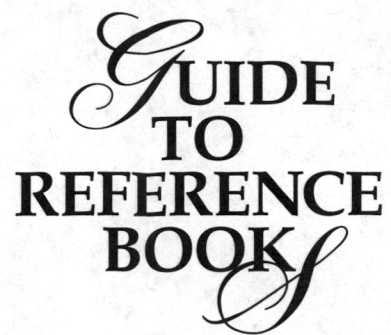

GUIDE TO REFERENCE BOOKS

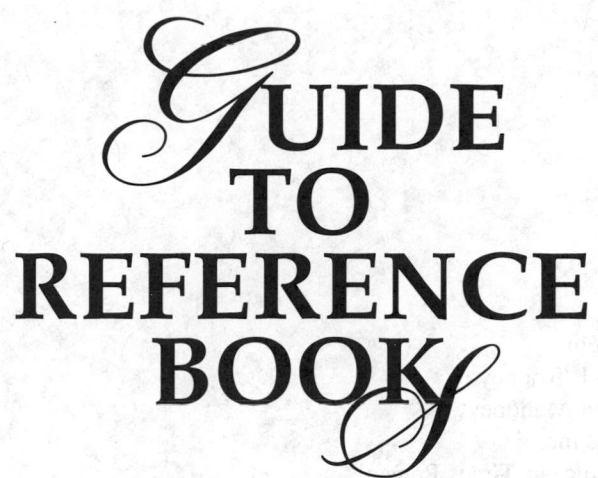

GUIDE TO REFERENCE BOOKS

Eleventh Edition

Edited by
Robert Balay

Associate Editor
Vee Friesner Carrington

With special editorial assistance by
Murray S. Martin

AMERICAN LIBRARY ASSOCIATION

CHICAGO AND LONDON 1996

Project Editor: David M. Epstein
Production Manager: Dianne M. Rooney
Manufacturing Manager: Eileen Mahoney
Cover Design: Tessing Design, Inc.
Composed by INFORONICS, Inc. in Times Roman
and Friz Quadrata.
Printed on 35-pound C-Brite, a pH-neutral stock, and
bound in Roxite B cloth by Edwards Brothers, Inc.

The paper used in this publication meets the minimum
requirements of American National Standard for Information Sciences—Permanence of Paper for Printed
Library Materials, ANSI Z39.48–1992.∞

Library of Congress Cataloging-in-Publication Data

Guide to reference books / edited by Robert Balay ;
    associate editor, Vee Friesner Carrington ; with
    special editorial assistance by Murray S. Martin. —
    11th ed.
        p.   cm.
    Includes bibliographical references and index.
    ISBN 0–8389–0669–9
    1. Reference books—Bibliography.   I. Balay,
Robert.   II. Carrington, Vee Friesner.   III. Martin,
Murray S.
    Z1035.1.G89   1996
    011'.02—dc20   95-26322
                                                        CIP

ISBN 0–8389–0669–9

Printed in the United States of America.

00 99 98 97 96   5 4 3 2 1

Contributors

Cheryl Abbott, *Harvard University*—Section AB

Cynthia Adams, *University of North Carolina at Chapel Hill*—Section BE

Mary Beth Allen, *University of Illinois at Urbana-Champaign*—Section BL

Janet Ayers, *Northwestern University*—Section EK

David S. Azzolina, *University of Pennsylvania*—Section CF

Bernice Bergup, *University of North Carolina at Chapel Hill*—Section BE

Phyllis B. Bischof, *University of California, Berkeley*—Section DD

Henri J. Bourneuf, *Harvard College*—Section AH

Wendy Bousfield, *Syracuse University*—Sections CA, AL

Barbara A. Burg, *Harvard University*—Section BB

Mary Cargill, *Columbia University*—Section AA

Bessie M. Carrington, *Duke University*—Section CH

Kathe Chipman, *Avery Architectural and Fine Arts Library, Columbia University*—Sections BF, BG

Diane Choquette, *Graduate Theological Union*—Section BC

Marie L. Clark, *Northwestern University*—Section AF

Elaine M. Coppola, *Syracuse University*—Section CJ

Philip N. Cronenwett, *Dartmouth College*—Section DG

Lloyd Davidson, *Northwestern University*—Section EG

Elizabeth A. Davis, *Columbia University*—Section BJ

Kevin J. Donnelly, *Harvard College*—Section BB

Cathryn Easterbrook, *John Crerar Library, University of Chicago*—Section EH

Ed Goodman, *Syracuse University*—Section CB

Robin Hanson, *Muskingum College*—Section AC

David P. Heighton, *Family History Library*—Sections AJ, AL

Thomas Holzmann, *Princeton University*—Section CG

Donald Clay Johnson, *University of Minnesota*—Section DE

Alfred Kagan, *University of Illinois at Urbana-Champaign*—Section DD

Regina Kammer, *University of California, Berkeley*—Section DD

Deborah Kelley-Milburn, *Harvard University*—Section AB

David A. Lincove, *Ohio State University*—Section AE

Eileen McIlvaine, *Columbia University*—Sections DA, DB, DC

Cheryl Knott Malone, *University of Texas at Austin*—Section DF

Robert C. Michaelson, *Northwestern University*—Sections ED, EE, EK

Christa M. Modschiedler, *John Crerar Library, University of Chicago*—Section EH

Rita W. Moss, *University of North Carolina at Chapel Hill*—Section CH

Fred Muratori, *Cornell University*   Section AD

Marjorie E. Murfin, *Ohio State University*   Section AE

Thomas J. Nixon, *University of North Carolina at Chapel Hill*—Section BE

Hugh Olmsted, *Harvard College*—Section BD

Kent C. Olson, *University of Virginia*—Section CK

Elizabeth Patterson, *Emory University*—Sections AG, CD

Lesley Pease, *Syracuse University*—Section CC

Maria A. Porta, *University of Illinois at Urbana-Champaign*—Section EJ

Brenda S. Rice, *John Crerar Library, University of Chicago*—Sections EB, EK

†Phillip A. Smith, *University of California, San Diego*—Section BH

Marcella Stark, *Southern Methodist University*—Section CC

Patricia F. Stenstrom, *University of Illinois at Urbana-Champaign*—Section AK

†Deceased

Barbara C. Swain, *University of Illinois at Urbana-Champaign*—Section EJ

Michael Van Fossen, *University of North Carolina at Chapel Hill*—Section AF

Mary Anne Waltz, *University at Albany, State University of New York*—Sections CE, CL

Kathleen A. Zar, *John Crerar Library, University of Chicago*—Sections EA, EC, EF

Referees

Mary Cargill, *Columbia University*—Section A

Scott Kennedy, *University of Nebraska*—Section B

Kevin Mulcahy, *Rutgers University*—Section C

Eileen McIlvaine, *Columbia University*—Section D

Robert C. Michaelson, *Northwestern University*—Section E

Project Directors

Patricia Sabosik, *Choice*—through April 1994

Francine Graf, *Choice*—April 1994–August 1995

The editors, contributors, and publishers record with sadness the death of their colleague, Phillip A. Smith, in May, 1995. We regret he did not live to see into print his work on the *Guide*.

Contents

This table of contents lists only the principal subdivisions in most sections.
In most cases, forms of publication (Bibliography, Dictionaries, etc.) are omitted.
For sections arranged geographically, the notation *(Subdivided geographically)* is used.
To locate specific subjects, consult the Index.

Abbreviations xvii

Foreword xxi

A

General Reference Works

AA Bibliography 1
Mary Cargill, Columbia University

General Works 1
  Guides and manuals 1
  Bibliography of bibliography 2
    (Subdivided geographically) 3
Universal 10
  Bibliography 10
    Books in series 11
  Library catalogs 11
    National libraries 11
    Nonnational libraries 15
    Union lists 16
  Festschriften 17
  Microforms and reproductions 17
  Translations 18
  Anonyms and pseudonyms 19
    (Subdivided geographically) 20
  Fictitious imprints 23
Ancient, Medieval, and Renaissance Manuscripts 24
  Diplomatics, handwriting, and scripts 26
Early and Rare Books 26
  Incunabula and early printed books 26
  Book collecting 28
    Historical children's books 29
  Printers' marks 29
    Watermarks 30
  Auction records 30
Printing and Publishing 31
  General works 31
  Copyright 36
  Copy preparation 36
Selection of Books 37
  Guides 37
    Current 37

Books for college students 37
Books for children and young people 38
Reference books 38
Book review indexes 40
Selection of Periodicals 42
Audiovisual Materials 42
National and Trade 43
  (Subdivided geographically) 44

AB Encyclopedias 105
*Deborah Kelley-Milburn and Cheryl Abbott,
Harvard College*

Guides 106
American and English 106
  Juvenile 108
Electronic 110
Foreign Language 110
  (Arranged by language)
Fact Books and Compendiums 118

AC Language Dictionaries 119
Robin Hanson, Muskingum College

English Language 119
  American 119
    Desk dictionaries 120
    Juvenile dictionaries 121
  English 122
    Desk dictionaries 123
  Abbreviations 124
  Etymology 124
  Idioms and usage 126
  New words 128
  Obsolete words 128
  Pronunciation 129

Punctuation 129
Rhymes 129
Slang 130
Synonyms and antonyms 131
Regional and dialect 132
Foreign words and phrases 136
Foreign Languages 136
(Arranged by language)

AD Periodicals 187

Fred Muratori, Cornell University

Bibliography 187
General works 187
By region 190
Union Lists 207
(Subdivided geographically) 208
Indexes 212
(Subdivided geographically) 213

AE Newspapers 224

David A. Lincove and Marjorie E. Murfin, Ohio State University

Bibliographies, Union Lists, and Directories 224
(Subdivided geographically) 226
Indexes 238
General works 238
(Subdivided geographically) 238
Features 241
Journalism 242
Press surveys and directories 243

AF Government Publications 244

Marie L. Clark, Northwestern University, and Michael Van Fossen, University of North Carolina, Chapel Hill

International 244
General works 244
International governmental organizations 247
European Communities 247
League of Nations 247
United Nations 248
United States 251
General works 251
Federal publications 252
Catalogs and indexes 254
Legislative branch 258
Executive branch 260
State publications 261
Municipal publications 262
Other Governments 262
General works 262
(Subdivided geographically) 262

AG Dissertations 274

Elizabeth Patterson, Emory University

Guides and Manuals 274
Bibliography 275
(Subdivided geographically) 275

AH Biography 281

Henri J. Bourneuf, Harvard College

General Works 281
International 283
(Subdivided geographically) 287

AJ Genealogy 317

David P. Heighton, Family History Library

North America 317
Europe 323
Asia 329
Australia and Oceania 329
Jewish 329
Heraldry 330
Names 331

AK Library and Information Science 334

Patricia F. Stenstrom, University of Illinois at Urbana-Champaign

General Works 334
Libraries, Archives, and Information Centers 343
(Subdivided geographically) 345
Acquisitions Work and Collection Development 349
Administration 350
Archives 351
Information Storage and Retrieval 351
Automated library systems 352
Cataloging codes 352
Classification 352
Database directories 353
Filing 354
Indexing and abstracting 354
Subject headings 354
Interlibrary Loan and Document Delivery 355
Library Instruction 356
Reference 356
Preservation 356
Reprography and Micrographics 357

AL Other General Reference Works 358

Wendy Bousfield, Syracuse University, and David P. Heighton, Family History Library

General Works 358
Associations, Societies, and Academies 358
(Subdivided geographically) 361
Secret societies 365
Research Centers 366
Museums 366
Foundations and Philanthropic Organizations 367
Holidays and Anniversaries 372
Etiquette 372
Prizes and Awards 373
Nobel Prizes 374
Orders and Decorations 375
Flags 376
Weights and Measures 376

B

Humanities

BA   General Works 378

BB   Philosophy 380

Barbara A. Burg and Kevin J. Donnelly, Harvard College

General Works   380
By Period   385
   Ancient   385
   Medieval   385
   Renaissance   386
   Modern   386
   Nineteenth century   387
   Twentieth century   387

BC   Religion 388

Diane Choquette, Graduate Theological Union

General Works   388
Sacred Books   397
   General works   397
   The Bible   398
      Versions   398
      Concordances   406
      Commentaries   407
      Hebrew Bible   408
   Koran   410
Prayers   411
Christianity   411
   General works   411
      Biography   415
         Saints   416
      Liturgy and ritual   417
   Church history and expansion   417
      Patrology   419
      Missions   420
   Creeds   421
   Costume   421
   Hymnology   421
   Protestant denominations   422
      Baptists   422
      Brethren churches   423
      Church of England   423
      Church of Ireland   424
      Church of Scotland   424
      Episcopal   424
         Book of Common Prayer   425
      Friends, Society of   425
      Lutheran   426
      Mennonite   426
      Methodist   426
      Mormon   427
      Pentecostal   427
      Presbyterian   428
      Reformed   428

      Shakers   428
      United Church of Christ   428
   Roman Catholic Church   429
      Liturgy and ritual   432
      Popes, cardinals, bishops   433
      Religious orders   434
   Eastern churches   435
   Coptic church   435
Buddhism   435
Hinduism   437
Islam   438
Jainism   440
Judaism   440
Native American Religions   446
Shintō   446
Sikhism   446
Zoroastrianism   446

BD   Languages, Linguistics, Philology 447

Hugh Olmsted, Harvard College

Languages: General Works   447
Linguistics   450
   General works   450
   Descriptive grammar   452
   Transformational grammar   453
   Analogy and metaphor   453
   Artificial and nonverbal languages   453
   Semantics   453
   Semiotics   454
   Creoles and pidgins   454
   Language origins   454
   Dialectology   454
   Other topics   454
Applied Linguistics and Related Fields   455
   Bilingualism; Second language acquisition   455
   Child language; First language acquisition   455
   Computational and mathematical linguistics   455
   Discourse analysis; Pragmatics   455
   History of linguistics   456
   Language study and teaching   456
   Psycho- and neurolinguistics   457
   Sociolinguistics   457
   Translation   458
English   458
Other Germanic Languages   461
Latin and Greek   463
Romance Languages   464
Celtic Languages   468
Slavic Languages   468
Baltic Languages   469
Indo-Iranian Languages   470
Other Indo-European Languages   470
Balkan Languages   470
Semitic Languages   471

CONTENTS

Finno-Ugric Languages 471
Turkic Languages 471
African Languages 472
Chinese 472
Japanese 473
Korean 473
South Asian Languages 473
Mainland Southeast Asian Languages 474
Malayo-Polynesian Languages 474
Australian Languages 474
Native American Languages 474

BE Literature 475

Cynthia Adams, Bernice Bergup, and Thomas J. Nixon,
University of North Carolina, Chapel Hill

General Works 475
Genres 497
    Biography 497
    Drama 498
    Essays 499
    Fiction 500
        Novels 501
        Short stories 502
        Detective and mystery fiction 502
        Science fiction, fantasy, the Gothic 504
    Poetry 508
    Romances, epics, etc. 511
Speech and Rhetoric 512
    Debating 514
Stylistics 514
Children's Literature 515
Literatures of the English-Speaking Countries 516
    United States 516
        General works 516
        Genres 524
            Drama 524
            Fiction 526
            Poetry 529
            Diaries, letters, autobiography 531
        Literature of ethnic groups 531
            African-American literature 531
            Asian-American literature 535
            Native American literature 535
            Latino literature 536
            Jewish-American literature 537
        Regional literature 537
    Great Britain 539
        General works 539
        Genres 546
            Ballads 546
            Drama 546
            Fiction 550
            Poetry 553
            Parodies 557
            Diaries, letters, autobiography 557
        By period 557
            Old English 557
            Middle English 558
            To 1660 558
            Restoration and 18th century 559

            19th century 560
            20th century 562
        Shakespeare 562
    Ireland 566
    Scotland 567
    Wales 568
    Commonwealth 568
    Canada 568
    Australia 571
    New Zealand 573
Literatures of Latin America 573
    General works 573
    Genres 576
Literatures of Central America 577
    (Subdivided geographically) 577
Literatures of South America 579
    (Subdivided geographically) 579
Literatures of the Caribbean 583
    (Subdivided geographically) 584
Literatures of Europe 584
    General works 584
    Regional literatures 585
        Classical literature 585
        Germanic literature 592
        Romance literature 593
        Slavic literature 594
        Yiddish literature 594
        Scandinavian literature 595
    (Subdivided geographically) 596
Literatures of Africa 637
    General works 637
    Literature in French 638
    Literature in Portuguese 639
    Regional literatures 639
    (Subdivided geographically) 639
Literatures of Asia 641
    Regional literatures 642
    (Subdivided geographically) 642

BF Art and Architecture 648

Kathe Chipman, Avery Architectural and Fine Arts
Library, Columbia University

General Works 648
    Sales 660
    Museums 660
    Exhibitions 661
    Artists' signatures 665
Symbolism and Iconography 666
    Buddhist 667
    Chinese 667
    Christian 667
    Classical 668
    Hindu 668
    Jewish 669
Art Reproductions 669
Restoration and Conservation 669
Architecture 670
    General works 670
    Restoration and conservation 677
    City planning 678
    Landscape architecture 679

Painting 681
Photography 684
Graphic Arts 688
Sculpture 691

BG   Design and Applied Arts **693**
Kathe Chipman, Avery Architectural and Fine Arts Library, Columbia University

General Works 693
Antiques 696
Ceramics and Glass 698
Clocks, Watches, and Jewelry 701
Costume and Fashion 702
Furniture and Interior Design 704
Metal Arts 706
Textiles 708
Coins, Numismatics, and Currency 710
Postage Stamps 712

BH   Theater and Performing Arts **714**
Phillip A. Smith, University of California, San Diego

Performing Arts (General) 714
Theater 717
    Stage history 718
    Stagecraft 719
Dance 727
Film 730
    Film catalogs 733
    Film guides 734
    Filmography 735
        Adaptations 737
        Themes and genres 737
    Prizes and awards 742
    Screen characters 743
Television and Radio 744
    Program catalogs 745
    Radio 746

BJ   Music **748**
Elizabeth A. Davis, Columbia University

General Works 748
    Bibliography: Books 748
    Bibliography: Scores 752
    Library catalogs: Books 756
    Library catalogs: Scores 757
    Music business 764
Musical Forms 769
    Themes 769
    Opera 769
    Musical theater 771
    Chamber music 772
    Songs 772
    Choral music 774
    Orchestral music 775
    Jazz 775
    Electronic music 776
    Folk and traditional music 777
    Popular music 778
    Music in films 780
Instruments 781
Recorded Music 782

BK   Sports and Recreation **784**
Mary Beth Allen, University of Illinois at Urbana-Champaign

Sports and Games 784
    General works 784
    Rules 787
    Individual sports 788
        (Arranged alphabetically)
    Other outdoor sports and recreation 792
        Parks and protected areas 793
    Board and card games 794
Crafts 795

C

Social and Behavioral Sciences

CA   General Works **796**
Wendy Bousfield, Syracuse University

CB   Education **803**
Ed Goodman, Syracuse University

General Works 803
Tests and Measurements 818
Educational Law and Legislation 819
Teachers and Teacher Education 819
Educational Technology 820
Educational Administration 821
Education of the Gifted 822

Special Education 822
Guidance 824
Higher Education 825
Adult Education 838
Fellowships and Scholarships 840
Academic Customs 843

CC   Sociology **844**
Lesley Pease, Syracuse University, and Marcella Stark, Southern Methodist University

General Works 844
Social Conditions and Social Welfare 846

General works   846
Social work   848
Aging   849
Alcoholism and drug abuse   854
Childhood and adolescence   856
Death and dying   860
Disabilities and the disabled   861
Homelessness and the homeless   862
Marriage and the family   863
Population planning   866
Poverty and the poor   867
Sex and sexual behavior   868
Urbanization   870
Ethnic Groups   871
General works   871
United States   876
African Americans   876
Asian Americans   880
Native Americans   881
Latinos   884
Canada   887
South America   887
International ethnic groups   887
Women   887
General works   887
Women in specific countries, regions, or ethnic groups   897

CD   Psychology 900

Elizabeth Patterson, Emory University

General Works   900
History and Theory   905
Research Methodology and Statistics   906
Tests and Measurements   906
Developmental Psychology   907
Educational Psychology   908
Social Psychology   909
Clinical Psychology   909
Cognition and Intelligence   910
Physiological and Comparative Psychology   911
Industrial and Organizational Psychology   911
Parapsychology   912

CE   Anthropology and Ethnology 913

Mary Anne Waltz, University at Albany, State University of New York

General Works   913
The Americas   920
Europe   922
Africa   923
Asia   923
Australia and Oceania   924

CF   Mythology, Folklore, and Popular Culture 924

David S. Azzolina, University of Pennsylvania

Mythology   924
Folklore and Popular Culture   927

CG   Statistics and Demography 933

Thomas Holzmann, Princeton University

General Works   933
Compendiums   937
(Subdivided geographically)   940

CH   Economics and Business 973

Bessie M. Carrington, Duke University, and Rita W. Moss, University of North Carolina at Chapel Hill

General Works   973
Economic Conditions and World Trade   982
General works   982
(Subdivided geographically)   987
Finance and Investment   991
General works   991
Finance   993
Public finance   994
Accounting   994
Money and banking   996
Investment   999
Company Information and Industry Analysis   1002
General works   1002
Business history   1008
Company information   1010
Industry analysis   1011
Commerce   1012
General works   1012
Commodities   1012
Transportation   1013
Communications   1017
International trade   1018
Insurance   1018
Real estate   1020
Marketing and Advertising   1022
General works   1022
Consumerism   1023
Public relations   1023
Advertising   1024
Marketing   1024
Organizational Behavior   1027
Management   1027
Labor and industrial relations   1028
Occupations   1035
Personnel   1036
Human resources   1037

CJ   Political Science 1038

Elaine M. Coppola, Syracuse University

General Works   1038
National Politics and Government   1045
General works   1045
The Americas   1048
North America   1048
United States   1048
Executive branch   1055
Congress   1058
Elections   1064
Political parties   1066
State and local government   1067

Confederate States of America   1070
Canada   1070
Mexico   1071
Latin America   1071
Central America   1072
South America   1072
Europe   1072
Great Britain   1074
Parliament   1076
Local government   1078
British Commonwealth   1078
Africa   1081
Asia   1082
Australia and Oceania   1085
Parliamentary Procedure   1086
Public Administration   1087
Public Opinion   1089
Communism and Socialism   1091
Intelligence and Espionage   1094
Terrorism   1096
Armed Forces   1097
General works   1097
Individual countries   1102
Arms Control and Peace Research   1108

CK   Law **1112**
Kent C. Olson, University of Virginia

General Works   1112

International Law   1120
Treaties   1121
National Legal Systems   1124
United States   1124
Constitutions   1130
Statutes   1130
Regulations   1132
Supreme Court   1132
(Other regions subdivided geographically)   1133
Religious Legal Systems   1138
Criminology   1138

CL   Geography **1141**
Mary Anne Waltz, University at Albany, State University of New York

General Works   1141
Gazetteers   1149
General works   1149
(Subdivided geographically)   1151
Geographical Names and Terms   1158
General works   1158
(Subdivided geographically)   1158
Atlases and Maps   1162
General works   1162
Regional and national   1168
Travel and Tourism   1177

D

History and Area Studies

DA   General History **1180**
Eileen McIlvaine, Columbia University

General Works   1180
Historiography   1185
Archaeology and Ancient History   1187
General works   1187
Classical studies   1190
Ancient Egypt   1194
Medieval and Renaissance   1195
General works   1195
Byzantine studies   1198
Crusades   1199
Modern   1199
General works   1199
The World Wars   1202
World War I   1202
World War II   1203
Holocaust   1205

DB   The Americas **1206**
Eileen McIlvaine, Columbia University

General Works   1206

North America   1207
United States   1207
General works   1207
17th and 18th centuries   1216
American Revolution   1216
19th century   1218
Civil War   1219
20th century   1221
Regional and local   1222
Canada   1226
General works   1226
Regional and local   1230
Mexico   1231
Latin America   1234
General works   1234
Central America   1239
(Subdivided geographically)   1240
South America   1241
Amazon River region   1241
(Subdivided geographically)   1242
Islands of the Caribbean and Western Atlantic   1249
General works   1249
(Subdivided geographically)   1250

DC   Europe **1254**
Eileen McIlvaine, Columbia University

General Works   1254
Reformation   1256
By Region   1257
    Europe, Eastern   1257
    Balkan states   1260
    Baltic states   1261
    Scandinavia   1261
By Country   1262
    (Subdivided geographically)   1262
        France   1268
            General works   1268
            Early to 1798 (including archaeology)   1271
            French Revolution   1272
            Napoleonic era   1273
            Since 1815   1274
            Regional and local   1275
        Germany   1276
            General works   1276
            To 1600   1277
            18th–20th centuries   1278
        Great Britain   1282
            General works   1282
            Early to 1485   1286
            16th–18th centuries   1287
            19th–20th centuries   1288
            British Empire and Commonwealth   1290
            Regional and local   1291
        Spain   1306
            General works   1306
            Spanish Civil War   1307
    Union of Soviet Socialist Republics   1310
        General works   1310
        Pre–1917   1313
        Post–1917   1315
        Regional and local   1316

DD   Africa **1318**
Alfred Kagan, University of Illinois at Urbana-Champaign, and Phyllis B. Bischof and Regina Kammer, University of California, Berkeley

General Works   1318
Africa *(by region)*   1326
    Africa, North   1326
    Africa, South of the Sahara   1327
    Africa, West   1330
    Africa, East   1330
    Africa, Central   1331
    Africa, Southern   1331
Africa *(by country)*   1333

DE   Asia **1346**
Donald Clay Johnson, University of Minnesota

General Works   1346
Asia *(by region)*   1348
    Asia, West   1348
    Asia, Central   1353
    Asia, South   1353
    Asia, Southeast   1354
    Asia, East   1355
Asia *(by country)*   1356

DF   Australia and Oceania **1371**
Cheryl Knott Malone, University of Texas at Austin

DG   Polar Regions **1376**
Philip N. Cronenwett, Dartmouth College

E

Science, Technology, and Medicine

EA   General Science **1378**
Kathleen A. Zar, John Crerar Library, University of Chicago

General Works   1378
Societies and Congresses   1400
Laboratories   1401
Scientific Expeditions   1402
Scientific Illustration   1402
History of Science   1402
Patents; Trademarks   1405
Standards   1406
Formulas and Recipes   1407

EB   Mathematics **1408**
Brenda S. Rice, John Crerar Library, University of Chicago

EC   Astronomy **1418**
Kathleen A. Zar, John Crerar Library, University of Chicago

General Works   1418
Stars   1423
Navigation   1424
Chronology   1425

ED Physics **1426**
Robert C. Michaelson, Northwestern University

General Works 1426
Color 1431

EE Chemistry **1432**
Robert C. Michaelson, Northwestern University

General Works 1432
Inorganic 1443
Organic 1444

EF Earth Sciences **1449**
Kathleen A. Zar, John Crerar Library, University of Chicago

General Works 1449
Geology 1451
Crystallography 1459
Geodesy 1459
Glaciology 1460
Hydrology 1460
Meteorology 1461
    Climatology 1462
Mineralogy 1464
    Meteorites 1467
Oceanography 1467
Paleontology 1469
    Fossil indexes 1469
Petrology 1471
Seismology 1471
Volcanology 1472

EG Biological Sciences **1472**
Lloyd Davidson, Northwestern University

General Works 1472
Ecology 1477
Natural History 1478
Botany 1480
    General works 1480
    Ferns 1487
    Flora 1487
    Fungi 1488
    Mosses 1489
    Trees 1489
Zoology 1490
    General works 1490
    Amphibians and reptiles 1494
    Birds 1494
    Fishes 1497
    Mammals 1497
    Shells 1499
Bacteriology 1499
Biochemistry 1499
Entomology 1500
Genetics 1501
Virology 1502

EH Medical and Health Sciences **1502**
Christa M. Modschiedler and Cathryn Easterbrook, John Crerar Library, University of Chicago

Medicine 1502
    History 1520
    Medical illustration 1524
Bioethics 1524
Dentistry 1525
Medical Jurisprudence 1527
Nursing 1527
Nutrition 1529
Pharmacology 1531
    Dispensatories and pharmacopoeias 1535
Psychiatry 1536
Public Health 1539
Toxicology 1541

EJ Agricultural Sciences **1542**
Maria A. Porta and Barbara C. Swain, University of Illinois at Urbana-Champaign

Agriculture 1542
    U.S. Department of Agriculture 1550
Animal Science 1552
Food Science 1556
Forestry 1559
Home Economics 1561
Horticulture 1564

EK Engineering **1567**
Janet Ayers and Robert C. Michaelson, Northwestern University, and Brenda S. Rice, John Crerar Library, University of Chicago

General Works 1567
Aeronautical and Space Engineering 1569
Automotive Engineering 1571
Biotechnology 1571
Chemical Engineering 1572
Civil Engineering 1573
    Environment and environmental problems 1574
    Hydraulic engineering and hydrodynamics 1577
    Structural engineering 1577
    Transportation engineering 1578
Electrical and Electronic Engineering 1579
    Television and radio 1581
Computer Science 1581
Energy 1587
Heating and Refrigeration 1588
Industrial Engineering 1588
Mechanical Engineering 1589
    Plant engineering and maintenance 1590
Mining Engineering 1590
Engineering Materials 1591
    Plastics 1594
Nuclear Engineering 1594
Petroleum Engineering 1595

Index 1599

Abbreviations

This list includes only abbreviations for which some explanation seems necessary. Shortened forms of publishers' names or other abbreviations that seem self-explanatory have been omitted.

aarg.: *aargang*

Abt.: *Abteilung, Abtheilung*

Admin.: Administration

afl.: *aflevering*

Ala.: Alabama

A.L.A.: American Library Association

Alta.: Alberta

Amer.: American

ampl.: *ampliata*

A.M.S.: American Mathematical Society

approx.: approximately

Apr.: April

årg.: *årgang*

Ark.: Arkansas

arr.: arranged, arranger

assoc.: associate

Assoc.: Association

Aufl.: *Auflage*

augm.: augmented

Aug.: August

Ausg.: *Ausgabe*

b.: born

B.C.: British Columbia

BCE: Before Common Era

Bd.: *Band, Bind*

bd.: *band, bind*

bearb.: *bearbeitet*

begr.: *begründet*

Bro., Bros.: Brother, -s

Buchdr.: *Buchdrucker, -ei*

bull.: bulletin

c: copyright

ca.: *circa*

Calif.: California

CAS: Chemical Abstracts Service

CD-ROM: compact disc–read-only memory

CE: Common Era

cent.: century

cf.: compare; confer

ch.: chapter, -s

Co.: Company

col.: column, -s

cm.: centimeter, -s

Colo.: Colorado

comp.: compiled, compiler

compl.: completed, completely

Cong.: Congress

Conn.: Connecticut

Corp.: Corporation

corr.: corrected, *corregido, corretto, corrigé*

CRC: Chemical Rubber Company

d.: *deel*

d.: *der*

d.: died

D.C.: District of Columbia

Dec.: December

Del.: Delaware

Dept.: Department

D.F.: *Distrito Federal*

distr.: distributed

Div.: Division

DNA: deoxyribonucleic acid

doc.: document

DOT: Department of Transportation (U.S.)

EC: European Community, -ies

ed.: edited, edition, editor, *edizione, edición*

éd.: *édition*

ed. in chief: editor in chief

eds.: editions

e.g.: *exempli gratia*

Eng.: English, England

enl.: enlarged

EPA: Environmental Protection Administration (U.S.)

erg.: *ergänzt*

Ergbd.: *Ergänzungsband*

erw.: *erweiterte*

estab. tip.: *establicimiento tipográfico*
et al.: *et alii*
etc.: *et cetera*

f.: *für*
facsim., facsims.: facsimile, -s
fasc.: fascicle, fascicule
FDA: Food and Drug Administration (U.S.)
Feb.: February
ff.: following
Fla.: Florida
fol.: folio

Ga.: Georgia
glav. red.: *glavnyi redaktor*
GmbH.: *Gesellschaft mit beschränkter Haftung*
Gos.: *Gosudarstvo, -vennii*
govt.: government
Govt. Print. Off.: Government Printing Office (U.S.)

Hft.: *Heft, Hefte*
hft.: *hefte*
Hlbbd.: *Halbband*
H.M.S.O.: Her (His) Majesty's Stationery Office
hrsg.: *herausgegeben*

i.e.: *id est*
IFLA: International Federation of Library Associations
Ill.: Illinois
ill.: illustrated, illustrations
ILO: International Labour Organization
impr.: *imprenta, impresión, imprimé, imprimerie, imprimeur*
in.: inch, -es
Inc.: Incorporated
incompl.: incomplete
Ind.: Indiana
Inst.: Institute, Institution
Internat.: International
Introd.: Introduction
ISBN: International Standard Book Number
ISSN: International Standard Serial Number
IUPAC: International Union of Pure and Applied Chemistry
izd.: *izdatel'*

jaarg.: *jaargang*
Jahrg.: *Jahrgang*
Jan.: January
JANAF: Joint Army-Navy-Air Force
JPRS: Joint Publications Research Service (U.S.)

Kan.: Kansas

l.: leaves

La.: Louisiana
Lfg.: *Lieferung*
libr.: *librairie;* library, -ies
Ltd.: Limited

Mar.: March
Mass.: Massachusetts
Md.: Maryland
Me.: Maine
Mich.: Michigan
Minn.: Minnesota
misc.: miscellaneous
Miss.: Mississippi
mm: millimeter, -s
Mo.: Missouri
Mont.: Montana
ms., mss.: manuscript, -s

Nachf.: *Nachfolger*
Nacht.: *Nachtrag*
nákl.: *náklad, nákladatel*
NAL: National Agricultural Library (U.S.)
Nat.: National
NATO: North Atlantic Treaty Organization
N.B.: New Brunswick
N.C.: North Carolina
n.d.: no date
Neb.: Nebraska
neubearb.: *neubearbeitet*
Nev.: Nevada
n.F.: *neue Folge*
N.H.: New Hampshire
N.J.: New Jersey
N.M.: New Mexico
NMR: nuclear magnetic resonance
no.: number, -s
nouv.: *nouveau, nouvelle*
Nov.: November
Nr.: *Nummer*
n.s.: new series
N.S.: Nova Scotia
N.S.W.: New South Wales
N.T.: New Testament
N.T.: Northern Territory
núm.: *número*
N.Y.: New York
N.Z.: New Zealand

Oct.: October
Okla.: Oklahoma
omarb.: *omarbetad*
Ont.: Ontario
Or.: Oregon

O.T.: Old Testament
OTC: over the counter

p.: page, -s
pa.: paper
Pa.: Pennsylvania
P.E.I.: Prince Edward Island
photo., photos.: photograph, -s
ports.: portraits
Pr.: Press
P.R.: Puerto Rico
Pref.: Preface
prelim.: preliminary
prep.: prepared
print.: printing
priv. print.: privately printed
pseud.: pseudonym
pt., pts.: part, *parte;* parts
Pub.: Public
publ.: publication, published, *publié*
Publ.: Publishers, Publishing

red.: *redaktor*
réd.: *rédigé*
repr.: reprinted
revid.: *reviderad*
rev.: *revisé, -e;* revised; *revisado*
R.I.: Rhode Island
RISM: *Répertoire internationale des sources musicales*
riv.: *riveduto*
R.S.F.S.R.: Russian Soviet Federated Socialist Republic

S.C.: South Carolina
S.D.: South Dakota
sec.: *sección*
Sep.: September
sér.: *série*
ser.: series
sess.: session
S.I.: *Système Internationale*
SIC: Standard Industrial Classification
s.l.: no place (of publication) [*sine loco*]
s.n.: no name (of publisher) [*sine nomine*]
Soc.: Society
sost.: *sostavitel'*

Stat.: Stationery
suppl.: supplement; *supplément*
supt.: superintendent
szerk.: *szerkesztette*

T.: *Teil, Theil*
t.: *tome, tomo*
Tenn.: Tennessee
Tex.: Texas
tip.: *tipografía, tipográfica*
t.p.: title page
tr.: *traduit;* translated; translator; *tryckt*
trad.: *traducido*

u.: *und*
u. A.: *und Andere*
udarb.: *udarbeidet*
uit.: *uitgaaf*
uitg.: *uitgegeven*
umgearb.: *umgearbeitete*
U.K.: United Kingdom
U.N.: United Nations
Univ.: University
uppl.: *upplaga*
U.S.: United States
USP: United States Pharmacopoeia
U.S.S.R.: Union of Soviet Socialist Republics
utarb.: *utarbeidet*
utg.: *utgave*

v.: volume, -s
v.: *von*
Va.: Virginia
verb.: *verbeterde, verbesserte*
verm.: *vermehrte*
vol.: volume, -s
Vt.: Vermont
vyd.: *vydání*

Wash.: Washington, D.C.
WHO: World Health Organization
Wis.: Wisconsin

yr.: year

Foreword

The present version of the *Guide* is the eleventh full edition in a record of continuing publication by the American Library Association that reaches back to the first edition of 1907. Like other full editions, this one represents an attempt to reassess the corpus of reference sources at present available and select those that have been found most useful. As one might expect, the *Guide,* in keeping with growth in the number and variety of reference sources, has itself increased in size with each edition.

This edition has been driven by two considerations: the need to assist information workers by selecting and describing the reference sources that have been found most useful in libraries in North America, and the desire to continue the tradition of excellence set by the compilers of earlier editions. We were constantly aware that we would be judged against the respect approaching reverence in which the *Guide* has been held by generations of librarians.

The shape of this particular edition was determined by discussions at a planning conference held at the Midwinter Meetings of A.L.A. in San Antonio in January 1992. Work on the supplement to the tenth edition had just been completed, with publication set for the spring of 1992. Those invited to the planning conference included contributors to the tenth edition supplement, prominent reference librarians, library educators, and representatives from the publishing community.

The editors asked this panel of advisors to consider how the *Guide* had been used in their libraries and to recommend any improvements that should be made in the eleventh edition. The following guidelines were agreed on:

- Since the *Guide* has been held in high esteem by generations of librarians, no dramatic changes in scope or arrangement would be warranted.
- The eleventh edition should continue to be published in a single volume.
- The number of titles listed in the eleventh edition should therefore be roughly the same as the tenth edition, about 15,500.
- Although the eleventh edition should continue to list primarily sources in printed format, those in machine-readable form should be included, recognizing the increasing importance of these sources.
- The eleventh edition should include a higher proportion of titles that support the study of non-Western cultures and of diverse viewpoints than did its predecessors.

The panel also insisted that, while the new edition continue to be primarily a printed product, it be produced in a manner that would allow it to be made available in machine-readable form as well as in print. This requirement was consistent with plans already made by Publishing Services and the *Guide* staff to produce the printed version from machine-readable copy.

Contributors

Contributors to this edition constitute a national cross-section of the reference profession as it is practiced in research libraries. For many decades, the *Guide* was compiled in the Reference Department of the Columbia University Library and was based on the reference collections of that library, supplemented by resources in nearby libraries, principally the New York Public Library. For some years, however, there has been recognition of the need to broaden the contributor base. With the supplements to the ninth edition and the full tenth edition, the science sections were compiled by librarians of the Kline Science Library at Yale University, and the supplement to the tenth edition was assembled by a much larger group of contributors, including sizable contingents from Syracuse University for the social sciences and from libraries at Northwestern University and the University of Chicago for the sciences.

The present edition has been compiled by 50 librarians from institutions ranging geographically from Harvard and Columbia in the east to the University of California and the Graduate Theological Union in the west, and from Dartmouth in the north to Emory and the University of Texas in the south. Many contributors are subject specialists whose knowledge is evident in the thorough recasting of a number of sections. Most contributors, however, are general reference librarians, a choice that constitutes, as it always has, one of the *Guide*'s strengths; the selection here represents the considered appraisal by librarians in general reference departments of the corpus of reference works currently available. Because they work daily with readers and make daily use of the reference collections available in their own libraries, the *Guide* contributors are uniquely qualified to assess the available resources.

By contrast, the staff of the *Guide* did their work in a publisher's office (the office of *Choice* magazine in Middletown, Connecticut), that offers, like most publishing offices, only a rudimentary collection of books and little contact with readers. Although the editors have had substantial reference experience, we were not in a position to select titles, to assess their usefulness, or to verify some details of bibliographic description (e.g., the contents of volumes published on continuations). By force of circumstance, we devoted most of our attention to editing annotations (usually with an eye to making them more concise), combining entries for related titles, resolving problems in entries, putting notes into standard order, and in general, attending to the thousands of details that arise in producing a book of this size and complexity. We interfered only infrequently in the choice of entries or the structure of sections.

For this edition, we also asked five experienced reference librarians (who are listed with the contributors) to read proof pages at an early stage and advise compilers and editors concerning the completeness, accuracy, balance, and stylistic felicity of the *Guide* sections as they stood at that point. The principal mission of these referees was to point out omissions and recommend deletions, based on their experience in reference work. Their comments proved extremely valuable to both editors and contributors.

Selection

This version of the *Guide* lists as entries 15,875 titles. Some entries that are of interest in more than one subject may appear several times; the full annotation for such entries appears only once, with other occurrences referring to that annotation. Other titles useful in reference work are mentioned in the notes and annotations; although we do not know the exact number of supplementary titles, we think it is nearly as large as the number of main entries.

To insure that this edition be about the same size as the tenth edition, the compiler of each section was given a specific number of titles at which to aim in selecting titles for the section. This target number was based on comparative section sizes in previous editions and on our understanding of present-day patterns in reference publishing. Although some contributors chafed under this restraint, most were careful to keep their sections close to the established limit. After closure of copy, the editors were able to allot slight increases to a number of sections. The science sections, which their compilers suspected had been underrepresented in previous editions of the *Guide,* turned out to be only slightly larger (14 percent of the total) than in the previous edition. The largest single section continues to be Literature, followed by Bibliography, Language Dictionaries, Economics and Business, and Political Science, but the discipline with the largest number of entries is still History and Area Studies.

Contributors were asked to base their selections principally on the collections of their own libraries, supplemented by resources in nearby research libraries or by materials requested through interlibrary loan. Since nearly all the contributors hold positions in research libraries, the eleventh edition, like its predecessors, emphasizes scholarly works, supplemented by titles intended for general readers to the extent those works would be useful in research libraries. Some topics that might seem to lie outside this definition (e.g., children's literature) were included because they are objects of scholarly interest and are important in the education of students (in the case of children's literature, the education of teachers). Contributors were asked to keep in mind that the specialist in one field is an amateur in another, and that users of research libraries have in common with general readers the need for advice concerning such matters as their personal health, education of their children, and laws of their state or city. This edition therefore includes a selection of titles that serve those needs.

It is appropriate on another ground to pitch the *Guide* toward research libraries. Such libraries commonly have collections characterized by breadth of scope and variety of materials, and readers with a broad range of interests. The reference collections needed to exploit such a library's holdings and serve its readers will be correspondingly wide and varied. If the *Guide* fulfills its intention to list the reference sources most useful to research libraries, it will also serve the needs of smaller libraries, which commonly have smaller collections and need reference sources that will lead to materials not available locally.

The sources contributors were asked to select are those needed to support reference service in the general reference department of a large university library that serves undergraduates, graduate students, faculty and other researchers (including visiting scholars and university administrators), and educated adults from the general populace, and that covers all subjects in the university curriculum. Works intended primarily or exclusively for the training of professionals (physicians, attorneys, clergy, etc.) or for use by highly specialized clientele (e.g., at pharmaceutical houses, hospitals, or architectural offices) were to be excluded.

In assessing titles for inclusion, contributors used standard qualitative criteria. Works selected had to meet high standards of accuracy, completeness, clarity, and scholarly authority; to have been put together by recognized compilers or groups of compilers and published by reputable publishers; and to have clearly stated purposes, to which their compilers adhered. In the end, however, the titles chosen met the single overriding test of having been found useful in providing reference service to readers. In the *Guide* context, that criterion is so important that works which fail other criteria can be included if they meet the test of usefulness.

It is sometimes said that inclusion in the *Guide* establishes a source's reputation as an outstanding work in its field. It is certainly true that authors and publishers are delighted to see their titles included here, but in this regard, the warning that has appeared in earlier editions bears repetition. The collection described here is a working collection drawn from the sources available at the time of the *Guide*'s publication. Although in many areas reference resources are well developed and include many titles that show high levels of excellence and scholarship and a keen appreciation of the needs of readers, in other areas there are gaps in coverage or adequacy. In the latter circumstance, we simply list a selection from what is available. It will be seen that in some instances, compilers are careful to warn readers about a work's shortcomings.

In choosing titles for inclusion, contributors used four basic sources: the tenth edition (1986), the tenth edition supplement (1992), titles published since the cutoff date for the supplement (the end of the 1990 imprint year), and titles of importance that had been omitted from previous editions of the *Guide*. For the first two categories, contributors were to screen all titles carefully, drop those that are outdated or no longer useful, record new editions, and bring continuations up to date. Annotations could be accepted as previously published if they adequately described the work, but contributors were advised that annotations, whether taken without change from previous editions, modified to fit new circumstances, or written anew, should represent their own view of the source.

The last two categories by necessity were based on each contributor's knowledge of recent reference materials and the collection at the contributor's own institution. Since competition for space in every section was intense, contributors had to think about a range of difficult questions; e.g., whether a newer work displaced an older one; whether it supplemented the older work and hence could be mentioned in the annotation; whether it was so slight or narrow in scope as not to deserve mention; whether it covered entirely new ground and so deserved a separate listing, and if so which title to drop in order to make room.

Contributors were also asked to keep in mind the various purposes for which the *Guide* will be used: to aid in developing reference collections, to refresh the memory of working reference librarians, and to help readers in locating reference sources. We also tried not to lose sight of the intention for which the *Guide* was first compiled—that it be a teaching resource for student librarians—and to ensure that it continue to serve that purpose.

Scope and Coverage

Since the *Guide* is intended for a North American audience, it emphasizes works published in North America. When the same title has been published both in North America and elsewhere at about the same time, the *Guide* favors the North American version, since it is more likely to be available to North American libraries. There is, however, no intention to exclude publishers elsewhere, and imprints from outside North America will be found in every section; the comprehensiveness in coverage that the *Guide* strives for could be met in no other way.

Similarly, sources in the English language are emphasized, but there is no theoretical restriction as to language of publication. Sources important in reference work are included without regard to language.

The dates of coverage extend back to the beginning of printing (although in fact no works earlier than the eighteenth century are listed) and come forward to the end of the 1993 imprint year. Although a scattering of works later than 1993 (chiefly new editions and continuations) will be found, they are not covered systematically, and contributors have attempted to select comprehensively only for titles published through 1993.

Like earlier editions, this version lists primarily titles in printed format, but the electronic revolution that has overtaken reference work is acknowledged by the inclusion of machine-readable sources. Contributors were asked to apply to electronic sources the same criteria they used in selecting those that are printed—authority, completeness, coverage, accuracy, and above all, usefulness.

Entries

So far as possible, entries here are based on MARC entries cataloged by the Library of Congress. When no LC entry could be found, we have used what seemed to us the best available record, but often ended by keyboarding the record directly into a MARC workform. We followed *Anglo-American cataloguing rules* (2nd ed., 1988 revision; AACR2R) in formulating entries or in converting older records. Entries will therefore resemble records readers are accustomed to seeing in library catalogs, whether card catalogs or OPACs, but the need for a standard printed format required some modifications. Among these are:

- Main entries (a term beginning to sound antique) print in boldface.
- The space-dash-space that separates sections of records is omitted for clarity.
- Many bibliographic notes (earlier editions, contents, continued titles) do not appear as part of the record proper but are appended as notes.
- Some parts of the description (size and bibliography and index notes) are omitted.
- Records for works in which a single personal author stands as the main entry do not repeat the author in the responsibility statement following the title.
- Some key parts of the description (LCCN, ISBN, ISSN, price) are suppressed, in keeping with longstanding *Guide*

tradition. These fields are included in most records, and will be searchable in electronic versions of the *Guide*.

We have retained AACR2R conventions that seemed useful in a printed bibliography; for example, a virgule (/) is used to separate the title from the responsibility statement; if a work has multiple authorship, the first author is listed as the main entry, with all authors listed in the responsibility statement.

But entries in the eleventh edition are by no means uniform. Some derive directly from MARC records and have been read virtually unchanged into the *Guide* record format. Some were already in machine-readable form from the tenth edition supplement, hence they largely conformed to both AACR2R and MARC. Some, however, were derived from the tenth edition, which predated full adoption of AACR2R; these records have been converted to *Guide* format and closely resemble modern records, although time did not permit changing some characteristics of these entries (for example, the practice, now abandoned, of bracketing publication dates when the date is not given on the title page).

We have also for convenience used publishers' series as the entry point for several large sets (*see,* for example, *African historical dictionaries* or *Dictionary of literary biography*). These so-called umbrella entries permitted us to list individual titles in the sets (or in the case of DLB to note where a list of volumes in the set may be found) rather than listing each title individually, which would have both inflated the significance of the set and left little room in the section for any other titles. AACR2R allows for entry under publishers' series, but in library catalogs entry by individual title is preferred.

Databases also presented special problems, and here we departed from library practice altogether. Some MARC records that describe databases (or "computer files" as they are quaintly called) include information such as system requirements that, in light of the increasing computer power available, no longer seems as important as it once was. Entry format for databases was discussed at several meetings between editorial staff and contributors, and we finally settled on an abbreviated form of entry that specifies title, material type (in our case, "[database]"), place, provider of data (not vendor), dates of coverage (not dates of availability), formats, and update frequency. It seemed to all of us that specifying additional information (e.g., file size) that was likely to change in a week or month, but certainly before the *Guide* was published, would not assist readers. As a result, although database records have been loaded into the standard *Guide* format, they do not resemble records found in any other source. Further information is best sought in directories of databases, where these sources are described more fully than in library catalogs. Machine-readable sources are flagged by a bullet (•). When the machine-readable version has a printed counterpart, it is attached to the entry for a printed version in a bulleted paragraph; when there is no printed counterpart, or when the electronic source combines two or more printed sources, it is given its own entry, with the entire entry preceded by a bullet. In the index, machine-readable sources are also preceded by a bullet.

Annotations

The annotations that accompany most entries are intended to enable users of the *Guide* to understand a source's scope and visualize its arrangement and features so that it can be used more easily at the shelf. In writing annotations, contributors were asked to consider a title's purpose, audience, scope, coverage, arrangement, and special features, and were invited to comment on its usefulness in reference work.

Contributors were urged to make their annotations as varied as possible (although in describing a group of similar sources such as German-English dictionaries, little variation is possible) and to keep annotations brief but long enough to describe the source adequately and give any necessary background. Readers of the *Guide* should not assume that a long annotation is an indication of a work's high reputation. Sometimes, an authoritative and useful work can be described in a few words, whereas in others, considerable detail is required to warn of a work's shortcomings. Some annotations are made long by the need to describe a work's publishing history or to provide a complicated contents list.

A few titles (e.g., the Bible) that were treated in a separate text section in the tenth edition are here given regular entries. The information about editions of the Bible that stood at the head of the Bible section in the tenth edition is here attached to an entry for the Authorized Version. This has been done in order for all the versions mentioned to be listed in the index.

Many entries contain a paragraph headed by a section device (§), which is used to separate from the annotation proper discussion of comparable works or other titles by the author of the work described in the entry. On the other hand, supplements, indexes, continuations, or titles bibliographically related to the entry title are not differentiated from the parent title. In many cases, the venerable but useful device of the dashed-on entry is used to indicate repetition of a preceding author or title, or both.

Classification

The general arrangement used for this edition resembles that used in all versions of the *Guide* since the eighth edition. We have kept the familiar five-part division: A, General Reference Works; B, Humanities; C, Social and Behavioral Sciences; D, History and Area Studies; and E, Science, Technology, and Medicine. For the most part the arrangement within each division closely resembles that of earlier editions. In A, Librarianship and Library Resources has been renamed Library and Information Science and has been moved near the end of the division in recognition that most sections in A represent forms of publication rather than topics; and a general section AL, Other General Reference Works, has been created as a place to locate titles of general interest that in earlier editions were forced into one of the topical divisions (usually C). In B, a general section BA, General Works, has been added that resembles those in divisions C, D, and E, making it necessary to redesignate all the other double-letter sections in B; BD has been renamed Languages, Linguistics, Philology, BF Art and Architecture, BG Design and Applied Arts, and BF Sports and Recreation (Travel and Tourism being moved to the Geography section). C is substantially unchanged except that CH is renamed Economics and Business. In D, two sections have been collapsed into DF, now called Australia and Oceania, and DG renamed Polar Regions. Finally, in E the order of sections has been revised to mirror the sequence of subjects in the LC classifications for science, agriculture, medicine, and engineering (Q, R, S, and T).

Some contributors have been content to keep the internal classification of their sections substantially unchanged from the tenth edition, but other sections have been thoroughly revised, reflecting the structure of the subject matter covered by the section and by its reference literature. Among those revised are Languages, Linguistics, Philology; Literature; Theater and Performing Arts; Education; Psychology; Economics and Business; and Law.

One change affecting many sections has been applied across the entire *Guide*. In recent editions, geographic headings have been arranged in alphabetical order by country, resulting in a certain randomness of sequence: Italy, Jamaica, Japan, Jordan, Korea, Latin America, for example. For this edition, we thought it would assist readers to group geographic headings by a classification based on continental land masses, so that readers interested in countries of Central America, for example, could find the countries of that region listed together. The classification uses the following large groupings:

North America
Central America
South America
Caribbean and Islands of the Western Atlantic
Europe
Africa
Asia
Australia and Oceania
Polar regions

Within each grouping, works that treat regions (e.g., East Asia) are listed first, followed by works about individual countries listed in alphabetical order by country. This arrangement has been invoked wherever a geographic arrangement is needed, so that from section to section, readers can look for a similar sequence of geographic entries. Even in Literature, which is more language-dependent than other sections, a modified geographic approach has been adopted. Sections that are arranged strictly by language (e.g., Language Dictionaries) continue to be in alphabetical order by language, since languages are no respecters of national boundaries.

This scheme has made necessary some surprising choices. Mexico, clearly part of the North American land mass, is classed with North America. Siberia, although it stretches east of Japan, is politically part of Russia and so is classed with Europe. Although most of its land mass is east of the Bosporus, Turkey classes with Europe because it is at least partly on the European continent, is a member of NATO, and lies west of the Urals. Latin America, on whose definition not even specialists can agree, sometimes includes South America (but often not all of it), sometimes Central America (but not all), sometimes parts of the Caribbean, and sometimes Mexico. It seemed best, therefore, to leave Latin America as an entirely separate designation. If the publisher or compiler of a reference work says it is about Latin America, that is where we class it.

Although this classification requires some choices that at first glance seem arbitrary, we think its groupings will be more useful to readers than a straight alphabetical listing by country and will collocate countries that are increasingly viewed as belonging together (e.g., Mexico is not separated from its North American neighbors by a line drawn in the desert).

Multicultural Concerns

In the early stages of planning for this edition, the editors and advisors heard criticism from the library community concerning the *Guide*'s failure to cover adequately materials relating to regions of the world outside Europe and North America, to ethnic groups inside North America, to gay men and lesbians, and to women. We addressed this concern in two ways. First, we asked specialists in the supposedly neglected regions, including some of those whose objections had been loudest, to become contributors; and second, editors and contributors alike were urged to keep in mind the need to give full representation to the regions and groups we were alleged to have ignored—a kind of across-the-board raising of consciousness.

Some of the newer contributors discovered that coverage of developing regions had been better than they imagined. The contributors for Africa, for example, found that materials concerning Africa were not confined to their section but were scattered through many sections of the tenth edition and its supplement, and concluded that coverage of the region was better than they had thought. The newer contributors were, however, diligent in recasting their sections and were able to make suggestions concerning titles treating their region that should be included in other sections.

With regard to women, there was discussion at several editorial meetings as to whether materials relating to women should be located in a separate section or should continue to be scattered among other sections by topic. Although contributors recognized the emergence of women's studies as a discipline, they recommended that works about women that were related to a specific topic or discipline (e.g., women scientists) should be classed with the topic or discipline. A discrete subsection relating to women in CC, Sociology, is a legacy from the tenth edition. All contributors have tried to include sources relating to women where such sources are available and their inclusion met *Guide* criteria.

We have also attempted to be careful in choosing terminology to describe non-Western parts of the world, ethnic groups, and women. Throughout this edition—in subject headings in the index, section heads in the text, and the language of annotations—we have tried to use terms that will avoid the stigma of Eurocentrism and give fair representation to groups whose members may have reason, now or in the past, to believe they are being treated dismissively. "Middle East" and "Near East," for example, although both will be found in titles of works cited here, were found to be Eurocentric ("East," "Middle," and "Near" all revealing a European standpoint) and have been dropped in favor of "Asia, West." "Far East" is gone for the same reason. New nations are listed under the names they presently use (e.g., Vanuatu, Sri Lanka, Burkina Fasu), although Burma poses a special political problem the *Guide* cannot resolve, so we have continued its former name. The four principal ethnic groups in the United States are here called African Americans, Asian Americans, Latinos, and Native Americans. Other ethnic groups are identified by their country or region of origin (e.g., Ethiopians, French); if they are submerged in another country or culture, they are given a subject heading that follows the pattern "Armenians (by country or region)—United States." We have tried to use up-to-date anthropological advice in assigning ethnic group names; for example, the groups variously identified as "Gypsies," "Rom," or "Travelers" are given the term "Peripatetics." We have also tried to assign the most specific group name that applies to a given work, even if the group belongs to a larger designation; "Inuit" is used in preference to "Native American" for works that treat only the Inuit. Native American names are used in preference to Anglo-European names: "Siksika" is preferred to "Blackfoot."

In subject headings used to describe women, we have tried to avoid such headings as "Women as artists," preferring "Women artists" and have attempted to be conscientious when using "Women artists" to add a heading for "Artists." Women in specific regions are assigned headings in both the following patterns: "Women (by country or region)—Nigeria" and "Nigeria (by subject)—women." We have also attempted to excise sexist language from the notes and annotations. "His" or "her" pronouns are allowed to stand only when a single sex is clearly referred to; elsewhere, we have tried to avoid the "his/her" awkwardness by recasting the text to plural so that "they" constructions can be substituted. In quoted matter, male pronouns are followed by a "[sic]" notation.

Index

The index, following *Guide* tradition, is in dictionary form. The differentiation of entries by means of typeface that began with the tenth edition supplement continues, with authors (both personal and corporate) printing in roman, titles in italic, and subjects in boldface. The index has entries both for authors and titles in the principal entries, and for authors or titles mentioned in the notes or in the annotations. We found it unnecessary to index every appearance of *Chemical abstracts* or *Oxford English dictionary,* since both are mentioned in passing in a number of entries; similarly, some references are so cursory and refer to sources so well known (e.g., Pollard and Redgrave) that index entries were often omitted. These exceptions are rare, however, and we have exercised great care in picking up index entries for works mentioned in the notes or annotations. The result is a very large index.

Subject entries posed the most difficult problems. Many subjects were assigned by contributors, and the editorial staff added other headings as necessary. To separate heavily posted entries such as "United States," parenthetical qualifiers have been used, in the following order:

Unqualified headings, subdivided by forms of publication:
    United States—bibliography
Headings qualified by country or region:
    Jews (by country or region)—Great Britain
Headings qualified by subject:
    Science (by subject)—history

Used more occasionally are qualifiers "(by language)," "(by occupation or profession)," and "(by period)." The authority used for subjects was an informal file that conflated headings used in the tenth edition and its supplement, to which we added supplementary headings drawn from *Library of Congress subject headings* or, when *LCSH* supplied no satisfactory term, from language suggested by contributors based on terms found in the works being cited. The experience of trying to control subject entries even in a file of limited size such as this one increases our appreciation for the difficulties catalogers routinely encounter.

Production

The records for this edition were derived from four sources: the tenth edition, its supplement, MARC files at the Library of Congress, and direct keyboarding. Because we wanted to create a file that could later be used in electronic access, we chose a fairly straightforward version of the MARC record format, since it is designed for computer manipulation and is widely recognized by the library community and by vendors who prepare electronic versions of bibliographic files. The record format uses MARC tags, and reserves most fields for the data they hold in other MARC versions (100 for personal author, 245 for title, 300 for collation, etc.). Some fields are used for special *Guide* needs and other fields were added to normal MARC format for such items as section heads and cross-references.

Records from the tenth edition supplement were already in a format much like the one developed for the eleventh edition, so these records, about 4,700 in number, could be converted with little difficulty. The 15,500 records for the tenth edition, on the other hand, existed only on paper and in a typesetting tape. Records on this tape were not fielded, hence could not be manipulated or treated individually. Our service bureau (Inforonics, Inc., of Littleton, Mass.) devised a program that converted the typesetting tape to individual records, formatted in the MARC record structure that had been devised for the *Guide.* We also obtained several hundred records, principally for new titles, by enrolling in the Library of Congress' Select-MARC program, which permitted us to use records from LC's machine-readable files. Finally, we keyboarded many records directly to workforms, basing our records largely on copy submitted by contributors.

We used a database management system called Infocat and an editorial system called Blue Sky, both proprietary to Inforonics, Inc. We leased equipment and software from Inforonics, and did all keyboarding in the office of *Choice* magazine in Middletown, Connecticut. At several points during compilation, we made a copy of the file on cassette tape, which we sent by courier to Inforonics. There, a compiler program selected records from the database and put them in order according to section heads, a number generator assigned *Guide* numbers, and an index program generated the index. A page makeup program formatted the data to pages, and proof pages were produced on a laser printer. Final pages were printed ready for the camera on a photocompositor.

The Infocat system manages a random-access database into which records may be entered in any order. All fields necessary for manipulation of records, collation, formatting, and indexing reside in each record. We attempted to keyboard as much information as possible on a record's first pass in order to make later revisions as simple as possible. Contributors submitted entries on paper, usually sending annotations and often supplying catalog copy from a local catalog or from a bibliographic utility. Usually, contributors suggested section heads and subject headings. We reviewed records as received, editing annotations and specifying section heads, added entries, and subject headings.

Contributors reviewed two sets of proof pages, and the first set was reviewed by the referees as well. *Guide* staff reviewed records on a continuing basis, seeing most records several times before final pages were printed.

Acknowledgments

My thanks go first to the contributors to this edition, all of whom were expected to assess their sections from the tenth edition and its supplement, and find which titles needed to be updated. They were also required to decide which titles should be carried forward to this edition, select new titles from works published since 1990, decide which electronic sources deserved inclusion, and find catalog copy for all of them. Beyond all that, they had to write annotations to describe the titles they chose in as much detail but as few words as possible, suggest section heads and subject headings, read and mark proof, and respond to queries from the various editors, conducting much of this labor in semi-isolation in the time permitted by their regular work. Some had unflinching support from their administrations, some had to do *Guide* work entirely on their own time. Either way, the task might well have daunted Heracles, but was carried out with dedication and skill. I am deeply grateful to them for agreeing to contribute to the *Guide* and for their hard, unremitting work. It is a tribute to their forbearance and psychological balance that, after all that has happened, they still consent to speak to me when I call on the telephone.

I owe a similar debt to the referees, who reviewed proof pages under very tight deadlines, wrote detailed reports, and brought their considerable experience to bear on the *Guide* at a time when most sections were incomplete and the contributors could benefit from the referees' advice.

I extend special thanks also to the Project Director, Pat Sabosik, who first arranged for the *Guide* to be edited at the *Choice* offices and handled negotiations with ALA Editions at the American Library Association and with the service bureau during early stages of the project. My thanks go also to her successor, Francine Graf, who managed the project to completion with aplomb and finesse while she was simultaneously learning the complexities of managing a magazine. To the staff of *Choice,* who are no doubt relieved to see this project come at last to an end, I offer a special note of thanks for their support and their willingness to listen patiently to months of complaint. The Executive Director of our parent organization, the Association of College and Research Libraries, Althea Jenkins, was helpful and supportive on a number of occasions. Personnel at ALA Editions have been very helpful during the entire period of compilation, and showed remarkable forbearance in the face of several extensions of the publishing schedule. I mention especially Donald Chatham, Associate Executive Director for Publishing, and David Epstein, Associate Publisher for Production.

The staff at Inforonics, Inc., were uniformly helpful, responded promptly to our distress signals (which included a power failure that caused a head crash, incomplete tape backups at critical moments, and lapsed communications over various system features), and displayed the characteristic that is indispensable in a service bureau—they cared how the book looked. Especially helpful were John Finni, Candy Verhulst, Steve Prowten, Beverly Steiner, Sandra Dennis, Jonathan Bourne (during the project's early stages), and the firm's president, Lawrence Buckland.

Early in this project, I received excellent and highly informed advice on our proposed use of terms to describe ethnic groups from David Levinson of Human Relations Files, Inc., and Sanford Berman of the Hennepin County Library. I have attempted to follow their recommendations, but they should be held blameless for any blunders I may have committed.

It should not be forgotten that the contributors did their work in the context of busy libraries, and the administrations of those libraries have our profound gratitude for their willingness to permit staff to contribute to the *Guide,* for use of their facilities and collections in compilation, and for the support, moral and tangible, they provided. The contributors also would like to express appreciation to the interlibrary loan units of libraries around the country who went to extraordinary lengths to locate materials and were willing to suspend normal lending restrictions to make reference materials available to *Guide* contributors.

This brings me finally to the staff at the *Choice* offices who actually produced the *Guide*. Three data entry personnel showed extraordinary skill and dedication. LaWanda Manzie, with no previous bibliographic experience, learned quickly and added to her fine keyboarding skills the ability to interpret instructions from the editors, becoming adept at the *Guide* format. Cheryl Stauning, a graduate librarian, understood at once the significance of the project and brought experience working with MARC records to bear on the *Guide,* becoming very accomplished and valuable in a short time. Diane Kuhn, who did much of the keyboarding in the early and middle stages of the project and returned near the end to help at a critical juncture in correcting second proofs, performed splendidly during her entire time with us, developing an instinct for quality control and pointing out hundreds of errors the editors had missed or had themselves committed. Murray S. Martin was able to give editorial time during the middle stages of the project at a time when his help was badly needed.

Vee Carrington, who worked with me on the tenth edition supplement, acted as Associate Editor for this edition, doing everything required to bring the book into print—screening records for completeness and correctness, editing annotations, suggesting changes, explaining intricacies of MARC records, reading copy, endlessly loading corrections. Those who have not worked on a large bibliographic project have no concept of the immense amount of sheer donkey work such a project demands—correcting misspellings, checking cross-references, fixing bad header codes, correcting field indicators, finding why diacritics misprint, or why records print entirely in Greek characters or half a record prints in italic. Vee did all this without complaint, worked patiently with data entry staff, made suggestions for improvement too numerous to remember, and kept up everyone's spirits. Not even the admiration and gratitude all of us feel toward her can repay the debt the Association and the profession owe her. Without Vee, there would be no *Guide;* it is as simple as that.

ROBERT BALAY
JUNE 1995

A

General Reference Works

AA

Bibliography

GENERAL WORKS

Guides and manuals

Bowers, Fredson Thayer. Principles of bibliographical description. Princeton, N.J. : Princeton Univ. Pr., 1949. 505 p.
AA1

Repr. : Winchester, U.K. : St. Paul's Bibliographies, 1986.

A full, detailed treatment of analytical bibliography, as applied to the description of books. Covers the principles of describing incunabula, and English and American books from the 16th to the 20th centuries. Most of the principles would be applicable to printing in other countries.   Z1001.B78

Esdaile, Arundell James Kennedy. Esdaile's manual of bibliography. 5th rev. ed. / by Roy Bishop Stokes. Metuchen, N.J. : Scarecrow, 1981. 397 p., [8] p. of plates : ill.   **AA2**

1st ed., 1931; 4th ed., 1967; earlier eds. had title: *A student's manual of bibliography.*

"Designed for the literary student, the student librarian, the embryo book collector."—*p. ix.* Offers chapters, each with a brief bibliography, on the the history and makeup of the book, collation, binding, illustration, etc. Includes a glossary of frequently used terms.
     Z1001.E75

Gaskell, Philip. A new introduction to bibliography. Oxford : Clarendon Pr. ; N.Y. : Oxford Univ. Pr., 1972. 438 p. : ill.
AA3

Repr. with corrections: Oxford : Clarendon Pr., 1985.

Intended as a successor to (but not a mere revision of) R. B. McKerrow, *Introduction to bibliography for literary students* (Oxford : Clarendon Pr., 1927), which remains useful for the period up to about 1800. Offers a survey of the mechanical and technical side of book production during both the hand-press period and the machine-press period to 1950. Covers printing type, composition, paper, imposition, press work, warehouse routines, binding, decoration and illustration, printing machines, patterns of production, processes of reproduction, and the book trade in Britain and America. Attention is given to bibliographical description, format of books, meaning of "edition," "impression," etc., dating of editions, variations in copies, cancels, and similar matters. Appendixes include McKerrow's "Note on Elizabethan handwriting"; specimen bibliographical descriptions; examples of transmission of text; and a bibliography. Detailed index.   Z116.A2G27

Harmon, Robert B. Elements of bibliography : a simplified approach. Rev. ed. Metuchen, N.J. : Scarecrow, 1989. 288 p.
AA4

1st ed., 1981.

A brief guide to the study of bibliography and methods of compilation; combines explanatory text with annotated suggestions for further reading. Name, title, and subject indexes.   Z1001.H29

Krummel, Donald William. Bibliographies : their aims and methods. London ; N.Y. : Mansell, 1984. 192 p.   **AA5**

A work for compilers and students of bibliography, with attention given to both theory and practice, characteristics of bibliographies, and

1

their functions. Bibliographies interspersed throughout the volume, plus a bibliography of "Major writings on the compiling of bibliographies 1883–1983," p. 161–81. Indexed.   Z1001.K86

Malclès, Louise-Noëlle. Manuel de bibliographie. 4e éd. rev. et augm. / par Andrée Lhéritier. Paris : Presses universitaires de France, 1985. 448 p.   **AA6**

1st ed., 1963; 3rd ed., 1976.

An annotated guide to the study and use of bibliographies. It lists selected general and specialized bibliographies and other reference works in all fields, and thus serves as an updated abridgment of the author's *Les sources du travail bibliographique* (AA352) for students and those not needing the larger set. Includes information on the new information technologies. International in scope, with emphasis on French materials. Indexed.   Z1002.M28

Masanov, ÍUriĭ Ivanovich. Teoriĭa i praktika bibliografii : ukazatel' literatury, 1917–1958 / pod red. ... E. I. Shamurina. Moskva : Izd-vo Vsesoiuznoi Knizhnoi Palaty, 1960. 479 p.   **AA7**

At head of title: Ministerstvo kul'tury SSSR. Vsesoĭuznaĭa knizhnaĭa palata.

A comprehensive guide to the literature in Russian published 1917–58 on the theory and practice of bibliography, including history of the book, publishing, library practice, classification and cataloging, and types of bibliographies. An appendix lists reviews of bibliographies.   Z1002.M45

Meze'r, Avgusta Vladimirovna. Slovarnyĭ ukazatel' po knigovedeniĭu. Moskva : Gos. Sotsialn'-ekon, 1931–34. 3 v. **AA8**

1st ed., 1924.

A bibliographical manual and index to the literature, covering such subjects as archive and manuscript lists, bibliographies, dictionaries, reference books, library science, etc. Supplements the 1924 ed. Serves as subject index to many articles related to Russian cultural history.   Z1002.M61

Schneider, Georg. Handbuch der Bibliographie. 4. gänzl. veränd. u. stark verm. Aufl. Leipzig : Hiersemann, 1930. 674 p.   **AA9**

Repr., 1959.

A guide to general bibliography, national bibliography, bibliographies of incunabula, newspapers, society publications, etc. Includes lists of biographical dictionaries. Offers comment and annotations. A basic work, though now out of date.

The first three editions (1923–26) contained an introductory theoretical-historical treatment of bibliography, which has been omitted in the 4th ed. An English translation of this portion of the 3rd ed. is available under the title: *Theory and history of bibliography*, tr. by R. R. Shaw (N.Y. : Columbia Univ. Pr., 1934. 306 p.). The "5. Aufl." (1969) is an unchanged reprint of the 4th ed.   Z1001.S35

Stein, Henri. Manuel de bibliographie générale = Bibliotheca bibliographica nova. Paris : Picard, 1897. 895 p.   **AA10**

Repr. : N.Y. : Kraus, 1962.

Includes universal bibliographies, national and regional bibliographies, subject bibliographies. Appendixes contain: (1) alphabetical list of places having printing presses before the 19th century, arranged by the modern name, with indication of the Latin name of each place, the date of establishment of its press, and references to sources of information; (2) indexes of periodicals; (3) printed catalogs of libraries. The main list and appendixes 2 and 3 were continued by the lists of new bibliographies, indexes, and catalogs given in each number of *Le bibliographe moderne*, 1897–1931, edited by Henri Stein.   Z1002.S81

Stokes, Roy Bishop. A bibliographical companion. Metuchen, N.J. : Scarecrow, 1989. 298 p.   **AA11**

Offers definitions, ranging in length from a paragraph to a page, of standard terms in the field of bibliography; many entries suggest additional sources. Prepared by a noted professor, "it is designed to meet the needs of students who are at an early stage in their bibliographical interests."—*Introd.*   Z1006.S73

Totok, Wilhelm. Handbuch der bibliographischen Nachschlagewerke / [Wilhelm] Totok, [Rolf] Weitzel ; hrsg. von Hans-Jürgen und Dagmar Kernchen. 6., erw., völlig neu bearb. Aufl. Frankfurt am Main : V. Klostermann, 1984–85. 2 v.   **AA12**

1st ed., 1954; 1977 repr. called 5th ed.

Contents: Bd. 1, Allgemeinbibliographien und allgemeine Nachschlagewerke; Bd. 2, Fachbibliographien und fachbezogene Nachschlagewerke.

A selective bibliography of bibliographies, less extensive than Louise-Noëlle Malclès, *Les sources du travail bibliographique* (AA352). Emphasis is on European and American publications. Vol. 1 includes chapters on library catalogs, national bibliographies (a major section, p. 42–175), periodicals, newspapers, book reviews, theses, official publications, incunabula and rare books, societies and organizations, encyclopedias, and biographical dictionaries. Vol. 2 has its own author, title, and subject index.   Z1002.T68

Vitale, Philip H. Bibliography, historical and bibliothecal : a handbook of terms and names. Chicago : Loyola Univ. Pr., [1971]. 251 p.   **AA13**

Intended "to make readily available ... an identification of those terms and persons that relate significantly to the history of writing, printing, and publishing; to the development of libraries and to the systems of classification which govern the storage of written and printed works in them; and to the concepts of theory and practice which make for the most fruitful use of the works themselves."—*Pref.* Terms and personal names are in separate alphabetical sections.   Z1006.V5

Bibliography of bibliography

Besterman, Theodore. A world bibliography of bibliographies : and of bibliographical catalogues, calendars, abstracts, digests, indexes, and the like. 4th ed., rev. and greatly enl. Lausanne : Societas Bibliographica, 1965–66. 5 v. (8425 columns).   **AA14**

1st ed., 1939–40; 2nd ed., 1947–49; 3rd ed., 1965–66.

A classified bibliography of separately published bibliographies of books, manuscripts, and patent abridgments. International in scope.

The index volume lists in one alphabet: (1) authors, editors, translators, etc.; (2) titles of serial and anonymous works; (3) libraries and archives, etc.; (4) patents (under "Patents," lists subjects covered by British patent specifications). "Bibliographies which would appear in the index under the same heading as in the text are excluded, unless they appear in the text under more than one heading."—*Pref.*

Although the 3rd ed. was to have been the final one, this edition records bibliographies published through 1963, with some later additions. It includes some 117,000 items grouped under about 16,000 headings and subheadings. Supplemented in part by AA20, Alice F. Toomey's work of the same title, covering 1964–74.   Z1002.B5685

Bibliographic index : a cumulative bibliography of bibliographies. v. 1 (1938)– . N.Y. : H.W. Wilson, 1938– .   **AA15**

Published in three forms: (1) permanent cumulated volumes, coverage varying; (2) annual volumes to supplement the permanent volumes; (3) current issues published quarterly 1938–June 1951, then semiannually in June and Dec. from Dec. 1951–1969. Beginning 1970, published in April and Aug., with a bound cumulation in Dec.

An alphabetical subject arrangement of separately published bibliographies and bibliographies included in books and periodicals. About 2,600 periodicals, including many in foreign languages, are now examined regularly. An extensive list, useful in itself and as a valuable complement to Theodore Besterman, *A world bibliography of bibliographies* (AA14).   Z1002.B594

Bibliographic services throughout the world. 1er et 2e rapports annuels (1951–52, 1952–53)– . Paris : Unesco, General Information Programme : UNISIST, 1954– . Biennial.   **AA16**

Frequency varies; biennial since volume for 1981–82.

Vol. for 1980 has title: Bibliographical services throughout the world.

The 1950/59 volume ed. by Robert L. Collison is a cumulative report covering materials derived from the volumes published 1951–59. In two main parts: pt. 1, Bibliographical activities in various countries and territories, arranged alphabetically by country and indicating whether or not there is a National Committee of Bibliography, and listing national bibliographies, periodical indexes, current bibliographies of special subjects, etc.; pt. 2, Bibliographical activities of international organizations.

The 1960/64 and 1965/69 volumes comp. by Paul Avicenne provide updated information and follow the general plan of the earlier work except that there is no section on international organizations. An introductory survey of the development of bibliographical services during the period precedes the individual countries section.

The 1960/64 volume first appeared in French (Paris, 1967) under the title: *Les services bibliographiques dans le monde.*

Both the 1970/74 and 1975/79 volumes were ed. by Marcelle Beaudiquez, the first covering 120 countries, the second 121. Those volumes were also published in French; they follow the general plan of the series.

————. *Supplement,* ed. by Marcelle Beaudiquez. Two have appeared: 1980 (publ. 1982); 1983–84 (Unesco, 1987).   Z1008.U55

Bibliographische Berichte. Jahrg. 1 (1959)–30 (1988). Frankfurt a. M. : Klostermann, 1959–88.   **AA17**

Frequency varies: quarterly, 1959–62; semiannual, 1963–69; annual, 1970–88.

Sponsorship varies: "Im Auftrag des Deutschen Bibliographischen Kuratoriums," 1959–69; "Hrsg. von der Staatsbibliothek Preussischer Kulturbesitz," 1970–88.

Vol. 4 and following, title also in English: *Bibliographical bulletin.*

Vols. 1–3 called "Neue Folge der *Bibliographischen Beihefte* zur *Zeit-schrift für Bibliothekswesen und Bibliographie.*"

A classified listing of recent bibliographies—those found in periodicals and books as well as those separately published. Coverage is international with, naturally, a high percentage of German titles; now lists more than 2,000 items per year. "Gesamtregister : Cumulated subject index" covering 1959/63 and 1964/68 publ. 1965–70; no subsequent annual indexes.

An "Ergänzungsband" publ. 1977 is entitled *Geisteswissenschaftliche Fortschrittsberichte : Titelnachweis 1965–1975* (Research progress reports in the humanities : titles registered 1965–1975).

Harvard University. Library. Bibliography and bibliography periodicals. Cambridge : Publ. by the Harvard Univ. Libr. ; distr. by the Harvard Univ. Pr., 1966. 1066 p. (Widener Library shelflist, no. 7).   **AA18**

For a note on the series, *see* AA115.

19,586 titles. The bibliography classification at Widener is similar to Class Z of the Library of Congress scheme and encompasses "works on the science of bibliography, general bibliographies, library catalogues, catalogues of publishers and booksellers, catalogues of manuscripts, the art of writing, the book arts (printing, binding, etc.), publishing and bookselling, the freedom of the press, copyright, library science, and the history of libraries."—*Note on the classification.*
    Z1002.H26

Internationale Personalbibliographie, 1800–1943 / bearb. von Max Arnim. 2. verb. und stark verm. Aufl. Leipzig : Hiersemann, 1944–52. 2 v.   **AA19**

A revised edition of a useful bibliography which was first publ. in 1936, covering the years 1850–1935. This edition has been extended to cover the first half of the 19th century as well as more recent years. It indexes bibliographies contained in books, periodicals, biographical dictionaries, academic annuals, festschriften, etc. In many cases the references lead to biographical as well as to bibliographical information. International in scope with the emphasis on German names. The 1st ed. should be consulted for many names which were dropped from the second for political reasons. Identification in this edition is simplified by the addition of occupations and, frequently, the date of death.

Internationale Personalbibliographie, begr. von Max Arnim, fortgef. von Franz Hodes. 2., völlig neubearb. Aufl. von Bd. III (Berichtszeit 1944–1959) in drei bis zum jeweiligen Erscheinungsjahr ergänzten Bänden III–V (Stuttgart : Hiersemann, 1978–87. 3 v.).

1st ed. of Bd. 3 publ. 1961–63.

Originally published in 19 Lfg. and numbered v. 3–5.

The 2nd ed. of Bd. 3 was originally planned to extend the period of coverage only through 1975, but from an early stage citations gathered up to time of publication of the individual Lieferungen have been included. Also incorporates new references for persons included in Bd. 1–2 of the set, those names being marked with an asterisk. Indexes to the full set are promised.   Z8001.A1I57

Toomey, Alice F. A world bibliography of bibliographies, 1964–1974 : a list of works represented by Library of Congress printed catalog cards : a decennial supplement to Theodore Besterman, A world bibliography of bibliographies. Totowa, N.J. : Rowman and Littlefield, 1977. 2 v. (1166 p.).
    AA20

Compiled as a supplement to the 4th ed. of Besterman (AA14). Limited to separately published bibliographies represented by Library of Congress printed cards, "including, however, some offprints of bibliographies which originally appeared as part of a larger work."—*Note.*
    Z1002.T67

North America

United States

Jones, Helen Gertrude (Dudenbostel). United States of America national bibliographical services and related activities in 1965–1967. Chicago : Reference Services Div., Amer. Libr. Assoc., 1968. 56 p.   **AA21**

"This publication represents a combination of three separate reports—one for each of the three years (1965, 1966, and 1967)—prepared in reply to a United Nations Educational, Scientific and Cultural Organization questionnaire" which is sent "to each country annually in order to keep up to date the information in its *Bibliographical Services Throughout the World* [AA16]."—*Pref.* Offers a guide to a variety of publications and bibliographical services; includes a section on interlibrary cooperation. Supplementary articles by M. J. Gibson (bearing the same title), covering the years 1968/69 and 1970–78, appeared annually in the Winter issue of the periodical *RQ*, 1970–80.   Z1002.J66

Canada

Lochhead, Douglas. Bibliography of Canadian bibliographies. 2nd ed., rev. and enl. [Toronto] : Univ. of Toronto, publ. in assoc. with the Bibliographical Society of Canada, [1972]. 312 p.   **AA22**

1st ed., 1960, comp. by Raymond Tanghe.

This edition lists more than 2,300 bibliographies, each of which has "some Canadian connection, either by subject, compiler, geographical location, etc."—*Introd.* It represents a thorough revision of the earlier edition, incorporating listings from the supplements thereto and new works to mid-1970. Follows an alphabetical author arrangement rather than the earlier classed listing. Index of subjects and compilers. There are some brief annotations in English or French according to the language of the title.   Z1365.A1L6

Mexico

Millares Carlo, Agustín. Ensayo de una bibliografía de bibliografías mexicanas : (la imprenta, el libro, las bibliotecas, etc.) / por Agustín Millares Carlo y José Ignacio Mantecón. México : Biblioteca de la II Feria del Libro y Exposición Nacional del Periodismo, 1943. 224 p.   **AA23**

At head of title: Departamento del Distrito Federal. Dirección de Acción Social. Oficina de Bibliotecas.

1,777 entries, arranged by class. Includes general bibliographies relating to America that have references to Mexico, and bibliographies relating to Mexico, including general, individual, regional, subject, periodicals, etc.   Z1411.A1M5

Latin America

Gropp, Arthur Eric. A bibliography of Latin American bibliographies. Metuchen, N.J. : Scarecrow, 1968. 515 p.   **AA24**

A greatly enlarged and updated version of a work of the same title compiled by Cecil K. Jones, published 1942. Retains about 2,900 items from the earlier work and adds more than 4,000 new references published through 1964. Emphasizes works of a purely bibliographic nature, excluding many of the general works listed by Jones. Arranged by subject field rather than by country as in the Jones work. Detailed index.

Supplemented by:

(1) ———. ———. *Supplement* (1971. 277 p.).

Adds more than 1,400 references from the 1965–69 period.

(2) Daniel Raposo Cordeiro, ed., *A bibliography of Latin American bibliographies : social sciences & humanities* (1979. v. 1 [272 p.]).

"Supplementing the original works by Arthur E. Gropp." —*t.p.*

A cumulation, with additional citations to articles gleaned from some 250 periodicals, of the annual working papers prepared for the Subcommittee on the Bibliography of Latin American Bibliographies of the Seminar on the Acquistion of Latin American Library Materials (SALALM) for the years 1969–74. Covers periodical publications 1966–74; monographs of 1969–74. Author and subject indexes.

(3) *A bibliography of Latin American bibliographies, 1975–1979 : social sciences & humanities*, ed. by Haydée Piedracueva (1982. 313 p.).

"Supplement No. 3 to Arthur E. Gropp's *A bibliography of Latin American bibliographies.*" —*t.p.*

Like the Cordeiro compilation, consolidates entries from the SALALM *Annual report on bibliographic activities* for the period; covers monographic and periodical publications.

(4) *A bibliography of Latin American bibliographies, 1980–1984 : social sciences & humanities*, ed. by Lionel V. Loroña (1987. 223 p.).

"Supplement No. 4 to Arthur E. Gropp's *A bibliography of Latin American bibliographies* —*t.p.*

Consolidates the entries in *Annual report on Latin American and Caribbean bibliographic activities* of the Seminar on the Acquisition of Latin American Library Materials for 1980–82, and its successor which appears in the SALALM *Bibliography and reference series* for 1983–85. Adheres to the format of the earlier volumes.

(5) *A bibliography of Latin American and Caribbean bibliographies, 1985–1989 : social sciences and humanities*, Lionel V. Loroña, ed. (1993. 314 p.).

Consolidates the annual bibliographies in *Bibliography of Latin American and Caribbean bibliographies* (Madison : SALALM Secretariat, Memorial Libr., Univ. of Wisconsin–Madison, 1986–). Expanded 1984–85 to include bibliographies of the Caribbean countries; supplemented by items from *HAPI : Hispanic American periodicals index* (AD296).

——————— A bibliography of Latin American bibliographies published in periodicals. Metuchen, N.J. : Scarecrow, 1976. 2 v. (1031 p.).   **AA25**

A companion to the same author's *Bibliography of Latin American bibliographies* (AA24).

A classed listing of more than 9,700 items, mainly from the period 1929–65, but including some earlier publications. Lists not only articles which are bibliographic in nature, but also articles which have substantial bibliographies appended. Fully indexed.   Z1601.A2G76

South America

Argentina

Geoghegan, Abel Rodolfo. Bibliografía de bibliografías argentinas, 1807–1970. Edición preliminar. Buenos Aires : Casa Pardo, 1970. 130 p.   **AA26**

A classified listing of the principal Argentinian bibliographies of the period. Brief annotations for most entries. No author index.

Z1611.A1G4

Bolivia

Siles Guevara, Juan. Bibliografía de bibliografías bolivianas / Juan Siles Guevara ; con adiciones de José Roberto Arze. La Paz, Bolivia : Universidad Mayor de San Andrés, Centro Nacional de Documentación Científica y Tecnológica, 1983. 52 p. (Serie bibliográfica [Centro Nacional de Documentación Científica y Tecnológica], no. 14).   **AA27**

Essentially two separate books, since it reprints the 1969 volume of the same title by Juan Siles Guevara, and adds an addendum of 154 items compiled by José Roberto Arze. Each section is arranged by subject, but there is a combined author index.   Z1641.A1S53

Brazil

Basseches, Bruno. A bibliography of Brazilian bibliographies = Uma bibliografia das bibliografias brasileiras. Detroit : Blaine Ethridge, c1978. 185 p.   **AA28**

In Portuguese; introductory matter in English and Portuguese.

An author (or other main entry) listing of nearly 2,500 Brazilian bibliographies published as separates, in periodicals, or as parts of books. Includes works published outside Brazil on Brazilian topics. Index of authors and subjects.   Z1671.B37

Colombia

Giraldo Jaramillo, Gabriel. Bibliografía de bibliografías colombianas. 2. ed. corr. y puesta al día por Rubén Pérez Ortiz. Bogotá : Inst. Caro y Cuervo, 1960. 208 p. (Colombia. Instituto Caro y Cuervo. Publicaciones. Serie bibliográfica, 1).   **AA29**

1st ed., 1954.

Lists bibliographies in books and periodicals in classed arrangement with author index.   Z1008.C685 no.1

Peru

Lostaunau Rubio, Gabriel. Fuentes para el estudio del Perú : bibliografía de bibliografías. Lima : [Impr. y Encuadernación Herrera Márquez], 1980. 500 p.   **AA30**

A classified, annotated bibliography of bibliographies relating to Peru, including separately published works and those appearing as periodical articles or parts of books. Index of names.   Z1851.A1L67

Uruguay

Musso Ambrosi, Luis Alberto. Bibliografía de bibliografías uruguayas : con aportes a la historia del periodismo en el Uruguay. Montevideo, 1964. 102 p. **AA31**
Lists bibliographies published in or about Uruguay from all periods of that country's history. Classed arrangement; author index.
Z1881.A1M8

Venezuela

Cardozo, Lubio. Bibliografía de bibliografías sobre la literatura venezolana en las bibliotecas de Madrid, Paris y Londres. Maracaibo : Centro de Estudios Literarios de la Univ. del Zulia [y] Centro de Investigaciones Literarias de la Univ. de Los Andes, 1975. 67 p. **AA32**
An annotated bibliography of about 100 bibliographies.
Z1911.A1C37

Caribbean and Islands of the Western Atlantic

Jordan, Alma. The English-speaking Caribbean : a bibliography of bibliographies / Alma Jordan and Barbara Comissiong. Boston : G.K. Hall, c1984. 411 p. **AA33**
A classified listing of "bibliographies produced up to April 1981 about the lands and peoples of the former British Caribbean territories, both island and mainland."—*Pref.* Includes separately published bibliographies and those appearing as parts of books, periodical articles, in conference proceedings, etc.; many are unpublished or issued in mimeographed form. More than 1,400 entries; many brief annotations. Locates copies. Name and subject indexes. Z1595.J67

Dominican Republic

Florén Lozano, Luis. Bibliografía de la bibliografía dominicana. Ciudad Trujillo : Roques Román, 1948. 66 p. **AA34**
A bibliography of bibliographies in all subjects, both those separately published and those included in books and periodicals.
Z1531.F57

Puerto Rico

Fowlie-Flores, Fay. Annotated bibliography of Puerto Rican bibliographies. N.Y. : Greenwood, 1990. 167 p. (Bibliographies and indexes in ethnic studies, no. 1). **AA35**
For annotation, *see* DB452. Z1551.F69

Europe

Austria

Stock, Karl F. Bibliographie österreichischer Bibliographien, Sammelbiographien und Nachschlagewerke / Karl F. Stock, Rudolf Heilinger, Marylène Stock. Graz : K. F. Stock [Selbstverlag], 1976–1992. Abt.1, bd. 1–9; Abt. 3, bd. 1–7. (In progress). **AA36**

Contents: Abt. 1, Bibliographien der österreichischen Bundesländer. Bd. 1. Burgenland. Bd. 2. Kärnten. Bd. 3. Niederösterreich. Bd. 4. Oberösterreich. Bd. 5. Salzburg; Bd. 6, Steiermark; Bd. 7, Tirol; Bd. 8, Vorarlberg; Bd. 9 (in 4 v.), Wien: Abt. 3, Personalbibliographien österreichischer Persönlichkeiten, Bd. 1–7, A–Horm.
A major undertaking that attempts to list all bibliographies relating to Austria—those separately published as well as ones appearing in books, dissertations, and articles. Abt. 1 covers geographic areas, Abt. 3 individuals. Abt. 2 will list bibliographies on Austria in general. Each volume has its own index. Z2101.A1S86

Bulgaria

Bibliografiiã na bŭlgarskata bibliografiiã. 1963– . Sofiia : Narodna Biblioteka "Kiril i Metodii", 1964– . Annual. **AA37**
Beginning with the issue for 1973 (publ. 1974) constitutes series 8 of the Bulgarian national bibliography (*Natsionalna bibliografiiã na NR Bulgariiã*, AA589).
A classed listing with author index. Includes bibliographies published in periodicals as well as in book form; relevant items published outside Bulgaria are also listed. Z2891.A1B8

Bibliografiiã na bŭlgarskata bibliografiiã, 1852–1944 / [Sustaviteli Khristo Trenkov ... et al.]. Sofiiã : Narodna Biblioteka "Kiril i Metodii", 1981. 311 p. **AA38**
A classed bibliography of nearly 2,600 items. Indexed.
This work's chronological successor is Zornitsa Malcheva Petkova, *Bibliografiiã na bŭlgarskata bibliografiiã, 1944–1969* (AA39). Z2891.A1B52

Petkova, Zornitsa Malcheva. Bibliografiiã na bŭlgarskata bibliografiiã, 1944–1969. Sofiia : Narodna Biblioteka "Kiril i Metodii", 1971. 603 p. **AA39**
Although published earlier, this serves as the chronological successor to *Bibliografiiã na bŭlgarskata bibliografiiã, 1852–1944* (AA38). Classed arrangement of more than 1,500 items. Indexed.
Z2891.A1P4

Denmark

Munch-Petersen, Erland. A guide to Danish bibliography / comp. by Erland Munch-Petersen ; assisted by Frederic J. Mosher. Copenhagen : Royal School of Librarianship, 1965. 140 p. **AA40**
An annotated bibliography of general and subject bibliographies of Danish publications and works relating to Danish topics. Arranged by broad Universal Decimal Classification with author index. Annotations are in English. Z2561.A1M8

Finland

Grönroos, Henrik. Finlands bibliografiska litteratur : kommenterad förteckning. Ekenäs : Ekenäs Tryckeri, 1975. 388 p. **AA41**
An annotated bibliography of Finnish bibliographies, both those published in Finland and works published abroad which include sections on Finland. In four main sections: (1) general bibliographies; (2) Finland in foreign literature and foreign countries in Finnish literature; (3) subject bibliographies; (4) author bibliographies. Indexed.

Germany

Bibliographie der Bibliographien. Jahrg. 7, Heft 1 (Jan. 1972)– . Frankfurt am Main : Deutsche Bibliothek, 1971– . Annual. **AA42**

Publisher varies: 1972–90, Leipzig : Deutsche Bücherei.

Frequency varies: 1972–90, monthly.

Numeric designation dropped after Jahrg. 25, Heft 12 (Dez. 1990).

Also referred to as: *BB*. Continues *Bibliographie der deutschen Bibliographien* (AA44).

An annual listing of separately published bibliographies, as well as those appearing in books and journals, primarily covering German publications, although other languages are included. Classed arrangement with author index.

Bibliographie der deutschen Bibliographien : Jahresverzeichnis der selbständig erschienenen und der in deutschsprachigen Büchern und Zeitschriften enthaltenen versteckten Bibliographien / bearb. von der Deutschen Bücherei. Jahrg. 1 (1954)–12 (1965). Leipzig : Verlag für Buch- und Bibliothekswesen, 1957–69. Annual.　　**AA43**

Continues *Bibliographie der versteckten Bibliographien* (AA45).

An annual listing that includes separately published bibliographies as well as those in periodicals and books.

A similar series was published as a monthly, 1966–71 (AA44). Continued by: *Bibliographie der Bibliographien* (AA42).　Z1002.B58

Bibliographie der deutschen Bibliographien : monatliches Verzeichnis …. Jahrg. 1–6. Leipzig : Verlag für Buch- und Bibliothekswesen, 1966–71. Monthly.　　**AA44**

Superseded *Bulletin wichtiger Literatur-Zusammenstellungen*.

A similar series with the same title was published annually, 1957–69 (AA43).

Continued by *Bibliographie der Bibliographien* (AA42).

Z2221.A1B5

Deutsche Bücherei (Germany). Bibliographie der versteckten Bibliographien : aus deutschsprachigen Büchern und Zeitschriften der Jahre 1930–1953. Leipzig : Verlag für Buch- und Bibliothekswesen, 1956. 371 p. (Sonderbibliographien der Deutschen Bücherei, 3).　　**AA45**

Repr.: Leipzig : Zentralantiquariat der Deutschen Demokratischen Republik, 1983.

Lists bibliographies published 1930–53, as parts of books or in periodicals. Aims to be comprehensive in listing bibliographies consisting of 60 titles or more. Arrangement is alphabetical by subject, with a classified index of subject headings.

Continued by *Bibliographie der deutschen Bibliographien* (AA43).　　Z1002.L42

Widmann, Hans. Bibliographien zum deutschen Schrifttum der Jahre 1939–1950. Tübingen : Niemeyer, 1951. 284 p.

AA46

Because of the breakdown of the well-organized bibliographical system of Germany due to war, this bibliography attempts to list bibliographies of the period dealing with German publications and includes: international bibliographies; bibliographies of books published in Germany; bibliographies of translations into German; regional and personal bibliographies; and bibliographies arranged by subject field.

Greece (Modern)

Phousaras, G. I. Bibliographia tōn Hellēnikōn bibliographiōn, 1791–1947. Athēna : Bibliopōleion tēs "Hestias", 1961. 284 p.

AA47

A classified listing of modern Greek bibliographies—1,614 numbered entries. Indexes by name, subject, date, and place.

Z2281.A1P48

Hungary

A magyar bibliográfiák bibliográfiája. 1956/57– . Budapest : Országos Széchényi Könyvtár, 1960– . Irregular.

AA48

Added title page in Latin: Bibliographia bibliographiarum hungaricarum.

A detailed listing of bibliographies published in Hungary, including those in books, periodicals, yearbooks, etc., as well as separately published ones. Arranged by Universal Decimal Classification with index of names and subjects.　　Z1002.M25

Ireland

Eager, Alan R. A guide to Irish bibliographical material : a bibliography of Irish bibliographies and sources of information. 2nd rev. and enl. ed. London : Libr. Assoc. ; Westport, Conn. : Greenwood, 1980. 502 p.　　**AA49**

1st ed., 1964.

A bibliography of bibliographies (including periodical articles and parts of books as well as separately published works) which "aims to serve as a quick reference guide to all who are interested in Irish studies and research work."—*Introd.* Classed arrangement with author and subject indexes. More than 9,500 items in this edition.　　Z2031.E16

Italy

Bosco, Giovanna. Bibliografia di bibliografie : edizioni italiane del XVI secolo / a dura di Giovanna Bosco e Alessandra Pesante. Pisa : Scuola Normale Superiore, 1988. 105 p. : ill. (Mnemosyne, ricerche sull'arte della memoria, 1).　　**AA50**

An annotated listing by broad subject of 177 bibliographies of early Italian books. Author index.　　Z155.3.B5

Fumagalli, Giuseppe. La bibliografia. Roma : Fondazione Leonardo, 1923. lxxxix, 169 p.　　**AA51**

Pages i–lxxxix contain a survey of Italian bibliography and bibliographers. The rest of the work is a classified bibliography of bibliographies in all fields with an author index. It includes a selection of titles from *Bibliotheca bibliographica italica*, by Fumagalli and Giuseppi Ottino (AA54) and additional works published from 1901 to 1923.

Z2341.A1F9

Istituto nazionale per le relazioni culturali con l'estero. La bibliografia italiana / a cura di Giannetto Avanzi. 2. ed. interamente rifatta con 3 appendici e una aggiunta. Roma, 1946. 570 p.　　**AA52**

Half title: Guida sistematica e analitica degli scritti principali di bibliologia, bibliografia, biblioteconomia pubblicati in Italia dal 1921 al 1946.

The 2nd ed. of *La bibliografia italiana*, a volume in the "Bibliografie del ventennio" series (AA53).

A work of first importance for the record of Italian bibliography. Covers history of the book; general, national, regional, and personal bibliography; libraries, graphic arts, etc.　　Z1002.I8

――――――――― Bibliografie del ventennio. Roma, 1941. 14 v.

AA53

A series of separately published bibliographies listing works published in Italy, 1922–41. Volumes cover: Archeologia, arti figurative, musica. 498 p.; La bibliografia italiana. 248 p. (*see* AA52 for revised edition); Filologia classica e romanza. 152 p.; Geografia e viaggi. 194 p.; Letteratura italiana. 238 p.; Letterature straniere. 455 p.; Medicina. 165 p.; Mussolini e il fascismo. 81 p.; Scienze economiche e sociali. 167 p.; Scienze fisiche, matematiche ed agrarie. 211 p.; Scienze naturali. 101 p.; Scienze religiose, filosofia, pedagogia. 173 p.; Studi storici militari, etnografia popolare. 214 p.; Il pensiero giuridico italiano. 5 v.

Ottino, Giuseppe. Bibliotheca bibliographica italica : catalogo degli scritti di bibliologia, bibliografia e biblioteconomia pub. in Italia e di quelli risguardanti l'Italia pub. all'estero / comp. da G. Ottino... e G. Fumagalli.... Roma : Pasqualucci, 1889 ; Torino : Clausen, 1895–1902. 2 v. and 4 suppl.   **AA54**

Repr., with supplements: Graz : Akademische Druck- u. Berlangsantalt, 1957.

Basic volumes, 6,450 entries; supplements—for 1895, 1896, 1896–99, 1900—entries no. 6451–8259.

Supplements 1 and 2 by Ottino; supplements 3 and 4 by Emilio Calvi.

The basic bibliography of Italian bibliographies, in classified order, covering: history of the book and printing; general, regional, local, personal bibliography; bibliographies of subjects; libraries and library economy.

Continued by Fumagalli's *La bibliografia* (AA51).

Z2341.A1O8

Luxembourg

Hury, Carlo. Luxemburgensia : eine Bibliographie der Bibliographien. 2., erw., völlig neue bearb. Aufl. München : K.G. Saur, 1978. 352 p.   **AA55**

1st ed., 1964.

A classed, annotated bibliography of bibliographies relating to Luxembourg. Nearly 700 items (books, parts of books, periodical articles). Indexed.

Netherlands

Library of Congress. Netherlands Studies Unit. A guide to Dutch bibliographies / prep. by Bertus H. Wabeke. Wash. : [Library of Congress], 1951. 193 p.   **AA56**

At head of title: Library of Congress, Reference Dept., General Reference and Bibliography Division.

Contents: pt. 1, Comprehensive bibliographies: general, Netherlands, overseas territories; pt. 2, Subject bibliographies; pt. 3, Other bibliographies: academic dissertations, government publications, pamphlets, periodical press, personal bibliographies.

Lists more than 750 bibliographies. If copies are not available in the Library of Congress, an effort has been made to locate at least one copy of every item in a library in the U.S.   Z2416.U6

Poland

Bibliografia bibliografii i nauki o ksiazce = Bibliographia Poloniae bibliographica. 1937/44–1980. Warszawa : Biblioteka Narodowa, Inst. Bibliograficzny, 1947–88.   **AA57**

Frequency varies.

A classified bibliography of Polish bibliographies in the fields of bookmaking, librarianship, documentation, etc., including monographs and periodical articles.

§ Continued in part by: *Bibliografia bibliografii polskich* (1981– . Warszawa : Biblioteka Narodowa, Instytut Bibliograficzny, 1988– . Annual). A classified bibliography of bibliographies, including monographs and periodical articles, published in Poland. Bibliographies published abroad dealing with Polish topics are also included.

Bibliographies in librarianship are now treated in: *Polska bibliografia bibliologiczna* (Warszawa : Biblioteka Narodowa, Instytut Bibliograficzny, 1988–).   Z2521.B54

Czachowska, Jadwiga. Przewodnik polonisty : bibliografie, słowniki, biblioteki, muzea literackie / Jadwiga Czachowska, Roman Loth. Wyd. 3., zmienione i uzup. Wrocław : Zakład Narodowy im. Ossolińskich, 1989. 850 p.   **AA58**

1st ed., 1974.

An extensive guide to Polish dictionaries, general bibliographies, and bibliographies of Polish literature and other fields, plus sections on libraries and museums. Classed arrangement with author and subject indexes.   Z2528.P5C95

Hahn, Wiktor. Bibliografia bibliografij polskich do 1950 roku. Wyd. 3 / uzupelnil Henryk Sawoniak. Wroclaw : Zaklad Narodowy im. Ossolińskich, 1966. 586 p.   **AA59**

1st ed., 1921; 2nd ed., 1956.

More than 7,500 bibliographic works published through 1950 are listed. Item numbers from the previous edition are retained, with added items given letter suffixes. Classed arrangement, with author and title indexes.   Z2521.A1H3

Sawoniak, Henryk. Bibliografia bibliografii polskich, 1951–1960. Wrocław : Zakład Narodowy im Ossolińskich, 1967. 483 p.   **AA60**

Added title page and introductory notes in English and Russian.

Extends the period of coverage of Wiktor Hahn's *Bibliografia bibliografij polskich* (AA59). Nearly 5,800 items in classed arrangement; author and subject indexes.

Continued by: *Bibliografia bibliografii polskich, 1961–1970*, by Maria B. Bienkowa and Barbara Eychlerowa (Warszawa : BN, 1992. 1440 p.).

Added title page and preface in English.

A list by broad subject of some 9,000 bibliographies produced in Poland or about Polish topics. Author and subject indexes.

Z2521.A1S3

Russia

Bibliografiia sovetskoĭ bibliografii. 1939, 1946– . Moskva : [Vsesoiuznaia Knizhnaia Palata] , 1941– . Annual.   **AA61**

Suspended 1940–45.

A section of the Soviet national bibliography comprising a classified annual index to bibliographies published separately or as parts of books or articles.

Gosudarstvennaia biblioteka SSSR imeni V.I. Lenina. Svodnyi ukazatel' bibliograficheskikh spiskov i kartotek, sostavlennykh bibliotekami Sovetskogo Soiuza. Obshchestvennye nauki. Khudozhestvennaia literatura / Iskusstvo. 1960–1973. Moskva : Izdatelstvo Kniga, 1961–74.   **AA62**

An annual subject cumulation of the information in *Informatsionnyi ukazatel' bibliograficheskikh spiskov i kartotek, sostavlennykh bibliotekami Sovetskogo Soiuza* (AA64). Ceased publication.   Z2491.A1M625

Gosudarstvennaia publichnaia biblioteka imeni M.E. Saltykova-Shchedrina. Obshchie bibliografi russkikh knig grazhdanskoĭ pechati, 1708–1955 : annotirovannyĭ ukazatel'. Izd. 2., perer. i dop. / pod. red. ... P. N. Berkova. Leningrad, 1956. 283 p. : ports., facsims., table.   **AA63**

Repr.: Cleveland : Bell and Howell, 1963.

At head of title: M. V. Sokurova.

1st ed., 1944.

A definitive guide to general bibliographies of Russian books. Gives full description, notes on authors and editors, and citations to pertinent literature and critical reviews. Includes an extensive list of sources, a name index, and chronological chart. The introductory essay on bibliography is by the general editor, P. N. Berkova.

Z2491.A1L43

Informatsionnyĭ ukazatel' bibliograficheskikh spiskov i kartotek, sostavlennykh bibliotekami Sovetskogo Soiuza. no. 1–23. Moskva : [Gosudarstvennaia biblioteka SSSR imeni V. I. Lenina], 1957–73. Monthly (frequency varies).   **AA64**

Continues *Vazhneishie bibliograficheskie raboty bibliotek*, issued 1943–48. Ceased publication.

Provides classified lists of currently published bibliographies and card indexes in various fields.

Issued in microfilm, 1989.

Cumulated as: *Svodnyi ukazatel' bibliograficheskikh spiskov i kartotek* (AA62). Z2491.A1M63

Kirpicheva, Iraida Konstantinova. Bibliografiĭa v pomoshch' nauchnoĭ rabote : metodicheskoe i spravochnoe posobie / pod red. i so vstup. stateĭ P. N. Verkova. Leningrad, 1958. 480 p. **AA65**

At head of title: Ministerstvo kul'tury RSFSR. Gosudarstvennaĭa publichnaĭa biblioteka imeni M. E. Saltykova-Shchedrina.

A guide and manual to Russian bibliographies, including a section on bibliographical technique followed by sections on general and subject bibliography.

§ An abridgment appeared in German translation as: *Handbuch der russischen und sowjetischen Bibliographien* (Leipzig : Verlag für Buch– und Bibliothekswesen, 1962. 225 p. [Bibliothekswissenschaftliche Arbeiten aus der Sowjetunion und den Ländern der Volksdemokratie in deutscher Übersetzung. Reihe B, Bd. 5]). Z1001.K6

Zdobnov, Nikolai Vasilevich. Istoriĭa russkoĭ bibliografii nachala XX veka. Izd. 3. Moskva : Gos. izd-vo kulturno-prosvetitelnoi lit-ry, 1955. 607 p. **AA66**

1st ed., 1944–47.

A history of Russian bibliography of the early 20th century. Includes bibliographical footnotes. Indexed.

§ Continued by: Mariĭa Vasil'evna Mashkova, *Istoriĭa russkoĭ bibliografii nachala XX veka : do oktĭabria 1917 goda* (Moscow : Kniga, 1969. 492 p.). Z2492.5.M36

Spain

Foulché-Delbosc, Raymond. Manuel de l'hispanisant / Raymond Foulché-Delbosc, Louis Barrau-Dihigo. N.Y. : Putnam, 1920–25. 2 v. **AA67**

For annotation, *see* AA801. Z2681.A1F7

Turkey

Başbuğoğlu, Filiz. 1928–1965 [i.e., Bin dokuz yüz yirmi sekiz, bin dokuz yüz altmışbeş] yılları arasında Türkiyede basılmış bibliyografyaların bibliyografyası / Hazırlıyanlar: Filiz Başbuğoğlu, Lâmia Acar [ve] Necdet Ok. Ankara : Ayyıldız Matbaası, 1966. 270 p. **AA68**

A classified, annotated bibliography of Turkish bibliographies. Nearly 500 items. Indexed. Z2831.A1B3

Yugoslavia

Savez društava bibliotekara FNRJ. Bibliografija jugoslovenskih bibliografija, 1945–55. Beograd : Bibliografski Inst. FNRJ, 1958. 270 p. **AA69**

Bibliographies on all subjects published in Yugoslavia, in classified arrangement with author and subject indexes. Entries are in Latin characters, with the indication "ćiril" if the work cited is in the Cyrillic alphabet.

A second volume, publ. 1975, covers 1956–1960 (295 p.). Z1002.B5688

Africa

Besterman, Theodore. A world bibliography of African bibliographies / by Theodore Besterman ; rev. and brought up to date by J. D. Pearson. Totowa, N.J. : Rowman and Littlefield, 1975. 241 col. **AA70**

Includes the entries for the various African subjects as found in the 4th ed. of Besterman's *World bibliography of bibliographies* (AA14), plus additional works published through 1972. Arranged by geographical division, with subdivisions by region and subject as pertinent. Indexed. Z3501.A1B47

Ethiopia

Girma Makonnen. A bibliography of Ethiopian bibliographies, 1932–1972. Addis Ababa : Addis Ababa Univ., Univ. Libraries, 1976. 53 p. (Ethiopian bibliographic series. Series minor, 2). **AA71**

A classed list with author index. Includes bibliographies appended to books and periodical articles as well as separately published works. 395 items. Z3521.A1G57

South Africa

Musiker, Reuben. South African bibliography : a survey of bibliographies and bibliographical work. 2nd ed. Cape Town : David Philip, 1980. 84 p. **AA72**

1st ed., 1970; suppls. 1975 and 1977.

Intended as a companion to Musiker's *South Africa* (note, AA353) which lists South African reference books. A discursive treatment of South African bibliographical activity, including "national and subject bibliographies, as well as lists of periodicals, newspapers, theses, official publications and manuscripts."—*Pref.* A main entry listing of the 585 items mentioned in the text gives the full bibliographic information. Most of the items are South African publications. Subject index. Z3601.A1M9

Asia

Besterman, Theodore. A world bibliography of Oriental bibliographies / by Theodore Besterman ; rev. and brought up to date by J. D. Pearson. Totowa, N.J. : Rowman and Littlefield, 1975. 727 columns. **AA73**

"Includes volumes cited in the 4th ed. of the author's *A world bibliography of bibliographies* [AA14], first published 1965–1966, plus additional volumes published down to 1973."—*verso of t. p.*

Lists some 11,000 separately published bibliographies arranged by area, then by topic. Title index. Z3001.A1B47

China

Tsien, Tsuen-Hsuin. China : an annotated bibliography of bibliographies / comp. by Tsuen-Hsuin Tsien, in collaboration with James K. M. Cheng. Boston : G.K. Hall, c1978. 604 p. **AA74**

Title also in Chinese: *Chung-kuo shu mu chien t'i hui pien.*

Lists "a selection of over 2500 bibliographies concerning China, mainly in English, Chinese, and Japanese, with some in French, German, Russian, and other European languages."—*Introd.* Includes separate publications, bibliographies in periodicals and monographs, surveys of the literature of specific fields, etc. In two sections, each with numerous subdivisions: (1) General and special bibliographies; (2) Subject bibliographies (e.g., classics and philosophy, religion, history, geography, literature, etc.). Author, title, and subject indexes. Z3106.T87

India

Kalia, D. R. A bibliography of bibliographies on India / D. R. Kalia, M. K. Jain. Delhi : Concept Publ. Co., 1975. 204 p. **AA75**

A bibliography of bibliographies arranged alphabetically by subject. 1,243 entries; index of authors and subjects. Numerous brief annotations. Z3201.A1K34

Kochukoshy, K. K. A bibliography of Indian bibliographies, 1961–1980. [Calcutta], India : Central Reference Library, Govt. of India, Dept. of Culture, 1985. 146 p. **AA76**

A listing by broad Dewey decimal classes of some 655 English-language bibliographies, with author/title and subject indexes. Based mainly on entries in *Indian national bibliography* (AA900), 1961–80. Z3201.A1K63

Indonesia

Filer, Colin. A bibliography of Melanesian bibliographies / Colin Filer and Papiya Chakravarti. University, NCD, Papua New Guinea : Univ. of Papua New Guinea, Dept. of Anthropology and Sociology, [1990]. 42 p. (University of Papua New Guinea, Department of Anthropology and Sociology. Occasional paper, 5). **AA77**

Includes the Indonesian province of Irian Jaya, as well as Papua New Guinea, the Solomon Islands, and Fiji. Lists separately published bibliographies in the fields of (1) National and regional bibliographies, (2) Culture and physical environment, and (3) Colonialism, independence, and development. Z4501.F54

Kemp, Herman C. Annotated bibliography of bibliographies on Indonesia. Leiden, Netherlands : KITLV Pr., 1990. 433 p. **AA78**

Based on the holdings of the Koninklijk Instituut vor Tal, Land, en Volkenkunde in Leiden, this well-documented bibliography lists 1,649 separately published bibliographies. It is divided into (1) General bibliographies, (2) Regional bibliographies, and (3) Subject bibliographies. The subject arrangement is primarily by academic discipline although some sections treat format (government publications, theses, etc.). Descriptive annotations. Author and subject indexes. Z3271.A1K46

Tairas, J. N. B. Indonesia : a bibliography of bibliographies = Daftar karya bibliografi Indonesia. N.Y. : Oleander Pr., c1975. 123 p. **AA79**

A revised edition of: *Daftar karya bibliografi Indonesia* publ. in Jakarta, 1973.

Foreword and subject headings in English and Indonesian.

A classified listing of 661 items. Includes: (1) all types of bibliographical works published in Indonesia; (2) bibliographies dealing wholly or partly with Indonesia, published outside Indonesia; (3) important bibliographical listings published as parts of books. Brief descriptive notes in English. Author-title-subject index. Z3271.A1T313

Iran

Tasbīḥī, Ghulām Ḥusayn. Nigarishī jāmiʿ bar jahān-i kitābshināsī hā-yi Īrān. Chāp-i 1. Tabrīz : Intishārāt-i Nīmā, 1365 [i.e., 1986]. 306 p. **AA80**

Title on added title page: *A comprehensive survey of Persian bibliographies in the world.*

A listing of bibliographies on all subjects published in Persian or about Iran appearing as books or journal articles. Arranged by subject; lacks an index.

Japan

Amano, Keitaro. Nihon shoshi no shoshi. Tokyo : Gannandō Shoten, 1973–84. v. 1–4. (In progress?). **AA81**

Added t. p.: *A Japan bibliography of bibliographies.*

Contents: v. 1, Generalia; v. 2–3, Subject bibliographies; v. 4, Personal bibliographies, index. Z1002.A455

Philippines

Bernardo, Gabriel Adriano. Bibliography of Philippine bibliographies, 1593–1961 / ed. by Natividad P. Verzosa. Quezon City : Ateneo Univ. Pr., 1968. 192 p. (Ateneo de Manila University. Dept. of History. Bibliographical ser., 2). **AA82**

A chronologically arranged bibliography of bibliographies, library and sales catalogs, and books and pamphlets containing bibliographical information on the Philippines. Many annotations; index.

Continued by: Lily O. Orbase, *Bibliography of Philippine bibliographies, 1962–1985*, comp. by Lily O. Orbase and Yolanda E. Jacinto (Manila : Bibliography Div., National Library, 1987. 128 p.).

Follows the arrangement of Bernardo's volume, but has no annotations. Author, title, subject, and series index. Z3291.A1B45

Thailand

Hart, Don Vorhis. Thailand : an annotated bibliography of bibliographies. [De Kalb] : Northern Illinois Univ., Center for Southeast Asian Studies ; Detroit : distr. by Cellar Book Shop, 1977. 100 p. (Northern Illinois University; Center for Southeast Asian Studies. Occasional paper, no. 5). **AA83**

Cites 205 bibliographies relating specifically to Thailand and more than ten pages in length. Arranged alphabetically by author or issuing body, with subject index. Annotations indicate number of entries, arrangement, kinds of indexes, languages of works cited, special features. DS563.5

Australia and Oceania

Australia

Borchardt, D. H. Australian bibliography : a guide to printed sources of information. [3rd ed.]. Rushcutter's Bay, N.S.W. : Pergamon Pr., 1976. 270 p. : ill. **AA84**

1st ed., 1963; 2nd ed., 1966.

A bibliographic survey of printed sources intended for serious students, much enlarged in this edition. Includes chapters on libraries and library catalogs, encyclopedias and general reference works, general bibliographies, subject bibliographies, sources of biographical information, and government publications. Indexed. Z4011.B65

Commonwealth National Library (Canberra). Australian Bibliographical Centre. Australian bibliography and bibliographical services. Canberra : Australian Advisory Council on Bibliographical Services, 1960. 219 p. **AA85**

Subject arrangement with author index. Lists "catalogues and bibliographies in the usual sense, indexes, abstracts, digests, union lists and catalogues, booksellers' lists, calendars of archives and manuscripts, and services designed for bibliographical ends."—*Pref.* Indicates location of copies in Australian libraries. Z4039.C3

New Zealand

Guide to New Zealand information sources. [Palmerston North] : Massey Univ., 1975–82. 7 v. (Massey University library ser., no.8, 10–11, 13–17).   **AA86**

Contents: v.1, Plants and animals (1975); v.2a, Farming, field and horticultural crops (1977); v.2b, Livestock farming, fisheries and forestry (1979); v.3, Education (1978); v.4, Religion (1980); v.5, Official publications (1980); v.6, History (1982); v. 7, Geography (1982).

Undertaken as an effort to compile a new work to replace John Harris' *Guide to New Zealand reference material* (1947; suppls. 1951 and 1957), the decision was later made to publish subject lists a section at a time. Listings are confined to monographic works except when the major source of information for a particular topic is a periodical article. Works included range from the introductory level to the specialized. Annotations are usually evaluative and indicate the level of scholarship.   Z4101.B37

New Zealand Library Association. A bibliography of New Zealand bibliographies. Prelim. ed. Wellington, 1967. 58 p.   **AA87**

A combination of previous annual lists. Limited to those bibliographies "concerned with aspects of New Zealand—its history, government and literature, its economic, industrial and scientific activities."—*Pref.* Index of names.   Z4101.A1N4

UNIVERSAL

Bibliography

Brunet, Jacques Charles. Manuel du libraire et de l'amateur de livres. 5. éd. originale entièrement refondue et augm. d'un tiers. Paris : Didot, 1860–80. 9 v. : ill.   **AA88**

Facsimile reprint: Berlin : Altmann, 1921–22 (6 v.); Paris : Dorbon-Aîní, 1928 (6 v.); Copenhagen : Rosenkilde & Bagger, 1966–67 (9 v.).

Contents: v. 1–5, Author and title list, A–Z; v. 6, Subject index; v. 7–8, Supplement, by P. Deschamps and G. Brunet, Author and title list, with subject index in v. 8; v. 9, Dictionnaire de géographie ancienne et moderne à l'usage du libraire et de l'amateur de livres, par P. Deschamps, 1870.

Brunet's *Manuel* is a general bibliography of rare, important, or noteworthy books not limited to those of any one period or language but especially strong for French and Latin titles and for publications before the 19th century. For each book listed it gives author, full title, place, publisher, date, size, number of volumes, but not generally paging, and, in the case of rare books, bibliographical and critical notes with mention of copies and prices at famous sales, and occasional facsimiles of title pages, printers' marks, etc. The arrangement of the main work (v. 1–5) is alphabetical by author and anonymous title, and there are two subject indexes: one in v. 6 to the main work and one in v. 8 to the supplement. Footnotes throughout v. 1–5 refer to titles omitted from the main author list but included in the subject volume (v. 6).

§ Covers much the same ground as Johann Georg Theodor Grässe's *Trésor de livres rares et précieux* (Dresden : Kuntze, 1859–69. 7 v. Repr. Geneva : Slatkine, 1993) but in general contains a larger portion of French books while Grässe lists more German titles. The two books must often be used together as each lists titles not given in the other.   Z1011.B9M5

Bulletin of bibliography. v.1 (1897)– . Boston : Faxon, 1897– . Quarterly.   **AA89**

Title varies: Apr. 1907–Jan. 1912, *Bulletin of bibliography and magazine subject-index*; Apr. 1912–May/Aug. 1953, *Bulletin of bibliography and dramatic index*; May/Aug. 1956–Oct./Dec. 1978, *Bulletin of bibliography & magazine notes*. Frequency has varied.

Originally devoted to brief bibliographical notes and announcements, reading lists on various topics, and brief bibliographies of interest to librarians, the publication later encompassed indexing features and eventually came to emphasize bibliographies of considerable length on topics in the humanities, social sciences and fine arts; bibliographies of literary figures tended to predominate at various periods. A section of "Births and deaths in the periodical world" (later called "Births, deaths, and magazine notes") quickly became a regular feature and continued through 1978.

A cumulative index to v. 1–32 (1897–1975), comp. by Eleanor C. Jones and Margaret L. Pollard, was published in 1977.   Z1007.B94

Checklist of bibliographies appearing in the Bulletin of bibliography 1897–1987 / ed. by Naomi Caldwell-Wood and Patrick W. Wood. Westport, Conn. : Meckler, c1989. 144 p.   **AA90**

"Covers articles, bibliographies, and selected book reviews as well as editorials of historical or continuing interest."—*Pref.*

Z1007.B94C45

Enciclopedia de orientación bibliográfica / Director: Tomás Zamarriego. Barcelona : J. Flors, 1963–65. 4 v.   **AA91**

Contents: v. 1, Introducción general; Ciencias religiosas; v. 2, Ciencias religiosas (continuación); Ciencias humanas; v. 3, Ciencias humanas (continuación); v. 4, Ciencias humanas (continuación); Ciencias de la materia y de la vida; Apéndice; Índices.

An annotated subject bibliography with author index; intended as a guide to the best material in all fields. International in scope, but with a heavy concentration of Spanish-language materials and an emphasis on the humanities and religion in particular.   Z1035.7.E5

Georgi, Theophilus. Allgemeines europäisches Bücher-Lexicon. Leipzig, 1742–53. 5 v. in 2.   **AA92**

Subtitle: In welchem nach Ordnung des Dictionarii die allgemeinen autores oder Gattungen von Büchern zu finden, welche ... noch ver dem Anfange des XVI. Seculi bis 1739 inclusive ... in dem europäischen Theile der Welt, sonderlich aber in Teutschland, sind geschrieben und gedruckt worden.

Vol. 5 has title: *Allgemeinen europäischen Bücher-Lexici fünfter Theil, in welchem die frantzösischen auctores und bücher ... so von dem XVI. Seculo an bis auf gegenwärtige Zeit geschrieben und gedrucket worden sind.*   Z1012.G35

Krieg, Michael O. Mehr nicht erschienen : ein Verzeichnis unvollendet gebliebener Druckwerke. Bad Bocklet, Wien : Walter Krieg Verlag, 1954–58. 2 v. (Bibliotheca bibliographica, Bd.II, 1.–2. Teil).   **AA93**

A bibliography of works supposed to have been published in several volumes which have never been completed. In the main, the listings are for European publications from the beginning of printing to the early 1930s with emphasis on German works, but some American works are included. In many cases, gives references to bibliographies where the titles are listed.   Z1033.U6K7

Peddie, Robert Alexander. Subject index of books published before 1880. London : Grafton, 1933–48. 4 v.   **AA94**

1st ser. (1933. 745 p.); 2nd ser. (1935. 857 p.); 3rd ser. (1939. 945 p.); new ser. (1948. 872 p.).

Each series furnishes an alphabetical subject list of some 50,000 books in various languages published before 1880 (1881), the date from which the British Museum subject indexes (AA104) continue the record. Includes many small and specific subject entries, e.g., place names, excluding, however, personal names.

The third series includes in its alphabetical arrangement every subject heading used in the three series, with cross-references to the first and second series. This record is not continued in the "new series." International in scope, but with a preponderance of English titles.   Z1035.P37

Books in series

Baer, Eleanora A. Titles in series : a handbook for librarians and students. 3rd ed. Metuchen, N.J. : Scarecrow, 1978. 4 v.   **AA95**

> 1st ed., 1953–60.
>
> Contents: v. 1–2, Titles in series; v. 3–4, Authors and titles index. Series title index. Directory of publishers.
>
> Lists 69,657 titles appearing in series published throughout the world prior to Jan. 1975. Both numbered and unnumbered series are included. Vols. 1–2 are arranged alphabetically by series title, with series contents listed numerically, chronologically, or alphabetically as appropriate. This edition supersedes earlier editions and their supplements.   AI3.T5

Books in series. 3rd ed.– . N.Y. : Bowker, 1980– . Quinquennial.   **AA96**

> 1st ed., 1977–2nd ed., 1979 had title: *Books in series in the United States.*
>
> "Original, reprinted, in-print, and out-of-print books, published or distributed in the U.S. in popular, scholarly, and professional series."—*t.p.*
>
> The 1st ed. and its supplement were concerned only with series published 1966 and later. Beginning with the 2nd ed., date of publication is no longer a criterion for inclusion. The 3rd ed. lists nearly 200,000 titles in over 21,000 series; the contents of that edition are: v. 1, Series; v. 2, Authors; v. 3, Titles.
>
> "In compiling *Books in Series* these sources of series information were reviewed: the Library of Congress *National Union Catalog* and MARC (Machine Readable Cataloging) files; the *Books in Print* Active and Out-of-Print files; series listings included in the *Publishers' Trade List Annual*; publishers' catalogs, brochures or publisher-supplied information; the *American Book Publishing Record 1950–1977* and *1978, 1979, 1980* database, and *Irregular Serials and Annuals*."—*Pref., 3rd ed.*
>
> For earlier publications in series, see: *Books in series, 1876–1949* (AA97).   Z1215.B65

Books in series 1876–1949 : original, reprinted, in-print, and out-of-print books, published or distributed in the U.S. in popular, scholarly, and professional series. N.Y. : Bowker, 1982. 3 v. (2562 p.).   **AA97**

> Contents: v. 1, Series heading index; Subject index to series; v. 2, Authors; v. 3, Titles.
>
> A chronological predecessor to the ongoing record of series publications (*see* AA96). For this compilation the publisher "surveyed all LC cataloging of United States titles back to the inception of LC cataloging, utilizing the resources of Bowker's *American Book Publishing Record 1876–1949* database" (*Pref.*) in order to provide a comprehensive record of publications issued in series. Works are grouped in volumes 2 and 3. An asterisk preceding a series title indicates that the series continues to be listed in the 3rd ed. of *Books in series.*   Z1036.B711

Library catalogs

Bibliography

Nelson, Bonnie R. A guide to published library catalogs. Metuchen, N.J. : Scarecrow, 1982. 342 p.   **AA98**

> Includes 429 numbered entries for published catalogs in 33 subject sections. Lengthy annotations; subject index and index of libraries.   Z710.N44

Winans, Robert B. A descriptive checklist of book catalogues separately printed in America, 1693–1800. Worcester : American Antiquarian Society, 1981. 207 p.   **AA99**

Lists and describes separately published book catalogs "issued in America prior to 1801 by booksellers, publishers, book auctioneers, circulating libraries, social libraries, college libraries, and private libraries."—*Introd.* Chronological arrangement. Lists 278 located items (plus eight others not known to be extant but for which there is good evidence of publication) and some 393 unnumbered entries for unlocated items, many or most of which "may be bibliographic ghosts." Indexed.   Z1029.W56

National libraries

France

Bernard, Annick. Guide de l'utilisateur des catalogues des livres imprimés de la Bibliothèque Nationale. Paris : Chadwyck-Healey France ; Alexandria, Va. : distr. by Chadwyck-Healey, 1986. 60 p.   **AA100**

> Offers a useful description of the history and arrangement of the printed and microfiche catalogs of the Bibliothèque Nationale (AA101).   Z927.P3

Bibliothèque Nationale (France). Catalogue général des livres imprimés : Auteurs. Paris : Impr. Nationale, 1900–81. 231 v.   **AA101**

> An important modern catalog, the value of which cannot be overestimated. An alphabetical author catalog, including only entries under names of personal authors, with the necessary cross-references; does not include title entries for anonymous books or entries for anonymous classics, periodicals or society transactions or government or corporate authors. The cataloging is excellent; the information given includes author's full name whenever possible, title, place, publisher, date, edition, paging or volumes, format, and occasional notes of contents, original publication in case of reprints from periodicals, etc. An important reference feature, in the case of authors whose works are voluminous, is the detailed alphabetical title index under the author's name, which indicates in what volumes or editions a given work may be found, and also indicates alternative and changed titles. In addition to its comprehensive coverage of French publications, the catalog is particularly strong in other Romance-language and classical materials.
>
> Originally each volume included titles acquired up to the date of publication of that particular volume, so that there is a wide spread in coverage between the first volumes published in 1900 and those issued half a century later. Beginning with v. 189, however, no imprints after 1959 have been included, and this policy continues through the end of the alphabet.
>
> Supplemented by:
>
> ———. *Catalogue général des livres imprimés, 1897–1959 : supplément sur fiches* [microform] (Paris : Chadwyck-Healey France, 1986. 2890 microfiches).
>
> Lists works added to the Bibliothèque Nationale through 1959; as in the printed catalog, only works under names of personal authors are included. Thus the catalog (which, before v. 189, listed works acquired at the time the individual volumes were published) now has uniform coverage.
>
> ———. *Catalogue général des livres imprimés : auteurs—collectivités-auteurs—anonymes, 1960–1969* (Paris : Impr. Nationale, 1972–78. 27 v.).
>
> Contents: Série 1, t. 1–23, Caractéres latins et caractéres grecs; Série 2, t. 1, Caractéres hébraïques; t. 2–3, Caractéres cyrilliques; t. 4, Caractéres arabes.
>
> Supersedes a 1960–64 supplement published 1965–67 in 12 v.
>
> ———. *Catalogue général des livres imprimés. Auteurs, Collectivités-auteurs, anonymes, 1970–1979. Série en caractéres latins* (Paris : La Bibliothèque, 1983–85. v. 1, pts. 1–3; v. 2–4; v. 5, pts. 1–2; v. 6–8; v. 9, pts. 1–3; v. 10 [In progress]).
>
> Contents: t. 1, Caractéres cyrilliques: russe (3 v.); t. 2, Caractéres cyrilliques: biélorusse, moldave, ukrainien, macédonien; t. 3, Caractéres cyrilliques: bulgare; t. 4, Caractéres grecs; t. 5, Caractéres hébraïques (2 v.); t. 6, Thaï, t. 7, Coréen; t. 8, Japonais; t. 9, Arabe (3 v.); t. 10, Persan.

The second volume of t. 5 and the third volume of t. 9 are indexes.

The basic set is further supplemented by:

———. *Anonymes 1501–1800 : état au 31 décembre 1986* [microform] (Paris : BN, Livres imprimés, 1986. 9 microfiches, negative).

User's guide has title: *Catalogue général des livres imprimés de la Bibliothèque nationale. Anonymes XVIe-XVIIIe siécles.*

A listing, arranged alphabetically by title, of some 175,000 anonymous printed books issued from 1501 to 1800 held by the Bibliothèque Nationale as of December 1986. It includes works published without a name on the title page; works issued under a pseudonym which is not a personal name, or under initials, or an occupation; and works by more than five authors. Excludes corporate publications, and anonymous works (e.g., legal documents, liturgical books) listed in special catalogs of the Bibliothèque Nationale. Z927.P2

Great Britain

British Library. The British Library general catalogue of printed books to 1975. London : C. Bingley ; London ; N.Y. : K.G. Saur, 1979–87. 360 v. **AA102**

On spine: *BLC to 1975.*

"The present printed edition of the *General Catalogue* has been designed to accommodate, in one alphabetic sequence, a complex series of earlier published catalogues: GK1, the first printed catalogue of real substance; GK2, the revision begun in 1931 for the letters A–DEZ; GK3, the photo lithographic cumulated edition begun in 1956 with its three Supplements. In addition, the present catalogue will incorporate the many thousands of additions and corrections inserted in the working copies."—*Foreword.*

The great advantage of this set is the cumulative aspect which obviates the need to consult supplements as well as the basic volumes, but libraries owning the earlier sets will need to weigh the frequency of use against the very considerable cost of the cumulation. An early review in *Times literary supplement* (Apr. 4, 1980): 398, mentions that a "D" prefixed to a shelfmark indicates that the book was destroyed during World War II, although this is not explained in the preface.

Two unnumbered indexes to the entries under England (v. 95–100) were published in 1982: an index to the subheadings used, and a title index. This edition is also available in CD-ROM.

Supplemented by:

———. *The British Library general catalogue of printed books to 1975: Supplement* (London; N.Y. : K.G. Saur, 1987–1988. 6 v.).

Lists some 85,000 entries "for books published before 1971 which were cataloged by the British Library too late for inclusion in the BLC, or are reprints of entries considerably revised from the form in which they appear there."—*Introd.* "Some *see* references which appear in the Supplement refer to authors and titles in the General Catalog."—*Note to users.* Items in the supplement are not included in the CD-ROM version of the catalog.

Continued by:

———. *The British Library general catalogue of printed books, 1976 to 1982*, (London; N.Y. : K.G. Saur, 1983. 50 v.).

———. *The British Library general catalogue of printed books, 1982 to 1985*, (London; N.Y. : Saur, 1986. 26 v.).

———. *The British Library general catalogue of printed books, 1986 to 1987* (London; N.Y. : K.G. Saur, 1988. 22 v.).

———. *The British Library general catalogue of printed books 1988 to 1989* (London : Saur, 1990. 28 v.).

Although not stated, numerals and diacritics (including some obvious mistakes) are filed before the letter A in the supplements issued 1976 on. The individual supplements and a 1976–85 cumulation are also available in microfiche.

•A machine-readable version with the same title is available on CD-ROM (no update). Z921.L553B74

British Museum. Department of Printed Books. General catalogue of printed books. Photolithographic edition to 1955. London : Trustees of the British Museum, 1959–66. 263 v. **AA103**

Vol. 1 publ. 1965.

Previous complete edition (entitled *Catalogue of printed books*), 1881–1900. 95 v.; Supplement, 1900–1905. 13 v. (Photographic reprint: Ann Arbor, Mich. : Edwards Bros., 1946–50).

Vols. 1–51, A–Dezw, of a new catalog were published between 1931 and 1954, but mounting costs caused its discontinuance. These volumes included entries cataloged up to the time of the publication of each volume and reflected much recataloging and revision of the previous catalog.

In 1959 the Trustees began to issue, by photo-offset lithography, the Working Catalogue of the Reading Room, covering books cataloged through 1955, without further editing but with the manuscript amendments which were contained in the volumes. Publication began with v. 52 and continued through the alphabet, after which v. 1–51 were brought up to 1955 to conform to the rest of the set and were reproduced in the same manner.

The catalog is a complete record of the printed books in the Library of the British Museum (now the British Library), which have appeared from the 15th century to the end of 1955, in all languages except those of Asia. The Library is particularly important because of the extent and richness of its collections in all fields and in all languages, and also because its possession of the copyright privilege helps make it the most comprehensive collection of British publications in existence. Its catalog, therefore, is an indispensable bibliographical source for the scholar and librarian. In the main, it is an author catalog only, with catchword title entries, cross-references for anonymous books, etc. Subject entries are included to a limited extent, principally for the following: (1) under personal names, biographical works are included; (2) under countries, e.g., England, France, etc., are entered official publications, some works about the country, and many titles in which the name of the country occurs; and (3) under names of sacred books, e.g., Bible, Kur'an, etc., are entered both texts and works about them. Two important reference features are: (1) the large amount of analytical material included (analysis of series, etc.), and (2) the many cross-references from names of editors, translators, or other personal names.

The amount of bibliographical information varies; titles taken from the 19th-century catalog usually include only author, title, editor, place, and date, whereas more recent cataloging adds publisher, paging, and size. Some cataloging for early printed books is fairly full.

Special sections to be noted include: Bible (3 v. with index); England (5 v. with index); Liturgies; London (3 v. with index); Periodical publications (3 v.). These serve as comprehensive bibliographies of these areas. For academies, *see* its *Catalogue of printed books : academies* (AL12).

———. ———. *Ten-year supplement, 1956–1965* (1968. 50 v.).

———. ———. *Five-year supplement, 1966–1970* (1971–72. 26 v.).

A series of annual volumes of *Additions* to the *General catalogue* began to appear in 1964, but covered the period 1963–65 only. Entries from those volumes were included in the 10-year supplement, 1956–1965.

Although the National Reference Library of Science and Invention (formerly the Patent Office Library) was amalgamated with the British Museum in 1966, its holdings are not recorded in the *General catalogue* nor in the 1966–70 supplement. Attention is called to some arrears in cataloging of United Kingdom materials published 1966–67, and the *British national bibliography* (AA689) will have to be consulted for those years. Greater conformity with the Anglo-American cataloging rules is evident in the supplements, and recently cataloged periodicals are entered under title instead of the uniform "Periodical publications" heading (although the latter is also employed). Z921.B87

——————— Subject index of the modern works added to the library, 1881–1900 / ed. by G. K. Fortescue. London, 1902–1903. 3 v. **AA104**

Supersedes earlier indexes published for this period. Continued by five-year supplements:

———. ———. 1901–05, 1906–10, 1911–15, 1916–20, 1921–25, 1926–30, 1931–35 (2 v.), 1936–40 (2 v.), 1941–45, 1946–50 (4 v.), 1951–55 (6 v.), 1956–60 (6 v.) (London, 1906–74).

Title varies slightly.

For works published before 1880, *see* Robert Alexander Peddie, *Subject index of books published before 1880* (AA94).

An alphabetical subject catalog of the modern works added to the library since 1881. Contains entries for well over 925,000 titles, but is sometimes difficult to use. Subjects are often general rather than specific, with many subheadings, and there is no table of headings used, although there are many cross-references. Arrangement under headings is neither alphabetical nor chronological. Bibliographical information usually includes author, brief title, pagination, place, and date. Personal names are not included as these are covered in the *General catalogue*.

Various changes were made in the subject heading terminology in the 1956–60 index, many new headings having been added, and some former subheads standing as subject headings in their own right.

Continued by:

British Library. Department of Printed Books. *Subject index of modern books acquired, 1961–1970* (London : British Library, 1982. 12 v.).

———. *Subject index of modern books acquired 1971–1975* (London : The Library, 1986. 14 v. [8366 p.]).

———. *The British Library general subject catalog, 1975–1985* (London ; N.Y. : K.G. Saur, 1986. 75 v.). Also available on microfiche.

———. *The British Library general subject catalogue 1986 to 1990* (London : Saur, 1991–92. 42 v.).

Spain

Biblioteca Nacional (Spain). Catálogo general de libros impresos, hasta 1981 [microform]. [Paris ; Alexandria, Va.] : Chadwyck-Healey, c1989. 4408 fiche.   **AA105**

———. *Catálogo general de libros impresos, 1982–1987* [microform]. (c1989. 579 microfiches).

These two sets list the nearly 2 million printed books in the Biblioteca Nacional. Arranged alphabetically by author, corporate author (since 1964 with place-name first), or title, if anonymous.

§ A 56-page *Catalogo de autores y orbra anonimas de la Biblioteca Nacional de Madrid : gúia de consulta* was published in 1990 by Chadwyck-Healey.   Z945.B53

United States

Library of Congress. A catalog of books represented by Library of Congress printed cards issued to July 31, 1942. Ann Arbor, Mich. : Edwards, 1942–46. 167 v.   **AA106**

Repr.: N.Y. : Rowman & Littlefield.

Because of the immensity of the collections, the excellence of the cataloging, and the full bibliographical descriptions, the *Catalog* of the Library of Congress has been for many years an invaluable work in any library and indispensable in those where research is done. Of first importance in cataloging, acquistion, and reference work, and for the bibliographer and research worker, it is valuable for author bibliography, verification of titles, bibliographical information, historical notes, location of copies, etc.

History: Until 1942, the catalog was produced only on cards, and to make the information available outside Washington, "depository sets" were placed in various large libraries in different sections of the country. These sets consisted of main entry cards only and were kept up to date by the addition of new cards as printed. To make the catalog even more generally accessible, the Association of Research Libraries, in 1942, sponsored the photographic reproduction of a depository catalog and its publication in book form. The cards were photographed and printed in reduced size. The main catalog includes all cards printed from 1898 to July 31, 1942.

Scope: It is an author and main entry catalog (with cross-references but not added entries) of books and other materials for which Library of Congress printed cards were available in: (1) the Library of Congress (as cards had not been printed for all the Library's books, the catalog is not a complete record of the Library's holdings, but does represent a large percentage); (2) many government department libraries; and (3) various libraries throughout the country, as a result of the cooperative cataloging program.

Information given is detailed and represents a high degreee of accuracy, usually including, as pertinent: full name of author, dates of birth and death; full title; place, publisher, and date; collation (paging, illustrations, maps, tables, size, etc.); series; edition; notes on contents, history, etc.; tracing for subject headings and added entries; LC class number, sometimes Dewey class number, and LC card number. Frequently a considerable amount of analysis is noted for composite books, sets, periodicals, etc.

———. ———. *Supplement : cards issued Aug. 1, 1942–Dec. 31, 1947* (Ann Arbor, Mich. : Edwards, 1948. 24 v. Repr.: N.Y. : Rowman & Littlefield, 1967).

At head of title: The Association of Research Libraries.

The *Supplement* and later cumulations contain cards issued during the periods covered regardless of the imprint date of the book recorded, and revised cards are treated in the same manner as new ones. The *Supplement* also includes some 26,000 title entries for anonymous and pseudonymous works for which the Library of Congress had supplied the authors—the so-called bracketed authors. The title entries were made by crossing out the author's name; the card was then filed under title. For those cards which were printed before Aug. 1942, the author card will be in the main set; for cards printed Aug. 1942–1947, in the *Supplement*.

Library of Congress author catalog : a cumulative list of works represented by Library of Congress printed cards, 1948–1952 (Ann Arbor, Mich. : Edwards, 1953. 24 v. Repr.: N.Y. : Rowman & Littlefield).

In this set and the *National union catalog* (AA111) that succeeded it, besides main entries and cross-references for books, pamphlets, maps, music scores, periodicals, and other serials, essential added entries are included. Motion pictures and filmstrips are grouped in v. 24.

——————— Library of Congress catalog : Motion pictures and filmstrips. Ann Arbor, Mich. : Edwards, 1955–73. .   **AA107**

Subtitle: A cumulative list of works represented by Library of Congress printed cards.

Quarterly, with annual and quinquennial cumulations. Quinquennial volumes issued as volumes of *National union catalog* (AA111).

Quinquennial volumes cover 1953–57, 1958–62, 1963–67, 1968–72.

1953–57 publ. as v. 28 and 1958–62 as v. 53–54 of *National union catalog*; 1963–67 and 1968–72 not numbered as part of *NUC* although included in the series. Preceded by v. 24 (Films) of *Library of Congress author catalog, 1948–52* (AA106).

"Includes entries for all motion pictures and filmstrips (but not for microfilms) currently cataloged or recataloged on L.C. printed cards … Attempts to cover all educational motion pictures and filmstrips released in the United States and Canada."—*Introd.* Other coverage varies.

Superseded by:

Library of Congress. *Films and other materials for projection* (Oct. 1972/June 1973–1978. Wash. : Library of Congress, 1973–78. 8 v.).

Quarterly, with annual and quinquennial cumulations.

The change of title is intended to "reflect the inclusion in 1973 of cataloging data for sets of slides and other transparencies."—*Foreword*.

Continued by:

Audiovisual materials (Jan.–Mar. 1979–1982. Wash. : Library of Congress, 1979–82).

Quarterly, with annual cumulations.

"Presents motion pictures, filmstrips, set of transparencies, slide sets, videorecordings, and kits currently cataloged by the Library of Congress, thus serving as an acquisition, reference, and research tool."—*Foreword, 1979*. Aims to list all items in the aforementioned categories "released in the United States or Canada which have educational or instructional value."

Continued by:

NUC. Audiovisual materials [microform] (Jan./Mar. 1983– . Wash. : Library of Congress, 1983?–). Microfiche.

Includes motion pictures, video recordings, filmstrips, transparancy sets, and slide sets released in the U.S. or Canada, and cataloged by the Library of Congress.   Z881.U49A25

———————— Main catalog of the Library of Congress. N.Y. : K.G. Saur, 1984– . [microfiche].   **AA108**

Reproduces some 25,000,000 cards in the Library of Congress' main card catalog, representing books in the Library's collections cataloged from 1898 through 1980, when the Library adopted AACR2 and closed its card catalog. Dictionary arrangement, with authors, titles, subjects, and cross-references interfiled. Unfortunately, for most of this time, subject headings were typed in red, not in uppercase, and are not always easy to discern in this format.

———————— Monographic series. Jan./Mar. 1974–82. Wash. : Library of Congress, 1974–83. Quarterly, with the fourth issue being an annual cumulation.   **AA109**

Superintendent of Documents classification: LC 30.8/9: .

At head of title: Library of Congress catalogs.

"Compiled and edited by the Catalog Publication Division of the Processing Department, Library of Congress."—*verso of t.p.*

Includes reproductions of Library of Congress printed cards on which a series statement appears in parentheses following the collation. Arrangement is according to series entry which is shown in capital letters preceding the reproduction of the cards for that series. Includes unnumbered as well as numbered series.

Ceased publication with the 1982 cumulation. Superseded by the microform edition of *National union catalog* (see AA111).

Z881.U49U54a

Library of Congress catalog. Books: subjects : a cumulative list of works represented by Library of Congress printed cards. 1950–54–1970–74. Ann Arbor, Mich. : Edwards, 1955–76.   **AA110**

Cumulations issued as: 1950–54 (Ann Arbor, Mich. : Edwards, 1955. 20 v.); 1955–59 (Paterson, N.J. : Pageant Books, 1960. 22 v.); 1960–64 (Ann Arbor, Mich. : Edwards, 1965. 25 v.); 1965–69 (N.Y. : Rowman & Littlefield, 1970. 42 v.); 1970–74 (1976. 100 v.).

Quinquennial cumulation of a publication of the same title issued by the Library of Congress on a quarterly basis, cumulating annually. An alphabetical subject arrangement of entries for publications which were cataloged or recataloged during the periods covered, by the Library of Congress and by libraries participating in the cooperative cataloging program, and which are represented by LC printed cards. Included are the types of material in the languages indicated for *National union catalog* (AA111). From 1950 to 1952, maps, motion pictures, and music scores were also included, but from 1953 on, these were issued separately. (*Maps and atlases*, issued separately 1953–55, was discontinued, and those entries are included in the 1955–59 cumulation.) Originally included entries for publications with imprint dates of 1945 or later which had been currently cataloged, but pre-1945 items newly cataloged or recataloged were subsequently added in the annual cumulations.

Continued by: Library of Congress. *Subject catalog* (Jan./Mar. 1975–1982. Wash., 1975–84. Quarterly, with annual cumulations).

At head of title: Library of Congress catalogs.

Ceased with the annual cumulation for 1982, being superseded by the microform edition of *National union catalog*.

National union catalog : a cumulative author list representing Library of Congress printed cards and titles reported by other American libraries, 1953–1957. Ann Arbor, Mich. : Edwards, 1958. 28 v.   **AA111**

Contents: v. 1–26, Authors; v. 27, Music and phonorecords; v. 28, Motion pictures and filmstrips.

The great innovation in the 1950s was the move toward a *National union catalog*, by the inclusion of monographs not represented by LC printed cards, reported by some 500 other North American libraries, together with the indication of location of titles by the symbols of libraries. Includes printed cards in all languages written in the Roman, Cyrillic, Greek, Gaelic, or Hebraic alphabets and contains entries for books, pamphlets, maps and atlases, periodicals, and other serials. *Motion pictures and filmstrips* and *The music catalog* were published sep-

arately (*see* AA107, BJ82). All serials represented by LC printed cards are included, but holdings of serials not cataloged by the Library of Congress are omitted and are listed in *New serial titles* (AD225).

————. *1958–1962* (N.Y. : Rowman & Littlefield, 1963. 54 v.).

Contents: v. 1–50, Authors; v. 51–52, Music and phonorecords; v. 53–54, Motion pictures and filmstrips.

Coverage was expanded to include cards in the Arabic and Indic alphabets and in Chinese, Japanese, and Korean characters. The number of libraries reporting holdings increased to about 750.

(As an aid to faster searching, the four series covering the 1942–62 period have been cumulated and published as: *Library of Congress and national union catalog author lists, 1942–1962 : a master cumulation*, comp. by the editorial staff of the Gale Research Company. Detroit : Gale, 1969. 152 v.).

————. *1963–1967* (Ann Arbor, Mich. : Edwards, 1969. 72 v.).

Contents: v. 1–59, Authors; v. 60–67, Register of additional locations; [v. 68–70], Music and phonorecords; [v. 71–72], Motion pictures and filmstrips.

National union catalog : a cumulative author list (Wash. : Library of Congress, Card Div., 1968?–82?).

Concurrent with, and following the publication of the pre-1956 and the 1956–67 segments of *NUC* (AA113, AA112), the catalog continued to appear monthly, with quarterly and annual cumulations. (Quinquennial cumulations were commercially published: 1968–72 by J. W. Edwards, Ann Arbor, Mich.; 1973–77 by Rowman & Littlefield, Totowa, N.J.; no 1978–82 cumulation has yet appeared.) Printed editions ceased with the 1982 issues.

The national union catalog, 1952–1955 imprints : an author list representing Library of Congress printed cards and titles reported by other American libraries (Ann Arbor, Mich. : Edwards, 1961. 30 v.).

This series, supplementary to the regular set, and not included in its chronological sequence, lists titles previously included in earlier catalogs with additional locations, as well as newly reported titles, many not represented by LC printed cards. The catalog is not fully edited, so that there may be some duplication under variant forms of entry, but cross-references are given whenever possible.

Beginning 1983, issued in microform as:

NUC : books [microform]. (Jan. 1983– . Wash. : Library of Congress, 1983– . Monthly).

Represents entries for works cataloged by the Library of Congress, together with catalog entries prepared by about 1,100 contributing libraries. Supersedes the paper editions of *National union catalog*, *Subject catalog* (AA110), *Chinese cooperative catalog* (AA892), and *Monographic series* (AA109). Includes books, pamphlets, some typescripts, map atlases, monographic microform publications, and monographic government publications. Priority of processing is given to post-1955 publications, but all imprints are included, regardless of date. Entries for nonroman language materials are given in romanized form only. For printed monographs, at least one library location is given.

Utilizes a "register/index" format. Full bibliographic citations (i.e., all information traditionally found on Library of Congress cards) appear in a separate register in a numbered sequence according to the order in which the items were entered. Access to the register is provided by separate indexes for (1) names used as main or added entry; (2) titles; (3) LC series; and (4) LC subjects. Indexes display a shortened form of the record, with reference to the register number for full information; the indexes are cumulative.

According to the *Library of Congress information bulletin* (18 June 1990 : 227), as of 1990, *NUC* will no longer list books from OCLC, the Research Libraries Information Network (RLIN), or the Western Library Network (WLN). The article states that *NUC* "will continue to include Library of Congress cataloging, reports from U.S. libraries that create records on local systems, reports from Canadian libraries, reports of microform masters and reports from other libraries that do not add their cataloging to the three bibliographic utilities."

For related microform publications of the Library of Congress see *National union catalog. Audiovisual materials* (AA381), *National union catalog. Cartographic materials* (CL252), and *National union catalog. Register of additional locations* (AA114).

National union catalog, 1956 through 1967 : a cumulative author list representing Library of Congress printed cards and titles reported by other American libraries. Totowa, N.J. : Rowman and Littlefield, 1970–72. 125 v.   **AA112**

"A new and augmented twelve-year catalog, being a compilation into one alphabet of the fourth & fifth supplements of the National union catalog, with a key to additional locations through 1967 and with a unique identifying number allocated to each title … The present compilation is the work of the Cataloging and Editorial staffs of Rowman and Littlefield."—*title page.*

Offers a cumulation of the 1958–62 and 1963–67 quinquennial supplements to *National union catalog* (AA111). Inasmuch as 1956–57 imprints were repeated in the 1958–62 supplement, this new set serves as a continuation to *National union catalog, pre-1956 imprints* (AA113). An important feature is the designation of those items for which further locations are given in *Register of additional locations* (AA114) as cumulated in the 1963–67 supplement. Added locations are cited in a separate section at the end of each volume of the new set.

National union catalog, pre-1956 imprints : a cumulative author list representing Library of Congress printed cards and titles reported by other American libraries. London : Mansell, 1968–80. 685 v.   **AA113**

"Compiled and edited with the cooperation of the Library of Congress and the National Union Catalog Subcommittee of the Resources Committee of the Resources and Technical Services Division, American Library Association."—*title page.*

Supersedes the basic Library of Congress *Catalog of books …* and its *Supplement, 1942–47* (AA106); *Library of Congress author catalog, 1948–1952*; *National union catalog, 1952–1955 imprints*; and *National union catalog … 1953–1957* (AA111). The 1953–57 cumulation is fully superseded because, in anticipation of the present compilation, 1956–57 imprints were repeated in the 1958–62 cumulation of *National union catalog.* However, the volumes for motion pictures, filmstrips, and phonorecords—v. 24 of the 1948–52 cumulation; v. 27–28 of the 1953–57 set—should not be discarded since these materials are not included in the new catalog.

In addition to cumulating the entries in the above-mentioned catalogs, this monumental work incorporates entries from the Union Catalog card file at the Library of Congress. Thus it is "a repertory of the cataloged holdings of selected portions of the cataloged collections of the major research libraries of the United States and Canada, plus the more rarely held items in the collections of selected smaller and specialized libraries."—*Introd.* The completed set encompasses some 10 million entries and indicates locations in more than 700 libraries. As the work progressed, pre-1956 imprints reported by participating libraries were added up to about a year before publication of the volume in which the work was entered.

Reference librarians will want to familiarize themselves with the introductory matter relevant to scope, form of entries, etc. In general, the catalog includes entries for books, pamphlets, maps, atlases, and music. Serials are listed if represented by an LC printed card or if separately reported by another library; similarly, individual manuscripts are represented if so reported. Works in Cyrillic, Hebrew, Chinese, Japanese, and other non-Latin alphabets are included only if represented by an LC printed card. *See* and *see also* references are provided; added entries are included in specified circumstances.

Vols. 53–56 (the Bible) did not appear until 1980. Vols. 609–24 have been reprinted with title: *United States government publications : an author index representing pre-1956 holdings of American libraries …* (London : Mansell, 1981. 16 v.).

An interesting account of the publishing history of the pre-1956 *NUC* may be found in W. J. Walsh's article, "Last of the monumental book catalogs," *American libraries* 12 (Sept. 1981): 464–68.

Supplementary volumes continue the numbering of the basic set:

———. *Supplement* ([London] : Mansell, 1980–81. v. 686–754).

The supplement is "designed to accommodate the mass of material that has accumulated since the editorial work was begun in 1967. Since then … over three million cards have cumulated in those parts of the alphabet previously published."—*Introd.* Entries represent reports from contributing libraries and cards generated by project editors; they comprise (1) new titles; (2) new editions of titles already listed; (3) added entries and cross-references supplied by the editorial staff. A separate section at the end of each supplementary volume records additional locations for items already listed (i.e., for items whose initial listings included less than one full line of location symbols). Reports from contributing libraries received to Aug. 1977 and Library of Congress cards received to Aug. 1979 are included.   Z881.A1U518

National union catalog. Register of additional locations. June 1965–1979. Wash. : Library of Congress, 1965–80. Annual.   **AA114**

Notes additional locations of titles included in *National union catalog* (AA111) reported after the annual or quinquennial cumulations have been published. A cumulation of the early volumes of the *Register* was issued as v. 60–67 of the 1963–67 quinquennial cumulation of *NUC* and included "additional locations for titles with post-1955 imprints in the 1958–62 and 1963–67 quinquennial cumulations."—*Introd.*

Comprises two lists: one arranged by Library of Congress card number; the other by main entry and representing only those titles for which no card number appears in the *Catalog.*

The 1979 annual was the last to appear in book form. Continued in microform:

———. ———. *Cumulative microform edition.* [microform]. (1968/79– . Wash. : Libr. of Congress, 1980– . Annual).

First publ. 1975 as 1968/75 ed. Sets for 1968/76 and 1968/77 not published.

"The cumulative microform edition includes the following: (1) the locations for the 68 to 79 card number series in the 1968–1972 quinquennial, (2) the locations published in the 1973 and later annuals, and (3) the locations currently in process that have been added to the automated file, but not yet published in hard copy."—*1968/79 cum., fiche 1.*

The 1979 annual was the last *RAL* to appear in book form. Using 1968 as the base year, each annual "Cumulative microform edition" provides an update of the complete file, replacing all earlier editions.

Nonnational libraries

United States

Harvard University. Library. Widener Library shelflist Cambridge : Publ. by the Harvard Univ. Lib.; distr. by the Harvard Univ. Pr., 1965–79. no. 1–60.   **AA115**

A series of computer-produced shelflists, each volume of which is devoted to a single classification or a segment of a large class of cataloged materials in the Widener Library. Most numbers are in four parts: (1) a copy of the classification schedule which serves as a key to the second part; (2) a list of the entries in call-number sequence; (3) an alphabetical listing by author or anonymous title; and (4) a chronological listing by date of publication.

Although originally intended primarily for use at the Widener Library, the rich resources of the Harvard collections make the lists useful elsewhere as good subject bibliographies.

Numbers published are: no. 1, Crusades (superseded by no. 32); no. 2, Africa (superseded by no. 34); no. 3, Twentieth century Russian literature; no. 4, Russian history since 1917; no. 5–6, Latin America and Latin American periodicals; no. 7, Bibliography and bibliography periodicals; no. 8, Reference collections (superseded by no. 33); no. 9–13, American history; no. 14, China, Japan, and Korea; no. 15, Periodical classes; no. 16–17, Education and education periodicals; no. 18, Literature: general and comparative; no. 19, Southern Asia; no. 20, Canadian history and literature; no. 21, Latin American literature; no. 22, Government; no. 23–24, Economics; no. 25, Celtic literatures; no. 26–27, American literature; no. 28–31, Slavic history and literatures; no. 32, General European and world history; no. 33, Reference collections shelved in the Reading Room and Acquisitions Department; (supersedes no. 8); no. 34, African history and literatures; (supersedes no. 2); no. 35–38, English literature; no. 39, Judaica; no. 40, Finnish and Baltic history and literatures; no. 41, Spanish history and literature; no. 42–43, Philosophy and psychology; no. 44, Hungarian history and literature; no. 45–46, Sociology; no. 47–48, French literature; no. 49–50,

German literature; no. 51–52, Italian history and literature; no. 53–54, British history; no. 55, Ancient history; no. 56, Archaeology; no. 57, Classical studies; no. 58, Ancient Greek literature; no. 59, Latin literature; v. 60, Geography and anthropology. A number of these works have more detailed entries in appropriate sections of the present *Guide*.

New York Public Library. Research Libraries. Dictionary catalog of the Research Libraries of the New York Public Library, 1911–1971. [N.Y.] : New York Public Library, Astor, Lenox, and Tilden Foundations (distr. by G. K. Hall), [1979–83]. 800 v.   **AA116**

The 1911 date of the title refers to the opening of the Central Building of the New York Public Library when the newly created card catalog (in preparation for many years) was first available to the public. Thus, this catalog "represents the holdings of book and book-like materials of The Research Libraries ... as they were developed between 1895 and 1971 [the date after which the book catalog was adopted], and includes entries for the holdings of three predecessor collections—those of the Astor Library, Lenox Library, and the library of Samuel Jones Tilden—that became part of the present Library upon their consolidation in 1895."—*p. xxiii.* Includes books, periodicals (together with some indexing of contents of periodicals), and other media in most fields of human knowledge—one of the world's great collections. Reproduces about nine million cards.

"The major part of the collections is represented ... , including materials for general research, history and the humanities, the social sciences, science and technology, history of the Americas, local history and genealogy, art and architecture, and rare books. It includes entries for parts of the collections of music, dance, theatre, Orientalia, Baltica, Slavonica, and Judaica. It does not include certain forms of material such as manuscripts, maps, prints, etc."—*p. xxiii.*

————. *Dictionary catalog of the Research Libraries : a cumulative list of authors, titles, and subjects representing books and booklike materials added to the collections since January 1, 1971.*

A computer-produced, ongoing record of materials (regardless of publication date) newly added to the research collection. Originally in monthly cumulative supplements, with annual re-cumulations of the full set. Publication was suspended after the July 1981 supplement. "Interim indexes" are issued irregularly for in-house use, but not made generally available.

A cumulation for 1972–80 was published in 1980 in 64 v. and a second cumulation covering 1981–88 in 1988 in 73 v.   Z881.N59

Germany

Bayerische Staatsbibliothek. Alphabetischer Katalog 1501–1840 : BSB-AK 1501–1840. Voraus-Ausg. München ; N.Y. : K.G. Saur, 1987–90. v. 1–60. (In progress).   **AA117**

Title on added t.p.: Alphabetical catalogue 1501–1840.

Introductory material in English and German.

An author and title listing of some 662,000 items held by the Bavarian State Library, excluding incunabula and journals. "The preliminary edition will contain about 80 percent of all titles edited and recorded during the first work phase. The bulk of the dissertations ... will only be included in the final edition."—*p. v.*   Z929.M98B38

Deutsche Bibliothekskataloge im 19. Jahrhundert : analytisches Repertorium / hrsg. von Paul Kaegbein ; bearb. von Martin Schenkel ... [et al.]. München ; N.Y. : K.G. Saur, 1992. 2 v.   **AA118**

Offers descriptions of several hundred catalogs of the holdings of academic, special, and official libraries, arranged alphabetically by city. Vol. 2 is a subject and institution index.

Great Britain

Bodleian Library. Catalogus librorum impressorum Bibliothecae Bodleianae in Academia Oxoniensi. .... Oxford : e Typographeo Academico, 1843–51. 4 v.   **AA119**

An author catalog. Vols. 1–3 included holdings to 1835, with the Gough, Douce, and Oppenheimer collections, academic dissertations, and music excluded. Vol. 4 is a supplementary volume listing accessions of the 1835–47 period.   Z921.O93

London Library. Catalogue / by C. T. Hagberg Wright and C. J. Purnell. London, 1913–14. 2v.   **AA120**

An author catalog of a library of more than 250,000 volumes. This edition incorporates the material of the 1st ed., 1903, and the eight annual supplements to that edition.

————. ————. *Supplement,* 1913–20, 1920–28, 1928–50 (London, 1920-53. 3 v.). The 3rd suppl. adds some 150,000 titles.

————. *Subject index of the London Library,* by C.T. Hagberg Wright (London, 1909-55. 4 v.). Contents: v. 1, Main subject list; v. 2, Additions, 1909–22, by C.T. Hagberg Wright and C.J. Purnell; v. 3, Additions, 1923–38; v. 4, Additions, 1938–53.

Union lists

Deutscher Gesamtkatalog : Neue Titel. Berlin : Staatsbibliothek, 1938–1944.   **AA121**

Issued weekly (frequently varies slightly) with quarterly and annual cumulations that supplement *Deutscher Gesamtkatalog* (AA122).

Continues *Berliner Titeldrucke,* 1910–1937. Originally publ. 1892.

Partially cumulated into Preussische Staatsbibliothek, *Berliner Titeldruke : fünfjahrs Katalog* (1930/34–1935/39. Berlin : Staatsbibliothek, 1935–40).

Each cumulation issued in 8 v. A–Z, paged continuously.

Title varies: 1935/39 called *Deutscher Gesamtkatalog. Neue Titel.*

Lists works published 1930–39 cataloged in more than 100 German libraries, thus supplementing the *Deutscher Gesamtkatalog.*

After World War II the *Berliner Titeldrucke* was continued in part by the following three series: (1) Berliner Titeldrucke. Neue Folge. Zugänge aus der Sowjetunion und den europäischen Ländern der Volksdemokratie. Jahreskatalog, 1954–59 (publ. 1956–62); (2) Berliner Titeldrucke. Neuerwerbungen ausländischer Literatur der wissenschaftlichen Bibliotheken der Deutschen Demokratischen Republik. Reihe, A, B, 1960–63; (3) Berliner Titeldrucke. Neuerwerbungen ausländischer Literatur wissenschaftlicher Bibliotheken der Deutschen Demokratischen Republik. Jahreskatalog, 1964–1988.

Deutscher Gesamtkatalog / hrsg. von der Preussischen Staatsbibliothek. .... Berlin : Preussische Druckerei– u. Verlags Aktiengesellschaft, 1931–39. 14 v.   **AA122**

Contents: v. 1–14, A–Beethordnung. No more published.

Repr.: Nendeln; Liechtenstein : Kraus, 1976. 14 v. in 7.

Vols. 1–8 had title *Gesamtkatalog der preussischen Bibliotheken* and listed books contained in about 18 important libraries. With v. 9, 1936, beginning the letter B, the scope was changed to include the contents of some 100 German and Austrian libraries—an ambitious undertaking, unfortunately suspended because of the war. The few volumes published show that, for the letters covered, the work is (1) indispensable for catalogers, reference workers, and bibliographical investigation generally, in the matter of German publications, and (2) useful for non-German subjects, also, as it contains much foreign material in many languages, including English works not listed in the British Museum catalog (AA103) and French works not listed in the catalog of the Bibliothèque Nationale (AA101).

Arranged alphabetically by author and anonymous title; includes books published up to 1930. The cataloging is detailed and exact, and for this reason the volumes issued are still useful.   Z929.A1D4

The Near East national union list / comp. by Dorothy Stehle under the direction of George N. Atiyeh. Wash. : Library of Congress, 1988. v. 1. (In progress?).   **AA123**

Contents: v. 1, A.

Superintendent of Documents classification: LC 1.2:N27.

"A guide to [pre-1979] publications in Near Eastern languages that have been reported to the National Union Catalog by some 240 libraries in the United States and Canada."—*Pref.* (Beginning with 1979 these titles are listed in *National union catalog.*) Arranged alphabetically by author or title, if anonymous. All forms of the authors' names are listed at the end of v. 1, with cross-references to the main alphabetical section. Title index.   Z3015.N4

Rome. Centro Nazionale per il Catalogo Unico delle Biblioteche Italiane e per le Informazioni Bibliografiche. Primo catalogo collettivo delle biblioteche italiane. Roma, 1962–79. 9 v.   **AA124**

Contents: v. 1–9, A–Barq. No more published.

A first effort toward a national union catalog for Italy. Locates copies in eight collections of the Biblioteche statali in Rome and in the Biblioteche Nazionali in Rome, Florence, Milan, and Naples. Includes works published 1500–1957. A main-entry catalog with entries for anonymous titles, academies, etc.; cross-references. Progress on the catalog was seriously delayed as a result of the Florence flood of 1966, and survival of numerous Florentine copies reported in at least the first six volumes is open to question.

§ A new publication, *Le edizioni italiane del XVI secolo* (AA731), is a partial continuation of this lapsed publication.   Z933.A1R6

Festschriften

Leistner, Otto. Internationale Bibliographie der Festschriften von den Anfängen bis 1979 : mit Sachregister = International bibliography of festschriften from the beginnings until 1979 : with subject-index. 2. erw. Aufl. Osnabrück : Biblio Verlag, 1984–89. 3 v.   **AA125**

1st ed., 1976.

The list of festschriften arranged by name of the personality or institution honoured (which provides the citations to the homage volumes) is followed by a subject index to the general content of the works cited. There is no list of the individual essays and their contributors and therefore no specific subject indexing of the contents. A list of frequently employed terms in foreign languages with German and English translations, and a section of general abbreviations completes the volume. Vol. 3 has a subject index and supplements v. 1–2.

§ Kept up to date by: *Internationale Jahresbibliographie der Festschriften... mit Verzeichnis aller Beiträge, einem Autorenregister und einem Sachregister zu den Festschriften* (Jahrg. 1 [1980]– . Osnabrück : Biblio Verlag, 1982– . Annual).

At head of title: IJBF.

Title (*International annual bibliography of festschriften*) and preface also in English.

Festschriften are listed alphabetically in the first section under the name of the person or institution honored, with full bibliographic information and a list of the contents of each. (A number of volumes are listed without contents, and these are to be analyzed in subsequent issues.) An author index of contributions gives reference to the name of the honoree, as does the subject index (i.e., subject entries refer to the overall content of the festschrift, not to specific contributions). A subject index using English terms gives reference to the corresponding German headings. A cumulated index to Jahrg. 1–10 was published in 2 v. in 1992.   Z1033.F4L43

New York Public Library. Research Libraries. Guide to festschriften. Boston : G. K. Hall, 1977. 2 v.   **AA126**

Contents: v. 1, The retrospective festschriften collection of the New York Public Library: materials cataloged through 1971; v. 2, A dictionary of festschriften in the New York Public Library (1972–1976) and the Library of Congress (1968–1976).

The first volume is a reproduction of the catalog cards for "over 6,000 *Festschriften* collected by NYPL over a fifty-year period, ending in December, 1971" (*Introd.*), and therefore includes some imprints prior to the 1920s. Unfortunately this is a main-entry arrangement only, with no cross-references from names of honorees, editors, etc., and no subject approach. Vol. 2, an infinitely more satisfactory compilation, is a computer-produced dictionary catalog of festschriften

added to the NYPL collections 1972–76, plus entries for festschriften available in the Library of Congress MARC data base 1968–76. It offers multiple access: main entry, secondary entries (for editors, persons honored, etc.), and subjects.   Z1033.F4N48

Taube, Gurli Elisa (Westgren). Svensk festskriftsbibliografi, åren 1891–1925. Uppsala : Appelbergs Boktr., 1954. 168 p. (Svenska bibliotekariesamfundets skriftserie, 2).   **AA127**

Festschriften are listed by name of honoree, with full contents notes for each volume. A second section groups the individual contributions by subject field. Index of contributors.

Continued by : Rosa Malmström, *Svensk festskriftsbibliografi, åren 1936–1960 = Bibliography of Swedish homage volumes 1936–1960* (Göteborg : Universitetsbiblioteket, 1967. 390 p. [Acta Bibliothecae Universitatis Gothoburgensis, 10]).

Follows the plan of the earlier volume, with a somewhat more refined breakdown in the subject section. The 1926–35 period remains to be covered.

Microforms and reproductions

Bibliographic guide to microform publications. 1986– . Boston : G.K. Hall, c1987– . Annual.   **AA128**

Brings together catalog records for microform publications in the New York Public Library and the Library of Congress, including books, government publications, and pamphlets. Lists microforms made in-house as well as commercial publications. Dictionary arrangement of author, title, and subject entries.   Z1033.M5B525

British Library. Lending Division. Microform research collections at the British Library Lending Division. [London] : The Library, 1985. 27 p.   **AA129**

1st ed., 1983.

A listing, complete as of July 1985, of the 199 microfilm collections available from the British Library Lending Division. Arranged by broad subject, with a title index.   Z921.L5545B75

Dodson, Suzanne Cates. Microform research collections : a guide. 2nd ed. Westport, Conn. : Microform Review, [1984]. 670 p. (Meckler Publishing series in library micrographics management, 9).   **AA130**

1st ed., 1978.

A title listing of about 375 microform research collections. As far as possible, information given for each includes publisher, date, format, price, reference to published reviews, notes on arrangement and bibliographic control, bibliographies or indexes which serve as keys to the collection, and notes on scope and content of the collection. Index of authors, editors, compilers, and titles (including variant titles) of the microform collections and of the bibliographies, indexes, etc., upon which they are based. A valuable work for reference librarians, acquisitions librarians, and catalogers.   Z1033.M5D64

Guide to microforms in print. Author, title. 1978– . Westport, Conn. : Microform Review, 1978– . Annual.   **AA131**

Guide to microforms in print. Subject (1978– . Westport, Conn., 1978– . Annual).

The *Author, title* and *Subject* guides are companion compilations replacing three earlier publications: *Guide to microforms in print* (1961–77), *Subject guide to microforms in print* (1962/63–77) and *International microforms in print* (1974/75). They provide "a cumulative annual listing of microform titles, comprising books, journals, newspapers, government publications, archival material, collections and other projects, etc. [excepting theses and dissertations], which are currently available from micropublishing organizations throughout the world."—*Introd.* Both have introductory matter in English, French, German and Spanish.

The author/title series is an alphabetical main-entry listing; the arrangement of the subject series is based on the Library of Congress classification system. Both include pertinent ordering information.

Beginning 1979, an interim supplement adds new listings in both main-entry and subject arrangements.   Z1033.M5G8

An index to microform collections / ed. by Ann Niles. Westport, Conn. : Meckler Pub., c1984. 891 p. (Meckler Publishing series in library micrographics management, no. 11). **AA132**

Each self-contained volume analyzes commercially published microform collections of monographs; v. 1 includes 26 sets with more than 9,000 monographs, and v. 2, 44 sets with more than 11,000 monographs. The author "chose smaller collections since the larger ones are more likely to be cataloged through the ARL Microform Project."—*Introd.* Contents are listed under each set; each volume has author and title indexes.   Z1033.M5I53

Library of Congress. Processing Department. British manuscripts project : a checklist of the microfilms prep. in England and Wales for the American Council of Learned Societies, 1941–1945 / comp. by Lester K. Born. Wash., 1955. 179 p. **AA133**

Repr.: N.Y. : Greenwood, 1968.

Lists the contents of 2,652 reels of microfilm containing reproductions of manuscripts and some rare printed materials found in libraries in England and Wales. The period covered is from medieval times to the 18th century. Copies of the films may be purchased from the Photoduplication Service of the Library of Congress.
                                          Z6620.G7U5

Modern Language Association of America. Reproductions of manuscripts and rare printed books. Short title list. (*In* PMLA : Publ. of the Modern Language Assoc. of America, 65 [Apr. 1950] : 289–338).   **AA134**

"Complete to January 1, 1950."—*p. 289.*

"Rotographs or microfilms of the … materials listed … are now on deposit in the Library of Congress."—*p. 289.* These are available for interlibrary loan, or microfilm copies may usually be purchased.
                                          Z1012.M6

National register of microform masters / comp. by the Library of Congress with the cooperation of the American Libr. Assoc. and the Assoc. of Research Libraries. Sept. 1965–1983. Wash. : Library of Congress, 1965–83. **AA135**

Lists and locates microfilm masters (those used only for making copies) from which libraries may acquire prints without the expense of making another master. Originally arranged by LC or NUC card numbers, with a separate section by main entry for those items for which cards are not available; a third section listed serial publications alphabetically by main entry. With the 1970 annual a single, alphabetical listing by main entry was adopted. Includes microform masters of "foreign and domestic books, pamphlets, serials, and foreign doctoral dissertations but excludes technical reports, typescript translations, foreign or domestic archival manuscript collections, U.S. doctoral dissertations, and masters' theses."—*Foreword.* Holdings of commercial microform producers as well as of libraries are represented.

A 1965–75 cumulation, with all reports for the period in a single alphabetical sequence (i.e., with the 1965–69 listings which were originally arranged by catalog card number integrated into the main-entry listing) was published 1976.   Z1033.M5N3

Philadelphia Bibliographical Center and Union Library Catalogue. Union list of microfilms. Rev., enl., and cumulated ed. Ann Arbor, Mich. : J. W. Edwards, 1951. 1961 col.
                                          AA136

Supersedes the 1942 edition and its 5 supplements. Lists some 25,000 titles held on microfilm by 197 institutions, reported through June 1949. Includes materials of all kinds, the fullness of information depending on what was furnished by the individual library. Arrangement is alphabetical, and each entry gives Library of Congress subject classification, bibliographical information, and the location of negative and positive microfilms and of the originals when available. Newspapers are listed by title, with full information on the years covered and the location of negatives and positives, except when the newspaper was included in *Newspapers on microfilm* (*see* headnotes, Section AE), in which case reference is given to the latter.

———. ———. 1949–59. (Ann Arbor, 1961. 2 v.).

A supplement to the basic list, including more than 52,000 entries for all types of materials, reported by 215 libraries during the period July 1, 1949–July 31, 1959. Lists all serials except newspapers.

Omits dissertations which are covered by *Dissertation abstracts international* (AG13) and various other materials listed in existing bibliographies (*see* Introd.).

Reviews

Microform review. v. 1, no. 1 (Jan. 1972)– . Weston, Conn. : [Microform Review], 1972– . Quarterly.   **AA137**

Allen B. Veaner, ed.

In addition to articles on microform projects and developments of interest to librarians and scholars, a large portion of each issue is devoted to reviews and evaluations of microform series, both current and retrospective.

Cumulative microform reviews (1972/76– . Westport, Conn. : Microform Review Inc., 1978–).

A periodic reprinting, with cumulated title index, of the reviews of micropublications appearing in v. 1–5 (1972–76) and subsequent volumes of *Microform review.*   Z265.M565

Translations

Bibliographia neerlandica. [New enl. ed.]. The Hague : Nijhoff, 1962. 598 p.   **AA138**

For annotation, *see* DC450.   Z2446.M64

Bibliographie der Übersetzungen deutschsprachiger Werke / Verzeichnis der in der Deutschen Bücherei eingegangenen Schriften, bearb. und hrsg. von der Deutschen Bücherei. Jahrg. 1 (1954)– Jahrg. 37 (1990). Leipzig : Verlag für Buch- und Bibliothekswesen, 1954–90. Quarterly. **AA139**

Subtitle varies.

A quarterly bibliography listing translations from German into other languages, published since 1951. Arranged by language, each subdivided by large class groups, with indexes: classified, author, and publisher. Bibliographic information is detailed; the translated title is followed by the original German title in brackets; and prices are included.

Absorbed by: *Deutsche Nationalbibliographie und Bibliographie der im Ausland erschienen deutschsprachigen Veröffentlichungen. Reihe G, Fremdsprachigen Germanica und Übersetzungen deutschsprachiger Werke* (AA142).   Z2234.T7B5

Canadian translations = Traductions canadiennes. 1984/ 85– . Ottawa : National Library of Canada = Bibliothèque nationale du Canada, 1987– . Annual.   **AA140**

Introductory and explanatory matter in English and French.

A record of translations published in Canada and cataloged by the National Library of Canada during the year of coverage. Arranged by broad Universal Decimal Classification, with author/title index incorporating cross-references and added entries. Includes translations in any language, although the great bulk of entries is in French or English.   Z1369.C28

Cumulative index to English translations, 1948–1968. Boston : G. K. Hall, 1973. 2 v.   **AA141**

Cumulates the entries from the annual volumes of the *Index translationum* (AA144) for those translations published in Australia, Canada, New Zealand, Republic of Eire, Republic of South Africa, U. K., and U. S. The overwhelming majority of entries is for translations into English, but a few translations into other languages are included. Entries are reproduced from the original volumes (n.s.v. 1–21) of *Index translationum* without reconciliation of variant entries, provision of adequate cross- references, or other re-editing.   Z6514.T7C8

Deutsche Nationalbibliographie und Bibliographie der im Ausland erschienenen deutschsprachigen Veröffentlichungen : Reihe G, Fremdsprachige Germanica und Übersetzungen deutschsprachiger Werke—Vierteljährliches Verzeichnis / bearb. und hrsg.: Die Deutsche Bibliothek. G01/02 (Juni 1992)– . Frankfurt am Main : Buchhändler-Vereinigung, 1992– . Quarterly.   **AA142**

Formed by the merger of *Bibliographie der Übersetzungen deutschsprachiger Werke* (AA139), and *Bibliographie fremdsprachiger Germanica*, publ. 1972–89.

A quarterly listing of German works translated into other languages: the original German title is provided. Arranged by broad subject. Each issue is indexed by author/title (including the original title)/keyword, by language, and by publisher; the indexes cumulate annually.

Fromm, Hans. Bibliographie deutscher Übersetzungen aus dem Französischen, 1700–1948 ... . Baden-Baden : Verlag für Kunst und Wissenschaft, 1950–53. 6 v.   **AA143**

Contents: Verzeichnis A, Alphabetical list of authors and titles of translations from French, A–Z; Verzeichnis B, Translations of French texts by German authors; Verzeichnis C, Alphabetical list of German collections, series, miscellanies, anthologies, etc., containing only translations from French. Index A, Alphabetical index of translators; Index B, Alphabetical index of German titles arranged in List A under the French titles.

Title pages and introductory matter in German, French, and English. The main list records books and some periodical articles under author and French title, followed by full bibliographical information of German translations.   Z2174.T7F7

Index translationum : Répertoire international des traductions = International bibliography of translations. no. 1 (juil. 1932)–31 (jan. 1940); nouv. sér., v. 1 (1948)–39 (1986). Paris : UNESCO, 1932–86. Annual.   **AA144**

Repr. (first series, no. 1–31): Nendeln : Kraus Repr., 1974, in 4 v. Suspended after v. 39 (1986).

Issued by the International Institute of Intellectual Co-operation, 1932–40; suspended Apr. 1940–47.

Frequency varies: the first series was quarterly; the new series, annual.

Entries are arranged by country, and under country name by the ten major headings of the Universal Decimal Classification. Complete bibliographical information, including the original language and title, are given when available. Both series include indexes of authors, publishers, and translators. The last issue of the first series, published in Jan. 1940, covered 12 countries including the USSR. The new series began with a coverage of 26 countries, which was increased to 75 in 1961, and varies slightly from year to year.

•Continued by: *Index translationum* [database] (Paris : UNESCO, 1979–). Available on CD-ROM; first disc covers 1979–94, update frequency not yet known.   Z6514.T7I42

Anonyms and pseudonyms

Bibliography

Taylor, Archer. The bibliographical history of anonyma and pseudonyma / Archer Taylor and Frederic J. Mosher. Chicago : Univ. of Chicago Pr. for the Newberry Libr., 1951. 288 p. : ill.   **AA145**

Preliminary chapters discuss homonyms, latinized names, pseudepigrapha, anonyma and pseudonyma, confusing titles, and fictitious facts of publication. A classified guide to dictionaries and lists of anonyma and pseudonyma, and an index to the historical chapters are included. Bibliography, p. 207–79.   Z1041.T3

International

Pseudonyms and nicknames dictionary / Jennifer Mossman, ed. 3rd ed. Detroit : Gale, c1987. 2 v. (2207 p.).   **AA146**
2nd ed., 1982.

Subtitle: A guide to aliases, appellations, assumed names, code names, cognomens, cover names, epithets, initialisms, nicknames, noms de guerre, noms de plume, pen names, pseudonyms, sobriquets, and stage names of contemporary and historical persons, including the subjects' real names, basic biographical information, and citations for the sources from which the entries were compiled. Covers actors, aristocrats, artists, athletes, authors, clergymen, criminals, entertainers, film stars, journalists, military leaders, monarchs, musicians, playwrights, poets, politicans, popes, rogues, saints, theatrical figures, and other prominent personalities of all nations throughout the ages.

Real names and nicknames are presented in a single alphabetical sequence, with cross-reference from the nickname or pseudonym to the real name (where the full information is given). About 135,000 entries.   CT120.P8

Writers in English

Atkinson, Frank. Dictionary of literary pseudonyms : a selection of popular modern writers in English. 4th enl. ed. London : Libr. Assoc. Publ. ; Chicago : Amer. Libr. Assoc., 1987. 299 p.   **AA147**

1st ed., 1975, had title: *Dictionary of pseudonyms and pennames.* 3rd ed., 1982.

"This dictionary is limited to writers in English and the selection has been made from those writing in the years 1900 to date."—*Introd.* In two sections: Real names; Pseudonyms. Sources of information are not indicated, although the preface states that both publishers and the writers themselves were queried in an effort to establish identities. About 11,500 names in this edition.   Z1065.A83

Clarke, Joseph F. Pseudonyms. London : Book Club Associates, [1977]. 252 p.   **AA148**

Not limited to pennames, but extends to "anyone well known who changed his or her name. Of the 3400 pseudonyms listed, pennames account for roughly half the collection, stage names a third; the remainder of the entries cover personalities in the various spheres of politics, sport, crime, painting and sculpture, and music."—*Introd.* Many entries include brief remarks on background and choice of pseudonym.   Z1041.C57

Cushing, William. Anonyms : a dictionary of revealed authorship. Cambridge, [Mass.] : Cushing, 1889. 829 p.   **AA149**

Includes both English and American works. In two alphabets: (1) anonymous titles followed by name of author; (2) index of authors found only in the *Anonyms.* Does not give authorities.

———. *Initials and pseudonyms : a dictionary of literary disguises* (N.Y. : Crowell, c1885–88. 2 v.).

In two series, together including about 18,500 initials and pseudonyms, principally English and American, with a few well-known Continental names. Each series is in two parts: (1) initials followed by real name; (2) real name followed by pseudonym or initials, with short biographical notices. Does not give authorities.   Z1045.C98A

Halkett, Samuel. Dictionary of anonymous and pseudonymous English literature / by Samuel Halkett and John Laing. New and enl. ed. / by James Kennedy, W. A. Smith and A. F. Johnson. Edinburgh : Oliver and Boyd, 1926–62. 9 v.   **AA150**

1st ed.: Edinburgh : Paterson, 1882–88. 4 v.

Contents: v. 1–6 (publ. 1926–34), A–Z. Supplement, v. 6, p. 273–449; v. 7, Index and 2nd suppl.; v. 8, 1900–50; v. 9 (*see* below).

Vols. 8–9 by Dennis E. Rhodes and Anna E. C. Simoni.

A comprehensive list, arranged alphabetically by first word of title not an article, giving for each item listed: title (sometimes shortened), size, paging, place, date, author's name, and (in some cases) the

AA151 — title

authority for attribution of authorship. The best list for English works, although since most of the authorities cited are general in character, the work is not final authority in cases of disputed authorship.

Vol. 8 aims to give the authorship of as many anonymous and pseudonymous works as possible, published in the English language between 1900 and 1949 inclusive.

From 1950 on, the same kind of information may usually be found in *British national bibliography* (AA689) for books published in Great Britain and in *National union catalog* (AA111).

Vol. 9, originally planned to "consist entirely of additions and corrections to the period before 1900" (*Pref.*), now includes also as many additional items for the 1900–50 period as possible.

A new edition has begun to appear as:

————. *A dictionary of anonymous and pseudonymous publications in the English language* (3rd [rev. and enl.] ed., John Horden, ed. [Harlow, Eng.] : Longman, [1980]– . [v. 1]– . In progress).

At head of title: Halkett and Laing.

Contents: [v. 1] 1475–1640.

A thorough revision for which each item in the 2nd ed. and its supplements was checked and revised, and the whole cast into a different form: i.e., the new edition is to be presented in three chronological segments (1475–1640, 1641–1700, and 1701–1800), each segment being an alphabetical title listing with indexes. Entries are numbered, and each entry now includes "full documentary evidence for the attribution of authorship made" (*Pref.*) Indication is given of erroneous attributions in the 2nd ed.; and items not truly anonymous which were entered in the 2nd ed. are carried forward with appropriate comment, so that no item from the previous edition is omitted. The first volume includes an index of writers' names, a list of pseudonyms (with supposed writer), a table of *STC* numbers, a table of Allison and Rogers numbers, and a table of Greg numbers.   Z1065.H17

North America

Canada

Amtmann, Bernard. Contributions to a dictionary of Canadian pseudonyms and anonymous works relating to Canada = Contributions à un dictionnaire des pseudonymes canadiens et des ouvrages anonymes relatifs au Canada. Montreal : Author, 1973. 144 p.   **AA151**

Text in English or French.

A listing by pseudonym or anonymous title, without indication of source of the attribution. Addenda, p.137–44.   Z1047.A47

Mexico

Ruiz Castañeda, María del Carmen. Catálogo de seudónimos, anagramas, iniciales y otros alias usados por escritores mexicanos y extranjeros que han publicado en México / María del Carmen Ruiz Castañeda ; Sergio Márquez Acevedo, coautor. México, D.F. : Universidad Nacional Autónoma de México, Instituto de Investigaciones Bibliográficas, 1985. lxxi, 290 p. (Instrumenta bibliographica, 6).   **AA152**

A single alphabetical list of authors (with dates and pseudonyms) and cross-references from pseudonyms to real names. Addenda and bibliography of works consulted.   Z1049.M6R84

Latin America

Medina, José Toribio. Diccionario de anónimos y seudónimos hispanoamericanos. Buenos Aires : Impr. de la Univ., 1925. 2 v. in 1. (Buenos Aires, Univ. Nacional. Inst. de Investigaciones Históricas. Publ. 26–7).   **AA153**

Many useful notes; sources of attribution sometimes given.

Supplemented by:

(1) Ricardo Victoria, *Errores y omisiones del Diccionario de anónimos y seudónimos hispoanoamericanos de José Toribio de Medina* (Buenos Aires : Viau & Zona, 1928. 338 p.).

An extensive critique by Guillermo Feliú Cruz appeared in *Boletin del Inst. de Investigationes Históricas* 8:254–59; 9:237–80 (abril-junio, oct-dic. 1929) and was reprinted as *Advertencias saludables a un criticastro de mala ley* (Buenos Aires, 1929).

(2) Victoria's "Verdades que levantan roncha. Belitras enfurecidos," *Gaceta del foro*, año 15 (11 Abr. 1930): 173–78.

Has about 16 columns of "Nuevas adiciones al 'Diccionario' de Medina," p. 274–78, in alphabetical order.

(3) Victoria's *Neuva epanortosis al Diccvionario de anónimos y seudónimos de J.T. Medina* (Buenos Aires : Rosso, 1929. 207 p.).

Entry is by title of the anonymous or pseudonymous work, with cross-references from the pseudonym and the true name of the author. Authorities not cited.   Z1049.A1M4

Sáenz, Gerardo. Diccionario de seudónimos y escritores Iberoamericanos : thesaurus, seudónimos, etc., de Iberoamérica. Miami, Fla. : Ediciones Universal, 1991. 405 p.   **AA154**

A well-documented dictionary of pennames of Latin American (including Cuban) writers. Pseudonyms are listed first, with references to the writer's real name. The second half is an alphabetical listing of authors, with their pseudonyms and sources for each attribution. A bibliography of further references is also provided.   Z1049.A1S3 1991

South America

Argentina

Cutolo, Vicente Osvaldo. Diccionario de alfónimos y seudónimos de la Argentina (1800–1930). Buenos Aires : Ed. Elche, 1962. 160 p.   **AA155**

1,100 entries; authority frequently cited.   Z1049.A7C8

Tesler, Mario. Diccionario argentino de seudónimos. Buenos Aires : Editorial Galerna, c1991. 277 p.   **AA156**

In two parts, the first listing pseudonyms, and the second the given names, with very brief biographical information (usually dates and occupation.) Sources not cited.   Z1049.A7T47

Brazil

Barros Paiva, Tancredo de. Achêgas a um diccionario de pseudonymos, iniciaes, abreviaturas e obras anonymas de auctores brasileiros e de estrangeiros, sobre o Brasil ou no mesmo impressas. Rio de Janeiro : J. Leite, 1929. 248 p.   **AA157**

More than 1,500 entries. Authorities not cited.   Z1049.B8B3

Colombia

Pérez Ortiz, Rubén. Seudónimos colombianos. Bogotá, 1961. 276 p. (Publicaciones del Inst. Caro y Cuervo. Ser. bibliográfica, 2).   **AA158**

In two parts: the first is a list by pseudonym, giving real name; the second is a list of Colombian authors indicating any pseudonyms which they have used.   Z1731.C6 no.2

Caribbean and Islands of the Western Atlantic

Dominican Republic

Rodriguez Demorizi, Emilio. Seudónimos dominicanos. Ciudad Trujillo : Ed. Montalvo, 1956. 280 p. **AA159**
Authorities sometimes cited. Z1049.D6R6

Europe (by region)

Slovak writers

Kormúth, Dezider. Slovník slovenských pseudonymov 1919–1944. Martin : Matica Slovenská, 1974. 594 p. **AA160**
The first section gives the pseudonym and the corresponding true name. A second section arranged by the Slovak authors' real names gives references to publications in which the pseudonyms were used. PG5402.K6

Writers in Yiddish

Chajes, Saul. Thesaurus pseudonymorum quae in litteratura hebraica et judaeo-germanica inveniuntur = Pseudonymen-Lexikon der hebräischen und jiddischen Literatur. Wien : Glanz, 1933. various pagings. **AA161**
Added title page in Yiddish.
In Yiddish, with index in romanized form of name. Z1069.5.C5

Europe (by country)

Belgium

Delecourt, Jules Victor. Dictionnaire des anonymes et pseudonymes, XVᵉ siècle–1900 / mis en ordre et enrichi par G. de LeCourt. Brussels : Académie Royale, 1960. v. 1 (1281 p.). **AA162**
At head of title: Bibliographie nationale. No more published.
A reworking and updating of the author's *Essai d'un dictionnaire des ouvrages anonymes et pseudonymes publiés en Belgique au XIVᵉ siècle et principalement depuis 1830* (Brussels, 1863. 548 p.). Z1071.D4

Montagne, Victor Alexander de la. Vlaamsche pseudoniemen : bibliographische opzoekingen. Roeselare : DeSeyn-Verhougstraete, 1884. 132 p. **AA163**
Includes some extensive notes, but does not cite sources of attributions. Z1071.M758

Bulgaria

Bogdanov, Ivan. Rechnik na bŭlgarskite psevdonimi : pisateli, nauchni rabotnitsi, prevodachi, karikaturisti, publitsisti, zhurnalisti. 3., osnovno prer. i dop. izd. Sofiia : "D-r Petŭr Beron", 1989. 528 p. **AA164**
1st ed., 1961; 2nd ed., 1978.
In three sections: (1) a listing of pseudonyms, (2) a listing of initials and abbreviations, and (3) a listing of nonalphabetical symbols used to sign works. Each entry provides the real name, when and where the pseudonym was used, and the source of the information; sections are divided into Cyrillic and Roman alphabets. Indexed by real name. Z1080.B8B6

Czechoslovakia

Ormis, Ján Vladimir. Slovník slovenských pseudonymov. [V Turč sv. Martine] : Slovenská Národná Knižnica, 1944. 366 p. (Knihy Slovenskej národnej knižnice v Turčianskom svätom Martine. Sväzok, I). **AA165**
Authorities cited. Z1066.5.O7

Denmark

Ehrencron-Müller, Holger. Anonym– og Pseudonym-Lexikon for Danmark og Island til 1920 og Norge til 1814. København : Hagerup, 1940. 391 p. **AA166**
Issued in parts. Sources not cited. Z1074.E5

Estonia

Kahu, Meelik. Eesti pseudonüümide leksikon. Tallinn : "Eesti Raamat", c1991. v. 1. (In progress?). **AA167**
Title on added t.p.: *Leksikon pseudonymorum Estonicorum.*
Contents: v. 1, 1821–1900.
A listing of pseudonyms used by Estonian writers from all fields, produced under the auspices of the Kreutzwald Literary Museum. Listed by pseudonym, citing the book or journal where the pseudonym was used, then by author, with the pseudonym(s) and an indication of profession. Z1073.6.K34

France

Brunet, Gustave. Dictionnaire des ouvrages anonymes [de Barbier] : suivi des Supercheries littéraires dévoilées [de Quérard] : supplément à la dernière édition de ces deux ouvrages (Edition Daffis). Paris : Féchoz, 1889. 310 col., cix p.; 122 col., xiv p. **AA168**
Repr.: Paris : Maisonneuve & Larose, 1964.
Contents: Dictionnaire des ouvrages anonymes (Supplément); Essai sur les bibliothèques imaginaires; Les devises des vieux poètes: étude littéraire et bibliographique, par M. Gustave Mouravit; Appel aux bibliophiles, aux érudits et aux curieux ["Désiderata," i.e., une liste d'anonymes et de pseudonymes dont le mystère n'a pas été découvert]; Les supercheries littéraires dévoilées (Supplément); Varia: Pseudonymes étrangers. Traductions supposées. Supercheries typographiques. Z1067.B92

Quérard, Joseph Marie. Les supercheries littéraires dévoilées. 2. éd. Paris : Daffis, 1869–[79]. 7 v. **AA169**
Vols. 1–3 repr.: Paris : Maisonneuve & Larose, 1964.
Subtitle: Galerie des écrivains français de toute l'Europe qui se sont déguisés sous des anagrammes, des astéronymes, des cryptonymes, des initialismes, des noms littéraires, des pseudonymes facétieux ou bizarres, etc. 2. éd., considérablement augm., pub. par Gustave Brunet et Pierre Jannet. Suivie 1ᵉ, Du Dictionnaire des ouvrages anonymes, par Ant.–Alex. Barbier. 3. éd., rev. et augm. par Olivier Barbier. ... 2ᵉ, D'une table générale des noms réels des écrivains anonymes et pseudonymes cités dans les deux ouvrages.
Contents: v. 1–3, J. M. Quérard. Les supercheries littéraires dévoilées. 2. éd., A–Z; v. 4–7, A. A. Barbier. Dictionnaire des ouvrages anonymes. 3. éd., A–Z. Anonymes Latins.
The same edition of Barbier was also issued separately (Paris : Féchoz. 4 v.; repr.: Hildesheim : Olms, 1963. 4 v.). The *Table générale des noms réels* was never issued.

Gives notes about the books and editions listed, but in general does not give authority for identification of authors. Supplemented by Brunet's *Dictionnaire des ouvrages anonymes* (AA168).　　Z1067.Q4S

Germany

Holzmann, Michael. Deutsches Anonymen-Lexikon / Michael Holzmann and Hanns Bohatta. Weimar : Gesellschaft der Bibliophilen, 1902–28. 7.　　**AA170**
> Repr.: Hildesheim : Olms, 1961.
> Contents: v. 1–4, 1501–1850; v. 5, supplement, 1851–1908; v. 6, 1501–1910, additions and corrections; v. 7, 1501–1926, additions and corrections.
> Includes, in the four lists, some 83,000 entries. Arranged alphabetically by title, with author's name supplied for each and the authority for the information indicated.　　Z1068.H76

———————— Deutsches Pseudonymen-Lexikon / Michael Holzmann and Hanns Bohatta. Wien : Akademie Verlag, 1906. 323 p.　　**AA171**
> Repr.: Hildesheim : Olms, 1961.
> Gives pseudonym, followed by real name, and indicates the authority for the information.　　Z1068.H77

Namenschlüssel zu Pseudonymen, Doppelnamen und Namensabwandlungen. 4. Ausg. Hildesheim : Olms, 1965–68. 2 v.　　**AA172**
> Contents: Bd. 1, Stand vom 1. Juli 1941; Bd. 2, Ergänzungen aus der Zeit vom 1. Juli 1941 bis 31. Dezember 1965.
> Bd. 1 is a reprint of the 3rd ed. of the Preussische Staatsbibliothek's *Namenschlüssel die Verweisungen der Berliner Titeldrucke zu Pseudonymen, Doppelnamen und Namensabwandlungen* (Berlin, 1941); Bd. 2 represents additional listings.　　Z695.1.P4N34

Weigand, Jörg. Pseudonyme : ein Lexikon : Decknamen der Autoren deutschsprachiger erzählender Literatur. Baden-Baden : Nomos, 1991. 282 p.　　**AA173**
> A guide to pseudonyms used in 20th-century German popular literature—detective novels, romances, children's books, etc. Arranged by the author's given name, with an index by pseudonyms. Sources not cited.　　PT741.W45

Greece

Ntelopoulos, Kyriakos. Neoellēnika philologika pseudonyma. Athenai : Kollegion Athenon, 1969. 143 p.　　**AA174**
> More than 1,400 pseudonyms of modern Greek authors. Approach is both from true name of author to pseudonym and from pseudonym to true name. Authority is noted for most entries.　　Z1069.N85

Hungary

Gulyás, Pál. Magyar írói álnév lexikon : a magyarországi írók álnevei és egyéb jegyei. Függelék: Néhány száz névtelen munka jegyzéke. Budapest : Akadémiai Kiadó, 1956. 706 p.　　**AA175**
> Added title page in Latin: Lexicon pseudonymorum hungaricum: pseudonyma et alia signa scriptorum regni hungariae.
> An alphabetical list of pseudonyms and initials with the author's name supplied for each, and authorities indicated. Includes also a list of anonymous works whose authors were identified.　　Z1069.7.G8

Sz. Debreczeni, Kornélia. Magyar írói álnév lexikon : a magyarországi írók álnevei és egyéb jegyei : Gulyás Pál lexikonának kiegészítése = Lexicon pseudonymorum Hungaricum : pseudonyma et alia signa scriptorum regni Hungariae. Budapest : Petőfi Irodalmi Múzeum, 1992. 688 p.　　**AA176**

Supplements and updates, but does not replace, Pál Gulyas, *Magyar írói álnév lexikon* (AA175); follows his format.　　Z1069.7.S78

Italy

Melzi, Gaetano. Dizionario di opere anonime e pseudonime di scrittori italiani : o come che sia aventi relazione all'Italia. Milano : Coi Torchi di L. di Giacomo Pirole, 1848–59. 3 v.　　**AA177**
> Repr.: N.Y. : Burt Franklin, 1960.
> Covers the 16th to 19th centuries. Many useful bibliographic notes; sources of attribution sometimes indicated.
> ———. *Supplemento*, comp. da Giambattista Passano (Ancona : Morelli, 1887. 517 p. [Repr. with Rocco, below: N.Y. : Burt Franklin, 1960]).
> *Supplemento al Melzi e al Passano*, di Emmanuele Rocco (Napoli : Chiurazzi, 1888. 16 p.).
> Repr.: N.Y. : Burt Franklin, 1960.

Netherlands

Doorninck, Jan Izaak van. Vermomde en naamlooze schrijvers : opgespoord op het gebiet der Nederlandsche en Vlaamsche letteren. 2. uitg. der "Bibliothek van anonymen en pseudonymen.". Leiden : Brill, 1883–85. 2 pts. in l v.　　**AA178**
> Contents: v. 1, Pseudonyms and initials. 671 col.; v. 2, Anonyms. 681 col.
> Many bibliographical notes and notes on sources are given.
> Supplemented by: A. de Kempenaer, *Vermomde Nederlandsche en Vlaamsche schrijvers, vervolg op J.I. van Doorninck's Vermomde en naamlooze schrijvers…* (Leiden : Sijthoff, [1928]).　　Z1072.D69B2

Norway

Pettersen, Hjalmar Marius. Norsk anonym– og pseudonym-lexikon. Kristiania : Steen, 1924. 690 col., [34] p.　　**AA179**
> 1st ed., 1890, had title: *Anonymer og pseudonymer i den norske literatur 1678–1890.*
> Added title page in English: Dictionary of anonyms and pseudonyms in Norwegian literature.
> Sources sometimes given.
> ———. ———. "Tilføielser og rettelser" (In: *Nordisk tidskrift fr bok–och biblioteksväsen* 12 [1925]:118–26.).　　Z1075.P49

Poland

Bar, Adam. Słownik pseudonimów i kryptonimów pisarzy polskich oraz Polski dotyczących / opracował Adam Bar … i Tad. Godłowskiego …. Kraków : [Nakł. Krakowskiego koła Związku Bibljotekarzy Polskich], 1936–38. 3 v. (Prace bibljoteczne Krakowskiego koła Związku Bibljotekarzy Polskich , VII–IX).　　**AA180**
> Vols. 1–2, Alphabetical list of pseudonyms, initials, etc., with full name, title, and source of attribution; v. 3, Real name followed by pseudonym.　　Z1073.5.B22

Portugal

Fonseca, Martinho Augusto Ferreira da. Subsidios para um diccionario de pseudonymos, iniciaes e obras anonymas de escriptores portuguezes, contribuição para o estudo da litteratura portugueza. Lisboa : Academia Real das Sciencias, 1896. 298 p.　　**AA181**

In three parts: (1) pseudonyms; (2) initials; (3) anonymous works. Z1078.F67

Romania

Straje, Mihail. Dictionar de pseudonime, alonime [sic], anagrame, asteronime, criptonime ale scriitorilor si publicistilor români. Bucuresti : Editura Minerva, 1973. 810 p. **AA182**

A dictionary of Romanian pseudonyms, etc., with references to sources of identification. Z1080.R6S8

Russia

Gosudarstvennaia publichnaia biblioteka imeni M.E. Saltykova-Shchedrina. Russkie anonimnye i podpisannye psevdonimami proizvedeniia pechati : 1801–1926: bibliograficheskiĭ ukazatel' / [sost. G. Z. Guseva et al.]. Leningrad : Gos. Publichnaia Biblioteka, 1977–79. 3 v. **AA183**

A listing by title of works published anonymously or pseudonymously, with indication of authorship and source of attribution. Does not include material covered in Ivan Filippovich Masanov's *Slovar' psevdonimov russkikh pisateleĭ, uchenykh i obshchestvennykh deiateleĭ* (AA184). Index of attributions and pseudonyms in v. 3.

Masanov, Ivan Filippovich. Slovar' psevdonimov russkikh pisateleĭ, uchenykh i obshchestvennykh deiateleĭ : V chetyrekh tomakh / Podgotovil k pechati IU. I. Masanov. Red. B. P. Koz'min. Moskva : Izd-vo Vses. knizh. palaty, 1956–60. 4 v. **AA184**

An enlarged edition of Masanov's dictionary of Russian pseudonyms (Moskva, 1941). Vol. 3 completes the Russian alphabet and lists Latin and Greek pseudonyms and other symbols used by Russian authors. Vol. 4 contains a name index and additions to v. 1–3. Z1073.M33

Spain

Rogers, Paul Patrick. Diccionario de seudónimos literarios españoles, con algunas iniciales / Paul Patrick Rogers and Felipe-Antonio Lapuente. [Madrid] : Gredos, [1977]. 608 p. (Biblioteca románica hispánica, 5). **AA185**

Entry is under pseudonym, with index of true names. Entries usually provide citations to one or more publications in which the pseudonym was used. Select bibliography. Z1077.R63

Sweden

Andersson, Per. Pseudonymregister. Lund : Bibliotekstjänst, [1967]. 184 p. **AA186**

Lists pseudonyms of Swedish writers, giving the true name but no biographical or bibliographical information. Z1076.A65

Bygdén, Anders Leonard. Svenskt anonym– och pseudonym-lexikon : bibliografisk förteckning öfver uppdagade anonymer och pseudonymer i den svenska litteraturen. Upsala : Berling, 1898–1915. 2 v. **AA187**

Includes a supplement, v. 2, col. 849–1052. Sources of attribution are usually given. Z1076.B98

Ukraine

Dei, Oleksii Ivanovych. Slovnyk ukrains'kykh psevdonimiv ta kriptonimiv (XVI–XX st.). Kyiv : Naukova Dumka, 1969. 557 p. **AA188**

A dictionary of about 10,000 pseudonyms; sources are given. Z1073.D4

Asia

Writers in Arabic

Dāghir, Yūsuf As'ad. Mu'jam al-asmā' al-musta 'ārah waaṣhābihā lā siyyama fī al-adab al-'Arabī al-hadīth. Bayrūt : Maktabat Lubnān, 1982. 291 p. **AA189**

A dictionary of pseudonyms of Arabic writers.

China

Shu, Austin C. W. Modern Chinese authors : a list of pseudonyms. East Lansing : Asian Studies Center, Michigan State Univ., 1969. 108 p. **AA190**

About 2,000 entries. Z1087.C6S56

India

Chatterjee, Amitabha. Dictionary of Indian pseudonyms. Calcutta : Mukherji Book House, [1977]. 170 p. **AA191**

A dictionary of about 3,500 pseudonyms used by Indian writers in all Indian languages and in English. Gives real name, an identifying phrase, and (when possible) date of birth. Index of real names giving reference to page number only—not to pseudonym. Sources not indicated. Z1087.I5C43

Virendra Kumar. Dictionary of pseudonmys [sic] in Indian literature. [Delhi] : Delhi Library Assoc., 1973. 163 p. (Delhi Lib. Assoc. English ser., no. 7). **AA192**

An initial attempt to provide a guide to the real names of pseudonymous Indian authors. Includes writers in various Indian languages. Under the pseudonym is indicated the real name, language, and year of birth of the writer. A second section provides a guide from original name to pseudonym. Z1087.I5V57

Australia and Oceania

Nesbitt, Bruce. Australian literary pseudonyms : an index, with selected New Zealand references / comp. by Bruce Nesbitt and Susan Hadfield. Adelaide : Libraries Board of South Australia, 1972. 134 p. **AA193**

Covers a literature that abounds in pseudonyms. Pseudonyms and real names are listed in a single alphabet, the pseudonym being entered as a *see* reference to the original name. Z1107.N47

Fictitious imprints

Brunet, Gustave. Imprimeurs imaginaires et libraires supposés : étude bibliographique, suivie de recherches sur quelques ouvrages imprimés avec des indications fictives de lieux ou avec des dates singulières. Paris : Tross, 1866. 290 p. **AA194**

Repr.: N.Y. : Burt Franklin, 1963.

Primarily a bibliography with some notes on variant editions, attributions, etc. Z1067.B9I

Parenti, Marino. Dizionario dei luoghi di stampa falsi, inventati o supposti in opere di autori e traduttori italiani : con un'appendice sulla data "Italia," e un saggio sui falsi luoghi italiani usati all'estero, o in Italia, da autori stranieri. Firenze : Sansoni, 1951. 311 p. : ill. (Biblioteca bibliografica italica, 1). **AA195**

Arranged alphabetically by place, and then chronologically, with an index of actual and pseudonymous authors. Many facsimiles.

Weller, Emil Ottokar. Die falschen und fingirten Druckorte : Repertorium der seit erfindung der Buchdruckerkunst unter falscher Firma erschienenen deutschen, lateinischen und französischen Schriften. 2. verm. und verb. Aufl. Leipzig : W. Engelmann, 1864. 2 v. **AA196**

Repr.: Hildesheim : Olms, 1970. 3 v.

Chronological arrangement within each volume, v. 1 dealing with German and Latin works, 1510–1862; v. 2 with French works, 1530–1863; each volume has its own index. Vol. 3 of the reprint edition was originally published 1867 with Weller's *Index pseudonymorum* as "Drittes Supplementheft: Neue Nachträge zu den 'Falschen und fingirten Druckorten,' 2. Aufl. (Leipzig, 1864)." It offers both additional listings and corrections to v. 1–2. Z1041.W43

ANCIENT, MEDIEVAL AND RENAISSANCE MANUSCRIPTS

Guides

Fitzgerald, Wilma. Ocelli nominum : names and shelf marks of famous/familiar manuscripts. Toronto : Pontifical Inst. of Mediaeval Studies, c1992. 170 p. (Subsidia mediaevalia, 19). **AA197**

"Earlier versions of this work were published as articles in *Mediaeval studies*; they have been thoroughly revised, corrected, collated and enlarged for this edition."—*Leaf before t.p.*

An alphabetical listing of common names for manuscripts, with their locations and class marks. Z6601.F58 1992

Bibliography

Braswell, Laurel Nichols. Western manuscripts from classical antiquity to the Renaissance : a handbook. N.Y. : Garland, 1981. 382 p. (Garland reference library of the humanities, v. 139). **AA198**

An annotated bibliography intended to serve as a guide to the study of early Western manuscripts. Arrangement is meant to proceed from "first steps in identifying a manuscript to its transcription and ultimately its edition."—*Introd.* Includes sections on incipits, paleography, diplomatics and archives, illumination, music, codicology, textual criticism, bibliographies and reference works. Indexed. Z105.B73

Ker, Neil Ripley. Medieval manuscripts in British libraries. Oxford : Clarendon Pr., 1969–92. v. 1–4. (In progress). **AA199**

Contents: v. 1, London; v. 2, Abbotsford–Keele; v. 3, Lampeter–Oxford; v. 4, Paisley-York (by Ker and A. J. Piper).

Intends to "provide information about manuscripts, other than muniments and binding fragments, written before 1500, in Latin or a Western European language, either by reference to an existing catalogue or by description."—*Pref.* Z6620.G7K4

Scriptorium : revue internationale des études relatives aux manuscrits = International review of manuscript studies. t. 1 (1946/47)– . Brussels : Centre d'etudes des manuscrits [etc.], 1947– . Two no. a year. **AA200**

Contributions in English, French, German, and Spanish.

Publisher and place of publication vary.

Includes current bibliographies of manuscript studies and facsimile editions. Z108.S35

Catalogs

Codices latini antiquiores : a palaeographical guide to Latin manuscripts prior to the ninth century / ed. by E. A. Lowe. Oxford : Clarendon Pr., 1934–71. 12 v. : facsims. **AA201**

Repr.: Osnabruck : Otto Zeller, 1982.

Edited under the auspices of the Union Académique Internationale for the American Council of Learned Societies and the Carnegie Institution of Washington.

Contents: pt. 1, Vatican City; pt. 2, Great Britain, Ireland; pt. 3–4, Italy; pt. 5, Paris; pt. 6, France; pt. 7, Switzerland; pt. 8–9, Germany; pt. 10, Austria, Belgium, Czechoslovakia, Denmark, Egypt, and Holland; pt. 11, Hungary, Luxembourg, Poland, Russia, Spain, Sweden, the United States, and Yugoslavia; pt. 12, Supplement.

Arranged by present location of manuscripts. Within date and language limits, this is the most comprehensive and detailed catalog of manuscripts ever published. It is far more than a "paleographical guide" as it includes notes about decoration, content, and history of the manuscripts. Prefaces point out items of particular paleographic or textual importance and discuss characteristics of significant book centers in various regions. The extensive references serve also as a general bibliography of manuscripts.

The supplement "contains newly found representatives from nearly every country" (*Introd.*), includes selected supplementary bibliography for the entire series, and provides an author index to all volumes. The introduction to the supplement notes that "Work is already in progress on a portable volume to contain, as an epilogue to the *C.L.A.* series, the editor's observations and reflections on the material that passed through his hands and along with that epilogue the numerous palaeographical indexes the twelve volumes call for"; however, the death of Lowe in 1969 puts publication of this volume in doubt.

Pt. 2, Great Britain and Ireland, was issued in a 2nd ed. in 1972, with some corrections and an effort to incorporate the findings of recent scholarship. Z114.C677

Bibliography

Bibliothèque Nationale (France). Les catalogues imprimés de la Bibliothèque Nationale : liste établié en 1943 suivie d'un supplément (1944–1952). Paris, 1953. 204 p., xxvii p. **AA202**

Catalogs of manuscripts: p. 4–57, iii–v. Lists some 250 catalogs of manuscripts in various languages, subjects, and collections.

§ Supplements Paul Oskar Kristeller, *Latin manuscript books before 1600* (AA207). Z927.P196

British Library. Department of Manuscripts. Catalogue of dated and datable manuscripts, c.700–1600 in the Department of Manuscripts, the British Library / Andrew G. Watson [comp.]. London : British Museum Pubns. [for] the British Library, [1979]. 2 v. : facsims. **AA203**

Contents: v. 1, The text; v. 2, The plates.

953 manuscripts, all but a few from before 1550, in the Cottonian, Arundel, Harley, Sloan, Lansdowne, Burney, King's, Egerton, Stowe, Yates Thompson, and Additional collections are listed alphabetically by collection, then by number. Entry gives collection, number, date and place of origin, author and title, and physical description. Notes cover evidence of date and origin, other manuscripts of the scribe, history of ownership, bibliographical references, and plate number in v. 2. List of rejected manuscripts; date index; name index.

———————— Index of manuscripts in the British Library. Cambridge, Eng. ; Teaneck, N.J. : Chadwyck-Healey, 1984–1986. 10 v. **AA204**

An alphabetical personal- and place-name index to manuscript collections acquired by the Library up to 1950. Entries are derived from more than 30 catalogs, both published and unpublished. Each entry includes the name of the manuscript item, the collection to which it belongs, its number within the collection, and its folio or article number (which may be used for ordering photocopies). Numerous cross-references from variant forms of names. Z921.L553B74

British Museum. Department of Manuscripts. The catalogues of the manuscript collections / [by T. C. Skeat]. Rev. ed. [London] : Trustees of the British Museum, 1962. 45 p. **AA205**

First issued in *Journal of documentation* 7 (1951): 18–60.

Annotated list of 176 printed and handwritten catalogs of the Museum's various collections of Western manuscripts.

§ Supplements Paul Oskar Kristeller's *Latin manuscript books before 1600* (AA207). Z6621.B844

Kristeller, Paul Oskar. Iter Italicum : a finding list of uncatalogued or incompletely catalogued humanistic manuscripts of the Renaissance in Italian and other libraries. London : Warburg Institute, 1963–93. v. 1–6 in 8. (In progress). **AA206**

Contents: v. 1, Italy: Agrigento to Novara; v. 2, Italy: Orvieto to Volterra. Vatican City; v. 3, Alia itinera I: Australia to Germany; v. 4, Alia itinera II: Great Britain to Spain; v. 5, Alia itinera III: Sweden to Yugoslavia. Utopia. Suppl. to Italy (A–F); v. 5 pt. 2, Index and addenda; v. 6, Italy III and Alia itinera IV. Suppl. to Italy (G–V). Suppl. to Vatican and Austria to Spain.

Originally intended to cover only italian repositories and collections, the work has been expanded to worldwide coverage. It was "conceived primarily as a finding list for certain texts, and the main emphasis is on the textual content of the manuscripts listed."—*Pref.* Geographical arrangement; v. 1 and v. 2 each has its own index; index to v. 3 published separately.

The section entitled "Utopia" in v. 5 "lists pertinent manuscripts owned by private collectors or antiquarian book dealers...[who] did not authorize me to disclose their name or address."—*Pref.* Z6611.H8K7

———————— Latin manuscript books before 1600 : a list of the printed catalogues and unpublished inventories of extant collections. 3rd ed. N.Y. : Fordham Univ. Pr., [1965]. 284 p. **AA207**

First published in *Traditio: studies in ancient and medieval history, thought and religion* 6 (1948):227–317 and 9 (1953):393–418. "New ed. rev." publ. 1960.

The 3rd ed. reprints the 1960 edition, adding a section of supplementary material (p. 233–84) which incorporates the addenda from previous edition with new listings.

Contents: A, Bibliography and statistics of libraries and their collections of manuscripts; B, Works describing manuscripts of more than one city; C, Printed catalogues and handwritten inventories of individual libraries, by cities.

A valuable guide to public collections in Europe and the U.S. Indicates the number of manuscripts included in a list, and analyzes lists covering more than one collection. Excludes archives and most private collections. Includes some lists of Greek and vernacular manuscripts since most collections are not divided according to language. Gives cross-references, but no index. Z6601.A1K7

A microfilm corpus of the indexes to printed catalogues of Latin manuscripts before 1600 A.D : based on P.O. Kristeller, Latin manuscript books before 1600, 3rd ed / prep. under the direction of F. Edward Cranz ; in consultation with P. O. Kristeller [microform]. New London, Conn. : Connecticut College Bookstore [distributor], 1982. 38 microfilm reels. **AA208**

Offers microfilms of "all the indexes to authors and works found in the catalogues listed in P. O. Kristeller's *Latin manuscripts before 1600* [AA207]" (*Pref.*) arranged in the order in which they appear in the Kristeller list. The accompanying printed guide, also arranged according to Kristeller, includes citations to additional locations of the indexes. The printed guide has several indexes, including an index of libraries and of private collections, and an index to specialized indexes to incipits, scribes, etc.

A microfilm corpus of unpublished inventories of Latin manuscripts through 1600 A.D / prep. under the direction of F. Edward Cranz [microform]. [N.Y. : Renaissance Society of America, 1988]. 340 pts. in 349 microfilm reels. **AA209**

Sponsored by the American Council of Learned Societies.

"The start toward a collection of unpublished inventories was made after World War II by a committee chaired by B. L. Ullman. The filming had after a time to be abandoned...but what had been obtained was deposited in the Library of Congress.... The present microfilm corpus builds upon the Ullman collection but does not attempt to duplicate it. It has, however, gone on to create as complete a collection as possible of all other inventories. The corpus also includes an appendix reel containing small lists from a large number of libraries... supplied by P. O. Kristeller."—*Pref.* The film is arranged alphabetically by city, then by library, as is the printed guide.

Richard, Marcel. Répertoire des bibliothèques et des catalogues de manuscrits grecs. 2. éd. Paris : Centre Nationale de la Recherche Scientifique, 1958. 276 p. (Institut de Recherche et d'Histoire des Textes, Pubn. 1). **AA210**

1st ed., 1948.

Contents: 1, Bibliographie; 2, Catalogues spécialisés; 3, Catalogues régionaux; 4, Villes.

Includes lists of manuscripts in periodicals as well as those published separately. Covers collections in Europe, the Middle East, Egypt, and North and South America, indicating size and character. Detailed index.

"Revues et Actes académiques cités," p. 253–60.

————. ————. *Supplément 1 (1958–1963)*. (Paris : CNRS, 1964. 76 p. Z6601.A1R39

Union Lists

Jeudy, Colette. Les manuscrits classiques latins des bibliothèques publiques de France / catalogue établi par Colette Jeudy et Yves-François Riou. Paris : Editions du Centre national de la recherche scientifique, 1989. v. 1 ; ill. (In progress). **AA211**

Contents: v. 1, Agen–Évreux.

Offers detailed physical descriptions and provenance of manuscripts of classical texts from the 8th to the 15th century. Arranged by city; excludes collections in private and academic libraries. Each entry has a bibliography of secondary literature. Many indexes, including authors and texts, scribes and illuminators, incipits, etc. Z6605.L3J48

Ricci, Seymour de. Census of medieval and Renaissance manuscripts in the United States and Canada / Seymour de Ricci, with the assistance of W. J. Wilson. N.Y. : Wilson, 1935–40. 3 v. **AA212**

Repr.: N.Y. : Kraus, 1961.

Published under the auspices of the American Council of Learned Societies.

Contents: v. 1, Alabama–Massachusetts; v. 2, Michigan–Canada. Errata and addenda; v. 3, Indexes: [1], General index of names, titles and headings; [2], Scribes, illuminators and cartographers; [3], *Incipits*; [4], Gregory numbers for Greek and New Testament manuscripts; [5], Present owners; [6], Previous owners.

Arranged alphabetically by states, cities, and libraries, including private collections. Brief descriptions include: probable date and place of origin, material on which written, size, number of leaves, kind of binding, former owners, and references to printed descriptions.

————. ————. *Supplement*, originated by C. U. Faye, continued and ed. by W. H. Bond. (N.Y. : Bibliographical Soc. of America, 1962. 626 p.).

Gives cross-references to the *Census* when additional or corrected information is supplied and for manuscripts whose ownership has changed.

Diplomatics, handwriting, and scripts

Brown, Michelle P. A guide to western historical scripts from antiquity to 1600. London : British Library, 1990. [144] p. : ill.   **AA213**

Aims "to provide an aid for a wide variety of readers who wish to trace the evolution of scripts in the West from the world of Antiquity to the early modern period."—*Introd.* Indexed.

Hector, Leonard Charles. The handwriting of English documents. [2nd ed.]. London : Arnold, [1966]. 136 p. : ill.   **AA214**

1st ed., 1958.

"The chief object of this book is to moderate as far as possible the difficulties of reading presented by the hands written in England for administrative, legal or business purposes during the past eight or nine centuries."—*Introd.* In addition to textual discussion of the writers' materials, languages, abbreviations, scribal conventions, etc., there is an extensive set of plates with transcriptions of the passages reproduced thereon.   Z115.E5H4

Martin, Charles Trice. The record interpreter : a collection of abbreviations, Latin words and names used in English historical manuscripts and records. 2nd ed. London : Stevens, 1910. 464 p.   **AA215**

Repr.: Hildesheim : Olms, 1969.

Contents: (1) Abbreviations of Latin words used in English records; (2) Abbreviations of French words used in English records; (3) Glossary of Latin words found in records and other English manuscripts, but not occurring in classical authors; (4) Latin names of places in Great Britain and Ireland; (5) Latin names of bishoprics in England; (6) Latin names of bishoprics in Scotland; (7) Latin names of bishoprics in Ireland; (8) Latin forms of English surnames; (9) Latin Christian names with their English equivalents.

The 1st ed., publ. 1892, was an amplification of the appendix to Andrew Wright's *Court-hand restored* (9th ed., 1879).   Z111.M23

Thompson, Edward Maunde. An introduction to Greek and Latin palaeography. Oxford : Clarendon Pr., 1912. 600 p. : 250 facsims.   **AA216**

Repr.: N.Y. : Burt Franklin, 1964.

An enlarged edition of the author's *Handbook of Greek and Latin palaeography* (3rd ed., 1906).

Gives transcription of each facsimile. Includes chapters on the history of Greek and Roman alphabets, materials and writing implements, forms of books, abbreviations, contractions, and numerals. Bibliography, p. 571–83, includes lists of published facsimiles.   Z114.T472

EARLY AND RARE BOOKS

Incunabula and early printed books

Guides

Berkowitz, David Sandler. Bibliotheca bibliographica incunabula : a manual of bibliographical guides to inventories of printing, of holdings, and of reference aids. Waltham, Mass., 1967. 336 p.   **AA217**

"With an appendix of useful information on place-names and dating, collected and classified for the use of researchers in incunabulistics."—*title page.*

An effort toward providing a bibliographic guide to the study of incunabula. A general section on guides to sources of information on the topic is followed by chapters on registers or catalogs of incunabula. Lacks an index.   Z240.A1B4

Stillwell, Margaret Bingham. Incunabula and Americana, 1450–1800 : a key to bibliographical study. N.Y. : Columbia Univ. Pr., 1931. 483 p. : facsims.   **AA218**

Repr.: N.Y. : Cooper Square Pub., 1961.

Contents: *Incunabula*: 1, Printed books of the 15th century; 2, Identification and collation; 3, Bibliographical reference material; *Americana*: 1, Preliminary survey of sources and methods; 2, Century of maritime discovery, 1492–1600; 3, Two centuries of colonial growth, 1500–1700; 4, Later Americana and the Revolutionary periods; 5, Early printing in America; *Reference sections*: 1, Notes and definitions; 2, Foreign bibliographical terms: French, German, Italian, and Spanish; 3, Latin contractions and abbreviations; 4, Place names of 15th-century printing towns; 5, Incunabula: selected bibliographies and monographs (600 items); 6, 15th-century woodcuts: selected monographs; 7, Americana: selected bibliographies and monographs (more than 600 items).

An indispensable reference work and guide for the collector or librarian. Important both for the text and for the extensive annotated bibliographies.   Z240.A1S8

Bibliography

British Museum. Department of Printed Books. Catalogue of books printed in the XVth century now in the British Museum. London, 1908–71. Pts. 1–10 : facsims.   **AA219**

Work supervised by A. W. Pollard.

Contents: pts. 1–2, Germany; pt. 3, Germany, German-speaking Switzerland and Austria-Hungary; pts. 4–7, Italy; pt. 8, France, French-speaking Switzerland; pt. 9, Holland, Belgium; pt. 10, Spain, Portugal.

Arranged under places by printers' names. Gives historical notes about printers, and full title, description, collation, and date of purchase of each book. Pt. 3 contains also an introduction by A. W. Pollard, a typographical map, facsimiles, and indexes to pts. 1–3 by (1) Hain's numbers, (2) concordance of Proctor's numbers, and (3) printers and towns. Covers the same ground as the first part of Robert Proctor's *Index to the early printed books...* (AA227) but with much fuller descriptions.   Z240.B85

Burger, Konrad. Supplement zu Hain und Panzer : Beiträge zur Inkunabelbibliographie, Nummernconcordanz von Panzers lateinischen u. deutschen Annalen u. Ludwig Hain's Repertorium bibliographicum. Leipzig : Hiersemann, 1908. 440 p.   **AA220**
Z240.H151

——————— Ludwig Hain's Repertorium bibliographicum : Register : Die Drucker des XV. Jahrhunderts. Leipzig : Harrassowitz, 1891. 428 p. (Centralblatt für Bibliothekswesen. Beihefte, Bd.2, Hft.8).   **AA221**
Repr.: Nendeln : Kraus, 1968.   Z671.C39B

Copinger, Walter Arthur. Supplement to Hain's Repertorium bibliographicum : or, Collections towards a new edition of that work. London : Sotheran, 1895–1902. 2 v. in 3.   **AA222**
Repr.: Leipzig : Lorentz, 1926.

Pt. 1, nearly 7,000 corrections of and additions to the collation of works described in Hain [AA223]; pt.2, list of nearly 6,000 volumes not in Hain: v. 1, A–O; v. 2, P–Z.

Vol. 2 includes "The printers and publishers of the XV century with lists of their works," by Konrad Burger (p. 319–670), which is an index to the *Supplement to Hain's Repertorium* and to the works of Campbell, Pellechet, and Proctor.   Z240.T15S

Hain, Ludwig Friedrich Theodor. Repertorium bibliographicum : in quo libri omnes ab arte typographica inventa usque ad annum MD.... Stuttgart : Cotta, 1826–38. 2 v. in 4.   **AA223**

Repr.: Berlin : Altmann, 1925.

A basic list arranged alphabetically, the items numbered serially throughout. The "Hain number" is referred to in many later bibliographies of incunabula.

Index: Konrad Burger, *Ludwig Hain's Repertorium bibliographicum : Register : Die Drucker des XV. Jahrhunderts* (Leipzig : Harrassowitz, 1891. 428 p. [Centralblatt für Bibliothekswesen. Beihefte, Bd. 2, Hft. 8]. Repr.: Nedeln : Kraus, 1968).

Supplement: Konrad Burger, *Supplement zu Hain und Panzer : Beiträge zur Inkunabelbibliographie, Nummernconcordanz von Panzers lateinischen u. deutschen Annalen u. Ludwig Hain's Repertorium bibliographicum* (Leipzig : Hiersemann, 1908. 440 p.).

Continued by Walter Arthur Copinger, *Supplement to Hain's Repertorium bibliographicum* (AA222).   Z240.H15

Harvard University. Library. A catalogue of the fifteenth-century printed books in the Harvard University Library / by James E. Walsh. Binghamton, N.Y. : Center for Medieval and Early Renaissance Studies, State Univ. of New York at Binghamton, 1991–1993. v. 1–2 : ill. (Medieval & Renaissance texts & studies, v. 84, 97). (In progress).   **AA224**

Contents: v. 1: Books printed in Germany, German-speaking Switzerland, and Austria-Hungary; v. 2: Books printed in Rome and Venice.

A listing of all the incunabula in the library system, not just those housed in its rare books collection. Arranged by town, printer, and date. Information provided includes details about the author, title and date, and the number and size of leaves; information about the binding; reference to standard catalogs; and information about the provenance. A review of v. 1 in *TLS* (April 17, 1992, p. 27) says it is "a model of scrupulous and authoritative scholarship" adding that the "catalogue will come to be recognized not just as a guide to the Harvard collection, but as a significant contribution to incunabula studies generally."   Z240.H37

Index Aureliensis : catalogus librorum sedecimo saeculo impressorum. Editio princeps. Aureliae Aquensis, 1965–93. 1a. pars, t. 1–10; 3a. pars, t. 1, 3. (Bibliotheca bibliographica Aureliana, 7 etc.). (In progress).   **AA225**

Issued in parts 1962– , as "Editio princeps" and in bound volumes 1965– , as "Editio altera."

An alphabetical main-entry listing of 16th-century imprints that has progressed partly through the letter C. Indicates locations for about 500 libraries throughout the world. Vol. 1 of pt. 3 has indexes to v. 1–2 of printers, personal names, and places.   Z1014.I5

Panzer, Georg Wolfgang Franz. Annales typographici ab artis inventae origine ad annum MD. Norimbergae : Zeh, 1793–97. 5 v.   **AA226**

Arranged by places, then chronologically under place.

Supplemented by: Panzer's *Annales typographici ab artis inventae origine ab anno MDI ad annum MDXXXVI* (Norimbergae : 1798–1803. 6 v.).

Numbered v. 6–11. v. 10–11, Indici.

Proctor, Robert. Index to the early printed books in the British Museum : with notes of those in the Bodleian Library. London : K. Paul, Trench, Trübner, 1898–1903 : B. Quaritch, 1938. Pts. 1–2 in 6 v.   **AA227**

Pt. 1 publ. 1898–99 (4 v.); pt. 2 publ. 1903–38 (2 v.).

Contents: Pt. 1, To 1500: v. 1, Germany; v. 2, Italy; v. 3, Switzerland to Montenegro, including France, Netherlands, Austria-Hungary, Spain, England, Scandinavia, Portugal; v. 4, Register. Pt. 2, 1501–20: sec. 1, Germany, sec. 2, Italy; Sec. 3, Switzerland and Eastern Europe (sec. 2–3 by Frank Isaac).

A chronological list under each country by names of presses. The index volume contains an alphabetical list of towns, printers, and publishers; a list of books mentioned in Ludwig Hain's *Repertorium bibliographicum* (AA223) and of those not in Hain; authors of books printed in the Low Countries; and books printed in England.

———. ———. *Supplements, 1898–1902* (London : 1890–1903. 5 pts.).

Contents: Pts. 1–4, Supplements; pt. 5, Register.

Reichling, Dietrich. Appendices ad Hainii-Copingeri Repertorivm bibliographicvm : additiones et emendationes. Monachii : Rosenthal, 1905–11. 7 v.   **AA228**

Repr. with suppl.: Milano : Görlich, 1953.

Pts. 1–6 in two sections each: I, Additions; II, Emendations; pt. [7], Indices fascicvlorvm I–VI.

———. ———. *Svpplementvm (maximam partem e bibliothecis Helvetiae collectvm) cvm indice vrbivm et typographorvm. Accedit index avctorvm generalis totivs operis.* (Monasterii Gvestphalorvm, Theissingianis, 1914. 109 p., cxxxv p.).

Union Lists

Biblioteca Nacional (Spain). Catalogo general de incunables en bibliotecas españolas / Biblioteca Nacional ; coordinado y dirigido por Francisco García Craviotto. Madrid : Ministerio de Cultura, Dirección General del Libro y Bibliotecas, 1989–90. 2 v.   **AA229**

A listing, arranged alphabetically by author, of incunabula published throughout Europe and held in Spanish libraries. Locates copies and provides citations to the standard bibliographies of incunabula. Several indexes, arranged (1) geographically by printer, (2) by printer and publisher, (3) by name, both personal and geographic, and (4) by title. Also includes a concordance to other standard incunabula catalogs.   Z240.B6154

Gesamtkatalog der Wiegendrucke / hrsg. von der Kommission für der Gesamtkatalog der Wiegendrucke. Leipzig : Hiersemann, 1925 40. v.1 8[1].   **AA230**

Contents: v.1–8[1], A–Federicis. No more published.

As far as published, the most comprehensive record of incunabula yet made, based on information collected during more than 20 years' work by the Kommission. The sections issued record nearly half again as many editions as Ludwig Hain, *Repertorium bibliographicum* (AA223), and the information given for each is much fuller, including: (1) author entry, title, date, etc.; (2) collation, types, capitals, and illustrations; (3) transcripts of title, colophon, and other extracts; (4) references to descriptions in Hain and other bibliographies; and (5) location of copies, which includes a complete record of all copies if not more than ten are known and, for commoner books, a selection of copies in representative libraries in different countries, both European and American. Indispensable in both cataloging and reference work in the scholarly library.

A new edition is appearing:

———. ———. (2. Aufl., durchgesehener Neudruck der 1. Aufl. Stuttgart : Hiersemann ; N.Y. : Kraus, 1968-92. Bd. 1–10[1]. [In progress]).

Contents: Bd. 1–10[1], Abano–Gresemundus.

The first seven volumes of the new edition are reprints of those published 1925–38. The first part of Bd. 8 (publ. 1940) is not reprinted for this edition, and revision and expansion begins with Bd. 8, Lfg. 1 (publ. 1972). New information is supplied as relevant for materials previously treated in the 1940 fascicle of v. 8. The list of locations now includes some 4,000 libraries and collections.

Reviews of new fascicles appear in *The Library*, ser. 5, v.30 (Dec. 1975): 339–44 and in *TLS*, (Aug. 15, 1980): 922.   Z240.G39

Goff, Frederick Richmond. Incunabula in American libraries : a third census of fifteenth-century books recorded in North American collections. N.Y. : Bibliographical Soc. of America, 1964. 798 p.   **AA231**

First census by the Bibliographical Society, 1919; *Second census* by Margaret Bingham Stillwell, 1940.

A much enlarged edition recording 47,188 copies of 12,599 titles held by 760 owners. Roughly 90% of the total registered are held by institutions. The method of listing follows closely that of the *Second census*, and the style is virtually the same. The entries have been re-numbered, but the Stillwell number is indicated in a subsidiary position.

Authors are listed alphabetically, in general conforming to Ludwig Hain's *Repertorium bibliographicum* (AA223), or to the form used in the British Museum *Catalogue of books printed in the XVth century* (AA219), or in *Gesamtkatalog der Wiegendrucke* (AA230). (Works in Hebrew are listed in a separate section under "Hebraica.") Information under each entry usually includes author (with variant spellings), short title, place, printer, date, size, references to descriptions in printed catalogs, and location of copies.

Additional sections include: Variant author-forms and entries; Index of printers and publishers; Concordances to the numbers used in the *Gesamtkatalog*, Hain, Robert Proctor's *Index to the early printed books in the British Museum* (AA227), and the *Second census* if the sequence of numbers has been changed; Deletions from the *Second census*; Addenda.

A reprinting of the 1964 edition (Millwood, N.Y. : Kraus Reprint, 1973) is "Reproduced from the annotated copy maintained by Frederick R. Goff, compiler and editor." It includes annotations and corrections in the text, and a new introduction and list of dealers.

————. ————. *A supplement* (N.Y. : Bibliographical Society of America, 1972. 104 p.).

Offers additions and corrections to the third census, the additions including 3,560 copies, of which "324 are new titles not previously represented in American ownership."—*Introd.*   Z240.G58

Incunabula in Dutch libraries : a census of fifteenth-century printed books in Dutch public collections / [Gerard van Thienen, ed. in chief]. Nieuwkoop : De Graaf, 1983. 2 v. (Bibliotheca bibliographica Neerlandica, 17).   **AA232**

An alphabetical listing of incunabula in nearly 90 libraries; indexes of printers and places of publication, and a detailed general index. A review appears in *Times literary supplement* (June 8, 1994) : 647.

Indice generale degli incunaboli delle biblioteche d'Italia / a cura del Centro nazionale d'informazioni bibliografiche. Roma : Istituto poligrafico dello Stato, 1943–1981. 6 v. : facsims. (Indici e cataloghi. Nuova serie, 1, etc.).   **AA233**

A union catalog of incunabula in the libraries of Italy. Vol. 6, Aggiunte, correzioni, indici, includes a list of Hebraic incunabula, p. 285–298, and a concordance to entries in Ludwig Hain's *Repertorium bibliographicum* (AA223) and the *Gesamtkatalog der Wiegendrucke* (AA230).   Z240.I5

Pellechet, Marie Léontine Catherine. Catalogue général des incunables des bibliothèques publiques de France. Paris : A. Picard et fils, 1897–1909. 3 v.   **AA234**

Repr.: Nedeln, Liechtenstein : Kraus-Thomson, 1970. 26 v.

Contents: v.1–3, A–Gregorius Magnus. No more published.

Reprinted (Nedeln, Liechtenstein : Kraus-Thomson, 1970) in 26 volumes. Vols. 1–3 constitute Louis Polain's working copy of Pellechet's *Catalogue* with Polain's corrections and amendments; v. 4–26, a reprint of the manuscript of later volumes by Polain continuing the work from Gregorius to Z and never published, but available in some libraries in microfilm copy.

Polain, Louis. Catalogue des livres imprimés au quinzième siècle des bibliothèques de Belgique. Bruxelles : Soc. des Bibliophiles, 1932. 4 v. : facsims.   **AA235**

Contents: v. 1–3, A–S; v. 4, T–Z; Supplément (no. 4070–4109). Additions. Tables: A, Facsimilés; B, Concordance des numéros avec ceux de Campbell, *Gesamtkatalog*, Hain, Pellechet, Voulliéme; C, Imprimeurs; E, Gravures; F, Table générale alphabétique des matières; (D, Table des bibliothèques, announced in the introduction, p.xxi, was not published).

————. ————. *Supplément.* (Bruxelles : Fl. Tulkens pour l'Assoc. des Archivistes et Bibliothécaires de Belgique, 1978. 615 p.).

Pages 1–286 are devoted to corrections and additions to items in v. 1–4. A section of "Nouvelles descriptions" adds items 4110–4804, continuing the item numbering of the basic set. A section of "Tables" provides concordances with standard catalogs of incunabula such as Hain (AA223), Goff (AA231), Copinger (AA222), etc.   Z240.P76

History

Bühler, Curt Ferdinand. The fifteenth-century book : the scribes, the printers, the decorators. Philadelphia : Univ. of Pennsylvania Pr., 1960. 195 p. : ill.   **AA236**

Gives an excellent survey of the development of the 15th-century book. Includes bibliographical notes and an index.   Z240.B924

Book collecting

Guides and manuals

Bradley, Van Allen. The book collector's handbook of values. 4th rev., enl. ed. N.Y. : Putnam, c1982. 640 p.   **AA237**

1st ed., 1972; 3rd ed., 1978.

Intended not only for general readers, but for the "serious and sophisticated collector," as well as libraries, scholars, and booksellers. Limited principally to 19th- and 20th-century American and English publications (with a few works published in Europe by English and American authors), having a retail value of at least $25 as of the date of publication of the *Handbook*. Alphabetical author or anonymous title listing. Price range for copies in good condition is indicated, with record of recent auction prices as applicable.

§ Supersedes the price index in the compiler's *New gold in your attic* (2nd ed. N.Y. : Fleet Pr., 1968), although the introductory matter in that volume may still prove valuable for beginning collectors.

Z1029.B7

Bibliography

British Library. Modern British and American private presses, 1850–1965 : holdings of the British Library. [London] : Publ. for the British Library by British Museum Pubns., [1976]. 211 p.   **AA238**

"The present list is based on entries in the General Catalogue of the British Library, arranged (i) alphabetically, by presses; (ii) chronologically within each press; (iii) alphabetically by author or other heading within each year under each press. The entries have been made over a long period, and consequently changes in catalogue practice are reflected by differences in style."—*Pref.* American presses are less fully represented than those of Britain. Indexed.   Z1028.B75

Brussel, Isidore Rosenbaum. Anglo-American first editions. London : Constable ; N.Y. : Bowker, 1935–36. 2 v. : ill. (Bibliographia; studies in book history and structure, no. 9–10).   **AA239**

Repr.: N.Y. : Sol Lewis, 1981.

Contents: pt. 1: East to West [1826–1900] describing first editions of English authors whose books were published in America before their publication in England (170 p.); pt. 2, West to East, 1786–1930, describing first editions of American authors whose books were published in England before their publication in America (131 p.).

Gives detailed bibliographical information with descriptive annotations.   Z2014.F5B9

Heard, J. Norman. Bookman's guide to Americana. 8th ed. Metuchen, N.J. : Scarecrow, 1981. 284 p.   **AA240**

1st ed., 1953.

"The eighth edition, like its predecessors, is an alphabetically arranged compilation of quotations gleaned from recent out-of-print booksellers' catalogs. It is intended to provide the bookseller or book buyer with a record of prices asked for out-of-print titles in the broad field of Americana, including factual or fictional works relating to America or written by Americans."—*Pref.* Z1207.H43

Howes, Wright. U.S.iana, 1650–1950 : a selective bibliography in which are described 11,620 uncommon and significant books relating to the continental portion of the United States. Rev. and enl. [i.e., 2nd] ed. N.Y. : Bowker, for the Newberry Libr., 1962. 652 p. **AA241**
This list of uncommon books relating to the continental U.S., compiled primarily for the use of the average collector, indicates their relative sales value in five categories from $10 to more than $1,000. For the rarer items indication is frequently given of the location of one or more perfect copies in American libraries. Z1215.H75

Johnson, Merle DeVore. Merle Johnson's American first editions. 4th ed., rev. and enl. by Jacob N. Blanck. N.Y. : Bowker, 1942. 553 p. **AA242**
Repr.: Waltham, Mass. : Mark Pr., 1969.
1st ed., 1929, planned as a continuation of Patrick K. Foley's *American authors, 1795–1895* (Boston, 1897).
Lists the first editions of more than 200 American authors having "collector interest." Z1231.F5J6

Private press books. v. 1 (1959)– . Pinner, Middlesex, Eng. : Private Libraries Assoc., 1959– . Annual. **AA243**
Publisher varies.
"Attempts to include the work of all private presses printing in English, and the more important of those printing in other languages."—*Note, v. 5, 1963.* Alphabetical by name of press, with the titles published during the year covered. A bibliography of "the literature of private printing" appears in each issue. Each year has an index by author and title. The 1970 issue includes a "Cumulative index to private press books 1959–70." Z1028.P7

Ricci, Seymour de. The book collector's guide : a practical handbook of British and American bibliography. Philadelphia : Rosenbach, 1921. 649 p. **AA244**
Repr.: N.Y. : Burt Franklin, 1970.
A guide for the collector and book buyer, covering the period from Chaucer to Swinburne and listing books which because of rarity, market value, etc., were most sought after by collectors, including first editions, illustrated books, 17th-century and 18th-century drama, and standard works. Arranged alphabetically by author, giving bibliographical descriptions, prices at sales, notes, etc. Z2001.R49

Historical children's books

Gumuchian et compagnie, booksellers, Paris. Les livres de l'enfance du XVᵉ au XIXᵉ siècle. Paris : Gumuchian, [1930]. 2 v. : ill. **AA245**
Repr.: London : Holland Pr., 1967.
Contents: v. 1, Text, i.e., Bibliography of 6,251 items, with full bibliographical description of each; v. 2, 338 plates, containing a total of 1,080 facsimiles of illustrations from books described in v. 1, beautifully reproduced, many of them hand-colored.
Important both for the careful description of rare books and for the wealth of illustration. May be supplemented by two simpler lists issued by the same firm (Catalogues 15 and 18): (1) *100 noteworthy firsts in juvenile literature* (1932. 30 p.) and (2) *500 early juveniles* (1933. 39 p.). Z1037.Z9G9

Library of Congress. Rare Book Division. Children's books in the Rare Book Division of the Library of Congress. Totowa, N.J. : Rowman and Littlefield, 1975. 2 v. **AA246**
Contents: v. 1, Author; v. 2, Chronological.

"As a result of the federal copyright regulations, the Library of Congress has assembled an immense collection of American children's books. For its period—the 19th and 20th centuries—and its country of origin—the United States—this collection outranks any other in the world. From these holdings the Rare Book Division has brought together on its shelves approximately 15,000 volumes of particular interest, maintaining them separately as a special collection, which this publication describes."—*Introd.* Also includes other children's books in the Rare Book Division which are not part of the separate children's book collection. Reproduces the catalog cards describing the books; includes numerous temporary entries for works not found in *National union catalog.* Z1037.U5U54

Rosenbach, Abraham Simon Wolf. Early American children's books : with bibliographical descriptions of the books in his private collection. Portland, Me. : Southworth Pr., 1933. 354 p. : ill. **AA247**
Includes: Foreword by A. Edward Newton; Introduction; Early American children's books, p. 3–287; Index of authors and titles; Index of printers and publishers; List of printers, publishers, and booksellers; Bibliography.

Welch, D'Alté Aldridge. A bibliography of American children's books printed prior to 1821. [Worcester, Mass.] : American Antiquarian Soc., 1972. 516 p. **AA248**
Originally published in the *Proceedings* of the American Antiquarian Society, April 1963–Oct. 1967
"This bibliography is primarily concerned with narrative books written in English, designed for children under fifteen years of age. They should be the type of book read at leisure for pleasure. The book must have been originally written for children or abridged for them from an adult version."—*p.liii.*
An alphabetical listing by author or other main entry. Locates copies. Index of printers, publishers, and imprints. (A 4-page supplement, "Index to titles listed under author without cross references," was published later for insertion into the book.) A detailed and scholarly work. Z1232.W44

Dictionaries

Carter, John. ABC for book-collectors. 6th ed. / with corrections and additions by Nicolas Barker. London ; N.Y. : Granada, 1980. 219 p. **AA249**
1st ed., 1952.
Repr.: New Castle, Del. : Oak Knoll Books, 1992.
An alphabetical dictionary of bibliographic and booksellers' terms with definitions as used in Great Britain and the U.S. Z1006.C37

Printers' marks

McKerrow, R. B. Printers' & publishers' devices in England & Scotland, 1485–1640. London : Bibliographical Soc., 1913. 216 p. 69 plates. **AA250**
Contains descriptions and facsimiles of 428 devices, a dictionary of certain printers' names with information about transfers of devices, and five indexes of devices and compartments by: (1) sizes, (2) printers and booksellers, (3) mottoes, (4) initials of designers and engravers, (5) subjects. Z236.G7M2

Polain, Louis. Marques des imprimeurs et libraires en France au XVᵉ siècle. Paris : Droz, 1926. 207 p. : ill. (Documents typographiques du XVᵉ siècle, t.1). **AA251**
Augments and corrects Silvestre's *Marques typographiques* (AA254). Z236.F8P7

Reilly, Elizabeth Carroll. A dictionary of colonial American printers' ornaments and illustrations. Worcester, Mass. : Amer. Antiquarian Soc., 1975. 515 p. : ill.   **AA252**

"The purpose of the dictionary is to aid both bibliographers and historians in their studies of the colonial period. Used judiciously, the listings may facilitate the bibliographer's identification of many books, pamphlets, and broadsides which lack imprints or colophons. The index of printers records the ornaments and illustrations used by each printer and thus provides the means for a study of the changes in his printing stock."—*Introd.*   Z208.R43

Roberts, William. Printers' marks : a chapter in the history of typography. London ; N.Y. : Geo. Bell, 1893. 261 p. : ill.   **AA253**

A chronological account describing the marks of the early and important printers of Europe. Includes some modern examples, mostly from England. Contains more than 200 illustrations.   Z235.R64

Silvestre, Louis Catherine. Marques typographiques. Paris : Jannet, successeur de L. C. Silvestre, 1853 : Impr. Renou, 1867. 2 v. : facsims.   **AA254**

Published anonymously in parts.

Subtitle: Recueil des monogrammes, chiffres, enseignes, emblèmes, devises, rébus et fleurons des libraires et imprimeurs qui ont excercé en France, depuis l'introduction de l'imprimerie, en 1470, jusqu'à la fin du seizième siècle: à ces marques sont jointes celles des libraires et imprimeurs qui pendant la même période ont publié, hors de France, des livres en langue française.

Includes more than 1,300 devices.   Z236.F8S5

Watermarks

The Briquet album : a miscellany on watermarks, supplementing Dr. Briquet's Les filigranes / by various paper scholars. Hilversum, Holland : Paper Publications Soc., 1952. 158 p. : ill. (Monumenta chartae papyraceae historia illustrantia, 2).   **AA255**

"Indexes to Charles Moïse Briquet's *Les filigranes* [AA256] in German, English and Italian," p.125–54.   TS1080.P183

Briquet, Charles Moïse. Les filigranes : dictionnaire historique des marques du papier dès leur apparition vers 1282 jusqu'en 1600 : facsimile of the 1907 ed. with supplementary material contributed by a number of scholars / ed. by Allan Stevenson. Amsterdam : Paper Publications Soc., 1968. 4 v. : ill.   **AA256**

Originally publ. Paris : Picard, 1907. 4 v.

A monumental work with reproductions of more than 16,000 watermarks. For the "New Briquet" Stevenson has contributed a general introduction entitled "How to use 'Les Filigranes'," followed by a group of "Bibliographical and historical illustrations"; a selective and annotated bibliography; and, most important, a section of "Addenda and corrigenda." A supplementary index is mainly an index to the new materials, plus some additional references to the original text. In the volumes with plates of watermark reproductions, the use date of each mark has been added in parentheses.   Z237.B845

Gravell, Thomas L. A catalogue of American watermarks, 1690–1835 / by Thomas L. Gravell and George Miller. N.Y. : Garland, 1979. 230 p. : ill. (Garland reference library of the humanities, v.151).   **AA257**

Identifies more than 700 watermarks, giving location of the manuscript, place and date of use, and a reproduction of the watermark. A brief history of each paper mill represented is given in a separate section. Select bibliography, proper name index, and a subject index which provides an approach through the devices used in the watermarks.   TS1115.G7

Auction records

American book-prices current : a record of literary properties sold at auction in England, the United States, and in Canada. v. 1 (1894/95)– . N.Y. : Amer. Book-Prices Current, 1895– . Annual.   **AA258**

Publisher varies.

Subtitle varies. Before v. 64, 1958, included only records of sales held in the U.S.

Arrangement and information given vary somewhat but usually include author, title, edition, place and date of publication, size, binding, condition, where sold, date of sale, catalog number of lot, and price. Includes autographs and manuscripts as well as printed materials of all periods and languages. Generally considered the most accurate of the auction record compilations.   Z1000.A51

Blogie, Jeanne. Répertoire des catalogues de ventes de livres imprimés. Bruxelles : Fl. Tulkens, 1982–92. v. 1–4. (Collection du Centre national de l'archéologie et de l'histoire du livre, 4). (In progress).   **AA259**

Contents: v. 1, Catalogues belges appartenant à la Bibliothèque royale Albert Iᵉʳ; v. 2, Catalogues français appartenant à la Bibliothèque royale Albert Iᵉʳ; v. 3, Catalogues britanniques appartenant à la Bibliothèque royale Albert Iᵉʳ; v. 4, Catalogues néerlandais appartenant à la Bibliothèque royal Albert Iᵉʳ.

The series is designed to present an inventory of sales catalogues of printed books found in Belgian libraries.   Z999.5.B55

Book-auction records : a priced and annotated annual record of London [and other] book-auctions. v. 1 (June 1902)– . London ; N.Y. : Henry Stevens, 1903– .   **AA260**

Subtitle: Giving instant clues to the contents ... and, incidentally, to anonymous authors, autographs, bibliophiles, binders, bindings, distinguished owners, editors, fore-edge paintings, holograph manuscripts, illustrators, notable presses, pseudonyms, translators, etc.

Frequency varies: Quarterly, 1902–40/41; annual since 1941/42.

Publisher varies.

Subtitle varies. From v. 12, Edinburgh, Glasgow, and Dublin auctions sometimes included. From 1939/40, also includes principal New York auctions.

Entries are "exact reproductions, abbreviated, of the auctioneers' catalogue-descriptions," and include date of sale, number of lot, price, and name of buyer.

When issued quarterly, each number was arranged alphabetically by author, with an index in each volume. Annual volumes are arranged alphabetically by author.

————. *General index, 1902–12, 1912–23, 1924–33, 1934–43, 1944–48, 1948–58, 1958–63, 1963–68.* (London, Stevens, 1924–71. 8v.).

Book-prices current. Dec. 1886–1956/58. London : Sergeants Pr., 1888–1959. Annual (irregular).   **AA261**

Publisher varies.

Subtitle: A record of the prices at which books have been sold at auction.

Vols. 1–27, 1886–1913, arranged by date of sale; v. 28–64, 1914–56/58, arranged alphabetically by author and some titles. Useful both as a record of market prices of secondhand books and as a supplement to the various general and national bibliographies for titles and editions not noted in such bibliographies.

————. *Index,* 1887–96, 1897–1906, 1907–16. (London : Stock, 1901–20. 3 v.).

Bookman's price index. v. 1 (1964)– . Detroit : Gale, 1964– . Annual (slightly irregular).   **AA262**

Editor: D. F. McGrath.

A main-entry list. Listings are based on descriptions of books and periodicals which were offered for sale by leading dealers in their catalogs of the period covered. Includes a list of dealers represented.   Z1000.B74

Catalogue bibliographique des ventes publiques. 1968/70– . Paris : Éditions Mayer, [1970]– . Irregular. **AA263**
At head of title: O. Matterlin.
Continues Matterlin's *La cote internationale des livres et manuscrits*, 1964/65–1966/68.
Subtitle varies. Volumes usually cover three years, with a year's overlap (e.g., 1978/80, 1980/82).
Provides a record of auction prices for books and manuscripts bringing 500 Fr. or more (100 Fr. in early volumes). A list of the sales and their dates is followed by an author listing of the works sold with full description, auction at which sold, and price. Coverage is most complete for France, but there is regular coverage of England, Belgium, the U.S., plus irregular coverage of Switzerland, Monaco, and Italy.

Jahrbuch der Auktionspreise für Bücher und Autographen : Ergebnisse der Auktionen in Deutschland, Holland, Österreich und der Schweiz. Bd. 1 (1950)– . Hamburg : E. Hauswedell, 1951– . Annual. **AA264**
Title varies slightly.
Supersedes *Jahrbuch der Bücherpreise*, Jahrg. 1–34, 1906–39.
Lists the auctions of the year covered, followed by a main-entry listing of the books, manuscripts, and autographs sold, with indication of price realized. Z1000.J235

McKay, George Leslie. American book auction catalogues, 1713–1934 : a union list / with introd. by Clarence S. Brigham. N.Y. : New York Pub. Libr., 1937. 540 p. : facsims. **AA265**
A "list of some 10,000 auction catalogues ... issued in what is now the United States, that list books, pamphlets, broadsides, newspapers, manuscripts, autographs and bookplates."—*Pref.* Arranged chronologically. Locates copies.
———. ———. Supplement no. 1–2, 1946–48 (Repr. from New York Public Library *Bulletin* 50 [1946]: 177–84; 52 [1948]: 401–12).

PRINTING AND PUBLISHING

General works

Bibliography

Bigmore, Edward Clements. A bibliography of printing, with notes and illustrations / Edward Clements Bigmore and Charles William Henry Wyman. London : Quaritch, 1880–86. 3 v. : ill. **AA266**
Repr.: N.Y. : P. C. Duschnes, 1945. 2 v.
Arranged alphabetically by author, with some subject references and form headings. Biographical, historical, and descriptive annotations. Z117.B59

Brenni, Vito Joseph. Book printing in Britain and America : a guide to the literature and a directory of printers. Westport, Conn. : Greenwood, 1983. 163 p. **AA267**
A selective bibliography with separate sections for Britain and America. Entries are grouped by form (printing manuals, type specimen books, etc.) or as history (subdivided chronologically). Includes sections for music, scientific publishing, writing, and calligraphy. The directory of printers, typographers, calligraphers, and book designers gives an identifying phrase and dates when known. Indexed. Z151.B68

Current

Annual bibliography of the history of the printed book and libraries. v. 1 (1970)– . The Hague : Nijhoff, 1973– . Annual. **AA268**
At head of title: ABHB.
Sponsored by IFLA.
Intends to record all books and articles of scholarly value that relate to the history of (1) printed books, (2) the arts, crafts, techniques, and equipment, and (3) the economic, social, and cultural environment as they relate to production, distribution, conservation, and description of books. A classed listing with name index. Writings on modern technical processes are excluded. Includes a section, Libraries, librarianship, scholarship, institutions, arranged geographically, then by century. Lists relevant dissertations and book reviews. Volumes appear late (v. 9, covering 1978, was published 1982). Z117.A55

Periodicals

Ulrich, Carolyn F. Books and printing : a selected list of periodicals, 1800–1942 / Carolyn Farquhar Ulrich and Karl Küp. Woodstock, Vt. : Wm. E. Rudge, 1943. 244 p. **AA269**
An annotated and selected bibliography of periodicals classed under such headings as history of printing, printing types, design, layout and typography, illustration, paper, binding, publishing, book trade, collecting, bibliography, libraries, directories, societies, etc. Z1002.U4

Encyclopedias

Lexikon des gesamten Buchwesens : LGB[2] / hrsg. von Severin Corsten, Günther Pflug und Friedrich Adolf Schmidt-Künsemüller, unter Mitwirkung von Bernhard Bischoff ... [et al.]. 2., völlig neubearbeitete Aufl. Stuttgart : A. Hiersemann, 1985–93. Bd. 1–4[4] : ill. (In progress). **AA270**
1st ed., 1935–37 (3 v.).
Contents: Bd. 1 4[4], A Koreanische Schrift.
An encyclopedia of concise articles, many with bibliographical references, on a great variety of subjects connected with books and the book arts; e.g., printers and printing, publishing, illustration, places of printing, organizations and societies, manuscripts, etc. Contains many biographies. The 2nd ed. is greatly revised and expanded, although some entries have been dropped; many articles have illustrations.
A revised version of the 1st ed., *Lexikon des Buchwesens*, hrsg. von Joachim Kirchner (Stuttgart : Hiersemann, 1952–56. 4 v.) was based on the 1st ed., but in somewhat briefer form. Vols. 1–2 include encyclopedic articles on subjects connected with the book, many with bibliographies; v. 3–4 contained plates showing illustrations, facsimiles of title pages, examples of book binding, printing presses, libraries, etc. Z1006.L464

Dictionaries

The bookman's glossary. 6th ed., rev. and enl. / ed. by Jean Peters. N.Y. : Bowker, 1983. 223 p. **AA271**
1st ed., 1925.
Provides "definitions of some 1,800 terms used in book publishing, book manufacturing, bookselling, the antiquarian trade, and librarianship."—*Pref.* Terms from printing, library science, etc., are those which would be likely to be encountered in publishing circumstances, not highly technical terms. Includes brief biographical sketches of "men and women of historic importance in bibliography, the graphic arts, and book publishing." Reflects the increasing use of computers in the book industry. Select reading list; table of proofreader's marks. Z118.B75

Brownstone, David M. The dictionary of publishing / by David Brownstone and Irene M. Franck. N.Y. : Van Nostrand Reinhold, [1982]. 302 p. **AA272**

Aims "to provide a modern, concise American dictionary of publishing and allied terms for all those involved in or pursuing work related to the publishing process."—*Pref.* Gives special attention to terms relating to new technologies (computer science, etc.) as they affect publishing. Z282.5.B76

Dictionary of the graphic arts industry : in eight languages, English, German, French, Russian, Spanish, Polish, Hungarian, Slovak / ed. by Wolfgang Müller. Amsterdam ; N.Y. : Elsevier, 1981. 1020 p. **AA273**

Arranged on an English base with equivalent terms from the other languages in parallel columns; indexes from the other languages. Intended "for interpreters, translators, engineers, technicians, students and scientists—indeed for anyone at all connected with the graphic arts."—*Pref.* Very wide-ranging in coverage. Z118.D523

Feather, John. A dictionary of book history. N.Y. : Oxford Univ. Pr., 1986. 278 p. **AA274**

Offers short articles, many with brief bibliographies, which explain the "technical language of bibliography ... derived largely from that of the book trade, and especially of printing."—*Introd.*
Z1006.F38

Multilingual dictionary of publishing, printing and bookselling / [editors, Alan Issacs, Elizabeth Martin, Fran Alexander]. London : Cassell : Publishers Association, 1992. 439 p. **AA275**

Aims to provide "a selection of the most commonly used terms in printing and publishing in seven languages (English, French, German, Italian, Portuguese, Spanish, and Swedish), with the addition of American English where it differs from British English."—*Pref.* All terms in these languages are arranged alphabetically, each with a list of the definitions in the other languages. Z282.5.M85 1992

Orne, Jerrold. The language of the foreign book trade : abbreviations, terms, phrases. 3rd ed. Chicago : Amer. Libr. Assoc., 1976. 333 p. **AA276**

1st ed., 1949.

Includes definitions from 15 languages, arranged by language with English equivalent supplied for each. Z1006.O7

The Oxford dictionary for writers and editors / comp. by the Oxford English Dictionary Department. Oxford : Clarendon Pr., 1981. 448 p. **AA277**

Reprint, with corrections: *The Oxford writers' dictionary* (N.Y. : Oxford University Pr., 1990).

"The present work is the successor to eleven editions of the *Authors' and printers' dictionary*, first published under the editorship of F. Howard Collins in 1905. The eleventh edition, published in 1973, has been thoroughly revised and extensively rewritten, and a great deal of new material ... has been incorporated to bring the book up to date in matters of vocabulary and usage and to give it an orientation and purpose that are reflected in its new name."—*Publisher's note.*

A dictionary of proper names, abbreviations, foreign words and phrases, and common words frequently misspelled or misused, with definitions and indication of correct or preferred usage, etc.
PE1628.C54

Directories

International

International literary market place. 1965– . N.Y. : Bowker, 1965– . Biennial. **AA278**

1965 called "Pilot ed." Annual, 1965–69/70. 1st–5th eds., 1965–69/70, called "European edition"; beginning with the 6th ed. (1971/72, publ. 1971) also includes Africa, Australia, New Zealand, Japan, Israel, and Latin America.

A directory of publishers and book-trade organizations arranged by country; now truly international. Z291.5.I5

Publishers' international ISBN directory / International ISBN Agency, Berlin. 16th ed. (1989/90)– . München : K.G. Saur ; N.Y. : R.R. Bowker, 1989– . Annual. **AA279**

Represents a merger of *Publishers' international directory* (1964–79) and its successor, *Publishers' international directory with ISBN index* (1982–88) with *International ISBN publishers' directory* (1980–88). These works are often listed under their original German titles: *Internationales Verlagsadressbuch* and *Internationales ISBN-Verlagsverzeichnis.*

Beginning in 1990/91, appeared in 3 v.

Contents: v. 1: Geographical section; v. 2: Numerical ISBN section; v. 3: Alphabetical section.

The 20th ed., 1993/94, includes 293,380 publishers from 206 countries. Z282.P7946

North America

United States

Alternative publications : a guide to directories, indexes, bibliographies, and other sources / ed. by Cathy Seitz Whitaker. Jefferson, N.C. : McFarland, c1990. 90 p. **AA280**

Prep. by the American Library Association's Social Responsibilities Round Table Task Force on Alternatives in Print.

Aims "to facilitate identifying and locating small press material."—*Introd.* Differs from the Task Force's earlier publication, *Alternatives in print* (1st–6th eds., 1971–80) "in that it does not list individual titles, but rather cites sources, many ongoing, which in turn list individual titles." A selective bibliography is followed by annotated lists of indexes and abstracts, review sources, subject and trade bibliographies, and alternative mail order outlets. Combined index of authors, titles, publishers, subjects, etc. Z1033.L73A45

American book trade directory. 1925– . N.Y. : R. R. Bowker Co. Annual. **AA281**

Frequency has varied: triennial, 1925–52, then biennial until 1980.

Continues: *American book trade manual*, begun 1915.

Coverage varies. 28th ed. (1982) includes: (1) Retailers & antiquarians in the U. S. & Canada; (2) Wholesalers of books & magazines in the U. S. & Canada; (3) Book trade information (auctioneers, appraisers of library collections, dealers in foreign language books, exporters and importers, rental library chains, national and regional associations); (4) Index to retailers & wholesalers in the U.S. & Canada. The section on U. S. and Canadian book publishers and the lists of former publishing companies which were a feature of earlier editions were discontinued with the 26th ed. (1980).

•Available on CD-ROM as part of *Library reference plus* (AK33). Z475.A5

Literary market place : LMP. 1989– . New Providence, N.J. : Bowker, c1988– . Annual. **AA282**

Continues: *Literary market place* (1st ed. [1940]–31st ed. [1971/72]), which merged with *Names and numbers* to form *Literary market place with names and numbers* (32nd ed. [1972/73]–48th ed. [1988]).

A useful directory of organizations, periodicals, publishers, etc., which might be helpful in the placing, promotion, and advertising of literary property. Lists officers and key personnel. Classified under such headings as: book publishing, book clubs, associations, book trade events, conferences and contests, agents and agencies, services and suppliers, direct mail promotion, review services, exporters and importers, book manufacturing, magazine and newspaper publishing, radio, television, and motion pictures.

From 1952–71 a supplementary "Names and numbers" volume was published, first as the *Book industry register* (1952/53–59/60), then as the *Book industry telephone directory*. This was an alphabetical listing of the names found in the matching annual volume of *LMP*, giving name, firm, address, telephone, and code number of the section of

LMP in which the name was listed. Beginning with the 1972/73 edition (publ. 1972) the "Names and numbers" section was included in *LMP* as the final section of the volume.

•Available in machine-readable form as part of: *Library reference plus* [database] (AK33). Available in CD-ROM; released annually with monthly updates. Each annual release contains the most recent version of *LMP*.   PN161.L5

Microform market place. 1974/75– . Weston, Conn. : Microfilm Review, 1974– . Biennial.   **AA283**

Subtitle: An international directory of micropublishing.

Publisher varies.

Contents, 1982/83: Directory of micropublishers; Subject index; Geographic index; Mergers & acquisitions, name changes; Organizations; Bibliography of primary sources; Names & numbers directory.

Micropublishers are listed alphabetically in the first section.   Z286.M5V43

Publishers directory. Ed. 5 (1984/85)– . Detroit : Gale, [1984]– . Irregular.   **AA284**

Subtitle: A guide to more than 9,000 new and established, commercial and nonprofit, private and alternative, corporate and association, government and institution publishing programs and their distributors; includes producers of books, classroom materials, reports, and databases.

Linda S. Hubbard, ed.

Supersedes *Book publishers directory*, eds. 1–4, 1977–83, and continues its numbering. Published in 2 v.

An alphabetical listing of directory information (address, telephone, ISBN, principal officials, subject specialties, etc.) with indexes of imprints and distributors, subjects, and geographic areas. Excludes vanity presses and publishers covered in *Literary market place*, (AA282).

Latin America

Editoriales, distribuidoras y librerías : directorio latinoamericano / Centro Regional para el Fomento del Libro en America Latina y el Caribe. [2a ed.]. Santafé de Bogotá, Colombia : CERLALC, 1992. 365 p.   **AA285**

A listing of 2,362 publishers, distributors, and booksellers for 21 Central and South American countries, including Cuba. Arranged by country, then by type of operation (publisher, distributor, or bookseller), then alphabetically. Provides, among other information, address, telephone and fax numbers, and specialties. Indexed by company and by subject interest. Includes a listing of firms involved in importing and/or exporting. Index.   Z490.E35 1992

Europe

Deutschsprachige Verlage, Deutschland, Österreich, Schweiz, sowie Anschriften weiterer ausländischer Verlage mit deutschen Auslieferungen. Ausg. 1991/92 (41. Jahrg.)– . Köln : Verlag der Schillerbuchhandlung H. Banger, 1991– . Annual.   **AA286**

Continues *Anschriften deutscher Verlage* (1952–90).

An alphabetical list of German language publishers, providing address, telephone and fax numbers, and ISBN prefixes. Includes indexes of ISBN prefixes and publishers' main subject interests.   Z317.A57

Directory of publishing : Continental Europe. 1992– . London, England : Cassell, c1991– .   **AA287**

A companion to the same publisher's directory for the U.K., Commonwealth, and overseas (AA290), providing the same type of information for the publishing industry in Continental Europe.   Z291.D57

France

Les editeurs et diffuseurs de langue française. 1979– . Paris : Cercle de la librairie, 1979– . Annual.   **AA288**

Also has title: Répertoire international des éditeurs et diffuseurs de langue française.

In two main sections: (1) Table générale des éditeurs, and (2) Table générale des organismes de diffusion. Classified index for the first and a geographical index for the second.   Z282.R46

Germany

Adressbuch für den deutschsprachigen Buchhandel. 1977/78– . Frankfurt am Main : Buchhandler-Vereingung GMBH, 1977– . Annual.   **AA289**

Subtitle: Buchhandels-Adressbuch für die Bundesrepublik Deutschland; Adressbuch des Österreichischen Buchhandels; Schweizer Buchhandel, Adressbuch; Verzeichnis des Buchhandels anderer Länder.

Continues: *Adressbuch des deutschsprachigen Buchhandels*, publ. 1954–75. With various changes of title (e.g., *Adressbuch des deutschen Buchhandels*), the series goes back to 1839.

Provides extensive coverage of German, Austrian, and Swiss publishers, book dealers, and related organizations, with selective coverage for other countries. Offers geographical approach, ISBN numbers, etc.   Z317.A26

Great Britain

Directory of publishing. United Kingdom, Commonwealth and overseas. 1992– . London : Cassell, c1991– . Annual.   **AA290**

Continues: *Cassell's directory of publishing in Great Britain, the Commonwealth, and Ireland*, 1960–76 (title varies); *Cassell & the Publishers Association directory of publishing* (London : Cassell, 1984–90. 7 v.). Vols. for 1992– also called 17th ed.– .

Gives information similar to that provided for the U. S. in *Literary market place* (AA282). lists of British and Commonwealth publishers, agents, associations, book clubs, prizes, etc.

Companion title: *Directory of publishing. Continental Europe* (1992– . London : Cassell, c1991–).

At head of title: Cassell, The Publishers Association and the Federation of European Publishers.

Provides similar information for the publishing industry in Continental Europe.   Z327.C37

Italy

Catalogo degli editori italiani / Associazione italiana editori. 1988– . Milano : Bibliografica, c1988– .   **AA291**

1st–5th eds., publ. 1976–86, entitled *Gli editori italiani*.

A directory of Italian publishers that gives, in addition to address and phone number, founding date, areas of specialization, number of titles in print, ISBN prefix, distributors, etc. Includes an introductory survey of Italian publishing, with statistical tables.   Z342.E32

Netherlands

Sijthoff's Adresboek voor Boekhandel, Uitgeverij, grafische Industrie, Gids voor Dagbladen en Tijdschriften. v. 1–103. Leiden : Sijthoff, 1855–1970. Annual (Irregular).   **AA292**

Title varies.

A directory of the newspaper and periodical press as well as of the book industry and trade. Z352.S58

Africa

The African book world and press : directory = Répertoire du livre et de la presse en Afrique. 4th ed. / ed. by Hans M. Zell. London : Zell, 1989. 306 p. **AA293**
1st ed., 1977; 3rd ed., 1983.
Comp. by *African book publishing record* (AA847).
Introduction and section headings in English and French; directory information in English or French. A country-by-country listing covering 51 African nations. For each country, gives information under as many of the following headings as applicable: (1) University, college, and public libraries; (2) Special libraries; (3) Booksellers; (4) Publishers; (5) Institutional publishers; (6) Periodicals and magazines; (7) Major newspapers; (8) Book industry associations and literary societies; (9) Printers; (10) the government printer of the country. Appendixes include subject index of special libraries; subject index of periodicals; a list of principal dealers in African books in Europe and the U.S.; book prizes and awards; African news agencies; and a directory of dealer and distributors of African studies material. Z857.A1

Asia

India

Directory of publishers and booksellers in India : based on actual mailing / comp. & ed. by Anand Sagar ; sponsored by the Federation of Indian Publishers. New Delhi, India : New Light Publishers, 1986. 1 v. (various pagings). **AA294**
"Sponsored by the Federation of Indian Publishers."—*t. p.*
A listing of some 25,000 publishers, booksellers, and distributors, arranged by state, then by city. Provides addresses, telephone, telex, and fax numbers, and areas of specialization. Indexed by city. Z455.D53

Handbooks

Balkin, Richard. A writer's guide to book publishing. 2nd ed., rev. and expanded. N.Y. : Hawthorn/Dutton, [1981]. 239 p. **AA295**
"With two chapters by Jared Carter."—*t.p.*
1st ed., 1977.
A commonsense guide to many aspects of book publishing, with good background information, recent statistics, and examples. Chapters include: How to approach a publisher, How a publisher evaluates a proposal or a manuscript, How to understand and negotiate a book contract, How to prepare a final manuscript, How a manuscript is processed by a publisher, How a manuscript is turned into a finished book, How a publisher markets a book. Gives attention to new technology in publishing, small presses, university presses, etc. Indexed. PN155.B3

Bell, Herbert W. How to get your book published. Cincinnati, Ohio : Writer's Digest Books, c1985. 250 p. : forms. **AA296**
Intended "to help authors through the complexities of book publishing: preparing acceptable projects, selecting the best publisher, negotiating favorable terms, and ensuring that their manuscripts are published in a satisfactory way."—*Pref.* Offers practical advice in brief chapters dealing with all stages of the work. Brief bibliography; appendix of sample publishing contracts; general index. PN155.B45

History

American literary publishing houses, 1638–1899 / ed. by Peter Dzwonkoski. Detroit : Gale, c1986. 715 p. (Dictionary of literary biography, v.49). **AA297**
American literary publishing houses, 1900–1980: trade and paperback, ed. by Peter Dzwonkoski (1986. [Dictionary of literary biography, v. 46]).
British literary publishing houses, 1820–1880, ed. by Patricia J. Anderson and Jonathan Rose (1991. [Dictionary of literary biography, v. 106]).
British literary publishing houses, 1881–1965, ed. by Jonathan Rose and Patricia J. Anderson (c1991. [Dictionary of literary biography, v. 112]).
These volumes offer signed articles on the history and character of American and British publishers of literary works in book format. Most articles include references to sources of further information. The series is described at BE200. Z479.A448

Book Subscriptions List Project. Book subscription lists : a revised guide / [Text] by F. J. G. Robinson and P. J. Wallis. Newcastle upon Tyne : H. Hill for The Book Subscriptions List Project, 1975. 120 p. **AA298**
Earlier, preliminary lists were issued in duplicated form.
An introductory section provides background and description of subscription lists and points out their potential uses. The "Catalogue of book subscription lists" is chronologically arranged within two main sections: "Lists to 1761" and "Lists 1761–1974." Author index; book trade index; provincial imprint index.

Columbia University. Libraries. The history of printing from its beginnings to 1930 : the subject catalogue of the American Type Founders Company Library in the Columbia University Libraries. Millwood, N.Y. : Kraus, [1980]. 4 v. **AA299**
Reproduces the subject cards (with some author and catchword title entries) for this outstanding collection. Nearly 45,000 entries. Z117.C65

Corsten, Severin. Der Buchdruck im 15. Jahrhundert : eine bibliographie. Stuttgart : A. Hiersemann, 1988. v. 1. (Hiersemanns bibliographische Handbücher, Bd. 7). (In progress). **AA300**
Contents: Teil 1, Bibliographie.
A useful classified bibliography covering such areas as the technical aspects of printing, works on individual authors, and publishing in different countries and cities. Includes books and articles written in the major European languages published from the 18th century to about 1982, the majority of citations being to 20th-century publications. Z127C826b

Fumagalli, Giuseppe. Lexicon typographicum Italiae : Dictionnaire géographique d'Italie pour servir à l'histoire de l'imprimerie dans ce pays .... Florence : Olschki, 1905. 587 p. : ill. **AA301**
Subtitle: Contenant l' l'indication de toutes les localités d'Italie géographique et politique, ou l'imprimerie à été introduite jusqu'à nos jours, avec la synonymie latine, française, etc., et celle des lieux supposés d'impression; 2e des notices bibliographiques sur les éditions principes de chaque ville, bourg, château, etc., et sur les faits les plus remarquables se rapportant à l'histoire de l'art typographique dans ces localités; 3e des notices biographiques sur les plus célèbres imprimeurs italiens; 4e des notices statistiques sur l'état présent de l'imprimerie en Italie; 5e des renseignements historiques sur les arts auxiliaires de l'imprimerie: lithographie, gravure, papeterie, fabrication des encres, des presses, des caractères, etc.
———. ———. *Giunte e correzioni = Additions et corrections.* (Florence : Olschki, 1939. 84 p.).

Joyce, Donald F. Black book publishers in the United States : a historical dictionary of the presses, 1817–1990. N.Y. : Greenwood, 1991. 256 p. **AA302**

"Designed for students, scholars, and researchers interested in cultural and intellectual black history who seek specific information on individual black publishers … relative to (1) publishing history, (2) books and other publications released by the publisher, (3) information sources about the publisher, (4) selected major titles issued by the publisher, (5) libraries holding titles produced by the publisher, and (6) officers of the publisher."—*p. xiv.* Arranged alphabetically by publishing house. Name, subject, and title index. Z471.J68

Lehmann-Haupt, Hellmut. The book in America : a history of the making and selling of books in the United States / by Hellmut Lehmann-Haupt … [et al.]. 2nd [rev. and enl. American] ed. N.Y. : Bowker, 1951. 493 p. **AA303**

Repr.: 1964.

1st American ed., 1939. Originally published in Leipzig as: *Das amerikanische Buchwesen*, 1937.

A survey history of book production and distribution in the U. S. from 1638 to mid-20th century. Bibliography, p.422–66. Z473.L522

Tebbel, John William. A history of book publishing in the United States. N.Y. : R. R. Bowker Co., [1972]–1981. 4 v. **AA304**

Contents: v. 1. The creation of an industry, 1630–1865; v. 2. The expansion of an industry, 1865–1919; v. 3. The golden age between two wars, 1920–1940; v. 4. The great change, 1940–1980.

The standard survey of American book publishing. Includes brief histories of many individual publishers as well as general information about trends and issues (censorship, copyright, book sales, regional publishing, etc.). Z473.T42

Biography

Ascarelli, Fernanda. La tipografia cinquecentina italiana. Firenze : Sansoni Antiquariato, 1953. 259 p. : ill. (Contributi alla Biblioteca bibliografica italica, 1). **AA305**

Intended to cover all printers active in Italy up to and including 1600. Arrangement is geographical by region, then alphabetical by city, and chronological by printer. Adequate indexes. Z155.A8

Bibliographical Society (London). [Dictionaries of printers and booksellers in England, Scotland and Ireland]. London : Soc., 1905–32. 5 v. **AA306**

Repr., 1949–68.

Comprises: *Century of the English book trade … 1457–1557*, by E. Gordon Duff (1905. 200 p.); *Dictionary of printers and booksellers in England, Scotland and Ireland and of foreign printers of English books, 1557–1640*, by R. B. McKerrow (1910. 346 p.); *Dictionary of the printers who were at work in England, Scotland and Ireland, from 1641 to 1667*, by H. R. Plomer (1907. 199 p.); *Dictionary of the printers and booksellers who were at work in England, Scotland and Ireland from 1668 to 1725*, by H. R. Plomer (1922. 342 p.); *Dictionary of the printers and booksellers who were at work in England, Scotland and Ireland from 1726 to 1775*; those in England by H. R. Plomer, Scotland by G. H. Bushnell, Ireland by E. R. McClintock Dix (1932. 432 p.).

Good, short biographies, with bibliographies. The different volumes in the series contain indexes as follows: 1457–1557, Index of Christian names, Index of London signs, Chronological index of foreign places, printers and stationers; 1557–1640, Indexes of (1) London signs, (2) London addresses, (3) Places other than London; 1668–1725, Index of printers and places to the two volumes, 1641–1667 and 1668–1725; 1726–1775, Indexes of (1) Places in England, Wales other than London, (2) Places in Scotland other than Edinburgh, (3) Places in Ireland, (4) Places abroad; Circulating libraries in England and Scotland arranged in order of date.

Geldner, Ferdinand. Die deutschen Inkunabeldrucker : ein Handbuch der deutschen Buchdrucker des XV. Jahrhunderts nach Druckorten. Stuttgart : A. Hiersemann, 1968–70. 2 v. : ill. **AA307**

Contents: v. 1, Das deutschen Sprachgebiet; v. 2, Die fremden Sprachgebiete.

Provides notes on the lives and works of German printers of the 15th century. A geographical-chronological arrangement is employed, designed to show the spread of printing from Mainz to other German cities and abroad. Indexed. Z240.G34

Lepreux, Georges. Gallia typographica : ou, Répertoire biographique et chronologique de tous les imprimeurs de France depuis les origines de l'imprimerie jusqu'à la Révolution. Paris : Champion, 1909–14. 5 v. **AA308**

Originally planned for 20 v. and a general index. Published as a supplement to *Revue des bibliothèques.*

In two series: (1) Série parisienne, and (2) Série départmentale.

Contents: Série parisienne, t. 1, Livre d'or des imprimeurs du roi; Série départmentale: t. l, Flandre, Artois, Picardie; t. 2, Champagne et Barrois; t. 3, Normandie (in 2 v.); t. 4, Bretagne.

A monumental work, containing full biographies with detailed bibliographical references. Each volume is in two parts: biographies and documents. Z144.L59

Muller, Jean. Dictionnaire abrégé des imprimeurs/éditeurs français du seizième siècle. Baden-Baden : Verlag Librairie Heitz, 1970. 150 p. (Bibliotheca bibliographica Aureliana, 30). **AA309**

Arrangement is alphabetical by place; then printers are listed chronologically by dates when they were active in that locality. (For the more important cities such as Paris and Lyons, an alphabetical arrangement of printers' names is used, with a chronological key.) For each printer a reference is given to bibliographical sources concerning his work. Alphabetical index of personal names, and a geographical table of variant place-names. Z144.M84

Renouard, Philippe. Imprimeurs & libraires parisiens du XVIe siècle / ouvrage publié d'après les manuscrits de Philippe Renouard. Paris : Service des travaux historiques de la ville de Paris, 1964–91. v. 1–5 : facsims. (In progress). **AA310**

Contents: v. 1–5, Abada-Bonamy.

First of a series to be devoted to the careers and works of 16th-century Parisian printers and booksellers. Primarily a biobibliography, the completed work will also serve as a bibliography of Parisian imprints of the period. Listings for printers predominate, and entries include descriptive notes on their editions; plates at the end of each volume illustrate their typographic traits. Detailed subject index. Useful both as a biographical and as a bibliographical tools.

Several unnumbered volumes have been published, initiating a new publication pattern: i.e., in addition to the continuing alphabetical sequence information on figures falling outside that sequence will be published as the completed articles become available: "Fasc. Breyer" (1982), "Fasc. Brumen" (1984), and "Fasc. Cavellat/Marnot & Cavellat" (1986). Z305.R4

——————— Répertoire des imprimeurs parisiens, libraires, fondeurs de caractères et correcteurs d'imprimerie : depuis l'introduction de l'imprimerie à Paris (1470) jusqu'à la fin du sizième siècle. Paris : M. J. Minard, 1965. 511 p. **AA311**

Contents: Libraires, imprimeurs, correcteurs et fondeurs de caractères; Auteurs qui vendaient eux-mêmes leurs ouvrages; Table des adresses classées par rues; Table des enseignes; Liste chronologique; Table des noms personnes.

First published in 1898 under title *Imprimeurs parisiens.* A new edition, with considerable additional material and new references to sources of information, was published in *Revue des bibliothèques*, v. 32–42 (1922–34). The present edition reprints the material for the revised 2nd ed. as it appeared in *Revue des bibliothèques*, with the addition of an index of printers' signs, etc.; an index of streets and landmarks; and a chronological table. Z305.R43

Copyright

Chickering, Robert B. How to register a copyright and protect your creative work / Robert B. Chickering and Susan Hartman. 1st pbk. ed. N.Y. : Scribner, 1987. 230 p.   **AA312**
1st ed., 1980.
Subtitle: A basic guide to the new copyright law and how it affects anyone who wants to protect creative work.
Outlines registration procedures and answers frequently asked questions about copyright. Also treats some special copyright situations. Index.   KF2995.C45

Copyright laws and treaties of the world. Paris : UNESCO ; Wash. : Bureau of Nat. Affairs, 1956– . 3 v. (loose-leaf).
          AA313
Kept current by supplements (originally annual, now irregular—e.g., 1979/80 suppl. publ. 1982).
Comp. by the United Nations Educational, Scientific and Cultural Organization and others.
Presents, either in the original English text or in specially prepared English translations, the laws and regulations of some 136 states.
In four parts: pt. 1, States, arranged alphabetically; for each state gives: (1) information primarily domestic in scope; (2) information primarily international in scope. Pt. 2, Territories. Pt. 3, Multilateral conventions, giving for each convention: the text of the Convention; the status of adherences to the Convention; and the states among which the Convention or portions thereof are applicable. Pt. 4, Rome Convention rights in two sections: (1) states, giving an index to national legislation; (2) multilateral conventions, giving the Rome Convention and regional conventions.

Fishman, Stephen. The copyright handbook : how to protect and use written works. Berkeley, Calif. : Nolo Pr., 1992. 1 v. (various pagings) : ill.   **AA314**
Designed as a practical handbook for writers and publishers. Includes a list of legal aid groups and sample forms.   KF2995.F53

Johnston, Donald F. Copyright handbook. 2nd ed. N.Y. : Bowker, 1982. 381 p.   **AA315**
1st ed., 1978.
Aims "to explain the 1976 Copyright Act and to report on legal developments that have taken place since it took effect at the beginning of 1978."—*Pref.* Provides information on kinds of works which are copyrightable, copyright duration, transfer of ownership, copyright notices and registrations, fair use, copyrights and teaching activities, library reproductions, limitations on rights of performance, etc. Appendixes include text of the 1976 Copyright Act, examples of application forms for registration of copyrights, and texts of various guidelines (e.g., for photocopying and interlibrary loan arrangements). Detailed table of contents; index.   KF2994.J63

Strong, William S. The copyright book : a practical guide. 2nd ed. Cambridge, Mass. : MIT Pr., [1984]. 223 p.   **AA316**
1st ed., 1981.
Aims "to make available to people whose lives and work are affected by the laws of copyright an understanding of their rights and responsibilities."—*Pref.* Includes chapters on ownership, transfer of copyright, registration of a copyright claim, infringement and fair use (with attention to library copying and home videotaping), etc.
          KF2994.S75

Copy preparation

Achtert, Walter S. The MLA style manual / by Walter S. Achtert and Joseph Gibaldi. N.Y. : Modern Language Association of America, 1985. 271 p.   **AA317**

A companion to the *MLA handbook* (AG2), which is intended for students, this guide "attempts to meet the scholar's need for comprehensive guide to publishing in the humanities."—*Pref.*   PN147.A28

Butcher, Judith. Copy-editing : the Cambridge handbook for editors, authors, and publishers. 3rd ed. Cambridge ; N.Y. : Cambridge Univ. Pr., 1992. 471 p. : ill.   **AA318**
1st ed., 1975; 2nd ed., 1981.
Based on the author's experience at Penguin Books and Cambridge Univ. Pr., but intended as a guide to copy editors in general. Covers much specialized material as well as general aspects of the work. Detailed index. Appendixes include a glossary and a good Checklist of copy-editing.   PN162.B86

The Chicago manual of style. 14th ed. Chicago : Univ. of Chicago Pr., 1993. 921 p. : ill.   **AA319**
A standard work, thoroughly revised and updated, which serves as a "how-to" book for authors and editors. In three main sections (Bookmaking; Style; Production and printing), offering practical information and advice on all aspects of manuscript preparation, copyediting, and seeing a work through the press. Glossary of technical terms; bibliography; index.   Z253.U69

Kline, Mary-Jo. A guide to documentary editing. Baltimore : Johns Hopkins Univ. Pr., c1987. 228 p.   **AA320**
At head of title: Prepared for the Association for Documentary Editing.
A unique and very useful work which provides chapters on the history, techniques, conventions, and applications of textual editing. Of interest to historians and others in nonliterary fields. Includes detailed instructions for preparing editions for printers and publishers, as well as sample form letters to libraries, collectors, and auction houses. General index.   Z113.3.K55

Luey, Beth. Handbook for academic authors. Rev. ed. Cambridge ; N.Y. : Cambridge Univ. Pr., 1990. 273 p. : ill.
          AA321
Covers a wide range of publishing practices, with chapters devoted to journal articles, revising a dissertation for publication, finding a publisher for scholarly books and college textbooks, as well as the mechanics of authorship and special problems relating to multiauthor books and anthologies. Classified bibliography p. 205–21; general index.   PN146.L84

Skillin, Marjorie E. Words into type / Marjorie E. Skillin ... [et al.]. 3rd ed., completely rev. Englewood Cliffs, N.J. : Prentice-Hall, [1974]. 585 p.   **AA322**
1st ed., 1948.
A reference source for writers, editors, copy editors, proofreaders, compositors, and printers. Includes sections on preparation of the manuscript, copy and proof, copy-editing style, typographical style, grammar, use of words, typography and illustration.   PN160.S52

United States. Government Printing Office. Style manual. Rev. ed. Wash. : U.S. Govt. Print. Off., 1973. 548 p.   **AA323**
First publ. 1908 under title: *Manual of style.* Frequently revised.
A useful and extensive manual giving the practices of the Government Printing Office on copy preparation, with rules for capitalization, punctuation, abbreviations, etc., and information on foreign languages, including alphabets, with pronunciation, special rules, lists of numbers, etc.
————. *Word division; supplement to Government Printing Office style manual* (6th ed.; 1962. 190 p).
This edition includes many new words, particularly scientific and technical words. Gives rules of word division and lists the syllabication of several thousand words.   Z253.U58

University of Chicago Press. Chicago guide to preparing electronic manuscripts : for authors and publishers. Chicago : Univ. of Chicago Pr., 1987. 143 p. : ill.   **AA324**
"This guide is addressed to authors and publishers who wish to use electronic manuscripts for typesetting ... . [The] focus is on manu-

script preparation ... and on the procedures that should be followed by author and publisher so that the author's electronic medium can be used for typesetting."—*Pref.* Indexed. Z286.E43U54

SELECTION OF BOOKS

Guides

Books for public libraries / PLA Starter List Comm., Public Libr. Assoc., Amer. Libr. Assoc. 3rd ed. Chicago : Amer. Libr. Assoc., 1981. 374 p. **AA325**
1st ed., 1971.
Intended "as an alternative book selection tool of representative subject suggestions for planning new public library collections or for assessing library collections being redeveloped."—*Pref.* Lists in-print books arranged according to the 19th ed. of the Dewey Decimal Classification. Includes publisher, date, price, ISBN and LC card numbers as available. Subject and author/title indexes. Z1035.B73

Good reading / prep. by the Committee on College Reading of the National Council of Teachers of English. 2nd ed.– . N.Y. : R.R. Bowker, 1934– . Irregular. **AA326**
1st publ. N.Y. : Weybright & Talley, 1933. New editions published and revised at frequent intervals. Publisher varies. 23rd ed., 1990.
Originally issued by Committee on College Reading and sponsored by the College English Association.
An annotated list of about 2,500 titles arranged under 34 subject headings. Aims "to lead an increasing number of people to savor the great or significant books."—*p. xix.* A very useful and inexpensive compilation. Z1035.G6

Hackett, Alice Payne. 80 years of best sellers, 1895–1975 / by Alice Payne Hackett and James Henry Burke. N.Y. : Bowker, 1977. 265 p. **AA327**
Earlier editions called *Fifty years of best sellers, 1895–1945; 60 years of best sellers, 1895–1955;* and *70 years of best sellers, 1895–1965.*
Includes dicussions of best-sellers, and of best-sellers in various subject fields, with lists of best-sellers arranged by number of copies sold, by subject, and by year. Z1033.B3H342

Public library catalog / ed. by Paula B. Entin and Juliette Yaakov. 9th ed. N.Y. : H.W. Wilson, 1989. 1338 p. **AA328**
1st–4th eds. (1934–58) publ. under title: *Standard catalog for public libraries.* 8th ed., 1984.
A very useful selection guide for medium-sized public and undergraduate college libraries, this is a carefully selected list of in-print titles with well-chosen descriptive notes drawn from introductory statements and reviews. In three parts: (1) classified cataloged, arranged by the abridged Dewey Decimal Classification; (2) author, title, subject, and analytical index; (3) directory of publishers and distributors. Does not include fiction; see *Fiction catalog* (BE245).
Kept up-to-date by annual supplements. Z1035.P934

The reader's adviser : a layman's guide to literature. 13th ed. N.Y. : Bowker, 1986–88. 6 v. **AA329**
1st–8th eds. had title: *Bookman's manual;* 9th ed., *Reader's adviser and bookman's manual.* 12th ed., 1974–77.
Contents: v. 1, Best in American and British fiction, poetry, essays, literary biography, bibliography, and reference; v. 2, Best in American and British drama and world literature in English translation; v. 3, Best in general reference literature, the social sciences, history, and the arts; v. 4, Best in the literature of philosophy and world religions; v. 5, Best in the literature of science, technology, and medicine; v. 6, Indexes.
Designed for nonspecialists, "provides annotated bibliographies arranged by subject, with brief biographies of authors, creative artists,

and scientists worthy of special mention; in addition it informs the reader of a book's availability, price, and purchasing source."—*Pref.* Each volume has its own name, title, and subject indexes. Vol. 6 has a directory of publishers and cumulated name, title, and subject indexes. Z1035.B7

Current

Booklist. v. 1 (1905)– . Chicago : Amer. Libr. Assoc., 1905– . Semimonthly (monthly in July and Aug.). **AA330**
The booklist and *Subscription books bulletin* were combined with v. 53, no. 1, Sept. 1, 1956, under title *The booklist and subscription books bulletin.* With v. 66, no. 1, Sept. 1, 1969, the publication reverted to the earlier title and with v. 73, no. 1, Sept. 1976 the title became simply *Booklist.*
Booklist is a selected, annotated list of recent publications recommended especially for small and medium-sized libraries. Arranged by broad classes, e.g., adult nonfiction and fiction, books for young adults, children's books, and paperback reprints. Beginning with v. 66 (1969) audiovisual materials are reviewed regularly. Microcomputer software is also reviewed. Complete bibliographical information is given for each entry, including price. Annotations describe, evaluate, and indicate the kind of library for which the book is recommended. Indexes are now published semiannually.
Reviews of reference materials appear in each issue, in a section titled "Reference books bulletin"(AA357). Z1035.A9

British book news : a monthly selection of recent books. London : British Council, 1940–1993. **AA331**
Title varies: no. 1–14, *A selection of recent books published in Great Britain.* Subtitle varies; publisher varies.
A useful, selective, annotated list of "best books" arranged according to the Dewey Decimal Classification. Each number has an index, and there is a separate cumulation of author and title indexes for the year. Z1035.B838

Bulletin critique du livre français. v.1– . Paris : Assoc. pour la Diffusion de la Pensée Française, 1945– . Monthly. **AA332**
Publisher varies.
A selected list of books in all subject fields published in France, with descriptive annotations. The index of authors cumulates annually. Z2165.B924

Deutsche Bibliographie : das deutsche Buch / bearb. von der Deutschen Bibliothek. 1954, Hft. 6–1984, Hft. 4. Frankfurt/ M. : Buchhändler-Vereinigung, 1954–84. Bimonthly. **AA333**
Continues: 1950–54, no. 5, *Das deutsche Buch: Neuerscheinungen der deutschen Verlage.* Subtitle varies.
A selective, classified list, with author index, of new German publications, including annotations. Z2221.D45

Libri e riviste d'Italia : rassegna bibliografica mensile. Anno 1, no. 1 (Marzo 1950)– . Roma : Capriotti, 1950– . Monthly. **AA334**
For annotation, *see* AA738. Z2345.L63

Books for college students

Books for college libraries : a core collection of 50,000 titles. 3rd ed. / [Virginia Clark, ed.]. Chicago : Amer. Libr. Assoc., 1988. 6 v. **AA335**
1st ed., 1967; 2nd ed., 1975.
Contents: v. 1, Humanities; v. 2, Language and literature; v. 3, History; v. 4, Social sciences; v. 5, Psychology, science, technology, bibliography; v. 6, Index.
"A project of the Association of College and Research Libraries."—*t.p.*

Offers a "core collection for undergraduate libraries."—*Introd.* Entries contain cataloging and classification information; titles are arranged by Library of Congress call number within each volume. Author, title, and subject indexes.   Z1039.C65B67

Current

Choice. v. 1– . Middletown, Conn. : Assoc. of College and Research Libraries, 1964– . Monthly (except bimonthly, July–Aug.).   **AA336**
Subtitle: Current reviews of academic books (varies). Earlier issues called: Books for college libraries.
A book review journal planned to assist college libraries in the selection of current books. Reviews are written by a large panel of faculty and librarians.   Z1035.C5

Books for children and young people

Best books for children : preschool through grade 6 / John T. Gillespie and Corinne J. Naden, editors. 5th ed. New Providence, N.J. : Bowker, 1994. 1 v.   **AA337**
1st ed., 1978–3rd ed., 1985, had subtitle: Preschool through the middle grades; 4th ed., 1990.
Aims "to provide a list of books, gathered from a number of sources, that are highly recommended to satisfy both a child's recreational reading needs and the demands of a typical school curriculum."—*Pref.* Classed arrangement with author/illustrator, title, and subject indexes, plus a list of biographical subjects.   Z1037.B547

Children's catalog. 16th ed. / ed. by Juliette Yaakov with the assistance of Anne Price. N.Y. : H.W. Wilson, 1991.   **AA338**
The most comprehensive bibliography in its field. Arranged in three parts: pt. 1, classified catalog, arranged by Dewey Decimal Classification, giving full bibliographic information and annotations; pt. 2, author, title, subject, and analytical index, pt. 3, directory of publishers. Titles especially recommended are starred. A listing by grades, which was a feature of earlier editions, was dropped with the 11th ed. (although grading is still indicated in pt. 1). Kept up to date by annual supplements.   Z1037.W76

Children's literature abstracts. no. 1 (May 1973)– . [Birmingham, Eng.] : Sub-section on Library Work with Children, International Federation of Library Associations, 1973– . Quarterly.   **AA339**
Includes brief abstracts of books about children's literature and reading as well as notes on books for children.   Z1037.C5446

Cianciolo, Patricia Jean. Picture books for children. 3rd ed. Chicago : Amer. Libr. Assoc., 1990. 230 p. : ill.   **AA340**
1st ed., 1973, prep. by the Picture Book Subcommittee of National Council of Teachers of English, Elementary Booklist Committee. 2nd ed., 1981.
Intended as "a resource and guide for teachers of children from nursery school through junior high school, for day-care center personnel, for librarians in school and public libraries, for parents, and for any other adult concerned with the selection of well-written, imaginitively illustrated picture books that are of interest to children of all ages and backgrounds."—*Pref.* Brief annotations comment on both text and illustrations. Age group indicated for each title. Author-title-illustrator index.   Z1037.C565

The elementary school library collection : a guide to books and other media, phases 1-2-3 / Lauren K. Lee, ed. ; Gary D. Hoyle, editorial assistant; assisted by Eileen Palmer Burke ... [et al.]. 18th ed. Williamsport, Pa. : Brodart Co., 1992. 1254 p.   **AA341**
1st ed., 1965.
A frequently revised and updated work "primarily designed to

serve as a resource to assist in the continuous maintenance and development of existing collections or for the establishment of new library media centers."—*Introd.* Classed arrangement, with author, title, and subject indexes.   Z1037.E4

National Association of Independent Schools. Ad Hoc Library Committee. Books for secondary school libraries. 6th ed. N.Y. : Bowker, 1981. 844 p.   **AA342**
1st ed., 1955. Title varies; 3rd ed., 1968, called *4000 books for secondary school libraries*.
This edition lists more than 9,000 nonfiction titles and series and is intended "as a comprehensive bibliographic guide and selection aid for librarians, teachers, administrators, and others involved in developing book collections to meet the needs of college-bound students."—*Pref.* Arranged by Dewey Decimal Classification, with author and title indexes; there are separate sections listing professional tools and reference works.   Z1035.N2

Peterson, Linda Kauffman. Newbery and Caldecott Medal and Honor books : an annotated bibliography / by Linda Kauffman Peterson and Marilyn Leathers Solt. Boston : G. K. Hall, 1982. 427 p.   **AA343**
Provides critical annotations of books chosen for the Newbery and Caldecott Medals (from 1922 and 1938, respectively) and the "Honor books" considered for the awards through 1981. Chronological arrangement with indexes.
§ Irene Smith's *A history of the Newbery and Caldecott medals* (N.Y. : Viking, 1957. 140 p.) provides a narrative account of the awards, together with lists of winners and runners-up.   Z1037.P45

Senior high school library catalog : ed. by Brenda Smith and Juliette Yaakov. 14th ed. N.Y. : H.W. Wilson, 1992. 1467 p.   **AA344**
1st ed., 1926–28; 2nd ed., 1932; now revised every five years. Kept up-to-date by annual supplements.
1st–8th eds. had title: *Standard catalog for high school libraries*. Beginning with the 9th ed., the work was revised for senior high school grades, with grades 7–9 being the province of the *Junior high school library catalog* (AA345).
In three parts: pt. 1, classified catalog, arranged according to the Dewey Decimal Classification number with full bibliographical information, suggested subject headings, and annotation; pt. 2, author, title, subject, and analytical index, arranged in one alphabet; pt. 3, directory of publishers and distributors.
Planned especially for school libraries, but useful also as a guide to selection of books for smaller public libraries. Many adult and young adult books are now included to reflect the more advanced and upgraded curricula now in effect in most high schools. Limited to in-print items.   Z1035.W77

Yaakov, Juliette. Junior high school library catalog. 6th ed. N.Y. : H.W. Wilson, 1990. 802 p.   **AA345**
1st ed., 1965. Revised every five years; kept up-to-date by annual supplements.
A relatively recent addition to the "Standard catalog series," assuming part of the coverage of the *Standard catalog for high school libraries* (AA344) and concentrating on books for the 7th through 9th grades. Follows the plan and arrangement of the publisher's other "Standard catalogs." Out-of-print books are not included. Indexed.   Z1037.W765

Reference books

American reference books annual. 1970– . Littleton, Colo. : Libraries Unlimited, [1970]– . Annual.   **AA346**
Ed. by Bohdan S. Wynar. Often referred to as *ARBA*.
Each issue covers the reference book output (including reprints) of the previous year (i.e., the 1970 volume covers 1969 publications). Offers descriptive and evaluative notes (many of them signed by contributors), with references to selected reviews. Limited to titles in English. Classed arrangement; author-subject-title index.

————. Cumulated indexes, v. 1–5, 6–10, 11–14; 15–20, publ. 1975–89. (4 v.)   Z1035.1.A55

Barteczko, Ewa. Polskie wydawnictwa informacyjne, 1945–1981 / Ewa Barteczko, Joanna Jarzyńska. Warszawa : Biblioteka Narodowa, 1985. 328 p.   **AA347**

At head of title: Biblioteka Narodowa. Dział Informacji i Udostępniania Zbiorów.

Attempts to list all major reference works published in Poland, 1945–81. Arranged by Universal Decimal Classification with an author/title index and an alphabetical list of subject headings.
Z1035.6.B37

Best reference books, 1986–1990 : titles of lasting value selected from American reference books annual / comp. by G. Kim Dority; ed. by Bohdan S. Wynar. Englewood, Colo. : Libraries Unlimited, 1992. 544 p.   **AA348**

Earlier versions covered 1970–76, 1970–80, and 1981–85.

Intended as a selection tool for librarians wishing to improve their collections or those building a new reference collection. Selections and annotations taken from *American reference books annual* (AA346), and thus limited to English-language titles.   Z1035.1.B534

Geoghegan, Abel Rodolfo. Obras de referencia de América Latina : repertorio selectivo y anotado de enciclopedias, diccionarios, bibliografías, repertorios biográficos, catálogos, guías, anuarios, índices, etc. [Buenos Aires : Impr. Crisol, 1965]. 280 p.   **AA349**

"Compiled with the assistance of Unesco."—*title page*.

Preface in Spanish, English, and French.

Includes "all types of reference works ... that refer to Latin America, regardless of subject matter and place of publication" (*Pref.*), thus differing in scope and purpose from Josefa Emilia Sabor's *Manual de fuentes de información* (Buenos Aires : Editorial Kapelusz, 1967). Lists 2,694 items arranged by Universal Decimal Classification, with analytical index. Many annotations.   Z1601.G4

Library of Congress. The Library of Congress main reading room reference collection subject catalog. 2nd ed. /comp. and ed. by Katherine Ann Gardner. Wash. : Library of Congress, 1980. 1236 p.   **AA350**

1st ed., 1975.

A computer-produced guide to the Library's Main Reading Room collection of some 17,315 titles (13,385 monographs, 3,930 serials) which constituted the collection on Aug. 15, 1980. Emphasizes the humanities, social sciences, and bibliography. Arranged alphabetically by subject heading, then by main entry.   Z1035.1.U526

Maichel, Karol. Guide to Russian reference books / ed. by J. S. G. Simmons. Stanford, Calif. : Hoover Inst., 1962–67. v. 1–2, 5. (Hoover Institute. Bibliographical series, 10, 18, 32).
AA351

No more published.

Contents: v. 1, General bibliographies and reference books (1962. 92 p.); v. 2, History, auxiliary historical sciences, ethnography, and geography (1964. 297 p.); v. 5, Science, technology, and medicine (1967. 384 p.).

The projected 6-v. series was expected to list more than 3,500 titles of reference works pertaining to all phases of Russian life. The parts published are classified, annotated guides to materials in Russian and other languages, with broad chronological coverage. Author, title, and subject indexes in each volume.   Z2491.M25

Malclès, Louise-Noëlle. Les sources du travail bibliographique. Genève : E. Droz ; Lille : Giard, 1950–58. 3 v. in 4.
AA352

Although now considerably out of date, this remains a notable contribution to bibliographical manuals, designed to serve as textbook and guide, with introductions and discussions in each chapter. Not limited to bibliographies; also includes dictionaries, encyclopedias, atlases, texts, important periodicals, collections, and other types of reference and source materials. While basic works of earlier dates are in-

cluded, emphasis lies on publications of the 25-year period preceding compilation, and particularly 1940–50. International in scope, with emphasis on French and European works.

Contents: t. 1, General bibliographical survey; bibliographies of bibliographies; universal bibliographies; the book of the 15th and 16th centuries; printed catalogs of libraries; union catalogs; national bibliographies; encyclopedias; biography; periodicals; society publications; periodical indexes; a special section on Slavic and Balkan countries; a section on encyclopedias of the book, and a list of technical dictionaries of publishing and library terms.

t. 2, pt. 1–2, Bibliographies spécialisées (Sciences humaines), covering prehistory, anthropology, ethnography, sociology; linguistics; history; languages and literatures; religions; geography; archaeology and art; music; political and social sciences; philosophy; and special sections on the language, literature, and history of Slavic and Balkan countries and the Near, Middle, and Far East.

t. 3, Bibliographies spécialisées (Sciences exactes et techniques), lists bibliographies, dictionaries, treatises, manuals, yearbooks, periodicals, etc., in the history of science and in the various sciences, including medicine and pharmacy but excluding agriculture.

A full index by author, subject, and title is included in v. 1; in v. 2, pt. 2; and in v. 3.   Z1002.M4

Musiker, Reuben. Guide to South African reference books. 5th rev. ed. Cape Town : A. A. Balkema, 1971. 136 p.
AA353

1st ed., 1955.

A guide to some 800 works used for reference purposes published, with a few exceptions, in South Africa. Arranged by subject in Dewey Decimal Classification order with author, title, and subject index. For those South African subject areas where standard reference books do not exist, more general sources have been substituted.

————. *4th cumulative supplement, 1970–1976 to 5th rev. ed.* (Johannesburg, The Library, Univ. of the Witwatersrand, 1977. 112 p.).

About 100 titles added in this supplement, bringing the total number of supplementary entries to 283.

————. *South Africa* (Santa Barbara, Calif. : Clio Pr., 1979. 194 p.) Meant to replace the 5th ed. (above). *See* DD18.

———————— South African reference books and bibliographies of 1979–1980. Johannesburg : Univ. of the Witwatersrand, Lib., 1981. 58 p.   **AA354**

Serves as a supplement to the compiler's *South Africa* (note, AA353) and his *South African bibliography* (AA72), listing some 200 items, mainly from the 1979–80 period.   Z3601.M82

Nihon no Sanko Tosho Henshu Iinkai. Guide to Japanese reference books. Chicago : Amer. Libr. Assoc., 1966. 303 p.
AA355

1st Japanese ed., 1962, had title: *Nihon no sankō tosho*.

A guide to basic Japanese reference works designed for the general reader. Each entry consists of author, title, imprint, collation, and, in most instances, a brief annotation.

In four sections: General works, Humanities, Social sciences, and Science-technology. Each section is broken down into specific subjects; within each subject, titles are listed according to the following general pattern, as applicable: bibliographies, dictionaries and encyclopedias, handbooks, chronological tables, biographical dictionaries and directories, pictorial works, yearbooks, statistical works, and documents. Included is an alphabetical index to authors, titles, and general subject headings.

This English-language edition provides transliteration of the entries as well as translations of the titles and annotations from the 2nd Japanese edition (Tokyo, 1966), which included materials published up to Sept. 1964; a revised Japanese edition of 1980 includes about 5,500 items published through 1977. The English- and Japanese-language editions were prepared simultaneously.

————. *Supplement.* (Wash.: Library of Congress, 1979. 300 p.).

An English-language edition of the Japanese supplement, adding about 1,700 items, most of them published from late 1964 through 1970. Includes a cumulated index to the main volume and the supplement.   Z3306.N5

Recommended reference books for small and medium-sized libraries and media centers. 1981– . Littleton, Colo. : Libraries Unlimited, Inc., 1981– . Annual.   **AA356**

A classified listing of items selected from *American reference books annual* (AA346) of the corresponding year.   Z1035.1.R438

Reference books bulletin. (*In* Booklist, 1983–). Chicago : Amer. Libr. Assoc., 1983– .   **AA357**

Semimonthly (monthly in July and Aug.).

Continues: *Subscription books bulletin* (v. 1 [1930]–27 [1956]. Chicago : American Libr. Assoc., 1930–56); *The booklist and subscription books bulletin* (v. 53 [1956]–65 [1969]); "Reference and subscription books reviews" section of *Booklist* (1970–83).

Consists of reviews, prepared by members of the Reference Books Bulletin Editorial Board and by guest reviewers, of "reference books likely to be of general interest (defining *reference book* as a publication designed by its arrangement and treatment to be consulted for definite items of information rather than to be read consecutively."—*Masthead.*

Cumulated reviews are reprinted annually as: *Reference books bulletin* (1984-85–).   Z1007.S94

Reference sources for small and medium-sized libraries / Jovian P. Lang, ed. 5th ed. / comp. by an ad hoc subcommittee of the Reference Sources Committee of the Reference and Adult Services Division, American Library Association. Chicago : Amer. Libr. Assoc., 1992. 317 p.   **AA358**

1st–3rd eds. (1968–79) had title *Reference books for small and medium-sized libraries;* the title change reflects "the growing number of reference sources available in microform and online formats" (*Pref.*) which are included in this edition along with traditional print materials. Nearly 2,000 items, part of the increased size of this edition accounted for by the inclusion of reference materials for children and young adults (works for those categories of readers being so marked). Intended as a guide for college and large secondary school libraries as well as for public libraries. Items are grouped in subject categories and further subdivided by type of reference source or other suitable subdivision. Sections were prepared by individual compilers or teams of compilers. Good annotations; coverage of various subject fields is unusually even for a work of this kind; index of names and titles.   Z1035.1.A47

RSR : reference services review. v. 1, no. 1 (Jan./Mar. 1973)– . Ann Arbor, Mich. : Pierian Pr., 1973– . Quarterly.   **AA359**

Vol. 1, no. 1 preceded by a "pilot issue" dated Nov./Dec. 1972.

Each issue includes a section of reviews, Recent reference books; a Reference book review index; and a section, Reference books in print.   Z1035.1.R43

Sharma, H. D. Indian reference sources : an annotated guide to Indian reference material / H. D. Sharma ; assisted by L. M. P. Singh, Ramji Singh, and G. C. Kendadamath. 2nd ed. Varanasi : Indian Bibliographic Centre, 1988–89. 2 v.   **AA360**

1st ed., 1972.

Contents: v. 1, Generalia and humanities; v. 2, Social sciences, pure sciences & applied sciences.

An annotated listing by broad subject of some 5,500 sources in print or readily available in 1985. Each volume has an author and title index.   Z3206.S483

Spanish-language reference books : an annotated bibliography / comp. by Bibliotecas para la Gente, Reference Committee. Berkeley, Calif. : Chicano Studies Library Publications Unit, Univ. of California at Berkeley, 1989. 45 *l*. (Chicano Studies Library publication series, no. 15.).   **AA361**

A classified list evaluating a core collection of Spanish-language reference books. Author and title index.   Z1035.1.S586

Teng, Ssu-yü. An annotated bibliography of selected Chinese reference works / Ssu-yü Teng, Knight Biggerstaff. 3rd ed. Cambridge : Harvard Univ. Pr., 1971. 250 p. (Harvard-Yenching Institute studies, 2).   **AA362**

For annotation, *see* DE123.   Z1035.T32

Walford's guide to reference material. 5th ed. London : Library Association, 1989–1991. 3 v.   **AA363**

Cover title: Guide to reference material.

1st ed., 1959; 4th ed., 1980–87.

Contents: v. 1, Science and technology, ed. by A.J. Walford ; with the editorial collaboration of Marilyn Mullay and Priscilla Schlicke; v. 2, Social and historical sciences, philosophy and religion, ed. by Alan Day and Joan M. Harvey, with the editorial collaboration of Marilyn Mullay; v. 3, Generalia, language & literature, the arts, ed. by Anthony Chalcraft, Ray Prytherch, and Stephen Willis.

Aims "to provide a signpost to reference books and bibliographies published in recent years. Although international in scope the material is principally in English."—*Introd.* Arranged by Universal Decimal Classification. Annotations often include critical comment, reference to related works not accorded a separate entry, and citations to reviews. Each volume has its own author/title and subject indexes; v. 3 has a cumulated subject guide referring to the volumes covering specific topics.

A 6th edition is in progress; *see* EA10.   Z1035.W25

Book review indexes

Bibliographie der Rezensionen. Leipzig : Dietrich, 1901–44.   **AA364**

Issues for 1901–10 inclusive (1 v. per year) index reviews of books printed in some 3,000 German periodicals. 1911–14, 2 v. per year: the first volume of each year indexes reviews in German periodicals, the second volume indexes reviews in about 2,000 periodicals in languages other than German. 1915 has 2 v. for German reviews and 1 v. for non-German. Volumes for 1916–24 index only German reviews except that v. 33 covers non-German publications for 1917–19. 1925–43 are annual volumes alternating German and *fremdsprachigen.* A very comprehensive list, especially useful in American and English research libraries as it indexes many American and English sets not included in the *Book review digest.* Does not give digests or quotations from the reviews listed. The volumes which index reviews in German periodicals cover the same list as the *Bibliographie der deutschen Zeitschriftenliteratur* (AD313) and supplement that work; the volumes indexing non-German periodicals do the same thing for the *Bibliographie der fremdsprachigen Zeitschriftenliteratur* (AD253).

Continued by *Internationale Bibliographie der Rezensionen wissenschaftlicher Literatur* (AA373).   AI9.B6

Book review digest. v. 1 (1905)– . N.Y. : Wilson, 1906– .   **AA365**

A digest and index of selected book reviews in about 75 English and American periodicals, principally general in character. Arranged alphabetically by author of book reviewed, with subject and title index. "To qualify for inclusion a book must have been published or distributed in the United States. A work of non-fiction must have received two or more reviews and one of fiction four or more reviews in the journals selected."—*Pref. note.* For each book entered, gives a brief descriptive note, quotations from selected reviews with exact reference to the periodical in which the review appeared, and references only—without quotation—to other reviews. Indicates length of review in number of words. Compiled mainly from the public library point of view, the reviews indexed being taken principally from the general journals and not to any great extent from the more specialized ones. Published monthly (except Feb. and July), with annual cumulations.

Cumulated subject and title indexes for the previous 5-year period are included in the annual volumes for 1921, 1926, 1931, 1936, 1941, 1946, 1951, 1956, and 1961; for the periods 1962–66 and 1967–71, the cumulated index was issued as a separate volume.

———. *Author/title index 1905–74*, ed. by Leslie Dunmore-Leiber. (N.Y. : Wilson, 1976. 4 v.).

Covers nearly 300,000 books. Variant forms of author entries have been reconciled and cross-references provided.

•Available in machine-readable format from H.W. Wilson: (1) as CD-ROM (also called *Wilsondisc book review digest*); (2) online, with twice weekly updates, through *Wilsonline*.   Z1219.C96

Book review index. v. 1 (1965)– . Detroit : Gale, 1965– . Bimonthly.   **AA366**

Originally published monthly, with quarterly and annual cumulations. Suspended 1969–71, then resumed with three issues covering 1972 and an annual cumulation for 1972 designated as v. 8. Beginning 1973, issued bimonthly, with alternate issues cumulating the preceding bimonthly issue, and an annual cumulation. Retrospective indexes covering 1969–71, were published 1974/75 as v. 5–7 of the series.

An author listing with abbreviated citations to reviews. Now intends to index all reviews appearing in about 450 publications. Reviews indexed are primarily in the fields of general fiction and nonfiction, humanities, social sciences, librarianship and bibliography, and juvenile and young adult books.

———. *A master cumulation 1969–79*, ed. by Gary C. Tarbert. (Detroit : Gale, [1980]. 7 v.).

Cumulates the citations for the years indicated. Vols. 6–7 are a title index (the title index was a new feature beginning 1976, but this cumulation includes title indexing for the full period).   Z1035.A1B6

Canadian book review annual. 1975– . Toronto : Peter Martin Associates, [1976]– . Annual.   **AA367**

Not an index to book reviews, but rather "an evaluative guide to Canadian English-language trade books."—*Pref.* Signed reviews of 200–400 words written for this publication. Classed arrangement; author and title indexes.   F1001.C224

Children's book review index. v. 1, no. 1 (Jan./Apr. 1975)– . Detroit : Gale, 1975– . Annual.   **AA368**

Citations are derived from the listings in the *Book review index* (AA366)—i.e., citations to reviews of works identified as children's books are repeated in this publication.

A cumulation has appeared as *Master cumulation, 1969–81*, ed. by Gary C. Tarbert. (Detroit : Gale, 1982. 4 v.).

Combined retrospective index to book reviews in scholarly journals, 1886–1974 / Evan Ira Farber, exec. ed. Arlington, Va. : Carrollton Pr., 1979–82. 15 v.   **AA369**

Contents: v. 1–12, Authors; v. 13–15, Titles.

Offers "author and title access to more than one million book reviews which appeared in the complete backfiles of 459 scholarly journals in History, Political Science and Sociology."—*Introd.* The author section is arranged alphabetically by author of the book reviewed, giving title of the book and citations to reviews (listed alphabetically by abbreviated journal title, with volume number, date, and initial page of the review); the titles section provides *see* references to the author part. In general, short notices are included as well as full-length reviews. Reviewers' names are not given.

A complementary set has appeared as *Combined retrospective index to book reviews in humanities journals, 1802–1974* (Woodbridge, Conn. : Research Publ., 1982–84. 10 v.). It indexes reviews in an additional 150 periodicals in the broad range of the humanities.   Z1035.A1C64

Guía a las reseñas de libros de y sobre Hispanoamérica. 1972– . Detroit : Blaine Ethridge-Books, [1976]– . Annual.   **AA370**

Added title page in English: A guide to reviews of books from and about Hispanic America.

Antonio Matos, comp. and ed.

Introductory matter in Spanish and English; annotations in English or Spanish.

Continues a publication of the same title published in Río Piedras, Puerto Rico, in 1965 covering the years 1960–64, and a second volume (published in Río Piedras in 1973) covering 1965. The intervening years have not yet been covered.

Provides summaries of the reviews as well as citations to reviews. "Hispanic America" as here defined "includes, in addition to Spanish-speaking countries, Brazil, French, Dutch, and English-speaking areas of the Caribbean."—*Pref.* Arranged alphabetically by author, with title index.

Index to Australian book reviews. v. 1–17 (1965–81). Adelaide : Libraries Board of South Australia, 1965–81. Quarterly with annual cumulation.   **AA371**

Indexes reviews of books by Australian authors (regardless of where published), books published in Australia, and books of Australian interest published abroad. A selected list of about 50 journals (mainly in the fields of literature, social sciences, and humanities) is regularly searched, and selected reviews from a number of other popular magazines are also included. Entry is by author of the book, with indexes by title and by reviewer.

Index to book reviews in the humanities. v. 1 (1960)– . Detroit : Phillip Thomson, 1960– . Annual.   **AA372**

Indexes several hundred periodicals, originally all in English, though a number of foreign-language titles were added in the 1970 volume. Several thousand book titles are now included in each issue. Vol. 1 originally had no cumulative index but was issued in cumulated form 1978; in v. 2–3, 1961–62, the quarterly issues are cumulated into an annual volume; from 1963– , published annually.

Originally "humanities" was here defined to include history and some aspects of the social sciences, but beginning with v. 11 (1970) the term was restricted to art and architecture; biography, personal narrative and memoirs; drama and dance; folklore; language; literature; music; philosophy; travel and adventure.   Z1035.A1I63

Internationale Bibliographie der Rezensionen wissenschaftlicher Literatur = International bibliography of book reviews of scholarly literature = Bibliographie internationale des recensions de la littérature savante. Jahrg. 1 (1971)–13, pt. 1 (1983). Osnabrück : F. Dietrich Verlag, 1971–1983. Semiannual.   **AA373**

Title varies.

Prefatory matter in German, English, and French.

In four parts: pt. A, Index of periodicals consulted; pt. B, Classified subject index of book reviews; pt. C, Index of book reviews by reviewed authors; pt. D, Index of book reviews by reviewing authors.

Serves both as a companion to *Internationale Bibliographie der Zeitschriftenliteratur aus allen Gebieten des Wissens* (AD255) and as a continuation, after the long hiatus, of *Bibliographie der Rezensionen* (AA364). Reviews cited in the first volume are mainly of 1968–69 books, but many from earlier in the decade are also included. The listing by reviewer is an unusual feature among ongoing book review indexes.

For 1984, published as *Internationale Bibliographie der Rezensionen* (v. 13, pt. 2), which was then continued as *Internationale Bibliographie der Rezensionen wissenschaftlicher Literatur* (v. 14, pt. 1– . Osnabrück : F. Dietrick, 1984– . Annual). Title also in English and French. Also called *I.B.R.*

Appears annually in two half-year parts. Each part contains five sections: pt. A, Index rerum/Subject index; pt. B, Index systematicus/Keyword index; pt. C, Opera recensa/Reviewed works; pt. D, Recensores/Reviewers; pt. E, Periodica/Periodicals.

From 1971–83, full information was given in pts. B, C, and D. Currently, citations to the book reviews are found only in Part A, the subject index; Part C and D refer the user to the subject heading.   Z5051.I64

SELECTION OF PERIODICALS

Ganly, John. Serials for libraries : an annotated guide to continuations, annuals, yearbooks, almanacs, transactions, proceedings, directories, services / ed. by John V. Ganly and Diane M. Sciattara. 2nd ed. N.Y. : Neal-Schuman Publishers, c1985. 441 p.   **AA374**

1st ed., 1979, ed. by Joan K. Marshall.

"Designed as a reference tool for the selection, acquisition, and control of serials. It provides current information on the contents, frequency, and price of serials of interest to school, junior and senior college, and public libraries."—*Introd.* The main section, a classified, annotated list of about 2,000 serials, is followed by a guide to about 125 serials available online, a "when to buy what" purchasing guide, and title and subject indexes.   Z1035.1.G34

Magazines for libraries. [1st ed.]– . N.Y. : Bowker, 1969– . Irregular.   **AA375**

1st–3rd eds. by Bill Katz and Berry G. Richards; 4th ed.– by Bill Katz and Linda Sternberg Katz.

The 7th ed., publ. 1992, annotates and evaluates more than 6,500 periodicals. Titles "have been selected to include: (1) some general, non-specialist periodicals of interest to the layperson; (2) the main English-language research journals sponsored by distinguished societies in the United States, Canada, and Great Britain, and (3) some high-quality commercial publications commonly found in academic/special libraries. Although titles cannot represent the full scope of research publications available for specialized collections, there has been an attempt to provide a balance, by discipline, between specialist versus layperson interests, student versus faculty use, and general science versus research concerns."—*Pref.* Classed arrangement with title and subject index. Names of consultants appear at the beginning of most sections.   Z6941.M23

Richardson, Selma K. Magazines for children : a guide for parents, teachers, and librarians. 2nd ed. Chicago : Amer. Libr. Assoc., 1991. 139 p.   **AA376**

1st ed., 1983.

An alphabetical title listing, with extensive annotations and subject index, of magazines intended primarily for children.   PN4878.R5

———————— Magazines for young adults : selections for school and public libraries. Chicago : Amer. Libr. Assoc., 1984. 329 p.   **AA377**

Together with the same compiler's *Magazines for children* (AA376), supersedes *Periodicals for school media programs* (1978). Offers annotated listings (with subscription information) of some 600 magazines, including all titles indexed in *Readers' guide* and a number of other magazines published primarily for adults but widely read by young adults. Also includes a few newspapers and periodical indexes. Title listing with subject index. A useful selection tool.

       Z6944.Y68R53

Serials review. v. 1, no. 1/2 (Jan./June 1975)– . Ann Arbor, Mich. : Pierian Pr., 1975– . Quarterly.   **AA378**

Aims "to provide evaluations of periodicals, newspapers, indexes, union lists, periodical bibliographies, other reviewing tools, as well as any literature which is primarily designed to support collection evaluation, development, and preservation."—*verso of t.p.* Also carries articles on periodical selection, problems of serials management and budgeting, etc. Cumulative index of titles reviewed in v. 1–5 (1975–79) appears in v. 6, no. 1 (1980).   PN4832.S47

AUDIOVISUAL MATERIALS

Audio video market place : AVMP. 1984– . N.Y. : Bowker, [1984]– . Annual.   **AA379**

Subtitle: A multimedia guide.

Continues *Audiovisual market place*, eds.1–13, 1969–83.

A directory for the AV industry presented along the lines of *Literary market place* (AA282). The major section, "Producers, distributors & services" is arranged geographically by state, then alphabetically by name of the company, organization, or agency; a classified index to that section is arranged under main headings such as cable programming services, equipment and facilities, libraries, production services, properties, software, and unions and guilds (each with numerous subheads). There are also sections for associations, awards and festivals, a calendar, lists of periodicals and reference books, and a "names and numbers" section.

Educational film & video locator of the Consortium of College and University Media Centers and R. R. Bowker. 4th ed. (1990/91)– . N.Y. : Bowker, c1990– .   **AA380**

For annotation, *see* CB31.   LB1044.Z9E37

Library of Congress. Audiovisual materials. Jan./Mar. 1979–1982. Wash. : The Library, 1979–83. Quarterly with annual cumulation.   **AA381**

Continues the Library's *Films and other materials for projection* (*note*, AA107) which ceased with the 1978 cumulation.

"*Audiovisual Materials* presents motion pictures, filmstrips, sets of transparencies, slide sets, videorecordings, and kits currently cataloged by the Library of Congress, thus serving as an acquisition, reference, and research tool."—*Foreword, 1979.* Aims to list all items in the aforementioned categories "released in the United States or Canada which have educational or instructional value."

Continued by: *NUC. Audiovisual materials* [microform] (AA107, *note*).

National Audiovisual Center. A reference list of audiovisual materials produced by the United States government, 1978. Wash. : The Center, 1978. 354 p.   **AA382**

1974 ed. had title: *A catalog of United States government produced audiovisual materials.*

"This is a list of over 6,000 audiovisual materials selected from over 10,000 programs produced by 175 Federal agencies covering a wide range of subjects. Major subject concentrations in the Center's collection include medicine, dentistry, and allied health; education; science; social studies; industrial/technical training; safety; and the environmental sciences."—*Introd.* A title section provides the full information on a given item, including availability through rental or sale; a subject section serves as an index to the titles. Price list included.

————. Supplement. (Wash. : The Center, 1980. 54 p.).

Lists about 600 titles recently added to the Center's collection.

National Information Center for Educational Media. NICEM media indexes. Los Angeles : Nat. Information Center, Univ. of Southern California. [various volumes].   **AA383**

Publisher varies.

The series of indexes issued by the Center covers a wide range of audiovisual materials; most of the volumes in the series are periodically revised. Titles include: *Index to educational audio tapes*; *Index to educational records*; *Index to educational videotapes*; *Index to 8mm motion cartridges*; *Index to health and safety education (multimedia)*; *Index to educational overhead transparencies*; *Index to producers and distributors*; *Index to psychology (multimedia)*; *Index to 16mm educational films*; *Index to 35mm educational filmstrips*; *Index to vocational and technical education (multimedia)*; *Index to educational slides*; *Index to environmental studies (multimedia)*.

The video source book. Syosset, N.Y. : National Video Clearinghouse, 1979– . Annual.   **AA384**

Compiled from video and film catalogs and from lists furnished by wholesale distributors. Title listing (giving full information on the programs) with "subject category" index and index of distributors or sources. Includes programs for home, business, and institutional use.

       PN1992.95.V52

Words on cassette. 7th ed. (1992)– . New Providence, N.J. : Bowker, c1992– . Annual.   **AA385**

Represents a merger of *Words on tape*, publ. 1984/85–1991, and *On cassette*, 1st ed., 1985; continues the numbering of the latter.

The 8th ed., publ. 1993, lists some 53,000 titles available on spoken-word cassette from more than 1,300 producers. Arranged by title, with author, reader/performer, subject, and producers and distributors indexes.   Z5347.W67

Reviews

Media review. v. 3, no. 3 (Nov. 1979)– . Pleasantville, N.Y. : Media Review, 1979– . Monthly (Sept.–June). Looseleaf.   **AA386**

Continues *Media index* (v. 1 [Apr. 1978]–3, no. 2 [Oct. 1979]).

Subtitle: Professional evaluations of instructional materials.

The looseleaf service includes a newsletter, evaluations, new releases, and a cumulative index.

Media review digest. [v. 1] (1973/74)– . Ann Arbor, Mich. : Pierian Pr., 1974– . Annual, with semiannual suppl.   **AA387**

Continues *Multi media reviews index*, 1970–72.

Frequency has varied.

Subtitle: The only complete guide to reviews of non-book media.

Provides citations, with descriptive notes, "to reviews of films and filmstrips; educational and spoken-word records and tapes; slides, transparencies, illustrations, globes, charts, media kits, games and other miscellaneous media forms."—*Introd. 1983*. Separate sections for (1) films and videotapes, (2) filmstrips, (3) records and tapes, and (4) miscellaneous media. Listing is by main entry within each section, with classified and alphabetical subject indexes to the volume as a whole.   LB1043.Z9M4

NATIONAL AND TRADE

Bibliography

Bell, Barbara L. An annotated guide to current national bibliographies. Alexandria, Va. : Chadwyck-Healey, 1986. 407 p.   **AA388**

A comprehensive worldwide guide to current national bibliographies, suitable substitutes, or alternative information when no current national bibliography exists. Information from 160 countries is arranged alphabetically by country; annotations provide complete information in a standardized format. "Selective bibliography on current national bibliographies" (p. 358 401) includes books, pamphlets, and periodical articles, and is divided into general guides and source materials, and by geographic areas. Analytical table of contents.

A new edition is in preparation.   Z1002.B4714

Commonwealth national bibliographies : an annotated directory / comp. by the IFLA International Office for UBC. 2nd ed. rev. London : Commonwealth Secretariat, 1982. 69 p.   **AA389**

1st ed., 1977.

Companion to *Commonwealth retrospective national bibliographies* (AA390).

A country-by-country listing, with full descriptions, of national bibliographies (plus some nationally produced serials lists and periodical indexes), published in Commonwealth countries. "Most of the bibliographies appearing in the directory have been produced nationally, but some regional publications have also been included so as to cover those Commonwealth states and dependencies that are too small to warrant their own national bibliographies. In addition, the Accessions

Lists, produced by Library of Congress Offices for the use of librarians in the U.S.A. have been included so as to supplement inadequate bibliographic coverage in some regions."—*Introd.*   Z2000.9.C653

Commonwealth retrospective national bibliographies : an annotated directory / comp. by the IFLA International Office for UBC. London : Commonwealth Secretariat, 1981. 128 p.   **AA390**

Companion volume to *Commonwealth national bibliographies* (AA389). Lists alphabetically, by the English name, publications that provide national bibliographic coverage antedating the member's current national bibliography.   Z2000.9.C58

Domay, Friedrich. Bibliographie der nationalen Bibliographien = Bibliographie mondiale des bibliographies nationales = A world bibliography of national bibliographies. Stuttgart : A. Hiersemann, 1987. 557 p. (Hiersemanns Bibliographische Handbücher, Bd. 6).   **AA391**

A useful annotated listing of retrospective and current national bibliographies and related works for more than 100 regions and countries. Arranged first by continent, then by region, then by country. Annotations in German. Name and title index.   Z1002.D65

Gorman, G. E. Guide to current national bibliographies in the Third World / G. E. Gorman and J. J. Mills. 2nd rev. ed. London ; N.Y. : Zell, 1987. 372 p.   **AA392**

1st ed., 1983.

Arranged alphabetically by country or region, this work discusses "twelve regional bibliographies and ninety-eight national bibliographies, complementary compilations or substitute services for 152 developing countries."—*Introd.* For each country, gives a bibliographical citation to the national bibliography or effective substitute, together with its history, scope, and content, plus an analysis or critique of the publication and its usefulness. Title index.   Z1002.G67

Guide to reprints. 1967– . Wash. : Microcard Eds., [1967]– . Annual.   **AA393**

Albert James Diaz, ed.

Originally an in-print listing for books, journals, and other materials issued in reprint form (i.e., through photographic reproduction of original text, not by resetting of type) by U.S. publishers; now international in scope, covering reprints from more than 400 publishers throughout the world.

During 1964–81, *Bibliographia anastatica* (bimonthly) and its successor, *Bulletin of reprints* (quarterly) provided an ongoing record of newly available reprints.   Z1000.5.G8

International books in print : English language titles published outside the U.S.A. and the United Kingdom. München, etc. : K. G. Saur, [1979]– . Irregular.   **AA394**

The subtitle explains the scope of this publication. Originally an author-title catalog, but beginning with the 1984 ed. (publ. 1983), published in two parts: pt. 1, Author-title list (in 2 v.) and pt. 2, Subject guide (v. 1, Classes; v. 2, Countries and persons). In the author-title section full information is given under main entry, with cross-references from added entries. Lists of participating publishers and central distributors (with addresses) appear in v. 2 of each part.

Inventaire général des bibliographies nationales rétrospectives = Retrospective national bibliographies : an international directory / ed. by Marcelle Beaudiquez. Munich ; N.Y. : K.G. Saur, 1986. 189 p. (IFLA publications, 35).   **AA395**

Introductory matter in English and French.

Offers brief annotations in English, French, or German of the retrospective national bibliographies of more than 100 countries. Author and anonymous title index.   Z1002.I58

Kuznetsova, T. R. Gosudarstvennye (natsional'nye) bibliograficheskie ukazateli sotsialisticheskikh stran : annotirovannyĭ bibliograficheskiĭ ukazatel' / [sostavitel' T.R. Kuznetsova ; redaktor N.V. Gavrilenko]. Moskva : Gos. biblioteka SSSR im. V.I. Lenina, 1984–1985. v. 1–2. (In progress).   **AA396**

Title on added t.p.: National bibliographical indexes of the socialist countries.

Contents: v. 1–2, Annotated bibliographical index.

Prefatory matter in Russian and English.

Vol. 1 deals with Bulgaria, Hungary, the German Democratic Republic, Cuba, Poland, the U.S.S.R., and Czechoslovakia; v. 2 with Yugoslavia and its individual republics. Each part lists and annotates the national bibliographies (current and retrospective) country by country, then by type of publication recorded: books, periodicals, periodical indexes, dissertations, maps, printed music, recorded music, bibliographies of bibliographies. Emphasizes bibliographical publications of the 1945–82 period, although publishing output of earlier periods is dealt with. Name, title, and corporate author indexes.   Z1975.K89

Library of Congress. General Reference and Bibliography Division. Current national bibliographies / comp. by Helen F. Conover. Wash., 1955. 132 p.   **AA397**

Repr.: N.Y. : Greenwood, 1968.

An annotated listing of the records of publishing in 67 countries. In addition, the work lists periodical indexes, government publications, and directories of periodicals and newspapers. Dated, but still useful.   Z1002.A2U52

Reprints

Books on demand : author guide. [v. 1]– . Ann Arbor, Mich. : Univ. Microfilms, 1977– . Irregular.   **AA398**

Books on demand : subject guide (1977– . Irregular).

Books on demand : title guide (1977– . Irregular).

The three volumes of *Books on demand*, offering variant approaches to the same 100,000 works, are available separately or as a set. The "on-demand" reprint program makes the works listed in the catalogs available by xerography as full-size bound books or in microfilm. The lists include many early and rare books, but also include books that have only recently gone out of print. Prices of the reprints are indicated.

A review of the 1977 ed. in *Library journal* 103 (July 1978) : 1384 concludes that the set is "essential for any acquisitions department," but warns that "some of the books listed here are still in *Books in Print* at more reasonable prices."

Internationale Bibliographie der Reprints = International bibliography of reprints / ed. by Christa Gnirss. München : Verlag Dokumentation, 1976–80. 2 v. in 4.   **AA399**

Contents: Bd. 1, Teil 1–2, Bücher und Reihen; Teil 3, Register; Bd. 2, Zeitschriften, Zeitungen, Jahrbücher, Konferenzberichte, usw.

Introductory matter in German and English.

"The term 'reprint' is here used to describe all reprinted works produced by photomechanical means in so far as the publisher is not identical with the publisher of the original work."—*Foreword*. Information was initially derived from publishers' catalogs, lists, and prospectuses, but additional searching in national bibliographies was done in order to supply full information, including original publication date where possible.   Z1033.R4I572

North America

United States

Tanselle, George Thomas. Guide to the study of United States imprints. Cambridge, Mass. : Belknap Pr. of Harvard Univ. Pr., 1971. 2 v.   **AA400**

An attempt to record "most of the published research which is relevant to the study of United States imprints."—*Introd*. Bibliographies, checklists, and supplementary studies are listed in nine main categories: (1) Regional lists; (2) Genre lists; (3) Author lists; (4) Copyright records; (5) Catalogues; (6) Book-trade directories; (7) Studies of individual printers and publishers; (8) General studies; and (9) Checklists of secondary material. Indexed.   Z1215.A2T35

Early

American Antiquarian Society. Library. A dictionary catalog of American books pertaining to the 17th through 19th centuries. Westport, Conn. : Greenwood, [1971]. 20 v.
                                                                                AA401

Reproduction of the catalog cards (author, title, and subject cards in dictionary arrangement) for the Society's collection of American imprints prior to 1821 and first editions of American literary authors through the 19th century.

Bibliography of American imprints to 1901 : compiled from the databases of the American Antiquarian Society and the Research Libraries Group, Inc. N.Y. : K.G. Saur Verlag, 1992. 92 v.   **AA402**

Contents: v. 1–42, Title listing; v. 43–56, Name index; v. 57–71, Subject index; v. 72–82, Place index; v. 83–92, Date index.

The main volumes are an alphabetical listing by title, with author, publisher, and imprint data, of "some 400,000 records of printed matter issued from presses located within the present borders of the United States of America during the years 1640 through 1900."—*Introd*. The listings are based on the databases of the American Antiquarian Society, a main contributor to the *Eighteenth century short title catalogue* (*see* AA681), and the Research Libraries Group. Since 19th-century listings in RLIN are sporadic "the work must be considered as a beginning or contribution toward a complete listing of American imprints." Its usefulness for libraries with access to RLIN is questionable.
                                                                                Z1215.B524

Bristol, Roger Pattrell. Supplement to Charles Evans' American bibliography. Charlottesville : publ. for the Bibliographical Society of America and the Bibliographical Society of the Univ. of Virginia by the Univ. Pr. of Virginia, [1970]. 636 p.
                                                                                AA403

A "checking edition" was issued in parts in 1962. As now published, the supplement adds about 11,200 entries to the Evans listings (AA405).

———. ——— *Index to Supplement…* (Charlottesville, [1971]. 191 p.).

———. *Index of printers, publishers and booksellers indicated by Charles Evans in his American bibliography* (Charlottesville : Bibliographical Soc. of the Univ. of Virginia, 1961. 172 p.). Under each name is indicated—chronologically and then by item number—references to be found in Evans.   Z1215.E92334

European Americana : a chronological guide to works printed in Europe relating to the Americas, 1493–1776 / ed. by John Alden with the assistance of Dennis C. Landis. N.Y. : Readex Books, 1980–1988. v. 1–2, 5–6. (In progress).
                                                                                AA404

At head of title: The John Carter Brown Library.

v. 1–2 ed. by John Alden and Dennis C. Landis; v. 5–6 ed. by Dennis C. Landis.

Contents: v. 1, 1493–1600 (1980. 467 p.); v. 2, 1601–1650 (1982. 954 p.); v. 5, 1701–1725 (1987. 597 p.); v. 6, 1726–1750 (1988. 852 p.).

Published out of sequence (v. 3–4 have yet to appear.).

When completed, the series is to cover the period 1493–1776; it "represents an effort to record in chronological form those works printed in Europe which depict the Americas in verbal terms."—*Pref.* For purposes of the bibliography "The Americas" are defined as "the area from Greenland to the Straits of Magellan, comprising the two Americas, Central America, and geologically related islands in the Caribbean and elsewhere." Bibliographic information for the individual items seeks to provide "a terse and unencumbered presentation of salient American content which at the same time permits identification of the work itself," and bibliographical references to works offering fuller descriptions are often given. Library locations are indicated.

Although Joseph Sabin's *A dictionary of books relating to America* (AA409) provided the starting point for compilation, non-Sabin items abound: of the approximately 4,300 entries in v. 1, only a fourth appear in Sabin. In addition to an author, title, and subject index, each volume offers a "Geographic index of printers and booksellers and their publications" and an "Alphabetical index of printers and booksellers and their geographic locations."   Z1203.E87

Evans, Charles. American bibliography : a chronological dictionary of all books, pamphlets and periodical publications printed in the United States of America from the genesis of printing in 1639 down to and including the year 1800; with bibliographical and biographical notes. Chicago : pr. for the author, 1903–1959. 14 v.   **AA405**

Repr.: N.Y. : Peter Smith, 1941–1967.

Publisher varies: v. 13–14 published by the American Antiquarian Society, Worcester, Mass.

The most important general list of early American publications, indispensable in the large reference or special library. Includes books, pamphlets, and periodicals, arranged chronologically by dates of publication; gives for each book author's full name with dates of birth and death, full title, place, date, publisher or printer, paging, size, and, whenever possible, location of copies in American libraries. Each volume has three indexes: (1) authors, (2) classified subjects, (3) printers and publishers.

Although Evans had originally hoped to continue to 1820, as indicated on the title pages of v. 1–12, 1639–1799 (publ. 1903–34), he finally decided to stop with 1800 and, in fact, carried through the letter M of 1799. Vol. 13 (publ. 1955) starts with the letter N for 1799 and continues through 1800 with author and subject indexes. In this volume, compiled by Clifford K. Shipton, the system used by Evans has been modified somewhat, e.g., titles have been shortened, and cross-references are given from the title when anonymous works are listed under author.

Vol. 14 (publ. 1959), edited by Roger Pattrell Bristol, is a cumulated author-title index to the whole work, including pseudonyms, attributed authors, other names appearing on the title page, governmental bodies, etc. Newspapers and almanacs are grouped under these respective headings and are not listed under specific title.   Z1215.E92

Federal copyright records, 1790–1800 / ed. and with an introd. by James Gilreath ; comp. by Elizabeth Carter Wills. Wash. : Lib. of Congress : for sale by U. S. Govt. Print. Off., 1987. 166 p. : facsims.   **AA406**

A listing of 779 titles from ledger books, copyright deposits, and title page deposits. Geographic arrangement. Each entry provides, where available, author, title, printer, bookseller, and publisher. Author and title index.   Z642.W54

Henry E. Huntington Library and Art Gallery. American imprints, 1648–1797, in the Huntington Library, supplementing Evans' American bibliography / comp. by Willard O. Waters. Repr. from: *Huntington Library Bulletin,* no. 3, Feb. 1933, p. 1–95.   **AA407**

Arranged chronologically, with author index. Lists 736 "titles of books, pamphlets, broadsides, maps, etc., supplementary to the Evans

bibliography. It comprises, besides items apparently not listed in that work, a number appearing there but with titles or imprints varying from the copies here described."—(*Prelim. note*).   Z1215.E92

New York Public Library. Rare Book Division. Checklist of additions to Evans' American bibliography in the Rare Book Division of the New York Public Library / comp. by Lewis M. Stark and Maud D. Cole. N.Y. : The Libr., 1960. 110 p.   **AA408**

1,289 entries. Lists originals, photostats, and facsimiles, for the latter frequently indicating the location of the original.   Z1215.E95

Sabin, Joseph. A dictionary of books relating to America, from its discovery to the present time / begun by Joseph Sabin, and continued by Wilberforce Eames for the Bibliographical Society of America. N.Y. : Sabin, 1868–1936. 29 v.   **AA409**

Repr.: Amsterdam : N. Israel, 1961–62.

Title on some volumes: Bibliotheca americana.

Begun by Joseph Sabin, and continued by Wilberforce Eames for the Bibliographical Society of America.

Imprint varies.

An important bibliography of Americana, including books, pamphlets, and periodicals printed in the Western hemisphere, and works about the region printed elsewhere. Comprises 106,413 numbered entries, but the actual number of titles recorded is much greater, as that total does not count the added editions and titles mentioned in the various notes. The arrangement is by author, with some title entries for anonymous works and many entries under names of places. Information given includes full title, place, publisher, date, format, paging, often contents and bibliographical notes with reference to a description or review in some other work, and, in many cases, names of libraries possessing copies. A list of library location symbols is given in v. 29, p. 299–305, which is more extensive than the partial list given in v. 1.

John Edgar Molnar's *Author-title index to Joseph Sabin's Dictionary of books relating to America* (Metuchen, N. J. : Scarecrow, 1974. 3 v. [3196 p.]) arranges authors and titles in a single sequence, with some identification of pseudonyms.   Z1201.S2

Shipton, Clifford Kenyon. National index of American imprints through 1800 : the short-title Evans / Clifford Kenyon Shipton and James E. Mooney. [Worcester, Mass.] : American Antiquarian Soc. and Barre Publs., 1969. 2 v. (1028 p.).   **AA410**

Offers an index to the Readex Microprint edition of *Early American imprints.* It eliminates the need to consult Charles Evans's *American bibliography* (AA405) to obtain the sequence number in the microprint edition, and also incorporates into the single alphabetical listing 10,035 additional items which have turned up since the publication of the Evans work. Most, but not all, the items in Roger Bristol's supplement to Evans (AA403) are included. Many corrections have been made in the Evans listings. Only one location (i.e., the copy used for the microprint edition) is noted; ghosts and unlocated items are so indicated. An important bibliographic source in its own right.   Z1215.S495

Thompson, Lawrence Sidney. The new Sabin : books described by Joseph Sabin and his successors, now described again on the basis of examination of originals, and fully indexed by title, subject, joint authors, and institutions and agencies. Troy, N.Y. : Whitston, 1974–86. 10 v.   **AA411**

Represents works from the Sabin period (not all are in Sabin, AA409) examined by the compiler either in the original or in microform, with descriptions mainly taken from Library of Congress cards. Items are numbered serially, and each volume is a separate author alphabet. The indexing is a salient feature. A cumulative index to v. 1–10 (entries 1–25946) appeared in 1986 (497 p.) and covers authors, titles, and some subjects. Most of the items cited are available on microcard from Lost Cause Press.   Z1201BT45

Wing, Donald Goddard. Short-title catalogue of books printed in England, Scotland, Ireland, Wales, and British America, and of English books printed in other countries, 1641–1700. 2nd ed., rev. and enl. N.Y. : Index Committee of the Modern Language Association of America, 1972–1988. 3 v.   **AA412**
For annotation, *see* AA683.   Z2002.W52

19th century

American catalogue ... 1876–1910. N.Y. : Publishers' Weekly, 1880–1911. 8 v. in 13.   **AA413**
Repr.: N.Y. : Peter Smith, 1941.
Cumulates *Annual American catalogue*, 1886–1910.
The basic work (1876, Author and title entries of books in print, July 1, 1876; Subject entries. 2 v.) is supplemented by volumes covering various periods (e.g., three, five, or eight years) usually with author/title and subject volumes.
The standard American list for the period covered; comprehensive and generally reliable although information given is based on reports from publishers and not, in most cases, on actual examination of the books themselves. Aims to include, with certain exceptions, all books published in the U.S. which were for sale to the general public.   Z1215.A5

A checklist of American imprints. Metuchen, N.J. : Scarecrow, 1972–1993. v. 1–16. (In progress).   **AA414**
Dates of coverage appear in title.
Contents: v. 1–16, 1830–1844.
Compiler varies: first volume comp. by Gayle Cooper; vols. for 1835–39 comp. by Carol Rinderknecht; vols. for 1840– comp. by Carol Rinderknecht and Scott Bruntjen.
When complete, will cover 1820–75.
Cumulative indexes published separately: 1820–29, Author index; corrections & sources (1973); 1830–39, Title index (1989. 2 v.); 1830–39, Author index (1989).   Z1215.C44

Kelly, James. The American catalogue of books (original and reprints), published in the United States from Jan. 1861 to Jan. 1871 : with date of publication, size, price, and publisher's name. N.Y. : Wiley, 1866–71. 2 v.   **AA415**
Repr.: N.Y. : Peter Smith, 1938. 2 v.
Continues the record of American bibliography from Roorbach's last volume (AA416), giving about the same kind of information. Each volume contains a list of societies and their publications. Vol. 1 also contains a list of pamphlets, sermons, and addresses on the Civil War, 1861–66.
Both Roorbach and Kelly are unsatisfactory, as they are far from complete and often inaccurate, but they must be used as they are the most general lists for the period 1820–70.   Z1215.A5

Roorbach, Orville Augustus. Bibliotheca americana : 1820–61. N.Y. : Roorbach, 1852–61. 4 v.   **AA416**
Repr.: N.Y. : Peter Smith, 1939.
Vol. 1, 1820–52, with a list of periodicals published in the United States; v. 2, Supplement, Oct. 1852–May 1855; v. 3, Addenda, May 1855–March 1858; v. 4, March 1858–Jan. 1861.
A trade catalog of American publications, including reprints, arranged alphabetically by author and title, giving publisher, size, price, and, in some cases, date.   Z1215.A5

Shaw, Ralph R. American bibliography : a preliminary checklist for 1801–1819 / [by] Ralph Robert Shaw and Richard H. Shoemaker. N.Y. : Scarecrow, 1958–66. 22 v.   **AA417**
Contents: v. 1–19, 1801–1819; [v. 20], Addenda; list of sources; library symbols; [v. 21], Title index; [v. 22], Corrections; author index. [v. 23], Printers, publishers, and booksellers index, geographical index, omissions, comp. by Francis P. Newton.
A preliminary checklist "gathered entirely from secondary sources," designed as a first step in filling the gap in American national bibliography between 1800, when Evans stops, and 1820, when Roorbach starts. The Preface explains purpose and procedure. Each

volume covers one year; the Addenda volume lists 1,768 additional items from the full 1801–19 period. Locations of copies are given when they were included in the original citations.   Z1215.S48

Shoemaker, Richard H. Checklist of American imprints for 1820–1829. N.Y. : Scarecrow, 1964–71. 10 v.   **AA418**
Vols. for 1826–29 comp. with the assistance of G. Cooper.
Designed as a continuation of Shaw-Shoemaker (AA417) to provide fuller coverage than Roorbach (AA416). Lists several times as many titles as the latter, with more complete information and location of copies.
————. ———— *Title index*, comp. by M. Frances Cooper (Metuchen, N.J. : Scarecrow, 1972. 556 p.).
Continued by: *A checklist of American imprints* (AA414).   Z1215.S5

Stevens, Henry. Catalogue of the American books in the library of the British Museum at Christmas MDCCCLVI. London : Chiswick Pr. for H. Stevens, 1866. 4 pts. in 1 v.   **AA419**
Contents: (1) American books printed in the United States. 628p.; (2) Catalogue of the Canadian and other British North American books. 14 p.; (3) Catalogue of the Mexican and other Spanish American and West Indian books. 62 p.; (4) Catalogue of the American maps. 17 p.
Includes some works not included in Roorbach and gives fuller titles for others that are included there.   Z1207.B862

20th century

American book publishing record cumulative 1876–1949. N.Y. : Bowker, 1980. 15 v.   **AA420**
Contents: v. 1–10, Dewey Decimal classes 000–999; v. 11, Fiction, Juvenile fiction; v. 12, Non-Dewey Decimal classified titles; v. 13, Author index; v. 14, Title index; v. 15, Subject guide.
For *American book publishing record* and its earlier cumulations *see* AA424.
Entries for this cumulation "were compiled from *A Catalog of Books Represented by Library of Congress Printed Cards* (cards issued from August 1898 through July 1942), *Supplement* (cards issued from August 1942 through December 1947), and *The Library of Congress Author Catalog, 1948–1952.*"—Pref. About 625,000 entries. Does not include "federal and other governmental publications (with the exception of some city and state government reports), subscription books, dissertations, new printings (as distinct from reprints, re-issues, and revised or new editions), quarterlies, and other periodicals, pamphlets under forty-nine pages, and specialized publications of a transitory nature or intended as advertising."

American book publishing record cumulative 1950–1977. N.Y. : Bowker, 1979. 15 v.   **AA421**
Contents: v. 1–10, Dewey Decimal classes 000–999; v. 11, Fiction, Juvenile fiction; v. 12, Non-Dewey Decimal classified titles; v. 13, Author index; v. 14, Title index; v. 15, Subject guide.
About 900,000 entries. Cumulates entries from the *American book publishing record* (AA424), 1960–77, together with "thousands of titles from the *National Union Catalog* [AA111] for the years 1950 to 1968 and from the Library of Congress MARC tapes for the years 1968 to 1977 that have not appeared in previous cumulations of the *American Book Publishing Record.*"—Pref.

Cumulative book index. Minneapolis ; N.Y. : Wilson, 1898– . Frequency varies; now monthly (except Aug.) with annual cumulations.   **AA422**
Subtitle : A world list of books in the English language.
Often referred to as *CBI*.
Through Jan. 1907, monthly issues and cumulations were considered supplements to *United States catalog*. From Jan. 1907 through July 1921, annual cumulations continued to be issued as supplements to *United States catalog*. Cumulations needed to supplement the 4th ed. of *United States catalog* are: 1928/32 (publ. 1933); 1933/37 (publ. 1938); 1938/42 (publ. 1945); 1943/48 (publ. 1950); 1949/52 (publ. 1953); 1953/56 (publ. 1959); biennial 1957–68; annual since 1969.

United States catalog (AA423) and *CBI* constitute a comprehensive record of American publications from 1898 to date that is indispensable for reference work in this field. The most frequently used parts will be the 4th ed. of *United States catalog* (1928) and the *CBI* cumulations listed above, but the earlier volumes must be used for: (1) books out-of-print by 1928; (2) fuller information, e.g., paging, date, etc., on some titles still in print.

Each volume is a dictionary catalog with entries under author, title, and subject. From Oct. 1982 the work is computer-produced.

The 4th ed. of *United States catalog* includes publications in the regular book trade; privately printed books; regular importations of American publishers; Canadian books (in English) not also published in the U.S.; publications of universities, societies, and scientific institutions, e.g., Smithsonian Institution; and a selected list of publications of the national and state governments. For each book, gives: author, short title, edition, publisher, price, and, generally but not always, date, paging, and illustration; gives also Library of Congress card numbers, and, for a book entered in *Book review digest* (AA365), its Dewey Decimal Classification number and a tracing of the subject headings used for it in *United States catalog*.

The *CBI* volumes covering 1928/32 and after have wider scope and include a comprehensive listing of books and pamphlets, in English, issued in the U.S. and Canada and a selection of publications from other parts of the English-speaking world: Australia, Great Britain, New Zealand, South Africa, etc. Omitted are government documents, maps, sheet music, paperbound editions, and ephemeral material. In proportion to the size of the catalog there are very few inaccuracies, although, as some of the entries have had to be made without examination of the books and are based on publishers' descriptions and lists, the work is not a final authority on bibliographical detail. As a first aid, it is indispensable: (1) in order department work; (2) as an adjunct to the library's own catalog; and (3) as a reference tool for many purposes: verification of titles, authors' names and dates, authorship when only the title or subject of a book is known, lists of books on a given subject, etc. Subject lists of fiction, e.g., ghost stories, sea stories, etc., and the use of the subhead "Fiction" under many subjects make it useful for certain types of questions about fiction. Each cumulation includes a list of publishers with addresses.

•Machine-readable version of the monthly *CBI* is available on CD-ROM (N.Y. : H.W. Wilson). Begun in 1987. Also called *Wilsondisc cumulative book index*. Z1219.M78

United States catalog : books in print, Jan. 1, 1928. 4th ed. N.Y. : Wilson, 1928. 3164 p. **AA423**

1st ed. 1899 (v. 1, Author list; v. 2, Title index); 2nd ed. 1902; 3rd ed. Jan. 1, 1912.

Supplements (entitled *Cumulative book index*) for intervening years were published as follows: [cumulation] 1902/1905; annual supplements, 1906–10; [cumulations] 1912/17, 1918/June 1921, June 1921/June 1924; annual supplements, July 1924–Dec.1927.

For full information, see *Cumulative book index*, AA422. Z1215.U6

Current

American book publishing record. v. 1 (1960)– . N.Y. : Bowker, 1960– . Monthly. **AA424**

At head of title: BPR.

Includes the same information as the weekly lists in *Publishers' weekly* and the successor publication, *Weekly record* (AA440), cumulated monthly and rearranged by subject according to Dewey Decimal numbers. Indexed by author and title. A separate annual index was published for 1962–64 only.

Since 1965 cumulates into: ———. *BPR annual cumulative*. 1965– . N.Y. : Bowker, 1966– . Annual.

Subtitle: A record of American book production in 1965 [etc.] as cataloged by the Library of Congress and annotated by Publishers' weekly in the monthly issues of the American book publishing record; arranged by subject according to the Dewey Decimal Classification and indexed by author and by title.

Cumulates the monthly listings from *BPR*, including author and title indexes.

Cumulates quinquennially as: ———. *BPR cumulative*. 1960/64– . N.Y. : Bowker, 1968– . Quinquennial.

The early cumulations (1960/64, 1965/69, 1970/74) are superseded by *American book publishing record cumulative 1950–1977* (AA421). Z1219.A515

Books in print. 1948– . N.Y. : Bowker, 1948– . Annual.
AA425

Prior to 1972, publ. with subtitle: An author-title-series index to the Publishers' trade list annual. After that date, *BIP* ceased its function as an index to *PTLA*.

Each multivolume annual includes an author index and a title index (since 1966 authors and titles appear in separate volumes), in each case giving publisher and price. In 1989, it began listing titles reported out of print or out of stock indefinitely; for the 1994/95 ed., more than 127,000 titles can be found in the OP/OSI volume.

A very valuable addition for both acquisitions and reference work in a library. Useful for finding the publisher and price of a book; for finding the author's name if only the title is known; and, for 1948–72, as an index to the vast amount of material in the *Publishers' trade list annual*.

Beginning 1973 the first of a series of annual mid-year supplements was issued as *Books in print supplement*, listing authors, titles, and subjects in separate sections. Issued about six months after the yearly *Books in print* volume, it lists new titles and provides updated information as available.

Inasmuch as there is no evident attempt to reconcile variant forms of an author's name, considerable care must be exercised in searching the author listings.

Beginning Apr. 1982, available in microfiche. The microfiche service provides a fully updated edition of *BIP* four times a year, each quarterly edition including all forthcoming titles six months prior to publication.

Books in print is complemented by *Subject guide to Books in print* (AA438).

•In machine-readable form as part of *Books in print plus* CD-ROM (AA426), *Books in print* online file, and by tape leasing. Z1215.P972

•**Books in print plus** [database]. N.Y. : Bowker, 1979– .
AA426

CD-ROM format. Updated bimonthly.

Includes *Books in print* (AA425), *Subject guide to Books in print* (AA438) *Forthcoming books* (AA432) as well as other Bowker publications. Searchable fields include author, title, publisher, subject, keyword, etc.

Books out-of-print. 1980/83– . N.Y. : Bowker, [1983]– . Annual. **AA427**

Subtitle: Titles which publishers have reported out-of-print or out-of-stock indefinitely in the years [1980/1983]– .

Contents: v. 1, Titles; v. 2, Authors; publishers.

A reference and book acquisitions tool intended to reduce the expense and time wasted on orders which are unfilled because items have gone out of print or are indefinitely out of stock at the publishers. Publishers were asked to verify the status of "o.p." and "o.s.i." items previously reported to the editors of *Books in print* since 1980, and this compilation is based on those reports. It is important to note that some 35 publishers elected not to participate; their names are listed in the preface.

Children's books in print. 1969– . N.Y. : Bowker, 1969– . Annual. **AA428**

Supersedes *Children's books for schools and libraries* (v. 1–3, 1966/67–1968/69) and provides expanded coverage for trade books, both paperbound and hard cover. Author, title, and illustrator sections.

Complemented by: *Subject guide to children's books in print* (1970– . N.Y. : Bowker, 1970– . Annual).

Books are entered in some 7,000 categories, with numerous *see* and *see also* references. Z1037.A1C482

The complete directory of large print books & serials. 1988– . N.Y. : R.R. Bowker, c1988– . Biennial.   **AA429**

Title page note: "General reading subject index, textbooks subject index, children's subject index, title index, author index, newspapers & periodicals, publishers & services."

"Provides a complete resource for what's available in the field of large print materials"—(*Foreword to the 1993 ed.*), including periodicals. Arranged by subject, using Library of Congress subject headings, author, and title.   Z5348.L37

Cumulative book index. Minneapolis ; N.Y. : Wilson, 1898– . Frequency varies; now monthly (except Aug.) with annual cumulations.   **AA430**

The monthly numbers of *CBI* constitute an ongoing record of current publications in English throughout the world. For full information see AA422.   Z1219.M78

El-Hi textbooks in print. 1970– . N.Y. : Bowker, 1970– . Annual.   **AA431**

Issued 1872–1926 as a number in *Publishers' weekly* under various titles; 1927–55, as the *American educational catalog*; 1956–69, as *Textbooks in print*.

Now a computer-produced bibliography with subject, title, author, and series sections. The 1982 volume is a list of 39,000 elementary, junior and senior high school textbooks and pedagogical books from about 453 publishers.   Z5813.A51

Forthcoming books : now including new books in print; a forecast of books to come .... v. 1 (1966)– . N.Y. : Bowker, 1966– . Bimonthly.   **AA432**

Supersedes *Publishers' weekly interim index*.

Beginning with v. 2, no. 6, each issue provides a cumulated list of all books published in the U.S. since the compilation of the current issue of *Books in print* (AA425) and continues to offer information on titles announced for publication in the next five months. Each issue overlaps and updates the preceding one. Separate author and title sections; publisher, price, and publication date are indicated. Beginning in 1987, includes a subject section which had been published separately 1966–86 as *Subject guide to forthcoming books*.

•Available in machine-readable form as part of *Books in print plus* database (AA426).

Library of Congress. Copyright Office. Catalog of copyright entries. 1891–1946. Wash. : U.S. Govt. Print. Off., 1891–1947.   **AA433**

Title varies. Before 1906 issued by the Treasury Dept.; 1906–46, issued by the Copyright Office as *New series*.

Contents: Arrangement differs slightly. Pt.1, *Books,* 1909–27 issued in two groups; 1928–46 in three groups as follows: group 1, v.25–43, *Books* proper (frequency varies; annual index); group 2, v.25–43, *Pamphlets,* etc., including lectures, sermons, maps, etc. (monthly, with annual index); group 3, v.1–19, *Dramatic compositions, motion pictures* (before 1920, motion pictures were included in pt.4; monthly, with annual index). Pt.2, v.1–41, *Periodicals and newspapers,* (quarterly, with annual index). Pt.3, v.1–41, *Musical compositions,* (monthly, with annual index; for full information *see* BJ81). Pt.4, v.1–41, *Works of art,* photographs, etc. (quarterly, with annual index).

For 1946 each part was issued as an annual.

———. ———. *Series 3* (Wash. : U.S. Govt. Print. Off., 1947–77).

With the third series the arrangement and the format were changed to make the contents of the set more easily available. The *Catalog* was subdivided into separate parts following the classification as given in the Copyright Act: pt.1, *Books and pamphlets,* including serials and contributions to periodicals (1947–Jan./June 1953, issued in two sections, pt.1A and pt.1B, which were combined to form the new pt.1 with v.7, no.2, July/Dec. 1953); pt.2, *Periodicals;* pt.3–4, *Dramas and works prepared for oral delivery;* pt.5, *Music* (1947–56, issued in two sections: pt.5A, Published music, and pt.5B, Unpublished music. From 1957, these are combined into pt.5; pt.6, *Maps and atlases;* pt.7–11A, *Works of art,* reproductions, scientific and technical drawings, photographic works, prints, and pictorial illustrations; pt.11B,

Commercial prints and labels; pts.12–13, *Motion pictures and filmstrips;* pt.14A, *Renewal registrations:* literature, art, film; pt.14B, *Renewal registrations:* music.

Each part was published semiannually and listed the works copyrighted during the period. The *Books* section included books published in the U.S. and, when copyrighted in this country, books in foreign languages published outside the U.S., and books in the English language first published abroad.

All types of books were included: literature, fiction, nonfiction, business reports and yearbooks, trade catalogs and directories, manuals, instruction books, research studies in many fields, etc.

———. ———. *4th series* (Wash. : U.S. Govt. Print. Off., 1978–).

Contents: Pt.1, Nondramatic literary works excluding serials and periodicals (quarterly); pt.2, Serials and periodicals (semiannual); pt.3, Performing arts (quarterly); pt.4, Motion pictures and filmstrips (semiannual); pt.5, Visual arts (semiannual); pt.6, Maps (semiannual); pt.7, Sound recordings (semiannual); pt.8, Renewals (semiannual).

This new series coincides with the implementation of the Copyright Act of 1976. Works are entered under title, with an index of authors, claimants, and other names associated with the work in each part; entries include bibliographic description plus information relating to the copyright claim. Entries for published and unpublished materials are interfiled. Although one or two copies must be deposited for registration of copyright, not all works deposited are selected for inclusion in the collections of the Library of Congress.

Issues covering 1978 were the last to be published in paper. The catalog is now published only on microfiche, with some parts available on fiche beginning 1978, other parts beginning 1979. The microfiche is issued in the same eight sections noted above, and each section has been cataloged separately by the Library of Congress (e.g., Library of Congress. Copyright Office. *Catalog of copyright entries, fourth series. Part 4, Motion pictures & filmstrips*).   Z1219.U58C

Paperbound books in print. Mar. 1971– . N.Y. : Bowker, 1955– . Semiannual.   **AA434**

Frequency varies; originally monthly. Now issued in two three-volume sets published in Spring and Fall: v. 1, Titles; v. 2, Authors; v. 3, Subjects and publishers.

Each issue now lists an average of about 200,000 titles of currently available paperbacks.   Z1033.P3P32

Publishers' catalogs annual. 1979– . Westport, Conn. : Meckler Publ., 1979– . Annual. Microfiche.   **AA435**

In view of the large number of publishers not represented in *PTLA* (AA436) in recent years, this is an attempt to complete the record by providing microform reproduction of all available catalogs from U.S. and Canadian publishers. While there is a good deal of overlap between this series and *PTLA*, each includes some catalogs not found in the other. A printed index of publishers accompanies the fiches, giving the address of each publisher and number of the fiche on which the catalog is found; a classified listing of publishers is also included in the accompanying pamphlet.

Publishers' trade list annual. 1873– . N.Y. : Bowker, 1873– . Annual.   **AA436**

A collection of publishers' catalogs, arranged alphabetically by publishers' names, and bound up in one, two, three or more large volumes per year. As the catalogs are not compiled on any uniform system, the amount of information given about books varies greatly, ranging from full information and occasional notes in some lists to only short title and price in others; in general, dates of publication are omitted. Lists only books in print. An alphabetical list of the publishers included is given in the first volume. In recent years an increasing number of important publishers have declined, for economic reasons, to have their catalogs included in *PTLA*. This unfortunate trend lessens both the comprehensiveness of *PTLA* and the effectiveness of its companion publication, *Books in print* (AA425), as a searching tool. However, with the improvements in electronic communictions with publishers, *Books in print* information no longer relies upon *PTLA* in the same manner.

Except for brief indexes in 1902–1904, no indexes were issued until 1948 when *Books in print* began publication, followed in 1957 by the *Subject guide to Books in print* (AA438).

The volumes for 1903–63 have been published in microform by Meckler Pub., Westport, Conn. (1980; 4100 fiches). An index to the microfiche set was compiled by Anthony Abbott (Westport, Conn. : Meckler Publ., 1980–84. 2 v. Contents: v. 1, 1903–63; v. 2, 1964–80). These volumes indicate the fiche number (and position on the fiche) of the catalog of a given publisher for a given year.   Z1215.P972

Publishers' weekly : the book industry journal. v. 1 (1872)– . N.Y. : Bowker, 1872– . Weekly.   **AA437**

Subtitle varies; publisher varies.

The standard American book-trade journal, containing lists of new publications, lists of books announced for publication, news notes, editorials and articles, advertisements of books wanted, etc. The principal bibliographical list was the weekly list of new publications, for which the amount of information, promptness of listing, and indexing have differed through the years. Beginning Sept. 1974, the *Weekly record* (AA440) was issued as a separate publication and not bound with *Publishers' weekly*.

Special numbers issued during the year vary but usually include: Spring announcement number in Jan.; Summer announcement number in Apr.; Fall children's book number in July; Fall announcement number in Aug.   Z1219.P98

Subject guide to Books in print. 1957– . N.Y. : Bowker, 1957– . Annual.   **AA438**

Volume for 1988–89 has title: *Books in print. Subject guide*.

A companion publication to *Books in print* (AA425), listing under subject the books to be found there. Conforms to the subject headings and cross-references set up by the Library of Congress. Works to which the Library of Congress does not assign subject headings (e.g., fiction, poetry, drama, and Bibles) are not indexed. A review appears in *Booklist* 79: 1294–96 (June 1, 1983).

•In machine-readable form as part of *Books in print plus* (AA426).   Z1215.P973

Vertical file index : subject and title index to selected pamphlet material. 1932/34– . N.Y. : Wilson, 1935– . Monthly (except Aug.), with annual cumulations.   **AA439**

Title varies: v. 1–23, 1935–54, *Vertical file service catalog*.

A list of free and inexpensive pamphlets, booklets, leaflets, and similar material considered to be of interest to general libraries. Subjects range from those suitable for school libraries to specialized technical reports. Arranged alphabetically by subject headings (deemed suitable for vertical file use) with title index.   Z1231.P2V48

Weekly record. Sept. 2, 1974–Dec. 23, 1991. N.Y. : Bowker, 1974–1991. Weekly.   **AA440**

Formerly issued as a section of *Publishers' weekly*.

A main-entry listing based mainly on Library of Congress cataloging and giving full title, imprint, collation, price, Library of Congress and Dewey Decimal classification numbers, subject headings and other tracings. Lists current American books and foreign books distributed in the U.S.; does not include federal and other government publications, subscription books, dissertations, new printings (as distinct from reprints), pamphlets, ephemera, and most elementary and high school textbooks. Listings for mass market paperbacks, annuals, yearbooks and reprints reflect only those sent to the editorial offices.

Serves as the basis for *American book publishing record* (AA424). An effort is made to supply any missing prices and to complete the information in C.I.P. entries prior to publication of *ABPR*.   Z1219.W4

Regional

Historical Records Survey. American imprints inventory / prep. by the Historical Records Survey, Division of Women's and Professional Projects, Works Progress Administration. Wash. : Historical Records Survey, 1937–42. no. 1–20, 23–26, 31–32, 36, 38–42, 44–45, 52, and unnumbered issue.   **AA441**

Nos. 21–22, 27–30, 33–35, 37, 43, 46–51 had not been published when the work of the *American imprints inventory* ceased.

Contents: no. 1, A preliminary check list of *Missouri* imprints, 1808–1850 (1937. 225 p.); no. 2, M. R. Martin, Check list of *Minnesota* imprints, 1849–1865 (1938. 219 p.); no. 3, A check list of *Arizona* imprints, 1860–1890 (1938. 81 p.); no. 4, Check list of *Chicago* ante-fire imprints, 1851–1871 (1938. 727 p.); no. 5, D. C. McMurtrie, Check list of *Kentucky* imprints, 1787–1810 (1939. 205 p.); no. 6, D. C. McMurtrie and A. H. Allen, Check list of *Kentucky* imprints, 1811–1820, with notes in supplement to the Check list of 1787–1810 imprints (1939. 235 p.); no. 7, A check list of *Nevada* imprints, 1859–1890 (1939. 127 p.); no. 8, Check list of *Alabama* imprints, 1807–1840 (1939. 159 p.); no. 9, Lucile M. Morsch, Check list of *New Jersey* imprints, 1784–1800 (1939. 189 p.); no. 10, Check list of *Kansas* imprints, 1854–1876 (1939. 773 p.); no. 11, Chicago Historical Society Library, A check list of the Kellogg collection of "patent inside" newspapers of 1876 (1939. 99 p.); no. 12, D. C. McMurtrie, A check list of the imprints of *Sag Harbor, L.I.*, 1791–1820 (1939. 61 p.); no. 13, A check list of *Idaho* imprints, 1839–1890 (1940. 74 p.); no. 14, A check list of *West Virginia* imprints, 1791–1830 (1940. 62 p.);

no. 15, A check list of *Iowa* imprints, 1838–1860, in supplement to those recorded by Alexander Moffit in the *Iowa journal of history and politics* for Jan. 1938 (1940. 84 [i.e., 85] p.); no. 16, List of *Tennessee* imprints, 1793–1840, in Tennessee libraries (1941. 97 p.); no. 17, A check list of *Ohio* imprints, 1796–1820 (1941. 202 p.); no. 18, A check list of *Wyoming* imprints, 1866–1890 (1941. 69 [i.e., 70] p.); no. 19, Lucy B. Foote, Bibliography of the official publications of *Louisiana*, 1803–1934 (1942. 579 p.); no. 20, Check list of *Tennessee* imprints, 1841–1850 (1941. 138 p.); no. 23–24, 41–42, A check list of *Wisconsin* imprints, 1833–1849, 1850–1854, 1855–1858, 1859–1863 (1942. 4 v.); no. 25, Check list of *New Mexico* imprints and publications, 1784–1876: imprints, 1834–1876; publications, 1784–1876 (1942. 115 p.); no. 26, A check list of *Nebraska* non-documentary imprints, 1847–1876 (1942. 132 p.);

no. 31, A check list of *California* non-documentary imprints, 1833–1855 (1942. 109 p.); no. 32, A check list of *Tennessee* imprints, 1793–1840 (1942. 285 p.); no. 36, A check list of *Utica, N.Y.*, imprints, 1799–1830 (1942. 179 p.); no. 38 (misnumbered 25), Supplemental check list of *Kentucky* imprints, 1788–1820, including the original printing of the original Kentucky copyright ledger, 1800–1854, and the first account of the run of Baptist minutes in the collection of Mr. Henry S. Robinson, ed. by John Wilson Townsend (1942. 241 p.); no. 39, A check list of *Arkansas* imprints, 1821–1876 (1942. 139 p.); no. 40 and 45, A check list of *Massachusetts* imprints, 1801–1802 (1942. 2 v.); no. 41–42, *see* no. 23–24; no. 44, A check list of *Washington* imprints, 1853–1876 (1942. 89 p.); no. 45, *see* no. 40; no. 52, Preliminary check list of *Michigan* imprints, 1796–1850 (1942. 224 p.); [unnumbered issue] A guide to *Wisconsin* newspapers, Iowa County, 1837–1940 (1942. 142 p.).   Z1215.H67

McMurtrie, Douglas Crawford. Locating the printed source materials for United States history : with a bibliography of lists of regional imprints. (*In* Mississippi Valley historical review 31 [Dec. 1944]: 369–406).   **AA442**

Lists of regional imprints, arranged alphabetically by state, p. 379–403; American imprints checklist, p. 403–406.

United States. Work Projects Administration. Bibliography of research projects reports : check-list of Historical Records Survey publications. Rev. Apr. 1943. Wash. : Federal Works Agency, W.P.A., 1943. 110 p. (W.P.A. Technical ser. Research and records bibliography, 7).   **AA443**

A final record of publications superseding all earlier listings. Lists inventories of federal archives in the states; inventories of county archives; inventories of municipal and town archives; transcriptions of public archives; vital statistics; church archives publications; manuscript publications; American imprints inventory; American portrait inventory; guides to civilian organizations; miscellaneous publications; microfilm records; depositories of unpublished material, etc.

The volumes published in these various series are not listed here, with the exception of the American imprints inventory (AA441).   Z1223.W85 no.7

Canada

Amtmann, Bernard. Contributions to a short-title catalogue of Canadiana. Montreal, 1971–1973. 4 v.   **AA444**
A main entry listing of books and pamphlets relating to Canada. Auction prices of recent date are indicated.   Z1365.A64

Canadian catalogue of books published in Canada, about Canada : as well as those written by Canadians, with imprint 1921–1949. Consolidated English language reprint edition, with cumulated author index. [Toronto] : Toronto Pub. Libraries, 1959. 2 v.   **AA445**
Contents: v. 1, 1921–39; v. 2, 1940–49.
Reprints of the English-language sections of the annual lists issued by the Toronto Public Libraries during this period, with a cumulative author index in each of the two volumes.
From 1921 to 1943, included books, pamphlets, and selected government documents; from 1944 to 1949, federal government publications were omitted. Usually each annual number was in two sections: (1) books in English, and (2) books in French. The reprint edition is of the English sections only.
Superseded by: *Canadiana* (AA456).   Z1365.C222

Canadiana, 1867–1900 : monographs [microform]. Ottawa, Ontario : National Library of Canada, 1988. 92 microfiches : negative.   **AA446**
A listing of monographs (including pamphlets, municipal and county government publications, sheet music; excluding federal, provincial, and territorial publications, serials, maps, and dissertations) published in Canada or by Canadians outside of Canada. Arranged by accession number, with indexes for author/title, publication date, publisher, place of publication, and subject. Locates copies in Canadian libraries. Accompanied by a printed guide.   Z1365.C25

Dionne, Narcisse Eutrope. Inventaire chronologique ... . Québec, 1905–1909. 4 v.   **AA447**
Repr.: N.Y. : AMS Pr., 1974, in 1 v. (including supplement, below).
Published by the Royal Society of Canada. Also issued in the Society's *Proceedings and transactions*, 2nd ser., v. 10–12, 14 (1904–1906, 1908), 3rd ser., v. 5 (1911).
Contents: [v. 1, pt. 1], Inventaire chronologique des livres, brochures, journaux et revues publiés en langue française dans la province de Québec, depuis l'établissement de l'imprimerie au Canada jusqu'à nos jours, 1764–1905; [v. 1, pt. 2], Tables des noms et des matières; v. 2, Québec et Nouvelle France, bibliographie; Inventaire chronologique des ouvrages publiés à l'étranger en diverses langues ... 1534–1906; v. 3, Inventaire chronologique des livres, brochures, journaux et revues publiés en langue anglaise dans la province de Québec ... 1764–1906; v. 4, Inventaire chronologique des cartes, plans, atlas, relatifs à la Nouvelle-France et à la province de Québec, 1508–1908.
Inventaire chronologique des livres, brochures, journaux et revues ... . 1. suppl., 1904–12 (1912. 76 p.).   Z1392.Q3D5

Haight, Willet Ricketson. Canadian catalogue of books, 1791–1897. Toronto : Haight, 1896–1904. 6 v.   **AA448**
Facsimile repr.: Vancouver : Devlin ; London : Pordes, 1958.
Basic volume, 1791–1895, pt. 1 of a projected list for that period (publ. 1896. 130 p.); Supplements 1–2, 1896–97, Annual Canadian catalogue, publ. 1898 (48 p.) and 1904 (57 p.).
No more published.   Z1365.H15

Martin, Gérard. Bibliographie sommaire du Canada français, 1854–1954. Québec : Secrétariat de la Province de Québec, 1954. 104 p.   **AA449**
A classified list of some 900 items concerning French Canada.   Z1377.F8M3

Morgan, Henry James. Bibliotheca canadensis : or, A manual of Canadian literature. Ottawa : G. E. Desbarats, 1867. 411p.   **AA450**

An alphabetical list of the authors of books, pamphlets, and contributions to the periodical press, with brief biographical notices and lists of their works. The biographical sketches are occasionally of some length and include, in addition to authors whose books are listed, sketches of Canadian journalists for whom no separate publications are noted.   Z1365.M84

Public Archives Canada. Catalogue of pamphlets in the Public Archives of Canada, with index / prep. by Magdalen Casey. Ottawa : Acland, 1931–32. 2 v. (Public Archives of Canada. Publication, no.13).   **AA451**
1st ed., 1903; 2nd ed., covering period 1611–1867, 1911; 3rd ed. 1916.
Contents: v. 1, 1493–1877; v. 2, 1878–1931.
The new edition lists a total of 10,072 items, arranged chronologically, with author and subject indexes in each volume. Includes material published in Canada and pamphlets about Canada published elsewhere.   Z1365.C21

Tod, Dorothea D. A check list of Canadian imprints, 1900–1925. Prelim. checking ed. / Dorothea D. Tod and Audrey Cordingley. Ottawa : Canadian Bibliographic Centre, Public Archives of Canada, 1950. 370 p.   **AA452**
Designed to fill the gap in Canadian national bibliography.
An alphabetically arranged checklist of books and pamphlets (of more than 50 p.). Government documents and serial publications are not included.   Z1365.T6

Tremaine, Marie. A bibliography of Canadian imprints, 1751–1800. Toronto : Univ. of Toronto Pr., 1952. 705 p.   **AA453**
A full record of what is known of the first 50 years of the provincial press. Books, magazines, pamphlets, newspapers, broadsides, and handbills are included, both those actually issued and those known to have been projected. Full bibliographical information is given for each item, and copies are located in Canadian, American, and foreign libraries. Good descriptive notes make this a guide to the society and thought of the period. A section on printing offices and a good general index to the volume.   Z1365.T7

Current

Canadian books in print : author and title index. 1975– . Toronto : Univ. of Toronto Pr., 1976– . Annual.   **AA454**
Continues an earlier series of the same title covering 1967–74 and which also carried a French title (*Catalogue des livres canadiens en librairie*) through 1972. Now includes only those French-language titles issued by predominantly English-language Canadian publishers (the French-language publications being covered by the irregularly published *Répertoire de l'édition au Québec*, 1972–). Beginning with the 1975 volume the subtitle, "Author and title index," appears on the title page. With the 1983/84 ed. (publ. 1984) the annual hardcover volume is supplemented by complete microfiche editions in April, July, and October of each year.
A companion publication appears as *Canadian books in print : subject index* (AA455).   Z1365.C2196

Canadian books in print : subject index. 1975– . Toronto : Univ. of Toronto Pr., 1976– . Annual.   **AA455**
Continues *Subject guide to Canadian books in print* 1973–74.
Offers a subject arrangement of the materials listed in *Canadian books in print: author and title indexes* (AA454). Includes an alphabetical list of subject headings and a list of publishers with addresses.   Z1365.S9

Canadiana. 1950– . Ottawa : Nat. Libr. of Canada, 1951– . Monthly, with annual cumulations.   **AA456**
Succeeds the *Canadian catalogue of books*, 1921–49 (AA445). For an account of the history of the publication of *Canadiana* and a chronology of the changes in the individual sections *see* Appendix A of Dorothy E. Ryder's *Canadian reference sources* (2nd ed. Ottawa : Canadian Libr. Assoc., 1981).

Coverage varies considerably. Beginning 1967, arranged in six sections: (1) Fully catalogued and classified material arranged by Dewey classes and including "publications of Canadian origin or interest"; (2) Pamphlet file material; (3) Microforms; (4) Films, filmstrips, etc.; (5) Publications of the Government of Canada; (6) Publications of the Provincial governments of Canada.

Annual volumes cumulate, with minor revisions, the monthly issues with complete indexes; since 1968 a single cumulative index has been published for all six parts.

Automation of the production of *Canadiana* proceeded in stages from 1973 and was completed at the end of 1977, with various changes during the transition period. Beginning 1974, the bibliography appeared in eight parts: (1) Monographs (fully catalogued and classified) [now includes sheet music and scores]; (2) Theses in microform; (3) Serials (fully catalogued and classified) [now includes monographic series]; (4) Pamphlet file material; (5) Sound recordings (fully catalogued and classified); (6) Films, filmstrips and videotapes [not included after the Dec. 1976 issue; thereafter these materials are listed in an annual publication, *Film Canadiana,* prepared by the Canadian Film Institute in cooperation with the National Library]; (7) Publications of the government of Canada; (8) Publications of the provincial governments of Canada. Indexing pattern has varied; in recent years there is an author/title/series index, and separate English and French subject indexes.

Also available on microfiche from 1978.

———. *1968–76 index.* (Ottawa : Nat. Lib. of Canada, 1978. 10 v.).

"This index is the cumulation of Index A information for all the manually-prepared text of CANADIANA for the years 1968 to 1976; for 1968 to 1973 this included all parts, for 1974 parts III–VIII, and for 1975 and 1976 parts V and VI only. It attempts to provide every type of specific entry under which a publication may be sought. It includes authors (personal and corporate), titles, added entries (i.e. associated names such as editors, joint authors, etc.) and series. It also includes cross-references from headings not used, and where relevant, histories of corporate bodies occurring as authors."—*v. 1 [p. 1].* Users are cautioned that changes in cataloging rules and filing procedures sometimes mean that separate alphabetical sequences must be searched for publications of given organizations.   Z1365.C23

Mexico

Andrade, Vicente de Paula. Ensayo bibliográfico mexicana del siglo XVII. 2nd ed. México : Impr. del Museo Nacional, 1899 [1900]. 803 p.   **AA457**

Reprinted in part from the *Memorias de la Sociedad Científica Antonio Alzate,* 1894. Also available in Readex Microprint.

Lists 1,228 titles, transcribed line for line. Arranged chronologically and followed by alphabetical indexes of authors and of anonymous works.   Z1412.A55

Anuario bibliográfico mexicano. 1931–1941/42. México : Secretaría de Relaciones Exteriores, 1931–1944.   **AA458**

Comp. 1931–33 comp. by Felipe Teixidor; 1940–1941/42 by Julián Amo.

1934–39 not published. Issuing agency varies.

The 1931–33 issues are alphabetical author listings based on the copyright accessions of the National Library; those for 1940–1941/42 are classified lists, with a combined author index for 1941–42.
                                                    Z1411.A62

Beristain de Souza, José Mariano. Biblioteca hispano americana septentrional : o, Catálogo y noticias de los literatos que o nacidos o educados, o florecientes en la América Septentrional Española, han dado a luz algún escrito, o lo han dejado prep. para la prensa, 1521–1850. [3rd. ed.]. México : Ed. Fuente Cultural, [1947]. 5 v. in 2. : ill., facsims.   **AA459**

1st ed., 1816–21; 2nd ed., 1883, in three volumes.

Vol. 1–5, A–Z. Also includes *Suplemento especial* to v. 5 (called v. 6?) and lists of anonyms, biobibliographical notes, and indexes. Based upon the 2nd ed., this is a reissue, with additions and corrections. Arrangement is confusing and must be studied with care.

———. ———. *Suplemento especial II–III* (México, Ed. Fuente Cultural, 1951. 2 v.; ill., facsims.). Also numbered as v. 7–8 of the main work.

García Icazbalceta, Joaquín. Bibliografía mexicana del siglo XVI : Catálogo razonado de libros impresos en México de 1539 á 1600, con biografías de autores y otras ilustraciones .... Nueva edición / por Augustín Millares Carlo. México : Fondo de Cultura Económica, 1954. 581 p. : ill., facsims. (Biblioteca americana, proyectada por Pedro Henríquez Ureña y publicada en memoria suya; Serie de literatura moderna: historia y biografía, [27]).   **AA460**

1st ed., 1886.

This edition uses the text of the original which listed 116 titles, transcribed line for line, without change of wording, but with additions and emendations resulting from later investigation. Additional titles are included, with an appendix, and an analytical index. Quotations and very full bibliographical and historical notes are given, with references to sources and, in many cases, location of copies.   Z1412.G2

González de Cossio, Francisco. La imprenta en México, 1594–1820 / cien adiciones a la obra de Don José Toribio Medina. México : Antigua Librería Robredo, 1947. 205 p.; facsims.   **AA461**

Includes full bibliographical information and line-by-line transcriptions.

———. *La imprenta en México, 1553–1820 : 510 adiciones a la obra de José Toribio Medina en homenaje al primer centenario de su nacimiento* (México : Univ. Nacional de México, 1952. 354 p. ; facsims.). Continues the earlier work, with the same format. Does not duplicate the entries given there.   Z1411.G6

León, Nicolás. Bibliografía mexicana del siglo XVIII. México : Francisco Díaz de León, 1902–08. 5 v. in 6. **AA462**

Publication first begun in *Anales del Museo Michoacano,* 1890. Planned to be issued in two parallel sections: one purely bibliographical (including reprints in whole or in part of the rarer works); the other (which remains unpublished) biographical, historical, and critical. Line-by-line transcription. Each part arranged alphabetically. Some sources cite pt. 6a (A–N) as unpublished.

———. *Índice[s]* arreglado por Roberto Valles (México : Ed. Vargas Rea, 1945–46. 3 v.). Contents: Índice de nombres (1945. 61 p.;) Índice de impresos, (1946. 29 p.); Índice de anónimos (1946. 44 p.).

Medina, José Toribio. La imprenta en México (1539–1821). Santiago de Chile : Autor, 1908/-12. 8 v. in ill.   **AA463**

Repr.: Amsterdam : N. Israel, 1965. Also in Readex Microprint.

Vol. 1, publ. 1912.

12,412 entries.

———. *La imprenta en Guadalajara de México (1792–1821) : notas bibliográficas* (Santiago de Chile : Impr. Elzeveriana, 1904. 104 p.).

Repr.: Amsterdam : N. Israel, 1964.

———. *La imprenta en la Puebla de Los Angeles (1640–1821)* (Santiago de Chile : Cervantes, 1908. 823 p. ; ill.

Repr.: Amsterdam : N. Israel, 1964.

———. *La imprenta en Mérida de Yucatán (1813–21) : notas bibliográficas* (Santiago de Chile : Impr. Elzeveriana, 1904. 32 p.).

Repr.: Amsterdam : N. Israel, 1964. Also in Readex Microprint.

Also publ. in an Ed. commemorativa del centenario de nacimiento del autor, con un prólogo y dis apéndices por Victor M. Suárez (Mérida : Ed. Suárez, 1956. 102 p).

———. *La imprenta en Oaxaca (1720–1820) : notas bibliográficas* (Santiago de Chile : Impr. Elzeveriana, 1904. 29 p.).

Repr.: Amsterdam : N. Israel, 1964.

———. *La imprenta en Veracruz (1794–1821) : notas bibliográficas* (Santiago de Chile : Impr. Elzeveriana, 1904. 34 p.).

Repr.: Amsterdam : N. Israel, 1964.   Z1411.M49

Valtón, Emilio. Impresos mexicanos del siglo XVI (incunables americanos) en la Biblioteca Nacional de México, el Museo Nacional y el Archivo General de la Nación : estudio bibliográfico precidido de una introducción sobre los orígenes de la imprenta en América. México : Impr. Universitaria, 1935. 244 p. : ill., facsims.   **AA464**
Detailed bibliographical descriptions of 16th-century Mexican imprints.   Z1412.V21

Current

Bibliografía mexicana / Biblioteca Nacional Instituto Bibliográfico Mexicano. Enero–Feb. 1967– . México : Biblioteca Nacional, 1967– . Bimonthly.   **AA465**
Frequency varies: originally bimonthly; annually 1986–88; monthly, 1989, nos. 1–6.
A classed bibliography with author, title, and subject index.
A note from the publisher indicates that issues after 1989, no. 6, will be available only in electronic format.

Biblioteca Nacional de México. Anuario bibliográfico. 1958–69. México : Biblioteca Nacional, 1967–76.   **AA466**
At head of title: Universidad Nacional Autonoma de México.
The first official Mexican national bibliography to appear since the *Anuario bibliográfico mexicano* (AA458) which covered through 1941/42. (1958 was chosen as the beginning date for the new annual since that is the point at which the law regarding legal deposit was made generally effective.) Classed arrangement with author-title-subject index.
Absorbed by: *Bibliografía mexicana* (AA465).   Z1411.M5

Boletín bibliográfico mexicano. Año 1, num. 1 (enero 31, 1940)– . México : [E.U. Mexicanos], 1940– . Bimonthly.   **AA467**
Some published with subtitle: Reseña bimestral de libros y folletos, impresos en los E. U. Mexicanos. A preliminary no. was issued with designation Año 1, num. 1 (10 de oct. de 1939).
Frequency varied: monthly to 1947.
A classified listing.   Z1415.B65

Latin America

British Museum. Department of Printed Books. Short-title catalogues of Portuguese books and of Spanish-American books printed before 1601, now in the British Museum / by H. Thomas. London : Quaritch, 1926. 55 p.   **AA468**
The Portuguese section was issued in an enlarged edition, *Short-title catalogue of Portuguese books printed before 1601, now in the British Museum* (AA775), but since no significant additions had been made to the Spanish-American section up to 1940, this part was not revised. A 19 p. volume of Spanish-American books was published 1944. See also *Catalogue of books printed in Spain and of Spanish books printed elsewhere …* (AA813) and *Short-title catalogues of Spanish, Spanish-American and Portuguese books printed before 1601 in the British Museum* (London : British Museum, [1966]).
    Z2712.B86

Historia y bibliografía de las primeras imprentas rioplatenses, 1700–1850 : misiones del Paraguay, Argentina, Uruguay / por Guillermo Fúrlong … [et al.]. Buenos Aires : Ed. Guaranía, 1953–75. 4 v. : ill.   **AA469**
Publisher varies.
Contents: t. 1, La imprenta en las reducciones del Paraguay, 1700–27. La imprenta en Córdoba, 1765–67. La imprenta en Buenos Aires, 1780–84; t. 2, La imprenta en Buenos Aires, 1785–1807; t. 3,

La imprenta en Buenos Aires, 1808–1810. La imprenta en Montevideo, 1807–1810; v. 4, La imprenta en Buenos Aires, 1810–1815. No more published?
Designed to furnish a complete record of printing in Argentina, Paraguay, and Uruguay from 1700 to 1850. A history of early printing in the area is followed by the bibliography. Information about each item is detailed, including transcript of title page or colophon, collation, location, contents, description of type, etc. Biographical notes on author and printer are often given, and references to other bibliographical sources.   Z213.A69H5

Medina, José Toribio. Biblioteca hispano-americana (1493–1810). Santiago de Chile : Impreso y grabado en casa del autor, 1898–1907. 7 v. : ill.   **AA470**
Repr.: Amsterdam : N. Israel, 1958–62; also Readex Microprint.
Contents: t. 1–5, 1493–1810; t. 6, Prólogo. Sin fecha determinada, siglo XVII–XIX. Adiciones. Ampliaciones. Dudosos. Manuscritos; t. 7, Algo más de Léon Pinelo. Nuevas adiciones. Sin fecha determinada. Ultimas adiciones. Ampliaciones. Notas biográficas. Índice alfabético.

———. *Historia y bibliografía de la imprenta en el antiguo vireinato del Rio de la Plata.* (La Plata : Taller de Publicaciones del Museo, 1892. 4 pts. in l v. ill. [Historia y bibliografía de la imprenta en la América Española, pt. 2]).
Publisher varies.
Added half-title: Anales del Museo de la Planta. Materiales para la historia fisica y moral del continente sub-americano. Publicados bajo la dirección de Francisco P. Moreno … Sección de historia americana. III.
Contents: pt. 1, Historia y bibliografía de la imprenta en el Paraguay (1705–1727); pt. 2, En Córdoba del Tuchumán (1766); pt. 3, En Buenos Aires (1780–1810); pt. 4, En Montevideo (1807–10). Indice alfabético.

———. *Notas bibliográficas referentes á las primeras producciones de la imprenta en algunas ciudades de la América Española (Ambato, Angostura, Curazao, Guayaquil, Maracaibo, Neuva Orleans, Nueva Valencia, Panamá, Popayán, Puerto España, Puerto Rico, Querétaro, Santa Marta, Santiago de Cuba, Santo Domingo, Tunja y otros lugares), (1754–1823).* (Santiago de Chile : Impr. Elzeviriana, 1904. 116 p.).   Z1601.M49

Pan American book shelf. v. 1 (Mar. 1938)–v. 11, no. 12 (Dec. 1948). Wash. : Pan Amer. Union, Columbus Memorial Lib., 1938–1948.   **AA471**
A useful monthly bibliography with annual author index. Listed books currently received in the Columbus Memorial Library—usually, but not always, recent material.
§ Succeeded by *LEA : librarians, editors, authors = libros, editores, autores* (Wash., 1949–50. no. 1–12) which in turn was superseded by *Revista interamericana de bibliografía* (AA476) in Jan. 1951.
    Z881.W3255

Zimmerman, Irene. Current national bibliographies of Latin America : a state of the art study. [Gainesville] : Center for Latin American Studies, Univ. of Florida, 1971. 139 p.
    AA472
Provides a brief but careful description of the state (as of 1969) of national bibliographical services of the individual countries of South America and the Caribbean. Attention is given to historical aspects and to future plans. Bibliography; index. Dated, but useful for historical information.   Z1602.5.Z55

Current

Boletín bibliográfico / Centro Regional para el Fomento del Libro en América Latina y el Caribe. v. 5, no. 2–4 (abr.-dic. 1978)–v. 11, 1984. Bogotá, Colombia : El Centro, 1978–84. Quarterly (irregular).   **AA473**
Continues *Boletín bibliografico CERLALC*, publ. 1974–77, and retains its numbering.

A regional bibliography covering Spanish and Portuguese publications of Bolivia, Colombia, Chile, Ecuador, Peru, and Venezuela. Classed listing with author and title indexes. Issues for 1985 are published in the 1985 issues of the journal *CERLALC noticias sobre el libro*; no more appear to have been published.   Z1601.U5a

Fichero bibliográfico hispanoamericano. v. 1 (1961)– . N.Y. ; Buenos Aires : Bowker, 1961– . Monthly.   **AA474**
Frequency varies; quarterly until Oct. 1964.

Attempts to list all new books published in the Americas in the Spanish language in all subjects and by all publishers. Arranged by Dewey Decimal Classification with an index by authors and titles, followed by a list of publishers.   Z1201.F5

Libros en venta en Hispanoamérica y España. 1964– . N.Y. : R.R. Bowker, 1964– .   **AA475**
An in-print record for books in the Spanish language, listing titles published in Spain, the U. S., and the Latin American countries. The 5th ed., publ. 1990, lists more than 150,000 titles currently available from some 6,000 publishers, and is in 3 v.: v. 1, Autores con guia de editores; v. 2, Titulos; v. 3, Materias. A directory of publishers appears at the end of v. 1. Vol. 3 is a subject index arranged according to the Dewey Decimal Classification. Kept up-to-date by supplements. Also available in microfiche.   Z1601.L59

Revista interamericana de bibliografía = Inter-American review of bibliography. v. 1 (Jan.-Mar. 1951)– . Wash. : Organization of American States, 1951– . Quarterly (frequency varies).   **AA476**
English title varies; originally, *Review of inter-American bibliography.* Issuing body varies.

Includes lists of recent books, bibliographies, and reviews. Annual index.   Z1007.R4317

Central America

Costa Rica

Biblioteca Nacional (Costa Rica). Boletín bibliográfico. 1935/38–1956. San José : Impr. Nacional, 1939–56. Annual.   **AA477**
Title page note: "Publicaciones nacionales correspondientes al año [date]."

§ Superseded by: *Anuario bibliográfico costarricense* (AA480).

Dobles Segreda, Luis. Indice bibliográfico de Costa Rica. San José : Lehmann, 1927–36. v. 1–9.   **AA478**
Contents: t. 1: sec.1, Agricultura y veterinaria; sec. 2, Ciencias físicas y naturales; t. 2: sec. 3, Filología y gramática; sec. 4, Geografía y geología, Lista de mapas de Costa Rica; t. 3: sec. 5, Matemáticas, ingeniería y finanzas; sec. 6, Psicología, filosofía y religión; t. 4: sec. 7, Novela, cuento y artículo literario; sec. 8, Teatro; t. 5, sec. 9, Historia hasta 1900; t. 6, sec. 10, Historia desde 1900 hasta 1933; t. 7, sec. 11, and t. 8, sec. 11 (cont.), Política y derecho desde 1831 hasta 1935; t. 8, sec. 12, Milicia; t. 9, sec. 13, Hígiene y Medicina.

Other volumes were projected to cover education, sociology and demography, and poetry, as well as an Indice alfabético de autores (Biográfico y bibliográfico), but have not been published.   Z1451.D63

Lines, J. A. Libros y folletos publicados en Costa Rica durante los años 1830–1849. San José : Univ. de Costa Rica, Facultad de Letras y Filosofía, 1944. 151 p. : ill.   **AA479**
Lists 103 titles arranged chronologically with author index.   Z1451.L5

Current

Anuario bibliográfico costarricense. 1956– . San José : Impr. Nacional., 1958– . Irregular.   **AA480**
Supersedes *Boletín bibliográfico* (AA477).

At head of title: Asociación costarricense de bibliotecarios. Comité nacional de bibliografía "Adolfo Bien."

Originally works were listed in two alphabets, one by author, the second classified by subject, with an index of specific subjects and of names not appearing as main entries. Beginning with the issue covering 1959–60, the bibliography became a classified list with author index.   Z1453.A65

Guatemala

Bibliografía guatemalteca : colleción bibliográfica del tercer centenario de la fundación de la primera imprenta en Centro América. Guatemala : Tipografía Nacional, 1960–63. 10 v.   **AA481**
Contents: v. 1, Juan Enrique O'Ryan. Bibliografía guatemalteca de los siglos XVII y XVIII. 2. ed. [1660–1800]. (Text is a reprint of *Bibliografía de la imprenta en Guatemala en los siglos XVII y XVIII.* Santiago de Chile, 1897.).

Vol. 2, José Toribio Medina. La imprenta en Guatemala, 1660–1821. 2. ed. 1960. 2 v. (Originally published in Santiago de Chile, 1910.) Includes two supplements of *Algunas adiciones*, one by Gilberto Valenzuela, v. 2, p. 637–72, published originally in *La imprenta en Guatemala* (1933. 72 p.), and the other by Arturo Taracena Flores, v. 2, p. 673–92.

Vol. 3–5, Gilberto Valenzuela. Bibliografía guatemalteca, y catálogo general de libros, folletos, periódicos, revistas, etc. (v. 3, 1821–1830, 2. ed. [1. ed. 1933]; v. 4, 1831–1840; v. 5, 1841–1860).

Vol. 6–10, Gilberto Valenzuela Reyna. Bibliografía guatemalteca, y catálogo general de libros, folletos, periódicos, revistas, etc. (v. 6, 1861–1900; v. 7, 1901–1930; v. 8, 1931–1940; v. 9, 1941–50; v. 10, 1951–60).

An attempt to provide a record of printing in Guatemala from 1660 to the present by combining older works covering the early periods with new compilations for more recent times.

These volumes give detailed bibliographical information with annotations about books, pamphlets, etc., and in many cases the texts of decrees, official notices, etc. No more published.

José Luis Reyes Monroy's *Bibliografía de la imprenta en Guatemala (Adiciones de 1769 a 1900)* (Guatemala : Editorial "José de Pineda Ibarra," 1969. 143 p.) supplements the early volumes of the series.

Figueroa Marroquín, Horacio. Apéndice a la Bibliografía guatemalteca. Guatemala : Tip. Nacional, 1988. 204 p. : ill. (Colección Guatemala, v. 47 ; Serie José Joaquín Pardo, 6).   **AA482**

A listing of items not included in *Bibliografía guatemalteca* (AA481). Offers detailed annotated descriptions in separate sections for: (1) books and pamphlets; (2) dissertations, mainly in the fields of medicine and pharmacology; and (3) journals published in Guatemala through 1960. Each section is arranged chronologically. Pt. 2 is a listing of undated works arranged by approximate publication date. Lacks an index.   Z1461.F54

Guatemala. Tipografía Nacional. Catálogo general de libros, folletos y revistas : editados en la Tipografía Nacional de Guatemala desde 1892 hasta 1943. Guatemala : [Tipografía Nacional], 1944. 352 p.   **AA483**
Alphabetical by year; no index.   Z1465.G8

Índice bibliográfico guatemalteco. 1951–52, 1958–59/60. Guatemala : Inst. Guatemalteco-Americano, 1952–61. Annual (irregular).   **AA484**
At head of title: Cooperación Interbibliotecaria.

Gonzálo Dardon Córdova, ed.

Volumes covering 1953–57 not published? Volume for 1959/60 published 1961. Ceased publication?

An author and subject catalog of books, periodical articles, and pamphlets published in Guatemala, together with some works about Guatemala published abroad.   Z1461.I5

Villacorta Calderon, José Antonio. Bibliografía guatemalteca : exposiciones abiertas en el Salón de historia y bellas artes del Museo Nacional, en los meses de noviembre de 1939, 40, 41 y 42. Guatemala : Tipografía Nacional, 1944. 638 p. : ill.   **AA485**

Based on the exhibit on the history of printing in Guatemala held at the Museo Nacional. Covers the period from the introduction of printing in 1660 to 1942, with extensive bibliographies, location of copies, facsimilies of title pages, etc.   Z1461.V5

Honduras

Anuario bibliográfico hondureño / preparado por Miguel Angel García. 1962–1963– . Tegucigalpa, D.C., Honduras, C.A. : Biblioteca Nacional de Honduras, 1966– . Annual.   **AA486**

Publisher varies. Suspended 1972–79.

Continues *Bibliografía hondureña* (AA489), covering 1620–1960, and *Anuario bibiográfico*, publ. 1963 to cover 1961.

Lists books, pamphlets, official and government publications, and dissertations deposited at the Biblioteca Nacional. Arranged alphabetically by author; issues covering a range of years (e.g., 1981–83) are arranged year by year, then alphabetically. No index.

Ten-year cumulation: *Anuario bibliográfico hondureño, 1961–71*, ed. by García, publ. 1973.   Z1471.H6

Durón, Jorge Fidel. Índice de la bibliografía hondureña. Tegucigalpa : Impr. Calderón, 1946. 211 p.   **AA487**

Attempts to list all works published in Honduras (alphabetized by first letter only). For these it largely supersedes the author's *Repertorio bibliográfico hondureño* (AA488), which includes some items not in the *Índice*.   Z1471.D77

——————— Repertorio bibliográfico hondureño. Tegucigalpa : Impr. Calderón, 1943. 68p.   **AA488**

At head of title: Instituto Hondureño de Cultura Interamericana.

The first tentative edition of a national bibliography covering all periods. Books exhibited at the Primera Exposición y Feria del Libro Hondureño y Americano are listed in the first three sections: (1) Repertorio bibliográfico hondureño; (2) Libros de autores norteamericanos; (3) Libros de autores chilenos. Sec. 4 is a list of books published in Honduras, and sec. 5, an "Índice de nombres." All sections and index are alphabetized by first letter only. Index is a list of names only, without page references.   Z1471.D8

García, Miguel Angel. Bibliografía hondureña. [Tegucigalpa] : Banco Central de Honduras, [1971–72]. 2 v.   **AA489**

Contents: v. 1, 1620–1930; v. 2, 1931–1960.

A chronological listing without indexes. Locates copies.

Coverage continues in *Anuario bibliográfico hondureño* (AA486).   Z1471.G37

Nicaragua

Biblioteca Americana de Nicaragua. Bibliografía de libros y folletos publicados en Nicaragua (en 1942, o antes según fecha de publicación) : que se encuentran en algunas bibliotecas particulares de Nicaragua = A bibliography of books and pamphlets published in Nicaragua (with 1942 or earlier as date of publication) to be found in certain private libraries of Nicaragua. [Managua] : Biblioteca Americana de Nicaragua, 1945. 157 p. (Biblioteca Americana de Nicaragua. Serie bibliográfica, no. 4, pt. 1).   **AA490**

Ed., 1943–44, Graciela González.

Ceased publication.

Continued by: *Bibliografía de trabajos publicados en Nicaragua ... = A bibliography of works published in Nicaragua. 1943–45/47.* ([Managua : Ed. Nuevos Horizontes], 1944–48. 3 v. [Serie bibliográfica, no. 1, 6, 7–9]).

Ed. 1943–44 by Graciela González.

No more published.

Nicaraguan national bibliography, 1800–1978 = Bibliografía nacional nicaragüense, 1800–1978 / Latin American Bibliographic Foundation [and] Ministerio de Cultura de Nicaragua. Redlands, Calif. : Latin American Bibliographic Foundation ; Managua : Biblioteca Nacional Rubén Darío, 1986–87. 3 v.   **AA491**

General ed., G. F. Elmendorf.

Contents: v. 1–2, A–Z; v. 3, Serials and indexes.

Prefatory matter in English and Spanish.

An ambitious compilation designed to compensate in part for the lack of an official ongoing national bibliography. "These volumes sum up the entire Nicaraguan bibliography, everything that has been published by Nicaraguans or about Nicaragua, whether inside the country or abroad, whether printed or mimeographed and whether a book or a flier, from the time the printing press was introduced into the country in 1829 until 1978."—*Prologue*. Monographs and serials are listed by main entry in separate sections. Only annuals and irregular serials are included, but a "serial history and holding records section" is issue-specific and locates copies in selected U.S. and Nicaraguan libraries. There are separate author, title, and subject indexes in English for both the monographs and the serials, plus an "encabezamientos de materia, monografias y publicaciones en serie" which gives cross-references to the English indexes.

Continued by: *Bibliografía nacional de Nicaragua, 1979–1989*, Biblioteca Nacional "Rubén Darío" [director y compilador general, Jorge Eduardo Arellano (Managua : Inst. Nicaragüense de Cultura, 1991. 452 p.).

An alphabetical listing by main entry of works published in Nicaragua or published elsewhere about Nicaragua. Includes government publications and dissertations; unlike the earlier compilation, this does not list serials. Author, corporate author, and title indexes. Provides selective locations in U.S. and Nicaraguan libraries.   Z1481.N53

Panama

Biblioteca Nacional (Panama). Bibliografía panameña. Panama, 1953. 66 p.   **AA492**

At head of title: Ministerio de Educación, Comité Nacional Pro-bibliotecas, Biblioteca Nacional.

An alphabetical listing, in preliminary form, of books, pamphlets, and documents printed in Panama in the 20th century, with a few titles on Panama published elsewhere.

Herrera, Carmen D. de. Bibliografía de libros y folletos, 1958–1960. Panama : Grupo Bibliográfico Nacional de Panamá, 1960. 44 l.   **AA493**

On cover: Universidad de Panamá, Biblioteca.

Arranged by year, then by main entry, with books and pamphlets in separate alphabets.

South America

Argentina

Anuario bibliográfico de la República Argentina. año [1] (1879)–9 (1887). Buenos Aires : [s.n.], 1880–88.   **AA494**
   Editors: 1879–84, Alberto Navarro Viola; 1885–87, Enrique Navarro Viola.
   A selected, critical annual list, classified by subject; author index.
                                                    Z1611.A63

Boletín bibliográfico nacional. no. [1] (1937)–33 (1954/56). Buenos Aires : Biblioteca Nacional, 1937–63.   **AA495**
   Title varies: 1937–49, *Boletín bibliográfico argentino*.
   Publisher varies.
   An annual (irregular) publication listing books in the original and in translation, translations of foreign books published in Argentina, and foreign books that deal with Argentina. Classified arrangement with author index.   Z1615.B69

Gutiérrez, Juan María. Bibliografía de la primera imprenta de Buenos Aires desde su fundación hasta el año 1810 inclusive .... Buenos Aires : Impr. de Mayo, 1866. 43 p., 34 p., 246 p.   **AA496**
   Pt. 1, Celebridades argentinas del siglo XVIII; pt. 2, Orijenes del arte de imprimir en la America Española; pt. 3, Bibliografía de la primera imprenta de Buenos Aires [215 imprints].
   Pts. 2–3, repr. from *Revista de Buenos Aires*, June 1865–Aug. 1866.   Z213.B92G9

Universidad de Buenos Aires. Bibliografía argentina : catálogo de materiales argentinos en las bibliotecas de la Universidad de Buenos Aires. Boston : G. K. Hall, 1980. 7 v.
                                                    AA497
   Added title page in English: Argentine bibliography : a union catalogue of Argentinian holdings in the libraries of the University of Buenos Aires.
   Photographic reproduction of the cards from the union catalog of Argentinian printed books maintained by the Instituto Bibliotecológico for the 17 central and 56 departmental libraries of the University of Buenos Aires. The purpose of the catalog is to create a national bibliography and it therefore contains author cards for Argentinian books and pamphlets published up to 1979, as well as for works by Argentine authors published abroad.   Z1611.U54

Current

Bibliografía argentina de artes y letras. no. 1–49/50. Buenos Aires : Fondo Nacional de las Artes, 1959–72. Quarterly (irregular).   **AA498**
   A selective, classified bibliography, including periodical articles as well as books. Author index in each issue with annual cumulated indexes of names and anonymous titles. Many issues include special bibliographic studies.   Z1611.B5

Libros argentinos. ISBN. Buenos Aires : Cámara Argentina del Libro, c1984– . Annual.   **AA499**
   On t.p. of 1984 vol.: La presente edición continene la producción registrada hasta 1984. On t.p. of the 1987 vol.: Producción editorial registrada entre 1982 y 1986.
   A classified listing (arranged by title within subject classes), with author and title indexes. Includes an alphabetical list of publishers with addresses and ISBN prefix, and another list by ISBN number.
                                                    Z1615.L73

Bolivia

Abecía, Valentín. Adiciones á la Biblioteca boliviana de Gabriel René-Moreno : con un apéndice del editor, 1602–1879. Santiago de Chile : Impr. Barcelona, 1899. 440 p.   **AA500**
   571 entries, of which no.1–350 are the work of Abecía, and the remainder form part of the appendix by the editor, Enrique Barrenechea.
   §Supplements Gabriel René-Moreno, *Biblioteca boliviana* (AA505).   Z1641.B58A

Bibliografía boliviana. 1962–74. Cochabamba : Los Amigos del Libro, 1963–75. Annual.   **AA501**
   Werner Guttentag Tichauer, ed.
   An alphabetical listing of books and pamphlets published in Bolivia, with title and subject indexes and a list of publishers.
   Superseded by *Bio-bibliografía boliviana* (AA502).   Z1641.B5

Bio-bibliografía boliviana. 1975– . La Paz : Los Amigos del Libro, 1976– . Annual.   **AA502**
   Werner Guttentag Tichauer, ed.
   Supersedes *Bibliografía boliviana* (AA501).
   The change of title reflects an increase in the practice of supplying dates and identifying notes for authors whose books are listed. A supplementary list of publications from 1962 to the year preceding the date of coverage appears in each volume.   Z1641.B5

Costa de la Torre, Arturo. Catálogo de la bibliografía boliviana : libros y folletos, 1900–1963. La Paz : [Editorial Universidad Mayor de San Andrés], 1966 [i.e., 1968]–73. v. 1–2.
                                                    AA503
   Contents: v. 1, Prolegomenos [etc.]; pt. 1, Escritores bolivianos: libros y folletos, 1908–1963 (1255 p.); v. 2, Adiciones al "Segundo suplemento de la Bibliografía boliviana" de Gabriel René Moreno—1900–1908; Folletos anónimos en general—1908–1963 (1069 p.).
   Continues chronologically Gabriel René-Moreno's *Biblioteca boliviana* and its supplements (AA505). Additions to the second supplement, 1900–1908, appear in v. 2 of the present work—hence the beginning date as indicated in the title. Vol. 1 provides an alphabetical listing of more than 3,000 Bolivian authors with some 8,700 bibliographical entries. An extensive introductory section (p. 1–237) provides a comprehensive survey of Bolivian bibliography.
   A third volume was to provide a bibliography of foreign authors, 1909–63.   Z1641.C66

Gutiérrez, José Rosendo. Datos para la bibliografía boliviana. 1. sección. La Paz : Arzadum, 1875. 255 p.   **AA504**
   Lists 2,203 items.
   ———. ———. *Supplemento : últimas adiciones y correcciones á la primera sección* (La Paz : Impr. de la Union Americana, 1880. 24 p., 126 p.).
   Items 2204–3089. No more published.

René-Moreno, Gabriel. Biblioteca boliviana : catálogo de la sección de libros i folletos. Santiago de Chile : Impr. Gutenberg, 1879. 880 p.   **AA505**
   Available from Readex Microprint.
   Arranged alphabetically by title with index of authors, translators, etc. Full bibliographical information, with annotations; 3,529 entries. The most important Bolivian bibliography of the period.
   ———. ———. *1. suplemento ... epítome de un Catálogo de libros y folletos, 1879–99* (Santiago de Chile : Impr. Barcelona, 1900. 349 p.), containing items 3,530–5,176; and *2. suplemento, 1900–1908* (Santiago de Chile : Impr. Univ., 1908. 349 p.), items 5,177–6,815.

Brazil

BBB : Boletim bibliográfico brasileiro. v. 6 (1958)–[Sept./Dec. 1967]. [Rio de Janeiro : Estante Publicações, 1957–67?]. Monthly (irregular). **AA506**
Frequency varies: bimonthly, 1952–57.
Title varies.
A classified list, commercially sponsored, claiming to include all Brazilian publications for the period covered and giving full bibliographical information and prices. Does not include serials. Title index in each issue. Z1671.B6

Bibliografia brasileira. 1938/39–1955, 1963–66. Rio de Janeiro : Instituto Nacional do Livro, 1941–67. Irregular. **AA507**
Publ. by Ministério da Educação e Cultura. Instituto Nacional do Livro (form of name varies).
1938/39 publ. 1941; 1940 publ. 1954; 1941 publ. 1952; 1942/45 publ. 1953 in 2 v.; 1946 publ. 1947; 1947/52 publ. 1957; 1953 publ. 1954; 1954 publ. 1956; 1955 publ. 1959; 1956–62 not publ.; 1963/65 publ. 1966; 1966 publ. 1967.
A comprehensive dictionary catalog, arranged by author, title, and subject in one alphabet. Includes trade books only. A list of publishers at the back of each volume.
Continued by: *Bibliografia brasileira mensal* (ano 1 [1967]–5 [1972]. Rio de Janeiro : Instituto Nacional do Livro). Z1671.B582

Moraes, Rubens Borba de. Bibliografia brasileira do período colonial : catalogo comentado das obras dos autores nascidos no Brasil e publicadas antes de 1808. São Paulo : Universidade de São Paulo, 1969. 437 p. : ill., facsims. **AA508**
Aims to list all books by Brazilian authors published before 1808; includes works after that date if a part was published pre-1908. Also includes early works about Brazil and unpublished manuscripts by classic authors written during the period. Arranged alphabetically by author (where possible, works published anonymously have the author supplied), then chronologically. Many entries have detailed annotations, some with reproductions of title pages. Indexed by author and anonymous title. Z1672.M6

Sacramento Blake, Augusto Victorino Alves do. Diccionario bibliographico brasileiro. Rio de Janeiro : Typ. Nacional, 1883–1902. 7 v. **AA509**
Repr.: Nendeln, Liechtenstein : Kraus, 1969, with *Indice* in v. 7. Arranged alphabetically by *first* names.
————. ————. Indice alphabetico, comp. pelo Jango Fischer. (Rio de Janeiro : Impr. Nacional, 1937. 127 p.). Provides an author approach by surname.

Current

Bibliografia brasileira / Biblioteca Nacional. v. 1, no. 1/2 (1o. e 2o. trim. 1983)– . Rio de Janeiro : A Biblioteca, 1984– . Quarterly (irregular). **AA510**
Supersedes *Boletim bibliográfico da Biblioteca Nacional*, publ. 1951–82.
Includes materials received on legal deposit. Classified arrangement using Dewey Decimal Classification; author, title, and subject indexes in each issue (with no cumulation). The fourth issue of each year includes a list of periodicals with addresses. Z1671.B52

Library of Congress. Library of Congress Office, Rio de Janeiro. Accessions list, Brazil and Uruguay. v. 15, no. 1 (Jan./Feb. 1989)– . Rio de Janeiro : Library of Congress Office, [1989]– . Bimonthly. **AA511**
Superintendent of Documents classification: LC 1.30/11: .
Supersedes *Accessions list, Brazil*, 1975–88 and continues its numbering.

"Encompasses current Brazilian and Uruguayan materials that are within the scope of the Library's acquisitions policies and hence is not intended to take the place of current national bibliographies."—*Introd.*
Divided by country, then by monographs and serials; arranged alphabetically by main entry with preliminary cataloging supplied by the Library's field office. Entries for serials cumulate annually in a supplement. Z1671.U53a

Chile

Anuario de la prensa chilena. 1877–1975. Santiago de Chile : Pub. por la Biblioteca Nacional, 1887–1979. Annual (Irregular). **AA512**
Annual, 1886–1916. Except for a volume covering 1877–85 (publ. 1952), publication was suspended 1928–62. Resumed with issues covering 5–year periods, though not cumulative: 1917–23, 1922–26, 1927–31 (all publ. 1963); 1932–36 (publ. in 2 pts., 1932–34 and 1935–36), 1937–41, 1942–46, 1947–51, 1952–56 (all publ. 1964); 1957–61 (publ. 1963); annual beginning with the issue for 1962 (publ. 1963).
Catalog of books deposited in the national library under the law of 1872. From 1891, includes books by Chilean authors or relating to Chile published in other countries. An author listing only.
Many volumes contain an appendix of *publicaciones omitidas* from previous volumes. Musical compositions are entered in volumes for 1896–1900.
§ *Servicio bibliográfico chileno,* a bookdealer's listing prepared primarily for foreign customers by the firm Zamorano y Caperan, was published monthly (then quarterly) 1940–71. Although it had no indexes or cumulative features, it served as a useful contemporary record during the long period when the *Anuario* was suspended.
Superseded by *Bibliografía chilena* (AA513). Z1705.A58

Bibliografía chilena. 1976/79– . Santiago, Chile : Ediciones de la Dirección de Bibliotecas, Archivos y Museos, 1981– . Annual. **AA513**
At head of title: Biblioteca Nacional.
Supersedes *Anuario de la prensa chilena* (AA512).
The first volume covers 1976–79; annual thereafter, listing materials received on legal deposit during the year of coverage. Annual volumes are arranged by Dewey Decimal Classification, with a general index. Citations include full bibliographic information and show catalog tracings. Z1701.S23

Biblioteca Nacional (Chile). Impresos chilenos, 1776–1818. Santiago de Chile, 1963. 2 v. : ill., facsims. **AA514**
Contents: v. 1, Bibliografía histórica de la imprenta en Santiago de Chile. Impresos chilenos, 1776–1818, textos. Indice cronológico de los impresos que posee la Biblioteca Nacional, 1776–1818; v. 2, Descripciones bibliográficas de los impresos chilenos, 1776–1818. Textos manuscritos … 1813–14. Indice cronológico de los impresos chilenos, 1776–1818. Indice cronológico de los textos manuscritos.
————. Bibliografía general de Chile, por Emilio Vaisse (Santiago de Chile : Impr. Univ., 1915–[18]. v. 1–2).
Repr. from *Revista de bibliografía chilena y extranjera*.
Contents: 1. pt. Diccionario de autores y obras (bio-bibliografía y bibliografía): t. 1, Bibliografía de bibliografías chilenas. por R. A. Laval. Diccionario; A–Barros Arana; t. 2, Barros Baeza–Bustos.
A biobibliographical dictionary, listing writings of Chilean authors. A supplement to t. 1 is: Ramón Arminio Laval, *Bibliografía de bibliografías chilenas* (*In* Santiago de Chile. Bibliografía general de Chile, 1915. v.1, p.i–lxix) and its *Suplemento y adiciones*, by Herminia Elgueta de Ochsenius (Santiago de Chile : Impr. Cervantes, 1930. 71 p.). Z1702.S3

Briseño, Ramón. Estadística bibliográfica de la literatura chilena / obra compuesta, en virtud de encargo especial del consejo de la Universidad de Chile. Santiago de Chile : Impr. Chilena, 1862–79. 2 v. **AA515**

Contents: t. 1, 1812–1859. Impresos chilenos. Obras sobre Chile. Escritores chilenos; t. 2, 1860–1876. Prólogo. Prensa chilena por órden alfabético. Prensa chilena por órden cronolójico. Prensa periodística chilena. Bibliografía chilena en el país, desde 1812 hasta 1859. Bibliografía chilena en el extranjero, desde 1860 hasta 1876. Curiosidades bibliográfico-chilenas.   Z1701.B85

Medina, José Toribio. Bibliografía de la imprenta en Santiago de Chile desde sus orígenes hasta febrero de 1817. Santiago de Chile : Autor, 1891. 179 p.   **AA516**

Available from Readex Microprint.

Includes no books printed in Chile, only books printed in Europe or America by Chileans or by Spaniards who wrote in Chile. Lists 876 titles chronologically, with critical and bibliographical notes and references to authorities. Locates copies.

————. *Adiciones y ampliaciones* (Santiago de Chile : Univ. de Chile, 1939. 140 p.; ill.).

————. *Biblioteca hispano-chilena (1523–1817)* (Santiago de Chile : Autor, 1897–99. 3 v.). Repr.: Amsterdam : N. israel, 1964.

Montt, Luis. Bibliografía chilena. Santiago de Chile : Impr. Univ., 1904–21. 3 v.   **AA517**

v. 1, 1780–1811 (1918); v. 2, 1812–1817 (1904); v. 3, 1817–1818 (1921).

Of v. 1, 264 pages were printed which the author intended to revise; of v. 3, 160 pages were printed; sheets of both of these were destroyed, but in 1918 and 1921, reprints of the pages as originally printed were issued.   Z1701.M82

Revista de bibliografía chilena / publ. por la Biblioteca Nacional, enero 1913–oct. 1918, 1927–29. Santiago de Chile : Impr. Univ., 1913–29. 9 v.   **AA518**

Quarterly, 1927–29 (1913–18, monthly); 1913–18, have title *Revista de bibliografía chilena y extranjera.* None issued Nov. 1918–26.

No more published.

A valuable contemporary bibliography, which included special bibliographics in addition to the current record.   Z1701.R4

Revista de bibliografía chilena / Biblioteca Nacional de Chile. Santiago de Chile : La Biblioteca, 1927–[29]. Quarterly.   **AA519**

See also the related publication *Revista de bibliografía chilena y extranjera (AA520).*

Revista de bibliografía chilena y extranjera. Año 1, no. 1 (enero 1913)–anako 6, no. 11/12 (nov./dic. 1918). Santiago de Chile : Imprenta Universitaria, 1913–1918.   **AA520**

Monthly. Reproduced in microform: Cambridge, Mass. : General Microfilm Co.

Title page note: "publicado mensualmente por la Sección de Informaciones de la Biblioteca Nacional."

A valuable contemporary bibliography that included special bibliographies in addition to the current record.

See also *Revista de bibliografía chilena (AA519).*

Current

El libro chileno en venta. 1950/75– . [Santiago de Chile] : Servicio de Extensión de Cultura Chilena, [1975]– . Irregular (1979/80 publ. 1982).   **AA521**

An in-print list for Chile. The first issue is intended as "a cumulative catalog of the bibliographical Chilean production between the years 1950–August 1975 ... available in the Chilean book market."— *Foreword.* Subject arrangement by broad Dewey classes, with author and title indexes. Includes prices.

Libros chilenos ISBN. 1989– . Santiago, Chile : Cámara Chilena del Libro, 1989– .   **AA522**

A listing of currently available titles with separate sections arranged by Universal Decimal Classification, by author, and by title. Includes a list of publishers arranged by ISBN.   Z1701.L52

Colombia

Bibliografía colombiana. t. 8 (jul.–dic. 1964)– t. 17 (1972). Gainesville, Fla. : Fermín Peraza, 1964–1972. Annual.   **AA523**

Frequency varies: semiannual, 1964–65; annual, 1966–72. Place of publication varies.

An alphabetical main-entry listing with an author-subject index.

Continues *Fichas para el anuario bibliográfico colombiano* (t. 1 [enero–jun. 1961]– t. 7 [erero–jun. 1964]. 1961 publ. Medellin, Colombia, comp. by Fermín Peraza Sarausa.

Vol. 2 (julio–dic. 1961) publ. in a 2nd ed., 1972.   Z1731.B5

Laverde Amaya, Isidoro. Bibliografía colombiana. Bogotá : M. Rivas, 1895. v. 1 (296 p.).   **AA524**

v. 1, A–O; no more published.

Biobibliography; includes mainly 19th-century publications, with a few of earlier date.   Z1740.L4

Medina, José Toribio. La imprenta en Bogotá (1739–1821) : notas bibliográficas. Santiago de Chile : Impr. Elzeviriana, 1904. 101 p.   **AA525**

Repr.: Amsterdam : N. Israel, 1964.

————. *La imprenta en Cartagena de las Indias (1809–1820) : notas bibliográficas* (Santiago de Chile : Impr. Elzeveriana, 1904. 70 p.).

Repr.: Amsterdam : N. Israel, 1964.

Both are chronological listings with descriptive notes.   Z213.B7M4

Posada, Eduardo. Bibliografía bogotana. Bogotá : Impr. Nacional, 1917–25. 2 v. : facsim. (Biblioteca de historia nacional, v.16, 36).   **AA526**

Arranged chronologically, 1738–1831, with author and subject indexes both alphabetical and by date.   Z1754.B7P8

Current

Anuario bibliográfico colombiano "Rubén Pérez Ortiz". 1963– . Bogotá : Inst. Caro y Cuervo, Dept. de Bibliografía, 1966– .   **AA527**

Continues *Anuario bibliográfico colombiano,* publ. 1951–62.

Lists books, pamphlets, and periodicals published in Colombia, and foreign publications dealing with Colombia. Volumes cover one or two years; publication is relatively current. Classified arrangement, with a name index.   Z1731.A58

Ecuador

Anuario bibliográfico ecuatoriano. 1975– . Quito : Universidad Central del Ecuador, 1976– . Annual.   **AA528**

At head of title: Universidad Central del Ecuador, Biblioteca General.

Represents a cumulation of issues of *Bibliografía ecuatoriana* and includes the 6th number of that series.

A classed listing in two sections: (1) Bibliografía monográfica, and (2) Bibliografía analítica, the latter providing analytics for collective works and selected periodicals. Indexes of names, titles, and subjects.

May have ceased publication.   Z1761.A68

Ecuador : bibliografía analítica. Año 1 (1979)–3 (1981). Cuenca : Centro de Investigación y Cultura del Banco Central del Ecuador, 1979–81.   **AA529**

An effort toward a current national bibliography. In two sections, each subdivided according to the Universal Decimal Classification: (1) Bibliografía monográfica; (2) Bibliografía analítica (which provides references to periodical articles and collective works). Indexes of names and topical subjects.

Continued on an annual basis by: *Anuario bibliográfico ecuatoriano* (AA532).   Z1761.E37

Espinosa Cordero, Nicolás. Bibliografía ecuatoriana, 1534–1809. Cuenca : Impr. del Colegio Nacional "Benigno Malo," 1934. 171 p.   **AA530**
Issued also as pt. 4 of the author's *Estudios literarios y bibliográficos* (Cuenca, 1934. p.93–256).
Includes brief biographical notes of authors.   Z1770.E76

Medina, José Toribio. La imprenta en Quito (1760–1818) : notas bibliográficas. Santiago de Chile : Impr. Elzeviriana, 1904. 86 p.   **AA531**
Repr.: Amsterdam : N. Israel, 1964.
A chronological listing with descriptive notes.   Z213.Q5M4

Current

Anuario bibliográfico ecuatoriano. 1982– . Cuenca : Banco Central del Ecuador, Centro de Investigación y Cultura, c1984– . Annual.   **AA532**
Continues *Ecuador : bibliografía analítica* (AA529).
A listing of books, pamphlets, and periodical articles arranged by broad subject, then alphabetically. Author and corporate author index; subject index. Volume for 1985 has "Indice alfabetico de revistas ... " and a name and corporate author index.   Z1761.E37

Guyana

Guyanese national bibliography. 1973– . Georgetown, Guyana : National Library, [1974]– . Quarterly with annual cumulation [i.e., the 4th issue of the year is the annual cumulation].   **AA533**
"A subject list of new books printed in the Republic of Guyana, based on the books deposited at the National Library, classified according to the Dewey Decimal Classification 16th edition, catalogued according to the British Text of the Anglo-American Cataloguing Rules, 1967 and provided with a full author, title and subject index and a List of Guyanese Publishers."—*t. p., 1973*.
Beginning 1975, includes nonbook materials; classification follows the 18th edition of Dewey; subject entries are omitted from the index; and a "List of single bills, acts, subsidiary legislation and parliamentary debates" forms an appendix to each issue.   Z1791.G88

Paraguay

Bibliografía nacional paraguaya : obras publicados entre los años 1971–1977 / compilada por alumnos y profesores de la Escuela de Bibliotecología. Edición preliminar. Asunción : Univ. Nacional de Asunción, Escuela de Bibliotecologia, 1978. 42 p.   **AA534**
A first attempt to provide retrospective coverage of works published in and about Paraguay. 523 items in an alphabetical subject arrangement.

Biblioteca Nacional (Paraguay). Bibliografía paraguaya : catálogo de la biblioteca paraguaya "Solano López.". Asunción : Talleres Nacionales de H. Kraus, 1906. 984 p. **AA535**
Rich in material relating to the early history of Paraguay.   Z907.A86

Fernández-Caballero, Carlos F. S. The Paraguayan bibliography : a retrospective and enumerative bibliography of printed works of Paraguayan authors. Asunción ; Wash. : Paraguay Arandú Books, 1970–83. 3 v.   **AA536**
Vol. 3 has title: La bibliografia paraguaya, prep. by Marianne Fernandez-Caballero.
Contents: v. 1, Aranduká ha kuatiañeé paraguái rembiapocué; v. 2, Paraguái tai hũme, tove paraguái arandu taisarambi ko yvy apére; v. 3, Paraguái rembiapokúe ha paraguái rehegúa tembiapo añembokuatiavaekúe.
Vol. 2 publ. by the Seminar on the Acquisition of Latin American Library Materials as its Bibliography, no. 3.
Vol. 1 is an author listing of some 1,423 items; v. 2, with some 2,363 entries, extends many of the author bibliographies in v. 1 and lists additional works by Paraguayans and works on Paraguay published from the 18th century to 1974; in addition to having its own subject index, v. 2 provides a separate subject index to v. 1. Vol. 3 is an author listing of some 3,550 unannotated entries that supplement v. 1–2. Includes additional works by Paraguayans and foreign works on Paraguay published 1975–82. Some earlier imprints not previously listed are also included; has its own subject index.   Z1821.F45

Paraguay ... años de bibliografía. Asunción, Paraguay : Cromos, 198?– .   **AA537**
Compiler: Margarita Kallsen.
Published at intervals: ... *cinco años de bibliografía, 1980–1984* (publ. 1986); ... *dos años de bibliografía, 1985–1986* (publ. 1987); ... *un año de bibliografía, 1987* (publ. 1988); ... *dos años de bibliografía, 1988–1989* (publ. 1990).
Serie Bibliografía paraguaya, 4–5, 7–8.
Publisher varies.
An annotated bibliography of books, journals, and official publications published in Paraguay or about Paraguay published abroad. The five-year list includes more than 1,400 titles, the first two-year list 450, the one-year list 289. Appendixes list publications omitted from prior lists.   Z1821.P37

Peru

Biblioteca Nacional (Peru). Bibliografía nacional. enero/marzo 1978–nov./dic. 1982. Lima : Biblioteca Nacional, Instituto Nacional de Cultura, 1978–1982.   **AA538**
On cover: Libros, artículos de revistas y periódicos.
A combined national bibliography and periodical index. Employs a classed arrangement, with separate sections for books and pamphlets and for periodical articles. Contents notes or brief annotations are provided for most entries. Index of names and broad subjects.
     Z1851.P47a

Biblioteca peruana : apuntos para un catálogo de impresos.... Santiago de Chile : Biblioteca del Inst. Nacional, 1896. 2 v.   **AA539**
Repr.: Naarden : Anton W. van Bekhoven, 1970.
Ed. by Gabriel René-Moreno.
Contents: v. 1, pts. 1–2, Libros y folletos peruanos de la Biblioteca del Instituto Nacional; v. 2, pts. 1–2, Libros y folletos peruanos de la Biblioteca Nacional y notas bibliográficas.
A basic work, fully annotated.   Z1851.B58

Medina, José Toribio. La imprenta en Lima (1584–1824). Santiago de Chile : Autor, 1904–07. 4v.   **AA540**
Repr.: Amsterdam : N. Israel, 1965; also Readex Microprint.
———. *La imprenta en Arequipa, el Cuzco, Trujillo y otros pueblos del Perú durante las campañas de la independencia (1820–1825) : notas bibliográficas* (Santiago de Chile : Impr. Elzeviriana, 1904. 71 p.). Repr.: Amsterdam : N. Israel, 1964; also Readex Microprint.   Z213.L5M4

Universidad de San Marcos (Lima). Biblioteca. Boletin bibliográfico. v. 1 (1923)–39 (1966). Lima : [Biblioteca?], 1923–66. Quarterly (irregular). **AA541**

Suspended 1930–Oct. 1934 and 1967–72; a cumulative issue for the latter period was planned for 1973 publication. Ceased publication.

Usually each year includes a list of books and pamphlets published in Peru, with full bibliographical information, and a list of articles from Peruvian periodicals. Z782.L77B

Vargas Ugarte, Rubén. Impresos peruanos. Lima : [Ed. San Marcos], 1949–57. 7 v. in 6. (Biblioteca peruana, t. 6–12). **AA542**

Contents: v. 1, Impresos peruanos publicados en el extranjero 1546–1825; v. 2–7, Impresos peruanos 1584–1825.

Aims to include all books and pamphlets published in Peru; arranged chronologically, with author index in each volume. Line-by-line transcription, with detailed bibliographical description. Locates copies. Vol. 1 is concerned with publications appearing outside Peru. Z1866.V3

Current

Anuario bibliográfico peruano. v. 1 (1943)–[1983?]. Lima : [Biblioteca Nacional], 1945–[1983?]. **AA543**

Frequency varies: annual 1943–48; biennial 1949/50–1953/54; triennial from 1955/57. (1970/72 publ. 1978).

A national bibliography that attempts to record books, pamphlets, and all other publications printed in Peru, as well as works of Peruvian authors and works relating to Peru printed abroad. Classified, with indexes of periodicals, authors, etc.

Each volume includes a section of periodicals and newspapers, and a separate biobibliographical section of Peruvian authors who died during the years covered. These bibliographies are extensive and are indexed separately.

Ceased 1983. Continued by *Bibliografía peruana* (1984–1986– . Lima : Biblioteca Nacional del Perú, Dirección General de Bibliografía National y Ediciones, 1992–). Z1851.A5

Biblioteca Nacional (Peru). Catalogo de autores de la colección peruana. Boston : G. K. Hall, 1979. 6 v. **AA544**

Added title page: Author catalog of the Peruvian Collection, National Library of Peru.

Contents: v. 1–5, Libros y folletos; v. 6, Publicaciones periódicas; Mapas y planos.

An author listing of some 94,000 books, pamphlets, periodicals, and maps, published 1553–1977; includes works by Peruvian authors and works about Peru. Z1879.P47

Uruguay

Estrada, Dardo. Historia y bibliografía de la imprenta en Montevideo, 1810–1865. Montevideo : Librería Cervantes, 1912. 318 p. **AA545**

Chronological arrangement.

Supplemented by: Horacio Arredondo, *Bibliografía uruguaya: contribución* (Montevideo : El Siglo Ilustrado, 1929. 182 p. ill.).

"Apartado de lo Revista del Instituto Histórico y Geográfico del Uruguay, t. 6, no. 2."—*t. p.*

Arranged chronologically, 1559–1865. Line-by-line transcription. Locates copies. Also available in Readex Microprint. Z213.M7E8

Current

Anuario bibliográfico uruguayo. 1946– . Montevideo : Biblioteca Nacional, 1947– . Annual. **AA546**

Volumes covering 1950–67 not published.

Lists books and pamphlets in classed arrangement with author index. Beginning with the volume covering 1968 a section for periodicals was added, with listings by title and subject classes. Supplements are issued periodically. Z1881.A5

Bibliografía uruguaya. v. 1 (1962)– . Montevideo : Biblioteca del Poder Legislativo, 1962– . Irregular. **AA547**

Frequency varies: began publication as a quarterly in 1962, annual volumes were issued for 1963–64, and a list of addenda for 1963 was publ. 1966. These issues are superseded by a cumulative volume covering 1962–68, publ. 1971 in two volumes. 1969/72 publ. 1977 in two volumes; 1973/77 published in 1983 in two volumes; 1978/80 publ. 1989; annual since 1989. Not publ. 1981–88?

Began publication during the hiatus of the *Anuario bibligrafico uruguayo* (AA546). Arrangement has varied; currently arranged by title with author, subject, publisher, and printer indexes. Z1881.M76

Venezuela

Anuario bibliográfico venezolano. 1942–54–1975–76. Caracas : Tipografía Americana, 1944–79. Irregular. **AA548**

At head of title: República de Venezuela. Biblioteca Nacional, Caracas.

Publisher varies.

Frequency varies. Suspended 1955–66.

Lists books, pamphlets, government publications, etc., and periodical articles. The second volume of the 1949/54 issue was devoted to material about Venezuela published abroad. A well-arranged classed list with author, subject, and title index, and an index of printers.

Replaced by *Bibliografía venezolana* (AA552). Z1881.A5

Bibliografía venezolana. Año 1, no.1 (enero/marzo 1970)–[5] (jul./sept. 1974). Caracas : Biblioteca Nacional, Centro Bibliográfico Venezolano, 1970–74. Quarterly. **AA549**

On cover: BV; Bibliografía venezolana.

Published concurrently with *Anuario bibliográfico venezolano* (AA548).

Classed arrangement. The first issue lists publications of the final months of 1969.

Replaced by *Bibliografía venezolana* (AA552). Z1881.M76

Drenikoff, Iván. Impresos venezolanos del siglo XIX. Caracas : Instituto Autónomo Biblioteca Nacional y de Servicios de Bibliotecas, 1984. 238 p. **AA550**

Offers an alphabetical listing of publications, excluding periodicals, but including broadsheets, leaflets, and books, produced in Venezuela, 1808 30. Gives locations in South American and major North American and European libraries. Chronological index and an index of printers arranged by city. Z213.V45D64

Villasana, Angel Raúl. Ensayo de un repertorio bibliográfico venezolano. Caracas, 1969–79. 6 v. (Banco Central de Venezuela. Colección cuatricentenario de Caracas, 8). **AA551**

On cover: (Años 1808–1950).

A bibliography for the period 1808–1950. Includes books and pamphlets by Venezuelans published both at home and abroad, and works by foreigners published in Venezuela. Works appearing in anthologies and collections are also noted. Concerned with works of literature, history and general culture; scientific and technical works are excluded. Many descriptive and explanatory notes.

Continued by: Villasana's *Nuevo repertorio bibliográfico venezolano : años 1951–1975* (Caracas : Inst. Autónomo Biblioteca Nacional y de Servicios de Bibliotecas ; Fundacíon para el rescate del Acervo Documental Venezolano, 1989. v. 1 [In progress]).

Like its predecessor, excludes scientific works. Offers extremely detailed contents and explanatory notes. Indicates the location of the copy described. A list of the major bibliographies consulted appears on p. 563–573. Z1921.V5

Current

Bibliografía venezolana. v. 1 (1980)– . [Caracas] : Instituto Autónomo Biblioteca Nacional y de Servicios de Bibliotecas, 1982– . Quarterly with annual cumulation.   **AA552**
  Continues: *Bibliografía venezolana* (AA549). The first issue lists publications of the final months of 1969. Also continues *Anuario bibliográfico venezolano* (AA548).
  Classed arrangement.   Z1911.B52

Boletín ISBN, Venezuela. No. 1 (1987)– . Caracas : Instituto Autónomo Biblioteca Nacional y de Servicios de Bibliotecas, Dirección de Formación de Colecciones, Agencia Nacional del ISBN, 1987– . Annual.   **AA553**
  A register of Venezuelan publications assigned International Standard Book numbers, the 1987 issue covering 1985–86. Arranged by Dewey Decimal Classification, with indexes by ISBN, authors, and titles. Useful list of publishers with addresses.   Z1911.B64

Caribbean and Islands of the Western Atlantic

Bibliografía actual del Caribe = Current Caribbean bibliography. v. 1 (1950)–23 (1973). Hato Rey, P.R. : Caribbean Regional Libr., 1951–1976. Annual (irregular).   **AA554**
  Title varies: early vols. called *Current Caribbean bibliography*. Publisher varies.
  Early issues have subtitle: An alphabetical list of publications issued in the Caribbean countries of France, Great Britain, the Netherlands, and the U. S.
  Cumulations have been published as follows: 1950–53, publ. 1955; 1954–58, publ. 1961; 1959–61 publ. 1968. Beginning with the 1959–61 cumulative issue, listing is by Universal Decimal Classification with author-title-subject index.   Z1595.C8

The CARICOM bibliography. v. 1 (1977)–v. 10, no. 1 & 2 (Jan.–Dec. 1986). Georgetown, Guyana : Caribbean Community Secretariat Library, 1977–86. Biennial.   **AA555**
  Subtitle: A cumulated subject list of current national imprints of the Caribbean Community member countries, arranged according to the Dewey Decimal Classification, 18th ed., and catalogued according to the British text of the Anglo-American rules (1967) and the International Standard Bibliographic Description for Monographs and Serials.
  Frequency varies; annual 1977–79.
  Aims "to list all material currently published" (*Pref.*) in Antigua, Bahamas, Barbados, Belize, Dominica, Grenada, Guyana, Jamaica, Montserrat, St. Kitts/Nevis/Anguilla, St. Lucia, St. Vincent, Trinidad and Tobago. Full information appears in the classified section; index of authors, titles, series. Excludes periodicals (except first issue, changes of title, and annual reports) and certain types of government publications. Vol. 1 covers mainly 1976 publications, with some of earlier date.   Z1501.C35a

University of Florida. Libraries. Catalog Dept. Caribbean acquisitions. 1957/58–1979. Gainesville : Univ. of Florida, 1959–80. Annual.   **AA556**
  Issued 1959–62 by Technical Processing Dept.
  Lists books, pamphlets, periodicals, newspapers, and microforms published in or about the Caribbean area, as well as books by authors from the area. Covers the West Indies and Bermuda; Colombia, Venezuela, and the Guianas; Central America and Mexico. Titles in the humanities and social sciences predominate. Classed arrangement with author index.   Z1601.F55

Barbados

The national bibliography of Barbados. Jan./Mar. 1975– . Bridgetown, Barbados : Public Library, 1975– . Quarterly, the 4th issue being an annual cumulation.   **AA557**
  Intends "to list all new works published in Barbados; as well as those works of Barbadian authorship published abroad."—*Pref.* Classed arrangement according to Dewey Decimal Classification, with author/title/series index.

Bermuda

Bermuda national bibliography. 1983– . [Hamilton] : Bermuda Lib., Tech. Serv., [1984]– . Quarterly, with annual cumulation.   **AA558**
  The 1983 volume was issued as an annual only; subsequent issues are to appear quarterly.
  A classed listing (by Dewey Decimal Classification) with an author/title/series index. Includes works about Bermuda and Bermudians, published both locally and abroad, works published in Bermuda on other subjects, and works published abroad by Bermudians. There is a separate listing of periodical publications; also lists published and unpublished government reports.

Cuba

Anuario bibliográfico cubano. 1937–66. Gainesville, Fla. : Anuario Bibliográfico Cubano, 1938–67. 30 v.   **AA559**
  Through 1959 (publ. 1960) published in Havana.
  Ed. by Fermín Peraza Sarausa.
  An annual with arrangement varying from year to year, but each issue giving excellent coverage. Beginning with the 1953 volume the series appeared with the cover title *Bibliografía cubana*, and that title is used in the prefaces, etc.
  The 1956 volume appeared in a 2nd ed. in 1966, adding 225 new entries and employing a different arrangement from the earlier edition.
  Bibliografía cubana. Complementos: 1937–61, compilados por Fermín Peraza [Sarausa]. (Gainsville, Fla. : Univ. of Florida Libraries, 1966. 233 p).
  Cumulates the addenda sections published in the *Annuario* for years 1937–59, together with previously unpublished entries for 1960–61.   Z1511.A61

Bachiller y Morales, Antonio. Catálogo de libros y folletos publicados en Cuba : desde la introducción de la imprenta hasta 1840. (*In his Apuntes para la historia de las letras y de la instrucción publica de la Isla de Cuba* [Havana : P. Mas-sana, 1861. v. 3, p. 121–241]).   **AA560**
  Repr. in his *Apuntes* ... (Havana : Cultural, 1936–37. v. 3, p. 243–457).
  Arranged chronologically. No index.
  ———. ——— *Suplementos y adiciones* (Revista de Cuba 7:354–64, 491–98; 8:71–78, 124–35, abril, mayo, julio, agosto 1880).

Medina, José Toribio. La imprenta en la Habana (1707–1810) : notas bibliográficas. Santiago de Chile : Impr. Elzeviriana, 1904. 199 p.   **AA561**
  Repr.: Amsterdam : N. Israel, 1964.
  Chronological listing with brief descriptive notes.   Z213.H2M4

Revolutionary Cuba : a bibliographical guide, 1966–68. Coral Gables, Fla. : Univ. of Miami Pr., 1967–70. Annual.   **AA562**
  Fermín Peraza Sarausa, ed., 1966–67.

Supersedes *Anuario bibliográfico cubano* (AA559). Scope broadened to include materials about, as well as those published in, Cuba since the establishment of the Castro regime. Main entry listing with analytical index.   Z1511.A653

Trelles y Govín, Carlos Manuel. Ensayo de bibliografía cubana de los siglos XVII y XVIII : seguido de unos apuntes para la bibliografía dominicana y portorriqueña. Matanzas : "El Escritorio," 1907–1908. 228 p., and suppl., 76 p.   **AA563**

Basic bibliography and related works below all available in microprint.

Continued by:

(1) ———. *Bibliografía cubana del siglo XIX* (Matanzas : Quirós y Estrada, 1911–15. 8 v.)

Contents: t.1, 1800–1825; t. 2, 1826–1840. Seguide de una relación de periódicos publicados en Cuba en el siglo XX, por F. Llaca, y unas Noticias curiosas referentes á escritores de los siglos XVII y XVIII, por M. Perez Beato; t. 3–8, 1841–1899. Ensayo de biblioteca cubana del siglo XIX; Indice.

(2) ———. *Bibliografía cubana del siglo XX (1900–1919)* (Matanzas : Quirós y Estrada, 1916–17. 2 v.)

These two volumes, with those cited above, make up what is termed the compiler's *Bibliografía cubana*.

(3) ———. *Biblioteca científica cubana* (Matanzas : J.F. Oliver, 1918–20. 2 v.).

Lists 9,500 titles of books and periodical articles.

(4) ———. *Biblioteca geográfica cubana* (Mantanzas : J.F. Oliver, 1920–25. 340 p. and suppl., 64 p.).

Main work and supplement list 3,900 titles of books and periodical articles.

(5) ———. *Biblioteca histórica cubana* (Mantanzas : J.F. Oliver, 1922–26. 3 v.).

Lists 17,000 titles of books and periodical articles.   Z1511.T85

Current

Bibliografía cubana. 1917/20– . La Habana : Consejo Nacional de Cultura, 1978– . Annual.   **AA564**

Continues Carlos Manuel Trelles y Govín, *Bibliografía cubana del siglo XX* (Matanzas : Quirós y Estrada, 1916–17).

Vols. for 1917/20–1963/64 issued by the Departamento Colección Cubana, Biblioteca Nacional José Martí; 1965– by the library. 1917–36 issued in 5 v., each covering four years; each volume provides annual main-entry lists of publications from the years of coverage, with a combined index for the full volume. Vols. for 1937–62 not yet published.   Z1511.B5

Dominican Republic

Anuario bibliográfico dominicano. 1946– . Santo Domingo [etc.] : Biblioteca Nacional, 1946– .   **AA565**

Not published 1948–77.

Supersedes *Boletín bibliográfico dominicano* of which only two numbers were published: no. 1, July–August 1945, which covered 1944, and no. 2, Sept.–Dec. 1945, which covered 1945.

Subject arrangement; author index. Not published after 1983?   Z1533.A58

Haiti

Bissainthe, Max. Dictionnaire de bibliographie haïtienne. Wash. : Scarecrow, 1951. 1052 p.   **AA566**

Includes three main bibliographic lists, each arranged alphabetically and covering: (1) works published in Haiti, or by Haitians abroad, Jan. 1804–Dec. 1949; (2) works published in Hispaniola and Santo Domingo, or concerning them, from the beginning to 1949; (3) newspapers and periodicals from Santo Domingo and Haiti, 1764–

1949, and an index of journalists working on them. Title and subject indexes. Many entries have brief annotations—both bio- and bibliographical—and library locations are given. Complements Ulrick Duvivier, *Bibliographie générale et méthodique d'Haiti* (AA567).

———. ———. *Supplement* (Metuchen, N.J. : Scarecrow, 1973. 269 p.).

Covers publications of the 1950–70 period, plus some older works.

§ Max Manigat's *Haitiana 1971–1975 (Bibliographie haïtienne)* (LaSalle, Quebec : Collectif Paroles, 1980. 83 p.) provides a year-by-year listing of publications by Haitians and others on Haiti, Santo Domingo, Hispaniola, and related subjects, plus an appendix of works not listed in the supplement to Bissainthe's bibliography.

Haitian publications : an acquisitions guide and bibliography by Lygia Maria F. C. Ballantyne (Wash. : Library of Congress, Processing Serv., Hispanic Acquisitions Project, 1979. 53 p.), in addition to supplying information on the book trade and noncommercial publishing, includes as appendixes directories of bookstores and publishers in Haiti, an annotated list of current serial titles, and a checklist of Haitian monographs, 1970–79.   Z1531.B5

Duvivier, Ulrick. Bibliographie générale et méthodique d'Haïti. Port-au-Prince, Haïti : Impr. de l'État, 1941. 2 v.   **AA567**

Covers material published in Haiti from the earliest period to date of publication. Classed arrangement; no index.   Z1531.D88

Jamaica

Jamaican national bibliography. v. 1 (Jan./Mar. 1975)– . Kingston, Jamaica : Institute of Jamaica, West India Reference Library, 1975– . Quarterly, with annual cumulations.   **AA568**

Vols. for 1978– issued by the National Library of Jamaica.

Lists books, pamphlets, first issues or changes of serials, annual reports, government publications, maps and atlases, and audiovisual materials published in Jamaica, as well as works about Jamaica or by Jamaicans published outside the country and received at the National Library of Jamaica. Not based on depository law. Indexed.

Continues a publication by the same title which ceased with v. 74, covering 1970. The earlier title superseded *Jamaican accessions* (1965–67) and, like that publication, was based on the accessions of the West India Reference Library, with additional entries (beginning 1967) from the Jamaica Library Service and the Library of the University of the West Indies.

Partially cumulated by: Institute of Jamaica, Kingston. *The Jamaican national bibliography, 1964–1974* (Millwood, N.Y. : Kraus International, [1981]. 439 p.).

"This bibliography represents a cumulation of the entries in the 1964–1970 *Jamaican National Bibliography*, which was published in 1973, and the titles of those Jamaican publications acquired and cataloged by the West India Reference Library, Institute of Jamaica, between 1971 and 1974."—*Pref.* In addition, works published in Jamaica in 1963 have been included, as have works by Jamaicans published outside Jamaica, and works about Jamaica published elsewhere. Arrangement is by broad subject categories, with an index of authors, editors, corporate bodies, and titles. Separate list of Jamaican periodicals and newspapers.   Z1541.J27

Puerto Rico

Anuario bibliográfico puertorriqueño. v. 1 (1948)– . San Juan, P. R. : Biblioteca General, Univ. de Puerto Rico, Recinto de Río Piedras, 1948– .   **AA569**

Publisher varies. Frequency varies.

An author, subject, and title listing of books, pamphlets, and periodicals. Publication frequently lags.   Z1551.A6

Trinidad and Tobago

Trinidad and Tobago national bibliography. v. 1 (Jan./June 1975)– . [Port of Spain] : Central Library of Trinidad and Tobago, 1975– . Quarterly, with annual cumulation.   **AA570**
"A subject list of material published and printed in Trinidad and Tobago, classified according to the Dewey Decimal Classification, 18th edition, cataloged according to the British Text of the Anglo-American Cataloguing Rules, 1967 and the International Standard Bibliographic Description for Monographs and Serials. It is provided with a full author, title and series index and a list of Trinidad and Tobago publishers."—*t. p., v. 1.*
    Aims to list all works published and printed in Trinidad and Tobago, omitting only certain government publications (e.g., acts, bills, gazettes).   Z1561.T7T74

Europe (by country)

Albania

Bibliografia kombëtare e librit që botohet në RPS të Shqipërisë / Biblioteka Kombëtare, Sektori i Bibliografisë. Viti 27, 1 (Jan.–Mar. 1986)– . Tiranë : Biblioteka, 1986– . Quarterly.   **AA571**
    Continues: *Bibliografia kombëtare e Republikës Popullore të Shqipërise : libri shqip*, 1958–85.
    The current national bibliography, listing books, pamphlets, and official publications. Classed listing with author index.
    Z2854.A5B53

Legrand, Emile Louis Jean. Bibliographie albanaise : description raisonnée des ouvrages pub. en albanais ou relatifs à l'Albanie du 15. siècle à l'année 1900 / oeuvre posthume, compl. et pub. par Henri Gûys. Paris : Welter, 1912. 228 p.   **AA572**
    Lists books in Albanian and other languages, published in or relating to Albania, 1474–1900. Chronological with author and subject indexes.
    Continued by: Jup Kastrati, *Bibliografi shqipe, 29.XI.1944–31.XII.1958* (Tiranë : N. Sh. Botimeve "Naim frashëri," 1959. 498 p.).
    A classified listing of Albanian publications of the period; author index.   Z2854.A5L3

Austria

Langer, Eduard. Bibliographie der österreichischen Drucke des XV. und XVI. Jahrhunderts / hrsg. von dr. Eduard Langer. Wien : Gilhofer & Ranschburg, 1913. 171 p. : facsim.   **AA573**
    Bd. 1, Hft. 1, Trient-Wien-Schrattenthal, bearb. von dr. Walther Dolch.
    No more published.   Z133.L27

Oesterreichische Bibliographie. 1945–1986. Wien : Verein des österr. Buch- Kunst-, Musikalien-, Zeitungs- und Zeitschriftenhändler, 1945–86.   **AA574**
    Publisher varies.
    Ed. by Österreichische Nationalbibliothek.
    Frequency varies: 1945, annual; 1946, quarterly; 1947–48, monthly; 1949–1986, semimonthly, with quarterly indexes and annual cumulated indexes.
    A listing of trade publications that also includes university and official publications, newspapers, periodicals, and music scores. Beginning in 1961, music was listed in an annual *Sonderheft* entitled "Praktische Musik." Classified, with author and subject index.

In 1987, split into three parts: Reihe A, *Verzeichnis der Österreichischen Neuerscheinungen* (AA575); Reihe B, *Verzeichnis der Österreichischen Hochschulschriften* (1987–); and Reihe C, *Neuere ausländische Austraiaca: Auswahlbibliographie* (1983–), a selective listing of foreign titles about Austria; vols. for 1983 and 1984 were published in 1991.

Current

Oesterreichische Bibliographie. Reihe A : Verzeichnis der österreichischen Neuerscheinungen. nr. 1/2 (15 Jän. 1987)– . Wien : Hauptverband der österreichischen Buchhandels, 1987– . Twice a month, with 3 quarterly indexes and annual index.   **AA575**
    Ed. by Österreichische Nationalbibliothek.
    A listing of current trade publications arranged by broad subject; excludes periodicals. Music continues to be listed in the annual *Sonderheft* "Praktische Music." Each issue has author and title index, which cumulate into three quarterly indexes and an annual index.
    Z2105.O33

Belgium

Bibliographie nationale : dictionnaire des écrivains belges et catalogue de leurs publications, 1830–80. Bruxelles : P. Weissenbruch, 1886–1910. 4 v.   **AA576**
    Aims to furnish a comprehensive record, for the period 1830–80, of works by Belgian authors (either citizens or residents of the country), published either in Belgium or abroad, with record also of earlier works by the same authors and of periodicals with which they were associated as either editors or regular contributors. Includes books, pamphlets, official publications, many reprints from periodicals and newspapers, name (frequently with brief biographical data), title, place, publisher, date, size, paging, illustrations, price. Contents and other notes are frequently included, especially notes of reprints from periodicals.   Z2401.B586

Bibliotheca belgica : bibliographie générale des Pays-Bas / fondée [par] Ferdinand van der Haeghen. Re-éditée sous la direction de Marie-Thérèse Lenger. Bruxelles : Culture et Civilisation, 1964–75. 7 v. : ill.   **AA577**
    Contents: v. 1–5, A–Z; v. 6, Supplément; v. 7, Index général.
    Originally published in irregular order in 240 *livraisons*, 1880–1967, now reassembled and published in quarto volumes in alphabetical sequence.
    Includes works of the 15th and 16th centuries (with some inclusion of important later works) printed in Belgium and Holland, and books by Belgian and Dutch authors printed elsewhere, giving for each work listed: full title, imprint and collation, location of copies, and often full bibliographical and historical notes with biographical notes about authors and references to sources. The new edition makes this valuable collection of material easily available for the first time, through the rearrangement and the addition of indexes of authors, editors, and printers in v. 6, and a detailed general index in v. 7.
    Z2401.B6

Cockx-Indestege, Elly. Belgica typographica, 1541–1600 : catalogus librorum impressorum ab anno MDXLI ad annum MDC in regionibus quae nunc Regni Belgarum partes sunt / Elly Cockx-Indestege, Geneviève Glorieux. Nieuwkoop : B. de Graaf, 1968–80. 2 v. (Nationaal Centrum voor de Archeologie en de Geschiedenis van het Boek, 2).   **AA578**
    No more published?
    A series designed to record all works published in Belgium to 1600. Vol. 1 deals with the collections of the Bibliothèque Royale de Belgique; v. 2 describes works of the period in 40 libraries throughout Belgium. Other Belgian and selected foreign libraries are to be sur-

veyed for future volumes. The work is part of a larger project to establish a catalog of all pre-1601 imprints from the Low Countries.

Z2402.C6

Coopman, Theophiel. Bibliographie van den Vlaamschen taalstrijd / Theophiel Coopman, Jan Broeckaert. Gent : Siffer, 1904–14. 10 v.   **AA579**
> Contents: v. 1–10, 1787–1886.
> A bibliography of Flemish-language materials.   Z2424.F5C7

Foppens, Jean François. Bibliotheca belgica : sive Virorum in Belgio vitâ, scriptisque illustrium catalogus, librorumque nomenclatura continens scriptores à clariss / viris Valerio Andrea, Auberto Miraeo, Francisco Sweetio, aliisque, recensitos, usque ad annum MDCLXXX. Bruxellis : P. Foppens, 1738. 2 v.   **AA580**
> Includes writers of the various Low Countries, arranged alphabetically by Latin form of the name, giving brief biographical notices and lists of their writings. Covers from earliest printing to 1680. Indexes by place and by religious order.   Z2410.F69

Vlaamsche bibliographie : lijst der boeken, vlug- en tijdschriften, muziekwerken, kaarten, platen en tabellen, in België van 1830 tot 1890 verschenen / uitg. op last der Koninklijke Vlaamsche Academie voor taal- en letterkunde door Fr. de Potter. Gent : Siffer, 1893–[1902]. 894 p.   **AA581**
> Lists the Flemish books published in Belgium. Classified, with author index. Incorporates material included in the various editions of the *Vlaamsche bibliographie*, by F. A. Snellaert (1851–88).

Z2424.F5V7

Current

Bibliographie de Belgique : liste mensuelle des publications belges ou relatives à la Belgique, acquises par la Bibliothèque Royale. année 1 (1875)– . Bruxelles : Bibliothèque Royale, 1875– . Monthly.   **AA582**
> Title (*Belgische bibliografie*) and headings also in Dutch.
> This bibliography has undergone many changes in title, scope, plan, editor, and publisher. For the history of these, and for a collation by volumes of the set to 1931, see "Histoire des transformations de la Bibliographie de Belgique," in *Bibliographie de Belgique* 57 (1931) : 356–98. As at present organized, aims to cover books, pamphlets, etc., issued in Belgium; books by Belgian authors published abroad; and books by foreigners relating to Belgium. For 1959–74, these latter were listed in a *Fascicule spécial*, "Liste annuelle des publications d'auteurs belges à l'étranger et des publications étrangères relatives à la Belgique …" with separate indexes. Periodicals are included in a separate part through 1926. Beginning with v. 108 (1982) the bibliography appears in 12 monthly issues with indexes, all parts cumulating annually, plus three supplements: A, Publications in series (also included in the monthly issues); B, Maps and atlases; C, Music. In 1984 a semi-monthly section entitled "Publications annoncées" was added; it provides CIP information on forthcoming publications some three or four months prior to their appearance; after publication, the full bibliographic information is published in the regular issue of the *Bibliographie*.
> A classified list with author, title, and subject indexes. Information given for each entry is in full catalog form and includes author's name, full title, place, publisher, date, size, illustrations, and usually price.   Z2405.B58

Bulgaria

Bŭlgarski knigopis : natsionalna bibliografiĭa na NR Bŭlgariĭa. Sofia : [Narodna Biblioteka], 1897–1973.   **AA583**
> Frequency varies: annual, 1897–1944; quarterly, 1945–48; monthly, 1949–68; biweekly, 1969–73.

Title varies; subtitle varies; publisher varies. From 1897 to 1952, issued by the National Library; 1953–63, by the Bulgarian Bibliographical Institute (Bulgarski Bibliografski Institut); 1964–73, by the National Library.
> Lists books and new periodicals. Classified arrangement with annual author indexes; beginning 1969 an annual cumulation superseded the biweekly issues. The 1973 annual bears the title of the new series.
> § Continued by: *Natsionalna bibliografiĭa na NR Bŭlgariĭa* (1974–90), then by *Natsionalna bibliografiĭa na Republika Bŭlgariĭa* (AA589).   Z2893.B85

Narodna biblioteka "Kiril i Metodiĭ". Bŭlgarska vŭzrozhdenska knizhnina : analitichen repertoar na bŭlgarskite knigi i periodichni izdaniĭa, 1806–1878 / sŭstavil Man'o Stoĭanov. Pod red. na Aleksandŭr K. Burmov. Sofia : Nauka i Izkustvo, 1957–59. 2 v.   **AA584**
> An exhaustive listing of books and periodical articles, with various indexes: chronological, subject, etc. Nearly 30,000 entries.

Z2898.A4S6

Narodna biblioteka "Kiril i Metodii". Bŭlgarski knigi, 1878–1944 : bibliografski ukazatel. Sofia : Narodna Biblioteka, 1978–1983. 6 v.   **AA585**
> An author listing of Bulgarian imprints.   Z2891.S64

Paprikoff, George I. Works of Bulgarian emigrants : an annotated bibliography : books, booklets, dissertations. Chicago : S.K. Paprikoff, 1985. 693 p., [1] leaf of plates : port.   **AA586**
> A chronological listing of 1,579 monographs, dissertations, and conference proceedings published in any language and in any country from 1944 through 1983. For each, gives author, title in original and English language, bibliographic details, and often the table of contents. Indexed by author, genre (biographies, calenders, dissertations) or broad topic, language, and country.   Z2891.P36

Pogorelov, Valerii Aleksandrovich. Opis na starite pechatani bulgarski knigi, 1802–1877 g. Sofiĭa : Dzhrzh. Pechatnitsa, 1923. 795 p.   **AA587**
> At head of title: Narodna biblioteka v Sofiĭa.
> A detailed bibliography of publications from the earliest period of Bulgarian printing. Chronological arrangement with author index.
> A list of additions compiled by Charles Jelavich from the Library of Congress collections appeared in that Library's *Quarterly journal of current acquisitions* 14 (1957): 93–94.   Z2891.P75

Teodorov-Balan, Aleksandŭr. Bŭlgarski knigopis za sto godini, 1806–1905. Sofia : Drzhavna Pcchatnitsa, 1909. 1667 p.   **AA588**
> A century of Bulgarian bibliography. More than 15,000 entries; author listing with classified subject index.   Z2891.T4

Current

Natsionalna bibliografiĭa na NR Bŭlgariĭa. Sofiia : Narodna Biblioteka "Kiril i Metodii", 1974–1990. [various numberings].   **AA589**
> Continues *Bŭlgarski knigopis : natsionalna bibliografiĭa na NR Bŭlgariĭa* (AA583).
> Beginning 1974, the various bibliographic services for Bulgaria are brought together under a general title and issued by the National Library. The following series are included:
> Ser. 1, *Bŭlgarski knigopis : knigi, notni, graficheski i kartigrafski izdaniĭa.* v. 78– . 1974– . Bi-weekly with annual cumulation. Subtitle also in English: Books, music, prints, maps. Supersedes, in part, *Bŭlgarski knigopis* and continues its numbering.
> Ser. 2, *Bŭlgarski knigopis : sluzhebni izdaniĭa i disertatsii.* v. 78– . 1974– . Monthly with annual index. Subtitle also in English: Official publications and dissertations. Supersedes, in part, *Bŭlgarski knigopis* and continues its volume numbering. The entries for dissertations are also included in *Bŭlgarski disertatsii.* 1973– (publ. 1974–). Annual.

Ser. 3, *Bŭlgarski gramofonni plochi*. 1972– (publ. 1974–). Annual.

Ser. 4, *Bŭlgarski periodichen pechat*. 1972– (publ. 1974–). Annual. Title also in English: Bulgarian periodicals, newspapers, journals, bulletins and periodical collections. Supersedes a publication of the same title covering 1965–71. Includes all periodical publications listed in the bi-weekly issues of Ser. 2 (above) as well as non-official serial publications. *See also* AD86.

Ser. 5, *Letopis na statiite ot bŭlgarskite spisaniĩa i sbornitsi*. v. 23– . 1974– . Bi-weekly. Title also in English: Articles from Bulgarian journals and collections. Supersedes and continues the volume numbering of a publication of the same title covering 1972–73, which in turn partially superseded *Letopis na periodichnaia pechat*.

Ser. 6, *Letopis na statiite ot bŭlgarskite vestnitsi*. v. 23– , 1974– . Monthly. Title also in English: Articles from Bulgarian newspapers. Supersedes and continues the volume numbering of a publication of the same title covering 1972–73, which in turn partially superseded *Letopis na periodichnaĩa pechat* (AD304); *see* AE46.

Ser. 7, *Bŭlgariĩa v chuzhdata literatura (Bŭlgarika)*. 1972– (publ. 1974–). Annual. Title also in English: Bulgaria in foreign literature. Continues a publication of the same title covering 1964–71.

Ser. 8, *Bibliografiia na bŭlgarskata bibliografiĩa*. 1973– (publ. 1974–). Annual. Title also in English: Bibliography of Bulgarian bibliographies. Continues a publication of the same title covering 1963–72.

Continued by: *Natsionalna bibliografiĩa na Republika Bŭlgariĩa* (Sofiĩa : Narodna Biblioteka "Kiril : Metodii," 1991– .).

Cyprus

Kypriakē vivliographia. 1983/84– . Leukōsia : Vivliographikē Hetaireia Kyprou, [1985]– . Annual.   **AA590**
Compiler: Nikos Panagiotou.
An annual listing of books, serials, government publications, etc.; excludes Turkish Cypriot publications. Arranged by broad subject; Greek entries are listed first. Author index.   Z3496.K95

Czechoslovakia

Bibliografia slovenskej kniznej tvorby. 1939/41–1945/55. Bratislava [etc.] : [s.n.], 1948–70. Irregular.   **AA591**
Title varies: 1939/41, *Bibliografický katalog slovenskej kniznej tvorby* (a rev. ed. of *Slovenský bibliografický súpis kníh za roky 1939/41*, publ. 1942).
Vol. for 1942/45 issued as *Slovenská bibliografia*, Ser. B, sv. 1; vol. for 1945/55 issued as *Slovenská národná retrospektívná bibliografia*, Ser. A, kn. IV.
A main entry listing of Slovak book production for the period.   Z2124.S56B5

Bibliograficky katalog / red. Lad. J. Zivný. roc. 1 (1922)–7 (1928). Praha : [the Institut], 1923–28. Weekly.   **AA592**
Half title in German and French.
Classified, with annual author index. Published by the Institut Bibliographique Tchécoslovaque à Prague.   Z2133.B58

Bibliograficky katalog Československé Republiky : literárni tvorba z roku, 1929–46. V Praze : Nákl. Ministerstva Školství a Národni Osvvěty, 1930–47. Annual.   **AA593**
Publisher varies.
A classified, annual catalog of books and pamphlets with indexes of authors and subjects. Does not include periodicals.   Z2133.B582

Bibliograficky katalog Československé Republiky : týdenní sešitové vydání. 1933–1959. V Praze : [National Library, et al.], 1933–59. Weekly (irregular).   **AA594**
From 1933 to 1947, published concurrently with the yearly bibliography of the same name (AA593), of which 1946 was the last volume published.

During 1946–50 the weekly was issued in three parts, the titles of which have varied. From 1951 through 1954 the bibliography was designated as *Bibliograficky katalog ČSR* and the three parts were titled: *Česká kniha* (weekly); *Slovenska kniha* (approximately 15 issues per year); *České a slovenské hudebniny* (about 10 issues per year). The first and third of these (Czech books, and Czech and Slovak music) were published by the National Library in Prague, the Slovak books section by the Slovak University in Bratislava; both were legal repositories.

Classified arrangement; annual author and subject indexes for most years; supplements accompany many numbers.

For the period 1955–59 the designations of the first two parts were changed to *České knihy* and *Slovenské knihy*. The third section was superseded by two separate parts: *České hudebniny* and *Slovenské hudebniny*.

Beginning 1960, the overall title of the bibliography became *Bibliograficky katalog ČSSR (AA600)*.

Čaplovič, Ján. Bibliografia tlačí vydaných na Slovensku do roku 1700. Martin : Matica Slovenská, 1972–1984. 2 v. (1408 p.). (Slovenská národná retrospektívna bibliografia. Séria A, Knihy 1). (In progress).   **AA595**
A bibliography of Slovak imprints to 1700. Listing is alphabetical by place of publication, then chronological.   Z2137.S6C36

Czechoslovak Republic. Komise pro knihopisn y soupis českých a slovenských tisků až do konce XVIII. století. Knihopis československých tisků : od doby nejstarší až do konce XVIII. století. V. Praze : Komisi Knihkupectví F. Topiče, 1925–67. 2 v. in 11.   **AA596**
Title and publisher vary.
Contents: v. 1, to 1500, A–Z and atlas of facsim.; v. 2, 1501–1800, pts. 1–9, A–Z.
A bibliography of Czech and Slovakian imprints from early times to the end of the 18th century.
Indexed by: *Příspěvky ke knihopisu*, by Petr Voit (Praha : Státní knihovna ČSR, 1985–1988. 10 v.).
At head of title: Státní knihovna ČSR-Nositelka rádu republiky.
Contents: v. 1, Rejstřík autorů, překladatelů a editorů; v. 2, Rejstřík anonymních záhlaví; v. 3, Rejstřík názvový; v. 4, Význam Bartoloměje Netolického pro český knihtisk 16. století; v. 5, Moravské prameny z let 1567–1568 k dějinám bibliografie, cenzury, knihtisku a literární historie; v. 6–10, Konkordance koniášových klíčů, indexu, Jungmanna a knihopisu.
Indexes for v. 1 (incunabula, A) and v. 2, pt. 1 (B–C) were included with the original set; remainder had not been indexed.

Matica Slovenská, Turčiansky sv. Martin. Knižnica. Katalog slovákumových kníh Knižnice : Matice slovenskeij do roku 1918. [Spracoval a zostavil kolektív pracovníkov Knižnice Matice Slovenskej: Božena Baricová et al.]. Martin, 1964. 3 v.   **AA597**
A main entry listing of Slovakian imprints and books relating to Slovakia in the library, with chronological and geographical (i.e., place/publisher) indexes in v. 3.
Supplemented by: ———. *Katalóg slovacikálnych kníh vydaných do roku 1918 v knižnici Matice slovenskej*, zost. Anna Polmanicka (Martin : Matica Slovenská, 1974. 2 v. [1205 p.] [Slovenské knižnice, zv. 10–11]).
Added title page in Latin: Catalogus librorum slovacicorum usque ad annum 1918 impressorum qui in Bibliotheca 'Matica slovenská' asservantur.
A listing by author or other main entry. Index by place of publication, subdivided by publisher.   Z926.M35

Rizner, L'udovít Vladimir. Bibliografia písomníctva slovenského na sposob slovníka od najstarších čias do konca r. 1900 : S pripojenou bibliografiou archeologickou, historickou ... vydáva matičná sprava. V Turcianskom Sv. Martine : ákl. Matice Slovenskej, 1929–34. 6 v.   **AA598**
An alphabetical catalog of Slovakian literature to 1900. Often gives brief biographical notices of authors.

Supplemented by: Ján Misianik, *Bibliografía slovenského písomníctva do knoca XIX* ... : *(Doplnky k Risnerovej bibliografii)* (Bratislava : Slovenská Akadémia vied a umení, 1946. 300 p.).

Z2137.S6R6

Soupis československé literatury za léta 1901–1925. V Praze : Nákl. Svazu Knihkupcú a Nakladatelú, 1931–38. 2 v. in 3.   **AA599**

Karel Nosovský and Vilém Pražák, eds.

Vols. 1–2, author list, A–Z; v. 3, classified subject index.

Z2131.S72

Current

Bibliografický katalog. České knihy = Bibliograficheskīi katalog. Cheshskie knigi = Bibliographical catalogue. Czech books. sěs. 29 (1960)–12 (1989). Praha : Státní knihovna ČSSR, Národní knihovna v Praze, 1960–89. 12 no. a year, 1983–89.   **AA600**

The parts making up the bibliography were designated as: *České knihy* (weekly); *Slovenské knihy* (V Martine : Matica Slovenská; monthly, irregular); *České hudebniny* (quarterly); and *Slovenské hudebniny* (V Martine : Matica Slovenská; annual). The Library of Congress has cataloged each part separately.

Beginning 1970 the designation of the Slovak book selection was changed to: *Slovenská národná bibliografia Séria A: knihy* (V Martine : Martica Slovenská; monthly). It continues the volume numbering of the earlier series.

Other series of *Bibliograficky katalog CSSR* were reorganized in 1980 as follows: Seria B, Periodiká [periodicals]; C, Mapy [maps]; D, Dizertačné práce [theses and dissertations]; E, Špeciáe tlače [special publications]; F, Firemná literatúre [trade catalogs and technical newsletters]; G, Grafika [grafic and fine arts]; H, Hudebniny [sheet music, books on music]; I, Oficiáe dokumenty [official documents]; J, Audiovizuáne dokumenty [audiovisual materials].

Arrangement of the bibliography remained basically the same within parts throughout the title changes.

With the dissolution of the U.S.S.R., the title changed to *Bibliografický katalog ČSRF* (1990–92); in 1993, it became *Národní bibliografie České republiky. Knihy.*   Z2131.C4

Denmark

Early

Bibliotheca danica : systematisk Fortegnelse over den danske Literatur fra 1482 til 1830, efter Samlingerne i det Store Kongeligc Bibliothek i Kjøbenhavn / udg. Christian Walther Bruun. Copenhagen : Gyldendal, 1877–1931. 4 v., suppl., and index.   **AA601**

A classified bibliography of Danish materials from 1482 to 1830. Vol. 4 includes a *Supplement* (1914) and a *Register* (1927–31) by Lauritz Nielsen. The index is in three parts: (1) authors; (2) anonymous works; (3) subjects.

A 5-v. reprint was issued 1961–63 (Copenhagen : Rosenkilde og Bagger); in that set v. 5 consists of the original supplement, published 1914, and an additional supplement covering 1914–62, by Eric Dal, together with the original indexes and an additional index to the new supplement.

———. *Supplement 1831–40 til Bibliotheca danica og Dansk bogfortegnelse*, udarb. af H. Ehrencron-Müller (København : Gad, 1943–48. Hft. 1–4 [1546 col.]).

Hft. 1, Alfabetisk Fortenelse, 1943, 422 col.; Hft. 2, Systematisk Fortegnelse, 1944, col. 425–860; Hft. 3–4, Supplement til Bibliotheca danica ... Bibliotheca slesvico-holsatica til 1840; Alfabetisk Fortegnelse, 1945, col. 863–1184; Systematisk Fortegnelse, 1948, col. 1187–1564.

Hft. 1–2 are designed to fill the gap in Danish bibliography between Bruun, which covers the period to 1830 and *Dansk Bogfortegnelse [for aarene]* ... (AA606), which starts with 1841. Hft. 3–4 form a catalog of Schleswig-Holstein literature from the earliest times to 1840.   Z2561.B58

Mitchell, Phillip Marshall. A bibliography of 17th century German imprints in Denmark and the duchies of Schleswig-Holstein. [Lawrence] : Univ. of Kansas Libraries, 1969. 2 v. (University of Kansas publications. Library series, 28).

AA602

"This bibliography records all publications with German title-pages (or titles) known or presumed to have been printed or published within the [17th century] Danish monarchy, including all items which bear an imprint of a printer or bookseller within the monarchy."— *Introd.* Chronological listing with full bibliographical information. Indexes of authors, printers, and titles.   Z2562.M55

Nielsen, Lauritz Martin. Dansk Bibliografi, 1482–1550, 1551–1600 : med saerligt hensyn til dansk bogtrykkerkunsts Historie. København : Gyldendal, 1919–35. 2 v. and Registre (126 p.). : ill.   **AA603**

Vol. [2] was issued in nine parts, 1931–33.

1482–1550, Author and title list, A–Z, no. 1–298 (1919. 247 p.); 1551–1600, Author and title list, A–AE, no. 299–1672. (1931–33. 677 p.); *Registre*: alphabetical author index, alphabetical title index, chronological index, subject index.

Two companion works listing together 1,672 items and giving for each item: title, detailed collation, bibliographical references, and location of copies. Indexes of places and of printers and publishers in each work.   Z2562.N67

19th and 20th centuries

Dania Polyglotta : répertoire bibliographique des ouvrages, études, articles, etc., en langues étrangères parus en Danemark de 1901 à 1944. Copenhague : Bibliothèque Royale, 1947–51. 3 v.   **AA604**

Publié par l'Institut Danois des Échanges Internationaux de Publications Scientifiques et Littéraires sous la rédaction de son directeur K. Schmidt-Phiseldeck avec la collaboration de Henning Einersen.

Contents: v. 1, Ouvrages; v. 2, Périodiques, études et articles; v. 3, Addenda, musique, index.

Includes books and articles published in Denmark in foreign languages by native and foreign scholars. Works in each volume are grouped under language and then arranged by class, with a general author index.

Continued by the annual *Dania Polyglotta,* (1.–24. année, 1945–68. Copenhague : Bibliothèque Royale, 1946–69).

Beginning in 1961 the subtitle of the annual, previously in French, appears in English: Annual bibliography of books, articles, and summaries, etc., in foreign languages printed in Denmark.

With 1969 a new series was begun: *Dania Polyglotta : literature on Denmark in languages other than Danish & books of Danish interest published abroad* (n.s.1 [1969]– . Copenhagen, 1970– . Annual.).

"An annual bibliography compiled by the Danish Department of the Royal Library."—*title page.* A classified subject listing with author and title index. Forms part of the Danish national bibliography; *see* AA605.   Z2574.F6D3

Dansk bogfortegnelse : Åarskatalog. 1976– . [Ballerup] : Bibliotekscentralens Forlag [etc.], 1977– . Annual.   **AA605**

Title on added title page: *The Danish national bibliography. Books.*

"*The Danish National Bibliography. Books* is compiled by Bibliotekscentralen on the basis of new books and reprints sent in directly from the publishers. The Danish Department of the Royal Library supplements this material with books deposited by printers according to the Act of Legal Deposit."—*verso of t.p.*

The annual volumes constitute a cumulation of materials from several sources, the cumulation pattern and contents varying slightly. The current pattern is as follows: a weekly alphabetical list appears in the periodical *Det danske bogmarked*. Separately published monthly lists entitled *Dansk bogfortegnelse* (containing a classified short-title list in addition to the alphabetical section) appear 12 times a year, every third issue constituting a quarterly cumulation. Annual cumulations (the *Årskatalog*) include the alphabetical and classified sections plus a Faroese book list, a Greenlandic book list, and a section of maps. The annuals will continue to cumulate quinquennially. A microfiche edition cumulated from 1976, is also available, but does not include the special lists.

Annual issues cumulate quinquennially in *Dansk bogfortegnelse [for aarene]* ... (AA606). Other titles that collectively make up the *Danish national bibliography* are: *Dansk anmeldelsesindeks* [reviews], 1979– ; *Dansk artikelindeks. Aviser og tidsskrifter* [articles, newspapers, and periodicals], 1981– (AD309); *Dansk billedfortegnelse* [visual recordings], 1984– ; *Danske grammofonplader og kassetteband* [gramophone records and tapes], 1985– ; *Dansk lydfortegnelse* [sound recordings], 1982– ; *Dansk musikfortegnelse* [music], 1972/73– ; *Bibliografi over Danmarks offentlige publikationer* [government publications], 1948– (AF166); *Dania polyglotta* [foreign publications about Denmark; AA604 *note*); *Dansk periodicafortegnelse* [serials], 1977– ; *Artikler i bøger* [articles in books]; *Grønlandsk avis- og tidsskriftindex* [Greenlandic newspapers and periodicals index], 1976– .

Z2561.D22

Dansk bogfortegnelse [for aarene] .... 1841/58–1981/85. Ballerup [etc.] : Bibliotekscentralens Forlag [etc.], 1861–1987.   **AA606**

Most recently publ. in 4 v.

Cumulates the author-title and classified lists from the annual volumes of the same title, which began publication in 1851. 19th-century cumulations vary in number of years covered. Quinquennial 1915–69; triennial 1970–75.

From 1915/19 to 1930/34 includes *Islandsk bogfortegnelse*.

Covers all material entered for copyright. Alphabetical author and title list, followed by classified list, with a subject index to the latter. Also available in microfiche with coverage beginning in 1976.

Continued by *Dansk bogfortegnelse* (AA605).   Z2561.D19

Ehrencron-Müller, Holger. Stikordsregister til den danske Skønlitteratur. 1841/1908–1909/40. København : Gad, 1918–41. 2 v.   **AA607**

Vol. for 1909/40 issued in 3 pts. and includes "Stikordsregister til den danske Skønlitteratur indtil 1840" (29 p. at end, with special t.p.) which is a title index to books in the field of belles lettres listed in *Bibliotheca danica* (AA601) and its supplement.

Provides a title index to books in the fields of belles lettres which are listed in *Dansk bogfortegnelse [for aarene]* ... (AA606) through 1940.   Z2561.D19

Estonia

Friedrich Reinhold Kreutzwaldi nimeline Eeste NSV Riiklik Raamatukogu (Tallinn). Nõukogude Eesti raamat, 1940–1954 : koondbibliograafia. Tallinn : Eesti Riiklik Kirjastus, 1956. 513 p.   **AA608**

One of three works of the same title, covering different time spans (*see* below). Together, they constitute a record of Estonian imprints from 1940 through 1970.

(1) E. Kuldkepp and P. Topovere, *Nõukogude Eesti raamat, 1955–1965 : koondnimestik* (Tallinn : Eesti Raamat, 1972. 1098 p.).

At head of title: Eesti NSV Ministrite Nõukogu, Riiklik Kirjastuskomitee; Eesti NSV Riiklik Raamatupalat.

(2) *Nõukogude Eesti raamat, 1966–1970 : koondnimestik*, [Koostaja P. Topovere; toitemus M. Sibul, L. Ploompuu ja A. Tann] (Tallinn : Eesti Raamat, 1978. 750 p.).

At head of title: Eesti NSV Ministrite Nõukogu Riiklik Kirjastuste, Polügraafia ja Raamatukaubanduse Komitee Eesti NSV Riiklik Raamatupalat. Title page also in Russian.   Z2533.T26

Finland

Lisäyksiä Fredrik Wilhelm Pippingin bibliografiaan Luettelo suomeksi präntätyistä kirjoista = Tillägg till Förteckning öfver i tryck utgifna skrifter på finska av Fredrik Wilhelm Pipping / redigerad av Irja Rämä. Helsinki : Helsingin Yliopiston Kirjasto, 1984. 84 p.   **AA609**

Lists more than 400 titles published 1543–1809. Indexes of authors, titles of anonymous works, and persons; list of library locations.

Pipping, Fredrik Wilhelm. Luettelo suomeksi präntätyistä kirjoista, kuin myös muutamista muista teoksista, joissa löytyy joku kirjoitus suomen, kielellä, tahi joku johdatus sitä tuntemaan. Helsingfors : Finska Litteratursällsks Truck, 1856–57. 756p. (Suomalaisen Kirjallisuuden Seuran. Toimituksia, 20).   **AA610**

Lists Finnish imprints in chronological order from 1542 to 1856. Author index.

Supplemented by: *Lisäyksiä Fredrik Wilhelm Pippingin bibliografiaan Luettelo suomeksi präntätyistä kirjoista* (AA609).

Suomessa ilmestyneen kirjallisuuden luettelo = katalog över i Finland utkommen litteratur. 1945–71. Helsinki : Kirjavälitys Oy, 1945–71. Annual.   **AA611**

Title varies; earliest issues called: *Suomessa ilmestyneen kirjallisuuden aineenmukainen uutuusluettelo*. Ceased publication.

Originally a quarterly classified catalog without index or cumulative features, 1945–48; annual, 1949–71.

Beginning 1949, lists new Finnish and Swedish books alphabetically in two sections with subject indexes, also divided by language until 1963. Books and parts of series in foreign languages published in Finland are listed as pt. 3, but have no subject index until 1963 and subsequent issues, when a single classified index serves for all three parts.

Beginning 1962, title also in German and English.

Current

Suomen kirjallisuus = Finlands litteratur = The Finnish national bibliography. 1544/1877– . Helsinki : Helsingin Yliopiston Kirjasto [etc.], 1878– .   **AA612**

1544/1877–1939/43 issued as *Suomalaisen Kirjallisuuden Seuran toimituksia*, 57 osa, 1.–16. lisävihko.

Frequency varies; now issued monthly (some double issues) with annual and quinquennial cumulations.

A basic volume, 1544–1877, by Valfrid Vasenius was followed by five supplements covering 1878–79, 1880–85, 1886–91, 1892–95, 1896–1900. Subsequent cumulative volumes; some issued in parts and in irregular order, cover three- or five-year periods, the 1964/66 cumulation being the latest published.

Monthly issues follow a classed subject arrangement, with author/title index; the annual cumulation is a main-entry listing with a classified section giving brief information within UDC classes. Information is furnished by three contributing libraries: the university libraries of Helsinki, Turku, and Jyväskylä.

From 1977, various categories of works previously found in the multi-year cumulations are to be excluded therefrom and published separately: serials, maps, printed music, and literature on Finland published abroad.

•Machine-readable version: *Fennica CD-ROM = Suomen kansallisbibliografia = Finlands nationalbibliografi = The Finnish national bibliography* [database] (Helsinki : Helsinki Univ. of Technology Library, 1961–). Available on CD-ROM, updated quarterly.

Z2520.S95

France

Bibliothèque Nationale (France). Catalogue général des livres imprimés : Auteurs. Paris : Impr. Nationale, 1900–81. 231 v.   **AA613**

The Bibliothèque Nationale has received copies of all books published in France since the establishment, by law, of the *dépôt légal* in the reign of Henri II. It has the largest collection of French books in existence, and its printed *Catalogue* is the most important general bibliography of French publications. For full description *see* AA101.
Z927.P2

Répertoire de bibliographie française : contenant tous les ouvrages imprimés en France et aux colonies et les ouvrages français publiés à l'étranger, 1501–1930. .... Paris : Letouzey, 1937–41. Fasc. 1–10.   **AA614**

v. 1 (fasc. 1–6), A–Angélique; v. 2 (fasc. 7–10), Angelis–Arthaud.

An attempt at a comprehensive record of French bibliography, 1501–1930, including, in general, books published in France and books in French published in French colonies and abroad with certain omissions. Unfortunately, no more published.
Z2161.R42

Early

British Museum. Department of Printed Books. Short-title catalogue of books printed in France and of French books printed in other countries from 1470 to 1600, now in the British Museum. London : Trustees, 1924. 491 p.   **AA615**

Books printed in France, p. 1–450; Books in French printed elsewhere, p. 451–91.

An important record of about 12,000 editions, including many items not found in the printed catalog of the Bibliothèque Nationale. Information given includes: author, brief title, editor, translator, etc., place, publisher, date, size.

§ *A short title catalogue of French books, 1601–1700, in the Library of the British Museum,* by V. F. Goldsmith (Folkestone : Dawsons of Pall Mall, 1969–73. 690 p.).

Publ. in 7 fascicles. Contains about 21,000 entries. Includes 17th-century books "written wholly or partly in French, no matter where published" and those "in no matter what language, published or printed at any place which today forms a part of metropolitan France."—*Foreword.* Lists works in the British Museum's *General catalogue of printed books* (AA103), works acquired since 1955, and some earlier accessions not found in the printed catalog. In addition, three extensive collections of "Mazarinades" (pamphlets and satires issued against Cardinal Mazarin) are here fully listed for the first time. Numerous indexes.
Z2162.B86

La Croix du Maine, François Grudé. Les bibliothèques françoises de La Croix du Maine et de Du Verdier / by François Grudé La Croix du Maine and Antoine Du Verdier. Nouv. éd. rev., corr., et augm. ... par Rigoley de Juvigny. Paris : Saillant & Nyon, 1772–73. 6 v.   **AA616**

The original edition of La Croix du Maine published Paris, 1584; of Du Verdier, Lyons, 1585. The two works complement each other and form a biobibliographical catalog of French publications to about the end of the 16th century. A valuable record although it includes many inaccuracies.
Z2162.L145

Le Petit, Jules. Bibliographie des principales éditions originales d'écrivains français du XVᵉ aux XVIIIᵉ siècle. Paris : Quantin, 1888. 583 p. : ill., facsims.   **AA617**

Repr.: Paris : Jeanne et Brulon, 1927.

Facsimiles of title pages with long, detailed descriptions of the original editions.
Z2174.F5L5

Moreau, Brigitte. Inventaire chronologique des éditions parisiennes du XVIᵉ siècle ... d'après les manuscrits de Philippe Renouard. Paris : Imprimerie Municipale, 1972–85. v. 1–3. (In progress).   **AA618**

At head of title: Service des Travaux Historiques de la Ville de Paris.

Contents: v. 1, 1501–1510; v. 2, 1511–1520; v. 3, 1521–30.

To be published in ten parts, each part covering a 10–year period. Intended as a short-title catalog of 16th-century books published or sold in Paris, with indication of variant editions and locations of examples.
Z305.M67

Répertoire bibliographique des livres imprimés en France au seizième siècle. Baden-Baden : Heitz, 1968–80. Fasc. 1–30. (Bibliotheca bibliographica Aureliana, 25, 27, 29, etc.).   **AA619**

A bibliography of 17th-century book publishing throughout France, with the exception of Paris. A cooperative effort of many scholars, the original project was completed in 30 fascicles, the last two of which are devoted to additions and corrections, and indexes. Listing is by place, then by publisher and date. Further additions, published "hors série" but consecutively numbered, are now appearing in "Bibliotheca bibliographica Aureliana," v. 80– , offering coverage of (1) Strasbourg, (2) miscellaneous provincial towns, (3) Troyes, (4) Douai, and (5) Poitiers; further numbers are planned for Lyon, Caen, and Rouen.
Z2162.R4

Répertoire bibliographique des livres imprimés en France au XVIIᵉ siècle. Baden-Baden : V. Koerner, 1978–1989. 16 v. (Bibliotheca bibliographica Aureliana, 75, etc.).   **AA620**

Continues the 16th-century coverage provided by *Répertoire bibliographique des livres imprimés en France au seizième siècle* (AA619); continued for the 18th century by *Répertoire bibliographique des livres imprimés en France au XVIIIe siècle* (AA623). Arranged by region, then chronologically. Each region begins with a Table des imprimeurs et librairies; each volume has author and title indexes and an abbreviations list. A cooperative effort by various scholars; many volumes are by Louis Desgraves.
Z2162.D47

Tchemerzine, Avenir. Bibliographie d'éditions originales et rares d'auteurs français des XVᵉ, XVIᵉ, XVIIᵉ et XVIIIᵉ siècles contenant environ 6000 facsimilés de titres et de gravures. Paris : Plée, 1927–34. 10 v. : ill.   **AA621**

Gives detailed bibliographical descriptions, line-by-line transcriptions, and many reproductions of title pages and engravings.
Z2174.F5T2

18th century

Conlon, Pierre M. Le siècle des lumières : bibliographie chronologique. Genève : Droz, 1983–93. v. 1–12. (Histoire des idées et critique littéraire, vol. 213, 222, 227, 239, 250, 266, 282, 299, 302, 309, 319, 323). (In progress).   **AA622**

Contents: v. 1, 1716–22; v. 2, 1723–29; v. 3, 1730–36, v. 4, 1737–42; v. 5, 1743–47; v. 6, 1748–52; v. 7, 1753–56; v. 8, 1757–60; v. 9, Supplement, 1716–60; v. 10, Index des titres, 1716–60; v. 11, Index des auteurs, A–K, 1716–60; v. 12, Index des auteurs, L–Z, 1716–60.

An attempt to fill partially a gap in 18th-century French national bibliography; the completed work is to list French imprints through 1789, together with French writings published outside France. Listing is by year, then by author or anonymous title. Library locations (including some outside France) are given.
Z7128.E55C66

Desgraves, Louis. Répertoire bibliographique des livres imprimés en France au XVIIIe siècle. Baden-Baden ; Bouxwiller : V. Koerner, 1988–91. v. 1–5. (Bibliotheca bibliographica Aureliana, 112, etc.). (In progress).   **AA623**

Contents: v. 1, Agen, Albi, Angouleme, Auch, Bayonne, Bergerac, Cahors, Castres, Condom, Dax, Fontenay-le-Comte, Limoges, Lucon; v. 2, Montauban, Perigeux, Rochefors-sur-Mer, Rodex, Daintes,

Saint-Jean-d'Angely, Sarlat, Tarbes, Tulle, Villeiranche-de-Rouergue; v. 3, La Rochelle; v. 4, Bordeaux, Premeire partie, 1701–60; v. 5, Bordeaux, seconde partie, 1761–89.

Continues the coverage of *Répertoire bibliographique des livres imprimés en France au seizième siècle* ... (AA619) and *Répertoire bibliographique des livres imprimés en France au XVIIe siècle* (AA620) into the 18th century. Arranged alphabetically by place, then chronologically. Indexed.   Z1016.D47

Quérard, Joseph Marie. La France littéraire : ou Dictionnaire bibliographique des savants, historiens et gens de lettres de la France, ainsi que des littérateurs étrangers qui ont écrit en français, plus particulièrement pendant les XVIIIᵉ et XIXᵉ siècles. Paris : Didot, 1827–64. 12 v.   **AA624**

Repr.: Paris : Maisonneuve, 1964.

Contents: v. 1–10, A–Z; v. 11–12, supplements containing: Corrections, additions; Auteurs, pseudonymes et anonymes; v. 11, A–Razy; v. 12, Re–Roguet.

Emphasizes humanities and pure science.

Vols. 11–12 (publ. 1854–64) list by real name the authors of pseudonymous and anonymous works, giving the pseudonyms under which each has written, with brief biographical information, titles of works, etc. They serve as an index to Quérard's *Supercheries littéraires dévoilées* (AA169).   Z2161.Q4

19th and 20th centuries

Biblio : catalogue des ouvrages parus en langue française dans le monde entier. 1934–1970. Paris : Service Bibliographique des Messageries Hachette, 1935–71. Annual.   **AA625**

Subtitle varies.

Began publication as a monthly (10 issues a year) in Oct. 1933. The first annual cumulation was that for 1934 (publ. 1935).

During its period of publication, the most easily used trade bibliography covering books published in France and French books published in Belgium, Switzerland, Canada, etc. A dictionary catalog, published monthly with annual cumulation, entering each book under author, subject, and title with many cross-references. Full information—given under author entry—includes author's name, full title, date, place (if other than Paris), publisher, paging, size, illustrations, series, price.

The monthly issues contained biobibliographical sketches, frequently of some length, brief book reviews, etc., which were not carried over into the annual volumes. These biobibliographies are indexed in *Biography index* (AH10).

Merged with *Bibliographie de la France* (AA626) in Jan. 1972 to form *Bibliographie de la France—Biblio* (AA627). Monthly issues of *Biblio* continued to be published through Dec. 1971, but the annual cumulation for 1971 appears under the merged title, *Les livres de l'année—Biblio* (AA629 *note*), with the extended coverage of the new series.   Z2165.B56

Bibliographie de la France : journal général de l'imprimerie et de la librairie. Paris : Cercle de la Librairie, 1811–1971. Année 1–160.   **AA626**

Arrangement and parts issued vary.

The standard weekly list, recording material received through the *dépôt légal*, including books, pamphlets, official publications, music, prints, and, in addition, a monthly record of gifts to the Bibliothèque Nationale. Beginning 1857, each number consisted of three main parts: (1) *Bibliographie officielle*, (2) *Chronique*, and (3) *Annonces* (to 1919, *Feuilleton*).

1. pt.: *Bibliographie officielle* contained *Livres*, a classed list of books, pamphlets, etc., recorded with full cataloging information which includes author, full title, place, publisher, date, size, paging, price (if information about price was supplied by publisher), and pressmark of the book in the Bibliothèque Nationale. The following supplements were published at irregular intervals and began at different dates: A, Périodiques; B, Gravures, estampes et photographies; C, Musique; D, Thèses; E, Atlas, cartes et plans; F, Publications officielles gouvernementales et administratives; G, Catalogues des ventes publiques. Special supplements were also issued from time to time. At the end of the year there was a general author and title index to the record of books and gifts, an alphabetical list of new periodicals, an index to musical works, and a table of illustrators. Coverage of these indexes varied somewhat from year to year.

2. pt.: *Chronique* contained publishing news, postal and copyright information, legal and government notes, occasional historical articles, obituaries, lists of literary prizes, etc.

3. pt.: *Annonces* section consisted of advertising pages with indexes as follows:

Les livres de la semaine, a classified list, which cumulated into *Les livres du mois*, also classified with indexes of authors and of titles. This, in turn, cumulated into the quarterly and semiannual indexes, *Les livres du trimestre* and *Les livres du semestre*, which were author and title lists rather than classified.

Les livres de l'année, which cumulated these indexes, was in three parts: (1) classified, (2) titles, and (3) authors. It included not only all the works listed in the *Annonces*, but also books listed in the *Bibliographie officielle* which did not appear in the *Annonces*.

Livres et matériel d'enseignement, consisting of publishers' announcements with annual indexes by author and by title under classified headings.

For a full description of the *Bibliographie* and all its parts *see* Louis-Noëlle Malclès, *Les sources du travail bibliographique* 1:122–26 (AA352).

Merged with *Biblio* (AA625) to form *Bibliographie de la France—Biblio* (AA627).   Z2165.B58

Bibliographie de la France—Biblio. Année 161–168 no.26. Paris : Cercle de la Librairie, 1972–Juin 1979. Weekly.   **AA627**

Continues *Bibliographie de la France* (AA626) and assumes its numbering. Originally the general plan of the publication in three parts continued as outlined for the earlier bibliography but certain changes were effected in the makeup and frequency of portions of Pt. 1, *Bibliographie officielle*. The weekly classed lists in the *Livres* section continued to cumulate monthly in a classed arrangement designated as *Les livres du mois*. In July 1979 the weekly *Livres* section was superseded by *Livres-hebdo* (AA636), while from 1976 other sections had reverted to the title *Bibliographie de la France. Livres : notices établies par la Bibliothèque nationale* (AA634).

The yearly subscription includes 25 semimonthly issues of *Livres*, 4 cumulative indexes, and 23 supplementary issues distributed as: I, Publications en série (12 issues and annual index); II, Publications officielles (6 issues and index); III, Musique (4 issues); and IV, Atlas, cartes et plans (1 issue).

The *Livres* section is a classed list according to the Universal Decimal Classification, and full cataloging information, price, and Bibliothèque Nationale shelf mark are given; separate author and title indexes in each issue cumulate quarterly and annually.

Continued by: *Bibliographie nationale française* (AA634).

Catalogue général des ouvrages en langue française, 1926–1929 / publié sous la direction de Bernard Dermineur. München ; N.Y. : K.G. Saur, 1987–89. 9 v.   **AA628**

Contents: Auteurs (3 v.); Titres (2 v.); Matières (4 v.).

———. 1930–1933, publié sous la direction de Bernard Dermineur (1993–94. 14 v.).

Contents: Auteurs (7 v.); Titres (3 v.); Matières (4 v.).

These two sets are an effort to close the gap in coverage between *Biblio* (AA625) and Otto H. Lorenz's *Catalogue général de la librairie française, 1840–1925* (AA630). They attempt to list all works published in French, from France as well as from other French-speaking areas or countries, including Canada, Belgium, and Switzerland. Full bibliographic descriptions are given in the author volumes; only title, place, and date of publication (along with the author's name in boldface) are given in the other sections.   Z2161.C357

Librairie française : catalogue général des ouvrages en vente au 1. jan. 1930. Paris : Cercle de la Librairie, 1931. 3 v.   **AA629**

Continued by compilations in the same form covering 1930–33, 1933–45, 1946–55, 1956–65.

Contents: v. 1–2, Répertoire par auteurs; v. 3, Répertoire par titres.

Compiled from the annual volumes of *Les livres de l'année* of *Bibliographie de la France* (AA626). Lists books, new periodicals, publications of corporate bodies, and some documents. Gives for each book listed: author, title, paging, date, publisher, binding, illustration, format, price.

Cumulated by: *Les livres de l'année* (1933–1938, 1946/48–1970. Annual).

Not published 1939–45?

Cumulated the listings in *Bibliographie de la France* and was itself cumulated into *Librairie française, catalogue général.*

Each volume is in three parts: pt. 1, Classified by the main divisions of the decimal classification; pt. 2, Titles; pt. 3, Alphabetical lists of authors, illustrators, publishers, booksellers, etc.

Superseded by: *Les livres de l'année—Biblio* (1971–1979. Paris : Cercle de la Libraire, [1972–80]. Annual).

Cumulates the listings in the *Bibliographie de la France—Biblio* (AA627), using the author-title-subject arrangement in dictionary form as *Biblio* (AA625). The volume for 1971 serves as the final cumulation for the monthly issues of *Biblio* as well as the annual cumulation of entries in *Bibliographie de la France.*   Z2161.L69

Lorenz, Otto Henri. Catalogue général de la librairie française, 1840–1925. Paris : Lorenz, 1867–1945. 34 v.   **AA630**

Repr.: Nendeln, Liechtenstein, 1966–67.

Publisher varies.

Usually cited as *Lorenz.*

Vols. 1–11, ed. by Otto Lorenz; v. 12–28, pt. 2 by D. Jordell; v. 28, pt. 3–v. 32, by Henri Stein; v. 33–34, by the Service Bibliographique Hachette.

The standard French list for the 19th and early 20th centuries. Covers French publications by periods ranging from 3 years to 25 years, the volumes for each period consisting of: (1) a main author and anonymous title list containing full information, i.e., author's full name, full title of book, edition, place (if other than Paris), date, publisher, paging, size, price, and occasional brief notes; and (2) a subject list arranged by broad subjects, with briefer information. Includes books, pamphlets, some theses and annuals, but not periodicals, and lists some Belgian and Swiss publications. Special features are: (1) the inclusion of brief biographical notes about the authors whose works are listed; (2) the linking together of all entries for the same author by cross-references from the later volumes to the earlier ones; (3) occasional brief notes which tell whether a book has been crowned by the French Academy; which refer, in case of reissues or later editions, to date of first edition; and which give, in case of books or pamphlets reprinted from periodicals, reference to volume or date of the periodical, etc. The information about original publication in periodicals is often very useful.   Z2161.L86

Quérard, Joseph Marie. La littérature française contemporaine, 1827–49 : dictionnaire bibliographique ... accompagné de biographies et de notes historiques et littéraires / Joseph Marie Quérard ... [et al.]. Paris : Daguin, 1842–57. 6 v.   **AA631**

Repr.: Paris : Maisonneuve, 1965.

Title varies.

A continuation of Quérard's *La France littéraire* (AA624) on the same general plan.   Z2161.Q41

Vicaire, Georges. Manuel de l'amateur de livres du XIXᵉ siècle, 1801–1893. Paris : Rouquette, 1894–1920. 8 v.   **AA632**

v. 1–7, A–Z, 1801–1893; v. 8, Table des ouvrages cités.

Crowned by the French Academy.

An attempt to do for 19th-century French literature what Jacques Charles Brunet's *Manuel du libraire et de l'amateur de livres* (AA88) does for general literature of an earlier period. Covers some of the same period as Otto Henri Lorenz (*Catalogue général de la librairie française, 1840–1925*, AA630), but with a selection of material, listing

fewer titles than Lorenz but giving fuller information and annotations for those listed. Gives full titles and bibliographical notes, original price, and, often, prices realized at various auction sales.   Z2161.V62

Current

Un an de nouveautés. 1980– . Paris : Éditions Professionnelles du Livre, 1981– . Annual.   **AA633**

Cumulates the quarterly and semiannual listings in the "Répertoires livres hebdo" series, which in turn supersede the monthly "Livres du mois" supplement to *Livres-hebdo* (AA636). Serves as a continuation of the annual cumulation of *Bibliographie de la France—Biblio* (AA625 *note*) which covers through 1979. Classified arrangement with author and title indexes.

Bibliographie nationale française. Livres : notices établies par la Bibliothèque Nationale. 1990, no. 1 (3 janv. 1990)– . Paris : Bibliothèque Nationale, Office général du livre, 1990– . Biweekly.   **AA634**

Also called 179. année– .

Represents a title change for *Bibliographie de la France—Biblio* (AA627); assumes its numbering. The indexes now cumulate three times a year on microfiche, with an annual printed cumulation. The four supplements still appear: I, Publications en série (monthly with an annual index); II, Publications officielles (bimonthly with an annual index); III, Musique (three times a year); and IV, Atlas, cartes, et plans (annually).   Z2165.B5725

Les livres disponibles. 1977– . [Paris] : Cercle de la Librairie, 1977– . Annual.   **AA635**

Also called *French books in print.*

Subtitle: La liste exhaustive des ouvrages disponibles publiés en langue française dans le monde. La liste des éditeurs et la liste des collections de langue française.

Originally issued in two parts: (1) Auteurs; (2) Titres; a subject volume arranged by Universal Decimal Classification was added with the 1978 edition.

Supersedes *Le catalogue de l'édition française* (éd. 1–5 publ. 1971–76). Includes books published in French regardless of place of publication. Excludes theses, pamphlets, periodicals, musical scores, and annuals of associations. The lists of publishers and distributors and of publishers' series appear in both volumes.

Tous les livres au format de poche: répertoire (Paris, Cercle de la Librairie, 1981– . Annual; formerly *Répertoire des livres au format de poche*) provides a record of French popular publications available in pocket (paperback) format.

Livres-hebdo. no. 1 (Sept. 4, 1979)– . [Paris : Éditions Professionelles du Livre], 1979– . Weekly.   **AA636**

Supersedes the weekly "Chronique" and "Annonces" sections of *Bibliographie de la France—Biblio* (AA627) (covers originally carried the designation "Bibliographie de la France. Bulletin du livre"). Includes a monthly supplement, *Les livres du mois,* and a quarterly supplement, *Trois mois de nouveautés* (formerly *Les livres du trimestre*), which cumulate the classed lists from the "Livres" sections of the weekly issues and add author and title indexes.

The publication has evolved as a kind of French equivalent of *Publishers' weekly,* with each issue usually in three sections: (1) publishers' announcements and advertisements, and notes on literary prizes and promotions; (2) a magazine section devoted to news notes and articles on the book trade, libraries, etc.; and (3) a classed list of new publications arranged by Universal Decimal Classification and which cumulates as noted.   Z2165.L8

Germany

Early

Borchling, Conrad. Niederdeutsche bibliographie : Gesamt-verzeichnis der niederdeutschen Drucke bis zum Jahre 1800 / von dr. Conrad Borchling, und dr. Bruno Claussen. Neumünster : K. Wachholst Verlag, 1931–1936. 2 v.   **AA637**

Repr.: Utrecht, Nethrelands : HES Publishers, 1976.

Issued in 21 parts, in double columns numbered continously.

Contents: v. 1, 1473–1600; v. 2, 1601–1800; Nachträge, 1481–1800; Ergänzungen u. Verbesserungen, col.1871–91; Indexes (of places, printers, names, first lines, catchwords, etc.), col.1893–2018; Letze Nachträge u. Verbesserungen, col.2019–20.

Arranged chronologically; lists more than 4,700 items, described in detail with line-by-line transcription and with some location of copies.   Z2235.B72

British Museum. Department of Printed Books. Short-title catalogue of books printed in the German-speaking countries and German books printed in other countries from 1455 to 1600, now in the British Museum. London : Trustees, 1962. 1224 p.   **AA638**

One of a series of short-title catalogs, similar in scope and arrangement. Arranged alphabetically by author and anonymous title, with some collective headings, as used in the Museum's *General catalogue of printed books* (AA103), followed by an index of publishers, with titles listed chronologically under publisher.

Supplemented by: British Library. *Short-title catalogue of books printed in the German-speaking countries from 1455 to 1600, now in the British Library. Supplement* (London : British Library, 1990. 141 p.).

Lists more than 1,300 books which were added to the Library after 1962. Includes a list of amendments to the earlier catalogue, and a list of books destroyed during World War II which have been replaced. Printers and publishers index.   Z2222.B73

Panzer, Georg Wolfgang Franz. Annalen der ältern deutschen Litteratur. Nürnberg : Grattenauer, 1788–1805. 2 v.   **AA639**

Contents: v. 1, to 1520; v. 2, 1521–26; Zusätze .... (Leipzig : Hempel, 1802. 198 p. [Suppl. to v. 1]).

Supplemented by Joseph Heller in *Serapeum*, 4. Jahrg. (1843) : 299–303, 6. Jahrg. (1845) : 312–20, 327–33; and by E. O. Weller's *Repertorium typographicum. Die deutsche Literatur im ersten Viertel des sechzehnten Jahrhunderts.* ... (Nördlingen, 1864. Added title page: George Wolfgang Panzers Annalen der älteren deutschen Literatur, MD–MDXXVI).

Now largely superseded by later compilations of incunabula, e.g., British Museum. Department of Printed Books, *Catalogue of books printed in the XVth century now in the British Museum* (AA219), pts. 2–3.   Z2222.P19

Verzeichnis der im deutschen Sprachbereich erschienenen Drucke des XVI. Jahrhunderts : VD 16 / hrsg. von der Bayerischen Staatsbibliothek in München in Verbindung mit der Herzog August Bibliothek in Wolfenbüttel. Stuttgart : Hiersemann, 1983–93. Abt. 1, Bd. 1–20; Abt 2, Bd. 21; Abt. 3, Bd. 22. (In progress).   **AA640**

Redaktion: Irmgard Bezzel.

Introductory matter in German, English, and French.

Contents: Abt. 1, Verfasser, Körperschaften, Anonyma, Bd. 1–20; Abt. 2, Herausgeber, Kommentatoren, Übersetzer, literarische Beitrage, Bd. 21; Abt. 3, Druckorte, Drucker, Verleger, Bd. 22.

A catalog of "books printed between 1501 and 1600 in whatever language in the German-speaking areas (Germany, Austria and German-speaking parts of Switzerland and Alsace)."—*Pref.* Reproduces the catalog cards (usually prepared from the book in hand, but sometimes supplied from printed sources or by contributing libraries); library locations are given. To be in some 40 volumes.   Z1014.V47

18th and 19th centuries

The 18th and 19th centuries are well covered by series of catalogs published by three German bookdealers: Heinsius, beginning with 1700; Kayser with 1750; and Hinrichs with 1850, thus overlapping each other but together providing a continuous record from 1700 to 1910, when the *Deutsches Bücherverzeichnis* superseded and carried on Kayser and Hinrichs, following the general bibliographical practices of Kayser. A cumulation of these and related bibliographies of the period have been published as *Gesamtverzeichnis der deutschprachigen Schrifttums* (AA643).

There are subject indexes to Kayser covering 1750–1832 and 1891–1910, and Karl Georg (AA642) provides a subject approach from 1883 to 1912, but there are no cumulated subject indexes for 1700–50 or 1833–82.

Fünfjahrs-Katalog der im deutschen Buchhandel erschienenen Bücher, Zeitschriften, Landkarten, etc. : Titelverzeichnis und Sachregister, 1851–1912. Leipzig : Hinrichs, 1857–1913. 13 v.   **AA641**

Title varies.

Commonly known as "Hinrichs," for the publishing firm.

Five-year cumulations of *Halbjahrsverzeichnis der im deutschen Buchhandel erschienen Bücher, Zeitschriften und Landkarten* (AA656) with additions and corrections. No more published.   Z2221.H658

Georg, Karl. Karl Georgs Schlagwort-katalog : Verzeichnis der im deutschen Buchhandel erschienenen Bücher und Landkarten in sachlicher Anordnung .... Hannover : Lemmerman [etc.], 1889–1913. 7 v. in 12.   **AA642**

Imprint varies. Issued in parts. Vols. 1–2 have subtitle abbreviated. Date of coverage appears in title.

Vol. 1 comp. by C. Georg and L. Ost.

Lists, under subject and form headings, works published during these periods.   Z2221.G34

Gesamtverzeichnis des deutschsprachigen Schrifttums (GV), 1700–1910 / bearb. unter d. Leitung von Hilmar Schmuck u. Willi Gorzny ; bibliograph. u. red. Beratung, Hans Popst u. Rainer Schöller. München ; N.Y. : K.G. Saur, 1979–1987. 160 v.   **AA643**

Contents: v. 1–160; Nachträge (1 v.), A–Z.

Also available in microfiche.

Forms a chronological predecessor to "*GV* 1911–1965" (AA647) and is similarly compiled: i.e., entries from existing printed bibliographies and book catalogs have been interfiled and photographically reproduced, not reset. Thus, the main entries, but not the indexes, from some 178 works published in about 560 volumes are here alphabetically arranged in a single alphabet. Among the better-known sets included are Heinsius (1700–1892); (AA644); Kayser (1750–1910); (AA645), and Hinrichs (1851–1912) (AA641), but numerous dissertation lists and specialized bibliographies are also represented.   Z2221.G469

Heinsius, Wilhelm. Allgemeines Bücher-Lexikon : oder vollständiges alphabetisches Verzeichniss der von 1700 bis zu Ende 1892 erschienenen Bücher. Leipzig : Brockhaus, 1812–94. 19 v.   **AA644**

Repr.: Graz : Akademische Druck, 1963.

No more published. Publisher varies.

Lists books, pamphlets, and periodicals alphabetically by author or catchword title in chronological periods: 1700–1810 in 4 v.; thereafter to 1892 in volumes usually but not always quinquennial. Gives author, title, paging, place, publisher, date, and price. Through 1867, prices are given in thalers and neugroschen, after 1867 in marks and pfennigs.

Supplementary lists: 1700–1827, Romane, Schauspiele; 1868–92, Karten und Pläne.   Z2221.H47

Kayser, Christian Gottlob. Vollständiges Bücher-Lexikon, 1750–1910. Leipzig : Tauchnitz, 1834–1911. 36 v.   **AA645**

Repr.: Graz : Akademische Druck, 1961–62.

No more published. Publisher varies.

1750–1832 in 6 v. Continued to 1910 by volumes published at irregular intervals.

Lists books, pamphlets, periodicals, etc., in an author list with some title entries, giving, for each book listed, author, title, place, publisher, date, volumes, paging, series, prices of different editions, etc. Entry is generally under the author's name, but works having such titles as Wörterbuch, Lexikon, Jahresverzeichnis, etc., are entered under title rather than compiler, and under that entry are alphabetized by the main subject word in the title, the filing word being indicated by a different type or spacing. Before 1870, prices were given in thalers and neugroschen, after that date in marks and pfennigs. Includes some Austrian and Swiss publications.

———. ———. *Sachregister* (Leipzig : Schumann, 1838. 511 p.). Indexes v. 1–6, 1750–1832.

———. ———. *Sach- und Schlagwortregister, 1891–1910* (Leipzig : Tauchnitz, 1896–1912. 5 v.). Each index covers 2 v. of the main work, as follows: v. 27–28, 1891–94; v. 29–30, 1895–98; v. 31–32, 1899–1902; v. 33–34, 1903–06; v. 35–36, 1907–10.

Thelert, Gustav. Supplement zu Heinsius', Hinrichs' und Kaysers Bücher-Lexikon … . Grossenhain ; Leipzig : Baumert & Rouge, 1893. 405 p.   **AA646**

Repr.: Leipzig : Zentralantiquariat der Deutschen Demokratischen Republik, 1973.

Subtitle: Verzeichniss einer Anzahl Schriften, welche seit der Mitte des neunzehnten Jahrhunderts in Deutschland erschienen, in den gennannten Katalogen aber garnicht oder fehlerhaft aufgeführt sind. Mit bibliographischen Bemerkungen.   Z2221.T38

20th century

From the end of World War II to the reunification in 1990 there were two bibliographic centers in Germany: the Deutsche Bücherei in Leipzig, in East Germany, and the Deutsche Bibliothek in Frankfurt am Main, in West Germany. Each attempted to list all books published in both parts of Germany and German books published in both parts of Germany and German books published elsewhere. There is, thus, much duplication, but some entries will be found listed in one work and not in the other. After reunification, the centers merged under the Deutsche Bibliothek, with branches in both Leipzig and Frankfurt am Main. The East and West German bibliographies are described separately under their different locations, and the new, joint bibliography, is listed as the current source.

Gesamtverzeichnis des deutschsprachigen Schrifttums (GV); 1911–1965 / hrsg. von Reinhard Oberschelp; bearb. unter der Leitung von Willi Gorzny, mit einem Geleitwort von Wilhelm Totok. München : Verlag Dokumentation, 1976–81. 150 v.   **AA647**

Represents a cumulation and integration of the main entries from some 15 series of German-language national bibliographies and dissertation lists. (Entries from the original publications have been interfiled and photographed, not reset). Citations are drawn from *Deutsches Bücherverzeichnis* (AA655) *Deutsche Bibliographie* (AA651), *Deutsche Nationalbibliographie* (AA657), and from the various German, Austrian, and Swiss dissertation lists. These publications are not, however, fully superseded since the subject indexes are not similarly cumulated and integrated, and all portions of some series are not represented in the new work.   Z2221.G47

Gesamtverzeichnis des deutschsprachigen Schrifttums ausserhalb des Buchhandels (GVB), 1966–1980 / bearb. unter der Leitung von Willemina van der Meer und Hilmar Schmuck. München ; N.Y. : K.G. Saur, 1988–1991. 45 v.   **AA648**

Contents: v. 1–28, A–Z; v. 29–42, Sachregister; v. 43–45, Autoren- und Körperschaften register.

Includes "all available German-language titles published outside the booktrade."—*Introd.* Arranged by title, with subject and author/corporate body indexes.

Verfasser- und Stichwortregister zu Deutsche Bibliographie : Wöchentliches Verzeichnis; Österreichische Bibliographie; Das schweizer Buch, Ausg. A. Juli 1960–. Frankfurt a. M. : Buchhändler-Vereinigung GmbH, 1960– . Monthly.   **AA649**

Serie A of *Das schweizer Buch* (AA839).

Comp. by the Deutsche Bibliothek, Frankfurt a. M.

Continues *Verfasser- und Sachregister*, 1953–60.

An author and catchword-title index to three current national bibliographies—German, Austrian, and Swiss.

Entries are arranged in a single alphabet, with symbols to indicate the Austrian and Swiss items. No cumulations of the monthly issues. Quarterly 1965 only.

Frankfurt-am-Main

Deutsche Bibliographie. Fünfjahres-Verzeichnis / unter Mitwirkung der Österreichischen Nationalbibliothek in Wien … der Schweizerischen Landesbibliothek in Bern … bearbeitet von der Deutschen Bibliothek Frankfurt a. M. 1. Teil, Lfg. 1 (1966–1970)–2. Teil, Bd. 17 (1981–1985). Frankfurt a. M. : Buchhändler-Vereinigung, 1974–1989. Quinquennial.   **AA650**

Continues *Deutsche Bibliographie. Fünfjahres-Verzeichnis. Bücher und Karten* (begun with 1945–1950 volume).

Represents five-year cumulations of the various sections of *Deutsche Bibliographie*. The publication it continues, for the 1945–65 period, attempted to list all publications for Germany; German-language trade books published in Austria and Switzerland; and various German-language publications of other countries. Periodicals and annuals were omitted during the 1956–65 period; for the 1966–75 period only a selection of the nontrade publications from Reihe B of the *Deutsche Bibliographie*, and no listings for maps were included. The 1976–80 cumulation includes only the trade publications found in Reihe A. Beginning 1981, the five-year cumulation is to include all listings from Reihe A. The 1981–85 cumulation includes all listings from Reihen A, B, and C.

Each chronological period is in two parts: T. 1, Alphabetisches Titelverzeichnis (alphabetical listing by author and anonymous title); T. 2, Stich- und Schlagwortregister (the subject listing).

For periodicals, see *Deutsche Bibliographie: Zeitschriften Verzeichnis* (AD98).

§ Continued by: *Deutsche Nationalbibliographie und Bibliographie der im Ausland erschienen deutschsprachigan Veröffentlichungen : Reihe E* (AA659).   Z2221.D47

Deutsche Bibliographie. Halbjahres-Verzeichnis / bearb. von der Deutschen Bibliothek. Jan.-Juni 1953–1990. Frankfurt a. M. : Buchhändler-Vereinigung GmbH, 1953–90. Semiannual.   **AA651**

1951–52 had title: *Bibliographie der Deutschen Bibliothek: Halbjahres Verzeichnis*.

This semiannual cumulation of the *Wöchentliches Verzeichnis* (AA652) issued in two parts: pt. 1, Titelverzeichnis; pt. 2, Stich- und Schlagwortregister.

Continued by: *Deutsche Nationalbibliographie und Bibliographie… Reihe D.* (AA658).   Z2221.F73

Deutsche Bibliographie. Wöchentliches Verzeichnis. Frankfurt a. M. : Buchhändler-Vereinigung GmbH, 1947– . Weekly.   **AA652**

Comp. by the Deutsche Bibliothek, Frankfurt am Main. From 1947 to 1952, entitled *Bibliographie der deutschen Bibliothek*.

Originally attempted to include a record of all books published in the German language either in Germany or in other countries. Includes prices.

Arrangement has varied slightly; now classified under broad subject groupings, with author, title, subject index.

Beginning with 1965 issues, the bibliography appears in three series: *Reihe A* lists publications available in the book trade (including atlases, but not maps) and is a weekly with indexes cumulating monthly and quarterly (the listings cumulate semiannually in *Deutsche Bibliographie. Halbjahres-Verzeichnis* (AA658), and quinquennially in the *Deutsche Bibliographie. Fünfjahres-Verzeichnis* (AA650); *Reihe B*, appearing semimonthly with cumulated annual index, lists publications not in the book trade, and selected titles from *Reihe B* appear in the regular semiannual and 5-year lists; *Reihe C*, quarterly, covers maps. Annual indexes for Reihen B and C were published through 1980; beginning 1981, the listings are cumulated in *Halbjahres-Verzeichnis* and *Fünfjahres-Verzeichnis*.

§ Continued by: *Deutsche Nationalbibliographie und Bibliographie der im Ausland erschienenen deutschsprachigen Veröffentlichungen* (AA657).   Z2221.F75

Deutsche Bibliographie. Wöchentliches Verzeichnis. Neuerscheinungen Sofortdienst (CIP) : Amtsblatt der Deutschen Bibliothek. (2. Juli 1975)–(20. Dez. 1990). Frankfurt a. M. : Buchhändler-Vereinigung, 1975–90. Weekly, with monthly and quarterly cumulations.   **AA653**

Gives information on forthcoming books. Weekly issues follow a classed arrangement, the cumulations are main entry listings with *see* references from titles, editors, etc. Entries are based on information supplied for "cataloging-in-publication." Full bibliographic information derived from examination of the book itself is provided in Reihe A of *Deutsche Bibliographie : Wöchentliches Verzeichnis* (AA652) following publication.

§ Continued by: *Deutsche Nationalbibliographie… Reihe N* (AA659).

Leipzig

Deutsche Nationalbibliographie : Reihe A, Reihe B. Jan. 1931–1990. Leipzig : Börsenverein der Deutschen Buchhändler, 1931–1990.   **AA654**

Continues, with changed title and scope, *Wöchentliches Verzeichnis*, 1842–1930.

Reihe A, Neuerscheinungen des Buchhandels (books in the book trade), weekly; Reihe B, Neuerscheinungen ausserhalb des Buchhandels (books outside the book trade, e.g., dissertations, society publications), monthly (formerly semimonthly).

Both sections are classified under broad subject groupings with author, title and catchword index in each issue. Separate quarterly indexes (Vierteljahrsregister) for each Reihe. Includes books, periodicals, and maps, but not music.

"Dissertationen und Habilitationsschriften" are listed in Reihe C, 1968–90.

———. *Ergänzung*, 1–2 (Leipzig : Börsenverein der Deutschen Buchhändler, 1949. 2 v.).

Contents: 1, Verzeichnis der Schriften, die 1933–1945 nicht angezeigt werden durften; 2, Verzeichnis der Schriften, die infolge von Kriegseinwirkungen vor dem 8. Mai 1945 nicht angezeigt werden konnten.   Z2221.H67

Deutsches Bücherverzeichnis. v. 1 (1911/14)–v. 90 (1981/85). Leipzig : VEB Verlag für Buch- und Bibliothekswesen, 1914–1985.   **AA655**

Subtitle varies; publisher varies. Issued in parts.

Five-year cumulations, claiming to include all titles listed in *Halbjahresverzeichnis* and *Jahresverzeichnis*. Each period is in two sections: (1) Titelverzeichnis (listing works by author and anonymous

title); (2) Stich- und Schlagwortregister (subject index). The period 1941–50 is covered in a single listing and includes works previously omitted because of Nazi proscription or war conditions.

A continuation of *Fünfjahrs-Katalog der im deutschen Buchhandel erschienenen Bücher* [Hinrichs] (AA641) and Christian Gottlob Kayser, *Vollständiges Bücher-Lexikon* (AA645); compiled on the same general plan as Kayser. Lists German-language publications of the book trade in Germany, Austria, and Switzerland; some works outside the book trade (but not theses or musical texts, as these have bibliographies of their own); the more important official publications; and books in other languages published in Germany. Includes books, periodicals, and maps.

Five-year cumulations have appeared through 1966–70 (i.e., through v. 58 of the series). No five-year cumulations will be published for 1971–80; instead, there will be four cumulations covering 1971–73, 1974–75, 1976–77, and 1978–80.

§ Continued by: *Deutsche Nationalbibliographie und Bibliographie … Reihe E* (AA659).   Z2221.K25

Halbjahrsverzeichnis der im deutschen Buchhandel erschienenen Bücher, Zeitschriften und Landkarten : mit Voranzeigen von Neuigkeiten, Verlags- und Preisänderungen. Leipzig : Börsenverein der Deutschen Buchhändler, 1798–1944. v. 1–292.   **AA656**

Title varies: until 1915 was *Hinrichs' Halbjahrs-Katalog*.

Ceased publication. Continued by: *Jahresverzeichnis des deutschen Schrifttums*, bearb. und hrsg. von der Deutschen Bücherei und dem Börsenverein der Deutschen Buchändler zu Leipzig (Leipzig : Börsenverein, 1948–74. Jahrg. 164 ([1945/46])–170 ([1967]).

An annual cumulation of Reihe A and B of the *Deutsche Nationalbibliographie* (AA657).

Each year in two sections: I, *Titelverzeichnis*, listing works by author or catchword title; II, *Stich- und schlagwortregister*, listing works under catchword title and subject.

Cumulated into *Deutsches Bücherverzeichnis* (AA655).

Continued in turn by: *Jahresverzeichnis der Verlagsschriften* (Jahrg. 171–173. Leipzig : VEB Verlag für Buch- und Bibliothekswesen, 1972–78).

Continues its numbering and pattern of publication.

Full title: Jahresverzeichnis der Verlagsschriften und einer Auswahl der ausserhalb des Buchhandels erschienenen Veröffentlichungen der DDR, der BRD und Westberlins sowie der deutsch-sprachigen Werke anderer Länder.

Publication was suspended 1971–80 (1981–83 not published?); beginning with 1984 coverage, superseded by an annual index to Reihe A of *Deutsche Nationalbibliographie* (AA657).   Z2221.H66

Current

Deutsche Nationalbibliographie und Bibliographie der im Ausland erschienenen deutschsprachigen Veröffentlichungen / bearb. und hrsg., Die Deutsche Bibliothek. Frankfurt am Main : Buchhändler-Vereinigung, 1991– .   **AA657**

Frequency varies.

Formed by the merger of the East and West German bibliographies: *Deutsche Nationalbibliographie*, Reihe A–C, which ceased in 1990; and *Deutsche Bibliographie. Wöchentliches Verzeichnis* (AA652), Reihe A–C, H, N, M, and T, which ceased 1990.

Titles of sections incorporate frequency; e.g., Wöchentliches Verzeichnis, Vierteljährliches Verzeichnis.

Being published in the following sections: Reihe A, Monographien und Periodika des Verlagsbuchhandels (1991– . Weekly); Reihe B, Monographien und Periodika ausserhalb des Verlagsbuchhandels (1991–); Reihe C, Karten (1991–); Reihe G, Fremdsprachige Germanica und Übersetzungen deutschsprachiger Werke (1992?– . Quarterly); Reihe H., Hochschulschriften (1991– . Monthly); Reihe M, Musikalien und Musikschriften (1991– . Monthly); Reihe N, Vorankündigungen Monographien und Periodika (CIP) (1991– . Weekly); Reihe T, Musiktonträger (1991– . Monthly).

•Machine-readable version: *Deutsche Nationalbibliographie DNB aktuelle*.   Z2221F7

Deutsche Nationalbibliographie und Bibliographie der im Ausland erschienenen deutschsprachigen Veröffentlichungen : Reihe D, Monographien und periodika — Halbjahresverzeichnis. Jan.–Juni 1991– . Frankfurt am Main : Buchhändler-Vereinigung, 1991– . Semiannual.   **AA658**

Continues: *Deutsche Bibliographie: Halbjahres-Verzeichnis* (AA651).

A semiannual cumulation of Reihen A, B, and C of *Deutsche Nationalbibliographie und Bibliographie ...* (AA657). Currently issued in two parts., each with 2 v.: (1) Alphabetisches Titelverzeichnis; (2) Schlagwort- und Stichwortregister. This in turn cumulates into *Deutsche Nationalbibliographie und Bibliographie ...: Reihe F, Monographien und periodika — Funfjahres-Verzeichnis* (AA659).

Z2221.F73

Deutsche Nationalbibliographie und Bibliographie der im Ausland erschienenen deutschsprachigen Veröffentlichungen : Reihe E, Monographien und periodika — Fünfjahresverzeichnis / Bearbeiter und Herausgeber : Die Deutsche Bibliothek. 1986–90– . Frankfurt am Main : Buchhändler-Vereinigung, 1992– . Quinquennial.   **AA659**

Represents a merger of *Deutsche Bibliographie : Fünfjahres-Verzeichnis* (AA650) and *Deutsches Bücherverzeichnis* (AA655).

Cumulates *Deutsche Nationalbibliographie und Bibliographie ...*, Reihen A, B, C, and H (BJ48). Issued in two parts: T. 1, Alphabetisches Titelverzeichnis, T. 2, Schlagwort- und Stichwortregister.

Verzeichnis lieferbarer Bücher. 1971/72– . Frankfurt am Main : Verlag der Buchhändler-Vereinigung GmbH, 1971– . Biennial.   **AA660**

Ed.5 (1975/76)– have title also in English: *German books in print*. On spine: VLB.

Originally published in two parts per year: "Bücherverzeichnis im Autorenalphabet" and "Titelregister mit Verweisung auf den Autor." Now issued in a single alphabetical sequence with subtitle: *Bücherverzeichnis im Autorenalphabet kumuliert mit Titel– und Stichwortregistr mit Verweisung auf den Autor*. Includes a list of publishers, with addresses. A spring supplement is included in the subscription price, and a separate *ISBN-Register* is also available.

──. *Schlagwort-Verzeichnis. Subject guide to German books in print* (1978 79 . Frankfurt am Main : Verlag de Buchhndler Verinigung GmbH, 1979–). Provides a subject arrangement of the items in *VLB*. A list of headings used now precedes the main text.

§ *WerWasWo? im Taschenbuch: Gesamtverzeichnis aller Taschenbücher* (München : Rossipaul, 1981– . Annual) provides an in-print record for German popular publications in pocket format.

Z2221.V47

Great Britain

British Museum. Department of Printed Books. General catalogue of printed books. Photolithographic edition to 1955. London : Trustees of the British Museum, 1959–66. 263 v.   **AA661**

The possession of the copyright privilege helps to make this the most comprehensive collection of British materials in existence, and therefore it serves as an extensive national bibliography. For full information on the *Catalogue* and its supplements *see* AA103.   Z921.B87

Corns, Albert Reginald. A bibliography of unfinished books in the English language, with annotations / Albert Reginald Corns, Archibald Sparke. London : Quaritch, 1915. 255 p.   **AA662**

Repr. : Detroit : Gale, 1968.

An alphabetical list of works which began publication but were never finished.   Z1025.C7

Lowndes, William Thomas. Bibliographer's manual of English literature : containing an account of rare, curious, and useful books, published in or relating to Great Britain and Ireland, from the invention of printing .... New ed. rev., corr., and enl. by H. G. Bohn. London : Bell, 1857–1864. 6 v. in 11.   **AA663**

Repr.: Detroit : Gale, 1967. 8 v.

Contents: v. 1–5 (in 10 pts.), A–Z; v.6, Appendix containing lists of publications of societies and printing clubs, books issued by private presses, lists of series, etc.

Arranged alphabetically by author, with many title and catchword entries. Lists about 50,000 works, giving for each: author, title, place, date, size, with occasional notes as to rarity, value, editions, reprints, etc., and often records of prices at various 19th-century sales. While the prices shown are now only of historical interest, and there are some inaccuracies, the work remains useful for other information. The title and catchword entries are sometimes helpful in verifying citations not easily located in other catalogs.   Z2001.L92

Watt, Robert. Bibliotheca britannica : or, A general index to British and foreign literature. Edinburgh : Constable, 1824. 4 v.   **AA664**

Vol. 1–2, Author list, arranged alphabetically, with author's full name and dates, very brief biographical data, and for each book brief information which generally includes title, date, size, number of volumes; v. 3–4, An alphabetical subject list, serving as an index to the author volumes, giving for each book its date and brief title, and referring to the section of the author list (indicated by number and letter) where somewhat fuller information can be found. Anonymous titles are listed in this section.

Often useful for material not given in more modern catalogs, but sometimes inaccurate and so must be used with some caution.

Z2001.W34

Before 1640

Allison, Antony Francis. Titles of English books (and of foreign books printed in England) : an alphabetical finding-list by title of books published under the author's name, pseudonym or initials / Antony Francis Allison, V. F. Goldsmith. [Folkestone, Eng.] : Dawson : Hamden, Conn. : Archon Books, [1976–77]. 2 v.   **AA665**

Contents: v. 1, 1475–1640; v. 2, 1641–1700.

Vol. 1 offers a title approach to the 1st edition of Pollard and Redgrave's *Short-title catalogue ... 1475–1640* and some references to the 2nd edition (AA671). Vol. 2 provides a similar approach to Wing's *Short-title catalogue* (AA683).

A review of v. 1 in *Times literary supplement* (24 Sept. 1976) : 1221 expresses reservations about the completeness of the work and the form of entry chosen for many titles.   Z2001.A44

Bibliographical Society, London. Hand-lists of books printed by London printers, 1501–1556 / by E. G. Duff, W. W. Greg ... [et al.]. London : The Society, 1913. 4 pts. in 1 v. : ill., facsims.   **AA666**

Lists of the books printed by 89 printers up to the grant of a charter to the Stationers' Company in 1557. Publication in parts began in 1895 and sections have no continuous paging, thus allowing the completed work to be bound either alphabetically by printers' names or chronologically by their dates. Prepared (and sold only to members of the Society) as a basis for further work in the English bibliography of the period.   Z152.L8B5

Bishop, William Warner. A checklist of American copies of "Short-title catalogue" books. 2nd ed. Ann Arbor : Univ. of Michigan Pr., 1950. 203 p.   **AA667**

Repr.: N.Y. : Greenwood, 1968.

Compiled as a convenient guide to the location of *STC* titles in American libraries, this is a record of *STC* numbers with indication of holdings in some 110 libraries and collections. The 2nd ed. includes corrections and additions to the list in the 1st ed., publ. 1944, and records the holdings of about ten more libraries.   Z2002.P772B5

British Museum. Department of Printed Books. Catalogue of books in the library of the British Museum printed in England, Scotland, and Ireland, and of books in English printed abroad to the year 1640. London : Trustees, 1884. 3 v.   **AA668**

Alphabetically arranged, with index by title, subject, and form, e.g., plays, poems, etc., and an index of printers, booksellers, and stationers.   Z2002.B86

Cambridge University Library. Early English printed books in the University Library, 1475–1640. Cambridge : Univ. Pr., 1900–1907. 4 v.   **AA669**

Repr.: N.Y. : Johnson Reprint, 1971.

Vol. 1, 1475–1500, Caxton to F. Kingston; v. 2, 1501–1640, E. Mattes to R. Marriot and English provincial presses; v. 3, Scottish, Irish, and foreign presses, with addenda; v. 4, Indexes.

Includes 8,083 titles, arranged by presses, with full indexes of authors and titles, printers and stationers, engravers and painters, towns, portraits, music.   Z2002.C17

Greg, Walter Wilson. A companion to Arber. Oxford : Clarendon Pr., 1967. 451 p.   **AA670**

Subtitle: Being a calendar of documents in Edward Arber's *Transcript of the registers of the Company of Stationers of London, 1554–1640;* with text and calendar of supplementary documents.

A chronological calendar of the documents and illustrative matter interpolated into Arber's *Transcript* (AA674), plus additional, similar documents not in Arber. Indexed.   Z151.3.G68

Pollard, Alfred W. A short-title catalogue of books printed in England, Scotland, & Ireland and of English books printed abroad, 1475–1640 / first comp. by A. W. Pollard & G. R. Redgrave. 2nd ed. rev. & enl. / begun by W. A. Jackson & F. S. Ferguson, completed by Katharine F. Pantzer. London : Bibliographical Society, 1976–91. 3 v.   **AA671**

1st ed., 1926.

Frequently cited as *STC*.

Contents: v. 1–2, A–Z; v. 3, Indexes, appendices, addenda, and corrigenda.

A listing by title (5 words minimum) of every book or broadside printed in England in any language, or in English anywhere in the world from 1475 through 1640. Arranged alphabetically by author and other main entries; gives, for each item, author, brief title, size, printer, date, reference to entry of the book in the Stationers' registers, extensive editorial information (variant titles, editions, etc.), detailed notes, and indication of libraries possessing copies (or photocopies when the original text has been lost). This last important feature aims to record all known copies of very rare items and, in the case of commoner books, a selection in some 500 representative British, American, Australian and New Zealand libraries. The compiler used David Ramage's *A finding-list of English books to 1640 in libraries in the British Isles* (AA672) and William Warner Bishop's *A checklist of American copies of "Short-title catalogue" books* (AA667) for many additional locations, but notes that "these two works can still be of use in finding extra copies of more common items."—*p. xlix.*

"Most items in the *STC* revision retain the number alloted to them in old STC, and generally there is a simple correspondence of old numbers with revised entries … . When an entry in old *STC* has been moved, the new entry contains a note of the old number, and the old number has been turned into a cross-reference to the new number."—*p. xxxi–xxxii.*

The 2nd ed. of the *STC* has been widely acclaimed; *see* the *TLS* reviews (v. 1, 13 Feb. 1978: 170; v. 2, 27 August 1976: 1061; v. 3, 13 Dec. 1991: 25). The reviewer of v. 1 states that the new *STC* has "now become the most meticulous and definitive extended work of bibliography, in any language and on any subject, ever achieved."   Z2002.P77

Ramage, David. A finding-list of English books to 1640 in libraries in the British Isles (excluding the national libraries and the libraries of Oxford and Cambridge) : based on the numbers in Pollard and Redgrave's Short-title catalogue of books printed in England, Scotland and Ireland & English books printed abroad, 1475–1640 / with assistance from Mrs. M. S. G. Macleod (Miss Hands), A. I. Doyle, and Donald Hill. Durham, Eng. : Council of the Durham Colleges, 1958. 101 p.   **AA672**

"A project of the Standing Conference of National and University Libraries."—*title page.*

Gives additional locations for some 14,000 items in *STC* (AA671), arranged by *STC* number, plus a supplementary list of titles not in *STC*.   Z2002.P772R3

Shaaber, Matthias Adam. Check-list of works of British authors printed abroad in languages other than English, to 1641. N.Y. : Bibliographical Soc. of America, 1975. 168 p.   **AA673**

"British authors" are here defined as "(1) all writers born in the British Isles, including those who spent most of their lives abroad, (2) all writers born elsewhere who spent considerable parts of their mature lives in the British Isles."—*Pref.* Anonymous works are included if there is "direct evidence" or a consensus of opinion that they are of British origin." Locates copies.   Z1012.S49

Stationers' Company (London). A transcript of the registers of the Company of Stationers of London, 1554–1640 / ed. by Edward Arber. London : Priv. Pr., 1875–77 ; Birmingham, 1894. 5 v.   **AA674**

In chronological order with no indexes, these are transcripts of the manuscript registers. Difficult to use and sometimes inaccurate. For the most part superseded by Pollard and Redgrave, *Short-title catalogue* (AA671).   Z2002.S79

17th and 18th centuries

Bibliographies with the title *London catalogue of books*, published first by Bent and later by Hodgson, were issued covering, with considerable duplication of years, books published in Great Britain, 1700–1855. The 19th-century volumes formed one of the sources from which the 1801–36 and 1835–63 volumes of the *English catalogue* (below) were compiled and for ordinary purposes are therefore not often needed; but libraries having the 18th-century volumes will still use them for material not included in Robert Watt's *Bibliotheca britannica* or William Thomas Lowndes's *Bibliographer's manual of English literature* (both above). For a record of editions of *London catalogue*, see Adolf Growoll, *Three centuries of English book-trade bibliography* (N.Y. : Dibdin Club, 1903. 195 p.).

Arber, Edward. Term catalogues, 1668–1709 A.D. with a number for Easter term, 1711 A.D. London : Arber ; N.Y. : Dodd, 1903–1906. 3 v.   **AA675**

Repr. : N.Y. : Johnson, 1965.

Subtitle: A contemporary bibliography of English literature in the reigns of Charles II, James II, William and Mary, and Anne; edited from the very rare quarterly lists of new books … issued by the booksellers of London.

Copies of contemporary records arranged chronologically, with indexes by titles, names, and subjects in each volume.   Z2002.A31

Bibliotheca annua : or, The annual catalogue for the year, 1699–[March 25, 1704]. London : J. Nutt, 1700–1703. no. 1–4.   **AA676**

Repr.: London : Gregg, 1964.

Subtitle [varies slightly]: Being an exact catalogue of all English and Latin books, printed in England from January, 169 $^8_9$, to [March 25, 1704]. To which is added the titles of French books imported within the said time; as also most of the prizes [sic] that they are generally sold for.

Classified annual catalogs, with indexes for some years, and for these years the work is easier to use than *Term catalogues* (AA675). Titles are quite full, and include edition, publisher, and price.

British Museum. Department of Printed Books. Thomason Collection. Catalogue of the pamphlets, books, newspapers, and manuscripts relating to the Civil War, the Commonwealth, and Restoration collected by George Thomason, 1640–1661. London : Trustees, 1908. 2 v.　　　　　**AA677**

Running title: The Thomason tracts.

A very rich collection for this period, arranged chronologically with author, anonymous title, and subject index. Newspapers, 1641–43, listed in v. 2, p. 371–440.　　　　**Z2018.B85**

Clough, Eric A. A short-title catalogue arranged geographically of books printed and distributed by printers, publishers and booksellers in the English provincial towns and in Scotland and Ireland up to and including the year 1700. London : Libr. Assoc., 1969. 119 p.　　　　**AA678**

Arranged by city. Based on the 1st ed. of Pollard and Redgrave's *Short-title catalogue ... 1475–1640* (AA671) and the 1st ed. of Wing's *Short-title catalogue, 1641–1700* (AA683). Designed to complement H. G. Aldis's *List of books printed in Scotland before 1700* (AA695), E. R. McC. Dix's *Catalogue of early Dublin-printed books, 1601–1700* (AA721), and Falconer Madan's *Oxford books* (Oxford, 1895–1931); it therefore omits items appearing in those lists.　　**Z2002.C62**

Early English books, 1641–1700 : a cumulative index to units 1–60 of the microfilm collection. Ann Arbor, Mich. : Univ. Microfilms, 1990. 9 v. (7386 p.).　　　　**AA679**

A cumulative index to units 1–32 was published 1981–82 as *Accessing early English books, 1641–1700*.

Contents: v. 1–2, Author index; v. 3–5, Title index; v. 6–8, Subject index; v. 9, Wing number and reel position index.

Provides indexes to the first 60 units (about 42,500 titles) of the microform series *Early English books ...*, the project designed to microfilm all available items listed in Donald Wing's *Short title catalogue* (AA683) and the Thomason tracts. The author index lists primary, secondary, and corporate authors; subject indexing is by Library of Congress subject headings.　　　　**Z2002.E22**

Eighteenth-century British books : an author union catalogue extracted from the British Museum general catalogue of printed books, the catalogues of the Bodleian Library, and of the University Library, Cambridge / by F. J. G. Robinson [et al.]. Folkestone, Eng. : Dawson, 1981. 5 v.　**AA680**

It is generally agreed that this compilation was a seriously misguided effort (*see* reviews in *The book collector* [Autumn 1981]: 413; *TLS* [Dec. 11, 1981]: 1450; and *The library*, [Dec. 1982]: 453); it is mentioned here to avoid possible confusion with the ongoing Eighteenth Century Short Title Catalogue project, (*see* AA681), records of which are currently available online through the RLIN network.
　　　　Z1016.E36

The eighteenth century short title catalogue 1990 [microform]. Microfiche edition. [London] : The British Library, [1990]. 220 microfiches.　　　　**AA681**

Supersedes the 1983 microfiche ed.

The *ESTC*, an ambitious project begun at the British Library, and now involving libraries in the U.S. and Germany, is an online union list of the holdings of more than 1,000 libraries throughout the world of material published in Great Britain and its dependencies (including the U.S.) and material in English wherever published from 1701 through 1800. "Publication" is broadly defined; the *ESTC* includes advertisements, shipping lists, society membership lists, transport timetables, the sessional papers of the House of Commons, etc. Periodicals published more than once a year, engraved music, separately published maps, and playbills are excluded. Although called a short-title catalog, it offers detailed bibliographic descriptions; all known locations are listed.

The new microfiche edition is a "snapshot" of the online file as of 1990, and includes nearly 300,000 records. It is arranged by author, or title if anonymous, with date and place of publication indexes, and five genre indexes listing advertisements, almanacs, directories, prospectuses, and single-sheet verse.

The *ESTC* is maintained as part of the RLIN database. The March 1987 issue of *Factotum* (the newsletter issued by the ESTC project), called "Occasional paper 5," is entitled "Searching the *ESTC* on RLIN," and provides a detailed description of the search capabilities and protocols. A rather discursive set of articles discussing various aspects of the *ESTC* appears in *Papers of the Bibliographical Society of America* (Oct./Dec. 1981): 371–400.

Works in this set are being reproduced on microfilm in a series entitled *The eighteenth century* (Woodbridge, Conn. : Research Publications, 1983– .).

In 1994, RLIN announced that *ESTC* will add earlier works (basically Pollard and Redgrave and Wing) and will be known as *English short title catalogue*.

Jefcoate, Graham. A catalogue of English books printed before 1801 held by the University Library at Göttingen / comp. by Graham Jefcoate and Karen Kloth ; ed. for the Library by Bernhard Fabian. Hildesheim ; N.Y. : Olms : Weidmann, 1987–1988. 3 v. in 7.　　　　**AA682**

Contents: Pt. 1, v. 1–2, 1470–1700; Pt. 2, v. 1–4, 1701–1800; Pt. 3, Indices.

At head of title: Niedersächsische Staats- und Universitätsbibliothek Göttingen.

Prepared in cooperation with *Eighteenth century short-title catalogue* (AA681; Göttingen's 18th-century titles are included in *ESTC*), this publication provides detailed bibliographic descriptions for nearly 20,000 titles in "one of the largest repositories of early English books outside the English-speaking world."—*Pref.* Pt. 1 contains "(1) Books, pamphlets, single sheets and periodical publications printed in any language in the British Isles or English colonies; (2) Books printed in English anywhere ... ; (3) Books by English-speaking authors or subjects of English-speaking states regardless of language or place of publication ... ; (4) Translations of works by English-speaking authors ... ; (5) Works with false imprints purporting to have been printed in an English-speaking country."—*Introd. to Pt. 1*. Arranged alphabetically by author or anonymous title; Pt. 1 includes indexes by Goff, STC, and Wing numbers. Pt. 2 adheres to the same criteria. It includes items published in the U.S. and India; advertisements and prospectuses are also listed. Pt. 3 has indexes to prospectuses, to advertisements, to dates of publication, and to places of publication.

　　　　Z2002.J44

Wing, Donald Goddard. Short-title catalogue of books printed in England, Scotland, Ireland, Wales, and British America, and of English books printed in other countries, 1641–1700. 2nd ed., rev. and enl. N.Y. : Index Committee of the Modern Language Association of America, 1972–1988. 3 v.　**AA683**

1st ed., 1945–51.

Published as a continuation of Alfred W. Pollard and G. R. Redgrave's *Short-title catalogue ... 1475–1640* (AA671). Items are located in more than 300 libraries; relatively common books are given five locations in Great Britain and five in the U.S. in as varied geographical areas as possible in order to provide convenient locations for scholars in various parts of the country. It is not a census of copies, and "it is only when less than five copies are located in either British or American libraries that any deduction can be drawn that copies mentioned are all that the editor has found."—*Pref.* Location symbols follow a system devised by Wing, and revised in the 2nd ed.

"Unfortunately, about seven or eight percent of the numbers in the revised first volume were shifted one or two numbers to fill gaps caused by moving entries elsewhere. Confusingly, some new entries appeared with numbers assigned to an entirely different work in the first edition. A complete list of these number changes, giving a correlation of old and new numbers and providing references for those items moved to places in the second and third volumes, is published [in v. 2]."—*Pref., v. 2.* Users of v. 2 "may be assured that no number has been reassigned in this volume, except those designated 'entry cancelled' in the first edition and thus never allocated in print for a specific book."

A review of v. 2 in *Times literary supplement* (Dec. 17, 1982) : 1403, points out certain shortcomings of the work.

The scope and method of selection and entry are described in the preface, which should be carefully read before the book is used in order not to misinterpret or misunderstand the information given.

§ For serials published during this period, *see* Carolyn Nelson and Matthew Seccombe, *British newspapers and periodicals, 1641–1700* (AD107).   Z2002.W52

19th and 20th centuries

The bookseller. no. 1455 (Oct. 6, 1933)– . London : Whitaker, 1933– . Weekly.   **AA684**

Continues *Bookseller and stationery trades' journal, Publisher and bookseller*, and other works of similar titles published monthly (1858–1908) and weekly (1909–).

Includes weekly alphabetical lists of new publications and reissues. Through 1969 the weekly lists cumulated monthly in the last issue of the month and these, in turn, cumulated into *Whitaker's cumulative book list*. Beginning Jan. 1970, the monthly cumulative feature was incorporated into *Whitaker's books of the month and books to come* (AA688), which ceased in 1992.   Z2005.B72

British paperbacks in print. 1982–1985. London : J. Whitaker & Sons, 1982–85. Annual.   **AA685**

Similar in format and arrangement to *Whitaker's books in print* (AA691).

Supersedes: *Paperbacks in print* (May 1961–1980/81. London : J. Whitaker & Sons, 1961–81. 21 v.).

Scope is limited "to books of 96 pages or more which are reprints of original hardback books, simultaneous publications, or originals, issued by firms recognised by the book trade as paperback publishers."—*Pref.* Includes English-language paperbacks published abroad but "available in the United Kingdom through a sole stock-holding agent." Computer produced.

English catalogue of books. London : Publishers' Circular, 1864–1966. [various volumes].   **AA686**

Repr.: N.Y. : Kraus, 1963.

Subtitle varies. Publisher varies (S. Low, 1864–1901).

Vols. 1–3, 1835/63–1872/80, comp. by Sampson Low.

Volume covering 1801–36, published in 1914 and unnumbered, includes authors and catchword titles in one alphabet. [v. 1] covers 1835–63. Later 19th-century volumes were published at irregular intervals; 1901–35 volumes cover 5-year periods; 1936–41; 1942–47; 1948–52; 1952–55; 1956–59; 1960–62; 1963–65.

The standard English trade list during its period of publication. Reasonably comprehensive for books and pamphlets issued at main publishing centers, but less complete for the provincial presses. Arrangement is alphabetical by author with title and catchword subject entries, except that from 1837 to 1889 the subject entries are in separate index volumes (*see* below). Information given varies, but usually includes author, title, publisher, date, size, and price.

Arrangement changed with the 1960–62 volume: (1) paperback section, authors and titles in one alphabet; (2) author section, giving full bibliographical information; (3) title section, including inverted titles; (4) maps and atlases; (5) list of publishers.

Cumulated the annual *English catalogue of books*, 1835–1965 (the 1966–68 volumes remain uncumulated).

Over the years, the information for the compilation was derived mainly from the weekly *Publishers' circular* ... (1837–1959). During the period 1959–66, this was incorporated into a monthly, *British books*, which continued the volume numbering of the earlier publication and offered articles, announcements, etc., as well as the listings of new books which served as the basis for the *English catalogue*. (In 1967, *British books* was absorbed by *The publisher*, which assumed the volume numbering of the former and, in turn, ceased with the issue of Dec. 1970.).

Index to the English catalogue of books, 1837–1889 (London : S. Low, 1858–93. 4 v.).

Forms a subject index to v. 1–4 of the author catalog. No more published, as from v. 5 on, the *English catalogue* includes authors and catchword subjects in one alphabet.   Z2001.E52

Nineteenth century short title catalogue : Series I, Phase I, 1801–1815. Newcastle-upon-Tyne, Eng. : Avero ; Teaneck, N.J. : dist. by Chadwyck-Healy, c1984– . Ser. 1, v. 1–5; ser. 2, v. 1–8, 10–32, 34–40. (In progress).   **AA687**

Ser. 1, phase 1, 1801–1815; ser. 2, phase 1, 1816–1870. A third series will cover 1871–1918.

"Extracted from the catalogues of the Bodleian Library, the British Library, the Library of Trinity College, Dublin, the National Library of Scotland, and the University Libraries of Cambridge and Newcastle."—*t.p.*

Pref. signed J. W. Jolliffe.

Contents: Ser. 1 (1801–1815), phase 1, v. 1–4, A–Z; v. 5, England, Ireland, Scotland, London, directories, ephemerides and periodical publications, Title index [to v. 5], 1st supplement [and] cumulative imprint and subject indexes to v. 1–4; v. 6, Title index [to v. 1–4 and 1st suppl.]; Ser. 2 (1816–1870), phase 1, v. 1–36, A–Sinclair; v. 30, Boston, Massachusetts, directories, ephemerides, and hymnals.

An attempt to provide a comprehensive bibliographic record of "British" books published during the 19th century. "British books are taken to include all books published in Britain, its colonies and the United States of America; all books in English wherever published; and all translations from English."—*Introd.*

The first series was compiled from the in-house and published catalogs of the six libraries named above; rarely were books themselves examined. The second series added the catalogs of the libraries of Harvard University and the Library of Congress. As far as possible, entries from those catalogs have been adapted to the form and order of the British Museum *General catalogue* (AA103), with cross-references from alternative entries; thus the listing is basically by author or anonymous title (although the latter often takes the form of keyword entry). Each entry carries a reference number and, as applicable, includes an author statement (with epithet or life span dates), short title, as many as three Dewey classification numbers, the edition statement (which gives date, place of publication other than London, number of parts, and the names of editors, translators, etc.), and library locations. Each volume of Series 1 has had an imprint index (i.e., by place of publication) and a subject index according to the broad Dewey class numbers assigned to the items. These indexes have cumulated in Series 1, v. 5. Series 2 has subject and imprint indexes in every fifth volume. The subject indexes only list very broad topics, and refer only to item numbers; subjects can often refer to hundreds of undifferentiated items. Thus far, the indexes in Series 2 have not cumulated.

Introductory and explanatory matter is disappointingly brief (e.g., there is no sample entry to illustrate the various components of a typical citation). The review in *Times literary supplement* (April 6, 1984) : 381 supplies a good deal of useful information on both the background of the catalog and the content of the entries.

Whitaker's books of the month and books to come. Jan. 1970–Sept. 1992. London : J. Whitaker, 1970–1992. Monthly.   **AA688**

A service designed "to provide a record of the past month's books, together with those announced for publication in the next two months."—*Introd.* Replaced the monthly cumulated list of "Publications of the month" previously appearing in *The bookseller* (AA684) and incorporated listings for forthcoming books. ("Publications of the week" remains a feature of *The bookseller*, and *Whitaker's book list*, AA690, provides the quarterly and annual cumulations).   Z2005.W56

Current

The British national bibliography. 1950– . London : British Library, Bibliographic Services Div., 1950– .   **AA689**

Published weekly (except at Easter and Christmas) with cumulations at intervals which have varied (currently Jan.–Apr. and May–Aug.), and an annual volume. (For 3- to 5-year cumulations, *see* below for *Cumulated subject catalogue* and *Cumulated index*.) Now printed "from computer-controlled typesetting."

Beginning 1976, the annual cumulation is issued in 2 v.: v. 1, Subject catalogue (arranged by Dewey class numbers); v. 2, Indexes (offering separate author/title and alphabetical subject approaches).

An excellently planned and executed national bibliography, prepared at the British Library and based upon the books deposited at the Copyright Office. It aims to list and describe every new work published in Great Britain with certain specific exceptions: periodicals (except the first issue of a new periodical or a periodical under a new title); music; maps; certain government publications; cheap novelettes, etc.

The main section in each issue is classified by the Dewey Decimal Classification. Each weekly issue has an author and title index, and the last issue for each month now has a cumulated author/title index and a cumulated subject index for the month. Each cumulation is now in three sections: (1) Classified subject section; (2) Author and title section; and (3) Subject index. The author/title section includes entries for editors, translators, and series.

Full cataloging detail is given in the classified section, including: author, title, place, publisher, date, paging, illustrations, centimeter size, series, and price. The author/title section provides briefer information, adequate for many purposes, giving author, title, publisher, price, and classification number (the latter serving as an index number for finding the more detailed information in the classified section). The subject index is an alphabetical subject approach to the classification numbers used during the period covered by the cumulation.

Annual volumes for the 1951–70 period are superseded by the *Cumulated subject catalogue* and the *Cumulated index. A Cumulated author & title index, 1971–1973* (publ. 1977) provides a single alphabetical sequence of author and title entries from the annual indexes for the period, but the annual volumes are not superseded.

Beginning in 1977 the *BNB* carries advance cataloging information in the form of CIP (cataloging in publication) records in the weekly lists, thus increasing the bibliography's usefulness as a current selection tool since the entries appear as much as two months in advance of publication of the books themselves. Such entries are identified in the annotations as "CIP entry." As titles are published and deposited in the Copyright Receipt Office the corresponding entries are expanded to include full cataloging information and the full form appears in subsequent interim cumulations and in the annual volume identified as "CIP rev."

————. *Cumulated subject catalogue, 1951/54–1968/70* (London, 1958–73).

1951–54, 2 v.; 1955–59, 3 v.; 1960–64, 3 v.; 1965–67, 3 v; 1968 70, 2 v.

Cumulations of the material appearing in the classified sections of the annual volumes, originally made by cutting and arranging the entries in classified sequence and reproducing by photo-offset printing; beginning with 1960–64 cumulation, rephotographing has been done by Fotolist camera. Information, therefore, is that current at the time of the annual volumes. (Material from the 1950 volume was omitted from the first cumulation due to difference in format, and that volume is not superseded.).

————. *Cumulated index, 1950/54–1968/70* (London, 1955–73).

Quinquennial 1950–64; triennial, 1965–70.

Each volume is a cumulation in one alphabetical sequence of the author, title, and subject sections of the annual volume. These indexes serve as keys to the *Cumulated subject catalogue* and thus together provide a comprehensive record of British publications for the period, superseding the annual volumes.

•Machine-readable version: *British national bibliography on CD-ROM* [database] (London : British Library, 1950–).   Z2001.B75

Whitaker's book list. 1987– . London : J. Whitaker & Sons, Ltd., [c1987]– . Annual.   **AA690**

Title varies: 1924–86, *Whitaker's cumulative book list*, issued quarterly, cumulating throughout the year, and eventually cumulating into *Whitaker's five-year cumulative book list*.

"Endeavours to provide the complete list of all books published in the United Kingdom during the period, giving details as to author, title, subtitle, size, number of pages, price, date, classification, Standard Book Number and publisher of every book, in one alphabetical ar-

rangement under author, title and subject, where this forms part of the title."—*Pref*. Kept up-to-date by weekly lists in *The bookseller* (AA684). Cumulated by *Whitaker's five-year cumulative book list* (AA692).   Z2005.W57

Whitaker's books in print. 1988– . London : J. Whitaker & Sons, c1988– . Annual.   **AA691**

Continues: 1874–1961, *The reference catalogue of current literature*; 1962–87, *British books in print*.

1874–1932, a collection of publishers' catalogs bound together alphabetically by name of firm, with a detailed alphabetical index in a separate volume. Published about every fourth year during that period. Thereafter, published at irregular intervals and consolidated into two lists, author and title. Beginning 1971, a computer-produced annual with authors, titles, and catchwords in a single alphabetical sequence.   Z2001.R33

Whitaker's five-year cumulative book list. 1939/1943– . London : J. Whitaker & Sons, 1945– . Quinquenniel.   **AA692**

Title varies; some volumes are 4-year cumulations; 1973–75 is a 3-year cumulation.

1939/43, authors and titles in one alphabet; 1944/47–1948/52, authors and titles in separate alphabets; 1953/57– , authors, titles, and some subjects in one alphabet.

Privately printed

Dobell, Bertram. Catalogue of books printed for private circulation / collected by Bertram Dobell and now described and annotated by him. London : Dobell, 1906. 238 p.   **AA693**

Repr.: Detroit : Gale, 1966.

An author list, with full descriptions, including author's name, title, size, paging, date, price, size of edition when known, and bibliographical and historical notes with occasional quotations from the books themselves. Includes some, but not all, of the books listed in John Martin's *Bibliographical catalogue of privately printed books* (AA694).

Some 939 titles from this list are now in the Library of Congress, having been acquired in the Dobell collection of privately printed books purchased in 1914.   Z1028.D63

Martin, John. Bibliographical catalogue of privately printed books. 2nd ed. London : publ. for the author by J. Van Voort, 1854. 593 p. : ill.   **AA694**

Repr.: N.Y. : Johnson Reprint, 1968.

The 1st ed., 1834, was in two parts: (1) List of books, omitting pamphlets, arranged chronologically 1672–1833, giving author's name, title, place and printer when known, date, size and paging, with many bibliographical and historical notes and occasional references to authorities and copies; (2) List of books printed at private presses and for distribution among members of literary clubs, arranged by presses. General index of authors and titles. The list by presses contains some material not found in the appendix volume of William Thomas Lowndes, *Bibliographer's manual of English literature* (AA663). The 2nd ed. is a revision of the first part only, correcting some errors, adding previously omitted titles, and extending the list to 1853, but omitting the section of private presses.   Z1028.M38

Regional

Scotland

Aldis, Harry Gidney. List of books printed in Scotland before 1700 : including those printed furth of the realm for Scottish booksellers, with brief notes on the printers and stationers. [Edinburgh] : Edinburgh Bibliographical Soc., 1904. 153 p.   **AA695**

A preliminary hand list of 3,919 titles, arranged chronologically with an alphabetical index, and an index of printers, booksellers, and stationers.   Z2051.A55

Bibliography of Scotland. 1976/77– . Edinburgh : H.M.S.O., 1978– . Annual.   **AA696**

At head of title: National Library of Scotland.

Subtitle: A catalogue of books published in Scotland and of books published elsewhere of Scottish relevance, prepared from accessions received by the National Library of Scotland.

Beginning in 1990, with the issue for 1988, issued on microfiche; the fiche cumulates from 1988.

The first volume lists items published after 1975 and processed by the National Library in 1976–77; subsequent annual volumes continue to list post-1975 items processed during the year of coverage. In addition to books as specified in the subtitle, selected periodical articles, theses on Scottish topics acquired by the National Library, and music are included. First issues of new periodicals and changes of title are recorded. In two sections: (1) Topographical; (2) Subject. Name index.   Z2069.B52

Ferguson, Mary. Scottish Gaelic union catalogue : a list of books printed in Scottish Gaelic from 1567 to 1973 / Mary Ferguson, Ann Matheson. Edinburgh : National Library of Scotland, 1984. 200 p.   **AA697**

Intended as a finding list rather than a full bibliography: "Since not all copies of works were individually examined, the Catalogue cannot be regarded as a totally reliable bibliographical tool" (*Introd.*), and information found in Donald Maclean's *Typographia Scoto-Gadelica* (Edinburgh : Grant, 1915. 372 p.), for example, is not fully superseded. More than 3,000 entries for items in Scottish and British libraries; plans call for a supplement of foreign library holdings. Z2039.G3F47

Wales

Bibliotheca celtica / National Library of Wales. 1909–1981-84. Aberystwyth : The Library, 1910–1990. Annual.   **AA698**

Frequency varies.

Vols. for 1929/33–1949/52 called n.s., v. 1–5; vols. for 1953–57 called ser. 3, v. 1–5.

Includes works written in one of the Celtic languages or relating to any of the Celtic peoples, and works written in English on non-Celtic subjects by Welshmen. Volumes covering 1909–28 are an author listing; volumes after that include subject headings. Beginning with 1953 (designated the 3rd series) periodical articles are included.

Continued by: *Llyfryddiaeth Cymru = A bibliography of Wales*, Llyfregell Genedlaethol Cymru / National Library of Wales (Aberystwyth : The Library, 1992– . Biennial), a merger of *Bibliotheca celtica* and *Subject index to Welsh periodicals* (AD290).   Z2071.B56

Rees, Eiluned. Libri Walliae : a catalogue of Welsh books and books printed in Wales, 1546–1820 = Catalog o lyfrau cymraeg a llyfrau a argraffwyd yng nghymru, 1546–1820. Aberystwyth : National Library of Wales, 1987. 2 v. (923, lxxxx p.) : ill.   **AA699**

Added title page in Welsh. Introductory matter in English and Welsh.

While admitting imperfections, the compiler offers this as "the most comprehensive catalogue to date of Welsh books and books printed in Wales before 1820. Periodicals, newspapers, ephemera and ballads are not included. Ballads are defined … as poems for which tunes are provided, although exceptions are made for elegies."—*Guide for the reader.* Arranged by author, issuing body, or key word in title, with five indexes: titles, names, chronological; the book-trade (Wales); the book-trade (outside Wales). Vol. 2 includes an essay on "The Welsh book-trade before 1820" and a section of reproductions of "Some ornaments used by printers of Welsh books." Does not locate copies.   Z2071.L5

Rowlands, William. Cambrian bibliography : containing an account of the books printed in the Welsh language, or relating to Wales, from the year 1546 to the end of the eighteenth century; with biographical notices / by the late Rev. William Rowlands (Gwilym Lleyn) ; ed. and enl. by the Rev. D. Silvan Evans. Llanidloes : J. Pryse, 1869. 754 p.   **AA700**

Repr.: Amsterdam : Meridian Publ. Co., 1970.

Annotations, etc., in Welsh; English preface.   Z2071.R88

Greece

Gkinēs, Dēmētrios S. Hellēnikē bibliographia, 1800–1863 : Anagraphē tōn kata tēn chronikēn tauten periodon opou depote Hellenisti ekdothēntōn bibliōn kai entypōn en genei/ … Brabeutheisa hypo tes Akadēmias Athenōn / Dēmētrios S. Gkinēs, Balērios G. Mēxa. En Athenais : Grapheion Demosieumatōn Akadēmias Athenōn, 1939–57. 3 v. (Pragmateiai tes Akadēmias Athenōn, Tomos 11).   **AA701**

Contents: T. I, 1800–1839; T. II, 1840–1855; T. III, 1856–1863, and supplement, 1800–1855.

Intended as a continuation of the bibliographies by Emile Louis Jean Legrand (AA703).

Ladas, Geōrgios G. Hellēnikē vivliographia : symbolē sto dekato ogdoo aiōna / [hypo] Geōriou G. Lada kai Athanasiou D. Chatzēdēou. Athēna, 1964/-76. 2 v.   **AA702**

"Prosthēkes dirothōseis stēn Hellēnikē vivliographia tōn Emile Legrand, Louis Petit kai Hubert Pernot."—*t.p.*

A listing of 18th-century publications. Serves as a supplement to Emile Louis Jean Legrand's *Bibliographie hellénique* (AA703) for the same period.

Continued by: ———. ——— (Athēna : Alpha Pr., 1970–76. 3 v.).

Contents: v. 1, Tōn etōn 1791–1795 (1970. 431 p.); v. 2, Tōn etōn 1796–1799 (1973. 415 p.); v. 3, Prostheamkeis kai symplērōseis (1976. 32 p.).   Z2292.L25

Legrand, Emile Louis Jean. Bibliographie hellénique : ou, Description raisonnée des ouvrages publiés en grec par des Grecs aux XVᵉ et XVIᵉ siècles. Paris : Leroux, 1885–1906. 4 v. : ill.   **AA703**

Repr.: Paris : Maisonneuve, 1963.

Publisher varies. Title varies.

Covers the period 1476–1600 as follows: v. 1–2, Works published in Greek by the Greeks, 1476–1599; v. 3, Works published in Latin by the Greeks, 1469–1599; v. 4, Works published in Greek and other languages, 1551–1600.

———. *Bibliographie hellénique : ou, Description raisonée des ouvrages publiés par des Grecs aux dix-septième siècle* (Paris : Picard, 1894–96 ; Maisonneuve, 1903. 5 v.).

Contents: v. 1, 1601–1644; v. 2, 1645–1690; v. 3, 1691–1700, Notices biographiques; v. 4–5, Notices biographiques [con'd.].

Broader in scope than the author's volumes for the 15th and 16th centuries, including *tout ouvrage ayant un Grec pour auteur ou éditeur, tout ouvrage auquel le nom d'un Grec est attaché d'une façon quelconque.*

———. *Bibliographie hellénique : ou, Description raisonnée des ouvrages publiés par des Grecs aux dix-huitiéme siécle,* oeuvre posthume, complétée et pub. par Louis Petit et Hubert Pernot (Paris : Garnier, 1918–28. 2 v. ; ill.).

Covers 1701–90.

Listings supplementary to the three Legrand bibliographies cited above appear in: M. I. Manousakas, "Prosthekai kai sympleroseis eis ten Helleniken bibliographian tou E. Legrand (Symbole prote)," Akademia Athenon. Mesaionikon Archeion. *Epeteris* 7 (1957): 34–83.

———. *Bibliographie ionienne : description raisonnée des ouvrages publiés par les Grecs des Sept-Iles ou concernant ces iles du 15. siècle á l'année 1900,* oeuvre posthume complétée par Hubert Pernot (Paris : Leroux, 1910. 2 v.).   Z2292.L511

Papadopoulos, Thōmas I. Hellēnikē vivliographia : 1466 ci.-1800. Athēnai : Grapheion Dēmosieumatōn tēs Akadēmias Athēnōn, 1984–86. 2 v. (Pragmateiai tēs Akadēmias Athēnōn, t. 48).   **AA704**

Contents: v. 1, Alphavétikè ai chronologiké anakatataxis; v. 2, Prosthetais_ymperoseis diorthoseis.

Introductory summary in English.

Includes and supplements items from Emile Legrand's *Bibliographie hellénique* (AA703) but does not supersede his descriptions. Vol. 1 is an alphabetical listing of titles published in Greece or in Greek throughout the world, followed by a chronological listing of short titles. Entries in the alphabetical section include brief bibliographic descriptions, reference to other bibliographies, and locations in selected libraries. Printer, place of publication, and country of issue indexes.

Vol. 2 contains detailed bibliographic descriptions with citations to catalogs and selected locations of newly identified titles (these titles are also included in v. 1.). It is arranged chronologically, with additions and corrections beginning on p. 351. Separate indexes for author, or title if anonymous; date; and name, including editors and printers.

Z2282.P36

Politēs, Nikolaos G. Hellēnikē bibliographia : katalogos tōn en Helladi ē hupo Hellēnōn allachou ekdothentōn bibliōn apo tou etous. Athens : P.D. Sakellarios, 1907–32. 3 v.   **AA705**

Imprint varies: v. 3, pt. 1, Athens : Spendone; v. 3, pt. 2, Thessalonika : M. Triantspullos. Vol. 3 ed. by Stilpōn P. Kyriakidēs.

Vols. 1–2 repr. from: *Athens. Ethnikon kai kapodistriakon panepistēmion. Epistēmonikē epetēris* 3 (1906–1907) : 393–504; 6 (1909–10) : 139–612; v. 3, issued in 2 pts., 1927–32.

Vols. 1–2 cover 1907–10 (with some additions going back to 1906 in v. 2); v. 3 covers 1911–20. Includes books published in Greece and books by Greeks published elsewhere.   Z2281.P77

Current

Bulletin analytique de bibliographie hellénique. 1945–73. Athènes : Inst. Français d'Athènes, 1947–80. Annual.   **AA706**

1945 (v. 6), fasc. 1, was published 1947; 1946 (v. 7) appeared in 3 fasc. in 1947; 1947 was published in 1948 in three issues (fasc. 1/2, 3/4, and 5); 1948 , annual. The earlier volumes (v. 1–5 for 1940–44, and v. 6, fasc. 2–3) and v. 24–27 (covering 1963–66) are not yet published.

In two sections: (1) books and pamphlets; (2) periodicals. Classified arrangement with author index. Full bibliographical detail, followed by abstracts or reviews.

Continued by: *Bulletin signalétique de bibliographie hellénique.* (v. 35 [1974]–39 [1978]. Athénes : Inst. Français d'Athènes, 1981–85. Annual.).

Supersedes *Bulletin analytique…* and assumes its numbering.

With the change of title, coverage is limited to books, pamphlets, and theses. Retains the classed arrangement with the name index. Annotations follow some entries.   Z2285.A75

Greek bibliography. v. 1–5[20]. Athens : Nat. Print. Off., 1960–69. Quarterly.   **AA707**

At head of title: Ministry to the Prime Minister's Office. General Direction of Press, Research and Cultural Relations Division.

A preliminary issue, designated no. 1, was issued in Feb. 1959. The publication is an English-language edition of a new Greek national bibliography, *Deltion hellēnikēs bibliographias,* same date, same numbering. Arrangement is classified, with indexes scheduled for the fourth quarterly issue of each year. An edition in French is also published, but content of the three editions is not identical. Appears to have ceased with v. 5, no. 20.

Hellēnikē vivliographia. 1972– . Athēnai : Vivliographikē Hetaireia tēs Hellados, 1975– . Annual.   **AA708**

Added t.p.: Greek national bibliography.

Issues for 1976– published in 2 v.

Includes books, pamphlets, periodicals, official and government publications, reprints, foreign language publications, and translations into Greek that are published in Greece, most of which are housed at the national library. Alphabetically arranged by subject. Indexes of persons, biographies, corporate bodies, publishers, printers and printing houses. An alphabetical table of contents by subject is given in both Greek and English. The annual volumes are late in appearing, and include addenda to earlier volumes.   Z2281.H44

Hungary

Magyar könyvészet, 1712/1860–1911/20. Budapest : Magyar Könyvkereskedök Országos Egyesülete, 1885–1971. 13 v.   **AA709**

Repr.: Budapest : Országos Széchényi Könyvtár, 1969.

Title varies; publisher varies.

Many volumes have added title page: Bibliographia Hungariae.

Contents: [ser.1], 1712–1860, by Géza Petrik. 4 v. publ. 1888–92; Suppl. to v. 1–4 publ. 1971 (561 p.); [ser. 2], 1860–75, by Géza Petrik. 467 p. publ. 1885; [ser. 3], 1876–85, by Sándor Kiszlingstein. 556 p. publ. 1890; [ser. 4], 1886–1900, by Géza Petrik. 2 v. publ. 1908–13; [ser. 5], 1901–10, by Géza Petrik and Imre Barcza. 2 v. publ. 1917–28; [ser. 6], 1911–20, by Sándor Kozocsa. 2 v. publ. 1942.

Arranged alphabetically by author and anonymous title.

Z2141.M23

Magyar könyvészet, 1921–1944 : a Magyarországon nyomtatott könyvek szakosított jegyzéke / özreadja az Országos Széchényi Könyvtár. Budapest : Országos Széchényi Könyvtár, 1980–89. v. 1–3, 5–7. (In progress).   **AA710**

Title on added t.p.: *Bibliographia hungarica, 1921–1944.*

Contents: v. 1, Általános müvek—Filozófia—Vallás (publ. 1983); v. 2–3, Társadalomtudományok; v. 5, Müvészet-sport-földrajz-électrajz-történelem (1989); v. 6, Nyelvészet—Irodalom; v. 7, Magyar irodalom.

A bibliography (arranged by Universal Decimal Classification) designed to fill the gap between the compilations for 1712–1920 and 1945–60 of *Magyar könyvészet* (AA709 and AA711). To be complete in 8 v., the final volume to be an alphabetical index to the set; v. 6 includes its own index.

The work will supersede "the bibliographical attempts broken off during the period between the two World Wars, combining into a unified whole the incomplete bibliographical fragments (1921–1935), the annual alphabetical bibliographies of the National Library (1936–1941) and the bibliographical quarterlies of the Hungarian Sociological Institute (1942–March 1944)."—*Pref., v. 1.* A retrospective bibliography for the 1961–75 period is also in preparation.   Z2141.M256

Magyar könyvészet, 1945–60 : a Magyarországon nyomtatott könyvek szakositott jegyzeke / közreadja az Országos Széchényi Könyvtár. Budapest, 1964–68. 5 v.   **AA711**

Added title page in Latin: Bibliographia Hungarica, 1945–60. Catalogus systematicus librorum in Hungaria editorum.

Contents: v. 1, Opera universalia, philosophia, theologia, sociologia, linguistica; v. 2, Scientia naturales, medicina, agronomia; v. 3, Technica; v. 4, Artes, litteratura, geographia, historia; v. 5, Index alphabeticus ad tomos 1–4; Additamenta ad tomos 1–4.

Represents a cumulation of *Magyar nemzeti bibliográfia* (AA712), with the addition of coverage for 1945. Arranged by Universal Decimal Classification, with author and anonymous-title index.

Z925.M29

Magyar nemzeti bibliográfia = Bibliographia Hungarica. Kiadja az Országos Széchényi Könyvtár. 1 füzet, január-március 1946–1977. Budapest : [Országos Széchényi Könyvtár], 1946–77. Monthly.   **AA712**

Issued by Kiadja az Országos Széchényi Könyvtár.

A classed listing with headings in Hungarian, Russian, English, and French. 1946, quarterly; 1947–77, monthly. Monthly and annual indexes until 1960. Thereafter, only monthly indexes, as it was cumulated in *Magyar könyvészet* (AA715).

Cumulation of issues from the early years was published as *Magyar könyvészet, 1945–60* (AA711).

Continued by: *Magyar nemzeti bibliográfia. Könyvek bibliográfiája* (AA716).   Z2143.M32

Magyar Tudományos Akadémia, Budapest. Régi magyarországi nyomtatványok, 1473–1600. Budapest : Akadémiai Kiadó, 1971. 928 p.   **AA713**

Added title page in Latin: Res litteraria Hungariae vetus operum impressorum, 1473–1600.

Borsa Gedeon, ed.

Augments and expands much of the data in Károly Szabó's *Régi magyar könyvtár* (AA714). Lists, describes, and locates copies of "the publications issued prior to the year 1601 in Hungary in any language or abroad completely or partly in Hungarian."—*Guide to the work.* References to citations in earlier bibliographies and to published descriptions or discussions of the works are given. Photoreproductions of title pages and selected pages from the volumes listed provide an additional aid to identification. Indexes of printers, places of publication, titles, subjects, etc.   Z2142.M34

Szabó, Károly. Régi magyar könyvtár. Budapest : A Magyar Tudományos Akadémia Könyvkiadó Hivatala, 1879–98. 3 v. in 4.   **AA714**

v. 1, Books in Hungarian, 1531–1711; v. 2, Non-Hungarian books published in Hungary, 1473–1711; v. 3, Hungarian authors, non-Hungarian books published outside Hungary: pt. 1, 1480–1670; pt. 2, suppl., 1671–1711 and author index.

Supplemented by: ———. ———. *Adalekok Szabó Károly Régi magyar köyvtár c. munkájának I–II kötetéhez / pótlások és igazitasok 1472–1711,* egybeáĺlitotta Sztripszky Hiador. [Az 1912. évikiad. uj kiadása] (Budapest : [Országos Széchényi Könyvtár], 1967. 621 p.).

An extensive supplement to Szabó, published in multigraphed form; it includes an index by town (then by printer) to the first two volumes of Szabó's bibliography. Sztripszky's work (*Appendix ad I–II tomos....*Budapest, 1912. 710 p.) has been retyped and is published here together with a reproduction of previously unpublished proofsheets of Lajos Dézsi's supplement of Szabó's work.

Z2142.S98

Current

Magyar könyvészet : A magyarországi könyvek, zeneművek és térképek cimjegyzéke. 1961/62– . Budapest : Országos Széchényi Könyvtár, 1963– . Annual.   **AA715**

Subtitle varies.

Annual cumulation (with variations) of material in *Magyar nemzeti bibliográfia* (AA716) with an author index.

Magyar nemzeti bibliográfia könyvek bibliográfiája. évf.32[16] (Aug. 31, 1977)– . Budapest : Országos Széchényi Könyvtár, 1977– . Semimonthly.   **AA716**

Represents a change of title for *Magyar nemzeti bibliográfia = Bibliographica hungarica* (AA712), and continues its volume numbering. Classed arrangement (with index) remains the same, and the issues will continue to be cumulated in *Magyar könyvészet* (AA715).

Iceland

Cornell University. Library. Catalogue of the Icelandic collection bequeathed by Willard Fiske / comp. by Halldór Hermannsson. Ithaca, N.Y. : [The Library], 1914. 755 p.   **AA717**

For annotation, see BE1284.

Islandsk bogfortegnelse / af Bogi T. J. Melsted. 1899–1910, 1912–1920. København : Gad, 1899–1922. Annual (irregular).   **AA718**

Supplement to *Dansk bogfortegnelse [for aarene]* ... (AA606) and bound with it as follows: 1899–1910 with volume for 1899–1910; 1912 with 1914; 1913–14 with 1915; 1915 with 1917; 1916–18 with 1918; 1919 with 1921; 1920 with 1922.

———. 1915/19–1930/34. [*In* Dansk bogfortegnelse, 1915/19–1930/34].

Five-year cumulations.   Z2561.D19

Universität Kiel. Bibliothek. Islandkatalog der Universitätsbibliothek Kiel und der Universitäts– und Stadtbibliothek Köln / bearb. von Olaf Klose. Kiel : Universitätsbibliothek, 1931. 423 p. (Kataloge der Universitätsbibliothek Kiel, hrsg. von Christoph Weber, 1).   **AA719**

Lists more than 7,900 titles, in classified arrangement with author and title index.

Current

Íslenzk bókaskrá = The Icelandic national bibliography. 1974– . Reykjavík : Landsbókasafn Íslands, 1975– . Annual.   **AA720**

Prefatory matter in Icelandic and English.

"The Icelandic National Bibliography is a continuation of two older bibliographies, the 'Íslenzk rit' which appeared in 'Arbok Landsbókasafns Íslands' (Year book of the National Library) 1945–75, and 'Bókaskrá Bóksalafélags Íslands' (Bookseller's association list) 1937–73. These two works had different functions, the first being a bibliographic source for Icelandic publications and the second a practical aid for booksellers; the new bibliography is intended to combine the two functions."—*Pref. 1974.*

An alphabetical author/main entry listing, with a classified section; separate sections for new serial titles, maps and charts and sound recordings (the latter now listed in a separately paged annual supplement); plus a statistical summary of the year's publishing output. Entries in the alphabetical section appear under an author's given name, not the surname.

"A preliminary edition appears in *Íslenzk bókatidindi,* published by the Society of Icelandic Publishers."—*Pref.*   Z2590.A3I84

Ireland

Dix, Ernest Reginald McClintock. Catalogue of early Dublin-printed books, 1601 to 1700 / with an historical introduction and bibliographical notes by C. Winston Dugan. Dublin : [O'Donoghue ; London : Dobell], 1898–1905. 4 v. and suppl., all paged continuously, 386 p.   **AA721**

———. ———. *Supplement of additions to pts. I–IV.* (Dublin, 1912. p. 325–86).

National Library of Ireland. List of publications deposited under the terms of the Industrial and Commercial Property (Protection) Act, 1927. no. 1 (Aug. 1927–Dec. 1929)–5 (1935/36). Dublin : Stat. Off., [1930–37]. Annual.   **AA722**

Contents: (1) Books and pamphlets; (2) Annuals; (3) Periodicals and publications of societies; (4) Official publications issued by the Stationery Office; (5) Newspapers; (6) Music; (7) Maps.   Z921.D82

Current

Irish books in print & Leabhair Gaeilge i gCló. 1984– . Wicklow [Wicklow] : S & J Cleary, c1984– .   **AA723**

Offers a listing of "current literature from and about Ireland, North and South."—*Introd.* Includes English and Irish titles, excluding textbooks, published in Ireland, and books about Ireland available in the U.S. and Great Britain. English and Irish titles are listed separately; English titles are arranged by author, by title, and by broad subject, Irish titles by author and by title. Includes a list of Irish publishers.   Z2031.I75

Irish publishing record. 1967– . Dublin : School of Librarianship, Univ. College Dublin, 1968– . Annual.   **AA724**
Publisher varies.

Originally undertaken as a bibliographical project by students in the School of Librarianship at University College, Dublin. Beginning with the 1970 issue (publ. 1972), comp. by the School of Librarianship on behalf of the Irish Association for Documentation and Information Services.

A classified list with indexes of names and of titles. Covers publications of both the Republic of Ireland and Northern Ireland, and includes books, pamphlets, the first number of new periodicals, yearbooks, musical scores and works on music, and government publications of general interest.   Z2034.I87

Italy

Bibliografia italiana : bollettino delle pubblicazioni italiane ricevute per diritto di stampa dalla Biblioteca Nazionale Centrale di Firenze. Anno 1 (1867)–67 (1933). Milano : [Biblioteca Nazionale, etc.], 1868–1933. Monthly (varies slightly).   **AA725**

Anno 1–37 (1867–1903) had subtitle: Giornale dell' Associazione tipografico-libraria italiana ... .

From 1886 to 1900 the *Bibliografia*, compiled at the Biblioteca Nazionale Centrale di Firenze, was also issued by the library under title *Bollettino delle pubblicazioni italiane ricevute per diritto di stampa* (AA727).

Published in two parts, 1867–69: I, Bibliografia; II, Avvisi. Published in three parts, 1870–87: 1, Catalogo delle pubblicazioni italiane; 2, Cronaca; 3, Avvisi. Beginning with 1888, the *Cronaca* and *Avvisi* were discontinued in that form, being superseded by the *Giornale della libreria* (AA732).   Z2345.B58

Bibliografia nazionale italiana. Pubblicazione mensile / Centro nazionale per il catalogo unico delle biblioteche italiane e per le informazioni bibliografiche [e] a cura della Biblioteca nazionale centrale di Firenze. Anno 1, fasc. 1 (genn. 1958)– . Firenze : [s.n.], 1958– . Monthly.   **AA726**

Issues are called also: *Nuova serie de Bollettino delle pubblicazioni italiane ricevute per diritto di stampa*, and are numbered Anno 73– in continuation of *Bollettino delle pubblicazioni italiane ricevute per diritto di stampa* (AA727).

———. *Catalogo alfabetica annuale*, (v. 1 (1958)– . Firenze : Biblioteca Nazionale Centrale, 1961– . Annual).

A national bibliography in two forms, monthly and annual. The monthly series is a successor to *Bollettino*, being a current record of books and pamphlets received by legal deposit. Entries are presented in catalog card form; arrangement is by Dewey Decimal Classification; bibliographical information is complete, usually including prices; and tracings for subject and added entries are indicated. Author-title index in each issue, but no cumulated index.

Publication was disrupted following the Nov. 1966 flood in Florence, and monthly issues were irregular for a time. Issues designated *Supplementi* (v. 1–7 [1971–73]–) include additional entries for the period beginning 1958. Publication was suspended at the completion of the 1984 volume to update automation procedures and adopt the UNIMARC format. Publication resumed 1987, with monthly issues in a classified arrangement, and the annual edition in an alphabetical arrangement with subject and classified indexes. Annual volumes for 1985 and 1986 still in process.   Z3241B5

Biblioteca nazionale centrale di Firenze. Bollettino delle pubblicazioni italiane ricevute per diritto di stampa. 1866–1957. Firenze : Biblioteca, 1886–1957. Monthly.   **AA727**
Classified, with annual indexes. During its span, the most complete current record of Italian publications, based on copyright deposit.

Continued by *Bibliografia nazionale italiana* (AA726).

A cumulation into one alphabet was published as *Catalogo cumulativo 1886–1957 del Bollettino delle pubblicazioni italiane ricevute per diritto di stampa dalla Biblioteca nazionale centrale di Firenze* (Nedeln, Liechtenstein : Kraus Reprint, 1968–69. 41 v.).

At head of title: Centro Nazionale per il Catalogo Unico delle Biblioteche Italiane e per le Informazioni Bibliografiche, Roma.

Vols. 1–39 are a cumulated author listing, A–Z; v. 40–41 comprise Indice degli autori secondari, and Aggiunte.

Computer-produced, this set represents a cumulation of the nearly 640,000 entries from the *Bollettino* and provides an important bibliographic tool for Italian publications. Attilio Pagliaini's *Catalogo generale della libreria italiana, 1847–99* (AA734) remains, of course, indispensable in the large reference collection.   Z2345.F63

British Library. Catalogue of seventeenth century Italian books in the British Library. London ; Wolfeboro, N.H. : The Library, c1986. 3 v.   **AA728**
Contents: v. 1–2, A–Z; v. 3, Indexes.

Continues and follows the pattern of *Short-title catalogue of books printed in Italy ... from 1465 to 1600 ...* (AA729). Aims to include "all those books now in the British Library which were either printed in Italy between 1601 and 1700, or printed outside Italy in the Italian language."—*Pref.* Includes "entries for books of printed and engraved music; for books which may be classified as atlases or roadbooks, though not for sheet maps; and for books of prints or engravings, with or without text."—*Introd.*

Vol. 2 includes an appendix, Books destroyed by enemy action, 1939–1945. There are indexes of publishers and printers; of places of publication; of places shown in imprint without printer or publisher (together with false and fictitious imprints); and of books with no place, printer, or publisher.   Z1015.B75

British Museum. Department of Printed Books. Short-title catalogue of books printed in Italy and of Italian books printed in other countries from 1465 to 1600, now in the British Museum. London : Trustees, 1958. 992 p.   **AA729**
An author catalog, giving shortened title, place, publisher, date, and size, similar in scope and arrangement to the Museum's other catalogs in this series. Appended is a lengthy list of printers and publishers, with titles printed by each, arranged chronologically.

———. ———. *Supplement* (London ; Wolfeboro, N.H. : The Library, c1986. 152 p.).

Spine title: *Catalogue of Italian books, 1465–1600.*

Lists more than "1,200 books which have either been added to the Library since 1958, or been found to have been omitted by oversight from the previous work."—*Pref.* A section of corrigenda to the 1958 catalog precedes the new listings. An index of printers and publishers is followed by three indexes which also apply to the main volume; (1)Towns in Italy (with publishers); (2) Non-Italian towns; and (3) False and fictitious imprints. There is also a brief list of books destroyed during World War II which have been replaced since 1958.   Z2342.B7

CLIO : catalogo dei libri italiani dell'Ottocento (1801–1900) = catalogue of nineteenth century Italian books (1801–1900). Milano : Editrice bibliografica, c1991. 19 v.   **AA730**
Contents: v. 1–6 Autori, A–Z; v. 7–12, Editori, A–Z; v. 13–18, Luoghi di edizione, A–Z; v. 19, Indici.

A listing of more than 400,000 19th-century books (considered to be publications longer than 12 p.), published in Italy and Ticino, the Italian-speaking province of Switzerland. Each work is located in one Italian public or university library; the Biblioteca Nazionale in Florence is the preferred location.

The author catalog is an alphabetical listing by author, or title if anonymous, by a corporate author, or by three or more authors; v. 7–12 provide a listing by printer or publisher, with works arranged by year, then by author; v. 13–18 provide a listing by place of publication, then by year. Indexed by editor, translator, illustrator, etc., and by brief title. Includes many more titles than Attilio Pagliaini's *Catalogo generale della libreria italiana, 1847–99*, (AA734) but lacks its subject indexing.   Z2341.C56

Le edizioni italiane del XVI secolo : censimento nazionale. Roma : Istituto centrale per il catalogo unico delle biblioteche italiane e per le informazioni bibliografiche, 1985– . v. 1–2. (In progress?). **AA731**

Contents: v. 1–2, A–B.

Primo catalogo collettivo delle biblioteche italiane (AA124) having ceased publication with v. 9, this represents a new effort toward a national union catalog of Italian publications of the 16th century. Some 550 Italian libraries were surveyed. Arranged by author or anonymous title; each volume has indexes of coauthors, translators and commentators, and of printers/publishers.

§ A 2nd ed. has begun to appear as: *Le edizioni italiane del XVI secolo: censimento nazionale* (1990–1993. In progress). Contents: v. 1, A; V. 3, C–Chiesa cattolica. The 2nd ed. of v. 1 has been enlarged (3,775 entries as opposed to 3,539 in the 1st ed.) and corrected. There have also been changes in the arrangement; there will be a table of concordances between the 1st and 2nd eds. As in the 1st ed., each volume has its own indexes. It is not clear whether a 2nd ed. of v. 2 will appear; it seems that all subsequent volumes will be designated as 2nd ed. Z1014.E35

Giornale della libreria. v. 1 (1888)– . Milano : Assoc. Italiana Editori, 1921?– . Monthly. **AA732**

Publisher varies.

Continues *Gionale della libreria, della tipografia, e delle arti ed industrie affini* (1888–1920), which superseded *Cronaca* and *Avvisi*, published until 1887 as pts. 2 and 3 of *Bibliografia italiana* (AA725).

Contains classified lists of recent publications and announcements of forthcoming publications. As it appears more promptly than *Bibliografia nazionale italiana* (AA726), it is useful for current information. Z2345.G49

Michel, Suzanne P. Répertoire des ouvrages imprimés en langue italienne au XVIIe siècle conservés dans les bibliothèques de France / [par] Suzanne P. Michel [et] Paul-Henri Michel .... Paris : Éditions du Centre national de la recherche scientifique, 1967–84. 8 v. **AA733**

Vol. 8 includes a supplement (p. 157–243) listing additions and corrections to v. 1–7. Indicates locations in French libraries. Z2342.M5

Pagliaini, Attilio. Catalogo generale della libreria italiana, 1847–99. Milano : Assoc. Tip.-Lib. Ital., 1901–22. 6 v. **AA734**

Author and title list, 3 v., 1901–1905; Subject index, 3 v., 1910–22.

The standard Italian list, covering a period of 53 years in its basic volume and continued by decennial supplements. The 1847–99 volumes include more than 200,000 titles, comprising the principal books and pamphlets of the period but omitting minor pamphlets, periodicals, separates, and government and society publications. Consists of: (1) Main author and title list, giving fairly full information, i.e., author's name, title (somewhat abridged), place, publisher, date, paging, size, illustrations, original price when obtainable; (2) Subject index to the author list. Based upon the catalogs of the large Italian libraries, catalogs of book dealers and publishers, and about 200 Italian bibliographies.

———. ———. *1.–4. supplemento.* (1912–1958. 11 v.).

1st suppl., 1900–10, Authors and titles. 2 v. 1912–14; 2nd suppl., 1911–20, Authors and titles. 2 v. 1925–28; Subject index to 1st–2nd suppl., 1900–20. 4 v. 1933–40; 3rd suppl., 1921–30, Authors and titles. 2 v. 1932–38; 4th suppl., 1931–40, Authors and titles. 2 v. 1956–58.

The supplements follow the arrangement, coverage, and format of the original set. Subject indexes have not been published for the 3rd and 4th supplements.

Short-title catalog of books printed in Italy and of books in Italian printed abroad, 1501–1600, held in selected North American libraries. Boston : G.K. Hall, 1970. 3 v. **AA735**

Contributing libraries checked their holdings against the British Museum's *Short-title catalogue of books printed in Italy ...* (AA729),

adding citations for items not listed therein. About 40 American libraries are represented, as is the Gennadius Library of the American School of Classical Studies in Athens. Z2342.S56

Current

Bollettino del Servizio per il diritto d'autore e diritti connessi. Anno 43, n. 4–6 (apr.-giugno 1987)– . Roma : Istituto poligrafico e zecca dello Stato, 1987– . Monthly. **AA736**

Continues *Bollettino dell'Ufficio della proprieta letteraria, artistica e scientifica* (1945–86) and retains its numbering.

Like the *Bollettino* of the Biblioteca Nazionale Centrale in Florence (AA727) and the *Bibliografia nazionale italiana* (AA726), this is a copyright depository listing; its book section, however, arranged by subject areas and with cumulated annual author indexes, is said to be not so complete as the Florence listings. Includes lists of phonograph records and moving pictures. KKH1160.A13B65

Catalogo dei libri in commercio. 1970– . Milano : Associazione Italiana Editori, 1970– . Biennial. **AA737**

1970 vol. had title: *Catalogo dei libri italiani in commercio*.

Known in the book trade as *Italian books in print*.

Eds. for 1970–75 each issued in 1 v.; eds. for 1976– issued in 3 v. each (Autori, Soggetti, Titoli).

An in-print listing for Italian publications. The 1991 volume lists about 244,000 titles from 2,344 publishers. Beginning in 1980, a supplement, *Catalogo dei libri in commercio. Aggiornamento* is published in alternate years.

Libri e riviste d'Italia : rassegna bibliografica mensile. Anno 1, no. 1 (Marzo 1950)– . Roma : Capriotti, 1950– . Monthly. **AA738**

On cover (varies): Edito sotto gli auspicii del Centro di documentazione della Presidenza del Consiglio dei Ministri. ....

Title varies; publisher varies.

Also published in English, French, German, and Spanish. English edition: *Italian books and periodicals*.

A selected list of current Italian publications covering all subject fields, with fairly long reviews. Each issue in three sections: (1) Libri, consisting of reviews of new books listed by class; (2) Riviste, giving annotated contents of journals arranged alphabetically by titles of the journals under broad classifications; (3) Rassegna bibliografica, a classified listing of new titles published in Italy, giving complete bibliographical information, including price. Indexes of subjects and authors cumulate annually. Z2345.L63

Latvia

Jēgers, Benjamins. Latviešu trimdas izdevumu bibliografija, 1940–1960. [Stockholm] : Daugava, [1968–1972]. 2 v. **AA739**

Added title page in English: Bibliography of Latvian publications published outside Latvia, 1940–1960.

Contents: v. 1, Books and pamphlets; v. 2, Serials, music, maps, programmes & catalogues. Vol. 2 includes indexes.

An alphabetical author listing of Latvian publications in exile.

———. ———. *1961–70.* ([Stockholm] : Daugava, 1977. 460 p.).

Added title page in English: Bibliography of Latvian publications published outside Latvia, 1961–70.

Continues the listings from the earlier compilation, with items numbered consecutive to the entries in the first two volumes. This volume covers books and pamphlets, serials, music, maps, etc., in separate listings. Indexes of subjects, places of publication, publishers, persons, and titles. Z2535.J4

Liechtenstein

Liechtensteinische Bibliographie. Jahrg.1 (1974)– . Vaduz : Liechtensteinische Landesbibliothek, 1975– . Annual.
AA740
A classed bibliography with author/anonymous title and subject indexes. Includes serials.
§ For works published 1960–73, *see* DC440.   Z2124.L53L53

Lithuania

Knygos lietuvių kalba / [red. kolegija . A. Ulpis (ats. red.) . et al.]. Vilnius : Mintis, 1969–88. v. 1; v. 2, pt. 1–2; in 3 : ill. (Lietuvos TSR bibliografija, serija A).   **AA741**
Contents: v. 1, 1547–1861; Papildymai [Supplement]; v. 2 (2 v.), 1862–1904; v. 3 (2 v.). 1905–1917.
Prefatory material for v. 2 in German, Polish, and Russian.
This set aims to be a comprehensive listing of everything published in Lithuania: books, pamphlets, maps, albums, music, etc. Arranged alphabetically by author. (Books are listed first, then other types of publications by genre.) Vols. 1 and 2 provide extensive information, brief biography and photographs of many authors, detailed bibliographic information, citations to appearances in other bibliographies, and locations in major Russian and Lithuanian libraries; in addition, many title pages are reproduced. Indexes include: classified subject, chronological, name, geographical, corporate body, title, publishers and printers, and series. A detailed set of statistical tables illustrating publishing patterns is also provided.
Vol. 3, the first of the set published, is less lavishly produced, though it, too, attempts to list everything published during the period covered. Books are listed first alphabetically by author, then other types of material by type. There are no author biographies, no illustrations, less detailed bibliographic descriptions, and generally only one library location is provided. Author and title indexes.   Z2537.K75

Luxembourg

Bibliographie luxembourgeoise. 1944/45– . Luxembourg : Bibliothèque Nationale, 1946– . Annual.   **AA742**
Pierre Frieden, comp., 1944–53.
The first issue covered Sept. 10, 1944–Dec. 31, 1945; subsequent issues cover the calendar year.
The national bibliography, listing all materials published in Luxembourg, including official publications, new periodicals, and newspapers. Coverage varies. Since 1958, includes outstanding articles in periodicals. Arrangement is classified and, since 1958, has author and subject indexes.
§ An earlier work by Martin Blum, *Bibliographie luxembourgeoise: ou, Catalogue de tous les ouvrages ou travaux littéraires publiés par des Luxembourgeois ou dans le Grand-Duché de Luxembourg* (Luxembourg, 1902–32. 2 v.) partially covered the period 1902–32.
Z2461.B5

Mallorca

Bassa, Ramon. Llibres [sic] editats à Mallorca (1939–1972) / Ramon Bassa, Jaume Bover, Pere Carlos. [Palma de Mallorca : Ed. J. Mascaró Pasarius, 1972]. 322 p.   **AA743**
A classified listing of Mallorcan imprints, with author and title indexes.   Z2704.M23B3

Malta

Bibljografija nazzjonali ta' Malta = Malta national bibliography. 1983– . Valletta : National Library of Malta, 1984– . Annual.   **AA744**
A classed list, arranged according to the Dewey Decimal Classification, of monographs, pamphlets, first issues and title changes of periodicals, and official and government publications published in Malta during the current year. Also includes works about the Maltese Islands and works by Maltese nationals published abroad. A "Select list of periodical articles" includes items from local sources as well as articles about Malta or those written by Maltese in foreign periodicals. Index of authors, titles, and series.

Netherlands

Early

British Museum. Department of Printed Books. Short-title catalogue of books printed in the Netherlands and Belgium and of Dutch and Flemish books printed in other countries from 1470 to 1600, now in the British Museum. London : Trustees, 1965. 274 p.   **AA745**
Comp. by A. F. Johnson and V. Scholderer.
"The series of short-title catalogues of books in the British Museum printed before 1601 now covers ... all those countries of the European continent where there was a considerable output of early printing ... and in addition Spanish America."—*Pref.*
An author catalog with index of printers and publishers.
Z2402.B7

Nijhoff, Wouter. Nederlandsche bibliographie van 1500 tot 1540. 'sGravenhage : Nijhoff, 1923. 1002p.   **AA746**
A comprehensive record of the imprints of this period, giving full titles and collation, with bibliographical references and location of copies.
———. ———. 1.–4. aanvulling (1925–34. 328 p.).
—, ———, 2. deel, door M.E. Kronenberg (1936–40. 1158 p.). Titles are numbered in continuation of the basic work.
———. ———. Inleiding tot een derde deel. Winst en verlies (1942. 175 p.).
———. ———. 3. deel, door M.E. Kronenberg (1951–71. 5 pts.). Pt. 3 of this 3rd series includes various indexes: of printers, names, etc.. Pts. 4–5 offer supplementary listings, bringing to 4,532 the total number of entries.

Peeters-Fontainas, Jean F. Bibliographie des impressions espagnoles des Pays-Bas Méridionaux. Nieuwkoop : B. De Graaf, 1965. 2 v. (Centre National de l'Archéologie et de l'Histoire du Livre. Publ., 1).   **AA747**
Prefatory matter in French and Spanish.
A 1933 ed. had title: *Bibliographie des impressions des Pays-Bas.*
Lists works by Spanish authors which were produced in the presses of the Spanish Netherlands, 1520–1785. Arranged alphabetically by author or anonymous title, with a chronological table at the end of v. 2. There is also an appendix showing illustrations of printers' marks. Bibliographical details are complete; locations are indicated.
Z2402.P44

17th-19th centuries

Abkoude, Johannes van. Naamregister van de bekendste en meest in gebruik zynde Nederduitsche boeken : welke sedert het jaar 1600 tot het jaar 1761 zyn uitgekomen / nu overzien, verb. en tot het jaar 1787 verm. door Reinier Arrenberg. 2. druk. Rotterdam : Arrenberg, 1788. 598 p.   **AA748**

First published 1743–56; revised and reissued by Arrenberg, 1773.

————. *Alphabetische naamlijst van boeken... 1790–1932, in Noord-Nederland zijn uitgekomen* ('sGravenhage : van Cleef, 1835. 755 p., 159 p.), by J. de Jong. Continued by: C.L. Brinkman, *Alphabetische naamlijst... 1833–1949* (AA749).

————. *Alphabetische naamlijst van fondsartikelen, voorkomende in het naamregister van Nederlandsche boeken, alsmede in de Alphabetische naamlijst van boeken*, achtervolgens uitg. bij R. Arrenberg en de Gebroeders van Cleef, en waarvan het regt van eigendom aan anderen is overgegaan ('sGravenhage : van Cleef, 1939. 122 p.).

Brinkman, Carel Leonhard. Alphabetische naamlijst van boeken : plaat- en kaartwerken, die ... 1833–1849 in Nederland uitg. of herdrukt zijn. Amsterdam : Brinkman, 1858. 792 p.   **AA749**
   ————. *Alphabetische naamlijst van boeken : plaat- en kaartwerken... 1850–1862 (1868. 1010 p.).*
   ————. *Alphabetische naamlijst van boeken : plaat- en kaartwerken... 1863–1875 (1878. 1249 p.).*
   ————. *Alphabetische naamlijst van boeken : plaat- en kaartwerken... Wetenschappelijk register ... 1850–1875, met alphabetische opgave der onderwerpen*, bewerkt door R. van der Meulen (1878. 464 p.).
   Superseded and continued by *Brinkman's catalogus van boeken en tijdschriften* (AA753).

British Library. Catalogue of books from the Low Countries 1601–1621 in the British Library / comp. by Anna Simoni. London : British Library, 1989. [400] p. : ill.   **AA750**
   Continues *Short-title catalogue of books printed in the Netherlands ... 1470–1600* (AA745).
   A listing of "books now in the British Library whose text is either wholly or to a large extent in Dutch or which, though in other languages, were printed or published in the Low Countries."—*Introd.* Arranged by author, with an index of printers and publishers and a general index of secondary authors, editors, artists, and translators.
   Includes an appendix, Chronological list of news reports, which lists "publications which form part or are assumed to form part of regularly published reports, regardless of variable titles."—*p. 721.* Appendix arranged alphabetically by city, then chronologically.

Pamphlets

Koninklijke Bibliotheek (Netherlands). Catalogus van de pamfletten-verzameling : berustende in de Koninklijke Bibliotheek / bewerkt, met aanteekeningen en een register der schrijvers voorzien, door W. P. C. Knuttel. 'sGravenhage : Algemeene Landsdrukkerij, 1889–1920. 9 v.   **AA751**
   Contents: v. 1–7, Chronological, 1486–1853; v. 8, Supplement; v. 9, Alphabetical subject index, 1486–1795.   Z2444.P18H2

Muller, Frederik. Bibliotheek van Nederlandsche pamfletten / naar tijdsorde gerangschikt en beschreven door P. A. Tiele. Amsterdam : Frederik Muller, 1858–61. 3 v.   **AA752**
   Chronological list, 1482–1702 (9,668 entries).   Z2444.P18M9

19th–20th centuries

Brinkman's catalogus van boeken en tijdschriften. [v. 1] (1850/82)– . Amsterdam : Brinkman, 1883–93 ; Leiden : Sijthoff, 1903– .   **AA753**
   Title varies slightly.
   1850–82, 1437 p.; 1882–91, 2 v.; 1891–1900, 2 v.; 1901–10, 2 v.; 1911/15– , published in 5-year cumulations, each in several sections with separate title pages.
   Supersedes the annual volumes of *Brinkman's cumulatieve catalogus van boeken* (AA756).

Each issue, except that for 1850–82 which has only the *Catalogus*, is in two main parts, separately paged: (1) *Catalogus*, or main author and title list, giving full information including author, title, editor or translator (if any), illustration, size, paging, publisher, date, price; (2) *Repertorium*, or subject index to the *Catalogus*, giving brief information only and referring to the word under which full information is found in the *Catalogus*. From 1891–1900 on, each *Repertorium* contains a *Titel-catalogus*, supplementary to *Brinkman's titel-catalogus* (AA754). In the issue for 1926–30, the scope of the work was enlarged to include: (1) separate lists of periodicals and (2) Dutch works published in Belgium. (In the 1926–30 volume this is a separate list; in later volumes such titles are incorporated into the main alphabet.).

   Beginning 1984, *Nederlandse bibliografie, B-lijst* (Alphen aan den Rijn : Samsom Uitg.) serves as a supplement to *Brinkman's*, listing publications of government agencies, scientific institutes, university reports and papers, and privately-published academic dissertations not generally distributed through the usual commercial channels.
   Z2431.A3

Brinkman's titel-catalogus : van de sedert het begin dezer eeuw tot 1888 in Nederland verschenen werken op het gebied der nieuwe letterkunde (romans, novellen, gedichten, tooneelstukken en kinder-boeken) ... / bewerkonder toezicht en met voorbericht van R. van der Meulen. Amsterdam : Brinkman, [1888–89]. 232 p.   **AA754**
   A title index—for works of fiction, poetry, drama, music, juvenile literature, etc.—to *Brinkman's catalogus van boeken en tijdschriften* (AA753). Gives brief title, date, and author's name, the latter supplying the cross-reference to the fuller description in *Brinkman's catalogus*. Continued by supplements included in *Brinkman's catalogus*.
   Z2431.A297

Nederlandse bibliografie 1801–1832 / uitgegeven door de Koninklijke Bibliotheek. Houten : Bohn Stafleu Van Loghum, 1993. 3 v.   **AA755**
   Contents: v. 1–2, A–Z; v. 3, Registers.
   A listing of some 32,500 titles of books published during the period; aims to be a complete record. Listed alphabetically by author or anonymous title, with extensive cross-references. Includes locations in major libraries. Indexes of subjects arranged by the Dewey classification schedule, illustrators, printers, and names.   Z2431.N45

Current

Brinkman, Carel Leonhard. Brinkman's cumulatieve catalogus van boeken. Leiden : Sijthoff, 1930– . Monthly, with annual cumulations.   **AA756**
   Publisher varies. Continues, with consecutive numbering, *Brinkman's alphabetische lijst van boeken* (1881–1929), which in turn continues *Alphabetische naamlijst van boeken* (1846?–1880, AA749).
   Before 1930, the annual list was compiled on the same plan as the main author list in *Brinkman's catalogus van boeken en tijdschriften* (AA753) with brief subject index to the author list. Since 1930, this work has been published at varying intervals with cumulations, the last number of the year covering 12 months and forming an annual volume.
   The annual cumulations are superseded by the quinquennial volumes of *Brinkman's catalogus*.   Z2431.A46

Norway

Early

Bibliotheca norvegica. Christiania : Cammeyer, 1899–1924. 4 v.   **AA757**
   Each volume has added title page in English. Individual volumes issued in parts.

Hjalmar Pettersen, ed.

Contents: v. 1, Norsk boglexikon, 1643–1813 = Descriptive catalogue of books printed in Norway, 1643–1813 (1899–1908. 621 p.); v. 2, Norge og nordmaend i udlandets literatur = Norway and the Norwegians in foreign literature; descriptive catalogue of books and papers relating to Norway (1908–17. 843 p.); v. 3, Norske forfattere før 1814 = Norwegian authors before 1814 : descriptive catalogue of their works (1911–18. 595 p.); v. 4, Norske forfattere efter 1814. 1. samling med suppl. til Bibliotheca norvegica I–III = Norwegian authors : descriptive catalogue of their works printed in foreign countries (1913–24. 798 p.).   Z2591.P49

19th–20th centuries

Hauff, Nils Selmer. Stikords-katalog over norsk literatur, 1883–1907. Kristiania : Cappelen, [1908–1909]. 93 p.   **AA758**

Issued in six parts.

A catchword-title index to Norwegian materials for this period.   Z2591.H23

Norsk bokfortegnelse = Norwegian national bibliography. Oslo : Norske Bokhandlerforening, 1953– . 1953– .   **AA759**

Title varies; publisher varies.

Compiled by the University Library, Oslo. Cumulates the issues of *Norsk bokfortegnelse: Årskatalog* (AA761).

19th-century cumulations vary in number of years covered. Decennial, 1891–1920; quinquennial, 1921– .

Includes books, pamphlets, periodicals, official publications, theses, and maps. Arranged alphabetically by author and title, giving full bibliographical description, followed by a classified section.   Z2591.N865

Universitetsforlaget. Norwegian scholarly books, 1825–1967 : complete alphabetical list. Oslo [etc.] : Universitetsforlaget, [1968]. 339 p.   **AA760**

Inasmuch as the Universitetsforlaget publishes nearly all Norwegian scholarly books and journals, this volume represents most of the scholarly output of the country for the long period indicated. Author-title listing.   Z2593.U53

Current

Norsk bokfortegnelse : Årskatalog = The Norwegian national bibliography. 1952– . Oslo : Norske Bokhandlerforening, 1953– . Annual.   **AA761**

Supersedes *Årskatalog over norsk litteratur*, 1893–1951. Quarterly issues cumulate into annual volumes, then into the quinquennial publications (see *Norsk bokfortegnelse*, AA759).

Arrangement is alphabetical by author and title; there are also series entries with contents. Maps are listed separately, and there is a classified index.

After 1980, printed music is listed separately in *Norsk bokfortegnelse. Musikktrykk.*

Poland

Estreicher, Karol Józef Teofil. Bibliografia polska. Kraków : Czionkami Drukarni Uniwersytetu Jagiellońskiego, 1870–1939; 1951. 34 v.   **AA762**

In three series: ser. 1, an alphabetical list covering 1800–70. 7 v. (v. 1–5, A–Z; v. 6–7, Supplement, A–Z); ser. 2, chronological lists, 1455–1880. 4 v. (v. 8–9, 1455–1799; v. 10, 1800–1870; v. 11, 1871–1889); ser. 3, alphabetical list, 15th–18th centuries, v. 1–23 (whole no. v. 12–34), A–Zalł.

An exhaustive bibliography of Polish imprints from 1455 to 1880.

Continued to 1900 by: Estreicher's *Bibliografia polska XIX stulecia : lata 1881–1900* (Kraków : Spólki Ksiegarzy Polskich, 1906–16. 4 v.).   Z2521.E82

──────── Bibliografia polska XIX stulecia / pod. red. Karola Estreichera. Wyd. 2. Kraków : Czcionkami Drukarni Uniwersytetu Jagiellońskiego, 1959–91. v. 1–16. : port. (In progress).   **AA763**

Polish, French, German, and Latin.

Added t.p. in French.

Contents: v. 1–16, A–Knaus.

On leaf facing t.p., v. 1–3: Polska Akademia Nauk; v. 4– : Uniwersytet Jagiellonski.

A 2nd ed. of this important 19th-century bibliography.   Z2521.E85

Wierzbowski, Teodor. Bibliographia polonica XV ac XVI ss. Varsoviae : Kowalewski, 1889–94. 3 v.   **AA764**

Repr.: Nieuwkoop : B. DeGraaf, 1961.

Vol. 1 contains titles of works in the Warsaw University Library (destroyed by fire); v. 2–3, works found in other libraries, Polish and foreign, with indication of location. Arranged chronologically with indexes of authors, subjects, persons, and places.   Z2522.W65

20th century

Bibliografia polska 1901–1939 = Polish bibliography 1901–1939 / pod redakcją Janiny Wilgat. Wrocław : Zakład Narodowy im. Ossolińskich, 1986–1991. v. 1–2. (In progress).   **AA765**

At head of title : Biblioteka Narodowa. Instytut Bibliograficzny.

Contents: v. 1–2, A–Bok.

Designed to fill the gap between Karol J. T. Estreicher's *Bibliografia polska XIX stulecia* (Kraków : Państwowe Wydawn. Naukowe, Oddzial w Krakowie, 1987) and *Przewodnik bibljograficzny* (AA769).

Lists works published in Poland regardless of language, and works by Polish writers and works about Poland published throughout the world, 1901–August 1939. Arranged by author or title, (if anonymous); provides brief bibliographic descriptions. If possible, copies are located in major Polish libraries. Each volume has a separately published index of names (excluding names used as main entries) and titles.   Z2521.B568

Dąbrowska, Wanda. 555 książek wydanych w okresie powojennym / Wanda Dąbrowska, J. Czarnecka, J. Słomczewska. Warszawa : Ludowy Inst. Oświaty i Kultury, 1946. 80 p.   **AA766**

Lists 555 books published in Poland, July 1944–May 1, 1946. Classified, with author and title index and subject index.   Z2526.D3

Polish University College (London, England). Bibliography of books in Polish or relating to Poland published outside Poland since Sept. 1st, 1939 / comp. by Janina Zabielska. London, 1953–85. 4 v. (In progress).   **AA767**

Vol. 4 ed. by Zdzisław Jagodziński. Vols. 2–4 publ. London : Polish Library.

Contents: v. 1, 1939–51; v. 2, 1952–57 and supplements to 1939–51; v. 3, 1958–63 and supplement to 1939–57; v. 4, 1964–67 and supplements to 1939–63.

Each volume arranged chronologically.   Z2528.A5P6

Przewodnik bibljograficzny. Kraków : Základ Narodowy Imienia Ossolinskich, 1878–1933. ser. 1–3.   **AA768**

Ser. 1, v. 1 (1878)–37, no. 6 (June 1914); ser. 2, v. 1 (1920)–9 (1928); ser. 3, v. 1 (1929)–5 (1933).

July 1914–19 not numbered in series; called *Bibliografia polska*, v. 1–6.

Continued by: *Przewodnik bibliograficzny* 1946– (AA769).   Z2523.P92

Current

Przewodnik bibliograficzny : urzedowy wykaz druków wydanych w Rzeczypospolitej Polskiej. R. 1 (13), nr. 1/3– . Warszawa : Biblioteka Narodowa, 1946– . Weekly (frequency varies). **AA769**

Supersedes *Urzedowy wykaz druków, 1928–39,* and continues its numbering in parentheses. Vol. 1 (publ. 1955) is a retrospective volume for 1944–45. Includes Polish imprints, books, pamphlets, new periodicals, and many government publications, and also foreign publications dealing with Poland which are in the National Library. Arrangement is classified, with an annual alphabetical index. Some volumes also have subject indexes.   Z2523.P93

Portugal

Boletim de bibliografia portuguesa. v. 1 (1935)–46 (1980). Lisboa : Biblioteca Nacional, 1937–80. Annual, 1935–51; monthly, 1955–80. **AA770**

Not published 1940–42; 1952–54.

The national bibliography for Portugal, listing books, pamphlets, some periodical articles, and government publications. The annual volumes were arranged alphabetically by author. Beginning in 1955, published monthly and arranged by Universal Decimal Classification.

§ Continued by: *Boletim de bibliografia portuguesa. Monografias* (AA778).

Livros de Portugal. no. 1 (Nov. 1940)–100 (Dec. 1956); n.s., no. 1 (1959)–[7] (1975). Lisboa : Grémio Nacional dos Editores e Livreiros, 1940–75. **AA771**

Publication suspended 1948–51.

Unnumbered 1970–75.

Contains notes, advertisements, etc., and a list of recent books.   Z2715.L783

Early

Academia das Sciencias de Lisboa. Bibliografia geral portuguesa. Lisboa : Impr. Nacional, 1941–42. v. 1–2. : ill. **AA772**

Date on cover of v. 2: 1944.

Contents: v. 1–2, Século XV.

Detailed bibliographical descriptions with introduction and notes, facsimiles, and the following indexes in each volume: Matérias, Gravuras, Impressores, Bibliotecas e arquivos, Toponímico, and Geral.   Z2711.A3

Anselmo, António Joaquim. Bibliografia das obras impressas em Portugal no século XVI. Lisboa : Oficinas Gráficas da Biblioteca Nacional, 1926. 367 p. : ill. **AA773**

Reprinted from *Anais das bibliotecas e arquivos,* sér. 2, v. 2–6, 1921–25.

Detailed bibliographical descriptions.   Z2712.A61

Barbosa Machado, Diogo. Bibliotheca lusitana historica, critica, e cronologica : na qual se comprehende a noticia dos authores portuguezes, e das obras, que compuseraõ desde o tempo da promulgaçaõ da ley da graça até o tempo prezente. Lisboa, 1741–59. 4 v. **AA774**

Repr.: Coimbra : Atlântida Editora, 1965–67; also Readex Microprint.

A biobibliographical work arranged by given names, providing much information not available in later works. Covers from early times to mid-18th century.

An abridgment by B. J. de Sousa-Farinha, entitled *Summario da Bibliotheca lusitana,* was published in Lisbon, 1786–87. 3 v.   Z2722.B23

British Museum. Department of Printed Books. Short-title catalogue of Portuguese books printed before 1601, now in the British Museum / by Henry Thomas. London : Trustees, 1940. 43 p. **AA775**

A revised and enlarged edition of the Portuguese section of the Museum's *Short-title catalogues of Portuguese books and of Spanish-American books printed before 1601* (AA468).

Manuel II, *King of Portugal.* Livros antigos portuguezes, 1489–1600 : da bibliotheca de Sua Majestade Fidelissima / descriptos por S. M. el-rei D. Manuel …. Cambridge : Univ. Pr., 1929–35. 3 v. : ill. **AA776**

Contents: v. 1, 1489–1539; v. 2, 1540–1569; v. 3, 1570–1600 e Supplemento 1500–1597.   Z2712.M29

Silva, Innocencio Francisco da. Dicionário bibliografico portuguêz : estudos aplicaveis a Portugal e ao Brasil. Lisboa : Impr. Nacional, 1858–1923. v. 1–22. : ill. **AA777**

Contents: v. 1–7, A–Z; v. 8–22 (also called suppl. 1–15), A–Z, A–Au.

Vols. 10–22, "Continuados e ampliados por Brito Aranha."

A biobibliography arranged alphabetically by *first* names of authors. Includes books published from the 15th to the 19th centuries.

———. ———. *Indice alfabético,* [por] José Soares de Souza ([São Paulo?], Dept. de Cultura, Divisião de Bibliotécas, 1938. 264 p.).   Z2720.S58

Current

Boletim de bibliografia portuguesa. Monografias. v.47 (Jan./Jun. 1981)– . Lisboa : Biblioteca Nacional, 1982– . Quarterly. **AA778**

Continues in part *Boletim de bibliografia portuguesa* (AA770) and assumes its numbering. (1981 issued in 3 fasc.: no.1/2, 3/4 and indexes.).

Also referred to as *BBP. Monografias.*

Arranged by Universal Decimal Classification, with author, title, and systematic indexes. Companion publications are *Boletim de bibliografia portuguesa. Publicações em série* (1981–) and *Boletim de bibliografia portuguesa. Documentos não textuais* (1981–).

Livros disponíveis. 1987– . Lisboa : Associação Portuguesa de Editores e Livreiros, 1987– . Annual. **AA779**

Issue for 1985–86 entitled *Catalogo dos livros disponíveis.*

Prepared by the Bibliographical Documentation Centre of the Portuguese Publishers' and Booksellers' Association.

Kept up-to-date with alternate year supplement: *Livros disponíveis, actualizacão e adenda.*

Introductory matter in Portuguese and English.

A listing of currently available books by title, author, and subject. Includes a list of publishers, distributors, and booksellers.   Z2715.C38

Romania

Bianu, Ioan. Bibliografia românească veche, 1508–1830 / de Ioan Bianu si Nerva Hodoş. Ediţiunea Academiei Române. Bucureşti : Atelierele Socec & Co., 1903–43. 4 v. : ill. **AA780**

Repr.: Nendeln, Liechtenstein : Kraus Reprint, 1968–69.

Issued in parts: v. 1, 1508–1716; v. 2, 1716–1808 (by Bianu and Dan Simonescu); v. 3, 1809–1830; v. 4, Additions et corrections (1943) by Bianu and Simonescu.

An exhaustive bibliography, arranged chronologically, with index of names and titles.

Continued by: *Bibliografia românească modernă, 1831–1918* (AA781).   Z2921.B58

Bibliografia românească modernă, 1831–1918 / prefață de Gabriel Ștrempel ; [coordonare generală, Gabriel Ștrempel ; autori Neonila Onofrei, et al.]. [Bucharest] : Editura Științifică și Enciclopedică : Societatea de Științe Filologice din R.S. România, 1984–1989. v. 1–3. (In progress). **AA781**

At head of title: Biblioteca Academiei Republicii Socialiste România.

Contents: [Partea I] v. 1–3, A–Q.

Designed as a continuation of *Bibliografia românească veche, 1508–1830* (AA780). Pt. 1 is primarily an author listing with some form headings for anonymous works (e.g., catalogs, catechisms) and cross-references. It includes works by Romanians published outside Romania. Z2921.B59

Veress, Endre. Bibliografia româna-ungara. București : Cartea Româneasca, 1931–35. 3 v. : ill. **AA782**

Contents: v. 1, Românii in literatura ungara și Ungurii in literatura româna (1473–1780); v. 2, 1781–1838; v. 3, 1839–78.

Records some 2,377 titles in chronological order with full description and location of copies. Each volume has added title page and preface in French. Z2928.R4V5

Current

Bucharest (Romania). Biblioteca Centrală de Stat. Anuarul cărții din Republica Populara Romînă : 1952–1954. București : Ed. Stiințifica, 1957. 410 p. **AA783**

Classed arrangement, with alphabetic index of authors and titles. No more published.

———. *Bibliografia Republicii Popular Romîne : cărți, albume, hărti, note muzicale* (Anul 1 [1951]– 16 [1967]. [București], 1951–67. Semimonthly).

Title varies. v. 1–5 issued by the Romanian Ministerul Culturii under title: *Buletinul bibliografic al cărții*.

The national bibliography. Lists books, maps, and some government publications in classified order, with indexes of names and titles in each issue. (Early volumes had quarterly cumulations of the indexes, but these were abandoned after 1964.).

Superseded by: *Bibliografia Republicii Socialiste Româna : cărți, albume, hărti* (Anul 17 [1968]–38 [1989]. [București] : Biblioteca Centrală de Stat a Republicii Socialiste România, 1968–89). With *Bibliografia Republicii Socialiste România : note muzicale, discrui*, supersedes the 1951–67 series and assumes its numbering.

Superseded by: *Bibliografia României : carți, albume, hărti* (Anul 39 [1990]– . București : Tip. Bibliotecii Naționale, 1990–). Title varies; Jan. 1991–May 1991 called *Bibliografia Naționala România : cârte, albume, hărti*. Supersedes the 1968–89 series, assuming its numbering and retaining its format. Z2921.B8

Russia and the U.S.S.R.

General

Library of Congress. Cyrillic union catalog [microform]. N.Y. : Readex Microprint Corp., 1963. 1244 cards in 7 boxes (Micro-opaque). **AA784**

Contents: pt. 1, Authors and added entries; pt. 2, Titles, with complete listing of library locations; pt. 3, Subjects.

A union catalog of more than 700,000 cards, representing 178,226 titles in Russian, Belorussian, Bulgarian, Serbian, and Ukrainian. Substantially complete for monographic holdings of the Library of Congress as of March 1956. Reported holdings of 185 other American libraries are also included, with the most complete information on locations in pt. 2. "The title catalog is a useful finding aid for the reader who knows the title of a given book but not its author. It is also useful to the reader unversed in the intricate rules of cataloging corporate authors."—*Introd.* Library of Congress card numbers, where available, appear in parentheses following title. English translations of titles, other than belles lettres, are given for all post-1917 publications. Sub-

ject catalog contains form headings for fiction, drama, poetry. The microform set is accompanied by a booklet: *Cyrillic union catalog of the Library of Congress : description and guide to the Microprint edition* (N.Y., 1964. 12 p.).

Pt. 1 is, in effect, superseded by: Library of Congress. Catalog Publication Division, *The Slavic Cyrillic union catalog of pre-1956 imprints* (AA785).

Library of Congress. Catalog Publication Division. The Slavic Cyrillic union catalog of pre-1956 imprints [microform]. Totowa, N.J. : Rowman & Littlefield, 1980. Microfiche (174 sheets, 48x). **AA785**

A successor to the *Cyrillic union catalog* (AA784), considerably expanded in scope. Reproduces the catalog cards from the Slavic Union Catalog at the Library of Congress for books, pamphlets, maps, atlases, periodicals, and other serials published before 1956 in the Cyrillic alphabet and in seven languages: Rssian, Church Slavic, Belorussian, Ukrainian, Bulgarian, Serbian, and Macedonian. It represents more than 350,000 entries (main and added entries and cross references) as cataloged by the Library of Congress and participating libraries, and held by 220 libraries in the United States and Canada. Arranged by main entry, with essential added entries and cross references (although the main entry must be consulted for locations). No attempt was made to edit contributed copy for conformity with LC practice, and the searcher should be aware that inconsistencies in form of entry are to be expected. Most entries use the Cyrillic alphabet rather than transliteration as in the *Cyrillic union catalog*. The latter catalog, of course, remains useful for subject and title approaches.

Semenovker, B. A. Retrospektivnaiã gosudarstvennaiã bibliografiiã SSSR : spravochnik. Moskva : Izd-vo "Knizhnaiã palata", 1990. 303 p. **AA786**

Offers detailed descriptions of retrospective bibliographies produced by the Soviet Union and its autonomous republics, covering publications from the 16th century to the present. Indexes by author, title, institution, language, place of publication, and genre.

Z2491.S45

16th and 17th centuries

Zernova, Antonina S. Knigi kirillovskoï pechati, izdannye v Moskve v XVI-XVII vekakh : svodnyi katalog / Antonina S. Zernova, pod. red. N. P. Kiseleva. Moskva, 1958. 150 p. **AA787**

At head of title: Ministerstvo kultura RSFSR. Gosudarstvennaiã ordena Lenina Biblioteka SSSR im. V. I. Lenina. Otdel redkikh knig.

A union catalog of 16th- and 17th-century Moscow imprints in *kirillitsa* printing type, the alphabet for Russian prior to reform under Peter I and continued for ecclesiastical printing. Describes copies in six of the largest libraries of Moscow and Leningrad. Z7044.C4Z4

18th century

Akademiiã Nauk URSR, Kiev. Biblioteka. Knigi grazhdanskoi pechati XVIII veka : katalog knig, khraniãshchiksiã v Gosudarstvennoi Publichnoi Biblioteke Ukrainskoi SSR / Sost.: S. O. Petrov. Kiev, 1956. 300 p. **AA788**

Catalog of the books and journals, printed between 1708 and 1800 in Russian, which are preserved in the State Library in Kiev. Arrangement is by author, or title of anonymous work, with indexes for translators, places of publication and publishers' names, and broad subject fields.

§ Continued by: Akademiiã Nauk URSR, Kiev. Biblioteka, *Knigi pervoi chetverti XIX veka* (AA842). Z2501.A4

Gosudarstvennaia publichnaia biblioteka imeni M.E. Saltykova-Shchedrina. Opisanie izdaniĭ, napechatannykh pri Petre Pervom : svodnyi katalog ... / [Sost. T. A. Bykova i M. M. Gurevich ; red. i vstup. stat'ia P. N. Berkova]. Moskva : Izd-vo Akademii Nauk SSSR, 1955–58. 2 v. : ill.   **AA789**

At head of title: Gosudarstvennaia Publichnaia Biblioteka M. E. Saltykova-Shchedrina i Biblioteka Akademii Nauk SSSR.

Each volume also has special title page.

Contents: v. 1, Opisanie izdaniĭ grazhdanskoi pechati, 1708–ianvar' 1725g. (625 p.); v. 2, Opisanie izdaniĭ napechatannykh kirillitsei 1689–ianvar' 1725g. (402 p.).

Vol. 1 is a descriptive bibliography with extensive annotations of works published in the Russian "civic" type introduced under Peter I. Locational symbols are given for libraries in Moscow and Leningrad. Appendixes list books in foreign languages published in Russia. Vol. 2 is a detailed, descriptive bibliography of Russian books printed in the pre-reform alphabet, *kirillitsa*, between 1689 and 1725; appendixes include foreign books pertaining to Russia.

These two volumes of a Russian union catalog are continued, chronologically, by *Svodnyi katalog russkoi knigi ... XVIII veka, 1725–1800* (AA791).

§ Supplemented by: *Dopolneniia i prilozheniia*, sost. T. A. Bykova ... [et al.] (Leningrad : Izdatel'skii otdel Biblioteki Akademii nauk SSSR : 1972. 269 p.).

At head of title: Biblioteka Akademii Nauk SSSR. Gosudarstvennaia ordena Trudovogo Krasnogo Znameni Publichnaia Biblioteka imeni M. E. Saltykova-Shchedrina. Leningradskoe Otdelenie Instituta Istorii SSSR. Akademii Nauk SSSR.

Scope has been extended to cover through December 1727, and information from sources not searched for compilation of the basic volumes is included here.   Z2492.B94

Sopikov, Vasiliĭ Stephanovich. Opyt rossiiskoi bibliografiĭ. [Izd. 2] / red., V. N. Rogozhin. St. Petersburg, 1904–06. 5 v.   **AA790**

Originally published 1813–21.

Vol. 1 is a classed arrangement of books under the heading "Church Slavic." Vols. 2–5 list other books in Russian to 1813. Although largely replaced by more recent bibliographies for the 18th century, the Sopikov number is often cited as part of the bibliographic description in later works.

Subject index in: P. O. Morozov, *Alfavitnyi ukazatel' imen* ... (St. Petersburg : Tipografiia Imperatorskoi Akademii Nauk, 1876. 47 p.); various indexes in: V. N. Rogoshin, *Ukazatel'* ... (St. Petersburg : Izdanii A.S. Suvarina, 1900. 253 p.).   Z2491.S71

Svodnyi katalog russkoĭ knigi grazhdanskoi pechati XVIII veka, 1725–1800 / red. kollegia: I. P. Kondakov i dr. Moska : Izd. Gos. Biblioteki SSSR im. Lenina, 1962–67. 5 v.   **AA791**

Forms a chronological section of a union catalog of Russian books from 1708 to the present. Includes works of five pages or more published in Russia or abroad. Entries are annotated, refer to entry numbers in earlier standard bibliographies, and give location symbols for copies in the major libraries of Leningrad and Moscow.

For bibliography of the first quarter of the 18th century, see *Opisanie izdaniĭ, napechatannykh pri Petre Pervom* (AA789).

———. *Dopolneniia, razyskivaemye izdaniia utochenenia*, red. kollegii: N. M. Sikorskii (Moskva : Kniga, 1975. 189 p.).

Lists acquisitions of participating libraries from 1967; corrections to v. 1–4; citations to reviews and indexes. Includes a list of unlocated books.

§ A complementary publication is *Svodnyi katalog knig na inostrannykh iazikakh, izdannykh v Rossii v XVII veke, 1701–1800*, red. kollegiia, V. A. Filov [et al.] (Leningrad : "Nauka," Leningradskoe otd-nie, 1984–86. 3 v.).

Lists foreign-language books published in Russia during the period. Supplements in v. 3 include: bookseller and library catalogs, St. Petersburg and Moscow; advertisements from St. Petersburg Academy of Sciences and Moscow University; material earlier thought to be published in Russia, including chronological index of materials; and publications with falsified publishing data. Bibliography; list of abbreviations.   Z2492.S85

19th and 20th centuries

Gracheva, Iia Borisovna. Gosudarstvennaia bibliografiia SSSR : Spravochnik / comp. by I. B. Gracheva and V. N. Frantskevich. Izd. 2-e, pererabotannoe i dopolnennoe. Moskva : Kniga, 1967. 111 p. : ill.   **AA792**

At head of title: Vsesoiuznaia Knizhnaia Palata.

1st ed., 1952, had title: *Gosudarstvennaia registratsionno-uchetnaia bibliografiia v SSSR*; comp. by Iu. I. Masanov.

Describes in detail the various publications forming the national bibliographies of Russia and the republics of the Soviet Union.

A translation appears in Thomas J. Whitby and Tanja Lorković, *Introduction to Soviet national bibliography* (AA794).   Z2492.5.G7

Library of Congress. Processing Department. Monthly index of Russian accessions. v. 10, no. 10 (Jan. 1958)–v. 22, no. 5 (May 1969). Wash. : U.S. Govt. Print. Off., 1958–69.   **AA793**

Continues *Monthly list of Russian accessions* (v. 1 [Apr. 1948]–v. 10 no. 9 [Dec. 1957]) and assumes its numbering.

A union list of Russian-language monographs and periodicals issued in and outside the Soviet Union, received by the Library of Congress and a group of cooperating libraries. Whenever possible, publications printed in other languages in the Soviet Union are also included. Each issue is in three parts: pt. A, Monographs; pt. B, Periodicals, with their tables of contents translated into English; pt. C, Alphabetical subject index to A and B under English subject headings. Pts. A and B are classified in 17 main subject groups. Beginning v. 21, no. 1 (April 1968) the subject headings previously used in pt. C were replaced by classes based on the Universal Decimal Classification.

All titles are given first in English, followed by the Russian title in transliteration. Beginning with v. 5, an author index to monographs and a periodical location index are included annually as appendixes to the first two issues of the following volume (varies slightly). These are preceded by a cumulative index to v. 1–3, April 1948–March 1951, issued in one volume (1953), and a cumulative index to v. 4, April 1951–March 1952 (1957). In each issue pt. C included a list of Russian periodicals available in English translation from cover to cover.

§ The Library's Processing Department also issued, in similar format, a monthly *East European accessions index* (1951–61. 10 v.) which covered monographs published after 1944, and periodicals after 1950, received by the Library of Congress and certain other American libraries, published in ten East European countries (except Russia) or elsewhere in their languages.   Z2495.U6

Whitby, Thomas Joseph. Introduction to Soviet national bibliography / by Thomas Joseph Whitby and Tanja Lorković. Littleton, Colo. : Libraries Unlimited, 1979. 229 p.   **AA794**

An introductory section, which traces the development of Soviet national bibliography from tsarist times to the present and describes the current activities of the All-Union Book Chamber, is followed by a translation of *Gosudarstvennaia bibliografiia SSSR : Spravochnik* (AA792), by Iia B. Gracheva and Valentina N. Frantskevich, under the title "Guide to the organs of national bibliography in the USSR." Appendixes include a glossary of terms (i.e., English equivalents of Russian terms) and a bibliography, p. 211–24. Indexed.   Z2492.5.W47

Current

Ezhegodnik knigi SSSR : sistematicheskiĭ ukazatel'. 1935– . Moskva : Izd-vo Vsesoiuznoi Knizhnoi Palaty, 1935– . Annual.   **AA795**

Continues *Ezhogodnik knigi Gosudarstvennaia TSentral'noi knizhnoi palaty RSFSR* (1925–29).

Suspended 1936–40.

Semiannual 1946–56. Issued in 2 v. beginning 1959: v. 1, social sciences and humanities; v. 2, science and technology. Beginning 1981, issued in volumes and parts.

The book annual of the Soviet national bibliography. Cumulates, in classified arrangement, a selection from the weekly *Knizhnaĭa letopis'* (AA796). Indexes for names, titles, languages other than Russian, translations from foreign languages, and subjects.   Z2401.E9

Knizhnaĭa letopis' : glavnago upravleniĭa po dielam pechati. 1907–77. Moskva : Upravlenie, 1907–1977. Weekly. **AA796**

Issued by Vsesoiuznaĭa Knizhnaĭa Palata.

Title varies: 1907–17, *Knizhnaĭa Palata*.

Available on microfilm from Library of Congress.

For a detailed history of the title with a list of indexes and bibliography, see *Obshchie bibliografiĭ russkikh knig grazhdanskoi pechati, 1708–1955*, p. 179–222 (AA63) and I. B. Gracheva and V. N. Frantskevich, *Gosudarstvennaĭa bibliografiĭa SSSR : Spravochnik*, p. 13–25 (AA792).

As the principal organ of Soviet national bibliography, this work listed, in Russian, books and pamphlets published in the USSR in all languages. Each issue contains a language index to non-Russian publications.

Arranged in 31 classes. Each entry includes a classification number based on a variant of the Universal Decimal Classification. Quarterly indexes: name, geographical, and subject. *Ukazatel' seriinykh izdaniĭ* is an annual index to publishers' series. An annual cumulation of a selection of titles appeared as *Ezhegodnik knigi SSSR* (AA795).

In 1978, changed title to:

Knizhnaĭa letopis' : osnovnoi vypusk (1978–92; Moskva : Kniga, 1978–92).

A monthly supplement to *Knizhnaĭa letopis'* 1907–77 was publ. as:

Knizhnaĭa letopis' : dopolnitel'nyi vypusk (1962–80; Moskva : Palata, 1962–80).

Issued by Vsezoiuznaĭa Knizhnaĭa Palata.

Includes certain types of publications formerly registered in the weekly, but categories transferred have varied. In general, lists small editions if printed in 101 copies or more and over five pages in length, and unpriced materials not intended for the book trade. List of dissertations, included in 1961, was omitted in 1962 and 1963, and resumed in 1964. Quarterly indexes (name, subject, and geographical) and annual index to publishers' series.

In 1980, split into: (1) *Knizhnaĭa letopis' : dopolnitel'nyi vypusk : avtoreferaty dissertatsiĭ* (1981–92; later became *Letopis' avtoreferatov dissertatsiĭ* [1993– . AG46]); and (2) *Knizhnaĭa letopis' : dopolnitel'nyi vypusk : knigi i broshiury* (1981–92).

In 1993, *Knizhnaĭa letopis' : osnovnoi vypusk* and *Knizhnaĭa letopis' : dopolnitel'nyi vypustk : knigi i broshiury* (both above) merged to form:

Knizhnaĭa letopis' : rossiskaĭa knizhnaĭa palata (1993– . Moskva : Izd-vo "Knizhnaĭa palata," 1993–).

Retains the format and indexing of the former titles, but lists only publications of the new Russian state.   Z2491.K5

Serbia

Srpska bibliografija : knjige, 1868–1944 / predsednik Radovan Samardžić ... et al. ; glavni i odgovorni urednik Milomir Petrović. Beograd : Narodna biblioteka Srbije, 1989–92. v. 1–8. (In progress).   **AA797**

Title page and introductory material in English and Serbian. Title on added t. p. : *The Serbian bibliography : books, 1868–1944*.

"Edited by the National Library of Serbia."—*t. p.*

Contents: v. 1–8, A–Km. To be complete in 20 v.

Constitutes pt. 4 of "Serbian retrospective bibliography," to be published under the auspices of the Council for Science and Culture of Serbia. Also planned are pt. 1, 1494–1700; pt. 2, 1701–1800; pt. 3, 1801–67.

Attempts to list Serbian books published in Serbia, books published by writers of Serbian origin throughout the world in any language, and "books published in Serbo-Croatian in other republics or outside Yugoslavia if they are intended for Serbs."—*p. xxiv.* Arranged alphabetically by author with detailed bibliographic descriptions. Pro-

vides locations in Yugoslavian and some European libraries. Each volume has indexes of names (including authors, coauthors, translators, editors, etc.) and subjects; indexes will be cumulated when pt. 4 is complete.   Z2951.S65

Slovenia

Simonic, Franc. Slovenska bibliografija : 1. del : Knjige (1550–1900). Ljubljani : Natisnila J. Blasnikova Tikarna, 1903–05. 627 p.   **AA798**

Alphabetical arrangement of books in Slovenian or by Slovenian authors. Additions were published annually in the periodical *Slovenska matica v Ljubljani, Zbornik*, v. 3–9 (1901–1906).   Z7041.S59

Spain

General

Aguiló y Fustér, Mariano. Catálogo de obras en lengua catalana impresas desde 1474 hasta 1860. Madrid : Rivadeneyra, 1923. 1077 p. : ill.   **AA799**

A classified catalog of books in the Catalan language, with a general index and an index of printers.   Z2704.C35A27

Boston Public Library. Ticknor Collection. Catalogue of the Spanish library and of the Portuguese books bequeathed by George Ticknor. Boston, 1879. 476 p.   **AA800**

A dictionary catalog of an important 19th-century collection. Includes also the collection of Spanish and Portuguese literature in the general library.

A 1970 reprint (Boston : G. K. Hall) includes an appendix, p. 477–550, listing material acquired since publication of the original catalog.   Z2691.B74

Foulché-Delbosc, Raymond. Manuel de l'hispanisant / Raymond Foulché-Delbosc, Louis Barrau-Dihigo. N.Y. : Putnam, 1920–25. 2 v.   **AA801**

Repr.: N.Y. : Kraus, 1970.

Vol. 2 publ. by the Hispanic Society of America, New York.

Contents: v. 1, Répertoires; v. 2, Collections.

A useful manual of Spanish bibliography including material on Portugal as well as on Spain. Vol. 1 lists bibliographies: national, regional, special; biographical works; bibliographies of special subjects; descriptions of public and private archives, libraries, and museums. Vol. 2 gives contents of printed collections and series published 1579–1923.   Z2681.A1F7

Heredia y Livermore, Ricardo. Catalogue de la bibliothèque de M. Ricardo Heredia. Paris : E. Paul, 1891–94. 4 v. : ill.   **AA802**

A sales catalog of this famous collection of Spanish and other rare works. For index *see*: Gabriel Molina Navarro, *Índice para facilitar el manejo y consulta de los catálogos de Salvá y Heredia* (AA805).   Z2709.H54

Hidalgo, Dionisio. Diccionario general de bibliografía española. Madrid : Impr. de las Escuelas Pias, 1862–81. 7 v.   **AA803**

A general list of works published in Spain, arranged alphabetically by title, with author and classed indexes.   Z2681.H63

Llordén, Andrés. La imprenta en Málaga : ensayo para una tipobibliografía malagueña. Málaga : Caja de Ahorros Provincial, [1973]. 2 v.   **AA804**

Arranged by printer or press; an historical note is followed by a bibliography of the works published by each.   Z174.M22L55

Molina Navarro, Gabriel. Índice para facilitar el manejo y consulta de los catálogos de Salvá y Heredia. Madrid : Molina, 1913. 162 p.   **AA805**

A combined index to the catalogs of Vicente Salvá y Pérez, *Catálogo de la biblioteca de Salvá* (AA807) and Ricardo Heredia y Livermore, *Catalogue de la bibliothèque de M. Ricardo Heredia* (AA802).   Z997.H54

Palau y Dulcet, Antonio. Manual del librero hispano-americano : bibliografía general española e hispano-americana desde la invención de la imprenta hasta nuestros tiempos, con el valor comercial de los impresos descritos. 2. ed. corr. y aum. por el autor. Barcelona : Librería Palau, 1948–77. 28 v.   **AA806**

1st ed. 1923–27. 7 v.

A very useful, comprehensive, alphabetical record, listing material under author, or under title for anonymous works. Covers material published in Spain and Spanish America from the beginning of printing to mid-20th century.

Indexed by: Agustín Palau Claveras, *Indice alfabético de títulos—materias, correcciones, conexiones, y adiciones del Manual del librero hispanoamericano de Antonio Palau y Dulcet* (Gerona : Palacete Palau Dulcet ; Oxford : Dolphin Book, 1981–87. 7 v.) The appendix in v. 7 includes in a single alphabet corrections, additional information, and some titles from the main body of the index under a second subject heading.

————. *Addenda y corrigenda o volumen complementario del tomo primero del Manual del librero hispanoamericano de Antonio Palau y Dulcet* (Barcelona : Editorial Palau y Dulcet, 1990. v. 1. [In progress]).

Contents: v. 1, A–Azzac.

A meticulous elaboration of information appearing in the 2nd ed. of Palau, supplying omitted material, corrections, and additional entries. Incorporates material from the appendix published with v. 7 of the *Indice*.   Z2681.P16

Salvá y Pérez, Vicente. Catálogo de la biblioteca de Salvá / escrito por Pedro Salvá y Mallen, y enriquecido con la descripción de otras muchas obras, de sus ediciones, etc. Valencia : Impr. de Ferrer de Orga, 1872. 2 v. : ill.   **AA807**

Repr.: Barcelona : Porter-Libros, 1963.

A classified catalog, with indexes, giving detailed descriptions of works published from the 16th to the mid-19th centuries.

For index, *see* Gabriel Molina Navarro, *Indice para facilitar el manejo y consulta de los catálogos de Salvá y Heredia* (AA805).   Z2709.S25

Simón Díaz, José. Impresos del siglo XVII : bibliografía selectiva por materias de 3.500 ediciones príncipes en lengua castellana. Madrid : Consejo Superior de Investigaciones Científicas, 1972. 926 p.   **AA808**

Classed arrangement modeled on the Dewey Decimal system. Author and detailed subject indexes.   Z2682.S543

University of California, Berkeley. Library. Spain and Spanish America in the libraries of the University of California : a catalogue of books. Berkeley, 1928–30. 2 v.   **AA809**

Contents: v. 1, General and departmental libraries; v. 2, The Bancroft Library.

A catalog of very rich collections. Each volume is arranged alphabetically with a subject index.   Z2709.C16

Vaganay, Hugues. Bibliographie hispanique extra-péninsulaire : 16e et 17e siècles. (*In* Revue hispanique 42 [1918] : 1–304).   **AA810**

A listing of 1,198 works of authors from the Hispanic peninsula, which were printed outside Spain from 1502 to 1700. Arranged chronologically.

15th–19th centuries

Antonio, Nicolás. Bibliotheca hispana vetus : sive, Hispani scriptores qui ab Octaviani Augusti aevo ad annum Christi MD. floruerunt. Matriti : J. Ibarra, 1788. 2 v. : facsims.   **AA811**

————. *Bibliotheca hispana nova : sive, Hispanorum scriptorum qui ab anno MD. ad MDCLXXXIV, floruere notitia* (Matriti : J. de Ibarra, 1783–88. 2 v.).

The date 1783 on the title page of v. 1 is a misprint for 1788.

2nd ed., edited by T. A. Sánchez, J. A. Pellicer, and R. Casalbón; 1st ed., published 1672 as *Bibliotheca hispana*.

Together these two works provide an indispensable record of the writings of persons born in the Spanish peninsula regardless of the language in which they wrote. The volumes covering to 1500 are in narrative form; those covering 1500–1684 are arranged as a bibliographical dictionary.   Z2681.A632

Biblioteca Nacional (Spain). Catálogo colectivo de obras impresas en los siglos XVI al XVIII existentes en las bibliotecas españolas. Ed. provisional. Madrid : [Instituto Bibliografico Hispanico], 1972–84. v. 1–15. (In progress).   **AA812**

Contents: Sección I, Siglo XVI, v. 1–15, A–Z.

A main-entry catalog reproducing the catalog cards for the relevant items and indicating library locations in Spain.   Z1012.M22

British Library. Catalogue of books printed in Spain and of Spanish books printed elsewhere in Europe before 1601 now in the British Library. 2nd ed. London : British Library, 1989. 294 p.   **AA813**

1st ed. had title: *Short-title catalogue of books printed in Spain …* (London, 1921).

"Very considerably revised and expanded, and for the first time includes comprehensive indexes of printers, booksellers and towns both within and outside Spain in which books in Spanish were printed."—*Pref.* Entries conform to new cataloging rules of the British Library so that some items appear under headings differing from those of the 1921 edition.   Z2682.B75

Catálogo colectivo del patrimonio bibliográfico español : siglo XIX. Madrid : Arco Libros, c1989–91. v. 1–4. (In progress).   **AA814**

Contents: v. 1–3, A; v. 4. Índices.

Follows the format of the earlier set. Vol. 4 is an index to the first 3 v.; includes separate indexes for authors (primary, secondary, and corporate), titles, illustrators, and publishers and printers.   Z1017.C37

Catálogo colectivo del patrimonio bibliográfico español : siglo XVII / Dirección General del Libro y Bibliotecas, Biblioteca Nacional. Madrid : Arco Libros, 1988–92. v. 1–3. (In progress).   **AA815**

Contents: v. 1–3, A–Ciz.

A listing by author, or title if anonymous, of books published in Spain or in Spanish during the 17th century held by major libraries in Madrid. Includes detailed bibliographic descriptions and Madrid locations.   Z1015.C37

Goldsmith, Valentine Fernande. A short title catalogue of Spanish and Portuguese books, 1601–1700, in the Library of the British Museum (The British Library—Reference Division). Folkestone : Dawsons of Pall Mall, 1974. 250 p.   **AA816**

Includes "1. Books written wholly or partly in Spanish or Portuguese, no matter where published; 2. Books, in no matter what language, published or printed at any place which today forms part of Spain or Portugal."—*Definitions.* Books lost or destroyed during World War II are listed whether or not the library has replaced them. Continues chronologically the Museum's *Short-title catalogue of books printed in Spain and of Spanish books printed elsewhere in Eu-*

rope before 1601 ... (London, 1921; 2nd ed., AA813). Errors and shortcomings of the work are pointed out in a review in *The Library*, ser. 5, 29 (Dec. 1974): 463–67. Z2686.G64

Haebler, Konrad. Bibliografía ibérica del siglo XV : enumeración de todos los libros impresos en España y Portugal hasta el año de 1500 con notas críticas. La Haya : Nijhoff; Leipzig : Hiersemann, 1903–17. 2 v. **AA817**
Each volume alphabetically arranged with detailed bibliographical information and annotations. Indexes of printers, etc. Z240.H1

Hispanic Society of America. Printed books, 1468–1700, in the Hispanic Society of America / a listing by Clara Louisa Penney. N.Y., 1965. 614 p. **AA818**
Two previous listings of the Society's early books were prepared by the same compiler: *List of books printed before 1601 in the Library of the Hispanic Society of America* (N.Y., 1929; Offset reissue, with additions, N.Y., 1955) and *List of books printed 1601–1700, in the Library* (N.Y., 1938).
This catalog combines the listings in the two earlier bibliographies and adds some 2,000 pamphlets and other additions to the Library since 1938. Alphabetical arrangement by main entry, with short title and usually a reference to another published source for additional information or a more complete description. Omits "Check list of Hispanic printing sites and printers, 1468?–1700" which appeared as Appendix II of the 1938 publication. Most of the pre-1701 items are not represented in the catalog of the Library published by G.K. Hall (Boston, 1962). Z1012.H58

Ribelles Comín, José. Bibliografía de la lengua valenciana. .... Madrid : "Rev. de Arch., Bibl. y Museos", 1915–31. 3 v. : facsim. **AA819**
Subtitle: O sea catálogo razonada por orden alfabético de autores de los libros, folletos, obras dramáticas, periódicos, coloquios, coplas, chistes, discursos, romances, alocuciones, cantares, gozos, etc., que escritos en lengua valenciana y bilingüe, han visto la luz pública desde el establecimiento de la imprenta en España hasta nuestros días.
Vol. 1, siglo XV (i.e., descriptions and notes of printed editions to 1918 of works in the Valencian dialect composed before the end of the 15th century); v. 2, siglo XVI; v. 3, siglo XVII. Z2704.V1R4

Vindel, Francisco. Manual gráfico-descriptivo del bibliófilo hispano-americano (1475–1850) / con un prólogo de Pedro Sáinz Rodríguez. Madrid : [Impr. Góngora], 1930–34. 12 v. in 13. : ill. **AA820**
Contents: v. 1–10, A–Z; v. 11, Tasación e índices; v. 12, Suplemento, siglo XV.
An author list of 3,442 books, mainly early. Information for each includes: author's name, title, place, publisher or printer, date, size, and, generally, paging. For each item, features a reproduction of some page of the work, usually title page or colophon. Z2681.V77

20th century

Anuario español e hispano-americano del libro y de las artes gráficas con el Catálogo mundial del libro impreso en lengua española. v. 1 (1944)–v. 10 (1957). Madrid : Editores del Anuario Maritimo Español, 1945–59. **AA821**
Vols. 1–2 had title: *Catálogo de los libros publicados en España en 1944 [en 1945]*; publ. 1945–46.
Arranged by decimal classification with author indexes. Vols. 5 and 9 include "Relación de las tesis doctorales manuscritas existentes en la biblioteca de la Universidad de Madrid"; v. 10 includes "Las tesis doctorales leídas en la Universidad de Chile." Some volumes have cumulated indexes. Z2681.A64

Bibliografía española : revista general de la imprenta, de la librería y de las industrias que concurren á la fabricación del libro. Madrid : Asociación de la Librería, 1901–22. 22 v. **AA822**

Subtitle varies.
Frequency varies; semimonthly, then monthly.
Continued by *Bibliografía general española e hispanoamericana* (1923–marzo/abril 1942. Madrid-Barcelona, 1923–42. 16 v.).
Monthly, 1923–36; bimonthly, 1941–42. Publication suspended July 1936–Jan. 1941. 1923–36 in three parts: (1) *Bibliografía*, a list of new publications, giving for each item author's name, title, place, date, publisher, paging, size, and price; (2) *Crónica*; (3) *Anuncios*. Vols. 1–9 have a general author index to the books listed in the monthly *Bibliografía*; v. 10 has, instead, a cumulated author list of the entries in v. 9–10.
Continued by: *Bibliografía hispánica* (año 1–16 [mayo/junio 1942–dic. 1957]. Madrid : Inst. Nacional de Libro Español, 1942–57).
Each monthly issue in two sections: (1) articles on the book trade, bibliographies, book reviews, etc.; (2) *Repertorio bibliográfico*, which is a classed list of books published, with an annual index of authors and titles. This section is usually paged separately and continuously, with a special title page, so that it may be bound separately. Variations are: v. 1, 1942, *Repertorio* paged separately in each issue but not continuously; v. 2–3, 1943, *Repertorio* is not separately paged; v. 8, 1948, *Bibliografía* published three times per year. *Repertorio* published separately monthly; v. 9, 1949–57, monthly issues containing both sections, paged separately.
Continued by: *El libro español* (AA826). Z2685.B58

Bibliotheca hispana : revista de información y orientación bibliográficas. v. 1–32. Madrid : Consejo Superior de Investigaciones Científicas, Inst. Nicolás Antonio, 1943–73. **AA823**
Originally issued in three sections; beginning with v. 13, issued in two sections, each of which had four issues per year and its own annual index. The sections contain the following subject materials: sec. 1, Letras: Obras generales, bibliografía, religión, filosofía, pedagogía, estadística y demografía, sociología y política, economía, derecho, filología, literatura, geografía, historia, arte (ceased with v. 30, no. 2/3); sec. 2, Ciencias: Ciencia en general, matemáticas, astronomía, física, química, ciencias naturales, medicina, ingeniería y construcción, ciencia y artes militares, agricultura y ganadería, industria, comercio, economía doméstica (ceased with v. 31, no. 1).
Entries are annotated, and periodical articles are also included. Z2685.B597

Catálogo general de la librería española e hispanoamericana, 1901–30 : Autores. Madrid : Inst. Nacional del Libro Español, 1932–51. 5 v. **AA824**
Publisher varies.
A comprehensive list giving full name of author, title, edition, place, publisher, date, paging, size, price.
Continued by: *Catálogo general de la librería española, 1931–1950* (Madrid : Inst. Nacional del Libro Español. 1957–65. 4 v.), which follows the same plan, but does not include Spanish-American imprints. Z2681.C35

Current

Bibliografía española. 1958– . Madrid : Ministerio de Educación Nacional, Dirección General de Archivos y Bibliotecas, Servicio Nacional de Informacíon Bibliográfica, 1959– . Annual (varies). **AA825**
At head of title: Ministerio de Educación Nacional. Dirección General de Archivos y Bibliotecas, Servicio Nacional de Información Bibliográfica.
Frequency varies: Annual 1958–68; monthly 1969–75; annual 1977–78; monthly 1982– .
Publication suspended 1979–81.
A national bibliography based on copyright receipts in the national library. Arranged by Universal Decimal Classification, with index of authors, titles, and subjects, and with supplementary lists of publishers, series, and periodicals. Z2685.B583

El libro español : revista mensual .... t. 1, núm. 1 (enero 1958)– . Madrid : Inst. Nacional del Libro Español, 1958– . Monthly; biweekly.   **AA826**

The merger of the Institute's two former titles: *Bibliografía hispánica* and the more popular *Novedades editoriales españolas* with its supplement *Libros del mes*. The new title is much like the former *Bibliografía*, the first half consisting of articles of interest to the book trade, bibliographic studies, etc., the other half being the list of new books, "Repertorio bibliográfico clasificado por materias." Annual author, title, and subject indexes are issued for the "Repertorio."

————. *Indices de la producción editorial española, 1968–72 : autores y obras anónimas, titulos y conceptos, editores* ([Madrid] : Instituto, 1972. 636 p.).

Provides cumulative indexes to v. 11–15 (1968–72) of *El libro español*.   Z2685.L5

Libros españoles en venta ISBN = Spanish books in print. 1983/84– . Madrid : Ministerio de Cultura, Instituto Nacional del Libro Español, c1984– . Irregular.   **AA827**

Continues *Libros españoles ISBN* (1974–82), which in turn continued *Libros españoles: catalogo ISBN* (1973).

Issued in 3 v.: Titulos, Autores, Materias.

Sweden

Early

Sveriges bibliografi intill år 1600 / av Isak Collijn. Uppsala : Svenska Litteratursällskapet, 1927–38. 3 v. : ill. (Svenska litteratursällskapet. Skrifter, 10: 5–18).   **AA828**

Published in parts.

Contents: Bd. 1, 1478–1530 (publ. 1934–38); bd. 2, 1530–82 (publ. 1927–31); bd. 3, 1583–99 (publ. 1932–33); Alfabetiskt register till bd. 1, bd. 2–3; Typografiska tabeller, 1483–1525, 1526–99.

Vol. 1 is a revision of *Sveriges bibliografi, 1481–1600*, by G. E. Klemming and Aksel Anderson (Uppsala : 1927. 216 p.).

Arranged chronologically, with alphabetical indexes. Gives full descriptions, with bibliographical references and location of copies.

Continued by: *Sveriges bibliografi, 1600-talet: bidrag till en bibliografisk förteckning*, av Isak Collijn (Uppsala : Almqvist, 1942–46. 2 v. [Svenska litteratursällskapet. Skrifter, 10: 19–23]).

Arranged alphabetically with no chronological approach. Gives brief biographical facts of authors, full description, and location of copies. Covers 17th century.   Z2622.S962

Swedish imprints, 1731–1833 : a retrospective national bibliography / prep. at the Center for Bibliographical Studies, Uppsala (CBSU). Uppsala : Dahlia Books, 1977–94. v. 1–38. (In progress).   **AA829**

Rolf E. DuRietz, gen. ed.

Title often abbreviated as *SWIM*.

An effort toward a comprehensive retrospective bibliography of works printed and/or published in the area constituting the sovereign territory of Sweden, 1731–1833. The bibliography is being published in parts, each part having its own index. Within each part arrangement is chronological-alphabetical. Supplementary entries in later parts correct and augment information appearing in the first entry for a given work. Cumulative indexes are published at intervals; the third cumulative index for v. 1–35 appeared in 1993; it offers separate indexes for personal names; printing, publishing and bookselling firms; entry headings; and supplementary entries which supersede all earlier lists and corrigenda.

Accompanied by a manual, *Basic information for users of SWIM*, (1977), and supplemented by information in v. 5. A revised ed. of the manual is expected in 1994. "The reader is expected to have digested the contents of *Basic Information* before making any serious use of the bibliography."—*p. 2, v. 37*.   Z2621.S975

19th-20th centuries

Linnström, Hjalmar. Svenskt boklexikon, 1830–65. Stockholm : Linnström, 1883–84. 2 v.   **AA830**

Alphabetical arrangement. Includes brief biographical data for most authors.

Continued by: *Svensk bok-katalog* (AA831).   Z2621.S95

Current

Svensk bok-katalog. 1866/75– . Stockholm : Liberförlag, 1875– . Quinquennial.   **AA831**

Continues Hjalmar Linnström, *Svenskt boklexikon, 1830–65* (AA830).

A cumulation of *Svensk bokförteckning* (AA832).

Beginning with the volumes for 1941/50, issued by the Bibliographical Institute of the Royal Library in Stockholm, with the parallel title, *The Swedish national bibliography*.

1866/75, 1876/85, 1886/95 published as 10-year volumes. Thereafter, published as 5-year cumulations except for 1941/50.

Includes books, pamphlets, periodicals, government publications, and theses. Each cumulation is in two parts: (1) alphabetical author and title list; (2) classed list. Scope of the cumulations varies slightly (e.g., treatment of sheet music, maps); cumulations list additional titles excluded from annual volumes (e..g., certain legal deposit material, state and local official publications, society and firm publications).   Z2621.S95

Svensk bokförteckning = The Swedish national bibliography. Jan. 1953– . Stockholm : Tidningsaktiebolaget svensk bokhandel [etc.], [1953]– . Six no. a year with annual cumulation.   **AA832**

Supersedes an earlier monthly publication with the same title, issued 1913–52, and *Årskatalog för Svenska bokhandeln*, 1861–1952.

Frequency varies; beginning 1977, published six times a year at intervals of one to three months, with an annual cumulation. The monthly issues are main-entry lists only; the cumulations include a classified section.

Cumulates into: *Svensk bok-katalog* (AA831).   Z2625.S952

Svensk bokhandel. arg. 1 ([4. jan.] 1952)– . Stockholm : Avenska Bokförläggareföreningen, 1952– .   **AA833**

Abbreviated title: SvB.

Official organ of Svenska Bokförläggareföreningen and Svenska Bokhandlareföreningen.

Frequency varies: every two weeks, Jan.–July; weekly, Aug.–Dec.

Formed by the union of *Bokhandlaren* and *Svensk bokhandelstidning*.

Offers news and announcements concerning the book trade, with a "Svensk bokförteckning" section which cumulates into the monthly publication of that title (AA832).   Z407.S84

Switzerland

Lonchamp, Frédéric Charles. Bibliographie générale des ouvrages publiés ou illustrés en Suisse et à l'étranger de 1475 à 1914 par des écrivains et des artistes suisses. Paris et Lausanne : Librairie des Bibliophiles, 1922. 500 p. : ill.   **AA834**

A list of 3,376 items giving for each: author, title, date, printer or publisher, size, paging, and note of illustrations, with name of artist. Indexes of titles and of artists.   Z1023.L835

Schweizer Bücherverzeichnis : Katalog der Schweizerischen Landesbibliothek = Répertoire du livre suisse : Catalogue de la bibliothèque nationale suisse = Elenco del libro svizzero : Catalogo della biblioteca nazionale svizzera. 1948/50–1976/80, pt. 2. Zürich : Schweizerischer Buchhändler- und Verlegerverein, 1951–[1980?]. Quinquennial. **AA835**

1976/80, pt. 1 never published.

Cumulates the titles listed in *Das schweizer Buch* (AA839) and supersedes *Katalog der Schweizerischen Landesbibliothek, Bern : Systematisches Verzeichnis* (AA838). Beginning with 1951/55, forms pt.1 of *Schweizerische Nationalbibliographie.*

Vols. for 1948/50–1961/65 issued in two parts: (1) Author catalog (including anonymous titles) with index of catchwords, editors, translators, etc.; (2) Subject catalog in German with an index from the French forms. Z949.B56

Das schweizerische Buch = Le livre en Suisse, 1896–1914. Bern : Kollektivausstellung Schweizer. Verleger, 1914. 287 p. **AA836**

Classed arrangement with author index.

Continued by: Schweizerischer Buchhändlerverein, *Das schweizerischer Buch, 1914–1930* (Zürich : Schweizerische Landesausstellung, 1939. 232 p.).

Both are classified listings with author indexes, and are complemented by:

Société des Libraires et Éditeurs de la Suisse Romande, Geneva, *Catalogue des éditions de la Suisse romande*, rédigé par Alex. Jullien… (Genéve : Jullien, 1902–12; Société, 1929. 3 v. and suppl.).

A record of books published in French Switzerland. An alphabetical listing by author or other main entry. The basic volume lists books in print in 1900 (publ. 1902. 280 p.); Supplements, 1901–09 (1912. 181 p.); 1910–27 (1929. 404 p.); *Supplément, correction… comprenant en particulier les éditions Edwin Frankfurter à Lausanne* (1929. 16 p.).

Continued by: Société des Libraires et F'aaditeurs de la Suisse Romande, Geneva, *Catalogue des ouvrages de langue francaise publiés en Suisse, 1928–1945*, red. par Alexandre Jullien (Neuchâtel : Impr. Delachaux et Niestle, 1948. 377 p.).

An alphabetical main-entry listing. Z2771.S42

Schweizerische Landesbibliothek. Catalogue de la Bibliothèque Nationale Suisse á Berne : Liste alphabétique des imprimés parus jusqu'en 1900. Bern : Francke, 1910. 2 v. **AA837**

Added title page in German. Preface in German and French.

Contents: Abt. A: Histoire et géographie (2 v. No more published). Z949.B54

———— Katalog der Schweizerische Landesbibliothek Bern : systematisches Verzeichnis der schweizerischen oder die Schweiz betreffenden Veröffentlichungen. Bern : Huber, [1927]–54. 4 v. **AA838**

Added title page: Catalogue de la Bibliothèque Nationale Suisse. Répertoire méthodique des publications suisses ou relatives à la Suisse.

Contents and preface in German and French.

In 4 v., covering 1901–20, 1921–30, 1931–40, 1941–47. The catalog for each period is in two volumes: v. 1, Classed list, arranged by the Decimal Classification; v. 2, Biographical and topographical catalog, each arranged alphabetically.

A subject list which serves both as a short-title catalog of the works listed and as an index to the fuller descriptions in *Das schweizer Buch: Bibliographisches Bulletin* (AA839) for the same years. Gives author, brief title, date of publication, and also the year of the *Bulletin*, if that differs from publication date, in which full description is given.

§ Continued by: *Schweizer Bücherverzeichnis* (AA835).

Z949.B552

Current

Das schweizer Buch : Bibliographisches Bulletin der Schweizerischen Landesbibliothek, Bern = Le livre suisse : bulletin bibliographique de la Bibliothèque nationale suisse, Berne. v. 43 (1943)– . Bern : Schweizerischer Buchhandler- und Verlegerverein, 1943– . Semimonthly. **AA839**

Continues: *Bibliographisches Bulletin der Schweiz*, 1901–42.

Introductory text in French and German; some years add title in Italian.

Issued in two series, 1943–75: Série A, semimonthly, listing publications in the book trade; Série B, bimonthly, listing publications outside the book trade, e.g., theses, institutional publications, etc. Each issue has classified arrangement with author, title, and subject index.

Beginning 1976, a single combined list is published semimonthly and covers all types of publications. The classified arrangement with author/title/subject index is retained. Indexes cumulate semiannually and annually. Issue no. 16 is a special issue devoted to music.

Cumulates into the 5-year *Schweizer Bücherverzeichnis* (AA835).

————. Série A … *Verfasser- und Stichwortregister zu Deutsche Bibliographie* (AA649). Z2775.S35

Turkey

Türkiye bibliyografyasi. [v. 1] (1934)– . Ankara [etc.] : Türk Tarih Kurumu Basimevi, 1935– . **AA840**

Frequency varies: annual, 1934; semiannual, 1935–38; quarterly, 1939–43; monthly, 1944–48; quarterly, 1949– . Publisher varies.

A classified catalog with author and title indexes in each issue 1934–43; annual indexes 1944– . Records books, pamphlets, and government publications in Turkish and other languages. Includes a separate section of new periodicals and newspapers.

Cumulative decennial volumes (publ. Istanbul: Devlet Basimevi): 1928/1938, publ. 1939 in 2 v.: v. 1, Official publications; v. 2, Non-official publications, arranged by Universal Decimal Classification.

1939/1948 in 3 v.: v. 1, arranged by Universal Decimal Classification, covering general, philosophy, religion, social sciences, and philology, publ. 1957; v. 2, covering abstract science, applied science, literature, history, geography, and biography, publ. 1962; v. 3, alphabetical index, publ. 1964. Z2835.T93

Yeni yayinlar : aylik bibliyografya dergisi. Cilt 1 (Temmuz 1956)– . Ankara : [s.n.], 1956– . Monthly. **AA841**

No numbers issued for Aug.–Oct. 1956.

Includes a classified list of recent publications. Z2835.Y4

Ukraine

Akademiíà Nauk URSR, Kiev. Biblioteka. Knigi pervoi chetverti XIX veka : katalog knig, khraniashchikhsia v Gosudarstvennoi Publichnoi Biblioteke Ukrainskoi SSR / sost.: S. O. Petrov. Kiev, 1961. 398 p. **AA842**

Continues the Library's catalog of 18th-century books, *Knigi grazhdanskoi pechati XVIII veka* (AA788), with 2,800 works published in the first quarter of the 19th century, primarily St. Petersburg and Moscow imprints. Arranged by author or anonymous title, with indexes for translators and editors, cities and publishers, and broad subject. Annotations include references to 19th-century bibliographic listings.

Z2503.A5

Yugoslavia

Kukuljevic-Sakcinski, Ivan. Bibliografia hrvatska : Dio prvi. Tiskane knijige. Zagreb : Brzotiskom : D. Albrechta, 1860. 233 p.   **AA843**

Added title page: Bibliografia jugoslavenska. Kn. I.

————. *Dodatak k prvomu dielu. Tiskane knije* (Zagreb : 1863. 31 p.). No more published.

The main volume and supplement list Croation books from early times to 1860.   Z2124.C7K9

Novakovic, Stojan. Srpska biblijografija za noviju književnost. Belgrade : Drzhavnoj Shtampariji, 1869. 644 p.   **AA844**

Covers the period 1741–1867.

Arranged chronologically with author and subject indexes.   Z2931.N89

Current

Bibliografija Jugoslavije : knjige, brošure i muzikalije. 1950– . Beograd : Bibliografski Inst. FNRJ, 1950– . Semimonthly.   **AA845**

Frequency varies; publ. monthly, 1950–52.

Caption title also in Serbian, English, and French.

Lists books, pamphlets, sheet music, and government publications in Serbian, Croatian, and other languages. Classified by Universal Decimal Classification with author/title and subject indexes.

§ The 1945–49 period is covered by *Jugoslovenska bibliografija* (Beograd : Direkcija za Informacije Vlade FNRJ, 1949–50. 5 v.).

For a companion section of the current Yugoslav national bibliography see *Bibliografija Jugoslavije* (AA846), which covers periodical articles.   Z2951.B37

Bibliografija Jugoslavije : Zbirke i monografske serije / Jugoslovenski bibliografski institut. 1984/1985– . Beograd : Institut, 1986– . Irregular.   **AA846**

A companion to *Bibliografija Jugoslavije : knjige, brošure i muzikalije* (AA845).

An alphabetical title listing of some 2,000 collections and monographic series published during the year. Gives place and publisher, but no indication of volume number or beginning date.   Z2951.B38

Africa

The African book publishing record. v. 1, no. 1 (Jan. 1975)– . [Oxford, Eng. : Hans Zell Ltd.], 1975– . Quarterly.   **AA847**

Now offers subject, author, and country lists of English, French, or African vernacular books recently published or in press on the African continent. Each issue includes articles on and news of the book trade in Africa, reviews of new magazincs or special issues of journals. Beginning with the Apr. 1977 issue, reviews of major publications are included. The second number for each year contains a selective annotated bibliography, "Africana reference works," with more than 200 works arranged by subject. A directory of publishers is a useful feature. Annual table of contents for the volume, but no index.   Z465.7.A35

African books in print. 1975– . London : Mansell Information Pub. Ltd., 1975– . Irregular.   **AA848**

Hans M. Zell, ed.

Aims "to provide a systematic, reliable and functional reference resource tool and buying guide to African published materials currently in print."—*Introd. to 4th ed.* Compiled from information supplied by publishers in response to a questionnaire; "a large proportion of African publishers are apparently still to be convinced of the value of having their titles listed."

4th ed., 1993, issued in two vols.: v. 1, Author index, Title index; v. 2, Subject index.   Z3501.A46

Algeria

Bibliographie de l'Algérie. Année 1, no. 1 (Oct. 1963)– . Alger : Bibliothèque Nationale, 1964– . Irregular.   **AA849**

Title also in Arabic.

The first issue is a classified bibliography of Algerian periodicals published in either French or Arabic. Later numbers offer a classed list of books and theses received on legal deposit at the national library.

Benin

Bibliographie du Bénin. Année 1, no.1 (1976/77)– . Porto-Novo : Bibliothèque Nationale, 1978– . Irregular.   **AA850**

At head of title: République Populaire du Bénin. Ministère de la Jeunesse, de la Culture Populaire et des Sports. Direction de la Bibliothèque Nationale.

A classed bibliography of works published in Bénin, together with works about the country published abroad. In four sections: (1) Books; (2) Articles from periodicals; (3) Official publications; (4) Other documents (e.g., maps). Indexed.   Z3686.B52

Botswana

The national bibliography of Botswana. v. 1 (1969)– . [Gaberones] : Botswana National Libr. Service, 1969– . 3 no. a year.   **AA851**

Vol. 1 had two numbers, the second being cumulative; beginning with v. 2, publ. three times a year, the first number covering Jan.–Apr., the second May–Aug., and the third a cumulative issue for the full year.

Listing is by Dewey class numbers, with an alphabetical index of authors, titles, and serials. The list excludes books on Botswana published in other countries, as well as those in the local languages of Botswana published elsewhere. Each issue of a serial appearing less than six times a year is noted, and notices of cessation of serials are included.   Z3559.N38

Côte d'Ivoire

Bibliographie de la Côte d'Ivoire. v. 1, (1969)– . Abidjan : Bibliothèque Nationale, 1970– . Annual.   **AA852**

A national bibliography with separate sections for books, periodicals, periodical articles (including selected articles in periodicals published outside the country), official publications, and a miscellaneous section for pamphlets, theses, etc. Classed arrangement within each section. Indexed.   Z3689.B5

Egypt

Nashrat al-īdā'. [1974]– . [al-Qāhirah] : Dār al-Kutub wa-al-Wathā'iq al-Qawmīyah, 1974– . Quarterly.   **AA853**

Also called *Legal deposit bulletin*.

Excludes serials. In two parts, English and Arabic, each part arranged by broad Dewey classification, with author, title, and subject indexes.   Z3651.N36

Nuṣayr, ʿĀydah Ibrāhīm. al-Kutub al-ʿArabīyah allatī nushirat fī Miṣr fī al-qarn al-tāsiʿ ʿashar. Ṭabʿah 1. al-Qāhirah : Qism al-Nashr bi-al-Jāmiʿah al-Amrīkīyah bi-al-Qāhirah, 1990. 14, 403 p. **AA854**

Introductory material in Arabic and English. Title on added t.p.: *Arabic books published in Egypt in the nineteenth century.*

"Covers the period from the first Egyptian printed book published in 1822 up until the end of 1900."—*Introd.* Arranged by Dewey Decimal Classification, with author, title, and subject indexes.

Chronological coverage continued by the author's *al-Kutub al-al-'Arabīyah allatī nushirat fī miṣrbayna amay 1926–1940* (1980); and by *Dalil al-matbuat al-miṣriyah, 1940–1956* (1975), all published al-Qāhirah : Qism al-Nashr bi-al Jāmiah al-Amrīkīyah bi-al-Qāhirah (American University in Cairo Pr.). Z3658.A4N87

Ethiopia

Ethiopian publications : books, pamphlets, annuals and periodical articles published in 1963 and 1964– . Addis Ababa : Haile Sellassie I Univ., Inst. of Ethiopian Studies, 1965– . Annual. **AA855**

"It is intended that subsequent numbers of this publication should appear annually and should become the current Ethiopian National Bibliography."—*Introd.* [v. 1] In the early issues, an Ethiopian-language section in alphabetical order is followed by a foreign-language section in classed arrangement with author index. Beginning with the issue covering 1970, both the Ethiopian and the foreign-language sections follow a classed arrangement. Vol. publ. July 1974 covers 1942–62. Z3521.E82

Höjer, Christianne. Ethiopian publications : books, pamphlets, annuals and periodical articles published in Ethiopia in foreign languages from 1942 till 1962. Addis Ababa : Haile Sellassie I Univ., Inst. of Ethiopian Studies, 1974. 146 p. **AA856**

Intends to fill the gap between Stephen G. Wright's *Ethiopian incunabula* (Addis Ababa, 1967) and the annual *Ethiopian publications* (AA855). A classified list with annual index. Z3521.H63

Solomon Gebre Christos. A decade of Ethiopian languages publications, 1959–1969. Addis Ababa : Haile Sellassie I Univ. Lib., 1970. 232 p. **AA857**

Title also in Amharic.
Nearly 1,300 items. Z3521.S65

The Gambia

National bibliography of the Gambia. v. 1, no. 1 (Jan./Dec. 1977)–1987. Banjul : National Library of the Gambia, 1978–1988. **AA858**

Title varies: *Gambia national bibliography.*

Frequency varies; generally, semiannual with the 2nd issue an annual cumulation.

Attempts to list all new books and pamphlets published in the Gambia, together with books about the Gambia and Gambians published elsewhere. Also lists first issues of new serials and first issue of a serial under a new title. Arranged by Dewey Decimal Classification, with index of authors, editors, titles, and series.

Ghana

Ghana national bibliography. 1965– . Accra : Ghana Library Board, 1966– . Annual. **AA859**

Intended as a current national bibliography for the country; includes official publications and, beginning 1966, periodical articles and theses. There is a separate section for publications in the various

Ghanian languages (e.g., Fante, Ewe, Twi, Ga). Inasmuch as books about Ghana published elsewhere are also included, the bibliography will serve to supplement Albert Frederick Johnson's *Bibliography of Ghana, 1930–1961* (DD162 *note*). Slow in appearing; vol. for 1976 was publ. 1985. Z3785.G45

Ghana national bibliography bi-monthly. v. 20, no. 1 (Jan./ Feb. 1987)– . [Accra, Ghana] : Research Library on African Affairs, 1987– . Bimonthly. **AA860**

Supersedes *Ghana : a current bibliography*, v. 1–19 (Sept./Oct. 1967–Nov./Dec. 1986), and assumes its numbering.

A classified list (according to Dewey Decimal Classification) of materials received on legal deposit, works by Ghaians or about Ghana published abroad, new serial titles, and selected articles about Ghana appearing in books, pamphlets, periodicals, and newspapers. Author/title/series and subject indexes. The promised annual cumulations have not been forthcoming. Z3785.G445

Kenya

Kenya national bibliography. 1980– . Nairobi : Kenya Nat. Lib. Serv., Nat. Reference & Bibliographic Dept., [1983]– . Annual. **AA861**

Subtitle: A classified subject bibliography of current publications produced in Kenya & foreign materials of interest to Kenya and/or written by Kenyans, arranged according to the Dewey Decimal Classification and catalogued according to the Anglo-American Cataloguing Rules, with a full author & title index.

Lists books, research reports, conference proceedings, pamphlets, maps, first issues of new serials (and subsequent title changes), selected audiovisual and nonprint materials published in Kenya. Foreign publications of interest to Kenya and works by Kenyans published abroad are marked with an asterisk.

Libya

Bibliyūghrāfiyah al-Waṭaniyah al-ʿArabiyah al-Lībiyah. 1982 . Benghāzī : al-Markaz al-Bibliūghrāfi al-Waṭani, Dār al-Kutub al-Waṭaniyah, 1983– . Annual. **AA862**

1972–81 publ. as: *al-Bibliyūghrāfiyah al-ʿArabiyah al-Lībiyah.*
Added t.p.: *Libyan national bibliography.*

Aims to list all Libyan publications issued in the year of coverage. In two sections, the first listing Arabic titles, and the second, Western language publications. Each section is further divided by type of publication, then arranged by Dewey classification scheme. Author and title indexes.

A 3-v. retrospective set covering 1866/71–1971 was published in 1972 as *al-Bibliyūghrāfiyah al-Waṭaniyah al-Lībiyah.*

Madagascar

Bibliographie annuelle de Madagascar. 1964–1969. Tananarive : Bibliothèque Universitaire et Bibliothèque Nationale, [1966–1973]. Annual. **AA863**

At head of title: Université de Madagascar.

A national bibliography which lists Madagascar imprints, new Madagascar periodicals, maps, etc., and also indexes Madagascar periodicals. In addition, books and periodical articles relating to Madagascar but published elsewhere are included. Classed arrangement with author index. Continues the listings in Guillaume Grandidier's *Bibliographie de Madagascar* (DD175) which covered 1500–1955, and Jean Roger Fontvieille's *Bibliographie nationale de Madagascar, 1956–1963* (AA865).

Continued by *Bibliographie nationale de Madagascar* (AA864). Z3701.B5

Bibliographie nationale de Madagascar. 1983– . Antananarivo : Bibliothèque Nationale, [1984]– . **AA864**

Supersedes a work of the same title publ. 1979–[83?], which continued the *Bibliographie annuelle de Madagascar* (AA863).

Alternate title: Rakitahirinkevi-Pirenen'i Madigasikara.

Frequency varies.

Being compiled in separate sections by the Bibliothèque Nationale, which is responsible for monographs ("ouvrages") and the Université d'Antananarivo, for periodical articles. No volumes have appeared so far from the Université. The Bibliothèque Nationale has issued mimeographed lists irregularly since 1983 that include monographs published in Madagascar as well as selected foreign titles. Classified order with author, series, and subject indexes. There is a lag between publication of the bibliography and the time period covered. Z3701.B5

Fontvieille, Jean Roger. Bibliographie nationale de Madagascar, 1956–1963. [Tananarive] : Univ. de Madagascar, [1971]. 511 p. **AA865**

Fills the gap between Guillaume Grandidier's *Bibliographie de Madagascar* (DD175) and *Bibliographie annuelle de Madagascar* (AA863). Classed arrangement with author-title index. Z3701.F66

Malawi

National Archives of Malawi. Malawi national bibliography. Ed. 1 (1967)– . Zomba : National Archives, 1968– . Annual (irregular). **AA866**

Continues the National Archives' *List of publications deposited in the Library of the National Archives*, 1965–66.

Lists books, pamphlets, and first issues of new serials as deposited with the National Archives in accordance with the "Printed publications ordinance." Employs the Dewey Decimal Classification. Author/title index beginning 1975. Titles in African languages are followed by an English translation. Z3577.N37a

Morocco

al-Bibliyūghrāfīyā al-waṭanīyah al-Maghrabīyah / al-Khizānah al-ʿAmmah lil-Kutub wa-al-Wathāïq. 1961– . Rabat : Bibliothèque générale et archives du Maroc, 1962– . **AA867**

Title on added t.p.: *Bibliographie nationale marocaine*.

Continues *Informations bibliographique marocaines*, publ. 1942–62.

Lists titles published in or about Morocco, deposited at the National Library. In two sections; Arabic, followed by Western languages. Each section has classified arrangements. Author, title, and subject indexes. Z3636.B53

Namibia

Strohmeyer, Eckhard. NNB : Namibische National Bibliographie = Namibian national bibliography. 1971–75–1979. Basel : Basler Afrika Bibliographien, 1978–81. **AA868**

Contents: [v.1] 1971–75; [v.2] 1976–77; [v.3] 1978–79.

In English and German.

These volumes represent an attempt by an individual compiler to provide a Namibian national bibliography in lieu of a governmental or institutional effort. Aims to include "all written materials of Namibian concern, no matter whether they are published inside the country or elsewhere."—*Foreword.* Materials in both European and African languages are listed; only items actually examined by the compiler are included. Classed arrangement with author/title index; some annotations. Many entries deal with natural sciences and related subjects. At least one library location is given for each item. Z3771.S77

Nigeria

Nigerian publications : current national bibliography. 1950/52–1972. Ibadan : Ibadan Univ. Pr., 1953–73. Annual. **AA869**

Early volumes carried subtitle: A list of works received under the Publications Ordinance by the Library, University College, Ibadan.

Lists books and pamphlets published in Nigeria, or about Nigeria or by Nigerians published abroad. Includes official publications and first issues of periodicals.

Superseded by: *The national bibliography of Nigeria.* (1973– . Lagos : National Library of Nigeria, 1974– . Annual.) Covers "books and pamphlets published in Nigeria and received under the legal deposit provisions…as well as those about Nigeria or by Nigerians published abroad. In addition, it includes a section on Nigerian periodicals and newspapers."—*Pref. 1974.* Originally arranged by author or other main entry within five sections: (1) works in English; (2) government publications; (3) works in vernacular (i.e., Nigerian languages); (4) Nigeriana published outside the country; (5) Nigerian periodicals and newspapers. Beginning with the issue covering 1976 a single classified sequence (with index) is used for types 1–4, and there is a separate listing of new Nigerian periodicals and newspapers. Z3553.N5N5

University of Ibadan. Library. Nigerian publications, 1950–1970 / comp. in the Ibadan University Library. [Ibadan] : Ibadan Univ. Pr., 1977. 430 p. **AA870**

Constitutes a partial cumulation of the annual issues of *Nigerian publications* (AA869) for the 1950–70 period; the 1971–72 issues of that series are not superseded, nor are the earlier volumes fully superseded since the lists of "Nigeriana published outside the country" are not cumulated. Arranged by main entry within three sections: (1) Nonofficial publications in English; (2) Official publications; (3) Publications in Nigerian languages (grouped by language).

A prefatory note states: "Throughout the period, 1950–1970, no single library could lay claim to having a comprehensive collection of all works produced in Nigeria. This twenty-year cumulation of works deposited at Ibadan University Library, should therefore be used along with two other annual lists, to obtain a complete picture of publications produced in Nigeria. They are: *Northern Nigeria Publications* (Zaria, Kashim Ibrahim Library, Ahmadu Bello University) 1965– and *A list of publications acquired under the Western Nigeria Publications Law no. 177 of 1957* (Ibadan, Western Regional Library) May 1959– ." Periodicals and newspapers are excluded, having been covered in *Nigerian periodicals and newspapers, 1950–70* (AD175). Z3597.U54

Rhodesia, Southern

See Zimbabwe.

Rwanda

Lévesque, Albert. Contribution to the national bibliography of Rwanda, 1965–1970 = Contribution à la bibliographic nationale du Rwanda. [2nd ed.]. Boston : G.K. Hall, [1979]. 542 p. **AA871**

1st ed., 1974, had limited circulation.

Prefatory matter in English and French; subject headings in French.

Offered as "a contribution to the future Bibliographie Nationale Rwandaise" (*Introd.*) as well as a supplement to Joseph R. A. M. Clément's *Essai de bibliographie Ruanda-Urundi* (Usumbura, 1959), to Théodore Heyse's *Bibliographie du Congo Belge et du Ruanda-Urundi* (DD244) and to Marcel Walraet's *Les sciences au Rwanda : bibliographie 1894–1965* (Bruxelles : Bibliothèque Royale de Belgique, 1966). Aims to list all works published in Rwanda during the period, together with writings about Rwanda published abroad. The compiler admits failure to achieve exhaustiveness in either category owing to lack of a copyright law, the size of the task, and the difficulty of locating ephemeral materials. Lists some 4,500 items in classed arrangement, with author/subject and title indexes.   Z3721.L48

Senegal

Bibliographie du Sénégal. no. 40 (1972)– . [Dakar : Archives du Sénégal], 1972– .   **AA872**
   Early volumes issued over agency's former name, Archives du Sénégal. Continues *Bulletin bibliographique des Archives du Sénégal* (Oct. 1964–1971).
   Includes publications received by legal deposit, Senegalese works acquired by the Archives, works about Senegal, and those by Senegalese published elsewhere. Beginning with no. 52, employs a classified subject arrangement. Some issues include supplements (e.g.: no. 48, Liste des périodiques Sénégalese reçus aux Archives; no. 52, Thèses et mémoires reçus aux Archives en 1980). Author and title indexes.   Z3711.A73a

Sierra Leone

Sierra Leone. Library Board. Sierra Leone publications. 1962/63– . Freetown : Sierra Leone Library Board, 1964– . Annual.   **AA873**
   A classified subject listing of books, pamphlets, first issues of periodicals, government publications, publications of international government organizations, maps and atlases, reports, and internal documents published in Sierra Leone during the year of coverage and received by the Library Board under depository law. Also includes works by Sierra Leoneans or about Sierra Leone published elsewhere. Author/title index.   Z3553.S5S5

South Africa

Africana nova. Sept. 1958–1969. Capetown : South African Public Libr., 1958–69. Quarterly.   **AA874**
   Subtitle: A quarterly bibliography of books currently published in and about the Republic of South Africa. Based on the accessions to the Africana Department, South African Public Library, including material received by Legal Deposit.
   In English and Afrikaans. Arranged by Dewey Decimal Classification, with author index in each issue, and annual index. Preceded by lists of current publications published in the *Quarterly bulletin* of the South African Public Library, Sept. 1946–June 1958.   Z3603.A65

Nienaber, Petrus Johannes. Bibliografie van Afrikaanse boeke. 2. druk, met'n aanvullende lijs. Deel 1 (1861–1943)–9 (1975–77). Johannesburg : s.n., 1954–1981.   **AA875**
   1st ed. 1943–54 in 3 v.; Deel 3 and following not designated as 2nd ed.
   Contents: Deel 1, 6 Apr. 1861–6 Apr. 1943 (1952); Deel 2, Apr. 1943–Okt. 1948 (1958); Deel 3, Nov. 1948–Okt. 1953 (1954); Deel 4, Nov. 1953–Junie 1958 (1958); Deel 5, Julie 1958–Feb. 1963 (1963); Deel 6, Maart 1963–Des. 1966 (1967); Deel 7, Jan. 1967–Des. 1970 (1971); Deel 8, Jan. 1971–Des. 1974 (1977); Deel 9, Jan. 1975–Des. 1977 (1981).
   A comprehensive bibliography. Each volume is in three main sections: (1) Author list; (2) Title list; (3) Classified list.   Z3601.N512

RSANB, 1926–1958 : retrospective South African national bibliography for the period, 1926–1958 = Retrospektiewe Suid-Afrikaanse nasionale bibliografie vir die tydperk, 1926–1958. Pretoria : State Library, 1985. 2 v. : ill. (Bibliographies / the State Library = Bibliografieë / die Staatsbiblioteek, no. 33).   **AA876**

Contents: v. 1, A–Z; v. 2, Index.
   Prefatory matter in English and Afrikaans.
   Intended to fill the gap between Sidney Mendelssohn, *A South African bibliography to the year 1925* (London : Mansell, 1979. 4 v.) and *South African national bibliography (SANB)* (AA878).
   Includes material published in South Africa and South West Africa (excluding the High Commission Territories); excludes material in Bantu languages, periodicals and government publications, technical reports, and highly ephemeral material. Arranged alphabetically by main entry. The index includes titles, series, personal and corporate names in a single alphabet.   Z3601.R77

S. A. Katalogus = S.A. catalogue. Johannesburg : Technical Books & Careers, 1956. [2 v.?].   **AA877**
   Vols. 1–14 (annual ed.) publ. 1939–1952. "5th complete ed." (publ. 1956) cumulated 1900–54.
   Title varies: earlier editions called *South African catalogue of books; Suid-afrikaanse katalogus von boeke.* Some editions have subtitle: And list of publishers in South Africa.
   An author-title listing of books published in South Africa since 1900. The cumulated editions do not always include all previously listed titles, and therefore earlier editions should be preserved.
          Z3601.S8

Current

South African national bibliography = Suid-Afrikaanse nasionale bibliografie. 1959– . Pretoria : State Libr., 1960– . Quarterly, with annual cumulation.   **AA878**
   At head of title: SANB.
   Replaces the State Library's monthly copyright list, *Publications received ...* , issued since 1938 in mimeographed form, unclassified and noncumulating. This new series, based on legal deposit, is arranged by Dewey Decimal Classification with a name and title index.
   A cumulation for the period 1968–71 was published 1973 in 2 v.
          Z3603.P7

Swaziland

Swaziland national bibliography. 1973/76– . Kwaluseni : Univ. of Botswana and Swaziland, Univ. College of Swaziland, 1977– . Irregular.   **AA879**
   The first volume covers 1973–76; 1977 was separately published; and 1978/82 appeared in 1 v. in 1984. Lists "all known publications issued in Swaziland ... with the exception of certain ephemeral items and those items which are regarded as confidential or restricted. In addition, all publications in Siswati, including those published outside Swaziland, are included in the bibliography."—*Pref.* Arranged by Dewey Decimal Classification with author/title index. Appendixes include a list of foreign publications on Swaziland, Swaziland legislation and law reports, and forthcoming books and works in progress.
   § Serves in part to supplement *Swaziland official publications, 1880–1972* (AF237).   Z3560.S93

Tanzania

Printed in Tanzania. 1969–73. [Dar es Salaam] : Tanganyika Lib. Services Board, 1970–76. Annual.   **AA880**
   On cover, 1969: A list of publications printed in mainland Tanzania during 1969 and deposited with the Tanganyika Library Service and the Library of the University of Dar es Salaam, together with some publications published in Tanzania but printed elsewhere.
   The 1969 issue represents a first attempt to produce a cumulative national bibliography, items received on legal deposit having previously been listed only in the *Bulletin* of the University of Dar es Salaam

Library. Arrangement is by Dewey Decimal Classification, with a full index. Plans call for a retrospective cumulative volume covering 1964–68.

Continued by *Tanzania national bibliography* (AA881).

Z3753.T3P74

Tanzania national bibliography / comp. by the Acquisitions Department, National Central Library, Dar es Salaam. 1974/75– . Dar es Salaam : Tanzania Library Service, 1975– . Annual.   **AA881**

Continues *Printed in Tanzania* (AA880). Employs the same classified arrangement, but has separate author and title indexes. Now includes various mimeographed materials, conference papers, and annual reports. Became a monthly publication in 1983, although some of the intervening annuals are not yet published.   Z3588.P74

Tunisia

Bibliographie nationale de la Tunisie : publications non officielles. 1956/68–1976. Tunis : Service Documentaire, 1974–77. 5 v.   **AA882**

Issued by the Bibliothèque Nationale of Tunisia.

Title varies slightly. Title also in Arabic.

An issue published 1970 as "Série II, Année 1, 1969" was superseded by retrospective compilations covering 1956/68 (publ. 1974) and 1969/73 (publ. 1975), and annual volumes for 1974–76. Each volume is a classed listing according to the Universal Decimal Classification system, with separate sections for Western language and Arabic publications.

Continued by: *Bibliographie nationale de Tunisie* (1977– . Tunis : Service du Depot Légal et des Publications, 1977– . Annual.).

At head of title: Ministére des Affaires Culturelles. Bibliothèque Nationale.

Frequency varies: originally bimonthly, then quarterly.

Added title page in Arabic.

Supersedes the earlier series of similar title (above). Now includes both official and nonofficial publications; separate sections for Arabic and Western language materials, with classified arrangement within sections.   Z3681.B529

Uganda

Uganda national bibliography. v. 1, no. 1 (Mar. 1987)– . [Kampala, Uganda] : Makerere Univ. Library Services, 1987– . Quarterly.   **AA883**

Lists books and first issues of serials published in Uganda, and books about Uganda or by Ugandan authors published in other countries. Arranged by Dewey Decimal Classification, with an author and title index. Does not cumulate.   Z3586.U37

Zaïre

Bibliographie du Zaire. 1987/88– . [Kinshasa/Gombé : Bibliothèque Nationale du Zaire, 1990]– . Annual.   **AA884**

A new attempt to record titles published in Zaïre or elsewhere about Zaïre. The initial volume lists internal publications only, and is arranged by Dewey Decimal Classification, with lists of publishers and journals and an author index. Beginning with the volume covering 1989, to be in three annual volumes: Imprimés; Les mémoires et thèses de doctorat; Les documents audio-visuels.

Zambia

The national bibliography of Zambia. 1970/71– . Lusaka : National Archives of Zambia, [1972]– . Annual (beginning with the issue covering 1972).   **AA885**

Attempts to list "all work published in Zambia and received by National Archives of Zambia under the Printed Publication Act" during the period covered. Includes "books, pamphlets, first issues of new serials, publications of statutory bodies and government publications, excluding Acts, Bills, Parliamentary debates and Gazettes."—*Introd.* Arranged by Dewey Decimal Classification, with author and title index.   Z3573.Z3N37

Zimbabwe

Hartridge, Anne. Rhodesia national bibliography, 1890 to 1930. Salisbury : National Archives, 1977. 50 p. (National Archives of Rhodesia. Bibliographical series, no. 2).   **AA886**

A first step toward providing coverage from 1890 (the date of "commencement of administration and modern commerce within Rhodesia"—*Foreword*) to 1961, the beginning date for annual bibliographic records for the area.

Classed arrangement according to the Dewey Decimal Classification, with index of authors, editors, etc. and titles. Lists books, pamphlets, maps, serials (including newspapers), and government publications published in Rhodesia.

Rhodesia national bibliography. 1967–78. Salisbury : Rhodesia Nat. Archives, 1968–79. Annual.   **AA887**

Subtitle: List of publications deposited in the Library of the National Archives.

Supersedes the National Archives of Rhodesia's *List of publications deposited in the library*, which covered 1961–66 (publ. 1963–67). The 1961 volume included the Federation of Rhodesia and Nyasaland; subsequent volumes are limited to items published in what was then Rhodesia (previously Southern Rhodesia, now Zimbabwe) and excludes those published in Northern Rhodesia and Nyasaland. Includes books, pamphlets, and first issues of new serials; official government publications and annual reports of local authorities are also listed. Classed arrangement (with index, beginning 1970).

Continued by: *Zimbabwe national bibliography* (AA888).

Z3573.R5R54

Zimbabwe national bibliography. 1979– . Salisbury : National Archives, 1980– . Annual.   **AA888**

Continues *Rhodesia national bibliography* (AA887).

The bibliography continues to list "books, pamphlets, maps and the first issues of new serials (periodicals, newspapers, etc.) published in Rhodesia and Zimbabwe Rhodesia."—*Introd.* Arranged by Dewey Decimal Classification with author/title/series index. Also notes serial cessations in a separate section.   Z3573.R5R54

Asia (by region)

Asia, South

Shaw, Graham. The South Asia and Burma retrospective bibliography (SABREB). London : British Library, 1987. v. 1. (In progress).   **AA889**

Contents: Stage 1: 1556–1800 (554 p.).

The "aim is ultimately to provide for the first time a comprehensive standard record of publishing in the subcontinent from the introduction of printing technology in the middle of the sixteenth century up to the close of the nineteenth."—*Pref.*

Stage 1 is based primarily on the collection of the British Library and includes almost all forms of printed material (excluding maps and prints) in any language. Arrangement is by date and place of publication, with indexes of names, titles, and subjects. For extant copies, location symbols are given.

Stage 2 is to cover 1802–67; Stage 3, 1868–1900. Z3185.S54

Arab states

The Arab bulletin of publications. 1982– . Tunis : [s.n.], 1984– . Annual? **AA890**

Prepared in collaboration with Tunisian National Library.

At head of title: Arab League Educational Cultural and Scientific Organization (ALECSO).

Title page and introductory matter also in Arabic.

An attempt to provide a bibliographic record of all books published in Arab countries. Separate sections for Arabic and non-Arabic publications; arranged by Dewey Decimal Classification within sections; author and title indexes. The volume for 1982 includes reports from Jordan-United Arab Emirates, Bahrein, Tunisia, Algeria, Syria, Saudi Arabia, Iraq, Oman, Qatar, Kuwait, Libya, Morocco, and Lebanon.

Asia (by country)

Bangladesh

Bangladesh national bibliography. 1972– . Dacca : Directorate of Archives and Libraries, Ministry of Education, 1974– . Annual. **AA891**

Title also in Bengali.

In two parts: (1) Bengali; (2) English. Publication runs well behind date of coverage.

"A subject catalogue of new books published in Bangladesh and received under the provision of Copyright Ordinance, 1962; classified with modification according to the Dewey Decimal Classification (16th edition), provided with a full author, title and subject index and a list of Bangladesh publishers whose books have been included in the Bibliography."—*1972 ed., p. 109.*

Title also in Bengali.

In two parts: (1) Bengali; (2) English. Publication runs well behind date of coverage.

Ceylon

See Sri Lanka.

China

Chinese cooperative catalog. Jan. 1975–1982. Wash. : Library of Congress, 1975–82. Monthly, with annual cumulation. **AA892**

Intended as an aid for libraries acquiring Chinese-language materials, this catalog presents "Library of Congress printed cards, preliminary cards prepared in the Library of Congress at the initial stage of cataloging, and catalog cards submitted by 12 of the larger Chinese collections in the United States. Although most of the entries are monographs, serials are also included."—*Foreword.* Arranged alphabetically by romanized title. Not to be considered a union catalog, since only a single location is usually indicated. 1978–82 issued in microfiche. Merged into *NUC : books* (AA111) in 1983. Z881.U49C49

Chüan kuo hsin shu mu. 1950– . Peking : Chung yang jen min cheng fu chü pan tsung shu, tü shu chï kǎn ssu, 1951– . **AA893**

Publisher and frequency vary. Suspended Aug. 1966–May 1972.

A classified listing of books, official publications, etc. Excludes serials. The last issue of the year includes a list of publishers and their addresses. Cumulated annually by *Quan-guo xinshumu*. Z3101.C54

Cordier, Henri. L'imprimerie sino-européenne en Chine : bibliographie des ouvrages publiés en Chine par les Européens au XVIIe et au XVIIIe siècles. Paris : Leroux, 1901. 73 p. : ill. (Publ. de l'École des Langues Orientales Vivantes, 5. sér., t. 3). **AA894**

Lists mainly works written in the Chinese language or translated into Chinese by missionaries.

First published in 1883 as "Essai d'une bibliographie des ouvrages publiés en Chine par les Européens au XVIIe et au XVIIIe siècles" in *Mélanges orientaux* (Publ. de l'École des Langues Orientales Vivantes, 2. sér., t. 9). Z3108.T7C7

Quarterly bulletin of Chinese bibliography. [English ed.], v. 1–4, 1934–37; n.s., v. 1–7, 1940–47. Peiping : Nat. Lib. of Peiping, 1934–47. Irregular. **AA895**

Includes general articles, book reviews, notes and news, and an annotated, selected list of new books published in China, divided into three sections: (1) Books in Chinese; (2) Books in foreign languages; (3) Government publications. Scope of contents varies. Z3103.Q23

India

Indian books. 1969–1984. Varanasi, India : Indian Bibliographic Centre, 1970–84. **AA896**

Vols. for 1975–82 never published.

Subtitle: A bibliography of Indian books published or reprinted … in the English language.

In view of the very considerable time lag in the appearance of *Indian national bibliography* (AA900), this series was intended as a current record of Indian publications in English. Author, title, and subject sections, plus a directory of publishers.

§ Three other attempts to provide a current record for Indian publications have been abandoned: *Impex reference catalogue of Indian books* (New Delhi : Indian Book Export and Import Co., 1960), an in-print listing of Indian books in English, with a 1960–62 supplement published 1962; *Books of India : a reference catalogue …* (Bombay : Publisher's World, 1964), covering 1963 only; and *Indian books* (Delhi : Researchco Reprints, 1972–76), an annual listing of Indian books in English, offering coverage for 1971–74/75. Z3201.I65

National bibliography of Indian literature, 1901–1953 / gen. editors, B. S. Kesavan, V. Y. Kulkarni. New Delhi : Sahitya Akademi, 1962–90. 5 v. **AA897**

Contents: v. 1, Assamese, Bengali, English, Gujarati; v. 2, Hindi, Kannada, Kashmiri, Malayalam; v. 3, Marathi, Oriya, Panjabi, Sanskrit; v. 4, Sindhi, Tamil, Telugu, Urdu; v. 5, Dogri, Konkani, Maithili, Manipuri, Nepali, Rajasthani.

This work aims to include "books of literary merit, and important and significant books" in the following categories: general works, philosophy and religion, social sciences, linguistics, arts, literature, history, biography and travel, and miscellaneous. "Initially, it was decided that the fifth volume … should also cover the same time-span as the earlier volumes, but it was later felt that the period 1901–1953 was not sufficient to be represented in a printed bibliography for these languages … . Besides it may also be noted that the *Indian National Bibliography* [AA900] … inadequately covers these languages."—*Introd. to v. 5.* In Roman script with annotations in English. Arranged by language then by broad subject. Each volume has its own author and title index. Z3201.N3

Current

Indian book industry : book production and distribution journal. v. 1, no. 1 (Oct. 1969)– . Delhi : Sterling Pub., 1969– . Monthly. **AA898**
    Patterned after *Publishers' weekly*. Includes a monthly listing of current Indian publications in English—an alphabetical author listing with Dewey Decimal class numbers indicated. Z457.I48

Indian books in print. 1955/67– . Delhi : Indian Bibliographies Bureau, [1969]– . Annual. **AA899**
    Subtitle: A bibliography of Indian books published in English language.
    Beginning with 1972–73 issued in 3 v. : (1) Authors; (2) Titles; (3) Subject guide (i.e. a classified listing according to Dewey Decimal Classification system). The 1992 ed. lists nearly 100,000 English-language books from Indian publishers.

Indian national bibliography / gen. ed., B. S. Kesavan. v. 1– . Calcutta : Central Reference Lib., 1958– . Quarterly, with annual cumulation, 1958–63; monthly, with annual cumulation, 1964– . **AA900**
    A five-year cumulation called "Cumulated index, 1958–1962" appeared in 1970. Monthly issues not published 1968–70; the annual volumes for those years are to be published.
    A national bibliography that attempts to list all new publications appearing in the 15 major languages of the country, including first issues of new periodicals but excluding musical scores, maps, and several categories of ephemera.
    Vernacular scripts have been transliterated into the Roman alphabet, and the text is in English. Each issue is in two parts: pt. 1, General publications; pt. 2, Government publications. In each section the entries are classified by Dewey Decimal Classification with a detailed index of authors, titles, and subjects.
    There is a very considerable time lag in publication of the annual cumulations. Z3201.A2I5

Indonesia

Catalogus dari buku-buku jang diterbitkan di Indonesia : 1870/1937–1954. Bandung, etc. : Gedung Buku Nasional, [1940]–55. 6 v. in 7. **AA901**
    Title varies slightly (also in Dutch: *Catalogus van boeken en tijdschriften uit. in Ned. Oost-Indië*). Publisher varies.
    G. Ockeloen, ed.
    1870–1937 issued in 2 v. (i.e., separate listings for Dutch and Indonesian publications); the Dutch listings for 1938–41 were published 1942, but the Indonesian listings were destroyed by war action; 1942–44 not published (although very few books were issued during the war and almost no bibliographic data on them exist); 1945–49 issued in 2 pts., the first covering Indonesian and Western language books, the second being a recompilation from original cards of the listings of Indonesian books for the 1937–41 period; further volumes cover 1950–51, 1952–53, and 1955.
    Superseded by *Berita bibliografi* (AA903). Z3278.A5C3

Projek Perpustakaan Nasional. Bibliografi nasional Indonesia : kumulasi, 1945–1963. Djakarta : Balai Pustaka, 1965. 2 v. **AA902**
    A main entry listing with subject and title indexes. Intends to include all works (excepting government documents) published in Indonesia during the period specified. The word "kumulasi" (cumulation) of the subtitle is meant to indicate that the work is based on three earlier bibliographies: G. Ockeloen's *Catalogus dari buku-buku jang diterbitkan di Indonesia* (AA901); *Berita bibliografi* of the Indonesian publishing house Gunung Agung (AA903); and *Berita bulanan* of the Kantor Bibliografi Nasional (AA904 *note*). Z3261.P76

Current

Berita bibliografi. 1955–1975. Djakarta : Gunung Agung, 1955–75. Monthly, with annual cumulations. **AA903**
    A commercially sponsored national bibliography. Lists books, pamphlets, periodicals, and newspapers published in Indonesia, as well as Indonesian books published overseas. In dictionary arrangement: author, title, and subject in one alphabet.
    Continued by *Berita Idayu bibliografi* (1976– . [Jakarta : Yayasan Idayu], 1976– . Monthly).
    Each issue usually includes one or more articles relating to the Indonesian book trade, Indonesian authors, etc., but a section called "Berita bibliografi" which serves as a continuation of the earlier series of that title (above) makes up the bulk of the publication; it is a classed listing with an author/title index which cumulates annually (beginning 1977, authors and titles cumulate separately) in the final issue of the year. Z3273.B44

Kantor Bibliografi Nasional (Indonesia). Bibliografi nasional Indonesia. no. 1, Th. XI (1963)– . [Djakarta] : [Kantor Bibliografi Nasional], 1963– . Quarterly (irregular). **AA904**
    A continuation of the Office's *Berita bulanan*, v. 1–10, 1953–62, monthly.
    Not published Oct.–Dec. 1964 (no. 4, Th. XII) and Apr.–Dec. 1965 (no. 2–5, Th. XIII); a cumulated issue called "Kumulasi 1964–1965" was published to fill the gap. Volumes for 1966–69 not yet published? Resumed with no. 1, Th. XVII, April 1970, the next issue for that year being no. 2, Th. XVII, Sept.–Dec. 1970.
    A classified list by Dewey Decimal Classification, with author index. Produced by the Office of National Bibliography; serves as the official list, but because it depends on the deposit of books (which is not required by law) it is not so comprehensive as the commercial list, *Berita bibliografi* (AA903). Z3261.A36

Iran

Kitābhā-ye Īrān. Tehrān : An-joman-e Ketab, 1955–69. Annual. **AA905**
    Title varies.
    In Persian. Ed. by Īraj Afshār.
    Some issues have added t. p. in English: *Bibliography of Persia: national bibliography*, publ. by the Book Society of Persia.

Kitābkhānah-i Millī-i Īrān. Kitābshināsī-i millī : Intishār-āt-i Īrān. no. 1 (1963)– . Teheran : [Kitābkhānah-i Millī], 1963– . Quarterly. **AA906**
    Not published for the years covering 1978–80.
    Frequency varies: originally annual.
    A classified subject listing, with an author index, of books, some government publications, and serials published in Iran. Z3366.T4

Mudabbirī, Maḥmūd. Farhang-i kitābhā–yi Fārsī : az qarn-i chahārum tā 1300. Chāp-i 1. Tihrān : Nashr-i Vīs, 1364 [1985]. v. 1–2. (In progress). **AA907**
    Added title page for v. 2: Bibliography of Persian books from 921 to 1921.
    Aims to list most of the books published in Persia from 921 to 1921. Does not include collected editions of an individual writer, pamphlets, or translations of European writers; the compilers hope to list the latter in a forthcoming volume. Arranged alphabetically by title, with an author index. A subject listing is planned. Z3366.M73

Iraq

al-Fihris al-waṭanī lil-maṭbūat al-ʿIrāqīyah. [Baghdād] : Wizārat al-ʿIlām, al-Maktabah al-Waṭanīyah, 1977– . quarterly. **AA908**

Added t.p.: *Iraqi national bibliography.*

Previously issued as *Deposit bulletin of Iraqi publications*, 1971–75, and as *al-Bibliyūghrāfīyah al-waṭanīyah al-ʿIrāqīyah*, 1976–77.

Aims to list all works published in Iraq, as well as works written by Iraqi authors published elsewhere. Includes titles in all languages. Divided into two sections, one for Western languages, one for Arabic languages; each section has a classified arrangement with its own author and title indexes.

Appears to cumulate annually as *al-Nitāj al-fikrī al-ʿIrāqī li-ām*, which has an added t.p. in English, *Iraqi national bibliography, annual cumulation for…*   Z3036.B5

Israel

Halevy, Shoshana Dyamont. Ha-Sefarim ha-ivriyim she-nidpesu bi-Yerushalayim … 1841–1891. [Jerusalem : Kiryath Sepher, 1963]. 202 p. : ill.   **AA909**

On verso of title page: The printed Hebrew books in Jerusalem during the first half century (1841–1891).   Z3478.J4H3

Current

Israel book news. no. 1 (Winter 1983)– . Tel Aviv : Israel Export Inst., Book and Printing Center, 1983– . Quarterly.   **AA910**

At head of title: IBN.

In English.

Includes articles on publishing and the book world, plus notes on a brief selection of new publications.

§ During the period Aug. 1970–Jan. 1980 the Center published the quarterly *Israel book world* which offered similar information. The Center also publishes *Books from Israel* (1964?–), an annual catalog of selected Israeli publications of interest to libraries and the book trade.   Z449.7.I83

Israeli books in print. Tel Aviv : Israel Book and Printing Center, Israel Export Institute ; Jerusalem : Halberstadt Communication, c1986– .   **AA911**

Intends to provide "a fair and representative picture of the range of subject matter and variety of languages" to be found in non-Hebrew books published in Israel 1970–86. Lists 1,260 books in classed arrangement with author/editor index. Directory of Israeli publishers.   Z3476.I86

Kirjath sepher : quarterly bibliographical review. 1924– . Jerusalem : Jewish Nat. and Univ. Lib., 1924– . Quarterly.   **AA912**

Each issue carries a classified listing of new publications. The list is now arranged in three sections: (1) Israel publications; (2) Hebraica and Judaica; and (3) Periodicals. Annual index.   Z6367.K57

Japan

Kokusho sōmokuroku. Tokyo : Iwanami Shoten, 1963–76. 9 v.   **AA913**

A very comprehensive listing of books written, edited, or translated by Japanese to 1867. About 500,000 titles which were checked against the holdings of 426 libraries in Japan. Vol. 9 is an author index.   Z3301.K8

Meiji zenki shomoku shūsei. Tokyo : Meiji Bunken Shiryo Kankokai, 1971–75. 20 v.   **AA914**

Reprints various copyright records and lists of trade publications from the 1876–99 period.

Samura, Hachiro. Kokusho kaidai. Rev. and enl. ed. Tokyo : Rikugōkan, 1926. 2 v.   **AA915**

Repr.: Kyoto : Rinsen Shoten, 1968.

An annotated bibliography of some 25,000 Japanese books published up to 1867.

Current

Kokuritsu Kokkai Toshokan (Japan). Zen nihon shuppan-butsu so-mokuroku. 1948–1976. Tōkyō : Kokuritsu Kokkai Toshokan, 1948–1976.   **AA916**

Added t.p. in English: *Japanese national bibliography.*

An annual cumulation of the National Diet Library's weekly list of current acquisitions, *Nōhon shūhō*, which began publication on an irregular basis in 1948.

A subject listing, including books, periodicals, newspapers, films, records, maps, etc. Government publications are listed by issuing agency. Title index. With v. 12, 1959, issued in two parts: pt. 1, Government publications; pt. 2, Nongovernment publications. 1948–69. Suppl. publ. 1975.

Superseded by: *Nihon zenkoku shoshi* [Japanese national bibliography] ([1977]– . Tōkyō : Kokuritsu Kokkai Toshokan, [1982]– . Annual).

Issued in 3 v.: [1], Kankocho shuppan; [2] Minkan shuppan; [3], Sakuin.

An annual index, with relatively full bibliographic information, to: *Nihon zenkoku shoshi shūkanban = Japanese national bibliography, weekly list* (1981– . Tōkyō : Kokuritsu Kokkai Toshokan, [1981]–).

Supersedes *Nōhon shūhō* (1948–80).

The current national bibliography, listing government publications by agency and nongovernment publications according to the Japanese decimal classification; includes separate sections for juvenile literature, braille and large-print books, technical reports, foreign-language publications, etc. Suppl. A, Pamphlets, is issued quarterly; Suppl. B, Periodicals, monthly. Quarterly author and title indexes. An annual index is provided by *Nihon zenkoku shoshi shomei choshamei sakuin.*

Nihon shoseki sōmokuroku. 1977   . Tokyo : Nihon Shoseki Shuppan Kyokai, 1977– . Annual.   **AA917**

A list of books currently available in the trade; similar to *Books in print.* The 1985 issue lists more than 359,000 items in title arrangement, with index volume offering author and series approaches, plus a directory of publishers and an appendix of pertinent statistical information.   Z3301.N53

Shuppan nenkan. [1950]– . Tokyo : Shuppan Nyūsusha, 1951– . Annual.   **AA918**

Includes information (with statistics) on publishing for the previous year; a classified listing of books published; new periodicals; lists of publishers, organizations, etc.; and laws and ordinances governing publication; excludes government publications. Title index.

§ This title supersedes *Nihon shuppan nenkan*, which appeared in 2 v. (1943–44/46 and 1947/48; no volume was issued for 1949), and was preceded by *Shuppan nenkan* (1930–41) and *Shoseki nenkan* (1942). A separate annual dealing with periodicals, *Zasshi nenkan*, was published from 1939 to 1942, when it merged with *Nihon shuppan nenkan.*

Jordan

Bibliyūghrāfiyā al-wataniyah al Urdunīyah. 1979– . Amman : Jordan Libr. Assoc., 1980– . Annual.   **AA919**

Added title page in English: The Jordanian national bibliography. Prefatory matter in Arabic and English.

Aims to list "all types of published materials produced in Jordan by individuals, private and official organisations excluding school text books and audio-visual aids."—*Pref.* Classified arrangement according to the Dewey Decimal Classification, with author-title and subject indexes. Separate section for English-language publications.

Z3471.B52

Korea

Taehan Min'guk ch'ulp'anmul ch'ongmongnok. 1963/1964– . Seoul : Kungnip chungang Tosŏgwan, 1965– . Annual.   **AA920**
　　Added title page: Korean national bibliography.
　　Continues *Han'guk sŏmok*, 1945/62 (Seoul : Kungnip Chungang Tosŏgwan, 1964).
　　Includes titles published in the Republic of Korea deposited at the national library. Separate sections for: official publications, general publications, theses and scholarly works, books for children, special publications, and serial publications. Sections for official publications, books for children and special publications are arranged by author or issuing agency; the others are alphabetically arranged under subject headings of the Korean Decimal Classification system. Western-language titles are listed at the end of each section. Title index.

Z3316.T3

Malaysia

Bibliografi negara Malaysia = Malaysian national bibliography. 1967– . Kuala Lumpur : Perkhidmatan Perpustakaan Negara, Arkib Negara Malaysia, 1969– . Quarterly. **AA921**
　　Issued annually 1967–74; 1975– , quarterly, the fourth issue being an annual cumulation.
　　Lists "materials published in Malaysia which are deposited in the National Library of Malaysia under the provisions of the *Preservation of Books Act, 1966*, and includes books, pamphlets, Government publications, new serial titles, maps and posters. However, it excludes popular magazines, comics, commemorative and travel brochures, souvenir programmes and trade catalogues."—*Pref., 1975 annual.*
　　In two sections: (1) a classified section according to Dewey Decimal Classification in which the full bibliographic information is given; and (2) an alphabetical author/title/series index. An alphabetical subject index to the Dewey class numbers is added in the annual cumulation.

Z3261.B5

Nepal

Nepalese national bibliography / [comp. by Tribhuvan University Central Library and Nepal Research Centre]. 1981– . Kathmandu : The Library and The Centre, 1983– . Annual.
AA922
　　Date of coverage appears in title.
　　A listing of Nepalese publications, excluding periodicals, newspapers, textbooks, and ephemeral publications such as trade catalogs. Arranged by Dewey Decimal Classification, with author, title, and subject indexes. A serial supplement is planned. Also appears in the *Journal of the Nepal Research Centre : JNRC*. Vols. 5–6 (1981/82) include the 1981 bibliography, v. 7 (1985) the 1982 bibliography, v.8 (1988) the 1983 bibliography, etc.   Z3210.N44

Pakistan

Books from Pakistan. 1969– . Karachi : Nat. Book Centre of Pakistan, 1970– . Annual.   **AA923**
　　Continues *Books from Pakistan published during the decade of reforms, 1958–1968* (AA924).
　　On cover: A bibliography of English language publications.
　　1969–70 called "annual supplement"; 1971– called "annual publication."
　　A classed listing with author and title indexes.   Z3191.N292

National Book Centre of Pakistan. Books from Pakistan published during the decade of reforms, 1958–1968. [2nd ed.]. Karachi, [1968]. 159 p.   **AA924**
　　1st ed. published 1967 under title: *English language publications from Pakistan.*
　　A classified list without author index.
　　Continued by: *Books from Pakistan* (AA923).   Z3191.N29

The Pakistan national bibliography. 1962– . Karachi : Govt. of Pakistan, Directorate of Archives & Libraries, Nat. Bibliographical Unit, [1967]– . Annual.   **AA925**
　　In accordance with the copyright ordinance of 1962, an attempt is being made to provide national bibliographic coverage from that date forward. Following publication of the 1962 annual in 1967 an effort was made to put the bibliography on a more current basis; thus, the 1968 volume was published 1970 and, apart from a 1970/71 hiatus, annual volumes have been appearing about two years after date of coverage.
　　Includes books and first issues of periodicals deposited according to the copy ordinance. Arranged by Dewey Decimal Classification, with author, title, subject index.
　　§ Pakistan Bibliographical Working Group. *The Pakistan national bibliography, 1947–1961* ([Karachi] : National Book Centre of Pakistan, 1973–75). A retrospective bibliography in two fascicles (General works to Islam, 001 to 297; Social sciences to Languages, 300 to 492), covering publications of 1947–61 (i.e., from the time Pakistan became an independent nation to 1962 when coverage of the annual volumes of the national bibliography begins). Some work has gone forward toward filling the 1963–67 gap.   Z3191.P33

Philippines

Bernardo, Gabriel Adriano. Philippine retrospective national bibliography, 1523–1699 / comp. by Gabriel A. Bernardo with the assistance of Natividad P. Verzosa ; ed. by John N. Schumacher. [Manila] : Nat. Libr. of the Philippines, [1974]. 160 p. : ill. (Occasional papers of the Department of History. Ateneo de Manila bibliographical series, no. 3).   **AA926**
　　Includes three categories of foreign and Philippine imprints: "(1) those which deal in whole or in part with the Philippines and were printed abroad, (2) all those printed in the Philippines of any nature, and (3) those written by Filipinos."—*Introd.* Chronological listing in two main sections, (1) Foreign imprints; (2) Philippine imprints. Author/subject index. 760 items.   Z3298.A35B47

Medina, José Toribio. Bibliografía española de las Islas Filipinas (1523–1810). Santiago de Chile : Impr. Cervantes, 1897–[98]. 556 p.   **AA927**
　　Repr. from *Anales de la Universidad de Chile*, 1897–98.
　　A list of 667 titles arranged chronologically, with author index.
　　——. *La imprenta en Manila desde sus orígenes hasta 1810* (Santiago de Chile : Autor, 1896. 280 p.; facsims. Repr. with *Adiciones*: Amsterdam : N. Israel, 1964.
　　——. ——. *Adiciones y ampliaciones* (1904. 203 p.).   Z3291.M40

Pérez, Angel. Adiciones y continuación de "La imprenta en Manila" de d. J. T. Medina : ó rarezas curiosidades bibliográficas filipinas de las bibliotecas de esta capital / por los pp. fr. Angel Pérez y fr. Cecilio Güemes, Agustinos. Manila : Santos y Bernal, 1904. 620 p.   **AA928**
    Available from Readex Microprint.   Z186.P5M6

Retana y Gamboa, Wenceslao Emilio. La imprenta en Filipinas : adiciones y observaciones á la Imprenta en Manila de d. J. T. Medina. Madrid : Minuesa de los Ríos, 1897. 276 cols.   **AA929**
    Also in Readex Microprint.
    ————. *Aparato bibliográfico de la historia general de Filipinas* (Madrid : Minuesa de los Ríos, 1906. 3 v.).
    Contents: v. 1, 1524–1800; v. 2, 1801–86; v. 3, 1887–1905.
    Includes: (1) Philippine imprints regardless of subject; (2) Books about the Philippines regardless of what language written in or where published; (3) Publications of Filipinos wherever printed.
    Arranged by years with the following indexes in v. 1: (1) Anónimos y principales materias, refundidos; (2) Publicaciones periódicas; 93) Biblioteca idiomática oriental; (4) Lugares geográficos; (5) Nombres propios de personas.
    ————. *Tablas cronológica y alfabética de imprentas e impresores de Filipinas (1593–1898)*. (Madrid : Victoriano Suárez, 1908. 114 p.).
    Also in Readex Microprint.   Z3291.M497

Current

Philippine bibliography. 1963/64–1970/72. Diliman, [Quezon] : Univ. of the Philippines Lib., 1965–73. 5 v.   **AA930**
    An effort toward establishing a national bibliography for the Philippines. Includes items published in the Philippines, works by Filipinos published elsewhere, and works by foreign authors treating solely, or in large part, Philippine subjects. Entries comprise books, pamphlets, government publications, and first issues of new periodicals. Nongovernment and government publications are listed in separate alphabetical sequences. Title and subject index.
    Superseded by *Filipiniana union catalog* (Jan./June 1976– . Quezon City : Univ. of the Philippines Library, 1976–).
    "An author list of Filipiniana materials currently acquired by the University of the Philippines Library and other libraries."—*t.p.*
    Gives full catalog entries for "Filipiniana materials including books, theses, music scores, phonodiscs, tapes, microfilms, new serial titles and other materials, or reproductions of any of these forms. It also includes government documents and publications except individual acts, bills and other ordinances. Pamphlets of less than five pages, unless of research value, are excluded."—*Introd.* Includes both current materials and older works recently acquired by participating libraries. Author listing with title and subject indexes.   Z3291.P48

Philippine national bibliography. Jan./Feb. 1974– . Manila : National Library of the Philippines, 1974– . Bimonthly with annual cumulations.   **AA931**
    Aims to list "new works published or printed in the Philippines, by Filipino authors, or about the Philippines, including unpublished materials."—*Pref., 1974.* Includes books, pamphlets, government publications, first issues of newspapers and periodicals, theses and dissertations. The "Book list or main sequence" is arranged by type of publication (e.g., books and pamphlets; periodicals, newspapers, annuals), then alphabetically by main entry. Author/title/series index and subject index.   Z3296.P53

Qatar

Qāʾimat al-intāj al-fikrī al-Qaṭarī li-ʿām / Dawlat Qaṭar, Wizārat al-Tarbiyah wa-al-Taʿlīm, Dār al-Kutub al-Qaṭarīyah. 1970– . al-Dawḥah [Qatar] : al-Dār, 1971– . Annual.   **AA932**
    Lists books, pamphlets, dissertations, serials, maps, music, official and government publications, and audiovisual materials written by Qataris and deposited in the National Library. Beginning in 1982, has sections for general publications, government publications, school publications, and children's books in non-Arabic languages. The general and school sections are arranged in classified sequence; the government publications by issuing agency. Author, title, subject, and publisher indexes.   Z3038.Q2Q24

Singapore

Singapore national bibliography. 1967– . Singapore : Nat. Lib., 1969– . Annual.   **AA933**
    Quarterly lists of deposit publications were previously published only in the Singapore *Government gazette*.
    Aims to list all works published in the Republic of Singapore; based on materials received at the National Library. Arrangement is by Dewey Decimal Classification, with author, title, and subject index.
    •Machine-readable version: *Singapore national bibliography* [database] (Singapore : National Library, 1967–). Available on CD-ROM, updated semiannually and cumulative from 1967.
    Z3248.S5A3

Sri Lanka

Ceylon national bibliography. v. 1 (1963)–v. 9 (1970). Nuwara Eliya, Ceylon : Nat. Bibliography Branch, Dept. of the Govt. Archivist, 1964–71.   **AA934**
    In Sinhalese, Tamil, and English.
    A current record of material deposited with the Registrar of Books and Newspapers. Each language division is in two parts (varies slightly): (1) Alphabetical author, title, and subject index; (2) Classified by Dewey Decimal Classification system. No cumulated indexes.
    Two preliminary numbers were issued (in English only), no. 1–2, Nov. and Dec. 1962, but they apparently are not counted in the subsequent voluming.
    § Continued by: *Sri Lanka jatika grantha namavaliya. Ilankait teciya nurpattiyal = Sri Lanka national bibliography* (AA935).

Sri Lanka jatika grantha namavaliya. Ilankait teciya nurpattiyal = Sri Lanka national bibliography. v. 10– . Colombo : Dept. of Nat. Archives, 1972– .   **AA935**
    Continues *Ceylon national bibliography* (AA934) and assumes its numbering.
    In Sinhalese, Tamil, and English.

Syria

al-Bibliyūghrāfīyā al-waṭanīyah al-Sūrīyah. 1984– . Dimashq : al-Maktabat al-Asad, 1985– . Annual.   **AA936**
    Continues: *al-Nashrah al-Maktabīyah bi-al-Kutub al-Ṣādirah fī al-Jumhūrīyah al-ʿArabīyah al-Sūrīyah* covering 1970–1973 (Ministry of National Culture and Guidance, 1971–1974).
    At head of title: Jumhuriyah al-ʾArabiyah al-Suriyah. Title on added t.p.: The Syrian national bibliography.
    A classified arrangement of Arabic-language books, pamphlets, serials, government publications, and theses published in Syria and deposited at the Assad Library. Includes some titles published since *al-Nashrah* ceased. Recent volumes include a section for periodicals,

newspapers, and irregular serials (alphabetically arranged), and a section for Western language books (in classified arrangement). Author, title, subject, and publisher indexes. An additional retrospective volume covering items published 1980–84 was issued in 1984. Z3028

Maktabat al-Asad (Damascus, Syria). al-Bībliyūghrāfiyā al-waṭanīyah al-Sūrīyah al-rāji'ah. Dimashq : al-Maktabah, 1987. v. 1. (In progress). **AA937**
Title on added t.p.: The Syrian national bibliography.
A retrospective bibliography of titles published in Syria prior to the current national bibliography; also includes titles by Syrians published abroad and titles from other languages translated into Syrian. Classified arrangement; author, title, subject, publisher indexes.
Z3481.M33

Taiwan

Chung-hua min kuo ch'u pan t'u shu mu lu. v. 1 (June 1970)– . [T'ai-pei] : Kuo li chung yang t'u shu kuan, 1970– . Monthly. **AA938**
Cover title: Chinese national bibliography.
Supersedes: *Hsin shu chien pao = The monthly list of Chinese books*, v. 1–9, 1960–69. Title varies.
Published monthly, with irregular annual and five-year cumulations.
Lists books and first issues of periodicals published in Taiwan and deposited at the National Central Library. Also includes books acquired by gift or purchase and earlier titles of research value not previously listed. Arrangement varies; recent issues arranged by broad subject. Title and author indexes. Z3111.C59

Thailand

Bannānukrom hāēng chāt = Thai national bibliography. 1975– . [Krungthēp, i.e. Bangkok, Thailand] : Hosamut hāēng Chat, Krom Sinlapakon, [1978]– . **AA939**
Introduction and table of contents in Thai and English.
Lists publications received by the National Library of Thailand under depository law and works of national interest published elsewhere. Since 1985, in two sections: books, arranged by Dewey Decimal Classification, with author, title, and cremation books indexes; and serials, arranged alphabetically by title.

Vietnam

Thư mục quôc gia / Cọng hòa xã hôi chủ nghĩa Viet Nam, Thư viẹn quôc gia. 1954– . Hà-nôoi : Cọng Hòa Xã Hôi Chủ Nghĩa Viet Nam, Thư viẹn qúoc gia, 1954– . Monthly (issues often combined), with annual index cumulation. **AA940**
Although coverage has varied, presently includes books, first issues of periodicals, official and government publications, annual reports, microforms, newspapers, photographs, and drawings deposited in the National Library. Arranged alphabetically within general subject categories. Author and title indexes. Z3226.T48

Australia and Oceania

Australia

Annual catalogue of Australian publications. no. 1 (1936)–[no. 25] (1960). Canberra : National Library of Australia, 1937–61. **AA941**

Generally includes books published in Australia, with supplements to previous issues; books of Australian interest published overseas; official publications of the Commonwealth and territories (although these are omitted for 1936 and 1941–44); selected list of Australian periodicals, annuals, and serial publications; and a directory of Australian publishers.
§ Superseded by: *Australian national bibliography* (AA944).
Z4011.C22

Australian national bibliography, 1901–1950. Canberra : National Library of Australia, 1988. 4 v. **AA942**
A retrospective bibliography that includes about 49,500 entries for books and pamphlets published in Australia, titles by Australian authors published elsewhere, or works with significant content on Australia. Bridges the period between John Ferguson's *Bibliography of Australia 1784–1900* (Sydney : Angus & Robertson, 1941–69) and *Annual catalogue of Australian publications* (AA941), the latter incomplete between 1936 and 1951. Serials and nonprint titles excluded. Arranged by main entry. Vol. 3 is an author/title/series index, v. 4 a subject index. Z4011.A94

Current

Australian books in print. [Ed.1]– . Melbourne : D. W. Thorpe, 1956– . Irregular, then annual. **AA943**
Eds. 1–5 called *Australian books in print*; 6th ed. called *Bookseller's reference book*; 7th ed. called *Bookbuyer's reference book*.
In addition to an author-title listing of books in print and a directory of publishers, recent issues include information on library and book trade associations, literary societies, literary awards and prizes.
Z4011.A85

Australian national bibliography. Jan. 1961– . Canberra : National Library of Australia, 1961– . Monthly issues superseded by annual cumulation. **AA944**
Supersedes *Annual catalogue of Australian publications* (AA941), its monthly supplement *Books published in Australia* ... , and *Monthly list of Australian government publications*.
Frequency and arrangement have varied. Cumulations are published on microfiche covering Jan.–Apr., Jan.–Aug., and Jan.–Dec.; the annual cumulation is available on microfiche and in paper.
Lists books and pamphlets published in Australia and those published overseas dealing with Australia. Includes government publications, and the first issue of new periodicals, newspapers, etc. Originally a monthly arranged alphabetically by main entry, with comprehensive bibliographic data for each item, prices, Dewey Decimal numbers, and a subject and title index. Z4015.A96

Fiji

Fiji national bibliography. Dec. 1979– . Lautoka, Fiji : Library Service of Fiji, Ministry of Social Welfare, 1979– . Annual. **AA945**
First issue covers 1970–78.
A classified listing of materials published in, as well as about Fiji. Author/title/series and subject indexes. Includes a list of government acts. Z4651.F54

New Zealand

Bagnall, Austin Graham. New Zealand national bibliography to the year 1960. Wellington : A.R. Shearer, Govt. Printer, 1970–85. 5 v. : ill. **AA946**
Often cited as "Bagnall".
Contents: v. 1, To 1889; v. 2–4, 1890–1960; v. 5, Supplement and index.

Primarily "a catalogue of printed books and pamphlets; periodicals and annual reports are omitted."—*Introd., v. 2*. Principles of inclusion and exclusion are carefully detailed in the introduction; it should be noted, in particular, that books published outside New Zealand are included if they contain some significant reference to the country, or if the author was a resident (as opposed to an expatriate) New Zealander; also excluded are New Zealand reprintings of books first published outside the country and with no New Zealand bibliographical association.

Publication of v. 1 (1980, in 2 pts.) was delayed until work was completed on the later period, both to take advantage of experience acquired in compilation of the other volumes and because of the reasonably adequate coverage of T. M. Hocken's *Bibliography of the literature relating to New Zealand* (Wellington : Government Printer, 1909 [repr. Wellington : Newrich Assocs., 1973]) and James Collier's *The literature relating to New Zealand* (Wellington : Government Printer, 1889). A wider range of materials is included in v. 1 than in the rest of the set (e.g., more Maori language items); annotations have been supplied for many items; but Bagnall does not include periodical articles as do Hocken and Collier. 6,229 entries in v. 1; about 32,000 in the complete work. Vol. 1 has its own index. Vol. 5 is in three sections: (1) Addenda and corrigenda to v. 2–4; (2) Index to v. 2–4, and (3) Addenda and corrigenda to v. 1. Some 2,500 new titles have been added are assigned numbers "in closest alphabetical sequence to their hypothetical position in volumes I–IV with the prefix 'S'."—*Note*.

Z4101.B28

New Zealand. General Assembly. Library. Copyright publications. 1933/34–66. Wellington : Govt. Printer, [193?]–66. **AA947**

Superseded by *New Zealand national bibliography* (AA949).

An annual list, supplemented by monthly lists in mimeographed form, of material received under the provisions of the Copyright Act. Full bibliographical information is given, including prices. There are sections listing government publications, overseas publications of New Zealand interest, maps, new periodicals, and periodicals that have ceased publication. Z975.W42

Current

New Zealand books in print. 1957– . Wellington : New Zealand Book Publishers Assoc., 1957– . Irregular. **AA948**

5th ed., 1970.

Title varies: 1957, 1961 issues called *A list of New Zealand books in print*; publisher varies.

Beginning with the 4th ed. (1968), sponsored by the New Zealand Book Publishers Association.

Originally a classified listing. Beginning 1968, the arrangement is alphabetical by main entry, with title and classified indexes.

New Zealand national bibliography. Feb. 1967– . Wellington : Nat. Lib. of New Zealand, 1967– . Monthly, with annual cumulation. **AA949**

Replaces *Current national bibliography of New Zealand books* (below) and *Copyright publications* (AA947). The first annual cumulation covers 1966 and was compiled from the records of the two earlier publications.

Each issue in three sections: (1) Books and pamphlets (including government publications as well as works published overseas dealing with New Zealand or by New Zealand authors); (2) Maps; (3) New periodicals (including notices of cessation). Main, added, subject, and title entries are all interfiled in the first section; tracings, price, and Dewey class number are given with most main entries.

Beginning 1983, the bibliography is available only on microfiche, and from 1984 is issued monthly in four sections (Register; Author/title; Subjects; and Non-books plus addresses) with annual cumulation.

§ Supersedes: *Current national bibliography of New Zealand books and pamphlets published in [1950–65]* in *Index to New Zealand periodicals*, 1950–65 (AD347). An alphabetical author, title, and subject list of all books and pamphlets published in New Zealand, and those published elsewhere by New Zealanders or having reference to New Zealand. Z4101.N57

Oceania

South Pacific bibliography. 1981– . Suva : Univ. of the South Pacific Library, Pacific Information Centre, 1982– . Annual. **AA950**

Supersedes *Pacific Collection accession list* (v. 1–8; 1975–82), which in turn superseded *Pacific Collection legal deposit accessions* (1972–74).

A cooperative regional bibliography which includes books, pamphlets, government publications, first issues of serials, maps, local language publications, and material related to social and cultural affairs published in the region or related thereto. Also includes titles on the Pacific and indigenous peoples in Australia, Hawaii, and New Zealand. Lists titles received at the Library regardless of date and place of publication, as well as titles published after 1975 not previously included. Monographs are arranged by Dewey Decimal Classification, with author/title and subject indexes. Separate list of periodicals and legal notices; directory of printers and publishers. Z4001.S65

Papua New Guinea

Papua New Guinea national bibliography. Mar. 1981– . Waigani : National Library Service of Papua New Guinea, 1981– . Quarterly with annual cumulation. **AA951**

Continues in part *New Guinea bibliography* publ. by University of Papua New Guinea, 1967–80. Material from Irian Jaya and the Solomon Islands (included in the earlier series) is now excluded.

Arranged by Dewey Decimal Classification with author/title/series and subject indexes. Lists monographs, first issues of serials (as well as subsequent name changes), maps, and audiovisual materials published in Papua New Guinea. Overseas publications dealing with Papua New Guinea or by Papua New Guineans are also included. Z4811.N48

AB

Encyclopedias

Although a good collection of encyclopedias is still basic to good reference service, there has been much excitement recently over encyclopedias in electronic format. Most are based on well-known printed sets, and most incorporate pictures, film clips, or sound. A few titles in electronic form are included here (*see* the Electronic section below), but most libraries will continue to rely on printed encyclopedia sets in reference work, applying to electronic encyclopedias the same criteria that are used in judging printed versions:

—Is the editor capable and experienced?

—Are the contributors outstanding in their fields, and are the articles signed?

—Is the publisher well known, reputable, and experienced?

—Does the length of articles match the importance of the topic? Do the articles show editorial balance and judgment?

—Is the information up to date?

—Does the work follow a continuous revision policy?

—Are there signs of bias or prejudice? Is there evidence of a strong national or political influence?

—How current and useful are bibliographies? Do bibliographies follow individual articles or is there a general bibliography? Do bibliographies supply full bibliographic information?

—How is the work arranged? If articles are very specific and for the most part brief, does the index associate related topics? If articles treat more general topics and tend to be longer and monographic, does the index point out specific topics? If in classified arrangement, does the index give access to topics?

—Is there a separate atlas and gazetteer? If not, are maps incorporated with the text?

—Are there sufficient illustrations and are they appropriately used? Are they of good quality?

—Are paper and binding of good quality, and will they stand up to heavy use?

—Does the work have special features that assist readers—appendixes, abbreviations lists, cross-references, special indexes, type face conventions, etc.?

—Is the work kept up-to-date by supplements or annuals?

For evaluations of individual encyclopedias, consult Kenneth F. Kister, *Kister's best encyclopedias* (AB1) or the annual encyclopedia review articles in "Reference books bulletin" (AA357).

GUIDES

Kister, Kenneth F. Kister's best encyclopedias : a comparative guide to general and specialized encyclopedias. 2nd ed. Phoenix : Oryx, 1994. 506 p.   **AB1**

Supersedes Kister's *Best encyclopedias: a guide to general and special encyclopedias* (1986) and *Kister's concise guide to best encyclopedias* (1988).

An excellent source that surveys and evaluates more than 1,000 encyclopedas, both print and electronic. While the emphasis is on works in English, major foreign-language encyclopedias are covered as well. Includes a title/topic index and a directory of publishers and distributors. Valuable for consumers and librarians.   AE1.K57

AMERICAN AND ENGLISH

Academic American encyclopedia. Princeton, N.J. : Aretê Publ. Co. 21 v. : ill.   **AB2**

Titles of other English-language editions: *Lexicon universal encyclopedia*, *Grolier academic encyclopedia*, *Academic international*, *Grolier international encyclopedia*.

First published in 1980. A relatively new work is intended "for students in junior high school, high school, of college and for the inquisitive adult."—*Pref.* Coverage is meant to be comprehensive throughout the various fields of knowledge and international in viewpoint. The stated intention of the set is to provide quick access to facts, readily intelligible concise overviews, a starting place for further research, and as many color maps and illustrations as possible.

Although treatment of individual topics is not exhaustive, the work falls somewhere between *World Book* and *Britannica* in scope and depth of treatment. Most of the articles are written and signed by scholars whose affiliations are listed in v. 1. Bibliographies of English-language books accompany many of the articles, emphasis here

being on recent and in-print materials within the understanding of the intended audience. *See* and *see also* references are employed, together with the use of small capitals within articles to signal related articles. The index volume notes bibliographies, illustrations, tables, and maps. Helpful pronunciation using simple respelling is indicated for difficult personal and place-names and for foreign words used as article headings.

According to most reviews, the encyclopedia meets its stated goals extremely well. The "1993 annual encyclopedia update" (*Booklist* 90: 172–173 [15 Sept. 1993] : 173) concludes that the *Academic American* "is an excellent quick-reference encyclopedia for high school and college students and adults. Librarians will find it useful at the reference desk. Its handsome illustrations and informative diagrams and tables combine with the up-to-date text to create a useful resource." *American reference books annual*, 1990, goes further, declaring that "for older audiences seeking concise, accurate, current, and informative articles at a reasonable price, Academic American takes its place among the best."

•Machine-readable version : *The Grolier multimedia encyclopedia* [database] (AB25).   AE5.A23

The Cambridge encyclopedia. Cambridge ; N.Y. : Cambridge Univ. Pr., 1990. 1334, 128 p., xvi p. of plates : ill. (some col.), some maps in color.   **AB3**

Ed. by David Crystal.

Aiming to "provide a succinct, systematic, and readable guide to the facts, events, issues, beliefs, and achievements which make up the sum of human knowledge" (*Pref.*), this encyclopedia was developed in collaboration between British publishers W. & R. Chambers and Cambridge Univ. Pr. First published in 1990, it was reprinted with updates and corrections in 1991 and 1992. It contains 25,000 entries in alphabetical order with an additional 127 pages of "Ready reference" tables and charts, including a useful list of political leaders 1900–91 arranged alphabetically by country. British emphasis.   AG5.C26

Chambers's encyclopaedia. New rev. ed. Oxford ; N.Y. : Pergamon, [1967]. 15 v. : ill.   **AB4**

History: 1st ed., ed. by Andrew Findlater, 1850–68; new ed., recast by David Patrick, 1888–92; 1923–27 rev. and reset; new ed. 1950. A "new rev. ed.," 1973, shows limited revisions.

Chambers's is a well-known British encyclopedia, with more than 23,000 signed articles and short bibliographies. With the bulk of the information now nearly 30 years old, this encyclopedia is seriously dated and useful only for historical purposes.   AE5.C443

Collier's encyclopedia. N.Y. : Collier. 24 v. : ill., maps. **AB5**

1st ed., 1949–51. 20 v.

Vol. 24, Bibliography and index.

Uses the continuous revision policy.

A usable, readable encyclopedia for students and general readers. Aimed at the high school and junior college level; is more advanced than the juvenile encyclopedias in its treatment and choice of subjects, but its coverage is not so great and information is not usually so detailed as in *Britannica* (AB8) or the *Americana* (AB9). However, emphasis on scholarly quality has increased somewhat over the years. The style is popular, clear, and concise. Many articles are long and well developed, others are short under very specific headings, but broad entries predominate. A high percentage of articles are signed with full names of contributors. Alphabetized letter by letter. Pronunciation is indicated by the international phonetic alphabet. Illustrations, both in color and black-and-white, are pertinent and well reproduced; maps are prepared by Rand McNally.

Bibliographies are not given at the ends of articles but are grouped together in the last volume, where they serve as reading lists in the various subject fields; they are updated at regular intervals. Arranged under broad subjects with subdivisions. Insofar as possible, within each subdivision, general and elementary subjects are treated first, followed by more advanced and specialized works. Titles, starting at high school level and progressing through college level and beyond, are selected with a view to their availability, and therefore most are of a recent date; all are in English. In recent printings, lists of "Further readings" have been appended to some articles, especially those of very current interest.

The consolidated index indexes text, illustrations, maps, and bibliography.

In its 1993 "Annual encyclopedia update" *Booklist* 90 (15 Sept. 1993): 174–175, concludes that "*Collier's*, with its lengthly detailed coverage, provides good historical information for the general layperson. Not all of its articles reflect the most current information, but progress is being made in the set's revision. Its appearance is improving as large numbers of new photographs added."

Collier's also publishes an annual *Year book* which serves as a supplement.   AE5.C683

The Columbia encyclopedia / ed. by Barbara A. Chernow and George A. Vallasi ; consultants, Peter J. Awn … [et al.]. 5th ed. [N.Y.] : Columbia Univ. Pr. ; [Boston] : Houghton Mifflin, 1993. 3048 p. : ill., maps.   **AB6**

1st ed., 1935; 4th ed., 1975, had title *The new Columbia encyclopedia*.

The first one-volume encyclopedia in English, *Columbia* has been justly popular for many years and this new edition continues the tradition. With more than 3,000 pages, 50,000 articles, and 65,000 cross-references, the 5th ed. is 60% revised, updated through Nov. 1, 1992. The emphasis is on text, authoritative and concise, with a few diagrams, tables and maps. A compact, reputable work for home, office, or library; an excellent source for quick reference.   AG5.C725

The concise Columbia encyclopedia. 2nd ed. N.Y. : Columbia Univ. Pr., c1989. 920 p.   **AB7**

1st ed., 1983.

This 2nd concise edition, based on *The Columbia encyclopedia* (AB6), is aimed at home reference libraries. The 1st ed. met with praise; this edition has "500 new articles … The remaining articles have been checked for accuracy … Those things that characterized the first edition are still evident here: authority, currency, readability, and conciseness."—*American reference books annual*, v. 21 (1990): 20. Also available in large print edition.

•Available in machine-readable form as part of *Microsoft bookshelf '94* [database] (AB27).   AG5.C737

Encyclopaedia Britannica : a new survey of universal knowledge. Chicago [etc.] : Encyclopaedia Britannica, 1768–1973. 1st–14th eds.   **AB8**

History: 1st ed., 1768–71, 3 v.; 9th ed., 1875–89, 25 v.; 10th ed., a supplement to the 9th ed., with a combined index to the main work and the supplement, 1902–1903, 10 v.; 11th ed., 1911, 29 v.; 12th ed., 1922, 3 v. and 13th ed., 1926, 3 v., not revisions of the whole work but supplements to the 11th ed.; 14th ed., 1929, 24 v. From 1929, used the continuous revision policy and did not number editions.

The most famous encyclopedia in English, and for some purposes the best. Until modified in the 20th-century editions, it differed from most European and American encyclopedias in its fundamental plan, which called for a collection of important monographs on large subjects by specialists, often very scholarly and of lasting importance, with good bibliographies, excellent illustrations, but no separate treatment of small topics and no biographical sketches of living persons. Narrow or very specific topics were treated only as parts of broader subjects and could be found only through the index. This plan, which was seen most typically in the 9th ed., was modified somewhat in the supplementary 10th ed. and still more, to meet modern demands, in the 11th ed. With the 14th ed. the traditional monographic policy was largely abandoned in favor of shorter articles under more specific headings.

Although the library fortunate enough to have sets of all editions of *Britannica* will still make occasional use of the early editions for older subjects or points of view, biographies, etc., the 1st–8th eds. are now mainly of historical interest. The 9th and 11th eds. and their supplements, however, still will be used. The 9th ed., under the able editorship of William Robertson Smith, was the high watermark of *Britannica,* and its scholarly articles may be used profitably for subjects where recent information is not essential. The 11th ed., although more popular in style than the great 9th, is scholarly and carefully edited, and should still keep its place on the shelves of the reference room.

Recent editions: The 14th ed., first published in 1929, was revised, reset, and reorganized to include short articles on small subjects as well as many long articles. Some of the latter have been carried over from the 9th and 11th eds., sometimes revised and abridged but still carrying the signature of the original author. Although now essentially an American work, the set still reflects traces of its British origins, e.g., in spelling, in some headings, and in the relative length of treatment of many British topics. As noted above, the continuous revision policy was followed from 1929, and editions were not numbered until publication of the new 15th ed.

A useful and generally well-made encyclopedia, with long, detailed articles on many subjects. Articles are signed with initials, the list of contributors being given in the index volume. Alphabetized letter by letter; pronunciation is not indicated. Maps are included in the index volume, with a separate index. Bibliographies appended to some articles include titles in various languages, and give place of publication and date. Frequently, even if the article has been rewritten, the bibliographies have not been brought up to date. In recent years the tendency has been to shorten the bibliographies and to omit scholarly works in favor of those easily available. Vol. 24 includes a comprehensive, detailed index which must always be used in order that all pertinent material may be found.

Because the 15th ed., appearing under the title *The new Encyclopaedia Britannica,* represents a radical departure from its predecessors in makeup and treatment, it is considered in a separate entry (AB12).   AE5.E363

Encyclopedia Americana. N.Y. ; Chicago : Encyclopedia Americana. 30 v. : ill.   **AB9**

History: 1st ed. 1903–1904, 16 v. unpaged; several partial revisions, especially an edition in 22 v., published 1912 under the title *The Americana,* which included some new articles and changes in others. The 1918–20 edition was a complete revision, reset throughout, with much new material; it is the basis of succeeding editions. Now uses the continuous revision policy.

A good, comprehensive encyclopedia for general use. Important articles are signed with full name and title of the contributor; some have bibliographies. Illustrations are numerous, maps are included with articles, and references to them are included in the index. Alphabetized word by word. Pronunciation is frequently indicated. For the most part, articles are short, and on very specific subjects, but many articles of some length and on broad topics are included.

Americana has always been particularly strong in its information about American towns and cities; and there is an abundance of biographical sketches (including numerous ones of living persons). Other special features are the evaluations of particular books, operas, musical compositions, works of art, etc.

Since 1943 the index volume (v. 30) has been an alphabetical index arranged in dictionary form, instead of the classed index of previous editions. It is kept up-to-date with each printing and should always be consulted in order that pertinent material treated in various parts of the work not be overlooked.

Comparative assessments of encyclopedias by ALA's Reference Books Bulletin Editorial Board conclude that *Americana* is "highly recommended for homes and libraries, for all readers from upper elementary grades upwards and for any readership which needs an up-to-date, general purpose, high-quality American encyclopedia."—*Booklist* 81 (15 Dec. 1984) : 570. The 1993 review concludes that "*Americana* one of the most comprehensive encyclopedias, and its excellent historical coverage of topics will make it useful in high school, college and public libraries. The board hopes that the conversion of the set to machine readable format will enable the publisher to deal with the problem of lack of currency by being more ambitious in the scope of yearly revisions."—*Booklist* 90 (15 Sept. 1993) : 178–80.

Americana annual : an encyclopedia of events, is a yearbook that serves both as an annual supplement to the encyclopedia and as a record of progress and events.

•Although the text of *Americana* is not available electronically, its index is searchable, together with the indexes to *Academic American encyclopedia* and *The new book of knowledge* in *The Grolier master encyclopedia index* (Danbury, Conn. : Grolier Educational Corp.). Available on diskette and CD-ROM.   AE5.E333

Funk & Wagnalls new encyclopedia / Joseph Laffan Morse, ed. in chief. N.Y. : Funk & Wagnalls. 27 v. : ill., maps. **AB10**

Editions prior to 1971 had title: *The new Funk & Wagnalls encyclopedia.*

A general encyclopedia for junior high school through adult audiences, designed to be sold in supermarkets throughout the U. S. and Canada. Kept up-to-date by a continuous revision policy. Articles range from a few lines of brief identification to several pages; some articles are signed. Index in v.26–27; classified bibliography in v.27.

The 1984 reassessment in *Booklist* 81 (15 Dec. 1984): 570 finds the set "a good, straightforward provider of facts on people, places, and things" and, while neither as scholarly or detailed as various larger works, offers excellent value. A useful, inexpensive choice for the home library.

•Machine-readable version: *Encarta* [database] (AB24). Also available as part of *Infopedia* [database] (AB26). **AE5.F83**

The Longman encyclopedia / ed. in chief, Asa Briggs. Burnt Mill, Harlow, Essex, England : Longman, 1989. 1178 p. **AB11**

Based on the 1st ed. of *The concise Columbia encyclopedia* (AB7). The editors "went on to review and update each existing article, to add thousands of new ones, and to delete some others."— *Foreword.* Contains alphabetically arranged entries varying in length from a paragraph to a column, many with illustrations. British emphasis. **AE5.L66**

The new Encyclopaedia Britannica. 15th ed. Chicago : Encyclopaedia Britannica. 30 v. : ill. **AB12**

Contents: Micropaedia (Ready reference), 12 v.; Macropaedia (knowledge in depth), 17 v.; Propaedia (Outline of knowledge), 1 v.; Index, 2 v.

Reduced to its simplest terms, the changed structure of this edition which first appeared in 1974 means that the long, monographic articles of the type that distinguished the 11th ed. have been brought together in the Macropaedia, while brief factual information best imparted through the more fragmented, direct entry approach of the 14th ed. is presented in the Micropaedia. Until the 1985 printing, the conventional index was eliminated and the Micropaedia indexed the Macropaedia with very unsatisfactory results. Thankfully, that situation has been remedied with an excellent 2-v. index, containing more than 702,000 references. *The Britannica electronic index* on CD-ROM expands the printed index by allowing users to search multiple terms, although it is awkward to combine a CD-ROM with a large print set.

The annual encyclopedia review in *Booklist* says of the most recent revision, "The Micropaedia features 64,128 articles (most of them unsigned) averaging about 300 words in length. [189] new articles were added ... with another 974 rewritten or revised. Biographies continue to be a strong feature ... accounting for about one-third of the entries. The Macropaedia contains 672 articles ranging in length from 2 to 309 pages. Seven ... are new ... 21 entries were replaced, 12 were revised, and 21 have updated text. All articles feature extensive bibliographies ... and [are] signed." *Booklist*: (15 Sept. 1993): 182.

Updating continues to be effected through *The Britannica book of the year* and through a continuous revision policy. The extent of the latter has been disappointingly slight to date, with the Micropaedia being generally more up-to-date than the Macropaedia.

All in all, *Britannica* remains the most comprehensive, authoritative, international encyclopedia in the English language. However, its unconventional arrangement makes it inconvenient to use for quick fact checking.

•Machine-readable versions: *Britannica CD* [database] (Chicago : Encyclopaedia Britannica, c1994), which includes the 44-million-word text of the printed encyclopedia together with unspecified versions of a Merriam-Webster dictionary and thesaurus; and *Britannica instant research system* [database] (Chicago : Encyclopaedia Britannica, c1994), which incorporates *Britannica book of the year* for 1993 and 1994 and is intended for businesses and publishers and is not available to the public. Both are available on CD-ROM. **AE5.E363**

The Random House encyclopedia / James Mitchell, ed. in chief; Jess Stein, ed. dir. New rev. 3rd ed. N.Y. : Random House, c1990. 2781, 130 p. : ill. (some col.), maps in color. **AB13**

2nd ed., 1983.

First published in 1977, and conceived "as a 'family bible' of knowledge for our times."—*Pref.* Its division of the text into Colorpedia (lengthy articles) and Alphapedia (brief, factual entries) has been criticized by librarians. However, the encyclopedia is popular in the home market.

•Machine-readable version : *The Random House encyclopedia* [database] (N.Y. : Random House, 1990). Available on computer diskettes. **AG5.R25**

Webster's new World encyclopedia. College ed. N.Y. : Prentice Hall, 1993. 1156 p. : ill. ; maps. **AB14**

Contains 20,000 articles in alphabetical arrangement, consisting of short entries with numerous maps, diagrams, and tables. A serviceable, small, 1-v. encyclopedia that identifies and briefly describes countries, events, and people, with particular strength in the contemporary and popular. **AG5.W386**

Bibliography

Walsh, S. Padraig. Anglo-American general encyclopedias : a historical bibliography, 1703–1967. N.Y. : Bowker, 1968. 270 p. **AB15**

More than 400 English-language general encyclopedias are included, with notes on the publishing history of each and indication of relationships to earlier or later sets. Evaluative statements are given for most titles; *Subscription books bulletin* reviews are cited as applicable. There is an index of originators, compilers, editors, etc.; a chronology; and a general bibliography, but not the full bibliographical detail and footnote references to be expected in a work of this kind.

Z5849.E5W3

Indexes

Ryan, Joe. First stop : the master index to subject encyclopedias. Phoenix : Oryx, 1989. 1582 p. **AB16**

A subject and keyword and index to nearly 430 English-language reference books, including specialized encyclopedias, dictionaries, and textbooks. Indexes sources of more detailed information for both scholarly and poplar topics is provided by general encyclopedias. Does not include biography or criticism.

"This index would be most useful in almost any public or academic library which has a reference collection containing many of the works indexed ... it has the opportunity to become a prime reference source."—*American Reference Books Annual 1990*, 21 (1990): 32.

Z5848.R93

Juvenile

Children's Britannica. 5th ed. ; Chicago : Encyclopaedia Britannica, c1993. 20 v. : ill. **AB17**

Children's Britannica was revised in 1988 for "the American market," and now supersedes *Britannica junior* (1934–84). First published in Britain in 1960, the purpose of the revised set is "to adapt the encyclopedia for young students living in the technological age of the late 20th century and to do so on a broad, international basis." Although some of the longest articles treat the U.S., *American reference books annual* 23 (1992) : 15 notes the lack of separate articles on all U.S. presidents.

Approximately 4,000 articles provide information on some 35,000 topics. Each of 19 volumes contains, alphabetically arranged,

320 pages, resulting in split letters, "something other sets for this age group avoid"—*Booklist* (1 Jan. 1989): 758. Articles are unsigned, although the final volume concludes with a list of more than 450 writers or advisors. Vol. 19 includes an atlas of 40 maps with a gazetteer, and v. 20 contains a "Reference index" (complete with six pages of directions) of 30,000 dictionary entries. The set is suitable for a slightly younger age group than *World book* and comparable children's encyclopedias.   AG5.B8

Compton's encyclopedia and fact-index. Chicago : Compton. 24 v. (varies) : ill.   **AB18**

Issued annually since 1922. Uses the continuous revision policy.

A good juvenile encyclopedia and one of the leading American works in this field. Planned especially for upper elementary and high school use; attempts to keep in close touch with school needs, but is useful for the adult who needs a somewhat simpler article than that given in the standard encyclopedias for adults.

General policy is to use long articles on large subjects, with smaller subjects analyzed or treated in the "Fact-index" (*see* below). Has a clear, direct style and pays especial attention to illustrations, charts, and maps. Indicates pronunciation of unusual words. Alphabetized letter by letter. For some of the longer articles, gives reference outlines for organized study, and certain articles include brief bibliographies, sometimes divided into lists of books for younger readers and books for advanced students and teachers.

Instead of a general index volume, a "Fact-index" at the end of each volume serves as a guide to all volumes for subjects beginning with the letter or letters covered in that volume. The "Fact-index" is not only an analytical index to all text and illustrative material in the main work, but also includes dictionary-type information, brief biographical sketches, etc., on subjects not treated elsewhere.

The 1989 revised edition includes 5,200 articles complemented by 2,000 maps and 20,000 illustrations (mostly black-and-white).

Supplemented by *Compton yearbook: an illustrative factual record of outstanding events.*

•*Booklist* (15 Sept. 1993): 176 notes that *Compton's* is available in several electronic versions, including *Compton's multimedia encyclopedia* [database] (AB23).   AG5.C73

Merit students encyclopedia. [N.Y.] : Macmillan Educational Corp. 20 v. : ill.   **AB19**

First published 1967.

Intended for the use of students from the 5th grade through high school. Emphasis is placed on the encyclopedia's "curriculum orientation," with individual articles written to be understood at the grade level at which the subject is taught. Material for younger readers is placed at the beginning of an article and more advanced information incorporated as the article is developed. Signed articles; only the longer ones include a bibliography or suggestions for further reading. Pronunciation is indicated. Vol. 20 includes an index.

Updated by *Colliers encyclopedia yearbook. Walford's guide to reference material* (5th ed., v. 3, p. 151) notes: "an established set in the US, but revision is not as diligent as in some comparable encyclopedias, bibliographies especially requiring more frequent updating." Suitable for children "aged 10 and upwards."   AE5.M38

The new book of knowledge : the children's encyclopedia. N.Y. : Grolier. 21 v. : ill. maps.   **AB20**

First published 1912 under title *The book of knowledge;* printings through 1965 had that title.

Intended to interest a wide range of readers from those in early childhood to students nearly ready to use an adult encyclopedia; thus, articles are written at various levels of understanding, with the main emphasis being for children in grades three to six. Longer articles are signed by contributors or consultants. Suggested activities or projects are incorporated into some articles to further the educational value. Alphabetical arrangement with *see* and *see also* references, plus a "dictionary index" at the back of each volume (i.e., with the index section corresponding to the portion of the alphabet dealt with in that particular volume) providing factual information as well as references to pertinent information in other volumes of the set. This fragmented arrangement of the index is not particularly effective, and a combined index has been added as v. 21 of recent editions. Bibliographies do not appear in the main set, but a bibliography keyed to topics in the encyclopedia (and with reading levels indicated) makes up the first part of a paperbound supplement entitled "Home and school reading and study guides." Illustrations make up about a third of the entire set. Continuous revision policy.

The *New book of knowledge annual* (1940–) includes a chronology of the year's events and entries from the main set.

•Index available in machine-readable form as part of : *The Grolier master encyclopedia index* [database] (Danbury, Conn. : Grolier). Available on CD-ROM, updated annually.   AG5.B64

Oxford children's encyclopedia / ed. by Mary Worrall. Oxford Univ. Pr., 1991. 7 v.   **AB21**

Beginning as a successor to *Oxford junior encyclopedia* of the 1950s—a "sober reference work of the pre-TV era"—the "child-friendly volumes" of this new set feature "slick design and up-to-date photos" intended "to appeal to children accustomed to the visual stimulation of television and computer."—*Publisher's weekly* (17 Feb. 1992) : 27. Articles are arranged alphabetically, grouped by category only in the biographical volume (v. 6). The editors conferred with their U.S. colleagues in an attempt to keep balance between, e.g., British and American history, but acknowledge that the text has not been systematically Americanized. Most useful for children 8 through 13.

World book encyclopedia. Chicago : Field Enterprises Educ. Corp. 22 v. (varies) : ill.   **AB22**

Issued annually. Uses the continuous revision policy.

A good juvenile encyclopedia, one of the leading American works in the field; approximates the form and treatment of the standard works for adults, so is especially good for the older child nearly ready to use adult material.

Offers 17,500 articles signed by 3,000 contributors and consultants, with 29,000 illustrations (24,000 in color) and 2,300 maps. Longer articles include bibliographies and study guides. Vol. 21 has a detailed analytical index. Vol. 22 is an "Index and research guide," which contains more than 200 "Reading and study guides," that supplement bibliographies in the main set. Vols. 23–24, marketed specifically in the British Isles, treat Britain and Ireland in greater detail than the main set; there is also a volume called "Australasia" that is marketed in Australia and New Zealand. Kept up-to-date by *World book year book* (1922–), which prints new and revised articles and reviews events of the previous year in a section called "The world on file."

Children's librarians generally agree that *World book* continues to be the most popular general encyclopedia for readers 10 years of age and older. *Booklist* (15 Sept. 1993) : 183 praises the "general updating" in this set, in particular its coverage of world events and a new feature, "What the newspapers say about the United States," that explains the 1990 census with charts and graphs.

•The complete text is available in machine-readable form as part of *World book information finder* [database] (AB28).   AE5.W55

ELECTRONIC

Besides the sources named below in this section, a new venture, *Britannica online*, makes the entire text of *The new encyclopaedia Britannica* (AB12) available through the Internet. Besides the 44-million-word text of the encyclopedia, *Britannica online* includes *Britannica classics* (important articles from earlier editions), *Britannica book of the year*, and *Merriam-Webster's collegiate dictionary*, 10th ed. (AC17). It also incorporates some graphics and illustrations, as well as new material not found in the printed version. The technology of World Wide Web enables *Britannica online* to provide hypertext links within the database and to outside resources on the Internet. It has a Wide Area Information Server search engine that readily comprehends natural language. Placing *EB* on the Internet provides several advantages over CD-ROM: there are no size limitations; continuous updating can be achieved more readily; and in MacIntosh or Windows environments, shifting from a working file to *Britannica online* and back again is simple.

•**Compton's multimedia encyclopedia** [database]. [Carlsbad, Calif.] : Compton's NewMedia.   **AB23**
     Compton's introduced the multimedia encyclopedia in 1989. This edition contains the complete text of the 26-v. *Compton's encyclopedia and fact-index* (AB18), including 35,000 articles, more than 15,000 illustrations, and better sound than its competitors. It has a fine user interface and a quasi-natural language search capability, "Idea search," that understands phrases and questions. A unique "editing room" feature allows users to create their own multimedia presentations. Best suited for elementary to middle school students.

•**Encarta** [database]. [Redmond, Wash.] : Microsoft Corp., 1994– .   **AB24**
     Beginning with the text of *Funk & Wagnalls new encyclopedia* (AB10), Microsoft has significantly revised some articles and added others, some signed, totalling 26,000, and claims a more scholarly content than previous editions. Has excellent search facilities that enable users to specify words, broad subjects, time period and place, and types of media desired. Keyword searching is possible, and the "Wizard" subroutine will go through the search process step by step. Main advantage is its multimedia content (9½ hours of sound, 29 videos, 8,000 pictures) and its smooth, elegant, stylish interface. Attractive and fun to use, it appeals most to middle and high school students.

•**The Grolier multimedia encyclopedia** [database]. Danbury, Conn. : Grolier, c1995– .   **AB25**
     Replaces the *The new Grolier multimedia encyclopedia* (1993). Other titles: *New Grolier electronic encyclopedia, Electronic encyclopedia*.
     The pioneer CD-ROM encyclopedia, first released in 1985 as *Academic American encyclopedia on CD-ROM*, and still one of the most respected. Appealing to older students and adults, it contains 33,000 articles—the full text of the 21-v. printed set of *Academic American encyclopedia* (AB2), plus additional articles written specifically for this product. The 1995 edition offers additional pictures, maps, sounds, animations, and video clips. Combines sophisticated text searching capability with excellent topic trees. In a new "Pathmakers" feature, experts introduce a series of articles on a topic; e.g., astronaut Buzz Aldrin narrates a section, "Explorers and the horizons of discovery." While the user interface is not the best, this is a solid product that can be used by both older children and adults.
     The text is available online through a number of vendors.

•**Infopedia** [database]. [s.l.] : Future Vision Multimedia, 1994.   **AB26**
     A new source that combines in one laser disc the full text of eight reference works, including *Funk & Wagnalls new encyclopedia* (AB10), *Roget's 21st century thesaurus* (Nashville, Tenn. : T. Nelson, c1992), *Hammond atlas of the world* (Maplewood, N.J. : Hammond,

c1993), *World almanac and book of facts* (AB110), *Webster's dictionary of English usage* (AC87), *Webster's compact dictionary of quotations* (Springfield, Mass. : Merriam-Webster, c1992), *Webster's new biographical dictionary* (AH38), and something identified by the producer only as *Merriam-Webster's dictionary*. Among its 200,000 entries are 39,000 full-length articles, the greatest number of the CD-ROM electronic encyclopedias. Hypertext links each word and cross-reference to each of the eight titles, providing ready-made cross-referenced entries from numerous sources. Has less impressive interface and far fewer visuals than other multimedia encyclopedias, but has an attractive price.

•**Microsoft bookshelf '94** [database]. Redmond, Wash. : Microsoft Corp., c1994.   **AB27**
     Similar in concept to *Infopedia* (AB26), containing the full texts of several standard reference sources: *The concise Columbia encyclopedia* (AB7), *The American heritage dictionary of the English language* (AC9), *Columbia dictionary of quotations* (BE97), *The world almanac and book of facts* (AB110), *The intermediate world atlas* (Maplewood, N.J. : Hammond, 1984), *Roget's international thesaurus* (AC144), and *The people's chronology*, by James Trager (DA39). Lacks the depth of information provided by *Infopedia*, which is based on a larger encyclopedia, but has an excellent interface that allows users to search any combination of the sources and move among them easily. A good complement to larger printed or electronic encyclopedias.

•**World book information finder** : a CD-ROM reference based on The World book encyclopedia [database]. Chicago : World Book, 1994.   **AB28**
     Offers the complete text of the excellent 22-v. *World book encyclopedia* (AB22), containing 17,000 full-text articles with illustrations and diagrams. Entries are indexed by subject and include reading lists. Also includes the complete text (139,000 entries) of *World book dictionary* (AC28). Not a multimedia encyclopedia; concentrates on providing in-depth, comprehensive information. There are plans to add sound and video in the next edition.

FOREIGN LANGUAGE

Chinese

Chung-kuo ta pai ko chuan shu. Pei-ching : Chung-kuo ta pai do chuan shushu pan she ; [Shanghai] : Hsin hua shu tien Shang-hai fa hsing fo fa hsing, 1982– . v. 1, pts 1–2; 2, pts. 1–2; 4; 7; 8, pts. 1–2; 10, pts. 1–2; 12–13; 14, pts. 1–2; 15–16; 19–20; 21, pts. 1–2; 22; 23, pt 1–2; 24–25; 29–31; pts. 1–3; 46–49, pts. 1–2; 50–51 : ill. (In progress).   **AB29**
     The "Great Chinese encyclopedia," with lengthy signed articles, well-illustrated with line drawings and photographs. Arranged by topic—e.g., 3 v. on Chinese history, 2 v. on Chinese literature, one each on sociology, geography, etc. Several indexes, including subjects (English and Chinese) and proper names. Uses pinyin romanization.
                                    AE17.C48

Czech

Malá československá encyklopedie / [hlavní redakce československé encyklopedie Bohumil Kvasil et al.]. Praha : Academia, 1984–1987. 6 v. : ill.   **AB30**
     Editors vary.
     The most complete of the Czech socialist encyclopedias, with comprehensive international coverage. There are more than 110,000 short unsigned articles arranged alphabetically. Good illustrations; many biographies of Czech nationals.   AE51.M25

Masarykův slovník naučný : lidová encyklopedie všeobecných vědomostí. V. Praze : Nákl. "Československého Kompasu", 1925–33. 7 v. : ill. **AB31**

Contains little bibliography but has many biographies, including those of persons still living at time of compilation. AE51.M3

Ottův slovník naučný : illustrovaná encyklopaedie obecných vědomostí. V Praze : Otto, 1888–1909. 28 v. : ill. **AB32**

Contents: v. 1–27, A–Z; v. 28, Supplement.

The standard Czech encyclopedia. Signed articles, many biographies, some bibliography (including works in many languages). Maps, many folded; town plans; illustrations include plates and line drawings in text.

Supplemented by *Ottův slovník naučný nové doby : dodatky k velikému Ottovu slovniku naučnému*, redakci vede B. Nemec (V Praze : "Novina," 1930–43. 6 v. ill.). Updates the previous work until World War II, when publication ceased. Never completed. AE51.O8

Danish

Gyldendals tibinds leksikon / hovedredaktør, Jørgen Bang… [et al.]. København : Gyldendalske boghandel, c1977–78. 10 v. : ill. **AB33**

Contains more than 75,000 short unsigned articles and 15,000 illustrations, mostly black-and-white. A supplement (1984) updates the set. AE41.G97

Hagerups Illustrerede Konversations Leksikon. 4. gennemsete og forøgede Udg. / redigeret af P. Engelstoft. København : Hagerup, 1948–53. 10 v. : ill. **AB34**

1st ed., 1892–1900; 3rd ed., 1921–25.

A general encyclopedia with short articles, most of them signed. Little or no bibliography. AE41.H3

Salmonsens Konversationsleksikon. 2. Udg. Copenhagen : Schultz, 1915–30. 26 v. : ill. **AB35**

1st ed. (1893–1911. 19 v.) had title: *Salmonsens Store illustrerede Konversationsleksikon*.

Contents: v. 1–25, A–Ø; v. 26, Supplement.

The standard Danish encyclopedia, with signed articles, bibliographies, maps, town plans, and illustrations. Marks pronunciation of proper names.

Supplemented by *Salmonsen Leksikon Tidsskrift* (Copenhagen : Schultz, 1941–57. Aarg. 1–15) which was monthly with biennial indexes. (No index for 1956–57; 10-year index, 1941–50, publ. 1951.). AE41.S2

Dutch

Eerste Nederlandse systematisch ingerichte encyclopaedie / Samengesteld onder leiding van H. J. Pos, J. M. Romem … [et al.]. Amsterdam : E.N.S.I.E., [1946–60]. 12 v. : ill. **AB36**

A classed encyclopedia, each article written by a specialist. Includes bibliographies.

Vol. 10, Lexicon en register; v. 11, Supplement; v. 12, Lexicon en register, beknopt overzicht der wereldgeschiedenis in synchronistische tabellen.

Vol. 10 includes, in the same alphabet with the index, much encyclopedic information not covered in the main set: e.g., biographical sketches, gazetteer information about places, definitions of historical terms; v. 12 is an index to v. 11 (the supplement) and also a lexicon adding new entries and bringing up to date material in v. 10. Includes much gazetteer information. AE19.E3

Grote Winkler Prins encyclopedie in 26 delen. 9. geheel nieuwe druk. Amsterdam : Elsevier, [1990–93]. 26 v. : ill., maps. **AB37**

1st ed. 1870–82; 5th ed., 1932–38, had title *Winkler Prins' algemeene encyclopaedie*; 6th ed. 1947–54 called *Winkler Prins encyclopedie*.

The standard Dutch encyclopedia, originally based on *Der grosse Brockhaus* (AB49) with well-balanced articles, some signed; some include bibliographies listing works in various languages. Illustrations and maps are good. Bibliographies include living persons.

A completely revised and updated edition. The format is smaller, but includes 85,000 entries in 16,000 pages of text with 173,000 cross-references. A completely new geographic volume (v. 26) has been added with color maps, gazetteer etc.

————. *Supplement 1994* (1994. 612 p.). AE19.W5262

Farsi

Dāyirat al-ma'ārif-i Fārsī / bi-sarparastī-yi Ghulām Husayn Musāhib. [Tihrān] : Firānklīn, 1345 [i.e., 1966 or 7]– . [v. 1]– . (In progress). **AB38**

A short-entry encyclopedia based on *The Columbia-Viking desk encyclopedia* (2nd ed., rev. and enl. N.Y. : Viking Pr., [1960]), but with much added material. AG36.D38

Finnish

Uusi tietosanakirja / Päätoimittaja: Veli Valpola. [4. painos]. Helsinki : Tietosanakirja, [1960–66]. 24 v. : ill. **AB39**

1st ed., 1931–39, had title *Iso tietosanakirja*.

Largest of the Finnish encyclopedias (more than 250,000 entries). A good general work, well printed and with numerous maps and illustrations. Signed articles; includes biographies of living persons. Final volume is an index.

§ A more recent work designed for the home market is *Kodin Suuri tietosanakirja* (Espoo : Weilin & Göös, 1975–80. 15 v.). AE21.I72

French

Encyclopaedia universalis. [3rd ed.]. Paris : Encyclopaedia Universalis France, c1990. 30 v. : ill. **AB40**

1st ed., 1968–74; [2nd ed.], 1985–88.

Contents: v. 1–23, A–Z; v. 24–26, Symposium; v. 27–30, Thesaurus-index.

Vols. 1–23 contain some 5,000 extended articles on all topics, more than 1,000 of which are new to this edition. The "Thesaurus-index" consists of shorter articles, providing brief factual information. The "Symposium" has nearly 200 essays on recent world developments, and current social, economic, and demographic statistics for all nations.

A 2-v. supplement to the 1st ed. was published in 1980, and a 2nd suppl., also 2 v. (called v. 21–22 of the 1st ed.), was published 1984–85. Another 2-v. suppl. was published in 1990, incorporating new information from the 3rd ed. of the encyclopedia. This can serve as either the 3rd suppl. to the 1968–74 ed., or as the 1st suppl. to the 1985–88 ed. The purpose is to allow libraries to have current information without having to buy a new edition every few years.

Universalia : les événements, les hommes, les problèmes en 1973– . (1974– . Paris : Encyclopaedia Universalis, 1974– . Annual).

At head of title: Encyclopaedia universalis.

A series of yearbooks supplementing *Encyclopaedia universalis*. Each volume in five sections: (1) La marche du temps (a brief summary of the year's events chronologically presented); (2) Points d'histoire (essays on contemporary events and problems); (3) Thèmes et problèmes (alphabetically arranged articles on events, countries, personalities, and special topics); (4) Vies et portraits (obituary notes on figures who died during the year covered); (5) Statistiques pour l'année (graphs, tables, and explanatory texts).   AE25.E3

Encyclopédie : ou Dictionnaire raisonné des sciences, des arts et des métiers, par une société des gens de lettres / mis en ordre & publié par m. Diderot; & quant à la partie mathématique, par m. d'Alembert. Paris : Briasson, [etc.], 1751–65. 17 v.
                                                            AB41
Repr.: Stuttgart : F. Frommann Verlag, 1969. 35 v. incl. suppl. and indexes.
Publ. in various eds. (e.g., Lausanne ; Berne : Sociétiés Typographiques, 1780–82. 36 v.).
Often cited as *Diderot.*
The famous 18th-century French encyclopedia, with emphasis on the arts, sciences, and mechanical trades, reflecting the philosophical concepts of the time. The articles contributed by Diderot are reprinted as v. 5–8 of Diderot's *Oeuvres complétes* (Paris : Hermann, 1975–).
Supplement and indexes:
(1) *Supplément á l'Encyclopedie* ... (Amsterdam : M. M. Rey, 1776–77. 4 v.).
(2) *Recueil de planches, sur les sciences, les art libéraux, et les arts méchaniques, avec leur explication* ... (Paris : Briasson, 1762–72. 11 v.).
(3) *Suite du Recueil des planches* ... (Paris : Panckoucke, 1777. 22 p.).
(4) *Table analytique et raisonnée des matieres contenues dans les XXXIII volumes in-folio du Dictionnaire ... et dans son supplément* ... (Paris : Panckoucke, 1780. 2 v.).

Grand dictionnaire encyclopédique Larousse. Paris : Libr. Larousse, 1982–85. 10 v. (11038 p.) : ill. (some col.).   **AB42**
Cover title: *GDEL.*
A 10-v. encyclopedic dictionary based on *La grande encyclopédie* (AB45), with more than 190,000 short articles. Includes some 25,000 illustrations and many bibliographies. Similar to *Grand Larousse encyclopédique en dix volumes* (AB43) and *Grand dictionnaire universel du XIXe siècle* (AB46), in effect updating them.   AE25.G63

Grand Larousse encyclopédique en dix volumes. Paris : Larousse, [1960–64]. 10 v. : ill.   **AB43**
Based on the series of earlier Larousse encyclopedias, i.e., a dictionary as well as an encyclopedia. Articles are brief, and entries specific. Some articles are based on those in older sets, but many are new or rewritten, information is brought up-to-date, and there are new illustrations and plates, which in general are superior to those previously used. Bibliographies, arranged by encyclopedia entry, are grouped at the back of each volume with *see* references at the ends of the appropriate articles; titles are almost entirely in French.
Largely supersedes *Nouveau Larousse illustré* (1898–1907. 8 v.) and *Larousse du XXe siècle* (1958. 6 v.).
———. *Supplément* (Paris : Larousse, [1968]. 918, cvi p. ill.).
Intends to provide information on recent political, social, and cultural events, together with biographical sketches of contemporary figures, many of whom have achieved prominence in recent years or were omitted from the main set. In general, updating does not extend beyond mid-1967, though some 1968 events are recorded. A bibliography of about 100 pages appears at the end of the volume; it is arranged by encyclopedia entry, as in the main set, and includes publications through 1967.
———. *2e supplément* (Paris : Larousse, [1975]. 1 v., unpaged).
Covers events, personalities, etc., of the 1968–75 period.
                                                            AE25.G64

La grande encyclopédie : inventaire raisonné des sciences, des lettres et des arts, par une société de savants et de gens de lettres / sous la direction de Berthelot, Derenbourg, [etc.]. Paris : Lamirault, [1886–1902]. 31 v. : ill.   **AB44**
Secrétaire général: v. 1–18, F. Camille Dreyfus; v. 19–31, André Berthelot.
Vols. 23–31 published by Société Anonyme de La Grande Encyclopédie.

The most important 19th-century French encyclopedia, with authoritative signed articles, excellent bibliographies, and many entries under small subjects. Out-of-date now for sciences, etc., but an excellent authority in many other fields, especially for medieval and Renaissance subjects, and for literature, history, etc., of continental Europe. Very good for French and other continental biographical and gazetteer information. The bibliographies are especially important. Has fewer illustrations and plates than recent English and American encyclopedias.
                                                            AE25.G72

La grande encyclopédie. Paris : Larousse, [1971–78]. 21 v.
                                                            AB45
A wholly new work comprising about 8,000 entries with admitted emphasis on technology and technological advances, the physical and social sciences, and political and social economy. Articles are signed with the initials of contributors. Many up-to-date bibliographies; numerous illustrations (most of them in color); charts; tables. Vol. 21 is an index.
———— *Supplément* (1981. 673 p.) covers events of 1971–76 and *2e supplément* (1985. 584 p.), events of 1977–82, with cross-references to the basic set and the first supplement. Additional supplements are planned at 5-year intervals.   AE25.G69

Larousse, Pierre. Grand dictionnaire universel du XIXe siècle. Paris : Larousse, [1865–90?]. 17 v.   **AB46**
Contents: v. 1–15, A–Z; v. 16, Suppl. A–Z; v. 17, Suppl. A–Z.
A famous encyclopedia, well edited and well written—one of first importance and still useful in many cases. Combines the features of dictionary and encyclopedia, and as an encyclopedia is an extreme example of entry under small subject, including many articles on individual works of literature (e.g., poems, plays, novels, romances, newspapers, periodicals, songs, etc., entered under their titles), and a very large amount of minor biography not included in other general encyclopedias. Gives words and music (melody only) of about 600 songs. Good for questions relating to European literature, biography, and history.   AE25.L32

German

Allgemeine Encyclopädie der Wissenschaften und Künste / von genannten Schriftstellern bearb. und hrsg. von J. S. Ersch und J. G. Gruber. Leipzig : Brockhaus, 1818–89. 167 v. : ill.
                                                            AB47
Contents: 1st sec., A–G. 99 v.; 2nd sec., H–Lig. 43 v.; 3rd sec., O–Phyx. 25 v.
Unfinished. Editors vary, but set is usually referred to as *Ersch und Gruber Encyclopädie.*
A scholarly work particularly useful for biography, bibliography, and geographical information.

Brockhaus Enzyklopädie : in vierundzwanzig Bänden. 19. völlig neu bearbeitete Aufl. Mannheim : F.A. Brockhaus, 1986–94. 25 v. : ill. (some col.). (In progress).   **AB48**
1st ed., *Brockhaus' Koversations-Lexikon* (1796–1808), frequently revised; first postwar ed., 16th, *Der grosse Brockhaus* (1952–63); 17th ed., 1966–81, completely revised; 18th ed., 1977–82, is a revision of the 16th ed.
The most recent revised edition of a standard German encyclopedia, earlier editions of which influenced work on encyclopedias in many countries. Contains 260,000 entries and 33,000 illustrations, many in color. The character of the work remains the same: predominantly short articles on a wide range of topics, inclusion of biographies of living persons, and bibliographies. There are longer articles for countries and major topics. A fine, scholarly work.
———. *Jahrbuch.* (1993– . Leipzig : F.A. Brockhaus, 1994– . Annual).   AG27.B861

Der grosse Brockhaus : in zwolf Bänden. 18. völlig neubearb. Aufl. Wiesbaden : Brockhaus, 1977–1982. 14 v. : ill.
                                                            AB49

1st ed., 1796–1808; frequently revised. Earlier editions called *Brockhaus' Konversations-Lexikon.*

Condensed and updated version of the 17th ed. of the *Brockhaus Enzyklopadie* (AB48). Characterized by short articles on very specific subjects; profusely illustrated, including many small illustrations in text. Articles are unsigned; many have bibliographies which are sometimes quite extensive. Illustrations include good maps, black-and-white and colored plates, many portraits, coats of arms of cities, etc. Includes biographies of living persons.

Briefer encyclopedic works issued by the Brockhaus firm include *Der neue Brockhaus* (6. völlig neubearb. Aufl. 1978–80. 6v.; a 7th ed. began to appear 1984) and *Der Brockhaus* (Völlig neu bearb. Aufl. 1984. 2v.). AE27.G67

Der Grosse Herder : Nachschlagewerk für Wissen und Leben. 5. neubearb. Aufl. von Herders Konversationslexikon. Freiburg : Herder, 1953–56. 10 v. **AB50**
1st ed., 1854–57; 4th ed. 1931–35 in 12 v.
Contents: v. 1–9, A–Z; v. 10, Der Mensch in seiner Welt.
A well-illustrated, well-made general encyclopedia with short articles and little bibliography, written from the Catholic viewpoint.
———. *Ergänzungsband* (1962. 2 v.).
Each of these two volumes includes material supplementary to the main work, and has additional sections on *Die Welt in unserer Zeit:* T. 1, Natur und Technik; T. 2, Geist und Kultur. AE27.H5

Grosses vollständiges Universal-Lexikon aller Wissenschaften und Künste. Halle : J. H. Zedler, 1732–50. 64 v. : ports. **AB51**
Vols. 19–64 ed. by Carl Günther Ludovici.
One of the great encyclopedias. Particularly useful for biography and bibliography of the 16th and 17th centuries.
———. *Nöthig Supplemente* ... (Leipzig, 1751–54. v. 1–4.).
Contents: v. 1–4, A–Caq. No more of the supplement published.
AE27.G7

Meyers enzyklopädisches Lexikon. 9., völlig neu bearb. Aufl. Mit 100 signierten Sonderbeiträgen. Mannheim : Bibliographisches Institut, 1971–81. 29 v. : ill., maps. **AB52**
1st ed., 1840–55.
Contents: Bd 1–25, A–Z; Bd.26, Nachträge; Bd.27, Weltatlas (CL283); Bd.28, Personenregister; Bd.29, Bildwörterbuch, Deutsch-Englisch-Französich.
This is the latest edition in a long line of encyclopedias bearing the name of Meyer and originally published in Leipzig. The 1st–8th eds. (1840/55–1936/42) carried the title (with slight variations) *Meyers Konversations-Lexikon.* (The 8th ed. was incomplete, only 9 v. having been published, and was strongly influenced by Nazi ideology.) The Meyer firm was liquidated in 1945, and the first postwar "Meyers" appeared as *Meyers neues Lexikon* (1961–64 in 8 v., with a 1969 suppl.); a new edition of that title was published 1978–81 (8 v. and atlas).
This edition marks a return to the quality and standards of the 6th and 7th eds. of the Meyer encyclopedias. While brief entries still abound, important topics receive very full treatment, and bibliographies are often extensive and generally up-to-date. Maps and charts accompany country articles, and there are thousands of diagrams and illustrations (both in color and in black-and-white), most of them small, but of high quality. Biographical sketches include living persons. Atlas and index volumes are promised, but are optional purchases.
A *Jahrbuch* series began publication 1974 with a "Berichtszeitraum 1973." The 1978 *Jahrbuch* includes a cumulated index 1974–78. AE27.M6

Greek

Ekpaideutikē Hellēnikē enkyklopaideia : thematikē kai alphavētikē enkyklopaideia. Athens : Ekdotikē Athēnōn, c1983–1992. v. 1–11, 14–15, 20–21, 23–25; in 20 : ill. (some col.). (In progress). **AB53**

Contents: v. 1–9, Pankosmio viographiko lexiko (10 v.), v. 10, Phytologia, v. 11, Zōologia, v. 14–15, Mathēmatika, physikē, chēmeia, v. 20, Pankosmia mythologia, v. 21, Thrēskeies, v. 23–24, Pankosmia historia, v, 25, Hellēnikē historia.
A well-illustrated, thematically arranged general encyclopedia. Some articles have brief bibliographies. To be complete in 35 vols., the last of which will be a general index. AE29.E55

Megalē hellēnikē enkyklopaideia. Ekdosis 2., enēmerōmenē dia symplērōmatōn. Athēnai : Ekdotikos Organismos "Ho Phoinix", [1959–64?]. 24 v. and suppl. v. 1–4. **AB54**
Ed. by Paulos Drandakēs.
1st ed., 1926–34. 24 v.
A general encyclopedia in modern Greek. Many articles are of some length and have bibliographies. Illustrations are poor. A supplement in 4 v. appeared 1959–63(?), and a complete revision of v.10 (on Greece) was published 1964(?). AE29.M42

Neōteron enkyklopaidikon lexikon : methodikē kai systēmatikē sympyknōsis kai eklaikeusis holōn tōn andrōpinōn gnōseōn. [2nd ed.]. Athēnai : Ekdosis tēs Enkyklopaidikēs Epitheōreseōs "Hēlios", [1957–59]. 18 v. : ill. **AB55**
A general encyclopedia in modern Greek, including many long articles as well as short ones, some of them signed. Includes very little bibliography. The poor quality of the paper results in poor reproduction of illustrations. AE29.N4

Hebrew

ha-Entsiḳlopedyah ha-Yiśre'elit ha-kelalit : ḥadashah, maḳifah / [rikuz meda' ṿa-'arikhah, Pozner u-vanaṿ (yo'atsim) be-'e. m.]. Yerushalayim : Keter, c1987–1988. v. 1–3 : ill. (some col.). **AB56**
Title on added t.p.: *The Israeli general encyclopedia.*
Contents: v. 1, A'eginah–hatashah; v. 2, Ṿagner–Natran; v. 3, Saba–Tat-Pituaḥ; v. 4, Yediòn.
A general, well-illustrated encyclopedia, with brief, unsigned entries.
•Machine readable version: *Israeli general encyclopedia* [database] (Jerusalem : C.D.I. Systems, 1993). Available on CD-ROM.
AE30.E515

ha-Entsiḳlopedyah ha-'ivrit : [Encyclopaedia hebraica]. Yerushalayim : Hevrah le-hotsaat entsiḳlopedyot, 709–741 [1949–1985]. 32 v. : ill. **AB57**
Repr.: [Tel Aviv] : Sifriyat póalim, 1988.
A general encyclopedia with articles contributed and signed by outstanding Jewish and non-Jewish scholars. Bibliographies include titles in many languages. Illustrated in black-and-white with occasional color plates. AE30E5

Hungarian

Akadémiai kislexikon / [a szerkesztőség vezetője, Szelle Béla ; főszerkesztők, Beck Mihály, Peschka Vilmos ; szerkesztő, Élesztős László]. Budapest : Akadémiai Kiadó, 1989–90. 2 v. : ill. (some col.). **AB58**
A well-illustrated general encyclopedia, with very brief entries. Particularly useful for biographical information. AE31.A38

Encyclopaedia Hungarica / főszerkesztő, Bagossy László. Calgary : Hungarian Ethnic Lexicon Foundation, 1992. v. 1. (In progress). **AB59**
Contents: v. 1, A–H. DB904.E

Révai nagy lexikona : az ismeretek enciklopédiája. Budapest : Révai Testvérek, 1911–27. 20 v. (v. 21, 1935) : ill. **AB60**

Unsigned articles, the longer ones with bibliographies of some length. Includes biographies of living persons. Illustrations in black-and-white, plus some good color plates; maps. Vol. 19, p. 769–863, and v. 20–21 are supplements.   AE31.R4

Uj magyar lexikon / [Szerkesztette az Akadémiai Kiadó lexi-konszerkesztösége. Szerkesztö bizottság: Berei Andor et al.]. Budapest : Akadémiai Kiadó, [1959–72]. 7 v.   **AB61**

A relatively new work, in dictionary arrangement, with generally brief articles. Strong in geographical and personal names, the latter including contemporaries. Point of view is stated in the preface as Marx-ist-Leninist. No bibliographies. Useful for current information, but does not replace older works. Vol. 7 is a supplement.   AE31.U44

Italian

Dizionario enciclopedico italiano. Roma : Istit. della Enciclo-pedia Italiana, [1955–61]. 12 v. : ill.   **AB62**

An encyclopedic dictionary, giving meanings of words with ety-mologies and examples of usage, and concise encyclopedic articles. These latter are not signed and have no bibliographies, but include a large number of biographies, characters of fiction, titles of individual works of literature, gazetteer information, detailed discrimination of word meanings, etc. Includes abbreviations. Illustrations are excellent, some in color, and more numerous than in many encyclopedias. Excel-lent maps.   AE35.D516

Enciclopedia / [Direzione Ruggiero Romano]. Torino : G. Einaudi, 1977–84. 16 v. : ill.   **AB63**

Half title: Enciclopedia Einaudi.

Offers long, signed articles on fairly broad topics; bibliographies include works in many languages. Following each article is a note on related articles with indication of how they elaborate or supplement the information which precedes. Charts and graphs are included in the arti-cles, but other illustrations are concentrated in sections of plates. Vol. 16 is an index with extensive charts and graphs showing interrelation-ships of topics as well as a conventional alphabetical index.
    AE35.E45

Enciclopedia del novecento. Roma : Istituto della Enciclo-pedia Italiana, [1975–84]. 8 v.   **AB64**

Serves as a complement to *Enciclopedia italiana di scienze, let-tere ed arti* (AB66) offering long, signed articles by an international roster of scholars surveying 20th-century developments on relatively broad topics and issues (e.g., anarchismo, armamenti, arte, astronomia e astrofisica, cattolicesimo, chemioterapia, cinema, consumi, criminal-ità). Bibliographies; charts and graphs; numerous illustrations, some in color.

Enciclopedia europea. [Milano] : Garzanti, [1976–84]. 12 v. : ill.; maps.   **AB65**

Contents: v. 1–11, A–Z; v. 12, Bibliografia, Repertorio, Statis-tiche.

A general encyclopedia. Brief articles under specific headings predominate, but there are numerous long, signed articles. Many illus-trations, small but clearly reproduced and presented in close proximity to the articles concerned. Occasional bibliographic references within articles, but bibliographies are not appended. The final volume in-cludes a classified bibliography.

Enciclopedia italiana di scienze, lettere ed arti. [Roma] : Is-tit. della Enciclopedia Italiana, fondata da Giovanni Treccani, 1929–37. 35 v. : ill.   **AB66**

An important encyclopedia with excellent long articles, many bib-liographies, and a wealth of illustrations of all types, i.e., excellent maps and colored plates, dark sepia plates of unusual quality, and many text illustrations, some of which are almost equal to plates. Some articles have a fascist viewpoint. All articles, even very short ones, are signed. Includes many biographical articles, genealogical ar-ticles containing additional biographies, and biographies of living per-sons. While all subjects are illustrated, the illustrations for localities and landmarks, and particularly for art subjects are most notable; many portraits.

Vol. 36, *Indice* (1939) is a detailed index to the set, including Ap-pendice I.

Supplemented by: —— *Appendice I* (1938. 1147 p.); *Appen-dice II, 1938–48* (2948–49. 2 v.); *Appendice III, 1949–60* (1961. 2 v.); *Appendice IV, 1961–78* (1979–81. 3 v.); *Appendice V, 1979–92* (1991– . [In progress]).

Supplements follow the same basic plan as the main work, i.e., an alphabetical arrangement of signed articles by authorities, with bibli-ographies. Well-illustrated, although the illustrations are neither so plentiful nor so beautifully reproduced as in the main work. Cross-references are used liberally when additions or corrections are made to articles in previous volumes. The final volume in each set includes an analytical index.

The material in a preliminary supplement, publ. 1934–36 cover-ing A-Pavia, was not entirely taken over in *Appendice I*, and therefore the earlier parts should be retained by libraries that received them.
    AE35.E5

Grande dizionario enciclopedico UTET / fondato da Pietro Fedele. 4th ed. [Torino] : Unione Tipografco-Editrice Torinese, 1984–c1991. 20 v.   **AB67**

1st ed., 1933–40; 3rd ed., 1966–79.

Contents: v.1–19, A–Z; v.20, Indici; Atlanti.

A fully revised and expanded edition. A good general encyclope-dia with many short articles and an abundance of good quality illustra-tions, both black-and-white and in color. A high percentage of articles are signed. Some of the longer entries carry quite extensive bibliogra-phies, and even the brief ones often cite one or more works on the sub-ject. Many biographical sketches, including some living persons.
    AE35.G7

Japanese

Ban'yu hyakka dai-jiten. Tokyo : Shôgakukan, 1972–76. 24 v. : ill.   **AB68**

A topically arranged general encyclopedia with entries arranged by Japanese phonetic alphabet within subject fields. Articles are gener-ally on specific topics; some have brief bibliographies. Vol. 21 is an index of some 400,000 entries plus a chronological table; v. 22–24 offer atlases of the world, Japan, and human anatomy.   AE35.2.B35

Dai-Nihon hyakka jiten. Tokyo : Shôgakukan, [c.1967–72]. 23 v. : ill.   **AB69**

Popularly known as *Japonica*.

A richly illustrated general encyclopedia with brief entries for topical subjects, proper names, titles of literary works, etc.; functions also as a dictionary. Includes bibliographies. There are two atlases, a dictionary of art treasures of Japan and the world (v. 20–21), and an index (v. 19) which is, in effect, a single-volume encyclopedia.

§ Kodansha's *Daijiten desuku* (*Encyclopedia of contemporary knowledge*. Tokyo, 1983. 1832 p.) is a one-volume work offering brief articles with color illustrations and good maps.   AE35.2.D3

Heibonsha dai-hyakka jiten = Encyclopedia Heibonsha. Tokyo : Heibonsha, 1984–85. 16 v. : ill.   **AB70**

A successor to the same publisher's *Sekai dai-hyakka jiten* first published 1955–59 and most recently issued 1981 in 37 v. plus a sup-plement, and with yearbooks through 1984.

Consists mainly of short articles, signed but usually without bibli-ographic references. Entries for about 7,000 topics and terms. Black-and-white illustrations.

§ *Dai-hyakka jiten* (Tokyo : Heibonsha, 1931–34. 26 v., with suppls. publ. 1934–50 in 4 v., and an index publ. 1935) is a compre-hensive general encyclopedia of pre-World War II Japan still of inter-est to historians.

Kodansha encyclopedia of Japan. [Tokyo] : Kodansha, [1983]. 9 v. : ill., maps.   **AB71**
A comprehensive survey of Japanese life and culture offering "9,417 entries covering 37 categories of information, from such standard ones as history, literature, art, religion, economy, and geography to less obvious fields, such as science, technology, law, women, folklore, plant and animal life, food, clothing, sports, and leisure."— *Introd.* Represents extensive international scholarly cooperation, with articles contributed by some 680 Japanese and 524 non-Japanese scholars from 27 nations. Bibliographies appended to many articles. Vol. 9 is an index.
§ *Japan : an illustrated encyclopedia* (Tokyo : Kodansha ; N.Y. : distr. by Kodansha America, 1993. 2 v. [1924 p.]). Based on the 1983 *Kodansha encyclopedia*, this compact edition updates the earlier work in a new format designed to reach a wider audience. Color illustrations, extensive chronology of Japanese history, and a bibliography for further reading. Entry words also in Japanese.   DS805.K633

Bibliography

Sogô, Masaki. Jisho kaidai jiten / Masaki Sogô, Haruhiko Asakura. Tokyo : Tokyodo, 1977. 538 p.   **AB72**
A guide to encyclopedias and dictionaries in all subject fields, arranged by title according to Japanese phonetic alphabet, but lacking a subject index.
§ Issued irregularly, *Jiten jiten sôgo mokuroku* (Tokyo : Shuppan nyûsusha) provides a comprehensive, in-print list of dictionaries and encyclopedias published or distributed in Japan; the 1985 volume lists works in print as of June 1984.   Z5849.J3S64

Norwegian

Aschehoug og Gyldendals store norske leksikon / [hovedredaktorer, Olaf Kortner, Preben Munthe, Egil Tveterås]. Oslo : Kunnskapsforl., 1978–1981. v. 1–9, 11–12 : ill. (In progress?).   **AB73**
International in scope, with primarily short articles. Well illustrated; index in each volume.

Aschehougs konversasjonsleksikon. 5. utg. / Red. Arthur Holmesland ... [et al.]. Oslo : Aschehoug, 1968–73. 20 v. : ill.   **AB74**
1st ed. published as *Illustreret norsk konversations-leksikon*, 1907–13. 6 v.; 4th ed. 1954–61. 18 v.
A complete revision of this standard work, adhering to the principles of the previous editions: i.e., short, popularly written articles, all but the briefest of them signed; numerous illustrations (some in color); maps; many biographies, including persons still living; very little bibliography. Particularly strong in contemporary Norwegian biography. Vol. 20 is an index.   AE43.I34

Norsk allkunnebok / redaktør: A. Sudman ... [et al.]. Oslo : Gonna, [1948–66]. 10 v. and atlas. : ill.   **AB75**
The first encyclopedia to be written entirely in the *nynorsk* (*landsmal*) language. Short articles, most of them signed. AE43.N6

Persian

See Farsi.

Polish

Encyklopedia powszechna PWN / [red. nacz. Henryk Bonecki... et al.]. Warszawa : Pa'nst. Wydaw. Naukowe, 1973–1976. 4 v. : ill.   **AB76**
A short-entry encyclopedia that in effect updates *Wielka encyklopedia powszechna PWN* (AB78). There are no bibliographies.
AE53.E57

Orgelbrand, Samuel. S. Orgelbranda Encyklopedja powszechna z ilustracjami i mapami. Warszawa : Orgelbrand, 1898–1912. 18 v. : ill.   **AB77**
Contents: v.1–16, A–Z (supplement included in v.16); v.17–18, Supplement.
Short, popularly written articles; many biographies.   AE53.O6

Wielka encyklopedia powszechna PWN / [Komitet redakcyjny; przewodniczacy: Bogdan Suchodolski]. Warszawa : Państwowe Wydawn. Naukowe, [1962–70]. 13 v. : ill.
AB78
A general encyclopedia of about 82,000 entries, mainly brief articles. Longer articles are signed; many include selective bibliographies. Vol. 13 is an index.
The part of v. 9 dealing exclusively with Poland has been issued separately as *Polska* (Warszawa, 1967. 230 p.).   AE53.W44

Portuguese

Enciclopédia Mirador internacional. São Paulo, Brasil : Encyclopaedia Britannica do Brasil Publicações Ltda., 1993. 20 v. (11,565 p.) : ill. some maps in color.   **AB79**
Spine title: Mirador.
The most up to date Portuguese encyclopedia. Lengthy signed articles include bibliographies and illustrations.   AE37.E487

Grande enciclopédia portuguesa e brasileira : ilustrada com cerce de 15.000 gravuras e 400 hors-textes a cores. Lisboa ; Rio de Janeiro : Ed. Enciclopédia, [1936–60]. 40 v. : ill.
AB80
Issued in parts.
Vols. 37, pt. 2–40, Apêndice.
The standard encyclopedia for Brazil and Portugal, with the emphasis on Portugal. Limited international coverage. Many short dictionary-style entries as well as longer descriptive articles make this an excellent source for the history and culture of Portugal. Most articles lack bibliographies.
———. *Actualizaçaõ* (Lisboa : Ed. Enciclopédia, 1981–87. 10 v.). Less biased toward Portugal. Particularly useful for contemporary biograhical information.

Verbo : enciclopédia luso-brasileira de cultura. Lisboa : Ed. Verbo, 1963–86. 21 v. : ill.   **AB81**
Excellent Portuguese-language encyclopedia. The articles are lengthy and signed, with short bibliographies. Richly illustrated with color photographs and diagrams, including many coats of arms. Emphasis on Portugal and Brazil, but international in coverage.
AE37.V4

Russian

Bol'shaíā sovetskaíā entsiklopedíīā. 3. izd. / glav. red. A. M. Prokhorov. Moskva : Izd. Sovetskaíā Entsiklopedíīā, 1970–78. 30 v. in 31 : ill.   **AB82**

A complete revision. Use of a smaller typeface and more stringent editing result in the lesser number of volumes in this edition. The quality of the work remains at the previous level, and the total number of entries (about 100,000) much the same. As might be expected, emphasis is on achievements in Communist-dominated areas and on those subjects (e.g., philosophy, economics, political science, sociology) that support Soviet ideology. Articles are signed by contributing scholars; bibliographies accompany many articles. Vol. 30 includes a supplement, p. 574–631.

An English translation has appeared as *Great Soviet encyclopedia* (AB87).   AE55.B623

———————— 2. izd. Moskva, [1949]–58. 51 v. : ill.   **AB83**

A new edition of the Soviet encyclopedia, revised and reset, with most of the articles new or rewritten; articles in the 1st ed. (AB84) were signed, in the 2nd they are not; etymological derivations are given much more freely in the 1st ed.; bibliographies are quite extensive and for the most part contain only Russian titles, although for articles on foreign subjects some titles in other languages are occasionally included. Illustrations and maps are more numerous and of better quality in the newer work, and the general makeup of the volume is more attractive.

The main alphabet ends with v. 49; v. 50 is devoted to the U.S.S.R., corresponding to the supplement to the first edition; v. 51 supplements the 2nd ed. as a whole, with some 950 articles, many of which are biographical, and it contains tables of weights and measures, currencies, and foreign words and phrases.

Vol. 50 has been translated into German as *Die UdSSR : Enzyklopädie der Union der Sozialistischen Sowjetrepubliken*, hrsg. W. Fickenscher unter Mitwirkung von H. Becker [et al.] (Leipzig : Verlag Enzyklopädie, 1959. 1104 p.).

————————. *Alfavitnyi ukazatel' ko vtoromu izdaniiu* ([Leningrad, 1960] 2 v.). An alphabetical index to subjects and authors.

Bol'shaíā sovetskaíā entsiklopedíīā / redaktsiei N. I. Bukharina, V. V. Kuibysheva ... [et al.]. Moskva : "Sovetskaíā Entsiklopedíīā", 1926–47. 65 v. : ill.   **AB84**

The most extensive of the Russian encyclopedias, Soviet in treatment, international in scope. Signed articles; extensive bibliographies.

§ *Soiuz sovetskikh sotsialisticheskikh respublik.* (1947. 1946 col., 1xxx p. ill.).

A historical supplement on the U.S.S.R. Classed arrangement, with no index and therefore difficult to use. Does not include government and politics. Chronology, p.-i-xi; bibliography, p. xli-1xxx.

Translated into German as *Enzyklopädie der Union der Sozialistischen Sowjetrepubliken*, hrsg. von S. I. Wawilor [u.A.] (Berlin : Verlag Kultur und Fortschritt, 1950. 2 v. ill.). This includes a personal name index.   AE55.B6

Entsiklopedicheskiĭ slovar' / pod red. I. E. Andreevskago ; izdateli F. A. Brokgauz [Leiptsig], I. A. Efron [S.-Peterburg]. S.-Peterburg : I.A. Efron, 1890–1907. 43 v. : ill., maps, some in color.   **AB85**

Repr.: Moskva : Terra, 1990– .

The great Russian *Brockhaus*, the equivalent of the 11th ed. of *Britannica*. While general articles were translated from German, French, or English, the articles pertinent to Russia were written by Russian scholars and are signed. "This and the 'Granat' are the two most historically important Russian general encyclopedias."—*Slavic studies : a guide to bibliographies, encyclopedias, and handbooks* (Wilmington, Del. : Scholarly Resources, 1993. p. 497).

Entsiklopedicheskiĭ slovar' / T-va "Br. A. i I. Granat' i Ko.". 7. sovershevnopere. izd. Moskva : Br. A. i I. Granat', 1910–48. v. 1–55, 57–58 and suppl.   **AB86**

Vol. 56 not published.

Some volumes have title: *Entsiklopedichesiĭ slovar' Russkogo bibliograficheskogo instituta Granat.*

For notes on publication schedule and content of specific volumes *see*: Isaak Mikhailovich Kaufman, *Russkie entsiklopedii* (AB90), p. 72–78; Karol Maichel, *Guide to Russian reference books* (AA351), p. 68–69; and John S. G. Simmons, *Russian bibliography, libraries and archives* (Columbus : Ohio State Univ. Pr., 1968. 367 p.), p. 61–62.

Uneven in treatment, but occasionally useful for material not included in the other encyclopedias.

Great Soviet encyclopedia : a translation of the third edition. N.Y. : Macmillan ; London : Collier Macmillan, [1973–83]. 31 v. and index.   **AB87**

A translation of the 3rd ed. of *Bol'shaíā sovetskaíā entsiklopedíīā* (AB84), "unannotated and as true as possible to the content and meaning intended by the editors of the original edition in Russian."—*Publisher's foreword.* Means "to convey the scope and point of view of the Great Soviet Encyclopedia and to bring to scholars and others with a serious professional interest in Soviet affairs a primary source through which they can gain a richer knowledge and understanding of the contemporary Soviet Union."

The work was translated on a volume-for-volume basis (only "certain articles that can be classified simply as dictionary or gazetteer entries" were omitted) and articles are arranged within each translated volume according to the English form of the entry or transliterated form of the personal and place names. Thus, while the preponderance of entries in v.1 begins with the letter A, terms such as "Diamond," "Highway," and "Zulu War" are also found in v. 1 because the Russian term begins with "A." (The index noted below makes the latter articles readily findable.) The advantage of this arrangement was that the English translation became available relatively soon after publication of the Russian original. Even so, some updating was deemed necessary, and articles which were substantially changed in this respect are marked as "updated." A complete list (in transliteration) of all articles in the Russian equivalent volume is given, with an asterisk preceding those entries for which the articles are not translated. Bibliographies are carried over into the translation, with Western-language citations given in the original language; Russian citations in transliteration.

Vol. 31 is a translation of the long country article on the U.S.S.R. contained in v. 24^2 of the 3rd ed. of *Bol'shaíā ...* ; additional, up-to-date information has been supplied with the translation.

Review: *Wilson library bulletin* 49: (June 1975): 728–40.

AE5.B5813

Malaíā sovetskaíā entsiklopedíīā / Glav. red. B. A. Vvedenskiĭ. 3. izd. [Moskva] : "Bol'shaíā Sovetskaíā Entsiklopedíīā", [1958–60]. 10 v. : ill.   **AB88**

1st ed., 1928–31.

A 3rd ed. of the shorter Soviet encyclopedia, containing some 50,000 articles as compared with 31,000 in the 2nd ed. (1933–47) of 11 volumes. A general encyclopedia with some emphasis on terms of non-Russian origin.

————————. *Alfavitnyi predmetno-imennoi ukazatel'.* [Index] (3. izd. [Moskva, 1961]. 600 p.).

Novyĭ entsiklopedicheskiĭ slovar' / izdateli F. A. Brokgauz (Leiptsig), I. A. Efron (S.-Petersburg). S.-Petersburg : Brokgauz-Efron, [1912–17?]. 29 v. : ill.   **AB89**

Contents: v. 1–29, A–Otto. No more published.

A revised edition, showing considerable change, of the great Russian *Brockhaus* (AB85). Valuable for historical subjects.   AE55.E62

Bibliography

Kaufman, Isaak Mikhailovich. Russkie entsiklopedii. Moskva, 1960. v. 1.   **AB90**

At head of title: Ministerstvo kul'tury RSFSR. Gosudarstvennaíā ordena Lenina Biblioteka SSSR im. V. I. Lenina.

Contents: v. 1, Obshchie entsiklopediĭ, bibliografiĭa i kratkie ocherki. No more publ.

Provides detailed bibliographic descriptions, with notes and commentary, for Russian encyclopedias. Vol. 1 describes 22 general encyclopedias of the pre-Revolutionary and Soviet periods, indicating the publishing date for each volume of each edition. Z2505.D55K3

Annuals

Bol'shaĭa sovetskaĭa entsiklopediĭa. Ezhegodnik. 1957– . Moskva : Ezhegodnik, 1957– . Annual. **AB91**

Records events, chiefly of the preceding year, by country (the U.S.S.R. and constituent republics, and other countries of the world) and under such headings as international organizations, science and technology, and international cultural events. Each volume contains a biographical directory of persons of various nationalities. A detailed table of contents, but no index. AE55.B64

Spanish

Diccionario enciclopédico abreviado : versiones de la mayoría de las voces en francés, inglés, italiano y alemán y sus etimologías. 6. ed. Madrid : Espasa-Calpe, 1954–55. 7 v. : ill. **AB92**

1st ed., 1940.

A general encyclopedia with, for the most part, brief articles and no bibliography. For many words gives equivalents in French, English, Italian, and German, plus etymologies. Illustrations not clearly reproduced.

———. *Apéndice* (Madrid : Espasa-Calpe, 1965. 1575 p.).

Includes many new entries in addition to updating articles from the main set through 1964. A special section at the end supplies information on new developments as late as Sept. 1965. AE61.D45

Enciclopedia hispanica. Barcelona : Encyclopaedia Britannica Publishers, c1990–91. 18 v. : ill., maps. **AB93**

Contents: v. 1–14, Macropedia; v. I–II [i.e., v. 15–16], Micropedia e índice; [v. 17], Temapedia; [v. 18], Datapedia y atlas.

Divided into Micropedia, a 2 v. ready reference tool; Macropedia, with in-depth articles; Temapedia, with essays on selected topics; and Datapedia, with an atlas and current statistical information for all nations. AE61.E52

Enciclopedia universal ilustrada europeo-americana. Barcelona : Espasa, [1907?–33]. 80 v. in 81 : ill. **AB94**

Often cited as *Espasa*.

Contents: v.1–70 in 71 v., A–Z; Apéndice, v.1–10, A–Z.

A useful encyclopedia for the large reference or special library. It has long articles, bibliographies, good illustrations and maps, and includes short articles on small subjects; especially strong in biography and in gazetteer information. Special features are the many maps (geographical, geological, historical, and statistical); the numerous plans of even small cities; colored plates of uniforms, flags, coins, etc. of each country; and the reproductions of paintings and other works of art (usually given under title, or sometimes under the artist's name). Useful for its large amount of Spanish and Spanish-American biography.

Etymologies are included, and equivalents of words are given in French, Italian, English, German, Portuguese, Catalan, and Esperanto.

———. *Suplemento anual* (1934– . Barcelona : Espasa-Calpe, 1936–).

Volumes cover 1934, 1935, 1936–39 (2 v.), 1940–41, 1942–44, 1945–48, 1949–52, 1953–54, 1955–56, 1957–58, 1959–60, 1961–62, 1963–64, 1965–66, 1967–68, 1969–70, 1972–72, 1973–74, 1975–76, 1977–78, 1979–80, 1981–82.

Arrangement of the supplementary volumes differs from that of the basic work; instead of a straight alphabetical arrangement of all material, articles are arranged alphabetically by large classes, e.g., Agricultura, Biografía, Geografía, Química, etc., with small topics in an alphabetical arrangement under some of these large classes, and a general alphabetical index to all classes and topics at the end of the volume. AE61.E6

Gran enciclopedia Rialp : GER. 5. ed. (revisada). Madrid : Ediciones Rialp, 1989. 25 v. : ill. (some col.). **AB95**

1st ed., 1971–76.

Contents: v. 1–23, A–Z; v. 24, Cartografia, Indices; v. 25, Suplemento, A–Z, 4th ed.

The 1st (1979), 2nd (1981), and 3rd (1984) reprintings were called the 2nd, 3rd, and 4th editions respectively.

A work featuring signed articles with bibliographies. Most articles are of considerable length; few run to less than half a column. Bibliographies emphasize Spanish-language materials. List of contributors and advisory editors (with indication of qualifications) in v.1. Elaborately illustrated with black-and-white and color photos; charts, maps, diagrams.

This edi. follows the format of the 1st ed. and in many cases reprints articles and bibliographies without revision. Vol. 25, called a supplement to the 4th ed., contains substantial articles, with brief bibliographies, emphasizing current geographical, political, and biographical information. The supplement has its own detailed subject index, and contains information not found in the main volumes.

Salvat universal diccionario enciclopédico / [dirección Juan Salvat]. 16a ed. Barcelona : Salvat, 1986. 20 v. : ill. **AB96**

1st ed. publ. under title *Diccionario Salvat*.

Previous eds. have title *Diccionario enciclopédico Salvat universal*.

A medium-sized, general encyclopedia. Articles are usually brief, but some are lengthy; they are unsigned, and include little or no bibliography. Illustrations and maps are good. AE61.D62

Swedish

Focus, uppslagsbok : Almqvist & Wiksells stora illustrerade bildnings- och uppslagsverk. Stockholm : Almqvist & Wiksell, [1958–60]. 5 v. : ill. **AB97**

A general encyclopedia with many short articles and small illustrations. Vol. 5 is an index with a section of synonyms and one of tables of statistics and miscellaneous information. AG45.F6

Nationalencyklopedin : ett uppslagsverk på vetenskaplig grund utarbetat på initiativ av Statens kulturråd / [divisionschef och chefredaktör, Kari Marklund]. Höganäs : Bra böcker, c1989–1993. v. 1–12 : ill. (some col.), some maps in color. (In progress). **AB98**

Contents: v. 1–12, A–Kag.

A new encyclopedia, international in scope. Consists primarily of short entries, some of which are signed and include bibliographies. The quality of the paper and illustrations is excellent, the information up-to-date. AE45.N38

Svensk uppslagsbok. 2. omarb. och utvidg. upplagan. Malmö : Förlagshuset Norden, 1947–55. 32 v. : ill. **AB99**

1st ed., 1929–37. 30 v. and suppl.

An excellent modern encyclopedia edited by a board of specialists; well printed and beautifully bound. Many articles are signed. Bibliographies are scant. Profusely illustrated with pertinent maps, city plans, portraits, and many fine photographs. Contains numerous biographical sketches, including living persons. AE45.S82

Swiss

Schweizer Lexikon 91 : in sechs Bänden. Lucerne : Verlag Schweizer Lexikon, 1992–93. 6 v. **AB100**

Supersedes *Schweizer Lexikon* (Zurich : Encyclios-Verlag, [1945–48]. 7 v.).

Very recent and attractive; international in scope, with excellent coverage of Swiss topics. There are brief articles and numerous color illustrations. Many articles are signed and include short up-to-date bibliographies.   AE27.S39

Turkish

Türk ansiklopedisi. Ankara : Millî Egitim Basimevi, 1946–84. 33 v. : ill., maps.   **AB101**

Vols. 1–4 had title *Inönü ansiklopedisi*; title changed with *fasikül* 34. Vols. 1–16 issued in parts.

Published under the auspices of the Turkish government. International and general in scope, with emphasis on Turkish and Islamic materials. Contains a large amount of biography, including living persons. Articles are usually short, unsigned, and without much bibliography. Illustrations and maps are plentiful.

Yeni Türk ansiklopedisi. [İstanbul] : Ötüken, [1985]. 12 v. : ill. (some col.).   **AB102**

A general encyclopedia, some of whose articles are quite long. While international in scope, the coverage of Turkish topics is particularly detailed. Articles are not signed and there is no bibliography. Well illustrated.   AE75.Y46

FACT BOOKS AND COMPENDIUMS

Drake, Milton. Almanacs of the United States. N.Y. : Scarecrow, 1962. 2 v.   **AB103**

Lists more than 14,000 almanacs published "from 1639 to 1850 … from states east of the Mississippi River, and from Missouri, Arkansas, Louisiana, and Texas; to 1875 for the rest of the states." —*Notes*. Also lists almanacs of the Confederate States of America. Entries are arranged by state and then chronologically and include library locations for copies. Bibliography: v. 2, p. 1374–97. No index.   Z1231.A6D7

Guinness book of records. N.Y. : Sterling, 1956– . Annual.   **AB104**

1st American ed. had title *Guinness book of superlatives*. Other eds. called *Guiness book of world records*.

Publisher varies.

A compendium of information concerning the longest, shortest, tallest, deepest, fastest, etc., in relation to natural features, manmade structures, people, events and achievements (in sports, politics, arts and entertainment), etc., grouped in topical sections (e.g., The human being; The animal and plant kingdoms; The scientific world; The business world). Indexed.

•Machine-readable versions called : *Guiness book of records on CD-ROM; Guinness CDTV disc of records; Guinness disc of records; Guinness multimedia disc of records*. All available on CD-ROM, most updated annually.   AG243.G87

Information please almanac, atlas and yearbook / Planned and supervised by Dan Golenpaul Associates. 1947– . N.Y. : Simon & Schuster, 1947– . Annual.   **AB105**

Publisher varies. Title varies.

An almanac of miscellaneous information, with a general topical arrangement and a subject index. Includes extensive statistical and historical information on the U. S.; chronology of the year's events; statistical and historical descriptions of the various countries of the world; sports records; motion picture, theatrical, and literary awards, etc.; and many kinds of general information. Sources for many of the tables and special articles are noted. A "People" section lists many celebrated

persons, giving profession, place and date of birth, and death date if deceased. Names in this section are not indexed individually in the general index.   AY64.I55

Kane, Joseph Nathan. Famous first facts : a record of first happenings, discoveries, and inventions in American history. 4th ed., expanded and rev. N.Y. : Wilson, 1981. 1350 p.   **AB106**

1st ed., 1933.

Aims to establish the earliest date of various occurrences, achievements, inventions, etc. Dictionary arrangement with many cross-references. Gives brief description or explanation together with the date; some references to sources. This edition "includes more than 9,000 firsts in American history. These pertain to Americans and to events that have occurred in the U.S."—*Pref.* Indexes by years, by days of the month, by personal name, and by geographical location.   AG5.K315

The New York Public Library desk reference. 2nd ed. N.Y. : Prentice Hall General Reference, 1993. 930 p. : ill.   **AB107**

First published in 1989, the *Desk reference* met with mixed reviews by librarians, (see *Choice* 27 [Jan. 1990] : 774). The 2nd ed. has 930 pages of information ranging from household hints to major world philosophers. Although not scholarly (sources are not cited), the *Desk reference* does contain much useful information on popular subjects.

•Available in machine-readable form as part of *Toolworks reference library* [database] (Novato, Calif. : The Software Toolworks, 1991). Available on CD-ROM.   AG6.N49

The people's almanac / ed. by David Wallechinsky and Irving Wallace. N.Y. : Doubleday, 1975. 1478 p. : ill.   **AB108**

In endeavoring to produce "a reference book to be read for pleasure," the editors admit to sacrificing "a small degree of comprehensiveness for detail."—*p.xv*. A general almanac with a good deal of unusual and out-of-the-way information. Contributions are signed (some material is reprinted from indicated sources); suggestions for further reading are sometimes given. Indexed.

Supplemented by:

The people's almanac #2, by Wallechinsky and Wallace (N.Y. : Morrow, 1978. 1416 p.), designed to be consulted alongside the first *Almanac*, hence carries new information, articles, etc., but some headings and subject sections have been carried forward.

The people's almanac #3, by Wallechinsky and Wallace (N.Y. : Morrow, 1981. 722 p.) has further supplementary information and updating.

§ Among the spin-offs from the original *Almanac* are *The book of lists* (1977) and *The people's almanac presents The book of predictions* (1980).   AG106.P46

Whitaker's almanack. 125th ed (1993)– . London : J. Whitaker, 1993– . Annual.   **AB109**

Former title: *An almanack for the year of our Lord*, but generally known as *Whitaker's almanack* through its history. Began publishing 1869.

Particularly strong in statistics of the British Commonwealth, with brief statistics for other countries. Index at front.   AY754.W5

World almanac and book of facts. v. 1– . N.Y. : World-Telegram, 1868– . Annual.   **AB110**

Title varies; publisher varies.

The most comprehensive and most frequently useful of the American almanacs of miscellaneous information. Contains statistics on social, industrial, political, financial, religious, educational, and other subjects; political organizations; societies; historical lists of famous events, etc. Well up-to-date and, in general, reliable; sources for many of the statistics are given. A useful handbook, and one with which reference workers should be thoroughly familiar. Alphabetical index at the front of each volume. Each issue before 1915 has also a short index of notable articles in preceding volumes.

•Available in machine-readable form as part of *Microsoft book-shelf '94* [database] (AB27) and as part of *Infopedia* [database] (AB26).   AY67.N5W7

AC

Language Dictionaries

ENGLISH LANGUAGE

Bibliography

Collison, Robert Lewis. Dictionaries of English and foreign languages : a bibliographical guide to both general and technical dictionaries with historical and explanatory notes and references. 2nd ed. [N.Y.] : Hafner, 1971. 303 p.   **AC1**
1st ed., (1955) had title: *Dictionaries of foreign languages.*
The earlier edition provided historical and critical notes on the general, special, and bilingual dictionaries of the languages of Europe, Asia, and Africa, together with special lists of French, German, Italian, Spanish, Russian, and Scandinavian dialect dictionaries, and an appendix listing technical dictionaries in various languages arranged by subject. The new edition, much revised and updated, adds new chapters on early and modern English-language dictionaries, the Celtic languages, and comparative philology.   Z7004.D5C6

Kister, Kenneth F. Kister's best dictionaries for adults & young people : a comparative guide. Phoenix : Oryx, 1992. 438 p.   **AC2**
Annotations for 300 English-language dictionaries provide consumers with evaluative information to aid in selection of an appropriate dictionary resource. 132 entries describe dictionaries for adults, 168 those for children. The entries range from picture dictionaries for preschoolers to unabridged dictionaries for adults and scholars. Each source reviewed gives: bibliographic citation (including price), purpose, scope, authority, treatment and extent of vocabulary, graphics, additional features, summary of strong and weak characteristics, and comparative notes among similar dictionaries. Author-title-subject index.   PE1611.K57

Loughridge, Brendan. Which dictionary? : a consumer's guide to selected English-language dictionaries, thesauri and language guides. London : Library Association, 1990. 177 p.
                                                        AC3
Evaluating "what seem to be the best and most popular English language dictionaries, thesauri and language guides currently available," (*Introd.*) this work emphasizes publications of the U.K. Annotations provide information on targeted readership, authority, scope, organization, definitions, linguistic information, currency, supplementary material and format.
§ *See also*: Kenneth F. Kister, *Kister's best dictionaries for adults & young people : a comprehensive guide* (AC2).   Z7004.D5L68

Mathews, Mitford McLeod. A survey of English dictionaries. Oxford : Univ. Pr. ; London : Milford, 1933. 123 p. : ill. **AC4**

Repr.: N.Y. : Russell & Russell, 1966.
A historical survey of English dictionaries from earliest times to the 19th century. Also includes chapters on: The historical principle in lexicography, Review of lexicographic methods, and Chief features of some modern dictionaries.   Z2015.D6M4

Murray, James Augustus Henry. Evolution of English lexicography. Oxford : Univ. Pr., 1900. 51 p.   **AC5**
Repr.: College Park, Md. : McGrath, 1970.
An interesting and authoritative survey of the history and development of English dictionaries.   PE1611.M9

O'Neill, Robert Keating. English-language dictionaries, 1604–1900 : the catalog of the Warren N. and Suzanne B. Cordell collection. N.Y. : Greenwood, 1988. 480 p. (Bibliographies and indexes in library and information science, no. 1).
                                                        AC6
A descriptive bibliography of more than 2,000 titles in the collection at Indiana State University (which includes subject as well as language dictionaries), representing "all but a few of the English language dictionary titles known to have been published prior to 1900."—*Pref.* Arranged by author, with a subject index.   Z2015.D6O53

Schäfer, Jürgen. Early modern English lexicography. Oxford : Clarendon Pr. ; N.Y. : Oxford Univ. Pr., 1989. 2 v.
                                                        AC7
Contents: v. 1, A survey of monolingual printed glossaries and dictionaries, 1475–1640; v. 2, Additions and corrections to the OED.
                                                        PE891.S34

Starnes, DeWitt Talmage. The English dictionary from Cawdrey to Johnson, 1604–1755 / DeWitt Talmage Starnes, Gertrude Elizabeth Noyes. Chapel Hill : Univ. of North Carolina Pr., 1946. 299 p. : ill.   **AC8**
Includes a bibliography and census of copies in American libraries of all known editions, p. 228–41.   PE1611.S68

American

The American heritage dictionary of the English language. 3rd ed. Boston : Houghton Mifflin, c1992. 2140 p. : ill. **AC9**
1st ed., 1969; new college ed., 1975; 2nd college ed., 1982.
Offers some 200,000 headwords, printed in boldface, with more than 350,000 senses. The strengths of the dictionary stem from its aim "to provide the user with comprehension and appreciation of the language in a readable manner."—*Introd.* Definitions are readable; etymological information is provided. Biographical and geographical entries are interfiled. Introductory sections treat the history of English and the mathematics of language, and there is an appendix of Indo-European roots. Pronunciation symbols are printed at the bottom of each double-page spread. Illustrations (mostly photographs or line drawings) appear in the margins throughout.
•Available in machine-readable form as part of *Microsoft book-shelf '94* [database] (AB27).   PE1628.A623

Funk & Wagnalls new international dictionary of the English language. Comprehensive ed. Chicago, Ill. : J. G. Ferguson Publ. Co., c1987. 2 v. (1930 p.) : ill., plates.   **AC10**
1st ed., 1893, had title *Standard dictionary. Funk & Wagnalls new standard dictionary,* first publ. 1913 (title varies), was a thorough revision of the 1893 edition, reset and printed from new plates throughout. Later issues or reprints of this edition show changes in the plates, insertion of new words, etc.; e.g., issues published since World War II include some new words inserted in their proper alphabetical place by cutting out or compressing old material, and recent editions include a supplement of new words.
Contents: (1) Dictionary, including in one alphabet all ordinary dictionary words and also the various proper names, i.e., biographical, geographical, mythological, biblical, etc.; Supplement of new words

and additional meanings, p. xxxvi–lxix; (2) Appendix: Disputed pronunciations, Rules for simplified spelling, Foreign words and phrases, Statistics of population.   PE1625.S7

New Century dictionary of the English language : based on matter selected from the original Century dictionary and entirely rewritten, with the addition of a great amount of new material / ed. by H. G. Emery and K. G. Brewster; revision ed., Catherine B. Avery. N.Y. : Appleton-Century-Crofts, [1963]. 2 v. (2832 p.).   **AC11**
   1st ed., 1927. Frequently reprinted without change.
   Title page note: With supplements of synonyms and antonyms, foreign words and phrases, biographical names, geographical names, etc.
   Not a revision of *Century dictionary and cyclopedia* (Rev. and enl. ed. N.Y. : Century, 1911. 12 v.), but a much smaller work including a smaller vocabulary selected from *Century* with new definitions and a different selection of quotations. More than 160,000 entries with more than 12,000 illustrative quotations.   PE1625.C4

The Random House dictionary of the English language / Stuart Berg Flexner, ed. in chief. 2nd ed., unabridged. N.Y. : Random House, c1987. 2478, 32 p. : ill. (some col.).   **AC12**
   1st ed., 1966.
   "Expanded by some 50,000 new entries and 75,000 new definitions. Sample sentences, Usage notes, Synonym Studies, Synonym and Antonym Lists, illustrations and locator maps have also been increased in number."—*Pref. to the 2nd ed.* This edition also indicates the dates words entered the vocabulary, identifies American words, and provides specific regional labeling for American dialects. Geographic and the somewhat eclectic biographical entries are interfiled with other terms. A supplement includes concise French, Spanish, Italian, and German dictionaries; a style manual; lists of words commonly confused and misspelled; and a world atlas.
   The illustrative sentences are not actual quotations but were written by the staff. The example from the publicity brochure illustrating "broadcast" as an adverb ("The vital news was sent broadcast to inform the entire nation") might make some users regret this policy.
   Unlike the 1st ed., this edition is completely descriptive, attempting to reflect the language as the editors believe it is actually used—an approach that has not found universal favor. The reviewer in *New York times book review*, Jan. 3, 1988, 8–9 concludes that "This dictionary is depressingly, even resolutely, antiliterary. If users want to use English with grace, power and precision ... this work is not for them."
                                                         PE1625.R3

Webster's new international dictionary of the English language : utilizing all the experience and resources of more than one hundred years of Merriam-Webster dictionaries / William Allan Neilson, ed. in chief; Thomas A. Knott, gen. ed.; Paul W. Carhart, managing ed. 2nd ed., unabridged [revised and reset]. Springfield, Mass. : Merriam, 1961. cxxxvi p., 3194 p. : ill.   **AC13**
   1st ed. of *Webster's dictionary*, 1828; *New international*, 1909; 2nd ed. of *New international*, 1934. Later printings show some changes and corrections in plates, mainly in spelling, punctuation, or pronunciation, but in some cases adding new information or revising the treatment. In 1939 a "New words" section was added at the front of the book, p. xcvii–civ; in 1961, this section was called "Addenda section," p. xcvii–cxxxv. It includes several thousand new words or words used with new or different meanings, including scientific and technical terms, slang, abbreviations, etc.
   Contents: (1) Dictionary, including in the same list both the usual dictionary words and also foreign phrases, abbreviations, proverbs, noted names of fiction, and all proper names except those in the biographical and geographical lists; (2) Appendix: (a) Abbreviations, (b) Arbitrary signs and symbols, (c) Forms of address, (d) Pronouncing gazetteer, (e) Pronouncing biographical dictionary. In addition to the foregoing, the "Reference history" edition contains a separately paged supplement "Reference history of the world" by A. B. Hart, c1934.
   The oldest and most famous American dictionary, well rounded, with no marked specialization or bias, ably edited, reliable, and noted

particularly for the clearness of its definitions. A special feature introduced in the 1909 edition and continued in the 2nd ed. (1934) is the divided page, containing in the upper part the main words of the language and in the lower part, in finer print, various minor words, e.g., different kinds of cross-references, reformed spellings, such biblical proper names as are entered only to show pronunciation, a few obsolete words and a few extremely rare words, and foreign-language quotations, proverbs, and longer phrases. Other special points to remember in using the work are: definitions given in historical sequence; pronunciation indicated by Webster phonetic alphabet (not by the international phonetic system); hyphenization indicated by single hyphen, division of syllables by either accent or centered period. Vocabulary claimed is "600,000 vocabulary entries."   PE1625.W3

Webster's third new international dictionary of the English language, unabridged / ed. in chief: Philip Babcock Gove and the Merriam-Webster editorial staff. Springfield, Mass. : Merriam, 1961. 2662 p. : ill.   **AC14**
   "A completely new work, redesigned, restyled and reset."—*Pref.* Vastly different from the 2nd ed. (AC13); it was probably the most controversial reference book of the generation, both attacked and defended in the newspaper and periodical press. Because of its departures from accepted dictionary practices thorough familiarity with the introduction is essential to efficient use of the text. A few of the major points to be observed are:
   Usage: This edition presents the language as currently *used*, with a novel concept of acceptability of usage, construction, pronunciation, etc.; therefore, much is included, often without qualification, which (particularly at the time of the work's original publication) was regarded by many as colloquial, vulgar, or incorrect.
   Scope: Some 100,000 new entries appear, with new scientific and technical terms especially well represented, but the total has been reduced from 600,000 to 450,000, meaning that many obsolete and rare words have been dropped; the divided page system has been abandoned; abbreviations are included in the main alphabet; the gazetteer and the biographical dictionary have been dropped; all proper nouns have been excluded, although proper adjectives remain, all in lower case. An 8-page "Addenda" section of new words was added to the 1966 printing; that section was increased to 16 pages in 1971, to 32 in 1976, to 48 in 1981, and to 56 in 1988.
   Treatment of words: Individual definitions are generally clear and to the point; meanings are given as before, chronologically, with eager usage first; etymologies have been expanded; pronunciations are given as used in "general cultivated conversational usage as well as in formal platform speech"; regional pronunciations are also frequently shown; indication of pronunciation is given by a newly devised system with the key only in the introduction, not on each page; the devices to indicate word division, stress, and hyphenization have been revised and are explained and illustrated in the introduction; punctuation and indentation are at a minimum.
   Quotations: Illustrative quotations are abundant, updated, and almost exclusively from recent sources, many of them popular. Citations are to author only.   PE1625.W36

Desk dictionaries

American college dictionary / Clarence L. Barnhart, ed. in chief; Jess Stein, managing ed.; assisted and advised by 355 authorities and specialists. N.Y. : Random House, 1962. 1444 p. : ill.   **AC15**
   1st ed., 1947; 1965 printing called "Newly revised" on dust jacket, but pagination unchanged.
   A modern, desk-size dictionary designed to provide an accurate guide to current usage. All entries are in one alphabet, including proper names of persons and places, abbreviations, foreign phrases, inflected forms of words in which the stem is changed, etc. Pronunciation is indicated by the "traditional textbook key," given on the endpapers and in abbreviated form at the bottom of every other page. Definitions are given in reverse chronological order, modern usage first. Etymologies follow. Typography is particularly good.   PE1628.A55

The American heritage illustrated encyclopedic dictionary. Boston : Houghton Mifflin, c1987. 1920 p. : ill. (some col.).
AC16

Offers definitions, etymologies, usage notes, illustrative quotations, and synonyms for some 200,000 words "with special emphasis on North America."—*Pref.* Includes geographical and biographical entries. Also published in 2 v. as *Reader's Digest illustrated encyclopedic dictionary* (Pleasantville, N.Y. : Readers Digest Association, 1987).
PE1628.A624

Merriam-Webster's collegiate dictionary. 10th ed. Springfield, Mass. : Merriam-Webster, c1993. 1559 p. : ill. **AC17**

1st ed., 1893.

Frequently reprinted.

9th ed., 1983, had title: *Webster's ninth new collegiate dictionary.*

The 10th ed. draws on *Webster's third new international dictionary*, unabridged (AC14), as does its predecessor, and on the collection of 14.5 million citations maintained by the publisher.

The format of entries within the dictionary has changed little. Pronunciation is indicated by diacritics and a phonetic transcription, a brief table of which is given at the bottom of each right-hand page. Etymologies are given at the beginning of each entry, and the date of first use follows, in most instances. Definitions appear in chronological order, the most recent sense or meaning coming last. Notes on synonyms discriminate from one another words of closely associated meaning. Illustrative quotations, though not dated, occur frequently. Trademarks or service marks are labeled, as are regional, dialectical, archaic and obsolete terms; selected abbreviations are included in the alphabet. Appended are sections for abbreviations and symbols for chemical elements, foreign words and phrases, biographical and geographical names, and signs and symbols.
PE1628.M36

Oxford American dictionary / ed. by Eugene H. Ehrlich and others. N.Y. : Oxford Univ. Pr., 1980. 816 p. **AC18**

Issued in paperback (N.Y. : Avon Books).

Based on *Oxford paperback dictionary* (comp. by Joyce M. Hawkins. Oxford ; N.Y. : Oxford Univ. Pr., 1979), but using American lexicographers and editors. "It has been compiled for everyday use in home, school, office, and library. It emphasizes concise and precise definitions presented in a straightforward way. It does not use synonyms to define words unless they help distinguish shades of meaning. It supplies the most common current meanings, spellings, and pronunciations. All spellings and pronunciations are American unless otherwise labeled."—*p. xvi.*

A review in *Library journal* 105 (1 Nov. 1980): 2318, notes that the dictionary's "appended matter is scant, etymologies are few, and its treatment of pronunciation leaves much to be desired. It is the body of the work which is important to most readers, however, and in this major respect it is highly recommended."
PE2835.O9

Random House Webster's college dictionary. N.Y. : Random House, c1991. 1568 p. : ill. **AC19**

1st ed., 1968, had title *The Random House dictionary of the English language, College edition*; rev. ed., 1975, had title *The Random House college dictionary*. Various reprintings.

A desk dictionary based on the unabridged *Random House dictionary of the English language* (AC12) and following its style. Includes synonyms, etymologies, etc.; proper names and abbreviations appear in the main alphabet. Appendixes include signs and symbols, directories of U. S. and Canadian universities and colleges, English given names, and a brief manual of style. More than 180,000 vocabulary words, including 4,000 biographical and 7,000 geographical entries. Includes historical and literary entries.
PE1628.R28

Webster's new World dictionary of American English / Victoria Neufeldt, ed. in chief ; David B. Guralnik, ed. in chief emeritus. 3rd college ed. N.Y. : Webster's New World ; distr. by Prentice Hall Trade, c1988. 1574 p. : ill. **AC20**

"A major revision of *Webster's new World dictionary*, 2nd college ed."—*verso of t.p.*

Format and arrangement of the prior edition have been retained, but the appendixes now consist of a family tree of Indo-European lan-

guages; a guide to editorial style; and a list of special signs and symbols. Some 5,000 words, mainly from the business and scientific fields, have been added.
PE1628.W5633

Juvenile dictionaries

The American heritage student's dictionary. Boston : Houghton Mifflin, c1986. 992 p. : ill. **AC21**

Intended for students in grades six through nine, the entry list for this dictionary is based on "textbooks, magazines, encyclopedias, workbooks, and other printed materials that are used in schools."—*Introd.* Over 2,000 illustrations.
PE1628.5.A46

Macmillan dictionary for children / Judith S. Levey, ed. in chief. Newly rev. ed., 2nd rev. ed. N.Y. : Macmillan ; London : Collier Macmillan, 1989. 32, 864 p. : col. ill. **AC22**

"Pages 1–832 of this dictionary are published in text edition under the title *Macmillan school dictionary 1*"—*t.p. verso.*

Contains 35,000 entries with 1,100 full color illustrations, 300 word histories, and language notes. Emphasis on nonsexist definitions. Designed for eight- to 11-year old students.
PE1628.5.M27

Scott, Foresman advanced dictionary / [comp.] by E. L. Thorndike, Clarence L. Barnhart. Glenview, Ill. : Scott, Foresman, c1988. 26, 1302 p. : ill. **AC23**

Prior ed. publ. 1979.

Designed for mature junior high and high school students. Contains 100,000 words, including 18,000 etymological studies. "Special care has been taken to update geographical and biographical entries."—*Pref.*
PE1628.5.T49

Scott, Foresman beginning dictionary / by E. L. Thorndike, Clarence L. Barnhart. Glenview, Ill. : Scott, Foresman, c1988. 770 p. : ill. **AC24**

Prior ed. publ. 1979.

Designed for lower elementary grades. Definitions may include example sentences for usage. One word for each two pages is highlighted with a word history section. A reference section contains maps, facts about states and presidents, and information about the earth. Illustrated.
PE1628.T64

Scott, Foresman intermediate dictionary / By E. L. Thorndike, Clarence L. Barnhart. Glenview, Ill. : Scott, Foresman, c1988. 1098 p. : ill. **AC25**

Prior ed. publ. 1983.

Designed for middle grades; "all material has been selected to reflect the pluralism in our society, and at the same time to avoid unfortunate stereotypes."—*Pref.* Includes 1,800 etymologies.
PE1628.5.S36

Webster's intermediate dictionary. Springfield, Mass. : Merriam-Webster, c1986. 14a, 943 p. : ill. **AC26**

Contains about 65,000 entries with 1,000 pictoral illustrations and 2,500 etymologies for junior high and middle school students. The entries were selected "chiefly on the basis of their occurrence in textbooks and other school materials."—*Pref.* Includes abbreviations, symbols for chemical elements, and biographical, biblical, and mythological names.
PE1628.5.W387

Webster's new World children's dictionary / Victoria Neufeldt, ed. in chief ; Fernando de Mello Vianna, project ed. Cleveland : Webster's New World, c1991. 16, 896 p. : col. ill. **AC27**

Written and produced by the lexicographical staff that prepared *Webster's new World dictionary* (AC20). For students aged eight to 11 years. Provides 13,700 main entry words.
PE1628.5.W3877

The World book dictionary / ed. by Clarence L. Barnhart, Robert K. Barnhart. Prep. in cooperation with World Book, Inc. Chicago : World Book, [1983]. 2 v. (124, 2430 p.) : ill.
AC28
1st ed., 1963; frequently revised (latest major revision 1976). An ed. with 1991 imprint date is identical to 1983 ed.

Designed as a companion to *World book encyclopedia* (AB22) and meant to be "useful to all members of the family and to students of various ages."—*p. 4.* About 225,000 terms and some 3,000 illustrations; definitions are clear and easy to understand, with careful consideration for younger readers; most common meanings are presented first. Examples of usage are frequently given. Pronunciation is indicated; a brief pronunciation key appears at the bottom of each right-hand page. Various educational materials, charts and lists occupy a separately paged section preceding the dictionary proper.
  ●Available in machine-readable form as part of *World book information finder* [database] (AB28).　　　PE1625.W73

English

Early modern English : additions and antedatings to the record of English vocabulary, 1475–1700 / Richard W. Bailey, ed. Hildesheim : Olms, 1978. 367 p.　　　**AC29**
Concerned with "words and senses ... overlooked or omitted by the editors of the *Oxford English Dictionary*" (*Pref.*), thus serving as a supplement to that work for the early modern period. For each word an excerpt illustrating usage is given, together with citation to the source. Appendixes: Early modern English texts cited; Secondary sources consulted.

The listings here "form an addition to the citations already published as part of *Michigan early modern English materials* [Ann Arbor : Xerox University Microfilms, 1975. 2 v.] and generally follow the editorial conventions of that work."—*Introd.*　　　PE891.E3

Murray, James Augustus Henry. New English dictionary on historical principles : founded mainly on the materials collected by the Philological Society. Oxford : Clarendon Pr., 1888–1933. 10 v. and suppl.　　　**AC30**
Contents: v. 1–10, A–Z; Supplementary volume: Historical introduction, p. vii–xxvi; Supplement A–K, 542 p.; L–Z, 325 p.; List of spurious words, p. 327–30; Bibliography, i.e., list of books most commonly quoted in the Dictionary, 91 p.

Known variously as *Murray's dictionary*, *New English dictionary*, and *Oxford dictionary*. Often cited as *NED* or *OED*. For history of the work *see* its Supplementary volume, p. vii–xxvi.

The great dictionary of the language, compiled on a different plan from any of the older standard English dictionaries and serving a different purpose. It is based upon the application of the historical method to the life and use of words, and its purpose is to show the history of every word included from the date of its introduction into the language, giving differences in meaning, spelling, pronunciation, usage, etc., at different periods of the last 800 years, and supporting such information by numerous quotations from the works of more than 5,000 authors of all periods, including all writers before the 16th century and as many as possible of the important writers since then. The vocabulary is very full, and is intended to include all words now in use or known to have been in use since 1150, excluding only words which had become obsolete by 1150. Within these chronological limits, aims to include: (1) all common words of speech and literature, and all words that approach these in character, the limits being extended further into science and philosophy than into slang and cant; (2) in scientific and technical terminology, all words English in form except those of which an explanation would be intelligible only to a specialist, and such words not English in form as are in general use or belong to the more familiar language of science; and (3) dialectal words before 1500, omitting dialectal words after that date except when they continue the history of a word once in general use, illustrate the history of a literary word, or have a literary currency.

Words included are classified as: (1) main words, 92) subordinate words, and (3) combinations; information for all main words is entered under the current modern or most usual spelling, or, if obsolete, under the most typical later spelling, with cross-references from all other forms. Information given about each main word is very full and includes: (1) identification, with (a) usual or typical spelling, (b) pronunciation, indicated by respelling in an amplified alphabet or, in case of obsolete words, by marking of stress only, (c) grammatical designation, (d) specification, e.g., musical term, etc., (e) status, if peculiar, e.g., obsolete, archaic, etc., (f) earlier spelling, (g) inflexions; (2) morphology, including derivation, subsequent form history, etc.; (3) signification, arranged in groups and historically, with marking of obsolete senses, erroneous uses, etc; (4) quotations, arranged chronologically to illustrate each sense of a word, about one quotation for each century, given with exact reference. The complete work has a total vocabulary of 414,825 words and includes 1,827,306 quotations.

The most important use of this dictionary is for historical information about a word, but it has many other secondary uses, e.g., while not intentionally encyclopedic, it has a good deal of encyclopedic information including some not given in other dictionaries, and while not specializing in slang, it does include many colloquial and slang words, Americanisms, etc. Where such words are included, the information is often better than in the special slang dictionaries.

The supplementary volume is a partial, not a complete, supplement, in that it does not comprise all supplementary material collected since the publication of the first parts of the original work but is limited in the main to new words and senses of the 50 years preceding publication, with inclusion of: (1) other items of modern origin and currency omitted in the main work; (2) earlier evidence of American uses; and (3) some correction or amplification of previous definitions to bring the work into line with more recent research. Recent words added include scientific and technical terms, colloquialisms, and slang—American, British, and colonial—and a larger proportion of proper names than in the original work. This volume is superseded by the multi-volume supplement which began to appear in 1972.

New English dictionary, large and comprehensive though it is, is necessarily selective, and could not include all words for the whole period covered or even all material collected during the compilation of the work. Since the completion of the dictionary in 1928, four period and regional dictionaries on the same extensive plan, either have been published or are in course of publication to supplement the *New English dictionary* by including words, uses, illustrations, etc. which could not be included in that dictionary. These are: *Middle English dictionary* (AC175), *Dictionary of American English on historical principles* (AC150), *Dictionary of the older Scottish tongue* (AC164), *Scottish national dictionary* (AC166).　　　PE1625.M7

————— The shorter Oxford English dictionary on historical principles / prep. by William Little, H. W. Fowler and Jessie Coulson ; rev. and ed. by C. T. Onions. 3rd ed. compl. reset with etymologies by G. W. S. Friedrichsen and with revised addenda. Oxford : Clarendon Pr., [1973]. 2672 p.
AC31
1st ed., 1933; 3rd ed., 1944, repr. with rev. addenda, 1956; frequently repr. with revisions. Also publ. in 1 v. as *Oxford universal dictionary* (1955. 2515 p.).

An authorized abridgment of *New English dictionary,* (AC30) which, while in the main an abridgment, also includes some additional material, especially new words too recent to have been included in the original work, or older words omitted there, with some later illustrative quotations. Important, therefore, in the library which already has the larger work, as well as in the small library which has not been able to afford the complete *Oxford English dictionary* (AC33).

"The aim of this Dictionary is to present in miniature all the features of the principal work. It is designed to embrace not only the literary and colloquial English of the present day together with such technical and scientific terms as are most frequently met with ... but also a considerable proportion of obsolete, archaic and dialectal words and uses."—*Pref.*

The reset version of 1973 is notable for two features: (1) etymologies of the words have been revised; and (2) there is a new Addenda section "drawn chiefly from the material assembled for the new Supplement to the *O.E.D.* ... , and presenting notable accessions to the English language in the period since the *O.E.D.* appeared."—*Publ. note.*　　　PE1625.L53

The Oxford English dictionary : being a corrected re-issue with an introduction, supplement, and bibliography of A new English dictionary on historical principles, founded mainly on the materials collected by the Philological Society and edited by James A. H. Murray [and others]. Oxford : Clarendon Pr., 1933. 13 v. **AC32**

Vol. 13, "Supplement and bibliography," unnumbered.

A reprint, on thinner paper and with somewhat smaller margins, from the plates of the original edition with the correction of such typographical errors as had been discovered.

In 1895 "a new name for the Dictionary was introduced, though no change was made on the title-page. On the cover of the section containing *Deceit* to *Deject* ... above the title, appeared for the first time the designation 'The Oxford English Dictionary,' which was repeated on every section and part issued after 1 July of that year. The new name, being more distinctive than the old, has steadily come more and more into use, and the abbreviation O.E.D. tends to supplant N.E.D. although the latter is still frequently employed."—*Historical introd., p. xx.* PE1625.N53

The Oxford English dictionary. 2nd ed. / prep. by J. A. Simpson and E. S. C. Weiner. Oxford : Clarendon Pr. ; Oxford : N. Y. ; Oxford Univ. Pr., 1989. 20 v. **AC33**

1st ed., 1888–1933; *Supplement,* v. 1–4, 1972–86.

Combines and partially revises Sir James Murray's *New English dictionary* and its *Supplement.* Adds some 5,000 words, mainly in the scientific and technical fields. Although the 2nd ed. omits the words "on historical principles" from the title, the purpose remains the same as that of the 1st ed. (*see* AC30). Briefly, both editions provide the history and development of English words through the last 800 years, excluding only those words which were obsolete by 1150, illustrating them with numerous quotations from the works of some 5,000 authors. A 143-page bibliography of the most frequently quoted works may be found at the end of v. 20.

The 2nd ed. reprints, with minor changes, the "Historical introduction" from the 1933 ed., but does not reprint Sir James Murray's preface nor the prefaces to the *Supplements.* The 2nd ed. has also eliminated Murray's unique pronunciation alphabet in favor of the International Phonetical Alphabet; in many cases pronunciations have been updated. An extensive and generally favorable review in *The review of English studies* n.s. 41 (Feb. 1990) : 76–88 notes that changes and additions to entries are not indicated, and that "the etymological sections leave much to be desired. We are never sure what belongs to the dictionary of 1882–1932, and what to the edition of 1989." After noting that some of the quotations have been dropped (and many added), the reviewer states that "a learned library must not sell its *OED* [1st ed.] and *Supplements.*"

———. *Additions,* ed. by J. A. Simpson and E. S. C. Weiner. Oxford; N.Y. : Oxford Univ. Pr., 1993– .

•Machine-readable version: *Oxford English dictionary on compact disc, 2nd ed.* [database] (Oxford : Oxford Univ. Pr.).

Available on CD-ROM, updated at irregular intervals.

A single CD contains the more than half a million searchable headwords from the 20-volume printed edition of the *OED.* Unlike the 1st CD-ROM ed., this version allows users to search the complete text of the dictionary and permits word searches to be limited to etymology, parts of speech, quotations, or date. Quotation and author searches may be executed as part of a word search or as stand-alone searches. Reading and understanding the manual that accompanies the CD is not required for successfully using the resource; extensive help screens are easy to use. However, the manual does explain precisely how to construct advanced searches. Results of searches may be saved to a field and redisplayed in a later part of the session. Users may also write comments and associate them with an entry; these comment files do not become a permanent part of the file. Results from searches are not text files and may not be edited or printed from the workstation. For this reason, though it is a powerful tool for research, the compact disc version of the *OED* does not replace the printed one. PE1625.O87

A supplement to the Oxford English dictionary / ed. by R. W. Burchfield. Oxford : Clarendon Pr., 1972–86. 4 v. **AC34**

"The vocabulary treated is that which came into use during the publication of the successive sections of the main Dictionary—that is, between 1884, when the first fascicle of the letter A was published, and 1928, when the final section of the Dictionary appeared—together with accessions to the English language in Britain and abroad from 1928 to the present day."—*Pref.* Includes additional uses, earlier and later examples, etc, of words appearing in the main set, together with corrections as in the earlier supplement. Contains approximately 50,000 main words. PE1625.N53

Desk dictionaries

BBC English dictionary / [ed. in chief, John Sinclair]. London : BBC English : HarperCollins, 1992. 1374 p. **AC35**

Includes 1,000 encyclopedic entries about people, places and events as an aid to understanding current affairs. Produced from the Bank of English (70 million words of English from the BBC World Service [radio] and 10 million words from National Public Radio in Washington, D.C.). PE1625.B34

Chambers English dictionary / editors, Catherine Schwarz ... [et al.] ; assistant editors, Pandora Kerr Frost ... [et al.]. Edinburgh : Chambers ; Cambridge ; N.Y. : Cambridge Univ. Pr., c1988. 1792 p. **AC36**

1st ed., 1901, had title *Chambers's twentieth century dictionary of the English language*; previous ed., 1983, entitled *Chambers 20th century dictionary.*

The reference dictionary for the National Scrabble Championships. This edition has added many new scientific and technical terms. Particularly useful for archaic words. Includes etymologies; British emphasis. PE1628.C43

Collins English dictionary. 3rd ed. Glasgow : Harper Collins, 1991. 1791 p. **AC37**

1st ed., 1979; 2nd ed., 1986, had title: *Collins dictionary of the English language.*

Aims to be a "fresh, revised and augmented description of contemporary English" (*Foreword*) for general readers. Coverage of terms from science and technology, life sciences, medicine, physics, chemistry is strong. One alphabetic list includes people and place-names. Cross-references to American and Canadian English. Includes updated geographical information, with special emphasis on unified Germany. PE1628.C548

The concise Oxford dictionary of current English. 8th ed. / ed. by R. E. Allen. Oxford : Clarendon Pr. ; N.Y. : Oxford Univ. Pr., 1990. 1454 p. **AC38**

1st ed. 1911, ed. by H. W. Fowler and F. G. Fowler.

Based on *The Oxford English dictionary,* 2nd ed. (AC33), this excellent desk dictionary shows "profound changes over previous editions."—*Pref.* Among improvements are: use of International Phonetic Alphabet; minimum use of special conventions and abbreviations; and reduced number of nested items. The vocabulary shows a marked emphasis on British English; equivalents for speakers in Africa, America, and Australia are listed but not cross-referenced. The vocabulary of science and technology is current. PE1628.F78C7

Longman dictionary of contemporary English / [ed. dir., Della Summers]. New ed. Harlow, Essex, England : Longman, 1987. F53, 1229, B29 p. : ill. **AC39**

Chart containing grammar codes and pronunciation and spelling table in pocket.

A readable dictionary of contemporary spoken English. The 56,000 entries, many with illustrative sentences, are intended for international English speakers. PE1628.L58

The Oxford encyclopedic English dictionary / ed. by Joyce M. Hawkins and Robert Allen. Oxford : Clarendon Pr. ; N.Y. : Oxford Univ. Pr., 1991. 1767 p. : ill., some maps in color. **AC40**

Scientific and technical vocabulary receive special attention in this dictionary of current English and concise world encyclopedia.

PE1625.O86

Oxford illustrated dictionary / text ed. by Jessie Coulson ... [et al.]. 2nd ed. Oxford : Clarendon Pr., 1975. 998 p. : ill.

AC41

An illustrated dictionary including much encyclopedic material in addition to the usual dictionary information, and various explanatory illustrations usually in the form of line drawings.

Vocabulary is "based on that of the *Concise Oxford dictionary*, and the definitions retain its historical ordering" (*Pref.*), but there is less full treatment of more familiar words in order to give a wider scope to the treatment of things, often by means of illustration. All terms are in one alphabet, including proper nouns, abbreviations, foreign phrases, etc. As far as possible, pronunciation is shown without respelling, by placing symbols over the letters; when respelling is necessary, a phonetic system is used. Little or no etymology.

A useful dictionary, from the English viewpoint.   PE1628.O9

Abbreviations

Acronyms, initialisms & abbreviations dictionary. Ed. 5– . Detroit : Gale, 1976– . Irregular.   **AC42**

1st ed., 1960, had title: *Acronyms dictionary;* 2nd–4th eds., *Acronyms and initialisms dictionary*. Now issued in three volumes, each volume separately titled: v. 1, *Acronyms, initialisms & abbreviations dictionary*; v. 2, *New acronyms, initialisms & abbreviations*; v. 3, *Reverse acronyms, initialisms & abbreviations dictionary*. Each part may be purchased separately. Vol. 1 of each ed. is kept up to date by a periodic supplement designated as v. 2 (i.e., *New acronyms. ...*).

Subtitle, v. 1, 14th ed., 1990: A guide to more than 480,000 acronyms, initialisms, abbreviations, contractions, alphabetic symbols, and similar condensed appellations. Covering aerospace, associations, banking, biochemistry, business, data processing, domestic and international affairs, economics, education, electronics, genetics, government, information technology, investment, labor, law, medicine, military affairs, periodicals, pharmacy, physiology, politics, religion, science, societies, sports, technical drawings and specifications, telecommunications, trade, transportation, and other fields.   P365.A28

De Sola, Ralph. Abbreviations dictionary. Expanded international 8th ed. N.Y. : Elsevier, c1992. 1300 p.   **AC43**

Subtitle: Abbreviations; acronyms; anonyms; appellations; computer terminology; contractions; criminalistic and data-processing terms; eponyms; geographical equivalents; government agencies; historical, musical and mythological characters; initialisms; medical and military terms; nations of the world; nicknames; parts of the world; short forms; shortcuts; signs and symbols; slang; superlatives; winds of the world; zip coding; zodiacal signs.

1st ed., 1958; 5th ed., 1978.

Anonyms, contractions, eponyms, geographical name equivalents, nicknames and short forms are interfiled with the abbreviations and acronyms. Numerous special lists (e.g., airlines of the world; astronomical constellations, stars and symbols; birthstones; diacritical and punctuation marks; numbered abbreviations) are appended.   PE1693.D4

The Oxford dictionary of abbreviations. Oxford : Clarendon Pr. ; N.Y. : Oxford Univ. Pr., 1992. 397 p.   **AC44**

A well-conceived and well-executed dictionary that emphasizes British English but includes abbreviations from other English-speaking countries such as Canada, the U.S., and India. Moreover, it offers abbreviations from other languages that travelers or those with contacts abroad might encounter. It indicates levels of usage from colloquial to specialized abbreviations used in scientific and technical fields. Index of symbols.   PE1693.O94

Paxton, John. Everyman's dictionary of abbreviations. Repr. with rev. suppl. London : Dent, [1983]. 393 p.   **AC45**

1st ed., 1974, had title: *Dictionary of abbreviations* (repr. with revisions and suppl. 1981).

Aims "to provide a representative selection of the old and the new ... to serve the purposes of the student and scholar, the administrator, the business man, the exporter and the community of the general reader at home and at work."—*Pref.* With 25,000 entries and a British English slant, it is less complete than Ralph De Sola's *Abbreviations dictionary* (AC43). An unnumbered supplement of eight pages follows the body of the book.   P365.P3

Wall, C. Edward. Abbreviations : the comprehensive dictionary of abbreviations and letter symbols for the computer era. Ann Arbor, Mich. : Pierian Pr., 1984. 2 v.   **AC46**

Contents: v. 1, Abbreviation to word; v. 2, Word to abbreviation.

"The main source ... has been primary documents designed for data processing purposes ... . This is the first major, comprehensive dictionary of abbreviated words for application in the computer era."—*Introd.*   PE1693.W35

Etymology

The American heritage dictionary of Indo-European roots / rev. and ed. by Calvert Watkins. Boston : Houghton Mifflin Co., c1985. 113 p.   **AC47**

A revised and expanded ed. of the "Appendix of Indo-European roots" from *American heritage dictionary of the English language* (1969 ed.; *see* AC9); published as a companion to *American heritage dictionary*, 2nd College ed. (1982).

"Designed and written for the general English-speaking public."—*Pref.* Arranged alphabetically by Indo-European root, with examples of English words derived from that root. Index of English words.   P615.A43

The Barnhart dictionary of etymology / Robert K. Barnhart, ed. ; Sol Steinmetz, managing ed. [Bronx, N.Y.] : H.W. Wilson Co., 1988. 1284 p.   **AC48**

"Traces the origins of the basic vocabulary of modern English. It contains over 30,000 entries ... [and] examines not only the antecedents of modern English, but emphasizes its development, especially from the point of view of American English."—*Explanatory note.* Includes two brief articles (Short history of the English language, and General statement of proto-Germanic forms and Indo-European roots) and glossaries of language names and linguistic terms and of literary works listed in etymologies. The review in *Language* 65 (Dec. 1989) : 848–52 stresses both its scholarship and its accessibility and concludes that it "appears to be the best etymological work now available."   PE1580.B35

Beeching, Cyril Leslie. A dictionary of eponyms. 3rd ed. Oxford ; N.Y. : Oxford Univ. Pr., 1990. 218 p.   **AC49**

1st ed., 1979; 2nd ed., 1983.

Offers 700 descriptions of " 'true' eponymic words which have become part of the language ... and are taken from the names of people who actually exist."—*Introd.* The areas of engineering, horticulture, and botany have been avoided, and eponyms of doubtful origin have been excluded. Subject index.   PE1596.B43

Byrne, Mary. Eureka! : a dictionary of Latin and Greek elements in English words. Newton Abbot : David & Charles, c1987. 224 p.   **AC50**

"Each entry consists of a number of examples derived from a particular Latin or Greek word ... . [Entries] are intended to show the route (sometimes obvious, sometimes tortuous) by which the modern meaning of an English word can be traced back to the basic meaning of its Latin or Greek ancestors."—*Introd.* Arranged by Greek and Latin roots.   PE1582.L3B97

Claiborne, Robert. The roots of English : a reader's handbook of word origins. N.Y. : Times Books, c1989. 335 p.

AC51

An alphabetical listing of Indo-European sources of English words, with illustrative examples, excluding "roots whose only English descendants are scholarly, rare, or archaic."—*Introd.* The compiler used *The American heritage dictionary of Indo-European roots* (AC47) and *The Oxford dictionary of English etymology* (AC58) and has emphasized the evolution from the root to the English word. Includes an index to English words.   PE1580.C56

The concise Oxford dictionary of English etymology / ed. by T.F. Hoad. Oxford ; N.Y. : Oxford Univ. Pr., 1986. 552 p.   **AC52**

This abridged version of *Oxford dictionary of English etymology* (AC58), has some 17,000 headwords as opposed to 24,000. Personal and mythological names, and medical and technical terms have been dropped. "The intention is that each entry should give a concise statement of the route by which its headword entered the English language, together with, where appropriate, a brief account of its development in English."—*Introd.*   PE1580.C66

Eponyms dictionaries index / ed. by James A. Ruffner. Detroit : Gale, [1977]. 730 p.   **AC53**

"A reference guide to persons, both real and imaginary, and the terms derived from their names, providing basic biographical identification and citing dictionaries, encyclopedias, word books, journal articles, and other sources for additional information: includes acts, analyses, awards, axioms, bills, cases, circles, codes, coefficients, collections, commissions, complexes, costumes, diseases, dynasties, effects, equations, expeditions, experiments, forces, formulas, functions, laws, maneuvers, medals, methods, mixtures, organs, paradoxes, phenomena, presses, prizes, processes, ratios, reactions, rebellions, rules, schemes, societies, solutions, styles, syndromes, systems, techniques, tests, theories, trophies, unity, and wars."—*t.p.*

A "1st ed. supplement" was publ. 1984, ed. by Ruffner and Jennifer Mossman.   PE1596.E6

Hendrickson, Robert. The Facts on File encyclopedia of word and phrase origins. N.Y. : Facts on File, c1987. 581 p.   **AC54**

Repr. as: *Henry Holt encyclopedia of word and phrase origins* (N.Y. : Holt, 1990).

Offers an alphabetical listing of some 7,500 words and phrases with definitions and origins. Intended for general readers rather than scholars.   PE1689.H47

——————— Human words : the compleat unexpurgated, uncomputerized human wordbook. Philadelphia : Chilton, [1972]. 342 p.   **AC55**

"Containing herein the true unadulterated stories of more than 3,500 unique and remarkably eponymous personalities: saints and sinners, losers and winners, lovers and hatemongers, murderers and masochists, scalawags and saviors … that have given their names to the language."—*title page.* It is "designed both for the general reader with a love for words and history and as a reference work that should be of particular value to the student."—*Introd.*   PE1596.H4

Klein, Ernest David. A comprehensive etymological dictionary of the English language : dealing with the origin of words and their sense development, thus illustrating the history of civilization and culture. Amsterdam ; N.Y. [etc.] : Elsevier, 1966–67. 2 v.   **AC56**

Also publ. in an unabridged one-volume edition, 1971.

The work of a Czech scholar and linguist. Contains substantially more entries than the *Oxford dictionary of English etymology* (AC58), including origins of mythological and given names and assigning some etymologies not found in the Oxford work. The *Oxford dictionary,* however, will prove adequate in all but the largest collections, and its dating of meanings by century offers a distinct advantage.   PE1580.K47

Morris, William. Morris dictionary of word and phrase origins / William and Mary Morris ; foreword by Isaac Asimov. 2nd ed. N.Y. : Harper & Row, c1988. 669 p.   **AC57**

1st ed., 1977.

Incorporates new material with that previously published in the 1st ed. and the three volumes of the same authors' *Dictionary of word and phrase origins* (N.Y. : Harper & Row, 1962–71). Popular treatment; index.   PE1580.M6

Oxford dictionary of English etymology / ed. by C. T. Onions with the assistance of G. W. S. Friedrichsen and R. W. Burchfield. Oxford : Clarendon Pr., 1966. 1025 p.   **AC58**

Repr. with corrections, 1969.

The first really comprehensive etymological dictionary of the English language since William Walter Skeat's *An etymological dictionary of the English language* (AC62), and sure to be the standard for years ahead. About 24,000 entries. For each entry, pronunciation is given, followed by a selection of meanings or senses in chronological sequence to show the general trend of development; the century in which the word or meaning is first recorded is indicated by a roman numeral. A thoroughly scholarly work, and, despite many space-saving symbols and abbreviations, very easy to use. Offers less information on various individual terms than does Eric Partridge's *Origins* (AC60), but breadth of coverage is much greater.   PE1580.O5

Partridge, Eric. Name into word : proper names that have become common property : a discursive dictionary. London : Secker & Warburg, 1949 ; N.Y. : Macmillan, 1950. 644 p.   **AC59**

Repr. : N.Y. : Ayer, 1977 (called 2nd ed.); Freeport, N.Y. : Books for Libraries Pr., [1970] (called 2nd ed., rev. and enl.).

Common words derived from personal, geographical, and other names, with "discursive" explanations.   PE1583.P35

——————— Origins : a short etymological dictionary of modern English. 4th ed. London : Routledge & Paul, [1966]. 972 p.   **AC60**

1st ed., 1958.

An etymological dictionary of the most common words in modern English. Omits dialect and slang, except in a few instances, and does not include many scientific and technical terms.   PE1580.P3

Rees, Nigel. Why do we say— ? : words and sayings and where they come from. Poole ; N.Y. : Blandford Pr. ; N.Y. : Distr. by Sterling Pub., 1987. (1988 printing). 224 p.   **AC61**

Aims to "sift through the lore and disentangle the misconceptions" (*Pref.*) of many common folk etymologies. Sources are frequently cited. British emphasis.   PE1574.R44

Skeat, Walter William. An etymological dictionary of the English language. New ed., rev. and enl. [4th ed.]. Oxford : Clarendon Pr., 1910. 780 p.   **AC62**

1st ed., 1882; 4th ed. frequently reprinted.

Contents: (1) Dictionary; (2) Appendix: Lists of Prefixes, Suffixes, Homonyms, Doublets, Indogermanic roots; Distribution of words according to languages from which they are derived.

A standard scholarly work giving full histories of more than 14,000 words, with references to sources.

A shorter version is the author's *A concise etymological dictionary of the English language* (New and corrected imprint. Oxford : Clarendon Pr., 1911. 663 p. Repr. 1958). Explanations, etymologies, histories, and quotations are much abbreviated.   PE1580.S5

Webster's word histories. Springfield, Mass. : Merriam-Webster, c1989. 526 p.   **AC63**

Offers one- to two-page articles on the origins and meanings of some 600 words selected "to catch the fancy of all readers, whatever their interests."—*Pref.* The etymology of each entry is represented in the style of *Webster's third new international dictionary* (AC14); however, cross-references are omitted.   PE1580.W35

Weekley, Ernest. Etymological dictionary of modern English. London : Murray ; N.Y. : Dutton, 1921. 1659 col.   **AC64**

Repr. : N.Y. : Dover, 1967.

A popular work, for the general reader rather than for the specialist, giving the histories of the literary and colloquial vocabulary, omitting most scientific terms.

Abridged version:————. *A concise etymological dictionary of modern English* ... (Rev. ed. London : Secker & Warburg ; N.Y. : Dutton, 1952. 480 p.).

Does not supersede the basic work. References to "remote languages" and illustrative quotations are omitted; some new words are added and others dropped.   PE1580.W5

Idioms and usage

Allusions—cultural, literary, biblical, and historical : a thematic dictionary / Laurence Urdang and Frederick G. Ruffner, Jr., editors, David M. Glixon, assoc. ed. 2nd ed. Detroit : Gale, c1986. 634 p.   **AC65**

For annotation, *see* BE74.   PN43.A4

Britannica book of English usage / ed. by Christine Timmons and Frank Gibney. Garden City, N.Y. : Doubleday/ Britannica Books, 1980. 655 p.   **AC66**

Made up in part by excerpts from articles in *Encyclopaedia Britannica* and partly by new contributions. In three main sections: (1) English today and how it evolved; (2) The basic tools [with subsections on grammar, spelling, pronunciation, words and dictionaries, the library, and abbreviations]; (3) Writing and speaking effectively. Bibliography; index.   PE25.B7

Bryant, Margaret M. Current American usage. N.Y. : Funk & Wagnalls, [1962]. 290 p.   **AC67**

A handbook which "attempts to bring together the most recent information about frequently debated points of usage in English speech and writing."—*Introd.* Debated points in current usage are discussed with citations to dictionaries, linguistic treatments, and articles in current periodicals, as well as to special investigations made especially for use in this book.   PE2835.B67

Clark, John Owen Edward. Word perfect : a dictionary of current English usage. N.Y. : H. Holt, 1990. 490 p.   **AC68**

"Originally published in Great Britain in 1987 by Harrap Ltd."—*verso of t.p.*

"A guide to current English usage, arranged alphabetically .... It is intended to be of help to learners of English, to writers and to editors."—*Pref.* British English is emphasized.   PE1460.C485

Copperud, Roy H. American usage and style : the consensus. N.Y. : Van Nostrand Reinhold, [1980]. 433 p.   **AC69**

"This book revises, brings up to date, and consolidates two earlier ones: *A dictionary of usage and style* and *American usage: the consensus.*"—*Pref.* Compares the judgments of various current dictionaries on disputed points and offers the compiler's own views on those points.   PE1460.C648

Evans, Bergen. A dictionary of contemporary American usage / Bergen Evans, Cornelia Evans. N.Y. : Random House, 1957. 567 p.   **AC70**

An informally written, scholarly, and sometimes witty dictionary reflecting the personal opinions of the authors. Arranged alphabetically, with explanations of grammar and rhetoric, word usage, literary concepts, clichés, phrases, idioms, figures of speech, etc. Informative and provocative.   PE2835.E84

Follett, Wilson. Modern American usage : a guide / ed. and completed by Jacques Barzun ... [et al.]. N.Y. : Hill & Wang, [1966]. 436 p.   **AC71**

While this work deals with many of the same terms as Margaret Nicholson, *Dictionary of American-English usage* (N.Y. : Oxford Univ. Pr., 1957) and Henry Watson Fowler, *Dictionary of modern English usage* (AC72), and although it includes a smaller number of entries, the individual style and the length of many of the discussions make it a worthwhile companion to those works. An extensive appendix on the use of *shall* and *will,* and another on punctuation.   PE2835.F6

Fowler, Henry Watson. Dictionary of modern English usage. 2nd ed. / rev. by Sir Ernest Gowers. Oxford : Clarendon Pr., 1965. 725 p.   **AC72**

1st ed., 1926.

Alphabetically arranged; definitions of terms—sometimes with disputed spellings and spelling of plurals, pronunciation, etc.—are interspersed with brief essays on the use and misuse of words and expressions, parts of speech, etc. Reflects the author's personal opinions, and comments are often astringent and witty. The revision by Sir Ernest Gowers aims to bring the work up-to-date without sacrificing the "Fowleresque flavour." It adds a classified guide to enable the reader to find items given by Fowler under enigmatic titles.   PE1628.F65

Freeman, Morton S. A handbook of problem words & phrases. Philadelphia : ISI Pr., c1987. 299 p.   **AC73**

Repr. under title *The wordwatcher's guide to good writing & grammar* (Cincinnati : Writer's Digest Pr., 1990).

An easy-to-use source "designed to present in concise and readable form a clear exposition of problems involving word usage, spelling and pronunciation—and their suggested answers."—*Pref.* No index.   PE1460.F654

Glazier, Stephen. Random House word menu. N.Y. : Random House, 1992. 977 p.   **AC74**

Concerned with relating words by subject, this book classifies entries into 7 major topics and 25 subdivisions. The "single overriding purpose is to help the writer or speaker find the mot juste—the indispensable word that the occasion calls for, no matter how arcane or specialized its references."—*Pref.*   PE1680.G58

Hobbs, James B. Homophones and homographs : an American dictionary. 2nd ed. Jefferson, N.C. : McFarland, c1993. 302 p.   **AC75**

1st ed., 1986.

Offers more than 7,000 homophones with brief definitions to distinguish them, and nearly 1,500 homographs with accurate pronunciation.   PE2833.H63

Horwill, Herbert William. Dictionary of modern American usage. 2nd ed. Oxford : Clarendon Pr., 1944. 360 p.   **AC76**

1st ed., 1935. Frequently reprinted.

Not a dictionary of standard American usage, but a handbook, by an English writer, intended primarily to assist English visitors in America or English readers of American books and magazines by explaining words or phrases which have a meaning or use in the U. S. different from that in England. Includes about 1,300 main words.   PE2835.H6

Maggio, Rosalie. The dictionary of bias-free usage : a guide to nondiscriminatory language. Phoenix : Oryx, 1991. 293 p.   **AC77**

1987 ed. had title: *The nonsexist word finder.*

Repr.: Boston : Beacon Pr., 1992, as *The bias-free word finder.*

Intended to assist in recognizing and avoiding biased language, not "to tell anyone how they must speak or write."—*User's guide.* Most of the 5,000 entries demonstrate some form of bias (e.g., based on gender or race), and 15,000 alternative expressions are offered. A few entries represent words commonly assumed to be biased, but Maggio explains why they are not. A section of guidelines for writing provides a good overview of biased language.   PE1689.M23

Morris, William. Harper dictionary of contemporary usage / William and Mary Morris. 2nd ed. N.Y. : Harper & Row, c1985. 641 p.   **AC78**

1st ed., 1975.

"With the assistance of a panel of 166 distinguished consultants on usage."—*t.p.*

The purpose of this source is prescriptive: to call attention to inaccuracies of usage and correct or eliminate them through discussion and example of the panel. Opinions of the panel, both pro and con, are offered.   PE1680.M59

-ologies & -isms / Laurence Urdang, ed. in chief ; Anne Ryle and Tanya H. Lee, editors. 3rd ed. Detroit : Gale, c1986. 795 p.   **AC79**

1st ed., 1978; 2nd ed., 1981.

Subtitle: A unique lexicon of more than 15,000 English words used of and about theories, concepts, doctrines, systems, attitudes, practices, states of mind, and branches of science, focusing especially on words containing the suffixes *-ology, -ism, -ics, -graphy, -metry, -archy, -cide, -philia, -phobia, -mancy, -latry*, et al., including derivative forms of these words, the entries conveniently arranged by thematic categories, and the whole supplemented by an alphabetical index.

Repr. as : *Dictionary of uncommon words: over 17,000 entries often omitted from standard dictionaries* (N.Y. : Wynwood Pr., 1991). This edition adds about 1,000 new words.   PE1680.O4

Oxford dictionary of current idiomatic English / comp. by A. P. Cowie and R. Mackin. London : Oxford Univ. Pr., 1975–83. 2 v.   **AC80**

Contents: v. 1, Verbs with prepositions & particles; v. 2, Phrases, clauses and sentence idioms.

Intends to provide a specialized dictionary of idiomatic usage "which is sufficiently broad in scope to answer the various practical requirements of the learner."—*Gen. introd.* Idiomatic phrases are defined in "concise and readily intelligible statements ... which do not assume an understanding of ... expressions given elsewhere in the dictionary." Examples of usage from contemporary speech and writing are given; caveats against wrong usage or wrong constructions are frequently included. A valuable work for the foreign-language speaker learning English.   PE1689.O94

Picturesque expressions : a thematic dictionary / Laurence Urdang, editorial director ; Nancy LaRoche, ed. in chief. Detroit : Gale, [1980]. 408 p.   **AC81**

"Designed to serve as a browsing book for word fanciers, as a reference book for language students, and as a resource for writers."—*How to use this book.* Includes old and new figurative expressions grouped in thematic categories. Phrases are defined, their origins explained, and the approximate date of appearance in the written language is indicated when possible. Examples of use are sometimes given.   PE1689.P5

Room, Adrian. Dictionary of changes in meaning. London ; N.Y. : Routledge & Kegan Paul, 1986. 292 p.   **AC82**

"The dictionary, in the main, deals with past senses of a word that are now obsolete, charting their approximate century of appearance and disappearance."—*Introd.* It offers histories of more than 1,300 words with quotations. Most quotations are taken from 1933 edition of *Oxford English dictionary.* No formal etymologies. British emphasis.   PE1580.R59

Schur, Norman W. British English, A to Zed. N.Y. : Facts on File, c1987. 477 p.   **AC83**

First publ. as *British self-taught* (N.Y. : Macmillan, 1973) and later as *English English* ([Essex, Conn.] : Verbatim, 1980).

Aims to be "a comprehensive glossary of Briticisms for Americans, rather than a dictionary of British English in general."—*Introd.* Briticisms appear in the left column, Americanisms in the right column; explanations follow. Appendixes: General differences between British and American English; Glossaries and tables. Indexed.   PE1704.S38

Shaw, Harry. Dictionary of problem words and expressions. Rev. ed. N.Y. : McGraw-Hill, c1987. 368 p.   **AC84**

1st ed., 1975.

"Selects, defines, explains, and illustrates more than 1500 of the most common mistakes made by speakers and writers of our language."—*To the reader.*   PE1460.S5158

Sparkes, Ivan George. Dictionary of collective nouns and group terms. 2nd ed. Detroit : Gale, c1985. 283 p.   **AC85**

Subtitle: Being a compendium of more than 1800 collective nouns, group terms, and phrases, that from medieval to modern times have described companies of persons, birds, insects, animals, professions, and objects.

1st ed., 1975.

Entries include definitions and dated examples. Index of "things collected"—items for which the book gives a collective term.   PE1689.S69

Todd, Loreto. International English usage / Loreto Todd & Ian Hancock. N.Y. : New York Univ. Pr., c1987. 520 p.   **AC86**

Originally publ. London : Croom Helm, 1986; repr.: London : Routledge, 1990.

Aims "to deal objectively with English as a world-wide language with many local varieties, and to distinguish legitimate regional practices from actual errors" (*Introd.*), striking "a balance between *description* and *prescription.*" Dictionary arrangement of grammatical terms, figures and parts of speech, specific words and phrases. Indexed.   PE1460.T64

Webster's dictionary of English usage. Springfield, Mass. : Merriam-Webster, c1989. [989 p.].   **AC87**

"Examines and evaluates common problems of confused or disputed English usage from two perspectives: that of historical background ... and that of present-day usage."—*Pref.* Not so prescriptive as to use the label "sub-standard." Some 500 words are discussed; usage is illustrated with quotations.

•Available in machine-readable form as part of *Infopedia* [database] (AB26).   PE1460.W425

Weiner, E. S. C. The Oxford guide to English usage. Oxford : Clarendon Pr., [1983]. 238 p.   **AC88**

Reprinted with corrections, 1984.

Paperback ed. publ. as: *The Oxford miniguide to English usage,* 1983.

"Intended for anyone who needs simple and direct guidance about the formation and use of English words—about spelling, pronunciation, meanings, and grammar—and who cannot claim any specialist training in these subjects."—*Pref.* Concerned with "correct and acceptable standard British English" with American variants noted, particularly in the section on pronunciation. Word index.   PE1091.W44

Williams, Stephen N. The dictionary of British and American homophones. London : Brookside Pr., c1987. 503 p.   **AC89**

Claims to be "the first and only comprehensive dictionary of British and American homophones."—*Introd.* More than 12,000 are listed, with brief definitions.   PE1595.W54

Wood, Frederick Thomas. English prepositional idioms. London : Macmillan ; N.Y. : St. Martin's, 1967. 562 p.   **AC90**

The alphabetical listing of prepositions and their various uses (with examples of usage) is followed by a section dealing with idiomatic phrases introduced by a preposition and with the idiomatic use of prepositions after verbs, adjectives, verbal nouns, etc., these phrases being arranged by key word and including many examples. A useful work for the native speaker as well as for the foreign student of English.   PE1335.W6

Indexes

Idioms and phrases index / Laurence Urdang, ed. in chief. Detroit : Gale, [1983]. 3 v. (1691 p.).   **AC91**

Subtitle: An unrivaled collection of idioms, phrases, expressions, and collocutions of two or more words which are part of the English lexicon and for which the meaning of the whole is not transparent from the sum of the meanings of the constituent parts, also including nominal, verbal, and other phrases which exhibit syntactic and semantic character peculiar to the English language, the entries gathered from more than thirty sources, each described in the bibliography provided, with all items arranged alphabetically both by first word and any significant words.

An index to the sources where definitions or discussions of the idioms may be found, not a dictionary of the terms. Source books range from compiliations such as *Brewer's dictionary of phrase and fable* (BE181) through various dictionaries of slang and idioms, and including *Words and phrases index* (AC155).   PE1689.I3

New words

12,000 words : a supplement to Webster's third new international dictionary. Springfield, Mass. : Merriam-Webster, c1986. [236] p.   **AC92**

Includes new words and "older words that for various reasons had been passed over in the earlier editing."—*p. 21a*. This appears as the "Addenda" in editions of *Webster's third new international dictionary of the English language, unabridged* (AC14) printed after 1985. Supersedes *6,000 words*, (1976), and *9,000 words*, (1983). PE1630.A17

Ayto, John. The Longman register of new words. Harlow, Essex, England : Longman, c1989–1990. v. 1–2. (In progress).   **AC93**

Vol. 1 defines some 1,200 words that appeared between 1986 and 1988, based primarily on usage in British newspapers and magazines. It "does not set out to be a record of every last coinage … but is a representative sample."—*Introd.*   PE1630.A97

The Barnhart dictionary companion : a quarterly to update "the" dictionary. v. 1, no. 1 (Jan. 1982)– . Cold Spring, N.Y. : Barnhart, 1982– . Quarterly.   **AC94**

Newsletter format. The bulk of each issue is devoted to new words and meanings not found in current dictionaries. Cumulated index in issues 2–4 of each volume.

Index: David K. Barnhart, *The Barnhart dictionary companion-index, 1982–1985* (Cold Spring, N.Y. : Lexik House, c1987. 102 p.). Arranged alphabetically with a broad subject index, various etymological lists, and a list of "Formative elements of words and phrases."

The Barnhart dictionary of new English since 1963 / [ed. by] Clarence L. Barnhart, Sol Steinmetz [and] Robert K. Barnhart. Bronxville, N.Y. : Barnhart/Harper & Row, [1973]. 512 p.   **AC95**

"By 'New English' we mean those terms and meanings which have come into the common or working vocabulary of the English-speaking world during the period from 1963 to 1972."—*Pref.* Includes old words in new applications, idiomatic phrases, figurative and transferred meanings of names, and scientific and technical terms which are not necessarily new but which have recently become part of the common vocabulary.

Pronunciation is indicated for hard or unfamiliar words; area labels (U.S., British, Canadian) are given for regional terms; usage labels (other than "slang") are not used. Illustrative examples of usage attempt to place the term in full context, and a complete citation to the source follows each quotation.

Continued by:

(1) *The second Barnhart dictionary of new English* / [ed. by] Clarence L. Barnhart, Sol Steinmetz, and Robert K. Barnhart (Bronxville, N.Y. : Barnhart/Harper & Row, [1980]. 520 p.).

Follows the basic editorial principles and practices of the basic work. In general, usage notes are fuller, and a date for "our earliest available evidence for use of a word or meaning" (*Pref.*) is supplied in brackets. The two volumes cover some 10,000 "words and meanings not entered or inadequately explained in standard dictionaries."

(2) *The third Barnhart dictionary of new English* / [ed. by] Robert K. Barnhart, Sol Steinmetz with Clarence L. Barnhart. (Bronx, N.Y. : H.W. Wilson, 1990. 565 p.).

Offers "a lexical index of new words of the past decade" (*Pref.*) and new uses of older words, illustrated by quotations. Many of the entries in the first two volumes have been revised, but have not been superseded. Entries include the word or phrase, part of speech, meaning, and at least one usage example with a citation and date of first appearance. Etymologies are added for many entries.   PE1630.B3

The Oxford dictionary of new words : a popular guide to words in the news / comp. by Sara Tulloch. Oxford ; N.Y. : Oxford Univ. Pr., 1991. 322 p.   **AC96**

Contains about "2,000 high-profile words and phrases which have been in the news during the past decade."—*Pref.* Entries explain the derivations of words or phrases and the events that brought them to prominence. Subject icons identify the field of use: drugs, environment, business and world, health and fitness, lifestyle and leisure, music, politics, weaponry, and youth culture. Illustrative quotations "aim to give a representative sample of recent quotations from a range of sources" rather than offer the earliest use.   PE1630.O94

Obsolete words

Halliwell-Philips, James Orchard. Dictionary of archaic and provincial words : obsolete phrases, proverbs, and ancient customs from the 14th century. 3rd ed. London : T. and W. Boone, 1855. 2 v. (960 p.).   **AC97**

Originally publ. 1847. This ed. frequently repr. in one volume, most recently N.Y. : AMS Pr., 1973.

Defines archaic and provincial words and gives many illustrative quotations showing their use.

Supplemented by: Thomas Lewis Owen Davies, *Supplementary English glossary* (London : Bell, 1881. 736 p. Repr.: Detroit : Gale, 1968).

"Originally intended as a supplementary glossary to Halliwell's *Dictionary of archaic and provincial words*, but containing also old and modern expressions, not noted in the best existing dictionaries."—*Pref.*   PE1667.H3

Lewis, Jack Windsor. A concise pronouncing dictionary of British and American English. London : Oxford Univ. Pr., 1972. 233 p.   **AC98**

Planned for "the benefit of users of English as a foreign or second language."—*Pref.* The 24,000 entries provide pronunciation for the English of Great Britain and the U.S.   PE1137.L43

Nares, Robert. Glossary of words, phrases, names, and allusions in the works of English authors, particularly of Shakespeare and his contemporaries. New ed., with considerable additions both of words and examples, by J. O. Halliwell and Thomas Wright. London : Routledge ; N.Y. : Dutton, 1905. 981 p.   **AC99**

Repr.: Detroit : Gale, 1966.

1st ed., 1822, publ. under title *A glossary; or Collection of words, phrases, names, and allusion to customs, proverbs, etc.* First Halliwell and Wright edition publ. 1867.

Rich in quotations.   PE1667.N3

Shipley, Joseph Twadell. Dictionary of early English. N.Y. : Philosophical Library, [1955]. 753 p.   **AC100**

Includes words that have been dropped from general use. Useful when the *OED* is too large and cumbersome for consulting.   PE1667.S48

Skeat, Walter William. Glossary of Tudor and Stuart words, especially from the dramatists / collected by Walter William Skeat ; ed. with additions by A. L. Mayhew. Oxford : Clarendon Pr., 1914. 461 p.   **AC101**

Repr. : Oxford : Clarendon Pr., [1986].

Quotations are brief, as are explanations, references, and etymologies for entries.   PE1667.S5

Pronunciation

BBC pronouncing dictionary of British names. 2nd ed. / ed. and transcribed by G. E. Pointon. Oxford : Oxford Univ. Pr., 1983. 274 p.   **AC102**
1st ed., 1971, ed. by G. M. Miller.
Indicates pronunciation (by both International Spelling Association symbols and English modified spelling) of "titles, family names (i.e., surnames), certain Christian names (or personal first names), place names, those of institutions and societies, and adjectival forms of proper names, drawn from England, Wales, Scotland, Northern Ireland, the Isle of Man, and the Channel Islands."—*Introd.*   PE1660.B3

Ehrlich, Eugene H. NBC handbook of pronunciation / Eugene H. Ehrlich, Raymond Hand. 4th ed., rev. and updated. N.Y. : Harper & Row, [1984]. 539 p.   **AC103**
1st ed., 1943, by James F. Bender; 3rd ed., 1964, rev. by Thomas L. Crowell, Jr.
Now a standard guide to "General American" speech, this edition includes more than 21,000 "commonly used words and proper names as well as perennially difficult names from history and the arts."—*Pref.* Employs a "readily understandable respelling system to indicate pronunciation"; primary and secondary stresses are also indicated; there is a brief pronunciation key at the bottom of facing pages.
PE1137.E52

Greet, William Cabell. World words : recommended pronunciations. 2nd ed. rev. and enl. N.Y. : Columbia Univ. Pr., 1948. 608 p.   **AC104**
A revised and much enlarged revision of the author's *War words* (1943) and *World words* (1944). Gives pronunciation of some 25,000 names and words including battlefields, places made familiar by the war, names of persons in the news, and difficult words. Pronunciation is given "by a simplified Websterian alphabet ... and by a phonetic respelling."—*p.lii.* Compiled especially for radio broadcasters of the Columbia Broadcasting System. Includes the pronunciation of many names not easily found elsewhere.   PE1660.G7

Jones, Daniel. Everyman's English pronouncing dictionary : containing over 59,000 words in international phonetic transcription. 14th ed. London : Dent, c1988. 576 p.   **AC105**
13th ed., 1977.
Earlier editions had title *An English pronouncing dictionary.*
"Extensively revised and edited by A. C. Gimson ... with revisions and Supplement by Susan Ramsaran."—*t.p.*
Words, including some proper names, are followed by pronunciation in the phonetic alphabet. No definitions.   PE1137.J55

Kenyon, John Samuel. A pronouncing dictionary of American English / by John Samuel Kenyon and Thomas Albert Knott. [2nd ed.]. Springfield, Mass. : Merriam, [1953]. 484 p. : ill.   **AC106**
1st ed., 1944.
A dictionary giving the pronunciation, by the phonetic alphabet, of the colloquial speech of cultivated Americans, recording the variant pronunciations in different parts of the country, as East, West, South, North. Besides the common words, includes proper names, especially for America; some British personal and place-names; a few foreign names of general interest; and names in literature and history likely to be encountered by college students in their reading. No definitions.
PE1137.K37

Lass, Abraham Harold. Dictionary of pronunciation / Abraham Harold Lass, Betty Lass. N.Y. : Quadrangle, [1976]. 334 p.   **AC107**
A guide to pronunciation of 8,000 English-language words which are frequently mispronounced or have one or more acceptable variant pronunciations. Pronunciations are given phonetically (and a "pronunciation key" appears on every right-hand page of the book) for each

variant accepted by four standard desk dictionaries; a small numeral beside each pronunciation serves to indicate consensus of preference.
PE1137.L38

Noory, Samuel. Dictionary of pronunciation : guide to English spelling and speech. 4th ed. N.Y. : Cornwall Books, [1981]. 517 p.   **AC108**
1st ed., 1965; 3rd ed., 1979.
Pronunciation is indicated according to a simplified system developed by the compiler. Syllabication and part of speech are also indicated. Separate section for personal and place names. About 45,000 words in the main section.
The review in *Booklist* 79 (15 Dec. 1982): 581 concludes: "Since Noory's word list has not changed since 1965, it seems appropriate to compare his book with the *NBC Handbook of Pronunciation* (3d. ed., 1964). *NBC* lists only about 20,000 words, including proper nouns, but it has a more thoroughly developed set of pronunciation symbols, and this makes it preferable. Libraries lacking an older edition of *Noory* should acquire this edition, but any library with an earlier edition still usable will want to give *Noory* a low priority."   PE1137.N65

Pronouncing dictionary of proper names : pronunciations for more than 23,000 proper names, selected for currency, frequency, or difficulty of pronunciation / ed. John K. Bollard ; assoc. editors, Frank R. Abate and Katherine M. Isaacs. Detroit : Omnigraphics, c1993. 894 p.   **AC109**
Designed to lessen the uncertainty of pronouncing names and proper nouns, this dictionary includes cross-references and variant spellings. Entries include origin, and pronunciation according to two systems: the familiar conventions used in English language dictionaries and the International Phonetic System.   PE1137.P82

Punctuation

Lauther, Howard. Lauther's complete punctuation thesaurus of the English language. Boston : Branden Publ., c1991. 341 p.
AC110
Punctuation is shown for categories of words, phrases, sentences, quotations, time, questions, lists, numbers, titles, names, punctuation marks, hyphenations, etc. An index includes prefixes, parts of speech, and punctuation marks with references to the text.   PE1450.C74

McDermott, John. Punctuation for now. London : Macmillan, 1990. 213 p.   **AC111**
Surveys "the current best practice in the use of punctuation by educated writers of English."—*Pref.* Each section treats a mark of punctuation and begins with a quotation about its nature. Entries include a description as well as examples of use. Index.   PE1450

Shaw, Harry. Punctuate it right! 2nd ed. N.Y. : HarperPerennial, c1993. 208 p. : ill.   **AC112**
1st ed., 1963.
A useful, well-arranged handbook explaining current practices of American punctuation. Includes many examples.   PE1450.S45

Rhymes

Espy, Willard R. Words to rhyme with : for poets and song writers. N.Y. : Facts on File Publications, c1986. 656 p.
AC113
Subtitle continues: "Including a primer of prosody, a list of more than 80,000 words that rhyme, a glossary defining 9,000 of the more eccentric rhyming words; and a variety of exemplary verses, one of which does not rhyme at all."
Organized by single, double, and triple rhymes. Index.
PE1519.E87

Johnson, Burges. New rhyming dictionary and poets' handbook. Rev. ed. N.Y. : Harper, 1957. 464 p.   **AC114**
   1st ed., 1931.
   Contents: Forms of English versification with examples; Rhyming dictionary, one-syllable rhymes, two-syllable rhymes, three-syllable rhymes.   PE1519.J6

Lathrop, Lorin Andrews. Rhymers' lexicon / comp. and ed. by Andrew Loring [pseud.] ... introd. by George Saintsbury. 2nd ed. rev. London : Routledge ; N.Y. : Dutton, 1905. xlviii, 879 p.   **AC115**
   Repr.: Detroit : Gale, 1971.
   Contents: pt. 1, monosyllables and words accented on the last syllable; pt. 2, words accented on the penult; pt. 3, words accented on the antepenult.   PE1519.L3

Wood, Clement. The complete rhyming dictionary and poet's craft book / ed. by Clement Wood ; rev. by Ronald J. Bogus. N.Y. : Doubleday, c1990. 627 p.   **AC116**
   Rev. ed. of *Wood's unabridged rhyming dictionary* (Cleveland ; N.Y. : World, 1943).
   Offers separate chapters for single, double, and triple rhymes; within each chapter words are arranged by vowel sounds, then alphabetically. "The poet's craft book" serves as an introduction to the technical aspects of writing poetry, but the introduction to the earlier edition is still useful for its examples and concise definitions of the different poetic genres.   PE1519.W6

Young, Sue. The new comprehensive American rhyming dictionary. N.Y. : W. Morrow, c1991. 622 p.   **AC117**
   Arranged by vowel sound according to American pronunciation. Includes phrases.   PE1519.Y68

Slang

Barrère, Albert. Dictionary of slang, jargon & cant : embracing English, American and Anglo-Indian slang, pidgin English, tinker's jargon and other irregular phraseology / comp. and ed. by Albert Barrère and Charles G. Leland ; with a new introd. by Eric Partridge. Detroit : Gale, 1967. 2 v.   **AC118**
   Reprint. Title pages include original imprint: [London] : Ballantyne Pr., 1889–90.   PE3721.B3

Berrey, Lester V. American thesaurus of slang : a complete reference book of colloquial speech / by Lester V. Berry and Melvin Van den Bark. 2nd ed. N.Y. : Crowell, 1953. 1272 p.   **AC119**
   1st ed., 1942.
   Arranged in two parts: general slang and colloquialisms subdivided into categories arranged according to dominant idea; and special slang of particular classes and occupations including such sections as underworld, trades and occupations, sports, military, western, etc. Includes an alphabetical word index. In the 2nd ed. new words have been added and outmoded terms omitted, so that the new edition does not entirely supersede the earlier one.   PE3729.A5B4

Chapman, Robert L. New dictionary of American slang. N.Y. : Harper & Row, c1986. 485 p.   **AC120**
   Based on Harold Wentworth and Stuart Berg Flexner's *Dictionary of American slang*, 2nd supplemented ed., 1975 (AC135), the content of that work having been " 'recycled' and its wealth of material retained, altered, or discarded according to the new policies" (*Pref.*) established for the present work, which is intended as "a dictionary of current general American slang." In addition to definitions and indication of parts of speech, entries sometimes include "impact symbols" (indicating social or emotional impact), pronunciation (for unusual pronunciations only), variant forms, dating labels, provenience labels, slang synonyms, examples (but omitting specific sources and dates),

and derivation. Although a considerable number of "non-current" terms have been retained, the Wentworth and Flexner volume will continue to be useful for many older terms.   PE2846.C46

Clark, Gregory R. Words of the Vietnam War. Jefferson, N.C. : McFarland, c1990. 604 p.   **AC121**
   Subtitle: the slang, jargon, abbreviations, acronyms, nomenclature, nicknames, pseudonyms, slogans, specs, euphemisms, doubletalk, chants, and names and places of the era of United States involvement in Vietnam.
   "The primary focus of this dictionary is the period of direct American involvement in Southeast Asia, from 1961 ... to the fall of Saigon in 1975."—*Introd.* Some 4,000 entries (plus about 6,000 references) compiled from printed material, interviews with veterans and antiwar antivists, and personal experience. Numerals are filed at the end of the alphabet. No index; liberal use of cross-references.
      PE3727.S7C57

Farmer, John Stephen. Slang and its analogues, past and present : a dictionary, historical and comparative of the heterodox speech of all classes of society for more than three hundred years, with synonyms in English, French, German, Italian, etc / comp. and ed. by John S. Farmer & W. E. Henley. London : Routledge, 1890–1904. 7 v.   **AC122**
   Repr. : N.Y. : Kraus, 1986. 7 v. in 3.
   An abridged edition was published 1905 (533 p.).
   An older and still useful slang dictionary, listing about 100,000 words. Gives explanation, derivation, kind of usage, illustrative quotations with references to sources, and synonyms in French, German, Italian, and Spanish.
   A "revised edition" with the title *Dictionary of slang and its analogues* was announced for publication in 8 v. by University Books, New Hyde Park, N.Y., but only volumes 1 and 8 have appeared (1966). Vol. 1 of that edition is a reprint (with the addition of two extensive introductory essays) of the only published volume of a revised edition. Vol. 8 contains Farmer's *Vocabula amatoria* (1896), on the erotic slang of the French language.   PE3721.F4

Green, Jonathon. Dictionary of jargon. London ; N.Y. : Routledge & Kegan Paul, in association with Methuen, 1987. 616 p.   **AC123**
   A greatly expanded edition of the author's *Newspeak*, (London ; Boston : Routledge & Kegan Paul, c1984. 263 p.). Offers "a collection of some 21,000 words and phrases, acronyms and abbreviations that have been collected from the jargons, or professional slangs and verbal shorthands, of a wide variety of occupations."—*Introd.* Each entry provides usage locale (e.g., U.S., U.K.), a subject or occupation in which the word is used, and a definition or explanation.   PE1689.G73

Henke, James T. Gutter life and language in the early "street" literature of England : a glossary of terms and topics, chiefly of the sixteenth and seventeenth centuries. West Cornwall, Conn. : Locust Hill Pr., 1988. 339 p.   **AC124**
   "Contains the gleanings from thousands of items of ephemeral British literature published chiefly in London and chiefly during the 16th and 17th centuries."—*Pref.* Dictionary arrangement with broad subject index.   PE3724.O3H44

Holder, R. W. The Faber dictionary of euphemisms. Rev. ed. London ; Boston : Faber and Faber, 1989. 408 p.   **AC125**
   1st ed. had title: *A dictionary of American and British euphemisms : the language of evasion, hypocrisy, prudery and deceit* (Bath : Bath Univ. Pr., 1987).
   Arranged alphabetically, with illustrative quotations. Broad subject index.   PE1449.H548

Landy, Eugene E. The underground dictionary. N.Y. : Simon and Schuster, [1971]. 206 p.   **AC126**
   Brief definitions of words drawn from the underground language of various subcultures. Definitions do not indicate what subculture coined the word or expression, nor whether the word is still in use.
      PE3721.L3

Lewin, Esther. The thesaurus of slang / Esther Lewin and Albert E. Lewin. N.Y. : Facts on File, c1988. 435 p.   **AC127**

Subtitle: 150,000 uncensored contemporary slang terms, common idioms, and colloquialisms arranged for quick and easy reference.

Repr. as *The Random House thesaurus of slang* (N.Y. : Random House, 1988).

Some 12,000 standard words are listed alphabetically, followed by their slang equivalents. No attempt is made to indicate a culture or group associated with the slang words. Access is only by standard words, not by slang expressions.   PE3721.L45

Major, Clarence. Dictionary of Afro-American slang. N.Y. : International Publ., [1970]. 127 p.   **AC128**

"A book of the words and phrases used by black people irrespective of their origin."—*Introd.* Dates are frequently inserted to indicate the period at which a word or phrase was most popular.

PE3727.N4M3

Maurer, David W. Language of the underworld / collected and ed. by Allan W. Futrell & Charles B. Wordell. [Lexington] : Univ. Pr. of Kentucky, [1981]. 417 p.   **AC129**

Essentially a reprinting of some 20 of Maurer's articles (with glossaries) which appeared in a variety of scholarly publications, each article dealing with the argot of a specific subcultural group. A key word index enables the user to locate terms in the individual glossaries.   HV6085.M38

McDonald, James. A dictionary of obscenity, taboo & euphemism. London ; N.Y. : Sphere, 1988. 167 p.   **AC130**

An "eclectic rather than comprehensive" (*p. xiii*) listing, providing brief histories and, in some cases, quotations from literary sources.   PE1691

The Oxford dictionary of modern slang / John Ayto, John Simpson. Oxford ; N.Y. : Oxford Univ. Pr., 1992. 299 p.   **AC131**

Includes about 8,000 entries of 10–12 lines each. Information includes the century in which the use of the word was first recorded.   PE3721.O94

Partridge, Eric. A dictionary of slang and unconventional English : colloquialisms and catch phrases, fossilised jokes and puns, general nicknames, vulgarisms and such Americanisms as have been naturalized / ed. by Paul Beale. London : Routledge & Kegan Paul, [1984]. 1400 p.   **AC132**

Previous editions of this work had reprinted the original 1937 publication and added a cumulated supplement of new terms. The present edition incorporates the supplementary entries into the main alphabet along with many entries, modifications, and corrections, a high percentage of which had been collected by Partridge prior to his death in 1979; post-1978 entries contributed by Beale carry the latter's initials. An appendix of "items too unwieldy to fit comfortably into the main text" (*Pref.*).

———. *A concise dictionary of slang and unconventional English,* ed. by Paul Beale (N.Y. : Macmillan, 1990. 534 p.), is based closely on the 8th ed., and intended as a supplement. It contains only those terms known to have originated in the 20th century. Specialized lists of slang terms are appended to the body of the work.

§ Partridge is also the author of several specialized slang dictionaries: *A dictionary of Forces' slang, 1939–1945* (London : Secker & Warburg; N.Y. : Saunders, 1948. 212 p.); *Slang, today and yesterday, with a short historical sketch and vocabularies of English, American and Australian slang* (London : Routledge, 1933. 476 p.); and *A dictionary of the underworld, British and American* (3rd ed. London : Routledge, 1968. 886 p.).   PE3721.P322

Rawson, Hugh. Wicked words : a treasury of curses, insults, put-downs, and other formerly unprintable terms from Anglo-Saxon times to the present. N.Y. : Crown, c1989. 435 p.   **AC133**

Offers detailed definitions and usage histories of some 1,600 words.   PE3721.R38

Spears, Richard A. Slang and euphemism : a dictionary of oaths, curses, insults, sexual slang and metaphor, racial slurs, drug talk, homosexual lingo, and related matters. Middle Village, N.Y. : David Publ., [1981]. 448 p.   **AC134**

Intended as "a record of the usage of prohibited words and subjects among speakers of English" (*Introd.*) since the beginnings of the English language. Entries include variant forms, definition, often a statement concerning origin or derivation, location of use and/or period of use as applicable. Some entries have long lists of synonyms and/or the source for the entry word. Cross-references.   PE3721.S67

Wentworth, Harold. Dictionary of American slang / comp. and ed. by Harold Wentworth and Stuart Berg Flexner. 2nd supplemented ed. N.Y. : Crowell, [1975]. 766 p.   **AC135**

The original (1960) edition was reprinted in 1967 and a 48-page supplement added. In this latest edition the main section again remains unchanged, but the new supplement includes "all of the material that appeared in the first supplement of 1967 plus about 1,500 new slang terms and definitions that have become current since then."—*Pref. to the Suppl.*

A very full listing, including many previously "taboo" expressions, with considerable explanation of usage, and a high percentage of references to source and date. The appendix includes various classified lists and an extensive bibliography. The best of the American slang dictionaries.   PE2846.W4

Synonyms and antonyms

Bernstein, Theodore Menline. Bernstein's reverse dictionary / with the collaboration of Jane Wagner. [N.Y.] : Quadrangle, [1975]. 277 p.   **AC136**

Not a "reverse dictionary" in the usual sense of the term. The intent here is to enable the user to work from a definition to the term; the work also functions as a dictionary of synonyms. The definitions derive from *Funk & Wagnalls standard college dictionary* (N.Y. : Funk & Wagnalls, [1973]).   PE1591.B45

Crabb, George. Crabb's English synonyms. Rev. and enl. by the addition of modern terms and definitions arranged alphabetically, with complete cross-references throughout. N.Y. ; London : Harper, 1917. 769 p.   **AC137**

At head of title: Centennial edition.

1st ed., 1817.

Reprinted 1974 (with corrections), 1977, and 1979, London : Routledge & Kegan Paul.

An alphabetical list arranged by the first word of a group of synonymous words, with explanation and differentiation of the use and meaning of the words in the group; cross-references from each of the words.   PE1591.C7

The Doubleday Roget's thesaurus in dictionary form / Sidney I. Landau, ed. in chief. Garden City, N.Y. : Doubleday, 1977. 804 p.   **AC138**

A dictionary of synonyms rather than a thesaurus in the sense of Roget's classified arrangement. "It is not based on any other thesaurus," (*Pref.*) and the entries are based on *The Doubleday dictionary for home, school, and office* (Garden City, N.Y. : Doubleday, c1975). A list of antonyms is given for many of the words.   PE1591.D6

Hayakawa, Samuel Ichiyé. Funk & Wagnalls modern guide to synonyms and related words. N.Y. : Funk & Wagnalls, [1968]. 726 p.   **AC139**

Reprinted as: *Choose the right word : a modern guide to synonyms* (N.Y. : Perennial Library, 1987).

Cover title: *Modern guide to synonyms and related words.*

Rev. ed. (London, 1971) publ. as: *Cassell's modern guide to synonyms & related words.*

A new dictionary of synonyms, with terms defined, compared, and contrasted in textual essays that are precise and highly readable.

Cross-references (mainly intended to show relationships rather than synonymy) and antonyms are given as appropriate. Index.

PE1591.F8

Longman synonym dictionary. Burnt Mill, Harlow, Essex, England : Longman, 1986. 1355 p.   **AC140**

A slightly expanded version of Jerome Irving Rodale's *The synonym finder*, rev. by Laurence Urdang and Nancy La Roche (Emmaus, Pa. : Rodale Pr., 1978. 1361 p.), which was based on Rodale's *The word finder* (1947. 1317 p.).

Offers more than a million words, synonymous or similar in meaning, in dictionary arrangement. Parts of speech are indicated for headwords and usage labels are given for some. Not all words in the synonym lists have their own entries, and there is no index of words.

PE1591.L66

March, Francis Andrew. March's thesaurus and dictionary of the English language / introd. by Clarence L. Barnhart ; under the editorial supervision of Norman Cousins ; with a new suppl. by R. A. Goodwin and Stuart B. Flexner. N.Y. : Abbeville Pr., [1980]. 1312 p.   **AC141**

1st ed., 1902, had title: *A thesaurus dictionary of the English language*.

A reprint, with a new supplement, of the 1958 ed., which had title: *March's thesaurus-dictionary*.

A standard work, giving for each word a definition and cross-references to key words under which will be found groups of words of related significance. The supplement (p. 1191–1312) has been considerably expanded and updated.

PE1625.M3

Merriam-Webster's collegiate thesaurus. Springfield, Mass. : G. & C. Merriam, [1993]. 868 p.   **AC142**

Repr. of 1976 ed., which had title: *Webster's collegiate thesaurus*.

"A wholly new book resulting from long study and planning and differing from existent thesauruses in a number of significant respects."—*Pref*. Employs a conventional dictionary arrangement, and gives synonyms, related terms, idiomatic equivalents, antonyms, and contrasted words as applicable. Cross-references in small capitals. Less full than *Webster's new dictionary of synonyms* (AC147).

PE1591.W38

The Random House thesaurus / ed. by Jess Stein and Stuart Berg Flexner. College ed. N.Y. : Random House, c1984. 812 p.   **AC143**

"Based upon the Reader's Digest family word finder, c1975."— *verso of t.p.*

Some 11,000 words are arranged alphabetically, with illustrative sentences and lists of synonyms and antonyms.   PE1591.R28

Roget's international thesaurus. 5th ed. / ed. by Robert L. Chapman. N.Y. : HarperCollins, c1992. 1141 p.   **AC144**

1st ed., [1990]; 4th ed., 1977.

Follows the pattern of the original "Roget's" (AC145 *note*). Organizes 325,000 words and phrases into 15 classes and 1,073 categories by topic. In the Foreword, the editor explains the addition of 30 categories and rearrangement of classes and categories. A comprehensive index of words and phrases refers to category numbers. Up to date; the best thesaurus available.

•Available in machine-readable form as part of *Microsoft bookshelf '94* [database] (AB27).   PE1591.R73

Roget's thesaurus of English words and phrases. New ed. / prep. by Susan M. Lloyd. [London] : Longman, [1982]. 1247 p.   **AC145**

1st ed., 1852 by Peter Mark Roget; frequently revised.

A grouping of words according to ideas within a classification scheme devised by Roget. Whereas a synonym dictionary "provides alternatives for a given word ... a thesaurus offers a variety of ways to express a given idea."—*Pref*. Within six main sections (abstract relations; space; matter; intellect; volition; emotion, religion and morality)

terms are grouped under 990 "heads" (reduced from 1,000 for the 1962 ed.) or ideas which the words express. An index facilitates use.

PE1591.R7

Urdang, Laurence. The Oxford thesaurus. N.Y. : Oxford Univ. Pr., 1992. 1005 p.   **AC146**

Includes 650,000 headwords selected on the basis of their frequency in the language. Example sentences illustrate "the uses of headwords, and their alternatives, in natural, idiomatic contexts."— *Introd*. Liberal cross-references and detailed index.   PE2832.U7

Webster's new dictionary of synonyms : a dictionary of discriminated synonyms, with antonyms and analogous and contrasted words. Springfield, Mass. : Merriam-Webster, c1984. 909 p.   **AC147**

First publ. 1942; previous editions had title: *Webster's dictionary of synonyms*.

A comprehensive dictionary of synonyms, including antonyms and lists of analogous words and their opposites. Words of like meaning are distinguished from one another by careful discrimination and illustrations from classical and contemporary writers. Includes an introduction on the history of English synonymy. This edition revised, updated, and reset. For many purposes the most useful of the dictionaries of synonyms.

§ *Webster's new World dictionary of synonyms*, prep. by Ruth Kimball Kent (N.Y. : Simon and Schuster, 1984. 255 p.), is intended as "a handy guide to distinguishing the subtle differences that exist" among groups of words "that have nearly the same meaning."— *Foreword*. It is based on material in *Webster's new World dictionary*, 2nd college ed. (N.Y. : World, 1970).   PE1591.W4

Regional and dialect

American

Adams, Ramon Frederick. Western words : a dictionary of the American West. New ed., rev. and enl. Norman : Univ. of Oklahoma Pr., [1968]. 355 p.   **AC148**

1st ed., 1944.

Coverage has been extended beyond the "cowman's language" of the earlier edition to include the vocabulary of "the sheepman, the freighter and packer, the trapper, the buffalo hunter, the stagecoach driver, the western-river boatman, the logger, the sawmill worker, the miner, the western gambler—and the Indian."—*Introd*. The appeal is for general readers; the definitions are informal and anecdotal.

PE2970.W4A3

Blevins, Winfred. Dictionary of the American West / Winfred Blevins ; Ruth Valsing, research assistant ; assisted further by the members of Western Writers of America. N.Y. : Facts on File, c1993. 400 p. : ill., maps.   **AC149**

Intends to record the vocabulary of people associated with the American West. Etymologies are given where possible.

PE2970.W4B5

Craigie, William Alexander. Dictionary of American English on historical principles / ed. by Sir William Craigie, with the collaboration of James R. Hulbert [et al.]. Chicago : Univ. of Chicago Pr. ; London : Oxford Univ. Pr. : Humphrey Milford, 1936–44. 4 v.   **AC150**

The bibliography (v. 4, p. 2529–52) gives "a record of the bulk of the reading done for the Dictionary," and expands into completeness the short-title references used in citations.

Compiled on historical principles, with explanations of meaning or use dated when period is clearly determined, and with illustrative quotations dated and arranged chronologically. Symbols indicate a word or sense found in English before 1600; a word or sense originating within the present limits of the United States; a term or sense known only from the passage cited.

Does not attempt to present a complete historical dictionary of every word which has been current since the settlement of the first English colonists but, instead, to show "those features by which the English of the American colonies and the U. S. is distinguished from that of England and the rest of the English-speaking world," including for that purpose "not only words or phrases which are clearly or apparently of American origin, or have greater currency here than elsewhere, but also every word denoting something which has a real connection with the development of the country and the history of its people."—*Pref., p. v.*

The period covered is to the end of the 19th century, with later information for some words established before that date. Includes names of plants, trees, and animals; names of natural or artificial products; and special terms, e.g., topographical, medical, legal, military, naval, business, educational, etc. Colloquialisms are included, but slang and dialect words are restricted to those of early date or special prominence.   PE2835.C72

Dictionary of American regional English / Frederic G. Cassidy, chief ed. ; Joan Houston Hall, assoc. ed. Cambridge, Mass. : Belknap Pr. of Harvard Univ. Pr., 1985–91. v. 1–2 : ill. (In progress).   **AC151**

Contents: v. 1, Introduction; A–C; v. 2, D–H.

Sponsored by the American Dialect Society. Compiled mainly from responses to a lengthy questionnaire (reprinted in the introduction) administered in 1,002 communities in the U.S. Concentrating on colloquialisms, regional usages, dialect and ethnic terms, and out-of-the-way meanings. "DARE does not treat technical, scientific, or other learned words or phrases—or anything else that could be considered standard."—*Introd.* Entries (mainly single words but including some phrases) indicate parts of speech, variant spellings, etc., and are illustrated with quotations. Many entries have maps indicating geographical distribution of usages. Five volumes are planned; v. 5 is to be a detailed bibliography of quoted sources.   PE2843.D52

Mathews, Mitford McLeod. A dictionary of Americanisms on historical principles. Chicago : Univ. of Chicago Pr., [1951]. 2 v. (1946 p.).   **AC152**

Bibliography, p. 1913–46.

More limited in scope than William A. Craigie's *Dictionary of American English on historical principles* (AC150); deals with "Americanisms," meaning "a word or expression that originated in the United States," (*Pref.*) including (1) outright coinages; (2) foreign words which first became English in the U. S.; and (3) words used in senses first given them in American usage. Compiled from sources up to time of publication, excluding manuscript material. Many of the quotations are the same as in Craigie, although the bibliographies vary widely. Definitions and illustrative quotations are given chronologically; usually only one pronunciation is indicated. Some variant spellings are given.

A selection of entries from this work has been published as *Americanisms* (Chicago : Univ. of Chicago Pr., 1966. 304 p.); it may prove useful in the small library unable to afford the 2 v. set.   PE2835.D5

Thornton, Richard H. An American glossary : being an attempt to illustrate certain Americanisms upon historical principles. London : Francis ; Philadelphia : Lippincott, 1912. 2 v.   **AC153**

A 3rd volume (*Supplement*, ed. by Louise Hanley), was first publ. in *Dialect notes* 6 (Madison, Wis. : American Dialect Society, 1939). It is separately paged and has its own title page, so that it can be bound to stand with v. 1–2. Reprinted as a set, N.Y. : Ungar, 1962.

Includes: (1) forms of speech now obsolete or provincial in England which survive in the U. S.; (2) words and phrases of American origin; (3) nouns indicating quadrupeds, birds, trees, etc., that are distinctly American; (4) names of persons, of classes of people, and of places; (5) words that have assumed a new meaning; (6) words and phrases of which there are earlier examples in American than in English writers.

The list of words is largely historical and includes little modern slang. For each word a definition and explanation are given as well as illustrative quotations with exact references to sources, chronologically

arranged. These quotations are numerous, some 14,000 in the first two volumes, and are taken from books, pamphlets, newspapers, and periodicals published in various parts of the country.

The *Supplement* is based on material collected by Thornton after the publication of his *Glossary* and later turned over by him to the American Dialect Society. Examples and illustrative quotations are from a wide general reading, but especially full for the *Congressional globe* and *Congressional record,* 1860–1900, with indication, for words taken from this source, of both the name of the speaker and the part of the country from which he came.   PE2835.T6

Wentworth, Harold. American dialect dictionary. N.Y. : Crowell, 1944. 747 p.   **AC154**

"American printed sources quoted," p. 737–47.

Includes more than 10,000 terms with 60,000 quotations showing usage. "Deals mainly with dialect in the sense of localisms, regionalisms, and provincialisms; folk speech, urban as well as rustic New England and Southern United States dialects viewed in their deviations from General Northern or Western. ..."—*Pref.*   PE2835.W4

Indexes

Wall, C. Edward. Words and phrases index / C. Edward Wall, Edward Przebienda. Ann Arbor, Mich. : Pierian Pr., 1969–70. 4 v.   **AC155**

Subtitle: A guide to antedatings, new words, new compounds, new meanings, and other published scholarship supplementing the *Oxford English Dictionary, Dictionary of Americanisms, Dictionary of American English* and other major dictionaries of the English language.

Vol. 1 lists unusual words, compound words, and phrases, with citations to pertinent articles or notes appearing in *American notes and queries* (1962–67), *American speech* (1925–66), *Britannica book of the year* (1945–67), and *Notes and queries* (1925–66); v. 2 indexes materials from the same publications, but in a different arrangement—by keyword nouns, verbs, adjectives, and adverbs; v. 3 includes about 50,000 references to *American notes and queries* (1941–49), *College English* (1939–68), *Dialect notes* (1890–1939), and the *Publications* of the American Dialect Society (1944–47); v. 4 includes material from the same sources as v. 3, again in different arrangement, plus new entries from *California folklore quarterly* (1942–47) and *Western folklore* (1948–67).   PE1689.W3

British

Wright, Joseph. English dialect dictionary : being the complete vocabulary of all dialect words still in use, or known to have been in use during the last 200 years; founded on the publications of the English Dialect Society .... London : Frowde, 1898–1905. 6 v.   **AC156**

Repr.: N.Y. : Hacker, 1962.

Contents: v. 1–6, A–Z; Supplement, Bibliography, Grammar.

Aims to cover the complete vocabulary of all English dialect words still in use, or known to have been in use from 1700 on, in England, Ireland, Scotland, and Wales, including words occurring in both the literary language and the spoken dialect. Gives for each word: (1) exact geographical area over which it extends; (2) pronunciation; and (3) etymology. Includes American and colonial words still in use in Great Britain or contained in early books and glossaries. Gives many illustrative quotations and, incidentally, considerable information about popular games, customs, and superstitions, with bibliographical references to sources of fuller information.   PE1766.W8

Commonwealth

Cassidy, Frederic Gomes. Dictionary of Jamaican English / Frederic G. Cassidy, R. B. Le Page. 2nd ed. Cambridge : Cambridge Univ. Pr., [1980]. 509 p.   **AC157**

A reprinting of the 1967 edition with the addition of a supplement, p. 491–509.

A "historical, descriptive dictionary of the English language in all forms it has taken in Jamaica since 1655."—*Gen. introd.*

PE3313.Z5C3

Dictionary of Canadianisms on historical principles / produced ... by the Lexicographical Centre for Canadian English, Univ. of Victoria ... Walter S. Avis, ed. in chief. Toronto : W. J. Gage, 1967. 926 p. : ill.   **AC158**

An important work designed "to provide a historical record of words and expressions characteristic of the various spheres of Canadian life during the almost four centuries that English has been used in Canada."—*Introd.* Gives meanings and, where relevant, etymologies and pronunciation (in International Phonetic Alphabet), together with dated examples from printed sources. Extensive bibliography, p. 882–926.   PE3243.D5

Dictionary of Newfoundland English / ed. by G. M. Story, W. J. Kirwin, J. D. A. Widdowson. Toronto : Univ. of Toronto Pr., c1990. 770 p.   **AC159**

1st ed., 1982.

"The core of the work is, of course, the alphabetical list of words, phrases and idioms derived from both printed and oral sources and presented with dated quotations in a manner familiar to users of historical dictionaries."—*Pref.* Additional material occurs only as a supplement of 1,500 entries appended to the text of the 1st ed. Indexed.

PE3245.N4D53

Dictionary of Prince Edward Island English / ed. by T. K. Pratt. Toronto ; Buffalo : Univ. of Toronto Pr., c1988. 192 p.   **AC160**

Intends to record words that are currently used, or were once used, on Prince Edward Island. The entries were compiled from observation, postal and fieldwork surveys, and tapes. Illustrative quotations are dated; cross-references.   PE3245.P75D53

Holm, John A. Dictionary of Bahamian English / by John A. Holm with Alison Watt Shilling. Cold Spring, N.Y. : Lexik House Publishers, c1982. 228 p. : maps.   **AC161**

Represents "the words Bahamians use when talking informally. It demonstrates that Bahamian English forms a link between the Caribbean creoles, such as Jamaican English, and the English spoken today by many Black people in the United States."—*Introd.* The 5,500 entries are words and expressions used in the Bahamas but are not generally in the current vocabulary of Great Britain or the U.S. PE3311.Z5H64

Yule, Henry. Hobson-Jobson : a glossary of colloquial Anglo-Indian words and phrases, and of kindred terms, etymological, historical, geographical and discursive / Henry Yule, A. C. Burnell. New ed. / by William Crooke. London : Murray, 1903. 1021 p.   **AC162**

Rcpr. (London ; Boston : Routledge & Kegan Paul, 1985) called "2nd ed., new ed." but without change in format or pagination. Frequently reprinted.

A standard work still not superseded.   PE3501.Y8

Scottish

The concise Scots dictionary / ed. in chief, Mairi Robinson. Aberdeen : Aberdeen Univ. Pr., 1985. 819 p. : ill.   **AC163**

Based mainly on the *Scottish national dictionary* (AC166) and William A. Craigie's *Dictionary of the older Scottish tongue* (AC164), this work "aims to include what is (or was) wholly or mainly Scots ...

[and] words and usages which ... were used at least 100 years earlier or later in Scots than in the English of England."—*Introd.* Provides pronunciations, parts of speech, definitions, dates of usage, and geographical distribution.   PE2106.C66

Craigie, William Alexander. A dictionary of the older Scottish tongue : from the twelfth century to the end of the seventeenth. Chicago : The Univ. of Chicago Pr. ; London : H. Milford, Oxford Univ. Pr., 1932–1991. pts. 1–42. (In progress).   **AC164**

Contents: pts. 1–42, A–Sanct.

"Intended to exhibit the whole range of the Older Scottish vocabulary, as preserved in literature and documentary records, and to continue the history of the language to 1700, so far as it does not coincide with the ordinary English usage of that century."—*Pref. note.*

PE2116.C7

Jamieson, John. Etymological dictionary of the Scottish language : to which is prefixed a dissertation on the origin of the Scottish language. New ed. / carefully rev. and collated, with the entire supplement incorporated, by John Longmuir and David Donaldson. Paisley : Gardner, 1879–82. 4 v. and suppl., 1887.   **AC165**

1st ed., 2 v., 1808; suppl. by Jamieson, 2 v., 1827; an edition incorporating the words of the supplement but omitting its quotations, ed. by J. Johnstone, 1840–41; the rev. ed. by Longmuir and Donaldson, as above.

A comprehensive work, now out-of-date for etymologies, but still useful for the number of words included, the definitions, and the large amount of incidental information on local usages, customs, etc.

Available in an abridged version as: *Jamieson's dictionary of the Scottish language*, abridged by J. Johnstone and rev. and enl. by Dr. Longmuir, with suppl. ... by W. M. Metcalfe (Paisley : Gardner, 1910. 2 v. in 1).

1st ed. of the Johnstone abridgment of Jamieson, 1840; ed. rev. by Longmuir, 2 v., 1867.

Contents: v. 1, The Johnstone-Longmuir abridgment (635 p.); v. 2, Supplementary dictionary, by W. M. Metcalfe (263 p.).   PE2106.J3

Scottish national dictionary : designed partly on regional lines and partly on historical principles, and containing all the Scottish words known to be in use or to have been in use since *c.* 1700 / ed. by William Grant and David Murison. Edinburgh : Scottish National Dictionary Association, [1931–75]. 10 v.   **AC166**

Scope: "The *Scottish National Dictionary* deals with (1) Scottish words in existence since *c.* 1700: (a) in Scottish literature, (b) in public records, (c) in glossaries and in dictionaries, (d) in private collections, (e) in special dialect treatises, and (2) Scottish words gathered from the mouth of dialect speakers by competent observers. The general vocabulary will include (1) Scottish words that do not occur in Standard English except as acknowledged loan words; (2) Scottish words the cognates of which occur in St. Eng.; (3) words which have the same form in Scots and St. Eng. but have a different meaning in Sc., *i.e.,* so-called Scotticisms; (4) legal, theological or ecclesiastical terms which within our period have been current in Scottish speech ... (5) words borrowed since *c.* 1700 (from other dialects or languages) which have become current in General Scots, or in any of its dialects, especially Gaelic words in counties on or near the Sc. Western limit and Gypsy words in the Border counties."—*Introd., p. xlv.*

Treatment: for each word gives variant spellings, grammatical function, status (e.g., obsolete, colloquial, etc.), pronunciation, illustrative quotations with exact references to sources, and origin of word, if known.

Vol. 10 includes a Miscellanea section giving lists of personal names, place-names, fairs and markets, Scottish currency, weights and measures; Supplement; List of works quoted in the Dictionary; and A list of scientific terms with Scottish connections.   PE2106.S4

Stevenson, James A. C. Scoor-oot : a dictionary of Scots words and phrases in current use / James A.C. Stevenson with Iseabail Macleod. London ; Atlantic Highlands, N.J. : Athlone Pr., 1989. 256 p., [10] p. of plates : ill. **AC167**

A dictionary, arranged under 15 broad subject headings, of "the most widely-used words and expressions."—*Foreword*. Alphabetical index. PE2106.S74

Anglo-Norman

Anglo-Norman dictionary. London : Modern Humanities Research Assoc., 1977–92. 1 v. (Publications of the Modern Humanities Research Association, v. 8). **AC168**

Issued in fascicles.

At head of title: Modern Humanities Research Association in conjunction with the Anglo-Norman Text Society.

Ed. by L. W. Stone, W. Rothwell [et al.].

"The purpose of this Dictionary is to facilitate the reading and understanding of a wide variety of texts written in the French used in the British Isles between the time of the Norman Conquest and the late fifteenth century. To this end, each separate sense of each word listed is illustrated by a quotation, chosen on semantic rather than on historical grounds."—*Introd*. PC2946.M6

Anglo-Saxon

Bessinger, Jess Balsor. A short dictionary of Anglo-Saxon poetry in a normalized early West-Saxon orthography. Toronto : Univ. of Toronto Pr., 1960. 87 p. **AC169**

"A gloss to the crucial 40 per cent of the poetic vocabulary—some 3000 parent words."—*Pref*. PE279.B4

Borden, Arthur R. A comprehensive Old-English dictionary. [Wash.] : Univ. Pr. of America, [1982]. 1606 p. **AC170**

Aims to provide as complete a list of Old English words as possible, including all those found in earlier dictionaries and those in glosses of standard texts and readers. Indicates part of speech and meaning. PE279.B48

Bosworth, Joseph. Anglo-Saxon dictionary : based on the manuscript collections of the late Joseph Bosworth / ed. and enl. by T. Northcote Toller. Oxford : Clarendon Pr., 1882–98. 1302 p. **AC171**

Repr., 1972.

1st ed., 1838.

Still the standard work, with many illustrative quotations and exact references to sources.

Supplement, by T. Northcote Toller (1908–21, 768 p.). Repr., 1972, with enl. addenda and corrigenda, below.

The letters A–G are extensively revised and enlarged.

Enlarged addenda and corrigenda, by Alistair Campbell (1972. 68 p.).

Dictionary of Old English [microform]. [Toronto] : Published for the Dictionary of Old English Project, Centre for Medieval Studies, Univ. of Toronto by the Pontifical Institute of Mediaeval Studies, [1986–1988]. Fasc. C–D; 10 microfiches. (In progress). **AC172**

When completed this will include all words from *A microfiche concordance to Old English* (Newark : Univ. of Delaware, 1980), excepting Latin words in a Latin context, partial and damaged spellings, and personal and place names. Thus, it complements the *Oxford English dictionary* (AC33), which excludes words not used after 1150. Arranged by late West Saxon spellings (with many cross-references), entries include: grammatical labels; brief definitions; number of occurrences in, and up to 12 citations to, the *Microfiche concordance*, and when appropriate, Latin equivalents and references to *Oxford English dictionary, Middle English dictionary* (AC175), etc. Etymologies are not provided. Note that line references in the citations to the *Micro-*

fiche concordance are to the beginning of the sentence in which the word occurs rather than to the line in which the word itself appears. A printed preface is available; there are no plans to publish the dictionary in printed form. PE279D53

Hall, John Richard Clark. Concise Anglo-Saxon dictionary. 4th ed., with a supplement by Herbert D. Meritt. Cambridge : Univ. Pr., 1960. 432 p., [20 p.]. **AC173**

1st ed. 1894; 3rd ed., rev. and enl., 1931.

Serves as a companion index to the Old English words included in *New English dictionary* (AC30) and its successors. References are given to the headings in the *NED* under which quotations are cited from Anglo-Saxon texts. The references also carry through to headwords in the 1st and 2nd editions of *Oxford English dictionary* (AC33). PE279.H3

Jember, Gregory K. English-Old English, Old English-English dictionary. Boulder, Colo. : Westview Pr., [1975]. 178 p. **AC174**

Each section provides equivalents for about 5,000 of the most common words. Intended to be a practical instrument toward the improvement of teaching Old English. Contains an outline of grammar. PE279.J4

Middle English

Middle English dictionary / Hans Kurath, ed. ; Sherman M. Kuhn, associate ed. Ann Arbor, Mich. : Univ. of Michigan Pr. ; London : G. Cumberledge, Oxford Univ. Pr., c1952–1992. Pts. A–S in 13 v. (In progress). **AC175**

Issued in fascicles.

Editor varies: A–F, 1946–61, Hans Kurath, G–P, 1961–83, Sherman M. Kuhn, Q– , 1984– , Robert E. Lewis.

This important dictionary, a research project of the University of Michigan, is based on a large collection of Middle English quotations, including those assembled for *New English dictionary* (AC30), both published and unpublished and unpublished, in addition to hundreds of thousands gathered for this work. It is to be completed in some 65 parts and about 10,000 pages. The bibliography and a full description of the editing plan appeared as a separate part in 1954 with the title *Plan and bibliography* (105 p.). Suppl. 1 to the *Plan and bibliography* was publ. in 1984.

Covers the language from 1100 to 1475; gives the history of each word, with many illustrative quotations arranged chronologically. Many cross-references. PE679.M54

Stratmann, Franz Heinrich. A Middle-English dictionary : containing words used by English writers from the twelfth to the fifteenth century. A new ed., re-arranged, rev. and enl. by H. Bradley. Oxford : The Clarendon Pr., 1891. 708 p. **AC176**

Frequently reprinted.

This standard work will remain useful until *Middle English dictionary* (AC175) is completed. Gives etymologies and references to sources. Detailed explanation of references and abbreviations. PE679.S7

Australian

The Australian concise Oxford dictionary of current English / ed. by George W. Turner. 1st Australian ed. Melbourne ; N.Y. : Oxford Univ. Pr., 1987. 1340 p. **AC177**

"A line-by-line revision, from an Australian point of view, of the seventh edition of the *Concise Oxford dictionary [of current English]* edited by J.B. Sykes [AC38]."—*Pref*. PE3601.Z5A863

The Australian national dictionary : a dictionary of Australianisms on historical principles / ed. by W.S. Ramson. Melbourne ; N.Y. : Oxford Univ. Pr., 1988. 814 p. **AC178**

"An Australianism is one of those words and meanings of words which have originated in Australia, which have a greater currency here than elsewhere, or which have a special significance in Australia ... . The aim of the dictionary is to provide as full an historical record of these as possible."—*Introd.* Includes pronunciations, etymologies, definitions, and illustrative quotations arranged chronologically. Select bibliography of works frequently quoted, p. 767–814.

An abridged version, with the entire word list minus some of the illustrative material, was published as *Australian words and their origins* (Melbourne : Oxford Univ. Pr., 1989).   PE3601.Z5A865

Morris, Edward Ellis. A dictionary of Austral English. [Sydney] : Sydney Univ. Pr., [1972]. 525 p.   **AC179**
Running title: Australasian dictionary.
First publ. in 1898 as: *Austral English*, this dictionary is fashioned after the *Oxford English dictionary* (AC30). Compiled on historical principles, it traces the influence of the Maori language on English in Australia.   PE3601.M8

Wilkes, G. A. A dictionary of Australian colloquialisms. 2nd ed., rev. and reset. [Sydney] : Sydney Univ. Pr. ; Portland, Ore. : distr., ISBS, 1985. 470 p.   **AC180**
1st ed., 1978.
Planned to record "the history of each word, through examples of usage."—*Introd.* Examples are dated, and citations to sources are given.
§ An older work, *Austral English* by Edward Ellis Morris (above), includes words, phrases and usages from Australasia in general.   PE3601.Z5W5

South African

Beeton, Douglas Ridley. A dictionary of English usage in Southern Africa / Douglas Ridley Beeton, Helen Dorner. Capetown ; N.Y. : Oxford Univ. Pr., 1975. 196 p.   **AC181**
Preliminary work was carried out through the journal *English usage in Southern Africa*. Aims to provide a glossary of local vocabulary and idiom; to indicate mistakes and problems which are characteristically South African, as well as those common to speakers of English in general; and to list departures from standard English encountered in South African speech.   PE3451.B36D5

Branford, Jean. A dictionary of South African English / Jean Branford with William Branford. 4th ed. Cape Town : Oxford Univ. Pr., 1991. 412 p.   **AC182**
1st ed., 1978.
The aims for this edition are "fairly extensive quotations from some sources previously banned; back dating some major items, e.g., *impi* to early appearances in English; stronger representation of some major South African authors."—*Introd.* In general, each entry gives pronunciation (for non-English terms), part of speech, definition, etymology, and illustrative quotations (usually drawn from fairly recent sources). Appendixes include "Word sources quoted."   PE3451.B7

Pettman, Charles. Africanderisms : a glossary of South African colloquial words and phrases, and of place and other names. London ; N.Y. : Longmans, 1913. 579 p.   **AC183**
Good definitions. Illustrative quotations are given with date and exact page reference.   PE3401.P4

Foreign words and phrases

Bliss, Alan Joseph. A dictionary of foreign words and phrases in current English. N.Y. : Dutton ; London : Routledge, 1966. 389 p.   **AC184**
Indicates language of origin (but not pronunciation), definition, and date (i.e., century) introduced into English. Literal translation is given if it differs substantially from the English application. An appendix lists all the words and phrases included in the dictionary and is arranged according to the language of origin and the date of introduction into English.   PE1670.B55

Guinagh, Kevin. Dictionary of foreign phrases and abbreviations. 3rd ed. N.Y. : Wilson, 1983. 261 p.   **AC185**
1st ed., 1965.
Lists, in a single alphabet, foreign phrases, proverbs, abbreviations, etc., frequently used in written and spoken English. Translations and, where necessary, brief explanatory notes are given. No pronunciation guide. Includes a list of phrases arranged by language.   PE1670.G8

Loanwords dictionary / Laurence Urdang, editorial dir. ; Frank R. Abate, ed. Detroit : Gale, c1988. 324 p.   **AC186**
Subtitle: a lexicon of more than 6,500 words and phrases encountered in English contexts that are not fully assimilated into English and retain a measure of their foreign orthography, pronunciation, or flavor.
Repr. as: *Dictionary of borrowed words : over 6,500 foreign words and phrases used in English contexts* (N.Y. : Wynwood Pr., 1991).
Aims to "focus on those terms that are likely to be encountered ... by a person who is attuned to literature, culture, and society."—*Pref.* Does not include botanical or zoological names, quotations, mottoes, or proverbs.   PE1670.L58

Mawson, Christopher Orlando Sylvester. The Harper dictionary of foreign terms : based on the original edition by C. O. Sylvester Mawson. 3rd ed. / rev. and ed. by Eugene Ehrlich. N.Y. : Harper & Row, c1987. 423 p.   **AC187**
1st ed., 1934, and 2nd ed., 1975, had title: *Dictionary of foreign terms*.
Repr. as *Le mot juste : the Penguin dictionary of foreign terms and phrases* (Harmondsworth : Penguin, 1990).
Aims "to create a single-volume source that explains foreign phrases and words likely to be encountered in American and English literature."—*Pref.* Some 7,500 foreign words and phrases are listed alphabetically, with brief explanations of English usage; indexed by English term.   PE1670.M3

Pei, Mario Andrew. Dictionary of foreign terms / Mario Andrew Pei, Salvatore Ramondino. N.Y. : Delacorte Pr., [1974]. 366 p.   **AC188**
Indicates the language from which the word or phrase derives, pronunciation, and meaning of "useful, interesting and timely" foreign terms frequently encountered in the English-speaking world.   PE1670.P44

FOREIGN LANGUAGES

Bibliography

Dictionaries, encyclopedias, and other word-related books / Annie M. Brewer. 4th ed. Detroit : Gale, c1988. 2 v. (1333 p.).   **AC189**
1st ed., 1975; 3rd ed., 1982.
Subtitle: A classed guide to dictionaries, encyclopedias, and similar works, based on Library of Congress MARC records, and arranged according to the Library of Congress classification system. Including compilations of acronyms, Americanisms, colloquialisms, etymologies, glossaries, idioms and expressions, orthography, provincialisms, slang, terms and phrases, and vocabularies in English and all other languages.
English and foreign language titles are interfiled. The characterization of the 2nd ed. from *Booklist* 76:(1980) 1079 as "expensive and difficult to use" is still applicable.   Z5848.D52

Haugen, Eva Lund. A bibliography of Scandinavian dictionaries. White Plains, N.Y. : Kraus Internat., [1984]. 387 p.
AC190

"Lists dictionaries published between 1510 and 1980 that are entirely in one of the Scandinavian languages (Danish, Faroese, Icelandic, Norwegian, or Swedish) or that translate one of the Scandinavian languages into one or more other languages."—*p.xvii*. Sections for monolingual, bilingual, and multilingual dictionaries are subdivided by subject matter or language, as appropriate. More than 2,500 items. Author and subject indexes.   Z2555.H39

Hendrix, Melvin K. An international bibliography of African lexicons. Metuchen, N.J. : Scarecrow, 1982. 348 p.   **AC191**

More than 2,600 entries relating to some 600 languages and about 200 dialects. As used here, "lexicon" refers to "any stock of words or word elements compiled for an African language in order to present materials of diverse linguistic interest."—*Introd*. Listed by language, semantic and etymological studies are included as well as dictionaries, vocabularies, word lists, conversation and phrase books, glossaries, etc. Some entries are annotated.   Z7106.H45

International bibliography of specialized dictionaries = Fachwörterbücher und Lexika, ein internationales Verzeichnis / [ed. by Helga Lengenfelder]. 6th ed. München ; N.Y. : K.G. Saur ; Detroit : Distr. by Gale, 1979. 470 p. (Handbook of international documentation and information, v.4).   **AC192**

1st ed.–3rd ed., 1960–66, publ. as: *Technik und Wirtschaft in fremden Sprachen: internationale Bibliographie der Fachwörterbücher*, by Karl Otto Saur. 4th ed., 1969, had title *Technik, Wissenschaft und Wirtschaft in Fremden Sprachen = Techniques, science and economics in foreign languages : international bibliography of dictionaries*. 5th ed., 1972, had title *International bibliography of dictionaries*.

About 5,700 entries in a classified subject arrangement, with separate indexes by (1) authors, compilers, translators, and editors; (2) distributors; and (3) subject fields. Emphasizes works published since 1970, but includes older works still in print. Includes both monolingual and multilingual works.   Z7004.D5I55

Lewanski, Richard Casimir. A bibliography of Slavic dictionaries. Bologna : Ist. Informatico Italiano, 1972–73. 4 v.
AC193

Vol. 1 first issued 1959 as *A bibliography of Polish dictionaries*; 1959–63 ed. issued by New York Public Library in 3 v.

Contents: v.1, Polish; v.2, Belorussian, Bulgarian, Czech, Kashubian, Lusatian, Old Church Slavic, Macedonian, Polabian, Serbo-Croatian, Slovak, Slovenian, Ukrainian; v.3, Russian; v.4, Supplement [covering Belorussian, Bulgarian, Czech, Kashubian, Lusatian, Macedonian, Old Church Slavic, Polabian, Russian, Serbocroatian, Slovak, Slovenian, Ukrainian; author, language, and subject indexes].

A comprehensive bibliography of Slavic dictionaries, not only dictionaries of language, but of abbreviations, biography, orthography, quotations, philosophy, science, etc.   Z70412b.L58

Wajid, Mohammad. Oriental dictionaries : a select bibliography. Karachi : Libr. Promotion Bureau, 1967. 54 p. (Library Promotion Bureau publication, no. 2).   **AC194**

Lists 345 dictionaries of the Arabic, Balochi, Bengali, Gujarati, Hindi, Hindustani, Kashmiri, Persian, Punjabi, Pushto, Sanskrit, Sinhi, Turkish, and Urdu languages. Some brief annotations.   Z7004.D5W3

Walford, Albert John. A guide to foreign language courses and dictionaries / ed. by A. J. Walford and J. E. O. Screen. 3rd ed., rev. and enl. London : Library Assoc. ; Westport, Conn. : Greenwood, 1977. 343 p.   **AC195**

1st–2nd eds. (1964–67) by A. J. Walford had title: *A guide to foreign language grammars and dictionaries*.

A complete revision, considerably expanded as to the number of languages covered. The work now "provides a running commentary on selected courses, audio-visual aids and dictionaries in most of the main European languages, plus Arabic, Chinese and Japanese. It is intended for teachers, students, graduates taking up a particular language for the first time, scientists (for acquiring a reading knowledge of a language on a minimum of grammar), tourists, business men and librarians (for book-selection and stock revision)."—*Introd*. Information is presented in sections according to type and level of user.   Z5818.L35

Zaunmüller, Wolfram. Bibliographisches Handbuch der Sprachwörterbücher : ein internationales Verzeichnis von 5600 Wörterbüchern der Jahre 1460–1958 für mehr als 500 Sprachen und Dialekte. Stuttgart : Hiersemann, 1958. 496 col.
AC196

A very useful annotated bibliography of language dictionaries attempting to be complete for those published during the 100 years prior to preparation of this work, with a selection of those published between 1460 and 1850. The first and the last editions are noted. The most important items are starred. Arranged alphabetically under language names with subdivisions for the large language groups. These subdivisions usually include as pertinent: (1) General (monolingual) dictionaries since 1850; (2) Bilingual or polylingual dictionaries; (3) Orthography, pronunciation, dictionaries of names; (4) Synonyms, style, usage, rhymes, etc.; (5) Slang, foreign words; (6) Dialect dictionaries; (7) Etymological dictionaries; (8) Dictionaries of old speech; (9) General dictionaries before 1850. Includes indexes of names and languages under each continent.   Z7004.D5Z3

Afrikaans

Bosman, Daniël Brink. Tweetalige woordeboek : Afrikaans-Engels, Engels-Afrikaans / Daniël Brink Bosman, I. W. van der Merwe, L. W. Hiemstra. 7., verb. uitg. Kaapstad : Tafelberg-Uitgewers, 1981. 1901 p.   **AC197**

1st ed., 1931–36 in 2 v. by Bosman and Merwe.

The word list for the English-Afrikaans section is based on the *Concise Oxford dictionary of current English* (AC38); the Afrikaans list was developed for this publication.   PF862.B617

Kritzinger, Matthys Stefanus Benjamin. Groot woordeboek : Afrikaans-Engels, [English-Afrikaans] / vroeëre samestellers, M. S. B. Kritzinger, P. C. Schoonees, U. J. Cronjé. 13e uitg. / versorg deur L. C. Eksteen. Pretoria : J.L. van Schaik, 1986. 1410 p.   **AC198**

"Revised by L. C. Eksteen."—*English t. p.*

Prior to 1937 published as: *Woordeboek Afrikaans-Engels, Engels Afrikaans*. 1st ed., 1927; 12th ed., 1981.

Proper nouns are included in the primary alphabetic listing. Abbreviations are appended.

Kritzinger's *Handige woordeboek : Afrikaans-Engels = Handy dictionary : English-Afrikaans* (Pretoria : J.L. van Schaik, 1976. 750 p.) is a shorter work including "most of the words which the intelligent reader uses and needs" (*Foreword*), but omitting proverbs, expressions, abbreviations, and some vocabulary found in the larger version.   PF862.K7

Terblanche, Hendrik Josephus. Nuwe praktiese woordeboek, Engels-Afrikaans, Afrikaans-Engels = New practical dictionary, English-Afrikaans, Afrikaans-English. 5., verb. en uitgebreide uitg. Johannesburg : Afrikaanse Pers-Boekhandel, 1966. 883 p.   **AC199**

1st ed., 1949; 4th ed., 1959.

Intends to represent the spoken and written language of everyday life, with emphasis on current idiom and general practice.

PF862.T43

Akkadian

Assyrian dictionary / editorial board: Ignace J. Gelb ... [et al.]. Chicago : Univ. of Chicago Oriental Institute, 1956–1989. v. 1–11, 13, 15–17[1], 21. (In progress).   **AC200**

Some volumes issued in parts.

Contents: v. 1–11, A–N; v. 13, Q; v. 15–17, pt. 1, S–Šap and Provisional list of bibliographical abbreviations; v. 21, Z.

Cited as *CAD* (*Chicago Assyrian dictionary*).

A scholarly Assyrian-English dictionary, giving meanings in English with examples and citations to literature. Of first importance.

      PJ3525.C5

Bezold, Carl. Babylonisch-assyrisches Glossar / von Carl Bezold; nach dem Tode des Verfassers unter Mitwirkung von Adele Bezold zum Druck gebracht von Albrecht Götze. Heidelberg : C. Winter, 1926. 343 p.   **AC201**

Based on historical, legal, and religious texts.   PJ3540.B4

Deimel, Anton. Šumerisches Lexikon / Anton Deimel, P. Felix Gössman. Rome : sumptibus Pontificii Instituti biblici, 1930–50. 4 v.   **AC202**

Issued in parts.

Contents: t. 1, Šumerische, akkadische und hethitische Lautwerte nach Keilschriftzeichen und Alphabet (3rd ed., 1947); t. 2, Vollständige Ideogramm-Sammlung (4 v.); t. 3, Bd. 1, Šumerisch-akkadisches Glossar; Bd. 2, Akkadisch-šumerisches glossar; t. 4, Bd. 1, Pantheon Babylonicum; Bd. 2, Planetarium Babylonicum, von P. Gössman.

      PJ4037.D35

Soden, Wolfram von. Akkadisches Handwörterbuch : unter Benutzung des lexikalischen Nachlasses von Bruno Meissner (1868–1947). 2., um Hinweise auf die Nachträge verm. Aufl. Wiesbaden : Harrassowitz, 1985. 3 v.   **AC203**

1st ed., 1959–81.

A scholarly work, somewhat less comprehensive than the *Assyrian dictionary* (AC200). This is a reprinting of the 1st ed. with the addition of markers in the text referring the reader to the supplement at the end of v. 3.   PJ3540.S63

The Sumerian dictionary of the University Museum of the University of Pennsylvania / ed. by Åke W. Sjöberg with the collaboration of Hermann Behrens ... [et al.]. Philadelphia : Babylonian Section of the Univ. Museum, 1984–92. v. 1–2. (In progress).   **AC204**

Contents: v. 1, pt. 1, A–A-zum; v. 2, B.

The first parts of a Sumerian-English dictionary modeled on the Univ. of Chicago Oriental Institute's *Assyrian dictionary* (AC200). "Entries are arranged according to the presumed Sumerian word unit. Readings represent transliterations rather than transcriptions, with segments, or signs, belonging to the same word being joined by hyphens."—*Foreword.*   PJ4037.S86

Albanian

Drizari, Nelo. Albanian-English and English-Albanian dictionary. 2nd enl. ed., with a suppl. of new words. N.Y. : Ungar, 1957. 320 p.   **AC205**

1st ed., 1934, had title: *Fjalór Shqip-Inglisht dhe Inglisht-Shqip.*

      PG9591.D7

Fjalor anglisht-shqip / punuar nga Ilo Stefanllari ; [redkatorë Xhevat Lloshi, Frida Idrizi]. Tiranë : Shtëpia Botuese "8 Nëntori", 1986. 441 p.   **AC206**

A desk dictionary with 30,000 entries.   PG9591.F4982

Kici, Gasper. English-Albanian dictionary / Gasper Kici, Hysni Aliko. [Roma : Tip. Editrice Romana, 1969]. 627p.

      AC207

Added title-page in Albanian: Fjalor anglisht-shqip.

Intended primarily for the Albanian immigrant to North America.

§ Another dictionary by Kici is *Albanian-English dictionary* (3rd ed. [Tivoli : 'f Tip. A. Picchi], 1986. 448 p.). It aims to provide a

"complete guide to students of literary Albanian."—*Pref.* Terms dealing with sciences are included; proper nouns are omitted.

      PG9591.K5

Mann, Stuart Edward. An historical Albanian-English dictionary. London : Longmans, 1948. 601 p.   **AC208**

A standard work concerned primarily with linguistics but useful as a bilingual dictionary.

Its counterpart, Mann's *An English-Albanian dictionary* (Cambridge : Univ. Pr., 1957. 434 p.) is "an attempt to express the essential vocabulary of the English literary language in modern literary Albanian."—*Pref.*   PG9591.M32

Amharic

Kane, Thomas Leiper. Amharic-English dictionary. Wiesbaden : O. Harrassowitz, 1990. 2 v. (2351 p.).   **AC209**

The emphasis is on current Amharic. Orthography follows the example set by Wolf Leslau in his *English-Amharic context dictionary* (AC211).   PJ9237.E7K35

Leslau, Wolf. Concise Amharic dictionary : Amharic-English, English-Amharic. Wiesbaden : Harrassowitz, 1976. 538 p.

      AC210

Intends to provide an up-to-date reference work for the student of Amharic. The order of entries is alphabetical by consonant, disregarding initial vowels.   PJ9237.E7L424

———— English-Amharic context dictionary. Wiesbaden : Harrassowitz, 1973. 1503 p.   **AC211**

The first modern English-Amharic dictionary in many years. The English term is followed by the Amharic equivalent, plus an English sentence using the word and an Amharic translation thereof.

      PJ9237.E7L43

Arabic

Badger, George Percy. English-Arabic lexicon : in which the equivalents for English words and idiomatic sentences are rendered into literary and colloquial Arabic. London : Paul, 1881. 1244 p.   **AC212**

Frequently reprinted.

A famous 19th-century work.   PJ6640.B3

Blachère, Régis. Dictionnaire arabe-français-anglais : (langue classique et moderne) = Arabic/French/English dictionary / par Régis Blachère, Moustafa Chouémi et Claude Denizeau. Paris : Maisonneuve et Larose, 1964–88. v.1–4 (fasc. 1–46). (In progress).   **AC213**

Vol. 4– titled *al-Kōil dictionnaire arabe-français-anglais.*

Beginning with fasc. 37, editorship was assumed by Moustafa Chouémi and Charles Pellat.

Intends "to comprise all the vocabulary that constitutes ... 'literary' Arabic."—*Foreword.* Meanings are given in French, then in English.   PJ6645.F6B6

A dictionary of Iraqi Arabic : Arabic-English / ed. by D. R. Woodhead and Wayne Beene ... [et al.]. Wash. : Georgetown Univ. Pr., 1967. 509 p. (Georgetown University. Institute of Languages and Linguistics. Arabic series, 10).   **AC214**

Repr., 1991.

1st ed., 1964.

A dictionary of the colloquial Arabic spoken in Baghdad; "designed to allow Americans to understand Iraqi Arabic."—*Introd.*

Elias, Elias Antoon. Elias' modern dictionary, English-Arabic / Elias Antoon Elias and Edward E. Elias. 16th ed. [Cairo : Elias], 1969. 816 p.   **AC215**

Frequently reprinted. About 68,000 words.

————. *Elias' modern dictionary : Arabic-English* (9th ed., with several additions and alterations. Cairo : Elias, 1962. 870 p. ill.).

"Containing about 64,500 words."—*verso of title page.*

PJ6640.E6

Hinds, Martin. A dictionary of Egyptian Arabic : Arabic-English / Martin Hinds, el-Said Badawi. Beirut : Librairie du Liban, 1986. 981 p. : ill.   **AC216**

Title on added t.p.: *Mu'jam al-lughah al-'Arabīyah al-Miṣrīyah.*

The intent is to document stable lexical items with the "primary purpose of fulfilling the needs of an English speaking user who requires a general, overall-descriptive, synchronic, comprehension dictionary of Egyptian Arabic at all levels of society."—*Introd.*

PJ6795.H54

Karmi, Ḥasan Saʿīd. al-Mughni al-akbar : a dictionary of classical and contemporary English : English-Arabic, with illustrations and coloured plates. Beirut : Librairie du Liban, c1987. 1710 p. : ill. (some col.).   **AC217**

Added t.p. in Arabic.

English words, phrases, and idioms are defined by "the correct equivalent from classical Arabic," followed "by either modern Arabic equivalents or by explanations in simple language."—*Pref.*

PJ6640.K35

Lane, Edward William. Arabic-English lexicon : derived from the best and the most copious eastern sources … . In two books: the first containing all the classical words and significations commonly known to the learned among the Arabs; the second, those that are of rare occurrence and not commonly known … . London ; Edinburgh : Williams and Norgate, 1863–93. 1 v. in 8 pts., paged continuously.   **AC218**

Repr. : Cambridge : Islamic Text Soc., 1984. 2 v.

Pts. 6–8 ed. by Stanley Lane-Poole.

The second book never published.

Includes references to the literature.

A review of the 1984 reprint appears in *Times literary supplement* (26 April 1985): 474.   PJ6640.L3

The Oxford English-Arabic dictionary of current usage / ed. by N. S. Doniach. Oxford : Clarendon Pr., 1972. 1392 p.   **AC219**

Frequently reprinted.

Intended both for English-speaking students of Arabic and for Arabic-speaking students of English. Includes formal literary English, colloquial, and slang usage, with the closest Arabic equivalent at the same level of usage.

The concise Oxford English-Arabic dictionary of current usage (London : Oxford Univ. Pr., 1982. 461 p.) is a condensed and updated version.   PJ6640.O93

Selim, George Dimitri. Arabic-English and English-Arabic dictionaries in the Library of Congress. Wash. : Library of Congress : for sale by the U.S. Govt. Print. Off., 1992. 213 p. (Near East series, no. 5).   **AC220**

Superintendent of Documents classification: LC 41.9:Ar 1/3.

Includes all "dictionaries, glossaries and vocabularies which the Library of Congress has acquired."—*Pref.* Multilingual dictionaries with Arabic and English are also represented. An appendix lists dictionaries not acquired by the Library of Congress. Indexed.

Z7052.S4

Spiro, Socrates. Arabic-English dictionary of the modern Arabic of Egypt. 2nd ed., rev. and considerably enl. Cairo : Elias' Modern Pr., 1923. 518 p.   **AC221**

Repr.: Beirut : Librairie du Liban, 1974, with its companion, *An English Arabic vocabulary of the modern and colloquial Arabic of Egypt* (3rd ed., rev. and considerably enl. 1929. 325 p.).

These dictionaries cover the colloquial Arabic of Egypt, with special attention to idiomatic usage.   PJ6767.S6

Wehr, Hans. A dictionary of modern written Arabic : (Arab.-Engl.) / Hans Wehr ; ed. by J. Milton Cowan. 4th ed., considerably enl. and amended. Wiesbaden : Harrassowitz, 1979. 1301 p.   **AC222**

The 1961 ed. was a translated, edited, and enlarged version of the author's *Arabisches Wörterbuch für die Schriftsprache der Gegenwart* (Leipzig : Harrassowitz, 1952. 2 v. ; Supplement, 1958).

This edition incorporates new words and usages as well as some older material not previously included. "The number of new entries, including lemmata as well as compounds, idiomatic phrases and new definitions of head words, runs to approximately 13,000" (*Pref.*), and in some 3,000 instances "smaller additions (new transcriptions, plural forms, prepositional government of verbs, cross-references, etc.) have been inserted, errors corrected, obsolete entries eliminated." Additions and deletions were accomplished by "cutting and pasting" rather than resetting, with some resulting inconsistencies in presentation and arrangement.   PJ6640.W43

Wortabet, John. English-Arabic and Arabic-English dictionary / John Wortabet and Harvey Porter, with a supplement of modern words and new meanings by John L. Mish. [Enl. ed.]. N.Y. : Ungar, 1954. 455 p., 423 p.   **AC223**

Repr.: Beirut : Librarie du Liban, 1984, and Beirut : Librarie du Liban; Troy, Mich : International Book Centre, 1991.

A basic dictionary, with a supplement containing modern words and expressions. The 1991 reprint contains a supplement of modern science terms.   PJ6640.W57

Wortabet, William Thomson. Wortabet's Arabic-English dictionary / with the collaboration of John Wortabet and Harvey Porter. 4th ed. Beirut : Librairie du Liban, 1968. 802 p.   **AC224**

Added title page in Arabic.

1st ed., 1888.

A reprint of the 3rd ed. published in Beirut, 1913, under title: *Arabic-English dictionary.*   PJ6640.W6

Wörterbuch der klassischen arabischen Sprache / unter Mitwirkung der Akademien der Wissenschaften in Göttingen, Heidelberg und Müchen und der Akademie der Wissenschaft und der Literatur in Mainz hrsg. durch die Deutsche Morgenländische Gesellschaft; begründet von Jörg Kraemer und Helmut Gätje; in Verbindung mit Anton Spitaler bearbeitet von Manfred Ullmann. Wiesbaden : Otto Harrassowitz, 1957–93. Lfg. 1–21. (In progress).   **AC225**

Manfred Ullman became editor with Lfg. 3.

Contents: Bd. 1, ka–kaiwana; Bd. 2, teil 1, (lfg. 1–11) la–ladama; Bd. 2, teil 2, (lfg. 12–20), latta–lakiya; Bd. 2, lfg. 21, lam–mulimmatun.

A scholarly work of classical Arabic with extensive references to the literature. The main words are translated into both German and English.

A 2nd rev. ed. of *Vorläufiges Literatur- und Abkürzungsverzeichnis zum zweiten Band (Lām)* was issued in 1989 (62 p.).   PJ6635.W63

Armenian

Aukerian, Haroutiun. A dictionary, English and Armenian / by Father Paschal Aucher; with the assistance of Joan Brand. 2nd ed. Venice : Armenian Academy of St. Lazarus, 1868. 815 p.   **AC226**

1st ed., 1821–25.

§ Companion volume: Matthias Bedrossian, *New dictionary : Armenian-English* (Venice : St. Lazarus Academy, 1875–79. 786 p. [Repr.: Beirut : Librarie du Liban, 1985]).   PK8091.A8

Kouyoumdjian, Mesrob G. A comprehensive dictionary, Armenian-English. Cairo : Sahag-Mesrob Pr., [1950]. 1158 p. **AC227**

Repr.: Watertown, Mass. : Baikar Armenian Daily, 1970.

A dictionary of modern Armenian, giving equivalents in English. Proper nouns and table of numbers appended.

§ Companion work by the same compiler: *A comprehensive dictionary of idioms, English-Armenian* (Cairo : Vozguedar, 1969. 668 p.) and *A practical dictionary for adults* (Cairo : Vozguedar, 1973. 544 p., 746.). PK8091.K6

Aryan

See Indo-European.

Assyro-Babylonian

See Akkadian.

Basque

Griera y Gaja, Antonio. Vocabolario vasco : (ensayo de una interpretación de la lengua vasca). Abadía de San Cugat del Vallés : Instituto Internacional de Cultura Románica, 1960. 2 v. (1111 p.). (Biblioteca filológica-histórica, 2-7). **AC228**

Gives Spanish equivalent and derivation of the Basque term.

PH5177.S7G7

Lhande, Pierre. Dictionnaire basque-français et français-basque : (dialectes labourdin, bas-navarrais et souletin) / d'après le Dictionnaire basque-espagnol-français de l'abbé R. M. de Askué [i.e., Azkué] et les dictionnaires manuscrits des abbés M. Harriet, M. Hiribarren et Pierre Foix. Paris : G. Beauchesne, 1926-38. 1 v. **AC229**

v. 1, Basque-français (1117 p.), publ. in 9 pts. No more published.

The standard work. PH5177.F8L5

Bilingual

Aulestia, Gorka. Basque-English dictionary. Reno : Univ. of Nevada Pr., c1989. 108, 558 p. : ill. **AC230**

Compiled at the Basque Studies Program of the Univ. of Nevada, this is the first Basque-English dictionary, listing some 50,000 words from Unified Basque and the five major Basque dialects. Includes a detailed discussion of Basque grammar. PH5177.E5A95

——————— English-Basque dictionary / Gorka Aulestia and Linda White. Reno : Univ. of Nevada Pr., c1990. 397 p. : map. **AC231**

A companion to the title described above. Provides Unified Basque equivalents for some 25,000 English words. PH5177.E5A96

Bengali

Dev, Ashu Tosh. Students' favourite dictionary, English-to-Bengali & English. 24th ed. Calcutta : S.C. Mazumder, 1970. 1614 p. : ill. **AC232**

1st ed., 1937.

Subtitle (varies): Etymological, explanatory, with pronunciations, compound words, phrases, current technical terms, ... foreign words and phrases, historical, mythological and classical allusions, proverbs, etc. PK1687.D45

Sen, Sukumar. An etymological dictionary of Bengali, c.1000-1800 A.D. Calcutta : Eastern Publ., [1971]. 2 v. (968 p.). **AC233**

Bengali-English (Bengali in roman script). About 15,000 entries.

PK1681.S4

Breton

Dictionnaire breton : breton-français, français-breton / sous la direction de Per Jakez Hélias ; [ont participé à rédaction, Joseph Abasq ... et al.]. Paris : Garnier, c1986. 816 p. **AC234**

Includes a brief section on grammar and appendixes of proper names and the conjugation of words. PB2837.D5

Ernault, Émile. Dictionnaire étymologique du breton moyen. (*In his* Le mystère de Sainte Barbe [Nantes : Soc. des Bibliophiles Bretons, 1885-87. p. 189-400]). **AC235**

An etymological dictionary of medieval Breton.

DC611.B842A6

——————— Glossaire moyen-breton. 2. éd. corr. et augm. Paris : Bouillon, 1895-96. 833 p. **AC236**

Supplement to the author's *Dictionnaire étymologique du breton moyen* (AC235).

Forms v. 2 of Henry d'Arbois de Jubainville and Émile Ernault's *Études grammaticales sur les langues celtiques* (Paris, 1881-96).

Includes words found in manuscripts and texts of the 12th to the 16th centuries inclusive, together with an etymological treatment of some modern terms.

Hemon, Roparz. Geriadur istorel ar brezhoneg = Dictionnaire historique du breton. Paris : Preder, 1958-79. 3232 p. **AC237**

Published in parts. Abbreviations of works cited, p.3219-30.

Hemon is also the compiler of *Dictionnaire français breton* (Nouv. éd. Brest : al Liamm, 1974. 420p.) and *Nouveau dictionnaire breton* (4e éd. Brest : al Liamm, 1970. 849 p.).

Vallée, François. Grand dictionnaire français-breton / avec le concours de É. Ernault et R. Le Roux. Rennes : Éd. de l'Impr. Commerciale de Bretagne, 1931 [i.e. 1934]. 814 p. **AC238**

——————. ——————. *Supplément* (La Baule : Skridou Breizh, 1948. 176 p.).

Bulgarian

Bŭlgarski-angliĭsko rechnik / T. Atanasova ... [et al.]. 3., sterotipno izd. s priturka. Sofiĭa : Izd-vo Nauka i izkustvo, 1990. 2 v. **AC239**

Title on added t.p.: *Bulgarian-English dictionary.*

Companion work: *Angliĭsko-bŭlgarski rechnik*, sustaviteli T. Atanasova, Marihiĭa Rankova, Ivanka Kharlakova. (3. izd. s d obavka. Sofiia : izd-vo Bŭlgarskata akademiĭa na naukite, 1985. 2 v.).

Title on added t.-p.: *English-Bulgarian dictionary.*

Both titles frequently reprinted.

Called "Atanasova" by scholars in the field. Has become the standard dictionary for the language. PG979.R36

Bŭlgarski etimologichen rechnik / sŭstavili V. I. Georgiev ... [et al. ; red. Vladimir I. Georgiev]. Sofiĭa : BAN, 1962-86. v. 1-3⁵. (In progress). **AC240**

At head of title: Bŭlgarska Akademiĭa na Naukite. Institut Bŭlgarski Ezik.

Contents: v. 1-3, A-Mingo.

An extensive etymological dictionary. Bibliography of sources, v. 1, p. xii-xcv.

Issued in fascicles; title page of t. 1 bears the date 1971.

PG963.B8

Mladenov, Stefan. Bŭlgarski tulkoven rechnik, s ogled kŭm narodnite govori / Stŭkmi Stefan Mladenov s donegdeshno uchastie na A. T. Balan. Sofii͡a : Decho Stefanov, 1951. v. 1. (In progress).   **AC241**

Contents: v. 1, A–K.

A scholarly dictionary, still unfinished.   PG975.M57

Rechnik na bŭlgarskiia ezik / [glav. redaktor Kristalina Cholakova ; sŭstaviteli Simeon Boi͡adzhiev ... et al.]. Sofii͡a : Izdvo na Bŭlgarskata akademii͡a na naukite, 1977–90. v. 1–6. (In progress).   **AC242**

Contents: v. 1–6, A–ň.

An extensive work with emphasis on examples of usage (and providing citations to sources of the examples). Includes many technical and specialized terms.

§ The Academy's *Rechnik na suvremennais bulgarski ezik* (Sofia : Bulgarska Akad. Naukite, 1955–59. 3 v.) remains useful while the present work is in progress.   PG975.R39

Abbreviations

Library of Congress. Slavic and Central European Division. Bulgarian abbreviations : a selective list / prep. by Konstantin Z. Furness. Wash. : U.S. Govt. Prt. Off., 1961. 326 p.   **AC243**

A listing of abbreviations culled from Bulgarian texts with the emphasis on governmental and other organizational titles, and some general terms. Each entry gives the Bulgarian abbreviation with its transliteration, and the expansion in Bulgarian and in English translation.   PG984.U5

Burmese

Judson, Adoniram. The Judson Burmese-English dictionary / rev. and enl. by Robert C. Stevenson; ed. by F. H. Eveleth. Rangoon : Amer. Baptist Mission Pr., 1921. 1123 p.   **AC244**

Repr.: Rangoon : Baptist Board of Publ., 1953.

Offers examples of colloquial and written usage of most entry words.   PL3957.J834

Stewart, John Alexander. A Burmese-English dictionary / comp. by J. A. Stewart and C. W. Dunn, from material supplied by a large number of contributors. London : Luzac, 1940–81. Pts. 1–6. (In progress?).   **AC245**

Imprint varies. Published under the auspices of the University of Rangoon until 1950 when sponsorship was transferred to the School of Oriental and African Studies, London University.

Vocabulary is drawn from Burmese literature from its beginning in the 15th century to the present; comprehensive bibliographies of sources are included. Although not strictly an etymological dictionary, etymological notes are given. An important scholarly work which will presumably supersede Adoniram Judson's *The Judson Burmese-English dictionary* (AC244).   PL3957.S8

Catalan

Aguiló y Fúster, Mariano. Diccionari Aguiló : materials lexicogràfics aplegats / rev. i publ. sota la cura de Pompeu Fabra i Manuel de Montoliu. Barcelona : Inst. d'Estudis Catalans, 1914–34. 8 v. in 6. (Biblioteca filològica de l'Inst. de la Llengua Catalana, III, VIII).   **AC246**

Repr.: Barcelona : Editorial Alta Fulla, 1988– (Documents de filologia catalana, v. 3–).

A scholarly work with illustrative quotations and references to the literature.   PC3889.A4

Alcover Sureda, Antonio Maria. Diccionari català-valencià-balear : inventari lexicogràfic i etimològic de la llengua catalana en totes les seves formes literáries i dialectals ... / Obra iniciada per mn. Antoni Ma. Alcover. 2. ed., corr. i posada al dia / Dibuixos de Josep Mill i Francesc de B. Moll. Palma de Mallorca : [Editorial Moll], 1964. 10 v.   **AC247**

Repr.: Barcelona, 1968–69; Palma de Mallorca, 1988.

1st ed., 1930–62.

A dictionary of the literary and spoken language as found in the various parts of Spain and the islands where Catalan is used. Gives etymologies and regional variations.   PC3889.A5

Corominas, Joan. Diccionari etimològic i complementari de la llengua catalana / per Joan Coromines, amb la col·laboració de Joseph Gulsoy i Max Cahner. Barcelona : Curial Edicions Catalanes : Caixa de Pensions La Caixa, 1980–91. 9 v.   **AC248**

Gives etymologies, with references to earlier dictionaries, grammars, linguistic studies, collections of documents, etc.   PC3883.5.C6

Diccionari de la llengua catalana / [director editorial, Joan Carreras i Martí]. 2a ed. corr. i rev. Barcelona : Fundació Enciclopèdia Catalana, 1983. 1677 p.   **AC249**

1st ed., 1982.

A comprehensive dictionary. Includes models for irregular verbs.   PC3889.D49

Diccionari enciclopèdic de la llengua catalana amb la correspondència castellana. Nova ed. Barcelona : Salvat, 1930–35. 4 v. : ill.   **AC250**

Title page note: "Redactada segons les normes de l' 'Institut d'Estudis Catalans,' la qual conté tots els vocables, modismes i aforismes, mots tècnics de ciències, arts i indústries, biografies de personatges cèlebres, antics i moderns, nom i descripció de poblacions, rius i muntanyes de les comarques on és parlat et català en qualsevol de les seves variants."

Previously published under title *Diccionari de la llengua catalana ab la correspondència castellana* (1888–89. 2 v.).   PC3889.D5

Fabra, Pompeu. Diccionari manual de la llengua catalana. Barcelona : Editorial EDHASA, 1983. 1331 p.   **AC251**

21st ed., 1986; text is identical to the earlier edition.

Based on Fabra's *Diccionari general de la llengua catalana* (1st ed., 1932).   PC3889.D49

Celtic

Holder, Alfred. Alt-celtischer Sprachschatz. Leipzig : Teubner, 1896–1913. 3 v.   **AC252**

Repr.: Graz, Austria: Akademsche Druck U. Verlagsanstalt, 1961.

Vol. 3 includes a *Nachträge* (incomplete) to v. 1.

PB1089.H6RR

Chinese

Han yü ta tz'u tien / chu pien Lo Chu-feng ; Han yü ta tz'u tien pien chi wei yüan hui, Han yü ta tz'u tien pien tsuan ch'u pien tsuan. Ti 1 pan. [Shanghai] : Shang-hai tz'u shu ch'u pan she : Fa hsing Shang-hai tz'u shu ch'u pan she fa hsing so, 1986–93. v. 1–10. (In progress).   **AC253**

Aims to be a comprehensive dictionary of classical and modern Chinese. Lists major people and places; includes etymologies.

PL1420.H349

Tz'u hai / [ed. by] Tz'u hai pien chi wei yüan hui. [Rev. and enl. ed.]. Taipei : Chung Hua shu chu, [1979]. 3 v. (4915 p.) : ill.   **AC254**

A standard encyclopedic dictionary published in various formats and frequently reprinted.   **PL1420.T86**

Wieger, Leon. Chinese characters : their origin, etymology, history, classification and signification / tr. into English by Leo Davrout. 2nd ed., enl. and rev. according to the 4th French ed. N.Y. : Paragon Book Repr. Corp., 1965. 820 p. : ill.   **AC255**
    "Unabridged and unaltered republication of the 2nd ed. ... 1927."—*verso of title page.*   **PL1171.W6**

Williams, Samuel Wells. A syllabic dictionary of the Chinese language : arranged according to the Wu-Fang Yuen Yin, with the pronunciation of the characters as heard in Peking, Canton, Amoy and Shanghai. Shanghai : Amer. Presbyterian Mission Pr., 1903. 1254 p.   **AC256**
    A reprint of the 1874 edition, with four pages of "Errata and corrections."   **PL1455.W65**

Bilingual

Chen, Janey. A practical English-Chinese pronouncing dictionary : English, Chinese characters, romanized Mandarin and Cantonese. Rutland, Vt. : Tuttle, 1970. 601 p.   **AC257**
    Repr., 1992.
    Contains 15,000 entries of conversational vocabulary in lists: the English word; Chinese characters with Chinese phonetics; the romanization in Mandarin with tone signs. Where the spoken word differs from the written word, the spoken form is present.   **PL1455.C579**

Chi, Wen-shun. Chinese-English dictionary of contemporary usage. Berkeley : Univ. of California Pr., [1977]. 484 p.   **AC258**
    A dictionary of some 1,200 entries for new words and words with new definitions resulting from the institutional and ideological changes of the last 40 years.   **PL1455.C59.**

Corbeil, Jean Claude. The Facts on File English/Chinese visual dictionary : look up the word from the picture, find the picture from the word / Jean-Claude Corbeil, Mein-ven Lee. N.Y. : Facts on File Publications, c1988. 823 p. : ill.   **AC259**
    This visual dictionary is "meant for the active member of the modern industrial society who needs to be acquainted with a wide range of technical terms" (*Introd.*) but who is not a specialist. Includes more than 25,000 English and Chinese terms.   **PL1455.C675**

Cowles, Roy T. The Cantonese speaker's dictionary. [Hong Kong] : Hong Kong Univ. Pr., 1965. 1318 p., 232p.   **AC260**
    "In Romanized Cantonese, being handled entirely from the standpoint of the speech and for the benefit of the foreign student."—*Foreword.* About 133,000 entries, with English equivalents. The romanized form is keyed to a "character code book" (which makes up the second part of the volume) to designate the Chinese characters.   **PL1736.C6**

Dictionary of spoken Chinese / comp. by the staff of the Institute of Far Eastern Langauges, Yale University. New Haven : Yale Univ. Pr., 1966. 1071 p. (Yale linguistic series, 8).   **AC261**
    "A revision of War Department Technical manual TM 30–933, *Dictionary of spoken Chinese,* published ... 1945."—*Acknowledgments.*
    Chinese-English and English-Chinese. Intended for the student of colloquial Mandarin. Yale romanization used throughout.   **PL1455.Y295**

Fenn, Courtenay Hughes. The five thousand dictionary : a Chinese-English pocket dictionary and index to the character cards of the College of Chinese Studies, California College in China / originally comp. by Courtenay H. Fenn ... with the assistance of Mr. Chin Hsien Tseng. 5th ed. with add. and rev. by George D. Wilder and Mr. Chin Hsien Tseng. [Peking : Union Pr.], 1940. 697 p.   **AC262**
    Repr. as: Fifth rev. Amer. ed. (Cambridge : Harvard Univ. Pr., 1940. 694 p.). Various later reprintings.
    1st ed., 1926.
    Standards and styles of pronunciation and the exposition of tones are described; neutral tones are marked in the entries.   **PL1455.F4**

Giles, Herbert Allen. Chinese-English dictionary. 2nd ed., rev. and enl. Shanghai : Kelly & Walsh ; London : Quaritch, 1912. 4 v. (84, 1711 p.).   **AC263**
    Repr. : Taipei : Ch'eng Wen Publ. Co., 1972 (distr., N.Y. : Paragon Repr. Corp.).
    Contains 10,926 characters. Illustrative phrases. List of family names.   **PL1455.G6**

Huang, Parker Po-fei. Cantonese dictionary : Cantonese-English, English-Cantonese. New Haven, Conn. : Yale Univ. Pr., 1970. 489 p.   **AC264**
    About 20,000 entries in the English-Cantonese section. The primary object of the work is "to help the English-speaking student understand and communicate in the oral-aural mode of Cantonese."—*Pref.*   **PL1736.H8**

Lin, Yutang. Chinese-English dictionary of modern usage. [Hong Kong] : Chinese Univ. of Hong Kong ; distr. N.Y. : McGraw-Hill, New York], 1972. 1720 p.   **AC265**
    Aims for idiomatic equivalents. Most useful for reading modern newspapers, magazines, and books. Detailed introduction is provided. Index of English terms is appended to the text.   **PL1455.L67**

Mathews, Robert Henry. Mathews' Chinese-English dictionary. Rev. Amer. ed. Cambridge : Harvard Univ. Pr., [1943]. 1226 p.   **AC266**
    Originally published in 1931 as *A Chinese-English dictionary,* comp. for the China Inland Mission by R. H. Mathews ; various reprintings.
    "Within the necessary limitations of a photographic edition, and as far as interstices of the original edition allow, errors have been corrected, pronunciations and definitions revised, and new entries inserted—in all amounting to some 15,000 items. A whole introduction on pronunciation has been added, and a list of the syllabic headings is included for quick reference. ... An additional feature of the new edition is that all cases of the neutral, i.e., unstressed, tone are indicated."—*Foreword* to American edition.
    ———. *A Chinese-English dictionary,* comp. for the China Inland Mission. Rev. English index publ. for the Harvard-Yenching Institute (Cambridge : Harvard Univ. Pr., 1944. 186 p.).   **PL1455.M34**

The pinyin Chinese-English dictionary / ed. in chief, Wu Jinrong. Beijing [etc.] : Commercial Pr. ; San Francisco : Pitman, [1979]. 976 p.   **AC267**
    A desk dictionary compiled by an editorial committee of the Beijing Foreign Languages Institute and representing contributions of some 50 people. "There are over 6,000 single-character entries, including a small number of characters with variant tones. There are over 50,000 compound-character entries and over 70,000 compound words, set phrases and examples. Apart from everyday words and expressions, a number of common classical Chinese words, dialect words, four-character idioms, proverbs and common scientific expressions from both the natural and social sciences have been included."—*Foreword.*
                                 PL1455.P55

Schuessler, Axel. A dictionary of early Zhou Chinese. Honolulu : Univ. of Hawaii Pr., c1987. 876 p.   **AC268**

Defines vocabulary of the Western Zhou Bronze Age in China and draws on inscription sources, 1250–771 BCE. The arrangement of entries is alphabetical according to pinyin transcription and among homophones according to the four tones. PL1077.S38

Bibliography

Chien, David. Lexicography in China : bibliography of dictionaries and related literature. [Exeter, England] : Univ. of Exeter, 1986. 237 p. (Exeter linguistic studies, 12). **AC269**
Pt. 1 is a 1,000-item bibliography. Pt. 2 offers 630 references to major dictionaries of the Chinese language, from ancient times to the present. Entries are not annotated, although languages are indicated.

Chinese dictionaries : an extensive bibliography of dictionaries in Chinese and other languages / comp. and ed. by the Chinese-English Translation Assistance Group, James Mathias, managing ed. Westport, Conn. : Greenwood, 1982. 446 p.
AC270
A compilation of Chinese dictionaries, comp. and ed. by S. Hixson and J. Mathias, was published under CETA sponsorship (New Haven, Conn. : Yale Univ. Pr., 1975).
Aims "to identify as many Chinese monolingual, bilingual, and polyglot dictionaries as possible."—*Pref.* A section of general dictionaries (p. 3–90) is followed by specialized dictionaries listed according to subject areas. Title and language indexes. (An appendix of additional titles has its own index.) More than 2,700 entries. Z3108.L5C483

Library of Congress. Chinese-English and English-Chinese dictionaries in the Library of Congress : an annotated bibliography / comp. by Robert Dunn. Wash. : Library of Congress, 1977. 140 p. **AC271**
In two main sections: (1) special subject dictionaries listed alphabetically by subject field; (2) general language dictionaries. Indexes of authors and titles, plus a Chinese-character author and title list. 569 items with annotations. Z3109.U53

Coptic

Černý, Jaroslav. Coptic etymological dictionary. Cambridge ; N.Y. : Cambridge Univ. Pr., 1976. 384 p. **AC272**
"My guiding principle in compiling this dictionary has been to adopt only etymologies which I considered certain, probable or at least possible."—*Pref.* Serves as a complement to W. E. Crum's *Coptic dictionary* (AC273) which omits etymologies. Gives bibliographic references to sources for the etymologies. Indexed.
For a review of this "great work of scholarship" see *Bulletin* of the School of Oriental and African Studies 41 (1978): 358–62.
PJ2163.C4

Crum, Walter Ewing. A Coptic dictionary. Oxford : Clarendon Pr., 1939. 953 p. **AC273**
Issued in 6 pts., 1929–39.
The standard Coptic-English dictionary compiled from published and unpublished manuscripts, ostraca, and inscriptions. 3,308 entries, including 309 words whose meanings are yet unknown. Includes illustrative quotations with references to sources. Indexes in English, Greek, and Arabic.
§ *A concise Coptic-English lexicon*, comp. by Richard Smith (Grand Rapids, Mich. : Eerdmans, 1983. 81 p.), is a useful work for the beginning student. PJ2181.C7

Cornish

Nance, Robert Morton. An English-Cornish dictionary. Marazion : printed for the Federation of Old Cornwall Societies by Worden, 1952. 200 p. **AC274**
1st ed., 1934, by R. M. Nance and A. S. D. Smith.
Relying on original manuscripts rather than printed editions as authority, this dictionary "aims at giving students of Cornish the means of expressing themselves in words which are either part of the Middle Cornish learnt [sic] by them in unified form, or where these fail, loans from Welsh and Breton or from Middle English, so spelt [sic] as to harmonise with it."—*Introd.*
————. A new Cornish-English dictionary (St. Ives : pr. for the Federation of Old Cornwall Societies by James Lanham, 1938. 209 p.).
PB2537.E5N3

Williams, Robert. Lexicon Cornu-Britannicum : a dictionary of the ancient Celtic language of Cornwall, in which the words are elucidated by copious examples from the Cornish works now remaining; with translations into English. Llan-dovery : Roderic, 1865. 398p. **AC275**
The aim was to "collect and explain all the remains of the ancient British language of Cornwall,"—*Pref.* "The synonyms are also given in the cognate dialects of Welsh, Amoric, Irish, Gaelic, and Manx"—*t.p.* PB2537.E5W6

Czech

Česká Akademie Věd a Uměni. Třída 3. Příruční slovník jazyka českého. V Praze : Státní Pedagogické Nakl., 1935–57. 8 v. in 9. **AC276**
The authoritative dictionary of the Czech language, with illustrative examples from standard authors. Issued by the Czech Academy.
PG4625.C4

Československá Akademie Věd. Ústav pro Jazyk Český. Slovník spisovného jazyka českého. Praha : Akademia Nakl. Československé Akademie Věd, 1971. 4 v. **AC277**
Contents: v. 1 3, A U; v. 4, V Ž, Doplňky a opravy.
Originally issued in parts, 1958–71. Also issued with title in Czech and English (*Dictionary of the Czech literary language*) by Univ. of Alabama Pr. (University, Ala., 1966–71. 4v.).
A smaller work based on *Příruční slovník jazyka českého* (AC276), but including more up-to-date words. PG4625.C45

Trávníček, František. Slovník jazyka českého. 4. přepr. a dopl. vyd. Praha : Slovanské Nakl., 1952. 1081 p. **AC278**
Earlier editions were by Pavel Vása and F. Trávníček (Prague : Borový, 1935–36; 3rd ed., 1946).
A standard work. PG4625.T7

Bilingual

Hais, Karel. Velký anglicko-český slovník / Karel Hais, Břetislav Hodek. 2nd rev. ed. Praha : Academia, 1991–1992. 3 v. **AC279**
Title on added t.p. : *English-Czech dictionary*.
1st ed., 1984–84.
Replaces Václav Jung's *Slovník anglicko-česky* (1st ed., 1911), previously the most comprehensive English-Czech dictionary available. Lists some 100,000 words, including slang and technical terms.
PG4640.H343

Poldauf, Ivan. Česko-anglický slovník / zpracoval Ivan Poldauf ; spolupracoval Robert Pynsent. 2. vyd. Praha : Státní Pedagogické Naakl., 1990. 1133 p. **AC280**

Added title page in English: *Czech-English dictionary.*

Czech to English only. Appendixes include: abbreviations, proper names, and an abstract of Czech grammar.   PG4640.C43

Procházka, Jindřich. Slovník anglicko-český a česko-anglický. 16th rev. and enl. ed. Prague : Artia, 1959. 423 p., 589 p.   **AC281**

Added title page: English-Czech and Czech-English dictionary : giving pronunciation of all English words, with special regard to idiomatic phrases and phraseology of commercial correspondence.

Frequently reprinted; editors vary.   PG4640.P73

Abbreviations

Library of Congress. Slavic and Central European Division. Czech and Slovak abbreviations : a selective list / ed. by Paul L. Horecky. Wash., 1956. 164 p.   **AC282**

"Entries for the most part denote governmental, political, economic, cultural, and social bodies" (*Pref.*) with some general terms that are commonly abbreviated. Needs to be updated.   Z663.47.C9

Etymology

Holub, Josef. Stručny etymologický slovník jazyka českého se zvlástním zřetelem k slovům kulturním a cizím / Joseph Holub, Stanislav Lyer. Vyd. 4. Praha : Státńi Pedag. Naklad., 1992. 483 p.   **AC283**

1st ed., 1967.

A brief etymological dictionary. Includes foreign words and phrases.   PG4580.H63

Machek, Václav. Etymologický slovník jazyka českého. 2. opr. a dopln. vyd. Praha : Academia, 1968. 866 p.   **AC284**

1st ed., 1957, had title *Etymologický slovník jazyka českého a slovenského.*

An etymological dictionary of the Czech and Slovak languages.   PG4580.M3

Danish

Danske sprog- og litteraturselskab. Ordbog over det danske sprog / grundlagt af Verner Dahlerup; med understøttelse af Undervisningsministeriet og Carlsbergfondet .... Copenhagen : Gyldendal, 1919–1956. 28 v.   **AC285**

Vol. 1 issued in 2 pts., 1918–19.

Vol. 28: Liste over forkortelser med en lydskrifttavle og en efterskrift.

The scholarly dictionary of the Danish language since 1700, giving etymologies, illustrative quotations, etc.

Supplemented by: *Liste over Forkortelser med en Lydskrifttavle og en Efterskrift* (Copenhagen, 1956. 113 p.).

Nudansk ordbog / [redaktion, Lis Jacobsen ... et al.]. 11. revid. og förgede udg. / ved Erik Oxenvad. Copenhagen : Politiken, 1982. 2 v. (1100 p.).   **AC286**

1st ed., 1953.

Concise definitions; derivation and part of speech indicated. About 50,000 terms.   PD3625.N8

Bilingual

Axelsen, Jens. Dansk-engelsk Ordbog / [af] Jens Axelsen ; grundlagt af Hermann Vinterverg. 9. udg., 8. opl. Copenhagen : Gyldendal, [1992]. 652 p.   **AC287**

1st ed., 1954–56. Frequently reprinted.

Based on the work first compiled by Hermann Vinterberg and Carl Adolf Bodelsen.

Examples of usage follow definitions. Proper nouns and abbreviations are included in a single alphabetic sequence.   PD3640.V5

Kjaerulff Nielsen, Bernhard. Engelsk-dansk ordbog. Anden udgave. [Copenhagen] : Gyldendal, 1981. 1273 p.   **AC288**

1st ed., 1964.

Frequently reprinted.

An excellent work giving grammatical details, pronunciation, variant meanings, and examples of usage.   PD3640.K4

The standard Danish-English, English-Danish dictionary = Dansk-engelsk, engelsk-dansk ordbok / ed. by Jens Axelsen. Eastbourne, East Sussex : Holt, Rinehart & Winston ; Copenhagen : Gyldendal, 1986. 581 p.   **AC289**

1st Gyldendal ed., 1984.

About 65,000 entries in each section, aiming "to cover the general contemporary vocabulary of the two languages" (*Pref.*) including idioms and phrases, slang words, and some terms from business, technology, etc.   PD3640.S74

Etymology

Falk, Hjalmar Sejersted. Norwegisch-dänisches etymologisches Wörterbuch : auf Grund der Übersetzung von H. Davidsen neu bearb. deutsche Ausg., mit Literaturnachweisen strittiger Etymologien sowie deutschem und alt-nordischem Wörterverzeichnis. Heidelberg : Winter, 1910–11. 2 v.   **AC290**

Translated from *Etymologisk ordbog over det norske og det danske sprog* (Kristiania, 1903–1906).

1st ed., 1910–11.   PD2683.F33

Dravidian

Burrow, Thomas. A Dravidian etymological dictionary / by T. Burrow and M. B. Emeneau. 2nd ed. Oxford : Clarendon Pr. ; N.Y. : Oxford Univ. Pr., 1984. 853 p.   **AC291**

1st ed., 1961; suppl., 1968.

The Dravidian languages are spoken in southeastern India and northern Ceylon. This dictionary gives etymologies of all known Dravidian languages with English equivalents. Treats the four major literary languages and many nonliterary ones. Incorporates material from the earlier edition and its supplement with results of new scholarship and information published elsewhere. Bibliography and list of sources.   PL4609.B8

Dutch

Geerts, Guido. Groot woordenboek der Nederlandse taal / door G. Geerts en H. Heestermans ... [et al.]. 12., herziene druk. Utrecht : Van Dale Lexicografie, c1992. 3 v.   **AC292**

1st ed., 1864; 11th ed., 1984.

At head of title : Van Dale.

An excellent, well-established dictionary. Words from the supplement to the previous edition are now incorporated into the body of the work.   PF625.D3

Woordenboek der nederlandsche taal. 's-Gravenhage [etc.] : M. Nijhoff [etc.], 1882–[1992?]. 1.–26$^{1-19}$ deel. (In progress).   **AC293**

Ed. by M. De Vries and others.

Contents: v. 1–26[1–19], A–Wraak.

———. *Supplement* (1942–56. v. 1.).

———. *Bronnenlijst*, bewerkt door C. H. A. Kruyskamp (1943. 144 p.).

———. ———. 1.–2. *Aanvulling* (1953–66. 2 v.).

The standard dictionary compiled on historical principles, with etymologies, references to sources, synonyms, etc. **PF625.W6**

Early

Verdam, Jacob. Middelnederlandsch handwoordenboek. 2. uitg. 'sGravenhage : Nijhoff, 1932. 811 p. **AC294**

Repr., 1979.

Enlarged from the 1st ed., 1911, with revision of section Sterne–Z by C. H. Ebbinge Wubben.

Supplemented by J. J. van der Voort van der Kleij, *Middelnederlandsch handwoordenboek : Supplement* (Leiden : Nijhoff, 1983. 354 p.). **PF776.V3**

Verwijs, Eelco. Middelnederlandsch woordenboek / Eelco Verwijs and Jacob Verdam. 'sGravenhage : Nijhoff, 1885–1953. 11 v. **AC295**

Contents: deel 1–9, A–Z; deel 10[1], Tekstcritiek van J. Verdam, en Bouwstoffen, eerste gedeelte (A–F) door Willem de Vreese; deel 10[2], Bouwstoffen, tweede gedeelte (G–Z) door G. I. Lieftinck; deel 11, afl. 1–5, Aanvullingen en verbeteringen op het gebied van dijken waterschapsrecht, bodem en water, aardrijkskunde, enz. door A. A. Beekman (A–Z).

A comprehensive dictionary of the older language. Vol. 10 includes an extensive bibliography of sources; v. 11, additions and corrections in the fields of water rights, geography, etc. **PF776.V3**

Bilingual

Bruggencate, Karel ten. Engels woordenboek. 19. druk / bewerkt door J. Gerritsen en N. E. Osselton ; met medewerking van R. W. Zandvoort. Groningen : Wolters, [1981–82]. 2 v. **AC296**

Repr.: Groningen : Wolters-Noordhof, 1989.

1st ed., 1895–96.

Contents: v. 1, Engels-Nederlands; v. 2, Nederlands-Engels. (v. 2 is a 5th printing of the 18th ed.).

A practical desk dictionary, reflecting current usage. **PF640.B8**

Cassell's English-Dutch, Dutch-English dictionary = Engels-Nederlands, Nederlands-Engels woordenboek / completely rev. by J. A. Jockin-La Bastide, G. van Kooten. London : Cassell ; N.Y. : Macmillan, 1981. 602 p., 729 p. **AC297**

Spine title: Cassell's Dutch dictionary.

Earlier editions of *Cassell's Dutch-English, English-Dutch dictionary* (first publ. 1951; last revision 1965) were ed. by F. P. H. Prick van Wely. The 1978 ed. of the present title by Jockin-La Bastide and Kooten corresponded to their 36th ed. of *Kramers' Engels woordenboek* (AC298); it was revised and reset in 1980.

A practical, up-to-date work for the student, business person, or general reader. **PF640.C375**

Kramers, Jacob. Kramers' Engels woordenboek. 36. geheel herziene en vermeerderde druk / bewerkt door J. A. Jockin-La Bastide en G. van Kooten. Amsterdam : Van Goor ; N.Y. : distr. by W. S. Heinman, 1978. 2 v. **AC298**

1st ed. 1917–19?

Frequently reissued.

Contents: v.1, Engels-Nederlands (602 p.); v.2, Nederlands-Engels (729 p.).

A standard bilingual dictionary. Pronunciation is indicated in the English-Dutch part. **PF640.K7**

Etymology

Franck, Johannes. Franck's Etymologisch woordenboek der Nederlandsche taal. 2. druk / door Dr. N. van Wijk. Met registers der Nieuwhoogduitsche woorden, enz. 'sGravenhage : Nijhoff, 1912. 897 p. **AC299**

Repr. with Suppl.: 1949.

Issued in 14 pts., 1910–12.

Contains an index that lists words by origin.

———. ———. *Supplement*, door C. B. van Haeringen (1936. 235 p.).

Bibliography

Claes, Frans M. A bibliography of Netherlandic dictionaries : Dutch-Flemish. München : Kraus Internat., [1980]. 314 p. **AC300**

Aims to list "all monolingual, bilingual and polyglot dictionaries with a Netherlandic text, specialized ... as well as general works, including dictionaries, vocabularies and glossaries of abbreviations, synonyms and homonyms, foreign words, individual authors, proverbs and quotations as well as etymological, orthographical, geographical, onomastic, rhyming, reverse, dialectical and slang lexicographic works."—*Introd.* In three main sections: (1) Monolingual (in classed arrangement); (2) Bilingual (arranged by language); and (3) Polyglot. Indexed. **Z2445.D6C49**

Egyptian

Budge, Ernest Alfred Thompson Wallis. An Egyptian hieroglyphic dictionary : with an index of English words, king list and geographical list, with indexes, list of hieroglyphic characters, Coptic and Semitic alphabets, etc. London : Murray, 1920. 1356 p. **AC301**

Repr.: N.Y. : Ungar, 1960; N.Y. : Dover, 1978. **PJ1425.B8**

A dictionary of Late Egyptian / Leonard H. Lesko, ed., Barbara Switalski Lesko, collaborating ed. Berkeley, Calif. : B.C. Scribe Pubns., [1982–89]. 4 v. **AC302**

A computer-generated work (with hieroglyphs) based on selected texts in readily available editions and translations. "For our *lexicographical* purposes we have generally restricted our period as the Nineteenth through the end of the Twenty-first Dynasties and we have included literary, some historical and almost no religious literature."—*Pref., v. 1.* The work is "not a complete concordance of every reference to each word, but is an attempt to collect all the significant variations in orthography in as many various translations as have been offered or seemed practical."—*Pref., v. 4.* **PJ1425.D53**

Erman, Adolf. Wörterbuch der aegyptischen Sprache : im Auftrage der Deutschen Akademien / von Adolf Erman und Hermann Grapow. Leipzig : Hinrichs, 1926–63. 7 v. **AC303**

Repr. : Berlin : Akademie Verlag, 1971.

Imprint varies.

An authoritative work in German, covering both the hieratic and the hieroglyphic vocabularies.

———. ———. *Die Belegstellen* (1940–59. Imprint varies. 5 v. Repr. in 6 v.: Berlin : Akademie-Verlag, 1971). **PJ1430.E65**

Faulkner, Raymond O. A concise dictionary of Middle Egyptian. Oxford : Printed for the Griffith Institute at the Univ. Pr. by V. Ridler, c1962. 327 p. **AC304**

Frequently reprinted.

Intended for third year undergraduate or epigraphist, the text draws from the language of Heracleopolitan period to the end of the Eighteenth Dynasty. A seven-page addendum was issued in 1972.

Estonian

Nurm, E. Õigekeelsuse sõnaraamat. Tallinn : Eesti Riiklik Kirjastus, 1960. 871 p.   **AC305**
> At head of title: Eesti NSV Teaduste Akadeemia, Keele ja Kirjanduse Instituut.   PH623.N8

Saareste, Andrus Kustas. Eesti keele môisteline sõnaraamat = Dictionnaire analogique de la langue estonienne : avec un index pourvu des traductions en français. Stockholm : Kirjastus Vaba Eesti, 1958–[68?]. 4 v. (Eesti Teadusiliku Seltsi Rootsis väljaane, 3).   **AC306**
> Issued in parts.
> An analogical dictionary of the Estonian language containing "the entire subject matter of [Ferdinand Johann] Wiedemann's Dictionary [AC309]; new words now commonly used … ; dialectal words … ; examples to make clear all nuances of meaning and style, taken from colloquial or standard Estonian; proverbs; and pictures of objects which cannot be described adequately or which are comparatively rare. At the end of the Dictionary there will be an alphabetical index in Estonian and French of all words to be found in it."—[*Descriptive statement*]. Addenda in v.4.   PH623.S2

Bilingual

Saagpakk, Paul Friidrih. Eesti-inglise sõnaraamat = Estonian-English dictionary. New Haven : Yale Univ. Pr., c1982. 1180 p.   **AC307**
> Prefatory matter in Estonian and English.
> The work "has two main objects: first to enable Estonians to find the British and American words and idioms most closely corresponding to those in Estonian; and second, to provide world philologists and students of language with a means of learning Estonian thoroughly, whether for purposes of philological research or with a view to reading Estonian literature."—*Pref.* Includes an introduction with "A grammatical survey of the Estonian language" by Johannes Aavik, p. xxxvii–lxxxvii.   PH625.S325

Silvet, J. Eesti-inglise sõnaraamat. 2. trükk. Tallinn : Valgus, 1980. 508 p.   **AC308**
> Added t.p.: *Estonian-English dictionary*.
> Previous ed., 1965.
> Separate appendix for proper names.
> ———. *Inglise-Eesti sonaraamat* (3. trükk. Tallinn : Valgus, 1989–90. 2 v.
> Added t.-p.: *English-Estonian dictionary*.
> About 80,000 items. Abbreviations and proper names are interfiled with other countries.   PH625.S49

Wiedemann, F. J. Eesti-saksa sõnaraamat kolmas muutmatu trük teisest, dr. Jakob Hurt'i poolt redigeeritud väljaandest / sissejuhatusega varustanud Albert Saareste. Eesti kaardiga. Tartu : Eesti kirjanduse seltsi kirjastus, 1923. 1406 col., cix p. : map.   **AC309**
> Title in German: Estnisch-deutsches worterbuch. 3. unveranderter druck nach der 2., von dr. Jakob Hurt redigierten aufl. Mit einer einleitung versehen von Albert Saareste. Mit einer karte Eestis. Dorpat : Estnische literaturgesellschaft, 1923.
> 1st ed., St. Petersburg, 1869.
> Repr.: Tallinn : "Valgus," 1973.
> The Estonian and German titles are printed side by side. Introduction in Estonian and German.   PH625.W5

Languages of Ethopia

Dillmann, August. Lexicon linguae Aethiopicae cum indice Latino. Lipsae : T.O. Weigel, 1865. 3 v. (1522 col.).   **AC310**
> Repr.: Osnabrück : Biblio Verlag, 1970.
> An appendix, ed. by Werner Munzinger, covers the vocabulary of the Tigré region, where a related language is spoken.   PJ9093.D5

Grébaut, Sylvain. Supplément au Lexicon linguae Aethiopicae … (1865) et édition du lexique de Juste d'Urbin (1850–1855). Paris : Impr. Nationale, 1952. 520 p.   **AC311**
> Words are identified by column numbers given in August Dillman's *Lexicon linguae Aethiopicae* (AC310).   PJ9093.G7

Leslau, Wolf. Comparative dictionary of Ge'ez (Classical Ethiopic) : Ge'ez-English, English-Ge'ez, with an index of the Semitic roots. Wiesbaden : Harrassowitz, 1987. 813 p.   **AC312**
> "A comprehensive dictionary of Geez."—*Introd.* Entries are in phonetic transcription followed by Ethiopic script. Includes etymologies and comparisons with other Semitic languages.   PJ9087.L37

Farsi

Āryānpūr Kāshānī, 'Abbās. The new unabridged English-Persian dictionary / by Abbas Aryanpur (Kashani), with the collaboration of Jahan Shah Saleh and numerous consultants, translators, etc. [Tehran : Amir-Kabir Publ. & Print. Inst., 1963–64]. 5 v. : ill.   **AC313**
> Title on added t.p.: *Farhang-i jadīd-i Inglīlisī Fārsī*.
> "This book is based on Webster's International Dictionary, and The Shorter Oxford Dictionary, attempting to give Persian equivalents of all the words of Oxford and all the key-words of Webster."—*Introd.*
> § Another work by 'Abbās and Manūchihr Āryānpūr Kāshānī is *Farhang-i nuvin-i payvastah-i Fārsī-Ingilīsī va Ingilisī-Fārsī* (*The combined new Persian-English and English-Persian dictionary*) (Lexington, Ky. : Mazdâ Publ., 1986. 45, 307, 273 p.).
> "A combination and rearrangement of our pocket English-Persian and Persian-English dictionaries plus an all-new Etymological Study and the pioneering Guide to Punctuation in Persian."—*Pref. to the first American ed.*   PK6379.A7

Hayyīm, Sulaymān. The larger English-Persian dictionary : designed to give the Persian meanings of 80,000 words, idioms, phrases and proverbs in the English language, as well as the transliteration of difficult Persian words. Téhéran : Bēroukhim, 1941–43. 2 v.   **AC314**
> Added t.p. in Farsi.
> Various reprintings.
> Each volume has Addenda, including some words omitted from the text, important proper names, foreign words and phrases, a few colloquial and slang expressions, abbreviations used in English literature, and Persian abbreviations.
> § Two other dictionaries by the same author:
> *New Persian-English dictionary* (Téhéran : Bēroukhim, 1960–62. 2 v.).
> Subtitle: complete and modern, designed to give the English meanings of over 50,000 words, terms, idioms, and proverbs in the Persian language as well as the transliteration of the words in English characters. Together with a sufficient treatment of all the grammatical features of the Persian language.
> First publ. 1934–36. Repr. 1975.
> "Designed to be the fullest, most-modern, and most accurate of all the Persian-English dictionaries hitherto compiled."—*Pref.*
> *The shorter Persian-English dictionary : treating 30,000 words and idioms used in modern Persian* (3rd ed., rev. and enl. Téhéran : Bēroukhim, 1963. 814 p.). 1st ed., 1954.   PK6379.H26

Montazem, Mir Ali Asghar. The new English-Persian dictionary : designed to give the Persian equivalents of the most important and the most common English words in International phonetic transcription. Téhéran : Ebn-e Sina Book-Store, 1967. 1407 p. **AC315**

 Repr.: Téhéran : Khoosheh Book, 1991.
 Title also in Persian.
 Includes examples of usage and a list of common abbreviations. PK6379.M6

Palmer, Edward H. A concise dictionary of the Persian language. London : Routledge & Paul, 1949. 726 col. **AC316**
 English-Persian and Persian-English. PK6379.P3

Razi, F. D. The modern Persian dictionary (Persian-Urdu-English) / comp. by F. D. Razi, assisted by M. Rasheed Ahmed. Lahore : Ripon Printing Pr., 1952. 240 p. **AC317**
 Repr. : New Delhi : Kitāb-i Bhavan, 1990.
 Title also in Farsi.
 Includes separate vocabulary sections for weights and measures, abbreviations, and military vocabulary. PK6379.R3

Wollaston, Arthur Naylor. A complete English-Persian dictionary : comp. from original sources. London : Murray, 1904. 1491 p. **AC318**
 Repr. : New Delhi : Publication India, 1988.
 First publ. 1889; publisher varies.
 Appendixes for numbers, names of persons and places, and a table for the Islamic calendar. PK6379.W7

Fijian

Capell, Arthur. A new Fijian dictionary / comp. by A. Capell for the government of Fiji. 4th ed. Suva, Fiji : Government Printer, 1973. 407 p. **AC319**
 1st ed., 1941; 3rd. ed., 1968.
 Fijian-English; English-Fijian.
 The vocabulary is limited to the Bau dialect. "The language taken as the standard in this work has been the normal educated Fijian, taught in schools, and printed in books and magazines." *Introd.* PL6235.Z5C3

Finnish

Suomalaisen Kirjallisuuden Seura. Nykysuomen sanakirja / Valtion toimeksiannosta teettänyt Suomalaisen Kirjallisuuden Seura ; [Päätoimittaja: Matti Sadeniemi]. 2. painos. Porvoo : Söderström, 1957–62. 6 v. **AC320**
 An authoritative dictionary of contemporary Finnish. PH275.S8

Bilingual

Alanne, Vieno Severi. Suomalais-englantilainen suursanakirja. [3rd ed.]. [Porvoo] : W. Söderström, 1956. 1111 p. **AC321**
 1st ed., 1919.
 Frequently reprinted.
 Added t.p.: Finnish-English general dictionary.
 Earlier editions had title: *Suomalais-englantilainen sanakirja.* PH279.A6

Hurme, Raija. Englanti-suomi suursanakirja = English-Finnish general dictionary / Raija Hurme, Maritta Pesonen, Olli Syväoja. 3. painoksen. Porvoo : Söderström, c1990. 1525 p. **AC322**

1st ed., 1973.; 2nd ed., 1978.
 "The editors have primarily had in mind a general dictionary to meet the needs of Finnish readers. ... Throughout the work, however, we have taken pains not to forget foreign users with their special problems."—*Foreword.* Gives pronunciation and examples of usage. PH279.H8

Särkkä, Heikki. Englantilais-suomalais-englantilainen yleiskielen käyttösanakirja = English-Finnish-English general dictionary. Helsingissä : Otava, c1992. 812 p. **AC323**
 The "Finnish-English portion contains the essential vocabulary of Standard Finnish, as well as the most commonly used vocabulary from tourism, technology, transportation, commerce and household affairs."—*Pref.*

Tuomikoski, Aune. Englantilais-suomalainen sanakirja / toimittaneet Aune Tuomikoski ja Anna Slöör. 6. painos. Helsinki : Suomalaisen Kirjallisuuden Seura, 1973. 1100 p. (Suomalaisen Kirjallisuuden Seuran Toimituksia, 212. osa). **AC324**

 Added t.p.: *English-Finnish dictionary.*
 Definitions given with examples and variant meanings. Abbreviations and proper nouns are appended. PH279.T8

Wuolle, Aino. The standard Finnish-English English-Finnish dictionary. Eastbourne [East Sussex] : Holt, Rinehart and Winston, 1986. 492, 512 p. **AC325**
 Combines Wuolle's *Suomalais-englantilainen sanakirja*, 1978 printing, and *Englantilais-suomalainen koulusanakirja*, 1981 printing, in a single volume.

Finno-Ugric

Collinder, Bjorn. Fenno-Ugric vocabulary : an etymological dictionary of the Uralic languages. Stockholm : Almqvist & Wiksell, [1955]. 211 p. **AC326**
 Entries are organized under three headings: Uralic words, genuine Finno-Ugric words, and Indo-European words. Index lists words under their language of origin

French

Davau, Maurice. Dictionaire du français vivant / Maurice Davau, Marcel Cohen, Maurice Lallemand. Nouv. éd., entièrement rev. et augm. [Paris] : Bordas, [1979]. 1344 p. **AC327**
 1st ed., 1972.
 A desk dictionary for the student and general reader. Gives pronunciation (in International Phonetic Alphabet), etymology, definitions, and examples of usage. Emphasis is on contemporary vocabulary and use. About 34,000 words. PC2625.D3

Dictionnaire de l'Académie française. 9e éd. Paris : Impr. nationale, 1986–1990. Fasc. 1–5. (In progress). **AC328**
 8th éd., 1931–35.
 Issued in fascicles.
 Contents: Fasc. 1–5, A–Encyclique.
 The standard conservative dictionary of the French language for spelling and usage. Does not include etymologies or show historical development. Primarily for the literary language; includes very few scientific and technical terms.
 This edition adheres to the form and purpose of the earlier editions; that is, to establish proper French usage. Some 10,000 words not listed in the earlier edition will be included, indicated by asterisks. PC2625.D455

Grand Larousse de la langue française / [sous la direction de Louis Guilbert, René Lagane et Georges Niobey]. Paris : Larousse, [1971–78]. 7 v. (6729 p.).   **AC329**

    Comparable in physical size to Paul Robert, *Dictionnaire alphabétique et analogique de la langue française* (AC334), but less comprehensive than that work. In addition to definition and transcription in International Phonetic Alphabet, each entry includes: etymology, examples of usage, indication of level of usage, synonyms and antonyms. Limited to words in use in the 19th and 20th centuries, including a generous number of current technical terms.

    Vol. 7 includes a "Bibliographie des matériaux utilisés pour la partie historique du dictionnaire," p. 6634–6730.   PC2625.G7

Hatzfeld, Adolphe. Dictionnaire général de la langue française : du commencement du XVIIe siècle jusqu'à nos jours. Précédé d'un traite de la formation de la langue / par Adolphe Hatzfeld et Arsene Darmesteter, avec le concourse de Antoine Thomas. 9. éd. Paris : Delagrave, 1932. 2 v.   **AC330**

    Repr.: Paris : Delagrave, 1964.

    1st ed. publ. in pts., 1890–1900; 8th ed., 1926.

    Gives etymologies, examples showing first usage, changes in meaning, etc.   PC2625.H4

Imbs, Paul. Trésor de la langue française : dictionnaire de la langue du XIXe et du XXe siècle (1789–1960). Paris : Éditions du Centre National de la Recherche Scientifique, 1971–92. v. 1–15. (In progress).   **AC331**

    Vol. 13–15 publ. by Gallimard, Paris. Vol. 8–15 publ. under the direction of B. Quemada.

    Contents: v. 1–15, A–Teindre.

    Originally planned as a comprehensive historical dictionary—a "French O.E.D."—for the 19th and 20th centuries and eventually covering all the earlier period as well. Vol. 1 includes definitions, illustrations from fully identified texts, history, etymology with sources, pronunciation in International Phonetic Alphabet, citations to books and articles for further information, frequency of occurrence in texts cited, and detailed indications of usage and syntax. Some compressions, notably in the number of textual examples, were made in v. 2. Beginning with v. 3, the scope was reduced drastically to permit completion in considerably fewer volumes than the 60 the original design would have demanded.   PC2625.I4

Littré, Émile. Dictionnaire de la langue française. Éd. intégrale. Paris : J. Pauvert, 1956–58. 7 v.   **AC332**

    Éd. intégrale: la seule complète des étymologies et des différents suppléments et additifs reclassés dans le texte selon les intentions de l'auteur.

    A reprint of the famous Littré (1873–78; 4 v. and suppl.) in modern format, in which the material in the supplement of the early work has been incorporated into the main alphabet. An older work still important for the history, etymology, and grammar of the French language. Includes many quotations from literature with exact references to sources.

    An abridgment was published as: *Dictionnaire de la langue française*, abrégé du dictionnaire de É. Littré par A. Beaujean. 12. éd. conforme pour l'orthographe à la dernière éd. du Dictionnaire de l'Académie Française (Paris : Hachette, 1914. 1295 p., 123 p. Repr.: Paris : Éds. Universitaires, 1950. 1294 p.).   PC2625.L3

Petit Larousse illustré, 1990. Paris : Larousse, c1989. 1680 p., [50] p. of plates : ill. (some col.), maps.   **AC333**

    Rev. ed. of *Nouveau petit Larousse* (1972). Repr., 1991.

    "83,500 articles, 3,600 illustrations, 269 cartes, et un atlas à la fin de l'ouvrage."—*t.p.*

    A popular desk dictionary that gives definitions of words, pronunciation in International Phonetic Alphabet, and usage, and is followed by a short section of foreign phrases. More emphasis is placed on computer science, biology, and medicine.   AG25.P43

Robert, Paul. Dictionnaire alphabétique et analogique de la langue française. 2e éd. entièrement rev. et enrichie / par Alain Rey. Paris : Le Robert, c1985. 9 v. : ill.   **AC334**

1st ed. issued in parts, 1951–64, then in 6 v., 1970.

    A historical dictionary of the French language, giving for each entry: etymology, definitions, synonyms, antonyms, and cross-references to words with related meaning. Extensive quotations from French writers, selected to clarify usage and trace historical changes in meaning. Sponsored by the Academie Française.   PC2625.R552

Bilingual

Collins-Robert French-English, English-French dictionary / by Beryl T. Atkins ... [et al.]. 2nd ed. / contributors, Edwin Carpenter, Françoise Morcellet. N.Y. : HarperCollins, 1993. 465, 570 p.   **AC335**

    1st ed., 1978; Nouv. ed., 1987.

    Added t.p.: Dictionnaire francais-anglais, anglais-francais.

    Includes a section of standard phrases and expressions.

    PC2640.R63

Collins Robert French-English, English-French dictionary, unabridged / by Beryl T. Atkins ... [et al.]. 3rd ed. London ; N.Y. : HarperCollins ; Paris : Dictionnaires Le Robert, 1993. 886, 72, 962, 46 p.   **AC336**

    Added title page in French: *Le Robert & Collins dictionnaire français-anglais, anglais-français, senior.*

    1st ed., 1978; 2nd ed., 1987.

    Designed to be "equally valid for French-speaking and English-speaking users."—*Introd.* Contemporary French terms; especially good for business terms and revised geographical terms.

    PC2640.C69

The concise Oxford French dictionary / French-English ed. by H. Ferrar ; English-French ed. by J. A. Hutchinson and J.-D. Biard. 2nd ed. Oxford : Clarendon Pr. ; N.Y. : Oxford Univ. Pr., 1980. 596 p., 267 p.   **AC337**

    1st ed. 1934–40 (2 v.) ed. by Abel Chevalley, M. Chevalley and G. W. F. R. Goodridge.

    2nd ed. with corr., 1984; repr.: 1992.

    About 40,000 headwords in the French-English section and about 30,000 in the English-French. The former ranges from classical to contemporary vocabulary; the latter relies heavily on the 6th ed. of the *Concise Oxford dictionary of current English* (AC38) for choice of vocabulary.   PC2640.C54

Corbeil, Jean Claude. The Facts on File English/French visual dictionary : look up the word from the picture, find the picture from the word / Jean-Claude Corbeil, Ariane Archambault. N.Y. : Facts on File, c1987. 924 p. : ill.   **AC338**

    Provides accurate terminology for objects, devices, machines, instruments, and tools of everyday life. It differentiates between the French of Canada and France, and between the English of the U.S. and Great Britain.   AG250.C64

Deak, Étienne. Grand dictionnaire d'américanismes : contenant les principaux termes américains avec leur équivalent exact en français / Étienne Deak, Simone Deak. 5. éd. augm. Paris : Éditions du Dauphin, 1973. 823 p.   **AC339**

    1st ed., 1956, by Étienne Deak had title *Dictionnaire d'américanismes.*

    Provides French equivalents of American slang terms, popular phrases, and idiomatic expressions.   PC2640.D4

Kirk-Greene, C. W. E. NTC's dictionary of faux amis. Lincolnwood, Ill. : National Textbook Co., c1990. 197 p. **AC340**

    Relates words in French and English that appear to derive from a common root but do not. Each entry gives a French word with its definition, and the English word that appears to be its cognate with the French equivalent.   PC2593.K48

Larousse modern French-English [English-French] dictionary / by Marguerite-Marie Dubois … [et al.]. N.Y. : McGraw-Hill, [c1960]. 2 v. in 1 (768, 751 p.) : ill.　　**AC341**

Frequently reprinted.

A desk dictionary, the work of several French, British, and American collaborators. Colloquial and slang expressions are included.　　PC2640.L3

New Cassell's French dictionary : French-English, English-French / completely rev. by Denis Girard … [et al.]. N.Y. : Funk & Wagnalls, [1962]. 762, 655 p.　　**AC342**

First published 1920 with title *Cassell's French-English, English-French dictionary*. Frequently reprinted.

A familiar and useful desk dictionary which has gone through five editions and many reprintings. This is a thoroughly revised work by different editors: many new words have been added, as well as new meanings; obsolete terms have been omitted; and errors have been rectified. Includes translations of phrases and expressions. Gives pronunciation.　　PC2640.C3

NTC's French and English business dictionary / Michel Marcheteau … [et al.]. Lincolnwood, Ill. : National Textbook Co., 1992. 620 p.　　**AC343**

For annotation, *see* CH61.　　HF1002.N93

The Oxford-Duden pictorial French-English dictionary. Oxford : Clarendon Pr., 1983. 1 v., various paging : ill.　　**AC344**

Like *The Oxford-Duden pictorial German-English dictionary* (AC420), this is based on the German *Bildwörterbuch* "published as Volume 3 of the ten-volume *Duden* series of monolingual German dictionaries."—*Foreword*. On the principle that certain kinds of information can better be conveyed by pictures than by description or explanation, the work employs a series of 384 plates in subject arrangement; each object illustrated is numbered, and the corresponding French terms and their English equivalents are given on the same or facing page. Indexes from both languages.　　PC2680.O93

Abbreviations

Carton, Jean. Dictionnaire de sigles nationaux et internationaux / Jean Carton avec la collaboration de François Carton et Bruno Iacono. 3e éd. rev., corr. et augm. et reg. / sur la base de la 2e éd. de 1977 élaborée par Michel Dubois. Paris : Maison du dictionnaire, c1987. [4], 379 p.　　**AC345**

First ed., 1973, had title: *Sigles nationaux & internationaux*; 2nd ed., 1977, tr. as *French and international acronyms & initialisms dictionary*.

Lists abbreviations in business and industry, economic and social activities, and politics and government from France, Spain, Germany, and the U.S. It provides addresses for many associations.　　AS8.D7813

Etymology

Baldinger, Kurt. Dictionnaire étymologique de l'ancien français / Kurt Baldinger ; avec la collaboration de Jean-Denis Gendron et Georges Straka. Québec : Presses de l'Université Laval ; Tübingen : Niemeyer ; Paris : Klincksieck, 1974–88. Fasc. G, pts. 1–5. (In progress).　　**AC346**

On cover: DEAF.

Fascicle G1 called "2. éd." replacing a provisional edition issued in 1971.

Contents: fasc. G1–G5, G–Glotonie.

An ambitious new dictionary, still in its infancy, based on Walther von Wartburg's *Französisches etymologisches Wörterbuch* (AC352) but restricted to the vocabulary of the mid-9th to mid-14th centuries.

One of the work's objectives is to correct inaccuracies found in Frédéric Eugéne Godefroy's *Dictionnaire de l'ancienne langue française* (AC378).　　PC2883.B3

Bloch, Oscar. Dictionnaire étymologique de la langue française / par Oscar Bloch et W. von Wartburg. 3. éd. / refondue par W. von Wartburg. Paris : Presses Universitaires de France, 1960. 674 p.　　**AC347**

Frequently reprinted; reprintings since 1960 based on this edition.

An etymological dictionary of contemporary French, giving date of earliest appearance, derivatives, etc.　　PC2580.B55

Dauzat, Albert. Nouveau dictionnaire étymologique et historique / par Albert Dauzat, Jean Dubois, Henri Mittterand. 3e éd. rev. et corr. Paris : Larousse, 1974. 804 p.　　**AC348**

Frequently reprinted.

1st ed., 1965; 2nd ed., 1971.

Based on Dauzat's *Dictionnaire étymologique de la langue française* (1st ed., 1938).

A work for general readers and students, giving brief etymological information, date of earliest usage, definition, derivatives, etc.　　PC2580.D35

Dictionnaire historique de la langue française : contenant les mots français en usage quelques autres délaissés / sous la direction de Alain Rey. Paris : Dictionnaires Le Robert, c1992. 2 v. (2383 p.) : ill.　　**AC349**

Includes words from 842 CE to the present. Entries provide a detailed history of each word and dated examples of use, earliest to most recent, with examples for each change in meaning. Icons are used to indicate the language of origin of each word. *See also* references link variant spellings to the main entry for a word. Bibliography. Chronological table of principal French texts.　　PC2580.D52

Gamillscheg, Ernst. Etymologisches Wörterbuch der französischen Sprache. 2. vollst. neu bearb. Aufl. Heidelberg : Winter, 1966–69. 1326 p. (Sammlung romanischer Elementar– und Handbücher. Reihe 3. Wörterbücher, Bd.5).　　**AC350**

Issued in 17 Lfg.

1st ed., 1928.

A scholarly dictionary in German with references to sources. Not as comprehensive as Walther von Wartburg's *Französisches etymologisches Wörterbuch* (AC352), but a useful one-volume work.　　PC2580.G32

Picoche, Jacqueline. Dictionnaire étymologique du français. [Nouv. éd.]. Paris : Robert, [1983]. 827 p.　　**AC351**

1st ed., 1979; frequently reprinted.

In addition to etymologies and dates of usage, for many words there are lists of variants and derived forms grouped as popular or learned (sometimes further subdivided for terms derived from Latin and from Greek).　　PC2580.P48

Wartburg, Walther von. Französisches etymologisches Wörterbuch : eine Darstellung des galloromanischen Sprachschatzes. Bonn, etc. : F. Klopp, etc., 1928–1992. v. 1–25 (v. 22, 23, 25 incomplete). (In progress).　　**AC352**

Imprint varies.

The great German dictionary of French etymology, giving the historical development of the meanings of the words with dates. Includes dialectal forms.

Published in *Lieferungen* (and now fascicles) numbered consecutively as issued but forming parts of different volumes. Lfg. 1–152 published to 1992; volumes completed are v. 1–14, A–Z; v. 15–17, Germanische Elemente; v. 18, Anglizismen; v. 19, Orientalia; v. 20, Entlehnungen aus den übrigen Sprachen; v. 21, Materialen unbekannten oder unsicheren Ursprugs, Teil 1; v. 24, Ganzlich neubearbeitete Ausgabe von Band 1 (Teil 1), A–apaideutos. Partially completed volumes are: v. 22, pt. 1^{1-3}, pt. 2^1, Materialen unbekannten unsicheren Ursprugs; v. 23^{1-3}, Materialen unbekannten oder unsicheren Ursprugs; and v. 25^{1-7}, Ganzlich neubearbeitete Ausgabe von Band 1 (Teil 2) Apaideutos–atrium.　　PC2580.W3

Slang

Bernet, Charles. Dictionnaire du français parlé : le monde des expressions familières / Charles Bernet, Pierre Rézeau. Paris : Seuil, c1989. 465 p.   **AC353**
   Offers definitions, with examples of usage, of more than 700 colloquial terms not found in other French dictionaries.   PC2689.B47

Cellard, Jacques. Dictionnaire du français non conventionnel / Jacques Cellard, Alain Rey. Paris : Hachette, c1991. 908 p.
                                             AC354
                    PC2689.C44

Colin, Jean-Paul. Dictionnaire de l'argot / Jean-Paul Colin, Jean-Pierre Mével, avec la collaboration de Christian Leclère. Paris : Larousse, c1990. 763 p.   **AC355**
   A scholarly dictionary partially based on Gaston Esnault's *Dictionnaire historique des argots français* (AC356). Offers etymologies and historical developments, with examples and sources, of some 6,500 words from the end of the 13th century to the present. "Glossaire français–argot," p. 677–726.   PC3741.C66

Esnault, Gaston. Dictionnaire historique des argots français. Paris : Larousse, [1965]. 644 p.   **AC356**
   More substantial than many French slang dictionaries. Indicates etymology in most instances, and cites examples of early usage.
                    PC3741.E8

Hérail, René James. Dictionary of modern colloquial French / René James Hérail, Edwin A. Lovatt. London ; Boston : Routledge & K. Paul, [1984]. 327 p.   **AC357**
   Repr. : London ; N.Y. : Routledge, 1990.
   Intends to bridge the gap between the kind of French learned in colleges and universities and that encountered in everyday French conversation. About 8,000 headwords. For each French term there is given, whenever possible, three English equivalents in decreasing levels of colloquiality.   PC2640.H47

Rheims, Maurice. Dictionnaire des mots sauvages (écrivains des XIXᵉ et XXᵉ siècles). Paris : Larousse, 1969. 605 p.
                                             AC358
   Repr., 1989.
   Includes words coined, obsolete terms revived, and provincialisms borrowed by French writers of the 19th and 20th centuries. Literary context of each term is shown, followed by a note on usage.
                    PC2460.R5

Synonyms

Bailly, René. Dictionnaire des synonymes de la langue française / par René Bailly, sous la direction de Michel de Toro. Éd. 1975, rev. et corr. Paris : Larousse, 1975. 626 p.
                                             AC359
   First publ. 1946; various reprints.
   A convenient, usable, alphabetically arranged dictionary giving definitions, discriminations in meanings, and examples of usage.
                    PC2591.B3

Batchelor, R. E. Using French synonyms / R. E. Batchelor and M. H. Offord. Cambridge [Eng.] : N.Y. : Cambridge Univ. Pr., 1993. 595 p.   **AC360**
   Clearly printed and easy to use, this dictionary "aims to present its material in an easily accessible manner, and is designed to promote easy assimilation and personal use of material."—*Introd.* Entries are categorized in French. Includes an index of English terms.
                    PC2591.B37

Bénac, Henri. Dictionnaire des synonymes, conforme au dictionnaire de l'Académie française. Paris : Hachette, [1983]. 1026 p.   **AC361**
   First publ. 1956.
   A dictionary of synonyms with explanations and examples showing discriminations in meaning. Cross-references provided.
                    PC2591.B4

Bertaud du Chazaud, Henri. Dictionnaire des synonymes. [Nouv. éd.]. Paris : Robert, [1983]. 516 p.   **AC362**
   1971 ed. had title: *Nouveau dictionnaire des synonymes.* Repr. by Robert, 1989.
   About 20,000 entry words.   PC2591.B44

Thésaurus Larousse : des mots aux idées, des idées aux mots / sous la direction de Daniel Péchoin. Paris : Larousse, c1991. 1146 p.   **AC363**
   A classed thesaurus with large sections for the world, individuals, and society, and 873 subcategories. Headwords with synonyms are listed alphabetically within categories. Index of all words listed.
                    PC2591.T47

Idioms and usage

Brueckner, John H. Brueckner's French contextuary. Englewood Cliffs, N.J. : Prentice-Hall, 1975. 613 p.   **AC364**
   Aims "to provide full contextual illustrations of over 11,500 basic English words used in combination and translated into idiomatic French. ... It also provides the native French speaker with a clear analysis of English meanings and many of the common uses of the same basic words."—*Gen. introd.* In four main sections: (1) adjectives, (2) nouns, (3) verbs, (4) adverbs and other parts of speech. English and French parallel columns.   PC2460.B78

Colin, Jean-Paul. Dictionnaire des difficultés du français. Nouv. éd. Paris : Dictionnaires Le Robert, c1978. 857 p.
                                             AC365
   Repr., 1989.
   1971 ed. had title *Nouveau dictionnaire des difficultés du français.*
   Concerned with words that pose problems in regard to pronunciation, conjugation, orthography, form gender, usage, and meaning. Often makes distinctions between similar or related terms that are likely to be confused.   PC2460.C58

Dournon, Jean-Yves. Dictionnaire d'orthographe et des difficultés du français. Paris : Hachette, [1974]. 648 p.   **AC366**
   Repr.: Paris : Librairie generale français, 1982.
   About 38,000 entries, with indication of part of speech, gender, etc, as applicable. Some 8,000 terms are marked with a dot and an explanation of the point of difficulty is provided.   PC2460.D65

Dupré, P. Encyclopédie du bon français dans l'usage contemporain : difficultés, subtilités, complexités, singularités. Paris : Éditions de Trévise, [1972]. 3 v.   **AC367**
   A guide to good usage of about 10,000 terms. Words are treated at some length, with definitions from standard dictionaries quoted, Academy strictures cited, and illustrations of usage given from published sources.   PC2460.D88

Gerber, Barbara L. Dictionary of modern French idioms / Barbara L. Gerber, Gerald H. Storzer. N.Y. : Garland, 1976. 2 v. (1228 p.). (Garland reference library of the humanities, v. 63).   **AC368**
   Intended "to serve both as a dictionary of expressions and as a handbook for colloquial usage."—*Pref.* In pt. 1 the idioms are presented topically (e.g., travel and transportation, dining, stores, apartments, schools), with sentences to illustrate meaning in context, and review

exercises at the end of each section. Pt. 2 is the dictionary proper, taking the form of French and English indexes to the idioms.

PC2460.G46

Girodet, Jean. Pièges et difficultées de la langue française. Paris : Bordas, 1990. 896 p. **AC369**

1st ed., had title *Dictionnaire du bon français* [Paris : Bordas, 1981].

Includes syntax, plurals, difficult agreement, pronunciation, and illustrative phrases. It aims to describe, without judgment, the variety of usages of spoken and written French.

Hanse, Joseph. Nouveau dictionnaire des difficultés du français moderne. [Paris] : Duculot, [1983]. 1014 p. **AC370**

Not merely a revised and updated edition of the author's *Dictionnaire des difficultés grammaticales et lexicologiques* (Paris : Baude, 1949), but a greatly expanded work based on new research and taking advantage of recent linguistic studies and new dictionaries published since 1949 (and often cited in the text). PC2630.H33

Rey, Alain. Dictionnaire des expressions et locutions / Alain Rey, Sophie Chantreau. Nouvelle éd. revue et augmentée. Paris : Robert, [1982]. 1035 p. **AC371**

1st ed., 1979.

Offers definitions of terms and phrases, giving examples of usage and datings. Entry is under keyword within the phrase or expression, and there is an index by first substantive word in the expression.

PC2460.R43

New words

Dictionnaire du français contemporain illustré / [Direction: Jean Dubois]. Paris : Larousse, c1980. 1263 p. : ill. **AC372**

Follows the plan and principles of *Dictionnaire du français contemporain*, by Jean Dubois [et al.] (Paris : Librairie Larousse, [1967?]). Repr. 1971 with "Livret methodologique" [47 p.] inserted); also issued under title *Larousse dictionnaire du français contemporain* in 1971. Defines terms and gives examples of contemporary usage. Incorporates new terms and meanings including those from the sciences. About 33,000 terms. PC2625.D46

Gilbert, Pierre. Dictionnaire des mots contemporains. Nouv. éd. Paris : Robert, 1989. 739 p. **AC373**

1st ed., 1980. A 1971 work by Gilbert was entitled *Dictionnaire des mots nouveaux*.

A dictionary of new words that have appeared in print, for the most part, after 1960. Entries include dated examples and references to sources. PC2630.G54

Old–17th century

Cayrou, Gaston. Le français classique : lexique de la langue du dix-septième siècle expliquant d'après les dictionnaires du temps et les remarques des grammairiens, le sens et l'usage des mots aujourd'hui vieillis ou différemment employés. 6. éd. rev. et corr. Paris : Didier, [1948]. 884 p. : ill. **AC374**

1st ed., 1923.

A dictionary of 17th-century French, with many quotations from the literature and exact references to sources. Includes some 2,200 words. PC2650.C3

De Gorog, Ralph Paul. Lexique français moderne-ancien français. [Athens] : Univ. of Georgia Pr., [1973]. 481 p.

AC375

An index in modern French to all the words in Frédéric Eugène Godefroy's abridged *Lexique de l'ancien français* (AC378 *note*).

Brings together the various old equivalents of modern words. Shares the limitation of the original by not showing the usage in Old French of words which have persisted. PC2889.D4

Dubois, Jean. Dictionnaire du français classique / Jean Dubois, René Lagane, Alain Lerond. [3 éd.]. Paris : Larousse, [1971]. 564 p. **AC376**

2nd ed., 1965, by Dubois and Lagane.
Repr., 1988, 1992.

A dictionary of the language of the great classical texts of the 17th century, providing definitions of words which have changed their meaning or have become obsolete; provides citations to writers of the period. PC2650.D83

Duchesne, Alain. L'obsolète : dictionnaire des mots perdus / Alain Duchesne, Thierry Leguay. Paris : Larousse, c1989. 267 p. : ill. **AC377**

An illustrative dictionary arranged by broad subject. Includes illustrative sentences, mainly from 17th- and 18th-century authors, although these examples are not dated. Lacks an index. PC2667.D83

Godefroy, Frédéric Eugène. Dictionnaire de l'ancienne langue française, et de tous ses dialectes, du IXe au XVe siècle : composé d'après le dépouillement de tous les plus importants documents, manuscrits ou imprimés / qui se trouvent dans les grandes bibliothèques de la France et de l'Europe, et dans les principales archives départementales, municipales, hospitalières ou privées, par Frédéric Godefroy. Publ. sous les auspices du Ministère de l'instruction publique. Paris : F. Vieweg, 1881–1902. 10 v. **AC378**

Various reprints.

Issued in parts. Publisher varies: v. 6–10 have imprint: Paris : E. Bouillon, 1889–1902.

Vol. 8 (last half) and v. 9–10 form supplement, first part of which has special t.p., dated 1893.

Contents: v. 1–7, A–Traioir; v. 8, Traire–Z; Complément, A–Carrefour; v. 9–10, Complément, Carrel–Z.

The standard dictionary of old French, with a wealth of illustrative quotations.

Godefroy's *Lexique de l'ancien français* / ed. by J. Bonnard and Am. Salmon (Paris : H. Welter, 1901. 544 p.) is an abridgment of the larger work, omitting the quotations and many of the words, but including some additional words. PC2889.G6

Grandsaignes d'Hauterive, Robert. Dictionnaire d'ancien français : moyen âge et renaissance. Paris : Larousse, 1947. 591 p. **AC379**

Gives spelling variations, meaning, modern approximation, etymology, time when current, etc. PC2889.G74

Greimas, Algirdas Julien. Dictionnaire de l'ancien français : le moyen age. Paris : Larousse, 1992. 630 p. **AC380**

Earlier version: *Dictionnaire de l'ancien français jusqu'au milieu du XIVe siecle* (Paris : Librairie Larousse, 1969).

Covers the period from *La chanson de Roland* to 1350. Provides the century of origin of a word, its meaning, examples of usage from original texts, and brief etymology. Entries for words that have variant spellings are found at the version most frequently seen, with *see* references provided for variants. PC2889.G76

———————— Dictionnaire du moyen français : la Renaissance / Algirdas Julien Greimas, Teresa Mary Keane. Paris : Larousse, c1992. xlv, 668 p. **AC381**

For each headword, cites the century in which it was used, and provides examples and sources. Abbreviated bibliography.

PC2650.G74

Huguet, Edmond Eugène Auguste. Dictionnaire de la langue française du seizième siècle. Paris : E. Champion, 1925–73. 7 v. **AC382**

Publisher varies; v. 3–7 have imprint: Paris : Librairie M. Didier.

A scholarly dictionary of 16th-century French, including words no longer in use and those whose meanings have changed. Rich in illustrative examples, with exact references to source.

§ Wilhelm Kesselring's *Dictionnaire chronologique du vocabulaire français: le XVIe siècle* (Heidelberg : C. Winter, 1981. 758 p.) lists words year-by-year according to first appearance in a French text, 1501–1600, and includes a bibliography of sources cited. PC2650.H7

Tobler, Adolf. Altfranzösisches Wörterbuch : Adolf Toblers nachgelassene Materialien / bearb. und hrsg. von Erhard Lommatzsch, weitergeführt von Hans Helmut Christmann. Stuttgart : F. Steiner Verlag Wiesbaden, 1925–1989. v. 1–11[1]. (In progress). **AC383**

At head of title: Tobler-Lommatzsch.

Imprint varies.

Contents: v. 1–11[1], A–Venteler. Vol. 11 ed. by Hans Helmut Christmann.

"Von der 25. Lieferung an mit Unterstützung der Akademie der Wissenschaften und der Literatur (Mainz)."—*t.p.*

An outstanding German work, which attempts to include all words of the 12th to the 14th centuries, being particularly strong in the literary language. Gives etymologies of each word with examples of usage and references to other treatments. PC2893.T6

Vandaele, Hilaire. Petit dictionnaire de l'ancien français. Paris : Garnier, [1940]. 536 p. **AC384**

Compiled to furnish students with a compact, convenient dictionary to Old French. Not a substitute for Frédéric Eugéne Godefroy, *Dictionnaire de l'ancienne langue française* (AC378), but useful as a small dictionary. PC2889.V3

Regional and dialect

Dictionnaire du français québécois : description et histoire des régionalismes en usage au Québec depuis l'époque de la Nouvelle-France jusqu'à nos jours incluant un aperçu de leur extension dans les provinces Canadiennes limitrophes. Volume de présentation / sous la direction de Claude Poirier ; rédacteurs principaux Lionel Boisvert ... [et al.] avec la collaboration de Micheline Massicotte. Sainte-Foy : Presses de l'Université Laval, 1985. 167 p., [3] p. of plates : ill. **AC385**

At head of title: Trésor de la langue française au Québec.

An extensive introduction describes the regional differences between the French spoken in France and in Quebec. Entries include dated quotations for usage. Extensive bibliography. Index. PC3645.Q4D52

Dulong, Gaston. Dictionnaire des canadianismes. [Montréal] : Larousse Canada, c1989. 461 p. **AC386**

The regionalisms of Québec, New Brunswick, Nova Scotia, Prince Edward Island, and Ontario are offered in 8,000 entries, providing part of speech, synonyms, and brief etymology for each headword. Phrases illustrate usage. PC3637.D82

Bibliography

Baldinger, Kurt. Introduction aux dictionnaires les plus importants pour l'histoire du français : recueil d'études. [Paris] : Klincksieck, 1974. 184 p. (Bibliothèque française et romane. Série D: Initiation textes et documents, 8). **AC387**

A collection of essays (one by Baldinger, the remainder by his seminar students) on the purpose, scope, strengths and weaknesses of the important etymological and historical French dictionaries from Walther von Wartburg's *Französisches etymologisches Wörterbuch* (AC352) to *Dictionnaire etymologique de l'ancien français (DEAF)* (AC346). PC2571.B3

Klaar, R. M. French dictionaries. [London : Centre for Information on Language Teaching and Research], 1976. 71 p. **AC388**

At head of title: Specialised bibliography.

An annotated list of French monolingual, French-English and English-French dictionaries available in Dec. 1975. Includes dictionaries of etymology, phonetics, place names, proper names, and slang. Z2175.D6K58

Levy, Raphael. Répertoire des lexiques du vieux français. N.Y. : Modern Language Assoc. of America, 1937. 64 p. **AC389**

Gives the titles of all printed alphabetical lists of words of Old French, with various indexes. The period studied covers from the 11th through the 15th centuries. Z2175.D6L6

Wartburg, Walther von. Bibliographie des dictionnaires patois galloromans (1550–1967) / [par] Walther von Wartburg, Hans-Erich Keller [et] Robert Geuljans. Nouv. éd. entièrement revue et mise á jour. Genéve : Droz, 1969. 376 p. : map. (Société de Publications Romanes et Françaises, v.8). **AC390**

1st ed., 1934, had title: *Bibliographie des dictionnaires patois*; suppl., 1955.

Incorporates corrections from the 1st ed. and supplement. A comprehensive listing of regional and dialect dictionaries from all parts of France and from Francophone countries. Z2175.D5W3

Friesian

Dijkstra, Waling. Friesch woordenboek : (Lexicon frisicum), met medewerking van anderen, benevens lijst van Friesche eigennamen / bewerkt door Johan Winkler ... Uitg. ingevolge besluit der Staten van Friesland, onder toezicht van de door Gedeputeerde staten benoemde commissie .... Leeuwarden : Meijer, [1896–1911]. 4 v. **AC391**

Repr.: Amsterdam : S. Emmering, 1971. 4 v. in 2.

Introd. by Y. Poortinga. Contains vocabulary from the 19th century, although quotations from the 17th and 18th centuries are occasionally cited. Personal and geographical names included. PF1493.D33

Frysk wurdboek / [Utjefte fan de Fryske Akademy]. Bolswert : A. J. Osinga, 1952–56. 2 v. **AC392**

Contents: v. 1 (publ. 1956), Frysk-Nederlânsk; v. 2, Nederlânsk-Frysk.

Replaces the Academy's *Lyts Frysk wirdboek* (Bolswert : A. J. Osinga, 1945–52). PF1493.F7

Gaelic

Dwelly, Edward. The illustrated Gaelic-English dictionary : containing every Gaelic word and meaning given in all previously published dictionaries, and a great number never in print before, to which is prefixed a concise Gaelic grammar. [7th ed.]. Glasgow : Gairm Publications, 1971. 1034 p. : 675 ill. **AC393**

1st ed., 1901–11.

"The first edition ... appeared in parts under the title of *Faclair gàidhlig le dealbahn,* and the nom-de-plume of 'Ewen MacDonald.' "—*Pref.*

Appendix: Proper names, and persons and places mentioned in old Gaelic folktales and poetry from R. A. Armstrong's *A Gaelic dictionary in two parts* (London : J. Duncan, 1825). PB1591.D8

Maclennan, Malcolm. A pronouncing and etymological dictionary of the Gaelic language : Gaelic-English, English-Gaelic. Edinburgh : Grant, 1925. 613 p. **AC394**

Repr. : Aberdeen : Aberdeen Univ. Pr., 1979.

Based on *A pronouncing Gaelic dictionary* by Neil MacAlpine (Edinburgh : N. MacAlpine, 1831).

Includes an extensive pronunciation guide. PB1591.M29

MacLeod, Norman. Dictionary of the Gaelic language : I. Gaelic and English; II. English and Gaelic / by the Rev. Dr. Norman Macleod, and the Rev. Dr. Daniel Dewar. Edinburgh : Grant, 1909. 1005 p. **AC395**
> First publ. 1833. Frequently reprinted.
> Uses Gaelic orthography as found in the Gaelic Bible.
> PB1591.M3

Ganda

Snoxall, R. A. Luganda-English dictionary. Oxford : Clarendon Pr., 1967. 357 p. **AC396**
> Intended for the speaker of English. Some 8,000 entries. Words are arranged alphabetically, but many words (especially nouns derived from verbs) appear also under the verb stem. Illustrative sentences given. PL8201.S6

Georgian

Cherkesi, E. Georgian-English dictionary. [Oxford] : pr. for the Trustees of the Marjory Wardrop Fund, Univ. of Oxford, 1950. 257 p. **AC397**
> An excellent dictionary, based on a textual comparison of the English and Georgian versions of the books of the Old and New Testaments and other sources. The *Russian-Georgian dictionary* of D. Chubinashvili (1886) and the works of early Georgian scholars were used as reference. Ancient as well as modern Georgian terms are included. PK9125.C47

Gvardzhaladze, Tamara. English-Georgian dictionary / comp. by Thamar and Isidore Gvarjaladze. [3rd ed.]. Tbilissi : Sabčota Sakartvelo, 1975. 1050 p. **AC398**
> 1st ed., 1948; 2nd ed., 1955.
> Added title page in Georgian.
> A concise dictionary. PK9125.G9

German

Althochdeutsches Wörterbuch / auf Grund der von Elias von Steinmeyer hinterlassenen Sammlungen im Auftr. d. Sächs. Akad. d. Wiss. zu Leipzig bearb. u. hrsg. von Elisabeth Karg-Gasterstädt u. Theodor Frings. Berlin : Akademie-Verlag, 1952–92. Bd. 1–4$^{1-11}$. (In progress). **AC399**
> Contents: Bd. 1–4$^{1-11}$, A–Heilida.
> A scholarly dictionary of Old High German, with many examples and exact references to the literature. Bd. 4, lfg. 1/2 includes supplementary lists of texts and sources of quotations. PF3975.K35

Brockhaus Wahrig : deutsches Wörterbuch / hrsg. von Gerhard Wahrig, Hildegard Krämer, Harald Zimmermann. Wiesbaden : Brockhaus ; Stuttgart : Deutsche Verlags-Anstalt, 1980–1984. 6 v. **AC400**
> Includes some 220,000 keywords and 550,000 definitions. Examples of usage are given; field of use is indicated for the many scientific and technical terms included. PF3625.B7

Frühneuhochdeutsches Wörterbuch / hrsg. von Robert R. Anderson, Ulrich Goebel, Oskar Reichmann. Berlin ; N.Y. : W. de Gruyter, 1986–1992. Bd. 1–2$^{1-2}$. (In progress). **AC401**
> Contents: Bd. 1–Bd. 2$^{1-2}$, A–Ausgang.
> A scholarly German-German dictionary covering the period 1350–1600; includes etymologies, illustrative quotations, and references to secondary sources. Lfg. 1 includes a "Verzeichnes der Quellen," p. 165–224, and a "Verzeichnis der Sekundarliteratur, p. 225–285. To be in 10 v.; v. 10 will be an index. PF4591.F78

Grimm, Jakob Ludwig Karl. Deutsches Wörterbuch / Jakob Ludwig Karl Grimm, Wilhelm Grimm. Leipzig : Hirzel, 1854–1960. 16 v. **AC402**
> On cover (varies): Im Auftrage des Deutschen Reiches und Preussens mit Unterstützung des Reichministeriums des Innern, des Preussischen Ministeriums für Wissenschaft, Kunst und Volksbildung, und der Preussischen Akademie der Wissenschaften.
> The great dictionary of the German language, completed in 1960 after more than 100 years in preparation. Since it was issued in *Lieferungen*, not in alphabetical sequence, but in various parts of the alphabet simultaneously, the volumes show wide divergence in dates of publication, as well as in scope and method of presentation.
> Compiled on historical principles. The design of the brothers Grimm "was to give an exhaustive account of the words of the literary language (New High German) from about the end of the 15th century, including their earlier etymological and later history, with references to important dialectal words and forms; and to illustrate their use and history abundantly by quotations. ..."—*Encyclopaedia Britannica*, 11th ed., 8:189.
> As the dictionary uses small letters throughout instead of capitals for common nouns, it is the main German authority for noncapitalization of nouns in German.
> ————. *Quellenverzeichnis*, bearb ... von A. Huber [et al.] (Leipzig : Hirzel, 1971. 1094 p.). Issued in 7 Lfg., 1966–71.
> A new edition is appearing as:
> ————. *Deutsches Wörterbuch*, hrsg. von der Deutschen Akademie der Wissenschaften zu Berlin in Zusammenarbeit mit der Akademie der Wissenschaften zu Göttingen (Neubearbeitung. Leipzig : Hirzel, 1965–90. Bd. 1, Lfg. 1–10, Bd. 2, Lfg. 1–3, Bd. 6, Lfg. 1–12, Bd. 7, Bd. 1–6. [In progress]).
> Contents: Hinweise; Bd. 1, Lfg. 1–10, A–Affrikata; Bd. 2, Lfg. 1–3, Affront–Allmenda; Bd. 6, Lfg. 1–12, D–D-zug; Bd. 7, Lfg. 1–6, E–Einschlagen.
> A revised and expanded edition, incorporating results of new research and carrying on the thorough scholarly traditions of the earlier work. PF3625.G7

Das Grosse Wörterbuch der deutschen Sprache in 6 Bänden / hrsg. und bearbeitet vom Wissenschaftlichen Rat und den Mitarbeitern der Dudenredaktion unter Leitung von Günther Drosdowski ; [Bearb., Rudolf Köster ... et al.]. Mannheim ; Wien ; Zürich : Bibliographisches Institut, 1976–1981. 6 v. **AC403**
> At head of title: Duden.
> The first 20th-century unabridged dictionary of the German language published in West Germany. Contains etymologies, grammatical information, usage labels, and illustrative quotations. An earlier unabridged dictionary, *Wörterbuch der deutschen Gegenwartssprache* (AC412), was published in East Germany; according to an extensive review comparing the two dictionaries in *Modern language review* 80 (April 1985) : 372–86, it has marked ideological bias. The review also discusses a number of serious errors in *Das grosse Wörterbuch* and concludes the two works are "monumental but flawed .... [T]here is still no comprehensive dictionary of German to which a user can turn for a reliable, objective account of the German lexis."
> § A one-volume abridgment, without quotations, of *Das grosse Wörterbuch* was published as *Duden, deutsches Universal-Wörterbuch* (1st ed., 1983; 2nd rev. ed., 1989). Many of the errors in the parent work have been corrected in the 2nd ed.
> A new edition with the same editorial forces has begun publication under the title *Duden, das grosse Wörterbuch der deutschen Sprache in acht Bänden* (2., völlig neu bearbeitete und stark erw. Aufl. Mannheim : Dudenverlag, 1993–).
> Contents: Bd. 1, A–Bim. PF3625.G75

Holthausen, Ferdinand. Altsächsisches Wörterbuch. 2. unveränderte Aufl. Köln : Böhlau, 1967 [c1954]. 95 p. (Niederdeutsche Studien, Bd. 1). **AC404**

1st ed., 1954.
The standard dictionary for Old Saxon.   PF3996.H65

Lexer, Matthias von. Matthias Lexers Mittelhochdeutsches Taschenwörterbuch. 37. aufl., mit neubearb. und erw. Nachträgen. Stuttgart : Hirzel, c1983. 504 p.   **AC405**
1st ed., 1879; frequently reprinted.
A standard small dictionary of Middle High German. The first section is a reprint of earlier editions. The Nachträge section was prepared by Ulrich Pretzel.
§ A larger work is the author's *Mittelhochdeutsches Handwörterbuch* (Leipzig, 1872–78. 3 v. and Nachträge).   PF4327.L42

Müller, Wilhelm. Mittelhochdeutsches Wörterbuch : mit Benutzung des Nachlasses von Georg Friedrich Benecke. Leipzig : S. Hirzel, 1854–66. 3 v. in 4.   **AC406**
Repr.: Hildesheim : G. Olms, 1963.
The standard dictionary for Middle High German of the 11th to 16th centuries.   PF4327.M8

Paul, Hermann. Deutsches Wörterbuch. 9., vollständig neu bearbeitete Aufl., von Helmut Henne und Georg Objartel unter Mitarbeit von Heidrun Kämper-Jensen. Tübingen : Max Niemeyer, 1992. 1130 p.   **AC407**
1st ed., 1897.
A standard work, strong in the historical development of words.   PF3625.P4

Schiller, K. Mittelniederdeutsches Wörterbuch / von Dr. Karl Schiller ... und Dr. August Lübben. Bremen : J. Kühtmann, 1875–81. 6 v.   **AC408**
Repr.: Schaan, Liechtenstein : Sändig Reprint Verlag; Hans R. Wohlwend, 1981.
The standard dictionary for Middle Low German.
§ A good companion title: August Lübben, *Mittelniederdeutsches Handwörterbuch* (Norden : D. Soltau, 1888. Repr. 1965, 1981).   PF5636.S3

Schulz, Hans. Deutsches Fremdwörterbuch. Berlin ; N.Y. : de Gruyter, 1913–88. v. 1–7. (In progress).   **AC409**
Continued by Otto Basler and completed in the Institut für Deutsche Sprache.
Vol. 1 originally publ. Strassburg : Trübner, 1913. Vol. 7, Quellenverzeichnis.
An authoritative work dealing with words of foreign origin, with examples and dated references to sources.   PF3670.S4

Der Sprach-Brockhaus : deutsches Bildwörterbuch. 8., völlig neubearb. und erw. Aufl. Wiesbaden : Brockhaus, 1972. 835 p. : ill.   **AC410**
1st ed., 1935; 7th ed., 1956. Frequently reprinted.
A practical desk-sized dictionary, which includes geographical names, technical terms, colloquialisms, etc. Small line drawings are used to illustrate the text.   PF3629.S65

Wahrig, Gerhard. Deutsches Wörterbuch : mit einem "Lexikon der Deutschen Sprachlehre" / Gerhard Wahrig ; hrsg. in Zusammenarbeit mit zahlreichen Wissenschaftlern und anderen Fachleuten. Völlig überarbeitete Neuausg. München : Mosaik, c1992. 1493 p.   **AC411**
1st ed., 1975, was a revised and updated ed. of Wahrig's *Das grosse deutsche Wörterbuch* (1966).
All reprints based on the 1987 ed. which contains about 225,000 words. The most recent additions are from the sciences. Includes a fairly detailed dictionary of grammatical terms by Walter Ludewig.   PF3625.W2

Wörterbuch der deutschen Gegenwartssprache / hrsg. von Ruth Klappenbach und Wolfgang Steinitz. Bearbeiter: R. Klappenbach und H. Malige-Klappenbach. Berlin : Akademie-Verlag, 1961–76. 6v.   **AC412**
At head of title: Akademie der Wissenschaft der DDR. Zentralinstitut für Sprachwissenschaft.

Later editions in progress; set may consist of volumes from several editions. Issued in parts.
A dictionary of the present-day language, with examples from and references to modern writers. The final volume contains "Alphabetisches Verzeichnis der Quellen."   PF3625.W62

Wörterbuch der mittelhochdeutschen Urkundensprache : auf der Grundlage des Corpus der altdeutschen Originalurkunden bis zum Jahr 1300 / unter Leitung von Bettina Kirschstein und Ursula Schulze. Berlin : E. Schmidt, c1986–1989. v. 1, pt. 1–7. (In progress).   **AC413**
Contents: v. 1, lfg. 1–7, Ab–Gesenden.
At head of title: Veröffentlichungen der Komission für Deutsche Literatur des Mittelalters der Bayerischen Akademie der Wissenschaften.
Limited to the approximately 10,000 words of the *Corpus der altdeutschen Originalurkunden bus zum Jahr 1300* (Lahr [Baden] : M. Schauenburg, 1929–), this scholarly German-German dictionary is based on legal and business rather than literary sources.
   PF4327.W67

Bilingual

Betteridge, Harold T. Cassell's German-English, English-German dictionary = Deutsch-englisches, englisch-deutsches Wörterbuch. Completely revised. London : Cassell ; N.Y. : Macmillan, [1978]. 1580 p.   **AC414**
Betteridge's first edition of this work, entitled *The new Cassell's German dictionary* (1958) was an almost completely rewritten edition of the work edited for many years by Karl Breul. This "first Macmillan revision" is an expanded edition, completely revised and reset, incorporating many new words and usages. Gives phonetic transcriptions of headwords. One of the most useful bilingual dictionaries.   PF3640.B453

Collins German-English, English-German dictionary / Peter Terrell ... [et al.]. 2nd ed. London : HarperCollins, 1991. 902 p.   **AC415**
1st ed., 1980.
The 280,000 headwords in this dictionary represent an in-depth treatment of contemporary German and English, with emphasis on ordinary language. Introductory and supplementary material (e.g., German noun endings, and a pronunciation guide) is in English and German.   PF3640.C68

Harrap's concise German and English dictionary : English-German/German-English in one volume / ed. by Robin Sawers. London : Harrap ; [Lincolnwood, Ill.] : National Textbook Co., [1982]. 499 p., 627 p.   **AC416**
Aims "to provide a dictionary slightly smaller than the existing medium-sized volumes, omitting obscure or literary usage, but with more generous treatment of the entries—full grammatical information and pronunciation and plenty of examples."—*Pref.* Introductory matter in English and German. Includes a list of common abbreviations for each language.   PF3640.H29

Langenscheidt's condensed Muret-Sanders German dictionary : German-English / Heinz Messinger, ed. Berlin : Langenscheidt, [1982]. 1296 p.   **AC417**
Based on the German-English part of *Langenscheidt's new Muret-Sanders encyclopedic dictionary of the English and German languages* (below), but "it is by no means simply the result of a systematic halving of the larger dictionary" (*Pref.*); rather, it involved "a word-for-word scrutiny and careful sifting of the original material." About 14,000 entry words.   PF3640.L25732

Langenscheidt's new Muret-Sanders encyclopedic dictionary of the English and German languages / ed. by Otto Springer. Compl. rev. 1962. N.Y. : Barnes & Noble, 1962–75. 2 pts. in 4 v.   **AC418**

Added title page: Der neue Muret-Sanders Langenscheidts enzyklopädisches Wörterbuch der englischen und deutschen Sprache.

German edition has title: *Langenscheidts enzyklopädisches Wörterbuch der englischen und deutschen Sprache.*

Contents: pt. 1, English-German; pt. 2, German-English.

The Muret-Sanders has long been an outstanding bilingual dictionary. The 1962 edition is, in effect, a new work although based on the old. Printed in roman type, each word has received new treatment, and thousands of new words have been added to make the work representative of 20th-century usage. "In pronunciation, spelling, and vocabulary, American English is treated with the same degree of completeness and accuracy as British English ..." (*Pref.*), but some reviewers feel that American usage has been emphasized. Includes scientific and technical terms; for biological terms, the Latin names are given following the German equivalent. Pronunciation is indicated; idiomatic phrases and colloquialisms are given. PF3640.L257

The Oxford-Duden German dictionary : English-German/German-English / ed. by the Dudenredaktion and the German Section of the Oxford Univ. Pr. Dictionary Dept. ; chief eds., W. Scholze-Stubenrecht, J.B. Sykes. Oxford : Clarendon Pr., 1990. 1696 p. : ill. **AC419**

Based on the databases maintained by the Oxford Univ. Pr. and by the Dudenredaktion of the Bibliographisches Institut, Mannheim, "this is the first bilingual dictionary ever to be produced by a team based in both language areas."—*Foreword*. Includes many examples illustrating usage and a number of appendixes discussing grammar, punctuation, etc. PF3640.O94

The Oxford-Duden pictorial German-English dictionary / ed. by the Dudenredaktion and the German Section of the Oxford University Press Dictionary Department. Oxford : Clarendon Pr. ; N.Y. : Oxford Univ. Pr., 1980. 677 p., 87 p., 96 p. : ill. **AC420**

A cooperative effort of two highly reputable publishers, "based on the third, completely revised edition of the German *Bildwörterbuch* published as Volume 3 of the ten-volume *Duden* series of monolingual German dictionaries. The English text represents a direct translation of the German original and follows the original layout as closely as possible."—*Foreword*.

The intention is to help the reader visualize the object denoted by a given word or term. Terms are grouped by subject and illustrated in some 384 plates (chiefly line drawings), with the German terms and English equivalents given on the same or facing page. German and English indexes allow the dictionary to be used as either German-English or English-German. Covers a wide range of technical and everyday vocabulary. PF3629.O9

The Oxford-Harrap standard German-English dictionary / ed. by Trevor Jones. Oxford : Clarendon Pr., 1977– . v. 1–3. (In progress). **AC421**

First publ. 1963 under title: *Harrap's standard German and English dictionary.*

A scholarly dictionary intended for general use. Each word is treated separately instead of under groupings. Scientific terms are included. Gives examples of usage. PF3640.H3

Schöffler, Herbert. The new enlarged Schöffler-Weis German and English dictionary : English-German/German-English. Completely rev., greatly expanded, and fully updated, by Erich Weis and Erwin Weis in collaboration with Heinrich Mattutat. Lincolnwood, Ill. : National Textbook, 1981. 500 p. : maps. **AC422**

Repr.: 1991.

Offers definitions for more than 150,000 terms. Abbreviations are appended. PF3640.S35

Spalding, Keith. An historical dictionary of German figurative usage. Oxford : Blackwell, 1952–90. fasc. 1–49. (In progress). **AC423**

Contents: Fasc. 1–49, A–Stehen [v. 1 fasc. 1–10, v. 2, fasc. 11–20, v. 3, fasc. 21–30 have been published separately as volumes].

Records figurative expressions, proverbs, quotations, and other established phrases appearing in German literature since approximately 1750, with explanations in English; the annotations illustrating use and change of meaning are often drawn from sources preceding this date. Equivalent English phrases or expressions are given for each entry. A complete list of sources is planned for the conclusion of the work. PF3440.S7

Wildhagen, Karl. The new Wildhagen German dictionary : German-English, English-German / Karl Wildhagen, Will Héraucourt ; eds.: Eva Ruetz and Richard Wiczell. Chicago : Follett, 1965. 1296, 1061 p. **AC424**

Subtitle: An encyclopedic and strictly scientific representation of the vocabulary of the modern and present-day languages, with special regard to syntax, style, and idiomatic usage.

Previous ed. in 2 v., 1962; the English-German part was first published 1938, the German-English part, 1953/54.

A single-volume edition of the 1962 publication in 2 v. It shows only minor changes in the German-English part, but there has been significant expansion (about 30 percent) in the English-German section. A well-edited desk dictionary. PF3640.W546

Bibliography

Kühn, Peter. Deutsche Wörterbücher : eine systematische Bibliographie. Tübingen : Niemeyer, 1978. 266 p. (Reihe germanistische Linguistik, 15). **AC425**

A classified bibliography of general and specialized German-language dictionaries and various other types of "word books" (including dictionaries of names, quotation books, concordances, etc.). Includes bilingual and multilingual dictionaries. About 2,700 items. Author index. Z2235.D6K83

Lemmer, Manfred. Deutscher Wortschatz : Bibliographie zur deutschen Lexikologie. Halle : Niemeyer, 1967. 123 p. **AC426**

A bibliography of German-language dictionaries and of works on German lexicography. Some brief annotations. Z2235.L4

Etymology

Etymologisches Wörterbuch des Deutschen / erarbeitet von einem Autorenkollektiv des Zentralinstituts für Sprachwissenschaft unter der Leitung von Wolfgang Pfeifer ; Autoren, Wilhelm Braun ... [et al.]. Berlin : Akademie-Verlag, 1989. 3 v. **AC427**

On added t.p.: Akademie der Wissenschaften der DDR. Zentralinstitut für Sprachwissenschaft.

Offers detailed etymologies of some 8,000 words. PF3580.E88

Kluge, Friedrich. Etymologisches Wörterbuch der deutschen Sprache. 22. Aufl. / unter Mithilfe von Max Bürgisser und Bernd Gregor völlig neu bearb. von Elmar Seebold. Berlin ; N.Y. : de Gruyter, 1989. lxv, 822 p. **AC428**

21. Aufl., 1975.

A standard work frequently reprinted. Especially strong in word development with dated examples of usage. This edition is a complete revision. The "Sachverzeichnis," a feature of the 21. Aufl., has been dropped but will be included in Seebold's forthcoming *Register und Auswertung zur 22. Auflage des Etymologischen Wörterbuch von Freidrich Kluge.* PF3580.K5

Slang

Küpper, Heinz. Illustriertes Lexikon der deutschen Umgangssprache. [Stuttgart] : Klett, [1982–84]. 8 v. : ill.
        AC429
    An extensive slang dictionary with indication of dates of origin or usage, derivation, etc. Heavily illustrated (mainly in color) with pictures drawn from a wide range of sources including contemporary advertising and newsphotos as well as various examples of world art. It generally supersedes the earlier *Wörterbuch der deutschen Umgangssprache* (1st ed., 1955).   PF3815.K87

—————————— Pons Wörterbuch der deutschen Umgangssprache. Stuttgart : Klett, c1987. 959 p.   **AC430**
Includes dates of usage.   PF5991.K85

Wolf, Siegmund A. Wörterbuch des Rotwelschen : deutsche Gaunersprache. 2., durchgesehene Aufl. Hamburg : H. Buske, 1985. 430 p.   **AC431**
    Previous ed., 1956.
    A historical dictionary of underworld slang, with dated references to the literature.

Synonyms

Dornseiff, Franz. Der deutsche Wortschatz nach Sachgruppen. 7. Aufl. mit alphabetischem Generalregister. Berlin : W. de Gruyter, 1970. 166, 922 p.   **AC432**
    1st ed., 1933–34; 6th ed., 1965.
    This edition considerably expanded, especially in supplementary material and index. The main part is arranged as a thesaurus in 20 main categories with many subdivisions. A detailed index refers to the appropriate sections.   PF3591.D6

Farrell, Ralph Barstow. Dictionary of German synonyms. 3rd ed. Cambridge : Univ. Pr., 1977. 412 p.   **AC433**
    1st ed., 1953; 2nd ed., 1971.
    Arranged by English word with German equivalents and definitions; differences in meaning are discussed and examples of German usage are given. Particularly useful for students.
    This edition "introduces no innovation except an appendix comprising a list of difficult German words—difficult because their meaning is not readily perceived or because they have no exact equivalent in English."—*Pref.* Some examples and explanations have been improved so long as extensive resetting of type was not involved.   PF3591.F37

Görner, Herbert. Synonymwörterbuch : sinnverwandte Ausdrucke der deutschen Sprache / Herbert Görner, Günter Kempcke. Aufl. 3. Leipzig : VEB Bibliographisches Institut, 1975. 643 p.   **AC434**
    Repr., 1987.
    1st ed., 1973.
    A dictionary of synonyms and synonymous expressions.   PF3591.G6

Wehrle, Hugo. Deutscher Wortschatz : ein Wegweiser zum treffenden Ausdruck / Wehrle-Eggers [i.e., Hugo Wehrle, Hans Eggers]. 12 Aufl. Stuttgart : Ernst Klett, 1961. 821 p.   **AC435**
    12th ed. of Anton Schlessing's *Deutscher Wortschatz* (1st ed. 1880–81), an outstanding work for many years.
    Frequently reprinted without change.
    This edition has been much enlarged, completely revised, and rearranged. The first part is arranged systematically by idea, in much the manner of *Roget's thesaurus* (AC145). The second part is an alphabetical list of words referring to the paragraph sections of the first part.   PF3591.W39

New words

Heberth, Alfred. Neue Wörter : Neologismen in der deutschen Sprache seit 1945. Wien : Verband der Wissenschaftlichen Gesellschaften Österreichs, 1977. 240 p.   **AC436**
    A dictionary of new words that have achieved currency in German speech since World War I. Indicates derivation of terms, country of origin for loan-words, etc.
    Supplemented by Heberth's *Neue Wörter 2 : Neologismen in der deutschen Sprache seit 1945* (1982. 75 p.).   PF3445.H4

Usage

Anderson, Beatrix. Cassell's colloquial German : a handbook of idiomatic usage / Beatrix Anderson, Maurice North. Completely rev. London : Cassell ; N.Y. : Macmillan, [1980]. 176 p.   **AC437**
    1st ed., 1968, had title: *Beyond the dictionary in German.*
    Aims to help guard against misinterpretations and to supply information on current usage.   PF3680.A5

Eggeling, Hans F. A dictionary of modern German prose usage. Oxford : Clarendon Pr., c1961. 418 p.   **AC438**
    Repr.: Oxford, 1974.
    This reliable guide illustrates the use of the language in difficult grammatical and syntactical constructions.   PF3640.E38

Mackensen, Lutz. Deutsches Wörterbuch : Rechtschreibung, Grammatik, Stil, Worterklärungen, Abkürzungen, Aussprache, Fremdwörterlexikon, Geschichte des deutschen Wortschatzes. 12., völlig neu bearbeitete und stark erw. Aufl. / unter Mitarbeit von Gesine Schwarz-Mackensen. München : Südwest, 1986. 1219 p.   **AC439**
    1st ed., 1952, had title: *Neues deutsches Wörterbuch.*
    Offers definitions, pronunciations, and usage.   PF3625.M25

Gothic

Lehmann, Winfred Philipp. A Gothic etymological dictionary / Winfred P. Lehmann ; with bibliography prepared under the direction of Helen-Jo J. Hewitt. Leiden : E.J. Brill, 1986. 712 p.   **AC440**
    Title page note: Based on the third edition of *Vergleichendes Wörterbuch der gotischen Sprache* by Sigmund Feist [Leiden : Brill, 1986].
    Entries have four parts: (1) Gothic data with brief morphological classification; (2) citation of cognates from other Germanic languages (3) non-Germanic cognates; and (4) words of special interest. Index and bibliography.   PD1193.L44

Grebo

Innes, Gordon. A Grebo-English dictionary. London : Cambridge Univ. Pr., 1967. 131 p. (West African language monographs, no.6).   **AC441**
    The first Grebo dictionary in a century. Based on the speech of an informant and incorporates all the identifiable words of J. L. Wilson's *Dictionary of the Grebo language* (1839). Intended for the speaker of English.   PL8821.I49

Greek

Estienne, Henri. Thēsauros tēs hellēnikēs glōssēs = Thesaurus graecae linguae / ab Henrico Stephano constructus. Post editionem anglicam novis additamentis auctum, ordineque alphabetico digestum tertio ediderunt Carolus Benedictus Hase, Guilielmus Dindorfius et Ludovicus Dindorfius. Paris : Didot, [1831–1865]. 8 v. in 9. **AC442**

1st ed., 1572.

An authoritative dictionary from its first publication, reedited by outstanding scholars in the 19th century. Still of first importance.

PA442.E8

•**Thesaurus Linguae Graecae** [database]. [Irvine, Calif.] : Univ. of California, Irvine, 1987. **AC443**

For annotation, *see* BE1036.

Bilingual

Liddell, Henry George. A Greek-English lexicon / comp. by Henry George Liddell and Robert Scott. A new ed. rev. and augm. throughout by Henry Stuart Jones with the assistance of Roderick McKenzie and with the cooperation of many scholars. Oxford : Clarendon Pr., [1925–40]. 2 v. (2111 p.). **AC444**

1st ed., 1843. This new (9th) ed. is revised throughout and enlarged by the addition of many words, including scientific and technical terms.

Issued in 10 pts., 1925–40. Frequently reprinted. A 1968 printing (2042 p., 153 p.) is available with the 1968 supplement bound in. Preliminary leaves include: List of authors and works; Epigraphical publications; Papyrological publications; Periodicals. General list of abbreviations. Addenda and corrigenda, p. 2043–2111.

The standard Greek and English lexicon, covering the language to about 600 CE, omitting Patristic and Byzantine Greek. Omits placenames, for which Franz Passow's dictionary (*Handwörterbuch der griechischen Sprache*, AC445) must be used.

———. ———. *Supplement*, ed. by E. A. Barber. (Oxford : Clarendon Pr., 1968. 153 p.).

Incorporates the "Addenda et corrigenda" section from the 9th ed., adds new words, and amends earlier articles. PA445.E5L6

Passow, Franz. Handwörterbuch der griechischen Sprache. Neubearb. und zeitgemäss umgestaltet von Val. Chr. Fr. Rost und Friedrich Palm. Des ursprunglichen Werkes 5. Aufl. Leipzig : Vogel, 1841–57. 2 v. in 4. **AC445**

Repr. : Darmstadt : Wissenschaftliche Buchgesellschaft, 1983.

The standard Greek and German lexicon, useful to the English reader also because it includes geographical names omitted from Henry George Liddell and Robert Scott's *Greek-English lexicon* (AC444). A new, much enlarged edition by Wilhelm Crönert was started, but only pts. 1–3 (A–An) were issued (Göttingen : Vandenhoeck, 1912–13). PA445.G3P3

Preisigke, Friedrich. Wörterbuch der griechischen Papyrusurkunden : mit Einschluss der griechischen Inschriften, Aufschriften, Ostraka, Mumienschilder usw. aus Ägypten / hrsg. von Emil Kiessling. Heidelberg : Selbstverlag des Erben, 1925–93. v.1–4¹ (In progress). **AC446**

Imprint varies.

Contents: Bd. 1–2, A–Ω; Bd.3, Besondere Wörterliste; Bd.4, Lfg.1–5, α – ξωφυτεω.

A Greek-German dictionary of words found in the papyrus documents, inscriptions, etc.

———. ———. *Supplement*, hrsg. von Emil Kiessling (Amsterdam : Hakkert, 1969–71. 450 p.). Covers 1940–66; issued in 3 Lfg.

———. ———. *Supplement 2 (1967–1976)*, hrsg. von Hans-Albert Rupprecht (Wiesbaden : Otto Harassowitz, 1991. 335 p.).

PA3369.P75

Snell, Bruno. Lexikon des frühgriechischen Epos / vorbereitet und hrsg. von Bruno Snell ; verantwortlicher Redaktor, Hans Joachim Mette. Göttingen : Vandenhoeck & Ruprecht, 1955–1991. v. 1–2. (In progress). **AC447**

Subtitle: In Zusammenarbeit mit dem Thesaurus linguae graecae und mit Unterstützung der UNESCO und der Joachim-Jungius-Gesellschaft, Hamburg.

Editor varies.

Contents: v. 1–2, Lfg. 1–14, α–λωφαω.

Issued in parts.

A new *Thesaurus linguae graecae* (BE1036), attempting to list all words in the texts of the earliest literary works up to, but not including, the works of Antimachos; covers Homer, Hesiod, and others. As planned, the Greek *Thesaurus* will consist of a series of dictionaries, each covering a different literary period. PA445.G4S6

Woodhouse, Sidney Chawner. English-Greek dictionary : a vocabulary of the Attic language. London : Routledge, 1910. 1029 p. **AC448**

Frequently reprinted.

Includes 30-page vocabulary of proper names. PA445.E5W6

Etymology

Boisacq, Émile. Dictionnaire étymologique de la langue grecque : étudiée dans ses rapports avec les autres langues indo-européennes. 4. éd., augm. d'un index par Helmut Rix. Heidelberg : Winter, 1950. 1256 p. **AC449**

1st ed., 1907–16.

This edition includes a useful index which lists the words in all languages cited in the text. The beginning source for etymological study. PA421.B6

Chantraine, Pierre. Dictionnaire étymologique de la langue grecque : histoire des mots. Paris : Klincksieck, [1968–80]. 4 v. **AC450**

Emphasizes the history of use of the vocabulary. Etymologies follow those of Hjalmar Frisk's *Griechisches etymologisches Wörterbuch* (AC451) for the most part, except when new evidence or recent scholarship indicates otherwise. Abbreviations for ancient authors follow those in Henry George Liddell and Robert Scott's *Greek-English lexicon* (AC444). Thorough bibliography. PA422.C5

Frisk, Hjalmar. Griechisches etymologisches Wörterbuch. Heidelberg : Winter, 1954–72. 3 v. (Indogermanische Bibliothek, II. Reihe. Wörterbücher). **AC451**

Issued in parts. A "2. unveränderte Aufl." appeared 1972–73.

An authoritative work tracing the etymologies of classical Greek with references to sources, etc.

Vol. 3: Nachträge, Wortregister, Corrigenda und Nachwort.

PA422.F7

Pronunciation

Allen, William Sidney. Vox Graeca : a guide to the pronunciation of classical Greek. 2nd ed. Cambridge : Univ. Pr., 1974. 174 p. **AC452**

A companion to the same author's *Vox latina* (AC594) and, like that volume, a guide to the principles of pronunciation rather than a pronouncing dictionary. PA267.A4

Christian and medieval

Arndt, William. A Greek-English lexicon of the New Testament and other early Christian literature : a translation and adaptation of the fourth revised and augmented edition of Walter Bauer's Griechisch-deutsches Wörterbuch zu den Schriften des Neuen Testaments und der übrigen urchristlichen Literatur / by William F. Arndt and F. Wilbur Gingrich. 2nd ed. / rev. & aug. by F. Wilbur Gingrich and Frederick W. Danker from Walter Bauer's 5th ed., 1958. Chicago : Univ. of Chicago Pr., 1979. 900 p.   **AC453**
     1st ed., 1957.
     This edition "contains Bauer's additions as well as a number of changes and additions" (*Foreword*) by the editors of the translation.
     A list of corrections in spellings, oversights in accents, etc., is included in the generally favorable review in *Classical philology* 76 (Apr. 1981): 153–59.
     A greatly condensed version, with some revision, is F. Wilbur Gingrich, *Shorter lexicon of the Greek New Testament* (2nd ed., rev. by Frederick W. Danker, Chicago : Univ. of Chicago Pr., 1983. 221 p.).   PA881.B38

Du Cange, Charles Du Fresne. Glossarium ad scriptores mediæ & infimæ graecitatis : in qvo græca vocabula novatæ significationis, aut usus rarioris, barbara, exotica, ecclesiastica, liturgica, tactica, nomica, jatrica, botanica, chymica explicantur, eorum notiones & originationes reteguntur ... E libris editis, ineditis veteribusque monumentis. Accedit Appendix ad Glossarium mediæ & Infimæ latinitatis, un'a c'um brevi etymologico linguae gallicæ ex utroque glossario / Auctore Carolo Dv Fresne, domino Dv Cange .... Lugduni : apud Anissonios, J. Posuel, & C. Rigaud, 1688. 2 v. [2426 col.].
     AC454
     Frequently reprinted.
     In spite of its age, still the authoritative dictionary of medieval Greek, including many quotations with exact reference to sources.
     PA1125.D8

Greek-English lexicon of the New Testament : based on semantic domains / Johannes P. Louw, Eugene A. Nida, editors. N.Y. : United Bible Societies, 1988. 2 v. : col. maps.   **AC455**
     Cover title: Greek-English lexicon.
     Containing 5,000 lexical items and more than 25,000 meanings, this dictionary is designed "for translators of the New Testament in various languages."—*Pref.* Vol. 2 contains a Greek-English index and an English index.   PA881.G68

Kittel, Gerhard. Theological dictionary of the New Testament / tr. and ed. by Geoffrey W. Bromiley. Grand Rapids, Mich. : Eerdmans, [1964–76]. 10 v.   **AC456**
     For annotation, *see* BC143.   PA881.K513

Lampe, Geoffrey William Hugo. A patristic Greek lexicon. Oxford : Clarendon Pr., 1961–68. 1568 p.   **AC457**
     Originally publ. in 5 pts.
     "The object of this work is primarily to interpret the theological and ecclesiastical vocabulary of the Greek Christian authors from Clement of Rome to Theodore of Studium."—*Pref.* It is complementary to Henry George Liddell and Robert Scott's *Greek-English lexicon* (AC444) in that common meanings of words noted there are not repeated by Lampe, though unusual usages may be. Biblical words and usages to be found in the Septuagint and the New Testament are also omitted. List of authors and works, p.xi–xlv.

Moulton, James Hope. Vocabulary of the Greek Testament / illustrated from the papyri and other non-literary sources by James Hope Moulton and George Milligan. London : Hodder, 1914–29. 835 p.   **AC458**
     Originally published in 8 pts., 1914–29, 835 p.; reprintings (1930, etc.) have 705 p.

This work shows the nature of the language of the Greek Testament in light of inscriptions and contemporary papyri.   PA881.M7

Sophocles, Evangelinus Apostolides. Greek lexicon of the Roman and Byzantine periods : (from B.C. 146 to A.D. 1100). Memorial ed. / ed. by J. H. Thayer. N.Y. : Scribner, 1887. 1188 p.   **AC459**
     1st ed., 1870. Various reprintings.
     A dictionary of the later classical Greek of the Roman and Byzantine periods. Useful for the Church Fathers.   PA1125.S7

Greek, Modern

Dēmētrakos, Dēmētrios B. Mega lexikon tēs Hellēnikēs glōssēs. Athens : Demetrákou, 1936–50. 9 v.   **AC460**
     Repr.: Athens : Efedoseis Domē, 1964 (15 v); Athens : Hellēnikē paideia, 1964 (9 v.).
     Covers all periods from ancient times to mid-20th century.
     PA441.D4

Penguin-Hellenews anglo-hellēnikon lexikon : Vasismeno eiz ten ekdosin The Penguin English dictionary, by G. N. Garmonsway / [genikos epimelētēs hylēs Lingrēs Nikolaos]. Athens : Hellenews-Paideia, 1975. 926 p.   **AC461**
     English-Greek only.
     A pocket dictionary designed for Greek speakers who are learning English. The vocabulary is based on Garmonsway and Jacqueline Simpson's *Penguin dictionary of English* (Baltimore : Penguin, [1965]).   PA1139.E5P34

"Proias" lexikon tēs neas Hellēnikēs glōssēs : orthographikon kai hermēneutikon / syntachthen hypo epitropēs philologōn kai epistēmonōn epimeleia Geōrgiou Zeugōlē. Ekd. 2. epeuxēmenē. Athēnai : Ekdot. Oikos S.P. Dēmētrakou, [196?]. 2 v.   **AC462**
     Previously publ. under title: *Lexikon Neas Hellēnikēs glōssēs* (195–?) and *Lexikon tēs Hellēnikēs glōssēs* (1933).
     Intended as a complete dictionary of all words written in Modern Greek.   PA1131.L42

Bilingual

Divry, George C. Divry's modern English-Greek and Greek-English desk dictionary = Meizon neōteron Angloellēnikon kai Hellēnoanglikon lexikon. N.Y. : D.C. Divry Publishers, 1988. 767 p.   **AC463**
     A thorough, easy-to-use desk dictionary for formal written modern Greek.   PA1139.E5D46

Kykkōtēs, Hierotheos. English-modern Greek and modern Greek-English dictionary : including English and Greek grammar, geographical and proper names, and abbreviations. [3rd ed.]. London : P. Lund, [1957]. 2 v. in 1 (644 p.).   **AC464**
     1st ed., 1942; 2nd ed., 1947.
     A pocket-sized dictionary for formal, written Greek. Out-of-date for modern spoken Greek.   PA1139.E5K85

Mega anglo-hellēnikon lexikon / syntachthen hypo epiteleiou epistēmonōn, technikōn kai logotechnōn. [Dieuthyntēs syntaxeōs, Th. N. Tsaveas]. Athēnai : "Odysseus", [1962?]. 4 v.
     AC465
     An English-Modern Greek dictionary giving examples of usage. Phonetic alphabet is used for pronunciation of English words. For formal, written modern Greek.
     § Updated by: D. N. Stavropoulos, *Oxford Greek-English learner's dictionary* (Oxford : Oxford Univ. Pr., 1988. 1019 p.).

Nathanail, Paul. NTC's new college Greek and English dictionary. Lincolnwood, Ill. : National Textbook Co., 1990. 556 p. **AC466**

Focuses on everday language spoken throughout Greece. Up-to-date definitions of technical, scientific, and business terms are included in the more than 50,000 entries. Lists 175 irregular Greek verbs and a short group of geographical names. PA1139.E5N37

Pring, Julian Talbot. The Oxford dictionary of modern Greek : Greek-English and English-Greek. Oxford : Clarendon Pr. ; N.Y. : Oxford Univ. Pr., 1982. 2 v. in 1 (222, 380 p.). **AC467**

Each volume first published separately: *Greek-English* in 1965; *English-Greek*, 1982.

This compact, up-to-date desk dictionary provides a practical selection of words and idiomatic expressions in common use. An appendix lists principal parts of verbs. PA1139.E5P77

Gujarati

Deśapāṇḍe, Pāṇḍuraṅga Ganeśa. Universal English-Gujarati dictionary / Pandurang Ganesh Deshpande with Bharati Deshpande. Bombay ; N.Y. : Oxford Univ. Pr., 1988. 960 p. **AC468**

Title also in Gujarati. *Sarvāṅgī Aṅgrejī-Gujarātī kośa.*

A new and slightly enlarged edition of the same compiler's *A modern English-Gujarati dictionary* (Bombay ; N.Y. : Oxford Univ. Pr., 1982. 809 p.). PK1846.D437

Hausa

See Xhosa.

Hawaiian

Pukui, Mary Kawena. Hawaiian dictionary : Hawaiian-English, English-Hawaiian / Mary Kawena Pukui, Samuel H. Elbert. Rev. and enl. ed. Honolulu : Univ. of Hawaii Pr., c1986. 572 p. **AC469**

Originally published in two volumes, the Hawaiian-English part first appearing in 1957 (3rd ed., 1965; suppl., 1966) and the English-Hawaiian part in 1964.

Based to some extent on Lorrin Andrews, *Dictionary of the Hawaiian language* revised by Henry H. Parker (Honolulu : Board of Commissioners of Public Archives of the Territory of Hawaii, 1922). The Hawaiian-English part now comprises 29,000 entries. It is the most comprehensive and up-to-date dictionary for the language. PL6446.P795

Hebrew

Ben-Yehuda, Eliezer. Milon ha-lashon ha-ivrit. Berlin-Schöneberg : Langenscheidt ; Jerusalem : Ben-Yehudah Hozaa-la'Or, 1908–1959. 16 v. **AC470**

Each volume has added t.p. in Latin : *Thesaurus totius Hebraitatis et veteris et recentioris.*

Added title pages also in German, French, and English : Gesamtwörterbuch der alt- und neuhebräischen sprache = Dictionnaire complet de la langue hebraique anciennne et moderne = A complete dictionary of ancient and modern Hebrew.

Vol. 8–13 ed. by Morris [i.e., Moses] Hirsch Segal; v. 15–16 ed. by N. H. Tur-Sinai.

All explanations given in Hebrew. PJ4830.B36

Klein, Ernest David. A comprehensive etymological dictionary of the Hebrew language for readers of English / Ernest David Klein ; [ed., Baruch Sarel]. N.Y. : Macmillan, c1987. 721 p. **AC471**

"The first etymological dictionary in the proper sense of Hebrew as a totality, comprising both the vocabulary current in present-day Hebrew ... as well as medieval words."—*Introd.* Includes transliteration rules for Hebrew, Arabic, and Greek. PJ4833.K54

Sokoloff, Michael. A dictionary of Jewish Palestinian Aramaic of the Byzantine period. Ramat Gan : Bar Ilan Univ. Pr., 1990. 823 p. (Dictionaries of Talmud, Midrash and Targum, 2). **AC472**

Aims "to provide students and scholars with a tool for an accurate understanding of the Aramaic dialect of the Jewish Palestinian literature of the Byzantine period [and] to provide a tool for the Aramaist and Semitic linguist by which to see the relationship of this Aramaic dialect to the other ones."—*Pref.* Includes etymologies. PJ5205.S6

Bilingual

Alcalay, Reuben. Milon angli-'ivri shalem. Tel Aviv : Masadah, 1959–61. 4 v. (4270 col.). **AC473**

Various reprintings in 1,2, and 4 v. by various publishers, including a large print ed., 1990.

Added t. p. in English: *The complete English-Hebrew dictionary.*

Title page and introduction in Hebrew. Vocabulary is extensive; gives equivalents only.

§ Companion volume: *Milon 'ivri-angli shalem*, me'et Re'uven Alkala'i (Tel Aviv : Masada, [1965]. 2884 col.). Added t.p. in English: *The complete Hebrew-English dictionary.* PJ4833.A4

Baltsan, Hayim. Webster's new World Hebrew dictionary. N.Y. : Prentice Hall, c1992. 827 p. **AC474**

Hebrew-English/English Hebrew.

Title on added t.p.: Milon 'ivri shimushi.

Aims to render modern Hebrew accessible to a wide range of people by presenting transliterated Hebrew words in Latin alphabetical order. Difficulties may arise because the transliterations, while they may be easily understood by English speakers, are not those prescribed by the Hebrew Language Academy. Entries include definition and usage, as well as the proper Hebrew spelling of each word. PJ4833.B26

Botterweck, G. Johannes. Theologisches Wörterbuch zum Alten Testament / hrsg. von G. Johannes Botterweck und Helmer Ringgren. Stuttgart : W. Kohlhammer, 1973–94. Bd. 1–8, Lfg. 4. (In progress). **AC475**

For annotation, *see* BC134. BS440.B57

Brown, Francis. The new Brown, Driver, Briggs, Gesenius Hebrew and English lexicon : with an appendix containing the biblical Aramaic / by Francis Brown ; with the cooperation of S. R. Driver and Charles A. Briggs. Peabody, Mass. : Hendrickson Publ., c1979. 1118, [4], 58 p. **AC476**

Repr. : Christian Copyrights, 1983.

"Based on the lexicon of William Gesunius, as translated by Edward Robinson; and edited with constant reference to the thesarus [sic] of Gesenius as completed by E. Rödiger, and with authorized use of the latest German editions of Gesenius' Handwörterbuch über das Alte Testament; with the numbering system from Strong's Exhaustive Concordance added, thus greatly increasing the usefulness of this lexicon by all serious students of the Bible, especially those knowing no Hebrew."—*t.p.*

Includes *Indexes to all editions of Brown-Driver-Briggs Hebrew lexicon*, comp. by Maurice A. Robinson.

Supplies etymological information. PJ4833.G33

Gesenius, Friedrich Heinrich Wilhelm. Hebräisches und aramäisches Handwörterbuch über das Alte Testament ... . 17. Aufl. Leipzig : Vogel, 1921. 1013 p.   **AC477**

Hebrew-German with German-Hebrew index.

Gives etymologies and references to sources. The standard in the field.

To be replaced by:

———. ———. Wilhelm Gesenius unter verantwortlicher Mitarbeit von Udo Rüterwörden ... (18. Aufl. Berlin ; N.Y. : Springer-Verlag, c1987. Lfg. 1. [In progress]).

Contents: Lfg. 1, Alef–Gimel.

A scholarly Hebrew-German dictionary, listing all words, including proper names, found in the Hebrew Bible. Provides etymologies.   PJ4835.G5G45

Goldberg, Nathan. New functional Hebrew-English, English-Hebrew dictionary : with illustrative sentences and derivative words and expressions. N.Y. : Ktav Publ. House, 1958. 355 p.   **AC478**

Title also in Hebrew: *ha-Milon ha-shimushi he-hadash.*

A dictionary for beginners. The English-Hebrew section is an index.   PJ4833.G6

Jastrow, Marcus. Dictionary of the Targumim, the Talmud Babli and Yerushalmi, and the Midrashic literature : with an index of Scriptural quotations. London : Luzac ; N.Y. : Putnam, 1903. 2 v.   **AC479**

Repr.: Brooklyn, Traditional Pr., 1975.

A photographic reprint was issued by Shapiro, Vallentine (London, 1926).

A standard English dictionary of Talmudic Hebrew.   PJ5205.J3

Kaufman, Judah. English-Hebrew dictionary / by Israel Efros, Judah Ibn-Shmuel Kaufman, Benjamin Silk, ed. by Judah Kaufman. Tel Aviv : Dvir, [1929]. 751 p.   **AC480**

Frequently reprinted.

Title also in Hebrew: Milon angli-ivri.   PJ4833.K2

Koehler, Ludwig Hugo. Hebräisches und aramäisches Lexikon zum Alten Testament. 3. Aufl. neu bearb. von Walter Baumgartner. Unter Mitarbeit von Benedikt Hartmann und E. Y. Kutscher. Leiden : Brill, 1967–90. Lfg. 1–4. (In progress).   **AC481**

Editors vary.

Earlier editions had title: *Lexicon in Veteris Testamenti libros* (AC482).

Completely revised and reset, with materials from the supplement incorporated.

§ A related work is William Lee Holladay, *A concise Hebrew and Aramaic lexicon of the Old Testament*, based upon the lexical work of Ludwig Koehler and Walter Baumgartner. (12th corrected impression. Grand Rapids, Mich. : Eerdmans ; Leiden : Brill, 1991, c1988. 425 p.).

Each successive impression incorporates new corrections.

Inasmuch as the 3rd ed. of the Koehler-Baumgartner lexicon (above) omits renderings in English, this is an effort to provide an English edition of that work in abridged format. It uses material from the 3rd ed. of Koehler-Baumgartner so far as available, and depends on the earlier editions for the remainder of the alphabet.   PJ4835.G5K58

——————— Lexicon in Veteris Testamenti libros = Wörterbuch zum hebräischen Alten Testament in deutscher und englischer Sprache = A dictionary of the Hebrew Old Testament in English and German / ed. by Ludwig Koehler. Wörterbuch zum aramäischen Teil des Alten Testaments in deutscher und englischer Sprache = A dictionary of the Aramaic parts of the Old Testament in English and German / ed. by Walter Baumgartner. Leiden : Brill, 1948–53. 1138 p.   **AC482**

Preface and introduction in German and English. Equivalents of terms also given in German and English. Includes quotations with exact references to sources.

———. ———. *Supplementum* (Leiden : Brill, 1958. 227 p.). Includes tables of scripts and transcriptions; abbreviations and signs; a German word list with Hebrew and Aramaic equivalents; additions and corrections.

A new edition is in progress: *Hebräisches und aramäisches Lexikon zum Alten Testament* (AC481).

Lazar, Yisrael. ha-Milion he-hadash : ʿIvri-Angli Angli-ʿIvri / arukh biyede Yisrael Lazar. London : Kuperard, 1990. 343, 419 p.   **AC483**

Title on added t.p. : The new dictionary Hebrew-English English-Hebrew.

This desk-size bilingual dictionary "contains words and concepts which are most commonly used in Hebrew and English in daily life, in the press, media education and in the realm of science and technology."—*Pref.* It uses the full spelling established by the Hebrew Language Academy.

Zilkha, Avraham. Modern Hebrew-English dictionary. New Haven, Conn. : Yale Univ. Pr., c1989. 305 p.   **AC484**

Aims to be easy to use and up to date. "Special attention was given to the language of the media; thus, political terms and names of institutions have been included in abundance."—*Pref.* The vocabulary is written as it is likely to be found in print.   PJ4833.Z57

Hindi

The Oxford Hindi-English dictionary / ed. by R. S. McGregor. Oxford : Oxford Univ. Pr., 1993. 1083 p.   **AC485**

Though this dictionary retains and supplements John Thompson Platts's treatment of the vocabulary of early Hindi literature [*Dictionary of Urdū, classical Hindī and English*, AC801], it treats the "spoken and written language of the twentieth century in which the broad standard of urban usage" (*Pref.*) is emphasized. More than 70,000 entries offer the headword in Devāngarī script and transliteration in roman script which serves as a guide to pronunciation, derivation, grammatical designation, examples of use, and modern regional variants. A brief history of the language is offered in the introduction.   PK1936O.93

Pathak, Ram Chandra. Bhargava's standard illustrated dictionary of the English language (Anglo-Hindi ed.). 12th ed., thoroughly rev. & enl. Varanasi : Bhargava, [1972]. 1432 p. : ill.   **AC486**

"All the words in literary and conversational Hindi, modern and ancient have been included in the work."—*Pref.*

A companion work is Pathak's *Bhargava's standard illustrated dictionary of the Hindi language* (Varanasi : Bhargava, 1964. 1280 p.).

Both works are frequently reprinted.   PK1936.P3

Bilingual

Raghu Vira. A comprehensive English-Hindi dictionary of governmental and educational words and phrases. Nagpur : International Academy of Indian Culture, 1955. 189 p., 1579 p. : ill. (Sarasvati-Vihara series, v. 35).   **AC487**

Repr.: New Delhi : International Academy of Indian Culture, 1976. Frequently reprinted.

"The most comprehensive dictionary of the modern Hindi language yet published."—*Library journal* 81 (15 Nov. 1956): 2694. Particularly strong in all aspects of governmental administration, law and political science, and the sciences.   PK1937.R3

Hindustani

Craven, Thomas. The new royal dictionary : English into Hindustani and Hindustani into English. 1932 ed. / rev. by Bishop J. R. Chitambar. Lucknow : Methodist Publ. House, 1932. 328, 372p. **AC488**
Contents: pt. 1, English-Hindustani; pt. 2, Hindustani-English.
Printed in the roman alphabet. PK1986.C8

Fallon, S. W. New Hindustani-English dictionary : with illustrations from Hindustani literature and folk-lore. Banāras : Medical Hall Pr. ; London : Trübner, 1879. 1216 p. **AC489**
Repr. : New Delhi : Asian Educational Services, 1989.
Provides "determinations of the roots and generic meanings of Hindi words, which are traced sometimes to older forms."—*Introd.* Part of speech is indicated. No pronunciation is offered.
The companion work: *New English-Hindustani dictionary : with illustrations from English literature and colloquial English, tr. into Hindustani* (Lahore : Gulab Singh, 1905. 703 p.) was completed under the supervision of Rev. J. D. Bate after Fallon's death. PK1986.F3

Hittite

Puhvel, Jaan. Hittite etymological dictionary. Berlin ; N.Y. : Mouton, 1984–1991. v. 1–3 in 2 v. (Trends in linguistics. Documentation, 5). (In progress). **AC490**
Contents: v. 1–2 in 1 v., Words beginning with A; Words beginning with E and I; v. 3, Words beginning with H.
A pioneering effort in which as many entries as possible are presented as "self-contained micro-essays of a format best suited to the item at hand. When no etymology is rated certain, the discussion often proceeds from the less likely possibilities and ends up with the most probable. When the preferred etymology is featured as virtually certain, it is usually stated and discussed first, and discarded alternatives, to the extent that they are deemed historically interesting, are mentioned in a coda."—*Pref.* P945.Z8

University of Chicago. Oriental Institute. The Hittite dictionary of the Oriental Institute of the University of Chicago / ed. by Hans G. Güterbock and Harry A. Hoffner. [Chicago] : The Institute, 1980–1989. v. 3, fasc. 1–4. (In progress). **AC491**
Contents: v. 3 fasc. 1–4, L–nutarnu.
A Hittite-English dictionary intended for English-speaking scholars and students; planned to be of intermediate length. Publication was begun "with the letter 'L' to avoid immediate overlap with Annelies Kammenhuber's Hittite-German work [*Hethitisches Wörterbuch.* 2. Aufl. Heidelberg : Winter, 1975–]."—*Foreword.* Aims "to give complete coverage of the representative occurrences of each Hittite word" (*Pref.*), but does not seek to be exhaustive. Attempts to give usable information that allows an understanding of the basis of the scholarly conclusions presented. Does not attempt to determine the proto-Indo-European origins of Hittite words, and is not, therefore, an etymological dictionary. Words borrowed from identifiable foreign sources are noted. P945.Z8

Hungarian

Magyar értelmező kéziszótár / szerk. Juhász József [et al.] ; készült a Magyar Todományos Akadémia Nyelvtodományi Intézetében. 2. változatlan kiad. Budapest : Akademiai Kiadó, 1975. 1550 p. : ill. **AC492**
1st ed., 1972.
Frequently reprinted, recently in 2 v.
About 70,000 entry words. PH2625.M27

A magyar nyelv értelmező szótára / szerkesztette a Magyar Tudományos Akadémia Nyelvtudományi Intézet ; Bárczi Géza, Országh László vezetésével szerkesztették Balázs János ... [et al.]. Budapest : Akadémiai Kiadó, 1959–62. 7 v. **AC493**
Repr., 1978–80.
A thorough and carefully edited dictionary of standard modern Hungarian. Usage is illustrated by copious quotations, with sources indicated. PH2625.M3

Szarvas, Gábor. Magyar-nyelvtörténeti szótár a legrégibb nyelvemlékektöl a nyelvújításig / Gábor Szarvas, Zsigmond Simonyi. Budapest : V. Hornyánszky, 1890–93. 3 v. **AC494**
Added title page in Latin: Lexicon linguae hungaricae aevi antiquioris, auspiciis Academiae Scientiarum Hungaricae.
A dictionary of the early Hungarian language compiled on historical principles. PH2625.S8

Bilingual

Magay, Tamás. A concise Hungarian-English dictionary / by T. Magay, L. Országh ; contributing ed., P. A. Sherwood. Oxford ; N.Y. : Oxford Univ. Pr. by permission of the Akadémiai Kiadó, 1990. 1152 p. **AC495**
A previous ed., 1973, ed. by László Országh, had title, *Magyar-angol kéziszótár.*
Introductory material in English and Hungarian. PH2640.M3

Országh, László. A concise English-Hungarian dictionary / ed. in chief, L. Országh ; editor, T. Magay. 14th ed., new impression of the 10th, completely rev. ed. Oxford ; N.Y. : Oxford Univ. Pr. ; Budapest : Akadémiai Kiadó, 1990. 1052, [1] p. **AC496**
8th ed., 1975; 10th completely rev. ed., 1981.
Some eds. publ. with Hungarian title: *Angol-magyar keziszotar.*
This edition, a new impression of the 10th ed., lists some 37,000 words. PH2640.O6513

Abbreviations

Library of Congress. Slavic and Central European Division. Hungarian abbreviations : a selective list / comp. by Elemer Bako. Wash. : U.S. Govt. Print. Off., 1961. 146 p. **AC497**
Approximately 2,500 abbreviations, followed by the full word or words in Hungarian and the English equivalent. Emphasis is on governmental and other organizational names; but terms frequently found in Hungarian publications are also included. PH2693.U5

Etymology

Gombocz, Zoltán. Magyar etymologiai szótár : lexicon critico-etymologicum linguae Hungaricae. A Magyar Tudományos Akadémia megbizásából / írta Gombocz Zoltán és Melich János. Budapest : Magyar Tudományos Akadémia, 1914/30–44. 17 pts. **AC498**
Contents: pts. 1–10, A–érdëm (1599 col.); pts. 11–17, erdö–gaz (1160 col.).
No more published. PH2580.G6

A magyar nyelv történeti-etimológiai szótára. Budapest : Akadémiai Kiadó, 1967–76. 3 v. **AC499**
Föszerkesztö: Benkö Loránd [et al.].
Introductory remarks also in German.

An important etymological dictionary. Gives derivation, earliest known date of occurrence, and examples of usage, plus bibliographical references to philological discussions and research. PH2580.M3

Bibliography

Halasz de Beky, I. L. Bibliography of Hungarian dictionaries, 1410–1963. Toronto : Univ. of Toronto Pr., [1966]. 148 p. **AC500**
1,025 entries in two main sections: language dictionaries, and subject dictionaries. Only the latest edition is cited in most instances. English translations of Hungarian titles are provided except where the title gives no information beyond the languages included. Z2148.L5H3

Ibo

Welmers, Beatrice F. Igbo : a learner's dictionary / Beatrice F. Welmers, William E. Welmers. Los Angeles : [African Studies Center, Univ. of Calif.], 1968. 396 p. **AC501**
"This dictionary has been prepared primarily for speakers of English who have acquired at least a minimum of competence in speaking Igbo, and who are aware of the major structural patterns of Igbo."— *Introd.* English-Igbo and Igbo-English. About 2,000 entries in each section. Represents colloquial speech. PL8261.Z5W4

Icelandic

Arngrímur Sigurðsson. Íslenzk-ensk orðabók. 4. utg. Reykjavík : Isafoldarprentsmiðja, c1983. 942 p. **AC502**
1st ed., 1970 ; 3rd ed., 1980.
Title on added title page: Icelandic-English dictionary.
Offers English equivalents only, without indication of parts of speech or examples of usage. PD2437.A7

Cleasby, Richard. An Icelandic-English dictionary / initiated by Richard Cleasby. Subsequently rev., enl., and compl. by Gudbrand Vigfússon. 2nd ed. with a suppl. by Sir William A. Craigie containing many additional words and references. Oxford : Clarendon Pr., 1957. 833 p. **AC503**
Repr.: Oxford : Clarendon Pr., 1969.
The original edition, first published in 1874, was started by Cleasby and completed by Vigfússon. This is a lithographic reprint with the addition of a 52-page supplement. The introduction and biographical sketch of Cleasby included in the first edition are omitted, but the section on grammar is reprinted. PD2379.C5

Fritzner, Johan. Ordbog over det gamle norsk sprog. Omar., forøget og forbedret udg …. Kristiania : Den Norske Forlagsforening ; Chicago : Relling, 1886–96. 3 v. **AC504**
———, ——— *Tillegg* … ved Didrik Arup Seip og Trygve Knudsen (Oslo : Møller, 1955. 155 p.).
Repr.: Oslo: T.J. Møller, 1954–72 with v. 4, "Rettelser og tillegg," by Finn Hødnebø (Oslo : Universitetforlaget).
1st ed., 1867.
Includes many references, quotations, variations in meaning, etc. A 4th ed. (Oslo : Universitetforlaget, 1972–) is in progress.

Íslenzk orðabók, handa skólum og almenningi / [Redaktører] Árni Böðvarsson. Reykjavík : Bókaútgáfa Menningarsjóðs, 1963. 852 p. **AC505**
A scholarly work which includes both old and new Icelandic, and which covers literary and written language as well as that of colloquial speech. PD2437.I83

Sigfús Blöndal. Íslandsk-dansk ordbog / hoved-medarbejdere: Björg Thorláksson Blöndal, Jón Ofeigsson, Holger Wiehe. Reykjavík : H. Aschehoug & Co., 1920–24. 1052 p. **AC506**
Repr. : Reykjavík : Íslensk-danskur orðabókarajóður ; Söluumboð : Íslenska bókmenntaféllag, 1980–81.
Added title page: Íslensk-dönsk orðabók.
Old Icelandic, including dialect and colloquial words.
———. ———. *Supplement,* Redaktører Halldór Halldórsson … [et al.] (Reykjavík : Islandsk-Dansk Ordbogsfond, 1963. 200 p.). PD2437.B5

Sören Sörensen. Ensk-Íslensk orðabók : með alfræðilegu ívafi / Sören Sörenson ; Jóhann S. Hannesson bjó til prentunar ásamt fleirum. [Reykjavík] : Örn og örlygur, 1984. 1241 p. : ill. **AC507**
On t.p. : "Byggð á Scott, Foresman advanced dictionary sem er endurskouðuð útgáfa af the Thorndike-Barnhart high school dictionary eftir E.L. Thorndike og Clarence L. Barnhart."
English vocabulary is derived from the Thorndike-Barnhart and Scott, Foresman dictionaries mentioned on the title page. Definitions in Icelandic, with some examples of English usage. PD2437.S6

Sverrir Hólmarsson. Íslensk-ensk orðabók / Sverrir Hólmarsson, Christopher Sanders, John Tucker ; ráðgjöf, Svavar Sigmundsson. Reykjavík : Iðunn, c1989. 536 p. **AC508**
Title on added t.p: Concise Icelandic-English dictionary.
Aims to meet the needs of both English-speaking students of Icelandic culture and Icelanders who need "a good dictionary of modern everyday Icelandic and its contemporary English equivalents."— *Foreword.* PD2437.S87

Zoëga, Geir Tómasson. A concise dictionary of old Icelandic. Oxford : Clarendon Pr., 1926. 551 p. **AC509**
Based on Richard Cleasby's *An Icelandic-English dictionary* (AC503).
Icelandic to English only. For "those whose interests chiefly centre in Old-Icelandic prose writings."—*Pref.* Purely poetic words are omitted. PD2379.Z6

Etymology

Jóhannesson, Alexander. Isländisches etymologisches Wörterbuch. Bern : A. Francke, 1951–56. 1406p. **AC510**
Issued in parts.
Contains some 20,000 words, including so-called poetic words and mythological names but omitting personal and place-names. Arrangement is by Indo-Germanic roots, with an index of Icelandic words. Draws on linguistic literature through 1950. PD2431.J6

Vries, Jan de. Altnordisches etymologisches Wörterbuch. Leiden : Brill, 1957–61. 689 p. **AC511**
Issued in 9 pts.
Repr., 1977.
Old Icelandic and Old Norwegian. Gives equivalents in other Scandinavian languages, references to sources, etc. PD1805.V7

Indo-European

Buck, Carl Darling. A dictionary of selected synonyms in the principal Indo-European languages : a contribution to the history of ideas. Chicago : Univ. of Chicago Pr., 1949. 1515 p. **AC512**
Repr., 1965, 1988.
Arranged by semantic groupings. Under each term the equivalent word is given in about 30 of the major Indo-European languages, followed by a description of its etymology and semantic history. P765.B8

Carnoy, Albert Joseph. Dictionnaire étymologique du proto-indo-européen. Louvain : Publications Universitaires, 1955. 223 p. (Bibliothèque du Muséon, v. 39). **AC513**

At head of title: Université de Louvain. Institut Orientaliste.

Words are listed under three main sections: Pelasgic, Proto-Indo-European, and Etruscan. P725.C3

Mann, Stuart Edward. An Indo-European comparative dictionary. Hamburg : H. Buske, c1984–87. 1682 col. **AC514**

"The object of the present work is to indicate what words in the living or the dead languages of the Indo-European family appear to have a common origin, and to give them an acceptable prototype form …. [T]he author has tried to avoid the German fault of overloading etymologies with irrelevancies, the French fault of trimming the evidence to achieve a neat pattern, and the Anglo-Saxon fault of being content with approximations."—*Introd.* P725.M36

Pokorny, Julius. Indogermanisches etymologisches Wörterbuch. Berne : A. Francke, 1948–69. 2 v. (1183 p., 495 p.). **AC515**

Issued in parts.

Repr., 1989.

A standard etymological dictionary of the various Indogermanic languages. More than a revision of Alois Walde and Julius Pokorny's *Vergleichendes Wörterbuch der indogermanischen Sprachen* (Berlin : de Gruyter, 1927–32), which was based on materials published only through 1923. The present work uses sources through 1947, and is arranged according to the European, rather than the Indian, alphabet. Vol. 2 contains indexes. P725.P63

Turner, Ralph Lilley. A comparative dictionary of Indo-Aryan languages. London ; N.Y. : Oxford Univ. Pr., 1966. 841 p. **AC516**

Published in 11 pts, 1962–1966.

A comparative dictionary of more than 50 of the related languages of India, which are descended from the tongue of the Aryan invaders, with English translations. Frequent references to the literature. Words are given in roman transliteration.

§ Supplementary works from the same publisher: *A comparative dictionary of Indo-Aryan languages : indexes,* comp. by Dorothy Rivers Turner (1969. 357 p.), which lists all the 140,000 headwords in the *Dictionary* for purposes of comparison, arranged by language or language group; *A comparative dictionary of Indo-Aryan languages : phonetic analysis,* [by] R. L. Turner and D. R. Turner (1971. 231 p.). PK175.T8

Indonesian

Echols, John M. An Indonesian-English dictionary / by John M. Echols and Hassan Shadily. 3rd ed. / rev. and ed. by John U. Wolff and James T. Collins in cooperation with Hassan Shadily. Ithaca, N.Y. : Cornell Univ. Pr., 1989. 618 p. **AC517**

1st ed., 1961; 2nd ed., 1963.

Repr.: Jakarta : Gramedia, 1989 and 1992 with added title in Indonesian: *Kamus Indonesia-Inggris.*

Intended as a comprehensive dictionary of modern Indonesian, incorporating many technical terms. Includes illustrative phrases and sentences. This edition is "much-revised and much-expanded."—*Editor's pref.*

§ A companion volume by the same authors: *An English-Indonesian dictionary* (Ithaca, N.Y. : Cornell Univ. Pr., [1975]. 660 p. Repr.: Ithaca, N.Y. : Cornell Univ. Pr.; Jakarta : Gramedia, 1989 and 1990). Added title in Indonesian: *Kamus Inggris-Indonesia.* Includes "the most common words and phrases in American English … with the Indonesian equivalent."—*Pref.* Intended primarily for use by Indonesians. PL5076.E35

Schmidgall Tellings, A. Ed. Contemporary Indonesian-English dictionary / by A. Ed. Schmidgall-Tellings and Alan M. Stevens. Chicago : Ohio Univ. Pr., c1981. 388 p. **AC518**

On title page: A supplement to the standard Indonesian dictionaries with particular concentration on new words, expressions, and meanings. PL5076.S34

Irish

Royal Irish Academy (Dublin). Dictionary of the Irish language : based mainly on Old and Middle Irish materials. [Dublin] : Royal Irish Academy, 1913–76. 4 v. **AC519**

Issued in fascicles; parts publ. irregularly as completed.

Some fascicles have title: *Contributions to a dictionary of the Irish language.*

The authoritative dictionary of the Irish language, based on materials collected for many years by the Academy from printed books, manuscripts, and the spoken language. Arranged on historical principles, with many quotations illustrating the development both of meanings of words and of their grammatical inflections. Begins with the letter D, leaving A–C to be published last, because the letters A–Dn were covered in Kuno Meyer's *Contributions to Irish lexicography* (Halle : Niemeyer; London : Nutt, 1906. 670 p.), of which the Academy's dictionary is a continuation.

Work on the *Dictionary* fascicles was abandoned after publication of the letter F in 1957, but earlier and later parts of the alphabet continued to be published as *Contributions.* In some libraries the fascicles of the *Dictionary* and those of the *Contributions* have been bound together and cataloged as a 4-volume set with title page (issued by the Academy) bearing the dates 1913–76 and carrying the title *Dictionary of the Irish language.* … This combined edition constitutes the full work and no further work on either series is planned.

The Academy has issued a *Dictionary of the Irish language … Compact edition* (Dublin, 1983. 632p.) which reproduces in a single alphabetical sequence the fascicles of both the *Contributions* and the *Dictionary.* Type size is greatly reduced in this photographic reproduction, four pages of the original fascicles appearing on each page of the "Compact edition." The "Historical note" by E. G. Quin, originally published 1976, serves as an overall introduction, and the "Additions and corrections" for the letters A, B, C and F are reproduced at the end of the volume. PB1291.R7

Bilingual

De Bhaldraithe, Tomás. English-Irish dictionary. Baile Átha Cliath : Oifig an tSoláthair, 1959. 864 p. **AC520**

"Made and printed for the Stationery Office by Hely's Ltd., Printers, Dublin."

"The aim of this dictionary is the practical one of providing Irish equivalents for English words and phrases in common use. It is not then to be regarded as an exhaustive word-store of modern literary Irish or of the current spoken language."—*Pref.* PB1291.D4

Dinneen, Patrick Stephen. Irish-English dictionary : being a thesaurus of the words, phrases and idioms of the modern Irish language. New ed., rev. and greatly enl. Dublin : publ. for the Irish Texts Society by the Educ. Co. of Ireland, 1927. 1340 p. **AC521**

1st ed., 1904; various reprintings.

Principal abbreviations and references, p. xxiii–xxx. Uses traditional Irish orthography. PB1291.D5

Etymology

Vendryes, Joseph. Lexique étymologique de l'irlandais ancien. Dublin : Dublin Institue for Advanced Studies, 1959–[1987?]. [fasc. 1–8?]. (In progress). **AC522**
Contents: pts. C, M–P, R–S, T–U.
Following each Irish word is a brief equivalent in French. Etymology is then presented in detail with exact references to sources.
Since the death of Vendryes in 1960, the work has been carried on by other hands. PB1288.V4

Italian

Accademia della Crusca (Florence). Vocabolario degli Accademici della Crusca. 5. impressione. Firenze : Tip. Galileiana di M. Cellini ecc., 1863–1923. 11 v. **AC523**
1st ed., 1612.
Contents: v.1–11, A–O.
The great dictionary of the Academy, published in various editions. The 5th ed. was never completed; but was to be replaced by: Accademia d'Italia, *Vocabolario della lingua italiana* (Milano : Soc. Anonima per la Pubblicazione del Vocabolario, 1941. v. 1, A–C. No more published.). PC1625.A32

Battaglia, Salvatore. Grande dizionario della lingua italiana / [Redazione, direttore: Giorgio Bárberi Squarotti]. [Torino] : Unione tipografico-editrice torinese, 1961–1992. v. 1–16. (In progress). **AC524**
Contents: v. 1–16, A–Roba.
Designed to replace as a new work, not a revision, the century-old standard *Dizionario della lingua italiana* of Nicolò Tommaseo and Bernardo Bellini (Torino : Unione tipografico-editrice, [1861–79]. 4 v. in 8).
A scholarly work, with the collaboration of many specialists; planned on historical principles, giving full definitions and examples of meanings and usages in chronological order.
Numerous citations to sources both early and modern are listed in the separate *Indice degli autori citati nei volumni 1–8* (1973. 121 p.).

Devoto, Giacomo. Nouvo vocabolario illustrato della lingua italiana / di Giacomo Devoto e Gian Carlo Oli. 1a ed. / edizione a cura de Gian Carlo Oli e Lorenzo Magini. Milano : Selezione dal Reader's Digest, 1987. 2 v. (3523 p.) : ill. **AC525**
1968 ed. had title: *Vocabolario illustrato della lingua italiana.*
An illustrated dictionary with an extensive, up-to-date vocabulary. Unusually find from the standpoint of both content and form (good typeface, paper, illustrations). PC1625.D4

Palazzi, Fernando. Novissimo dizionario della lingua italiana / Fernando Palazzi ; edizione a cura di Gianfranco Folena. [Ed. riv. e aggiornata]. Turin : Loescher, 1986. 1648 p. : ill. **AC526**
1st ed., 1939; rev. ed., 1974.
A dictionary of contemporary Italian. Proper nouns and abbreviations are appended. PC1625.P17

Vocabolario della lingua italiana. Roma : Istituto della Enciclopedia Italiana, Fondata da Giovanni Treccani, 1986–91. v. 1–3 : ill. (some col.). (In progress). **AC527**
Contents: v. 1–3 [pt. 2] : A–R.
A comprehensive dictionary with etymology. Illustrations, some in color. PC1625.V53

Bilingual

Cassell's Italian-English, English-Italian dictionary / prep. by Piero Rébora with the assistance of Francis M. Guercio and Arthur L. Hayward. 7th ed., with rev. suppl. London : Cassell, 1977. 1128 p. **AC528**
First publ. 1958.
A general dictionary of the Italian language as written and spoken today. PC1640.C33

Dizionario inglese/italiano, italiano-inglese. Torino : Società Editrice Internazionale, [1981]. 1894 p. **AC529**
"Adattamento e ristrutturazione dell' originale 'Advanced Learner's Dictionary of Current English' [publ. 1963] della Oxford University Press."—*t.p.*
Later printings (e.g., 14a ed., Torino, 1991) are reprints.
Intended as an up-to-date bilingual dictionary based on a practical, functional vocabulary. Pronunciation is indicated in the English-Italian section; examples of usage are given; and British and American forms are indicated where usage differs between those countries.
A review in *Library journal* (15 Apr. 1982): 800, calls this a "superb bilingual dictionary" for speakers of Italian who want access to English, but not the other way around: "Those who don't know Italian will be better served by another dictionary, such as the *Concise Cambridge Italian Dictionary* [AC535] or the *Cambridge Italian Dictionary* [AC534]." PC1640.D54

Hofmann Cortesi, Livio. I segreti dell'inglese : bidizionario di falsi sinonimi e vere equivalenze tra italiano e inglese / Livio Hofmann Cortesi, Bona Schmid. Firenze : Sansoni, 1988. 264 p. **AC530**
Arranged by English word accompanied by the similar Italian word (which may or may not have the same meaning); definitions in Italian for both are provided. PC1640.H64

Inglese-italiano, italiano-inglese / realizzato dal Centro lessicografico Sansoni ; sotto la direzione di Vladimiro Macchi. 3. ed. riv. e ampliata. Firenze : Sansoni, 1988. 2227 p. **AC531**
Title on added title page: English-Italian, Italian-English.
1st ed., 1950–75, and 2nd ed., 1985, had title: Dizionario delle lingue italiana e inglese.
More than 150,000 entries in the Italian-English section; proper nouns and abbreviations are interfiled. Weights and measures, mathematical symbols, and phonetic alphabets are appended. PC1640.D47

Il nuovo dizionario Hazon Garzanti : inglese-italiano, italiano-inglese. [Milan] : Garzanti, 1990. 2429 p. **AC532**
Publ. 1961 under title: *Dizionario inglese-italiano, italiano-inglese.* Publ. 1963 as *Garzanti comprehensive Italian-English, English-Italian dictionary,* both ed. by Mario Hazon. Other reprints appeared as *Grande dizionario* (e.g., 27 ed. Milan : Garzanti, 1981. 2099 p.). Later editions (1991, 1994) may be reprints.
Well-edited and useful. Coverage is excellent, including technical and colloquial words, proper names, personal and geographical. PC1640.N85

Ragazzini, Giuseppe. The Follett Zanichelli Italian dictionary : English-Italian, Italian-English / by Giuseppe Ragazzini with the collaboration of Adele Biagi and Camilla Roatta. Chicago : Follett Publ. Co., [1968]. 1864 p. **AC533**
First publ., 1967, with title: *Dizionario inglese-italiano, italiano-inglese.*
A work of about 250,000 terms including technical terms and a broad selection of scientific terms. Includes proper nouns. Numerous examples of usage, with many colloquialisms. PC1640.R26

Reynolds, Barbara. The Cambridge Italian dictionary. Cambridge : Univ. Pr., 1962–81. 2 v. **AC534**
Contents: v. 1, Italian-English (899 p.); v. 2, English-Italian (843 p.).

"First, and underlying all its criteria, is the fact that [the *Dictionary*] has been compiled, selected, and arranged from the point of view of the English-speaking user."—*Introd.*

Emphasis is on inclusiveness and elucidation of vocabulary for both the literary scholar and the student of the spoken language. Thus, many little-used and obsolete words are included, together with numerous items from specialized vocabularies; the editors have relied on subject specialists for the selection of these terms and for their definitions. Etymological derivation is not usually given, but etymologically related words are often grouped together, with cross-references from the alphabetical listings of the individual terms.

Although Alfred Hoare's *Italian dictionary* (2nd ed. Cambridge : The University Press, 1925) is an acknowledged predecessor of v. 1, the present work is not to be considered a mere revision. The word list for v. 2 reflects British usage, including Americanisms only if current in Britain. The vocabulary of specialties—such as economics, sociology, political science, philosophy—are well represented.   PC1640.R4

———————— The concise Cambridge Italian dictionary. [London] : Cambridge Univ. Pr., [1975]. 792 p.   **AC535**
"The Italian-English section is based on *The Cambridge Italian Dictionary* (AC534), which it follows closely in style and conventions. The English-Italian section represents a selection of material compiled in preparation for the English-Italian volume of that publication."—*Introd.*   PC1640.R44

Etymology

Battisti, Carlo. Dizionario etimologico italiano / Carlo Battisti, Giovanni Alessio. Firenze : G. Barbèra, 1950–57. 5 v.   **AC536**
Sponsored by the Istituto di Glottologia of the Università di Firenze.
The first extensive etymological dictionary in Italian, giving derivations, similar words in other languages, definitions, etc. Coverage is comprehensive including archaic and modern terms, scientific and technical words, and some dialectal forms.   PC1580.B3

Cortelazzo, Manlio. Dizionario etimologico della lingua italiana / [di] Manlio Cortelazzo, Paolo Zolli. Bologna : Zanichelli, 1979–1988. 5 v.   **AC537**
Definitions and examples of usage (with date and author of illustrative quotation) accompany etymological information of each term.   PC1580.C67

Pfister, Max. Lessico etimologico italiano : LEI. Wiesbaden : Reichert, 1979–90. fasc. 1–39. (In progress).   **AC538**
Contents: v. 1–4, fasc. 1–39, A–Balanus.
An ambitious and scholarly work on the etymology of the Italian language and its dialects (excluding those areas covered by Walther von Wartburg's *Französisches etymologisches Wörterbuch* [AC352] and M. L. Wagner's *Dizionario etimologico sardo* [Heidelberg, 1960–64]). Not only provides sources and datings of usage, but cites other dictionaries, linguistic atlases, and provides references to linguistic studies.
————. ————. *Supplemento bibliografico* (1991) contains a key to abbreviations used in the fascicles and in citations to primary and secondary sources. An index to v. 1–3 also was published in 1991.   PC1580.P38

Pianigiani, Ottorino. Vocabolario etimologico della lingua italiana. 4a. ed. La Spezia : Melita, 1991. 1651 p.   **AC539**
1st ed., 1907.
Includes bibliographical sources, *see also* references.   PC1580.P4

Synonyms

Cinti, Decio. Dizionario dei sinònimi e dei contrari. Nuova ed. Novara : Istituto Geografico De Agostini, 1980. 587 p.   **AC540**
1st ed., 1947; 13th ed., 1965.
A compact and useful dictionary of synonyms and antonyms.   PC1591.C5

Dizionario Garzanti dei sinonimi e dei contrari : con generici, specifici, analoghi, inversi e 207 inserti di sinonimia ragionata / diretto da Pasquale Stoppelli. [Milano] : Garzanti, 1991. 815 p.   **AC541**
Levels of usage and fields of use (e.g., sciences, zoology) are indicated; some *see also* references.   PC1591.D59

Giocondi, Michele. Dizionario dei sinonimi e dei contrari / Michele Giocondi con la collaborazione di Piero Marovelli. Firenze : Paradigma, 1988. 725 p.   **AC542**
Lists synonyms and antonyms for each entry. Indicates parts of speech.   PC1591.G5

Pittàno, Giuseppe. Sinonimi e contrari : dizionario fraseologico delle parole equivalenti, analoghe e contrarie. Bologna : Zanichelli, c1987. 863 p.   **AC543**
A useful and current guide.   PC1591.P58

Usage

Pekelis, Carla. A dictionary of colorful Italian idioms. N.Y. : Braziller, [1965]. 226 p.   **AC544**
Subtitle: A treasury of expressions most commonly found in Italian speech and writing today, with their American equivalents.   PC1640.P4

Japanese

Daijiten. Tokyo : Heibonsha, 1974. 2 v.   **AC545**
1st ed. 1934–36 in 26 v.; reduced-size repr. 1953–54 in 13 v.
More than 700,000 words; arranged in phonetic alphabet order (*gojū-on*) and indexed by ideograms.   AG35.2.D3

Gakken kokugo daijiten. Tokyo : Gakushū Kenkyūsha, 1978. 2270p.   **AC546**
14th printing 1985.
Kindaichi Haruhiko and Ikeda Yasaburō, eds.
A dictionary of current usage with examples taken from works by 250 contemporary writers. Includes synonyms.   PL675.G27

Iwanami kogo jiten. Tokyo : Iwanami Shoten, 1982. 1488 p.   **AC547**
Ed. by Ono Susumu, Satake Akihiro, and Maeda Kingoro.
First published 1974.
More than 40,000 words, covering from ancient times through the first half of the Edo period. Rich in examples of usage. Includes a guide to historical grammar, old calendar, etc.   PL675.O63

Kōjirin. [6th ed.]. Tokyo : Sanseido, 1983. 2111 p., 46 p., 48 p.   **AC548**
1st ed., 1925, was a revised and enlarged ed. of *Jirin* by Kanazawa Shōzaburo (first publ. 1907); successive editions updated to reflect current usage.
Includes a section on grammar, a pronunciation guide to difficult-to-read ideograms, and a dictionary of abbreviations in roman alphabet that are currently used in Japanese.   PL675.K595

Ōtsuki, Fumihiko. Dai-genkai. Tokyo : Fuzambo, 1932–37. 5 v.   **AC549**

A revised and enlarged edition of *Genkai* (1890). A revised edition of v. 1–4 (i.e., without v. 5, the index), *Shintei genkai*, was published 1956.

Basically a dictionary of classical Japanese. Words are arranged in phonetic alphabet order. Gives pronunciation, etymology, examples of usage (with sources), as well as definitions. The indexes in v. 5 include a separate index for foreign words.   PL675.O79

Shinmura, Izuru. Kōjien. [3rd ed.]. Tokyo : Iwanami Shoten, 1983. 2667 p.   **AC550**

1st ed., 1935, had title: *Jien*.

A standard single-volume work.   PL675.S49

Bilingual

Basic Japanese-English dictionary = [Kiso Nihongo gakushū jiten] / the Japan Foundation. Tokyo : Bonjinsha Co., c1986. 958 p., [1] leaf of plates : ill.   **AC551**

Repr.: Oxford ; N.Y. : Oxford Univ. Pr., 1989.

This desk dictionary provides basic vocabulary for the daily use of those learning Japanese. The nearly 2,900 entries are written in Roman letters followed by Kanji and/or Kana. Example sentences are included.   PL679.B37

Kodansha's compact Kanji guide : a new character dictionary for students and businessmen. N.Y. : Kodansha International, 1992. 894 p.   **AC552**

An up-to-date dictionary of *Jōyō Kanji*, the 1,945 most commonly used characters in modern Japanese writing. Examples of use.   PL679K567

Koine, Yoshio. Kenkyūsha's new English-Japanese dictionary. Rev. and enl. 5th ed. Tokyo : Kenkyūsha, 1980. 2477 p.   **AC553**

1st ed., 1927.

More than 140,000 words. Indicates American and British pronunciation; gives etymology. Some illustrative drawings. Includes a thesaurus of synonyms and a foreign phrase list. A standard English-Japanese dictionary.   PL679.K39

Masuda, Koh. Kenkyūsha's new Japanese-English dictionary = Kenkyūsha shin Wa-Ei daijiten. Rev. 4th ed. Tokyo : Kenkyūsha, 1974. 2110 p.   **AC554**

1st ed., 1918. Various printings.

About 80,000 words, with 160,000 derivatives. Numerous examples of usage. Arranged according to roman alphabet; transliteration is by Hepburn system. Numerous appendixes.   PL697.K4

Nakajima, Fumio. Iwanami Ei-Wa daijiten = Iwanami's comprehensive English-Japanese dictionary. Tokyo : Iwanami Shoten, 1970. 2124 p.   **AC555**

More than 110,000 words. Includes pronunciation (British and American), etymology, idiomatic phrases. Supplement includes geographic and personal names, abbreviations and symbols. One of the standard works.   PL697.I83

O'Neill, Patrick Geoffrey. Japanese names : a comprehensive index by characters and readings. N.Y. ; Tokyo : Weatherhill, 1972. 359 p.   **AC556**

Title also in Japanese: *Nihon jinmei chimei jiten*.

A pronouncing dictionary for Japanese proper names in two parts: (1) From characters to readings (with ideograms arranged by number of strokes); (2) From readings to characters.

A similar guide by Araki Ryōzō is *Nanori jiten* (Tokyo : Tokyōdō, 1959. 306 p. Repr., 1981).   PL683.O5

Shōgakukan Randamu Hausu Ei-Wa daijiten / henshou Shōgakukan Randamu Hausu Ei-Wa Daijiten Henshou Iinkai. Tōkyō : Shōgakukan, [1973–1974]. 4 v.   **AC557**

Title page reads: Shōgkukan Random House English-Japanese dictionary.

Vol. 1 is accompanied by suppl. (32 p.).

Also issued in two volumes.

A joint project of the Japanese and American publishing houses. The supplement includes a history of the English language and a comparative study of British and American pronunciation.   PL679.S64

Spahn, Mark. Kan-Ei jukugo ribāsu jiten = Japanese character dictionary with compound lookup / Mark Spahn, Wolfgang Hadamitzky, with Kimiko Fujie-Winter. Tokyo : Nichigai Asoshiētsu : Hatsubai Kinokuniya Shoten, 1989. 1669 p.   **AC558**

Intends "to make it as easy as possible to look [for] the readings and meanings of Japanese words written in Chinese characters."— *Pref.* Contains 5,906 characters (7,054 counting variants) and nearly 47,000 multicharacter compounds.   PL677.5.S6

Javanese

Horne, Elinor McCullough Clark. Javanese-English dictionary. New Haven, Conn. : Yale Univ. Pr., 1974. 728 p. **AC559**

Intended "to be a general-purpose dictionary of Javanese as it is now used by educated urban speakers from central Java, the area of the standard language."—*Introd.* The introduction offers the following sections: Background, Phonology and spelling, Summary of Javanese morphology, Dictionary entries, Social styles, Degree words, Guide to local variants, Symbols, and Abbreviations.   PL5166.H64

Zoetmulder, P. J. Old Javanese-English dictionary / P. J. Zoetmulder with the collaboration of S. O. Robson. 's-Gravenhage : M. Nijhoff, 1982. 2 v. (2368 p.).   **AC560**

Vocabulary is arranged in 25,500 main entries according to Latin alphabetical order.   PL5156.Z63

Kazakh

Shnitnikov, Boris Nikolayevich. Kazakh-English dictionary. The Hague : Mouton, 1966. 301 p. (Indiana University. Uralic and Altaic series, v. 28).   **AC561**

Research performed as a project of the American Council of Learned Societies.

Kazakh to English only.   PL65.K44S4

Khmer

Cambodian-English dictionary / [ed. by] Robert K. Headley, Jr. ... [et al.]. Wash. : Catholic Univ. of Amer. Pr., 1977. 2 v. (1495 p.) : ill. (Publications in the languages of Asia, 3).   **AC562**

Intended as a "reasonably comprehensive, accurate, and, above all, usable" (*Pref.*) compilation including "not only current literary and standard spoken forms of Khmer, but also archaic, obsolete, obsolescent, dialectal, and argot forms." Gives etymologies "for almost all known or suspected Indo-European loan words as well as for most of the Chinese, Thai, and Vietnamese borrowings."   PL4326.C3

Huffman, Franklin E. English-Khmer dictionary / Franklin E. Huffman, Im Proam. New Haven : Yale Univ. Pr., 1978. 690 p.   **AC563**

"The primary objective of this dictionary is to provide a corpus of basic words and phrases which it would be useful for Western students of Khmer to know how to say (or write) in standard Khmer. The dictionary contains some 40,000 English entries and subentries."—*Introd.* Also intends to offer complete coverage of basic American English vocabulary for Khmer students learning English. PL4326.H85

Jacob, Judith M. A concise Cambodian-English dictionary. London ; N.Y. : Oxford Univ. Pr., 1974. 242 p. **AC564**
Aims "to provide a handy reference book of basic modern Khmer vocabulary for the English-speaking reader. Every effort has been made to cover the recurrent vocabulary of 20th-century prose publications—newspapers, novels, articles, etc.—as well as that of the spoken language."—*Introd.* PL4326.J3

Korean

Martin, Samuel Elmo. A Korean-English dictionary / Samuel Elmo Martin, Yang Ha Lee, Sung-Un Chang. New Haven : Yale Univ. Pr., 1967. 1902 p. **AC565**
An important work attempting "to give a full and accurate portrayal of the basic native Korean vocabulary."—*Introd.* PL937.E5M3

The new World comprehensive English-Korean dictionary / [p'yonja Min Chae-sik]. Sŏul T'ŭkpyŏlsi : Si-sa-yong-o-sa, 1988. 2959 p. : ill. **AC566**
Earlier editions from 1970.
Title also in Korean.
Aims to be a manual for Koreans who live in an English-speaking world. Includes bibliographical references. PL937.K67N49

Kurdish

McCarus, Ernest Nasseph. A Kurdish-English dictionary : dialect of Sulaimania, Iraq. Ann Arbor : Univ. of Michigan Pr., [1967]. 194 p. **AC567**
The language of this work "is strictly that of Sulaimania, Iraq, predominantly literary, but including spoken language as well."—*Introd.* PK6902.M3

Wahby, Taufiq. A Kurdish-English dictionary / Taufiq Wahby, Cecil John Edmonds. Oxford : Clarendon Pr., 1966. 179 p. **AC568**
"The Kurdish of this Dictionary is the standard language of belles-lettres, journalism, official and private correspondence, and formal speech as it has developed, on the basis of the Southern-Kirmanj dialect of Sulamani in Iraq, since 1918."—*Introd.* Kurdish words are given in roman transliteration. Words borrowed from other languages are indicated. PK6906.W3

Lao

Kerr, Allen D. Lao-English dictionary / Allen D. Kerr ; assisted by Sing Bourommavong [et al.]. Wash. : Consortium Pr., Catholic Univ. of America Pr., 1972. 2 v. (1223 p.). (Publications in the languages of Asia, 2). **AC569**
Repr.: Wash. : Catholic Univ. of America Pr., 1982; Bankok : White Lotus Pr., 1992.
Vocabulary was drawn from earlier dictionaries and from current vernacular publications. PL4251.L34K4

Lappish

Nielsen, Konrad. Lappisk (samisk) ordbok : grunnet på dialektene i Polmak, Karasjok og Kautokeino = Lapp dictionary, based on the dialects of Polmak, Karasjok and Kautokeino / Konrad Nielsen, Asbjørn Nesheim. Cambridge : Harvard Univ. Pr. ; London : Williams, 1932–56. 4 v. (Inst. for Sammenlignende Kulturforskning. [Publikasjoner] ser. B: Skrifter, 17). **AC570**
Lappish, English, and Norwegian. Preliminary matter in Norwegian and English in parallel columns.
Vols.1–3 publ. 1932–38. Vol. 4, the vocabulary classified according to the meanings of the words, with many illustrations of Lappish life and customs, publ. 1956; a supplement was issued as v. 5, 1962. A 2nd ed. was published Oslo : Universitetsforl., 1979 (5 v.).
PH725.N5

Latin

Thesaurus linguae latinae : editus autoritatae et consilio academiarum quinque germanicarum Berolinensis, Gottingensis, Lipsiensis, Monacensis, Vidobonensis. Lipsiae : Teubner, 1900–92. v.1–8, v.9^2, v.10$^{1-6}$. (In progress). **AC571**
Contents: v. 1–8, A–M; v.9^2, O; v.10$^{1-6}$, P–Praesuscipio.
The great dictionary of the language, in Latin; indispensable in the university or large reference library. Plans to record, with representative quotations from each author, every word in the text of each Latin author down to the Antonines, with a selection of important passages from the works of all writers to the 7th century.
In the section A–B, proper names are included in the main alphabet, but from C on they are given in: *Supplementum nomina propria [Onomasticon]* (Lipsiae : Teubner, 1907–23; v. 2–3$^{1-2}$, C–Don). Additions and corrections are found in: Antonio Ferrua, *Note al Thesaurus linguae latinae : addenda et corrigenda* (Bari : Edipuglia, [1986]; v. 1, A–D.

Thesaurus linguae latinae : Index librorum scriptorum inscriptionum ex quibus exempla afferuntur / editus iussu et auctoritate consilii ab academiis societatibusque diversarum nationum electi. Editio altera. Lipsiae : B.G. Teubneri, 1990. 228 p. **AC572**
Cumulates the 1904 index and its 1958 supplement. PA2361.T4

Thesaurus linguae latinae : Praemonenda de rationibus et usu operis / editus iussu et auctoritate consilii ab academiis societatibusque diversarum nationum electi. Lipsiae : B.G. Teubneri, 1990. 72 p. **AC573**
An introduction to and explanation of the dictionary in Latin, German, English, French, Italian, Spanish, and Russian.
PA2361.T47

Bilingual

Andrews, Ethan Allen. Harper's Latin dictionary : a new Latin dictionary founded on the translation of Freund's Latin-German lexicon. Rev., enl., and in great part rewritten by Charlton T. Lewis and Charles Short. N.Y. ; Cincinnati : American Book Co., 1907. 2019 p. **AC574**
1st ed., 1879. Frequently reprinted under title *A latin dictionary*.
Often referred to as "Lewis and Short." The most generally useful of the older Latin-English dictionaries. PA2365.E5A7

Cassell's Latin dictionary : Latin-English, English-Latin / by D. P. Simpson. [6th ed.]. London : Cassell ; N.Y. : Macmillan, 1977, 1959. 883 p. **AC575**

5th ed. published in 1968 under title: *Cassell's new Latin dictionary*.

Popular and reliable desk dictionary.   PA2365.L3C3

Levine, Edwin B. Follett world-wide Latin dictionary : Latin-English, English-Latin (American English). Chicago : Follett, 1967. 767 p.   **AC576**

About 40,000 entries. Offers Latin equivalents for many modern terms and idioms. Includes a Guide to practical Latin. A useful desk dictionary for students.   PA2365.E5L65

Oxford Latin dictionary / ed. by P. G. W. Glare. Combined ed. Oxford : Clarendon Pr. ; N.Y. : Oxford Univ. Pr., 1982. 2126 p.   **AC577**

Originally issued in parts, 1968–82.

In Latin and English.

An important scholarly work; the standard reference for Classical Latin. Treats classical Latin from its beginnings to the end of the second century CE and includes words from both literary and nonliterary sources. Etymological notes are brief; quotations illustrating usage are arranged in chronological order.   PA2365.E5O9

Smith, William. Chambers/Murray Latin-English dictionary / by Sir William Smith and Sir John Lockwood. Edinburgh : Chambers ; London : J. Murray, 1976. 817 p.   **AC578**

1st ed., 1855. Frequently reprinted.

Previous editions had title: *A smaller Latin-English dictionary*.

Includes tables of the Roman calendar, measures, weights, and monetary units.   PA2365.E5S6

Etymology

Ernout, Alfred. Dictionnaire étymologique de la langue latine : histoire des most / par A. Ernout et A. Meillet. 4. éd., 4. tirage augm. d'additions et de corrections nouv, par Jacques André. Paris : Klincksieck, 1985. 833 p.   **AC579**

1st ed., 1932. 4th ed. first publ. 1959–60; various printings.

One of the best of the modern etymological dictionaries.   PA2342E7

Maltby, Robert. A lexicon of ancient Latin etymologies. Leeds : Cairns, 1991. 609 p.   **AC580**

Provides "as comprehensive a list as possible of explicit etymologies of Latin words to to be found in Latin (and Greek) writers."—*Introd.* The list covers the time of Varro and his teacher, Aelius Stilo, to the time of Isidore of Seville (second century BCE to early 7th century CE). "Vocabula graeca ex quibus latina derivantur," p. 661–669.   PA2342.M35

Early Christian era

Blaise, Albert. Dictionnaire latin-français des auteurs chrétiens / revu spécialement pour le vocabulaire théologique par Henri Chirat. Turnhout : Éd. Brepols, 1967. 914 p.   **AC581**

Reprint of the Strasbourg, 1954, edition with the addition of "Addenda et corrigenda."

Covers from Tertullian to the end of the Merovingian period, i.e., from the end of the first to the seventh century, and includes new terms and classical terms with new meanings. Many quotations with exact reference to sources. Bibliography of works cited, p. 9–29.   PA2308.B6

Sleumer, Albert. Kirchenlateinisches Wörterbuch. 2. sehr verm. Aufl. des "Liturgischen Lexikons" unter umfassendster Mitarbeit von Joseph Schmid, hrsg. von Albert Sleumer. Limburg a.d. Lahn : Steffen, 1926. 840 p.   **AC582**

Repr.: Hildesheim ; N.Y. : G. Olms, 1990.

Subtitle: Ausführliches Wörterverzeichnis zum Römischen Missale, Breviarium, Rituale, Graduale, Pontificale, Caeremoniale, Martyrologium, sowie zur Vulgata und zum Codex juris canonici; desgleichen zu den Proprien der Bistümer Deutschlands, Öster-reichs, Ungarns, Luxemburgs, der Schweiz und zahlreicher kirch-licher Orden und Kongregationen.

For specialists in church history.   BX1970.S55

Souter, Alexander. Glossary of later Latin to 600 A.D.. Oxford : Clarendon Pr., 1949. 454 p.   **AC583**

Frequently reprinted.

Covers the Christian literature from 180 CE to 600 CE, and thus was planned to supplement the *Oxford Latin dictionary* which treats classical Latin, omitting Christian Latin authors.   PA2308.S6

Walde, Alois. Lateinisches etymologisches Wörterbuch. 3. neubearb. Aufl. von J. B. Hofmann. Heidelberg : Winter, 1938–56. 3 v. (Indogermanische Bibliothek, II. Reihe, Wörterbücher).   **AC584**

Vol. 3 (1956): Registerband, zusammengestellt von Elsbeth Berger.

A "4. Aufl.," (1965) and "5., unveränderte Aufl." (1982) are reprints of the 3rd ed.

A scholarly etymological dictionary which indicates the first appearance of each Latin word with references to documents and usage.

Medieval

Arnaldi, Francesco. Latinitas italicae medii aevi inde ab a. CDLXXVI usque ad a. MXXII lexicon imperfectum cura et studio Francisci Arnaldi. Brussels : Secrétariat Administratif de L'Union Académique Internationale Bulletin du Cange, 1936–67. 4 v. in 2.   **AC585**

Repr. : Torino : Bottega d'Erasmo, 1970.

Originally published in *Bulletin Du Cange*, v. 10–34 (1936–67) without separate paging.

Continued by: *Addenda*, fasc. 1–6. (*In: Bulletin Du Cange*, v. 35–36, 38, 40, 42, 44/45, 48/49, 50 [1967–91]. [In progress]).

Contents: fasc. 1–9, A–Mediator.

Blaise, Albert. Dictionnaire latin-français des auteurs du moyen-age = Lexicon latinitatis medii aevi : praesertim ad res ecclesiasticas investigandas pertinens. Turnholti : Typographi Brepols, 1975. lxviii, 970 p.   **AC586**

A companion to Blaise's *Dictionnaire latin-français des auteurs chrétiens* (AC581). Gives special attention to the vocabulary of history, hagiography, liturgy, philosophy, theology, ascetic writers, and canon law, 7th–13th centuries. List of authors and works cited, p. [xiv]–lxviii.   PA2893.F7B6

Du Cange, Charles Du Fresne. Glossarium mediae et infimae latinitatis / conditum a Carolo Du Fresne, domino Du Cange; auctum a monachis Ordinis S. Benedicti, cum supplementis integris D. P. Carpenterii, Adelungii, aliorum, suisque digessit G. A. L. Henschel; sequuntur Glossarium gallicum, Tabulae, Indices auctorum et rerum, Dissertationes. Ed. nova, aucta pluribus verbis aliorum scriptorum a Léopold Favre. Niort : L. Favre, 1883–87. 10 v. : ill.   **AC587**

Repr. : Paris : Librairie des Sciences et des Arts, 1937–38 ; Graz : Akademische Druck– & Verlagsanstalt, 1954. 10 v. in 5.

Contents: v. 1–8, A–Z; v. 9, Glossaire français; v. 10, Indices.

The great dictionary of medieval Latin, originally published 1678 and several times revised. This is the latest edition but is very little changed from the edition of 1840–57 (8 v.), which is still usable and as good for general purposes as the later edition.

Schmidt, Charles. *Petit supplément au Dictionnaire de Du Cange*. (Strasbourg : Heitz, 1906. 71 p.).

Latham, Ronald Edward. Dictionary of medieval Latin from British sources / prep. by R. E. Latham under the direction of a committee appointed by the British Academy. London : Publ. for the British Academy by Oxford Univ. Pr., 1975–89. fasc. 1–4. (In progress). **AC588**

Vol. 4 prepared by D. R. Howlett and others.

Contents: fasc. 1–4, A–H.

"This dictionary is designed to present a comprehensive picture of the Latin language current in Britain from the sixth century to the sixteenth. … Sources later than 1550 are normally excluded, though some use has been made of Latin records in the Medieval tradition as late as the seventeenth century."—*Pref.* Three categories of material are distinguished, with varying fullness of treatment: "(a) The use by British authors of CL words in approximately their basic classical meanings" is afforded fairly brief treatment; "(b) Words and usages that belong to the post-classical development of Latin as a whole are dealt with more fully"; and "(c) The fullest treatment is reserved for what is distinctively British, either because of its links with Anglo-Saxon, Anglo-Norman, or some other vernacular … , or because it reflects the growth of institutions with specifically British features." Etymology is indicated where not self-evident. Quotations are dated in boldface type. Bibliography of sources cited in fasc. 1, p. xvi–xlv; bibliography supplement in fasc. 2. PA2891.L28

————— Revised medieval Latin word-list from British and Irish sources. London : publ. for the British Academy by Oxford Univ. Pr., 1965. 524 p. **AC589**

A revision and enlargement of James Houston Baxter and Charles Johnson, *Medieval Latin word-list from British and Irish sources* (London : Oxford Univ. Pr., 1934. 466 p.). A word list rather than a formal dictionary. Gives brief information, i.e., Latin word, date, and equivalent English word or phrase. PA2891.L3

Maigne d'Arnis, W. H. Lexicon manuale ad scriptores mediae et infimae latinitatis : ex glossariis Caroli Dufresne, D. Ducangii, D. P. Carpentarii, Adelungii et aliorum, in compendium accuratissime redactum; ou, Recueil de mots de la basse latinité. Paris : Migne, 1866. 2336 col. **AC590**

Repr.: Hildesheim ; N.Y. : Olms, 1977.

Gives definitions in Latin and in French. PA2889.M3

Mittellateinisches Wörterbuch bis zum ausgehenden 13. [i.e. dreizehnten] Jahrhundert / in Gemeinschaft mit den Akademien der Wissenschaften zu Göttingen, Heidelberg, Leipzig, Mainz, Wien, und der Schweizerischen Geisteswissenschaftlichen Gesellschaft, hrsg. von der Bayerischen Akademie der Wissenschaften und der Deutschen Akademie der Wissenschaften zu Berlin. München : Beck, 1959–1991. Bd. 1–2⁹. (In progress). **AC591**

Contents: Bd. 1–2⁹, Abkürzungs–Conigium.

A number of German-speaking Latinists are collaborating to produce this scholarly dictionary of medieval Latin. Designed to extend the scope of the standard *Thesaurus linguae latinae* (AC571), i.e., to cover the centuries from the decline of classical Latin to the end of the 13th century, it follows generally the plan of the *Thesaurus* in its treatment of individual words. Among many sources drawn upon for vocabulary, the extensive series *Monumenta germaniae historica* (DA145) is particularly heavily utilized. PA2893.G3M48

Niermeyer, Jan Frederik. Mediae latinitatis lexicon minus : lexique latin médiéval—français/anglais; a medieval Latin-French/English dictionary / composuit J. F. Niermeyer, perficiendum curavit C. van de Kieft. Leiden : Brill, 1976. 2 v. **AC592**

Originally issued in parts, 1954–76. Vol. 2 entitled "Abbreviationes et index fontium."

A scholarly and succinct dictionary designed to be less bulky than Du Cange, *Glossarium mediae et infimae latinitatis* (AC587), but more extensive than the word lists. It is Latin of the Vulgate and the Christian fathers. Explanations of meanings are given both in French and in English. Variant forms are cross-referenced to the basic forms. Quotations appear when the meaning is rare and are from sources between 550 and 1150 CE. PA2364.N5

Novum glossarium mediae latinitatis : ab anno DCCC usque ad annum MCC / ed. curavit Consilium Academiarum Consociatarum. Hafniae : Munksgaard, 1957–87. 4 v. (In progress). **AC593**

Issued in parts.

Contents: L–Nysus, ed. by Franz Blatt; O, ed. by Franz Blatt and Yves Lefèvre; P–Panis, ed. by Yves Lefèvre; Paniscardus–Parrula, ed. by Jacque Monfrin.

Designed to cover the "general" language of authors from the 9th to the 13th centuries. Word treatment is primarily lexicographic rather than historical or encyclopedic. Supplements but does not replace Du Cange's *Glossarium mediae et infimae latinitatis* (AC587).

—————. *Index scriptorum novus mediae latinitatis ab anno DCCC usque ad annum MCC qui afferuntur in Novo glossario ab Academiis Consociatis iuris publici facto* (1973. 246 p. Fasc. unnumbered).

An earlier list was published 1957.

A long list of periodicals and collections precedes the index of abbreviations (with full citations to sources). Useful not only in connection with the dictionary, but for identifying medieval texts generally. A supplement was publ. in 1989 (62 p.). PA2893.F7N65

Pronunciation

Allen, William Sidney. Vox Latina : a guide to the pronunciation of classical Latin. 2nd ed. Cambridge : Cambridge Univ. Pr., 1978. 132 p. **AC594**

1st ed., 1965.

An explanation of the rules and principles of classical pronunciation; not a pronouncing dictionary. PA2117.A5

Bibliography

Starnes, DeWitt Talmage. Renaissance dictionaries : English-Latin and Latin-English. Austin : Univ. of Texas Pr., 1954. 427 p. : ill. **AC595**

A history of English-Latin and Latin-English lexicography down to the 18th century, particularly of the period 1500–1660. Includes a bibliography of references pertaining to the history of Latin-English lexicography, p. 393–94, and a short-title list of Latin-English and English-Latin dictionaries (1500–*ca.* 1800) in American libraries, with location of copies. PA2353.S7

Latvian

Anglu-latviešu vārdnīca : ap 7500 vārdu. 2. izdeveums. Rīgā : Liesma, 1966. 575 p. **AC596**

Added t.p.: *English-Latvian dictionary.*

English text from English-Russian dictionary by O. Benyuch and G. Chernov. Latvian text by I. Juhņēviča and A. Klētniece.

Contains 42,000 entries. Appendixes for proper names and for abbreviations. PG8979.A47

Dravnieks, Jēkabs. Angliski-latviska vārdnīca = English-Latvian dictionary. [Riga] : Grāmatu Draugs, [1957]. 606 p. **AC597**

1st ed., Riga, 1933.

22,000 entries. PG8979.D7

Metuzāle-Kangere, Baiba. A derivational dictionary of Latvian = Latviešu valodas atvasinājumu vārdnīca. Hamburg : H. Buske, c1985. 355 p. (Bayreuther Beitrage zur Sprachwissenschaft, Bd. 5). **AC598**
Provides detailed information of the morphological system. Entries are arranged in three columns: the roots of Latvian; the words that contain each root; and the English equivalent. PG8861.M47

Turkina, Eiženija. Latviešu-anglu vārdnīca : ap 30,000 vā. 4. pārstrādāts izdevums. Rīga : "Avots", 1982. 638 p. **AC599**
Added title page in English: Latvian-English dictionary.
1st ed., 1948; 3rd ed., 1964.
Approx. 30,000 entries. PG8979.T83

Lithuanian

Bilingual

Anglu-lietuvių kalbų žodynas : Apie 30,000 žodžiu ir posakių / redagavo A. Laučka ir A. Dantaitė. 2., pataisytas ir papildytas leidimas. Vilnius : Valstybinė politinės ir mokslinės literatūros leidykla, 1961. 595 p. **AC600**
1st ed., 1958. Frequently reprinted.
At head of title: V. Baravykas.
English-Lithuanian dictionary of 30,000 entries. PG8679.A57

Lalis, Anthony. Lietuviškos ir angliškos kalbu žodynas. 3., isnaujo taisytas ir gausiai papildytas, spaudimas. Chicago : Turtu ir spauda "Lietuvos", 1915. 2 pts. in 1 v. **AC601**
1st ed., 1903; 3rd ed., 1911.
Added title page in English: *Dictionary of the Lithuanian and English languages*, 3rd rev. and enl. ed. PG8679.L33

Niedermann, Max. Wörterbuch der litauischen Schriftsprache, litauisch-deutsch / Max Niedermann, Alfred Senn, Anton Salys. Heidelberg : C. Winter, 1926–68. 5 v. (Indogermanische Bibliothek, II. Reihe, Wörterbücher). **AC602**
Published in parts. Editors vary.
A dictionary of the modern literary language, giving examples of usage. PG8681.N6

Peteraitis, Vilius. Lietuviškai angliškas žodynas = Lithuanian-English dictionary. 4. laida. Chicago : Lietuviškos knygos klubas, 1985. 576 p. **AC603**
1st ed., 1948; 3rd ed., 1980.
Prepared for the use of Lithuanians in English-speaking countries. PG8679.P38

Piesarskas, Bronius. Lietuvių-anglų kalbų žodynas = Lithuanian-English dictionary / Bronius Piesarskas, Bronius Svececicius. 2-asis pataisytas leidimas. [Vilnius : Mokslas, 1991]. 832 p. **AC604**
Gives English equivalents, with frequent examples of usage.
§ Companion work: A. Laucka, B. Piesarkas, E. Stasiuleviciute, *Anglu-lietuvių kalbų žodynas : apie 60,000 zodzi = English-Lithuanian dictionary : about 60,000 words* (2. stereotipinis leidimas. Vilnius : Mosklas, 1978. 1094 p. Repr., 1992, called 4. stereotipinis leidimas. 2 v.). PG8679.P5

Etymology

Fraenkel, Ernst. Litauisches etymologisches Wörterbuch. Heidelberg : C. Winter, 1962–65. 2 v. (1560 p.). (Indogermanische Bibliothek, II. Reihe, Wörterbücher). **AC605**
Issued in parts 1955–65. Bd. 1, A–Prive, appeared in 8 pts., 1955–58; a new title page and preliminary matter issued 1962.
An extensive etymological dictionary. PG8663.F7

Malay

Wilkinson, Richard James. Malay-English dictionary (romanised). Mitylene, Greece : Printed by Salavopoulos and Kinderlis ; Singapore : Kelly and Walsh, 1932. 2 v. **AC606**
Repr.: London : Macmillan, 1957 (2 v. in 1).
Includes examples of use. PL5125.W62

Winstedt, Richard Olof. An unabridged Malay-English dictionary. 6th ed., enl. Kuala Lumpur, Malaysia : Marican, [1965]. 390 p. **AC607**
Companion volume by the same compiler: *A practical modern English-Malay dictionary* (6th ed. with an appendix. [1963]. 421 p.).
Both dictionaries are intended for the Malay speaker learning English. Single alphabetic sequence includes proper nouns. PL5125.W7

Maori

Biggs, Bruce. The complete English-Maori dictionary. [Auckland] : Auckland Univ. Pr. : Oxford Univ. Pr., [1981]. 227 p. **AC608**
"The scope of this Dictionary does not include examples of the use of the Maori words. [William L.] Williams's Maori to English dictionary [7th ed., 1979] remains an indispensable source for such information."—*Introd.* PL6465.Z5B5

Reed, A. W. Concise Māori dictionary : Māori-English, English-Māori. New rev. ed. / rev. by T.S. Kāretu. Wellington : Reed, 1984. 124 p. **AC609**
1st ed., 1948.
Compound words are not included. PL6465.Z5R4

Williams, Herbert William. A dictionary of the Maori language. 7th ed., rev. and augm. by the Advisory Committee on the Teaching of the Maori language, Dept. of Education. Wellington : A. R. Shearer, Govt. printer, 1971. 499 p. **AC610**
1st ed., by William Williams, publ. 1844 under title: *Dictionary of the New Zealand language.*
Repr. : Wellington : GP Publications, 1992.
The standard work for Maori. Words are illustrated by examples drawn from Maori use. PL6465.Z5W58

Mende

Innes, Gordon. A Mende-English dictionary. London : Cambridge Univ. Pr., 1969. 155 p. **AC611**
Intended for the speaker of English. Based on the Eastern dialect (of Sierra Leone). Approximately 6,500 entries with tones indicated by letters. PL8511.Z5I5

Mongolian

Boberg, Folke. Mongolian-English dictionary. Stockholm : Förlaget, Filadelfia, [1954–55]. 3 v. **AC612**
Contents: v. 1–2, Mongolian-English, A–Vivangkhirit; v. 3, English-Mongolian, A–Zodiac and Index to v. 1–2.
The first Mongolian dictionary "published to a Western language since 1849."—*Pref.* PL406.B6

Hangin, John G. A concise English-Mongolian dictionary. Bloomington : Indiana Univ. Pr., 1970. 287 p. (Indiana University. Uralic and Altaic series, v. 89). **AC613**

"About 10,000 words in English together with their equivalents in modern Mongolian."—*Foreword.* Examples of usage are given for frequently occurring verbs, prepositions, and common expressions.

PL406.H34

———————— A modern Mongolian-English dictionary / by Gombojab Hangin with John R. Krueger … [et al.]. [Bloomington] : Indiana Univ., Research Institute for Inner Asian Studies, 1986. 900 p. (Indiana University. Uralic and Altaic series, v. 150). **AC614**

Aims to enable readers to "read current Mongolian newspapers, belles-lettres, and texts in the humanities and social sciences."—*Pref.*

PL406.H35

Lessing, Ferdinand D. Mongolian-English dictionary / Ferdinand D. Lessing, ed. ; comp. by Mattai Haltod … [et al.]. Berkeley : Univ. of California Pr., 1960. 1217 p. **AC615**

"Excluding the strictly archaic language, the dictionary contains the vocabulary of all periods from 1940 on, including the modern terminology developed since sovietization … strictly technical Buddhist terms and expressions are presented in a special Supplement."—*Introd.*

Selected bibliography of dictionaries and grammars, p. xiv.

PL406.L4

Navajo

Young, Robert W. The Navajo language : a grammar and colloquial dictionary / Robert W. Young and William Morgan, Sr. Rev. ed. Albuquerque : Univ. of New Mexico Pr., c1987. 437, 1069 p. **AC616**

1st ed., 1980.

Designed to "reflect, in detail, morphological features of the Navajo language—an objective that includes the identification and description of a corpus of about 1,130 roots."—*Introd.* Contains 20,700 entries.

PM2007.Y75

Norse, Old

See Icelandic.

Norwegian

Knudsen, Trygve. Norsk riksmålsordbok / Trygve Knudsen, Alf Sommerfelt. Oslo : Aschehoug, 1930–57. 2 v. in 3. **AC617**

Issued in parts, 1930–57.

The standard Norwegian dictionary of the "literary" language—the language of the educated class—with many illustrative quotations showing usage, primarily since 1870.

PD2688.K6

Bilingual

Bjerke, Lucie. English-Norwegian dictionary / Lucie Bjerke, Haakon Soraas. London : Harrap, 1964. 562 p. **AC618**

"First published in Norway 1963 by H. Aschehoug & Co. (W. Nygaard) Oslo."—*verso of t.p.*

PD2691.B48

Cappelens store engelsk-norsk ordbok. 2. utg. / revidert og utvidet ved Herbert Svenkerud. Oslo : Cappelen, c1988. 1302 p. **AC619**

1st ed., 1968.

English-Norwegian only. Entries include pronunciation in phonetic spelling, examples of usage, and variant forms.

PD2691.C3

Kirkeby, Willy. English-Norwegian dictionary = Engelsknorsk ordbok. [Oslo, Norway] : Norwegian Univ. Pr. ; Oxford : Distr. world-wide excluding Scandinavia by Oxford Univ. Pr., c1989. 809 p. **AC620**

Prefatory material in English and Norwegian. Confined to standard Norwegian. Includes guidance in current usage.

PD2691.K49

Norwegian English dictionary : a pronouncing and translating dictionary of modern Norwegian [Bokmål and Nynorsk] with a historical and grammatical introduction / Einar Haugen, ed. in chief. Oslo : Universitetsforlaget ; Madison : Univ. of Wisconsin Pr., 1965. 500 p. **AC621**

Added title page in Norwegian.

Primarily intended "as a tool for the learning of Norwegian by American students."—*Pref.* Introduction includes historical background of Norwegian. Contains both Dano-Norwegian (Bok-mål) and New Norwegian (Nynorsk).

PD2691.N6

Etymology

Torp, Alf. Nynorsk etymologisk ordbog. Kristiania : Aschehoug, 1919. 886 p. **AC622**

Repr.: Oslo : Aschehoug, 1963.

Treats Nynorsk or Landsmål, the language of the "country people."

PD2683.T6

Nubian

Armbruster, Carl Hubert. Dongolese Nubian, a lexicon : Nubian-English, English-Nubian. Cambridge : Univ. Pr., 1965. 268 p. **AC623**

Intended for the English speaker. In the Nubian-English section, words are arranged under main word; the English-Nubian section is alphabetical. Part of speech, etymology, and illustrative sentences are given.

PL8573.A7

Pali

Buddhadatta, Ambalangoda Polvattē. English-Pali dictionary. [Colombo, Ceylon] : Pali Text Society, [1955]. 588 p. **AC624**

In Romanized alphabet, these dictionaries were designed for students in schools and colleges. Does not include non-Asian plants or animals.

Companion volume by the same compiler: *Concise Pali-English dictionary* ([2nd ed.]. Colombo : Colombo Apothecaries Co., 1968. 294 p.).

PK1091.B8

Pali Text Society. Pali-English dictionary / ed. by T. W. Rhys Davids and William Stede. London : Publ. for the Pali Text Society by Luzac, 1921–25. 4 v. **AC625**

Repr. in 1 v. (738 p.): London : Pali Text Society ; Boston : Routledge & Kegan Paul, 1986.

Issued in 8 pts.

A standard dictionary with references to sources. Includes a list of works consulted for vocabulary.

PK1091.P33

Trenckner, Vilhelm. A critical Pali dictionary / begun by V. Trenckner ; rev., cont. and ed. by Dines Andersen, Helmer Smith and Hans Hendriksen. Copenhagen : Commissioner : Munksgaard, 1924/48,1960–1992. v. 1–3¹. (In progress).
AC626

Editor varies; publisher varies.

Contents: v. 1–3¹, A–Kanha. Epilegomena to v. 1, by Helmer Smith, publ. 1948 (97 p.), containing abbreviations, bibliography, concordances, devices of transliteration.

Vol. 1 and Epilegomena published 1924–48; publication resumed in 1960, again from the beginning of the alphabet, but not duplicating the work previously published.

A scholarly critical dictionary with English definitions and many references to sources. PK1091.T7

Panjabi

Singh, Maya. The Panjábí dictionary. [2d ed.]. Patiala : Language Dept., 1961. 1221 p. **AC627**

"Reproduced from the 1st ed. (Lahore : Munshi Gulab Singh, 1895)."—*verso of title page.*

Repr., 1972.

Panjabi-English.

Persian

See Farsi.

Pidgin

Mihalic, Francis. The Jacaranda dictionary and grammar of Melanesian Pidgin. [Milton, Queensland] : Jacaranda, [1971]. 375 p. **AC628**

A 1957 version had title: *Grammar and dictionary of Neo-Melanesian.* This revised and expanded edition takes into account changes to the language Includes Melanesian Pidgin to English and bibliography, p. 52–54. PM7891.Z5M5

Polish

Polska Akademia Nauk. Słownik staropolski / [Komitet redakcyjny: Kazimierz Nitsch ... et al.]. Warszawa : [Polska Akademia Nauk], 1953–1990. v. 1–10⁶. **AC629**

Contents: v. 1–10¹–6, A–Wyjsc.

A scholarly dictionary of Old Polish. PG6729.P6

Skorupka, Stanisław. Maly słownik języka polskiego / Stanisław Skorupka, Halina Anderska, Zofia Łempicka. Warszawa : Państwowe Wydawnictwo Naukowe, 1968. 1033 p. **AC630**

Repr., 1989.

About 35,000 terms. PG6625.S83

Słownik języka polskiego. Wyd. 2. / Red. nauk. Mieczysław Szymczak. Warszawa : Państwowe Wydawn., Nauk., 1982–83. 3 v. **AC631**

1st ed., 1978–81.

About 80,000 entries. PG6625.S523

Słownik języka polskiego / redaktor naczelny Witold Doroszewski. Warszawa : Wieda Powszechna, 1958–69. 11 v. **AC632**

A major scholarly dictionary of the Polish language, with many references to the literature. Vol. 11 is a supplement.

———. *Indeks a tergo do Słownika jezyka polskiego pod. red. Witolda Doroszewskiego,* [oprakowal zespól pod kierunkiem Renalty Grzegorczykowej i Jadwigi Puzininy] (Warszawa : Panstwowe Wydawn. Naukowe, 1973. 558 p.).

Bilingual

Jáslan, Janina. Wiedza Powszechna compact Polish and English dictionary : English-Polish Polish-English / Janina Jáslan, Jan Stanisławski. 9th ed. Lincolnwood, Ill. : National Textbook Co., 1993. 712 p. **AC633**

More than 12,000 entries for each language. Each section has introductory information, a pronunciation guide, and an appendix of abbreviations. PG6640.J38

Kościuszko Foundation dictionary : English-Polish, Polish-English. The Hague : Mouton, 1959–61. 2 v. **AC634**

Repr. : Warszawa : Paśtwowe Wydaw. Naukowe, 1972.

Contents: v. 1, English-Polish, by K. Bulas and F. J. Whitfield; v. 2, Polish-English, by K. Bulas, L. L. Thomas and F. J. Whitfield.

The second volume emphasizes "twentieth century standard Polish"; the first volume includes some English dialect and slang. Examples of usage are given. A substantial bilingual dictionary.

PG6640.K65

Stanisławski, Jan. Wielki słownik angielsko-polski / Red. naukowy, Wiktor Jassem. Warszawa : Wiedza Powszechna, 1964. 1175 p. **AC635**

Added title page: *The great English-Polish dictionary.*

"Comprises over 100,000 words, phrases and expressions commonly used in the English language of the 19th and 20th centuries."—*Pref.* Includes terms in technology, medicine and science, colloquialisms, Americanisms, etc. Scholars consider this and its companion below the best available.

———. *Wielki słownik polsko-angielski : z suplementum,* red. naukowy: Wiktor Jassem. Wyd. 5, Supl. 3. (Warszawa : Państwowe Wydawnictwo Wiedza Powszechna, 1980. 2 v.).

Added title page: *The great Polish-English dictionary, supplemented.*

1st ed., 1969; suppl., 1977.

A reprinting of the 1969 ed. with the corresponding portions of the 1977 supplement reprinted at the end of each volume. About 180,000 entries in the basic work, plus about 10,000 in the supplement. PG6640.S3

Abbreviations

Library of Congress. Slavic and Central European Division. Polish abbreviations : a selective list / comp. by Janina Wojcicka. 2nd ed. rev. and enl. Wash., 1957. 164 p. **AC636**

1st ed., 1955.

Lists some 2,600 abbreviations which have gained currency in Poland since 1945—particularly names of government agencies, societies, companies, and institutions—but with some general abbreviations as well. Z663.47.P6

Paruch, Józef. Słownik skrótów. Wyd. 2. Warszawa : Wiedza Powszechna, [1992], c1970. 647 p. **AC637**

1st ed., 1970 (389 p.).

Has entries for abbreviations in Polish, French, English, and other languages. Expressions in the original language are followed by explanations in Polish. PG6693.P3

Etymology

Brückner, Alexander. Słownik etymologiczny języka polskiego. [2. wyd.]. Warszawa : Wiedza Powszechna, 1957. 805 p. **AC638**
Repr., 1970.
A reprint, with new introduction, of a work published: Kraków : Nakład i Własność Krakowskiej Spółki Wydawniczej, 1927.
The only complete etymological dictionary for Polish.
PG6580.B7

Sławski, Franciszek. Słownik etymologiczny języka polskiego. Kraków : Nakł. Tow. Miłośników. Polskiego, 1952–82. v. 1–5⁵. (In progress?). **AC639**
Contents: v. 1–5⁵, A–łżywy. PG6580.S5

Pronunciation

Słownik wymowy polskiej PWN = The dictionary of Polish pronunciation / Redakcja naukowa Mieczyslaw Karas, Marla Madejowa. [Warszaw] : Państwowe Wydawnictwo Naukowe, 1977. 564 p. **AC640**
Title also in French, German, and Russian; preface in Polish, English, French, German, and Russian.
Aims to show the pronunciation of "Standard Polish ... the common medium of expression among Poles."—*p.XL.* Uses the International Phonetic Alphabet. PG6137.S6

Portuguese

Dicionário contemporâneo da língua portuguesa Caldas Aulete. 3.a ed. brasileira. .... [Lisboa] : Editora Delta, 1974. 5 v. : ill. **AC641**
2nd. ed., Rio de Janeiro: Edição Brasilerira, 1968.
Subtitle: Novamente rev., atualizada e aumentada pela introd. de termos da tecnologia recente, pelo registro dos vocábulos usados no Brasil e pela extensão dos apêndices por Hamílcar de Garcia, com estudos sobre a origem e evolução da língua portuguesa, sua expansão no Brasil, e uma exposição da pronúncia normal brasileira por Antenor Nascentes.
Various printings.
Based on F. J. Caldas Aulete's *Diccionario contemporâneo da língua portugueza,* first published 1881. PC5327.D515

Ferreira, Aurélio Buarque de Holanda. Novo dicionário da língua portuguesa / Aurélio Buarque de Holanda Ferreira ; assistentes, Margarida dos Anjos ... [et al.] ; auxiliar, Giovani Mafra e Silva ; colaboração especializada, Ademar Bezerra Ferreira Lima ... [et al.]. 2a. ed., rev. e aum. Rio de Janeiro : Editora Nova Fronteira, c1986. 1838 p. **AC642**
1st ed., 1975.
Emphasis is on Brazilian Portuguese. Bibliography.
PC5327.F44

Lima, Hildebrando de. Pequeno dicionário brasileiro da língua portuguêsa / Hildebrando de Lima [and] Gustavo Barroso. 11. ed. 4. impr. / supervisionada e considerávelmente aum. por Aurélio Buarque de Holanda Ferreira com a assistência de José Baptista da Luz, e revista e aumentada por inúmeros especialistas. Rio de Janeiro : Civilizaçao Brasileira, 1969. 1301 p. : ill. **AC643**
Frequently reprinted.
1st ed. ed. by Hildebrando de Lima and revised by various editors through the years.
A standard and practical dictionary of Brazilian Portuguese.
PC5327.L5

Moraes Silva, António de. Grande dicionário da língua portuguesa. 10. ed. rev., corrigida, muito aumentada e actualizada segunda as regras do Acordo Ortográfico Luso-Brasileiro de 10 de agosto de 1945, por Augusto Moreno, Cardoso Júnior e José Pedro Machado. [Lisboa] : Ed. Confluéncia, 1949–59. 12 v. **AC644**
Earlier editions published under title *Diccionário da lingua portugueza.*
Contents: v. 1–11, A–Z. Vol. 12 consists of a number of special sections: an epitome of Portuguese grammar; a statement of the Acordo Ortografia and its decisions; and various word lists: foreign words and phrases, place-names, irregular verbs, root words, abbreviations, addenda, etc.
A famous dictionary, first published in 1789. Of first importance and generally considered to be the best Portuguese dictionary. Includes quotations from the literature in chronological order and showing usage.
This edition takes into account the Portuguese-Brazilian *Acordo Ortográfico* of 1945, which aimed at instituting a uniform system of orthography for the Portuguese language. PC5327.M733

Bilingual

Dicionário inglês-português / Antônio Houaiss, ed. ; Ismael Cardim, co-ed. ; Peônia Viana Guedes ... [et al.], redatores. [Rio de Janeiro, Brasil] : Record, 1982. 928 p. **AC645**
Contains a useful section of common abbreviations, including initialisms, used in English. PC5333.D537

Ferreira, Julio Albino. Dicionário inglês-português. Nova ed. / rev. e melhorada pelo Dr. Armando de Morais. Porto : Editorial Domingos Barreira, [1952–54]. 2 v. in 1. **AC646**
Contents: [Pt. 1], Dicionário inglês-português; [Pt. 2], Dicionário português-inglês.
One of the better bilingual dictionaries. PC5333.F

Houaiss, Antônio. The new Appleton dictionary of the English and Portuguese languages / Antônio Houaiss and Catherine B. Avery. N.Y. : Appleton, 1964. 636 p., 665 p. **AC647**
Added title page in Portuguese. Various printings.
Contents: pt. 1, English-Portuguese; pt. 2, Portuguese-English.
Each part contains approximately 60,000 words and expressions. Particular emphasis is on Portuguese as it is spoken and written in Brazil. Equivalents are given or, when necessary, explanations or definitions. Includes a large general vocabulary as well as a wide selection of words from specialized fields. Pronunciation is indicated by the phonetic system. PC5333.H6

Michaelis, Henritte. Novo Michaelis : dicionário ilustrado / Baseado em material selecionado do antigo dicionário Michaelis e inteiramente remodelado, revisto e aumentado pela Seção Lexicográfica das Edições Melhoramentos, sob a orientação de Fritz Pietzschke. São Paulo : Ed. Melhoramentos ; Wiesbaden : Brockhaus, [1958–61]. 2 v. : ill. **AC648**
Added title page in English.
On spine: Brockhaus picture dictionary.
Contents: v. 1, English-Portuguese; v. 2, Portuguese-English.
English subtitle: Comprehensive modern vocabulary; idiomatic phrases, pronunciation key, numerous plates with more than 4,000 conceptions, based on matter selected from the original Michaelis dictionary and completely reorganized, revised, and enlarged.
Based on the *Novo dicionário da língua portugueza e ingleza* by Henriette Michaelis ([8.ed.] Leipzig : Brockhaus, 1945), frequently reprinted and long a standard work of current Portuguese. Includes technical terms used in commerce and industry, the arts and sciences, etc.
PC5333.M582

The Oxford-Duden pictorial Portuguese-English dictionary. Oxford : Clarendon ; N.Y. : Oxford Univ. Pr., 1992. 384, 69, 96 p. : ill. (some col.). **AC649**

Preface in Portuguese; foreword in English.

Based on the 3rd rev. ed. of v. 3 of the Duden series of German dictionaries.

200 illustrations arranged in 11 broad subject areas. "Each double page contains a plate illustrating the vocabulary of a whole subject, together with the exact English names and their Portuguese translation."—*Foreword*. No pronounciation guide. Alphabetical index for Portuguese and for English. PC5328.O9

Taylor, James Lumpkin. A Portuguese-English dictionary. Rev., with corrections and additions by the author and Priscilla Clark Martin. Stanford, Calif. : Stanford Univ. Pr., 1970. 655 p. **AC650**

Repr. : Rio de Janeiro : Record, 1982.

1st ed., 1958 (655 p.); rev. edition shows limited revisions.

Contains some 60,000 entries, including Brazilian Portuguese. Planned "to provide an everyday working tool for as large a number of persons as possible."—*Introd*. Gives not only English equivalents, but often one or more synonyms and, in some cases, examples of usage. Includes many technical and scientific terms, particularly the names of Brazilian fauna and flora. PC5333.T3

Etymology

Dicionário etimológico da língua portuguesa : com a mais antigua documentação escrita e conhecida de muitos dos vocábulos estudados / [por] José Pedro Machado. 2. ed. [Lisboa] : Editorial Confluência, [1967–73]. 3 v. **AC651**

First issued 1956–59 in 2 v. A 3rd ed. was publ. 1977 in 5 v.

Issued in fascicules.

Most entries indicate origin of word with dated examples.

PC5305.D52

Synonyms

Costa, Agenor. Dicionário de sinônimos e locuções da língua portuguêsa. [3. ed.]. [Rio de Janeiro] : Editôra Fundo de Cultura, [1967]. 5 v. (2370 p.) : ill. **AC652**

1st ed., 1950, and 2nd ed., 1960, in 2 v.

A thorough list of synonyms and idiomatic expressions.

PC5315.C6

Nascentes, Antenor. Dicionário de sinónimos. 3a. ed. / rev. por Olavo Anibal Nascentes. Rio de Janeiro : Editora Nova Fronteira, 1981. 485 p. **AC653**

1st ed., 1957.

There is an index of entry words and synonyms rather than cross-references within the text. PC5315.N3

Provençal

Alibert, Louis. Dictionnaire occitan-français d'après les parlers languedociens. Nouv. éd. Toulouse : Institut d'Etudes Occitanes, [1977]. 699 p. **AC654**

A corrected reprint of the 1966 edition.

Entries offer part of speech, illustrative examples, and brief etymology. PC3376.A4

Levy, Emil. Petit dictionnaire provençal-français. 5. ed. Heidelberg : C. Winter, 1973. 387 p. **AC655**

1st. ed., 1909; 4th ed., 1966.

A pocket-sized but useful dictionary.

Romanian

Academia Română, Bucharest. Dicţionarul limbii române / intocmit şi publicat după îndemnul şi cu cheltuiala Maiestătii Sale Regelui Carol I … . Bucureşti : Librariile Socec & comp. si C. Sfetea, 1913–40. v. [1–2]. **AC656**

Contents: v. 1^1, A–B; v. 1^2, C–Cojoaică; v. 2^1, F–I; v. 2^{1-3}, J–Lojnită.

A scholarly dictionary compiled on historical principles, including literary, obsolete, and regional terms; etymologies; and examples of usage. Definitions and explanations are in Romanian, but French equivalents are also given.

Resumed publication in a new series as: *Dicţionarul limbii române : (DLR)* (AC660).

Breban, Vasile. Dicţionar general al limbii române. Editie revžită si adăaugită. [Bucureşti] : Editura Enciclopedică, 1992. 2 v. **AC657**

1st ed. had title *Dicţionar al limbii române contemporane : de uz curent* (Bucureşti : Editura Stiintifică, 1980).

Emphasis is on contemporary vocabulary. PC775.B7

Costinescu, Mariana. Dicţionarul limbii române literare vechi, 1640–1780 : termeni regionali / Mariana Costinescu, Magdalena Georgescu, Florentina Zgraon. Bucureşti : Editura Ştiinţifică şi Enciclopedică, 1987. 330 p. **AC658**

Includes brief etymologies. PC782.C67

Dicţionarul explicativ al limbii române / Conducătorii lucrării: Ion Coteanu, Luiza Seche, Mircea Seche. [Bucureşti] : Editura Academiei Republicii Socialiste România, 1975. 1049 p. : ill. **AC659**

At head of title: Academia Republicii Socialiste România. Institutul de Lingvistică din Bucureşti.

About 60,000 entries with definitions, parts of speech, areas of usage. PC775.D46

Dicţionarul limbii române : (DLR). Serie nouă. / [redactori responsabili: Iorgu Iordan şi Ion Coteanu]. Bucureşti : Editura Academia Republicii Populare Române, 1965–1987. v. 6; v. 7, pts. 1–2; v. 8, pts. 1–5; v. 9; v. 10, pts. 1–2; v. 11, pts. 2–3. (In progress). **AC660**

At head of title: Academia Republicii Populare Romîne.

Contents: t. 6, M; t. 7, pts. 1–2, N–O; t. 8, pts. 1–5, P–Puzzolana; t. 9, R; t. 10, pts. 1–2, S–Semintarie; t. 11,pts. 1–3, T–Twist. (T. 6 issued in fascicules; t. 7–8 issued in bound volumes).

A continuation in a slightly changed format of: Academia Romana, Bucharest. *Dicţionarul limbii romane* (AC656). French equivalents are no longer given as they were in the A–L parts. PC775.D48

Dicţionarul limbii romîne literare contemporane. [Bucureşti] : Editura Academiei Republicii Populare Romîne, 1955–57. 4 v. **AC661**

Includes examples of 20th-century usage, with references to the literature. List of sources in v. 4.

Abridged version: *Dicţionarul limbii romîne moderne* (1958. 961 p.). PC775.D5

Bilingual

Dicţionar englez-român. [Bucureşti] : Editura Academiei Republicii Socialiste România, 1974. 825 p. **AC662**

At head of title: Academia Republicii Socialiste România. Institutul de Lingvistică Bucureşti.

A comprehensive English-Romanian dictionary (about 120,000 entries); gives pronunciation of the English entry word in phonetic transcription. PC779.D485

Leviţchi, Leon. Dicţionar român-englez / Ediţia a 3–a revizuită de autori şi de Andrei Bantaş. Bucureşti : Editura Ştiinţifică, 1973. 1088 p. **AC663**

1st ed., 1960.

Companion volume: Leon Levitchi and Andrei Bantaś, *Dictionar englez-român* (1971. 1068 p.).

Both parts give pronounciation of the English headwords in phonetic transcription.

Bantaś is also compiler of *Dictionar de buzunar englez-român, român-englez* (Editia a 2-a; Bucaresti : Editura Stiintifica, 1973. 1133 p.). PC779.L4

Romansh

Società Retorumantscha. Disciunari rumantsch grischen / publichà da la Società retorumantscha cul agüd da la Confederaziun, dal chantun Grischen e da la Lia rumantscha. Fundà da Robert de Planta e Florian Melcher; redacziun: Chasper Pult [et al.]. Cuoira : Bischofberger, 1939–1993. v. 1–v. 9¹. (In progress). **AC664**

Publisher varies.

Contents: v. 1–9¹, A–Infragante.

A scholarly work giving etymologies, references to sources, and explanations in German. PC937.G5S6

Velleman, Antoine. Dicziunari scurznieu da la lingua ladina = Ladinisches Notwörterbuch mit deutscher, französischer und englischer Übersetzung. = Abridged dictionary of the Ladin (or Romansh) language, with German, French and English translation and numerous indications referring to topography and population. Samaden : Engadin Pr., 1929. 928 p. **AC665**

Romansh-German-French-English dictionary. PC937.A1V4

Russian

Akademiiǎ Nauk SSSR. Institut IAzykoznaniiǎ. Slovar' russkogo iǎzyka. Moskva : Gos. Izd-vo Inostrannykh i Natsional'nykh Slovarei, 1957–61. 4 v. **AC666**

Vols. 2–4 issued by the Academy's Institut Russkogo IAzyka.

A general dictionary of the Russian language. Emphasis is on current usage with examples quoted from Russian literature of the 19th and 20th centuries. Intended for more general use than the larger, specialized lexicon *Slovar' sovremennogo russkogo literaturnogo iǎzyka* (AC667). PG2625.A4

Akademiiǎ Nauk SSSR. Institut Russkogo IAzyka. Slovar' sovremennogo russkogo literaturnogo iǎzyka. Moskva : Izd-vo Akad. Nauk SSSR, 1950–65. 17 v. **AC667**

Issuing body varies.

The major dictionary for modern literary Russian, based on the vocabulary used in literary, artistic, social, political, and general scientific works of the 19th and 20th centuries. Entries include the field in which the word is used, variant meanings, some variant forms, derivations, references to other dictionaries, and—in most cases—extensive illustrative quotations with their sources. Loan words from other languages are numerous. PG2625.A533

Dal', Vladimir Ivanovich. Tolkovyi slovar' zhivogo velikorusskago iǎzyka / pod red. I. A. Boduena-de-Kurtene. S. Peterburg : Izd. T-va. M. O. Vol'f, [1904–12?]. 4 v. **AC668**

Edition note varies: v.1–3; 4th ed., stereotype; v. 4; 3rd ed. Various reprintings.

The standard pre-Revolutionary dictionary for Russian and dialect vocabulary, including slang. The 3rd and 4th eds. include revisions made by J. Baudouin de Courtenay. PG2625.D316

Daum, Edmund. A dictionary of Russian verbs : bases of inflection; aspects; regimen; stressing; meanings / Edmund Daum, Werner Schenk. Leipzig : VEB Verlag ; N.Y. : Hippocrene Books, [1974]. 750 p. **AC669**

"With an essay on the syntax and semantics of the verb in present-day Russian by Professor Rudolf Ruzicka.—*t.p.*

A translation of *Die russischen Verben* (München, 1963).

About 20,000 verbs in alphabetical order, with inflected forms, etc. PG2271.D313

Institut russkogo IAzyka (Akademiiǎ nauk SSSR). Slovarnyǐ sektor. Slovar' russkikh narodnykh govorov / Sostavil F. P. Filin. Leningrad : Nauka [Leningradskoe otd-nie], 1965–1990. v. 1–25. **AC670**

Contents: v. 1–25, A–Pervachok.

A dictionary of 19th-century and 20th-century vocabulary of Russian dialects. All Russian dialects, even those spoken in nonnative Russian areas, are represented. PG2735.A48

Lunt, Horace Gray. Kratkii slovar' drevnerusskogo iǎzyka (XI–XVII vekov). München : W. Fink, 1970. 85 p. **AC671**

Added title page, cover title (*Concise dictionary of Old Russian*) and prefatory matter in English.

An earlier version *A short vocabulary of Old Russian*, (Cambridge, Mass. : Harvard Univ. Pr., 1954) was itself based on a mimeographed preliminary working list available to Harvard students in 1950. It is "intended for the student who is ready to read extensively in medieval Russian cultural works."—*Pref.* The equivalent term or definition is given in modern Russian. PG2743.L8

Ozhegov, Sergei Ivanovich. Slovar' russkogo iǎzyka : Okolo 57000 slov / pod red. ... N. IU. Shvedovoi. Izd. 10e, stereotip. Moskva : Sov. Entsiklopediiǎ, 1973. 847 p. **AC672**

1st ed., 1949. PG2625.O9

Slovar' russkogo iǎzyka XI-XVII vv / [glav. redaktor S.G. Barkhudarov]. Moskva : Nauka, 1975–1990. v. 1–16. (In progress). **AC673**

At head of title : Akademiiǎ nauk SSSR. Institut russkogo iǎzyka.

Vols. 9–10 ed. by F. P. Filin; v. 11–14 by D. N. Shmelev; v. 15–16 by G. P. Romanova.

Contents: v. 1–16, A–Pomanuti.

When complete, this dictionary of obsolete Russian words will contain about 60,000 terms, listing their first appearance and subsequent development. An extensive review in *Language 52* (Sept. 1976): 708–17 praises the "rich documentation for the 15–17th centuries," but calls the scholarship on the whole "disappointing." PG2742.S5

Tolkovyi slovar' russkogo iǎzyka / sostavili: G. O. Vinokur [i dr.] : pod red. D. N. Ushakova. Moskva : Gos. Izd-vo Inostrannykh i Natsional'nykh Slovarei, 1935–40. 4 v. **AC674**

Repr.: Moscow, 1948; Ann Arbor, 1948.

Editors vary. Publisher varies.

This general dictionary, published earlier than the Akademiiǎ Nauk's *Slovar' russkogo iǎzyka* (AC666) retains value for the inclusion of words and definitions of contemporary political significance. PG2625.T6

Bilingual

Bol'shoǐ anglo-russkiǐ slovar' / pod obshchim rukovodstvom I.R. Gal'perina i E.M. Mednikovoǐ. Izd. 4–e, ispr., s dopolneniem. Moskva : "Russkiǐ iǎzyk", 1987–1988. 2 v. **AC675**

1st ed., 1972.

Title on added t.p.: *New English-Russian dictionary.*

"Fourth improved edition with a supplement."—*added t.p.*

Though intended primarily for Russians reading English-language texts, numerous features recommend it for use by English-speaking students of Russian: prefatory material appears in both languages;

stress is marked for Russian words; many compound and idiomatic expressions are allotted separate entries; and emphasis is on the modern language. One of the best resources.   PG2640.G3

Katzner, Kenneth. English-Russian, Russian-English dictionary. N.Y. : Wiley, [1984]. 904 p.   **AC676**

"This dictionary constitutes a first in many respects. It is the first full-size English-Russian or Russian-English dictionary to be compiled and published in the United States. It is the first to be based on American, rather than British, English. And it is the first full-size dictionary published anywhere, including the Soviet Union, to contain English-Russian and Russian-English sections in the same volume."—*Pref.* For English words having more than one meaning, a synonym or "label" is given in parentheses to indicate which meaning is being rendered into Russian.   PG2640.K34

Macura, Paul. Elsevier's Russian-English dictionary. Amsterdam ; N.Y. : Elsevier ; N.Y. : distr. [by] Elsevier Science Publ. Co., 1990. 4 v. (3208 p.).   **AC677**

"Contains approximately 240,000 key entries, constituting the most extensive listing of vocabulary to date in the areas of humanities, social sciences, and fine arts. It also contains scientific terminology."—*Pref.* Appears to rely heavily on the Marcus Wheeler, *The Oxford Russian-English dictionary* (AC683), although that work is not cited as a source.   Q123.M182

Marder, Stephen. A supplementary Russian-English dictionary. Columbus, Ohio : Slavica Publishers, 1992. 522 p.   **AC678**

With 350,000 words in 29,000 entries, this dictionary is intended to supplement Aleksandr Ivanovich Smirnitskiĭ's *Russian-English dictionary* (AC681) and Marcus Wheeler's *The Oxford Russian English dictionary* (AC683), and contains words these sources lack. Strong vocabulary for slang, as well as business and computer terms.   PG2640.M34

Müller, Vladimir Karlovich. English-Russian dictionary. 7th ed., new rev. ed. completely reset. N.Y. : Dutton, [1965]. 1192 p.   **AC679**

1st American ed., 1944.

The English-Russian portion of the earlier Müller dictionaries, re-edited by the Moscow State Pedagogical Inst. of Foreign Languages. This edition runs to 70,000 words, and incorporates extensive revisions and additions. Corresponds to the 11th ed. publ. in Moscow, 1965 (912 p. ; various reprintings).   PG2640.M813

Russko-angliiskii slovar' : Okolo 34000 slov / A. M. Taube [i dr.] ; pod red. R. S. Daglisha. Izd. 7-e, ispr. i dop. Moskva : "Russkiĭ iazyk", 1987. 623 p.   **AC680**

Added title page in English: Russian-English dictionary.

1st ed., 1965.

The aim is to provide "the fullest possible picture of present-day written and spoken Russian rendered correctly and idiomatically into English."—*Pref.* Contains 34,000 entries.   PG2640.R84

Smirnitskiĭ, Aleksandr Ivanovich. Russian-English dictionary : 50,000 words approx / comp. by O. S. Akhmanova [et al.] under the general direction of A. I. Smirnitsky. 7th ed. N.Y. : Dutton, [1966]. 766 p.   **AC681**

Added title page in Russian: *Russko-angliiski slovar'.*

The 3rd ed., 1959, was an American printing of the 3rd Russian ed. first published 1952. The 7th ed., 1966, represents the first resetting since the 3rd ed.

Although certain features favor the Russian-speaking user, this is a useful up-to-date general dictionary.

The 1973 printing (N.Y. : Dutton. 766 p.) is called "9th ed." as published by "Sovetskaia Entsiklopediia," Moscow, 1971.

Most recent Russian edition: *Russko-angliiskiĭ slovar' : okolo 55,000 slov.* / pod obshchim rukovodstvom A.I. Smirnitskogo ; s prilozheniem kratkikh svedeniĭ po angliĭskoĭ grammatike i orforêpii, sos-

tavlennykh A.I. Smirnitskim ; [avtory O.S. adhmanova … et al.] (Izd. 16., ispr. / pod red. O.S. Akhmanovoĭ. Moskva : "Russkiĭ iazyk," 1991. 758 p.).   PG2640.S5

Transliterated dictionary of the Russian language : an abridged dictionary consisting of Russian-to-English and English-to-Russian sections / Eugene Garfield, ed. Philadelphia : ISI Pr., 1979. 382 p.   **AC682**

An unorthodox dictionary which gives the Russian word in transliteration rather than in the Cyrillic alphabet, and with the entries arranged according to the Roman alphabet in both the Russian and English sections. Gives equivalent terms and indicates prt of speech for the Russian terms. About 17,000 entries in the Russian-to-English section. Transliteration system used is that of the British Standards Institute.   PG2640.T7

Wheeler, Marcus. The Oxford Russian-English dictionary. 2nd ed. Oxford ; N.Y. : Oxford Univ. Pr., 1984. 930 p.   **AC683**

1st ed., 1972.

"This work is intended as a general-purpose dictionary of Russian as it is written and spoken. It is designed primarily, though not exclusively, for the use of those whose native language is English."—*Introd.* About 50,000 entries. To a large extent this is a reprinting, with corrections, of the 1972 ed., but some new entries and additional meanings have been inserted; an "Index of supplementary material" has been supplied to signal those additions. An appendix of Russian geographical names with English equivalents has also been added.

Companion work: *The Oxford English-Russian dictionary*, ed. by P. S. Falla (Oxford : Clarendon Pr. ; N.Y. : Oxford Univ. Pr., 1984. 1052 p.). Includes "over 90,000 words, vocabulary items and illustrative phrases."—*Pref.* The English vocabulary is based mainly on the most recent editions of *The concise Oxford dictionary of current English* (Oxford : Clarendon Pr.) and *Oxford advanced learner's dictionary of current English* (3rd ed. London : Oxford Univ. Pr., 1974).   PG2640.W5

Wilson, Elizabeth A. M. The modern Russian dictionary for English speakers : English-Russian / by Elizabeth A. M. Wilson ; Russian editor, Popova, L. P. … [et al.]. Oxford ; N.Y. : Pergamon Pr., 1982. 715 p.   **AC684**

Intended as a practical dictionary "for the student whose approach to the Russian language will be through English … The vocabulary comprises the words which the average educated man might want to use in speaking or writing Russian, including the simple technical terms in common use."—*Introd.*   PG2640.W54

Abbreviations

Alekseev, Dmitriĭ Ivanovich. Slovar' sokrashcheniĭ russkogo iazyka : okolo 17,700 sokrashcheniĭ / D.I. Alekseev, I. G. Gozman, G. V. Sakhorov ; pod red. D. I. Alekseeva. Izd. 3-e, sprilozheniem novykh sokr. Moskva : Russkiĭ iazyk, 1983. 485 p.   **AC685**

1st ed., 1963 ("12,500 sokrashcheniĭ"); 2nd ed., 1977 ("15,000 sokrashcheniĭ").

In addition to full expansion of the term, shows pronunciation, stress, and, for those abbreviations and acronyms used substantively, grammatical gender. The more important journals are included, as well as Russian forms of abbreviations for international and foreign organizations.   PG2693.A4

Crowe, Barry. Concise dictionary of Soviet terminology, institutions, and abbreviations. Oxford ; N.Y. : Pergamon, [1969]. 182 p.   **AC686**

"The purpose of this dictionary is to provide a glossary of 'Sovietisms,' by which is meant the host of abbreviations, neologisms, portmanteau words and references to institutions which readers of Soviet literature constantly come across."—*Pref.*   PG2693.C7

Kramer, Alex A. Sokrashcheniĭa v sovetskikh izdaniĭakh = Abbreviations in Soviet publications. [Trenton, N. J. : Scientific Russian Translating Service, 1965]. 396 p. **AC687**

> Some 19,500 Russian abbreviations with expansion and English translation are given. There is an added section for signs and symbols. Supplements 1 and 2 publ. 1970 (178 p.) and 1972 (167 p.).
> PG2693.K72

Library of Congress. Aerospace Technology Division. Glossary of Russian abbreviations and acronyms. Wash. : Library of Congress, 1967. 806 p. **AC688**

> 23,600 entries. Abbreviations and their meanings are given in Cyrillic alphabet, and transliteration and translation are provided in parallel columns. PG2693.U47

Scheitz, Edgar. Dictionary of Russian abbreviations : containing about 40,000 abbreviations. Amsterdam ; N.Y. : Elsevier, 1986. 695 p. **AC689**

> Originally published in Russian as *Russische Abkürzungen* (Berlin : Verlag Technik, 1985).
> Text in Russian.
> Includes abbreviations for state authorities, institutions of the Academy of Science, serials, measurements, etc. PG2693.S28

Zalucky, Henry K. Compressed Russian : Russian-English dictionary of acronyms, semiacronyms and other abbreviations used in contemporary standard Russian, with their pronunciation and explicit correlates in Russian, and equivalents in English. Amsterdam ; N.Y. : Elsevier, 1991. 890 p. **AC690**

> A "lexicon of up-to-date Russian contractions with their pronunciation, including stress, and English equivalents."—*Foreword*. More than 40,000 Russian abbreviations are included. Among the types of entries are: acronyms, semiacronyms, eponyms, typo-geographical appellations, clips, intraphrasal deletion and suffixed contractions and graphicisms, and abridgements of military terminology. PG2693.Z28

Etymology

Vasmer, Max. Russisches etymologisches Wörterbuch. Heidelberg : C. Winter, [1950–58]. 3 v. (Indogermanische Bibliothek, II Reihe, Wörterbücher). **AC691**

> Issued in parts.
> A dictionary of importance for the etymology of the Russian language, its dialects, and foreign words used in Russian. Bibliography of sources, v. 1, p.xi–xliii.
> ———. *Etimologicheskiĭ slovar' russkogo ĭazyka*, perevod s memetskogo i dopolneniĭa O. N. Trubacheva; pod red. i s predisl. B. A. Larina (Moskva : Progress, 1964 73. 4 v.).
> Added t.-p.: *Russisches etymologisches Wörterbuch*.
> A Russian translation of the Heidelberg edition (above) that indicates additions and corrections by the Russian editors. PG2580.V3

Synonyms

Aleksandrova, Zinaida Evgen'evna. Slovar' sinonimov russkogo ĭazyka / Zinaida Evgen'evna Aleksandrova ; pod red. L. A. Chesko. 3–e stereotip. Moskva : Izd. Sovetskaĭa Entsiklopediĭa, 1971. 600 p. **AC692**

> 1st ed., 1968.
> About 9,000 terms. PG2591.A43

Slovar' sinonimov russkogo ĭazyka. V 2–kh t./ [Avt. vved. i glav. red. A. P. Evgen'eva]. Leningrad : Nauka, 1970–71. 2 v. **AC693**

> At head of title: Akademiĭa Nauk SSSR. Institut Russkogo Ĭazyka. PG2591.S6

Usage

Jaszczun, Wasyl. A dictionary of Russian idioms and colloquialisms : 2,200 expressions with examples / Wasyl Jaszczun, Szymon Krynski. [Pittsburgh] : Univ. of Pittsburgh Pr., [1967]. 102 p. **AC694**

> Russian idioms with English definitions. PG2460.J3

Kunin, Aleksandr Vladimirovich. Anglo-russkiĭ frazeologicheskiĭ slovar'. Izd. 4–e, pererab. i dop. Moskva : Russkiĭ Ĭazyk, 1984. 942 p. **AC695**

> Added t.p. in English: *English-Russian phraseological dictionary*. 1st ed., 1955.
> About 20,000 English idioms with Russian equivalents. Examples from English sources are given with Russian translation to illustrate usage in context. PE1129.S4K8

Bibliography

Aav, Yrjö. Russian dictionaries : dictionaries and glossaries printed in Russia, 1627–1917. Zug, Switz. : Inter Documentation, [1977]. 196 p. **AC696**

> Lists "general dictionaries and vocabularies published separately or printed in Russian newspapers, periodicals and series in Russia before the year 1918."—*Pref*. Technical and specialized dictionaries are not included. Z2505.D6A18

Aissing, Alena. Russian dictionaries : selected bibliography, 1960–1990. Monroe, N.Y. : Library Research Associates, 1991. 61 p. **AC697**

> A listing of more than 300 Russian monolingual, bilingual, and multilingual dictionaries in all subjects. Entries in these three sections are subdivided by content and appear alphabetically within each subdivision. No annotations or evaluations; subject index. Z2505.D6A38

Akademiĭa Nauk SSSR. Institut Russkogo Ĭazyka. Slovari, izdannye v SSSR : bibliograficheskiĭ ukazatel', 1918–1962 / [sostaviteli: M. G. Izhevskaĭa i dr. Redaktory: V. V. Veselitskiĭ, N. P. Debets]. Moskva : Nauka, 1966. 231 p. **AC698**

> A bibliography of Russian dictionaries and bilingual dictionaries of which one language is Russian. Classed arrangement within language groupings. Author and language indexes. Z7004.D5A55

Kaufman, Isaak Mikhailovich. Terminologicheskie slovari : bibliografiia. Moskva : Sovetskaĭa Rossiĭa, 1961. 419 p. **AC699**

> An annotated bibliography of glossaries and subject dictionaries, primarily Russian, published from the 18th century through 1961. Classified arrangement, with alphabetical indexes for authors and titles, and subjects. The 1,755 entries include lists of specialized terminology in periodical literature, as well as separately published dictionaries. Z7004.D5K3

Samoan

Allardice, R. W. A simplified dictionary of modern Samoan. Auckland : Polynesian Pr., 1985. 228 p. **AC700**

> A concise dictionary intended as a supplement to George Bertram Milner's *Samoan dictionary* (AC701). PL6501.Z5A44

Milner, George Bertram. Samoan dictionary : Samoan-English, English-Samoan. London ; N.Y. : Oxford Univ. Pr., 1966. 464 p. **AC701**

> Intended to "serve as an up-to-date standard work of reference in matters of spelling and translation."—*Pref*. PL6501.Z5M5

Sanskrit

Apte, Vaman Shivaram. The practical Sanskrit-English dictionary / eds.-in-chief: P. K. Gode and C. G. Karve. Rev. and enl. ed. Poona : Prasad Prakashan, 1957–59. 3 v.   **AC702**
1st ed., 1890.
A revision of the earlier text with the addition of new words, changes of meaning, and more quotations.   PK933.A65

Böhtlingk, Otto von. Sanskrit-Wörterbuch / hrsg. von der Kaiserlichen Akademie der Wissenschaften ; bearb. von Otto Böhtlingk und Rudolph Roth. St. Petersburg : Buchdr. der K. Akademie der Wissenschaften, 1855–75. 7 v.   **AC703**
Repr.: Osnabrück : Zeller ; Wiesbaden : Harrossowitz, 1966.
Verbesserungen und Nachträge zu Theil 1–5, Bd. 5, col. 941–1678; Verbesserungen und Nachträge zum ganzen Werke, Bd. 7, col. [1685]–1822.   PK935.G5B7

————— Sanskrit-Wörterbuch in kürzerer Fassung. St. Petersburg : Buchdr. der K. Akademie der Wissenschaften, 1879–89. 7 v. in 1.   **AC704**
Frequently reprinted. Also available in microform.
—————. —————. *Nachträge* ... bearb von Richard Schmidt (Leipzig : Harrossowitz, 1928. 396 p.).

An encyclopaedic dictionary of Sanskrit on historical principles / gen. ed., A. M. Ghatage. Poona : Deccan College Post Graduate and Research Institute, 1976–1988. v. 1–3 issued in 3 pts. each. (In progress).   **AC705**
Contents: v. 1–3³, A–an-anuviddha.
A work (in progress since 1948) "based on an entirely new reading of the original texts and a fresh extraction of the material without relying on the earlier lexicons."—*Pref.*
A review of the first two published parts in the *Bulletin* of the London University School of Oriental and African Studies (v. 41 [1978] : 388) calls this "a monumental glossary which offers fuller concordances of Vedic and classical Sanskrit than have been available heretofore, together with a massive and long overdue attack upon the medieval literature, including epigraphy and traditional grammer, both fairly fully exploited for the first time."   PK933.E5

Monier-Williams, Monier. A Sanskrit-English dictionary : etymologically and philologically arranged with special reference to cognate Indo-European languages .... New ed., greatly enl. and improved, with the collaboration of Prof. E. Leumann ... Prof. C. Cappeller, and other scholars. Oxford : Clarendon Pr., 1899. 1333 p.   **AC706**
Various reprintings.
Sanskrit-English, with etymologies and references to the literature. The introduction contains a detailed explanation of the plan of the work and the extent of Sanskrit literature. Provides a list of works and authors.
§ By the same author: *A dictionary, English and Sanskrit* (Lucknow : Akhila Bharatiya Sanskrit Parishad, 1957. 859 p.).
"1st ed. 1851; reprinted lithographically in India from sheets of the 1st ed. by Bureau of Agricultural Information, Uttar Pradesh, Lucknow, 1957."—*verso of title page.* 1982 repr. (Delhi : Motilal Banarsidass) called 4th ed.   PK933.M6

Etymology

Mayrhofer, Manfred. Etymologisches Wörterbuch des Altindoarischen. Heidelberg : C. Winter, 1986–1993. Bd. 1–2[11–13]. (Indogermanische Bibliothek, II. Reihe, Wörterbücher). (In progress).   **AC707**
Issued in parts.
Contents: Bd. 1, 2[11–13], A-bhanga-².
A scholarly German-Sanskrit dictionary that updates but does not supersede the author's *Kurzgefasstes etymologisches Wörterbuch des Altindischen* (AC708). This work concentrates on word origins, not historical development, and does not include English glosses. A list of words cited in the text appears on p. 7–31 of Lfg. 1, with additions on the back cover of subsequent Lfg.
To be in 3 v. Each volume will be in two sections, the first covering the original Vedic Sanskrit vocabulary, and the second, post-Vedic vocabulary.   PK905.M28

————— Kurzgefasstes etymologisches Wörterbuch des Altindischen = A concise etymological Sanskrit dictionary. Heidelberg : C. Winter, 1953–80. 4 v. (Indogermanische Bibliothek, II. Reihe. Wörterbücher).   **AC708**
Issued in parts.
A Sanskrit-German etymological dictionary. The base language is German, but all Sanskrit catchwords are translated also into English, the substance of the introduction is summarized in English, and the list of abbreviations is in German and English. Vol. 4 contains indexes in various languages.

Serbo-Croatian

Jugoslavenska akademija znanosti i umjetnosti. Rječnik hrvatskoga ili srpskoga jezika / Obraduje Đ. Daničić. U Zagrebu : U knížarnici L. Hartmana, 1880–1976. 23 v.   **AC709**
Issued in parts.
Editors vary; publisher varies.
The standard dictionary of the Yugoslavian Academy. Includes specialized usage, e.g., law, and includes extensive references to dictionaries and other sources. The only full, complete work available. Copies may be in fragile condition.   PG1374.R5

Bilingual

Benson, Morton. An English-SerboCroatian dictionary. 3rd ed. Cambridge ; N.Y. : Cambridge Univ. Pr., 1990. xlix, 722 p.   **AC710**
1st ed., 1979; 2nd ed., 1986.
Title on added title page: *Englesko-srpskohrvatski rečnik.*
Introductory material in English and Serbo-Croatian.
Basic vocabulary is standard contemporary American English, based on the speech of educated Americans and on the press. This edition adds many new scientific and technical terms.
A companion work: *SerboCroatian-English dictionary* / by Morton Benson with the collaboration of Biljana Šljivić-Šimšić. (3rd ed. Cambridge ; N.Y. : Cambridge Univ. Pr., 1990. lxv, 769 p.).
1st ed., 1971; 2nd ed., 1981.
Title on added title page: *Srpskohrvatsko-engleski rečnik.*
Introductory material in English and Serbo-Croatian.
About 60,000 entries, emphasizing the "speech of educated Yugoslavs and the daily press."—*Introd., 1st ed.* This edition adds technical, mainly computer-related words to the scientific and technical vocabulary included in earlier editions. A careful and scholarly work.   PG1376.B38

Bogadek, Francis Aloysius. New English-Croatian and Croatian-English dictionary : with an appendix comprising a short grammar of the English language; foreign words and phrases; Christian names and other information. 3rd ed. enl. and corr. N.Y. : Hafner, [1944]. 2 v. in 1.   **AC711**
Various reprints; 1985 reprint (N.Y. : Macmillan) titled *Cassell's new English-Croatian and Croatian-English dictionary.*
1st ed., 1926.   PG1377.B72

Bujas, Željko. Hrvatsko ili srpsko-engleski enciklopedijski rječnik. Zagreb : Grafički zavod Hrvatske, 1983–1989. v. 1–2. (In progress?).   **AC712**
Title on added title page: *Croatoserbian-English encyclopedic dictionary.*

Contents: v. 1, A–LJ; v. 2, M–O.

Defines some 150,000 words in the Croatian variant of Serbo-Croatian. Includes colloquial and slang terms and selected scientific and technical terms.   PG1377.B82

Drvodelić, Milan. Englesko-hrvatski ili srpski rječnik / preradio Željko Bujas. 7. izd. Zagreb : Školska Knjiga, 1983. 880 p.   **AC713**

Added title page: *English-Croatian or Serbian dictionary.*

1st ed., 1954 had title: *Englesko-hrvatski rječnik*; 2nd–3rd eds. (1962–70), *Englesko-hrvatskosrpski rječnik.*

A companion work by the same author: *Hrvatsko ili srpasko engleski rječnik*, preradio Željiko Bujas (6. izd. Zagreb : Školska Knjiga, 1989. 847 p.).

Added title page: *Croatian or Serbian-English dictionary.*

1st ed., 1953, had title: *Hrvatsko-engleski rječnik.*   PG1377.D77

The Oxford-Duden pictorial Serbo-Croat & English dictionary / Croatian text ed. by Vjekoslav Boban ; English text ed. by John Pheby [et al.]. Oxford : Clarendon Pr., 1988. 677, 78, 96 p. : ill.   **AC714**

Produced by Cankarjeva Založba in collaboration with the Oxford University Press Dictionary Department and Bibliographisches Institut in Mannheim.

Foreword and all introductory material in English and Serbo-Croatian.

Encompasses "the most diverse areas of daily life and scientific activity" (*Foreword*) through 384 plates. Detailed line drawings illustrate the vocabulary identified for both languages. An alphabetical index for each language follows the plates.   PG1377.O94

Abbreviations

Plamenatz, Ilija P. Yugoslav abbreviations : a selective list. 2nd enl. ed. Wash. : Slavic and Central European Div., Reference Dept., Libr. of Congress, 1962. 198 p.   **AC715**

1st ed., 1959.

"Intended ... to include the more common abbreviations which have come into use since World War II, especially names of government institutions and official bodies, industrial and trade establishments and the more important newspapers and periodicals. ..." *Introd.*

The main list contains nearly 3,000 abbreviations; the 2nd ed. adds some 200 newly identified abbreviations in an appendix.   PG1386.P55

Shona

Hannan, M. Standard Shona dictionary / comp. for the Literature Bureau by M. Hannan. Rev. ed. with addendum. [Harare : College Pr. in conjunction with the Literature Bureau, 1984]. 1014 p.   **AC716**

1st ed., 1959; 2nd ed., 1974.

Repr., 1987.

A Shona-English dictionary with an English index of words that appear in the definitions. This edition offers minor revisions to the 2nd ed. and a brief addendum.   PL8681.4.H3

Siksika

Frantz, Donald. Blackfoot dictionary of stems, roots, and affixes / Donald G. Frantz and Norma Jean Russell. Toronto ; Buffalo : Univ. of Toronto Pr., c1989. 470 p.   **AC717**

Entries include Blackfoot stem, root, or affix, as header; morphological type; meaning; and examples of usage.   PM2343.F7

Slovak

Konuš, Joseph James. Slovak-English phraseological dictionary. [Passaic, N.J.] : Slovak Catholic Sokol, 1969. 1664 p.   **AC718**

Added t.p.: Slovensko-anglický frazeologický slovník.

Written for "all those who are interested in learning or studying the Slovak language, Slovak history or culture."—*Foreword.* Includes thousands of the most common Slovak phrases and expressions.   PG5379.K58

Simko, Ján. Anglicko-slovenský slovník. 3. vyd. Bratislava : SPN, 1971. 1443 p.   **AC719**

1st ed., 1967.   PG5379.S5

Slovenian

Inštitut za slovenski jezik (Slovenska akademija znanosti in umetnosti). Slovar slovenskega knjižnega jezika : [Glavni uredniški odbor / Anton Bajec in dr.]. Ljubljana : Slovenska akademija znanosti in umetnosti, Inštitut za slovenski jezik; Državna založba Slovenije, 1970–1991. 5 v.   **AC720**

An important scholarly work.   PG1888.S5

Bilingual

Grad, Anton. Veliki angleško-slovenski slovar / Anton Grad, Ružena Škerlj, Nada Vitorovič. Ljubljana : Državna Založba Slovenije, 1984. 1377 p.   **AC721**

Added t.p. in English: The great English-Slovene dictionary.

Various printings.

Includes pronunciation of the English words.

§ A small, "two way," dictionary is Daša Komac's *Angleško-slovenski in slovensko-angleški slovar; English-Slovene and Slovene-English dictionary* (Ljubljana : Cankarjeva Založba, 1981. 787 p.).   PG1891.G73

Kotnik, Janko. Slovensko-angleški slovar. 8. izd. Ljubljana : Državna Založba Slovenije, 1978. 831 p.   **AC722**

Added title page: Slovene-English dictionary.

1st ed., 1945, had title: *Slovenian-English dictionary.*   PG1891.K6

Škerlj, Ružena. Angleško-slovenski slovar. Ljubljana : Državna založba Slovenije, 1965. 812 p.   **AC723**

Added t.p. : English-Slovene dictionary.

A reliable desk dictionary.   PG1891.S48

Somali

Abraham, Roy Clive. English-Somali dictionary. London : Univ. of London Pr., [1967]. 208 p.   **AC724**

English vocabulary in alphabetical order, but for compactness, cross-references are used liberally, with Somali equivalents given under the related word to which readers are directed. Standard orthography is used.

———. *Somali-English dictionary* ([London] : Univ. of London Pr., [1966]. 322 p.).

Approximately 8,000 entries, in transcription, with tone indicated by numbers. Intended for speakers of English. Illustrative sentences. Includes a grammatical outline.   PJ2533.A18

Zorc, R. David Paul. Somali-English dictionary. 2nd rev. and expanded ed. / R. David Zorc with Madina M. Osman and Virginia Luling. Kensington, Md. : Dunwoody Pr., 1991. 530 p.
AC725
1st ed., 1987.
Gives clear English translations and examples of use. Variant forms of words have separate entries. Offers thorough grammatical description of the language.   PJ2533.Z67

Spanish

Alonso Pedraz, Martin. Enciclopedia del idioma : diccionario histórico y moderno de la lengua española (siglos XII al XX), etimológico, tecnológico, regional e hispano-americano. Madrid : Aguilar, 1958. 3 v.   **AC726**
Intended to be more comprehensive in number of words listed but less detailed in treatment of individual words than the Real Academia Española's *Diccionario histórico de la lengua española* (AC728). For many words, treatment is full, giving etymology, morphology, definitions with citations of usage, examples of phrasal combinations, and dates of appearances in early dictionaries. For other words for which there are no new or specialized meanings, the standard definitions from the Academia's *Diccionario* are often used almost verbatim.   PC4667.A4

Diccionario de la lengua española. 21. ed. Madrid : Real Academia Española, 1992. 1513 p.   **AC727**
1st ed., 1726–39 had title: *Diccionario de la lengua castellana*. 20th ed., 1984.
A standard work which includes etymologies. This edition has 83,500 entries; it modifies more than 12,000 entries from previous editions.   PC4625.A3

Real Academia Española. Diccionario histórico de la lengua española / Seminario de Lexicografía: Director, Julio Casares .... Madrid, 1960–92. v. 1–2. (In progress).   **AC728**
Contents: v. 1–2, A–Antigrapho.
A new attempt at a major historical dictionary of the language to replace the earlier unfinished work with the same title (Madrid : Hernando, 1933–36. v. 1–2, A–Cevilla).
Each word is treated in scholarly detail, with variations in meaning illustrated by numerous quotations, chronologically listed. Citations are given to exact source. Extensive list of works consulted.

Bilingual

American heritage Larousse Spanish dictionary. Boston : Houghton Mifflin, c1986. 532 p., 572 p.   **AC729**
Repr. 1992 as: *The American heritage Spanish dictionary. Spanish/English, English/Spanish*.
Based on *American heritage dictionary* (AC9). Introductory material in English and Spanish. Emphasizes "U.S. and Latin American usage."—*Pref*. Contains notes on grammar and usage, verb table, numerals, and weights and measures tables.   PC4640.A54

Cassell's Spanish-English English-Spanish dictionary = Diccionario Español-Inglés, Inglés-Español. Completely rev. / by Anthony Gooch, Ángel García de Paredes. London : Cassell ; N.Y. : Macmillan, c1978. 1109 p.   **AC730**
1st ed., 1959.
A standard desk dictionary, second only to *Collins Spanish-English, English-Spanish dictionary* (AC731). Definitions are concise; proper names are interfiled with other entries.   PC4640.C35

Collins Spanish-English, English-Spanish dictionary = Collins diccionario español-inglés, inglés-español / [contributors, Teresa Alvarez García ... et al.]. 2nd ed. N.Y. : HarperCollins Publ., 1993. 1 v. (various pagings).   **AC731**

Rev. ed. of *Collins concise Spanish-English, English-Spanish dictionary*, 1985.
Abridged from *Collins Spanish-English, English-Spanish dictionary*, 3rd ed. (AC738). "The user whose aim is to learn, read, and understand Spanish will find this dictionary, with its wide-ranging and up-to-date coverage of current usage, an invaluable companion."—*Introd*. The vocabulary is Spanish and English from both Europe and America. 135,000 references and 220,000 translations.   PC4640.C53

Cuyás, Arturo. Appleton's new Cuyás English-Spanish and Spanish-English dictionary / Rev. and enl. by Lewis E. Brett (pt. 1) and Helen S. Eaton (pt. 2) with the assistance of Walter Beveraggi-Allende. Revision ed., Catherine B. Avery. 5th ed., rev. N.Y. : Appleton-Century-Crofts, 1972. 2 v. in 1 (698, 589 p.).   **AC732**
Added t.p. in Spanish.
First publ. in 1928 under title: *Appleton's new English-Spanish and Spanish-English dictionary*. Frequently reprinted.
A standard desk dictionary. In this latest revision the compilers have "added new words from all fields of interest; dropped those words that are no longer of frequent use; and modified those that have acquired new meanings of more precise equivalents in Spanish or in English."—*Pref*.   PC4640.C8

García-Pelayo y Gross, Ramón. Gran diccionario moderno : español/inglés [y English/Spanish] Larousse / Ramón García-Pelayo y Gross, Micheline Durand. México, D.F. [etc.] : Ediciones Larousse, [1984]. 1542 p.   **AC733**
Introductory matter in Spanish and English.
An extensive new work in the Larousse tradition. Its principal aim "is to gather together all the words, classic and *modern*, which go to make up the rich Anglo-Hispanic cultural heritage. Special care has been taken with the new technical and scientific terms progress brings, and which appear in our newspapers and periodicals and on radio and television every day. Equally, attention has been devoted to neologisms and foreign words in common use and to more recent colloquialisms."—*Foreword*. Pronunciation is indicated in the English-Spanish part. Numerous examples of usage are given. Americanisms appear frequently in both parts: "Amer." designates Latin American words or phrases, "U.S." precedes North American ones.
A shorter version has been published as *Diccionario general español-inglés [y English-Spanish]*, ed. by Ramón García-Pelayo y Gross (Paris, etc. : Ediciones Larousse, 1984. 431 p., 499 p.).

Harrap's concise Spanish and English dictionary : English-Spanish/Spanish-English in one volume. London : Harrap ; N.Y. : distr. by Prentice Hall, 1992. 526 p., 557 p.
AC734
"An entirely new dictionary, the first modern English-Spanish bilingual dictionary to adopt the latest Spanish alphabetical order in which the digraphs Ch and Ll cease to be considered separate letters and, as its name implies, one which manages to compress a wealth of information into the relatively small space."—*Pref*. 115,000 main entries offer definitions, examples of uses, common expressions, and idioms. English from North America and Spanish from Central and South America have ample treatment.   PC4640.H33

Martínez Amador, Emilio M. Diccionario inglés-español, español-inglés = Spanish-English, English-Spanish dictionary. Nueva ed. Barcelona : Sopena, 1985. 2 v.   **AC735**
1st ed., 1946; 3rd ed., 1958, had title: *Standard English-Spanish and Spanish-English dictionary*.
Contains more than 80,000 entries for each part. Proper nouns and geographical names are included in main alphabetical sequence. Offers a glossary of terms used in computing.

The Oxford-Duden pictorial Spanish-English dictionary. Oxford : Clarendon Pr. ; N.Y. : Oxford Univ. Pr., 1985. 672, 112, 96 p. : ill.   **AC736**
Like other dictionaries in the Duden pictoral series, consists of line drawings in which terms in the object language are identified. Particularly good for technical and specialized terminology. Indexes

for Spanish and for English enable readers to locate charts in which a term and other terms associated with it may be found. Although British English is emphasized, attempt has been made to include American Spanish parts of Latin America."—*Foreword.* PC4629.O94

Simon and Schuster's international dictionary = Diccionario internacional Simon and Schuster. English/Spanish, Spanish/ English / Tana de Gámez, ed. in chief. N.Y. : Simon and Schuster, [1973]. 1605 p. **AC737**

Prefatory matter in Spanish and English.

Publ. in 1975 under title: *Simon and Schuster's concise international dictionary.*

Desk dictionary with more than 200,000 entries. Includes scientific and technical terms, vulgarisms, loan words. Extensive use of illustrative phrases to indicate usage and idioms. Distinguishes meanings and usage of Spanish words as they are used in Latin American countries. Numerous proper and place-names and abbreviations are listed in the main alphabetical sequences. Pronunciation of English entry words is indicated according to International Phonetic Alphabet, with distinction made where American and British pronunciation differs; distinction is also made between American and British usage. PC4640.S48

Smith, Colin. Collins Spanish-English, English-Spanish dictionary / by Colin Smith in collaboration with Diarmuid Bradley ... [et al.]. 3rd ed., unabridged. Glasgow ; N.Y. : HarperCollins, 1993. 775, 908 p. **AC738**

1st ed., 1971; 2nd ed., 1988.

Introductory material in English and Spanish.

Reliable and current. "The fact that this new edition appears so shortly after the second (1988) has a particular motive. While on the one hand there is a permanent need to modernize such works of reference, ... the author and publishers have seized the opportunity offered by 1992 to salute both the Single European Act and the Spanish speaking worlds."—*Pref.* Includes sections on "Pronunciation of European Spanish" and "Pronunciation of Spanish in America."

§ A revised edition of *Collins concise Spanish-English, English-Spanish dictionary* confusingly has the same title as the unabridged version; *see* AC731. PC4640.S595

The University of Chicago Spanish dictionary / comp. by Carlos Castillo & Otto F. Bond, with the assistance of Barbara M. García. 4th ed, rev. and enl. by D. Lincoln Canfield. Chicago : Univ. of Chicago Pr., 1987. 475 p. : maps. **AC739**

Subtitle: A new concise Spanish-English and English-Spanish dictionary of words and phrases basic to the written and spoken languages of today, plus a list of 500 Spanish idioms and sayings, with variants and English equivalents.

3rd ed., 1977.

New World usages, as found in the U.S. and Spanish America, receive special references. PC4640.U5

Velázquez de la Cadena, Mariano. New revised Velázquez Spanish and English dictionary / comp. ... with Edward Gray and Juan L. Iribas; newly revised by Ida Navarro Hinojosa, Manuel Blanco-González and R. J. Nelson. New rev. 1985 ed. Piscataway, N.J. : New Century, [1985]. 698 p., 34 p., 788 p. **AC740**

First published 1852 under title *A pronouncing dictionary of the Spanish and English languages*; frequently reprinted with revisions. 1973 ed. had title *New pronouncing dictionary of the Spanish and English languages.*

A useful and authoritative Spanish-English dictionary for general purposes. This edition includes a "1985 supplement" to the Spanish-English part comprising "Contemporary additions of scientific, technological, commercial, and colloquial terms to maintain the authority of this work for accurate modern Spanish as used in Latin America and Spain."—*Suppl., p.1.* PC4640.V55

Vox: new college Spanish and English dictionary : English-Spanish/Spanish-English / comp. by Carlos F. MacHale and the editors of Biblograf, S.A. ; North American ed. prep. by the editors of National Textbook Co. Lincolnwood, Ill. : Nat. Textbook Co., [1984]. 1456 p. : maps. **AC741**

1st ed., 1966.

Repr.: 1992.

Examples of usage are offered in entries for more than 250,000 headwords. The center section, separating the Spanish and English sections, offers 3,500 of the most frequently used idiomatic expressions in both Spanish and English. PC4640.V68

Etymology

Corominas, Joan. Diccionario crítico etimológico de la lengua castellana. Madrid : Gredos, [1954–57]. 4 v. (Biblioteca románica hispánica, 5. Diccionarios etimológicos). **AC742**

Frequently reprinted.

Vol. 4 includes *Adiciones y rectificaciones,* p. 897–1092, and *Indices,* p. 1093–1224.

A comprehensive etymological dictionary giving dates of origin of words, with quotations showing usages and derivations. Covers the languages of both Spain and Spanish America and includes the ancient languages, such as pre-Roman Iberian and vulgar Arabic, as well as dialects and Latin-American influences.

§ Corominas has also compiled *Breve diccionario etimológico de la lengua castellana* (3rd ed. Madrid : Grados, 1973. 627 p.). PC4580.C59

García de Diego, Vicente. Diccionario etimológico español e hispánico. 2a ed. Madrid : Espasa-Calpe, 1985. 1091 p. **AC743**

1st ed., 1954.

"Considerablemente aumentada con materiales inéditos del autor a cargo de Carmen García de Diego."—*t.p.*

Repr. without change as the 3rd ed., 1989. PC4580.G33

Gómez de Silva, Guido. Elsevier's concise Spanish etymological dictionary : containing 10,000 entries, 1,300 word families. Amsterdam ; N.Y. : Elsevier, 1985. 559 p. : ill. **AC744**

Aims "to trace each Spanish word as far back as possible in order to acquaint the reader with the story of the evolution of the Spanish language."—*Introd.* Includes prefixes, suffixes, inflectional endings, and proper names. Definitions and explanations are in English. The etymologies do not generally give dated information. PC4580.G65

Idioms and usage

Harrap's diccionario de expresiones idiomáticas : inglés español/español-inglés = Harrap's dictionary of idioms : English-Spanish/Spanish-English / Louis J. Rodrigues, Josefina Bernet de Rodrigues. London : Harrap, 1991. 466 p. **AC745**

Preface in English and Spanish.

Aims to "provide a reasonable range of useful idiomatic expressions in both English and Spanish, together with their corresponding translations."—*Pref.* Entries include sentences showing usage.

Moliner, María. Diccionario de uso del español. Madrid : Editorial Gredos, [1966–67]. 2 v. (Biblioteca románica hispánica, 5. Diccionarios [5]). **AC746**

Various printings.

Synonyms and related terms are given; derivation is indicated for many words. PC4625.M6

Synonyms

Casares y Sánchez, Julio. Diccionario ideológico de la lengua española : desde la idea a la palabra, desde la palabra a la idea. 2. ed., corr., aumentada y puesta al día. Barcelona : Ed. G. Gili, 1959. 1xxv , 482, 887 p.   **AC747**

First published 1942. Frequently reprinted (3. tirada 1966).

Contents: pt. 1, Parte sinóptica; pt. 2, Parte analógica; pt. 3, Parte alfabética.

Pt. 2 consists of lists of words grouped by association of ideas; pt. 3 is an alphabetical dictionary defining these words.   PC4625.C3

Vox diccionario manual de sinónimos y antónimos. 8. ed. Barcelona : Bibliograf, 1992. 647 p.   **AC748**

7th ed., 1984, had title: *Diccionario manual de sinónimos y antónimos.*

Entries include part of speech, special usage labels (e.g. ironical, vulgar), alternative words, and an explanation of the definition, if necessary.   PC4591.V793

Medieval–18th century

Boggs, Ralph Steele. Tentative dictionary of medieval Spanish / by Ralph Steele Boggs ... [et al.]. Chapel Hill, N.C., 1946. 2 v. (537 p.).   **AC749**

A preliminary work, issued in multigraph form, sponsored by the Old Spanish Group of the Modern Language Association. Useful until a complete dictionary for this period is published.

Müller, Bodo. Diccionario del español medieval. Heidelberg : C. Winter, 1987–1993. fasc. 1–9. (Sammlung romanischer Elementar- und Handbücher, 3. Reihe, Wörterbücher). (In progress).   **AC750**

Contents: fasc. 1–9, A–Achar.

"Bibliografía provisional," fasc. 1, p. viii–xxxii.

A scholarly etymological and historical dictionary, based on some 500 literary and nonliterary texts. Sponsored by the Heidelberger Akademie der Wissenschaften.   PC4715.Z5M8

Bibliography

Espinosa Elerick, María Luz. Annotated bibliography of technical and specialized dictionaries in Spanish-Spanish and Spanish-English, with commentary. Troy, N.Y. : Whitston, 1982. 100 p.   **AC751**

Title also in Spanish.

An alphabetical listing of 86 Spanish and bilingual and polyglot technical dictionaries of which one of the languages is Spanish. Full descriptions and annotations appear in both Spanish and English in parallel columns. Index of descriptors.   Z2695.D6E43

Fabbri, Maurizio. A bibliography of Hispanic dictionaries : Catalan, Galician, Spanish, Spanish in Latin America and the Philippines. Imola : Galeati, 1979. 381 p. (Collana bibliografica, 1).   **AC752**

Lists some 3,500 "dictionaries, vocabularies, glossaries and word-lists of a general character—synonyms, etymologies, homonyms, foreign words, dialects, slangs, proverbs, verbs, etc.—as well as of texts dealing with technical and scientific micro-languages and the highly specialized terminology of these fields."—*Pref.* Separate sections for monolingual (subdivided for dialects, etymology, etc.), bilingual, and polyglot dictionaries. Arranged by author within sections. Appendix: A bibliography of Basque dictionaries. Author, language, and subject indexes.   Z2695.D6F32

Indexes

Romera-Navarro, Miguel. Registro de lexicografía hispánica. Madrid : Consejo Superior de Investigaciones Científicas, 1951. 1013 p.   **AC753**

Supplement to *Revista de filología española* (Anejo LIV).

An alphabetical index of 50,000 Spanish words, with 80,000 references to etymologies, linguistic studies, etc., in monographs, treatises, and scholarly journals.   PC4580.R75

Regional and dialect

Galván, Roberto A. El diccionario del español chicano = The dictionary of Chicano Spanish / comp. by Roberto A. Galván, Richard V. Teschner. Lincolnwood, Ill. : Voluntad Publishers, c1985. 145 p.   **AC754**

Reprint of the 1977 ed. (Silver Spring, Md. : Institute of Modern Languages), which was a revised and expanded ed. of Galván's *El diccionario del español de Tejas*, (Silver Spring, Md. : Institute, 1975).

Repr. : Lincolnwood, Ill. : National Textbook Co., 1989.

Contains almost 8,000 words and phrases, including slang, some with citations, from conversational Spanish of Texas, California, Arizona, New Mexico, Colorado, and Florida, which are "not included, as yet, in the more readily available reference lexicons."—*Pref.* Intended as a supplement to standard dictionaries of Spanish.   PC4827.G35

Raluy Poudevida, Antonio. Diccionario Porrúa de la lengua española / prepardo por Antonio Raluy Poudevida ; revisado por Francisco Monterde. 33. ed. México : Editorial Po rrúa, 1992. 848 p. : map in color.   **AC755**

1st ed., 1969.

Basic idiomatic expressions and general Spanish as spoken in Mexico.

Sumerian

See Akkadian.

Swahili

Inter-territorial Language (Swahili) Committee to the East African Dependencies. A standard English-Swahili dictionary : (founded on Madan's English-Swahili dictionary) / by the Inter-territorial Language Committee of the East African Dependencies under the direction of the late Frederick Johnson. London : Oxford Univ. Pr., H. Milford, 1939. 635 p.   **AC756**

Frequently reprinted. Also available in microform.

A revision of the dictionaries by Arthur C. Madan and Bishop Edward Steere.

Its counterpart is *A standard Swahili-English dictionary : (founded on Madan's Swahili-English dictionary)*, publ. by the same committee (London : Oxford Univ. Pr., 1939. 548 p.).

§ Another work of interest is J. L. Krapf, *A dictionary of the Swahili language : with introduction containing an outline of a Suahili grammar*, (London : Trübner and Co., 1882. 433 p.).

Repr.: N.Y. : Negro Univ. Pr., 1969. Also available in microform.

Primary technical dictionary English-Swahili / comp. by Rajmund Ohly ; standardized by the National Kiswahili Council (BAKITA) ; with a foreword by His Excellency Ali Hassan Mwinyi. Dar es Salaam, Tanzania : Institute of Production Innovation IPI, Univ. of Dar es Salaam, 1987. 243 p.   **AC757**

Contains 10,000 technical terms with brief definitions from areas such as agriculture, architecture, automotive and building industries, etc. It "serves primarily to assist in the translation of technical texts into Swahili and aid oral instruction."—*Introd.*   PL8703.P75

Rechenbach, Charles William. Swahili-English dictionary / Charles W. Rechenbach, assisted by Angelica Wanjinu Gesuga ... [et al.]. Wash. : Catholic Univ. of America Pr., 1967. 641 p.   **AC758**

A comprehensive dictionary intended for speakers of English. Built on *A standard Swahili-English dictionary* (AC756), bringing the vocabulary up-to-date and including extensive developments since World War II. Includes loan words and lists of derivative words.   PL8703.R4

Snoxall, R. A. A concise English-Swahili dictionary = Kamusi ya Kiingereza-Kiswahili. [Repr., rev.]. London : Oxford Univ. Pr., [1961]. 325 p. : ill.   **AC759**

Intended for speakers of Swahili. About 8,000 entries and illustrations. Phonetic transcription, part of speech, level of style and equivalent Swahili word or sentence given.   PL8703.S6

Swedish

Gibson, Haldo. Svensk slangordbok. 2. uppl. [S.l.] : Esselte Studium, 1983. 243 p.   **AC760**

1st ed., 1969.

A concise dictionary that attempts to cover all areas of the vocabulary of slang.   PD5921.G52

Illustrerad svensk ordbok / Redaktör: Bertil Molde. Medarbetare: Daniel Andreae [et al.]. 3. revid. uppl. Stockholm : Natur och Kultur, [1964]. 1917 p. : ill.   **AC761**

1st ed., 1955; 2nd ed., 1958. Various printings.

A modern Swedish dictionary with line drawings.   PD5625.I4

Östergren, Olof. Nusvensk ordbok. Stockholm : Wahlström & Widstrand, 1919–72. 10 v.   **AC762**

Issued in parts.

An important dictionary of modern Swedish.   PD5625.O4

Söderwall, Knut Fredrik. Ordbok öfver svenska medeltidsspråket. Lund : Berlingska Boktryckeri, 1884–1918. 2 v. in 3. (Samlingar utgifna af Svenska fornskrift-sällskapet, häfte 85 [etc.]).   **AC763**

Issued in 29 pts.

A dictionary of the Swedish of medieval times.

——. ——. *Supplement*, 1925–73 (Hft. 1–35. 1149 p.) continues the work of the basic set.

Svenska akademien. Ordbok öfver svenska språket. Lund : C.W.K. Gleerup, 1898–1989. v. 1–30². (In progress).   **AC764**

Contents: v. 1–30², A–Strutshar.

The great Academy dictionary of modern Swedish; includes etymologies, and references to the literature with dates.

——. ——. *Supplement 1–2* (1899–1975). Offer bibliographies of sources cited in the dictionary.   PD5625.S8

Bilingual

Kärre, Karl. Engelsk-svensk ordbok : skolupplaga / av Karl Kärre [et al.] under medverkan av Grenville Grove. 3., omarb. uppl. Stockholm : Svenska Bokförlaget, Norstedt, [1953]. 973 p.   **AC765**

1st ed., 1935; 2nd ed., 1949. Frequently reprinted.

Added t. p.: *English-Swedish dictionary.*

A standard work that includes proper names.   PD5640.K3

Petti, Vincent. English-Swedish Swedish-English dictionary / Vincent Petti and Kerstin Petti. N.Y. : Hippocrene Books, 1990. 747 p.   **AC766**

A compact dictionary with 18,500 entries for the English-Swedish portion, and 23,300 entries for Swedish-English.

Prisma's Swedish-English and English-Swedish dictionary. Minneapolis : Univ. of Minnesota Pr. ; Stockholm : Bokförlaget Prisma, 1988. 622, 613 p.   **AC767**

Comp. by Eva Gomer and Mona Morris-Nygren.

Swedish-English part, 1st ed., 1970; English-Swedish part, 1st ed., 1964. 1st American ed., 1984, had title : *Prisma's modern Swedish-English and English-Swedish dictionary*; Swedish ed. had title: *Modern engelsk-svensk och svensk-engelsk ordbok.*

Emphasizes modern usage of both languages. 54,000 headwords with 15,000 phrases, expressions and other language constructions.   PD5640.M564

Stora engelsk-svenska ordboken = A comprehensive English-Swedish dictionary / [red., Rudolf Santesson, et al.]. [Nacka] : Esselte Studium, 1980. 1071 p.   **AC768**

Introductory material in Swedish and English.

Presents "a very wide range of English words and phrases with exact and idiomatic Swedish translation."—*Introd.*   PD5640.S8

Svensk-engelsk ordbok / leksikonred. chef: Rudolf Santesson. Nacka : Esselte Studium, 1980. 979 p.   **AC769**

First publ. 1968.

Illustrative Swedish sentences with English translations frequently follow definitions.

Companion work: *Stora engelsk-svensk ordboken = A comprehensive English-Swedish dictionary* / Red. Rudolph Santesson ... [et al.] (AC768).

Etymology

Hellquist, Elof. Svensk etymologisk ordbok. Ny omarb. och utv. uppl. Lund : C. W. K. Gleerup, [1939]. 2 v.   **AC770**

Issued in 18 pts., 1935–39. Previous ed. publ. 1920–22. A reprint of this edition with minor changes and corrections was published as a 3rd ed., 1948. (Repr. 1957, 1970).

A standard work including personal and place-names, with etymologies and cognate words in various western European languages.   PD5580.H42

Syriac

Brockelmann, Carl. Lexicon syriacum. Ed. 2, aucta et emendata. Halis Saxonum : Niemeyer, 1928. 930 p.   **AC771**

Repr. : Hildesheim ; N.Y. : G. Olms, 1982.

1st ed., 1895.

Issued in parts, 1923–28.

In Latin and Syriac.

Includes a Latin index of words, addenda, and a list of abbreviations with the bibliography.   PJ5493.B7

Oraham, Alexander Joseph. Oraham's dictionary of the stabilized and enriched Assyrian language and English. [Chicago : Consolidated Pr. (Assyrian Pr. of America), 1943]. 576 p.   **AC772**

Added title page and preface in Syriac.

Not a dictionary of classical Assyrian but of that language sometimes called by scholars "Nestorian Syriac"; includes "the ancient, medieval and the modern literary phases of this language."—*Foreword.*   PJ5491.O7

Payne Smith, Robert. Thesaurus syriacus / collegerunt Stephanus M. Quatremere, Georgius Henricus Bernstein … [et al.]. Oxford : Clarendon Pr., 1879–1901. 2 v. (4515 p.). **AC773**

Repr.: Hildsheim ; N.Y. : Georg Olms, 1981. 2 v. plus suppl.

Vol. 2 also ed. by D. S. and J. P. Margoliouth.

———. ———. *Supplement*, coll. and arranged by … J. P. Margoliouth (Oxford : Clarendon Pr., 1927. 345 p.).

Issued in abridged form as: *Compendious Syriac dictionary*, ed. by J. Payne Smith (Mrs. Margoliouth) (Oxford : Clarendon Pr., 1903. 626 p.).

Tagalog

Ramos, Teresita V. Tagalog dictionary. Honolulu : Univ. of Hawaii Pr., 1971. 330 p. **AC774**

Tagalog-English only. About 4,000 entries, representing "the high frequency words that are necessary for a non-Tagalog speaker to be able to communicate effectively in day-by-day conversational situations."—*Introd.* PL6056.R3

Tamil

English-Tamil dictionary / chief ed.: A. Chidambaranatha Chettiar. [Madras] : Univ. of Madras, 1963–65. 3 v. **AC775**

Publ. in 1965 as a single volume.

Preface and hints for using the dictionary are in English and Tamil. PL4756.E55

Tamil lexicon / published under the authority of the University of Madras. [Madras] : Univ. of Madras, 1924–36. 6 v. **AC776**

Repr., 1982.

Issued in 24 pts., with various imprints, 1924–36.

Gives transliterations and English translations for more than 100,000 Tamil words. All previous dictionaries in the language were drawn upon, and many outstanding scholars collaborated in the compilation. Terminology of special fields—e.g., law, architecture, medicine—is included. The outstanding dictionary of the language. Does not include etymologies.

———. ———. *Supplement* (1938–39. 2 v.). PL4756.M3

Thai

Haas, Mary Rosamond. Thai-English student's dictionary / comp. by Mary R. Haas, with the assistance of George V. Grekoff … [et al.]. Stanford, Calif. : Stanford Univ. Pr., 1964. 638 p. **AC777**

Intended for the English-speaking student of Thai. Distinguishes among levels of usage and provides examples of a variety of uses. Lists synonyms and antonyms. PL4156.H3

McFarland, George Bradley. Thai-English dictionary. Stanford, Calif. : Stanford Univ. Pr. ; London : H. Milford, Oxford Univ. Pr., [1944]. 1019 p., 39 p. **AC778**

Repr., 1982.

A photolithographic reprint of the first edition originally published in Bangkok in 1941.

Based on earlier dictionaries, this is a new work reflecting modern usage. Gives Thai script, transliteration, and definition in English. Includes scientific terms. In the addenda the scientific Latin names of flora, birds, fishes, shells, and snakes are translated into Thai. PL4187.M18

Plang Phloyphrom. Pru's standard Thai-English dictionary / Plang Phloyphrom and Robert Dorne Golden, with the cooperation of Brother Urbain-Gabriel. [Bangkok] : Āthōn Banpraditt; agent: Pricha Co., 1955. 1774 p. **AC779**

Gives Thai script, transliteration, and equivalent word in English. PL4187.P5

So Sethaputra. New model English-Thai dictionary. [4th] Library ed. Bangkok : Thai Watana Panich, [1979]. 2 v. **AC780**

1st ed., 1940. Publ. in various eds.

Aims to illustrate rather than define; gives illustrative phrases and sentences rather than equivalents and definitions. PL4187.S4

Tibetan

Bell, Charles Alfred. English-Tibetan colloquial dictionary. 2nd ed. Calcutta : Bengal Secretariat Book Depot, 1920. 562 p. **AC781**

Repr.: Calcutta : Firma KLM Private, 1977.

Originally published as the second part of Bell's *Manual of colloquial Tibetan*, 1905.

Tibetan words in Tibetan and also in romanized type. PL3637.B4

Buck, Stuart H. Tibetan-English dictionary : with supplement. Wash. : Catholic Univ. of America Pr., 1969. 833. (Publications in the languages of Asia, 1). **AC782**

"The primary purpose of the present dictionary is to provide full and accurate definitions of the vocabulary used in current publica-tions in the Tibetan language, especially those appearing in Communist China."—*Introd.* PL3637.B8

Das, Sarat Chandra. A Tibetan-English dictionary with Sanskrit synonyms. Rev. and ed. under the orders of the government of Bengal, by Graham Sandberg … and A. William Heyde …. Calcutta : Bengal Secretariat Book Depot, 1902. 1353 p. **AC783**

Added title page in Tibetan. Various printings.

With Sanskrit equivalents of the respective Tibetan words, selected by native Indian scholars of medieval and later days, in collaboration with Tibetan lotsawas or translators, and supplemented by Pandit Satis Chandra Acharya Vidyabhusan. —*Revisors' pref.* PL3637.D3

Goldstein, Melvyn C. English-Tibetan dictionary of modern Tibetan / comp. by Melvyn C. Goldstein with Ngawangthondup Narkyid. Berkeley : Univ. of California Pr., 1984. 485 p. **AC784**

Sponsored by the Department of Education's Division of International Education and the National Endowment for the Humanities.

Distributed to depository libraries in microfiche.

Since it was assumed "that this dictionary will be used primarily by teachers, students, and scholars, we have included not only 'basic' English lexical items … but also terms that might be useful in research or scholarly communication."—*Introd.* Emphasis is on spoken rather than literary language. PL3637.T52G65

——————— Tibetan-English dictionary of modern Tibetan. [2nd ed.]. Kathmandu : Ratna Pustak Bhandar, 1978. 1234 p. (Bibliotheca Himalayica, ser. 2, v. 9). **AC785**

1st ed., 1975.

About 40,000 entries. Vocabulary was drawn mainly from modern textual sources, with heavy emphasis on that used in newspapers and magazines.

Jäschke, Heinrich August. Tibetan-English dictionary : with special reference to the prevailing dialects, to which is added an English-Tibetan vocabulary. London ; Berlin : Printed by Unger Brothers (T. Grimm), 1881. 671 p. **AC786**

Prepared and published at the charge of the secretary of state for India in council.

"This work represents a new and thoroughly revised edition of a Tibetan-German dictionary, which appeared in a lithographed form between the years 1871–1876."—*Pref.* Frequently reprinted.

PL3637.J2

Turkish

Eren, Hasan. Türkçe sözlük / [hazırlayanlar, başkan, Hasan Eren ; Nevzat Gözaydın ... et al.]. Yeni baskı. Ankara : Atatürk Kültür, Dil, ve Tarih Yüksek Kurumu, Türk Dil Kurumu, 1988. 2 v. (1679 p.) : ill. **AC787**
An excellent dictionary of modern Turkish. PL189.E68

Karşılaşrmalı Türk lehceleri sözlüğü / Komisyon başkanı, Ahmet Bican Ercilasun. Ankara : Kültür Bakanlığı, 1991. 2 v. **AC788**
In Turkish, Azerbaijani, Başkurt, Kazak, Kırgız, Uzbek, Tatar, Turkemen, Uighur, and Russian (in transliteration).
A useful dictionary for dialects. Vol. 1 contains a section on the grammar of each language. The body of the dictionary contains ten columns (split into two pages) with the equivalent word for each language listed. Vol. 2 is an index by language; the word lists refer to page numbers in v. 1. PL27.K37

Bilingual

Akdikmen, Resuhi. Langenscheidt's standard Turkish dictionary / by Resuhi Akdikmen ; assistant lexicographers, Ekrem Uzbay, Necdet Özgüven. N.Y. : Langenscheidt, c1986. 622 p., 422 p. **AC789**
Contents: pt. 1, English-Turkish; pt. 2, Turkish-English.
80,000 entries. Uses the International Phonetic Alphabet as a pronunciation guide. "The vocabulary reflects that used in the modern everyday Turkish. The dictionary furthermore contains the most important terminology from such specialist areas as trade and commerce, technology, and medicine."—*Foreword.* PL191.A35

Alderson, Anthony Dolphin. The concise Oxford Turkish dictionary / Anthony Dolphin Alderson and Fahir İz. Oxford : Clarendon Pr., 1959. 807 p. **AC790**
Abridged edition of *A Turkish-English dictionary* by H. C. Hony (2nd ed. Oxford : Clarendon Pr., 1957) and *An English-Turkish dictionary* by Hony and F. İz (Oxford : Clarendon Pr., 1952). Suitable for student use.
Reduces the original volumes to about one-third of their length. Omits close synonyms, geographical and scientific terms easily recognizable and "those Arabic and Persian forms now commonly replaced by Turkish ones."—*Pref.* Suitable for student use. PL137.A4

İz, Fahir. The Oxford Turkish dictionary / Fahir İz, H. C. Hony, A. D. Alderson. Oxford ; N.Y. : Oxford Univ. Pr., c1992. 526, 619 p. **AC791**
A reprinting in 1 v. of: *The Oxford Turkish-English dictionary* (3rd ed., 1984) and *The Oxford English-Turkish dictionary* (2nd ed., 1978).
A modern work with emphasis on common terms and idioms. "A great deal of the obsolete Arabic-Persian heritage has been omitted ... balanced by the incorporation of the Turkish neologisms and of the European loan-words."—*Pref.* Spellings conform to the 1977 recommendations of the Turkish Language Institute. The English-Turkish section was "compiled mainly with a view to the needs of the Turkish student." PL191.H6

Redhouse yeni Türkçe-İngilizce sözlük = New Redhouse Turkish-English dictionary. [1. baskı]. [İstanbul : Redhouse Yayınevi, 1968]. 1292 p. **AC792**
Frequently reprinted.

"A new dictionary based largely on the Turkish-English Lexicon prepared by Sir James Redhouse and published in 1890 by the Publication Department of the American Board."—*half-title page.*
"The intention has been to include every word, and as nearly as possible every set phrase or locution, that has been used in standard Turkish as it has been spoken within the geographical area now called Turkey in the last two hundred years."—*Pref.*
Gives indications of the old spelling in the Ottoman alphabet.
PL191.R55

Redhouse, James William. Turkish and English lexicon : shewing in English the significations of the Turkish terms. Constantinople : pr. for the Amer. Mission by A. H. Boyajian, 1890. 2224 p. **AC793**
Repr.: Beirut : Librairie du Liban, 1974.
Provides approximately 93,000 "Turkish words of Turkish, Arabic, Persian, and European origin, in the Turkish character, with their pronunciation in European letters."—*Pref.* PL191.R52

Twi

Christaller, Johann Gottlieb. Dictionary of the Asante and Fante language, called Tshi (Twi) / Johann Gottlieb Christaller; [ed. by J. Schweizer]. 2nd ed., rev. and enl. Basel : pr. for the Basel Evangelical Missionary Society, 1933. 607 p. **AC794**
First published 1881.
"Based on the Akuapem dialect which was reduced to writing about 1838, and became afterwards the literary form."—*Pref.* This edition adds new words, meanings, and phrases in addition to the contents of the earlier edition. PL8751.Z5C5

Ukrainian

Akademiia Nauk URSR, Kiev. Instytut movoznavstva. Ukrainsko-russkii slovar' / glav. redaktor I. M. Kyrychenko. Kiev : Izd-vo Akademii Nauk Ukr. SSR, 1953–63. 6 v. **AC795**
Added title page in Ukrainian.
A major Ukrainian-Russian dictionary, giving examples of usage in Ukrainian from literary and other sources. PG3893.R8A54

Andrusyshen, C. H. Ukrains'ko-anhliis'kyi slovnyk = Ukrainian-English dictionary / C. H. Andrusyshen, J. N. Krett. Toronto : publ. for the Univ. of Saskatchewan by Univ. of Toronto Pr., 1957. 1163 p. **AC796**
First published by the Univ. of Saskatchewan, 1955.
Approximately "95,000 words with full definitions plus about 35,000 ... phrases."—*Foreword.* The orthography, based on a system of 1928, "does not differ radically" from the system accepted officially in the Ukrainian SSR in 1946.

Podvez'ko, M. L. Ukraïns'ko-angliïskyĭ slovnyk = Ukrainian-English dictionary : blyz'ko 60 000 sliv. 2nd ed. rev. N.Y. : Saphrograph Co., 1973. 1018 p. **AC797**
1st ed., 1952.
Also publ. Kiev : Radianska shkola, 1957.
A reliable desk dictionary. Appendixes for abbreviations and proper names. PG3891.P62

Slovnyk ukraïns'koi movy / [red. kolehiia: I. K. Bilodid (holova), ta inshi]. Kyiv : Nauk. Dumka, 1970–80. 11 v. **AC798**
The first general language academy dictionary for spoken and literary Ukrainian. Includes specialized terms from science, law, linguistics, journalism, etc. Extensive illustrations of usage from end of the

18th century to the present. Includes a long list of sources, with full bibliographical information. Vol. 11 includes a supplement.

PG3888.S6

Urdu

Ferozsons English to English and Urdu dictionary. New ed. Lahore : Ferozsons, [1973]. 1123 p.   **AC799**
   Cover title: English to English and Urdu dictionary.
   Combined edition of an English-to-English and English-to-Urdu dictionary containing "50,000 words, phrases, idioms, terms and expressions in English with their synonyms and equivalents in Urdu."—*Pref.*   PK1976.F4

Ferozsons Urdu-English dictionary : Urdu words, phrases & idioms with English meanings and synonyms. 4th ed. Lahore : Ferozsons, [1964]. 831 p.   **AC800**
   1st ed., 1960.
   Contains "30,000 words, phrases, idioms, maxims, proverbs, and technical words with their English meanings."—*Pref.* Intends to give English synonyms of Urdu words and phrases.   PK1976.F42

Platts, John Thompson. Dictionary of Urdū, classical Hindī and English. London : Oxford Univ. Pr., 1960. 1259 p.
                              AC801
   "Reprinted ... from sheets of the 5th (1930) impression."—*verso of title page.*
   First published 1884.   PK1986.P4

Uzbek

Waterson, Natalie. Uzbek-English dictionary. [Oxford] : Oxford Univ. Pr., 1980. 190 p.   **AC802**
   "This dictionary was planned primarily for English users but with Uzbek learners also in mind. ... The aim was to cover the essential vocabulary of modern spoken Uzbek."—*Introd.* Gives examples of usage as well as meanings of the words.   PL55.U84W3

Vietnamese

Nguyên, Dình-Hòa. Essential English-Vietnamese dictionary / by Dình-Hòa Nguyên with the assistance of Patricia Nguyen Thi My-Huong. Rutland, Vt. : C. E. Tuttle, c1983. 316 p.
                              AC803
   Title also in Vietnamese.
   Originally published as: *Hoà's essential English-Vietnamese dictionary* (Carbondale, Ill. : Asia Books, 1980).
   English terms with indication of parts of speech and the Vietnamese equivalents. Compiled with the needs of students of English-as-a-second-language in mind.   PL3476.N34

——————— Vietnamese-English student dictionary. Rev. and enl. ed. Saigon : Vietnamese-American Assoc., [1967] ; Carbondale : Southern Illinois Univ. Pr., [1971]. 675 p.
                              AC804
   1st ed., 1959, had title: *Vietnamese-English dictionary.*
   "Efforts have been made to glean abundant compounds from newspapers and periodicals, government releases and modern textbooks."—*Pref.*   PL4376.N355

Welsh

Evans, H. Meurig. Y geiriadur mawr : the complete Welsh-English, English-Welsh dictionary / H. Meurig Evans, W. O. Thomas ; [consulting ed.], Stephen J. Williams. 11th ed. Llandybie [Pembrokeshire] : C. Davies, 1983. 492 p., 367 p.
                              AC805
   1st ed., 1958. Frequently reprinted.
   Based on the compilers' *New Welsh dictionary* (1953), but greatly enlarged and improved. Includes technical terms along with a great many obsolete words.
   ———. *Welsh-English, English-Welsh dictionary* (N.Y. : Hippocrene Books, 1993. 611 p.). A concise version.   PB2191.E685

Geiriadur Prifysgol Cymru : a dictionary of the Welsh language / Golygydd: R.J. Thomas. Cyhoeddwyd ar ran Bwrdd Gwybodau Celtaidd, Prifysgol Cymru. Caerdydd : Gwasg Prifysgol Cymru, 1967–90. pts. 1–39.   **AC806**
   Contents: v. 1 (pts. 1–21), v. 2 (pts. 22–36), v. 3 (pts. 37–39); A–Obo.
   A scholarly historical Welsh-English dictionary that follows the same general pattern as *Oxford English dictionary.* Each entry gives etymology, definition in Welsh, English equivalent, and date of earliest use of the word. Most entries also give illustrative quotations drawn from an extensive bibliography of sources.   PB2191.G45

Spurrell, William. Geiriadur saesneg a chymraeg = Spurrell's English-Welsh dictionary / ed. by J. Bodvan Anwyl, aided by the late Sir Edward Anwyl ... [et al.]. 11th ed. rev. and enl. Carmarthen : W. Spurrell, 1937. 2 v. in 1.   **AC807**
   In two parts: pt. 1, English-Welsh; pt. 2, Welsh-English.
   Vol. 2 has special title page: Geiriadur cymraeg a saesneg = Spurrell's Welsh-English dictionary ... 13th ed. thoroughly rev.
                              PB2191.S75

Xhosa

Abraham, Roy Clive. Dictionary of the Hausa language. 2nd ed. London : Univ. of London Pr., [1962]. 992 p.   **AC808**
   1st ed., 1949.
   A comprehensive Xhosa-English dictionary intended for the speaker of English. Tones are marked by diacritics; part of speech is indicated. Includes illustrative phrases and sentences.   PL8233.A7

Fischer, A. English-Xhosa dictionary / A. Fischer ... [et al.]. Cape Town ; N.Y. : Oxford Univ. Pr., 1985. 738 p.   **AC809**
   For the English-speaking student learning Xhosa, this dictionary "will help make Xhosa accessible to anyone who wishes to learn the language, and encourage the Xhosa-speaking population to use the English language well."—*Pref.*   PL8795.4.F57

McLaren, James. A new concise Xhosa-English dictionary. First rev. by W. G. Bennie and put into standard orthography by J. R. R. Jolobe. [New ed. in standard orthography]. [Cape Town] : Longmans, [1963]. 194 p.   **AC810**
   Repr., 1975.
   First published under title *A concise Kaffir-English dictionary.*
   Aims to present "clear, concise, accurate definitions of the words" (*Pref.*) for those who wish to acquire or improve knowledge of the language.   PL8323.M35

Newman, Roxana Ma. An English-Hausa dictionary. New Haven, Conn. : Yale Univ. Pr., c1990. 327 p.   **AC811**
   Intended to be "a practical dictionary designed for the English-speaking user who wishes to acquire an active control of the modern vocabulary and structure of the Hausa language."—*User's guide.* In-

cludes a guide to pronunciation of Xhosa personal names, an index of Nigerian and international organizations, and a description of currencies in Nigeria and Niger. PL8233.N49

Yiddish

Groyser verterbukh fun der Yidisher shprakh = Great dictionary of the Yiddish language / editors in chief, Judah A. Joffe, Yudel Mark … [et al.]. N.Y. : Yiddish Dictionary Committee, 1961–80. v. 1–4 : ill. (In progress). **AC812**
Contents: v. 1–4, A–esrog.
Main title page and text in Yiddish.
A scholarly, inclusive Yiddish-Yiddish dictionary covering the language from the earliest extant records to the living Yiddish of today and in all countries where Yiddish was or is spoken. Includes scholarly and dialectic words, and slang. To be in 12 v. PJ5117.G7

Bilingual

Galvin, Herman. The Yiddish dictionary sourcebook : a transliterated guide to the Yiddish language / by Herman Galvin & Stan Tamarkin. Hoboken [N.J.] : Ktav, 1986. 317 p. **AC813**
For more than 8,000 entries, this introductory guide provides English transliterations of Yiddish, English equivalents to Yiddish expressions, phonetic renderings of Yiddish pronunciation, and Hebrew spellings of Yiddish words. PJ5117.G34

Harduf, David Mendel. Transliterated English-Yiddish dictionary = Transliterirter English-Yidisher verterbukh. Willowdale, Ont., Canada : Harduf Hebrew Books, c1989–90. 2 v. **AC814**
——. *Transliterated Yiddish-English dictionary = Transliterirter Yidish-Englisher verterbukh* (c1987. 185 p.).
——. *Harduf's transliterated Yiddish-English dictionary* (c1992. 270 p.).
The first two volumes, English-Yiddish, are arranged according to the English alphabet. The last two volumes, called "Third volume" and "Fourth volume," are arranged according to the Yiddish alphabet and the English alphabet, respectively. PJ5117.H25

Harkavy, Alexander. English-Yiddish [Yiddish-English] dictionary. 22nd ed. rev. and enl. N.Y. : Hebrew Pub. Co., [1953?]. 2 v. in 1. **AC815**
1st ed., 1898–1900?
Originally publ. as 2 v., English-Yiddish and Yiddish-English. Frequently reprinted. PJ5117.H5

Weinreich, Uriel. Modern English-Yiddish, Yiddish-English dictionary. N.Y. : YIVO Institute for Jewish Research, 1968. 789 p. **AC816**
Repr. : New York : Schocken Books, 1977.
"The Dictionary is designed in the main for persons who have a firm grounding in English and at least a rudimentary command of Yiddish. … Accordingly, the Yiddish rather than the English material has been phonetically and grammatically analyzed, and English glosses have been used, wherever appropriate, to specify semantic detail."—*Author's pref.* A scholarly and useful work. PJ5117.W4

Yoruba

Abraham, Roy Clive. Dictionary of modern Yoruba. London : Univ. of London Pr., [1958]. 776 p. : ill. **AC817**
A comprehensive Yoruba-English dictionary intended for speakers of English. Includes idioms, current phrases, proverbs, riddles, de-

scriptions of flora and fauna with illustrations. Historical, religious and ethnological background facts of the vocabulary are explained and extensively cross-referenced. PL8823.A2

Delano, Isaac O. A dictionary of Yoruba monosyllabic verbs. [Ile-Ife, Nigeria] : Institute of African Studies, Univ. of Ife, 1969. 2 v. **AC818**
A preliminary edition produced in 1965 was entitled *A modern dictionary of Yoruba usage.*
"Intended for those who already have a fair knowledge of Yoruba but need help in speaking it correctly and writing it with taste and accuracy."—*Introd.* PL8822.D45

Yugoslavian

See Serbo-Croatian.

Zulu

Doke, Clement Martyn. English-Zulu Zulu-English dictionary. 1st combined ed. Johannesburg : Witwatersrand Univ. Pr., 1990. 1 v. **AC819**
Combines the author's *Zulu-English dictionary* (1953) and his *English-Zulu dictionary* (1958).
"While recognizing the need to revise and update both volumes, a task that will be the work of several years, the publishers are convinced that these invaluable works must be kept in print."—*Pref. note.*

AD

Periodicals

BIBLIOGRAPHY

General Works

Benn's media. 141st ed. (1993)– . Tonbridge, Kent : Benn Business Information Services. Annual. **AD1**
Title varies: *Newspaper press directory,* 1846–1977; *Benn's press directory,* 1978; *Benn's media directory,* 1986–92.
1993– issued in three vols. : United Kingdom, Europe, and World. The Europe and World sections were formerly combined in an International volume, 1986–92. Each volume is available separately.
Vol. 1, United Kingdom, lists publishing houses, national newspapers, regional newspapers, consumer periodicals, business and professional periodicals, reference publications, broadcasting services, other advertising media, media organizations, and media services. Master index.
Vol. 2, Europe, contains country-by-country lists of newspapers (by place of publication); periodicals (by consumer or business and professional classification); useful contacts and media; inflight (arranged by parent company of airline) and international media; selected

international organizations and their official periodicals; and U.K. advertisement representatives for European media. Classified index to periodicals; master index.

Vol. 3, World, contains eight sections, the first four of which are divided by geographical region (the Americas, Africa, Asia, Australasia and the Pacific Islands) and by smaller geographical units within each region. For each country, major media organizations, embassies, newspapers, periodicals, and broadcast media are listed. Other sections list inflight and international media, U.K. advertisement representatives, and periodicals by subject classification. Periodical entries provide addresses, telephone, telex, and fax numbers, frequency, and circulation figures. Master index.   Z6956.E5M6

Books and periodicals online. v. 1 (1987)– . N.Y. : Library Alliance, 1987– . Annual, with 2 supplements.   **AD2**

Before 1993, had subtitle: *A guide to publication contents of business and legal databases.*

Publisher varies.

Issued in two cumulative issues for 1987. Annual, 1989– . None published for 1988. 1993 ed. issued without volume designation.

1993 ed. incorporates *Directory of periodicals online* (AD6), which was issued in subject-based "editions."

Lists more than 43,000 titles available full-text in more than 1,800 databases, both online and on CD-ROM. Divided into five sections, alphabetical listings are by: (1) publication title, (2) publisher name (includes address), (3) producer or vendor name (includes address), (4) database (including list of publications included), and (5) journal titles available in CD-ROM format. Discontinued titles listed if still available in databases.   Z7164.C81725

British Museum. Department of Printed Books. General catalogue of printed books. Photolithographic edition to 1955. London : Trustees of the British Museum, 1959–66. 263 v.   **AD3**

Vol. 184–186 list periodical publications, arranged alphabetically by place of publication. Vol. 185 is devoted to London. No title index. This new catalog includes 20th-century publications, but loses some of its value because of the lack of a title index. For full information, *see* AA103.   Z921.B87

——————— Catalogue of printed books : periodical publications. 2nd ed. London : [The Museum], 1899–1900. 2 v. (1716 col., 508 col.).   **AD4**

Repr. as v. 41 of the Edwards reprint of the British Museum *Catalogue of printed books.*

Arranged alphabetically by place of publication with an index of titles. Gives brief information about each title, i.e., title, dates, place, and note of changed titles. For the verification of titles this is an important general list for the period before 1900 because of the great number of periodicals included and the convenient double arrangement by place and by title.   Z6945.B86

Deutsche Forschungsgemeinschaft. Verzeichnis ausgewählter wissenschaftlicher Zeitschriften des Auslandes : VAZ. Wiesbaden : Franz Steiner, 1957. 749 p.   **AD5**

An attempt to present a critical selection of the most important titles of the world's periodical literature. Those considered fundamental for a given field are designated "A," those serving more specialized research purposes "B." Classed arrangement with alphabetical index by title.

——————. ——————. *Register* (Wiesbaden, 1957. 333 p.).

Directory of periodicals online. 1st–6th ed. Wash. : Federal Document Retrieval, 1985–1991. Annual.   **AD6**

Contents: v. 1, News, law & business; v. 2, Medicine & social science (planned but not published); v. 3, Science & technology.

Published in Toronto by Info Globe, 1990–1991.

Kept up to date by supplements.

An "alphabetical listing of periodicals available online in North American (English and French) and English language commercial databases worldwide ... [bringing] together in one comprehensive source current information about the availability of periodicals in online databases, in full-text, abstracted, or indexed formats."—*Introd.* Lists more

than 9,500 periodical titles represented in 1,070 databases. Indexes periodical titles by subject and database, and includes a chart showing the availability of titles online (coverage, update frequency, format, vendor).

Absorbed by *Books and periodicals online* (AD2).   Q1.A1D57

Directory of world Jewish press and publications. Jerusalem : The Directory, 1984.   **AD7**

1st ed. (Mar. 1984) only one published?

Aims to provide a "current, reliable and comprehensive worldwide listing" (*Introd.*) of some 900 bulletins, newsletters, newspapers, and journals. Based on responses to a questionnaire, the directory provides for each title the mailing address, editor, date founded, publisher, language, frequency, and circulation. Arranged by continent, then country, then alphabetically by title. U.S. publications are subdivided by state. Title index. Effectively supersedes Josef Fraenkel's *The Jewish press of the world* (AE6).

Duprat, Gabrielle. Bibliographie des répertoires nationaux de périodiques en cours / Gabrielle Duprat, Ksenia Liutova, and Marie-Louise Bossuat. London ; Paris : Fédération Internationale des Associations de Bibliothécaires and UNESCO, 1969. 141p. (Manuels bibliographiques de l'UNESCO, 12 ; IFLA/FIAB manuels internationaux, 3).   **AD8**

Identifies and describes on a country-by-country basis the directories and bibliographies of current periodicals available at the end of 1966. Now useful mainly as a research source concerning older materials.   AS4.U8A154

Gremling, Richard C. English language equivalent editions of foreign language serials. [2nd ed.]. Bound Brook, N.J. : Literature Service Associates, [1966]. Various paging.   **AD9**

1st ed., 1959.

Lists periodicals by original title and gives title and beginning date of cover-to-cover translations or other English-language equivalent editions. An English title index enables the user to relate the translated title to its foreign-language source.   Z1007.G7

Harvard University. Library. Periodical classes : classified listing by call number, alphabetical listing by title. Cambridge : Harvard Univ. Lib.; distr. by Harvard Univ. Pr., 1968. 758 p. (Widener Library shelflist, 15).   **AD10**

For a note on the Widener shelflist series, *see* AA115.

Nearly 26,000 titles.   Z6945.H34

Hebrew Union College—Jewish Institute of Religion. American Jewish Periodical Center. Jewish newspapers and periodicals on microfilm available at the American Jewish Periodical Center / ed. by Herbert C. Zafren. Augm. ed. Cincinnati : The Center, 1984. 158 p.   **AD11**

1st ed., 1957; Supplement, 1960.

Arranged by state and city, with some South American and Canadian titles. This edition does not include editors' names or characterization of editorial policy. English and Hebrew title indexes.

    Z6367.H48

International directory of little magazines & small presses. Ed. 9 (1973/74)– . Paradise, Calif. : Dustbooks, 1973– . Annual.   **AD12**

Supersedes *Directory of little magazines* (eds. 1–8, publ. 1965–72 with slightly varying titles) and continues its numbering.

Ed. by Len Fulton and others.

Entries for little magazines and for small presses appear in a single alphabetical listing. In addition to the expected directory information, listings usually include comments by the editors regarding policies and types of material published, and lists of recent contributors. State, country, and subject indexes.   Z6944.L5D5

Irregular serials and annuals : an international directory. 1st ed. (1967)–13th ed. (1987/88). N.Y. : Bowker, 1967–88.

    AD13

Irregular, 1967–72; biennial, with annual supplements, 1974/75–1980/81; annual, 1982–1988.

A companion to *Ulrich's international periodicals directory* (AD18); kept up to date between editions by *Ulrich's quarterly*. Followed the general format and classified arrangement of *Ulrich's* and attempted the same international coverage. The two publications were issued in alternate years. Provided publication information on serials issued annually, less frequently than once a year, or irregularly. Listed a wide range of foreign and domestic yearbooks, transactions, proceedings, etc., including the many "advances" and "progress in" series in the pure and applied sciences.

Content varied. Later editions included a list of cessations and suspensions since the prior edition, an index of serial publications of international organizations, and an index by ISSN numbers (in addition to the expected title index).   Z6941.I78

Kressel, Getzel. Guide to the Hebrew press. Zug, Switzerland : Inter Documentation, [1979]. 151 p.   **AD14**

Offers descriptive notes and publication information on nearly 140 periodicals and newspapers selected for inclusion in the publisher's "Jewish Studies Microform Project."   PN5650.K69

The serials directory : an international reference book. 1986– . Birmingham, Ala. : EBSCO, c1986– . Annual.
                                                            AD15

Updated twice yearly by *Serials directory update*.

Compiled from four sources: the international EBSCO Subscription Services database, the Library of Congress' CONSER file, the ISSN Register, and correspondence with publishers. The 8th ed. (1994) lists approximately 155,000 titles: periodicals classed by subject in three volumes, and newspapers—both domestic and foreign, listed by location—in one volume. Entries may contain up to 51 elements of information, including variant titles; dates of publication; ISSN; language; frequency; price; publisher and address; telephone; editor; indexing or abstracting services covering the title; circulation figures; and other data.

An alphabetical title index for the set is included in the newspaper volume, while a fifth volume contains nine separate indexes for ISSN, peer-review, CD-ROM availability, acceptance of advertising, controlled circulation, Copyright Clearance Center titles, new titles, etc.

•*The serials directory* [database] (Birmingham, Ala. : EBSCO, [1990]–). CD-ROM format, updated quarterly. Like its printed counterpart, contains current information, with full CONSER MARC records for each citation.   Z6941.S464

Singerman, Robert. Jewish serials of the world : a research bibliography of secondary sources. N.Y. : Greenwood, 1986. 377 p.   **AD16**

Aims to identify "pertinent source materials for writing a world history of the Jewish press."—*Introd*. General and multinational sections are followed by geographical sections listing studies of the Jewish press on a country-by-country basis. Author and subject indexes.
                                                            Z6366.S526

Sources of serials. 1st ed. (1977)–2nd ed. (1981). N.Y. : Bowker.   **AD17**

"International serials publishers and their titles, with copyright and copy availability information."—*t.p., 2nd ed. 1981*.

Based on a name authority file developed by Bowker in connection with publication of *Ulrich's international periodicals directory* (AD18), *Irregular serials and annuals* (AD13), and *Ulrich's quarterly*. The 2nd edition "includes 65,000 publishers and corporate authors arranged under 180 countries, listing 96,600 current serial titles they publish or sponsor."—*Pref*. Entry is by name of publisher or sponsoring body and includes address, co-publisher information if any, distributor information, and lists of titles of serials with indication of frequency and ISSN designation; copyright information is indicated by symbols. Publisher imprints and subsidiaries of publishing houses are interfiled as entries for publishers. Cross-references; index of publishers and corporate authors.   Z6941.S74

Ulrich's international periodicals directory. [1st] ed. (1932)– . N.Y. : Bowker, 1932– . Biennial.   **AD18**

Title varies: 1932–38, *Periodicals directory*; 1943–63, *Ulrich's periodicals directory*.

Frequency varies; beginning with 13th ed. (1969/70; publ. 1969), biennial.

With 27th ed. (1988), absorbed *Irregular serials and annuals* (AD13).

Kept up to date by *Ulrich's update* (AD19).

A very useful classified list of periodicals from many countries (more than 140,000 titles in the 32nd ed. [1993/94]). Coverage has varied in the different editions. Titles are grouped in subject classifications arranged alphabetically. Entries usually include, as pertinent: title, subtitle, sponsoring group, date of origin, frequency, price, editors, publisher, place of publication, annual and cumulative indexes. International Standard Serial Number (ISSN) and Dewey Decimal Classification number are now included with the entry, as is information about bibliographies, book reviews, film reviews, music and record reviews, illustrations, maps, charts, advertisements, statistics, circulation, etc. An especially useful feature is the indication of the indexing and abstracting services in which titles are included. Includes a list of periodicals that have ceased since the previous edition of the directory; index of titles and subjects. Recent editions include an Index to publications of international organizations.

With the 11th ed. (publ. 1965–66) "International" was added to the title to emphasize "the broad scope of its coverage which limits the selection of entries only to those in the Roman alphabet or with subtitles and abstracts in English."—*Pref., 11th ed*. Both the 11th and 12th eds. had separate volumes (publ. in alternate years) for science and technology and for the humanities and social sciences. In the 13th ed. the directory reverted to the earlier plan of a single alphabetical arrangement for all subject classes.

With the 28th ed. (1989/90), refereed titles are indicated by an italicized note at the end of the entry. The 29th ed. (1990/91) adds an index of refereed serials and an index of publications available in CD-ROM. Beginning with the 32nd ed. (1993/94), a volume listing newspapers has been added.

Earlier issues continue to be useful, both for the listing of periodicals which have ceased publication and for special lists included (e.g., "A list of clandestine periodicals of World War II", by Adrienne Florence Muzzy, in the 5th ed. [1947]).

•Available in machine-readable form as: *Ulrich's plus* [database] (N.Y. : Bowker). Incorporates materials from both *Ulrich's international periodicals directory* and *Ulrich's update*. Searchable fields include title, publisher, subject, abstracting/indexing services. Available in CD-ROM, updated quarterly, and online as *Ulrich's international periodicals directory*, updated monthly.   Z6941.U5

Ulrich's update. v. 1, no. 1 (Sept. 1988)– . N.Y. : Bowker, [c1988]– . Publ. in Feb., May, Nov.   **AD19**

Supersedes earlier versions: 1972–76, *Bowker serials bibliography supplement*; Spring 1977–Sept. 1985, *Ulrich's quarterly*; Dec. 1985–1987, *The Bowker international serials database update*.

Provides a record of new serial titles, title changes, and cessations between issues of *Ulrich's international periodicals directory* (AD18). Includes title and subject indexes.

•Available in machine-readable form as *Ulrich's plus* [database] (N.Y. : Bowker). Incorporates materials from both *Ulrich's international periodicals directory* and *Ulrich's update*. Available in CD-ROM, updated quarterly, and online as *Ulrich's international periodicals directory*, updated monthly.

UMI article clearinghouse catalog. Ann Arbor, Mich. : Univ. Microfilms International, [1984]– .   **AD20**

Title varies; early issues called UMI article clearinghouse.

The 1991 edition provides information on pricing, availability and coverage of more than 12,000 periodicals "for which the Clearinghouse has copy permission from the publisher" (*p. 9*) as well as details regarding use of UMI's document delivery service, its policies on pricing and payment. Titles of publications available are listed alphabetically. Not published in 1992.

Union of International Associations. Directory of periodicals published by international organizations = Répertoire des périodiques publiés par les organisations internationales. 3rd ed. Brussels : [The Union], [1969]. 240p.   **AD21**

1st ed. 1953.
English and French.
"The present edition describes 1734 periodicals: 1475 published by 1071 non-governmental organizations and 259 published by 125 intergovernmental organizations."—*Introd.* AS8.U38

Abbreviations

Leistner, Otto. ITA : internationale Titelabkürzungen von Zeitschriften, Zeitungen, wichtigen Handbüchern, Wörterbüchern, Gesetzen usw. = International title abbreviations of periodicals, newspapers, important handbooks, dictionaries, laws, etc. 4. erw. Aufl. Osnabrück : Biblio Verlag, 1990. 2 v. (1367 p.). **AD22**
1st ed. 1967–70; 3rd ed., 1981.
A very useful guide to the full form of thousands of abbreviations for periodicals, newspapers, and related works published throughout the world and in all subject fields. Z6945.A2L4

Periodical title abbreviations. [1st ed.]– . Detroit : Gale, 1969– . Irregular. **AD23**
Subtitle: International coverage of periodical abbreviations in science, the social sciences, the humanities, law, medicine, religion, library science, engineering, education, business, art, and many other fields.
8th ed., 1992.
Contents: v. 1, Periodicial title abbreviations: by abbreviation; v. 2, Periodical title abbreviations: by title.
Kept up to date since the 3rd ed. by an annual supplement (also called v. 3): *New periodical title abbreviations.*
Vol. 1 of the 8th ed. includes more than 130,000 entries. Z6945.A2P47

Rust, Werner. Verzeichnis von unklaren Titelkürzungen deutscher und ausländischer Zeitschriften. Leipzig : Harrassowitz, 1927. 142 p. **AD24**
A world list of initial abbreviations, arranged alphabetically. Gives full name of periodical and alternate abbreviation. Z6945.A2R

Translations

Journals in translation. 5th ed. Boston Spa, U.K. : British Library Document Supply Centre ; Delft, The Netherlands : International Translations Centre, c1991. 286 p. **AD25**
Complemented by *World translations index* (EA63).
1st ed., 1976, publ. by the British Library Lending Division; the 1978 rev. ed. publ. jointly by the BLLD and the International Translations Centre, replaced both the earlier edition and the Centre's *Translations journals* (1970–1974/75); 4th ed., 1988.
Provides bibliographic information on cover-to-cover translation journals and those offering selected articles in translation; most are translations into English. Journals published in two or more languages simultaneously are not included. Title listing with keyword index. Indicates those titles held by the BLLD and sources (such as NTIS) from which copies may be ordered. Z6944.T7J68

Guides for authors

Birkos, Alexander S. Academic writer's guide to periodicals / Alexander S. Birkos and Lewis A. Tambs. [Kent, Ohio] : Kent State Univ. Pr., [1971–75]. 3 v. **AD26**
Publisher varies; v. 3 publ. by Libraries Unlimited, 1975.
Contents: v. 1, Latin American studies; v. 2, East European and Slavic studies; v. 3, African and black American studies.

Each volume is intended as a guide for academic authors desiring to place an article for journal publication. Lists and provides directory information on periodicals and monograph series that publish at least part of their articles in English or accept manuscripts in English.

Directory of publishing opportunities in journals and periodicals. 5th ed. Chicago : Marquis Academic Media, 1981. 844 p. **AD27**
1st ed., 1971; 4th ed., 1979. Title varies.
This edition "includes more than 3,900 specialized and professional journals, over 450 of which appear for the first time with this edition."—*Pref.* Entries are arranged alphabetically within 73 subject fields. Gives address, beginning date, changes of title, subscription data, editorial description, and information for submitting manuscripts for each journal. Indexes of (1) periodicals; (2) subjects; (3) sponsoring organizations; (4) editorial staff. Z6944.S3D57

By region

North America

United States

Bibliography and history

American humor magazines and comic periodicals / ed. by David E.E. Sloane. N.Y. : Greenwood, 1987. 648 p. **AD28**
"Seeks to provide a comprehensive survey of its field, assessing over two hundred years of publication in this genre through examination of the individual magazines."—*Pref.* Pt. 1 describes more than 100 titles, listed alphabetically. Brief bibliographies, detailed publication histories, and selected locations follow each article. Pt. 2 has 400 briefer entries, again arranged alphabetically by title. Pt. 3 contains two lists: unexamined titles compiled from *Catalog of copyright entries: serials and periodicals* and a list of other unexamined titles. Pt. 4 contains essays on college humor magazines, scholarly humor magazines, and humor in American almanacs. Name and title index. PN4880.A46

American mass-market magazines / ed. by Alan Nourie and Barbara Nourie. N.Y. : Greenwood, 1990. 611 p. **AD29**
Offers profiles, arranged alphabetically by title, of 106 "of the most significant mass-market or general U.S. periodicals... for the most part originating in the late nineteenth and twentieth centuries."—*Introd.* A bibliography, indexes, selected locations, and publication history follow each entry. Also includes a selected bibliography of books and articles discussing American magazines in general. Name and title index. PN4877.A48

Children's periodicals of the United States / ed. by R. Gordon Kelly. Westport, Conn. : Greenwood, 1984. 591 p. **AD30**
Intends "to provide brief, authoritative descriptions of a broad sample of American periodicals for children" (*Pref.*) and thereby supplement the brief accounts found in Frank Luther Mott's *History of American magazines* (AD40). Signed articles on individual magazines discuss history and content, and are followed by notes on sources of additional information and details of publication history. Appendixes: selected bibliography of American children's periodicals; chronological and geographical listings of magazines. Indexed. PN4878.C48

Edgar, Neal L. A history and bibliography of American magazines, 1810–1820. Metuchen, N.J. : Scarecrow, 1975. 379 p. **AD31**
The major portion of the work is an annotated bibliography of American magazines (p. 85–257), giving very full information about

more than 200 periodicals of the period. Appendixes include a list of exclusions, a chronological list, a register of printers, and a selected bibliography. Indexed.   PN4877.E3

The ethnic press in the United States : a historical analysis and handbook / ed. by Sally M. Miller. N.Y. : Greenwood, 1987. 437 p.   **AD32**

Offers ten- to fifteen-page signed articles, each with a brief bibliography, on the press of 28 ethnic groups. Name and title index.   PN4882.E84

Goldwater, Walter. Radical periodicals in America, 1890–1950 : a bibliography with brief notes ; with a genealogical chart and a concise lexicon of the parties and groups which issued them. 3rd ed. N.Y. : University Place Book Shop, 1977. 56 p.   **AD33**

1st ed., 1964, and rev. ed., 1966, published by Yale Univ. Library.

A list of titles with information on volumes and dates, and with brief annotations.   Z7164.S67G57

Guide to special issues and indexes of periodicals / ed. by Miriam Uhlan and Doris B. Katz. 4th ed. Wash. : Special Libraries Association, c1994. 240 p.   **AD34**

1st ed., 1962; 3rd ed., 1985.

Covers more than 1,700 U.S. and Canadian periodicals which publish special issues (directories, buyers' guides, convention issues, statistical outlooks or reviews, and other features or supplementary issues appearing on a continual, annual or other basis). Arranged alphabetically by title. Each entry contains a list of special issues published by the periodical, giving the date and any special pricing information. Most titles listed are in the areas of business, commerce, and industry. Subject index.   Z7164.C81G85

Hoffman, Frederick John. The little magazine : a history and a bibliography / Frederick John Hoffman, Charles Allen, Carolyn F. Ulrich. Princeton, N.J. : Princeton Univ. Pr., 1946. 440 p. : ill.   **AD35**

"A little magazine is a magazine designed to print artistic work which for reasons of commercial expediency is not acceptable to the money-minded periodicals or presses."—*Introd.*

In two sections: (1) History, p. 1–230; (2) Bibliography, p. 233–398, followed by a detailed index to titles, change of titles, editors, contributors, etc. The history gives a general survey of little magazines from about 1910, with discussion of the more important ones, many of which included the first works of writers who later achieved prominence, and thus have a definite place in the literary history of the period. The annotated bibliography gives, in chronological order, detailed information about a long, selected list of these little magazines which will be of particular use to libraries in determining titles, number of issues published, outstanding contributors, etc.

A "Second printing" of the work (Princeton, 1947. 450 p.) incorporates a few corrections, but changes "consist primarily of additional titles of magazines either started since May, 1945, or discovered by the authors since that date."—*p.ix.* The index was also revised to reflect the changes in this printing.   PN4836.H6

Hoornstra, Jean. American periodicals, 1741–1900 : an index to the microfilm collections: American periodicals, 18th century; American periodicals, 1800–1850; American periodicals, 1850–1900, Civil War and Reconstruction / Jean Hoornstra, Trudy Heath. Ann Arbor, Mich. : Univ. Microfilms International, 1979. 341 p.   **AD36**

Offers cumulative title, editor, subject and reel number indexes to the three microfilm collections mentioned in the subtitle. The title index (with cross-references for title changes, etc.) provides full bibliographic information and notes on character and content. The subject index lists relevant periodical titles under the Library of Congress subject headings assigned during cataloging.   Z6951.H65

Humphreys, Nancy K. American women's magazines : an annotated historical guide. N.Y. : Garland, 1989. 303 p. (Garland reference library of the humanities, vol. 789).   **AD37**

For annotation, *see* CC522.   Z6944.W6H85

Lewis, Benjamin Morgan. A history and bibliography of American magazines, 1800–1810. Ann Arbor, Mich. : Univ. Microfilms, [1956]. 333 *l.*   **AD38**

Dissertation, Univ. of Mich., 1955.

"The primary goal of this study is a bibliographical investigation of all known magazines published in the United States between January 1, 1800 and December 31, 1809 .... The basic list of magazines, one hundred and twenty-five in all, is found in the University Microfilms' *American Periodical Series, 1800–1825.*"—*Author's abstract.* Bibliography beginning on p. 99 is alphabetical by title. Appendixes include a chronological list, a register of editors, printers, etc., and an index to illustrations listed by magazine title.

The little magazine in America : a modern documentary history / ed. by Elliott Anderson and Mary Kinzie. [Yonkers, N.Y.] : Pushcart, [1978]. 770 p. : ill.   **AD39**

Intended as a companion to *The little magazine* (AD35). "Rather than a historical overview, or even a collaboration between historians," this volume offers "a large collection of essay-memoirs by prominent and representative little magazine editors, publishers, and contributors, including a generous selection of photo-documents and an annotated bibliography of 84 important magazines of the period."—*Pref.* Indexed.   PN4878.3.L5

Mott, Frank Luther. A history of American magazines. Cambridge : Harvard Univ. Pr., 1938–68. 5 v. : ill.   **AD40**

Contents: v. 1, 1741–1850; v. 2, 1850–65; v. 3, 1865–85; v. 4, 1885–1905; v. 5, Sketches of 21 magazines, 1905–30, with a cumulative index to the 5 v.

A comprehensive history with many bibliographical footnotes throughout and a chronological list of the magazines at the end of v. 1–3. Because of these and the detailed indexes, the publication is of great value in reference work.

Left unfinished at the author's death, v. 5 appeared without the projected general discussion of magazine publication for the period, which Mott had proposed to include. Nonetheless, the sketches included in the final volume and the overall index make a valuable addition to the set.   PN4877.M63

Paine, Fred K. Magazines : a bibliography for their analysis with annotations and study guide / by Fred K. Paine and Nancy E. Paine. Metuchen, N.J. : Scarecrow, 1987. 690 p.   **AD41**

Intended as a supplement to J.H. Schacht's *Bibliography for the study of magazines* (Urbana : College of Communications, Univ. of Illinois, 1979), "this bibliography lists more than 2,200 magazine, newspaper and journal articles, books, and dissertations written about [American] magazines" (*Pref.*), 1979–86. Arranged by broad topic, then alphabetically by author. Subject and magazine title index. Lacks an author index.   Z6940.P24

Periodical directories and bibliographies / Gary C. Tarbert, ed. Detroit : Gale, c1987. 195 p.   **AD42**

Subtitle: An annotated guide to approximately 350 directories, bibliographies, and other sources of information about English-language periodicals, from 1850 to the present, including newspapers, journals, magazines, newsletters, yearbooks, and other serial publications.

" ... identifies approximately 350 directories, bibliographies, and other publications that furnish facts about English-language periodicals, from 1850 to the present .... Emphasis is on U.S. and Canadian sources with some representation of foreign materials."—*Introd.* Arranged alphabetically by title; subject index.   Z6941.P47

Regional interest magazines of the United States / ed. by Sam G. Riley and Gary W. Selnow. N.Y. : Greenwood, 1991. 418 p.   **AD43**

Provides information about American magazines with a geographic emphasis. "Our focus is on magazines that direct their attention to a particular city or region and that reach a fairly general consumer audience, providing their readers with entertainment and information".—*Introd.* Entries are arranged alphabetically by title. Appendixes provide chronological and geographical listings. Most titles listed began publication after 1900.   Z6944.R44R44 1990

Riley, Sam G. Magazines of the American South. N.Y. : Greenwood, 1986. 346 p.   **AD44**

Offers profiles, arranged alphabetically by title, of some 85 general interest magazines published in the South between 1764 and 1982. Each article discusses the history and contents of the journal, and includes a bibliography of secondary sources and a detailed publishing history. Name and title index.   PN4893.R54

Skidmore, Gail. From radical left to extreme right : a bibliography of current periodicals of protest, controversy, advocacy, or dissent, with dispassionate content-summaries to guide librarians and other educators. 3rd ed., completely rev. / by Gail Skidmore and Theodore Jurgen Spahn. Metuchen, N.J. : Scarecrow, 1987. 491 p.   **AD45**

1st ed., 1967.

Arranged by broad subject with a geographical index; an index of titles, editors, and publishers; and a subject index.

§ Does not fully supersede the 2nd ed., by Robert H. Muller, Theodore Jurgen Spahn, and Janet M. Spahn (Ann Arbor, Mich. : Campus Publishers ; Metuchen, N.J. : Scarecrow, 1970–76. 3 v.), which contains many titles omitted from the 3rd ed. The 2nd ed. is greatly expanded, v. 3 being a supplement. Periodicals are grouped under such headings as: Radical left, Marxist-Socialist left, Underground, Anarchist, Libertarian, Utopian, Liberal, Civil rights, Sex, Peace, Conservative, Anti-communist. In addition to directory information, a summary of content and editorial policy (based on examination of at least three issues) is given for each title. Vol. 3 includes a title index for the set.   Z7165.U5S473

University of Wisconsin-Madison. Libraries. Catalog of little magazines : a collection in the Rare Book Room, Memorial Library, University of Wisconsin-Madison / comp. and ed. by Robert F. Roeming. [Madison] : Univ. of Wisconsin Pr. ; Ann Arbor, Mich. : distrib. on demand by Univ. Microfilm International, 1979. 137 p.   **AD46**

A catalog of "one of the largest and most complete collections of little magazines in the United States" (*Foreword*)—about 3,650 titles. Arrangement is by title with cross-references from variant titles. Addenda list of titles added Nov. 1977–June 1979.   Z6944.L5W57

Varona, Esperanza Bravo de. Cuban exile periodicals at the University of Miami Library : an annotated bibliography. Madison : Secretariat, Seminar on the Acquisition of Latin American Library Materials, Memorial Library, Univ. of Wisconsin-Madison, c1987. 203 p. (Seminar on the Acquisition of Latin American Library Materials bibliography and reference series, 19).   **AD47**

Lists 665 alphabetically arranged entries giving for each a complete bibliographic citation and notes on frequency, language, and editors. Brief annotations accompany many entries. List of directors (i.e., publishers); chronological index; geographic index subdivided into city and country; subject index. The preface provides a brief history of publishing among Cuban émigrés.   Z1361.C85D4

White, Cynthia Leslie. Women's magazines, 1693–1968. London : Michael Joseph, [1970]. 348 p.   **AD48**

Primarily a survey of the history, growth, and character of British and American women's magazines, but includes useful lists of women's magazines and a bibliography.

§ *Women's periodicals and newspapers from the 18th century to 1981*, ed. by James P. Danky, comp. by Maureen E. Hady and others in association with the State Historical Society of Wisconsin (Boston : G.K. Hall, 1982. 376 p.), is a union list of holdings of libraries in Madison, Wis.   PN5124.W6W5

Directories

Directory of literary magazines / prep. in cooperation with the Council of Literary Magazines and Presses. 1984– . Mt. Kisco, N.Y. : Moyer Bell, c1984– . Annual.   **AD49**

Former title: *CCLM literary magazine directory* (1983). Publisher varies; name of issuing agency varies (Coordinating Council of Literary Magazines).

Includes little magazines. The 1992/93 edition lists more than 500 magazines alphabetically by title. Information provided includes editor, address, description, beginning publication date, price, and advertising rates.   Z6513.C37

Encyclopedia of associations. Association periodicals. Detroit : Gale, c1987.   **AD50**

Contents: v. 1, Business, finance, industry, and trade; v. 2, Science, medicine, and technology; v.3, Social sciences, education, and humanities.

A listing of more than "12,000 periodical publications of national nonprofit membership organizations in the United States ... arranged alphabetically by assigned primary subject keywords."—*Introd.* Each volume has its own association index and title and keyword index.   Z5055.U4E53

Gale directory of publications and broadcast media. 122nd ed. (1990)– . Detroit : Gale, c1990– . Annual.   **AD51**

For annotation, *see* AE23.   Z6951.A97

Ireland, Sandra L. Jones. Ethnic periodicals in contemporary America : an annotated guide. N.Y. : Greenwood, 1990. 222 p. (Bibliographies and indexes in ethnic studies, no. 3).   **AD52**

A list, alphabetical by ethnic group, of 234 current magazines, newspapers, and newsletters "published for and about an audience identified as interested in the social, cultural, religious, economic, education, geographic and political information associated with people who align themselves with a specific ethnic group."—*p. xvii.* Includes detailed information on publication requirements. Title, subject, and editor index.   Z6953.5.A1I74

MIMP, magazine industry market place : the directory of American periodical publishing. v. 1 (1980)–8 (1987). N.Y. : Bowker, [1979–87]. Annual.   **AD53**

Provided for the magazine industry the type of directory information which the *Literary market place* (AA282) supplies for the book publishing world. The first part of the work is an alphabetical title listing of periodical publications with full directory information. Periodical titles are then classified by type of publication (e.g., Business, Consumer, Farm, Literary, News, Professional, Religious) and again by subject matter (e.g., Advertising, Agriculture, Art, Current events, Education, Law, Military, Poetry, Women). There are numerous additional lists of specialized publishers (micropublishers, newsletters and reference books for the trade, etc.), magazine organizations and associations, agents and agencies, special services (consultants, market research, translators, photographers, mailing lists, subscription agents, distributors, publication printers, back-date periodical dealers). A Names and numbers section on colored paper completes the volume.   Z475.M18

Murphy, Dennis D. Directory of conservative and libertarian serials, publishers, and freelance markets. 2nd ed. [Tucson : The Author], 1979. 64 p.   **AD54**

1st ed., 1977.

Gives directory information and policies of "organizations which publish or distribute, and some bookstores and book clubs which specialize in libertarian or conservative works."—*Introd.* Entries for serials predominate.   Z475.M87

The national directory of magazines. 1988– . N.Y. : Oxbridge Communications, c1988– . Annual.   **AD55**

Claims to be the "largest single source of information available on the U.S. & Canadian magazine industry."—*Pref.* Includes addresses, circulation figures, and advertising rates. Arranged by subject with a title index.   Z6941.N28

The standard periodical directory. 1st ed. (1964/65)– . N.Y. : Oxbridge Communications. Annual.   **AD56**

Subtitle, 16th ed. (1993): The largest authoritative guide to United States & Canadian periodicals ... information on more than 75,000 publications.

Frequency varies: biennial, 1977–87; annual since 1989.

Alphabetical subject arrangement with index of titles and subjects. Information given includes name and address of publisher, editorial content and scope, year founded, frequency, subscription rate, total circulation, advertising rate, etc.   Z6951.S78

Working press of the nation. Ed. 1 (1947)– . Chicago : National Research Bureau, [1945]– .   **AD57**

First issue was entitled: *Working press of New York City.*

Frequency varies: irregular, 1947–57; annual, 1959– . Publisher and place of publication vary.

Content has varied; recently issued in 5 v. per year. Contents of the 1993 ed.: v. 1, Newspaper directory (listing daily and weekly newspapers of the United States, feature syndicates, news and photo services, with index of editorial personnel by subject, index of Sunday supplements, etc.); v. 2, Magazine directory (listing some 5,000 magazines grouped by subject area, with title index); v. 3, TV and radio directory (listing about 9,500 radio and television stations, plus some 25,700 local programs by subject); v. 4, Feature writer and photographer directory (giving home addresses and fields of interest of about 2,000 writers and photographers); v. 5, Internal publications directory (not included in 1995 ed.). Vol. 5 gives information on publications of more than 2,600 U.S. companies, government agencies, etc.; for the 1952–74 period this information appeared in the *Gebbie Press house directory.*   Z6951.W6

Wynar, Lubomyr Roman. Guide to the American ethnic press : Slavic and East European newspapers and periodicals. Kent, Ohio : Center for the Study of Ethnic Publications, School of Library Science, Kent State Univ., 1986. 280 p.   **AD58**

An "annotated encyclopedic directory to current Slavic and East European newspapers and periodicals published in the United States."—*Pref.* Based on answers to a questionnaire; lists some 580 titles alphabetically by ethnic group. Includes address, frequency, circulation, and price. Geographic and title indexes.   Z6953.5.S62W96

Canada

Beaulieu, André. Les journaux de Québec de 1764 à 1964. Québec : Presses de l'Université Laval ; Paris : A. Colin, 1965. 329 p. (Les cahiers de l'Institut d'Histoire, 6).   **AD59**

Lists, by place of publication, magazines and newspapers published in the province of Quebec. Gives beginning and closing dates, frequency, founder when known, locations in Quebec libraries if any, and, often, notes on the publication's history. Chronological and alphabetical title indexes.   Z6954.A21Q33

Canadian serials directory = Répertoire des publications sériées canadiennes / ed. by Gordon Ripley. 3rd ed. Toronto : Reference Pr., 1987. 396 p.   **AD60**

1st ed., 1972; 2nd ed., 1977.

Text in English and French.

An alphabetical listing of serials (magazines, annuals, yearbooks, proceedings and transactions of societies, special interest newspapers) published in Canada. Subject index and index of publishers and sponsoring bodies. Indicates type of publication, frequency, format, price, circulation, etc.   Z6954.C2C258

Mexico

Directorio de publicaciones periódicas mexicanas : 1981 / Universidad de Guanajuato, Dirección General de Bibliotecas, Departmento de Investigaciones Bibliotecológicas. Guanajuato, Gto. : El Departamento, c1982. 200 p.   **AD61**

A title listing with subject and geographic indexes. Gives beginning date, address, frequency, subscription price, and circulation.

Mendoza-López, Margarita. Catálogo de publicaciones periódicas mexicanas. México, 1959. 262 p.   **AD62**

At head of title: Centro Mexicano de Escritores.

Listing is by place of publication, then alphabetical by title. Detailed directory information is given, with auxiliary lists of titles for which full information was not available.   Z6954.M6M4

Orozco Tenorio, José. Las publicaciones periódicas mexicanas. México : Instituto Tecnológico Autónomo de México, 1986. 190 p.   **AD63**

An alphabetical listing of 546 currently published Mexican journals. Includes address, price, frequency, and circulation. Subject and variant title indexes. A section of statistical tables provides data on subscription costs, geographical distribution of titles, periodicity, etc.   PN4968.O769

Latin America

Committee on Latin America. Literature with language, art and music / ed. by L. Hallewell. London : Committee on Latin America, 1977. 253 p. (Latin American serials, v. 3).   **AD64**

A listing by country of publication of Latin American periodicals on linguistics, literature, art and music held in British libraries.   Z5961.L3C65

Levi, Nadia. Guía de publicaciones periódicas de universidades latinoamericanas. México : Universidad Nacional Autónoma de México, 1967. 406 p.   **AD65**

At head of title: Unión de Universidades de América Latina. Hemeroteca Universitaria Latinoamericana.

A title listing within country divisions is followed by a classified index by faculty or subject field and a university index.   Z6944.S3L4

Liste mondiale des périodiques spécialisés dans les sciences sociales = World list of social science periodicals. 1st ed. (1953)– . [Paris] : UNESCO, 1953– . Irregular.   **AD66**

Provides directory and brief descriptive information on nearly 400 periodicals devoted to Latin America (regardless of where published). For complete information, *see* CA18.   Z7163.L523

Pan American Union. Repertorio de publicaciones periódicas actuales latinoamericanas = Directory of current Latin American periodicals = Répertoire des périodiques en cours publiés en Amerique latine. [Paris] : UNESCO, [1958]. 266 p. (Unesco bibliographical handbooks, [8]).   **AD67**

Lists 3,375 titles, arranged by Universal Decimal Classification, with geographical index and subject indexes in Spanish, English, and French. No title index.   Z6954.S8P3

Zimmerman, Irene. A guide to current Latin American periodicals : humanities and social sciences. Gainesville, Fla. : Kallman Publ. Co., 1961. 357 p.   **AD68**

"Primarily an annotated, evaluative bibliography ..."—*Introd.* Lists 668 active periodicals and 117 on a "casualty list." Includes periodicals published in South and Central America, Mexico, and the West Indies, together with those published in the U.S. by Latin Americans and those dealing with Latin-American languages and literatures, etc.

Main arrangement is alphabetical by country, followed by a classified section and a chronological listing. The annotations, given in the first section, are full in descriptive and evaluative information. The "casualty list" records those periodicals from which the author had not been able to elicit recent information.   Z6954.S8Z5

South America

Universidad Nacional de La Plata. Biblioteca. Catálogo de periódicos sudamericanos existentes en la Biblioteca Pública de la Universidad (1791–1861). La Plata : [Imprenta López], 1934. 231 p.   **AD69**

    Detailed bibliographical information concerning Latin American periodicals published 1791–1861.   Z6954.A6L25

Argentina

Ferreira Sobral, Eduardo F. Publicaciones periódicas argentinas, 1781–1969. Buenos Aires : Ministerio de Agricultura y Ganadería de la Nación, 1971. v. 1.   **AD70**

    Vol. 2 never published?

    An alphabetical list of Argentinian periodicals for the period indicated.

Publicaciones periódicas argentinas : registradas para el sistema internacional de datos sobre publicaciones seriadas (ISDS). Buenos Aires : Centro Argentino de Información Cientifica y Tecnológica del CONICET, 1981. 217 p.   **AD71**

    Lists some 1,457 Argentinian periodicals registered for the ISDS by late 1980, a considerable number of which are no longer current. Listing is by ISSN, with a title index. A 58-p. supplement was published 1983.   Z6954.A6P93

Brazil

Guia de publicações seriadas brasileiras / MCT-Ministério da Ciência e Tecnologia, CNPq-Conselho Nacional de Desenvolvimento Científico e Tecnológico, IBICT-Instituto Brasileiro de Informação em Ciência e Tecnologia. Brasília : IBICT, 1987. 671 p.   **AD72**

    Issued by Instituto Brasileira de Bibliografía e Documentação as : *Periódicos brasileiros de cultura* (Rio de Janeiro, 1968).

    Supersedes *Periódicos brasileiros de ciência e technologia* (Rio de Janeiro : IBICT, [1977]); rev. ed. of *ISSN, publicações periódicas brasileiras* (Brasília : DTI, Departamento de Tratamento da Informaçao, 1983).

    Lists more than 1,500 currently published titles by broad subject category. Subject, title, and ISSN indexes. Includes an alphabetical list of publishers and their addresses.   Z6954.B8G84

Colombia

Bogotá. Biblioteca Nacional. Catálogo de todos los periódicos que existen desde su fundación hasta el año de 1935, inclusive. Edición oficial. Bogotá : El Gráfico, 1936. 2 v.   **AD73**

    Contents: t. 1, Periódicos nacionales, A–P; t. 2, Periódicos nacionales, R–Z. Periódicos extranjeros, A–Z.

    A listing of the issues of periodicals in the National Library. Does not give bibliographical information beyond title, place of publication, and numbers and dates of issues held.   Z6954.C7B6

Caribbean and Islands of the Western Atlantic

Cuba

Directorio de revistas y periódicos de Cuba. 1942–1968. Gainesville, Fla. : [Dr. Fermin Peraza], 1963–68. Annual.   **AD74**

    Ed., Fermín Peraza y Sarausa.

    Publ. 1942–53, La Habana : Anuario Bibliográfico Cubano.

    Publication suspended, 1954–62.

    The 1965 edition lists more than 200 titles of periodicals published in Cuba, with a special section of more than 100 titles of Cuban periodicals published outside Cuba.   Z6954.C9D5

University of Pittsburgh. University Libraries. Cuban periodicals in the University of Pittsburgh libraries / by Eduardo Lozano. 5th ed. Pittsburgh : Univ. of Pittsburgh Libraries, Center for Latin American Studies, 1991. 172 p.   **AD75**

    1st ed., 1971; 4th ed., 1985.

    An alphabetical listing of 495 titles currently received or inactive. "Although the list includes many periodicals, some serials such as annual reports, yearbooks, and statistical serials have been included."— *Preface.* Entries include title or corporate author, source of publication, place of publication, beginning and ending dates of publication, frequency, and notes. Subject index.   Z6954.C9P5

Europe (by region)

Dietzel, Thomas. Deutsche literarische Zeitschriften, 1880–1945 : ein Repertorium / Thomas Dietzel, Hans-Otto Hügel ; hrsg. vom Deutschen Literaturarchiv, Marbach am Neckar. München ; N.Y. : K.G. Saur, 1988. 5 v.   **AD76**

    Continues Alfred Estermann's *Die deutschen Literatur-Zeitschriften, 1850–1880* (AD77); does not list titles covered in that set.

    The 3,341 titles, listed alphabetically, include literary, cultural, and general interest journals published in German throughout Europe. Information for each title includes dates, editors, publication history, detailed collation, selected locations, and in many cases, names of the major contributors. Selected bibliographies of secondary sources are provided for many titles. Indexed by editor, by contributor, by publisher, by place of publication, and by type of publication (literary, political, women, film, etc.).   Z2233.D37

Estermann, Alfred Adolph. Die deutschen Literatur-Zeitschriften, 1850–1880 : Bibliographien, Programme. München : K.G. Saur, c1988–1989. 5 v.   **AD77**

    Continues the author's *Die deutschen Literatur-Zeitschriften, 1815–1850* (Nendeln : KTO Press, 1977–1981. 10 v.), and is continued by Thomas Dietzel's *Deutsche literarische Zeitschriften, 1880–1945* (AD76).

    An alphabetical listing of nearly 3,000 literary, cultural, and general interest journals published in German throughout Europe. Each entry includes the title, any variant titles, dates and places of publication, selected locations and call numbers in German and other European libraries, and a detailed collation. In many cases introductions or prospectuses are reprinted. Separate indexes for editors, places of publication, and publishers.   Z2225.E87

Schatoff, Michael. Half a century of Russian serials, 1917–1968 : cumulative index of serials published outside the USSR / comp. by Michael Schatoff ; ed. by N. A. Hale. N.Y. : Russian Book Chamber Abroad, 1970–72. 4 v. (697 p.).   **AD78**

    Contents: pts. 1–3, 1917–1956, A–Z; pt. 4, 1957–1968, A–Z.

    Pt. 1 (1917–56, A–M) appeared in a 2nd ed., rev., 1972.

Lists newspapers and magazines published in Russian outside the USSR. Indicates place and dates of publication, and editor if known.
Z6956.R9S35

Sgard, Jean. Bibliographie de la presse classique, 1600–1789. Genève : Slatkine, 1984. 226 p. : ill.   **AD79**
An alphabetic listing of 1,138 French-language general interest titles published throughout Europe. Information provided includes titles, with variants and subtitles, publication dates, frequency, and editors and founders. Locations and call numbers in major French libraries are also given. Chronological and name indexes.   Z6956.F8S48

Scandinavia

Media Scandinavia. [Ed. 1]– . København : Danske Reklamebureauers Brancheforening, 1967– . Annual.   **AD80**
Title varies: 19?–59, Eberlins Bladliste; 1960–61, Bladlisten; 1962–70, Media.
"Published by the Danish Association of Advertising Agencies (DEB)."—*Pref.*
"Media Scandinavia contains—in Danish and English—information on advertising media in Denmark, Greenland, the Faroe Islands, Norway, Sweden, Finland and Iceland, besides a number of international publications."—*t.p. Ed. 39, 1990.* Lists daily newspapers, weeklies and magazines, as well as trade papers, yearbooks, directories, television and radio stations, and other advertising media, associations, etc. Arranged by country.

Europe (by country)

Austria

Presse Handbuch / Verband Österreichischer Zeitungsherausgeber und Zeitungsverleger. 1985– . Wien : Der Verband, 1985– . Annual.   **AD81**
Continues *Österreichs Presse, Werbung, Graphik Handbuch*, 1967–84. First published as *Handbuch Österreichs Presse, Werbung, Graphik*, 1953–66.
Gives statistical and directory information on Austrian newspapers and periodicals. Classified with title index.

Belgium

Annuaire officiel de la presse belge = Officieel jaarboek van de belgische pers / éd. par l'Association générale de la presse belge. [1950?]– . [Bruxelles] : L'Association. Irregular.   **AD82**
In Dutch and French.
In addition to directory information on Belgian newspapers and periodicals, there are extensive sections devoted to journalists, professional associations, specialist groups, and much miscellaneous information useful to the Belgian journalist.   PN4709.A48

Catalogus van Belgische en Luxemburgse periodieken. 6. uitg. Brussel : Nederlandsche Kamer van Koophandel voor België en Luxemburg, 1988. 187 p.   **AD83**
1st ed. (1962) and 2nd ed. publ. under title *Catalogus van Belgische en Luxemburgse tijdschriften.*
In two parts: (1) a classified section which lists the periodical titles under 114 subject headings, and (2) an alphabetical title list giving full information about each periodical.

Hove, Julien van. Répertoire des périodiques paraissant en Belgique. Bruxelles : Librairie Encyclopédique, 1951. 358 p.   **AD84**

Added title page: Repertorium van de België verschijnende tijdschriften.
Alphabetical listing of more than 2,000 periodicals published in Belgium, with full bibliographical data. Indexes by subject, editorial bodies, and place of publication.
———. ———. *Supplement* 1–4 (1955–72) list periodicals published through 1968, as well as omissions from the previous volumes, changes in title, and cessations.

Marechal, Yvon. Répertoire pratique des périodiques [belges] édités en langue française. 3ᵉ éd. Bruxelles : Les Auteurs Réunis, 1982. 267 p.   **AD85**
1st ed., 1970.
A classed listing of current serials, with addresses and indication of periodicity. Title index.   Z6956.B4M27

Bulgaria

Bŭlgarski periodichen pechat. 1972– . Sofiia : Narodna Biblioteka "Kiril i Metodii.". Annual.   **AD86**
An earlier series of the same title covered 1965–71 (AA589 *note*).
Provides an annual record of periodical publications with indication of numbers or issues actually published, new titles, etc.

Bŭlgarski periodichen pechat 1844–1944 : anotiran bibliografski ukazatel. Sofiia : Nauka i Izkustvo, 1962–69. 3 v.   **AD87**
Added title page in German: *Bŭlgarische periodika 1844–1944 : annotiertes bibliographisches Verzeichnis.*
Comp. by Dimitur P. Ivanchev.
Vol. 1–2 are an exhaustive alphabetical listing of Bulgarian periodicals, with notes on the history, editors, etc., of each. Vol. 3 lists foreign-language periodicals published in Bulgaria, includes a section of additions and corrections, and provides full indexing for the set.
§ Continued by Mariia Vladimirova Spasova, *Bŭlgarski periodichen pechat, 1944–1969 : bibliografski ukazatel* (Sofia : Narodna Biblioteka "Kiril i Metodii," 1975. 3 v.). Added title page in German: *Bŭlgarische periodika.* Vol. 3 comprises indexes and tables.
Z6956.B9B88

Czechoslovakia

Malec, Karel. Soupis bibliografí novin a časopisů, vydávaných na území Československé republiky. Praha : Orbis, 1959. 216 p.   **AD88**
Bibliography of bibliographies of Czechoslovak periodicals and newspapers from the 18th century through 1958.   Z2131.A1M3

Finland

Kurikka, Jussi. Suomen aikakauslehdistön bibliografia 1782–1955 = Bibliografi över Finlands tidskriftslitteratur 1782–1955 = Bibliography of Finnish periodicals, 1782–1955 / Jussi Kurikka, Marketta Takkala. Helsinki : [Helsingin yliopiston kirjasto], 1983. 463 p. (Helsingin yliopiston kirjaston julkaisuja, 47.).   **AD89**
Continued by: *Suomen aikakauslehdistön bibliografia 1956–1977 = Bibliografi över Finlands tidskriftslitteratur 1956–1977 = Bibliography of Finnish periodicals, 1956–1977* / Marketta Takkala, Anna-Maija Ortamo, Päivi Tommila (Helsinki : Helsingin yliopiston kirjasto, 1986. 632 p.).
A listing of all periodicals issued at least twice a year published in Finland through 1977. Arranged by title; indexes of editors and publishers.   Z6956.F5K87

France

Arbour, Roméo. Les revues littéraires éphémères paraissant à Paris entre 1900 et 1914 : répertoire descriptif. Paris : Librairie José Corti, 1956. 93 p.   **AD90**

Lists 154 "little magazines" published in Paris which lived less than four years, with locations in Parisian libraries. Gives full bibliographical description, with names of editors, etc., as well as the names of the principal contributors. Index of personal names and an appendix of 31 titles not found in the libraries of Paris.

Bibliothèque Nationale (France). Catalogue des périodiques clandestins diffusés en France de 1939 à 1945 : suivi d'un catalogue des périodiques clandestins diffusés à l'étranger / preparé et redigé successivement par Renée Roux-Fouillet et Paul Roux-Fouillet. Paris : Bibliothèque Nationale, 1954. 282 p.   **AD91**

Lists clandestine periodicals to be found in the Bibliothèque Nationale, either in the original or in photostatic copies. In three sections: Periodicals distributed in France (about 1,015 titles); Periodicals distributed in other countries (about 71 titles); Supplement. Index.

Bibliothèque Nationale (France). Département des Périodiques. Bibliographie de la presse française politique et d'information générale, 1865–1944. Paris : Bibliothèque Nationale, 1964–1992. 89 pts. (In progress).   **AD92**

Chronologically, a successor to Louis Eugène Hatin's *Bibliographie historique et critique de la presse périodique française* (AD95). Limited mainly to dailies and weeklies. In 89 fascicles, each covering a *département* (and numbered alphabetically by *département* name), issued as they are completed; the finished work is to comprise 4 v., with a general preface and a title index. Each fascicle includes a preface or historical note, an alphabetical listing with bibliographical details, and a chronological table of titles. Gives locations in the Bibliothèque Nationale, municipal libraries, or other archives.

Z6956.F8P32

——————— Répertoire national des annuaires français, 1958–1968 : et supplément signalant les annuaires reçus en 1969 / par Monique Lambert. Paris : Bibliothèque Nationale, 1970. 311 p.   **AD93**

"Ouvrage publié avec le concours du Syndicat national des annuaires et supports divers de publicité"—*t.p.*

A classed list with alphabetical title index.   Z2174.Y4P29

Caron, Pierre. Répertoire des périodiques de langue française, philosophiques, historiques, philologiques et juridiques / Pierre Caron et Marc Jaryc. Paris : Fédération des sociétés françaises de sciences philosophiques, historiques, philologiques et juridiques., 1935. 351 p.   **AD94**

Contents: Alphabetical list, p. 1–278, no. 1–1421; Supplément, p. 279–92, no. 1421–76; IIe supplément, no. 1477–96.

With its supplements (below) forms an important list of French periodicals existing in the 1930s, giving exact title, date of founding, names and addresses of chief editors, periodicity, average number of pages per volume, size, price, etc. Indexes of persons, places, and subjects.

Supplements:

——————. ——————. *1. supplément, no. 1477–1686* (1937. 68 p.). Incorporates, in regular alphabetical order and numbering, the titles (no. 1477–96) of the original IIe supplément.

——————. ——————. *2. supplément, no. 1687–1900* (Paris : Maison du livre françaises, 1939. 62 p.).

Hatin, Louis Eugène. Bibliographie historique et critique de la presse périodique française. Paris : Firmin-Didot, 1866. cxvii, 660 p. : ill.   **AD95**

Repr.: Hildesheim : Olms, 1965.

Subtitle: Catalogue systématique et raisonné de tous les écrits périodiques de quelque valeur publiés ou ayant circulé en France depuis l'origine du journal jusqu'à nos jours, avec extraits, notes historiques, critiques, et morales, indication des prix que les principaux journaux ont atteints dans les ventes publiques, etc.

A retrospective bibliography with detailed bibliographical and historical notes about each periodical listed. Covers 1631–1865. Useful for historical information, though not complete.   Z6956.F8H36

Place, Jean-Michel. Bibliographie des revues et journaux littéraires des XIXe et XXe siècles / par Jean-Michel Place et André Vasseur. Paris : Éditions de la Chronique des lettres françaises, 1973–77. 3 v.   **AD96**

Gives detailed descriptions of French literary journals of the period, contents of each issue published, and illustrative extracts. Chronologically arranged by starting date of publication, with some overlap in v. 1–2 (covering 1840–99); v. 3 is designated as covering 1915–30 and includes an index of names cited. About 15 titles in each volume.

PQ2.P5

Répertoire de la presse et des publications périodiques françaises, 1977/1978. 6e éd / préparée par le Service français du Département des Périodiques. Paris : Bibliothèque Nationale, 1981. 2 v. (1599 p.).   **AD97**

Contents: v. 1, Répertoire systématique des périodiques vivants; v. 2, Index alphabétique des titres, Index alphabétique des collectivités, Liste des périodiques disparue entre le 1er octobre 1965 et 31 décembre 1976.

1st–5th eds. covered 1956/57, 1957/60, 1960/63, 1963/66, 1966/71, and were publ. by Documentation française. The 5th ed. departed from the policy of earlier ones (which listed periodicals which began publication during the period of coverage) in that it combined the listings from the 4th ed. with new titles of the 1966–71 period. Vol. 1 of the 6th ed. is a comprehensive, classified list of periodicals (with full details of publication) which were current Jan. 1977–Mar. 1978. About 20,400 titles in this edition; earlier editions remain useful, of course, for reference purposes.

Germany

Deutsche Bibliographie. Zeitschriften-Verzeichnis / bearbeitet von der Deutschen Bibliothek, Frankfurt a. M. 1953–1957– . Frankfurt am Main : Buchhändler-Vereinigung. Irregular.   **AD98**

Title varies slightly.

Coverage varies: 1945–52; 1953–57; 1958–70; 1971–76; 1977–80; 1981–85.

Volume for each period issued in parts.

A comprehensive list of German-language publications appearing in Germany and other countries. Editor, publisher, size, price, frequency, irregularities, and title changes are usually given. Issued in two parts, a classified section and an index. Indexed by editor, title, publishers, society or sponsoring organization, and subject.

Z6956.G3F67

Diesch, Carl Hermann. Bibliographie der germanistischen Zeitschriften. Leipzig : Hiersemann, 1927. 441 p. (Modern Language Association of America. Germanic Section. Bibliographical publications, v. 1).   **AD99**

Repr.: Stuttgart : Hiersemann, 1970.

A chronological, classed arrangement covering from the 18th to the 20th centuries. Lists more than 4,600 titles with information on full title, editor, volumes and years published, place, publisher, etc. Title and name indexes.   Z7037.A1D5

Kirchner, Joachim. Bibliographie der Zeitschriften des deutschen Sprachgebietes bis 1900. Stuttgart : Hiersemann, 1966–89. v. 1–4. (In progress).   **AD100**

Contents: Bd. 1, Von den Anfängen bis 1830; Bd. 2, 1831–1870; Bd. 3, 1871–1900; Bd. 4, Teil 1, Alphabetisches Titleregister ed. by Edith Chorherr. Teil 2 is projected to be an index of publishers, places of publication, and editors.

Published in parts.

A bibliography of periodicals from German-speaking regions for the period to 1900. Arrangement is by subject, then chronological. Editors and changes of title are noted. Each volume has its own detailed index in addition to the cumulative index (Bd. 4).   Z6956.G3K53

Maas, Lieselotte. Handbuch der deutschen Exilpresse 1933–1945 = Handbook of the German exile press 1933–1945 / Lieselotte Maas ; hrsg. von Eberhard Lämmert. München : C. Hanser, 1976–90. v. 1–4. (Sonderveröffentlichungen der Deutschen Bibliothek, 2, 3, 9). (In progress).   **AD101**

Vol. 4 lacks series statement.

A very full record of German periodicals published outside Germany during the Nazi regime. Provides lists of contributors and locations of files of the publications in addition to bibliographic details of more than 400 serials. Indexes of names and pseudonyms, organizations, countries and places of publication. Bd. 4 contains descriptive essays about individual titles and the organizations that published them, as will a projected Bd. 5.   Z6956.G3M27

Current

Rösch-Sondermann, Hermann. Bibliographie der lokalen Alternativpresse : vom Volksblatt zum Stadtmagazin. München ; N.Y. : K.G. Saur, 1988. 156 p.   **AD102**

An alphabetical listing of 930 titles published in West Germany in the 1970s and 1980s. Lists place of publication, beginning and cessation dates as applicable, frequency, and periodical type. Indexed by place of publication.   PN5214.U53R6

Stamm Leitfaden durch Presse und Werbung = Annual directory through press and advertising. 29 Ausg. (1976)– . [Essen : Stamm Verlag], 1976– . Annual.   **AD103**

Title also in English and French. Introduction and tables of contents in German, English, and French.

At head of title: Presse– und Medien-Handbuch.

Continues *Stamm-Leitfaden für Presse und Werbung* (ed. 25–28, 1972–75), which in turn superseded *Die Leitfaden für Presse und Werbung* (ed. 1–24, 1947–71), and assumes its numbering.

Issued in two vol. beginning with Ausg. 45, 1992, the second being *Tarife (Rates)*, containing advertisement-related data for the print media.

Arrangement and coverage has varied slightly, but content has been fairly consistent throughout the changes of title. Ausg. 46, 1993, contains information on newspapers; free-distribution papers; magazines and annual publications; press and information services; press and diplomatic information for foreign countries; broadcasting and cinema; outdoor advertising; miscellaneous information related to advertising and the press. Despite the broad scope, the section on magazines is substantial.

Great Britain

before 1800

Bodleian Library. A catalogue of English newspapers and periodicals in the Bodleian Library, 1622–1800 / by R. T. Milford and D. M. Sutherland. Oxford : Oxford Bibliographical Society, 1936. [163]–346 p.   **AD104**

Repr. : Nendeln : Kraus Reprint, 1969.

Reprinted from Oxford Bibliographical Society. Proceedings & papers, v. IV, pt. 2.

An alphabetical title catalog, p. 171–344; index to editors, authors, and contributors, p. 345–46.   Z1008.O98

Couper, William James. The Edinburgh periodical press : being a bibliographical account of the newspapers, journals, and magazines issued in Edinburgh from the earliest times to 1800. Stirling : E. Mackay, 1908. 2 v. : facsims.   **AD105**

Contents: v. 1, Introduction and bibliography, 1642–1711; v. 2, Bibliography, 1711–1800.

Full bibliographical information with historical sketches.   PN5139.E39C7

Crane, Ronald Salmon. Census of British newspapers and periodicals, 1620–1800 / by R S. Crane and F. B. Kaye, with the assistance of M. E. Prior. Chapel Hill : Univ. of North Carolina Pr. ; London : Cambridge Univ. Pr., 1927. 205 p.   **AD106**

Repr. : London : Holland, 1979.

Contents: (1) British periodicals, 1620–1800, accessible in American libraries; (2) British periodicals, 1620–1800, not found in American libraries; (3) Chronological index; (4) Geographical index of periodicals published outside of London.

Lists 970 papers and periodicals, with indication of the holdings in 62 American libraries.   Z6956.E5C8

Nelson, Carolyn. British newspapers and periodicals, 1641–1700 : a short-title catalogue of serials printed in England, Scotland, Ireland, and British America / comp. by Carolyn Nelson and Matthew Seccombe. N.Y. : Modern Language Association of America, 1987. 724 p.   **AD107**

Subtitle continues: With a checklist of serials printed 1701–March 1702 and chronological, geographical, foreign language, subject, publishers, and editor indexes, 1641–1702.

The 700 titles are listed alphabetically with detailed bibliographic information for each issue. Includes issue-specific locations in a number of British and American Libraries. "Designed ... to be compatible with Pollard and Redgrave's *STC* [AA671], which includes serials published before 1641, and with Wing's *Catalogue* [AA683], which includes annuals but excludes serials published at shorter intervals ... . [The authors] have excluded annuals."—*Pref.*   Z6956.G6N44

Ward, William Smith. British periodicals & newspapers, 1789–1832 : a bibliography of secondary sources. [Lexington] : Univ. Pr. of Kentucky, [1972]. 386 p.   **AD108**

A companion to Ward's *Index and finding list of serials published in the British Isles, 1789–1832* (Lexington, 1953). Offers a bibliography of writings about the magazines and newspapers listed in that work, including writings on their editors, publishers, and readership. Topical arrangement; author and subject indexes.   Z6956.G6W37

Weed, Katherine Kirtley. Studies of British newspapers and periodicals from their beginning to 1800 : a bibliography / by Katherine Kirtley Weed and Richmond Pugh Bond. Chapel Hill : Univ. of North Carolina Pr., 1946. 233 p. (Studies in philology, extra series, no. 2).   **AD109**

Repr. : N.Y. : Johnson Reprint Corp., 1970.

Contents: Bibliographies and bibliographical studies; Beginnings of the newspaper; General studies; Individual newspapers and periodicals; Editors, authors, and publishers; Towns and counties; Special subjects; Newspapers and periodicals in Europe and in America.

Lists some 2,100 books and periodical articles printed mainly 1800–1940, arranged by subject with author index.   P25.S82 no.2

19th century and after

Madden, Lionel. The nineteenth-century periodical press in Britain : a bibliography of modern studies, 1901–1971 / comp. by Lionel Madden & Diana Dixon. N.Y. : Garland, 1976. 280 p. (Garland reference library of the humanities, v.53).   **AD110**

An expanded version of the 1975 publ. (Toronto : Victorian Periodicals Newsletter. 76 p.).

A relatively brief section, Bibliographies, finding lists and reports on bibliographical projects, is followed by a fairly long one, General history of periodicals and newspapers; both are arranged chronologically by date of publication. The bulk of the volume is devoted to section C, Studies of individual periodicals and newspapers, and section D, Studies and memoirs of proprietors, editors, journalists and contributors, each arranged alphabetically by title/name, then chronologically by date of the study. Author index; some brief annotations. About 2,600 items.

Updated by: *The nineteenth-century periodical press in Britain : a bibliography of modern studies, 1972–1987*, comp. by Larry K. Uffelman, with assistance from Lionel Madden and Diana Dixon (Edwardsville, Ill. : Victorian Periodicals Review, 1992. 124 p.). Issued as a supplement to the Summer 1992 issue of *Victorian periodicals review*; retains the scope and arrangement of the earlier title.

Z6956.G6M3

Noyce, John L. The directory of British alternative periodicals, 1965–1974. Hassocks, [Eng.] : Harvester Pr. ; Atlantic Highlands, N.J. : Humanities Pr., [1979]. 359 p.   **AD111**

A title listing of British underground and alternative periodicals of the period indicated, giving publication information, description (including many historical notes), format, library locations when available, and references to directory listings, reviews, notices, etc. In general, excludes "poetry and traditional politics—though entries have been included for those titles which were an important part of the underground and alternative press. In the absence of any other listing, and in view of their importance in the counter-culture of the time" (*Introd.*), anarchist and libertarian periodicals have been included. Indexed.

Z6956.G6N69

Spiers, John. The underground and alternative press in Britain : a bibliographical guide with historical notes. [Brighton, Eng.] : Harvester Pr., 1974. 77 p.   **AD112**

"Published with a title and chronological index as a companion to the Underground/Alternative Press collection prepared for microfilm publication by Ann Sexsmith and Alastair Everitt."—*t.p.*

Offers bibliographic and historical notes on sixty-odd British underground and alternative press periodicals included in the publisher's basic microform set for the 1961–73 period. The microform series, which carries the same title, has been continued on an annual basis with printed guides for the individual years.   Z6944.U5S64

Victorian periodicals : a guide to research / Scott Bennett ... [et al.] ; ed. by J. Don Vann and Rosemary T. VanArsdel. N.Y. : Modern Language Association of America, 1978–1989. 2 v.   **AD113**

Vol. 2 has series title, *Reviews of research*.

Presents chapters by specialists on resources for research and special problems encountered in work with Victorian periodicals, giving attention to bibliographic control, finding lists, biographical sources, histories of the periodical press, and identification of authors. Also covers topical matters such as women's serials, the radical and labor press, publishers' archives, magazines for children, religious periodicals, the Welsh periodical press, and serialized novels. Indexed.

PN5124.P4V5

Wolff, Michael. The Waterloo directory of Victorian periodicals, 1824–1900 / Michael Wolff, John S. North, Dorothy Deering ; sponsored by the Research Society for Victorian Periodicals and Waterloo Computing in the Humanities. [Waterloo, Ont.] : Wilfrid Laurier Univ. Pr., [1976]. 1187 p.   **AD114**

Called Phase I.

An attempt to make "conveniently available in one alphabetical listing the newspaper and periodical titles published in England, Ireland, Scotland, and Wales at any time between 1824 and 1900."—*Pref.* Includes some 29,000 entries (about 4,400 of them cross-references), covering all fields of publication: government, church, trade, the professions, the sciences and humanities. Titles were gleaned chiefly from the *British union-catalogue of periodicals* (AD236), the *Union list of serials* (AD226), the British Museum's *Newspapers published in Great Britain and Ireland, 1801–1900* (London : Clowes, 1905), and the Times's *Tercentenary handlist of English and Welsh newspapers, magazines and reviews* (AE59). Information available on many titles is admittedly sketchy, but the following points are covered to the extent possible: subtitle, numbering, publication dates, editor, place of publi-

cation, publisher, printer, price, size, frequency, illustrations, circulation, sponsoring body, indexing, mergers, alternate titles, and descriptive or explanatory notes. Discrepancies between earlier listings are also noted.

Phase II volumes for Irish (AD124) and Scottish (AD119) titles contain more entries, fuller bibliographic descriptions, more library holdings, and subject indexes. A Phase II directory of English titles is planned as a 50-v. set of approximately 100,000 entries.

Z6956.G6W63

Current

Current British journals : a bibliographic guide. [3rd ed.] (1982)– . Boston Spa [England] : publ. jointly by the British Library Document Supply Centre and the UK Serials Group, 1982– . Irregular.   **AD115**

1st–2nd eds. (1970–1973) had title: *Guide to current British journals.*

Editor varies; 6th ed. (1992), Mary Toase.

Arranged by Universal Decimal Classification, with alphabetical indexes for titles, subjects, recent cessations, and sponsoring bodies. Entries include title, first year of issue, previous title, recent subscription price, number of issues per year, brief subject statement, number of pages per issue, presence of advertising and book reviews, frequency of index, sponsoring body, ISSN, additional formats available, where abstracted or indexed, publisher, publisher's address, telephone and fax numbers. Entries are based on information supplied by publishers.   Z6956.G6G84

Serials in the British Library. No. 1 (June 1981)– . London : British Library, Bibliographic Services Division, c1981– . Quarterly.   **AD116**

Subtitle, 1981–1986: "together with locations and holdings of other British and Irish libraries."

Supersedes in part the quarterly *British union-catalogue of periodicals* (AD237) which ceased with the 1980 ed.

Three quarterly issues consist of new serial entries; the fourth cumulates the previous three.

After 1986, lists alphabetically "titles (including new British serials received through legal deposit) that have been newly acquired for the London-based reference collections of the British Library."—*Pref.* Since 1987, no longer lists additional locations. Entries include title, dates, publisher, frequency, ISSN, and price. Keyword-in-title index. Also available in microfiche. Beginning 1987, published in three quarterly issues and annual printed cumulation.

A cumulation, *Serials in the British library, 1976–1986*, was issued in 1988 on 57 microfiche.   Z6945.B874

Walford's guide to current British periodicals in the humanities and social sciences / ed. by A.J. Walford with the assistance of Joan M. Harvey. London : Library Association, 1985. 473 p.   **AD117**

A classified listing of current British periodicals in the broad range of humanities and social sciences. In addition to publication information, there is a brief listing of representative articles and notes on sponsorship, coverage, etc. Subject sections begin with a short survey of the range of publications included, plus listings of abstracting, indexing, and online services in the field. Indexed.   Z7165.W36

Willing's press guide. v. 1– . East Grinstead, Eng. : Reed Information Services, 1874– . Annual.   **AD118**

Beginning 117th ed. (1991) publ. in 2 vol. : United Kingdom and Overseas.

Publisher varies.

Principal contents of 120th ed., 1994: v. 1, alphabetical list of nearly 14,000 newspapers and periodicals published in the U.K., classified index to periodicals, regional and local index of U.K. newspapers, list of titles ceased or begun during the prior year, and listing of U.K. publishers and their titles; v. 2, alphabetical and classified listings of 14,085 overseas serials (entries arranged by region—Europe, the Americas, Africa, etc.), alphabetical list of U.K. representatives overseas, list of more than 1,122 overseas publishers and their titles. Advertisement rates are included with entries when known.

Z6956.E5W5

Scotland

North, John S. The Waterloo directory of Scottish newspapers and periodicals, 1800–1900. Waterloo, Ont. : North Waterloo Academic Pr., 1989. 2 v. (2199 p.) : ill. (Waterloo directory series of newspapers and periodicals, England, Ireland, Scotland and Wales, 1800–1900, v. 1–2).   **AD119**

Forms part of Phase II of "Waterloo directory series of newspapers and periodicals, England, Ireland, Scotland and Wales, 1600–1900".

Offers "an alphabetical listing, description, and finding list of publications issued in Scotland in all fields."—*Pref.* Lists more than 7,000 titles, including daily and annual publications. The extremely detailed annotations include collation statements, printers, descriptions of content, locations in Great Britain, etc. More than 2,000 title pages are reproduced. Subject, name, and place of publication indexes.

Z6956.S36N67

Hungary

Budapest. Országos Széchényi Könyvtár. A magyar sajtó bibliográfiája, 1945–1954 / Dezsényi Béla, Falvy Zoltán [és] Fejér Judit. Budapest : "Müvelt Nép", 1956. 159 p. (Az Országos Széchényi Könyvtár kiadványai, 36).   **AD120**

Alphabetical listing of periodicals and newspapers published in Hungary between 1945 and 1954.   Z6956.H8D4

Dezsényi, Béla. A magyar hirlapirodalom elsö százada, 1705–1805 / Kiadja a Magyar Nemzeti Múzeum Országos Széchényi Könyvtára. Budapest : Magyar Nemzeti Múzeum Országos Széchényi Könyvtara, 1941. 66 p. (Magyarország idöszaki sajtójának könyvészete, 1).   **AD121**

Lists, with location, periodicals and newspapers published in Hungary from 1705 to 1805.   PN5168.H8D4

Kemény, György. Magyarország idöszaki sajtója, 1911–töl 1920–ig. Budapest : Magyar Nemzeti Múzeum Országos Széchényi Könyvtára, 1942. 474 p. (Magyarország idöszaki sajtójának könyvészete, 4).   **AD122**

An alphabetical list of periodicals and newspapers published in Hungary from 1911 to 1920.

Magyar nemzeti bibliográfia. Idöszaki kiadványok bibliográfiája. 1981– . Budapest : Országos Széchényi Könyvtár, 1983– . Annual.   **AD123**

Continues: *Kurrens idöszaki kiadványok,* 1976–80.

Introductory matter in Hungarian, English, and Russian.

A comprehensive record of current periodicals (including yearbooks and directories, professional and local publications, etc.) and newspapers. Title listing with index of corporate bodies.

A cumulated index for 1981–85 was published in 1988 in 2 v.: v. 1, Címmutató; v. 2, Testületi mutató. The first is a cumulative title index, including title changes and variant titles; the second a cumulative index to the corporate bodies issuing periodicals during the period. Both refer to the appropriate annual volumes.

Ireland

North, John S. The Waterloo directory of Irish newspapers and periodicals, 1800–1900. Waterloo, Ont. : North Waterloo Academic Pr., 1986. 838 p. (Waterloo directory series of newspapers and periodicals, England, Ireland, Scotland and Wales, 1800–1900, Phase II, v. 1).   **AD124**

Phase II of the Waterloo directory series. For description of Phase I, *Waterloo directory of Victorian periodicals, 1824–1900,* see AD114.

"An alphabetical listing and description of publications in Ireland in all fields … . The editor has sought to list every newspaper and periodical published in the century."—*Pref.* The 3,932 titles, most examined by the compilers, include the 1,100 Irish titles listed in Phase I. The listings include, when available, title, subtitle, publisher, printer, dates and volume numbers, price, circulation, indexes, description of the contents, and a bibliography of secondary sources. At least one British or Irish location is given for most titles. Includes subject, personal name, and place of publication indexes.   PN5144.W2

Italy

Annuario della stampa italiana / a cura della Federazione Nazionale della stampa italiana. 1954/55–59/60. Milan ; Rome : Fratelli, Bocca, 1954–59. Irregular.   **AD125**

A continuation of the annual of the same title publ. 1916–42.

Includes texts of laws of the press, professional organizations, material on journalism in Italy, and lists of periodicals and newspapers, Italian journalists, associations, etc.   Z6956.I8A6

Consiglio nazionale delle ricerche (Italy). Periodici italiani scientifici, tecnici e di cultura generale. 5. ed. interamente rinnovata, 1939. Roma : Arti Grafiche Trinacria, 1939. 3 v. in 1.   **AD126**

Gives detailed information about Italian periodicals current in the 1930s.   Z7403.I88

Majolo Molinari, Olga. La stampa periodica romana dell' Ottocento. Roma : Istituto di studi romani, 1963. 2 v. (xcvi, 1188 p.).   **AD127**

A comprehensive bibliography of some 1,700 Italian 19th-century periodicals with bibliographical details and descriptive annotations. Arranged alphabetically; chronological, subject, and name. Indexes.

Z6956.I8M3

Periodici italiani, 1886–1957. Roma : Istituto centrale per il catalogo unico delle biblioteche italiane e per le informazione bibliografiche, 1980. 940 p.   **AD128**

A list of Italian periodicals extracted from the *Catalogo cumulativo 1886–1957 del Bollettino delle pubblicazioni italiane* of the Biblioteca Nazionale Centrale, Florence (AA727).

§ Continued by: *Periodici italiani, 1968–1981,* a cura di Maria Barachino, Giovanna Merola, Carla Stocco (Roma : Istituto centrale per il catalogo unico delle biblioteche italiane e per le informazione bibliografiche, 1983. 612 p.).

A title listing with indexes of title changes, supplements, editors, and corporate bodies.

Repertorio analitico della stampa italiana : quotidiani e periodici, 1964–69. Milano : Messaggerie Italiane, 1963–69. 6 v.   **AD129**

Lists periodicals in a simplified Dewey Decimal Classification with title index. The main list gives title, frequency, and city of publication; the title index indicates subscription prices. An *Indirizzi* volume was published 1965 and 1966, listing the periodicals in alphabetical order with addresses.   Z6956.I8R4

Current

Catalogo dei periodici italiani. 1981– . Milano : Editrice Bibliografica, 1980– .   **AD130**

Ed. by Roberti Maini, 1981– .

The 4th ed., current as of Dec. 1991, lists more than 10,000 titles of periodicals published in Italy. In four parts: title index, subject index, geographical index, and cessation list. Includes a section of tables presenting statistical data on periodical publishing in Italy. Indivi-

dual entries note title, subtitle, editor's name, publisher's address, telephone and fax numbers, frequency, subscription price, and ISSN.
Z6956.I8C18

Luxembourg

Catalogus van Belgische en Luxemburgse periodieken. 6. uitg. Brussel : Nederlandsche Kamer van Koophandel voor België en Luxemburg, 1988. 187 p.   **AD131**
For annotation, *see* AD83.

Netherlands

Handboek van de Nederlandse pers en publiciteit. 42 Uitg. (Sept. 1974)– . Schiedam : "Publiciteit" Schiedam, 1974– . Semiannual.   **AD132**
Continues *Handboek van de Nederlandse pers* (1964–74) which continued a looseleaf ed. of the same title, publ. 1956–63.
Publ. in April and September.
Since 1984, issued in two vols.: (1) Gedruckte media; (2) Algemene gegevans.
Tables of contents and section headings also in English.
The first volume is a directory of periodicals and newspapers, arranged alphabetically by title. Includes lists of title changes, ceased publications, and previously unlisted titles. Also includes indexes by subject category and by town of publication. The second volume is a directory of organizations in the fields of publishing, advertising, audiovisual production, market research, and other media related services.
Z6956.N45H352

Poland

Bibliografia wydawnictw ciągłych = Bibliography of Polish serials / Biblioteka Narodowa, Instytut Bibliograficzny. 1981– . Warsaw : Biblioteka, 1984– . Annual.   **AD133**
Continues *Bibliografia czasopism i wydawnictw zbiorowych* (Warsaw : Biblioteka, 1960–), which last appeared in 1978, covering 1972/74.
Lists, alphabetically by title, all Polish serials—including newspapers, annuals, and irregular issues—legally deposited at the Biblioteka Narodowa during the year. Classified, organization, and editor indexes.
Z6956.P7B5

Biblioteka Jagiellońska. Katalog czasopism polskich Biblioteki Jagiellońskiej / [pod red. Stanisława Grzeszczuka]. Wyd. 2. Kraków : Nakładem Uniwersytetu Jagiellońskiego, 1974–86. 9 v. in 10. (Varia, zesz. 94, 116, 131, 139, 144, 153, 162, 174, 214).   **AD134**
Contents: v. 1–5, A–N; v. 6¹–6², O–Q; v. 7–8, R–Wiadomsci zeglarskie; v. 9, Wiadukt–Żywienie. Vol. 9 also includes corrections to v. 1–8. Includes various editions of some volumes.
A main-entry catalog of Polish periodicals in the Library, with an issue-specific record of holdings.   Z6956.P7K72

Kowalik, Jan. Bibliografia czasopism polskich wydanych poza granicami Kraju od września 1939 roku = World index of Polish periodicals published outside of Poland since September 1939. Wyd. 1. Lublin : Katolicki Uniwersytet Lubelski, 1976–88. 5 v. : ill.   **AD135**
Introductory matter in Polish and English.
The first four volumes, publ. 1976, provide "... information about more than 3000 Polish periodicals published around the world in some sixty countries from September 1939 through September 1972."—*Introd.* Vol. 5 lists 361 titles published 1973–84, and 354 titles supplementing earlier volumes. Arranged by title, with indexes by subject, editor, and place of publication. Locates copies.   Z6956.P7K59

Polish Library (London, England). Catalogue of periodicals in Polish or relating to Poland and other Slavonic countries, published outside Poland since September 1st, 1939 / comp. by Maria Danilewicz and Barbara Jabłońska. 2nd ed. London : The Polish Library, 1971. 126 ł.   **AD136**
Added title page and preface in Polish.
1st ed., 1964, by Danilewicz and Genowefa Sadowska.
Lists more than 1,000 titles in alphabetical sequence.
Z6956.P7L6

Polska Akademia Nauk. Pracownia Historii Czasopiśmiennictwa Polskiego XIX–XX Wieku. Bibliografia prasy polskiej, 1944–1948 / Prace krajowa. [Opracował Jerzy Myśliński przy udziale zespołu Pracowni]. Warszawa : Państwowe Wydawnictwo Naukowe, [1966]. 323 p. (Polska Akademia Nauk. Materiały i studia do historii prasy i czasopiśmiennictwa polskiego, zesz. 1).   **AD137**
A chronological bibliography of the Polish press, with indexes by journal title, editor, and place of publication.   Z6956.P7P62

Portugal

Boletim de bibliografia portuguesa. Publicações em série / Biblioteca Nacional. Jan./Dez. 1981– . Lisboa : Biblioteca, [1981]– . Irregular.   **AD138**
Alternate title: *BBP. Publicações em série*.
None published 1983–86?
A companion publication to the *Boletim de bibliografia portuguesa. Monografias* (AA778).
An alphabetical title listing of new serial publications, with full bibliographical information; indexes by issuing/sponsoring bodies, by subjects, and by places of publication.

Romania

Newspapers and periodicals from Romania = Journaux et périodiques de Roumanie = Zeitungen und Zeitschriften aus Rumänien. Bucharest : ILEXIM, Pr. Dept., 1980. 142 p.   **AD139**
Publisher varies.
Earlier eds. publ. 1958, 1964, 1971.
Text in English, French, and German.
A classified listing with alphabetical index. 1980 latest published?
Z6956.R8N48

Publicaţiunile periodice româneşti (ziare, gazete, reviste) / cu o introducere de Ioan Bianu. Bucureşti : Socec, 1913–87. 3 v.   **AD140**
Vol. 1 issued by Socec. At head of title for v. 3: Biblioteca Academiei Republicii Socialiste România.
Contents: v. 1, Catalog alfabetic, 1820–1906, descriere bibliografica de Nerva Hodoş şi Al.-Sadi Ionescu; v. 2, Catalog alfabetic, 1907–1918; Supplement, 1790–1906, descriere bibliografica de George Baiculescu, Georgeta Radvica şi Neonila Onofrei; v. 3, Catalog alfabetic, 1919–1924, descriere bibliografică de Ileana Stancu Desa, Dulcia Morărescu, Ioana Patriche, Adriana Paliade şi Iliana Sulică.
Periodicals and newspapers listed alphabetically by title with full bibliographical information, notes on title changes, editors, supplements issued, etc.   Z2923.P9

Russia and the U.S.S.R.

Center for Research Libraries. Soviet serials currently received at the Center for Research Libraries. 1st ed. (1981)– . Chicago : The Center, 1981– .   **AD141**

The 4th ed. (1990) offers an alphabetical listing of "1287 titles of Soviet periodicals, irregular serials, annuals, and numbered monographic series received at CRL as of June 1, 1990."—*Introd.* Monographic series, nonacademic serials, and broad subject indexes.

Gosudarstvennaia publichnaia biblioteka imeni M.E. Saltykova-Shchedrina. Bibliografiia periodicheskikh izdanii Rossii 1901–1916 / pod obshchei red. V. M. Barashenkova, O. D. Golubevoĭ, N. IA. Morachevskogo. Leningrad, 1958–61. 4 v. **AD142**

Repr.: Neldeln : Kraus, 1975.

Title also in English (*Bibliography of periodicals of Russia, 1901–1916*), German, and French.

Full bibliographic description of periodicals, other than illegal publications, published within the territory of pre-1917 Russia. Includes newspapers; excludes annuals and almanacs. Entries are arranged alphabetically, with numerous indexes in v. 4.

Supersedes the checking edition, *Predvaritel'nyi spisok periodicheskikh izdanii Rossii, 1901–1916* (Leningrad, 1949).

Z6956.R9L353

———————— Obshchie bibliografii russkikh periodicheskikh izdanii, 1703–1954, i materialy po statistike russkoĭ periodicheskoĭ pechati : annotirovannyĭ ukazatel' / pod red. P. N. Berkova. Leningrad, 1956. 189 p. **AD143**

At head of title: M. V. Mashkova i M. V. Sokurova.

General bibliographies, annotated, of the Russian periodical press, together with statistical material. Supplements the bibliography of book bibliographies by Sokurova (*Obshchie bibliografi russkikh knig grazhdanskoĭ pechati, 1708–1955* (AA63). Z2491.A1L44

Library of Congress. Russian imperial government serials on microfilm in the Library of Congress : a guide to the uncatalogued collection / comp. by Harold M. Leich with the assistance of staff members of the Library of Congress European Division and Preservation Microfilming Office. Wash. : The Library, 1985. 135 p. **AD144**

For annotation, *see* AF214. Z6956.S65L52

Lisovskiĭ, Nikolai Mikhailovich. Russkaia periodicheskaia pechat' 1703–1900 gg : (Bibliografiia i graficheskiia tablitsy). Petrograd : Tip. G. A. Shumakhera i B. D. Brukera, 1915. 267 p. : tables. **AD145**

Repr. Petrograd, 1915, in smaller format without tables; Leipzig : Zentral-Antiquariat der Deutschen Demikratischen Republik, 1965.

The standard bibliography for 18th- and 19th-century Russian journals and newspapers. Chronologically arranged, with indexes. See also: *Russkaia periodicheskaia pechat'* (AD146). Z6956.R9L39

Russkaia periodicheskaia pechat' : spravochnik. Moskva : Gos. izd-vo polit. lit-ry, 1957–59. 2 v. **AD146**

Vol. 1, publ. 1959, ed. by A. G. Dement'ev, A. V. Zapadov, M. S. Cherepakhov; v. 2, publ. 1957, ed. by Cherepakhov and E. M. Fingerit.

A chronologically arranged, well-indexed handbook giving extensive factual information, with political commentary, on the major social and literary periodicals (journals, almanacs, and newspapers) published in and outside Russia between 1702 and October 1917. Included are editors' names, major contributors, special features, and references to supplements and indexes. PN5274.C43

Smits, Rudolf. Half a century of Soviet serials, 1917–1968 : a bibliography and union list of serials published in the USSR. Wash. : Library of Congress : For sale by U.S. Govt. Print. Off., 1968. 2 v. (1661 p.). **AD147**

Supersedes: Library of Congress. Cyrillic Bibliographic Project, *Serial publications of the Soviet Union, 1939–1957 : a bibliographic checklist*, comp. by Smits (Wash., 1958. 459 p.).

Scope is extended to include "all known serial publications appearing in the Soviet Union at regular or irregular intervals since 1917, in all except oriental languages such as Armenian, Georgian, Kirghiz, etc."—*Pref.* More than 29,700 entries. Symbols for U.S. and Canadian

libraries are given whenever a title is known to be represented in a collection, but no exact record of individual holdings is attempted.

Z6956.R9S58

Vsesoiuznaia Knizhnaia Palata. Periodicheskaia pechat' SSSR 1917–1949 / bibliograficheskiĭ ukazatel'. Moskva, 1955–63. 10 v. in 11. **AD148**

[v. 1[1-2]], Zhurnaly, trudy i biulleteni po obshchestvenno-politicheskim i sotsial'no-ekonomicheskim voprosam. 1958. 317 p., 267 p.

[v. 2] ———— po estestvennym naukam i matematike. 1956. 219 p.

[v. 3] ———— po tekhnike i promyshlennosti. 1955. 315 p.

[v. 4] ———— po transporty, sviazy i kommunal'nomu delu. 1955. 124 p.

[v. 5] ———— po sel'skomu khoziaistvu. 1955. 230 p.

[v. 6] ———— po kul'turnomy stroitel'stvu, narodnomu obrazovaniiu i prosveshcheniiu. 1956. 198 p.

[v. 7] ———— po zdravookhraneniiu, meditzine, fizicheskoi kul'ture i sportu. 1956. 170 p.

[v. 8] ———— po iazykoznaniiu, literaturovedeniiu, khudozhestvennoi literature i iskusstvu. 1958. 218 p.

[v. 9] ———— po voprosam pechati, bibliotechnogo dela i bibliografii. 1959. 191 p.

[v. 10], Svodnye ukazateli. 1963. 863 p.

The major retrospective bibliography of periodicals, other than newspapers, published in the U.S.S.R. in all languages from Nov. 1917 through 1949. Includes numbered series appearing irregularly. Gives full bibliographic information as to periodicity, numbering, title changes, etc. Each volume contains alphabetical index of titles, index of journals in languages other than Russian, index by place of publication, and index of publishers and issuing organizations; master indexes in the last volume.

Continued chronologically by the quinquennial cumulations of *Letopis' periodicheskikh izdanii SSSR* (AD150). Z6956.R9V8

Current

Letopis' periodicheskikh i prodolzhaiushchikhsia izdanii. Sborniki. 1971– . Moskva : Kniga, 1976– . Annual. **AD149**

Issued by: Gosudarstvennyi Komitet SSSR po Delam Izdatelstv, Poligrafii i Knizhnoi Torgovli [i] Vsesoiuznaia Knizhnaia Palata.

A comprehensive listing of periodical publications; newspapers are listed in a biennial *Biulleteni* section (AE74). A separate *Novye* section is issued annually, beginning with an issue covering Jan. 1976–Mar. 1977 (publ. 1977).

Cumulates as: *Letopis' periodicheskikh i prodolzhaiushchikhsia izdanii* (1971/75– . Moskva : Kniga, 1977– . Quinquennial).

Issued in two parts: v.1, Zhurnaly; v.2, Gazety. (1971/75 publ. 1977–81 in 2 v.; 1976/80, chast 1, publ. 1983; 1981/85, chast. 2, publ. 1989). Z6956.S65L474

Letopis' periodicheskikh izdanii SSSR. 1933–70. Moskva : Izd-vo Vsesoiuznoi Knizhnoi Palaty, 1933–75. Annual. **AD150**

Suspended 1940–45.

Continued by: *Letopis' periodicheskikh i prodolzhaiushchikhsia izdanii* (1971– . Moskva : Kniga, 1976–).

Title varies: 1933, *Spisok periodicheskikh izdanii RSFSR*; 1934–37, *Letopis' periodicheskikh izdanii SSSR*; 1938–59, *Ezhegodnik periodicheskikh izdanii SSSR*; 1946–50, *Letopis' periodicheskikh izdanii SSSR*.

Lists all Soviet periodical publications, using classified subject arrangement under which entries are listed by type of publication, then alphabetically by title within the grouping. From 1938, issued in two parts, the first covering journals, the second newspapers. Arrangement varies in earlier editions.

Annual, 1933–39, 1946–49. Beginning with coverage for 1950, split into two annual supplements to the quinquennial eds.: *Novye, pereimenovannye i prekrativshiesia zhurnaly i gazety* (indexing journals and newspapers which began, ceased, or changed title during the year), and *Trudy, uchennye zapiski, sborniki i drugie prodol-zhaiuschiesīa izdaniīa* (covering transactions and other irregular serials). *Trudy* for 1959 not published.

Novye continues to appear annually, but beginning with 1971, *Trudy* split into *Sborniki* (covering periodical publications; published annually. AD149), and *Biulleteni* (covering newspapers; published biennially. AE74).

The primary matter of the index continued in quinquennial cumulations for 1950/54, 1955/60 (in 2 v.), 1961/65 (2 pts. in 3 v.), and 1966/70 (2v.), which were issued in two parts, *Zhurnaly* (periodicals) and *Gazety* (newspapers) beginning with the 1955/60 coverage. Quinquennial cumulations issued under new title beginning with 1971/75 (2v).

With coverage for 1981/85, the numerical arrangement has been simplified somewhat, the various parts numbered as follows: ch. 1, *Zhurnaly*; ch. 2, *Gazety*; ch. 3, *Sborniki*; ch. 4, *Biulleteni*. Ch. 2 and ch. 4 pub. 1989.

For a detailed history of this publication from its beginnings to the mid-1970s, see Thomas J. Whitby and Tanja Lorković, *Introduction to Soviet national bibliography* (AA794).   Z6956.R9L36

Spain

Anuario de la prensa española. v. 1– . Madrid : Editora Nacional, 1943– . Irregular.   **AD151**
1970 vol. last published?
Some eds. published in 2 v.: pt. 1, newspapers; pt. 2, periodicals.
Edited for the Ministerio de Informacíon y Turismo, dirección General de Prensa.
v. 1, 1943; v. 2, 1945/6; v. 3–5, 1953–62; vols. for 1965 and 1970 issued without *año* number.
Gives detailed information, including address, personnel, format, size, number of copies printed, etc.   Z6956.S7S65

Biblioteca Nacional (Spain). Publicaciones periódicas existentes en la Biblioteca Nacional : catálogo redactado y ordenado por Florentino Zamora Lucas y María Casado Jorge. Madrid : Dirección General de Archivos y Bibliotecas, Servicio de Publicaciones del Ministerio de Educación Nacional, 1952. 718 p. : ill. (Publicaciones de educación nacional, obra no. 16).   **AD152**
A classed list of almost 9,000 titles with alphabetical index of titles. Indicates place of publication, holdings of the library, and (sometimes) frequency.   Z6945.M14

Givanel Mas, Juan. Bibliografía catalana : premsa. Barcelona : [Impr. Altés], 1931–37. 3 v. : ill.   **AD153**
Gives detailed bibliographical information about periodicals published in Catalonia, 1792–1925, arranged chronologically under cities. Vol. 3 is an alphabetical index with historical notes and many facsimiles.   Z6956.S7G4

Hemeroteca Municipal de Madrid. Catálogo de las publicaciones periódicas madrileñas existentes en la Hemeroteca Municipal de Madrid, 1661–1930. Madrid : Artes Gráficas Municipales, 1933. 360 p.   **AD154**
Arranged chronologically; alphabetical and chronological indexes.   Z6956.S7M16

Instituto Bibliográfico Hispánico. Revistas españolas, 1973–1978 : repertorio bibliográfico. Madrid : El Instituto, 1978–79. 2 v. (487 p.; 165 p.).   **AD155**
At head of title: Ministerio de Cultura, Dirección General del Libro y Bibliotecas, Subdirección General de Bibliotecas.
Contents: [v. 1] 1973–77; [v. 2] 1977–78.
An alphabetical title listing of Spanish periodicals published during the periods indicated, plus listing by place of publication.
Continued by *Bibliografía española* (AA825 and AD159).
Z6956.S7I56

Instituto de Cultura Hispánica (Spain). Departamento de Información. Catálogo de revistas españolas. Madrid : Ediciones Cultura Hispánica, 1948. 216 p.   **AD156**
A classified list of periodicals, omitting those of very limited interest. Gives detailed information for each, including editors, publishers, contributors, size, frequency, etc., but not dates. Subject and title indexes.   Z6956.S7S67

Periódicos y revistas españolas e hispanoamericanas. Barcelona : C.I.L.E.H., 1989. 2 v. (1153 p.).   **AD157**
Prefatory matter in English, French, German, and Italian.
Aims to list all currently published Spanish-language periodicals, including newspapers and irregular serial titles. Titles in Catalan, Basque, and Galician are listed separately. Information provided includes frequency, beginning date, price, editor, address, and subject. Includes brief biographical entries for editors where possble. Subject index.   Z6956.S7P47

Ruiz de Gauna, Adolfo. Catálogo de publicaciones periódicas vascas de los siglos XIX y XX. San Sebastián : Eusko Ikaskuntza ; Vitoria-Gasteiz : Eusko Jaurlaritza, Kultura eta Turismo Saila, 1991. 710 p. : ill.   **AD158**
An alphabetical listing of 2,200 Basque periodicals published between 1803 and 1975. In addition to title and subtitle, entries include beginning date, frequency, subject, political affiliation, language/dialect, bibliographic notes, and library holdings both inside and outside Spain. Includes geographical, chronological, ideological, subject, and library indexes. Tables and maps relating to the diffusion of periodicals are appended.   Z6956.S7R85

Current

Bibliografía española : suplemento de publicaciones periódicas. 1979– . Madrid : Dirección General del Libro y Bibliotecas, Instituto Bibliográfico Hispánico, [1980]– . Annual.   **AD159**
A classed listing of new periodical publications, giving full bibliographic information, frequency, etc.   Z2685.B572

Sweden

Lundstedt, Bernhard Wilhelm. Sveriges periodiska litteratur : bibliografi. Stockholm : Iduns Tryckeri, 1895–1902. 3 v. in 2.   **AD160**
v. 1, 1645–1812; v. 2, Stockholm, 1813–94; v. 3, Landsorten, 1813–99.
Gives detailed bibliographical information about Swedish periodicals and newspapers of the period. Each volume has its own title index; v. 3 includes a systematic index for the set.   Z6956.S9L9

Svensk tidskriftsförteckning = Current Swedish periodicals. 1967/68– . Stockholm : Tidningsaktiebolaget Svensk Bokhandel, 1968– . Triennial.   **AD161**
"Redigerad av Bibliografiska Institutet vid Kungl. Biblioteket i Stockholm."—*t.p.*
In English and Swedish.
An alphabetical listing giving full bibliographic information on current periodicals, followed by a classed listing of the titles. Kept up to date by information in *Svensk bokförteckning* (AA832).

Switzerland

Schweizer Zeitschriftenverzeichnis = Répertoire des périodiques suisses = Repertorio dei periodici svizzeri, 1951/55– . Zürich : Schweizerisches Buchhändler– und Verleger-Vereins, 1956– . Quinquennial.   **AD162**

1986–90 vol. publ. in Bern by the Schweizerische Landesbibliothek and distr. by Eidgenössische Drucksachen- und Materialzentrale, 1992.

With *Schweizer Bücherverzeichnis* (AA835), forms part of the *Schweizerische Nationalbibliographie.*

Introductory matter and section headings in German and French.

Periodicals are listed alphabetically by title in classified arrangement. Entries include relatively complete bibliographic descriptions along with addresses. Title index. KWIC index on microfiche also provided. 1986–90 vol. lists 5,463 titles published in Switzerland.

Z6956.S92S33

Schweizerische Landesbibliothek. Verzeichnis der laufenden schweizerischen Zeitschriften = Catalogue des périodiques suisses, revues, journaux, annuaires, almanachs, collections, etc / reçus par la Bibliothèque Nationale à Berne. 2. éd. refondue et considérablement augm., publ. par la direction de la Bibliothèque. Bern-Bümpliz : Benteli, [1925]. 217 p.   **AD163**

A classified list with title index.

————. ————. *Nachtrag, 1926-30* (Bern-Bümpliz : Benteli, 1926–31. 5 v.).

Schweizerischer Zeitschriften- und Zeitungskatalog = Catalogue des revues et journaux suisses. Olten : Schweizerisches Vereinssortiment, [1952]. 329 p.   **AD164**

Classed list with title index of periodicals currently published in Switzerland and information on complete title, publisher, address, beginning date, frequency, size, general coverage, etc. Title and subject/keyword indexes.   Z6956.S92S35

Current

Katalog der Schweizer Presse : Zeitschriften, Fachblätter = Catalogue de la presse suisse: périodiques, journaux professionnels. 1969– . [Zürich] : Verband Schweizerischer Werbegesellschaften, 1969– .   **AD165**

Subtitle varies.

Supersedes *Zeitungskatalog der Schweiz*, publ. 1950–68.

Introductory matter in German and French. Information is presented in tabular form.   HF6023.K36

Ukraine

Knyzhkova Palata Ukraïns'koi RSR. Periodychni vydannīa URSU, 1918–1950 : zhurnaly. Bibliohrafichnyĭ dovidnyk / [Vidpovidalnyĭ redaktor Kravchenko G. O.]. Kharkiv : [s.n.], 1956. 461 p. : ill.   **AD166**

A bibliography of Ukrainian periodicals of the period.

Updated by: *Periodychni vydannīa URSU, 1951–1960 : zhurnaly*, ed. by V. M. Skachkov (Kharkiv : Redaktsīino-vydavnychyĭ viddil Knyzhkovoï palaty URSR, 1964. 180 p.).   Z6956.U4K5

Yugoslavia

Bibliografija Jugoslavije : serijske publikacije. jan./mart 1975– . Beograd : Jugoslovenski Bibliografski Institut, 1975– . Quarterly with annual index.   **AD167**

Continues *Bibliografija jugoslovenske periodike* publ. 1956–74.

Front matter and index in Serbo-Croatian.

A current listing of periodicals and newspapers published in the republics of Serbia (inc. Kosovo and Vojvodina) and Montenegro. Entries include fairly complete bibliographic information. Arranged alphabetically. Subject index. 1992 annual vol. lists 938 titles.

Z6956.Y9B48

Jugoslovenski casopisi (izbor). Ed. [1]–2. Beograd : Jugoslovenski Centar za Tehničku i Naučnu Documentaciju, 1953–55. .   **AD168**

Title also in English (*Yugoslav periodicals : selection*), French, and German.

A classified list with title index. All headings are given in the four languages: Yugoslavian, English, French, German. Titles are also translated into the four languages. Gives publisher, address, beginning date, frequency, price, language of text, etc.   Z6956.Y9J8

Africa

Directory of scholarly journals published in Africa / comp. by African Association of Science Editors. 1990– . Nairobi, Kenya : Academy Science Publishers, c1990– . Annual.   **AD169**

Subtitle for 1990 issue: "a preliminary survey, 1990."

Includes indexes.   Z6944.S3D54

Thomassery, Marguerite. Catalogue des périodiques d'Afrique noire francophone (1858–1962) conservés à l'IFAN. Dakar : Institut Français d'Afrique Noire, 1965. 117 p. (Institut Français d'Afrique Noire. Catalogues et documents, 19).   **AD170**

Includes official serial publications as well as periodicals of general interest.   Z3503.T48

Congo

Berlage, Jean. Répertoire de la presse du Congo Belge (1884–1958) et du Ruanda-Urundi (1920–1958) … . [Rev. ed.]. Bruxelles : Commission belge de bibliographie, 1959. 193 p. (Bibliographia belgica, 43).   **AD171**

Title also in Flemish.

Continues an earlier edition (1955) whose coverage ended with 1954.

662 titles in alphabetical arrangement with four indexes: (1) chronological, (2) place names, (3) broad subject classification, and (4) publisher.   Z2407.B57

Kenya

Kenyan periodicals directory. 1984–85– . Nairobi : Kenya National Library Service, National Reference & Bibliographic Dept., c1984– . Biennial.   **AD172**

Attempts "to list all serial titles published in Kenya. Foreign serials of interest to Kenya, by subject or otherwise, and periodicals produced locally by international and regional intergovernmental and private organizations based in Kenya are also listed."—*Pref.* Classified arrangement with title/agency index. Separate classified list of cessations; directory of publishers.   Z6960.K4K43

Nigeria

Ogbondah, Chris W. The press in Nigeria : an annotated bibliography. N.Y. : Greenwood, 1990. 127 p. (African special bibliographic series, no. 12).   **AD173**

Includes "scholarly journal articles, books, conference papers and reports on Nigerian mass communication" (*Introd.*) published from the 1950s to about 1985. Arranged alphabetically by author. Subject index.   Z6940.O34

Serials in print in Nigeria / comp. by the staff of the National Library of Nigeria. 1967–68. Lagos : National Library of Nigeria, 1967–69.   **AD174**

No more published?

Includes newsletters, annuals, and government serials as well as magazines and newspapers.

University of Ibadan. Library. Nigerian periodicals and newspapers, 1950–1970. [Ibadan] : Ibadan Univ. Lib., 1971. 122 p.   **AD175**

Subtitle: A list of those [periodicals and newspapers] received by Ibadan University Library under the country's various deposit legislations from April 1950 to June 1970.

Supersedes the edition covering 1950–55 (publ. 1956). Includes periodicals which were already being published in 1950 when deposit legislation went into effect.   Z6960.N5I2

Senegal

Bibliothèque Nationale (France). Les publications en série éditées au Sénégal, 1856–1982 : liste provisoire / par Marie-Elisabeth Bouscarle. Paris : Bibliothèque Nationale, 1987. 107 p. (Collection Etudes, guides et inventaires, no 7).   **AD176**

At head of title: Bibliothèque Nationale. Département des livres imprimés. Département des entrées étrangères.

An alphabetical listing of 692 journals, newspapers, and serial government publications held in the Bibliothèque Nationale and in the libraries of Versailles and the Société de Géographie. Detailed holdings and call numbers are given, but publication dates are not included. Subject, editor, and sponsoring body index.   Z3715.B54

South Africa

Marketing mix promodata : promotion, marketing and advertising data. 1985– . Johannesburg : Systems Publishers (Pty) Ltd, 1985– . Annual.   **AD177**

Ceased 1986?

Continues: *Promodata : promotion, marketing & advertising data* (1981–85), which superseded *Advertising & press annual of Southern Africa* (1977–80) and *Advertising & press annual of Africa* (1966–76).

"Press guide" section contains basic data on South African newspapers, trade, technical, professional, and consumer publications, as well as data on annuals and directories. Emphasis on advertising and marketing information.

Saul, C. Daphne. South African periodical publications, 1800–1875 : a bibliography. Capetown : Univ. School of Librarianship, 1949. 45 p.   **AD178**

Lists periodicals, almanacs, directories, and yearbooks; excludes newspapers, government publications, and annual reports of societies. Gives the usual bibliographical information and locates copies in South African libraries.   Z6960.S6S33

Tunisia

Abdeljaoued, Mohamed. Répertoire de la presse et des publications périodiques tunisiennes. Tunis : École Normale Supérieure, 1979. 78 p.   **AD179**

A classed listing, with title index, of periodicals (including annual and irregular publications as well as those appearing more frequently) published in Tunisia. Indicates beginning date, address, frequency, etc. Includes both French and Arabic publications. Some periodicals known or thought to have ceased between 1975 and 1979 are still included with a note on cessation.

Bibliyūghrāfiyā al-qawmīyah al-Tūnisīyah. Dawrīyāt al-'Arabīyah. al-Bibliyūghrāfiyā al-qawmīyah al-Tūnisīyah. al-Dawrīyāt al-'Arabīyah / Wizārat al-Shu'ūn al-Thaqāfīyah, Dār al-Kutub al-Waṭanīyah, Maṣlaḥat al-Dawrīyāt. v. 1 (1860–1975)– . Tūnis : al-Maṣlaḥah, 1975– . Decennial.   **AD180**

Contents: v. 1, 1860–1975; v. 2, 1975–1985 (publ. 1987).

An alphabetical listing of Arabic periodicals published in Tunisia. Information provided includes title, place of publication, publisher and printer, dates, and frequency. Separate indexes for subject, sponsor and/or publisher, date of first publication, printer, and place of publication (excluding Tunis). Vol. 2 lacks place and printer indexes.

Ḥamdān, Muḥammad. Dalīl al-dawrīyāt al-ṣādirah bi-al-bilād al-Tūnisīyah : min sanat 1838 ilā 20 Mārs 1956. Qarṭaj : al-Muássasah al-Waṭanīyah lil-Tarjamah wa-al-Taḥqīq wa-al-Dirāsāt, Bayt al-Ḥikham, 1989. 2 v.   **AD181**

Vol. 2 in French.

Title on added t.p.: *Guide des périodiques parus en Tunisie de 1838 au 20 mars 1956.*

Contents: v. 1, Guide des periodiques in Arabe et en Judéo-Arabe; v. 2, Guide des periodiques in langues Européennes.

An alphabetic list of periodicals published during the European occupation of Tunisia, until independence in 1956. Vol. 1 lists 340 titles; v. 2 lists 977. Each entry includes title, dates, type of publication (e.g., almanac, bulletin, journal, etc.), frequency, affiliation or tendency (political, social, religious), editors, address, publisher, format, size, price, circulation, number of issues published, where archived, publication history (e.g., "continues," "continued by" references). Indexed by chronology, frequency, subject, languages, affiliation/tendency, type, editor, and place of publication.   Z6960.T82

Asia (by region)

Asia, West

Ahmed-Bioud, Abdelghani. 3200 revues et journaux arabes de 1800 à 1965 : titres arabes et titres translittérés / répertoire établi par Abdelghani Ahmed-Bioud avec la collaboration de Hassan Hanafi et Habib Feki. Paris : Bibliothèque Nationale, 1969. 252 p.   **AD182**

At head of title: Maison des sciences de l'homme.

Locates files of the periodicals listed in 20 libraries throughout the world (e.g., Harvard and Princeton locations are noted). Alphabetical title listing, with index by transliterated form. Entries include place of publication and general subject headings. Includes a supplement of "230 revues et journaux tunisiens."—*Table des matières.* Z6957.A34

Aman, Mohammed M. Arab periodicals and serials : a subject bibliography. N.Y. : Garland, 1979. 252 p. (Garland reference library of social science, v. 57).   **AD183**

A subject listing of "serials and periodicals in Arabic, English, French and other European languages published in the Arab countries or in the Western hemisphere."—*Introd.* Includes current publications and some which have ceased; daily and weekly newspapers, irregular serials, and annuals are included along with monthly and quarterly magazines and government-sponsored series. Subject categories (such as Agriculture, Biological sciences, Business and industry, Children and youth, Economics, General periodicals, Middle East studies, Public administration) are in alphabetical order, with titles arranged alphabetically therein. About 2,700 items. No index.   Z3013.5.A42

Bloss, Ingeborg. Zeitschriftenverzeichnis Moderner Orient : Stand 1979 = Union list of Middle East periodicals (up to 1979) / Ingebord Bloss und Marianne Schmidt-Dumont. Hamburg : Deutsches Orient-Institut, Dokumentations-Leitstelle Moderner Orient, 1980. 657 p. (Dokumentationsdienst Moderner Orient, B, 1).   **AD184**

Prefatory matter in German and English.

A union list of Middle East periodicals in the libraries of the Federal Republic of Germany and West Berlin. Limited to those periodicals which were current in 1918 or which have begun publication since that date. Titles in nonroman alphabets are given in transliteration.

Z3015.B57

Asia, Southeast

Library of Congress. Southeast Asia : Western-language periodicals in the Library of Congress / comp. by A. Kohar Rony. Wash. : Library of Congress ; U.S. Govt. Print. Off., 1979. 201 p.   **AD185**

A main-entry listing of nearly 2,300 periodicals in the Library of Congress collections that contain "information on Southeast Asia, including Brunei, Burma, Cambodia, Indochina, Indonesia, Laos, Malaysia, the Philippines, Portuguese Timor, Singapore, Thailand, and Vietnam, and on Melanesia and Polynesia."—*Pref.* Includes Western-language publications both from and outside those areas, and some which only occasionally deal with the region. Indicates holdings. Index by geographical area.   Z3221.U524

Nunn, Godfrey Raymond. Southeast Asian periodicals : an international union list. [London] : Mansell, [1977]. 456 p.

AD186

A union list of "some 26,000 periodicals published since the beginning of the nineteenth century."—*Introd.* Arrangement is by country (Burma; Cambodia; Indonesia; Laos; Malaysia, Singapore and Brunei; Philippines; Thailand; Timor; Vietnam), then by title or other main entry. In addition to locations in libraries of the countries covered, selected libraries in Australia, Canada, France, India, Great Britain, Netherlands, Portugal, Spain, and the U.S. are represented.

Z6958.S6N85

Asia (by country)

China

Chung-kuo pao k'an ta ch'ûan / "Chung-kuo pao k'an pao" pien chi pu, Yü tien pu pao k'an fa hsing chü shen chiao. Peiching : Jen min yü tien ch'u pan she, [1986?]– . Annual.

AD187

Offers listings of newspapers and magazines currently published in China; both sections are arranged by subject. Each entry provides frequency, beginning date, any title changes, issuing body, distribution, and a brief description of the contents. Province and title indexes.

Z6958.C5C5834

Library of Congress. Chinese periodicals in the Library of Congress : a bibliography / comp. by Han-chu Huang and David H. G. Hsu. Wash. : Library of Congress : for sale by the U.S. Govt. Print. Off, 1988. 814 p.   **AD188**

1st ed., 1978.

"The present work records more than 8,000 Chinese periodical titles in [LC's Chinese Collection] published from 1868 to 1986 .... Like its predecessor, this volume includes Chinese periodicals covering all subjects relating to the humanities, social sciences, natural sciences, and technology; it excludes Chinese legal serials in the custody of the Far Eastern Law Division of the Law Library of the Library of Congress, as well as periodicals in specialized fields of technical agriculture and clinical medicine which are held in the National Agricultural Library and the National Library of Medicine, respectively .... Also not listed are the holdings of some 400 periodicals on microfilm or microfiche that are in the Chinese Collection .... An added feature of the edition is that the location and call numbers of the serials are given."—*Foreword.* Titles are listed alphabetically and romanized according the Wade-Giles system. Wade-Giles to pinyin and pinyin to Wade-Giles romanization tables are appended.   Z6958.C5U53

Tung, Julia. Bibliography of Chinese academic serials, pre-1949 : material in Hoover Institution on War, Revolution, and Peace. Stanford, Calif. : East Asian Collection, Hoover Inst., Stanford Univ., [1982]. 107 p.   **AD189**

Titles are listed alphabetically by romanized title (Wade-Giles system) followed by Chinese title and bibliographic details in Chinese characters; Hoover Institution call numbers and holdings are indicated. Index of Chinese titles.   Z6944.S3T86

India

Gandhi, H. N. D. Indian periodicals in print, 1973 / H. N. D. Gandhi, Jagdish Lal, Suren Agrawal. Delhi : Vidya Mandal, [1973]. 2 v.   **AD190**

An alphabetical title list of periodicals (including newspapers) which indicates language, title changes, beginning date, frequency, sponsoring body and address, and price. Sponsor and subject indexes. Serves as an extensive bibliography, though out of date as an in-print list.   Z6958.I4G35

Gidwani, N. N. Current Indian periodicals in English : an annotated guide / N. N. Gidwani, K. Navalani. 2nd rev. enl. ed. Jaipur : Saraswati Publ., 1978. 403 p.   **AD191**

1st ed. (1969) had title: *Indian periodicals.*

A classified listing of about 5,000 English-language periodicals published in India. Index of titles and subject headings. Brief annotations (indicating scope, indexing, etc.) accompany many of the entries.

Z6958.I4G5

Nagar, Murari Lal. TULIP : the universal list of Indian periodicals / offered by Murari Lal Nagar and Sarla Devi Nagar. Columbia, Mo. : International Library Center, 1986–89. 8 v.

AD192

An alphabetical listing of Indian periodicals, including those from Pakistan and Bangladesh, issued in English, Hindi, or Sanskrit before 1980. "It does not locate a title in a specific library, but in some major union catalogs which report the title."—*Introd.*   Z6958.I4N33

Susheel Kaur. Directory of periodicals published in India, 1991 / comp., Susheel Kaur and Dr. P. Sapra. 2nd ed. New Delhi : Sapra and Sapra, c1991. 515 p.   **AD193**

1st ed. (1988) had title: *Directory of periodicals published in India, 1986–87 : a classified guide.* Updates and expands N. N. Gidwani and K. Navalani, *Current Indian periodicals in English* (Delhi : Vidya Mandal, 1973. 2 v.).

Lists by broad subject approximately 7,200 titles published in India in any language, excluding newspapers, house organs, most annual reports, and "most of the delayed, and irregular publications of Government departments (Centre as well as State)."—*Introd.* Discontinued and ceased titles are noted, as are those from the earlier edition that remain unverified. Main entries specify title information, ISSN, language, year first published, frequency, price, publisher name and address, editor's name, presence of advertising or book reviews, etc., circulation, and cross-references. Title index.

Indonesia

Perpustakaan Nasional (Indonesia). Katalog majalah terbitan Indonesia : kumulasi 1779–1980 (A–Z) = Catalogue of Indonesian serials. [Jakarta] : Perpustakaan Nasional, Departemen Pendidikan dan Kebudayaan, [1985]. 412 p.   **AD194**

From verso: "[D]isusen oleh Wartini Santoso."

Previous ed. published 1984.

Introduction in Indonesian and English.

A list of journals published in Indonesia from the late 18th through the 20th century, arranged alphabetically by title (the previous edition had classified arrangement, no title index). Entries include title, subtitle, dates of first and last issues held by the National Library, place of publication, publisher, and first year of publication, along with annotations related to binding, sequence, and Javanese script.

Z6958.I45I53

Reid, Anthony. Indonesian serials, 1942–1950, in Yogyakarta libraries : with a list of government publications in the Perpustakaan Negara, Yogyakarta / [Anthony Reid, Annemarie Jubb, and J. Jahmin]. Canberra : Australian National Univ. Pr. in association with the Faculty of Asian Studies, Australian National Univ., 1974. 133 p. (Oriental monograph series, no. 15). **AD195**

Includes newspapers as well as periodicals. Listing is by place of publication. Indexed.   Z3275.R44

Thung, Yvonne. A checklist of Indonesian serials in the Cornell University Library (1945–1970) / comp. by Yvonne Thung and John M. Echols. Ithaca, N.Y. : Southeast Asia Program, Cornell Univ., 1973. 225 p. (Cornell University. Southeast Asia Program. Data paper, no. 89). **AD196**

Supersedes *A guide to Indonesian serials (1945–1965) in the Cornell University Library* (Ithaca, N.Y., 1966), which supplanted Benedict R. Anderson, *Bibliography of Indonesian publications … 1945–1958* (Ithaca, N.Y., 1959).

Lists title, place of publication, beginning date, frequency, local holdings, and call numbers for 2,269 serials, alphabetically arranged.

Z6958.I45T5

Zulkarjono, Maesarah. Daftar majalah Indonesia yang telah mempunyai ISSN. Jakarta : Pusat Dokumentasi Ilmiah Nasional, Lembaga Ilmu Pengetahuan Indonesia, 1984. 87 p.

AD197

A list of currently published Indonesian periodicals arranged alphabetically by publisher. Title index.   Z460.4.Z84

Iran

A directory of Iranian periodicals. 1969–78/79. Tehran : Tehran Book Processing Centre, 1969–79? Irregular. **AD198**

Poori Soltani, comp.

Publisher varies. Also published in Persian.

On t.p.: "Institute for Research and Planning in Science and Education."—*1978–79 ed.*

Each issue lists magazines appearing at least twice per year during the period covered. Alphabetical title listing, with subject and name indexes. Introduction in English.

Continued under a similar title?

Cumulated ed. : *A directory of Iranian periodicals, 1968–1989* (Tehran : National Library of Iran, 1989) by the same compiler, assisted by Reza Eqtedar. Title also in Persian.   Z6958.I65D55

Union catalogue of Persian serials & newspapers in British libraries / Middle East Libraries Committee ; ed. by Ursula Sims-Williams. London : Ithaca Pr., 1985. 149 p. **AD199**

"Attempts to record all Persian language serials in national, university and government libraries in Great Britain. It includes details of periodicals and newspapers, whether wholly or partially in Persian, Dari, or Tajik, published throughout the world."—*p. xii.* Arranged alphabetically by title. Holdings are issue-specific.   Z6958.I65U54

Israel

Tronik, Ruth. Israeli periodicals & serials in English & other European languages : a classified bibliography. Metuchen, N.J. : Scarecrow, 1974. 193 p. **AD200**

"Broadly speaking, this bibliography records materials emanating from scientific institutions, institutions of higher learning and learned societies to the scientific world at large."—*Introd.* Includes both current and defunct publications.

A supplement, "Israeli periodicals and serials in English and other European languages, 1974–78 : a classified bibliography" appeared in *The serials librarian* 4 (Summer 1980): 427–462.   Z6985.I8T76

Japan

Nihon zasshi sōran. 1963– . Tokyo : Shuppan Nyūsu-sha, 1963– . Irregular. **AD201**

Periodicals are grouped in six categories: general; scholarly journals; government publications; association publications; literary society publications; and publicity or corporate in-house publications. Arrangement varies within categories. Title index; publishers' directory.

Z6958.J3N56

Zasshi shimbun sōkatarogu = Periodicals in print. 1979– . Tokyo : Media Research Center, 1979– . Annual. **AD202**

The 15th ed. lists 15,834 periodicals and 3,718 newspapers current as of early 1993. Classified arrangement with indexes of titles and classification codes.

§ Although not as complete as *Nihon zasshi sōran* (AD201) for periodicals or *Nihon shimbun nenkan* (*Japanese newspaper annual*; Tokyo : Nihon Shimbun Kyōkai), this has the advantage of annual updating as well as coverage of both periodicals and newspapers in one volume.   Z6958.J3Z37

Malaysia

Harris, L. J. Guide to current Malaysian serials. Kuala Lumpur : Univ. of Malaya Libr., 1967. 73 p. **AD203**

Classified list with title and subject index. Descriptive and bibliographical notes.   Z6958.M3H3

Perpustakaan Negara Malaysia. Terbitan bersiri kini Malaysia (bukan kerajaan) = Malaysian current serials (non-government). 1981– . Kuala Lumpur : Perpustakaan Negara Malaysia, 1981– . **AD204**

In Chinese, English, and Malay.

"Lists all current serial publications received by the National Library of Malaysia under the provisions of the Preservation of Books Act, 1966."—*Pref.* Government publications are not included. Lists 1,526 titles arranged alphabetically; entries contain place of publication, beginning date, frequency, corporate source and, where available, English title, subscription price, and ISSN. Transliterated headings are provided for entries in Jawi, Chinese, and Tamil. A list of publishers' addresses is included.   Z6958.M3P47a

Roff, William R. Bibliography of Malay and Arabic periodicals published in the Straits Settlements and peninsular Malay states 1876–1941 : with an annotated union list of holdings in Malaysia, Singapore and the United Kingdom. London : Oxford Univ. Pr., 1972. 74 p. (London oriental bibliographies, 3).

AD205

A revision and expansion of the same compiler's *Guide to Malay periodicals, 1876–1941* (Singapore, 1961). In addition to new and updated information on holdings, locations, and availability of microfilms, some new titles have been added, U.K. locations supplied, and historical or explanatory notes appended for most entries. A chronological listing with indexes of titles and of proper names.

Z6958.M3R64

Pakistan

Mahmud ul-Hassan. Pakistani serials : bibliographic control list, 1990 / Mahmud ul-Hassan, Zamurad Mahmud. [Islamabad] : M. Hassan : Z. Mahmud ; Rawalpindi : distr. by Federal Book Corp., 1990. 290 p. **AD206**

"The aim of this ... list is to provide a full guide to the English periodicals published from Pakistan up to 1989."—*Introd.* Most entries cover the period 1947–89, although some earlier titles are included. Arranged alphabetically by title, entries specify place of publication, editor or publisher, first year published, frequency, language other than English (if bilingual), price, publication changes, microform availability, address if known, and broad subject field. Cessation and suspension information is also given. Z6958.P2M35

Moid, A. A guide to periodical publications and newspapers of Pakistan / by A. Moid and Akhtar H. Siddiqui. Karachi : Pakistan Bibliographical Working Group, [1953]. 60 p. (Pakistan Bibliographical Working Group. Publication, no. 2). **AD207**

A classified arrangement with very brief information: title, address, frequency, and price. Z3193.M6

Philippines

Golay, Frank H. An annotated guide to Philippine serials / Frank H. Golay and Marianne H. Hauswedell. Ithaca, N.Y. : Southeast Asia Program, Dept. of Asian Studies, Cornell Univ., 1976. 131 p. (Southeast Asia Program, Dept. of Asian Studies, Cornell University. Data paper, no. 101). **AD208**

Based on the holdings of the Cornell University Library. Arranged as two lists, each with its own index: (1) nongovernmental serials; (2) government serials. Z6958.P5G64

National Library (Philippines). Filipiniana and Asia Division. Checklist of rare Filipiniana serials (1811–1944). [Manila] : Filipiniana and Asia Div., National Library, 1976. pt. 1. (TNL Research guide series, no. 10). **AD209**

Contents: pt. 1, 1811–1944.

An alphabetically arranged "preliminary checklist of rare serial titles available in the Filipiniana and Asia Division of the National Library."—*Pref.* Includes 271 titles of Filipino magazines, newspapers, provincial newspapers, and school publications published between 1811 and 1944. Entries contain basic bibliographic information and National Library holdings. A planned pt. 2 covering the period beginning with 1945 had not yet been published. Z6958.P5M35

Taiwan

Annotated guide to Taiwan periodical literature, 1972 / ed. by Robert L. Irick. Rev. and enl. / by K. M. Ho. [Taipei : Che'eng-Wen Pub. Co.], 1972. 174 p. (Chinese Materials and Research Aids Service Center, Occasional series, no. 15). **AD210**

1st ed., 1966.

Provides directory information concerning 1,070 periodicals published in Taiwan. Entries are arranged alphabetically by romanized title. Annotations in English. Subject and stroke count title indexes are provided, as is a brief listing of English and bilingual periodicals. Z6958.F6A75

Vietnam

Pham, Henry Thuoc V. A bibliography of Vietnamese magazines, newspapers and newsletters published in the United States and other countries = Mục-lục tạp-chí, báo-chí, thông-tin xut-bản ở hoa-kỳ và thế-Giới. [Aurora, Colo. : Vietnamese-American Cultural Alliance of Colorado, 1988?]. 21 *l.* **AD211**

Compiler's pen name: Xûan-Tuòn.

Title, foreword, and section headings also in Vietnamese. Collection held by Auraria Library, Denver, Colo.

Alphabetical title listings in sections: magazines published in the U.S., newspapers published in the U.S., newsletters published in the U.S., and Vietnamese serials published in other countries. Basic bibliographic information is given. Z6944.E8P54

Reference aid : data on serial publications of Vietnam, Laos, and Cambodia. [s.l.] : Foreign Broadcast Information Service ; Springfield, Va. : [distr. by] National Technical Information Service, [1986]. 159 p. **AD212**

"This report replaces JPRS Report 77846 DATA ON SERIAL PUBLICATIONS OF VIETNAM dated 16 April 1981"—*Introd.* Compiled by the Foreign Broadcast Information Service (FBIS), this listing provides bibliographic information about periodicals and newspapers published in the three countries, including English title, periodicity, language, publisher, address, description of contents, circulation, and other data. "All the information is derived from the publications themselves or from references to those publications in other printed or radio sources." Entries for Laos and Cambodia make up only about 5% of the total. PN5449.V5R436

Australia and Oceania

Press, radio & TV guide : Australia, New Zealand and the Pacific Islands. v. 1 (1914)– . Sydney : Country Pr. Ltd., 1914– . Irregular. **AD213**

Publisher varies; frequency varies.

Title varies: 1914–68, *The press directory of Australia and New Zealand.*

A listing of newspapers, periodicals, and radio and television stations arranged geographically. Gives directory information, including considerable statistical and gazetteer information about places. Alphabetical index.

Australia

Australian periodicals in print. 1987– . Melbourne : D. W. Thorpe, 1987– . Annual. **AD214**

Continues *Australian serials in print,* 1981–86, which replaced *Current Australian serials* (Canberra: National Library of Australia, 1963–75).

Aims to list any serial publication "that is produced in Australia, no matter how frequently or infrequently, regularly or irregularly, under the same name, and available to the public."—*Introd.* An alphabetical title listing includes newspapers, magazines, directories, yearbooks, newsletters, society proceedings, etc. The 1988 ed. indicates serials available in microform. Distributors' names and addresses are included in the listings. Z6961.C8

UNION LISTS

International

The bibliography of South Asian periodicals : a union-list of periodicals in South Asian languages / comp. by Graham W. Shaw, Salim Quraishi. [Brighton] Sussex : Harvester Pr. ; Totowa, N.J. : Barnes & Noble, 1982. 135 p. **AD215**

A union catalog for six British libraries. South Asia is defined as encompassing India, Pakistan, Bangladesh, Nepal, Bhutan, Sikkim, Sri Lanka and Afghanistan. Aims to record all serials written wholly or partly in a South Asian language and published anwhere in the world which can be found in the cooperating libraries. Listing is by language. Z6958.S57B5

Moon, Brenda Elizabeth. Periodicals for South-East Asian studies : a union catalogue of holdings in British and selected European libraries. London : Mansell, 1979. 610 p.   **AD216**
   At head of title: South-East Asia Library Group.
   Originally undertaken as a union catalog of British library holdings of Southeast Asian periodicals, the published checklist extends to periodicals for which no holdings were reported and includes not only British resources, but also those of a number of libraries in France, Germany, and the Netherlands. Attempts "to include all periodicals, both current and extinct, of Asian or East Asian interest if they are considered to be of substantial value for South-East Asian studies, whether published in South-East Asia or outside these areas."—*p.ix.* Serves as a useful complement to G. R. Nunn's *Southeast Asian periodicals* (AD186).
   Arrangement is by title (or issuing body in the case of bulletins, etc.); publications in nonroman scripts are entered in romanized form. Periodicals of all frequencies are included, but those appearing irregularly or less than annually are not comprehensively covered.
                                                          Z3221.M59

Nunn, Godfrey Raymond. Japanese periodicals and newspapers in Western languages : an international union list. London : Mansell, 1979. 235 p.   **AD217**
   An international list of some 3,500 periodicals and newspapers held by libraries in Great Britain, Canada, the U.S., and Japan.
                                                          Z6958.J3N86

Ossorguine-Bakounine, Tatiana. L'émigration russe en Europe : catalogue collectif des périodiques en langue russe. Paris : Institut d'Études Slaves, 1976–77. 2 v. (Bibliothèque russe de l'Institut d'études slaves , t. 40$^{1-2}$.).   **AD218**
   Contents: [v. 1.] 1855–1940 (340 p); [v. 2] 1940–1970, établi par Anne-Marie Volkoff (139 p); [v. 2, 2e éd.] 1940–1979 (second ed. of v. 2 published 1981, 147 p).
   Lists and locates files of Russian émigré publications published in the Russian language in European countries other than Russia. Vol. 1 is in two sections: 1855–Feb. 1917, and Mar. 1917–1939, each being an alphabetical title listing. Entries are given in Cyrillic characters, with notes on holdings, etc., in French. Indexes of transliterated titles and of names cited. Serves as the basis for *Russian émigré journals, 1855–1917* [microform] (Leiden, IDC Microform Publishers, 1988–), a full-text microfiche set of the titles listed in v. 1.
   A 2nd ed. of v. 2, comp. by Volkoff and covering 1940–79, was publ. 1981.   Z6955.V64

North America

United States

Bibliography

Library of Congress. General Reference and Bibliography Division. Union lists of serials : a bibliography / comp. by Ruth S. Freitag. Wash. : U.S. Govt. Print. Off., 1964. 150 p.
                                                          AD219
   Updates the bibliography compiled by Daniel C. Haskell and Karl Brown which appeared in the 2nd ed. (1943) of the *Union list of serials in libraries of the United States and Canada*, p. 3053–65. Lists more than 1,200 union lists, arranged geographically by region and country. Includes both separately published works and lists published in journals or as parts of books.   Z6945.U5U53

Lists

Balys, John P. Lithuanian periodicals in American libraries : a union list. Wash. : Libr. of Congress, 1982. 125 p.   **AD220**

Lists and locates files of "newspapers, periodicals, and serial publications in the Lithuanian language published anytime and anywhere; periodicals on Lithuanian matters in other languages; and periodicals published in the territory of Lithuania in any language and at any time."—*Introd.* Only titles found in U.S. and Canadian libraries are included.   Z6956.S65B34

Danky, James Philip. Undergrounds : a union list of alternative periodicals in libraries of the United States and Canada. Madison : State Historical Soc. of Wis., 1974. 206 p.   **AD221**
   "The purpose of this list is to bring a heterogeneous group of often little-known periodicals to the attention of North American researchers and librarians."—*Introd.*
   An alphabetical listing, with geographic index. Gives title, place of publication, and library location, but no indication of holdings or dates of publication. Indicates availability on microfilm, indexing in *Alternative press index* (AD259), and citations in other lists or directories.   Z6944.U5D3

Fulton, Richard D. Union list of Victorian serials : a union list of selected nineteenth-century British serials available in United States and Canadian libraries / Richard D. Fulton and C.M. Colee, general editors ; editorial board, Christopher C. Dahl ... [et al.]. N.Y. : Garland , 1985. 732 p. (Garland reference library of the humanities, vol. 530).   **AD222**
   Aims to provide a finding list for selected Victorian periodicals in nearly 500 North American libraries. Selection was "based on the list of periodicals included in Volume III of the *New Cambridge bibliography of English literature*, with about 100 titles added in science and technology."—*Introd.* More than 300 librarians and scholars assisted in compiling detailed holdings information and doing actual shelf checks; where only published lists or regional guides had to be relied on, the library name is marked with an asterisk. In addition to libraries with major Victorian collections, local and regional libraries were selected to give broad geographical representation.   Z6956.G6F85

Indiana University. Libraries. Current Japanese serials in the humanities and social sciences received in American libraries. Bloomington : Indiana Univ. Lib., East Asian Collection, 1980. 337 p.   **AD223**
   "Sponsored by the Japan-U.S. Friendship Commission."—*t.p.*
   "The primary purpose of this listing ... is to provide a tool for making judgments on curtailing and adding Japanese subscriptions."—*Pref.* A romanized title listing of nearly 4,400 serials. Symbols for holding libraries are given without indication of actual holdings.   Z6958.J3I5

———————— Union list of little magazines. Chicago : Midwest Inter-Libr. Center, 1956. 98 p.   **AD224**
   Subtitle: Showing holdings of 1037 little magazines in the libraries of Indiana University, Northwestern University, Ohio State University, State University of Iowa, University of Chicago, University of Illinois.

New serial titles / prep. under the sponsorship of the Joint Committee on the Union List of Serials. Jan. 1953– . Wash. : Library of Congress. ·   **AD225**
   Superintendent of Documents classification: LC 1.23/4: .
   Monthly with annual cumulations (beginning 1969, in 8 monthly issues, 4 quarterly issues, and annual cumulation), which are self-cumulative through periods of three or more years.
   Cumulations include 1950–70 in 4 v.; 1971–75 in 2 v.; 1976–80 in 2 v.; 1981–83 in 3 v.; 1981–1985 (6 v.); 1986–1989 (6 v.).
   Prepared under the sponsorship of the Joint Committee on the Union List of Serials; serves as a continuation of the *Union list of serials* (AD226).
   Lists periodicals which began publication in 1950 and later, giving place of publication and statement of beginning date (and closing date if pertinent) with record of holdings in about 700 U.S. and Canadian libraries. Additional locations are published in each cumulation. Through 1980, a section at the back of each cumulation listed "Changes in serials" and noted changes for all serials regardless of their begin-

ning date. These changes included title changes, changes in the name or catalog entry of corporate authors, cessations, suspensions, resumptions and the like.

The 1950–1970 cumulation (publ. 1973) was compiled with Bowker's computerized publication system, and incorporates thousands of revisions, additional library locations, and ISSNs. Some irregularities in filing order of corporate entries. A two-volume *Subject guide* (publ. 1975) provides a subject approach according to the Dewey Decimal Classification.

In 1981, *NST* became a product of the CONSER (CONversion of SERials) Project, an online cooperative database, with coverage including reports of all serials contributed to the CONSER file, regardless of beginning date of publication. Information is now presented in traditional "card catalog" format, with the fullness of the record depending on the amount of data available in the CONSER record. Catalog "tracings" are included along with bibliographic information and library locations. Generally speaking, records appear as "open" entries; there is no indication of holdings of individual libraries. The "Change in serials" feature last appeared in the 1976–80 cumulation.

New serial titles. 1950–1970 cumulative (Wash. : Libr. of Congress; N.Y. : Bowker, 1973. 4 v.).

New serial titles. 1950–1970, subject guide (N.Y. : Bowker, 1975. 2 v. [3692 p.]) offers a subject approach, according to the Dewey Decimal Classification. Z6945.U5S42

Union list of serials in libraries of the United States and Canada. 3rd ed. / ed. by Edna Brown Titus. N.Y. : Wilson, 1965. 5 v. (4649 p.). **AD226**

History: 1st ed., 1927 (Supplements, Jan. 1925–Dec. 1932. 2v.); 2nd ed., 1943 (Supplements, Jan. 1941–Dec.1949. 2v.), ed. by Winifred Gregory. (For a history of the *Union list* and its predecessors, *see* Preface by Howard Rovelstad.).

The 1st ed. contained entries for some 75,000 serial titles with location of holdings in 225 libraries in the U.S. and Canada. The 2nd ed. was enlarged to some 115,000 titles with locations in 650 libraries. The two supplements brought this record up to Dec. 1949 with additional titles. These two editions proved that this comprehensive union list was indispensible in American libraries doing research and reference work with periodicals. Therefore, under the sponsorship of the Joint Committee on the Union List of Serials, with the cooperation of the Library of Congress, and funded by a grant from the Council on Library Resources, a 3rd ed. was prepared.

The 3rd ed. follows closely the pattern of the 2nd, listing the entries in the 2nd ed., plus those in the two supplements, with the addition of almost 12,000 new titles which began publication before 1950, thus listing more than 156,000 titles, with holdings in 956 cooperating libraries. For the titles acquired by cooperating libraries since the 2nd ed. and its supplements, additional locations are reported for "significant titles only—titles not commonly held. Additional locations were not to be listed whenever ten or more locations had already been listed in the second edition and supplements unless considered both desirable and necessary—e.g., geographical considerations."—*Introd.*

Each entry gives catalog description of title (under *latest* form name), a statement of what constitutes a complete set, and indicates changes of title and exact holdings in reporting libraries, with cross-references from all changed titles and alternate entries. Includes all types of serial publications except: government publications (other than periodicals and monograph series issued by governments); U.S. publications; administrative reports of societies, universities, corporations, etc.; almanacs; gift books; American newspapers; English and other foreign newspapers after 1820; law reports and digests; publications of agricultural and other experiment stations; local religious, labor, and fraternal organizations; boards of trade; chambers of commerce; national and international conferences and congresses, etc.; house organs (unless of technical and scientific value); alumni, undergraduate, and intercollegiate fraternal publications; trench papers; and in general all titles having a highly limited or ephemeral value.—cf. *Introd.* It was found to be impractical to incorporate entries for titles in the Far Eastern languages.

This edition, covering to Dec. 1949, was the last in this form. Continued for periodicals begun after 1950 by *New serial titles* (AD225). Z6945.U45

Willging, Eugene Paul. Catholic serials of the nineteenth century in the United States : a descriptive bibliography and union list. First series / Eugene Paul Willging, Herta Hatzfeld. Wash. : Catholic Univ. of America Pr., 1968. 2 v. **AD227**

First published as a series of 15 articles in *Records* of the American Catholic Historical Society, Philadelphia, from 1954 to 1963. Information was revised and updated for this publication.

Covers 29 states in alphabetical order. For each state, gives: historical background, description of publications with library locations, special bibliography, alphabetical and chronological tables, etc.

States having longer histories and more extensive lists of Catholic publications are covered in:

————. ————. *Second series* (Wash. : Catholic Univ. of America Pr., 1959–68. 15 pts.).

Contents: pt. 1, Minnesota, North Dakota and South Dakota; pt. 2, Wisconsin; pt. 3, Illinois; pt. 4, Indiana; pt. 5, Pennsylvania; pt. 6, Iowa; pt. 7, Michigan; pt. 8, California; pt. 9, Missouri; pt. 10, Massachusetts; pt. 11, Maryland and District of Columbia; pt. 12, Kentucky and Ohio; pt. 13, Louisiana, Mississippi, Texas; pt. 14, v. 1, New York City; pt. 14, v. 2, New York State; pt. 15, Statistical analysis of 1st ser., pts. 1–2 and 2nd ser., pts. 1–14.

The second series follows the arrangement of the first.

Canada

National Library of Canada. Periodicals in the social sciences and humanities currently received by Canadian libraries = Inventaire des périodiques de sciences sociales et d'humanités possèdent les bibliothèques canadiennes. [Ottawa : Queen's Printer], 1968. 2 v. **AD228**

Preface and explanatory matter in French and English.

Offered as an "interim publication" pending publication of a proposed full-scale union list for Canadian libraries. Lists about 12,000 titles held by 179 libraries. Z6945.O895

Mexico

Velásquez Gallardo, Pablo. Catálogo colectivo de publicaciones periódicas existentes en bibliotecas de la República Mexicana / Pablo Velásquez Gallardo, Ramon Nadurille. México : Instituto Nacional de Investigaciones Agrícolas, 1968. 2 v. **AD229**

A union list of the periodical holdings of about 130 cooperating libraries. Z6945.V4

Europe

Belgium

Bibliothèque Royale de Belgique. Catalogue collectif belge et luxembourgeois des périodiques étrangers en cours de publication / rédigé sous la direction de A. Cockx. Bruxelles : Culture et Civilisation, 1965. 2 v. (1982 p.). **AD230**

Title and introductory matter in Flemish and French.

Provides a finding list in libraries of Belgium and Luxembourg of periodicals currently published outside those areas. Some 400 libraries reported holdings, and the list of these forms a useful directory indicating accessibility, hours, and special services. Z6945.B907

France

Bibliothèque Nationale (France). Département des Périodiques. Catalogue collectif des périodiques du début du XVIIᵉ siècle à 1939 : conservés dans les bibliothèques de Paris et dans les bibliothèques universitaires des départements. Paris : Bibliothèque nationale, 1967–81. 5 v.   **AD231**

Contents: v. 1–4, A–Z; v. 5, Additions et corrections; Tables des collectivités citées.

An important union list of periodicals held by some 73 libraries in France. Unfortunately, coverage has been limited to serials which began publication before 1940. Excluded are: daily papers after 1849; almanacs; annual directories; administrative publications of limited interest (e.g., local church bulletins, alumni magazines). Slavic periodicals in the Cyrillic alphabet are also excluded since these are listed in *Périodiques slaves en caracatères cyrilliques* (AD232).

Entry is under first word of the title not an article. Thus, there are a great number of entries under "Proceedings," "Bulletin," etc., but the "Tables des collectivités citées" in v. 5 enables the user to identify the publications of specific societies, organizations, and similar issuing bodies. Entries include dates of publication, notes on title changes, issuing body, supplements, cumulative indexes, and library locations with indication of exact holdings.   Z6945.P236

——————— Périodiques slaves en caractères cyrilliques : état des collections en 1950. Paris, 1956. 2 v.   **AD232**

A union list of periodical holdings of 46 libraries of Paris and of French universities. Russian, Ukrainian, Belorussian, Bulgarian, and Serbian titles are listed in one alphabet. Newspapers are excluded. Slavic periodicals in Latin characters are listed in the general section of the Bibliothèque Nationale's *Catalogue collectif des périodiques* (AD231).

——. ——. *Supplément, 1951–1960* (Paris : 1963. 495 p.).
——. ——. *Addenda et errata, é tat général des collections en 1960* (Paris, 1965. 222 p.).

Inventaire des périodiques étrangers et des publications en série étrangères reçus en France par les bibliothèques et les organismes de documentation en 1965. [4. éd.]. Paris : Bibliothèque Nationale, 1969. 1207 p.   **AD233**

At head of title: Direction des Bibliothèques et de la Lecture Publique. Inventaire Permanent des Périodiques Étrangers en Cours (I.P.P.E.C.).

1st ed., 1956; 3rd ed., 1962. Earlier editions had title: *Inventaire des périodiques étrangers reçus en France*.

Lists about 43,000 publications received in some 2,300 participating libraries and other repositories. Covers all subject fields. Gives title, subtitle, place of publication, and locations of files, but not dates of publication.

Germany

Bruhn, Peter. Gesamtverzeichnis russischer und sowjetischer Periodika und Serienwerke / hrsg. von Werner Philipp. Wiesbaden : In Kommission bei O. Harrassowitz, [1960–76]. 4 v. (Berlin. Freie Universität. Östeuropa Inst. Bibliographische Mitteilungen, 3).   **AD234**

Locates files of Russian and Soviet periodicals in libraries of the Federal Republic of Germany and West Berlin. Notable for its broad chronological, linguistic, and geographical coverage. Includes newspapers, yearbooks, almanacs, and numbered series; also publications of official and semiofficial Russian and Soviet groups abroad. Title listing, with a "Nachtrag" in v.3; v.4 is an index.

Gesamtverzeichnis ausländischer Zeitschriften und Serien 1939–1958 : (GAZS) / bearb. und hrsg. von der Staatsbibliothek der Stiftung Preussischer Kulturbesitz. Wiesbaden : Harrassowitz, 1959–68. 5 v.   **AD235**

Sponsoring body varies. Issued in parts.

An earlier series, *Gesamtverzeichnis der ausländischen Zeitschriften (GAZ) 1914–1924*, was issued by the Prussian Auskunftsbureau der deutschen Bibliotheken (Berlin, 1927–29).

An extensive list of non-German periodicals, with holdings in German libraries indicated in detail. Unfortunately, there is no key to the symbols used to indicate libraries; for this, reference must be made to Wolfgang Voigt's *Sigelverzeichnis für die Bibliotheken der Bundesrepublik Deutschland* (Wiesbaden : Harrassowitz, 1960).

——. *Nachträge* (Marburg an der Lahn : Staatsbibliothek der Stiftung Preussische Kulturbesitz, 1966–78. 30 pts.).

Great Britain

British union-catalogue of periodicals : a record of the periodicals of the world, from the seventeenth century to the present day, in British libraries / ed. for the Council of the British Union-Catalogue of Periodicals by James D. Stewart, with Muriel E. Hammond and Erwin Saenger. N.Y. : Academic Pr. ; London : Butterworths Scientific Publs., 1955–58. 4 v.   **AD236**

Lists more than 140,000 titles contained in about 440 libraries with indication of holdings; an important addition to any library's collection of union lists. Includes many periodicals not in the *Union list of serials* (AD226), and the difference in form of entry makes possible a different approach in identifying titles.

Periodicals are listed under the first word of the title that is not an article, except that periodicals issued by an organization are entered under the name of the organization unless the title is specific in itself. All periodicals are entered under their *earliest* known names, followed by particulars of all changes of name in chronological sequence. References are given from all later names to the original name. Similarly all academies, societies, and other organizations are entered under their *original* names, with particulars of alternate names, and all changes of organization. References from all variants are given to the original name.

Alphabetization is by the words printed in heavy type; all minor words, articles, prepositions, conjunctions, etc., are printed but ignored in filing. Variant spellings such as "Bollettino" and "Bullettino" are amalgamated. Other details are explained at the beginning of v. 1.

All locations for commonly held periodicals are not necessarily given, but in the case of rare periodicals all reported holdings, fragmentary or otherwise, have been included.

——. *Supplement to 1960*, ed. for the Council of the British Union-Catalogue of Periodicals by James D. Stewart with Muriel E. Hammond and Erwin Saenger (London : Butterworths, 1962. 991 p.).

Includes entries for new periodicals reported as first appearing since publication of the main volumes, some expanded or amended entries, and some entries for earlier periodicals not previously reported.

Supersedes for most purposes the *Union catalogue of the periodical publications in the university libraries of the British Isles* (London : Nat. Central Lib., 1937. 712p.).

British union-catalogue of periodicals : incorporating World list of scientific periodicals. New periodical titles. 1960/68–1980. London : Butterworths, 1964–81. Quarterly; annual cumulations.   **AD237**

Ed. for the National Central Library by Kenneth I. Porter.

A cumulative issue for 1960–68, ed. by Kenneth I. Porter and C. J. Koster, was published 1970.

Aims to list periodicals and serials which began in or after 1960, changed title, began a new series, or ceased publication. Serves as a continuing supplement to both the *British union-catalogue of periodicals* (AD236) and the *World list* (EA46). Lists library holdings in British libraries.

§ Continued by *Serials in the British Library* (AD116).
    Z6945.B874

Travis, Carole. Periodicals from Africa : a bibliography and union list of periodicals published in Africa / comp. and ed. by Carole Travis and Miriam Alman. Boston : G. K. Hall, 1977. 619 p. **AD238**

Aims to present "as comprehensive a list as possible of periodicals published in Africa, and at the same time, to give locations for those titles held in libraries in the United Kingdom."—*Introd.* (Egypt is excluded, and only those South African periodicals held in U.K. libraries are listed.) Arrangement is alphabetical by country of publication, then by title; comprehensive title index. Holdings of "some 60 university, national, government and private libraries, representing the major African collections in the United Kingdom" are recorded, but bibliographic information on many titles not located in those libraries is also given.

————. *First supplement*, comp. and ed. by David Blake and Carole Travis (Boston : G.K. Hall, 1984. 217 p.). At head of title: Standing Conference on Library Materials on Africa. Z3503.T73

Italy

Catalogo collettivo nazionale delle pubblicazioni periodiche. Roma : Istituto di studi sulla ricerca e documentazione scientifica, 1990. 2 v. (2460 p.). **AD239**

At head of title: Consiglio nazionale delle ricerche. Istituto di studi sulla ricerca e documentazione scientifica.

Alphabetical title listing of more than 70,000 periodicals in all disciplines reported to be held in 1,730 Italian libraries. Entries contain very basic bibliographic and holdings information. Z7403.C385

Netherlands

Koninklijke Bibliotheek (Netherlands). Centrale catalogus van periodieken en seriewerken in Nederlandse bibliotheken (CCP). 3. uitg. 'sGravenhage : De Bibliotheek, 1983. 14 v. **AD240**

1st ed., 1971–73.

"Abridged introduction" in English.

A union list of periodicals and serial publications in libraries of the Netherlands. Main entry listing; about 200,000 titles; holdings are specific. Z6945.H16

Spain

Spain. Dirección General de Archivos y Bibliotecas. Catálogo colectivo de publicaciones periódicas en bibliotecas españolas. [Madrid, 1971–76]. v.1–5[1]. **AD241**

Contents: v. 1, Derecho y administración [pública]; v. 2, Medicina; v. 3, Agricultura y veterinaria; v. 4, Ciencias de la educación; v. 5, Humanidades, tomo 1: Ciencias historicas.

A union list of serials in Spanish libraries as of 1969. Within each volume periodicals are listed alphabetically by title with library location and indication of holdings. At the end of the volume, titles are grouped by subclasses (e.g., in v. 1, under headings for canon law, civil law, military law, etc.; in v. 2, anatomy, pathology, internal medicine, etc.). Libraries in more than 50 cities are represented.
Z6945.S694

Switzerland

Vereinigung Schweizerischer Bibliothekare. Verzeichnis ausländischer Zeitschriften und Serien in schweizerischen Bibliotheken = Répertoire des périodiques étrangers reçus par les bibliothèques suisses. 6. Aufl. Bern : Vereinigung Schweizerischer Bibliothekare, 1981. 1355 p. **AD242**

1st ed., 1904.

A union list of foreign periodicals in Swiss libraries. The 4th ed. (1955) listed some 34,000 titles. This edition is concerned with serials published after World War II (i.e., those which began publication after Dec. 31, 1945 and older series which continued or resumed publication after that date); for titles which ceased before 1946, the user is referred to the 4th ed. The list of cooperating libraries precedes the main-entry listing; holdings information is precise. Z6945.V8

Africa

South Africa

PISAL : Periodicals in South African libraries = TISAL : Tydskrifte in Suid-Afrikaanse biblioteke [microform]. 2nd ed. Pretoria : The State Library, 1985. Microfiche, accompanied by booklet. **AD243**

Earlier eds. issued 1961, 1972–73, 1977, and 1980.

Comp. for South African Council for Scientific and Industrial Research and Human Sciences Research Council.

Updated by cumulative *PISAL* supplement issued twice per year, in May and November. 1986 and 1987 supplements do not wholly replace *PISAL 1985*, though holdings information is cumulative.

Entries alphabetically arranged by author/title; includes locations and holdings information contributed by more than 384 South African libraries. No subject index. Excludes certain types of publications, such as newspapers, some annual reports, and government publications with nondistinct titles. Accompanying booklet has introductory matter in Afrikaans and English, and contains code list for contributing libraries. Z6945.P452

Asia (by country)

Philippines

University of the Philippines. Inter-Departmental Reference Service. Union list of serials of government agency libraries of the Philippines / comp. by Maxima M. Ferrer ... [et al.]. Rev. and enl. ed. Manila, 1960. 911 p. **AD244**

1st ed., 1955.

Includes nearly 8,000 entries of foreign and domestic periodicals, representing the holdings of 79 libraries in the Philippines.

The alphabetical list, which gives full information, is followed by a classified list of the serials included. Z6945.Q4

University of the Philippines. Library. Union checklist of Filipiniana serials / prep. by the serials project staff. Provisional ed. Quezon City : Univ. of the Philippines Library, 1980. 925 p. **AD245**

Earlier eds. published 1963, 1968.

A list, alphabetical by title, of approximately 6,000 serials in all subjects published in the Philippines. Entries contain basic bibliographic information and summarized holdings for the 42 libraries in the Philippines Library System. Both a classified subject index and a final edition have been planned. Z3299.U54

Thailand

Rúam ráichou̓ wárasán nai Prathét Thai = Union list of periodicals in Thailand / dói Khana ʿAnukammakán Klum Wárasán læ ʿÉkkasán Bannárak ʿHóngsamut Sathában ʿUdommasu̓ksá. Chabap sombún. [Bangkok] : Khana ʿAnukammakán Klum Wárasán læ ʿÉkkasán Bannárak ʿHóngsamut Sathában ʿUdommasu̓ksá, [1987]. 512 *l.* **AD246**
Listing of Thai periodicals held in Thai libraries, with holdings information. Entries include English titles where appropriate.

Australia and Oceania

New Zealand

National Library of New Zealand. Union list of serials in New Zealand libraries. 3rd ed. Wellington : Nat. Lib. of New Zealand, 1969–70. 6 v.   **AD247**
1st ed. 1953; 2nd ed. 1964–68. Section 2, "Conferences, symposia, etc." (Wellington, 1968. 244p.) of the 2nd ed. is not superseded by the 3rd.   Z6945.N285

INDEXES

Bibliography

Covington, Paula Hattox. Indexed journals : a guide to Latin American serials. Madison, Wis. : Secretariat, Seminar on the Acquisition of Latin American Library Materials [SALALM], Memorial Lib., Univ. of Wisconsin, 1983. 458 p. (Seminar on the Acquisition of Latin American Library Materials. Bibliography series, 8).   **AD248**
Both an aid for determining where articles in a given journal are indexed or abstracted and an evaluative guide to the indexing and abstracting services. More than 100 indexes are listed by subject discipline with an indication of their coverage and relevance to Latin American research interests. Journals are listed by title, then by subject, then by country of publication; in each list the abbreviations for the pertinent indexing/abstracting services follow the individual titles. Journals relating wholly to Latin America or published in Central or South America or the Caribbean (except those concerned with pure and applied sciences) are included.
§ Elena Ardissone has compiled a *Bibliografía de índices de publicaciones periódicas argentinas* (Buenos Aires : Univ. de Buenos Aires, Inst. Bibliotecologico, 1984. 52 p.) listing more than 150 indexes, mainly for individual periodicals.

The index and abstract directory : an international guide to services and serial coverage. 1st ["Premier"] ed.– . Birmingham, Ala. : EBSCO Pub., c1989– . Irregular.   **AD249**
2nd ed. publ. 1990.
Aims "to provide one complete reference source to locate (1) all serials … in the EBSCO Publishing database which are covered by one or more index/abstract services and (2) all international index/abstract services available to us [i.e. EBSCO].—*Pref., 2nd ed.*
Section 1 of the 2nd ed. lists more than 35,000 serial titles arranged by subject, then alphabetically by title. Fairly full bibliographic entries are followed by lists of services covering the title. Section 2 is an alphabetical list of more than 700 indexing/abstracting services, with each entry listing the serial titles covered. Services listed include

online and CD-ROM as well as print. Provides a title index for both serials and services, a subject index to the services, and a combined ISSN index.   Z695.93.I52

Kujoth, Jean Spealman. Subject guide to periodical indexes and review indexes. Metuchen, N.J. : Scarecrow, 1969. 129 p.   **AD250**
Offers a subject approach to lists of periodical indexes and reviewing media.   Z6293.K84

Marconi, Joseph V. Indexed periodicals : a guide to 170 years of coverage in 33 indexing services. Ann Arbor, Mich. : Pierian Pr., 1976. 416 p.   **AD251**
"An alphabetically arranged listing of those periodical and serial titles identified as being indexed in some 33 (counting title changes) American, British and Canadian periodical indexes, showing the indexes in which they were covered and the dates indexed. … The overall scope of this volume ranges from 1802 into mid-1973, consisting of approximately 11,000 periodical and serial titles, title changes, and cross references."—*Introd.*

New York Public Library. A check list of cumulative indexes to individual periodicals in the New York Public Library / comp. by Daniel C. Haskell. N.Y. : Library, 1942. 370 p.   **AD252**
An alphabetical list of thousands of cumulative indexes to periodicals in various languages, mainly of the 19th and 20th centuries, which are available in the New York Public Library, with the addition of a few not available there.
"A cumulative index is to be understood as one which indexes at least 3 volumes … and makes at least a slight attempt at the classification of the periodical's contents, either an arrangement by authors or by subjects."—*Pref.*   Z6293.N45

International

Bibliographie der fremdsprachigen Zeitschriftenliteratur = Répertoire bibliographique international des revues = International index to periodicals. v. 1 (1911)–Bd. 22 (1921/25); n.F. v.1 (1925/26)–51 (1962/64). Leipzig : Dietrich, 1911–64.   **AD253**
Repr.: N.Y. : Kraus Reprint, 1961.
An important index, similar in general plan and arrangement to the *Bibliographie der deutschen Zeitschriftenliteratur* (AD313). Indexes about 1,400 periodicals and general works in the principal non-German languages. The first series is a subject index only; the second series includes, in addition, author indexes. Beginning with n.F.v.4, some supplementary indexing of material earlier than the covering date of the volume is included.
With its wide coverage, this index is very useful for finding materials in American and English periodicals, as well as in French, Italian, and other European publications. Because of the lack of French periodical indexes, it is particularly important for French articles.
N.F.v.26–29 (1944–48) not published. Merged into *Internationale Bibliographie der Zeitschriftenliteratur aus allen Gebieten des Wissens* (AD255).   AI9.B7

FRANCIS. Bulletin signalétique. v. 1 (1947)– . Paris : Centre de Documentation du C.N.R.S. [Centre National de la Recherche Scientifique], 1947– . Quarterly.   **AD254**
Title and pattern of organization vary.
A large, multisectioned indexing and abstracting source that scans hundreds of journals in the humanities and social sciences worldwide. *PASCAL*, a similar series by the same publisher covering the world's literature in science and technology, is treated at EA72.
Began as *Bulletin analytique. Philosophie* with v. 1, no. 1 (1947), including, under the broad umbrella of philosophy, sections on religion, psychology, the history of science, and sociology. Author indexes were included from the first volume onward, with annual subject indexes added beginning with v. 5 (1951).

With v. 10 (1956), the title changed to *Bulletin signalétique : philosophie, sciences humaines*. The word order of the subtitle was reversed with v. 15 (1961), reflecting the growing scope of the index. Also in that year, the title was incorporated into the overall scheme of the science series and numbered as its section 19.

Beginning with v. 18 (1964), the section numbering was expanded to account for subject areas, as follows: Sec. 19, Philosophie. Sciences religieuses; Sec. 20, Psychologie. Pédagogie; Sec. 21, Sociologie. Ethnologie. Sciences du langage; Sec. 22, Histoire des sciences et des techniques; Sec. 23, Esthétique. Archéologie. Arts. The following year, with v. 19 (1965), "Sciences du langage" was removed from Sec. 21 and added as a separate Sec. 24. An unnumbered "Domaines complémentaires" covering nonclassical archaeology, prehistory, and ancient art was added with v. 20, no. 4 (1966). For one volume only, v. 22 (1968), section numbers were preceded by the letter "C."

With v. 23 (1969), the individual sections within *Sciences humaines* were split into separately published titles, renumbered, and reorganized as follows: Sec. 519, Philosophie. Sciences religieuses; Sec. 520, Pédagogie (retitled Sciences de l'education in 1970); Sec. 521, Sociologie. Ethnologie. Préhistoire et archéologie; Sec. 522, Histoires des sciences et des techniques; Sec. 523, Histoire et sciences de la littérature. Arts du spectacle; Sec. 524, Sciences du langage. With this change, coverage of psychology appears to have ceased.

The organization was further modified with v. 24 (1970), which saw the addition of Sec. 525, Préhistoire (retitled Préhistorie et protohistorie with v. 34) [1980]), Sec. 26, Art et archéologie, and Sec. 527, Sciences religieuses. Sec. 528, Science administrative, was added with v. 25 (1971).

Beginning with the issues for 1991, all the sections began to be issued under the general title *FRANCIS. Bulletin signalétique*. Also in 1991, *Bibliographie géographique internationale* was subsumed within the series and numbered as Sec. 531 beginning with its v. 96 (1991).

An associate index cosponsored by C.N.R.S., *Répertoire d'art et d'archéologie* (now called *Bibliography of the history of art*) has sometimes been advertised as Sec. 530, although this designation does not appear on the publication itself.

● All the above sections are parts of *FRANCIS* (French Retrieval Automated Network for Current Information in Social and Human Sciences) [database] (Paris : C.N.R.S., 1972–), available online and on CD-ROM, updated quarterly.

With completion of issues for 1994, the publisher intends to issue *FRANCIS* only in machine-readable form, terminating the printed version.

Internationale Bibliographie der Zeitschriftenliteratur aus allen Gebieten des Wissens = International bibliography of periodical literature covering all fields of knowledge. Jahr. 1 (1964)– . Osnabrück : F. Dietrich, 1965– . Two no. a year.
AD255

Often referred to as *IBZ*.

Frequency has varied.

Merges and continues: *Bibliographie der deutschen Zeitschriftenliteratur* (AD313) and *Bibliographie der fremdsprachigen Zeitschriftenliteratur* (AD253).

A subject index to world periodical literature. The subject headings are in German with cross-references from English and French forms. Author index.

An index of key-words used in this and its predecessor series has been published as:

Register der Schlagwörter 1896–1974, hrsg. von Otto Zeller (Osnabrück : F. Dietrich, 1975. 2 v.).

Title also in English (*Index of key-words 1896–1974*) and French.

Indicates whether a given index term has ever been used in the long series, but references to specific volumes are given only for the 1965–74 period. A second keyword index covers 1975–90 (3 v.).

● Machine-readable version: *IBZ CD-ROM* [database]. From user's guide: *Internationale Bibliographie der Zeitschriftenliteratur aus allen Gebieten des Wissens = International bibliography of periodical literature covering all fields of knowledge*, ed. by Otto and Wolfram Zeller (Osnabrück : F. Dietrich). 1st covered 1989–93; next issued as 1994/1– ; frequency unknown. AI9.I61

North America

United States and Great Britain

Abridged readers' guide to periodical literature. July 1935/Aug. 1936– . N.Y. : H.W. Wilson Co., 1936– . **AD256**

Monthly except June–Aug., cumulating annually. Biennial cumulations were publ. through v. 14 (triennial, 1935/38).

Currently an index of nearly 70 periodicals, designed especially for schools and small public libraries unable to afford the regular *Readers' guide* (AD285). For the public library which is growing and can possibly afford the greater expense, the unabridged *Readers' guide* is the better investment. AI3.R494

Abstracts of popular culture. v. 1–3^A-B. Bowling Green, Ohio : Bowling Green Univ. Popular Pr., 1976–82. Biannual.
AD257

For annotation, *see* CF41. Z7164.S66A27

Access : the supplementary index to periodicals. Jan./Apr. 1975– . Syracuse, N.Y. : Gaylord Professional Pubs., 1975– .
AD258

John Gordon Burke and Ned Kehde, editors.

Publisher and place of publication vary.

An "index designed to complement the *Readers guide to periodical literature*. Its purpose is to provide information about the contents of magazines not presently indexed in the *Readers guide*... [*Access*] indexes regional and city magazines as well as a balanced subject-oriented list of general and special interest periodicals.... As a principle of editorial policy, magazines which are voted into the *Readers guide to periodical literature* are dropped by *Access—Introd*.

A companion publication, *Access: the index to literary magazines*, indexing primarily poetry, fiction, and essays, was published for 1977 and 1978.

● Current year available to subscribers in a machine-readable online version. A CD-ROM version is planned for 1994 with coverage back to Oct. 1987. A retrospective online version is also planned as part of the Library Corporation's Universal index. AI3.A23

Alternative press index. v. 1, no. 1/2 (July/Dec. 1969)– . Baltimore : Alternative Pr. Center, [1970]– . Quarterly.
AD259

Publisher varies.

Subtitle on cover: An index to alternative and radical publications.

Provides a subject index to liberal, radical, alternative lifestyle, and "underground" periodicals, most not indexed elsewhere, some from outside the U.S. July–Sept. 1993 issue lists articles from 124 titles. "Most articles are listed under at least two subject headings, except fiction and some reviews."—*How to use the index*. Lists special issues. New periodicals added regularly. Lists addresses and subscription information. AI3.A27

The American humanities index. v.1, no.1/2 (Spr./Sum. 1975)– . Troy, N.Y. : Whitston, 1975– . Annual. **AD260**
For annotation, *see* BA2. AI3.A278

Annual literary index. 1892–1904. N.Y. : Publishers' Weekly, 1893–1905. Annual. **AD261**

Subtitle continues, 1895–1904: Including periodicals, American and English; essays, book-chapters, etc.; with author-index, bibliographies, necrology, and index to dates of principal events.

§ *Annual library index: including periodicals, American and English; essays, book-chapters, etc.* (1905–10. N.Y. : Publishers' Weekly, 1906–11. 6 v.).

Subtitle continues, 1905–07: With author-index, bibliographies, necrology, and index to dates of principal events. For 1908–09, adds: And select list of libraries in the United States. 1910 adds: And selected lists of public libraries in the United States and Canada and of private collectors of books.

These two indexes, although differing slightly in arrangement, served as a continuation of *Poole's index to periodical literature* (AD282), forming the basis for the 5-year supplements, but added author indexing never incorporated in *Poole's*. Except for this indexing, they were largely superseded by *Poole's* and by *The A.L.A. index : an index to general literature ....* (BE239).   AI3.A5

Annual magazine subject index, 1907–49 : a subject index to a selected list of American and English periodicals and society publications. Boston : Faxon, 1908–52. 43 v.   **AD262**

Vol. 1 had title *Magazine subject index* and is a basic volume indexing 79 periodicals (44 from their first issues to Dec. 31, 1907, and 35 for the year 1907).

An index of subjects only, not of authors or titles, except that fiction when included is indexed under author's name. Indexes material with exact references and indication of illustrations, maps, etc. Intended as a supplement to other indexes and so aims to include no periodicals indexed in established indexes. While the list of periodicals is general in character, about half the titles relate to history, especially local history; the index specializes also in travel, mountaineering, exploration, outdoor life, and fine arts. Indexes all important articles in the periodicals covered but omits short articles, poetry, and most fiction, although continued stories and short stories by notable writers are included.

Includes many local history titles, especially transactions of local history societies indexed in Appleton Prentiss Clark Griffin, *Bibliography of American historical societies (the United States and the Dominion of Canada)* (2nd ed. rev. and enl. Wash. : U.S. Govt. Print. Off., 1907. 1374 p. [*In* American Historical Assoc. Annual report, 1905. v. 2]. Repr.: Detroit : Gale, 1966). As these are often indexed back to the date when Griffin stopped, the index constitutes an informal continuation of Griffin. The only exception to the rule not to index material included elsewhere is in the case of these history periodicals.

The entries in the 43 v. are cumulated into one alphabet in: *Cumulated magazine subject index* (AD270).   AI3.M26

Bloomfield, Barry Cambray. An author index to selected British 'little magazines,' 1930–1939. [London] : Mansell, 1976. 153 p.   **AD263**

Indexes 73 periodicals of the period, less than a dozen of which are included in Marion Sader's *Comprehensive index to English-language little magazines, 1890–1970* (AD287). With the exception of *Caravel* (published in Majorca, but containing "a considerable amount of poetry by young British writers"—*Pref.*) all were published in the U.K. With a few exceptions noted in the preface, all magazines are fully indexed. This is an author index only, although the form heading "Films reviewed" provides cross-references to film reviews, and cross-references to book reviews are provided under the name of the author of the book reviewed.   AI3.B56

British humanities index. 1962– . London : Lib. Assoc., 1963– . Quarterly, with annual cumulations.   **AD264**

Publisher varies.

Often referred to as *BHI.*

A continuation in part of *Subject index to periodicals* (AD289), "providing a guide to articles in over 300 journals and newspapers published in Britain. The term 'humanities' is interpreted broadly to include the arts, music, philosophy, religion, literature, economics, politics, history and society. In addition, selected non-specialist articles of popular interest in science and technology" (*Guide for users*) are also included.

Beginning 1993, includes abstracts. In four sections: numbered abstracts arranged alphabetically by subject heading, alphabetical subject index, full author index, and index by source journal.   AI3.B7

Catholic periodical and literature index. v. 14 (1967/68)– . Winona, Minn. : Catholic Libr. Assoc., [1968]– . Quarterly, including annual cumulation.   **AD265**

Place of publication varies.

Bimonthly, v. 14–v. 28, n. 1.

Beginning July 1968, *Catholic periodical index* (BC395) and *The guide to Catholic literature* (BC390) were combined in a single publi-

cation under this title, which continues the volume numbering of the *Index*. Coverage of both the earlier publications is maintained. Regularly indexes about 135 periodicals as well as about 250–300 book titles per issue. Also lists Papal documents. Beginning with v. 28, no. 2 (Apr./May/June 1993), consists of four sections (subject index, author and editor index, book title index, and book review author index) instead of a single alphabetical listing.   AI3.C32

Catholic periodical index : a cumulative author and subject index to a selected list of Catholic periodicals. v. 1 (1930)–13 (1966). N.Y. : Catholic Lib. Assoc., 1939–67. Quarterly, with biennial cumulations.   **AD266**

For annotation, *see* BC395.   AI3.C32

Chicano periodical index : a cumulative index to selected Chicano periodicals published between 1967 and 1978 / produced by the Committee for the Development of Subject Access to Chicano Literatures ; dir., Richard Chabrán, associate dir., Francisco García. Boston : G.K. Hall, 1981. 972 p.   **AD267**

For annotation, *see* CC456.   Z1361.M4C47

Children's magazine guide. v.34, no.1 (Sept. 1981)– . New Providence, N.J. : Bowker, 1981– . Monthly Aug.–Mar.; bimonthly Apr.–May.   **AD268**

Feb. and Aug. issues are semi-annual cumulations.

Publ. Madison, Wis. : Rowland, 1981–93.

Indexes by subject some 40–50 magazines useful to elementary and junior high school libraries.

§ Continues *Subject index to children's magazines* (v. 1 [1948]–v.33 [1981]; Madison, 1948–81) and assumes its numbering.

The cover story index, 1960–1991 / Robert Skapura, ed. Fort Atkinson, Wis. : Highsmith Pr., 1992. 521 p.   **AD269**

Ed. covering 1960–89 publ. 1990.

Subject index and chronology to cover stories appearing in 12 U.S. magazines, nine of which are new with this edition. However, only *Newsweek, Time,* and *U.S. news & world report* are covered from 1960; the others are covered from 1981.   AP2.C68

Cumulated magazine subject index, 1907–1949 : a cumulation of the F. W. Faxon Company's Annual magazine subject index / cumulated by G. K. Hall & Co. Boston : G. K. Hall, 1964. 2 v.   **AD270**

A photographic reproduction of the actual entries originally printed in *Annual magazine subject index*, clipped and rearranged in one alphabetical sequence. For coverage *see* AD262.   AI3.C76

Fulltext sources online / BiblioData. Winter 1989– . Needham, Mass. : BiblioData, 1989– . Semiannual.   **AD271**

Subtitle: For periodicals, newspapers, newsletters & newswires. Covers titles in science, technology, medicine, law, finance, business, industry, the popular press, etc.

Ed. by Ruth M. Orenstein.

"Each edition is complete in itself and replaces all previous editions. Complete new editions are published twice yearly in January and July."—*p.i.* Titles are listed alphabetically, each entry listing the databases in which that title appears. Subject index.

Index to American periodicals of the 1700's : keyed to University Microfilms APS I. [Indianapolis : Computer Indexed Systems, 1989. 2 v.   **AD272**

Contents: v. 1, Reels 1–16; v. 2, Reels 17–33.   Z6951.I533

Index to American periodicals of the 1800's : keyed to University Microfilms APS II. Indianapolis : Computer Indexed Systems, 1989– . v. 1–11. (In progress).   **AD273**

Contents: v. 1–3, 1800–09; v. 4–11, 1810–25.

A detailed subject index to articles in the magazines included in the microfilm sets *American periodicals : series I, 1741–1800* and *American periodicals : series II, 1800–1850* (both Ann Arbor, Mich. : Univ. Microfilms International). The index refers to the reel number of the microfilm set, the title and volume of the journal, and the page number of the article. Jean Hoornstra and Trudy Heath's *American periodicals, 1741–1900 : an index to the microfilm collection* (AD36) is an index to the periodical titles in the microfilm series, rather than to their contents.

The index is "a 'Key Word' article-level index. Typically 2 to 3 key words, in the form of names, places, subjects or phrases have been taken from the title of the article or from the article itself to form a topic … . In some of the more popular periodical titles, the indexing goes beyond article level and actually indexes all names, places, subjects and phrases mentioned within the article."—*Operation Guide, (for 1989 ed.) p. 3.*

•Both indexes available on CD-ROM as: *Index to American periodicals of the 1700's and 1800's* [database] (Indianapolis : Computers Indexed Systems). Z6951.I533

Index to black periodicals. 1984– . Boston : G. K. Hall & Co., 1988– . Annual. **AD274**

Continues: *Index to periodical articles by and about blacks, Index to periodical articles by and about negroes*, and *Index to selected periodicals*. 1950–1959 cumulation entitled: *Index to selected periodicals in the Hallie Q. Brown Library*. 1960–1970 cumulation entitled: *Index to periodical articles by and about negroes.*

"An index to Afro-American periodicals of general and scholarly interest. The 1991 volume [publ. 1993] covers articles in a total of 33 black American journals."—*Pref.* Because it was no longer possible for the Hallie Q. Brown Library (Central State Univ. Wilberforce, Ohio) to continue work on the index, G. K. Hall assumed editorial responsibility in mid-1984. Combined author/subject index. AI3.04

Index to Commonwealth little magazines. 1964/65–1990/92. N.Y. : Johnson Reprint Corp., 1966–1992. Biennial (irregular). **AD275**

Stephen H. Goode, ed.

"An author-subject index of a selected list of English-language little magazines published in Commonwealth and ex-Commonwealth countries …. Review articles are entered under the reviewer (an author), under the author of the work reviewed (as subject), and under the subject of the reviewed work."—*Pref.* 1990–92 vol. indexes 15 titles, mostly literary. AI3.I48

Index to little magazines. Denver : Alan Swallow, 1949–70. **AD276**

Publisher varies; compilers vary.

Frequency varies; began publication with volume for 1948 (publ. 1949). Annual, 1948–52; 1953/55 publ. in 1 v., 1957; biennial, 1956/57–66/67. Retrospective volumes have been issued covering 1900–19 and 1920–39 (publ. 1969–74 with title *Index to American little magazines*), 1940–42 (publ. 1967) and 1943–47 (publ. 1965). The 1966/67 volume (publ. 1970) was the last to appear.

Indexes a selective list of from 31 to more than 50 titles. Periodicals are mainly literary; indexing is by author and subject (many of the subjects being quite broad). Coverage varies from volume to volume, as does treatment of book reviews. AI3.I54

Index to U.S. government periodicals. 1970–1987. [Chicago] : Infordata International, 1974–87. Quarterly, the 4th issue being an annual cumulation. **AD277**

Began publication with quarterly issues for 1974; retrospective annual volumes published subsequently.

"A computer-generated guide to 156 selected titles by author and subject."—*t.p., 1976.* The number of periodicals listed varied from year to year. Included various titles not sent to depository libraries, many of which were distributed directly by department or issuing agency rather than through the Government Printing Office. Z1223.Z9I5

Magazine index [microform]. 1976– . [Menlo Park, Calif. : Information Access Corp], 1976– . Monthly. **AD278**

Also called: *IAC magazine index.*

Indexes about 435 popular periodicals, with each monthly microfilm being a cumulation for the preceding three years. After three years, citations are dropped from the microfilm and cumulated on microfiche. Cumulations date back to 1979.

Subjects, names, titles, etc. are indexed in one alphabet. Information on using the index and the list of periodicals indexed appears at each end of the microfilm reel. Full titles of periodicals, rather than abbreviations, are given in the citations.

Two printed looseleaf services are included in the subscription: (1) *Hot topics* lists recent articles on subjects of current topical interest; (2) *Product evaluations* lists recent product reviews as found in the microform index.

•Machine-readable versions: *Magazine index* [database] (Foster City, Calif. : Information Access Co., 1959–70; 1973–). Available online, updated weekly. Also available on CD-ROM: *Magazine index plus* [database] as part of InfoTrac II (1980–), updated monthly. An online file, *Magazine ASAP* [database] offers full text of selected articles covered by *Magazine index*, 1983– .

The new periodicals index. v. 1, no. 1 (Jan./June 1977)–v. 4 (Jan.–Dec.1980). Boulder, Colo. : Mediaworks Ltd., 1977–1983. **AD279**

Frequency varies: semiannual, 1977–78; annual 1979–80.

Although covering only four years before ceasing, indexed alternative and new age magazines (i.e., those dealing with "spritual life, lifestyles, energy, ecology, health, diet, feminism, community [etc.]" (*Introd., v. 1, no. 1*), newspapers and newsletters not well covered elsewhere. Comparison of v. 4, 1980 (publ. 1983) with *Alternative press index* (AD259) for the same year shows overlap of only 13 titles out of the 52 indexed. Author and subject indexes, no cumulations.

Nineteenth century readers' guide to periodical literature, 1890–1899 : with supplementary indexing, 1900–1922 / ed. by Helen Grant Cushing and Adah V. Morris …. N.Y. : H.W. Wilson, 1944. 2 v. **AD280**

An author, subject, and illustrator index to the material in 51 periodicals (1,003 volumes) mainly in the period from 1890 to 1899. Some indexing has been done for volumes published after 1899 "in order to make the indexing of each title complete from the year 1890 to the time when it was added to the list of one of the Wilson indexes. Fourteen of the 51 titles included have been indexed beyond 1899, some as far as 1922."—*Pref.*

Periodicals indexed are mainly general and literary, but some are included from special fields. Book reviews are listed under author entry only. More than 13,000 poems are listed under "Poems" by title. Full entry is under author's name. Poems on particular persons, events, etc., are also under subject.

In some 19th-century periodicals the editorial practice was to publish articles anonymously, e.g., in the *Edinburgh review* and the *Quarterly review*. For many of these articles the authors' names have been ascertained from the publishers' records and are indicated in this index.

These two volumes were planned as part of a larger project to cover the whole 19th century by a modern periodical index in dictionary form, but no further volumes have been published. For a similar effort, see *Wellesley index to Victorian periodicals, 1824–1900* (AD292). AI3.R496

Poole's index : date and volume key / by Marion V. Bell and Jean C. Bacon. Chicago : Assoc. of College and Research Libraries, 1957. 61 p. (ACRL monograph, 19). **AD281**

In this "key the 479 periodical titles indexed in the various volumes of *Poole's Index* are thrown into one alphabet" (p.19) and the date is shown, in tabular form, for each volume number, thus obviating the necessity for checking a title in the "Chronological conspectus" in each volume of *Poole's.*

§ A similar aid is Vinton A. Dearing's *Transfer vectors for Poole's Index to periodical literature*, no.1, Titles, volumes, and dates (Los Angeles : Pison Pr., 1967. 95p.) which lists the periodicals alphabetically by abbreviation, with full title, dates indexed, and the volume number of *Poole's* in which a given date appears.

Poole's index to periodical literature, 1802–81. Rev. ed. Boston : Houghton, 1891. 2 v. **AD282**

Originally ed. by William Frederick Poole, continued by him and William I. Fletcher, with the cooperation of members of the American Library Assoc.

Repr.: N.Y. : P. Smith, 1938 ; Gloucester, Mass. : P. Smith, 1963.
———. *Supplements*, Jan. 1882–Jan 1, 1907. Boston : Houghton, [c1887–1908]. 5 v.

Contents: v. 1, 1802–81; 1st suppl., 1882–86; 2nd suppl., 1887–91; 3rd suppl., 1892–96; 4th suppl., 1897–1901; 5th suppl., 1902–1906.

The pioneer index and, though long discontinued, still an important index to American and English periodicals, since it covers the longest period (105 years) and indexes the large total of about 590,000 articles in 12,241 volumes of 479 American and English periodicals. A subject index only; includes *no author entries.* Authors' names appear frequently as entries, but only as subject entries for biographical or critical articles about them. To make intelligent use of the index the user should remember the following four points: (1) no author entries; (2) all articles having a distinct subject are entered under that subject; (3) articles having no subject, i.e., fiction, poems, plays, are entered under first word of the title not an article; (4) book reviews are entered in two ways: (a) reviews of a book which has a definite subject are entered under subject of the book; (b) reviews of a book which does not have a distinct subject, i.e., a novel, poetry, a drama, are entered under the name of the author reviewed. Approximately complete for the periodicals covered, except in the following respects: (1) very brief articles, notes, etc. are generally omitted; (2) minor book reviews are not included; and (3) some English periodicals noted in v. 1 are incompletely indexed because of failure in collaboration between English and American indexers. Information given about each article includes its title, author's name in parentheses when it was known or could be ascertained, abbreviated title of periodical, and volume and page reference. Neither inclusive paging nor date is given, but the date (year only) can be ascertained from the "Chronological conspectus" in each volume. Indexes principally periodicals of a general nature, but a few selected periodicals on special subjects are included. In general, the work of both indexing and printing is very accurate, with comparatively few typographical errors. For lists of errata, see *Bulletin of bibliography* 2:24–25, 40–41, 56–58, 75–76, 133–34; 3:25; 4:11–12, 72 (Jan. 1900–Oct. 1905).

Cumulative author index for Poole's index to periodical literature, 1802–1906, comp. and ed. by C. Edward Wall (Ann Arbor, Mich. : Pierian Pr., 1971. 488 p.).

Popular periodical index. no. 1 (Jan./June 1973)– . [Camden, N.J. : Rutgers Univ., Camden Library], 1973– . Quarterly, including annual cumulation.   **AD283**

Frequency varies; semiannual, 1973–88, with no cumulations.

A subject index (with some author entries) now indexing 35–40 American periodicals not covered in standard periodical indexes. Separate section for book reviews.   AI3.P76

Readers' guide abstracts. Aug. 1988– . N.Y. : H.W. Wilson, 1989– .   **AD284**

Monthly and semiannual eds.

Issues for Sept. 1991–May 1992 have ed. statement: *School and public library edition*; issues from Sept. 1992 have ed. statement: *Select edition.*

Indexes and abstracts articles selected from 240 core periodicals indexed in *Reader's guide to periodical literature* (AD285), based on their perceived research value.

Also available on microfiche, eight cumulative issues per year; retrospective indexing and abstract coverage available back to Sept. 1984. Microfiche edition contains more than twice as many abstracts per year as the printed edition. However, microfiche access is to be discontinued in March 1994.

•Machine-readable versions: *Readers' guide abstracts* [database] (N.Y. : H.W. Wilson, 1983–). Available online, updated twice weekly (indexing) and weekly (abstracting), and on CD-ROM, updated monthly.   Z6941.R38

Readers' guide to periodical literature. [Cumulated ed.]. v. 1 (1901)– . N.Y. : Wilson, 1905– .   **AD285**

A cumulative index made up of three forms or sections: (1) cumulated volumes covering two to five years (i.e., 1935–Feb. 1965, two years to a volume; previous volumes covered from three to five years); (2) annual cumulations (beginning with v.25, Mar. 1965–Feb. 1966,

these are final cumulations); and (3) issues published semimonthly in March, Oct., and Dec., monthly in Jan., Feb., April, May, June, July, August, Sept., and Nov., with a bound cumulation each year.

The *Readers' guide* began in 1901 as an index for the small library, covering at first only 15 of the more popular periodicals, and gradually extended until in 1903 it absorbed *Cumulative index* (1896–1903) and in 1911 took over the work of *Annual library index.* List of periodicals indexed varies from volume to volume. Beginning with v.19, 1953, *Readers' guide:* (a) indexes U.S. periodicals of broad, general, and popular character, and (b) aims to provide a well-balanced selection of U.S. popular, nontechnical magazines representing all the important scientific and humanistic subject fields. About 174 periodicals of general interest are now included.

Special features are: (1) full dictionary cataloging of all articles, i.e., their entry under author, subject, and (when necessary) title; (2) uniformity of entries, due to the fact that the work is done by a few professional indexers rather than by many voluntary collaborators; (3) use of catalog subject headings instead of catchword subject; (4) full information in the references, i.e., exact date and inclusive paging, illustrations, portraits, etc.; (5) cumulative features which keep the index up to date without multiplying alphabets to be consulted; (6) indexing of all book reviews, through 1904, under author reviewed; after 1905, reviews are generally omitted because included in the *Book review digest* (AA365), although a listing of citations to book reviews follows the main body of the index; (7) indexing, in the second and third cumulated volumes, of some 597 composite books, thus forming an unofficial continuation of the *A.L.A. index ... to general literature.* This book indexing was abandoned after 1914.

§ *Readers' guide abstracts* (AD284) offers abstracts of some 40% of the articles indexed by *Readers' guide.*

•Machine-readable version: *Readers' guide to periodical literature* [database] (Bronx, N.Y. : H.W. Wilson, 1983–). Machine-readable version. Available online (updated twice weekly), on tape, and on CD-ROM (updated quarterly).   AI3.R48

Review of reviews : index to the periodicals of [1890–1902]. [v. 1]–13. London ; N.Y. : Review of Reviews, 1891–1903. Annual.   **AD286**

Title varies: v. 1, *Annual index of periodicals and photographs for 1890*; v. 2–4, *Index to the periodical literature of the world.*

Primarily a subject index, but contains a fair number of author entries also, especially in the later volumes. Indexes material under broad subjects and gives full bibliographical information with reference to the volume, month, and page of *Review of reviews* where a summary or other notice of the article is to be found. Indicates maps and illustrations. Number of periodicals indexed varies from 117 in 1890 to 195 in 1902. Principally useful because it covers many English periodicals (about 100 in the later volumes) not indexed in *Poole's index to periodical literature* (AD282).   AI3.R5

Sader, Marion. Comprehensive index to English-language little magazines, 1890–1970 : Series one. Millwood, N.Y. : Kraus-Thomson, 1976. 8 v.   **AD287**

An index to 100 English-language little magazines of the period indicated, 59 of which are "partly or totally American"—*Pref.* It aims to index complete files of defunct publications; magazines which were still current are completely indexed through 1970, with some 1971 issues included. Selection of titles for this first series—it is indicated that work had begun on a second series—was made by Felix Pollak, formerly of the University of Wisconsin Libraries, with the advice of Charles Allen, well-known authority on the American little magazine. Indexing is by personal name only, with designation of "Works by" and/or "Works about" under each name. Book reviews are entered under both the author of the book and the name of the reviewer, with an additional subject entry if the book is a biography or a critical work devoted to an individual writer or artist, etc. In addition to the expected details of pagination, date, etc., each contribution has been categorized as to type (article, poem, excerpt, illus., etc.).   Z6944.L5S23

Social sciences and humanities index. v. 1 (1907/15)–61 (1974). N.Y. : H.W. Wilson, 1916–1974.   **AD288**

Title varies: v. 1–2, *Readers' guide to periodical literature supplement*; v. 3–52, *International index to periodicals* (with various subtitles); v. 53, no. 1, June 1965–Mar. 1974, *Social sciences and humanities index*. (Volume numbering of the cumulations differs from that of the quarterly issues; e.g., v. 3–18 of the cumulated set called *International index.*).

A cumulative index made up of permanent cumulative volumes covering four, three, or two years, with annual volumes from 1964 onward.

An important index for the large or scholarly library. An author and subject index on the same plan as *Readers' guide* (AD285) but covering more scholarly journals in the humanities and social sciences. Coverage varies, with the transfer of titles to new Wilson subject indexes, etc., and the addition of new titles. Before World War II a number of foreign titles were included, e.g., in v. 8 (1937–40), 221 titles were indexed: 125 American, 39 English, three Canadian, 25 French, 20 German, four Oriental, two Italian, one each Dutch, Irish, and Spanish. Since the war, foreign titles have been dropped, as have psychological and scientific periodicals. In 1973, indexed about 200 American and English periodicals.

Continued by: *Social sciences index* (CA29) and *Humanities index* (BA5). AI3.R49

Subject index to periodicals. 1915–1961. London : Libr. Assoc., 1919–62. **AD289**

Frequency varied: annual through 1953; quarterly, 1954–61, with annual cumulations. 1923–25 not published.

An English index, begun in 1915 under the title *Athenaeum subject index;* title changed in 1919 to *Subject index*. The 1915–16 volume has an author subject arrangement cumulated from preliminary class lists. Continued by class lists 1917–19, in one set, with a general author index, and 1920–22, one volume per year, with no author index.

The form was changed in 1926, becoming an alphabetical subject list (with no author index) to articles on definite subjects. Magazine fiction, poetry, and essays not on definite subjects were omitted. Until the time of World War II (approximately 1940), it indexed more than 500 periodicals, principally British and American but including a number of foreign titles. Though duplicating much of the indexing in *Readers' guide* (AD285) and *International index* (later *Social science and humanities index*; see AD288), it indexed many periodicals not covered by those indexes, including British local-history periodicals, antiquarian society proceedings, etc.

During World War II, the indexing of foreign titles was discontinued, and with the 1947 volume (publ. 1949), the indexing of American periodicals was also dropped. Later volumes indexed more than 300 titles, entirely British.

Regional lists, including entries of local interest, were collected and issued annually by county, with Scotland as a separate issue.

Ceased publication in this form with the 1961 volume. Continued by indexes covering special subjects: *British humanities index* (AD264) and *British technology index* (now *Current technology index*, EK6). AI3.A72

Subject index to Welsh periodicals. 1968–1984. Aberystwyth : National Library of Wales., 1978–1984. **AD290**

Continues a work of the same title (1931–1946/55. Swansea : Library Association, Wales and Monmouthshire Branch, 1934–64).

Indexes periodicals (excluding newspapers and some denominational publications) published in Wales, in both Welsh and English, and periodicals published elsewhere which include material of Welsh and general Celtic interest. Indexes approximately 90 titles. Subject and author indexes. "It is hoped to bridge the gap between the present volume and the last in the previous series ... as soon as possible" (*Introd.*, 1968–70 volume), an objective not yet accomplished as of this writing.

Merged with *Bibliotheca celtica* (AA698) to form *Llyfryddiaeth Cymru = A bibliography of Wales* (AA698 note).

U.S. government periodicals index. v. 1 (1994)– . Bethesda, Md. : Congressional Information Service, 1994– . Quarterly. **AD291**

Indexes "artices in approximately 180 federal publicaations that have major research, reference, or general interest value."—*CIS catalog, 1994–95, p. 5* Access by subject and author; includes cross-references.

•Machine-readable version: *U.S. government periodicals index* [database] (Bethesda, Md. : CIS, 1993?–). Available on CD-ROM and magnetic tape, both updated quarterly. Z1223.Z7.U8

The Wellesley index to Victorian periodicals, 1824–1900 / Walter E. Houghton, ed. [Toronto] : Univ. of Toronto Pr. ; [London] : Routledge & K. Paul, [c1966–c1989]. 5 v. **AD292**

Vols. 2–4 have subtitle: Tables of contents and identification of contributors with bibliographies of their articles and stories and an index of initials and pseudonyms.

Vol. 5, Epitome and index, ed. by Jean Harris Slingerland, has subtitle: Dated bibliographies of all identified authors and their contributions to major quarterlies and monthlies of the period with a separate bibliography of identified pseudonyms and initials.

Indexes 43 major 19th-century British monthlies and quarterlies. Pt. A of the first four volumes offers issue-by-issue tables of contents for each magazine included, with identification of the frequently anonymous contributors and references to the evidence for attribution. Original English-language poetry is omitted, but translated poetry is included from v. 3 onward. Pt. B for vols. 1–4, an author/contributor index, varies slightly in format volume to volume. Vol. 5, largely an author index for the set, also contains appendixes listing corrections and additions to the previous volumes. Because editorial methodologies and formatting varied over the life of the project, serious researchers are encouraged to consult the introduction to v. 5 before making any assumptions based on the characteristics of any prior volume.

AI3.W45

Canada

Canadian periodical index. 1928–1947. Toronto : Public Libraries Branch, Ontario Dept. of Educ., 1928–47. **AD293**

Publisher varies.

Frequency varies. Set consists of: quarterly issues, 1928–30; annual cumulation, 1931 (publ. 1932); quarterly issues, 1932; not published 1933–37; annual volumes (being cumulations of the quarterly indexes published in the *Ontario library review*), 1938–47.

An author and subject index to Canadian periodicals, most of which are not indexed in other periodical indexes. Covers a varying number of titles, usually between 30 and 40.

§ Continued by: *Canadian index to periodicals and documentary films : an author and subject index Jan. 1948–Dec. 1959*, ed. by Margaret E. Wodehouse [and] Ruth Mulholland (Ottawa : Canadian Library Association, 1962. 1180 p.).

Added title page in French: *Index de périodiques et de films documentaires canadiens*. Cumulation, superseding annual volumes published as *Canadian index : a guide to Canadian periodicals and films*. A bilingual index by author and subject to some 60 to 80 Canadian periodicals. Subject headings are in English, but French cross-references are given to the English headings. Includes documentary films. Book reviews are listed under the form heading "Book reviews." Kept up-to-date by monthly and annual volumes, 1960–63 (v. 13–16).

Also continued by: *Canadian periodical index = Index de périodiques canadiens* (v. 17– . Ottawa : Canadian Library Assoc., 1964– . Monthly, with annual cumulations). An author and subject index to Canadian periodicals, following the plan of *Canadian index to periodicals and documentary films* (above). The listing of films has been taken over by the National Library and appears in *Canadiana* (AA456). Now indexes about 135 periodicals.

Earlier materials are indexed by: *Canadian periodical index, 1920–1937 : an author and subject index*, by Grace F. Heggie ... [et al.] (Ottawa : Canadian Library Assoc., 1988. 567 p.). "A retrospective index to twenty Canadian periodicals covering the years 1920 to 1937" (*Pref.*), the period preceding the annual cumulative volumes of *Canadian periodical index*. Follows the format of that index. AI3.C262

Point de repère : index analytique d'articles de periodiques de langue française. v. 1, no. 1 (janv.–févr. 1984)– . Montréal, Quebec : Services Documentaires Multimedia (SDM), Bibliothèque nationale du Québec, 1984– . Monthly, with two bimonthly issues and an annual cumulation.   **AD294**

Formed by merger of *Périodex* and *RADAR: Rèpertoire analytique d'articles de revues du Québec*, each of which covered 1972–83, succeeding *Index analytique*, which covered 1966–72.

Also available on microfiche.

As of late 1993 indexed 200 periodicals from Quebec, 12 other Canadian titles, and more than 70 French-language periodicals from Europe. Contains a detailed, classified subject index and a book review index. Most entries are annotated. An abridged bimonthly edition covering 130 periodicals is also available.

•Machine-readable version: *REPÉRE* [database] (Montréal : Services Documentaires Multimedia, Inc. [SDM], 1972–). Available online, updated bimonthly.   AI7.P65

Latin America

Columbus Memorial Library (Washington, D.C.). Index to Latin American periodical literature, 1929–1960. Boston : G.K. Hall, 1962. 8 v.   **AD295**

Photoreproduced from catalog cards, this set is compiled from index cards prepared at the Library of the Pan American Union and includes "approximately 250,000 entries of authors, subjects and other secondary entries. Until 1951 … only entries by subject were made, except for well-known authors and authors of articles having literary value."—*Pref.* Indexing is on a broad, selective basis from an estimated 3,000 different titles mainly of Latin-American origin.

———. *1st suppl., 1961–1965* (Boston : G.K. Hall, 1968. 2 v.).

Materials indexed in the *Índice general de publicaciones periódicas latino-americanas* (AD298) are not included in this supplement.

———. *[2nd suppl.] 1966–70* (Boston : G.K. Hall, 1980. 2 v.).

Adds about 51,000 entries.   Z1601.P16

HAPI : Hispanic American periodicals index. 1970/74– . Los Angeles : UCLA Latin American Center Publ., Univ. of California, 1977– . Annual.   **AD296**

Barbara G. Cox, ed.

Began publication on an annual basis with the 1975 volume (publ. 1977); a set of three retrospective volumes covering 1970/74 was published 1984 (v. 1–2, Subjects; v. 3, Authors), bridging the gap between the cessation of *Index to Latin American periodical literature, 1929–1960* (AD295) and the first published volume of *HAPI*.

HAPI "lists annually by subject and author articles, documents, reviews, bibliographies, original literary works, and other items appearing in nearly two hundred and fifty journals published throughout the world which regularly contain information on Latin America … Most journals published in Mexico, Central and South America, and the Caribbean area are indexed in full. Items from journals published in other countries are cited only if they concern Latin America or Hispanics in the United States."—*Introd., p. 1, 1992 vol.* Subject, author, and book review indexes.

§ *Hispanic American periodicals index : articles in English 1976–1980*, ed. by Barbara G. Valk, (Westwood, Mass. : Faxon, 1984. 403 p.) is a spin-off from the annual volumes of *HAPI*. It has the advantage of offering a cumulation of the English-language articles indexed and simplifies the search process for those who read only English.

•In machine-readable form (1970–) online from publisher and through Research Libraries Group's *CitaDel*. Also available as part of *Latin American studies. Volume 1* [database] (Baltimore, Md. : National Information Services Corp.) on CD-ROM, updated semiannually.
          Z1605.H16

Índice de artículos de publicaciones periódicas en el área de ciencias sociales y humanidades : acumulado 1974–1979. Bogotá : Instituto Colombiano para el Fomento de la Educación Superior, 1983. 2 v.   **AD297**

Also called v. 5, no. 1, 1983.

Cumulates the issues of the index of the same title which appeared irregularly beginning July 1975 and which, in turn, continued *Índice latinoamericano de ciencias sociales y humanidades, 1970–1973* (Bogotá : Instituto Colombiano para el Formento de la Educacíon Superior, Div. de Documentacíon e Informacíon, 1978. 3 v.).
          AI17.I48

Índice general de publicaciones periódicas latino-americanas : humanidades y ciencias sociales = Index to Latin American periodicals : humanities and social sciences. v. 1 (1961)–10 (1970). Boston : G.K. Hall, 1962–71. Quarterly, with annual cumulations.   **AD298**

Prep. by the Columbus Memorial Library of the Organization of American States. Jorge Grossmann, ed.

"A guide to articles appearing in selected Latin American periodicals in the humanities and social sciences."—*Introd.* Originally an author and subject index; arrangement was changed with v. 3 to an alphabetical listing by subject. Entries are under the Spanish form of the subject heading, with an auxiliary list of corresponding English terms. The annual volume for 1963 is a single alphabetical subject listing with author and title indexes. Annual volumes for 1964–69 (v. 4–9) reprint the quarterly subject listings without interfiling of entries, but add a cumulated author index.

Ceased with v. 10, no. 2, and no cumulation of v. 10 was published.   Z1605.I55

Leavitt, Sturgis Elleno. Revistas hispanoamericanas : índice bibliográfico, 1843–1935 / recopilado … con la colaboración de Madaline W. Nichols y Jefferson Rea Spell. Santiago de Chile : Fondo Histórico y Bibliográfico José Toribio Medina, 1960. 589 p.   **AD299**

"Homenaje al Sesquicentenario de la independencia nacional, 1810–1960."—*t.p.*

A classified index to the material in 56 Spanish-American periodicals, primarily in literature, linguistics, and folklore. Name index. An appendix lists those libraries in the U. S. holding complete sets of the periodicals indexed.

A list of "Errata" compiled by Leavitt appeared as: Univ. of Kentucky. Library. *Occasional contribution*, no. 123. 6 p.   AI17.L4

Europe

L'emigration russe : revues et recueils, 1920–1980 : index général des articles / [ouvrage édité sous la direction de Tatiana Gladkova, Tatiana Ossorguine]. Paris : Institut d'études slaves, 1988. 661 p. (Bibliothèque russe de l'Institut d'études slaves, t. 81).   **AD300**

Title on added t.p.: Russkaîa émigratsiîa : zhurnaly i sborniki na russkom îazyke, 1920–1980 : svodnyĭ ukazatel' stateĭ = The Russian emigration : journals and miscellanea, 1920–1980 : general index of articles.

"Publié par la Bibliothèque russe Tourguenev et la Bibliothèque de documentation internationale contemporaine."—*t.p.*

Text in Russian; introductory material in French, English, and Russian.

An author index to the "contents of 45 Russian language periodicals and 16 collections of general historical and cultural interest" (*Pref.*) published 1920–80, mainly in Paris. Gives the title of the article, the source, and the year and volume number. Index of names mentioned in the articles.   Z6955.E56

Albania

Bibliografia kombëtare e RPS të Shqipërisë : Artikujtë periodikut shqiptar / Biblioteka Kombëtare, Sektoriï Bibliografië. Viti 26, 1 (Janar 1986)– . Tiranë : Biblioteka, 1986– . Monthly.　　　　　　　　　　　　　　　　**AD301**

Continues: *Bibliografia kombëtare e Republikës Popullore të Shqipërisë : Artikujt e perioikut shqip*, 1966–76, and *Bibliografia kombëtare e Republikës Popullore Socialiste të Shqipërisë : Artikujt e periodikut shqip* 1977–85.

In Albanian, English, French, and Russian.

An index to periodical articles; classed arrangement with author index.　　　　　　　　　　　　　　　　Z6956.A5B53

Belgium

Bibliographie de Belgique : 2ème partie, Sommaire des périodiques. 1897–1914. Bruxelles : Van Oest, 1897–1914.　　　　　　　　　　　　　　　　**AD302**

Title and frequency vary. 1899–1911 issued as third part of *Bibliographie de Belgique* with title *Bulletin des sommaires;* 1912–13 issued as second part, with title *Sommaire des périodiques;* 1899–1911 issued at irregular intervals, usually monthly (sometimes bimonthly or quarterly) with annual author index; 1912–14 semiannual with annual author and subject indexes. Each number is a classed subject index arranged by the Universal Decimal Classification numbers. Indexes a large number of periodicals, giving fairly full information for each article. A cumbersome but usable index supplying material not easily found in any other way.

Discontinued 1915 because of World War I. Continued by: *Bibliographie de Belgique : 2ème partie, Bulletin mensuel des articles de fond parus les revues belges* (n.s., v. 47 [Janv.1921]–v.51 [1925]. Bruxelles : Service de la Bibliographie de Belgique, 1921–25). No more published.

Roemans, Robert. Bibliographie van de moderne Vlaamsche litteratuur, 1893 1930. 1. deel. Kortrijk : Steenlandt, 1930–34. Afl. 1–10.　　　　　　　　　　　　　　　　**AD303**

No more published.

1. deel: De Vlaamsche tijdschriften.

An index to the literary articles in Flemish periodicals, indexed periodical by periodical, with cumulated author indexes to poetry, prose, and critical articles.

§ Continued by: *Bibliografie van de Vlaamse tijdschriften*, door Robert Roemans en Hilda van Assche (Hasselt : Heideland, 1960–71. Reeks I–III).

Contents: Reeks I, Vlaamse literaire tijdschriften van 1930 tot en met 1965; Reeks II, Vlaamse niet-literaire tijdschriften van 1886 tot en met 1961; Reeks III, Vlaamse literaire tijdschriften vanaf 1969.

Reeks I indexes literary periodicals, poetry, prose, theater, and critical articles; some issues are devoted to a single periodical, while others index several. Reeks II indexes periodicals in the fields of linguistics, philology, folklore, history, etc. Reeks III indexes literary journals.

Reeks III continued by: *Bibliografie van de literaire tijdschriften in Vlaanderen en Nederland : de tijdschriften verschenen* (1972– . Antwerp : Roemans-Stichting, 1974– . Annual).

Journals are listed individually in separate sections for Flemish and Dutch periodicals. Gives full information for each journal, including names of editors, number of issues published, etc., followed by lists of authors and their contributions grouped as poetry, prose, criticism, etc. Author and subject indexes. Coverage is somewhat broader than literature, many of the journals encompassing areas such as art, music, or photography.　　　　　　　　　　Z2424.F5R7

Bulgaria

Letopis na periodichniia pechat / Bŭlgarski bibliografski institut Elin Pelin. god. 1 (1952)–god. 20 (1971). Sofia : [Narodna Biblioteka], 1952–71.　　　　　　　　　　**AD304**

Arranged by a classified scheme, with author indexes. Annual cumulated author index.

Beginning 1972, continued in two sections: *Letopis na statiie ot bŭlgarskite spisaniia i sbronitsi* (god. 21 [1972]–god. 23 [1973]), which indexed periodicals, and *Letopis na statiie ot bulgarskite vestnitsi* (god. 21, 1972– . AE46), which indexes newspapers. Both assume the volume numbering of the earlier series, and both are issued by the Narodna Biblioteka.　　　　　　　　　　AI15.L37

Letopis na statiite ot bŭlgarskite spisaniia i sbornitsi. god. 21 (1972)–god. 23 (1973). Sofiia : Narodna biblioteka "Sv. sv. Kiril i Metodii", 1972–73.　　　　　　　　**AD305**

Beginning 1974, issued as "seriia 5" of the *Natsionalna bibliografiia na NR Bŭlgariia* (AA583 note). Title in English: *Bulgarian national bibliography. Series 5. Articles from Bulgarian journals and collections.*

Continues in part: *Letopis na periodichniia pechat* (AD304), assuming its organization and numbering.　　　　　AI15.L375

Croatia

Bibliografija rasprava, članaka i književnih radova u časopisima Narodne Republike Hrvatske za godunu. 1945-1946–1952. Zagreb : Jugoslovenska Akademija Znanosti i Umjetnosti, [1948–56].　　　　　　　　　**AD306**

Index to Croatian periodicals; classified, with alphabetical indexes by author and subject. The first volume covers the years 1945–46; subsequent issues are annual.

§ More current: *Bibliografija rasprava, članaka i književnih radova u časopisima SR Hrvatske* (1979– . U Zagrebu : Biblioteka. 12 no. a year).　　　　　　　　　　　　　　　　AI15.B5

Czechoslovakia

Članky v českých časopisech. roč. 1 (1953)– . V Praze : Národní Knihovna, [1953]– . Monthly.　　　　　　**AD307**

Title varies.

Constitutes a part of the *Bibliograficky katalog ČSSR* (AA600 note). A classified index with annual cumulative indexes for some years.　　　　　　　　　　　　　　　　AI15.C55

Denmark

Dansk artikelindeks : aviser og tidsskrifter. 1979– . Ballerup : Bibliotekscentralens Forlag, 1981– . Monthly with annual cumulations.　　　　　　　　　　　　　　　　**AD308**

Added title page in English: *The Danish national bibliography: articles, newspapers and journals.* Forms a part of the Danish national bibliography; *see* AA605.

Formed by merger of *Dansk Tidsskrift-Index* (AD309) and *Avis-kronik-index* (København : Munksgaard, 1940–78).

Introductory matter in Danish and English.

Serves as a continuation of both *Dansk tidsskrift-index* and *Avis-kronik-index*, providing indexing of substantive articles from 25 newspapers and about 550 periodicals published in Denmark (including the Faroe Islands). Full citations are given in a classified section according to the Danish Decimal Classification; author and subject indexes refer to the classified section. Book reviews are excluded. The annual cumulation may be purchased without the monthly issues.

Dansk Tidsskrift-Index. v. 1 (1915)–64 (1978). København : Dansk Bibliografisk Kontor, 1916–79.   **AD309**
Publisher varies.

A classified subject index. Later volumes include subject and author indexes. Number of periodicals indexed varies: v. 1, 165; about 300 in the 1970 issue. Each volume contains a section, "Personal historie," listing biographical articles.

Biographical material for the years 1915-49 indexed by: Sven Houmøller, *Biografiske tidsskriftartikler* (Copenhagen : Bibliotekscentralen, 1971).

Cumulated index: *Stedregister til Dansk Tidskrift-Index 1915–1970*, [af] Torben Sorensen, Hans Michelsen ([Ballerup] : Bibliotekscentralen, 1978. 231 p.).

§ Merged with *Avis-kronik-index* (København : Munksgaard, 1940–78) to form *Dansk artikelindeks* (AD308).   AI13.D3

Thomsen, Svend. Danske blandede Tidsskrifter, 1855–1912 : inholdsoversigt til 27 danske Tidsskrifter / udarb. af Ellen Bruun ... [et al.]. Copenhagen : Bianco Lunos, 1928–29. 2 v.   **AD310**

At head of title: Københavns Kommunebiblioteker.

A classified subject index of articles contained in 27 general periodicals, arranged by a decimal classification, with author and alphabetical subject indexes. Useful for its indexing of some material earlier than that covered by the more comprehensive *Dansk Tidsskrift-Index*, 1915–1978 (AD309). Later indexing of 5 of the 27 periodicals covered is given in the *Dansk Tidsskrift-Index*.

Biographical material indexed by: Sven Houmøller, *Biografiske tidsskriftartikler* (Copenhagen : Bibliotekscentralen, 1971).   AI13.T4

Finland

Suomen aikakauslehti-indeksi = Index to Finnish periodicals. 1959–1981. Turku : Turun Yliopiston Kirjasto, 1961–1984. Annual.   **AD311**
A classified subject listing with author index. The 1981 vol. lists nearly 8,000 articles from 162 periodicals.

A retrospective volume of the same title by Maija Palperi covering 1803–63 was published 1974 (211 p.).

§ Continued by: *Suomalaisia aikakauslehtiartikkeleita, uutuusindeksi = Finlandanska tidskriftsartiklar, nyhetsindex* (1982– . Helsinki : Kirjastopaloelu oy, 1984– . Quarterly). In Finnish and Swedish.
AI19.F5N8

France

French periodical index. 1973/74– . Morgantown, W. Va. : Ponchie & Co., 1976– . Annual.   **AD312**
Publisher varies.
Subtitle: *Répertoriex* (1977–).
Comp. by Jean-Pierre Ponchie.
Preface and table of contents in English and French.

Intended for students of French who need to locate articles in general interest French-language periodicals. Though most titles indexed are published in France, some Canadian titles are also included. 1991 volume indexes 50 titles. Alphabetical subject index in French only. Headings are rather broad.   AI7.F7

Germany

Bibliographie der deutschen Zeitschriftenliteratur. v.1 (1896)–128 (1964). Leipzig : Fr. Andra's Nachfolger, 1897–1964. Semiannual.   **AD313**
Title varies slightly.
Bd. 95–96 (1945–46) never published.

A comprehensive index valuable because of the large number of important German periodicals, transactions, yearbooks, and other composite works indexed. Semiannual volumes with no cumulation necessitate the consultation of many alphabets. Except in the case of v. 34–35, 40, 40a–41, and 43–46, for which combined author indexes in three separate volumes have been published, each volume consists of: (1) a subject index arranged alphabetically by rather broad subjects, giving for each article indexed its title, author's name in parentheses when known, reference to periodical by key number (instead of title), page, and sometimes volume; and (2) an author index to the subject part (omitted in some volumes). The number of periodicals indexed is large, ranging from 275 in the first volume to some 4,500 in later volumes. The retrospective indexing of the *Ergänzungsbände* carries the work back to 1861. Important in university work and in large libraries which have many German periodicals, but not generally recommended for other libraries. Often especially useful for biography because it indexes many yearbooks of learned societies containing obituary notices.

In 1965 merged into *Internationale Bibliographie der Zeitschriftenliteratur aus allen Gebieten des Wissens* (AD255).

————. *Gesamt-register der Schlagworte aus Bd. 66–75, 76–85.* Leipzig : Dietrich, 1940–43. 2 v.

————. *Gesamt-register der Schlagworte zu Abt. A. Bibliographie der deutschen Zeitschriftenliteratur.* Bd. 97–113, und Abt. B. *Bibliographie der fremdsprachigen Zeitschriftenliteratur*, n.F., Bd. 30–39. Osnabrück : Dietrich, 1957. 533 p.

————. *Ergänzungsband 1–20* (Gautzsch b. Leipzig : Dietrich, 1908–42. v. 1–20.).

Numbered in set as v. 22A, 24A, 28A, 30A, 32A, 33A, 35A, 35B, 36B, 37A, 39B, 41A, 42A, 72A, 78A, 80A, 82A.

Contents: Ergbd. 1, 1896–98; 2, 1896–1908; 3, 1893–95; 4, 1891–92; 5, 1889–90; 6, 1911–13; 7, 1887–88; 8, 1913–14; 9, 1885–86; 10, 1914–15; 11, 1883–84; 12, 1881–82; 13, 1915–17; 14, 1879–81; 15, 1876–78; 16, 1873–75; 17, 1870–73; 18, 1868–70; v. 19, 1865–67; v. 20, 1861–67.   AI9.B512

Gesamtinhaltsverzeichnis der wissenschaftlichen Zeitschriften der Universitäten und Hochschulen der Deutschen Demokratischen Republik. 1951/52–1978. [Leipzig : Leipziger Druckhaus], 1959–1982. Annual, with quinquennial cumulations.   **AD314**
"Im Auftrage des Ministeriums für Hoch- und Fachschulwesen zusammengestellt un herausgegeben von der Universitätsbibliothek der Humboldt-Universität zu Berlin."—*title page*.

Frequency varies: quinquennial issues cover 1951/56–1957/76; after that, volumes are either biennial or annual.

Indexes scholarly periodicals issued by selected universities and Hochschulen of the former Eastern Germany. Classified arrangement with author index.

Hocks, Paul. Index zu deutschen Zeitschriften der Jahre 1773–1830. Nendeln, Liechtenstein : KTO Pr., 1979. Abt.I.   **AD315**
Contents: Abt. I, Bd. 1–3, Zeitschriften der Berliner Spätaufklärung.

Abt.I indexes 14 journals published during the late years of the "Berlin enlightenment" (i.e., journals ranging in dates from 1783 to 1811). Bd.1 provides an issue-by-issue listing of the contents of each journal; Bd.2 offers indexes of names (*Namenregister*) and of specific types of contributions or titles with recurring phrases (*Guttungsregister*); and Bd. 3 is a *Stichwortregister* or catchword index.   AI9.H54

Index deutschsprachiger Zeitschriften, 1750–1815 / erstellt durch eine Arbeitsgruppe unter Leitung von Klaus Schmidt [microform]. Hildesheim : Olms Neue Medien, c1990. 28 microfiches, with printed user's guide and list of titles indexed.   **AD316**
Title from cover of guide.
At head of title: Akademie der Wissenschaften zu Göttingen.
Fiche provide separate indexes by author, subject keyword, subject name, geographical subject, and illustration (including portraits, maps, and music), as well as book reviews. Nearly 200 titles are covered.   AI9.I45

Hungary

Magyar folyóiratok repertóriuma : Repertorium bibliographicum periodicorum Hungaricorum / Kiadja az Országos Széchényi Könyvtár. 1946–1977. Budapest : Országos Széchényi Könyvtár, 1946–77. Semimonthly.   **AD317**

A supplement to *Magyar nemzeti bibliográfia* (AA712). Originally appeared quarterly, then monthly, then semimonthly.

A classified index to Hungarian literary and scientific periodicals, with semimonthly and annual author indexes.

§ Continued by *Magyar nemzeti bibliográfia. Időszaki kiadványok repertóriuma* (AD123).   AI19.H8M22

Italy

Italy. Parlamento. Camera dei Deputati. Biblioteca. Catalogo metodico degli scritti contenuti nelle pubblicazioni periodiche italiane e straniere : Parte 1. Scritti biografici e critici. Roma : Tip. della Camera dei Deputati, 1885–1935. 10 v. and index.   **AD318**

Contents: v.1, to 1883; suppl.1, 1884–87 and earlier; suppl. 2, 1887–88 and earlier; suppl.3, 1889–94; suppl.4, 1895–1900; suppl.5, 1901–06; n.s. v.1, 1907–12; n.s. v.2, 1913–18; n.s. v.3, 1919–24; n.s. v.4, 1925–30. Indice generale, a tutto l'anno 1906 (publ. 1909. 117 p.).

Not a general index but a subject catalog of biographical articles in the sets of periodicals (19,785 volumes) contained in the library of the Italian Chamber of Deputies. Each volume has: (1) a main subject list, arranged by name of biographee, which gives for each article indexed the title, author, and the title and volume or year of the periodical in which it is to be found, and (2) a brief author index referring to the subject list. The supplements index the volumes added during the period covered and earlier material omitted from the first volume. The *Indice generale* refers to all names included in the subject lists of the first volume and supplements 1–5. Sets indexed include the principal Italian periodicals and society transactions and also many important English, French, German, and Spanish titles.   AI11.I8

Italy. Provveditorato Generale dello Stato. Pubblicazioni edite dallo stato o col suo concorso : Spoglio dei periodici e delle opere collettive 1901–40. Roma : Libreria dello Stato, 1926–42. [8 v.].   **AD319**

Basic work, 1901–25, 2v. (publ. 1926); 1926–30, 2v. (publ. 1931); 1931–35, 2v. (publ. 1937); 1936–40, 2v. (publ. 1942).

A subject index to more than 200 Italian periodicals and collected works which are either government publications or issued under government auspices or aid. Each volume in two parts: (1) Index to biographical and critical articles arranged alphabetically by name of person written about, and (2) Subject index, arranged by large classes, e.g., agriculture, archaeology, etc., with subdivisions under each, and an alphabetical index of small topics referring to the large classes. Entries in the biographical section are repeated in the classed section. Information given about each article is full, including author and title of article, and title, volume, inclusive paging, and date of the volume in which it appears.   AI11.I82

Netherlands

Nijhoff's Index op de Nederlandse en Vlaamse periodieken. v. 1 (Sept. 1909)–60 (1970). 'sGravenhage : Nijhoff, 1910–73. Monthly.   **AD320**

Title varies.

A monthly index to general periodicals, including a few newspapers. Each number contains authors and subjects in one alphabet with a separate list of book reviews at the end. No cumulations, but begin-

ning with the volume for 1925, there is an annual author index and a catchword subject index. The number of periodicals indexed varies from 19 in the earlier volumes to more than 60.   AI5.N4

Norway

Deichmanske Bibliotek, Oslo. Register til en del norske tidsskrifter. Kristiania : Arnesens Bog & Accidenstrykkeri, 1908–11. 2 v.   **AD321**

Contents: v. 1, Topografi; v. 2, Norsk biografi.

Arranged by subject, each volume indexes one topic. Vol. 1 (1908) indexes the topographical articles in 75 periodicals of varying dates from about the beginning of the 19th century to 1907; v. 2 indexes nearly 15,000 biographical articles in more than 700 periodicals of the 19th and the first part of the 20th century, giving not only references to periodicals, but also dates of birth and death and very brief characterization for each name indexed. The list of periodicals included in v. 2 furnishes a nearly complete bibliography of Norwegian periodicals for the 19th and early 20th centuries.   Z2595.D32

Norsk tidsskriftindex. Årg. 1 (1918)–46 (1965). Oslo : Steenske Forlag, 1919–71. Annual.   **AD322**

Subtitle: Systematisk fortegnelse over indholdet av norske periodiske skrifter (varies); publisher varies.

A classified subject index with an alphabetical subject index to some 250 Norwegian periodicals.

Issued in annual volumes, with a general title page, list of abbreviations and periodicals indexed, and alphabetical subject index to the classed lists for v. 1–3 (1918–20), v. 4–8 (1921–25), v. 9–13 (1926–30), v. 14–18 (1931–35), v. 19–23 (1936–40), v. 24–25 (1941–42), v. 26–28 (1943–45), v. 29–33 (1946–50); thereafter, only annual issues were published. Superseded by the annual *Norske tidsskriftartikler* which began publication 1981 with a volume covering 1980.

Beginning with v. 18 (1935), the publisher changed and the index became a part of the bibliographical series *Norsk bibliografisk bibliotek*, v. 18 being numbered as bd. 1, hft. 5 in that series (with retrospective numbering of v. 14–17 as bd. 1, hft. 1–4), and v. 19–23 as bd. 4. The detailed indexing of articles of individual biography, formerly a feature of the index under the heading "Personalhistorie," is omitted from 1931 and included, instead, in a separate series, the first volume of which is *Biografiske artikler i norske tidsskrifter 1931–35*, numbered as bd. 2, hft. 3 of the *Norsk bibliografisk bibliotek*.   AI13.N6

Romania

Bibliografia Republicii Socialiste România : Articole din publicatii periodice şi seriale. v. 13, no. 16 (Aug. 16/31 1965)– . [Bucureşti] : Biblioteca Centrală de Stat a Republicii Socialiste România. Semimonthly.   **AD323**

Continues: *Bibliografia Republicii Populare Romîne : Articole din publicatii periodice seriale* (1963–65), which continued *Bibliografia, periodicelor din Republica Populara Romîna* (1957–62) and *Buletinul bibliografic. Seria B. Articole si recenzii din presa.*

Issues for 1988 index approximately 85 Romanian serial titles. Classified subject arrangement and author index.   AI19.R8B8

Lupu, Ioan. Bibliografia analitică a periodicelor româneşti / Ioan Lupu ... [et al.]. Bucureşti : Editura Academiei Republicii Socialiste România, 1966–70. 2 v. in 6.   **AD324**

Contents: v. 1, pts. 1–3, 1790–1850; v. 2, pts. 1–3, 1851–58.

An annotated bibliography of Romanian periodical articles relating to political, economic, and cultural matters. Arranged by Universal Decimal Classification.   Z2929.L86

Russia and the U.S.S.R.

Letopis' zhurnal'nykh stateĭ. T. 1 (1926)– . Moskva : Izd. Gos. tsentral'no knizhoi palaty, 1926– . Weekly.   **AD325**
> Frequency varies.
> Title varies: 1926–37, *Zhurnal'naĩa letopis'*.
> A weekly index of wide scope covering more than 1,700 journals, series, and continuing publications of academies, universities and research institutes in humanities, science, and the social sciences. Excluded are popular magazines, children's literature, and government publications. Entries, averaging some 3,500 an issue, are arranged in the 31 sections of the Soviet classification scheme. Each issue identifies the specific journal numbers indexed; the annual *Spisok zhurnalov* ... cumulates this information. Indexes of names and localities were published quarterly 1956–77; starting 1978, indexes are issued bimonthly.   AI15.L4

Masanov, ĨUriĭ Ivanovich. Ukazateli soderzhaniĩa russkikh zhurnalov i prodolzhaĩushchikhsĩa izdaniĭ 1755–1970 gg / U. I. Masanov, N. V. Nitkina, Z. D. Titova. Moskva : "Kniga", 1975. 437 p.   **AD326**
> At head of title: Gosudarstvennaĩa publichnaĩa biblioteka im. M. E. Saltykova-Shchedrina.
> A bibliography of indexes to individual Russian journals. Arranged alphabetically by title of the journal. Indexed.   Z6956.R9M37

Spain

Coleccíon de índices de publicaciones periódicas. [t.] 1– . Madrid : Consejo Superior de Investigaciones Científicas, Instituto Miguel de Cervantes, 1946– .   **AD327**
> Each volume is an index to an individual periodical, usually from the 19th century. In some cases extracts from articles or annotations are included. Usually gives: name, place, subject, title, first-line index, and a selection of plates or illustrations.

Indice español de humanidades. v. [0, no. 1], [July–Dec. 1975]–v. 6 (1981). Madrid : Instituto de Información y Documentación en Ciencias Sociales y Humanidades, Centro Nacional de Informatión y Documentación, C.S.I.C., 1978–81. Annual.   **AD328**
> Semiannual, 1976.
> Reproduces tables of contents of the journals indexed and provides author and keyword subject indexing.
> Split into four parts: Serie A, *Bellas artes*, Serie B, *Ciencias históricas*, Serie C, *Linguistica y literatura*, and Serie D, *Filisofía*.
>   AS1.I5

Tortajada, A. Materiales de investigación : índice de artículos de revistas (1939–1949) / A. Tortajada, C. de Amaniel. Madrid : Consejo Superior de Investigaciones Científicas, Biblioteca General, 1952. 2 v.   **AD329**
> Arranged alphabetically by author and subject. Indexes some 125 periodicals in both the humanities and the sciences.   AI17.T6

Switzerland

Studer, Maja. Analytische Bibliographie der Gesamtregister schweizerischer Zeitschriften = Bibliographie analytique des tables générales des périodiques suisses. Bern : Schweizerische Landesbibliothek, 1974. 125 p.   **AD330**
> A classed listing of Swiss periodicals having one or more cumulative indexes, with indication of type of index and period covered. Alphabetical title index.   Z6293.S87

Turkey

Türkiye makaleler bibliyoğrafyasĭ. Mart 1952– . Ankara : Türk Tarih Kurumu Basimevi, 1952– . Monthly.   **AD331**
> Place, publisher, series and frequency vary.
> Volumes before 1976 also have French title, *Bibliographie des articles parus dans les périodiques turcs*. Prefatory matter in Turkish and English.
> Indexes periodical articles and reviews, as well as conference and seminar papers that have been received by the National Library. Classified subject arrangement and author index, with a cumulative author index issued annually. Older volumes give titles in both Turkish and French.

Yugoslavia

Bibliografija Jugoslavije : Članci i književni prilozi u časopisima / Bibliografiski institut FNRJ. G. 1, br. 1 (jan.-mart 1950)–G. 2 (1951). Beograd : Institut, 1950–1951.   **AD332**
> A classified index to Yugoslav periodicals in all fields. Beginning with the first issue of 1952, it appears in sections:
> Series A, social sciences (most recently *Bibliografija Jugoslavije : Clanci i prilozi u serijskim publikacijama: Serija A : Društvene nauke*. G. 28, br. 1 [jan. 1977]– . Monthly).
> Series B, natural and applied sciences (most recently *Bibliografija Jugoslavije : Clanci i prilozi u serijskim publikacijama: Serija B : Prirodne, primenjene, medicinske i tehničke nauke* (1985, 1-2– . Monthly).
> Series C, philology, art, sport, literature, music (most recently *Bibliografija Jugoslavije : Clanci i prilozi u serijskim publikacijama: Serija C : Umetnost, sport, filologija, književnost* (G. 36, br. 1 [jan. 1985]– . Monthly).
> Coverage, titles, and frequencies have changed. Issuing agency: Jugoslovenski bibliografski institut.   AI15.B59

Jugoslavenski leksikografski zavod. Bibliografija rasprava, članaka i književnih radova. Zagreb : Jugoslavenski leksikografski zavod, 1956– . v. 1–8. (In progress).   **AD333**
> Beginning with v. 4, volumes have title *Bibliografija rasprava i članaka*.
> A retrospective periodical index, planned to be in 25 v., to form a comprehensive record of articles published in Yugoslavia since 1800 in magazines, newspapers, yearbooks and collections. Arrangement is by broad classification, with indexes. The first 4 v. (in 7 pts.) are devoted to various categories of literature: v. 4 (in 4 pts.) is concerned with history, v. 5 with the plastic arts, and v. 6 (2 pts.) with music.   Z2951.Z3

Africa

Nigeria

Index to Nigeriana in selected periodicals. 1965–67. Lagos : Nat. Libr. of Nigeria, 1967–70. Annual.   **AD334**
> Issue for 1965 had title: *Index to selected Nigerian periodicals*.
> An author (or anonymous title) and subject index to articles of Nigerian interest appearing in a selection of periodicals, most of them published in Nigeria. 28 journals are indexed in the 1967 issue (publ. 1970).   Z965.N38

South Africa

Index to South African periodicals. v. 1 (1940)– . Johannesburg : Johannesburg Public Lib., 1941– . Annual.   **AD335**
  Added title page in Afrikaans.
  1940–42 issued by the South African Library Association.
  Cumulations issued for the periods 1940–49 (4 v.), 1950–59 (3 v.), 1960–69 (microfiche), 1970–74 (microfiche). Annual volumes issued on microfiche 1980–86. Author and subject entries. Includes book reviews. Ceased microform publication with 1986 ed.
  •Resumed coverage with: *Index to South African periodicals 1987+* [database] ([Pretoria] : Information Services, State Library, South Africa, 1987–). Available on CD-ROM.   AI3.I65

Asia (by region)

Asia, Southeast

Index to periodical articles relating to Singapore, Malaysia, Brunei, ASEAN : humanities & social sciences / comp. by the Humanities/Social Sciences/Management Reference Department. 1980–1982– . [Singapore] : National Univ. of Singapore Library, 1984– . Annual.   **AD336**
  Covers approximately 150 periodicals, most of which are published in Singapore, Malaysia, and Burnei. Classified subject arrangement, with author and book review indexes. Includes list of journals covered and subject headings used.   Z3221.I54

Asia (by country)

India

Guide to Indian periodical literature. v. 1 (1964) . Gurgaon : Indian Documentation Service [etc.], 1964– . Quarterly.   **AD337**
  Originally appearing as a monthly, publication was suspended after eight issues. With the issue for Jan.–Mar. 1967 (v.4, no.1), publication was resumed on a quarterly basis with annual cumulations. A cumulated volume covering 1964 has since been published, and annual volumes were issued to fill the 1965–66 gap. A retrospective volume covering 1963 was published in 1978 as *Index to Indian periodical literature*. Now indexes about 400 Indian journals. Author and subject entries in dictionary arrangement.   Z6958.I4G8

Index India. v. 1 (Jan./Mar. 1967)– . Jaipur : Rajasthan Univ. Libr., 1967– . Quarterly. (irregular).   **AD338**
  Frequency varies : 1986–87, Semiannual. Issued in annual, two-part vols. since 1988.
  Subtitle and editors vary. Current subtitle: *A documentation list on India of documents in English.*
  Classified arrangement with alphabetical subject and author indexes. Beginning with v. 2, no. 1, essays and studies in collections of works by diverse hands are also indexed. 1990 vol. (publ. 1993) covers approximately 1,000 periodical titles and 18 collections. Coverage is worldwide, though only English-language items pertaining to India are included.

India (Republic). Parliament. House of the People. Abstracts and index of articles. v. 1 (1958)–12 (1962). New Delhi : Lok Sabha Secretariat, 1958–62. Monthly.   **AD339**
  Incorporates the "Abstracting service" and the "Monthly list of selected articles" which were previously issued as separate periodicals.

In two parts: pt. 1, Abstracts, giving "digests of important articles on political, economic, social, legal, parliamentary, and other subjects"; pt. 2, an index to the contents of periodicals and newspapers received in the Parliament Library.
  Ceased publication and merged with its *Abstracts of reports* to form its *Abstracts of books, reports and articles* (AF245).   AI3.I7

Israel

Mafteaḥ le-khitve-ѐt be-ʿIvrit / ba-àrikhat Elḥanan Adler, Yosef Yerushalmi, ʿKarniyaḥ Flaisher. 1977– . Yerushalayim : Yotse le-or àvur Universitat ʿHefah, 1978– . Annual.   **AD340**
  Added title page in English: *Index to Hebrew periodicals.*
  At head of title: University of Haifa. Library.
  An index of authors (or other main entry) and subjects, with a separate section for book reviews. Beginning 1982, also available on microfiche.   PN5650.M28

Japan

Current contents of academic journals in Japan : the humanities and social sciences. 1970– . Tokyo : Center for Academic Publications Japan, 1971– . Annual.   **AD341**
  Indexes nearly 300 scholarly Japanese journals. Articles may be written in any one of a dozen languages, but the titles of Japanese-language items are translated into a western language—often English—making this index quite useful for non-Japanese speakers. Original languages of articles and their abstracts are indicated. Classified subject arrangement (but no subject index) with author index. Lists bibliographic data for indexed journals.
  •"The data on titles listed in the preceding (from vol. 15) and present volumes can be obtained in floppy disk form as an MS-DOS text-file and a Japanese dBase III data-file."—*Pref., Vol. 19 (1992).*   AI19.J3C85

Zasshi kiji sakuin = Japanese periodicals index. [Tokyo] : Kokuritsu Kokkai Toshokan, 1948–49. Monthly   **AD342**
  Subtitle varies; sponsoring body varies; frequency varies.
  Now published quarterly in three parts: *Jimbun shukai hen* (Humanities and social science, 1948–); *Kagaku gijutsu hen* (Science and technology, 1950–); *Igaku yakugaku hen* (Medical science and pharmacology, 1978–). A classified subject arrangement with author index, personal and corporate name index, schedule of subject classification, and list of periodicals indexed. Annual index supplements published for some years in the 1970s. Cumulations for humanities and social sciences published for 1948–54, 1955–64, and for each five-year period following (1985–89 ed. publ. 1993).   AI19.J3Z38

Malaysia

Indeks majalah Malaysia = Malaysian periodicals index. 1973– . Kuala Lumpur : Perpustakaan Negara Malaysia, 1974–   **AD343**
  Frequency varies: from 1980 issued semiannually with two parts to each issue (pt.1, Classified section with subject index; pt.2, Author/title section).
  Supersedes in part: *Indeks majallah kini Malaysia Singapura dan Brunei* (Index to current Malaysian, Singapore and Brunei periodicals) publ. 1969–71 and covering 1967–68.
  Introductory matter in Malay and English.
  Now indexes about 180 periodicals in Malay, English, Chinese and Tamil. The subject section is arranged by Dewey Decimal Classification with subject indexing in English. Also indexes working papers from conferences held in the area.   AI3.I26

Philippines

Index to Philippine periodicals. v. 1 (Oct. 1955/Sept. 1956)– . Manila : Inter-Departmental Reference Service, Inst. of Public Administration, Univ. of the Philippines, 1956– . Quarterly.   **AD344**

Frequency varies. Originally a quarterly. 1970–79, varies among annual, semiannual, and quarterly schedules. 1980–84 issues not published, although a retrospective index for those years is promised "as soon as additional budgetary support becomes available."—*Pref. v. 26, Jan.–Mar. 1985–1986* (publ. 1988). Issues for 1985–86 combined in four quarterly vols. Semiannual, 1987–88. Resumed publishing quarterly, 1989.

Combined alphabetical author/subject index.   AI3.I63

Singapore

Singapore periodicals index. 1969/70– . Singapore : Nat. Libr., [1973]– . Annual.   **AD345**

Supersedes in part *Index to current Malaysian, Singapore and Brunei periodicals*, 1967–68, publ. 1969–71.

Classed arrangement with author and subject indexes. Separate author index of Chinese entries. Now indexes about 110 periodicals.   AI3.S57

Australia and Oceania

Australia

Mitchell Library, Sydney. Index to periodicals. Jan. 1944/June 1949– . Sydney : Mitchell Library, 1950– .   **AD346**

Title varies: 1944/49–52/55 called *Index to periodicals*.

A preliminary issue covering 1944–49 was published in 1950 as *The Mitchell Library index to periodicals*. Subsequent volumes cover varying periods, and from 1956 represent annual cumulations of monthly indexes issued as part of the *NSW Library bulletin*.

A subject index only.

New Zealand

Index to New Zealand periodicals. 1966–1986. Wellington : National Library of New Zealand, 1966–1986.   **AD347**

Continues: *Index to New Zealand periodicals, 1940–49; Index to New Zealand periodicals and current national bibliography of New Zealand books & pamphlets, 1950–65*.

History: 1940 issue, prep. by the Otago Branch of the Library Association as a preliminary index to 12 periodicals; v.1–2, 1941–42, issued quarterly, cumulated annually; v.3, no.1, Jan.–June 1943; publication suspended July 1943–Dec. 1946; 1941–46 cumulation published 1949; 1947–49 published semiannually with annual cumulation; annual volumes have appeared since 1957, with irregular cumulations as noted below. From 1979, publ. 3 times a year with annual cumulation. The periodical index sections for 1958–60 inclusive were cumulated into one volume (publ. 1961) with the *Current national bibliography* for 1960, but the national bibliography sections were not cumulated. 1961–62 also cumulated into one volume.

This is a subject index with cross-references from author entries to the subject listing. Indexed about 220 New Zealand periodicals on a selective basis, plus some articles on New Zealand published elsewhere.   Z6962.N5I5

Papua New Guinea

New Guinea periodical index. v. 1 (1968)–v. 15, no. 2 (1983). Boroko, Papua New Guinea : Univ. of Papua New Guinea Library, 1968–1983.   **AD348**

Frequency varied: typically quarterly with annual cumulation.

Aims to bring together references to "all major articles published anywhere in the world about any aspect of New Guinea."—*Introd.* Based on the periodical acquisitions of the New Guinea Collection in the University of Papua New Guinea Library (and includes some noncurrent and photocopied material from journals not in that library). Originally an author/subject arrangement; beginning 1981, a topical listing with author and people/places indexes.   Z4811.U54a

AE

Newspapers

Scope. Although this section lists works primarily concerned with newspapers, many bibliographies that treat both newspapers and periodicals will have full entries in the Periodicals section (AD). Works that deal with the broader subject of the press—broadcast media as well as newspapers—are listed under Journalism (below). Foreign press surveys for a particular country or area, however, will be included with newspaper bibliographies for that country or region. Directories or other sources pertaining to the media may also be found in the section on Mass media in the Economics section (CH).

This section also lists a selection of bibliographies and indexes for ethnic or other special interest papers. These works are not grouped together, and the index should be consulted under subject—e.g., "Ethnic press"—for a complete listing.

Newsletter bibliographies are listed in this section, but information concerning them may also be found under Periodicals. *Standard periodicals directory* (AD56) contains many listings for newsletters, but does not so identify them. Bibliographies of newspapers and newletters in special subjects will be listed with those subjects.

BIBLIOGRAPHIES, UNION LISTS, AND DIRECTORIES

International

Current: Among important international sources giving bibliographical, circulation and other information about current newspapers are: *Benn's media directory* (AD1) *Willing's press guide* (AD118), *Europa world year book* (CJ94), *Editor and Publisher international yearbook* (AE22), *International media guide: newspapers worldwide* (AE9) and *Gale international directory of publications* (Detroit : Gale Research, c1989). For availability of current newspapers, a listing of current newspapers being microfilmed can be found in *Serials in microform* (the newspaper portion was formerly *Newspapers on microfilm*, Ann Arbor, Mich.: University Microfilms, 1984–85). A list of newspapers to which the Center for Research Libraries currently subscribes and that are available for loan to member libraries, can be found in *Serials and newspapers currently received at the Center for Research Libraries* (Chicago : CRL, [1991]). Unpublished lists of newspapers currently being received are sometimes available from the Center. See also *Newspapers received currently in the Library of Congress* (AE11) below.

Retrospective: In addition to the sources listed below, earlier editions of the current directories noted above may be useful for past information. Older editions of *Newspapers received currently in the Library of Congress* may also have retrospective information.

Arndt, Karl John Richard. The German language press of the Americas / Karl John Richard Arndt, May E. Olson. München : Verlag Dokumentation, [1973–80]. 3 v. **AE1**

Added title page in German: *Die deutschsprachige Presse der Amerikas*.

Publisher varies.

Contents: v. 1, 1732–1968: United States of America (3rd rev. ed., enl. by an appendix, publ. 1976); v. 2, 1732–1968: Argentina, Bolivia, Brazil, Canada, Chile, Colombia, Costa Rica, Cuba, Dominican Republic, Ecuador, Guatemala, Guyana, Mexico, Paraguay, Peru, USA (addenda), Uruguay, Venezuela (publ. 1973); v. 3, German-American press research from the American Revolution to the Bicentennial (publ. 1980).

Vol. 1 was first published 1965 with title: *German-American newspapers and periodicals, 1732–1955*; it was reprinted 1965 with an appendix of additional newspapers.

The U.S. section is arranged by state, then by city, while other sections are by country, then by city. Gives title changes, names of editors and publishers, etc., for each newspaper and locates files in American and European libraries.

Vol. 3 is a selection of essays in German or English, chiefly reprints, relating to the history and influence of the German-language press in America. Z6956.G3A75

Benn's media. 141st ed. (1993)– . Tonbridge, Kent : Benn Business Information Services. Annual. **AE2**

For annotation, *see* AD1. Z6956.E5M6

Center for Research Libraries. Foreign newspapers held by the Center for Research Libraries / comp. by Kristine Smets and and Adriana Pilecky-Dekajlo. Chicago : Center for Research Libraries, 1992. 2 v. **AE3**

Contents: v. 1, Title list; v. 2, Geographic list.

Lists 5,562 titles from 156 countries published from the 1600s to the present. 328 titles are currently received by the Center; information is current as of Oct. 1992. Vol. 1 is arranged alphabetically by title and for each paper gives place and date of publication, cross-references to earlier and later titles, OCLC number, language of text, frequency, summary of holdings, and format. In v. 2, titles are arranged by country and city. Z6945.C43

Feuereisen, Fritz. Die Presse in Afrika : ein Handbuch für Wirtschaft und Werbung = The press in Africa: a handbook for economics and advertising / bearb. von Fritz Feuereisen [und] Ernst Schmacke. 2. Aufl. Pullach/München : Verlag Dokumentation, 1973. 280 p. **AE4**

1st ed., 1968.

The same publisher has released companion volumes under the same editorship except as noted: *Die Presse in Asien und Ozeanien* (1968; 2. Aufl., 1973. 376 p.); *Die Presse in Lateinamerika* (1968; 2. Aufl., 1973. 268 p.); *Die Presse in Europa*, bearb. von Fritz Feuereisen (1971. 328 p.).

All four volumes have text in German and English, and have similar format and organization. For each country, newspapers are presented in tabular format, giving each title: address, frequency, circulation, type of readership, and advertising information. Title and geographic indexes in each volume.

§ Lists more countries and more newspaper titles for Europe, for example, than *Benn's media* (AD1). Z6959.F47

Foreign newspaper report. 1973–1975. [Wash.] : Libr. of Congress, 1973–75. **AE5**

Title varied: *Foreign newspaper and gazette report*, 1974–75.

Carried information previously included in the ARL Foreign Newspaper Microfilm Project *Circular letter*, which ceased publication with no. 21 (Feb. 1971).

Newsletter of the Foreign Newspaper Microfilming Coordinator's office. Contains information on foreign newspapers being microfilmed, particular dates being filmed, and by whom. Also describes important newspaper collections, newspaper microfilming projects being undertaken, and gives occasional newspaper bibliographies with locations.

Superseded by *Newspaper and gazette report* (Wash. : Libr. of Congress, 1976–78), which included information on both foreign and domestic newspapers. Beginning 1977, the December issue contained an annual index; a cumulative index covering 1973–76 was publ. 1978. Continued in part by *National preservation report*, which was itself continued by *National preservation news* (Wash. : National Preservation Program Office of the Library of Congress, 1985– . Quarterly.). Z663.2F66

Fraenkel, Josef. The Jewish press of the world. 7th ed. London : Cultural Dept. of the World Jewish Congress, [1972]. 128 p. **AE6**

1st ed., 1953.

Begins with an essay on the history of the Jewish press. Directory section gives information on more than 950 Jewish newspapers and periodicals published throughout the world. Concludes with a statistical summary indicating linguistic and geographic distribution of the papers.

§ For a very similar updated publication, *see Directory of world Jewish press and publications* (AD7). Z6367.F7

Hewitt, Arthur Reginald. Union list of Commonwealth newspapers in London, Oxford and Cambridge. [London] : publ. for the Institute of Commonwealth Studies by the Athlone Pr., Univ. of London, 1960. 101 p. **AE7**

Based on the holdings of the British Library; indicates files—in 62 British and Commonwealth libraries and newspaper offices—of newspapers published in the Commonwealth nations. (Irish Free State newspapers are not included; newspapers published in Anglo-Egyptian Sudan pre-1955 are included, though this was never part of the Commonwealth.) Arrangement is alphabetical by country and territory of origin. Title index. Z6945.H55

Iben, Icko. The Germanic press of Europe : an aid to research. Münster : Fahle, 1965. 146 p. (Studien zur Publizistik. Bremer Reihe, Bd.5). **AE8**

An attempt to list and locate files of the most significant newspapers of the Benelux countries (Belgium, Netherlands, and Luxembourg) and Scandinavia for the guidance of researchers. Also includes selected pre-1949 newspapers from the Dutch East Indies (Indonesia) and from the Netherlands West Indies. Discusses history and political background of major papers for each country, along with a chronological chart of holdings in European libraries. Indexes of names and titles. PN5110.I2

International media guide. 1983– . N.Y. : Directories International, 1983– . Annual. **AE9**

Title varies: some issues called *Media guide international*, some *IMG*.

Consists of three parts: *Newspapers worldwide, Consumer magazines worldwide*, and *Business and professional publications*.

Newspapers worldwide begins with a section on multicontinental papers (e.g., "The world paper, International herald tribune"), then is arranged by region—Asia/Pacific, Europe, Latin America, Middle East/Africa, North America. Each section begins with a chart giving an overview of the region and a list and description of regional papers, then is arranged by country subdivided by city. For each paper, gives address, description, circulation, and information needed to place advertisements (e.g., U.S. representative, advertising rates, size of columns). Concludes with an alphabetical list of all titles with country codes.   Z6941.M44

Library of Congress. Periodical Division. A check list of foreign newspapers in the Library of Congress / newly comp. under the direction of Henry S. Parsons, chief, Periodical Division. Wash. : U.S. Govt. Print Off., 1929. 209 p.   **AE10**
1st ed., 1904.

Arranged geographically by country of publication, and under each city alphabetically by title of newspaper. Gives for each paper exact statement of Library of Congress files. Includes almost 2,700 titles, published in 79 countries in 21 languages. Title index.   Z881.U5

Library of Congress. Serial and Government Publications Division. Newspapers received currently in the Library of Congress / comp. by the Serial and Government Publications Division. 7th ed.– . Wash. : U. S. Govt. Print. Off., 1980– . Biennial.   **AE11**

Supersedes *Newspapers currently received & permanently retained in the Library of Congress*, (1968–70) and *Newspapers received currently in the Library of Congress* (1972–78).

The 12th ed. (1990) lists 359 U.S. and 1,134 foreign newspapers retained on a permanent basis and an additional 120 U.S. and 43 foreign newspapers retained on a current basis only.   Z6945.U5N42

Library of Congress. Serial Division. Postwar foreign newspapers : a union list. Wash., 1953. 231 p.   **AE12**

Includes Russian but not Latin American newspapers (for Latin American newspapers *see* Steven M. Charno, *Latin American newspapers in United States libraries*, AE40.) Locations holding files of less than a three-month period are excluded, except for those in the Philippines. Alphabetical by country, then by city, with a title index. Frequency and date of establishment are given where known. Reports volume-specific holdings of 76 U.S. libraries.   Z6945.U5N44

Newspapers in microform : foreign countries, 1948–1983 / comp. and ed. by the Catalog Management and Publication Division, Library of Congress. Wash. : Library of Congress, 1984. 504 p.   **AE13**

At head of title: Library of Congress catalogs.

Supersedes previous cumulations in the foreign countries section of *Newspapers in microform* (1948–72), the 1973–1977 quinquennial, the annual issues for 1978–82, and reports received in 1983. Annual issues are no longer compiled or published.

A union list of newspapers arranged by country, then city, that provides library locations and holdings and availability of files for libraries and commercial firms in the U.S. and Canada. Entries include brief publication history, library holdings, and indication of the type of microform held. Title index. Includes (1) countries outside the 50 states of the U.S. and (2) territories and possessions of the U.S. (e.g., Guam, Puerto Rico).

For U.S. titles, *see* AE27.   AP1.25.U525A43

Webber, Rosemary. World list of national newspapers : a union list of national newspapers in libraries in the British Isles. London : Butterworths, [1976]. 95 p.   **AE14**

Comp. under the auspices of the Standing Conference of National and University Libraries in contract with the Social Science Research Council.

A title listing with index by country. For British and Irish newspapers, "all newspapers having national circulation have been listed" (*Introd.*), as have regional newspapers which regularly carry a significant amount of national news; all foreign newspaper holdings are reported. Holdings of the British Library's Newspaper Library at Colindale have *not* been included.   Z6945.W385

North America

Campbell, Georgetta Merritt. Extant collections of early black newspapers : a research guide to the black press, 1880–1915; with an index to the Boston *Guardian,* 1902–1904. Troy, N.Y. : Whitston, 1981. 401 p.   **AE15**

A research guide that begins with a historical essay on the African-American press which includes a brief bibliography, and a list of sources used in compilation. A union list follows, arranged by state, city, and title, giving holdings and microform availability. The *Guardian* index occupies p. 216–385. The work concludes with an Afterword on the historical context of the African-American press and a note outlining bibliographic coverage of African-American newspapers in the 20th century prior to 1981.

§ Campbell's work is the culmination of previous efforts to locate, collect, and preserve African-American newspapers, beginning with Armistead Scott Pride's *Negro newspapers on microfilm : a selected list* (Wash. : Library of Congress, 1953), a forerunner in providing a register of 19th-century African-American papers. Campbell consolidates Pride's listings, adding many collections and locations. Pride's work provided the impetus for developing both *Negro newspapers on microfilm* (Wash. : Library of Congress, 1947–), 200 papers, mid-1800s to mid-1900s, and *Black newspaper collection* [microform] (Ann Arbor, Mich. : University Microfilms International, 1987– . 2038 microfilm reels), covering 1893–1983. A revised guide for the former is: *Guide to Negro newspapers on microfilm : a selected list* (Wash. : Library of Congress, 1972).

Other sources for African-American newspapers: *Survey of black newspapers in America*, by Henry La Brie III (Kennebunkport, Me. : Mercer House Pr., 1979); *Black press handbook : sesquicentennial 1827–1977* (Wash. : National Newspapers Publishers Assoc., 1977); *The black press periodical directory* (Newark, N.J. : The Black Press Clipping Bureau, 1974); *Black list : the concise guide to black journalism, radio, television, educational and cultural organizations in the USA, Africa and the Caribbean*, (N.Y. : Black List, [1975]). v. l, *Afroamerica* (USA); *National black media directory* (Ft. Lauderdale, Fla. : Alliance Publ., 1989); *Black Americans information directory* (CC388) lists 95 African-American newspapers.   Z6944.N39C35

Native American periodicals and newspapers, 1828–1982 : bibliography, publishing record, and holdings / ed. by James P. Danky ; comp. by Maureen E. Hady. Westport, Conn. : Greenwood, 1984. 532 p. : ill.   **AE16**

"In association with the State Historical Society of Wisconsin."—*t.p.*

Lists 1,164 periodical and newspaper titles, both current and ceased, by and about Native Americans. Intended to be comprehensive for the Northern Hemisphere. Bibliographic descriptions of current titles and holdings for all titles are based on collections of the State Historical Society of Wisconsin, but holdings of many other repositories are also listed (e.g., Newberry Library, National Library of Canada). Titles are listed alphabetically, with complete bibliographic information, holdings, and often a reproduction of the title page. A foreword and introduction summarize the history of Native American periodical and newspaper bibliography. Concludes with multiple indexes: subjects, publishers, editors, geographic, catchwords and subtitles, chronological.

§ Other important works: *American Indian and Alaska native newspapers and periodicals* (CC424), covering 1826–1985, and *Newspapers and periodicals in the American Native Press Archives* (Little Rock, Ark. : American Native Press Archives, Univ. of Arkansas at Little Rock, 1987).   Z1209.2.U5N37

United States

Current and retrospective. Besides the current sources listed below, *Ulrich's international periodical directory* (AD15) includes, beginning with the volumes for 1993–94, a separate volume for U.S. newspapers. Current papers being microfilmed are listed in *Serials on microfilm*. Earlier issues of current directories can be used for retrospective information.

Ethnic press: Selected bibliographies of newspapers published by and for ethnic or special interest groups are scattered throughout this section. For a complete listing, see under "Ethnic press" in the index. Other sources for ethnic papers include: *Gale directory of publications and broadcast media* (AE23), which lists current African American, Latino, Jewish, women's and foreign-language titles; *Editor and publisher international yearbook* (AE22), which lists foreign-language, religious, and African American publications; *Oxbridge directory of ethnic periodicals and newspapers* (CC336); *Guide to the American ethnic press : Slavic and East European newspapers and periodicals* (AD58); *Ethnic periodicals in contemporary America* (AD52); and Paul Wasserman's *Ethnic information sources of the United States* (2nd ed. Detroit : Gale, 1983. 2 v.). *Ethnic forum* (Kent, Ohio: Kent State Univ. School of Library Science, 1980–) frequently carries bibliographies of ethnic publications. *See also* sections for Ethnic groups and Women in Sociology (section CC) below.

State and regional: Useful in locating state and regional checklists and union lists of U.S. newspapers are: *A bibliography of U.S. newspaper bibliographies* (AE29); *Journalism : a guide to the reference literature* (AE132); and *United States Newspaper Program national union list* (AE32). Since 1983, many state bibliographies of newspapers have been completed or are in progress as part of the United States Newspaper Program (*see* AE32); as they are completed, these bibliographies will be accessible through OCLC.

The American-Jewish media directory. 1989– . Rego Park, NY : R.K. Associates, c1989– . Biennial. **AE17**

Title varies to include date; first issue called *The 1989 American-Jewish media directory*.

A substantial portion of this work consists of a directory of Jewish newspapers. Major sections list Jewish news serivces; the metropolitan Jewish press of N.Y., Los Angeles, and Washington, D.C.; and Jewish newspapers published throughout the U.S. in various languages. The directory of newspapers is arranged by national or regional focus, and by state or city for papers with a local focus. Other sections include Canadian newspapers, student newspapers, and a large number of printed periodicals and electronic media.

Supplement: ———. *1990 press update: American-Jewish media directory*, ed. by Ray Kestenbaum (Rego Park, N.Y. : R. K. Associates, 1990. 16 p.), notes major changes from the full edition and lists new periodicals.
PN5650.A47

American newspapers, 1821–1936 : a union list of files available in the United States and Canada / ed. by Winifred Gregory under the auspices of the Bibliographical Society of America. N.Y. : Wilson, 1937. 791 p. **AE18**

Repr. : N.Y. : Kraus, 1967.

A union list of first importance which lists the exact holdings of newspapers in nearly 5,700 depositories, such as libraries, county courthouses, newspaper offices, and private collections. In addition to the main union list, contains (p. 787–89) "A bibliography of union lists of newspapers," compiled by Karl Brown and Daniel C. Haskell.
Z6945.A53

Brigham, Clarence Saunders. History and bibliography of American newspapers, 1690–1820. Westport, Conn. : Greenwood, 1976. 2 v. (1508, 50 p.). **AE19**

Reprint of the 1947 ed. (Worcester, Mass. : American Antiquarian Soc.), which was a revision of a work first issued in *Proceedings* of the American Antiquarian Society, 1913–27 under title: "Bibliography of American newspapers, 1690–1820." The 1976 reprint incorporates additions and corrections originally published in *Proceedings*, April 1961.

A vital reference work. Arranged alphabetically by state, then by town, it lists 2,120 newspapers published 1690–1820, with locations and holdings for libraries in all parts of the U.S. Historical notes for each paper give title, date of establishment, exact dates of title changes, editors and publishers, frequency, etc. The bibliography is followed by lists of libraries and private owners and by indexes of titles and printers.

§ With *American newspapers, 1821–1936* (AE18), forms a comprehensive record of American newspaper files, 1690–1936. Serves as the working bibliography for *Early American newspapers, 1704–1820* [microform] (N.Y. : Readex, 19??–), which reproduces full text of the Brigham titles in microopaque format (some titles converted to microfilm).
Z6951.B86

A check list of American 18th century newspapers in the Library of Congress / originally comp. by John Van Ness Ingram. New ed. rev. and enl. / under the direction of Henry S. Parsons. Wash. : U.S. Govt. Print. Off., 1936. 401 p. **AE20**

Repr.: N.Y. : Greenwood, [1968].

At head of title: Library of Congress.

1st ed., 1912.

Arranged alphabetically by state, subdivided by town. Gives for each newspaper: date of establishment; changes in title; names of printers, publishers, and editors; and a statement of the Library of Congress file. Title index; index to printers, publishers, and editors.
Z6951.U47

Circulation / American Newspaper Markets. 1962– . Northfield, Ill. : American Newspaper Markets, Inc., 1962– . Annual. **AE21**

Absorbed: Standard Rate & Data Service, *SRDS newspaper circulation analysis* (Skokie, Ill. : 1959–90).

Analyzes, by means of lists and tables, newspaper circulation in metropolitan areas, television market areas, counties, principal market areas, and city zones. Provides basic demographic data for metropolitan areas, TV market areas, and counties. Monthly updates give rate and circulation changes.

§ One source of retrospective statistics is: Simon Newton Dexter North, *History and present condition of the newspaper and periodical press of the United States* (AE28).
HF5905.A57

Editor and publisher international yearbook. 1959– . N.Y. : Editor and Publisher, 1959– . Annual. **AE22**

Issued from 1920/21–1958 in January as a regular number, or section of a regular number, of *Editor and publisher*.

Contains a large amount of useful statistical and directory information in the field of American and foreign journalism.

Intends to be a complete listing of all U.S. daily newspapers, with circulation, rates, executive personnel, departmental managers, and editors; weekly newspapers; printing equipment and its suppliers; syndicated services; organizations; schools of journalism; foreign correspondents; etc.; as well as listings of daily newspapers of Canada and of countries throughout the world.
PN4700.E4

Gale directory of publications and broadcast media. 122nd ed. (1990)– . Detroit : Gale, c1990– . Annual. **AE23**

Subtitle: An annual guide to publications and broadcasting stations including newspapers, magazines, journals, radio stations, television stations, and cable systems.

Title varies: Ed. 119–121 (1987–89) called: *Gale directory of publications*.

Covers U.S. and Canada. Arranged alphabetically by state (for Canada, by province), then by city. For print media, information includes publisher, address and telephone, beginning date, description, advertising rates, circulation, etc.; for broadcast media, call letters and frequency, address, format, advertising rates, etc. Special features include: detailed subject index to print media, including type of publication (college, black, women, trade, etc.); subject index to radio station format; list of feature editors of daily newspapers with at least 50,000 circulation, arranged alphabetically by state, then by city. Name and keyword index. "A single-volume directory of new or changed media will be sent to subscribers midway between editions."—*Introd.*

Supersedes and assumes the edition numbering of:

(1) *Ayer directory of publications* (v. 1–114. Philadelphia : Ayer, 1880–1982. Annual).

Title varies: 1930–69. *N. W. Ayer and Son's directory of newspapers and periodicals*; 1970–71, *Ayer directory : newspapers, magazines ....*

Absorbed *Rowell's American newspaper directory* (N.Y. : G. P. Rowell, 1869–1908. 40 v.) in 1910.

For decades, the standard American list; comprehensive, listing newspapers and periodicals, but not claiming completeness, since it intentionally omitted certain classes of papers (e.g., publications of schools and smaller colleges, local church papers, and most house organs issued merely to exploit goods of their firms). The main list gave: (1) some statistical and descriptive matter about each state; a list of its counties (originally marking those that had no newspapers); and considerable gazetteer information about each city (e.g., its distance and direction from some important place, its railroads, leading manufactures, products, and institutions; and (2) detailed information about each paper or periodical listed, including its name, frequency, character or politics, date of foundation, size of column and page, subscription price, circulation, editors and publishers. Has many good maps, at least one for each state.

(2) *The IMS ... Ayer directory of publications* (Ed. 115 [1983]–117 [1985]. Fort Washington, Pa. : IMS Pr., 1983–85. Annual).

Ed. 118 (1986) called: *The IMS directory of publications.*

Arrangement and content continued to be much the same. Principal contents 1984: (1) General information; (2) Maps; (3) Catalog of publications (U.S. publications arranged by state or territory, then city; Canadian by province, then city; Bermuda, Philippines, and Bahamas); (4) Cross-reference sections (alphabetical index to subject classifications; newspaper feature editors; lists of agricultural, college, foreign-language, Jewish, fraternal, black, and religious publications; newsletters; general circulation magazines grouped by classification; trade and technical publications grouped by classification; lists of daily newspapers, daily periodicals, and weekly, semiweekly, and triweekly newspapers); (5) Title index, with place of publication for each title.

The earlier titles continue to be valuable for verification and research, and should be retained.   Z6951.A97

Hady, Maureen E. Asian-American periodicals and newspapers : a union list of holdings in the Library of the State Historical Soc. of Wisconsin and the Libraries of the Univ. of Wisconsin-Madison / comp. by Maureen E. Hady and James P. Danky. Madison : The Society, 1979. 54 p.   **AE24**

A guide to the location of 104 periodicals and newspapers relating to Asian Americans, including current and ceased literary, political, and historical journals, general newspapers, and feature magazines. For each title, gives publishing history, editors by date, subject focus, microfilm availability, and holding libraries. For campus libraries, specific volume holdings are given. Concludes with indexes (geographic, name, subject) and a chronological listing.

§ Retrospective lists of Asian-American newspapers can be found in *Asian-American journalism : a brief historical analysis*, by David Heiser (Thesis [M. A.]—Univ. of Texas at Austin, 1982) and current papers in *Asian Americans information directory* (Detroit : Gale, 1990–), which lists 14 Asian-American newspapers and 56 newsletters.   Z1361.O7H34

————————— Women's periodicals and newspapers from the 18th century to 1981 : a union list of the holdings of Madison, Wisconsin, libraries / ed. by James P. Danky ; comp. by Maureen E. Hady, Barry Christopher Noonan, Neil E. Strache. Boston : G.K. Hall, c1982. 376 p. : ill.   **AE25**

A bibliography with library holdings of 1,461 publications, many of which are newspapers.

§ For other retrospective lists of women's newspapers, see: *Reel guide to Herstory : supplementary set and title index* (Berkeley, Calif. : Women's History Research Center, 1976–), which lists issues of newsletters included in full text in the microform set, *Herstory* ([Wooster, Ohio] : Micro Photo Division, Bell & Howell, 1972); and *Feminist newspapers, 1970–1980 : an index to holdings in Lake Forest College Library* (Lake Forest, Ill. : Lake Forest College, 1985. 77 p.). Current women's newspapers and newsletters are listed in: *Women's information directory* (Detroit : Gale, 1993–) and *DWM : a directory of women's media* (CC549).   Z7965.H3

Lathem, Edward Connery. Chronological tables of American newspapers, 1690–1820 : being a tabular guide to holdings of newspapers published in America through the year 1820. Barre, Mass. : Amer. Antiquarian Soc. and Barre Publ., [1972]. 131 p.   **AE26**

A companion to Clarence S. Brigham's *History and bibliography of American newspapers* and his *Additions and corrections* to that work (AE19). Intended to serve as an aid "in approaching, on a chronological basis, available issues of American newspapers for the period through 1820."—*Introd.*   Z6951.L3

Newspapers in microform : United States, 1948–1983 / comp. and ed. by the Catalog Management and Publication Division, Library of Congress. Wash. : Library of Congress, 1984. 2 v.   **AE27**

Supersedes previous cumulations in the U.S. section of *Newspapers in microform* (1948–72), the 1973–1977 quinquennial, the annual issues for 1978–82, and reports received in 1983. Annual issues are no longer compiled or published.

A union list of newspapers arranged by state and city that provides library locations and holdings and availability of files for libraries and commercial firms in the U.S. and Canada. Title entries are based on masthead titles. Title index. Includes religious, collegiate, labor, and other special interest papers excluded from earlier cumulations.

For foreign titles, *see* AE13.   AP1.25.U525A44

North, Simon Newton Dexter. History and present condition of the newspaper and periodical press of the United States : with a catalogue of the publications of the census year. Wash. : U.S. Govt. Print. Off., 1884. 446 p. : maps.   **AE28**

In U.S. Census Office. 10th Census, v. 8.

Provides a detailed history of the newspaper and periodical press, 1639–1880. Organized by period with special segments on topics such as the colonial press in Pennsylvania and New York, newspaper typography, libel, political parties and the press, ethnic press, newspaper stereotyping, postal laws, and how news was transmitted with particular emphasis on the influence of the telegraph. Regional maps illustrate the distribution of newspapers throughout the U.S. 15 tables of contemporary statistics about newspapers are provided. Also included are a catalog of periodicals issued 1879–80; a chronological history of U.S. newspapers arranged by state and city; and a catalog of bound American newspapers held at the American Antiquarian Society in Worcester, Mass.   PN4855.N6

Pluge, John. A bibliography of U.S. newspaper bibliographies. [Wash. : Library of Congress, Serial & Government Publications Division], 1984. 92 *l.*   **AE29**

An unannotated bibliography that gives for each entry: author, title, imprint, date of 1st ed., pagination, and LC class number. In two sections.

Section 1 lists 202 bibliographies for the U.S. as a whole and for regions. Includes union lists, general newspaper directories, bibliographic histories, and bibliographies of special newspapers (e.g., frontier, colonial, tabloid, lilliputian). Also has a subsection of 81 U.S.-wide bibliographies of ethnic papers.

Section 2, arranged by state and city, lists 652 bibliographies, each pertaining to newspapers originating in a particular state or city (e.g., Montana, Baltimore). Includes many holdings lists and histories of individual papers, as well as ethnic newspaper bibliographies.

A valuable starting point for historical research. The arrangement requires that readers looking for bibliographies of papers from a given locale, or for ethnic papers, search in both sections.

§ Also helpful are: Jo A. Cates, *Journalism : a guide to the reference literature* (AE132), which provides detailed annotations for many kinds of newspaper bibliographies, and Richard Allen Schwarzlose, *Newspapers, a reference guide* (AE146), which lists many newspaper bibliographies, union lists, and directories. Z6951.P6

Special Libraries Association. Newspaper Division. Newspaper libraries in the U.S. and Canada : an SLA directory / Elizabeth L. Anderson, ed. 2nd ed. N.Y. : Special Libraries Assoc., c1980. 321 p. **AE30**

1st ed., 1976, ed. by Grace D. Parch, had title: *Directory of newspaper libraries in the U.S. and Canada.*

A directory of libraries maintained by newspaper publishers. This edition is based on questionnaire responses from 314 newspapers and follows the plan of the 1st ed., arranged by state or province and city. Gives basic information, date the library was established, services, resources, microfilm holdings of the newspaper, and automated files. Notes whether the library maintains an index for its newspaper.

§ Also of interest: *Newspaper libraries : a bibliography, 1933–1985* by Celia Jo Wall (Wash. : Special Libraries Assoc., 1986. 126 p.). Z675.N4D57

State Historical Society of Wisconsin. Library. Hispanic Americans in the United States : a union list of periodicals and newspapers held by the Library of the State Historical Soc. of Wisconsin and the Libraries of the Univ. of Wisconsin-Madison / comp. by Neil E. Strache and James P. Danky. Madison : The Society, 1979. 77 p. **AE31**

English and Spanish.

A guide to the location of 129 periodicals and newspapers relating to Latinos. Includes older and ceased titles. For each title, gives publishing history, editors by date, subject focus, microfilm, availability, and libraries holding the title. For campus libraries, gives specific volume holdings. Concludes with multiple indexes (geographic, name, subject) and chronological chart of papers 1808–1979.

§ Other directories of Latino media are *Hispanic media, USA* (Wash. : The Media Institute, 1987), and *Burrelle's Hispanic media directory* (Livingston, N.J. : Burrelle's Media Directories, 1989). Current listings of Latino newspapers can be found in the general current ethnic sources listed at the beginning of this section. Other sources are *Hispanic Americans information directory, 1950–1991* (Detroit : Gale, 1990–) which lists newspapers, and *Hispanic resource directory* (CC463). Z1361.S7W57

United States Newspaper Program national union list [microform]. 4th ed. Dublin, Ohio : OCLC, 1993. 70 microfiches + 1 booklet in binder. **AE32**

1st ed., 1985; 2nd ed., 1987; 3rd ed., 1990.

A title listing with volume-specific holdings for more than 100,000 U.S. newspapers held by American libraries participating in the United States Newspaper Program. The information is maintained as part of the OCLC database. Arranged by title, augmented when necessary by place and starting date. Bibliographical information is given, plus volume-specific holdings, format, notes and variant and related titles. Also provided are separate indexes by subject, geographic area covered, place of publication, and beginning-ending date. An indispensable source by virtue of its comprehensive coverage, and a worthy successor to *American newspapers* (AE18).

§ For more information on the U.S. Newspaper Program, see *United States Newspaper Program planning guide and resource notebook* (Wash. : Library of Congress, 1991) and *Guide to sources in American journalism history* (AE144). Z6945.U6115

University of Notre Dame. Library. Directory of Roman Catholic newspapers on microfilm : United States. Notre Dame, Ind. : Memorial Libr., Univ. of Notre Dame, 1982. 69 p. **AE33**

A catalog of the Library's holdings—"one of the finest collections of Roman Catholic newspapers in the United States."—*Pref.* Lists 307 titles, arranged by state and city of publication. For certain states, notes that Notre Dame holds no newspapers. Gives volume holdings and OCLC numbers. Title index.

§ For updated and retrospective listings of Roman Catholic newspapers, see: *Catholic press directory* (N.Y. : Catholic Pr. Assoc., 1923–). Z7837.5.U54

Wynar, Lubomyr Roman. Encyclopedic directory of ethnic newspapers and periodicals in the United States / Lubomyr Roman Wynar, Anna T. Wynar. 2nd ed. Littleton, Colo. : Libraries Unlimited, 1976. 248 p. **AE34**

1st ed., 1972.

Covers 43 ethnic groups that have continued to publish in their native languages. Groups are of European, Asian, West Asian, and Latin American extraction. Excluded are African-American, Native American, or other ethnic groups (e.g., Irish-Americans), whose papers are primarily in English. Limited to newspapers current in 1970–71. Begins with a bibliographical essay on the ethnic press in the U.S., including statistical tables and discussion of bibliographical control. Entries are arranged by ethnic group with address, editor, date started, sponsor, language, circulation, frequency and price, and a note describing content. Both native language and English-language papers are listed for the 43 ethnic groups. An appendix gives a statistical analysis of of newspapers for each ethnic group. Concludes with a title index. An essential title.

§ Complementary work: Sally M. Miller, ed., *The ethnic press in the United States : a historical analysis and handbook* (AD32) which consists of bibliographic essays, with notes and bibliography, on the history of the press in 27 American ethnic groups. An introduction provides an historical analysis of the ethnic press in general. Limited to European, Asian, West Asian, and some Latin American groups. Z6953.5.A1W94

Newsletters

Information concerning newsletters may also be found under Periodicals (Section AD). *The standard periodical directory* (AD56) contains many listings for newsletters but does not identify them as newsletters.

Hudson's subscription newsletter directory. 1989– . Rhinebeck, N.Y. : Hudson's Subscription Newsletter Directory, c1989– . **AE35**

Continues: *Hudson's newsletter directory* (1986–88).

Lists more than 4,200 business, professional and consumer newsletters worldwide under 158 subject categories. Gives address, telephone, fax, editor, price, frequency, and year founded. Codes indicate type of news published, e.g., financial, personnel changes, industrial, new products. Index of publishers; geographic, editorial, and title indexes.

§ See also *The newsletter yearbook/directory* (1st–5th ed. [Rhinebeck, N.Y.] : Newsletter Clearinghouse, 1977–85). PN4784.N5N48

Newsletters in print. 4th ed. (1988–89)– . Detroit : Gale, c1988– . Annual. **AE36**

1st ed., 1966, had title: *National directory of newsletters and reporting services*; 3rd ed., 1987, had title *Newsletters directory.*

Subtitle (varies): A descriptive guide to more than 11,000 subscription, membership, and free newsletters, bulletins, digests, updates, and similar serial publications issued in the United States and Canada, and available in print or online.

Arranged by five broad topics—business and industry, family and everyday life, information and communication, agriculture and science, community and world affairs—each subdivided for a total of 33 subjects. For each title, gives address, frequency, circulation, price, description. Title, publisher, and subject indexes. Z6941.N3

Oxbridge directory of newsletters. 1979– . N.Y. : Oxbridge Communications, 1979– . Annual. **AE37**

Continues: *Standard directory of newsletters* (1971).

The 9th ed., 1991, lists 21,000 newsletters, including 812 newsletters for investors. Entries are arranged under some 200 subject categories, and include address, personnel, subscription and advertising information, where indexed, circulation, brief editorial description, and whether list of subscribers can be rented. Additional indexes include: publishers of multiple newsletters, publishers by state, names and telephone numbers of contact persons, and titles.   Z6944.N44S82

Canada

For current Canadian newspapers, see *Gale directory of publications and broadcast media* (AE23). Retrospective information may be found in earlier volumes of the same source and in *McKim's directory of Canadian publications* (1892–1942). An additional retrospective source is André Beaulieu's *Les journaux de Québec de 1764 à 1964* (AD59).

National Library of Canada. Newspaper Section. Union list of Canadian newspapers held by Canadian libraries = Liste collective des journaux canadiens disponibles dans les bibliothèques canadiennes. Ottawa : The Library, 1977. 483 p.
AE38

New ed. : *ULCN : union list of Canadian newspapers = LCJC : Liste collective des journaux canadiens* [microform] (Ottawa, 1988).

Text in English and French.

The 1977 edition reflects the Canadian newspaper holdings of more than 125 Canadian libraries; both original and microfilm files are represented. Arranged by province, then by city, with an alphabetical listing of titles under city; title index. Includes titles for which bibliographical information was available but no location reported.

A union list of non-Canadian newspapers held by Canadian libraries was issued by the Reference Branch of the National Library in 1968 (69 p).   Z6954.C2N36

Sotiron, Minko. An annotated bibliography of works on daily newspapers in Canada, 1914–1983 = Une bibliographie annotée des ouvrages portant sur les quotidiens canadiens, 1914–1983 / Gordon Rabchuk, indexation. Montréal : M. Sotiron, 1987. 288 p.   **AE39**

Includes 3,750 annotated entries for books and articles. A general section is followed by sections arranged by province, then alphabetically by author. Emphasizes 20th-century newspapers. Author and subject indexes.   PN904.S68

Latin America

Latin American newspapers in United States libraries : a union list compiled in the Serial Division, Library of Congress / by Steven M. Charno. Austin : publ. for the Conference on Latin American History by the Univ. of Texas Pr., [1969, c1968]. 619 p. (Conference on Latin American History. Publication, no. 2).   **AE40**

Lists about 5,500 Latin American newspapers held by 70 reporting libraries. Arrangement is by place of publication, first by country, then by city. A detailed record of holdings is provided; both original and microfilm copies are recorded. Includes official gazettes before 1900; excludes specialized papers whose nature is evident from the title. Covers Puerto Rico and the 20 Latin American republics.

§ An earlier list by Arthur E. Gropp, *Union list of Latin American newspapers in libraries in the United States* (Wash. : Pan American Union, 1953) listed about 5,000 titles held by 56 libraries.   Z6947.C5

Caribbean and Islands of the Western Atlantic

Pactor, Howard S. Colonial British Caribbean newspapers : a bibliography and directory. N.Y. : Greenwood, c1990. 144 p. (Bibliographies and indexes in world history, no. 19).   **AE41**

Lists 677 newspapers, published from the 18th century through the gaining of independence, alphabetically by colony, then chronologically. Includes publication dates; editors, publishers and proprietors when they can be determined; and issue-specific locations when available. Notes the existence of microfilmed copies. An introduction includes an essay on colonial British and Caribbean newspapers. Bibliography of selected sources and title and name indexes.   Z6941.P26

Europe (by region)

Europe, Eastern

Estafy, George D. The East European Newspaper Collection of the Slavic and Baltic Division, the New York Public Library. N.Y. : Slavic and Baltic Division, NYPL, 1989. 53 p.
AE42

Includes current and ceased titles on microfilm. Newspaper titles are arranged in alphabetical order. Each entry includes the city of publication, frequency, language, dates held by the library, and an indication of positive or negative master microfilm.

§ Also useful is: *Current Slavic, Baltic and East European periodical and newspaper titles in the Slavic and Baltic Division, the Periodicals Division, and the branch libraries of the New York Public Library*, prep. by Robert H. Davis [et al.] (2nd rev. and exp. ed. N.Y., 1989).

Library of Congress. Slavic and Central European Division. Newspapers of east central and southeastern Europe in the Library of Congress / ed. by Robert G. Carlton. Wash. : Library of Congress, 1965. 204 p.   **AE43**

Provides detailed holdings of post-World War I newspapers (both newsprint and microform files) in alphabetical arrangement by country, then by city. Covers countries of Eastern Europe outside the former Soviet Union, including Albania, Bulgaria, Czechoslovakia, Hungary, Poland, Romania, and Yugoslavia, and includes the Baltic countries (Estonia, Latvia, and Lithuania) but only to the date of initial occupation by the Soviet Union in the summer of 1940. From 1940 through 1962, Baltic papers are covered by *Newspapers of the Soviet Union in the Library of Congress* (AE75).   Z6955.U52

Scandinavia

Recent Scandinavian newspapers can be found in the directory *Media Scandinavia* (AD80), covering Denmark, Greenland, Faroe Islands, Norway, Sweden, Finland, and Iceland.

Europe (by country)

Austria

See also *Presse Handbuch* (AD81).

200 Jahre Tageszeitung in Österreich, 1783–1983 : Festschrift und Ausstellungskatalog / herausgegeben von Franz Ivan, Helmut W. Lang und Heinz Pürer. Wien : Österreichische Nationalbibliothek : Verband Österreichischer Zeitungsherausgeber und Zeitungsverleger, 1983. 473 p. : ill. (some col.). **AE44**

Prepared as a catalog of an exhibition held in April 1983 at the Austrian National Library. Begins with 27 essays on the history of the Austrian press during this period, many focusing on specific Austrian papers. Continues with a catalog of the exhibition oriented around periods and subjects. Altogether, some 573 exhibits of newspapers are described along with facsimile pages and mastheads. The exhibits, in addition to the holdings of the Nationalbibliothek, were lent by 24 libraries in Austria and Hungary. Alphabetical title index.

PN5164.A14

Belgium

Bertelson, Lionel. La presse d'information : tableau chronologique des journaux belges. [Bruxelles, 1974]. 287 p. **AE45**

At head of title: Institut pour Journalistes de Belgique.

In two parts: (1) Newspapers of the past, "Les journaux disparus," divided into sections for newspapers published in Belgium, and for those published outside Belgium. Within each section newspapers are arranged in periods, 1605–1830, 1830–1914, 1914–18, and within these periods by province and city in Belgium or by outside place. (2) Newspapers of the present, "Les journaux actuels," divided into sections for dailies and weeklies, then arranged in periods, 1918–40, 1940–44, and after 1944. Within periods, newspapers are arranged by province and city. Each entry gives brief historical notes on issues published. No holdings. Index of titles and geographical index.

§ For current Belgian newspapers, see: *Annuaire officiel de la presse belge = Officieel jaarboek van de belgische pers* (AD82).

Z6956.B4B43

Bulgaria

Natsionalna bibliografiía na NR Bŭlgariía : Seriía 6 : Letopis na statiite ot bŭlgarskite vestnitsi = Bulgarian national bibliography. Series 6 : Articles from Bulgarian newspapers. [v. 1] (1991)– . Sofiía : Narodna Biblioteka Sv. sv. Kiril i Metodii, [1991]– . Monthly with annual index supplement. **AE46**

Continues: *Letopis' na periodichniía pechat* (AD304); *Letopis' na statiíte ot bulgarskite vestnitsi* (Sofiia : Narodna biblioteka Sv. sv. Kiril i Metodii, 1972–73); *Natsionalna bibliografiia NR Bulgariia* (1974–90, AA583).

References are arranged by topic and include author, article title, newspaper title, date of publication, and page numbers. Some referenc-

es include brief annotations. Each issue also includes indexes for authors, places, subjects, newspapers indexed, and a guide to abbreviations. AI15.L377

Czechoslovakia

Potemra, Michal. Bibliografia slovenských novín a časopisov do roku 1918. V. Martine : Matica Slovenská, 1958. 145 p. (Slovenská národná bibliografia, Séria B. Periódiká, zväzok 1a). **AE47**

At head of title: Štátna vedecká knižnica v Košiciach.

Bibliography, with library locations, of Slovak newspapers and journals up to 1918, including those of the resistance movement abroad and handwritten publications. Geographical, name, and chronological indexes. Concludes with brief overview, in English, Russian, French, and German of the compilation of this work and the history of the Slovak press during the period.

§ A similar survey and bibliography of foreign newspapers and journals of Slovakia up to 1918: *Bibliografia inorečových novín a časopisov na Slovensku do roku 1918*, by Michal Potemra (V. Martine : Matica Slovenska, 1963. 818 p. [Slovenská národná bibliografia, Série B. Periódiká, zväzok 1b]). See also: *Soupis bibliografi novín a casopisu vydanvanych na uzemi Ceskoslovenske republiky* (AD88) covering the 18th century through 1958.

Denmark

Minerva mikrofilm a/s, Copenhagen. Topografisk, kronologisk fortegnelse over danske, færøske og grønlandske aviser 1648–1975 / [udg. af Helge Tønnesen]. København 27] : Minerva Mikrofilm, 1977. 47 p. **AE48**

Revised and enlarged ed. of *Topografisk kronologisk fortegnelse over danske aviser 1648–1970*, 1971 (rev. 1973).

A guide to newspapers on microfilm in the Danish language held by Minerva Mikrofilm Aps. Arranged by region and city in Denmark. Also there are separate lists of Danish newspapers from Greenland, Slesvig-Holstein, Faeroe Islands, and English-language papers from the islands of St. Croix and St. Thomas. Dates of holdings are included. Alphabetical index of all the newspapers listed. AI13.M52

Finland

Kaarna, Väinö. Suomen sanomalehdistön bibliografia, 1771–1963 = Bibliografi över Finlands tidnings-press, 1771–1963 = Bibliography of the Finnish newspapers, 1771–1963 / Vaino Kaarna, Kaarina Winter. Helsinki : Helsingin Yliopisto Kirjasto, 1965. 130 p. (Helsingin Yliopiston Kirjaston julkaisuja, 31). **AE49**

Lists about 1,250 Finnish newspapers alphabetically by title. Places and dates of publication, names of editors, party affiliations, etc., are indicated. Indexes: chronological, place of publication, and personal names. Bibliography of general sources. Z6956.F5K2

France

Bibliothèque Nationale (France). Département des Périodiques. Bibliographie de la presse française politique et d'information générale, 1865–1944. Paris : Bibliothèque Nationale, 1964–1992. 89 pts. (In progress). **AE50**

For annotation, *see* AD92. Z6956.F8P32

———————— Répertoire collectif des quotidiens et hebdomadaires : publiés dans les départements de la France métropolitaine de 1944 à 1956 et conservés dans les archives et bibliothèques de France. Paris : Univ. de Paris, Inst. Français de Presse, 1958. 153 p.   **AE51**

    Cover title: Journaux français, 1944–1956.

    Gives title, place of publication, date of first issue, and location of files.

    Continued by *Catalogue collectif des journaux quotidiens d'information générale publiés en France métropolitaine de 1957 à 1961* (Paris, 1962. 129 p.).   Z6956.F8P34

Histoire générale de la presse française / publiée sous la direction de Claude Bellanger [et al.]. Paris : Presses Universitaire de France, 1969–1976. 5 v. : ill.   **AE52**

    A comprehensive history of the French newspaper and periodical press from its origins to the mid-1970s. Gives attention to provincial and specialist publications as well as those at the national level. Includes notes on the history, scope, and influence of numerous individual newspapers and periodicals. Each volume has its own indexes, and bibliographies in v. 1–3 follow the text; bibliography for v. 4, covering 1940–58, is included in v. 5.

    § Additional retrospective sources of interest: Bibliothèque Nationale, *Catalogue général des périodiques du début du XVIIᵉ siècle à 1959* [microform] ([Paris] : Chadwyck-Healy France S.A.R.L., 1988. 1419 microfiches) and *Le presse quotidienne française*, by Emmanuel Derieux and Jean C. Texier (Paris : A. Colin, 1974).   PN5174.H5

Germany

For current listings of German newspapers, see: *Stamm Leitfaden durch Presse und Werbung* (AD103). Sources of retrospective information on German newspapers, in addition to those listed below, are *ADW Zeitungskatalog* (Frankfurt am Main : ADW Verband deutscher Werbeagenturen und Werbungsmittler, 1960–83), and *Sperlings Zeitschriften- und Zeitungs-Adressbuch : Handbuch der deutschen Presse* (Leipzig : Börsenvereins der Deutschen Buchhändler, 1926–).

Hagelweide, Gert. Deutsche Zeitungsbestände in Bibliotheken und Archiven. Düsseldorf : Droste Verlag, [1974]. 372 p. (Bibliographien zur Geschichte des Parlamentarismus und der politischen Parteien, Hft. 6).   **AE53**

    Added title page in English: *German newspapers in libraries and archives: a survey.*

    Introductory matter in German and English.

    "Hrsg. von der Kommission für Geschichte des Parlamentarismus und der politischen Parteien und dem Verein Deutscher Bibliothekare e. V."—*t.p.*

    An effort to provide reasonably up-to-date information on files of German newspapers. "For the period from 1700 to 1969 (with several supplements up to 1972), it covers a total of 2,018 German newspapers with an overall number of 4,411 titles arranged according to 222 German places of publication, within the German frontiers of 1939, which have been and are of special historic interest as far as the press is concerned."—*Publisher's pref.* Gives holdings in German libraries and archives, in major British and European libraries, and in the Library of Congress. An introductory essay treats the history of the German press and bibliographic control of German newspapers. Title index.

    § For additional retrospective information, see: *Literatur zur deutschsprachigen Presse: eine bibliographie* (München ; N.Y. : K.G. Saur, 1985–89. v. 1–3) and *The German language press of the Americas* (AE1).   Z6956.G3H33

Lindemann, Margot. Geschichte der deutschen Presse. Berlin : Colloquium Verlag, 1966–86. 4 v. (Abhandlungen und Materialen zur Publizistik, Bd.5–7, 10).   **AE54**

    Contents: v.1, Deutsche Presse bis 1815, von Margot Lindemann; v.2, Deutsche Presse im 19. Jahrhundert, von Kurt Koszyk; v.3, Deutsche Presse 1914–1945, von Kurt Koszyk; v. 4, Pressepolitik für Deutsche, 1945–1949, von Kurt Koszyk.

    Each volume includes an extensive bibliography and its own index. Thorough and scholarly.   PN5204.L5

Great Britain

Bibliography of British newspapers / [gen. ed., Charles A. Toase]. London : Libr. Assoc., Reference, Special and Information Section, 1975–1991. 6 v. : maps.   **AE55**

    County editors vary.

    Contents: v. 1, Wiltshire; v. 2, Nottinghamshire; v. 3, Kent; v. 4, Durham and Northumberland; v. 5, Derbyshire; v. 6, Cornwall and Devon.

    Aims to provide a complete list of all British newspapers, county by county, with brief notes on dates of publication, title changes and issue-specific holdings in British and eight American libraries. The entry for each paper also gives bibliographical citations to any published historical accounts about the paper. Each county volume is arranged by local area, then by title, and is accompanied by a title index. A valuable source for historical research.   Z6956.G6B5

British Library. Newspaper Library, Colindale. Catalogue of the Newspaper Library, Colindale. London : Publ. for the British Library Board by British Museum Publ. Ltd., 1975. 8 v.   **AE56**

    Contents: v. 1, London; v. 2, England and Wales, Scotland, Ireland; v. 3–4, Overseas countries; v. 5–8, Alphabetical title catalogue.

    "The Newspaper Library at Colindale (formerly the British Museum Newspaper Library) contains about half a million volumes and parcels of daily and weekly newspapers and periodicals, including London newspapers and journals from 1801 onward, English provincial, Scottish and Irish newspapers from about 1700 onward, and large collections of Commonwealth and foreign newspapers. It contains no London newspapers published before 1801 (which are in the Burney Collection at Bloomsbury), no newspapers in oriental languages (which are in the Department of Oriental Manuscripts and Printed Books at Bloomsbury), and very few periodicals which appear monthly or less frequently."—*Introd.*

    Effectively supersedes the 1905 supplement to the British Museum's *Catalogue of printed books* entitled *Newspapers published in Great Britain and Ireland, 1801–1900* (London : Clowes, 1905. 532 col.).

    § Other sources for historical bibliography and locations of British newspapers: *A bibliography of English corantos and periodical newsbooks, 1620–1642*, by Folke Dahl (London : Bibliographical Soc., 1952 ; repr. : Boston : Longwood Pr., 1977); *British newspapers and periodicals, 1641–1700 : a short title catalogue* (AD107); *British newspapers and periodicals, 1632–1800 : a descriptive catalog of a collection at the University of Texas*, by Powell Stewart (Austin : Univ. of Texas at Austin, 1950. 172 p.); *A census of British newspapers and periodicals, 1620–1800* (AD106), listing titles available in U.S. libraries; and *Checklist of newspapers of the British Isles, 1665–1800, in the American Antiquarian Society* (Worcester, Mass. : American Antiquarian Soc., 1956; also publ. in American Antiquarian Society *Proceedings*, v. 65, pt. 2). Also of interest: *Local newspapers & periodicals of the nineteenth century : a checklist of holdings in provincial libraries*, comp. by Diana Dixen (rev. ed., Leicester : Univ. of Leicester, Victorian Studies Centre, 1976. 2 v.).

Cox, Susan M. Early English newspapers : bibliography and guide to the microfilm collection / comp. by Susan M. Cox and Janice L. Budeit. Woodbridge, Conn. : Research Publications, 1983. 80 p.   **AE57**

    A reel guide and finding list for the microform set *Early English newspapers* [microform] (Woodbridge, Conn. : Research Publ., 1983– . 3715 microform reels. [In progress]). The microfilm set merges the holdings of two collections, the Burney Collection at the British

Library and the Nicholls collection at the Bodleian Library, covering 1603–1818. "These newspapers form a significant record of the social, intellectual and political history of modern Europe."—*Introd.*

The guide covers the first 24 units of the microfilm set. Entries give publication dates and reel locations and title changes. Numerous cross-references.

§ A continuation of the guide was published as: *Early English newspapers : cumulative guide to the microfilm collection, units 25–72* (Woodbridge, Conn. : Research Publ., [1992]). Guides to additional units will be issued as microfilming progresses. Z6956.G6C68

Linton, David. The newspaper press in Britain : an annotated bibliography / ed. by David Linton and Ray Boston. London ; N.Y. : Mansell, 1987. 361 p. **AE58**

Lists (alphabetically by author) books, dissertations, and articles discussing the history of British newspapers from the 17th century through the mid-1980s. Two appendixes: (1) Chronology of British newspaper history, 1476–1986; (2) Locations of journalists' papers, and certain newspaper titles (e.g., files of *The Grub Street journal* are at Queen's College, Oxford).

§ Complementary works: *Studies of British newspapers and periodicals from their beginning to 1800* (AD109), and *British periodicals & newspapers, 1789–1832 : a bibliography of secondary sources* (AD108). Z6956.G6L56

The Times, London. Tercentenary handlist of English & Welsh newspapers, magazines & reviews. London : The Times, 1920. 324 p. **AE59**

Repr.: London : Dawsons of Pall Mall, 1966.

Comp. by J. G. Muddlman.

Contents, arranged chronologically by date of the first known issue: Sec. I: London and suburban press, 1620–1919; Sec. II: The provincial press, 1801–1919. Each section has a separate list of periodicals in languages such as Armenian, Hebrew, Yiddish, Russian, and Turkish, and a title index.

Begins with essays on early press laws, origin of newspapers, the first English newspaper, newsbooks, etc. Sec. II also has a brief essay on the history of the provincial press. Presents a chronological bibliography of English periodicals 1620–1919, attempting to include all types of periodicals except: (1) official periodicals issued during the war; (2) annuals and yearbooks; (3) publications of societies classed as academies in the British Library; and (4) local church periodicals. While avowedly incomplete for the difficult period of the 18th century, claims to be nearly exhaustive for the 17th and 19th centuries. Based on the collections of the British Library. Each title is listed under the date of the earliest copy found for examination, and the information given for it includes: number and date of the earliest issue; date of discontinuance, if known; and in some cases name of printer, editor, distributor, and a reference to the library or collection if it is other than the British Library's general collection.

Useful as a means of identifying titles, and of showing, by its chronological arrangement, what periodicals and newspapers are available for a given date. Additions and corrections by Rowland Austin appeared in *Notes and queries*, 12th ser., 8 (1921) and 10 (1922). Z6956.E5T5

Weed, Katherine Kirtley. Studies of British newspapers and periodicals from their beginning to 1800 : a bibliography / by Katherine Kirtley Weed and Richmond Pugh Bond. Chapel Hill : Univ. of North Carolina Pr., 1946. 233 p. (Studies in philology, extra series, no. 2). **AE60**

For annotation, *see* AD109. P25.S82 no.2

Ireland, Northern

Northern Ireland newspapers, 1737–1987 : a checklist with locations. 2nd rev. ed. Belfast : Libr. Assoc. (Northern Ireland Branch) : Public Record Office of Northern Ireland Working Party on Resources for Local Studies, 1987. 63 p. **AE61**

1st ed., 1979.

"A detailed listing of all Northern Ireland newspapers known to have existed together with details of the holdings of the major collections of them."—*Pref.* Represents a consolidation of two previous lists, the first a comprehensive checklist by J. R. R. Adams in 1979 and the second a checklist of microfilm titles by the Working Party in 1983. Arranged alphabetically by title. Lists holdings of both microfilm and hard copy in 26 libraries mostly in Ireland and Northern Ireland, and in the National Library in Dublin, the British Newspaper Library, and the Cambridge University Library. Z6956.G6N67

Scotland

Ferguson, Joan P. S. Directory of Scottish newspapers. [2nd ed.]. Edinburgh : National Library of Scotland, 1984. 155 p. : ill. **AE62**

Lists "Scottish newspaper holdings of 57 Scottish libraries and of many Scottish newspaper publishers, as well as approximately 80% of the Scottish newspaper holdings of the British Library Newspaper Library."—*Introd.* 1,178 newspapers published from the 1700s through 1979 are arranged alphabetically by title. Includes detailed holdings and existence of microfilm editions. Indexed by place of publication.

§ See also John S. North, *The Waterloo directory of Scottish newspapers and periodicals, 1800–1900* (AD119). Z6956.G6F47

Ireland

Munter, Robert LaVerne. A hand-list of Irish newspapers, 1685–1750. London : Bowes and Bowes, 1960. 35 p. (Cambridge Bibliographical Society. Monograph, no. 4). **AE63**

Begins with brief history of the Irish periodical press. Listing is by place of publication, then chronological. Locates files of the papers in Irish and English libraries. Gives brief historical notes and issue-specific information for each paper. Lists some newspapers known to exist for which no copies have been traced. Indexes of printers and altered titles.

§ Munter has also published *History of the Irish newspaper, 1685–1760* (London : Cambridge Univ. Pr., 1967. 217 p.).

Z6956.I7M8

Italy

Current italian newspapers can also be found in *Annuario della stampa italiana* (AD125).

Storia della stampa italiana / a cura di Valerio Castronovo e Nicola Tranfaglia. Roma ; Bari : Laterza, 1976–80. 6 v. **AE64**

Contents: v. 1, La stampa italiana dal cinquecento all'ottocento (1976. 566 p.); v. 2, La stampa italiana del risorgimento (1979. 601 p.); v. 3, La stampa italiana nell'età liberale (1979. 429 p.); v. 4, La stampa italiana nell'età fascista (1980. 385 p.); v. 5, La stampa italiana dalla resistenza agli anni sessanta (1980. 330 p.); v. 6, La stampa italiana del neocapitalismo (1976. 608 p.).

This essential source covers the Italian press from the cinquecento through the period of neocapitalism. Separate indexes for each volume. Occasional appendixes provide data and statistics.

§ An additional source with retrospective data on Italian newspapers 1964–69, is: *Repertorio analitico della stampa italiana* (AD129). Retrospective information may also be found in *Guida della stampa periodica italiana*, comp. by Nicola Bernardini (Lecce : R. Tipografia editrice salentina dei fratelli Spacciante, 1890). PN5242.S86

Netherlands

Handboek van de Nederlandse pers en publiciteit. 42 Uitg. (Sept. 1974)– . Schiedam : "Publiciteit" Schiedam, 1974– . Semiannual.   **AE65**

For complete annotation, *see* AD132. For retrospective listings, *see* Koninklijke Bibliotheek (Netherlands), *Centrale catalogus van periodieken en seriewerken in Nederlandse bibliotheken (CCP)* (AD240). For current and retrospective sources, *see also* International section, above.   Z6956.N45H352

Poland

Biblioteka Narodowa (Poland). Polska prasa konspiracyjna (1939–1945) i powstania warszawskiego w zbiorach Biblioteki Narodowej : katalog / Jadwiga Cieślakiewicz, Hanna Falkowska, Andrzej Paczkowski. Warszawa : Biblioteka Narodowa, 1984. 205 p.   **AE66**

At head of title: Biblioteka Narodowa. Zakład Czasopism Zakład Zbiorów Mikrofilmowych.

Lists 713 Polish underground newspapers and periodicals published during World War II and held at the National Library in Warsaw in print or microfilm. Arranged alphabetically by title, giving place of publication, publisher, dates, and inclusive dates of the Library's holdings.

§ See also: *Bibliografia prasy polskiej, 1944–1948* (AD137).
    Z6514.U5B53

"Prasa," Robotnicza Spółdzielnia Wydawnicza, Warsaw. Zakład Badań Prasoznawczych. Materiały do bibliografii dziennikarstwa i prasy w Polsce, w latach 1944–1954 : wybór / [Opracował Zespół Biblioteki Stowarzyszenia Dziennikarzy Polskich: Maria Bzowska ... (et al.) ; Pod redkcja Jana Halperna]. Warsaw : Państwowe Wydawnictwo Naukowe, 1957. 788 p.   **AE67**

An extensive bibliography of more than 10,000 titles on the history and organization of journalism and the press in Poland.
    Z6956.P7P7

Russia and the U.S.S.R.

Current digest of the post-Soviet press. v. 44 (5 Feb. 1992)– . Columbus, Ohio : Current Digest of the Soviet Pr., 1992– . Weekly.   **AE68**

v. 1 (1949)–43 (1991) had title: *Current digest of the Soviet press.*

Founded 1949 by American Council of Learned Societies and Social Science Research Council. Originally publ. by Joint Committee on Slavic Studies, then by American Association for the Advancement of Slavic Studies. *Current digest* continues to be affiliated with AAASS, ACLS, and The Ohio State University.

Provides English translations of selected Russian-language publications reflecting major political, economic, social, and cultural developments in Russia and the former Soviet republics. Each article begins with a brief outline followed by the title, author, source, date of publication, pages and an indication of whether the article is translated completely, in condensed form, or in excerpts. No comment or elaboration is offered by *Current digest* staff. A list, "Some publications from which translations in the *Current digest* are drawn," is included in several issues throughout each volume. Subject and name indexes are available quarterly (paper only) or annually (paper and microfiche).

§ Through v. 25 (1973), each issue included a complete index to the two leading Soviet dailies, *Pravda* and *Izvestiia*. A separate index to *Pravda* was published as: *Index to Pravda* (1975–77. [Columbus, Ohio] : AAASS, 1975–78. Monthly with annual cumulations) and later

as *Pravda index* (Ann Arbor, Mich. : Univ. Microfilms Internat., 1986–87. Quarterly with annual cumulations). The UMI version indexed the English translation.   D839.C87

Gosudarstvennaia publichnaia biblioteka imeni M.E. Saltykova-Shchedrina. Gazetnyi otdel'. Alfavitnyĭ sluzhebnyĭ katalog russkikh dorevoliutsionnykh gazet, 1703–1916. Leningrad, 1958. 279 p.   **AE69**

The Leningrad Public Library's holdings of Russian newspapers published between 1703 and 1916, listed alphabetically, with a geographical-chronological index. Omitted are illegal publications included in the Library's *Volnaia russkaia pechat'* (Sankt-Peterburg : [Nezavisimaia Obshchestvennaia Biblioteka], 1920), and newspapers published abroad in Russian, except those published in Harbin and Port Arthur.   Z6956.R9L357

Hoover Institution on War, Revolution, and Peace. Soviet and Russian newspapers at the Hoover Institution : a catalog / comp. by Karol Maichel. [Stanford, Calif.], 1966. 235 p. (Hoover Institution bibliographical series, 24).   **AE70**

1,108 entries in alphabetical title arrangement. Includes émigré papers. In addition to Hoover holdings, reference is made to files of the newspapers in the Library of Congress and the Columbia University Libraries.   Z6945.S7983

Horecky, Paul Louis. Russian, Ukrainian, and Belorussian newspapers, 1917–1953 : a union list. Wash. : Library of Congress, Reference Dept., Slavic and East European Div., 1953. 218 p.   **AE71**

An expansion of a working paper issued by the Division in 1952 under title: *Preliminary checklist of Russian, Ukrainian, and Belorussian newspapers published since January 1, 1917 ... preserved in United States libraries.*

Holdings as of May 1953 are given for 39 participating U.S. libraries. Arranged by place of publication, with title index and a guide to places of publication by Union Republics. Degree of completeness of holdings is indicated as poor, moderate, substantial, or extensive, without listing of actual issues held. Microfilm files are included.
    Z6956.R9U66

Knyzhkova palata Ukraïns'koi RSR. Periodychni vydannia URSR, 1917–1960 : hazety, bibliohrafichnyi dovidnyk / [A. I. Kozlova, V. M. Skachkov]. Kharkiv : Redaktsiinovydavnychyi viddil Knyzhkovoi palaty URSR, 1965. 575 p.
    AE72

A detailed bibliography of the Ukrainian newspapers of the period.   Z6956.U4K52

Kuznetsov, Ivan Vasil'evich. Gazetnyi mir Sovetskogo Soiuza, 1917–1970 gg / Ivan Vasil'evich Kuznetsov, Efim Markovich Fingerit. Moskva : Izd-vo Moskovskogo universiteta, 1972–76. 2 v. : ill.   **AE73**

Contents: v. 1, Tsentral'nye gazety; v. 2, Respublikanskie, kraevye, oblastnye i okruzhnye gazety.

A listing of Russian newspapers of the period, with extensive notes on the publishing history of each. In v. 1 newspapers are arranged in chronological sections; v. 2 is arranged by individual Soviet republics, then by title. Volumes are separately indexed.   PN5274.K8

Letopis' periodicheskikh i prodolzhaiushchikhsia izdanii. Biulleteni / Gosudarstvennuă komitet SSSR po delam izdatel'stv, poligrafii i knizhnoĭ torgovli [i] Vsesoiuznaia palata. 1971/72– . Moskva : Kniga, 1978– . Biennial.   **AE74**

Continues in part: *Letopis' periodicheskikh izdanii SSSR* (AD150).

A comprehensive listing of Russian newspapers and similar publications. For cumulative listings of newspapers, see *Letopis' periodicheskikh i prodolzhaiushchikhsia izdanii. Sborniki* (AD149).
    Z6956.S65L473

Library of Congress. Newspapers of the Soviet Union in the Library of Congress : (Slavic, 1954–1960; non-Slavic, 1917–1960) / prep. by Paul L. Horecky … [et al.]. Wash. : Slavic and Central European Div., and Serial Div., Reference Dept., Library of Congress : [for sale by the U.S. Govt. Print. Off.], 1962. 73 p.   **AE75**

Includes some pre-1954 titles added to the Library's collection since 1954, and therefore not included in *Russian, Ukrainian, and Belorussian newspapers, 1917–1953*, ed. by Paul Horecky (AE71). Also lists Baltic newspapers from 1940 to 1960. Arranged alphabetically by place of publication; title index. Includes microfilm files.

§ For a more recent list of Soviet, post-Soviet, and Russian newspapers in the Library of Congress, see: *Newspapers received currently in the Library of Congress* (AE11) which is updated annually.

Z6956.R9U55

Spain

Sinclair, Alison. Madrid newspapers, 1661–1870 : a computerized handbook based on the work of Eugenio Hartzenbusch. Leeds : W. Maney, 1984. 964 p., [1] folded leaf of plates : map. (Compendia, v. 11).   **AE76**

Entries for 2,345 newspapers, arranged in chronological order, with bibliographic information, editor or founder's name, and subject focus or character of the newspaper. Includes indexes arranged by printers, editor names, prices, paper sizes, frequency, title, and holdings in the Hemeroteca Municipal (Madrid), the Biblioteca Nacional (Madrid), and the British Library.

§ Supplements and updates *Apuntes para un catálogo de periódicos madrileños desde el año 1661 al 1870*, by D. Eugenio Hartzenbusch (Madrid : Estab. tip. Sucesores de Rivadeneyra, 1894). See also: *La presse periodique madrilène entre 1871–1885*, by Gisèle Cazottes (Montpellier : Université Paul Valéry, 1982). Retrospective listings of Spanish newspapers can also be found in *Catalogo de las publicaciones periodicas madrilenas* and *La Empress periodistica en España* (Alfonso Nieto. Pamplona : Ediciones Universidad de Navarra, 1973. 265 p.).   Z6956.S7S58

Switzerland

Blaser, Fritz. Bibliographie der schweizer Presse : mit Einschluss der Fürstentums Liechtenstein = Bibliographie de la presse suisse = Bibliografia della stampa svizzera. Basel : Birkhäuser Verlag, 1956–58. 1 v. in 2 (1441 p.). (Quellen der Schweizer Geschichte, n.F. 4.Abt. : Handbücher, Bd. 7).   **AE77**

Title and introductory material in German, French, and Italian, with the annotation in the language of the publication.

An extensive listing of the Swiss and Liechtenstein press that attempts to include all dailies and periodicals published before 1803 and all political papers and periodicals after 1803; omits scientific and literary periodicals. Gives detailed information about each title. Arranged alphabetically with chronological and geographical indexes.

DQ3.Q35

Turkey

Duman, Hasan. İstanbul kütüphaneleri Arap harfli süreli yayınlar toplu kataloğu, 1828–1928 = Union catalogue of the periodicals in Arabic script in the libraries of Istanbul, 1898–1928. Beşiktaş, İstanbul : İslâm Tarih, Sanat, ve Kültür Araştırma Merkezi, İslâm Konferansı Teşkilâtı, 1986. 602, 24 p. (Research Centre for Islamic History, Art, and Culture. Bibliographical series, 3).   **AE78**

In Turkish; introductory material also in Arabic and English.

Lists newspapers and periodicals that appear daily, weekly, biweekly, quarterly, semiannually, and annually in Ottoman Turkish, Arabic, Persian, and Urdu, and are printed in Arabic script. Many titles are published in several languages, including some from outside the region. Of 1,804 publications from 32 countries, 1,493 were published in Turkey, and most of the remainder in the former U.S.S.R., Greece, Egypt, and Bulgaria. Entries are arranged alphabetically by transliterated title, followed by publisher, place of publication, publishing history, languages of publication, and holdings in libraries in Istanbul.

§ For Turkish newspapers printed in Arabic script, see also *Eski harfli Türkçe yayınlar toplu kataloğu* (Ankara : Kültür ve Türkism Bakanlığı, 1987–), which gives bibliographic information and library holdings for 2,325 newspapers and periodicals published 1831–1928.

Z6958.T8D86

Africa

Library of Congress. Serial Division. African newspapers in selected American libraries. 3rd ed. Wash. : [Library of Congress], 1965. 135 p.   **AE79**

[1st ed.], 1956.

Records volume-specific holdings in 33 libraries known for their African collections. Lists 708 current and retrospective titles, both positive microfilm and hard copy. Gives full bibliographic information, including starting date and cross-references. Country/city arrangement; title index. Never updated.

§ See also: *African newspapers in the Library of Congress* (DD26 note); *African newspapers available on positive microfilm* (DD26 note); Mette Shayne, *African newspapers currently received by American libraries* (DD26 note); *African newspapers held by the Center for Research Libraries* (Chicago : CRL, 1992. 128 p.); *African newspapers on microfilm : a checklist of sub-Saharan titles held by institutions in the United States, United Kingdom, and Africa* (New Haven, Conn. : Yale Univ. Library, 1977. 57 l); M.D. McGee, comp., *African newspapers on microfilm* ([London] : Standing Conference on Library Materials on Africa, 1973. 58 p.).   Z6959.Z9U5

South Africa

Coetzee, J. C. South African newspapers on microfilm / comp. by J. C. Coetzee ; ed. by Hester van der Walt. 2nd ed., rev. and expanded. Pretoria : The State Libr., 1991. 93 p. (Contributions to library science, no. 35).   **AE80**

1st ed., 1975.

Provides information on microform editions of South African newspapers through 1989 held by international institutions. Arranged alphabetically by title; each entry provides bibliographic and historical information, dates held, number of reels, and the location of microfilm negatives. Geographic and title indexes. There is also a list of newspapers available at the State Library in Pretoria, and a list of sources consulted.

Z6960.S6P73

A list of South African newspapers, 1800–1982, with library holdings. Pretoria : State Library, 1983. 253 p.   **AE81**

Includes holdings of a number of libraries outside South Africa. Indicates microfilm files in the reporting libraries and a given library's intention to film at a future date. Title listing, with index by place of publication.

PN5471.L57

Asia (by region)

Center for Research Libraries. A checklist of Southeast Asian newspapers and other research materials in microform held by the Center for Research Libraries / Daniel F. Doeppers. 9th ed. Madison : Center for Southeast Asian Studies, Univ. of Wisconsin, 1989. 15 p. (Wisconsin papers on southeast Asia. Bibliography, no. 1).   **AE82**

Lists current and retrospective newspapers and other research materials on Southeast Asia acquired by the Southeast Asia Microform Project, and similar materials acquired by the Foreign Newspaper Microfilm Project. Covers 11 Southeast Asian nations. Gives holdings.

Z6957.Z9C46

The-Mulliner, Lian. Southeast Asia microforms project resources : draft listing. Athens, Ohio : Ohio Univ. Libraries, 1989. 16 p.   **AE83**

A "preliminary attempt to list materials owned by SEAM [Southeast Asia Microforms Project] or which SEAM members are permitted to use."—*Pref.* The materials are available through the Center for Research Libraries. Listing is by country and includes theses and dissertations, microform sets, newspapers, and gazettes. Not indexed.

§ See also: *A checklist of Southeast Asian newspapers and other research materials in microform held by the Center for Research Libraries*, comp. Daniel F. Doeppers (AE82).

Arab states

Auchterlonie, Paul. Union catalogue of Arabic serials and newspapers in British libraries / James Paul Crawford Auchterlonie, Yasin H. Safadi. London : Mansell, 1977. 146 p.   **AE84**

Added title page in Arabic.

Covers 1,021 serials and newspapers written wholly or partially in Arabic and located in British "national and university libraries with substantial holdings of Arabic materials with the exception of Leeds and Glasgow."—*Introd.* The arrangement is first by country of origin and then in alphabetical order by transliterated title. Gives languages of publication, some publication history, and library holdings.

Z6958.A6A93

Library of Congress. Arab-world newspapers in the Library of Congress / prep. by George Dimitri Selim. Wash. : Library of Congress, 1980. 85 p.   **AE85**

Lists both those newspapers held by the Library of Congress "that are published in the Arab countries in either Arabic or Latin scripts and those published outside the Arab countries in Arabic script."—*Pref.* Separate sections for Arabic, English, French, German, Italian, and Spanish-language newspapers. Listing is by country and city of publication, then by title. Indexed.

Asia (by country)

China

For recent Chinese newspapers, see *Chung-kuo pao k'an ta ch'üan* (AD187).

King, Frank H. H. A research guide to China-coast newspapers, 1822–1911 / Frank H. H. King, Prescott Clarke. [Cambridge] : East Asian Research Center, Harvard Univ., 1965. 235 p. (Harvard East Asian monographs, 18).   **AE86**

Begins with essays on the history, development, character, and use of China-coast newspapers, and a historical survey by city. An annotated list of newspapers follows, arranged by language and city, with

many brief historical essays and notes. Includes biographies of China-coast editors and publishers and a finding list of extant copies of the papers in repositories in Europe and the U.S. Includes three indexes: chronological, title, and general. Also has a Chinese-English glossary of titles, and lists of other China-coast periodicals and Japanese-language newspapers in China.   Z6958.C5K5

Library of Congress. Chinese newspapers in the Library of Congress : a bibliography = [Kuo hui t'u shu kuan ts'ang Chung wen pao k'an mu lu] / comp. by Han-chu Huang and Hseo-chin Jen. Wash. : Library of Congress : for sale by the U.S. Govt. Print. Off., 1985. 206 p.   **AE87**

Superintendent of Documents classification: LC 17.9:C44.

Lists newspapers from the 1870s to the present, both original and microform files. About 1,200 titles; holdings are issue-specific. Title listing with index by place of publication.   Z6958.C5L52

India

Press in India. 9th (1965)– . New Delhi : Ministry of Information and Broadcasting, Govt. of India, 1965– .   **AE88**

From 1956–64, issued as the *Report* of the Registrar of Newspapers for India; 1965– , also called the *Annual report of the Registrar of Newspapers for India.*

Useful for both recent and retrospective listings. Pt. 1 is an extensive statistical analysis of the newspaper and periodical press covering 93 languages and dialects, circulation, newsprint, chronology, and many other aspects. Pt. 2 is a geographically arranged directory of newspapers and periodicals. Under place, serials are listed by frequency, i.e., dailies, etc., and then by language. Listings give publisher's name and address, editor, price, circulation figures, field of interest, etc. Very comprehensive. Title index.

§ Another source listing newspapers: *Indian periodicals in print, 1973* (AD190), by H. N. D. Gandhi. For listings of early Indian newspapers, see *Newspaper holdings of the India Office Library and Records* (London : Oriental and India Office Collections, 1993).

Z6958.I4A25

Indonesia

Perpustakaan Nasional (Indonesia). Katalog surat kabar : koleksi Perpustakaan Nasional, 1810–1984 = Catalogue of newspapers / disusun oleh Wartini Santoso. Ed. rev. [Jakarta] : Perpustakaan Nasional, Departemen Pendidikan dan Kebudayaan, [1984]. 246 p.   **AE89**

Rev. ed. of *Katalogus surat-karab, koleksi Perpustakaan Museum Pusat 1810–1973* (1973).

An alphabetical listing of approximately 1,600 newspapers published 1810–1984 held by the National Library of Indonesia; the majority are Indonesian titles. Indexed by place of publication. Includes an essay in English, "A short history of the newspaper in Indonesia."

§ See also: *Indonesian newspapers : an international union list,* by Godfrey R. Nunn (Taipei : Chinese Materials and Research Aids Service Center, 1971).   Z6958.I45I53

Iran

Pourhadi, Ibrahim Vaqfi. Persian and Afghan newspapers in the Library of Congress, 1871–1978. Wash. : Library of Congress, 1979. 101 p.   **AE90**

An alphabetical title listing of 326 Iranian and 23 Afghani newspapers in the Library of Congress collections. Gives publication dates, place of publication, frequency, publisher or owner of license, LC holdings, and a brief annotation indicating the character of the publication. Titles are given in transliteration and in English translation. Indexed.

§ See also: *Union catalogue of Persian serials & newspapers in British libraries* (AD199).   Z6958.I65P875

Iraq

Ibrāhīm, Zāhidah. Dalīl al-jarā'id wa-al-majallāt al-'Irāqīyah, 1869–1978. al-Ṭab'ah 2., munaqqaḥah wa-mazīdah. al-Kuwayt : Dār al-Nashr wa-al-Maṭbū'āt al-Kuwaytīyah, 1982. 712 p.   **AE91**
In Arabic.
Lists Arabic-language newspapers and periodicals published in Iraq. The first section lists alphabetically by title 802 newspapers published 1869–1978. Indexes: names and organizations, chronology, geography, and political parties. Also offers a list of Iraqi journalists.
§ For a guide to Arabic newspapers published in Lebanon see: *Qāmūs al-siḥāfah al-Lubnānīyah, 1858–1974 : wa-huwa mujam yuàrrif wa-yuŕrikh lil-ṣuḥuf wa-al-dawrīyāt al-latī aṣdarahā al-Lubnāniyūn fī Lubnān wa-al-khārij,* talīf Yūsuf Asàd Dāghir (Bayrūt : al-Jāiàh al-Lubnānīyah : al-Tawzī, al-Maktabah as-Sharqīyah, 1978. 526 p.). Title may be translated as: Dictionary [i.e., encyclopedia] of the Lebanese press. Includes historical account of Lebanese journalism and bibliography of 2,145 periodicals and newspapers published in Lebanon in Arabic (2,032 titles), French (71), and English (42), 1858–1974. Arranged alphabetically by title. Indexed by publisher and subject. Information is also given about publishing laws.   Z6958.I7I27

Israel

Israel. Lishkat ha-'itonut ha-memshaltit. Newspapers and periodicals appearing in Israel. [1966]– . [Jerusalem] : Govt. Press Offices of the State of Israel, [1966]– . Irregular.   **AE92**
Although not an official census, attempts to include all daily newspapers and the majority of other periodical publications. Newspapers are listed by frequency (daily to quarterly or irregular). Each entry gives language of paper, political or other sponsor, special subject (if applicable) and addresses and telephone numbers.   Z6958.I8A32

Japan

Japanese press. 1949– . [Tokyo] : Japan Newspaper Publishers' and Editors' Assoc., 1949– . Annual (irregular).   **AE93**
Title varies.
Articles surveying the current state of the Japanese press are followed by a directory of newspapers, news agencies, broadcasting stations, television newsreel agencies, and overseas correspondents.   PN5401.J36

Kokuritsu Kokkai Toshokan (Japan). Etsuranbu. Kokuritsu Kokkai Toshokan shozo shinbun moruroku / [henshu Kokuritsu Kokkai Toshokan Etsuranbu]. Tokyo : Kokuritsu Kokkai Toshokan, 1981. 248 p.   **AE94**
Lists newspapers collected by the National Diet Library. Includes 4,758 foreign and domestic titles, with indication of format.
Updated by: *Kokuritsu Kokkai Toshokan shozo kokunai chikuji kankobutsu mokuroku* [National Diet Library catalog of Japanese periodicals] (Tokyo : 1969–) for Japanese and Western-language journals and newspapers published in Japan; and *Kokuritsu Kokkai Toshokan shozo Gaikoku chikuji kankobutsu mokuroku* [National Diet Library catalog of foreign serials] (Tokyo : 1987–), which lists newspapers, journals, and annuals published in countries other than Japan, Korea, or China.

Nihon shinbun nenkan / Nihon Shinbun Kyōkai. Tokyo : Dentsu, 1947– . Annual.   **AE95**
In addition to directory information on individual newspapers and broadcasting companies, includes texts of codes relating to the press and radio; a general survey of the press; lists of awards, newspaper directories, university courses in journalism; and a who's who of the press.   PN4709.N52

Zenkoku maikuro shinbun shozō ichiran : Shōwa 62-nen 11-gatsumatsu genzai / [henshū Kokuritsu Kokkai Toshokan Chikuji Kankōbutsubu]. Tōkyō : Kokuritsu Kokkai Toshokan, [1988]. 235 p.   **AE96**
A union list of Japanese newspapers on microfilm held by more than 1,200 libraries and institutions in Japan updated as of Nov. 1987. Approximately 1,300 newspapers published in Japan, China, Korea, and Western countries are included. A portion of the guide is arranged by holding institutions with a list of the newspapers held.   Z6945.Z444

Pakistan

National Archives of Pakistan. Holdings of the newspapers and periodicals. Islamabad : Dept. of Archives, Govt. of Pakistan, 1988. v. 1. (In progress).   **AE97**
Cover title.
Organized by frequency of publication. Each of 597 entries (17 daily, 89 weekly, 419 monthly, and 19 quarterly) gives title, years held, and place of publication.   Z6958.P2N27

Philippines

Saito, Shiro. Philippine newspapers : an international union list / Shiro Saito and Alice W. Mak. Honolulu, Hawaii : Philippine Studies Program, Center for Asian and Pacific Studies, Univ. of Hawaii, 1984. 273 p. (Philippine Studies occasional paper, 7).   **AE98**
Constitutes a revised, enlarged and updated edition of Saito's *Philippine newspapers in selected American libraries* (1966). This edition includes newspapers published in the Philippines and held by libraries in Australia, Canada, England, the Philippines, and the U.S. In two parts: (1) listing by place of publication (with title index) and (2) listing by repository.

Australia and Oceania

For the most current listings of Australian newspapers, see *Australian periodicals in print* (AD214). Newspapers published earlier were listed in *Press, radio & TV guide : Australia, New Zealand and the Pacific islands* (AD213).

Australia

Newspapers in Australian libraries : a union list. 4th ed. Canberra : National Library of Australia, 1985. 2 v.   **AE99**
Contents: pt. 1, Overseas newspapers; pt. 2, Australian newspapers.
A list with library location of more than 4,000 overseas and more than 6,000 Australian papers in 114 Australian libraries. Geographic arrangement, with a title index for each volume. Includes both original and microfilm files. Gives holdings and indication of current subscription.   Z6945.N63

New Zealand

Harvey, D. R. Union list of New Zealand newspapers before 1940 : preserved in libraries, newspaper offices, local authority offices, and museums in New Zealand. Wellington : National Library of New Zealand, 1985. [98] p.   **AE100**

Based on a survey conducted in 1983. Arranged by place of publication, then by latest title as of 1940. For each title, includes dates of first and (if ceased) last issues, place of publication, previous titles, frequency, available indexes, and holding libraries with an indication of microform availability. Title index.

§ The two editions of: New Zealand. Parliament. Library, *A union catalogue of New Zealand newspapers preserved in public libraries, newspaper offices, etc.* (Wellington : [Govt. Printer], 1938. 38 p. 2nd ed., 1961. 74 p.) give holdings both in New Zealand and in research libraries in Great Britain and Australia. See also: *A checklist of newspapers in New Zealand libraries 1938–1959 : a provisional supplement to the Union catalogue of New Zealand newspapers, 1938* (Wellington, 1959).   Z6962.N5H37

INDEXES

Listed here are indexes that vary from broad subject listings to machine-readable versions that provide full-text searching. Indexes that treat only certain features (e.g., obituaries) are omitted, but these features are included in many of the general indexes. Indexes covering newsletters will be found under Periodicals (Section AD).

Bibliographic control over newspaper indexes has lagged but is receiving increased attention. Ongoing indexes, U.S. and foreign, are listed in *Ulrich's international periodicals directory* (AD18) under "Journalism"; *Index and abstract directory* (AD249) lists newspapers in a special section and notes where they are indexed; and current and retrospective indexes are listed in *Serials on microfilm* (Ann Arbor, Mich. : Univ. Microfilms International, 1994–).

Computerized indexes. Computers, by facilitating the indexing process and providing full-text access to the content of newspapers, have brought dramatic changes over the past ten years in the number and kinds of newspaper indexes available. Also, groups such as the U.S. Newspaper Program have made considerable progress in indexing state newspapers. Hundreds of index titles from the last decade are accessible through OCLC's *Worldcat* database.

Machine-readable indexes and full-text databases for newspapers are available—e.g., *British newspapers index* (BNI) on CD-ROM, *Current digest of the post-Soviet press* online and on CD-ROM, *NewsBank reference service plus* on CD-ROM—and a large number of newspapers are incorporated in full-text format in such vendor systems as LEXIS/NEXIS, DIALOG, and Datatimes.

General works

Bibliography

Milner, Anita Cheek. Newspaper indexes : a location and subject guide for researchers. Metuchen, N.J. : Scarecrow, 1977–82. 3 v.   **AE101**

Primarily a guide to indexes for U.S. newspapers, but also provides valuable information concerning foreign newspaper indexes. For the most part, entries report card files and unpublished indexes, and were gathered by questionnaires sent to libraries, newspapers, and his-

torical and genealogical societies. The first part of v. 1 lists by state and county the newspapers indexed, indicates dates and special topics covered, and gives location of the index; the second part lists indexes by repository, with notes on type of indexes maintained. Vols. 2–3 offer data on newspaper indexes of various kinds in repositories not covered in v. 1, plus some updating of earlier entries. Since each volume is indexed separately, all three must be consulted.

§ Other bibliographies of newspaper indexes: (1) *Lathrop report on newspaper indexes: an illustrated guide to published and unpublished newspaper indexes in the United States & Canada*, comp. by Norman M. and Mary Lou Lathrop (Wooster, Ohio : Norman Lathrop Enterprises, 1980), originally issued as a loose-leaf service to be updated annually, appeared only in a 1979/80 edition. It provides information on the scope, method of compilation, availability, etc., of a wide range of newspaper indexes, including card, electronic, microform, and special subject indexes, but clipping files are excluded. (2) *Indexes in the Newspaper and Current Periodicals Room*, by John Pluge (AE102), which lists 271 general and subject indexes to U.S. papers and 94 to foreign papers.   Z6951.M635

Pluge, John. Newspaper indexes in the Newspaper and Current Periodical Room. [Wash.] : Library of Congress, Serial and Government Publications Division, Newspaper Section, 1987. 102 p.   **AE102**

First issued 1985, comp. by William E. Laing and Pluge.

An annotated list of indexes to both U.S. and foreign newspapers. Indexes of a general nature with U.S. coverage are listed first, including ethnic and general historical indexes, followed by state and city listings. There are 271 U.S. and 94 foreign listings.

§ For U.S. and foreign retrospective indexes, supplements Anita Cheek Milner's *Newspaper indexes* (AE101) and *Lathrop report on newspaper indexes* (Wooster, Ohio : Norman Lathrop Enterprises, 1980). Includes many indexes in existence for only short periods and specialized compilations of birth and death records from newspapers, making it a valuable resource for genealogy.   Z881.U5

International

Letopis' gazetnykh stateĭ. 1936– . Moskva : Vsesoiuznaīa knizhnaīa palata, 1936– . Monthly.   **AE103**

Frequency varies; monthly since 1977.

Indexes the most important articles from numerous metropolitan, regional, and subject newspapers. Classified subject arrangement. Personal and geographical name indexes in each issue. Annual indexes were published 1948–55.   AI15.L35

United States

[Bell & Howell/UMI newspaper indexes]. Wooster, Ohio : Bell & Howell, 1972– . [various volumes].   **AE104**

Frequency and cumulation pattern varies.

In 1972, Bell & Howell's Newspaper Indexing Center began to issue indexes to four regional newspapers, *Chicago tribune, Los Angeles times, New Orleans times-picayune*, and *Washington post*. In 1982, Bell & Howell acquired University Microfilms International and transferred its newspaper indexing operation to UMI, continuing to issue indexes over the UMI imprint, and adding other newspapers. Indexes are now published for the following titles:

Chicago tribune (1972–).
Los Angeles times (1972–).
New Orleans times-picayune (1972–).
Washington post (1971–).
St. Louis post-dispatch (1975–).
Denver Post (1976–).
Detroit news (1976–).
Houston post (1976–).

San Francisco chronicle (1976–).
Wall Street journal (1976–).
USA today (1982–).
Atlanta constitution and journal (1983–).
Boston globe (1983–).
Washington times (1986–).

§ UMI also publishes *Black newspapers index* (AE105) and has published the index to *Christian Science monitor* since 1987 (AE106).

Black newspapers index. 1971– . Ann Arbor, Mich. : Univ. Microfilms International, 1971– . Quarterly, with annual cumulation. **AE105**

Imprint varies: 1971–86, Wooster, Ohio : Bell & Howell.

An index to eleven African-American newspapers: *Afro American* (Baltimore, Md. and Wash.), *Amsterdam news* (N.Y.), *Argus* (St. Louis, Mo.), *Atlanta daily world*, *Call & post* (Cleveland, Ohio), *Chicago defender* and *Muslim journal* (Chicago), *Los Angeles sentinel*, *Michigan chronicle* (Detroit), *New Pittsburgh courier*, and *Journal & guide* (Norfolk, Va.). For most papers, coverage begins around 1977.

§ Indexes to newspapers of earlier periods include:

(1) Donald M. Jacobs … [et al.], *Antebellum black newspapers : indices to New York Freedom's journal (1827–1829), The rights of all (1829), The weekly advocate (1837), and The colored American (1837–1841)* (Westport, Conn. : Greenwood, c1976. 587 p.).

(2) James de T. Abajian, *Blacks in selected newspapers, censuses and other sources: an index to names and subjects* (Boston : G.K. Hall, 1977. 3 v. Suppl., 1985. 2 v.).

(3) Georgetta Merritt Campbell, *Extant collections of early black newspapers* (AE15). AI3.I46

The Christian Science monitor index. Jan. 1987– . Ann Arbor, Mich. : Publ. under agreement with the Christian Science Publ. Soc. by Univ. Microfilms Internat., 1987– . Monthly, with quarterly and annual cumulations. **AE106**

Continues: 1945–78, *Index to the Christian Science monitor*; 1979–83, *Bell & Howell's index to the Christian Science monitor*; 1984–87, *Bell & Howell's newspaper index to the Christian Science Monitor*.

Provides comprehensive indexing, continuous with its predecessors, from 1945, of all significant articles, including news, editorials, cartoons, commentaries, sports, business and finance, book reviews, art exhibitions, dance, movies, music, restaurants, theater, and television. Advertising and the daily religious column are omitted. Coverage of regional editions has varied over the years; format of all editions was made uniform as of Apr. 1, 1975, so that page positions are thereafter uniform for all editions, but references to special regional sections are identified.

In early volumes, 1945–78, personal names were included in the regular alphabet; from 1979 through 1986, indexes were in two sections for subjects and personal names. Beginning in 1987, personal names were again included with subjects in one alphabet and each entry was accompanied by a brief abstract. Like *New York times index* (AE110), the abstracts themselves provide a chronological record of events; but unlike the *Times*, articles solely about persons, rather than being cross-referenced to subject, are entered under the person's name. All articles with bylines are indexed by author. AI21.C46

•**Ethnic newswatch** [database]. Stamford, Conn. : Softline Information, Inc., Aug. 1991– . **AE107**

Available on CD-ROM, updated monthly (quarterly subscription available).

"A comprehensive collection of newspapers and other periodicals published by the ethnic and minority press for the Americas."— *database screen*. Not available in printed form. Provides full-text access, with searching in English and Spanish, to about 90 newspapers and periodicals, in English and Spanish, published for the most part by the ethnic press for ethnic groups in the U.S. Includes a directory of publications indexed. Groups covered: African Americans, European Americans, Chicanos, Hispanics, Latinos, Native Americans, Asian Americans, Jews, Arab Americans.

Falk, Byron A. Personal name index to "The New York times index," 1851–1974 / Bryon A. Falk, Jr., Valerie R. Falk. Verdi, Nev. : Roxbury Data Interface, c1976–88. 22 v. **AE108**

Vol. 1–20 publ. in Succasunna, N.J.

An index to the volumes of the *New York times index* rather than to the newspaper itself; i.e., references are to the date and page of the *Index* volumes. Brings together in a single alphabetical sequence names found throughout the *Index* volumes, including names appearing in index categories such as Book reviews, Concerts, Deaths, Disappearances, etc.

Kept up to date by periodic supplements, each of which supersedes and extends the coverage of its predecessor. The most recent, *1975–1989 Supplement* (Verdi, Nev. : Roxbury Data Interface, 1990–91, 5 v.) includes all errata entries from the *Index* 1851–1989, names missed previously, and new names 1975–89. The 1975–79 supplement is also numbered as v. 23–25 of the original set. Z5301.F28

New York daily tribune index. 1875–1906. N.Y. : Tribune Assoc., 1876–1907. 32 v. **AE109**

Repr. : N.Y. : Kraus, 1976. 10 v.

Annual.

Much briefer than the *New York times index* (AE110), but useful for the period covered. See also: *Bell & Howell/UMI newspaper indexes* (AE104). AI21.N5

New York times index. v. 1 (1913)– . N.Y. : Times, 1913– . **AE110**

Frequency varies; 1913–29, quarterly with no cumulations, the four quarterly parts constituting a volume; 1930, monthly with quarterly cumulations and an annual cumulated volume; 1931–47, monthly with annual cumulations; 1948– , semimonthly with annual cumulations.

A carefully made subject index giving exact reference to date, page, and column, and plentiful cross-references to names and related topics. The brief synopses of articles answer some questions without need to refer to the paper itself. Indexes the Late City edition of the *New York times*, the edition that is microfilmed and used for bound files, but also serves as an independent index to dates and even as a guide to the reporting of current happenings in other newspapers (and thereby justifying the subtitle, "Master-key to the news").

Users of the *Index* should be aware that in recent years the weekday editions of the newspaper have special feature sections ("Sports Monday," "Living," etc.) with parts designated by the letters A, B, C and D, but these are represented in the *Index* by the Roman numerals I, II, III and IV, respectively.

Beginning 1978, quarterly cumulations of the *Index* are issued for the first three quarters of the year, with the annual volume "serving, in effect, as the fourth quarterly cumulation covering the entire year."

Before publication of the "Prior series" (below), an "in-house" index covering 1851–58, 1860, 1863–June 1905 had been made available on microfilm.

———. *Prior series* (N.Y. : Bowker, [1966–76]. 15 v.).

Publisher varies.

Contents: v. 1, Sept. 1851–Dec.1862; v. 2, 1863–1874; v. 3, 1875–1879; v. 4, 1880–1885; v. 5, 1886–1889; v. 6, 1890–1893; v. 7, 1894–1898; v. 8, 1899–June 1905; v. 9, July 1905–Dec. 1906; v. 10–15, 1907–1912.

The "Prior series" is designed to provide index coverage in book form from 1851 to 1912. Some volumes represent new indexing, others are reprintings of existing indexes originally prepared for staff use; i.e., the handwritten index for Sept. 1851–Aug. 1858 is reproduced in facsimile; the index for the remainder of 1858 through 1862 and the volumes for July 1905–1912 are newly prepared (though they are presented year by year rather than in cumulated form); the other volumes are reprinted from indexes previously printed for staff use. When the older indexes cover only three- or six-month periods they have not been cumulated, and users of the index must be careful to check a number of alphabets within a given volume.

§ For more detailed information on the *Index*, see: Grant W. Morse, *Guide to the incomparable New York times index* (N.Y. : Fleet

Academic Editions, 1980). Describes filing rules, headings, subheadings, cross-references, special features, and calls attention to changes in the *Index* over the years.   AI21.N44

NewsBank index. Jan. 1982– . [New Canaan, Conn.] : News-Bank, 1982– . Monthly, with quarterly and annual cumulations.   **AE111**
Continues *NewsBank urban affairs library* issued in various sections 1970–81.

A current awareness service issued in conjunction with, and serving as an index to, a microfiche set of the articles indexed (known as *NewsBank*). Articles, selected from more than 100 newspapers throughout the U.S., focus on socioeconomic, political, international, and scientific areas. (Separate NewsBank services, *Review of the arts* and *Names in the news*, cover articles on film and television, fine arts, performing arts and literature, and material on individuals and specific groups, respectively.) Indexing is by broad subject headings (with some entries for individuals and organizations, and numerous cross-references) with geographical subdivisions; index references (which do not include dates) are to the microfiche, which is arranged in 14 broad subject categories.

Not properly a newspaper index since it is tied to the microfiche service, but useful for its regional approach to news events and its countrywide coverage.

•Machine-readable version: *NewsBank reference service plus* [database] (New Canaan, Conn. : NewsBank, 1992–). Available on CD-ROM, updated monthly.

Incorporates *NewsBank* (Jan. 1981–), *NewsBank review of the arts* (July 1980–), *NewsBank names in the news* (Aug. 1981–), and *NewsBank index to periodicals* (Jan. 1988–).

•**Newspaper abstracts ondisc** [database]. Louisville, Ky. : UMI/Data Courier, 1985– .   **AE112**
Indexes *New York times, Washington post, Christian Science monitor, Boston globe, Los Angeles times, Chicago tribune, Atlanta constitution, Atlanta journal, Wall Street journal,* and *USA today*. The database includes citations to articles, brief descriptive abstracts, and subject headings. The titles indexed vary with the part of the service purchased. In CD-ROM, updated monthly. Also available online as part of *Newspaper and periodical abstracts,* updated monthly. A tape version is also available that includes some ethnic group papers.

Newspapers online : a guide to searching daily newspapers whose articles are online in full text : includes geographic indexes / comp. and ed. by Susanne Bjørner. 2nd ed. Needham Heights, Mass. : BiblioData, [1993]. 1 v. (looseleaf).   **AE113**
1st ed., 1992.
Subtitle varies.

Lists alphabetically some 125 daily newspapers whose full texts are available online. If titles lack a geographic term, one is supplied and is used in filing (e.g., *Sun* is filed as *Baltimore sun*). Entries give: address; telephone; editor; description of region served; key businesses; brief history, including circulation; online services that offer full text, with coverage and types of articles included or excluded. Vendors included: DIALOG, DataTimes, Mead Data Central (NEXIS), Vu/Text (whose titles have migrated to DIALOG).

A 3rd ed. is planned for 1995 publication.

§ See also: *Fulltext sources online* (v. 1 [Winter 1989]– . Needham Heights, Mass. : BiblioData, 1989– . Semiannual), which includes more than 3,000 sources in science, technology, medicine, law, finance, business, industry, the press, etc.   Z699.5.N47N4

USA today index. Jan. 1987– . Ann Arbor, Mich. : Univ. Microfilms International, c1983– . Monthly, with quarterly and annual cumulations.   **AE114**
Publisher varies: 1983–86, Wooster, Ohio : Bell & Howell.

Provides abstracts and comprehensive indexing for all significant articles in the newspaper. Indexed material includes news items, feature articles, editorials, editorial cartoons, obituaries, commentaries, sports articles, business and financial news, book reviews, art exhibitions, dance, movies, music, restaurants, theatre, and TV programs. Not indexed are: articles from other UMI newspapers, society announcements, self-help columns, meeting announcements, horoscopes,

ads, TV schedules, comic strips, and routine weather reports. Special entries include books, recordings, deaths, editorials, and theater. Signed articles have entries for author's name under "Bylines."

Wall Street journal. Index. 1958– . [N.Y.] : Dow Jones, 1959– . Monthly, with annual cumulations.   **AE115**
Based on the final Eastern edition of the newspaper. Each issue has two parts: (1) corporate news indexed by company name; (2) general news indexed by topic. Includes special sections for book reviews, personalities, deaths, and theater reviews. The last section of the index includes the daily Dow Jones averages for each month of the year. Since 1981, v. 1 includes *Barron's index* (green pages), a subject and corporate index to *Barron's business and financial weekly*.
                          HG1.W26

The Washington post index. v. 1 (Jan. 1989)– . Ann Arbor, Mich. : publ. under agreement with the *Washington post* by Univ. Microfilms International, 1989– . Monthly, with quarterly and annual cumulations.   **AE116**
Continues: *The Washington post : newspaper index* (Wooster, Ohio : Newspaper Indexing Center, Micro Photo Div., Bell & Howell, 1971–78. 7 v.) and *The official Washington post index* (Woodbridge, Conn. : Research Publ., 1979–88. 10 v.).

Canada

Burrows, Sandra. Checklist of indexes to Canadian newspapers = Liste de contrôle des index de journaux canadiens / by Sandra Burrows and Franceen Gaudet. Ottawa : National Library of Canada, 1987. 148, 154 p. : ill.   **AE117**
In English and French.

Based on responses to a survey sent to Canadian libraries, archives, newspaper offices, and genealogical and historical societies. Lists in-house indexes, including clipping files, of 19th- and 20th-century newspapers. Arranged by province, then by city, organization, and newspaper. Geographic and title indexes are included.
                          Z69.54.C2B87

Canadian index. v. 1 (1993)– . Toronto : Micromedia, 1993– . Monthly, with semi-annual cumulations.   **AE118**
Formed by merger of the publisher's *Canadian news index* (v. 1 [1980]–16 [1992]), *Canadian magazine index* (v. 1 [1985]–8 [1992]), and *Canadian business index* (v. 6 [1980]–18 [1992]. Formerly *Canadian business periodicals index*).

Follows *Canadian news index* in covering English-language newspapers and periodicals. Separate indexes by subjects, names, and corporations. Includes book reviews. Entries arranged chronologically.

•The resources available in *Canadian index* are available online through Infomart Online, which also provides full-text searching of more than 20 Canadian papers. *Canadian NewsDisc* [database] on CD-ROM offers on French-language discs the full text of five Canadian papers and on English-language discs the full text of six.   AI3C34

Denmark

Dansk artikelindeks : aviser og tidsskrifter. 1979– . Ballerup : Bibliotekscentralens Forlag, 1981– . Monthly with annual cumulations.   **AE119**
For annotation, *see* AD308.

France

Le Monde [Index]. Janv. 1985– . Reading, England : Research Publications Ltd., 1988– . Monthly with annual cumulations.   **AE120**

A detailed subject index with brief annotations, referring to date, page, and column. Lists reviews by type (livre, film, etc.). The publisher is extending coverage backward to close the gap from 1969; retrospective volumes for 1985–87 have appeared so far; the volume for 1984 is expected in 1994.

Earlier years are indexed by: *Le Monde. Index analytique* (Paris : Le Monde, 1967–80). Years indexed: 1944–51, 1958, 1965–68. An alphabetical subject index referring to date of issue only. Names of persons within entries are printed in boldface capitals; most do not have separate entries, but appear in a "List of names cited" at the end of each letter of the alphabet. Obituaries, reviews of books and films, etc., are grouped under appropriate headings. Important for research libraries.

Tables du journal Le temps. Paris : Éditions du Centre national de la recherche scientifique, 1966–83. 10 v.   **AE121**

Contents: v. 1, 1861–1865; v. 2, 1866–1870; v. 3, 1871–1875; v. 4, 1876–1880; v. 5, 1881–1885; v. 6, 1886–1888; v. 7, 1889–1891; v. 8, 1892–1894; v. 9, 1895–1897; v. 10, 1898–1900. No more published?

Issued by: Institut Français de presse et des sciences de l'information. Section d'Histoire.

Covers *Le temps*, 1861–1900. Originally planned to extend to 1942.

Like the index to its successor *Le monde* (Paris : Le Monde, 1969–80), this is an important tool for research in French history, literature, and related subjects. Each volume is in the form of a series of annual indexes arranged topically within broad geographical sections (Africa, Asia, Americas, Oceania, and Europe). Under these areas topics are grouped broadly according to generalities, politics, economics, society and religion, and regional and cultural aspects. Each volume is also accompanied by five-year indexes for authors of signed articles, personal names, and specific subjects and countries. Articles giving accounts of great events and appearing contemporaneously with those events are not indexed since it is assumed that they can easily be located through the date.   AI21.T375

Germany

Monatliches Verzeichnis von Aufsätzen aus deutschen Zeitungen in sachlich-alphabetischer Anordnung : mit Jahres-Gesamt-Sach-und-Verfasser-Register. Gautzsch bei Leipzig : Dietrich, 1909–44. 31 v. (Bibliographie der deutschen Zeitschriftenliteratur, Abt. A. Beilage Bde.).   **AE122**

Weekly, 1928–29; fortnightly, 1909–22, 1930–33; monthly, 1934–44.

An index to the principal articles in German and some Austrian papers. For each volume year, there are subject and author indexes. Not published 1923–27; during that period indexing of the same papers was included in *Bibliographie der deutschen Zeitschriftenliteratur* (AD313).

For an earlier period, an index that includes newspapers: *Zeitschriften-Index, 1750–1815* [microform], [sponsored by] Akademie der Wissenschaft zu Göttingen, under the direction of Klaus Schmidt (Hildesheim : Olms Neue Medien, 1989. 28 microfiches).   AI9.B513

Zeitungs-Index. Jahrg. 1, nr.1 (Jan./März 1974)– . Pullach bei München : Verlag Dokumentation, 1974– . Quarterly.   **AE123**

"Verzeichnis wichtiger Aufsätze aus deutschsprachigen Zeitungen."—*t.p.*

Willi Gorzny, ed.

A subject index to 21 German-language newspapers (mainly weeklies), including two Zürich publications and one from Vienna. Listing is chronological under topical headings. Entry includes author's name (for the high percentage of signed articles), title of article, newspaper abbreviation, volume number, date, and page. Issues do not cumulate, but an annual Register issue includes Verfasser-register, Systematisches Register, and Geographisches Register.   AI9.Z44

Great Britain

The Guardian index. v. 1 (Jan. 1986)– . Ann Arbor, Mich. : Univ. Microfilms International, c1986– . 8 monthly and 4 quarterly issues, with annual cumulations.   **AE124**

A detailed alphabetical index referring to date, page, and column, with illustration and article length indicators. Provides brief "abstracts and comprehensive indexing of all significant articles" (*Users' guide*), including editorials and editorial cartoons. Entries are arranged chronologically under each subject heading. Reviews are indexed under form (books, moving pictures, etc.) subdivided by author and by title. Also indexes *Guardian weekly*. Available in microform for 1842–1985 from Adam Matthews Publications.   AI21.G8G82

Times (London). The Times index. Jan./Mar. 1973– . Reading, Eng. : Newspaper Archive Developments, 1973– . Monthly, with annual cumulation beginning 1977.   **AE125**

Frequency varies: 1973–76, quarterly.

Also called *London Times index*.

Now indexes *The Times, The Sunday Times, The Times literary supplement, The Times educational supplement,* and *The Times higher education supplement*. Indexing practices of the preceding series (below) are continued—e.g., book reviews are listed under both author and "book reviews"; obituaries under name of the deceased; theater reviews under "theatre"; motion picture reviews under "films."

Predecessors:

(1) *Index to the Times* (1906–72. London : Times, 1907–73).

Title varies: 1906–13, *The annual index*; 1914–Jan./Feb. 1957, *The official index*. Frequency varies: 1906–June 1914, monthly with annual cumulations 1906–13 and semiannual cumulation Jan.–June 1914; July 1914–56, quarterly; 1957–72, bimonthly with no cumulations.

A detailed alphabetical index that refers to date, page, and column. Indexes the final edition of *The Times* and material from earlier editions that were dropped from the final.

(2) *Palmer's index to the Times newspaper, 1790–June 1941* (London : Palmer, 1868–1943. Repr. : N.Y. : Kraus, 1965).

Quarterly, beginning with the index covering Oct.–Dec. 1867, publ. 1868. Coverage 1906–43 overlaps *Index to the Times*. *Palmer's* is much less detailed but useful because of the long period of coverage. Indexing of obituary, death, and funeral notices under "Deaths" frequently supplies biographical material difficult to find elsewhere. Available on CD-ROM (1790–1905) from Chadwyck-Healey Inc.   AI21.T46

Spain

El país. Indice. 1984– . Madrid : Ediciones El País, 1984– .   **AE126**

Publisher varies: 1991– publ. by Diario Sociedad Anonima.

An index by broad subjects with subheadings under which entries are arranged chronologically. Entries consist of a citation with brief descriptive note and give date, edition (Madrid, Barcelona, Madrid-Barcelona) and section.

Other indexes to Spanish papers: *Diario de Barcelona (1792–1929) : monografia bibliografica del decano actual de la prense periodica española* (Madrid : Imprenta Municipal, 1929. 44 p.); *Vienticuatros diarios, Madrid, 1830–1900 : articulos y noticias de escritores españoles del siglo XIX* (Madrid : Consejo Superior de Investigaciones Cientificas, Instituto Miguel de Cervantes, 1986).   AI21.P32P34

FEATURES

Editorials on file. v.1 (Jan. 1970)– . N.Y. : Facts on File, 1970– . Looseleaf. Semimonthly.   **AE127**

Brief introductory information on editorial subjects (drawn from the weekly *Facts on file* news service) is followed by a selection of approximately 15–25 editorials reprinted in their entirety from U.S. and Canadian newspapers of the preceding half-month. Monthly subject indexes cumulate quarterly and annually. Cartoons on selected subjects are often included.   D839.E3

News bureau contacts. 1990– . N.Y., N.Y : BPi Media Services, c1990– . Annual.   **AE128**
Continues: *News bureaus in the U.S.* (N.Y. : R. Weiner, 1969–89. Irregular).

An aid for publicists, journalists, etc. Arranged by state, with major publications listed according to the city in which its editorial headquarters is located. Gives address, telephone number, and name of person in charge, plus helpful notes on many of the larger publications. Index by publication title, giving location of news bureau that handles each publication.   Z6951.N626

Syndicated columnist contacts. 1990– . N.Y. : BPi Media Services, c1990– . Annual. with monthly updates.   **AE129**
1st–3rd eds., 1975–79, had title: *Syndicated columnists*, by Richard Weiner (N.Y. : Weiner).

Lists syndicated columns by broad subjects. Indexes for author, title, syndicator (organizations), and "package" (combination media packages). Includes a list of columns available in Spanish. Comics, other nontext features, local columnists ommitted.

§ A similar source is: *Syndicate directory : annual directory of syndicated services* (N.Y. : Editor and Publisher, 1985–). Arranged by 51 broad subjects (e.g., advice, environment, etiquette, family, gardening). Features are listed by title, then by author or artist. Entries give full description and address.   PN4888.S9S93

JOURNALISM

Guides

Block, Eleanor S. Communication and the mass media : a guide to the reference literature / Eleanor S. Block, James K. Bracken. Englewood, Colo. : Libraries Unlimited, 1991. 198 p.   **AE130**
Intended to provide a broader approach to supplement, but not supersede other specialized guides, such as Jo A. Cates *Journalism : a guide to the reference literature* (AE132). Arranged by type of reference source.

Bibliography

Blum, Eleanor. Mass media bibliography : an annotated guide to books and journals for research and reference / Eleanor Blum and Frances Goins Wilhoit. 3rd ed. Urbana : Univ. of Illinois Pr., c1990. 344 p.   **AE131**
2nd ed., 1980, had title: *Basic books in the mass media*.

Covers some 1,947 titles on the mass media and "enables the reader to piece together an informal history of the literature of mass communication in the English-speaking areas of the world."—*Pref.* Many, but not all, of the titles are reference works. Chapters cover general communication, broadcasting and print media, film, advertising and public relations, bibliographies, directories and handbooks, journals, and indexes to the mass communications literature. Author, title, and subject indexes.   Z5630.B55

Cates, Jo A. Journalism : a guide to the reference literature. Englewood, Colo. : Libraries Unlimited, 1990. 214 p. **AE132**
"A selected, annotated bibliography and reference guide to the English-language reference library of print and broadcast journalism"

(*Introd.*), listing sources published from the late 1960s through 1988. Some earlier standard works are included. Arranged by broad topic. Author, title, and subject indexes. Essential for reference work in journalism.   Z6940.C38

Merrill, John Calhoun. The world's great dailies : profiles of fifty newspapers / John Calhoun Merrill, Harold A. Fisher. N.Y. : Hastings House, [1980]. 399 p. : ill.   **AE133**
Offers profiles—historical notes, discussions of policies, strengths and weaknesses—of those newspapers which the editors believe "represent the very best in the world's journalism, regardless of how differently this journalism may manifest itself in different cultures and ideological contexts."—*Pref.* Opens with essays defining and discussing the context and hallmarks of newspaper greatness, global patterns of great dailies, history, and statistics. Gives front-page illustrations of each paper. Bibliographical footnotes; selected bibliography; index.   PN4731.M446

Price, Warren C. An annotated journalism bibliography, 1958–1968. Minneapolis : Univ. of Minnesota Pr., [1970]. 285 p.   **AE134**
Forms a supplement to Price's *The literature of journalism* (AE135), adding nearly 2,200 items (a few of them from the earlier period). Alphabetically arranged by author or other main entry, with a detailed subject index.   Z6940.P69

——————— The literature of journalism : an annotated bibliography. Minneapolis : Univ. of Minnesota Pr., [1959]. 489 p.   **AE135**
Intended to fill the gap between Carl L. Cannon, *Journalism : a bibliography* (N.Y. : N.Y. Public Library, 1924) and 1958. Lists more than 3,000 items (in English), most annotated. "The base of the work is frankly historical and biographical, with more than two-fifths of all titles in these two categories."—*Foreword.* Sections are included for selected works on press management, public opinion, radio and television, foreign press, etc. Classified arrangement with author, subject, and anonymous title index.

§ A classic bibliography providing historical information on journalism and law is: *A bibliography of law and journalism*, by William F. Swindler (N.Y. : Columbia Univ. Pr., 1947. 191 p.).   Z6940.P7

Wolseley, Roland Edgar. The journalist's bookshelf : an annotated and selected bibliography of United States print journalism / Roland E. Wolseley and Isabel Wolseley. 8th ed. Indianapolis : R.J. Berg, 1986. 400 p.   **AE136**
1st ed., 1939; 7th ed., 1961.

Provides annotated entries for 2,368 titles. Arranged in 42 broad subject areas that include books in certain categories not in other general bibliographies of journalism, such as Warren C. Price's *The literature of journalism* (AE135) (e.g., high school journalism and fiction relating to journalism). Author and title indexes. The 7th ed. was intended to supplement Carl L. Cannon's *Journalism : a bibliography* (N.Y. : N.Y. Public Library, 1924. 360 p.).   Z6940.W64

Dissertations

Journalism abstracts. v. 1 (1963)– . Minneapolis : Assoc. for Education in Journalism, 1963– . Annual.   **AE137**
Imprint varies.

On cover: M.A., M.S., and Ph.D. theses in journalism and mass communication.

Master's and doctoral theses are listed in separate alphabets by author. Subject index.

§ Annual listings of dissertations in journalism have also appeared in *Journalism quarterly*, 27–48 (1950–71). Title and coverage of these reports have varied from year to year: some are reports of research in progress by staff members and graduate students in American schools of journalism; others are limited to reports of doctoral dissertations completed.   PN4725.J67

Encyclopedias

Paneth, Donald. The encyclopedia of American journalism. N.Y. : Facts on File, [1983]. 548 p. : ill.   **AE138**

Attempts to cover all aspects of the field—history of journalism, types of media, the news-gathering process, people, organizations, styles, technology, court cases—with emphasis on "the idea and ideal of freedom of the press."—*Introd.* Cross-references, bibliographic references. A subject index groups entry words into broad subject categories (e.g., black journalists, comic strip artists, muckrakers, issues).
    PN4755.P26

Dictionaries

Kent, Ruth K. The language of journalism : a glossary of print-communication terms. [Kent, Ohio] : Kent State Univ. Pr., [1971, c1970]. 186 p. : ill.   **AE139**

Covers journalistic jargon, technical terms, graphic arts terms, and abbreviations most commonly used by the journalist. Lists sources of reference; partially annotated bibliography.   PN4728.K4

Koszyk, Kurt. Wörterbuch zur Publizistik / Kurt Koszyk, Karl Hugo Pruys. München-Pullach : Verlag Dokumentation, 1970. 539 p.   **AE140**

Originally publ. 1969 under title *DTV-Wörterbuch zur Publizistik.*

A dictionary of terms, many of the entries including extensive background information and bibliographic references. Indexes of names, subjects, and newspapers and periodicals mentioned in the text. Classed bibliography, p. 435–539.   PN4728.K67

Press surveys and directories

Works that treat broader aspects of the press—broadcast media as well as newspapers, historical as well as current material and world press surveys—are listed here. Foreign press surveys for particular countries or areas will be found under that country or area. Sources pertaining to the media may be found under Mass Media in the Economics section (CH).

Merrill, John Calhoun. The foreign press : a survey of the world's journalism / by John C. Merrill, Carter R. Bryan, [and] Marvin Alisky. Baton Rouge : Louisiana State Univ. Pr., [1970]. 365 p.   **AE141**

Previous ed., 1964: Merrill's original *Handbook of the foreign press* was publ. 1959.

Begins with surveys of the press in large areas (e.g., Africa, Asia, Europe) followed by surveys of individual countries. Each narrative survey covers statistics, information about lending newspapers, censorship and freedom of the press, legal position of journalists, news agencies, etc. The 1970 ed. includes an overview of the U.S. press and expansion of the African section.   PN4736.M39

World press encyclopedia / ed. by George Thomas Kurian. N.Y. : Facts on File, [1982]. 2 v. (1202 p.); graphs.   **AE142**

Aims to present "a definitive survey of the state of the press in 180 countries."—*Pref.* In four sections: International press; World's developed press systems; Smaller and developing press systems; Minimal and underdeveloped press systems. Essays consider a country's press on the economic, political, professional, and philosophic levels. For each country treats such topics as the economic framework, press laws, censorship, news agencies, education and training. Bibliographies, chronologies, and appendixes.   PN4735.W6

The world's news media : a comprehensive reference guide / ed. by Harry Drost. Detroit : Gale, c1991. 604 p.   **AE143**

Arranged by country, giving for each: brief history; factual information (literacy, newspaper circulation, numbers of radio receivers and television sets); news sources, press, and broadcasting; directory of newspapers and radio and television stations. After countries are sections on regional media in Africa, Asia-Pacific, Europe, and Middle East and North Africa, and a section on world media. Appendixes: (1) primary sources of information for each country (e.g., address of its Ministry of Information) and where one exists, the title of the country's official bulletin or journal; (2) newspapers publishers' associations; (3) journalists' associations; (4) international dialing codes.
    P90.W65

History

Guide to sources in American journalism history / ed. and comp. by Lucy Shelton Caswell. N.Y. : Greenwood, 1989. 319 p. (Bibliographies and indexes in mass media and communications, no. 2).   **AE144**

"Prepared under the auspices of the American Journalism Historians Association"—*t.p.*

In two parts, the first a collection of essays, most with bibliographies, discussing various aspects of research in the history of American journalism. The second part is a guide, arranged by state, to archival and manuscript sources, including many collections of personal papers. The archival guide has a subject index.   Z6951.G83

Mott, Frank Luther. American journalism : a history, 1690–1960. 3rd ed. N.Y. : Macmillan, [1962]. 901 p. : ill.   **AE145**

1st ed., 1941; 2nd ed., 1950.

A detailed history with bibliographical notes. The 3rd ed. includes a section on electronic media and the growth of the "mass audience" as it relates to U.S. journalism.   PN4855.M63

Schwarzlose, Richard Allen. Newspapers, a reference guide. N.Y. : Greenwood, 1987. 417 p.   **AE146**

Discusses the core literature about newspapers and journalism in brief essays written from historical perspective. Topics include newspaper histories, biographies, technologies, newspapers in society, and newspaper production. Discusses reference sources and periodicals, and includes a selected chronology of newspaper history.   Z6951.S35

Sloan, W. David. American journalism history : an annotated bibliography. N.Y. : Greenwood, 1989. 344 p. (Bibliographies and indexes in mass media and communications, no. 1).
    AE147

Books, articles, and dissertations written primarily in the 20th century and covering all aspects of American journalism history, are arranged by broad topic, and within each topic, alphabetically by author. Includes an annotated list of research guides and reference works on contemporary media, 1945 to the present. Author and subject index.   Z6951.S54

Biography

American magazine journalists, 1741–1850 / ed. by Sam G. Riley. Detroit : Gale, 1988. 430 p. : ill. (Dictionary of literary biography, v. 73).   **AE148**

§ Other volumes in this subseries, all ed. by Riley and publ. by Gale: *American magazine journalists, 1850–1900* (1989. 387 p. [Dictionary of literary biography, 79]); *American magazine journals, 1900–1960* (1990. 401 p. [Dictionary of literary biography, 91]).

These volumes in the *DLB* series offer biographical articles ranging in length from three to ten pages on 133 magazine journalists. The biographical and critical treatment of these subjects includes lists of their major writings, bibliographies of works about them, and the location of their manuscripts and papers.   PN4871.A47

American newspaper journalists, 1690–1872 / ed. by Perry J. Ashley. Detroit : Gale, 1985. 527 p. : ill. (Dictionary of literary biography, v. 43).   **AE149**

§ Other volumes in this subseries, all ed. by Ashley and publ. by Gale: *American newspaper journalists, 1873–1900* (1983. 392 p. [Dictionary of literary biography, 23]); *American newspaper journalists, 1901–1925* (1984. 385 p. [Dictionary of literary biography, 25]); *American newspaper journalists, 1926–1950* (1984. 410 p. [Dictionary of literary biography, 29]).

These volumes in the *DLB* series offer biographical articles ranging in length from three to ten pages on 214 journalists. The biographical and critical treatment of these subjects includes lists of their major writings, bibliographies of works about them, and the location of their manuscripts and papers.   PN4871.A49

Biographical dictionary of American journalism / ed. by Joseph P. McKerns. N.Y. : Greenwood, 1989. 820 p.   **AE150**

The alphabetically arranged entries of one to two pages cover "nearly 500 persons who contributed to the development of American journalism" (*Introd.*) in the fields of newspapers, magazines, radio, and television, from 1690 to the present. Each entry includes a brief bibliography. Appendixes include lists of women in journalism, minority and ethnic journalists, winners of major awards, and an index to journalists by specialty. Subject index.   PN4871.B56

Journalist biographies master index / Alan E. Abrams, ed. Detroit : Gale, [1979]. 380 p. (Gale biographical index series, no. 4).   **AE151**

Subtitle: A guide to 90,000 references to historical and contemporary journalists in 200 biographical directories and other sources.

In addition to the standard biographical sources referred to in the subtitle, "indexes textual references to individuals which appear in about 15 historical studies of the field of journalism."—*Introd.* A review in *Booklist* 88 (1 May 1981): 1209–11 notes "flaws in coverage"—e.g., spotty coverage of journalists listed in *Biography index*.
                    Z6940.J58

Taft, William H. Encyclopedia of twentieth-century journalists. N.Y. : Garland, 1986. 408 p. (Garland reference library of the humanities, vol. 493).   **AE152**

Contains biographical information on some 600 post-World War II newspaper, magazine, and television journalists. "The majority of persons here are alive" (*Introd.*) and the emphasis is on Americans. Subject index.   PN4871.T34

Who was who in journalism, 1925–1928. Detroit : Gale, [1978]. 664 p. (Gale composite biographical dictionary series, no. 4).   **AE153**

"A consolidation of all material appearing in the 1928 edition of *Who's who in journalism*, with unduplicated biographical entries from the 1925 edition of *Who's who in journalism*, originally compiled by M. N. Ask (1925 and 1928 editions) and S. Gershanek (1925 edition)."—*t.p.* The 1928 edition is reprinted as the main portion of the book; biographical sketches from the 1925 edition which were not updated or repeated in the 1928 edition are brought together in a separate alphabetical section printed on colored paper at the back of the volume.

Provides biographical sketches concerning 4,000 American and Canadian journalists active 1925–28. Indexed by specialty and geographic area.   PN4871.W65

AF

Government Publications

Important reference material may be found in publications issued by national, state, and municipal governments and by international governmental organizations. Government publications (often called government documents) chronicle the workings of governmental units, both currently and historically; provide information on many other subjects as well, including economics, history, education, health, labor, agriculture, and the arts; and contain large collections of national statistics.

The bibliographic control of government publications and access to the information in them are tied to their publishing and printing channels. Government printing cycles are determined by the creation and dissolution of political administrations and regimes, and by the organization and reorganization of governmental agencies and units. This uncertain publishing and printing situation, combined with the fact that most libraries have not included government publications in their catalogs, has fostered the creation of a government publications reference literature designed to assist readers and librarians in finding what they need in a voluminous body of material. This literature consists of catalogs, bibliographies, indexing and abstracting journals, and guides that help unravel the publishing trail of a title or agency and suggest research methods. The availability of machine-readable cataloging data for U.S. government publications, beginning in 1976, has made these materials more accessible as some libraries integrate records for government publications with records for other materials. Much information generated by government agencies is itself available in CD-ROMs or online bulletin boards that contain both bibliographic citations and the full texts of documents.

Greater user awareness of government publications has resulted in the creation of more sophisticated government reference tools. Benjamin Poore's *Descriptive catalogue of the government publications of the United States, 1774–1881* (AF97), while still necessary, stands alongside the multitude of Congressional Information Service (CIS) paper and CD-ROM indexes to congressional hearings. Joe Morehead and Mary Fetzer's *Introduction to United States government information sources* (AF73) provides an overview of U.S. government publications and a framework for research, while Jean Sears and Marilyn Moody's *Using government information sources : print and electronic* (AF62) gives guidance in the new technology.

For research in state publications, Susan Dow's *State document checklists : a historical bibliography* (AF140) is essential; its completeness makes it unnecessary for the present *Guide* to list state documents checklists. Likewise, Gloria Westfall's *Guide to official publications of foreign countries* (AF8) should be consulted in addition to the individual country listings found here. For indexes and bibliographies relating to special subjects, *see* those subjects.

INTERNATIONAL

General works

Guides

Emerging as a medium of information exchange concerning government publications is *Govdoc-L : online discussion of government document issues*, a discussion forum that takes place across computer networks through electronic mail. Topics discussed include: the Depository Library Program, reference needs, management of documents collections, and legislation affecting access to government information.

Baer, George W. International organizations, 1918–1945 : a guide to research and research materials. Rev. ed. Wilmington, Del. : Scholarly Resources Inc., 1991. 212 p.   **AF1**

General chapters cover archives of international organizations; state archives, published documents and private papers; and other collections and resources. There are topical chapters on planning for peace, 1919; disarmament; crises of the 1930s; mandates; minorities and refugees; and social and humanitarian activities. Additional chapters cover individual organizations (e.g., League of Nations), or groups of organizations. Index by author.   Z6464.A1B33

The bibliographic control of official publications / ed. by John E. Pemberton. Oxford : Pergamon, 1982. 172 p. : ill. (Guides to official publications, v. 11).   **AF2**

A collection of contributed essays by librarians from Australia, Canada, Ireland, the U.S., and the U.K. describing the systems developed in specific libraries for bibliographic control of official publications from international organizations as well as individual countries). The aim is to stimulate work toward a system which would be universally applicable.   Z1001.B5146

Cherns, J. J. Official publishing : an overview. An international survey and review of the role, organisation and principles of official publishing. Oxford : Pergamon, [1979]. 527 p. (Guides to official publications, v. 3).   **AF3**

Examines official publishing of 22 countries, the U.N. and its principal agencies, and a few other international bodies. Provides introductory information on the scope and importance of official publishing, a survey by country and international organization, and reviews the growth and control of publishing. Indexed.   Z286.G69C47

International information : documents, publications, and information systems of international governmental organizations / ed. by Peter I. Hajnal. Englewood, Colo. : Libraries Unlimited, 1988. 339 p. : ill.   **AF4**

A guide to aid researchers and librarians in understanding, selecting, organizing, and using a collection of publications of international intergovernmental organizations. The chapters, written by specialists, cover the organizational setting, intergovernmental organizations as publishers, bibliographic control, collection development, arrangement of collections, reference and information work, citation forms, documentation in microform, computerized information systems, and the user's perspective. Includes bibliography and an index by author, title, and subject.   Z688.I57I56

Reference service for publications of intergovernmental organizations : papers from an IFLA workshop, Paris, August 24, 1989 / Section on Government Information and Official Publications, Section on Bibliography, Section on Social Sciences Libraries, ed. by Alfred Kagan. München ; N.Y. : K. G. Saur, c1991. 158 p.   **AF5**

Topics of the nine papers range from general information on bibliographic services of international intergovernmental organizations to papers on specific organizations such as the World Bank, Organization for Economic Co-operation and Development, the U.N., the Organiza-

tion of American States, the World Health Organization, UNESCO, and the Vienna International Centre Library. Most papers include bibliographical references.

Roberts, John E. A guide to official gazettes and their contents. Wash. : Library of Congress, 1985. [204] p.   **AF6**

Superintendent of Documents number: LC42.8.G25.

On cover: Revised ed.

Aims "to create a reference tool to assist researchers unfamiliar with the legal publications of foreign jurisdictions in identifying and using official gazettes."—*Introd.* Includes entries for all sovereign nations and some semi-dependent entities. Gives current data only, not changes of title or references to earlier titles. Arranged alphabetically by country name, giving title of the gazette, commonly used abbreviation, frequency, language(s) of publication, list of gazette contents (with indication of whether or not international agreements and court decisions are included), frequency and arrangement of indexes, if any.   K520.R63

Bibliography

Dimitrov, Théodore Delchev. World bibliography of international documentation. Pleasantville, N.Y. : UNIFO, 1981. 2 v.   **AF7**

Contents: v. 1, International organizations; v. 2, Politics and world affairs.

First publ. under title: *Documents of international organisations* (London : Internat. Univ. Publ. ; Chicago : Amer. Libr. Assoc., 1973).

Vol. 1 provides a bibliography of secondary literature on the principal international organizations, as well as a list of their basic primary documents; references to collection development, cataloging, indexing, and other aspects of bibliographic control are also included. Vol. 2 provides bibliographic references on world politics, arms issues, and relevant journal titles. Appendixes list major U.N. conferences and holidays. Indexed by author, corporate body, and subject.   Z6481.D57

Guide to official publications of foreign countries / American Library Association, Government Documents Round Table. [Bethesda, Md.] : Congressional Information Service, c1990. 359 p.   **AF8**

Gloria Westfall, ed. in chief.

An extremely useful, selective, annotated bibliography of official publications issued by 157 countries that includes guides, directories, statistical sources, legislative proceedings, development plans, court reports, etc. Includes acquisition information. Arranged alphabetically by country, then by subject.   Z7164.G7G83

International bibliography. v. 1 (1973)–v. 19 (1991). N.Y. : Bowker and UNIPUB, 1973–91. Quarterly.   **AF9**

Continues: v. 1–10, 1973–Winter 1982, *International bibliography, information, documentation,* also referred to as *IBID.* Publ. by Kraus Internat., 1988–91.

An index to publications of international intergovernmental organizations, including the U.N. and related agencies. Includes sales publications, unpriced material issued by public information offices and selected other unpriced material available to the public. Entries for monographs are arranged by subject category and annotated. "Periodicals record" section lists the table of contents for each issue. Indexes by organization, title, and subject included in each issue; fourth quarterly issue has cumulative indexes for the year.   Z6482.I55

New York Public Library. Research Libraries. Catalog of government publications in the Research Libraries : the New York Public Library, Astor, Lenox & Tilden Foundations. Boston : G.K. Hall, 1972. 40 v.   **AF10**

Photoreproduction of the catalog cards of a collection of more than a million volumes of government publications. While the collection started in the late 1840s, it includes a group of American legislative publications printed before 1800. Arranged by political jurisdiction. Serials and monographs are listed separately under each agency; serials are arranged alphabetically, monographs according to publication date. Census material is arranged by numbered census. No subject entries.

———. ——— *Supplement 1974* (Boston : G.K. Hall, [1976]. 2 v.).

Continued by two annual series, *Bibliographic guide to government publications—U.S.* (AF83) and *Bibliographic guide to government publications—foreign* (AF148).   Z7164.G7N54

Palic, Vladimir M. Government publications : a guide to bibliographic tools. 4th ed. Wash. : Library of Congress, 1975. 441 p.   **AF11**

3rd ed., 1942, by James B. Childs, had title: *Government document bibliography in the United States and elsewhere.*

"This guide outlines bibliographic aids in the field of official publications issued by the United States, foreign countries, and international government organizations. It is intended to be a practical guide directing the researcher, the student, and, last but not least, the reference librarian to bibliographic tools which may help him to identify or locate the materials needed."—*Pref.* In three main sections: (1) United States of America; (2) International governmental organizations; (3) Foreign countries. Indexed.   Z7164.G7C5

Library resources

Directory of official publications in Scotland. Edinburgh : SWOP, Scottish Working Group on Official Publications, 1991. 110 p.   **AF12**

A guide to the main collections of official publications of national governments or international organizations in 14 major Scottish libraries. Arranged by library, the first section provides information about the library and the second indicates collection strengths for publications of national governments or international organizations. Collection strengths are labeled basic, intermediate, or extensive. Index by name of international organization or geographic term.

   Z7164.G7D56

Union lists

List of the serial publications of foreign governments, 1815–1931 / ed. by Winifred Gregory, for the American Council of Learned Societies, American Library Association, National Research Council. N.Y. : Wilson, 1932. 720 p.   **AF13**

Repr. : N.Y. : Kraus, 1966.

A union list, on the same general plan as the *Union list of serials* (AD226), for a type of serial publication excluded from that list, i.e., government serials, including only genuine government serials and omitting publications of universities, societies, etc., which are subsidized by a government. Arranged alphabetically by country name (except that Russia is in a separate list at the end), with subarrangement by government departments, bureaus, etc., and with indication of holdings of the various publications in some 85 American libraries.

   Z7164.G7L7

Periodicals

Government information quarterly. v. 1 ([Feb.] 1984)– . Greenwich, Conn. : JAI Pr., c1984– . Quarterly.   **AF14**

Intended for "documents librarians, government administrators, library administrators, record managers, students, and others interested in the role of government information."—*Editors.* Articles discuss government information issues on both the theoretical and the practical levels, and present current research findings. Reviews of government information reference works in each issue.   Z688.G6G68

Journal of government information : an international review of policy, issues and resources. v. 21, no. 1 (Jan./Feb. 1994)– . Tarrytown, N.Y. : Pergamon, 1994– . Bimonthly.   **AF15**

Continues: *Government publications review*, (v. 1 [1973]–v. 6 [1979]); split into: *Government publications review, Part A, Research*

articles (v. 7A, no. 1 [1980]–v. 8A, no. 6 [1981]) and *Government publications review, Part B, Acquisitions guide to significant government publications at all levles* (v. 7B, no. 1 [1980]–v. 8B, no. 6 [1981]); two parts merged to form: *Government publications review : an international journal of issues and information resources* (v. 9 [1982]–20 [1993]).

Covers "the field of documents production, distribution, library handling and use of documents at all levels of government: federal, state, and municipal, U.N. and international agencies and all countries."—*inside cover.* Articles, book reviews, bibliographies, and news updates describe the information activities of governmental units. The final issue of each year lists and annotates "Notable documents of the year," a selection and acquisitions tool.   Z7164.G7G69

Yearbooks

Yearbook of international organizations = Annuaire des organisations internationales. 1st ed. (1948)– . Brussels : Union of Internat. Assoc., 1948– . Irregular.   **AF16**

Publisher varies: 20th ed. (1983)– , Munich : K.G. Saur.

In English and French, varying with editions, 1951–80.

A comprehensive guide to international intergovernmental organizations. Vol. 1 : Organizational descriptions and cross-references. Arranged alphabetically by title; each description gives addresses, aims, structure, languages, staff, finance, consultative status, IGO relations, NGO relations, activities, events, publications, and members. Appendixes include a publications index and statistics on international organizations. Vol. 2 : Countries. Arranged by country, lists the organizations of which each country is a member. Vol. 3 : Subject guide and index.   JX1904.A42

Collections

International organization and integration : annotated basic documents and descriptive directory of international organizations and arrangements / Board of eds., P. J. G. Kapteyn ... [et al.]. 2nd, completely rev. ed. The Hague : Nijhoff, [1981–84]. v. 1–2 in 6 v. (In progress?).   **AF17**

1st ed. 1969.

Contents: v. I.A, The United Nations organization; v. I.B, Organizations related to the United Nations; v.II.A, European Communities; v. II.B–II.D, Organizations and arrangements of the northern hemisphere; v. II.E–II.J, Organizations and arrangements outside the northern hemisphere; v. II.K, Functional organizations and arrangements.

A large collection of documents relating to international organizations. The directory section of each volume describes the organizational structure of organizations or the background of treaties and includes a short bibliography. Full texts of treaties (that have been entered into force) and U.N. resolutions are in the documents section. Each volume includes an index.   JX171.I54

Peaslee, Amos Jenkins. International governmental organizations : constitutional documents. Rev. 3rd ed. / prep. by Dorothy Peaslee Xydis. The Hague : Nijhoff, 1974–[79]. pts. 1–5 in 5 v.   **AF18**

1st ed., 1956.

Contents: pt. 1, General and regional, political, economic, social, legal, defense (2 v.); pt. 2, Agriculture, commodities, fisheries, food, plants (1 v.); pts. 3–4, Education, culture, copyright, science, health (1 v.); pt. 5, Communications, transport, travel (1 v.).

Each volume, arranged alphabetically by organization, contains the basic constitutional documents of more than 200 "international organizations created by governments, and themselves of a governmental nature."—*Foreword.* Unofficial private organizations are not included.

Brief summaries of the history and constitutional development, membership, functions, organs, headquarters, etc., are given for each organization; selective bibliographies.

International governmental organizations

Clements, Frank A. Arab regional organizations. New Brunswick, N.J. : Transaction Publishers, c1992. 198 p. (International organizations series, v. 2).   **AF19**

An annotated bibliography covering major Arab regional organizations including the Arab League, Arab Monetary Fund, Organization of Arab Petroleum Exporting Countries, and the Gulf Cooperation Council. Also includes Arab aid organizations and international organizations that operate in the region. Index by author, title, and subject.   Z7165.A67C58

Fredland, Richard A. A guide to African international organisations. London ; N.Y. : Zell, 1990. [432] p. : ill., maps.   **AF20**

Provides information on 400 international intergovernmental organizations that have appeared in Africa during the 20th century. Eight sections, including background, analysis of international organizations, directory, biographical data and chronology, tables and appendixes, maps, bibliography. Includes index.   JX1995.F67

Speeckaert, Georges Patrick. Bibliographie sélective sur l'organisation internationale, 1885–1964 = Select bibliography on international organization. Brussels : Union des associations internationales, 1965. 150 p. (International Federation for Documentation. Publication, no. 361 ; Union of International Associations. Publication, no. 191).   **AF21**

A revision of the author's *International institutions and international organization* (1956), dropping numerous citations from the earlier work and adding many new ones. In two parts, the first listing references on international organization in general; the second devoted to materials on individual organizations. More than 1,000 entries; author index.   Z6464.I6S68

European Communities

The Arthur Andersen European Community sourcebook : the most comprehensive, authoritative reference guide ever assembled on the European market / Arthur Andersen & Co. ; Iain P.A. Stitt, consulting ed.; John J. McGonagle, Jr., ed. Chicago : Triumph Books, 1991. 499 p.   **AF22**

Intended to serve as "a comprehensive guide to the Single Market program and the vast array of information sources available."—*Introd.* In five parts: (1) The European Community and the single market of 1991, considers both the EC's history and key institutions, strategies, and legislation; (2) Profiles of the European Community member states, includes, in addition to standard background information, data on establishing businesses and business taxation practices in each member country; (3) Sources on EC 1992 by topic (e.g., employment and labor, regulation of business and competition); (4) Sources on EC 1992 by industry, with information on 11 different industry sectors; and (5) Appendixes and indexes, with eight appendixes (e.g., bibliographies, list of acronyms and abbreviations, contact directories), an index of associations and organizations, and a general subject index.   HC241.2.A755

Euro who's who : who's who in the European Communities and in the other European organizations. 4th ed. (1991–92)– . Bruxelles : Editions delta, 1991– .   **AF23**

Biographical information on people who work in the European Communities and other European organizations. Arranged in one alphabetical sequence. No indexes.   JN15.W47

Paxton, John. European Communities. New Brunswick, N.J. : Transaction Publishers, c1992. 182 p. : map. (International organizations series, v. 1).   **AF24**

An annotated, comprehensive bibliography on the European Communities. Chapters cover history, biography, publications, periodicals, directories, bibliographies and databases, as well as topics such as energy policy, transport policy, etc. Index by author, title, subject.   Z7165.E8P34

•SCAD+ CD : multilingual European Community bibliographic database [database]. [Bruxelles] : Commission of the European Communities : EPMS bv : Context Ltd., 1992– .   **AF25**

Issued quarterly.

SCAD (Système Communautaire d'Accèss á la Documentation) is the primary bibliographic file of European Community publications. Includes references to the main community legal texts and preparatory documents, official publications and European institution documents, articles relating to the community taken from more than 2,000 journals, and statements and opinions from industry, employers' organizations and trade unions. Two search modes: Subject search form, and a more advanced Full form searching. Searchable fields include subject, title, abstract, document type, source language, publication year, personal and corporate authors, and references to related publications.

Thomson, Ian. The documentation of the European Communities : a guide. London ; N. Y. : Mansell, 1989. 382 p.   **AF26**

Describes the current range of publications produced by organs of the European Community, including primary and secondary legislation and explanatory and background materials. In two parts: an introduction to the EC and its publications; individual chapters on organs of the EC (e.g., European Parliament, Council of Ministers, Court of Justice), providing for each a description of its structure and a list of publications. Appendixes include lists of depository libraries, information offices, and online services, as well as a table of regularly published series with references to their discussion in the text. General subject index.   Z7165.E8T47

League of Nations

Aufricht, Hans. Guide to League of Nations publications : a bibliographical survey of the work of the League, 1920–1947. N.Y. : Columbia Univ. Pr., 1951. 682 p.   **AF27**

Repr. : N.Y. : AMS Pr., 1966.

A selective bibliography of publications of the League, including confidential items and some that were never put on public sale as well as publications of the International Labor Office and the Permanent Court of International Justice. Arranged by broad subject with an author and subject index. Appendixes include documents relating to the League, documents relating to the International Labor Organization and the Permanent Court of International Justice, and documents relating to the transfer of League assets and functions to the U.N.   Z6473.A85

Birchfield, Mary Eva. Consolidated catalog of League of Nations publications, offered for sale. Dobbs Ferry, N.Y. : Oceana, 1976. 477 p.   **AF28**

Consolidates the entries from the League's *Catalog of publications, 1930–35* and its supplements, and includes additional material from M. J. Carroll's *Key to League of Nations documents* (1920–29, with supplements through 1947). Arrangement is by category (e.g., Assembly, Council, Library, Health, Social Questions, Legal, etc.), then chronologically unless some other arrangement is dictated for ease of use. Indexes by official number, sales number, and subject/title.   Z6479.Z9B57

Reno, Edward A. League of Nations documents, 1919–1946 : a descriptive guide and key to the microfilm collection. New Haven, Conn. : Research Publ., 1973–75. 3 v.   **AF29**

Contents: v. 1, Subject categories IA through IV; v. 2, Subject categories V through VII; C.P.M. documents; Minutes and reports of the Permanent Mandates Commission; and 19/F/– , 19/6/– , 20/6/– ,

21/6/– , Documents; v. 3, Subject categories VIII through General, serial publications reel index, Minutes of the Directors' meetings reel index.

A guide prepared for use with the microfilm edition of League of Nations documents published by Research Publications, Inc. This microfilm set is presumably as complete as any that is likely to be assembled. The guide should, however, be independently useful.

Documents have been grouped in 18 categories for the microfilm edition: IA, Administrative Commissions; IB, Minorities; IIA, Financial questions; IIB, Economic questions; III, Health; IV, Social questions; V, Legal questions; VIA, Mandates; VIB, Slavery; VII, Political questions; VIII, Communications and transit; IX, Disarmament; X, Financial administration of the League of Nations; XI, Traffic in opium and other dangerous drugs; XIIA, Intellectual cooperation; XIIB, International Bureaux; XIII, Refugees; G, General. v.3 includes a consolidated index for subject categories IA through G, "followed by separate listings for the Permanent Mandates Commission (C.P.M.) Documents, the Minutes and Reports of the Permanent Mandates Commission, and the collection of Secretariat communications known as the 19/F/– , 19/6/– , 20/6/– , and 21/6/– Series."—*p. v.*

For each item is given: the document number, place of issue if other than Geneva, subject title of the document, and a descriptive abstract. Listings in the guide follow the filming sequence, and reel indicators are provided at appropriate intervals.   Z6473.R45

United Nations

Birchfield, Mary Eva. The complete reference guide to United Nations sales publications, 1946–1978. Pleasantville, N.Y. : UNIFO Publ., 1982. 2 v.   **AF30**
Contents: v.1, The catalogue, comp. and ed. by Mary Eva Birchfield; v.2, Indexes: sales number index, title index, comp. by Mary Eva Birchfield; key word in context index, comp. by Jacqueline Coolman.

"The body of the Catalogue text is a listing of publications arranged alphabetically from A/– (Assembly) to WFC/– (World Food Council). ... Information for each publication includes titles, dates ... , languages of publication, pagination, and sales number."—*Introd.* Title index includes complete and shortened version, and subtitles. Subject approach is through key-word-in-context index.

Z6485.Z9B57

Brimmer, Brenda. A guide to the use of United Nations documents : including reference to the specialized agencies and special U.N. bodies / Brenda Brimmer [et al.]. Dobbs Ferry, N.Y. : Oceana, 1962. 272 p. (New York University. Libraries. Occasional papers, no. 3.).   **AF31**
A guide for the researcher or librarian who works with U.N. publications. Explains the documentation system, and how to research in various size libraries. Basic tools and guides for research by U.N. organ, specialized and related agency, or subject are explained.

Z674.N47 no. 3

A chronology and fact book of the United Nations. 1941-1961– . Dobbs Ferry, N.Y. : Oceana Publ., 1961– . Triennial.   **AF32**
An earlier publication (1959) had title: *A chronology of the United Nations, 1941–1958.*

Issued as a supplement to *Annual review of United Nations affairs.*

New editions with extended period of coverage issued at irregular intervals. 8th ed., 1992, covers 1941–91.

Three parts: Chronology (lists major events in the history of the U.N.), Tables (contain basic information), Documents (provides texts of major U.N. publications).   JX1977.A1C48

A comprehensive handbook of the United Nations : a documentary presentation in two volumes / comp. and ed. by Minchuan Ku. N.Y. : Monarch Pr., 1978. 2 v. : ill.   **AF33**
Vol. 1 covers background material, organizational documents and procedural rules of the principal organs of the United Nations; v. 2

treats the specialized agencies, nongovernmental organizations having relations with the U.N., trusteeship agreements, regional agencies, and General Assembly resolutions. Bibliography; indexed.

JX1977.C6123

Hajnal, Peter I. Guide to United Nations organization, documentation & publishing for students, researchers, librarians. Dobbs Ferry, N.Y. : Oceana, 1978. 450 p.   **AF34**
In five parts: (1) structure, functions and evolution of the U.N. and its relation to other organizations within and outside the U.N. system; (2) publishing and documentation patterns; (3) use, acquisition, and organization of U.N. publications; (4) a select, annotated bibliography of works by and about the U.N.; (5) a selection of important documents. Concludes with an appendix describing intergovernmental organizations related to the U.N.   JX1977.H22

Hüfner, Klaus. The United Nations system, international bibliography = Das System der Vereinten Nationen, internationale Bibliographie / Klaus Hüfner, Jens Naumann. München : Verlag Dokumentation, 1976–[1991?]. v. 1–5 in 8. (In progress).   **AF35**
A publication of the Research Unit of the German United Nations Association, Bonn/Berlin.

Prefatory matter and headings in English and German.

Contents: v. 1, The United Nations system: an international bibliography ... 1945–65; v. 2A, Learned journals, 1965–70; v. 2B, Learned journals, 1971–75; v. 3A, Monographs and articles in collected volumes 1965–1970; v. 3B, Monographs and articles in collective volumes, 1971–1975; v. 4A, Learned journals, 1976–1980; v. 4B, Learned journals, 1981–1985; v. 5A, Monographs and articles in collective volumes 1976–1980.

A bibliography of secondary literature published in English, German, and French on the U.N. and its specialized agencies. Vol. 1 is a reprint of Hüfner's *Zwanzig Jähre Vereinte Nationen ... 1945–1965.* Vols. 2–3 cover articles produced between 1965 and 1975 in about 360 journals and 13,300 books and essays. The classification scheme is in four sections: (1) The United Nations as part of the empirical solutions for four main functional problems of world society [polity, adaptation, normative integration, cultural problems]; (2) The United Nations system and its internal structures and processes; (3) The United Nations system—institutional and organizational arrangements; (4) The United Nations system—actual and potential areas of activity. Detailed table of contents; author index.   Z6481.H83

Index to proceedings of the Economic and Social Council. 1st spec. sess., 14th sess., 14th sess., resumed (24 Mar. 1952, 20 May to 1 Aug 1952, 16 and 19 Dec. 1952)– . N.Y. : United Nations, 1953– . Annual.   **AF36**
An index to the published meeting records of the U.N. Economic and Social Council. Several sessions may be included in each issue. For each session there is a checklist of meetings, agenda, subject index, index to speeches, a list of resolutions, documents, and reports of the sessional committees.   Z7161.I5

Index to proceedings of the General Assembly. 5th session (19 Sept. 1950 to 5 Nov. 1951)– . N.Y. : United Nations, 1953– . Irregular.   **AF37**
An index to the published meeting records of the U.N. General Assembly. Issued in two parts: (1) includes sessional information, checklist of meetings, agenda, subject index, list of documents, reports of the main and procedural committees, list of resolutions, and voting chart of resolutions adopted by recorded or roll-call vote; (2) index to speeches by corporate name/country, speaker, or subject.

JX1977.A44

Index to proceedings of the Security Council / Dag Hammarskjöld Library. 19th year (1964)– . N.Y. : United Nations, 1965– . Annual.   **AF38**
An index to the published meeting records of the U.N. Security Council. Includes organizational information, checklist of meetings, agenda, subject index, index to speeches, list of documents, resolutions adopted, and voting chart of resolutions.   JX1977.A5

Index to proceedings of the Trusteeship Council. 11th session (June to 24 July 1952 and 20 Nov. to 3 Dec. 1952)– . N.Y. : United Nations, 1953– . Annual.   **AF39**

Issued by the United Nations Headquarters Library, 1952–1963; by the Dag Hammarskjöld Library since 1964.

An index to the published meeting records of the U.N. Trusteeship Council. Includes sessional information, checklist of meetings, agenda, subject index, index to speeches and list of documents.

JX4021.U32

•**Index to United Nations documents and publications** [databasc]. New Caanan, Conn. : Newsbank/Readex, 1990– .   **AF40**

Available on CD-ROM, updated monthly, each disc being cumulative.

In two sections: (1) The index to U.N. documents and publications; contains references to official records, documents, mimeographed items, and periodicals. (2) The full-text U.N. resolutions and decisions section; includes texts of resolutions as well as voting records on them. Provisional verbatim records are from full meetings of the U.N. General Assembly and the Security Council. Two levels of searching are offered and searches can be made on all fields, subjects, session, author, title, document date, document number, U.N. sales number, document type, and country.

Osmańszyk, Edmund Jan. The encyclopedia of the United Nations and international agreements. 2nd ed. London ; N.Y. : Taylor & Francis, 1990. 1220 p.   **AF41**

1st ed., 1985.

A compendium of political, economic, and social information. Describes the structure of the U.N., its specialized agencies and the organizations that cooperate with it. Reprints treaties, international agreements, and conventions from the late 19th and 20th centuries in part or in their entirety. Explains terminology from politics, economics, the military, geography, sociology, diplomacy, and international law. Arranged in one alphabetical sequence. Most entries conclude with bibliographical references.   JX1977.O8213

Who's who in the United Nations and related agencies. 2nd ed. / Stanley R. Greenfield, ed. Detroit : Omnigraphics, Inc., c1992. 850 p.   **AF42**

A biographical directory of the U.N. system during 1991. Includes many Ambassadors to the U.N. and the offices in New York, Geneva, and Vienna. Biographical entries are in one alphabetical sequence. Numerous appendixes list U.N. depository libraries, World Federation of U.N. Associations, U.N. Associations, Presidents of the General Assembly, etc. Index by organization and nationality.

JX1977.W467

General works

Guides

Directory of United Nations databases and information systems / compiled by the Advisory Committee for the Co-ordination of Information Systems (ACCIS). 1985– . N.Y. : United Nations, 1984– .   **AF43**

4th ed. (1990)– have title: *Directory of United Nations databases and information services.*

A directory of 872 selected information services and databases operated directly by or in association with the organizations of the U.N. system. Section 1 describes each organization, listing its information services and databases. Section 2 is a subject list of services. Section 3 lists databases under broad subject categories. Index by name/acronym and subject.   JX1977.8.D6D573

Everyone's United Nations. Ed. 9– . N.Y. : United Nations, 1979– . Irregular.   **AF44**

Continues *Everyman's United Nations* (1948–68).

A basic reference work describing the work of the U.N. and the 18 intergovernmental agencies associated with it. Pt. 1 describes the structure of the U.N., pt. 2 its work. The latter part has chapters on U.N. functions, such as peacemaking, human rights, etc. Appendixes include the U.N. Charter, the Statute of the International Court of Justice, and the Universal Declaration of Human Rights. Index by author and subject.   JX1977.A37E9

Hajnal, Peter I. Directory of United Nations documentary and archival sources. [Hanover, N.H.] : Academic Council on the United Nations System ; Millwood, N.Y. : Kraus Internat. ; [N.Y.] : United Nations, 1991. 106 p.   **AF45**

Prepared in co-operation with the United Nations' Dag Hammarskjöld Library.

Introductory chapters cover U.N. publishing and distribution in general. Subject chapters range from environment to peace and security. Research resources include collections of documents; statistics; archival resources; and catalogs, indexes, guides, and other bibliographic tools. Author and title indexes.   JX1977.8.D6H34

Bibliography

Books in print of the United Nations system. 1st ed. (1992)– . N.Y. : United Nations, c1992– .   **AF46**

Comp. by the Advisory Committee for the Co-ordination of Information Systems.

A comprehensive list of more than 14,000 publications available from the U.N. system sales offices, copublishers, and external publishers who publish for the system. Includes publications of specialized agencies, such as the ILO, FAO, IMF, World Bank, etc. Each publication has one entry in the "Descriptive list of publications" section, which is arranged by topic. Index by title, series, organization, and ISBN. Also includes a list of sales office/agents and publishers.

Z6485.B6

Directory of United Nations serial publications / comp. by the Advisory Committee for the Co-ordination of Information Systems (ACCIS). 1988– . N.Y. : United Nations, 1988– .   **AF47**

A source of ordering and bibliographic information for 4,000 serial titles published by 38 U.N. organizations. Some of those organizations include the U.N. itself, and U.N. specialized agencies such as FAO, GATT, IAEA, IMO, IMF, etc. Each serial is thoroughly described. Earlier and later titles, and other language editions are listed. Arranged by title; includes organization, subject, and ISSN indexes. Addresses of U.N. headquarters publications offices are included.

Z6482.R43

Catalogs and indexes

UNDOC : current index ; United Nations documents index. v. 1 (Jan./Feb. 1979)– . N.Y. : United Nations, 1979– . Quarterly with annual microfiche cumulation.   **AF48**

Successor to *UNDEX.*

Frequency varies; 10 nos. per yr.; annual cumulation (1979–83).

Each issue is composed of: (1) checklist of documents and publications; (2) list of official records; (3) list of sales publications; (4) list of documents republished; (5) new document series symbols; (6) U.N. maps included in documents; (7) U.N. sheet maps; and (8) subject, personal/corporate name, and title indexes. Annual cumulative index includes (1) documents and publications; and (2) subject, name, and title indexes.   JX1977.A2

United Nations. UNDEX : United Nations documents index. Series A: Subject index. v. 1 (Jan. 1970)–9 (1978). N.Y. : United Nations, 1970–80. Monthly (except July and Aug.).   **AF49**

ST/LIB/SER.1/A.

Provides the information needed for locating a document on a given topic through its U.N. document symbol. Includes "references to the subject matter of documents and publications issued by the United Nations for which analytical annotations have been stored in computer-based files."—*Introd. note.* The index entry contains the subject (given in fairly precise terminology), type of document (e.g., Decisions, Meeting records, Voting), and document symbol.

—————. —————. *Series B: Country index* (v. 1–9, Jan. 1970–Dec. 1978. N.Y., 1970–78. Monthly [except July and Aug.] [ST/LIB/SER. 1/B]).

An alphabetical listing by member states, indicating participation in U.N. activities. Name of country is followed by type of action or participating (voting, statements in debates, documents submitted, etc.), subject on which action was taken, and document symbol.

—————. —————. *Series C: List of documents issued* (v. 1–6, Jan. 1974–Jan 1979. N.Y., 1974–79. Monthly [except July and Aug.] [ST/LIB/SER.1/C]).

Prepared by conventional methods rather than computer techniques used for Series A and B (above). The three series supersede the *United Nations documents index, 1950–73* (AF54).

Series C "contains a listing and the bibliographical description of all documents and publications of the United Nations, except restricted material and internal papers, and all printed publications of the International Court of Justice."—*Introd. note.* Coverage of each issue is limited to specific series of documents, following a set pattern outlined in the prefatory note. Entry is by series symbol; gives full information on language versions, etc.

A partial cumulation was published as: *UNDEX Series "C": cumulative edition, 1974–77* (White Plains, N.Y. UNIFO Publ., [1979–80]. 4 v.).

Contents: v. 1, General Assembly; v. 2, ECOSOC, Secretariat, and Regional Economic Commissions; v. 3, Security Council, Trusteeship Council, International Court of Justice, and miscellaneous; v. 4, [Supplement] 1978.

Comp. and ed. by Milton Mittleman and Mina Pease.

Cumulates 40 issues of *UNDEX series C* published between 1974 and 1978. Listings are by agency and document series number, with microfiche availability indicated.

United Nations. Dag Hammarskjöld Library. United Nations documents index : cumulative checklist. v. 14 (1963)–24 (1973). N.Y. : United Nations, 1964–75. Annual.   **AF50**
ST/LIB/SER.E/CUM.

Supersedes the monthly issues of *United Nations documents index* (AF54); also indexed by that publication's annual cumulative index.

Contains consolidated lists, by symbol, of all documents and publications issued by the U.N. and the International Court of Justice during the year.

§ Beginning 1974, *United Nations document index* was superseded by: *UNDEX* (AF49).

United Nations documents index : United Nations and specialized agencies documents and publications. Cumulated index, volumes 1–13, 1950–1962. N.Y. : Kraus-Thomson, 1974. 4 v.   **AF51**

Cumulates in a single alphabetical sequence the author and subject indexes for the first 13 v. of the series.

—————————— Checklist of United Nations documents, 1946–49. N.Y., 1949–53. ST/LIB/SER.F.   **AF52**

Originally intended to be "a complete list of the documents issued by the organs of the United Nations" (*Pref.*), printed and mimeographed. Issued in parts, each one devoted to the documents of a particular unit. Every part issued in consecutive numbers, the initial numbers covering 1946–49.

Very detailed indexing, with information as to original publication and where documents were republished, if any. Detailed subject index.

Continued in part by *United Nations documents index* (AF54).
                                                                    JX1977.A2

—————————— List of United Nations document series symbols. Sept. 1952– . N.Y. : United Nations, 1952– . Irregular.
                                                                    AF53

Title varies: 1952, *Consolidated list of United Nations document series symbols*; 1955, *United Nations document series symbols*; 1978, *United Nations document series symbols, 1946–1977.*

The 1984 edition is entitled *United Nations document series symbols, 1978–1984* and consists of (1) List of symbols, which identifies issuing body, subsidiary organization, and title of conference or meeting with date that series symbol was first used; (2) Subject index, (3) Corporate name index, and (4) Series title index.   JX1977.A24

—————————— United Nations documents index. v.1 (Jan. 1950)–24 (Dec. 1973). [N.Y.] : United Nations. Dag Hammarskjöld Library, 1950–73. Monthly.   **AF54**
ST/LIB/SER.E.

Often referred to as *UNDI.*

Indexes to v.23–24 not published.

Each volume includes an annual cumulative index which supersedes indexes of the monthly issues; beginning with v.14 (1963) the monthly issues were superseded at the end of the year by the index and the annual *United Nations documents index: cumulative checklist* (AF50).   JX1977.A2

Periodicals

International documents review : the weekly newsletter on the United Nations. 1990– . N.Y. : Impact Communications Consultants. 46 no. a year.   **AF55**

A weekly newsletter devoted to happenings in the U.N. The "Documents" section describes U.N. reports issued that week and includes their U.N. symbol numbers. The "Communications" section describes letters and reports from U.N. member countries and includes their U.N. symbol numbers. These two sections are useful for finding U.N. symbol numbers for very current publications. Other sections include "Meetings" and "Secretary General."   JX1977.A1I58

Yearbooks

United Nations. Yearbook of the United Nations. 1946/47– . N.Y. : United Nations, Dept. of Public Information, 1947– . Annual.   **AF56**

The third yearbook covered Sept. 21, 1948 to Dec. 31, 1949. Each succeeding volume covers a calendar year.

Summarizes the activities, proceedings, and decisions of the U.N. Vol. 1, 1946/47, covers the origin and the evolution of the U.N., the 1st General Assembly, and the organization and work of subsidiary and allied organizations. Includes documentary bibliography, subject index, index of names, aand texts of important resolutions.

                                                                    JX1977.A37Y4

International Monetary Fund

Salda, Anne C. M. The International Monetary Fund. New Brunswick, N.J. : Transaction Publishers, c1992. 295 p. (International organizations series, v. 4).   **AF57**

An annotated bibliography that includes sections on history, organization, policies and regulatory functions, statistics, periodicals, and bibliographies. A "Relations with areas and countries" section includes listings for 64 individual countries. Index by author, title, and subject.   Z7164.F5S2 1

UN Educational, Scientific & Cultural Organization

Hajnal, Peter I. Guide to Unesco. London ; N.Y. : Oceana, 1983. 578 p.   **AF58**

In three main parts: background, structure, activities and financing; modes of action; annotated bibliography of selected works by and about Unesco. Appendixes; index.   AS4.U83H33

•**UNESCO databases** [database]. [Lanham, Md.? : UNIPUB?].   **AF59**

Available on CD-ROM.

A collection of 10 bibliographic and reference databases, in English, Spanish, or French. Includes: UNESBIB, records of Unesco publications 1946 to the present; AIDS, sources to use for AIDS prevention in schools; IAUDOC, references on higher education worldwide; IBEDOCS, references on education, literacy; ICOMMOS, references to worldwide literature on all aspects of museum works; DARE, references to social science research and training institutions worldwide; ENERGY, references on sources of energy; UNESDATA, a description of databases produced at Unesco headquarters; ISISDIF, a list of national distributors of Micro CDS/SIS software; and UNESIS, a description of 33 Unesco regional information services. Two search modes, assisted and expert. Searchable fields include author, institution, keyword, title, document type, language, country of publication, and date of publication.

United Nations Educational, Scientific and Cultural Organization. Bibliography of publications issued by Unesco or under its auspices : the first twenty-five years, 1946 to 1971. Paris, 1973. 385 p.   **AF60**

Title page also in French; introductory matter and captions in French and English.

More than 5,000 books and journals are arranged according to the Universal Decimal Classification and indexed by author and title. Official records and publications are grouped separately at the beginning of the classification, and are not repeated in the bibliography.

————. *Unesco list of documents and publications* ([Paris] : Unesco, 1972– . Quarterly with annual cumulation).

First two cumulative volumes covered 1972–76 and 1977–80; thereafter, cumulative volumes cover three years.

A comprehensive bibliography of all documentation produced by Unesco during the period of coverage. In two parts: (1) Masterfile listing for all items includes bibliographic description, descriptors, identifiers, and subject headings; (2) Indexes by subject, personal name, meeting and corporate body, and title and series.   Z6483.U5U47

UNITED STATES

General Works

Guides

Management of government information resources in libraries / ed. by Diane H. Smith. Englewood, Colo. : Libraries Unlimited, 1993. 260 p. : ill.   **AF61**

Designed "as a textbook for those learning about government information resources and the management of such collections."—*Introd.* Reviews recent changes in technology and economics and discusses their impact on government documents reference service and collection processing. Chapters are by practitioners in the field and cover collection development, acquisitions, bibliographic control and access, reference service, staff training, bibliographic instruction, the politics of documents librarianship, and costs and benefits of running a depository collection. Selected bibliography. Author, subject, title index.   Z675.D63S6

Sears, Jean L. Using government information sources : print and electronic / by Jean L. Sears and Marilyn K. Moody. 2nd ed. Phoenix : Oryx, 1994. 539 p. : charts, facsims.   **AF62**

A revision of the authors' 1985/86 ed., *Using government publications* (2 v.).

Contains substantial coverage of electronic formats for government information. The book's "purpose is ... to provide a guide to the most commonly used government information sources and an introduction to related research strategies."—*Pref.* Divided into four main sections: the subject search, the agency search, the statistical search, and special techniques. Checklists of sources in each section include title, issuing agency, Superintendent of Documents classification number, item number, and *American statistics index (ASI)* (CG96) abstract number if the item is available in that source. Appendix contains agency and publisher addresses. Author, title, subject index.   Z1223.Z7S4

Williams, Wiley J. Subject guide to major United States government publications. 2nd. ed., rev. and expanded. Chicago : Amer. Libr. Assoc., 1987. 257 p.   **AF63**

An alphabetical subject guide listing nearly 1,000 major government information resources. Annotations include title, issuing agency, date of publication, pagination, and Superintendent of Documents classification number. Updates Ellen Jackson's *Subject guide to major United States publications* (Chicago : Amer. Libr. Assoc., 1968), and supplements other guides, many of which are listed in Williams's Appendix I. Title index.   Z1223.Z7J32

Bibliography

•**CQ's Washington alert** [database]. [Wash.] : Congressional Quarterly Inc.   **AF64**

Available online, updated daily. Accompanied by a looseleaf reference guide.

An online legislative tracking service containing multiple databases. Contains the texts of bills, *Congressional record* (AF127), Congressional committee reports, *Congressional Quarterly weekly report* (CJ209), *CQ researcher*, selected hearing transcripts, and *Federal register* (CK182 note). Also provides access to European Community news, state legal citations, and major American newspapers.

The federal data base finder. [1st ed.] (1984–85)– . Potomac, Md. : Information USA, Inc., c1984– .   **AF65**

Subtitle: A directory of free and fee-based data bases and files available from the federal government.

Issue for 1987 has title: *Federal database finder.*

Place of publication and compilers vary; comp. by Matthew Lesko, 1990– .

Lists "thousands of data bases and data files from ... Federal departments ... independent agencies, and the legislative, executive and judicial branches."—*Introd.* Departmental and agency entries are arranged alphabetically. Annotations generally include technical specifications, equipment requirements, and ordering information. Subject index.   QA76.9.D32F4

Huls, Mary Ellen. United States government documents on women, 1800–1990 : a comprehensive bibliography. Westport, Conn. : Greenwood, 1993. 2 v. (Bibliographies and indexes in women's studies, no. 17–18).   **AF66**

For annotation, *see* CC494.   Z7964.U49H85

•**Legi-Slate** [database]. [Wash. : Legi-Slate, Inc., 1980?]– .   **AF67**

Accompanied by a looseleaf reference manual.

An online legislative tracking service providing bill status, legislative histories, and voting records. Contains the texts of bills, committee reports, selected hearings, *Congressional record* (AF127), *United*

States code (CK177), *Federal register* (CK182 *note*), and *Code of federal regulations* (CK182). Other files include information on members of Congress and several news services.

Periodicals

DttP. Documents to the people. v. 3 (Sept. 1974)– . [College Park, Md.] : American Libr. Assoc., Government Documents Round Table. Quarterly.   **AF68**

Frequency varies; quarterly since 1984.

The official publication of the Government Documents Round Table (GODORT) of the American Library Association. Contains articles on all aspects of documents librarianship and reports on the organization's activities. Reviews current local, state, national, foreign, and international government publications. Annual indexes.

Style manuals

Garner, Diane L. The complete guide to citing government information resources : a manual for writers & librarians. Rev. ed. / by Diane L. Garner, Diane H. Smith. Bethesda, Md. : Congressional Information Service, c1993. 222 p.   **AF69**

A revised and expanded edition of Garner and Smith's *Complete guide to citing government documents* (1984).

Publ. for the Government Documents Round Table, American Library Association.

Intended to supplement standard style and citation manuals. Provides specific examples for citing government information resources of U.S., state, local, and regional governments, international/intergovernmental organizations, foreign governments, and government information in electronic format. Appendixes list other style manuals and reference sources for government information. Includes a brief glossary of terms. Indexed.   Z7164.G7G37

Federal publications

Guides

Boyd, Anne Morris. United States government publications. 3rd ed. / rev. by Rae Elizabeth Rips. N.Y. : Wilson, 1949. 627 p.   **AF70**

Repr., with corrections: N.Y. : Wilson, 1952.

1st ed., 1931; 2nd ed., 1940.

An invaluable guide for information on the history, organization, and duties of government agencies up to July 1948. After a discussion of the nature, printing, and distribution of catalogs and indexes of U.S. government publications, the arrangement of material then follows that of the organization of the government, i.e., the legislative, judicial, and executive branches. Lists and describes the important and typical publications of Congress, the courts, the departments, and independent agencies and institutions, but does not attempt to be complete. Extensive index by subject, agency, and title.   Z1223.Z7B7

D'Aleo, Richard J. FEDfind : your key to finding federal government information : a directory of information sources, products, and services. 2nd ed. Springfield, Va. : ICUC Pr., 1986. 480 p. : ill.   **AF71**

Designed to help individuals locate both products and services, and information from the federal government. Arranged by department with brief descriptions of the different branches and their services and publications. Subject and organization index.   Z1223.Z7D3

Hernon, Peter. Developing collections of U.S. government publications / by Peter Hernon, Gary R. Purcell. Greenwich, Conn. : Jai Pr., c1982. 289 p. (Foundations in library and information science, v. 12).   **AF72**

Intended for "practicing librarians, library educators, and library science students."—*Pref.* Chapters outline collection development principles to be applied to government publications collections. Includes the texts of collection development policies in use in government publications departments in seven academic institutions. Bibliography; author, title, subject indexes.   Z688.G6H468

Morehead, Joe. Introduction to United States government information sources / Joe Morehead and Mary Fetzer. 4th ed. Englewood, Colo. : Libraries Unlimited, 1992. 474 p.   **AF73**

1st ed., 1975. Morehead's 3rd ed. (1983) had title: *Introduction to United States public documents.*

A guide for librarians, library school students, and the public. Intends "to provide an introductory account of the general and specialized sources in print and nonprint formats that compose the bibliographic structure of federal government information."—*Pref.* Sections on Government Printing Office, Superintendent of Documents, depository library system, technical report literature, reference sources for federal government publications, publications of the presidency and the judiciary, legislative branch publications, administrative law, statistical sources, executive agency and independent agency publications, geographical information sources, and government periodicals and serials. Appendix contains "Principles of government information." Indexed.   Z1223.Z7M665

Robinson, Judith Schiek. Subject guide to U.S. government reference sources. Littleton, Colo. : Libraries Unlimited, 1985. 333 p.   **AF74**

Rev. ed. of Sally Wynkoop's *Subject guide to government reference books* (Littleton, Colo. : Libraries Unlimited, 1972).

More than half the entries are new. Selective and significant resources are arranged by four broad categories: General reference, Social sciences, Science and technology, Humanities. Includes machine-readable data bases. Detailed annotations include Superintendent of Documents classification numbers and acquisitions information. Agency-title-subject index.

Government reference books (AF79) serves as a continuing supplement.   Z1223.Z7R63

——————— Tapping the government grapevine : the user-friendly guide to U.S. government information sources. 2nd ed. Phoenix : Oryx, 1993. 227 p. : ill.   **AF75**

A practical handbook intended for all levels of users on how to find government information. Brief explanations of government processes provide background for the descriptions of major publications. Includes mostly U.S. print, electronic, and archival resources with some coverage of foreign, international, and state materials. Contains quick reference tables and short bibliographies. Indexed.

Z1223.Z7R633

Schmeckebier, Laurence Frederick. Government publications and their use / Laurence F. Schmeckebier, Roy B. Eastin. 2nd rev. ed. Wash. : Brookings Institution, [1969]. 502 p.   **AF76**

1st ed., 1936; rev. ed., 1961.

Although now considerably out of date, this remains a useful guide to government publications with descriptions, including classification and distribution, of catalogs and indexes, bibliographies, Congressional publications, constitutions (federal and state), laws (federal and state), court decisions, administrative regulations, presidential papers, foreign affairs, reports, organization and personnel, maps, etc. Includes list of government periodicals, and microfacsimile editions of government publications. Answers many questions as to what was published, when, by whom, in what form, etc.   Z1223.Z7S3

Bibliography

Bailey, William G. Guide to popular U.S. government publications. 3rd ed. Englewood, Colo. : Libraries Unlimited, 1993. 289 p. **AF77**

Lists titles publ. July 1989–Dec. 1992, retaining some publications from the 2nd ed. (1990). Rev. ed. of LeRoy C. Schwarzkopf's *Guide to popular U.S. government publications* (1986), which revised Walter L. Newsome's *New guide to government publications* (1978).

Arranged by subject with brief annotations and subject and title indexes. Contains a section on using and acquiring government publications; lists publications catalogs. Z1223.Z7B35

Body, Alexander C. Annotated bibliography of bibliographies on selected government publications and supplementary guides to the Superintendent of Documents classification system. [Kalamazoo] : Western Michigan Univ., 1967. 181 p. **AF78**

A bibliography of bibliographies arranged by Superintendent of Documents classification. Subject index in addition to guides to the classification system; list of government agency abbreviations and symbols.

————. ———— *Supplement*, 1st–4th ([Kalamazoo], 1968–74).

Continued by: Gabor Kovacs, *Annotated bibliography of bibliographies on selected government publications and supplementary guides to the Superintendent of Documents classification system : supplement*, 5th–9th ([Greeley, Colo. : Univ. of Northern Colorado], 1977–86). Each supplement includes a cumulative index (on microfiche) to volumes in the set.

Government reference books. 1st ed. (1968/69)– . [Englewood, Colo.] : Libraries Unlimited, 1970– . Biennial. **AF79**

Compiler varies.

An annotated listing of bibliographies, directories, dictionaries, statistical works, handbooks, almanacs, and similar reference sources published by the United States government. Author/title/subject index. Includes Superintendent of Documents classification numbers.

§ Beginning with the 1984/85 ed., most serial titles were withdrawn and listed in LeRoy C. Schwarzkopf's *Government reference serials* (AF84). Z1223.Z7G68

Guide to U.S. government publications. 1973– . McLean, Va. : Documents Index, 1973– . Annual. **AF80**

Imprint and format vary: 1973–76, looseleaf with quarterly updates; 1976–85, multiple vols. each year; 1986– , annual single volumes.

Available in microfiche; 1981 publ. on microfiche only.

Editor varies: 1973– , John L. Andriot; later issues, Donna Andriot.

Purpose is "to provide an annotated guide to the important series and periodicals currently being published by the various U.S. Government agencies ... and a complete listing of the Superintendent of Documents classification numbers issued since the turn of the century ... to December 31 [of the year preceding each annual volume]."— *Foreword*. Contains an extensive explanation of the Superintendent of Documents classification system, brief notes on the creation and authority of government agencies, and annotations for some titles. Agency and title indexes; recent volumes also have keyword-in-title index.

§ Supersedes: *Guide to U.S. government serials and periodicals* (McLean, Va. : Documents Index, 1959–1972).

Comp. by John L. Andriot. Frequency and coverage varied. Some issues had supplements offering updated information. 1959, called "pilot ed.," had title: *U.S. government serials & periodicals*. Offered an annotated listing of "important current Government publications issued on a recurring basis."—*Foreword, 1972 ed.* Z1223.Z7A574

Kanely, Edna A. Cumulative subject guide to U.S. government bibliographies, 1924–1973 / comp. by Edna A. Kanely ; with an introd. by Joseph Morehead. Wash. : Carrollton Pr., c1976. 7 v. **AF81**

Contains more than 40,000 entries by subject, alphabetically arranged, taken from 50 years of *Monthly catalog of U.S. government publications* (AF111). Expands coverage found in the *Cumulative subject index to the Monthly catalog of United States government publications, 1900–1971* (AF103) by including entries that describe both individually published bibliographies and "publications which have addended bibliographies or lists of references."—*Introd. and user's guide.* Citations include full title, personal author, issuing agency, size, pagination, and Superintendent of Documents classification number. Entries are keyed to a microfiche full-text collection of the bibliographies. A separate index volume is arranged by Superintendent of Documents classification number. Z1223.Z7K25

Major studies & issue briefs of the Congressional Research Service : cumulative index. 1916–1989. Frederick, Md. : Univ. Publication of Americas, c1989. 2 v. **AF82**

"The Congressional Research Service (CRS) ... [in] the Library of Congress ... works exclusively as a reference and research arm for members, committees, and staff of the United States Congress .... [CRS] produces policy ... scientific, economic, and legislative analyses; legal research; and legislative histories [for the Congress] ... [This] index covers over 5,000 [CRS] documents (most from 1975 to 1989) reproduced in the companion UPA microfilm collection."— *Introd.* Vol. 1 is an annotated list of the documents, arranged in the order in which they appear on the reels, and includes indexes by title and report numbers. Vol. 2 is an index of names and subjects.

Continued by quarterly and annual supplements. Z733.U63C653

New York Public Library. Research Libraries. Bibliographic guide to government publications—U.S. 1975– . Boston : G.K. Hall, 1976– . Annual. **AF83**

Issued in two or more vols. per year.

Serves as a partial supplement to the Library's *Catalog of government publications ...* (AF10), listing relevant publications cataloged by the Research Libraries during the year of coverage, plus additional entries from the Library of Congress MARC tapes. A dictionary catalog employing the format of *Dictionary catalog of the Research Libraries* (AA116).

For publications of other governments, *see* the Library's *Bibliographic guide to government publications—foreign* (AF148). Z7164.G7N54

Schwarzkopf, LeRoy C. Government reference serials. Englewood, Colo. : Libraries Unlimited, 1988. 344 p. **AF84**

"A companion and supplementary guide to *Government reference books* [AF79]."—*Introd.* Lists serial titles previously listed in *Government reference books* through 1984/85. Titles published less frequently than biennially are excluded; only titles distributed to depository libraries are described. Classified arrangement under four main categories: General library reference, Social sciences, Science and technology, and Humanities. Entries, based on the latest issue of the serial available, provide complete bibliographic information and include Superintendent of Documents and *Monthly catalog* numbers, complete publishing history, and detailed annotation. Title, SuDoc class number, author, and subject indexes. Z1223.Z7S338

Zink, Steven D. United States government publications catalogs. 2nd ed. Wash. : Special Libraries Assoc., [1988]. 292 p. **AF85**

1st ed., 1982.

Lists 370 catalogs and bibliographies published by various government agencies. Annotated entries are arranged by issuing agency and include complete title, Superintendent of Documents classification number, and acquisitions information. Title and subject indexes. Z1223.A12Z56

Library resources

Directory of government document collections & librarians. 1974– . Wash.: Congressional Information Service, c1974– . Irregular.   **AF86**

Publ. for the Government Documents Round Table, American Library Association ; ed., Judy Horn.

The 6th ed. (1991) commemorates the 20th anniversary of the Government Documents Round Table (GODORT). Section 1 is a geographic guide to libraries, documents collections, and staff. Indexes list institutions by documents collections type—state, foreign, international—and by subject specialty. Contains names and addresses for library schools offering government documents instruction, state data centers, professional organizations, and government offices. Personal name index.   Z1223.Z7D57

Catalogs and indexes

Serial set

The collected edition of U.S. government publications is known as the *Congressional edition* or *Serial set*. It includes Senate and House journals (through the 82nd Congress, 1952), Senate and House documents, and Senate and House reports. The documents include a large variety of reports from executive departments and independent bodies which are printed in the set by order of Congress. The reports include Congressional committee recommendations on public bills and Senate executive reports. For further description of this set, *see* Morehead and Fetzer, *Introduction to United States government information sources* (AF73).

For purposes of easy arrangement, each bound volume is given a serial number (a volume may include from one to several individual items). Volumes are numbered consecutively beginning with the 15th Congress (1817). In many libraries documents are arranged on the shelves by these serial numbers, and the number must be ascertained in order to find a particular document. These serial numbers are included in many of the lists and indexes noted below, sometimes in numerical lists and sometimes under specific entries. A complete record, with some overlapping, can be found in the following: 15th–60th Congress (1817–1909) in *Checklist* (AF99); 54th–76th Congress (1895–1940) in *Document catalog* (AF110) under "Congressional documents" list; 73rd–96th Congress (1933/34–80) in *Numerical lists* (AF88); 97th Congress (1981/82) in *Monthly catalog—U.S. Congressional serial set supplement* (AF89); 98th Congress (1983/84–) in *United States Congressional serial set catalog : numerical lists and schedule of volumes* (AF91), and 15th–91st Congress, 1st session in *CIS U.S. serial set index* (AF87).

American state papers, which contain reprints of the documents of the first 14 Congresses (1789–1817), grouped by class into 38 v., have been assigned special serial numbers 01–038. The numbers can be found in *Checklist* (AF99) and in *CIS U.S. serial set index*, pt. 1 (AF87).

Congressional Information Service. CIS U.S. serial set index. Wash.: Congressional Information Service, [1975–79]. 12 pt.   **AF87**

Published in 3 v. per part.

Contents: Pt. 1, American state papers and the 15th–34th Congresses, 1789–1857 (1977); Pt. 2, 35th–45th Congresses, 1857–1879 (1977); Pt. 3, 46th–50th Congresses, 1879–1889 (1978); Pt. 4, 51st–54th Congresses, 1889–1897 (1978); Pt. 5, 55th–57th Congresses, 1897–1903 (1978); Pt. 6, 58th-60th Congresses, 1903–1909 (1979); Pt.

7, 61st–63rd Congresses, 1909–1915 (1979); Pt. 8, 64th–68th Congresses, 1915–1925 (1979); Pt. 9, 69th–73rd Congresses, 1925–1934 (1975); Pt. 10, 74th–79th Congresses, 1935–1946 (1976); Pt. 11, 80th–85th Congresses, 1947–1958 (1976); Pt. 12, 86th–91st Congress, 1st session, 1959–1969 (1976). Each part consists of a 2 v. "Index of subjects and keywords" and a volume of "Finding lists" (i.e., "Private relief and related actions—Index of names of individuals and organizations"; "Numerical list of reports and documents"; "Schedule of serial volumes").

An index to the U.S. Serial Set for the period 1789–1969. Designed to be used either with printed volumes of the Serial Set or with CIS's *U.S. serial set on microfiche.*

Titles and reference numbers of Serial Set documents were converted to machine-readable form, "making extensive use of existing secondary sources of this information such as the Government Printing Office's *Numerical Lists and Schedule of Volumes* and its predecessor, the *Document Index."—User guide.* Accuracy was verified through cross-checking with the Serial Set volumes themselves, and a subject and keyword index was computer-generated. Editorial effort was focused "on careful review and revision of the subject-keyword index, to increase its ease of use, to structure extensive listings into meaningful breakdown, to reduce distracting redundancy, to eliminate meaningless terms, and to improve the thoroughness of the coverage."

The "Private relief and related actions" section of each part is "a separate index for documents concerned with … actions of Congress affecting specified individuals in specific circumstances. Such separate coverage provides access to reports on specific legislation, and at the same time allows exclusion of voluminous listings from the Index of Subjects and Keywords."—*User guide.* It is an alphabetical index to names of persons and organizations cited as recipients of proposed relief or related action. It is important to remember that the distinction between public actions (which are covered in the "Subject and keywords index") and private actions cannot always be clealy made, and both indexes should be consulted for thorough research.

Although the enriched keyword and subject indexing of this compilation should obviate the use of government publications catalogs by Benjamin Perley Poore (AF97) and John G. Ames (AF98), the *Document catalog* (AF110), and the *Monthly catalog* (AF111) for locating Serial Set publications of the relevant periods, those earlier indexes are not superceded for listings of the many other publications not included in the Serial Set. Moreover, because of variations in indexing practice between the earlier publications and the CIS set, the former may sometimes provide a more satisfactory approach to a given topic, since the CIS indexing appears to be mainly keyword-in-context.

•Available in machine-readable form as part of CIS's *Congressional masterfile 1* [database] (AF118).   Z1223.Z9C65

Numerical lists and schedule of volumes of the reports and documents of the … Congress, … session / comp. under the direction of the Superintendent of Documents. 73rd Congress (1933/34)–96th Congress, 2nd Session (Jan. 3–Dec. 16, 1980). Wash.: U.S. Govt. Print. Off., 1934–80. Annual.   **AF88**

Superintendent of Documents classification: GP 3.7/2: .

Numeric designation of Congress and dates of session appear in title.

A separate volume usually publ. for each session.

Prior to 1941, volumes were superseded by "Congressional documents" tables in the *Document catalog* (AF110). From the 77th Congress, 1st Sess., Jan. 3, 1941 through the 96th Congress, 2nd Sess., 1980, the *Numerical lists* had to be used to obtain serial numbers for Congressional reports and documents that were listed in the *Monthly catalog* (AF111) without serial numbers. The *Numerical lists* can now be bypassed altogether by using *CIS U.S. serial set index* (AF87) and *CIS index* (AF126).

For the 97th Congress, 1981/82, Serial Set numbers will be found in the *United States congressional serial set supplement to the Monthly catalog* (AF89). Beginning with the 98th Congress, 1983/84, full bibliographic records for reports and documents are found in *U.S. congressional serial set catalog : numerical lists and schedule of volumes* (AF91).   Z1223.A15

United States. Superintendent of Documents. Monthly catalog of United States government publications. United States congressional serial set supplement. 97th Congress (1981/82). Wash. : U.S. Govt. Print. Off., 1985. **AF89**

Also issued in microform.

Provides access to the *Serial set*, replacing the *Numerical list*. Arranged according to type of publication: Senate documents, Senate treaty documents, Senate reports, Senate executive reports, House documents and House reports. Gives complete bibliographic citations. Author, title, subject, series/report, bill number, stock number, and title keyword indexes.

§ Superseded by: *United States congressional serial set catalog : numerical lists and schedule of volumes* (AF91).

——————— Tables of and annotated index to the congressional series of United States public documents. Wash. : U.S. Govt. Print. Off., 1902. 769 p. **AF90**

In two parts: (1) tables of the American state papers and the documents of the 15th through the 52nd Congress (1817–93), arranged by serial number; and (2) an alphabetical subject and name index to these documents. The first part is superseded by the third edition of the *Checklist of United States public documents, 1789–1909* (AF99). The index is useful as a key to the Congressional set before 1893; however, it is incomplete and one should also consult the *CIS U.S. serial set index, 1789–1969* (AF87). Z1223.A 1902

United States congressional serial set catalog. 98th Congress (1983–1984)– . Wash. : Classification and Cataloging Branch, Library Division, Library Programs Service, Supt. of Docs. : For sale by U.S. Govt. Print. Off., 1988– . Biennial. **AF91**

Superintendent of Documents classification: GP 3.34.

Subtitle: Numerical lists and schedule of volumes.

"Through the 96th Congress, this index had been issued as the *Numerical lists and schedule of volumes* [AF88]. In 1985, the title for the records of the 97th Congress was changed to *Monthly catalog—U.S. congressional serial set supplement* [AF89] and made part of the *Monthly catalog of United States government publications*. That publication was reviewed and evaluated by the Congressional Serial Set Committee, which issued its report and recommendations to the Public Printer in 1987 .... This catalog was prepared using bibliographic records which originally appeared in various issues of the *Monthly catalog of United States government publications*."—*Pref.* Follows the format of the traditional numerical lists, but includes detailed author, title, subject, series, and bill number indexes. Z1223.A18

Early period to 1893

Greely, Adolphus Washington. Public documents of the first fourteen Congresses, 1789–1817 : papers relating to early Congressional documents. Wash. : U.S. Govt. Print. Off., 1900. 903 p. (56th Congress, 1st session. Senate document, no. 428). **AF92**

Repr. : N.Y. : Johnson, 1973 (includes *Supplement*, below).

A chronological listing by Congress number, then by type (e.g., Senate documents, Senate reports), with index of names.

———. ———. *Supplement* (Wash. : U.S. Govt. Print. Off., 1904). Reprinted from the *Annual report* of the American Historical Association, 1 (1903): 343–406.

Kanely, Edna A. Cumulative index to Hickcox's monthly catalog of United States government publications, 1885–1894. Arlington, Va. : Carrollton Pr., [1981]. 3 v. (2292 p.). **AF93**

"Now, with the completion of this index set, cumulative subject and author access is at last provided to the ten annual catalogs of U.S. Government publications which were compiled and published privately by John H. Hickcox."—*Foreword.* For Hickcox's catalog *see United States government publications : a monthly catalogue, 1885–1894* (AF100). Z1233.A1823

——————— Cumulative subject index to the Monthly catalog of United States government publications, 1895–1899. Wash. : Carrollton Pr., 1977. 2 v. **AF94**

Provides a single-alphabet subject index to the *Monthly catalog* (AF111) issues from 1895–99, including new indexing for the previously unindexed issues of Jan. 1895 Nov. 1897. Entries were coordinated with those from Dec. 1897–Dec. 1899. Z1223.A1K36

Lester, Daniel W. Checklist of United States public documents, 1789–1976 : indexes / [comp. by Daniel W. Lester and Marilyn A. Lester]. Arlington, Va. : U.S. Historical Documents Inst., c1978. 5 v. **AF95**

"A dual media edition of the U.S. Superintendent of Documents' public documents library shelflists with accompanying indexes."—*t.p.*

Originally publ. 1972, with coverage through 1970. Vol. 4 comp. by the staff of the United States Historical Documents Institute.

Contents: v. 1, pt. 1, Supt. of Docs. classification number index; pt. 2, Table of contents of microfilm reels; v. 2, U.S. government author-organization index; v. 3, Department keyword indexes to U.S. government author-organizations; v. 4, U.S. government serial titles (comp. by the staff of the U.S. Historical Docs. Inst.); v. 5, Master keyword index to the publication issuing offices of the U.S. Government, 1789–1970, and Supplemental master keyword index, 1971–76. Z1223.Z7L46

——————— Cumulative title index to United States public documents, 1789–1976 / comp. by Daniel W. Lester, Sandra K. Faull, and Lorraine E. Lester. Arlington, Va. : United States Historical Documents Institute, 1979–82. 16 v. **AF96**

Provides a listing of the titles contained in the Public Documents Library of the Government Printing Office. "Indexed titles include all items classified and cataloged in the Superintendent of Documents Classification System since it was created in 1895, through June of 1976, plus all earlier materials in the collection."—*Introd.* Entries include title, publication date, Superintendent of Documents number and microfilm reel code. Z1223.Z7L47

Poore, Benjamin Perley. A descriptive catalogue of the government publications of the United States, Sept. 5, 1774–March 4, 1881 / comp. by order of Congress. Wash. : U.S. Govt. Print. Off., 1885. 1392 p. (48th Congress, 2nd session. Senate. Misc. doc., 67). **AF97**

Repr. : Ann Arbor, Mich. : Edwards, 1953 ; N.Y. : Johnson Reprint, 1970 (2 v.).

Arranged chronologically, with general index. For each document gives full title, author, date, and a brief abstract of contents. Exact reference is given to the series in which each document appears. Contains much valuable material, but is difficult to use for quick reference because the index is not sufficiently complete, detailed, or specific. Z1223.A 1885

United States. Department of the Interior. Division of Documents. Comprehensive index to the publications of the United States government, 1881–1893 / by John G. Ames. Wash. : U.S. Govt. Print. Off., 1905. 2 v. (1590 p.). (58th Congress, 2nd session. House. Doc., 754). **AF98**

Repr. : Ann Arbor, Mich. : Edwards, 1953 ; N.Y. : Johnson Reprint, 1970.

The *Comprehensive index*, 1889–93, by J. G. Ames, publ. 1894, is superseded by this work.

Bridges the gap between Benjamin Perley Poore's *Descriptive catalogue* (AF97) and the first volume of the *Document catalog* (AF110).

Arranged in three columns. The first gives the author of the document or the department by which it was issued; the second, a list of the documents arranged alphabetically by the key word in the title; the third, if the document is in the serial set, a reference to the Congress, session, and volume of the series in which each is embraced, and the number of the document. Personal name index.

Although not entirely complete, a good usable index, but less minute and detailed than the *Document catalog*. Indicates the different editions in which a document was issued and gives serial numbers in a table under the heading "Congressional documents."　Z1223.A 1905

United States. Superintendent of Documents. Checklist of United States public documents, 1789–1909. 3rd ed. rev. and enl. Wash. : U.S. Govt. Print. Off., 1911. v. 1 (1707 p.).
AF99

Repr.: N.Y. : Kraus, 1962.

Vol. 1: Lists of Congressional and departmental publications; v. 2 was to have been an index, but was never issued.

A checklist, not a catalog, covering Congressional documents through the 60th Congress, and department and bureau publications to the end of 1909. Lists (1) American state papers, with serial numbers; (2) Congressional documents, 15th–60th Congresses, with serial numbers; (3) Department publications arranged alphabetically by government author; (4) Proceedings of Congress; (5) Miscellaneous publications of Congress, committee reports, etc.; (6) Papers of Revolutionary period and first 14 Congresses. The list of departmental publications gives, for periodical publications, a statement of the volumes and dates which constitute a complete set, and the serial numbers if the publication is contained also in the serial set; for separate publications the full title and date are given, and the serial number if the document appears also in the serial set. The preface contains a list and description of previous indexes and catalogs of the U.S. documents. This edition replaces the 2nd ed. of the *Checklist* and the tables of the *Tables and index* (AF90), but not its index section.

A brief errata list is printed in the *Monthly catalog*, May, 1912, p. 720–21.

§ For an index to the executive branch documents published in the *Checklist*, see: *CIS index to U.S. executive branch documents, 1789–1909* (AF129).　Z1223.A113

United States government publications : a monthly catalogue, 1885–1894 / by John H. Hickcox with Superintendent of Documents classification numbers added by Mary Elizabeth Poole. Repr. ed. Arlington, Va. : Carrollton Pr., [1978]. 10 v. in 6.　**AF100**

Reprint of the edition published in Washington, D.C., by J. H. Hickcox, 1885–89; W. H. Lowdermilk Co., 1889–94.

This catalog was privately published and includes both congressional and executive department publications. Arrangement is by author and subject in one alphabet, with numerous cross- references. Indexed. The reprint edition is enhanced by the addition of Superintendent of Documents classification numbers.　Z1223.Z7U523

1893 to date

A machine-readable bulletin board, *Federal depository library program bulletin board*, available by means of various telecommunications programs, provides for federal depository libraries: information concerning the Depository Library Program, access to selected federal databases, an order service for GPO products, participation in online forums, and the ability to download files.

Bernier, Bernard A. Popular names of U.S. government reports : a catalog / comp. by Bernard A. Bernier, Jr., Karen A. Wood. 4th ed. Wash. : Library of Congress : For sale by the U.S. Govt. Print. Off., 1984. 272 p.　**AF101**

Superintendent of Documents classification: LC 6.2:G74/984.

1st ed., 1966. Compilers vary.

Provides bibliographic records for 1,555 reports of U.S. executive, legislative, and judicial bodies. Arrangement is under popular name by which reports are generally known; a corporate author and subject index is included.　Z1223.A199U54

Bibliography-index to current U.S. JPRS translations. v. 1 (July/Sept. 1962)–v. 8 (July 1969–June 1970). [N.Y.] : R & M Pubs., CCM Info Corp., [1962–70]. Monthly.　**AF102**

Issued as a series of four indexes: (1) Soviet Union; (2) China & Asia exclusive of Near East; (3) East Europe; Albania, Bulgaria, Czechoslovakia, East Germany, Hungary, Poland, Romania, Yugoslavia; (4) International developments; Africa, Latin America, Near East, international communist developments. Titles and dates of coverage vary slightly.

Superseded by *Transdex* (AF108) which assumed its volume numbering.　Z2483.B52

Cumulative subject index to the Monthly catalog of United States government publications, 1900–1971 / comp. by William W. Buchanan and Edna A. Kanely. Wash. : Carrollton Pr., 1973–75. 15 v.　**AF103**

Merges the numerous annual indexes of the *Monthly catalog* (AF111) with the two decennial and one 6-month index (July–Dec. 1934), plus new indexing for the previously unindexed issues of June 1906–Dec. 1908, thus providing a subject approach in one alphabet to over 800,000 government publications from a 72-year period. Cross-references have been included, but variant subject entries and spellings were considered too numerous to be integrated. Therefore, the user must consult both "aeroplanes" and "airplanes" as well as "aircraft," etc. Chronological and numerical subheadings are used when deemed more appropriate than an alphabetical arrangement within large topics. "Major segments" such as states, larger U.S. government organizations, and other extensive, self-contained subject areas such as "Bibliographies" are set off from surrounding entries by special half-title pages.

Citation is to year of the *Monthly catalog* and page (prior to Sept. 1947) or item number. Unfortunately, libraries holding only the biennial *Document catalog* (AF110) from 1895 to 1940 will not be able to turn directly from the index to the appropriate page. Although the large number of entries under the broader headings will still necessitate considerable searching in the cited issues of the *Monthly catalog*, librarians and researchers working in a documents collection arranged according to the Superintendent of Documents classification and relying on the *Monthly catalog* as their main approach to this collection will find the *Cumulative subject index* a useful tool.

§ For an earlier period, *see*: Kanely's *Cumulative subject index to the Monthly catalog of United States government publications, 1895–1899* (AF94).

Directory of U.S. government datafiles for mainframes and microcomputers / prep. by the Federal Computer Products Center, National Technical Information Service, Technology Administration, U.S. Department of Commerce [microform]. Jan. 1991– . Springfield, Va. : U.S. Dept. of Commerce, National Technical Information Service, c1991– . Annual.
AF104

Superintendent of Documents classification: C 51.19:D 26/ .

Also available in printed form from NTIS.

"The only complete record of government-produced machine readable data files.—*Introd*. Lists more than 1,600 data files in three subject areas: economics, social studies, and science and technology. Summarizes briefly the content of each file, including technical information. Files are issued by more than 50 federal agencies and are available from NTIS. Subject and author indexes.

●**FedWorld Gateway** [database]. Springfield, Va. : National Technical Information Service, [1993].　**AF105**

Connects the user to more than 100 U.S. government computer bulletin board systems. Available through a communications software package or via Internet. Provides names, voice and data telephone numbers, and brief contents information for numerous other U.S. government online systems. Users can access White House documents released electronically, order products online, and obtain electronic delivery of selected items.

•**Index to the Foreign Broadcast Information Service (FBIS) daily reports** [database]. New Canaan, Conn. : News-Bank/Readex, 1983– . **AF106**

Available on CD-ROM, updated monthly, each disc being cumulative. Also called *Foreign Broadcast Information Service daily reports electronic index.*

Merges and cumulates several NewsBank/Readex paper indexes to FBIS daily reports: (1) Central Eurasia; (2) East Asia; (3) East Europe; (4) Latin America; (5) Near East & South Asia; (6) Sub-Saharan Africa; and (7) West Europe.

Consists of translations by the U.S. Foreign Broadcast Information Service, a government agency which monitors and translates newspapers, radio and television broadcasts, and statements of foreign governments. The *Daily reports* are available in microfiche through the Depository Library Program, in paper from NTIS, and in microfiche from NewsBank/Readex. Titles of *Daily reports* and indexes vary.

SIGCAT CD-ROM compendium. Apr. 1992– . Wash. : Office of Electronic Information Dissemination Services : for sale by U.S. Govt. Print. Off., 1992– . Annual. **AF107**

Superintendent of Documents classification: GP 3.22/6: .

A catalog of in-process and completed CD-ROMs containing federal government information. Most discs are issued by federal agencies. Entries include abstracts of disc contents, vendor and source data, and technical specifications. Includes a "Selected list of resources about CD-ROM." Z286.O68S552

Transdex : bibliography and index to the United States Joint Publications Research Service (JPRS) translations. v. 9 (1970/71)–12 (1974). N.Y. : CCM Info Corp., 1971–74. Monthly with semiannual cumulations. **AF108**

Bibliographic listings are in order by JPRS Accession numbers. Country and title, subject, publications, and author indexes.

Supersedes the *Bibliography-index to current U.S. JPRS translations* (AF102) and assumes its numbering.

Superseded by *Transdex index* (AF109). AS36.U574

Transdex index. 1975– . Wooster, Ohio : Micro Photo Div., Bell and Howell Co., 1975– . Monthly printed issues with annual cumulations in microfiche. **AF109**

Annual cumulation has header title: *Index to transdex.*

Title varies slightly.

Continues *Transdex: bibliography and index to the U.S. Joint Publications Research Service (JPRS) translations* (AF108) and *Bibliography-index to current U.S. JPRS translations* (AF102).

Lists and indexes all JPRS translations. Arranged in four major divisions: Series and *ad hoc* title section; Bibliographic section; Keyword section; Personal names section.

United States. Superintendent of Documents. Catalog of the public documents of Congress and of other departments of the government of the United States for the period March 4, 1893–Dec. 31, 1940. Wash. : U.S. Govt. Print. Off., 1896–1945. 25 v. **AF110**

The "comprehensive index" provided for by the act approved Jan. 12, 1895. Publication terminated with v. 25.

This index, which is generally referred to by its binder's title as the *Document catalog*, forms for the years 1893 to 1940 the permanent and complete catalog of all government publications from Congressional and departmental. It is a dictionary catalog in form, listing all documents under author (governmental or personal), subject, and, when necessary, title; gives full catalog information for each book or pamphlet included. Includes a large amount of analysis; refers to all editions in which a document has appeared; and gives serial numbers for documents in the serial set, as follows: in v. 1–4, serial numbers are given only in the table under the entry "Congressional documents"; beginning with v. 5, serial numbers are *also* given throughout the list under the main (i.e., author) entry for each document, but not under the analytical entries. Z1223.A13

———— Monthly catalog of United States government publications. no. [1] (Jan. 1895)– . Wash. : U.S. Govt. Print. Off., 1895– . Monthly. **AF111**

Superintendent of Documents classification: GP 3.8: .

Title varies: 1895–June 1907, *Catalogue of the United States public documents;* July 1907–1939, *Monthly catalog, United States public documents;* 1940–50, *United States government publications: monthly catalog.*

A current bibliography of publications issued by all branches of the government, including both the Congressional and the department and bureau publications. Each issue contains general instructions for ordering documents, and, prior to 1976, a list of documents published arranged by the department and bureau. An annual subject and agency index appeared in each volume and, beginning with July 1945, a monthly index in each issue until 1974 when separate personal author and title indexes were added.

Beginning with the issue for July 1976, the catalog was converted to MARC format, with full cataloging according to Anglo-American cataloging rules provided for each item. "The *Monthly Catalog* utilizes AACR and Library of Congress main entries. Subjects are derived from *Library of Congress Subject Headings* 8th edition and its supplements. The catalog consists of text and four indexes—author, title, subject, and series/report number."—*Pref., July 1976.* Up-to-date information regarding sales status ("in stock," "out of print," etc.) is provided by the *GPO sales publications reference file* (Wash. : U.S. Govt. Print. Off., Feb. 1977– . Monthly. Microfiche).

A reprint edition for the period 1895–1940, with Superintendent of Documents classification numbers added, was published by Carroll-ton Pr., Wash., D.C., 1975–78 (40 v. in 58).

A directory of United States government periodicals and subscription publications (title varies) was published semiannually 1951–60 (usually Feb. and Aug.); annually 1961–76 (in Feb. issue). It was replaced by an annual *Serials supplement*, 1977–84 which was in turn superseded by the *Periodicals supplement* (AF112 note).

Supplements: 1941–42, 1943–44, 1945–46 (Wash. : U.S. Govt. Print. Off., 1947–48 3 v.).

These supplements include publications received by the Public Documents Division Library, not listed previously in any Superintendent of Documents catalog. No further supplements published, as, beginning in April 1947, all documents are listed in the *Monthly catalog* as received, regardless of publication date.

Indexes.

(1) *Decennial cumulative index, 1941–1950* (Wash. : U.S. Govt. Print. Off., 1953. 1848 p.). "Index to the monthly issues from January 1941 to December 1950 and the Supplements for 1941–42, 1943–44, and 1945–46."—*title page.*

(2) ————. ————. *1951–1960* (Wash. U.S. Govt. Print. Off., 1968. 2 v.).

(3) Cumulative indexes covering 1961–65 (1976. 2 v.); 1966–70 (1978. 2 v.); 1971–76 (1981. 2 v.); 1976–80 (Phoenix : Oryx, [1987]. 6 v.); 1981–85 (Phoenix : Oryx, 1988. 7 v.).

(4) *Decennial cumulative personal author index, 1941–1950, 1951–1960,* ed. by Edward Przebienda (Ann Arbor, Mich. : Pierian Pr., 1971. 2 v.).

(5) *Quinquennial cumulative personal author index, 1961–65, 1966–1970, 1971–1975,* ed. by Edward Przebienda (Ann Arbor, 1971–79. 3 v.).

(6) *Cumulative subject index to the Monthly catalog of United States government publications, 1900–1971,* comp. by William W. Buchanan and Edna A. Kanely (AF103).

•Machine-readable versions:

(1) *GPO monthly catalog* [database] (Wash. : U.S. Govt. Print. Off., 1976–). Available online or on CD-ROM (both updated monthly).

(2) *LC MARC : GPO monthly catalog* [database] (Wash. : Library of Congress, 1976–). Available on magnetic tape (updated monthly).

(3) CD-ROM versions, variously titled *Government documents catalog service* [database], *Government publications index on IN-FOTRAC* [database], and *GPO on SilverPlatter* [database], all offering the *Monthly catalog* entries, variously enhanced, 1976 to the present, usually updated monthly. Z1223.A18

——————— Monthly catalog of United States government publications. Periodicals supplement. 1985– . Wash. : U.S. Govt. Print. Off., 1985– . Annual.   **AF112**

Superintendent of Documents classification: GP 3.8/5: .

Also available in microform.

Continues the annual *Serials supplement* published 1977–84, which replaced the *Directory of United States government periodicals and subscription publications* published semiannually, 1951–60 (usually Feb. and Aug.), and annually 1961–76 (Feb. issue).

——————— [Subject bibliographies]. Wash. : U.S. Govt. Print. Off., 1975– . Irregular.   **AF113**

Supersedes the *Price lists* that were published irregularly 1898–1975.

"There are over 21,000 different publications, periodicals, and subscription services for sale by the Superintendent of Documents. Topics range from accidents and accident prevention to zoology and touch on nearly every facet of human life. Since an average of 3,000 new titles enters the sales inventory each year, and a similar number of titles become outdated or superseded by revised editions, it is impractical to issue a single catalog listing all of the titles sold.

"Instead, we have created over 250 Subject Bibliographies which list publications on a single subject or field of interest."—*Index, Mar. 15, 1982.*

Most entries in the bibliographies are briefly annotated and include order information. Each bibliography carries an "SB" number and the subject indexing refers to those numbers. A subject index is issued periodically.

Price list 36, "Government periodicals and subscription services," (101st ed., [Feb. 1961]–227th ed. [Fall 1992]), listed more than 500 subscription services published by more than 450 federal agencies and available from the Superintendent of Documents. It also listed new subscription services, discontinued subscriptions, title changes, and latest prices.

United States government publications (non-depository) [microform]. Jan. 1953– . N.Y. : Readex Microprint, 1953– . Monthly.   **AF114**

Imprint varies: 1981– , New Canaan, Conn. : Readex.

Format varies: 1953–80, issued on micro-opaque cards; 1981– on microfiche.

Arranged by *Monthly catalog* entry number (AF111).

§ A companion series, *United States government depository publications,* is also available in microform.

U.S. government periodicals index. v. 1 (1994)– . Bethesda, Md. : Congressional Information Service, 1994– . Quarterly.   **AF115**

For annotation, *see* AD291.   Z1223.Z7.U8

U.S. government subscriptions. Ed. 228 (winter 1993)– . Wash. : U.S. Govt. Print. Off., 1993– . Quarterly.   **AF116**

Superintendent of Documents classification: GP 3.9: .

Continues *Government periodicals and subscription services.*

"Lists government periodicals and subscription services offered for sale by the U.S. government."—*Introd. page.* Alphabetical listing of items available in print, on diskette, or on magnetic tape. Gives title, frequency, price, and ordering information. Agency and subject indexes.   Z1223.A1U15

Legislative branch

CIS index to U.S. Senate executive documents & reports : covering documents and reports not printed in the U.S. serial set, 1817–1969. Wash. : Congressional Information Service, c1987. 2 v.   **AF117**

Contents: [v. 1] Reference bibliography; [v. 2] Indexes.

"Assembles, describes, and indexes comprehensively all [Senate executive] documents and reports from the earliest items through 1969 .... The majority of materials in this collection concern Senate consideration of treaties with foreign governments [including Indian

tribes]."—*Introd.* The documents are listed by accession number and have brief annotations. Subject, personal name, and document and report number indexes. A companion microfiche collection, *Senate executive documents and reports,* is available; most of these items have not been previously available.

•Available in machine-readable form as part of CIS's *Congressional masterfile 1* [database] (AF118).   KF40.C57

•**Congressional masterfile 1** : 1789–1969 [database]. Bethesda, Md. : Congressional Information Service, c1988.   **AF118**

A machine-readable version of the following CIS indexes: *CIS U.S. serial set index, 1789–1969* (AF87); *CIS U.S. congressional committee hearings index, 1833–1969* (AF123); *CIS index to unpublished U.S. Senate committee hearings 1823–1964* (AF122); *CIS index to unpublished U.S. House of Representatives committee hearings, 1833–1936* and its supplements for 1937–46 and 1947–54 (AF121); *CIS index to U.S. Senate executive documents & reports, 1817–1969* (AF117); and *CIS U.S. congressional committee prints index, from the earliest publications through 1969* (AF124).

Available on CD-ROM, or online as *CIS.*

•**Congressional masterfile 2** [database]. Bethesda, Md. : Congressional Information Service, 1970– .   **AF119**

Machine-readable version of *CIS/index to publications of the United States Congress* (AF126).

Available online and on CD-ROM, both updated quarterly.

Includes CIS indexes covering from 1970 (*Congressional masterfile 1* contains coverage of the major CIS historical indexes). Accompanied by reference manual.

Zwirn, Jerrold. Congressional publications and proceedings : research on legislation, budgets, and treaties. 2nd ed. Englewood, Colo. : Libraries Unlimited, 1988. 299 p.   **AF120**

For annotation, *see* CJ200.   JK1067.Z85

Congressional hearings and committee prints

CIS index to unpublished U.S. House of Representatives committee hearings, 1833–1936. Bethesda, Md : Congressional Information Service, c1988. 2 v.   **AF121**

Contents: v. 1, Reference bibliography; v. 2, Index.

Indexes 1,400 House Committee hearings transcripts, 1833–1936 (22nd–74th Congresses) that were never published. At the time of publication of this index, transcripts for the last 50 years were not available under the rules of the House. Vol. 1 lists the hearings in chronological order and includes complete bibliographical data, names of witnesses, and page numbers of testimony. Vol. 2 includes subject, name (including witnesses), title, and bill number indexes. A companion collection of the hearings on microfiche is available.

Supplemented by:

——————— *. 1937–1946* (1990. 2 v.).

Contents: v. 1, Reference bibliography; v. 2, Index.

Lists approximately 4,550 hearings transcripts made available after the House of Representatives modified its rules to allow access to hearings more than 30 years old. Companion microfiche set available.

——————— *. 1947–1954* (1992. 2 v.).

Contents: v. 1, Reference bibliography; v. 2, Index.

Lists an additional 4,660 hearings transcripts. Companion microfiche set available.

•All three indexes are included as part of *Congressional masterfile 1* [database] (AF118).   KF40.C54

CIS index to unpublished U.S. Senate committee hearings : 18th Congress–88th Congress, 1823–1964. Bethesda, Md. : Congressional Information Service, c1986. 5 v.   **AF122**

Contents: [v. 1–2], Index by subjects and organizations; [v. 3], Index by personal names; [v. 4–5], Reference bibliography.

Lists some 7,300 unpublished hearings found in the National Archives and in the papers of former senators; texts of the hearings are available in the companion set, *CIS unpublished U.S. Senate committee hearings on microfiche.* Arranged by microfiche accession number. Information provided for each hearing includes title, date, collation, related bill numbers, issuing committee and subcommittee, and witnesses. Separate subject, name (mainly witnesses), title, and bill number indexes.

Supplemented by *CIS index to unpublished U.S. Senate committee hearings : 89th Congress–90th Congress, 1965–1968* (c1989. 255 p.). Lists approximately 690 hearings not previously printed or published. As with the main set, texts of the hearings are reproduced in the accompanying microfiche set.

•Available in machine-readable form as part of CIS's *Congressional masterfile 1* [database] (AF118). KF40.C55

Congressional Information Service. CIS U.S. congressional committee hearings index. Wash. : C.I.S., [1981–85]. 42 v.
AF123
Contents: pt. 1, 23rd–64th 64th Congress (1833–Mar. 1917) (1985. 5 v.); pt. 2, 65th–68th Congresses (Apr. 1917–Mar. 1925) (1984. 5 v.); pt. 3, 69th–73rd Congresses (Dec. 1925–1934) (1984. 5 v.); pt. 4, 74th–78th Congresses (1935–1944) (1983. 6 v.); pt. 5, 79th–82nd Congresses (1945–1952) (1983. 6 v.); pt. 6, 83rd–85th Congresses (1953–1958) (1982. 5 v.); pt. 7, 86th–88th Congresses (1959–1964) (1982. 5 v.); pt. 8, 89th–91st Congresses (1965–1969) (1981. 5 v.).

Each part contains the following sections: (1) Reference bibliography (giving full bibliographic data on hearings from the period covered, notes on subject content, subject descriptors, names of witnesses, etc.); (2) Index by subject and organizations; (3) Index by personal names; (4) Supplementary indexes (e.g., bill number, report and document numbers, titles, and Superintendent of Documents classification number).

•Also issued as part of *Congressional masterfile 1*, a CD-ROM product (AF118). A companion collection of full texts of the hearings on microfiche is available with the additional option of purchasing MARC-format basic catalog records for the microfiche. KF40.C56

———— CIS U.S. congressional committee prints index from the earliest publications through 1969. Wash. : Congressional Information Service, [1980]. 5 v. **AF124**
Contents: [v. 1–2] Reference bibliography; [v. 3–4] Index by subjects and names; [v. 5] Finding aids.

Serves as a guide to the publisher's *U.S. congressional committee prints on microfiche* series and as an independent bibliography and index of committee prints from 1830 (when the first known print was issued) through 1969. (Committee prints are included in the *CIS/index to publications of the United States Congress* [AF126] beginning 1970.) The "Reference bibliography" volumes provide bibliographic data on some 14,000 committee prints, virtually all of which are included in the microfiche series. In addition to the 2-volume index of subjects and names, the "Finding aids" volume includes indexes by title, by Congress and Committee, by bill number, and by Superintendent of Documents number.

•Available in machine-readable form as part of CIS's *Congressional masterfile 1* [database] (AF118). Z1223.Z7C66

———— CIS/annual. 1970– . Wash. : CIS, 1970– . Annual. **AF125**
2 v. per year, 1970–83. Contents: (1) Abstracts of Congressional publications and legislative histories; (2) Index to Congressional publications and public laws.

3 v. per year, 1984– . Contents: (1) Abstracts of Congressional publications; (2) Legislative histories of U.S. public laws; (3) Index to Congressional publications and public laws.

Cumulates the abstracts of hearings, reports, committee prints, and other Congressional papers from the monthly issues of *CIS index to publications of the U.S. Congress* (AF126), and offers a cumulative index to them. Before 1984, the abstracts volume included brief descriptions and legislative histories of public laws enacted during the period covered. From 1984, the legislative histories are considerably expanded and published in a separate volume. A microfiche library of publications is available for all years; MARC-format catalog records are available for the microfiche.

Multiyear cumulations have appeared as: *CIS five-year cumulative index, 1970–1974* (Wash., 1975. 2 v.).
CIS four-year cumulative index, 1975–1978 (Wash., 1979. 3 v.).

————. *1979–1982* (Bethesda, Md., 1983. 3 v.).
————. *1983–1986* (Bethesda, Md., 1987. 4 v.).
————. *1987–1990* (Bethesda, Md., 1991. 4 v.).
These volumes revise and supersede the *CIS/annual* index volumes for the years indicated and are designed to be used with the annual abstract volumes. The subject index includes topical subjects and names, while the supplementary indexes cover titles; bill, report, and document numbers; and committee and subcommittee chairs.
KF49.C62

———— CIS/index to publications of the United States Congress. v. 1, no. 1 (Jan. 1970)– . Wash. : C.I.S., 1970– . Monthly with quarterly index cumulations. **AF126**
Monthly issues in two parts, Abstracts and Indexes. Bound cumulations have title *CIS annual* (AF125).

A service offering detailed indexing and brief abstracts of the following types of Congressional publications: committee hearings, committee prints, House and Senate documents and reports, Senate treaty documents. Indexes by subjects and names (including names of witnesses at hearings, etc.); titles; bill, report, and document numbers; and committee and subcommittee chairs. A microfiche collection providing full text of the publications is available.

•In machine-readable form as part of *Congressional masterfile 2* [database] (AF119). KF49.C62

Legislative debates

United States. Congress. Congressional record. v. 1– . Wash. : U.S. Govt. Print. Off., 1873– . **AF127**
Title page: Containing the proceedings and debates of Congress. Covers 43rd Congress, March 4, 1873– .

Issued daily while Congress is in session. Each issue usually has four parts: Proceedings of the House; Proceedings of the Senate; Extension of remarks; and beginning with March 17, 1947, Daily digest.

The daily issues are revised and published in bound form at the end of each session of Congress. Each session is numbered as a single volume and paged continuously, although bound volumes are issued in several parts. Pagination of daily issues and bound volumes differ. Daily issues are indexed every two weeks; bound volumes have a cumulative index that is sometimes bound separately, sometimes bound into the last part. Publication of the bound volumes and cumulative index lag by several years.

Each index is in two parts: (1) Alphabetical index of names and subjects, giving (under subject) bills and bill numbers, and (2) History of bills and resolutions, arranged by number. The second index can be used to find full information about a bill, since it gives page references to all material in the *Record* concerning the bill, from introduction to final passage and signing.

The *Record* contains presidential messages, Congressional speeches and debates in full, and records of votes. Texts of bills will sometimes be included. The appendix to the bound *Record*, containing the "Extension of remarks," was not included in the volumes for the 83rd Congress, 2nd Session, through the 90th Congress, 1st Session (although the Appendix from the daily issues was available on microfilm and continued to be indexed in the bound set cumulative indexes). Beginning with the 90th Congress, 2nd Session, this material was again included in the bound volumes, where it is continuously paged and indexed.

•A CD-ROM version was issued by the Government Printing Office for the 99th Congress only.

§ Prior to 1873, the following should be consulted for a record of congressional debates:

(1) *Debates and proceedings in the Congress of the United States, with an appendix, containing important state papers and all the laws of a public nature: with a copious index* (Wash. : Gales and Seaton, 1834–56. 42 v.).

Generally known by its binder's title, *Annals of Congress.* A retrospective compilation of summaries of House and Senate activities and debates, 1st–8th Congresses, 1789–1824.

(2) *Register of debates in Congress* (Wash. : Printed and publ. by Gales and Seaton, 1825–37. 14 v. in 29).

Covers 18th Congress, 2nd Session through 25th Congress, 1st Session. A compilation of summaries of the debates, not a verbatim record.

(3) *Congressional globe* (Wash. : Blair and Rives, 1834–73. 46 v. in 108).

Covers 23rd Congress through 42nd Congress, 1833–73. Overlapped publication of the *Register* for several years, eventually becoming more of a verbatim record of Congressional debates.   JR11.R5

Executive branch

CIS index to presidential executive orders & proclamations. Wash. : Congressional Information Service, c1987. 2 v. in 22.   **AF128**

Contents: Pt. 1, George Washington to Woodrow Wilson (v. 1–10); Pt. 2, Warren Harding to Ronald Reagan (v. 11–20).

Lists more than "75,000 orders and proclamations … together with related descriptive attachments and oversized maps acquired and filmed separately. The collection is as comprehensive and complete as it has been possible to make it based upon thorough review and screening of all key source groups of records in major federal archives and public government documents collections."—*User guide*. Each part consists of a reference bibliography, arranged in accession order (roughly chronological), giving the title, date, and other related information; and an index by subject and organization, a chronological list of orders, an index of personal names, an index of interrelated executive orders and proclamations, and an index of site and document numbers. The "User guide" describes the various printed sources of the available texts; the texts are also available in the companion microfiche collection. The *Supplement* covers "two large series of 1921–1983 presidential pardons and military orders that were discovered by CIS editors subsequent to the original publication of Part II."—*User guide*.   KF70.A55

CIS index to U.S. executive branch documents, 1789–1909 : a guide to documents listed in Checklist of U.S. public documents, 1789–1909, not printed in the U.S. serial set. Bethesda, Md. : Congressional Information Service, c1990. pts. 1–4. (In progress).   **AF129**

Contents: Pt. 1, Treasury Dept., Commerce and Labor Dept.; Pt. 2, War Dept.; Pt. 3, Interior, Justice, and Labor Depts, Interstate Commerce Commission, Library of Congress; Pt. 4, Agriculture Dept., American Republics Bureau, Dist. of Columbia, Civil Service, Geographic Board, Government Printing Office, and others.

Indexes the executive branch materials in *Checklist of United States public documents, 1789–1909* (AF99). Each part contains four detailed indexes: subjects and names, titles, Superintendent of Documents classification numbers, and agency report numbers. The reference bibliography provides full bibliographic data. To be issued in 6 pts. A microfiche set of the collection is available.   CD3030.C57

Cumulated indexes to the public papers of the Presidents of the United States. Millwood, N.Y. : KTO Pr., 1977–83. [v. 1–8].   **AF130**

Contents: Herbert C. Hoover, 1929–1933 (1980); Harry S. Truman, 1945–1953 (1979); Dwight D. Eisenhower, 1953–1961 (1978); John F. Kennedy, 1961–1963 (1977); Lyndon B. Johnson, 1963–1969 (1978); Richard M. Nixon, 1969–1974 (1978); Gerald R. Ford, 1974–1977 (1980); Jimmy Carter, 1977–1981 (1983).

For each of the Presidents, combines and integrates into one volume the separate indexes appearing in the annual volumes of the *Public papers* series (AF136).

O'Hara, Frederic J. A guide to publications of the Executive branch. Ann Arbor, Mich. : Pierian Pr., 1979. 287 p.   **AF131**

"Intended to provide an understanding of the function and operation of … government agencies."—*Introd.* Arranged by department; includes a short essay about each agency, SuDocs classification numbers, and descriptions of useful publications such as agency catalogs,

bibliographies, career literature, dictionaries, statistical compilations, and directories. Agency, personal name, title, and subject indexes.   Z1223.Z7O48

Tollefson, Alan M. A bibliography of presidential commissions, committees, councils, panels, and task forces, 1961–1972 / comp. and ed. by Alan M. Tollefson and Henry C. Chang. Minneapolis : Govt. Publications Div., Univ. of Minnesota Libraries, 1973. 30 p.   **AF132**

Lists 243 reports selected from the *Monthly catalog* (AF111) and *Popular names of U.S. government reports* (AF101). Arranged alphabetically by main entry, with indexes by personal name, title, and subject-keyword.

§ *See also*: Steven D. Zink, *Guide to the Presidential advisory commissions, 1973–1984* (CJ186).   Z1223.Z7T66

United States. Congress. Senate. Library. Presidential vetoes, 1789–1988. Wash. : U.S. Govt. Print. Off., 1992. 595 p.   **AF133**

Previous ed., 1978.

Arranged chronologically by Congresses and the administrations in which the vetoes occurred. Index of names and subjects. Includes a statistical summary.

Supplemented by: *Presidential vetoes, 1989–1991*. (Wash. : U.S. Govt. Print. Off., 1992. 12 p.).   KF42.2

United States. President. Codification of presidential proclamations and executive orders. 1961/77– . Wash. : Office of the Federal Register, National Archives and Records Service : For sale by the U.S. Govt. Print. Off., [1979]– . Irregular.   **AF134**

Superintendent of Documents classification: GS 4.113/3: .

Volume covering April 13, 1945–Jan. 20, 1989 publ. [1989] (1122 p.).

"Provide[s] in one convenient reference source proclamations and Executive orders with general applicability and continuing effect."—*Foreword.* Arranged in 50 chapters according to the title designations of the *Code of federal regulations* and the *United States code*. Contains text and all amendments in effect. Disposition tables and subject index.   KF70.A473

———————— A compilation of the messages and papers of the Presidents : (with additions and encyclopedic index by private enterprise). N.Y. : Bureau of Nat. Literature, [1917?]. 20 v.   **AF135**

Vols. 1–18 paged continuously: v. 19–20, Encyclopedic index.

Originally published: Wash. : U.S. Govt. Print. Off., 1896–99. 10 v. (House misc. doc. 210, 53rd Cong., 2nd sess.), covering 1789–1897. Published by authority of Congress by James D. Richardson.

Continued officially by *Public papers of the Presidents of the United States* (AF136).   J81.B96g

———————— Public papers of the presidents of the United States : containing the public messages, speeches, and statements of the President. Wash. : Federal Register Div., National Archives and Records Service : For sale U.S. Govt. Print. Off., 1958– . Annual.   **AF136**

Superintendent of Documents classifications: GS 4.113: ; AE 2.114: .

Contents: Herbert Hoover, 1929–33. 4 v. (publ. 1974–77); Harry S. Truman, 1945–53. 8 v. (publ. 1961–66); Dwight D. Eisenhower, 1953–61. 8 v. (publ. 1958–61); John F. Kennedy, 1961–63. 3 v. (publ., 1962–64); Lyndon B. Johnson, 1963–69. 7 v. (publ. 1964–70); Richard M. Nixon, 1969–74. 6 v. (publ. 1969–75); Gerald R. Ford, 1974–76/77. 6 v. (publ. 1975–79); Jimmy Carter, 1977–81. 9 v. (publ. 1977–82); Ronald Reagan, 1981–89. 15 v. (publ. 1982–91); George Bush, 1989–93. 8 v. (publ. 1990–93).

Begun in 1957. Papers of presidents Hoover, Truman, and Eisenhower were published retrospectively. Compilations for F. D. Roosevelt and earlier presidents have been published commercially. Annual volumes are published soon after the close of each calendar year. Beginning with volumes for the Carter administration, coverage was expanded to include materials published in the *Weekly compilation of presidential documents* (below).

§ *Weekly compilation of presidential documents.* (v. 1, no. 1 [Aug. 2, 1965]– . [Wash. : Office of the Federal Register, National Archives and Records Service, General Services Administration], 1965. Weekly).

Publishes "transcripts of the President's news conferences, messages to Congress, public speeches, and statements, and other Presidential materials released by the White House up to 5 p.m. on each Friday."—*v. 1, no. 1, p. 2.* Cumulative index in each issues; also provides quarterly, semiannual, and annual indexes.   **J80.A283**

State publications

See Susan Dow, *State document checklists : a historical bibliography* (AF140) for state documents checklists.

Lane, Margaret T. State publications : depository distribution and bibliographical programs / comp. for the State and Local Documents Task Force, Government Documents Round Table, American Library Association. [Austin] : Texas State Publications Clearinghouse, Texas State Library, 1980. 178 p. (Documents monograph series, no. 2).   **AF137**

Attempts to survey the distribution and bibliographical control of state documents. Information, supplied by the individual states, includes name of agency, legal authority, place of agency within state and parent organization, depository libraries (if any), document distribution, dissemination of cataloging data, availability of microforms, checklists and other publications available, and budget. A *Supplement* (1981. 49 p.) contains reports from states not included in the basic volume, plus reports from the Center for Research Libraries and the Library of Congress.

Guides

Lane, Margaret T. Selecting and organizing state government publications. Chicago : Amer. Libr. Assoc., 1987. 254 p. : forms.   **AF138**

A guide for librarians on organizing and maintaining a state publications collection. The various chapters cover characteristics and history of state publications, state agencies, distribution, acquisition, state checklists and bibliographies, information services, cataloging and classification, and processing documents in the library. Includes a bibliography, "Guidelines for state documents," and a list of depository and state agency manuals. Index by author, title, and subject.

                Z688.G6L35

——————— State publications and depository libraries : a reference handbook. Westport, Conn. : Greenwood, [1981]. 573 p.   **AF139**

Intended mainly for "administrators of state document distribution programs and librarians attempting to establish depository library programs."—*Pref.* Pt. I, Characteristics of depository library legislation, provides an overview and comparative study of the situation; pt. II, State publications—the literature, offers a bibliography and survey of the literature; pt. III, The states, cites pertinent legislation (current as of mid-1980) for each state, followed by commentary and bibliography. Indexed.   **Z688.G6L36**

Bibliography

Dow, Susan L. State document checklists : a historical bibliography. Buffalo, N.Y. : W.S. Hein, 1990. 224 p.   **AF140**

"Serves as a reference tool for librarians who acquire materials and librarians that provide reference services."—*p. 48.* Arranged alphabetically by state, then chronologically by date covered; title index. Sources consulted, p. [201]–210.   **Z1223.5.A1D68**

Guide to the publications of interstate agencies and authorities / comp. by Jack Sulzer and Roberta Palen. Chicago : Amer. Libr. Assoc., 1986. 48 p.   **AF141**

A list of the types and availability of publications issued by interstate agencies, based on the agencies included in the Council of State Governments' *Interstate compacts and agencies* (Lexington, Ky., 1983). Arranged by broad topic with an index of agencies by states, and an index of agency names.   **JK2445.I57G85**

Library of Congress. Exchange and Gift Division. Monthly checklist of state publications. v. 1 (1910)– . Wash. : U.S. Govt. Print. Off., 1910– . Monthly.   **AF142**

Title varies: 1910–21: *Monthly list of state publications.*
Sponsoring division of the Library of Congress varies.
A record of publications of states, territories, and insular possessions of the U.S., received by the Library of Congress. Monographs, annual publications and monographs in series are arranged by state, then issuing agency. This is followed by publications of associations of state officials and regional organizations, then state library surveys, studies, manuals, and statistical reports. Beginning in 1963, periodicals are listed in the June and December issues; the December list is cumulative for the year. From 1987, each issue includes a subject index with a cumulative annual index issued the following year. College and university catalogs, looseleaf additions, slip laws, blank forms and publishers' announcements are not included.   **Z1223.5.A1U5**

Parish, David W. A bibliography of state bibliographies, 1970–1982. Littleton, Colo. : Libraries Unlimited, c1985. 267 p.   **AF143**

A bibliography of bibliographies that were issued as state documents; a high percentage of entries relate to the state in which the bibliography was published, but many items have no geographical focus or limitation. Arranged by state, then by subject categories; title and subject indexes. Includes some important pre-1970 imprints.

                Z1223.5.A1P36

——————— State government reference publications : an annotated bibliography. 2nd ed. Littleton, Colo. : Libraries Unlimited, 1981. 355 p.   **AF144**

1st ed., 1974.
Annotated entries are arranged by bibliographic classifications, then by state. Classifications include official state bibliographies; blue books; legislative manuals and related references; state government finances; statistical abstracts and other data sources; directories; tourist guides; audiovisual guides, atlases and maps; bibliographies and general references. Appendixes include Suggested readings; Reference tools; Subject core of state publications; and Agency addresses. Indexed by title, subject, and personal author.   **Z1223.5.A1P37**

State government research checklist / the Council of State Governments. Feb. 1979– . Lexington, Ky. : The Council, 1979– . Bimonthly.   **AF145**

Arranged by subject; includes references to publications produced by the 50 states. Also indexes publications of the Council of State Governments (CSG) and other national, nonprofit organizations. Publications listed may be borrowed from the CSG's States Information Center.

Subject index for v. 24–29 in v. 30, no. 1.

State reference publications. 1991–92– . Topeka, Kan. : Government Research Service, c1991– . Annual.   **AF146**

Continues Lynn Hellebust's *State blue books, legislative manuals, and reference publications* (Topeka, 1990).
Under each state are listed: blue books and general reference; legislative manuals and handbooks; directories and biographies; statistical abstracts; government and politics texts; and other reference sources. The appendix lists a number of general state reference books and directories and a list of periodicals that deal with state issues.

                Z7165.U5S679

Municipal publications

Index to current urban documents. v. 1 (July/Oct. 1972)– .
Westport, Conn. : Greenwood, 1972– . Quarterly with annual
cumulation.   **AF147**
An index to publications of cities, counties, regional organizations, special districts, quasi-public organizations (such as local citizens' groups) and state publications that treat a specific city or county.
Covers large U.S. and Canadian cities. Arranged by place-name, then
by issuing agency and title. Geographic and subject indexes.
Urban documents microfiche collection [microform] (Westport,
Conn. : Greenwood, 1973–) reproduces most of the documents cited
in the *Index*. The *Index* provides information for locating publications
within the *Collection*.   Z7165.U5I654

OTHER GOVERNMENTS

See Gloria Westfall, *Guide to official publications of foreign
countries* (AF8) for expanded coverage of documents catalogs
from other nations.

General Works

Bibliography

New York Public Library. Research Libraries. Bibliographic guide to government publications—foreign. 1975– . Boston : G.K. Hall, 1976– . Annual.   **AF148**
Serves as a partial supplement to the Library's *Catalog of government publications in the Research Libraries* (AF10), listing relevant
publications cataloged by the Research Libraries during the year of
coverage, plus additional entries from the Library of Congress MARC
tapes. A dictionary catalog employing the format of the *Dictionary
catalog of the Research Libraries* (AA116).
§ For the NYPL catalog of U.S. government publications *see*
AF83.   Z7164.G7N54

Library resources

Turner, Carol A. Directory of foreign document collections /
Government Documents Round Table, American Library Association. N.Y. : UNIPUB, [1985?]. 148 p.   **AF149**
Compiled from results of a questionnaire sent to 200 libraries.
Has two major sections: directory of collections and an alphabetical
country list. Library listings include scope notes describing the collections and availability and accessibility of documents within the libraries.   Z675.D63T87

North America

Canada

Guides

Bishop, Olga B. Canadian official publications. Oxford ;
N.Y. : Pergamon, 1981. 297 p. : ill. (Guides to official publications, v.9).   **AF150**

Aims "to introduce the student to the various types of publications
issued by both Parliament and the departments and agencies of the federal government as well as the types of information which may be
found in the various documents."—*Pref.* Chapters deal with specific
types of publications, cite examples, and provide background information. Indexed.   Z1373.3.B48

Bibliography

Henderson, George Fletcher. Federal royal commissions in
Canada, 1867–1966 : a checklist. [Toronto] : Univ. of Toronto
Pr., 1967. 212 p.   **AF151**
A chronological listing of nearly 400 Canadian federal royal commissions, with notes on the appointment of the commission and indication of whether or not the report was printed; if so, in what form; and
whether or not the report has been located. Index of subjects, names of
commissioners, and authors and titles of special studies.   Z1373.H4

Higgins, Marion Villiers. Canadian government publications : a manual for librarians. Chicago : Amer. Libr. Assoc.,
1935. 582 p. : ill.   **AF152**
Beginning with the French regime, 1608–1760, lists Canadian
government publications to 1935, including a historical summary of issuing bodies. Arrangement is by department with subject and author
index.   Z1373.C2H6

Catalogs and indexes

Government of Canada publications = Publications du
gouvernement du Canada. v. 27 (Jan./Mar. 1979)– . Ottawa :
Canadian Government Publishing Centre, 1979– . Quarterly,
with annual index.   **AF153**
Continues *Catalogue of official publications of the Parliament
and government of Canada*, 1928–48; *Canadian government publications: catalogue*, v. 1–17, 1953–69. Earlier volumes of the present series (with slight variations in the subtitle) were published by different
agencies: 1954–70 by Dept. of Public Printing and Stationery; 1971–75
by Information Canada; 1976–78 by Dept. of Supply and Services; beginning 1979 issued by the Canadian Government Publishing Centre.
In three parts: pt. 1, Parliamentary publications; pt. 2, Departmental publications; pt. 3, Index. Pts. 1 and 2 are in two sections: English
and French; the index is bilingual.

Provincial publications

Maillet, Lise. Provincial royal commissions and commissions
of inquiry, 1867–1982 : a selective bibliography = Commissions royales provinciales et commissions d'enquête, 1867–
1982 : bibliographie sélective. Ottawa : National Library of
Canada, 1986. 254 p.   **AF154**
For annotation, *see* CJ303.   Z1373.3.M34

Pross, Catherine A. Guide to the identification and acquisition of Canadian government publications : provinces and territories. 2nd ed. Halifax, N.S. : Dalhousie Univ., Univ. Libraries, School of Libr. Serv. ; London : Vine, 1983. 103 p. (Dalhousie University Libraries. Occasional paper, 16, rev.).
                                             AF155
1st ed., 1977.
Arranged by province or territory. In addition to providing information about publication activity and how to purchase the documents,
indicates collection strengths of various libraries in order to facilitate
interlibrary borrowing.
§ Records of Canadian provincial publications are provided by:
Publications of the government of British Columbia, 1871–1947, by
Marjorie C. Holmes (Victoria, 1950. 254 p.); *Publications of the government of the Province of Canada, 1841–1867*, by Olga B. Bishop

(Ottawa : National Library of Canada, 1963. 351 p.); *Publications of the governments of the Northwest Territories, 1876–1905*, by Christine MacDonald (Regina : Legislative Library, 1952. 109 p.); *Publications of the governments of Nova Scotia, Prince Edward Island, New Brunswick, 1758–1952*, by Olga B. Bishop (Ottawa : National Library, 1957. 237 p.); *Publications of the government of Ontario, 1867–1900*, by Olga B. Bishop (Toronto : Ministry of Government Services, 1976. 409 p.); *Publications of the government of Ontario, 1901–1955*, by Hazel I. MacTaggart (Toronto : Univ. of Toronto Pr., 1964. 303 p.); *Publications of the government of Ontario, 1956–1971*, by Hazel I. MacTaggart (Toronto : Ministry of Government Services, 1975. 410 p.); *Ontario royal commissions and commissions of inquiry, 1867–1978*, by Susan Waintman and Ana Tampold (Toronto : Legislative Library, 1980. 74 p.); and *Répertoire des publications gouvernementales du Québec de 1867 à 1964*, by André Beaulieu, Jean-Charles Bonenfant and Jean Hamelin (Québec : Impr. de la Reine, 1968. 554 p.; *Supplément, 1965–68*, 1970. 388 p.). Mohan Bhatia's *Canadian provincial government publications* (Rev. & enl. ed. Saskatoon : Univ. of Saskatchewan Libr., 1971. 19 p.) is a bibliography of relevant bibliographies. Z1373.3.P7

Collections

Documenting Canada : a history of modern Canada in documents / Dave De Brou and Bill Waiser, editors. Saskatoon, Sask. : Fifth House Publishers, c1992. 702 p. **AF156**
For annotation, *see* DB206. F1033.D63

Mexico

Fernández de Zamora, Rosa María. Las publicaciones oficiales de México : guía de publicaciones periódicas y seriadas, 1937–1970. México : Universidad Nacional Autónoma de México, Instituto de Investigaciones Sociales, 1977. 238 p. (Universidad Nacional Autónoma de México. Instituto de Investigaciones Bibliográficas. Ser. guías, 5). **AF157**
Continues *Mexican government publications* by A. M. Rei (Wash. : U.S. Govt. Print. Off., 1940).
Introductory chapters on official publications, their production and distribution, are followed by detailed listings of official serial publications for the period indicated. The lists are arranged by issuing agency and include contents notes for many of the series. Index of subjects and titles. Z1419.F4

Latin America

Latin American serial documents : a holdings list / comp. by Rosa Quintero Mesa. Ann Arbor, Mich. : Univ. Microfilms, Xerox Education Group, 1968–1976. 12 v. : ill. **AF158**
Prepared under a grant from the Ford Foundation to the University of Florida Libraries.
Contents: v. 1, Colombia; v. 2, Brazil; v. 3, Cuba; v. 4, Mexico; v. 5, Argentina; v. 6, Bolivia; v. 7, Chile; v. 8, Ecuador; v. 9, Paraguay; v. 10, Peru; v. 11, Uruguay; v. 12, Venezuela.
Each volume provides a bibliography with locations for as many serial documents as could be identified for each country from the time of its formation or date of independence. Lists are based on the holdings of the University of Florida Library, but each has been checked in those libraries which once had Farmington Plan assignments for the area in question. In addition, individual lists have been checked in other libraries having special collections or special interest in a given country.

Library of Congress. A guide to the official publications of the other American republics. Wash. : U.S. Govt. Print. Off., [1945–48]. 19 v. (Library of Congress. Latin American series, no. 9 [etc.]). **AF159**
Superintendent of Documents classification: LC1.16: .
Repr. : N.Y. : Johnson Reprint Corp., [1964].
James B. Childs, gen. ed. 1945; Henry V. Besso, gen. ed. 1946–49.
Contents: v. 1, Argentina (1945); v. 2, Bolivia (1945); v. 3, Brazil, comp. by John De Noia (1948, 1949); v. 4, Chile, comp. by Otto Neuburger (1947); v. 5, Colombia, [comp. by] James B. Childs (1948); v. 6, Costa Rica, comp. by Henry V. Besso (1947); v. 7, Cuba (1945); v. 8, Dominican Republic, comp. by John De Noia (1947); v. 9, Ecuador, comp. by John De Noia (1947); v. 10, El Salvador, comp. by John De Noia (1947); v. 11, Guatemala, comp. by Henry V. Besso (1947); v. 12, Haiti (1947); v. 13, Honduras (1947); v. 14, Nicaragua, comp. by John De Noia (1947); v.15, Panama, comp. by John De Noia (1947); v. 16, Paraguay, [comp. by] James B. Childs (1947); v. 17, Peru, comp. by John De Noia (1948, 1949); v. 18, Uruguay, comp. by John De Noia and Glenda Crevenna (1948, 1949); v. 19, Venezuela, comp. by Otto Neuburger (1948, 1949).
A series of guides, each of which gives information about general publications, including official gazettes, session laws, codes, constitution, etc., followed by the publications of the legislative, executive, and judicial branches. Time period covered starts with independence and ends at date of compilation. Includes index by author, title.
Z1605.U64

South America

Brazil

Lombardi, Mary. Brazilian serial documents : a selective and annotated guide. Bloomington : Indiana Univ. Pr., 1974. 445 p. **AF160**
Sponsored by the Indiana University Latin American Studies Program.
Listing is by issuing agency, with index of titles and agencies. A detailed table of contents serves as an outline of government structure. About 1,400 entries with full bibliographical details and notes on the agencies. Z1679.L65

Chile

Publicaciones oficiales de Chile, 1973–1983 / dirigida por María Teresa Sanz con la colaboración de Manuel Cornejo A., Héctor Gómez F. ; compilada por Manuel Cornejo A. ... [et al.]. Santiago, Chile : Instituto Profesional de Santiago, Escuela de Bibliotecología y Documentación, 1985. 196 p. **AF161**
Lists more than 4,000 government publications by agency. Author and agency indexes, but no detailed subject approach.
Z1709.P83

Uruguay

Musso Ambrosi, Luis Alberto. Bibliografía del Poder Legislativo desde sus comienzos hasta el ano 1965. Montevideo : [Centro de Estudios del Pasado Uruguayo], 1967. 236 p. **AF162**
A bibliography of the major official publications of Uruguay's National Congress from 1830 through 1965, plus some earlier publications of provincial bodies for 1825–30. Includes author, geographic and subject indexes.

Venezuela

Instituto Autónomo Biblioteca Nacional. Sección de Publicaciones Oficiales. Catálogo de publicaciones oficiales, 1840–1977 / por Beatriz Martínez de Cartay. Mérida : Imprenta Oficial del Estado Mérida, 1978. 445 p.   **AF163**
    A listing by ministry or other issuing body of Venezuelan official publications on file at the Biblioteca Nacional. Full bibliographical citations are given; indexed.   Z1919.I55

Europe (by region)

Europe, Western

Official publications of Western Europe / ed. by Eve Johansson. London : Mansell ; Bronx, N.Y. : H.W. Wilson, 1984–88. 2 v. : ill.   **AF164**
    Contents: v. 1, Denmark, Finland, France, Ireland, Italy, Luxembourg, Netherlands, Spain, and Turkey; v. 2, Austria, Belgium, Federal Republic of Germany, Greece, Norway, Portugal, Sweden, Switzerland, and United Kingdom.
    Designed to give "an overview of the main publications, their indexing and bibliographic control, the languages in which they appear, and their availability."—*Pref.* Arranged by country; indexes of organizations and titles, and of subjects.   Z291.O38

Europe, Eastern

Official publications of the Soviet Union and Eastern Europe, 1945–1980 : a select annotated bibliography / ed. by Gregory Walker. London : Mansell ; Bronx, N.Y. : Distr. by H.W. Wilson, 1982. 620 p.   **AF165**
    Covers Albania, Bulgaria, Czechoslovakia, German Democratic Republic, Hungary, Yugoslavia, Poland, Romania, and the U.S.S.R., each country being dealt with by an individual contributor. Each chapter has an introduction outlining postwar political and administrative developments and the state of official publishing. "Official publications" has been interpreted broadly and contributors "were asked to include what they regarded as the most important material within the general guidelines for coverage …, and to give details of any existing bibliographies which offered useful data on official publications."—*Pref.* Within country sections publications are grouped topically under such headings as: Constitutional documents, General party documents, General statistics, Military affairs, Economic affairs. "Where documents are available in Western published sources, these are stated."—*Introd.* The lists of bibliographies and general reference works are not limited to official publications of the country concerned. The U.S.S.R. is accorded much fuller treatment than the other countries. Indexed.   Z2483.W34

Europe (by country)

Denmark

Bibliografi over Danmarks offentlige Publikationer. Årg. 1 (1948)– . København : Dansk Bibliografisk Kontor, 1949– . Annual.   **AF166**
    Title varies: 1948–59, *Bibliografisk, Fortegnelse over statens Tryksager og statsunderstøttede Publikationer*. Forms part of the Danish national bibliography; *see* AA605.

At head of title: Impressa publica Regni Danici 1948– .
    Begins with a section on parliamentary publications, then is arranged by issuing ministry. Indexes by periodical and serial title, name of institution, subject, author, and a brief English index of subjects and corporate authors.   Z2569.A25

Finland

Valtion virallisjulkaisut = Statens officiella publikationer = Government publications in Finland. 1961– . Helsinki : Kirjasto., 1962– . Annual.   **AF167**
    An index of government publications arranged by Finnish names of agencies with cross-references from the Swedish names. Name index and separate subject indexes for publications in Finnish, in Swedish, and in other languages (the latter index being in English).   Z2520.A3F25

France

Bibliographie nationale française : publications officielles : bibliographie etablie par la Bibliothèque nationale. no. 1 (26 fevr. 1992)– . Paris : Bibliothèque nationale, Office général du livre, 1992– . Bimonthly.   **AF168**
    Continues:
    (1) The "Publications officielles" section of *Bibliographie de la France* designated as "Supplement F" during the 1950–71 period and continued as a supplementary publication during the time the national bibliography was entitled *Bibliographie de la France-Biblio* (AA627).
    (2) *Bibliographie de la France. Supplement II, Publications officielles; notices établies par la Bibliotheque nationale* (1977–89; AA626).
    (3) *Bibliographie nationale française. Supplement II, Publications officielles: notices établies part la Bibliothéque nationale* (1990–91).
    Lists publications from the national to the local level; entries are classed in several sections listed at the beginning of each issue. Index in each issue, cumulating annually.   Z2165.B592

Dampierre, Jacques de. Les publications officielles des pouvoirs publics : étude critique et administrative. Paris : Picard, 1942. 628 p.   **AF169**
    The most authoritative source on French government publications before 1943. A detailed discussion of the main types of publications, their productions and distribution. Other topics covered include copyright law, training of librarians, legal deposit and the work of various commissions that studies administrative documents. The full texts of many of the reports cited appear in the appendix. Includes bibliographies of publications. There is no index, but an analytic table of contents is included.   Z7164.G7D3

France. Journal officiel de la République française. [Éd. complete]. 2e année, no. 244 (5 sept. 1870)– . Paris : [s.n.], 1870– .   **AF170**
    Preceded by: *Gazette nationale, ou Moniteur universel*, 1789–1810; *Moniteur universel, journal officiel*, 1811–68; *Journal officiel de l'Empire français*, 1869–4 sept. 1870.
    From 1881, in several parts, the main ones being: (1) Lois et décrets; (2) Débats parlementaires: (a) Sénat, and (b) Assemblée Nationale; (3) Documents administratifs; (4) Impressions; (5) Avis et rapports du Conseil Economique et Social.
    Designations vary. Édition du matin began at date given above; Édition du soir began with no. 245, 6 sept. 1870.
    Appears daily except Mondays and holidays; contains texts of national laws and decrees, important administrative orders and proclamations, and parliamentary debates and committee reports.
    Indexes (Tables) published annually.
    For more complete information, *see* Gloria Westfall's *French official publications* (AF172).

Répertoire des publications officielles (séries et périodiques) : Administrations centrales françaises, établissements public. 1985–[198?]. [Paris] : Documentation Française, 1985–[198?]. **AF171**

Supersedes *Répertoire des publications officielles : séries et périodiques* (Paris : Documentation Française, 1979–80. 3 v.); and *Répertoire des publications périodiques et de serie de l'administration française* (Paris: Documentation Française, 1973).

Issued by the Commission de Coordination de la Documentation Administrative as a separate issue of *Bulletin signalétique d'information administrative* for April 1985.

Lists 893 periodicals issued by government ministries and other public institutions, including scientific and cultural organizations. Provides title, address of issuing agency, frequency, summary of the contents, etc. Arranged by ministry, with subject, abbreviation, agency, and title indexes.

Continued by: *Répertoire des publications en série de l'administration française (périodiques et collections)*, Commission de coordination de la documentation administrative (4th ed. [1990]– . Paris : Documentation française, 1990–).

Westfall, Gloria. French official publications. Oxford ; N.Y. : Pergamon, 1980. 209 p. : ill. (Guides to official publications, v. 6). **AF172**

Offers a survey of French official publishing, with discussion of official publications and their issuing bodies and the problems of bibliographic control, dissemination, and acquisition of French government documents. Attention is given to the publishing history of various series and to available guides, indexes and bibliographies. Devotes a separate chapter to the *Journal officiel* (AF170). Indexed.

Z2169.W47

Germany

Childs, James Bennett. German Federal Republic official publications, 1949–1957 : with inclusion of preceding zonal official publications; a survey. Wash. : Library of Congress, Reference Dept., Serial Div., 1958. 2 v. in 1 (887 p.). **AF173**

Contents: v. 1, Bundespräsident—Bundesministerium der Justiz; v. 2, Bundesministerium für das Post– und Fernmeldewesen—Zonal period.

Describes the agencies of the Federal Republic and of the zonal organization with lists of their publications. Publications of the Länder are not included. Publications are organized under issuing body, then serials, monographs, and maps. Library of Congress holdings as of Oct. 1957 are indicated. Index of agency headings. Z663.44.G4

Deutsche Bücherei. Monatliches Verzeichnis der reichsdeutschen amtlichen Druckschriften. v. 1 (1928)–v. 17, no. 6 (1944). Berlin : Reichs– und Staatsverlag GmbH., 1928–44. Monthly with annual cumulative index. **AF174**

Lists federal, state, and city publications. Indexes by subject, author, agency.

Great Britain

Guides

Bond, Maurice F. Guide to the records of Parliament. London : H.M.S.O., 1971. 352 p. **AF175**

At head of title: House of Lords Record Office.

"Describes the complete range of records preserved within the Palace of Westminster: the records of both Houses of Parliament; all documents which have been presented to the two Houses or purchased by them; and the papers which have accumulated in the various Parlia-mentary and non-Parliamentary offices of the Palace."—*Pref.* Deals with both manuscript and printed records. Includes historical notes pertinent to the various types of records. Indexed. CD1063.B63

Butcher, David. Official publications in Britain. 2nd ed. London : Libr. Assoc., 1991. 192 p. **AF176**

Covers the scope and structure of official publishing in Britain, parliamentary publications, government department publishing, national and regional public bodies, bibliographic control and selection sources, avaliability of official publications and local government publishing. Index by organization, type of publication and title.

Z2009.B93

Ford, Percy. A guide to parliamentary papers : what they are; how to find them; how to use them / Percy Ford, Grace Ford. 3rd ed. Shannon, Ireland : Irish Univ. Pr., 1972. 87 p. **AF177**

1st ed., 1955.

A useful introductory guide, giving a brief history and description of the contents of the papers and indexes. The appendix includes notes on collections of papers, and lists of indexes, catalogs, and official guides to sources. Z2009.A1F6

Richard, Stephen. Directory of British official publications : a guide to sources. 2nd ed. London : Mansell, [1984]. 431 p. **AF178**

1st ed., 1981.

"Attempts to solve problems facing librarians, members of the public and booksellers who find considerable difficulty not only in hearing of official publications that are of interest ... but in obtaining copies of known publications."—*Introd.* Not a bibliography of official publications, but a directory of the organizations that issue and distribute them. Organizations are grouped geographically (i.e., United Kingdom, Great Britain, England and Wales; Northern Ireland; Scotland, etc.) then by type (central government; libraries, museums, galleries; research council establishments, etc.). Entries provide information on the types of publications issued, the subjects covered, and availability of the publications. Indexed. Z2009.R533

Rodgers, Frank. A guide to British government publications. N.Y. : H.W. Wilson, 1980. 750 p. **AF179**

A guide to British parliamentary and other government publications giving background information on the issuing body and the types of publications issued. Three main sections: General; Parliamentary; Executive agencies. Emphasizes the central departments but includes many committees, boards, councils, and other agencies that actively publish. Includes glossary and index. Z2009.R62

Bibliography

Catalogue of British official publications not published by HMSO. 1980– . Cambridge, Eng. : Chadwyck-Healey, 1981– . Bimonthly, with annual cumulations. **AF180**

"The majority of the publications listed in the Catalogue are available on microfiche from Chadwyck-Healey."—*t. p.*

A listing of the publications of some 350 organizations "financed or controlled completely or partially by the British Government, which are *not* published by Her Majesty's Stationery Office (HMSO)."—*Scope.* Includes periodicals, pamphlets, technical reports, memoranda, publicity material, audiovisual aids, etc. Entry is by issuing agency; subject index. Keyword index on microfiche, 1989– .

Check list of British official serial publications. 1967–. [London] : British Museum, State Paper Room, [1967?]– . Annual. **AF181**

1975–78, issued by British Library, Official Publications Library; 1979– , issued by British Library, Reference Division.

A listing of serial publications of the British government, arranged by title, except in cases where the issuing body is considered an essential part of the title—e.g., annual reports, bulletins, etc.—and is entered first. Indicates issuing body, availability, frequency, latest part received in the British Library. Z2009.B87

Catalogs and indexes

•**Catalogue of the United Kingdom official publications** : (UKOP) [database]. Cambridge, Eng. : Chadwyck-Healey, 1980– . **AF182**

 Available on CD-ROM, updated quarterly.

 Includes H.M.S.O. publications, non-H.M.S.O. publications of official organizations, and publications of international organizations available through H.M.S.O.

Great Britain. Stationery Office. Catalogues and indexes of British government publications, 1920–1970. Bishops Stortford : Chadwyck-Healey, 1974. 5 v. **AF183**

 Reprint of the catalogs published by H.M.S.O., London.

 Contents: v. 1, Consolidated indexes to British government publications, 1936–1970; v. 2, Annual catalogues of British government publications, 1920–1935; v. 3, Annual catalogues of British government publications, 1936–1950; v. 4, Annual catalogues of British government publications, 1951–1960; v. 5, Annual catalogues of British government publications, 1961–1970. Z2009.G85

——————— Cumulative index to the annual catalogues of Her Majesty's Stationery Office publications, 1922–1972 / comp. by Ruth Matteson Blackmore. Wash. : Carrollton Pr., 1976. 2 v. **AF184**

 Represents "a merger of twenty-three separate annual and quinquennial indexes" *(User's guide)* into a single alphabet, giving references to entries in the original catalogs. Variant forms of subject headings used at different periods have not been reconciled and cross-references from such forms are not always provided. Basic purpose of the cumulation was to provide an index to the microfilm edition of documents for the period published by United States Historical Documents Institute. Z2009.G85

——————— HMSO agency catalogue. 1986–87– . London : H.M.S.O., c1988– . Annual. **AF185**

 Previously: 1955–64, *International organisations publications*, a supplement to the Stationery Office's *Government publications* (AF190); 1965–1975, *International organisations and overseas agencies publications*; 1976–1984, *International organisations publications*; 1985, *International organisations catalogue*.

 "Lists items placed on sale by HMSO ... for the British, European and international organizations for which HMSO is the United Kingdom agent."—*Introd.* Arranged alphabetically by issuing agency; author and keyword index. Z6464.I6I62

HMSO annual catalogue. [London] : H.M.S.O., 1986– . **AF186**

 Also available in microfiche.

 Continues: Great Britain. Stationery Office. *Government publications*, issued under various titles 1922–84 (AF190).

 The annual cumulation of the *HMSO monthly catalogue* (AF187). Includes Parliamentary publications, public general acts, local actas, measures of the General Synod, list of publications by agency, Northern Ireland publications. Alphabetical index; ISBN index.

 Z2009.G822

HMSO monthly catalogue. Feb. 1986– . London : H.M.S.O., c1986– . Monthly. **AF187**

 Continues: Great Britain. Stationery Office. *Government publications monthly list* (AF190 *note*).

 Contains listings of parliamentary publications, agency publications (arranged by agency), Northern Ireland publications, and publications of international intergovernmental organizations for which HMSO is an agent. The index is cumulative in each issue and has entries for subjects, authors, chairmen and editors in one alphabetical sequence. Cumulated by: *HMSO annual catalogue* (AF186).

Printing for Parliament, 1641–1700 / ed. by Sheila Lambert. London : Swift Printers (Sales), 1984. 323 p. (Special series / List & Index Society, v. 20). **AF188**

A chronological list of items ordered to be printed by Parliament. "The loss of titles for the period 1641–48 is of the order of 25%. To minimise this distortion ... this list makes reference to all papers known to have been printed for parliament, whether or not copies have been found."—*p.i.* Detailed bibliographic information, including reference to available copies, is provided. Includes a checklist of titles arranged by Wing number. Z2018.P75

19th and 20th centuries

Great Britain. Stationery Office. Consolidated index to government publications. 1936/40–1976/80. London : H.M.S.O., 1952–1982. Quinquennial. **AF189**

 These 5-year indexes consolidate the indexing of the annual lists, which are consecutively paged in anticipation of the publication of the indexes. Z2009.G822

——————— Government publications. 1922–Jan. 1986. London : H.M.S.O., 1923–1986. Annual. **AF190**

 Title varies: *Consolidated list of parliamentary and Stationery Office publications*, 1922; *Consolidated list of government publications*, 1923–50; *Government publications: consolidated list*, 1951–53; *Government publications: catalogue*, 1954–55; *Catalogue of government publications*, 1956–71; *Government publications listed during ...*, [1971?]–1976; *Government publications*, 1976–84. Continued by: *HMSO annual catalogue* (AF186), cumulating issues of *HMSO monthly catalogue* (AF187).

 Continues the *Quarterly list ... of official publications* (London : Stat. Off., 1897–1922).

 Arranged by Parliamentary Papers, then by issuing agency. Index by author, title, series, agency.

 § *Government publications monthly list*, also titled *Government publications of ...* (monthly, 1939–Jan. 1986). Issues were intended primarily as sales catalogs; these were superseded by *Government publications*. Continued by *HMSO monthly catalog* (AF187).

——————— The sale catalogues of British government publications, 1836–1921. Dobbs Ferry, N.Y. : Oceana, 1977. 4 v. **AF191**

 Reprint of the catalogs published by H.M.S.O., London, 1836–1921.

 Contents: v. 1, 1836–1889; v. 2, 1890–1900; v. 3, 1901–1911; v. 4, 1912–1921. Z2009.G85

Maltby, Arthur. Ireland in the nineteenth century : a breviate of official publications / by Arthur Maltby and Jean Maltby. Oxford ; N.Y. : Pergamon, 1979. 269 p. : facsims. (Guide to official publications, v. 4). **AF192**

 Covers 600 19th-century reports relating to Ireland. Arranged by topic. All publications are annotated; some annotations are quite lengthy. Includes a "Select list of annual or other recurring reports." Index to topics. DA950.M25

Richard, Stephen. British government publications : an index to chairmen and authors. London : Libr. Assoc., 1974–[84]. 4 v. **AF193**

 Subtitle varies.

 Coverage begins with 1800.

 Vol. 3 is a cumulation of A. M. Morgan's index covering 1941–66 (2nd ed., 1973) and A. M. Morgan and L. R. Stephen's index for 1967–71 (1976), plus additional indexing through 1978; v. 4 includes pre-1979 reports discovered since publication of v. 1–3.

 Provides access to British government reports popularly referred to by name of the chairman of the committee or author of the report. Each volume arranged by name of chairman or author, with citation to the report (including Command Paper number or reference to House of Lords papers). Vol. 2 includes an "Alphabetical list of Royal Commissions and distinctive titles of committees, 1900–1940," with the name of the chairman listed. Z2009.R53

Parliamentary papers

Cockton, Peter. Subject catalogue of the House of Commons Parliamentary papers, 1801–1900. Cambridge, England ; Alexandria, Va. : Chadwyck-Healey, 1988. 5 v.   **AF194**

Contents: v. 1, Central government and administration; national finance and financial institutions; population and demography; statistics, agriculture and rural society; v. 2, Industry and industrial society; trade and commerce; transport and communication; v. 3, Law and order; local government and local finance; poverty and social administration; education; information and recreation; v. 4, Health and housing; Ireland; the churches and religious affairs; India, Ceylon, Burma and Afghanistan; v. 5, The dominions and colonies; slavery and the slave trade; defence and the armed services; foreign affairs and diplomacy.

Aims "to provide a comprehensive listing of the entire output of nineteenth century Parliamentary Papers in the form of a thematic subject catalog."—*Introd.* Earlier indexes generally exclude some areas. Offers a detailed, although somewhat confusing, classified arrangement. Titles "have been slightly shortened in some cases .... Others have been expanded by the insertion of added words, within brackets." Provides citations to both the bound set and the publisher's microfiche set. Includes an index, with cross-references, to the headings used in the classified section.

A review in *Government publications review* 16 (Sept./Oct., 1989) : 516 concludes that "The *Subject catalogue* complements but does not replace the existing indexes to the nineteenth century Sessional Papers .... Libraries whose research is done in this area will consider this a basic purchase."   Z2019.C63

Di Roma, Edward. A numerical finding list of British command papers published 1833–1961/62 / by Edward Di Roma and Joseph A. Rosenthal. [N.Y.] : New York Public Libr., 1967. 148 p.   **AF195**

Designed to allow researchers to find Command Papers that have been published in the British sessional papers. In order by Command Paper number; indicates the volume and beginning page.

§ Supplemented by Elizabeth A. McBride's *British command papers* (AF206).   Z2009.D5

Ford, Percy. Select list of British parliamentary papers, 1833–1899 / Percy Ford and Grace Ford. Oxford : Blackwell, 1953. 165 p.   **AF196**

Rev. repr.: Shannon : Irish Univ. Pr., 1969.

Arranged by subject, with an alphabetical index. Includes the "reports and all other material issued by committees and commissions or similar bodies of investigation into economic, social and constitutional questions, and matters of law and administration."—*Introd.* Supplements *Catalogue of parliamentary reports and a breviate of their contents ...* (AF198).

Continued by:

———. *A breviate of parliamentary papers, 1900–1916 : the foundation of the welfare state* (Oxford : Blackwell, 1957. 470 p. [Repr.: Shannon : Irish Univ. Pr., 1969]).

A guide, with abstracts, to 1,048 reports of British royal commissions and other committees of inquiry in the fields on constitutional, economic, financial, and social policy and legal administration. Arranged by broad subject list of individual documents. Index by title keywords and chairman or author.

———. *A breviate of parliamentary papers, 1917–1939* (Oxford : Blackwell, 1951; N.Y. : Macmillan, 1952. 571 p. [Rev. repr.: Shannon : Irish Univ. Pr., 1969]).

A guide to 1,200 reports, arranged like its predecessors.

———. ———. *1940–1954 : war and reconstruction* (Oxford : Blackwell, 1961. 515 p.).

"Follows the same pattern as the two previous breviates."—*Introd.*

———. *Select list of British parliamentary papers, 1955–1964*, by Percy Ford and Diana Marshallsay (Shannon : Irish Univ. Pr., [1970]. 117 p.).

———. *Ford list of British parliamentary papers, 1965–1974 : together with specialist commentaries*, ed. by Diana Marshallsay and J. H. Smith (Nedeln, Liechtenstein : KTO Pr., 1979. 452 p.).

Broad subject arrangement; subject/title index and chairman/author index.   J301.M3

Great Britain. Parliament. House of Commons. Catalogue of papers printed by order of the House of Commons from the year 1731 to 1800, in the custody of the Clerk of the Journals. [London], 1807. 101 p. in various pagings.   **AF197**

Repr.: London : HMSO, 1953.

Consists of three chronological lists, each with its own subject index: (1) Bills; (2) Reports; and (3) Accounts and Papers.   J301.A2

———————— Catalogue of parliamentary reports and a breviate of their contents : arranged under heads according to the subjects, 1696–1834. [London, 1836]. 220 p.   **AF198**

Repr.: Oxford : Blackwell, 1953.

Indexes the "1st series" of parliamentary reports (15 v.), the reports in the *Journals*, and those in the *Sessional papers*, 1801–34.

The reprint (entitled *Hansard's Catalogue and breviate ...*) includes a "Select list of House of Lords papers not in this breviate" by P. Ford and G. Ford.   J301.K62

———————— General alphabetical index to the bills, reports, estimates, accounts and papers printed by order of the House of Commons and to the papers presented by command, 1801–1948/49. London : Stat. Off., 1853–1960. 4 v.   **AF199**

Consists of the following unnumbered volumes: (1) General index to the accounts and papers, reports of the commissioners, estimates, etc., 1801–1852; (2) Indexes to bills and reports, 1801–1852, in two sections: General index to the bills, and General index to the reports of select committees; (3) General index, 1852–1899; and (4) General index, 1900–1948/49.

An index to the documents included in the parliamentary papers of the House of Commons, not including the papers of the House of Lords except insofar as these are duplicated in the Commons papers, and not including the publications of the bureaus and departments. Arranged alphabetically by rather large subjects; does not include many analytical entries. Gives fairly full information about each paper, including its full title, date, and bill, document, or command number, and a reference to the year and volume of the sessional papers in which it is to be found, and the paging as made up for the House of Commons set.

For most purposes these indexes supersede the decennial and annual indexes for the periods covered, although the latter may still be useful for analyses of comprehensive series and for the numerical list of command papers.

———. *General alphabetical index to the bills, reports, estimates, accounts and papers printed by order of the House of Commons and to the papers presented by command, 1950–1958/59–* (London : Stat. Off., 1963–).

Decennial cumulation of the annual indexes. Does not include the numerical lists. A continuation of the decennial indexes, 1870–1949, now superseded by the 50-year indexes.

———————— House of Commons sessional papers of the eighteenth century / ed. by Sheila Lambert. Wilmington, Del. : Scholarly Resources, Inc., [1975]. 2 v.   **AF200**

A session-by-session list; within each session entries are grouped as bills, reports, or accounts and papers. An index in v. 2 (p. 425–83) provides a subject approach. The papers have been reproduced on microfilm by Scholarly Resources, Inc.   J301.K625

———————— List of the bills, reports, estimates, and accounts and papers printed by order of the House of Commons and of the papers presented by command ... : with a general alphabetical index thereto. 1801– . London : Stat. Off., 1802– . Annual.   **AF201**

Issued annually as the final volume for each session of the *Sessional papers* of the House of Commons.

From 1828, contains not only an index, but also a list of bills and papers in their numerical order; in 1834, a list of Command Papers is added, and, in 1867, a preliminary list showing the makeup of the set for each session.

The index section is superseded through 1958/59 by the general indexes described above, but the numerical lists are still the only ones available for the period prior to 1833. Command Papers of the 1833–1961/62 period, asked for by number only, can be identified through Edward Di Roma and Joseph A. Rosenthal's *A numerical finding list of British command papers published 1833–1961/62* (AF195).

Great Britain. Parliament. House of Lords. General index to sessional papers printed by order of the House of Lords or presented by special command. London : Eyre, 1860–86. 3 v.
AF202

Publisher varies. Vol. 1 repr.: London : Stat. Off., 1938.
Contents: v. 1, 1801–59; v. 2, 1859–70; v. 3, 1871–85.
Arranged in one alphabetical sequence including subjects and personal names.　　　　　　　　　　　　　　　　　　J301.J6

•Index to House of Commons parliamentary papers [database]. Cambridge : Chadwyck-Healey, 1992– . 　**AF203**

Issued quarterly on CD-ROM. Each disc is cumulative from the 1991/92 session.

The House of Commons Library's *POLIS* database is used to prepare this index. House of Commons bills, papers, and Command Papers published from the beginning of the 1991/92 session to date are included. Includes also all papers ordered to be printed by Commons but not necessarily yet published. Subject terms used in the index are taken from the House of Commons *Library thesaurus*. There are two search modes: expert and novice. Searches can be done by categories: all, bills, command papers, House of Commons papers. Browse options are: all keywords, title, title keyword, subject, subject keyword, paper number, session, and date.

Irish University Press. Checklist of British parliamentary papers in the Irish University Press 1000-volume series, 1801–1899. Shannon : Irish Univ. Pr., [1972]. 218 p.　　**AF204**

A chronological and subject index to the contents of the selected papers reprinted in the Irish University Press subject sets. Includes a keyword title index and an index to chairmen and individual authors of reports and papers.　　　　　　　　　　　　　　Z2019.I73

Irish University Press series of British parliamentary papers : Indexes. Shannon : Irish Univ. Pr., [1968]. 8 v.　**AF205**

Title on spine: British parliamentary papers.
Contents: v. 1, 1696–1834, Hansard's Catalogue; v. 2, 1801–1852, Reports of select committees; v. 3, 1801–1852, Accounts and papers; v. 4, 1852–1869, Bills, reports, estimates, and papers; v. 5, 1801–1852, Bills, printed by order of the House of Commons; v. 6, 1870–1879, Bills, reports, estimates, accounts, and papers; v. 7, 1880–1889, Bills, reports, estimates, and papers; v. 8, 1890–1899, Bills, reports, estimates, accounts, and papers.

A reprint of existing indexes (e.g., those noted in AF198, AF199), not new indexing prepared specifically for the Irish University Press "1000-volume series." On each index page there is "an overprinted heading at the top of the outside margin" (*verso of t.p.*) so that keying to the IUP set can be added by hand or by pasting in slips supplied "from time to time" by the publisher.　　　　　　Z2019.I73

McBride, Elizabeth A. British command papers : a numerical finding list 1962/63–1976/77. Atlanta, Ga. : Emory General Libraries, c1982. 35 p.　　　　　　　　**AF206**

Supplements Edward Di Roma and Joseph A. Rosenthal, comps., *A numerical finding list of British command papers published 1833–1961/62* (AF195). Lists the session, volume number, and beginning page number for some 5,000 Command papers.　　Z2009.D5

Rodgers, Frank. Serial publications in the British parliamentary papers, 1900–1968 : a bibliography. Chicago : Amer. Libr. Assoc., 1971. 146 p.　　　　　　**AF207**

Lists some 1,300 serial publications which have appeared in the House of Commons Sessional Papers since 1900. Arranged by issuing agency, with useful historical notes on the principal agencies.
Z2009.R63

Parliamentary debates

Great Britain. Parliament. Parliamentary debates. London, 1804– . v. 1 (1803)– .　　　　　　　　　　**AF208**

Generally cited as *Hansard* or *Hansard's parliamentary debates* after its 19th-century printers, Luke and T.C. Hansard. Publisher varies.

Contents:
[1st series.] v. 1 (1803)–v. 41 (1820).
n.s. [new series]. v. 1 (1820)–v. 25 (1830).
3rd. series. v. 1 (1830)–v. 356 (1890–91).
4th series. v. 1 (1892)–v. 199 (1908).

In the first four series, debates in Commons and Lords were published under the same cover. Beginning with the 5th series, they were divided:

5th series : Lords, v. 1 (1909)– .
5th series : Commons, v. 1 (1909)–v. 999 (1980–81).
6th series : Commons, v. 1 (1980–81)– .

There is a general index to the 66 v. of the 1st–2nd series (London : Baldwin, 1834. 2 v.); for series 3–5 the sessional indexes—sometimes in separate volumes, sometimes included in the last volume of debates of the session—must be used.

The 1st through 4th series were unofficial; their reports of debates are neither complete nor verbatim, and not all division lists are given in full. The 5th series is official and contains complete and verbatim reports of debates, and all division lists. For an interesting account of parliamentary debates of the 19th to the 20th century *see* H.D. Jordan, "Reports of parliamentary debates 1803–1908," *Economica* 11 (Nov. 1931) : 437–49.

The period before 1803 is covered by William Cobbett's *Parliamentary history of England from the earliest period to the year 1803* (London : Hansard, 1806–20. 36 v.), which is a retrospective compilation rather than a current record. For an account of sources on which it is based, or which are available for the earlier period, *see* "General collections of reports of parliamentary debates for the period since 1660," *Bulletin of the Institute of Historical Research* [Univ. of London], 10 (Feb. 1933) : 171–77.　　　　　　　　　　J301.H22

Jones, David Lewis. Debates and proceedings of the British parliaments : a guide to printed sources. London : H.M.S.O., 1986. 152 p. (House of Commons Library document, no. 16).
AF209

Based on holdings of the House of Commons and House of Lords Libraries. Intends "to provide as complete a record as possible of the printed sources" (*Introd.*) for the debates and proceedings from 1278 to the 1980s for the British Parliament; from the 13th century to 1800 for the Parliament of Ireland; and from the 12th century to 1704 for the Parliament of Scotland. Citations to *STC*, Wing, *Eighteenth century short title catalogue*, etc., are noted. Author and title index.
Z2009.J65

Ireland, Northern

Maltby, Arthur. The government of Northern Ireland, 1922–72 : a catalogue and breviate of Parliamentary papers. Dublin : Irish Univ. Pr. ; N.Y. : Barnes & Noble, 1974. 235 p.　**AF210**

Includes parliamentary papers considered to have lasting interest. Some publications issued by government dpeartments are included. Arranged by 16 different subject classes. Lengthy annotations for each publication. Two appendixes: Westminster reports (concerning Northern Ireland) and Select list of annual and other recurring reports. Index by title, chairmen, and authors.　　　　　　Z2035.M34

Ireland

Maltby, Arthur. Irish official publications : a guide to Republic of Ireland papers, with a breviate of reports 1922–1972 / by Arthur Maltby and Brian McKenna. Oxford ; N.Y. : Pergamon, 1980. 377 p. (Guides to official publications, v.7).   **AF211**

    The "Guide" section describes how to find and acquire various types of Irish official publications. Includes background information and an explanation of terms and symbols. A list of libraries with good collections is included. The "Breviate" section lists publications arranged in ten subject areas, from agriculture to transport and communications. Name and subject index.   Z2035.M345

Netherlands

Bibliografie van in Nederland verschenen officiële uitgaven bij rijksoverheid en provinciale besturen. v. 49 (1977)– . 's-Gravenhage : Koninklijke Bibliotheek, 1978– . Annual.   **AF212**

    Continues: *Nederlandsche overheidsuitgaven* (v. 1 [1929]–v. 12–13 [1940–41]. 's-Gravenhage : Algemeene Lnadsdrukkerij, 1930–43); *Nederlandse overheidesuitgaven* (v. 14–18 [1942–46]–v. 24 [1952]. 's-Gravenhage : Staatsdrukkerij ; Nijhoff ; 1947–53); *Bibliografie van in Nederland verschenen officiële en semiofficiële uitgaven* (v. 25 [1953]–v. 48 [1976]. 's-Gravenhage : Staatsdrukkerij, 1954–77).

    Vols. 1–45 list government publications by agency with personal name and subject indexes. Vol. 46– list publications by personal author or title with title and subject indexes and list of titles arranged by agency.

    Includes provincial publications. 1929–39 includes publications of Dutch East and West Indies.

Norway

Bibliografi over Norges offentlige publikasjoner / Utgitt av Universitetsbiblioteket i Oslo. [1. arg.] (1956)–35. arg., del 2 (1990). Oslo : Universitetsforlaget, 1956–1991. Annual.   **AF213**

    Listings by agency, down to the local level. Includes government publications and publications produced with grants from the government. Pt. 1 has serials and monographs, pt. 2 ministerial and departmental circulars.   Z2599.O8

Russia

Library of Congress. Russian imperial government serials on microfilm in the Library of Congress : a guide to the uncatalogued collection / comp. by Harold M. Leich with the assistance of staff members of the Library of Congress European Division and Preservation Microfilming Office. Wash. : The Library, 1985. 135 p.   **AF214**

    Superintendent of Documents classification: LC 43.8:R92.

    The 967 titles include "publications of pre-revolutionary Russian governmental bodies and units at various levels ... publications of a large number of general and specialized societies, associations, and institutions ... [and] a group of miscellaneous serials" (*Introd.*) arranged alphabetically by romanized title. It does not include titles which the Library of Congress has cataloged. Information provided includes statement of responsibility, place of publication, related titles, and dates which the Library of Congress has filmed; does not give beginning and ending dates. Indexed by issuing body and by place of publi-

cation. (There is a broad subject arrangement under cities with more than 12 titles). Also includes a summary guide to reels.   Z6956.S65L52

Sweden

Årsbibliografi över Sveriges offentliga publikationer / utg. av Riksdagsbiblioteket. 1931/33–1974/75. Stockholm : Beckmans, 1934–1979. Annual.   **AF215**

    A listing by department or issuing agency, with personal name and subject indexes.

    Continued by: *Sveriges statliga publikationer, bibliografi* (Årg. 46–48 [1976–1978]–årg. 54 [1984]. Stockholm : Riksdagsbibliotek, 1983–85. Annual.) and by *Statliga publikationer, årsbibliografi* (AF216).   Z2629.S94

Statliga publikationer, årsbibliografi. 1985– . Stockholm : Riksdagsbiblioteket, 1987– . Annual.   **AF216**

    Added title: Swedish government publications, annual bibliography.

    Continues *Årsbibliografi över Sveriges offentliga publikationer* and *Sveriges statliga publikationer, bibliografi* (AF215).

    Arranged by agency, then alphabetically by title. Subject and personal name indexes.   Z2629.S94

Switzerland

Bibliographie der schweizerischen Amtsdruckschriften = Bibliographie des publications officielles suisses. Bd. 1 (1946)– . Bern : Schweizerische Landesbibliothek, 1947– . Biennial.   **AF217**

    Frequency varies; annual, 1946–62.

    Originally this listing of official publications was drawn from *Das schweizer Buch* (AA839). Beginning with Bd. 22/23 (1967/68) the list attempts to be as comprehensive as possible in its coverage of monographic publications of the cantons and municipalities of Switzerland as well as of federal government publications regularly listed in the national bibliography. Index by author, title.   Z2779.B4

Africa

Balima, Mildred Grimes. Botswana, Lesotho, and Swaziland : a guide to official publications, 1868–1968 / comp. by Mildred Grimes Balima, African Section. Wash. : General Reference and Bibliography Div., Library of Congress, 1971. 84 p.   **AF218**

    Superintendent of Documents classification: LC 2.8: B65/ 868–968 .

    "This bibliography includes citations to documents of the former High Commission Territories during British protection and since independence, together with reports prepared by agencies or individuals with official authorization and funds. ... To increase the usefulness ... , a number of relevant British official papers have been included, some of which pertain to Bechuanaland (Botswana) and Swaziland before the establishment of British protectorates."—*Pref.*   Z3559.B3

Boston University. Libraries. Catalog of African government documents. 3rd ed., rev. & enl. Boston : G. K. Hall, 1976. 679 p.   **AF219**

    1st–2nd eds., 1960–64, had title: *Catalog of African government documents and African area index.*

    Reproduces the catalog cards in classed arrangement (based on the Library of Congress schedule J700–881). This edition lists more than 13,000 titles, many of them serials. A classed catalog with country index; listing under country is by main entry only. The "African area index" does not appear in this edition.   Z3507.5.B67

Gibson, Mary Jane. Portuguese Africa : a guide to official publications / comp. [in the] African Section. Wash. : General Reference and Bibliography Div., Reference Dept., Library of Congress, 1967. 217 p.   **AF220**
Superintendent of Documents classification: LC 2.8:P83.
Covers documents from 1850 to 1964, listing "publications of the governments of Angola, the Cape Verde Islands, Mozambique, Portuguese Guinea, and the São Thomé e Principe Islands and also of Portugual pertaining to its African possessions."—*Pref.* Arranged by geographical area; index of subjects and individual authors. American library location indicated for many items.   Z3871.G5

Howell, John Bruce. East African community : subject guide to official publications. Wash. : Library of Congress : For sale by the U.S. Govt. Print. Off., 1976. 272 p.   **AF221**
Superintendent of Documents classification: LC 1.12/2:Af8.
"This is a subject guide to official publications of the East African Community and its predecessors for the period 1926 to 1974 and of the East African region (including Kenya, Tanzania, and Uganda) for the period 1859 to 1974 issued by Great Britain or one of the three partner states."—*Pref.* Includes author, title, and subject index.   Z3582.H69

Library of Congress. African Section. Madagascar and adjacent islands : a guide to official publications / comp. by Julian W. Witherell, African Section. Wash. : General Reference and Bibliography Div., Reference Dept., Library of Congress : [For sale by the U.S. Govt. Print. Off.], 1965. 58 p.   **AF222**
Superintendent of Documents classification: LC 2.8:M26.
Includes "materials dating from the establishments of French administrations in Madagascar, the Comoro Islands, and Réunion, and the British administrations in Mauritius and Seychelles."—*Pref.* Arranged geographically. Includes index by author, subject.   Z3702.U5

——————— Official publications of British East Africa / comp. by Helen F. Conover and Audrey A. Walker. Wash. : General Reference and Bibliography Division, Reference Dept., Library of Congress, 1960–63. 4 v.   **AF223**
Superintendent of Documents classification: LC2.2:Af8/4/pt. 1–4.
Contents: pt. 1, The East Africa High Commission and other regional documents. (67 p.); pt. 2, Tanganyika. (134 p.); pt. 3, Kenya and Zanzibar. (162 p.); pt. 4, Uganda. (100 p.).
Pts. 2–4 include government publications as well as publications about the country by the East Africa High Commission, Great Britain, the League of Nations, and the U. N. All parts have an index by author, subject.   Z3582.U5

——————— Official publications of French Equatorial Africa : French Cameroons, and Togo, 1946–1958 / comp. by Julian W. Witherell, African Section. Wash. : General Reference and Bibliography Division, Reference Dept., Library of Congress, 1964. 78 p.   **AF224**
Superintendent of Documents classification: LC 2.8: Af8/11/946-958.
A list of publications of the various governments concerned with AEF (Afrique Equatoriale Française)—Chad, Gabon, Middle Congo, Ubangi-Shari, French Cameroons, Togo, France, and French Union. U.N. publications dealing with French Cameroons and Togo are also listed. Subject and author index.   Z3961.U5

——————— Official publications of Sierra Leone and Gambia / comp. by Audrey A. Walker. Wash. : General Reference and Bibliography Div., Reference Dept., Library of Congress, 1963. 92 p.   **AF225**
Superintendent of Documents classification: LC 2.2:Si 1/2.
Also available in microfilm: Cambridge, Mass. : General Microfilm Co.
Materials included date from the establishment of the central government in each country. Pt. 1 includes publications of the Sierra Leone Company, the central government of Sierra Leone, and significant British papers. Pt. 2 includes publications of the government of Gambia as well as publications issued by Great Britain. Index by author and subject.   Z3533.S5U5

——————— The Rhodesias and Nyasaland : a guide to official publications / comp. by Audrey A. Walker. Wash. : General Reference and Bibliography Div., Reference Dept., Library of Congress, 1965. 285 p.   **AF226**
Superintendent of Documents classification: LC 2.8:R34.
Also available in microfilm: Cambridge, Mass. : General Microfilm Co.
Covers "as comprehensively as possible, the published records of administration in the former Federation of Rhodesia and Nyasaland and in the three territorial governments of Northern Rhodesia, Southern Rhodesia, and Nyasaland from 1889 to 1963."—*Pref.* Includes author, title, and subject index.   Z3573.R5U5

Rishworth, Susan Knoke. Spanish-speaking Africa : a guide to official publications. Wash. : Library of Congress : for sale by the U.S. Govt. Print. Off., 1973. 66 p.   **AF227**
Superintendent of Documents classification: LC 2.8:Af8/4.
Includes "Equatorial Guinea, Spanish Sahara, Ifni, and that part of northern Morocco known as the Spanish Zone until it was united with the rest of the country when Morocco became independent from France in 1956."—*Pref.* Lists published official records of those areas and publications of the Spanish government issued on behalf of its African territories. Includes author, title, subject index.   Z2689.R57

Westfall, Gloria. French colonial Africa : a guide to official sources. London ; N.Y. : Hans Zell Publishers, 1992. 226 p.   **AF228**
Attempts to improve access to official records treating political, economic, social, and cultural conditions in the former French colonies in tropical Africa. There are chapters on guides and bibliographies, archives, publications of the central administration, semiofficial publications, and publications of colonial governments. Index by personal and corporate author, subjects, and distinctive title.   DT532.W47

Witherell, Julian W. French-speaking central Africa : a guide to official publications in American libraries. Wash. : General Reference and Bibliography Div., Library of Congress : [For sale by the U.S. Govt. Print. Off.], 1973. 314 p.   **AF229**
Superintendent of Documents classification: LC 2.8:Af8/3.
Includes "documents of former Belgian and French possessions from the beginning of colonial rule to the time of independence as well as publications of national governments and regional and provincial administrations from independence to 1970. Also included are League of Nations and United Nations documents on Ruanda-Urundi and Cameroon, selections of Belgian and French official publications pertaining to their former territories, and material published by government-sponsored organizations."—*Pref.* Arranged by country; index of personal names and subjects.   Z3692.W5

——————— French-speaking West Africa : a guide to official publications. Wash. : General Reference and Bibliography Div., Library of Congress : [For sale by the U.S. Govt. Print. Off.], 1967. 201 p.   **AF230**
Superintendent of Documents classification: LC 2.2:Af8/3.
Lists as comprehensively as possible the published government records from the mid-19th century to date of compilation, including "publications of the federation of French West Africa, its eight component colonies (later territories), the French administration in the mandated territory (later trust territory) of Togo, and documents of the autonomous and national governments of each state."—*Pref.*
§ An earlier guide, *Official publications of French West Africa, 1946–1958,* was compiled by Helen F. Conover and issued by the General Reference and Bibliography Division, Library of Congress (Wash., 1960).   Z3672.W5

Ghana

Witherell, Julian W. Ghana : a guide to official publications, 1872–1968 / comp. by Julian W. Witherell and Sharon B. Lockwood, African Section. Wash. : General Reference and Bibliography Div., Reference Dept., Library of Congress : [For sale by the U.S. Govt. Print. Off.], 1969. 110 p. **AF231**
Superintendent of Documents classification: LC 2.8:G34/872- .
Includes "publications of the Gold Coast (1872–1957) and Ghana (1957–68) and a selection of British Government documents relating specifically to the Gold Coast, Ghana, and British Togoland. Also included are League of Nations and United Nations publications on British Togoland. The emphasis of the guide is on official documents held by the Library of Congress and other American libraries represented in the National Union Catalog."—*Pref.* Includes author, subject index.
Z3785.W5

Kenya

Howell, John Bruce. Kenya : subject guide to official publications. Wash. : Library of Congress : For sale by the U.S. Govt. Print. Off., 1978. 423 p. **AF232**
Superintendent of Documents classification: LC 2.7/2:K42.
A subject guide to official publications of Kenya, 1886–1975. Included are citations to documents by the Republic of Kenya (1963–75), the Kenya Colony and Protectorate, (1920–1963), and the East Africa Protectorate (1895–1920), Great Britain (1886–1975), and the East African Community and its predecessors (1926–75). Arranged by subject. Includes author, title, and subject index. Z3587.H68

Kenya National Archives. A guide to government monographs, reports, and research works / Republic of Kenya, Office of the Vice-President and Ministry of Home Affairs, Department of Kenya National Archives. [Nairobi] : The Archives, 1984. 157 p. **AF233**
In four chapters: (1) Government monographs, arranged alphabetically by title; (2) Reports and other documents from government ministries, departments, and other institutions; (3) Provincial and district annual and quarterly reports, both arranged alphabetically by department; (4) Theses, dissertations and other research reports (including works about Kenya prepared anywhere in the world), arranged alphabetically by author. Lacks an index. Z3587.K467

Mauritius

Deerpalsingh, S. A bibliography of Mauritian government publications, 1955–1978. Moka, Mauritius : Mahatma Gandhi Institute Library, 1979. 61 p. **AF234**
Covers government publications of the pre-independence period (1955–68) as well as those published after independence (1968–78). In two sections: (1) serials; (2) non-serial publications. Indexed.

Nigeria

Library of Congress. African Section. Nigeria : a guide to official publications / comp. by Sharon Burdge Lockwood. [Rev. ed.]. Wash. : General Reference and Bibliography Div., Reference Dept., Library of Congress, 1966. 166 p. **AF235**
A revision of: *Nigerian official publications, 1869–1959 : a guide*, comp. by Helen F. Conover (Wash. : Library of Congress, 1959).
Covers publications of Nigerian governments 1861–1965. Also includes documents that pertain to Nigeria and the British Cameroons

published by British government offices, the League of Nations and the U.N. Does not include publications issued by Nigerian provincial and municipal bodies. Z3553.N5U48

Stanley, Janet L. Nigerian government publications, 1966–1973 : a bibliography. Ile-Ife, Nigeria : Univ. of Ife Pr., [1975]. 193 p. **AF236**
Serves as a continuation of Sharon Burdge Lockwood's *Nigeria: a guide to official publications* (AF235). Includes all publications of the federal government, and the four regional governments. Index by author, personal name, subject, and title. Z3597.S73

Somalia

Library of Congress. General Reference and Bibliography Division. Official publications of Somaliland, 1941–1959 : a guide / comp. by Helen F. Conover. Wash. : The Library, 1960. 41 p. **AF237**
Superintendent of Documents classification: LC 2.2:So5.
Also available in microfilm: Cambridge, Mass. : General Microfilm Co.
Has separate sections for Somaliland under Italian administration, British Somaliland, and French Somaliland. Subject index. Lists about 170 titles, including a bibliography of chief sources. Z3516.U5

Swaziland

Swaziland official publications, 1880–1972 : a bibliography of the original and microfiche edition. Pretoria : State Libr., 1975. 190 p. (State Library bibliographies, no.18). **AF238**
A classed bibliography, with the first four sections "arranged in a sort of logical development-of-the-Territory order: historical background, concessions, constitutional development and parliament."—*Notes.* Includes both official and semiofficial publications. Indexed.
Microfiche supplements were issued for 1973–75 (1980) and for 1976 (1981).

Tunisia

Dar al-Kutub al-Qawmiyah (Tunisia). Récapitulation des périodiques officiels parus en Tunisie de 1881 à 1955 / par Hélène Pilipenko et Jean Rousset de Pina. Tunis : Royame de Tunis, Ministère de l'Éducation Nationale, Bibliothèque Nationale de Tunisie, 1956. 108 p. **AF239**
A detailed listing of official periodical publications arranged by issuing agency, with title, name, and agency indexes. Z6960.T8T8

Uganda

Gray, Beverly Ann. Uganda : subject guide to official publications. Wash. : Library of Congress : For sale by the U.S. Govt. Print. Off., 1977. 271 p. **AF240**
Also available in microfilm: Cambridge, Mass. : General Microfilm Co.
Comp. in the African Section, General Reference and Bibliography Division, Library of Congress.
A topical listing of "official publications of Uganda for the period 1893 to 1974. Every attempt was made to include documents issued by Uganda, Great Britain, and the East African Common Services Organization and its predecessors before October 1962, and by Uganda, the East African Common Services Organization, and the East African Community after independence. Included also are publications prepared by organizations and individuals on behalf of the Uganda government."—*Pref.* Indexed. Z3586.G7

Zimbabwe

Wilding, Norman W. Catalogue of the parliamentary papers of Southern Rhodesia and Rhodesia, 1954–1970, and the Federation of Rhodesia and Nyasaland, 1954–1963. Salisbury : Univ. College of Rhodesia, 1970. 161 p. (University College of Rhodesia. Source book, no.6). **AF241**
   In two sections: (1) Southern Rhodesia and Rhodesia; (2) Federation of Rhodesia and Nyasaland. Within each section, numbered series, series of select and standing committees, and petitions are first listed in chronological order, followed by a classified listing of those items plus additional papers not belonging to the preceding categories. Indexed.
                                                       Z3573.R5

Willson, Francis Michael Glenn. Catalogue of the parliamentary papers of Southern Rhodesia, 1899–1953 / Francis Michael Glenn Willson, Gloria C. Passmore. Salisbury, S. Rhodesia : Dept. of Government, Univ. College of Rhodesia and Nyasaland, 1965. 484 p. **AF242**
   "A catalogue of most of the papers [i.e., reports and papers, other than legislative documents] laid before the Legislative Council and Legislative Assembly of Southern Rhodesia during the years from the first meeting of the Legislative Council in 1899 until the creation of the Federation of Rhodesia and Nyasaland in 1953."—p.v.
   § Continued by: Norman W. Wilding, *Catalog of the parliamentary papers of southern Rhodesia and Rhodesia, 1954–1970* (AF241).
                                                       JQ2921.A23

Asia

China

Tsai, David W. A study of modern Chinese government publications, 1912–1949. Chicago : Univ. of Chicago, 1979. 429*l* : ill. **AF243**
   A comprehensive work that describes Chinese government publications and offers an annotated bibliography of publications. Includes chapters on printing and distribution of government publications; Chinese Imperial documents; Peking government publications, 1912–49; Nationalist government publications 1927–49; and Nationalist Party publications 1927–49.   Z3105.T73

India

Government books in print. 1986– . Delhi : Bookwell Publications, 1987– . **AF244**
   Arranged by ministry. Index by title.   Z3205.G68

India (Republic). Parliament. House of the People. Abstracts of books, reports and articles. v. 13 (Jan./Mar. 1975)– . New Delhi : Parliament Libr., 1975– . Quarterly. **AF245**
   Supersedes *Abstracts and index of reports and articles* (1963–Jan. 1975) which was formed by the merger of the *Abstracts of reports* (1955–62) and *Abstracts and index of articles* (AD339), both issued by the Indian Parliament's House of the People.
   Abstracts are listed by broad subject areas (agriculture, economic growth, Parliament, etc.) with subject and author indexes in each issue. Beginning with 1977, cumulative subject and author indexes are located in the fourth quarterly issue for each year.   AS472.I44A27

Macdonald, Teresa. Union catalogue of the serial publications of the Indian government, 1858–1947, held in libraries in Britain. [London] : Mansell, 1973. 154 p. **AF246**
   At head of title: Centre of South Asian Studies, University of Cambridge.

"The scope of the catalogue is limited to English-language material published in India, by the Central or Provincial Governments, and the Governments of the major Princely states, and appearing within the period 1858 to 1947."—*Introd.* Arrangement is by subject within sections for Central government, Provinces, etc.   Z3205.M15

Singh, Mohinder. Government of India publications. New Delhi : Budua, 1982. 176 p. **AF247**
   The introduction covers the general organization of the government as well as types of government publications. The other chapters treat major publications and sponsoring agencies, publishing and distribution, bibliographies and accession lists, and acquisition and access. The bibliography is arranged by agency. Name and subject indexes.   Z3205.S62

——————— Government publications of India : a survey of their nature, bibliographical control and distribution systems, including over 1500 titles / Mohinder Singh, assisted by J. F. Pandya. Delhi : Metropolitan Book Co., [1967]. 270 p. **AF248**
   Chapters, arranged by issuing agency, include major serials and monographs. Includes information on how the agency's publications are distributed. Does not include state publications. Index by agency.   Z3205.S63

——————— State government publications in India, 1947–1982. Delhi : Academic Publications, c1985. 2 v. (659 p.). **AF249**
   Vol. 1 includes a discussion of government publishing in India and the beginning of the state government publications bibliography. Within each state, publications are arranged by issuing agency, then title. Vol. 2 continues the state government publications bibliography and includes a bibliography of publications of the Union Territories. Personal name index.   Z3205.S64

Israel

Israel government publications / comp. by the State Archives. 1948/64– . Jerusalem : Govt. Printer, 1952– . Frequency varies. **AF250**
   Title also in Hebrew.
   Some published out of order; volume for 1948/64 publ. 1972.
   Volumes for 1952–56 comp. by the State Archives and Library and publ. under title *List of government publications.*
   Separate sections for European-language publications and for Hebrew publications.   Z3477.A56

Japan

Kuroki, Tsutomu. An introduction to Japanese government publications / tr. by Masako Kishi. Oxford ; Elmsford, N.Y. : Pergamon, 1981. 204 p. (Guides to official publications, v.10). **AF251**
   A guide to the contents and characteristics of Japanese government publications. Pt. 1 describes the structure of government publications; pt. 2 discusses publication and distribution; pt. 3 explains retrieval of government documents; pt. 4 contains an annotated bibliography of government publications. Indexed.   Z3305.K8713

Library of Congress. Japanese national government publications in the Library of Congress : a bibliography / comp. by Thaddeus Y. Ohta. Wash. : The Library : for sale by the U.S. Govt. Print. Off., 1981. 402 p. **AF252**
   Superintendent of Documents classification: LC 1.12/2:J27/3.
   A guide to the extensive collection of Japanese government publications in the Library of Congress. 3,376 title entries arranged in four main sections: (1) legislative branch; (2) executive branch; (3) judicial branch; and (4) public corporations and research institutes. A high per-

centage of entries is for serial publications; some 350 bilingual or English-language publications are included. Index of romanized Japanese titles and one of non-Japanese titles. Z3305.U54

Malaysia

Malaysia. Jabatan Cetak Kerajaan (Sabah). Senarai penerbitan-penerbitan lengkap. Kota Kinabalu, Sabah : Jabatan, 1982?– . Annual. **AF253**

In Malay and English.

Title varies slightly.

Preceded by a quarterly *Current list of publications* (Kuala Lumpur : Govt. Print. Dept., 1955?–66); an annual *Senarai penerbitan lengkap : Current list of publications* (Kuala Lumpur : Jabatan Chetak Kerajaan, 1965–75); and an annual *Senarai penerbitan: List of publications* (Kuala Lumpur : Jabatan Cetak Kerajaan, 1976?–81?).

A classified list. Z3247.M356a

Pakistan

Moreland, George B. Publications of the government of Pakistan, 1947–1957 / George B. Moreland, Akhtar H. Siddiqui. [Karachi] : Inst. of Public and Business Admin., Univ. of Karachi, 1958. 187 p. **AF254**

Cumulates and indexes the irregularly published issues of the *Catalogue of the government of Pakistan publications* (AF255). adding some additional listings. Includes sales publications as well as listing and indexing many government publications not for sale by the Manager of Publications. Arranged by Ministry. Includes a subject index. Z3195.M6

Pakistan. Catalogue of the government of Pakistan publications. 1947?– . Karachi : Manager of Publications, 1947?– . Irregular. **AF255**

Arranged by departments; lists publications available for sale. Includes a separate list of periodicals.

———. ———. *Supplement ... (corrected up to 5-7-66)*. Publ. 1966? Z3195.A22

Siddiqui, Akhtar H. Pakistan government publications : their nature, content, production, and distribution. [Lahore] : Vanguard Books, [1981]. 97 p. **AF256**

Describes the types of government publications, their bibliographic control, acquisition, production and distribution; includes brief descriptions of the various agencies and the nature and content of their publications. Lists government periodical publications. One appendix includes a list of subjects covered by various ministries, divisions, and departments. Z3195.S5

Philippines

Checklist of exchange materials. 1974/75– . Manila : National Library. Public Documents, Exchange and Gifts Division, 1975– . Annual. **AF257**

A main entry listing of government publications available on exchange. No index.

Continues in part *Philippine government publications*, comp. by Documents, Gifts & Exchange Section, Bureau of Public Libraries (v. 1 no. 1 [Jan. 1958]–v. 2 no. 11 & 12 [Nov.–Dec. 1959]. Manila : The Bureau, 1958–59), the first current record of government publications, and its successor, the Division's *Checklist of Philippine government publications* (1961–1972/73. Manila : 1962–75). This listing is by issuing agency. Volumes for 1962–63 included only items available on exchange. No index.

Manila (Philippines). National Library. Legislative Reference Division. Checklist of publications of the government of the Philippine Islands Sept. 1, 1900 to Dec. 31, 1917 / comp. by Emma Osterman Elmer, chief of the Public documents section ; Macario Adriatico, director, Philippine library and museum. Manila : Bureau of Printing, 1918. 288 p. **AF258**

A "nearly complete" checklist of government publications. Lists publications from the legislative, executive, and judicial branches of government; the provinces; municipalities; the Univ. of the Phillippines; and from various offices, boards, and committees. Includes some citations to U.S. Congressional Serial Set items. Index to government authors. Subject, author, and agency index.

§ Continued by the Bibliographical Society of the Philippines' *Checklist of Philippine government publications, 1917–1949*, comp. by Consolacion B. Rebadavia (Quezon City: Univ. of the Philippines Libr., 1960. 817 p.), which contains more than 6,000 items, and by a supplementary *Checklist of Philippine government documents, 1950* (Wash. : Libr. of Congress, 1953. 62 p.) containing 755 items.

University of the Philippines. Institute of Public Administration. Library. List of Philippine government publications, 1945–1958 / comp. by Andrea C. Ponce and Jacinta C. Yatco. Manila, 1959–60. 2 v. **AF259**

Contents: pt. 1, Publications of agencies under the Dept. of Agriculture and Natural Resources, Dept. of Commerce and Industry, Dept. of Education, and Dept. of Labor (Pt. 1 has subject, title, author index); pt. 2, Publications of agencies under the Depts. of Finance, Foreign Affairs, Health, and Justice. Z3295.Q5

Saudi Arabia

Ma'had al-Idārah al-'Āmmah (Riyadh, Saudi Arabia). Markaz al-Wathā'iq. Qism al-Maṭbū'āt al-Rasmīyah. al-Maṭbū'āt al-rasmīyah fī al-Mamlakah al-'Arabīyah al-al-Sa'ūdīyah : bibliyūjrāfiyah mukhtārah min majmū'āt Qism al-Maṭbū'āt al-Rasmīyah fī Markaz al-Wathā'iq. al-Riyāḍ : al-Mamlakah al-'Arabīyah al-Sa'ūdīyah, Ma'had al-Idārah al-'Āmmah, al-Idārah al-'Āmmah lil-Maktabāt, Markaz al Wathā'iq, 1984. 552 p. : ill. **AF260**

A retrospective, selective bibliography of government publications, including those issued by public companies, held by the Dept. of Official Publications of the Documentation Center, Riyadh. Arranged by agency with subject and title indexes. Z3027.M34

Australia and Oceania

Australia

Australian government publications [microform]. Sept. 1988– . Canberra : National Library of Australia, 1988– . Quarterly, with annual cumulations. **AF261**

Includes entries for local, federal, state, and territorial publications. Microfiche sets arranged in two sequences: author/title, and subject.

Continues: *Australian government publications* (1961–70. Canberra : National Library of Australia, 1971–87). Supersedes the Library's *Monthly list of Australian government publications* (1952–60) and the annual cumulation in its *Annual catalogue of Australian publications*.

Australian official publications / ed. by D. H. Borchardt. Melbourne : Longman Cheshire, 1979. 365 p. **AF262**

A series of essays by specialists presents an overview of national, state, and municipal/shire/county publications. Parliamentary and judicial publications are treated separately, followed by topical sections on general and administrative publications, publications in the social sciences, science and technology, and local government publications. The final section discusses bibliographic control, distribution, and access to government publications. Index by subject, title.   Z4019.A97

Cook, John. A guide to commonwealth government information sources / John Cook, Nancy Lane, Michael Piggott. Sydney [Australia] : Pergamon, 1988. 89 p.   **AF263**

     "Serves as a guide to the unpublished information ... available through Commonwealth [i.e. Australian] departments, statutory authorities and agencies. Excluded, however, is the unpublished information extracted and provided by the Parliament, the Courts, Royal Commissions and other enquiries."—*Introd.* Indexed.   Z674.5.A8C66

Coxon, Howard. Australian official publications. Oxford ; N.Y. : Pergamon, 1981. 211 p. : ill. (Guides to official publications, v. 5).   **AF264**

     A guide to the types of publications issued by official organizations and agencies. An introductory essay on the framework of the Australian government is followed by sections for (1) the Commonwealth Parliament; (2) Commonwealth departments and statutory authorities; (3) distribution and availability of publications; (4) the states of Australia; (5) the internal territories. Brief bibliography of Australian official publications; index.   Z4019.C69

Harrington, Michael. The guide to government publications in Australia. Canberra : Australian Government Publishing Service, c1990. 164 p.   **AF265**

     General chapters on printing and publishing in Australia are followed by specific chapters on parliamentary publications, executive publications, judicial publications and publications of intergovernmental organizations. Each chapter has extensive lists of publications. Includes bibliography and index by topic, agency, and title.   Z4019.H37

New Commonwealth government books from AGPS. Jan.–Feb. 1988– . Canberra : Australian Government Publishing Service, 1988– . Monthly.   **AF266**

     Arranged in two sections: (1) New and recent books, a short section with annotation for all titles; (2) Departmental titles, arranged by title of publication.   Z4019.N49

New Zealand

Guide to government information / Government Printing Office. v. 1, no. 1 (Mon., 13 Apr. 1987)–v. 6, no. 13 (Mon., 29 June 1992). [Wellington] : The Office, 1987–1992. Biweekly.   **AF267**

     Title from caption; publisher varies.

     Lists Parliamentary materials (acts, bills, regulations, parliamentary papers) and official departmental reports and periodicals. Current materials only.   Z4109.G85

Guide to New Zealand information sources. [Palmerston North] : Massey Univ., 1975–82. 7 v. (Massey University library ser., no.8, 10–11, 13–17).   **AF268**

     Pt. 5, Official publications. In addition to dealing with current official publications and early provincial papers, there are sections on British and Australian parliamentary papers relating to New Zealand and on New Zealand statistical publications. For annotation, *see* AA86.   Z4101.B37

Papua New Guinea

Government publications of Papua New Guinea. no. 14 (Jan./June 1973)– . Port Moresby [Papua New Guinea] : Administrative College, 1973?– . Quarterly.   **AF269**

     Continues: *Government publications of Papua and New Guinea* no. 1/2 (Jan./June 1968)–no. 13 (Jan./Mar. 1971).

No. 14 last issue published? A listing by issuing agency.   Z4812.G66

AG

Dissertations

GUIDES AND MANUALS

This section includes a selection of general aids for writers of research papers as well as guides and manuals relating to doctoral research and preparation of dissertations. Specialized guides and manuals are available for some disciplines.

Campbell, William Giles. Form and style : theses, reports, term papers / William Giles Campbell, Stephen Vaughan Ballou, Carole Slade. 8th ed. Boston : Houghton Mifflin, c1990. 279 p.   **AG1**

     1st ed., 1939, had title: *A form book for thesis writing.*

     Incorporates the style of *MLA handbook* (AG2), the *Chicago manual of style* (AA319), and the *Publication manual of the American Psychological Association* (CD42). Eight chapters focus on topics such as style and mechanics, emphasizing forms for bibliographies and works cited, including computer software and online databases. Glossary of terms and abbreviations and subject index.   LB2369.C3

Gibaldi, Joseph. MLA handbook for writers of research papers / Joseph Gibaldi, Walter S. Achtert. 3rd ed. N.Y. : Modern Language Association of America, 1988. 248 p. : ill.   **AG2**

     1st ed., 1977; 2nd ed., 1984.

     Designed "as a supplementary text in writing courses or as a reference book for students."—*Pref.* Includes details on using and citing computer software, online databases, and other nonprint sources. A brief summary of this handbook, not officially endorsed by the MLA, was published by Joseph Trimmer as *A guide to MLA documentation* (Boston : Houghton Mifflin, 1989).   LB2369.G53

Madsen, David. Successful dissertations and theses : a guide to graduate student research from proposal to completion. 2nd ed. San Francisco : Jossey-Bass, 1992. 216 p.   **AG3**

     1st ed., 1983.

     Offers chapters on preparing the research proposal, conducting research, and writing and defending the thesis. Special emphasis is given the use of computers in the research and composition process. Focuses on the humanities and social sciences.   LB2369.M32

Meyer, Michael. The Little, Brown guide to writing research papers. 3rd ed. N.Y. : HarperCollins College Publ., 1994. 311 p.   **AG4**

     1st ed., 1982.

     Intended for both undergraduate and graduate research papers in a variety of disciplines, covering print and electronic resources. Bibliography and topical index.   LB2369.M42

Stock, Molly. A practical guide to graduate research. N.Y. : McGraw-Hill, c1985. 168 p. : ill. **AG5**

Emphasizes study in the sciences. Thesis-oriented, but includes some information on preparing grant proposals and presentations. Bibliography and subject index. Q180.55.M4S86

Turabian, Kate L. A manual for writers of term papers, theses, and dissertations. 5th ed. / rev. and exp. by Bonnie Birtwistle Honigsblum. Chicago : Univ. of Chicago Pr., 1987. 300 p. **AG6**

1st ed., 1937; 4th ed., 1973.

A standard publication, well-organized and widely used. This edition contains extensive additional materials on computer word processing, graphics, software use, and forms of citation for all the above. Detailed subject index. LB2369.T8

BIBLIOGRAPHY

The number and type of publications available to identify dissertations by country vary widely. This section presents a selective list, representing a broad cross-section of countries and languages of the numerous contemporary and historical guides and checklists available in printed and electronic forms.

Bibliography of bibliography

Reynolds, Michael M. Guide to theses and dissertations : an international bibliography of bibliographies. Rev. and enl. ed. Phoenix : Oryx, 1985. 263 p. **AG7**

1st ed., 1975.

Covers works published through 1984, providing a retrospective international listing of bibliographies of theses and dissertations, including serial and monograph publications. Arranged both by country and by broad subject heading, with indexes of institutions, names and titles, and specific subjects. Z5053.A1R49

International

Bibliothèque Nationale (France). Département des Imprimés. Catalogue des dissertations et écrits académiques provenant des échanges avec les universités étrangères et reçus par la Bibliothèque Nationale, 1882–1924. Paris : Klincksieck, 1884–1925. T. 1–43. **AG8**

Dissertations received by the Bibliothèque Nationale from numerous European universities, arranged by university. Z5053.P22

Bodleian Library. Catalogus dissertationum academicarum : quibus nuper aucta est Bibliotheca Bodleiana. Oxford : Typographeo Academico, 1834. 448, [63] p. **AG9**

A listing of dissertations from various institutions held by the Bodleian Library in 1832. Arranged by name of praeses (academic moderator), each entry also gives the name of the respondent (the author and defender of the dissertation). An index of respondents also is included. Z921.O95D5

Gesamtverzeichnis deutschsprachiger Hochschulschriften (GVH), 1966–1980 / hrsg. von Willi Gorzny. München ; N.Y. : K.G. Saur, 1984–91. 40 v. **AG10**

A list of dissertations and theses written in German, compiled from dissertation lists in Germany, other Eastern and Western European countries, Great Britain, the U.S., and Canada. Vols. 25–40 constitute an index register of authors. Z5055.G4G47

North America

United States

American doctoral dissertations. 1955/56– . Ann Arbor, Mich. : Univ. Microfilms, 1957– . Annual. **AG11**

Comp. for the Assoc. of Research Libraries.

Title varies: 1955/56–1963/64 called: *Index to American doctoral dissertations.* Through 1964/65, issued annually as no. 13 of *Dissertation abstracts international* (AG13), and continues *Doctoral dissertations accepted by American universities.*

Lists "dissertations accepted for the Ph.D. and other doctoral degrees by American and Canadian degree-granting institutions."— *Introd.* Arranged by general subject and institution. An author index is included, and UMI publication information is provided for most entries.

●Also available in machine-readable versions of *Dissertation abstracts international.* Z5055.U49A62

Comprehensive dissertation index, 1861–1972. Ann Arbor, Mich. : Xerox Univ. Microfilms, 1973. 37 v. **AG12**

Contents: v. 1–4, Chemistry; v. 5, Mathematics and statistics; v. 6–7, Astronomy and physics; v. 8–10, Engineering; v. 11–13, Biological sciences; v. 14, Health and environmental sciences; v. 15, Agriculture; v. 16, Geography and geology; v. 17, Social sciences; v. 18–19, Psychology; v. 20–24, Education; v. 25–26, Business and economics; v. 27, Law and political science; v. 28, History; v. 29–30, Language and literature; v. 31, Communication and the arts; v. 32, Philosophy and religion; v. 33–37, Author index.

A computer-generated index arranged by subject and author, listing virtually all dissertations accepted by American educational institutions. Some Canadian and European dissertations are included, but no claim for completeness is made for universities outside the U.S. This work cumulates entries in *American doctoral dissertations* (AG11), and *Dissertation abstracts international* (AG13). Full citations appear in both the author and subject listings, and include references to *Dissertation abstracts international* or other printed lists and to University Microfilms publication number when available.

————. *Supplement* (1973– . Ann Arbor, Mich. : Univ. Microfilms Internat., 1974– . Annual). Follows the arrangement of the main set.

Ten-year and five-year cumulations covering 1973–82 and 1983–87 supersede earlier annual volumes and include some citations to earlier dissertation titles for which information was erroneous or unavailable. Beginning 1988, *CDI* includes citations to some British dissertations and has continued to expand its listings of foreign dissertations to include most entries cited in *Dissertation abstracts international* Section C : Worldwide. Z5053.C64

Dissertation abstracts international. v. 1 (1938)– . Ann Arbor, Mich. : Univ. Microfilms, 1938– . Sections A and B, monthly; Section C, quarterly. **AG13**

Title varies: v. 1 (1938)–v. 11 (1951), *Microfilm abstracts*; v. 12 (1952)–v. 29 (June 1969), *Dissertation abstracts.*

Beginning 1961/62, an annual cumulative author and subject index has been publ. as pt. 2 of the June issue. With v. 30 (1969/70), author and keyword-title indexes cumulated separately for each section.

Issued July 1966– in two sections: A, The humanities and social sciences; B, The sciences and engineering. In Autumn 1976, Section C, European abstracts, was added; with v. 50 (1989), Section C was expanded to include institutions in all countries and renamed Worldwide.

A compilation of author-prepared abstracts of doctoral dissertations submitted to University Microfilms International for publication in microform. Extensive coverage of many recent U.S. and foreign dissertations. Arranged by classed topic, with keyword and author indexes. Each entry gives title, author, degree date, institution, pagination, advisor, UMI order number, and abstract.

•Machine-readable version: *Dissertation abstracts online* [database] (Ann Arbor, Mich. : UMI, 1861–). Available online (updated monthly) and in CD-ROM as *Dissertations abstracts ondisc* (updated semiannually). Formerly called *Comprehensive dissertation index online*. More than 1.1 million records, corresponding to entries in *Dissertation abstracts international, American doctoral dissertations* (AG11), *Comprehensive dissertation index* (AG12), and *Masters abstracts international* (AG15). Since 1980, the database has included full abstracts for all entries. The CD-ROM version excludes masters essays.　　　　　　　　　　　　　　　　Z5053.D57

Master's theses

Black, Dorothy M. Guide to lists of master's theses. Chicago : Amer. Libr. Assoc., 1965. 144 p.　　　**AG14**
　In two main sections: (1) master's theses in special fields; and (2) master's theses of specific institutions. Based only on printed sources (of which a list is given); provides descriptive annotations for each entry. Information on lists published in series is unusually detailed.　　　　　　　　　　　　　　Z5055.U49B55

Masters abstracts international : a catalog of selected master's theses on microfilm. Ann Arbor, Mich. : Univ. Microfilms Internat., 1962– . Quarterly.　　　**AG15**
　Title varies: v. 1 (1962)–24 (1985), *Masters abstracts*. Absorbed *Research abstracts* (AG16) in 1991.
　Includes masters theses, educational specialist materials, and other projects accepted for degrees by accredited institutions. Follows the subject classifications and format used by *Dissertation abstracts international* (AG13).
　•Available online in machine-readable versions of *Dissertation abstracts international*.　　　　　Z5055.U49M3

Research abstracts. v. 1 (1976)–15 (1990). Ann Arbor, Mich. : Univ. Microfilms Internat., 1973–1990. Quarterly.　　　　　　　　　　　　　　　　　**AG16**
　Continues *Monograph abstracts*, publ. 1973–76. Absorbed in 1991 by *Masters abstracts international* (AG15).
　A fine source for specialized pre- and post-doctoral research monographs and reports, following the same subject classifications and format used by *Dissertation abstracts international* (AG13).
　　　　　　　　　　　　　　　　　AS36X4415

Canada

Canadian Bibliographic Centre (Ottawa). Canadian graduate theses in the humanities and social sciences, 1921–1946. Ottawa : E. Cloutier, printer to the King, 1951. 194 p.　**AG17**
　More than 3,000 theses arranged by subject and institution, with an author index and English and French subject indexes.
　Continued by:
　(1) National Library of Canada, *Canadian theses = Thèses canadiennes, 1947–1960* (Ottawa : National Library of Canada, 1973. 2 v.). Text in English and French. Arranged by subject and institution, with an author index.
　(2) *Canadian theses = Thèses canadiennes* (1960/61–1976/77/1979/80. Ottawa : National Library of Canada, 1961–80. 15 v.). Arranged by broad classification based on Dewey Decimal Classification, subdivided by university, with author index.
　(3) Continued in microfiche: *Canadian theses = Thèses canadiennes* [microform] (1980/81– . Ottawa : National Library of Canada, 1984–). Semiannual with five cumulating indexes.　　Z5055.C2O88

South America

Argentina

Universidad de Buenos Aires. Instituto Bibliotecológico. Tesis presentadas a la Universidad de Buenos Aires. 1961/62– . Buenos Aires : Universidad. Instituto Bibliotecológico, 1966– . Biennial (varies).　　　　　**AG18**
　Title varies: occasionally issued as part of Instituto Bibliotecológico "Publicacion" series.
　Theses are listed by faculty sponsor; author index.
　　　　　　　　　　　　　　Z5055.A69B947

Bolivia

Guía nacional de tesis. La Paz, Bolivia : SYFNID, 1981–82. 2 v.　　　　　　　　　　　　　　**AG19**
　At head of title: Ministerio de Planeamiento y Coordinación, Sistema y Fondo Nacional de Información para el Desarrollo (SYFNID); Centro Internacional de Investigaciones para el Desarrollo (CIID–Canada).
　Contents: v. 1, 1960–77; v. 2, 1978–82.
　For the period 1960–82, lists more than 3,500 theses completed at major universities in Bolivia. Arranged by university and faculty, with author and subject indexes.　　　　Z7409.G84

Brazil

Catálogo do banco de teses. v. 1 (1976)– . Brasília : Ministério da Educação e Cultura, Secretaria Geral [etc.], 1976– . Annual.　　　　　　　　　　　　　**AG20**
　1976/77 issued by the Conselho Nacional de Desenvolvimento Científica e Technológico.
　Lists more than 20,000 theses and dissertations completed in Brazil. Arranged by subject, entries list the advisor and objectives, and provide an abstract. Author and subject indexes.　Z5055.B8C38

Europe

Répertoire des thèses de doctorat européennes. [1969/70–1974/75]. Louvain : A. Detwallens, 1970–76.　**AG21**
　Arranged under social sciences, medicine, and science, provides an alphabetical author listing and KWIC index of dissertations received by the University of Liége library. Includes many French and German works, and since 1971/72 also includes Belgian and British dissertations not actually received by the library. Indexes in English, French, German, and other languages supplement the main author and KWIC indexes.　　　　　　　　Z5055.B5R45

Austria

Gesamtverzeichnis österreichischer Dissertationen. v. 1 (1966)–v. 19 (1984). Wien : Verlag Notring der Wissenschaftliche Verbände Österreichs, 1967–1989.　　**AG22**
　A index to Austrian dissertations arranged by university, then by faculty. Includes subject indexes for names and places. Authors and complete titles are not included in later volumes.　Z 5055.A9 G389

Universität Wien. Philosophische Fakultät. Verzeichnis über die seit dem Jahre 1872 an der Philosophischen Fakultät der Universität in Wien eingereichten und approbierten Dissertationen. Wien, 1935–37. 4 v. **AG23**

Arranged by large subjects, with a catchword subject index at end of each group and an author index at end of each volume.

Updated by: *Verzeichnis der an der Universität Wien approbierten Dissertationen*, ed. by Lisl Alker and H. Alker (Wien : Kerry, 1954–69. 5 v.). In classified order, with combined author and subject index. Z5055.A9V6

Bulgaria

Bŭlgarski disertatsii. 1973– . Sofiia : Narodna Biblioteka "Kiril i Metodiĭ", 1974– . Annual. **AG24**

An annual cumulation of dissertations listed monthly in *Bŭlgarski knigopis*, Ser. 2 : *Sluzhebni izdaniﬁa disertatsii* (AA589). Table of contents in Bulgarian, English, and Russian, with theses and dissertations listed under broad subject. Author index. Z5055.B87B84

Czech Republic

Bibliografický katalog ČSFR : České disertace a autoreferáty. 1989– . V Praze : Národní knihovna v Praze., 1993– . Irregular. **AG25**

Continues: *České disertace*, zpracovala Marie Nedvídková (1979–1986. Praha : Státní knihovna ČSR v Nakl. a vydavatelství Panorama, 1980–88. Annual). 1964–78, dissertations were listed in *Bibliografický katalog ČSSR. České knihy* (AA600).

Covers dissertations completed in major universities in the Czech Republic and before the division in the former Czechoslovakia. Z5055.C917C46

France

Catalogue des thèses de doctorat soutenues devant les universités françaises / Ministère de l'éducation nationale. Direction des bibliothèques de France. Année 1959–année 1978. [Paris] : Cercle de la librairie, 1960–85. Annual. **AG26**

At head of title: Ministère de l'Éducation Nationale. Direction Générale des Enseignements Supérieurs et de la Recherche.

Called "nouv. sér."

Issued in three sections per year: (1) Droit, sciences économiques, sciences de gestion; Lettres, sciences humaines, théologies; (2) Médecine, médecine vétérinaire, odontostomatologie, pharmacie; (3) Sciences.

Within each discipline theses are listed by university, then alphabetically by author; author index for each section, plus an "index des spécialités" in sections (1) and (3). Beginning 1973, issues include author, university, and subject indexes.

Catalogue des thèses et écrits académiques / Ministère de l'instruction publique. T. 1, fasc. 1–5 (année scolaire 1884–85)–t. 15, fasc. 75 (1958). Paris : Librairie Hachette, 1885–1958. Annual. **AG27**

Publisher and issuing agency vary.

The official listing of French dissertations. Annual issues, 1885–1913, are arranged alphabetically by university subdivided by faculty, and follow the academic calendar; annual issues, 1914–58, cover the calendar year and are arranged by faculty, subdivided by university. Five-year author and subject indexes are provided through 1928.

§ Continued by:

(1) *Catalogue des thèses de doctorat soutenues devant les universités françaises* (AG26).

(2) *Inventaire des thèses de doctorat soutenues devant les universités françaises* (1981– . Paris : Université de Paris I, Bibliothéque de

la Sorbonne, Direction des bibliothéques, des musées et de l'information scientifique et techniques, 1982– . Annual). Issued in three series: Droit, sciences économiques, sciences de gestion, lettres, sciences humaines, théologies; Sciences; and Médecines, médecine vétérinaires, odontostomatologie, pharmacie (1981 only; replaced by Médecine, pharmacie, chirurgie dentaire, odontologie et médecine vétéinaire [microform], 1983–). In each series, theses are listed by subject, then alphabetically by author, with author and university indexes. Z5055.F79C37

Maire, Albert. Répertoire alphabétique des thèses de doctorat ès lettres des universités françaises, 1810–1900. Paris : A. Picard et fils, 1903. 226 p. **AG28**

More than 2,000 theses arranged alphabetically by author. Entries provide author, title, place, publisher, pagination, date, university, and whether published in any other form. Includes rejected theses. Subject index and chronological list by university. Z5055.F79M22

Mourier, Athénaïs. Notice sur le doctorat ès lettres suivie du Catalogue et de l'analyse des thèses françaises et latines admises par les facultés des lettres depuis 1810 / Athénaïs Mourier [et] F. Deltour. 4. éd., corr. et considérablement augm. Paris : Delalain, [1880]. 442 p. **AG29**

With the annuals (below) covers virtually the same material as Albert Maire's *Répertoire alphabétique des thèses de doctorat ès lettres des universités françaises* (AG28) but arranges entries by year and university rather than alphabetically. In addition to title and pagination, provides contents of each thesis and brief biographical data. Subject and author index.

Continued by: *Recueil Mourier-Deltour : catalogue et analyse des thèses latines et françaises ...* (Année scolaire 1880/81–[1901/02]. Paris : Delalain, [1882–1902]). Z5055.F79M8

Germany

Deutsche Nationalbibliographie und Bibliographie der im Ausland erschienenen deutschsprachigen Veröffentlichungen / bearb. und hrsg., Die Deutsche Bibliothek. Frankfurt am Main : Buchhändler-Vereinigung, 1991– . **AG30**

Reihe H. Hochschulschriften, provides a classified listing of theses, published and unpublished, from German universities, together with some dissertations written in Germany but submitted in other countries (mainly Switzerland). It was formed by the merger of Reihe C, Dissertationen und Habilitationsschriften, and *Deutsche Bibliographie. Hochschulschriften-Verzeichnis*. Author and subject index in each issue. For more information on the complete work, *see* AA657. Z2221F7

Jahresverzeichnis der Hochschulschriften der DDR, der BRD, und Westberlins. 1. Jahrg. (1884)–87 Jahrg. (1971). Leipzig : VEB Bibliographisches Institut, 1887–1987. **AG31**

Minor variations in title.

The standard official German list of dissertations accepted at German universities, 1884–1971. Arranged by university, with an author index for each volume, a separate subject index for Jahrg. 1–5, and a subject index in each volume for Jahrg. 6–85. Numbering has been continuous throughout the title variations and coverage remains the same.

Mundt, Hermann. Bio-bibliographisches Verzeichnis von Universitäts- u. Hochschuldrucken (Dissertationen) vom Ausgang des 16. bis Ende des 19. Jahrhunderts. Leipzig : Carlsohn, 1934–80. 4 v. **AG32**

Publisher varies.

Contents: Bd. 1–3, A–Z; Bd. 4, Personenregister.

A list of theses containing brief biographical data about persons connected with them, arranged alphabetically by respondent (author). Includes some Dutch and Scandinavian titles, but focuses chiefly on German works. Z5053.M89

Great Britain

Index to theses with abstracts accepted for higher degrees by the universities of Great Britain and Ireland and the Council for National Academic Awards. v. 35 (Nov. 1986)– . London : Aslib, c1986– . Quarterly.   **AG33**

Continues *Index to theses accepted for higher degrees by the universities of Great Britain and Ireland* (v. 1 [1950/51]–17 [1966/67]) and *Index to theses accepted for higher degrees by the universities of Great Britain and Ireland and the Council for National Academic Awards* (v. 18 [1967/68]–34 [1986]), and assumes their numbering, arrangement, and coverage.

Classified arrangement, subdivided by university. Subject and author indexes. Now includes abstracts.

•In machine-readable form as: *Index to theses* [database] (London : Aslib, 1950–). Available in CD-ROM, updated annually.

Z5055.G69A84

Oxford. University. Committee for Advanced Studies. Abstracts of dissertations for the degree of doctor of philosophy. v. 1 (1924/28)–v. 13 (1940). Oxford : Univ. Pr., 1928–47.   **AG34**

Continued by: *Successful candidates for the degrees of D.Phil., B.Litt., and B.Sc., with the titles of their theses* (v. 1 [1940/49]– . Oxford : Oxford Univ. Pr., 1950– . Annual). Title varies.   AS122.09

Retrospective index to theses of Great Britain and Ireland, 1716–1950 / Roger R. Bilboul, ed. Santa Barbara, Calif. : ABC-Clio, [1975–77]. 5 v.   **AG35**

Contents: v. 1, Social sciences and humanities; v. 2, Applied sciences and technology; v. 3, Life sciences; v. 4, Physical sciences; v. 5, Chemical sciences.

Provides retrospective coverage for dissertations completed before 1950, when Aslib began its annual *Index to theses* ... (AG33). Concentrates on manuscripts and typescripts and "does not attempt to list the earlier printed theses whether they be full texts of theses by individuals or the broadsheets announcing the propositions to be disputed and the names of the candidates"—*Foreword*. Each volume is in two parts: an alphabetical subject arrangement based on index headings used in the *British humanities index* (AD264) and an author index. Both parts give the full citation.

University of Cambridge. Abstracts of dissertations approved for the Ph.D., M.Sc., and M.Litt. degrees in the University of Cambridge during the academical year. 1925/26–1956/57. Cambridge : The Cambridge Univ. Pr., 1927–59. Annual.   **AG36**

Continued by: *Titles of dissertations approved for the Ph.D., M.Sc., and M. Litt. degrees in the University of Cambridge.* v. 1 (1957/58)– . [Cambridge] : Cambridge Univ. Pr., 1958– . Annual.   AS122.C3

Hungary

Magyar Tudományos Akadémia. Kézirattár. A Magyar Tudományos Akadémia Könyvtára Kézirattárának katalógusai. no. 1 (1966)– . Budapest : [Magyar Tudományos Akadémia], 1966– .   **AG37**

Absorbed *Kandidátusi és doktori disszertációk katalógusa*, which covered 1952/61–1968/70.

Title and prefatory matter in Hungarian and Russian.

A catalog of unpublished theses in the Academy's library. Board subject classification, with author index.   Z6621.M25125

Netherlands

Rijksuniversiteit te Utrecht. Bibliotheek. Catalogus van academische geschriften in Nederland verschenen. jaarg. 1 (1924)–37/38 (1960/61); Nieuwe reeks, jaarg. 1/2 (1962/63)–15 (1976). Utrecht : Bibliotheek dur Rijksuniversiteit te Utrecht, 1925–79.   **AG38**

Publisher varies: 1924–1960/61, Nederlandsche Vereeniging van Bibliothecarissen. Through 1945 included Nederlands Indie. 1954/61 not publ.

Arranged by university. Combined author and subject index for jaarg. 1–5, 1924–28, which form v. 1; later volumes have author index only.

Continued by: *Bibliografie van Nederlandse proefschriften = Dutch theses* ([Jaarg.] 1 [1977]– . Utrecht : Bibliotheek der Rijksuniversiteit, 1980– . Annual).

Theses are listed under the sponsoring faculty department. Author index, but no detailed subject approach.   Z5055.N59U8

Poland

Katalog rozpraw doktorskich i habilitacyjnych / Ministerstwo Szkolnictwa Wyższego. 1959/61– . Warszawa : Państwowe Wydawn. Naukowe, 1962– . Annual.   **AG39**

Vols. for 1965–[1969] issued by Ministerstwo Oswiaty i Szkolnictwa Wyższego; vols. for [1974–1990] issued by Ministerstwo Nauki, Szkolnictwa Wyższego i Techniki; vols. for 1991– issued by Osrodek Przetwarzania Informacji.

Classified entries list major advisor and provide abstracts. Author index.   Z5055.P69

Romania

Teze de doctorat : lucrări susţinute iñ ţără de autori români şi străini şi lucrări susţinute în străinătate de autori romanî / [lucrare elaborată in cadrul Serviciului de Informare şi Documentare condus de Ileana Băncilă ; redactor responsabil, Silvia Maruţa]. Bucureşti : Biblioteca Centrală Universitară Bucureşti, 1973–1982. v. 1–4. (In progress?).   **AG40**

Compilations have been published covering 1948–1970, 1971–1973, 1974–76, and 1977–79.

A classed subject listing of dissertations completed at Romanian universities or by Romanians abroad. Author, advisor, and title indexes.   Z5055.R64B878

Spain

Universidad de Madrid. Catálogo de las tesis doctorales manuscritas en la Universidad de Madrid. Madrid : Graficas González, 1952. 36 p.   **AG41**

Covers dissertations completed at the University of Madrid and other Spanish universities. Arranged alphabetically by author under broad subject headings. No separate author or subject index.

§ Continued by:

(1) *Tesis doctorales leidas en la Universidad de Madrid* (1954– . Madrid : Editorial de la Universidad complutense de Madrid, [1954]– . Annual).

Title varies. Some issues publ. in more than one volume. 1973/74–1975/76 publ. both as part of *Revista de la Universidad Complutense* and as *Publicaciones de la Universidad Complutense de Madrid*. An alphabetical listing of completed dissertations, with abstracts.

(2) *Tesis doctorales : 1976–77/1988–89* (Madrid : Ministerio de Educacion y Ciencia, Consejo de Universidades, Secretaria General, c1990–). Contents: T. 1, Ciencias y technica; T. 2, Ciencias medicas y de la vida; T. 3, Ciencias humanas. Z5055.S5M57

Sweden

Josephson, Aksel Gustav Salomon. Avhandlingar ock program utgivna vid svenska ock finska akademier ock skolor under aren 1855–1890. Uppsala : Lundequistska bokhandeln, [1891–97]. 2 v. **AG42**
Author list with classified index.
§ Continued by:
(1) Axel Herman Nelson, *Akademiska avhandlingar vid Sveriges universitet och högskolor läsåren 1890/91–1909/10 jämte förteckning öfver svenskars akademiska afhandlingar vid utländska universitet under samma tid* (Uppsala : Akademiska bokhandeln, [1911–12]. 149 p.). Author list with broad subject index. 2 v. in 1.
(2) John Tuneld, *Akademiska avhandlingar vid Sveriges universitet och högskolor läsåren 1910/11–1939/40; bibliograpfi* (Lund : [H. Ohlssons boktryckeri], c1945. 336 p.). Author list with broad subject index. Z5055.S79J8

Switzerland

Jahresverzeichnis der schweizerischen Hochschulschriften = Catalogue des écrits académiques suisses. Bd. 1 (1897/98)– . Basel : Verlag der Universitätsbibliothek, 1898– . Annual. **AG43**
Publisher and title vary. Entries in French and German.
Arranged by university, with author and general subject indexes.
Index: *Verfasser-register zu den Jahrgägen 1897/98 1922/23* (Basel : Universitätsbibliothek, 1927. 87 p.). Z5055.S89.J21

Turkey

Orta Doğu Teknik Üniversitesi (Ankara, Turkey). Graduate theses / Middle East Technical University, Ankara, Turkey. Ankara : METU, 198?– . Annual. **AG44**
Abstracts of theses completed at Graduate Schools of Natural and Applied Sciences, Social Sciences, and Marine Sciences.
AS348.A57A2

Union of Soviet Socialist Republics

Gosudarstvennaia biblioteka SSSR imeni V.I. Lenina. Katalog doktorskikh i kandidatskikh dissertatsiĭ, postupivshikh v Gosudarstvennuiu biblioteku SSSR imeni V. I. Lenina. vyp. 1 (1990)– . Moskva : Biblioteka, 1990– . 25 issues per year. **AG45**
Continues:
———. *Katalog kandidatskikh i doktorskikh dissertatsiĭ, postupivshikh v Biblioteku imeni V. I. Lenina i Gosudarstvennuiu tsentral'nuiu nauchnuiu meditsinskuiu biblioteku* (Moskva : Biblioteka, 1957–1974).
———. *Katalog Kandidatskikh i doktorskikh dissertacij, postupivshikh v Gosudarstvennuiu biblioteku SSSR imeni V. I. Lenina i Gosudarstvennuiu tsentral'nuiu nauchnuiu meditsinskuiu biblioteku* (vyp. 5 [1974]–35 [1989]. Moskva : Biblioteka, 1975–1989).
A listing by topic of theses and dissertations accepted in the U.S.S.R., including some completed prior to 1957. Non-Cyrillic titles are transliterated. Author, name, and university indexes.
Z5055.R89M63

Letopis' avtoreferatov dissertatsiĭ / Rossiĭskaia knizhnaia palata. 1 (1993)– . Moscow : Izd-vo "Knizhnaia palata", 1993– . Monthly. **AG46**
Continues "Avtoreferaty dissertatsiĭ " [1954–1960], in *Knizhnaia letopis'* (Moskva, 1907– . AA796); "Avtoreferaty dissertatsiĭ" in *Knizhnaia letopis' : dopolnitel'nyi vypusk* (1961–80. Moskva : Palata, 1962–80. 19 v.); "Avtoreferaty dissertatsiĭ," in *Knizhnaia letopis' : dopolnitel'nyi vypusk* (1981–92). Moskva : Palata, 1981–92. 19 v.).
A classified listing of published abstracts of theses and dissertations accepted in Russia (and earlier, in the Soviet Union). Listed with other publications, with quarterly and annual author, subject, and geographical indexes. Z22945.K68

Africa

Nigeria

Nigerian universities dissertation abstracts : NUDA. A comprehensive listing of dissertations and theses undertaken in the universities of Nigeria / [ed., Stephen A. Osiobe]. Vol. 1 (1960–1975)– . Port Harcourt : Univ. of Port Harcourt Pr., c1989– . Irregular. **AG47**
A classified listing with author and subject indexes.
Z5055.N83N5

Ofori, Patrick E. Retrospective index to Nigerian doctoral dissertations and masters theses, 1895–1980 / Patrick E. Ofori, Stephen A. Amune. Zaria : Gaskiya Corp., 1984. v. 1. (In progress). **AG48**
Contents: v.1, Science and technology.
Lists, by broad subject categories, dissertations and theses accepted by Nigerian universities and those by Nigerians completed at in American and British universities. Covers Nigerian universities through 1977, and foreign and selected Nigerian universities through 1980. Author and detailed subject indexes. Z5055.O37

South Africa

Robinson, Anthony Meredith Lewin. Catalogue of theses and dissertations accepted for degrees by the South African universities = Katalogus van proefskrifte en verhandelinge vir grade deur die Suid-Afrikaanse universiteite goedgekeur, 1918–1941. Cape Town : [Publ. with the assistance of the National Research Board], 1943. 155 p. **AG49**
Includes more than 1,700 completed theses and dissertations. Subject and author indexes.
§ Continued by:
(1) Stephanus I. Malan, *Gesamentlike katalogus van proefskrifte en verhandelinge van di Suid-Afrikaanse universiteite = Union catalogue of theses and dissertations of the South African universities, 1942–1958.* (Potchefstroom : Univ. for Christian Higher Education, 1959. 216 p.). Title page and introductory materials in Afrikaans and English. A classified list with author index.
(2) *Gesamentlike katalogus van proefskrifte en verhandelinge van die Suid-Afrikaanse universiteite : Aanvulling. Supplement* (no. 1 (1959)– . Potchefstroom : Potchesfstroomse Universiteit vir C.H.D., 1959– . Annual).
Since 1961 compiled by Ferdinand Posta Library.
A cumulated catalog covering 1918–84 is available in microform from the Potchefstroom University. Follows the same arrangement as Malan. Z5055.S45R6

Zambia

Mwanza, Ilse. Bibliography of Zambiana theses and dissertations, 1930s–1989. [Lusaka, Zambia] : Univ. of Zambia, Inst. for African Studies, Office of the Research Secretary, 1990. 95 p.   **AG50**

First issued 1984.

A 4th updated version, listing more than 1,200 entries in alphabetical order by author, with no annotations.

Subject access is provided in part by: *Subject guide to Zambiana theses*, by Ilse Mwanza ([s.l. : s.n., 1993?]. 58*l*.). Available on diskette from Herskovitz Library of African Studies, Northwestern Univ. Provides limited subject access to most dissertations cited in Mwanza's bibliography.

Asia (by region)

Arab states

Jāmiåt al-Kuwayt. Qism al-Tawthīq. Dalīl al-risālāt al-ʿArabīyah : darajāt al-duktūrāh wa-al-mājistūr al-latī manahaṭha al-Jāmiåt al-ʿArabiyah mundhu 1930–1970. [Kuwait] : Jamiåt al-Kuwayt, 1972. 510 p.   **AG51**

Added t.p.: Kuwait University. Libraries Department. Documentation Division. Arab dissertation index.

An index to more than 3,000 dissertations completed in Arab universities 1930–70, written in English and other languages. Arranged by broad subject, with an author index.   Z5055.A63J34

Asia

India

Inter-University Board of India and Ceylon. A bibliography of doctoral dissertations accepted by Indian universities, 1857–1970. New Delhi : [The Board], 1972–75. 24 v.   **AG52**

Contents: [v. 1] Education, library science, journalism; [v. 2] Psychology; [v. 3] Political science, law, public administration; [v. 4] Sociology; [v. 5] Economics, commerce, management; [v. 6] Mathematics, astronomy, statistics; [v. 7] English, Chinese, French, German; [v. 8] Geography; [v. 9] Physics; [v. 10] Hindi; [v. 11] Kannada, Malayalam, Tamil, Telugu; [v. 12] Assamese, Bengali, Gujarati, Marathi, Oriya, Punjabi; [v. 13] Earth sciences; [v. 14] History, the arts; [v. 15] Engineering, technology; [v. 16] Pali, Prakrit, Sanskrit; [v. 17] Botany; [v. 18] Chemistry; [v. 19] Philosophy, religion; [v. 20] Urdu, Persian, Arabic; [v. 21] Agriculture, animal husbandry; [v. 22] Zoology; [v. 23] Palaeontology, anthropology, biology; [v. 24] Medical sciences.

Classed arrangement within volumes, with author index.

§ Continued in part by *Bibliography of doctoral disserations* (New Delhi : Assoc. of Indian Universities, 1975/76– . Irregular).

Supplements and continues coverage, beginning with 1970. Lists doctoral dissertations accepted by Indian universities in three volumes per year: Biological sciences; Natural and applied sciences; Social sciences and humanities. Titles in non-English languages have been transliterated. Classed arrangement, with subject and author indexes.

Z5055.I57I56

Israel

Ilsar, Nira. Bibliyografyah shel ʿalvodot dokṭor be-madaʿe ha-ruaḥ yeha-ḥevrah she-nikhtevu be-universiṭaʾot Yiśraʾel. Yerushalayim : Bet ha-sefarim ha-leʾumi yeha-universiṭaʾi, 1992. 284 p. (Pirsume Bet ha-sefarim, mis. 8).   **AG53**

Hebrew and English.

Title on added t.p.: Bibiliography [sic] of doctoral dissertations in the humanities and the social sciences submitted to Israeli universities.

Lists 1,975 doctoral dissertations in the social sciences and humanities completed at Israeli universities from 1936 through 1990. Arranged by academic department, then alphabetically by Hebrew name of author. Entries include title, year, and university. Indexed by author's name (English and Hebrew).   Z5055.I753I45

Japan

Nihon hakushiroku. Shōwa 31(1956)–51 (1975). Tōkyō : Kyōiku Gyōsei Kenkyūsho, 1956–75. Irregular.   **AG54**

Publisher varies.

Lists dissertations conferred under both the old and new system for awarding doctorates. Early volumes cover a particular time period and are arranged by major subjects, subdivided chronologically, with an author index. Beginning in 1957, volumes are arranged by year, subdivided by institution and subject area. Includes indexes by type of degree and author.

Continued in part by: *Nihon hakushi gakuiroku* (Shōwa 52-nenban [1977]– . Kyōto : Shōraisha, 1980– . Annual). A classified listing of Japanese dissertations, with subject indexes in Japanese and English.   Z5055.J3N53

Philippines

Philippine national bibliography. Jan./Feb. 1974– . Manila : National Library of the Philippines, 1974– . Bimonthly with annual cumulations.   **AG55**

Pt. 4 includes an alphabetical listing of theses and dissertations. Author, title, and broad subject indexes. For complete annotation, *see* AA931.   Z3296.P53

Philippines. National Science Development Board. Compilation of graduate theses prepared in the Philippines. Manila : National Science Development Board, 1964–80. v. 1–3. (In progress?).   **AG56**

Contents: [v. 1], 1913–1960; [v. 2], 1961–1965; v. 3, 1966–1969. Listing is by subject, with author index.   Z5055.P47P47

Saudi Arabia

Ali, Kamāl Muḥammad. Ph.D. Saudi dissertation abstracts. [Cairo] : al-Arabi, [1979]. 512, 71 p.   **AG57**

Title on added t.p.: Mustakhlaṣāt rasāïl al-duktūrāh al-Saūdīyah.

Text in Arabic and English. An alphabetical listing of 20th-century dissertations, with abstracts.   Z5055.S333A45

Taiwan

Kuo li Tåi-wan ta hsöueh po shu shih lun wen ,mu lu : 38 chih 73 hsöueh nien tu / Kuo li tåi-wan ta hsöueh tu shu kuan pien yịn. Chung-hua min kuo tåi-pei shih : Kuo li Tåi-wan ta hsüeh tu shu kuan, min kuo 74 [1985]. 513 p.   **AG58**

Title in English: *Catalog of the National Taiwan University theses and dissertations; 1949–85.*

Continued in part by: *Chüan kuo po shuo shih lun wen mu lu / Kuo li cheng chich ta hsüeh, she hui ko hsüeh tzu liao chung hsin pien yin* 1986– . (Taipei : Kai Ta Hsüeh, [1986–]. Annual. Continues format of above, but expands coverage of universities.

Z5055.T28K885A

Australia and Oceania

Australia

Union list of higher degree theses in Australian university libraries : cumulative edition to 1965 / [ed. by Enid Wylie]. Hobart : Univ. of Tasmania Libr., 1967. 568 p. **AG59**

Supersedes the edition by M. J. Marshall (Hobart, 1959), supplementing and extending the period of coverage.

A union list from ten university libraries, including both masters and doctoral theses in classified arrangement with author and subject indexes.

————. *Supplement, 1966–72/73* (Hobart : Univ. of Tasmania Libr., 1971–76. 3 v.).

————. *Supplement* (1974–89. Hobart : Univ. of Tasmania Libr., 1976 91.). Arranged by subject field, with author and keyword indexes. Z5055.A698U5

New Zealand

Jenkins, David Lloyd. Union list of theses of the University of New Zealand, 1910–1954. Wellington : New Zealand Libr. Assoc., 1956. 1 v. (unpaged). **AG60**

Arranged by subject, then chronologically. Author index.

§ Supplemented by:

(1) Donald Graham Jamieson, *Union list of theses of the universities of New Zealand; supplement 1955–1962, with some additions and corrections to the 1910–1954 list* (Wellington : New Zealand Libr. Assoc. 1963. 86 p.).

(2) *Union list of higher degree theses of the universities of New Zealand : supplement* ([no. 2], 1963/67– . Wellington : The Association, 1969– . Irregular). Comp. by Catherine G. Swift, 1969–80; by John Cochrane, 1984– .

Both follow the general arrangement of the basic list. In the 1963–67 and 1968–71 supplements, the arrangement within subject categories is alphabetical by author rather than chronological.

Z5055.N72N484

AH

Biography

Collective biographies are central to any general reference collection. The trustworthy identification of a person, together with biographical data and, where possible, citation of additional sources, is vital to a broad range of research activity.

This section lists general international and national biographical works, retrospective and current. Collective biographies for specialized fields (e.g., a who's who in medicine) will be found in the appropriate section of the *Guide*. The heading Contemporary has been reserved for works that list persons active in the late 20th century. Older works that treat celebrities of that particular time have been deleted as ephemeral, unless they form part of a series whose publication run was sufficiently long to give the set significant temporal depth.

The key works needed by almost any American library include: *Dictionary of American biography* (AH62), the latest edition of *Who's who in America* (AH72), *Current biography* (AH44), and *Webster's biographical dictionary* (AH38). These might be supplemented by the appropriate regional who's who and by *Biography index* (AH10). Many libraries will need professional or occupational works such as *American men and women of science* (EA170), *Directory of American scholars* (AH76), or *Baker's biographical dictionary of musicians* (BJ203). Research libraries will need many collective biographies.

GENERAL WORKS

Bibliography

ARBA guide to biographical dictionaries / Bohdan S. Wynar, ed. Littleton, Colo. : Libraries Unlimited, 1986. 444 p. **AH1**

Generous critical annotations for some 700 English language works selected from more than 2,500 reviews in *American reference books annual (ARBA)*. In two parts: Universal and national biographies; Professional fields. Whenever possible, dictionaries in print at the time of publication were selected. Z5301.A82

Biographical books, 1876–1949. N.Y. : Bowker, [1983]. 1768 p. **AH2**

A companion to the previously published volume for 1950–80 (AH3). Entries were derived from the database used to produce the *American book publishing record cumulative 1876–1949* (AA420). A "vocation index" which lists the names of the biographees by vocation or areas of interest (with cross-references) precedes the "name/subject index" in which topical subject headings and entries for names of the biographees are interfiled, and which provides the full Library of Congress cataloging information; author and title indexes follow. More than 40,000 titles are included. Z5301.B48

Biographical books, 1950–1980 : vocation index; name/subject index; author index; title index; biographical books in print index. N.Y. : Bowker, [1980]. 1557 p.   **AH3**

Derived from the database used to produce the *American book publishing record* (AA424) and its various cumulations. The "name/subject" index reproduces the full cataloging information as found in *ABPR* for biographies, autobiographies, collective biographies, letters, diaries, journals, biographical dictionaries, and directories published or distributed in the United States since 1950. Includes reprints, paperbacks, and juvenile literature. The name/subject section is arranged by the name of the biographee, with form headings such as Poets, American interfiled among the personal names. The vocation index lists names under field or profession; author and title indexes refer to page numbers in the name/subject section. The "in print" index with its list of publishers, addresses, etc., has lost whatever slight value it may have once possessed. Seriously flawed by a great number of duplicate entries and other evidence of careless editing.   Z5301.B68

Cimbala, Diane J. Biographical sources : a guide to dictionaries and reference works / by Diane J. Cimbala [Diane J. Graves], Jennifer Cargill, and Brian Alley. Phoenix : Oryx, 1986. 146 p.   **AH4**

A classified, annotated listing of English-language biographical sources. Author/title/subject index. Despite its brevity, lists useful works not included in *ARBA guide to biographical dictionaries* (AH1) or Robert B. Slocum's *Biographical dictionaries and related works* (AH6).   Z5301.G72

Jarboe, Betty. Obituaries : a guide to sources. 2nd ed. Boston : G.K. Hall, 1989. 362 p.   **AH5**

1st ed., 1982.

A bibliography of books, periodical articles, scrapbooks, clipping files, and some manuscript sources which include obituary notices or provide indexing to such notices. In three sections: (1)International sources; (2) United States sources (subdivided by state); (3) Foreign sources. Appendix of obituary card files. Many annotations; detailed subject index. The 2nd ed. more than doubles the number of sources listed in the 1st ed.   Z5305.U5J37

Slocum, Robert B. Biographical dictionaries and related works. 2nd ed. Detroit : Gale, c1986. 2 v.   **AH6**

Subtitle: An international bibliography of more than 16,000 collective biographies, bio-bibliographies, collections of epitaphs, selected genealogical works, dictionaries of anonyms and pseudonyms, historical and specialized dictionaries, biographical materials in government manuals, bibliographies of biography, biographical indexes, and selected portrait catalogs.

1st ed., 1967; supplements, 1972, 1978.

Devoted principally to biographical dictionaries. More than 16,000 entries are grouped as universal, national, and vocational biography, with appropriate subdivisions. Author, title, and subject indexes. Aims to represent all languages and cultures. The 2nd ed. conflates titles from the 1st ed. and its two supplements and adds new materials.   Z5301.S55

St. James guide to biography / ed., Paul E. Schellinger. Chicago : St. James, 1991. 870 p.   **AH7**

Consists of signed articles with bibliographies that review the English-language biographical literature concerning more than 700 noted persons from all fields and time periods about whom more than one full-dress biography has been written. Weighted toward Anglo-Americans but with reasonable coverage of Europeans. Arranged alphabetically by the subjects of the biographies, and includes brief biographic sketch of each subject. Does not attempt to be exhaustive. Essays are critical and evaluative.   CT21.S68

Indexes

Bio-base [microform]. 1978– . [Detroit] : Gale. Irregular.
   AH8

The current master cumulation and its annual update contain nearly 8,500,000 biographical citations, corresponding to the total number found in *Biography and genealogy master index* and its *Cumulations* and *Supplements*. Includes a separate booklet describing the set and giving full citations for the abbreviated references found in the indexes.   Z5301

Biography and genealogy master index / ed. by Miranda C. Herbert and Barbara McNeil. 2nd ed. Detroit : Gale, 1980. 8 v. (Gale biographical index series, 1).   **AH9**

Subtitle: A consolidated index to more than 3,200,000 biographical sketches in over 350 current and retrospective biographical dictionaries.

1st ed., 1975, had title: *Biographical dictionaries master index.*

A review in *Booklist* 78 (15 Mar. 1982): 978–79 recommends this edition "for very large public and academic libraries and for the central collections of cooperative reference service systems."

————. *Supplement* (1981/82– . Detroit : Gale, 1982– . Annual).

————. *Cumulation* (1981–85. Detroit : Gale, 1985–). Published at five-year intervals.

The basic set and its *Supplements* and *Cumulations* are available in consolidated form on microfiche as *Bio-base* (AH8).

    Z3505.U5B56

Biography index : a cumulative index to biographical material in books and magazines. v. 1 (1946)– . N.Y. : Wilson, 1947– .   **AH10**

A comprehensive index to English language biographical material found in periodicals, individual and collective biographical books, selected obituaries in the *New York times*, and other sources. Currently published quarterly with annual and biennial cumulations. Includes index by profession.

•Available on CD-ROM, with coverage July 1984– .   Z5301.B5

Chevalier, Cyr Ulysse Joseph. Répertoire des sources historiques du Moyen Âge : bio-bibliographie. Nouv. éd. refondue, corr. et condidérablement augm. Paris : Picard, 1903–1907. 2 v.   **AH11**

Repr. : N.Y. : Kraus, 1960.

The most complete and important work for the medieval period, arranged alphabetically, giving under the French form of each name: (1) brief biographical data, i.e., characterizing phrase and dates of birth and death, and (2) references to books, periodicals, society transactions, etc., where some account of the personage may be found. Very useful for out-of-the-way names, or for complete lists of references on more familiar names; less useful for quick reference work on more familiar names because too much material is given for the ordinary reader. For the large and university library.

For complete set, *see* DA130.   Z6203.C53

Essay and general literature index. v. [1] (1900/33)– . N.Y. : H.W. Wilson, 1934– . Frequency varies.   **AH12**

Contains a large amount of analytical material for biography and criticism of individuals and thus often serves as an index of biography. For full description *see* BA4.   AI3.E752

Hyamson, Albert Montefiore. A dictionary of universal biography of all ages and of all peoples. 2nd ed., entirely rewritten. N.Y. : Dutton, 1951. 679 p.   **AH13**

Repr. : Detroit : Gale, 1981.

1st ed., 1916.

Not a biographical dictionary in the general sense of the term, but an index to the persons appearing in 24 standard biographical dictionaries of various countries. Most of the entries consist of a single line, giving name, dates, nationality, profession, and symbol for source.
    CT103.H9

Internationale Personalbibliographie, 1800–1943 / bearb. von Max Arnim. 2. verb. und stark verm. Aufl. Leipzig : Hiersemann, 1944–52. 2 v.   **AH14**

Bd. 3 of the 2nd ed. of this work extends its coverage and incorporates new references. For complete annotation, *see* AA19 *note*.

Z8001.A1I57

Ireland, Norma Olin. Index to women of the world from ancient to modern times : biographies and portraits. Westwood, Mass. : Faxon, 1970. 573 p. (Useful reference series, no. 97).

AH15

A companion to the compiler's *Index to scientists* (1962. EA195). Provides references to biographical sketches of about 13,000 women which appear in 945 collective biographies and a few series, such as *Current biography*. Indicates location of portraits.

————. *Supplement* (Metuchen, N.J. : Scarecrow, 1988. 774 p.) analyzes some 380 collective biographies published from 1971 to about 1985.

Z7963.B6I73

Lobies, Jean-Pierre. IBN : Index bio-bibliographicus notorum hominum. Osnabrück : Biblio Verlag, 1972–92. Pt. B; pt. C., v. 1–58. (In progress).

AH16

Edited 1990– by Otto and Wolfram Zeller.

Contents: Pt. B and Suppl. and pt. C, v. 1–58, A–Duarte, Felipe.

To be in five parts: (A) General introduction; (B) List of the evaluated biobibliographical works; (C) Corpus alphabeticum; (D) Supplement; (E) General index of references. Pts. A, D, and E not yet published.

Designed as an index to biobibliographical information in 2,000 collective works covering all periods and countries, it will also serve as a bibliography of such works. Originally issued in fascicules (later in bound volumes). The end of this monumental project seems nowhere in sight; 20 years and 58 v. have brought the general section from A to Felipe Duarte.

In pt. B, universal biographical works are listed first, followed by listings according to geographical, historical, or linguistic principles. Each source listed in pt. B is assigned an identifying number; in the alphabetical list of biographees in pt. C, reference is made to these numbers as a means of locating the biobibliographical information.

Pt. C includes separately numbered subsections for Chinese/Korean and Armenian entries. Supplementary additions to the primary alphabetical sequence of pt. C are found in v. 10–12, 29–30, 44–47 of pt. C. Additional lists of sources (supplements to pt. B) are found in v. 23–25, and 40 of pt. C.

Z5301.L7

The New York times obituaries index, 1858–1968. N.Y. : New York Times, 1970. 1136 p.

AH17

A very useful work which "brings together, in a single alphabetical listing, all the names entered under the heading 'Deaths' in the issues of the *New York times index* from September 1858 through December 1968, … a total of over 353,000 names."—*Introd.* It must be kept in mind that indexing policies regarding accidental deaths, suicides, etc., have varied over the years and that the names of certain prominent persons do not, therefore, appear in this index.

CT213.N47

The New York times obituaries index, 1969–1978. N.Y. : New York Times, 1980. 131 p. ill.

AH18

Designated in the introduction as *Obituaries index II*.

Forms a 10–year supplement to the 1858–1968 index (AH17). Adds references to *New York times* obituaries of some 36,000 persons. Unlike the earlier volume, this one includes "certain well known persons whose deaths are listed in the 'Murders' and 'Suicides' sections of *The New York Times Indexes* for the years covered."—*Introd.* In addition, full-text reprints of *New York times* obituaries of 50 notable figures precede the index section. There is also a section of addenda and errata for the first volume of the series.

CT213.N47

People in world history : an index to biographies in history journals and dissertations covering all countries of the world except Canada and the U.S. / Susan K. Kinnell, ed. Santa Barbara, Calif. : ABC-CLIO, 1988. 2 v.

AH19

Complementary in scope and arrangement to *People in history* (AH54). Drawn from *Historical abstracts* 1983–88.

Z5301.P5

Phillips, Lawrence Barnett. Dictionary of biographical reference : containing over 100,000 names; together with a classed index of the biographical literature of Europe and America. New ed. rev., corr., and augm. with supplement to date / by Frank Weitenkampf [i.e., 3rd ed.]. London : Low ; Philadelphia : Gebbie, 1889. 1038 p.

AH20

Repr.: Detroit : Gale, 1981.

1st ed., 1871; 2nd ed., under title *Great index of biographical reference*, 1881.

International in scope and covering all periods. Gives full name, identifying phrase, dates, and reference to collections where biographical material can be found. Indexes some 40 biographical collections and other works.

CT108.P56

Riches, Phyllis M. Analytical bibliography of universal collected biography : comprising books published in the English tongue in Great Britain and Ireland, America and the British dominions. London : Libr. Assoc., 1934. 709 p.

AH21

Repr.: Detroit : Gale, 1980.

An index to biographies of persons of various periods and nationalities in collected works in the English language. In four sections: (1) analytical index, arranged alphabetically by biographee; (2) a bibliography of the works analyzed; (3) a chronological list of the biographees; and (4) a list arranged by profession or trade.

Z5301.R53

INTERNATIONAL

Biographie universelle (Michaud) ancienne et moderne. Nouv. éd., publiée sous la direction de M. Michaud, rev., corr. et considérablement augm. d'articles omis ou nouveaux; ouvrage rédigé par une société de gens de lettres et de savants. Paris : Madame C. Desplaces, 1843–65. 45 v.

AH22

Repr.: Graz : Akademische Druck- u. Verlagsanstalt, 1966–70.

2nd ed. of the work founded by J. F. Michaud and his brother, L. G. Michaud; v. 13–45 ed. by E. E. Desplaces. Vols. 21–45 undated.

Usually cited as *Michaud*.

The 1st ed., in 84 v. including supplements, was published 1811 57. Issue of the new edition, revised and enlarged, was begun in 1843. Its publication was interrupted in 1852 by a lawsuit undertaken by Mme. Desplaces, its publisher, against the firm of Didot Frères, which had started a rival dictionary, the *Nouvelle biographie universelle ancienne et moderne*, ed. by J. C. F. Hoefer (AH31), and had incorporated many articles taken in whole or in part from *Michaud*. After various decisions and reversals, the suit was finally won by Mme. Desplaces in 1855, Didot was forbidden to copy any more of the biographical sketches, and the publication of *Michaud* was resumed. The Didot dictionary, under a changed title and without the pirated articles, was also continued. For an interesting account of this famous suit, by R. C. Christie, see *Quarterly review* 157:204–26 (repr. in his *Selected essays and papers*. London : Longmans, 1902).

The most important of the large dictionaries of universal biography, still very useful. While *Michaud* and the rival work by Hoefer cover much the same ground, there are definite and well-recognized differences. In spite of various inaccuracies, *Michaud* is more carefully edited; its articles, signed with initials, are longer and often better than those in *Hoefer;* its bibliographies (except in one respect, as noted below) are better; and it contains more names in the second half of the alphabet, N–Z. *Hoefer* contains more names, especially minor ones, in the part A–M; has some articles which are better than the corresponding articles in *Michaud;* and in the bibliographies gives titles in the original language, whereas *Michaud* translates into French.

CT143.M5

Biographisches Lexikon zur Geschichte Südosteuropas. München : Oldenbourg, 1970–81. 4 v.

AH23

Vol. 1 issued in parts.

Covers figures from Hungary, Romania, Yugoslavia, Bulgaria, Albania, Greece, Turkey, and areas of the Ottoman Empire. Signed articles with bibliographic references on persons from all periods prior to 1945. "Personenregister" in v. 4. DR33.B56

Cambridge biographical dictionary / gen. ed., Magnus Magnusson, assistant ed., Rosemary Goring. Cambridge ; N.Y. : Cambridge Univ. Pr., c1990. 1604 p. **AH24**

Rev. ed. of *Chambers biographical dictionary*, 1969.

"Published in the U.K. under the title *Chambers biographical dictionary*"—*verso t.p.*

"One of our priorities for this edition was to broaden the work's international coverage. We have also focused far more attention on women, at the same time giving greater prominence to 20th century figures and to personalities from more popular spheres such as sports, media, and jazz."—*Pref.* Some names have been dropped from the earlier edition, but this volume "contains a third more entries than previously." CT103.C4

The Continuum dictionary of women's biography / comp. and ed., Jennifer S. Uglow ; assistant ed. on first edition (for science, mathematics, and medicine), Frances Hinton. New expanded ed. N.Y. : Continuum, 1989. 621 p. : ill. **AH25**

1st ed., 1982, had title: *The international dictionary of women's biography*.

Publ. in U.K. as *The Macmillan dictionary of women's biography*.

Brief entries treat women of all periods, but there are no bibliographical references. Includes a "subject index" listing biographees by various categories. The 2nd ed. adds approximately 250 entries and deletes only a few. CT3202.C66

Dupuy, Trevor Nevitt. The Harper encyclopedia of military biography / Trevor N. Dupuy, Curt Johnson, and David L. Bongard. N.Y. : HarperCollins, c1992. 834 p. **AH26**

Concise signed sketches of some 3,000 world military leaders from antiquity through the Kuwait War, usually ending with a paragraph evaluating the individual's character, abilities, and contributions. Brief bibliographies of primarily English-language sources. U51.D87

Heinzel, E. Lexikon historischer Ereignisse und Personen in Kunst, Literatur und Musik. Wien : Hollinek, [1956]. 782 p. : ill. **AH27**

Confines its listings to those historically important persons and events of many countries that have subsequently received substantial treatment in literature, music, or art. For each person or event, gives a statement of biographical or historical background and a summary of the extent and nature of the treatment the subject has received in the arts. These are followed by a list of the literary, musical, and artistic works concerning the subject (e.g., poems, novels, dramas, operas, symphonies, portraits, busts, etc.). D9.H48

Jöcher, Christian Gottlieb. Allgemeines Gelehrten-Lexikon : darinne die Gelehrten aller Stände sowohl männ– als weiblichen Geschlechts, welche vom Anfange der Welt bis auf ietzige Zeit gelebt, und sich der gelehrten Welt bekannt gemacht, nach ihrer Geburt, Leben, merckwürdigen Geschichten, Absterben und Schriften aus en glaubwurdigsten Scribenten in alphabetischer Ordnung beschrieben werden. Leipzig : Gleditsch, 1750–51. 4 v. **AH28**

A comprehensive and still very useful compilation of biographical sketches of scholars of many nationalities and periods but particularly strong for the Middle Ages. Includes persons living before 1750.

§ A supplement, *Fortsetzung und Ergänzungen* ... (Leipzig : Gleditsch, 1784–87 ; Delmenhorst : Jöntzen, 1810 ; Bremen : Heyse, 1813–19 ; Leipzig : Selbstverlag der Deutschen Gesellschaft, 1897. 7 v.) adds more names from the period covered by the original, as well as others of a slightly later date. In both, references are given to sources, and bibliographies, especially in the supplement, are quite full. The 7 v. of the supplement cover A–Romuleus (no more were published); v. 1–2 are by J. C. Adelung, v. 3–6 by H. W. Rotermund, v. 7 by Otto Günther. The supplement was reprinted, Hildesheim : Georg Olms Verlagsbuchhandlung, 1961.

New Century cyclopedia of names / ed. by Clarence L. Barnhart with the assistance of William D. Halsey ... [et al.]. N.Y. : Appleton, 1954. 3 v. **AH29**

Repr.: Englewood Cliffs, N.J. : Prentice-Hall, [1977?].

A complete modernization and revision of the *Century cyclopedia of names* originally issued as v. 11 of the *Century dictionary and cyclopedia* (AC11 *note*).

More than twice as large as the previous work, this edition contains entries for more than 100,000 proper names: "persons, places, historical events, plays and operas, works of fiction, literary characters, works of art, mythological and legendary persons and places and any other class of proper names of interest or importance today."—*Pref.* Pronunciation is indicated; articles vary in length from two lines to more than half a page. Numerous appendixes, including a chronological table of world history, lists of rulers, genealogical charts, and a list of prenames with pronunciations. PE1625.C43

Nobel prize winners : an H.W. Wilson biographical dictionary / ed., Tyler Wasson ; consultants, Gert H. Brieger ... [et al.]. N.Y. : H.W. Wilson, 1987. 1165 p. : ports. **AH30**

For annotation, *see* AL170. AS911.N9N59

Nouvelle biographie générale depuis les temps plus reculés jusqu'à nos jours : avec les renseignements bibliographiques et l'indication des sources à consulter / publiée par MM. Firmin Didot Frères, sous la direction de M. le Dr. Hoefer. Paris : Firmin Didot, 1853–66. 46 v. **AH31**

Repr.: Copenhague : Rosenkilde & Bagger, 1963–69. 46 v. in 23.

Usually cited as *Hoefer*.

Begun in 1852 under the title *Nouvelle biographie universelle*; title later changed to *Nouvelle biographie générale*. There are three editions of v. 1–2: (1) edition with the title *Nouvelle biographie universelle ancienne et moderne,* containing the 405 pirated articles from *Biographie universelle (Michaud) ancienne et moderne* (AH22); (2) edition with title *Nouvelle biographie universelle depuis les temps les plus reculés,* with those articles omitted; (3) edition with title *Nouvelle biographie générale.* This last is the one usually found in libraries.

Planned to be more concise and more comprehensive than *Michaud,* to include names of people then living, and to list many minor names omitted from *Michaud.* It does include more names in the first part of the alphabet. For other points of comparison see *Michaud* (AH22). CT143.H5

Obituaries from the Times 1951–1960 : including an index to all obituaries and tributes appearing in the Times during the years 1951–1960. [Reading, Eng.] : Newspaper Archive Developments Ltd. ; Westport, Conn. : Meckler Books, [1979]. 896 p. **AH32**

Frank C. Roberts, comp.

Although the third volume published, this is chronologically the first of the series of *Times* obituary compilations, providing full text of selected obituaries from the *Times* of London plus an index to all obituaries and tributes appearing in that newspaper during the period covered.

"In this volume there are 1,450 entries. There is of course some overlap with the relevant volume of the *Dictionary of National Biography.* ... , but twenty-eight per cent of the notices refer to British subjects who do not appear in the *Dictionary of National Biography* and twenty-nine per cent are foreign subjects."—*Pref.* CT120.O16

Obituaries from the Times 1961–1970 : including an index to all obituaries and tributes appearing in the Times during the years 1961–1970. Reading, Eng. : Newspaper Archive Developments Ltd., [1975]. 952 p. **AH33**

Frank C. Roberts, comp.

In two parts: "The second contains an index of all entries appearing in the obituary columns of the *Times* between January 1, 1961 and December 31, 1970. The first part reprints in full an alphabetically-arranged selection of about 1,500 obituary notices of the period. The selection has been made with regard to the public importance of the subject of the obituary, the intrinsic interest of what was written about him, and the need to reflect the wide range of nationalities and walks of life which the *Times* obituary columns encompass."—*Pref.*

CT120.O15

Obituaries from the Times 1971–1975 : including an index to all obituaries and tributes appearing in the Times during the years 1971–1975. [Reading, Eng.] : Newspaper Archive Developments Ltd. ; [Westport, Conn.] : Meckler Books, [1978]. 647 p.   **AH34**

The first of a promised series of five-year supplements to the volume covering 1961–70. Reprints a selection of about 1,000 obituaries from the 1971–75 period, and provides an index to all obituaries and tributes appearing in the *Times* during those years.

Oettinger, Eduard Maria. Moniteur des dates : Biographisch-genealogisch-historisches Welt-Register enthaltend die Personal-Akten der Menschheit, d. h. den Heimaths- und Geburts-schein, den Heirathsakt und Todestag von mehr als 100,000 Geschichtlichen persönlichkeiten aller Zeiten und nationen von Erschaffung der Welt bis auf den heutigen Tag, mit Zahlreich eingestreuten Noten aus allen zweigen der Curiosität. Leipzig : Denicke, 1869. 6 v. in 1.   **AH35**

Contents: v. 1–6, A–Z.

Publ. in 33 monthly parts, 1866–68, with title *Moniteur des dates, contenant un million de renseignements biographiques, généalogiques et historiques.*

Articles are very brief, usually three or four lines, but the work is very comprehensive and includes some names not easily found elsewhere.

———. *Supplément*, ed. by Hugo Schramm, was originally publ. in 19 parts numbered 34–52 (Leipzig : B. Hermann, 1873–82. 3 v. in 1).

The 9 v. were reprinted as two in 1964 (Graz : Akademische Druck -u. Verlagsanstalt).   CT154.O3

Thomas, Joseph. Universal pronouncing dictionary of biography and mythology. 5th ed. Philadelphia ; London : Lippincott, [1930]. 2550 p.   **AH36**

Repr. : N.Y. : AMS Press, 1972.

Usually cited as *Lippincott's biographical dictionary.* Cover title: *Lippincott's pronouncing biographical dictionary.*

1st ed., 1870 (repr. ; Detroit : Gale, 1976).

A useful general biographical dictionary in English. Includes men and women of all nations and periods, and names from the Greek, Roman, Teutonic, Sanskrit, and other mythologies. Articles in general are brief, though a few are long; particular attention is given to pronunciation; and there is some bibliography, though this is a minor feature. Appendixes: (1) Vocabulary of Christian (or first) names, with pronunciation, and equivalents in the principal foreign languages; (2) Disputed or doubtful pronunciations.   CT103.L7

Ungherini, Aglauro. Manuel de bibliographie biographique et d'iconographie des femmes célèbres. Turin : Roux ; Paris : Nilsson, 1892–1905. 3 v., [i.e. main work, 896 col. ; 1st suppl., 634 col. ; 2nd suppl., 758 col.].   **AH37**

Republ. in microform: *History of women* (New Haven, Conn. : Research Publications, 1976), reel 613, no. 4874.

A useful index to material about women of all countries and all periods. Gives an identifying phrase with dates of birth and death, lists monographic biographies in various languages, and cites portraits, autographs, etc. A cumulated index is in the 2nd supplement.

Z7963.B6U5

Webster's new biographical dictionary. Springfield, Mass. : Merriam-Webster, c1988. 1130 p.   **AH38**

1st ed., 1943. Editions before 1983 entitled *Webster's biographical dictionary.*

A pronouncing dictionary with brief factual entries; editions published from 1983 do not include living persons. The 1988 edition lists some 30,000 names, and has greatly expanded the coverage of Africans and Asians.

•Available in machine-readable form as part of *Infopedia* [database] (AB26).   CT103.W4

Bibliography

Zubatsky, David S. Jewish autobiographies and biographies : an international bibliography of books and dissertations in English. N.Y. : Garland, 1989. 370 p. (Garland reference library of the humanities, vol. 722).   **AH39**

A listing of autobiographies and biographies of Jews, including converts to Judaism, living from the 1st century CE to the present. Arranged alphabetically by biographee. Topical index.   Z6374.B5Z78

Indexes

Marquis Who's Who index to Who's Who books. 1985– . Chicago : Marquis Who's Who, Inc., c1985– . Annual.

AH40

Continues *Marquis Who's Who publications : index to all books* (1974–84).

An index to the names of all persons whose biographical sketches appear in current editions of 14 Marquis biographical directories, with reference to the work in which the biography appears.   Z5301.M37a

Spradling, Mary Mace. In black and white : a guide to magazine articles and books concerning more than 15,000 black individuals and groups. 3rd ed. Detroit : Gale, [1980]. 2 v.   **AH41**

1st ed., 1971.

This edition provides references to biographical information about some 15,000 individuals and groups throughout the world. Includes many citations to newspaper articles (including papers from Chicago, Detroit, St. Louis, San Francisco, New York, Boston, Toronto, etc.). Index of occupations and bibliography of books, magazines, and newspapers cited.

———. *Supplement* (Detroit : Gale, 1985) has 6,797 additional entries.   Z1361.N39S655

Contemporary

Contemporary authors : a bio-bibliographical guide to current authors and their works. v. 1– . Detroit : Gale, 1962– . Annual.   **AH42**

Frequency varies. Indexes cumulate at frequent intervals.

Published to give an up-to-date source of biographical information on current authors in many fields—humanities, social sciences, and sciences—and from many countries. Sketches attempt to give, as pertinent: personal facts (including names of parents, children, etc.), career, writings (as complete a bibliography as possible), work in progress, sidelights, and occasional biographical sources.

A number of related titles incorporate revised and updated biographies, or provide new information:

(1) *1st revision* (Detroit : Gale, [1976–79]. v. 1–44 in 11 v.). These volumes represent both an updating and a cumulation of the corresponding volumes of the original series; none of the earlier sketches has been omitted. Continued as:

(2) *New revision series* (v. 1– . Detroit : Gale, [1981]– . Irregular).

Subtitle: A bio-bibliographical guide to current writers in fiction, general nonfiction, poetry, journalism, drama, motion pictures, television, and other fields.

Ann Evory, ed.

This series represents a major change from the method of preparation and policy for inclusion of the *1st revision* series. "No longer will all of the sketches in a given *Contemporary authors* volume be updated and published together as a revision volume. Instead, sketches from a number of volumes will be assessed, and only those sketches requiring *significant change* will be revised and published" (*Pref.*) in the *New revision series* volumes. Updated sketches from previous revisions will also be included. The latest *Contemporary authors* cumulative index also serves as the index to the *New revision series*.

(3) *Permanent series* : a bio-bibliographical guide to current authors and their works (v. 1– . Detroit : Gale, [1975]– . Irregular).

Clare D. Kinsman, ed.

"The *Permanent series* will consist of biographical sketches which formerly appeared in regular volumes of *Contemporary authors*. Sketches ... have been removed from regular volumes at the time or revision for one of two reasons: (1) The subject of the sketch is now deceased; (2) The subject of the sketch is approaching or has passed normal retirement age and has not reported a recently published book or a new book in progress."—*Pref.* Some revision and updating is done prior to publication of a sketch in this series. The cumulative index to the current series of *Contemporary authors* includes references to sketches in the *Permanent series*.

(4) *Autobiography series* (v. 1– . Detroit : Gale, c1984– . Irregular.).

Offers substantial autobiographical sketches as long as 50 p. with numerous photographs, and bibliographies by both well-known and obscure writers. Cumulatively and comprehensively indexed.

(5) *Bibliographical series* (Detroit : Gale, c1986–89. v. 1–3).

•Machine-readable version: *Contemporary authors* [database] (Detroit : Gale). Available on CD-ROM, updated annually.

Z1224.C6

Contemporary black biography. v. 1– . Detroit : Gale, c1992– . Twice a year.   **AH43**

Substantial articles (two to six pages), with bibliographic references on predominantly American subjects. Each volume has about 70 articles. Many entries have photographs or interviews. Covers primarily (but not exclusively) living persons; about 80% are Americans. Indexed by nationality, occupation, subject, and name.   E185.96.C66

Current biography. v. 1 (1940)– . N.Y. : Wilson. Monthly (except Dec.).   **AH44**

Published monthly, with a bound annual cumulation, *Current biography yearbook* (1955–), which includes all biographical sketches and obituary notices revised and brought up to date. Each monthly issue carries a cumulative index for all issues of the current year, and each yearbook includes a cumulated index to all preceding volumes for ten-year periods.

Now includes about 150 biographies annually of persons of various nationalities, professions, and occupations, who are currently prominent in their particular fields. Information given generally includes: full name, dates of birth and death, occupation and reason for newsworthiness, address, a biographical sketch of about 2,500 words, with portrait and references to sources for further information. Each cumulation contains a classified list by occupations.

Cumulated indexes are published at intervals. The most recent is: *Cumulated index, 1940–1990*, ed. by Jill Kadetsky (N.Y. : Wilson, 1991. 133 p.).   CT100.C8

International who's who. 1935– . London : Europa Publ. and Allen & Unwin, 1935– . Annual (slightly irregular).   **AH45**

Offers brief biographical data on prominent persons throughout the world.

See also *Who's who in the world* (AH51).   CT120.I5

The international who's who of women. 1st ed.– . London : Europa Publications Limited, c1992– .   **AH46**

Provides the expected biographical facts concerning nearly 5,000 women who have been "under-represented" (*Foreword*) in works such as *International who's who* (AH45). Information was derived from responses to questionnaires and was verified by the publisher. Substantial coverage of women from Third World and non-Western European/North American countries. Index, by broad career categories, identifies nationality of subjects.   CT3202.I58

Lewytzkyj, Borys. Who's who in the socialist countries : a biographical encyclopedia of 10,000 leading personalities in 16 communist countries / Borys Lewytzkyj, Juliusz Stroynowski. N.Y. : K.G. Saur ; München : Verlag Dokumentation, 1978. 736 p.   **AH47**

Offers biographical sketches of contemporary figures (a few recently deceased persons are included) in socialist countries, compiled mainly from information in the editors' personal archives. In addition to political leaders, figures from the fields of economics, the arts and sciences, the military, and religion are included. The prefatory matter does not specify countries covered, but the list includes Albania, Bulgaria, China, Cuba, Czechoslovakia, East Germany, Estonia, Hungary, Laos, Latvia, Lithuania, Poland, Romania, U.S.S.R., Vietnam, and Yugoslavia; country representation and depth of coverage varies widely.

CT120.L44

New York times biographical service. v. 5, no. 12 (Dec. 1974)– . Ann Arbor, Mich. : Univ. Microfilms Internat. Monthly.   **AH48**

Continues the *New York times biographical edition*, v. 1 (Jan. 1970)–v. 5 no. 11 (Nov. 1974).

Offers photomechanical reproduction of major biographical articles (both obituaries and special, news-oriented biographical sketches) which have appeared in issues of the *New York times*. Index of names cumulates annually.   CT120.N45

Vernoff, Edward. The international dictionary of 20th-century biography / Edward Vernoff and Rima Shore. N.Y. : New American Library, c1987. 819 p.   **AH49**

A convenient source for quick identification of 5,560 living and deceased subjects who have achieved celebrity in any of a wide range of activities. Comparatively balanced coverage given to the world beyond North America and Western Europe. Provides succinct references to book-length biographies. Subject index, subdivided geographically.   CT103.V38

Who's who in international organizations. Brussels : Union of International Associations.   **AH50**

Ceased with 1964/65?

Contents: v. 1–2, A–Z; v. 3, Index.

An index to personal names listed in *Yearbook of international organizations* (AF16). Biographical information on 12,000 people, giving information on main field of work, career, education, interests, publications. Mailing address is included; residence address is included for most entries. The index volume includes a survey of countries, a name index arranged by country, a survey of professions, a name index arranged by professions, and a name index arranged by organizations.

Who's who in the world. Ed. 1 (1971/72)– . Chicago : Marquis, [1970]– . Biennial.   **AH51**

Approximately 29,000 biographies in the current edition are drawn from "virtually every nation"—*Pref.* Invites comparison with *International who's who* (AH45) and includes many of the same names, though there is far less overlap than one might expect.

CT120.W5

Who's who in world Jewry. 1955– . N.Y. : Pitman.   **AH52**

Frequency varies; publisher varies.

Although international in scope, a very high percentage of biographees are from the U.S.   DS125.3.A2W5

European Communities

European biographical directory. 8th ed. (1989–1990)– . Waterloo-Belgique : Editions Database, c1989– .   **AH53**

1st–7th eds., 1965–88, had title: *Who's who in Europe*.

Brief sketches, with addresses, of more than 30,000 prominent citizens of nations in the European Community. Generally ignores celebrities, for whom information is readily found elsewhere, in favor of those unlikely to be found in pan-national sources.   CT759.E93

NORTH AMERICA

Indexes

People in history : an index to U.S. and Canadian biographies in history journals and dissertations / Susan K. Kinnell, ed. Santa Barbara, Calif. : ABC-Clio, c1988. 2 v. (425 p.). **AH54**

For more than 6,000 people, provides 7,600 citations drawn from *America : history and life*, 1976–88 (DB24). Includes exhaustive rotated subject index and author index. Regular supplements are planned. See also *People in world history* (AH19). Z5305.U5P46

United States

See also *American reformers* (CC38).

African American women : a biographical dictionary / Dorothy C. Salem, ed. N.Y. : Garland, 1993. 622 p. (Biographical dictionaries of minority women, v. 2 ; Garland reference library of social science, v. 706). **AH55**

Signed, scholarly biographies, often running to several pages, on approximately 300 women from colonial times to the present. Includes living subjects. Exhaustive bibliographies, with extensive descriptions of archival resources as well as secondary materials. Includes a categorical index and an extremely thorough general index. E185.96.A45

American biographical archive : a one-alphabet cumulation of almost 400 of the most important English-language biographical reference works on the United States and Canada originally published between the 18th and the early 20th centuries / managing ed., Laureen Baillie ; ed., Gerry Easter. Worters [microform]. London : Bowker-Saur Ltd. ; N.Y. : K.G. Saur, [1986?-1990]. 1842 microfiches : negative, ill. **AH56**

Its subtitle notwithstanding, this set includes an appendix arranged in a second alphabetical roster on fiche, 1807–42. Does not include the *Dictionary of American biography*.

Indexed by: *American biographical index*, ed. by Laureen Baillie, compilers, Anthea Batty [et al.] (London; N.Y. : K.G. Saur, 1993. 6 v.). Useful both an an index to the microfiche set and as an independent resource. Entries provide dates, occupations, and citations to printed sources.

American women, 1935–1940 : a composite biographical dictionary / ed. by Durwood Howes. Detroit : Gale, [1981]. 2 v. (Gale composite biographical dictionary series, 6). **AH57**

"A consolidation of all material appearing in the 1939–40 edition of *American women*, with a supplement of unduplicated biographical entries from the 1935–1936 and 1937-1938 editions."—*t.p.*

Constitutes a reprint (complete with all prefatory matter) of the 1939–40 edition (Los Angeles, 1939), with the unduplicated sketches from the two earlier volumes reproduced in a single sequence printed on yellow paper at the back of v. 2.

Includes approximately 12,000 women born between 1842 and 1929. Statistical summary at front of v. 1 provides numerical breakdowns by a broad range of categories, including politics, religion, hobbies, etc. CT3260.A473

Appleton's cyclopaedia of American biography / ed. by J. G. Wilson and John Fiske. N.Y. : Appleton, 1894–1900. 7 v. : ill. **AH58**

Repr.: Detroit : Gale, 1968.

Contents: v. 1–6, A–Z, suppl. A–Z, analytical index; v. 7, suppl. A–Z; Pen names, nicknames, sobriquets; Lists of deaths in v. 1–6; Signers of the Declaration of Independence, presidents of the Continental Congress, presidents, vice-presidents, unsuccessful candidates for those offices, cabinets, 1789–1897; analytical index to v. 7.

Includes names of native and adopted citizens of the United States (including persons living at time of compilation) from time of earliest settlement; eminent citizens of Canada, Mexico, and other countries of North and South America; and names of men of foreign birth closely identified with American history.

Contains fairly long articles; little bibliography; many portraits, principally small insets in the text; and many facsimiles of autographs. Note that under each family name arrangement is not alphabetical but by seniority in the family. The analytical index is useful for subjects and for names not treated separately. Practically superseded by the *Dictionary of American biography* (AH62), but still useful for names and certain types of information not given there. Not entirely accurate; for interesting accounts of some curious fictitious biographies *see*: (1) J. H. Barnhart, "Some fictitious botanists," *Journal of the N.Y. Botanical Garden* 20 (Sept. 1919) 171–81; (2) Margaret Castle Schindler, "Fictitious biography," *American historical review* 42 (July 1937) 680–90; (3) "84 phonies," *Letters* 3, no.19 (14 Sept. 1936) 1–2.

No cumulated index for the set.

An edition entitled *Cyclopedia of American biography* (N.Y. : Press Assoc. Compilers, 1915. 6 v.), purportedly a new enlarged edition, is printed from the same plates as the original edition, with the omission of some of the older articles, the inclusion of some new ones, and the addition of a supplementary list at the end of each volume. Six supplementary (nonalphabetical) volumes to this edition, numbered as v. 7–12, 1918–31, were sold separately. E176.A659

Black biographical dictionaries, 1790–1950 [microform]. Alexandria, Va. : Chadwyck-Healey Inc., 1987. 1068 microfiches : ill. **AH59**

Sponsored by the W.E.B. DuBois Institute for Afro-American Research at Harvard University, the microfiches reproduce some 300 American collective biographies published before 1951. "We have also included all separately published books or pamphlets, whether histories, handbooks, yearbooks, or other works ... that have an identifiable chapter, section, or appendix devoted to collective biographies .... We have also sought to include all variant editions of each title where different biographical sketches are included or new information is given."—*Introd. to the Index.*

§ Indexed by: *Black biography, 1790–1950 : a cumulative index* / editors, Randall K. Burkett, Nancy Hall Burkett, Henry Louis Gates, Jr. (Alexandria, Va. : Chadwyck-Healey, 1991. 3 v.). Vol. 1–2, A–Z; v. 3, Indexes.

An alphabetical listing of all African Americans included in the collective biographies reproduced in the microfiche set. The editors included the names of individuals when it could not be determined whether they were African Americans. A list of sources in given at the beginning of v. 3. Includes indexes by place of birth, occupation, and religion, and an index of women. A useful source, independent of the microfiche set.

Concise dictionary of American biography. 4th ed. complete to 1970. N.Y. : Scribner's, c1990. 1536 p. **AH60**

1st ed., 1964; 3rd ed., 1980.

Presents the essential facts of every article in the *Dictionary of American biography* (AH62) and its eight supplements. Bibliographical sources are omitted, but this edition adds an occupational index.

§ A more selective single-volume work (about 1,000 entries) is the *Encyclopedia of American biography*, ed. by John A. Garraty and Jerome L. Sternstein (N.Y. : Harper & Row, 1974. 1241 p.) which includes brief interpretive essays along with factual accounts of the subjects' lives. *Webster's American biographies*, by Charles Van Doren and Robert McHenry (Springfield, Mass. : Merriam, 1975. 1233 p.) offers brief sketches (averaging 350 words) of some 3,000 persons. E176.D564

Dexter, Franklin Bowditch. Biographical sketches of the graduates of Yale college. N.Y. : Holt, 1885–1912. 6 v. **AH61**

Covers 1701–1815. Good biographies with full bibliographies of works by biographees and references to authorities.

§ Sketches for graduates of later years found in: Yale University, *Obituary record of graduates ... 1859–1951*. No. 1–111 (New Haven, Conn. : [Yale Univ. Pr.], 1860–1952. Annual).

Supplemented retroactively by: Yale University, *Biographical notices of graduates of Yale College, including those graduated in classes later than 1815, who are not commemorated in the annual obituary records : issued as a supplement to the Obituary record* / by Franklin Bowditch Dexter (New Haven, Conn. : [Yale Univ. Pr.], 1913. 411 p.). Covers 1815–84.   LD6323.D5

Dictionary of American biography / publ. under the auspices of the American Council of Learned Societies. N.Y. : Scribner ; London : Milford, 1928–37. 20 v. and Index.   **AH62**

Repr.: N.Y. : Scribner, 1943 (21 v.); 1946 (11 v. on thin paper).

Editors: v. 1–3, Allen Johnson; v. 4–7, Allen Johnson and Dumas Malone; v. 8–20, Dumas Malone.

The scholarly American biographical dictionary designed on the lines of the English *Dictionary of national biography* (AH226) with signed articles and bibliographies. Planned to include noteworthy persons of all periods who lived in the territory now known as the U.S., excluding British officers serving in America after the colonies declared their independence. More than 13,600 biographies in the basic set. Does not include living persons.

As compared with the other principal dictionaries in this field, *DAB* is narrower in scope than *Appleton's cyclopaedia of American biography* (AH58), which includes Canadian and Latin American names, and less inclusive than the *National cyclopaedia of American biography* (AH65), which includes many more minor names. However, it has articles of greater distinction than either of those works and much fuller bibliographies. In most cases, the articles are excellent, but there are occasional inaccuracies in both articles and bibliographies.

The reprint edition has a list of errata, v.1, p.xiii–xxxi, with this note: "In making this reprinting of the [*DAB*], such corrections as have so far come to the attention of the editors have been made either in the plates or in the following list."

———. *Supplements* 1–8 (N.Y. : Scribner, 1944–88 8 v.).

Contents: Suppl. 1, to Dec. 31, 1935, ed. by Harris E. Starr; Suppl. 2, 1936–40, ed. by Robert L. Schuyler and Edward T. James; Suppl. 3, 1941–45, ed. by Edward T. James; Suppl. 4, 1946–50, ed. by John A. Garraty and Edward T. James; Suppl. 5, 1951–55, ed. by John A. Garraty; Suppl. 6, 1956–60, ed. by John A. Garraty; Suppl. 7, 1961–1965, ed. by John A. Garraty; Suppl. 8, 1966–70, ed. by John A. Garraty and Mark C. Carnes.

The dates of each supplement refer to the death dates of its subjects. Beginning with Suppl. 5, the preface states that "certain 'standard' facts not necessarily important for the individual … [which were included in earlier supplements] for the benefit of sociologists and other scholars interested in collective biography" are generally omitted from the supplements. Such information, however, was gathered on data sheets which will be on file with *DAB* papers at the library of Congress.

———. *Comprehensive index.* N.Y. ; Scribner, 1990. 1001 p.

Covers the original set and Suppl. 1–8. Contains six separate indexes: (1) Names of subjects of biographies, with authors; (2) Contributors, with subjects of their articles; (3) Birthplaces, arranged alphabetically by (a) states and (b) foreign countries; (4) Schools and colleges attended by persons included in the dictionary; (5) Occupations; (6) Topics.

Dockstader, Frederick J. Great North American Indians : profiles in life and leadership. N.Y. : Van Nostrand Reinhold, [1977]. 386 p. : ill.   **AH63**

Offers biographical sketches of about 300 notable Native Americans. List of books for further reading, p. 355–369. Tribal listing, chronology, and an "Index of names" which includes names of all people mentioned in the text, together with variants of the Indian names. Many portraits.   E89.D55

Logan, Rayford W. Dictionary of American Negro biography / Rayford W. Logan and Michael R. Winston. N.Y. : Norton, [1982]. 680 p.   **AH64**

Intended to meet the need for a comprehensive biographical dictionary based on scholarly research. Includes only persons who died prior to Jan. 1, 1970. Signed articles with notes on sources. "Historical significance," rather than eminence or achievement per se, was the principal criterion and numerous figures of regional or local importance are included "as illustrations of the broad participation of Negroes in the development of the United States."—*Introd.* E185.96L6

National cyclopaedia of American biography. N.Y. : White, 1898–1984. 63 v. : ill.   **AH65**

Vol. 53–v. N-63 have title *National cyclopedia of American biography.*

Some volumes issued in revised editions. Not issued consecutively.

Ceased with v. N-63, published in 1984.

The most comprehensive American work, less limited and selective than the *Dictionary of American biography* (AH62), and more up to date than *Appleton's cyclopaedia of American biography* (AH65). Articles are unsigned, in general being written by members of an editorial force from questionnaires and other information supplied by families of the biographees. No bibliographies. Not alphabetically arranged, so must be used through the general indexes (below). Each volume is also separately indexed.

The final volume, issued in 1984 and designated "N-63," includes biographies of both deceased and living persons (the latter having been treated theretofore only in the "Current" or "lettered" volumes).

———. *Current volumes.* (N.Y. : J.T. White, 1930–78. Vol. A–M. ill.).

Includes only persons living at the time of compilation, the biographies given being considerably longer than those in *Who's who in America* (AH82). Each volume is separately indexed, and all are cumulatively indexed in the general index as noted below. *See* note in main entry for set concerning v. N-63.

———. *Index* (Clifton, N.J. : J.T. White, 1984. 576 p.).

Supersedes the earlier indexes issued in looseleaf form and the bound volumes published 1971 and 1979. Covers the entire set as published 1891–1984: i.e., the permanent series, v.1–62; the current series, v. A–M; and v. N-63, which includes both living and deceased persons. Indexes not only the main biographical articles, but also names, institutions, events, and other subjects mentioned in the articles.

E176.N27

Notable American women : a biographical dictionary. Cambridge, Mass. : Belknap Pr. of Harvard Univ. Pr., 1971–1980. 4 v.   **AH66**

Editors: v. 1–3, Edward T. James, ed.; Janet Wilson James, assoc. ed.; v. 4: Barbara Sicherman.

Contents: v. 1–3, 1607–1950; v. 4, The modern period.

Prep. under the auspices of Radcliffe College.

Biographical sketches of more than 1,800 women, the great majority of whom are not included in *Dictionary of American biography* (AH62). A fairly significant number of those found in *DAB* were purposely excluded from this work. With few exceptions, the scholarly articles are signed and all include extensive bibliographies giving particular attention to unpublished sources. Includes classified index. Vol. 4 covers women who died during 1951–75.   CT3260.N57

Notable black American women / Jessie Carney Smith, ed. Detroit : Gale, c1992. xlvii, 1334 p. : ill.   **AH67**

Substantial signed biographies of 500 subjects born 1730–1958. Articles include bibliographical references and, in many instances, information on archival collections. Selection portrays the diversity of the subjects' contributions to American life, as well as their fundamental distinction. Includes an "Area of endeavor" index and an unusually detailed subject index.   E185.96.N68

Notable names in American history : a tabulated register. 3rd ed. of White's Conspectus of American biography. [Clifton, N.J.] : James T. White & Co., 1973. 725 p.   **AH68**

An expanded and updated edition of the work which first appeared as the "Conspectus" part of the "Conspectus and index" volume (1906) of the *National cyclopaedia of American biography* (AH65). 2nd ed. publ. 1937 as *White's conspectus of American biography.*

Includes many chronological lists of officeholders of various kinds—e.g., presidents, cabinet members, congressmen, judges, governors of the states, leaders of the Confederacy, foreign service representatives, mayors of selected cities, presidents of universities and colleges, church dignitaries, business executives, recipients of awards, prizes, etc. An index of names is provided in this edition, but references to volume and page in the *National cyclopaedia* are not included. Inasmuch as a number of lists (e.g., "Americans in fiction, poetry, and the drama," "Pseudonyms and sobriquets," "Anniversary calendar") have been dropped, libraries having the 2nd ed. will want to retain it on the reference shelf. E176.N89

Research guide to American historical biography / Robert Muccigrosso, ed. ; Suzanne Niemeyer, editorial director. Wash. : Beacham Publ., c1988–c1992. v. 1–5 : ill. (In progress). **AH69**
Brief biographies with evaluative bibliographical essays that include thorough discussion of primary and archival sources. Also lists museums, historical landmarks, and societies associated with each entrant. Vol. 5 has a cumulative name index to the set idiosyncratically placed at the front and a disappointingly brief cumulative bibliography at the back. Each volume has appendixes grouping subjects by era and museums (etc.) by location. CT214.R47

Sibley's Harvard graduates. Boston : Massachusetts Historical Society, 1873– . v.1 (1642/58)– . (In progress). **AH70**
Vols. 1–3 have title: *Biographical sketches of graduates of Harvard University.*
Vols. 1–3 by John Langdon Sibley; v. 4–6 ed. by C. K. Shipton. Imprint varies.
Vols. 1–17 (1873–1975) cover 1642–1771. LD2139.S53

Wakelyn, Jon L. Biographical dictionary of the Confederacy. Westport, Conn. : Greenwood, 1977. 601 p. **AH71**
Provides biographical information on "the political, business, and intellectual figures of Rebel society" *(Pref.)* as well as the military leaders. Five appendixes offer lists and tables showing: (1) Geographical mobility before and after the Civil War; (2) Principal occupations; (3) Religious affiliation; (4) Education; (5) Prewar and postwar political party affiliation. Bibliography; index. E467.W2

Who was who in America : historical volume, 1607–1896 : a component volume of Who's who in American history. Chicago : Marquis, 1963. 670 p. **AH72**
Subtitle: A compilation of sketches of individuals, both of the United States of America and other countries, who have made contribution to, or whose activity was in some manner related to the history of the United States, from the founding of the Jamestown Colony to the year of continuation by volume 1 of *Who was who.*
Includes tables of presidents and vice-presidents of the U.S., cabinet officers, justices of the Supreme Court, first governors and years of admission of the several states, some major events in U.S. history, etc. A revised edition (1967. 689 p.) includes about 200 additional sketches.
Who was who in America : a companion biographical reference work to Who's who in America. Chicago : Marquis, 1942–89. v. 1–9. (In progress).
Contents: v. 1, 1897–1942; v. 2, 1943–50; v. 3, 1951–60; v. 4, 1961–68; v. 5, 1969–73; v. 6, 1974–76; v. 7, 1977–81; v. 8, 1982–85; v. 9, 1985–89.
Includes sketches removed from *Who's who in America* because of death of the biographee; date of death and, often, interment location is added. With the historical volume, these volumes form a series entitled "Who's who in American history." Vol. 6 includes a cumulated index to the series.
Who was who in America with world notables : index, 1607–1989, volumes I–IX and historical volume. Wilmette, Ill. : Marquis Who's Who, c1989. 272 p. E176.W64

Who's who among black Americans. Ed. 1 (1975/76)– . Detroit : Gale, 1976– . **AH73**
Publisher varies.
"Reference value" is cited as the prime basis of selection. "Individuals became eligible for listing by virtue of positions achieved through election or appointment to office and by distinguished

achievement in meritorious careers."—*Pref.* As far as possible, information was collected by questionnaires to the biographees. About 10,000 entries in the first edition; this was increased to about 19,000 in the 7th ed. (1992/1993).
§ An earlier work: *Who's who in colored America : a biographical dictionary of notable living persons of Negro descent in America* (Ed. 1 (1927)–7 (1950). Yonkers, N.Y. : Burckell, 1927–50.).
Publ. at irregular intervals; publisher and subtitle vary. Biographical sketches of African Americans outstanding in all fields and professions. Includes a geographical listing and a vocational listing.
E185.96.W52

Willard, Frances Elizabeth. A woman of the century : 1470 biographical sketches accompanied by portraits of leading American women in all walks of life / Frances Elizabeth Willard and Mary A. Livermore. Buffalo, N.Y. : Charles Wells Moulton, 1893. 812 p. : ill. **AH74**
Repr.: Detroit : Gale, 1967.
Useful for biographies of American women of the 19th century, many of whom do not appear in other biographical reference works.
E176.W691

Contemporary

American Catholic who's who. 1934/35–1980/81. Wash. [etc.] : NC News Service [etc.], 1911–1980. **AH75**
None published between 1911 and 1934/35, or for 1974/75.
Published biennially. Ceased publication.
Although the clergy predominate, lay Catholics are well represented. Includes geographical index and necrology. E184.C3A6

Directory of American scholars. 1st (1942)–8th (1982). N.Y. : Bowker, 1942–[1982?]. Irregular. **AH76**
Publisher varies: Lancaster, Pa. : Science Pr., 1942–[1956?].
Beginning with the 4th ed., published in several vols., each devoted to a specific academic area.
Contents, 8th ed.: v.1, History; v.2, English, speech and drama; v.3, Foreign languages, linguistics and philology; v.4, Philosophy, religion and law.
About 37,500 biographies of United States and Canadian scholars in the 8th ed. Achievement in research, publication of scholarly works, and attainment of position of substantial responsibility are among the chief criteria for inclusion. Scholars in fields that cross the discipline groupings are given a full entry in only one volume, with cross references in others, as necessary. Geographic index in each volume and a name index to the full set in v.4. Continues to be an important biographical source in large academic libraries. LA2311.C32

Leavitt, Judith A. American women managers and administrators : a selective biographical dictionary of twentieth-century leaders in business, education, and government. Westport, Conn. : Greenwood, 1985. 317 p. **AH77**
For annotation, *see* CH101. HC102.5.A2L37

Notable Hispanic American women / Diane Telgen and Jim Kamp, editors. Detroit : Gale, c1993. 448 p. : ill. **AH78**
Entries of 500–2,500 words on nearly 300 individuals, all but a few of whom are living. Includes bibliographies of sources and, where appropriate, publications. Indexes by occupation and nationality of origin or descent and by an extensive subject index. E184.S75N68

Polner, Murray. American Jewish biographies. N.Y. : Facts on File, [1982]. 493 p. **AH79**
Offers approximately 400 biographical sketches as long as a page or more, with occasional bibliographic references. E184.J5P625

Who's wealthy in America. 1st ed. (1990)– . Rockville, Md. : Taft Group, c1990– . Annual. **AH80**
Issued in two volumes. Vol. 1 lists individuals with an estimated net worth of at least $1 million. The brief entries, arranged alphabeti-

cally, may include name, address, and telephone; year of birth or age range; life-style indicators (e.g., ownership of art or a yacht, involvement in a business limited partnership); estimated net worth; alma mater(s); recent political contributions; and additional references. Vol. 2 lists people from v. 1 who are officers, directors, or 10% principal stockholders in publicly traded companies. Entries include name, address, and telephone; name of company/security; number of shares held; and nature of the individual's affiliation with the company. Also has insider stock/security, political contribution, and geographic indexes.   E154.7.W45

Who's who among Hispanic Americans. 1st ed. (1991–92)– . Detroit : Gale, 1991– . Biennial.   **AH81**
   Provides information "on more than 5,000 of today's prominent Hispanic leaders."—*Pref.* Entries give biographical and occupational information, note honors and awards, and may provide home or business addresses. Sources of additional information accompany many entries. Two pages of obituaries. Geographic, occupational, and ethnic/culture heritage indexes.

Who's who in America : a biographical dictionary of notable living men and women. v. 1– . Chicago : Marquis, 1899– . Biennial.   **AH82**
   The standard dictionary of contemporary biography, containing concise biographical data, prepared according to established practices, with addresses and, in the case of authors, lists of works. Issued biennially and constantly expanded since 1899. The standards of admission are high, aiming to include the "best-known men and women in all lines of useful and reputable achievement," including (1) those selected on account of special prominence in creditable lines of effort, and (2) those included as a matter of policy on account of official position.
   The 47th ed. (1992/1993) lists more than 80,500 persons, and has a section of "Biographies in Marquis who's who regional editions" providing reference to names in those volumes. Includes the names of leading government officials of Canada and Mexico, and recipients of major national and international awards. Inclusion of non-Americans has varied over the years. Each edition is thoroughly revised, new biographies added, and others dropped. For names of persons dropped because of death, see *Who was who in America* (AH72); for those dropped for other reasons, *see* "Non-current listings" in *Indices and necrology* (3 v. 1952–58). A "Retiree index" now lists names deleted because the biographee retired from active work; it gives reference to the last sketch published in this set. Beginning with the 39th, each edition includes a "Necrology" listing.
   A separately published volume designated "Geographic index; professional area index" was made available beginning with the 42nd ed. (1982/83).
   Kept up-to-date by supplements, 1989– .
   During Dec. 1939–Aug. 1959 a *Monthly supplement and international who's who* was published as a supplementary service, giving sketches concerned with "who's who in world news—and why." A cumulated index to v. 1–10 (1939–49) of this series was published separately and also in *Who was who* 2:605–54.
   ————. *Indices and necrology*. [v. 1], 1952; [v. 2], 1954; [v. 3], 1958.
   Contents: Non-current listings from v. 1–22, 23–26 (1899–1950/51) in [v. 1]; from v. 27–30 (1952/53–1958/59) in [v. 3].
   Vocational-geographical index to v. 26 (1950/51) in [v. 1]; to v. 28 (1954/55) in [v. 2]; to v. 30 (1958/59) in [v. 3].
   Necrology, v. 28 (1954/55) in [v. 2]; v. 29 (1956/57) in [v. 3].
                                                      E176.W642

Who's who in American Jewry. 1980 ed. Los Angeles : Standard Who's Who, [1980]. 726 p.   **AH83**
   "Incorporating The directory of American Jewish institutions."—*t.p.*
   An earlier series with the same title appeared 1926–38 in 3 v.
   Offers biographical sketches of some 6,000 "Jewish men and women who have achieved distinction in a particular field of human endeavour or who hold leadership positions in the Jewish or national community."—*Pref.*

The directory section lists about 10,000 "American Jewish organizations, synagogues, educational institutions, youth groups, libraries, periodicals, hospitals and camps in the United States and Canada," giving address, telephone, and executive officer.   E184.J5W62

Who's who in the East : a biographical dictionary of leading men and women of the eastern United States. v. 1 (1942/43)– . Chicago : Marquis, 1943– . Biennial.   **AH84**
   Publisher varies; subtitle varies; coverage varies. 1964/65 called 9th ed. and scope broadened to include eastern Canada.
   Now covers Connecticut, Delaware, the District of Columbia, Maine, Maryland, Massachusetts, New Hampshire, New Jersey, New York, Pennsylvania, Rhode Island, Vermont, and the Canadian provinces of New Brunswick, Nova Scotia, Prince Edward Island, Quebec, and the eastern half of Ontario.   E747.W643

Who's who in the Midwest : a biographical dictionary of noteworthy men and women of the central and midwestern states. [1st ed.] ([1949])– . Chicago : Marquis, 1949– . Biennial.   **AH85**
   Subtitle varies; coverage varies. With the 9th ed. (1965/66) coverage was extended to include central Canada.
   Now covers Illinois, Indiana, Iowa, Kansas, Michigan, Minnesota, Missouri, Nebraska, North Dakota, Ohio, South Dakota, and Wisconsin, and the Canadian provinces of Manitoba and western Ontario.
                                                      E747.W644

Who's who in the South and Southwest : a biographical dictionary of noteworthy men and women of the southern and southwestern states. 1st ed. (1947)– . Chicago : Marquis Who's Who [etc.]. Biennial.   **AH86**
   Subtitle varies; coverage varies.
   Issue for 1950 called 2nd ed., but is first under Marquis editorship. An earlier volume of the same title was published 1947 by Larkin, Roosevelt & Larkin of Chicago.
   Now covers Alabama, Arkansas, Florida, Georgia, Kentucky, Louisiana, Mississippi, North Carolina, Oklahoma, South Carolina, Tennessee, Texas, Virginia, West Virginia, Puerto Rico, and the Virgin Islands, together with some figures from Mexico. ("Notables of Mexico" were first included in the 11th ed., 1969/70.).

Who's who in the West. 12th ed. (1970/71)– . Chicago : Marquis Who's Who, Inc., c1970– . Biennial.   **AH87**
   Title varies: *Who's who in the West*, 1949–64 (also published as *Who's who on the Pacific coast*, 1949–51); *Who's who in the West (and Western Canada)*, 1966–1970.
   Subtitle varies; coverage varies. Beginning with the 9th ed. (1965/66) coverage extended to include western Canada.
   Now covers Alaska, Arizona, California, Colorado, Hawaii, Idaho, Montana, Nevada, New Mexico, Oregon, Utah, Washington, and Wyoming, and the Canadian provinces of Alberta, British Columbia, and Saskatchewan.   E176.W646

Who's who of American women : a biographical dictionary of notable living American women. 1st ed. (1958/59)– . Chicago : Marquis, 1958– . Biennial.   **AH88**
   17th ed. 1991/92.
   Subtitle varies. 7th ed. and later publ. without subtitle. Coverage varies; some eds. include Canadian women and "world notables."
   Selection is based on individual achievement and general reference interest, conforming to the pattern and standards of other Marquis publications.
   An earlier work, by a different publisher, entitled *American women* was published in three editions (Los Angeles : American Publ., 1935–39). Unduplicated entries from those volumes were reprinted as *American women, 1935–1940* (AH57).   E176.W647

Bibliography

A bibliography of American autobiographies / comp. by Louis Kaplan … [et al.]. Madison : Univ. of Wisconsin Pr., 1961. 372 p. **AH89**

Arranges 6,377 numbered entries alphabetically by author. The subject index indicates occupation, locale, and important historical events, as well as some other categories. Many headings are subdivided by period—e.g., Doctors: to 1800, 1800–50, 1850–1900, 1900–45.

Continued by *American autobiography, 1945–1980 : a bibliography* / Mary Louise Briscoe, ed. ; Barbara Tobias and Lynn Z. Bloom, assoc. editors. ([Madison] : Univ. of Wisconsin Pr., 1982. 365 p.).

Lists more than 5,000 autobiographies published in book form 1945–80; some pre-1945 items not cited in Kaplan have been included. Main entry listing; annotations; subject index. Z1224.K3

Indexes

Herman, Kali. Women in particular : an index to American women. Phoenix : Oryx, 1984. 740 p. : ill. **AH90**

An index to biographical articles on women to be found in some 54 works of collective biography. In five sections offering a variety of approaches to the information: (1) Field and career index; (2) Religious affiliation index; (3) Ethnic and racial index; (4) Geographical index; and (5) Alphabetical index. Biographees are entered in as many of the first four sections (and subsections) as are applicable, with full information (name, dates, occupation or field of activity, places of residence, religion, ethnicity, and references to biographical sources) repeated at each entry. The alphabetical index refers to section and entry numbers in the earlier parts. HQ1412.H47

Canada

Allaire, Jean Baptiste Arthur. Dictionnaire biographique du clergé canadien-français. St.-Hyacinthe, [Québec] : Impr. de "La Tribune", 1908–20. 4 v. : ill. **AH91**

Contents: v. 1, Les anciens; v. 2, Les contemporains; v. 3, Suppléments, 1–6; v. 4, Le clergé canadien-français, revue mensuelle; Table générale des quatre volumes.

Consists of two main volumes—six supplements forming one volume—and 24 monthly numbers. The general index at the end of v. 4 links together these 32 alphabets. Short articles; many small portraits. F1005.A41

Creative Canada : a biographical dictionary of twentieth-century creative and performing artists. [Toronto] : Univ. of Toronto Pr., [1971–72]. 2 v. **AH92**

Contains approximately 1,000 entries on both living and deceased figures in the creative arts including print, film, and electronic media, but excluding such categories as architecture, journalism, and handcrafts. Each vol. is arranged in a separate alphabet with a combined index in v. 2. NX513.A1C7

Dictionary of Canadian biography. Toronto : Univ. of Toronto Pr., 1966–90. 12 v. **AH93**

Also published in French under title *Dictionnaire biographique du Canada*, (Québec : Presses de l'Université Laval, 1966–).

Contents: v. 1–12, 1000–1900.

A monumental reference work, offering signed articles ranging from 200 to 10,000 words with comprehensive bibliographic references to manuscripts as well as printed sources. Articles were submitted in English or French, according to the preference of the contributor, then translated for the alternate edition. Arranged in chronological sequence by volume with an index and bibliography at the end of each. Vol. 12, which covers individuals who died between 1891 and 1900, culminates the first series in this project.

Cumulative index to all names mentioned, and to subjects in articles in the work to date has been published as: *Index, volumes I to XII, 1000–1900* (Toronto: Univ. of Toronto Pr., 1991). F1005.D49

The Macmillan dictionary of Canadian biography / ed. by W. Stewart Wallace. 4th ed. rev., enl. and updated by W. A. McKay. Toronto : Macmillan, [1978]. 914 p. **AH94**

Repr.: Toronto : Macmillan of Canada, 1985.

"Canadians who died before 1976."—*verso of t.p.*

1st ed. 1926; earlier eds. had title: *The dictionary of Canadian biography*.

Except for the now-complete *Dictionary of Canadian biography* (AH93), this is the best general dictionary of Canadian biography of all periods and classes, exclusive of living persons. Contains concise biographical sketches with bibliographies. CT283.D52

Morice, Adrien Gabriel. Dictionnaire historique des Canadiens et des Métis français de l'Ouest. 2. éd., augmentée d'un supplement. Québec : Garneau, 1912. 355 p. **AH95**

1st ed., 1908.

A historical biographical dictionary of the French explorers of the Canadian Northwest. Z1060.3.M85

Standard dictionary of Canadian biography : the Canadian who was who / Charles G. D. Roberts and Arthur L. Tunnell, editors. Toronto : Trans-Canada Pr., 1934–38. 2 v. **AH96**

Contains fairly long biographies, with bibliographies, of Canadians who died 1875–1937. Articles are signed with initials. Each volume is arranged alphabetically, with a list in v. 2 of the sketches in v. 1. F1005.S82

Contemporary

See also AH84, AH85, and AH87.

Canadian who's who. v.1 (1910)– . Toronto : Univ. of Toronto Pr. Annual, 1980– . **AH97**

Publisher varies prior to 1980.

Brief sketches based on questionnaires provided by the biographees, thus very similar to *Who's who in America* (AH82). Includes biographies of some persons in *Who's who in Canada* (Toronto : Internat. Pr., 1922–), but each work includes names not in the other. F1033.C23

McMann, Evelyn de R. Canadian who's who index, 1898–1984 : incorporating Canadian men and women of the time. Toronto ; Buffalo : Univ. of Toronto, c1986. 528 p. **AH98**

Provides a cumulated index to biographical sketches found in *Canadian who's who* (AH97), 1910–84, together with those appearing in Henry J. Morgan's *Canadian men and women of the time* (1st ed., Toronto: W. Briggs, 1898; 2nd ed., 1912). F1033.C23

Mexico

Beristain de Souza, José Mariano. Biblioteca hispano americana septentrional : o, Catálogo y noticias de los literatos que o nacidos o educados, o florecientes en la América Septentrional Española, han dado a luz algún escrito, o lo han dejado prep. para la prensa, 1521–1850. [3rd. ed.]. México : Ed. Fuente Cultural, [1947]. 5 v. in 2. : ill., facsims. **AH99**

Includes biobibliographical information about authors. For full record, *see* AA459.

Garcia Granados, Rafael. Diccionario biográfico de historia antigua de Méjico. Méjico : Instituto de Historia, 1952–53 [i.e. 1955]. 3 v. (Publicaciones del Instituto de Historia, 1. serie, no. 23). **AH100**

Biographical information on Aztec (v. 1–2) and christianized (v. 3) native Mexicans drawn directly from the contemporary Spanish and indigenous sources. Coverage extends from before the Spanish conquest through the 17th century. Vol. 3 contains a bibliography, detailed name and geographical indexes, dynastic tables, etc.   F1219.G27

Mestre Ghigliazza, Manuel. Efemérides biográficas (defunciones-nacimientos). México, D.F. : Antigua librería Robredo, J. Porrúa e hijos, 1945. 347 p.   **AH101**

A chronological arrangement, by year of death, of outstanding Mexicans who died between 1822 and 1945. Gives field of activity or title, place and date of birth and death. Alphabetical index.
          F1205.M37

Peral, Miguel Angel. Diccionario biográfico mexicano. México : Ed. P.A.C., [1944]. 894 p.   **AH102**

Cover title: Diccionario biográfico mexicano de 544 á 1944.

Gathers much material in one place, but with certain shortcomings, e.g., date of birth and death are frequently omitted and no bibliographical data or references to sources are given.

————. ————. *Apéndice* (465 p.) was also publ. 1944.
          F1205.P42

Sosa, Francisco. Biografías de Mexicanos distinguidos. Edición de la Secretaría de Fomento. México : Oficina Tipográfica de la Secretaría de Fomento, 1884. 1115 p.   **AH103**

Republished (Editorial Porrúa, 1985) in 670 p., with spine title *Mexicanos distinguidos.*

Sketches, averaging more than three pages, on almost 300 figures from Mexican history. Lacks bibliographies.   F1205.S71

Valverde Tellez, Emeterio. Bio-bibliografía eclesiástica mexicana (1821–1943). México : Ed. Jus, 1949. 3 v.   **AH104**

Contents: v. 1–2, Obispos; v. 3, Sacerdotes.

Biographical sketches with long bibliographies of the bishops and other clergy of the Catholic Church in Mexico.   Z7778.M4V3

Woods, Richard Donovon. Mexican autobiography : an annotated bibliography = La autobiografía mexicana : una bibliografía razonada / comp. by Richard Donovon Woods ; translated by Josefina Cruz-Meléndez. N.Y. : Greenwood, 1988. 228 p. (Bibliographies and indexes in world history, no. 13).
          AH105

Annotations in Spanish and English.

A listing, arranged alphabetically by author, of 332 autobiographies, "memoirs, collections of letters, diaries, oral autobiographies, interviews, the autobiographical novel, as well as the autobiographical essay."—*Introd.* Title, subject, profession, genre, and chronological indexes.   Z5305.M6W6618

Contemporary

Camp, Roderic Ai. Mexican political biographies, 1884–1935. Austin : Univ. of Texas Pr., 1991. 458 p.   **AH106**
For annotation, *see* CJ305.   F1235.5.A2C35

———————— Who's who in Mexico today. Boulder, Colo. : Westview, 1988. 183 p.   **AH107**
Summary biographies of some 600 men and women prominent in business, government, and cultural activities. Gives references to sources.   CT552.C36

Who's notable in Mexico. v. 1 (1972)– . [Mexico City] : Who's Who in Mexico.   **AH108**
An English-language biographical directory with brief sketches on approximately 1,200 figures.   CT556.W48

Bibliography

Iguíniz, Juan Bautista. Bibliografía biográfica mexicana. México : Universidad Nacional Autónoma de México, Instituto de Investigaciones Históricas, 1969. 431p. (Instituto de Investigaciones Históricas. Serie bibliográfica, 5).   **AH109**
1st ed., 1930, was intended to be in two parts; only t.1, Repertorios biográficos, was published.

Analyzes more than 1,300 collective biographical works, listed by editor. Includes exhaustive name index.   Z5305.M6I22

LATIN AMERICA

See also AH287.

Biographical dictionary of Latin American and Caribbean political leaders / ed. by Robert J. Alexander. N.Y. : Greenwood, 1988. 509 p.   **AH110**
For annotation, *see* CJ306.   F1414.2.B48

Who's who in Latin America : government, politics, banking & industry. 3rd ed. (1993)– . N.Y. : Norman Ross Publ., 1993– . Annual.   **AH111**
For annotation, *see* CJ310.   F1407.W52

Bibliography and indexes

Mundo Lo, Sara de. Index to Spanish American collective biography. Boston : G.K. Hall, 1981–1985. v. 1–4. (In progress).
          AH112

Contents: v. 1, The Andean countries; v. 2, Mexico; v. 3, The Central American and Caribbean countries; v. 4, The River Plate countries.

Essentially a bibliography of works of collective biography (including encyclopedias, anthologies, general and specialized histories, as well as biographical dictionaries and "who's who" type publications), with annotations and detailed contents notes, followed by an index of persons mentioned in the notes. In general, works containing information on fewer than 300 people are fully analyzed; more comprehensive works are not analyzed. Locates copies in U.S. and Canadian libraries. Volumes on Brazil and on general Spanish American sources are planned.   Z1609.B6M86

Toro, Josefina de. A bibliography of the collective biography of Spanish America. Río Piedras, P.R. : The Univ., 1938. 140 p. (University of Puerto Rico. Bulletin, ser. IX, no.1, Sept. 1938).   **AH113**
Repr.: Detroit : Ethridge Books, 1971; spine title, *Collective biography of Spanish America.*

A very useful annotated list of 488 works of collective biography, arranged by country with author index.   Z1609.B6T6

CENTRAL AMERICA

Costa Rica

Creedman, Theodore S. Historical dictionary of Costa Rica. 2nd ed. Metuchen, N.J. : Scarecrow, 1991. 338 p. : maps. (Latin American historical dictionaries, no. 16).   **AH114**
          F1542.C7

Who's who in Costa Rica. 1979/80. [San José, Costa Rica : Lubeck S.A.], [1979]. **AH115**
   Series apparently ceased with this edition. Publisher no longer listed in standard directories.
   Short career summaries followed by a business and government directory with information given in both English and Spanish. Includes personal, business, and institutional indexes with complex subject cross-reference tables. Cultural leaders are in evidence, despite its clear business/government orientation. CT586.W47

El Salvador

García, Miguel Angel. Diccionario histórico-enciclopédico de la República de El Salvador. San Salvador : Tipografía "La Luz", 1927–1951. 13 v. **AH116**
   Includes biographies. For complete annotation, *see* DB306.
   F1483.G21

SOUTH AMERICA

Argentina

Nuevo diccionario biografico argentino (1750–1930) / Vicente Osvaldo Cutolo. Buenos Aires : Editorial Elche, 1968–1985. 7 v. **AH117**
   A scholarly dictionary of national biography in the manner of its British and American counterparts. Its completion makes redundant several earlier works. CT653.C87

Sosa de Newton, Lily. Diccionario biográfico de mujeres argentinas. Buenos Aires : [Author], 1972. 414 p. **AH118**
   Brief biographical sketches of outstanding Argentinian women, including living persons. CT3290.S67

Udaondo, Enrique. Diccionario biográfico colonial argentino / Enrique Udaondo ; obra prologada por Gregorio Araoz Alfaro. Buenos Aires : Ed. Huarpes, 1945. 980p. : ll. **AH119**
   Covers the colonial period of Argentina from the discovery and conquest of the Rio de la Plata to 1810. F2805.U37

Contemporary

Quién es quién en América del Sur : diccionario biográfico argentino. Ed. 1 (1982/83)– . [Buenos Aires] : Publicaciones Referenciales Latinoamericanas, [1982]– . Biennial? **AH120**
   A who's who of contemporary Argentinians in the broad range of academic and professional life, arts and communication, government, religion, politics, etc. CT652.Q53

Quién es quién en la Argentina : biografías contemporáneas. [Ed.1] (1939)– . Buenos Aires : Kraft, [1939]– . Irregular.
   AH121
   9th ed., 1968. Latest published? F2805.Q55

Bolivia

Arze, José Roberto. Diccionario biográfico boliviano. La Paz : Editorial Los Amigos del Libro, 1984–91. v. 1–5. (In progress?). **AH122**

Contents: v. 1, Figuras bolivianas en las ciencias sociales; v. 2, Figuras eclesiásticas en Bolivia; v. 3, Géografos, exploradores y figuras en la ciencia; v. 4, Historiadores y cronistas; v. 5, Figuras centrales en la historia de Bolivia : épocas precolonial y colonial.
   Short sketches of both living and deceased individuals with bibliographical references. Individual volumes include indexes by birthplace and field of endeavor. CT676.A79

Quién es quién en Bolivia. [La Paz] : Ed. Quién es Quién en Bolivia, 1942– . Irregular. **AH123**
   1959 latest published?
   Provides short sketches of approximately 500 Bolivians prominent at mid-20th century. F3305.Q5

Brazil

Dicionário histórico-biográfico brasileiro, 1930–1983 / coordenação de Israel Beloch e Alzira Alves de Abreu. Rio de Janeiro-RJ : Forense-Universitária : FINEP, 1984. 4 v. (3634 p.) : ports. **AH124**
   Entries range from a few lines to several double-columned pages and include bibliographical references. Coverage is devoted almost exclusively to politicians and the military. Articles on political parties and other institutions are interfiled among biographies. F2504.D53

Quem é quem no Brasil : biografias contemporaneas. Ed. 1 (1948)– . São Paulo : Sociedade Brasileira de Expansão Commercial. Irregular. **AH125**
   10th ed. 1972 last published?
   Biographies are grouped according to profession or subject field, with an alphabetical index of names. F2505.Q4

Segadas Machado-Guimarães, Argeu de. Diccionario bio-bibliographico brasileiro : de diplomacia, politica externa e direito internacional. Rio de Janeiro : Autor, 1938. 482 p.
   AH126
   At head of title: Argeu Guimarães.
   A biographical dictionary of Brazilian statesmen and a bibliography of Brazilian foreign relations, all in one alphabetical arrangement. Primarily 19th and 20th centuries but includes some earlier material.
   Z1680.S4

Contemporary

Who's who in Brazil. Ed. 1 (1968/69)–6 (1976/77). São Paulo : [s.n.], [1968–76?]. Biennial. **AH127**
   Biographies appear in English and Portuguese (Ed. 6 in Portuguese only).
   Continued by *The international registry of who's who* (Ed. 7 [1978/79]– . São Paulo : Intercontinental de Promoções, 1978?– . Irregular). The edition for 1978/79 was issued in 3 v. with sketches in English and Portuguese; an "Ed. especial" (publ. 1980? in 2 v.) is in Portuguese only. CT683.W5

Chile

Figueroa, Pedro Pablo. Diccionario biográfico de Chile. 4th ed. Santiago : Impr. y Encuadernación Barcelona, 1897–1902. 3 v. : ill. **AH128**
   4th ed. repr: Nendeln, Liechtenstein : Kraus Reprint, 1974.
   1st ed., 1887; 2nd ed., 1888; 3rd ed., 1891.
   Earlier editions include names dropped from later editions, and the later editions add new names and incorporate corrections and additional information for sketches previously included. Primarily 19th century with a few earlier names. F3055.F48

——————— Diccionario biográfico de estranjeros en Chile. Santiago : Impr. Moderna, 1900. 258 p.   **AH129**
> Biographies of foreigners who lived in Chile.   F3055.F49

Figueroa, Virgilio. Diccionario histórico, biográfico y bibliográfico de Chile / por Virgilio Figueroa (Virgilio Talquino), 1800–1930. Santiago de Chile : Establecimientos gráficos "Balcells & co.", 1925–31. 5 v. in 4. : ill.   **AH130**
> Repr. : Nendeln, Liechtenstein : Kraus Reprints, 1974. 5 v.
> Title varies: v. 1 has title *Diccionario histórico y biográfico de Chile, 1800–1925.*
> Arranged alphabetically by family name and then by seniority in the family rather than alphabetically. Most articles conclude with bibliographies of source materials.   F3055.F56

Medina, José Toribio. Diccionario biográfico colonial de Chile. Santiago : Impr. Elzeviriana, 1906. 1004 p. : ill.   **AH131**
> A biographical dictionary covering from the age of discovery through the 18th century.
> Corrections are supplied by: Prieto del Rio, Luis Francisco. *Muestras de errores y defectos de "Diccionario biográfico colonial de Chile por José Toribio Medina."* (Santiago : Impr. y Encuadernación Chile, 1907. 124 p.).   F3055.M49

Contemporary

Diccionario biográfico de Chile. 1936– . Santiago : Empresa Periodistica Chile, 1936– . Triennial (irregular).   **AH132**
> Offers short entries typical of most other "who's who" reference works.   F3055.D45

Colombia

Ospina, Joaquín. Diccionario biográfico y bibliográfico de Colombia. Bogotá : Editorial de Cromos, 1927–39. 3 v. : ill.   **AH133**
> Imprint varies.
> Covers from the Spanish conquest to the 20th century. Includes persons of many professions who contributed to the development of the country.   F2255.O84

Quién es quién en Colombia, 1978 : Biografías contempora1neas. Bogotá : Temis, 1978. 400 p. : ill.   **AH134**
> An earlier series with the same title appeared in four editions (Bogotá : Oliverio Perry, 1944–70).
> The first, and to date, sole edition of an intended who's who series. A Clasificación por profesiones (p. 387–400) groups the names of the biographees by occupation.   CT706.Q53

Ecuador

Pérez Marchant, Braulio. Diccionario biográfico del Ecuador. Quito : Escuela de Artes y Oficios, 1928. 515 p. : ill.   **AH135**
> Covers all periods, but is mainly 19th century.   F3705.P43

Pérez Pimentel, Rodolfo. Diccionario biográfico del Ecuador. [Guayaquil, Ecuador] : Litografía e Impr. de la Universidad de Guayaquil, 1987–[1988]. v. 1–5. (In progress).   **AH136**
> Contains two- to three-page essays, most of which previously appeared in Ecuadorian newspapers, concerning individuals from all areas and periods of Ecuadorian life; no living people are included. Each volume is arranged alphabetically; v. 5 includes a cumulative index, p. ii–xii.   CT712.D53

Contemporary

Diccionario biográfico ecuatoriano. 2nd ed. Quito, Ecuador : R 2 M Producciones Editoriales, 1985/86 [i.e. 1986]. 2 v.   **AH137**
> 1st ed., 1975.
> Brief who's who entries on more than 10,000 prominent figures from all fields. Includes addresses and telephone numbers.
>   CT712.D53

Paraguay

Benítez, Luis G. Breve historia de grandes hombres. [S.l. : s.n., 1986]. (Asunción, Paraguay : Industrial Gráfica Comuneros). 390 p. : ports.   **AH138**
> One-page articles, without bibliographical references, on almost 400 primarily historical figures. Arranged in chapters by category of achievement, then by birth date.   CT726.B46

Quién es quién en el Paraguay? v. 1– . Buenos Aires : Ed. F. Monte Domecq, 1941– . Irregular.   **AH139**
> Successive volumes omit names included in earlier ones and add new names, making it necessary to consult all volumes. Includes government and commercial directory information. Ed. 9, 1990, latest published.   F2665.Q5

Peru

Diccionario histórico y biográfico del Perú, siglos XV–XX / dirección, producción, revisión, ilustración, epígrafes, diagramación y edición, Carlos Milla Batres. Lima : Editorial Milla Batres, 1986. 9 v. : ill.   **AH140**
> Comprised almost entirely of short biographical articles, most including brief bibliographical references. For annotation *see* DB387.
>   F3404.D53

Mendiburu, Manuel de. Diccionario histórico-biográfico del Perú. 2. ed. / con adiciones y notas bibliográficas publicada por Evaristo San Cristóval ; estudio biográfico del general mendiburo por el dr. d. José de la Riva-Agüero y Osma. Lima : "Enrique Palacios", 1931–35. 11 v. : port.   **AH141**
> "Catálogo de las obras y manuscritos que deben consultarse para la historia de la América latina y particularmente del Perú."—*v. 1, p. 15–52.*
> Historical and biographical articles in one alphabet, with a subject index in each volume and a general index at the end. Includes fairly long articles with references to sources.
> ———. *Apéndice* (Lima : Gil, 1935–38. 4 v.).
> The first volume of a third edition covers Abad–Amat (Lima : Editorial Arica, 1976).

Contemporary

Requejo, Juan Vicente. Quién es quién en el Peru. Lima, Peru : Centro de Documentación Andina, [1990]. 95 p.   **AH142**
> Subtitle on cover: Los personajes de 1990.
> Extremely brief identifications of approximately 2,600 prominent Peruvians.   F3448.3.R45

Uruguay

Diccionario biográfico de la mujer en el Uruguay / Osvaldo A. Fraire [ed.]. [Montevideo, Uruguay : Impr. Rosgal], 1983. 163 p.   **AH143**

Biographies, averaging about one page, on approximately 250 living Uruguayan women. Gives addresses and telephone numbers. Includes an appendix of additional entries.   CT3290.D53

Fernández Saldaña, José María. Diccionario uruguayo de biografías, 1810–1940. Montevideo : Editorial Amerindia, 1945. 1366 p.   **AH144**

Sketches range in length from a single column to several pages and include figures from many fields—diplomats, military men, writers, artists, etc. Few references to sources.   F2705.F38

Quién es quién en el Uruguay / editado por Central de Publicaciones S.R.L. ; promoción de Panamérica Uruguaya S.A. [Montevideo] : Central de Publicaciones, [1980]. 688 p. : ill.   **AH145**

On cover: Arte, banca, ciencias, comercio, industria, profesiones. Personas, empresas e instituciones, 1979–1980.

Ed. by Osvaldo A. Fraire.

A "Perfil [profile] del Uruguay" precedes the biographical section; a separate classified section provides information on major corporations and industrial enterprises.   CT742.Q53

Venezuela

Diccionario biográfico de Venezuela / editores: Garrido Mezquita y Compania ; publ. bajo la dirección técnica de Julio Cárdenas Ramírez ; director de recopilaciones Carlos Sáenz de la Calzada. Madrid : Bláss, 1953. li, 1558 p. : ports. (part col.), fold. col. maps.   **AH146**

Besides biographical sketches, contains much statistical and gazetteer information interspersed with the who's who. Persons, associations, and states are arranged in a single alphabet, with a commercial and industrial directory by trade, and indexes by profession to the biographical section. Lists mainly living persons, but has some full-page articles on Venezuelans of historic importance. In spite of the confusing arrangement, this is useful for the great amount of information included.   F2305.D5

Quién es quién en Venezuela. 1988– . Caracas : Editorial Quiénes Somos en Venezuela, 1988– .   **AH147**

No more published?

Includes a separate listing of government officials and a section illustrating and describing official medals.

CARIBBEAN AND ISLANDS OF THE WESTERN ATLANTIC

The directory of Caribbean personalities in Britain and North America / ed., Roy Dickson. Kingston, Jamaica : Gleaner Co., 1985. 333 p., [1] leaf of plates : map, ports.   **AH148**

Based entirely on information provided by the biographees, the sketches include brief biographical information and a current address. Limited to individuals from the English-speaking islands. Divided into sections for those living in Britain, in Canada, and in the U.S. Lacks an index.   CT366.D57

Personalities Caribbean. Ed. 1 (1962)– . Kingston, Jamaica : Personalities Ltd., 1962– . Biennial.   **AH149**

Subtitle: The international guide to who's who in the West Indies, Bahamas and Bermuda.

Ed. 1 had title: *Personalities in the Caribbean.*

Arranged by countries and islands with a General listings section for individuals from the rest of the world with links, often of an academic nature, to the Caribbean area.   F2175.P4

Cuba

Calcagno, Francisco. Diccionario biográfico cubano. N.Y. : N. Ponce de Leon, 1878. 727 p.   **AH150**

Articles from a few lines to several pages on figures from the time of Columbus through those living at date of publication. A significant number of entries are ignored by Fermín Peraza Sarausa, *Diccionario biográfico cubano* (AH151).   F1755.C263

Peraza Sarausa, Fermín. Diccionario biográfico cubano. Habana : Ed. Anuario Bibliográfico Cubano, 1951–68. 14 v.   **AH151**

Imprint varies; v. 12 publ. in Gainesville, Fla., v. 13–14 publ. in Coral Gables, Fla.

Contents: v. 1–7, Abad–Z; v. 8–11, A–Iz; v. 12–14 *see* below.

Vols. 1–11 were a re-issue (1951–60), in mimeographed form, of a collection of Cuban biographies which originally appeared in *El mundo* (Havana). Only persons no longer living are included.

Because information files for the project were destroyed after the Communist takeover in Cuba, the original scheme of the publication had to be abandoned. Vol. 12 offers a new series of biographies in alphabetical sequence, A–L, plus a general index to v. 1–12; v. 13–14 each presents new biographies in a complete alphabet. Sketches vary from several lines to several pages and lack bibliographic references beyond the subject's own publications.   F1755.P4

————— Personalidades cubanas. Gainesville, Fla., 1964–68. 10 v.   **AH152**

Imprint varies.

Vols. 1–7 are reprints of volumes publ. in Havana by Ediciones Anuario Biobibliográfico Cubano, 1957–59; v. 8–10 have subtitle *Cuba en el exilio.*

A companion work to the author's *Diccionario biográfico cubano* (AH151); gives brief sketches of living persons. Vol. 10 includes a general alphabetical index to the series.   F1755.P45

Dominican Republic

Martínez, Rufino. Diccionario biográfico-histórico dominicano, 1821–1930. Santo Domingo : Ediciones de la Universidad Autónoma de Santo Domingo, 1971. 541 p. (Universidad Autónoma de Santo Domingo. Publicaciones., 152 ; Colección historia y sociedad, 5).   **AH153**

Offers extensive coverage of historical figures up to the time of the rise of Trujillo. Articles vary from brief identifications to essays of several pages. No bibliography.   F1933.M37

Contemporary

Clase, Pablo. 50 biografías de figuras dominicanas. Santo Domingo, R.D. : Libreros Dominicanos Unidos, 1990. 241 p. : ill. (Colección Dominicanos célebres, t. 3).   **AH154**

Offers two- to three-page biographies of living persons. Many of the biographies were originally published in the magazine *Hoy* and the newspaper *Listin diario.*   CT542.C57

Personalidades dominicanas. 1988–89– . Santo Domingo, República Dominicana : Molina Morillo & Asociados, [1989?]– .   **AH155**
Provides brief biographies, but no current addresses, for individuals in all fields living at the time of compilation.   CT542.P47

Jamaica

Guy, Henry A. Women of distinction in Jamaica : a record of career women in Jamaica, their background, service, and achievements / comp. and ed. by Henry A. Guy and Lavern Bailey. [Kingston, Jamaica : Caribbean Herald], c1977. 164 p. : ill.   **AH156**
Brief sketches followed by a short directory of general information about the country.   HQ1517.G89

The Jamaica directory of personalities. 1981–82– . Kingston, Jamaica : Selecto Publ., 1982– .   **AH157**
Publisher varies.
Short "who's who" sketches on prominent living Jamaicans.
CT366.J35

Who's who, Jamaica, British West Indies. 1941–1946– . Kingston, Jamaica, B.W.I. : Who's Who (Jamaica). Irregular.
AH158
Published 1934/35–1939/40 as *Who's who and why in Jamaica : containing biographical records of outstanding personalities in the official, professional, intellectual, commercial and political life in Jamaica*.   F1865.W63

Puerto Rico

Fowlie-Flores, Fay. Index to Puerto Rican collective biography. N.Y. : Greenwood, 1987. 214, [1] p. (Bibliographies and indexes in American history, no. 5).   **AH159**
Indexes some 140 collective biographies—"reference works, collections of essays, histories, and some anthologies, all published before or during 1985 ... [of] Puerto Ricans living on the island or on the mainland ... as well as Americans and other nationals who have lived on the island."—*Pref.* Excludes journal articles.   Z5305.P9F68

Reynal, Vicente. Diccionario de hombres y mujeres ilustres de Puerto Rico y de hechos históricos. Rio Piedras : Editorial Edil, 1988. 256, [3] p. : ill. (some col.).   **AH160**
Offers brief biographies of people in all fields from the earliest period to the present day. Dictionary arrangement.   CT522.R49

Rosa-Nieves, Cesáreo. Biografías puertorriqueñas : perfil histórico de un pueblo / Cesáreo Rosa-Nieves, Esther M. Melón. Sharon, Conn. : Troutman Pr., [1970?]. 487 p.   **AH161**
Biographees are mainly contemporary and early 20th-century figures.   F1955.R6

EUROPE (by region)

Research guide to European historical biography, 1450–present / ed., James A. Moncure. Wash. : Beacham Publ., 1992–93. v. 1–5 (5075 p.). (In progress).   **AH162**
Contents: v. 1, A-Col, Appendices 1–9, Maps; v. 2, Coo–Khr; v. 3, Koh–Pet; v. 4, Phi–Z, Appendices 10–14, Index; v. 5, A–Z.
Treats "400 prominent men and women who shaped European civilisation since 1450."—*Pref.* For each gives: biographical chronology and synopsis; activities of historical significance (i.e., issues upon which the biographee had an impact); overview and evaluation of biographical sources (annotated bibliography); overview and evaluation of primary sources (museums, historical landmarks, societies which have collections pertinent to the subject); any other sources; place in broader historical context (describing works). Uses English-language material wherever possible. Numerous appendixes for such topics as lines of succession of European royalty; boundary maps; names groups by periods, by wars, by treaties, etc. Index to biographees for v. 1–4 in v. 4. Vols. 5–8, currently in progress, are to treat scientists, philosophers, political theorists, theologians, popes, artists, writers, and musicians.
§ Similar to *Research guide to American historical biography* (AH69).   Z5304.C44R47

Europe, Eastern

Who's who in the socialist countries of Europe / ed. by Juliusz Stroynowski. München ; N.Y. : K.G. Saur, 1989. 3 v. (lx, 1367 p.).   **AH163**
Subtitle: A biographical encyclopedia of more than 12,600 leading personalities in Albania, Bulgaria, Czechoslovakia, German Democratic Republic, Hungary, Poland, Romania, Yugoslavia.
A companion to Jeanne Vronskaya's *A biographical dictionary of the Soviet Union, 1917–1988* (*see* AH179).
Offers brief entries for "individuals from the spheres of party, government, military, diplomacy, economics, sciences, literature, religion, art and press."—*Pref.* "Name index arranged by country," p. xv–lx.   CT1195.W46

Scandinavia

Scandinavian biographical archive [microform]. London ; N.Y. : K.G. Saur, 1990– . microfiches : negative, ill. **AH164**
Ed. by David Metherell and Paul Guthrie.
Reproduces entries from more than 350 biographical sources for Denmark, Finland, Iceland, Norway, and Sweden published from the earliest period through the early 20th century. Divided into two alphabetical sections, the first covering Denmark, Norway, and Iceland, and the second Sweden and Finland. Includes a printed list of sources.

Who's who in Scandinavia. 1st ed. (1981)– . [Wörthsee?] : Who's Who, 1981– . Semiannual.   **AH165**
Very brief. English-language career sketches, with addresses, on approximately 13,000 prominent Scandinavians. Arranged in a single alphabet. An appendix gives institutional directories for each country.   CT1253.W47

EUROPE (by country)

Austria

Ackerl, Isabella. Österreichisches Personen Lexikon / Isabella Ackerl, Friedrich Weissensteiner. Vienna : Ueberreuter, c1992. 551 p. : ill.   **AH166**
Brief entries concerning approximately 1,600 individuals prominent in a broad range of endeavor, 1918 to the present. Bibliographic references are very limited.   DB96.A35

Kleindel, Walter. Das grosse Buch der Österreicher : 4500 Personendarstellungen in Wort und Bild : Namen, Daten, Fakten / zusammengestellt von Walter Kleindel unter Mitarbeit von Hans Veigl. Wien : Kremayr & Scheriau, c1987. 615 p. : ill. (some col.).   **AH167**

A lavishly illustrated dictionary of Austrians, as well as other nationals who lived and worked in Austria, in all fields, from the earliest period to the present day. Many of the entries are quite brief, but some run to several columns. Many cite additional sources.   CT905.K57

Neue österreichische Biographie ab 1815. Wien : Amalthea-Verlag, 1923–87. Abt. 1, Bd. 1–23; Abt. 2, Bd. 1. (In progress).   **AH168**

Bd. 1–8 had title *Neue österreichische Biographie, 1815–1918*. Bd. 10–23 have subtitle *Grosse Österreicher* (varies slightly).

Long, signed articles with bibliographies—and in many cases, portraits—of 19th- and 20th-century Austrians. Not alphabetically arranged, but with a cumulated index at the back of each volume beginning with v. 8.

Abt. 2, Bd. 1 is a bibliography listing biographical dictionaries and collective biography in two parts: (1) by subject or specialty; and (2) by geographical division.   CT912.N4

Österreichisches biographisches Lexikon 1815–1950 / hrsg. von der Österreichischen Akademie der Wissenschaften unter der Leitung von Leo Santifaller, bearb. von Eva Obermeyer-Marnach. Graz : H. Böhlaus Nachf., 1954–1992. Lfg. 1–48. (In progress).   **AH169**

Contents: Bd. 1–10 (Lfg. 1–48), A–Schmidt, Maximilian.

Designed to continue Constantin Wurzbach, *Biographisches Lexikon des Kaiserthums Oesterreich* (AH170) and *Neue österreichische Biographie* (AH168). Includes sketches of prominent persons of the former Austro-Hungarian Empire and the succeeding state of Austria who were active in the arts, sciences, and politics, and who died prior to 1951. Sketches are brief and unsigned, but include bibliographies of works both by and about the subject.   CT903.O4

Wurzbach, Constantin. Biographisches Lexikon des Kaiserthums Oesterreich : enthaltend die Lebensskizzen der denkwürdigen Personen, welche seit 1750 in den österreichischen Kronländern geboren wurden oder darin gelebt und gewirkt haben. Wien : Zamarski, 1856–91. 60 v.   **AH170**

Subtitle and imprint vary.

The standard Austrian work covering the period from 1750. Contains 24,254 biographies of inhabitants of the various lands included in the former Austrian Empire. Gives biographies of some length, with bibliographies.

Index to supplements: *Register zu den Nachträgen in Wurzbachs 'Biographischen Lexikon d. Kaiserthums Österreich'* ... (Wien : Gilhofer, 1923. 16 p.).

Contemporary

Who's who in Austria : a biographical dictionary ... of prominent personalities from and in Austria. v. 1 (1954)– . [Montreal] : Intercontinental Book and Pub. Co., 1954– .   **AH171**

Subtitle varies; some issues lack subtitle.

Note on cover and half title: Sutter's international red series.

Imprint varies: 1954–55, Zurich : Central European Times Publ. Co., Ltd. ; 1957/58–?, N.Y. : Intercontinental Book and Publ. Co., Ltd. ; 1983– , Zurich : Who's Who The International Red Series Verlag AG.

Frequency varies: earlier issues, biennial; 1983– , triennial.

In English. Each volume in two parts: (1) Who's who section; and (2) in earlier issues, directory of organizations, institutes, associations, enterprises; in later issues, directory of political, economic, cultural, and social life.   DB36.W45

Belgium

Académie royale des sciences, des lettres et des beaux-arts de Belgique. Biographie nationale. Brussels : H. Thiry-van Buggenhoudt, 1866–1986. 44 v.   **AH172**

Vol. 29–44 also called *Supplément 1–16*.

Contents: v. 1–27, A–Z; v.28, Table générale; v. 29–35, Supplément 1–7; v. 36, Supplément 8: Table générale (supersedes v. 28); v. 37–44, Supplément 9–16.

Vol. 1–27 are arranged in a single alphabet; subsequent volumes are not. Vol. 36 comprises an index to v. 1–35. Vol. 44 contains an index to v. 37–44.

Long, signed articles by specialists, with bibliographies. Includes no living persons and, as names were not selected for inclusion until a person had been dead ten years, the earlier volumes contain mainly persons who died before 1850. The supplement includes both early names and names of the 19th and 20th centuries.

§ For names of more recent date the *Biographie* may be supplemented by the long, signed obituaries, with detailed bibliographies, in the *Annuaire* of the Académie Royale. For these obituaries published to 1914, the general index *Table des notices biographiques publiées dans l'Annuaire (1835–1914)* (Brussels : Hayez, 1919. 55 p.) is helpful. It is also publ. in the issue of the *Annuaire* for 1915–1919, p. 113–167. An addenda for 1915–1926 is in the *Annuaire* for 1926, p. 129–133.

Additional information is supplied by the Academie's *Notices biographiques et bibliographiques concernant les membres, les correspondants et les associés* (Brussels : Hayez. 1st ed., 1855; 5th ed., 1909).

The *Notices* include brief biographical sketches with long bibliographies. Each edition repeats some names from the previous edition, but also omits others and provides additional entries.   CT1163.A2

Académie royale des sciences d'outre-mer. Biographie coloniale belge = Belgische koloniale biografie. Bruxelles : Académie, 1948–68. v. 1–6 : ill. (In progress?).   **AH173**

Publisher varies.

Vol. 6 has title: *Biographie belge d'outre-mer*.

Devoted to persons, mostly but not exclusively Belgians, who contributed to the history and development of the Belgian Congo. No name is chosen for inclusion until at least ten years after the person's death. Sketches vary in length, but all are signed and dated, and many include bibliographies. Each volume is a separate alphabetical listing, with a cumulative index to the preceding volumes.   DT663.A2A6

Nationaal biografisch woordenboek / Red. J. Duverger. Brussels : Paleis der Academiën, 1964–90. v. 1–13. (In progress).   **AH174**

At head of title: Koninklijke Vlaamse Academiën van Belgie.

A Flemish biographical dictionary which includes sketches of numerous persons who were omitted from the Belgian *Biographie nationale* (AH172). Each volume is an alphabetical listing with a cumulative index in each successive volume. Bibliographical references are appended to each article.   CT1163.N37

Nouvelle biographie nationale. Brussels : Académie royale des sciences, des lettres et des beaux-arts de Belgique : Diffusion, P. Mardaga, 1988–90. v. 1–2 : ill. (some col.). (In progress).   **AH175**

This new series appears to be intended to entirely recast the Académie's *Biographie nationale* (AH172). Again, subjects are deceased Belgians or others who figured largely in the area's history from the middle ages to the present century. Entries are typically a page or more and include substantial bibliographies and occasionally portraits or other illustrations. Each volume is a complete alphabet of entries without reference to period or other organizing principle. A cumulative name index at the end of each volume will maintain access to the work as a whole.   CT1163.A2N68

Seyn, Eugène de. Dictionnaire biographique des sciences, des lettres et des arts en Belgique. Bruxelles : Éd. l'Avenir, 1935–36. 2 v. : ill.   **AH176**

Covers all periods, and included living persons. Articles are brief, with many portraits but little or no bibliography about the names included, although, in the case of writers, lists of works are given. Many of the biographies of authors are adapted from the articles in the compiler's *Dictionnaire des écrivains belges* (BE1102). Many of its subjects are not found in *Biographie nationale* (AH172).   CT1163.S4

Contemporary

Decan, Rik. Wie is wie in Vlaanderen, 1989–1993 : biografisce encyclopedie. 3. uitg. [Brussels] : BRD, 1989. 1455 p.   **AH177**

1st ed., 1980; 2nd ed. covered 1985–89.

Offers biographical sketches of some 15,000 contemporary figures.

§ Complemented by *Qui est qui en Belgique francophone* (Brussels : Editions BRD, 1981–).

Bibliography

Dhondt, Jan. Instruments biographiques pour l'histoire contemporaine de la Belgique / Jan Dhondt and Solange Vervaeck. 2. éd. Louvain : Éd. Nauwelaerts, 1964. 88 p. (Centre Inter-universitaire d'Histoire Contemporaine. Cahiers, 13).   **AH178**

1st ed., 1960.

A bibliography of general and specialized sources for Belgian biography.

Commonwealth of Independent States

Vronskaya, Jeanne. A biographical dictionary of the former Soviet Union : prominent people in all fields from 1917 to the present / Jeanne Vronskaya with Vladimir Chuguev. London ; New Jersey : Bowker-Saur, c1992. 643 p. : ports., map.   **AH179**

Previously published under title: *A biographical dictionary of the Soviet Union, 1917–1988* (London ; N.Y. : K.G. Saur, 1988. 525 p.).

Short biographies of 6,550 prominent figures from all fields of endeavor, including those who recently came to prominence in the newly independent republics. A major step toward filling the tremendous gaps and elisions that plagued Soviet-era biographical works. The Library of Congress transliteration system is pedantically applied, with the consequence that Yeltsin is found as Eltsin and Tchaikovsky as Chaikovskii. A lack of cross-references magnifies the problem. Indexed by profession.   CT1213.V76

Who's who in Russia and the new states / ed. by Leonard Geron and Alex Pravda. [Rev. ed.]. London ; N.Y. : I.B. Tauris, c1993. 77, ca. 525 p.   **AH180**

Contents: Pt. 1, Governments; pt. 2, Biographical entries.

Includes prominent individuals from many fields, but politicians are predominant. The presence of businessmen marks the most obvious departure from the Soviet era. Addresses for most entrants, and telephone and fax numbers for many, are further indicators of the recent changes in these societies.   CT1203.W47

Czechoslovakia

Biographisches Lexikon zur Geschichte der böhmischen Länder / hrsg. im Auftrag des Collegium Carolinum von Heribert Sturm. München : R. Oldenbourg, 1974–91. Bd. 1–3⁶. (In progress).   **AH181**

Contents: Bd. 1, A–H; Bd. 2, I-Me; Bd. 3, Lfg. 1–6, Me–Ri.

Short sketches accompanied by unusually copious bibliographical references. The completed work is expected to include about 20,000 articles on a broad spectrum of prominent Czechs and Slovaks from the earliest times through the latter 20th century, excluding living persons.   CT933.B56

Kdo je kdo : 91/92 : Česká republika : federální orgány ČSFR / [zpracovalo a vydalo nakladatelství Kdo je kdo]. Praha : Nakl. Kdo je kdo, 1991. 2 v.   **AH182**

"Who's who" entries on approximately 5,000 citizens of the short-lived Czech and Slovak Federal Republic, with a clear bias towards the Czech component. Includes an appendix of directories to government, cultural, and commercial entities.   CT933.K39

Denmark

Dansk biografisk leksikon. 3. Udg, redaktør Sv. Cedergreen Bech. København : Gyldendal, 1979–84. 16 v.   **AH183**

"Grundlagt 1887 af C. F. Bricka og videreført 1933–44 af Povl Engelstoft under medvirken af Svend Dahl."—*t.p.*

The latest edition of this standard Danish biographical dictionary contains signed articles with thorough bibliographies on figures from early history through the present. Some names found in previous editions no longer appear, but numerous additions, including some early figures, as well as those who have come to prominence since the last edition (1933–44). An asterisk after the contributor's name indicates that the article has been carried over from the previous edition without substantial change. A list of additions and corrections, an index of contributors, a comprehensive name index (including references to entries found only in the ealier editions), and a chronological index are found in v. 16.   CT1263.D33

Contemporary

Kraks blå bog : nulevende danske maends og kvinders levnedsløb. v. 1– . Copenhagen : Krak, 1910– . Annual.   **AH184**

The standard Danish who's who. A necrology and list of abbreviations is found at back of volumes.

Kraks blå bog 1989 : register over 15.229 [i.e., 15,229] personer, der er biograferet i Kraks blå bog 1910–1988. (Copenhagen : Krak, 1989.) Index referring to last annual appearance for 15,229 people covered in this series.   DL144.K7

Bibliography

Erichsen, Balder. Dansk personalhistorisk bibliografi : systematisk Fortegnelse over bidrag til Danmarks personalhistorie (i Tilslutning til Bibliotheca danica) / Balder Erichsen, Alfred Krarup. København : Gads, 1917. 806 p.   **AH185**

Vol. 3 of the authors' *Dansk historisk bibliografi* (DC131).

Includes books and analytical material, indexing many articles in periodicals. Lists more than 15,000 references. As it usually gives dates of birth or death and some characterizing phrase, it can be used for such direct biographical information, as well as for its bibliographical references.

Continued informally by the indexing of biographical articles, also with dates and characterizing phrases, given in the *Dansk Tidsskrift-Index* (AD309) under the heading *Personalhistorie*.

Z2576.E68

Finland

Finsk biografisk handbok / under medvärken af fackmän utg. af Tor Capelan. Helsingfors : Edlunds Förlag, 1903. 2 v. **AH186**

Issued in parts, 1895–1903.

Signed biographical sketches in Swedish, of roughly 5,000 individuals averaging about a half page in length. Bibliographic references only to the subjects own works. CT1220.F5

Heikinheimo, Ilmari. Suomen elämäkerrasto. Helsinki : Werner Söderström, [1955]. 855 p. : ill. **AH187**

Fairly brief sketches of personalities of all periods, with many portraits. Particularly strong for the 18th and 19th centuries.

DK448.H4

Kansallinen elämäkerrasto. Porvoo : Söderström, 1927–1934. 5 v. **AH188**

A scholarly national biography produced under the auspices of the Finnish Historical Society. Signed biographies average about one page and include extensive bibliographic references. CT1220.K13

Contemporary

Kuka kukin on = Who's who in Finland. 1920– . Helsingissä : Kustannusosakeyhtiö Otava. Irregular. **AH189**

Title varies: 1920–41, *Aikalaiskirja*.

"Henkilötietoja nykypolven suomalaisista."

1990 latest published.

Outlines biographies on over 4,000 living Finns. A table of English equivalents to common words and abbreviations, found at the front, gives a degree of accessibility to those unfamiliar with Finnish. CT1220.K8

Vem och vad? : biografisk handbok. 1920– . Helsingfors : H. Schildt, 1920– . Irregular. **AH190**

1992 latest published.

Published quinquennially through 1941, but because of the war the volume due in 1946 was not published until 1948; irregular thereafter.

As the language of the title suggests, this is devoted largely to Finns of Swedish extraction. The text of the nearly 3,000 entries is also Swedish. Only limited overlap with *Kuka kukin on* (AH189).

CT1220.V4

France

Académie des Sciences (France). Index biographique de l'Académie des Sciences du 22 décembre 1666 au 1^{ier} octobre 1978. [4. éd.]. Paris : Gauthier-Villars, 1979. 513 p. **AH191**

Earlier eds. appeared 1939, 1954 and 1968.

Lists, with brief biographical information, all persons who have been members or *correspondants* of the Academy since its origin in 1666. Q46.A163

Archives biographiques françaises / [ed. by Susan Bradley] [microform]. London : Bowker-Saur Ltd., c1988–90. 1065 microfiches : negative, ill. **AH192**

Reproduces entries from nearly 180 biographical sources published from the earliest time to 1914. Includes an A–Z supplement on fiche 1049–1065.

Caratini, Roger. Dictionnaire des personnages de la Révolution. [Paris] : Le Préaux Clercs, c1988. 576 p. : ill. **AH193**

Short sketches on 3,000 men and women who participated in the Revolution, 1789–95. Includes a summary history of the period and a very selective general bibliography and chronology. DC147.C37

Dictionnaire de biographie française / sous la direction de J. Balteau ... M. Barroux ... M. Prévost ... avec le concours de nombreux collaborateurs. Paris : Letouzey et Ané, 1933–92. v. 1–18 (fasc. 1–106). (In progress). **AH194**

Issued in parts, 1929– . Editors vary.

Publisher varies; early volumes issued by Letouzey.

Contents: v. 1–18 (fasc. 1–106), A–Jumelle.

An important dictionary of national biography; planned to be a much more extensive work than the corresponding dictionaries of English and American biography. Articles, for the most part shorter than those in *Dictionary of national biography* (AH226), are signed, and nearly all have bibliographies, some of which are very extensive.

CT143.D5

Dictionnaire des maréchaux de France : du Moyen Age à nos jours / coordination de Geneviéve Maze-Sencier ; avec la collaboration de Christophe Brun ... [et al.] ; introduction de Joseph Valynseele. [Paris] : Perrin, c1988. 452 p., [32] p. of plates : ports. (some col.). **AH195**

Sketches average about one page, with short bibliographies on the 337 Marshals of France who flourished from the 12th through the 20th century. Preceded by a chronological roster and historical summary.

DC44.5.D53

Fierro, Alfred. Bibliographie analytique des biographies collectives imprimées de la France contemporaine : 1789–1985. Paris : Libr. H. Champion, 1986. 376 p. (Bibliothèque de l'Ecole des hautes études, IVe section, Sciences historiques et philologiques, fasc. 330.). **AH196**

A bibliography of collective biographies of French figures of the period 1789–1985. Works of international coverage are excluded if less than 25% of the entries are for French persons; and each work must include three or more biographies. More than 2,500 citations, many with brief descriptive notes, are arranged in three main sections: (1) general works of collective biography subdivided by period; (2) biographical works grouped by profession (with chronological and other subdivisions as appropriate); and (3) works of local and regional coverage. Index of authors and titles. AS162.B6

Hommes et destins : dictionnaire biographique d'outre-mer. Paris : Académie des sciences d'outre-mer, [1975–89]. 9 v. (Académie des sciences d'outre-mer. Publications. Travaux et mémoires, n.s., no.2, etc.). **AH197**

A biographical series concerned with outstanding figures in French colonial territories, including citizens of the new nations, explorers, administrators, missionaries, doctors, anthropologists, engineers, etc., who made significant contributions in those areas. Includes about 500 signed biographies, mainly of 20th century figures. Bibliographies include writings by and about the individual. Vol. 3 comprises some 250 sketches of deceased persons of prominence in Madagascar; the 35 sketches of Madagascar personalities included in v. 1–2 are not repeated, but are listed in the front matter of v. 3. Vol. 4 adds 264 sketches from various territories and includes a name index for v. 1–4. Vol. 5 covers Africa and the French West Indies; v. 6, Asia; v. 7, Northern Africa; v. 8, Colonial governors, administrators, and magistrates; and v. 9, Africa south of the Sahara. Each volume has a cumulative index. CT1014.H65

Kuscinski, August. Dictionnaire des conventionnels. Paris : Au Siège de la Société, 1916–19. 615 p. **AH198**

Issued in parts.

Biographical sketches of the members of the National Convention, 1792–95.

Maurepas, Arnaud de. Les grands hommes d'état de l'histoire de France / Arnaud de Maurepas, Hervé Robert, Pierre Thibault. Paris : Larousse, c1989. 527 p. : ill. **AH199**

Page-length biographies with chronologies for 120 French heads of state from Clovis to Mitterand, with shorter sketches for another 780 major political figures associated with each. No bibliographical references.   DC36.1

Robert, Adolphe. Dictionnaire des parlementaires français : comprenant tous les membres des assemblées françaises et tous les ministres français depuis le 1er mai 1789 jusqu'au 1er mai 1889, avec leurs noms, état civil, états de services, actes politiques, votes parlementaires, etc / Adolphe Robert, Edgar Bourloton, and Gaston Cougny. Paris : Bourloton, 1891. 5 v. : ill.   **AH200**

For annotation, *see* CJ329.   JN2771.R7

Contemporary

Who's who in France : dictionnaire biographique. Ed. 1 (1953/54)– . Paris : Lafitte, 1953– . Biennial.   **AH201**

1st ed., 1953/54, had title *Who's who in France: Paris,* and was restricted to persons living in Paris.

Later editions cover all of France, as well as French persons overseas and French-speaking peoples in African nations, etc. Sketches are of the usual who's who type. In spite of the English title, sketches and explanatory text are in French. In addition to the biographical sketches, there is a section listing government officials, information about large business firms, etc.

An earlier, similar publication, *Qui êtes-vous?* (Paris : Delagrave), appeared in three editions: 1908, 1909, 1924.

DC705.A1W46

Germany

Allgemeine deutsche Biographie / hrsg. durch die Historische Commission bei der K. Akademie der Wissenschaften. Leipzig : Duncker, 1875–1912. 56 v.   **AH202**

Contents: v. 1–45, A–Z; v. 46–55, Nachträge bis 1899, Andr–Z (A–Ad included in v. 45); v. 56, General Register.

The outstanding German biographical dictionary, containing long, signed articles, with bibliographies, on persons from early times to the end of the 19th century. Does not include living persons. As there are supplementary sections in many volumes, it is essential that the index be used to find the complete record.

§For biographies of persons deceased since the compilation of this work, several publications may be used as informal supplements: *Biographisches Jahrbuch und deutscher Nekrolog, 1896–1913* (AH204), continued by *Deutsches biographisches Jahrbuch* (AH207), and *Deutsches biographisches Archiv* (AH206).   CT1053.A5

Biographisches Handbuch der deutschsprachigen Emigration nach 1933 / Leitung und Bearbeitung, Werner Röder, Herbert A. Strauss, unter Mitwirkung von Dieter Marc Schneider, Louise Forsyth ; Autoren, Jan Foitzik [et al.] ; Redaktion, Sybille Claus und Beatrix Schmidt. München ; N.Y. : K.G. Saur ; Detroit : Distr. by Gale, 1980–1983. 3 v. in 4.   **AH203**

"International biographical dictionary of Central European emigrés 1933–1945, sponsored by Research Foundation for Jewish Immigration, Inc., New York, and Institut für Zeitgeschichte München, directed by Herbert A. Strauss and Werner Röder."—*half-t.p.*

Vol. 1 has title in German; v. 2 has title in English.

Contents: v. 1, Politik, Wirtschaft, Öffentliches Leben; v. 2, The arts, sciences, and literature (in 2 v.); v. 3, Gesamtregister; Index.

Offers some 8,700 biographical sketches of persons (living and deceased) who emigrated from Central European areas during the period of the Third Reich. Vol. 3 offers indexes by names, pseudonyms, cover names and name changes, by countries of intermediate emigration and final settlement, by occupations, plus selected references to parties, associations, and institutions mentioned in the text.

DD68.B52

Biographisches Jahrbuch und deutscher Nekrolog, 1896–1913 / hrsg. von Anton Bettelheim. v. 1 (1896)–v. 18 (1913). Berlin : Reimer, 1897–1917. Annual.   **AH204**

Each volume contains: (1) section of long, signed articles, with bibliographies, on prominent Germans who died during the year; (2) a necrology of briefer notices; and (3) index. A separate volume indexes v. 1–10 (1896–1905).

Continued by: *Deutsches biographisches Jahrbuch* (AH207).

CT1050.B5

Bode, Ingrid. Die Autobiographien zur deutschen Literatur, Kunst und Musik, 1900–1965 : Bibliographie und Nachweise der persönlichen Begegnungen und Charakteristiken / Ingrid Hannich-Bode. Stuttgart : Metzler, [1966]. 308 p.   **AH205**

More than 500 autobiographies and diaries are listed in the first section. A second section offers an index to the names of persons appearing in the autobiographies cited.

Deutsches biographisches Archiv : eine Kumulation aus 254 der wichtigsten biographischen Nachschlagswerke für den deutschen Bereich bis zum Ausgang des neunzehnten Jahrhunderts / hrsg. von Bernhard Fabian, bearb. unter der Leitung von Willi Gorzny [microform]. München ; N.Y. : K. G. Saur, 1982. 1447 microfiches.   **AH206**

Advertised under title: *German biographical archive.*

Quellenverzeichnisse: microfiche 1–16.

Reproduces in a single alphabetical sequence about 400,000 entries on 225,000 individuals from 267 biographical sources published between 1700 and 1910, plus a supplement of omissions on microfiches 1422–1431.

Indexed by: *Deutscher biographischer index,* bearb. von Hans-Albrecht Koch, Uta Koch und Angelika Koller (München ; N.Y. : K.G. Saur, 1986. 4 v.). Useful both as an index to the microfiche set and as an independent resource. Entries provide dates, occupations, and citations to both the printed sources and the microfiche set.

Continued by: *Neue Folge bis zur Mitte des 20. Jahrhunderts: eine Kumulation aus 284 der wichtigsten biographischen Nachschlagewerke für den deutschsprachigen Bereich* [microform], hrsg. von Willi Gorzny ([München ; N.Y.] : K.G. Saur, [c1990?]– . 760 microfiches. In progress?).

Drawn from 284 reference works published between 1800 and the mid-1960s. When complete, expected to include some 280,000 subjects.

Deutsches biographisches Jahrbuch / hrsg. vom Verbande der Deutschen Akademien. Bd. 1 (1914/16)–Bd. 11 (1929). Stuttgart : Deutsche Verlags-Anstalt, 1925–1932.   **AH207**

Contents: v. 1, 1914–16; v. 2, 1917–20; v. 3, 1921; v. 4, 1922; v. 5, 1923; v. 10, 1928; v. 11, 1929. Vol. 6–9 not publ.

Contains long, signed articles, many with bibliographies, and a necrology list of briefer notices.

———. *Reg. zu Bd. 1–5, 10 u. 11,* by Heinrich Ihme. (München ; N.Y. ; London ; Oxford ; Paris : Saur, 1986. 99 p.). Indexes the cumulated volumes.

Die grossen Deutschen : deutsche Biographie / hrsg. von Hermann Heimpel, Theodor Heuss, Benno Reifenberg. Berlin : Propyläen-Verlag, [1956–57]. 5 v. : ill.   **AH208**

Signed biographies several pages in length on 234 major figures in German cultural, religious, and political history from 672 through mid-20th century. Arranged chronologically with a cumulative index in v. 5. Profusely illustrated with portraits, artists' works, and manuscript facsimiles. Based on an earlier edition edited by Willy Andreas and Wilhelm von Scholz (Berlin : Propyläen-Verlag, [1937]) but largely reworked.   CT1054.G72

Kürschners deutscher Gelehrten-Kalender. 1. Ausg. (1925)– . Berlin ; N.Y. : W. de Gruyter. Irregular. **AH209**

A biographical dictionary of German scholars in nonliterary fields, an offshoot of *Kürschners deutscher Literatur-Kalender* (BE1060). The editions vary considerably in size and content, both as to names included and as to supplementary information. The 16th ed. (1992) is in 3 v., treating 62,998 personalities including, for the first time since World War II, scholars from the former East Germany. Extensive bibliographical listings. Z2230.K93

Neue deutsche Biographie / hrsg. von der Historischen Kommission bei der Bayerischen Akademie der Wissenschaften. Berlin : Duncker & Humblot, 1953–1990. v. 1–16. (In progress). **AH210**

Contents: v. 1–16, Aachen–Melanchthon.

A newly compiled work, not intended to supersede the *Allgemeine deutsche Biographie* (AH202), although many of the same names appear in it along with persons who have died since the older work was published and some additional names from earlier periods. Articles are signed, and bibliographies, including materials by and about biographees, are given at the end of each article. References to portraits are sometimes noted. An index in each volume, covering the part of the alphabet contained therein, includes references to all entries in the *Allgemeine ...*, thus calling attention to articles omitted from the newer work. CT1053.N4

Contemporary

Wer ist wer? v. 11 (1950)– . Lübeck [etc.] : Schmidt Rönhild [etc.]. Irregular. **AH211**

Subtitle : Das deutsche who's who.

Title varies: v. 1–9, *Wer ist's?*; v. 10, 1935, *Degeners Wer ist's?*. Imprint and editors vary; v. 1–10 ed. by H. A. L. Degener.

The standard German who's who, offering sketches of personalities in all fields. Beginning with the 14th ed. (publ. 1962–65), issued in 2 parts, the first covering "Bundesrepublik Deutschland und West Berlin," the second, the German Democratic Republic. Later eds. were concerned with personalities of the German Federal Republic and West Berlin, with some Swiss and Austrian figures included in recent volumes. The 31st ed. (1992) contains about 40,000 entries. Inclusion of the former German Democratic Republic is largely limited to those currently occupying government posts. "If anything, this serves as a reminder that the number of those able to lay claim to remarkable achievements in these regions over a large period is still very low."—*Pref.* DD85.W3

Who's who in Germany. 1956– . Munich : Intercontinental Book and Pub. Co., German editor R. Oldenbourg Verlag, 1956– . Irregular. **AH212**

Publisher varies; subtitle varies. Beginning 1988, publ. Essen : Who's Who the International Red Book Series Verlag (Sutter's international red series). In 2 v. beginning with 3rd ed.

Another in the English-language series of who's whos of European countries. Includes biographical sketches and a directory of businesses, organizations, associations, and institutions. The 1992 ed. includes about 13,000 biographies of prominent persons. DD85.W45

Who's who in the arts and literature. 3rd ed.– . [Zürich] : Who's who, the International Red Series Verlag, 1982– . **AH213**

Formed by the union of *Who's who in literature* (Wörthsee, Germany) and *Who's who in the arts*, continuing the numbering of the latter. Issued in parts: v. 1–2, Fine arts; v. 3, Literature; v. 4, Applied arts and music.

Includes artists and authors from Germany, Austria, and Switzerland.

Bibliography

Jessen, Jens Christian. Bibliographie der Autobiographien. München ; N.Y. : K.G. Saur, 1987–1989. v. 1–3. (In progress). **AH214**

Contents: v. 1, Selbstzeugnisse, Erinnerungen, Tagebücher und Briefe deutscher Schriftsteller und Künstler; v. 2, Selbstzeugnisse, Erinnerungen, Tagebücher und Briefe deutscher Geisteswissenschaftler; v. 3, Selbstzeugnisse, Erinnerungen, Tagebücher und Briefe deutscher Mathematiker, Naturwissenschaftler und Techniker. Projected for 6 v.

A listing, arranged alphabetically by author, of published autobiographies, diaries, and letters. Most entries have abbreviated citations to standard biographical sources, the keys to which appear at the end of each volume. Although the author disclaims comprehensiveness, this series should present a fairly complete enumeration of German autobiographical works from the late renaissance through the twentieth century. Z5961.G4J47

Rössler, Hellmuth. Biographisches Wörterbuch zur deutschen Geschichte. 2., völlig neubearb. und stark erw. Aufl. bearb. von Karl Bosl, Günther Franz, Hanns Hubert Hofmann. München : Francke Verlag, [1973–75]. 3 v. **AH215**

1st ed., 1952, included some 2,000 individual biographies, in all fields and from Roman times to 1933, mainly of Germans but also of some foreigners important in the history of Germany.

This is a new and enlarged edition, with numerous articles added and bibliographies updated. The work now extends to the period of publication, and about four-fifths of the material is either new or rewritten. Name index in v. 3. DD85.R572

Germany (East)

Wer war wer, DDR : Ein biographisches Lexikon / [Hrsg. von Jochen Černý ; unter Mitwirkung von Lothar Berthold ... et al.]. 2. durchgesehene Aufl. Berlin : Ch. Links, 1992. 538 p. **AH216**

Summary biographies of 1,510 figures, both living and deceased, who played a prominent part in East German history, 1949–1990. DD281.5.W47

Contemporary

Buch, Günther. Namen und Daten wichtiger Personen der DDR. 4., überarb. u. erw. Aufl. [Berlin] : Dietz, [1987]. 399 p. **AH217**

1st ed., 1973; 3rd ed., 1982.

Provides brief career outlines on prominent persons of the German Democratic Republic. Nekrolog, p. 375–99. CT1099.2.B82

Great Britain

Banks, Olive. The biographical dictionary of British feminists. N.Y. : N.Y. Univ. Pr., 1985–1990. v. 1–2. (In progress?). **AH218**

Contents: v. 1, 1800–1930; v. 2, Supplement, 1900–45.

Aims "to provide biographical sketches of those women and, occasionally, men, who contributed their time, effort and money, and sometimes their health and happiness to forwarding the progress of the women's movement."—*Introd. to v. 1*. Women whose feminist careers began after 1930 or whose main work belongs to the later generation of feminists are not included in v. 1. Vol. 2 focuses on "the years between 1920 and 1945 ... . Women whose feminist activity did not appear to begin until after 1945 have been excluded."—*Introd. to v. 2.* Principal sources of information are indicated at the end of each article. Alphabetical arrangement; each volume has an index of names (with cross-references) and a topical index.   HQ1123.B36

Barrows, Floyd D. A dictionary of obituaries of modern British radicals / Floyd D. Barrows, David B. Mock. N.Y. : Harvester Wheatsheaf, 1989. 490 p.   **AH219**

Reprints contemporary obituaries "of individuals who have sought to introduce far-reaching change to the political, social, economic, or religious institutions of Great Britain" (*Introd.*) since the 1780s. The radicals chosen are those included in *Biographical dictionary of modern British radicals* (AH221) for whom obituaries were available. Sources of obituaries include *Gentleman's magazine*, *Western mail*, the *Times*, the *New York times*, and *Spectator*. Each entry concludes with a few bibliographical citations. Not indexed.

Bellamy, Joyce M. Dictionary of labour biography / Joyce M. Bellamy, John Saville. [London] : Macmillan ; [Clifton, N.J.] : A. M. Kelley, [1972–93]. v. 1–9. (In progress).   **AH220**

An ambitious biographical dictionary which intends to include "not only the national personalities of the British labour movement but also the activists at regional and local level."—*Introd.* Indeed, "everyone who made a contribution, however modest, to any organisation or movement, provided that certain basic details of their career can be established," is to be included. The period of coverage is from 1790 to the present, but excluding living persons. It is expected that 15 to 20 volumes will be required to treat figures down to 1914. Each volume is alphabetically arranged and includes biographies without regard to date of the biographee's activity. A consolidated index appears in each successive volume; a system of cross-references is also provided, referring to both earlier and later volumes. Vol. 6 includes a list of additions and corrections for v. 1–5.   HD8393.A1B44

Biographical dictionary of modern British radicals / ed. by Joseph O. Baylen and Norbert J. Gossman. [Hassocks, Sussex] : Harvester Pr. ; [Atlantic Highlands, N.J.] : Humanities Pr., [1979]–83. 3 v.   **AH221**

Contents: v. 1, 1770–1830; v. 2, 1830–70; v. 3, 1870–1914.

"For the purpose of this biographical dictionary, the term 'Radical' has been interpreted to include those persons whose programmes and work involved something more than a moderate adjustment of policy or minor change in the operation of political, social and economic institutions. More specifically, our primary interest is in two categories of Radicals: (1) those who hoped to change in some fundamental way the old order in which Britain was dominated by the landed aristocracy and the established Church; and (2) those who sought to alter the social and economic structure of society through positive state action, to achieve a more equitable distribution of wealth and social welfare legislation."—*Introd.*

Supplements the *Dictionary of national biography* (AH226), including many persons not found therein and correcting sketches in the *DNB* as necessary. Complements the *Dictionary of labour biography* (AH220) and provides cross-references to sketches of individuals which also appear in that work. Articles are of substantial length, are signed with the names of contributing scholars, and include bibliographic references.   IIN400.R3B56

Boase, Frederic. Modern English biography : containing many thousand concise memoirs of persons who have died since 1850, with an index of the most interesting matter. Truro : Netherton, 1892–1921. 6 v.   **AH222**

Repr. : N.Y. : Barnes & Noble, [1965].

Contents: v. 1–3, A–Z, Index; v. 4–6 (Suppl. v. 1–3), A–Z. Supplement title varies slightly.

A useful work, particularly for minor 19th-century names not included in the *Dictionary of national biography* (AH226). Good subject index, including such interesting headings as Deaths under peculiar circumstances, and Names, fancy (i.e., sobriquets), as well as the more usual categories.   CT773.B6

British and Irish biographies, 1840–1940 / David Lewis Jones, ed. Microfiche ed. Teaneck, N.J. : Chadwyck-Healey Inc., 1984–92. Pt.1–27. (In progress).   **AH223**

A reproduction on microfiche of some 272 biographical dictionaries (totalling about 1,200 volumes). The biographical works, many of them multivolume sets, annuals, etc., are reproduced in full as published and a computer-produced index of names is provided; i.e., the biographical sketches are not cumulated into a single alphabet as in the *British biographical archive* (AH224).

British biographical archive : a one-alphabet cumulation of 324 of the most important English-language biographical reference works originally published between 1601 and 1929 / managing ed., Laureen Baillie ; ed., Paul Sieveking [microform]. London ; N.Y. : K.G. Saur, c1984. 1236, 16 microfiches : negative.   **AH224**

Reproduces in one alphabetical sequence entries from some 320 biographical sources. Entries from the *Dictionary of national biography* (AH226) are cited but not reproduced.

Indexed by *British biographical index*, ed. by David Bank and Anthony Esposito (London ; N.Y. : K.G. Saur, 1990. 4 v.). Useful both as an index to the microfiche set and an independent resource. Entries provide dates, occupations, and citations to both the printed sources and the microfiche set.

Supplemented by: *British biographical archive. Series 2* [microform], managing ed., David Bank; ed., Anthony Esposito (London ; N.Y. : K.G. Saur, 1991– , 1550 microfiche, A–Hogbin. [In progress]). Drawn from 268 additional biographical dictionaries. Covers the period treated by the original set and extends coverage to 1960.

Catholic who's who. 29th ed.–35th ed. London : Burns, Oates & Washbourne, 1936–1952.   **AH225**

Published 1908–1935 as *Catholic who's who and yearbook*. Publication suspended 1943–52. Supplement to the 1941 ed. and volume for 1952 called 35th ed.   DA28.8C3C33

Dictionary of national biography / ed. by Sir Leslie Stephen and Sir Sidney Lee. London : Smith, Elder, 1908–09. 22 v.   **AH226**

Frequently reprinted, most recently 1967–68.

Contents: v. 1–21, A–Z; v. 22, 1st suppl., Additional names, 1901.

History: Founded by George Smith of the London firm of Smith, Elder and Co., and originally published by that firm as follows: Main work and 1st suppl., 63 v. 1885–1901; Index and epitome to v. 1–63. 1903. 1456 p.; Errata for v. 1–63. 1904. 299 p.; 2nd suppl., 3 v. 1912; Index and epitome to 2nd suppl., 1913. 129 p.; Reissue of 63 v. ed., on thinner paper, with the incorporation in the text of the material in the Errata volume. 22 v. 1908–1909. Presented, 1917, by the heirs of George Smith, to the Oxford University Press, to be continued by that institution. In 1920 the Press reissued the 2nd supplement, on thin paper, in one volume and has continued the work by publishing the 3rd–10th supplements and *The concise dictionary*. Though the original work has not been revised by the present publisher, an informal revision of many articles is to be found in the Errata notes published in the *Bulletin* of the Institute of Historical Research of London University; a cumulation of those notes for the 1923–63 period was published by G. K. Hall in 1966 (below).

Constitutes the most important reference work for English biography, containing signed articles by specialists, and excellent bibliographies; important names are treated at great length, minor names more briefly, and all are generally reliable and scholarly. Scope includes all noteworthy inhabitants of the British Isles and the Colonies, exclusive of living persons; also noteworthy Americans of the colonial period. The supplements bring the record down to 1990. Each supplement includes a cumulative index covering all entries from 1901 in one alphabetical sequence.

The main *Dictionary* includes those deceased prior to the 20th century. Supplements cover those who died within the periods indicated.

Supplementary volumes published as follows: 1st suppl., Additional names, (1901); 2nd suppl., 1901–11, ed. by Sir Sidney Lee (1912); 3rd suppl., 1912–21, ed. by H. W. C. Davis and J. R. H. Weaver (1927); 4th suppl., 1922–30, ed. by J. R. H. Weaver (1937); 5th suppl., 1931–40, ed. by L. G. Wickham Legg (1949); 6th suppl., 1941–50, ed. by L. G. Wickham Legg and E. T. Williams (1959); 7th suppl., 1951–60, ed. by E. T. Williams and Helen M. Palmer (1971); 8th suppl., 1961–70, ed. by E. T. Williams and C. S. Nicholls (1981); 9th suppl., 1971–80, ed. by Lord Blake and C. S. Nicholls (1986); 10th suppl., 1981–85, ed. by Lord Blake and C. S. Nicholls (1990).

Associated volumes include:

(1) *Index and epitome*, ed. by Sir Sidney Lee (London : Smith, Elder, 1903–13. 2 v.).

Contents: Index and epitome to main set and 1st suppl. (22 v.) 2nd ed., 1906. 1456 p.; Index … to 2nd suppl., 1913. 129 p.

(2) *The concise dictionary* (London : Oxford Univ. Pr., 1953–61. 2 v.).

A reprinting of the *Index and epitome* (above) with corrections and additions extending coverage through 1950.

Contents: pt. 1, From the beginning to 1900: being an epitome of the main work and its supplement. 1503 p. [The reprint lists, on p. 1457–1503, corrections and additions]; pt. 2, 1901–1950: being an epitome of the 20th century *DNB* down to the end of 1950. 528 p. [Includes a "Select subject index," p. 485–528.].

The concise dictionary serves a double purpose, i.e., it is both an index and also an independent biographical dictionary (since it gives abstracts, each about one-fourteenth of the length of the original article).

Vol. 2 is superseded by:

(3) *The concise dictionary. Part II, 1901–1970* (Oxford : Oxford Univ. Pr., 1982. 747 p.).

Supersedes the "Part II, 1901–1950" volume published 1961. Adds epitomes through 1970, but omits the Select subject index found in the earlier volumes.

(4) *Corrections and additions to the Dictionary of national biography : cumulated from the Bulletin of the Institute of Historical Research, University of London, covering the years 1923–1963* (Boston : G.K. Hall, 1966. 212 p.).

At head of title: Institute of Historical Research, London.

Assembles the "Corrections and additions" from the *Bulletin* in alphabetical sequence, providing a convenient and essential supplement to the *DNB*.

(5) *Missing persons*, ed. by C. S. Nicholls (Oxford : Oxford Univ. Pr., 1993. 768 p.).

Biographies of 1,086 persons whom the editors believe were overlooked by the original *DNB* and its supplements through 1985, selected from over 100,000 suggested candidates. The criterion for inclusion remains that enunciated in the preface to the 1st supplement: "the probability that his [or her] career would be the subject of intelligent enquiry on the part of an appreciable number of persons a generation or more hence." Includes an occupational index, and bibliographical references.

(6) Gillian Fenwick, *The contributors' index to the Dictionary of national biography, 1885–1901* (Winchester : St. Paul's Bibliographies ; Detroit : Omnigraphics, 1989. 413 p.).

An alphabetical roster of contributors to the *Dictionary of national biography*, excluding the supplements, with a list of their subjects.

The Europa biographical dictionary of British women : over 1000 notable women from Britain's past / ed. by Anne Crawford … [et al.]. Detroit : Gale, c1983. 436 p.   **AH227**

Also publ. London : Europa, 1983.

Short biographies with limited bibliographical references on women from the earliest historical periods through those recently deceased, ranging from feminists to women whose notability rests on that of their husbands, with every variety of celebrity in between.

CT3320.E94

Gillow, Joseph. A literary and biographical history : or, Bibliographical dictionary of the English Catholics from the breach with Rome, in 1534, to the present time. London : Burns ; N.Y. : Catholic Publication Society, [1885–1902]. 5 v.

AH228

Repr. : N.Y. : Burt Franklin, 1961.

Gives some 2,000 biographies. Useful for names not included in the *Dictionary of national biography* (AH226) and for more information about some names which are there. Especially useful for the bibliographies which are very full.

Indexed by: *Index and finding list to Joseph Gillow's Bibliographical dictionary of the English Catholics*, comp. by John Bevan (Ross-on-Wye : J. Bevan, 1985. 275 p.). Provides index for names (excluding main entries) and works mentioned in the above.

Z2010.G483

Valentine, Alan Chester. The British establishment, 1760–1784 : an eighteenth-century biographical dictionary. Norman : Univ. of Oklahoma Pr., [1970]. 2 v.   **AH229**

About 3,000 entries, nearly half of which do not appear in *Dictionary of national biography* (AH226). "Though these skeleton biographies profess a reasonably thorough coverage only of the period from 1760 to 1784, their usefulness extends beyond that period. The biographical data about many of the individuals go back to 1700 or forward into the 19th century."—*Foreword.*   CT781.V3

Ward, Thomas Humphry. Men of the reign : a biographical dictionary of eminent persons of British and colonial birth who have died during the reign of Queen Victoria. London : Routledge, 1885. 1020 p.   **AH230**

Repr. : Graz : Akad. Druck– u. Verlagsanstalt, 1968.

A concise biographical dictionary of 19th-century personalities, containing some names included in neither the *Dictionary of national biography* (AH226) nor Frederic Boase, *Modern English biography* (AH222).   DA581.1.W2

Wedgwood, Josiah Clement. History of Parliament, 1439–1509 / by Colonel the Right Honourable Josiah C. Wedgwood in collaboration with Anne D. Holt. London : H. M. S. O., 1936–38. 2 v. : coats of arms, facsim.   **AH231**

Vol. 1 contains biographical materials; for complete information, *see* CJ355.   JN505.W4

Who was who : a companion to Who's who; containing biographies of those who died during the period. London : A. & C. Black, 1920–1991. 8 v.   **AH232**

Also published in a New York edition by St. Martin's.

Dates for each volume appear in the title.

Contents: v. 1, 1897–1915 (6th ed., 1988); v. 2, 1916–28 (5th ed., 1992); v. 3, 1929–40 (2nd ed., 1967); v. 4, 1941–50 (5th ed., 1980); v. 5, 1951–60 (4th ed., 1984); v. 6, 1961–70 (2nd ed., 1979); v. 7, 1971–80 (1981); v. 8, 1981–90 (1991).

For the most part the original sketches as they last appeared in *Who's who* (AH233) are reprinted with the date of death added, but in a few instances additional information has been incorporated. Entries for those whose death came to the editors' attention after previous editions of a volume were published are found in an addemdum preceding the main alphabet.

Indexed by: *Who was who : a cumulated index, 1897–1990* (London : Black ; N.Y. : St. Martin's Pr., 1991. 801 p.). Provides an index to v. 1–8 of the series. Death dates which did not appear in *Who was who* have been added in the index when available.   DA28.W65

Contemporary

Who's who. N.Y. : St. Martin's Press. Annual.   **AH233**

American ed. of work published in London since 1849.

The pioneer work of the who's who type and still one of the most important. Until 1897, it was a handbook of titled and official classes and included lists of names rather than biographical sketches. With 1897, called "First year of new issue," it changed its character and became a biographical dictionary of prominent persons in many fields. It has been developed and enlarged along these lines ever since. It is principally British, but a few prominent names of other nationalities are included. Biographies are reliable and fairly detailed; they give main facts, addresses, often telephone numbers and, in case of authors, lists of works.

For a compilation of biographies of deceased persons selected from the volumes 1897–1990, see *Who was who* (AH232).

DA28.W6

Bibliography

Hart, Hester E. R. Bibliography of the registers (printed) of the universities, inns of court, colleges and schools of Great Britain and Ireland / Hester E. R. Hart, Marjorie Johnston. (*In* University of London. Institute of Historical Research. *Bulletin*, 9 [June, Nov. 1931; Feb. 1932] 19–30, 65–83, 154–70; 10 [Nov. 1932] 109–13).   **AH234**
A bibliography of registers, most of which include some biographical material. Pt.1, Universities, inns of court, colleges, and other similar institutions; pt.2, Schools; Addenda and corrigenda.

Hepworth, Philip. Select biographical sources : the Library Association manuscripts survey. London : Library Association, 1971. 154 p. (Library Association Research Publication, 5).   **AH235**
A preliminary effort to indicate location of manuscripts of biographical interest in British repositories. Similar to *American literary manuscripts* (BE430), but not limited by nationality (e.g., some Americans are included).   Z6616.A2H4

Matthews, William. British autobiographies : an annotated bibliography of British autobiographies published or written before 1951. Berkeley : Univ. of California Pr., 1955. 376 p.   **AH236**
Information given includes full name of author, abbreviated title, and date of publication with brief and pithy annotations. Arranged alphabetically by author with an index under headings indicating professions and occupations, places and regions, reminiscences, wars, and general topics.   Z2027.A9M3

Musgrave, William. Obituary prior to 1800 : (as far as relates to England, Scotland, and Ireland) / comp. by Sir William Musgrave ... and entitled by him "A general nomenclator and obituary, with reference to the books where the persons are mentioned, and where some account of their character is to be found." Ed. by Sir George J. Armytage .... London : [s.n.], 1899–1901. 6 v.   **AH237**
Half title: Publication of the Harleian Society, v. 44–49.
Vol. 1 and 2, repr.: West Jordan, Utah : Stemmons Publishing, 1986.
An alphabetical index to a large number of obituaries and biographies found in some 85 works. Gives name, date of death, sometimes a characterizing word or phrase, and reference to the book or other publication where a biography or obituary notice may be found. Very useful, especially for names not included in the *Dictionary of national biography* (AH226).

Royal Commonwealth Society. Library. Biography catalogue of the Library of the Royal Commonwealth Society / by Donald H. Simpson. London : Royal Commonwealth Society, 1961. 511 p.   **AH238**
An index of biographical materials contained in the Society's library about persons in the Empire and the Commonwealth, and those in the United Kingdom and elsewhere connected with British imperial affairs. Books and periodical articles are both included. There is an extensive listing and index, by country, of works of collective biography, and an index of authors.   Z5301.R6

Stauffer, Donald Alfred. The art of biography in 18th century England : bibliographical supplement. Princeton, N.J. : Princeton Univ. Pr., 1941. 293 p.   **AH239**
A subject and author index of biographies and autobiographies written or translated in England 1700–1800, with a chronological table of the most important biographical works in England, 1700–1800.

A supplement to the author's *The art of biography in 18th century England* (Princeton, 1941). Preceded by the author's *English biography before 1700* (Cambridge : Harvard Univ. Pr., 1930), which included a bibliography of early biographies published before 1700, p. 289–372.   CT34.G7S67

Sweeney, Patricia E. Biographies of British women : an annotated bibliography. Santa Barbara, Calif. : ABC-Clio, c1993. 410 p.   **AH240**
Cites 2,014 books, published from the 17th century through 1992, on more than 700 British women. Annotations are evaluative as well as descriptive. Includes a categorical index and an author/title index.   CT3320.S85

Indexes

Farrar, Robert Henry. An index to the biographical and obituary notices in the Gentleman's magazine, 1731–1780. London : [British Record Society], [1886–91]. 677 p. (Publications of the British Record Society, Index Society, v. 15).   **AH241**
Issued in parts. Pt. 1–2 issued by the Index Society, 1886–89; pt. 3, by the British Record Society, 1891.
A brief identifying phrase usually appears with the name.
§ Continued by: Benjamin Christie Nangle, *The Gentleman's magazine biographical and obituary notices, 1781–1819 : an index* (N.Y. : Garland, 1980. 422 p. [Garland reference library of the humanities, v. 212]). As in the *Index*, an identifying word or phrase is given with most names.   AI3.I4

Scotland

Anderson, William. The Scottish nation : or, The surnames, families, literature, honours and biographical history of the people of Scotland. Edinburgh [etc.] : Fullarton, [1859]–63. 3 v. in 9 : fronts., ill., ports., coats of arms.   **AH242**
Frequently republished during the 1800s, often in three volumes.
Fairly long articles giving the histories of families and biographies of individuals, illustrated by woodcuts and steel engravings and often with facsimiles of autographs.   CT813.A6

Chambers Scottish biographical dictionary / ed., Rosemary Goring. Edinburgh ; N.Y. : Chambers, 1992. 468 p.   **AH243**
Previous ed.: *Lives of illustrious and distinguished Scotsman*, by Robert Chambers (Glascow : Blackie & Son, 1932–1935).
Biographical sketches of some 2,500 figures, both living and deceased, with an emphasis on the 20th century. A subject index precedes the biographical entries.   CT813.C42

Contemporary

Who's who in Scotland. 1st ed. (1986)– . Ayr : Carrick, 1986– .   **AH244**
About 5,000 entries, most with addresses and telephone numbers.   CT810.W56x

Wales

Y Bywgraffiadur Cymreig hyd 1940 / Paratowyd dan nawdd Anrhydeddus Gymdeithas y Cymmrodorion. [Golygyddion: Syr John Edward Lloyd, R. T. Jenkins ; cydolygydd: Syr William Llewellyn Davies]. Llundain, 1953. liv, 1110 p.   **AH245**
A biographical dictionary in Welsh planned on the lines of the *DNB* and covering CE 400–1940, but not including living persons. Articles are written by specialists; are signed; and include references to sources and, for writers, extensive bibliographies.

Largely supersedes earlier works, but, if needed, the list of abbreviations, p. xxx–lii, serves as a bibliography of these.

An English translation with additions and corrections appeared as: *Dictionary of Welsh biography down to 1940*, under the auspices of the Honourable Society of Cymmrodorion (Oxford : Blackwell, 1959. 1157 p.).

"The present English edition is not a mere translation of the Welsh volume. The intervening years have enabled the Editors to pick up the fruits of later research and to make many corrections."—*Pref.*

DA710.A1B9

Greece

Viographiko lexiko prosōpikotētōn = who's who 1979. Athena : Ekdotikos Organismos Viographiko Lexiko Prosōpikotētōn, Who's Who, 1979. 768 p. : ill.   **AH246**

About 2,500 short biographies of contemporary figures in all fields.

Hungary

Gulyás, Pál. Magyar írók : élete és munkái. Új sorozat. Budapest : Magyar Könyvtárosok és Levéltárosok Egyesülete, 1939–1944. 6 v.   **AH247**

Contents: v. 1–6, A–Dzurányi. Ceased publication.

Supplements József Szinnyei's work of the same title (AH250) for late 19th- and early 20th-century writers.

§ Constantin Wurzbach's *Biographisches Lexikon des Kaiserthums Oesterreich* (AH170) includes biographies of 3,344 Hungarians.

PH3028.G8

Jásznigi, Alexander. Das geistige Ungarn : biographisches Lexikon / hrsg. von Oskar von Krücken [pseud.] und Imre Parlagi. Wien ; Leipzig : W. Braumüller, [1918]. 2 v.   **AH248**

Includes principally writers, artists, and men in public life.

C1950.J3

Magyar életrajzi lexikon : Föszerkesztō Kenyeres Ágnes / [Szerkesztō bizottság: Bortnyik Sándor, et al.]. Budapest : Akadémiai Kiadó, 1967–81. 3 v. : ill.   **AH249**

Brief biographical sketches of Hungarians of all periods (excluding living persons). Includes some bibliographical references. Many small portraits. Vol. 3 is a supplement.   DB922.M25

Szinnyei, József. Magyar írók : élete és munkái a Magyar Tudományos Akadémia megbizásából. Budapest : Hornyánszky V., 1891–1914. 14 v.   **AH250**

Repr.: Budapest : Magyar Könyviadók e/aas Könyvterjesztók Egyesülése, 1980–81.

A biobibliographical dictionary of Hungarian literature from its beginnings through the 19th century.

Continued by: Pál Gulyás, *Magyar írók : élete és munkái. Új sorozat* (AH247).   Z2141.S9

Szy, Tibor. Hungarians in America : a biographical directory of professionals of Hungarian origin in the Americas. [2nd ed.]. N.Y. : Kossuth Foundation, [1966]. 488 p. (East European biographies and studies, v.2).   **AH251**

1st ed., 1963.   E184.H95S9

Contemporary

Fekete, Márton. Prominent Hungarians : home and abroad. 5th ed. Budapest : [s.n.], 1991. 504 p.   **AH252**

1st ed., 1966; 4th ed., 1985. Imprint varies.

About 5,000 very brief entries, often identifying only position. Many lack addresses. Text in English.   CT963.F44

Magyar ki kicsoda 1990 : több mint 6000 élő magyar személy életrajza / Biográf Szerkesztőség. [Budapest] : TEXOFT : Láng, [1990?]. 667 p.   **AH253**

Career sketches of approximately 6,000 Hungarians, living at home and abroad. Many entries include addresses and telephone numbers.   CT963.M34

Iceland

Ólason, Páll Eggert. Íslenzkar æviskrár frá landnámstímum til ársloka 1940. Reykjavík : Íslenzka Bókmenntafélags, 1948–52. 5 v.   **AH254**

A national biographical dictionary covering up to 1940. Living persons are not included. Entries are brief but include bibliography. Biographees are entered under first name according to Icelandic usage.

Continued by: *Íslenzkar æviskrár frá landnámstímum til ársloka 1965*, Jón Guðnason, tók saman; Ólafur Þ. Kristjánsson, sá um útgáfu. (Reykjavík : Birt Á Kostnaðð Hins Íslenzka Bókmenntafélags, 1976).

Also designated as v. 6 of the main work.

Includes those who died after 1940 but before 1965, as well as individuals from earlier periods who were omitted from the main work.   CT1280.O55

Ireland

See also AH223, AH234.

Boylan, Henry. A dictionary of Irish biography. 2nd ed. N.Y. : St. Martin's, 1988. 420 p.   **AH255**

1st ed., 1978.

Aims to provide the important facts for individuals born in Ireland or those born abroad who "had an Irish parent, or were of Irish descent, lived or worked in Ireland or made a considerable contribution to Irish affairs" (*Pref.*); excludes living people. Intended as a successor to John Smyth Crone's *Concise dictionary of Irish biography* (AH256), this work attempts to steer a middle course between the brevity of that work and the diffuseness of A. J. Webb's *A compendium of Irish biography* (Dublin : M.H. Gill & Son, 1878. Repr.. N.Y. : Lemma Publ. Corp., 1970) by "giving the important facts and events of the subject's career in chronological order and including, where possible, a sentence or quotation 'to give the flavour of the man'"—*Introd., 1st ed.*   CT862.B69

Crone, John Smyth. A concise dictionary of Irish biography. Rev. and enl. ed. Dublin : Talbot Pr. ; N.Y. : Longmans, 1937. 290 p.   **AH256**

Repr.: Nendeln : Kraus, 1970.

1st ed., 1928.

Brief biographical sketches of "notable Irish men and women in every sphere of activity," from the early days to the 20th century. Does not include living persons. Appendix, p. 271–90.   DA916.C7

Contemporary

Cairnduff, Maureen. Who's who in Ireland : the influential 1,000. Updated 2nd ed. Dun Laoghaire, Co. Dublin : Hibernian Publ. Co., c1991. 249 p. : ill.   **AH257**

1st ed., 1984.

Career outlines of people prominent in a broad array of activities in the Republic of Ireland. An appendix lists about 300 individuals under age 30, giving only their occupations.   CT862.C35

Italy

Archivio biografico italiano / a cura di Tommaso Nappo ; curatore consigliere Silvio Furlani [microform]. [München ; N.Y.] : Saur, c1987–[1990]. 1024 microfiches : ill., negative.
AH258
Reproduces in one alphabetical sequence more than 200,000 articles from 321 Italian language biographical dictionaries publ. 1646–1931.
Indexed by: *Indice biografico italiano = Italian biographical index*, comp. by Tommaso Nappo, Paolo Noto. (München ; N.Y. :K.G. Saur, 1993. 4 v.).
The *Archivio* is continued by: *Archivio biografico italiano II = Italian biographical archive II* [microfiche] (München : K.G. Saur, 1992– . In progress.).
Contents: Microfiche 1–260. A–Galeffi.
Drawn largely from 20th-century publications and covering from earliest history up to the late 1950s. When complete will include more than 180,000 people from approximately 110 sources.

Chi à? 1. ed.–7. ed. Roma : A. F. Formíggini Editore, 1928–1961. Irregular.
AH259
Subtitle: Dizionario degli Italiani d'oggi.
Ed. 1–4 ed. by A. F. Formíggini; ed. 5–7 ed. by Filippo Scarano.
Another work with the same title was issued in 1908 by Guido Biagi.
A who's who of Italian personalities.
DG463.C53

Dizionario biografico degli Italiani / [direttore, Alberto M. Ghisalberti]. Roma : Istituto della Enciclopedia Italiana, 1960–91. v. 1–39. (In progress).
AH260
Contents: v. 1–39, Aaron–Di Falco.
A scholarly dictionary of national biography with signed biographies of Italians from the 5th century to the present, exclusive of living persons. A bibliography of source material is included for each sketch.
CT1123.D5

Enciclopedia biografica e bibliografica "Italiana" / Direttore generale : Almerico Ribera …. Milano : E. B. B. I., Istituto editoriale italiano B. C. Tosi, s. a., [1936–44]. ser. 4–50. : ill.
AH261
Announced for publication in 48 series, each devoted to a special class, e.g., writers, soldiers, scientists, actors, etc. Includes biographies of short to medium length, unsigned, but supplied with bibliographies and with illustrations taken from contemporary sources. Planned on a large scale but never carried to completion. Series were published in irregular order, and many were never issued.
CT1123.E6

Il movimento operaio italiano : dizionario biografico, 1853–1943 / [a cura di] Franco Andreucci, Tommaso Detti. [Roma] : Editori Riuniti, [1975–79]. 6 v. : ill.
AH262
Offers signed articles of substantial length, with bibliographies, on persons active in the Italian workers' movement.
Vol. 6 is an index and includes a general bibliography, p. 159–308.
HD8483.A1M68

Savino, Edoardo. La nazione operante : albo d'oro del fascismo profili et figure, 3000 illustrazioni. 3. ed. riveduta e ampliata. Novara : Istituto geografico De Agostini, 1937. 784 p. : ill.
AH263
Contains some 2,150 biographies of prominent Fascists in all fields.
DG574.S3

Contemporary

Le donne italiane : il chi e del '900 / a cura di Miriam Mafai ; con interventi di Natalia Aspesi … [et al.]. Milano : Rizzoli, 1993. 403 p.
AH264

The first portion of the book contains a series of general essays on the participation of Italian women in sports, politics, the arts, etc. Beginning on p. 127 are 900 short biographies of prominent 20th century Italian women, a high percentage of whom are living. No addresses.
CT3540.D66

Who's who in Italy. [Ed. 1] (1957/1958)– . Milano : Intercontinental Book and Publ., 1958– . Irregular.
AH265
Publisher varies.
The biographical section includes more than 9,000 entries (1986 ed.), followed by more than 400 pages of directory information on political, commercial, and cultural institutions.
DG578.W5

Bibliography

Manzoni, Cesare. Biografia italica : saggio bibliografico di opere italiane a stampa per servire alla biografia italiani. Osnabrück : Biblio Verlag, 1981. 592 p.
AH266
Introductory matter in Italian, English and German.
Includes general biographical dictionaries and works of collective biography, volumes of local and regional biography, etc. Works are grouped by type, subdivided geographically as appropriate. Index of authors, editors, and anonymous titles.

Lithuania

Biržiška, Vaclovas. Aleksandrynas : biographies, bibliographies, and bio-bibliographies of old Lithuanian authors to 1865. Chicago : Lithuanian-American Cultural Fund, 1960–65. 3 v.
AH267
Added title page and text in Lithuanian.
Contents: v. 1, 16th–17th centuries, with a preface in English; v. 2, 18th–19th centuries; v. 3, 19th century.
PG8703.B53

Luxembourg

Biographie nationale du pays de Luxembourg depuis ses origines jusqu'à nos jours / collection présentée par Jules Mersch. Luxembourg : Impr. de la Cour Victor Buck, 1947–75. 11 v. : ill.
AH268
Fasc. 1 was published in a revised and corrected edition, 1957.
Nonalphabetical. Each fascicule includes some six to nine long articles on persons or families of various periods in the history of Luxembourg, often with bibliographies and many illustrations. Two fascicules form a volume, continuously paged and including an index to the names appearing in the articles in each volume. The final fascicule, a personal name index, indicates birth and death dates and an identifying note as well as giving reference to volume and page for the biographical sketch.
DH904.B5

Netherlands

Aa, Abraham Jacobus van der. Biographisch woordenboek der Nederlanden : bevattende levensbeschrijvingen van zoodanige personen, die zich op ennigerlei wijze in ons vaderland hebben vermaard gemaakt. Haarlem : Brederode, 1852–78. 21 v. in 17 : ill.
AH269
Repr. : Amsterdam : B. M. Israël, 1969–70, in seven volumes.
Vol. 7–8, 10–21, voortgezet door K. J. R. van harderwijk en Dr. G. D. J. Schotel.
An earlier ed., publ. 1839–51, was in 13 volumes.
Vol. 2 in in four parts; vol. 8, 12, and 17 in two parts each, with continuous paging.

A valuable work including sketches on persons from medieval times to mid-19th century. The length of articles varies from a few lines to two or three columns. Includes considerable bibliography both by and about the biographees.

Biografisch archief van de Benelux = Archives biographiques des pays du Benelux = Biographical archive of the Benelux countries = Biographisches Archiv der Benelux-Länder (BAB) / bearb. von Willi Gorzny und Willemina van der Meer. Microfiche-Ed. München : Saur, [1992?]–[1994]. 593 microfiches : negative, ill. (In progress). **AH270**
In Dutch, French, and German.
Reproduces in a single alphabet biographical entries on citizens of Belgium, the Netherlands, and Luxembourg from 122 sources, covering the period from the late 16th through the early 20th centuries.
CT1163

Biografisch woordenboek van Nederland / onder eindredactie van J. Charité ; redactiecommissie I. Schöffer ... [et al.]. 's-Gravenhage : Nijhoff, 1979–89. v. 1–3. (In progress). **AH271**
Publ. under the auspices of the Bureau der Rijkscommissie voor Vaderlandse Geschiedenis, 'sGravenhage.
A chronological successor to the *Nieuw Nederlandsch biografisch woordenboek* (AH272), providing biographical sketches of persons deceased since 1910. Signed articles; bibliographies of writings by and about the biographee, and indication of collections of papers and archival materials. Each volume is arranged alphabetically with a cumulative index to all preceeding volumes. Additional volumes are planned every four years. CT1143.B56

Molhuysen, Philip Christiaan. Nieuw Nederlandsch biografisch woordenboek / Philip Christiaan Molhuysen, P. J. Blok, F. K. H. Kossman. Leiden : Sijthoff, 1911–37. 10 v. **AH272**
Repr.: Amsterdam : B. M. Israel, 1974. 11 v.
Each volume is arranged alphabetically and has a cumulated index to all previous volumes. Vol. 10 has an index to the set. Articles vary from several lines to more than a page; frequent bibliographic references. CT1143.M7

Wie is dat? 1. utg. (Sep. 1931)– . 's-Gravenhage : Nijhoff. Irregular. **AH273**
Subtitle (varies): Biografische gegevens van Nederlanders die een vooraanstaande plaats in het maatschappelijk leven innemen met vermelding van adressen.
6th ed., 1956. No more published?
An earlier vol. with different subtitle appeared in 1902.
The Netherlands who's who. DJ103.W62

Norway

Deichmanske Bibliotek, Oslo. Register til en del norske tidsskrifter. Kristiania : Arnesens Bog & Accidenstrykkeri, 1908–11. 2 v. **AH274**
Vol. 2, Norsk biografi. For complete annotation, *see* AD321. Continued informally in *Norsk tidsskriftindex*, 1921–30 (AD322), under the heading Personalhistorie. Also continued by: *Biografiske artikler i norske tidsskrifter*, 1931–1935, 1936–1940 (Oslo : Fabritius, 1936–47. 2 v. [Norsk bibliografisk bibliotek, bd. 2, hft. 3; bd. 7]). Editors: 1931/35, W. P. Sommerfeldt; 1936/40, Vilhelm Haffner. Z2595.D32

Norsk biografisk leksikon. Oslo : H. Aschehoug, 1923–83. 19 v. **AH275**
Imprint and editors vary; early volumes ed. by Edvard Bull [et al.].

Signed articles, typically several pages in length and containing substantial bibliographies, on approximately 5,000 Norwegians from the earliest times to the present, including some living at the time of publication. Cumulative index in v. 19. CT1293.N6

Contemporary

Hvem er hvem? v. 1 (1912)– . Oslo : H. Aschehoug, 1912– . Irregular. **AH276**
The Norwegian who's who. The 13th ed. (1984) includes 4,300 biographical sketches. DL444.H8

Bibliography

Andresen, Harald. Norsk biografisk oppslagsliteratur : katalog utarbeidet for Norsk slektshistorisk forening. [Oslo] : Cammermeyer, [1945]. 218 p. **AH277**
A bibliography of Norwegian sources for biographical materials, arranged by occupation.

Poland

Biogramy uczonych polskich : materiały o życiu i działalności członków AU w Krakowie, TNW, PAU, PAN / opracowali Andrzej Śródka, Paweł Szczawiński. Wrocław : Zakład Narodowy im. Ossolińskich, 1983–90. v. 1–6, pt. 1 : ill. (In progress). **AH278**
At head of title: Polska Akademia Nauk. Ośrodek Informacji Naukowej.
Contents: cz. 1, Nauki społeczne; cz. 2, Nauki biologiczne; cz. 3, Nauki ścisłe; cz. 4, Nauki techniczne; cz. 5, Nauki rolnicze i leśne; cz. 6, v. 1, Nauki medyczne, A–L.
Offers biographical information for members of four 19th- and 20th century scholarly societies (the Polska Akademia Umiejętności w Krakowie, the Towarzystwo Naukowe Warszawskie, the Polska Akademia Umiejętności, and the Polska Akademia Nauk); no living members are included. Information provided includes mentors, most important publications, and important students, as well as standard biographical information. Each part is arranged alphabetically; each volume (including those with partial alphabetical sequences) has its own name and discipline index. To be complete in 7 volumes. CT1230.B56

Polski słownik biograficzny / komitet redakcyjny: Władysław Konopczyński [et al.]. Kraków : Skład głowny w ksieg, Gebethnera i Wolffa, 1935–93. v. 1–34³. (In progress). **AH279**
Publisher varies.
Contents: v. 1–34³, A–Sanguszko, Dymitr.
A scholarly dictionary with signed articles and full bibliographies; only deceased persons are included. CT1230.P65

Contemporary

Krzyzanowska, Jadwiga. Członkowie Polskiej Akademii Nauk : informator. Wyd. 5, uaktualnione. Wrocław : Zakład Narodowy im. Ossolińskich, 1990. 194 p. : ports. **AH280**
1st ed., 1979; 4th ed., 1987.
A directory of current Polish members of the Polish Academy of Sciences, arranged by division (social sciences, biological sciences, etc.). Entries include a photograph, birth date, position, degrees, awards, and current addresses. Foreign and deceased members are listed separately with brief entries. Name index. AS248.W37K79

Kto jest kim w Polsce : informator biografiszny / [redaguje zespół Lidia Becela … et al.]. Edycja 2. Warszawa : Wydawn. Interpress, 1989. 1584 p.   **AH281**
1st ed., 1984.
Provides brief biographical information and current addresses for some 4,500 contemporary individuals in the fields of government, science, and the arts.

Who's who in Poland / ed. by Interpress Publishers, Warsaw. 1st ed. (1982)– . Zurich : Who's Who the International Red Series Verlag, 1982– . Biennial.   **AH282**
Subtitle: A biographical directory comprising about 4,000 entries on leading personalities in Poland and information on major state, political, diplomatic, scientific and artistic institutions, and organizations.
Following the section of biographical sketches is an index which gives directory information on some 800 institutions, organizations, associations, foreign embassies, etc.   CT1230.W46

Portugal

As there is no national biographical dictionary for Portugal, Portuguese encyclopedias should be consulted for biographical articles. *See* AA777 for the biographical notes given for authors, and AH287 for collective works.

Russia

Deĭateli revolĭutsionnogo dvizheniĭa v Rossii : bio-bibliograficheskii slovar' : ot predshestvennikov dekabristov do padeniĭa tsarizma. Moskva : [s.n.], 1927–34. v. 1–2, 3^{1–2}, 5^{1–2} : ill.   **AH283**
Repr. : Leipzig : Zentralantiquariat der Deutschen Demokratischen Republik, 1974.
Various editors.
At head of title: Vsesoĭuznoe obshchestvo politicheskikh katorzhan i ssyl'no-poselentsev.
Vol. 4 not published; v. 3 and v. 5 incomplete.
A biographical dictionary of the Revolutionary movement, 1825–1917.   DK188.3.D45

Russkiĭ biograficheskiĭ slovar' …. S.-Peterburg' [etc.] : Izdanie Imperatorskago Russkago istoricheskago obshchestva, 1896–1918. 25 v.   **AH284**
Editors: A. A. Polovtsova … [et al.].
Publisher varies.
Arranged alphabetically but not published in that order, some volumes in the last of the alphabet appearing before earlier letters; parts of the alphabet not yet covered when work was discontinued are the letters V, Gog–Gia, E, M, Nik–Nia, Tk–Tia, U; volumes after v. 2 are not numbered.
Contains signed articles of some length, with bibliographies. Especially strong for material about the upper and ecclesiastical classes of pre-Revolutionary Russia.
A preliminary list with additional names and brief identification appeared in *Sbornik* (St. Petersburg : Russkoe istoricheskoe obshchestvo), v. 60–62.   CT1203.R7

Slovakia

Slovenský biografický slovník : od roku 833 do roku 1990 / [hlavná redakcia Vladimír Mináč, hlavný redaktor … et al.]. Martin : Matica slovenská, 1986–1992. v. 1–5. (In progress).   **AH285**
Contents: v. 1–5, A–Š.

Introductory material in Slovak, Russian, English, and German.
Gives articles typically running to several paragraphs on figures who played a part in Slovak history and Slovakians abroad from the early middle ages up to the present time. Includes citations to published and archival sources.   CT945.S56S55

Contemporary

Kto je kto na Slovensku 1991? / zostavili Vladimír Adamec … [et al.]. Bratislava : Konzorcium Encyklopédia, 1991. 236 p.   **AH286**
Short career outlines for approximately 1,400 citizens of the area that has now become Slovakia. Includes a government, business, and cultural directory that focuses exclusively on the Slovak element of what was the Czech and Slovak Federal Republic, except when forced to acknowledge the reality of the then central government.

     CT945.S56K79

Spain

No general modern dictionary of national biography is available for Spain. The large Spanish encyclopedias, especially *Espasa* (AB94), include many biographies of Spaniards and Spanish-Americans. For names and information not found there, works of collective biography and the numerous regional and special biographical dictionaries should be consulted. A useful bibliography of older regional and special works is given in Raymond Delbosc-Foulché and Louis Barrau-Dihigo, *Manuel de l'hispanisant* (AA801).

Archivo biográfico de España, Portugal e Iberoamérica = Arquivo biográfico de Espanha, Portugal e Ibero-América / direccíon y redaccíon Victor Herrero Mediavilla, L. Rosa Aguayo Nayle [microform]. [München ; N.Y. : K.G. Saur, 1990?]. 1,144 microfiches : negative.   **AH287**
Text of microfiche in Spanish or Portuguese; text of manual in Spanish, Portuguese, English, and German.
Reproduces in one alphabetical sequence entries from 300 works of collective biography published from the 17th to the early 20th century. Includes more than 300,000 individuals. Extends to other countries colonized by Iberians, such as the Phillippines and Macao.
Indexed by: *Indice biográfico de España, Portugal y Iberoamérica* (München ; N.Y. : K.G. Saur, 1990. 4 v. [1429 p.]).
Useful both as an index to the microfiche set and as an independent resource. Entries provide dates, occupations and references to printed sources.
Supplemented by: *Archivo biográfico de España, Portugal e Iberoamérica. Nuevo serie* (München ; N.Y. : K.G. Saur, [1990]–), which includes biographies of 180,000 individuals drawn from 250 sources for the 19th–20th centuries.

Diccionari biogràfic. Barcelona : Alberti, 1966–70. 4 v. : coats of arms, facsims., geneal. tables, maps.   **AH288**
A biographical dictionary for Catalonia. Mainly brief sketches of figures from all periods, including some living persons. No principal editor or editorial board is indicated; articles are unsigned and without bibliographies.   DP302.C58D5

Esperabé Arteaga, Enrique. Diccionario enciclopédico ilustrado y crítico de los hombres de España. [Nueva ed., reformada, ampliada y completada]. Madrid : Gráficas Ibarra, [1957?]. 530 p. : ports.   **AH289**
1st ed. covers 1946–47.
Brief biographical sketches of Spaniards of various periods including living persons. Illustrations are poor; no bibliographies.

     DP58.E82

Foulché-Delbosc, Raymond. Manuel de l'hispanisant / Raymond Foulché-Delbosc, Louis Barrau-Dihigo. N.Y. : Putnam, 1920–25. 2 v. **AH290**

Vol. 1 includes a list of general biographies; regional biographies, arranged by place; and a list of biographical works on special classes (e.g., artists). For full annotation, *see* AA801. Z2681.A1F7

Contemporary

Who's who in Spain. 1987– . Milano : Who's Who in Italy S.r.l., c1987– . Biennial. **AH291**

The 1992 ed. provides entries on some 7,500 individuals, giving addresses and, in many cases, telephone numbers. A directory of business, government, and other Spanish institutions is appended, followed by its own index. Entries are in English.

Sweden

See also AH164.

Svenska män och kvinnor : biografisk uppslagsbok. Stockholm : Bonnier, [1942–55]. 8 v. : ports. (part col.). **AH292**

Vols. 1–2 ed. by Nils Bohman; v. 3–8, Oscar Wieselgren, Bengt Hildebrand, Torsten Dahl.

Covers from the earliest times to the present and includes living persons. Articles are brief but are signed. Almost no bibliography except for the titles of books written by persons included. Differs from the *Svenskt biografiskt lexikon* (AH293) in the brevity of its sketches and its lack of bibliography. Should be useful in libraries which do not need the extensive information given in the larger work, and in all libraries until that set is completed. CT1313.S58

Svenskt biografiskt lexikon. Stockholm : A. Bonnier, 1917–92. v. 1–28[1] : ill. (In progress). **AH293**

Ed. by Bertil Boëthius and others.

Contents: v. 1–28[1], A–Olavus Petri.

An excellent work with long, signed articles, bibliographies, and many portraits. Includes persons of all periods but no longer covers living persons, although these were considered in v. 1–10. Chronological index to v. 1–10 is included in v. 10, p. 769–94. CT1313.S8

Vem är det? : Svensk biografisk handbok. 1912– . Stockholm : Norstedt, [1912]– . Biennial. **AH294**

Subtitle varies.

The standard Swedish who's who. About 10,000 sketches in v. 41, 1993, which includes a necrology for 1982–92. DL644.V4

Bibliography

Ågren, Sven. Svensk biografisk uppslagslitteratur : biografisk förteckning. Uppsala : Almqvist & Wiksell, 1929. 423 p. **AH295**

Added t.p.: Svenska bibliotekariesamfundets skriftserie. I.

Classified, with author and subject index. Includes material dealing with Swedish Finland (to 1809) and other Swedish possessions, as well as with Swedes in foreign countries. Lists more than 2,000 biographical dictionaries, registers, collective biographies, etc., which include Swedish biography. Z5305.S9A2

Switzerland

Dictionnaire historique et biographique de la Suisse. Neuchâtel : Admin. du Dictionnaire, 1921–34. 9 v. : ill., maps. **AH296**

Contains a large amount of genealogy and biography, including information on persons still living at the time of compilation. For full description, *see* DC529. DQ51.D5

Who's who in Switzerland, including the Principality of Liechtenstein. 1950/51– . Zurich : Central European Times Publ., 1952– . Biennial. **AH297**

Imprint varies: publ. later in Geneva, Switzerland, by Nagel Publishers, Inc.

In English. The 1992/93 ed. contains 3,030 biographies. Includes a "who's who" section. DQ52.W5

Bibliography

Barth, Hans. Bibliographie der schweizer Geschichte enthaltend die selbständig erschienenen Druckwerke zur Geschichte der Schweiz bis Ende 1912. Basel : Basler Buch– und Antiquariatshandlung, 1914–15. 3 v. (Quellen zur schweizer Geschichte hrsg. von der Allgemeinen Geschichtforschenden Gesellschaft der Schweiz. n. F., 4. Abt. Handbücher). **AH298**

A very full bibliography of separately published biographies is given in vol. 2, p. 116–404. For full description, *see* DC522. Z2786.B28

Bibliographie der Schweizergeschichte = Bibliographie de l'histoire suisse. Jahrg. 1913– . [Bern : Eidegenössische Drucksachen- und Materialzentrale], 1914– . Annual (some years combined). **AH299**

This current bibliography has a section entitled Personengeschichte which, particularly in its earlier volumes, provides a very complete index of biographical and obituary articles on natives and residents of Switzerland. For full description, *see* DC528. Z2786.B38

Brandstetter, Josef Leopold. Repertorium über die in Zeit- und Sammelschriften der Jahre 1812–1890 enthaltenen Aufsätze und Mitteilungen schweizergeschichtlichen Inhaltes / hrsg. von der Allgemeinen Geschichtforschenden Gesellschaft der Schweiz von Josef Leopold Brandstetter .... Basel : A. Geering, 1892. 467 p. **AH300**

Contains a list of biographical articles and obituaries in more than 300 periodicals and other collective works, which—because the entry gives dates of birth and death and, in many cases, a brief characterizing phrase—furnishes some direct information as well as the references to the articles indexed. For full description, *see* DC523. Z2786.B81

Schweizerische Landesbibliothek. Katalog der Schweizerische Landesbibliothek Bern : systematisches Verzeichnis der schweizerischen oder die Schweiz betreffenden Veröffentlichungen. Bern : Huber, [1927]–54. 4 v. **AH301**

Lists of biographical works published in Switzerland during the period are arranged alphabetically by the name of the biographee. For complete description, *see* AA838. Z949.B552

Turkey

Günümüz Türkiyesinde kim kimdir = Who's who in Turkey. 1985/86– . İstanbul : Profesyonel, c1986– . **AH302**

Includes Turks living in the U.S. and Cyprus. CT1906.G86

Union of Soviet Socialist Republics

See also AH47.

Biographical dictionary of dissidents in the Soviet Union, 1956–1975 / comp. and ed. by S. P. de Boer, E. J. Driessen and H. L. Verhaar. The Hague ; Boston : Nijhoff ; Hingham, Mass. : Kluwer Boston, 1982. 679 p.   **AH303**
Outgrowth of a project initiated at the Institute of Eastern European Studies, Univ. of Amsterdam.
Provides biographical sketches of dissidents active during the period of coverage. Criteria for inclusion and method of presenting the biographical data are carefully spelled out in the introduction. Glossary; select bibliography.   DK275.A1B56

Institut zur Erforschung der UdSSR. Who was who in the USSR : a biographic directory containing 5,015 biographies of prominent Soviet historical personalities. Metuchen, N.J. : Scarecrow, 1972. 677 p.   **AH304**
Comp. by the Institute for the Study of the USSR, Munich, Germany. Ed. by Heinrich E. Schulz, Paul K. Urban, Andrew I. Lebed.
Concerned with deceased persons active in the period 1917–67 and including "a certain number of biographies of people who actively campaigned against the Soviet regime or were later exiled or put to death by the Soviet authorities."—*Pref.*
§ Complemented by: *Prominent personalities in the USSR : a biographic directory containing 6,013 biographies of prominent personalities in the Soviet Union* / comp. by the Institute for the Study of the USSR, Munich, Germany (ed. by Edward L. Crowley, [et al.]. Metuchen, N.J. : Scarecrow, 1968. 792 p.).   CT1212.I57

Kaufman, Isaak Mikhailovich. Russkie biograficheskie i biobibliograficheskie slovari. Moskva : Gos. izd-vo kul'turno-prosvetitel'noi lit-ry, 1955. 751 p.   **AH305**
1st ed., 1950.
A valuable guide to Russian biography and biobibliography from the 18th century through 1954.   Z5305.R9K32

Who's who in the Soviet Union : a biographical encyclopedia of 5,000 leading personalities in the Soviet Union / ed. by Borys Lewytzkyj. München : Saur, 1984. 428 p.   **AH306**
Updates the information about Soviet figures found in the same editor's *Who's who in the socialist countries* (AH47) and, like that work, is based on information in the editor's private archives. "All changes in the biographies of Party, State, Komsomol, and Trade Union leaders and functionaries between the end of 1976 and 1982 are fully noted. Less completely noted are changes in the biographies of authors, artists, and other groups. ..."—*Foreword.* Extensive indexes list party, government, and military leaders (including officials of the individual republics), plus lists of authors, scientists, artists, etc. There are also lists of persons who died and who were relieved or dismissed since publication of the earlier volume.   DK37.W48

Yugoslavia

Hrvatski biografski leksikon / [glavni urednik Nikica Kolumbić]. Zagreb : Jugoslavenski leksikografski zavod, 1983–89. v. 1–2 : ill. (some col.). (In progress).   **AH307**
Ivo Cecić, direktor, v. 1; Vladimir Pezo, direktor, v. 2.
Contents: v. 1–2, A–C.
Covers figures from all periods, including persons living at time of compilation. Extensive bibliographies.   CT1457.C76H78

Jugoslovenski savremenici : Ko je ko u Jugoslaviji / redakcioni odbor: Milan Joksimović ... [et al.]. Beograd : "Hronometar", 1970. 1208, [66] p.   **AH308**
The Yugoslav who's who. An early work of the same title was published in 1928. The first postwar edition appeared in 1957, and a new edition by a different publisher was published 1968.
                          DR316.K63

Slovenski biografski leksikon / uredila Izidor Cankar in Franc Ksaver Lukman s sodelovanjem uredniškega odbora. Ljubljana : Založila Zadružna gospodarska banka, 1925–91.   **AH309**
Issued in fascicules. Publisher varies.
Long, signed articles on Slovenians, many with bibliographies.
§ Indexed by: *Osebno kazalo* / uredil Jože Munda s odeljovanjem uredniškega odbora (Ljubljana : Slovenska akademija znanosti in umetnosti : Znanstvenoraziskovalni center SAZU, Inštitut za slovensko literaturo in literarne vede, 1991.   DR381.S66S58

AFRICA

Lipschutz, Mark R. Dictionary of African historical biography / Mark R. Lipschutz & R. Kent Rasmussen. 2nd ed., expanded and updated. Berkeley : Univ. of California Pr., c1986. 328 p.   **AH310**
1st ed., 1978.
Provides biographical information and brief bibliographies for major figures, primarily political, from Africa south of the Sahara, including South Africa, from the earliest period. Besides updating and revising many of the entries in the 1st ed., the authors have included African leaders, 1960–80, in a supplement, p. 258–290. Includes a bibliography of secondary sources, a subject index, and a name index.
                          DT352.6.L56

Rosenthal, Eric. Southern African dictionary of national biography. London : Warne, [1966]. 430 p.   **AH311**
The work of a single compiler rather than a cooperative effort. About 2,000 brief biographical sketches of deceased persons who figure in the history of the Republic of South Africa, South West Africa, Rhodesia, Zambia, Malawi, Mozambique, Swaziland, Bechuanaland, and Basutoland. A classified list of entries by profession or occupation precedes the dictionary proper. No bibliographies.   CT1923.R6

Contemporary

Africa who's who. 1st ed. (1981)– . [London] : Publ. by Africa Journal Ltd. for Africa Books Ltd., 1981– .   **AH312**
On spine: *Know Africa.*
A companion to the same publisher's *Makers of modern Africa* (London, 1981), a retrospective collection of some 500 biographies of deceased Africans, and *Africa today* (London, 1981), a reference work dealing with 54 African countries. Offers biographical sketches on about 7,000 Africans from all nations and professions.
An earlier effort under the auspices of *Africa journal* was the *Africa yearbook and who's who* (1st ed., London : Africa Journal, 1976), which included a biographical section.

The black who's who of Southern Africa today. Ed. 1 (1979)– . Johannesburg : African Business Publ., 1979– . Irregular.   **AH313**
A general reference section (lists of government officials, etc.) and a list of universities and their staffs precede the biographical section. The 2nd ed. (1982) includes some 2,000 brief sketches of non-white residents.

Dictionary of African biography. N.Y. : Reference Publs. Inc., [1977–79]. 2 v. : ill.   **AH314**

At head of title: The encyclopaedia Africana.

Contents: v. 1, Ethiopia, Ghana; v. 2, Sierra Leone, Zaïre.

The idea for the dictionary originated with W. E. B. DuBois and has been carried forward as a cooperative effort of the African states. Articles deal with "the personalities of the past who ... influenced the history and development of their various countries."—*Introd.* Living persons are excluded. Each country section is preceded by a historical introduction. Articles are signed by the contributors (including some European and American, as well as African, scholars) and carry bibliographies. Originally projected to be in 20 volumes. No more published?
DT18.D55

Who's who of southern Africa : (incorporating South African who's who and the Central African who's who). 1907– . Johannesburg : Wootton & Gibson, 1907– . Annual.　**AH315**

Subtitle (1988–89): An illustrated biographical record of prominent personalities in the Republic of South Africa, Botswana, Mauritius, S.W.A./Namibia, Swaziland, Zimbabwe, and neighbouring countries in Southern Africa.

The 1988/89 edition generally reflects the existing apartheid of South Africa, while including more nonwhites for surrounding nations.
DT752.S5

Wiseman, John A. Political leaders in Black Africa : a biographical dictionary of the major politicians since independence. Aldershot, Hants., England ; Brookfield, Vt. : E. Elgar, c1991. 248 p.　**AH316**

For annotation, *see* CJ409.　DT352.8.W57

AFRICA (by country)

Algeria

Les élites algériennes. 1re éd. Paris : Ediafric, La Documentation africaine, 1985. 2 v. (311 p.).　**AH317**

Contents: v. 1, Les élites politiques; v. 2, Les élites économiques.

Identifies approximately 1,000 government and business figures, with brief biographical outlines for key officials. Arranged by departments or areas of activity, with a personal name index in v. 2.
JQ3221.E43

Ethiopia

The dictionary of Ethiopian biography / editors: Belaynesh Michael, S. Chojnacki, Richard Pankhurst. [Addis Ababa : Inst. of Ethiopian Studies, 1975]. v. 1. (In progress?).　**AH318**

Contents: v. 1, From early times to the end of the Zagwe dynasty c.1270 A.D.

"Because of the limited historical sources available for the early period covered [in v. 1] ... the majority of entries are devoted to kings, religious leaders, warriors and other personalities who appear on coins, inscriptions and in manuscripts."—*Pref.* Includes persons "irrespective of nationality who, for good or ill, played a significant rôle in the area." Signed articles; bibliographies.　CT2153.D53

Ghana

Ghana who's who. 1972/73– . Accra : Bartels, 1972– . Irregular.　**AH319**

Subtitle: A biographical dictionary of prominent men and women in the country, including an encyclopaedia of useful information.
DT510.6.A1G45

Kenya

Who is who in Kenya. 1982/83– . Nairobi : Africa Book Services, [1982]– . Irregular?　**AH320**

A biographical dictionary of contemporary figures arranged by occupational or professional categories. Many entries provide only an address, not a biographical sketch.

Madagascar

Hommes et destins : dictionnaire biographique d'outre-mer. Paris : Académie des sciences d'outre-mer, [1975–89]. 9 v. (Académie des sciences d'outre-mer. Publications. Travaux et mémoires, n.s., no.2, etc.).　**AH321**

For annotation, *see* AH197.　CT1014.H65

Nigeria

Orimoloye, S. A. Biographia Nigeriana : a biographical dictionary of eminent Nigerians. Boston : G.K. Hall, [1977]. 368 p.　**AH322**

An attempt to provide a who's who of contemporary Nigerians and other prominent figures living and working in Nigeria. Information was gathered from questionnaires; there is some emphasis on academic figures.　CT2526.O74

Who's who in Nigeria / ed., Nyaknno Osso. Lagos, Nigeria : Newswatch, 1990. 803 p.　**AH323**

The most substantial biographical work yet published for Nigeria, with brief career sketches of more than 2,500 Nigerians, giving addresses and telephone numbers.

§ Another important source listing nearly 1,000 professionals: *Who's who in science and technology in Nigeria*, ed. by Adetunji Akinyotu (Akure : Federal University of Technology, 1989).
CT2522.W45

Sierra Leone

See also AH312 and AH314.

Who's who in Sierra Leone. [Ed. 1]– . [Freetown : Lyns Publicity Inc., 1980?]– . Annual.　**AH324**

Mallyveen Roy Johnson, comp.

The 1981 ed. (latest published?) contains approximately 250 short entries.　CT2446.W48

South Africa

Dictionary of South African biography / ed. in chief W.J. de Kock. [Pretoria] : Nasional Boekhandel Bpk. for National Council for Social Research, Dept. of Higher Education, 1968–87. v. 1–5. (In progress).　**AH325**

Also published in Afrikaans. Publisher varies; editor varies.

A scholarly work designed to present biographies "of all those who have since the earliest European contact with the southern extremity of Africa made a contribution of importance to the course of South African history."—*Introd.* There is no overall alphabetical or chronological sequence: arrangement is alphabetical within each volume, and each volume includes whatever sketches were available at the time it was readied for press. Persons who have had a significant influence on South African affairs and events are included even though they may never have visited South Africa. Articles are signed with the initials of contributors; bibliographies are appended; and there are usually notes on iconography.

Vols. 1–4 include about 3,400 biographies and cover "all the important figures who lived before the twentieth century."—*Pref., v. 4.* Although the original plan was to include only those who died before 1950, that date was extended through 1959 for v. 2, through 1965 for v. 3, and through 1970 for v. 4. Vol. 5 includes some 1,100 biographies, the majority of which treat 20th-century individuals who died before 1983. It includes a cumulative name index to v. 1–5.

CT1924.D53

Sudan

Hill, Richard Leslie. A biographical dictionary of the Sudan. 2nd ed. [London] : Frank Cass, 1967. 409 p.   **AH326**

1st ed., 1951, had title: *A biographical dictionary of the Anglo-Egyptian Sudan.* It included short notices of some 1,900 people who died before 1948. This volume reprints the earlier edition, adding a section of notes and corrections. An asterisk added to a name in the main body of the work signals a reference to the additions and corrections section.   DT108.05.A2H5

Zimbabwe

Mitchell, Diana. Who's who, 1981–82 : nationalist leaders in Zimbabwe. Causeway, Zimbabwe : D. Mitchell, [1982]. 170 p. : ill.   **AH327**

At head of title: Makers of history.

Label on cover states: Contains updated 1982–83 supplement, 24 pages including Cabinet reshuffle and 80 new entries.

Constitutes a rev. ed. of *African nationalist leaders in Rhodesia who's who* by Robert Cary and Diana Mitchell (1977). Biographies are presented in narrative form, often in the words of the biographee.

DT962.6.M57

ASIA (by region)

Arab states

The international who's who of the Arab world. [Ed.1] (1978/79)– . London : Internat. Who's Who of the Arab World Ltd., [1978–]. Irregular.   **AH328**

3rd ed., 1987–88.

Aims to present up-to-date information on "leading personalities of the Arab World in all walks of life" (*Pref.*), including "prominent Arabs living outside their countries of birth." A directory at the end of the volume lists the biographees by country, then by occupation or field of activity.   CT1860.I57

Who's who in the Arab world. Ed.1 (1965/66)– . Beirut : Éditions Publitec, [1965–]. Irregular.   **AH329**

The 11th ed. (1993–94) includes short biographies with addresses and telephone numbers of "about 6,000 outstanding personalities and leading national figures in 19 Arab Countries"—*Contents.* Also offers succinct country surveys of the 19 nations providing political and economic summaries and directories of key institutions.   D198.3.W5

Who's who in U.A.R. and the Near East : the greatest biographical work in the Middle and Near East. Ed. 1–24. Cairo : [s.n.], [19?–59]. Annual.   **AH330**

Title varies: 19?–47, *Le mondain égyptien, The Egyptian who's who;* 1948–51, *Who's who in Egypt and the Middle East;* 1952–1957/58, *Who's who in Egypt and the Near East.* Title also in Arabic and in French: *Le mondain égyptien et du Proche-Orient.*

Includes U.A.R., Sudan, Iran, Libya, Cyprus, Lebanon, Jordan, Iraq, Saudi Arabia, India, Pakistan, Ceylon, Indonesia, Ethiopia, and Aden.

The first section is arranged by country, giving brief descriptive information with names of governmental officials, diplomatic representatives, and business firms, followed by an alphabetical listing of persons with addresses and brief biographical information.

DT44.W47

Bibliography

Auchterlonie, Paul. Arabic biographical dictionaries : a summary guide and bibliography. Durham : Middle East Libraries Committee, 1987. 60 p. (Middle East Libraries Committee research guides, 2.).   **AH331**

Offers a classified listing of "the best-known, fullest and most useful biographical dictionaries" (*p. 1*) for the classical and modern periods. Author, editor, translator, and title index.   DS39.2.A2A93

ASIA (by country)

Afghanistan

Adamec, Ludwig W. Historical and political who's who of Afghanistan. Graz : Akademische Druck– u. Verlagsanstalt, 1975. 385 p.   **AH332**

Title on spine: Who's who of Afghanistan.

Offers concise biographical information on about 1,500 persons. In four parts: Who is who, 1945–1974; Who was who, 1747–1945; Afghan government positions, 1901–1974; Genealogies of important Afghan families in 92 tables.   DS355.A3

———————   First supplement to the Who's who of Afghanistan : Democratic Republic of Afghanistan. Graz : Akademische Druck– u. Verlagsanstalt, 1979. 53p.   **AH333**

The who's who section is followed by a diplomatic list, corrections to the first edition, addenda, and a list of "Afghan government positions, 1978–1979."   DS355.A3

Bangladesh

Who's who in Bangladesh. 1982– . Dhaka, Bangladesh : Times Publications, 1982– .   **AH334**

Gives short career outlines on some 400 living Bangladeshis, arranged in chapters by category of distinction. Lacks a name index.

Who's who in Bangladesh art, culture, literature, 1901–1991 / [comp. and ed. by] Abul Fazal Shamsuzzaman. Dhaka : Tribhuj Prakashani, 1992. 303 p. : ill.   **AH335**

Short biographical sketches on 573 notables, both living and deceased. Predominantly literary figures.   NX576.8.B3W47

China

Association for Asian Studies. Ming Biographical History Project Committee. Dictionary of Ming biography, 1368–1644 / L. Carrington Goodrich, ed. N.Y. : Columbia Univ. Pr., 1976. 2 v. (1751 p.) : ill.   **AH336**

Substantial signed articles with extensive bibliographies referring to predominantly Chinese-language sources. Indexed selectively by names appearing in the biographies as well as their subjects, also by topics and titles of books.   DS753.5.A84

Bartke, Wolfgang. Chinaköpfe : Kurzbiographien der Partei- und Staatsfunktionäre der Volksrepublik China. Hannover : Verlag für Literatur und Zeitgeschehen, [1966]. 454 p. (Schriftenreihe des Forschungsinstituts der Friedrich-Ebert-Stiftung, B. Historisch-politische Schriften).   **AH337**

In addition to the biographical sketches of political personalities, there are sections on the organization of the Chinese Communist party and the government agencies of the Chinese People's Republic, together with a list of the various party and government officials as of Oct. 1966.   DS778.A1B3

Biographical dictionary of Republican China / Howard L. Boorman, ed. N.Y. : Columbia Univ. Pr., 1967–79. 5 v.   **AH338**

Intended as a supplement to the Library of Congress Orientalia Division's *Eminent Chinese of the Ch'ing period* (AH340) and concentrating on figures of the period 1911–49. Includes both living and deceased persons; about 600 biographies in the complete set. The final volume includes an extensive bibliography which lists the writings by the subject of each article in the dictionary, together with the sources (books, periodicals, manuscripts) used in preparing the article. Vol. 5 is a personal name index. A substantial and scholarly work.   DS778.A1B5

Giles, Herbert Allen. A Chinese biographical dictionary. London : Quaritch ; Shanghai : Kelly and Walsh, 1898. 1022 p.   **AH339**

A standard dictionary of figures from the earliest, and even legendary, times to the date of publication. Not completely superseded by the Library of Congress Orientalia Division's *Eminent Chinese of the Ch'ing period* (AH340). May be supplemented and corrected on certain points by the use of the following: E. von Zach, "Einige Verbesserungen zu Giles' Chinese biographical dictionary," *Asia major* 3 (1926): 545–68; Paul Pelliot, "A propos du 'Chinese biographical dictionary' de M. H. Giles," *Asia major* 4 (1927): 377–89; Paul Pelliot, "Les Yi nien lou," *T'oung pao* 25 (1927): 65–81.

§ Indexed by *Supplementary index to Giles' "Chinese biographical dictionary"*, by Irvin Van Gorder Gillis and Yü Ping-yüeh (Beijing, 1936. 88 p. Repr.: San Francisco : Chinese Materials Center, 1978.).   DS734.G46

Library of Congress. Orientalia Division. Eminent Chinese of the Ch'ing period (1644–1912) / ed. by Arthur W. Hummel. Wash. : U.S. Govt. Print. Off., 1943–44. 2 v.   **AH340**

Designed to include some 800 sketches of eminent Chinese of the last 300 years, primarily of the epoch ruled by the Ch'ing dynasty (1644–1912). A very useful reference work, with detailed, authoritative, signed articles and references to sources. "No independent sketches are included for persons who died after 1912; but it was found possible to incorporate information, sometimes in considerable detail, of many men who lived after that date, and of not a few who are still living."—*Editor's note.*   DS734.U65

Perleberg, Max. Who's who in modern China : (from the beginning of the Chinese Republic to the end of 1953). Hong Kong : Ye Olde Printerie, 1954. 428 p. : ill.   **AH341**

Subtitle continues: Over two thousand detailed biographies of the most important men who took part in the great struggle for China, including detailed histories of the political parties, government organizations, a glossary of new terms used in contemporary Chinese together with a double index in Chinese and English and two charts.

Includes persons both living and dead. Now badly out of date, but may be useful for the period covered. Entries are of the usual who's who type, with much additional information on government structure and personnel for both Nationalist and Communist China. The indexes cover only the biographical sections.   DS734.P4

Who's who in China : biographies of Chinese leaders. Shanghai : China Weekly Review, 1918–50. 6 v. : ill.   **AH342**

Publisher varies; subtitle varies.

1st ed. 1918; 2nd ed. 1920; 3rd ed. 1925; 3rd ed. Suppl. [1928?]; 4th ed. 1932; 4th ed. Suppl. 1933; 5th ed. 1936; 5th ed. Suppl. 1940; 6th ed. 1950.

The 5th ed. is the first in the series to include biographies of women.   DS734.W5

Who's who in Communist China. [Rev. ed.]. Kowloon : Union Research Institute, [1969–70]. 2 v. (897 p.).   **AH343**

1st ed., 1966.

Biographies of major personalities in contemporary political, diplomatic, military, cultural, and scientific affairs. Information was drawn from the biographical files of the Union Research Institute and from major Chinese Communist and foreign publications. Text is in English, with Chinese characters added for personal and place-names. About 1,600 biographies in the 2d ed., earlier sketches having been reviewed and updated as necessary; biographies of some recently deceased persons were retained because of continuing influence.   DS778.A1W46

Contemporary

See also AH47.

Bartke, Wolfgang. Who's who in the People's Republic of China. 3rd ed. München ; N.Y. : K.G. Saur, 1991. 2 v. : ports.   **AH344**

1st ed., 1981; 2nd ed., 1987.

Intended as a guide to the currently active leaders of China; information was drawn "primarily from the daily Chinese press...and reports from the Summary of World Broadcasts of the BBC."—*Pref.* Includes government and mass organization officials at levels specified in the standards for inclusion. Names are entered according to the pinyin system of transliteration; Chinese characters are also given. Details concerning date and place of birth, education, etc., were often not available and numerous entries consist only of positions held and a chronology of appointments and official activities. Many entries include a photograph. An extensive appendix offers background tables, lists of party, government, and mass organization officials, etc.

The 3rd ed. "contains 4,120 biographies and includes only 40% of the contents of the 2nd ed." (*Pref.*) A list of 1,340 cadres who were deceased or lost their official positions since the 2nd ed. with dates of death or "last appearance" is appended to v. 2.   DS779.28.B37

Goldfiem, Jacques de. Personnalités chinoises d'aujourdui. Paris : L'Harmattan, c1989. 377 p.   **AH345**

Apparently the only current Western-language work to include prominent Chinese in the arts, commerce, education, and dissident movements, as well as the Party élite. Also distinguished by providing fleshed-out sketches frequently running to a page or more that seek to describe the subjects and their place in the Chinese socio-political matrix, rather than simply a career outline. Approximately 300 biographies are accompanied by a complete name index, an index to fields of endeavor, and a bibliography of sources.   CT1822.G65 1989

Who's who in China. Current leaders / comp. by the Editorial Board of Who's who in China = [Chung-kuo jen ming ta tz'u tien. Hsien jen tang cheng chün ling tao jen wu chüan / "Chung-kuo jen ming ta tz'u tien" pien chi pu pien]. Beijing : Foreign Languages Pr. : China International Book Trading Corp. [distributor], c1989. 1126 p. : ill.   **AH346**

In English and Chinese.

Offers biographies and photographs of more than 2,100 "current senior officials at the central level and in the provinces, municipalities and autonomous regions."—*Publishers' note.* Each entry provides birth date, present position, and career summary; current addresses are not listed. Includes an appendix of major organizations and their leading officials, p. 1037–1078.   DS779.28.W46

Bibliography

Wu, Eugene. Leaders of twentieth-century China : an annotated bibliography of selected Chinese biographical works in the Hoover Library. Stanford, Calif. : Stanford Univ. Pr., 1956. 106 p. (Hoover Institution on War, Revolution, and Peace. Bibliographical series, 4).   **AH347**

Approximately 500 items, including collections, dictionaries, and serials, as well as individual biographies. Names are listed in Wade-Giles romanization followed by Chinese characters. A list of publishers giving full names for the abbreviations found in the bibliography and an index to biographees, authors, and book titles is included.   Z3106.W8

Hong Kong

Who's who in Hong Kong. 1984– . Hong Kong : Data Base Publ., 1984– .   **AH348**

Title varies slightly.

Publ. by South China Morning Post, 1979–84.

Based on response to questionnaires. English text; index in Chinese and English.   DS796.H753A28

India

Buckland, Charles Edward. Dictionary of Indian biography. London : Sonnenschein, 1906. 494 p.   **AH349**

Repr.: N.Y. : Greenwood, 1969.

Contains about 2,600 concise biographies of persons noteworthy in the history, service, or literature of India since 1750. Most biographees are English, but Indian and other nationalities are included.   DS434.B8

Eminent Indians who was who, 1900–1980, also annual diary of events. New Delhi : Durga Das Pvt. Ltd., 1985. 420 p. : ill.   **AH350**

Spine title: Who was who, 1900–1980.

Short biographies of Indians prominent in a broad range of activity, many of whom are not found in Siba Pada Sen's *Dictionary of national biography* (AH351).   CT1502.E54

Sen, Siba Pada. Dictionary of national biography. Calcutta : Inst. of Historical Studies, 1972–74. 4 v.   **AH351**

Approximately 1,400 signed articles, on persons, both native and foreign, who played a prominent role during 1800–1947. Includes those living at the time of publication. Entries are typically one or two pages and include bibliographies.

Supplement, ed. by N. R. Ray. (Calcutta : Institute of Historical Studies, 1986. v. 1. [In progress]).

Contents: v. 1, A–D.

Updates and expands the coverage. Four volumes, with some 1,400 entries, are planned. Athletes and figures in the performing arts, generally omitted from the main work, are to be included here.   CT1502.S46

Who's who in India, Burma and Ceylon. [Ed.1]–9. Poona : Sun Publ. House, 1911–38. Irregular.   **AH352**

Title varies: *Who's who in India.* Imprint varies.

The 9th ed. (1938) includes sections on the royal family and provincial governors, Indian princes and chiefs, and a "Who's who in Indian industries and commerce."   DS434.W43

Contemporary

India who's who. 1969– . New Delhi : INFA Publs. Annual.   **AH353**

Biographical sketches of prominent Indians are presented under professional categories. Index of biographees.   CT1506.I53

Who's who, Indian personages / [comp. and ed. by P. Chavda and H. L. Sagar]. New Delhi : Crystal Ship Pub., 1986. v. 1 : ports. (In progress).   **AH354**

Vol. 1 contains short biographies of more than 1,000 subjects in an alphabetic arrangement. Most are academics or physicians; the balance are business people. Future volumes are intended to expand coverage rather than update existing entries.   CT1502.W48

Iran

Iran who's who. 1st ed. (1972)–3rd ed. (1976). Tehran : Echo of Iran. Biennial.   **AH355**

Biographical sketches, in English, of "important Iranian personalities in political, social, administrative, cultural, scientific, art, literature and sports fields."—*Introd.*   CT1886.I7

Israel

Who's who in Israel and Jewish personalities from all over the world. 20th biennial English ed. (1985–86)– . Tel-Aviv : Bronfman, 1985– . Biennial.   **AH356**

Continues *Palestine and Transjordan who's who* (1945/6), *Palestine personalia* (1947), *Who's who in the State of Israel* (1949), *Who's who, Israel* (ceased with 1968), and *Who's who in Israel and in the work for Israel abroad* (1970–1981).

In addition to the biographical sketches there are lists of government officials and a section on public and private organizations, etc.   DS125.3.A2W53

Japan

Dai-Nihon hakushiroku = Who's who in "Hakushi" in great Japan / Kurō Iseki, ed. Tōkyō : Hattensha, [1921–30]. 5 v. : ill.   **AH357**

Title varies slightly.

A dictionary of contemporary biography of Japanese who are *Hakushi,* or holders of the doctor's degree in various fields. Articles are in Japanese and English. Arranged by subjects: v. 1, Law, Pharmacology; v. 2–4, Medicine; v. 5, Engineering.

§ Supplemented for the period 1888–1955 by *Nihon hakushiroku* (Tōkyō : Kyoiku Gyosei Kenkyu-jo, 1956–64. 8 v.), with annual supplements through 1962. A 4 v. work of the same title (Tōkyō : Teikoku Chiho Gyoseigakkai, 1967) lists recipients of the doctorate during the period 1957–65.   CT1836.I8

The Japan biographical encyclopedia and who's who / comp. and ed. by the staff of the Japan Biographical Research Department, The Rengo Press. Tokyo : Rengo Pr., 1964. 105, 2377 p. : maps in color.   **AH358**

1st ed., 1958; 2nd ed., 1961.

Gives, in English, concise biographical sketches of notables in all fields, of all periods, living and dead, with names of religious, mythical, and legendary beings and a very few foreigners. Appendixes offer chronological lists of emperors, government officials, diplomatic representatives from other countries, etc., as well as a glossary defining Japanese terms. An "Inseki," indicating familial relationships between two or more of an selected group of Japanese notables, is printed on green paper.　　　　　　　　　DS834.J7

Contemporary

Who's who in Japan. 1984/85– . Hong Kong : International Culture Institute, c1984– . Biennial.　　　　**AH359**
Copublished, Tokyo : Asia Press, 1991–92– .
Includes figures "from the fields of government, commerce and industry, medicine, journalism, visual and performing arts and cultural areas such as literature and education."—*Introd*. Information is very brief, often no more than birth date, education, current position, and address. The 1991/1992 ed. lists approximately 28,000 entries, and includes an index by very broad professional categories and a classified business directory.
§ An earlier work of the same title (v. 1 [1912]–21 [1940/41]. Tokyo : Who's Who in Japan Publ. Off., 1911–1940) is still useful for retrospective coverage. It includes a section on Europeans in Japan.　　　　　　　　　CT1836.W47

Lebanon

Who's who in Lebanon. 1. éd. (1963/64)– . Beyrouth : Les Éditions Publitec, 1964– . Biennial.　　　　**AH360**
Volumes for 1963/64–1973/74 in French, with imprint: Beyrouth, Editions Publitec; beginning with the 6th ed. (1975/76), in English, with imprint: Beirut, Publitec Publications.
The 12th ed. (1993/94) contains approximately 1,500 brief biographies and more than 200 pages of descriptive and directory information.　　　　　　　　　D380.75.W5

Malaysia

New Malaysian who's who. Kuala Lumpur : Kasuya Publ., 1989/1990 [i.e. 1989?]–1990. 2 v. in 3 : ill., map, ports.　　　　　　　　　**AH361**
Contents: Pt. 1, Sabah & Sarawak; pt. 2. West Malaysia (2 v.).
Provides more than 400 pages of useful information on government and business as well as outline biographies of several thousand Malaysians. Gives addresses and telephone numbers. May prove difficult to use for those unfamiliar with Malay names.　　　CT1566.N48

Who's who in Malaysia & Singapore. 15th ed. (1983–4)– . [Petaling Jaya, Selangor] : Who's Who Publications, [c1983]– .　　　　　　　　　**AH362**
Each ed. issued in two volumes: v. 1, Malaysia; v. 2, Singapore.
Publisher varies. Title varies: 1956–1959/60, *Leaders of Malaya and who's who*; 1963–67, *The who's who in Malaysia*; 1969–71/72, *The who's who—Malaysia and Singapore*; 1973/74–77/78, *Who's who in Malaysia and guide to Singapore*; 1978/79, *Who's who in Malaysia, Singapore & Brunei*; 1979/80, *Who's who in Malaysia & Singapore*; 1982, *Who's who in Malaysia & profiles of Singapore*.
Includes sections on rulers and government officials and a section of obituary notices in addition to the regular who's who portions.　　　　　　　　　CT1566.W47

Nepal

Aryal, Deepak Kumar. SAARC women : Nepal, 1988–1990. Kathmandu, Nepal : Research Centre for Communication and Development, 1990. 1 v. (various pagings) : ill.　　**AH363**
Subtitle: Biographical dictionary of selected women in Nepal.
Gives career outlines for several hundred prominent Nepalese women. Includes relevant statistical tables and general information on the role of women in this society. Intended to be the first in a series of such works on women of the SAARC (South Asian Association for Regional Cooperation).　　　　　　　　　CT3739.A79

Who's who—Nepal, 1992 / ed., Nirmal Nath Rimal. Kathmandu, Nepal : National Research Associates, 1992. 335 p.　　　　　　　　　**AH364**
Brief biographical outlines of approximately 1,200 individuals prominent in a variety of endeavors, based on information supplied by subjects. Includes addresses, and, in most instances, telephone numbers. An addendum gives a substantial number of entries omitted from the main alphabetical sequence.　　　　　CT1529.W49

Pakistan

Biographical encyclopedia of Pakistan. Ed. 1 (1955/56)– . [Lahore] : Biographical Research Inst., Pakistan, [1956?]– .　　　　　　　　　**AH365**
Chief ed., Khan Tahawar Ali Khan.
5th ed., 1971/72 (erroneously called "4th edition" in Preface) latest published?
Biographical data on important contemporary figures in Pakistan. Arranged in broad occupational groups with alphabetical index.　　　　　　　　　DS381.B5

Persons who shape our destiny : a compendium of bio-datas of those persons who are rendering important services in various fields of national activity / comp. and ed. by S. Mohammad Reza. Karachi : Dar Publications, 1990. v. 1 : ports. (In progress).　　　　　　　　　**AH366**
Sketches varying from a few lines to several pages on 448 prominent Pakistanis, arranged by occupation, with an alphabetical index at the front. A planned second volume will cover additional fields.　　　　　　　　　CT1513.P47

Philippines

Manuel, E. Arsenio. Dictionary of Philippine biography. Quezon City : Filipiniana Publications, 1955–86. v. 1–3. : ill., ports., facsims. (In progress).　　　　　　　　　**AH367**
Covers deceased individuals who have contributed significantly to Philippine history or culture. Articles are extremely varied in length and are arranged alphabetically within each volume. Fairly extensive bibliographies of works by and about the persons. Each volume has its own name and subject index; no cumulative index to date.　　　　　　　　　DS653.7.M3

Saudi Arabia

See also AH329 and AH330.

Who's who in Saudi Arabia. [Ed. 1] (1976/77)– . Jeddah, Saudi Arabia : Tihama, [1977]– .　　　　　　**AH368**

An English language who's who. The third ed. (1983/84) offers almost 1,000 brief sketches, including addresses and telephone numbers. Includes an index by field of endeavor.   CT1890.W47

Singapore

Who's who in Malaysia & Singapore. 15th ed. (1983–4)– . [Petaling Jaya, Selangor] : Who's Who Publications, [c1983]– .   **AH369**
   For annotation, *see* AH362.   CT1566.W47

Vietnam

See also AH47.

Who's who in Vietnam. 1967/68– . Saigon : Vietnam Pr., 1967– . Irregular.   **AH370**
   3rd ed., 1974, latest published.
   Persons selected for inclusion are "those who are holding elected positions, high-ranking government posts, and those who have scored outstanding achievements in social, cultural and economic domains."—*3rd ed., 1974.*   DS557.A5A555

AUSTRALIA AND OCEANIA

Australia

Australian dictionary of biography. [Melbourne] : Melbourne Univ. Pr. ; London ; N.Y. : Cambridge Univ. Pr., [1966]–1991. 13 vol.   **AH371**
   Editors: v. 1–6. Douglas Pike; v. 7–10, Bede Nairn, Geoffrey Serle; v. 12–[13], John Ritchie.
   Contents: v. 1, 1788–1850, A–H; v. 2, 1788–1850, I–Z; v. 3, 1851/–1890, A–C; v. 4, 1851–1890, D–J; v. 5, 1851–1890, K–Q; v. 6, 1851–1890, R–Z; v. 7, 1891–1939, A–Ch; v. 8, 1891–1939, Cl–Gib; v. 9, 1891–1939, Gil–Las; v. 10, 1891–1939, Lat–Ner; v. 11, 1891–1939, Nes–Smi; v. 12, 1891–1939, Smy–Z; v. 13, Index: v. 1–12, 1788–1939.
   Modeled on the British *Dictionary of national biography*. The index contains 10,442 individuals whose names are given substantial notice in the 7,211 major entries. While most entries are of obvious significance, some in the earlier period were chosen merely as examples of the "Australian experience." The index gives a name, occupation, and birthplace key, a consolidated corrigenda, and a select bibliography to v. 1–12. "Four volumes covering those whose *floruit* was after 1939 and who died before 1981 will be published subsequently."—*Pref., v.12.*   CT2802.A95

Gibbney, H. J. A biographical register, 1788–1939 : notes from the name index of the Australian dictionary of biography / comp. and ed. by H.J. Gibbney and Ann G. Smith. Canberra : Australian Dictionary of Biography, Australian National Univ., 1987. 2 v.   **AH372**
   Contains brief biographical information and citations to further sources for individuals about whom the staff of the *Australian dictionary of biography* (AH371) and found material, but who were not included in that work. "Readers must be cautioned against taking the *Biographical register* entries as fully researched statements … rather they should be used as the basis for individual research."—*Introd.* Includes an occupational index.   CT280B.G53

Contemporary

Debrett's handbook of Australia and New Zealand. 1st ed. (1982)– . Sydney : Debrett's Peerage, c1982– .   **AH373**
   Includes numerous entries for individuals of palpable distinction not found in the standard *Who's whos* of the two countries.

Lofthouse, Andrea. Who's who of Australian women / comp. by Andrea Lofthouse; based on research by Vivienne Smith. North Ryde, [Australia] : Methuen Australia, 1982. 504 p.   **AH374**
   Contains brief biographical entries derived from questionnaires returned by 1,425 noteworthy living Australian women. Includes an index by occupation.   CT3800.L63 1982

Who's who in Australia. v. 1 (1922)– . Melbourne : Herald and Weekly Times.   **AH375**
   Title varies slightly. Publisher varies.
   The 29th ed. (1993) gives summary sketches for 8,200 subjects, registries of titled Australians and of senior government officials, and an obituary drawn from entrants in the previous edition. Currently scheduled for annual publication.   DU82.W5

Fiji

Berwick, Sam. Who's who in Fiji : Fiji's golden book of record. Suva, Fiji : Berwicks Publishing House, 1990. 307 p. : ill.   **AH376**
   Includes a directory of government and other institutions, along with general background information on Fiji. An appendix, Who was who in Fiji, gives short biographical essays, lacking bibliographic references, on historical figures.   DU600.B47

New Zealand

The book of New Zealand women = Ko kui ma te kaupapa / ed. by Charlotte Macdonald, Merimeri Penfold, and Bridget Williams. Wellington, N.Z. : B. Williams Books, 1991. 772 p.   **AH377**
   Gives biographical sketches, most averaging about three pages, of more than 300 New Zealand women. Some entries include transcripts of oral history interviews, especially for the Maori women included. Each biography ends with a list of sources. Illustrated with photographs. Name, author, and subject indexes.   CT3805.B66

The dictionary of New Zealand biography. Wellington : Dept. of Internal Affairs : Allen & Unwin, 1990–93. v. 1–2. (In progress).   **AH378**
   Contents : v. 1, 1769–1869; v. 2, 1870–1900.
   Vol. 1 includes 572 signed biographical essays arranged in alphabetical order by name. Entries often run to a double columned page or more and give extensive bibliographic references. Nearly one third of the entrants are Maori and one fifth women. Indexing by personal name, occupation, and tribe. Five or six volumes are projected.
   A Maori version is under way: *Ngā Tāngata taumata rau* (Wellington : Allen & Unwin ; Te Tari Taiwhenua, 1990– . v. 1. In progress).   CT2886.S35

New Zealand who's who, Aotearoa. v. 1 (1992)– . Auckland : New Zealand who's who Aotearoa Ltd., 1992– . Annual.   **AH379**
   Includes career outlines and addresses of 4,500 individuals, with particular reference to women, Maori, Polynesian, and other ethnic minorities. "Aotearoa" is the Maori name for New Zealand.

Scholefield, Guy Hardy. A dictionary of New Zealand biography. Wellington : Dept. of Internal Affairs, 1940. 2 v.

AH380

A national biographical dictionary, modeled on the *DNB* (AH226), of persons who have distinguished themselves in the history of New Zealand since organized European migration began. Bibliographic references are given in most cases and a bibliography of major sources is found in v. 1, p. xviii–xxix. Maori figures are represented only to a limited extent. CT2886.S35

Contemporary

See also AH373.

Who's who in New Zealand. 5th ed. (1951)– . Wellington : A.H. & A.W. Reed, 1951– . Irregular. **AH381**

1st ed. (1908)–4th ed. (1941) publ. as *Who's who in New Zealand and the western Pacific.*

12th ed., 1991.

Contains preliminary directory material, including lists of officials of government, church, and education, and diplomatic representatives; election returns; titles and dignities, etc. Biographies are of the usual who's who type. DU402.W5

South Pacific

O'Reilly, Patrick. Calédoniens : répertoire bio-bibliographique de la Nouvelle-Calédonie. 2ᵉ éd. Paris : Société des Océanistes, Musée de l'Homme, 1980. 416 p. : ill. (Société des Océanistes, no. 41). **AH382**

Includes persons living and deceased who have contributed to the growth and prosperity of the colony: administrators, scientists, engineers, travelers, missionaries, etc., and also the principal Caledonian chiefs. Gives titles of works by authors, and occasional references to sources. DU720.O74

———————— Hébridais : répertoire bio-bibliographique des Nouvelles-Hébrides. Paris : Musée de l'Homme, 1957. 289 p. : ill., ports. (Société des océanistes. Publications, no. 6).

AH383

Several hundred biographical sketches of people of all periods connected with the life of the New Hebrides (now Vanuatu), European as well as native. Gives titles of works by authors, but no references to sources. Includes an index by professions. DU760.O7

———————— Tahitiens : répertoire bio-bibliographique de la Polynésie française / Patrick O'Reilly, Raoul Teissier. Paris : Musée de l'Homme, 1962. 534 p. : ill., ports. (Société des océanistes. Publications, no. 10). **AH384**

Includes fairly long articles on people of all periods connected with Tahiti, native and European, and an index by professions.

§ Updated by a *Supplement* (1966. 103 p.). DU870.O6

Who's who in Oceania, 1980–1981 / comp. by Robert D. Craig and Russell T. Clement. Laie, Hawaii : Brigham Young Univ., Inst. for Polynesian Studies, [1980]. 219 p. **AH385**

"The majority of entries … deal with personalities in the fields of government, education, science, and religion. Admission was based on subjective decisions regarding the position of responsibility held and the level of achievement attained by the individual."—*Pref.* In most cases, information was supplied by the biographee. Serves as a successor to the who's who section which appeared in the *Pacific Islands yearbook* (Syndey, Australia : Pacific Publications, 1932–84) through 1968. CT2775.W48

AJ

Genealogy

Genealogy, the study of family history, may require special techniques and the searching of records of many kinds. Guides such as Doane and Bell's *Searching for your ancestors* (AJ7), Greenwood's *Researcher's guide to American genealogy* (AJ11), and Croom's *Unpuzzling your past* (AJ6) may be helpful, but the average library will not find it possible to have available the materials necessary for detailed genealogical research, including the genealogies of individual families, local histories, parish registers, etc. A bibliographic guide to many such sources is Filby's *American and British genealogy and heraldry* (AJ28). Some large libraries have extensive genealogical collections, notably the Library of Congress, the New York Public Library, the Newberry Library in Chicago, the Los Angeles Public Library, and the Allen County Public Library in Fort Wayne, Ind. Some special libraries are also devoted to this work, such as the Family History Library of the Church of Jesus Christ of Latter-Day Saints in Salt Lake City. Local libraries often collect material relating to their own community or area, and may have sources not available in larger collections. When a library cannot supply readers with genealogical material, they should be referred to specialized libraries. Lists will be found in the library directories, e.g., *Subject collections* by Lee Ash (AK100).

This section includes some of the guides, bibliographies and other sources useful in American and English genealogy; a selection of peerages and other compilations of European nobility; and reference works on heraldry and personal names. The increased interest of Americans in genealogy in recent years is reflected in the newer guides (e.g., AJ2, AJ141) which, though describing sources in foreign countries, are written for Americans interested in tracing the antecedents of immigrant ancestors.

NORTH AMERICA

United States

Guides

Ancestry's red book : American state, county, and town sources / ed. by Alice Eichholz. Rev. ed. Salt Lake City, Utah : Ancestry, 1991. 858 p. **AJ1**

A guide to state and local records of genealogical interest, arranged alphabetically by state with brief descriptions of records. Counties (or, for the New England states, towns) listed alphabetically under state, giving for each: address of the courthouse, year of county formation, parent county, beginning dates for genealogical records (births, marriages, deaths), and land, probate, and court records. County outline maps are provided for each state.

§ Expands and updates much of the information in the 7th ed. of George B. Everton's *Handy book for genealogists* (8th ed., AJ9).
CS49.A55

Baxter, Angus. In search of your European roots : a complete guide to tracing ancestors in every country in Europe. Baltimore : Genealogical Pub. Co., 1985. 289 p. **AJ2**

Describes genealogical resources in 30 European countries, giving information on archival repositories from the national to the municipal level, and on the historical and political background that has affected or created the records. Includes a chapter on the Mormon records (i.e., those microfilmed in Europe) in Salt Lake City, and another on Jewish record repositories.

§ Similar but more specialized titles by Baxter are: *In search of your Canadian roots* (Baltimore : Genealogical Publ. Co., 1989. 350 p.), which covers Canada with briefer attention to some foreign countries; *In search of your British & Irish roots* (AJ96), which describes English, Welsh, Scottish, and Irish sources; and *In search of your German roots* (AJ90).

A work intended more for background than for the actual search is Noel Currer-Briggs, *Worldwide family history* (London : Routledge & Kegan Paul, 1982. 230 p.), which gives brief descriptions of the types of records to be found in European and Islamic countries, China, and Japan, together with chapters on migration from many countries to the U.S. and other English-speaking countries. CS403.B39

Blockson, Charles L. Black genealogy / by Charles L. Blockson with Ron Fry. Englewood Cliffs, N.J. : Prentice-Hall, [1977]. 232 p. **AJ3**

Includes chapters on the use of family and public documents, slave records, and other sources useful in tracing African-American genealogy. Two appendixes: A "directory of research resources" listing names and addresses of record and information centers in the U.S. and abroad; a list of newspapers important in black genealogical searching. Index; bibliography. CS21.B55

Cerny, Johni. Ancestry's guide to research : case studies in American genealogy / by Johni Cerny and Arlene Eakle. Salt Lake City, Utah : Ancestry, 1985. 364 p. : ill. **AJ4**

A companion volume to the authors' *The source* (AJ23). Offers "research instruction through applying the basics in case studies," with emphasis on "familiarizing the novice researcher with primary and original sources" (*Introd.*) necessary for tracing American ancestors. One short chapter on two ethnic groups (Cherokee and slave) and another on immigrant ancestors. Indexed. CS49.C46

Computer genealogy : a guide to research through high technology / ed. by Richard A. Pence. Rev. ed. Salt Lake City, Utah : Ancestry, 1991. 258 p. : ill. **AJ5**

Rev. ed. of: *Computer genealogy*, by Paul A. Andereck and Richard A. Pence (1985).

"The book clarifies ... what computers do, how they do it, and in what ways other family researchers use their computers."—*Introd.* Chapters on hardware, software, and suggestions on helping in getting started. Glossary; index. CS14.A52

Croom, Emily Anne. Unpuzzling your past : a basic guide to genealogy. 2nd ed. White Hall, Va. : Betterway Publications, c1989. 136 p. : ill., map, port. **AJ6**

1st ed., 1983.

One of the best guides for beginners. Introduces family history as well as genealogy, explores family sources and interviewing, and briefly introduces major record types. CS47.C76

Doane, Gilbert Harry. Searching for your ancestors : the how and why of genealogy / Gilbert Harry Doane and James B. Bell. [6th ed.]. Minneapolis : Univ. of Minnesota Pr., [1992]. 334 p. **AJ7**

1st ed., 1937 ; 5th ed., 1980.

In two parts: (1) a manual and guide to genealogical searching, with chapters on such subjects as the finding and use of family papers, town records, cemeteries, church records; how to arrange a genealogy;

(2) chapters on ethnic origins and research in some 20 foreign countries. Includes a useful bibliography of the most used guides and materials. CS16.D6

Ethnic genealogy : a research guide / ed. by Jessie Carney Smith. Westport, Conn. : Greenwood, [1983]. 440 p. : ill. **AJ8**

In three main sections: (1) General information on sources, procedures, and genealogical research; (2) Utilizing major repositories for genealogical research; (3) Sources available to specific ethnic groups (Native Americans, Asian Americans, Latinos, and African Americans). Each section has chapters by contributing scholars discussing methods and procedures, and listing pertinent bibliographic sources, repositories, etc. Numerous illustrative forms and sample records. Indexed. CS49.E83

Everton, George B. The handy book for genealogists : United States of America / by George B. Everton, Jr., and Louise Mathews Everton. 8th ed. Logan, Utah : Everton Publishers, c1991. 378 p. **AJ9**

1st ed., 1949; 7th ed., 1981.

For every U.S. county, lists the parent county and date organized and notes available records. Similar to the 7th ed. except this edition covers only the U.S. Includes a nationwide county index, new county boundary maps showing rivers and lakes, and several maps of migration trails. CS47.E9

Genealogical research : methods and sources / ed., Milton Rubincam. Rev. ed. Wash. : Amer. Soc. of Genealogists, 1980–83. 2 v. **AJ10**

1st ed., 1960–71.

Vol. 1 offers chapters by various authors on methods, interpretation, rules of evidence, materials for research (original sources, public and institutional records, secondary materials), regional genealogy of Eastern U.S. and of Canada, pre-American ancestry and special subjects (heraldry, law, names). Vol. 2 covers regional genealogy of states to the Mississippi, Florida, and special subjects (Ontario, Huguenots, Jewish migrations, black genealogy). CS16.G43

Greenwood, Val D. The researcher's guide to American genealogy. 2nd ed. Baltimore : Genealogical Pub. Co., 1990. 609 p. : ill. **AJ11**

1st ed., 1973.

Aims "to provide a meaningful and comprehensive guide to the records used in American genealogical research."—*Pref.* Pt. 1, "Background to research," deals with various aspects, problems, and tools of research; pt. 2, "Records and their use," treats specific types of records, such as birth and death records, census reports, wills, deeds, land records, court records, church records, military records, etc. Indexed. The new edition adds chapters on proper research methodology, computers, and expansion of genealogy into family history.
CS47.G73

Kemp, Thomas Jay. International vital records handbook. 3rd ed. Baltimore : Genealogical Pub. Co., c1994. 417 p. **AJ12**

1st ed., 1990.

Provides guidance in requesting birth, marriage, and death certificates. Gives for each state or country cost, addresses of vital records offices, and application forms. Emphasizes the U.S., but scope is international; describes procedures for obtaining vital records from many foreign countries. CS24.K44

Kurzweil, Arthur. From generation to generation : how to trace your Jewish genealogy and personal history. N.Y. : Morrow, 1980. 353 p. **AJ13**

Repr.: N.Y. : Schocken, 1982.

In two parts: pt. 1 gives a lively account of the author's investigation of his own family history; pt. 2 identifies and describes sources for Jewish genealogy, with instructions on methods and procedures. Bibliographical references throughout; index. CS21.K87

The library : a guide to the LDS Family History Library / ed. by Johni Cerny & Wendy Elliott. Salt Lake City, Utah : Ancestry, c1988. 763 p. : ill. **AJ14**

A guide to some of the records at the Family History Library, with emphasis on how to use its catalog to obtain the records. It lists key records of each state and country and is helpful for preparing to visit the Family History Library or a family history center. Z733.C55L53

National Archives and Records Service. Guide to genealogical research in the National Archives. Rev. ed. Wash. : Nat. Archives Trust Fund Board, 1985. 304 p. : ill. **AJ15**

Supersedes *Guide to genealogical records in the National Archives* by M. B. Colket and F. E. Bridgers (1964).

A brief introduction stresses the value and limitations of federal records for genealogical research and offers remarks about "the organization of records in general, finding aids, microfilm, and research facilities and special programs at the National Archives Building and the Federal Archives and Records Centers."—*Introd.* Individual chapters (grouped by broad subject areas such as population and immigration, military records, etc.) deal with specific groups of records, their extent, general content, and finding aids. Indexed. Z5313.U5U54

Neagles, James C. Confederate research sources : a guide to archive collections. Salt Lake City, Utah : Ancestry, c1986. 286 p. : ill. **AJ16**

Intended to help the researcher "track down information about his confederate ancestor whether in a state archive, the National Archives in Washington, D.C., or in a state or other genealogical library."—*Introd.* Offers descriptions of archives and lists of publications.
Z1242.N3

———————— The Library of Congress : a guide to genealogical and historical research / by James C. Neagles ; assisted by Mark C. Neagles. Salt Lake City, Utah : Ancestry, c1990. 381 p. : ill. **AJ17**

For annotation, *see* DB143. Z1250.N4

———————— U.S. military records : a guide to federal and state sources, Colonial America to the present. Salt Lake City, Utah : Ancestry, 1994. 441 p. : ill. **AJ18**

Both useful and easy to use. Chapters describe the types of records that exist, resources available at the National Archives and other repositories, and published sources for each state and for the U.S. in general. Appendix includes a summary of America's military history. Z1249.M5N43

Parker, J. Carlyle. Library service for genealogists. Detroit : Gale, [1981]. 362 p. (Gale genealogy and local history series, 15). **AJ19**

Aims to provide guidance to the librarian in administration, collection development and reference work in the many aspects of genealogy. Bibliography with full information in each chapter. Indexed.

§ A British counterpart of the Parker work is Richard Harvey's *Genealogy for librarians* (AJ101), which describes sources for English, and to a lesser extent, Welsh, Scottish and Irish, genealogical sources. Z5313.U5P37

A practical guide to the "misteaks" made in census indexes / ed. by Richard H. Saldana. [Salt Lake City, Utah : R. H. Saldana & Co., c1987]. 63 p. : ill. **AJ20**

Repr., 1989.

Explains how census indexes are made, the types of errors usually found, and how to overcome some errors. Census indexes now exist for most states from 1790 (or date of admission to the union) to 1870; some are to 1910.

Rottenberg, Dan. Finding our fathers : a guidebook to Jewish genealogy. N.Y. : Random House, [1977]. 401 p. **AJ21**

Repr.: Baltimore : Genealogical Publ. Co., 1986.

An introductory guide to research in Jewish genealogy, with emphasis on "American Jews of European ancestry, and especially East

European ancestry."—*Pref.* Chapters on methods, archives and general sources are followed by "A source guide to Jewish family genealogies" (p. 141–375), an alphabetical listing of family names (including cross-references from variant and related forms) with references to sources of information. Bibliography, p. 376–401. CS21.R58

Smith, Clifford Neal. Encyclopedia of German-American genealogical research / Clifford Neal Smith, Anna Piszczan-Czaja Smith. N.Y. : Bowker, 1976. 273 p. **AJ22**

Attempts to "survey the material available to the genealogist seeking to link American lineages with their origins in German-speaking Europe" (*Pref.*) through bibliographical essays. Includes some background material on German customs, sociological stratification and governmental organization useful to the genealogist. Indexed.
E184.G3S66

The source : a guidebook of American genealogy / ed. by Arlene Eakle and Johni Cerny. Salt Lake City, Utah : Ancestry, 1984. 786 p. : ill. **AJ23**

Aims to provide "a solid introduction to the major American record types from their beginnings to 1910."—*Introd.* Following a general introduction to records and techniques, 23 chapters (each by an expert) describe in some detail: (1) Major record sources (e.g., censuses; church, court, and business records, etc.); (2) Published sources (city directories, newspapers, reference books); and (3) Special resources (for immigrant origins, records of various ethnic groups; use of databases). Appendixes of sources of genealogical information, societies, and publishers; glossary; bibliographic index and subject index. Numerous illustrations of typical documents and records. Valuable to the historian as well as the genealogist. CS49.S65

Szucs, Loretto Dennis. The archives : a guide to the National Archives field branches / by Loretto Dennis Szucs & Sandra Hargreaves Luebking. Salt Lake City, Utah : Ancestry, 1988. 340 p. : ill. **AJ24**

For annotation, *see* DB37. CD3026

Tepper, Michael. American passenger arrival records : a guide to the records of immigrants arriving at American ports by sail and steam. Updated and enl. Baltimore : Genealogical Pub. Co., 1993. 142 p. **AJ25**

1st ed., 1988.

An in-depth discussion of colonial and federal immigration lists, both reprinted and original. CS49.T46

Thorndale, William. Map guide to the U.S. federal censuses, 1790–1920 / William Thorndale and William Dollarhide. Baltimore : Genealogical Pub. Co., 1987. 420 p. : maps ; 23 x 30 cm. **AJ26**

For annotation, *see* CL306. G1201.F7T5

Wright, Norman Edgar. Preserving your American heritage : a guide to family and local history. Provo, Utah : Brigham Young Univ. Pr., [1981]. 285 p. **AJ27**

1974 ed., had title: *Building an American pedigree.*

A basic guide to genealogy and family history, with detailed descriptions of important sources and repositories. Bibliography; index.
CS47.W68

Bibliography

Filby, P. William. American & British genealogy & heraldry : a selected list of books. 3rd ed. Boston : New England Historic Genealogical Soc., 1983. 736 p. **AJ28**

1st ed., 1970.

Aims "to present to American and Canadian libraries a comprehensive bibliography through Fall 1981."—*Introd.* Within sections for the U.S., Latin America, Canada, England, Ireland, Scotland, Wales, British dominions and former dominions, and World, works are grouped by type/topic (e.g., bibliographies; records, guides, indexes; biographies; manuals and aids; immigration; religions) or by individual country; there are separate subsections for the individual states and provinces of the U.S. and Canada. Heraldry and chivalry are accorded separate sections. Many items are briefly annotated, and relationships between publications are noted. 9,773 entries, all but a few in English; detailed index.

A supplement covering 1982–85 was publ. 1987.   Z5311.F55

──────────────── Passenger and immigration lists bibliography, 1538–1900 : being a guide to published lists of arrivals in the United States and Canada / by P. William Filby & Dorothy M. Lower. 2nd ed. Detroit : Gale, c1988. 324 p.   **AJ29**

1st ed., 1981; suppl., 1984.

Includes entries from 1st ed. and its supplement plus more than 750 new lists. Indexed.   Z5313.U5F54

Horowitz, Lois. A bibliography of military name lists from pre-1675 to 1900 : a guide to genealogical sources. Metuchen, N.J. : Scarecrow, 1990. 1080 p.   **AJ30**

A monumental annotated bibliography designed to help genealogists identify individuals through their military service in America through 1900. Includes war records, rolls of soldiers, reports, journals, histories, lists of veterans and pensioners. Arranged by time period and locality. Not comprehensive, but valuable for locating published or typescript U.S. military records. No index.   Z5313.U5H67

Kaminkow, Marion J. A complement to genealogies in the Library of Congress : a bibliography. Baltimore : Magna Carta Book Co., 1981. 1118 p.   **AJ31**

"Identifies genealogies on individual families, produced up until the end of 1976 that are *not* listed" (*Introd.*) among the Library of Congress holdings (AJ32), and locates copies in 24 American libraries. About 20,000 entries. Index of secondary names.   Z5319.K35

Library of Congress. Genealogies in the Library of Congress : a bibliography / ed. by Marion J. Kaminkow. Baltimore : Magna Carta Book Co., 1972. 2 v.   **AJ32**

Updates and expands the Library's *American and English genealogies in the Library of Congress* (2nd ed., 1919). "This new edition can … be considered as three tools in one: a guide to genealogical monographs which may be found in the Library of Congress and in other libraries; the Library's own particular index [i.e., the "Family name index," a card file in the Local History and Genealogy Room] to genealogies in sources not primarily genealogical in nature; and a guide to the unique collection of nonprinted genealogies held by the Library, other than those in its Manuscript Division."—*Editor's note.* About 20,000 entries. *See also* Kaminkow's *A complement to genealogies in the Library of Congress* (AJ31).

Supplements: (1) *Supplement 1972–1976* (1977. 285 p.); (2) *Second supplement, 1976–1986* (1987. 861 p.); (3) *Genealogies cataloged by the Library of Congress since 1986: with a list of established forms of family names and a list of genealogies converted to microform since 1983* (Wash. : Cataloging Distribution Service, Library of Congress, 1991. 1349 p.).   Z5319.U53

Sperry, Kip. A survey of American genealogical periodicals and periodical indexes. Detroit : Gale, [1978]. 199 p. (Gale genealogy and local history series, v.3).   **AJ33**

Introductory chapters on basic genealogical research sources and procedures, American genealogical periodical literature (value, types, and limitations), and access to the periodical literature are followed by individual indexes or groups of indexes. Appendixes offer a list of additional indexes (with brief annotations) and a select list of periodicals. Indexed.   Z5313.U5S65

Yantis, Netti Schreiner. Genealogical and local history books in print. 4th ed. [Springfield, Va.], Genealogical Books in Print, 1985–1992. 5 v.   **AJ34**

Vols. 4–5 are supplements 1–2.

1st ed., 1975, had title *Genealogical books in print.*

A classified list with prices and sources of more than "30,000 books and microforms valuable to those tracing their ancestry."—*Cover.* The "Family genealogies" section is indexed.   Z5313.U5Y35

Indexes

American genealogical-biographical index to American genealogical, biographical and local history materials. Middletown, Conn. : Godfrey Memorial Library, 1952–93. v. 1–175. (In progress).   **AJ35**

Editor: v. 1–53, Fremont Rider.

Contents: v. 1–175, A–Thurston.

Often referred to as "Rider."

"Should be the first tool to be used by every genealogical researcher in seeking an answer for every question."—*Introd.* Will eventually replace the initial series (below).

Supersedes:

The American genealogical index, Fremont Rider, ed. (Middletown, Conn. : publ. by a committee representing the cooperating subscribing libraries, 1942–52. 48 v.

Only v. 40–48 need to be retained.   Z5313.Z15A55

Daughters of the American Revolution. DAR patriot index. [1st ed.]. Wash., 1966–86. 3 v.   **AJ36**

An alphabetical list of more than 100,000 persons whose service has been established by the Daughters of the American Revolution. Vol. 3 is an alphabetical list of the spouses of persons named in the first two volumes. Corrections have been published in *DAR magazine*, starting with the May 1983 issue.

Kept up to date by supplements. Centennial edition publ. 1994.   E255.D38 1967

The famine immigrants : lists of Irish immigrants arriving at the port of New York, 1846–1851 / Ira A. Glazier, ed. Baltimore : Genealogical Publ. Co., 1983–86. 7 v.   **AJ37**

Contents: v.1–7, Jan. 1846–Dec. 1851.

Transcribes names of Irish passengers as recorded in ship manifests. Arranged chronologically by ship list. Data includes name, age, sex, occupation, ship's name, port of origin and date of arrival. Name index.   E184.I6F25

Genealogical abstracts of Revolutionary War pension files / abstracted by Virgil D. White. Waynesboro, Tenn. : National Historical Publ. Co., 1990–92. 4 v.   **AJ38**

Includes alphabetical name index (v. 4) of all persons mentioned in the abstracts.

Supersedes: National Genealogical Society, *Index of Revolutionary War pension applications in the National Archives* (Bicentennial ed., rev. & enl. Wash., 1976. 658 p.). 1st ed., 1966; originally published in parts as supplements to the Society's *Quarterly*, 1943–62.   CS42.N43

Genealogical periodical annual index. 1962– . Bowie, Md. : Heritage Books, 1963– . Annual.   **AJ39**

1990 vol. publ. 1992.

Editor and publisher vary.

Indexes genealogical periodicals and includes some articles of genealogical interest from other periodicals. The 1990 vol. indexed 308 periodicals.

Germans to America : lists of passengers arriving at U.S. ports / ed. by Ira A. Glazier and P. William Filby. Wilmington, Del. : Scholarly Resources, c1988–c1994. v. 1–42 : ill. (In progress).   **AJ40**

Contents: v.1–42 : Jan. 1850–May 1887.

Transcriptions of passenger lists for ships arriving at major Atlantic coast ports as well as New Orleans, Galveston, and San Francisco. For 1850–55 includes only lists that contained 80% German passengers; thereafter, covers all ships with German passengers. Age, sex, occupation, place of origin, and destination are provided for each passenger; for some the home town is given, for others only the province of origin. Indexed by surname.

§ Supplemented by Gary J. Zimmerman's *German immigrants* (AJ49).   E184.G3G38

Index to American genealogies : and to genealogical material contained in all works such as town histories, county histories, local histories, historical society publications, biographies, historical periodicals, and kindred works, alphabetically arranged. 5th ed. rev., improved, and enl. Albany, N.Y. : Munsell, 1900. 352 p. **AJ41**

Repr.: Baltimore : Genealogical Publ. Co, 1984 (includes supplement).

Cover title: *Munsell's genealogical index.*

The basic volume (1900) indexes about 50,000 references; a supplement (1908. 107 p.) continues indexing for 1900–1908.

Z5313.U515

Jacobus, Donald Lines. Index to genealogical periodicals. Rev. ed. / by Carl Boyer. Newhall, Calif. : C. Boyer, 1983. 373 p. **AJ42**

1st ed., 1932–53.

This revision cumulates the six indexes of the original work. Arranged in three sections: name index, place index, topic index. The "Key to genealogical periodicals" adds useful notes on various periodical indexes of a genealogical nature. Z5313.U5J22

Olsson, Nils William. Swedish passenger arrivals in New York, 1820–1850. Stockholm : Kungl. Bibl. ; Chicago : Swedish Pioneer Historical Soc., 1967. 391 p. : il. (Acta Bibliothecae Regiae Stockholmiensis, 6). **AJ43**

Both this work and the author's *Swedish passenger arrivals in U.S. ports 1820–1850 (except New York)* (1979. 139 p.) transcribe passengers' names, with age, sex and occupation, from ship manifests for the period. Many names are annotated with further information culled from archival sources in Sweden and the United States. For each ship are given name, date of arrival and port of origin. Place and name indexes.

§ Olsson is also the author of the instructional guide addressed to Americans: *Tracing your Swedish ancestry* (Rev. ed. Stockholm : Ministry for Foreign Affairs, 1974. 27 p.; repr. 1977). E184.S23O43

Passenger and immigration lists index : a guide / ed. by P. William Filby with Mary K. Meyer. Detroit : Gale, [1981]. 3 v. (2339 p.). **AJ44**

"A guide to published arrival records of about 500,000 passengers who came to the United States and Canada in the seventeenth, eighteenth and nineteenth centuries."—*t.p.*

A "preliminary edition" was published 1980.

This work "brings together in one alphabet citations to information about passengers ... whose names appear in a broad collection of published passenger lists or naturalization records."—*Introd.* Some 500,000 names from about 300 sources, with many duplications (since a name may appear in more than one record). Entry usually gives name, age, place and year of arrival or of naturalization record.

Supplements are published annually and cumulated as:

————. *1982–85 cumulated supplements* (1985. 4 v.).

————. *1986–90 cumulated supplements* (1990. 3 v.).

Annual supplements have appeared for 1991, 1992, 1993, and 1994. The 1994 suppl. listed more than 127,000 names, bringing the total for the set to 2,283,000. Cumulated supplements are promised every five years. CS68.F537

Periodical source index / prep. by the staff of the Allen County Public Library, Genealogy Department, Fort Wayne, Indiana. Fort Wayne, Ind. : Allen County Public Library Foundation, c1988– . Annual. **AJ45**

Also known as *PERSI.*

A valuable surname, subject, and locality index to more than 2,000 genealogical and local history periodicals. Essential for genealogical research. Currently includes annual volumes, covering 1986–92, and a retrospective 12 v. set, 1847–1985. CS1.P47

Schenk, Trudy. The Wuerttemberg emigration index / by Trudy Schenk, Ruth Froelke, and Inge Bork. Salt Lake City, Utah : Ancestry, 1986–1990. 6 v. **AJ46**

Contains names of emigrants from Wuerttemberg to other countries in Europe and elsewhere, ca. 1808–1890; many listed the U.S. as their destination. Provides names, birthdates, birthplaces, emigration dates, destinations, and the call numbers of microfilms from the Family History Library (Salt Lake City, Utah) used in the project. CS627.W86S34

Sperry, Kip. Index to genealogical periodical literature : 1960–1977. Detroit : Gale, [1979]. 166 p. (Gale genealogy and local history series, v.9). **AJ47**

A selective list of major "periodical articles describing research techniques and procedures, genealogical and historical sources and collections, as well as international genealogical subjects."—*Pref.* Pt. 1 is the subject index (a list of subject headings with citations to sources, but without authors and titles). Pt. 2 lists alphabetically by author the articles indexed in the first part. Z5313.U5S64

White, Virgil D. Index to War of 1812 pension files / transcribed by Virgil D. White. Waynesboro, Tenn. : National Historical Publ. Co., 1992. 3 v. **AJ48**

1st ed., 1989.

§ A related title transcribed by White: *Index to old wars pension files, 1815–1926* (Rev. ed., 1993. 844 p.). E359.4.W45

Zimmerman, Gary J. German immigrants : lists of passengers bound from Bremen to New York [1847–1871], with places of origin / comp. by Gary J. Zimmerman & Marion Wolfert. Baltimore : Genealogical Pub. Co., 1985–1993. 4 v. **AJ49**

Contents: v. 1–4, 1847–1871.

Vol. 4 comp. by Marion Wolfert.

Contains approximately 100,000 names (about 21% of the total) of passengers outbound from Bremen to New York during this period. Provides name, age, residence, year of emigration, and ship name. Lists only passengers who gave a town or district of origin. Valuable because the Bremen passenger lists were destroyed. Supplements *Germans to America* (AJ40) which does not cover the period 1847–49 and is incomplete for 1850–55. E184.G3Z56

Dictionaries

Evans, Barbara Jean. The new A to Zax : a comprehensive genealogical dictionary for genealogists and historians. 2nd ed. Champaign, Ill. : B.J. Evans, 1990. 323 p. **AJ50**

1st ed. publ. 1987 as *A to zax.*

A valuable list of genealogically significant terms and their meanings. Includes a list of nicknames and their usual given names. Stong on Dutch given names. CS6.E9

Directories

Bentley, Elizabeth Petty. County courthouse book. Baltimore : Genealogical Pub. Co., c1990. 386 p. **AJ51**

A genealogical guide to U.S. courthouses. Gives background on the court system for each state, name of courthouse, address, brief summary of holdings, etc. KF8700.A19B46

———— Directory of family associations. 1993–94 ed. Baltimore : Genealogical Pub. Co., 1993. 318 p. **AJ52**

1st ed., 1991/92.

Attempts to include all family associations engaged in genealogical research. CS42.B46

———— The genealogist's address book. Baltimore : Genealogical Pub. Co., c1992. 391 p. **AJ53**

A useful directory, giving names and addresses of genealogical and historical societies, state libraries and archives, public libraries, ethnic organizations, and many other institutions. CS44.B46

Filby, P. William. Directory of American libraries with gene-alogy or local history collections. Wilmington, Del. : Scholarly Resources Inc., 1988. 319 p.   **AJ54**

Identifies most libraries with genealogical collections in the U.S. and Canada. Arranged alphabetically by state or province; entries show address, telephone number, and a brief description of collections and services available. Omitted are genealogical and family history collections housed at libraries that did not return the questionnaire. A helpful feature is the index of libraries with significant out-of-state collections. Locality of library must be known, since there is no central index of libraries.   Z675.G44F56

Meyer, Mary Keysor. Meyer's directory of genealogical soci-eties in the U.S.A. and Canada. 1st ed. (1976)– . Pasadena, Md. : M. K. Meyer, [1982]– .   **AJ55**

Arranged alphabetically by state, or for Canada, by province. Compiled partially from responses to a questionnaire; gives fuller in-formation about publications, areas of interest, etc., for organizations that responded. Includes a list of specialized, surname, and independ-ent genealogical periodicals that gives address and scope.   CS44.M44

——————— Who's who in genealogy & heraldry / Mary Keyson Meyer and P. William Filby, eds. [2nd ed.]. Savage, Md. : Who's Who in Genealogy & Heraldry, [1990]. 331 p.   **AJ56**

Presents in "who's who" format information (personal, career, publications, special interests) concerning some 100 genealogists, chiefly American.   CS.M49

Where to write for vital records. May 1982– . Hyattsville, Md. : U.S. National Center for Health Statistics ; Wash. : U.S. Govt. Print. Off., 1982– . Triennial.   **AJ57**

For anotation, *see* CK157.   HA38.A493

Compendiums

Burke's distinguished families of America : the lineages of 1600 families of British origin now resident in the United States of America. London : Burke's Peerage, 1948. p. 2529–3021 : col. coats of arms.   **AJ58**

Originally publ. as the American section of Burke's *Genealogical and heraldic history of the landed gentry*, 16th ed., 1939. (Repr. as *Prominent families in America with British ancestry*. N.Y. ; London : House & Maxwell, 1971.).   CS45.B8

Burke's presidential families of the United States of Amer-ica. 2nd ed. London : Burke's Peerage, 1981. 597 p., 94 p. : ill.   **AJ59**

Hugh Montgomery-Massingberd, ed.

1st ed., 1975.

A chapter is devoted to each of the 39 presidents, Washington through Reagan, each chapter divided into sections for: (1) biography; (2) portraits; (3) chronology; (4) writings; (5) lineage; (6) descendants; (7) brothers and sisters; and (8) notes. Indexed.   CS69.B82

Coldham, Peter Wilson. The complete book of emigrants. Baltimore : Genealogical Publ. Co., 1987–c1993. 4 v. : ill.   **AJ60**

Contents: v. 1, 1607–1660; v. 2, 1661–1699. v. 3, 1700–1750. v. 4, 1751–1776.

Contains the names of approximately 50,000 emigrants to Ameri-ca taken from published and manuscript sources available in England. Entries are arranged chronologically and there is an index of persons and ships at the end of each volume. Bibliography of sources.   E184.B7C59

——————— The complete book of emigrants in bondage, 1614–1775. Baltimore : Genealogical Publ. Co., 1983. 9 v. in 3. : ill.   **AJ61**

Title varies: 1st ed. (1974–76?) called *English convicts in colonial America* (2 v.?); 2nd ed., 1983, called *Bonded passengers to America* (9 v. in 3).

Contents: v. 1, History of transportation, 1615–1775; v. 2, Mid-dlesex, 1617–1775; v. 3, London, 1656–1775; v. 4, Home counties, 1655–1775; v. 5, Western Circuit, 1664–1775; v. 6, Oxford Circuit, 1663–1775; v. 7, Norfolk Circuit, 1663–1775; v. 8, Northern Circuit, 1665–1775; v. 9, Midland Circuit, 1671–1775.

"Intended as a key to sources from which further information may be obtained."—*Introd., v. 2*. Vols. 2–9 list names alphabetically with reference to specific British court records.

——————— . Supplement to The complete book of emigrants in bond-age, 1614–1775 (c1992. 86 p.).   CS61.C62

Dobson, David. Directory of Scottish settlers in North Ameri-ca, 1625–1825. Baltimore : Genealogical Pub. Co., 1984–86. v. 1–6. (In progress).   **AJ62**

Drawing on archival sources and such contemporary publications as government documents and Scottish newspapers, this compilation "brings together ... the names of all Scots emigrants appearing in ships' passenger lists before 1825."—*Introd.* Alphabetical by name, with (typically) age, occupation, names and ages of family members, port of embarkation, destination, date and source of data.

§ Dobson has published a similar work for a shorter period: *Di-rectory of Scots banished to the American plantations, 1650–1775* (Baltimore : Genealogical Publ. Co., 1983. 239p.).   E184.S3D63

Hotten, John Camden. The original lists of persons of quali-ty, emigrants, religious exiles, political rebels ... and others who went from Great Britain to the American plantations. N.Y. : Bouton ; London : Chatto, 1874. 580 p.   **AJ63**

Repr.: Baltimore : Genealogical Publ. Co., 1983.

Supplemented by: *Omitted chapters from Hotten's original lists of persons of quality and others who went from Great Britain to the American plantations, 1600–1700: census returns, parish registers, and militia rolls from the Barbados census of 1679/80*, ed. by James C. Brandow (Baltimore : Genealogical Publ. Co., 1982. 245 p.).

Supplements the earlier work by listing the Barbados registers submitted by Hotten, and by transcribing the militia rolls and other lists in the Public Record Office.   E187.5.H795

Italians to America : lists of passengers arriving at U.S. ports, 1880–1899 / ed. by Ira A. Glazier and P. William Filby. Wil-mington, Del. : Scholarly Resources, 1992. v. 1–4. (In pro-gress).   **AJ64**

Contents: v. 1–4, Jan. 1880–Oct. 1890.

Similar in scope and arrangement to the same compilers' *Ger-mans to America* (AJ40). When complete, will include some 750,000 names. Taken from original passenger lists.   E184.I8I844 1992

Savage, James. A genealogical dictionary of the first settlers of New England : showing three generations of those who came before May, 1692, on the basis of the Farmer's Register. Boston : Little, 1860–62. 4 v.   **AJ65**

Repr.: Baltimore : Genealogical Publ. Co., 1981; includes in v. 4: *Genealogical notes and errata to Savage's genealogical dictionary ...* by C. H. Dall (Lowell, Mass. : Elliot, 1881. 8 p.) and *A genealogical cross index of ... the Genealogical dictionary of James Savage*, by O. P. Dexter (N. Y. : Dexter, 1884. 38 p.).   F3.S2

Stern, Malcolm H. First American Jewish families : 600 ge-nealogies, 1654–1977. Cincinnati : Amer. Jewish Archives ; Waltham, Mass. : Amer. Jewish Historical Society, 1978. 419 p.   **AJ66**

A revision and expansion of the author's *Americans of Jewish de-scent* (1960), offering genealogies of Jewish families established in the U.S. by 1840. Schematic charts for each family show names, dates and places of birth, marriage and death, military service in America's wars, and interrelationships. Almost 40,000 individuals are included. Sources of data indicated for each genealogy. Name index; bibliogra-phy of sources.   CS59.S76

Swierenga, Robert P. Dutch emigrants to the United States, South Africa, South America, and Southeast Asia, 1835–1880 : an alphabetical listing by household heads and independent persons. Wilmington, Del. : Scholarly Resources, [1983]. 346 p.   **AJ67**

Offers coded information from emigration lists in Dutch archives, including name, occupation, sex, age, religion, presumed reason for emigrating, economic status, tax assessment class, number of women, children and servants in household, destination, year of departure, province and municipality of origin. 21,800 names.   CS827.A1S89

——————— Dutch immigrants in U.S. ship passenger manifests, 1820–1880 : an alphabetical listing by household heads and independent persons. Wilmington, Del. : Scholarly Resources, [1983]. 2 v.   **AJ68**

Coded information includes person's name, sex, age, occupation, place of origin, ship's name, port of origin, port and date of arrival. Indication of specific source of citation enables searcher to locate the record readily.   E184.D9S95

Whyte, Donald. A dictionary of Scottish emigrants to the U.S.A. Baltimore : Magna Carta Book Co., 1972. 504 p.
                                                                       AJ69

A listing of Scottish emigrants prior to 1855. Gives birth and death dates as available and brief notes of genealogical interest.
                                                                   El84.S3W49

Canada

Genealogist's handbook for Atlantic Canada research / ed. by Terrence M. Punch. Boston : New England Historic Genealogical Society, 1989. 142 p. : maps.   **AJ70**

Explains research sources and procedures for New Brunswick, Newfoundland, Nova Scotia, and Prince Edward Island. Includes Acadia.   Z5313.C22A884

Jetté, René. Dictionnaire généalogique des familles du Québec ... : avec la collaboration du programme de recherche en démographie historique de l'Université de Montréal. Montréal : Presses de l'Univ. de Montréal, 1983. 1176 p.   **AJ71**

A thorough reworking and expansion of Cyprien Tanguay's *Dictionnaire généalogique des familles canadiennes* (AJ73). compiled with the aim of reconstructing the history of early Quebec families. Data drawn chiefly from parish registers of baptism, marriage and burial. When complete, the work will supersede Tanguay and supplements to or revisions of that work (e.g., Archange Godbout, *Nos ancêtres au XVIIᵉ siècle*). This volume covers 1621 to 1730, and no schedule of publication for further parts is mentioned although the compiler refers to the work as "la première partie." Alphabetically arranged by family name. Indexes of persons about whom little is known, and of variant names.   CS88.Q4J47

Merriman, Brenda Dougall. Genealogy in Ontario : searching the records. [2nd ed.]. [Toronto] : Ontario Genealogical Society, c1988. 168 p. : ill.   **AJ72**

1st ed., 1984.

A genealogical guide to the land, census, probate, civil, and church records of the province of Ontario, Canada.   CS88.O6M46

Tanguay, Cyprien. Dictionnaire généalogique des familles canadiennes : depuis la fondation de la colonie jusqu'à nos jours. Montréal : E. Senécal, 1871–90. 7 v.   **AJ73**

Repr.: N.Y. : AMS Pr., 1969.

1st ser., v. 1, 1608–1700; 2nd ser., v. 2–7, 1701–1763.

The 2nd series includes some entries later than 1763 (belonging to a projected 3rd series).

Complément au Dictionnaire généalogique Tanguay, [par] J.-Arthur Leboeuf. (Montréal : Société Généalogique Canadienne-Française, 1957–77. 2 v. in 1).

Contents: v. 1, Première série (1957); v. 2, Nouvelle deuxième série (1977). Contains additions and corrections to Tanguay.
                                                                      CS81.T3

Latin America

Platt, Lyman De. Genealogical historical guide to Latin America. Detroit : Gale, [1978]. 273 p. (Gale genealogy and local history series, v.4).   **AJ74**

Publ. in Spanish as *Una guía genealógico-histórica de Latinamérica* (Ramona, Calif. : Acoma Books, 1978).

Aims to provide basic information for Latin American genealogical research. Covers the 20 countries of Central and South America and the Caribbean once under Spanish or Portuguese dominion. Ten chapters on common problems (research standards, ecclesiastical organization and records, paleography, research aids, etc.) are followed by chapters on the history, records and archives of the individual countries. Some countries' records are covered in greater detail than others. Indexed.   CS95.P58

EUROPE

Many annual registers of the nobility of the various countries of Europe have been published, although most were suspended or discontinued before World War II. Some of the most important were the various series of the *Gothaisches genealogisches Taschenbuch* (Gotha : Justus Perthes) issued to cover various periods from 1765–1944. They included series on the Fürstliche Häuser, Adelige Häuser, Freiherrliche Häuser, Gräfliche Häuser, etc.

Others include: *Annuaire de la noblesse de France* (Paris; London, 1843– ; title varies; publisher varies); *Noblesse belge* (Bruxelles, 1847–1941; title varies); *Annuario della nobilità italiana* (Bari, 1879–1905); *Nederlands adelsboek* ('sGravenhage, 1903–); *Sveriges ridderskap och adels kalender* (Stockholm, 1854–); *Danmarks adels Aarbog* (København, 1884–); *Anuario de la nobleza de España* (Madrid, 1908–14).

Almanach de Gotha : annuaire généalogique, diplomatique et statistique, 1763–1959/60. Gotha : Perthes, 1763–1960. Annual.   **AJ75**

Not published 1945–58.

A standard handbook in which coverage varies, with extensions and additions. For many years, until 1940, included two main sections: (1) Annuaire généalogique, which gave genealogies of the royal and princely houses of Europe, and (2) Annuaire diplomatique et statistique, which gave statistical and descriptive information about the various countries of the world, with lists of the principal executive, legislative, and diplomatic officials of each.

Publication began in 1763 as the French edition of the *Gothaischer Hof-Kalender zum Nutzen und Vergnügen eingericht*. Publisher varies: 1823–1944 by Justus Perthes.

Title varies: 1942–44, *Gothaisches Jahrbuch für Diplomatie, Verwaltung und Wirtschaft*.

Année 182, 1959/60, also called *Nouvel almanach du corps diplomatique*, issued in separately paged parts, each covering an individual country. Parts issued: Afghanistan (1960); Albanie (1960); Amérique, États-Unis (1959); Belgique (1959). These parts include general information about governmental organization, diplomatic and consular representatives, statistics, genealogies of the royal or governing houses, and biographical notices of government officials; also bibliographies.

The first section was very useful for the genealogies of the royal and princely houses of Europe up to 1940; this is now, for the most part, continued in the *Genealogisches Handbuch des Adels* (AJ79). Ceased publication.   CS27.A2

Burke's royal families of the world. London : Burke's Peerage, 1977–80. 2 v.   **AJ76**
Contents: v. 1, Europe and Latin America; v. 2, Africa and the Middle East. A third volume was planned but not published.

A work on royal genealogy. Scope is restricted to "families which have reigned, at one time or another, since the middle of the nineteenth century."—*Pref*. Entries are alphabetical by country, with a historical sketch of the monarchy and of each royal family, followed by the genealogy of that family. Bibliography and index in each volume.

Europäische Stammtafeln : Stammtafeln zur Geschichte der europäischen Staaten. Neue Folge / hrsg. von Detlev Schwennicke. Marburg : Stargardt, 1978–85. v. 1–4, 6–8 (in 9 v.; v. 1 publ. 1980). (In progress).   **AJ77**
1st ed., 1936, by Wilhelm Karl Prinz von Isenburg.
Contents: Bd. 1, Die deutschen Staaten (160 tables); Bd. 2, Die ausserdeutschen Staaten (206 tables); Bd. 3, T1.1, Herzogs- und Gräfenhäuser des Heiligen Römischen Reiches, andere europäische Fürstenhäuser (tables 1–200); Bd. 3, T 1.2, Nichtstandesgemässe und illegitime Nachkommen der regierenden Häuser Europas (tables 201–400); Bd. 3, T1.3, Andere grosse europäische Familien illegitime Nachkommen spanischer und portugiesischer Konigshäuser (tables 401–600); Bd. 4, Standesherrliche Häuser I (168 tables); Bd. 6–7, Familien des Alten Lotharingien I–II (160, 168 tables); Bd. 8, West- Mittel- und Nordeuropäische Familien (163 tables).

Offers genealogical tables, with sources indicated, of kings, rulers and noble houses of Europe. This *Neue Folge* expands and supersedes earlier editions by Wilhelm Karl Prinz von Isenburg and Frank Baron Freytag von Loringhoven.

Genealogical guide to German ancestors from East Germany and Eastern Europe / ed. by Arbeitsgemeinschaft ostdeutscher Familienforscher e.V., Herne, Germany ; tr. by Joachim O. R. Nuthack and Adalbert Goertz. AGoFF-Wegweiser, English ed. Neustadt/Aisch, Germany (West) : Degener, 1984. 158 p. : maps.   **AJ78**
Tr. of the 2nd ed. (1982) of *Wegweiser für die Forschung nach Vorfahren aus den ostdeutschen und sudetendeutschen Gebieten sowie aus den deutschen Siedlungsbebieten in Ost– und Südosteuropa.*

A section of "Supraregional information" lists family research societies, vital statistics sources, relevant archives and libraries, and various other research aids, together with suggestions for working with certain types of records or in particular localities. A "Regional information" section (with helpful maps) offers similar listings of aids and resources for genealogical research in former German territories and German settlements in Central, Eastern and Southeastern Europe. Indexed.   CS684.W4413

Genealogisches Handbuch des Adels / bearb. unter Aufsicht des Ausschusses für adelsrechtliche Fragen der deutschen Adelsverbände in Gemeinschaft mit dem Deutschen Adelsarchiv, Limburg a.d. Lahn : C. A. Starke, 1951–85. v. 1–86. : ill. (In progress).   **AJ79**
Issued in five series: the first treats the reigning houses of Europe, the others include German families only. Information is detailed, and lineage is indicated from the earliest dates.
Contents: Fürstliche Häuser (Royal houses), v. 1–12, 1951–84 (the reigning houses of Europe); Adelslexikon, v. 1–5, 1972–84, A–I; Adelige Häuser (Nobility): A, v. 1–17, 1953–83; B, v. 1–16, 1954–85; Freiherrliche Häuser (Barons): A, v. 1–13, 1952–82; B, v. 1–8, 1954–82; Gräfliche Häuser (Counts): A, v. 1–7, 1952–73; B, v. 1–4, 1953–73; v. 8–11. 1976–83.
Each volume has an index of all names in that volume; most have also an index of families in previously published volumes of their series.   CS617.G45

International register of nobility. Bruxelles : Internat. Off. of Publicity, 1955–61. 2 v.   **AJ80**
Publisher varies.
Contents: v. 1, 1955 (223 p.); v. 2, 1959–1960 (1604 p.).
Vol. 2 bears the subtitle: Dictionnaire généalogique de la noblesse européenne, and is in four parts: (1) Maisons souveraines; (2) Maisons ex-souveraines; (3) Noblesse européenne; (4) Ordres de chevalerie.
Text in French.

Ruvigny and Raineval, Melville Amadeus Henry Douglas Heddle de la Caillemotte de Massue de Ruvigny, *9th Marquis of*. Titled nobility of Europe : an international peerage, or "Who's who," of the sovereigns, princes and nobles of Europe. London : Harrison, 1914. 1598 p. : ill. (coats of arms).   **AJ81**

Repr. : London : Burke's Peerage, 1980.
Contains fairly full accounts of existing titles of nobility and biographies of living members (in 1914) of each family included in one international list, arranged alphabetically under the chief title borne by the head of the house. With a full index to surnames, variant spellings, merged titles, and titled members of a family whose names differ from that of the head of the house. Claims to be fairly complete for all British, Spanish, Belgian, and Portuguese titles; for French ducal titles; and for Austrian, German, Hungarian, Swedish, Dutch, Danish, and Finnish titles above the rank of baron.   CS404.R8

France

Arnaud, Etienne. Répertoire de généalogies françaises imprimées. [Paris] : Berger-Levrault, [1978–82]. 3 v.   **AJ82**
Provides about 150,000 references from 50,000 French family names to genealogical accounts in published genealogical sources. More than 1,400 genealogical works are cited, with references to them given in abbreviated form under the individual family names. Vol. 3, p. 73–181, is the *Supplément aux tomes 1 et 2* (i.e., A–M).
Z5305.F7A75

Aublet, Robert. Nouveau guide de généalogie. Rennes : Ouest-France, c1986. 189 p. : ill., map.   **AJ83**
A basic guide to the methods and resources for genealogical research in France. Covers the roles of archives, libraries, and government offices in the research process. Brief appendixes describe paleography, heraldry, computer genealogy, calendars, emigrant genealogy, and vital records. Bibliography; index.   CS10.A93

Bernard, Gildas. Les familles protestantes en France : XVIe siècle–1792 : guide des recherches biographiques et généalogiques. Paris : Archives nationales : Diffusé par La Documentation française, 1987. 699 p. : maps.   **AJ84**
Describes records in France that name Protestants. A personal and place name index simplifies searches for specific families and localities. Chapters on colonial records will help those tracing Protestant emigrants; bibliographies provide an introduction to the subject of Protestant family history in France.   Z5313.F8B46

———— Guide des recherches sur l'histoire des familles. Paris : Archives nationales : diffusé par La Documentation française, 1981. 335 p.   **AJ85**
Describes genealogical sources in France and indicates where these materials are found. The bibliographies list book titles about archives and records seldom cited elsewhere. No index.   Z5313.F8B47

La Chesnaye-Desbois, François Alexandre Aubert de. Dictionnaire de la noblesse ... de la France .... 3. éd. Paris : Schlesinger, 1863–76. 19 v.   **AJ86**
Repr.: Nendeln : Kraus, 1969.
Subtitle: Contenant les généalogies, l'histoire & la chronologie des familles nobles de la France, l'explication de leurs armes et l'état des grandes terres du royaume. ... On a joint à ce dictionnaire le tableau généalogique et historique des maisons souveraines de l'Europe et une notice des familles étrangères, les plus anciennes, les plus nobles

et les plus illustrés. 3.éd. entièrement refondue ... & augm. d'une table générale de tous les noms de familles, de terres, de fiefs, d'alliances cités dans le cours de l'ouvrage ... .

Vols. 1–19 in A–Z arrangement. According to Otto Henri Lorenz, *Catalogue générale de la librairie française* (AA630) the work was to extend to 22 v., with an armorial; v. 20–22 and the armorial were, however, never published.

Saffroy, Gaston. Bibliographie généalogique, héraldique et nobiliaire de la France : des origines à nos jours, imprimés et manuscrits. Paris : G. Saffroy, 1968–1988. 5 v. : ill. **AJ87**

Contents: v. 1, Généralités (nos. 1–16008); v. 2, Provinces et colonies françaises, orient latin, réfugiés (nos. 16009–33963); v. 3, Recueils généalogiques généraux, monographies familiales et études particulières (nos. 33964–52222); v. 4, Table générale: auteurs, titres anonymes, matières. v. 5, Supplement 1969–1983 (by Genevieve Saffroy).

A comprehensive classed bibliography of published and manuscript writings relating to French genealogy. Z5305.F7S22

Sereville, Etienne de. Dictionnaire de la noblesse française / Etienne de Sereville, François de Saint Simon. Paris. : Soc. Française au XX⁰ siècle, [1976?]. 1214 p. : ill. ; plates. **AJ88**

The main portion of the work is an alphabetical listing of "Notices sur les familles nobles," giving place of origin, description of arms, and a historical note on the family, documenting its elevation to noble status. Includes statistics on the French nobility in 1975; a bibliography, p. 65–89; a glossary; and an "Index des noms de terre."

Supplemented by: François de Saint Simon, *Dictionnaire de la noblesse française : supplément* (Paris : Éditions Contrepoint, 1977. 668 p.).

Offers additions and corrections to the basic volume and two new sections, "La noblesse pontificale" and "La noblesse étrangére" (i.e., titles held by French families, but originating abroad). CS587.S47

Woelmont, Henri de. Notices généalogiques. 1–8. sér. Paris : Champion, 1923–35. v. 1–8 and suppl. **AJ89**

The eight series contain notices of 1,200 noble French families, some still in existence and some extinct, giving for each: description of the arms, bibliography, brief history of the family, and the genealogy. Each volume is arranged alphabetically by family names. Each volume has its own index to all names mentioned in articles as well as those used for headings; index of family names for the set in série 8. The supplementary volume contains additions and corrections to ser. 1–4. CS583.W62

Germany

Baxter, Angus. In search of your German roots : a complete guide to tracing your ancestors in the Germanic areas of Europe. 2nd ed. Baltimore : Genealogical Pub. Co., 1991. 116 p. **AJ90**

1st ed., 1987.

Describes German records commonly used by genealogists and indicates where to find them. Best used in conjunction with Larry O. Jensen's *A genealogical handbook of German research* (AJ92) and Clifford Neal Smith and Anna Piszczan-Czaja Smith's *Encyclopedia of German-American genealogical research* (AJ22), both of which treat research methods, historical background, and information sources not included here. This edition reflects changes brought by German unification. Indexed. CS614.B39

Familiengeschichtliche Bibliographie / hrsg. unter dem Schutze der Arbeitsgemeinschaft der deutschen familien- und wappenkundlichen Vereine, 1900– . Leipzig : Zentralstelle für Familiengeschichte, 1932–79. v. 1–7, 11¹⁻³, 16¹. (In progress). **AJ91**

Repr.: v. 1–6, Wiesbaden : Sändig, 1969; v. 7, Neustadt an der Aisch : V. Degener, 1967.

Vol. 1, 1900–20, by Friedrich Wecken, is a basic volume for that period and contains 13,912 entries. Vol. 2, 1921–26, by Friedrich Wecken, comprises annual lists, the six lists totalling 8,033 entries. Vol. 3, 1927–30, by Johannes Hohlfeld, is also made up of annual lists. Vol. 4, 1931/32, 1933, 1934, by Johannes Hohlfeld. Register. Vol. 5, pt. 1, Bibliographie, 1935, by Johannes Hohlfeld; pt. 2, Bibliographie, 1897–99, by Gunther Preuss-Tantzen; pt. 3, Heraldischer Bibliographie, by Egon *Freiherr* von Berchem. Vol. 6, pt. 1–2, Bibliographie, 1936/37, by Johannes Hohlfeld; pt. 3, Gesamtregister zur familiengeschichtlichen Bibliographie 1897–1937 und zur Heraldischen Bibliographie, Bd. 1, by Johannes Hohlfeld und Fritz Ranitzsch. Vol. 7, pts. 1–7, 1938–45, by Johannes Hohlfeld. Vol. 11, pts. 1–3, 1960–62, by Heinz F. Friedrichs. Vols. 8–15 not yet published. Vol. 16, pt. 1, 1975–77, Bücher und Broschüren, by Heinz F. Friedrichs, 1979. CS610.F3

Jensen, Larry O. A genealogical handbook of German research. Rev. ed. Pleasant Grove, Utah : Jensen Publ., c1978, 1983. 2 v. (205 p.) : ill. **AJ92**

Explains the use of German sources to reconstruct families from the 17th century to the present. Emphasizes genealogical research methods and solving specific research problems. Bibliography; index. CS614.J46

Kludas, Arnold. Die Geschichte der deutschen Passagierschiffahrt. Hamburg : E. Kabel, c1986–1990. 5 v. : ill. (some col.). (Schriften des Deutschen Schiffahrtsmuseums, Bd. 18, etc.). **AJ93**

Contents: v. 1, Die Pionierjahre von 1850 bis 1890; v. 2, Expansion auf allen Meeren 1890 bis 1900; v. 3, Sprunghaftes Wachstum 1900 bis 1914; v. 4, Vernichtung und Wiedergeburt 1914 bis 1930; v. 5, Eine Ära geht zu Ende 1930 bis 1990.

A history of German passenger ship trade, 1850–1990. Contains photographs of ships with charts outlining their specifications and history. Indexed. HE601.G3K58

Kneschke, Ernst Heinrich. Neues allgemeines deutsches Adels-Lexicon im Vereine mit mehreren Historikern. Leipzig : Voigt, 1859–70. 9 v. **AJ94**

Repr.: Hildesheim : Olms, 1973.

An older biographical dictionary of the German nobility with bibliographies. Alphabetically arranged. CS617.K6

Taschenbuch für Familiengeschichtsforschung / Wolfgang Ribbe, Eckart Henning ; begründet von Friedrich Wecken. 10., erw. und verb. Aufl. Neustadt an der Aisch : Degener, 1990. 479 p. : ill. **AJ95**

A comprehensive handbook, essential for genealogical research in Germany. Manuscript and published sources are discussed as are the uses of genealogy in other disciplines. There are extensive bibliographies on the subject for Europe, North and South America. Other chapters cover terminology, chronology, paleography, genealogical symbols, heraldry, and onomastics. Addresses of archives, libraries, genealogical, and historical societies add to the work's usefulness. CS18.T36

Great Britain

Guides

Baxter, Angus. In search of your British & Irish roots : a complete guide to tracing your English, Welsh, Scottish, and Irish ancestors. Rev. and updated. Baltimore : Genealogical Pub. Co., 1989. 310 p. : ill. **AJ96**

Explains how to find British, Scottish, Irish, and Welsh records containing information about families and individuals. Bibliography; index. CS414.B38

Cox, Jane. Tracing your ancestors in the Public Record Office / Jane Cox and Timothy Padfield. 4th ed. / by Amanda Bevan and Andrea Duncan. London : H.M.S.O., 1990. 244 p. (Public Record Office handbooks, no. 19).   **AJ97**

1st ed., 1981; 3rd ed., c1983.

Briefly describes genealogical records (e.g., court and criminal records, occupational records, military records) housed at the Public Record Office. Makes brief mention of records in other repositories (e.g., census, church, and probate records).   Z5313.G69C69

Foster, Janet. British archives : a guide to archive resources in the United Kingdom / Janet Foster & Julia Sheppard. 2nd ed. N.Y. : Stockton Pr., 1989. lviii, 834 p.   **AJ98**

For annotation, *see* AK145.   CD1040.F67

Gardner, David E. Genealogical research in England and Wales / David E. Gardner, Frank Smith. Salt Lake City, Utah : Bookcraft Pub., [1956–64]. 3 v.   **AJ99**

Individual volumes have appeared in various editions: v. 1, 7th ed., 1967; v. 2, 4th ed., 1970; v. 3, 2nd ed. 1966.

Notes on the principal genealogical sources for England and Wales (but excluding Scotland and Ireland) for the period 1538 to the present are followed by chapters on birth, marriage, and death records; parish records; records of religious groups; military records; county records; apprenticeship records; poll books; etc. Vol. 3 is concerned with paleography and the reading of ancient documents.   CS414.G3

Gibson, Jeremy Sumner Wycherley. Record offices : how to find them / Jeremy Gibson and Pamela Peskett. 6th ed. Birmingham, Eng. : Federation of Family History Societies, 1993. 60 p. : chiefly maps.   **AJ100**

1st ed., 1981; 5th ed., 1991.

Lists all major record repositories in England. Includes street maps showing record offices in cities.   CD1040.G53

Harvey, Richard. Genealogy for librarians. 2nd ed. London : Library Assoc. Pub., 1992. 194 p.   **AJ101**

1st ed., 1983.

A guide to books and original records, intended for librarians providing reference service to genealogical patrons of English ancestry. Indexed.   CS9.H35

Hey, David. Family history and local history in England. London ; N.Y. : Longman, 1987. 276 p. : ill.   **AJ102**

Presents a newly popular approach to genealogy that incorporates methods and sources used by local and social historians. The chapter on the Middle Ages covers ground ignored in most recent handbooks. Bibliography; index.   CS414.H49

Kitzmiller, John M. In search of the "Forlorn hope" : a comprehensive guide to locating British regiments and their records (1640–WW I). Salt Lake City, utah : Manuscript Pub. Foundation, c1988. 2 v. (1583 p., 28 p. of plates) : ill.   **AJ103**

A guide to locating British regiments around the world. Helpful when using military records.

———. ———. Supplement (268 p.).   UA649.K56

Moulton, Joy Wade. Genealogical resources in English repositories. Columbus, Ohio : Hampton House, 1988. 614 p. : ill., maps.   **AJ104**

A guide to repositories (records offices, libraries, and family history societies) and their records of genealogical value. Arranged by county. Indexed.

———. ———. Supplement (1992) provides updated information and addresses.   Z5313.G69M94

Richardson, John. The local historian's encyclopedia. 2nd ed. New Barnet, [Eng.] : Historical Publications Ltd., 1986. [312] p. : ill.   **AJ105**

1st ed., 1974.

A guide to terms, institutions, and records. Useful in genealogical work. Bibliographies; index. Includes new section on paleography.   DA34.R53

Rogers, Colin Darlington. Tracing your English ancestors : a manual for analysing and solving genealogical problems in England and Wales, 1538 to the present day. Manchester ; N.Y. : Manchester Univ. Pr. : Distr. by St. Martin's Pr., 1989. 1 v.   **AJ106**

Explains which records and methods solve specific research problems encountered in identifying English ancestors. Bibliography; index.   CS414.R64

Steel, D. J. National index of parish registers / D.J. Steel, A.E.F. Steel, and C.W. Field. London : Soc. of Genealogists, 1966–89. v. 1–6^2, 7, 8^1, 11^1, 12. (In progress).   **AJ107**

Subtitle: A guide to Anglican, Roman Catholic and nonconformist registers before 1837, together with information on marriage licences, bishop's transcripts, and modern copies.

Editors vary.

Contents: v. 1, Sources of births, marriages and deaths before 1837, pt. 1 (1967); v. 2, Sources for nonconformist genealogy and family history (1973); v. 3, Sources for Roman Catholic and Jewish genealogy and family history, index v. 1–3 (1974); v. 4, South East England: Kent, Surrey and Sussex (1980); v. 5, South Midlands and Welsh Border, comprising the counties of Gloucestershire, Herefordshire, Oxfordshire, Shropshire, Warwickshire, and Worcestershire (1976); v. 6, North Midlands, pt. 1: Staffordshire (1982); v. 6, pt. 2, Nottinghamshire (1988); v. 7, East Anglia, Cambridgeshire, Norfolk and Suffolk (1983); v. 8, pt. 1, Berkshire (1989); v. 11, North East England, pt. 1: Durham and Northumberland (1979; 2nd ed., 1984); v. 12, Sources for Scottish genealogy and family history (1970).   CD1068.A2S8

Bibliography

Kaminkow, Marion J. Genealogical manuscripts in British libraries : a descriptive guide. Baltimore : Magna Carta Book Co., 1967. 140 p.   **AJ108**

A listing of 279 libraries with indication of whether or not they hold genealogical manuscripts. Brief notes are provided on the types of manuscripts held, and reference is made to any published guides or descriptions of the collections. Indexes of family names, of places, and of authors and subjects.   Z5305.G7K3

Marshall, George William. The genealogist's guide : reprinted from the last ed. of 1903 [i.e., 4th] with a new introduction by Anthony J. Camp. Baltimore : Genealogical Pub. Co., 1967. 880 p.   **AJ109**

Repr., 1980.

1st ed., 1879.

A standard work which provides an alphabetical index to pedigrees "contained in every important genealogical and topographical work, as well as those in many of minor importance."—*Pref.*

Continued by:

John Beach Whitmore, *A genealogical guide: an index to British pedigrees, in continuation of Marshall's "Genealogist's guide (1903)"* (London : Walford, 1953. 658 p.). Originally publ. in parts in Harleian Society *Publications* 99, 101–102, 104 (1947–53).

Geoffrey Battiscombe Barrow, *The genealogist's guide: an index to printed British pedigrees and family histories, 1950–1975* (London : Research Publ. Co.; Chicago : Amer. Libr. Assoc., 1977. 205 p.). Updates Marshall and Whitmore by including books they omitted. Cites surname and abbreviated title of source of information.

    Z5313.G69M42

Thomson, Theodore Radford. A catalogue of British family histories. [3rd ed. with addenda]. London : Research Pub. Co., [1980] ; Rutland, Vt. : Tuttle, 1981. 229 p.   **AJ110**

1st ed., 1928.

"This book purports to be a complete list of British Family Histories, that is, books written as histories of families generally acknowledged to be English, Scots, Welsh or Irish."—*Pref.* Does not include reprints from periodicals, collections of pedigrees, biographies, histories of businesses, books dealing with more than one family, or books published in America. The 1980 reprint (of 3rd ed. 1976) adds some 400 recent or previously omitted titles, with date (but rarely place) of publication. Z5315.G69T4

Dictionaries

FitzHugh, Terrick V. H. The dictionary of genealogy. 4th ed. / rev. by Susan Lumas on behalf of the Society of Genealogists. London : A. & C. Black : distr. in the U.S. by Talman, 1994. 304 p. : ill. **AJ111**

3rd ed., 1991, ed. by FitzHugh and Brian Christmas.

Contains more than 1,000 entries detailing essential information on records useful for genealogical research. CS6.F58

Smith, Frank. A genealogical gazetteer of England. Baltimore : Genealogical Pub. Co., 1968. 599 p. **AJ112**

Repr., 1982.

Subtitle: An alphabetical dictionary of places, with their location, ecclesiastical jurisdiction, population, and the date of the earliest entry in the registers of every ancient parish in England.

Effectively supersedes older works of similar content, e.g., A. M. Burke's *Key to the ancient parish registers of England and Wales* (1908). DA640.S6

Atlases

The Phillimore atlas and index of parish registers / ed. by Cecil R. Humphery-Smith. Baltimore : Genealogical Publ. Co., 1984. 282 p. : some maps in color ; 29 cm. **AJ113**

Simultaneously published: Chichester, Sussex : Phillimore & Co., 1984.

Includes reproductions of topographical maps from James Bell's *A new and comprehensive gazetteer of England and Wales* (1834).

Contains detailed maps of English parishes and dioceses, indexed for easy use. Bibliography. Essential for locating English parishes. G1816.E42P5

Compendiums

Burke, John Bernard. Burke's genealogical and heraldic history of the peerage, baronetage, and knightage. v. 1– . London : Burke, 1826– . Quadrennial. **AJ114**

Title and publisher vary.

Frequency varies: annual, 1851–1940; quadrennial (slightly irregular) since 1949.

Contents vary; 1970: Special articles; Royal family; Peerage and baronetage, arranged alphabetically by title, giving brief account of present holder of title, names of wife, children, heir, lineage, date of creation, arms (both illustration and description), residence; Archbishops and bishops; Knightage; Peerages in order of precedence, Extinct titles, etc.

The only modern peerage which gives full lineage.

The 2nd impression of this edition (1975; with abridged supplement, elimination of some special articles, but otherwise unchanged) announced that future editions are to be issued "once every generation (i.e., every fifteen to twenty years)."—*Pref.* CS420.B85

——— Genealogical and heraldic history of the colonial gentry. London : Harrison, 1891–95. 2 v. : ill. **AJ115**

Repr.: Baltimore : Genealogical Pub. Co. ; London : Heraldry Today, 1970.

Gives pedigrees and coats of arms of leading families in British Colonies. Indexed. CS425.B7

——— Genealogical history of the dormant, abeyant, forfeited, and extinct peerages of the British Empire. New ed. London : Harrison, 1883. 642 p. : coats of arms. **AJ116**

Repr.: London : Wm. Clowes for Burke's Peerage, 1969.

1st ed., 1831. CS422.B88

Cokayne, George Edward. Complete baronetage. Exeter : Pollard, 1900–1909. 5 v. and index volume. **AJ117**

Repr.: Gloucester : A. Sutton, 1983, in one volume including index.

Contents: v.1, English baronetcies, 1611–25, and Irish, 1619–25; v.2, English, Irish and Scottish, 1625–49; v.3, English, Irish and Scottish, 1649–64; v.4, English, Irish and Scottish, 1665–1707; v.5, Great Britain and Ireland, 1707–1800, and Jacobite, 1688–1788. Index volume: Index and appendix. CS424.C68

——— The complete peerage : or, A history of the House of Lords and all its members from the earliest times ... rev. and much enl. London : St. Catherine Pr., 1910 59. 13 v. in 14. **AJ118**

Compact repr.: N.Y. : St. Martin's Pr., 1984. 13 v. in 6.

Title and editors vary.

Vols. 1–5 had title *Complete peerage of England, Scotland, Ireland, Great Britain, and the United Kingdom, extant, extinct, or dormant.*

Contents: v. 1–12, 14, A–Z; v. 13 (1940), *Peerage creations and promotions from 22 Jan. 1901 to 31 Dec. 1938.*

The most complete record of the British peerage, giving full accounts, with bibliographical references to sources of information and many biographical details. Important as a supplement to biographical dictionaries as well as for genealogical information. CS421.C71

Debrett's peerage and baronetage : with Her Majesty's royal warrant holders. 1976– . Kingston upon Thames : Kelly's Directories, Ltd., 1976– . Irregular. **AJ119**

Publisher varies.

Latest ed. publ. 1990.

"Comprises information concerning the royal family, the peerage, privy counsellors, Scottish Lords of Session, baronets, and chiefs of names and clans in Scotland."—*t.p., 1976.* "In future, Debrett will be published at longer intervals than previously."—*p.14, 1976.* Users are referred to *Kelly's handbook to the titled, landed, and official classes* (AJ120) for information on the knightage and companionage.

§ Supersedes in part: *Debrett's peerage, baronetage, knightage and companionage : with Her Majesty's Royal warrant holders* (London : Kelly's Directories, 1713–1974).

Title varies slightly; editors and publishers vary.

Subtitle, 1973/74: Comprises information concerning the peerage, Privy Counsellors, baronets, knights, knights; widows, and companions of orders.

Gives biographical data, arms (illustration and description), living children, living collateral branches, predecessors, etc.

Kelly's handbook to the titled, landed, and official classes. v. 1–101. London : Kelly Directories, 1880–1977. Annual. **AJ120**

Brief biographical sketches of those who have hereditary or honorary titles; members of Parliament; government officials; landed proprietors; distinguished members of the dramatic, literary, and artistic worlds; and leaders in commerce and industry. CS419.K5

Scotland

Ferguson, Joan P. S. Scottish family histories / comp. by Joan P. S. Ferguson, assisted by Dennis Smith and Peter Wellburn. [2nd ed.]. Edinburgh : National Library of Scotland, 1986. 254 p.   **AJ121**

1st ed., 1960.

Locates copies of published works and a few manuscripts. Arranged by family name. The 2nd ed. includes holdings of the National Library.   Z5313.S4F4

Hamilton-Edwards, Gerald Kenneth Savery. In search of Scottish ancestry. 2nd ed. Chichester, Sussex : Phillimore, 1983 ; Baltimore : Genealogical Pub. Co., 1984. 252 p.   **AJ122**

A guide to the sources of Scottish genealogical information, prefaced by "An outline of Scottish history." Changes in this edition include information on new calendars, indexes, etc., and on the transfer of documents to various repositories.   CS463.H35

Moody, David. Scottish local history. London : B.T. Batsford, 1986. 178 p. : ill.   **AJ123**

Repr.: Baltimore : Genealogical Pub. Co., 1994.

Describes sources of local history and how to do research. A very good introductory guide.   DA759.M66

Sinclair, Cecil. Tracing your Scottish ancestors : a guide to ancestry research in the Scottish Record Office. Edinburgh : H.M.S.O., 1990. 153 p.   **AJ124**

Written specifically to assist in tracing ancestors through documents preserved in the Scottish Record Office, a primary location of records for family research.   CS463.S56

Clans and tartans

Adam, Frank. The clans, septs, and regiments of the Scottish Highlands. 8th ed. / rev. by Sir Thomas Innes of Learney. Edinburgh, London : Johnston and Bacon ; Baltimore : Genealogical Publ. Co., 1970. 624 p. : ill.   **AJ125**

Repr., 1975.

Includes colored plates of tartans.

Covers the history and structure of the clan system, Celtic culture, the Highland regiments, clan insignia and heraldry, clan lists and statistics, etc.   DA880.H6A6

Innes, Thomas. The tartans of the clans and families of Scotland. 8th ed. Edinburgh : Johnston & Bacon, [1971]. 300 p. : ill. (116 col. plates of tartans).   **AJ126**

1st ed., 1938.

Introductory chapters discuss the clan system, order of succession, etc., followed by clans arranged alphabetically, with one-page histories, and colored plates of the tartans.   DA880.H76I5

Wales

Rawlins, Bert J. The parish churches and nonconformist chapels of Wales : their records and where to find them. Salt Lake City, Utah : Celtic Heritage Research, c1987. v. 1 : ill., maps. (In progress?).   **AJ127**

Contents: v. 1, Carmarthenshire, Cardiganshire, and Pembrokeshire.

Lists Church of England parishes and nonconformist chapels. Provides brief notes about the history and records of each parish or chapel, and includes numerous photographs. Bibliography; denominational index; general index. More comprehensive than C.J. Williams's *Parish registers of Wales* (AJ130).   CD1068.A2R39

Richards, Melville. Welsh administrative and territorial units, medieval and modern. Cardiff : Univ. of Wales Pr., 1969. 228 p., 229–324 p. of 104 maps.   **AJ128**

Intended to locate units of civil administration at various periods in the history of Wales. Maps indicate medieval and modern boundaries for the shires.   JS4012.L7R5

Welsh family history : a guide to research / ed. by John Rowlands [et al.]. [Aberystwyth] : Assoc. of Family History Societies of Wales in conjunction with the Federation of Family History Societies, 1994. 316 p. : ill., facims., maps.   **AJ129**

A comprehensive guide to family history research in Wales.

Williams, C. J. Cofrestri plwyf Cymru = Parish registers of Wales / comp. by C.J. Williams & J. Watts-Williams. [Aberystwyth, Dyfed] : National Library of Wales & Welsh County Archivists' Group in association with the Society of Genealogists, 1986. 217 p., [12] p. of plates : ill.   **AJ130**

Identifies Church of England parishes in Wales, the time periods covered by their records, and where records are kept. County maps show parishes but not their boundaries. Index.   CD1068.A2W55

Ireland

Burke's Irish family records / Ed., Hugh Montgomery-Massingberd. [5th ed.]. London : Burke's Peerage ; N.Y. : distr. by Arco Pub. Co., 1976. 1237 p.   **AJ131**

1st ed., 1899.

Represents a change of title for *Burke's landed gentry of Ireland* issued in four editions, 1899–1958.

Contains "genealogical histories of 514 Irish families from their earliest recorded male ancestor down to the present day, set out in narrative style, with biographical entries for each member of the family."—*Contents*. Does not supersede earlier editions since not every family appearing in preceding editions is contained herein.   CS482.B87

Grenham, John. Tracing your Irish ancestors : the complete guide. Baltimore : Genealogical Pub. Co., 1993. 281 p. : maps.   **AJ132**

Originally publ. Dublin : Gill and Macmillan, 1992.

A very comprehensive and authoritative guide for researchers of Irish family history.   CS483.G74

Helferty, Seamus. Directory of Irish archives / ed. by Seamus Helferty and Raymond Refaussé. 2nd ed. Dublin : Irish Academic Pr., 1993. 112 p.   **AJ133**

1st ed., 1988.

Lists addresses of record offices, libraries, and genealogical offices.   CD1101.D57

Irish genealogy : a record finder / ed. by Donal F. Begley. Dublin, Ireland : Heraldic Artists, c1981. 256 p. : ill.   **AJ134**

A guide to Irish sources, particularly the census, census substitutes, and directories. Includes information on surname locations and cemetary inscriptions.   CS483.I74

MacLysaght, Edward. Irish families : their names, arms, and origins. 4th ed. Blackrock, Co. Dublin : Irish Academic Pr., 1985. 366 p. : ill.   **AJ135**

MacLysaght's *More Irish families* ([rev. and enl. ed.]; 1982. 254 p.) is "in effect an enlarged second volume" of the 3rd ed. of *Irish families*, consisting of the author's *More Irish families* (1960) and *Supplement* to *Irish families* (1964) "carefully revised and in many cases added to, all the entries [now] integrated into the text."—*Pref.* An essay on the Irish chieftainries and additions to the first volume is included. Indexed.   CS498.M3

Mitchell, Brian. A guide to Irish parish registers. Baltimore : Genealogical Pub. Co., 1988. 134 p.   **AJ136**

Contains charts that facilitate identification of taxing districts and parishes in Ireland. Charts, arranged by country, are keyed to: (1) maps in Mitchell's *A new genealogical atlas of Ireland* (AJ137), and (2) maps prepared by the National Library of Ireland for use with the principal collection of Irish land tax records, called "Griffith's" or "Primary valuation of Ireland." The tax records themselves, some parish records, and the National Library maps are available in microfilm copy at several libraries in the U.S. and Britain.   CD1118.5.A1M58

——————— A new genealogical atlas of Ireland. Baltimore : Genealogical Pub. Co., 1986. 123 p. ; 26 cm.   **AJ137**
An atlas of church and civil jurisdictions in Ireland and Northern Ireland. Includes brief descriptions of sources created by church and state that are essential to the study of genealogy in Ireland. No index; meant to be used "in conjunction with ... *General alphabetical index to the town lands and towns, parishes, and baronies of Ireland* [Dublin : Tham, 1861; repr. Baltimore : Genealogical Pub. Co., 1984]."—*Introd.*   G1831.F7M5

Ryan, James G. Irish records : sources for family & local history. Salt Lake City, Utah : Ancestry, c1988. 562 p. : ill., maps.   **AJ138**
Indicates content and whereabouts of family history/genealogical sources in the Republic of Ireland and Northern Ireland. Bibliographies and index.   Z5313.I7R83

Italy

Spreti, Vittorio. Enciclopedia storico-nobiliare italiana : famiglie nobili e titolate viventi riconosciute dal R. governo d'Italia compresi: città, communità, mense vescovili, abazie, parrocchie ed enti nobili c titolati riconosciuti. Milano : Ed. Encic. Stor.–Nob. Ital., 1928–35. 6 v. and Appendix, v. 1–2. : ill.   **AJ139**
Repr.: Bologna : Forni, 1981.
A historical biographical encyclopedia of titled Italian families.
Supplemented by: *Saggio di bibliografia araldica italiana : supplemento a l'Enciclopedia storico-nobiliare italiana,* by Vittorio Spreti and Giustiniano degli Azzi Vitalleschi (1936. 230 p. Repr.: Bologna, Forni, 1974). A bibliography of Italian heraldry and nobility.   CS757.S7

Spain

Instituto Internacional de Genealogía y Heráldica. Índice nobiliario español / recop. y redac. por Vicente de Cardenas y Vicent [et al.]. Madrid : Ed. Hidalguía, 1955. 754 p.   **AJ140**
Brief listings of the Spanish nobility indicating titles, etc., and a section on military orders, societies of nobles, etc.
——————. ——————— *Supplemento 1957–1960,* recop. y redac. por el Barón de Cobos de Belchite. (Madrid : Ed. hidalguía, 1960. 87 p.).

Ryskamp, George R. Tracing your Hispanic heritage. Riverside, Calif. : Hispanic Family History Research, 1984. 954 p. : ill.   **AJ141**
Includes sections for: (1) Techniques and principles: organizing and evaluating information, language, handwriting, names, etc.; (2) Record types (church, civil, census, military, etc.); (3) Spain (geography, archives, reference works on Spain). Glossary; data forms; abbreviations; index. Concerns genealogy research chiefly in Spain, but includes examples and descriptions for many Hispanic countries. Numerous bibliographical references.

Switzerland

Familiennamenbuch der Schweiz = Répertoire des noms de famille suisses = Register of Swiss surnames / bearb. im Auftrag der Schweizerischen Gesellschaft für Familienforschung von der Arbeitsgemeinschaft Schweizer Familiennamen, Emil und Clothilde Meier ... [et. al.]. 3., verb. und korrigierte Aufl. Zürich : Schulthess, c1989. 3 v. (2082 p.).   **AJ142**
A register of Swiss surnames from a 1962 survey. Identifies communities where each surname was found and other towns where the name existed in the past. No bibliography or index.   CS2625.F34

ASIA

Israel

Sack, Sallyann Amdur. A guide to Jewish genealogical research in Israel. Baltimore : Genealogical Pub. Co., 1987. 110 p. : ill., maps.   **AJ143**
Spine title: *Genealogical research in Israel.*
Designed for those of Ashkenazi descent visiting Israel to do genealogical research. Provides detailed instruction on how to find and use genealogical sources in Israel. No bibliography or index.   Z6374.B5S23

AUSTRALIA AND OCEANIA

Australia

Vine Hall, Nick. Tracing your family history in Australia : a guide to sources. 2nd ed. Adelaide, Australia : Rigby, 1994. 657 p. . ill.   **AJ144**
1st ed., 1985.
An excellent guide to research materials for Australia. Arranged by record type for each state. Truly a national guide, covering all states and territories of European settlement as well as dealing with records of indigenous peoples. Includes addresses of record repositories.   CS2002.V56

New Zealand

Bromell, Anne. Tracing family history in New Zealand. Wellington, N.Z. : Govt. Print. Off., 1988. 196 p. : ill.   **AJ145**
Excellent basic guide for New Zealand genealogy.   CS2172.B77

JEWISH

Zubatsky, David S. Jewish genealogy : a sourcebook of family histories and genealogies / David S. Zubatsky, Irwin M. Berent. N.Y. : Garland, 1984–1990. 2 v. (Garland reference library of social science, 214, 510).   **AJ146**
Vol. 2 by Zubatsky only.
Aims to provide a comprehensive listing of sources, published and unpublished, for Jewish genealogies, family histories, and individual family names. A bibliography of general works is followed by an

alphabetical listing of family names with citations to genealogies, family histories, family trees, etc.; includes many references to papers in foreign archives (mainly English and Israeli), but not to private collections. Numerous cross-references.   Z6374.B5B47

HERALDRY

Bolton, Charles Knowles. Bolton's American armory : a record of coats of arms which have been in use within the present bounds of the United States. Boston : Faxon, 1927. 223 p.   **AJ147**
Repr.: Baltimore : Genealogical Pub. Co., 1969.   CR1209.B6

Boutell, Charles. Boutell's heraldry. [Rev. ed.] / rev. by J. P. Brooke-Little. London : N.Y. : Warne, [1983]. 368 p. : ill.
AJ148
Based on Boutell's *Manual of heraldry* (1863) and *English heraldry* (1867).
A standard work covering all aspects of the subject. Minor revisions and updating in this edition. A new chapter, "How to use arms," one on recent trends, and a revised critical bibliography are included.
CR21.B7

Burke, John Bernard. The general armory of England, Scotland, Ireland, and Wales : comprising a registry of armorial bearings from the earliest to the present time. With a supplement. London : Harrison, 1884. 1185 p. : ill.   **AJ149**
Repr.: London : Wm. Clowes for Burke's Peerage, 1961; Baltimore : Genealogical Publ. Co., 1976.
An enlarged edition (first publ. 1842) of *Encyclopaedia of heraldry : or, General armory of England, Scotland, and Ireland*, published in many editions. Lists names alphabetically, giving for each a blazon and brief explanatory text. Has glossary and a few sample black-and-white coats of arms.
Supplemented by: Cecil R. Humphery-Smith, *General armory two : Alfred Morant's additions and corrections to Burke's general armory* (London : Tabard Pr., 1973; Baltimore : Genealogical Publ. Co., 1974. 230 p.).
Contains all the "extra material and corrections"—*(Introd).* that Morant made to the original work and an appendix of names and information on coats of arms drawn from sources later than Burke and Morant.   CR1619.B73

Burke's family index. London : Burke's Peerage Ltd. : distr. by Arco Publ. Co., N.Y., 1976. 171 p. : ill.   **AJ150**
"Provides a guide to the most complete and up-to-date version of a family's narrative pedigree in a Burke's publication since 1826."—*p. xxxi.* Includes "A bibliography of Burke's, 1826–1976," by Rosemary Pinches, p. xii–xxx.   Z5305.G7B87

Fairbairn, James. Book of crests of the families of Great Britain and Ireland. 4th ed. / rev. and enl. by A. C. Fox-Davies. Edinburgh : Jack, 1905. 2 v. : ill.   **AJ151**
1st ed., 1859; rev. ed., 1860, in 2 v. (American ed.: N.Y., 1911 had title *Fairbairn's crests*).
Frequently reprinted.
A volume of plates with an index to crests arranged by surnames; a glossary; and a section of mottoes.   CR57.G7F2

Fox-Davies, Arthur Charles. Armorial families : a directory of gentlemen of coat-armour. 7th ed. London : Hurst and Blackett, 1929. 2 v. : ill.   **AJ152**
Repr.: Rutland Vt. : Tuttle, 1970; Newton Abbot : David & Charles, 1970.
Arranged by families with descriptions of coats of arms, mottoes, etc.   CR1618.F6

——————— The book of public arms : a complete encyclopaedia of all royal, territorial, municipal, corporate, official and impersonal arms. New ed., containing over 1300 drawings. London ; Edinburgh : Jack, 1915. 876 p. : ill.   **AJ153**
CR492.F7

——————— A complete guide to heraldry. [New ed.] / rev. and annotated by J. P. Brooke-Little. London : Nelson, 1969. 513 p. : ill.   **AJ154**
Founded upon the author's *Art of heraldry* (1904; repr.: London : Orbis, 1985). First published 1909. Later reprintings with revisions by C. A. H. Franklyn.
An annotated edition rather than a revision of Fox-Davies's original text. The editor has tried, "by detailing twentieth-century official heraldic practice, to make the book as valuable to the student of heraldry today as when it was first published," with the added advantage that "the reader will be able to see exactly how heraldry and heraldic thought has evolved during the past half century."—*Pref.* Only obvious anachronisms in the text have been changed.   CR21.F73

Haydn, Joseph Timothy. The book of dignities ... . 3rd ed. London : W.H. Allen, 1894. 1170 p.   **AJ155**
Repr.: Baltimore : Genealogical Publ. Co., 1970.
1st ed., 1851.
Subtitle: Containing lists of the official personages of the British Empire, civil, diplomatic, heraldic, judicial, ecclesiastical, municipal, naval and military ... with the sovereigns and rulers of the world from the foundation of their respective states; the orders of knighthood of the United Kingdom and India, etc.   DA34.H3

Henning, Eckart. Bibliographie zur Heraldik : Schrifttum Deutschlands und Österreichs bis 1980 / by Eckart Henning and Gabriele Jochums. Köln : Böhlau, 1984. 1 v. (Bibliographie der historischen Hilfswissenschaften, Bd.1).   **AJ156**
Presents an extensive systematic bibliography of books and articles on the basis, history and law of heraldry and on the arms of Germany and Austria, their provinces, counties, cities, towns, and families. Author, subject, and name indexes.

Innes, Thomas. Scots heraldry. [New ed.] / rev. by Malcolm R. Innes. London : Johnston and Bacon, 1978. 131 p. : ill.
AJ157
1st ed., 1934; 2nd ed., 1956.   CR1652.I5

Jougla de Morenas, Henri. Grand armorial de France : catalogue général des armoiries des familles nobles de France. Paris : Éd. Héraldiques, 1934–49. 6 v. : ill.   **AJ158**
——————. ——————. *Supplément.* (Paris : Soc. du Grand Armorial de France, 1952. 447 p. ill.).

Louda, Jiří. Lines of succession : heraldry of the royal families of Europe / tables by Jiří Louda ; text by Michael Maclagan. 2nd ed. N.Y. : Macmillan, 1991. 300 p. : ill. (some col.), maps.   **AJ159**
1st ed., 1981, titled *Heraldry of the royal families of Europe*.
Covers the genealogy of royal families of Europe and includes detailed lineage arranged by country, coats of arms, and heraldic shields of all European royal families.   CR1605.L68

Rietstap, Johannes Baptist. Armorial général : armoiries des familles contenues dans l'Armorial général. Paris : Inst. Héraldique Universel, 1903–26. 6 v. : ill.   **AJ160**
Vols. 5–6 have imprint: La Haye : Nijhoff, 1921–26.
Plates of coats of arms (blazons) described in Rietstap's *Armorial générale* (AJ161), arranged in alphabetical order.
A 3rd ed. with text in English was published as *General illustrated armorial*, by V. and H. Rolland (Lyon : Soc. de Sauvegarde Historique, [1953?]. 6 v.). Repr. as: *V. & H. Rolland's illustrations to the Armorial générale* (Baltimore : Heraldic Book Co., 1967).
CR1179.R55

———————— Armorial général : précédé d'un Dictionnaire des termes du blason. 2. éd., refondue et augm. Gouda : van Goor, [1884]–87. 2 v. : ill.   **AJ161**

Repr.: N.Y. : Barnes & Noble, 1965.

Publisher varies.

A general work on European arms, dealing with more than 100,000 families entitled to hereditary honors.

————. ———— Supplément, par V. [and] H. Rolland (La Haye : Nijhoff, 1926–54. 7 v. in 8). The supplements include both illustrations and blazons. Vol. 1–2 issued in 36 parts, 1904–26; v. 2 bound in 2 v. An index to v. 1–6 of the *Supplément* was issued as *Table du supplément*, par Henri Rolland (Lyon : Soc. de Sauvegarde Historique, 1951. 1 v., unpaged). The 6 v. of the *Supplément* (bound as 7) are called v. 1–7 in the index.   CR1179.R52

Terminology

Brooke-Little, John Philip. An heraldic alphabet. New and rev. ed. London : Macdonald and Jane's, [1975]. 226 p. : ill.   **AJ162**

Definitions prefaced by an essay on heraldry as "seen through the eyes of a herald rather than purely historically or academically."— *Foreword.* Recommended as an inexpensive substitute for libraries unable to afford Julian Franklyn and John Tanner's *Encyclopaedic dictionary of heraldry* (AJ163). This edition includes corrections, additions, and some new illustrations.   CR13.B76

Franklyn, Julian. An encyclopaedic dictionary of heraldry / Julian Franklyn, John Tanner. Oxford ; N.Y. : Pergamon, [1970]. 367 p. : ill.   **AJ163**

Provides definitions of terms employed in heraldry, usually with some indication of usage. Major terms used in foreign heraldry are also included.   CR13.F7

Parker, James. A glossary of terms used in heraldry. New ed. Rutland, Vt. : Tuttle, [1970]. 659 p. : ill.   **AJ164**

"Originally published in 1894 and based on H. Gough's A glossary of terms used in British heraldry, which was published in 1847."—*L.C. card.*

Still one of the more useful glossaries.   CR1618.G6

Stalins, Gaston Ferdinand Laurent. Vocabulaire-atlas héraldique en six langues : français-English-deutsch-español-italiano-Nederlandsch / par le baron Stalins avec la collaboration de René le Juge de Segrais ... [et al.]. Paris : Soc. du Grand Armorial de France, 1952. 119 p. : ill.   **AJ165**

At head of title: Académie Internationale d'héraldique.

Pt. 1 (p. 10–39) gives the principal terms used in heraldry, in six languages, in table form and numbered; the numbers correspond to the illustrations in the plates. Pt. 2 (p. 42–71) gives an alphabetical listing of terms for each of the six languages, with the number of its representation in the plates. Pt. 3 (p. 75–119) consists of 23 black-and-white plates, each containing several small but clear figures representing the heraldic terms in pts. 1–2. A clear, concise guide to heraldic terminology.   CR13.S8

NAMES

Bibliography

Smith, Elsdon Coles. Personal names : a bibliography. N.Y. : New York Pub. Libr., 1952. 226 p.   **AJ166**

Repr.: Detroit : Gale, 1965.

Reprinted from the *Bulletin* of the New York Public Library, 1950–51.

A classified bibliography of 3,415 monographs and periodical articles on names, with brief, critical annotations. Library locations are given. Alphabetical index.   Z6824.S55

Personal Names

Bahlow, Hans. Unsere Vornamen im Wandel der Jahrhunderte. Limburg a.d. Lahn : Starke, 1965. 113 p. (Grundriss der Genealogie, 4).   **AJ167**

Indicates derivation and changes in form of given names; cross-references are provided from variant forms.   CS2375.G3B26

Chuks-orji, Ogonna. Names from Africa : their origin, meaning, and pronunciation / Ogonna Chuks-orji ; ed. and with a commentary by Keith E. Baird. Chicago : Johnson, 1972. 89 p.   **AJ168**

A dictionary of given names, indicating pronunciation, meaning, language and country of origin.   CS2375.A33C48

Dunkling, Leslie. Everyman's dictionary of first names / by Leslie Dunkling and William Gosling. London : Dent, [1983]. 304 p.   **AJ169**

Publ. in U.S. as *The Facts on File dictionary of first names* (N.Y., 1984).

In addition to explaining where various first names come from, the dictionary indicates "when they have been most used, and if possible, why they were most used at that particular time."—*Introd.* Includes references to other name dictionaries, to literary uses, popularity of a name occasioned by film stars and other prominent personalities, diminutive forms, cross-references, etc. Information on popularity and continued use of specific names was derived from numerous surveys and sources cited in the introduction. "Since this dictionary has some 4,500 entries, dealing with more than 10,000 names, we feel justified in claiming that the first names borne by at least 95% of the English-speaking population are in this book."   CS2367.D837

Egger, Carl. Lexicon nominum virorum et mulierum. 2. ed. Romae : Studium, [1963]. 263 p.   **AJ170**

A dictionary of personal names, each given in Italian, French, Spanish, English and German, with their Latin equivalents and etymologies.   P769.E3

Kolatch, Alfred J. Complete dictionary of English and Hebrew first names. Middle Village, N.Y. : Jonathan David, [1984]. 488 p.   **AJ171**

1st ed., 1948, had title: *These are the names*; rev. ed. 1967 entitled *The name dictionary.*

Masculine and feminine names are given in separate alphabets. Hebrew characters are included for the Hebrew names.   CS2367.K63

———————— The Jonathan David dictionary of first names. Middle Village, N.Y. : Jonathan David, [1980]. 1 v.   **AJ172**

A more comprehensive list than the author's *Complete dictionary of English and Hebrew first names* (AJ171); i.e., not restricted to Hebrew names. Gives meaning and etymology, variant forms, contemporary examples, etc. Masculine and feminine names in separate alphabets.   CS2367.K64

Loughead, Flora Haines Apponyi. Dictionary of given names, with origins and meanings. 2nd ed. rev. and corr. Glendale, Calif. : A. H. Clark, 1958 [c1933]. 248 p.   **AJ173**

1st ed., 1933.   CS2367.L

Puckett, Newbell Niles. Black names in America : origins and usage / ed. by Murray Heller. Boston : G. K. Hall, [1975]. 561 p.   **AJ174**

At head of title: Newbell Niles Puckett Memorial gift, John G. White Department, Cleveland Public Library.

Chapters 1–4 offer background material, chronological and regional lists of names, and various types of statistics. Chapter 5 is a "Dictionary of African origins." There is also an "Index of unusual names" and a bibliography of principal sources.

§ *See also* Ihechukwu Madubuike, *A handbook of African names* (AJ188).   E185.89.N3P82

Stewart, George Rippey. American given names : their origin and history in the context of the English language. N.Y. : Oxford Univ. Pr., 1979. 264 p.   **AJ175**

A historical sketch of the use, frequency, etc., of given names in America is followed by a dictionary arrangement (p. 43–258) of selected names, indicating whether each is usually applied to male or female, the language from which derived, meaning, and (in most cases) a "history" of the name as it occurs in U.S. usage, with indication of popularity, etc.

A contemporary review concluded that this is "the best available reference book on American personal nomenclature."—*Booklist* 76 : 997–98.   CS2375.U6S74

Wells, Evelyn. What to name the baby : (a treasury of names). 15,000 names to choose from. Garden City, N.Y. : Doubleday, [1953]. 326 p.   **AJ176**

1st ed., 1946, had title *A treasury of names*.

A useful guide for quick reference to foreign equivalents of American forenames.

§ Another dictionary of this type, addressed "to the general, rather than to the learned, public" (*Author's note*), is Eric Partridge's *Name this child* (3rd ed., rev. & much enl. London : H. Hamilton, 1951. 296 p.); it is a dictionary of British and American given or Christian names.   CS2367.W43

Withycombe, Elizabeth Gidley. The Oxford dictionary of English Christian names. 3rd ed. Oxford ; N.Y. : Clarendon Pr., [1977]. 310 p.   **AJ177**

1st ed., 1945.

"The present edition contains about forty names not included in the previous editions, as well as a number of new cross-references. The main work of revision, as before, consists of many small corrections, emendations, and additions to existing articles, many of which reflect the changes in usage, frequency, and status of names…"—*Pref.* Gives sources for earliest usage.   CS2375.G7.W5

Woods, Richard D. Hispanic first names : a comprehensive dictionary of 250 years of Mexican-American usage. Westport, Conn. : Greenwood, [1984]. 224 p. (Bibliographies and indexes in anthropology, 1).   **AJ178**

For each name or variant the appropriate parent form was determined and under this form (or "main entry") is given the full information: phonetic transcription, gender, English equivalent (if any), derivation or meaning, diminutives and variants. *See* references are provided from all variant forms.   CS2375.U6W66

Yonge, Charlotte Mary. History of Christian names. New ed. rev. London : Macmillan, 1884. 476 p.   **AJ179**

Repr.: Detroit : Gale, 1966.

1st ed., 1863.

Contains a glossary of Christian names (*Preface*, p. 19–144) which gives the meaning and refers to the body of the book where a full description will be found with derivations, forms in various languages, etc.   CS2367.Y6

Nicknames

Sifakis, Carl. The dictionary of historic nicknames : a treasury of more than 7,500 famous and infamous nicknames from world history. N.Y. : Facts on File, [1984]. 566 p.   **AJ180**

Nicknames and real names are interfiled in a single alphabet, the nickname providing a *see* reference to the real name (where full information regarding origin of the nickname is given). An index groups the names by occupation or other identifying category.   CT108.S53

Twentieth century American nicknames / ed. by Laurence Urdang ; comp.by Walter C. Kidney and George C. Kohn. N.Y. : Wilson, 1979. 398 p.   **AJ181**

Nicknames and the formal names of persons, places, etc., are entered in a single alphabet; variant nicknames are given with the entry.   CT108.T83

Surnames

British and American

Cottle, Basil. The Penguin dictionary of surnames. 2nd ed. [London] : Allen Lane, [1978]. 444 p.   **AJ182**

1st ed., 1967.

Concerned with surnames of the British Isles and those of British ethnic stock in the Commonwealth and the U.S. This edition enlarged from about 8,000 to about 12,000 names.   CS2505.C67

Hanks, Patrick. A dictionary of surnames / Patrick Hanks and Flavia Hodges ; special consultant for Jewish names, David L. Gold. Oxford ; N.Y. : Oxford Univ. Pr., 1988. 826 p.   **AJ183**

Provides the origin and meaning of nearly 70,000 surnames in the English-speaking world.   CS2385.H27

Reaney, Percy Hide. A dictionary of British surnames. 2nd ed. with corrections and additions by R. M. Wilson. London : Routledge and K. Paul, 1976. 398 p.   **AJ184**

1st ed., 1958.

Gives etymologies, origins, different forms, and references to sources. Now includes about 10,700 entries. To some extent supersedes Charles W. Bardsley, *Dictionary of English and Welsh surnames* (London : Frowde, 1901. 837 p.), although this may still be useful.   CS2385.R4

————— The origin of English surnames. London : Routledge & K. Paul ; N.Y. : Barnes & Noble, [1967]. 415 p.   **AJ185**

Repr., 1980.

Aims "to give a general account of the development of English surnames, their classification, changes in pronunciation and spelling, and the gradual growth of hereditary family names."—*Pref.* Based largely on the author's *Dictionary of British surnames* (AJ184), but with the addition of some new material.   CS2505.R4

Smith, Elsdon Coles. New dictionary of American family names. N.Y. : Harper & Row, [1972]. 570 p.   **AJ186**

An earlier edition (1956) had title: *Dictionary of American family names*. The new edition is greatly enlarged and, in addition to the most common American surnames, includes many less common but interesting names. Indicates national origin and meaning of the name without attempt to provide etymological origins and bibliographic references.

§ The same author's *American surnames* (Philadelphia : Chilton, 1969) offers a running account of the origins of the most common American family names, with special attention to social conditions and customs surrounding the adoption of surnames in England and in Europe.   CS2481.S55

Woods, Richard D. Spanish surnames in the Southwestern United States : a dictionary / Richard Donovon Woods, Grace Alvarez-Altman. Boston : G. K. Hall, [1978]. 154 p.   **AJ187**

Gives information on origin and meaning of the more common Spanish surnames found in the Southwest. Sources of information are cited.   CS2745.W66

African

Madubuike, Ihechukwu. A handbook of African names. Wash. : Three Continents Pr., [1976]. 233 p. **AJ188**

The author acknowledges that "the work in its present form and content is tentative."—*Pref.* Sections are devoted to specific ethnic groups, and a brief discussion of naming conventions and practices for each is followed by a selected list of typical names and their meanings. There is an "Alphabetical list of some African names," p. 181–227.

CS375.A33M3

French

Dauzat, Albert. Dictionnaire étymologique des noms de famille et prénoms de France. Édition rev. et augm. / par Marie-Thérèse Morlet. Paris : Larousse, [1980]. 624 p. **AJ189**

Cover title: Noms et prénoms de France.

Frequently reprinted.

Reprint of the 1951 ed. with a new supplement, p. 605–[26.].

CS2691.D3

Gonzalez, Pierre-Gabriel. Le livre d'or des noms de famille. Alleur, Belgique : Marabout, c1990. 507 p. : ill. **AJ190**

Lists more than 10,000 surnames of French derivation, giving places they are most often found.

Le petit Robert 2 : dictionnaire universel des noms propres alphabétique et analogique / sous la direction de Paul Robert ; rédaction dirigée par Alain Rey. Nouv. éd. rev., corr. et mise à jour. Paris : Le Robert, c1987. 1952 p. : ill. (some col.). **AJ191**

First published 1974. 3rd ed., 1977 (frequently reprinted; 1983 called 8th ed.).

An abridgment of Robert's *Dictionnaire universel des noms propres, alphabétique et analogique*, ed. by Alain Rey and Josette Rey-Debove (Paris : Société du Nouveau Littérature, 1974. 6 v.), forming a companion volume to the language dictionary commonly known as *Le petit Robert* (Paris : Le Robert, 1984. 2171 p.).

AG5.P53

German

Bach, Adolf. Deutsche Namenkunde. Heidelberg : C. Winter, 1952–1956. 3 v. in 5 : ill. **AJ192**

Bd. 1 is devoted to personal names; for complete annotation, *see* CL189.

PF3576.B33

Bahlow, Hans. Deutsches Namenlexikon : Familien- und Vornamen nach Ursprung und Sinn erklärt. [Neu bearb.]. Bayreuth : Gondrom, [1980]. 576 p. **AJ193**

Frequently reprinted, showing minor changes in text and updated bibliography. 1984 (Frankfurt : Suhrkamp. 598 p.) called 7th ed.

Includes family names, forenames, and some place-names. 15,000 entries.

CS2541.B3

Brechenmacher, Josef Karlmann. Etymologisches Wörterbuch der deutschen Familiennamen. 2., von Grund auf neubearb. Aufl. der "Deutschen Sippennamen". Limburg/Lahn : Starke, 1957–63. 2 v. (Sippenbücherei, Bd. 5–9). **AJ194**

Also issued in 21 parts, 1957–63.

The most comprehensive dictionary of German family names, including more than 28,500 names.

CS2545.B73

Gottschald, Max. Deutsche Namenkunde : Unsere Familiennamen nach ihrer Entstehung und Bedeutung. 4. ufl. / Mit e. Nachw. u. e. bibliograph. Nachtr. von Rudolf Schützeichel. Berlin : de Gruyter, 1971. 646 p. **AJ195**

1st ed., 1932; 3rd ed., 1954.

Gives origins and meanings of German surnames. CS2545.G6

Jones, George Fenwick. German-American names. Baltimore : Genealogical Pub. Co., c1990. 268 p. : ill. **AJ196**

A dictionary of German given and surnames, including spelling variations found in North America. A 60-page introduction discusses the origins of German names and how they were changed when their bearers emigrated to the U.S.

CS2487.J66

Irish

MacLysaght, Edward. Surnames of Ireland. 6th ed. [Dublin] : Irish Academic Pr., [1985]. 312 p. : map. **AJ197**

1st ed., 1964, had title *Guide to Irish surnames.*

Presents "an epitome of essential facts" (*Pref.*) contained in the "Irish families" series. Brief entries give origin, meaning and principal locality of name, often with reference to longer treatment in the author's *Irish families* (AJ135). There has been little change from edition to edition.

CS2411.M25

Italian

De Felice, Emidio. Dizionario dei cognomi italiani. Milano : Mondadori, 1978. 351 p. (Gli Oscar studio, 59). **AJ198**

Lists surnames with variants, totaling more than 14,000 names, and giving derivation, geographic origin, and distribution. Indexed.

CS2715.F44

Fucilla, Joseph Guerin. Our Italian surnames. Evanston, Ill. : Chandler's, 1949. 299 p. **AJ199**

Includes bibliographies. CS2715.F8

Jewish

Kaganoff, Benzion C. A dictionary of Jewish names and their history. N.Y. : Schocken Books, [1977]. 250 p. **AJ200**

The "history," p. 1–115, is concerned with both first names and family names; the "Dictionary of selected Jewish names," p. 117–211, gives brief information on the origin and meaning of family names. Indexes of names and of subjects.

CS3010.K28

Singerman, Robert. Jewish and Hebrew onomastics : a bibliography. N.Y. : Garland, 1977. 132 p. **AJ201**

Presents "the first attempt at bringing under bibliographic control all significant literature on the etymology, history and folklore of Jewish and Hebrew personal names."—*Introd.* Lists books, parts of books and articles concerning biblical, ancient, and modern names of many countries. 1,195 entries. Indexed. Z6824.S5

Portuguese

Guérios, Rosário Farâni Mansur. Dicionário etimológico de nomes e sobrenomes. 2. ed., rev. e ampl. São Paulo : Editora Ave Maria, 1973. 231 p. **AJ202**

1st ed., 1949.

An introductory essay on names (p.13–43) precedes the dictionary section. Includes both given names and surnames. CS2761.G8

Russian

Benson, Morton. Dictionary of Russian personal names : with a guide to stress and morphology. [2nd ed., rev.]. Philadelphia : Univ. of Pennsylvania Pr., [1967]. 175 p.   **AJ203**
    1st ed., 1964.
    A chapter on the stress and declension of surnames is followed by a list of surnames with accents; a chapter on Russian given names with lists and explanations of diminutives; and a brief bibliography. Only minor changes and corrections in this edition.   CS2811.B4

Unbegaun, Boris Ottokar. Russian surnames. Oxford : Clarendon Pr., 1972. 529 p.   **AJ204**
    Aims "to discuss the modern system of Russian surnames in both its morphological and its semantic aspects."—*Pref*. Historical data are included "whenever they throw useful light on the modern system," but the work is not a history of Russian surnames. More than 10,000 surnames are cited. Bibliography; indexes of all quoted surnames and of surname-terminations.   PG2576.U5

Scottish

Black, George Fraser. The surnames of Scotland : their origin, meaning, and history. N.Y. : New York Pub. Libr., 1962. 838 p.   **AJ205**
    Repr. from the New York Public Library *Bulletin*, Aug. 1943–Sept. 1946.
    Revision of the 1946 ed., with new amendments and additions, p. 831–34, by Mary Elder Black.
    A monumental work giving origin, meaning, and history of Scottish surnames from the earliest times, with references to sources.

Spanish

Gosnell, Charles Francis. Spanish personal names : principles governing their formation and use which may be presented as a help for catalogers and bibliographers. N.Y. : Wilson, 1938. 112 p. (Inter-American bibliographical and library association. Publ., series I, v. 3).   **AJ206**
    Repr.: Detroit : Ethridge-Books, 1971.
    Originally written as a master's thesis at the School of Library Service, Columbia University.
    Bibliography, p. 89–101.   Z695.G67

AK

Library and Information Science

GENERAL WORKS

Guides

Prytherch, Raymond John. Sources of information in librarianship and information science. 2nd ed. Aldershot, England ; Brookfield, Vt. : Gower, c1987. 153 p.   **AK1**
    1st ed., 1983.
    A narrative description, illustrated with sample entries, of the principal sources and services (Encyclopedic tools; Theses, dissertations, and reports; Current awareness; and Abstracting and indexing services) that provide access to the literature and to professional knowledge of the field. Emphasis is on English-language materials. Indexed.   Z666.P935

Purcell, Gary R. Reference sources in library and information services : a guide to the literature / Gary R. Purcell with Gail Ann Schlachter. Santa Barbara, Calif. : ABC-Clio, c1984. 359 p.   **AK2**
    An annotated bibliography of separately published, commercially available library-related reference sources. Emphasizes titles issued from the early 1900s through the first half of 1983 in the U.S., Canada, the U.K., Australia, and New Zealand. Some foreign-language titles are also included. In two parts: Pt. 1, General, is divided by type of publication (e.g., bibliographies; biographical and membership directories; sources of library statistics), with subdivisions for format, language, and geographic region, as applicable. Pt. 2 lists, under 103 alphabetically arranged subject sections, 500 reference works that concentrate on one or more library issues, processes, institutions, or techniques. Numerous cross-references; separate author, title, and geographic indexes.   Z666.P96

User's guides

Gates, Jean Key. Guide to the use of libraries and information sources. 7th ed. N.Y. : McGraw-Hill, c1994. 304 p. : ill. **AK3**
    1st ed., 1962; 6th ed., 1989.
    An introduction to the resources and characteristics of libraries directed at students, especially undergraduates. Provides basic explanations of the library, library catalogs, indexes, and other reference works. Includes annotated lists of standard reference works both by form and subject. The final chapter offers guidance in the preparation of research papers. Although electronic sources are included, the author's approach to the library is very traditional.   Z710.G27

Research methods

Beasley, David R. How to use a research library. N.Y. : Oxford Univ. Pr., 1988. 164 p. **AK4**

Provides beginners with a basic instruction in the use of research libraries. Describes procedures at the New York Public Library as illustrative of procedures at other research libraries. An appendix gives short descriptions of nine research libraries: New York Public Library; Harvard University Library; British Library; Bibliothèque Nationale; State V. I. Lenin Library of the USSR; Saltykov-Schchedrin State Public Library; National Library of China; National Diet Library (Japan); Library of Congress. Z675.R45B42

Library data collection handbook / Mary Jo Lynch, ed. Chicago : Amer. Libr. Assoc., 1981. 228 p. : ill. **AK5**

Outlines the types of data useful in describing library resources and library programs, and defines the terms involved. Aims to provide "library managers, boards of trustees, and other library decision makers with guidance in identifying factual and comparative data useful in developing policies and making decisions."—*Introd.* Z670.L717

Mann, Thomas. Library research models : a guide to classification, cataloging, and computers. N.Y. : Oxford Univ. Pr., 1993. 248 p. **AK6**

Aimed at researchers who use large libraries and the professional staff who work in them. Discusses various research models (e.g., "the subject specific model," "the traditional library science model," and the "computer workstation model"). Describes the strengths and weaknesses of each and argues for a combination of models. Contains a helpful explanation of Library of Congress subject headings. Complements the author's earlier, more conventional research handbook, *A guide to library research methods* (N.Y. : Oxford Univ. Pr., 1987. 199 p.). Z711.M36

Powell, Ronald R. Basic research methods for librarians. 2nd ed. Norwood, N.J. : Ablex Publ. Corp., c1991. 213 p. : ill. **AK7**

Explains methods and statistics that can be used in basic library research or for administrative decision making. Although it emphasizes quantitative methods, qualitative and historical research are also included. Contains chapters on writing proposals and writing reports.

§ *Qualitative research in information management*, ed. by Jack D. Glazier and Ronald R. Powell (Englewood, Colo. : Libraries Unlimited, 1992) explains the application of qualitative methodology covering, e.g., participant observation and focus interviews. Annotated bibliography. Z669.7.P68

Bibliography

ARBA guide to library science literature, 1970–1983 / ed. by Donald G. Davis, Jr. and Charles D. Patterson. Littleton, Colo. : Libraries Unlimited, 1987. 682 p. **AK8**

A comprehensive, evaluative listing of some 1,700 works in library science, both reference and nonreference, arranged under four broad categories: general works, reference works, works dealing with types of libraries, and works dealing with library services and special topics. Comprises reviews published in *American reference books annual* (AA346) and summary reviews prepared specifically for this work; most are signed. Author/title and limited subject indexes. Z666.A73

Barr, Larry J. Libraries in American periodicals before 1876 : a bibliography with abstracts and an index / Larry J. Barr, Haynes McMullen, Steven G. Leach. Jefferson, N.C. : McFarland, 1983. 426 p. **AK9**

A bibliography of nearly 1,500 articles about libraries appearing in American periodicals prior to 1876. Articles of more than 150 words are abstracted; those with 150 or less are included in their entirety. Arranged geographically, the bibliography has a comprehensive author, title, subject index.

§ For articles after 1876, consult Harry George Turner Cannons, *Bibliography of library economy* (AK12). Z666.B33

British Library. Research and Development Dept. Complete list of reports published by the British Library R&D Department / ed. by Margaret Mann. Boston Spa : British Library Research and Development Dept. : distr. by British Library Publications, c1988. 316 p. (British Library information guide, 9). **AK10**

An annotated list of the publications of the British Library Research and Development Department from the department's inception in 1974 to the end of 1987. Author, title, institution, subject indexes. Z666.B84

Burton, Margaret. A bibliography of librarianship : classified and annotated guide to the library literature of the world (excluding Slavonic and oriental languages) / selected by Margaret Burton ... and Marion E. Vosburgh .... London : Lib. Assoc., 1934. 176 p. **AK11**

An annotated bibliography that covers the early literature of librarianship. Arranged by subject classification. Subjects covered include: library history, special libraries, libraries for children, library practice, the library profession, law, architecture, cooperation, bibliography, the book, paleography and archives, general bibliographies of librarianship. Although selective, an invaluable source of information about library literature before 1934. Author and subject index.

Cannons, Harry George Turner. Bibliography of library economy : a classified index to the professional periodical literature in the English language relating to library economy, printing, methods of publishing, copyright, bibliography, etc. from 1876 to 1920. Chicago : Amer. Libr. Assoc., 1927. 680 p. **AK12**

Repr. : N.Y. : B. Franklin, 1970.

1st ed., 1910.

Includes English-language articles published in 65 professional periodicals and some articles from general periodicals. Classified index, supplemented by an alphabetical subject index.

Continued by: *Library literature* (AK32).

For author index, see: *Cannons' bibliography of library economy, 1876–1920 : an author index with citations*, ed. by Anne Harwell Jordan and Melbourne Jordan (Metuchen, N.J. : Scarecrow, 1976). All the entries in Cannons that bore the author's personal name are indexed alphabetically by name, then by title. Since citations are complete, it is not necessary to refer to Cannons. Z666.C21

Danton, Joseph Periam. Index to festschriften in librarianship / Joseph Periam Danton, with the assistance of Ottilia C. Anderson. N.Y. : Bowker, 1970. 461 p. **AK13**

An index to approximately 3,300 articles in 283 festschriften published 1864–1966. Authors, editors, subjects, and cross-references appear in a single alphabet.

Continued by: Joseph Periam Danton and Jane F. Pulis, *Index to festschriften in librarianship, 1967–1975* (München ; N.Y. : K.G. Saur, 1979. 354 p.). "This volume covers approximately 1,500 articles in 143 works, 104 published from 1967 to 1975 inclusive" (*Introd.*), the remainder being from the earlier period. Dictionary arrangement. Z666.D35

Heim, Kathleen M. On account of sex : an annotated bibliography on the status of women in librarianship, 1977–1981 / Kathleen Heim and Katharine Phenix. Chicago : Amer. Libr. Assoc., 1984. 188 p. **AK14**

Continues: *The role of women in librarianship, 1876–1976* (AK73).

A chronological bibliography of articles and other publications that discuss or define women's status in librarianship. A few entries before 1975 are included. Author, title, and subject indexes.

Updated by:

———. ———. *1982–1986*, by Katharine Phenix … [et al.] for the Committee on the Status of Women in Librarianship, Amer. Libr. Assoc. (1989. 136 p.).

———. ———. *1987–1992*, Lori A. Goetsch and Sarah B. Watstein, gen. editors (Metuchen, N.J. : Scarecrow, 1993. 244 p.). Both follow the plan of the earlier work. The introduction to the later update consists of a citations analysis of the 1976–89 entries.   Z682.4.W65H44

Herring, Mark Youngblood. Controversial issues in librarianship : an annotated bibliography, 1960–1984. N.Y. : Garland, 1987. 698 p. (Garland reference library of social science, v. 342).   **AK15**

Coverage extends to controversies regarding collections, library facilities, human factors in libraries, technology, cooperation and networking, library education, reference services, library management, librarians and society, and the profession. Non-English material is excluded. Annotations describe the controversy in question and whenever possible, trace it to a conclusion. Entries are arranged alphabetically by subject. Author/name and title indexes.   Z666.H44

Wei, Karen T. Library and information science in China : an annotated bibliography. N.Y. : Greenwood, 1988. 273 p. (Bibliographies and indexes in library and information science, no. 3).   **AK16**

"Designed to meet the needs of scholars, researchers, librarians, and library school students in their search for sources in the field."—*Pref.* About 1,000 entries, with emphasis on English-language materials and titles of great importance in Chinese, French, German, and Japanese published during the past 100 years. 11 topical sections: (1) Bibliography and reference, (2) Books and printing, (3) History, (4) Types of libraries, (5) Technical services activities, (6) Automation and information services, (7) Education for librarianship, (8) Publishing and trade, (9) General works, (10) International exchange and activities, and (11) Librarians. Author and subject indexes.   Z845.C5W45

Current

Annual bibliography of the history of the printed book and libraries. v. 1 (1970)– . The Hague : Nijhoff, 1973– . Annual.   **AK17**

For annotation, *see* AA268.   Z117.A55

Bibliographie der Buch- und Bibliotheksgeschichte : BBB. Bd. 1 (1980/81)– . Bad Iburg Germany : H. Meyer, 1982– . Annual.   **AK18**

Often referred to as: *BBB*.

An international bibliography that includes articles and books on libraries and librarianship. There is a name index.   Z4.B54

Library hi tech bibliography. v. 1– . Ann Arbor, Mich. : Pierian Pr., c1986– .   **AK19**

Each issue offers bibliographies on topics primarily but not exclusively related to technology in libraries. "All bibliographies emphasize recent literature, supplementing previous volumes of *Library hi tech bibliographies* and *Automation in libraries : a LITA bibliography, 1978–1982* [AK190]"—*Introd.*   Z666.L43

Periodicals

Bowman, Mary Ann. Library and information science journals and serials : an analytical guide. Westport, Conn. : Greenwood, c1985. 140 p. (Annotated bibliographies of serials, no. 1.).   **AK20**

An alphabetically arranged, annotated list of 311 periodicals (including annuals), international in scope but limited to materials in Eng-

lish. Information was drawn mainly from responses to questionnaires. An appendix lists 56 additional titles for which full information was not available. Geographical, classified title, and publisher indexes.   Z666.B64

Janzing, Grażyna. Library, documentation, and archives serials / comp. by Grażyna Janzing ; ed. by K. R. Brown. 4th ed. The Hague : Internat. Federation for Documentation, 1975. 203 p.   **AK21**

1st ed. 1956, had title: *Library and documentation periodicals*; 3rd ed., 1968, had title: *Library and documentation journals.*

Lists about 950 serials, with subscription information. A section for publications of international organizations is followed by country lists; a section for abstracting, indexing, and current awareness services; and a list of ceased titles. Information was drawn mainly from responses to questionnaires. Now very dated, but still the only publication with extensive international coverage. Title index and a selected list of titles arranged by subject specialty.   Z666.I55

Library periodicals : an annual guide for subscribers, authors, publicists. 1993– . Alameda, Calif. : Periodical Guides Pub. Co. Annual.   **AK22**

A directory of some 150 U.S. and Canadian library journals. Entries include a description of the content of the publication, the publisher and publisher's address, editor, ISSN, beginning date, frequency, size, page count, price and where indexed. Authors are given information about submissions and publicists about acceptance of news releases. There is an index to refereed journals, as well as indexes by subject and publisher.

Dissertations

Library and information studies in the United Kingdom and Ireland, 1950–1974 : an index to theses / ed. by Peter J. Taylor. [London] : Aslib, [1976]. 69 p.   **AK23**

A bibliography of theses in librarianship and information work which "seeks to bring together in one list all of those theses accepted in full or partial requirement for [higher] degrees, either in library schools or other departments of the universities."—*Introd.* Chronological listing with author and detailed subject indexes.   Z666.L374

Library Association. Library. FLA theses : abstracts of all theses accepted for the fellowship of the Library Association from 1964 / comp. by L. J. Taylor. London : British Libr., Libr. Assoc. Libr., [1979]. 90 p.   **AK24**

A subject listing, with abstracts. 297 entries; author and detailed subject indexes. Complements *Library and information studies in the United Kingdom and Ireland* (AK23), which does not include FLA theses.   Z666.L39

Magnotti, Shirley. Master's theses in library science, 1960–1969. Troy, N.Y. : Whitston, 1975. 366 p.   **AK25**

Lists about 2,500 master's theses from 31 accredited library schools. An author listing with subject index.

Supplements by the same compiler: *Master's theses in library science, 1970–74* (Troy, N.Y. : Whitston, 1976. 198 p.). Adds some 700 titles from 24 schools (plus a few titles from the earlier period). An author listing that repeats the full citation in a subject section. *Library science research, 1974–1979* (Troy, N.Y. : Whitston, 1982. 179 p.). Serves as a continuation of the earlier titles. The change of title reflects the inclusion of "final research reports" accepted by many schools in lieu of the master's thesis. About 750 items.

Schlachter, Gail Ann. Library science dissertations, 1925–1972 : an annotated bibliography / Gail A. Schlachter, Dennis Thomison. Littleton, Colo. : Libraries Unlimited, 1974. 293 p. (Research studies in library science, no. 12).   **AK26**

A chronological listing, with author and subject indexes. Drawing their citations from the standard American dissertation lists, the compilers have listed "those doctoral studies which were either accepted by library schools or concerned with areas bearing a close relationship to the field of librarianship (e.g., communications, information services, education, etc.)."—*Introd.* So far as possible, each entry is annotated as to purpose, procedure, and findings.

Supersedes an earlier list by Nathan M. Cohen [et al.], *Library science dissertations, 1925–60* (Wash. : U.S. Govt. Print. Off., 1963).

Supplement by the same compilers: *Library science dissertations, 1973–1981 : an annotated bibliography* (Littleton, Colo. : Libr. Unlimited, 1982. 293 p. [Research studies in library science, no. 18]). Adds about 1,000 dissertations. Partially updated by *Library and information science annual* (AK80). **Z674.R4**

Young, Arthur P. American library history : a bibliography of dissertations and theses. 3rd rev. ed. Metuchen, N.J. : Scarecrow, 1988. 469 p. **AK27**

Rev. and updated ed. of: Michael Harris, *A guide to research in American library history* (2nd ed. Metuchen, N.J. : Scarecrow, 1974).

An annotated subject guide to masters theses, doctoral dissertations and some research reports about American library history. Indexes more than 1,150 items and extends coverage of the earlier edition to late 1986. Author and subject indexes. **Z666.Y68**

Indexes; Abstract journals

Current index to journals in education : (CIJE). v. 1, no. 1/2 (Jan./Feb. 1969)– . Phoenix : Oryx, 1969– . Monthly, with semiannual cumulations. **AK28**

For annotation, *see* CB54.

Current research in library & information science. v. 1 (March 1983)– . London : Bowker-Saur, 1983– . Quarterly. **AK29**

Continues: *Radials bulletin* (1974–82). Formerly published by the Library Association.

Indexes and abstracts library and information science research in progress. International in scope.

•Machine-readable versions: *Library and information science abstracts* (LISA) [database] (London : Bowker-Saur, 1969–) available online, updated monthly; and *LISA plus* [database] (London ; N.Y. : Bowker-Saur, 1969–), available on CD-ROM, updated quarterly. Coverage of *CRLIS* begins with 1981. **Z669.7.C87**

Information science abstracts. v. 1 (Mar. 1966)– . N.Y. : Plenum Pr., 1969– . Monthly. **AK30**

Continues: *Documentation abstracts*, v. 1–3 (Mar. 1966–1968); *Documentation abstracts and information science abstracts*, v. 3 no. 3 (Sept. 1968)–v. 3 no. 4 (Dec. 1968).

Publisher varies: 1966–68, American Documentation Institute (after 1967 called American Society for Information Science), Division of Chemical Literature of the American Chemical Society, and Special Libraries Association; 1968–83?, Documentation Abstracts, Inc.; 1984– , Plenum Pr.

Frequency varies: 1966–77, quarterly; 1977–83, bimonthly; 1984– , monthly.

A classified indexing and abstracting service, covering books, journals, conference proceedings, reports, and patents in library and information science and related fields. A core list of journals is indexed completely, and several hundred more are indexed selectively. Monthly author and subject indexes; annual cumulative index.

•*Information science abstracts* [database] (Alexandria, Va. : IFI/Plenum Data Corp., 1966–). Available online; updated monthly. **Z699.A1I575**

Library & information science abstracts. no. 1 (Jan./Feb. 1969)– . London : Bowker/Saur, 1969– . Monthly. **AK31**

Continues and expands the scope of *Library science abstracts* (AK34).

Publisher varies: 1969–90, Libr. Assoc.

Frequency varies: 1969–81, bimonthly.

Provides, in classified order, abstracts of journal articles and a few selected reports in fields of interest to librarians and information workers. International in scope. Titles are given in the original language with English translation; abstracts are in English. Author and subject index in each issue, and beginning 1991, index by journal title; annual cumulative index.

•*Library and information science abstracts (LISA)* [database] (London : Bowker/Saur, 1969–). Available online (updated monthly) and in CD-ROM as *LISA* (updated annually). Abstracts are available in the online file from 1976 onward. **Z671.L6**

Library literature. 1921/32– . N.Y. : Wilson, 1934– . Bimonthly, with annual cumulation. **AK32**

Subtitle and publisher vary.

Frequency varies; formerly quarterly, with annual and triennial cumulations.

An index to current books, pamphlets, periodical literature, films, microforms, and theses relating to librarianship, arranged alphabetically by author and subject. More than 200 journals are covered. Includes foreign material. Abstracts and digests appearing in earlier issues were discontinued after 1958.

Prior to 1978 book review citations were listed under the book's main entry in the body of the index; thereafter they appear in a separate section. Reviews of audiovisual materials and periodicals are cited only in the body of the index.

•*Library literature* [database] (N.Y. : H.W. Wilson, 1984–). Available online (updated twice weekly) and in CD-ROM (updated quarterly). **Z666.L69**

•**Library reference plus** [database]. [New Providence, N.J.] : Bowker, 1989– . **AK33**

Available on CD-ROM; Annual (with monthly, bimonthly, or quarterly updates); current coverage, disc replaced annually.

A directory of libraries and librarians, book publishing and publishers, distributors, and wholesalers, drawn from: *American book trade directory* (AA281); *American library directory* (AK122); *Literary market place* (AA282); *International literary market place* (AA278); *Publishers, distributors and wholesalers of the United States*; and the complete text of *The Bowker annual library and book trade almanac* (AK77).

Library science abstracts. 1950–68. London : Libr. Assoc., 1950–68. **AK34**

Classified abstracts taken from some 200 periodicals, books, pamphlets, reports, etc. Annual indexes by author and by name and subject. International in scope.

§ Continued by: *Library & information science abstracts* (AK31). **Z671.L617**

Resources in education / Educational Resources Information Center. v. 10, no. 1 (Jan. 1975)– . Wash. : Office of Educational Research and Improvement : distr. by U.S. Govt. Print. Off., [1975]– . Monthly. **AK35**

An important source for report literature, conference proceedings, and unpublished papers in library and information science. For complete annotation, *see* CB61. **Z5813.R4**

Encyclopedias

Encyclopedia of library and information science / Allen Kent and Harold Lancour, editors. N.Y. : Dekker, 1968– . v. 1–48. (In progress). **AK36**

Some volumes also ed. by J. E. Daily and W. Z. Nasri.

Contents: v. 1–33, A–Z; v. 34–35, Author and subject indexes; v. 36–45, Supplements 1–10; v. 46–47, Author and subject indexes, v. 1–45; v. 48– , Supplements 11– .

International in scope. Signed articles in dictionary arrangement, most of them of considerable length and carrying bibliographies. Articles on all aspects of library work and related aspects of the book world, together with survey articles on libraries and library service in individual countries and major cities. Includes biographies of deceased persons in the field of librarianship.

Supplements include signed articles on topics of current professional interest, as well as an occasional biography. Articles in the supplements are indexed in *Library literature* (AK32).   Z1006.E57

Landau, Thomas. Encyclopaedia of librarianship. 3rd rev. ed. London : Bowes & Bowes ; N.Y. : Hafner, [1966]. 484 p.
AK37

1st ed., 1958.

An alphabetical work covering all aspects of librarianship, with entries varying in length from a few words to signed articles of several pages. Usage covered is almost entirely British. Some articles include bibliographies.   Z1006.L3

Milkau, Fritz. Handbuch der Bibliothekswissenschaft. 2. verm. und verb. Aufl. / hrsg. von Georg Leyh. Wiesbaden : Harrassowitz, 1950–65. 4 v. in 5.   **AK38**

1st ed., 1931–42 (3 v. and index).

Contents: v. 1, Schrift und Buch; v. 2, Bibliotheksverwaltung; v. 3, Geschichte der Bibliotheken (2 v.); Registerband, bearb. von Renate Bellmann.

A scholarly work on the history of books, libraries, and librarianship with emphasis on German and Western European aspects of the subject. Long, signed articles with many bibliographical footnotes.
Z670.M642

World encyclopedia of library and information services / [Robert Wedgeworth, ed.]. 3rd ed. Chicago : Amer. Libr. Assoc., c1993. 905 p.   **AK39**

Title varies: 1st ed., 1980, and 2nd ed., 1986, had title: *ALA world encyclopedia of library and information services.*

Signed articles on the concepts, condition, history, and personalities of library services. Library education, organizations, archives, and services are included but not information science. International in scope; includes articles concerning the condition of libraries and librarianship in 160 countries written by contributors from these countries, as well as 216 biographies of important library figures, living and dead. Articles are enhanced by hard-to-locate statistical data, many excellent illustrations, and selective bibliographies. This edition also contains separate entries on five major libraries: the Bibliothèque National, British Library, Harvard University Library, Library of Congress, and New York Public Library. Dictionary arrangement with a comprehensive index.   Z1006.W67

Dictionaries

The ALA glossary of library and information science / Heartsill Young, ed. Chicago : Amer. Libr. Assoc., 1983. 245 p.   **AK40**

Succeeds: American Library Association. Committee on Library Terminology. *A.L.A. glossary of library terms : with a section of terms in other fields* / by Elizabeth H. Thompson (Chicago : Amer. Libr. Assoc., 1934. 159 p.).

Compiled with the assistance of specialists in various areas, this edition is seen as "a contribution toward the development of standard terminology, or a set of terms, which will enable librarians and other information scientists better to communicate with each other and with specialists in related fields."—*Foreword.* In addition to library and information science, terms are drawn from printing and publishing, graphic arts, computer science, telecommunications, reprography, educational technology, administrative science, and archives administration.   Z1006.A48

Bürger, Erich. Dictionary of information science. Amsterdam ; N.Y. : Elsevier, 1989. 2 v. (903 p.).   **AK41**

A listing of information science terms without definitions, arranged on an English base with equivalent terms in German, French, and Russian. Covers computer architecture, hardware and software components, systems engineering, interactive and batch processing,

programming, data mangement, artificial intelligence, expert systems, databases, etc. Vol. 2 consists of German, French, and Russian indexes.   Z1006.B94

Harrod's librarians glossary : 9,200 terms used in information management, library science, publishing, the book trades, and archive management / comp. by Ray Prytherch. 8th ed. Aldershot, England ; Brookfield, Vt. : Gower, c1995. 1 v.
AK42

Title and subtitle vary slightly in previous editions.
1st ed., 1938; 6th ed., 1987.

Includes the terminology of librarianship, information science, archives, the book trade, information technology, and relevant applications of automation. Definitions and/or descriptions are given of associations, awards, and significant library collections. Acronyms are included. Although British in origin, attention is given to American institutions, organizations etc., and to the differences between British and American terminology.   Z1006.H32

Rosenberg, Kenyon C. Dictionary of library and educational technology / Kenyon C. Rosenberg and John J. Elsbree. 3rd and enl. ed. Englewood, Colo. : Libraries Unlimited, 1989. 196 p.   **AK43**

[1st ed.] (1976) called *Media equipment : a guide and dictionary,* by Rosenberg and J. S. Dosky; 2nd ed., 1983.

A work for librarians, teachers, and students responsible for the selection, use, and care of equipment used for computing, telecommunications, and audiovisual media. A section on criteria for equipment selection precedes the dictionary, which includes terms and organizations related to the equipment. Acronyms, abbreviations, and initialisms file at the beginning of each letter.   TS2301.A7R66

Watters, Carolyn. Dictionary of information science and technology. Boston : Academic Pr., c1992. 300 p. : ill. **AK44**

"The breadth of terms included … reflect the interdisciplinary nature of the study of information and its uses."—*Pref.* Each term in the alphabetically arranged dictionary includes a key to a subject outline and a notation to the list of references, both at the end of the volume. The aim of the work is to make highly technical and specialized language more understandable.   Z1006.W35

Abbreviations

Sawoniak, Henryk. New international dictionary of acronyms in library and information science and related fields / Henryk Sawoniak, Maria Witt. 2nd rev. and enl. ed. München ; N.Y. : K.G. Saur, 1992. 497 p.   **AK45**

1st ed., 1988.

Lists acronyms (including variant and equivalent forms) in library and information science, publishing, printing, archival management, journalism, and reprography. Global coverage. Acronyms are expanded in the language of the official name, when known, otherwise an English form is given and in the case of lesser-known languages, an English translation; Cyrillic alphabet entries are transliterated. For organizations, there are notes concerning country, dates, and, in some instances, focus. Tables of country and language codes precede the principal list. This edition contains about 5,000 more entries than the 1st ed.   Z1006.S344

Foreign terms

Allen, Charles Geoffry. A manual of European languages for librarians. [2nd impression (with minor corrections)]. London ; N.Y. : Bowker in assoc. with the London School of Economics, [1977]. 803 p.   **AK46**

For annotation, *see* BD11.   P380.A4

Keitz, Saiedeh von. Dictionary of library and information science : English/German, German/English = Wörterbuch Bibliotheks- und Informationswissenschaft : Englisch/Deutsch, Deutsch/Englisch / Saiedeh von Keitz und Wolfgang von Keitz. 2nd rev. ed. Weinheim, FRG ; N.Y. : VCH, c1992. 527 p. **AK47**
  Notable for its inclusion of many recent information technology terms. Z1006.K4

Pipics, Zoltán. Dictionarium bibliothecarii practicum : Ad usum internationalem in XXII linguis = Wörterbuch des Bibliothekars in zweiundzwanzig Sprachen = The librarian's practical dictionary in twenty-two languages. 7. correcta et aucta editio. Budapest : Akadémiai Kiadó, 1977. 385 p. **AK48**
  6th ed. (Münich, 1974) also 385 p.
  Based on the author's *A könyvtáros gyakorlati szótára* (Budapest, 1963), using German rather than Hungarian as the base language. Presents library terms in 22 languages. Z1006.P67

Thompson, Anthony. Vocabularium bibliothecarii : English, French, German, Spanish, Russian / collaborator for Russian, E. I. Shamurin; collaborator for Spanish, Domingo Bonocore. 2nd ed. [Paris] : UNESCO, 1962. 440 p. **AK49**
  1st ed., 1953; suppl., 1958.
  About 2,800 terms are included; definitions are given only where a word has two meanings, or where there is no equivalent in one of the languages. Terms are arranged in columns by Universal Decimal Classification number on an English base with indexes by each language to classification number.
  Mu'jam al-mustalahāt al-maktabīyah (1965. 692 p.) is a photo-offset reproduction of this edition with an introduction and index in Arabic, and with the Arabic vocabulary inserted in the right-hand column of the pages of the glossary.
  Supplemented by: Pipics Zoltán, *Vocabularium bibliothecarii : supplementum hungaricum* (Budapest : Akadémiai Kiadó, 1954. 251 p. Repr. 1971). Z1006.T47

Von Ostermann, Georg Frederick. Manual of foreign languages for the use of librarians, bibliographers, research workers, editors, translators, and printers. 4th ed., rev. and enl. N.Y. : Central Book Co., 1952. 414 p. : ill. **AK50**
  For annotation, *see* BD17. Z253.V94

Quotations

Krummel, Donald William. A librarian's collacon : an anthology of quotations and aphorisms reflecting moral philosophy of the library profession. Prelim. ed. Urbana : [Univ. of Illinois], 1971. 223 p. **AK51**
  Quotations, arranged by subject, about or relevant to libraries, librarians, and books. List of sources. Z1003.K75

Directories

Medical Library Association. MLA directory. 1983–84– . Chicago : M.L.A., [1984]– . Annual. **AK52**
  Continues: *Directory of medical libraries belonging to the Medical Library Association, Directory of the Medical Library Association,* and *Medical Library Association directory.* Formerly publ.: Hamden, Conn. : Shoe String Pr.
  Provides general information about the association and a listing of personal and institutional members.

International

Directory / IFLA. 1977– . [The Hague, Netherlands : International Federation of Library Associations and Institutions], 1977– . Biennial. **AK53**
  Former title: *IFLA Directory.* Frequency varies; formerly annual.
  Continues: International Federation of Library Associations, *Répertoire des associations de bibliothécaires membres de la Fédération internationale.*
  Lists officers, committees, members, and publications of the association. International and national associations, and institutional members are listed alphabetically by country and town. Includes addresses, telephone, telex, and fax numbers for members. Index of personal names. Z673.I58485

International guide to library and information science education : a reference source for educational programs in the information fields world-wide / ed. by Josephine Riss Fang and Paul Nauta with the assistance of Anna J. Fang. München ; N.Y. : K.G. Saur, 1985. 537 p. (IFLA publications, 32). **AK54**
  Arranged alphabetically by country. For each country, gives a brief introductory sketch of the general educational system, followed by individual library and information science educational institutions alphabetically arranged by place. The profile for each institution includes: name, address, head, year founded, administrative structure, sources of finance, program, teaching staff, physical resources, continuing education, and accreditation information. Index of place names. Z668.I574

World guide to library, archive, and information science associations / Josephine Riss Fang and Alice H. Songe ; with the assistance of Anna J. Fang and Alexandra Herz. München ; N.Y. : K.G. Saur, 1990. 516 p. (IFLA publications, 52/53). **AK55**
  1st ed., 1976, and 2nd ed., 1980, had title: *International guide to library, archival, and information science associations.*
  Offers information on nonprofit national and international associations. Following an alphabetical list of international associations, national associations are arranged alphabetically by country. Each entry includes address, officers, goals, publications, etc. Many entries include bibliographies. Z673.A1F33

North America

United States

American Library Association. ALA handbook of organization and membership directory. 1980/81– . Chicago : Amer. Libr. Assoc., 1980– . Annual. **AK56**
  Formed by the union of *A.L.A. handbook of organization* (publ. 1971–) and *A.L.A. membership directory* (publ. 1949–79). In addition to describing organization and committee structure of the association, the handbook also contains the full text of important ALA documents and an index to ALA-approved standards. The handbook portion is also published separately.
  The directory includes institutional as well as personal memberships. Z673.A5H37

American Society for Information Science. ASIS handbook & directory. 1968/69– . Wash. : American Society for Information Science, 1969– . **AK57**
  Besides an alphabetical list of members, also includes officers, committees, publications, history of the association, etc. Z673.A47

Association for Library and Information Science Education. Directory of the Association for Library and Information Science Education. 1983– . State College, Pa. : The Association, 1983– . Annual.   **AK58**

Issues for 1983– also called Directory issue and published as a special edition of the *Journal of education for library and information science.*

Continues a directory issued by the association under its earlier name: Association of American Library Schools.

Includes institutional and affiliate members. Institutional members are listed alphabetically; entries include institution address and telephone number together with names of faculty and their telephone and e-mail numbers. Alphabetic index of personal names and an index to subject areas and instructors.   Z668.A78a

The Burwell directory of information brokers. 1991– . Houston, Tex. : Burwell Enterprises, c1991– . Annual.
     AK59

Continues: *The directory of fee-based information services* (Woodstock, N.Y. : Information Alternatives, 1984–90).

Comp. and ed. by H.P. Burwell.

An international directory. The U.S. section is arranged by state, the international section by country. U.S. listings include: addresses; telephone, telex, and fax numbers; contact person; professional memberships; subjects; services; hours; fees. The 1993 ed. has nearly 1,400 entries. Indexes by city, company name, contact person, subjects, services.   Z674.5.U5D57

Directory of telefacsimile sites in North American libraries. 4th ed. (1989)– . Buchanan Dam, Tex. : CBR Consulting Services, Inc., c1989– . Annual.   **AK60**

At head of title, 1990– : The library fax directory.

Continues: *Directory of telefacsimile sites in libraries in the United States and Canada*, 1986–89.

A geographically arranged listing of telefax numbers for libraries in Canada, Mexico and the U.S. Index by institution name.

    Z713.5.U6D57

Who's who in special libraries. N.Y. : Special Libraries Association, 1981– . Annual.   **AK61**

Continues: Special Libraries Association, *Directory of members.*

A handbook of the Association as well as a list of personal members.   Z673.S81D5

Africa

The African book world and press : directory = Répertoire du livre et de la presse en Afrique. 4th ed. / ed. by Hans M. Zell. London : Zell, 1989. 306 p.   **AK62**

For annotation, *see* AA293.   Z857.A1

Australia and Oceania

New Zealand

Szentirmay, Paul. DILSI, NZ : a directory of information and library services in New Zealand / comp. by Paul Szentirmay and Thiam Ch'ng Szentirmay. Wellington : New Zealand Library Association, 1988. 145 p.   **AK63**

Arranged alphabetically by library name. Includes 540 special, academic, major public libraries, and the National Library of New Zealand. Gives address and telephone numbers, hours, services, special collections, and publications. Exceptionally well-indexed by parent organization, type of organization, subject, publications, named and special collections, names of personnel, locality, and library symbol.

Grants

National guide to funding for libraries and information services / ed. by Stan Olson & Ruth Kovacs ; Zoe Waldron, project coordinator. 2nd ed. [New York] : Foundation Center, c1993. 190 p.   **AK64**

Lists 602 foundations and corporate direct giving programs with a history of awarding grants to libraries and related organizations. Arranged alphabetically by state, entries include: donor(s); foundation type; financial date; purpose; fields of interests; type of support; application information; officers; and recent library/information services grants. Indexed by donors, officer, trustee; geography; type of support; subject; foundations and corporate giving program. There is a glossary, bibliography, and a list of participants in the Foundation Center Cooperating Collections Network.   Z683.N38

Handbooks

Crawford, Walt. Technical standards : an introduction for librarians. 2nd ed. Boston : G.K. Hall, 1991. 333p. : ill. **AK65**

The first part explains library standards and the organizations that create them; the second part lists current National Information Standards Organization (NISO) standards together with description, details, and status. An appendix provides a selective list of standards from International Organization for Standardization (ISO).   Z678.85.C7

How libraries must comply with the Americans with Disabilities Act (ADA) / comp. and ed. by Donald D. Foos and Nancy C. Pack. Phoenix : Oryx, 1992. 168 p.   **AK66**

Outlines legal requirements for libraries of the Americans with Disabilities Act and discusses its implementation and impact. Includes lists of related organizations and bibliographies of relevant books, pamphlets, databases, and videos.   Z711.92.H3H68

Intellectual freedom manual / comp. by the Office for Intellectual Freedom of the American Library Association. 4th ed. Chicago : Amer. Libr. Assoc., 1992. 283 p. : ill.   **AK67**

Provides basic library policies and statements relevant to intellectual freedom. In addition to major documents such as the "Library Bill of Rights," provides a history and interpretation of American libraries' positions regarding censorship and advice on handling censorship disputes. Indexed.   Z711.4.I57

Library and information science education statistical report / Association for Library and Information Science Education. 1983– . State College, Penn. : ALISE, 1983– . Annual.
     AK68

Presents detailed information on faculty, students, curriculum, income and expenditures, and continuing professional education for ALA accredited programs. Some information on nonaccredited programs is also included. The best source for information on American library education.   Z668.L495

Compendiums

Eberhardt, George M. The whole library handbook 2 : current data, professional advice, and curiosa about libraries and library services. Chicago : Amer. Libr. Assoc., 1995. 521 p. : ill.   **AK69**

1st ed., 1991.

A compendium of miscellaneous facts and figures about libraries and librarians. In ten sections: Libraries; People; The profession; Material; Operations; Special populations; Public relations; Technology; Issues; and Librariana. The place to find an explanation of MARC; the dates of National Library Week to 2001; an explanation of "what makes a book rare," and a list of professional grants and scholarships. Sources of data are cited; some short articles include bibliographies.

Z665.2.U6E24

Histories

British library history : bibliography. 1962–1968– . Winchester, Eng. : St. Paul's Bibliographies, 1972– . Quadrennial. **AK70**

Each edition covers a four-year period; 1985–88 publ. 1991.

Publisher varies: 1972–87, Library Association.

Ed. by Denis F. Keeling; comp. by a committee of the Library Association's Library History Group.

An annotated bibliography covering librarians, librarianship, libraries, reading, and the study of library history. Continuously numbered from one edition to the next. Contains obituaries and references to biographical information. Author and subject indexes.

Z791.A1B75

Davis, Donald G. American library history : a comprehensive guide to the literature / Donald G. Davis, Jr., John Mark Tucker. Santa Barbara, Calif. : ABC-Clio, c1989. 471 p.   **AK71**

A revised and expanded version of Michael H. Harris's *American library history : a bibliography* (Austin : Univ. of Texas Pr., 1978).

Includes 7,150 entries, published through 1986, consciously written as history, about libraries and closely related subjects in the U.S. In 15 sections: (1) Historiography and sources, (2) General studies, (3) Private libraries and reading tastes, (4) Predecessors of the public library, (5) Public libraries, (6) Academic libraries, (7) School libraries, (8) State libraries, (9) Special libraries, (10) Archival enterprise, (11) Education for librarianship, (12) Library associations, (13) Special aspects of librarianship, (14) Women in librarianship, (15) Biographies of individual librarians and library benefactors. Indexes of authors, institutions, and essays.

Z731.D38

Encyclopedia of library history / ed. by Wayne A. Wiegand and Donald G. Davis. N.Y. : Garland, 1993. 707 p. (Garland reference library of social science, v. 503).   **AK72**

Signed articles of varying length describe the historical development of libraries as institutions without geographic or time limitations. There are entries by country, by type of library, and by period, as well as on topics such as education for librarianship, library equipment, and censorship. Histories of more than 50 famous libraries are also included, but biographies have been excluded. Preliminary tables of contents arrange the entries by geographic location and by subject. Subject index.

Z721.E54

The role of women in librarianship, 1876–1976 : the entry, advancement, and struggle for equalization in one profession / by Kathleen Weibel and Kathleen M. Heim, with assistance from Dianne J. Ellsworth. Phoenix : Oryx, 1979. 510 p. **AK73**

Following a series of chapters that provide a historical overview of the status of women in librarianship is a chronologically organized bibliography of 1,000 items. There are subject, author, and title indexes to the bibliography.

Continued by Kathleen Heim and Katharine Phenix, *On account of sex* (AK14).   Z682.2.U5R64

Yearbooks and current surveys

Advances in librarianship. v. 1 (1970)– . N.Y. : Academic Pr., 1970– . Annual.   **AK74**

None published 1987–89.

Each volume contains eight to ten chapters on subjects of current interest in librarianship, such as document delivery or strategic quality management. The chapters, written by experts in the field, review and summarize current writing and research.   Z674.A4

The ALA yearbook of library and information services. v. 9 (1984)–v. 15 (1990). Chicago : Amer. Libr. Assoc., 1984–90. Annual.   **AK75**

Continues: *Library and information science today* (v. 1–3); *Library and information services today* (v. 4 [1974]– v. 5 [1975]; American Library Assoc., *The ALA yearbook* (v. 1 [1976]–v. 8 [1983]).

An annual record of events in American librarianship, focusing especially on activities of the American Library Association. Although no longer published, it is still a useful source for biographies and other information about libraries and librarianship. With the exception of 1980–81, each yearbook includes an index which partially cumulates until 1986.   Z673.A5A14

Annual review of information science and technology. v. 1 (1966)– . Medford, N.J. [etc.] : Learned Information, Inc. [etc.] for the American Society for Information Science, [1966]– . Annual.   **AK76**

v. 1–2 issued by the society under its earlier name: American Documentation Institute.

Editor: 1966–75, C. A. Cuadra.

Each issue presents bibliographic essays on topics in information science or technology. In the first few years, subjects were repeated frequently with the latest essay updating those earlier. More recently the range of subjects has been broader; e.g., the 1992 edition included: The impact of information technology on the individual, Data representations for geographic systems, and Education and training for information science in the Soviet Union. Chapters end with bibliographies. Indexes of individual names, corporate bodies, geographic locations, and authors. A cumulative keyword author and title index is also included. A separate cumulative index was published for v. 1–10 (1966–75).   Z699.A1A65

The Bowker annual library and book trade almanac. Ed. 1– . N.Y. : Bowker, 1956– . Annual.   **AK77**

Title varies: 1956–58, *American library annual* [new series]; 1959–61, *American library and book trade annual*; 1962–88, *The Bowker annual of library and book trade information*.

A compendium of descriptive, statistical, and directory information about libraries and publishing. Significant features of this work include: directories of library networks, consortia and other cooperative agencies; national, international, state and regional library associations, and book trade associations; statistics on placement and salaries of beginning librarians; lists of toll-free numbers; summaries of federal grant programs; statistics on the average prices of books; lists of literary prizes; and reports on topics of current interest.

•Available on CD-ROM as part of *Library reference plus* [database] (AK33).   Z731.A47

British librarianship and information work. 1976–80– . London : Libr. Assoc., 1982– .   **AK78**

Continues the Association's *Year's work in librarianship* (v. 1 (1928)–v. 17 (1950); *Five years' work in librarianship*, 1951/55–1961/65; and *British librarianship and information science*, 1966/70–1971/75.

Contents: v. 1, General libraries and the profession; v. 2, Special libraries, materials and processes.

A literature review of professional activity and research in the U.K. during the period covered. Volumes are divided into chapters on topics such as Library cooperation, Public libraries, and Audiovisual librarianship. Each chapter, written by a specialist, summarizes events and provides a lengthy list of references. Volumes have subject indexes.   Z666.F5

Librarianship and information work worldwide. 1991– . London ; N.Y. : Bowker-Saur, c1991– . Annual.   **AK79**

Editors: 1991– , Maurice B. Line, Graham Mackenzie, and Raymond Prytherch.

A survey, primarily based on published literature, of events in library and information science during the previous year. Topical chapters include extensive bibliographies. Although international in coverage, the literature reviewed is mostly in English. Author and subject indexes.   Z671.L59

Library and information science annual. v. 1 (1985)–v. 5 (1989). Littleton, Colo. : Libraries Unlimited, 1985–89.   **AK80**

Title varies: 1985–86, *Library science annual.*

Intended as an annual update to *ARBA guide to library science literature* (AK8), providing articles about and book reviews on library and information science literature. Although some of the same reviews were included in *American reference books annual* (AA346), coverage of library literature was more extensive in this title. Reviews the previous year's English-language monographs, reference books, and periodicals; provides abstracts of the year's most significant doctoral dissertations; and presents essays on current trends and issues in library and information science. Author/title and subject indexes.   Z666.L45

Biography

American Association of Law Libraries. Biographical directory / ed. and produced by Shackelford & Associates Systems Design. 5th ed. St. Paul, Minn. : publ. for The Association with the compliments of West Pub. Co., 1992.   **AK81**

1st ed., 1964; 4th ed., 1984.

Biographical information about some 2,500 members of AALL. Two indexes: Subjects taught and areas of expertise; Colleges and universities attended.   Z720.A4B53

Biographical dictionary of Australian librarians / Géza A. Kósa, ed. 4th ed. Melbourne : Academia Pr., 1990. 252 p.   **AK82**

1st ed., 1968, had title: *Who's who in Australian libraries*; 3rd ed., 1984.

Includes biographical information for 2,052 Australian librarians, obtained from questionnaires. Entries from the 3rd ed. that were not updated are included but marked with an asterisk.   Z720.A46A85

A biographical directory of librarians in the United States and Canada / Lee Ash, ed. ; B. A. Uhlendorf, assoc. ed. 5th ed. Chicago : Amer. Libr. Assoc., 1970. 1250 p.   **AK83**

1st ed. (1933)–4th ed. (1966) had title: *Who's who in library service* (N.Y. : H.W. Wilson).

Sponsored by the Council of National Library Associations.

Although now seriously dated, this directory continues to be valuable because it includes many librarians not included in *Who's who in library and information services* (AK93) and provides biographical information about librarians for whom only abbreviated information is given in the *Directory of library & information professionals* (AK88).   Z720.A4W47

Carroll, Frances Laverne. Biographical directory of national librarians / ed. by Frances Laverne Carroll and Philip J. Schwartz. London ; N.Y. : Mansell, 1989. 134 p.   **AK84**

Arranged alphabetically by country; provides biographical information about the chief executive of each country's national library. Many entries also include a "Recommended source of the history and description of the library."   Z720.A1C37

Dale, Doris Cruger. A directory of oral history tapes of librarians in the United States and Canada. Chicago : Amer. Libr. Assoc., 1986. 103 p.   **AK85**

A list of 205 recorded interviews held by 40 institutions, arranged alphabetically by institution, then by name of librarian. Entries include a brief biographical sketch of the interviewee, name of interviewer, date and length of interview, subjects covered and names of other librarians mentioned, as well as information regarding copyright, availability of transcript, and permission to cite. Personal name and subject indexes.   Z720.A4D34

Dictionary of American library biography / editorial board: George S. Bobinski, Jesse Hauk Shera, Bohdan S. Wynar. Littleton, Colo. : Libraries Unlimited, 1978. 596 p.   **AK86**

A collection of biographical sketches (about 1,000 to 6,000 words each) of 302 outstanding men and women of the library field. Emphasis is on "figures of national importance, based on the following criteria: contributions of national significance to library development; writings that influenced library trends and activities; positions of national importance … ; major achievements in special fields of librarianship; significant scholarly, philanthropic, legislative, or governmental support or activity that affected American libraries. To ensure proper historical perspective, only those people deceased as of June 30, 1976, were considered for inclusion."—*p. xxxi.* Articles are signed and include bibliographies.

§ The *Supplement to the dictionary of American library biography* / ed. by Wayne A. Wiegand (Englewood, Colo. : Libraries Unlimited, 1990. 184 p.) uses the same selection criteria. A majority of the biographies are of individuals who died between June 30, 1976, and June 30, 1987, the *Supplement*'s original cutoff date. Includes individuals overlooked in the original edition. A cumulative name index covers both publications.   Z720.A4D5

The directory of ethnic professionals in LIS (library and information science) / comp. by George C. Grant. Winter Park, Fla. : Four-G Publishers, 1991. 254, 60 p.   **AK87**

Includes 1,600 biographies of ethnic librarians, including African Americans, Asian Americans, Latinos, and Native Americans. Some librarians from Africa and the Phillipines are included. Biographical entries contain ethnic heritage, employment history, education, professional activities, publications, specialization, and areas of consulting.   Z720.A4D54

Directory of library & information professionals. Woodbridge, Conn. : Research Publ., c1988. 2 v.   **AK88**

Vol. 1 presents biographical data on 23,000 individuals who are employed in the information field at a professional level or in education or training, or who are members of library and information professional associations. Entries appear in alphabetical order and include some or all of the following information: biographee's name, current position, previous positions, education, publications, achievements, honors, memberships, language proficiency, professional expertise or subject specialty, and consulting availability. Name, employer, and address are supplied for an additional 20,000 individuals based on information from the American Library Association's membership files. Vol. 2 contains specialty, employer, consulting/freelance, and geographical indexes.

•Available in machine-readable form as: *Directory of library & information professionals : (DLIP)* [database] (Chicago : Amer. Libr. Assoc., 1988).

Originally compiled jointly by ALA and Research Publications. Entries date to 1986–87.

There are no plans to update either the printed or machine-readable versions.   Z720.A4D57

Engelbarts, Rudolf. Librarian authors : a bibliography. Jefferson, N.C. : McFarland, 1981. 276 p. : ill.   **AK89**

Begins with chronologically arranged descriptions of the careers of 105 famous librarian authors or influential friends of the library, such as Sir Thomas Bodley and Andrew Carnegie and concludes with a general bibliography on librarianship, librarians as authors, and an alphabetically arranged bibliography of works by and about the authors discussed in the volume. Most of the contemporary authors are American. Biographical information is incomplete.   Z720.A1E53

Frati, Carlo. Dizionario bio-bibliografico dei bibliotecari e bibliofili italiani dal sec. XIV al XIX / raccolto e pubblicato da Albano Sorbelli. Firenze : Olschki, 1933. 705 p. : ill. (Biblioteca de bibliografia italiana, v. 13).   **AK90**

A biographical dictionary of Italian librarians and bibliophiles with detailed lists of works by and about each of them. Includes index by place of libraries mentioned and author index to the works cited.

Munford, William Arthur. Who was who in British librarianship, 1800–1985 : a dictionary of dates with notes. London : Libr. Assoc., 1987. 91 p. **AK91**

Entries (arranged alphabetically) give, where available, birth and death dates, dates and places of positions held, and other significant achievements. Abbreviations table. Appendix of persons with information limited to place and date of office held. Includes librarians in senior positions who have died, or must be presumed to have died, by December 1985. Z720.A46G7

New York State Library School Association. New York State library school register, 1887–1926. James I. Wyer memorial ed. [i.e. 6th ed.]. N.Y. : Assoc., 1959. 175 p. : ill. **AK92**

A biographical directory of students who attended the school 1887–1926. Arranged chronologically by class, entries include library experience, retirement, marriages, other sources of biographical information, elective offices, publications, and death. Information is current to the approximate time of publication. Name index provides cross-references for women's married names. Important because so many pioneer library leaders graduated from the school.

Who's who in library and information services / Joel M. Lee, ed. in chief. Chicago : Amer. Libr. Assoc., 1982. 559 p. **AK93**

Forms a successor to *A biographical directory of librarians in the United States and Canada* (AK83) and its predecessor, *Who's who in library service* (N.Y. : H.W. Wilson Co., 1933–1966.).

Although requirements for inclusion were somewhat more stringent than was the case for the earlier series, scope for this volume extends to "librarians and information scientists; archivists; library school faculty and other educators; scholars in subject specialties associated with libraries or library education programs; publishers, editors, and journalists whose primary activity is in librarianship and information fields; trustees; others who have made notable contributions to library and information services."—*p. ix.* Z720.A4W45

Who's who in New Zealand library and information service. 1990– . Wellington : New Zealand Libr. Assoc., 1991– . **AK94**

Title varies: 1951– , *Who's who in New Zealand libraries.* Z720.A4N4

Statistics

ACRL university library statistics. 1978–79– . Chicago : Association of College and Research Libraries, 1980– . Biennial. **AK95**

Title varies: earlier issues called *ACRL statistics: University library statistics.* Absorbed: *100 libraries statistical survey 1985–86.*

Provides data on more than 100 U.S. and Canadian academic libraries of research universities and doctorate-granting colleges and universities. Statistical tables present information on collections, interlibrary loan, personnel, and expenditures. Complements *ARL statistics* (AK96) by providing similar data on additional colleges and universities. Z675.U5A36

Association of Research Libraries. ARL statistics. 1974/75– . Wash. : Association of Research Libraries. Annual. **AK96**

Continues: *Academic library statistics*, 1963–1973.

Reports fiscal year statistics for the 108 university and 12 independent U.S. and Canadian research libraries that are members of the association. Includes statistics on collections, interlibrary loan, personnel, and expenditures. Complemented by *ACRL university library statistics* (AK95). Z675.U5A78

LISU annual library statistics. 1992– . [Loughborough, Eng.] : Library and Information Statistics Unit, Dept. of Information and Library Studies, Loughborough Univ., 1992– . **AK97**

Includes statistics on library holdings, staffing and other expenditures by type of library. Emphasis is on trends. Gives an academic book price index for the U.K.

Lynch, Mary Jo. Sources of library statistics, 1972–1982. Chicago : Amer. Libr. Assoc., 1983. 48 p. **AK98**

An annotated guide to sources of library statistics for all types of American libraries. Sources are also included for networks, state library agencies, and special topics, such as buildings, library education, salaries, and prices. Three appendixes: Commentary of library statistics; Library statistics from state government sources; and Library statistics published before 1972. Z721.L96

Statistical report ... Public Library Data Service / Prep. by Public Library Assoc., a div. of the American Library Assoc. 1992– . Chicago : The Assoc., 1992– . Annual. **AK99**

Continues: *Public Library Data Service statistical report* (Chicago : American Library Assoc., 1988–91).

The 1993 report provides data concerning 630 public libraries. Statistics, arranged by population size, include data on income, salaries, and operating expenditures. Gives demographic information about each library community. A directory, arranged alphabetically, lists population service area, address, director, person completing survey, presence of a central library, number of branches. Z731.P937

LIBRARIES, ARCHIVES, AND INFORMATION CENTERS

Resources

Ash, Lee. Subject collections / comp. by Lee Ash and William G. Miller ... [et al.]. 7th ed., rev. & enl. New Providence, N.J. : Bowker, 1993. 2 v. (2466 p.). **AK100**

Subtitle: A guide to special book collections and subject emphases as reported by university, college, public, and special libraries and museums in the United States and Canada.

1st ed., 1958; 6th ed., 1985.

Arranged alphabetically by subject, then geographically. Information is based on questionnaires completed by holding libraries, resulting in some unevenness. Z731.A78

British Library. The British Library : past, present, future / [text, R. C. Alston ; photography, Anne Gilbert ... et al.]. London : British Library, c1989. 64 p. : col. ill. **AK101**

This lavishly illustrated work describes history, collections and services of the British Library. Z792.B85932B74

Burton, Dennis A. A guide to manuscripts in the presidential libraries / comp. and ed. by Dennis A. Burton, James B. Rhoads, Raymond W. Smock. College Park, Md. : Research Materials Corp., c1985. 451 p. : ill. **AK102**

For annotation, *see* CJ176. CD3029.82.B87

Downs, Robert Bingham. American library resources : a bibliographical guide. Chicago : Amer. Libr. Assoc., 1951. 428 p. **AK103**

A bibliography of sources of information about library collections. Catalogs, bibliographies, articles that describe special collections, and the like are included. This work and its decennial supplements are arranged by subject. A full index by author, subject, and library helps in locating individual titles as well as special collections on particular subjects. However, it must be borne in mind that other libraries may have collections of equal or greater importance for which no lists are available.

Updated by three supplements: 1950–61 (1962. 226 p.); 1961–70 (1972. 244 p.); 1971–1980 (1981. 209 p.).

American library resources cumulative index, 1870–1970, ed. by Clara D. Keller (1981. 89 p.), provides an author/subject index.

————————— Australian and New Zealand library resources. London : Mansell ; Melbourne : Thorpe, 1979. 164 p.

AK104

Records the results of a survey of Australian and New Zealand libraries. Arrangement is by general subjects and types of material, with brief descriptions of those collections having significant resources for advanced study and research. References are given to published bibliographies, descriptions of collections, etc. Bibliography, p. 121–45. Indexed.   Z870.A1D6

East Central and Southeast Europe : a handbook of library and archival resources in North America / Paul L. Horecky, chief ed. ; David H. Kraus, assoc. ed. Santa Barbara, Calif. : Clio Pr., 1976. 466 p. (Joint Committee on Eastern Europe. Publications series, no.3).   **AK105**

For annotation, *see* DC47.   Z2483.E2

Grant, Steven A. The Russian Empire and the Soviet Union : a guide to manuscripts and archival materials in the United States / Steven A. Grant and John H. Brown ; Kennan Institute for Advanced Russian Studies, the Wilson Center. Boston : G.K. Hall, 1981. 632 p.   **AK106**

For annotation, *see* DC560.   Z2491.G66

Histoire des bibliothèques françaises / sous la direction d'André Vernet. [Paris] : Promodis-Editions du Cercle du librairie, 1988–92. 4 v. : ill.   **AK107**

Editors vary.

Contents: [v. 1], Les bibliothèques médiévales, du VIe siècle à 1530; [v. 2], Les bibliothèques sous l'Ancien Régime, 1530–1789; [v. 3], Les bibliothèques de la Révolution et du XIXe siècle, 1789–1914 [v. 4], Les bibliothèques au XXe siècle, 1914–1990.

A definitive history of French libraries that includes much information about individual libraries and their collections, and biographical information about important librarians. Includes bibliographies.   Z797.A1H57

Lee, Thomas H. A guide to East Asian collections in North America. N.Y. : Greenwood, c1992. 158 p. (Bibliographies and indexes in world history, no. 25).   **AK108**

A directory of East Asian collections arranged alphabetically by institution. Entries for 55 libraries include address, hours, holdings by language, areas of strength, special collections, and access. Subject index.   Z3001.L4

Lewanski, Richard Casimir. Eastern Europe and Russia/Soviet Union : a handbook of West European archival and library resources. N.Y. [etc.] : K.G. Saur, 1980. 317 p. (American Council of Learned Societies/Social Science Research Council. Joint Committee on Eastern Europe. Publications series, 3).   **AK109**

For annotation, *see* DC50.   Z2483.L48

Library of Congress. Special collections in the Library of Congress : a selective guide / comp. by Annette Melville. Wash. : Library of Congress, 1980. 464 p. : ill.   **AK110**

An alphabetical guide, by name of collection, to the 269 special collections at the Library of Congress. Collections composed entirely of microforms, personal papers, nonmusic manuscripts within the scope of the *National union catalog of manuscript collections* (DB34), and "format collections" such as miniature books, globes, and piano rolls are excluded. An appendix explains the collections and services of LC divisions. There is a subject index.   Z733.U58U54

Macdonald, Roger. Libraries and special collections on Latin America and the Caribbean : a directory of European resources / by Roger Macdonald and Carole Travis. 2nd ed. London ; Atlantic Highlands, N.J. : publ. for the Inst. of Latin American Studies, Univ. of London [by] the Athlone Pr., 1988. 339 p. (Institute of Latin American Studies monographs, 14).

AK111

1st ed., 1975: *Directory of libraries and special collections on Latin America and the West Indies*, by Bernard Naylor, Laurence Hallewell, and Colin Steele.

Concentrates on collections of printed material in 468 European repositories. Based on results of a questionnaire and, for those institutions not responding, on secondary sources. Arranged by country and city; for each gives name and address (including telephone and fax numbers), names of specialist librarians, brief description of the collection, hours and access, copying facilities, publications. Name, subject, format (e.g., videotapes, press cuttings) index.   Z1601.M25

National inventory of documentary sources in the United States [microform]. Teaneck, N.J. : Chadwyck-Healey, 1983– . [ca.23,000 fiche]. (In progress).   **AK112**

Known as *NIDS*.

Contents: pt. 1, Federal records; pt. 2, Manuscript Division, Library of Congress; pt. 3, State, academic and regional repositories (formed by the merger of pt. 3, State archives, libraries and historical societies, and pt. 4, Academic libraries and other repositories).

Reproduces "published and unpublished finding aids to archives and manuscript collections" (*Index, v. 1*) in the U.S., beginning with the National Archives and the Library of Congress. The finding aids are reproduced and issued in no particular order, about ten units per year. Cumulative name indexes appear on fiche which usually file first.

The first two parts have printed indexes: *Federal records*, comp. by V. Agee [et al.] (1985. 260 p.) and *Manuscript Division, Library of Congress*, comp. by V. Agee (1983. 219 p.). Each lists the finding aids reproduced in the microfiche set and indexes their contents by subject and by personal, corporate, institutional, and geographic names.

•The publisher has issued an index on CD-ROM that covers all of pts. 1–2 and units 1–45 of pts. 3–4. Searching is by keyword or by browsing titles, subjects, names of repositories, and NUCMC or microfiche numbers.

For a description of the project, see *American historical review* 93 (Feb. 1988): 224-25. For a comparison of NUCMC, NIDS, and RLIN, see "Finding manuscript collections : NUCMC, NIDS, and RLIN," *National Genealogical Society quarterly*, 77 (Sept. 1989) : 208–18.

Special collections in children's literature / ed. by Carolyn W. Field. Chicago : Amer. Libr. Assoc., 1982. 257 p. : ill.

AK113

Represents a revised and updated edition of Field's *Subject collections in children's literature* (N.Y. : Bowker, 1969).

Comp. in consultation with the National Planning for Special Collections Committee, Association for Library Service to Children.

Provides a subject approach to special collections of children's books at 267 institutions in the U.S. and Canada. Within the alphabetical subject arrangement, repositories are listed and an indication is given of the type and extent of holdings. A directory of collections lists the repositories by state; appendix of references to descriptive articles, catalogs of the collections, etc. Indexed.   Z688.C47S63

United States. National Archives and Records Administration. Guide to the National Archives of the United States / new pref. by Frank B. Evans. Wash. : The Archives, 1987. 896 p.

AK114

For annotation, *see* DB38.   CD3023.U53

Williams, Sam P. Guide to research collections of the New York Public Library. Chicago : Amer. Libr. Assoc., 1975. 336 p.   **AK115**

Supersedes Karl Brown's *Guide to the reference collections of the New York Public Library* (N.Y., 1941).

A guide to the principal resources and special collections in this vast library system. In four main sections, each with numerous subdivisions: (1) General materials; (2) The humanities; (3) The social sciences; (4) The pure and applied sciences. Index of subjects and collections.   Z733.N6W54

Wynar, Lubomyr Roman. Slavic ethnic libraries, museums and archives in the United States : a guide and directory. Chicago : Amer. Libr. Assoc., 1980. 164 p.   **AK116**

At head of title: Association of College and Research Libraries, American Library Association and Center for the Study of Ethnic Publications, School of Library Science, Kent State University.

Arranged by ethnic group (Bulgarian-American through Yugoslavian-American). Gives information on size and scope of the collections, staff, access, publications, etc. Includes societies, associations, fraternal organizations, etc., which maintain libraries or archival collections.   Z1361.S5W9

Directories

International

Directory of libraries and information centers of the academies of sciences of socialist countries / [J. Boldis ... et al.]. Moscow : General Editorial Board for Foreign Publications, Nauka Publishers, 1986. 119 p.   **AK117**

Translation of: Biblioteki i tsentry informatsii akademiĭ nauk sotsialisticheskikh stran.

At head of title: Library of the USSR Academy of Sciences.

An expanded version of the Russian-language edition publ. 1984. Arranged geographically by country. Academies of sciences of Bulgaria, Hungary, Vietnam, German Democratic Republic, Mongolia, Poland, Romania, USSR, Czechoslovakia, and Yugoslavia are included. Entries contain information about staff, collections, catalogs, and publications.   Z789.5.B5313

Esdaile, Arundell James Kennedy. National libraries of the world : their history, administration and public services. 2nd ed. compl. rev. by F. J. Hill. London : Libr. Assoc., 1957. 413 p.   **AK118**

1st ed., 1934.

Describes the national libraries of 32 countries. Each library is treated in a separate chapter giving history, description of buildings, catalogs, departments, staff, finances, etc., and a brief bibliography.   Z721.E74

Lewanski, Richard Casimir. Subject collections in European libraries. 2nd ed. London ; N.Y. : Bowker, [1978]. 495 p.   **AK119**

1st ed., 1965.

Designed as a companion to Lee Ash and William G. Miller's *Subject collections* (AK100) for the U. S. and Canada, this directory concentrates chiefly on libraries of northwestern Europe. Entries are arranged by Dewey class numbers, with an alphabetical subject index to the classification. Within classes the arrangement is alphabetical by country. Indicates size and character of collection, restrictions, photocopy facilities, etc.   Z789.L4

Steele, Colin. Major libraries of the world : a selective guide. London ; N.Y. : Bowker, c1976. 479 p. : ill.   **AK120**

Although now dated, this book continues to be a useful guide to major research library collections. national, special, and academic libraries are included. Provides information about history, special collections, exhibition areas, hours, parking, admission, services, catalogs, etc. Arranged by country, then by city.   Z721.S82

World guide to libraries = Internationale Bibliotheksadressbuch / [ed. by Helga Lengenfelder]. 9th ed.– . München ; N.Y. : K.G. Saur, 1989– .   **AK121**

Issued as Bd. 8 of *Handbuch der internationalen Dokumentation und information* (München : Verlag Dokumentationen der Technik, 1956–).

Provides name of institution, address, telephone, telex and fax numbers, year founded, name of director, important holdings, and size of collection for more than 40,000 libraries in about 170 countries, including special libraries with more than 5,000 volumes, or national, academic, research, government, school, ecclesiastical, and public libraries with more than 30,000 volumes. Arranged alphabetically by country, then by type of library. Index of libraries.

North America

United States

American library directory : a classified list of libraries in the United States and Canada, with personnel and statistical data. 1923– . N.Y. : Bowker, 1923– . Annual.   **AK122**

Subtitle, compiler, place of publication, and frequency vary. 1951– called Ed. 19– ; 1992–93 is 45th ed.

Earlier lists were a feature of *American library annual* (N.Y. : Office of the Publishers' Weekly, 1912–18. 7 v.).

Libraries are arranged alphabetically by state and then by city. Gives name, librarian (and usually names of department heads), number of volumes, circulation, income, budget, special collections. For large libraries information is more detailed. Statistical information regarding public libraries precedes each state, region and province division. Additional lists include networks, consortia and other cooperative library organizations; library schools and training courses; library systems; libraries for the blind and physically handicapped; libraries serving the deaf and hearing impaired; state and provincial public library agencies; state school library agencies; national and model interlibrary loan codes; United States Armed Forces libraries overseas; United States Information Agency centers. Indexed.

•Available in machine-readable version as: *American library directory (ALD)* [database] (N.Y. : Bowker). Available online and in CD-ROM as part of of *Library reference plus* (AK33). Database version, replaced annually, lists only entries for current edition.   Z731.A53

Directory of special libraries and information centers. 1st ed., (1963)– . Detroit : Gale, [1963]– . Irregular.   **AK123**

Subtitle, 2nd ed. (1968)– : A guide to special libraries, research libraries, information centers, archives, and data centers maintained by government agencies, business, industry, newspapers, educational institutions, nonprofit organizations, and societies in the field of science and engineering, technology, medicine, law, art, religion, history, social sciences and humanities.

Lists more than 20,000 special libraries in the U.S. and Canada. Libraries are listed by name, sponsoring body, or institution in a single alphabetical sequence, with a subject index in v. 1. Appendixes list networks and consortia, regional and subregional libraries for the blind and physically handicapped, patent and trademark depository libraries, regional government depository libraries, U.N. depository libraries, World Bank depository libraries, and European Community depository libraries. Vol. 2 offers geographic and personnel indexes.

Vol. 1 is kept up-to-date between editions by *New special libraries* (1971–), which lists new or previously overlooked libraries.   Z731.D56

Evinger, William R. Directory of federal libraries. 2nd ed. Phoenix : Oryx, 1993. 373 p.   **AK124**

Lists more than 2,500 U.S. government libraries throughout the world. Entries include: address and telephone number; name or names of administrative staff; library size; special subjects; automated services; circulation and reference policies; and publications. Arranged by federal administrative structure; indexes by type of library, subject, and geographic location.   Z731.E93

Special collections in college and university libraries / comp. by Modoc Press, Inc. N.Y. : Macmillan ; London : Collier Macmillan, c1989. 639 p.   **AK125**

"A compilation of detailed, descriptive information concerning special collections, rare books, and manuscripts to be found in the libraries of colleges and universities throughout the United States."— *Pref.* Describes collections at 1,805 four- and two-year institutions. Alphabetically arranged by state, then by institution. General index (personal names, subjects, geographic place names, and titles of books and magazines) and institutional index.   Z731.S73

Subject directory of special libraries and information centers. 1st ed.– . Detroit : Gale, 1975– .   **AK126**

Frequency varies: annual beginning with the 10th ed. (1987).

Number of volumes and subject coverage vary: 17th ed. (1994) in three volumes (v. 1: Business, government, and law libraries; v. 2: Computers, engineering, and science libraries; v. 3, Health sciences libraries).

Entries from *Directory of special libraries and information centers* (AK123), reorganized by subject.   Z675.A2S83

Canada

See also *American library directory* (AK122) and *Directory of special libraries and information centers* (AK123).

Directory of Canadian archives = Annuaire des dépôts d'archives canadiens. [Ottawa] : Bureau of Canadian Archivists, [1981]. 130 p.   **AK127**

Ed. by Judith Beattie [et al.].

A joint project of the Association of Canadian Archivists and the Association des Archivistes du Québec. Represents a revised and updated edition of the 1977 *Directory of Canadian records and manuscript repositories.*

Gives address, hours of opening, etc., and brief notes on holdings. Federal repositories are listed first, with others listed by province or territory. Indexed.

National Library of Canada. Research collections in Canadian libraries. Ottawa : Information Canada, 1972–1984. 2 v. in 15 pts. : maps. (In progress).   **AK128**

Contents: Section I, Universities: v. 1, Prairie provinces; v. 2, Atlantic provinces; v. 3, British Columbia; v. 4. Ontario; v. 5, Quebec; v. 6, Canada. Section II, Special studies: v. 1, Theatre resources in Canadian collections; v. 2, Federal government libraries; v. 3, Law library resources in Canada; v. 4, Slavic and east European resources in Canadian academic and research libraries; v. 5. Collections of official publications in Canada; v. 6. Fine arts library resources in Canada; v. 7, Music resources in Canadian collections; v. 8, Dance resources in Canadian libraries; v. 9, Resources for native peoples study.   Z735.A1N37

Mexico

Guía de archivos y bibliotecas. [Mexico, D.F.] : Universidad Iberoamericana, Departamento de Historia : Ediciones El Caballito, [1984, i.e. 1985]. 167 p. : maps.   **AK129**

Lists 24 institutions housing major historical collections. Each entry gives the name of the institution, address, hours, access policy, historical sketch and mission statement, description of holdings, services provided, organizational structure, and situates the institution on a local map.   CD3677.M4G85

Latin America

Nauman, Ann Keith. A handbook of Latin American & Caribbean national archives = Guía de los archivos nacionales de America Latina y el Caribe. Detroit : Blaine Ethridge–Books, [1983]. 127 p.   **AK130**

Intended for "the potential first-time user of archival collections in Mexico, Central and South America, the Outer Islands and nations of the Caribbean. It is designed to provide pertinent data relative to what the user may expect to encounter in the way of materials and services, and what, if any, requirements and restrictions apply."— *Introd.* Information for most countries was derived from questionnaires completed at the respective national archives; text appears in English and Spanish in separate sections.

§ An article by Ron L. Seckinger, "A guide to selected diplomatic archives of South America" (*Latin American research review* 10 no. 1 [1975] : 127–53), provides a supplement for major diplomatic archives in Argentina, Bolivia, Brazil, Chile, Colombia, Peru, and Uruguay.   CD3680.N38

Europe

Directory of special collections in Western Europe / ed. by Alison Gallico. London ; N.Y. : Bowker-Saur, 1993. 146 p.   **AK131**

Aims "to make known substantial collections in specific subjects which are held in large general collections"—*Introd.* Arranged geographically by the 11 countries treated. Entries contain information about interlibrary loan and photocopying. Institution index; subject index in English, French, and German.   Z789.D56

Guide to libraries in Western Europe : national, international and government libraries / ed. by Peter Dale. London : British Library, 1991. 122 p.   **AK132**

A directory of government, national, and British Council libraries, and national library associations in Western Europe and the U.K. Organized in four geographic sections, with indexes by name, organization, and subject.

Benelux countries

Brogan, Martha L. Research guide to libraries and archives in the Low Countries. N.Y. : Greenwood, 1991. 546 p. (Bibliographies and indexes in library and information science, no. 5).   **AK133**

This comprehensive guide to research collections in the Benelux countries (Belgium, Luxembourg, and the Netherlands) has two parts. Pt. 1 lists national bibliographies, union catalogs, directories and guides to the collections, as well as many subject guides and bibliographies; pt. 2 is a directory of libraries and archives. The directory is arranged geographically, and each entry contains information about collections, catalogs, use of the collection, and services. Some entries also list publications and provide a bibliography for further reading. Author/title, institution, and subject indexes.

§ Companion to others in the series commissioned by the Council of European Studies: Erwin K. Welsch, *Archives and libraries in France* and, with Jürgen Danyel and Thomas Kilton, *Archives and libraries in a new Germany* (AK136 and AK139), and Rudolf J. Lewanski, *Guide to Italian libraries and archives* (AK151).   813.A1B76

Finland

Liinamaa, Matti. Suomen tieteellisten Kirjastojen opas / [by] Matti Liinamaa and Marjatta Heikkilä. 6. uusittu ja täydennetty painos. Helsinki : Suomen Tieteellinen Kirjastoseura, 1981. 175 p. **AK134**

Title also in English: *Guide to research libraries and information services in Finland.*

In English, Finnish, and Swedish.

1st ed., 1950, by Eino Nivanka. Z829.A1L54

France

Chauleur, André. Bibliothèques et archives : comment se documenter? 2ème éd. Paris : Économica, [1980]. 334 p. **AK135**

"Guide pratique à l'usage des étudiants, des professeurs, des documentalistes et archivistes, des chercheurs ..."–*t.p.*

"Publié pour l'Institut National de Recherche Pédagogique."–*t.p.*

1st ed., 1978.

A guide for students and research workers in the libraries and archives of France. An "Introduction bibliographique" has been provided in this edition; it is followed by separate sections for libraries and for archives, each section providing directory information for the repositories (which are grouped by type). There are extensive sections on the Bibliothèque Nationale and the Archives Nationales. Indexed. Z797.A1C47

Welsch, Erwin K. Archives and libraries in France : with 1991 supplement. N.Y. : Council for European Studies, 1991. 147 p. **AK136**

1st ed., 1973, and rev. ed., 1979, had title *Libraries and archives in France : a handbook.*

Intended as "a compact and portable source of basic information of the kind most frequently needed by students and scholars working in France for the first time."—*Introd.* Emphasis is on resources for modern French history and the social sciences. In three sections. (1) Libraries in the Paris region; (2) Archives in the Paris region; (3) Departmental archives and libraries. Gives address, hours of opening, size of collections, terms of access, etc., and references to published descriptions of the collections. Z797.A1W44

Germany

Archive : Archive im deutschsprachigen Raum. Berlin ; N.Y. : de Gruyter, 1974. 2 v. (1418 p.). **AK137**

At head of title: Minerva-Handbücher.

Aufl. 1, 1932, published as *Minerva-Handbücher*: 2. Abt. Die Archive, Bd.1.

Offers information on about 8,000 archives in Germany (both East and West Germany), Austria, Switzerland, Luxembourg and Lichtenstein, together with a few archives in Czechoslovakia and Poland. Indexes by type of archive, by country, and by city. Includes private as well as public archives. CD1000.A72

Handbuch der Bibliotheken Bundesrepublik Deutschland, Österreich, Schweiz / [hrsg. von Helga Lengenfelder]. München : K. G. Saur, 1984. 329 p. **AK138**

Listing is by type of library within separate sections for Germany, Austria, and Switzerland. Subject index. Z801.A1H35

Welsch, Erwin K. Archives and libraries in a new Germany / Erwin K. Welsch and Jürgen Danyel, with Thomas Kilton. N.Y. : Council for European Studies, 1994. 372 p. **AK139**

Based on an earlier work, *Libraries and archives in Germany* (1975).

"Intended as an introductory guide and handbook for researchers in the fields of German history, German social science, and German literature, who are planning their initial research trips to Germany."—*Introd.* With the exception of national and governmental libraries and archives, arranged geographically by state. Entries include holdings, provisions for use, directions to the library or archive, and bibliography of catalogs, guides and other publications. There is an extensive bibliography and subject index. Z675.R45W45

Great Britain

Academic libraries in the United Kingdom and the Republic of Ireland / ed. by Ann Harrold. 3rd ed. London : Libr. Assoc., 1994. 148 p. **AK140**

1st ed., 1987, called: *Libraries in colleges of further and higher education in the UK.*

Each entry includes: controlling authority, name of chief librarian, hours of opening, size of stock, relationship within the institution, and special collections. In some cases a short history is also given. Alphabetical arrangement. Indexed by institution, subject, special collections, and geography. The institutional index provides valuable cross-references from former names to current names. Z675.U5

Aslib directory of information sources in the United Kingdom / ed. by Ellen M. Codlin and Keith W. Reynard. 7th ed. London : Aslib, 1992. 2 v. **AK141**

1st ed., 1928; 6th ed., 1970.

Vol. 1 is an alphabetical list of over 6,800 institutions in the U.K. that contain subject collections. Entries include address information, subject coverage, and publications. Vol. 2 is the index to the subjects and a list of acronyms. Z791.A1A82

Directory of library and information organizations in the United Kingdom / comp. by Peter Dale. London : Library Association, 1993. 180 p. **AK142**

An alphabetical listing of library-related organizations not only in the U.K. but also in Europe and the Commonwealth. Entries include geographic scope, contact person, group activities, publications, and membership criteria. Subgroups of major associations (e.g., Library Association) as well as independent organizations are listed. Z674.5.P6D5

A directory of rare book and special collections in the United Kingdom and the Republic of Ireland / ed. by Moelwyn I. Williams for the Rare Books Group of the Library Association. London : The Association, 1985. 664 p. **AK143**

"The basic aim of the directory is to bring to the notice of scholars and researchers the location of rare book collections in the United Kingdom and Republic of Ireland."—*Introd.* Rare books are defined as all printed matter before 1851 and later material such as first editions, limited editions, and ephemera. Many special collections are also included. Arranged geographically, listings contain address, phone number, business hours, conditions of admission, and research facilities. A brief history and description of the collection is also given. Comprehensive index. Z791.A1D58

Downs, Robert Bingham. British and Irish library resources : a bibliographical guide / Robert B. Downs, assisted by Elizabeth C. Downs. London : Mansell, 1981. 427 p. **AK144**

"A rev. and updated ed. of *British library resources*, first published in 1973."—*t.p.*

Intends to "record all published library catalogs—general and special; all checklists of specialized collections in libraries; calendars of manuscripts and archives; exhibition catalogs; articles descriptive of library collections; guides to individual libraries and their holdings; directories of libraries—both general and in specialized fields; union lists of periodicals, newspapers, and other serials; and any other records, descriptive, analytical, or critical, that may guide the scholar, research worker, or advanced student in finding significant materials to meet his needs."—*Introd.* Includes libraries of the U. K. and Eire. Classed arrangement with index. Z791.A1D68

Foster, Janet. British archives : a guide to archive resources in the United Kingdom / Janet Foster & Julia Sheppard. 2nd ed. N.Y. : Stockton Pr., 1989. lviii, 834 p.   **AK145**

  1st ed., 1982.

  Publ. in U.K. : London : Macmillan, 1989.

  Arranged geographically by town. Gives for each repository address, telephone, hours of access, facilities, organization, major collections finding aids, and publications. Alphabetical indexes by name of institution, county, collections, and subjects. Appendixes list institutions that have placed their archives elsewhere; institutions reporting no archives; and institutions that did not respond to the questionnaire. Contains 1,048 entries, a substantial increase from the 1st ed.

  CD1040.F67

The libraries directory. 1988–90– . Cambridge : James Clarke & Co., c1991– . Biennial.   **AK146**

  Dist. in the U.S. and Canada by Gale.

  Title varies: 1985–87, *Libraries year book.*

  Continues: *Libraries, museums and art galleries year book.*

  A directory for the U.K. and the Republic of Ireland comparable to *American library directory* (AK122). Following a directory of the British Library are geographically arranged sections for public and special libraries in the U.K. with separate similarly arranged sections for the Republic of Ireland. Entries include address, hours, size of collection, special collections, publications etc. Academic libraries are entered in the "special libraries" section. Combined index by institution name.   Z791.L7

Libraries in the United Kingdom and the Republic of Ireland. 1960– . London : Libr. Assoc., 1960– . Annual beginning 1985.   **AK147**

  Title varies: 1960–1969, *Address list of public library authorities.* Frequency varies.

  Gives address, telephone number, and name of librarian for public, university and college, polytechnic, and selected national, government and special libraries. Includes a section for schools of librarianship. Indexed.   Z791.A1L43

Taylor, L. J. Library resources in London and South East England / ed. by L. J. Taylor and E. A. Taylor. 2nd ed. London : Library Assoc., Reference, Special and Information Section, 1979. 275 p.   **AK148**

  1st ed., 1969, ed. by S. Eagle.

  A directory for the area, with a subject index to the special strengths of the various collections. One of a series of directories published by the Reference, Special and Information Section of the Library Association; other volumes deal with library resources of the East Midlands (1979), the North East (1977), North West England (1980), South West England and the Channel Isles (1978), Wales (1975), West Midlands (1977), and Yorkshire and Humberside (1980).   Z791.L6E2

Italy

Annuario delle biblioteche italiane. Roma : Palombi, 1969–81. 5 v.   **AK149**

  Publ. under the direction of the Direzione Generale delle Accademie e Biblioteche e per la Diffusione della Cultura.

  Earlier editions with the same title were publ. 1949–54 (3 v. plus suppl.) and 1956–59 (3 v.).

  University, public, and other libraries are arranged alphabetically under towns, and described with considerable detail, including historical information. Contains bibliographic references.   Z809.A6

Guida generale degli archivi di Stato italiani / direttori, Piero D'Angiolini, Claudio Pavone. Roma : Ministero per i beni culturali e ambientali, Ufficio centrale per i beni archivistici, 1981–86. v. 1–3. (In progress?).   **AK150**

  An extensive inventory of government archives, both federal and local, with long descriptions, notes on finding aids, and lists of contents. A section on the Archivio Centrale dello Stato (v. 1) is followed

by descriptions of state archives arranged alphabetically by city. Sections on the individual city archives are usually subdivided by historical period, then by office or agency, with notes on the principal collections. Each archive has its own table of contents and index.

  CD1424.G84

Lewanski, Rudolf J. Guide to Italian libraries and archives. N.Y. : Council for European Studies, [1979]. 101 p.   **AK151**

  A directory of major archives and libraries, arranged by city and furnishing brief information on holdings, special collections, hours of opening, etc., together with references to published descriptions, catalogs, and finding aids. A section entitled "Subject collections" lists the repositories by subject field.   Z809.A1L48

Poland

Lewanski, Richard Casimir. Guide to Polish libraries and archives. Boulder, Colo. : East European Quarterly (distr. by Columbia Univ. Pr.), 1974. 209 p. (East European monographs, no. 6).   **AK152**

  Aims "to provide American and other English-reading scholars and researchers a comprehensive guide to materials in Polish repositories of manuscript and printed records."—*Introd.* Emphasis is on resources for study of Polish history, civilization, and society. Listing is by city, then by repository. A "subject profile" for each library is usually supplemented by a listing of special collections or unique features. Published catalogs and descriptions of the libraries or special collections are noted. Subject index.   Z817.A1L48

Russia and the U.S.S.R.

Grimsted, Patricia Kennedy. Archives and manuscript repositories in the USSR : Moscow and Leningrad. Princeton : Princeton Univ. Pr., [1972]. 436 p.   **AK153**

  For this and other handbooks on archives and manuscript repositories in Russia and the U.S.S.R., *see* DC561.   CD1711.G7

Africa

Directory of documentation, libraries and archives services in Africa = Répertoire des services de documentation, de bibliothèque et d'archives d'Afrique. 2. éd. by Dominique Zidouemba, rev. and enl. by Éric de Grolier. Paris : Unesco, 1977. 311 p. (Documentation, libraries and archives: Bibliographies and reference works, 5).   **AK154**

  "Replaces and supersedes the Directory of archives, libraries and schools of librarianship in Africa, published in 1965 ... prepared by E. W. Dadzie and J. T. Strickland."

  Information in English or French.

  A directory of libraries, archives, and information centers in 40 countries. A section of general references and notes on international cooperative arrangements and associations precedes the country listings. Indexes in English and French.   Z857.A1D57

Sitzman, Glenn L. African libraries. Metuchen, N.J. : Scarecrow, 1988. 486 p.   **AK155**

  An overview of African libraries. Pt. 4, "Angola to Zimbabwe : a nation-by-nation survey," contains brief data about specific libraries. Extensive bibliography.   Z857.A1S57

Asia

China

Chung-kuo tŭ shu kuan ming lu = Directory of Chinese libraries / Wang Enguang, Wu Renyong, Xie Wanruo. Peiching : Chung-kuo hsüeh shu chu pan she ; Detroit : Distr. by Gale, 1982. 428 p. : ill. (World books reference guide, no.3).   **AK156**

In two main sections: (1) a selected list of about 500 libraries with foreign-language holdings (with indication of subject fields) and (2) a list of about 2,700 libraries (public, academic, and special) with addresses. All entries appear in both Chinese and English.
Z845.C5C493

India

Directory of special and research libraries in India / comp. by IASLIC. 2nd ed. Calcutta : Indian Association of Special Libraries & Information Centres, 1985. 90 p.   **AK157**
1st ed., 1962.

Lists about 250 libraries alphabetically by institution, including some academic and public. Entries include name, address, librarian, subjects, and holdings. Geographic, subject, and name indexes.
Z845.I4D57

Indian library directory / comp. and ed. by Joginder Singh and A.R. Sethi. 4th ed. Delhi : Indian Libr. Assoc., 1985. 251 p.   **AK158**
1st ed., 1938; 3rd ed., 1951.

Lists 1,610 university, college, special, government, and public libraries. Arrangement is alphabetical within each category, except for public libraries which are first grouped by state. Entries include name of library, address, founding date, head librarian, size of staff, size of budget, size of collection, special collections, access policy, services, and library hours. Institution, librarian, and state indexes.
Z845.I4I42

Japan

Directory of information sources in Japan, 1986 / ed. by Japan Special Libraries Association. Tokyo : Nichigai Associates : Distr. by Kinokuniya Book-Store, c1986. 378 p.
AK159
Previous ed., 1980.

Organized in sections by type of institution (national; public corporation and government organizations; local government; universities and colleges; learned societies and independent organizations; private enterprises; and international organizations and foreign government institutions) then by subject. Address, staff, budget, collection size, and subject are given for 1,778 institutions. In English and Japanese with an alphabetical index by institution name in both languages.
Z845.J4D57

Librarianship in Japan / ed. by International Relations Committee of Japan Library Association. Rev. ed. Tokyo : Japan Library Association, 1994. 107 p. : ill.   **AK160**
A detailed overview of Japanese libraries first prepared for the 1986 IFLA General Conference held in Tokyo. Describes all types of libraries and includes many statistics. Resources and services of specific important libraries are given. Includes a directory of Japanese library and information associations and societies.   Z845.J3L4

Australia and Oceania

Australia

ALIAS, Australia's library, information, and archives services : an encyclopaedia of practice and practioners / ed., Harrison Bryan. Sydney : Library Association of Australia, 1988–1991. 3 v. : ill.   **AK161**
A compendium of information about libraries and librarianship in Australia. Signed articles include biographies, descriptions of libraries, histories of associations, and discussions of national information policies and practices. Many photographs. Vol. 3 includes a comprehensive index.   Z870.A1A45

Directory of Australian academic and research libraries. 4th ed. (1989)– . Blackwood, S. Aust. : Auslib Pr., 1989– .
AK162
Continues: *Directory of Australian academic libraries* (1st–3rd ed., 1978–85).
Editors, 1989– , Judith and Alan Bundy.
Includes libraries of universities, colleges of advanced education, and colleges of technical and continuing education, as well as state libraries.

New Zealand

Rogers, Frank. Archives New Zealand : a directory of archives and manuscript repositories in New Zealand, the Cook Islands, Fiji, Niue, Tokelau, Tonga, and Western Samoa. Plimmerton, N.Z. : Archives Pr., c1992. 65 p. : 2 maps.   **AK163**
"Designed to be complementary to the vastly more extensive *National register of archives and manuscripts in New Zealand* (Wellington, N.Z. : National Library, 1979–83. 2 v. [loose-leaf]).
Geographically arranged list of archives and manuscript collections. Entries include hours open, materials solicited, holdings, and collection description. There is an index to repositories and a general index to collections.   CD2770.R7

ACQUISITIONS WORK AND COLLECTION DEVELOPMENT

American Library Association. Collection Development Committee. Guidelines for collection development / David L. Perkins, ed. Chicago : The Association, [1979]. 78 p.   **AK164**
Offers guidelines for the formulation of collection development policies, for the evaluation of the effectiveness of library collections, for the review of library collections, and for the allocation of library materials budgets.
§ A revision of the chapter, "Guidelines for the formulation of collection development policies" was published as: American Library Association. Subcommittee on Guidelines for Collection Development, *Guide for written collection policy statements*, ed. by Bonita Bryant. (2nd ed. Chicago : The Association, 1989. 29 p. ; ill.). Concentrates on policy statements; additional sections on the conspectus apparatus, collection levels, language codes and definitions, narrative statements, and analysis of special collections. Glossary.   Z687.A518

Kim, David U. Policies of publishers : a handbook for order librarians / by David U. Kim and Craig A. Wilson. 4th ed. Metuchen, N.J. : Scarecrow, 1989. 279 p.   **AK165**
1st ed., 1975; 3rd ed., 1982.

Indicates policies of approximately 600 publishers regarding such matters as prepayments, discounts, returns, shipping and billing, back orders, standing orders, and approval plans. Information was gathered by questionnaire.   Z689.K55

Lane, Alfred H. Gifts and exchange manual. Westport, Conn. : Greenwood, [1980]. 121 p.   **AK166**
A manual of practical procedures for maintaining a gifts and exchange program in a library. Includes a special chapter on exchange work in academic libraries. Sample forms and letters; index.   Z690.L36

Magrill, Rose Mary. Acquisitions management and collection development in libraries / Rose Mary Magrill and John Corbin. 2nd ed. Chicago : Amer. Libr. Assoc., 1989. 285 p.   **AK167**
1st ed., 1984.
A basic guide to both collection development and acquisitions work. Each chapter includes an excellent bibliography; particularly noteworthy is that for the chapter on collection evaluation.   Z689.M19

Understanding the business of library acquisitions / Karen A. Schmidt, ed. Chicago : Amer. Libr. Assoc., 1990. 322 p. : ill.   **AK168**
Intends "to answer questions [that] concern publishing and the decisions that affect the cost and life of the book, the publication of serials and their cost and procurement, the world of vendors and how one decides if a vendor is performing well for the library, vendor librarian ethics, handling gift and exchanges, dealing with other parts of the bookselling world, approval plans, and basic information on accounting principles, audits and business practices."—*Introd.*   Z689.U53

United Nations Educational, Scientific and Cultural Organization. Handbook on the international exchange of publications / ed. by Frans Vanwijngaerden. 4th ed. Paris : UNESCO, 1978. 165 p. (Documentation, libraries, and archives: Bibliographies and reference works, 4).   **AK169**
1st ed., 1950.
Aims to provide: "(a) a guide on the methodology, organization and management of the international exchange of publications ... (b) a detailed up-to-date directory of exchange centres with a national responsibility, providing practical information on their activities and services...."—*Pref.*   Z690.U454

Wilkas, Lenore. International subscription agents. 6th ed. Chicago : Amer. Libr. Assoc., 1994. 410 p.   **AK170**
5th ed., 1986, by Wilkas and Wayne R. Perryman.
Directory information—address, telephone and fax numbers, material supplied, countries served, and computerized operations—of international subscription agents. A subject and geographic index.   Z286.P4W53

ADMINISTRATION

ALA survey of librarian salaries. 1982– . Chicago : Office for Research and Office for Library Personnel Resources, Amer. Libr. Assoc., 1982– . Annual.   **AK171**
Frequency varies: biennial, 1982–88; annual, 1989– .
Based on a stratified sample of public and academic libraries, this survey reports average salaries by geographic region for six positions commonly found in libraries. The six positions are director, deputy/associate/assistant director, reference/information librarian, cataloger/classifier, children's/young adult services librarian, and beginning librarian.   Z682.3.A4

American library laws / Alex Ladenson, ed. 5th ed. Chicago : Amer. Libr. Assoc., 1983. 2009 p.   **AK172**

Library laws, effective December 31, 1982, compiled and reprinted from the original statutes. In three sections: federal government, states (listed alphabetically), and territories. Each set of laws is arranged by type of library or by subject. Subject index.   KF4315.A4

Association of Research Libraries. ARL annual salary survey. [1972/73]– . Wash. : Association of Research Libraries, [1973]– .   **AK173**
Vol. for 1966/67 issued as *ARL newsletter*, no. 23; 1967/68– as part of its *Academic library statistics*; first publ. separately in 1973, covering 1972/73.
Compiled from data submitted by member institutions. Average and median salaries for the Association and by institution are included for the current and next fiscal years. Data is also broken into categories such as beginning salaries, minority salaries, salaries by selected positions, and by region. Categories are broken down by gender.   Z682.3.A79a

Kohl, David F. Administration, personnel, buildings and equipment : a handbook for library management. Santa Barbara, Calif. : ABC-Clio, 1985. 304 p. (Handbooks for library management, [1]).   **AK174**
First in a planned series of six "Handbooks for library management" (called "Library administrator's handbook series" in the introduction) which, "rather than abstracting complete studies or providing only citations to research, instead presents summaries of individual research findings grouped by subject."—*Introd.* Within the three categories mentioned in the title, topics are arranged alphabetically; there is a detailed table of contents, but no subject index. Covers studies from the period 1960–83. A "Bibliography of articles," p. 239–94, gives full citations and references from the text are by number; index of authors of articles.
§ *Library management* by Robert D. Stueart and John T. Eastlick (4th ed. Littleton, Colo. : Libraries Unlimited, 1993. 402 p.) is intended both as a textbook for the student and a guide for the practicing librarian.   Z678.K63

Leighton, Philip D. Planning academic and research library buildings. 2nd ed. / by Philip S. Leighton and David C. Weber. Chicago : Amer. Libr. Assoc., 1986. 630 p. : ill.   **AK175**
1st ed., 1965, by Keyes D. Metcalf.
Three appendixes—program examples, formulas and tables, and list of equipment—make this standard text useful in reference work. Includes formulas and tables to determine volumes per shelf, seating and space requirements, and collection growth.   Z679.5.L45

Library management consultants list / ed. by Robert F. Moran, Jr., for the Library Organization and Management Section, Library Administration and Management Association. Chicago : The Association, 1990. 36 p.   **AK176**
Alphabetical list by consultant's name. Gives address, education, years as a consultant, number of projects completed, fees, and lists previous projects.
§ LAMA also publishes two other lists of consultants, *Library buildings consultants list (1993)* and *Library personnel consultants list (1990)*.   Z682.4.C65L53

Library technology reports. v. 12 (Jan. 1976)– . [Chicago] : Amer. Libr. Assoc., 1976– . Bimonthly.   **AK177**
Continues the supplementary material to: American Library Assoc. Library Technology Program, *Library technology reports* (1965–75) and assumes its volume numbering.
Evaluates library systems, equipment and supplies. Objective reviews contain specifications, features, costs, as well as comparisons and ratings of different products or systems, such as computer printers, integrated library systems, bibliographic utilities, and local area networks. Each issue has an index that generally covers the current and previous year. A cumulative microfiche edition called *The sourcebook of library technology* is published every other year.   Z684.L75

Rubin, Richard. Human resource management in libraries : theory and practice. N.Y. : Neal-Schuman Publ., c1991. 430 p. : ill.   **AK178**

A basic guide for personnel practices in libraries. Includes bibliographies and federal laws governing employment practices.

§ Another book covering some of the same topics is *Personnel administration in libraries* ed. by Sheila D. Creth and Frederick Duda (2nd ed. N.Y. : Neal-Schuman, 1989. 343 p.).   Z682.R83

SLA biennial salary survey / Special Libraries Association. 1991– . Wash. : The Association, 1991– .   **AK179**

Continues *SLA triennial salary survey*, 1967–89. Surveys for 1959, 1967, 1970, 1973, 1976, 1979 were published in *Special libraries*.

This survey of members of the Special Library Association provides median and rank order salaries according to a wide range of variables including: gender, geographic region, type of institution, primary responsibility, number of employees supervised, and education level.   Z682.4.S65S59

Stephenson, Mary Sue. Planning library facilities : a selected, annotated bibliography. Metuchen, N.J. : Scarecrow, 1990. 249 p.   **AK180**

Lists 800 references to documents published primarily in the U.S. and Canada, 1970–mid-1988. Three major sections: (1) Facility planning, design, evaluation and renovation; (2) Housing and serving the user; (3) Environmental, mechanical, electrical and security systems. Entries are arranged alphabetically by title within sections. Subject and author indexes.   Z679.5.S73

White, Herbert S. Managing the special library : strategies for success within the larger organization. White Plains, N.Y. : Knowledge Industry Pubns., [1984]. 152 p.   **AK181**

In effect, supersedes *Special libraries: a guide for management* (2nd ed., 1981) by Janet Ahrensfeld, Elin Christianson and David King.

A management guide for the practicing special librarian and for the library school student at the master's level. Select bibliography; index.   Z675.A2W45

ARCHIVES

Basic international bibliography of archive administration = Bibliographie internationale fondamentale d'archivistique / comp. by Michel Duchein. N.Y. : K.G. Saur, 1978. 250 p. (Archivum, v.25).   **AK182**

Introductory matter and explanatory notes in English and French.

Aims to include "only works or articles, general in interest and permanent in nature."—*Pref.* International in scope and intended for the professional archivist. Emphasizes "the problems of collecting, sorting, arranging, listing, making accessible and preserving, looked at from the archivist's point of view." Classed arrangement with author and subject indexes.   CD1.A18 v.25

Dictionary of archival terminology = Dictionnaire de terminologie archivistique : English and French, with equivalents in Dutch, German, Italian, Russian and Spanish / ed. by Peter Walne. 2nd rev. ed. München ; N.Y. : K.G. Saur, 1988. 212 p. (International Council on Archives. ICA handbooks series, v. 7.).   **AK183**

1st ed., 1984.

Terms "in common use throughout the archival profession" (*Introd.*) are arranged in alphabetical order by English form of the word, with the corresponding French terms in parallel columns; definitions are given in both English and French; Dutch, German, Italian, Russian and Spanish equivalent terms appear after the definitions. Austrian terms appear alongside the German equivalents and are identified as such. Indexes from all languages other than English.   CD945.D53

A glossary for archivists, manuscript curators, and records managers / comp. by Lewis J. Bellardo and Lynn Lady Bellardo. Chicago : Society of American Archivists, 1992. 45 p.   **AK184**

Defines nearly 1,000 terms used by archivists, manuscript curators, and records managers. Reflects Canadian and U.S. usage.   CD945.G56

International directory of archives = Annuaire international des archives / International Council on Archives. München ; N.Y. : K.G. Saur, 1992. 427 p. (Archivum, v.38).   **AK185**

1st ed., 1975; previous ed., 1988.

Alphabetically arranged by country, entries contain name of director, address, telephone, historical periods covered, and approximate linear feet of the collection. Covers national, state, regional, and some local archives. Expands geographical coverage over previous editions; now includes countries of Eastern Europe.   CD941.I61

Maher, William J. The management of college and university archives. Metuchen, N.J. : Society of American Archivists and Scarecrow Pr., 1992. 430 p.   **AK186**

Treats archival theory and practice in academic repositories. Emphasizes practical methods and technique. Includes bibliographies, The Society of American Archivists' "Guidelines for college and university archives" (1979), and examples of model archival forms.   CD3065.M34

Modern archives administration and records management : a RAMP reader / comp. by Peter Walne with the assistance of a working group of the International Council on Archives ; General Information Programme and UNISIST. Paris : UNESCO, 1985. 587 p. : ill.   **AK187**

A compilation of reading on basic archival and records management topics reprinted from the major journals in the field. International in scope; intended to supplement existing textbooks and manuals, with special applicability to training programs in the developing countries. No index.   CD950.M62

O'Toole, James M. Understanding archives and manuscripts. Chicago : Society of American Archivists, 1990. 79 p. : ill.   **AK188**

One of seven titles in the Society of American Archivists' "Archival fundamentals series," this work offers an overview of the history, purpose, and organization of archives.

§ Other titles in the series are: *Selecting and appraising archives and manuscripts* by F. Gerald Ham (1992); *Arranging and describing archives and manuscripts* by Frederic M. Miller (1990); *Preserving archives and manuscripts* by Mary Lynn Ritzenthaler (1993); *Providing reference services for archives and manuscripts* by Mary Jo Pugh (1992); *Managing archival and manuscript repositories* by Thomas Wilsted and William Nolte (1991); and *Glossary for archivists, manuscript curators, and records managers* by Lewis J. and Lynn Lady Bellardo (AK184).   CD950.O88

INFORMATION STORAGE AND RETRIEVAL

Pask, Judith M. User education for online systems in libraries : a selective bibliography, 1970–1988. Metuchen, N.J. : Scarecrow, 1990. 212 p.   **AK189**

A 550-entry annotated bibliography of books, articles, and reports that describe user education for online systems. Includes author and subject index.   Z699.2.P37

Automated library systems

Automation in libraries : a LITA bibliography, 1978–1982 / comp. by Anne G. Adler ... [et al.]. [Ann Arbor, Mich.] : Pierian Pr., 1983. 177 p. (Library hi tech series, no. 1).   **AK190**
A classified bibliography of more than 2,500 citations. Name index.
§ Earlier coverage is provided by Maxine MacCafferty's *An annotated bibliography of automation in libraries and information systems, 1972–1975* (London : Aslib, 1976. 147 p.) which was intended as a continuation of *An annotated bibliography of library automation 1968–1972*, compiled by Lynne Tinker (London : Aslib, 1973).
Z678.9.A2A96

Directory of library automation software, systems, and services. 1993– . Medford, N.J. : Learned Information Inc., c1993– . Annual.   **AK191**
Editor: Pamela Cibbarelli.
An alphabetical listing of software for library use. Entries contain system requirements, programming language, components and application, update modes, features, support, potential users, installations, and price. Also includes listings of retrospective conversion services; automation consultants; database hosts; CD-ROM distributors; conferences and meetings; and library automation periodicals. Comprehensive index.   Z678.9.A3D6

Information industry directory. 11th ed. (1991)– . Detroit : Gale, c1991– . Annual.   **AK192**
Continues: *Encyclopedia of information systems and services* (1st–10th ed., 1971–90). Issued in 2 v.: v. 1, Descriptive listings; v. 2, Indexes.
A comprehensive directory of information-related companies, products and services. Listings include database producers and products, online services, networks, bibliographic utilities, information retrieval software, and related companies and products. Vol. 1 is an alphabetical listing; v. 2 contains a master index and separate indexes to databases, publications/microforms, software, function or classification, personal name, geographic location, and subject.   Z674.3.E53

Teaching technologies in libraries : a practical guide / Linda Brew MacDonald ... [et al.]. Boston : G.K. Hall, c1991. 275 p.   **AK193**
Describes techniques, such as on-screen help, computer-aided instruction, expert systems, and audiovisuals, that could be employed to instruct patrons in the use of library technology. Includes bibliographical references.   Z711.2.T44

Cataloging codes

Anglo-American cataloguing rules / prep. under the direction of the Joint Steering Committee for Revision of AACR, a committee of the American Library Association, the Australian Committee on Cataloguing, the British Library, the Canadian Committee on Cataloguing, the Library Association, the Library of Congress ; ed. by Michael Gorman and Paul W. Winkler. 2nd ed., 1988 revision. Ottawa : Canadian Libr. Assoc. ; Chicago : Amer. Libr. Assoc., 1988. 677 p.   **AK194**
2nd ed., 1978.
This revision corrects errors, modifies wording, changes inadequate rules, and adds rules and examples. "It is not a new edition; it has not changed basic concepts."—*Pref.* Includes sets of already published rule revisions from 1982, 1983 and 1985, as well as authorized unpublished revisions since 1985. Appendixes cover capitalization, abbreviations, numerals, and glossary. Index.
§ Guidelines for applying the rules contained in this revision can be found in Margaret Maxwell's *Handbook for AACR2 1988 revision : explaining and illustrating the Anglo-American cataloguing rules* (Chicago : Amer. Libr. Assoc., 1989. 436 p.).   Z694.15.A56A53

Cataloging service bulletin. no. 1 (Summer 1978)– . Wash. : Library of Congress, Processing Services, [1978]– . Quarterly.   **AK195**
Contains interpretations and revisions of *Anglo-American cataloguing rules* (2nd ed., rev.; AK194), as well as additions or revisions of Library of Congress subject headings.
Cataloging service bulletin index (1978/82– . Lake Crystal, Minn. : Soldier Creek Pr., c1982– . Annual. Comp. by Nancy Olson). Each edition is cumulative and supersedes each previous edition.
Z693.A15C37

Gorman, Michael. The concise AACR2, 1988 revision. Chicago : Amer. Libr. Assoc., 1989. 161 p.   **AK196**
An abridgment "intended to convey the essence and basic principles of *AACR2 1988 Revision* [AK194] without many of that comprehensive work's rules for out-of-the-way and complex materials."—*General introd.*   Z694.15.A56G67

Library of Congress rule interpretations / [ed., Robert M. Hiatt; formulated by the Office for Descriptive Cataloging Policy, Library of Congress]. [2nd ed.]. Wash. : Cataloging Distribution Service, Library of Congress, 1990– . 2 v.   **AK197**
Kept up-to-date by replacement pages.
A cumulation of interpretations that first appeared in *Cataloging service bulletin* (AK195).

Classification

Bliss, Henry Evelyn. Bibliographic classification. 2nd ed. / J. Mills and Vanda Broughton, with the assistance of Valerie Lang. London : Bowker-Saur ; New Providence, N.J. : distr. by K.G. Saur/Reed Reference Publishing, 1977–94. 12 v. (In progress).   **AK198**
Publisher varies; originally publ. London : Butterworths; vols. issued by Butterworths now available from Bowker-Saur.
This new and completely revised edition of Bliss, now in progress, will ultimately replace the earlier edition (Bliss's *A bibliographic classification, extended by systematic auxiliary schedules for composite specification and notation* [N.Y. : H.W. Wilson, 1940–53. 4 v. in 3]).
Schedules to date include: Introduction and auxiliary schedules; Class A/AL, Philosophy and logic; Class AM/AX, Mathematics, probability, and statistics; Class H, Anthropology, human biology, life sciences; Class I, Psychology and psychiatry; Class J, Education; Class K, Society; Class P, Religion, the occult, morals, and ethics; Class Q, Social welfare; Class R, Politics and public administration; Class S, Law; Class T, Economics, management of economic enterprises.
Z696.B635

Chan, Lois Mai. Immroth's guide to the Library of Congress classification. 4th ed. Englewood, Colo. : Libraries Unlimited, 1990. 436 p.   **AK199**
3rd ed., 1989.
Reflects changes in general policies as well as changes and revisions in classification schedules. Follows the plan of the previous edition with the exception of Chapter 4, on tables, which has been reorganized. Examples in the book employ call numbers from LC MARC records. One consolidated bibliography.   Z696.U4C47

Dewey, Melvil. Dewey decimal classification and relative index / devised by Melvil Dewey. Ed. 20 / ed. by John P. Comaromi ... [et al.]. Albany, N.Y. : Forest Pr., a division of OCLC Online Computer Library Center, 1989. 4 v.   **AK200**
19th ed., 1979.
First published anonymously in 1876 under title: *A classification and subject index*, 2nd–14th eds. published under title: *Decimal classification and relative index*.
"The aim of Edition 20 is user convenience: clearer instructions, more explanations, greater accessibility through expanded summaries, elimination of duplicate provisions for classing single subjects, and the

inclusion of a Manual to guide the classifier … . The Manual describes policies and practices of the Decimal Classification Division of the L of C, offers advice on classing in difficult areas, and explains how to choose between related numbers."—*New features*. The number of summaries and notes have been increased. Reflects international assistance in the development of the DDC. Both tables and schedules have been revised. This edition's "Relative index" is smaller than the previous edition's as a result of the elimination of unlikely entries and the removal of *see* references.   Z696.D519

International classification and indexing bibliography : ICIB 1. Frankfurt : Indeks Verlag, 1982. 3 v.   **AK201**

Contents: v. 1: Classification systems and thesauri; v. 2: Reference tools and conferences in classification and indexing; v. 3: Classification and indexing systems theory—structure—methodology.

Comp. and ed. by Ingetraut Dahlberg.

Each bibliography covers 1950–82. A very thorough and well-indexed set of bibliographies containing more than 11,000 references.   Z696.A3I57

Library of Congress. Subject Cataloging Division. Classification. Wash. : U.S. Govt. Print. Off., 1911– . 48 v.   **AK202**

Contents: LC classification outline (6th ed. 1990); Class A, General works (4th ed. 1973); Class B, subclasses B–BJ: Philosophy, psychology (4th ed. 1989); Class B, subclasses BL, BM, BP, BQ: Religion–relations, Hinduism, Judaism, Islam, Buddhism (3rd ed. 1984); Class B, subclasses BR–BV: Religion, Christianity, Bible (1987); Class B, subclass, BX: Christian denominations (1985); Class C, Auxiliary sciences of history (4th ed. 1993); Class D, subclasses D–J: History (general). History of Europe, Part 1 (3rd ed. 1990); Class D, subclasses, DJK–DK: History of Eastern Europe (general); Soviet Union, Poland (1987); Class D, subclasses DL–DR: History of Europe, Part 2 (3rd ed. 1990); Class D, subclasses DS: History of Asia (1987); Class D, Subclasses DT–DX: History of Africa, Australia, New Zealand, etc. (3rd ed., 1989).

Class E–F: History: America (3rd ed. 1958, repr. with suppl. pages 1965); Class G: Geography, maps, anthropology, recreation (4th ed. 1976); Class H, subclasses H–HJ: Social sciences, economics (4th ed. 1981); Class H, HM–HX: Social sciences, sociology (4th ed. 1980); Class J: Political science (2nd ed. 1991); Class K: Law (general) (1977); Class K, subclass KD: Law of the United Kingdom and Ireland (1973); Class K, subclasses, KDZ, KG–KH: Law of the Americas, Latin America, and the West Indies (1984); Class K, subclass KE: Law of Canada (1976); Class K, subclass KF: Law of the United States (Prelim. ed. 1969); Class K, subclasses KJ–KKZ: Law of Europe (1989); Class K, subclasses KJV–KJW: Law of France (1985); Class K, subclasses KK–KKC: Law of Germany (1982); Class K, subclasses KL–KWX: Law of Asia and Eurasia, Africa, Pacific Area and Antarctica (1st ed. 1993).

Class L: Education (4th ed. 1984); Class M: Music and books on music (3rd ed. 1978); Class N: Fine arts (4th ed. 1970); Class P, subclasses P–PA: Philology, linguistics, classical philology, classical literature (1928, repr. with suppl. pages 1968); Class P, subclasses PB–PH: Modern European languages (1933, repr. with supplementary pages, 1966); Class P, subclass PG: Russian literature (1948, repr. with suppl. pages, 1965); Class P, subclasses PJ–PK: Oriental philology and literature, Indo-Iranian philology and literature (2nd ed. 1988); Class P, subclasses PL–PM: Languages of Eastern Asia, Africa, Oceania; Hyperborean, Indian, and artificial languages (2nd ed. 1988); Class P, subclasses, P–PM, Supplement: Index to languages and dialects (4th ed., 1991); Class P, subclasses PN, PR, PS, PZ: General literature, English and American literature, fiction in English, juvenile belles lettres (3rd ed. 1988); Class P, subclass PQ, pt. 1: French literature (2nd ed. 1992); Class P, subclass PQ, pt. 2: Italian, Spanish, and Portuguese languages (1937, repr. with suppl. pages, 1965); Class P, subclass PT, pt. 1 (2nd ed., 1989); Class P, subclass PT, pt. 2: Dutch and Scandinavian literature (2nd ed. 1992); Class P, subclasses P–PZ: Language and literature tables (1982).

Class Q: Science (7th ed. 1989); Class R: Medicine (5th ed. 1987); Class S: Agriculture (4th ed. 1982); Class T: Technology (5th ed. 1971); Class U: Military science (5th ed. 1992); Class V: Naval science (4th ed. 1993); Class Z: Bibliography and library science (5th ed. 1980).

Published in 48 v. representing divisions and subdivisions of the classification. Volumes are revised and published in new editions periodically. The entire classification is summarized in: Library of Congress. Office for Subject Cataloging Policy, *LC classification outline* (6th ed. Wash. : Library of Congress, 1990. 47 p.).

Changes are announced in: Library of Congress. Subject Cataloging Div., *LC classification, additions and changes* (Wash. : Library of Congress, 1941– . Quarterly). The latest edition of the classification, incorporating additions and changes adopted since the last revision, is published as: *Super LCCS : Gale's Library of Congress classification schedules combined with additions and changes through 1993*, Rita Runchock and Kathleen Droste, eds. (Detroit : Gale, 1994. 48 v.).

National Library of Medicine (U.S.). National Library of Medicine classification : a scheme for the shelf arrangement of books in the field of medicine and its related sciences. 4th ed., rev. 1981. Bethesda, Md. : U.S. Dept. of Health and Human Services ; Wash. : for sale by the U.S. Govt. Print. Off., 1981. 397 p. : ill. (NIH publication, no. 81-1535).   **AK203**

Superintendent of Documents classification: HE 20.3602:C 56/ 981.

Notation was developed from the block of letters, QS–QZ and W, unused by the Library of Congress and assigned to the National Library of Medicine.   Z697.M4N37

Scott, Mona L. Conversion tables : LC-Dewey, Dewey-LC / Mona L. Scott, with the assistance of Christine E. Alvey. Englewood, Colo. : Libraries Unlimited, 1993. 365 p. **AK204**

Consists of tables that covert LC class numbers to class numbers in the 20th ed. of Dewey Decimal Classification and vice versa. Although LC to Dewey conversion is more successful, both sets of tables are useful.   Z696.U4S36

Universal decimal classification = Classification décimale universelle = Dezimalklassifikation. International medium ed. English text, edition 2. London : BSi Standards, 1994. 2 v.   **AK205**

2nd English full ed., 1977; this ed. previously issued 1985–88.

Contents: pt. 1, Systematic tables; pt. 2, Alphabetical subject index.

English text published by arrangement with the International Federation for Documentation (FID) as part of the International Medium Edition of the UDC.

Represents a selective edition of UDC that includes modifications authorized in "Extensions and corrections to the UDC" through series 9, no. 3 (June 1977).   Z696.U862

Database directories

•**CD-ROM databases** [database]. Boston : Worldwide Videotex, 1987– .   **AK206**

Available online; updated monthly.

Provides descriptive information concerning CD-ROM databases in all subject areas.

CD-ROMs in print. 1987– . Westport, Conn. : Meckler, c1987– . Annual.   **AK207**

Includes more than 3,500 titles of commercially available CD-ROMs. An "Optical product directory" lists titles in alphabetical order, giving title, providers, drives, hardware/software, subscription, and description. Indexes of data providers, publishers, U.S. distributors, non-U.S. distributors, software providers, and subjects.   TK7882.C56C34

Gale directory of databases. Jan. 1993– . Detroit : Gale, c1993– . Semiannual.   **AK208**

Contents: v. 1 Online databases; v. 2, CD-ROM, diskette, magnetic tape, handheld, and batch access database products.

Formed by the merger of: *Computer-readable data bases*; *Directory of online databases*; and *Directory of portable databases*.

Vol. 1 consists of an alphabetical list of online databases, with separate directories of producers and online services. Database entries include: database name and acronym; producer with address and telephone number; contact person or department; type of database; updating; online availability; online available as part of another database; alternative electronic formats; and other historic background information. Geographic and subject indexes. Vol. 2 consists of separate alphabetical directories for each format, but content and organization are similar to v. 1.

•Machine-readable version: *Gale directory of databases* (Detroit : Gale). Current file. Available on CD-ROM, updated quarterly.

QA76.9.D32G36

OPAC directory. 1993– . Westport, Conn. : Meckler, c1993– . Annual.   **AK209**
Continues: *Dial in* (Westport, Conn. : Meckler, 1991–92).
Geographically arranged directory of online public access catalogs. Includes information about collection size and strengths, system data, and dialing instructions. Indexed by area code, type of system, institution (including Internet address), and subject and collection strength.   Z699.22.D5

Filing

American Library Association. Filing Committee. ALA filing rules. Chicago : Amer. Libr. Assoc., 1980. 50 p.   **AK210**
This publication is the "successor to *A.L.A. Rules for Filing Catalog Cards* (1942) and *ALA Rules for Filing Catalog Cards*, second edition (1968)."—*Introd.* It is to be considered a new work rather than a new edition "since the new rules are applicable to bibliographic displays in other than card formats." Glossary; index.   Z695.9.C63

Rather, John Carson. Library of Congress filing rules / John Carson Rather, Susan C. Biebel. Wash. : Libr. of Congress, 1980. 111 p.   **AK211**
A provisional version was publ. 1971 under title: *Filing arrangement in the Library of Congress catalogs.*
Supersedes *Filing rules for the dictionary catalogs in the Library of Congress* (1956).
Sets forth the rules applied in 1981 along with the adoption of AACR 2. Thus, "these filing rules were written to arrange headings formulated under various cataloging rules and practices. In those situations in which AACR 2 and pre-AACR 2 headings have contradictory characteristics, the filing rules were written to accommodate the new [i.e., 'Add-on'] catalog, which will include only AACR 2 and AACR 2-compatible headings."—*Introd.* The rules apply to the Library's computer-produced bibliographic products.   Z695.95.R37

Indexing and abstracting

Cleveland, Donald B. Introduction to indexing and abstracting / Donald B. Cleveland, Ana D. Cleveland. 2nd ed. Englewood, Colo. : Libraries Unlimited, 1990. 329 p. : ill.   **AK212**
1st ed., 1983.
A comprehensive guide for students and practitioners to the fundamentals of indexing and abstracting. There are chapters on the nature of information, the nature and types of indexes, vocabulary control, indexing methods and procedures, book indexes, index evaluation, nature and types of abstracts, abstracting methods and procedures, automatic methods, indexing and abstracting services, as well as examples of how to index and abstract a document. Includes a glossary, bibliography, and an index.   Z695.9.C592

Lancaster, F. Wilfrid. Indexing and abstracting in theory and practice. Champaign, Ill. : Univ. of Illinois, Graduate School of Library and Information Science, 1991. 328 p. : ill. **AK213**

Stresses similarities of indexing and abstracting. Covers principles, practice, pre-coordinate indexing, consistency, quality, writing abstracts, evaluation, indexing and abstracting services, natural language, and automatic indexing. Includes indexing and abstracting exercises, a glossary, and an extensive bibliography.

Register of indexers. Wash. [etc.] : American Society of Indexers, [197?]– . Annual.   **AK214**
Frequency varies; annual since 1986.
Lists members of ASI, including freelance indexers, providing name, address, telephone number and self-described qualifications. Indexed by subject, language specialty, related services (e.g., abstracting), types of material, and geographic location.   Z695.94.U5R43

Rowley, Jennifer E. Abstracting and indexing. 2nd ed. London : Bingley, 1988. 181 p. : ill.   **AK215**
1st ed., 1982.
"This book attempts to lay the groundwork for abstracting and indexing practice."—*Pref.* Emphasizes technique rather than theory. Covers the role of computers in abstracting and indexing. Includes an appendix on editing and proofreading an abstracting or indexing publication, a section on further readings and an index.   Z695.9.R68

Thesaurus guide : analytical directory of selected vocabularies for information retrieval, 1985 / prep. by Gesellschaft für Information und Dokumentation for the Commission of the European Communities. Amsterdam ; N.Y. : North-Holland ; Luxembourg : Office for Official Publications of the European Communities, 1985. 749 p.   **AK216**
A guide to thesauruses available in at least one of the official languages of the European Communities. Thesauruses are listed alphabetically within ten subject areas. Indexes to personal and organization names and subject areas. Indexes to personal and organization names and subject indexes in English, French, and German.
•Machine-readable version: *Thesauri* [database]. Luxembourg : Eurobrokers S.A.R.L. Current coverage. Available online, updated annually.   Z695.A1T46

Wellisch, Hans H. Indexing and abstracting : an international bibliography. Santa Barbara, Calif., ABC-Clio, [1980]. 308 p.
                                                         AK217
"Publ. in cooperation with the American Society of Indexers and the Society of Indexers (U.K.)"—*t.p.*
A topically arranged bibliography of nearly 2,400 items, most of them annotated. Nearly all items published before 1950 were included, but a more selective policy was followed for later publications. Author and subject indexes.
———. *Indexing and abstracting, 1977–1981: an international bibliography* (Santa Barbara, Calif. : ABC-Clio, 1984. 276 p.) Adds more than 1,400 items, including some publications from the earlier period.   Z695.9.W44

Subject headings

Aitchison, Jean. Thesaurus construction : a practical manual / Jean Aitchison, Alan Gilchrist. 2nd ed. London : Aslib, 1987. 173 p.   **AK218**
1st ed., 1972.
Concise step-by-step manual showing how to construct a thesaurus. Extensive bibliography.   Z695

Chan, Lois Mai. Library of Congress subject headings : principles of structure and application. 2nd. ed. Littleton, Colo. : Libraries Unlimited, 1986. 511 p. (Research studies in library science, 19).   **AK219**
1st ed., 1978.
Describes basic principles of LC subject headings, derived from *Library of Congress subject headings* (AK220) and from *Subject cataloging manual : subject headings* (AK221).

Also available: "Annotated version," prep. by Chan for the Library of Congress (Wash. : Cataloging Distribution Service, Library of Congress, 1990. 65 p.). Superintendent of Documents classification: LC 30.2: Su 1/3. Z695.Z8L5228

Library of Congress. Cataloging Policy and Support Office. Library of Congress subject headings / prep. by the Cataloging Policy and Support Office, Collections Services. 16th ed.– . Wash. : Library of Congress, Cataloging Distribution Service, 1993– . Annual. **AK220**

Superintendent of Documents classification: LC 26.7: .

Commonly referred to as: The red book; LCSH.

Issued in 4 or more volumes.

Continues the same title issued by the Subject Cataloging Division and, later, the Office for Subject Cataloging Policy.

The list of subject headings most widely used in U.S. libraries. Has adopted the format of many subject thesauruses, using BT (broader term), NT (narrower term), UF (use for), and Use to explain the syndetic structure of the headings. Use and interpretation of the headings may require that *Subject cataloging manual : subject headings* (AK221) or Lois Mai Chan's *Library of Congress subject headings : principles of structure and policies for application* (AK219) be consulted. Kept up-to-date by weekly lists and quarterly cumulative supplements. Available on microfiche.

•Machine-readable versions:

LC MARC : subject authorities [database] (Wash. : LC Information Systems, 1986– .). Available online, updated daily. Contains the complete LC subject authority file.

CDMARC subjects [database] (Wash. : LC, 1986–). Available on CD-ROM, cumulated every three months. Also contains the complete LC subject authority file. Z695.Z8L524a

Library of Congress. Office for Subject Cataloging Policy. Subject cataloging manual : subject headings / prep. by the Office of [sic] Subject Cataloging Policy, Library of Congress. 4th ed. Wash. : Cataloging Distribution Service, Library of Congress, 1991– . 2 v. (loose-leaf). **AK221**

Superintendent of Documents classification: LC26.8/4: 991/ v.1-2.

Explains the rules that govern the formulation of Library of Congress subject headings and defines and explains the use of terms in these headings. Z695.L695

Sears, Minnie Earl. Sears list of subject headings / ed. by Joseph Miller. 15th ed. N.Y. : Wilson, 1994. 758 p. **AK222**

14th ed., 1991.

Continues the updating and revision of existing headings, with particular attention to headings in health and environment, computer services, space technology, changing family relationships, minorities and consumerism. Uses new expanded Dewey Decimal Classification schedules as found in the 12th abridged edition of the DDC for data processing and computer science, and computer engineering. Revised and expanded list of subdivisions. Z695.S43

INTERLIBRARY LOAN AND DOCUMENT DELIVERY

Barwick, Margaret M. A guide to centres of international lending and copying. 4th ed. Boston Spa, England : IFLA Office for International Lending : British Library Lending Division, 1990. 139 p. **AK223**

First to third editions called: *A brief guide to centres of international lending and photocopying.*

A country-by-country guide to national or other significant libraries that lend internationally. Information is given about each country's system of bibliographic control and procedures for making an interlibrary request or a request for a photocopy or microform reproduction. Z672.B67

Borchardt, D. H. Guide to the availability of theses / D. H. Borchardt, J. D. Thawley. München ; N.Y. : K. G. Saur, 1981. 443 p. (IFLA publications, 17). **AK224**

Compiled for the International Federation of Library Associations and Institutions Section of University Libraries and other General Research Libraries.

Provides information on the availability of theses and dissertations at 698 individual institutions in 85 countries. Includes reference to each country's "national thesis bibliography," if any.

Supplemented by *Guide to the availability of theses II : non-university institutions,* comp. by G. G. Allen and K. Deubert (München ; N.Y. : K.G. Saur, 1984. 124 p. [IFLA publications, no. 29]). Entries are arranged alphabetically by country, then alphabetically by the official name of the institution. Subject, geographic, and institution indexes. Z5053.B67

Boucher, Virginia. Interlibrary loan practices handbook. Chicago : Amer. Libr. Assoc., 1984. 195 p. : ill. **AK225**

Serves as a successor to S. K. Thomson's *Interlibrary loan procedure manual* (Chicago : Amer. Libr. Assoc., 1970. 116 p.). Intended "for those without interlibrary loan experience who seek advice on how to proceed" and describes "the procedures outlined in interlibrary loan codes."—*Pref.* Includes chapters on both borrowing and lending, reproduction and copyright concerns, dissertations and masters' theses, international interlibrary loan, and managing the interlibrary loan operation. Appendixes of codes, forms, policy statements, etc. Bibliography of verification sources; index. Z713.B7

Interlibrary loan policies in Canada. Jan. 1993– . Ottawa : National Library of Canada, 1993– . Annual. **AK226**

Merger of: *Interlibrary loan services manual. Directory of interlibrary loan;* and *Interlibrary loan services manual. Envoy index.*

The main section consists of a list of Canadian libraries arranged geographically by province and alphabetically by library symbol within each province. Entries include address, telephone and fax numbers, and lending regulations, including fees. A library name index includes the library symbol, ENVOY 100 (Telecom Canada's electronic mail services) addresses, and a separate index for UTLAS codes. Z713.5

Morris, Leslie R. Interlibrary loan policies directory / Leslie R. Morris and Sandra Chass Morris. 4th ed. N.Y. : Neal-Schuman, c1991. 785 p. **AK227**

1st ed., 1975; 3rd ed., 1988.

Sets forth the interlibrary loan policies of more than 1,550 academic, public, and special libraries in the U.S. and Canada. The U.S. section is arranged alphabetically by state and then by name of library. Entries include: address and telephone number; acceptable methods of transmission; average turnaround time; loan regulations; duplication services, billing procedures; and mailing requirements. The section on Canada is brief and consists exclusively of academic libraries. Name index, index of fax numbers, index of libraries charging for loans. Z713.5.U6M67

Processing

Guide to technical services resources / Peggy Johnson, ed. ; with chapters by Sheila S. Intner ... [et al.]. Chicago : Amer. Libr. Assoc., 1994. 313 p. **AK228**

Organized in ten lettered sections very like the present *Guide,* this work aims to be a "comprehensive and practical guide to the principal information sources for technical services practitioners, educators, and students."—*Introd.* Provides annotations for a full range of reference books and for appropriate articles from current literature. Includes an author/title index. Z731.G9

LIBRARY INSTRUCTION

Beaubien, Anne K. Learning the library : concepts and methods for effective bibliographic instruction / Anne K. Beaubien, Sharon A. Hogan, and Mary W. George. N.Y. : Bowker, 1982. 269 p.   **AK229**

A guide for developing and implementing an academic bibliographic instruction program. Intended as a companion volume to *Theories of bibliographic education : designs for teaching* by Cerise Oberman and Katina Strauch (N.Y. : Bowker, 1982).   Z710.B37

The LIRT library instruction handbook / ed. by May Brottman and Mary Loe. Englewood, Colo. : Libraries Unlimited, 1990. 125 p. : ill.   **AK230**

Intends "to provide practical, step-by-step advice to enable institutions to develop programs based on sound theory and to enable practicing instruction librarians to evaluate and improve their own programs."—*Pref.* In six parts: (1) Planning and managing library instruction; (2) Academic libraries; (3) Public libraries; (4) School libraries; (5) Special libraries; (6) Bibliography. Index.   Z711.2.L77

Sourcebook for bibliographic instruction / Katherine Branch, chair, editorial board ; Carolyn Dusenbury, consulting ed. Chicago : Bibliographic Instruction Section, Assoc. of College and Research Libraries, c1993. 89 p.   **AK231**

Provides "an overview of bibliographic instruction and points readers to other sources of information, such as important publications, clearinghouses and associations." —*Introd.*

§ Two companion volumes have also been published: *Learning to teach* (Chicago : Bibliographic Instruction Section, Assoc. of College and Research Libraries, 1993. 76 p.) and *Read this first: an owner's guide to the new model statement of objectives for academic bibliographic instruction* (1991. 45 p.).

Wheeler, Helen Rippier. The bibliographic instruction-course handbook : a skills and concepts approach to the undergraduate, research methodology, credit course : for college and university personnel. Metuchen, N.J. : Scarecrow, 1988. 626 p.   **AK232**

Intended for librarians and library educators, this is primarily a detailed outline (including model assignments, handouts, instructor's text, and other supporting course materials) for a college-level bibliographic instruction course. Also includes a bibliographic instruction course case study, an extensive bibliography, and lists of pertinent clearinghouses and audiovisuals. Index.   Z711.2.W48

REFERENCE

Katz, William A. Introduction to reference work. 6th ed. N.Y. : McGraw-Hill, c1992. 2 v.   **AK233**

1st ed., 1969; 5th ed., 1987.

Contents: v. 1, Basic information sources; v. 2, Reference services and reference processes.

Long both a standard textbook and handbook for reference services, each edition has increasingly focused upon electronic sources in the reference process. Vol. 1 is essentially a discussion of important reference works grouped by form; v. 2 is concerned with principles and practice. Chapters include annotated bibliographies.   Z711.K32

Murfin, Marjorie E. Reference service : an annotated bibliographic guide / Marjorie E. Murfin, Lubomyr R. Wynar. Littleton, Colo. : Libraries Unlimited, 1977. 294 p.   **AK234**

A bibliographic guide to the literature of reference service, covering publications on all aspects of library reference work appearing during the period 1876–1975. Topically arranged in 14 chapters, with author and title indexes.

———. ———. *Supplement, 1976–82* (1984. 353 p.).

Updates the main volume to 1982. Organization is similar with emphasis on computer applications to reference work.   Z711.M86

Reference and information services : an introduction / gen. editors, Richard E. Bopp, Linda C. Smith. Englewood, Colo. : Libraries Unlimited, 1991. 483 p. : ill., maps.   **AK235**

In pt. 1, chapters discuss the history and practice of reference service. In pt. 2, they describe important typical reference works. Includes many of the same topics as William A. Katz, *Introduction to reference work* (AK233) but emphasizes not only electronic sources but their integration into the reference process. Chapters include sample questions and additional readings. Includes examples reproduced from reference sources.   Z711.R443

Reference and online services handbook : guidelines, policies, and procedures for libraries / ed. by Bill Katz and Anne Clifford. N.Y. : Neal-Schuman, 1982–86. 2 v.   **AK236**

Vol. 1 ed. by Bill Katz and Anne Clifford; v. 2, ed. by Bill Katz.

Primarily a collection of reference services policy statements encompassing "the essential guidelines, procedures, and policies necessary in the day-to-day operations of an effective reference operation in the academic, public, and, to a lesser extent, special library."—*Introd.* An overview of policy statements (with sections by contributing librarians) is followed by policy statements from academic and public libraries, and a further section of online policy statements from academic, public, and special libraries. Indexed.   Z711.K33

PRESERVATION

Banks, Paul Noble. A selective bibliography on the conservation of research library materials. Chicago : Newberry Libr., 1981. 198 p.   **AK237**

A classed listing with author index. The primary aim of the selection is "to provide the information available in English that is most useful to librarians and archivists concerned with conservation, and to conservators of bibliothecal and archival materials."—*Pref.*

Z701.B26

Darling, Pamela W. Preservation planning program : an assisted self-study manual for libraries / prep. by Pamela W. Darling with Duane E. Webster. Rev. 1993 ed. / rev. by Jan Merrill-Oldham and Jutta Reed-Scott. Wash. : Association of Research Libraries, c1993. 138 p. : ill.   **AK238**

1st ed., 1982.

Designed to help libraries determine steps to be taken before implementing a formal study of preservation needs.

§ Part of a series of publications, supported by the National Endowment for the Humanities, that also includes seven resource guides: *Options for replacing and reformatting deteriorated materials*, ed. by Jennifer Banks (1993); *Collection conservation*, ed. by Robert DeCandido (1993); *Organization preservation activities*, ed. by Michele Cloonan (1993); *Disaster preparedness*, ed. by Constance Brooks (1993); *Managing a library binding program*, ed. by Jan Merrill-Oldham (1993); *Collection maintenance and improvement*, ed. by Sherry Byrne (1993); *Staff training and user awareness in preservation management*, ed. by Wesley L. Boomgaarden (1993).

Z701.3.R48D37

DePew, John N. A library, media, and archival preservation handbook. Santa Barbara, Calif. : ABC-Clio, c1991. 441 p. : ill.   **AK239**

Describes basic environmental controls, materials, processes, and techniques for library conservation. Includes bibliographies, and alphabetical and subject directories of preservation sources.

§ Companion volume: *A library, media, and archival preservation glossary* by John N. DePew with C. Lee Jones. (Santa Barabara, Calif. : ABC-Clio, 1992. 192 p.).   Z701.D45

Greenfield, Jane. Books, their care and repair. N.Y. : H.W. Wilson, 1983. 204 p. : ill.   **AK240**

Explains how to repair and care for books. Directed at librarians, archivists, and others who have not been trained in book repair. Includes many simple diagrams.   Z701.G73

Kyle, Hedi. Library materials preservation manual : practical methods for preserving books, pamphlets, and other printed materials. Bronxville, N.Y. : N. T. Smith, [1983]. 160 p. : ill.   **AK241**

An introduction to the techniques of preservation "geared to the needs of the aspiring preservation librarian or layman."—*Introd.* Describes basic treatments for many commonly encountered preservation problems, combining explanatory text and illustrations. List of supply sources; selected bibliography; index.   Z701.K94

Morrow, Carolyn Clark. The preservation challenge : a guide to conserving library materials / Carolyn Clark Morrow, Gay Walker. White Plains, N.Y. : Knowledge Industry Pubns., [1983]. 231 p. : ill.   **AK242**

A work which "reviews the physical causes of deterioration, summarizes what has been learned thus far about controlling or even reversing the process, [and] describes procedural and organizational strategies for prolonging the life of record materials."—*Introd.* Includes chapters on developing preservation programs in libraries, case studies of preservation programs, and technological solutions to preservation problems. Select bibliography; index.

§ *Conservation treatment procedures : a manual of step by step procedures for the maintenance and repair of library materials*, by Carolyn Clark Morrow and Carole Dyal (2nd ed. Littleton, Colo. : Libraries Unlimited, 1986. 225 p.), offers a combination of brief text and photographs illustrating the basic techniques for repair and maintenance of books, pamphlets, etc.   Z701.M547

An ounce of prevention : a handbook on disaster contingency planning for archives, libraries and record centres / John P. Barton, Johanna G. Wellheiser, editors. Toronto : Toronto Area Archivists Group Education Foundation, 1985. 192 p.   **AK243**

Although written for use in Canadian libraries, the detailed standards and guidelines for disaster prevention and the clear instructions for handling disaster are applicable anywhere. Lengthy bibliography.   Z679.7.O95

REPROGRAPHY AND MICROGRAPHICS

Directory of library reprographic services. 8th ed. / comp. and ed. by Joseph Z. Nitecki. [Westport, Conn.] : Publ. for the Reproduction of Library Materials Section, RTSD-Amer. Libr. Assoc., by Meckler Publishing, [1982]. 540 p.   **AK244**
1st ed., 1959.

Title of earlier editions varies: 4th ed. called *Directory of institutional photocopying services*. Compiler varies.

Provides information on copying and duplicating services available in 428 U.S. and 92 non-U.S. libraries. Information (presented in tabular form and showing photoduplication services offered by each library, address, charges, etc.) is based on responses to questionnaires. Geographical arrangement.   Z265.N56

Gabriel, Michael. Micrographics, 1900–1977 : a bibliography. Mankato, Minn. : Scholarly Pr., [1978]. 266 p.   **AK245**

Aims to bring together "all known English references to monographic, periodical, and technical report literature for the years 1900–1977."—*Introd.* Citations are grouped in categories such as Microforms and libraries, Cataloging and classification, Computer-output-microform (COM) in libraries, Business micrographs, Microphotography, Micrographics equipment, User studies. Author index.   Z265.A1G32

Glossary of imaging technology. Silver Spring, Md. : Assoc. for Information and Image Management, c1992. 79 p. : ill.   **AK246**

A revised edition of National Micrographics Assoc., *Glossary of micrographics* (6th ed. Silver Springs, Md. : The Assoc., 1980).

Defines more than 1,600 micrographic and electronic image management (EIM) terms.   TR835.G58

Information management sourcebook : the AIIM buying guide and membership directory. 1987– . Silver Spring, Md. : Association for Information and Image Management, 1987– . Annual.   **AK247**

Continues: Association for Information and Image Management. *Buying guide* (1984).

In four sections: Trade listing, an alphabetical directory of companies listed in the Products and services section; Company profiles, one-page descriptions of companies that chose to be included; Products and services, covering electronic imaging, micrographics, multimedia systems, furniture, storage supplies, services, trade publications; and AIIM directory, an alphabetical directory and geographical listing of members.   HD9999.M47A39

International imaging source book : including micrographics and optical imaging. 1992– . Larchmont, N.Y. : Microfilm Publ., c1992– . Biennial.   **AK248**

Continues: *International micrographics sourcebook*.

Covers the software, hardware, and services of micrographics and electronic imaging. Includes products, services, dealers, consultants, and associations. Lists imaging journals and newsletters; annotated bibliography.   TR835.I53

Keene, James A. Planning, equipping, and staffing a document reprographic service : a RAMP study with guidelines / prep. by James A. Keene and Michael Roper [for the] General Information Programme and UNISIST. Paris : UNESCO, 1984. 84 p. : ill.   **AK249**

Intends "to provide archivists ... with a survey of current relevant reprographic technology and with guidelines and standards which they can apply in selecting and introducing the technology [most appropriate to their own specific situations]."—*Introd.* Written with the problems of developing countries (especially those in tropical areas) firmly in mind; in four parts: Basic technology; Issues in planning, equipping, and staffing; A three-stage program for establishing an archival reprographic service; and Guidelines. Eight appendixes include job descriptions, facility plans, list of manufacturers and suppliers, glossary, and bibliography.   Z48.K43

Saffady, William. Micrographics. 2nd ed. Littleton, Colo. : Libraries Unlimited, 1985. 254 p. : ill.   **AK250**
1st ed., 1978.

"A text designed for practicing librarians and library school students who want a systematic presentation of the basic facets of micrographics as applied to library work."—*Pref.* Describes the basic types of microforms and discusses production of microform from source documents as well as from machine-readable data (COM—Computer Output Microform). Also treats micropublishing, microform display and printing equipment, bibliographic control of microforms, and microform storage and retrieval. Illustrations; index.   Z692.M5S24

Vilhauer, Jerry. Introduction to micrographics. Silver Spring, Md. : Association for Information and Image Management, c1991. 38 p.   **AK251**

Explains all aspects of microfilming, including processing, equipment, and storage. Covers both source document and computer output microfilming.   Z265.V5

AL

Other General Reference Works

GENERAL WORKS

Directories

Atkins, Peter Joseph. The directories of London, 1677–1977. London ; N.Y. : Mansell, 1990. 732 p. : ill.   **AL1**
Revision and update of *The London directories, 1677–1855* by Charles Goss (London : Archer, 1932. 146 p.). Following a general discussion of compilations and development of London directories, the principal list is subdivided as series and nonseries, specialized, suburban and local. Lists source libraries and archives with holdings. Indexed by title, publisher, and topic.
§ Complemented by: *British directories : a bibliography and guide to directories published in England and Wales (1850–1950) and Scotland (1773–1950)*, by Gareth Shaw and Allison Tipper (Leicester : Leicester Univ. Pr., 1989. 440 p.) and J. E. Norton's *Guide to the national and provincial directories of England and Wales excluding London, published before 1856* (AL7).   Z5771.4.G7A85

Current British directories. 1953– . London : publ. for C.B.D. Research Ltd. by Jones & Evans Bookshop Ltd., 1953– .   **AL2**
Subtitle: A guide to the directories published in the British Isles.
12th ed., 1993.
Lists more than 4,000 directories alphabetically; indexed by publisher and by subject.   Z5771.C97

Directories in print. 6th ed. (1989)– . Detroit : Gale, c1989– . Annual.   **AL3**
11th ed., 1994.
Continues: *Directory of directories*, which ceased with the 5th ed., 1988.
Vol. 1 lists about 15,900 directories, arranged in broad subject areas. Vol. 2 indexes directories by detailed subject, title, and keyword, and lists directories issued in alternate formats, such as online, diskette, or magnetic tape.
•Machine-readable version: *Directories in print (DIP)* [database] (Detroit : Gale). Available online; corresponds to latest printed version.   Z5771.D55

Guide to American directories. 1954– . N.Y. : B. Klein Publ., 1954– . Irregular.   **AL4**
Publisher varies.
Title varies: 1954–58, *Guide to American directories for compiling mailing lists*. Subtitle varies; 1994, A guide to the major directories of the U.S. with major foreign directories included, covering all trade, professional and industrial categories.
13th ed., 1994, lists about 10,000 U.S. directories and about 1,000 major foreign directories in a topical arrangement. Indexed by subject and by title.   Z5771.G8

Henderson, George P. Current European directories. Ed. 2. Beckenham, Eng. : C.B.D. Research Ltd., [1981]. 413 p.   **AL5**
1st ed., 1969.
Subtitle: A guide to international, national, city and specialised directories and similar reference works for all countries of Europe, excluding Great Britain and Ireland.   Z57712.H39

The national directory of internships. 1984– . Raleigh, N.C. : National Society for Internships and Experiential Education, 1984– . Irregular.   **AL6**
For annotation, *see* CB385.

Norton, Jane Elizabeth. Guide to the national and provincial directories of England and Wales, excluding London, published before 1856. London : Offices of the Royal Historical Soc., 1950. 241 p. (Royal Historical Society. Guides and handbooks, 5).   **AL7**
Repr. 1984.
Includes national, local, and Welsh directories. Complements: Peter Joseph Atkins, *The directories of London, 1677–1977* (AL1) and *British directories : a bibliography and guide to directories published in England and Wales (1850–1950) and Scotland (1773–1950)*, by Gareth Shaw and Allison Tipper (Leicester : Leicester Univ. Pr., 1989. 440 p.).   Z2034.N67

Spear, Dorothea N. Bibliography of American directories through 1860. Worcester, Mass. : Amer. Antiquarian Soc., 1961. 389 p.   **AL8**
Repr.: Westport, Conn. : Greenwood, 1978.
A geographical listing, with locations of 1,647 business directories, city and county directories, etc. Many annotations. Works listed are available in the microfilm collection, *City directories of the United States* from Research Publications.   Z5771.22b.S68

ASSOCIATIONS, SOCIETIES, AND ACADEMIES

General Works

Avery, Barbara Brower. Guide to sources of professional ethics. Monticello, Ill. : Vance Bibliographies, [1986]. 29 p. (Public administration series—bibliography, P-1901).   **AL9**
Lists sources of professional codes of ethics (or notes their absence) for 74 professional societies and associations.   Z7164.A2P72

Ott, J. Steven. The Facts on File dictionary of nonprofit organization management / J. Steven Ott and Jay M. Shafritz. N.Y. : Facts on File, c1986. 407 p.   **AL10**
"Presents a comprehensive set of definitions for terms and phrases related to the purpose, structures, functions, law, codes, ethics, and financing (especially fund raising) of nonprofit organizations."—*Pref.* Also defines relevant terms drawn from other fields of business and management. Includes charts and other illustrations and a brief, unannotated bibliography.   HD62.6.O88

Wennrich, Peter. International encyclopedia of abbreviations and acronyms of organizations = Internationale Enzyklopädie der Abkürzungen und Akronyme von Organisationen / Peter Wennrich, Paul Spillner. 3rd rev. and enl. ed. München ; N.Y. : K.G. Saur, 1990–94. v. 1–7, 9–10. (In progress).   **AL11**
1st ed., ed. by Spillner, had title: *Ullstein-Abkürzungslexikon* (Frankfurt : Ullstein, 1967); 2nd ed., also ed. by Spillner, had title: *Internationales Wörterbuch der Abkürzungen von Organisationen = International dictionary of abbreviations of organizations* (München-Pullach : Verlag Dokumentation, 1970–72).

Contents: Pt. 1, Abbreviations and acronyms, v. 1–6, A–Z; pt. 2, Organizations and institutions, v. 7, A–Comma, v. 9–10, Instr–Z.

Title page and prefatory material in English and German.

Includes organizations, contemporary and historical, of all kinds—clubs, research centers, corporations, etc.   AS8.W46

Bibliography

British Museum. Department of Printed Books. Catalogue of printed books : Academics. London : Clowes, 1885–86. 1018 col., 100 col.   **AL12**

Published as part of the Museum's *General catalogue of printed books* (AA103); included in alphabetical sequence under "Academies" in v. 1 of the Edwards reprint of the *Catalogue*.

A useful historical record. In two parts: (1) Catalogue of the publications of societies, arranged alphabetically by place with subarrangement by name of society; (2) Alphabetical index of names of societies.

The listings for academies in the newer British Museum *Catalogue* (AA103 *note*) are scattered throughout rather than being collected in a single volume.

World of learning. 1947– . London : Allen & Unwin, 1947– . Annual.   **AL13**

Lists learned societies, research institutions, libraries, museums, and institutions of higher education in nearly 200 countries. For the latter, the information provided varies; for most, gives address and phone number, founding date, and number of teachers and students; for others, names administrators, deans, and the institution's publications; for some, all professors are listed. Arranged alphabetically by country, and within the U.S., by state. A separate section gives information on international organizations, including addresses and descriptions of structure and activities. Index of institutions.   AS2.W6

Abbreviations

Swinbank, Jean C. M. Buttress's world guide to abbreviations of organizations / revised by Jean C.M. Swinbank and Henry J. Heaney. 10th ed. London ; N.Y. : Blackie Academic & Professional, 1993. 1048 p.   **AL14**

Title varies: 1st ed., 1954, and 2nd ed., 1960, had title: *World list of abbreviations of scientific, technological and commercial organizations*. 3rd ed., 1966, had title: *World list of abbreviations*. 4th ed, 1971, through 8th ed., 1988, had title: *World guide to abbreviations of organizations*.

Some 60,000 entries, arranged alphabetically by acronym, followed by organization name. Includes international, national, governmental, and individual organizations. For national organizations, country follows in parentheses. Cross-references refer from defunct organizations to their successors. In the 10th ed., special attention is paid to the Far East, Australasia, Latin America, and the People's Republic of China, areas covered sparsely in earlier editions.   AS8.S88

International

An alternative directory of nongovernmental organizations in South Asia / ed. by Todd Nachowitz. Rev. ed. Syracuse, N.Y. : Maxwell School of Citizenship and Public Affairs, Syracuse Univ., c1990. 82 p. (Foreign and comparative studies. South Asian series, no. 14).   **AL15**

A directory for India, Bangladesh, Nepal, Pakistan, and Sri Lanka, of grassroots organizations that provide alternatives to international aid agencies and multilateral development banks. Arranged alphabetically by subject (e.g., alternative travel and tourism, animal rights, Bhopal gas victims, tribals, women), then by country. Profiles include: address, keywords describing primary activities, description,

and contact. English translation is given for names in vernacular. Index of organizations, contact persons, and agency publications.

AS408.A48

Directory of European professional & learned societies = Répertoire des sociétés professionnelles et savantes en Europe. Beckenham, Kent, England : CBD Research, c1989– . Irregular.   **AL16**

Continues pt. 2 of *Directory of European associations* (Beckenham, Kent : CBD Research ; Detroit : Gale, 1971–84).

Companion to *Directory of European industrial and trade associations* (Beckenham, Kent : CBD Research, 1991). Provides information on professional, learned, scientific, and technical associations in Europe (excluding the U.K. and Ireland), Iceland, Malta, and Cyprus. Arranged by topic (e.g., Napoleonic studies, robotics, tropical medicine), then by country. Entries include address, telephone and telex numbers, areas of interest, membership, activities, and publications. Subject index, classified directory of organizations, index of abbreviations of organizations, and alphabetical index of organizations.

HD6497.E85D57

Encyclopedia of associations. International organizations. 23rd ed. (1989)– . Detroit : Gale, c1989– . Annual, with midyear supplement.   **AL17**

Issued in 2 pts.

Similar in format to the parent work (AL41).   AS8.E53

Encyclopedia of women's associations worldwide : a guide to over 3,400 national and multinational nonprofit women's and women-related organizations / Jacqueline K. Barrett, ed. ; Jane A. Malonis, assoc. ed. London ; Detroit : Gale, c1993. 471 p. : maps.   **AL18**

Prefatory material in English, French, German, and Spanish.

Guide to women's and women-related nonprofit, national and multinational organizations. Eight sections, each covering a region (e.g., Africa, Europe, North America); organizations are listed alphabetically under country. Entries provide directory information, contact, brief mission statement, and, if appropriate, conventions, publications, description of library, awards, and committees. Index of organizational activities.   HQ1883.E53

International encyclopedia of learned societies and academies / ed. by Joseph C. Kiger. Westport, Conn. : Greenwood, 1993. 377 p. : ill.   **AL19**

Includes descriptions of 103 of the most prestigious national learned societies and academies in 50 countries. Profiles, arranged alphabetically by country, discuss history, organizational structure, membership, publication programs, research activities, and affiliations. Bibliographies. Appendixes include a chronological list of organizations, a "genealogy" (name changes from founding to present day), and listing by general area of concern. Index.   AS8.I637

Organizations master index / Denise M. Allard, ed. Detroit : Gale, c1987. 1120 p.   **AL20**

Subtitle: A consolidated index to approximately 50 directories, handbooks, yearbooks, encyclopedias, and guides providing information on approximately 150,000 national and international associations, government agencies and advisory organizations, foundations, research centers, museums, religious groups, political organizations, labor unions, and other organizations, institutions, and programs of all kinds in the U.S., Canada, and worldwide.

Organizations are listed alphabetically, followed by sponsoring or parent organization (if any), geographic location, and codes for information sources. Bibliography of sources with annotations describing arrangement, types of organizations included, and information provided.   Z5051.O73

Schiavone, Giuseppe. International organizations : a dictionary and directory. 3rd ed. N.Y. : St. Martin's, 1993. 337 p.   **AL21**

1st ed., 1983; 2nd ed., 1986.

Introduction discusses the expanding roles of international organizations that face such challenges as human rights, drugs, sustainable development, and the environment. Organized alphabetically by name of organization. Substantial profiles with bibliographies describe purpose, history, responsibilities of member nations, structure, and links with other bodies. Subsequent sections classify organizations in various ways: e.g., by date, subject, membership. Indexes of acronyms and organization names.   JX1995.S325

Union of International Associations. The 1,978 international organizations founded since the Congress of Vienna : chronological list / with an introduction by G. P. Speeckaert. Brussels, 1957. 204 p. (Documents, no.7).   **AL22**
   Title page, introduction, and subject index in French and English.
   A chronological list for the period 1815–1956 (with two earlier listings for 1693 and 1783). Entries include name of organization with place and date founded. Introduction traces, by subject area (e.g., welfare, health, law, commerce), the history of organized international exchange and cooperation from earliest times to the mid-1950s.
                                                        AS5.U5 no.7

Who is who in service to the earth. 1st ed.– . Waynesville, N.C. : VisionLink, c1991– . Annual.   **AL23**
   Subtitle: Over 8,000 listings and cross-indexes of people, projects and organizations, dedicated to a sustainable future.
   Organizations worldwide are listed in alphabetical order with contact, directory information, project, and description of mission. Besides agricultural and ecological topics, areas of concern include abortion rights, attitudinal healing, legal aid, and labor unions. Indexed by primary contact person, project title, country, and keyword.
   § See also *World directory of environmental organizations* (EK77).   GE1.W47

World guide to scientific associations and learned societies / ed. by Michael Sachs. 5th ed. Munich ; N.Y. : K.G. Saur, 1990. 672 p. (Handbook of international documentation and information, 13).   **AL24**
   Title varies: 1st ed., 1974, had title: *World guide to scientific organizations.* 4th ed., 1984.
   Lists some 18,000 active national and international organizations in science, culture, and technology. Arranged alphabetically by country, entries include the official name; address; numbers for telephone, telefacsimile, telex, and cable; official personnel listings; areas of activity; and publications. Title, prefatory matter, and headings in English and German. An index to 12,000 association and society periodical titles has been added to the 5th ed. Subject index.   Q145.W9267

Meetings

Association meeting planners & conference/convention directors. N.Y. : The Salesman's Guide, [198?]. Annual. Looseleaf.   **AL25**
   Organized by state, then city; lists national associations that regularly hold conventions at hotels or other commercial facilities. The 1993 edition lists 9,195 organizations, providing names of executive director and convention planner, dates and places of past and future conventions, smaller meetings held in conjunction with conventions, number of attendees, number of days held, etc. List of for-profit association management companies with their clients. Groups companies by number of attendees. Alphabetical, acronym, and speaker index.

British Library. Document Supply Centre. Index of conference proceedings. ICP 256 (Jan. 1989)– . Boston Spa, U.K. : The Centre, 1989– . Monthly, with annual cumulation.
                                                        AL26
   Coverage extends to all conference publications regardless of subject, language, or format with the exception of audiovisual material. About 18,000 titles are added each year. The arrangement is alphabetical by keyterms which are derived from the conference title and/or sponsoring agency. Within a heading, entries are arranged by the date of the meeting. Information for each conference consists of title, sponsor, date, meeting location, and Document Supply Centre identifier code.

Continues: (1) British Library. Lending Division, *BLL conference index, 1964–1973.* (Boston Spa : BLLD, 1974. 1220 p.).
   (2) British Library. Lending Division, *Index of conference proceedings received* (no. 69 [1973]–no. 255 [1988]. Boston Spa : BLLD, 1973–88).
   (3) Cumulations publ. as: *Index of conference proceedings, 1964–1988* (London ; N.Y. : K. G. Saur, 1989–90. 26 v); and as: British Library. Document Supply Centre, *Index of conference proceedings, 1964–1988* [microform] (Boston Spa : The Centre, [1989]. 138 microfiches).
   •Machine-readable versions: (1) *Conference proceedings index (CPI)* [database] (Boston Spa : British Library Document Supply Centre, 1964–). Available online; updated monthly. Lists some conferences dating back to the 19th century. (2) *Boston Spa conferences* [database] (Boston Spa : British Library Document Supply Centre, 1787–). Available on CD-ROM; updated quarterly. Covers conferences held 1787– .   Z5051.B862

Directory of published proceedings. Series SSH : Social sciences/Humanities. v. 1/4 (1968/71)– . Harrison, N.Y. : InterDok Corp., 1971– . Quarterly.   **AL27**
   At head of title: InterDok.
   Final issue of each volume contains cumulative index for issues in the volume.
   Lists published proceedings of congresses, conferences, symposia, etc., in the social sciences and humanities. Arranged chronologically by date of the meeting. Acronym list. Editor, location, and subject/sponsor indexes.
   § Companion work: *Directory of published proceedings. Series SEMT : Science, engineering, medicine, and technology* (EA209).
                                                        Z7161.D56

Event line. 1990– . Amsterdam ; N.Y. : Elsevier, 1989– .
                                                        AL28
   Lists conventions, symposia, exhibitions, trade fairs, and major sporting events. Includes dates and locations, organizers, scope (size and topic), as well as standard directory information.
   •Machine-readable version: *EventLine* [database] (Amsterdam : Elsevier, 1989–). Available online, updated monthly.   AS8.E94

Index to social sciences and humanities proceedings. no. 1 (Jan./Mar. 1979)– . Philadelphia : Institute for Scientific Information, 1979– . Quarterly, with annual cumulation. **AL29**
   An index to papers read at conferences that are published as books, reports, preprint sets, or journal literature. The main section provides full bibliographic information. Indexed by category (broad subject area), author/editor, sponsor, meeting location, keyword, and corporate (geographic location and organization).

International congresses and conferences, 1840–1937 : a union list of their publications available in libraries of the United States and Canada / ed. by Winifred Gregory under the auspices of the Bibliographical Society of America. N.Y. : Wilson, 1938. 229 p.   **AL30**
   Repr. : N.Y. : Kraus, 1967.
   Arranged alphabetically by name of congress or conference. Excludes diplomatic congresses and those sponsored by the League of Nations. In the case of proceedings and reports not separately published, entries include abstracts and excerpts from reviews. Lists holdings in more than 100 libraries. Subject index.   Z5051.I58

Union of International Associations. Les congrès internationaux de 1681 à 1899 : liste complète = International congresses, 1681 to 1899, full list. Bruxelles, 1960. 76 p. (Documents pour servir à l'etude des relations internationales nongouvernementales, no. 8. Publication no. 164).   **AL31**
   Title page, introduction, and subject index in French and English.
   A chronological list of 1,414 congresses, all but one from the 19th century, with meeting places and dates.

§ *Les congrès internationaux de 1900 à 1919: liste complète* (Bruxelles : Union of International Associations, 1964) continues coverage, treating 2,528 congresses in an identical format. Cumulative subject index for both volumes. As5.U5 no. 8

World meetings : social & behavioral sciences, human services & management. v. 7, no. 2 (Apr. 1977)– . N.Y. : World Meetings Publications : Macmillan, [c1977]– . Quarterly. **AL32**

Publisher varies; subtitle varies.

In each issue, data on meetings is presented in eight sections, one for each quarter of a two-year period. Each new issue drops the first quarter of the preceding issue and adds a new quarter; changes and new listings are added in all other sections as necessary. Indexes: subject, date, location, publication, deadline, and sponsor. AS8.W75

Yearbook of international congress proceedings : bibliography of reports arising out of meetings held by international organizations. Brussels : Union of International Associations, 1969–1970. 2 v. **AL33**

Contents: v. 1, 1960–67; v. 2, 1962–69.

Also known by its subtitle.

Although some entries for meetings during the overlapping years appear in both, each lists congresses that the other lacks. Arranged chronologically. For each meeting, dates, place, name, and documentation (report, proceedings, or summary) are provided. Address list of publishers of meeting reports. Indexes of organizations and subject/keyword.

Continues the listings in the *Bibliography of proceedings of international meetings* (Brussels : Union of International Associations, 1963–66. 3 v.), covering 1952–59. Z5051.B52

North America

Cross-border links : a directory of organizations in Canada, Mexico, and the United States / ed. by Ricardo Hernández & Edith Sánchez. Albuquerque, N.M. : Inter-Hemispheric Education Resource Center, 1992. 257 p. **AL34**

Bi- and tri-national organizations, as well as national organizations that address issues raised by the North American Free Trade Agreement, are listed under eight categories: Fair trade, Labor, Environment, Advocacy (human rights and social justice), Academic institutions, Government agencies, Business groups, and Electronic networks. Headnotes discuss the manner in which the three nations have organized to address each area of concern. Includes mailing address, phone, contact person, and, when available, e-mail address, history and description, activities, affiliations, and publications. Index of organizations. HS61.A2C76

Directory of Central America organizations. Spring 1984–1987. Austin, Tex. : Central America Resource Center, 1984–1987. Annual. **AL35**

The 3rd ed. lists 1,075 U.S. organizations concerned with Central American issues such as human rights, peace, displacement of natives, and poverty. Arranged by state, then by city. Entries provide address, contact, brief description, countries of interest, and activities. Indexed by organization name, acronym, and activity. HS17.D57

Schmidt, Alvin J. Fraternal organizations / Alvin J. Schmidt ; advisory ed., Nicholas Babchuk. Westport, Conn. : Greenwood, [1980]. 410 p. (Greenwood encyclopedia of American institutions, v. 3). **AL36**

Provides information on more than 450 fraternal organizations, active and defunct, of the U. S. and Canada: e.g., American Legion of Honor, Elks, Ku Klux Klan. An introductory chapter, "The Fraternal Context," discusses the nature, prevalence and function of American fraternal orders from the mid-19th century to the present. Entries are alphabetically arranged and include founding date and place, history, goals and activities, membership requirements, size, rituals, emblems,

publications, and sources of further information. Appendixes arrange organizations chronologically, geographically, and by ethnic and religious affiliation. Index. HS17.S3

United States

American Council of Learned Societies. Directory of constituent societies of the American Council of Learned Societies. Arlington, Va. : Carrollton Press. **AL37**

Profiles the 51 constituent organizations for which the ACLS serves as national representative (e.g., African Studies Association, American Dialect Society, American Psychological Association, and Society for Cinema Studies). Entries provide address and telephone, names of officers and staff, number of members, criteria for membership, dues, meetings, publications, and activities. Appendixes list constituent societies with membership figures, ACLS Board of Directors, Executive Committees, and other administrative bodies.

Bowker, Richard Rogers. Publications of societies : a provisional list of the publications of American scientific, literary, and other societies from their organization. N.Y. : Publishers' Weekly, 1899. 181 p. **AL38**

An alphabetical listing of more than 1,000 19th-century American organizations that issued publications: e.g., scientific and historical societies, universities, and professional associations at the state and national levels. Entries include date of founding, address, and a chronologically arranged bibliography of publications. Z5065.U39B7

Dewey, Patrick R. Fan club directory : 2000 fan clubs and fan mail addresses in the United States and abroad. Jefferson, N.C. : McFarland & Co., 1993. 104 p. **AL39**

Aimed at those wishing to share fanzines, conventions, and correspondence with other aficionados, this directory may also interest students of popular culture. Provides mailing addresses for fan clubs devoted to such topics as television and movie personalities, cartoon characters, vampires, sports, and many science fiction topics. All but a few clubs are located in the U.S. Subject and organization name index. AS8.D46

Directory of American youth organizations : a guide to 500 clubs, groups, troops, teams, societies, lodges, and more for young people / Judith B. Erickson. 4th ed., updated and revised. Minneapolis, Minn. : Free Spirit Pub., c1991. **AL40**

1st ed., 1983.

Aimed at children and young adults and adult volunteers. Nonprofit, adult-sponsored organizations that enroll youths are grouped under topical headings. Provides background information concerning youth organizations and lists organizations and clearinghouses providing support for volunteers. Annotated bibliography; index. HS3260.U5D57

Encyclopedia of associations. 3rd– . Detroit : Gale, 1961– . Annual. **AL41**

Continues *Encyclopedia of American associations*, 1956–59.

Frequency varies; irregular, 1961–73; annual since 1975.

Subtitle, content, and number of volumes vary. Currently publ. in 3 v.

Contents: v. 1, National organizations of the U.S.: pts. 1–2, Sections 1–18, pt. 3, Name/keyword index; v. 2, Geographic and executive indexes; v. 3, Supplement: New associations and projects (issued four months after v. 1, lists additional associations not included in v. 1).

The most comprehensive guide to U.S. nonprofit organizations. Vol. 1 lists associations by 18 broad fields (e.g, Education, Public affairs, Fan clubs). Entries include acronym, address, telephone, contact, date founded, membership, staff, budget, description, affiliations, committees, publications, and conventions. An updating service, issued twice a year since 1985, lists changes to associations listed in v. 1 and 3. Rankings indexes issued since the 21st ed. provide ranked listings by membership size, staff size, annual budget, and founding date for organizations listed in v. 1.

Companion publications:
———. *Association periodicals* (AD50).
———. *International organizations* (AL17).
———. *Regional, state, and local organizations* (AL42).
•Machine-readable version: *Encyclopedia of associations (EA)* [database] (Detroit : Gale). Available online, on CD-ROM, on diskettes, or magnetic tape, all updated semiannually. Current coverage.
AS22.E5

Encyclopedia of associations. Regional, state, and local organizations. 1st ed. (1988–89)– . Detroit : Gale, c1987– . Biennial.   **AL42**
Contents: v. 1, Great Lakes states; v. 2, Northeastern states; v. 3, Middle Atlantic states; v. 4, Western states; v. 5, Southeastern states; v. 6, Southwest and South Central states; v. 7, Northwestern and Great Plains states.
Similar in format to the parent work (AL41).   AS22.E53

Focus Japan II : a resource guide to Japan-oriented organizations : a joint project of National Planning Association [and] University of Maryland at College Park / presented by Gateway Japan ; ed. by Erland Heginbotham, Gretchen Shinoda. Wash. : Gateway Japan, c1993. 691 p.   **AL43**
"Grew out of a request for an inventory of Japan-focused organizations based in North America. [Lists] over 500 organizations classified by type, activity, products or services."—*Executive summary*. Primarily academic programs and libraries; does include foundations. Ten appendixes include information on Japan-related databases, outreach activities, sister cities, etc. No index.   DS801.F625

Gardner, Richard. Alternative America. Cambridge, Mass. : Copies from Resources, c1990. 1 v.   **AL44**
Directory of: groups promoting radical causes, alternative lifestyles, educational approaches to the arts; religious sects; specialized bookstores; small press publications; galleries; and food cooperatives. Name, address, telephone, and descriptor are listed by zip code. Name and subject indexes.   L901.G27

National trade and professional associations of the United States. 17th annual ed. (1982)– . Wash. : Columbia Books, [1982]– . Annual.   **AL45**
Supersedes *Directory of national trade and professional associations of the United States* (1966–71) and *National trade and professional associations of the United States, and labor unions*, and continues their numbering.
Entries for more than 7,500 trade and professional associations and labor unions, with directory information, historical notes, membership information, lists of publications and annual meetings. Separate directory lists association management companies with the names of the organizations they manage. Indexes: subject, geography, budget size, executive name, and acronyms.
§ Companion publication: *State and regional associations of the United States* (AL47).   HD2425.D53

Spectrum : a guide to the independent press and informative organizations. 19th ed. (1989)– . Olathe, Kan. : Editorial Research Service, 1989– .   **AL46**
1st ed. (1971)–18th ed. (1988?) had title: *Censored*.
Publisher varies.
A directory of organizations, periodicals, specialized bookstores, and publishers serving as alternative sources of current information on such topics as animal rights, euthanasia, and holistic medicine. Entries include directory information, publications, and brief statement of purpose or political viewpoint.   D839.C46

State and regional associations of the United States. 1st annual ed. (1989)– . Wash. : Columbia Books, 1989– . Annual.   **AL47**
The 4th ed. (1992) lists 6,900 major trade associations, professional societies, and labor organizations that have state or regional memberships. Fraternal, patriotic, charitable, hobby, and small organizations are excluded, making *SRA* about one-tenth the size of *Encyclopedia of associations. Regional, state, and local organizations* (AL42),

which includes all types of nonprofit groups. Entries include address, telephone, fax, president, number of members and of staff and, when available, annual budget, historical note, publications, and annual meetings. Arranged geographically with the following indexes: subject, budget, executive, acronym, and management firm.
§ For associations with national memberships, consult the companion directory: *National trade and professional associations of the United States* (AL45).   HD2425.S68

Walls, David. The activist's almanac : the concerned citizen's guide to the leading advocacy organizations in America. N.Y. : Simon & Schuster, c1993. 431 p. : ill.   **AL48**
Lists organizations that are national in scope, supported by individual contributions, open to the general public, nonprofit, and dedicated to changing public policy. Groups are arranged by order of founding in the following categories: environmental; peace and foreign policy; human rights; multi-issue (subdivided into progressive and conservative). Entries include directory information, statement of purpose, historical background, generalizations about membership, structure, finances, publications, and services. Bibliography; index.   HN55.W35

Washington information directory. 1975/76– . [Wash.] : Congressional Quarterly Inc., 1975– . Annual.   **AL49**
Topical chapters (e.g., Congress and politics, Employment and labor, Energy) list executive agencies, congressional committees and subcommittees, and private organizations as information sources. Each entry gives address, telephone, fax, director, and brief description of agency. "Ready Reference Lists" give directory information for Congress, foreign embassies, labor unions, regional federal information sources, governors, lieutenant governors, secretaries of state, attorneys general, and mayors of cities. Name and subject indexes.
§ A similar source, *Washington : a comprehensive directory of the key institutions and leaders of the national capital area* (Wash. : Columbia Books, 1985– . Annual) describes approximately 4,000 Washington area public and private institutions. Both directories are arranged by topical chapters, but there is less overlap between them than might be expected. Only *WID* has chapters on agricultural, transportation, and energy organizations; only *Washington* has sections on religious associations and on social, recreational, and professional clubs. Another difference is that *Washington* lists officers and trustees under each agency and includes them in a combined index of organizations and individuals that occupies half the volume.   F192.3.W33

Who's doing what? : a directory of U.S. organizations & institutions educating about development and other global issues. 2nd ed.– . N.Y. : National Clearinghouse on Development Education of the American Forum for Global Education, c1991– . Biennial.   **AL50**
1st ed., 1988, had title: *Who's doing what in development education?*
Describes 249 U.S. organizations concerned with "development education"; i.e., promoting worldwide justice, sensitivity toward cultural diversity, and an appreciation of the global interconnectedness of issues and systems. Includes Africa World Press, Greenpeace, League of Rural Voters, Peace Corps, Save the Children, and U.N. Development Programme. Entries provide acronym, type of organization (advocacy, federal, nonprofit, religious), history/goals, educational program, audience, geographic focus, services, and funding. Organizations indexed by state and geographic focus of educational activities.   LC1090.W56

Canada

Associations Canada : an encyclopedic directory = un répertoire encyclopédique. 1991– . Toronto : Canadian Almanac & Directory Pub. Co., c1991– . Annual.   **AL51**
Text in English and French.
Includes more than 20,000 Canadian organizations and 1,000 foreign organizations of interest to Canadians. Lists industrial, commercial, and professional associations, registered charities, special or common interest groups, foundations, research institutes, labor unions, political parties, and fraternal organizations. Profiles include acronym,

former and "popular" names, founding date, directory information, executive names, scope of activity, membership criteria, mission statement, affiliation with other organizations, membership fees, library services, serial publications, and conventions. Indexed by subject, geographic location, executive name, publications, acronym, speaker and mailing list availability.

§ Similar in size and scope to *Directory of associations in Canada* (AL52), but each directory includes organizations lacking in the other. AS40.A86

Directory of associations in Canada = Répertoire des associations du Canada. [1st] ed. (1973)– . [Toronto] : Univ. of Toronto Pr., 1973– . Annual. **AL52**

Introductory and explanatory matter in English and French. Publisher varies.

Brief directory information on approximately 18,000 nongovernmental, nonprofit organizations. New to the 11th ed. are discontinued listings of organizations that have become inactive or defunct since the previous edition. Detailed subject index with numerous *see* and *see also* references to activities, services and interests. AS40.D49

Latin America

Barreiro, Fernando. Organizaciones no gubernamentales de Uruguay : análisis y repertorio / Fernando Barreiro, Anabel Cruz. Montevideo : Instituto de Comunicación y Desarrollo ; [Madrid] : ICI, 1990. 195 p. **AL53**

Devoted to groups that promote democracy, excluding organizations that are primarily cultural or philanthropic. An introductory essay describes the role of social action groups in Uruguayan society. Arranged alphabetically by organization name, profiles include acronym, address, telephone, director, objectives, areas of interest, activities, publications, staff, and information resources (e.g., libraries, archives, databases). Indexed by theme (e.g., condition of women, human rights, ecology) and acronym. List of institutions that make databases available, with descriptions of the databases. HC232.B378

Directorio de organizaciones indígenas de América. no. [1]– . Madrid : Comisión Nacional "Quinto Centenario", 1988– . **AL54**

Prints responses to a 25 question survey sent to organizations of indigenous peoples south of the Rio Grande. (One U.S. organization, National Indian Youth Council, is also included.) Arranged alphabetically under country, self-descriptions of 26 organizations include directory information; facts about members (e.g., ethnicity, languages spoken, geographic areas inhabited); aims; social problems addressed; and organizational structure. E54.5.D57

Europe

Former Soviet Republics

Akademiĭa Nauk SSSR. Biblioteka. Bibliografiĭa izdaniĭ Akademii nauk SSSR. v. 1 (1956)–v. 34 (1989). Moskva ; Leningrad : Izd-vo AN SSSR, 1957–1991. Annual. **AL55**

English translation on verso of t.p.: *Bibliography of publications of the Academy of Sciences of the USSR.*

All publications of the U.S.S.R. Academy of Sciences for a given year are recorded under departments and institutes of the Union Academy and its affiliates. Publications of republic academies are not included. Articles in symposia and irregular serials (transactions, learned papers, etc.) are analyzed by author and title. The name index includes authors of articles in regularly appearing journals, with abbreviation of periodical title and number. Subject and journal indexes.

Continued by: Rossĭiskaĭa Akademiĭa Nauk. Biblioteka. *Bibliografiĭa izdaniĭ Akademii nauk* (v. 35 [1990]– . Sankt-Peterburg : BAN, 1992– . Annual). Z5055.R8A3726

Moskva : spravochnik : 132 obshchestvennye organizatsii. Moskva : SMOT, IAS, 1991. 25 p. **AL56**

Directory of nongovernmental organizations with headquarters in Moscow, including religious, political, and social agencies. Listings are in alphabetical order and include date of founding, number of members, brief description, and names and telephone numbers of contacts. No index. HS71.S652M6

Neformalniye : a guide to independent organizations and contacts in the Soviet Union. Seattle, Wash. : World Without War Council, c1990. 103 p. **AL57**

Compiled before the breakup of the Soviet Union, this directory lists *neformalniye*—informal grass-roots movements demanding legal status and freedom from censorship. Established mostly in the late 1980s and after, *neformalniye* address a wide range of concerns: e.g., art, film, peace, sports, ecology, political prisoners, freedom of emigration, legal review, freedom of the press. Arranged by state with separate listings for Moscow and Leningrad, entries include organization name in English translation and Russian transliteration, contact, telephone, address, description of activities, and publications. Alphabetical list of organizations. Index by city. DK14.N44

Raising the curtain : guide to independent organizations and contacts in Eastern Europe. 2nd ed. Seattle, Wash. : World Without War Council, c1990. 77 p. **AL58**

1st ed., 1989.

The compilers believe that Americans who work with Eastern European independent organizations have an opportunity to support democratic reconstruction and economic development in the region. The 2nd ed. includes Lithuania, Latvia, and Estonia, (omitted from the 1st ed.). Organizations are arranged by country under English name. Entries briefly describe history and activities and list names of leading figures. A Resources section contains a list of U.S. and Western European organizations involved with Eastern Europe, an annotated list of periodicals, and a bibliography of books and essays concerned with Eastern Europe and the Soviet Union. Index to organizations. JX1905.5.R35

A scholars' guide to humanities and social sciences in the Soviet successor states / Institute of Scientific Information in the Social Sciences (INION), Russian Academy of Sciences [and] Kennan Inst. for Advanced Russian Studies, Woodrow Wilson International Center for Scholars. 2nd ed. Armonk, N.Y. : M.E. Sharpe, c1993. 228 p. **AL59**

1st ed., 1985, had title: *A scholars' guide to humanities and social sciences in the Soviet Union.*

The purpose of this directory is to promote international cooperation by providing information about the work of Russian research institutes and researchers. The first part is devoted to the Russian Academy of Science and its administrative divisions. The second part, arranged alphabetically by country name, profiles the research institutes of the Soviet successor states. Descriptions provide address, telephone, history, administrative structure, staff, priority research, international cooperation, publications, library, archives, and technical equipment. Four indexes: subject, city, administrators, and supervisors of priority research projects. AS258.S36

Upjohn, Richard. Channels : a guide to service opportunities in the newly independent states formerly a part of the Soviet Union. Seattle, Wash. : Center for Civil Society International, c1993. 68 p. **AL60**

Designed for Americans wishing to travel and work in the NIS (newly independent states of the former Soviet Union). Alphabetically arranged entries describe U.S.-based "Volunteer placement organizations," including ethnic associations (e.g., Ukrainian National Association); religious groups (e.g., National Council of Churches); educational institutions (e.g., Russian American School of Business Administration); professional associations (e.g., American Bar Association); and others. A resources section lists directories of foreign study and travel opportunities, language study resources, English-language newspapers and periodicals, NIS government ministries, etc. Indexes to organizations and publications. HN530.Z9V64

France

Caron, Pierre. Répertoire des sociétés françaises de sciences philosophiques, historiques, philologiques et juridiques / publié par la Fédération des Sociétés Françaises de Sciences Philosophiques, Historiques, Philologiques et Juridiques. Paris : Maison du Livre Français, 1938. 280 p.   **AL61**

A companion to *Répertoire des périodiques de langue française, philosophiques, historiques, philologiques et juridiques* (AD94). For 563 learned societies in the human sciences, provides date of founding, address, officers, number of members, and publications. Arranged geographically. General index combines proper nouns and subject disciplines; separate indexes for persons and places.   AS155.C3

Germany

German institutions : designations, abbreviations, acronyms = Deutsche Einrichtungen : Bezeichnungen, Abkürzungen, Akronyme. Berlin ; N.Y. : W. de Gruyter, 1990. 119 p. (Terminological series, v. 3).   **AL62**

Title page and prefatory material in English, German, French, and Spanish.

Designed to aid translators needing equivalent names for German institutions in other languages. Includes German associations, foundations, political parties, and other public organizations, arranged alphabetically by German name, followed by equivalents in other languages, including English, French, Spanish, Italian, Dutch, Polish, Portuguese, Russian, and Serbo-Croatian. Indexed by keywords, abbreviations, and institutions.   AS178.G47

Müller, Johannes. Die wissenschaftlichen Vereine und Gesellschaften Deutschlands im neunzehnten Jahrhundert : Bibliographie ihrer Veröffentlichungen seit ihrer Begründung bis auf die Gegenwart. Berlin : Asher, 1883/87 ; Behrend, 1917. 2 v.   **AL63**

A record of 19th-century learned societies and their publications, consisting of: (1) a short classified list of societies; (2) a main list arranged alphabetically by place then by society, giving for each society a list of its publications, including published library catalogs; (3) a general index listing in alphabetical order titles of serials, names of societies, editors, and authors (with titles of their monographic publications).   Z5055.G29M9

Vademecum deutscher Lehr- und Forschungsstätten : Stätten der Forschung / ed. in cooperation with DUZ-Universitäts-Zeitung, Universitäts Bonn. 9. Aufl. Stuttgart : Raabe, c1989. 1621 p.   **AL64**

Title varies: 1st ed., 1953, and 2nd ed., 1957, had title: *Vademecum deutscher Forschungsstätten*; 3rd ed.: *Taschenbuch für das Wissenschaftliche Leben*. 8th ed., 1988.

Preface in German, English, and French.

Lists German research institutes and learned societies. Entries arranged by field, giving address, names of key staff, subject area, research projects, etc. Indexed by name, place, and subject.   AS178.S7

Great Britain

Anderson, Ian Gibson. Councils, committees, and boards : a handbook of advisory, consultative, executive & similar bodies in British public life. 8th ed. Beckenham, Kent, Eng. : CBD Research, 1993. 398 p.   **AL65**

1st ed., 1970 ; 7th ed., 1989.

A directory of national or regional bodies in the U.K. which exist as government advisory committees, departmental committees of inquiry, public boards and authorities, royal and other forms of commissions, and other groups of experts brought together in a similar advisory capacity. Provides name, address, description, activities, and publi-

cations. Alphabetically arranged; indexed by abbreviations, executive personnel, and subject. Conceived as a companion volume to *Directory of British associations & associations in Ireland* (AL66).   AS118.A5

Directory of British associations & associations in Ireland. Ed. 4 (1974–75)– . Beckenham, Kent : CBD Research Ltd, 1974– .   **AL66**

1st ed., 1965, and 2nd ed., 1970, had title: *Directory of British associations*.

Provides brief information on national and regional voluntary organizations in the U.K. and the Republic of Ireland. Alphabetical by name of the association, with indexes of abbreviations and subjects. New to the 9th and continued in subsequent editions is a list of "Unverified and lost associations," about which information is solicited.

§ See also *Directory of social research organisations in the United Kingdom*, by Wendy Sykes, Martin Bulmer, and Marleen Schwerzel (CA56).

Ireland

Alternative Ireland directory. [4th ed.]. Cork, Ireland : Quay Co-op (Cork) Limited, [1990]. 246 p. : ill.   **AL67**

Divided into sections for social movements, e.g., women, environment, gaeilege (Irish language), alternative medicine, animal rights. Each chapter opens with introduction describing the history of the movement in Ireland, followed by a list of relevant organizations, arranged by city. Entries give address and telephone number and often a brief description. No index.   DA906.A44

Italy

Doc Italia. 1978– . Roma : Editoriale Italiana, [1979]– . Irregular.   **AL68**

Subtitle: Annuario degli enti di studio, cultura, ricerca e informazione.

At head of title: Istituto Nazionale dell'Informazione.

Continues: *Doc : documentazione* (Rome : Editoriale Italiana, (1972).

A directory of learned societies, institutions, and associations in Italy. Arranged by organization name, entries include founding date, description of activities, officers, and periodical publications. Subject index.   AS218.D6

Maylender, Michele. Storia delle accademie d'Italia. Bologna : Cappelli, [1926–30]. 5 v.   **AL69**

Describes Italian academies, many of them obscure, that were devoted to literature, the Italian language, science, religion, or the arts, and that flourished from the late 15th through 19th centuries. For each academy, typically gives dates, relation to other societies, interests and activities, members, bibliography, and quotations (many from contemporary sources). Arranged alphabetically by keywords in academy names, but with no list either by date or complete name. Index of locations.   AS215.M3

Poland

Informator nauki polskiej. 1958– . Warszawa : Państwowe Wydawnictwo Naukowe, 1958– . Annual.   **AL70**

English-language edition: *Polish research guide* (Warszawa : publ. for the National Science Foundation on the order of Centralny Instvut Informacji Naukowo-Technicznejni Ekonomicznej by Państwowe Wydawn. Naukowe, 1964–).

In two parts: v. 1, directory of Poland's learned societies, universities and other institutions of higher education, scientific institutes, museums, and archives. Entries give addresses, names of directors and other personnel, and serial publications. Vol. 2, name index of Polish scientists, with addresses. Recent volumes include index to names of institutions. AS256.P7I5

Słownik polskich towarzystw naukowych / red. naukowy Leon Łoś ... [et al.]. Wrocław : Zakład Narodowy imienia Ossolińskich, 1978–1990. v. 1–3. (In progress). **AL71**

At head of title: Polska Akademia Nauk. Biblioteka PAN w Warszawie.

Contents: v. 1, Towarzystwa naukowe działające obecnie w Polsce; v. 2, pt. 1, Towarzystwa naukowe i upowszechniające naukę działające w przeszłości na ziemiach polskich; v. 3, Towarzystwa upowszechniające naukę działające obecnie w Polsce.

Vol. 1 (not updated since 1978) is a directory of scholarly institutions and learned and professional societies in Poland, arranged by subject fields and disciplines. Lengthy, signed entries for 172 institutions provide information on history, location, areas of specialization, library and archives, staff, publications, statutes, catalogs, and secondary literature on institution. Vol. 2, pt. 1, describes scholarly organizations and societies for the dissemination of learning in Polish territories in the past. Vol. 3, arranged by province, lists regional societies devoted to the popularization of learning and culture. Each volume indexed by personal and organization name. AS248.A7S58

Australia

Directory of Australian associations. 1st ed. (1978/79)– . Auckland, N.Z. : Australasia Reference Research Publications, 1979– . Quarterly. **AL72**

Frequency varies; first publ. annually.

Includes international and foreign associations with offices in Australia, as well as national, state, and metropolitan associations. Organizations are listed alphabetically within broad subject categories. Entries include directory information, year founded, contact, membership data, purpose, and publications. Subject and alphabetical indexes. AS718.D57

Secret societies

Hall, Manly Palmer. An encyclopedic outline of Masonic, Hermetic, Qabbalistic, and Rosicrucian symbolical philosophy : being an interpretation of the secret teachings concealed within the rituals, allegories, and mysteries of all ages. Los Angeles : Philosophical Research Society, 1977. [245] p., [42] leaves of plates (2 fold.) : ill. **AL73**

Repr. of subscriber's ed. (San Francisco : H.S. Crocker, 1928) with new preface and foreword.

Besides the topics in the title, the 45 chapters of this work, in rough chronological order, include other related topics (e.g., Gnosticism, alchemy, mathematical symbolism, and the symbolism of animals, plants, and the human body). Liberally illustrated. Bibliography of sources consulted; general index. Little of the information on the Masons and Rosicrucians can be easily found elsewhere. Useful for research in literature and the fine arts. BF1411.H3

Heckethorn, Charles William. The secret societies of all ages and countries ... : a comprehensive account of upwards of one hundred and sixty secret organizations religious, political, and social from the most remote ages down to the present time. New ed., throughly rev. and greatly enl. London : G. Redway, 1897. 2 v. **AL74**

Repr.: New Hyde Park, N.Y. : Univ. Books, 1965; Kita, Mont. : Kessinger, [1992?].

Subtitle: Embracing the mysteries of ancient India, China, Japan, Egypt, Mexico, Peru, Greece, and Scandinavia, the Cabbalists, early Christians, heretics, Assassins, Thugs, Templars, the Vehm and Inquisition, mystics, Rosicrucians, Illuminati, Freemasons, Skopzi, Camorristi, Carbonari, nihilists, and other sects.

1st ed., 1875; rev. ed., 1897.

Traces the evolution of secret societies from the ancient world to the present in Asia, Europe, and the New World. Societies are grouped in topical sections, e.g., Ancient mysteries, Anti-social societies, Social regeneration. Within these sections, societies are treated either chronologically or geographically. Index and bibliography for each volume. HS125.H45

Mariel, Pierre. Dictionnaire des sociétés secrètes en Occident. [Paris : Culture, art, loisirs, 1971]. 478 p. : ill. **AL75**

Devoted to secret societies throughout history that have nonmaterialistic concerns. Substantial entries on persons, organizations, key texts, and mystical topics are alphabetically arranged and include bibliographies. More selective than Arthur Preuss's *A dictionary of secret and other societies* (AL76); resembles in scope Manly P. Hall's *An encyclopedic outline of Masonic, Hermetic, Qabbalistic and Rosicrucian symbolical philosophy* (AL73). No index, but terms defined elsewhere are underlined, and page references to related articles appear at the beginning of entries. HS12.M35

Preuss, Arthur. A dictionary of secret and other societies. St. Louis, Mo. ; London : Herder Book Co., 1924. 543 p. **AL76**

Subtitle: Comprising Masonic rites, lodges, and clubs; concordant, clandestine, and spurious Masonic bodies; non-Masonic organizations to which only Freemasons are admitted; mystical and occult societies; fraternal, benevolent and beneficiary societies; political, patriotic, and civic brotherhoods; Greek letter fraternities and sororities; military and ancestral orders; revolutionary brotherhoods, and many other organizations.

Arranged by name of society, profiles range in length from brief paragraphs to four or five pages and include bibliographies. Information is based on responses to questionnaires. Intended for Catholic clergymen; excludes Catholic societies and comments on the appropriateness of Catholic membership. Appendix with descriptions of additional organizations. Index. HS122.P7

Stevens, Albert Clark. The cyclopaedia of fraternities. 2nd ed., rev to date. N.Y. : E.B. Treat and company, 1907. 444 p. : ill. **AL77**

Subtitle: A compilation of existing authentic information and the results of original investigation as to the origin, derivation, founders, development, aims, emblems, character, and personnel of more than six hundred secret societies in the United States supplemented by family trees of groups of societies, comparative statistics of membership, charts, plates, maps, and names of many representative members.

Traces the development of secret societies in the U.S. from 1787 to 1907. Emphasizes the Freemasons, the direct or indirect source of American secret societies of all types. Societies are grouped by category (e.g., Masonic bodies, military orders and societies, patriotic and political orders, mystical and theosophical) then alphabetically. Profiles of groups list influential members and, in many instances, officers, national and regional, at the time of publication. Indexes: maps, plates and charts; organizations; proper names. HS119.S85

Whalen, William Joseph. Handbook of secret organizations. Milwaukee : Bruce, [1966]. 169 p. **AL78**

Essays on 45 U.S. organizations with secret rituals and initiation ceremonies, including benevolent societies; "animal" lodges (e.g., Elks); and organizations based on religion (Knights of Columbus), nationality (Hibernians), or profession (Fraternal Order of Police). Chapters on college fraternities and on "Negro lodges." Except for two criminal associations, the Ku Klux Klan and Mafia, Whalen emphasizes positive aspects of the secret societies that have proliferated in America. Selected bibliography; subject index. HS204.W45

RESEARCH CENTERS

Directory of development research and training institutes in Europe = Inventaire des instituts de recherche et de formation en matière de développement en Europe / International Development Information Network. Paris : Organisation for Economic Co-operation and Development ; [Wash. : OECD Publications and Information Centre], 1991. 237 p.   **AL79**

In English and French.

Describes 540 research and training institutes concerned with economic development and social policies in Europe and the U.S.S.R. Profiles include affiliation, address, telephone, date founded, director, number of personnel, description of library, research areas, activities (including conferences), and publications.   HD82.O666

Government research directory. 3rd ed.– . Detroit : Gale, 1985– .   **AL80**

Continues *Government research centers directory* (Detroit : Gale, 1980–82) and assumes its edition numbering.

Subtitle: A descriptive guide to approximately 3,900 U.S. and Canadian government research and development centers, institutes, laboratories, bureaus, test facilities, experiment stations, data collection and analysis centers, and grants management and research coordinating offices in agriculture, commerce, education, energy, engineering, environment, the humanities, medicine, military science, and basic and applied sciences.

Lists entries by category: U.S. legislative, judicial, and executive offices; U.S. federal government departments; U.S. independent agencies; and Canadian government. Data for each entry includes name, address, telephone and fax number, director, organizational notes, research activities and fields, special resources, publications, and services. Subject, geographic, and master (acronym, name, keyword in name) indexes.

•Available as part of: *Research centers and services database (RCSD)* [database] (Detroit : Gale). Available online, on diskettes, or magnetic tape, updated semiannually; current coverage.

Q179.98.G68

International research centers directory. 1st ed., no.1 (Jan. 1982)– . Detroit : Gale, 1982– . Annual.   **AL81**

Subtitle: A world guide to government, university, independent nonprofit, and commercial research and development centers, institutes, laboratories, bureaus, test facilities, experiment stations, and data collection and analysis centers, as well as foundations, councils, and other organizations which support research.

Beginning with 1986/87 (3rd ed.), issued annually, with supplements published between editions.

The 1992–93 ed. describes more than 7,200 research programs and facilities worldwide. Excludes the U.S., represented in three companion publications: *Research centers directory* (AL82), *Research services directory* (AL84), *State government research directory* (CJ280). Arranged alphabetically by country. Includes address; phone; fax; organization notes (parent organization, staff, date founded, etc.); research activities and fields; publications and services. Subject, country, and master (name and acronym of research unit, keyword) indexes.   AS25.I8

Research centers directory. 2nd ed. (1965)– . Detroit : Gale, 1965– . Irregular.   **AL82**

Subtitle: A guide to over 12,000 university-related and other nonprofit research organizations established on a permanent basis and carrying on continuing research programs in agriculture, astronomy and space sciences, behavioral and social sciences, biological sciences and ecology, business and economics, computers and mathematics, education, engineering and technology, government and public affairs, humanities and religion, labor and industrial relations, law, medical sciences, physical and earth sciences, and regional and area studies.

1st ed., 1960, had title: *Directory of university research bureaus and institutes*.

The 16th ed. (1992) includes descriptions of 12,548 U.S. and Canadian organizations involved in a wide range of research topics: e.g., autism, groundwater, hazardous waste management, exercise physiolo-

gy, business ethics. Arranged by subject; organizational notes, research activities and fields, publications, and services. Subject, geographic, and master indexes.

Supplemented between editions by: *New research centers* (Detroit : Gale, 1965– . Quarterly). Renumbers with each edition of *Research centers directory*. Cumulative indexes in each issue.

AS25.D5

Research institutions and learned societies / Joseph C. Kiger, ed. Westport, Conn. : Greenwood, 1982. 551 p. (Greenwood encyclopedia of American institutions, 5).   **AL83**

Presents historical sketches of 164 American institutions devoted to the advancement of knowledge in the humanities, physical/biological sciences, and social sciences. Entries range from two to four pages and include suggestions for further reading. Appendixes provide classification (learned society, council, or research institution); chronology of organizations by founding date; name changes; areas of disciplinary interest; and affiliation with other institutions. Index.

AS25.R47

Research services directory. 1st ed. (1981)– . Detroit : Gale, 1981– .   **AL84**

5th ed. (1993) has subtitle: A one-stop guide to commercial research activity.

More than 4,400 for-profit firms throughout the U.S. and Canada that provide research services. Includes defense contractors, information brokers, biotechnology and pharmaceutical developers, and forensic investigators. Examples of research topics are cryogenics, day care centers, fusion, fungicides, and hypertension. Arranged alphabetically by company name; provides address, phone, fax, chief officer and contact, company description, research and technical services, and publications. Indexed by firm, state or city, name of chief executive and contact, and subject.   Q179.98.R47

Ruble, Blair A. Soviet research institutes project : final report / prep. for the United States International Communication Agency by Blair A. Ruble ; with the assistance of Mark H. Teeter ... [et al.]. [Wash.] : Office of Research, International Communication Agency, 1980–81. 4 v.   **AL85**

Superintendent of Documents classification: ICA 1.14:So 8/v.

Contents: v. 1, The policy sciences; v. 2, The social sciences; v. 3, The humanities; v. 4, Supplement to v. 1–2.

This study by the Kennan Institute for Advanced Russian Studies intends to provide detailed information on the history and organzation of Soviet research. An introductory essay describes the complex relationships between the Communist Party bureaucracy and the research it oversees. Each discipline is introduced by an essay describing Soviet research, followed by a selected bibliography. Profiles of more than 1,500 Soviet research institutes and institutions of higher education performing nonclassified research are grouped by union republic, then by city.   H62.5.S67R82

MUSEUMS

Works about museums collecting in a specific area, such as art museums, may be found with other works on that subject.

Clapp, Jane. Museum publications : a classified list and index of books, pamphlets and other monographs, and of serial reprints. N.Y. : Scarecrow, 1962. 2 v.   **AL86**

Contents: pt. 1, Publications in anthropology, archaeology, and art (4,416 publications); pt. 2, Publications in biological and earth sciences (9,231 publications).

"A classified bibliography of the publications available from 276 museums in the United States and Canada."—*Foreword.*   Z5051.C5

Directory of museums in Africa = Répertoire des musées en Afrique / Unesco-ICOM Documentation Centre ; ed. by Susanne Peters ... [et al.]. London ; N.Y. : Kegan Paul International, 1990. 1 v. **AL87**

The 503 entries are arranged by country, place, and museum name, and include some illustrations. Indexes: museum name, place, subject (archaeology, contemporary art, ethnography, folk art, geology, history, military history, oceanography, prehistory, transportation, zoology).

§ For additional information consult an earlier source, *Museums in Africa : a directory*, comp. by Gundolf Seidenspinner (N.Y. : Africana, [1970]). AM80.D57

Hudson, Kenneth. The directory of museums & living displays / Kenneth Hudson and Ann Nicholls. 4th ed. N.Y. : Stockton Pr., 1993. 1 v. **AL88**

First publ. as: *The directory of world museums.*

1st ed., 1975; 3rd ed., 1985.

Includes some 35,000 entries, incorporating zoos, aquaria, botanical gardens, and living history farms. Arrangement is alphabetical within country and the vernacular form of each museum name is supplied after the name in English. Introductory information covers scope and plan of the work, a note on languages and addresses, museums in the context of population and national income, glossary of terms used. Lacks an index. AM1.H78

Murray, David. Museums, their history and their use : with a bibliography and list of museums in the United Kingdom. Glasgow : Maclehose, 1904. 3 v. **AL89**

Contents: v.1, History. List of museums in the United Kingdom; v.2–3, Bibliography.

International in scope. Still valuable for its extensive bibliography, which lists (1) works about museums and museum work, and (2) catalogs and other works relating to particular museums. AM5.M9

The official museum directory. 1971– . Wash. : American Association of Museums, 1971– . Annual since 1980. **AL90**

Supersedes *Museums directory of the United States and Canada* (ed. 1–2, 1961–65). Publisher and place of publication vary.

Provides information (address, principal staff, type of museum and scope of collection, notes on facilities, activities and publications, hours of opening) for museums of art, history, and science. The 23rd edition (1993) profiles more than 7,000 U.S. museums and includes a Products and services section, also published separately. In four main sections: (1) Institutions by state (alphabetically by city or town and then by institution); (2) Institutions by name alphabetically; (3) Institution directors and department heads; (4) Institutions by category. Canada was included through 1983.

§ Related older or regional titles include: *Art museums of America* (N.Y. : Morrow, 1980), *The art museums of New England*, rev. ed. (Boston : D.R. Godine, 1982), *Museums in New York*, 5th ed. (N.Y. : St. Martin's Pr., 1990), and the Canadian Museums Association's *Directory of Canadian museums and related institutions = Répertoire des musées Canadian et institutions conneyes* (Ottawa, 1990–). AM10.A2O4

FOUNDATIONS AND PHILANTHROPIC ORGANIZATIONS

Guides

The Foundation Center's user-friendly guide : grantseeker's guide to resources / comp. by Public Service staff of the Foundation Center ; Judith B. Margolin, ed. Rev. ed. N.Y. : The Center, c1992. 39 p. : ill. **AL91**

Responds to ten concerns of beginning grantseekers—e.g., researching appropriate funding sources, securing tax-exempt status for one's organization, writing a grant proposal. Annotated bibliography of relevant reference books, periodicals, and databases. Glossary.

Hall, Mary S. Getting funded : a complete guide to proposal writing. 3rd ed. Portland, Ore. : Continuing Education Publ., Portland State Univ., c1988. 206 p. : ill., forms. **AL92**

1st ed., 1971, and 2nd ed., 1977, had title: *Developing skills in proposal writing.*

In three parts: (1) The preproposal phase, dealing with developing grant ideas, assessing one's own competitiveness and organizational support, and selecting a funding source; (2) The proposal phase, outlining the elements of a successful proposal and the processes of submission and renewal; and (3) Proposal development checklist, reinforcing the points made in the other chapters.

§ Similar step-by-step guides: *From idea to funded project : grant proposals that work*, by Jane C. Belcher and Julia M. Jacobsen (Phoenix : Oryx 1992. 138 p.); and Robert Lefferts, *Getting a grant in the 1990s : how to write successful grant proposals* (N.Y. : Prentice Hall, c1990. 239 p.). LB2825.H223

Mackey, Philip English. The giver's guide : making your charity dollars count. Highland Park, N.J. : Catbird Pr., c1990. 275 p. **AL93**

Aimed at persons wishing to make well-informed contributions, this guide explains how to find charities active in a field that interests the giver, how to evaluate a charity's use of funds, types of nonmonetary contributions, etc. Most of the book consists of Directory of Charitable Organizations. Grouped under such headings as: Health—visual handicaps; International relief; Minorities; Social action; Advocacy. Profiles of agencies include address, telephone, brief financial data, purpose, program, and miscellaneous comments. Indexes to text and to directory. HV91.M25

Bibliography

The literature of the nonprofit sector. v. 1– . N.Y. : The Foundation Center, c1989– . Annual. **AL94**

Vol. 1 is a bibliography of the the Foundation Center collection. Subsequent editions include the Foundation Center's current acquisitions, as well as other current literature. Includes citations, many with abstracts, to historical and current literature, arranged in subject chapters. Among the topics covered are the theory and philosophy of philanthropy, lives of philanthropists, histories of foundations, fictional accounts of philanthropy, administration of nonprofit organizations, fundraising, proposal development, impact of government policies, and volunteerism. Subject, author, and title indexes. List of Foundation Center libraries, publications, and services. Z7164.C4L57

Philanthropic studies index. v. 1, no. 1 (Sept. 1991)– . Indianapolis : Indiana Univ. Center on Philanthropy, c1991– . Three times a year, with annual cumulations. **AL95**

Subtitle: A reference to literature on voluntarism, nonprofit organizations, fund raising and charitable giving.

Subject and author index to *Chronicle of philanthropy, Philanthropy monthly, Responsive philanthropy*, and *The practical philanthropist*, as well as English-language dissertations, popular and scholarly books and periodicals treating aspects of philanthropy. Complements *The literature of the nonprofit sector* (AL94). HV85.P47

Directories

International

Hague Club, The. Foundation profiles. 4th ed. [Netherlands] : Bernard van Leer Foundation, 1988. 55 p.   **AL96**
1st ed., 1979.
Profiles 27 of the largest foundations in Europe and Israel, including origin, purpose, source of funds, annual expenditures, types of grants, restrictions, application procedures, trustees, and publications. List of chief executives.   HV41.H33

International encyclopedia of foundations / Joseph C. Kiger, ed. in chief. N.Y. : Greenwood, 1990. 355 p.   **AL97**
Presents essays on 145 of the most significant foundations in the world, excluding the U.S. The preface provides a historical overview of European and Asian foundations. Profiles, some written by foundation officers, include history, structure, types of projects supported, cooperative projects with other organizations, publications, and sources of further information. Complements the more inclusive work, *The international foundation directory* (AL98). Three appendixes: a chronological listing of foundations by date established; earlier names; and families associated with foundation giving. Index.   HV12.I58

The international foundation directory. [1st ed]– . Detroit : Gale ; London : Europa, 1974– . Irregular.   **AL98**
Includes international foundations and national foundations with a worldwide scope. Arranged by country; profiles include such information as founding date, mission, activities, publications, finances, names of officers and trustees, address, telephone, and fax. The introduction traces the history of foundations from medieval times to the present. Indexed by foundation name and main activity.   HV7.I56

United States

America's new foundations. 5th ed. (1991)– . Rockville, Md. : Taft Group, c1990– . Annual.   **AL99**
1st ed., 1986, 2nd ed., 1988, and 3rd ed., 1989, had title: *America's newest foundations*; 4th ed., 1990.
Provides current contact information for more than 3,300 new foundations (for 5th ed., those founded since 1986) with total giving or assets above $100,000. New foundations are often overlooked due to their brief giving histories. Profiles are listed by state, in alphabetical order, and give information that ranges from minimal (address and year started) to comprehensive (major grants given, recipients, and a catchall category, "Other things you should know"). An appendix lists foundations that appeared in the preceding edition but are no longer eligible for inclusion. Five indexes: foundations by grant and by recipient type, names of decision makers, recipient locations, and a list of all funders.   HV87.A6

Annual register of grant support. 1969– . Chicago [etc.] : Marquis Academic Media, Marquis Who's Who [etc.], 1969– . Annual.   **AL100**
Supersedes *Grant data quarterly* (v. 1 [1967]–2 [1968]).
Groups grants from government agencies, public and private corporations, and other organizations in 11 broad categories (e.g., multiple special purpose, humanities, special populations), subdivided by subject. The 26th ed. (1993) has 3,070 entries, describing a broad spectrum of programs, including academic and scientific research, project development, travel, publication support, and competitive awards. Profiles of agencies outline areas of interest, type of support, restrictions, information about past awards, trustees, and application information. Four indexes: subject, organization and program, geographical, and personnel.   AS911.A2A67

Assistance and benefits information directory. Detroit : Omnigraphics, c1992. 2 v.   **AL101**
Subtitle: A guide to programs and printed materials describing assistance programs, benefits, and services offered to individuals by federal and state agencies, national associations, and other organizations in the areas of cultural affairs, education, employment and training, health and social services, housing and home energy, and law.
Contents: v. 1, Programs, ed. by Kay Gill; v. 2, Publications, ed. by Mary Emanoil.
Vol. 1 describes more than 2,000 programs, including compensation for crime victims, veterans' benefits, mortgages for lower income families, and pharmaceutical assistance for senior citizens. Indexed by agency type: federal, state, association/organization, and combined. Vol. 2 describes some 1,200 publications that provide information about benefits and services. Indexed by agency, special interest (e.g., minority, youth, women); and publication/publisher. Neither volume has a subject index.   HC110.P63A77

Charitable organizations of the U.S. 1st ed. [1991–92]– . Detroit : Gale, c1991– .   **AL102**
Profiles nearly 800 public charities, concerned, among other causes, with AIDS, animal protection, right-to-life, gun control, fathers' rights, homelessness, and literacy. Aimed at persons wishing to make charitable contributions, this directory includes a preface explaining how to evaluate charities and the regulations governing them. Profiles include the charity's history, purpose, programs, administration and staff, fundraising activities, procedure for applying for aid, prominent supporters, tax status, financial data, and source where information was obtained. Three indexes: personal names, geographic, and subjects.   HV89.C48

Corporate and foundation grants. 1st ed. (1992)– . Rockville, Md. : Taft Group, c1992– . Annual.   **AL103**
Subtitle: A comprehensive listing of more than 80,000 recent grants to nonprofit organizations in the United States.
Contents: v. 1, Grants by category; v. 2, Funding organizations and indexes.
Lists grants awarded by more than 5,500 private and corporate foundations and corporate direct givers. Vol. 1 lists grant recipients, amount received, and grantmaking organization by category: arts and humanities, civic and public affairs, education, health, international, religion, science, social services. Vol. 2 is an alphabetical list of grantmaking organizations, with a paragraph on application procedure. Three indexes: grant recipients, funding organizations by recipient type, funding organizations by grant recipient location.   HG4028.C6C66

Corporate foundation profiles. 1st ed. (1980)– . N.Y. : Foundation Center, c1980– . Irregular.   **AL104**
The 6th (1990) ed. describes 251 of the largest company-sponsored foundations in the U.S., 63 of them new to this edition. Provides information identical to that in *National directory of corporate giving*, also compiled by the Foundation Center (AL121), adding background information about each foundation and a detailed analysis of annual grant spending, including major recipients, percentage and dollar amount of support awarded to various types of projects, geographic distribution, etc. Pt. 1 lists foundations alphabetically, pt. 2 in descending order by total amount awarded. Three indexes: subject of grant, type of support, geographic.   HV89.C68

Corporate giving directory. 12th ed. (1991)– . Rockville, Md. : Taft Group, c1991– . Annual.   **AL105**
Subtitle: Comprehensive profiles of America's major corporate foundations and corporate charitable giving programs.
Continues *Taft corporate directory* and *Taft corporate giving directory*.
Arranged alphabetically by company, entries include such information as foundation name, facts about sponsoring company, contact, total gifts for three most recent years, grant types, typical recipients, corporate officers, philosophy, application procedure, and lists of recent grants organized by category. Provides more detailed information

than the Foundation Center's comparable publication, *National directory of corporate giving* (AL121), but covers half the number of giving programs.   HV97.A3T29

Corporate giving yellow pages. 1992– . Rockville, Md. : The Taft Group, c1992– . Annual.   **AL106**
Continues: *Corporate giving yellow pages* (1st ed., 1983–5th ed., 1988) and *Taft guide to corporate giving contacts* (1989–91).
Lists addresses, telephone numbers and contact persons for more than 3,900 direct giving programs. Arranged alphabetically by company name. Corporations indexed by headquarters (state), operating locations (states), and SIC code.   HV89.C683

The directory of corporate and foundation givers. 1992– . Rockville, Md. : Taft Group, c1992– . Annual.   **AL107**
Subtitle: A national listing of 8,000 major funding sources for nonprofits.
Profiles of private and corporate foundations and direct giving programs including contact and application information, program descriptions, and information on the top ten recent grants. Similar in scope and organization to *The foundation directory* (AL112). Unique in supplying biographical information for trustees, foundation and corporate officers. Arranged alphabetically by name of organization with nine indexes: headquarters state; operating location; grant type; nonmonetary support type; recipient type; major products/industry; officers; grant recipients by state; and master index to corporations and foundations.   HG4028.C6D567

Directory of grants in the humanities. [1986]– . Phoenix : Oryx, c1986– . Annual.   **AL108**
For annotation, *see* BA9.   AZ188.U5D56

Directory of international corporate giving in America and abroad. 1st ed. (1989)– . Rockville, Md. : Taft Group, 1989– .   **AL109**
Editions prior to 1992 had title: *Directory of international corporate giving in America.*
Section 1 provides information about the charitable activities of 350 foreign-owned U.S. companies and has ten indexes: headquarters state, grant type, etc. Section 2, with eight indexes, describes international giving programs of more than 100 U.S. companies. Profiles in both sections are arranged alphabetically by company and include contact, summary of giving activities, types of support, etc. Bibliography; master index to companies.

Directory of research grants. [v. 1 (1975)]– . [Phoenix] : Oryx, [1975]– . Annual.   **AL110**
The 17th ed., 1992, lists nearly 6,000 programs funding research projects, scholarships, fellowships, conferences, and internships in medicine, the physical and social sciences, the arts, the humanities, and education. Alphabetically arranged by program name, profiles include goals, restrictions, eligibility requirements, funding amounts, deadlines, *Catalog of federal domestic assistance* page number (for federal programs), name and address of sponsor. The subject index is composed of terms from *The GRANTS subject authority guide* (Phoenix : Oryx, 1991). Indexes for sponsoring organization and sponsor type (e.g., corporation, federal, university).
•GRANTS [database] (Phoenix : Oryx, [n.d.]). Machine-readable version, available online. Covers current year's data; updated monthly.   LB2338.D57

The Foundation 1000 / comp. by the Foundation Center. 1992/1993– . N.Y. : The Center, c1992– . Annual.   **AL111**
Continues *Source book profiles*, publ. semiannually 1977–91.
Describes the 1,000 largest foundations, based on annual giving. Arranged alphabetically by foundation name; provides address, telephone, contact, purpose, limitations, and financial data. Grants awarded are analyzed by geographic area, subject, recipient type, type of support, and population group. Indexes: Donors, officers and trustees; Subjects; Types of support; and Geographic.   HV97.F65F67a

The foundation directory. 1st ed. (1960)– . N.Y. : Foundation Center ; Distr. by Columbia Univ. Pr., 1960– . Annual.   **AL112**
Replaces *American foundations and their fields* (N.Y. : American Foundation Information Service, 1931–55).
Provides detailed information concerning independent, corporate, community, and private foundations (15th ed. lists 6,334) with assets of at least $2 million or annual giving of at least $200,000. Geographical arrangement. Entries give date founded; names of officers, contact, and donors; foundation type; financial data; fields of interest; types of support; limitations; application information; and number of staff. Six indexes: Donors, officers, and trustees; Geographic; Types of support; Subject; Foundations new to edition; Foundations name index.
Supplemented by: *The foundation directory, Part 2 : a guide to grant programs, $50,000–$100,000* (1991–92 ed.– . N.Y. : Foundation Center, 1990–), similar in organization to the parent directory, listing more than 4,300 mid-sized foundations; and by *Directory of new and emerging foundations* (2nd ed., N.Y. : Foundation Center, 1991), which describes 1,050 recently formed foundations with annual grant programs of $25,000 or more.
•Available in machine-readable form as: *Foundation directory* [database] (N.Y. : Foundation Center). Available online, updated annually. Provides data for current year only.

The foundation grants index. [1st] ed. (1970/71)– . N.Y. : Foundation Center; distr. by Columbia Univ. Pr., 1970– . Annual.   **AL113**
Produced from a database maintained by the Foundation Center, the annual volume is a cumulated record of grants reported in the *Foundation grants index quarterly*. The 1993 ed. includes more than 58,000 grants of $10,000 or more from 846 foundations. Grants are listed under 28 subjects, such as Animals and wildlife, Religion, Youth development. Within subjects, foundations are listed alphabetically by state, each with a list of grants awarded for the time period covered. Indexes provide various ways of accessing information about grants, foundations, and recipients. Concludes with an alphabetical list of foundations with addresses and limitations.   AS911.A2F66

Foundation grants to individuals / comp. by the Foundation Center. [1st ed.]– . N.Y. : Foundation Center, 1977– . Biennial.   **AL114**
Provides data on scholarships and loans, fellowships, internships, awards, etc., from foundations or companies which accept applications directly from individuals. 8th ed. (1993) contains information on 2,275 private U.S. foundations. Useful annotated bibliography on sources of information on grants to individuals. Indexed.   LB2336.F599

Foundation reporter. 22nd ed. (1991)– . Rockville, Md. : Taft Group, c1991– . Annual.   **AL115**
Continues: *Taft foundation reporter* (1980–90).
Lists the leading 1,000 private foundations, including directory information; financial summary; contributions summary; donors, foundation philosophy/mission; contributions analysis; typical recipients; officers and directors; application and review process; "Other things you should know"; grants analysis; and listing of recent grants. Five foundation indexes and five indexes to biographical information about officers, trustees, donors, and staff.   HV97.A3T323

Foundations / editors in chief, Harold M. Keele and Joseph C. Kiger. Westport, Conn. : Greenwood, 1984. 516 p. (Greenwood encyclopedia of American institutions, 8).   **AL116**
Offers histories of 230 foundations with assets in excess of $30 million. Although dated, provides useful historical background on Coors, Bush, Hearst, Rockefeller and other venerable foundations. Appendixes arrange foundations in decreasing order by assets, by family name, and by date founded. Index.
§ Foundations that do not make grants to organizations and individuals, but use their own staff to complete projects, may be found in *Research institutions and learned societies* (AL83).   HV88.F68

Fund raiser's guide to human service funding. 1st ed. (1988)– . Rockville Md. : Taft Group, 1988– .   **AL117**

Editor, Susan E Elnicki.

More than 1,110 foundations and companies with a history of funding nonprofit organizations in the human services are listed in the 4th ed. (1993). Arranged alphabetically by name of funding agency, profiles provide contact, financial, and application information. The most substantial of the seven indexes is the index by recipient type, which lists philanthropic organizations under topical headings, e.g., Aged, Animal protection, Emergency relief, and Legal aid.

Guide to private fortunes : descriptive profiles of the wealthiest and most philanthropic individuals and families. 1993– . Rockville, Md. : Taft Group, c1993– .   **AL118**

Continues *Fund raiser's guide to private fortunes* (1st ed. [1987]–2nd ed. [1989]).

Biographical, historical, and financial information on philanthropists in the U.S. and, in a few instances, abroad. Profiles of 1,250 individuals, each with a minimum net worth of $25 million. Arranged alphabetically, biographies include contact address, affiliations, and charitable activities. Seven indexes: birthplace; place of residence; alma mater; corporate, nonprofit, philanthropic, and club affiliations. A necrology lists individuals deceased since the 2nd ed.   HV27.F86

Guide to U.S. foundations, their trustees, officers, and donors / comp. by the Foundation Center. [17th ed.] (1993)– . N.Y. : The Center, 1993– . Annual.   **AL119**

Continues: *The Foundation Center national data book*, 1st–4th eds., 1975–79; *National data book*, 5th–12th eds., 1981–88; *National data book of foundations*, 13th–16th ed., 1989–92.

Issued in 2 v.

The most comprehensive listing of U.S. grantmaking foundations, including more than 20,000 small foundations not covered elsewhere. In v. 1, foundations are listed twice, first in descending order by total grants paid, then in descending order by assets. Entries include address, telephone, affiliated persons, limitations, financial and application information. Name and community indexes to foundations. Vol. 2 lists trustees, officers, and donors alphabetically with the number assigned to their foundation in v. 1. Alphabetical list of foundations followed by state listings.

Money for visual artists / researched by Douglas Oxenhorn. New expanded 2nd ed. N.Y. : American Council for the Arts : Allworth Pr., 1993. 317 p.   **AL120**

For annotation, *see* BF105.   N347.M59

National directory of corporate giving / comp. by the Foundation Center. 1st ed.– . N.Y. : The Center, c1989– .   **AL121**

The 3rd ed., 1993, describes 2,050 firms that provided information to the Foundation Center or whose gift-giving activities were verified through public records. Entries, arranged alphabetically by company, include general descriptions of the firms and their "giving mechansims"; types of programs funded; limitations (e.g., geographic, type of recipient); and relevant publications. Six indexes: officers, donors, and trustees; geographic; type of support; subject; types of business; and corporation, foundation, and giving programs by name.

§ Two comparable publications include fewer than half the firms listed here: *Corporate 500 : the directory of corporate philanthropy* (San Francisco : Public Management Inst., 1980– ; distr. Detroit : Gale) and *Guide to corporate giving in the arts 4* (N.Y. : ACA Books, c1987).

See also *Search for security : the Access guide to foundations in peace, security, and international relations*, ed. by Anne Allen (CJ50); and *The national directory of arts & education support by business corporations*, by Nancy A. Fandel and editors of the Washington Int'l Arts Letter (BA10).   HV89.N26

●**Prospector's choice** : the electronic source profiling 8,000 corporate and foundation grantmakers [database]. Rockville, Md. : Taft Group, 1994.   **AL122**

Available in national and in five regional versions, on diskette or CD-ROM.

Provides the following information on independent and corporate foundations: contact, financial summary, types of projects supported, officers (with brief biographies), application information, financial

analysis of grants awarded, specific recent grants. Searchable by foundation or company names, officers' names, and geographic location or corporate sponsor. "Query" feature permits Boolean searching of such categories as grantmaker location, grant type, or recipient type. User manual.

Volunteerism : the directory of organizations, training, progams, and publications. 1991– . New Providence, N.J. : Bowker, c1991– . Irregular.   **AL123**

For annotation, *see* CC35.   HN90.V64C65

Who gets grants/who gives grants : nonprofit organizations and the foundation grants they received / Ruth Kovacs, ed. ; Daniel Hodges, assistant ed. [N.Y.] : Foundation Center, 1993. 1353 p.   **AL124**

Lists 16,934 nonprofit organizations and 48,554 grants awarded to them. In four sections of lists: (1) nonprofit organizations, first U.S., then international; (2) nonprofit organizations receiving grants by subject, then by U.S. state or foreign country; (3) nonprofit organizations under foundation state, then under foundation name; (4) addresses of 837 foundations, giving limitations on support provided. In each list, organizations are arranged alphabetically within categories.

HV97.A3W46

Canada

A Canadian directory to foundations. 6th ed. (1985)– . Toronto : Canadian Centre for Philanthropy, c1985– .   **AL125**

1st ed., 1966, had title: *Guide to foundations and granting agencies*.

Profiles more than 600 family, corporate, community and special interest foundations with grant programs available to Canadian individuals and charitable organizations. Information about foundations varies, often including source of funds, purpose, geographic scope, financial data, application procedure, and contact person. Indexes of foundation names, individuals, geographic location, and fields of interest.

AS911.A2C36

Japan

Inside Japanese support : descriptive profiles and other information on Japanese corporate giving and foundation giving programs. 1992– . Rockville, Md. : Taft Group, c1992– . Annual.   **AL126**

Intended to help U.S. nonprofit organizations seeking support from Japanese foundations or corporations. An introductory essay surveys Japanese foundations and charitable giving, emphasizing recent trends. Section 1 profiles 40 major Japanese grant-making foundations, while section 2 describes the contribution programs of 300 Japanese-affiliated U.S. companies. Section 2 has nine indexes, including headquarters state, grant type, Japanese parent company, and officers and directors. Master index to organizations profiled in both sections.

HG4028.C6I57

Australia

Philanthropic trusts in Australia. 5th ed. Hawthorn [Australia] : Australian Council for Educational Research, 1987. 168 p.   **AL127**

Published for the Association of Australian Philanthropic Trusts. 1st ed., 1968; 4th ed., 1983.

This edition profiles 275 philanthropic trusts (all but 12 Australian), 17 fewer than the previous edition. Alphabetically arranged profiles include address, telephone, history, functions, amounts disbursed, and application information. Excluded are trusts disbursing less than

$3,000 per year, those not wishing publicity, and those with local or exceedingly restricted beneficiaries. Index of subjects, scholarships, and institutions.   HV473.A2P48

New Zealand

Fieldhouse, Arthur E. A directory of philanthropic trusts in New Zealand. 3rd ed. Wellington : New Zealand Council for Educational Research in assoc. with J.R. McKenzie Trust Board, 1987. 126 p.   **AL128**
1st ed., 1964, and 2nd ed., 1978, had title: *Directory of philanthropic trusts.*

Descriptions of 179 trusts, listed under the following categories: general charitable purposes (trusts funding local projects are listed under the region served), education, health promotion, and conservation. Profiles include address, history, purpose and activities, disbursements, and application timetable and procedures. This edition excludes trusts that support activities outside New Zealand, includes trusts giving less than $1,000 yearly, and adds guidelines for prospective applicants. Alphabetical index of trusts.   HV515.5.F54

Handbooks

See also CA52.

Bauer, David G. Administering grants, contracts, and funds : evaluating and improving your grants system / by David G. Bauer ; with contributions by Mary L. Otto. N.Y. : American Council on Education : Macmillan, c1989. 234 p.   **AL129**
Aimed at the fund-raisers of nonprofit organizations, this guide recommends engaging staff in intensive organizational assessment. After defining mission and assessing needs, grants officers need to encourage proposal development and establish a preposal review system. Subsequent chapters deal with grant administration: e.g., The role of the grants office in the administration of private funds, Indirect cost recovery, and The role of the grants office in the politics of the funding process. Numerous checklists and sample forms. Index.
HG4027.65.B38

———— The "how to" grants manual : successful grantseeking techniques for obtaining public and private grants. 2nd ed. N.Y. : American Council on Education : Macmillan ; London : Collier Macmillan, c1988. 229 p. : ill.
AL130
Repr. : Phoenix : Oryx, 1993.
Bauer believes that to be successful in securing grants, nonprofit organizations need to tailor their image to what the funding source wants. Accordingly, this manual emphasizes public relations techniques. Bauer recommends that fund-raisers assess organizational needs, create a system for generating proposal ideas, research what projects potential funding sources have supported, determine the personal interests of its board and reviewers, and approach the contact diplomatically. Grants resource bibliography; index.
§ Two companion works, both by Bauer: *The complete grants sourcebook for higher education* (CB372); and *The complete grants sourcebook for nursing and health* (N.Y. : American Council on Education, 1988). Both begin with a condensed version of Bauer's approach described above, followed by profiles of relevant foundation, corporate, and federal funding sources.   HG177.B38

Blum, Laurie. The complete guide to getting a grant : how to turn your ideas into dollars. N.Y. : Poseidon Pr., c1993. 368 p.
AL131
Provides basic information about obtaining grants: generating ideas, marketing oneself, preparing a funding campaign, writing the proposal, and following up after a grant has been awarded. Chapters

are devoted to foundations, corporations, government agencies, and individual donors as funding sources. Appendix lists books and organizations useful to grant-seekers. Index.   HV41.9.U5B58

Carson, Emmett Devon. The charitable appeals fact book : how black and white Americans respond to different types of fund-raising efforts. Wash. : Joint Center for Political Studies, c1989. 60 p.   **AL132**
Reports results of a 1985 Joint Center for Political Studies nationwide survey of 896 blacks and 916 whites. Consists of an introductory chapter summarizing the findings and seven chapters individually treating responses to the appeals of specific types of organizations (e.g., religious, educational). Data in tabular form indicates percentages of subjects who contributed after solicitation. Includes breakdowns by type of appeal, (e.g, letter, phone call, solicitation by acquaintances), race, age, economic status, demographic characteristics, and educational background. No index, but detailed table of contents.
HV41.9.U5C37

The complete guide to corporate fund raising / ed. by Joseph Dermer and Stephen Wertheimer. Rockville, Md. : Taft Group, c1982. 110 p.   **AL133**
With examples from campaigns they have conducted, fund-raising councellors offer advice on drafting letters of solicitation, identifying and assessing prospective donors, and choosing fund-raising personnel. Chapters on fund-raising for universities, small institutions, and the arts. No index.   HG177.C65

The corporate contributions handbook : devoting private means to public needs / James P. Shannon, ed. San Francisco : Jossey-Bass Publishers, 1991. 410 p. : ill.   **AL134**
"A publication of Council on Foundations"—*t.p. verso.*
Addresses such concerns as the enhancement of a business's role in the community through wisely chosen contributions, the relationship between a company's mission and its giving program, measurable standards of accountability, and the administration of corporate grants. Appendixes include documents on charitable giving from such organizations as Council of Better Business Bureaus, Council on Foundations, and National Charities Information Bureau on Philanthropy.
Index.   HV91.C677

Council on Foundations. Evaluation for foundations : concepts, cases, guidelines, and resources. San Francisco : Jossey-Bass, c1993. 320 p.   **AL135**
Consists of nine case histories of actual evaluations carried out by foundations. Also explains why systematic evaluation is needed; lists questions evaluators need to ask; describes types of evaluation; describes the kind of information needed by evaluators; and discusses matching evaluation to type of project. Annotated bibliography; reference list; index.   HV97.A3C68

Foundations today. 1st ed. (1981)– . [N.Y.] : Foundation Center. Annual.   **AL136**
Drawn from the Foundation Center's databases, this compendium concerns U.S. foundations, mainly in the mid-1980s. Includes statistical tables of assets and awards by particular foundations and types of foundations, subjects supported, categories of recipients, and kinds of support. Discusses the history of foundations and trends in foundation giving.   HV85.F68

Margolin, Judith B. Foundation fundamentals : a guide for grantseekers / ed. by Judith B. Margolin ; contributors, Lorna Aikman ... [et al.]. 4th ed. N.Y. : Foundation Center, 1991. 222 p. : ill.   **AL137**
1st ed., 1980; 3rd ed., 1986. Editors vary.
A guide to the mechanics of grantsmanship. Describes various types of foundations and the regulations governing them, as well as the relationship between foundations and other funding sources. Includes worksheets to help grantseekers through the process of identifying appropriate funders. Gives an outline of the funding proposal. Extensive

bibliography is based on Foundation Center's New York library. Appendixes list Foundation Center publications and resources and directories of state and local funders. No index. HV41.9.U5M37

Miner, Lynn E. Proposal planning and writing / by Lynn E. Miner and Jerry Griffith. Phoenix : Oryx, 1993. 153 p. : ill. **AL138**

Cover title: Proposal planning & writing.

Takes grant seekers through the process of identifying funding sources, refining ideas, developing, evaluating, and submitting a proposal. Separate chapters treat public and private funding sources and the different strategies in applying to each. Unique in its emphasis on using computers in the grant development process: i.e., electronic sources of funding information, word processing and database programs, spreadsheets, etc. Bibliography; index. HG177.5.U6M56

Nonprofit almanac. 1992–1993– . San Francisco : Jossey-Bass Publ., c1992– . Biennial. **AL139**

1st ed., 1984, and 3rd ed., 1989, had title: *Dimensions of the independent sector.*

A massive compilation of statistics concerning the approximately 983,000 philanthropic (i.e., voluntary, advocacy, religious) groups in the U.S. and the individuals who donate time and money to them. Chapters with statistical tables provide information on such topics as earnings and operating expenses of nonprofit organizations; number of hours contributed by and demographic information about volunteers; and corporate contributions by region and state. Three appendixes: (1) methodology in compiling profiles, sources of financial information; (2) description of National Taxonomy of Exempt Entities (NTEE); and (3) glossary. Index. HD2769.2.U6D55

Practical guide to planned giving. 1991– . Rockville, Md. : The Taft Group, c1991– . Annual. **AL140**

This guide is aimed at financial professionals and fund-raisers for small nonprofit organizations. Discusses such topics as the tax consequences of charitable giving, implementation of a new giving program, upgrading existing programs, noncash gifts (e.g., art, patents, real estate), and solicitation methods. Over half the volume consists of appendixes, including bibliographies, lists of consultants, state agencies regulating charitable giving, sample tax and other forms, ethics statements, and tax laws and rulings. Index.

Williams, M. Jane. Big gifts : how to maximize gifts from individuals, with or without a capital campaign. Rockville, Md. : Fund Raising Institute, c1991. 330 p. : ill. **AL141**

Explains how to cultivate wealthy donors. After discussing what motivates philanthropists, pt. 1 outlines identification, cultivation, and solicitation, pt. 2 describes an organization's interaction with a funding prospect over a period of years, and pt. 3 describes a capital campaign aimed at specific major needs. Includes numerous examples of innovative gifts programs at particular educational and cultural institutions. Brief bibliography; no index. HV41.9.U5W55

HOLIDAYS AND ANNIVERSARIES

Chambers, Robert. Book of days : a miscellany of popular antiquities in connection with the calendar, including anecdote, biography, and history, curiosities of literature, and oddities of human life and character. Philadelphia : Lippincott, 1899. 2 v. **AL142**

1st ed., 1862–64. Later editions show little change.

Arranged by day, giving anecdotes and descriptions of popular customs and observances. A standard work. DA110.C52

Collison, Robert Lewis. Hamlyn dictionary of dates and anniversaries. 2nd rev. ed. / general ed., J. M. Bailie. London ; N.Y. : Hamlyn, 1978. 415 p. **AL143**

Represents a revision and expansion (especially in the number of biographical entries) of Collison's *Newnes dictionary of dates* (1st ed., 1962; rev. ed., 1966). In two sections: (1) an alphabetical listing of

12,000 persons, place-names and events, etc., with their dates and a brief identifying remark; and (2) a listing of 6,000 events by month and day through the years. No index; some cross-references.

§ The paperback *Dictionary of dates* by Cyril Leslie Beeching (N.Y. : Oxford Univ. Pr., 1993. 305 p.) is also a very useful record of day-by-day events. Each month and day is accompanied by a narrative of events that occurred and people born on that day. Index for names of people, events, and a few topics. The chronologies of world events and of scientific developments are not indexed. British outlook. D11.5.C6

The folklore of American holidays / Hennig Cohen and Tristram Potter Coffin, editors. Detroit : Gale, c1987. 431 p. : music. **AL144**

As the subtitle indicates, this is "a compilation of more than 400 beliefs, legends, superstitions, proverbs, riddles, poems, songs, dances, games, plays, pageants, fairs, foods, and processions associated with over 100 American calendar customs and festivals." Includes bibliographical references and indexes. GT4803.F65

The folklore of world holidays / Margaret Read MacDonald, editor. Detroit : Gale, c1992. 739 p. **AL145**

In order by days of the year. For each holiday or festival, a description and English-language references are provided. Indexed by subject and location. GT3930.F65

Gregory, Ruth W. Anniversaries and holidays. 4th ed. Chicago : Amer. Libr. Assoc., 1983. 262 p. **AL146**

1st ed., 1928, by Mary E. Hazeltine.

In three main parts: (1) Calendar of fixed days (arranged by month and day); (2) Calendars of movable days (with sections for the Christian church calendar, the Islamic calendar, the Jewish calendar, and other "feasts, festivals, and special events days"); (3) Books related to anniversaries and holidays (in classed arrangement). The book citations are annotated. Indexed. A very useful guide. GT3930.G74

Hatch, Jane M. The American book of days. 3rd ed. N.Y. : Wilson, 1978. 1214 p. **AL147**

Based on George W. Douglas' work of the same title (1st ed., 1937).

"Like its predecessors, this new edition profiles the lives of many of the United States' distinguished citizens, explores the richness of its religious traditions, describes the variety of its holidays, customs and festivities, samples its folklore, and reports its ways … of marking anniversaries and commemorating achievements."—*Pref.* Aims "to tell what happens or did happen on every day of the year and how, where, and by whom these events are (and have been) observed in this country." Indexed. GT4803.D6

Shemanski, Frances. A guide to fairs and festivals in the United States. Westport, Conn. : Greenwood, [1984]. 339 p. **AL148**

A selective guide to fairs and festivals in the 50 states and territories—American Samoa, Puerto Rico and the U.S. Virgin Islands. Narrative descriptions include history, special features, achievements, awards, financing, and date. Arranged by state and city; the calendar of fairs lists them chronologically within state, and an appendix lists fairs by broad type. Indexed. A companion guide to world festivals is in preparation. GT3930.S4

ETIQUETTE

Bibliography

Bobbitt, Mary Reed. A bibliography of etiquette books published in America before 1900. N.Y. : New York Public Library, 1947. 35 p. **AL149**

Repr. from New York Public Library *Bulletin*, Dec. 1947.
Arrangement is by author, or title when author is unknown. Includes title index. Locates copies. Z5877.B6

Hodges, Deborah Robertson. Etiquette : an annotated bibliography of literature published in English in the United States, 1900 through 1987. Jefferson, N.C. : McFarland, c1989. 182 p. **AL150**
Lists 1,075 books and periodical articles by author, with a title and subject index. A prefatory "Overview of the literature" provides a history of the genre. Z5877.H6

Newberry Library. A check list of courtesy books in the Newberry Library / comp. by Virgil B. Heltzel. Chicago, 1942. 161 p. **AL151**
Contains 1,539 entries, for various editions of works on "courtesy literature" written before 1775. Z5873.N5

Handbooks

Baldrige, Letitia. Letitia Baldrige's complete guide to the new manners for the 90's. N.Y. : Rawson Associates, c1990. 646 p. : ill. **AL152**
Emphasizes social issues and changes in the roles of women, men, and children. Detailed table of contents and index. Distinguishes between etiquette and manners: "Etiquette is protocol, rules of behavior that you memorize and that rarely bend to encompass individual concerns and needs. Manners embrace socially acceptable behavior, of course, but also much more than that."—*p. 4.* BJ1853.B35

Debrett's etiquette and modern manners / Elsie Burch Donald, ed. London : Debrett's Peerage ; N.Y. : Viking Pr., [1981]. 400 p. : ill. **AL153**
British orientation. Aims to give "detailed information about ceremonies and events which are part of the British tradition," to eliminate obsolete conventions, and to establish "as 'correct form' useful new practices that have emerged to suit new circumstances."—*Introd.* Indexed. BJ1873.D34

Martin, Judith. Miss Manners' guide to excruciatingly correct behavior. N.Y. : Atheneum, 1982. 745 p. : ill. **AL154**
A humorously presented, but determinedly correct, guide to modern social behavior. Incorporates questions and answers from the United Feature Syndicate column by "Miss Manners." Indexed. BJ1853.M294

McCaffree, Mary Jane. Protocol : the complete handbook of diplomatic, official, and social usage / Mary Jane McCaffree, Pauline B. Innis. Englewood Cliffs, N.J. : Prentice-Hall, [1977]. 414 p. : ill. **AL155**
"The purpose of this book is to help the newcomer to official life ... to learn and understand the rules of protocol and to serve as a reference for the person whose life is governed ... by the practices and policies of protocol."—*Pref.* Stresses everyday usage of protocol in the U.S., covering order of precedence, titles and forms of address, calling and calling cards, invitations and replies, official entertaining and private parties, places to entertain, table seating arrangements, White House entertaining, the diplomatic corps, ceremonies, flag etiquette, and women in public and official life. Bibliography. Subject index. BJ1853.M23

Post, Emily. Emily Post's etiquette. 15th ed. / rev. by Elizabeth L. Post. N.Y. : Harper/Collins, 1992. 783 p. : ill. **AL156**
First published in 1922 under title: *Etiquette in society, in business, in politics, and at home.*
Long a standard work. Particularly useful for formal occasions. BJ1853.P6

Swartz, Oretha D. Service etiquette. 3rd ed. Annapolis, Md. : Naval Institute Pr., [1977]. 582 p. : ill. **AL157**

1st ed., 1959.
A guide to service etiquette, or "aspects of everyday good manners combined with the traditions and customs of the various branches of the armed forces."—*Introd.* Includes male and female uniform charts, forms of military and civilian address, business and social correspondence, entertaining, traditional military ceremonies, flag etiquette, etc. Indexed. U766.M2

Vanderbilt, Amy. The Amy Vanderbilt complete book of etiquette : a guide to contemporary living / rev. and expanded by Letitia Baldrige. Garden City, N.Y. : Doubleday, 1978. 879 p. : ill. **AL158**
1st ed., 1952, had title *Amy Vanderbilt's etiquette*; 1972 ed. called *New complete book of etiquette.*
This latest revision emphasizes "good manners" in contemporary American society, offering options in many social situations rather than merely hard and fast rules (although attention is still given to formal etiquette). Includes a section "manners in business." Indexed. BJ1853.V27

Forms of address

Lists somewhat similar to those below are included in certain more comprehensive reference works, e.g.: modes of addressing persons of title are included regularly in the introductory parts of the peerages; sections on forms of address are included in various books on etiquette. A useful list for American forms is found in Mary De Vries, *Complete secretary's handbook* (CH86); another is in *Webster's third new international dictionary*, p. 51a–54a, under "Forms of address."

Montague-Smith, Patrick W. Debrett's correct form : an inclusive guide to everything from drafting wedding invitations to addressing an archbishop. [Rev. ed.]. [Kingston upon Thames] : Debrett's Peerage Ltd., [1976]. 423 p. **AL159**
1st ed., 1970.
Besides revision of existing text, new sections have been added for American usage and usage in other foreign countries. CR3891.M65

Titles and forms of address : a guide to their correct use. 17th ed. London : Black, [1980]. 190 p. **AL160**
First published, 1918, as *Titles, being a guide to the right use of British titles and honours.*
A useful handbook to correct English usage for the titled classes and for the church, the armed services, the law, the universities, the government services, etc. Also includes lists of abbreviations and of the pronunciation of names. CR3891.T58

PRIZES AND AWARDS

Awards, honors, and prizes. 1st ed.– . Detroit : Gale, [1969]– . **AL161**
Beginning with 3rd ed., issued in two vols.: v. 1, U.S. and Canada; v. 2, International and foreign awards.
Original ed.: Paul Wasserman.
Describes "more than 22,000 awards bestowed in all subject areas and by more than 8,000 organizations, foundations, corporations, universities and government bodies."—*Introd.* International in scope. Omits scholarships, grants, and fellowships for study toward degrees, but includes "the major fellowship programs given for research." The main section, arranged alphabetically by awarding body, provides addresses of awarding organizations, names of specific awards given, descriptive material on the award's purpose, eligibility requirements, etc. Organization, award, and subject indexes.

§ Complements *World of winners* (AL163), which lists award winners but does not include descriptive material.   AS8.A93

World dictionary of awards and prizes. London : Europa, [1979]. 386 p.   **AL162**

An alphabetical arrangement of entries for some "2,000 international and national awards from 62 countries," with emphasis in selection "on achievement of an intellectual nature and of truly national and international standing."—*Foreword*. Includes "prestigious lectureships" but not prizes for heroism, voluntary service, or sport. Gives descriptive information, awarding body, and selected list of recipients. Indexed. Numerous omissions.   AS911.A2W58

World of winners. 1st ed.– . Detroit : Gale, c1989– . Annual.   **AL163**

Subtitle: A current and historical perspective on awards and their winners.

Lists 100,000 past and present winners of 2,882 awards honoring achievement in "all areas of human endeavor that are bestowed worldwide and in which the general public has knowledge or interest."—*Introd*. Includes such fields as sports, entertainment, literature, scientific research, and public service. Entries are arranged alphabetically by the last name of the person for whom the award is named, followed by presenting organization and the listing, in reverse chronological order, of the winners. Some entries include the award's alternative or popular name, a brief description of the winning achievement, and the winner's affiliation or country. Includes user's guide and four indexes: award index arranged alphabetically by exact, rather than last, names; subject index; organization index, listing the award-granting groups; and winner's index.   AS8.W76

Nobel Prizes

Abrams, Irwin. The Nobel Peace Prize and the laureates : an illustrated biographical history, 1901–1987. Boston : G.K. Hall, c1988. 269 p. : ports.   **AL164**

Essays on the origins and development, mechanics, and evaluation of the prize are followed by profiles of the recipients. In four chronological sections (each beginning with a historical overview); the chronologically arranged profiles are 2,000–3,000 words in length, describe the lives and peace activities of the laureates, provide bibliographies of primary and secondary sources (some briefly annotated), and include portraits. Among the appendixes are Alfred Nobel's will and listings of the laureates by category and country. The second printing includes the 1988 award. General index.   JX1962.A2A25

Farber, Eduard. Nobel prize winners in chemistry, 1901–1961. Rev. ed. London ; N.Y. : Abelard-Schuman, 1963. 341 p. : ill.   **AL165**

1st ed., 1953.

For each person gives a biographical sketch, a description of the prize-winning work, and an estimate of its consequences in theory and practice.   QD21.F37

Nobel laureates in chemistry, 1901–1992 / Laylin K. James, ed. [Wash.] : American Chemical Society : Chemical Heritage Foundation, 1993. 798 p. : ill.   **AL166**

Articles on Nobel Prize winners in chemistry, arranged in chronological order from the first prize through 1992; entries include photographs of the laureates, an article on the laureate and his or her scientific work, and a bibliography. The volume ends with a brief bibliographic guide to the Nobel Prize in Chemistry. Indexed.

§ The similarities to Frank N. Magill's *The Nobel prize winners : chemistry* (AL171) are more pronounced than the differences; some authors contributed entries to both works. Magill's entries follow a rigid formula; here, authors were given somewhat more latitude. The entries in Magill are, on average, somewhat longer; its bibliographies are annotated, whereas here bibliographies are unannotated but longer. Magill has an overview on the history of the Nobel Prize in chemistry; here, there is only an annotated bibliography on that subject. Many li-

braries will decide between the works on the basis of price; the ACS publication is far less expensive, particularly in the paperback edition.   QD21.N63

Nobel laureates in economic sciences : a biographical dictionary / ed. by Bernard S. Katz. N.Y. : Garland, 1989. 339 p. (Garland reference library of the humanities, vol. 850).   **AL167**

Contains biographical essays on each of the recipients of the Nobel Prize in economic sciences since the award was first given in 1969. Entries, written by colleagues, are several pages long and generally include descriptions of the recipients' backgrounds and careers, main contributions, specific achievements for which the awards were given, and bibliographies of works by and about the laureates. A brief introduction describes the award itself and is followed by a list of recipients by year. Indexed.   HB76.N63

Nobel laureates in literature : a biographical dictionary / ed. by Rado Pribic. N.Y. : Garland, 1990. 473 p. (Garland reference library of the humanities, vol. 849).   **AL168**

Presents signed essays and selected bibliographies on laureates from 1901 through 1988. Arranged alphabetically by laureate, with a chronological list of prizewinners and a general index.   PN452.N6

Nobel laureates in medicine or physiology : a biographical dictionary / ed. by Daniel M. Fox, Marcia Meldrum, and Ira Rezak. N.Y. : Garland, c1990. 595 p. (Garland reference library of the humanities, vol. 852).   **AL169**

Contains scholarly biographical articles on prize winners, 1901–89. Articles are signed and "written to be accessible to students and general readers as well as to specialists in medical science and history."—*Pref*. Following a brief chronological listing, entries are arranged alphabetically by laureates' names. Index of laureates and scientists named in the articles, including names occuring in bibliographies appended to each article. No subject index.   R134.N63

Nobel prize winners : an H.W. Wilson biographical dictionary / ed., Tyler Wasson ; consultants, Gert H. Brieger … [et al.]. N.Y. : H.W. Wilson, 1987. 1165 p. : ports.   **AL170**

Contains "profiles of all 566 men, women, and institutions that have received the Nobel Prize between 1901 and 1986."—*Pref*. The two- to three-page essays, which have a photograph of the recipient, include a list of selected writings and a brief bibliography of secondary sources. "Nobel Prize winners by prize category and year," p. xii–xix. There is a *1987–1991 supplement* (N.Y. : H.W. Wilson, 1992. 143 p.).

§ *The who's who of Nobel Prize winners, 1901–1990*, ed. by Bernard S. Schlessinger and June H. Schlessinger (2nd ed. Phoenix : Oryx, 1991. 234 p.) gives brief summaries, is arranged chronologically under prize categories, and has indexes by name, education, nationality, and religion.   AS911.N9N59

The Nobel Prize winners : chemistry / ed. by Frank N. Magill. Pasadena, Calif. : Salem Pr., c1990. 3 v. (1246 p.) : ill.   **AL171**

A collection of articles on Nobel Prize winners in chemistry, arranged chronologically from the first prize through 1989. Articles follow a fixed pattern and include a picture of the chemist; summaries of the award presentation, the Nobel lecture, and the critical reception of the award; a biography of the prize winner; and a brief bibliography. Unlike the series in chemistry issued by the Nobelstiftelsen (AL174) these volumes do not include the full texts of presentation speeches or Nobel lectures, but the additional material they include makes this a useful source for the history of chemistry which both supplements and updates Edward Faber's *Nobel prize winners in chemistry, 1901–1961* (AL165). Vol. 1 includes an overview of the history of the Nobel Prize in chemistry, and each volume has an alphabetical list of prize winners. The index includes names, subjects, and institutions mentioned in the articles, and nationalities of the prize winners.   QD35.N64

The Nobel Prize winners : physics / ed. by Frank N. Magill. Pasadena, Calif. : Salem Pr., c1989. 3 v. (1364 p.) : ports. **AL172**

For physics, observes the scope and arrangement of the same series for chemistry (AL171) from the first prize through 1988. The full texts of the Nobel lectures are published in the series in physics issued by the Nobelstiftelsen (AL175). QC25.N63

The Nobel Prize winners : physiology and medicine / ed. by Frank N. Magill. Pasadena, Calif. : Salem Pr., c1991. 3 v. : ports. **AL173**
R134.N633

Nobelstiftelsen. Chemistry. Amsterdam : Elsevier, 1964–92. v. 1–6 : ill. (In progress). **AL174**

Publisher varies: v. 5– publ. Singapore ; Edge River, N.J. : World Scientific.

Contents: v. 1, 1901–21; v. 2, 1922–41; v. 3, 1942–62; v. 4, 1963–70; v. 5, 1971–80; v. 6, 1981–90.

Texts of laureates' acceptance speeches and presentation speeches, with biographies of laureates. Vols. 1–4 have name and subject indexes. QD39.N735

──────── Physics. Amsterdam : Elsevier, 1964–[1992?]. v. 1–6 : ill. (In progress). **AL175**

Publisher varies: v. 5– publ. Singapore ; Edge River, N.J. : World Scientific.

Contents: v. 1, 1901–21; v. 2, 1922–41; v. 3, 1942–62; v. 4, 1963–70; v. 5, 1971–80; v. 6, 1981–90.

Texts of Nobel lectures and presentation speeches, with biographies of the laureates. Texts have been translated into English when not originally in that language. Name and subject indexes in v. 1–4. QC71.N64

──────── Physiology or medicine. Amsterdam ; N.Y. : Elsevier, 1964–72. 4 v. : ill. **AL176**

Contents: [v. 1] 1901–21 (1967); [v. 2] 1922–41 (1965); [v. 3] 1942–62 (1964); [v. 4] 1963–70 (1972).

At head of title: Nobel lectures, including presentation speeches and laureates' biographies.

Text in English. QH311.N6

Sourkes, Theodore L. Nobel prize winners in medicine and physiology, 1901–1965. [New and rev. ed.]. London ; N.Y. : Abelard-Schuman, [1967]. 464 p. : ill. **AL177**

Previous ed. by Lloyd G. Stevenson, covering 1901–50, published 1953.

Short biographical sketches of each prize winner, followed by a description of the prize discovery and an explanation of its meaning and importance. In addition to new chapters for the 1951–65 period, earlier biographies have been brought up-to-date in this edition, and some explanatory matter in the earlier chapters has been changed. Entries are chronologically arranged; name and subject indexes. R149.S6

ORDERS AND DECORATIONS

American orders & societies and their decorations / comp. by Jennings Hood and Charles J. Young. Philadelphia : Bailey, Banks & Biddle Co., c1917. 107, [18] p. col. plates : ill. **AL178**

Subtitle: The objects of the military and naval orders, commemorative and patriotic societies of the United States and the requirements for membership therein, with illustrations in colored relief.

Devoted to military/patriotic societies (e.g., Army and Navy Medal of Honor Legion, Sons of Veterans, Military Society of the War of 1812) and to organizations with genealogical requirements (e.g., Daughters of the Revolution, Society of the Colonial Dames of America). Arranged alphabetically by organization name, profiles include "objects" (goals) and membership requirements. Glossy colored plates with representations of decorations and insignia. E172.7.H77

Burke, John Bernard. The book of orders of knighthood and decorations of honour of all nations : comprising an historical account of each order, military, naval, and civil, from the earliest to the present time, with lists of the knights and companions of each British order. London : Hurst and Blackett, 1858. 411 p. : 100 col.pl. **AL179**
CR4653.B8

The Congressional Medal of Honor : the names, the deeds. Forest Ranch, Calif. : Sharp & Dunnigan Publications, 1984. 1105 p., [1] leaf of plates : 1 col. ill. **AL180**

Lists recipients of the medal from its foundation during the Civil War through the Vietnam conflict. Short entries giving accounts of the acts of bravery that led to each bestowal are organized by military campaign in reverse chronological order. Includes chapters giving historical and documentary background. Lists of numbers of medals by wars/campaigns; awards by special legislation; recipients by state; and foreign born recipients. Name index. UB433.C65

Hieronymussen, Poul Ohm. Orders, medals and decorations of Britain and Europe in colour / translated [from the Danish] by Christine Crowley. 2nd ed. London : Blandford, 1970. 256 p. : ill. **AL181**

Repr., 1975.

Originally publ. as *Europaeiske ordner i farver* (Copenhagen, 1966). 1st English ed., 1967.

Illustrates and describes present-day international European orders. CR4515.H513

Jocelyn, Arthur. Awards of honour : the orders, decorations, medals and awards of Great Britain & the Commonwealth from Edward III to Elizabeth II. London : A. & C. Black, 1956. 276 p. : ill. ; col. plates. **AL182**

Contains description of the orders, decorations, etc.
CR4529.G7J6

Kerrigan, Evans E. American badges and insignia. N.Y. : Viking, [1967]. 286 p. : ill. **AL183**

Depicts and describes badges signifying personal attainments (e.g., for marksmanship) and insignia denoting rank, branch of service, etc. (e.g., shoulder patches). Bibliography; index.

────. *American war medals and decorations* (Newly rev. and expanded. N.Y. : Viking Pr., [1971]. 173 p.). A companion to the above. Describes decorations awarded for individual achievement (e.g., Navy Cross); medals given for service in a particular campaign, expedition, etc.; and civilian awards (e.g., Medal of Freedom). Bibliography; index. UC533.K45

Mĕřička, Václav. The book of orders and decorations / [trans. from the Czech by Ruth Shepherd and Eliška Říhová ; photographs by Jindřich Marco; ed. by Alec A. Purves]. London ; N.Y. : Hamlyn, [1976]. 248 p. : ill. (some col.) ; ports. **AL184**

A "further development" of the author's *Orders and decorations* (London : Hamlyn, 1967. 316 p.).

Histories and photographs of decorations, emphasizing those of continental Europe. Duplicates some material found in the earlier work. CR4509.M39

National Geographic Society. Insignia and decorations of the United States armed forces / by Gilbert Grosvenor ... [et al.]. Rev. ed., December 1, 1944. Wash. : Nat. Geographic Soc., 1945. 208 p. : ill. **AL185**

"2,476 reproductions in color and 159 illustrations from photographs"—*t.p.*

1st ed., 1943.

Useful for historical research. Contains descriptions and illustrations (many in color) of decorations, medals, service ribbons, badges, and other insignia of the U.S. armed forces. Emphasizes World War II era. No index.   UC533.N3

Robles, Philip K. United States military medals and ribbons. Rutland, Vt. : C.E. Tuttle, [1971]. 187 p. : ill.   **AL186**

Provides answers (through descriptive and historical text and colored illustrations) to "most of the questions concerning eligibility for award and wear of the medals of the United States Armed Forces."—*Pref.* Merchant Marine awards are also included. Appendix lists precedence of awards when worn and gives information on how to apply for earned medals. Bibliography. Index of medals and ribbons.   UC533.R62

United States. Adjutant General's Office. American decorations : a list of awards of the Congressional Medal of Honor, the Distinguished-Service Cross, and the Distinguished-Service Medal, awarded under authority of the Congress of the United States, 1862–1926. Wash. : U.S. Govt. Print. Off., 1927. 845 p.   **AL187**

Entries are arranged alphabetically by recipient, and are occasionally grouped by nationality. For each recipient, describes the acts or services rendered that led to the award. Provides more historical information than *The Congressional Medal of Honor* (AL180), due to coverage of the two additional awards.

————. ————. *Supplement*, no. 1–5 (Wash. : U.S. Govt. Print. Off., 1937–1941). Also available in microform (N.Y. : Columbia Univ. Libraries, 1986). In addition to updating information through June 30, 1941, the supplements include recipients of the Distinguished Flying Cross.

Werlich, Robert. Orders and decorations of all nations : ancient and modern, civil and military. 2nd ed. [Wash. : Quaker Pr., 1974]. 476 p. : ill.   **AL188**

1st ed., 1965.

Illustrates and describes the major awards of all countries. Arranged by country; general index.   CR4509.W4

Wyllie, Robert E. Orders, decorations and insignia, military and civil : with the history and romance of their origin and a full description of each ... with 367 illustrations (over 200 in colour). N.Y. ; London : Putnam, [1921]. 269 p. : ill.   **AL189**

Contains historical and descriptive information, with many excellent illustrations of the medals, ribbons, badges, etc., of the U. S., Britain, Belgium, China, Cuba, Czechoslovakia, France, Greece, Hawaii, Italy, Japan, Monaco, Montenegro, Panama, Poland, Portugal, Rumania, Russia, and Serbia. Includes information on shoulder insignia, insignia of rank, and insignia and colors of arms of service of the World War I period.   CR4509.W9

FLAGS

Flags of the world / ed. by E. M. C. Barraclough and W. G. Crampton. 2nd ed. [of 1978 ed.] with revisions and supplement. London ; N.Y. : F. Warne, [1981]. 262 p. : ill.   **AL190**

Based on *The flags of the world: their history, blazonry, and associations,* by F. Edward Hulme, publ. 1897. Editions by H. G. Carr publ. 1953 and 1961. First publ. under Barraclough's editorship 1965.

Offers histories and descriptions of the flags and standards of the various countries of the world, with special emphasis on British flags. In this edition newer material (1978–81) appears in the supplement, p. 241–52, and is cross-referenced to the main text.   CR109.F554

Shankle, George Earlie. State names, flags, seals, songs, birds, flowers and other symbols. Rev. ed. N.Y. : Wilson, 1941 [i.e., 1951, c1938]. 524 p. : ill.   **AL191**

Repr.: Westport, Conn. : Greenwood, 1970.

1st ed., 1938.

Subtitle: A study based on historical documents giving the origin and significance of the state names, nicknames, mottoes, seals, flags, flowers, birds, songs, and descriptive comments on the capitol buildings and on some of the leading state histories, with facsimiles of the state flags and seals.   E155.S43

Shearer, Benjamin F. State names, seals, flags, and symbols : a historical guide / Benjamin F. Shearer and Barbara S. Shearer. Rev. and expanded. Westport, Conn. : Greenwood, 1994. 438 p. : ill.   **AL192**

1st ed., 1987.

Origins of state names and symbols (e.g., mottoes, seals, flowers, trees, birds, songs) are arranged alphabetically by state under the type of symbol. Selected bibliography of state histories. The revised edition has four new chapters and extends coverage to the District of Columbia and five U.S. territories overseas. Excellent coverage of flags.   E155.S44

Smith, Whitney. Flags and arms across the world. N.Y. : McGraw-Hill, [1980]. 256 p. : ill.   **AL193**

"A field guide to the flags of the 174 nations of the world. National flags, coats of arms, state and provincial flags, presidential and ministerial banners—nearly 1,000 full-color illustrations, with maps, history, and thorough documentation."—*verso of t.p.*

Revises and updates the international section of the author's *Flags through the ages and across the world* (AL194). Indexed.   JC345.S56

————. Flags through the ages and across the world. N.Y. : McGraw-Hill, [1975]. 357 p. : col. ill.   **AL194**

In three main sections: (1) Flags through the ages (History of flags; Flags that made history; Customs and etiquette; National flag histories); (2) Flags across the world (Flags of the world's 157 nations and their subdivisions; International flags; Ethnic minority flags); (3) Symbols. A good deal of background information and explanatory text accompanies the illustrations. Glossary of terms; index.   JC345.S57

Talocci, Mauro. Guide to the flags of the world / rev. and updated by Whitney Smith; tr. from the Italian by Ronald Strom. N.Y. : Morrow, 1982. 271 p. : ill.   **AL195**

1977 Italian ed. had title: *Guida alle bandiere di tutto il mondo.*

Arranged by continent, then by country, with an added section for international flags. Flags and coats of arms are illustrated in color, with brief notes on historical background and symbols depicted. Glossary; index.   CR101.T3413

WEIGHTS AND MEASURES

Chisholm, L. J. Units of weight and measure : international (metric) and United States customary. Definitions and tables of equivalents. .... Wash. : U.S. Dept. of Commerce. Nat. Bur. of Standards, 1967. 251 p. (National Bureau of Standards. Misc. publ., 286).   **AL196**

Title of earlier eds. varies: 1903, *Table of equivalents of the customary and metric weights and measures*; 1906–13, *Tables of equivalents of the United States customary and metric weights and measures.*   QC100.U57 no.286

Doursther, Horace. Dictionnaire universel des poids et mesures : anciens et modernes, contenant des tables des monnaies de tous les pays. Bruxelles : Hayez, 1840. 604 p.   **AL197**

Repr.: Amsterdam : Meridian Publ. Co., 1965.

Out-of-date, but useful for questions involving historical information, since it includes many old and unusual terms.   QC82.D6

Elsevier's lexicon of international and national units : English/American, German, Spanish, French, Italian, Japanese, Dutch, Portuguese, Polish, Swedish, Russian / comp. and arr. by W. E. Clason. Amsterdam : Elsevier, 1964. 76.   **AL198**

A guide to the meaning and value of internationally and nationally used units. Includes: International units, arranged alphabetically by unit; Units used in different countries, arranged by country; Words and indexes; Bibliography.   QC82.E37

Naft, Stephen. International conversion tables : weights, measures, gauges, currencies, conversion equivalents and factors, technical units, alphabets, other useful information / expanded and rev. by Ralph De Sola. N.Y. : Duell, [1961]. 372 p.   **AL199**

1st ed. had title: *Conversion equivalents in international trade.*
HF5714.N3

The world measurement guide. [4th ed., rev.]. [London : Economist Newspaper ; Detroit : Gale, 1980]. 240 p. : ill.
AL200

1st ed., (1954) had title *The Economist guide to weights and measures*; 3rd ed. (1975), called *The Economist measurement guide and reckoner.*

Provides tables and data on: measurement systems for most countries; conversion tables; measurements in space and time, agriculture, fishing, forestry, and industry; definitions and formulae for accountancy, economics, finance, and mathematics; interest rate tables, etc. Indexed.   HF5712.W67

Zupko, Ronald Edward. A dictionary of weights and measures for the British Isles : the Middle Ages to the twentieth century. Philadelphia : American Philosophical Society, 1985. 520 p. (Memoirs of the American Philosophical Society, v. 168).   **AL201**

An expansion of the author's *A dictionary of English weights and measures from Anglo-Saxon times to the nineteenth century* (Madison : University of Wisc. Pr., 1968. 224 p.).

Gives etymology of the term, explanation of the unit and its variants, citing sources from the medieval period to modern times. Bibliography of sources and other reference works.   QC82.Z8

———————— French weights and measures before the Revolution : a dictionary of provincial and local units. Bloomington : Indiana Univ. Pr., [1978]. 208 p.   **AL202**

A dictionary of premetric terms giving definitions, periods and places of use, etymologies, equivalencies, and references (with dates) to manuscript and printed sources. Bibliography of sources cited, p. 189–208.   QC89.F8Z86

B

Humanities

BA

General Works

Bibliography

Black arts annual. v. 1 (1987/88)–v. 3 (1989/90). N.Y. : Garland, 1989–92. **BA1**

No longer publ. annually; presumed to have ceased with v. 3.

Sections treat art, photography, literature, popular music, jazz and classical music, dance, theater, movies, and television. Each section begins with an overview of the season in general, followed by annotated lists "spotlighting individual pieces of work."—*Introd., v. 2.* The purpose is "to examine and explore, probe and scrutinize, dissect and analyze ... and report on the year's important events in the arts in the African-American community." NX512.3.A35B58

Indexes; Abstract journals

The American humanities index. v.1, no.1/2 (Spr./Sum. 1975)– . Troy, N.Y. : Whitston, 1975– . Annual. **BA2**

Frequency varies: quarterly with annual cumulations, 1975–87; annual since 1988.

An "index to creative, critical, and scholarly journals in the arts and humanities. Most of the journals included are indexed exclusively by the *AHI*. At the present time [1993] we are indexing over 500 journals."—*Pref.*

A particularly good source for locating poems, essays, fiction, and book reviews appearing in little and literary magazines. Combined alphabetical author and subject arrangement. Book reviews listed under both author and reviewer. AI3.A278

Arts & humanities citation index. 1976– . Philadelphia : Inst. for Scientific Information, 1978– . Semiannual. **BA3**

Publ. semiannually in hardcover. Each issue in three physical parts: (1) Citation index; (2) Source and corporate index; (3) "Permuterm" subject index. One five-year cumulation (1975–79) available. Source/corporate index volume contains the primary entry: a full bibliographic description, author's address where known, and a list of works cited in the article's bibliography.

Patterned on *Science citation index* (EA75) and *Social sciences citation index* (CA27), and using the same general format and approach to indexing, "A&HCI is a multidisciplinary index to the literature of the arts and humanities ... Of the 6,100 journals indexed, approximately 1,000 are fully covered and 5,100 are selectively covered."—*Introd., 1993 first semiannual, v. 1.* The only materials omitted from fully-indexed journals are advertisements, news notices, and meeting agendas. Selectively covered journals are drawn from the databases for the two indexes mentioned above, which are reviewed for relevance to the arts and humanities. Titles of articles are enhanced by adding subject terms to improve subject access.

•Machine-readable versions: *Arts & humanities search* [database] (Philadelphia : ISI, 1980–). Available online, updated weekly. *Arts & humanities citation index : compact disc edition* [database] (Philadelphia : ISI, 1990–). Available on CD-ROM; triennial, publ. in two triennial cumulative updates and one annual cumulation. Single-year cumulations available, 1990– . A ten-year cumulation, 1980–89, includes records not indexed previously in the printed version. AI3.A63

Essay and general literature index. v. [1] (1900/33)– .
N.Y. : H.W. Wilson, 1934– . Frequency varies.   **BA4**
    Kept up-to-date by supplements: (1) 7-year cumulations, 1934–
1940, 1941–1947, 1948–1954; (2) 5-year cumulations, 1955/1959– ;
and (3) semiannual and annual cumulations.
    Frequently cited as *Essay index.*
    The basic volume is a detailed index by authors, subjects, and
some titles, to essays, festschriften and articles published 1900–33 and
also to earlier essays if included in collections published since 1900.
Emphasizes humanities and social sciences. Indexing is given with
exact reference; in the case of many essays first printed in periodicals,
the reference to the periodical is given also, and variant titles for the
same essay are indicated.
    As a reference aid, it serves many purposes, showing, for exam-
ple, (1) a list of essays by a given author; (2) authorship of an essay
when only the title is known; (3) analytical material on a given subject,
particularly small, unusual, or intangible subjects not covered by
whole books; (4) biographical and critical matter about persons; (5)
criticisms of individual books; and (6) different places or collections in
which an essay is printed. For purposes of book selection, the list of
books indexed serves as a good guide to worthwhile essay and other
composite-book materials.
    The various cumulated supplements, 1934–89, index more than
270,000 essays and articles in more than 15,700 collections.
    Essay and general literature index : works indexed 1900–1969
(N.Y. : Wilson, 1972) is a main entry and title listing of the 9,917
works analyzed in the *Index* during that period.
    •The *Index* is available in machine-readable form as: *Essay and
general literature index* [database] (N.Y. : H. W. Wilson, 1985–);
available on CD-ROM, updated annually, and online, updated semiannually.   AI3.E752

Humanities index. v. 1, no. 1 (June 1974)– . N.Y. : H.W.
Wilson, 1974– . Quarterly with annual cumulations.   **BA5**
    Supersedes in part *Social sciences and humanities index*
(AD288).
    "Subject fields indexed include archaeology and classical studies,
area studies, folklore, history, language and literature, performing arts,
philosophy, religion and theology, and related subjects."—*Prefatory
note, v. 20, n. 3.* Originally indexed 117 of the titles from *Social sciences and humanities index* plus 143 titles elected by subscribers to the
index; in 1993, indexed 345 English-language titles. Author and subject entries; a separate book review section has been added, with entry
under author of the book reviewed.
    •Machine-readable version: *Humanities index* [database] (Bronx,
N.Y. : H.W. Wilson, 1984–). Available online (updated twice weekly), on CD-ROM (updated quarterly) and on magnetic tape.   AI3.H85

Subject index to periodicals. 1915–1961. London : Libr. Assoc., 1919–62.   **BA6**
    For annotation, *see* AD289.   AI3.A72

Book reviews

**Combined retrospective index to book reviews in humani-
ties journals, 1802–1974** / executive ed., Evan Ira Farber, senior ed., Stanley Schindler. Woodbridge, Conn. : Research Publications, 1982–1984. 10 v.   **BA7**
    Contents: v. 1–9, Authors; v. 10, Title.
    "Offers author and title access to about 500,000 book reviews that
appeared in the complete backfiles of over 150 [English and Ameri-
can] humanities journals."—*Introd.* Reviewers' names are included in
the citations when they could be identified.   Z6265.C65

Directories

Current research in Britain : the humanities : CRB. 1st
ed.– . Boston Spa : British Library Lending Division, 1985– .
Annual.   **BA8**
    Each edition is in four parts: *Physical sciences* (EA138); *Biologi-
cal sciences* (EG47); *Social sciences* (CA46); *The humanities.*
    Supersedes *Research in British universities, polytechnics and col-
leges.*
    Provides information on more than 60,000 research projects at
some 300 British institutions. The main arrangement is by institutional
and departmental code numbers; within code numbers, listings are in
alphabetical order by the name of the principal investigator and include
the names of all researchers, a brief description of the project, project
dates, sponsors, and publications. Departmental addresses and the
names of department heads are also included. Institution/department
index.   AZ188.G7

Financial aids; Grants

Directory of grants in the humanities. [1986]– . Phoenix :
Oryx, c1986– . Annual.   **BA9**
    Describes more than 3,000 funding programs from public and pri-
vate sources supporting research and performance in the humanities
and the visual and performing arts. Entries include each program's
goals, restrictions, funding amounts, deadlines, and *Catalog of federal
domestic assistance* number when appropriate. Like *Directory of research grants* (BA9), this is a product of the *GRANTS* database
(grb91-5395), which is updated monthly and should be consulted for
changes or additions to programs.   AZ188.U5D56

**The national directory of arts & education support by
business corporations** / by Nancy A. Fandel and editors of
the Washington Int'l Arts Letter. 3rd ed. Wash. : Washington
International Arts Letter, 1988. 150 p. (Arts patronage series,
no. 14).   **BA10**
    1st ed., 1980, had title: *National directory of arts support by busi-
ness corporations, 1;* 2nd ed., 1982.
    This edition lists more than 600 companies that support nonprofit
arts organizations, educational institutions, and individual artists, the
latter indicated by asterisks. Arranged alphabetically by name of corporation, entries include address, contact person, officers, description
of business, types or projects supported and, in most cases, recipients
or recent grants, total contributions, and other figures pertaining to
gift-giving activities. No index.
    § Other titles in the series include *National directory of arts sup-
port by private foundations* (5th ed., 1983) and *National directory of
grants and aid to individuals in the arts, international* (7th ed., 1989).
        NX711.U5N3

Park, Karin R. Publication grants for writers & publishers :
how to find them, win them, and manage them / by Karin R.
Park & Beth Luey. Phoenix : Oryx, 1991. 105 p. : ill.   **BA11**
    Written "to help authors and publishers find outside funding for
their publications."—*Introd.* Organized in chapters that describe publication costs, governmental and nongovernmental sources, institutional
sources, and grant writing techniques. Brief bibliography; general
index.   Z283.P37

BB

Philosophy

GENERAL WORKS

Guides

Bynagle, Hans E. Philosophy : a guide to the reference literature. Littleton, Colo. : Libraries Unlimited, 1986. 170 p. **BB1**

A bibliography and handbook, "compiled and written with a diversity of users in mind."—*Pref.* Less exhaustive than R. T. De George's *Philosopher's guide* (BB2), but covers much the same ground, containing lengthy annotations and citations to more recent works. Organized by resource type (e.g., general and specialized dictionaries; indexes, abstracting and reviewing journals and serial bibliographies; concordances), with entries arranged alphabetically within each chapter. Core journals and professional societies are also listed. Reference sources are cited for specific philosophical schools, countries, periods, and individuals, but citations to standard editions of philosophical works are not included. Emphasis is on English-language materials. Author/title and subject indexes.   Z7125.B97

De George, Richard T. The philosopher's guide to sources, research tools, professional life and related fields. Lawrence : Regents Pr. of Kansas, c1980. 261 p.   **BB2**

Represents a reworking, updating, and expansion of the author's *Guide to philosophical bibliography and research* (1971). Now in three main sections: (1) Philosophy; (2) General research tools; and (3) Related fields (Religion; Humanities; Fine arts; Social sciences; Physical sciences, mathematics, and engineering; Professions). The first section (p. 1–166) has major subdivisions for (a) general works, (b) sources for the history of philosophy (further subdivided by period and with sections for individual philosophers), (c) branches, movements and regions of systematic philosophy, and (d) serials, publishing, and professional life. Many entries are annotated. Index of authors, subjects, and most titles.   Z7125.D445

Tice, Terrence N. Research guide to philosophy / Terrence N. Tice and Thomas P. Slavens. Chicago : Amer. Libr. Assoc., 1983. 608 p. (Sources of information in the humanities, no. 3).   **BB3**

In three main sections: (1) The history of philosophy (offering bibliographic essays on specific chronological periods, with subsections for individual philosophers); (2) Areas of philosophy (with similar essays on epistemology, logic, metaphysics, philosophy of history, etc.); and (3) Reference works (p. 503–15; listing reference works by type, with annotations). Indexed.   B52.T5

Bibliography

Barth, Else M. Women philosophers : a bibliography of books through 1990. Bowling Green, Ohio : Philosophy Documentation Center, 1992. 213, [22] p.   **BB4**

Includes books that are: (1) listed as philosophical by the publisher; (2) written by someone from a university philosophy department; or (3) on a topic satisfying one or more of the current definitions of "philosophy." Entries lack annotations, and are arranged alphabetically by author within a philosophical classification system used in the Netherlands. The majority of the works are in English. Name index.   Z7125.B34

Bibliographische Einführungen in das Studium der Philosophie / hrsg. von I. M. Bochenski. Bern : Francke, 1948–53. 23 no. in 20 v.   **BB5**

Contents: (1), I. M. Bochenski and F. Monteleone, Allgemeine philosophische Bibliographie (42 p.); (2) Ralph B. Winn, Amerikanische Philosophie (32 p.); (3) E. W. Beth, Symbolische Logik und Grundlegung der exakten Wissenschaften (28 p.); (4) Régis Jolivet, Kierkegaard (33 p.); (5) Olaf Gigon, Antike Philosophie (52 p.); (6) P. J. de Menasce, Arabische Philosophie (49 p.); (7) M. F. Sciacca, Italienische Philosophie der Gegenwart (36 p.); (8) M. D. Phillippe, Aristoteles (48 p.); (9) Régis Jolivet, Französische Existenzphilosophie (36 p.); (10) M. F. Sciacca, Augustinus (32 p.); (11) Karl Dürr, Der logische Positivismus (24 p.); (12) Olaf Gigon, Platon (30 p.); (13/14) Paul Wyser, Thomas von Aquin (78 p.); (15/16) Paul Wyser, Der Thomismus (120 p.); (17) F. van Steenberghen, Philosophie des Mittelalters (52 p.); (18) Othmar Perler, Patristische Philosophie (44 p.); (19) Georges Vajda, Jüdische Philosophie (40 p.); (20/21) C. Régamey, Buddhistische Philosophie (86 p.); (22) Odulf Schäfer, Johannes Duns Scotus (34 p.); (23) Otto Friedrich Bollnow, Deutsche Existenzphilosophie (40 p.).

A series of brief bibliographies on various aspects of philosophy; features 20th-century materials for the most part.

Harvard University. Library. Philosophy and psychology. Cambridge, Mass. : Harvard Univ. Lib., distr. by Harvard Univ. Pr., 1973. 2 v. (Widener Library shelflist, 42–43).   **BB6**

For a note on the series, *see* AA115.

Contents: v.1, Classification schedule; Classified listing by call number; Chronological listing; v.2, Author and title listing.

Lists materials in "the *Phil* classification, which contains nearly 59,000 books, periodicals, and pamphlets concerning metaphysics in general, cosmology, ontology, epistemology, logic, aesthetics, and psychology."—*Pref.*   Z7130.H3

The philosopher's index : a retrospective index to non-U.S. English language publications from 1940. Bowling Green, Ohio : Philosophy Documentation Center, Bowling Green State Univ., [1980]. 3 v.   **BB7**

A companion to the volumes for U.S. publications from 1940 (BB8).

Provides author and subject approaches to "original philosophy books published outside of the United States in English between 1940 and 1978, and articles published in philosophy journals outside of the United States in English between 1940 and 1966."—*Pref.* Includes about 12,000 articles and some 5,000 books.

Offers retrospective indexing for journal articles published prior to the beginning of the quarterly *Philosopher's index* (BB25).   Z7127.P473B72

The philosopher's index : a retrospective index to U.S. publications from 1940. Bowling Green, Ohio : Philosophy Documentation Ctr., Bowling Green State Univ., 1978. 3 v.   **BB8**

Contents: v.1–2, Subject index; v.3, Author index.

A companion to the above for U.S. publications; indexes "approximately 15,000 articles from U.S. journals published during the 27 year period, 1940–1966, and approximately 6,000 books published during the 37 year period, 1940–1976."—*p.vii.* It thus offers retrospective indexing for journal articles published prior to the beginning of the quarterly *Philosopher's index* (BB25), and complementary coverage for book publications from the longer period.   Z7127.P474

Totok, Wilhelm. Bibliographischer Wegweiser der philosophischen Literatur. 2. Aufl. / bearb. von Horst-Dieter Finke. Frankfurt am Main : Klostermann, 1985. 53 p.   **BB9**

1st ed., 1959.

Lists 200 citations to reference works, annuals, and periodicals by subject or publication type. Author/editor and title indexes.

Z7125.A1T67

World philosophy : a contemporary bibliography / ed. by John R. Burr ; Charlotte A. Burr, research ed. Westport, Conn. : Greenwood, 1993. 380 p. (Bibliographies and indexes in philosophy, no. 3). **BB10**

Supplements John Burr's *Handbook of world philosophy : contemporary developments since 1945* (BB81).

The purpose of this bibliography is to "give a representative sample of the books and monographs in philosophy that have been published throughout the world since 1976."—*Introd.* Does not include journal articles. Entries are arranged by geographical region (e.g., Africa, Middle East, etc.), and then alphabetically by country. Most entries are not annotated, although the editor points out important features such as bibliographies and translations. Author and subject indexes. Z7125.W87

Bibliography of bibliography

Guerry, Herbert. A bibliography of philosophical bibliographies. Westport, Conn. : Greenwood, 1977. 332 p. **BB11**

In two parts: (1) Bibliographies of individual philosophers (alphabetical by philosopher); (2) Subject bibliographies (alphabetical by subject). 2,353 items, with selective, brief annotations. In general, includes "only bibliographies that have been published separately or appeared as contributions to journals," but lists "a few significant bibliographies which were published as appendixes to monographs or as parts of larger bibliographies."—*Introd.* Author index.

Z7125.A1G83

Current

Bibliographie de la philosophie : bulletin trimestriel = Bibliography of philosophy : a quarterly bulletin. v.1– . Paris : Vrin, 1954– . Quarterly. **BB12**

Published for the International Federation of Philosophical Societies under the auspices of the International Council of Philosophy and Humanistic Studies with the aid of Unesco and of the French National Centre for Scientific Research.

Title page and preliminary matter in French and English.

An international bibliography, dealing with books only. Presents abstracts, usually in the language of the original work, but with translations into either English or French.

Continues *Bibliographie de la philosophie* ([Année 1] 1937–[année 10] 1952/53. Paris : Vrin, 1937–58).

Publication suspended, juil. 1939–déc. 1945; resumed with année 4, 1946. Includes books, periodicals, and dissertations. Z7127.B5

Répertoire bibliographique de la philosophie. t. 1 (fév. 1949)– . Louvain : Éd. de l'Inst. Supérieur de Philosophie, 1949– . Quarterly. **BB13**

With v. 43 (1991), title became: International philosophical bibliography = Répertoire bibliographique de la philosophie = Bibliografisch repertorium van de wijbegeerte.

Continues: "Répertoire bibliographique" that appeared quarterly as a supplement to *Revue philosophique de Louvain*, 1943–48.

Publ. under auspices of the International Institute of Philosophy with the support of UNESCO.

A comprehensive international bibliography of books and articles on philosophy. An index to book reviews appears annually in the Autumn number. Z7127.R42

Periodicals

Ruben, Douglas H. Philosophy journals and serials : an analytical guide. Westport, Conn. : Greenwood, 1985. 147 p. **BB14**

An annotated list of 335 journals, yearbooks, newsletters, and bulletins, compiled from responses to a survey mailed to the editors of philosophy serials listed in *Ulrich's international periodicals directory* (AD18). Arranged alphabetically with geographic and subject indexes.

Z7127.R83

Dissertations

Bechtle, Thomas C. Dissertations in philosophy accepted at American universities, 1861–1975 / Thomas C. Bechtle, Mary F. Riley. N.Y. : Garland, 1978. 537 p. (Garland reference library of the humanities, v.112). **BB15**

An author listing of more than 7,500 doctoral dissertations accepted at 120 U.S. and Canadian universities. "As a rule, only those authors have been included whose dissertations are primarily concerned with philosophy and whose degrees have been earned in a department of philosophy."—*Pref.* There were, however, numerous variant situations wherein content of the dissertation (i.e., whether or not it was "essentially concerned with philosophical concepts") determined its inclusion or exclusion. Detailed subject index. Z7125.D38

Marti, Hanspeter. Philosophische Dissertationen deutscher Universitäten 1660–1750 : eine Auswahlbibliographie / Hanspeter Marti, unter Mitarbeit von Karin Marti. Münich : K. G. Saur, 1982. 705 p. **BB16**

Arranged by name of the *Präses,* then by name of *Respondent* (i.e., author of the dissertation). Indexes of place names, authors, and subjects. Locates copies. Z7126.M37

Congresses and meetings

Geldsetzer, Lutz. Bibliography of the International Congresses of Philosophy : proceedings, 1900–1978 = Bibliographie der Internationalen Philosophie Kongresse : beiträge, 1900–1978. Münich : K. G. Saur, 1981. 207 p. **BB17**

Cites the publication of the first 16 meetings of the International Congress of Philosophy. Lists individual papers and provides author and subject indexes. Z7125.G4513

By topic

Encyclopedia of Indian philosophies : bibliography / comp. by Karl H. Potter. [Rev. ed.]. Princeton, N.J. : Princeton Univ. Pr., [1983]. 1023 p. **BB18**

A revised and expanded edition of the 1970 *Bibliography of Indian philosophies* (designated as v.1 of *Encyclopedia of Indian philosophies,* BB33), incorporating the supplementary lists published irregularly in *Journal of Indian philosophy* and much new material. In four main sections: (1) Sanskrit texts and authors whose dates are known; (2) Sanskrit texts, authors' dates unknown; (3) Sanskrit texts, authors and dates unknown; (4) Secondary literature (subdivided by philosophical school; omits material in non-Western languages). About 13,700 entries. Indexes of names of persons, of titles of texts, and topical index to books and articles. Z7129.I5E52

Fu, Charles Wei-Hsün. Guide to Chinese philosophy / by Charles Wei-Hsün Fu and Wing-Tsit Chan. Boston : G. K. Hall, [1978]. 262 p. **BB19**

"Prepared as part of the Asian Philosophies and Religions Project of the Council for Intercultural Studies and Programs, undertaken by the Foreign Area Materials Center, University of New York/State Education Department."—*Pref.*

Intended primarily for college instructors and students; limited mainly to English-language sources, with some important French and German material included. Topical arrangement; author and title index.
    Z7129.C5F8

Inada, Kenneth K. Guide to Buddhist philosophy. Boston : G.K. Hall, c1985. 226 p.   **BB20**

A companion to Frank E. Reynolds's *Guide to Buddhist religion* (BC472), this annotated bibliography is intended for undergraduates and their instructors. Lists primarily English-language books, articles, and dissertations on Buddhist philosophy, as well as English translations of Buddhist texts. Arranged in 16 chapters that treat such topics as logic, ethics, history, and comparative philosophy. Author/title and subject indexes.
    Z7128.B93I53

Potter, Karl H. Guide to Indian philosophy / Karl H. Potter with Austin B. Creel and Edwin Gerow. Boston : G.K. Hall, c1988. 159 p.   **BB21**

An annotated bibliography of 884 citations to English-language books and articles from the 20th century. Entries are arranged alphabetically by author and include primary texts translated into English, as well as secondary literature from all areas of philosophy, including "epistemology, logic, metaphysics and ethics, works on aesthetics, philosophy of religion, and social, legal, and political philosophy, and philosophy of education."—*Pref.* Name and subject indexes.
    Z7129.I5P68

Tobey, Jeremy L. The history of ideas : a bibliographical introduction. Santa Barbara, Calif. : Clio Books, 1975–1976. 2 v.   **BB22**

Contents: v.1, Classical antiquity; v.2, Medieval and early modern Europe.

Vol. 1 offers a series of bibliographic essays on "the important research and reference tools and scholarly works on the history of ideas and its related fields of philosophy, science, aesthetics, and religion in antiquity."—*Postscript.* A similar plan is followed in v. 2.
    Z7125.T58

Wainwright, William J. Philosophy of religion : an annotated bibliography of twentieth-century writings in English. N.Y. : Garland, 1978. 776 p. (Garland reference library of the humanities, v. 111).   **BB23**

"Addressed to professional philosophers and graduate students who work in the analytic tradition and who are primarily interested in the solution of philosophical problems rather than in the investigation of the systems of individual philosophers or the history of philosophical movements."—*Introd.* More than 1,100 items grouped in categories—The divine attributes, Arguments for the existence of God, The problem of evil, Mysticism and religious experience, etc. Index of authors, editors, and reviewers.
    Z7821.W34

Indexes; Abstract journals

FRANCIS. Bulletin signalétique. v. 1 (1947)– . Paris : Centre de Documentation du C.N.R.S. [Centre National de la Recherche Scientifique], 1947– . Quarterly.   **BB24**

Includes Sec. 519, *Philosophie*. For full description, *see* AD254.

The philosopher's index : an international index to philosophical periodicals and books. v. 1, no. 1 (Spring, 1967)– . Bowling Green, Ohio : Bowling Green Univ., 1967– . Quarterly, with annual cumulations.   **BB25**

Since 1980 this essential periodical index has included English-language monographs, dissertations, and translations. Books in other languages were included in 1984. Currently the index covers material in English, French, German, Italian, and Spanish, while selectively in-

cluding books and journals in other languages. Related interdisciplinary publications are indexed as well. Abstracts have been included when available since 1969, and book reviews since 1970.

•Machine-readable version: *DIALOG OnDisc : Philosopher's index* [database] (Bowling Green, Ohio : Philosophy Documentation Center, Bowling Green Univ., 1940–). Available on CD-ROM, updated quarterly.
    Z7127.P47

Encyclopedias

Baldwin, James Mark. Dictionary of philosophy and psychology : including many of the principal conceptions of ethics, logic, aesthetics, philosophy of religion, mental pathology, anthropology, biology, neurology, physiology, economics, political and social philosophy, philology, physical science and education, and giving a terminology in English, French, German and Italian. N.Y. : Macmillan, 1901–05. 3 v. in 4. : ill.
    BB26

Repr.: Gloucester, Mass. : Peter Smith, 1960.

Contents: v. 1–2, A–Z; indexes of Greek, Latin, German, French, and Italian terms; v. 3, Bibliography of philosophy, comp. by Benjamin Rand.

The first encyclopedia of the subject in English, excellent and authoritative when issued and still useful for many topics though now out-of-date for modern developments. Concise rather than exhaustive in treatment, with signed articles by specialists and many bibliographies. Covers the whole field but is fuller for modern than for earlier aspects of the subject and does not attempt to cover the whole of Greek and scholastic philosophy. Includes very brief biographies of men no longer living. Special features are the inclusion of French, German, and Italian equivalents of English terms used as entries, and the indexes of foreign terms used in the articles.

A new edition, 1910, differed from the original only in the correction of a few typographical errors.

Vol. 3 consists of an unannotated bibliography that includes some 60,000 English-language journal articles, books, and reviews. Its primary strength is its comprehensive coverage of 19th-century writers.
    B41.B3

A companion to aesthetics / ed. by David E. Cooper ; advisory eds., Joseph Margolis and Crispin Sartwell. Oxford ; Cambridge, Mass. : Blackwell Reference, 1992. 465 p. : ill. **BB27**

An encyclopedic guide of more than 130 signed articles and essays on concepts and individuals significant to the study of philosophy of art, including literature. Although essentially concerned with Western studies, there are articles dealing with Chinese, Japanese, and Indian aesthetic philosophy. Bibliographies; cross-references; index.
    BH55.C65

A companion to epistemology / ed. by Jonathan Dancy and Ernest Sosa. Oxford ; Cambridge, Mass. : Blackwell Reference, 1992. 541 p. : ill.   **BB28**

A substantial guide to theories, concepts, and individuals concerned with the study and theory of knowledge. Comprised of alphabetically arranged articles by contributors from Australia, Canada, Israel, South Africa, the U.K., and the U.S. Although intended to appeal to a broad readership, it is geared toward undergraduate and graduate students as well as professional philosophers. Each article concludes with a bibliography. Cross-references; subject index.   BD161.C637

Dictionary of the history of ideas : studies of selected pivotal ideas / Philip P. Wiener, ed. in chief. N.Y. : Scribner, [1973–74]. 5 v.   **BB29**

Articles of substantial length, covering a wide range of topics in intellectual history, have been contributed by an international roster of scholars. Emphasizes interdisciplinary, cross-cultural relations, to help "establish some sense of unity of human thought and its cultural manifestation in a world of ever-increasing specialization and alienation."—*Pref.*

As set forth in the "Analytical table of contents," the areas forming the basic framework for the selected topics are: (1) the history of ideas about the external order of nature studied by the physical and biological sciences, ideas also present in common usage, imaginative literature, myths about nature, metaphysical speculation; (2) the history of ideas about human nature in anthropology, psychology, religion, and philosophy as well as in literature and common sense; (3) the history of ideas in literature and the arts in aesthetic theory and literary criticism; (4) the history of ideas about or attitudes to history, historiography, and historical criticism; (5) the historical development of economic, legal, and political ideas and institutions, ideologies, and movements; (6) the history of religious and philosophical ideas; and (7) the history of formal mathematical, logical, linguistic, and methodological ideas.

Articles appear in alphabetical sequence; bibliographies are included; and a series of *see also* references at the end of each article serves to link related topics. Vol. 5 is a separate index volume (published after the appearance of the main set) that greatly facilitates use of the work. CB5.D52

Enciclopedia filosofica. 2. ed. interamente rielaborata. [Firenze] : Sansoni, [1968–69]. 6 v. : ill. **BB30**
At head of title: Centro di Studi Filosofici di Gallarate.
1st ed., 1957, in 4 v.
A scholarly encyclopedia with signed articles and bibliographies. Treats philosophical concepts and schools and relevant matters in literature, science, law, etc. Includes many biographical articles. The 2d ed. is a complete revision: bibliographies have been updated, numerous new entries appear, and many entries have been revised or expanded. Vol. 6 includes three main indexes: (1) classified by theoretical concept; (2) classified by historical development; and (3) an analytical index of terms and personal names referred to in the text but not used as entries. B44.E52

The encyclopedia of Eastern philosophy and religion : Buddhism, Hinduism, Taoism, Zen / Ingrid Fischer-Schreiber [et al.] ; editors, Stephan Schuhmacher, Gert Woerner. Boston : Shambhala, 1989. 468 p. : ill. **BB31**
For annotation, *see* BC57. BL1005.L4813

The encyclopedia of ethics / Lawrence G. Becker, ed. ; Charlotte B. Becker, co-editor. N.Y. : Garland, 1992. 2 v. (1462 p.). (Garland reference library of the humanities, v. 925). **BB32**
Contains 435 signed articles by 267 distinguished academic philosophers, covering a wide variety of ethical concepts (e.g., theories of the good) as well as ethical questions raised by contemporary social issues (capital punishment). Substantial survey articles describe both Eastern and Western ethical traditions as well as specialized areas such as environmental ethics. Includes a number of biographies. Each article contains a bibliography and references to related articles. Subject index; index of authors or editors cited in the bibliographies. BJ63.E55

Encyclopedia of Indian philosophies / Ram Shankar Bhattacharya ... [et al.]. [Princeton, N.J.] : Princeton Univ. Pr., 1977–89. v. 1–5. **BB33**
Contents: v. 1, Bibliography, comp. by Karl H. Potter (rev. ed., 1983; *see* BB18; [v. 2], Indian metaphysics and epistemology, ed. by Karl H. Potter; [v. 3], Advaita Vedānta up to Samkara and his pupils, ed. by Karl H. Potter; v. 4, Sāmkhya : a dualist tradition in Indian philosophy, ed. by Gerald James Larson and Ram Shankar Bhattacharya; v. 5, The philosophy of the grammarians, ed. by Harold G. Coward and K. Kunjunni Raja.
The encyclopedia draws on an international team of scholars in an "attempt to provide a definitive account of current knowledge about each of the systems of classical Indian philosophy."—*Pref., v. 1.* B131.E5

Encyclopedia of philosophy / Paul Edwards, ed. in chief. N.Y. : Macmillan, [1967]. 8 v. **BB34**
An important work, broader in scope than James Mark Baldwin's *Dictionary of philosophy and psychology* (BB26) and with articles generally more substantial in length. Designed "to cover the whole of philosophy as well as many of the points of contact between philosophy and other disciplines. The *Encyclopedia* treats Eastern and Western philosophy; it deals with ancient, medieval, and modern philosophy; and it discusses the theories of mathematicians, physicists, biologists, sociologists, psychologists, moral reformers, and religious thinkers where these have had an impact on philosophy."—*Introd.* Nearly 1,500 signed articles—about 900 of them on individual philosophers—were contributed by an international group of some 500 scholars. The final volume includes an index. B41.E5

Encyclopédie philosophique universelle / publié sous la direction d'André Jacob. Paris : Presses universitaires de France, 1989–1992. v. 1–3 : ill. **BB35**
Contents: v. 1, L'universe philosophique (ed. André Jacob); v. 2 (in 2 v.), Les notions philosophique (ed. Sylvain Auroux); v. 3, Les oeuvres philosophiques dictionnaire (ed. Jean-Francois Mattein); t. 1, Philosohie occidentale: IIIe millenaire av. J.-C.—1889; t. 2, Philosophie occidentale: 1889–1990; Pensees asiatiques; Conceptualisation des societes traditionelles; Repertoires, index, tables.
A comprehensive work with emphasis on current scholarship. In v. 1, chapters by leading scholars, such as Paul Ricoeur and Jacques Ellul, discuss the major themes and problems of philosophical thought, with numerous illustrations, charts, bibliographic references, and concept/theme and personal name indexes. Vol. 2 contains signed essays on concepts and terms; "Pensées asiatiques" are listed alphabetically by transliterated term with some Chinese and other vernacular characters and the French translation. "Conceptualizations" includes topics from African, South American, and other cultures. The tables list terms from all traditions under broad subjects, such as moral or political philosophy. B51.E52

Handbook of philosophical logic / ed. by D. Gabbay and F. Guenther. Dordrecht ; Boston : D. Reidel ; Higngham, Mass. : distr. by Kluwer Academic Publ., 1983–89. 4 v. **BB36**
Contents: v. 1, Elements of classical logic; v. 2, Extensions of classical logic; v. 3, Alternatives in classical logic; v. 4, Topics in the philosophy of language.
Designed to provide a systematic overview of the essential areas of philosophical logic. Lengthy articles include bibliographies. Although each volume is independent of the other, v. 1 provides background for the material in the other volumes. BC6.H36

Dictionaries

Angeles, Peter Adam. The HarperCollins dictionary of philosophy. 2nd ed. N.Y. : HarperPerennial, c1992. 342 p. **BB37**
1st ed., 1981, had title: Dictionary of philosophy.
This 2nd ed. is intended for students, general readers, and teachers. Contains more than 100 biographical entries about major philosophers. Many cross-references to other relevant articles.

Austeda, Franz. Lexikon der Philosophie. [6. erw. Aufl.]. Wien : Hollinek, 1989. 409 p. **BB38**
1st ed., 1954; 5th ed., 1979. Some previous editions entitled *Wörterbuch der Philosophie.*
The biographical section includes philosophers from earliest times to the present. Includes cross-references. B43.A86

Grimes, John A. A concise dictionary of Indian philosophy : Sanskrit terms defined in English. Albany, N.Y. : State Univ. of New York Pr., c1989. 440 p. **BB39**
An "introduction to the basic terms found in the major schools of Indian philosophy."—*Pref.* Headwords, printed in Sanskrit and in transliteration, are listed in alphabetical order with literal translations and, when necessary, further explanations of usage in various philosophical systems or schools. Includes transliteration and pronunciation guides, an index of major terms, and a useful series of charts depicting the relationships of works, concepts, and categories of individual schools.

§ A similar title, B. N. Singh's *Dictionary of Indian philosophical concepts* (Varanasi : Asha Prakashan, 1988. 340 p.), includes bibliographic citations to source texts along with the definitions.
                                                                    B131.G67

Historisches Wörterbuch der Philosophie / unter Mitwirkung von mehr als 700 Fachgelehrten in Verbindung mit Günther Bien … [et al.] ; hrsg. von Joachim Ritter. Völlig neubearbeitete Ausg. des Wörterbuchs der philosophischen Begriffe von Rudolf Eisler. Basel : Schwabe, 1971–1992. v. 1–8. (In progress).   **BB40**
    Vols. 4–8 ed. by J. Ritter and K. Gründer.
    Contents: v. 1–8, A–Sc. Vol. 8 contains errata for v. 1–8.
    A complete revision of Rudolf Eisler's *Wörterbuch der philosophischen Begriffe* (4th ed., 1927–30). Some entries, notably in psychology, have been dropped while others have been expanded. Overall there is much new material written by more than 1,200 scholars.
                                                                    B43.R59

Lalande, André. Vocabulaire technique et critique de la philosophie. 13ᵉ éd. Paris : Presses Universitaires, 1980. 1323 p.
                                                                    BB41
    1st ed., 1926.
    A standard work that first appeared in parts in *Bulletin* of the Société Française de Philosophie, 1902–23. In addition to definitions of terms, examples of use by philosophers, and bibliographic notes, etymologies are usually given, as are equivalents in German, English, and Italian.
                                                                    B42.L3

Peters, Francis Edwards. Greek philosophical terms : a historical lexicon. N.Y. : New York Univ. Pr., 1967. 234 p.
                                                                    BB42
    Intended for the "intermediate student" of Greek philosophy rather than for the beginner or the advanced scholar. Cross-references are used liberally throughout, as are textual citations to the philosophers. English-Greek index.
                                                                    B49.P4

Wörterbuch der philosophischen Begriffe / Johannes Hoffmeister. 2. Aufl. Hamburg : Felix Meiner, 1955. 687 p. (Die Philosophische Bibliothek, Bd. 225).   **BB43**
    1st ed., 1944.
    Based on the work originally edited by Friedrich Kirchner and Carl Michaelis (6th ed., 1911).
    Concise articles on philosophical terms and concepts with some bibliography. Does not include biography.   B43.H6

Directories

Directory of American philosophers. Ed. 1 (1962/63)– . Bowling Green, Ohio : Philosophy Documentation Center, Bowling Green Univ., 1962– . Biennial.   **BB44**
    Publisher varies.
    U.S. and Canadian universities appear in separate sections. Listing is alphabetical by state or province, then by institution, with a listing of philosophy faculty members at each institution. Also includes sections for societies, institutes, publishers, and journals in the field. Indexes of philosophers, institutions, pubishers, etc.   B935.D5

International directory of philosophy and philosophers. Ed. 1 (1966)– . Bowling Green, Ohio : Philosophy Documentation Center, Bowling Green Univ., 1966– . Irregular. **BB45**
    Publisher varies.
    1st ed., published under auspices of the International Institute of Philosophy with the aid of Unesco, had an added title page in French, introductory matter in English and French, and text in English or French. Beginning with 2nd ed. (1972/73) issued as a companion volume to *Directory of American philosophers* (BB44).
    Pt. 1 is a list of international philosophical organizations; pt. 2, arranged by country or territory, lists colleges and universities (with names of members of the philosophy staffs), institutes and research

centers, philosophical associations and societies, philosophy journals, and publishers who specialize to some degree in philosophical works. Indexed.   B35.I55

History

Bréhier, Émile. Histoire de la philosophie … . 9ᵉ éd. rev. et bibliographie mise à jour par Pierre-Maxime Schuhl. Paris : Presses Universitaires de France, 1981–91. [v. 1–3]. (In progress).   **BB46**
    Originally published 1926–32 (2 v. in 7) with the following contents: t. 1, L'antiquité et le moyen âge: I. Période hellénique. II. Période hellénistique et romaine. III. Moyen âge et renaissance; t. 2, La philosophie moderne: I. Le dix-septième siècle. II. Le dix-huitième siècle. III. Le XIXᵉ siècle—Période des systèmes (1800–1850); IV. Le XIXᵉ siècle aprés 1850. Le XXᵉ siècle; Fascicule supplémentaire (Paris, Alcan, 1938–49. 2v.).
    The 9th ed. remains incomplete. "Éd. revue et mise à jour" have been publ. (1981, 1987, 1991) in 3 v. with the following contents: v. 1, Antiquité et Moyen-âge; v. 2, 17ᵉ–18ᵉ siècles; v. 3, 19ᵉ–20ᵉ siècles.
    A standard history with selective bibliographies.
    An English translation has appeared as *The history of philosophy*, tr. by Joseph Thomas. (Chicago : Univ. of Chicago Pr., [1963–69]. 7 v.).   B77.B7212

A history of women philosophers / ed. by Mary Ellen Waithe. Dordrecht, Netherlands ; Boston : Kluver Academic Publ., 1987–1994. 4 v. : ill.   **BB47**
    Contents: v. 1, Ancient women philosophers, 600 B.C.–500 A.D.; v. 2, Medieval, Renaissance, and Enlightenment women philosophers, A.D. 500–1600; v. 3, Modern women philosophers, 1600–1900; v. 4, Contemporary women philosophers, 1900–today.
    The set evolved from the Project on the History of Women in Philosophy; *see* the introduction in v. 1 for more information, including criteria for inclusion and research methods.
    Scholarly essays on individual philosophers provide biographical information, discussion of works, and philosophical positions. Each volume begins with an overview and provides a comprehensive bibliography that includes the works cited in each essay and additional works of interest. In addition, each volume includes a timeline of the philosophers included, showing chronological overlap with contemporary male philosophers.   B105.W6.H67

Kersey, Ethel M. Women philosophers : a bio-critical source book / Ethel M. Kersey ; Calvin O. Schrag, consulting ed. N.Y. : Greenwood, 1989. 230 p.   **BB48**
    Approximately 150 biographical sketches and articles on women who have "seriously thought or written in the traditional fields of philosophy, including metaphysics, ethics, aesthetics, and logic."—*Pref.* Entries contain primary and secondary bibliographies, and the lengthy introductory essay provides an overview of women in the history of philosophy and a general bibliography. The appendix consists of an alphabetical table of women, indicating their countries, dates, and disciplines. Personal name index.   B105.W6K47

Totok, Wilhelm. Handbuch der Geschichte der Philosophie : unter Mitarbeit von Helmut Schröer. Frankfurt am Main : V. Klostermann, 1984–90. 6 v.   **BB49**
    Contents: v.1, Altertum. Indische, chinesische, griechischrömische Philosophie. Helmut Schröer, ed.; v.2, Die Philosophie des Mittelalters, unter Mitarbeit von Hiltraut Helderich und Helmut Schröer; v.3, Renaissance, unter Mitarbeit von Erwin Schadel [et al.]; v.4, Frühe Neuzeit, 17. Jahrhundert, unter Mitarbeit von Erwin Schadel [et al.]; v. 5, Bibliographie 18. und 19. Jahrhundert, unter Mitarbeit von Horst-Dieter Finke [et al.]; v. 6, Bibliographie 20. Jahrhundert, unter Mitarbeit von Horst-Dieter Finke [et al.].
    An extensive bibliographic listing, international in scope. Vol. 1 lists publications for the years 1920–60 in subject arrangement with author index; v.2 includes materials published 1920–66; v.3, 1920–75; v.4, 1920–78.   B82.T6

BY PERIOD

General

Ueberweg, Friedrich. Grundriss der Geschichte der Philosophie. 11.–12. Aufl. / hrsg. von Karl Praechter. Berlin : Mittler, 1923–28. 5 v. **BB50**
Repr.: Basel : B. Schwabe, 1957.
Each volume also has special title page.
1st ed., 1862–66 in 3 v.
Contents: v.1, Die Philosophie des Altertums. 12. Aufl., hrsg. von Karl Praechter; v.2, Die patristische und scholastische Philosophie. 11. Aufl., hrsg. von Bernhard Geyer; v.3, Die Philosophie der Neuzeit bis zum Ende des 18. Jahrhunderts. 12. Aufl., hrsg. von Max Frischeisen-Köhler und Willy Moog; v.4, Die deutsche Philosophie des neunzehnten Jahrhunderts und der Gegenwart. 12. Aufl., hrsg. von Traugott K. Oesterreich; v.5, Die Philosophie des Auslands vom Beginn des 19. Jahrhunderts bis auf die Gegenwart. 12. Aufl., hrsg. von Traugott K. Oesterreich.
An important history of philosophy particularly useful for its full bibliographies, which include periodicals and monographs, and for its biographical information. Covers ancient, patristic and scholastic, and modern philosophy. The English translation, *History of philosophy* (N.Y. : Scribner's, 1892. 2 v.) is from the 4th German ed. and does not include extensive bibliographies.
A new edition is in progress: *Grundriss der Geschichte der Philosophie*, begr. von Friedrich Ueberweg. (Völlig neubearbeite Ausgabe. Basel : Schwabe, 1983–).
Contents: Die Philosophie der Antike, hrsg. von Hellmut Flashar. Bd. 3, Ältere Akademie. Aristoteles. Peripatos. Die Philosophie des 17. Jahrhunderts, hrsg. von Jean-Pierre Schobinger. Bd. 3, England (2 v.). B82.U19

Ancient

Aristotle dictionary / ed. by Thomas P. Kiernan. N.Y. : Philosophical Lib., 1962. 524 p. **BB51**
"References are made to the appropriate *loci* of the quotations ... in the Bekker edition of the Greek published in 1831."—*p.162*.
Introduction by Thedore E. James, p. 7–163.
Arranged by subject word in English, with exact references to sources. PA3926.Z8K53

Ast, Friedrich. Lexicon Platonicum : sive, Vocum Platonicarum index. Lipsiae : Weidmann, 1835–38. 3 v. **BB52**
Repr.: N.Y. : B. Franklin, 1969.
Josef Zürcher's *Lexicon academicum* (Paderborn : Verlag F. Schöningh, 1954. 36 p.) serves as a supplementary dictionary of Greek proper names. B351.A72

Bonitz, Hermann. Index Aristotelicus. Berlin : Reimer, 1870. 878 p. **BB53**
Repr.: Graz : Akademische Druck– und Verlagsanstalt, 1955.
Forms part of v. 5 of the Bekker edition of Aristotle (Berlin, 1831–70). PA3926.Z8B6

Dictionnaire des philosophes antiques / publié sous la direction de Richard Goulet. Paris : Éditions du Centre national de la recherche scientifique, 1989–94. v. 1–2 : ill. (some col.). (In progress). **BB54**
Contents: v. 1–2, Abam(m)on–Dyscolius.
A comprehensive biographical encyclopedia of philosophers from the beginnings until about the 6th century CE. Signed articles range in length from a paragraph to more than 100 pages (e.g., Aristotle). Most include dates, citations to articles in Pauly-Wissowa (DA104), a biographical sketch with numerous citations to both ancient and modern sources, a list of works with standard editions and translations and tex-

tual histories, and a discussion of the subject's philosophy and influence. An appendix to v. 1, "Académie topographie et archéologie," p. 692–787, provides an overview of the situation, history, religious significance, and importance of the Academy, with several maps and charts. Name, Greek word, and subject indexes in each volume.
B112.D53

McKirahan, Richard D. Plato and Socrates : a comprehensive bibliography, 1958–1973. N.Y. : Garland, 1978. 592 p. (Garland reference library of the humanities, v.78). **BB55**
Supplements the bibliography "Plato (1950–1957)" by H. F. Cherniss which appeared in *Lustrum* 4–5 (1959–60). Separate sections for Plato and Socrates, each topically subdivided. About 4,600 items. Author index. Z8696.M34

Navia, Luis E. Socrates : an annotated bibliography / Luis E. Navia, Ellen L. Katz. N.Y. : Garland, 1988. 536 p. : ill. (Garland reference library of the humanities, vol. 844). **BB56**
Although by no means as comprehensive as R.D. McKirahan's *Plato and Socrates* (BB55), this volume contains almost 2,000 annotated citations to primary and secondary books, articles, and dissertations on the life, philosophy, and influence of Socrates. Arranged alphabetically within broad subject divisions, including a section on the portrayal of Socrates in fiction, poetry, and drama. Author index.
Z8824.34.N38

Organ, Troy Wilson. An index to Aristotle in English translation. Princeton, N.J. : Princeton Univ. Pr., 1949. 181 p. **BB57**
Repr.: N.Y. : Gordian Pr., 1966.
Based on the translation by W. D. Ross and J. A. Smith (Oxford : Univ. Pr., 1908–31. 11 v.). Does not include *Fragments* or *Constitution of Athens*. B401.O7

Paquet, Léonce. Les présocratiques : bibliographie analytique, 1879–1980 / par L. Paquet, M. Roussel, Y. Lafrance. Montréal : Éditions Bellarmin, 1988–1989. 2 v. **BB58**
Contents: v. 1, Des Milésiens à Héraclite; v. 2, D'Alcméon aux auteurs de la Collection hippocratique.
This comprehensive work lists, alphabetically by author, with annotations, books, dissertations, journal articles, and conference proceedings in all languages within a classified arrangement with sections devoted to general studies, specific themes, and individual schools or philosophers. Index of modern authors. Z7129.G7P36

Yale University. Library. The Plato manuscripts : a new index / prep. by the Plato Microfilm Project of the Yale University Library under the direction of Robert S. Brumbaugh and Rulon Wells. New Haven : Yale Univ. Pr., 1968. 163 p. **BB59**
"This *Index*, based on a new cataloguing from microfilm of the extant pre-1500 manuscripts containing Plato's works in whole or part, is a necessary first step toward the complete reediting of a new edition of Plato's works."—*Introd*. Manuscripts are listed by library and by dialogue. Z6616.P57Y35

Medieval

Andresen, Carl. Bibliographia Augustiniana. 2., völlig neubearb. Aufl. Darmstadt : Wissenschaftliche Buchgesellschaft, 1973. 317 p. **BB60**
Preface in German and Latin. Includes material by and about St. Augustine. Classified arrangement; indexed. Z8047.7.A53

Bourke, Vernon J. Thomistic bibliography, 1920–1940. St. Louis : The Modern Schoolman, 1945. 312 p. **BB61**
Supplements Pierre Félix Mandonnet and J. Destrez's *Bibliographie thomiste* (BB66).
Lists more than 6,660 books and periodical articles in various languages. Classified arrangement with indexes. Z8870.B67

Deferrari, Roy Joseph. A complete index of the Summa theologica of St. Thomas Aquinas / by Roy J. Deferrari and Sister M. Inviolata Barry. [Baltimore? : Catholic Univ. of America Pr., 1956]. 386 p.   **BB62**
    An *index verborum*, prepared in conjunction with the authors' *Lexicon of St. Thomas Aquinas* (BB63).   BX1749.T6D4

——————— A lexicon of St. Thomas Aquinas based on the Summa theologica and selected passages of his other works / by Roy J. Deferrari and Sister M. Inviolata Barry, with the technical collaboration of Ignatius McGuiness. [Wash. : Catholic Univ. of America Pr., 1948–53]. 1185 p.   **BB63**
    Issued in 5 fascicles.
    Arranged by Latin words, with their different English meanings and with Latin quotations from the *Summa theologica* and indications of exact sources.   B765.T54D38

Index Thomisticus : Sancti Thomae Aquinatis operum omnium indices et concordantiae in quibus verborum omnium et singulorum formae et lemmata cum suis frequentiis et contextibus variis modis referuntur quaeque auspice Paulo VI Summo Pontifice consociata plurium opera atque electronico IBM automato usus digessit Robertus Busa. Stuttgart-Bad Cannstatt : Frommann-Holzboog, 1974–80. 49 v.   **BB64**
    Provides for the scholar a sophisticated computer-produced linguistic analysis of 118 writings of St. Thomas Aquinas and of 61 other works associated with the *corpus thomisticum*, documenting the vocabulary and usage of 179 Latin works from the 9th to the 16th century. Introductory matter in Latin. Main set in three parts: Sectio I, Indices (i.e., tables of all works included, with specifying codes), 10 v.; Sectio II, Concordantiae operum Thomisticorum, 31 v.; Sectio III, Concordantiae operum aliorum auctorum, 8 v.
    Sancti Thomae Aquinatis Opera omnia : ut sunt in Indice Thomistico, additis 61 scriptis ex aliis medii aevi auctoribus curante Roberto Busa (1980. 7 v.). Half title: Indicis Thomistici supplementum. Contains the text of all works analyzed.
    § A further example of computer applications in the field of philosophy and religion is provided by *A concordance to the works of St. Anselm*, ed. by G. R. Evans (Millwood, N.Y. : Kraus Internat. Publ., 1984. 4 v.).   B765.T53Z85

Institut des Études Augustiniennes. Fichier augustinien. Boston : G. K. Hall, 1972. 2 pts. in 4 v.   **BB65**
    Added title page in English; preface in French and English.
    Contents: [pt. I] v. 1–2, Fichier-auteurs; [pt. II] v. 1–2, Fichier-matières.
    Aims to list both primary works and "all published studies on Augustine and related subjects."—*Pref.* In the author section writings by Augustine are followed by an alphabetically arranged author list of works about him. Studies include books, parts of books, and articles. In the subject section the secondary works are rearranged in a topical scheme; here the table of contents showing the detailed breakdown must serve as an index. Covers through 1970.
    ——————. —————— *Supplement 1* (Boston : G. K. Hall, 1981. 516 p.).
    Extends coverage through 1978, adding some older works, corrections and improvements.
    § Terry L. Miethe's *Augustinian bibliography, 1970–1980 : with essays on the fundamentals of Augustinian scholarship* (Westport, Conn. : Greenwood, 1982. 218 p.) lists earlier bibliographies, works on the life of Augustine, and (in classed arrangement) Augustinian studies.

Mandonnet, Pierre Félix. Bibliographie thomiste / Pierre Félix Mandonnet, J. Destrez. 2. éd. rev. et completée par M. D. Chenu. Paris : J. Vrin, 1960. 119 p. (Bibliothèque thomiste, 1).   **BB66**
    1st ed., 1921.
    A classified bibliography of 2,283 books and articles published before 1921, the appendix to this edition adding only earlier works omitted from the original edition. Includes materials on the life, works, philosophy, theology and influence of Aquinas. Indexed.

    § Supplemented by Vernon J. Bourke, *Thomistic bibliography, 1920–1940* (BB61).   Z8870.M27

Medieval philosophers / ed. by Jeremiah Hackett. Detroit : Gale, c1992. 465 p. : ill. (Dictionary of literary biography, v. 115).   **BB67**
    Contains signed biographical articles on representative thinkers of the Christian, Islamic, and Jewish traditions in Western philosophy, 400–1500. Includes bibliographies of philosophers' works and of secondary sources. Aimed at students to graduate level.   B721.M45

Miethe, Terry L. Thomistic bibliography, 1940–1978 / by Terry L. Miethe and Vernon J. Bourke. Westport, Conn. : Greenwood, [1980]. 318 p.   **BB68**
    Continues Bourke's *Thomistic bibliography, 1920-1940* (BB61). Lists nearly 4,100 items in classed arrangement, with personal name index. Detailed table of contents, but no subject index.   Z8870.M53

Renaissance

The Cambridge history of Renaissance philosophy / gen. ed., Charles B. Schmitt ; editors, Quentin Skinner, Eckhard Kessler ; associate ed., Jill Kraye. Cambridge [Eng.] ; N.Y. : Cambridge Univ. Pr., 1988. 968 p.   **BB69**
    Discusses the background and advancement of Renaissance philosophy, metaphysics, psychology, and related fields. Chapters by contributing scholars are organized in three parts: (1), The intellectual context, which includes sections on humanism, manuscripts, and printing; (2), Philosophy and its parts, the main body of text; and (3), appendixes on ancient texts and a history of textbooks, biobibliographies of Renaissance philosophers, and lengthy bibliographies of primary and secondary literature. Name and subject indexes.   B775.C25

Riedl, John Orth. Catalogue of Renaissance philosophers (1350–1650) / comp. by Robert A. Baker ... [et al.] under the direction of John O. Riedl. Milwaukee : Marquette Univ. Pr., 1940. 179 p.   **BB70**
    Arranged by schools with alphabetical author index. Gives biographical notes and bibliographies of writings.   Z7125.R54

Modern

Attig, John C. The works of John Locke : a comprehensive bibliography from the seventeenth century to the present. Westport, Conn. : Greenwood, 1985. 185 p. (Bibliographies and indexes in philosophy, no. 1).   **BB71**
    Lists all the editions and translations of Locke's works, arranged chronologically. Includes biographical notes on the controversial context of each work and selected references to early responses to them. Name and title indexes.   Z8513.45.A87

Chappell, V. C. Twenty-five years of Descartes scholarship, 1960–1984 : a bibliography / Vere Chappell and Willis Doney, eds. N.Y. : Garland, 1987. 183 p.   **BB72**
    Alphabetical list by author of 2,500 books and articles. Includes book reviews and review articles on books listed. Subject index.
    Continues Gregor Sebba, *Bibliographia Cartesiana* (BB76).   Z8277.7.C48

Hall, Roland. Fifty years of Hume scholarship : a bibliographical guide. Edinburgh : Univ. Pr., 1978. 150 p.   **BB73**
    Supersedes an earlier Hume bibliography by Hall (1971). Lists Hume literature from 1925 to 1976, together with a list of the principal writings on Hume for the 1900–1924 period. Chronological arrangement with author, language, and subject indexes.
                    Z8427.3.H34

Jessop, Thomas Edmund. A bibliography of David Hume and of Scottish philosophy from Francis Hutcheson to Lord Balfour. London : A. Brown, 1938. 201 p.   **BB74**

Repr.: N.Y. : Russell and Russell, 1966; N.Y. : Garland, 1983.

Lists works by and about Hume, p. 5–71; other Scottish philosophers, p. 75–189.   Z8427.3.J58

Leibniz-Bibliographie : die Literatur über Leibniz bis 1980 / Begründet von Kurt Müller, hrsg. von Albert Heinekamp. 2. neu bearb. Aufl. Frankfurt am Main : Vittorio Klostermann GmbH, 1984. 742 p. (Veröffentlichungen des Leibniz-Archivs, 10).   **BB75**

1st ed., 1967.

A comprehensive bibliography of writings about Leibniz.

§ The writings of Leibniz are listed in Emile Ravier's *Bibliographie des oeuvres de Leibniz* (Paris : Alcan, 1937. 703 p. Repr.: Hildesheim : Olms, 1966). Dissertations are listed in Gernot U. Gabel's *Leibniz : eine Bibliographie europäischer und nordamerikanischer Hochschulschriften 1875–1975* (Köln : Gemini, 1983. 46 p. [Bibliographien zur Philosophie, 7]).   Z8496.18.H44

Sebba, Gregor. Bibliographia Cartesiana : a critical guide to the Descartes literature, 1800–1960. The Hague : Nijhoff, 1964. 510 p. (International archives of the history of ideas, 5).   **BB76**

Contents: pt. 1, Introduction to Descartes studies; pt. 2, Alphabetical bibliography, 1800–1960; pt. 3, Indices: systematic and analytical.

Lists books and periodical articles in many languages. Supersedes the author's *Descartes and his philosophy: a bibliographical guide ... 1800–1958* (Athens, Ga., 1959. 1 v.).   Z8227.7.S38

Yolton, Jean S. John Locke, a reference guide / Jean S. Yolton and John W. Yolton. Boston : G.K. Hall, c1985. 294 p.   **BB77**

Primarily a descriptive list of secondary works about Locke, 1689–1982. Arranged chronologically. Includes name and subject indexes.   Z8513.45.Y64

Nineteenth century

Reichert, Herbert William. International Nietzsche bibliography / comp. and ed. by Herbert W. Reichert, Karl Schlechta. Rev. and expanded. Chapel Hill : Univ. of North Carolina Pr., 1968. 162 p. (University of North Carolina. Studies in comparative literature, 45).   **BB78**

1st ed., 1960.

Lists more than 4,500 items—books and periodical articles—about Nietzsche. Arranged by language, then alphabetically by author within each language group. New listings since the 1960 edition are grouped mainly in a separate sequence (again by language of the article) at the end, items 4001–4566. A subject index has been added.   Z8628.N5R4

Steinhauer, Kurt. Hegel bibliography : background material on the international reception of Hegel within the context of the history of philosophy. Munich : K. G. Saur, 1980. 894 p.   **BB79**

Title also in German. Introductory and explanatory matter in English and German.

A bibliography of Hegel's own works is followed by a chronological listing of secondary works from the period 1802–1975. Keyword index.

§ A *Hegel-Lexikon* by Hermann Glockner (2. verb. Aufl. Stuttgart, F. Frommann, 1957. 2 v.) was published as part of Glockner's edition of Hegel's *Sämtliche Werke*.   Z8394.6.S83

Twentieth century

Frongia, Guido. Wittgenstein : a bibliographical guide / Guido Frongia and Brian McGuinness. Oxford ; Cambridge, Mass. : Basil Blackwell, 1990. 438 p.   **BB80**

Rev. and updated translation of: *Guida alla letteratura su Wittgenstein.*

Provides annotated bibliographic references to discussions of Wittgenstein's works in chronological order. Indexes include a proper name index and another of reviews of Wittgenstein's writings.   Z8979.4.F7613

Handbook of world philosophy : contemporary developments since 1945 / ed. by John R. Burr. Westport, Conn. : Greenwood, 1980. 641 p.   **BB81**

"The comprehensive object of this book is to provide an internationally representative sample since 1945 of the characters, directions, wealth, and varieties of the reflections and activities called 'philosophic' as described, interpreted, and evaluated by philosophers particularly knowledgeable about the region or country being discussed; to exhibit the increasingly international development of philosophy; and to point to future possibilities."—*Introd.* Twenty-eight essays by contributing scholars treat developments in an individual country, pair of countries, or broad geographic area. Essays are grouped in six sections (Western Europe, Australia, and Israel; Eastern Europe; The Americas; Africa and the Republic of South Africa; Islamic countries; Asia); each ends with a select bibliography of books and articles, and a list of journals. Appendixes: (1) Directory of philosophical associations; (2) Congresses and meetings. Indexed.   B804.A1H36

Sass, Hans-Martin. Martin Heidegger : a bibliography and glossary. Bowling Green, Ohio : Philosophy Documentation Center, Bowling Green State Univ., c1982. 513 p.   **BB82**

Lists Heidegger's works in chronological order, with translations. Secondary sources are arranged alphabetically by author. The glossary provides translations of 100 technical terms into seven languages.   Z8394.95.S282

Shanker, V. A. A Wittgenstein bibliography / ed. by V. A. and S. G. Shanker. London ; Wolfeboro, N.H. : Croom Helm, 1986. 361 p. : ports.   **BB83**

Lists more than 6,000 books, articles, critical notices, and book reviews, arranged alphabetically by author. Includes a bibliography of Wittgenstein's own works with translations, and a reprint of G. H. Wright's study, "The Wittgenstein papers." Subject and name indexes.   B3376.W564.L77

BC

Religion

In the field of religion, reference materials are very extensive. They include encyclopedias, dictionaries, directories, and bibliographies in English and other languages. Although a great number of publications are related to Christianity and its various denominations, good English-language reference sources for primal religions, Native American religions, new religious movements, Buddhism, Judaism, and other religions, are increasing.

Libraries should acquire materials according to need, but a basic working collection of reference sources in English might include: *Encyclopedia of religion* (BC58); the *New Catholic encyclopedia* (BC401); *Encyclopedia Judaica* (BC546); one or more versions of the Bible and concordances to them; the *Anchor Bible dictionary* (BC125); *Encyclopedia of American religions* (BC66); Burton Egbert Stevenson, *Home book of Bible quotations* (BC156); *World Christian encyclopedia* (BC233); *Yearbook of American and Canadian churches* (BC324); and whatever denominational yearbooks are needed.

Large libraries, and libraries specializing in religious materials, will need to add many of the more specialized general works and works on the various religions.

GENERAL WORKS

Guides

Adams, Charles J. A reader's guide to the great religions. 2nd ed. N.Y. : Free Pr., [1977]. 521 p.   **BC1**
1st ed., 1965.
A bibliographic guide to the history and traditions of the world's principal religions. Chapters by specialists on primitive religion, the ancient world, Mexico, Central and South America, Hinduism, Buddhism, Sikhs, Jainas, religions of China and Japan, Judaism, Christianity, Islam. Somewhat outdated, but still provides helpful guidance. Appendix: "The history of the history of religions," by C. H. Long. Author and subject indexes.   Z7833.A35

Kennedy, James R. Library research guide to religion and theology : illustrated search strategy and sources. 2nd ed., rev. Ann Arbor, Mich. : Pierian Pr., 1984. 60 p. : ill. (Library research guides series, no. 1).   **BC2**
1st ed., 1974.
A manual, principally for undergraduates, on methods of searching in religion and theology and on writing term papers. Includes information on the use of the card catalog, basic reference tools, computerized searching, choosing a research topic, evaluating sources.
BL41.K45

Wilson, John Frederick. Research guide to religious studies / John F. Wilson, Thomas P. Slavens. Chicago : Amer. Libr. Assoc., 1982. 192 p. (Sources of information in the humanities, v. 1).   **BC3**
In two parts: (1) Introduction to religious scholarship (a series of bibliographic essays on various aspects of the study of religion) and (2) Reference works (with general works grouped by type, followed by works on particular religions subdivided by type; all entries are annotated). Indexed.   BL41.W5

Bibliography

Barrow, John Graves. A bibliography of bibliographies in religion. [Ann Arbor, Mich. : Edwards Bros., 1955]. 489 p.
BC4
Based on the author's doctoral dissertation, Yale University, 1930.
A comprehensive work attempting "to bring together all separately published bibliographies in the field of religion" (*Pref.*), from the 15th century to the mid-20th century, and in many languages. Primarily Christian, but with a brief section on non-Christian religions. Brief annotations. Chronological listing under subject fields, with author and subject index. Locates copies in numerous American and European libraries.   Z7751.B33

Beit-Hallahmi, Benjamin. Psychoanalysis and religion : a bibliography. Norwood, Pa. : Norwood Eds., 1978. 182 p.
BC5
"This work covers those writers that follow psychoanalysis as formulated by Freud and his recognized disciples.... Works inspired by the theories of Jung and Adler were not included."—*Introd.* Emphasis is on works which have religion as their main topic; "most works included are attempts to relate religion and psychoanalysis in a meaningful way." Items are first listed in a classed arrangement, then citations are repeated in full in a so-called "Alphabetical listing and index."
Z7204.P8B43

Bibliographie zur alteuropäischen Religionsgeschichte. Berlin ; N.Y. : W. de Gruyter, 1967–85. v. 1–3. (Arbeiten zur Frühmittelalterforschung, Bd. 2, 5, 16). (In progress).   **BC6**
Subtitle varies.
Contents: v. 1, 1954–64, ed. by Peter Buchholz; v. 2, 1965–69, ed. by Jürgen Ahrendts; v. 3, 1970–75, ed. by Wilfried Flüchter, with the assistance of Thomas Wefelmeyer.
Contains 5,298 items in v. 1; 7,628 items in v. 2; 7,548 items in v. 3. Classed arrangement within geographical divisions. Author and subject indexes.   Z7757.F9B5

Blasi, Anthony J. The sociology of religion : an organizational bibliography / Anthony J. Blasi, Michael W. Cuneo. N.Y. : Garland, 1990. 459 p. (Garland library of sociology, vol. 18 ; Garland reference library of social science, v. 612.).   **BC7**
Entries for 3,207 books, articles, and dissertations published through 1988 (some 1989 imprints are included), arranged under names of religions, denominations, and small religious bodies and movements. Most have brief annotations. Materials are in Western languages, for the most part English, and largely reflect North American scholarship. Provides convenient access to a substantial body of research. Author and subject indexes.
§ The authors' *Issues in the sociology of religion: a bibliography* (N.Y. : Garland, 1986) is a companion volume covering literature published through 1984. Entries are listed under issues within three broad categories: Structure, Processes, and Disciplinary conceptualizations. Author and alphabetical contents index.
The amount of overlap between the two volumes is unclear; different arrangement and subject access within each volume make each useful.   Z7831.B54

Bowman, Mary Ann. Western mysticism : a guide to the basic works. Chicago : Amer. Libr. Assoc., 1978. 113 p. **BC8**

A selective bibliography "designed as a guide to the literature for reference librarians in academic, public, and church-related libraries; undergraduate students; and general readers."—*Pref.* Classed arrangement. Author-title and subject indexes. Z7819.B68

Capps, Donald. Psychology of religion : a guide to information sources. Detroit : Gale, [1976]. 352 p. (Philosophy and religion information guide series, v. 1). **BC9**
A section of general works in psychology of religion is followed by sections for each of the six "dimensions" of religion: the mythological, ritual, experiential, dispositional, social, and directional. Each section has four to eight subsections, and there are author, title, and subject indexes. Materials are largely limited to publications from the period 1950–74, with fuller coverage for 1960–74 inasmuch as William W. Meissner's *Annotated bibliography in religion and psychology* (N.Y. : Academy of Religion and Mental Health, 1961) is very comprehensive for the earlier years. Books and articles of special merit are annotated. Z7204.R4C36

Finson, Shelley Davis. Women and religion : a bibliographic guide to Christian feminist liberation theology. Toronto ; Buffalo : Univ. of Toronto Pr., c1991. 207 p. **BC10**
Lists materials published 1975–88 under topics such as Ethics, Homiletics, Ordination discussion, within broad categories, e.g., Bible, Ministry, Theology, Language. Within each topic materials are organized by type: monographs, articles, and other sources. Includes selected materials on women in Judaism, the Jewish/Christian feminist dialogue, and goddess/wicca. Important as the first comprehensive bibliography on the subject, but suffers from the lack of a subject index, and the separation of monographs from articles has questionable value. Author index.
§ For a comprehensive treatment of contemporary goddess worship, wicca, and related aspects of feminist spirituality, *see* Anne Carson, *Feminist spirituality and the feminine divine : an annotated bibliography* (Trumansburg, N.Y. : Crossing Pr., 1986) and her supplementary *Goddesses & wise women : the literature of feminist spirituality 1980–1992* (Freedom, Calif. : Crossing Pr., 1992). Each employs a topical arrangement and has a subject index. Z7963.R45F56

International bibliography of the history of religions = Bibliographie internationale de l'histoire des religions .... Leiden : Brill, 1954–79. 20 v. **BC11**
Under the supervision of C. J. Bleeker. Published in connection with the periodical *Numen*, with the support of Unesco and under the auspices of the International Council for Philosophy and Humanistic Studies, by the International Association for the History of Religions.
Lists books and articles published during the year on the history of the various religions of the world. Classified arrangement. No author indexes until 1958/59.
Continued by: *Science of religion* (BC48). Z7833.I53

Kepple, Robert J. Reference works for theological research / Robert J. Kepple and John R. Muether. 3rd ed. Lanham, Md. : University Pr. of America, 1991. 250 p. **BC12**
1st ed., 1978; 2nd ed., 1981 (supplements: 1981/82, 1983, 1986).
A guide for students, teachers, and librarians. General works are grouped by type in pt. 1; pt. 2 arranges specialized works under Subject area lists. This edition adds a significant number of new titles and editions and a chapter on computer-assisted research. Since they are covered in James McCabe's *Critical guide to Catholic reference books* (BC391), Roman Catholic works are included on a very selective basis. Index to authors, editors, titles, and alternative titles. Z7751.K46

Melton, J. Gordon. Religious information sources : a worldwide guide / by J. Gordon Melton and Michael A. Köszegi. N.Y. : Garland, 1992. 569 p. (Garland reference library of the humanities, v. 1593 ; Religious information systems series, v. 2). **BC13**
Lists 2,527 reference sources in a classified arrangement according to type of religious body, preceded by a section of general sources. A brief introduction covers nonprint resources. Treats all religions (more than half the entries are related to Christianity) and is particu-

lary useful for its coverage of Christian denominations, esoteric and occult groups, Eastern religions, and other non-Christian traditions. Within topical sections, items are listed by material type; most chapters include lists of research centers and professional organizations, those for Christian denominations include archival depositories.
§ James McCabe's *Critical guide to Catholic reference books* (BC391), Joseph A. Fitzmyer's *Introductory bibliography for the study of scripture* (BC110), and Robert Kepple and John R. Muether's *Reference works for theological research* (BC12) all provide annotations and will be more useful for Christianity and the Bible. Z7751.M45

O'Brien, Betty A. Religion index two : festschriften 1960–1969 / Betty A. O'Brien and Elmer J. O'Brien. [Philadelphia] : Amer. Theological Libr. Assoc., [1980]. 741 p. **BC14**
Includes 821 volumes of festschriften with subject and author indexing on the pattern of *Religion index two* (BC45). Z7751.O23

Politics and religion : a bibliography selected from the ATLA religion database / ed. by Paul D. Petersen ; Ruth F. Frazer, gen. ed. 2nd rev. ed. Chicago : Amer. Theological Libr. Assoc., 1984. 774 p. **BC15**
1st ed., 1981; rev. ed., 1982.
Presents citations selected from the ATLA (American Theological Library Association) religion database that treat religion and its relationship with politics (e.g., church and state, politics and Islam, Zionism). Includes articles, conference proceedings, and essays in collections, 1949–84, and book reviews for titles published in the 1970s and 1980s. Citations are divided into three sections (each alphabetically arranged): (1) Subject index, (2) Author index (some with annotations), (3) Book review index. Z7776.72.P6

Religious books, 1876–1982. N.Y. : Bowker, [1983]. 4 v. (4389 p.). **BC16**
Contents: v. 1–3 Subject index; v. 4, Author and title indexes.
The most comprehensive record of religious publishing in the U.S. Provides a subject approach, with author and title indexes, to more than "one hundred years of Library of Congress cataloging on religious titles published or distributed in the United States."—*Pref.* Lists about 130,000 items in core religious subjects and peripheral areas selected from the *American book publishing record* database which contains all U.S. *National union catalog* and MARC tape monographs, plus titles cataloged at Bowker. Cataloging information is complete, including LC and Dewey class marks, tracings, notes, etc., but variations reflect changes in Library of Congress cataloging practice; similarly, LC subject headings no longer in current use are included in the Subject index section. Z7751.R385

Shermis, Michael. Jewish-Christian relations : an annotated bibliography and resource guide. Bloomington : Indiana Univ. Pr., c1988. 291 p. **BC17**
A comprehensive listing of books, pamphlets, important articles, journals, congresses, media, syllabi, organizations, and speakers. Covers Jewish-Christian relations from antiquity through the present. Classified arrangement, with critical annotations. Indexes of subjects, names and organizations, titles, and media. Z6370.S53

Speaking in tongues : a guide to research on glossolalia / ed. by Watson E. Mills. Grand Rapids, Mich. : Eerdmans, c1986. 537 p. **BC18**
A historical introduction by the editor, and a survey of the literature and a bibliography, are followed by 25 reprinted essays, written 1954–80 by theologians, biblical scholars, historians, and psychologists. Indexes of names and of Bible references. Does not "advocate a personal or theological position" (*Pref.*), but rather explores "the available methods for evaluating" this phenomenon. BL54.S64

Turner, Harold W. Bibliography of new religious movements in primal societies. Boston : G. K. Hall, [1977–92]. 6 v. **BC19**
Contents: v. 1, Black Africa; v. 2, North America; v. 3, Oceania; v. 4, Europe and Asia; v. 5, Latin America; v. 6, The Caribbean.
"The religious movements with which this bibliographic series is concerned are defined as those which arise in the interaction of a pri-

mal society with another society where there is great disparity of power or sophistication."—*Introd.* About two-thirds of the materials are deposited in the Centre for New Religious Movements at the Selly Oak Colleges in Birmingham, England. Most of the collection is available for purchase on microfiche. Each volume has a geographical arrangement with an index of authors and sources. Brief descriptive annotations for most items.

Vol. 1 is designed to "correct, cumulate and update" Turner and Robert Cameron Mitchell's *Comprehensive bibliography of modern African religious movements* (Evanston, Ill. : Northwestern Univ. Pr., 1966) and its two supplements which appeared in the *Journal of religion in Africa* (1968 and 1970). While the new work is more selective and omits some material from the earlier lists, some Islamic movements are now included. Vol. 2 subdivides the U. S. by Indian tribe, cult or group and includes indexes of (1) films and records and tapes, and (2) main movements and Indian individuals. Vols. 3–6 each have a section for particular movements that escape the boundaries of the geographical arrangement. Each volume also includes an index of main movements and individuals.   Z7833.T87

Vande Kemp, Hendrika. Psychology and theology in Western thought, 1672–1965 : a historical and annotated bibliography / Hendrika Vande Kemp and H. Newton Malony. Millwood, N.Y. : Kraus Internat., [1984]. 367 p.   **BC20**

A historical bibliography on the integration of psychology and theology in Judeo-Christian thought, listing book-length publications, monographs, and pamphlets (but not periodical articles) providing "information on earlier, less accessible sources."—*Pref.* 1,047 entries. Name, institution, title, and subject indexes.   Z7204.R4V36

Wainwright, William J. Philosophy of religion : an annotated bibliography of twentieth-century writings in English. N.Y. : Garland, 1978. 776 p. (Garland reference library of the humanities, v. 111).   **BC21**

For annotation, *see* BB23.   Z7821.W34

Current

Religious & inspirational books & serials in print. 1985– . N.Y. : Bowker, c1985– . Biennial.   **BC22**

Continues *Religious books and serials in print* (N.Y. : Bowker, 1978–1982/83), but excludes its helpful "Sacred works index" of in-print editions of the Bible and sacred books of other religions.

Covers all areas of religion, including devotional and self-help literature.   Z7751.R387

Periodicals

Cornish, Graham P. Religious periodicals directory. Santa Barbara, Calif. : ABC-Clio, c1986. 330 p.   **BC23**

Provides bibliographic information, contents notes, and indexing sources for 1,763 journals in religion/theology and many related fields. Arranged by six geographic regions, by country of publication within each region, and alphabetically by title within each country. Title and subject/geographic indexes.

§ *See also* Eugene C. Fieg, *Religion journals and serials : an analytical guide* (N.Y. : Greenwood, 1988. 218 p.) for similar information on 328 English-language journals.   Z7753.C75

Lippy, Charles H. Religious periodicals of the United States : academic and scholarly journals. Westport, Conn. : Greenwood, 1986. 607 p.   **BC24**

Essays by 50 specialists profile more than 100 academic and scholarly journals representative of various religious perspectives and ecclesiastical bodies. Essays, arranged alphabetically by journal title, are followed by endnotes, information sources, and publication history for the journal. Appendixes list journals chronologically by date of first publication and by sponsoring organization or religious orientation. Index of names, titles, and subjects. Serves as a survey of religious publishing in the U.S.   PN4888.R4L5

Schwertner, Siegfried M. IATG = Internationales Abkürzungsverzeichnis für Theologie und Grenzgebiete : Zeitschriften, Serien, Lexika, Quellenwerke mit bibliographischen Angaben = International glossary of abbreviations for theology and related subjects : periodicals, series, encyclopedias, sources with bibliographical notes. 2., uberarbeitete und erw. Aufl. Berlin ; N.Y. : W. de Gruyter, 1992. 488 p.   **BC25**

1st ed., 1974.

Title also in French, Italian and Spanish. Introduction in German, English, French, Italian and Spanish.

Also known as *IATG2.*

Greatly enlarged, the new edition of this very useful work lists abbreviations for about 14,000 periodicals, serials, dictionaries, and other source works. In two main sections: (1) by abbreviation, with full title; and (2) by full title, with abbreviation and bibliographical notes. The sections are preceded by various lists: Biblical books; Sources and versions of the Bible; Deuterocanonical books; Qumran; and Rabbinic texts.

Reprinted, with minor variations, in *Theologische Realenzyklopädie* (BC69).   Z6945.A2S35

Dissertations

Council on Graduate Studies in Religion. Doctoral dissertations in the field of religion, 1940–1952 : their titles, location, fields, and short précis of contents. [N.Y.] : Columbia Univ. Pr. for the Council, [1954]. 194 p.   **BC26**

Published as a supplement to *Review of religion,* v.18.

Title varies: 1964–77 called *Dissertation title index.*

The main work is an alphabetical list by author of 425 dissertations with brief abstracts. The supplements are annual author lists only; most include a list of dissertations in progress. Classified lists now appear in the Council of Societies for the Study of Religion's quarterly, *Religious studies review.*

————. ————. Supplement. 1952–77. Annual.   Z7751.C7

By country or region

North America

Burr, Nelson Rollin. A critical bibliography of religion in America. Princeton, N.J. : Princeton Univ. Pr., 1961. 2 v. (Princeton studies in American civilization, no. 5).   **BC27**

Also publ. as v. 4 of the set, *Religion in American life,* ed. by James Ward Smith and A. Leland Jamison (Princeton, N.J. : Princeton Univ. Pr., 1961–).

A very comprehensive bibliography in classified arrangement with running commentary. Main divisions: pt. 1, Bibliographical guides, general surveys and histories; pt. 2, Evolution of American religion; pt. 3, Religion and society; pt. 4, Religion in the arts and literature; pt. 5, Intellectual history, theology, philosophy, and science. Tables of contents; author index, but no subject index.

§ The author's *Religion in American life* (N.Y. : Appleton-Century-Crofts, 1971. 171 p.) is a selective bibliography intended "for graduate and advanced undergraduate students" *(Pref.)* of American civilization. Emphasis is on 20th-century research and on the sociology of religion.

Choquette, Diane. New religious movements in the United States and Canada : a critical assessment and annotated bibliography. Westport, Conn. : Greenwood, 1985. 235 p. (Bibliographies and indexes in religious studies, no. 5).   **BC28**

An annotated, classified bibliography of monographic and serial literature, dissertations, and unpublished papers documenting the new religious and human potential movements in North America from the 1960s through 1983. Author/title and subject indexes.   Z7834.U6C46

Lippy, Charles H. Bibliography of religion in the South. Macon, Ga. : Mercer Univ. Pr., c1985. 498 p.   **BC29**
A comprehensive work, identifying and critically appraising scholarly secondary literature, mostly published since 1960. Includes articles, monographs, dissertations, theses. Arranged in chapters dealing with religious groups and other topics such as art and literature; each chapter opens with a commentary on the literature, followed by a classified bibliography. Detailed table of contents, but no index.
Z7778.S59L56

Religion and society in North America : an annotated bibliography / Robert deV. Brunkow, ed. Santa Barbara, Calif. : ABC-Clio, [1983]. 515 p. (Clio bibliography series, 12).
BC30
Cites 4,304 periodical articles, with abstracts, relating to "the history of religion in the United States and Canada since the seventeenth century."—*Pref.* Includes Native American religions only if they have been affected by European contact. Items were drawn from v. 11–18 of *America : history and life* (DB24). Classed arrangement; indexed by author and subject.   Z7831.R44

Sandeen, Ernest Robert. American religion and philosophy : a guide to information sources / Ernest Robert Sandeen and Frederick Hale. Detroit : Gale, [1978]. 377 p. (American studies information guide series, v.5).   **BC31**
Intends "to provide students and scholars of religion and philosophy in the United States with a general introduction to recent secondary sources and key primary documents."—*Pref.* Serves in part as a supplement to Nelson Rollin Burr's *Critical bibliography of religion in America* (BC27), being designed especially to survey the literature which has appeared since that work was published in 1961. Classed arrangement with author, title, and subject indexes.   Z7757.U5S25

Shupe, Anson D. The anti-cult movement in America : a bibliography and historical survey / Anson D. Shupe, David G. Bromley, and Donna L. Oliver. N.Y. : Garland, 1984. 169 p. (Garland reference library of social science, v.130).   **BC32**
Lists 1,001 items on religious counter-movements and opposition to religious cults in America. Presented in seven topical chapters, each with an introductory essay. Author index.   Z7835.C86S55

Williams, Ethel L. The Howard University bibliography of African and Afro-American religious studies : with locations in American libraries. Wilmington, Del. : Scholarly Resources, [1977]. 525 p.   **BC33**
Some 13,000 entries (books, periodical articles, parts of books) in five main sections: African heritage; Christianity and slavery in the New World; The black man and his religious life in the Americas; Civil rights movement; The contemporary religious scene. Appendix 1 is a selected listing of manuscripts; Appendix 2 is an autobiographical and biographical index which includes references to biographical material in periodical articles and parts of books. Author index. No standards for inclusion are mentioned, and works listed range from scholarly works to popular accounts appearing in national weeklies.
Z1361.N39W555

Africa

Ofori, Patrick E. Black African traditional religions and philosophy : a select bibliographic survey of the sources from the earliest times to 1974. Nendeln, Liechtenstein : KTO Pr., 1975. 421 p.   **BC34**
"This bibliography covers all the major ethnic groups of black Africa. Black Africa, as used in the context of this bibliography, means Africa south of the Sahara, and it includes all the major ethnic groups drawn roughly from Senegal in the West, along the southern boundary of the Sahara desert, through Central Ethiopia to Somalia in the East,

through west, central, eastern and Southern Africa, including Madagascar."—*Introd.* Arranged by geographic area (Africa in general, West Africa, Central Africa, East Africa, Southern Africa), then by country and by ethnic groups within country sections. Some of the larger ethnic sections are subdivided according to such categories as Religious beliefs and conceptions; Birth, initiation and funeral rites; Festivals; Myths, superstitions, taboos, etc. Author and ethnic indexes.
§ See also '*Ashe, traditional religion and healing in Sub-Saharan Africa and the diaspora : a classified international bibliography* (N.Y. : Greenwood, 1989. 518 p.). Includes 3,187 entries for books, dissertations, unpublished papers, periodical and newspaper articles, and films and videotapes. Reference works, archives, and research centers are listed in appendixes. Ethnic group, subject, and author indexes.   Z7834.A3O34

Young, Josiah U. African theology : a critical analysis and annotated bibliography. Westport, Conn. : Greenwood, 1993. 257 p. (Bibliographies and indexes in religious studies, no. 26).   **BC35**
609 entries for articles, books, and essays, primarily in English with some French titles. Arranged in four chapters: (1) Historical and social analysis; (2) African traditional religion and religio-cultural analysis; (3) African theology; and (4) Black South African theology. Materials have been selected to provide a comprehensive picture of African theology. Indexes of names, titles, and subjects.
BT30.A438Y68

Asia

Earhart, H. Byron. The new religions of Japan : a bibliography of western-language materials. 2nd ed. Ann Arbor : Center for Japanese Studies, Univ. of Mich., 1983. 213 p. (Michigan papers in Japanese studies, 9).   **BC36**
1st ed., 1970.
Expands the earlier edition to include about 1,450 books, articles and dissertations on nineteenth- and twentieth-century religions of Japan. Classified arrangement; author and subject indexes.
Z7834.J3E2

Thompson, Laurence G. Chinese religion in Western languages : a comprehensive and classified bibliography of publications in English, French, and German through 1980. Tucson, Ariz. : Publ. for the Association for Asian Studies by the Univ. of Arizona Pr., c1985. 302 p. (Monographs of the Association for Asian Studies, no. 41).   **BC37**
Updated ed. of Thompson's *Studies of Chinese religion* (Encino, Calif. : Dickenson, 1976).
An extensive unannotated list of monographs and serials with an index of authors, editors, compilers, translators, photographers, and illustrators. Covers Chinese Buddhism as well as Chinese religion exclusive of Buddhism. Intended for specialists.
Supplemented by *Chinese religion : publication in Western languages, 1981 through 1990*, comp. by Laurence G. Thompson, ed. by Gary Seaman (Ann Arbor, Mich. : Assoc. for Asian Studies, 1992. 288 p. [Monographs of the Association for Asian Studies, v. 47]).
Z7757.C6T55

Yu, David C. Guide to Chinese religion / David C. Yu with contributions by Laurence G. Thompson. Boston : G.K. Hall, c1985. 200 p.   **BC38**
A critically annotated, selected bibliography of books, journal articles, and essays through 1977, primarily in English. Deals with religions indigenous to China: Taoism, Confucianism, Lao Tzu, Maoism, archaic religions and folk beliefs; excludes Chinese Buddhism. Detailed classified arrangement, with author/title and subject indexes. Intended for undergraduate and beginning graduate students.
Z7757.C6Y8

Union of Soviet Socialist Republics

Korsch, Boris. Religion in the Soviet Union : a bibliography, 1980–1989. N.Y. : Garland, 1992. 639 p. (Garland reference library of social science, v. 659.). **BC39**

Lists 5,858 publications, mostly in Russian, chosen to "present Soviet religious policies as illustrated by propaganda in a socio-political and ideological context."—*Pref.* Includes state- and denomination-sponsored writings, and censored and uncensored religious publications. Entries are arranged by type of publication (e.g., Reviews, Dissertations, Censored religious publications); English translations are provided for titles. Brings together a great deal of material of value to the researcher, but the work's organization and subject index do not provide sufficient access. Z7757.S65K67

Library catalogs

Union Theological Seminary (New York, N.Y.). Library. Alphabetical arrangement of main entries from the shelf list. Boston : G. K. Hall, 1960 [i.e., c1965]. 10 v. **BC40**

The catalog cards previously reproduced (1960) in shelflist sequence are here rearranged by main entry. The volumes in shelflist arrangement can be used for subject searching, following the classification scheme outlined in *The Prussian instructions : rules for the alphabetical catalogs of the Prussian libraries* (Ann Arbor : Univ. of Michigan Pr., 1938). An important theological bibliography. Z881.N4

Indexes; Abstract journals

In addition to those noted below, there are other indexes in this field which may prove useful in the very large or specialized collection: *Guide to social science and religion in periodical literature* (Flint, Mich. : National Periodical Library, 1964–); *Theology in context* (Aachen, Germany : Institute of Missiology Mission, 1984–); *Repertoire bibliographique des institutions chretiennes* (Strasbourg, 1967–); and the "Elenchus bibliographicus" section of the journal *Ephemerides theologicae lovanienses.*

•**ATLA religion database on CD-ROM** [database]. Evanston, Ill. : Amer. Theological Libr. Assoc., 1993– . **BC41**

Began with Issue 1993.1. Updated annually.

Machine-readable version of: *Religion index one : periodicals* (BC44); *Religion index two : multi-author works* (BC45); *Research in ministry* (Chicago : ATLA, 1982–); *Index to book reviews in religion* (BC53); and *Methodist reviews index 1818–1885* (Nashville : Board of Higher Education and Ministry, The United Methodist Church, 1989).

•*Religion indexes : RIO/RIT/IBRR 1975– on CD-ROM* includes *Religion index one*, *Religion index two*, and the *Index to book reviews in religion* citations since 1975.

Australasian religion index. v. 1, no. 1 (June 1989)– . [Wagga Wagga, NSW] : Australian and New Zealand Theological Libr. Assoc. and Centre for Information Studies, Charles Sturt Univ., 1989– . Semiannual; the second issue is the annual cumulation. **BC42**

Also called *ARI.*

Lists articles and book reviews from selected religious and theological serials published in and representative of the religions of Australia and New Zealand. Includes reviews of new serial titles. Author, subject, scripture passage, and book review indexes. Z7753.A87

Christian periodical index : (a selected list) / prep. by Librarians of the Association of Christian Librarians. v. 1 (1958)– . [Buffalo, N.Y.] : The Association, 1958– . Three times a year with annual cumulations. **BC43**

Subtitle varies: 1983– , An index to subjects and authors and to book and media reviews.

Frequency has varied; originally an annual with 5-year cumulations.

An index by authors and subjects to about 95 evangelical and fundamentalist periodicals, chiefly from the U.S. Reviews are listed in a separate section. Z7753.C5

Religion index one : periodicals. July/Dec. 1977– . [Chicago] : Amer. Theological Libr. Assoc., 1977– . Semiannual, with 2nd issue every year being an annual cumulation. **BC44**

Supersedes *Index to religious periodical literature* (1949–1975/76); vol. 1–4, 1949–59; v. 5–6, 1960–65; v. 7–9, 1965–69; and v. 10–11; 1970–74 issued in single volumes, revised and expanded, under the current title. Cumulations vary; annual since 1985.

Indexes religious and archaeological periodicals from the U. S., Canada, England, France, Germany, Japan, Scotland, and other countries. Coverage and number of periodicals indexed vary; now includes 460 titles. Book reviews in v. 12 (1975/76)–v. 17 (1985). Protestant in viewpoint, but indexes some Catholic and Jewish titles and titles from other religions. Employs a three-part arrangement introduced in 1986: (1) Subject index; (2) Author/editor index; and (3) Scripture index.

§ *Religion index two: multi-author works* (BC45) and *Index to book reviews in religion* (BC53) are companion publications.

•Included as part of *ATLA religion index on CD-ROM* [database] (BC41). Z7753.A5

Religion index two : multi-author works. 1976– . [Chicago] : Amer. Theological Libr. Assoc., 1978– . Annual, with quinquennial cumulations. **BC45**

A companion to *Religion index one : periodicals* (BC44). Indexes composite works by various authors published during the year covered. Includes Western-language publications which are collections by more than one author, which are intended to be scholarly, and which have a religious or theological subject focus. 514 books are indexed in the 1991 volume. Subjects and authors in separate sections; a scripture index was introduced in the 1985 volume.

•Included as part of *ATLA religion index on CD-ROM* [database] (BC41). Z7751.R35

Religious and theological abstracts. v.1 (Mar. 1958)– . Myerstown, Pa. : Theological Pub., 1958– . Quarterly. **BC46**

Currently indexes about 340 periodicals, primarily Christian, but Jewish titles and a small number of titles from other religions are also included. Journals are in various languages, but abstracts are in English. Classified arrangement with author, subject, and biblical indexes. The classified arrangement must be used for locating the primary articles on a subject, since the subject index fails to duplicate that access.

•A machine-readable version, *R & TA on CD-ROM*, is available on CD-ROM, updated annually. BR1.R286

Richardson, Ernest Cushing. An alphabetical subject index and index encyclopaedia to periodical articles on religion, 1890–1899. N.Y. : C. Scribner for the Hartford Seminary Pr., 1907. 1168 p. **BC47**

Companion volume: *Periodical articles in religion, 1890–1899 : author index*, comp. and ed. by Ernest Cushing Richardson ... [et al.]. (N.Y. : C. Scribner's Sons for the Hartford Seminary Pr., [c1911]. 876 p.).

Indexes 58,000 articles by 21,000 writers, in more than 600 periodicals and transactions in English and the principal foreign languages, on the religions of the world. The subject volume, arranged alphabetically, has a special feature not ordinarily found in indexes, i.e., each heading used is briefly defined, or a person or place is identified and followed by a reference to some encyclopedia article. The author volume indexes the same articles as the subject volume. Z7753.R55

Science of religion : abstracts and index of recent articles. v. 5 (1980)– . Amsterdam : Inst. for the Study of Religion, Free Univ. ; Dept. of Theology and Religious Studies, Univ. of Leeds. Quarterly. **BC48**

Vols. 1–4, 1976–79, publ. under title: *Science of religion bulletin: abstracts and index of recent articles.*

Published under the auspices of the International Association for the History of Religions on the recommendation of the International Council for Philosophy and Humanistic Studies with the financial support of Unesco. Continues *International bibliography of the history of religions* (BC11).

A "systematic bibliography of articles contributing to the academic study of religions" *(Scope statement),* covering religions of both East and West, ancient and modern. Analyzes about 250 journals. Quarterly author and subject indexes cumulate in the final issue of each volume; cumulated author and subject indexes for 1976–80 publ. in v. 5, no. 4. Beginning with v. 7, 1982, indexes for each volume cumulate with each quarterly issue.

South African theological bibliography = Suid-Afrikaanse teologiese bibliografie / editors, C.F.A. Borchardt & W.S. Vorster. Pretoria : Univ. of South Africa, 1980– . Annual. **BC49**

Vol. 4–7 ed. by C.F.A. Borchardt, J. Kilian, W.S. Vorster. Now annual; v. 1, 1980; v. 2, 1983; v. 3, 1988.

An index, with some abstracts, of theological journals and multi-author works published in South Africa. Includes dissertations and theses submitted to South African institutions. Vols. 1–4 constitute a retrospective bibliography; v. 5 achieves currency. Published annually beginning with v. 4; with that volume, subject, author, and book review sections provide improved access over the classified arrangement of v. 1–3. Z7757.S6S68

Bibliography

Walsh, Michael J. Religious bibliographies in serial literature : a guide / comp. by Michael J. Walsh ... [et al.] on behalf of the Assoc. of British Theological and Philosophical Libraries. Westport, Conn. : Greenwood, 1981. 216 p. **BC50**

Lists in alphabetical order 178 bibliographical tools, mainly periodical indexes and journals, devoted entirely to, or including entries for, topics in religion. Excellent full descriptions of bibliographical information, arrangement, and coverage; critical comment included. Subject and title indexes. Z7753.W34

Book reviews

Critical review of books in religion. 1988– . Atlanta : Journal of the American Academy of Religion and the Journal of Biblical Literature. Annual. **BC51**

A few long, critical reviews of a single work or type of work (e.g., *Encyclopedia of religion* in 1989, feminist studies of religion in 1991) fill the first portion of each annual volume. The balance contains shorter book reviews by specialists of works selected from the spectrum of religious studies literature. A bibliography of translations, new editions, and reference works is appended. Indexes of authors and reviewers. BL1.C75

Index to book reviews in religion : cumulated and revised edition of the book reviews from Index to religious periodical literature / ed. by Douglas W. Geyer. Evanston, Ill. : Amer. Theological Libr. Assoc., c1990–93. 3 v. **BC52**

Subtitle: IBRR : an author, title, and classified index to reviews of books published in and of interest to the field of religion.

Editor varies: v. 2, Janet M. Hackett; v. 3, Lowell K. Handy.

A cumulated and revised reprinting of the book review index sections of *Index to religious periodical literature* (v. 1 [1949]–v. 13 [1977]. Chicago : Amer. Theological Libr. Assoc.).

•The data in these volumes are available on CD-ROM as part of: *ATLA religion database on CD-ROM* (BC41). Z7753.I5

Index to book reviews in religion. Feb. 1986– . Chicago : Amer. Theological Libr. Assoc., c1986– . Bimonthly, with Dec. constituting the annual cumulation. **BC53**

Supersedes the book review index section of *Religion index one* (BC44), which last appeared in v. 17 (1985). Contains author/editor, title, reviewer, and series indexes to book reviews, review essays, and review articles published in more than 400 periodicals in the field of religion or of interest to it. The annual index, besides cumulating quarterly indexes, adds a classified index.

•Indexes to book reviews are included as part of *ATLA religion index on CD-ROM* [database] (BC41). Z7753.I5

Encyclopedias

For many questions asked by English-speaking readers, *Encyclopedia of religion* (BC58), *New Catholic encyclopedia* (BC401), and *New Schaff-Herzog encyclopedia of religious knowledge* (BC67) will be adequate. In the large reference library it will often be necessary to use some of the foreign works, especially for topics in foreign church history, foreign religious biography, etc. The most extended modern work of reference in the field of theology is the great French series now in course of publication under the general title *Encyclopédie des sciences religieuses*, composed of the following separate works: *Dictionnaire d'archéologie chrétienne et de liturgie* by Fernand Cabrol (BC246); *Dictionnaire d'histoire et de géographie ecclésiastiques* by Alfred Baudrillart (BC412); *Dictionaire de théologie catholique* by A. Vacant and E. Mangenot (BC398); *Dictionnaire de la Bible* by Fulcran Grégoire Vigouroux (BC152); and *Dictionnaire de droit canonique* (Paris : Letouzey, 1935–65. 7 v.). These are listed separately under their subjects. Parts of this series contain the finest material on the subject published in any language, and the work as a whole represents the highest level of French Catholic scholarship. The price of the sets puts them beyond the reach of the small or medium-sized library, and the work is too specialized to be of much use except in a theological library, a large general reference library, or a library specializing in medieval and ecclesiastical history and literature.

Dictionnaire de spiritualité : ascétique et mystique, doctrine et histoire / publié sous la direction de Marcel Viller, S.J., assisté de F. Cavallera, et J. de Guibert, S.J., avec le concours d'un grand nombre de collaborateurs .... Paris : G. Beauchesne et ses fils, 1937–1994. Fasc. 1–106/107. (In progress). **BC54**

Often cited as *DSp.*
Editors vary.
Contents: v. 1–15 (fasc. 106/107), A–Zypaeus.
Offers long, signed articles with bibliographies and references to sources; includes many bibliographies. BX841.D67

Encyclopaedia of religion and ethics / ed. by James Hastings, with the assistance of John A. Selbie and Louis H. Gray. Edinburgh : Clark ; N.Y. : Scribner, 1908–27. 12 v. and index. : ill. **BC55**

This comprehensive work covers all religions; ethical systems and movements; religious beliefs and customs; philosophical ideas; moral practices; related subjects in anthropology, mythology, folklore, biology, psychology, economics, and sociology; and names of persons and places connected with any of these subjects. Now largely updated by *The encyclopedia of religion* (ed. in chief, Mircea Eliade, BC58), but still important for historical purposes and for locating information not included in its successor. Signed articles; full bibliographies.

BL31.E4

Encyclopedia of African American religions / ed. by Larry G. Murphy, J. Gordon Melton, Gary L. Ward. N.Y. : Garland, 1993. lxxvi, 926 p. (Religious information systems series, v. 9 ; Garland reference library of social science, v. 721). **BC56**

Primarily compiled from the Black Studies Collection and the American Religions Collection at the Univ. of California, Santa Barbara.

Articles, with brief bibliographies, on people, churches, schools, and associations relating to African-American religious life in the U.S. Of some 1,200 entries, almost two-thirds are biographies. Also provides a basic bibliography, directory of churches and religious organizations, lists of religious leaders by religious affiliation, and a detailed chronology beginning at the year 1618. Index. BR563.N4E53

The encyclopedia of Eastern philosophy and religion : Buddhism, Hinduism, Taoism, Zen / Ingrid Fischer-Schreiber [et al.] ; editors, Stephan Schuhmacher, Gert Woerner. Boston : Shambhala, 1989. 468 p. : ill. **BC57**

Also published as: *The Rider encyclopedia of Eastern philosophy and religion* (London : Rider, [1989]).

Translation of: *Lexikon der östlichen Weisheitslehren* (Bern : O.W. Barth, [1986]).

Written by specialists but intended for general readers; attempts to present "the basic terminology and doctrinal systems of the four great wisdom teachings of the East."—*Introd.* Contains approximately 4,000 unsigned definitions and biographical sketches, arranged alphabetically. Longer entries often include discussions of historical and cultural significance, explanatory parables or *koans*, or references to important translations or studies. A "Ch'an/Zen lineage chart" following the text shows the transmission of the Buddhist tradition through various masters, texts, sects, and philosophies. Concludes with a lengthy classified bibliography that lists primary and secondary sources. No index, but entries contain numerous cross-references and illustrations. BL1005.L4813

The encyclopedia of religion / [ed. in chief, Mircea Eliade ; editors, Charles J. Adams ... et al.]. N.Y. : Macmillan, c1987. 16 v. : ill. **BC58**

Intended to "introduce educated, non-specialist readers to important ideas, practices and persons in the religious experience of humankind from the Paleolithic past to our day."—*Foreword.* Treats theoretical (e.g., doctrines, myths, theologies, ethics), practical (e.g., cults, sacraments, meditations), and sociological (e.g., religious groups, ecclesiastical forms) aspects of religion; includes extensive coverage of non-Western religions. Signed articles by some 1,400 contributors worldwide end with bibliographies. Many composite entries treat two or more related topics. Vol. 16 provides an alphabetic list of entries, a synoptic outline of contents, and an extensive general index. Has quickly become the standard work, updating *Encyclopaedia of religion and ethics*, James Hastings, ed. (BC55). BL31.E46

Encyclopedia of the American religious experience : studies of traditions and movements / Charles H. Lippy and Peter W. Williams, editors. N.Y. : Scribner, c1988. 3 v. (1872 p.). **BC59**

Consists of 105 long, interpretive essays by leading scholars in the fields of history, religion, theology, American studies, sociology, and philosophy. Arranged logically and topically under nine broad subjects: Approaches to religion in America; North America: contexts and backgrounds; Jewish and Christian traditions; Religions outside the Jewish and Christian traditions; Movements in American religion; American religious thought and literature; Liturgy, worship and the arts; Religion and the political and social orders; The dissemination of American religion. A selected bibliography and cross-references follow each essay. An extensive index provides quick access to topics discussed in one or many articles; there is also an alphabetical list of articles and a list of contributors, with institutional affiliations. A comprehensive, authoritative work. BL2525E53

Encyclopedic dictionary of religion / ed. by Paul Kevin Meagher, Thomas C. O'Brien, Sister Consuelo Maria Aherne. Wash. : Corpus Publ. [for] Sisters of St. Joseph of Philadelphia, [1979]. 3 v. **BC60**

Compiled under Catholic auspices (and stemming from an effort to keep together and further utilize the expertise developed for the *New Catholic encyclopedia*, BC401) but ecumenical in its coverage. Signed articles, usually including bibliographic references. Many biographical entries and entries for institutions, religious orders, etc. Entries relate chiefly to Christianity; viewpoint is Roman Catholic. BR95.E494

Ferguson, John. An illustrated encyclopaedia of mysticism and the mystery religions. N.Y. : Seabury, 1977. 228 p. : ill. **BC61**

First publ. London : Thames and Hudson, 1976.

Brief articles on names, terms, and movements relating to various forms of mysticism. Demonology, magic, and witchcraft are excluded. Bibliography of secondary sources, p. 217–27. BL625.F44

Leach, Marjorie. Guide to the gods / Marjorie Leach ; ed. by Michael Owen Jones, Frances Cattermole-Tally. Santa Barbara, Calif. : ABC-Clio, 1992. 995 p. **BC62**

Entries for deities throughout the world and in various time periods, arranged by function or attribute (e.g., nature, love, fortune) within eight categories: Cosmogonical deities, Celestial deities; Atmospheric deities; Terrestrial deities; Life/death cycle deities; Economic activities; Socio-cultural concepts; and Religion. Material, derived from more than 1,600 works, consists of brief descriptions of the functions of deities, principal charactaeristics, location, related deities or alternate names, and citations to sources of information. Bibliography; name index.

§ Martha Ann and Dorothy Myers Imel's *Goddesses in world mythology* (CF2) includes many entries from *Guide to the gods*, in addition to entries from other sources. BL473.L43

Lexikon für Theologie und Kirche / begründet von Michael Buchberger. 3. völlig neubearb. Aufl. ... hrsg. von Walter Kasper und Konrad Baumgartner ... [et al.]. Freiburg : Herder, 1993–94. v. 1–2. (In progress). **BC63**

1st ed., 1930–38; 2nd ed., 1957–65.

Projected to be in 10 v., with a separate index.

Signed articles, some of considerable length and containing bibliographies, covering various religions, practices, faiths, and rituals. Many brief biographies. An important German work, written from the Roman Catholic point of view. BR95.L48

Man, myth & magic : the illustrated encyclopedia of mythology, religion, and the unknown / ed. in chief, Richard Cavendish ; editorial board, C.A. Burland ... [et al.]. New ed. / ed. and comp. by Yvonne Deutch. N.Y. : Marshall Cavendish, 1983. 12 v. (3201 p.) : ill. (some col.). **BC64**

A unique resource for topics and themes not usually covered in standard reference works. Interdisciplinary and comprehensive in scope, ranging from prehistory to the newest cults. Includes entries for deities, significant individuals, and cross-cultural themes (e.g., water, birds, human body) as well as religious movements (e.g., Vishnu, Voodoo, Zen). Many illustrations; easily understood by the general reader. Vol. 1 includes a series of long bibliographies on general subjects supplementing the short bibliographies that accompany each article throughout the work; v. 12 is a detailed general index.

BF1411.M25

Mead, Frank Spencer. Handbook of denominations in the United States. New 9th ed./ rev. by Samuel S. Hill. Nashville : Abingdon, [1990]. 316 p. **BC65**

1st ed., 1951; 8th ed., 1985.

Brief sketches describe background, beliefs, governance, and membership of more than 200 religious groups. An appendix gives three classification schemes used by evangelical bodies, followed by: (1) Headquarters of denominations; (2) Glossary; (3) Bibliography; (4) Index.

§ For religious groups not found in Mead, consult J. Gordon Melton, *The encyclopedia of American religions* (BC66) and Arthur Carl Piepkorn, *Profiles in belief* (BC270). BR516.5.M38

Melton, J. Gordon. The encyclopedia of American religions. 4th ed. Detroit : Gale, c1993. 1217 p. : ill. **BC66**
1st ed., 1978; 3rd ed., 1989.

An authoritative source for information on prominent and obscure North American religious groups. Includes two extensive introductory essays on the history of religion in the U.S. and Canada; 22 essays on religious families (e.g., Catholic, Protestant, Jewish, Spiritualist, Middle Eastern), and a directory providing historical and contemporary information on individual religious bodies, arranged by families. Essays and many directory entries have bibliographies. Three indexes: geographic, subject, and name and keyword.

§ For obtaining addresses, lists of periodicals, and brief descriptions of U.S. religious groups, Melton's *Religious bodies in the United States : a directory* (2nd ed. N.Y. : Garland, 1992. 313 p.) is a handy resource. BL2525.M449

New Schaff-Herzog encyclopedia of religious knowledge : embracing biblical, historical, doctrinal and practical theology and biblical, theological and ecclesiastical biography, from the earliest times to the present day; based on the 3d ed. of the Realencyklopädie founded by J. J. Herzog and ed. by Albert Hauck / S. M. Jackson, ed. in chief. N.Y. : Funk & Wagnalls, 1908–12. 13 v. **BC67**
Repr. : Grand Rapids, Mich. : Baker Book House, 1969.
Vols. 2–12 have abbreviated title which varies slightly; v. 13, Index by George William Gilmore.

One of the most important reference books on its subject in English. Based upon Johann Jakob Herzog's *Realencyklopädie für protestantische Theologie und Kirche* (3rd ed., ed. by Albert Hauck. Leipzig : Hinrichs, 1896–1913), and thus Protestant in tone, it is not a mere translation of the German work since much of the material has been condensed, fresh material added, and the bibliographies extended and improved. Not limited to the Christian religion but includes articles on other religions and religious leaders. Covers the whole field of biblical and historical theology, including separate articles of all sects, denominations and churches, organizations and societies, missions, doctrines, controversies, etc. Biographical notices include those of men living at the time the work was published. The bibliography is in three forms: (1) general bibliographical survey, with critical comment, in the preface (p. xii–xiv); (2) bibliographical appendix at the beginning of each volume, listing recent (at time of publication) literature; and (3) bibliographies appended to each article.

Twentieth century encyclopedia of religious knowledge : an extension of the New Schaff-Herzog encyclopedia of religious knowledge, ed. in chief, Lefferts A. Loetscher (Grand Rapids, Mich. : Baker Book House, 1955. 2 v.).

May be used as a supplement to *New Schaff-Herzog* or independently. Includes biographical sketches of persons both living and dead; articles on newer subjects; and articles which update subjects previously treated. Articles are signed and usually include bibliographies. BR95.S43

Die Religion in Geschichte und Gegenwart : Handwörterbuch für Theologie und Religionswissenschaft. 3. völlig neubearb. Aufl. ... hrsg. von Kurt Galling. Tübingen : Mohr, 1957–65. 7 v. : ill. **BC68**
1st ed., 1909–13.
Cited as *RGG*. An authoritative work containing long, signed articles by specialists. From a liberal Protestant point of view but includes articles on Catholic doctrines. Full bibliographies. Many biographical sketches, including articles on living persons. Vol. 7 is the *Registerband*, containing biographies of contributors, index and corrections. BL31.R42

Theologische Realenzyklopädie / in Gemeinschaft mit Horst Robert Balz ... [et al.] ; hrsg. von Gerhard Krause u. Gerhard Müller. Berlin ; N.Y. : de Gruyter, 1976–1994. Bd. 1–24; Abkürzungsverzeichnis [v. 26]. (In progress). **BC69**

Contents: v. 1–24, A–Obrigkeit.
To be in 30 volumes of about 800 pages (five *Lieferungen*) each.
2nd ed. of *Abkürzungsverzeichnis*, ed. by Siegfried M. Schwertner, publ. 1994.

In some respects a successor to the *Realencyklopädie für protestantische Theologie und Kirche* (Leipzig : Hinrichs, 1896–1913), ed. by Johann Jakob Herzog and Albert Hauck, but a new work employing a broader interpretation of "theology" and less concerned with the strictly Protestant point of view. Long, scholarly articles (typically many pages in length) signed by the contributors, and including extensive bibliographies. Each volume has its own index, there is an index for v. 1–17, and a general index is promised as the final volume of the set. BR95.T47

Dictionaries

Abingdon dictionary of living religions / Keith Crim, gen. ed. Nashville : Abingdon, [1981]. 830 p. : ill. **BC70**
Repr. as: *The perennial dictionary of world religions* (San Francisco : Harper & Row, c1989).

Intended as a guide to the historical development, beliefs, and observances of religions which are being practiced today. Each major religious tradition has an extensive article devoted to it, and there are briefer articles on more specific topics and aspects of each, including entries for regional developments in religions which have spread to various geographical locations. Signed articles; bibliographies; cross-references. BL31.A24

The dictionary of Bible and religion / William H. Gentz, ed. Nashville : Abingdon, c1986. 1147 p. : ill. **BC71**
Brief articles with cross-references, initialed by 28 contributors, treat principally the Bible, but also the history of Christianity, Christian doctrine, world religions, and contemporary religions. Ecumenically Christian in origin; intended for the general reader. Contains photographs, illustrations, charts, maps in color, and a brief bibliography. BR95.D46

Dictionary of comparative religion / S. G. F. Brandon, gen. ed. London : Weidenfeld & Nicolson ; N.Y. : Scribner, [1970]. 704 p. **BC72**
Brief, signed articles intended "to treat the various religions proportionately to their significance in the history of human culture."— *Pref.* Bibliographies follow most articles. Scholar specialists served as sectional editors for articles dealing with aspects of Buddhism, Hinduism, Islam, and the religions of China and the Far East. There is both a general index and a synoptic index which lists articles relating to a specific religion or an individual country. BL31.D54

The Facts on File dictionary of religions / ed. by John R. Hinnells. N.Y. : Facts on File, 1984. 550 p. : ill., maps. **BC73**
Also publ. (London : Allen Lane), as *The Penguin dictionary of religions*.

The work of an international team of 29 scholars from a variety of academic disciplines. Emphasis is on "living religions," but ancient religions, astrology, magic, and the occult are also treated. Basically a dictionary of terms, but entries go well beyond brief definitions. Includes an extensive classed bibliography (p. 381–446), a synoptic index (which lists all articles relating to a given religion or group of religions), and a general index. BL31.P38

MacGregor, Geddes. Dictionary of religion and philosophy. N.Y. : Paragon House, 1989. 696 p. **BC74**
Intended for students. Emphasizes the Judeo-Christian tradition and philosophical topics related to it, but also includes information on Eastern religions. Brief articles in alphabetical order, without bibliographies or cross-references. Selected classified bibliography at the end of the work. BL31.M23

Parrinder, Edward Geoffrey. Dictionary of non-Christian religions. 2nd ed. [i.e., rev. repr.]. Amersham, Bucks : Hulton, 1981. 320 p. : ill.   **BC75**
     1st ed., 1971.
     "Covers the whole field of the religions of the world, with the exception of Christianity and the Bible."—*Introd.* Brief entries for gods, heroes, cults, beliefs, places, etc., especially for Hinduism, Buddhism and Islam. No bibliography; short reading list appended.   BL31.P36

Rice, Edward. Eastern definitions. Garden City, N.Y. : Doubleday, 1978. 433 p. : ill.   **BC76**
     Subtitle: A short encyclopedia of religions of the Orient; a guide to common, ordinary, and rare philosophical, mystical, religious, and psychological terms from Hinduism, Buddhism, Sufism, Islam, Zen, Taoism, the Sikhs, Zoroastrianism, and other major and minor Eastern religions.
     "The terms encountered in this work are in most cases those most likely to be met by the average curious reader of both popular and scholarly works written in or translated into English."—*Foreword.* Articles range in length from a few lines to several pages. Cross-references; no bibliography.   BL31.R52

Directories

Directory of departments and programs of religious studies in North America. Valparaiso, Indiana : Council of Societies for the Study of Religion. Valparaiso Univ., 1978– . Annual.   **BC77**
     At head of title: Council of Societies for the Study of Religion.
     Issued annually beginning in 1987. Prior to that, editions were publ. 1978, 1981, 1985. Place of publication varies.
     Provides detailed information on undergraduate and graduate programs in religious studies at four-year colleges, universities, and theological schools. Lists faculty members with their graduate degrees and fields of specialization. Includes geographical directory of schools and index of faculty members.   BL41.D57

Foundation guide for religious grant seekers / Kerry A. Robinson, ed. 4th ed. Atlanta : Scholars Pr., [c1992]. 287 p.   **BC78**
     1st ed., 1979; 3rd ed., 1987, ed. by Francis J. Butler.
     Provides brief information on 588 Protestant, Catholic, Jewish, and interfaith foundations with a history of religious grant making. Short chapters on sources of information, the grant-seeking process, religious philanthropy, and building constituency support. Appendixes give locations of Foundation Center libraries and list area foundation directories.   BV774.5.B87

Guide to schools and departments of religion and seminaries in the United States and Canada : degree programs in religious studies / comp. by Modoc Press, Inc. N.Y. : Macmillan, c1987. 609 p.   **BC79**
     Gives detailed information on 703 regionally or nationally accredited four-year and graduate institutions. Separate sections for U.S. and Canada. Arranged alphabetically by state or province, then by name of institution. Denomination and institution indexes.   BV4030.G85

Melton, J. Gordon. Directory of religious organizations in the United States / J. Gordon Melton ... [et al.]. 3rd ed. Detroit : Gale, c1993. 728 p.   **BC80**
     1st ed., 1977; 2nd ed., 1982.
     An alphabetical listing of 2,500 general organizations (exclusive of religious orders and departments of national churches) which have a religious purpose—professional associations, volunteer groups, religious publishers, ecumenical and interfaith organizations, medical ministries, fraternal societies, etc. Indicates religious affiliation, contact person, address, description of activities, founding date, membership, and publications. This edition adds 900 new groups and four indexes: personnel, function, religious affiliation, and name and keyword.   BL2530.U6D57

Handbooks

Religion in the Soviet republics : a guide to Christianity, Judaism, Islam, Buddhism, and other religions / Igor Troyanovsky, ed. [San Francisco, Calif.] : HarperSanFrancisco, c1991. 210 p. : ill. (some col.).   **BC81**
     Includes historical documents and recent legislation related to religion in the period of *glasnost;* biographies of clergy elected to the Congress of People's Deputies; articles on religious groups; directory of religious organizations. The articles on religious groups provide statistics, organization, history, and current situation. Index.
                           BL980.S65R34

Biography

Bowden, Henry Warner. Dictionary of American religious biography. 2nd ed., rev. and enl. Westport, Conn. : Greenwood, 1993. 686 p.   **BC82**
     1st ed., 1977.
     With a view to correlating "information on American religious figures from all chronological periods and most denominational or theological affiliations" (*Pref.*), the new edition presents biographical sketches of 550 deceased persons, thoroughly updating most of the original articles and adding 125 new biographies. For each biographee, available details of vital statistics, education, and career are briefly noted preceding a discussion of the life work and influence of the figure. Bibliographies at the end of the articles cite works both by and about a person. Appendixes: Denominational affiliation and Listing by birthplace.   BL72.B68

Religious leaders of America. [1st ed.]– . Detroit : Gale, c1991– . Triennial.   **BC83**
     Ed. by J. Gordon Melton.
     Provides "biographical profiles on more than 1000 American and Canadian religious figures whose impact on the religious community has occurred since 1865"—*Pref.* Includes living leaders. Covers persons from all types and sizes of religious and ecumenical bodies, and includes humanists, agnostics, and atheists. Excludes missionaries, with the exception of some home missionaries; includes some contemporary foreign religious leaders who have followings in the U.S. Sources appended to each entry. Religious affiliations appendix; index.   BL2525.R47

Who's who in religion. 4th ed. Chicago : Marquis Who's Who, 1992.   **BC84**
     1st ed., 1975; 3rd ed., 1985.
     Contains more than 15,600 biographies of North American religious leaders and professionals in the field of religion. Names of persons included were drawn from the following general categories: (1) church officials (both lay and clergy); (2) clergy, selected for outstanding contributions to activities of their respective faiths; (3) religious educators in the field of higher education; (4) lay leaders. Information was supplied by the biographees; a few sketches compiled by Marquis editors are marked with an asterisk.   BL2530.U6W48

Atlases

Halvorson, Peter L. Atlas of religious change in America, 1952–1971 / Peter L. Halvorson, William M. Newman ; cartography by Mark C. Nielsen. Wash. : Glenmary Research Center, 1978. 95 p. : maps.   **BC85**
     "In the early 1950's the National Council of Churches sponsored a unique county level census-type study of religious adherence [*Churches and church membership in the United States,* BC88]. Nearly twenty years later, a similar study was jointly sponsored by the Glenmary Research Center, the National Council of Churches, and the Lutheran Church-Missouri Synod [*Churches & church membership in*

the United States, BC87]. This *Atlas* presents time-series data from these two landmark and several supplemental data sources."—*Introd.* 35 religious denominations are represented; for each is given a summary statement and four maps showing changes by county, 1952–71.

Continued by: *Atlas of religious change in America, 1971–1980*, by Halvorson and Newman (Atlanta : Glenmary Research Center, 1987).

§ Edwin Scott Gaustad's *Historical atlas of religion in America* (Rev. ed. N.Y. : Harper & Row, 1976. 189 p.) uses maps, charts, tables, and text to show the expansion and development of the churches and membership of the various denominations from 1650 to 1970. Indexes to places, religious bodies, and names and subjects.

G1201.E4H3

Statistics

Churches and church membership in the United States, 1990 : an enumeration by region, state and county, based on data reported by 133 church groupings / Martin B. Bradley ... [et al.]. Atlanta : Glenmary Research Center, 1992. 456 p. : map.   **BC86**

An earlier work, publ. 1982, covered data reported as of 1980.

Presents data for "133 Judaeo-Christian church bodies or groupings."—*Pref.* Tables provide national, regional, and state summaries; number of churches and church membership by county and denomination; and churches and church membership by metropolitan area.

BR526.C48

Johnson, Douglas W. Churches & church membership in the United States : an enumeration by region, state, and county; 1971 / Douglas W. Johnson, Paul R. Picard, Bernard Quinn. Wash. : Glenmary Research Center, [1974]. 237 p. : maps.   **BC87**

"This report contains statistics by region, state and county on Christian churches and church membership for 1971. Fifty-three denominations are included, representing an estimated 80.8 percent of church membership in the United States."—*Pref.*

Offers tables for (1) churches and church membership by denomination; (2) churches and church membership by region, state and denomination; and (3) churches and church membership by state, county and denomination.   BR526.J64

National Council of the Churches of Christ in the U.S.A. Bureau of Research and Survey. Churches and church membership in the United States : an enumeration and analysis by counties, states and regions. N.Y. : Council, 1956–58. 80 no. : diagrs.   **BC88**

Contents: Ser. A, no.1–4, Major faiths by regions, divisions, and states; Ser. B, no.1–8, Denominational statistics by regions, divisions, and states; Ser. C, no.1–59, Denominational statistics by states and counties; Ser. D, no.1–6, Denominational statistics by metropolitan areas; Ser. E, no.1–3, Socio-economic characteristics.   BR526.N3

SACRED BOOKS

See also sections for individual religions.

General works

Quotations

Champion, Selwyn Gurney. The eleven religions and their proverbial lore : a comparative study. N.Y. : Dutton, 1945. 340 p.   **BC89**

Subtitle: A reference book to the eleven surviving major religions of the world, with introductions by thirteen leading authorities.

A book of quotations arranged under religion by keyword, with subject-matter index and alternative chief-word index. Bibliography, p. 336–60.   BL80.C337

Hume, Robert Ernest. Treasure house of the living religions : selections from their sacred scriptures. N.Y. : Scribner, 1932. 493 p.   **BC90**

A classified anthology of 3,074 selected quotations from the sacred books of the 11 great historical religions—Buddhism, Christianity, Confucianism, Hinduism, Islam, Jainism, Judaism, Shintō, Sikhism, Taoism, and Zoroastrianism—with exact indication of source of each quotation; a full "Bibliography showing the canonical order of constituent documents of the several sacred scriptures together with the English translations of each document," p. 405–43; and an alphabetical topical index. A work of wide and precise scholarship, useful to the general reader for the interest of the selections and to the specialist for both selections and bibliographical materials.   BL70.H8

Collections

The Bible of the world / ed. by Robert O. Ballou in collaboration with Friedrich Spiegelberg ... N.Y. : Viking, 1939. 1415 p.   **BC91**

Brings together "the scriptural essence of eight great living source religions."—*Introd.* Selections are intended to convey the concepts of each religion. Translations were chosen based on scholarship and readability. Notes; bibliography; index.   BL70.B5

Sacred books of the East / tr. by various oriental scholars and ed. by F. Max Müller. Oxford : Clarendon Pr., 1879–1910. 51 v.   **BC92**

Repr.: N.Y. : Dover, 1962–69.

Contents: v. 1, 15, The Upanishads, tr. by F. Max Müller; v. 2, 14, The sacred laws of the Âryas, tr. by Georg Bühler; v. 3, 16, 27, 28, The sacred books of China, the texts of Confucianism, tr. by James Legge; v. 4, 23, 31, The Zend-Avesta, tr. by James Darmesteter and L. H. Mills; v. 5, 18, 24, 37, 47, Pahlavi texts, tr. by E. W. West; v. 6, 9, The Qurân, tr. by E. Palmer; v. 7, The Institutes of Vishnu, tr. by Julius Jolly; v. 8, The Bhagavadgîtâ, with the Sanatsugâtîya and the Anugîtâ, tr. by Kâshinâth Trimbak Telang; v. 10, The Dhammapada, tr. from Pâli by F. M. Müller; The Sutta-nipâta, tr. from Pâli by V. Fausböll; v. 11, Buddhist suttas, tr. from Pâli by T. W. Rhys Davids; v. 12, 26, 41, 43, 44, The Satapathabrâhmana, tr. by Julius Eggeling; v. 13, 17, 20, Vinaya texts, tr. from the Pâli by T. W. Rhys Davids and Hermann Oldenberg;

v. 19, The Fo-sho-hing-tsan-king by Asvaghosha, tr. by Samuel Bael; v. 21, The Saddharma-pundarîka, tr. by H. Kern; v. 22, 45, Gaina sûtras, tr. from Prâkit by Herman Jacobi; v. 25, The laws of Manu, tr. by G. Bühler; v. 29, 30, The Grihya-sûtras, tr. by Hermann Oldenberg; v. 32, 46, Vedic hymns, tr. by F. M. Müller and H. Oldenberg; v. 33, The minor law books, pt. 1, tr. by Julius Jolly; v. 34, 38, 48, The Vedânta sûtras, tr. by George Thibaut; v. 35, 36, The questions of King Milinda, tr. by T. W. Rhys Davids; v. 39, 40, The sacred books of China, the texts of Tâoism, tr. by James Legge; v. 42, Hymns of the Atharva-veda, tr. by Maurice Bloomfield; v. 49, 50, Buddhist Mâhâyana texts, tr. by E. B. Cowell; v. 51, General index, by M. Winternitz.

Includes all the most important works of the seven non-Christian religions that have influenced the civilization of Asia: the Vedic-Brahmanic system, Buddhism, Jainism, Islam, Confucianism, Taoism, and the Parsi religion. The excellent and detailed general index can be used for both large and small topics, beliefs, myths, names of deities, etc.

Index also issued separately: Moriz Winternitz, *Concise dictionary of Eastern religion, being the index volume to the Sacred books of the East* (Oxford : Clarendon Pr., 1910. 683 p.) Published also under the title *A general index to the names and subject matter of the Sacred books of the East.*

The Bible

Versions

Anchor Bible. Garden City, N.Y. : Doubleday, 1964–93. v. 1–[v. 44]. (In progress).   **BC93**

Contents: v. 1, Genesis; v. 3, Leviticus 1–16; [v. 4a] Numbers 1–20; v. 5, Deuteronomy 1–11; v. 6, Joshua; [v. 6a] Judges; v. 7, Ruth; [v. 7a] Lamentations (2nd ed.); [v. 7b] Esther; [v. 7c] Song of Songs; v. 8, I Samuel ; v. 9, II Samuel; v. 11, II Kings; [v. 12] I Chronicles; [v. 13] II Chronicles; [v. 14] Ezra. Nehemiah; [v. 15] Job; [v. 16] Psalms I (1–50); [v. 17] Psalms II (51–100); [v. 17a] Psalms III (101–150); [v. 18] Proverbs. Ecclesiastes; v. 20, Second Isaiah; [v. 21] Jeremiah; v. 22, Ezekiel 1–20; v. 23, Daniel; v. 24, Hosea; v. 24a, Amos; v. 24b, Jonah; v. 25b, Haggai, Zechariah 1–8; v. 25c, Zechariah 9–14; [v. 26] Matthew; v. 27, Mark; v. 28, Luke (I–IX) ; [v. 29] The Gospel according to John (I–XII); [v. 29a] The Gospel according to John (XIII–XXI); v. 30, The Epistles of John; [v. 31] Acts of the Apostles; [v. 32] I Corinthians; v. 32a, II Corinthians; v. 33, Romans [v. 34] Ephesians, 1–3; [v. 34a] v. 35, Letter to Titus; [v. 36] To the Hebrews; [v. 37] Epistles of James, Peter and Jude; v. 37c, 2 Peter, Jude; [v. 38] Revelation; v. 39, Wisdom of Ben Sira; [v. 41] I Maccabees; v. 41a, II Maccabees; [v. 42] I and II Esdras; v. 43, Wisdom of Solomon; [v. 44] Daniel, Esther and Jeremiah: the additions.

A project of Protestant, Catholic, and Jewish scholars. Offers new translations of the books of the Bible with extensive commentary.

BS192.2.A1 1964.G3

Bible. *English*. The Holy Bible : containing the Old & New Testaments translated out of the original tongues, and with the former translations diligently compared and revised by His Majesty's special command ; appointed to be read in churches. London ; N.Y. ; Toronto : Oxford Univ. Pr., [n.d.]. 1018 p.

BC94

Although the Bible is not usually thought of as a reference book, at least one copy should be in even the small reference collection, and others should be acquired as needed. The Bible will be found useful not only in religious or theological research, but in queries related to many other disciplines, especially literature, art, music, philosophy, and history.

In recent years, many new translations and versions have been made directly from the original Hebrew and Greek manuscripts, and take into account modern archaeological discoveries. For a bibliography of English Bibles, *see* Margaret T. Hills, *The English Bible in America* (BC101) or William J. Chamberlin, *Catalogue of English Bible translations* (BC97).

The principal versions in English at present are:

(1) *Authorized* or *King James* version (1611), still heavily used in churches and for private reading, especially by Protestants. The effect of the Authorized version on the faith of believers and on the English language and its literature is incalculable. Many allusions in various fields can be traced to the language of the Authorized version. Frequently reprinted. The *New King James* version (Nashville, Tenn. : T. Nelson, c1982) introduces "present-day vocabulary, pronunciation, and syntax" where necessary, but strives to preserve "the legacy of the original translators."—*Introd.*

(2) *American Revised* or *American Standard* version (N.Y. : T. Nelson & Sons, [c1901]), which differs on some points from the *Revised Version* (Oxford at the Univ. Pr., 1881–85). Revised to provide "a more current English idiom" (*Pref.*) and published as *New American standard Bible* (La Habra, Calif. : Foundation Press Publ., [1971]; it is more literal than other modern translations.

(3) *Revised Standard* version (N.Y. : Nelson. 1952). The New Testament appeared first, in 1946. Translated into modern English by a group of American scholars under the general editorship of Luther A. Weigle. *The Oxford annotated Bible, with the Apocrypha*, ed. by Herbert G. May and Bruce M. Metzger (N.Y. : Oxford Univ. Pr., 1977.

1564 p., 340 p.) uses the text of the *Revised Standard* version. The *New Revised Standard Version* (Nashville, Tenn. : T. Nelson, c1990) attempts to be as literal as possible while following standard American English usage. It uses inclusive language "as far as this can be done without altering passages that reflect the historical situation of ancient patriarchal culture."—*To the reader.*

(4) *New English Bible* (N.Y. : Oxford Univ. Pr. ; Cambridge Univ. Pr., 1970. 3 v.). Undertaken to provide a faithful rendering of the best available texts into contemporary English idiom, the work was "planned and directed by representatives of the Baptist Union of Great Britain and Ireland, the Church of England, the Church of Scotland, the Congregational Church in England and Wales, the Council of Churches for Wales, the Irish Council of Churches, the London Yearly Meeting of the Society of Friends, the Methodist Church of Great Britain, the Presbyterian Church of England, the British and Foreign Bible Society, the National Bible Society of Scotland."—*p. ii.* The Oxford study edition, Samuel Sandmal gen. ed., M. Jack Suggs, New Testament ed., and Arnold J. Tkacik, Apocrypha ed. (N.Y. : Oxford Univ. Pr., 1976. 1036 p., 257 p., 333 p.) includes introductions to individual books and groups of books as well as general background articles on Scripture; there are also annotations throughout "dealing with literary, historical, theological, geographical, and archaeological aspects of the text, and … cross-references" (*Pref.*) to related passages. An index of people, places, and themes in the Bible is provided, as well as maps with index.

A substantial revision, *The revised English Bible with the Apocrypha* (N.Y. : Oxford Univ. Pr. ; Cambridge Univ. Pr., 1989. 828 p., 205 p., 236 p.) was based on scholarship of the 1980s. It attempts to use idiomatic English while maintaining a fluent style with appropriate dignity for liturgical use, and to employ "more inclusive gender reference where that has been possible without compromising scholarly integrity or English style."—*Pref.*

(5) *Douay Bible*, also known as *Douay-Rheims Bible*. The 17th-century Roman Catholic translation of the Latin Vulgate. It differs from Protestant versions in the number and order of books, and in the fact that the Apocryphal books are accepted as canonical and are interspersed with the other books. Frequently reprinted; a recent version is: *The Holy Bible : Old Testament, Douay version ; New Testament, Confraternity version* / first publ. by the English college at Douay, A.D. 1609 ; New Testament rev. and ed. by Catholic scholars under the patronage of the Confraternity of Christian Doctrine (N.Y. : Kenedy, [c1961]. 1086 p.).

(6) *New American Bible* (N.Y. : Kenedy ; London : Collier-Macmillan, 1970), "translated from the original languages with critical use of all the ancient sources by members of the Catholic Biblical Association of America; sponsored by the Bishops' Committee of the Confraternity of Christian Doctrine."—*Pref.* A new translation intended for contemporary American readers. Incorporates (with certain revisions) those portions of the Old Testament published in the "Confraternity edition" (Paterson, N.J. : St. Anthony Guild Pr., 1952–69). The first part of a new edition has begun to appear: *Revised New Testament* (Northport, N.Y. : Costello Pub. Co. ; Grand Rapids, Mich. : Eerdmans, 1988. 774 p.). This literal translation conforms to contemporary American English usage and is intended for Roman Catholic liturgical proclamation and for private reading and study. Introduces some inclusive language. The introductions and notes have been rewritten and expanded, and the cross-references revised.

(7) *Jerusalem Bible* (Garden City, N.Y. : Doubleday, 1966). Derives from the French version edited at the Dominican École Biblique de Jerusalem and known as *La Bible de Jerusalem* (Paris : Éditions du Cerf, 1956, etc.). The introductions and notes are "a direct translation from the French, though revised and brought up to date in some places" (*Foreword*), but translation of the biblical text goes back to the original languages. A new edition, *New Jerusalem Bible* (Garden City, N.Y. : Doubleday, 1985) is based on the original texts and is considered to be an improvement over its predecessor.

(8) The Hebrew Bible. Good reference editions of English translations of the Hebrew Bible are available in various printings. A new translation by leading contemporary Jewish scholars was first published as *The Torah* (Philadelphia : Jewish Publication Soc., 1962 ; 2nd ed., 1967), *The Prophets* (1978), and *The Writings* (1982). The three sections were reissued in a single volume as: *Tanakh : a new translation of the Holy Scriptures according to the traditional Hebrew text* (Philadelphia : Jewish Publication Soc., 1985. 1624 p.).

A convenient collection of various English translations of the New Testament is the *New Testament octapla*, ed. by Luther A. Weigle (N.Y. : Nelson, 1962). Versions represented are: Tyndale, Great Bible, Geneva Bible, Bishops' Bible, Rheims, King James, American Standard, Revised Standard.

Among other good modern translations of the Bible, the following are notable: *Moffatt Bible* (N.Y. : Harper, 1925); *Complete Bible, an American Translation*; the Old Testament, tr. by J. M. Powis Smith, and the Apocrypha and New Testament, tr. by Edgar J. Goodspeed (Chicago : Univ. of Chicago Pr., 1939); *New Testament in modern English*, tr. by J. B. Phillips (N.Y. : Macmillan, 1958; rev. ed., 1972); *The translation from the Latin Vulgate*, by Ronald A. Knox (N.Y. : Sheed & Ward, 1954); and the *New International Version*, publ. under the sponsorship of the New York Bible Society International (Grand Rapids, Mich. : Zondervan. New Testament, 1973 ; Old Testament, 1978).

Herbert Dennett's *A guide to modern versions of the New Testament: how to understand and use them* (Chicago : Moody Pr., 1966) provides historical and descriptive notes on the various versions, together with some assessment of the quality of each. Similarly, for the Bible as a whole, *The word of God : a guide to English versions of the Bible*, ed. by Lloyd R. Bailey (Atlanta : J. Knox Pr., 1982) presents essays by biblical scholars on English translations to help readers choose a Bible for themselves. Another book with the same purpose is Jack Pearl Lewis, *The English Bible, from KJV to NIV : a history and evaluation* (2nd ed. Grand Rapids, Mich : Baker, 1991) which examines the strengths and weaknesses of 14 major translations, including the NRSV and Revised English version.

In larger libraries bilingual or polyglot editions are sometimes needed. Three recent publications of this type are: (1) *NIV interlinear Hebrew-English Old Testament*, ed. by John R. Kohlenberger (Grand Rapids, Mich. : Zondervan, 1979–85. 4 v.), which interlines Hebrew and English, with the text of the New International Version in the right-hand margin. (2) *NIV triglot Old Testament* (Grand Rapids, Mich. : Zondervan, 1981. 1 v., unpaged) which presents in parallel columns "the two most important ancient texts of the Old Testament—the Hebrew according to the Masoretic Text and the Greek according to the Septaugint—together with the modern English of the New International Version."—*Introd*; (3) *NASB interlinear Greek-English New Testament*, ed. by Alfred Marshall (Grand Rapids, Mich : Regency Reference Library, 1984. 1027 p.) which offers an interlinear arrangement of the *Novum Testamentum Graece* text (Nestle, 21st), and a literal English translation by the editor, the English equivalent appearing directly beneath the Greek original, thus "illustrating an essential stage" (*Foreword*) in translation; the *NASB* text appears in a narrow left-hand column; and (4) *The New Greek-English interlinear New Testament : a new interlinear translation of the Greek New Testament, United Bible Societies' third, corrected edition with the New Revised Standard Version, New Testament* trans. by Robert K. Brown and Philip W. Comfort, ed. by J. D. Douglas (3rd corr. ed. Wheaton, Ill. : Tyndale House, 1990).

The Apocrypha.

Listed below are some important editions and versions of the apocrypha and pseudepigrapha. *The New Testament Apocrypha and Pseudepigrapha : a guide to publications, with excursuses on Apocalypses*, by James H. Charlesworth (BC107) provides a comprehensive list of the New Testament apocryphal books.

(1) *The Old Testament pseudepigrapha*, ed. by James H. Charlesworth (Garden City, N.Y. : Doubleday, 1983–85. 2 v.). "Designed for the scholar and for the interested non-specialist."—*Pref*. A wide selection, with some texts translated into English for the first time. Each work is preceded by an introduction covering text, manuscripts, provenance, significance, and select bibliography.

(2) *The Apocryphal Old Testament*, ed. by H. F. D. Sparks (Oxford : Clarendon Pr., 1984. 990 p.). Presents new (or revised) translations of the more important noncanonical Old Testament books, the selection smaller than Charlesworth (above) and intended for general rather than strictly academic use.

(3) *The Apocrypha according to The authorized version*, ed. by Robert H. Pfeiffer (N.Y. : Harper, 1953. 295 p.). The apocryphal books originally printed in the Authorized Version, but often omitted from modern editions.

(4) *Apocrypha of the Old Testament : Revised Standard Version* (N.Y. : Nelson, 1957. 250 p.). *The Oxford annotated Apocrypha*

(N.Y. : Oxford Univ. Pr., 1965. 298 p.) also uses the Revised Standard Version, and has been reprinted as part of the *Oxford annotated Bible* (above).

(5) *New Testament Apocrypha*, ed. by Wilhelm Schneemelcher; English trans. ed. by R. McL. Wilson. (Cambridge : J. Clarke, 1991–92. 2 v.). Vol. 1, Gospels and related writings; v. 2, Writings related to the apostles, apocalypes and related subjects.

(6) *The apocryphal New Testament : a collection of apocryphal Christian literature in English tranlsation*, ed. by J. K. Elliott (Oxford : Clarendon Pr. ; N.Y. : Oxford Univ. Pr., 1993. 747 p.). A revised and newly translated edition of *Apocryphal New Testament*, trans. by Montague Rhodes James (Oxford : The Clarendon Pr., 1924. 584 p.).

Bibliography

British and Foreign Bible Society. Library. Historical catalogue of the printed editions of Holy Scripture in the library of the British and Foreign Bible Society / comp. by T. H. Darlow and H. F. Moule. London : Bible House, 1903–11. 2 v. in 4. **BC95**

Repr. : N.Y. : Kraus, 1963.

Contents: v. 1, English; v. 2, Polyglots and languages other than English: pt. 1, Polyglots, Acawoio–Grebo; pt. 2, Greek–Opa; pt. 3, Ora–Zulu; Indexes.

An indispensable catalog of editions of the Bible, arranged chronologically under each language; annotated. Five indexes: (1) Languages and dialects (more than 600); (2) Translators, revisers, editors, etc.; (3) Printers, publishers, etc; (4) Places of printing; (5) General subjects (names of Bibles, etc.).

§ For a revision of v. 1, *see* Arthur Sumner Herbert, *Historical catalogue of printed editions of the English Bible, 1525–1961* (BC100); of the African sections, *see* Geraldine Elizabeth Coldham, *A bibliography of Scriptures in African languages* (BC99). Z7770.B73

British Library. The British Library general catalogue of printed books to 1975. London : C. Bingley ; London ; N.Y. : K.G. Saur, 1979–87. 360 v. **BC96**

Vols. 28–31 cover the Library's extensive collection of the Bible: (1) Complete editions by language, chronologically under language; (2) Selections; (3) Old Testament, followed by sections and individual books; (4) Books of the Apocrypha; (5) New Testament, sections, individual books, N.T., Apocrypha; (6) Appendix. Contents list and index of headings and languages. Recent additions are listed in the microfiche supplements. *See* AA102 for information on the complete set and its supplements. Z921.L553B74

Chamberlin, William J. Catalogue of English Bible translations : a classified bibliography of versions and editions including books, parts, and Old and New Testament Apocrypha and Apocryphal books. N.Y. : Greenwood, 1991. 898 p. (Bibliographies and indexes in religious studies, no. 21). **BC97**

Entries, some with annotations, are arranged chronologically within sections for the whole Bible and its parts. Includes chapters for Dead Sea scrolls, Koran, the works of Josephus, and collections of patristic writings. Reprints are listed under their original publication dates. Index of translators, editors, and translation names.

§ Chamberlin's work is more up-to-date than Arthur Sumner Herbert's *Historical catalogue of printed editions of the English Bible, 1525–1961* (BC100) and Margaret Thorndike Hills's *The English Bible in America* (BC101), but lacks the extensive descriptive notes and indexes those works provide. Z7771.E5C43

Chambers, Bettye Thomas. Bibliography of French Bibles : fifteenth- and sixteenth-century French-language editions of the scriptures. Genève : Droz, 1983. 548 p. : ill. (Travaux d'humanisme et renaissance, no.192). **BC98**

Aims to "present ... a standardized, comprehensive bibliographical description of 'ideal copy' of every French-language edition of the

Bible and New Testament published in the fifteenth and sixteenth centuries."—*Introd.* Lists in chronological order 551 entries, with full bibliographical description and notes, together with library locations.

Z7771.F8C48

Coldham, Geraldine Elizabeth. A bibliography of Scriptures in African languages. London : British and Foreign Bible Soc., 1966. 2 v.   **BC99**

Contents: v. 1, Polyglot; Acholi–Mousgoum; v. 2, Mpama–Zulu; Indexes.

"A revision of the African sections of the Darlow and Moule 'Historical Catalogue of the Printed Editions of Holy Scripture' [BC95], with additions to 1964."—*title page.*

———. ———. *Supplement, 1964–1974* (London : British and Foreign Bible Soc., 1975. 198 p.) is intended for use with the 1966 volume, which it supplements, and not as a separate work. Includes Scriptures published 1964–74 and editions of earlier years omitted from the basic work. Long lists of Language name corrections and Geographical name corrections help update a rapidly changing nomenclature.   Z7771.A4C6

Herbert, Arthur Sumner. Historical catalogue of printed editions of the English Bible, 1525–1961 : rev. and expanded from the edition of T. H. Darlow and H. F. Moule, 1903. London : British and Foreign Bible Society ; N.Y. : American Bible Society, [1968]. 549 p.   **BC100**

A revision and expansion of v. 1 of the Darlow and Moule *Historical catalogue of the printed editions of Holy Scripture in the library of the British and Foreign Bible Society* (BC95). This edition is not based solely on the collection in the British and Foreign Bible Society Library, but draws on the holdings of other outstanding collections in both Britain and the U.S. and indicates locations.

§ *See* William J. Chamberlin's *Catalogue of English Bible translations* (BC97) for a basic bibliography that updates Herbert, but lacks extensive historical notes and indexes.   Z7771.E5H47

Hills, Margaret Thorndike. The English Bible in America : a bibliography of editions of the Bible & the New Testament published in America, 1777–1957. N.Y. : American Bible Society, 1961. 477 p.   **BC101**

Repr., with corrections and revisions, 1962 (475 p.).

A chronological, annotated listing of Bibles in the English language published in the U.S. and Canada, with indication of locations of copies. Six indexes: (1) geographical index of publishers and printers; (2) alphabetical of publishers and printers; (3) translations, translators, and revisers; (4) editors and commentators; (5) edition titles; and (6) general index.   Z7771.A5H5

National union catalog, pre-1956 imprints : a cumulative author list representing Library of Congress printed cards and titles reported by other American libraries. London : Mansell, 1968–80. 685 v.   **BC102**

Vols. 53–56 of the *National union catalog* constitute an important bibliography of manuscripts, "texts and translations of the Bible and its component parts."—*Introd.* About 63,000 entries representing some 700 languages are arranged according to the English Authorized version (names of groups of books come before the first book of each group), followed by: (1) language; (2) date of publication; (3) version. *NUC* supplements 1956–67, v. 12; 1968–72, v. 10; 1973–77, v. 12, and subsequent annual cumulations record recently cataloged texts.

Z881.A1U518

North, Eric McCoy. The book of a thousand tongues : being some account of the translation and publication of all or part of the Holy Scriptures into more than a thousand languages and dialects with over 1100 examples from the text / publ. for the American Bible Society. N.Y. : Harper, 1938. 386 p. : ill.   **BC103**

Repr.: Detroit : Gale, 1971.

Descriptive notes and facsimiles of extracts from printed Bibles in more than a thousand languages. Useful for identifying Bibles in

varying tongues, including many versions in English. Includes chronological lists of the languages in which the Bible has been published in whole or in part.   P352.A2N6

Rumball-Petre, Edwin A. R. Rare Bibles : an introduction for collectors and a descriptive check list. [2nd ed., rev.]. N.Y. : Philip Duschnes, 1954. 53 p.   **BC104**

Repr., 1963.

1st ed., 1938.

An annotated bibliography of rare copies of the Bible in various languages.   Z7770.R89

Bibliography

Belle, Gilbert van. Johannine bibliography 1966–1985 : a cumulative bibliography on the Fourth Gospel. Louvain : Leuven Univ. Pr. : Uitgeverij Peters, 1988. 563 p. (Bibliotheca Ephemeridum theologicarum Lovaniensium, 82).   **BC105**

Contains 6,300 citations, with cross-references, to monographs, multiauthor works, articles, dissertations, and book reviews in detailed classified arrangement. Indexes of miscellanea, festschriften and collected essays; periodicals; biblical references; subjects; and names. Continues coverage provided by Edward Malatesta's *St. John's Gospel, 1920–1965* (Rome : Pontifical Biblical Institute, 1967).

Z7772.M1

Burchard, Christoph. Bibliographie zu den Handschriften vom Toten Meer. Berlin : Alfred Töpelmann, 1957–65. 2 v. (Beihefte zur Zeitschrift für die alttestamentliche Wissenschaft, 76, 89).   **BC106**

A bibliography of books and periodical articles on the Dead Sea Scrolls, in various languages. Author arrangement with sigla index.

Z6371.D4B8

Charlesworth, James H. The New Testament apocrypha and pseudepigrapha : a guide to publications, with excursuses on Apocalypses / by James H. Charlesworth, with James R. Mueller. [Chicago] : Amer. Theological Libr. Assoc. ; Metuchen, N.J. : Scarecrow, 1987. 450 p. (ATLA bibliography series, no. 17).   **BC107**

The first comprehensive bibliography of monographic and serial publications on the 99 major works forming the complex New Testament Apocrypha and Pseudepigrapha. Includes three introductory essays: (1) Defining the New Testament Apocrypha and Pseudepigrapha and the history of its study; (2) The theology and impact of the Apocalypse of John; (3) Subsequent apocalypses in the Jewish and Christian traditions. Author index. An invaluable tool for general readers and specialists alike.

§ Maurice Geerard's *Clavis apocryphorum Novi Testamenti* (Brepols : Turnhout, c1992) is an important complementary work for locating a wider range of Christian apocryphal texts, specifically those anonymous texts and pseudepigraphs in which the main subjects are characters named in the Bible or present at events described therein.

Z7772.Z5C45

Cully, Iris V. A guide to biblical resources / Iris V. Cully and Kendig Brubaker Cully. Wilton, Conn. : Morehouse-Barlow, [1981]. 153 p.   **BC108**

Aims "to offer ... guidance into the rich resources of meaning, scholarship, and interpretation which biblical study entails."—*Pref.* Presents chapters, with English-language bibliographies, on background materials, reference books, translations, versions, adults' and children's courses, and the Bible in worship, in literature and the arts. Popular in tone; addressed to the general reader.

§ For a helpful introduction to New Testament study, *see* Erasmus Hort, *The Bible book : resources for reading the New Testament* (N.Y. : Crossroad, 1983. 209 p.).   BS600.2.C796

École biblique et archéologique française (Jerusalem). Bibliothèque. Catalogue de la Bibliothèque de l'École biblique et archéologique française = Catalog of the Library of the French Biblical and Archeological School, Jerusalem, Israel. Boston : G.K. Hall, 1975. 13 v.   **BC109**

The catalog of an important collection strong in scripture studies, archaeology, papyrology, linguistics, etc. Includes both books and articles in a single alphabet of authors and subjects. Subject headings in French.   Z7770.J36

Fitzmyer, Joseph A. An introductory bibliography for the study of scripture. 3rd ed. Roma : Editrice Pontificio Istituto Biblico, 1990. 216 p. (Subsidia Biblica, 3).   **BC110**

1st ed., 1961, by George S. Glanzman and Fitzmyer; rev. ed., 1981.

A guide for students beginning serious study of the Bible or theology. Classified arrangement of basic titles and the most important secondary works. Evaluative annotations mention book reviews. Index of modern authors.   Z7770.F57

The Gospel of Mark : a cumulative bibliography, 1950–1990 / comp. by F. Neirynck … [et al.]. Leuven : Leuven Univ. Pr. : Peeters, 1992. 717, 5 p. (Bibliotheca Ephemeridum theologicarum Lovaniensium, 102).   **BC111**

An extensive bibliography compiled from some 500 periodicals and series, and including references to *New Testament abstracts* (BC123) and *Dissertation abstracts international* (AG13). Entries are listed by author, followed by an index of Gospel passages and a detailed classified subject index. Provides lists of festschriften and commentaries, in chronological order, publ. before 1950.   Z7772.M1G67

La Sor, William Sanford. Bibliography of the Dead Sea Scrolls, 1948–1957. Pasadena, Calif. : Library, Fuller Theological Seminary, 1958. 92 p. (Fuller Library Theological Seminary bibliographical series, 2 ; Fuller Library bulletin, 31).   **BC112**

A classed bibliography of almost 3,000 entries. In three sections: General works; Texts of Qumran; Interpretation of the Qumran literature. Author index.

§ Supplemented by Bastiaan Jongeling's *A classified bibliography of the finds in the desert of Judah* (Leiden : Brill, 1971) and by the bibliographies in each quarterly issue of *Revue de Qumran*.   Z6371.D4L3

Langevin, Paul-Emile. Bibliographie biblique = Biblical bibliography = Biblische Bibliographie = Bibliografia biblica = Bibliografía bíblica. Québec : Presses de l'Université Laval, 1972–1985. v. 1–3. (In progress?).   **BC113**

Contents: v. 1, 1930–70; v. 2, 1930–75; v. 3, 1930–83.

Citations are arranged in five main sections (Introduction to the Bible; Old Testament; New Testament; Jesus Christ; Biblical themes) with numerous subdivisions. Author and cumulative subject indexes in each volume. Vol. 1 cites articles gleaned from 70 Roman Catholic periodicals and a selection of Catholic books. Vol. 2 adds 50 journals (many non-Catholic), 1930–75, and includes references to some 800 books analyzed chapter by chapter. Vol. 3 adds 43 new titles, many related to Near Eastern studies, 1930–83, and also includes chapters of 450 books.   Z7770.L35

Mills, Watson E. A bibliography of the periodical literature on the Acts of the Apostles, 1962–1984. Leiden : E.J. Brill, 1986. 115 p. (Supplements to Novum Testamentum, v. 58).   **BC114**

Lists relevant articles from approximately 300 scholarly journals, many not covered by Günter Wagner's *Exegetical bibliography of the New Testament* (BC118). Entries are arranged alphabetically by author. Scripture and subject indexes.   Z7772.N1M55

Powell, Mark Allan. The Bible and modern literary criticism : a critical assessment and annotated bibliography / comp. by Mark Allan Powell with the assistance of Cecile G. Gray and Melissa C. Curtis. N.Y. : Greenwood, 1992. 469 p. (Bibliographies and indexes in religious studies, no. 22).   **BC115**

A classified bibliography "of works that draw on modern literary criticism for a scholarly study of the Bible."—*Pref.* 1,749 entries in six sections: (1) Basis (foundational works in fields other than relgion); (2) Theory; (3) Method; (4) Criticism (studies arranged by book of the Bible); (5) Evaluation (of the types of titles in pt. 4); (6) Implications. The Criticism section includes all materials publ. through 1990 that the author could locate; all other sections are selective. Generous use of cross-references in annotations and at the beginning of sections. Author, title, and subject indexes.

§ Mark Minor's *Literary-critical approaches to the Bible: an annotated bibliography* (West Cornwall, Conn. : Locust Hill Pr., 1992, 520 p.) is a complementary work of 2,254 citations. Although there is much duplication, both will be wanted by research collections.   Z7770.P68

Repertorium Biblicum Medii Aevi / Fridericus Stegmüller. Madrid : Consejo Superior de Investigaciones Científicas, Inst. Francisco Suárez, 1940 [i.e., 1950]–80. 11 v. (In progress?).   **BC116**

Repr., 1981–89.

Contents: v. 1, Initia biblica. Apocrypha. Prologi; v. 2–5, Commentaria: Auctores; v. 6–7, Commentaria: Anonyma (arranged alphabetically by place of publication); v. 8, Supplementum; v. 9, Supplementi altera pars glossa ordinaria; v. 10, Initia graeca. Initia latina A–K; v. 11, Initia latina L–Z.

Vol. 1 contains a long treatment of apocryphal writings and a list of prefaces to the Bible. Vols. 2–7 list patristic and medieval commentaries on the Bible, with *incipits* and *explicits*, editions, manuscripts, and bibliography. Vols. 8–9 list supplementary materials in the same arrangement as v. 1–7. Vols. 10 and 11 are indexes. A projected 12th volume will provide additional indexes.   Z7770.S835

Society for Old Testament Study. Book list. [Sheffield, etc., Eng. : The Society].   **BC117**

Annual classified list of books on the Old Testament and related subjects, with annotations written by contributing scholars. Author index.

§ Some years reprinted with cumulated author indexes: (1) *Eleven years of Bible bibliography : the books lists of the Society for Old Testament Study, 1946–56*, ed. by H. H. Rowley. (Indian Hills, Colo. : Falcon's Wing Pr., 1957).

(2) *A decade of Bible bibliography : the book lists of the Society for Old Testament Study, 1957–1966*. G. W. Anderson, ed. (Oxford : Blackwell, 1967).

(3) *Bible bibliography, 1967–1973. Old Testament*, ed. by Peter R. Ackroyd. (Oxford : Blackwell, 1974).   Z7772.A1S65

Wagner, Günter. An exegetical bibliography of the New Testament. Macon, Ga. : Mercer Univ. Pr., c1983–1987. v. 1–3. (In progress).   **BC118**

A compilation from the looseleaf ed. (Zürich : Rüschlikon, 1973–).

Contents: v. 1, Matthew and Mark; v. 2, Luke and Acts; v. 3, John and 1, 2, 3 John.

Entries are arranged in the order of chapters and verses of the biblical text, then chronologically. References cite many discussions hidden within more comprehensive works. Most citations refer to publications in English or German, 1950s to time of publication. No indexes. An outstanding contribution to biblical scholarship, but should be used with other standard bibliographies (e.g., *New testament abstracts*, BC123). A fourth volume, on the major Pauline epistles, is in preparation.

§ Earlier material may be found in *Bibliography of New Testament literature, 1900–1950*, prep. by the Graduate Seminar in New Testament (San Anselmo, Calif. : San Francisco Theological Seminary, 1953. 312 p.), under the direction of John Wick Bowman, and ed. by Tadashi Akaishi. A classified, annotated bibliography of nearly 2,400 books and some periodical articles in English.   Z7772.M1W33

Indexes; Abstract journals

Elenchus of Biblica. 1985– . Roma : Pontificio Istituto biblico, 1988– . Annual.   **BC119**
Prior to v. 49, appeared as part of the journal *Biblica*. Continues *Elenchus bibliographicus biblicus* (v. 49 [1968]–v. 58/59 [1977/78]) and *Elenchus bibliographicus biblicus of Biblica* (v. 60 [1979]–65 [1984]).
Provides, in a classed arrangement, the most comprehensive, although not most timely, indexing of journal and monographic literature for biblical studies. Author, Greek and Hebrew word, and Scripture indexes in each volume. Prior to v. 60, a detailed subject index and author index appeared in each volume.   Z7770.E63

Internationale Zeitschriftenschau für Bibelwissenschaft und Grenzgebiete = International review of biblical studies = Revue internationale des études bibliques. Bd. 1 (1951/52)– . Stuttgart : Verlag Katholisches Bibelwerk, 1952– . Annual.   **BC120**
An international bibliography and abstract journal. Classed arrangement with author indexes. Most of the abstracts are in German.   Z7770.I57

Metzger, Bruce Manning. Index of articles on the New Testament and the early church published in festschriften. Philadelphia : Society of Biblical Literature, 1951. 182 p. (Journal of Biblical literature. Monograph series, v. 5).   **BC121**
An index to some 2,350 articles to be found in 640 collections of festschriften published up to the end of 1950 in various languages. From these collections only articles pertinent to the subject have been included.
A 20-page supplement was published by the Society in 1955.

────────── Index to periodical literature on Christ and the Gospels. Leiden : Brill, 1966. 602 p. (New Testament tools and studies, v. 6).   **BC122**
Indexes pertinent articles from 160 periodicals in 16 languages, each periodical being indexed from beginning date through 1961. Classed arrangement; author index.
§ Another bibliography in the same series is Andrew J. Mattill and Mary B. Mattill's *A classified bibliography of literature on the Acts of the Apostles* (Leiden : Brill, 1966. 513 p.).   Z7772.M1M4

New Testament abstracts. v. 1 (1956)– . Cambridge, Mass. : Weston School of Theology, 1956– . 3 times a year.   **BC123**
Imprint varies.
Presents abstracts in English of articles on the New Testament which have appeared in Catholic, Protestant, and Jewish periodicals in many languages. Similar in size to *Old Testament abstracts* (BC124).
Each volume includes an index of Scripture texts and an index of authors, plus a separate list of book reviews.   BS410.N35

Old Testament abstracts. v. 1 (Feb. 1978)– . Wash. : Catholic Biblical Association of America, 1978– . 3 times per yr.   **BC124**
Subtitle: A thrice-yearly bibliography of literature relating to the Old Testament.
Covers about 300 journals (1992) offering annually some 1,500 abstracts of articles on all phases of Old Testament scholarship. Separate book review section in each issue. Annual indexes (of authors, scripture texts, and words in Hebrew and other ancient languages) in the third issue of each volume.   BS410.O42

Encyclopedias

The Anchor Bible dictionary / David Noel Freedman, ed. in chief ; associate editors, Gary A. Herion, David F. Graf, John David Pleins ; managing editor, Astrid B. Beck. N.Y. : Doubleday, c1992. 6 v. : ill., maps.   **BC125**
"Every generation needs its own Dictionary of the Bible" (*Introd.*) and this work fills that need admirably. 1,000 contributors, mostly North American, have provided 6,200 entries, some as long as 40 pages; most have bibliographies. Entries cover every proper name, major words, each book of the Bible, Apocryphal texts, Dead Sea scrolls, and Nag Hammadi codices. Gives much attention to cultural history, social institutions, and method. In the area of word studies, this work does not attempt to supplant important previous publications such as *The interpreter's dictionary of the Bible* (BC132). Uses cross-references, but an index would improve access.   BS440.A54

Catholic biblical encyclopedia / by John E. Steinmueller and Kathryn Sullivan. N.Y. : J. F. Wagner, [1956]. 2 v. in 1. : ill., maps in color.   **BC126**
Contents: [pt. 1], Old Testament; [pt. 2], New Testament (publ. separately in 1950).
Intended "for the great majority of educated people" rather than for the biblical specialist. Articles vary in length from a few lines to several pages, and include biographical, geographical, archaeological, and dogmatic subjects. Pronunciation is indicated. A special chapter on Mariology is appended to the volume.
§ For more recent Catholic theological interpretation, see the *Encyclopedia of biblical theology : the complete Sacramentum verbi*, ed. by Johannes B. Bauer (BC130).   BS440.C36

A dictionary of Biblical interpretation / ed. by R. J. Coggins and J. L. Houlden. London : SCM Pr. ; Philadelphia : Trinity Pr. Internat., 1990. 751 p.   **BC127**
Signed articles by British scholars, with bibliographies, on a wide range of topics dealing with the history of biblical interpretation and current issues in biblical scholarship. Includes a select index of subjects and an index of biblical references. Provides access to many subjects not treated in most Bible dictionaries.   BS500.D5

Dictionary of Jesus and the Gospels / editors, Joel B. Green, Scot McKnight ; consulting ed., I. Howard Marshall. Downers Grove, Ill. : InterVarsity Pr., c1992. 933 p. : ill.   **BC128**
Signed articles, with ample bibliographies and scripture references, cover important Gospel themes and concepts; the Gospels themselves; types of biblical interpretation; aspects of Jesus' life and ministry. A work of Protestant scholarship that attempts to be "both critically responsible and theologically evangelical" (*Pref*), this dictionary is the first of its kind since James Hastings' *Dictionary of Christ and the Gospels* (N.Y. : Scribner; Edinburgh : Clark, 1906–1908). Scripture and subject indexes.   BS2555.2.D53

Encyclopaedia biblica : thesaurus rerum bibliocarum alphabetico ordine digestus / ediderunt Institutum Bialik Procurationi Iudaicae pro Palaestina (Jewish Agency) Addictum et Museum Antiquitatum Iudaicarum ad Universitatem Hebraicam Hierosolymitanam Pertinens. Hierosolymis : Instituti Bialik, 1950–88. 9 v. : ill.   **BC129**
Added title page in Hebrew: Entsiklopediyah mikra'it.
Some volumes credit the Jewish Agency under the name Institutum Bialik Procurationi Iudaicae pro Israel (Jewish Agency) Addictum.
The product of modern Hebrew scholarship, published under the auspices of the Jewish Agency of Palestine and the Museum of Jewish Antiquities of the Hebrew University in Jerusalem. The contributors are, for the most part, Israeli scholars and are authorities in their fields. The articles, written entirely in modern literary Hebrew, are signed with initials, and usually are accompanied by bibliographies which list books both in Hebrew and in western European languages. Vol. 9 indexes the set.   BS440.E5

Encyclopedia of biblical theology : the complete Sacramentum verbi / ed. by Johannes B. Bauer. N.Y. : Crossroad, 1981. 1141 p.   **BC130**

Translated from the 3rd enl. and rev. ed. (1967) of Bauer's *Bibeltheologisches Wörterbuch*. Publ. 1970 as *Sacramentum verbi* and repr. 1976 as *Bauer encyclopedia of biblical theology*.

An important work of Roman Catholic biblical scholarship, providing articles on theologically significant words. A supplementary bibliography created for this translation includes English-language titles. Analytical index of articles and cross-references, index of biblical references, and index of Greek and Hebrew words.   BS440.B46713

The international standard Bible encyclopedia / gen. ed., Geoffrey W. Bromiley ... [et al.]. Fully rev. Grand Rapids, Mich. : Eerdmans, 1979–c1988. 4 v. : ill (some col.), maps.   **BC131**

1st ed., 1915; rev. 1930.

"Although some of the most durable of the original material" has been retained, this new edition, thoroughly updated in "both matter and format" is "to all intents and purposes a new, or at least a completely reconstructed encyclopedia."—*Pref*. Addressed to teachers, students, pastors, and general readers; contains an alphabetical arrangement of articles which define, identify, and explain terms and topics in the Bible and in biblical studies. Includes all personal and geographical names in the Bible, together with entries for subjects that bear on transmission of texts, interpretation, biblical theology, etc. "Great care has been taken to maintain what the preface of the first edition described as the attitude of 'a reasonable conservatism'." Entries range in length from a line or two to several pages; all except the shortest are signed, and most have bibliographies. No index.   BS440.I6

The interpreter's dictionary of the Bible : an illustrated encyclopedia identifying and explaining all proper names and significant terms and subjects in the Holy Scriptures, including the Apocrypha, with attention to archaeological discoveries and researches into the life and faith of ancient times. N.Y. : Abingdon, [1962]. 4 v. : ill.   **BC132**

George Arthur Buttrick, ed.

A scholarly encyclopedic dictionary designed for the preacher, scholar, student, teacher, and general reader, referring to both the King James Version and the Revised Standard Version, to the Apocrypha, the Pseudepigrapha, the Dead Sea Scrolls, and other ancient manuscripts. Articles have been contributed by scholars from many countries, are signed, and usually include bibliographies. The illustrations, both color and black-and-white, are good and pertinent, and there is a section of colored maps, as well as outline maps inserted in the text. Important for modern biblical study.

―――. *Supplementary volume*. Keith Crim, gen. ed. (Nashville : Abingdon, [1976]. 998 p.).

Updates articles in the 1962 publication and adds new articles on topics not previously treated. Provides cross-references to earlier articles where appropriate.

Dictionaries

In addition to the dictionaries listed below, there are available a number of smaller dictionaries, generally popular in tone, concerning specific aspects of the Bible. Among these are *Who's who in the Bible* (N.Y. : Bonanza, 1980. 448 p.), originally published in 2 v.: *Who's who in the Old Testament* by Joan Comay (1971) and *Who's who in the New Testament* by Robert Brownrigg (1971); *All of the women of the Bible* by Edith Deen (N.Y. : Harper, 1955. 410 p.), *Encyclopedia of Bible creatures* by Vilhelm Møller-Christensen and Karl Eduard Jordt Jørgensen, tr. from the Danish by Arne Unhjem (Philadelphia : Fortress Pr., 1965. 302 p.); *Plants of the Bible* by Michael Zohary (Cambridge : Cambridge Univ. Pr., 1982. 223 p.), which identifies and describes biblical plants and includes excellent illustrations; and an "All series" by Herbert Lockyer which includes among its dozen or more titles *All the men of the Bible* (Grand Rapids, Mich. : Zondervan, 1958. 381 p.) and *All the trades and occupations of the Bible* (Grand Rapids, Mich. : Zondervan, 1969. 327 p.).

While some glossaries are included here, standard dictionaries of Hebrew, of biblical Greek, and of Latin are listed with foreign language dictionaries in section AD.

Armstrong, Terry A. A reader's Hebrew-English lexicon of the Old Testament / Terry A. Armstrong, Douglas L. Busby, Cyril F. Carr. Grand Rapids, Mich. : Zondervan, 1980–88. 4 v.   **BC133**

Contents: v. 1, Genesis–Deuteronomy; v. 2, Joshua–2 Kings; v. 3, Isaiah–Malachi; v. 4, Psalms–2 Chronicles.

The main part of each volume lists Hebrew terms used 50 times or less, "verse by verse in the order of their occurrence."—*Pref*. Gives English translation, frequency and page reference to *The new Brown, Driver, Briggs, Gesenius Hebrew and English lexicon* (AC476). Each volume has an appendix of words occuring more than 50 times. Vol. 4 has an appendix of Aramaic words. Useful as a quick reference tool, but is not intended to replace standard lexicons.   PJ4833.A69

Botterweck, G. Johannes. Theologisches Wörterbuch zum Alten Testament / hrsg. von G. Johannes Botterweck und Helmer Ringgren. Stuttgart : W. Kohlhammer, 1973–94. Bd. 1–8, Lfg. 4. (In progress).   **BC134**

Issued in *Lieferungen* beginning 1970; title page of Bd. 1 is dated 1973. To be in about 8 v.

Contents: Bd. 1–8, Lfg. 4, 'āb–šāṭāh.

An important scholarly work presenting not only the theological meaning of Hebrew and Aramaic Old Testament words, but also their Near Eastern background. Arranged alphabetically according to the Hebrew term.

§ An English translation is appearing as *Theological dictionary of the Old Testament*, John T. Willis, translator. (Grand Rapids, Mich. : Wm. B. Eerdmans, 1974–90. v. 1–6. In progress). Contents: v. 1–6, 'abh–yāṭar.   BS440.B57

Bridges, Ronald. The Bible word book : concerning obsolete or archaic words in the King James version of the Bible / Ronald Bridges, Luther A. Weigle. N.Y. : Nelson, [1960]. 422 p.   **BC135**

For the general reader. Contains articles on 827 obsolete or archaic words used in the King James version. Explains the original meaning and shows what words have been used to replace them in the Revised Standard Version. Indexes the words and phrases from the RSV.   BS186.B7

The Eerdmans Bible dictionary / revision ed., Allen C. Myers. Grand Rapids, Mich. : Eerdmans, 1987. 1094 p., [12] p. of plates : ill. (some col.).   **BC136**

1st ed., (Kampen : Kok, c1950); 2nd ed., c1976.

A revised, augmented translation of *Bijbelse encyclopedie*, by North American scholars, that is evangelical Protestant in orientation, but treats other viewpoints fairly. Bibliographical references for selected articles. Limited number of black-and-white photographs, line drawings, and maps in color.   BS440.G7613

Exegetical dictionary of the New Testament / ed. by Horst Balz and Gerhard Schneider. Grand Rapids, Mich. : Eerdmans, c1990–c1993. 3 v.   **BC137**

Translation of: *Exegetisches Wörterbuch zum Neuen Testament* (Stuttgart : Kohlhammer, 1980–83).

Gives definition and English translation for every Greek word in the New Testament and discusses significant words in greater depth. Signed entries were contributed by Catholic and Lutheran scholars from the German-speaking world. Cannot replace Gerhard Kittel's *Theological dictionary of the New Testament* (BC143) but provides more recent material than that detailed work. English word index.   BS2312.E913

Gehman, Henry Snyder. The new Westminster dictionary of the Bible. Philadelphia : Westminster Pr., [1970]. 1027 p. : ill.   **BC138**

Based on: John D. Davis, *The Westminster dictionary of the Bible*, rev. and rewritten by Henry Snyder Gehman (Philadelphia : Westminster Pr., [c1944]).

A thorough reworking of the 1944 ed. in the light of later biblical scholarship and research.   BS440.G4

Harper's Bible dictionary / gen. ed., Paul J. Achtemeier. San Francisco : Harper & Row, c1985. 1178 p.   **BC139**

1st ed., 1952; 8th ed., 1973.

Sponsored by Society of Biblical Literature.

A thoroughly revised edition that presents in a form accessible to general readers the consensus of biblical scholarship from a nonsectarian perspective. Signed articles with cross-references by 179 leading scholars treat all the important personal and place- names in the Bible, every book of the Bible including the Apocrypha, all major archaeological sites, and all important theological terms. There are also major articles with bibliographies on such topics as: Jerusalem; Sociology of the Old and New Testaments; Moses; Bible texts, versions, manuscripts, and editions. Well-illustrated with numerous black-and-white photographs, some color photographs, and line drawings. Maps in color and an index appear at the end of the volume. An excellent one-volume source.   BS440.H237

Harper's Bible pronunciation guide / gen. ed., William O. Walker, Jr. ; associate editors, Toni Craven, J. Andrew Dearman, with the Society of Biblical Literature. San Francisco : Harper & Row, c1989. 170 p.   **BC140**

Gives the pronunciation of every proper name in the English Bible (including the Apocrypha), many proper names from the ancient world, and technical terms important for biblical study. Words appear in alphabetical order in two sections: Biblical terms and Nonbiblical terms. The pronunciation key is printed at the bottom of each page.   BS435.H35

Hastings, James. Dictionary of the Bible. Rev. ed. / by Frederick C. Grant and H. H. Rowley. N.Y. : Scribner, [1963]. 1059 p. : ill.   **BC141**

1st ed., 1909. Frequently reprinted.

The revisions cover Bible scholarship up to the time of publication. References are to the Revised Standard Version of the Bible with cross-references from the Authorized Version and the Revised Version.   BS440.H5

Illustrated dictionary & concordance of the Bible / [gen. ed., Geoffrey Wigoder ; editors, Shalom M. Paul, Old Testament, Benedict T. Viviano, New Testament, Ephraim Stern, biblical archeology]. N.Y. : Macmillan, c1986. 1070 p. : ill. (some col.).   **BC142**

A Bible dictionary with entries for every place and person mentioned in the Old and New Testaments and for major religious concepts and general topics. Brief articles by specialists reflecting current scholarship are free of technical jargon. Numerous illustrations in color, but few cross-references and no bibliography. Bible references related to each subject are listed in the margin next to the entry, hence the word "concordance" in the title.   BS440.I36

Kittel, Gerhard. Theological dictionary of the New Testament / tr. and ed. by Geoffrey W. Bromiley. Grand Rapids, Mich. : Eerdmans, [1964–76]. 10 v.   **BC143**

Editor varies: v. 5–9, ed. by Gerhard Friedrich, v. 10 by R. E. Pitkin.

Translated from *Theologisches Wörterbuch zum Neuen Testament* (Stuttgart : W. Kohlhammer, 1932–72. 9 v.).

A scholarly work of great importance, with signed contributions by many German biblical scholars, treating every word of religious or theological significance in the New Testament. Covers the secular Greek background for each word listed, and its role in the Old and New Testaments and in related texts. Vol. 10 contains indexes of English keywords, Greek keywords, and biblical references, as well as a list of contributors with their contributions and an essay on biblical scholarship, Pre-history of the *Theological dictionary of the New Testament*.

Abridged version: *Theological dictionary of the New Testament*, ed. by Gerhard Kittel and Gerhard Friedrich; tr. and abridged in 1 v. by Geoffrey W. Bromiley (Grand Rapids, Mich. : Eerdmans, c1985. 1356 p.).

Reduced to one-sixth the size of the parent set. Theological material has been retained so far as possible; philological, archaeological, and other supporting materials have been drastically reduced; footnotes and bibliographies are excluded. Volume and page references at the end of each article direct readers to the article in the parent set. Access is facilitated by transliteration of all Greek words, bracketed English translations in the running heads, and alphabetical tables of English and Greek keywords.

§ For new, although less detailed material, see *Exegetical dictionary of the New Testament* (BC137).   PA881.K513

Léon-Dufour, Xavier. Dictionary of biblical theology. 2nd ed. rev. and enl. N.Y. : Seabury Pr., [1973]. 711 p.   **BC144**

Translation of *Vocabulaire de théologie biblique* (1st ed., 1962; 2nd ed., 1970); 1st ed., in English translation, 1967.

Major theological themes of the Bible are presented in signed articles contributed by outstanding Catholic biblical scholars and exegetes. In the new edition some 40 articles have been added, and there are additional cross-references. Intended for the laity as well as for the clergy.   BS543.A1L413

——————— Dictionary of the New Testament / tr. from 2nd French ed. by Terrence Prendergast. N.Y. : Harper & Row, [1980]. 458 p. : ill., maps.   **BC145**

More than 1,000 entries of theological, historical, literary significance. Explanations include original Greek term (often with its Hebrew antecedent) and citations to scriptural use. Many cross-references. A lengthy introduction supplies the context of the New Testament, covering the land and its people, culture, politics and law, domestic life, the faith of Israel, the Scriptures, worship and morality.   BS2312.L4513

Mercer dictionary of the Bible / gen. ed., Watson E. Mills ; associate ed., Roger Bullard … [et al.]. Macon, Ga. : Mercer Univ. Pr., c1990. 987 p., 62 p. of plates : ill. (some col.).   **BC146**

Signed articles by 225 members of the National Association of Baptist Professors of Religion, intended for college, university, and seminary students. Reflects a broad range of viewpoints. Most articles have bibliographies. Well-illustrated throughout; 62 center plates have maps and photographs in color.   BS440.M429

New Bible dictionary. 2nd ed. / organizing ed., J. D. Douglas; revision ed., N. Hillyer. Leicester, Eng. : Inter-Varsity Pr. ; Wheaton, Ill. : Tyndale House, [1982]. 1326 p. : ill., maps. **BC147**

1st ed., 1962.

A thoroughly revised work of evangelical scholarship. Offers signed articles by predominantly British members of the Tyndale Fellowship for Biblical Research; some brief bibliographies. Bible references are to the Revised Standard Version. The text is that of the same publisher's *Illustrated Bible dictionary* (1980. 3 v.); maps and illustrations are drawn from that edition. Indexed.

The new international dictionary of New Testament theology / [German text] Lothar Coenen, Erich Beyreuther and Hans Bietenhard, eds.; trans., with additions and revisions, from the German, ed. by Colin Brown. Exeter : Paternoster Pr., 1975–[82]. 3 v. **BC148**

A translation, with additions and revisions, of *Theologisches Begriffslexikon zum Neuen Testament* (Wuppertal : Brockhaus, 1970–71. 3 v.). Also publ. Grand Rapids, Mich. : Zondervan, 1975–78.

Reissued in 4 v. (Grand Rapids, Mich. : Regency Reference Library, c1986); v. 4, the index volume, includes Townsley's *Scripture index* (below).

Treats New Testament terminology of theological importance. Material from the original is rearranged in this translation so as to group related New Testament Greek terms under concepts arranged alphabetically by English word. Greek terms are treated in their classical, Old Testament and New Testament meanings. Each volume indexed. Vol. 3 includes indexes (of Hebrew and Aramaic words; of Greek words; of subjects) for all three volumes. An *Addenda* volume (1982. 20 p.) updates the bibliographies of the set.

§ Intended as a companion volume to *The new international dictionary of the Christian church* by James Dixon Douglas (BC236). Supplemented by David Townsley, *Scripture index to The new international dictionary of New Testament theology, and index to selected extrabiblical material* (Grand Rapids, Mich. : Regency Reference Library, c1985). BS2397.N48

Odelain, O. Dictionary of proper names and places in the Bible / O. Odelain, R. Séguineau ; tr. and adapted by Matthew J. O'Connell. Garden City, N.Y. : Doubleday, 1981. 479 p. : maps. **BC149**

Translated and adapted from *Dictionnaire des noms propres de la Bible* (Paris : Cerf et Desclée de Brouwer, 1978).

Intended as a companion to the Jerusalem Bible (*see* BC94). Identifies all proper names and places in both the Old and New Testaments, with reference to Bible chapter and verse. Includes: Lists (e.g., Women, Sons of David, etc.); Indexes of Hebrew, Aramaic, and Syriac words and English equivalents; Chronological tables. BS435.O3313

Richardson, Alan. A theological word book of the Bible. London : SCM Pr., 1950 ; N.Y. : Macmillan, [1951]. 290 p. **BC150**

Repr.: London : SCM Pr., 1985.

Aims "to elucidate the distinctive meanings of the keywords of the Bible" (*Pref.*) from the theological point of view. Articles are written by specialists, mainly British, and are signed. BS440.R53

Theological wordbook of the Old Testament / R. Laird Harris, ed. Chicago : Moody Pr., [1980]. 2 v. **BC151**

A work for the "busy pastor or earnest Christian worker who has neither the time nor background for detailed technical study," but who needs "a tool for the study of the significant words of the Hebrew Bible."—*Introd.* Essays on the words selected for extensive treatment were contributed by 46 evangelical scholars of various denominations and are signed with the contributors' initials. Words not chosen for essay treatment are given one-line definitions. Arrangement is according to the consonants of the Hebrew alphabet; related words are presented with the root from which they derive. Bibliographies accompany many of the articles. An index employing the numbers from James Strong's *Exhaustive concordance of the Bible* (see BC165) facilitates access. BS440.T49

Vigouroux, Fulcran Grégoire. Dictionnaire de la Bible : contenant tous les noms de personnes, de lieux, de plantes, d'animaux mentionnés dans les Saintes Écritures, les questions théologiques, archéologiques, scientifiques relatives à l'Ancien et au Nouveau Testament et des notices sur les commentateurs anciens et modernes. Paris : Letouzey, 1907–1912. 5 v. : ill., maps, plans, etc. **BC152**

The standard Bible dictionary from the French Catholic point of view, containing long, signed articles by Catholic scholars, good bibliographies, and excellent illustrations. Includes separate biographical articles, with bibliographies, on the various commentators on the Bible, ancient, modern, Catholic, Protestant, and Jewish.

——. ——. *Supplément*, ed. by Louis Pirot [et al.] (Paris, 1928–1994. v.1–12² [fasc. 1–69], A–sexualité [In progress]). l'écriture). BS440.V7

Ziefle, Helmut W. Dictionary of modern theological German. 2nd ed. Grand Rapids, Mich. : Baker Book House, c1992. 354 p. **BC153**

1st ed., 1982.

Offered as an aid in the study of theological German. The new edition has an enlarged theological vocabulary of about 20,000 German entries with English equivalents "for reading the Bible and German theological texts."—*Pref.* Includes scripture references to Luther's translation of the Bible. BR95.Z53

Quotations

Biblical quotations / ed. by Jennifer Speake. N.Y. : Facts on File, 1983. 203 p. **BC154**

Also publ.: London : Hamlyn, 1982. Repr.: Secaucus, N.J. : Chartwell, 1990, as *A treasury of Biblical quotations.*

Arranged by book of the Bible, from Genesis to Revelation, with index of key words and thematic headings. Text used is that of the Authorized Version. BS391.2.S63

Ehrlich, Eugene H. Mene, Mene, Tekel / Eugene H. Ehrlich, David H. Scott. N.Y. : Harper & Row, 1990. 306 p. **BC155**

Lists in alphabetical order significant words and phrases from the Authorized (King James) Version of the Bible (1611), that have gained wide currency in English. Identifies the source and explains the context and meaning of each entry. Index to scriptural passages. PE1689.E36

Stevenson, Burton Egbert. The home book of Bible quotations. N.Y. : Harper, [1949]. 645 p. **BC156**

Quotations are arranged under subject with many cross-references; there is a word concordance index to the whole. Based on the King James Version, with a few references to variations in the Revised Version. Includes the Apocrypha of both the Old and the New Testaments. Exact citation is given to book, chapter, and verse. BS432.S667

Concordances

Listed below are concordances of English translations of the Bible which are commonly used in reference work. Large research and specialized collections will have need of concordances of the Hebrew, Latin, and Greek biblical texts. The standard concordance of the Hebrew Bible is *Veteris Testamenti concordantiae hebraicae atque chaldaicae* (Berlin : Margolin, 1937. 1532 p., 16 p. Repr.: Jerusalem ; Tel Aviv : Margolin; Graz : Akademische Druck- und Verlagsanstalt, 1955. 2 v.), by Salomon Mandelkern. Also in Hebrew, following the Masoretic text and including translation of many words into German, Latin, and English, is Gerhard Lisowsky's *Konkordanz zum hebräischen Alten Testament* (Stuttgart : Privilagierte Württembergische Bibelanstalt, [1958]. 1672 p. 3rd ed., rev. by Hans Peter Rüger, publ. 1993). *A concordance to the Septuagint and the other Greek versions of the Old Testament (including the Aprocryphal books)* (Oxford : Clarendon Pr., 1897–1906. 2 v. Repr: Graz : Akademische Druck- und Verlagsanstalt, 1975. 3 v. in 2, with a supplement by Henry A. Redpath. 272 p.), by Edwin Hatch and Henry A. Redpath, gives original Hebrew words for all Greek words listed.

For the New Testament, the most important concordance is *Vollständige konkordanz zum griechischen Neuen Testament* (Berlin ; N.Y. : De Gruyter, 1975–83. 2 v.), which is based on the 26th ed. of the Nestle-Aland *Novum Testamentum Graece* (Stuttgart : Deutsche Bibelgesellschaft, 1979). It lists every Greek word and its contexts, and gives all the variants from the other modern critical editions of the New Testament. Those who know little Greek will find *A concordance to the Greek Testament, according to the texts of Westcott and Hort, Tischendorf and the English revisers* (5th ed., rev. by H. K. Moulton. Edinburgh : Clark, 1978. 1110 p.) convenient because of its use of numbers from James Strong's *New Strong's exhaustive concordance of the Bible* (BC165).

Novae concordantiae Bibliorum sacrorum iuxta Vulgatam versionem critice editam quas digessit Bonifatius Fischer OSB ([Stuttgart-Bad Cannstatt] : Frommann-Holzboog, [1977]. 5 v.) is a computer-produced concordance to a new text of the Vulgate based on the important manuscripts and two modern critical editions.

Day, A. Colin. Roget's thesaurus of the Bible. San Francisco : Harper San Francisco, c1992. 927 p.   **BC157**
Intended for use in locating Bible verses and passages by subject. Biblical passages have been paraphrased and arranged in categories based on those of *Roget's thesaurus of English words and phrases* (AC145), allowing easy browsing of passages with similar meanings. A Bible verse index provides access from known passages to those on the same or related topics. Index.
§ See *Modern concordance to the New Testament* (BC161) for a similar treatment which employs the Greek text and modern English translations.
Harper's topical concordance by Charles Rhind Joy (Rev. and enl. ed. N.Y. : Harper, 1962. 628 p.) uses the King James text. Some 33,200 texts are arranged under 2,775 topics, with cross-references. *Harper's* is preferred when biblical text is required, but *Roget's* better satisfies needs for locating like and related passages.   BX432.D34

Ellison, John William. Nelson's complete concordance of the Revised Standard Version Bible. N.Y. : Nelson, [1957]. 2157 p.   **BC158**
The concordance lists the context and location of each word, except for some 150 frequently used words which would seldom, if ever, be the keywords in a passage. Inasmuch as the Apocrypha were omitted from the Revised Standard Version of 1952, they are not included here.

§ A useful companion is *A concordance to the Apocrypha/ Deuterocanonical books of the Revised Standard Version* ([Grand Rapids, Mich.] : Eerdmans ; [London] : Collins, 1983), which has "an entry for every word that appears in the 1977 edition of the RSV Apocrypha/Deuterocanonicals."—*Introd.*
The Oxford concise concordance to the Revised Standard Version of the Holy Bible, by Bruce Manning Metzger and Isobel M. Metzger (N.Y. : Oxford Univ. Pr., 1962. 158 p.), was prepared for the general reader. The selection of words and passages was planned to include the most significant and noteworthy. Proper names are included in the main alphabet, and brief digests of biographical or geographical facts are often given.   BS425.E4

Goodrick, Edward W. The NIV exhaustive concordance / Edward W. Goodrick, John R. Kohlenberger III. Grand Rapids, Mich. : Zondervan Pub. House, c1990. 1853 p.   **BC159**
Identifies the original Hebrew, Aramaic, and Greek words for which the English object words are translations, and lists in a separate sequence, with biblical citations, the articles, conjunctions, particles, prepositions, and pronouns. Gives frequency count for each word and contexts for each keyword. Contains Hebrew, Aramaic, and Greek concordances and indexes correlating this work to James Strong's *Exhaustive concordance of the Bible* (BC165).
§ The same editors also compiled *The NIV complete concordance* (Grand Rapids, Mich. : Zondervan, 1981).   BS425.G62

Hazard, Marshall Custiss. A complete concordance to the American Standard Version of the Holy Bible. N.Y. : Nelson, [c1922]. 1234 p.   **BC160**
Subtitle: Contains about 300,000 references, arranged under 16,000 headings and subheadings; includes the alternative marginal readings; gives the pronunciation and meaning of all proper names and places, with biographical and geographical information which make it serve as a Bible dictionary as well as a concordance.   BS425.H3

Modern concordance to the New Testament / ed. and rev. following all current English translations of the New Testament by Michael Darton. Garden City, N.Y. : Doubleday ; London : Darton Longman & Todd, [1976]. 786 p.   **BC161**
"Based on the French *Concordance de la Bible, Nouveau Testament* produced under the aegis of the Association de la Concordance française de la Bible."—*t.p.*
A thematic and verbal concordance in English and Greek designed to serve as a guide to the themes, subjects, and ideas of the New Testament as well as to specific words occurring therein. Its underlying purpose is to lead the student to the Greek text on which modern English translations are founded. "The presentation is by subject matter: 341 themes subdivided under their Greek roots according to sense."—*p. xii.* Headings are in English, with the Greek words given at the beginning of each subsection and with English and Greek indexes.   BS2305.M6

Nelson's complete concordance of the New American Bible / Stephen J. Hartdegen, gen. ed. Nashville : Thomas Nelson, [1977]. 1274 p.   **BC162**
A verbal concordance to the text of the New American Bible. Employs small, but very legible type on a three-column page, with keywords set in boldface capitals to make for ease of use.
          BS425.N36

New American standard exhaustive concordance of the Bible : Hebrew-Aramaic and Greek dictionaries / Robert L. Thomas, gen. ed. Nashville : Holman, [1981]. 1695 p. **BC163**
A concordance using the text of the New American standard Bible. Not only indicates the verse in which a word is to be found, but "also notes the original Hebrew, Aramaic or Greek word from which the English word was translated."—*Pref.* The latter is accomplished by keying the English words in the body of the concordance to numbered entries in the abridged dictionaries of the original languages at the back of the volume.   BS425.N385

NKJV exhaustive concordance : new King James version. Complete and unabridged. Nashville : T. Nelson Publishers, c1992. 1251 p.   **BC164**

Indexes all words and 32 key phrases such as Son of God; Angel of the Lord. Provides number of occurences for each word and places 100 words (e.g., conjunctions, articles) in a separate section without context lines. Includes cross-references for variant spellings of proper names, for variant names for the same person or place, to different forms of words, and from some 1,000 King James version words to their NKJV equivalents.

§ *The complete concordance to the Bible : New King James version* (Nashville : Nelson, 1983) will meet the common need of locating particular scripture passages. It indexes all but 363 less significant words and employs cross-references, but excludes KJV words and their equivalents.   BS425.N55

Strong, James. The new Strong's exhaustive concordance of the Bible : with main concordance, appendix to the main concordance, key verse comparison chart, dictionary of the Hebrew Bible, dictionary of the Greek Testament. Nashville : T. Nelson Publishers, c1990. 1260, 85, 126, 79, 219 p.   **BC165**

Rev. ed. of: *Exhaustive concordance of the Bible*, by James Strong (London : Hodder ; N.Y. : Hunt, 1894 [c1890]). Frequently reprinted.

The most complete biblical concordance, giving every word of the text of the King James version; brief dictionaries of the Hebrew and Greek words of the original texts, with references to the English words; and cross-references from variant spellings of proper names as they appear in the Revised Standard, New International, and New American Standard versions. 47 very common words are cited separately in an appendix. The new edition corrects errors in the 1st ed. and adds 200 pages of topical scripture passages indexes, but omits the comparative concordance of the Authorized and Revised versions.

§ For a concordance to the Apocrypha, *see* Alexander Cruden, *Cruden's complete concordance of the Old and New Testaments*, ed. by A. D. Adams, C. H. Irwin, S. A. Waters, a well-known older concordance issued in many editions by various publishers (first publ. 1737).   BS425.S8

Whitaker, Richard E. The Eerdmans analytical concordance to the Revised Standard Version of the Bible / Richard E. Whitaker, with James E. Goehring and research personnel of the Institute for Antiquity and Christianity. Grand Rapids, Mich. : Eerdmans, c1988. 1548 p.   **BC166**

The only analytical concordance of the whole Revised Standard Version, in that it indicates what word in an original language is being translated in each context. Omits many frequently used prepositions and conjunctions and all personal pronouns. Has main concordance, concordance of proper names, and concordance of numbers. Hebrew, Aramaic, Greek, and Latin indexes at the end of the volume include all words in those languages that are cited in the main concordance and in the concordance of proper names.   BS425.W48

Young, Robert. Analytical concordance to the Bible. 22nd American ed. / rev. by W. B. Stevenson. N.Y. : Funk & Wagnalls, [1955]. 1090 p., 93 p., 23 p., 51 p.   **BC167**

Subtitle: about 311,000 references, subdivided under the Hebrew and Greek originals with the literal meaning and pronunciation of each … Also index lexicons to the Old and New Testaments … and a complete list of Scripture proper names.

1st ed., 1879; rev. ed., rev. by W. B. Stevenson, 1902; editions of later date (by various publishers) are reprints of this, with some slight revision, and include varying supplementary material, such as "The canon of scripture," by R. K. Harrison and Everett F. Harrison. Uses the King James text.   BS425.Y7

Commentaries

Black, Matthew. Peake's commentary on the Bible / Old Testament editor, H. H. Rowley. London ; N.Y. : Nelson, 1962. 1126 p. : maps.   **BC168**

1st ed. by Arthur Samuel Peake, 1919; Supplement, 1936.

In addition to commentary on each book of the Bible, includes over 250 pages of signed general and introductory articles, with bibliographies by specialists from the British Commonwealth and the U.S. Gives the student and general reader the benefit of scholarship while avoiding technical language. Index.   BS491.B57

The books of the Bible / Bernhard W. Anderson, ed. N.Y. : Scribner's, c1989. 2 v.   **BC169**

Contents: v. 1, Old Testament, subject index; v. 2, New Testament, apocryphal writings, comprehensive subject index.

A series of interpretive essays, each followed by a select bibliography, on books of the Bible arranged according to the order of the biblical canon. Focuses on the text as it now stands rather than its historical development. Written from an ecumenical perspective mainly by American and British scholars. Intended for general readers.

BS540.B62

The Broadman Bible commentary / gen. ed. Clifton J. Allen. Nashville : Broadman Pr., [1969–1972]. 12 v.   **BC170**

Vol. 1 revised 1973.

Written for the minister and general reader by a group of Baptist scholars, mainly in the U.S. Signed commentaries and general articles are based on the Revised Standard Version.   BS491.2.B67

Guthrie, Donald. The new Bible commentary, revised / Donald Guthrie and J. A. Motyer, eds. [3rd ed., completely rev. and reset]. Grand Rapids, Mich. : Eerdmans, [1970]. 1310 p.   **BC171**

1st ed., 1953, ed. by Francis Davidson. 2nd ed., 1954.

Repr. as: *The Eerdmans Bible commentary* (Grand Rapids, Mich. : Eerdmans, 1987).

A work of Protestant scholarship based on the Revised Standard Version. More than half the contributions to this edition are new, and the rest have been revised.   BS491.2.G8

Harper's Bible commentary / gen. ed., James L. Mays, with the Society of Biblical Literature. San Francisco : Harper & Row, c1988. 1326 p.   **BC172**

Prior ed., ed. by William Neil, 1962.

The work of 82 contributors and six editors, representing Jewish and Christian scholarship. Designed "to make the best current scholarship available to general audiences for reading and studying the books of the Bible."—*Pref.* Contains numerous introductory essays on the whole Bible and on the seven parts into which the *Commentary* divides it, and provides an introductory essay, concise commentary, and current bibliography for each book, including the Apocrypha. Cross-references to *Harper's Bible dictionary* (BC139). Black-and-white illustrations; plates and maps in color. Index.   BS491.2.H37

The international critical commentary on the Holy Scriptures of the Old and New Testaments. Edinburgh : T. & T. Clark, 1975–94. v. 1–8. (In progress).   **BC173**

1st ed., ed. by Rev. Samuel Rolles Driver, Rev. Alfred Plummer and Rev. Charles Augustus Briggs (Edinburgh : Clark ; N.Y. : Scribner, 1896–1951).

Contents: Romans 1–8 (Romans, v. 1), 1975; Romans 9–16 (Romans, v. 2), 1979, both by C. E. B. Cranfield; Jeremiah 1–25 (Jeremiah, v. 1), 1986, by William McKane; Matthew 1–7 (Matthew, v. 1), 1988; (Matthew, v. 2), 1991, both by W. D. Davis and Dale C. Allison; Acts of the Apolstles 1–14 (Acts., v. 1), 1994, by C. K. Barrett; Second Epistle to the Corinthians 1–7 (II Corinthians, v. 1), 1994, by Margaret E. Thrall.

The previous edition of this important work was never completed; various volumes have been reprinted, and as recently as 1951 a completely new volume was published (*Kings I and II*, by J. A. Montgomery and H. S. German). This new edition constitutes an extension and revision of the earlier set. Under the new editors, "commentaries on books of the Bible which have not appeared in the ICC before are now in preparation and new editions of many existing volumes are in preparation."—*Publisher's catalog.* The newer works continue the critical and philological emphasis of the earlier titles. BS491.I6

Interpreter's Bible : the Holy Scriptures in the King James and Revised Standard versions with general articles and introduction, exegesis, exposition for each book of the Bible. N.Y. ; Nashville : Abingdon, [1951–57]. 12 v. **BC174**
A guide and commentary to the Bible by some 125 scholars, prepared for the general reader, the teacher, and the preacher. Includes long introductions with bibliographies to the whole Bible, to each Testament, and to each book. Each is written and signed by an individual scholar. Includes the text of both versions, exegesis and exposition.
§ *The new interpreter's Bible* (Nashville : Abingdon, 1994– . v. 1. [In progress]), a completely new work; began publication in 1994 and scheduled for 12 v., with a new volume appearing approximately every six months. Contributors represent diverse Protestant and Roman Catholic perspectives. The New Revised Standard and New International versions will replace the Revised Standard and Authorized versions used in the earlier edition. BS491.2.I55

Interpreter's one-volume commentary on the Bible : introd. and commentary for each book of the Bible including the Apocrypha, with general articles / ed. by Charles M. Laymon. Nashville : Abingdon Pr., [1971]. 1386 p. : ill., maps. **BC175**
Includes contributions by American, British and Canadian scholars. Intended for "ministers, lay and nonprofessional persons engaged in studying or teaching in the church school, college students, and those who are unequipped to follow the more specialized discussions of biblical matters, but who desire a thoroughly valid and perceptive guide in interpreting the Bible."—*Pref.* General articles include the geographical and historical setting, the languages of the Bible, measures and money, and a chronology. Subject index. BS491.2.I57

The literary guide to the Bible / ed. by Robert Alter and Frank Kermode. Cambridge, Mass. : Belknap Pr. of Harvard Univ. Pr., 1987. 678 p. **BC176**
The only commentary now available on the entire Bible that uses the methods of literary rather than historical criticism, emphasizing such matters as allusion, imagery, narrative structure, symbolism, and poetic form. Contributors are Christian, Jewish, and secular scholars affiliated with major universities in the U.S., Great Britain, and Israel. Has sections on individual books and on groups of related books (e.g., The Pauline epistles), followed by seven general essays (e.g., The characteristics of ancient Hebrew poetry), a glossary of biblical and literary terms, and a subject index. Intended for general readers. BS535.L54

A new Catholic commentary on Holy Scripture / Reginald Cuthbert Fuller, gen. ed. [Rev. ed.]. [London] : Nelson, [1969]. 1377 p. **BC177**
A new and updated edition of the *Catholic commentary,* ed. by Bernard Orchard (London : Nelson, 1953). A thorough revision, with only about a fifth of the material from the earlier volume retained. Bibliographies include citations as late as 1968. Numbering of chapters and verses now follows that of the Revised Standard Version. Includes general introductory articles to the whole work, to the Old Testament, and to the New Testament, each signed by a scholar; the commentaries are also signed. Detailed index. BS491.2.N48

The new Jerome biblical commentary / ed. by Raymond E. Brown, Joseph A. Fitzmyer, Roland E. Murphy. Englewood Cliffs, N.J. : Prentice-Hall, 1990. 1484 p. **BC178**
Earlier ed. had title *The Jerome biblical commentary* (Englewood Cliffs, N.J. : Prentice-Hall, [1968]. 2 v. in 1).
Two-thirds new material, contributed by some 70 Catholic scholars, laymen and women as well as clergy, primarily North Americans, who exemplify the sophistication of biblical scholarship and range of exegetical variation in the Catholic Church today. Intended for educat-

ed readers, seminarians and clergy. Contains commentary on all the books of the Bible, numerous cross-references to the 20 topical and introductory articles, scholarly bibliographies, a suggested basic bibliography, and an extensive index of subjects and persons.
BS491.2.N485

The new layman's Bible commentary in one volume / eds., G. C. D. Howley, F. F. Bruce, H. L. Ellison. Grand Rapids, Mich. : Zondervan, [1979]. 1712 p. **BC179**
Publ. in England as *The Bible commentary for today* (London : Pickering & Inglis, 1979. 1712 p.).
The New Testament section (p. [1059]–1712) was first published as *A New Testament commentary* (London : Pickering & Inglis, 1969). References in the Old Testament section of the 1979 one-volume edition to *A New Testament commentary* refer to the 1969 edition; the number 1046 must therefore be added to the page number to obtain the relevant page in the one-volume edition.
Based on the Revised Standard Version, contributions are from British Commonwealth scholars expressing a conservative Protestant viewpoint. Intended "to appeal to the non-expert in theology as well as those with a fuller training and insight in that field of study."—*Pref.*
BS491.2.N49

The women's Bible commentary / Carol A. Newsom and Sharon H. Ringe, editors. London : SPCK ; Louisville, Ky. : Westminster/John Knox Pr., 1992. 396 p. **BC180**
"The first comprehensive attempt to gather some of the fruits of feminist biblical scholarship on each book of the Bible."—*Introd.* Contributors are Jewish, Catholic, and Protestant women scholars from the U.S. The commentaries focus on those portions of each book related to women and their status and condition. Four articles: (1) Women in Old Testament times; (2) Women in New Testament times; (3) Women in early nonbiblical Christian literature; (4) Feminist hermeneutics. Short bibliographies follow each article. BS491.2.W66

Hebrew Bible

The Babylonian Talmud / tr. into English with notes, glossary, and indices under the editorship of Isidore Epstein. London : Soncino Pr., 1935–52. 35 v. **BC181**
Repr., 1961 (18 v.).
An important unabridged and annotated translation of the Babylonian Talmud, using the text of the Vilna Romm edition with variant texts noted and occasionally used. Extensive notes throughout employ the work of standard Hebrew commentators. Each volume includes a glossary and scriptural and general indexes. A separate index volume for the entire set includes a glossary, detailed general index, and rabbinical index. BM500.E57

Kasher, Menachem Mendel. Encyclopedia of biblical interpretation : a millenial anthology / tr. under the editorship of Rabbi Dr. Harry Freedman. N.Y. : American Biblical Encyclopedia Soc., [1953–79]. v. 1–9. (In progress?). **BC182**
Contents: v. 1–6, Genesis; v. 7–9, Exodus, 1–20:23.
A monumental collection of Jewish interpretations of the Bible, based on the author's *Humash Torah Shelemath* giving the text of the Pentateuch and an anthology of passages drawn from the Talmudic-Midrashic literature pertaining to each verse of the Bible, with indication of sources, and a commentary containing exegetical passages from ancient and modern sources with notes, bibliographies and subject indexes. BS1225.K363

The Pentateuch and Haftorahs : Hebrew text, English translation and commentary / ed. by J. H. Hertz. 2nd ed. London : Soncino Pr., 1960. 1067 p. **BC183**
1st ed., 1929–36; frequently reprinted.
Added title page in Hebrew.
Presents the Hebrew text with the Jewish Publication Society's English translation; commentary aims for "exposition … of the 'plain sense' of the Sacred Text; and … of its religious message as affecting everyday problems of human existence."—*Pref.* General index of names and subjects.

Plaut, W. Gunther. The Torah : a modern commentary. N.Y. : Union of American Hebrew Congregations, 1981. 1787 p. **BC184**

Contents: Commentaries on Genesis, Exodus, Numbers, Deuteronomy, by W. G. Plaut; Commentary on Leviticus, by B. J. Bamberger; Essays on Near Eastern literature (preceding each commentary), by W. W. Hallo. Also includes original Hebrew text and the Jewish Publication Society's English translation of the Pentateuch and of the Haftaroth.

A modern commentary reflecting the liberal point of view.

BS1225.3.P55

Handbooks

The Bible almanac / ed. by James I. Packer, Merrill C. Tenney, William White, Jr. Nashville : Thomas Nelson, [1980]. 765 p. : ill. **BC185**

Aims "to present in plain terms the information that is most helpful in interpreting the Bible accurately" (*Pref.*)—i.e., information on the "coinage, weights and measures, foods, means of travel, animal and vegetable life, chronology, social manners and customs, languages and literary forms, and many other aspects of human life" in biblical times. Information is presented in 46 sections, with illustrations, maps, and tables to elucidate the text. References to scripture appear throughout; occasional bibliographic citations; index. BS635.2.B48

Blair, Edward Payson. The illustrated Bible handbook. Nashville : Abingdon Pr., c1987. 538 p. : ill. **BC186**

A new edition of Blair's *Abingdon Bible handbook* (1975).

Provides background and introductory information to aid serious Bible study. In three sections: The Bible today; The Bible in history (with sections on the Old Testament, the Apocrypha, the New Testament, and the background of the Bible); and The Bible and faith and life. Includes bibliographies. Indexed. BS475.2.B5

Fitzmyer, Joseph A. The Dead Sea Scrolls : major publications and tools for study. Rev. ed. Atlanta : Scholars Pr., 1990. 246 p. (Resources for biblical study, 20). **BC187**

1st ed., 1975; with addendum, 1977.

This handbook, originating in a course taught by the author, aims to explain the sigla of the Scrolls, indicate place of publication of texts, explain contents of texts; and introduce the student to tools of study. Also notes major secondary publications: bibliographies, surveys, concordances, dictionaries, translations, and materials on selected topics. Indexes of modern authors, biblical and extra-biblical passages, and sigla. Z6371.D4F58

Hughes, John J. Bits, bytes & biblical studies : a resource guide for the use of computers in biblical and classical studies. Grand Rapids, Mich. : Academie Books, c1987. 643 p. : ill. **BC188**

Contains critical reviews of a wide variety of computer programs, arranged in chapters on word processing, Bible concordances, language learning, communications/online services, study of archaeology, and ancient texts, with a bibliography appended to each chapter. Also has an introductory chapter on computers, a list of computer abbreviations and acronyms, a list of trademarks, a glossary, and indexes of proper names and topics. A unique and highly useful encyclopedic work for beginners and specialists. Updated by the newsletter, *Bits & bytes review* (Whitefish, Mont. : Bits & Bytes Computer Resources, 1986–). BS600.2.H83

The Oxford companion to the Bible / ed. by Bruce M. Metzger, Michael D. Coogan. N.Y. : Oxford Univ. Pr., 1993. 874 p. : col. maps. **BC189**

Signed articles, written by 250 contributors, represent a wide range of perspectives, and cover "key persons, places, events, concepts, institutions, and realities of biblical times."—*Introd.* Most articles are brief; some are four to five pages in length, and a small number (e.g., "Literature and the Bible") are 20 pages or more. Entries include bibliographic citations, and employ biblical references selectively and cross-references extensively. A short, general bibliography at the end is followed by maps and an index. BS440.M434

Soulen, Richard N. Handbook of biblical criticism. 2nd ed. (rev. and augm.). Atlanta : John Knox Pr., [1981]. 239 p. **BC190**

1st ed., 1976.

For the beginning student and nonspecialist. Described as a "pocket reference ... to be used whenever a name, a term, or an abbreviation is met for the first time unidentified, unexplained, or without a clarifying illustration; or, when its meaning is simply forgotten."—*Introd.* Includes entries for methodologies, technical terms and phrases, research tools and texts, names (chiefly deceased biblical scholars), theological terms, and abbreviations.

§ Similarly, Nicholas Turner's *Handbook for biblical studies* (Philadelphia : Westminster ; Oxford : Blackwell, [1982]. 145 p.) offers a glossary of technical terms peculiar to biblical studies (including foreign words usually left untranslated), brief summaries of the books of the Bible, sources, authors, and manuscripts commonly referred to in biblical scholarship. Aims to enable the reader "to become sufficiently familiar with the terminology of scholarly argument to learn from it and to participate in it."—*Final word.* Tables of chronologies, alphabets, and a "Theological who's who" of the Fathers and modern scholars. BS511.2.S68

History

Cambridge history of the Bible. Cambridge : Univ. Pr., 1963–70. 3 v. **BC191**

Contents: v. 1, From the beginnings to Jerome, ed. by P. R. Ackroyd and C. F. Evans; v. 2, The West, from the Fathers to the Reformation, ed. by G. W. H. Lampe; v. 3, The West, from the Reformation to the present day, ed. by S. L. Greenslade.

Vol. 3, treating the most recent period, was the first to appear. The Ackroyd-Evans volume "represents the logical extension back into the beginnings of the biblical literature and sets out to trace the essential features of the process by which the Bible as we know it came into being, and how it came to be canonized and interpreted under Judaism and in the early years of the Christian Church."—*Pref.* The Lampe volume is primarily concerned with the history of the Bible in medieval western Europe; that by Greenslade (publ. 1963) carries the history forward to mid-20th century, treating translations of the Bible into Western languages, and its various versions. The Greenslade volume was designated as v. 3 after publication of the other volumes in 1970.

§ A one-volume history of English Bibles, covering translations from Anglo-Saxon times to the 1970s is F. F. Bruce's *History of the Bible in English* (3rd ed. N.Y. : Oxford Univ. Pr., 1978).

BS445.C26

Biblical archaeology

Archaeological encyclopedia of the Holy Land / ed. by Avraham Negev. 3rd ed. N.Y. : Prentice Hall, 1990. 419 p. : ill., maps. **BC192**

1st ed., 1972; rev. ed., 1986.

Brief articles concerned chiefly with "the geographical names mentioned in the Bible, both places in the Holy Land and countries and cities in other parts of the Middle East, identifying them as far as possible, describing the excavations that have been carried out at or near them, and analysing the importance of the finds they have yielded."—*Pref.* Includes entries on artifacts, ancient customs, etc. References to specific Bible passages and to early writers such as Josephus and Strabo are made, but there is no bibliography of modern sources.

DS111.A2N38

Corswant, Willy. A dictionary of life in Bible times / completed and illustrated by Édouard Urech. N.Y. : Oxford Univ. Pr., 1960. 308 p. : ill. **BC193**
  A translation of *Dictionnaire d'archéologie biblique* (Neuchâtel ; Paris : Delachaux et Niestlé, [1956]. 324 p.).
  Planned especially as an aid to teachers of the Bible. Concerned with the private, civil, and religious life of the Jews and early Christians, and with the flora, fauna, and minerals of Israel. Written in nontechnical language, illustrated with line drawings. At the end of each article, references are given to the biblical texts.

The new encyclopedia of archaeological excavations in the Holy Land / Ephraim Stern, ed. ; Joseph Aviram, editorial director. Jerusalem : Israel Exploration Society & Carta ; N.Y. : Simon & Schuster, c1993. 4 v. (1552 p.) : ill. **BC194**
  Updates *Encyclopedia of archaeological excavations in the Holy Land*, ed. by Michael Avi-Yonah (Englewood Cliffs, N.J. : Prentice-Hall, 1975–78 ; London : Oxford Univ. Pr., 1976–78).
  A comprehensive, authoritative summary of Palestinian archaeology. Articles, many published here for the first time, on excavated sites, specific areas, and collective subjects (e.g., Churches, Megaliths). Coverage through the end of 1991. Richly illustrated throughout with photographs (some in color), line drawings, and maps. A map indicating all sites covered is repeated on endpapers of each volume. Chronological tables, glossary, and indexes of persons, places, and Biblical references. DS111.A2E5813

The new international dictionary of biblical archaeology / Edward M. Blaiklock, R. K. Harrison, gen. editors. Grand Rapids, Mich. : Regency Reference Libr. : Zondervan, [1983]. 485 p. : ill., maps. **BC195**
  Offers entries for personal and place names, deities, terms, texts, etc., important in biblical archaeology. Except for some brief definitions, all articles are signed with the initials of the contributors; bibliographic references follow most articles; numerous cross-references. A section of 33 colored maps (on unnumbered pages) has its own index. Intended for a broad readership: "Our object has not been primarily polemical or evidential. We have sought, within prescribed limits, to present basic facts. Those who use the book must, for the most part, draw their own theological conclusions."—*Pref.* BS622.N48

Pfeiffer, Charles F. The Biblical world : a dictionary of Biblical archaeology. Grand Rapids, Mich. : Baker Book House, [1966]. 612 p. : ill. **BC196**
  Articles on biblical topics as related to archaeological studies and research. More than 40 contributors are listed, but articles are unsigned. Bibliographies accompany many entries. BS622.P4

Atlases

Aharoni, Yohanan. The Macmillan Bible atlas / Yohanan Aharoni and Michael Avi-Yonah ; designed and prep. by Carta, Jerusalem. Completely rev. 3rd ed. / Anson F. Rainey, Ze'ev Safrai. N.Y. : Macmillan, c1993. 215 p. : ill. ; 30 cm. **BC197**
  1st ed., 1968; 2nd ed., 1977.
  Aims "to show, as far as possible through maps of each event, the changes and historical processes in the lands of the Bible."—*Pref.* 271 maps of various sizes, with explanatory text, are arranged chronologically and cover events such as battles, journeys, trade routes, development of cities, etc., from the 4th millenium BCE to the 2nd century CE. Nearly all texts in the Old Testament section and the texts about Herodian Jerusalem (Second Temple section) have been rewritten in the light of recent archaeological discoveries. Scriptural key to maps; chronological tables; index. G2230.A2

Grollenberg, Luc H. Atlas of the Bible / Luc H. Grollenberg ; tr. and ed. by Joyce M. H. Reid and H. H. Rowley. [London] ; N.Y. : Nelson, 1956. 165 p. : ill., maps ; 36cm. **BC198**

A translation of the 2nd Dutch edition, *Atlas van de Bijbel* (Amsterdam : Elsevier, 1954), published with Catholic imprimatur. A scholarly work, with a wealth of illustrations and a text summarizing biblical history, geography, and archaeology, including a discussion of the Dead Sea Scrolls. 35 maps, well conceived and executed. A gazetteer index contains the names of geographical features, towns, and peoples, and the names of individuals who played especially important roles in biblical history. BS620.G752

The Harper atlas of the Bible / ed. by James B. Pritchard. N.Y. : Harper & Row, c1987. 254 p.; 37 cm. **BC199**
  Published in the U.K. as: *The Times atlas of the Bible* (London : Times Books, c1987).
  Some 50 scholars worldwide present the results of recent scholarship in an accessible and highly attractive form. Maps, illustrations, charts, and graphs, all in color, accompanied by concise commentary and notes, chronicle war and conquest, and everyday life and custom. A color-coded chronological chart extending from prehistoric times to 150 CE provides the context for the maps which follow. An index of people who play an important role in the Bible lists biblical citations for each. An index of place-names identifies each by area/country, variant name, Arabic name, modern Hebrew name, and map location.
  § *The Harper concise atlas of the Bible* is also ed. by Pritchard (N.Y. : Harper Collins, c1991. 151 p. ; 31 cm.). A condensed version, retaining many attractive illustrations, charts, and graphs and much of the commentary while providing new maps (not equal to those of the parent work) and indexes of biblical references and of personal names. G2230.H47

Oxford Bible atlas / ed. by Herbert G. May, with the assistance of G. N. S. Hunt. ; in consultation with R. W. Hamilton. 3rd ed. / rev. for the 3rd ed. by John Day. N.Y. : Oxford Univ. Pr., 1984. 144 p. : ill., maps in color; 26cm. **BC200**
  1st ed., 1962; 2nd ed., 1974.
  Attractive maps and photographs, accompanied by concise textual explanations, focus on the most important biblical and extra-biblical material. This edition revised to incorporate recent biblical research and archaeological data. A useful, inexpensive atlas. BS630.O96

Rasmussen, Carl. Zondervan NIV atlas of the Bible. Grand Rapids, Mich. : Regency Reference Library, c1989. 256 p. : ill. **BC201**
  Offers clear, concise, attractive maps, charts, diagrams, and pictures (most in color), accompanied by text. Bible quotations are drawn from the *New International Version* (NIV) (Grand Rapids, Mich. : Zondervan, 1973–78). Geographical section concentrates on areas within Israel and Jordan, but also covers the entire Middle East; historical section covers from the prepatriarchal period to the fall of Jerusalem. Appendixes include endnotes, bibliography, timeline of biblical history, glossary, index of scripture references, index of persons, and gazetteer with index. Intended for the general reader. BS630.R37

Smith, George Adam. Atlas of the historical geography of the Holy Land. London : Hodder, 1915. 60 p., 12 p. ; 57 col. : maps. **BC202**
  Although not abreast of modern scholarship, this standard atlas is still useful for its excellent maps of the Holy Land from biblical times through the 1800s. Also includes "conceptions of the land and of the world to which it belongs, prevalent at former periods of its history."—*Pref.* G2230.S6

Koran

Kassis, Hanna E. A concordance of the Qur'an. Berkeley : Univ. of Calif. Pr., [1983]. 1444 p. **BC203**
  Utilizes the English text of A. J. Arberry's *The Koran interpreted* (BC204). Arranged alphabetically by transliterated form of the Arabic root term, with indexes of English words. BP133.K37

The Koran interpreted / by Arthur J. Arberry. London : Allen & Unwin ; N.Y. : Macmillan, [1955]. 2 v.   **BC204**
Repr. : N.Y. : Collier, 1986; frequently reprinted.
A translation which seeks "to imitate, however imperfectly, those rhetorical and rhythmical patterns which are the glory and the sublimity of the Koran."—*Pref.*   BP109.A7

Mir, Mustansir. Dictionary of Qur'ānic terms and concepts. N.Y. : Garland, 1987. 244 p. (Garland reference library of the humanities, vol. 693).   **BC205**
Brief articles are arranged alphabetically by English translation or transliteration of Arabic words or phrases. Most entries contain cross-references. No bibliography.   BP133.M57

al-Qur'ān : a contemporary translation / by Ahmed Ali. 2nd rev. ed., Corr. ed. Princeton, N.J. : Princeton Univ. Pr., 1988. [572 p.].   **BC206**
1st ed., Karachi : Akrasu, 1984.
An elegant contemporary English translation of the Koran, with English and Arabic in parallel columns. Occasional explanatory footnotes. Subject index and index of the prophets give English and Qur'anic forms of their names.   BP109.1988

PRAYERS

The Oxford book of prayer / gen. ed., George Appleton. Oxford ; N.Y. : Oxford Univ. Pr., 1985. 397 p.   **BC207**
An anthology of prayers, selected mainly from the Bible and individuals and church liturgies representing the various branches of the Christian tradition, but including a long chapter with prayers from ten other traditions of belief (e.g., Jewish, Indian, Buddhist). An appendix contains "Notes on the development of eucharistic prayers," and the acknowledgements list all the sources from which selections were made. Indexes of authors and sources, and of subjects.   BV245.O94

CHRISTIANITY

General Works

West, Edward N. Outward signs : the language of Christian symbolism. N.Y. : Walker, 1989. 237 p. : ill.   **BC208**
Discusses the origin and meaning of Christian symbols used in liturgy, vestments, and architecture. Classified arrangement. Contains 455 line drawings, glossary, bibliography, and subject index. Intended for general readers.   BV150.W418

Guides

Bollier, John A. The literature of theology : a guide for students and pastors. Philadelphia : Westminster Pr., [1979]. 208 p.   **BC209**
Intended "to help the reader become independent in finding the books, the journal articles, or the information needed in the pursuit of either academic study or professional ministry."—*Pref.* Concentrates on reference works—bibliographies, encyclopedias, dictionaries, indexes, abstracts, handbooks, guides, manuals, commentaries, etc.—with considerable attention given to English-language Bible versions. 543 entries, topically arranged, with descriptive and evaluative annotations. Author/title index.   Z7751.B67

Bibliography

Berkhout, Carl T. Medieval heresies : a bibliography, 1960–1979 / Carl T. Berkhout, Jeffrey B. Russell. Toronto : Pontifical Institute of Mediaeval Studies, 1981. 201 p. (Subsidia mediaevalia, 11).   **BC210**
Consists of more than 2,000 items about popular social heresies from the 8th–15th centuries. Lists books (with references to reviews) and periodical articles in a classed arrangement, with author, subject, and manuscript indexes.   Z7779.H3B52

Birney, Alice L. The literary lives of Jesus : an international bibliography of poetry, drama, fiction, and criticism. N.Y. : Garland, 1989. 187 p. : ill. (Garland reference library of the humanities, vol. 735).   **BC211**
Lists "separately published poetry, drama, and fiction about the life of Jesus Christ and literary criticism on those poems, plays, and stories."—*Pref.* The 1,424 items, written from late antiquity to 1984, are arranged in chapters by genre and time period, with some annotations. Author/editor index.
§ Warren S. Kissinger's *Lives of Jesus* (N.Y. : Garland, 1985) is a discursive bibliography that focuses specifically on biographical, rather than literary, works.   Z6514.C5J473

Blumhofer, Edith Waldvogel. Twentieth-century evangelicalism : a guide to the sources / Edith L. Blumhofer, Joel A. Carpenter. N.Y. : Garland, 1990. 384 p. (Garland reference library of social science, v. 521).   **BC212**
Contains 1,572 citations, critically annotated by nine specialists, to the literature and the repositories essential for the study of all aspects of American Evangelicalism. Employs a classified arrangement with indexes of authors, institutions and organizations, and subjects.   BR1644.U6B48

Church and state in postwar eastern Europe : a bibliographical survey / comp. by Paul Mojzes. N.Y. : Greenwood, [1987]. 109 p. (Bibliographies and indexes in religious studies, no. 11).   **BC213**
For annotation, *see* DC31.   Z7776.72.C5

Crumb, Lawrence N. The Oxford Movement and its leaders : a bibliography of secondary and lesser primary sources. Metuchen, N.J. : Amer. Theological Libr. Assoc. : Scarecrow, 1988. 706 p. (ATLA bibliography series, no. 24).   **BC214**
Contains 5,432 entries on the "Tractarian" generation (1833–50) of the Oxford Movement. Includes books, pamphlets, theses, parts of books, periodical articles, manuscripts, microforms, and tape recordings. Arranged by year, by the form of literature within each year, and alphabetically within each form. Author, periodical, and subject indexes.
———. ———. *Supplement* (1993. 303 p.) adds 1,267 citations, two-thirds of which were published before 1984 with the remainder published 1984–90. Includes appendix of additions and corrections to the main volume. Author, periodical, and subject indexes.   Z7845.O83C78

Eisen, Sydney. Victorian science and religion : a bibliography with emphasis on evolution, belief, and unbelief, comprised of works published from c.1900–1975 / Sydney Eisen and Bernard V. Lightman. [Hamden, Conn.] : Archon Books, 1984. 696 p.   **BC215**
Lists in classified arrangement 6,267 books, articles and dissertations "dealing with ideas and institutions in Victorian science and religion" and concentrates "on the period from about 1830 to 1900."—*Introd.* In three parts: Main currents; Natural theology, geology and evolution; Religion—ideas and institutions. Many subdivisions for leading Victorian philosophers, theologians and scientists. Author and subject indexes.   Z5320.E57

Evans, James H. Black theology : a critical assessment and annotated bibliography / comp. by James H. Evans, Jr., G.E. Gorman, advisory ed. N.Y. : Greenwood, 1987. 205 p. (Bibliographies and indexes in religious studies, no. 10). **BC216**
An introductory essay is followed by an annotated bibliography of 461 entries listing both monographs and periodical articles. Materials are arranged alphabetically by author in one of three sections: Origins and development of black theology; Liberation, feminism and Marxism; Cultural and global discourse. Indexes of names, titles and subjects. Z7774.E9

Gorman, G. E. Theological and religious reference materials / G.E. Gorman and Lyn Gorman. Westport, Conn. : Greenwood, 1984–1986. v. 1–3. (Bibliographies and indexes in religious studies, no. 1, 2, 7). (In progress). **BC217**
Contents: v. 1, General resources and biblical studies; v. 2, Systematic theology and church history; v. 3, Practical theology.
A comprehensive bibliography intended for students, scholars, and clergy. Materials in all Western languages are arranged alphabetically by author in broad categories, subdivided by form. The length of sections makes browsing awkward. Many annotations are evaluative and provide useful cross-references. Each volume has author, title, and subject indexes. A fourth volume on comparative and non-Christian religions is planned. Z7770.G66

McLean, George F. A bibliography of Christian philosophy and contemporary issues. N.Y. : Ungar, [1967]. 312 p. (Philosophy in the 20th century: Catholic and Christian, v. 2). **BC218**
A selective, classified listing of books and periodical articles, 1934–66. An appendix lists the philosophy dissertations presented in Catholic universities in the U.S. and Canada. Indexed. Z7821.M26

Musto, Ronald G. Liberation theologies : a research guide. N.Y. : Garland, 1991. 581 p. : ill. (Garland reference library of social science, v. 507). **BC219**
Contains 1,295 critically annotated entries, primarily for books published in English since 1970, when liberation theology clearly emerged in Latin America. Initial chapters trace the historical roots of liberation theologies from biblical theology through Pope John Paul II. Entries for contemporary expressions are organized geographically: Africa, Asia, Latin American, and North America, with a final chapter on feminist theology. Most chapters begin with bibliographies followed by entries arranged topically, with writings of important liberation theologians given under their names. Title and author/editor indexes. Z7809.M87

O'Brien, Elmer J. Theology in transition : a bibliographical evaluation of the "decisive decade," 1954–1964. [N.Y.] : Herder and Herder, [1965]. 282 p. **BC220**
A bibliographic survey, by a group of Catholic theologians, of publications in biblical studies, liturgics, patristics, and theology.
§ A briefer, annotated guide to the literature is Urban J. Steiner's *Contemporary theology: a reading guide* (Collegeville, Minn. : Liturgical Pr., [1965]. 111 p.). BT28.O2

Ofori, Patrick E. Christianity in tropical Africa : a selective annotated bibliography. Nendeln, [Liechtenstein] : KTO Pr., 1977. 461 p. **BC221**
Brings together in a classified arrangement books, articles, pamphlets, theses, and unpublished mimeographed materials in many languages and "from numerous scattered sources from 1841–1974" (*Introd.*) to provide a basic guide to African Christianity. Arranged by broad region, then alphabetically by country. 2,859 entries. Author index. Z7757.A24O36

Robinson, Thomas A. The early church : an annotated bibliography of literature in English / by Thomas A. Robinson with Brent D. Shaw ... [et al.]. [Philadelphia] : Amer. Theological Libr. Assoc. ; Metuchen, N.J. : Scarecrow, 1993. 493 p. (ATLA bibliography series, no. 33). **BC222**
Includes books and articles selected for their value and accessibil-

ity to students; entries offer evaluative, useful annotations and employ symbols to indicate sourcebooks, summary articles, general works, and book reviews. Chapters, with informative introductions, cover (1) Reference works; (2) General works and collections; and (3) topics (e.g., Theology, Ethics and sexuality, Church and state). Excludes specifically New Testament materials; includes important materials on the Roman empire. Modern author index and general index.
BR162.2.R63

Sheldon, Joseph Kenneth. Rediscovery of creation : a bibliographical study of the church's response to the environmental crisis. Metuchen, N.J. : Amer. Theological Libr. Assoc. : Scarecrow, 1992. 1 v. (ATLA bibliography series, no. 29). **BC223**
A survey of English-language popular, scientific, and theological literature, published primarily since 1970. Materials listed represent viewpoints from the Christian tradition, with a small number added to represent Judaism, Islam, and Buddhism. Arrangement is by author; a preceding subject reference guide lacks useful specificity. Includes a list of Christian organizations with a focus on creation, and a list of curriculum materials. Z7799.8.S44

Soukup, Paul A. Christian communication : a bibliographical survey. N.Y. : Greenwood, 1989. 400 p. (Bibliographies and indexes in religious studies, no. 14). **BC224**
Annotates 1,311 books, journal articles, reports, and dissertations on communication history, theory, and current practice in Christian churches. Treats such topics as rhetoric, interpersonal communication, and mass communication, but excludes homiletics because of its coverage elsewhere. Classified arrangement; name, title, and subject indexes. Z5633.R45S66

Theologische Literaturzeitung. 1. Jahrg. (1876)– . [Berlin, etc. : Evangelsiche Verlagsanstalt, etc.]. Monthly. **BC225**
Publisher and place of publication vary.
Frequency varies: biweekly, 1876–1938; monthly since 1939.
A comprehensive survey of book and periodical material in many languages.
§ Supplemented by: *Bibliographisches Beiblatt : die theologische Literatur des Jahres 1922–42* (Leipzig : Hinrichs, 1922–43). Frequency varies: biweekly, 1922–24; semiannual, 1925–35; annual, 1936–42. Z7753.T39

Theologischer Jahresbericht. v. 1 (1881)–v. 33 (1913). Tübingen : Mohr, 1882–1916. **BC226**
Later volumes issued in parts. Vol. 33, pts. 4 and 7 never published.
An important serial bibliography of books and periodical material; for the university, theological, or large reference library. Discontinued after the outbreak of World War I.

Library catalogs

Union Theological Seminary (New York, N.Y.). Library. Catalogue of the McAlpin collection of British history and theology / comp. and ed. by Charles Ripley Gillett. N.Y. : [Union Theological Seminary], 1927–30. 5 v. **BC227**
Contents: v. 1–4, 1500–1700; v. 5, Index.
A rich collection of material including many pamphlets on British theology and history. Chronologically arranged. Alphabetical index.
———. ———. *Acquisitions 1924–1978* (Boston : G.K. Hall, 1979. 427 p.). Reproduces the catalog cards for 3,000 British imprints of the 16th and 17th centuries. In two sections, the first a dictionary arrangement of author, title, and subject entries, the second a chronological arrangement of the main entry cards by date of publication.
Z7757.E5N5

Manuscripts; Archives

Women religious history sources : a guide to repositories in the United States / ed. by Evangeline Thomas, CSJ. N.Y. : Bowker, 1983. 329 p.   **BC228**

"The all-inclusive term *women religious* in the title refers to women called *sisters* in the active orders and *nuns* in the contemplative orders of the Catholic, Orthodox, and Episcopal churches and to those called *deaconesses* in the Lutheran, Methodist, and Mennonite churches."—*Pref.* Repositories are listed by state, then city, and notes on background and holdings are given. Bibliography, p.143–68. A "Table of U.S. founding dates" (chronological rather than by name of order) and a "Biographical register of foundresses and major superiors" (giving personal dates, order, and entry number for the repository) are useful appendixes. Indexed. Makes a useful companion to Andrea Hinding's *Women's history sources* (DB39).   Z7839.W65

Encyclopedias

The Blackwell encyclopedia of modern Christian thought / ed. by Alister McGrath. Oxford ; Cambridge, Mass. : Blackwell, 1993. 701 p. : 26 cm.   **BC229**

"Designed as an authoritative, readable and reliable reference source for all those who are interested in, or wish to learn about, the main features of modern Christian thought" (*Introd.*) since 1700. Includes survey essays on major themes and movements both within Christianity and in its relation to culture, politics, science, etc. (e.g., Ethics, Marxism, Feminist theology, Protestant theology); articles on influential theologians; and many short entries on other significant thinkers. The essays are signed and often provide substantial bibliographies; brief biographies end with two or three references. Many cross-references; well-prepared index; glossary of theological terms.   BR95.B58

Dictionary of the ecumenical movement / ed. by Nicholas Lossky ... [et al.]. Geneva : WCC Publications ; Grand Rapids, Mich. : Eerdmans, 1991. 1196 p. : ill.   **BC230**

"By enlisting contributions from Protestants, Orthodox and Roman Catholics, the dictionary seeks to show how the ecumenical movement has been perceived and lived within various confessional perspectives" (*Introd.*) throughout the 20th century. Although studies and activities of the World Council of Churches command the greatest attention, Roman Catholic ecumenical interests are given substantial consideration. Useful articles indicate areas of convergence and divergence among the major religious bodies on doctrine (e.g., Sin, Salvation, Grace); views on social, political, legal, and ethical issues (e.g., Abortion, Land use, Torture); liturgy; and biblical interpretation. Also offers brief biographies of leaders in ecumenism. Ample cross-references; brief bibliographies at the ends of articles. Subject and name indexes.   BX6.3.D53

Encyclopedia of theology : the concise Sacramentum mundi / ed. by Karl Rahner. N.Y. : Seabury Pr., [1975]. 1841 p.   **BC231**

"This volume contains revised versions of the major articles on theology, biblical science and related topics from *Sacramentum Mundi* [BC405], together with a large number of articles from the major German works *Lexikon für Theologie und Kirche* [BC63] and *Theologisches Taschenlexikon,* and entirely new articles on topics of major importance written for the occasion by Professor Rahner and others."—*Pref. note.*   BR95.E48

Evangelisches Kirchenlexikon : EKL : internationale theologische Enzyklopädie / [hrsg. von Erwin Fahlbusch ... et al.]. 3 Aufl., Neufassung. Göttingen : Vandenhoeck & Ruprecht, c1986 [i.e. c1985]–1992. v. 1–3. (In progress).   **BC232**

1st ed. 1955–61; 2nd ed., 1961–62.

Contents: v. 1–3, A–R.

An entirely new edition, to be complete in four volumes. A German Protestant work on the life and teachings of the Christian churches, but ecumenical and international in outlook and with strong emphasis on contemporary issues, Third World churches, Roman Catholicism, and Eastern Orthodoxy. Long signed articles, in alphabetical order, contain cross-references and updated bibliographies arranged in chronological order. All articles on individuals and some historical surveys have been omitted. For this reason, v. 4 of the previous edition is useful for its 15,000 brief biographies of persons connected with Christianity through the ages.   BR95.E89

World Christian encyclopedia : a comparative study of churches and religions in the modern world, AD 1900–2000 / ed. by David B. Barrett. Oxford : Oxford Univ. Pr., 1982. 1010 p. : ill., maps.   **BC233**

A topical and comparative encyclopedia of many aspects of Christianity as found in about 20,800 denominations "spread among some 8,990 peoples speaking 7,010 languages in the modern world."—*Pref.* Offers country-by-country surveys, numerous statistical tables, chronologies, directory information, etc.; information is based on the research efforts of an international network of collaborators, contributors and local editors. The work "includes information on all the types and activities of organized Christianity, gives the data in an interdenominational or ecumenical presentation, and sets the whole in the context of all other religions including new religions and atheism."—*Introd.* Select bibliography; atlas section; dictionary of terms. Indexes.   BR157.W67

Dictionaries

Corpus dictionary of Western churches / Thomas C. O'Brien, ed. Wash. : Corpus Publications, [1970]. 820 p.   **BC234**

Concerned with "the Churches that have developed throughout the history of Western Christianity" (*Pref.*), with special attention to North American churches in the Western tradition. In addition to entries for the various denominations, there are subsidiary articles on events and personalities in church history, doctrines, documents, practices, etc. Some 2,300 concise, unsigned articles representing the contributions of more than 100 scholars and specialists of many faiths. Compiled under Roman Catholic auspices, but ecumenical in intent.   BR95.C67

Dictionary of Christianity in America / coordinating ed., Daniel G. Reid ; consulting editors, Robert D. Linder, Bruce L. Shelley, Harry S. Stout. Downers Grove, Ill. : InterVarsity Pr., c1990. 1305 p.   **BC235**

Authoritative articles by some 500 scholars cover religious bodies, movements, and individuals and institutions in North America (especially the U.S.). Gives special attention to the Protestant evangelical tradition. Emphasis is historical rather than contemporary. "Does not attempt to arbitrate in matters of religious convictions, but to report fairly, accurately and objectively the beliefs and practices of the respective groups."—*Pref.* The only work of its kind to date.   BR515.D53

Douglas, James Dixon. The new international dictionary of the Christian church. Rev. ed. Exeter, [Eng.] : Paternoster Pr. ; Grand Rapids, Mich. : Zondervan, [1978]. 1074 p.   **BC236**

1st ed., 1974.

An international group of some 180 scholars has contributed signed articles on a wide range of topics relating to the history, development, and practices of the Christian church. Many biographical sketches. Some articles include bibliographical references. Cross-referencing is effected both through conventional *see* references and use of an asterisk following a name or term in the text of an article. Strong in American church history and evangelical movements. Minor revisions in this edition.   BR95.D68

Harvey, Van Austin. A handbook of theological terms. N.Y. : Macmillan, [1964]. 253 p.　　**BC237**
"My aim has not been to provide definitions of obscure theological terms but to indicate how such terms, ancient and modern, have been variously used in differing circumstances and what is at issue in these various uses."—*Pref.*　　BR95.H32

Metford, J. C. J. Dictionary of Christian lore and legend. [London] : Thames and Hudson, [1983]. 272 p. : ill.　**BC238**
Aims "to provide, in convenient and concise form, a guide to the essentials of [the] Christian tradition in the arts, music and literature."—*Foreword.* Entries for saints, biblical figures and events, liturgical terms, etc. For the non-specialist.　　BR95.M396

New dictionary of theology / editors, Sinclair B. Ferguson, David F. Wright ; consulting ed., J. I. Packer. Downers Grove, Ill. : InterVarsity Pr., c1988. 738 p.　　**BC239**
Offers concise, signed articles, each with numerous cross-references and a select bibliography. The more than 200 British and North American contributors represent the Protestant evangelical viewpoint.　　BR95.N39

The Oxford dictionary of the Christian church. 2nd ed., repr. (with corrections and some revisions) / ed. by F. L. Cross and E. A. Livingstone. Oxford ; N.Y. : Oxford Univ. Pr., 1983. 1520 p.　　**BC240**
1st ed., 1957; 2nd ed., 1974.
A useful work of more than 6,000 articles. Coverage is broad, including historical and doctrinal development, biographies, and definitions of ecclesiastical terms and customs. About half the entries were written by contributing scholars, but all are unsigned. This edition provides minor revisions to entries and bibliographies and some new articles.　　BR95.O8

The Westminster dictionary of Christian ethics / ed. by James F. Childress and John Macquarrie. Philadelphia : Westminster Pr., c1986. 678 p.　　**BC241**
Rev. ed. of *A dictionary of Christian ethics*, ed. by John Macquarrie, 1967.
Contains signed articles, with numerous cross-references and brief bibliographies, by approximately 350 scholars from a wide range of traditions, including Protestant, Anglican, Roman Catholic, Orthodox, and Jewish. Articles provide factual information and indicate major options in Christian ethical debate. 60% of the articles are new; the remainder were retained, with revision, from the previous edition. Subject areas include: basic ethical concepts; biblical ethics; theological ethics; philosophical traditions in ethics; major non-Christian religious traditions in ethics; psychological, sociological and political concepts important for Christian ethics; and substantial ethical problems (e.g., abortion, war, unemployment). Individual thinkers are discussed in the context of articles on major traditions, movements, or themes, such as "Aristotelian ethics" or "Augustinian ethics." Index of names. A highly useful tool for general readers and specialists alike.
§ *Baker's dictionary of Christian ethics*, ed. by Carl F. H. Henry (Grand Rapids, Mich. : Baker Book House, 1973. 726 p.), provides various evangelical perspectives in signed articles, many with bibliographic references appended.　　BJ1199.W47

The Westminster dictionary of Christian spirituality / ed. by Gordon S. Wakefield. Philadelphia : Westminster Pr., c1983. 400 p.　　**BC242**
Also publ. as: *A dictionary of Christian spirituality* ([London] : SCM Pr., [1983]).
Attempts "to give direct access to the whole development and present state of the subject."—*Pref.* Contains concise articles, with cross-references and bibliographies, by more than 150 contributors. Ecumenical in perspective, international in scope; useful for students and scholars.　　BV4488.W47

The Westminster dictionary of Christian theology / ed. by Alan Richardson and John Bowden. Philadelphia : Westminster Pr., 1983. 614 p.　　**BC243**

Published simultaneously as *A new dictionary of Christian theology* (London : SCM Pr., 1983).
Based on Alan Richardson's *Dictionary of Christian theology* (Philadelphia : Westminster Pr. ; London : SCM Pr., 1969).
Relatively brief, signed articles (with bibliographies) on contemporary theological issues, terms, etc. Focus "is on theological thinking against a historical background rather than on historical events or figures."—*Pref.*　　BR95.W494

Westminster dictionary of church history / ed.: Jerald C. Brauer. Philadelphia : Westminster Pr., [1971]. 887 p.　**BC244**
Offers definitions and explanations "concerning the major men, events, facts and movements in the history of Christianity"—*Pref.* Alphabetically arranged.　　BR95.W496

White, Richard Clark. The vocabulary of the church : a pronunciation guide. N.Y. : Macmillan, 1960. 178 p.　　**BC245**
Emphasis is on proper nouns and biblical words; gives word and pronunciation only. "The standard pronunciation is American religious usage."—*Introd.*　　BR95.W53

Early church period

See also *Encyclopedia of the early church* (BC275) and *Encyclopedia of early Christianity* (BC274).

Cabrol, Fernand. Dictionnaire d'archéologie chrétienne et de liturgie. Paris : Letouzey et Ané, 1907–53. 15 v. : ill.　**BC246**
Vol. 3–15 ed. by Cabrol and Henri Leclercq; v. 14–15 ed. by Henri Marrou.
Issued in parts.
Excellent signed articles, with full bibliographies, on institutions, manners, and customs of primitive Christianity, and on the architecture, Christian art, iconography, symbols, epigraphy, paleography, numismatics, liturgy, rites, and ceremonies of the early church to the time of Charlemagne. Covers much of the same ground as William Smith and Samuel Cheetham, *Dictionary of Christian antiquities* (Hartford, Conn. : J. B. Burr Publ. Co., 1880. 2 v.), but with fuller and more up-to-date treatment.　　BR95.C2

Kelly, Joseph F. The concise dictionary of early Christianity. Collegeville, Minn. : Liturgical Pr., c1992. 203 p.　　**BC247**
Brief entries, intended for quick reference, cover people, movements, and terms from the first six centuries of Christianity. A bibliographic essay provides information on related reference sources.　　BR95.K395

Reallexikon für Antike und Christentum : Sachwörterbuch zur Auseinandersetzung des Christentums mit der antiken Welt / In Verbindung mit Franz Joseph Dölger und Hans Lietzmann und unter besonderer Mitwirkung von Jan Hendrik Wasznik und Leopold Wenger hrsg. von Theodor Klauser. Stuttgart : Hiersemann, 1950–1994. v. 1–16. (In progress).　　**BC248**
Editors vary.
Contents: Bd. 1–16, A–Ianus.
Presents long, signed articles by many scholars dealing with the relationship of the ancient world to Christianity up to the sixth century CE.
———. *Supplement*, ed. by Theodor Klauser ... [et.al] (Stuttgart, 1985–1992. [In progress]).
Contents: Lfg. 1/2, 3/4, 5/6, Aaron–Barbar II.
Contains selected articles reprinted from *Jahrbuch für Antike und Christentum* (1959–), new articles on topics not in the main work, and bibliographic essays updating articles in the main work.　　BR131.R4

Smith, William. Dictionary of Christian biography : literature, sects and doctrines / Sir William Smith, Henry Wace. London : Murray ; Boston : Little, 1877–87. 4 v.　　**BC249**

Repr.: N.Y. : AMS Pr., 1967.

A companion work to William Smith and Samuel Cheetham, *Dictionary of Christian antiquities* (Hartford, Conn. : J. B. Burr Publ. Co., 1880. 2 v.).

Aims to supply an adequate account, based upon original authorities, of all persons connected with the church—down to the age of Charlemagne—about whom anything is known, of all literature connected with them, and of the controversies about doctrine and discipline in which they were engaged. Pays special attention to subjects and names in English, Scottish, and Irish church history. Signed articles; bibliographies.

§ *The dictionary of Christian biography and literature to the end of the sixth century* A.D. (Boston : Little, 1911), by Henry Wace and William C. Piercy, is a revised and abridged edition of Smith's work. Adds some references, but covers only the first six centuries.
BR95.S65

Directories

Handbook, member churches / World Council of Churches ; ed. by Ans J. van der Bent. Fully rev. ed. Geneva : The Council, c1985. 289 p. : maps.   **BC250**
1st ed., 1982.

Descriptions of member churches include statistics, brief historical surveys, and notes on current activities. Arranged by continent, then by region and country. An introductory section covers national and regional councils and conferences to which member churches belong. A section on Christian world communities describes ecumenical activities of various traditions during the past 40 years. Indexes of countries, church names, and English-language versions of church names.
BX6.W78H26

UK Christian handbook. 1980?– . London : Evangelical Alliance, 198?– .   **BC251**
Editor: P. Brierley.
1994/95, publ. 1993.

Statistical and directory information for churches in the U.K.; directories of missionary societies, theological colleges and bible schools, religious publishers and bookstores, retreat houses, and religious organizations. Geographic, personnel, and organization indexes.
BV2420.U3

Handbooks

A new handbook of Christian theology / Donald W. Musser and Joseph L. Price, editors. Nashville : Abingdon, c1992. 525 p.   **BC252**
Catholic and Protestant scholars have contributed 148 articles, with short bibliographies. Updates standard theological topics included in *A handbook of Christian theology*, ed. by Marvin Halverson and Arthur A. Cohen (Cleveland : World Publ. Co., 1958) and adds articles on such newer theologies as black, confessional, liberation, narrative, feminist, and womanist.
BR95.N393

Biography

Most of the encyclopedias listed above include biographies, in some cases of considerable reference importance. In some instances, the yearbooks (e.g., BC333, BC415) include contemporary biography. The following entries are limited to biography and include many names not given in the more general works.

Bautz, Friedrich Wilhelm. Biographisch-bibliographisches Kirchenlexikon. Hamm : Verlag Traugott Bautz, 1970–1994. v. 1–8. (In progress).   **BC253**
Contents: v. 1–8, Aalders–Schenute von Atripe.
Issued in fascicles.

Biographical sketches are followed by lists of works by and about the individuals. Biographees include saints, popes, bishops, clergymen, theologians, church historians, hymn writers and composers of church music, literary authors of religious significance, etc.   BR1700.2.B38

Moyer, Elgin Sylvester. Wycliffe biographical dictionary of the church. Rev. and enl. by Earle E. Cairns. Chicago : Moody Pr., [1982]. 449 p.   **BC254**
Represents a revision of Moyer's *Who was who in church history* (rev. ed., 1968).

Offers "brief biographies of over two thousand men and women of all races, from all parts of the world, who have made major contributions to the cause of Christ."—*Pref.*   BR1700.2.M66

Sprague, William Buell. Annals of the American pulpit : or, commemorative notices of distinguished American clergymen of various denominations, from the early settlement of the country to the close of the year 1855. With historical introductions. N.Y. : R. Carter, 1857 [69]. 9 v. : ill.   **BC255**
Repr. : N.Y. : Arno Pr., 1969.
Contents: v. 1–2, Trinitarian Congregational; v. 3–4, Presbyterian; v. 5, Episcopalian; v. 6, Baptist; v. 7, Methodist; v. 8, Unitarian Congregational; v. 9, Lutheran; Reformed Dutch; Associate; Associate Reformed; Reformed Presbyterian.

A useful work of sketches, averaging two or three pages in length, with extensive bibliographies of the publications by the biographee. Alphabetical index for each denomination but no general index.

§ Another useful series for biographical information on early American clergy comprises the following works by Frederick Lewis Weis: *The colonial clergy of the Middle Colonies: New York, New Jersey, and Pennsylvania, 1628–1776* (Worcester, Mass. : Amer. Antiquarian Soc., 1957); *The colonial clergy of Maryland, Delaware and Georgia* (Lancaster, Mass., 1950); *The colonial clergy of Virginia, North Carolina, and South Carolina* (Boston, 1955); and *The colonial clergy and the colonial churches of New England* (Lancaster, Mass., 1936). These lists give only brief biographical information.
BR569.S7

Williams, Ethel L. Biographical directory of Negro ministers. 3rd ed. Boston : G.K. Hall, 1975. 584 p.   **BC256**
1st ed., 1965; 2nd ed., 1970.

Furnishes biographical data on living African-American ministers active and influential in local or national affairs. Geographical index. This edition includes 1,442 "who's who" type biographical sketches.
BR563.N4W5

Saints

Many questions regarding saints are related to feast days, legends, names, and patronage, and will be answered by the English-language sources listed below. For research use and to locate information on saints not included in the English sources, the indispensable works are *Acta sanctorum* and other publications of the Bollandists described below.

Acta sanctorum quotquot toto orbe coluntur : vel a catholicis scriptoribus celebrantur / quae ex Latinis et Graecis, aliarumque gentium antiquis monumentis collegit, digessit, notis illustravit Joannes Bollandus … operam et studium contulit Godefridus Henschenius …. Editio novissima / curante Joanne Carnandet …. Parisiis : Palmé, 1863–1940. 67 v. : ill., plates, ports., maps, tables.   **BC257**

Title and imprint vary.

Contents: Jan.–Apr., 3 v. each; May, 7 v. and Propylaeum; June–July, 7 v. each; Aug., 6 v.; Sept., 8 v.; Oct., 13 v. in 14; Nov., 4 v. and Propylaeum; Dec., Propylaeum.

Important source material collected from European libraries, with annotations and commentaries. For an account of the *Acta sanctorum*, see *Catholic encyclopedia* 2 : 630–39.

Supplemented by: (1) *Ad Acta sanctorum … supplementum, volumen complectens Auctaria Octobris et Tabulas generales. Scilicet ephemerides et indicem alphabeticum decem priorum mensium* …. cura et opera L. M. Rigollot.

(2) *Supplément aux Acta sanctorum pour des vies de saints de l'époque mérovingienne* par M. l'Abbé C. Narbey.

(3) *Analecta bollandiana* (BC258).   BX4655.A2

Analecta bollandiana. v. 1– . Bruxelles : Soc. des Bollandistes ; Paris : Picard, 1882– . Quarterly.   **BC258**

Imprint varies.

Gives the current bibliography of the subject, with critical reviews of new publications, and supplements the *Acta sanctorum* (BC257) by printing texts, commentaries, etc., not included in the *Acta*.

Indexed by:

———. *Indices in tomos I–XX (1882–1901), XXI–XL (1902–1922), XLI–LX (1923–1942)* (Bruxelles : Soc. des Bollandistes, 1904–45) 3 v.).

———. *Table générale des articles publiés en 80 ans, 1882–1961* (Bruxelles, 1962. 33 p.).

In addition, there are indexes to authors and saints in each volume.   BX4655.A3

Bibliotheca hagiographica graeca. 3. éd. mise à jour et considérablement augmentée par François Halkin. Brussels : Société des Bollandistes, 1957. 3 v. (Subsidia hagiographica, no. 8a).   **BC259**

Various reprints. The Société issued a one-volume repr. in 1986. 1st ed., 1895; 2nd ed., 1909.

Contents: t. 1–2, A–Z; t. 3, Supplément, appendices, et tables.

Lists, under names of saints, pre-16th century Greek writings, with references to printed versions.

Auctarium bibliotheca hagiographica graeca (1969. 386 p. [Subsidia hagiographica, no. 47]), and *Novum auctarium bibliothecae hagiographicae graeca* (1984. 430 p. [Subsidia hagiographica, no. 65]), both by François Halkin, offer corrections and additions to the 3rd ed.

§ The following two works cover materials in Latin and Middle Eastern and North African languages: (1) *Bibliotheca hagiographica latina antiquae et mediae aetatis* (1898–1901. 2 v. [1304 p.] [Subsidia hagiographica, no. 6]). Various reprints. The Société issued a one-volume repr. in 1992. A *Supplementi* was publ. in 1911 (355 p. [Subsidia hagiographica, no. 12]) and *Novum supplementum* in 1986 (Henryk Fros, ed. 959 p. [Subsidia hagiographica, no. 70]).

(2) *Bibliotheca hagiographica orientalis* (1910. 287 p. [Subsidia hagiographica, no. 10]. Repr. : Brussels : Société des Bollandistes, 1954).   Z7844.B53

Bibliotheca sanctorum. [Rome] : Istituto Giovanni XXIII nella Pontificia Università Laterense, [1961–69]. 12 v. : ill.   **BC260**

Repr. : Rome : Città nouva, 1987–91. A separate index volume was publ. in 1970.

Offers signed articles, with bibliographies, on figures of the Old and New Testaments, angels, saints, persons declared blessed or venerable or whose cause for canonization has been introduced. Four indexes: general name index, feast days, patronage, names of contributors.

A "prima appendice" was publ. in 1987.   BX4655.8.B5

The book of saints : a dictionary of servants of God / comp. by the Benedictine monks of St. Augustine's Abbey, Ramsgate. 6th ed., entirely rev. and re-set ; 1st American ed. Wilton, Conn. : Morehouse Pub., 1989. 605 p. : ill.   **BC261**

1st ed., 1921; 5th ed., 1966.

An entirely new edition, reflecting changes in the General Calendar of the Roman Catholic Church promulgated in 1969. Notes the removal from the canon of certain saints now considered nonhistorical, and the addition of others, including those recently canonized. Brief biographies include all saints in the Roman martyrology and some others, particularly those who have given place-names to towns and villages in the British Isles. Includes photographs; short bibliography; index of emblems; list of patron saints of various professions, trades, arts, states of life; and list of the twelve Sibyls (prophetesses) of the ancient world.   BX4655.2.B66

Butler, Alban. A dictionary of saints : based on Butler's Lives of the saints, complete ed / comp. by Donald Attwater. N.Y. : Kenedy, [1958]. 280 p.   **BC262**

2,500 brief entries, each with reference to the fuller treatment in the 1956 ed. of Butler's *Lives* (BC263).   BX4654.B8

———— Lives of the saints. Complete ed., rev. and supplemented by Herbert Thurston and Donald Attwater. N.Y. : Kennedy, [1956]. 4 v.   **BC263**

Repr. : Westminster, Md. : Christian Classics, 1981.

A standard source providing, in calendar order, readable, short biographies of saints. Gives legendary and factual information. Brief bibliographies for entries include references to *Acta sanctorum quotquot toto orbe coluntur* (BC257) and other sources. Name indexes for each volume; v. 4 index covers all volumes.

For brief sketches of lesser saints, see the earlier, 12-volume edition (London : Burns ; N.Y. : Kennedy, 1926–38).

A brief version was published as *Butler's lives of the saints*, ed. by Michael J. Walsh (Concise ed., rev. and updated. San Francisco : Harper, 1991).

Delaney, John J. Dictionary of saints. Garden City, N.Y. : Doubleday, 1980. 647 p.   **BC264**

Offers brief entries on some 5,000 "saints and *beati* about whom … the modern reader would be most likely to seek information."—*Introd.* Intended for the general reader "seeking a concise resume of the pertinent facts in particular saints' lives." Includes lists of saints as patrons and intercessors, patrons of countries and places, and their symbols in art; a chronological chart of popes and world rulers; and calendars of the Roman and Byzantine rites. No bibliography.   BX4655.8.D44

Farmer, David Hugh. The Oxford dictionary of saints. 3rd ed. Oxford ; N.Y. : Oxford Univ. Pr., 1992. 530 p.   **BC265**

1st ed., 1978; 2nd ed., 1987.

Offers brief accounts of some 1,000 saints of English origin, saints of foreign origin who died in England, and those who were known and venerated there. Select bibliographies give citations to official sources, to the best hagiographical studies, and sometimes to popular works. Appendixes list principal patronages, and principal iconographical emblems. Index of places; calendar of feasts.

BX4659.G7F37

The saints : a concise biographical dictionary / ed. by John Coulson. N.Y. : Hawthorn, [1958]. 496 p. : ill.   **BC266**

Contains brief biographies of more than 2,200 saints. Many of the articles, although not signed, are contributed by authorities in the field. Profusely illustrated with colored and black-and-white plates.

BX4655.S28

Liturgy and ritual

Johnson, Matthew. Bibliographia liturgica = Bibliographie der Nachschlagwerke für Liturgiewissenschaft = Bibliographie liturgique = Reference bibliography for liturgics. Rome : C.L.V. Edizioni Liturgiche, 1992. 114 p.   **BC267**

Introduction, table of contents, and headings in Latin, German, French, and English.

A selective list of standard reference works, periodicals, and series required for study and research in the history and theology of liturgics. Omits contemporary liturgical texts, exclusively pastoral works, and works on liturgical spirituality. Emphasis on Roman Catholic, Anglican, and Lutheran religions. Graduate student level. Indexes: author and editor, periodicals and series.

The new Westminster dictionary of liturgy and worship / ed. by J.G. Davies. Philadelphia : Westminster Pr., c1986. 544 p. : ill.   **BC268**

Publ. in U.K. as *A new dictionary of liturgy & worship* (London : S.C.M. Pr., 1986). Rev. ed. of *The Westminster dictionary of worship* ([1979], c1972), publ. in U.K. as *A dictionary of liturgy & worship* (London : S.C.M. Pr., 1972).

About half the articles have been updated from the earlier edition, 70 new articles added, and 50% more space made available; bibliographies have been updated. Numerous cross-references; 90 black-and-white illustrations. Most contributors are British. Not definitive for specialists in liturgical studies, but provides introduction and clarification for general readers.

§ *A dictionary of liturgical terms* by Philip H. Pfatteicher (Philadelphia : Trinity Pr. Internat., c1991) is a handy resource for pronunciation, etymology, and brief definitions of Eastern and Western Christian liturgical words and phrases.   BV173.N49

The study of liturgy / ed. by Cheslyn Jones ... [et al.]. Rev. ed. London : SPCK ; N.Y. : Oxford Univ. Pr., 1992. 601 p. : ill.   **BC269**

1st ed., 1978.

Serves as an introduction to the study of Christian liturgy and a guide to more advanced study of the subject. Thoroughly revised in the light of new rites and advances in liturgical scholarship. Chapters were contributed by British and American specialists and include bibliographies. In three main sections: (1) Theology and rite; (2) The development of the liturgy (general introduction; initiation; the Eucharist; ordination; the Divine Office; the calendar; the setting of the liturgy); (3) Pastoral orientation. Indexed.

§ A specialized bibliography is Richard W. Pfaff's *Medieval Latin liturgy : a select bibliography* (Toronto : Univ. of Toronto Pr., [1982]), which includes approximately 1,000 studies of the Latin liturgy from the late fourth century to the Reformation.   BV176.S76

Church history and expansion

General works

Piepkorn, Arthur Carl. Profiles in belief : the religious bodies of the United States and Canada. N.Y. : Harper & Row, 1977–79. 4 v. in 3.   **BC270**

Contents: v. 1, Roman Catholic, Old Catholic, Eastern Orthodox; v. 2, Protestant denominations; v. 3–4 (in 1 v.), Evangelical, fundamentalist, and other Christian bodies.

Arranged by "families" of churches, with an introductory essay which carries notes and bibliography. Articles on individual religious bodies include history, basic beliefs, practices, statistics, and address of the group's headquarters. Each volume is indexed.

BL2530.U6P53

Bibliography

Revue d'histoire ecclésiastique. v. 1– . Louvain : Université Catholique de Louvain, 1900– . Quarterly.   **BC271**

Vol. 1–55, "Bibliographie" issued as pt. 2 of the *Revue*; v. 56– , "Bibliographie" issued as a separately paged section in each issue.

An extensive classified bibliography of books, articles, and reviews published throughout the world on the history of the church including political history and philosophy. In four main sections, subdivided by topic: (1) Sciences auxiliaires; (2) Publications de sources et critique des sources; (3) Travaux historiques proprement dits; (4) Compte rendus d'ouvrage précédement annoncés. Name index.

BX940.R5

Vekene, Emil van der. Bibliotheca bibliographica historiae sanctae inquisitionis = Bibliographisches Verzeichnis der gedruckten Schrifttums zur Geschichte und Literatur der Inquisition. Vaduz : Topos Verlag, [1982–92]. 3 v.   **BC272**

Foreword and explanatory notes in Spanish, German, and English.

Constitutes a revised and expanded edition of the compiler's *Bibliografía de la Inquisición* (1963).

More than 7,000 publications relating to the Inquisition are listed chronologically within topical and geographical sections. Index of authors and anonymous publications and index to periodicals and festschriften.   Z7805.V43

World Council of Churches. Library. Classified catalog of the ecumenical movement. Boston : G.K. Hall, 1972. 2 v.   **BC273**

Reproduction of the catalog cards for a collection of some 11,000 items published since 1500, mainly in English, but international in scope.

————. *1st supplement* (Boston : G.K. Hall, 1981. 517 p.) adds materials from 1973–80, as well as publications of earlier years accessioned since publication of the basic set.

§ *International ökumenische Bibliographie* (Mainz : Matthias-Grünewald ; München : Kaiser, v. 1/2 [1962/63]–v. 17/18 [1978/79]), an important international bibliography, covers only 1962–79, but includes periodical articles.   Z7845.1.W63

History

Encyclopedia of early Christianity / Everett Ferguson, ed. ... [et al.]. N.Y. : Garland, 1990. 983 p. : ill. (Garland reference library of the humanities, vol. 846).   **BC274**

Covers persons, places, doctrines, practices, art, liturgy, heresies, and schisms from the time of Jesus to approximately 600 CE. Articles by 135 specialists include bibliographies and cross-references. Extensive subject index. Intended for general readers, students, and professionals in fields outside religion who want information concerning early Christianity.   BR162.2.E53

Encyclopedia of the early church / produced by the Institutum Patristicum Augustinianum and ed. by Angelo Di Berardino. N.Y. : Oxford Univ. Pr., 1992. 2 v. (1130 p.) : ill., maps.
                                                                  BC275
Translation of: *Dizionario patristico e di antichità cristiane*.
Concise, authoritative, signed articles, written by an international team of 167 scholars, cover topics in archaeology, philosophy, linguistics, history, theology, and geography to about 750 CE. Special attention is given to the relationship between Christianity and the pagan world. Bibliographies have been updated to 1991. Includes a synoptic table of secular, ecclesiastical, cultural, and doctrinal matters. Separate section of maps and illustrations; index.   BR66.5.D5813

A history of the ecumenical movement / ed. by Ruth Rouse and Stephen Charles Neill. 3rd ed. Geneva : World Council of Churches, 1986. 2 v.   **BC276**
Contents: v. 1, 1517–1948; v. 2, 1948–1968.
Vol. 1 first publ. 1954; v. 2, first publ. in the 2nd ed. of the work (1967–70), includes an updated bibliography and is edited by Harold E. Fey.
A survey history from the period of the Reformation to 1968, each section written by a specialist. Vol. 1 has a classed bibliography, p. 745–801; the bibliography in v. 2, p. 447–553, is arranged in chapters corresponding to the chapters of the text, followed by a classed bibliography of works published from 1968 through 1985.
§ Two earlier bibliographies of the ecumenical movement are *The ecumenical movement in bibliographical outline* by Paul A. Crow (N.Y. : Dept. of Faith and Order, Nat. Council of the Churches of Christ, 1965. 80 p.) and *Critical bibliography of ecumenical literature* by Josephus F. Lescrauwaet (Nijmegen : Bestel Centrale V.S.K.B., 1965. 93 p.).   BX6.5.R62

Jedin, Hubert. Handbook of church history / ed. by Hubert Jedin and John Dolan. N.Y. : Herder & Herder, etc., [1965–81]. 10 v.   **BC277**
Title varies: v. 5–10 publ. as *History of the church*. Also publ. by Crossroads, 1980–82, under title *History of the church*.
Contents: v. 1, From the apostolic community to Constantine, by Karl Baus; v. 2, The imperial church from Constantine to the early Middle Ages, by Karl Baus [et al.]; v. 3, The church in the age of feudalism, by Friedrich Kempf [et al.]; v. 4, From the High Middle Ages to the eve of the Reformation, by Hans-Georg Beck [et al.]; v. 5, Reformation and Counter Reformation, by Erwin Iserloh [et al.]; v. 6, The church in the age of absolutism and enlightenment, by Wolfgang Müller; v. 7, The church between Revolution and Restoration, by Roger Aubert [et al.]; v. 8, The church in the age of liberalism, by Roger Aubert [et al.]; v. 9, The church in the Industrial Age, by Roger Aubert [et al.]; v. 10, The church in the modern age, by Gabriel Adriányi [et al.].
Tr. from Jedin's *Handbuch der Kirchengeschichte,* (3rd ed. Freiburg : Herder, 1962–79. 7 v. in 10).
A scholarly history written from a Catholic viewpoint, which "examines not only the Church's external career in the world but also her inner life, the development of her doctrine and preaching, her ritual and devotion."—*Pref.* Bibliographies for each chapter indicate sources, general literature, and special studies.   BR145.2.J413

Oxford history of the Christian church. Oxford : Clarendon Pr. ; N.Y. : Oxford Univ. Pr., 1976–1990. v. 1–[6]. (In progress).   **BC278**
Contents: A history of the churches in the United States and Canada, by Robert T. Handy (1976. 471 p.); The Popes and European revolution, by Owen Chadwick (1981. 646 p.); The Frankish church, by John Michael Wallace-Hadrill (1983. 463 p.); Religion in England, 1688–1791, by Ernest Gordon Rupp (1986. 584 p.); The papal monarchy : the Western church from 1050 to 1250, by Colin Morris (1989. 673 p.); The Orthodox church in the Byzantine Empire, by Joan Mervyn Hussey (1990. 408 p.).

A monograph series with useful bibliographies. To be in about 20 volumes; only the first volume carries a series number.

The Oxford illustrated history of Christianity / ed. by John McManners. Oxford ; N.Y. : Oxford Univ. Pr., 1990. 724 p.
                                                                  BC279
A popular history written by 18 scholars, mostly British. Essays in the first section are arranged chronologically from the earliest Christian communities to 1800. The second section, 1800 to the present, is arranged geographically by continent. A third section treats current issues and future prospects. Includes illustrations, color plates, maps, a chronology, an annotated bibliography for further reading, and a comprehensive subject index.   BR145.2.O86

Schaff, Philip. History of the Christian church. New ed., thoroughly rev. and enl. N.Y. : Scribner, 1882–1910. 7 v. in 8. : ill.
                                                                  BC280
1st ed., 1867; various reprintings.
A detailed, documented history written from a Protestant viewpoint.   BR145.S3

Sourcebooks

Ayer, Joseph Cullen. A source book for ancient church history : from the apostolic age to the close of the conciliar period. N.Y. : Scribner, 1913. 707 p.   **BC281**
Repr.: N.Y. : AMS Pr., 1970.
A standard work.

Documentary history of faith and order, 1963–1993 / ed. by Günther Gassmann. Geneva : WCC Publications, c1993. 325 p. (Faith and order paper, no. 159).   **BC282**
A sequel to *A documentary history of the faith and order movement 1927–1963*, ed. by Lukas Vischer (St. Louis : Bethany Pr., 1963).
Includes statements on unity from assemblies of the World Council of Churches, documents from world conferences on faith and order, and other documents related to the aim of the WCC's Commission on Faith and Order to challenge and assist the churches to achieve "visible unity."—*Introd.*   BX6.W77.D63

Documents on Christian unity / George K. A. Bell, ed. London ; N.Y. : Oxford Univ. Pr., 1929–58. 4 v.   **BC283**
Contents: 1st series, 1920–24 (1924); 2nd series, 1924–30 (1930); 3rd series, 1930–48 (1948); 4th series, 1948–57 (1958).
The 1st and 2nd series were republished in 1930 as "2nd ed."
A collection of documents designed to illustrate the growth of the ecumenical movement throughout the world.
§ *Documents on Christian unity : a selection from the first and second series* was published in 1955 (271 p.).   BX8.A1D6

Gee, Henry. Documents illustrative of English church history, comp. from original sources / Henry Gee and William John Hardy. London ; N.Y. : Macmillan, 1896. 670 p.   **BC284**
Repr.: N.Y. : Kraus, 1966.
Covers 314–1700 CE, with most documents from the period after 1066.   BR741.G3

Kidd, Beresford James. Documents illustrative of the history of the church. London : Society for Promoting Christian Knowledge ; N.Y. : Macmillan, 1920–41. 3 v.   **BC285**
Contents: v. 1, to 313 CE; v. 2, 313–461; v. 3, ca. 500–1500.
Partially superseded by *A new Eusebius: documents illustrative of the history of the church to A.D. 337*, ed. by James Stevenson (London : SPCK, 1957. 427p.).
§ Kidd also edited *Documents illustrative of the continental Reformation* (Oxford : Clarendon Pr., 1911).   BR45.T66K5

Sweet, William Warren. Religion on the American frontier : a collection of source material. Chicago : Univ. of Chicago Pr., 1931–1946. 4 v. : ill.   **BC286**

Contents: [v. 1], The Baptists, 1783–1830 (N.Y.: Henry Holt, 1931); v. 2, The Presbyterians, 1783–1840 (N.Y.: Harper, 1936); v. 3, The Congregationalists, 1783–1850 (1939); v. 4, The Methodists, 1783–1840 (1946).

Each volume includes a bibliography.

Atlases

Anderson, Charles S. Augsburg historical atlas of Christianity in the Middle Ages and Reformation. Minneapolis: Augsburg, [1967]. 61 p.: ill. **BC287**

Maps with accompanying text; intended as a study aid for church history. G1796.E4A5

Atlas zur Kirchengeschichte: die christlichen Kirchen in Geschichte und Gegenwart; Kommentare Ausführliches Register / hrsg. von Hubert Jedin, Kenneth Scott Latourette, Jochen Martin. Aktualisierte Neuausg. / [bearb. und hrsg. von Jochen Martin]. Freiburg: Herder, c1987. 83, 152 p.: maps in color. **BC288**

1st ed., 1970.

Presents 257 maps and charts and 70 pages of commentary, with bibliographies following each section of commentary. An outstanding church history atlas. G1046.E4A8

Freitag, Anton. The twentieth century atlas of the Christian world: the expansion of Christianity through the centuries. N.Y.: Hawthorn, [1963, i.e., 1964]. 199 p.: ill., maps. **BC289**

A revision and translation of *Atlas du monde chrétien: l'expansion du christianisme à travers les siècles* (Paris; Brussels: Elsevier, 1959).

A pictorial atlas from the Catholic point of view. The historical maps are far outnumbered by photographs (of people, places, works of art) and explanatory text. Index of proper names. BV2100.F713

Meer, Frederik van der. Atlas of the early Christian world / Frederik van der Meer, Christine Mohrmann; tr. and ed. by Mary F. Hedlund and H. H. Rowley [London]: Nelson, 1958. 215 p.: ill., maps. **BC290**

A translation of the work originally published as *Atlas van de oudchristelijke wereld* (Amsterdam: Elsevier, 1958).

Includes 620 plates illustrating the history of Christianity for the first six centuries, covering sculpture, architecture, mosaics, Christian cities, etc. The 42 maps show in great detail the various parts of the Roman Empire, with plans of important cities and regions, churches, monuments, dioceses, etc. The text comments on the historical and geographical background and describes the illustrations. Indexed. G1046.E4M6

Statistics

United States. Bureau of the Census. Religious bodies: 1936. Wash.: U. S. Govt. Print. Off., 1941. 3 v. **BC291**

Contents: v. 1, Summary and detailed tables; v. 2–3, Separate denominations: statistics, history, doctrine, organization, and work.

Statistics given are, as nearly as possible, those for the year 1936, and cover, for the continental U.S.: membership, church edifices and parsonages, value of church property and debt on same, expenditures, and Sunday schools. Previous full reports for this century covered 1906, 1916, and 1926.

Since 1936, full reports have not been made by the Bureau of the Census, although very abbreviated statistics are given in its *Current population reports: Population characteristics*, Ser. P-20, no. 79 (1957). More detailed figures are included in *Yearbook of American and Canadian churches* (BC324). HA201.1936.A32

World Christian encyclopedia: a comparative study of churches and religions in the modern world, AD 1900–2000 / ed. by David B. Barrett. Oxford: Oxford Univ. Pr., 1982. 1010 p.: ill., maps. **BC292**

For annotation, *see* BC233. BR157.W67

Patrology

For certain kinds of reference work—especially in large reference libraries, theological libraries, and in college and university work in medieval history, literature, and philosophy—the writings of the Fathers of the Church are required. The important collections of the Latin and Greek texts are *Series latina* ("Patrologia latina"), and *Series graeca* ("Patrologia graeca") of Jacques Paul Migne's *Patrologiae cursus completus* (Paris: Migne, 1844–64 and 1857–66, respectively) and the various series of *Corpus Christianorum* (Turnholti: Typographi Brepols, 1953–), whose critical texts supersede Migne. Vols. 6–21, 52–76, 78–79, 102–129, and 158–185 of Migne's *Series latina* are also available on CD-ROM as the *Patrologia latina database* (Release 3. Alexandria, Va.: Chadwyck-Healey, c1994). The *CETEDOC library of Christian latin texts* on CD-ROM (Turnhout: Brepols, c1991–) contains a set of forms representing the entirety of volumes published in the *Corpus Christianorum*, both the *Series latina* and the *Continuatio mediaevalis*, the opera omnia of major authors such as Augustine, Jerome, and Gregory the Great, as well as several works not yet available in the *Corpus Christianorum* but included in the *Corpus scriptorum ecclesiasticorum latinorum* of Vienna, the Patrologia latina, or other collections.

Ancient Christian writers (N.Y.: Paulist Pr., 1945) and *Fathers of the church* (Wash.: Catholic Univ. of America Pr., 1947–) are two modern series preferred for their fresher English translations. They will be less useful, however, for most reference purposes than the works listed below, which have extensive indexes.

Texts

Ante-Nicene Fathers: translations of the writings of the Fathers down to A.D. 325 / Alexander Roberts and James Donaldson, eds. American repr. of the Edinburgh ed., rev. and chronologically arranged with brief prefaces and occasional notes by A. C. Coxe. Buffalo, N.Y.: Christian Literature Co., 1885–96. 10 v. **BC293**

Frequently reprinted.

The Edinburgh edition, with title *Ante-Nicene Christian library*, was publ. by Clark, 1867–72, in 24 volumes.

A collection of the writings of the Apostolic Fathers down to 325 CE, in English translation. Contents of American edition: v. 1–8, Text; v. 9, Additional volume, containing early Christian works ... and selections from the commentaries of Origen, etc., Allen Menzies, ed.; v. 10, Bibliographical synopsis, by E. C. Richardson. General index to v. 1–8, by Bernard Pick. BR60.A5

Select library of Nicene and post-Nicene Fathers of the Christian church / ed. by Philip Schaff. 1st–2nd series, trans. into English. N.Y.: Christian Literature Co., 1886-1900. 28 v. **BC294**

Repr.: Grand Rapids, Mich.: Eerdmans, 1961.

English translations of the "most important works of Greek Fathers from Eusebius to Photius, and of the Latin Fathers from Ambrose to Gregory the Great."—*Pref.* Lacks a general index, but has subject and scripture indexes in each volume. BR60.S4

419

Bibliography

Bibliographia patristica = Internationale patristische Bibliographie. v. 1 (1956)– . Berlin : W. de Gruyter, 1959– .
BC295

Issued annually, beginning with v. 28, 1983. Publication date lags date of coverage, typically by about five years.

A committee of patristic scholars of various confessions contributes to this listing of studies about the early Christian Fathers and related historical and theological topics. Each volume contains more than 3,000 entries in a classed arrangement, with entries repeated under appropriate subjects. Includes book reviews and author index.

———. *Supplementum : voces: eine Bibliographie zu Wörtern und Begriffen aus der Patristik (1918–1978)*, H. J. Sieben, ed. (Berlin : W. de Gruyter, 1980. 461 p.).

This supplementary volume is in two sections, Greek and Latin. Each has an alphabetical list of words and concepts in the writings of the Church Fathers, with citations to books, parts of books, journal articles, festschriften and encyclopedia contributions. Indexed.

Z7791.B5

Dekkers, Eligius. Clavis patrum latinorum : qua in novum Corpus Christianorum edendum optimas quasque scriptorum recensiones a Tertulliano ad Bedam / commode recludit Eligius Dekkers ; opera usus qua rem praeparavit et iuvit Aemilius Gaar. Ed. altera, aucta et emendata. Steenbrugis : In Abbatia Sancti Petri, 1961. 640 p. (Sacris erudiri; jaarboek voor godsdienstwetenschappen, 3).
BC296

1st ed., 1951.

A key to the Latin writings of the Church Fathers that have appeared in collections and periodicals. Three indexes: (1) Index nominum et operum; (2) Index systematicus; (3) Initia.

Geerard, Maurice. Clavis Patrum Graecorum. Turnhout : Brepols, 1974–87. 5 v.
BC297

Added t.p.: Clavis Patrum Graecorum : qua optimas quaeque scriptorum Patrum Graecorum recensiones a primaevis saeculis usque ad Octavum commode recluduntur.

Contents: v. 1, Patres antenicaeni; v. 2, Ab Athanasio ad Chrysostomum; v. 3, A Cyrillo Alexandrino ad Iohannem Damascenum; v. 4, Concilia. Catenae; v. 5, Indices, initia, concordantae.

A key to the writings of the Greek fathers and to related works. Primary bibliography (editions, manuscript sources, versions) and critical materials.

Z7791.G43

Stewardson, Jerry L. A bibliography of bibliographies on patristics. Evanston, Ill. : Garrett Theological Seminary Libr., 1967. 52 p.
BC298

Lists almost 200 bibliographies published as books, parts of books, journal articles, in encyclopedias, etc. Most entries are annotated and reviews are often noted. Armenian, Ethiopian, Georgian and Arabic literature are excluded; Syriac literature was not searched exhaustively.

Indexes

Biblia patristica : index des citations et allusions bibliques dans la littérature patristique / Centre d'analyse et de documentation patristiques, équipe de recherche associée au Centre national de la recherche scientifique, J. Allenbach ... [et al.]. Paris : Editions du Centre national de la recherche scientifique, 1975–1991. v. 1–5. (In progress).
BC299

Contents: v.1, Des origines à Clément d'Alexandrie et Tertullien; v.2, Le troisième siècle (Origène excepté); v.3, Origène; v. 4, Eusèbe de Césarée, Cyrille de Jérusalem, Epiphane de Salamine; v. 5, Basile de Césarée, Grégoire de Nazianze, Grégoire de Nysse, Amphiloque d'Iconium.

Offers correspondence tables arranged according to books of the Old Testament and listing (in abbreviated form): biblical book, chapter and verse, together with relevant patristic author, work, book chapter, paragraph, page and line.

———. *Supplement, Philon d'Alexandre*, publ. 1982.

BR66.5.U53

Manuals

Altaner, Berthold. Patrologie : Leben, Schriften u. Lehre d. Kirchenväter / Berthold Altaner, Alfred Stuiber. 8., durchges. u. erw. Aufl. Freiburg [etc.] : Herder, 1978. 672 p.   **BC300**

1st ed., 1938, by Altaner.

An extensive bibliographical work with comments on the lives, writings, and teachings of the Church Fathers. Translated into French, Spanish, and Italian; and into English (based on the 5th German ed.) as *Patrology*, tr. by Hilda C. Graef (2nd ed. N.Y. : Herder, 1961. 659 p.).

In this edition, the text of the 7th ed. (1966) is reprinted, unchanged, with additional bibliography (to 1977) placed in the *Anhang*, p. 535–662, and keyed to original entries. A 1980 printing is called "9. Aufl."
BR67.A37

Quasten, Johannes. Patrology. Utrecht : Spectrum ; Westminster, Md. : Newman, 1950–86. 4 v.
BC301

Frequently reprinted.

Contents: v. 1, The beginnings of patristic literature; v. 2, The Ante-Nicene literature after Irenaeus; v. 3, The golden age of Greek patristic literature: from the Council of Nicaea to the Council of Chalcedon; v. 4, The golden age of Latin patristic literature from the Council of Nicea to the Council of Chalcedon.

Vol. 4, ed. by Angelo di Berardino, is a translation of *Patrologia*, v. 3.

"A new Patrology that strives to place at the disposal of the English-reading public a solid introduction to Early Christian literature."—*Pref.* Extensive bibliographies list critical editions, translations into modern languages, and articles and monographic studies of the writings discussed.

Vol. 4 contains a brief introduction by the ailing Quasten and is designated as the final volume of his monumental work. "While following in its general outlines the methodological criteria of Quasten, the work attempts to see the Fathers in their political and social context and to give more space to the problematics of contemporary patristic research."—*Pref.* Indexes: scripture, ancient writers, authors, subjects.
BR67.Q32

Missions

No single comprehensive bibliography of Protestant missions is available comparable to P. Robert Streit's *Bibliotheca missionum* (BC304) which treats Catholic missions. For a listing of various bibliographies, largely specialized, *see*: John G. Barrow, *A bibliography of bibliographies in religion*, p. 286–301 (BC4).

Amistad Research Center. Author and added entry catalog of the American Missionary Association Archives : with references to schools and mission stations. Westport, Conn. : Greenwood, [1970]. 3 v.
BC302

A catalog of about 105,000 items, mainly letters, from the extensive American Missionary Association collections (approximately 350,000 manuscript pieces). Provides materials for a detailed history of the Association and its evangelistic and reform activities in America. The archive has accumulated valuable materials relating to abolition, the Underground Railroad, the Civil War, Reconstruction, etc. The Amistad Research Center is at Tulane Univ., New Orleans.
Z7817.A45

Bibliografia missionaria / Unione missionaria del clero in Italia. v. 1–49. Roma : L'Unione, 1935–1986. **BC303**
Publisher varies; editors vary.
Vols. for 1936–85 also called Anno 3–anno 49.
Vol. 1 covers Jan. 1, 1933–June 30, 1934; v. 2, July 1, 1934–Dec. 31, 1935; v. 10, 1943–46. Other volumes are annual, with 4-year cumulated indexes; after v. 37 (1973), includes annual index.
Aims to be a comprehensive bibliography of Catholic missions, covering history, theology, methodology, and cultural and pastoral aspects. Classified arrangement; author and subject indexes; separate section of book reviews. From 1961–83, provided an appendix, "Documenti e problemi missionari."
§ Superseded by: *Bibliographia missionaria* / Pontifical Missionary Library of the Congregation for the Evangelization of Peoples (Anno 50 [1986]– . Vatican City : Pontifical Urban University, 1987– . Annual). Annotations and other explanatory text chiefly in English; citations in various languages. Z7838.M6B5

Bibliotheca missionum / begonnen von P. Robert Streit, fortgeführt von P. Johannes Dindinger. Freiburg : Herder, 1916–74. 30 v. **BC304**
Imprint varies; editors vary.
Contents: v. 1, Grundlegender und allgemeiner Teil; v. 2–3, Amerikanische Missionsliteratur, 1493–1699, 1700–1909; v. 4–5, Asiatische Missionsliteratur, 1245–1599, 1600–1699; v. 6, Missionsliteratur Indiens, der Philippinen, Japans und Indochinas, 1700–1799; v. 7, Chinesische Missionsliteratur, 1700–1799; v. 8, Missionsliteratur Indiens und Indonesiens, 1800–1909; v. 9, Missionsliteratur der Philippinen, 1800–1909; v. 10, Missionsliteratur Japans und Koreas, 1800–1909; v. 11, Missionsliteratur Indochinas, 1800–1909; v. 12–14, Chinesische Missionsliteratur, 1800–1884, 1885–1909, 1910–1950; v. 15–20, Afrikanische Missionsliteratur, 1053–1599, 1600–1699, 1700–1879, 1880–1909, 1910–1940; v. 21, Missionsliteratur von Australien und Ozeanien, 1525–1950; v. 22, Grundlegender und allgemeiner Teil, 1910–1935, und Nachtrag zu Bd.1; v. 23, Grundlegender und allgemeiner Teil, 1936–1960; v. 24–26, Amerikanische Missionsliteratur, 1910–24, 1925–44, 1945–60; v. 27, Missionsliteratur Indiens, 1910–1946, und Nachtrag zu B.M. IV bis VIII; v. 28, Missionsliteratur Südasiens (Indien, Pakistan, Birma, Ceylon), 1947–68; v. 29, Missionsliteratur Südostasiens, 1910–1970; v. 30, Missionsliteratur Japans und Koreas, 1910–1970 und Nachtrag zu B.M. IV, V, VI, X.
The great Catholic bibliography of missions. Includes voyages, relations, official documents, etc. Gives full bibliographical details, critical estimates, annotations, references to sources, and (in many cases) location of copies in European libraries. Z7838.M6S9

Christianity in China : a scholars' guide to resources in the libraries and archives of the United States / Archie R. Crouch ... [et al.]. Armonk, N.Y. : M.E. Sharpe, c1989. lvi, 709 p. **BC305**
Lists and describes primary and secondary resources located in 554 repositories. Entries are arranged alphabetically by state, then by city. Also includes: union lists of more than 700 serial titles; 650 oral history interviews; 500 dissertations/theses; bibliography of archival guides and directories; and indexes by subject, personal name, and repository. Z7757.C6C46

Latourette, Kenneth Scott. A history of the expansion of Christianity. N.Y. : Harper, 1937–45. 7 v. : maps. **BC306**
A comprehensive survey of missions from the earliest times to the 1940s, with an extensive bibliography in each volume. BR145.L3

Laures, John. Kirishitan bunko : a manual of books and documents on the early Christian missions in Japan. 3rd rev. and enl. ed. Tokyo : Sophia Univ., 1957. 536 p. : ill. (Monumenta Nipponica monographs, 5). **BC307**
Subtitle: With special reference to the principal libraries in Japan, and more particularly to the collection at Sophia University, Tokyo. With an appendix of ancient maps of the Far East, especially Japan.
1st ed., 1940. Supplements issued 1941 and 1951.
A bibliography of documents (books, articles, manuscripts) relating to the Christian missions from their beginnings in the 16th century to the first years after the reopening of Japan to relations with the West. Presents a Catholic viewpoint.

Mission handbook : U.S.A./Canada Protestant ministries overseas. 14th ed. (1989)– . Monrovia, Calif. : Missions Advanced Research and Communication Center, c1989– . **BC308**
1st ed., 1953, had title: *Check list of foreign missionary agencies in the United States*. Subtitle varies.
15th ed., 1993, ed. by John A. Siewert and John A. Kenyon.
Provides directory information, both descriptive and statistical (on finances and personnel) for more than 800 Protestant mission agencies engaged in, or supporting, ministries outside North America. BV2050.D55

Missionary Research Library (New York, N.Y.). Dictionary catalog of the Missionary Research Library, New York. Boston : G.K. Hall, 1968. 17 v. **BC309**
Approximately 273,000 entries by author, title, and subject. Includes many entries for periodical articles by important authors. Missionary journals held by the library are listed in v. 17. Z817.N54

Neill, Stephen Charles. Concise dictionary of the Christian world mission / Stephen Charles Neill, Gerald H. Anderson, John Goodwin. London : Lutterworth ; Nashville : Abingdon Pr., [1971]. 682 p. **BC310**
Brief, signed articles on the spread of Christianity in various countries of the world, biographies of missionary leaders, and topics and problems relating to missionary work. Covers the period since 1492. Bibliographic references accompany most entries.
BV2040.N44

Creeds

Schaff, Philip. Bibliotheca symbolica ecclesiae universalis : the creeds of Christendom, with a history and critical notes. [Rev. ed.]. N.Y. ; London : Harper, [1919]. 3 v. **BC311**
1st ed., 1877. Various reprintings and revisions of individual volumes.
Contents: v.1, History of creeds (church by church, with many bibliographical references) v.2, Creeds of the Greek and Latin churches (giving for each the full Greek or Latin text and an English translation in parallel columns, with an index of subjects) v.3, Creeds of the Evangelical Protestant churches (in language of original with parallel English translation); index of subjects. BT990.S4

Costume

Norris, Herbert. Church vestments : their origin & development. London : Dent, 1949. 190 p. : ill. **BC312**
Illustrated with plates and line drawings. Based on the author's *Costume and fashion*, it treats the history and development of the classical garments used in the church. BV167.N67

Hymnology

Analecta hymnica medii aevi / hrsg. von Guido Maria Dreves und Clemens Blume. Leipzig : Reisland, 1886–1922. 55 v. **BC313**
Repr. : N.Y. : Johnson Reprint Corp., 1961; also available in microform from Microcard Editions, Wash., D.C.
A very comprehensive collection, giving texts of hymns and detailed historical and bibliographical notes.
———. *Register*, in Zusarb. mit Dorothea Baumann [et al.] ; hrsg. von Max Lütolf (Bern : Francke, 1978. 3 v.). Indexes the set.
Contents: v. 1 (in two volumes), Verzeichnis der Textanfängen; v. 2, Gattungen, Liturgische Bestimmungen, Verfasser.

Indexes in v. 2 refer to entry numbers in the first-line index in v. 1; which in turn gives volume and page in the set. BV468.A622A5

Claghorn, Charles Eugene. Women composers & hymnists : a concise biographical dictionary. Metuchen, N.J. : Scarecrow, 1984. 272 p. **BC314**
For annotation, *see* BJ207. BV325.C58

Dictionary of American hymnology : first line index : a project of the Hymn Society of America / Leonard Ellinwood, project director and ed. [microform]. N.Y. : Univ. Music Editions, 1984. 179 reels microfilm with looseleaf guide. **BC315**
Microfilm reproduction of more than a million alphabetically arranged data cards of the first-line hymn index compiled by the Hymn Society. Indexes 4,634 American hymnals and general gospel songbooks from 1640 to the present. Gives data for source hymnal, first line, title, author. Hymnals are listed in numerical code sequence on Reel 001.
§ *Bibliography of American hymnals*, by Ellinwood and Elizabeth Lockwood, associate ed. (N.Y. : University Music Editions, 1983. 27 microfiche), provides an alphabetical list of the works indexed in the *Dictionary*, plus nearly 3,000 other hymnals.

Diehl, Katharine Smith. Hymns and tunes : an index. N.Y. : Scarecrow, 1966. 1185 p. **BC316**
Indexes the hymns from 78 hymnals by first lines, variant first lines, and authors. The hymn tunes are indexed by names and variants, by composers, and by a systematic index to the melodies. BV305.D5

Hughes, Charles William. American hymns old and new : notes on the hymns and biographies of the authors and composers. N.Y. : Columbia Univ. Pr., 1980. 621 p. **BC317**
Arranged by first line, provides information about authors, tunes, and composers of hymns presented in the companion volume, *American hymns old and new*, by Albert Christ-Janer, Charles W. Hughes, and Carleton Sprague Smith (N.Y. : Columbia Univ. Pr., 1980). A substantial section of biographies is followed by a bibliography. Indexes to first lines/titles, and authors and composers from the companion volume. ML3270.H8

Julian, John. A dictionary of hymnology : setting forth the origin and history of Christian hymns of all ages and nations. Rev. ed. with new supplement. London : Murray ; N.Y. : Scribner, 1907. 1768 p. **BC318**
Repr. : Grand Rapids, Mich. : Kregel, 1985. 2 v.
1st ed., 1892; the revised edition corrects some typographical errors and adds a supplement of 131 pages.
Contents: (1) Dictionary; (2) Cross-reference index to first lines in English, French, German, Latin, etc.; (3) Index of authors, translators, etc.; (4) Appendix, A–Z, late articles; (5) Appendix, A–Z, additions and corrections to articles in main part; (6) New supplement; (7) Indexes to appendixes and supplement.
Deals with Christian hymns of all ages and nations, with special reference to those in the hymnbooks of English-speaking countries. Articles on subjects in hymnology, hymn writers, and separate hymns—all in one alphabet; important subjects are treated at considerable length. Signed articles; bibliographies. BV305.J8

McDormand, Thomas Bruce. Judson concordance to hymns / Thomas Bruce McDormand, Frederic S. Crossman. Valley Forge, Pa. : Judson Pr., [1965]. 375 p. **BC319**
Provides a subject approach to hymns as well as a kind of concordance. Lines from hymns are arranged by keyword with reference to the table of first lines. Includes 2,342 hymns. BV305.M3

Parks, Edna D. Early English hymns : an index. Metuchen, N.J. : Scarecrow, 1972. 168 p. **BC320**
Hymns are listed alphabetically by first line, with indication of meter, number of stanzas or lines, author's name, publication date and page reference in a collection, and indication of composer's name and the tune when available. Includes numerous items not found in John Julian's *A dictionary of hymnology* (BC318). Publication dates are mainly 17th century. Bibliography; indexes of authors and of composers. BV305.P37

Perry, David W. Hymns and tunes indexed by first lines, tune names, and metres, compiled from current English hymnbooks. Croydon, England : Hymn Society of Great Britain & Ireland ; Royal School of Church Music, 1980. 310 p. **BC321**
Locates hymns in 37 British hymnbooks "in wide current use for adult congregational worship."—*Introd.* BV305.P47

Poultney, David. Dictionary of Western church music. Chicago : Amer. Libr. Assoc., 1991. 234 p. : ill. **BC322**
For annotation, *see* BJ155. ML102.C5P77

Protestant denominations

General works

Yearbooks

Many denominations publish annuals or directories; only a few of the larger denominations are listed here, and many of these have been formed by mergers of various bodies. For information about other denominations see: *Yearbook of American and Canadian churches* (BC324), and the annual reports or yearbooks of individual denominations; the latter are useful for denominational facts and figures, lists of ministers, etc.

Fédération protestante de France. Annuaire de la France protestante. 1979– . Montauben [France] : imprimerie Lormond, [1979]– . Annual. **BC323**
Formerly *Annuaire protestant*, 1862–1978.
Directory and institutional information for France and overseas French-speaking regions. No biographies.

Yearbook of American and Canadian churches. 1916– . N.Y. : Publ. by the National Council of the Churches of Christ in the U.S.A. Annual. **BC324**
Title, publisher, and frequency vary: v. 1–2, *Federal Council year book*; v. 3–8, *Year book of the churches*; v. 9 (1927) *Handbook of the churches*; 1933–72, *Yearbook of American churches*. Current title and publisher, 1973– .
Includes directories of religious bodies of all faiths, theological seminaries and Bible colleges, ecumenical agencies, religious periodicals, international congregations, depositories of church history materials. A brief statistical section is followed by indexes to individuals and to organizations. BR513.Y4

Baptists

Encyclopedia of Southern Baptists. Nashville : Broadman, 1958–82. 4 v. : ill. **BC325**
Offers signed articles with bibliographies; includes many biographical sketches. Covers the history, methods, and work of Southern Baptists, including organizations, institutions, colleges, newspapers, etc., as well as articles on their viewpoint on religious beliefs and practices. Vols. 3 and 4 (also called supplements) update and expand the first two volumes, covering developments of 1956–70 and 1970–80, respectively. Each provides a system of cross-references to the earlier volumes.
———. *Index to volumes I–IV* (1982. 36 p.) lists articles in the full set. BX6211.E5

Starr, Edward Caryl. A Baptist bibliography : being a register of printed material by and about Baptists, including works written against the Baptists. Rochester, N.Y. : American Baptist Historical Society, 1947–76. 25 v.　　　**BC326**
Imprint varies.
Arranged alphabetically by author. Each volume has an index to joint authors, translators, Baptist publishers, distinctive titles, and subjects. Locates copies.　　　Z7845.B2S8

Whitley, William Thomas. A Baptist bibliography : being a register of the chief materials for Baptist history, whether in manuscript or in print, preserved in Great Britain, Ireland, and the colonies / comp. for the Baptist Union of Great Britain and Ireland. London : Kingsgate Pr., 1916–22. 2 v.　　　**BC327**
Repr. : Hildesheim : Olms, 1984. 2 v. in 1.
Contents: v. 1, 1526–1776; v. 2, 1777–1837. Addenda, 1613–53. Indexes: (1) Anonymous pamphlets, (2) Authors, (3) Places, (4) Subjects.
Locates copies in 31 libraries, mainly British.　　　Z7845.B2W6

Yearbooks

American Baptist Churches in the U.S.A. Yearbook. 1973– . Valley Forge, Pa. : [American Baptist Churches], 1973– . Annual.　　　**BC328**
Continues the *Yearbook* of the American Baptist Convention, 1950–72. Issued 1908–49 as *Yearbook* of the Northern Baptist Convention, which absorbed the *American Baptist yearbook* in 1941. (Issuing agency changed name to American Baptist Convention in 1950; to American Baptist Churches in the U.S.A. in 1973.).
Includes records of the biennial meeting of the association and reports of activities of the national boards.
§ Beginning in 1973, directory and statistical information published separately in *Directory of the American Baptist Churches in the U.S.A.* (Valley Forge, Pa. : Judson Pr., 1973–).　　　BX6207.A3

Southern Baptist Convention. Annual. 1st ed. (1845)– . Nashville : [The Convention], 1845– . Annual.　　　**BC329**
Includes proceedings, reports, statistics, directory information, etc.

Brethren churches

The Brethren encyclopedia. Philadelphia : Brethren Encyclopedia, Inc., 1983–84. 3 v. (2126 p.) : ill.　　　**BC330**
Offers signed articles, with bibliographies, on the "life, belief, practice and heritage" of "those religious bodies that trace their origin to the Brethren movement."—*Introd.* Included are the Brethren Church, the Church of the Brethren, the Dunkard Brethren, the Fellowship of Grace Brethren Churches, and the Old German Baptist Brethren. Strong in biography. Vol. 3, Lists—maps, contains statistical data, a list of ministers and elders, 1708–1980, extensive bibliography, chronology, maps, and corrections and additions to v. 1–2. BX7821.2B74

Church of England

History

Le Neve, John. Fasti ecclesiae Anglicanae : or, A calendar of the principal ecclesiastical dignitaries in England and Wales, and of the chief officers in the universities of Oxford and Cambridge, from the earliest time to the year MDCCXV / comp. by J. Le Neve, corrected and continued to the present time by T. Duffus Hardy. Oxford : Univ. Pr., 1854. 3 v.
　　　BC331

Lists of ecclesiastical dignitaries, bishops, archdeacons, prebendaries, etc., arranged by diocese, with alphabetical indexes of names. Some biographical information.
Le Neve's work first appeared in 1716 in 1 v. The LeNeve-Hardy compilation is being revised and expanded in three series, covering different time periods.
———. *Fasti ecclesiae Anglicanae, 1066–1300* (London : Univ. of London, Inst. of Historical Research ; Athlone Pr., 1968–91. 4 v. [In progress]).
Contents: v. 1, St. Paul's, London, comp. by D. E. Greenway; v. 2, Monastic cathedrals (Northern and southern provinces), comp. by D. E. Greenway; v. 3, Lincoln, comp. by D. E. Greenway; v. 4, Salisbury, comp. by D. E. Greenway.
———. *Fasti ecclesiae Anglicanae, 1300–1541* (London : Univ. of London, Inst. of Historical Research ; Athlone Pr., 1962–67. 12 v.).
Contents: v. 1, Lincoln Diocese, comp. by H. P. F. King; v. 2, Hereford Diocese, comp. by J. M. Horn; v. 3, Salisbury Diocese, comp. by J. M. Horn; v. 4, Monastic cathedrals, comp. by B. Jones; v. 5, St. Paul's, London, comp. by J. M. Horn; v. 6, Northern province, comp. by B. Jones; v. 7 Chichester Diocese, comp. by J. M. Horn; v. 10, Coventry and Lichfield Diocese, comp. by B. Jones; v. 11, The Welsh Dioceses, comp. by B. Jones; v. 12, Introduction, errata and index, comp. by J. M. Horn.
———. *Fasti ecclesiae Anglicanae, 1541–1857* (London : Univ. of London, Inst. of Historical Research ; Athlone Pr. ; distr. by Oxford Univ. Pr., N.Y., 1971–92. [In progress]).
Contents: v. 1, St. Paul's, London, comp. by J. M. Horn; v. 2, Chichester Diocese, comp. by J. M. Horn; v. 3, Canterbury, Rochester and Winchester Dioceses, comp. by J. M. Horn; v. 4, York Diocese, comp. by J. M. Horn and D. M. Smith; v. 5, Bath and Wells Diocese, comp. by J. M. Horn and D. S. Bailey; v. 6, Salisbury Diocese, comp. by J. M. Horn; v. 7, Ely, Norwich, Westminster and Worcester Diocese, comp. by J. M. Horn.　　　BX5197.L5

Ollard, Sidney Leslie. Dictionary of English church history / ed. by Sidney Leslie Ollard, Gordon Crosse, Maurice F. Bond. [3rd rev. ed.]. London : A.R. Mowbray ; N.Y. : Morehouse-Gorham, [1948]. 698 p.　　　**BC332**
1st ed., 1912; 2nd ed., 1919.
Scope of this work is strictly that of the English church, i.e., the provinces of Canterbury and York, and does not include discussion of the church in Ireland, Scotland, or America. Good signed articles with brief bibliographies (usually undated) on history, beliefs, controversies, architecture, costume, music, etc., of the church. Many biographies of persons deceased. A special feature is the list of bishops under the name of each see. High Church point of view.　　　BX5007.O5

Yearbooks

Church of England. General Synod. The Church of England year book. 88th (1971-72)– . [London] : Church Information Office, 1971– . Annual.　　　**BC333**
Title, subtitle, and issuing body vary: 1883–1921, *The official year-book of the Church of England*, publ. by the Society for Promoting Christian Knowledge; 1922–62, *The official year-book of the National Assembly of the Church of England*, publ. by the Church Assembly and the Society; 1963–1970, publ. under current title by the Church Information Office and the Society, with added title, *The official year book of the National Assembly of the Church of England*. Current added title: *The official year book of the General Synod of the Church of England*.
Provides general directory information for churches and provinces in the Anglican Communion throughout the world. Gives brief biographies of members of the General Synod, of bishops, deans, provosts, archdeacons, and Lambeth Palace staff.　　　BX5015.C45

Crockford's clerical directory. 1st (1858)– . London : Oxford Univ. Pr., 1858– . Biennial.　　　**BC334**
Frequency varies.
Subtitle varies: 1991–92, A directory of the clergy of the Church of England, the Church in Wales, the Scottish Episcopal Church, the Church of Ireland.

Includes biographical sketches for Anglican clergy in the British Isles and overseas, as well as statistical and directory information.

BX5031.C7

Service books

Church of England. The alternative service book of 1980 : services authorized for use in the Church of England in conjunction with the Book of Common Prayer, together with the Liturgical Psalter. Chichester [England] : Clowes, 1980. 1292 p. **BC335**

The service book of revised liturgical forms. "Intended to supplement the Book of Common Prayer, not to supersede it."—*Pref.*

BX5145.A55

———————— The annotated Book of Common Prayer : being an historical, ritual and theological commentary on the devotional system of the Church of England / ed. by the Rev. John Henry Blunt. With an introductory notice by the Rev. Frederick Gibson. New impression, 1899; reissue, with additions, and corrections. London : Longmans ; N.Y. : Dutton, 1903. 732 p. **BC336**

BX5145.B6

———————— The Book of Common Prayer : with the additions and deviations proposed in 1928. Oxford : Oxford Univ. Pr., [1928]. 778 p. **BC337**

Includes the Daily Offices, sacraments and other rites, Psalter and Ordinal. Supplemented by the *Alternative service book* (BC335).

§ For a history of the development of the *Book of Common Prayer*, see *Oxford dictionary of the Christian church* (BC240), p. 320–321.

Bibliography

Benton, Josiah Henry. The Book of Common Prayer and books connected with its origin and growth : catalogue of the collection of Josiah Henry Benton. 2nd ed. prep. by William Muss-Arnolt. Boston : Priv. print [D.B. Updike], 1914. 142 p. **BC338**

1st ed., 1910.

A collection of books of common prayer of the Churches of England, Ireland, and Scotland; the Protestant Episcopal church of the U.S.; and others. Z7813.B41

Muss-Arnolt, William. The Book of Common Prayer among the nations of the world : a study based mainly on the collection of Josiah Henry Benton. London : Society for Promoting Christian Knowledge, 1914. 473 p. **BC339**

Subtitle: A history of translations of the prayer book of the Church of England and of the Protestant Episcopal Church of America. Includes bibliographies and index to names and subjects.

BX5145.M8

Church of Ireland

Phillips, Walter Alison. History of the Church of Ireland : from the earliest times to the present day. London : Oxford Univ. Pr., 1933–34. 3 v. **BC340**

Contents: v. 1, The Celtic church; v. 2, The movement towards Rome, The medieval church and the reformation; v. 3, The modern church.

Bibliography and index in each volume. Succession of bishops of the Church of Ireland in v. 3. BX5500.P5

Church of Scotland

Macgregor, Malcolm B. The sources and literature of Scottish church history. Glasgow : J. McCallum, 1934. 260 p. **BC341**

Repr. : Merrick, N.Y. : Richwood Publ. Co., 1976.

An annotated bibliography of sources and secondary materials. Includes biographical sketches of outstanding persons in Scottish religious history from the earliest times. Z7778.S3M2

Scott, Hew. Fasti ecclesiae Scoticanae : the succession of ministers in the Church of Scotland from the Reformation. New ed., rev. and continued to the present time under the superintendence of a committee appointed by the General Assembly. Edinburgh : Oliver and Boyd, 1915–81. v. 1–10. (In progress). **BC342**

1st ed., 1866–71 (3 v. in 6).

Publisher varies.

Contents: v. 1–7, 1560–1914; v. 8, 1914–28, addenda and corrigenda for 1560–1949; v. 9, 1929–54; v. 10, 1955–75. Vol. 9 ed. by J. A. Lamb; v. 10 ed. by D. F. M. Macdonald.

A brief historical sketch of each minister is given, with a list of his writings and bibliographical references where such are available. Each volume has a bibliography of local and parish histories. More than 15,000 biographies. BX9099.S4

Congregational

See United Church of Christ.

Episcopal

Caldwell, Sandra M. The history of the Episcopal Church in America, 1607–1991 : a bibliography / by Sandra M. Caldwell and Ronald J. Caldwell. N.Y. : Garland, 1993. 528 p. (Garland reference library of the humanities, v. 1635 ; Religious information systems series, v. 13). **BC343**

Includes more than 3,800 entries, some with annotations, for works concerning the history of the Episcopal Church in the U.S. and the influence it has had on U.S. history. Emphasis is on secondary writings; only the most important primary sources are included. Offers comprehensive coverage of local histories (more than 1,500), and access to some 1,300 biographies of individuals, with the remainder of the entries arranged topically. Index. Z7845.A5C34

Clerical directory of the Protestant Episcopal church in the United States of America. N.Y. : Church Hymnal Corp., 1898–1968. 27 v. : ill. **BC344**

Previous titles: *Lloyd's clerical directory* and *Stowe's clerical directory*.

Contains biographical sketches of the clergymen of the Protestant Episcopal church throughout the world. Issued approximately every third year (none issued between 1941 and 1947); updated by supplements.

Continued by: *Episcopal clerical directory* (Ed. 24 [1972]– . N.Y. : Church Hymnal Corp. Biennial), which continues the numbering of the earlier publication.

Ed. 24 (1972) had title: *Episcopal clergy directory*.

Offers who's-who type "biographical data for all Episcopal clergy in good standing, both active and retired."—*Foreword, 1991.*

BX5830.S8

Dictionaries

Harper, Howard V. The Episcopalian's dictionary : church beliefs, terms, customs, and traditions explained in layman's language. N.Y. : Seabury Pr., [1975, c1974]. 183 p. **BC345**
    Ample definitions include historical information and provide Latin and Greek derivations of terms.   BX5007.H37

Yearbooks

The Episcopal church annual. 1953– . Wilton, Conn. [etc.] : Morehouse-Barlow, 1953– . Annual.   **BC346**
    Established in 1830 as *The churchman's almanac*; continued as *Churchman's year book and American church almanac* and *The living church annual*. In 1953 assumed the present title.
    General directory and institutional information, with clergy list.
                                BX5830.L5

Book of Common Prayer

The *Book of Common Prayer* of the Episcopal Church of the United States was adopted after the Revolution and put into use in 1790. There have been three revisions: in 1892, 1928, and 1979. The 1928 revision made numerous changes in arrangement of material, added new prayers, and rewrote others. In 1934 a standardized paging was approved for the main part of the book, i.e., from Morning Prayer to the end of the Articles of Religion. In 1943, additional material was added to the prefatory paging, which uses roman numerals. The *Analytic index* noted below (BC348) is based on these revisions. In 1977 a revised "proposed" text was published for a trial period and was adopted in 1979.

Episcopal Church. The Book of Common Prayer and administration of the sacraments and other rites and ceremonies of the church : together with the Psalter or Psalms of David according to the use of the Episcopal Church. N.Y. : Church Hymnal Corp. ; [Greenwich, Conn.] : Seabury Pr., [1979?]. 1001 p.   **BC347**
    The most recent revision, now in use in the U.S. A detailed commentary on this edition is Marion Hatchett's *Commentary on the American prayer book* (N.Y. : Seabury Pr., 1980. 670 p.); the prayer book text is not included, but page references to it are provided.
    For the previous edition (with issuing body given as Protestant Episcopal Church in the U.S.A.) and commentary, *see* BC349.
    § Galen Bushey's *Prayer book concordance* (N.Y. : Church Hymnal Corp., 1988) is a general context concordance in two sections: (1) spoken text; (2) words in rubrics, notes, and historical texts.
                                BX5943.A1

Pepper, George Wharton. An analytical index to the Book of Common Prayer and a brief account of its evolution : together with a revision of Gladstone's concordance to the Psalter. Philadelphia : J. C. Winston, [1948]. 251 p.   **BC348**
    Based on the 1928 revision, with the prefatory matter paged according to the resolution of 1943 and the remainder upon the pagination provided for by the resolution of 1934. Includes a table showing the principal changes in the Psalter made in the revision of 1928, and a concordance to the Psalter.
    § The *Concordance to the American Book of Common Prayer*, ed. by Milton Huggett (N.Y. : Church Hymnal Corp., 1970. 470 p.) provides a general context concordance to the text.   BX5945.P43

Protestant Episcopal Church in the U.S.A. Book of Common Prayer and administration of the sacraments and other rites and ceremonies of the church : according to the use of the Protestant Episcopal Church in the United States of America, together with the Psalter or Psalms of David. N.Y. : Oxford Univ. Pr., 1944. lvii, 611 p.   **BC349**
    Available in numerous editions.
    The 1928 revision is paged according to the Standard prayer book.
    § *The Oxford American prayer book commentary,* by Massey Hamilton Shepherd, Jr. (N.Y. : Oxford Univ. Pr., 1950) is a facsimile of the Oxford (1944) edition, with commentary on facing pages.
                                BX5943.A1

Friends, Society of

Friends Historical Library of Swarthmore College. Catalog of the book and serials collections of the Friends Historical Library of Swarthmore College. Boston : G. K. Hall, 1982. 6 v.
                                BC350
    Photographic reproduction of the catalog cards for a notable Quaker collection (more than 40,000 volumes) which includes imprints from the 17th century to the present. Arrangement is a single alphabet of authors, titles and subjects. Vol. 6 contains lists of serials, broadsides, and tracts.   Z7845.F8F8

Friends World Committee for Consultation. Section of the Americas. Friends directory : meetings for worship in the western hemisphere. 1975/76– . Philadelphia : Friends World Committee for Consultation. Section of the Americas, [1975] . Biennial.   **BC351**
    Directory information for Friends meetings and churches, schools, retirement communities, and other organizations. Covers groups affiliated with Conservative, Evangelical Friends, International, Friends United Meeting, and Friends General Conference, as well as eleven independent yearly meetings.   BX7613.F69

Smith, Joseph. Bibliotheca anti-Quakeriana : or, A catalogue of books adverse to the Society of Friends, alphabetically arranged, with biographical notices of the authors, together with the answers which have been given to some of them by Friends and others. London : J. Smith, 1873. 474 p.   **BC352**
    Includes the definitive "Muggletonian" bibliography (on Ludowick Muggleton, an English sectarian and critic of Quakerism).
    § Smith also compiled: *Bibliotheca Quakeristica : a bibliography of miscellaneous literature relating to the Friends (Quakers), chiefly written by persons not members of their society; also of publications by authors in some way connected; and biographical notices* (London : J. Smith, 1883. 32 p.). This was bound with the earlier work in a 1968 reprint (N.Y. : Kraus).   Z7845.F8S6

————— Descriptive catalogue of Friends' books : or books written by members of the Society of Friends ... from their first rise to the present time ... with critical remarks and occasional biographical notices. London : J. Smith, 1867. 2 v.
                                BC353
    Repr. : N.Y. : Kraus, 1970.
    An alphabetical catalog of books about Quakers, or written by Quakers, including "all, writings by authors before joining, and by those after having left the society."—*t. p.* Full entries, sometimes with annotations. Many biographical notes.
    ————. *Supplement* (London : Hicks, 1893. 364 p.) also was reprinted by Kraus in 1970.

Lutheran

Biographical directory of clergy : Evangelical Lutheran Church in America. Minneapolis : Augsburg Publ. House/Fortress Pr., 1988. 1498 p. : ill.   **BC354**

Rev. ed. of *A biographical directory of clergymen of the American Lutheran Church,* 1972.

Provides brief biographical entries in alphabetical order, many with photographs, for the approximately 17,000 clergy who, as of August 31, 1987, were on the clergy rosters of the three uniting American Lutheran church bodies (the American Lutheran Church, Association of Evangelical Lutheran Churches, and Lutheran Church in America), which in 1987 merged to form the Evangelical Lutheran Church in America.   BX8048.3.B56

Bodensieck, Julius. The encyclopedia of the Lutheran church / ed. by Julius Bodensieck for the Lutheran World Federation. Minneapolis : Augsburg Publ. House, [1965]. 3 v. (2575 p.).   **BC355**

Signed articles, generally scholarly in tone, treating Lutheran doctrine, history, and activity, together with brief descriptions of other religions and beliefs as related to Lutheranism. Some articles include bibliographies.   BX8007.B6

Evangelical Lutheran Church in America. Yearbook. 1988– . Minneapolis : Publishing House of the Evangelical Lutheran Church in America, 1988– . Annual.   **BC356**

Supersedes: The American Lutheran Church, *Yearbook* (1961–87); and Lutheran Church in America, *Yearbook* (1963–87).

The official statistical and directorial publication of the ELCA, the church created in 1987 by merger of the American Lutheran Church, the Lutheran Church in America, and the Association of Evangelical Lutheran Churches.

Lutheran annual. St. Louis, Mo. : Concordia Pub. House, [1939]– .   **BC357**

Includes statistics and directory information for congregations, ministers, schools, service agencies, etc. in the U.S.

§ For more detailed statistics, *see* Lutheran Church— Missouri Synod, *Statistical yearbook* (St. Louis, Mo. : Concordia Publ. House, 1884–).   BX8009.L83

Lutheran book of worship / prep. by the churches participating in the Inter-Lutheran Commission on Worship—Lutheran Church in America, the American Lutheran Church, the Evangelical Lutheran Church of Canada, the Lutheran Church–Missouri Synod. Minneapolis : Augsburg Publ. House ; Philadelphia : Board of Publication, Lutheran Church in America, c1978. 960 p. : music.   **BC358**

A hymnal for congregational use that includes the major services, complete with musical settings. Other editions are the "Ministers ed.," with supplementary materials for leaders of worship; and the "Accompaniment ed.," with keyboard settings for the music of the liturgy.

§ Philip H. Pfatteicher's *Commentary on the Lutheran book of worship : Lutheran liturgy in its ecumenical context* (Minneapolis : Augsburg/Fortress, 1990), gives, for each service, references to parallel services in the liturgies of other principal denominations and discussion of the purpose, history, and text of the rite.   BX8067.A3L76

Lutheran cyclopedia / Erwin L. Lueker, ed. Rev. ed. St. Louis : Concordia Publ. House, [1975]. 845 p.   **BC359**

1st ed., 1954.

The previous edition was prepared under the auspices of the General Literature Board of the Lutheran Church, and drew upon materials from an earlier (1927) *Concordia cyclopedia*. This edition does not mention official church sponsorship, but the cooperation of various affiliates is noted.

Offers brief articles on important aspects of the history, thought, and teachings of the Lutheran church and various related matters. For the revised edition, the number of entries has been substantially increased, various articles have been reworked, new bibliographic refer-

ences supplied, and special efforts made "to improve objectivity."—*Pref.* Although biographies of persons of various denominations and periods are included, it is understandably strong for Lutherans; for the most part, living persons are omitted.   BX8007.L8.

Mennonite

Annotated bibliography of Mennonite writings on war and peace, 1930–1980 / ed. by Willard M. Swartley and Cornelius J. Dyck ... [et al.]. Scottdale, Pa. : Herald Pr., 1987. 740 p.   **BC360**

Prepared by the Institute of Mennonite Studies, Elkhart, Indiana.

Includes 10,000 entries, topically arranged, by Mennonites or appearing in Mennonite publications. Writings limited to those in English and from North America. Author index.   Z7845.M4A56

The Mennonite encyclopedia : a comprehensive reference work on the Anabaptist-Mennonite movement. Hillsboro, Kan. : Mennonite Brethren Publ. House, 1955–90. 5 v. : ill., ports., maps, facsims.   **BC361**

Vol. 1–4 publ. 1955–59; v. 5 ed. by Cornelius J. Dyck and Dennis D. Martin (Scottsdale, Pa. : Herald Pr., 1990).

Treats historical and contemporary topics relating to the Anabaptist-Mennonite movement from its beginning in the 16th century to the present time. Covers theology, ethics, history, and biography with special emphasis on existing and extinct congregations and institutions. Articles vary in length from a few lines to several columns, are signed, and include bibliographies. Vol. 5 offers new material and additional topics, in particular those related to worldwide Mennonitism.   BX8106.M37

Springer, Nelson P. Mennonite bibliography, 1631–1961 / comp. by Nelson P. Springer and A. J. Klassen. Scottdale, Pa. : Herald Pr., 1977. 2 v.   **BC362**

Comp. under the direction of the Institute of Mennonite Studies.

Contents: v. 1, International, Europe, Latin America, Asia, Africa; v. 2, North America, Indexes.

Continues Hans J. Hillerbrand's *Bibliography of Anabaptism, 1520–1630* (Elkhart, Ind. : Inst. of Mennonite Studies, 1962 ; 2nd ed. St. Louis : Center for Reformation Research, c1991).

Aims "to report published materials of Mennonite authorship and statements about Mennonites by non-Mennonites. These include periodicals, books, pamphlets, dissertations, festschrifts, symposia, and encyclopedia and periodical articles."—*Pref.* Topical arrangement within geographical divisions; indexes of authors, subjects, and books reviewed. More than 28,000 items.   Z7845.M4S67

Methodist

The encyclopedia of world Methodism / sponsored by the World Methodist Council and the Commission on Archives and History of the United Methodist Church ; Nolan B. Harmon, gen. ed. Nashville : United Methodist Publ. House, c1974. 2 v. (2814 p.) : ill.   **BC363**

Aims "to give helpful information regarding the history, doctrines, institutions, and important personages, past and present, of World Methodism."—*Pref.* Inasmuch as expenses of the project were underwritten by the United Methodist Church in America, and because that "is the largest organized body among Methodist Churches of the world," a proportionately greater part of the work is devoted to that church. Articles are signed; many include bibliographies. Very strong in biography.   BX8211.E5

Rowe, Kenneth E. Methodist union catalog : pre-1976 imprints. Metuchen, N.J. : Scarecrow, 1975–1994. v. 1–7. (In progress).   **BC364**

Contents: v. 1–7, A–Le.

A preliminary edition, ed. by Brooks Little, appeared in 1967.

Represents holdings relating to Methodism of some 200 libraries "that have been reported to the editor or recorded in printed catalogs."—*Introd.* Main entry listing with locations. Includes variant editions. Some British and European libraries are represented.   Z7845.M5R69

United Methodist Church (U.S.). General minutes of the annual conferences of the United Methodist Church. 1968– . Evanston, Ill. : Section of Records and Statistics, 1968– . Annual.   **BC365**

Supersedes *General minutes of the annual conferences* issued by the Dept. of Research and Statistics of the Methodist Church, 1940?– 67.

Directory and statistical information.   BX8382.2.A1U57b

United Methodist studies : basic bibliographies / comp. and ed. by Kenneth E. Rowe. 3rd ed. Nashville : Abingdon Pr., c1992. 128 p.   **BC366**

1st ed., 1982; 2nd ed., 1987.

The purpose is "to provide a selected list of the basic resources for students and instructors of seminary-level courses in United Methodist history, doctrine, and polity, and to indicate minimum standards for libraries."—*Pref.* Index to authors and editors.   Z7845.M5U54

Who's who in the Methodist church / comp. by the editors of Who's who in America and the A. N. Marquis Co., Inc., with the cooperation of the Council of Secretaries of the Methodist Church. [2nd ed.] Nashville : Abingdon, [1966] 1489 p.   **BC367**

1st ed., 1952, entitled *Who's who in Methodism.*

About 25,000 biographies of officials, etc., of the church and its related organizations and of Methodists prominent in all fields of activity.   BX8213.W52

Mormon

Bitton, Davis. Guide to Mormon diaries & autobiographies. Provo, Utah : Brigham Young Univ. Pr., c1977. 417 p.   **BC368**

An author list, with descriptive notes and locations, of 2,894 diaries, journals, and memoirs of the 19th and 20th centuries. Many of the diaries were written by Mormon missionaries. Subject index.   Z7845.M8B58

Brigham Young University. College of Religious Instruction. A catalogue of theses and dissertations concerning the Church of Jesus Christ of Latter-Day Saints, Mormonism and Utah / [comp. by Wayne E. Brickey]. Provo : Brigham Young Univ. Printing Service, [1971]. 742 p.   **BC369**

Includes master's theses and doctoral dissertations from institutions throughout the U.S. through 1969. Classed arrangement with detailed subject index.

Clement, Russell T. Mormons in the Pacific : a bibliography. Laie, Hawaii : Inst. for Polynesian Studies, 1981. 239 p. : ill.   **BC370**

Subtitle: Holdings at the Brigham Young University-Hawaii Campus, Brigham Young University-Utah Campus and the Church Historical Department.

Offers "a concentrated attempt to list all books, pamphlets, periodicals, personal diaries, journals, mission histories, ephemera, and selected periodical articles concerning Mormons and the Mormon experience"(*Introd.*) in Polynesia, Micronesia and Melanesia. Author listing with name and geographic/subject indexes. 2,873 entries; annotations.

§ Biographical information on Mormons in the western and southwestern U.S. and southwestern Canada, 1820–1981, is indexed in Marvin E. Wiggins, *Mormons and their neighbors* (Provo, Utah : Harold B. Lee Libr., Brigham Young Univ., 1984. 2 v.) which analyzes 194 published volumes containing 75,000 biographical sketches.

Encyclopedia of Mormonism / ed. by Daniel H. Ludlow. N.Y. : Macmillan, c1992. 5 v. : ill.   **BC371**

More than 700 Latter-Day Saints lay scholars and others contributed signed articles, most with brief bibliography, on all aspects of the Church of Jesus Christ of the Latter-Day Saints. Emphasis is placed on the Church's history, doctrine, and procedures, but ample attention is given to biographies and Mormon lifestyle, folklore, literature, and art. Vol. 4 includes a glossary, index and appendixes (e.g., Biographical register of general church officers, Chronology of church history, Selection of LDS hymns). *The Book of Mormon*, *The Doctrine and covenants*, and *The pearl of great price* (a collection of materials translated and produced by Joseph Smith), comprise v. 5.   BX8605.5.E62

Flake, Chad J. A Mormon bibliography, 1830–1930 : books, pamphlets, periodicals, and broadsides relating to the first century of Mormonism. Salt Lake City : Univ. of Utah Pr., 1978. 825 p. : ill., facsims.   **BC372**

A main entry listing of more than 10,000 items pertaining wholly or partly to the first century of Mormonism: "books, periodicals, Mormon newspapers or predominantly Mormon newspapers ... pamphlets, and broadsides."—*Pref.* Not intended as a complete union catalog of Mormonism, but aims "to include adequate locations where an item could be found." Principles of inclusion and exclusion, form of entry, etc., are carefully stated in the preface. Chronological index.

Related publications, comp. by Flake and Larry W. Draper: *Ten year supplement* (1989. 413 p.) and *Indexes to A Mormon bibliography and Ten year supplement.* (1992. 208 p.)   Z7845.M8F55

University of Utah. Libraries. Holdings of the University of Utah on Utah and the Church of Jesus Christ of Latter-Day Saints / L. H. Kirkpatrick, ed. Salt Lake City : [The University], 1954. 285 p.   **BC373**

Entries for Mormonism and for Utah are in separate sections. Most of the Mormon entries are briefly annotated.   Z7845.M8U8

Pentecostal

Jones, Charles Edwin. Black holiness : a guide to the study of black participation in Wesleyan perfectionist and glossolalic Pentecostal movements. [Chicago] : Amer. Theological Libr. Assoc. ; Metuchen, N.J. : Scarecrow, 1987. 388 p. (ATLA bibliography series, no. 18).   **BC374**

Lists in classified order nearly 2,400 books and journal articles on the many church bodies and individuals in the U.S., Canada, Africa, the West Indies, and the U.K. that are identified with the Holiness Movement. Library locations often given. Historical and biographical notes introduce sections and subsections. Index of subjects and authors.   Z1361.N39J66

————— A guide to the study of the Pentecostal movement. Metuchen, N.J. : Scarecrow ; [Chicago] : Amer. Theological Libr. Assoc., 1983. 2 v. (ATLA bibliography series, no.6).   **BC375**

An extensive English language bibliography on Pentecostalism in many parts of the world and according to many traditions and churches. In four parts: pt. 1 lists literature of the movement without reference to doctrinal tradition; pt. 2 classifies materials by doctrinal emphasis, divided and subdivided by church or group, with each subsection preceded by a historical sketch; pt. 3 is a list of Bible schools, colleges, seminaries (with directory information); pt.4, Biography, identifies persons in the movement, citing sources of information about them. Indexed.   Z7845.P4J66

Presbyterian

Benedetto, Robert. Guide to the manuscript collections of the Presbyterian Church, U.S. / Robert Benedetto ; assisted by Betty K. Walker. N.Y. : Greenwood, 1990. 570 p. (Bibliographies and indexes in religious studies, no. 17). **BC376**

Published for the Presbyterian Historical Society.

Provides two guides useful for studying Presbyterianism in the South: (1) a guide to the unpublished papers of Presbyterian ministers located in the Church's Department of History (Montreat); (2) a guide to selected manuscript resources from the Antebellum period and from other Presbyterian denominations located in other repositories. Includes a lengthy introduction to the Department of History (Montreat) and to major areas of research in its collections. Index of names and subjects.

§ A companion is Harold B. Prince's *A Presbyterian bibliography* (BC379). Z6611.P74B46

Parker, Harold M. Bibliography of published articles on American Presbyterianism, 1901–1980. Westport, Conn. : Greenwood, 1985. 261 p. (Bibliographies and indexes in religious studies, no. 4). **BC377**

Lists almost 3,000 articles from U.S. periodicals, both religious and secular, excluding denominational journals, house organs, or serials published monthly or weekly. Entries are arranged alphabetically by author. Detailed topical index. Z7845.P9P37

Presbyterian Church (U.S.A.). General Assembly. Minutes. 195th (1983)– . [N.Y. ; Atlanta] : Office of the General Assembly, c1983– . Annual. **BC378**

Contents: pt. 1, Journal; pt. 2, Statistics.

Supersedes annuals published by two denominations which merged in 1983: *Minutes of the General Assembly* of the United Presbyterian Church in the U.S.A. (ceased with volume for 1982, but its numbering is continued by the new series) and *Minutes* of the Presbyterian Church in the U.S. (ceased with the volume that covered its 123rd General Assembly).

Prince, Harold B. A Presbyterian bibliography : the published writings of ministers who served in the Presbyterian Church in the United States during its first hundred years, 1861–1961, and their locations in eight significant theological collections in the U.S.A. Metuchen, N.J. : Scarecrow ; [Philadelphia] : Amer. Theological Libr. Assoc., 1983. 452 p. (ATLA bibliography series, no.8). **BC379**

A union list of published materials by and about Presbyterian ministers. 4,187 entries arranged alphabetically by author. Indexed. Z7845.P9P83

Reformed

Gasero, Russell L. Historical directory of the Reformed Church in America, 1628–1992. Grand Rapids, Mich. : Eerdmans Pub. Co., c1992. 440 p. (The historical series of the Reformed Church in America, no. 23). **BC380**

1st ed., 1966; 2nd ed., ed. by Peter N. VandenBerge, 1978. A successor to Charles E. Corwin's *Manual of the Reformed Church in America* (5th ed., 1922; suppl. 1933).

Lists of ordained ministers, missionaries, presidents of the General Synod, leaders of educational institutions, professors of theology, and all congregations organized since 1928. Omitted from this edition are the section for "other ministers" and the publications of the Ministers of the Word. BX9507.G37

Shakers

Henry Francis du Pont Winterthur Museum. The Edward Deming Andrews Memorial Shaker Collection / comp. by E. Richard McKinstry. N.Y. : Garland, 1987. 357 p., [22] p. of plates : ill., ports. (Garland reference library of social science, v. 410). **BC381**

A detailed guide to an extensive Shaker collection. Printed materials by and about the Shakers are arranged alphabetically by author; manuscripts, written mostly by Shakers, are arranged under 16 subject headings. Includes brief descriptive essays on the collection's photographic materials and artifacts and on the archives of Edward Deming Andrews and Faith Andrews, who assembled this collection. Extensive title, name, and subject index. Z7845.S5H46

Richmond, Mary L. Hurt. Shaker literature : a bibliography. Hancock, Mass. : Shaker Community ; distr. by Univ. Pr. of New England, 1977. 2 v. **BC382**

Contents: v. 1, By the Shakers; v. 2, About the Shakers.

About 4,000 entries, with annotations and library locations. Each volume in two main parts: (1) Books, pamphlets, broadsides; (2) Periodical articles. Each part is arranged by author or other main entry. Index of titles and joint authors in v. 2. Z7845.S5R52

United Church of Christ

Dexter, Henry Martyn. The Congregationalism of the last 300 years, as seen in its literature : with special reference to certain recondite, neglected, or disputed passages. In twelve lectures, delivered on the Southworth Foundation in the Theological Seminary at Andover, Mass., 1876–1879. With a bibliographical appendix. N.Y. : Harper, 1880. 2 v. (716, 326 p.). **BC383**

Repr. : N.Y. : B. Franklin, [1970]. Also available in microform: Louisville, Ky. : Lost Cause Pr., 1978.

Entries in chronological order, with an author/title index. Still the most extensive bibliography on Congregationalism. Includes *Collections toward a bibliography of Congregationalism*, v. 2 (326 p., 7,250 entries). BX7131.D4

On the trail of the UCC : a historical atlas of the United Church of Christ / comp. and ed. by Carolyn E. Goddard. N.Y. : United Church Pr., [1981]. 127 p. : maps. **BC384**

Intended "to help readers become acquainted with" the various "branches that have come together to form the United Church of Christ."—*Introd.* Offers a map for each of the 39 Conferences of the UCC showing locations of churches (about 6,000 in all) with brief historical notes. BX9884.O6

Peel, Albert. The Congregational two hundred, 1530–1948. London : Independent Pr., [1948]. 288 p. **BC385**

Incorporates: *A hundred eminent Congregationalists*, 1927.

Biographical sketches of 200 outstanding Congregationalists in England and America. BX7259.P4

United Church of Christ. Year book. 1962– . N.Y. : [The Church], 1962– . Annual. **BC386**

Imprint varies.

Offers statistical and directory information. Each yearbook contains statistics for the previous year (e.g., 1993 ed. gives 1992 statistics).

Corporate body united, in 1957, the Congregational Christian churches with the Evangelical and Reformed Church. Continues the *Year book of the Congregational Christian Churches*, which had been a continuation of the *Congregational yearbook* and the *Christian annual.* BX9884.A1U55

Youngs, J. William T. The Congregationalists. N.Y. : Greenwood, c1990. 376 p. (Denominations in America, no. 4). **BC387**

Consists of a history of Congregationalism from 16th-century England to 20th-century America and a biographical dictionary of approximately 85 Congregational leaders. Bibliography appended to each biographical entry. Includes a chronology, an extensive bibliographical essay, and a subject index. Useful for both general readers and specialists. BX7135.Y68

Roman Catholic church

Bibliography

Allison, Antony Francis. The contemporary printed literature of the English Counter-Reformation between 1558 and 1640 : an annotated catalogue / by A. F. Allison and D. M. Rogers. Aldershot, England : Scolar Pr. ; Brookfield, Vt. : Gower Publ. Co., 1989–1994. 2 v. **BC388**

Contents: v. 1, Works in languages other than English, with the collaboration of W. Lottes; v. 2, Works in English, with addenda and corrigenda to v. 1.

Vol. 1 contains 1,619 bibliographic entries with library location symbols and frequent descriptive notes. It lists "religious literature in Latin and other foreign languages [including translations from English] published abroad by the English Catholics."—*Foreword*. Pt. 1 (entries 1–1428) is arranged alphabetically by personal name, Pt. 2 (entries 1429–1619) by 19 subjects, with entries in chronological order, then alphabetically by name under each subject. Separate indexes for titles, publishers and printers, dates of publication, proper names. Vol. 2 is a revised and expanded version of the same editors' *A catalogue of Catholic books in English printed abroad or secretly in England, 1558–1640* (Bognor Regis [England] : Arandel Pr., 1956). Z7830.A46

Ellis, John Tracy. A guide to American Catholic history / John Tracy Ellis, Robert Trisco. 2nd ed., rev. and enl. Santa Barbara, Calif. : ABC-Clio, [1982]. 265 p. **BC389**

1st ed., 1959.

About 1,250 annotated entries in classed arrangement, with author/title/subject index. Covers through 1979. Omits the section on manuscript repositories found in the first edition. Z7778.U6E38

The guide to Catholic literature. v. [1] (1888–1940)–8 (1964/67). Haverford, Pa. [etc.] : Catholic Library Association [etc.], 1940–68. Issued annually, cumulating quadrennially. **BC390**

Subtitle, v. 1: An author-subject-title index in one straight alphabet of books and booklets, in all languages, on all subjects by Catholics or of particular Catholic interest, published or reprinted during the fifty-two years, January 1, 1888 to January 1, 1940, with more than a quarter of a million biographical, descriptive, and critical notes, each with complete reference to its authoritative source for further reference, reading, and study.

Under the author entry, material is entered in this order: (1) biography of the author, (2) books by the author, (3) books and appreciable parts of books about the author and the author's works, and (4) magazine articles about the author and the author's works. Critical annotations and brief extracts from reviews, with exact citations, are included. Subject and title entries are cross-references to the author entry. Annual volumes, issued 1940–67, were cumulated in the quadrennial supplements as v. 2–8.

§ Beginning with coverage for 1968, merged with *Catholic periodical index* (BC395) to form *Catholic periodical and literature index* (AD265). Z8737.G9

McCabe, James Patrick. Critical guide to Catholic reference books. 3rd ed. Englewood, Colo. : Libraries Unlimited, 1989. 323 p. (Research studies in library science, no. 20). **BC391**

1st ed., 1971; 2nd ed., 1980.

Provides "a critical introduction to over fifteen hundred of the most important reference works in English and foreign languages whose contents or point of view relate in some way to Catholicism."—*Introd.* Areas covered: general works, theology, the humanities, social sciences, and history. Annotations frequently cite critical reviews. All titles were available in the U.S. at the time of publication. Appendixes list typical diocesan reference publications and bibliographies consulted. Author, title and subject indexes. Z7837

Parsons, Wilfrid. Early Catholic Americana : a list of books and other works by Catholic authors in the United States, 1729–1830. N.Y. : Macmillan, 1939. 282 p. **BC392**

Repr.: Boston : Longwood, 1977. Also available in microform.

Includes 1,187 numbered entries, in chronological arrangement, with author index. Locates copies.

§ Supersedes, except for the notes and comment, the *Bibliographia Catholica Americana* of J. M. Finotti (N.Y. : The Catholic Publication House, 1872. 318 p. Repr. : N.Y. : B. Franklin, [1971]).

Continued by: *List of additions and corrections to Early Catholic Americana: contribution of French translations (1724–1820)*, by Forrest Bowe (N.Y. : Franco-Americana, 1952). Z7837.P24

Vollmar, Edward R. The Catholic church in America : an historical bibliography. 2nd ed. N.Y. : Scarecrow, 1963. 399 p. **BC393**

1st ed., 1956.

Lists, alphabetically by author, books and periodical articles covering the period 1850–1961, including master's essays and doctoral dissertations dealing with the history of the Catholic church in America. Only theses from the regular degree-granting Catholic colleges have been included. Subject index. Z7778.U6V6

Indexes; Abstract journals

Catholic periodical and literature index. v. 14 (1967/68)– . Winona, Minn. : Catholic Libr. Assoc., [1968]– . Quarterly, including annual cumulation. **BC394**

For annotation, *see* AD265. AI3.C32

Catholic periodical index : a cumulative author and subject index to a selected list of Catholic periodicals. v. 1 (1930)–13 (1966). N.Y. : Catholic Lib. Assoc., 1939–67. Quarterly, with biennial cumulations. **BC395**

1930–33 forms the first permanent volume in a series of 4-year cumulations to June 1948; thereafter cumulated biennially.

Indexes, by author and subject, 50 to more than 200 periodicals published mainly in the U.S., Canada, England, and Ireland.

Continued as *Catholic periodical and literature index* (AD265). AI3.C32

Encyclopedias

Addis, William E. A Catholic dictionary : containing some account of the doctrine, discipline, rites, ceremonies, councils, and religious orders of the Catholic church / by William E. Addis and Thomas Arnold ; rev. by T. B. Scannell ... [et al.]. 17th ed., rev. London : Routledge and Paul, [1960?]. 860 p. **BC396**

1st ed., 1883; 16th ed., 1957.

Prepared by British scholars. Many articles are two or three pages long and include footnotes and references. BX841.A3

Catholic encyclopedia : an international work of reference on the constitution, doctrine, discipline and history of the Catholic church. N.Y. : Encyclopedia Pr., [c1907–22]. 17 v. : ill. **BC397**

Contents: v. 1–15, A–Z. Errata; v. 16, Additional articles. Index; v. 17, Supplement.

In 1936, v. 1 of a revised and enlarged edition was published by the Gilmary Society in New York, but no further volumes appeared in that edition.

Authoritative work with long, signed articles by specialists, and good bibliographies and illustrations. Very useful for many questions on subjects in medieval literature, history, philosophy, art, etc., as well as for questions of Catholic doctrine, history, biography. Long a standard work in English, but in some respects not so complete as the great French Catholic works, and is now somewhat out-of-date. Despite the appearance of the *New Catholic encyclopedia* (BC401), the set continues to be useful and should be retained in the reference collection.

———. *Supplement II*, ed. by Vincent C. Hopkins (N.Y. : Gilmary Soc., [1950–58]. 2 v. [looseleaf]) is also called v. 18.

Serves as a record of events since the original publication in 1913 and the first Supplement in 1922, and consists of signed articles by scholars from many countries, dealing with events arranged by country. Other articles treat dogmas, orders, persons, etc. Bibliographies.

BX841.C25

Dictionnaire de théologie catholique : contenant l'esposé des doctrines de la théologie catholique : leurs preuves et leur histoire / commencé sous la direction de A. Vacant et E. Mangenot continué sous celle de E. Amann. Paris : Letouzey, 1909–50. 15 v. in 23 : ill.   **BC398**

Issued in 150 parts. Frequently reprinted.

Authoritative; long, signed articles and excellent bibliographies. More exhaustive in treatment than the English-language Catholic encyclopedias. Good for topics and names in scholastic and medieval philosophy. More recent information on topics treated in earlier volumes is frequently given under allied subjects in later volumes.

———. *Tables générales*, by Bernard Loth and Albert Michel (Paris : Letouzey, 1951–72. 3 v. [4503 p.]. Issued in 18 fascicles).

A synthesis of materials in the encyclopedia brought together under specific headings arranged alphabetically. In some cases new material, principally bio-bibliographical, has been inserted in the index in order to bring the matter in earlier volumes up-to-date.

BX841.D68

Enciclopedia cattolica. Vatican City : Enciclopedia Cattolica, [1948–54]. 12 v. : ill.   **BC399**

A work of major importance. Written in Italian and mainly by Italian scholars, it deals with all matters pertaining to the Catholic church up to the time of publication. Articles vary in length from a few lines to several pages, are signed, and include long bibliographies which give dates and exact references. Profusely illustrated. Vol. 12 includes an *Indice sistematico*, col. 1840–2134.   BX841.E47

Migne, Jacques Paul. Encyclopédie théologique. Paris : [Migne], 1844–73. 168 v. in 171.   **BC400**

Title varies: 2nd series, *Nouvelle encyclopédie théologique*; 3rd series, *Troisième et dernière encyclopédie théologique*.

Publ. in three series: 1st series, v. 1 (1844)–50 (1862); 2nd series ("nouvelle"), v. 1 (1851)–52 (1866); 3rd series, v. 1 (1854)–66 (1873).

The various dictionaries in this set are unequal in value—some of them were uncritical even when new—and many are now entirely superseded by later and more scholarly works. They cover a wide field, however; include some subjects for which there are no comprehensive modern dictionaries (e.g., the *Dictionnaire des mystères*); and some of them contain a large amount of minor biography. Such dictionaries may still be useful even though they do not give the latest critical information. For complete contents *see* Bibliothèque Nationale, *Catalogue général des livres imprimés*, v. 114, col. 948–62 (AA101), Otto Henri Lorenz, *Catalogue général*, v. 3 and 6 (AA630), or *National union catalog : pre-1956 imprints* (AA113), v. 383, p. 118–19.

BL31.M5

New Catholic encyclopedia / prep. by an editorial staff at the Catholic University of America. N.Y. : McGraw-Hill, [1967–89]. 18 v. : ill.   **BC401**

Subtitle: An international work of reference on the teachings, history, organization, and activities of the Catholic Church and on all institutions, religions, philosophies, and scientific and cultural developments affecting the Catholic Church from its beginnings to the present. Imprint varies.

Not merely a revision of the *Catholic encyclopedia* (BC397), but a new work intended to be "abreast of the state of knowledge and reflecting the outlook and interests of the second half of the 20th century."—*Pref.* About 17,000 signed articles contributed by some 4,800 scholars, both Catholic and non-Catholic. Emphasis is on the Catholic church in the United States and the English-speaking world, but scope is international (e.g., special attention has been given to the church in Latin America). Biographies of living persons are excluded, although works of outstanding living figures are often discussed in pertinent survey articles. Good-quality illustrations and maps are numerous; bibliographies accompany most of the articles. Vol. 15 is an index. Two supplements (v. 16, publ. 1974, and v. 18, publ. 1989) cover developments of 1967–74 and 1978–88, respectively. Vol. 17, "Supplement : Change in the Church" (publ. 1979) is an alphabetical arrangement of articles which are self-contained, but also designed to reflect the "impact of post conciliar thought and life" on entries in the basic set. Scope is outlined in the preface, and topics are listed therein. Bibliographies for most articles. The earlier set will continue to be useful on various counts: more extensive treatment of certain topics, some entries do not appear in the new work, different bibliographic citations are given, etc.   BX841.N44

The new dictionary of Catholic spirituality / ed., Michael Downey. Collegeville, Minn. : Liturgical Pr., c1993. 1083 p.   **BC402**

Articles, contributed mainly by North American scholars, range in length from a few paragraphs to about 12 pages (e.g., Faith, Holiness, Christ), and treat "spirituality in light of the reform and renewal that the Second Vatican Council set in motion."—*Pref.* Articles focus on Roman Catholic spirituality, but include the results of ecumenical and interreligious dialogues where appropriate. Each article has a bibliography; cross-references to related articles are generous. Topical index lists articles under broad subjects (e.g., Prayer; Types and schools of spirituality). Also contains index of names.

BX2350.65.N49

O'Carroll, Michael. Theotokos : a theological encyclopedia of the Blessed Virgin Mary. Rev. ed. with suppl. Wilmington, Del. : M. Glazier, 1983. 390 p.   **BC403**

Repr. : Collegeville, Minn. : Liturgical Pr., 1990.

1st ed., 1982.

Offers a dictionary arrangement of names, doctrines, devotions and biblical references that bear on Marian theology. A large proportion of entries are names of theologians, past and present, whose writings on Mary are outlined in brief. Bibliography for each article.

BT599.O22

Our Sunday Visitor's Catholic encyclopedia / Peter M. J. Stravinskas, ed. Huntington, Ind. : Our Sunday Visitor Publ., c1991. 1007 p. : ill.   **BC404**

Articles, without bibliographies, on beliefs and teachings, sacraments, and Catholic practice, for Catholics and non-Catholics.

Sacramentum mundi : an encyclopedia of theology / ed. by Karl Rahner ... [et al.]. N.Y. : Herder & Herder, 1968–70. 6 v.   **BC405**

Also publ. in Dutch, French, German, Italian, and Spanish.

The work of an international roster of Catholic theologians which attempts "to formulate present-day developments of the understanding of the faith, basing itself on modern theological investigations of the key themes of the theological disciplines."—*Gen. pref.* Includes signed articles of substantial length, bibliographies, and cross-references. General index in v. 6.   BR95.S23

Dictionaries

A Catholic dictionary : (The Catholic encyclopaedic dictionary) / ed. by Donald Attwater. 3rd ed. N.Y. : Macmillan, 1958. 552 p. **BC406**
Originally published in 1931 under title: *The Catholic encyclopaedic dictionary*; 2nd ed., 1953.
Includes definitions and meanings of terms, names, and phrases in the philosophy, theology, canon law, liturgy, institutions, etc., of the Catholic church. Omits biography except for the saints in the general calendar of the Roman church. BX841.C35

The new dictionary of theology / editors, Joseph A. Komonchak, Mary Collins, Dermot A. Lane. Wilmington, Del. : M. Glazier, 1987. 1112 p. **BC407**
Repr. : Collegeville, Minn. : Liturgical Pr., 1991.
Marking the 25th anniversary of the opening of the Second Vatican Council, this work "represents the first collaborative attempt in English to take stock of the remarkable developments in the church and in theology since the Council."—*Pref.* Clearly written articles summarize the present state of Catholic theology while demonstrating ecumenical sensitivity. Includes many articles of 10–15 pages on the 24 topics the editors believe constitute "principal themes of the Christian vision of faith," together with numerous articles on liturgy, the Bible, and theology. Articles are signed (most of the 165 contributors are from North America) and most include cross-references and bibliography. Intended for those engaged in secondary and college-level teaching and in preaching. BR95.N38

Rahner, Karl. Dictionary of theology / Karl Rahner, Herbert Vorgrimler ; tr. by Richard Strachan ... [et al.]. 2nd ed. N.Y. : Crossroad, 1981. 541 p. **BC408**
1st ed., 1965, had title *Theological dictionary*.
A translation of the authors' *Kleines theologisches Wörterbuch* (10th ed., 1976). 2nd English ed. has title *Concise theological dictionary* (London : Burns & Oates, 1983. 541 p.).
Intends "to provide brief explanations, in alphabetical order, of the most important concepts of modern Catholic dogmatic theology for readers who are prepared to make a certain intellectual effort."—*Pref.* BR95.R313

Directories

Annuario pontificio. 1912– . Vatican City : Tipografia Poliglotta Vaticana, 1912– . Annual. **BC409**
Publ. 1716–1858 as *Notizie*; 1860–71, *Annuario pontifico*; 1872–1911, *Gerarchia cattolica*. None publ. 1813–14, 1848–50, 1859?
Contains list of popes from St. Peter on; Roman Catholic hierarchy at Rome and throughout the world, with brief biographical notes; institutions and offices at Rome; list of religious orders with dates of founding and name of present head; Latin names of sees according to the Roman Curia, with classical Latin and vernacular names; Latin names of religious orders; index of personal names, etc. BX845.A75

The Catholic directory of England and Wales. 1973– . Liverpool : Publ. for the Hierarchy by The Universe, 1973– . Annual. **BC410**
Imprint varies.
Continues: *Catholic directory*, 1838–1970. None publ. 1971–72.
Gives directory information on churches, clergy, institutions, schools, etc. BX1491.A1C25

Official Catholic directory. 1886– . N.Y. : Kenedy, 1886– . Annual. **BC411**
Title varies; imprint varies.
Contains a large amount of useful and detailed directory, institutional, and statistical information about the organization, clergy, churches, missions, schools, religious orders, etc., of the Catholic church in the U.S. and its possessions. Coverage varies. BX845.C5

History

Baudrillart, Alfred. Dictionnaire d'histoire et de géographie ecclésiastiques / commencé sous la direction de Mgr. Alfred Baudrillart, continué par A. de Meyer et Ét. van Cauwenbergh, avec le concours d'un grand nombre de collaborateurs. Paris : Letouzey, 1912–[94]. v. 1–25¹ : ill. (In progress). **BC412**
Issued in parts, beginning 1909; title page of v. 1 dated 1912.
Editors vary; since v. 16, R. Aubert.
Contents: v. 1–25¹ (fasc. 1–145), A–Hyacinthe de Saint-Vincent.
Scope of the work covers all subjects in the history of the Roman Catholic church, and other churches as they affect the Roman church, from the beginning of Christianity to the present time. The geographical material includes separate articles on towns and other small divisions, past and present, indicating the connection of the place with ecclesiastical history, its present ecclesiastical status, a list of its religious institutions, and (in case it is or has been an episcopal see) a list of the bishops, etc. Includes biographical articles on: all important and some minor names in the Roman Catholic church; members of other churches who have had any effect on the Roman church; ecclesiastical and theological writers; saints in the Russian and other churches; ecclesiastical musicians, artists, etc. Signed articles; good bibliographies. BR95.B3

Catholicism in early modern history : a guide to research / John W. O'Malley, ed. St. Louis : Center for Reformation Research, c1988. 342 p. (Reformation guides to research, 2). **BC413**
Contains 16 essays by specialists, five on geographical areas in Europe (e.g., Germany, France, Spain) and the rest on various topics (e.g., popular piety, spirituality, preaching). Covers from about mid-16th–late 17th century. Each essay reviews current scholarship and includes an extensive bibliography. Index of names. BX946.C37

Ellis, John Tracy. Documents of American Catholic history. Wilmington, Del. : M. Glazier, 1987. 3 v. **BC414**
1st ed., 1959; rev. ed., 1967.
Vols. 1–2 are reprints of the 1967 ed.; vol. 3 is a new work.
"Document" is "broadly interpreted to include any written record that would illustrate an event from a contemporary point of view."—*Pref.* Includes papal documents, laws, charters and also private writings, printed letters, etc., arranged chronologically. Covers 1493–1986. Source is cited in introductory note to each section. Indexed. BX860.C37

Yearbooks

Catholic almanac. 65th ed. (1969)– . Huntington, Ind. : Our Sunday Visitor, Inc., 1969– . Annual. **BC415**
Publisher varies.
Represents a change of title for the *National Catholic almanac* (previously *St. Anthony's almanac* and *Franciscan almanac*), 1904–68.
Includes much miscellaneous information, e.g., annual survey of news, ecclesiastical calendar, glossary of terms in Catholic use, the Catholic church in various countries of the world, statistics, directory of information, etc. AY81.R6N3

Biography

American Catholic who's who. 1934/35–1980/81. Wash. [etc.] : NC News Service [etc.], 1911–1980. **BC416**
For annotation, *see* AH75. E184.C3A6

Catholic who's who. 29th ed.–35th ed. London : Burns, Oates & Washbourne, 1936–1952. **BC417**
For annotation, *see* AH225. DA28.8C3C33

Delaney, John J. Dictionary of American Catholic biography. Garden City, N.Y. : Doubleday, 1984. 621 p.   **BC418**
Aims "to provide in straightforward fashion factual information about the lives and activities of those Catholic men and women in the United States from the times of the explorers to the present time."—*Introd.* Presents brief information without bibliographies of sources. About 1,500 entries; no living persons included.   BX4670.D45

——————— Dictionary of Catholic biography / John J. Delaney and James Edward Tobin. Garden City, N.Y. : Doubleday, [1961]. 1245 p.   **BC419**
Includes biographical sketches of some 15,000 persons who have contributed to the development of the Catholic church from the beginning to 1961, but does not include living persons.   BX4651.2.D4

Atlases

Emmerich, Heinrich. Atlas hierarchicus : descriptio geographica et statistica ecclesiae catholicae tum occidentis tum orientis. Mödling bei Wien : St. Gabriel-Verlag ; Aachen : Missionswissenschaftl. Inst., Mission e.V., 1976. [126], 107 p. : maps in color ; 45cm.   **BC420**
1st publ. 1913, Karl Streit, ed.
Gives hierarchical boundaries for the Catholic Church, current as of 1975. Locates other significant points, such as seminaries and institutes. Text (in English, French, German, Italian, and Spanish) gives descriptive and historical information. "Principal statistical data of the ecclesiastical territories, on 31 December 1973," (50 p.) inserted.   G1046.E4E4

Liturgy and ritual

The history of liturgical texts in the Church (through the mid-1960s) is briefly described in the article "Liturgical books of the Roman rite" in the *New Catholic encyclopedia*, 8:890–92 (BC401). A much earlier, but more detailed description of the subject is the article "Liturgical books" in the *Catholic encyclopedia*, 9:296–302 (BC397). The "Catholic Church. Liturgy and ritual" section of v. 99 of the *National union catalog—pre-1956 imprints* (AA113) constitutes an excellent bibliography of these pre-Vatican II works.

The more important of these pre-Vatican II texts, of value in answering historical questions, are the *Rituale Romanum Pauli V ...* Editio quinta post typicam (Turonibus : Typ. A. Mame; N.Y. : Benziger, 1928. 710 p., 29 p.) and the *Brevarium Romanum ...* Editio vigesima juxta typicam (Rome ; Paris : Desclee & Socii, [1948–49]. 4 v.). English translations are *The Roman ritual, in Latin and English*, tr. and ed. by Philip T. Weller (Milwaukee : Bruce, [1947–52]. 3 v.); and *Roman breviary in English*, ed. by Joseph A. Nelson [N.Y. : Benziger, [1950–51]. 4 v.).

The new liturgical books, published in accordance with the reforms of the Second Vatican Council, and now in the vernacular, are cited in the article "Liturgical books of the Roman rite" in the *New Catholic encyclopedia*, 17:352–54, and are described in that volume under individual entries (e.g., Sacramentary. Lectionaries). Recent developments are noted under "Liturgical developments" in each volume of the *Catholic almanac* (BC415). The most important of the new liturgical books used in the U.S. are listed below.

Catholic Church. [Missal]. Saint Andrew Bible missal / tr. and adapted from Missel Dominical de l'Assemblée, prep. by the Benedictines of Saint-Andre d'Ottignies, Brepols, 1981. [Wash.] : American Editorial Commission, Center for Pastoral Liturgy, Catholic Univ. of America ; Brepols : Hirten, 1982. 1015 p.   **BC421**
Readings are from the *New American Bible*.   BX2130.S34

——————— Lectionary for Mass : English translation [i.e., version] approved by the National Conference of Catholic Bishops and confirmed by the Apostolic See; with the New American version of Sacred Scripture .... N.Y. : Catholic Book Publ. Co., 1970. 1122 p.   **BC422**
At head of title: The Roman missal, revised by decree of the Second Vatican Council and published by authority of Pope Paul VI.
Contains the three-year cycle of scripture readings for the eucharistic liturgy for Sundays and solemn feasts; the two-year cycle for weekdays; the one-year cycle for saints' feasts; responsorial psalms; gospel or alleluia verses; and readings for a wide variety of other Masses. Index.
§ The edition publ. by Liturgical Press (Collegeville, Minn., 1970) uses the RSV Catholic edition of Scripture; that publ. by Benziger (N.Y., 1970), uses the Jerusalem Bible text.   BX2003.A4

——————— The liturgy of the hours : according to the Roman rite. N.Y. : Catholic Book Publ. Co., 1975–76. 4 v.   **BC423**
At head of title: The Divine Office, revised by decree of the Second Vatican Ecumenical Council and published by authority of Pope Paul VI.
English translation prep. by the International Commission on English in the Liturgy.
Contents: v. 1, Advent season, Christmas season; v. 2, Lenten season, Easter season; v. 3, Ordinary time, weeks 1–17; v. 4, Ordinary time, weeks 18–34.
The new breviary revised according to modern liturgical norms. Biblical readings are from the New American Bible.   BX2000.A4

—————— The sacramentary : approved for use in the dioceses of the United States of America by the National Conference of Catholic Bishops and confirmed by the Apostolic See. [Rev. ed.]. Collegeville, Minn. : Liturgical Pr., 1985. 1182 p. : music.   **BC424**

At head of title: The Roman missal, revised by decree of the Second Vatican Council and published by authority of Pope Paul VI.

1st ed., 1974. Revised according to the second typical edition of the *Missale Romanum* (1975), March 1, 1985.

Translation by the International Commission on English in the Liturgy. Also publ. by the Catholic Book Publishing Co.

Contains all the texts proper to the priest for the celebration of the Eucharist and other sacraments or rites celebrated at Mass. Together with the *Lectionary for Mass* (BC422) replaces the Roman missal.

BX2037.A4

Catholic Church. Liturgy and Ritual. The rites of the Catholic Church : the Roman ritual as revised by decree of the Second Vatican Ecumenical Council and published by authority of Pope Paul VI / English translation prep. by the International Commission on English in the Liturgy. N.Y. : Pueblo Publ. Co., c1990–91. 2 v.   **BC425**

Updated and modified edition of work previously publ. with the same title in 1976–80.

Vol. 1 publ. separately by Pueblo Publ., 1983 (818 p.). Vol. 2 publ. Collegeville, Minn. : Liturgical Pr., [1991?].

Selected sections of the new Rituale Romanum and Pontificale Romanum.

Brings together in one compilation the revised texts of administration of the sacraments and other rites which were published individually starting in 1969. Includes pertinent excerpts from the Constitution on the Sacred Liturgy for each section.   BX2033.A4

Catholic Church. Martyrology. The Roman martyrology : in which are to be found the eulogies of the saints and blessed approved by the Sacred Congregation of Rites up to 1961. An English tr. from the 4th edition after the typical edition (1956) approved by Pope Benedict XV (1922) / ed. by J. B. O'Connell. Westminster, Md. : Newman Pr., [1962]. 412 p.   **BC426**

In calendar order, with several, but not all, saints mentioned for each day. Index of about 5,000 names.   BX2014.A4O3

The new dictionary of sacramental worship / ed., Peter E. Fink. Collegeville, Minn. : Liturgical Pr., c1990. 1351 p.   **BC427**

Signed articles, many several pages long, place the revised Roman Catholic liturgical texts within their historical contexts and address questions of implementation. "While most of the contributors come from the Latin rite of the Roman Catholic Church, the voices of almost all the sacramental churches are present here speaking from the ecumenical church to the ecumenical church."—*Pref.* A topical index provides a classified approach to the articles.

§ Jovian Lang's *Dictionary of liturgy* (N.Y. : Catholic Book Publ. Co., c1989) is a popular treatment intended for general and nonspecialist readers.   BV173.N485

Podhradsky, Gerhard. New dictionary of the liturgy. English ed. / ed. by Lancelot Sheppard. Staten Island, N.Y. : Alba House, [1967, c1966]. 208 p. : ill.   **BC428**

An enlarged translation of the author's *Lexikon der Liturgie* (Innsbruck : Tyrolia-Verlag, 1962).

Definitions include function, historical notes, and ecclesiastical regulations.   BV173.P613

Weale, William Henry James. Bibliographia liturgica : catalogus missalium ritus latini, ab anno M.CCCC.LXXIV impressorum / collegit W. H. Iacobus Weale, iterum edidit H. Bohatta. London : Quaritch, 1928. 380 p.   **BC429**

1st ed., 1886.

A listing of Latin missals by (pt. 1) place-name; (pt. 2) order. Chronological and typographical indexes.   Z7838.L7W3

Popes, cardinals, bishops

Hierarchia catholica medii aevi : sive, Summorum pontificum S.R.E. cardinalium, ecclesiarum antistitum series ab anno 1198 usque ad annum [1605] perducta e documentis tabularii praesertim Vaticani collecta, digesta / edita per Conradum Eubel .... Padua : "Il Messaggero di S. Antonio", 1898–1978. v. 1–8. (In progress).   **BC430**

Title varies slightly. Vols. 1–3 publ. "Monasterii sumptibus et typis librariae Regensbergianae" and ed. by Konrad Eubel; reissued 1913–23. Vol. 4 ed. by P. Gauchat; v. 5–8 ed. by R. Ritzler and P. Sefrin.

Also available in microform (Wash. : Library of Congress).

Chronological lists of the popes and cadinals, and of the bishops in all countries, arranged alphabetically by the Latin name of the diocese. Covers 1198–1903. Index by modern place name in each volume; personal name index beginning with v. 4 (1592–1667).

§ *Series episcoporum ecclesiae catholicae : ab initio usque ad annum MCXCVIII*, ed. by Odilo Engels and Stefan Fachgelehrten (Stuttgart : Anton Hiersemann, c1982–), includes bishops of each see from the beginning to 1198.   BX4651.E8

Kelly, J. N. D. The Oxford dictionary of Popes. Oxford ; N.Y. : Oxford Univ. Pr., 1986. 347 p.   **BC431**

Offers biographical sketches, arranged chronologically, of all 268 popes and 39 antipopes, from St. Peter to John Paul II. Bibliography of primary and secondary sources follows each entry. An alphabetical list of popes and antipopes precedes the text. Subject index.

BX955.2.K45

Mann, Horace Kinder. The lives of the popes in the early Middle Ages. 2nd ed. London : Kegan Paul, 1925–32. 18 v. in 19.   **BC432**

Repr. : Vaduz : Kraus, 1964–69.

1st ed., 1902.

Also available in microform: Wash. : Microcard Editions, 1972. 92 fiche.

Vol. 1–12 are 2nd ed.; v. 6–18 have title: *Lives of the popes in the Middle Ages*.

A documented history covering 590–1305.

§ For the period 1305–1799, *see* Ludwig Pastor, *History of the popes*, ed. by Frederick Ignatius Antrobus (London : Hodges, 1891–1953. 40 v.). An English translation of Pastor's *Geschichte der Päpiste*.   BX1070.M3

Papal and conciliar documents

Carlen, Claudia. Papal pronouncements : a guide : 1740–1978. Ann Arbor, Mich. : Pierian Pr., c1990. 2 v. (957 p.).   **BC433**

Provides, in chronological order, descriptions of all encyclicals, most addresses, and a selection of other papal documents, 1740–1978 (Benedict XIV to John Paul I). Entries for some 5,000 documents include: type of document; length in words; abstract; sources for original and English language texts. An important source that organizes and locates documents previously difficult to find. Sources, bibliography, general and title indexes.   Z7838.P53C37

Catholic Church. Pope. The papal encyclicals / [comp. by] Claudia Carlen. [Wilmington, N.C.] : McGrath, 1981. 5 v.   **BC434**

Aims "to provide a collection to which students and scholars can turn ... for a specific text or ... the entire corpus of papal teaching."—*Introd.* 280 papal encyclicals in English translation, chronologically arranged, from Benedict XIV to John Paul II (i.e., 1740–1981), each with citation to Latin text and with source of translation. Index of titles and subjects.   BX860.C37

Commentary on the documents of Vatican II / [tr. by Lalit Adolphus, et al.]. N.Y. : Herder and Herder, c1967–69. 5 v.
BC435

Repr. : N.Y. : Crossroad, 1989.
Translation of: *Das zweite Vatikanische Konzil : Dokumente und Kommentare* (Freiburg : Herder, 1966–68. 3 v.).   BR95.L48

Decrees of the ecumenical councils / ed. by Norman P. Tanner. London : Sheed & Ward ; Wash. : Georgetown Univ. Pr., 1990. 2 v.   **BC436**

Contents: v. 1, Nicaea I to Lateran V; v. 2, Trent to Vatican II.
An English translation, by 29 British Jesuits, of the decrees of all the Ecumenical Councils of the Catholic Church as they appear in the critical edition, *Conciliorum oecumenicorum decreta* (1972). The original text in Latin or Greek and the English translation appear on facing pages. Ten separate indexes in v. 2: chronological, Bible, councils, Roman Magisterium, Fathers and early church, liturgical books, canon law, proper names, authors, subjects.   BX825.A1990

Vatican Council (2nd : 1962–1965). Documents of Vatican II / Austin P. Flannery, ed. Grand Rapids, Mich. : Eerdmans, 1975–82. 2 v.   **BC437**

Subtitle varies.
Vol. 1 offers English translations of the 16 Vatican Council II documents, together with 49 subsequent "Roman documents which amplify, elucidate or apply the major themes" (*Pref.*) of the Council's work. Vol. 2 adds 58 more postconciliar constitutions, directives, etc., on liturgy, ecumenism, religious life, ministry, current problems, and education, 1966–82. Cites Latin sources. Indexed.
§ Locating papal and conciliar documents often proves a complex task. Contemporary documents will usually be found through the *Catholic periodical and literature index* (AD265). Some appear in *The Pope speaks* (Huntington, Ind., etc. : Our Sunday Visitor, 1954– . Bimonthly), *Origins* (Wash. : National Catholic News Service, 1971–), and virtually all of them appear in *L'Osservatore romano. Weekly edition in English* (Vatican City, 1968–). For description of collections of papal documents prior to 1740, *see* "Bullarium" in the *Catholic encyclopedia*, v. 3, p. 48–51 (BC397). In the same volume, the entry "Bulls and briefs" (p. 52–58) gives a useful history of papal documents, noting their characteristic features during each time period.
Beyond the sources listed above, there are many important works of use only in specialized or large research collections. *See* "The papacy" and "Councils" sections (p. 230–242) in James Patrick McCabe's *Critical guide to Catholic reference books* (BC391) for a thorough discussion of such works.   BX830 1962.A3F55

Religious orders

Bibliographies and biobibliographies for the individual religious orders have great usefulness in the large research library. Among the numerous works of this type are: *Bibliographia Augustiniana* by David Aurelio Perini (Florence, 1929–37. 4 v.); *A Benedictine bibliography*, by Oliver L. Kapsner (2nd ed. Collegeville, Minn., 1962–82. 2 v. and Suppl.); *Bibliotheca Carmelitana*, ed. by Gabriel Wessels (Rome, 1927. 2 v. in 1); *Bio-bibliographia Franciscana Neerlandica*, by Benjamin de Troeyer (Nieuwkoop, 1969–70. 2 v.) and his *Bio-bibliographia franciscana neerlandica ante saeculum XVI* (Nieuwkoop, 1974. 3 v.); *Bibliothèque de la Compagnie de Jésus* (Brussels, 1890–1932. 12 v.) and *Bibliothèque des écrivains de la Compagnie de Jésus* (Liège, 1869–76. 3 v.), both by Augustin de Backer; *Bibliographie sur l'histoire de la Compagnie de Jésus, 1901–1980*, by László Polgár (Rome : Institutum Historicum S.I., 1981–90. 3 v. publ. to date; to be in 7 v.).

For a comprehensive listing of bibliographies and biobibliographies of religious orders of all periods, *see*: John G. Barrow, *A bibliography of bibliographies in religion*, p. 236–56 (BC4).

Cottineau, L. H. Répertoire topo-bibliographique des abbayes et prieurés. Mâcon : Protat, 1935–70. 3 v.   **BC438**

Vols. 1–2 issued in parts, 1935–38; v. 3, Tables, publ. 1970.
Arranged by the place where the religious house is situated; gives variant forms of name, location with reference to larger places, order to which religious house belongs, sometimes brief history of the house, and references to sources of information.   Z7839.C84

Dizionario degli istituti di perfezione / diretto da Guerrino Pelliccia e da Giancarlo Rocca. [Roma] : Edizione Paoline, [1974–88]. v. 1–8. (In progress).   **BC439**

Contents: v. 1–8, A–Spirituali. Planned to be in nine volumes.
Offers signed articles ranging from a paragraph to many pages on the history and structure of about 4,000 Catholic religious orders, societies, etc., of the past and present, on monasticism of the East and West, and on religious life and institutions other than Roman Catholic. Many biographical articles on founders of religious orders, and entries on related material such as terminology of religious life, monastic architecture, etc. All but the shortest essays have bibliographies. Contributors are identified and their credentials listed. Indexes are planned.   BX2420.D58

Kapsner, Oliver Leonard. Catholic religious orders : listing conventional and full names in English, foreign language, and Latin, also abbreviations, date and country of origin and founders. 2nd ed., enl. Collegeville, Minn. : St. John's Abbey Pr., 1957. 594 p.   **BC440**

1st ed., 1948.
A listing of names of orders primarily for the use of library catalogers, but with its many cross-references from the variant forms it may also serve as a handy guide for others. Information under the main entry includes variant forms of name, abbreviation, founder, date, and country of founding.   BX2420.K3

Knowles, David. Medieval religious houses, England and Wales / by David Knowles and R. Neville Hadcock. [Rev. ed.]. N.Y. : St. Martin's, [1972, c1971]. 565 p. : maps.
BC441

A revised, expanded and corrected edition of the 1953 work of the same title which, in turn, was based on Knowles's *Religious houses of medieval England* (London : Sheed & Ward, 1940).
Includes religious houses, hospitals, cathedrals, and secular colleges. Houses are grouped by religious order, with information given on history, wealth, numerical strength of the resident community, architectural remains, etc. Extensive documentation, index, tables, maps.

§ *Medieval religious houses, Ireland : with an appendix to early sites*, by Aubrey Osborn Gwynn and Richard Neville Hadcock (Harlow, [Eng.] : Longman, 1970. 479 p.) and *Medieval religious houses, Scotland : with an appendix on the houses in the Isle of Man*, by Ian Borthwick Cowan and David E. Easson (2nd ed. London ; N.Y. : Longman, 1976. 246 p.) are companion volumes.   BX2592.K56

Molette, Charles. Guide des sources de l'histoire des congrégations féminines françaises de vie active. Paris : Éditions du Paris, 1974. 475 p.   **BC442**
"Ouvrage publié avec le concours du Centre National de Recherche Scientifique."—*t.p.*
In two main sections: (1) Introduction historique; (2) Sources et bibliographie (p. 107–379). The latter part lists nearly 400 religious congregations alphabetically by name of the order and indicates address, founding date, etc., information on the order's archives, publications, and bibliographical references to writings about an order and its members. Indexes of names, of places, and of groups (societies, congregations, etc.).   BX4210.M6

Eastern churches

Atiya, Aziz Suryal. A history of eastern Christianity. Enl. and updated by the author with new preface, supplement to pt. 1, supplementary bibliography. Millwood, N.Y. : Kraus, c1980. 492 p., [12] p. of plates : ill., maps.   **BC443**
1st ed., 1968.
Surveys the "Coptic and Ethiopic, Jacobite, Nestorian, Armenian, Indian, and Maronite [churches] and the vanished churches of Nubia and North Africa."—*Pref.* This edition adds a chapter, Copts abroad, and supplementary bibliography.   BX103.2.A8

Attwater, Donald. The Christian churches of the East. [New ed.]. Leominster, [Eng.] : Thomas More Books, 1961–62. 2 v.   **BC444**
Contents: v. 1, Churches in communion with Rome; v. 2, Churches not in communion with Rome.
A revision of the author's *The Catholic Eastern churches* (1935) and *The dissident Eastern churches* (1937).
For each church, offers a brief history, present state, organization, description of the liturgy, and a bibliography. Glossary and index in each volume.   BX230.A78

Day, Peter D. The liturgical dictionary of Eastern Christianity. Collegeville, Minn. : Liturgical Pr., c1993. 334 p.   **BC445**
Entries for vestments, rites, objects, ceremonies and other liturgical terms related to Eastern Christian traditions. Nontechnical descriptions use appropriate Eastern terminology, often include comparative information on rites, and employ ample cross-references. A handy reference guide offers Eastern Christian equivalents for English terms; comparative tables provide languages of liturgical books and names of vestments used in each rite.   BX106.2.D38

Eastern Christianity : a bibliography selected from the ATLA religion database / ed. by Paul D. Petersen ; Ruth F. Frazer, gen. ed. Rev. ed. Chicago : Amer. Theological Libr. Assoc., 1984. 781 p.   **BC446**
1st ed., 1982.
Includes journal articles 1949–59 and 1975 to mid-1983; chapters in multi-author works since 1970; festschriften articles 1960–69 and articles from *Research in ministry* since 1981. Three indexes: author/editor, subject, and book review.

Greek Orthodox Archdiocese of North and South America. Yearbook. 1967– . [N.Y. : The Archdiocese], 1967– .   **BC447**
Includes directory information, ecclesiastical calendars, and vital statistics.   BX240.N63

King, Archdale Arthur. The rites of Eastern Christendom. Rome : Catholic Book Agency, 1947–48. 2 v.   **BC448**
Repr. : N.Y. : AMS Pr., 1972.
A history and description of the development of nine Eastern liturgies: Syrian, Byzantine, Chaldean, Maronite, Syro-Malankara, Coptic, Ethiopic, Syro-Malabar, and Armenian. Index of names and places.   BX4710.K5

Langford-James, Richard Lloyd. A dictionary of the Eastern Orthodox church. London : Faith Pr., [1923]. 144 p.   **BC449**
Repr. : N.Y. : B. Franklin, 1976.
Covers rites, customs, and ceremonies of the Eastern Orthodox church. Anglican perspective.   BX230.L3

Orthodox Eastern Church. Service book of the Holy Orthodox-Catholic Apostolic church / comp., tr. and arr. from the Old Church-Slavonic service books of the Russian church, and collated with the service books of the Greek church, by Isabel Florence Hapgood. 6th ed. Englewood, N.J. : Antiochian Orthodox Christian Archdiocese of North America, 1983. 615 p. : ill.   **BC450**
1st ed., 1906; 5th ed., 1975.
Intended primarily for the use of the Russian church in America, but adapted for use by other Eastern Orthodox churches.   BX350.A5H3

Patrinacos, Nicon D. A dictionary of Greek Orthodoxy = Lexikon Hellenikes Orthodoxias. Pleasantville, N.Y. : Hellenic Heritage Publ., c1984. 391 p. : ill.   **BC451**
Parallel title romanized from Greek.
Topics address "the need of the English speaking Greek Orthodox to know precisely not only that which is going on during the Liturgy, the Sacraments, and other services of personal or communal import, but the meaning and historical development as well of church furnishings, sacred implements, vestments, and other articles used in Orthodox worship."—*How to consult this dictionary.* English-Greek index.

Coptic Church

The Coptic encyclopedia / Aziz S. Atiya, ed. in chief. N.Y. : Macmillan : Maxwell Macmillan International, c1991. 8 v. (lxxiii, 2372, 371 p.) : ill.   **BC452**
Provides a wealth of information on early Christian history; saints and other important Coptic church figures, art and architecture, and archaeology of the lands currently called Egypt, Nubia/Sudan, and Ethiopia. An international group of scholars contributed 2,800 signed articles, ranging in length from a brief paragraph to several pages and including cross-references, bibliographies, and many illustrations. More than 400 entries are devoted to monasteries. Vol. 8 consists of an appendix of articles on the current knowledge of the origins of the Coptic language and its dialects, 12 maps, and the index.   BX130.5.C66

The future of Coptic studies / ed. by R. McL. Wilson. Leiden : Brill, 1978. 253 p. (Coptic studies, v.1).   **BC453**
For annotation, *see* BE1520.   PJ2015.F88

Kammerer, Winifred. A Coptic bibliography / comp. ... with the collaboration of Elinor Mullet Husselman and Louise A. Shier. Ann Arbor : Univ. of Michigan Pr., 1950. 205 p. (University of Michigan. General library publ., no. 7).   **BC454**
For annotation, *see* BE1521.   Z7061.K3

BUDDHISM

Buddhist America : centers, retreats, practices / ed. by Don Morreale. Santa Fe, N.M. : John Muir Publications ; N.Y. : Distr. by W.W. Norton, 1988. 349 p. : ill.   **BC455**

Arranged in sections: Theravada; Mahayana; Vajrayana; Nonsectarian Buddhism; Other new directions. Each section includes a few short articles describing the writers' retreat experiences, followed by a directory of centers arranged geographically by state. Appendix of unconfirmed centers.   BQ724.B83

Prebish, Charles S. Historical dictionary of Buddhism. Metuchen, N.J. : Scarecrow, 1993. 387 p. : map. (Historical dictionaries of religions, philosophies, and movements, no. 1).
                                                                BC456

Dictionary entries include texts, events, doctrines, practices, institutions, movements, and significant places and people. Preceded by: introductory essay; overview of Indian, Chinese, and Tibetan Buddhist scriptures; chronology of Buddhist history. These are followed by a lengthy, detailed, classified bibliography. Intended for the general reader and as an introduction to the subject. Lacks index. BQ130.P74

Sacred books of the Buddhists / tr. by various Oriental scholars and ed. by F. M. Müller. London : H. Frowde, Oxford Univ. Pr., 1895–1978. 33 v.   **BC457**
Title page, publisher, editor vary.
Vols. 23–24, 30–34, 37–39– issued by Pali Text Society, London.
Begun under the editorship of F. M. Müller; similar in plan to *Sacred books of the East* series (BC92). Each volume has an index.

Snelling, John. The Buddhist handbook : a complete guide to Buddhist schools, teaching, practice, and history. Rochester, Vt. : Inner Traditions : American International Distribution Corp., c1991. 337 p. : ill.   **BC458**
Provides an historical overview of the development and spread of Buddhism throughout Asia and the West. Appendixes: Useful addresses (a selection of Buddhist centers in the U.S. and Canada); Major Buddhist festivals; Who's who in Buddhism; Further reading. Index.
                                                                BQ4012.S64

Yoo, Yushin. Buddhism : a subject index to periodical articles in English, 1728–1971. Metuchen, N.J. : Scarecrow, 1973 [c1972]. 162 p.   **BC459**
Broad subject arrangement, with author/subject and title indexes.
                                                                Z7860.Y65

Bibliography

550 books on Buddhism : translations, studies, and general readings / [ed. by Elizabeth Cook and Ruth Fellhauer]. Berkeley, Calif. : Nyingma Inst. : Dharma Publ., c1985. 95 p. : ill.
                                                                BC460
Cover title: Books on Buddhism.
Lists in classified order and often briefly annotates primary and secondary sources in English. Indicates availability and provides ordering information. Intended for beginners.   Z7860.A12

Beautrix, Pierre. Bibliographie du bouddhisme. Brussels : Institut belge des hautes études bouddhiques, [1970]. v. 1. (Institut belge des hautes études bouddhiques. Publications. Séries bibliographies, 2). (In progress?).   **BC461**
Contents: v. 1, Éditions de textes.
Entries for published editions of Buddhist texts are arranged by editor or commentator. Subject and title index. A proposed second volume will include translations into Western languages. Z7860.3.I5

———————— Bibliographie du bouddhisme Zen. Brussels : Institut belge des hautes études bouddhiques, [1969]. 114 *l.* (Institut belge des hautes études bouddhiques. Séries bibliographies, 1).   **BC462**
More than 700 entries grouped as: (1) Généralités; (2) Textes et commentaires; (3) Doctrine et philosophie; (4) Histoire et biographie; (5) Art; (6) Littérature; (7) Études comparatives. Author index.

————. ————. *Premier supplément* ([1975]. 119 *l.* [Institut belge des hautes études bouddhiques. Sér. bibliographies, 4]). 836 additional entries, following the classed order of the basic volume. Author index.   Z7864.Z4

Bibliographie bouddhique. 1928/29–1954/58. Paris : Librairie d'Amérique et d'Orient, 1930–67.   **BC463**
Vols. 1–3 issued as: *Buddhica : documents et travaux pour l'étude du bouddhisme.*
Indexes: v. 1–6, 1928–34, in v. 6; v. 7–23, 1934–50, in v. 23 suppl.; v. 24–31, 1951–58, issued as v. 32.
An important annotated bibliography which includes both books and the indexing of some 200 periodicals in many languages. Some issues include special retrospective author bibliographies.

A bibliography on Japanese Buddhism / ed. by Bandō Shōjun [et al.]. Tokyo : CIIB Pr., 1958. 180 p.   **BC464**
A classified bibliography listing books and periodical articles (1,660 numbered items) written mainly in Western languages up to July 1958. Locates copies in Japanese libraries.   Z7835.B9B63

Bussho kaisetsu daijiten / comp. by Ono Gemmyō. Tokyo : Daitō Shuppansha, [1964–78]. 14 v.   **BC465**
1st ed., 1933–36 in 12 v.
A comprehensive annotated list of books and manuscripts on Buddhism in Japanese and Chinese. More than 72,000 entries. The 1st ed. listed publications up to 1932. This ed. reprints those volumes with two supplements (v. 12–13) which add materials of 1932–65. Vol. 14 is a revision of v. 12 of the earlier ed., a discussion of sources.
                                                                Z7860.B87

Conze, Edward. Buddhist scriptures : a bibliography / Edward Conze ; ed. and rev. by Lewis Lancaster. N.Y. : Garland, 1982. 161 p. (Garland reference library of the humanities, v. 113).   **BC466**
A bibliographic guide to the editions, translations, and studies of the Buddhist scriptures. Title index and comparative catalog indexes for Tohoku-Conze and Taisho-Conze numbers.   Z7862.C66

Gardner, James L. Zen Buddhism : a classified bibliography of Western-language publications through 1990. [Salt Lake City] : Wings of Fire Pr., 1991. 412 p.   **BC467**
Sections cover Zen in Asia, the West, and the influence of Zen on Asian and Western literature, drama, the arts, and other aspects of culture. Includes books, essays within books, dissertations, and journal articles; excludes popular publications. Offers the most up-to-date listing on the subject, but must be used with care because of inconsistent editing and some incomplete citations. Author and subject indexes.
                                                                Z7864.Z4G37

Grönbold, Günter. Der buddhistische Kanon : eine Bibliographie. Wiesbaden : Harrassowitz, 1984. 70 p.   **BC468**
A bibliography of editions of the Pali, Sanskrit, Chinese, Japanese, Korean, Tibetan, Mongolian, Manchurian, and Tangut canons; ancient and modern canon catalogs; and selected secondary works on Buddhist literature publications. Indexed.

Hanayama, Shinsho. Bibliography on Buddhism / ed. by the Commemoration Committee for Prof. Shinsho Hanayama's sixty-first birthday. Tokyo : Hokuseido Pr., 1961. 869 p.
                                                                BC469
An extensive bibliography of 15,073 numbered entries, arranged alphabetically. Lists books and articles in Western languages primarily of the 19th–20th centuries—prior to 1928 when the *Bibliographie bouddhique* (BC463) was started. Subject index.   Z7835.B9H3

Inada, Kenneth K. Guide to Buddhist philosophy. Boston : G.K. Hall, c1985. 226 p.   **BC470**
For annotation, *see* BB20.   Z7128.B93I53

Powers, John. The Yogācāra school of Buddhism : a bibliography. [Philadelphia?] : Amer. Theological Libr. Assoc. ; Metuchen, N.J. : Scarecrow, 1991. 257 p. (ATLA bibliography series, no. 27).   **BC471**

Comprehensive list of primary and secondary sources in many Asian and Western languages. Functions as a tool for locating sutras and philosophical and historical texts in canonical sources, critical editions, and Western language translations. Indexes of Modern authors and technical terms; Traditional Indian authors; Titles of Sanskrit works; Tibetan authors and titles; Traditional Chinese and Japanese authors and works.   Z7864.Y64P69

Reynolds, Frank E. Guide to Buddhist religion / Frank E. Reynolds, with John Holt and John Strong ; arts section by Bardwell Smith ... [et al.]. Boston : G.K. Hall, c1981. 415 p.   **BC472**

One of a series of guides prep. by the Project on Asian Philosophies and Religions. Its companion is Kenneth K. Inanda, *Guide to Buddhist philosophy* (BB20).

Although undertaken as a guide for teachers of religion at the advanced undergraduate level, the work is also meant to be useful to those engaged in Buddhological research and as a means of pointing out "older materials which are presently inaccessible and need to be made more available, as well as areas in which new scholarly work needs to be done."—*Pref.* Includes both books and periodical articles. Materials are mainly in English, but some French items of first importance are listed; includes publications through the early 1970s only. Classed arrangement; annotations; author/title and subject indexes.

§ *Focus on Buddhism : a guide to audio-visual resources for teaching religion,* ed. by Robert A. McDermott ([Chambersburg, Pa.] : Anima Books, 1981) is a complementary volume covering films, slide sets, and recordings.   Z7860.R48

Satyaprakash. Buddhism : a select bibliography. 2nd ed., enl. and rev. Gurgaon : Indian Documentation Service, 1986. 247 p. (Subject bibliography series, 1).   **BC473**

1st ed., 1976.

Includes "3,271 articles, research papers, notes, news and book reviews" (*Pref.*) from 134 journals (mostly Indian) and *Times of India* and *Economic times* (both daily publications), 1962–85. Arranged in a single alphabet of authors and subjects.   Z7860.S28

Vessie, Patricia Armstrong. Zen Buddhism : a bibliography of books and articles in English, 1892–1975. Ann Arbor, Mich. : Univ. Microfilms Internat., 1976. 81 *l*.   **BC474**

"Publ. under the aegis of the East Asia Library, University of Washington."—*t.p.*

Some 760 items in classed arrangement. Pt. 1 includes: General, Historical, Texts and commentaries, Zen sects. Sections in Pt. 2 relate Zen to such topics as archery, the arts, food, and psychology. Lacks an index.   Z7864.Z4V47

Yoo, Yushin. Books on Buddhism : an annotated subject guide. Metuchen, N.J. : Scarecrow, 1976. 251 p.   **BC475**

A classed listing of some 1,300 items, with author and title indexes.   Z7860.Y64

Encyclopedias

Encyclopaedia of Buddhism / ed. by G. P. Malalasekera. Colombo : Govt. of Ceylon, 1961–93. v. 1–5⁴ : ill. (In progress).   **BC476**

Editor varies.

Contents: v. 1–5⁴, A–Japan.

Issued in parts.

Publ. by the Govt. of Sri Lanka since v. 3, fasc. 3.

Designed as a scholarly and definitive work with articles on all aspects of Buddhist thought, history, and civilization, including personal and place-names, literary works, and religious and moral concepts. With v. 4, in an effort to speed the progress of the work, articles

focus on concepts of doctrine, philosophy, and civilization; many personal and place-names and names of texts which may be found elsewhere are excluded. Articles vary in length; many are signed. For some, bibliographies are appended; references are cited only within the text of many other articles.   BL1403.E5

Dictionaries

Humphreys, Christmas. A popular dictionary of Buddhism. 2nd. ed. London : Curzon Pr. ; Totowa [N.J.] : Rowman and Littlefield, 1976. 223 p.   **BC477**

1st ed., 1962.

Originally based on *A brief glossary of Buddhist terms* by Arthur Charles March (London : Buddhist Lodge, 1937), later expanded by Humphreys for inclusion in *A Buddhist students' manual* (1956).

Designed for the English-speaking student of Buddhism who is not a trained scholar. Includes those terms of special meaning found in books on Buddhism. This edition incorporates corrections, minor additions and improved cross-referencing.   BQ130.H85

Inagaki, Hisao. A glossary of Zen terms. Kyoto : Nagata Bunshodo, Heisei 3 [1991]. 529 p.   **BC478**

Seeks to meet the need of serious students of Zen for a dictionary of technical terms, persons, names of temples, texts, and idiomatic expressions described in English and including Chinese and Japanese characters. 5,500 entries include references to sources.

§ The author, in collaboration with P. G. O'Neill, has similarly prepared *A dictionary of Japanese Buddhist terms : based on references in Japanese literature* (Kyoto : Nagata Bunshodo, 1984).   BQ9259.I54

The Shambhala dictionary of Buddhism and Zen / tr. by Michael H. Kohn. Boston : Shambhala ; N.Y. : Random House, 1991. 280 p. : ill.   **BC479**

Buddhism by Ingrid Fischer-Schreiber; Tibetan Buddhism by Franz-Karl Ehrhard; Zen by Michael S. Diener.

More than 1,500 entries extracted from *Encyclopedia of Eastern philosophy and religion* (BC57). Includes a Ch'an/Zen lineage chart and bibliography.   BQ130.I.492513

Soothill, William Edward. A dictionary of Chinese Buddhist terms : with Sanskrit and English equivalents and a Sanskrit-Pali index / comp. by William Edward Soothill ... and Lewis Hodous .... London : K. Paul, Trench, Trubner & Co., 1937. 510 p.   **BC480**

Repr. : Taipei : Ch'eng-Wen, 1968.

Definitions in English.   BL1403.S6

HINDUISM

Bibliography

Dell, David. Guide to Hindu religion / David Dell ... [et al.]. Boston : G.K. Hall, [1981]. 461 p.   **BC481**

A classified, annotated bibliography intended for "undergraduate teachers of Hinduism and others who may wish to pursue Hinduism's study on their own."—*Pref.* Mainly books, but includes some significant periodical articles. Section 12 is devoted to research aids. Appendixes list periodicals on Hinduism and related topics. Author index.

§ A complementary volume including films, videotapes, slides, filmstrips and recordings is: *Focus on Hinduism : a guide to audio-visual resources for teaching religion,* ed. by Robert A. McDermott (2nd ed., rev. by H. Daniel Smith. [Chambersburg, Pa.] : Anima Books, 1981).   Z7835.B8D44

Holland, Barron. Popular Hinduism and Hindu mythology : an annotated bibliography. Westport, Conn. : Greenwood, [1979]. 394 p.   **BC482**

A classed bibliography intended for "anyone interested in aspects of popular Hinduism, both general and specific, whether students, research scholars, teachers, devotees, or merely interested persons."—*Pref.* Entries, many with brief annotations, for nearly 3,500 books, articles, and dissertations, cover ethnographic and cultural aspects of contemporary Hindu religious practices and mythology. Excludes material on Karma, Yoga, reincarnation, and popular philosophy. Limited to English and other European languages; "does not include works on Hinduism beyond the confines of peninsular India." Indexed.

Z7835.B8H64

Kapoor, Jagdish Chander. Bhagavad-Gītā : an international bibliography of 1785–1979 imprints. N.Y. : Garland, 1983. 371 p. (Garland reference library of the humanities, v. 306).   **BC483**

"Includes all translations, commentaries, commentaries on commentaries, and books on or about the Bhagavad-Gītā" (*Foreword*) for the period specified; notes locations in libraries in many parts of the world. Arranged by language, then by date of publication. 50 languages are represented. Indexes of translators, of authors, of titles and subjects.   Z7835.B8K36

Renou, Louis. Bibliographie védique. Paris : Adrien-Maisonneuve, 1931. 339 p.   **BC484**

A classed bibliography listing materials in many languages on the Vedas and the history of Hinduism, primarily of the 19th and 20th centuries.

§ R. N. Dandekar's *Vedic bibliography* (Poona, India : Bhandarkar Oriental Research Inst., 1946–1985. v. 1–4. [In progress]) is regarded as the continuation of Renou's work. Publisher varies.

Z7090.R41

Encyclopedias

Walker, George Benjamin. Hindu world : an encyclopedic survey of Hinduism. London : Allen & Unwin ; N.Y. : Praeger, [1968]. 2 v.   **BC485**

Information "is derived largely from standard works of recognized authorities, supplemented by material drawn from traditional Indian sources."—*Pref.* Dictionary arrangement, plus a subject index. Bibliographies are appended to many articles.   BL1105.W34

Dictionaries

Dowson, John. A classical dictionary of Hindu mythology and religion, geography, history, and literature. 12th ed. London : Routledge & Kegan Paul, 1972. 411 p.   **BC486**

1st ed., 1879. Frequently reprinted with very little change.

Includes names of gods, personal and geographical names, and subjects.   BL1105.D6

Feuerstein, Georg. Encyclopedic dictionary of yoga. N.Y. : Paragon House, 1990. 430 p. : ill. (The Paragon living traditions series, v. 1).   **BC487**

Defines and discusses yogic terms, concepts, sages, history, and literature. Arranged alphabetically by English words or by words transliterated from nonroman alphabets. Numerous cross-references and illustrations; select annotated bibliography. Intended for general readers.   B132.Y6F46

Stutley, Margaret. Harper's dictionary of Hinduism : its mythology, folklore, philosophy, literature, and history / Margaret and James Stutley. San Francisco : Harper & Row, 1977. 372 p.   **BC488**

Publ. in London as: *A dictionary of Hinduism.*

Designed to "meet the requirements of the modern student and general reader."—*Pref.* Most entries are brief, although some run to several columns. References to texts and sources are often given; bibliography, p. 353–68.   BL1105.S78

Concordances and indexes

Bloomfield, Maurice. A Vedic concordance. Cambridge, Mass. : Harvard Univ. Pr., 1906. 1078 p. (Harvard oriental series, v. 10).   **BC489**

Repr. : Delhi : Motilal Banarsidass, 1964.

Subtitle: Being an alphabetic index to every line of every stanza of the published Vedic literature and to the liturgical formulas thereof; that is, an index to the Vedic mantras, together with an account of their variations in the different Vedic books.   PK3009.B6

Macdonnell, Arthur Anthony. Vedic index of names and subjects / Arthur Anthony Macdonnell and Arthur Berriedale Keith. London : Murray, publ. for the Govt. of India, 1912. 2 v. : folded map in color.   **BC490**

Repr.: Delhi : Motilal Banarsidass, 1982.

An index by proper name and subject to Vedic literature from its earliest forms (ca.1200 BCE) to the rise of Buddhism (ca.500 BCE). Entries include personal and geographical names and subjects (e.g., agriculture, caste, economic conditions, customs, law, position of women) given in Sanskrit transliterated into the Roman alphabet. Sanskrit and English indexes.   PK3009.M3

ISLAM

Islam in North America : a sourcebook / ed. by Michael A. Kőszegi and J. Gordon Melton. N.Y. : Garland, 1992. 414 p. (Religious information systems series, v. 8 ; Garland reference library of social science, v. 852).   **BC491**

Includes articles and documents (some reprinted here because of their historical value), a bibliography of English-language materials, and a directory of Muslim organizations, mosques, centers, and research/study facilities. Also covers Sufism and Sufi-inspired movements. Index of authors and periodical titles.   BP67.A1I82

Bibliography

Arab Islamic bibliography : the Middle East Library Committee guide ; based on Giuseppe Gabrieli's Manuale di bibliografia musulmana / ed. by Diana Grimwood-Jones, Derek Hopwood, J. D. Pearson ... [et al.]. Hassocks, Eng. : Harvester Pr. ; Atlantic Highlands, N.J. : Humanities Pr., 1977. 292 p.   **BC492**

A comprehensive, classified bibliography of reference materials, in many languages, on all phases of Arab Islamic life and culture. Most entries have short critical annotations; chapters have introductions. Follows the format of Giuseppe Gabrieli's *Manuale di bibliografia musulmana. Parte 1. Bibliografia generale* (Roma : Tipografia dell' Unione Editrice, 1916. 491 p.), retaining useful titles from that work and supplementing them with later titles. Index of authors and titles of anonymous works.   Z3013.A66

Geddes, Charles L. An analytical guide to the bibliographies on Islam, Muhammad, and the Qur'an. [Denver, Colo.] : American Inst. of Islamic Studies, [1973]. 102 p. (American Institute of Islamic Studies. Bibliographic series, no. 3).   **BC493**

Attempts to describe all relevant bibliographies in any language published 1658–1972. Arabic, Persian, and Russian titles appear in original script with English translations. Author/title/subject index, with transliterated titles for non-Western languages. Z7835.M6A54

———— Guide to reference books for Islamic studies. Denver, Colo. : American Inst. of Islamic Studies, c1985. 429 p. (American Institute of Islamic Studies. Bibliographic series, no. 9.). **BC494**

An annotated, classified bibliography of some 1,200 books and articles on Muslim history, culture, society, and faith from the time of Muhammad to the abolition of the caliphate in 1924. Covers geographical expanse from Spain to China. Titles in non-Western languages appear in their original script with transliterations and English translations. Author/title/subject index. Z7835.M6A54

Guide to Islam / David Ede ... [et al.]. Boston : G.K. Hall, [1983]. 261 p. **BC495**

A bibliography of nearly 3,000 items (books and periodical articles) which aims "to introduce the English-language reader to significant publications on Islam as a religion and a civilization."—*Pref.* Intended mainly for the undergraduate and graduate student; a few basic works in French and German have been included. Most entries are briefly annotated. Cutoff date is 1976. Classed arrangement; detailed table of contents; author and subject indexes. Z7835.M6G84

Haddad, Yvonne Yazbeck. The contemporary Islamic revival : a critical survey and bibliography / Yvonne Yazbeck Haddad, John Obert Voll, and John L. Esposito. N.Y. : Greenwood, 1991. 230 p. (Bibliographies and indexes in religious studies, no. 20). **BC496**

Concentrates on academic studies and primary sources published 1970–88. 1,225 entries (some annotated) are classed by geographic area. General materials form separate sections: Interpretive studies, Economics, and Women. Three essays precede the bibliography. Author, title, and subject indexes. Z7835.M6H23

Ofori, Patrick E. Islam in Africa south of the Sahara : a select bibliographic guide. Nendeln, [Liechtenstein] : KTO Pr., 1977. 223 p. **BC497**

Lists 1,170 books, pamphlets, articles, and theses, chiefly in European languages, arranged by broad geographic region, then by country. No Arabic-language material included. Some entries are annotated. Author index.

§ *See also* Samir M. Zoghby's *Islam in sub-Saharan Africa : a partially annotated guide* (Wash. : Library of Congress, 1978).

The compiler has two other guides to religions in Africa: *Black African traditional religions and philosophy* (BC34), and *Christianity in tropical Africa* (BC221). Z7835.M6O36

Pfannmüller, Gustav. Handbuch der Islam-Literatur. Berlin : W. de Gruyter, 1923. 436 p. **BC498**

A comprehensive, critical manual with bibliographies listing materials in various languages on Islamic religious literature. Now largely out of date, but still valued for its essays. Z7835.M6P5

The quarterly Index Islamicus. v. 1 (Jan. 1977)– . London : Mansell, 1977– . **BC499**

Issued as a supplement to *Index Islamicus* (BC502); five-year cumulations form the supplements to that publication. Also available on microfiche.

Subtitle: Current books, articles and papers on Islamic subjects.

Includes citations to books as well as to periodical articles. Analyzes more than 1,300 periodicals, festschriften, and other collections. Personal name and subject indexes in each issue. With v. 7, no. 4 (Nov. 1983) the classification scheme was revised to reflect expanded interest in social sciences of the Middle East and Islam. Z3013.Q34

Sauvaget, Jean. Introduction to the history of the Muslim East : a bibliographical guide / based on the second edition as recast by Claude Cahen. Berkeley : Univ. of California Pr., 1965. 252 p. **BC500**

Repr.: Westport, Conn. : Greenwood, 1982, as *Jean Sauvaget's introduction to the history of the Muslim East.*

Translation of *Introduction à l'histoire de l'Orient musulman.*

Not merely an English translation of Cahen's 1961 revision of the French text, but actually a new edition incorporating changes, corrections, and new materials. A scholarly and useful bibliographic survey. Z3013.S314

Shinar, Pessah. Essai de bibliographie sélective et annotée sur l'Islam maghrébin contemporain : Maroc, Algérie, Tunisie, Libye (1830–1978). Paris : Éditions du Centre National de la Recherche Scientifique, 1983. 506 p. **BC501**

At head of title: Centre de Recherches et d'Études sur les Sociétés Méditerranéennes.

An annotated bibliography of Islam in the countries of Northwest Africa mentioned in the subtitle. Islam is here considered as a "total phenomenon," so that social, cultural, ethical, educational, etc., aspects are included along with religious matters. Classed arrangement within geographical sections. Indexes of authors, subjects, people, and places. About 2,000 entries in French, English, Arabic, Spanish, Italian, and German. Z7835.M6S5

University of London. School of Oriental and African Studies. Library. Index Islamicus, 1906–1955 : a catalogue of articles on Islamic subjects in periodicals and other collective publications, comp. by J. D. Pearson, with the assistance of Julia F. Ashton. Cambridge, Eng. : W. Heffer, [1958]. 897 p. **BC502**

Repr.: London : Mansell, 1972.

Indexes more than 26,000 articles appearing in periodicals, festschriften, and other collected works, published 1906–55. Periodicals devoted to the field of Islam are indexed completely; other periodicals in many languages are indexed for articles on Islamic subjects. Articles are arranged by a detailed classification system with an author index.

Index Islamicus. Supplement. Issued with coverage for five-year periods (1956–60, 1961–65; 1966–70; 1971–75; 1976–80; 1981–85 [publ. 1991]). Currently compiled as five-year cumulations of *The quarterly Index Islamicus* (BC499); uses a revised classification scheme for monograph and article entries, begun in 1983 in the quarterly index. Subject and author indexes.

Encyclopedias

The encyclopaedia of Islam. New ed. / prep. by a number of leading orientalists ; ed. by an editorial committee consisting of H. A. R. Gibb [et al.]. Leiden : Brill, 1954–93. v. 1–7 ; Suppl., fasc. 1/2–5/6 : ill., plates, fold. maps in color; diagrs., plans. (In progress). **BC503**

1st ed., 1911–38, in four volumes and supplement.

Contents: v. 1–7, A–al-Naẓẓā; *Supplement*, fasc. 1/2–5/6, al-'Abbās–al-'Irāķī.

A completely new edition of the most important reference work in English on Islamic subjects. A work of high scholarship and authority, containing signed articles, with bibliographies, on subjects in biography, history, geography, religious beliefs, institutions, manners and customs, tribes, industries, sciences, and terms of different sorts. Special emphasis in the new edition on economic and social topics and on artistic production. Geographical material includes separate articles on towns and larger political divisions in the Ottoman Empire, and in foreign countries in which Islam is of importance. More cross-references in English and French have been introduced to facilitate usage. Until this edition is completed, it will be necessary to continue use of the 1st ed.

————. *Index of subjects* for v. 1–7 and *Supplement* (fasc. 1–6), comp. by P. J. Bearman; *Index of proper names* for v. 1–7 and *Supplement* (fasc. 1–6), comp. by E. van Donzel. DS37.E523

Glasse, Cyril. The concise encyclopedia of Islam. San Francisco : Harper & Row, 1989. 472 p. : col. ill. **BC504**

Offers articles of moderate length with cross-references, arranged alphabetically by English words or transliterations of Arabic words. From a Sunni perspective; focuses on outward religious forms (e.g., commandments, observances, and texts), and on inner religious and metaphysical truths. Contains three sections of photographic color plates and four appendixes: maps illustrating Islamic history; Mecca and the Hajj; branches of Islam; genealogical tables. Chronology and bibliography of primary and secondary sources.   BP40.G42

Shorter encyclopaedia of Islam / ed. on behalf of the Royal Netherlands Academy by H. A. R. Gibb and J. H. Kramers. Leiden : Brill ; London : Luzac, 1953. 671 p. : ill.   **BC505**

Consists mainly of articles on the religion and law of Islam taken from the first edition of the *The encyclopaedia of Islam* (1911–38; *see* BC503), with the addition of some new entries and the revision of some of the older material. Bibliographies have often been updated, and there is a useful Register of subjects, which indexes the entries under English-language headings.   DS37.E52

JAINISM

Guérinot, Armand Albert. Essai de bibliographie Jaina : répertoire analytique et méthodique des travaux relatifs au Jainisme. Paris : Leroux, 1906. 568 p. : ill. (Ministère de l'Instruction Publique. Annales Musée Guimet. Bibliothèque d'études, t.22).   **BC506**

A classed annotated bibliography of 852 works on Jainism. Author, title, place name, periodical, and subject indexes.

Supplemented by: "Notes de bibliographie jaina" in *Journal asiatique*, 10. sér., 10 (1909): 47–148.   Z7835.J2G9

Jain, Chhotelal. Chhotelal Jain's Jaina bibliography / ed., rearranged, rev. and aug. in collaboration with the author, by Satya Ranjan Banerjee. 2nd rev. ed. New Delhi : Vir Sewa Mandir, 1982. v. 1–2. (In progress).   **BC507**

1st ed., 1945.

Covers the entire field of Jainism, listing books, parts of books, reports, censuses, journal articles published from about 1800 to 1960, in English and European languages. About 3,000 entries in classed arrangement on art, history, biography, religion, philosophy, language and literature, etc. Annotations often summarize the work cited. An index is to be published as v. 3.   Z7835.J2J33

JUDAISM

Bibliography

Antisemitism : an annotated bibliography / the Vidal Sassoon International Center for the Study of Antisemitism, the Hebrew University of Jerusalem ; ed. by Susan Sarah Cohen. N.Y. : Garland, 1987–94. v. 1–3. (Garland reference library of social science, v. 366, etc.). (In progress).   **BC508**

A comprehensive, classified bibliography of books, dissertations, masters' theses, articles from periodicals, and collections about anti-Semitism from the ancient period to the present. Vol. 1 covers material published 1984–85; appendixes list current anti-Semitic periodicals and bibliographies on anti-Semitism published before 1984. Vols. 2–3 extend coverage through 1988. Includes materials in English, other European languages, Hebrew, and Yiddish. Author index and detailed subject index.

§ *See* Robert Singerman's *Antisemitic propaganda* (N.Y. : Garland, 1982. 448 p.) for materials that reflect "for the most part ... extreme ideological antisemitism."—*Foreword*. Most entries are for U.S and British materials, published 1871–1981.   Z6374.A56A57

Benjacob, Isaac. Ozar ha-sepharim : Thesaurus libororum hebraicorum tam impressorum quam many scriptorum = Ozar ha-seraphim (bücherschatz) : Bibliographie der gesammten hebraeischen Literatur mit Einschluss der Handschriften (bis 1863). Wilna : Benjacob, 1880. 678 p.   **BC509**

Title pages in Hebrew, Russian, German, and Latin. Text in Hebrew.

Issued in three parts.

Notes on entries by Moritz Steinschneider.

Arranged alphabetically. Includes entries for 17,000 Hebrew books and manuscripts published up to 1863.   Z7070.B33

Berlin, Charles. Index to festschriften in Jewish studies. Cambridge, Mass. : Harvard College Libr. ; N.Y. : Ktav Publ. House, 1971. 319 p.   **BC510**

Indexes 259 volumes of festschriften dealing with Jewish studies published primarily since 1936. Articles are first listed in an alphabetical author section, then by subject under specific topical headings.

§ For festschriften published before 1936, see Jacob Rader Marcus and Albert Bilgray's *An index to Jewish festschriften* (Cincinnati : Hebrew Union College, 1937. Repr.: N.Y. : Kraus, 1970).

Z6366.B45

Bibliographical essays in medieval Jewish studies. [N.Y.] : Anti-Defamation League of B'nai B'rith, [1976]. 392 p. (The study of Judaism, v. 2).   **BC511**

Six bibliographic essays by specialists, addressed primarily to the non-specialist. Brief contents: The Jews in Western Europe; The church and the Jews; The Jews under Islam; Medieval Jewish religious philosophy; Medieval Jewish mysticism; Minor Midrashim.

Z6368.B53

Brisman, Shimeon. Jewish research literature. Cincinnati : Hebrew Union College Pr., 1977–87. v. 1–2. (Bibliographica Judaica, 7, etc.). (In progress).   **BC512**

Contents: v. 1, A history and guide to Judaic bibliography; v. 2, A history and guide to Judaic encyclopedias and lexicons.

Offers thorough bibliographic histories and descriptions of the works considered. Each volume provides extensive analytical notes and many references to reviews. Indexes.   Z6366.B8

Cutter, Charles. Judaica reference sources : a selective, annotated bibliographic guide / Charles Cutter, Micha Falk Oppenheim. 2nd ed. Juneau, Alaska : Denali Pr., c1993. 224 p.
                    BC513

Covers 900 titles, emphasizing publications 1970–92, with critical earlier titles. Reference sources on all aspects of Jewish history, religion, and culture, arranged by subject, with author and title indexes. Although not definitive, provides useful information for students, researchers, and librarians.   Z6366.C87

Griffiths, David B. A critical bibliography of writings on Judaism. Lewiston, N.Y. : E. Mellen Pr., 1988. 2 v. (804 p.). (Jewish studies, v. 2).   **BC514**

Contents: Pt. 1, Resource apparatus; Judaism in antiquity; Medieval to early modern times; Thought and culture. Pt. 2, Modern Jewish history: The Holocaust; Studies of Zionist thought and history; Modernity and modern thought.

A comprehensive annotated bibliography of mainly English-language monographic and journal literature, most published since World War II. Arranged in classified order; absence of an index severely impedes access.   Z6370.G75

Kaplan, Jonathan. 2000 books and more : an annotated and selected bibliography of Jewish history and thought. Jerusalem : Magnes Pr. : Hebrew Univ., [1983]. 483 p.   **BC515**

At head of title: Rothberg School for Overseas Students, Hebrew University; Dor Hemschech Institutes, The World Zionist Organization.

Introductory matter and section headings in English and Hebrew.

Aims "to furnish the educator, the student and the librarian with a basic list of books that are of major importance for the study of Jewish

History and the History of Jewish Thought, and to assist them in the selection of books best suited to their respective needs and interests."—*Introd.* Includes works in Hebrew, English, German, Spanish, Portuguese and French. Arranged by historical period (subdivided topically), with a separate section on Jewish communities. Index of names.   Z6366.K33

Lubetski, Edith. Building a Judaica library collection : a resource guide / Edith Lubetski, Meir Lubetski. Littleton, Colo. : Libraries Unlimited, 1983. 185 p.   **BC516**
    Intends "to provide a resource tool for the acquisition librarian."—*Introd.* In two parts: (1) a classified list of well annotated selection aids for current and retrospective Judaic materials in many formats (including general tools wherever specialized sources are meager); (2) an international directory of publishers, bookdealers, antiquarian bookdealers and media publishers and distributors.
                                                                    Z688.J48L82

Roth, Cecil. Magna bibliotheca anglo-judaica : a bibliographical guide to Anglo-Jewish history. New ed. rev. and enl. London : Jewish Historical Soc. of England, 1937. 464 p. **BC517**
    A revised edition of *Bibliotheca anglo-judaica,* comp. by Joseph Jacobs and Lucien Wolf (London : Office of the "Jewish Chronicle," 1888). In two parts: pt.1, Histories, consists largely of secondary works; pt.2, Historical material, lists primary sources usually up to the year 1837, though material on the reform movement is extended to 1842 and on Jewish emancipation to 1858. Classified arrangement.
    § Pt. 1 was updated by Ruth P. Goldschmidt-Lehmann's *Nova bibliotheca anglo-judaica : a bibliographical guide to Anglo-Jewish history, 1937–1960* (London : Jewish Historical Society of England, 1961. 232 p.). The same compiler has continued to extend the coverage of writings on Jews in Great Britain and the Commonwealth in *Anglo-Jewish bibliography, 1937–1970* (London : Jewish Historical Society of England, 1973. 364 p.) and *Anglo-Jewish bibliography, 1971–1990,* ed. and augmented by Stephen W. Massil and Peter Shmuel Salinger (1992. 377 p.). Goldschmidt-Lehmann's works follow the basic arrangement of Roth's *Magna bibliotheca,* with the addition of new sections and subsections in each volume which reflect growing interest in cultural and literary history, novels and plays, biography, education, sociological research, communal history, and conferences and exhibitions.   Z6373.G7R4

The Schocken guide to Jewish books : where to start reading about Jewish history, literature, culture, and religion / ed. by Barry W. Holtz. N.Y. : Schocken Books, c1992. 357 p. : ill.
                                                                    BC518
    Bibliographic essays on topics such as Bible, Talmud, Women's studies, etc., focus on titles in print and of interest to the general reader. Written by experts, the essays are readable and informative and will also be useful to beginning students. Author/title index.
    § *The book of Jewish books : a reader's guide to Judaism,* ed. by Ruth S. Frank and William Wollheim (San Francisco : Harper & Row, c1986) provides similar material in an annotated, classified bibliography, and includes children's books.   Z6366.S39

Shunami, Shlomo. Bibliography of Jewish bibliographies. 2nd ed., enl. Jerusalem : Magnes Pr. : Hebrew Univ., 1965. 997 p.   **BC519**
    Repr. with corrections, 1969.
    Added title page in Hebrew; prefatory matter in English and Hebrew.
    1st ed., 1936.
    Of the 4,700 entries, about one-quarter cover the Bible and its parts, Talmudic and Midrashic literature, Sects, Dead Sea Scrolls, and related topics. The remainder of the entries are for bibliographies on the history and religion of Israel, Jewish literature, etc. Classed arrangement with name and subject index.
    ———. ——— *Supplement* (1975. 464 p.) adds about 2,000 entries, mainly publications from the 10-year period following appearance of the main volume.   Z7070.A1S5

Spector, Sheila. Jewish mysticism : an annotated bibliography on the Kabbalah in English. N.Y. : Garland, 1984. 399 p. (Garland library of social science, v. 210).   **BC520**
    "Provides access to the sources available to English readers from the seventeenth century on" (*Introd.*) and to secondary materials of both Jewish and Christian authorship. Due to the language restriction the bibliography primarily reflects attitudes of English-speaking Jews and Christians towards Jewish mystical practices. 1,500 entries for books and articles in a classified arrangement; chapters are subdivided for primary and secondary works, then chronologically by publication date. Includes books and articles. Indexes of primary sources, of authors, of subjects.   Z6371.C2S67

The study of Judaism : bibliographical essays / contributors: Richard Bavier ... [et al.]. N.Y. : publ. by Ktav Publ. House for Anti-Defamation League of B'nai B'rith, [1972]. 229 p. (The Study of Judaism, v. 1).   **BC521**
    Contents: Judaism in New Testament times, by Richard Bavier; Rabbinic sources, by John T. Townsend; Judaism on Christianity: Christianity on Judaism, by Frank Talmage; Modern Jewish thought, by Fritz Rothschild and Seymour Siegel; The contemporary Jewish community, by Lloyd Gartner; The holocaust: anti-Semitism and the Jewish catastrophe, by Henry Friedlander.   Z6370.S8

By country or region

United States

Brickman, William W. The Jewish community in America : an annotated and classified bibliographical guide. N.Y. : B. Franklin, [1977]. 396 p. (Burt Franklin ethnic bibliographical guides, 2).   **BC522**
    Aims "to present to scholars, teachers, and other interested persons a descriptively and, in part, critically annotated collection of over 800 basic and specialized writings in English, Hebrew, Yiddish, Ladino, German, French, Hungarian, Polish, and Russian" which "throw light on the Jewish experience in America from the Colonial period to the present."—*Pref.* Classified arrangement; entries are organized by type (e.g., Autobiographies, General histories), or by subject (e.g., Education, Religious life, Immigration). Appendix of reprints of documents and relevant articles. Main entry index.   Z6373.U5B75

Gurock, Jeffrey S. American Jewish history : a bibliographical guide. N.Y. : Anti-Defamation League of B'nai B'rith, 1983. 195 p.   **BC523**
    Aims "to identify which are the most useful volumes extant for studying and exploring the major issues in American Jewish history."—*p. 1.* Comprises a series of bibliographic essays (e.g., The era of German migration, The era of East European migration) with bibliography and suggestions for further research. Indexed.   Z6373.U5G87

Karkhanis, Sharad. Jewish heritage in America : an annotated bibliography. N.Y. : Garland, 1988. 434 p. (Garland reference library of social science, v. 467).   **BC524**
    A critically annotated, classified bibliography of 1,100 books and articles published in English 1925–87 on all aspects of Jewish life in America. A list of periodical sources and separate indexes by author, title, and subject are appended. The compiler, a Hindu, intends the work "for the use of students, scholars and general readers—both Jewish and non-Jewish."—*Introd.*   Z6373.U5K37

Singerman, Robert. Judaica Americana : a bibliography of publications to 1900. N.Y. : Greenwood, c1990. 2 v. (1335 p.). (Bibliographies and indexes in American history, no. 14).
                                                                    BC525
    Contents: v. 1, Chronological file 1676–1889; v. 2, Chronological file 1890–1900; Union list of nineteenth-century Jewish serials published in the United States; English, French, German, Hebrew, Yiddish serials; Index [of subjects].

"Sponsored by the Center for the Study of the American Jewish Experience, Hebrew Union College—Jewish Institute of Religion"—*t.p.*

A comprehensive work listing 6,512 books, pamphlets, and serials with NUC location symbols and some annotations. Supersedes and augments earlier bibliographies of U.S. publications on Jews and Judaism. Gazetteer of Jewish publishers and printers included in the index. Subject access is impeded by broad index categories.   Z6373.U5S58

Latin America

Elkin, Judith Laikin. Latin American Jewish studies : an annotated guide to the literature / comp. by Judith Laikin Elkin and Ana Lya Sater. N. Y. : Greenwood , 1990. 238 p. (Bibliographies and indexes in ethnic studies, no. 4).   **BC526**

Includes titles in Spanish, Portuguese, Yiddish, Hebrew, and English, concerning Jews in South and Middle America, the West Indies, and the Caribbean. In pt. 1, entries for monographs, dissertations, and articles published from 1970 through 1986 are arranged by subject. In pt. 2, more than 200 serial publications located in several U.S. libraries are described and evaluated. Author and titles indexes to pt. 1; subject index to pt. 2.

§ For earlier titles on this subject *see* Martin Sable's *Latin American Jewry* (Cincinnati : Hebrew Union College Pr. ; N.Y. : Ktav, 1978).   Z6373.L3E44

Europe

Blumenkranz, Bernhard. Bibliographie des Juifs en France / Bernhard Blumenkranz en collaboration avec Monique Lévy. [Toulouse] : Privat, [1974]. 349 p.   **BC527**

Offers more than 4,000 entries covering history, law, economics, social history, religion, culture. Classified arrangement. Author and subject index. Table of contents at the end.

An earlier work by the same author and with the same title was publ. 1961 (Paris : Centre d'Études Juives, 188 p.).   Z6373.F7B5

Eichstädt, Volkmar. Bibliographie zur Geschichte der Judenfrage : Bd. 1, 1750–1848. Hamburg : Hanseatische Verlagsanstalt, 1938. 267 p.   **BC528**

Repr. : [Farnborough, Eng. : Gregg, 1969].

No more published.

A classified bibliography of more than 3,000 books and articles, publ. 1750–1848, on the treatment of Jews in the German states, Austria, and France during that time. Entries provide library and archive locations in Germany and Austria. Index.   Z6372.E34

Kisch, Guido. Judaistische Bibliographie : Ein Verzeichnis der in Deutschland und der Schweiz von 1956–1970 erschienenen Dissertationen und Habilitationsschriften. Basel ; Stuttgart : Helbing & Lichtenhahn, 1972. 104 p.   **BC529**

Entries for 381 dissertations written in Germany and Switzerland on all aspects of Jewish religion and history, in a classified arrangement preceded by an introductory essay on German Jewish bibliography since the 19th century. Author index.

§ Another work by Kisch, with Kurt Roepke, *Schriften zur Geschichte der Juden : eine Bibliographie der in Deutschland und der Schweiz 1922–1955 erschienenen Dissertationen* (Tubingen : Mohr, 1959), lists 508 earlier dissertations. For Austrian dissertations on the same subject, *see* Wolfdieter Bihl, *Bibliographie der Dissertationen über Judentum und jüdische Persönlichkeiten, die 1872–1962 an österreichischen Hochschulen (Wien, Graz, Innsbruck) approbiert wurden* (Vienna : Notring der Wissenschaftlichen Verbände Österreichs, 1965).   Z6366.K54

Milano, Attilio. Bibliotheca historica italo-judaica. Firenze : Sansoni Antiquariato, 1954. 209 p. (Contributi alla Biblioteca bibliografica italica, 6).   **BC530**

Arranges 1,597 items on Jews in Italy, in many languages, by material type (e.g., encyclopedia articles, monographs). Author, subject, and locality indexes.

———. ———. *Supplemento 1954–1963* (Firenze : Sansoni, 1964. 82 p. [Contributi alla Biblioteca bibliografica italica, 26]).

§ For Jewish Italian works only, *see* Giorgio Romano's *Bibliografia italo-ebraica (1848–1977)* (Firenze : Olschki, 1979. 208 p. [Biblioteca di bibliografia italiana, 88]).

Singerman, Robert. Spanish and Portuguese Jewry : a classified bibliography. Westport, Conn. : Greenwood, 1993. 720 p. (Bibliographies and indexes in world history, no. 30).   **BC531**

A classified arrangement of 5,446 titles concerning the history and culture of the Jews in Spain and Portugal from antiquity to the present day. "Pays close attention to local Jewish history, Jewish-Christian polemics, and the portrayal of Spanish and Portuguese Jews in literature."—*Introd.* Excludes Hebrew literature and poetry, Rabbinical writings, biblical exegesis, philosophy, and general works on the Inquisition. Supplements and corrects, and adds titles omitted from the author's *The Jews in Spain and Portugal : a bibliography* (N.Y. : Garland, 1975). Together the two works list more than 10,000 titles, providing the most comprehensive, up-to-date bibliography on the subject. Index.   Z6373.S7S56

Stadtbibliothek Frankfurt am Main. Katalog der Judaica und Hebraica. Frankfurt am Main : M. Lehrberger, 1932. v. 1 (646 p.).   **BC532**

Contents: v. 1, Judaica, ed. by A. Freimann.

No more published.

Repr. : Graz : Akademische Druck- u. Verlagsantalt, 1968.

An extensive classified bibliography of primarily German materials on Jews and Judaism published before 1930. Includes many biblical commentaries and theology titles. Originally published as the catalog of an important collection, many volumes of which were destroyed in World War II.   Z6375.F83

Szajkowski, Zosa. Franco-Judaica : an analytical bibliography of books, pamphlets, decrees, briefs and other printed documents pertaining to the Jews in France, 1500–1788. N.Y. : Amer. Academy for Jewish Research, 1962. 160 p.   **BC533**

An annotated bibliography of more than 1,700 entries arranged topically. Those related to the history of Jews in French provinces are arranged under province name, with the remainder of the entries under headings such as Taxation, Bankrupticies, Marriage, and Credit. Many materials are related to legal status and court cases. Entries include archive and library locations.   Z6373.F7S9

Union of Soviet Socialist Republics

Fluk, Louise R. Jews in the Soviet Union : an annotated bibliography. N.Y. : American Jewish Committee, Inst. of Human Relations, [1975]. 44 p.   **BC534**

Nearly 300 books, pamphlets, periodicals, and articles in English, published between 1967 and 1974, selected for their significance and accessibility. Bibliographies, periodicals, books, and pamphlets are arranged by type. Articles are arranged under broad topics: History; Current situation; Response from abroad; and Emigration. Author index.   Z6373.R9F58

Kohen, Yitsḥaḳ Yosef. Jewish publications in the Soviet Union, 1917–1960 / bibliographies comp. and arr. by Y. Y. Cohen, with the assistance of M. Piekarz ... ed. by Kh. Shmeruk. Jerusalem : Historical Soc. of Israel, 1961. 143, 502 p.   **BC535**

In Hebrew; added title page, preface, and table of contents in English.

Lists Hebrew and Yiddish publications of the Soviet Union for the period indicated.

§ Supplemented by: *Russian publications on Jews and Judaism in the Soviet Union, 1917–1967 : a bibliography,* by B. Pinkus and A. A. Greenbaum; ed. by Mordechai Altshuler (Jerusalem : Soc. for Research on Jewish Communities, 1970. 273, 113 p.). Z7070.C68

Luckert, Yelena. Soviet Jewish history, 1917–1991 : an annotated bibliography. N.Y. : Garland, 1992. 271 p. (Garland reference library of social science, v. 611). **BC536**
For annotation, *see* DC587. Z6373.R9L83

Library catalogs

Harvard University. Library. Catalogue of Hebrew books. Cambridge : distr. by Harvard Univ. Pr., 1968. 6 v. **BC537**
Contents: v. 1–4, Authors and subjects (includes Bible, Talmud, Mishnah and other anonymous titles); v. 5–6, Titles.
Photoreproduction of catalog cards for the 40,000 Hebrew titles in the Harvard Judaica collection, which numbered approximately 100,000 volumes at the time of publication.
——. ——. *Supplement 1* (Cambridge, 1972. 3 v.).
Contents: v. 1, Classified listing. Appendix: Judaica in the Houghton Library; v. 2, Authors and selected subjects; v. 3, Titles.
§ Complemented by the Library's *Judaica : classification schedule, classified listing by call number, chronological listing, author and title listing* (Cambridge, 1971. 302 p. [Widener Library shelflist, v. 39]).
Lists about 9,000 titles in common European languages in the collection. An additional 1,725 items of rare Judaica from the Houghton Library (the cards for which are reproduced in the *Supplement*) are included in the chronological and alphabetical listings. For additional information concerning Widener shelflists, *see* AA115.

Hebrew Union College—Jewish Institute of Religion. American Jewish Archives. Guide to the holdings of the American Jewish Archives / by James W. Clasper and M. Carolyn Dellenbach. [Cincinnati] : American Jewish Archives, [1979]. 211 p. (American Jewish Archives. Publications, no. 11). **BC538**
Manuscript catalog of the American Jewish Archives was published 1971 (Boston . G. K. Hall. 4 v.) with 1978 (1 v.) and 1991 (51 microfiche) supplements, reproducing the catalog cards for the collection. The present volume provides a brief descriptive guide to that collection. In four sections: (1) Manuscript collections; (2) Microfilms from other repositories; (3) Theses, dissertations, and essays; and (4) Special files. Detailed index. Z6373.U5H43

Hebrew Union College—Jewish Institute of Religion. Library. Dictionary catalog of the Klau Library, Cincinnati. Boston : G. K. Hall, 1964. 32 v. **BC539**
Reproduces the catalog cards for this outstanding collection (about 200,000 items) with particular strengths in Bible, ancient Near East, Jewish music, Spinoza, and 15th and 16th century Judaica and Hebraica. The first 27 volumes represent the dictionary catalog of the collection; v. 28–32 offer a Hebrew-title catalog of all books and periodicals printed in Hebrew characters.
——. —— *Supplement—Hebrew titles. 1964–1971* [microform] (Cincinnati : The Library, 1981. 6 reels). Z6375.H4

New York Public Library. Reference Department. Dictionary catalog of the Jewish collection. Boston : G.K. Hall, 1960. 14 v. **BC540**
A photographic reproduction in book form of the cards from the catalog of one of the great Jewish collections of the world. Contains some 250,000 entries for books, periodicals, and analytics. Lists works in Hebrew and Yiddish, and in European languages, on the history and traditions of Jewish people in all times and countries.
——. ——. *Supplement 1* (Boston : G.K. Hall, 1975. 8 v.) adds materials cataloged through 1971, but with many omissions. Publications added to the collection through January 1, 1972, that were not listed in the 1960 catalog will be found in *Dictionary catalog of the*

Research Libraries of the New York Public Library (AA116). Cards for Hebrew-character titles that were omitted in photographing cards for the 1975 supplement are included in *Hebrew-character title catalog of the Jewish collection* (Boston : G.K. Hall, 1981. 4 v.), as are Hebrew-character titles from the 1960 dictionary catalog (v. 12–14) and the 1975 supplement (v. 7–8). Z6375.N6

Wiener Library, London. German Jewry : its history, life and culture. London : Vallentine, Mitchell, 1958–78. 2 v. (Wiener Library, London. Catalogue series, no. 3, 6). **BC541**
Contents: [Pt. 1], Publications (acquired by December 1956) on the history of German Jewry until 1945, ed. by Ilse R. Wolff; pt. 2, Additions and amendments, 1959–1972, ed. by Helen Kehr.
A detailed, classified bibliography of materials relating to the history and life of the German-speaking Jews of Germany, Austria, Czechoslavakia, and Switzerland. Although earlier works are included, most of the titles have been published since World War I. Pt. 2 adds 3,383 items, incorporates a new section on emigrant and expatriate Jews, and excludes materials on anti-Semitism and its defense, which may be found in the Wiener Library's catalog no. 5, *Prejudice : racist-religious-nationalist* (London : Vallentine, Mitchell [for the] Institute of Contemporary History, 1971), comp. and ed. by Helen Kehr. Index in each volume. Z6375.W5

Indexes

Index to Jewish periodicals. v. 1 (June 1963)– . [Cleveland Heights, etc. : Index to Jewish Periodicals, etc.], 1963– . Annual. **BC542**
Subtitle: An author and subject index to selected English language journals of general and scholarly interest.
Frequency varies; formerly semiannual. Numbered as a quarterly, but issues are double numbers, 1/2 covering July–Dec., 3/4 covering Jan.–June. Cumulated volume covers June 1963–May 1964; no further cumulations published. Vol. 26 (1988) publ. 1992; v. 27 (1989) publ. 1993. Volumes for subsequent years publ. in the year following coverage date.
Now indexes about 60 periodicals. Includes book reviews. Z6367.I5

Marcus, Jacob Rader. An index to scientific articles on American Jewish history. Cincinnati : American Jewish Archives, 1971. 240 p. (Publications of the American Jewish Archives, no. 7). **BC543**
An author-title-subject index to "the important articles in the scholarly Jewish periodicals dealing with the life, culture, and history of the American Jew."—*Pref.* Includes references to 13 periodicals from various periods, ranging from 1892–1968. Z6372.M35

Reshimat ma'arim be-mada'e ha-yahadut. Hov. 1 (726 [1966])– . Yerushalyim : Hotsaat sefarim al shem Y.L. Magnes-ha-Universitah ha Ivrit, 729 [i.e., 1968/69]– . Annual. **BC544**
Title also in English: Index of articles on Jewish studies.
In English and Hebrew.
An important index to materials in many languages, compiled from "thousands of periodicals and collections of articles … mainly from the holdings of the Jewish National and University Library."—*Foreword.* Strives to include all important articles published throughout the world on Judaica. Classified arrangement; author and subject indexes in Hebrew and English.

Schwab, Moïse. Index of articles relative to Jewish history and literature published in periodicals, from 1665 to 1900. Augm. ed. with an introd. and edited list of abbreviations, by Zosa Szajkowski. N.Y. : Ktav Publ. House, [1972]. 539, 409–613 p. **BC545**
A reprinting with additions, of Schwab's *Répertoire des articles relatifs à l'histoire et à la littérature juives, parus dans les périodiques, de 1665 à 1900* (Paris, 1914–23), an extensive bibliography of

articles in many languages arranged alphabetically by author. In addition to new introductory material, this edition includes a reproduction of the handwritten index of subjects and Hebrew words which appeared in a lithographed edition of 1900, but which was omitted from the later, printed volume. An errata list has also been added.

Z6366.S413

Encyclopedias

Encyclopaedia Judaica. [N.Y.] : Macmillan, [1971–72]. 16 v. : ill. **BC546**

An important work stemming from the unification of efforts to complete the old *Encyclopaedia Judaica : das Judentum in Geschichte und Gegenwart* (Berlin : Verlag Eschkol, [1928–34]. 10 v.). and to produce a new Jewish encyclopedia in English. Offers a comprehensive and up-to-date view of world Jewry in about 25,000 articles by an international list of contributors. Most articles are signed with initials; those contributed by internal editors are so designated. All but the briefest entries carry bibliographies (with preference given to English-language materials when quality studies are available in English). Living persons are included among the many biographees. Index of about 200,000 entries. A special section of supplementary entries incorporating new and updated information appears in v.16. Corrigenda section also in v. 16.

———. *Decennial book, 1973–1982 : events of 1972–1981* (Jerusalem : Encyclopedia Judaica, [1982]. 684 p.).

Covers the ten-year period subsequent to the publication of the *Encyclopaedia*, "incorporating the material of the *Year Books* along with a great deal of the new material."—*Introd.* Includes feature articles; new and updating articles, the latter with cross-references to the basic set; diary of events, 1973–81; necrology, Indexed.

———. *Yearbook* (1973– . Jerusalem : Encyclopaedia Judaica, [1973]– . Frequency varies).

1973 volume covers events of 1972, etc. Recent volumes cover two years.

In each volume, a section of feature articles is followed by an alphabetically-arranged section of "New facts, new entries," which offers supplementary information on matters treated in the basic work, as well as wholly new entries. The feature articles are lengthy essays by specialists on a wide range of topics, many of which are of special interest at the time of publication. Indexed.

§ Another earlier standard encyclopedia in English, with signed articles by specialists and with bibliographies, is *Jewish encyclopedia*, prep. under the direction of Cyrus Adler [et al.] ; Isidore Singer, managing ed. (N.Y. : Funk & Wagnalls, 1901–1906. 12 v. : ill.). Now out-of-date, but still useful for its biographies and other historical information. Repr.: N.Y. : Ktav, [1964?]. DS102.8.E496

The encyclopedia of Judaism / ed. in chief Geoffrey Wigoder. N.Y. : Macmillan ; London : Collier Macmillan, c1989. 768 p. : ill. (some col.). **BC547**

Concise articles on aspects of Jewish religious life and development contributed, but not signed, by 78 authorities. Intended for students and general readers. Attempts to give a balanced picture of various trends, schools of thought, and religious practices. Includes only those "outstanding individuals who have contributed to the development of Judaism."—*Pref.*

§ *The encyclopedia of the Jewish religion*, ed. by R. J. Zwi Werblowsky and Geoffrey Wigoder (New rev. ed. N.Y. : Adama Books, c1986) offers similar information, but is stronger in biography. BM50.E63

Encyclopedia of Zionism and Israel / Raphael Patai, ed. N.Y. : Herzl Pr., 1971. 2 v. : ill. **BC548**

Concerned with the history and development of the Zionist movement and its constituent organizations throughout the world. With the exception of a general historical survey article, the material on Israel concentrates on the modern period (i.e., beginning with the latter half of the 19th century). There are brief entries for places in Israel. Biographies are limited mainly to Zionist leaders and Israeli statesmen and

public officials; articles on persons who achieved fame in other areas deal primarily with their Zionist activities. About 3,000 articles; most of the longer ones are signed. Selective bibliography at the end of v. 2.

DS149.E597

Encyclopedia Talmudica : a digest of halachic literature and Jewish law from the Tannaitic period to the present time, alphabetically arr[anged] … / ed.: Shlomo Josef Zevin … ; English tr. and ed. by Isidore Epstein and Harry Freedman. Jerusalem : Talmudic Encyclopedia Inst., [1969–1992]. v. 1–4. (In progress). **BC549**

Contents: v. 1–4, 'Aleph–B'reyah.

A translation of *Entsiklopedyah talmudit*.

Intended as a "comprehensive presentation … of all Halakhic subjects dealt with in the Talmud and in post-Talmudic Rabbinic literature" (*Introd.*), with indication of sources, reasonings, and variations of opinion relevant to each subject. Arrangement is according to the Hebrew alphabet of the original work, but an English table of contents and subject index are supplied in each volume. BM500.5.E613

Encyclopédie de la mystique juive. Paris : Berg International, [1977]. 1528 col. : ill. **BC550**

"Ouvrage réalisé sous la direction de Armand Abécassis et Georges Nataf."—*t.p.*

Offers articles on various aspects of Jewish mysticism. French translations of relevant texts accompany the articles, and bibliographies are appended. BM723.E58

Jewish-American history and culture : an encyclopedia / ed. by Jack Fischel and Sanford Pinsker. N.Y. : Garland, 1992. 710 p. : music. (Garland reference library of social science, v. 429.). **BC551**

People, organizations, events, and topics have been selected for their importance and "to survey the distinctive experience of Jews in America."—*Pref.* Signed articles, with brief bibliographies, vary in length, substance and style. An introductory table arranges entries thematically. Fills a needed gap, but is not truly comprehensive. Index.

E184.J5J48

The new standard Jewish encyclopedia / Geoffrey Wigoder, ed. in chief. 6th new rev. ed. N.Y. : Facts on File, 1992. 1001 p. : ill. **BC552**

1st ed., 1959; 5th ed., 1977. Earlier eds. had title: *The standard Jewish encyclopedia*. Edition statement taken from book preface; elsewhere called 7th ed.

A compilation of concise factual and biographical information, intended primarily as a work of contemporary reference, places special emphasis on recent developments in Jewish history, and on the American community and the state of Israel, but also "covering every phase of Jewish life, literature, and thought from their beginning."—*Pref.* Biographical sketches include living persons.

§ Articles and biographies related to Jewish artistic, literary, musical, and intellectual activity may also be found in *The Blackwell companion to Jewish culture : from the eighteenth century to the present*, ed. by Glenda Abramson (Oxford ; Cambridge, Mass. : Blackwell Reference, c1989. 853 p.). DS102.8.S73

Dictionaries

Cohn-Sherbok, Dan. The Blackwell dictionary of Judaica. Oxford : Blackwell Reference, 1992. 597 p. : maps. **BC553**

Brief definitions of terms, places, and concepts from Jewish history, civilization, and religion; intended to provide information most commonly sought. Includes many short biographies for persons whose lives or work are connected to Judaism. BM50.C615

A dictionary of the Jewish-Christian dialogue / ed. by Leon Klenicki and Geoffrey Wigoder. N.Y. ; Ramsey, N.J. : Paulist Pr., c1984. 213 p. **BC554**

Brief essays, presented in pairs, by Jewish and Christian specialists, on 34 English words, such as "covenant," "law," and "messiah," which are used in both religious traditions, but understood differently. The headwords, with their interpretive essays, are arranged in alphabetical order. Index of Hebrew terms and subject index. BM50.D53

Unterman, Alan. Dictionary of Jewish lore and legend. N.Y. : Thames and Hudson, 1991. 216 p. : ill. **BC555**
Seeks to contribute to a fuller picture of Judaism as "it is lived by the traditional scholar and layman alike."—*Introd.* Material has been drawn from "Midrashic, Talmudic, Zoharic, Kabbalistic, Chasidic, halakhic and magical texts ... [and the] stores of localized folklore which are the life-blood of the Ashkenazi and Sephardi cultures." 222 black-and-white photographs. BM50.U58

Concordances

Charlesworth, James H. Graphic concordance to the Dead Sea scrolls / by James H. Charlesworth with R. E. Whitaker ... [et al.]. Tübingen : J.C.B. Mohr (P. Siebeck) ; Louisville : Westminster/John Knox Pr., c1991. 529 p. **BC556**
Introductory material in English; concordance in the original Hebrew and Aramaic.
Presents Qumran words, forms, and phrases as they actually appear in all sectarian texts published before 1990, a total of 223 texts and some 3,500 fragments. The "concordance furnishes an important databank for Hebrew Bible scholars who specialize in late biblical Hebrew and for rabbinic scholars who do research in Mishnaic Hebrew."—*Pref.* When new translations and critical editions are completed an analytical concordance will be prepared. BM487.G66

Handbooks

Birnbaum, Philip. A book of Jewish concepts. Rev. ed. N.Y. : Hebrew Publ. Co., [1975]. 722 p. **BC557**
1st ed., 1964.
Also publ. under title: *Encyclopedia of Jewish concepts* (N.Y. : Hebrew Publ. Co., c1979. Repr., 1991).
Aims "to provide in a single handy volume the essential teachings of Judaism."—*Introd.* Arrangement is alphabetical according to the Hebrew form of the term, with an English translation or transliteration provided for each term; Hebrew and English indexes. Articles range in length from a brief paragraph to two or more pages. Intended for rabbis, teachers, students and laymen. BM50.B55

Himelstein, Shmuel. The Jewish primer : questions and answers on Jewish faith and culture. N.Y. : Facts on File, c1990. 254 p. : ill. **BC558**
Addresses many common questions concerning beliefs and practices related to topics such as ritual objects, fast days, clothing, the Sabbath, dietary laws, and holy days. Intended to aid Jews and non-Jews in understanding the tenets of traditional Judaism. Topical arrangement with subject index. BM51.H49 1990

Reform Judaism in America : a biographical dictionary and sourcebook / ed. by Kerry M. Olitzky, Lance J. Sussman, and Malcolm H. Stern. Westport, Conn. : Greenwood, 1993. 347 p. **BC559**
Provides a short history of Reform Judaism; essays on its primary institutions; lists of the presidents of the denomination's organizations; biographies of national leaders who have emerged since 1976. The biographies include references to works by and about the biographee. Index.
§ Companion to Pamela S. Nadell's *Conservative Judaism in America: a biographical dictionary and sourcebook* (N.Y. : Greenwood, c1988). These works are two of a projected three-volume series, "Jewish denominations in America." BM750.R39

Trepp, Leo. The complete book of Jewish observance. N.Y. : Summit Books, [1980]. 370 p. : ill. **BC560**
Intended as an aid to Jews in studying their heritage and in performing the commandments, practices, ceremonies, and rituals of Judaism. In two main sections, the first following the Jewish year, the second the cycle of life. Individual festivals, rites, and ceremonies are discussed in their historical context; attention is given to modern developments and to variations in practice among Orthodox, Conservative, Reform, and Reconstructionist Jews. Indexed.
§ See also Isaac Klein's *Guide to Jewish religious practice* (N.Y. : Jewish Theological Seminary of America ; distr. by Ktav Publ. House, 1979. 588 p.) for Conservative Jewish practice. Includes "all the rules and regulations that observant Jews regard as norms, and on which they usually seek guidance from their rabbis."—*Pref.* Bibliography; index. BM690.T73

History

Baron, Salo Wittmayer. A social and religious history of the Jews. 2nd ed., rev. and enl. N.Y. : Columbia Univ. Pr., 1952–83. 18 v. **BC561**
1st ed., 1937, in 3 v.
Contents: v. 1–2, Ancient times; v. 3–8, High Middle Ages, 500–1200; v. 3, Heirs of Rome and Persia; v. 4, Meeting of East and West; v. 5, Religious controls and discussions; v. 6, Laws, homilies, and the Bible; v. 7, Hebrew language and letters; v. 8, Philosophy and science; v. 9–18, Late Middle Ages and era of European expansion: v. 9, Under Church and Empire; v. 10, On the Empire's periphery; v. 11, Citizen or alien conjurer; v. 12, Economic catalyst; v. 13, Inquisition, Renaissance, and Reformation; v. 14, Catholic restoration and wars of religion; v. 15, Resettlement and exploration; v. 16, Poland-Lithuania 1500–1650; v. 17, Byzantines, Mamelukes, and Maghribians; v. 18, The Ottoman Empire, Persia, Ethiopia, India, and China.
Covers from ancient times to 1650. Studies the history of the Jews in the various countries and societies in which they have lived. Each volume includes "Notes" (explanations, descriptions, and references to sources).
Indexes to v. 1–8 and v. 9–18 published separately. DS112.B315

The Cambridge history of Judaism / ed. by W.D. Davies, Louis Finkelstein. Cambridge ; N.Y. : Cambridge Univ. Pr., 1984–89. v. 1–2. (In progress). **BC562**
Contents: v. 1, The Persian period; v. 2, The Hellenistic age.
Presents a scholarly history incorporating the "new data provided by archaeology, new knowledge of the Apocryphal, Pseudepigraphical, Qumranic and Gnostic writings, and recent critical work on the Rabbinic sources" in chapters by scholars chosen "from various religious and non-religious backgrounds, and from various countries, so that the work may be truly ecumenical and international."—*Pref.* To cover from the Babylonian exile to the codification of the Mishnah, and to include extensive background on the context in which Judaism developed. Footnotes appear with the text; chapter bibliographies are at the back of the book. To be in four volumes; succeeding volumes are to cover the Roman period to CE 70, and CE 70 to CE 235. Index; chronological tables. BM155.2.C35

Yearbooks

American Jewish year book. v. 1 (1899/1900)– . Philadelphia [etc.] : American Jewish Committee, 1899– . Annual. **BC563**
Volumes for 1899/1900–1948/49 issued by the Jewish Publication Society of America.
1899/1900–1948/49 also called 5660–5709.
Contains important directory and statistical information, and a review of the year's events relating to Jewish matters in America and

other countries. Each volume contains special articles, biographies, necrologies, and bibliographies. Many of these from earlier issues continue to have reference value. Vol. 40 includes a subject index to special
articles in v. 1–40; v. 86 a similar index for v. 51–85. Each subsequent
volume includes a ten-year index.   E184.J5A6

Jewish year book : an annual record of matters Jewish. v. 1
(1896)– . London : Jewish Chronicle Publ., 1896– . Annual.
       BC564
    Contains statistical and institutional information for the British
Commonwealth, bibliographies, and a who's who.   DS135.E5A3

Biography

The concise dictionary of American Jewish biography /
Jacob Rader Marcus, ed. ; Judith M. Daniels, assoc. ed. Brooklyn, N. Y. : Carlson Publ., 1994. 1 v.   **BC565**
    "Consists of almost 24,000 brief biographies of American Jews. It
is by far the largest such biographical dictionary ever undertaken. All
of these individuals are notable in that their names were taken from
standard sources for American Jewish biography."—*How to use The
concise dictionary.* "Jewish" names were also selected from sources
such as *Who was who in America* and *Notable American women.* The
very short entries include conflicting information from sources consulted, along with references to all sources used. Originally intended to
include only individuals deceased through 1985, coverage has been extended to hundreds of individuals for whom obituaries were not found.
       E184.J5C653

Wininger, Salomon. Grosse jüdische National-Biographie :
mit mehr als 8,000 Lebensbeschreibungen namhafter jüdischer
Männer und Frauen aller Zeiten und Länder / ein Nachschlagewerk für das jüdische Volk und dessen Freunde. Nendeln :
Kraus, 1979. 7 v.   **BC566**
    Reprint of the edition publ. in Cernăuti (Ukraine) by various pub-
lishers between 1925 and 1936.
    Issued in parts.
    Contents: v. 1–5, A–St; v. 6, St–Z, Nachträge, A–Geldern; v. 7
(incomplete), Geiler–Z, 2. Nachträge, A–Fink. No more published.
    An international biographical dictionary of Jews primarily from
the Middle Ages to the 20th century, with a few of earlier date. The
number of sketches noted in the title varies from 8,000 to 12,000.
       DS115.W5

NATIVE AMERICAN RELIGIONS

Hirschfelder, Arlene B. The encyclopedia of Native Ameri-
can religions / Arlene Hirschfelder, Paulette Molin. N.Y. :
Facts on File, c1992. 367 p. : ill.   **BC567**
    In response to the "lack of reliable information about Native
American religion in conventional reference books" (*Pref*), the authors
present introductory information, from published sources, on many
Canadian and U.S. Native ceremonies and rituals, sacred sites, and
practitioners, and Christian missionaries who have influenced Native
American spiritual traditions. Cosmologies, stories of deities, chants,
prayers, etc., are not included. Entries emphasize contemporary religious forms, but include historical information. Out of respect for Native peoples, articles avoid detailed descriptions of rituals and ceremonies, even in cases where such information has been previously published. Entries omit bibliographies; a lengthly bibliography appears at
the end of the volume. Useful as an introductory resource.
       E98.R3H73

SHINTŌ

Herbert, Jean. Bibliographie du Shintô et des sectes shintôistes. Leiden : Brill, 1968. 73 p.   **BC568**
    An author listing of more than 1,100 books and articles in many
languages. Japanese titles are given also in French. Subject index.
       Z7835.S5H4

Holtom, Daniel Clarence. The national faith of Japan : a
study in modern Shinto. London : K. Paul, Trench, Trubner,
1938. 329 p.   **BC569**
    Printed in Japan.
    A good historical survey with bibliographical footnotes.
       BL2220.H58

Kato, Genchi. A bibliography of Shinto in Western languages : from the oldest times till 1952 / comp. by Genchi Kato,
Karl Reitz, and Wilhelm Schiffer. Tokyo : Meiji Jingu
Shamusho, 1953. 58 p.   **BC570**
    Books and articles publ. to 1940 are listed alphabetically, with a
subject index. Appendix, prep. by Rev. Wilhelm Schiffer, lists books
and articles on Shintō publ. 1941–52.   Z7835.S5K3

Schwade, Arcadio. Shintō-bibliography in western languages : bibliography on Shintō and religious sects, intellectual
schools and movements influenced by Shintōism. Leiden :
Brill, 1986. 124 p.   **BC571**
    Lists in alphabetical order 2,006 monographs and articles, most
published in English, French, or German in the 20th century. Topical
index.   Z7835.S5S38

SIKHISM

See also BC576.

Cole, W. Owen. A popular dictionary of Sikhism / W. Owen
Cole and Piara Singh Sambhi. London : Curzon ; Glenn Dale,
Md. : Riverdale Co, 1990. 163 p. : maps.   **BC572**
    Offers information on major concepts, beliefs, practices, histori-
cal events and important persons.   BL2018

Rai, Priya Muhar. Sikhism and the Sikhs : an annotated bibliography. N.Y. : Greenwood, 1989. 257 p. (Bibliographies and
indexes in religious studies, no. 13).   **BC573**
    A classified, annotated bibliography of 1,150 scholarly books and
articles written in English since 1965. Includes material on immigrant
Sikhs in the U.S., but lacks references to such groups as Sikh Dharma,
which have attracted many American followers. Author, title, and subject indexes.   Z7835.S64R34

ZOROASTRIANISM

Boyce, Mary. Zoroastrians : their religious beliefs and practices. London ; Boston : Routledge & Kegan Paul, 1979. 252 p.
       BC574
    Presents the history of Zoroastrianism from its beginnings to the
20th century. Offered as an introduction to the subject for university
religion students. Short bibliography, chiefly of English-language
sources. Indexed.
    § A more detailed work by the same author, to be in several vol-
umes, has begun publication as *A history of Zoroastrianism* (Leiden :
Brill, 1975–1991. v. 1–3. (In progress]).   BL1525.B695

Oxtoby, Willard Gurdon. Ancient Iran and Zoroastrianism in festschriften : an index. Waterloo, Ont. : Council on the Study of Religion, Waterloo Lutheran Univ. ; Shiraz, Iran : Asia Institute of Pahlavi Univ., 1973. 207 p. (Bibliographic studies in religion, no. 1 ; Asia Institute of Pahlavi University. Monograph series, no. 3). **BC575**

"Lists 1808 articles," chiefly in Western languages, "which have appeared in 421 Festschriften between 1875 and 1973."—*Introd.* Classified subject arrangement with author index and list of the festschriften fully identified. Outline of subject headings defines topics and aids in reference use. Besides religion, includes history, archaeology, and language. Z7835.Z8O95

Textual sources for the study of Zoroastrianism / ed. and tr. by Mary Boyce. Totowa, N.J., Barnes & Noble; Manchester, Univ. Pr., 1984. 166 p. : ill. **BC576**

Repr. : Chicago : U. of Chicago Pr., c1990.

Presents a selection of "ancient texts … retranslated for this anthology" (*Foreword*), together with some modern texts that bear on Zoroastrianism. Includes an introductory background chapter, bibliography, and glossarial index.

§ A companion work is the editor's *Zoroastrians* (BC574).

W.H. McLeod has translated and edited the similar *Textual sources for the study of Sikhism* (Manchester, Eng. : Univ. Pr., c1984). His selection of scriptural and liturgical texts provides new authoritative translations for students. BL1571.T44

Zaehner, Robert Charles. The dawn and twilight of Zoroastrianism. London : Weindenfeld and Nicolson, [1961]. 371 p. : ill. **BC577**

Scholarly in tone, but intended as a work for nonspecialist readers on the history and essential features of Zoroastrianism. A critical bibliography reviews translations of sacred texts and secondary writings. Index. BL1571.Z3

BD

Languages, Linguistics, Philology

LANGUAGES: GENERAL WORKS

Bibliography

Bibliographie Linguistischer Literatur : BLL. Bd.4 (1978)– . Frankfurt am Main : V. Klostermann, 1979– . Annual. **BD1**

Subtitle: Bibliographie zur allgemeinen Linguistik und zur anglistischen, germanistischen und romanistischen Linguistik.

Issued by Sondersammelgebiet Linguistik der Stadt- und Universitätsbibliothek, Frankfurt am Main.

Introductory matter and section headings in English and German.

In four main sections: (1) General linguistics; (2) German linguistics; (3) English linguistics; and (4) Romance linguistics, with appropriate subdivisions for each. International in scope, with coverage of a long list of periodicals and analysis of numerous collective works.

§ Continues: *Bibliographie unselbständiger Literatur-Linguistik (BUL-L)*, bearb. von Elke Suchan (Bd. 1–3 ([1971/75–77]. Frankfurt am Main : V. Klostermann, [1976–78]). A classed bibliography of periodical articles, essays in collections, proceedings of congresses, etc., arranged by language with detailed subject arrangement within each language. Author and subject indexes. Concerned only with Western languages.

•Machine-readable version: *Bibliographie Linguistischer Literatur : (BLL)* [database] (Frankfurt am Main : Stadt- und Universitätsbibliothek Frankfurt, 1971–). Available online, updated annually. Includes both printed counterparts above.

Bibliographie Sprache und Literatur : deutschsprachige Hochschulschriften und Veröffentlichungen ausserhalb des Buchhandels 1966–1980 / [Redaktion, Irene Butt und Monika Eichler]. München ; N.Y. : Saur, 1992. 8 v. (3226 p.). **BD2**

A bibliography of German-language grey literature related to language and literature for 1966–80, part of a series in various subject areas covering material distributed outside normal book trade channels. Includes dissertations, publications of institutes, private imprints, book club editions, and the like.

Geographical coverage is for all of German-speaking Europe, including both Germanys, Austria, and Switzerland, as well as German-language publications identified elsewhere. Lists some 42,000 titles in alphabetical order by title, subarranged by author or other responsible body, year and place of publication, etc. Introduction in German and English. Two indexes: persons/corporate bodies, and subjects (permuted keywords from titles).

DeMiller, Anna L. Linguistics : a guide to the reference literature. Englewood, Colo. : Libraries Unlimited, 1991. 256 p. **BD3**

An annotated list of 708 selected bibliographies and other reference sources, published primarily 1957–89, in three main sections with subdivisions: (1) General linguistics, subdivided by format and genre (e.g., biographies, online/CD-ROM databases, core periodicals); (2) Allied areas (Anthropological, Applied, Mathematical/computational, Psycholinguistics, Semiotics); (3) Languages (beginning with general and multilanguage works, followed by language families and areal aggregates such as Indo-European and Uralo-Altaic, concluding with artificial and Pidgin/Creole languages). Includes bibliographies of dictionaries. Author, title, and subject indexes.

Intended for a variety of users—students, librarians, specialists in linguistics and language. Annotations are thorough, helpful, and evaluative, frequently making comparisons between similar sources. A core reference work. Some peculiarities: works on Semitic languages are listed under "Afro-Asiatic," which includes one work on Semitic, two on Arabic, one each on Berber and Ethiopian Semitic, but none on Hebrew; and listings under individual languages and language families are highly selective. For better coverage of the latter, *see* Rudolph C. Troike, *Bibliography of bibliographies of the languages of the world* (BD8). Z7001.D45

Gazdar, Gerald. A bibliography of contemporary linguistic research / comp. by Gerald Gazdar, Ewan Klein, Geoffrey K. Pullum. N.Y. : Garland, 1978. 425 p. (Garland reference library of the humanities, v. 119). **BD4**

An author list of some 5,000 entries covering the period 1970–78, listing articles and short notes drawn from scholarly journals, conference proceedings, specialist anthologies and litho-printed books, chiefly on the central topics of linguistics: syntactic, semantic, philological and pragmatic theory. Language and subject indexes. Z7001.G38

Girke, Wolfgang. Handbibliographie zur neueren Linguistik in Osteuropa / Wolfgang Girke, Helmut Jachnow, Josef Schrenk. München : Wilhelm Fink Verlag, c1974–1988. 3 v. in 4. **BD5**

Contents: Bd. 1, covers 1963–65 (1974); Bd. 2, 1966–71; Bd. 3, pts. 1–2. 1972–77 (1988).

Title on spine varies: Bd. 1, Linguistiche Bibliographie, 1963–1965; Bd. 2–3, Handbibliographie der Linguistik in Osteuropa. Bd. 2–3 have title: Handbibliographie zur slavistischen und allgemeinen Linguistik in Osteuropa.

A classed unannotated listing of monographs and articles published in Eastern Europe and the U.S.S.R., primarily in Slavic and other East European languages (titles in Cyrillic are romanized). Vol. 1 contains nearly 6,000 entries; v. 2, more than 18,000; v. 3, more than 27,000. Covers a broad range of subjects in general and applied linguistics, but is particularly strong in Slavic linguistics. Classed arrangement by some 26–30 categories (e.g., History of linguistics, Phonology, Grammatical categories). The number and nature of categories vary slightly over the three volumes published to date; they are subdivided into detailed subsections. Headings in the tables of contents and in the listings are given in German, Russian, and English. Author indexes only (v. 1 includes persons as the subjects of studies; v. 1–3 list authors only). Since there is no indexing by language or other subject, the only subject access is through the classified arrangement.

Z7001.G57

Gosudarstvennaĭa biblioteka SSSR imeni V.I. Lenina. Bibliografiĭa bibliografiĭ po ĭazykoznaniĭu : annotirovannyĭ sistematicheskiĭ ukazatel' otechestvennykh izdaniĭ / [Sost.: E. I. Kukushkina i A. G. Stepanova]. Moskva, 1963. 411 p. **BD6**

A classified Russian-language list of more than 2,000 monograph and article-length bibliographies in the fields of general and applied linguistics, individual languages and language families, the history of linguistics, and biobibliography of linguistics. A general section covering both theoretical areas is followed by a larger section on languages of the world arranged by language family or geographical area. Also includes separate bibliographic lists covering individual situations, indexes and surveys of the contents of periodicals, and dissertations. Access to the numbered entries is through the classified arrangement, or through two indexes: one of personal names (including persons as subjects) and titles, and another of languages. Z7001.M65

Obshchee i prikladnoe ĭazykoznaniye : ukazatel' literatury, 1968–1977 gg / [sostaviteli B. A. Malinskia, M. TS. Shabat]. Moskva : Institut Nauchnoi Informatsii po Obshchestvennym Naukam, Akademiĭa Nauk SSSR, 1981–86. 13 pts. (In progress). **BD7**

Title translated: General and applied linguistics : an index for the literature for 1968–1977.

A Russian-language list of books and articles in general and applied linguistics published in the Soviet Union, 1968–77. Each part is devoted to a thematic area in a classed arrangement with a detailed table of contents. Pt. 13 contains addenda and general indexes consisting of tables of contents to all parts and a general subject index.

§ Continues a series of bibliographies; volumes previously published:

Obshchee iazikoznaniye : bibliograficheskii ukazatel' literatury, izdannoi v SSSR s 1918–1962 [General linguistics : bibliography of literature published in the USSR in 1918–1962] (1965).

Strukturnoe i prokladnoe iazykoznanie : bibliograficheskii ukazatel' literatury, izdannoi v SSSR s 1918–1962 [Structural and applied linguistics : bibliography of literature published in the USSR in 1918–1962] (1965).

Obshchee i prikladnoe iazikoznanie : ukazatel' literatury, izdannoi v SSSR s 1963 po 1967 [General and applied linguistics : bibliography of literature published in the USSR in 1963 through 1967], sost. B. A. Malinskaĭa i M.TS. Shabat (1972). Z7001.M33

Troike, Rudolph C. Bibliography of bibliographies of the languages of the world. Amsterdam ; Philadelphia : J. Benjamins Publ. Co., 1990. v. 1. (Amsterdam studies in the theory and history of linguistic science. Series V, Library and information sources in linguistics, v. 19). (In progress). **BD8**

Contents: v. 1, General and Indo-European languages of Europe.

An extensive annotated listing of bibliographies on individual languages and language families published through 1985, with some handbooks and historiographic works; focus is on languages, not linguistics. Excluded are: bibliographies of language teaching, semiotics, history of linguistics or general linguistic theory, catalogs of library collections, fugitive works, and works dealing only with language. Vol. 1 consists of 2,562 numbered entries that focus mainly on bibliographies for the Indo-European languages of Europe. Entries give full bibliographic data. English translation is added for most titles in Slavic, Baltic, and Albanian. Annotations attempt to indicate for each listed title: number of entries, arrangement, extent and type of annotation, indexes, relation to other entries (continuation, superseding, etc.). Sections are prefaced with helpful scope and *see also* notes. Particularly useful for reference and research collections. Vol. 2 is to complete the set with coverage of "all of the remaining 4,500 languages of the world."—*Introd.*

§ For coverage of theoretical linguistics, *see*: Anna L. DeMiller, *Linguistics : a guide to the reference literature* (BD3). Z7001.T78

Wares, Alan Campbell. Bibliography of the Summer Institute of Linguistics. Dallas, Tex. : The Institute ; distr. by International Academic Bookstore, 1992. 603 p. **BD9**

Lists publications directly sponsored by the Institute or those published elsewhere by Institute members, 1935–91, in the areas of lingusitics, anthropology, literacy, and community development. Also registers Bible translations and other Bible-related publications in all vernaculars. In two sections: Academic, arranged alphabetically by author, and Vernacular, arranged by language of publications; each section has its own list of abbreviations. Indexes by language and subject.

Supersedes the previous edition, which covered 1935–82 (1979–85).

§ Incorporates an updated version of Wares's *Bibliography of the Wycliffe Bible Translators* (Santa Ana, Calif. : Wycliffe Bible Translators, 1970), giving access to Bible texts and related material, which were omitted from the previous edition. Z7005.S86

Handbooks

ALA-LC romanization tables : transliteration schemes for non-Roman scripts / approved by the Library of Congress and the American Library Association ; tables comp. and ed. by Randall K. Barry. Wash. : Cataloging Distribution Service, Library of Congress, 1991. 216 p. : ill. **BD10**

Contains transliteration tables of recommended Roman-alphabet equivalences for 140 languages of the world that use other writing systems, e.g., Arabic, Chinese, Greek, Hebrew, Japanese, Russian, Sanskrit. The schemes are in alphabetical order by language (including an extended summary of modified versions of the Cyrillic alphabet used for non-Slavic languages of the former Soviet Union); they were developed as part of an ongoing process for use at the Library of Congress and in other U.S. libraries, in cooperation with a variety of language specialists and the American Library Association. Earlier versions of the majority of these schemes have been published previously in LC's *Cataloging service bulletin*; this edition supersedes all earlier versions.

In addition to transliteration proper, other related information is included as relevant for a given language, such as characteristics of capitalization and word division. Includes a complete list of basic and modified characters needed for transcription, together with Hex Codes (for encoding the characters in USMARC records) and standard names of the characters. Instructions are also given for differentiating similar characters, and for handling character-modifying diacritics. Detailed index by alphabet.

§ A bibliography of various transcription and transliteration systems which is still useful is: Hans Wellisch, *Transcription and transliteration : an annotated bibliography on conversion of scripts* (Silver Spring, Md. : Inst. of Modern Languages, 1975).

For phonetic transcription, *see* G.K. Pullum and W.A. Ladusaw, *Phonetic symbol guide* (BD15). P226.A4

Allen, Charles Geoffry. A manual of European languages for librarians. [2nd impression (with minor corrections)]. London ; N.Y. : Bowker in assoc. with the London School of Economics, [1977]. 803 p. **BD11**

1st impression, 1975.

Intended as an aid for librarians responsible for interpreting publications in less familiar languages. Gives basic orthographic, grammatical, syntactic, and lexical information for each of 38 languages of Western, Central, and Eastern Europe and some peripheral areas, including Latin/Greek (classical, post-classical, and modern), selected languages of the Romance, Germanic, Celtic, Slavic, Baltic, Finno-Ugric families, and Albian, Maltese, Turkish, and Basque, with a note on Esperanto. For each language a general brief introduction is followed by an analysis of title-page usage, conventions for authors' names, titles, numeration, edition and imprint statements, series and periodicals, with a short systematic grammar and a glossary of basic words and grammatical endings. For Greek and Cyrillic orthographies romanization is covered as well. For the languages it covers, generally more detailed than Georg F. Von Ostermann's *Manual of foreign languages for the use of librarians* ... (BD17) but the latter sometimes provides useful added detail.   P380.A4

Campbell, George L. Compendiums of the world's languages. London ; N.Y. : Routledge, 1991. 2 v. (1574 p.).   **BD12**

Summarizes grammatical structures of about 300 languages and language families modern and ancient, listed alphabetically (language families are interfiled with individual languages). In general, articles follow a standard format: introduction (affiliation, location, speakers, dialects, literature), script, phonology (given in International Phonetic Alphabet notation for living languages), morphology and syntax, and an illustrative text. Includes an "Appendix of scripts," 48 writing systems depicted in alphabetical order by English name.

§ An older work that still retains value is: Antoine Meillet and Marcel Cohen, *Langues du monde* (Nouv. ed. Paris : Centre National de la Recherche Scientifique, 1952).   P371.C36

Ethnologue. 1951– . Dallas, Tex. : Summer Institute of Linguistics, [1951]– . Irregular.   **BD13**

A list by country and geographic region of the known languages and dialects of the world (6,528 in the 12th ed.) and all their variant name forms, with many accompanying maps. The separate index volume gives an alphabetical listing of all language and dialect names and their alternate forms. Also given for each language: estimated number of mother-tongue speakers; primary country of location; dialects; linguistic affiliation; multilingualism of speakers; Bible translation status; and other relevant demographic and sociolinguistic information. Includes extensive bibliography, country index, tables of maps, and guide to "Languages of special interest" (Gypsy languages, etc.). Pie charts show geographical distribution of living languages (by continent and other major geographic region) and Bible translation status. The data are all drawn from a computerized sociolinguistic database maintained by the Summer Institute of Linguistics.

§ For equivalent names of languages and dialects in English, German, French, Italian and Russian, *see*: A. Klose, *Sprachen der Welt = Languages of the world : a multi-lingual concordance of languages, dialects and language-families* (München ; N.Y. : K.G. Saur, 1987). A greater range of sociolinguistic information can be found in *Written languages of the world : a survey of the degree and modes of use* (Quebec : Presses de l'Univ. Laval ; Forest Grove, Ore : distr. by ISBS, 1978– . [In progress]).   P371.E83

Gilīarevskii, R. S. Languages identification guide / R. S. Gilyarevsky, V. S. Grivnin. Moscow : Nauka; Central Dept. of Oriental Literature, 1970. 343 p.   **BD14**

Translation of: *Opredelitel' īazykov mira po pis'mennostīam.*

A field guide to identifying languages by samples of writing. Gives identifying features of some 200 of the world's languages, living and dead, by alphabet and peculiarities of orthography, combinations of diacritic marks or other letterforms, frequently occurring letter combinations, or other characteristic written features. The Introduction includes a recommended step-by-step identification procedure. Languages are listed by geographic and national location (languages of the former USSR grouped first, followed by languages of Europe, Asia and Oceania, Africa, and America and International artificial languages), with a sample of printed text and a model alphabet or other writing system for each. Includes an inventory of writing systems with accompanying lists of languages that use each; lists of Cyrillic and Roman alphabet letters, of characteristic letter combinations, and of characteristic auxiliary words; varying book hands and print types; number systems; guides to languages by geographic location and by genetic classification; a table of name equivalents; and an index by language name.   P213.G4913

Pullum, Geoffrey K. Phonetic symbol guide / Geoffrey K. Pullum and William A. Ladusaw. Chicago : Univ. of Chicago Pr., 1986. 266 p. : ill.   **BD15**

A guide to phonetic transcription of sounds of the languages of the world. Includes listings of phonetic symbols, with a letter-by-letter survey of standard and proposed uses of basic and modified letters of the Latin alphabet, a list of diacritic marks with their conventional names, a glossary of basic phonetic terminology, and structural symbol charts of typical vowel and consonant systems according to the International Phonetic Alphabet and other transcriptions. List of bibliographic references; initial table of entries.   P221.P85

Ruhlen, Merritt. A guide to the world's languages. Stanford, Calif. : Stanford Univ. Pr., 1987. v. 1. (In progress).   **BD16**

A detailed study of the genetic interrelationship and classification of the languages of the world. Amplifies and brings up to date the author's *Guide to the languages of the world* (Stanford : Stanford Univ. Pr., 1976) and incorporates and updates information from Charles Frederick Voegelin and Florence M. Voegelin, *Classification and index of the world's languages* (N.Y. : Elsevier, [1977]. 658 p.).

In addition to a detailed language classification, includes extended discussion of the history of discovery and reconstruction of the interrelationship among languages, and methodological issues and problems in doing so. Three volumes are projected; v. 2 will treat "language data ... for a broad sample of the world's languages," and v. 3 will survey "basic linguistic patterns that characterize human language around the world."—*Pref.* Intended for educated general readers. Topical bibliographies; indexes of personal names, language families and other groups, individual languages and dialects.   P203.R8

Von Ostermann, Georg Frederick. Manual of foreign languages for the use of librarians, bibliographers, research workers, editors, translators, and printers. 4th ed., rev. and enl. N.Y. : Central Book Co., 1952. 414 p · ill   **BD17**

A useful manual of concise information about some 130 languages and dialects, giving: the alphabet in the original letters or characters in varying forms, with transliteration into English and indication of pronunciation; brief rules for punctuation, capitalization, syllabication, transliteration, phonetics, and grammar; cardinal and ordinal numbers; years, seasons, months, days, etc.

In some particulars has lost its currency (e.g., Soviet-era Cyrillic Mongolian is not reflected) and is weak on some areas of the world, e.g., the Middle East, Central Asia, and parts of Africa (with languages either not mentioned or accorded little detail). Nevertheless, remains a rich repository of information; usually gives information about such features of each language as: writing system (with transliteration in case of nonroman orthographics), common abbreviations, word division, capitalization, parts of speech, numbers, measures of time, non filing articles and special individual features.

§ For greater detail on European languages, *see also*: Charles Geoffry Allen, *A manual of European languages for librarians* (BD11).   Z253.V94

Wemyss, Stanley. The languages of the world, ancient and modern. Philadelphia : author, 1950. 237 p.   **BD18**

Subtitle: The alphabets, ideographs, and other written characters of the languages of the world in sound and symbol.

Focuses on information about the writing systems of languages of the world. Languages are somewhat arbitrarily organized partly by language family and partly by geographic region. Lists of variant language-names, of "five hundred languages written in the Roman alphabet," and indexes of characters in which the languages of the world are written and of languages/dialects. Organized more to provide useful information by language and area, less towards identifying the language of an unknown sample of writing.

§ For the latter, *see*: R. S. Giliarevskii, *Languages identification guide* (BD14). P213.W4

The world's major languages / ed. by Bernard Comrie. N.Y. : Oxford Univ. Pr., 1987. 1025 p. : ill., maps. **BD19**

Gives a basic picture of the affinities, history, structure, and social situation for each of some 50 languages and language groups. Organized by genetically affiliated language family, with an introductory discussion on the history and interrelationship of the family as a whole. Each section concludes with a list of bibliographic references. "Major languages" are defined by criteria such as number of speakers, official national status, international use, and weight of literary tradition; European languages make up somewhat under half the total. Individual contributors were asked "to include a least some material on both the structure of their language and its social background," but to describe what they considered to be "the most interesting facts" (*Pref.*) about their languages. P371.W6

Atlases

Atlas of the world's languages / gen. editors, Chris Moseley and R. E. Asher. London ; N.Y. : Routledge, 1993. 372 p. : maps in color. **BD20**

This first attempt at comprehensive mapping of the world's languages divides the world into eight areas, each treated in a section by a recognized specialist. Each section begins with a basic but substantial text written for nonspecialists that covers general linguistic history of the area, genetic relationships and some structural features of the languages, statistical and sociolinguistic information, and a selected bibliography. An index map at the beginning of each section shows coverage of the more detailed maps that follow. Color is used in the maps to show both the locations of languages and relationships among them; a numbered color key is printed in the margins. Hatched areas show overlapping linguistic zones, and national boundaries are shown by dotted lines. There is an index of languages and genetic language groups. The editors have attempted to "map the location of every single living language on earth, no matter how small the number of its speakers."—*Introd.* For Australia and the Americas, historical maps are included that represent a reconstruction at the time of contact with European settlers. Maps are attractive and easy to use. Although specialists have raised questions about this edition (e.g., the placement of certain Native American languages and variations in language names), this is a most valuable source when used with care.

Sukhachev, N. L. Lingvisticheskie atlasy : annotirovannyi bibliograficheskii ukazatel'. Leningrad : Biblioteka Akademii nauk SSSR, 1984. 157 p. ; 20 cm. **BD21**

At head of title: Institut iazykoznaniia Akademii nauk SSSR. Leningradskoe otdelenie.

An annotated listing, by language family and language, of 234 linguistic atlases, including publications in progress and some prospectuses for planned projects (marked with asterisks). Regional atlases covering more than one language group are treated in a separate section at the end. Covers languages of the entire world; since citations are in the original language, it is possible to use this work without knowledge of Russian. Excludes toponymic atlases and ethnographic atlases that do not show the spread of linguistic phenomena. Annotations include such points as: the territory treated in the atlas, number and nature of sampled or surveyed points, questionnaire on which the work is based, linguistic maps, commentaries, indexes and other apparatus, nature of vocabulary or other material studied (if not evident in the atlas's title), principles of transcription of dialect speech, related publications resulting from the particular project. Indexes: titles of atlases, languages and dialects, geographical names, and personal names. Z7004.G3S84

LINGUISTICS

General works

Gipper, Helmut. Bibliographisches Handbuch zur Sprachinhaltsforschung / [von] Helmut Gipper and Hans Schwarz ; hrsg. von Leo Brandt. Köln : Westdeutscher Verlag, 1962–89. 2 pts. in 9 v. (Wissenschaftliche Abhandlungen der Arbeitsgemeinschaft für Forschung des Landes Nordrhein-Westfalen, Bd. 16a). (In progress). **BD22**

Contents: Teil 1 [Alphabetical listing by author], Bd. 1–4 (Lfrg. 1–32), A–Z; Teil 2, Systematischer Teil (Register), Pt. A, Name index; Pt. B, Classified index of topics; Pt. C, 1st half, Subject index to author listings L–Z; Pt. D, Index of dictionaries. Vocabulary lists by language. List of errata. Afterword on completion of the edition.

A voluminous partially annotated listing of 30,744 monographs, dissertations, and articles concerned with "language content," broadly defined to include (besides semantics) lexicography, etymology, comparative and historical philology, biblical philology, psycholinguistics, stylistics, some literary and cultural history, etc. Materials treating exclusively the formal structures of languages are excluded. Covers materials in English, languages of Western Europe, Slavic languages (Cyrillic citations are transliterated), and other languages of Central and Eastern Europe. Chronological scope ranges from the mid-19th century through the 1960s (for earlier Lieferungen) to the early 1980s (for later). Not all citations are annotated; some annotations are lengthy. Brief contents are sometimes indicated for English-language citations; reviews and related bibliography are sometimes cited. The voluminous introductory and concluding materials and reference apparatus (all in German) are detailed and discursive.

Bibliography

Current

Analecta linguista. 1971– . Budapest : Akadémiai Kiadó, 1971– . Two issues yearly. **BD23**

A selected, international bibliography on linguistic subjects. Based on monographs and offprints received in Hungarian libraries or reported to the editorial office during the period preceding publication of the bibliography. Also reproduces tables of contents of current linguistic journals, and periodically publishes specialized bibliographies on linguistic subjects. Author index.

§ See also *Current contents Linguistik* (Frankfurt am Main : Stadt- und Universitätsbibliothek, 19??–), which reproduces the tables of contents from current issues of some 275 journals in pure and applied linguistics and philology. Z7003.A5 P121

FRANCIS. Bulletin signalétique : 524, Sciences du langage. v. 45, no. 1 (1991)– . Nancy, France : Institut de l'Information Scientifique et Technique, 1991– . Four issues per year, plus an annual index. **BD24**

Continues: *Bulletin signalétique - Centre nationale de la recherche scientifique : 524. Sciences du langage* (v. 23 [1969]–44 [1990]. Paris : Centre de Documentation Sciences Humaines, 1969–90).

For more complete information concerning *FRANCIS. Bulletin signalétique*, see AD254.

A current bibliography without abstracts. Coverage has varied; currently includes the physiology, pathology, psychology, and sociology of language, linguistic theory, historical linguistics and comparative grammar, philology, and stylistics. Classified arrangement; author and subject indexes. P2.B84

Linguistic bibliography for the year [...] and supplement for the years [...] / Permanent International Committee Linguists. 1939–1947– . The Hague ; Boston : Martinus Nijhoff, 1948– . Annual.   **BD25**

Added title page in French: *Bibliographie linguistique de l'année ... et complément des années ...* .

Title varies slightly.

Issued also by the International Council for Philosophy and Humanistic Studies.

A major international bibliography of articles, dissertations, monographs, and reviews (the vol. for 1991 [publ. late 1993] contains 19,474 entries), covering more than 1,700 journals, and 820 conference proceedings, festschriften, and other collections. Classified arrangement, with general linguistic topics followed by sections for Indo-European languages, then other language families and areas. Preface, section headings, tables of contents and other apparatus are in both English and French; "Directions for use / Directives pratiques" directly precedes the entries. Journals are cited in abbreviated form, listed at the beginning. World coverage is thorough, although publication lags about 2–3 years.

§ The first volume, covering 1939–47, was published separately as a monograph in 1949.   Z7001.P4

Modern Language Association of America. MLA international bibliography of books and articles on the modern languages and literatures. 1921– . [N.Y.] : Modern Language Assoc. of America, [1921]– . Annual.   **BD26**

For annotation, *see* BE39.   Z7006.M64

Novaĭa Otechestvennaĭa literatura po obshchestvennym naukam / Rossĭiskaĭa nauk, Institut nauchnoĭ informatsii po obshchestvennuym naukam. 1992– . Moskva : RAN INION, 1992– . Monthly.   **BD27**

Continues: *Novaĭa sovetskaĭa literatura po obshchestvennym naukam : Ĭazykoznanie* (1976–91) and *Novaĭa sovetskaĭa literatura po ĭazykoznaniĭu* (1954–75).

The major Russian journal for current bibliography in linguistics, listing articles and monographs published in the USSR, then in Russia and former Soviet territories, mostly but not exclusively in Russian. Classified arrangement beginning with general linguistic topics followed by sections on individual languages and language families, with a table of contents in Russian and English. Each issue includes author, source journal, and subject index. The subject index lists only additional subjects beyond the thematic rubric under which entry is printed. No cumulations of listings or indexes.

The year's work in modern language studies. v.1 (1929/30)– . London [etc]. : Modern Humanities Research Association [etc.], 1930– . Annual.   **BD28**

A discursive, highly selective annual survey of recent work in some of the major European (non-English) languages and literatures, with signed articles, variously descriptive and evaluative, by specialists. Coverage has varied; as of 1991, there are sections for Latin, Romance, Celtic, Germanic, and Slavonic. Most sections have subdivisions for language studies and for various chronological periods of literary studies. Indexes: subject, name (both contributors and persons as subjects). Coverage lags somewhat.   PB1.Y45

Library catalogs

Center for Applied Linguistics. Library. Dictionary catalog of the Library of the Center for Applied Linguistics, Washington, D.C. Boston : G. K. Hall, 1974. 4 v.   **BD29**

Reproduces the catalog cards for the Center's collection. The library maintains "a predominantly contemporary acquisitions policy with only limited retrospective purchase and limited systematic book selection."—*Introd.*   Z7004.A6S46

Indexes; Abstract journals

Linguistics abstracts. v. 1, no. 1– . Oxford : Basil Blackwell, 1985– . Four no. a year.   **BD30**

Descriptive (not evaluative) abstracts concentrating on general linguistic theory, arranged in a classified system by major thematic categories. Areas excluded: applied linguistics (e.g., language teaching, speech pathology), and descriptive or historical works on particular languages or language families. Authors of abstracts are identified. Indexes: author, subject, and list of source journals; articles are numbered sequentially. Indexes are cumulative through each issue during the course of the year, with a final cumulation for the year.

Linguistics and language behavior abstracts : LLBA. v. 19, no. 1 (Apr. 1985)– . La Jolla, Calif. : Sociological Abstracts, Inc., 1985– . 5 no. a year.   **BD31**

Continues *LLBA: Language and language behavior abstracts* (v. 1–18 [1967–84]) and assumes its volume numbering.

One of the major abstract journals in linguistics and related areas. Abstracts are arranged under some 20 major subject areas (each with subdivisions). Abstracts are descriptive, not evaluative, arranged alphabetically by main author within each subject category. Some 1,500 sources are covered; foreign language materials are well represented (with English translations of titles as well as citations in the original). Indexes: subject, source, author, with cumulation for each volume. Coverage and scope have varied, tending towards greater inclusivity over time.

•Also available online as *LLBA* [database] (since 1973), updated 5 times a year; for information and a guide to use, see: *LLBA user's reference manual*, prep. by Michelle Blackman and Miriam Chall (3rd ed. San Diego, Calif. : Sociological Abstracts, 1987).   Z7001.L15

Encyclopedias

Crystal, David. The Cambridge encyclopedia of language. Cambridge, Eng. ; N.Y. : Cambridge Univ. Pr., 1987. 472 p. : ill.   **BD32**

"In 11 Parts, comprising 65 thematic sections. Each section is a self-contained presentation of a major theme in language study, with cross-references included to related section and topics."—*Contents.* Thematic sections cover subjects such as sounds, speech development, and language families, and include numerous illustrations, graphs, charts, and abbreviations, a table of world languages, and bibliographies of suggested readings. Language, author/name, and subject indexes.   P29.C64

An encyclopaedia of language / ed. by N.E. Collinge. London ; N.Y. : Routledge, 1990. 1011 p. : ill.   **BD33**

Presents 26 signed chapters that discuss current scholarship and provide bibliographies on the nature and social, scientific, logical, and geographical aspects of language. Topics/terms and personal name indexes.   P106.A46

The encyclopedia of language and linguistics / ed. in chief, R.E. Asher; coordinating ed., J. M. Y. Simpson. Oxford ; N.Y. : Pergamon, 1994. 10 v. (5644 p.) : ill.   **BD34**

A massive work, covering a particularly broad range of topics in linguistics or peripheral to it. Tends to promote many topics to individual entries rather than treating them under larger thematic entries. Features a list of articles, a glossary, a list of languages of the world (with number of speakers, genetic affiliation, and geographic location), abbreviations, transcriptional conventions and the International Phonetic Alphabet, a classed list of entries, and name and subject indexes.

§ Complements *International encyclopedia of linguistics* (BD35), but tends to give more detailed coverage to theoretical topics, including those peripheral to linguistics (e.g., Bats: acoustic behavior; Bible), to offer numerous entries on the language situation of various countries, and to provide more biographical information. Both works have international rosters of distinguished contributors and provide varying coverage and emphasis. P29.E48

International encyclopedia of linguistics / William Bright, ed. in chief. N.Y. : Oxford Univ. Pr., 1992. 4 v. **BD35**

Up-to-date and well-organized. The editors intend to cover all branches of linguistics, primarily for students and scholars of linguistics and related fields. Signed articles by recognized specialists cover both languages and linguistics. Gives particularly detailed coverage of languages and language families, with frequent use of maps. Tends to treat theoretical topics in synthetic, comprehensive articles rather than in individual smaller entries. Features an introduction, a sizeable glossary (by David Crystal, compiler of *Dictionary of linguistics and phonetics* [BD36] and *Encyclopedic dictionary of language and languages* [BD37]), list of contributors, a synoptic outline of contents that lists the authors of articles, and a general index of topics and persons that includes contributors, cited authors, and persons.

§ Complements *Encyclopedia of language and linguistics* (BD34), but Bright tends to give more detailed coverage of languages and fewer but more comprehensive theoretical articles. P29.I58

Dictionaries

Crystal, David. A dictionary of linguistics and phonetics. 3rd ed. Oxford ; Cambridge, Mass. : B. Blackwell, c1991. 389 p. : ill. **BD36**

1st ed., 1980, had title: *A first dictionary of linguistics and phonetics*; 2nd ed., 1985.

Now twice revised and expanded, this volume is intended both for general readers or undergraduates and for advanced scholars from other related disciplines. Definitions include bibliographic citations for further information. P29.C65

—————— An encyclopedic dictionary of language and languages. Oxford ; Cambridge, Mass. : Blackwell, 1992. 428 p. : ill. **BD37**

Intended as a dictionary of terms and concepts in linguistics with enough explanation to be useful to general readers, including besides definitions some substantive information, and covering also a number of peripheral popular and applied areas of related interest— e.g., "language-teaching and learning, speech therapy, stylistics, desk-top publishing, philology, writing systems, language names, and the many everyday notions which relate to the use of language."—*Pref.*

§ Intended to be broader and more accessible than Crystal's *Dictionary of linguistics and phonetics* (BD36), and more focused and convenient than his *Cambridge encyclopedia of language* (BD32). P29.C68

Ducrot, Oswald. Encyclopedic dictionary of the sciences of language / by Oswald Ducrot and Tzvetan Todorov; tr. by Catherine Porter. Baltimore : Johns Hopkins Univ. Pr., [1979]. 380 p. **BD38**

Translation based on the 2nd ed. of *Dictionnaire encyclopédique des sciences du langage* (Paris, 1973).

An overview of the sciences of language "organized, not on the basis of a list of words, but according to a conceptual division of the domain under examination."—*Introd.* Thus, terms are defined and explained within topical essays on various aspects of language grouped in four main sections: (1) Schools; (2) Fields; (3) Methodological concepts; (4) Descriptive concepts. The French original has been revised as needed, bibliographical material updated, and English-language publications substituted for the French when practicable. Index of terms defined and index of authors cited in the text. P29.D813

Hamp, Eric P. A glossary of American technical linguistic usage, 1925–1950. Utrecht : Spectrum Publ., 1963. 67 p. **BD39**

A publication of the Committee for Terminology, Permanent International Committee of Linguists.

The glossary is "designed to reflect terminology in use by linguists in America which may offer difficulty to linguistic workers in other countries. It includes technical terms which in form or in sense are peculiar to American usage."—*Introd.* It concentrates on terminology reflecting the structuralist traditions of Sapir and Bloomfield; pre-Sapirian and generative-transformational traditions are excluded. P29.H3

Jung, Heidrun. The dictionary of acronyms and abbreviations in applied linguistics and language learning / Heidrun and Udo O. H. Jung. Frankfurt am Main ; N.Y. : Peter Lang, c1991. 2 v. (802 p.). (Bayreuth contributions to glottodidactics, v. 1). **BD40**

More than 13,000 entries in major languages of Europe (English, French, German, Spanish, Dutch, Italian, Russian, Portuguese, Swedish, and occasional others). Includes additional information beyond simple resolution of shortened forms: genre (e.g. whether the abbreviation or acronym refers to a journal, place-name, publisher, textbook, or series); addresses, telephones, fax numbers, major periodical publications (given as available in the case of institutions); addresses of ministry of culture and tourist authority (in the case of countries); bibliographic references to further sources of information; a list of similar or thematically related other entries (signaled by @); and new words derived from the acronym or abbreviation.

Knobloch, Johann. Sprachwissenschaftliches Wörterbuch. Heidelberg : Winter, 1961–91. Lfg. 1–9. (Indogermanische Bibliothek, II. Reihe. Wörterbücher). (In progress). **BD41**

Contents: v. 1 (fasc. 1–11), A–E; v. 2 (fasc. 1–2), F–Frianlisch.

A scholarly dictionary of general and comparative linguistics, with emphasis on German terms and scholarship. Includes considerable international terminology, primarily English, French, Latin, Italian, and, to a lesser extent, Russian. Entries under terms in these languages give cross-references to German entries, where the information is gathered and controlled.

Nash, Rose. Multilingual lexicon of linguistics and philology : English, Russian, German, French. Coral Gables, Fla. : Univ. of Miami Pr., [1968]. 390 p. (Miami linguistics series, no. 3). **BD42**

Title on title page also in Russian, German, and French.

Lists more than 5,000 English terms with Russian, German, and French equivalents. "Designed specifically for the linguist who wishes to read the works of foreign scholars."—*Pref.* Based on a variety of sources, including technical and general dictionaries, reference grammars, language-teaching materials, indexes to textbooks on introductory linguistics, running text in representative linguistics publications, and comparisons of translations of important works with their originals. Covers traditional and modern terms, and includes specialized vocabulary of subdisciplines and fields related to linguistics. Introductory and explanatory apparatus in all four languages; indexes for each of the other three languages. P29.N34

Descriptive grammar

Morphology

Beard, Robert. Bibliography of morphology, 1960–1985 / comp. by Robert Beard and Bogdan Szymanek. Amsterdam ; Philadelphia : J. Benjamins, 1988. 193 p. (Amsterdam studies in the theory and history of linguistic science. Series V, Library and information sources in linguistics, v. 18). **BD43**

"Rather than an attempt at an exhaustive bibliography of morphology, this is a collection of major and selected minor works of theoretical interest in the broadest sense."—*Introd.* Emphasizes English-language works. Articles and books are listed alphabetically by author, with subject and language indexes. Z7004.M67B43

Syntax

Ostler, Rosemarie. Theoretical syntax 1980–1990 : an annotated and classified bibliography. Amsterdam ; Philadelphia : J. Benjamins Publ. Co., 1992. 192 p. (Amsterdam studies in the theory and history of linguistic science. Series V, Library & information sources in linguistics, v. 21). **BD44**

Lists 914 monographs and articles on syntactic theory; among them the transformationalist approach is prominent but not exclusive. Limited to publications assumed to be reasonably accessible to a variety of researchers (hence unpublished dissertations and working papers are excluded), and to those written in English. Books represent a wide variety of sources, but journal articles are taken from only 14 journals the compiler considers particularly "influential, widely available, and often cited."—*Pref.* Entries are organized in 10 thematic sections, of which the largest is "General studies"; others are devoted to introductions to syntax, to various specialized aspects of the discipline, or to syntactic studies of individual languages, subdivided alphabetically by language. Indexes: authors, topics, and languages.   Z7004.S94O88

Transformational grammar

Bibliography

Krenn, Herwig. Bibliographie zur Transformationsgrammatik. Heidelberg : Winter, 1968. 262 p.   **BD45**

An author listing of books, periodical articles, research reports, dissertations, reviews. 2,459 entries.

§ A keyword index is provided by Ulrich Knoop, Manfred Kohrt, and Christophr Küper, *An index of Bibliographie zur Transformationsgrammatik by H. Krenn and K. Müllner* (Heidelberg : C. Winter, 1971).   Z7004.G7K72

Dictionaries

Ambrose-Grillet, Jeanne. Glossary of transformational grammar. Rowley, Mass. : Newbury House, c1978. 166 p.   **BD46**

"An attempt to provide students, teachers and other interested people with a tool which will help them proceed through the work of Noam Chomsky and other linguists who write in the field of transformational grammar."—*Introd.* An appendix explains basic transformations.   P158.A4

Analogy and metaphor

Noppen, J. P. van. Metaphor : a bibliography of post-1970 publications / comp. by J. P. van Noppen, S. de Knop, R. Jongen, with the assistance of B. Nitelet, A Nysenholc, and W. Shibles. Amsterdam ; Philadelphia : J. Benjamins Pub. Co., 1985. 497 p. (Amsterdam studies in the theory and history of linguistic science, Series V ; Library and information sources in linguistics, v. 17).   **BD47**

Intended to supplement Warren Shibles's *Metaphor: an annotated bibliography and history* (Whitewater, Wis. : Language Pr., 1971). An alphabetical list of more than 2,300 citations, some with annotations. Indexed by name and subject, by theories and uses of metaphor, and by metaphor types. A supplementary index lists recommended texts on various topics for the beginning student.

Continued by: J. P. van Noppen and Edith Hols, *Metaphor II : a classified bibliography of publications, 1985 to 1900* [i.e., 1990] (Amsterdam ; Philadelphia : Benjamins, 1990), with similar indexes plus a new index of intellectual/academic disciplines. *See also* Raimo Anttila and Warren A. Brewer, *Analogy : a basic bibliography* (Amsterdam : Benjamins, 1977).   Z7004.M4N66

Artificial and nonverbal languages

Dulichenko, A. D. Mezhdunarodnye vspomogatel'nye iazyki. Tallinn : "Valgus,", 1990. 444 p.   **BD48**

(Title in English: International auxiliary languages).

A chronology and bibliography, subarranged under year by language name, of attempts to create universal artificial languages, including sign languages and derivative modifications of natural languages. Introduction and reference apparatus in Russian, although language names and the bibliography (mostly in European languages and English) are given in the original, which renders the book usable to those without Russian. Résumé in Estonian, French, German, and Esperanto. Indexes by language, chronology, personal name, and country.   Pm8009.D85

Federlin, Tom. A comprehensive bibliography on American sign language : a resource manual. N.Y. : Federlin, 1979. 84 p.   **BD49**

A classified bibliography of books, articles, reports, dissertations, and some unpublished manuscripts on various aspects of the discipline and practice, including some works on foreign sign languages. Organized in thematic sections (Linguistics; Pedagogy, including American and foreign sign language texts; Sign language with deaf populations; and General), each with 5–10 subdivisions, within which entries are alphabetical by author. Index of authors.   Z5721.F37

Stojan, Petro E. Bibliografio de internacia lingvo : kun bibliografia aldona de Reinhard Haupenthal. Hildesheim ; N.Y. : G. Olms, 1973. 560 p. : ports.   **BD50**

Repr. of 1929 ed. publ. by Bibliografia servo de Universala Esperanto-asocio, Geneva, with bibliographic addenda to 1973.

An unannotated bibliography of works on all aspects of international, universal, and artificial languages from antiquity to modern times. Contains 6,333 entries in a classed listing, in three main sections by subject: [1] International and universal languages (about 30% of the entries); [2]. Esperanto, subdivided by country and subject (about 60%); [3]. Other artificial languages (about 10%). Concludes with short sample passages in 64 artificial languages (34 represent the beginning of the Lord's Prayer, the remaining 30 other texts). Preface in French, German, and English, with a separate introduction in Esperanto. Indexes: of subjects (with terms in Esperanto), of artificial languages, and of authors.   Z7123.S87

Semantics

Gordon, W. Terrence. Semantics : a bibliography, 1986–1991. Metuchen, N.J. ; London : Scarecrow, 1992. 280 p.   **BD51**

A classified annotated listing of books, articles, dissertations, festschriften, conference papers, etc., in English, German, and the major Romance languages, organized in 23 topical sections. In addition to linguistics, includes relevant works from philosophy, psychology, and anthropology. Has a glossary of terms used in annotations and indexes of words/lexemes and authors.

Continues coverage provided by Gordon's two previous bibliographies that covered 1965–78 (entries 1–3326, publ. 1980) and 1979–85 (entries 3327–6034, publ. 1987). This third volume contains entries 6035–7385.   Z7004.S4G69

Semiotics

Encyclopedic dictionary of semiotics / gen. ed., Thomas A. Sebeok. Berlin ; N.Y. : Mouton de Gruyter, c1986. 3 v. (Approaches to semiotics, 73).   **BD52**

Vols. 1–2 contain signed essays with bibliographic references on terms, themes, persons, and schools of thought. Vol. 3 is a bibliographic companion to the work, arranged alphabetically by author.

§ *See also:* A. J. Greimas and J. Courtés, *Semiotics and language : an analytical dictionary* (Bloomington : Indiana Univ. Pr., c1982), tr. from the original French ed.: *Semiotique : dictionnaire raisonné de la théorie du language* (Paris : Hachette, c1979–86. 2 v.).

P99.E65

Eschbach, Achim. Bibliography of semiotics, 1975–1985 / comp. by Achim Eschbach & Viktoria Eschbach-Szabó with the collaboration of Gabi Willenberg. Amsterdam ; Philadelphia : J. Benjamins Pub. Co., 1986. 2 v. (948 p.). (Amsterdam studies in the theory and history of linguistic science. Series V, Library and information sources in linguistics, v. 16).

BD53

Intended to continue and supplement two of Eschbach's earlier works, *Semiotik-Bibliographie I* (Frankfurt am Main : Antoren- and Verlagsgesellschaft Syndikat, 1976) and *Zeichen, Text, Bedeutung* (München : Fink, 1974). Lists 10,839 monographs, articles, reviews, dissertations, conference proceedings, and translations in alphabetical order by main entry with subject/name and journal indexes.

Z7004.S43E76

Nöth, Winfried. Handbook of semiotics. Bloomington : Indiana Univ. Pr., c1990. 576 p. : ill.   **BD54**

Translation of *Handbuch der Semiotik* (Stuttgart : Matzler, 1985) with substantial revision and expansion.

"Aims at the adventurous goal of a topographical survey of the main areas of theoretical and applied semiotics ... [and] intends to be systematic, comprehensive, and up to date."—*Pref.* In eight chapters: (1) History and classics of modern semiotics; (2) Sign and meaning; (3) Semiosis, code, and the semiotic field; (4) Language and language-based codes; (5) From structuralism to texts, semiotics: schools and major figures; (6) Text semiotics: the field; (7) Nonverbal communication; (8) Aesthetics and visual communication. Each chapter is further subdivided into essays on particular problems, individuals, theories, or concepts. Within the text are numerous cross-references to the extensive bibliography at the end of the volume. Subject/term and name indexes.

P99.N6513

Creoles and pidgins

Reinecke, John E. A bibliography of pidgin and creole languages / comp. by John E. Reinecke, in collaboration with David DeCamp ... [et al.]. Honolulu : Univ. Pr. of Hawaii, [1975]. 804 p. (Oceanic linguistics special publications, no.14).   **BD55**

A substantial classified listing of some 11,000 entries, mostly annotated, by language, dialect, or language group; within each language alphabetically by author. 120 sections (three for non-language-specific types of entries). Indexes: of authors, Christian scripture translations, anonymous works, and pidgin/creole-language periodicals.

§ Coverage continued to 1982 by: *Bibliographie des études créoles languages et littératures* by Comité International des Études Créoles, ed. by Albert Valdman, Robert Chaudenson, and Marie-Christine Hazael-Massieux ([s.l.] : Agence de Coopération Culturelle et Technique, [1983]).

Z7124.R43

Language origins

Hewes, Gordon Winant. Language origins : a bibliography. 2nd rev. and enl. ed. The Hague : Mouton, 1975. 2 v. (Approaches to semiotics, 44).   **BD56**

1st ed., 1971.

Aims "to cover all works on the origins of language, and related topics, to the middle of 1972."—*Foreword.* About 11,000 items, including works from the disciplines of psychology, anthropology, philosophy, speech pathology, animal communication behavior, anatomy of the larynx, and anatomy and neurophysiology of the brain, as well as linguistics. International in scope; entries are mainly for books and periodical articles, but a few manuscripts are included. Author listing with topical index; publication dates are included in the index citations to facilitate use.

Z7004.O75H46

Dialectology

Pop, Sever. La dialectologie : aperçu historique et méthodes d'enquêtes linguistiques. Louvain, [1950]. 2 v. (1334p.). : ill., maps. (Université de Louvain. Recueil de travaux d'histoire et de philologie, 3. sér., fasc. 38–39).   **BD57**

Contents: 1. pt., Dialectologie romane: Le français, Le domaine franco-provençal, Le provençal, Le catalan, L'espagnol, Le portugais, L'italien, Le romanche, Le dalmate, Le roumain; 2. pt., Dialectologie non romane. Langues germaniques: Allemagne, Suisse, Grand-Duché de Luxembourg, Belgique et Pays-Bas. Les pays scandinaves, Grande-Bretagne, États-Unis et Canada. Langues celtiques, Langues slaves, Langues finno-ougriennes. Le grec modern. L'albanais. Le domaine berbère. Le domaine bantou. Le domaine arabe. Le chinois. Les langues de l'Inde. Le coréen.

A comprehensive historical survey covering dialectal research and methods employed. Fully documented throughout text and in footnotes. Detailed indexes by year, place, persons, geographical names, and subjects. List of illustrations. Table of contents. Chronological list of linguistic atlases, 1880–1948, p. 1194–97.

P375.P6

Other topics

International bibliography of terminological literature / Infoterm. Wien : TermNet, 1989. 284 p. (TermNet bibliographical series, 1).   **BD58**

"This bibliography covers literature on terminology science and research, terminology standardization, terminology training, and related fields... publications dealing with computerized terminology have also been included."—*Introd.*

This edition lists nearly 3,900 entries, concentrating on publications since 1981 and updating the 1984 bibliography by G. Rondeau and H. Felber, *Bibliographie sélective, terminologie et disciplines connexes = Selective bibliography, terminology and related fields* ([Ottawa] : Direction de la terminologie, c1988). Each entry indicates language of subject and publication, and subject content according to a classification system developed for this bibliography, and to the Universal Decimal Classification (UDC). Indexes: subjects (terms according to UDC) and authors.

APPLIED LINGUISTICS AND RELATED FIELDS

General works

Bibliography

Koerner, E. F. K. Western histories of linguistic thought : an annotated chronological bibliography 1822–1976. Amsterdam : Benjamins, 1978. 113 p. (Amsterdam studies in the theory and history of linguistic science. Series III, Studies in the history of linguistics, v. 11). **BD59**

A listing in chronological order of book-length studies or other individual publications, with occasional significant articles or contributions to collective volumes. Works devoted to specific authors or narrow time periods are excluded. Gives detailed substantive annotations, with frequent evaluative comments and cross-references to other relevant works. Index of authors of cited works.

§ Subsequent publications in the history of linguistics continue to be reviewed in the journal *Historiographia linguistica*, (v. 1 [1974]–) whose founder and editor is Koerner. Z7004.H56K64

Bilingualism; Second language acquisition

Afendras, Evangelos A. Le bilinguisme chez l'enfant et l'apprentissage d'une langue seconde : bibliographie analytique = Child bilingualism and second language learning : a descriptive bibliography / Evangelos A. Afendras, Albertina Pianarosa. Québec : Presses de l'Université Laval, 1975. 401 p. (Travaux du Centre international de recherche sur le bilinguisme, F-4). **BD60**

An alphabetical author listing of 1,661 items dealing with children and bilingualism from a variety of perspectives and disciplines. Each entry includes a summary subject analysis consisting of terms from a thesaurus of subject descriptors ("conceptual fields"), which are also registered in a subject index. Also has index of languages, countries, and peoples. All reference apparatus is in both English and French. Z7004.C45A44

Bibliographie internationale sur le bilinguisme : avec index analytique sur microfiches / préparée sous la direction de William F. Mackey. 2e éd. rév. et mise à jour. Québec : Les Presses de l'Université Laval, 1982. 575 p. (International Center for Research on Bilingualism, series F : Bibliographies, no. 3). **BD61**

1st ed., 1972.

A major international bibliography covering studies on bilingualism and bilingual education, including books, articles, reviews, dissertations, conference papers, and less formal reports and unpublished manuscripts. Excluded are pedagogical and language reference materials (such as language dictionaries, textbooks and other pedagogical materials, and works addressed exclusively to language teachers); included are language learning studies (both native- and foreign-language acquisition), studies of language contrast and interference, developmental studies, sociolinguistic and sociocultural studies, studies on language vis-à-vis ethnicity, and the psycholinguistics of bilingualism. Consists of two primary alphabetical author sections: the first (entries no. 1–11006) reproducing the listings from the 1st ed., the second (entries 11007–19030), citing added material for the original time period (1940–67) and new material through mid-1979. Cumulative author and subject (key-word descriptor) indexes, on microfiches in pockets at the end. All introductory material and other reference apparatus is in both French and English. Z7004.B5B52

Child language; First language acquisition

Abrahamsen, Adele A. Child language : an interdisciplinary guide to theory and research. Baltimore : Univ. Park Pr., c1977. 381 p. **BD62**

A topically arranged, annotated bibliography of about 1,500 items. Author and subject indexes. Z7004.C45A27

Higginson, Roy. CHILDES/BIB : an annotated bibliography of child language and language disorders / [comp. by] Roy Higginson, Brian MacWhinney. Hillsdale, N.J. : L. Erlbaum Associates, 1991. 1162 p. **BD63**

A printed version of the *CHILDES/BIB* bibliographic database maintained by one of the compilers at Carnegie Mellon University; the printed bibliography registers some 7,500 entries, and covers materials to 1990. An alphabetic author listing of partially annotated entries, with author and subject indexes (the latter includes names of languages).

Coverage has been extended by about 3,000 new entries in a supplement (1993. 693 p. Repr., 1994) that "covers North American research since late 1990 and international research published outside North America since 1970. It also includes a few North American items published prior to 1990 that were omitted from the earlier work."—*Pref.*

•Desktop machine readable versions of the *CHILDES/BIB* database, as well as versions for VAX- and UNIX-based mainframes, are available from the publisher. Z5814.C5H54

Computational and mathematical linguistics

Natural language processing in the 1980s : a bibliography / Gerald Gazdar ... [et al.]. Stanford, Calif. : Center for the Study of Language and Information, c1987. 240 p. (CSLI lecture notes, no. 12). **BD64**

An unannotated author listing of 1,764 entries on computational linguistics and natural language processing. Less complete coverage is given certain subject areas (lexicostatistics, stylistic and other identification of authors, and concordance generation); and languages of publication other than English are excluded outside a body of core publications. Indexes of added authors and of keyword terms from titles.

§ For those with Russian, can be supplemented with a 1986 work by V.A. Chizhakovskiĭ, K.B. Bektaev, and P.M. Alekseev: *Statistika rechi, 1957 1985 : bibliograficheskiĭ ukazatel'* (Statistics of speech, 1957–1985 : a bibliographic guide) (Kishinev : "Shtintsa," 1986). Z7004.L3N37

Discourse analysis; Pragmatics

Nuyts, Jan. A comprehensive bibliography of pragmatics / comp. by Jan Nuyts and Jef Verschueren ; under the auspices of the International Pragmatics Assoc. Amsterdam ; Philadelphia : J. Benjamins Pub. Co., 1987. 4 v. (2197 p.) : ill. **BD65**

Contents: v. 1, Introduction, abbreviations, indexes; v. 2–4, Annotated bibliography, A–Z.

An annotated alphabetic author listing of works in pragmatics, defined to include "all the functional, psychological, biological, and social phenomena which play a part in the use of language."—*Introd.* International coverage concentrates primarily on works in English, German, French, and Dutch; others, such as languages of Eastern Europe, Spanish, and Italian, are covered less completely and remain a priority for future versions of the bibliography. The cutoff date for inclusion is 1984, with only a few exceptions. Indexes in v. 1 : subjects, words (as subjects of studies), languages, and persons (as subjects of studies).   Z7004.P73N89

History of linguistics

Bio-bibliographisches Handbuch zur Sprachwissenschaft des 18. Jahrhunderts : die Grammatiker, Lexikographen und Sprachtheoretiker des deutschsprachigen Raums mit Beschreibungen ihrer Werke / hrsg. von Herbert E. Brekle … [et al.]. Tübingen : Niemeyer, 1992–1993. v. 1–2. (In progress).   **BD66**
    Cover title: BBHS.
    Contents: Bd. 1 (1992), A–Br; Bd. 2 (1993), Bu–E.
    An alphabetical register of persons involved in linguistic, lexicographic, grammatical speculation, or other endeavors in German-speaking territories in the 18th century. Only those whose relevant work was published strictly within the period 1700–1800 are included. Under each entry, as appropriate, the following subsections are given: Biography; Characterization of work; Bibliography (works about language; other works; secondary literature; biographical and bibliographical sources). Each volume concludes with an appendix (Anhang I) listing persons who were considered for inclusion, but were excluded, with reasons for the exclusion. Introduction and all other reference apparatus is in German.   Z7002.B56

Renaissance linguistics archive, 1350–1700 : a print-out from the secondary-sources data-base / ed. by Mirko Tavoni … [et al.]. Ferrara : Istituto di studi rinascimentali, 1987–1990. v. 1–3. (In progress).   **BD67**
    Subtitle varies.
    Vol. 2 ed. by Pierre Lardet and Mirko Tavoni [et al.].
    A bibliographical project in collaboration with the Henry Sweet Society for the History of Linguistic Ideas (Oxford) and the Société d' histoire et d'épistémologie des sciences du langage (Paris).
    The result of a cooperative bibliographic project to facilitate "an international and interdisciplinary exchange of bibliographical information among scholars in this large and complex field of research."—*Foreword.* Each of the first three volumes from the RLA database lists approximately 1,000 books, articles, conference proceedings, and book collections published in the 19th and 20th centuries that address the development and study of European languages during the early modern period. Entries are arranged alphabetically, with subject/names, keyword, geographic, and language indexes. Each volume also contains a list of periodicals and collective works that are indexed in the main bibliography. Further volumes are expected as the database grows.   Z7001.R46

Research guide on language change / ed. by Edgar C. Polomé. Berlin ; N.Y. : Mouton de Gruyter, 1990. 564 p. : ill. (Trends in linguistics. Studies and monographs, 48).   **BD68**
    A handbook consisting of brief synthetic, historiographic, or bibliographic essays devoted to a particular topic, area, methodology, or theoretical model of relevance in studying language change. Each essay is accompanied by a list of bibliographic references. Indexes of subjects, languages, and authors.   P142.R47

Salus, Peter H. Pāṇini to Postal : a bibliography in the history of linguistics. Edmonton, Alberta : Linguistic Research, Inc., c1971. 75 p. (Linguistic bibliography series, 2).   **BD69**
    A selective, unannotated classified register of 666 journal articles, monographs, and some dissertations, listed by cultural area and historic epoch, covering (with varying thoroughness) the entire world and all the history of speculation about language from the earliest times. Includes primarily historical studies of persons, theories, methodologies, national traditions of study, organizations, etc. Author index only (authors of articles and books, not historical authors as subjects). Much biographical material is included, but biographical subjects must be looked for in appropriate cultural and historical sections.   Z7004.H56S24

Sebeok, Thomas Albert. Portraits of linguists : a biographical source book for the history of western linguistics, 1746–1963. Bloomington : Indiana Univ. Pr., [1966]. 2 v.   **BD70**
    An anthology of 90 biographical studies of linguists born before 1900. Articles are reprinted from journals, yearbooks, etc.; some are in French or German. Index of names in v. 2.   P83.S4

Language study and teaching

Center for Applied Linguistics. A survey of materials for the study of the uncommonly taught languages / Dora E. Johnson … [et al.]. Arlington, Va. : Center for Applied Linguistics, c1976. 8 v.   **BD71**
    Previous ed. : *A provisional survey of materials for the study of neglected languages,* by Birgit A. Blass, Dora E. Johnson, and William W. Gage (Wash. : Center for Applied Linguistics, c1969. 414 p.).
    Contents: v. 1, Languages of Western Europe: pidgins and creoles (European based); v. 2, Languages of Eastern Europe and the Soviet Union; v. 3, Languages of the Middle East and North Africa; v. 4, Languages of South Asia; v. 5, Languages of eastern Asia; v. 6, Languages of sub-Saharan Africa; v. 7, Languages of Southeast Asia and the Pacific; v. 8, Languages of North, Central, and South America.
    An annotated bibliography of pedagogical and reference materials (grammars, dictionaries, etc.) that are intended primarily for English-speaking students of languages of the world. Excludes English itself and the most commonly taught European languages. A thorough revision of the previous edition. In each volume, materials are listed by genre under headings for each language. Indicates availability through ERIC Document Reproduction Service. Index in each volume by language.
    Chronological coverage is continued in Debora Hatfield, *Survey of materials for the study of the uncommonly taught languages : supplement, 1976–1981* (1982. 1 v.).   Z7001.C45

Centre for Information on Language Teaching. A language-teaching bibliography / comp. and ed. by the Centre for Information on Language Teaching and the English-Teaching Information Centre of the British Council. 2nd ed. Cambridge [Eng.] : Univ. Pr., 1972. 242 p.   **BD72**
    1st ed., 1968.
    In eight main divisions: (1) Language; (2) Language teaching; (3–8) English for speakers of other languages, French, German, Italian, Russian, and Spanish. Lists books only; annotated entries register both methodological studies and practical reference materials such as dictionaries and grammars (pedagogical materials are not included). Author index.   Z5814.L26C45

Jung, Udo O. H. An international bibliography of computer-assisted language learning with annotations in German. Frankfurt am Main ; N.Y. : P. Lang, c1988–93. 2 v.   **BD73**
    Vol. 2 by Udo O. H. Jung and Gothild Lieber.
    Together, the volumes present 3,051 partially annotated author entries for monographs, articles, and a few dissertations, covering from about 1980 (with a few earlier entries) to 1991. Gives rich international coverage, including Arab, Hungarian, Eastern European, and Russian sources. Annotations are in German, but most reference apparatus is in English. Each volume has its own indexes of proper names (types of computer, software applications, programming languages, organizations, institutions) and subjects; in v. 1, the latter is in German only, but v. 2 has one in English as well.
    § For citations to earlier works, see: *A bibliography of computer-aided language learning,* by Vance Stevens, Roland Sussex, and Walter Vladimir Tuman (N.Y. : AMS Pr., 1986. 140 p.).   Z5818.L35J86

Language teaching. [v. 15, no. 1] (Jan. 1982)– . Cambridge : Cambridge Univ. Pr., 1982– . Quarterly.   **BD74**
    For annotation, *see* CB58.   PB35.L32

Nostrand, Howard Lee. Research on language teaching : an annotated international bibliography, 1945–1964 / Howard Lee Nostrand, David William Foster, Clay Benjamin Christensen. 2nd ed. rev. Seattle : Univ. of Washington Pr., 1965. 373 p. **BD75**

1st ed., 1962.

An annotated, classified listing of books and periodical articles on methods, material, equipment, psychology of language learning, teaching at various levels, etc. Includes a list of bibliographies and one of periodicals and serials. In this edition a special effort was made to justify the "international" of the title by including more references to research outside the U.S. Author and subject indexes. Z7001.N6

Petrov, Julia A. Foreign language, area, and other international studies : a bibliography of research and instructional materials completed under the National Defense Education Act of 1958, title VI, section 602: list no. 9 / comp. by Julia A. Petrov ; ed. by John P. Brosseau. [9th ed.]. [Wash.] : U.S. Dept. of Education, Office of Education, 1980. 79 p. **BD76**

Dept. of Education Publ. no. E-80-14017. Superintendent of Documents classification: ED 1.17: F76/no.9.

Citations are presented in two categories: (1) General reports (studies and surveys, conferences, linguistic studies, research in language-teaching methods) and (2) Specialized materials (commonly taught languages, uncommonly taught languages, foreign area studies). Indexed. Z5818.L35P47

Richards, Jack C. Longman dictionary of language teaching and applied linguistics / Jack C. Richards, John Platt, Heidi Platt. New ed., 2nd ed. Essex, England : Longman, 1992. 423 p. : ill. **BD77**

1st ed., 1985, published under title *Longman dictionary of applied linguistics.*

This edition is expanded to reflect language teaching in greater detail. "Includes the core vocabulary of both language teaching and applied linguistics. The field of language teaching is concerned with the development of language programmes and courses, teaching methodology, materials development, testing, teacher training and related areas... 'Applied linguistics' includes terms from... introductory linguistics... discourse analysis... sociolinguistics... [and] psycholinguistics, including first and second language acquisition, contrastive analysis, error analysis and learning theories."—*Introd.*

Intended for students, teachers, and others in the above areas; concentrates on the English language, but has universal application. Contains 2,000 entries, including many not in the 1st ed., for terms important in the covered subject disciplines and characterized by specialized meanings not likely to be explained in other dictionaries. Definitions are clear, succinct, and accompanied by helpful examples, illustrations, and cross-references.

Psycho- and neurolinguistics

Dingwall, William Orr. Language and the brain : a bibliography and guide. N.Y. : Garland, 1981. 2 v. (1017 p.). **BD78**
For annotation, *see* CD117. Z6663.B8D56

Handbook of applied psycholinguistics : major thrusts of research and theory / ed. by Sheldon Rosenberg. Hillsdale, N.J. : L. Erlbaum Assoc., c1982. 615 p. **BD79**

"The chapters of this handbook contain critical integrative reviews of research and theory in the major areas of the field of applied psycholinguistics."—*Pref.* Each survey chapter concludes with a substantial bibliography. The 11 chapters cover: an introductory overview; psycholinguistic approaches to reading, writing, and language-learning (second-language learning and bilinguilism); discourse processes; disorders of first-language development (in children); and adult language disorders. Author and subject indexes. P37.H3

Sociolinguistics

Dechert, Hans W. Transfer and interference in language : a selected bibliography / comp. by Hans W. Dechert, Monika Brüggemeier & Dietmar Fütterer. Amsterdam ; Philadelphia : J. Benjamins Pub. Co., 1984. 488 p. (Amsterdam studies in the theory and history of linguistic science. Series V, Library & information sources in linguistics, v. 14). **BD80**

An unannotated alphabetic author listing of monographs, articles, dissertations, and reports in the general areas of "contact and interaction of languages in the speaker/hearer and learner, in language acquisition contexts, as well as in society in general."—*Pref.* The perspectives of various disciplines are represented, including psycholinguistics, sociolinguistics, applied linguistics (including language teaching, translation, and contrastive analysis), and neurolinguistics. The preface includes a useful bibliography of bibliographies in these areas. Indexes of languages and classified topics. A guide to the classification (called "Topic index") precedes the index itself (which is called "List of topics").

§ Can be usefully supplemented for English-language works on error analysis by: R. Palmberg, *Select bibliography of error analysis and interlanguage studies* (Abo, Finland : Abo akademi, 1980). Z7004.L34D43

Fernández, Mauro. Diglossia : a comprehensive bibliography, 1960–1990 : and supplements. Amsterdam ; Philadelphia : J. Benjamins, 1993. 472 p. (Amsterdam studies in the theory and history of linguistic science. Series V, Library and information sources in linguistics., v. 23.). **BD81**

"Diglossia" generally refers to language situations in which two or more significantly different language varieties complement each other in various functions within a single linguistic community. This bibliography is a partly annotated alphabetical author listing of works (monographs, articles, dissertations, and conference papers) devoted to various aspects and understandings of the topic, including works whose titles simply mention the term. Although 1960-90 is intensively covered, works actually range from 1885 to 1992 and altogether number more than 2,500. Six indexes: Languages; Diglossia in literature; Historically oriented works; Pedagogically oriented works; Theoretical works; Theses and dissertations. Z7004.D53F47

Henley, Nancy. She said / he said : an annotated bibliography of sex difference in language, speech, and nonverbal communication / comp. by Nancy Henley and Barrie Thorne. Pittsburgh : Know, Inc., 1975. p. 205–311. **BD82**

An extensively annotated bibliography of monographs, articles, dissertations, reports, etc., in classified arrangement by general thematic categories (Comprehensive sources; Language and speech; Vocabulary and syntax; Phonology; Conversational patterns; Women's and mens's languages, dialects, varieties; Multilingual situations; Language acquisition; Verbal ability; Nonverbal aspects of communication), with subdivisions; within each section or subdivision alphabetically by author. In addition to more neutral perceived sex-linked "differences," this work pays considerable evaluative attention to sexism in language and languages; includes references to more general sociolinguistic works as well. Includes cross-references to works whose relevance extends over multiple areas. Author index.

Reprinted with original pagination from the compilers' *Language and sex: difference and dominance* (Rowley, Mass. : Newbury House, 1975), where it was printed as the accompanying bibliography.

§ A functional continuation in coverage to 1980 is provided by: *Language, gender, and society* (Rowley, Mass. : Newbury House, 1983), ed. by Barrie Thorn, Cheris Kramarae, Nancy Henley.

Horvath, Barbara M. Community languages : a handbook : studies of languages used in prodominantly English-speaking countries / Barbara M. Horvath and Paul Vaughan. Clevedon, England ; Philadelphia : Multilingual Matters, c1991. 276 p. (Multilingual matters, 67). **BD83**

A handbook of basic information for policymakers and others who deal with foreign language communities in English-speaking host countries, with bibliographic references. After an introductory overview called "Sociolinguistic profiles : a guide for multicultural policymakers," the book consists of 68 chapters devoted to individual language communities alphabetically by language name, surveying the basic affiliation, linguistic and cultural history, traditions, standardization, education, and literacy of the parent country, and giving basic bibliographic references on these subjects. No indexes.   **P40.H69**

Jarrard, Mary E. W. Women speaking : an annotated bibliography of verbal and nonverbal communication, 1970–1980 / Mary E. W. Jarrard, Phyllis R. Randall. N.Y. : Garland, 1982. 478 p. (Garland reference library of social science, v. 108).
BD84

    For annotation, *see* CC495.   **HQ1426.J37**

Pogarell, Reiner. Minority languages in Europe : a classified bibliography. Berlin ; N.Y. : Mouton, c1983. 208 p.   **BD85**
    The subtitle not withstanding, this is a main-entry listing with indexes by (1) languages, regions, states, and (2) by keywords. About 2,400 entries in many languages for books, parts of books, and periodical articles.   **Z7004.L54P63**

Translation

Briamonte, Nino. Saggio di bibliografia sui problemi storici, teorici e pratici della traduzione. [Italy?] : Libreria sapere, [1984]. 253 p.   **BD86**
    Lists books, articles, conference proceedings, and special journal articles published for the most part 1960–80. Arranged in a classified scheme, with a name index.   **Z7004.T72B74**

Congrat-Butlar, Stefan. Translation & translators : an international directory and guide. N.Y. : Bowker, 1979. 241 p.
BD87
    Approximately half the volume is a "Register of translators & interpreters" which lists: agencies; industrial, scientific and technical translators; humanistic/literary translators; conference translators; and conference interpreters. Individual translators are classified by language at the end of each category. Preliminary matter includes much information useful to translators and concerning translating as a profession. Annotated list of books and journals in the field, p. 75–87.
        P306.A2C6

Delisle, Jean. Guide bibliographique du traducteur, rédacteur et terminologue = Bibliographic guide for translators, writers, and terminologists / compilé par Jean Delise et Lorraine Albert. Ottawa : Éditions de l'Univ. d'Ottawa, 1979. 207 p. (Cahiers de traductologie, no. 1).   **BD88**
    Introductory matter in French and English.
    An earlier version appeared in 1976 under title: *Répertoire bibliographique de la traduction.*
    Intended for students of translation, professional translators, and those interested in the study of terminology and its methodology. Includes citations to general materials on translation and interpretation, theory and history of translation, automatic translation, French and English linguistics, etc. There is an extensive section (p. 87–186) of specialized dictionaries (both mono- and multilingual) and thematic encyclopedias. Author index.   **Z7004.T72D44**

Olmsted, Hugh M. Translations and translating : a selected bibliography of bibliographies, indexes, and guides. Binghamton : Center for Translation and Intercultural Communication, Dept. of Comparative Literature, State Univ. of N. Y. at Binghamton, 1975. 54 p.   **BD89**
    Some three-quarters of the work lists bibliographies of translations from and into individual languages, by language, with special categories for Bible translation, Greek and Latin, and as needed for language groups, nationalities, and individual cultural and geographic areas of the world. Bibliographies in this section cover primarily literary translations, and are preferentially listed under "source" language,

unless the sources are multiple. Individual author bibliographies are excluded. Other sections cover bibliographies of works on the theory and practice of translation; listings of translated journals; translations from the press (current events, politics); and major international serial bibliographies, technical translations, announcement bulletins, etc. A revised version is in preparation.   **Z7004.T72O45**

ENGLISH

General works

Bibliography

Annual bibliography of English language and literature. Vol. 4 (1923)– . Cambridge : Bowes & Bowes, 1924– . Annual.   **BD90**
    For annotation, *see* BE588.   **Z2011.M69**

Höhlein, Helga. Auswahlbibliographie zum Studium der anglistischen Sprachwissenschaft : mit Kommentaren / Helga Höhlein, Peter H. Marsden, Clausdirk Pollner. Tübingen : M. Niemeyer, 1987. 155 p. (Forschung & Studium Anglistik, 2).
BD91
    Lists books and articles in a classed arrangement; most sections include a few titles (one to ten) with lengthy annotations and a longer, supplementary list without annotations. Author/title index.
    Annotations and reference apparatus are entirely in German; nevertheless this focused, highly selective listing can be useful to English speakers since most citations are in English.
    § *See also* the selective listing in H. B. Allen, *Linguistics and English linguistics* (2nd ed. Arlington Heights, Ill. : AHM Publ. Corp., 1977).   **Z5818.E5H64**

Scheurweghs, Gustave. Analytical bibliography of writings on modern English morphology and syntax, 1877–1960. Louvain, Belgium : Nauwelaerts, 1963–79. 5 v.   **BD92**
    Publisher varies.
    Contents: v. 1, Periodical literature and miscellanies of the United States of America and western and northern Europe. With an appendix on Japanese publications by Hideo Yamaguchi (Fukui, Japan); v. 2, Studies in book form, including dissertations and *Programmabhandlungen* published in the United States of America and western and northern Europe. With appendixes on Japanese publications by Hideo Yamaguchi, and on Czechoslovak publications by Ján Simko (Bratilava); v. 3, Soviet research on English morphology and syntax; English studies in Bulgaria, Poland, Rumania and Yugoslavia; v. 4, Addenda and general indexes; v. 5, Articles in periodicals, 1961–1970, comp. by E. Vorlat.
    Annotated, classified bibliographies with author and subject indexes. Vol. 5 is a listing by periodical (then chronologically by publication date of the articles) and includes abstracts.   **Z2015.A1S33**

Directories

Handbook of English and Celtic studies in the United Kingdom and Republic of Ireland / ed. by N.H. Keeble. [London] : Stirling Univ. Pr., 1988. 379 p.   **BD93**
    A faculty directory listing departments of English and Celtic language, literature, and linguistics by institution. Compiled by survey; many entries include an individual's birthdate, academic degrees, title of thesis, current position, areas of academic interest and publications, but some list only names of faculty members and their appointments. Name and topic indexes.   **PE68.G5H27**

Handbooks

The Oxford companion to the English language / ed., Tom McArthur; managing ed., Feri McArthur. Oxford ; N.Y. : Oxford Univ. Pr., c1992. 1184 p. : ill., map.   **BD94**

A rich and up-to-date encyclopedic dictionary on many aspects of the English language. It consists of three types of entries, arranged in one alphabet: essay entries; brief dictionary entries for definitions or other explanations; and biographical entries. Among the topics treated: the geography, history, biography, literature, style, language teaching, grammar, writing, speech, lexicology, usage, and varieties of the English language worldwide. Gives special emphasis to local, regional, and international variation in usage and to stylistic varieties (standard and nonstandard). A system of cross-references and "theme lists" (listing of all entries on selected major themes) allows use of the work for systematic study. Includes a chronology of the language, Roman times to 1990 (following the entry "History of English"); etymologies; sources; quotations; and bibliographies. Concludes with an index of persons.

Style manuals

An annotated bibliography of texts on writing skills : grammar and usage, composition, rhetoric, and technical writing / Shannon Burns ... [et al.]. N.Y. : Garland, 1976. 259 p.   **BD95**

An alphabetic listing of 443 titles designed primarily for teachers of writing who are searching for textbook materials, with extensive annotations intended to give a sense of the purpose, content, and intended audience. The listings are preceded by an introduction, How to use this bibliography, which explains the following section, Guide, which is in effect a subject index by categories (Grammar and basic usage, Handbooks/reference, Various levels of composition, Readers/source books, Language/style, etc.). Index of titles.   Z2015.R5A55

Harbrace college handbook / John C. Hodges ... [et al.]. 11th ed. San Diego, Calif. : Harcourt Brace Jovanovich, c1990. 576, 24 p.   **BD96**

1st ed., 1941 ; 10th ed., 1986.

Intended both as a reference source for writers and a textbook for class use. Offers sections on basic English grammar, punctuation, spelling and diction, sentence structure, planning and writing compositions (including library use, notetaking, footnotes, etc.). The 11th ed. (a "complete revision of the Tenth Edition" [*Pref.*]) offers significant additions to the sections concerning résumés, style sheets, and reasoning.

A 12th ed. was publ. 1994. Spine title: Hodges' Harbrace college handbook.

§ Similar guides to English style and usage include: Maxine Hairston and John Ruszkiewicz, *The Scott, Foresman handbook for writers* (3rd ed. N.Y. : HarperCollins, c1993); and Ian Dear, ed., *Oxford English : a guide to the language* (Oxford; N.Y. : Oxford Univ. Pr., 1989), which contains essays on usage vocabulary, grammar, slang, authors, and dialects, as well as specialized vocabulary lists.   PE1112.H6

History

Alston, R. C. A bibliography of the English language from the invention of printing to the year 1800 : a systematic record of writings on English, and on other languages in English, based on the collections of the principal libraries of the world. Leeds, Eng. : printed for the author by E. J. Arnold, 1965–87. v. 1–12. (In progress).   **BD97**

Contents: v. 1, English grammars written in English and English grammars written in Latin by native speakers; v. 2, Polyglot dictionaries and grammars; Treatises on English written for speakers of French,

German, Dutch, Danish, Swedish, Portuguese, Spanish, Italian, Hungarian, Persian, Bengali, and Russian; v. 3, pt. 1, Old English, Middle English, early modern English miscellaneous works; Vocabulary; v. 3, pt. 2, Punctuation; Concordances; Works on language in general; Origin of language; Theory of grammar; v. 4, Spelling books; v. 5, The English dictionary; v. 6, Rhetoric, style, elocution, prosody, rhyme, pronunciation, spelling reform; v. 7, Logic, philosophy, epistemology, universal language; v. 8, Treatises on short-hand; v. 9, English dialects; Scottish dialects; cant and vulgar English; v. 10, Education and language teaching; v. 11, Place names and personal names; v. 12, pt. 1, The French language : grammar, miscellaneous treatises, dictionaries; v. 12, pt. 2, The Italian, Spanish, Portuguese, and Romansh languages : grammars, dictionaries, miscellaneous treatises.

Planned to be complete in 20 v., the last of which is to contain indexes.

Covers all aspects of the English language, including language-teaching. Lists and locates copies in libraries throughout the world, though chiefly in British and American collections.

A corrected reprint of v. 1–10 "reproduced from the author's annotated copy with corrections to 1973" was published in 1974 in 1 v. by Janus Pr., Ilkey, Eng.

———. ———. *Supplement : additions and corrections, v. I–X ; list of libraries ; cumulative indexes* (Leeds : Arnold, 1973. 117 p.).   Z2015.A1A4

Baugh, Albert Croll. A history of the English language / Albert C. Baugh, Thomas Cable. 4th ed. Englewood Cliffs, N.J. : Prentice-Hall, 1993. 444 p. : ill., maps.   **BD98**

1st ed., 1957, by A. C. Baugh; 3rd ed., 1978.

Primarily a textbook for college students, which aims to present the historical development of the English language against a background of the political, social, and intellectual history of England from early times to the present. Includes English language in America. Along with minor additions and changes, this edition takes note of advances in scholarship and offers updated bibliographies.

Thomas Cable's *A companion to Baugh & Cable's History of the English language* (4th ed. Englewood Cliffs, N.J. : Prentice-Hall, 1993) is a study guide with exercises.   PE1075.B3

Cameron, Angus. Old English word studies : a preliminary author and word index / Angus Cameron, Allison Kingsmill, Ashley Crandell Amos. Toronto ; Buffalo : Published in association with the Centre for Medieval Studies, Univ. of Toronto by Univ. of Toronto Pr., c1983. 192 p. (Toronto Old English series, 8).   **BD99**

Word index: 5 microfiche in pocket.

A useful by-product of the *Dictionary of Old English* (AC172), this bibliography lists "etymological, phonological, morphological, or syntactic studies of Old English vocabulary."—*Introd.* Entries are arranged alphabetically by author, with an index by word on microfiche. The editors plan to publish a revised set of the microfiche index, with cross-references to dictionary entries, after the *Dictionary of Old English* has been completed.   Z2015.S4C35

Fisiak, Jacek. A bibliography of writings for the history of the English language. 2nd ed. Berlin ; N.Y. : Mouton de Gruyter, 1987. 216 p.   **BD100**

1st ed., 1983.

Lists 3,641 citations to books, articles, and dissertations in a classed arrangement. Author/editor index.   Z2015.A1F57

Pulsiano, Phillip. An annotated bibliography of North American doctoral dissertations on Old English language and literature. East Lansing, Mich. : Colleagues Pr., 1988. 317 p. (Medieval texts and studies, no. 3).   **BD101**

For annotation, *see* BE730.   Z2012.P85

Tajima, Matsuji. Old and Middle English language studies : a classified bibliography, 1923–1985. Amsterdam ; Philadelphia : J. Benjamins Publ. Co., 1988. 391 p. (Amsterdam studies in the theory and history of linguistic science. Series V, Library and information sources in linguistics, v. 13).   **BD102**

Intended to supplement in part A. G. Kennedy's *A bibliography of writings on the English language from the beginning of printing to the end of 1922* (Cambridge : Harvard Univ. Pr. ; New Haven, Conn. : Yale Univ. Pr., 1927. 517 p. Repr.: Freeport, N.Y. : Books for Libraries Pr., [1973]). Lists 3,913 books, monographs, dissertations, and articles in a classed arrangement. Most book entries include citations to reviews. Name index.　　　　Z2015.A1T3

Varieties and dialects

Brasch, Ila Wales. A comprehensive annotated bibliography of American Black English / [by] Ila Wales Brasch and Walter Milton Brasch. Baton Rouge : Louisiana State Univ. Pr., [1974]. 289 p.　　　　**BD103**

A partly annotated listing, arranged alphabetically by author, of books, articles, dissertations, reviews, and other materials on black American English. The range of genres covered is wide, including in addition to research studies, popular, pedagogical, memoir, and oral historical materials. Related subjects are also covered, including folklore, slave narratives, and a variety of creole dialects. Usefulness is hampered by the absence of any indexes.

§ *See also* the briefer: Dolores C. Leffall and James P. Johnson, *Black English : an annotated bibliography* (Wash. : Minority Research Center, [1973]. 75 p.).　　　　Z1234.D5B7

Fischer, Andreas. An index to dialect maps of Great Britain / by Andreas Fischer and Daniel Ammann. Amsterdam ; Philadelphia : J. Benjamins Pub. Co., 1991. 150 p. (Varieties of English around the world. General series, v. 10).　　　**BD104**

Intended as a key to the various atlases of English dialects, based on a computerized database maintained at the Universität Zürich by Andreas Fischer, from which individual printouts may be requested. Begins with an initial descriptive survey of the various general and areal survey projects of dialects, then gives a detailed index of individual words and phrases keyed to the maps and atlases in which they are registered, as well as a key to the particular questions in the surveys that elicited those items. Extensive list of printed sources. Excludes surveys of Ireland, still in progress.　　　PE1705.F57

Lougheed, W. C. Writings on Canadian English, 1976–1987 : a selective, annotated bibliography. Kingston, Ont. : Strathy Language Unit, Queen's Univ., [1988]. 66 p. (Queen's University (Kingston, Ont.). Strathy Language Unit. Occasional papers, no. 2.).　　　　**BD105**

§ Updates Walter Avis' *Writings on Canadian English, 1792–1987* (Toronto : Fitzhenry & Whiteside, c1978). Lists alphabetically by main entry approximately 300 items with cursory annotations. Subject index.　　　　Z1379.L68

McMillan, James B. Annotated bibliography of Southern American English / James B. McMillan and Michael B. Montgomery. Tuscaloosa : Univ. of Alabama Pr., c1989. 444 p.　　　　**BD106**

1st ed. by J. B. McMillan, 1978.

A classified listing of monographs, articles, and dissertations up to 1989, with coverage of peripheral, as well as central, southern areas (including the southern sections of such states as Indiana, Illinois, and Missouri; also Central and West Texas, Oklahoma, the Missouri Ozarks, the District of Columbia, and Delaware). Includes materials on black English, creoles, literary dialects, and place-name studies. Entries are classed by genres and topical themes, not by geographical region. Sections include Historical and creole studies; Lexical studies; Phonetics and phonology; Place-name studies; Literary dialect; Figurative language, exaggerations, and word-play; etc. *See also* references to materials spanning more than one subject. Index of authors only; no access by region.　　　　Z1251.S7M37

Mencken, Henry Louis. The American language : an inquiry into the development of English in the United States. 4th ed. corr., enl. and rewritten. N.Y. : Knopf, 1936. 796 p.　　**BD107**

──────. ──────. *Supplements 1–2* (N.Y. : Knopf, 1945–48).
Frequently reprinted.

A historical treatment of the development of the English language in the U.S. covering such topics as: the two streams of English; the beginning and growth of the American language; pronunciation and spelling; the common speech; proper names in America; American slang, etc. Appendix: Non-English dialects in America. List of words and phrases. Index.

The supplements follow the same plan as the original work.

──────. ──────. *The 4th ed. and the supplements, abridged, with annotations and new material,* by Raven I. McDavid, Jr., with the assistance of David W. Maurer ([1st abridged ed.]. N.Y : Knopf, 1963. 777, cxxiv p.).

Not a revision but a briefer form of the 3-v. work with some modifications required by recent changes in the language "and in the civilization which the language reflects."—*Introd.*

Viereck, Wolfgang. A bibliography of writings on varieties of English, 1965–1983 / comp. by Wolfgang Viereck, Edgar W. Schneider, and Manfred Görlach. Amsterdam ; Philadelphia : Benjamins, 1984. 319 p.　　　　**BD108**

Consists of three bibliographies, each prepared by one of the three compilers: on varieties of English in the British Isles (Viereck); on American and Canadian English (Schneider); and on English as a world language (Görlach). Entries are listed alphabetically by author within each section. Although homogeneity among them is the norm, they vary in some details which are explained in individual prefaces accompanying the three secions.

§ Coverage is continued to 1993 by: Beat Glauser, Schneider, and Görlach, *New bibliography of writings on varieties of English* (Amsterdam ; Philadelphia : Benjamins, 1993).　　　Z2015.V27V54

English as a second language

Cooper, Stephen. Graduate theses and dissertations in English as a second language / Stephen Cooper ; prep. by Clearinghouse on Languages and Linguistics. 1975/76–1978/79. [Arlington, Va.] : Center for Applied Linguistics, [1977–80]. Annual.　　　　**BD109**

Vols. for 1976/77, 1978/79 publ. as *Language in education: theory and practice,* no. 3, 15.

Classed listing with author index. Brief abstract for many entries. Includes author's address current at time of compilation.

Continued by: *ESL theses and dissertations, 1979–80* (Wash. : Center for Applied Linguistics, 1981. 20 p.).　　　Z5818.E5C66

Goldstein, Wallace L. Teaching English as a second language : an annotated bibliography. N.Y. : Garland, 1975. 218 p.　　　　**BD110**

A classed listing of 852 items, with descriptive annotations. Works are grouped under such headings as: Curriculum, Grammar, Reading, Spoken English, Teaching aids, Testing and evaluation, Texts, Writing. Key-word index and author index. A supplement appeared in 1975.

──────. *Teaching English as a second language 2 : an annotated bibliography* (N.Y. : Garland, 1984. 323 p.).

Serves as a supplement, adding more than 900 items, primarily 1975–82 publications.　　　　Z5818.E5G64

Maclin, Alice. Reference guide to English : a handbook of English as a second language. N.Y. : Holt, Rinehart and Winston, [1981]. 405 p.　　　　**BD111**

Intended either for classroom use or for independent study by non-native speakers and students of English. Employs a dictionary arrangement with the expectation that students can thus use it as a ready reference source to identify and correct their problems without consulting an instructor, but many of the headings (such as "determiners," "interrupters," "subordinating and reducing") seem sufficiently unusual as to make reference to the index essential. Cross-references are also provided.　　　　PE1128.M3254

OTHER GERMANIC LANGUAGES

General and comparative

Bibliography

Germanistik in Festschriften von den Anfängen (1877) bis 1973 : Verz. germanist. Festschriften u. Bibliographie d. darin avgedr. germanist. Beitr. / bearb. von Ingrid Hannich-Bode; in Zusammenarb. mit d. Ins. of Germanic Studies (Univ. of London). Stuttgart : Metzler, c1976. 441 p. **BD112**

Lists and analyzes about 800 volumes of festschriften. The analytical section is in nine main divisions, each with numerous subsections: (1) Allgemeines; (2) Allgemeine Sprachwissenschaft; (3) Germanische Sprachen; (4) Deutsche Sprache; (5) Allgemeine und deutsche Literaturwissenschaft; (6) Germanische Dichtung und Kultur; (7) Deutsche Literatur in einzelnen Zeitabschnitten; (8) Weltliteratur und vergleichende Literatur; (9) Nachbarwissenschaft. Indexes by author, title, broad subject, and personal names as subjects. Z7036.G47

Markey, Thomas L. Germanic and its dialects : a grammar of proto-Germanic / T. L. Markey, R. L. Kyes, Paul T. Roberge. Amsterdam : John Benjamins, 1977. v. 1. (In progress). **BD113**

An unannotated alphabetic listing of 8,298 entries covering a wide range of studies on early Germanic languages and dialects (monographs, articles, dissertations, and manuscript sources) up through 1976. The first of a 3-v. set, whose other volumes are to contain discursive presentation, maps, commentaries. Indexes of words treated (by languages), subjects, authors. PD76.M3

McKay, John C. A guide to Germanic reference grammars : the modern standard languages. Amsterdam ; Philadelphia : Benjamins, 1984. 239 p. (Amsterdam studies in the theory and history of linguistic science. Series V, Library and information sources in linguistics, v. 15.). **BD114**

A classed listing of grammars by language, preceded by an introductory chapter on the theoretical and methodological stances represented by various grammars. Living languages are covered, including Afrikaans, Faroese, Friesian, and Yiddish, as well as English, German, Dutch, and the Scandinavian languages. Each entry is annotated evaluatively and in detail; bibliographic citations accompany each entry as relevant. Includes also a bibliography of general linguistic and other non-Germanic works, and a general index both of subjects and of authors of Germanic grammars and syntactic works mentioned in the entries. Z7036.M38

Seymour, Richard K. A bibliography of word formations in the Germanic languages. Durham : Duke Univ. Pr., 1968. 158 p. **BD115**

An author listing of about 2,000 articles and monographs dealing with word formation in the Germanic languages (including English), through 1964. Omits studies on loan words, place-names, and personal names. Z7038.W6S4

German

General works

Bibliography

Bibliographie der deutschen Sprach- und Literaturwissenschaft. 9. Bd. (1969)– . Frankfurt am Main : V. Klostermann, [c1970]– . **BD116**

For annotation, *see* BE1235. Z2231.B5

Eisenberg, Peter. Bibliographie zur deutschen Grammatik : 1965–1986 / Peter Eisenberg, Alexander Gusovius. 2., überarbeitete und erw. Aufl. Tübingen : G. Narr, 1988. 412 p. (Studien zur deutschen Grammatik, Bd. 26). **BD117**

Supersedes the compilers' *Bibliographie zur deutschen Grammatik : 1965–1983* (1985).

An unannotated alphabetic author listing, covering "grammar" in the sense of works on all aspects of the structure of the languages. Entries in various languages. Subject index (called C. Systematischer Teil). Z2235.G7E39

Jahresbericht für deutsche Sprache und Literatur / bearb. unter Leitung von Gerhard Marx. 2 v. Berlin : Akademie-Verlag, 1960–66. **BD118**

For annotation, *see* BE1226. Z2235.A2J3

Jahresbericht über die Erscheinungen auf dem Gebiete der germanischen Philologie / hrsg. von Gesellschaft für Deutsche Philologie in Berlin. 1879–1936/39. Berlin : W. de Gruyter, 1880–1954. **BD119**

Useful annual bibliography, listing the new book, pamphlet, and dissertation literature, and also indexing articles in a large number of important periodicals. The 1936/39 volume (publ. 1954) brings the record up to the beginning of World War II.

§ Superseded by *Jahresbericht für deutsche Sprache und Literatur* (BE1226). Z7037.J25

Jahresbericht über die wissenschaftlichen Erscheinungen auf dem Gebiete der neueren deutschen Literatur / hrsg. von der Literaturarchivgesellschaft in Berlin. n.F., v.1 (1921)–16/19 (1936/39). Berlin : W. de Gruyter, 1924–56. **BD120**

For annotation, *see* BE1225. Z2231.J26

Jahresberichte für neuere deutsche Literaturgeschichte. v. 1 (1890)–v. 26, pt. 1 (1915). Berlin : Behr, 1892–1919. 1890–1915. **BD121**

For annotation, *see* BE1224. Z2231.J25

Pasierbsky, Fritz. Deutsche Sprache im Reformationszeitalter : eine geistes- und sozialgeschichtlich orientierte Bibliographie / Fritz Pasierbsky ; bearb. und hrsg. von Edeltrud Büchler und Edmund Dirkschnieder. Tübingen : Niemeyer, 1988. 2 v. (1088 p.). **BD122**

Lists books, dissertations, and articles on German philology and the German language in the medieval and early modern periods. Arranged alphabetically by author, with a section that analyzes collective works. Subject index. Z2235.A2P37x

University of London. Institute of Germanic Studies. German language and literature : select bibliography of reference books / by L. M. Newman. 2nd enl. ed. London : Inst. of Germanic Studies, Univ. of London, 1979. 175 p. **BD123**

1st ed., 1966.

A guide for students and research workers, listing and annotating reference works for German language and literature and reflecting the trend toward German studies as a discipline. Sections for research method, German language and literature, German literature, German language and linguistics, Germanic subjects, general rapid reference books, and other subjects. In general the cutoff date is Dec. 1976. Indexed. Z2235.A2L6

Encyclopedias

Deutsche Sprache : kleine Enzyklopädie / [hrsg., Wolfgang Fleischer ... et al.]. Leipzig : Bibliographisches Institut, 1983. 724 p., : ill., maps. **BD124**

Organized systematically (not alphabetically by individual subject), according to a scheme presented in the table of contents. Covers history of the language, current description, dialects and other variation, and sociolinguistic aspects; less attention to areas of applied linguistics (such as contrastive linguistics, study and teaching of German as a foreign language, etc.). Concludes with a general alphabetical bibliography and a subject index.

§ Another helpful encyclopedic source, covering an even wider range of subjects with signed articles by specialists, is: *Lexikon der Germanistischen Linguistik*, hrsg. von H. P. Althaus, H. Henne, H. E. Wiegand (2. Aufl. Tübingen : Niemeyer, 1980).   PF3073.D42

History

Sprachgeschichte : ein Handbuch zur Geschichte der deutschen Sprache und ihrer Erforschung / hrsg. von Werner Besch, Oskar Reichmann, Stefan Sonderegger. Berlin ; N.Y. : W. de Gruyter, 1984–1985. 2 v. (2251 p.) : ill, maps. (Handbücher zur Sprach- und Kommunikationswissenschaft, Bd. 2).   **BD125**

A very thorough handbook on various aspects of the history of the German language: on all its stages and precedents, its interrelationships with other Germanic languages, its variants, registers, and other aspects. Rich in historiography, with numerous maps, charts, and other illustrations. Indexes of subjects and authors.

Varieties and dialects

Dialektologie : ein Handbuch zur deutschen und allgemeinen Dialektforschung / hrsg. von Werner Besch … [et al.]. Berlin ; N.Y. : Walter de Gruyter, 1982– . v. 1– . (Handbücher zur Sprach- und Kommunikationswissenschaft, Bd. 1).   **BD126**

A voluminous detailed survey, with chapters consisting of discussion and bibliography thematically, not geographically, focused, covering linguistic and other issues across all the dialects. Devotes attention to such aspects of the field as historiography, theoretical and methodological approaches, and computational and other automated work. Extends enough into general principles of dialectology to be useful for work beyond the scope of German itself. Many maps, charts, and other illustrative material. Subject index (including access by geographic and dialect areas), but no author index.

§ Complements Peter Wiesinger's *Bibliographie zur Grammatik der deutschen Dialekte* (BD127), which is arranged geographically. For a much briefer handbook in English, see C. A. M. Noble's *Modern German dialects* (N.Y. : P. Lang, 1983).   PF5011.D52x

Wiesinger, Peter. Bibliographie zur Grammatik der deutschen Dialekte : Laut-, Formen-, Wortbildungs- und Satzlehre, 1800 bis 1980 / von Peter Wiesinger und Elisabeth Raffin. Bern ; N.Y. : P. Lang, 1987. 195 p.   **BD127**

A bibliography of "grammar" of the German dialects in a broad sense, including phonology, inflectional and derivational morphology, and syntax that excludes the large areas of lexicology and lexicography, sociolinguistics, etc. A classed listing, organized by geographic and dialect area, subdivided by grammatical and other linguistic categories. Author index, separate volume of maps.

———. ———. *1981 bis 1985 und Nachträge aus früheren Jahren* (Bern ; N.Y. : Lang, 1987). Continues the coverage. May be used with *Dialektologie*, by Werner Besch (BD126), whose focus is thematic, not geographic.   Z2235.D5W54

Dutch

Bibliography

Haeringen, Coenraad Bernardus van. Netherlandic language research : men and works in the study of Dutch. 2nd ed. Leiden : Brill, 1960. 120 p.   **BD128**

1st ed., 1954.

A survey of 20th-century research on the history of the language of the Netherlands, with some critical evaluation of selected works in the field. Includes a chapter on reference works and periodicals.

Scandinavian

General works

Bibliography

Bekker-Nielsen, Hans. Old Norse-Icelandic studies : a select bibliography. [Toronto] : Univ. of Toronto Pr., [1967]. 94 p.   **BD129**

For annotation, *see* BE1083.   Z2556.B4

Haugen, Einar. A bibliography of Scandinavian languages and linguistics, 1900–1970. Oslo : Universitetsforlaget, [1974]. 527 p.   **BD130**

Aims to present "a selection of articles, brochures, monographs, books, and series relating to the scientific and practical study of the Scandinavian languages" (*Pref.*), including "all the standard and nonstandard forms of Danish, Faroese, Icelandic, Norwegian, and Swedish, as well as older attested and unattested forms of these." The body of the work is an alphabetical author listing. Each entry is followed by a set of "descriptors," i.e., letters and numerals used to indicate the language or languages dealt with and the type of subject matter (grammar, syntax, language teaching, etc.). The index follows the numerical/alphabetical sequence of the descriptors.

Supplemented by: *Bibliography of Scandinavian linguistics* ([no.] 1 [1925/26]– . In *Acta philologica scandinavica*. Annual).

Title varies: early issues called *Bibliographie der nordischen Philologie*.

A bibliography of Scandinavian philology and linguistics, listing books and periodical articles. Some issues cover more than one year.   Z2555.H38

Danish

Hansen, Erik. Bibliografi over moderne dansk rigssprog, 1850–1978 / Erik Hansen og Nana Riemann. [København] : Gjellerup, [1979]. 94 p.   **BD131**

A classed bibliography of books, parts of books, and periodical articles. Detailed table of contents, but no index.

§ Supplemented by H. G. Jacobsen, *Dansk sprogrøgtslitteratur, 1900–1955* (København : [Gyldendal], 1974), which also contains subject and author indexes.   Z2575.A2H36

Other Germanic

Afrikaans

Nienaber, Petrus Johannes. Bronnegids by die studie van die Afrikaanse taal en letterkunde. Johannesburg : Nienaber, 1947. 422p.   **BD132**

A bibliography of Afrikaans literature and language.

Continued by: *Bronnegids by die studie van die Afrikaanse taal en letterkunde* ([Deel 1, 1947]–deel 7A [1969] ; Nuwe reeks, deel 1 [1970]–1985. Johannesburg : P.J. Nienaber, 1947–86). Irregular, 1947–53; annual, 1954–85.

Friesian

Bremmer, Rolf H. A bibliographical guide to Old Frisian studies. [Odense] : Odense Univ. Pr., 1992. 197 p. (North-Western European language evolution. Supplement, v. 6.). **BD133**

An alphabetic author listing, including much material relevant for Old English studies (Friesian being the closest relative of English). Contains an unusually detailed and structured "Analytical subject index," giving access to lexical studies by individual word, names of individual scholars active in the history of Old Friesian studies, geographic areas, linguistic and historical topics, numbered by a scheme listed in an initial "Contents Part III." Includes also an index of the authors of book reviews. Z7038.F75B74

Yiddish

Bratkowsky, Joan Gloria. Yiddish linguistics : a multilingual bibliography. N.Y. : Garland, 1988. 407 p. (Garland reference library of the humanities, v. 140). **BD134**

Intended to supplement Uriel and Beatrice Weinreich's *Yiddish language and folklore* ('sGravenhage : Mouton, 1959). Lists almost 2,200 items in a classed arrangement of 12 main chapters: general works, structure of Yiddish, history of Yiddish, dialectology, interaction with other languages, onomastics, stylistics, semiotics, history and biography of linguistics and linguists, sociolinguistics, psycholinguistics, and applied linguistics. Name index. Z7038.Y53B7

LATIN AND GREEK

Greek

General (including classical)

Bibliographical bulletin of the Greek language = Deltion vivliographias tēs Hellēnikēs glōssēs. v. 1 (1973)–v. 3 (1975/76). Athens : Spoudastērion Glossologias tou Panepistemiou Anthēon. Annual. **BD135**

At head of title: Department of Linguistics of the Univ. of Athens.

George Babiniotis, ed.

Introductory and explanatory matter in English and Greek.

Each issue is an international, classified listing (with author index) of the year's publications on "the entire Greek language (Ancient, Byzantine, Modern)."—*Pref.* No more published. Z7021.D44

Cirac Estopañan, Sebastian. Sintesis bibliografica de filologia griega. (*In* Logos : monografías y síntesis bibliográfica de filología griega [Barcelona : Univ. de Barcelona, 1960]). **BD136**

Issued as Parte II of v. 1 of the journal *Logos*, of which no more volumes appear to have been published.

A classed, unannotated listing of 4,605 entries for works on periods from antiquity through modern times, with subject coverage broader than the title suggests: not only philology, but also textology, numismatics, history, art history, science, mythology, religion (both Christian and other), philosophy, and law. Indexes: Greek forms; modern persons, journals, institutions; and general subjects (in Spanish). Z7022.L6

Householder, Fred W. Greek : a survey of recent work / by Fred W. Householder and Gregory Nagy. The Hague : Mouton, 1972. 105 p. (Janua linguarum. Series practica, 211). **BD137**

A first version, covering 1839–1968, was published in T. A. Sebeok, ed. *Current trends in linguistics*, v. 9 (1972) : 800–816.

A discursive, highly focused handbook concentrating on a survey of selective research issues in the entire prehistory and history of Greek. The compilers describe their work as "eclectic: it is neither a bibliographical survey nor an exhaustive chronicle of progress. ... the main attempt here is simply to outline given trends, either dynamic or routine, in the study of Greek."—*Introd.* A Generalities section (pt. 1), with broad outlines of research trends and many examples of Greek linguistic problems studied, is followed by Specifics (pt. 2, with subsections Phonology, Morphology, Syntax, Etymology and Vocabulary, and Dialectology), Conclusions (pt. 3), and an appendix, Towards a wider perspective on the Greek language, by Gregory Nagy, with examples in dialectology and diachrony, suggestive for a holistic approach to the language. Concludes with a bibliography (1839–1968) and a supplementary bibliography through 1972. No indexes.

PA231.H6

Prozorov, P. Sistematicheskiĭ ukazatel' knig i stateĭ po grecheskoĭ filologii, napechatannykh v Rossii s XVII stolĕtiĭa po 1892 god na russkom i inostrannykh ĭazykakh : S pribavleniem za 1893, 1894 i 1895 gody. Sanktpeterburg : Imperatorskaĭa akademiĭa nauk, 1898. 374 p. **BD138**

Title translated: Systematic bibliography of books and articles on Greek philology printed in Russia from the 17th century through 1892 in Russian and foreign languages : with a supplement for 1893–1895.

A classed, unannotated listing, with the basic bibliography for works published through 1892 followed in continuous pagination by a cumulative supplement for 1893–95; both are covered by a single table of contents. Records works on the period from antiquity through the end of the 5th century CE, with focus on non-Christian authors and subjects. Besides language and literature, contains sections for epigraphy, numismatics, philosophy, geography, history, and "antiquities" (archaeology, mythology, religion, ethnography, society). Each section is subdivided into more specific subsections, within which the entries are in chronological order by date of publication; entries are given a consecutive numeration throughout each general section. Index of authors and translators.

Mycenean

Baumbach, Lydia. Studies in Mycenaean inscriptions and dialect, 1965–1978. Roma : Edizioni dell'Ateneo, 1986. 516 p. (Incunabula Graeca, 86.). **BD139**

"A complete bibliography and index incorporating the contents of volumes XI-XXIII [of the annual bibliographic journal *Studies in Mycenaean inscriptions and dialect*] published between 1965 and 1978 by the Institute of Classical Studies of the University of London and the British Association of Mycenaean Studies compiled by Lydia Baumbach, from the volumes prepared by L. J. D. Richardson ... [et al.]."—*t.p.* An earlier volume (1968) cumulated the bibliographies from v. 1–10 (1953–64). Citations are listed alphabetically by author, subarranged chronologically. The basic bibliographic listing is called "Index A." Other indexes: "Interpretations of vocabulary words and placenames," a detailed word index (giving syllabic and phonetic transcriptions with inflectional variants in order of their nominatives, etc., their Attic equivalents, and a summary of the conjectures and interpretations in the citations); studies of tablets (by site of discovery); and subjects (classified by a scheme analyzed in the table of contents, at the end). Z7023.I5B38

Biblical

Tov, Emanuel. A classified bibliography of lexical and grammatical studies on the language of the Septuagint. Jerusalem : Academon, 1980. 46 p.   **BD140**
A classed unannotated listing of monographs, articles, (including review articles) in Western European languages on various linguistic aspects of the Greek Old Testament. Index of Greek forms is included, but there is neither an author index nor a list of the abbreviations of journal and series titles used; however, the abbreviations used are relatively standard and straightforward.   Z7023.B5T56

Medieval and modern

Swanson, Donald Carl Eugene. Modern Greek studies in the West : a critical bibliography of studies on modern Greek linguistics, philology, and folklore, in languages other than Greek. N.Y. : New York Pub. Lib., 1960. 93 p.   **BD141**
Includes books and periodical articles, with brief annotations and references to reviews. Indexes to authors, words discussed, Greek regions, etc.   Z2291.S9

Latin

General

Bibliographie zur lateinischen Wortforschung / hrsg. von Otto Hiltbrunner. Bern : Francke, c1981–1992. v. 1–4. (In progress).   **BD142**
Contents: v. 1–4, A–Cura.
Lists studies on etymology, word forms, and usage alphabetically by Latin word. Lengthier entries conclude with a brief discussion of the works cited and the history of scholarship on that particular word.   Z7028.E88B52

Cousin, Jean. Bibliographie de la langue latine, 1880–1948. Paris : Soc. d'Édit. "Les Belles-Lettres", 1951. 375 p.   **BD143**
A classified bibliography, in many languages, of books and periodical articles on the Latin language. Lists publications 1880–1948. Indexes of Latin words and classical authors; no author index.
Z7026.C6

Steitz, Lothar. Bibliographie zur Aussprache des Latein. Saarbrücken : [Institut für Phonetik, Universität des Saarlandes], 1987. 148 p. (Phonetica Saraviensia, Nr. 9).   **BD144**
In German, Czech, English, French, Hungarian, Italian, Polish, Russian, Spanish, and Ukrainian.
More than 1,400 citations to books, articles, and dissertations on the pronunciation of Latin, arranged alphabetically by author within chapters on particular topics. Author index.   Z7028.P75S73

Medieval and late

McGuire, Martin Rawson Patrick. Introduction to medieval Latin studies : a syllabus and bibliographical guide / by Martin R.P. McGuire and Hermigild Dressler. 2nd ed. Wash. : Catholic Univ. of Amer. Pr., 1977. 406 p.   **BD145**
1st ed., 1964.
Aims "to give the beginning graduate student a comprehensive, solid, and up-to-date orientation" (*Pref.*) in the field. "The *Syllabus* and *Select Bibliography* are broader in scope than their titles might indicate, for they include references to, or even initial orientation in, a number of other disciplines—e.g., Classical, Patristic, Celtic, German-

ic, Romance, Byzantine and Islamic Studies—insofar as these disciplines have connections with Medieval Latin Studies." Syllabus, with suggested readings, p. 1–241; Select bibliographies, p. 245–379. Indexed.   PA2816.M24

Sanders, Gabriel. Bibliographie signalétique du latin des chrétiens / par Gabriel Sanders et Marc Van Uytfanghe. Turnholti : Typographi Brepols editores pontificii, 1989. 188 p. (Corpus Christianorum. Lingua patrum, 1).   **BD146**
A list of books and articles on texts, vocabularies, and language use of early Christian authors. Index of Latin words.   BR67.L55 v.1

Tremblay, Florent A. Bibliotheca lexicologiae Medii Aevi. Lewiston, N.Y. : Edwin Mellen Pr., c1988–[1989?]. 10 v.
          BD147
Contents: v. 1, Classics in the Middle Ages. Education in the Middle Ages; v. 2, Lexicons (A–F) in the Middle Ages; v. 3, Lexicons (G–Z) in the Middle Ages; v. 4, Grammars in the Middle Ages; v. 5, Rise of vernacular languages; v. 6, Influence of vulgar Latin; v. 7, Lexicographical manuscripts (A–L); v. 8, Lexicographical manuscripts (M–Z), Journals and periodicals; v. 9, Author index, Title index; v. 10, Geographical index, Abbreviation index, Chronological index, Index on [sic] incipits.
Intended as a companion to Rodrigue LaRue's *Clavis scriptorum Graecorum et Latinorum* (Trois-Rivières : Université du Québec à Trois-Rivières, Service de la Bibliothèque, c1985. 4 v.), this computer-generated bibliography lists publications and manuscripts from all time periods that relate to the use and study of Latin in the Middle Ages. The citations, arranged alphabetically by author or main entry in the topical volumes (v. 1–8), include references to reviews for modern works, bibliographic descriptions and some holdings information for early printed works, and references to censuses or textual analyses for manuscripts. Although v. 9–10 contain numerous indexes, the lack of a comprehensive subject index, combined with the awkward use of abbreviations instead of volume numbers, makes this comprehensive tool suitable only for advanced scholars and researchers.   Z7028.L47T74

ROMANCE LANGUAGES

General and comparative

Lexikon der Romanistischen Linguistik : LRL / hrsg. von Günter Holtus, Michael Metzeltin, Christian Schmitt. Tübingen : M. Niemeyer, c1988–94. v. 3–6, pt. 2. (In progress).   **BD148**
Contents: v. 3 pt. 6 (1989), Die einzelnen romanischen Sprachen und Sprachgebiete von der Renaissance bis zur Gegenwart. Rumänisch, Dalmatisch/Irtroromanisch, Friaulisch, Ladinisch, Bünderromanisch; v. 4 (1988), Italienisch, Korsisch, Sardisch; v. 5 pt. 1–2 (1990–91), Französisch, Okzitanisch, Katalanisch; v. 6 pt. 1–2 (1992–94), Aragonesisch, Navarresisch, Spanisch, Asturianisch/Leonesisch, Galegisch, Portugesisch.
Table of contents in French and German; text in French, German, and Italian.
Although called "Lexikon," this major set, projected for 8 v., represents a comprehensive guide to and history of the Romance languages. It is, in effect, a revision of Gustav Gröber's *Grundriss der romanischen Philologie* (1st–2nd ed. Strassburg : Trübner, 1897–1906. 2 v. in 4) and its *Neue Folge* (Berlin : W. de Gruyter, 1933–38. v. 3–5). Arranged in signed chapters with detailed bibliographies, illustrations, charts, and maps both in color and black-and-white.   PC43.L49

Bibliography

Bach, Kathryn F. Romance linguistics and the romance languages : a bibliography of bibliographies / by Kathryn F. Bach and Glanville Price. London : Grant & Cutler, 1977. 194 p. **BD149**

"Lists, with brief critical or descriptive notes, some 650 bibliographical items relating to Romance linguistics in general or to one or more of the individual Romance languages or dialects."—*Pref.* Classed arrangement following the plan of *Linguistic bibliography for the year* (BD25). Index of names. Z7031.A1B33

Bibliographie sélective de linguistique romane et française / Willy Bal, Jean Germain, Jean-Rene Klein et Pierre Swiggers. Paris ; Louvain-la-Neuve : Duculot, c1991. 268 p. **BD150**

Based on Bal and Germain's *Guide bibliographique de linguistique romane* (Louvain : Éd. Peeters, 1978), but considered a separate work, not a new edition.

"The subject of the work is Romance linguistics and all the Romance languages; French is mentioned in the title only so that the French-speaking readership would understand that French is not excluded, as is sometimes implied by the phrase 'linguistique romane'."—*Introd.* A classed, unannotated listing of monographs. Includes intital sections on Indo-European lingusitics and Latin, followed by 11 sections devoted to individual Romance languages. In addition to the more commonly covered members of the family, also individually treated are: Dalmatian, Sardinian, Romansh ("Rhétoroman"), Occitan, and Catalan. Each section begins with a brief introduction to the particular language, a map, and a short list of features distinguishing it within the Romance family, followed by bibliographic citations. Each section has several levels of subdivision, including typically Bibliographies, Journals and guides, Synchronic studies, Historical studies, Onomastics, Versification, Anthologies of texts; the scheme is detailed in the "Table des matiéres" at the beginning. Index of author names.

McKay, John C. A guide to romance reference grammars : the modern standard languages. Amsterdam : Benjamins, 1979. 126 p. (Library and information sources in linguistics, v. 6). **BD151**

Describes and evaluates "the best reference grammars and comprehensive works on syntax of contemporary Catalan, French, Italian, Portuguese, Spanish, and Rumanian."—*Pref.* Indexed. Z7031.M32

Palfrey, Thomas Rossman. A bibliographical guide to the Romance languages and literatures / comp. by Thomas R. Palfrey, Joseph G. Fucilla, William C. Holbrook. 8th ed. Evanston, Ill. : Chandler, 1971. 122 p. **BD152**

For annotation, *see* BE1073. Z7031.P15

Romanische Bibliographie = Bibliographie romane = Romance bibliography. 1961–62– . Tübingen : Max Niemeyer, 1965– . Biennial. **BD153**

Publisher varies.

Title varies: until issue for 1961/62 (publ. 1965–68) publ. as "Supplementheft : Bibliographie" to *Zeitschrift für romanische Philogolie.*

Vols. 39–43, 1914–23, never published. 1940–50 issued in 1 v. (14 Lfg.), publ. 1952–57; 1951–55 issued in 1 v. (2 Lfg.), publ. 1961; 1956–60 issued in 1 v. (2 Lfg.), publ. 1964. Began separate publication with 1961/62; issued biennially in parts.

A major international serial bibliography for Romance philology. Now issued in three parts: (1) indexes (authors, reviewers, persons, subjects) and other general reference materials; (2) bibliography of language and linguistics studies; (3) bibliography of literature (editions, history, criticism) and intellectual/cultural history. Each volume includes a general table of contents. Listings are numbered, unannotated, and in classed arrangement. The volume for languages and linguistics has a general section divided by subject, followed by sections for the various languages also divided by subject. The literature volume begins with theoretical and comparative sections, followed by sections for the various literatures with topical subdivisions. For 1991 (publ. 1993), the language volume lists 3,326 entries, the literature volume 8,538. PC3.Z5

Wexler, Paul. Judeo-Romance linguistics : a bibliography (Latin, Italo-, Gallo, Ibero-, and Rhaeto-Romance except Castilian). N.Y. : Garland, 1989. 174 p. (Garland reference library of the humanities, v. 890). **BD154**

Lists 1,638 works on "all the Judeo-Romance languages attested before the expulsions of the Jews from the Kingdom of France and the Iberian Peninsula (1394 and 1492–8 respectively)—with the exception of Judezmo and Sephardic Ladino."—*Introd.* Arranged in a classified scheme of chapters on Latin, Italian, Gallic, Iberian forms, and comparative studies. Author index. Z7033.J48W49

Dissertations

Flasche, Hans. Die Sprachen und Literaturen der Romanen im Spiegel der deutschen Universitätsschriften, 1885–1950 : eine Bibliographie. Bonn : H. Bouvier, 1958. 299 p. (Bonner Beiträge zur Bibliotheks- und Bücherkunde, Bd. 3). **BD155**

For annotation, *see* BE1071. Z7031.F55

French

Bibliography

Bassan, Fernande. French language and literature : an annotated bibliography / Fernande Bassan, Donald C. Spinelli, Howard A. Sullivan. N.Y. : Garland, 1989. 365 p. (Garland reference library of the humanities, v. 954). **BD156**

1st ed., 1976.

Intended as a guide for the student, the scholar, and the librarian, although emphasis is on general materials rather than scholarly studies. In three main sections: (1) General bibliographies and reference works; (2) General studies on the French language; and (3) Bibliographies and studies of literature. Organization of sections and subsections is detailed in the table of contents containing 1,253 numbered entries, covering publications through the first half of 1988. Author and title index; titles are listed both for author and for title main entries. Z2175.A2B39

Chervel, André. Les grammaires françaises, 1800–1914 : répertoire chronologique / André Chervel. Paris : Institut national de recherche pédagogique, Service d'histoire de l'éducation, 1982. 223 p. **BD157**

A chronological numbered listing of 2,037 grammars of French, continuing the coverage of Edmund Stengel, *Chronologisches Verzeichnis französischer Grammatiken : vom Ende des 14. bis zum Ausgange des 18. Jahrhunderts ...* (Oppeln : Franck, 1890. Repr. : Amsterdam : Benjamins, 1976). Subarranged by author under year of publication. Various types of grammar and other reference works are indicated by letter codes accompanying each entry. Includes an "Annexe" listing grammars published outside France, by country; and another giving the call numbers of anonymous works in the Bibliothèque Nationale. Index of authors. Z2175.G7C45

Griffin, Lloyd W. Modern French literature and language : a bibliography of homage studies / comp. by Lloyd W. Griffin, Jack A. Clarke, and Alexander Y. Kroff. Madison : Univ. of Wisconsin Pr., 1976. 175 p. **BD158**

For annotation, *see* BE1134. Z2175.F45G74

Varieties and dialects

Oukada, Larbi. Louisiana French : an annotated, linguistic bibliography. Lafayette, La. : Center for Louisiana Studies, Univ. of Southwestern Louisiana, c1979. 133 p. **BD159**
Covers "the three varieties of French commonly recognized in the state—namely, Colonial-French, spoken by the descendents of the first settlers who came directly from Europe; Acadian-French, the speech of those who were expelled from Nova Scotia in 1755 and settled [in] … Louisiana; and finally, the Creole … spoken mainly, though not exclusively, by blacks."—*Introd.* The 924 numbered entries are classed by type of material: masters' theses, dissertations, articles, books, selected Louisiana French-language periodicals, selected and unannotated newspaper and popular magazine articles, and selected studies on the sociocultural characteristics of French-speaking Louisianians. General index of authors and subjects. Z2175.D5O93

Italian

Bibliography

Golden, Herbert Hershel. Modern Italian language and literature : a bibliography of homage studies / by Herbert Hershel Golden and Seymour O. Simches. Cambridge : Harvard Univ. Pr., 1959. 207 p. **BD160**
For annotation, *see* BE1293. Z2355.A2G6

Hall, Robert Anderson. Bibliografia della linguistica italiana. 2. ed. riv. e aggiornata. Firenze : Sansoni, 1958. 3 v. (Biblioteca bibliografica italica, 13–15). **BD161**
A major revision of the 1941 edition, published as *Bibliography of Italian linguistics* (Baltimore : Linguistic Soc. of America). This 2nd ed. contains some 6,900 numbered items, about twice the number in the 1st ed.
Includes material published since about 1860, arranged in four major sections: (1) History of the Italian language; (2) Description of the Italian language; (3) Italian dialectology; (4) History of Italian linguistics. Five indexes: author and title, regions and dialects, words, etyma, general subjects.
Continued by ten-year supplements, which continue the entry numbering of the 2nd ed.:
———. ———. *Primo supplemento decennale (1956–1966)* (1969. 524 p.). Through entry 9284.
———. ———. *Secondo supplemento decennale (1966–1976)* (Pisa : Giardini, [1980]. 388 p.). Through entry 12,961.
———. ———. *Terzo supplemento decennale* (1976–1986) (Firenze : Sansoni, 1988. 620 p.). Through entry 18,796.
Z2355.A2H315

Varieties and dialects

Sabourin, Conrad. La francité canadienne / Conrad F. Sabourin, Rolande M. Lamarche. Montréal : Université de Montréal, Faculté des sciences de l'éducation, 1985–1987. v. 1–2. (In progress). **BD162**
Vol. 2 by Conrad F. Sabourin, Rolande M. Lamarche, and Elca Tarrab.
Contents: v. 1, Aspects linguistiques : bibliographie; v. 2, Sociologie et politicologie de la langue.
Lists books, essays, journal articles, theses, dissertations, and government reports in alphabetical order by main entry. Subject index.
§ *See also*: G. Dulong, *Bibliographie linguistique du Canada français* (Québec : Presses de l'Univ. Laval ; Paris : Klincksieck, 1966). Z1380.S22

Portuguese

Chamberlain, Bobby J. Portuguese language and Luso-Brazilian literature : an annotated guide to selected reference works. N.Y. : Modern Language Association of America, 1989. 95 p. (Selected bibliographies in language and literature, 6). **BD163**
A classed, annotated, selective bibliography of bibliographies, indexes, catalogs, guides, directories, dictionaries, and other reference works on the varieties of Portuguese spoken in Portugal, Brazil, and Africa; and on the literatures of those areas. Excludes certain specialized dictionaries (technical, orthographic), grammars, histories of literature, and specialized linguistic or literary studies. Index of authors, editors, and compilers. Z2725.A2C45

Ferreira, José de Azevedo. Bibliografia selectiva da língua portuguesa. Lisboa : Instituto de Cultura e Língua Portuguesa, Ministério da Educação, 1989. 332 p. **BD164**
A classed unannotated listing under 41 section rubrics of 2,217 numbered entries representing monographs, articles, and dissertations in a wide range of areas of Portuguese language studies. These include structural and historical linguistic studies; practical language reference tools such as dictionaries and grammars; teaching of Portuguese both as native and as foreign language; dialectology; Portuguese creoles; textual criticism; etc. Indexes of persons (both authors and persons as subjects) and subjects.
§ Somewhat similar, though it lacks indexes: *Bibliografia de linguística portuguesa* (Lisboa : Litoral Edições; distr. Sodilivros, [1987?]. 147 p.). Z2725.A2F47

Spanish

General works

Bibliography

Dworkin, Steven Norman. Lexical studies of medieval Spanish texts : a bibliography of concordances, glossaries, vocabularies and selected word studies. 2nd ed., rev., expanded. Madison, Wis. : Hispanic Seminary of Medieval Studies, 1993. 116 p. (The Hispanic Seminary of Medieval Studies. Bibliographic series, 11). **BD165**
Indexes "the numerous glossaries, vocabularies, concordances, and word indices appended to or based on scholarly editions of medieval texts."—*Pref.* Intended to point to works that can partially fulfill the need for a comprehensive medieval Spanish lexicon, "the majority of the compilations included in this volume are alphabetically arranged glossaries restricted to words no longer used or which display a meaning unknown in the modern language." Citations to these glossaries, published as journal articles, books, appendixes, and theses, are arranged chronologically be century covered, with separate sections for Judeo-Spanish and Aljamiado texts. Indexes of author/editors, reviewers, and titles. Contains 802 entries, compared with 513 in the original edition, David J. Billick and Steven N. Dworkin, *Lexical studies of medieval Spanish texts* (1987. 116 p.). PC4715.Z5B54

Golden, Herbert Hershel. Modern Iberian language and literature : a bibliography of homage studies / by Herbert H. Golden and Seymour O. Simches. Cambridge, Mass. : Harvard Univ. Pr., 1958. 184 p. **BD166**
For annotation, *see* BE1436. Z7031.G6

Heydenreich, Titus. Bibliographie der Hispanistik in der Bundesrepublik Deutschland, Österreich und der deutschsprachigen Schweiz / Zusammenstellung, Titus Heydenreich; Redaktion, Christoph Strosetzki, im Auftrag des Deutschen Hispanistenverbandes. Frankfurt am Main : Vervuert, 1988–1990. 3 v. (Editionen der Iberoamericana. Reihe II, Bibliographische Reihe, 4–6). **BD167**

Contents: v. 1, 1978–81; v. 2, 1982–86; v. 3, 1987–88.

Lists publications on Spanish, Portuguese, Catalan, Basque, and Galician linguistics, philology, and literature in a classed arrangement. Name index. Z2695.A2H49

Nuessel, Frank H. Theoretical studies in Hispanic linguistics (1960–) : a selected, annotated research bibliography. Bloomington : Indiana Univ. Linguistics Club, c1988. 355 p. **BD168**

"The primary purpose of this reference guide is to provide the scholar in Hispanic linguistics with a basic research tool that will be a starting point for the examination of some of the fundamental issues in the field."—*Pref.* The lengthy introduction and list of "related bibliographies" furnishes an overview of the preceding 30 years of Spanish linguistic research. Organized alphabetically by author with subject and name indexes. Z2695.A2N84

Serís, Homero. Bibliografía de la lingüística española. Bogotá, 1964. 981 p. (Publicaciones del Instituto Caro y Cuervo, XIX). **BD169**

Nearly 8,000 items (periodical and book materials) on all aspects of Spanish linguistics, including sections for individual dialects and for the various Spanish-American countries. Fully indexed. Item numbers continue in sequence from the author's *Manuel de bibliografía de la literatura española* (BE1438) to emphasize the close relationship between language and literature and to facilitate cross-references to the earlier work. Z2695.A1S4

Viñaza, Cipriano Muñoz y Manzano. Biblioteca histórica de la filología castellana. Madrid : Manuel Tello, 1893. 1112 p. **BD170**

Repr. : Madrid : Atlas, 1978 (in 3 v.).

An extensive bibliography—covering the years 1492–1893—on Castilian philology. Classified arrangement, and then chronological. A valuable historical work. Z2695.A1V7

Woodbridge, Hensley Charles. Guide to reference works for the study of the Spanish language and literature and Spanish American literature. N.Y. : Modern Language Association of America, 1987. 183 p. (Selected bibliographies in language and literature, 5). **BD171**

For annotation, *see* BE1430. Z2695.A2W66

Varieties and dialects

Bleznick, Donald W. A sourcebook for Hispanic literature and language : a selected, annotated guide to Spanish, Spanish-American, and Chicano bibliography, literature, linguistics, journals, and other source materials. 2nd ed. Metuchen, N.J. : Scarecrow, 1983. 304 p. **BD172**

For annotation, *see* BE1426. Z2695.A2B55

Viudas Camarasa, Antonio. Dialectología hispánica y geografía lingüística en los estudios locales (1920–1984) : bibliografía crítica y comentada. Cáceres : Institución cultural "El Brocense," Excma. Diputacíon Provencial de Cáceres, 1986. 347 p. (Colección Plenos de la Confederación Espanola de Centros de Estudios Locales, 4). **BD173**

Arranged in sections by dialect, this bibliography lists primarily Spanish-language books, articles, dissertations, and conference proceedings in a classified scheme. Each section contains citations with sometimes lengthy annotations and a more inclusive "Bibliografía complementaria." Subject, geographical, and author indexes.

PC4700.Z9V854

Spanish American

Bibliografía sobre el español del Caribe hispánico / Rafael Angel Rivas D. ... [et al.]. Caracas : Instituto Universitario Pedagógico de Caracas, Departamento de Castellano, Literatura y Latín : Centro de Investigaciones Lingüísticas y Literarias "Andrés Bello", 1985. 294 p. **BD174**

A classed listing of 2,406 numbered entries representing books, articles, symposium and conference reports, and dissertations. Occasional brief annotations on contents. Classed by general subject or country; further subdivided by subject. The classification scheme is detailed in a table of contents at the end, called "Indice de materias." No author index. Z1609.L3B53

Solé, Carlos A. Bibliografía sobre el español de América, 1920–1986. Bogotá : Instituto Caro y Cuervo, 1990. 348 p. (Publicaciones del Instituto Caro y Cuervo, 88). **BD175**

A partially annotated classed list of monographs, articles, and dissertations on the Spanish language of North, Central, and South America. An international listing, with entries primarily in Spanish and English. Arranged by subject (in the case of general and multiple-country studies), otherwise by country; arrangement is detailed in a table of contents ("Indice general") at the end. Includes an index of abbreviations used in citations; no author index. Extends the coverage of the previous edition (Wash. : Georgetown Univ. Pr., 1970), which covered 1920–67.

§ For an annotated listing with good coverage of earlier material on Spanish throughout the Americas, *see also* M. W. Nichols, *Bibliographical guide to materials on American Spanish* (Cambridge, Mass. : Harvard Univ. Pr., 1941. 114 p.). Z1609.L3S65

Teschner, Richard V. Spanish and English of United States Hispanos : a critical, annotated, linguistic bibliography / Richard V. Teschner, gen. ed. ; Garland D. Bills and Jerry R. Craddock, associate editors. Arlington, Va. : Center for Applied Linguistics, c1975. 352 p. **BD176**

A thoroughly annotated listing of 675 monographs, articles, dissertations and other contributions "relating in full or in part to the speech and language behavior of United States residents / citizens of Hispanic background, chiefly Chicanos (Mexican Americans) and mainland Puerto Ricans but also Cubans, Sephardic Jews, peninsulares (Spaniards) and isleños (Canary Islanders in Louisiana)."—*Pref.* Within its specified limits, aims to be a complete listing. Includes issues of language education and bilingualism, including the English of the groups named. Classed arrangement by country of residence or of origin as relevant, with each section subdivided by linguistic categories described in an initial table of contents. Author index. Z2695.D5T47

Other Romance

Provençal

Bibliography

Klingebiel, Kathryn. Bibliographie linguistique de l'ancien occitan (1960–1982). Hamburg : H. Buske, c1986. 185 p. (Romanistik in Geschichte und Gegenwart, Bd. 19). **BD177**

Lists alphabetically 802 dictionaries and linguistic and stylistic studies of Provençal language and literature. A "Supplément lexicographique" lists older dictionaries that have been reissued or revised between 1960 and 1982, as well as some reviews of those works. Subject index. Z7033.P8K57

CELTIC LANGUAGES

Irish

Baumgarten, Rolf. Bibliography of Irish linguistics and literature, 1942–71. Dublin : Dublin Institute for Advanced Studies, 1986. 776 p. **BD178**
In effect, supplements and continues Richard I. Best, *Bibliography of Irish philology and manuscript literature* (Dublin : Dublin Inst. for Advanced Studies, 1942. 253 p.) and its predecessor, National Library of Ireland (Dublin), *Bibliography of Irish philology and of printed Irish literature* (Dublin : Stationery Off., 1913. 307 p. Repr. : N.Y. : Johnson, 1970). Contains citations to more than 9,000 books, articles, theses, and conference proceedings in a classed arrangement. Irish word/name, first line, source, and author indexes.
Z7012.I73B38

Edwards, John. The Irish language : an annotated bibliography of sociolinguistic publications, 1772–1982. N.Y. : Garland, 1983. 274 p. (Garland reference library of the humanities, v. 300). **BD179**
"Represented here are articles, chapters, books, and pamphlets bearing upon social, historical, psychological, and educational aspects of Irish—including the decline of the language, the restoration effort, the relationship of language to nationality and religion, and studies of important figures in the language movement."—*Introd.* Main entry listing, with subject, date, and journal indexes. Z7011.E38

SLAVIC LANGUAGES

General and comparative

Brang, Peter. Kommentierte Bibliographie zur slavischen Soziolinguistik / Peter Brang, Monika Züllig, unter Mitwirkung von Karin Brang. Bern : Lang, c1981. 3 v. (Slavica Helvetica, Bd. 17). **BD180**
A classed, partly annotated international register of 15,061 entries for monographs, scholarly and popular articles, and reviews from the 19th century through 1977, with selected added material from 1978–79. Vols. 1–2 are organized in six main thematic sections (not by language) divided into 158 subsections, some devoted to individual Slavic languages as relevant. A rich source for materials on the periphery of traditional linguistic study, including the jargons of professional, underworld, or age-group subcultures, written versus spoken speech, language acquisition, interaction among different languages, various registers and functions of language (national, international, cultural, social, political, artistic, tabu). Covers not only materials on Slavic sociolinguistics, but also works in Slavic languages on other sociolinguistic subjects.
Vol. 3 contains the indexes: Bibliographic abbreviations used in citations, Names (of authors, reviewed authors, and persons as subjects), and Subjects (including countries, ethnic groups, and languages, as well as sociolinguistic and other topics). Z7004.S65B7

De Bray, R. G. A. Guide to the Slavonic languages. 3rd ed., rev. and expanded. Columbus, Ohio : Slavica Publishers, 1980. 3 v. **BD181**
Contents: pt. 1, Guide to the south Slavonic languages; pt. 2, Guide to the west Slavonic languages; pt. 3, Guide to the east Slavonic languages. (Each volume may be purchased separately.).
1st ed., 1951.
An attempt to give an overall view of the Slavonic languages to those who are already familiar with one of the group. Each language is treated in a separate section, introduced by a brief history of the language and followed by a more or less detailed examination of the al-

phabet, pronunciation, morphology, word order, features characteristic of the language, and brief passages from its literature. Each volume includes a selected bibliography listing grammars, dictionaries, and other aids to study for the languages under consideration in that particular volume. Detailed table of contents for each volume, but no indexes.
PG53.D4

Schaller, Helmut Wilhelm. Bibliographie der Bibliographien zur slavischen Sprachwissenschaft. Frankfurt am Main : Lang, c1982. 115 p. (Symbolae Slavicae, Bd. 15). **BD182**
An unannotated classified bibliography of bibliographies, subarranged within each section alphabetically by author. Consists of 1,333 entries in various languages representing monographs, sections in monographs, and articles. Indexes of subjects, persons (subjects of biobibliographies), authors, and titles in the case of cumulative serial bibliographies. Z7041.A1S3

Slavi︠a︡nskoe ︠i︡azykoznanie : bibliograficheskiĭ ukazatel' literatury, izdannoĭ v SSSR c 1918 po 1960 gg. / [redakt︠s︡ionna︠i︡a killegi︠i︡a S.B. Bernshteĭn, D.E. Michal'chi, V.I. Shundov. Moskva : Izd-vo Akademii nauk SSSR, 1963. 2 v. **BD183**
Title translated: Slavic linguistics : bibliography of literature published in the USSR from 1928 through 1960.
A bibliography of books, articles, surveys, and reviews published in the Soviet Union on the subject of linguistics.
Continued by supplements covering 1961–65 (1969. 465 p.) and 1966–81 (1973–88). Z7041.A39

Stankiewicz, Edward. A selected bibliography of Slavic linguistics / by Edward Stankiewicz and Dean S. Worth. The Hague : Mouton, 1966–70. 2 v. (Slavistic printings and reprintings, 49). **BD184**
Intended as a bibliographical guide to all Slavic languages, but selective in that emphasis is on 20th-century linguistic research and on those studies "inspired by a structural approach."—*Introd.* Vol. 1 deals with Slavic cultural prehistory, Balto-Slavic, Common Slavic, Comparative Slavic, Old Church Slavonic, and the South Slavic languages (Bulgarian, Macedonian, Serbo-Croatian, Slovenian); v. 2 includes sections for general West Slavic linguistics, Polish, Pomeranian, Polabian, Lusatian, Czech, Slovak, general East Slavic linguistics, Belorussian, Russian, Ukranian, and a bibliography of bibliographies for the study of Slavic linguistics. Z7041.S82

Russian; Ukrainian; Belorussian

Institut ︠i︡azykoznani︠i︡a (Akademi︠i︡a nauk SSSR). Bibliograficheskiĭ ukazatel' literatury po russkomu ︠i︡azykoznani︠i︡u s 1825 po 1880 god / Sostavili: N.S. Avilova ... [et al.] ; Glav. red. V.V. Vinogradov. Moskva : Izd-vo Akademii nauk SSSR, 1954–59. 8 v. **BD185**
Title translated: Bibliography of literature on Russian linguistics from 1825 through 1880.
An annotated bibliographic index to the literature on linguistics published in Russia between 1825 and 1880. Vol. 8 contains a general index. Z2505.A55

An introduction to Russian language and literature / ed. by Robert Auty and Dimitri Obolensky. Cambridge ; N.Y. : Cambridge Univ. Pr., [1977]. 300 p. (Companion to Russian studies, 2). **BD186**
Intended as a first guide for university students, but also meant to be useful to general readers. Chapters on the Russian language and Russian writing and printing are followed by chapters on the main periods of Russian and Soviet literature, plus chapters on the theater. Each chapter was contributed by a specialist and ends with a select bibliography intended as a guide for further study (and listing both Russian and English sources). Indexed. PG2051.I5

Schaller, Helmut Wilhelm. Bibliographie zur russischen Sprache. Frankfurt a. M. ; Bern ; Cirencester/U.K. : Lang, 1980. 204 p. (Symbolae Slavicae, Bd. 8). **BD187**

A classed bibliography of more than 2,700 items with author and subject indexes. Includes books, periodical articles, and dissertations. Russian-language publications predominate, but other Western-language materials are well represented. Z2505.A2S33

Unbegaun, Boris Ottokar. A bibliographical guide to the Russian language / by B. O. Unbegaun ; with the collaboration of J. S. G. Simmons. Oxford : Clarendon Pr., 1953. 174 p. **BD188**

A practical guide to publications dealing with the Russian language and its history, listing 1,043 titles, many of them annotated, under three main divisions: (1) General (works of a general bibliographical nature); (2) Historical (works relating to the prehistory and history of the Russian language); and (3) Descriptive (grammar and vocabulary of modern literary Russian, and works on dialects, slang, jargon, etc.). Titles are given in full in the original language. Index.
Z2505.U5

South Slavic languages

Lenček, Rado L. A bibliography of recent literature on Macedonian, Serbo-Croatian, and Slovene languages / by Rado L. Lenček and Miloš Okuka. München : Slavica, 1990. 95 p. (Geschichte, Kultur und Geisteswelt der Südslaven, neue Ser. 1. Bd.). **BD189**
Z7041.L54

Milivojević, Dragan Dennis. Yugoslav linguistics in English, 1900–1980 : a bibliography / ed. by Dragan Milivojević and Vasa D. Mihailovich. Columbus, Ohio : Slavica Publishers, c1990. 122 p. **BD190**

An unannotated classed bibliography of English-language publications on Serbo-Croatian, Slovenian, and Macedonian—the languages of the former Yugoslavia. Registers books, articles, and reviews, and includes materials such as textbooks, language manuals, readers, and dictionaries, and areas such as stylistics and poetics, sociolinguistics, contrastive linguistics, onomastics, orthography/orthogeny, and dialectology, in addition to traditional synchronic and diachronic descriptions. Organized by general theme and genre, subdivided by language covered. Indexes of authors and of periodical titles. Z7041.M55

Mozhaeva, Inessa Evgen'evna. I͡Uzhnoslavi͡anskie i͡azyki : Annot. bibliogr. ukazatel' literatury opubl. v Rossii i v SSSR s 1835 po 1965 gg. Moskva : "Nauka", 1969. 183 p. **BD191**

Title translated: South Slavic languages : annotated bibliography of literature published in Russia and the USSR from 1835 through 1965.

A classed listing of 1,636 numbered entries for Russian-language publications (monographs, articles, and in-house mimeographed works) on the South Slavic languages: Bulgarian and the languages of the former Yugoslavia—Macedonian, Serbo-Croatian, and Slovenian. Organized by language, with subdivisions for more specific topics (detailed in a table of contents at end). Includes scholarly studies of the languages, scholarly-popular works, paleographic and philological studies, editions of manuscripts and other historical documents, catalogs, and manuscript descriptions featuring South Slavic manuscripts, bibliographies, book reviews. Works on Old Church Slavonic are excluded unless directly relevant for the South Slavic languages named. Index of names. Z7041.M64

Polish

Encyklopedia języka polskiego / [pod redakcją Stanisława Urbańczyka]. Wyd. 2., popr. i uzup. Wrocław : Zakład Narodowy im. Ossolińskich, 1991. 455 p. : ill., maps. **BD192**

Title translated: Encyclopedia of the Polish language.

1st ed. called *Encyklopedia wiedzy o języku polskim* (1978).

Contains articles on the history, structure, dialectology, sociolinguistics, and other aspects of the Polish language; includes definitions of some basic general linguistic terms in Polish. Good biobibliographical coverage of significant persons in the history of Polish linguistics and philology. Some themes are grouped together—e.g., individual dialects are gathered under the word *gwary* (dialects), with cross-references from the individual names. After the basic alphabetic section there is a section of maps of Polish dialects, a classed international bibliography of revelant sources, and a systematic guide to subjects and entries ("Wykaz rzeczowy haseł"), including a list of biographic entries. PG6031.E53

Paryl, Władysław. Językoznawstwo polonistyczne : przewodnik naukowo-bibliograficzny dla studentów i nauczycieli polonistów. Wrocław : Wydawn. Uniwersytetu Wrocławskiego, 1992. 240 p. **BD193**

Title translated: Polish linguistics : scholarly-bibliographic guide for Polonists—students and teachers.

A classed, unannotated bibliography of works mostly in Polish on various aspects of the Polish language. Works published since 1970 are emphasized. Organized in 59 sections, some with subdivisions (detailed in a table of contents, "Spis tresci," at the beginning); within these, arranged alphabetically by author. Covers descriptive, historical, comparative, dialectal, sociolinguistic, and philological-literary aspects of the language.

§ Useful for coverage of works published 1900–70 is K. Handke and E. Rzetelska-Feleszko *Przewodnik po językoznawstwie polskim* (Wrocław : Zakł. Narodowy Imienia Ossolińskich Wydawnnictwo, 1977. 474 p.). Z2528.L5P37

BALTIC LANGUAGES

Kubicka, Weronika. Języki bałtyckie : bibliografia = Baltic languages : bibliography. Łódź, 1967– . v. 1–4. (In progress?). **BD194**

Preface also in English.

Contents: v. 1, Baltic linguistics (in general); v. 2, Onomastics; v. 3, Latvian; v. 4, Lithuanian.

A classed, unannotated listing of works on Lithuanian, Latvian, and other Baltic languages and dialects, totaling more than 9,000 entries. The compiler's intention was to assemble a complete listing from the beginnings of comparative linguistics through 1966, including broader comparative and historical work that is relevant for Baltic linguistics. Most reference apparatus is in Polish and English (Introduction, Section headings) with the exception of terms in the subject indexes, which are in Polish only. Each volume has its own indexes: v. 1, has indexes of subjects and personal names, as do v. 2–4, which also have indexes of words. Z7044.6.A38

INDO-IRANIAN LANGUAGES

Iranian

Nawabi, Y. M. A bibliography of Iran : a catalogue of books and articles on Iranian subjects, mainly in European languages. [Tehran] : Cultural Studies & Research Institute, 1969–[1987?]. v. 1–8. (Iranian Culture Foundation, v. 53 [etc.]). (In progress?).   **BD195**
    For annotation, *see* DE186.   Z3366.N38

Oranskiĭ, I. M. Die neuiranischen Sprachen der Sowjetunion / von I. M. Oranskij ; übersetzt [aus dem Russischen] von Werner Winter. The Hague : Mouton, 1975. 2 v. (266 p.). (Janua linguarum : Series critica, 12).   **BD196**
    Contents: Bd. 1, Geschichte und Stand der Forschung; Bd. 2, Bibliographie.
    A handbook and bibliography on Tajik, Ossetian, Kurdish, and other modern Iranian languages of the former Soviet Union; covers their history, relationship to Persian, and interrelationship among themselves, as well as their structure, dialectology, and other aspects. The original Russian text evidently remains unpublished (cf. editor's note before the *Vorwort*). The handbook occupies v. 1; the bibliography, v. 2. The latter is in two sections, the first for Cyrillic citations and the second for Roman; within each section alphabetically by author. No indexes.   PK6079.O7

Indic

Sanskrit

Lakshminarasimha Moorty, C. Reasearch [sic] trends in Sanskrit : a bibliography of doctoral dissertations presented to various Indian universities. Trivandrum : CBH Publications, c1991. 17, 210 p.   **BD197**
    Lists more than 3,500 PhD dissertations in Sanskrit studies presented 1857–1988 in universities of India. Arranged by 14 general thematic sections within Sanskrit studies (History of literature, Classical literature, Vedas, Grammar, etc.), each subdivided. Titles in languages other than English are given also in English translation. Concludes with what is functionally a subject index, Index of works and authors, "authors" referring only to Sanskrit authors studied. The index includes also a number of subject-like terms (e.g., aborigines, arts, dictionaries, folk songs), which are, however, poorly controlled and inconsistently used, rendering the subject coverage inconsistent and weak. The index must be used together with the classified arrangement.   Z7090.L35

Satyaprakash. A bibliography of Sanskrit language and literature. Gurgaon, Haryana : Indian Documentation Service, 1984. 296 p. (Subject bibliography series, 5).   **BD198**
    Lists more than 3,500 scholarly and popular articles published from 1962 through 1983 in 137 journals and two daily newspapers (*Times of India* and *Economic times*). Consists of two sections: a classified listing by major subjects with subdivisions, and an alphabetical author listing. Since citations are given in full in both sections, each title is cited twice. The classified system must be used by browsing, since there is no table of contents, no list of section headings, and no index.   Z7090.S27

Hindi

Aggarwal, Narindar K. A bibliography of studies on Hindi language and linguistics. Rev. and enl. ed. Gurgaon : Indian Documentation Service, 1985. 321 p.   **BD199**
    1st ed., 1978.
    A classified listing of 2,926 monographs, articles, dissertations, and some unpublished materials produced from ca.1950 to 1982. Partially annotated. Index of authors.   Z7071.A34

Urdu

Mahmud, Shabana. Urdu language and literature : a bibliography of sources in European languages. London : Mansell, 1992. 331 p.   **BD200**
    A classed bibliography that "aims at covering the whole range of European language sources of Urdu language and literature. It includes monographs and articles from journals, Festschriften, symposiums, proceedings from conferences, and encyclopedias."—*Introd*. Organized into sections for Works of reference, Language, General literature, Poetry, Drama, and Dastan, each with subdivisions; within each subdivision alphabetically by author. Each of the sections on literature begins with a subsection on individual authors; under each author are subsections as relevant for Bibliography and catalogues, Editions of translated works, and Studies. Citations contain occasional brief notes on contents of cited works, bibliographic history, etc. Index of scholarly authors, editors, translators at end; at the beginning, after the introduction, is a separate index of literary authors treated.   Z7099.U7

OTHER INDO-EUROPEAN LANGUAGES

General and comparative

Indogermanische Chronik. v. 1 [1967]–v. 34 [1988/90]. (*In* Die Sprache : Zeitschrift für Sprachwissenschaft, 1967–1991. Semiannual).   **BD201**
    Subsequent issues planned as separate publication (note, v. 35 Heft 2 [1991/93]).
    An international classed serial bibliography of recent work on comparative and historical Indo-European linguistic topics. In 13 major sections (General studies, reference and historiography; Anatolian (Hittite, etc.); Tokharian; Indo-Iranian; Armenian; Albanian; Greek; Italic; Celtic; Germanic; Baltic; Slavic; Other). Some sections are subdivided by language or by linguistic topics. Indexes of linguistics forms studied (by language) and reviews or evaluative notices. No author index; no subject access apart from the classified listing.   P3.S6

BALKAN LANGUAGES

Schaller, Helmut Wilhelm. Bibliographie zur Balkanphilologie. Heidelberg : Winter, 1977. 109 p.   **BD202**
    A topically arranged bibliography with author and subject indexes. In addition to general studies of the Balkans as a linguistic area, includes materials on Bulgarian, Macedonian, Serbo-Croatian, Albanian, Romanian, and Modern Greek. About 1,500 items.   Z2845.A2S32

SEMITIC LANGUAGES

General and comparative

A basic bibliography for the study of Semitic languages / J. H. Hospers, ed. Leiden : Brill, 1973–74. 2 v.   **BD203**
Intends "to list as completely as possible and in the relevant contexts everything really needed by students in the Semitic languages, and other persons interested in these studies, in such a way that they can use the bibliographic information as an aid to discover for themselves more detailed material."—*Pref.*
In v. 1 there are sections for each language or group of languages (e.g., Akkadian, Sumerian, Anatolian languages, Ancient Persian, Hebrew, Samaritan Hebrew, Syriac and Aramaic, etc.) compiled by specialists; each has subsections for philology, literature, cultural history, etc., as applicable. There is a final section on comparative Semitics. Vol. 2 brings together "the bibliographic material in the fields of the study of Pre-Classical, Classical and Modern Literary Arabic … and the Modern Arabic Dialects." No indexes.   Z7049.S5B35

Arabic

Bakalla, M. H. Arabic linguistics : an introduction and bibliography. [2nd rev. ed.]. [London] : Mansell, [1983]. 741 p.   **BD204**
1st ed., 1975, had title *Bibliography of Arabic linguistics.*
Lists about 5,500 items in some 20 languages, with separate sections for materials in Occidental and Oriental languages. Introductory essays on various aspects of Arabic linguistics precede the bibliography. Indexes of subjects and names.   Z7052.B35

Aramaic

British Museum. Department of Oriental Printed Books and Manuscripts. Catalogue of Syriac printed books and related literature in the British Museum / comp. by Cyril Moss. London : Museum, 1962. 1174 col., 206 col., 272 col.   **BD205**
Not merely a catalog but an extensive listing of Syriac texts and of books and periodical articles on Syriac studies. The first published record of Syriac materials in the British Museum.   Z7094.B74

Fitzmyer, Joseph A. An Aramaic bibliography / Joseph A. Fitzmyer and Stephen A. Kaufman, with the collaboration of Stephan F. Bennett and Edward M. Cook. Baltimore : Johns Hopkins Univ. Pr., c1992. v. 1.   **BD206**
Contents: pt. 1, Old, official, and biblical Aramaic.
Covers scholarly literature on Aramaic from the earliest period through ca.300 CE. Intended "to be as comprehensive as possible. We have attempted to include every known text, no matter how small or fragmentary, and substantive secondary discussions of such texts."—*Pref.*
Planned for several parts: pt. 1 (v. 1) covers Aramaic to 200 BCE; pt. 2 (v. 2–) is to include texts from the middle period of the language (200 BCE to 300 CE). In v. 1, the main bibliographical list (a single alphabetical author-date list) is called "Part two: references." Pt. 1 has three chapters (A, Aramaic studies—general; B, Texts [old and official Aramaic]; C, Biblical Aramaic) and is in essence a detailed systematic subject index to pt. 2, providing author-date references to be looked up in pt. 2. Entries in the Texts section, which is ordered by geographic origin and date, consist of: an alphanumeric identifier for the text; a physical description; information about the *editio princeps* and other, readily available editions; and secondary literature. Other details concerning scope, organization, and definitions are discussed in the preface. Two appendixes: Aramaica? (for questionable texts) and Textual concordances (with tables that collate texts using the alphanumeric identifiers). Subject access is thus provided in pt. 1 and author access in pt. 2. No further indexes.   Z7053.F57

Hebrew

Waldman, Nahum M. The recent study of Hebrew : a survey of the literature with selected bibliography. Cincinnati : Hebrew Union College Pr., 1989. 464 p. (Bibliographica Judaica, 10).   **BD207**
A historical and thematic survey, together with a bibliography, of scholarly works from the end of World War II to the middle 1980s; covers studies on various aspects of the Hebrew language from the Biblical period through modern Israeli Hebrew. The 3,700 unannotated bibliographic entries are given in a single alphabetic author listing; subject access is provided through the initial survey. Index of names.   Z7070.W34

FINNO-UGRIC LANGUAGES

General and comparative

Bibliographie der uralischen Sprachwissenschaft 1830–1970 / hrsg. von Wolfgang Schlachter und Gerhard Ganschow. München : W. Fink, 1974 [i.e. 1979]–1986. 3 v.   **BD208**
Issued in fascicles; issued also in bound volumes.
A major bibliography covering all the Uralic languages (Hungarian, Finnish, Estonian, and the other Finno-Ugric languages) with more than 23,000 consecutively numbered, unannotated entries for works in many languages. The classed system of subdivided sections is parallel from language to language; and the subsections have their own numbered keys, summarized in the beginning of each volume. The introduction, section headings, and other reference apparatus are all in German.
The first volume covers materials on Hungarian, in addition to Uralic generalities; v. 2, Finnish, Estonian, and other Finnic languages; v. 3 contains an author index. The index gives a double number: the first refers to the sequential entry number, the second to the numbered thematic section.   Z7045.A18

TURKIC LANGUAGES

General and comparative

Loewenthal, Rudolf. The Turkic languages and literatures of Central Asia : a bibliography. 'sGravenhage : Mouton, 1957. 212 p. (Central Asiatic studies, I).   **BD209**
A classified list of 2,093 books and articles. Author index. Covers Old, Middle, and Modern Turkic languages.   Z7049.U5C4 no.1

Sovietico-Turcica : Beiträge zur Bibliographie der türkischen Sprachwissenschaft in russischer Sprache in der Sowjetunion, 1917–1957. Budapest : Akadémiai Kiadó, 1960. 319 p. (Bibliotheca orientalis hungarica, IX).   **BD210**
Ed. by György Hazai.
More than 2,700 items, alphabetically listed by main entry in Russian, with German translation of title following each listing. Subject index in German.

Bibliography

Hazai, György. Bibliographisches Handbuch der Turkologie : eine Bibliographie der Bibliographien vom 18. Jahrhundert bis 1979 / zusammengestellt von György Hazai und Barbara Kellner-Heinkele. Budapest : Akadémiai Kiadó, 1986. v. 1. (Bibliotheca orientalis Hungarica, v. 30). (In progress). **BD211**

    For annotation, *see* DE31.   Z7049.T87H39

Turkish

Handbuch der türkischen Sprachwissenschaft / hrsg. von György Hazai. Budapest : Akadémiai Kiadó : Vertrieb, Kultura, 1990. v. 1. (Bibliotheca orientalis Hungarica, 31). (In progress?). **BD212**

    A handbook consisting of 13 chapters on various aspects of the Turkish language, its structure, history, dialectology, interrelationships with other languages, etc., written by acknowledged specialists. Extensive bibliographic references. Chapters are in English or German, and vary in style and emphasis.   PL113.H36

AFRICAN LANGUAGES

Bibliography

Bibliographie analytique des langues parlées en Afrique subsaharienne, 1970–1980 / realisée par Jean-François Bourdin, Jean-Pierre Caprile, Michel Lafon. Paris : Assoc. d'Études Linguistiques Interculturelles Africaines, etc., [1983]. 555 p. **BD213**

    At head of title: "Les langues parlées en Afrique: études, documents et bibliographies" et "Bulletin bibliographique du CIRELFA [Conseil International de Recherche et d'Étude en Linguistique Fondamentale et Appliquée]."

    In three sections: (1) Sciences du language; (2) Ethnologie; (3) Sciences de l'éducation. Chronological arrangement within sections; indexes of authors, languages and ethnic groups, geographical names, and concepts. Entries include analytical notes; periodical citations predominte.   Z7106.B68

Meier, Wilma. Bibliography of African languages. Wiesbaden : Harrassowitz, 1984. 888 p.   **BD214**

    Title also in German, French, and Russian; introductory matter in English, German, French, and Russian.

    An author listing (with titles in chronological order) is followed by two indexes, one being an alphabetical arrangement of languages with authors and abbreviated indication of their topics thereunder, the other an alphabetical arrangement of the languages with publication dates of the studies listed chronologically and indicating author's name and abbreviated topic.   Z7106.B53

Library catalogs

African language materials in the Boston University Libraries / comp. by Gretchen Walsh and Jenny Hochstadt. [Updated ed.]. Boston : Boston Univ., African Studies Center, [1988]. [99 p.].   **BD215**

    1st ed., comp. by Andrea M. Van Hoosen, had title: *African language materials in the collection of Boston University's African Studies Library* (Boston, [1979]).

Includes a cross-reference table for various dialects and language families.   Z7106

University of Rhodesia. Library. Catalogue of the C. M. Doke collection on African languages in the Library of the University of Rhodesia. Boston : G. K. Hall, 1972. 546 p. (University of Rhodesia. Library. Bibliographical series, no. 2).   **BD216**

    Approximately 7,000 entries (i.e., reproductions of catalog cards) representing a collection of some 3,000 titles on more than 200 African languages. Separate author and subject sections.   Z7106.U54

Handbooks

Mann, Michael. A thesaurus of African languages : a classified and annotated inventory of the spoken languages of Africa : with an appendix on their written representation / by Michael Mann and David Dalby. London ; N.Y. : Zell, 1987. 325 p.   **BD217**

    Conceived in part as a companion to David Dalby's *Language map of Africa and the adjacent islands* (London : International African Inst., 1977). Dalby's earlier work contained a "Checklist of African languages" to provide a classified index to the language and dialect names recorded on the map, and an alphabetical index to those names; this follows that work's classification scheme. In four main sections: (1) an inventory listing languages, names, synonyms, and dialects and giving bibliographic references to grammars and studies; (2) a second inventory arranged geographically; (3) a discussion of the universal African alphabet; (4) a complete bibliography of cited sources. Language index.   PL8005.M36

CHINESE

Bibliography

Kim, T. W. A bibliographical guide to the study of Chinese language and linguistics / T. W. Kim and A. Wawrzyszko. Carbondale, Ill. : Linguistic Research, Inc., 1980. 89 p. (Current inquiry into language & linguistics, 39).   **BD218**

    An annotated bibliography of textbooks, dictionaries, and works on linguistics, the Chinese writing system, and bibliographies of the subject. Author index.   Z3108.L5K55

Yang, Paul Fu-mien. Chinese dialectology : a selected and classified bibliography = Chung-kuo fang yen hsüeh fen lei ts'an k'ao shu mu. Hong Kong : Chinese Univ. Pr., c1981. 189 p.   **BD219**

    Classified by dialect area, with sections also on: Bibliography/ biography and other general works; History of Chinese dialectology; Methodology; Archaic and old dialects; and Modern dialects in general. Altogether contains 2,275 entries. Romanized transcriptions and English translations are provided for Chinese, Japanese, or Korean-language titles, and brief characterizations are added if title is unclear. Roman indexes of publishers and of authors.

    § Intended as a companion to the compiler's *Chinese linguistics : a selected and classified bibliography* (BD221).   Z3108.L5Y285

————————— Chinese lexicology and lexicography : a selected and classified bibliography = Chung-kuo tzu huei hsueh chitzutien hsueh fen lei tsan kao shu mu. Hong Kong : Chinese Univ. Pr., c1985. 361 p.   **BD220**

    Consists of 4,165 entries, some annotated, for works in Asian and Western languages, in two main sections (lexicology and lexicography) with subdivisions. The organization is spelled out in the table of contents. Covers various aspects of Chinese semantics, lexicon, and word formation, and various sorts of dictionaries (including bilingual, both to and from Chinese, by language). In the entries, romanized transcriptions and English translations are provided for Chinese, Japanese, or Korean titles, and brief characterizations are added if the title is unclear. Uses the Wade-Giles system of transcription for Chinese titles. Includes roman-alphabet indexes of publishers and authors.

§ For lexicography of Chinese dialects, more thorough coverage is provided by the compiler's *Chinese dialectology : a selected and classified bibliography* (BD219). *See also* the compiler's more general *Chinese linguistics : a selected and classified bibliography* (BD221).

——————— Chinese linguistics : a selected and classified bibliography. [Hong Kong] : Chinese Univ. of Hong Kong, c1974. 292 p. **BD221**

Provides romanized transcriptions and English translations for Chinese, Japanese, or Korean-language titles, and adds brief characterizations (single phrases or sentences) in case the title is unclear. Roman indexes of publishers and of authors, plus Oriental character-index of Asian authors and Asian names for Western authors.

§ Omits works on dialectology; these are covered in a companion title by the same compiler: *Chinese dialectology : a select and classified bibliography* (BD219).

For an older but still valuable bibliography of works largely in English and other Western languages, with attention to pedagogical materials, see: Winston L. Y. Yang and Teresa S. Yang, *Bibliography of the Chinese language* (N.Y. : American Assoc. of Teachers of Chinese Language and Culture ; distr. by Paragon Book Gallery, 1966).
Z7059.Y286

JAPANESE

Yoshizaki, Yasuhiro. Studies in Japanese literature and language : a bibliography of English materials. Tokyo : Nichigai Associates ; distr. by Kinokuniya Book Store, [1979]. 451 p. (Nijisseiki bunken yōran taikei, 8). **BD222**
For annotation, *see* BE1596. Z7072.Y67

KOREAN

Lucas, Alain. Linguistique coréenne : bibliographie, 1960–1965 / Alain Lucas ; avec la collaboration de Yim Seong-sook et le concours de L. R. Kontsevich pour les publications d'URSS. [Paris] : Centre d'études coréennes, Collège de France, 1989. 234 p. (Mémoires du Centre d'études coréennes, v. 8). **BD223**
Title on added t.p.: Han'guk ŏhak nonjŏ mongnok.
A classed listing of 1,781 entries for monographs, articles, and dissertations in Oriental and Western languages. In addition to descriptive, historical, and comparative aspects of the language, covers problems of language teaching, psycholinguistics, sociolinguistics, rhetoric, stylistics and poetics, orthography, translations, and transliteration. Unusually good representation of the Russian/Soviet traditions of scholarship. Within each section, entries are arranged chronologically by date of publication. Names of authors are romanized (those in Chinese, in the pinyin transcription); titles of cited works are given in original characters. Indexes: journals and authors. Z3319.L5L83

SOUTH ASIAN LANGUAGES

General and comparative

Geetha, K. R. Classified state bibliography of linguistic research on Indian languages. Mysore : Central Institute of Indian Languages, 1983. v. 1. (CIIL occasional monographs series, 28). (In progress?). **BD224**
Contents: v. 1, Hindi speaking states (Bihar, Haryana, Himachal Pradesh, Madhya Pradesh, Rajasthan, Uttar Pradesh, Delhi). No more published?
Planned to be in five volumes, this work lists citations to linguistic studies by geographic area and language. Vol. 1 contains more than 4,250 citations in a classed arrangement with author and journal indexes. Appendixes include tables of languages spoken and sources consulted. Z7049.I3G44

Sakuntala Sharma, J. Classified bibliography of linguistic dissertations on Indian languages / compiler, J. Sakuntala Sharma; supervisers, D. P. Pattanayak, E. Annamalai. Mysore : Central Institute of Indian Languages, 1978. liv, 288 p. **BD225**
Lists 489 masters and 1,192 doctoral dissertations, primarily from Indian universities, presented 1921–78 and treating a wide variety of Indian languages and linguistic topics. In two major sections: Master's dissertations and Doctoral dissertations, both in classified order. English translations are provided for titles in other languages. Indexes of scholars, languages and dialects, and authors/titles of analyzed texts.
§ Continued for dissertations to 1983 by: Central Institute of Indian Languages, *Dissertations in Indian linguistics and on Indian languages*, comp. by B. A. Sharada (Mysore : the Institute, 1983).
Z7049.I3.S27

Dravidian languages

Agesthialingom, S. A bibliography of Dravidian linguistics / S. Agesthialingom and S. Sakthivel. Annamalainagar : Annamalai Univ., 1973. 362 p. (Annamalai University. Department of Linguistics. Publication, no. 30). **BD226**
An author listing of about 3,700 articles and books is followed by sections citing dictionaries and book reviews. No index.
§ *See also* Busnagi Rajannan, *Dravidian languages and literatures : a contribution toward a bibliography of books in English and in a few other European languages, on, about, and translated from the Dravidian languages* (Madurai : Madurai Univ., 1973. 279 p.). Partly annotated, classified listing by language, registering works from the 16th–20th centuries. Usefulness is somewhat hampered by lack of indexes. Z7049.D7A35

Nepali

A bibliography of Nepalese languages and linguistics / ed. by Sueyoshi Toba. Kathmandu : Linguistic Society of Nepal, Tribhuvan Univ., 1991. 120 p. **BD227**
An alphabetical author listing (with titles subarranged chronologically) of books, articles, dissertations, and various unpublished works. Indexes of language families treated; individual languages; subjects; and, by language of publication of works written in languages other than English. Contemporary, international work is well reflected, and the contents are well indexed. PK2595.B54

MAINLAND SOUTHEAST ASIAN LANGUAGES

General and comparative

Huffman, Franklin E. Bibliography and index of mainland Southeast Asian languages and linguistics. New Haven, Conn. : Yale Univ. Pr., c1986. 640 p. **BD228**
    Lists some 10,000 publications, 1960–85, on the Austroasiatic, Tibeto-Burman, Tai-Kadai, Miao-Yao, and mainland Austronesian language families. Arranged alphabetically by author and chronologically within each author listing. Subject index.   Z3221.H82

South-East Asia : languages and literatures : a select guide / ed. by Patricia Herbert & Anthony Milner. Honolulu : Univ. of Hawaii Pr., c1989. 182 p. : ill.   **BD229**
    For annotation, *see* BE1550.   PL3501.S66

Mon-Khmer; Tai

Shorto, H. L. Bibliographies of Mon-Khmer and Tai linguistics / comp. by H. L. Shorto, Judith M. Jacob and E. H. S. Simonds. London ; N.Y. ; Oxford Univ. Pr., 1963. 87 p. (London oriental bibliographies, v. 2)   **BD230**
    Consists of two separate bibliographies: H. L. Shorto and Judith M. Jacob, *Bibliography of Mon-Khmer linguistics* (436 entries dating through 1961) and E. H. S. Simonds, *Bibliography of Tai linguistics* (495 entries dating through 1959). Entries are numbered consecutively through both parts. Arranged by language group and geographic area. Indexes: Mon-Khmer languages and dialects, and authors.

Vietnamese

Nguyên, Dình Thâm. Studies on Vietnamese language and literature : a preliminary bibliography. Ithaca, N.Y. : Southeast Asia Program, Cornell Univ., 1992. 227 p.   **BD231**
    A classified bibliography of more than 2,500 entries (books and articles). Apart from materials in Vietnamese, mostly in English and French. In four sections on Vietnamese language, literature, folk literature, and the language and literature of ethnic minorities in Vietnam, subdivided by theme and genre into subsections within which entries are arranged alphabetically by author. Index of personal names; detailed table of contents.   Z3226.N48

MALAYO-POLYNESIAN LANGUAGES

General and comparative

Klieneberger, H. R. Bibliography of Oceanic linguistics. London : Oxford Univ. Pr., 1957. 143 p. (London oriental bibliographies, v. 1).   **BD232**
    Includes "printed books, periodical articles, and reviews dealing with Oceanic (i.e., Polynesian, Micronesian, Melanesian, and Papuan) languages ... [and] dictionaries, vocabularies, grammars, and other linguistic contributions but excludes writings in the individual languages themselves."—*Pref.* Arranged by region, subdivided by language. Contains 2,166 entries in a classed arrangement. Indexes of languages and of personal and corporate authors.   Z7111.K5

Languages of the Philippines

Cook, Marjorie. Bibliography of the Summer Institute of Linguistics, Philippines, 1953–1984 / comp. by Marjorie Cook, Heather Kilgour, Jeanne Miller. Manila, Philippines : The Institute, [1986?]. 212 p.   **BD233**
    Lists books, articles, government reports, and dissertations on some 78 languages of the Philippines in a classed arrangement. An appendix lists language name changes; author index.   Z7049.P45C66

Makarenko, Vladimir A. A preliminary annotated bibliography of Pilipino linguistics (1604–1976) / Vladimir A. Makarenko ; ed. by Andrew Gonzalez and Carolina Nemenzo Sacris. [Manila, Philippines] : De La Salle Univ. Libraries and Linguistic Soc. of the Philippines, 1981. 257 *l.*   **BD234**
    A partly annotated listing of nearly 1,800 works, limited in scope to the national language of the Philippines, Pilipino (based on, or otherwise known as, Tagalog); other Philippine languages are excluded. Divided by language of publication into two alphabetical sections: the first for works in Russian; the second, for those in Tagalog or European languages. Subject index.   Z7101.T33M34

Micronesian languages

Kunz, Egon F. An annotated bibliography of the languages of the Gilbert Islands, Ellice Islands and Nauru. Sydney : Trustees of the Pub. Lib. of New South Wales, 1959. 202p.   **BD235**
    Locates copies, some in libraries outside Australia.   Z7111.K8

AUSTRALIAN LANGUAGES

South-East Asia : languages and literatures : a select guide / ed. by Patricia Herbert & Anthony Milner. Honolulu : Univ. of Hawaii Pr., c1989. 182 p. : ill.   **BD236**
    For annotation, *see* BE1550.   PL3501.S66

NATIVE AMERICAN LANGUAGES

General and comparative

Edward E. Ayer Collection. A bibliographical check list of North and Middle American Indian linguistics in the Edward E. Ayer Collection. Chicago : Newberry Library, 1941. 2 v.   **BD237**
    A short-title checklist of the Library's holdings, arranged alphabetically by language, and within each of these categories alphabetically by author. Lists materials on 328 languages and dialects. Index of personal and corporate authors.   PM108.E393

Native languages of the Americas / ed. by Thomas Sebeok. N.Y. : Plenum Pr., c1976–1977. 2 v. : maps.   **BD238**
    Contents: v. 1, p. 1: North America: General chapters, area groupings; v. 2, p. 2: Central and South America. p. 3: Checklists [of languages].
    In 25 thematic chapters, each written by a specialist, consisting of a solid overview of the subject and its historiography and a substantial bibliography. Earlier versions of most of these chapters were previously published in the series "Current trends in linguistics" ('sGravenhage : Mouton, 1963–70), also ed. by Sebeok; they are here

published with varying but frequently substantial revisions, "... so the book, as a whole, may be viewed as a reasonable fresh and certainly comprehensive panoptic conspectus of the field in the last quarter of our century."—*Foreword.* Each volume has its own index of names.

PM108N.3

Pottier, Bernard. Bibliographie américaniste, linguistique amérindienne / Société des américanistes. 1 (1967)–9 (1980). Paris : Musée de l'homme, 1967–1982. Annual. **BD239**

A bibliography covering current linguistic work on native languages of all North, Central, and South America during the period it was issued. Works cited are in a variety of languages; reference apparatus is in French. The main section is an alphabetical author listing, each entry accompanied by alphanumeric codes representing geographical area, language, and subject of the cited work. These are used in three corresponding indexes: géographique, linguistique, and thématique. The nine volumes cover 1965–79, with a few titles from 1980.

E51.B54

North America

Bibliography

Evans, G. Edward. North American Indian language materials, 1890–1965 : an annotated bibliography of monographic works / G. Edward Evans and Jeffrey Clark. Los Angeles : American Indian Studies Center, Univ. of Calif., c1980. 154 p. (American Indian bibliographic series, 31). **BD240**

Intended as an updating of J. C. Pilling, *Bibliographies of the languages of the North American Indians* (N.Y. : AMS Pr., 1973. 3 v. Repr. from Smithsonian Inst. Bureau of Ethnology *Bulletin* [1887–94]), and as an aid in Native American education programs. Aims to list all "dictionaries, grammars, orthographies, primers, readers, and the like concerning those Native American languages whose main province lies north of the Mexican border."—*Introd.* Arranged by language, then by author; in addition to the annotation there is an indication of subject content (e.g., dictionary, grammar) and educational level. Indexed.

Marino Flores, Anselmo. Bibliografía lingüística de la República Mexicana. México : Inst. Indigenista Interamericano, 1957. 95 p. : diagrs. **BD241**

Lists books and articles on the native languages and dialects of Mexico. An unannotated listing by language, valuable for its registry of older material. Also includes tables and maps with selected sociolinguistic information (density, distribution, bilingualism). Z7120.M3

Marken, Jack W. The American Indian language and literature. Arlington Heights, Ill. : AHM Publ. Corp., c1978. 204 p. **BD242**

A bibliography of the languages and literatures of the Indians of North America, excluding the Indians of Mexico and Central America, as well as the Eskimo. In the matter of literatures, focus is on the writings of Indians (although critical works discussing literary writings about Indians by non-Indian authors are included). General sections on bibliography, autobiography, general literature, and general language are followed by geographical sections with subdivisions for individual tribes. Indexed. Z7118.M27

South America

Tovar, Antonio. Catálogo de las lenguas de América del Sur : con clasificaciones, indicaciones tipológicas, bibliografía y mapas / Antonio Tovar, Consuelo Larrucea de Tovar. Nueva ed. refundida. Madrid : Gredos, c1984. 632 p. : maps. **BD243**

1st ed., 1961.

A handbook reflecting recent research on the classification and interrelationship of South American languages. An initial section presents a series of discussions of the classification and typology, with bibliographical references; an extended bibliography follows, arranged alphabetically by author. Devotes some attention to Spanish and Portuguese, with some 350 references to relevant works in the bibliography. Includes an index of languages and dialects, and maps of language areas.

§ *See also*: Tovar's *Catálogo de las lenguas de América del Sur : enumeracíon, con indicaciones tipológicas, bibliografía y mapas* (Buenos Aires : Ed. Sudamericana, [1961]). PM5008.T6

BE

Literature

In general libraries, many inquiries pertain to some aspect of literature, e.g., biographies of authors, book reviews, literary criticism and analysis, quotations, characters, plots, history and development of literature by form or nationality. The needs of individual libraries will vary, but to answer effectively the range of literary inquiries, libraries will need an array of general and specialized reference works. This section intends to suggest as many sources, covering as wide a range of needs, as space will permit. Special attention has been given to sources for the literatures of individual countries outside North America, Great Britain, and Europe.

Two substantial changes in this section should be noted. Sources devoted to individual writers have been dropped, with the exception of a selective section on Shakespeare, which is included to serve as an example of the range of sources that may be found for other writers. Second, the section has been reorganized to reflect geographic rather than linguistic realities. Brazilian literature, for example, will be found among other literatures of South America rather than as a subset of Portuguese literature; literatures of Africa are arranged in a unified section, as are the English and French literatures of Canada; and Indian literatures, whether in English or in indigenous languages, will be found under India.

GENERAL WORKS

Guides

Altick, Richard Daniel. The art of literary research / Richard D. Altick and John J. Fenstermaker. 4th ed. N.Y. : Norton, c1993. 353 p. **BE1**

1st ed., 1963.

A general introduction to literary research, with discussions of the spirit of scholarship and its practical applications: for example, textual study, problems of authorship, finding materials, using libraries, and taking notes. Includes suggestions for further reading and exercises for practice. Indexed. Updated from earlier editions to reflect current literary scholarship.   PR56.A68

Baker, Nancy L. A research guide for undergraduate students : English and American literature. 3rd ed. N.Y. : Modern Language Assoc. of America, 1989. 60, [1] p.   **BE2**

Although brief, this guide is noteworthy for its lucid explanations of basic literary research tools and how to use them, taking a topical approach. Well-illustrated with examples from texts, it includes computerized sources such as *Oxford English dictionary* and online catalogs. The appendix is a selective bibliography of reference sources for English and American literature.

§ Another guide for undergraduates is R. H. Miller's *Handbook of literary research* (Metuchen, N. J. : Scarecrow, 1987) which presents chapters on basic reference sources and selected topics in literature and criticism, in a suggested order of consultation. Indexed by author and title.   PR56.B34

Feldman, Paula R. The wordworthy computer : classroom and research applications in language and literature / Paula R. Feldman and Buford Norman. N.Y. : Random House, c1987. 228 p. : ill.   **BE3**

As with many reference works on new technology, this volume is sadly out of date only a few years after publication. However, it still offers an idea of the broad range of applications which computers may have in both research and teaching, including bibliographic databases, concordances, stylistic analysis, and scholarly publishing. Selected bibliography; glossary of terms.   PN73.F44

Introduction to scholarship in modern languages and literatures / ed. by Joseph Gibaldi. 2nd ed. N.Y. : Modern Language Assoc. of America, 1992. 377 p. : ill.   **BE4**

Made up of 15 signed scholarly essays on linguistics and literary theory. Among the topics are: Language and composition; Language, culture and society; Canonicity and textuality; Historical and textual scholarship; Cross-disciplinary, interdisciplinary, and cultural studies; Feminist, gender, minority and ethnic studies; and The role of the scholar in society. Essays survey topics, outline major issues and provide bibliographies for further reading.   PB35.I57

Kaske, Robert Earl. Medieval Christian literary imagery : a guide to interpretation / R. E. Kaske, in collaboration with Arthur Groos and Michael W. Twomey. Toronto ; Buffalo : Univ. of Toronto Pr., c1988. 247 p. (Toronto medieval bibliographies, 11).   **BE5**

Designed for "the graduate student or young scholar who is interested in ... interpreting medieval literature but has little or no guidance in it."—*Introd.* Chapters provide bibliographical essays and suggest research methods on topics such as biblical exegesis, hymns, mythography, and major authors. Medieval encyclopedias are discussed in an appendix. Subject/medieval author, modern author/editor/translator, manuscript, and translation indexes.   PN671.Z99K37

Oakman, Robert L. Computer methods for literary research. Rev. ed. Athens : Univ. of Georgia Pr., 1984. 235 p. : ill.   **BE6**

1st ed., 1980.

Although somewhat dated, especially in its bibliographical references, this provides a basic introduction to the fundamentals of literary computing and to the use of computers in literary research. Includes chapters on concordances, historical dictionaries and scholarly bibliographies, textual editing, stylistic analysis, and archival considerations.

§ For articles on related topics consult *Literary research : a journal of scholarly method and technique* (v. 11, no. 1 [Winter 1986]– . College Park, Md. : Literary Research Assoc., c1986–), or its predecessor, *Literary research newsletter* (v. 1 [1976]–v. 10 [1985]).   PN73.O24

Research guide to biography and criticism / [ed. by] Walton Beacham. Wash. : Research Publ., c1985–c1991. 6 v.   **BE7**

Vol. 4–6 publ. by Beacham Publ.; v. 5–6 ed. by Walton Beacham, Erica Dickson, Charles J. Moseley.

"Designed to assist students in narrowing and researching topics for term papers and essay exams, and to provide librarians with a tool that will help them lead students to valuable, accessible resources."— *Pref.* [v. 5].

Vols. 1–2 treat British, American, and Canadian writers from *Beowulf* to the present; v. 4 updates these volumes with materials published since 1985. Vol. 3 covers the whole range of world drama beginning with the Greeks. Vols. 5–6 cover modern writers and some 19th-century authors currently the subject of critical study.

For each author, gives a chronology or biographical sketch, select bibliography, overview and evaluation of biographical sources, autobiographical sources, and an overview and evaluation of critical works.   Z2011.R47

Rudall, Brian H. Computers and literature : a practical guide / B. H. Rudall and T. N. Corns. Cambridge, Mass. ; Tunbridge Wells, Kent : Abacus Pr., 1987. 129 p. : ill.   **BE8**

Though much of the information is now outdated, this volume provides a guide for those doing literary research who wish to adapt "the power and convenience of data management and word-processing procedures" (*Pref.*) to their work. Chapters cover using the computer, programming and the choice of language, managing a bibliographic database, concordances, etc. Glossary of terms. An index is listed in the table of contents, but none is included.   PN73.R83

Stevens, Bonnie Klomp. A guide to literary criticism and research / Bonnie Klomp Stevens, Larry L. Stewart. 2nd ed. Fort Worth, Tex. : Harcourt Brace Jovanovich College Publ., c1992. 192 p.   **BE9**

Like the first edition (1987), attempts to offer "upper-level students a concise but adequate guide to the range of modern literary criticism and to basic methods of research."—*Pref.* Presents chapters on particular kinds of criticism, (e.g., Formalist studies, Structuralist studies), the influence of other fields upon criticism (e.g., Feminist studies, Psychological studies), elements of critical essays, and methods of literary research. Each chapter includes bibliographies of cited or recommended works. Appendixes provide an annotated bibliography of basic research sources and guidelines and advice on documentation. General index.   PN81.S73

Thorpe, James. The use of manuscripts in literary research : problems of access and literary property rights. 2nd ed. N.Y. : Modern Language Assoc. of America, 1979. 40 p.   **BE10**

1st ed., 1974.

A guide written from the scholar's point of view. Includes information on locating manuscripts, obtaining access to collections, permissions to photocopy and publish, and literary property rights. This edition takes into account provisions of the 1976 U.S. copyright law.   Z692.M28T47

The writer's advisor / comp. by Leland G. Alkire, Jr. ; Cheryl I. Westerman, associate ed. Detroit : Gale, c1985. 452 p.   **BE11**

Subtitle: A guide to books and articles about writing novels, short stories, poetry, dramatic scripts, screenplays, magazine articles, biographies, technical articles and books, as well as a guide to information about literary agents, marketing, and a wide range of legal and business materials of interest to full- and part-time writers.

About 4,250 entries are grouped mainly according to the categories mentioned in the subtitle. Some annotations. Author, title, and subject indexes.   Z5165.W74

Bibliography

See also Reuss, *Repertorium Commentationum*, EA21.

Baldensperger, Fernand. Bibliography of comparative literature / Fernand Baldensperger and Werner P. Friederich. Chapel Hill : Univ. of North Carolina Pr., 1950. 701 p. (Univ. of North Carolina studies in comparative literature, no. 1).   **BE12**

Repr. : N.Y. : Russell & Russell, 1960.

An extensive compendium attempting to cover literary influences from early to modern times. Arranged in four books: the first and third dealing with generalities (including themes, motifs, genres, international literary relations, etc.); the second and fourth with specific literatures and their contributions, listed according to country or author exerting influence. Bibliographical citations are very brief. A detailed table of contents, but no index.

§ For continuation, see: *Yearbook of comparative and general literature* (BE41). Z6514.C7B3

Betz, Louis Paul. La littérature comparée : essai bibliographique. 2. éd. augm. / pub., avec un index méthodique, par Fernand Baldensperger .... Strasbourg : Trübner, 1904. 386 col., 389–410 p. **BE13**
Repr. : N.Y. : Greenwood, 1969.

A bibliography of books and periodical articles on comparative literature from the Middle Ages through the 19th century. Still useful for the large amount of 19th-century material not included in Fernand Baldensperger and Werner P. Friederich, *Bibliography of comparative literature* (BE12). Z6514.C7B6

Doll, Howard D. Oral interpretation of literature : an annotated bibliography with multimedia listings. Metuchen, N.J. : Scarecrow, 1982. 489 p. **BE14**
About 4,200 entries. Chronological arrangement within separate sections for books, chapters in books, journal articles, specialized periodicals, theses and dissertations, filmstrips, and videotapes. Author and subject indexes. With the exception of theses and dissertations, entries are briefly annotated. Z6514.S7D64

Harvard University. Library. Literature : general and comparative : classification schedule, classified listing by call number, alphabetical listing by author or title, chronological listing. Cambridge : Harvard Univ. Library, dist. by the Harvard Univ. Pr., 1968. 189 p. (Widener Library shelflist, no. 18). **BE15**
For a note on the series, *see* AA115.

Includes "general works on the art of literature, histories of comparative literature, and anthologies which contain a wide variety of literature."—*Pref.* Z697.L45H3

Hebel, Udo J. Intertextuality, allusion, and quotation : an international bibliography of critical studies. N.Y. : Greenwood, 1989. 175 p. (Bibliographies and indexes in world literature, no. 18). **BE16**
Lists 2,033 articles, books, chapters, and dissertations alphabetically by author with indexes to writers and anonymous texts and to subjects. Scope is limited to three specific concepts of literary poststructuralism. Z6514.C97H4

International Federation for Modern Languages and Literature. Répertoire chronologique des littératures modernes / publié par la Commission internationale d'histoire littéraire moderne sous la direction de Paul Van Tieghem. Paris : Droz, 1935. 413 p. **BE17**
Issued in parts, 1935–37.

Arranged chronologically; under each year lists the principal writings and literary events by country. Covers 1455–1900. Index.
Z6519.I61

Internationale bibliographie zu Geschichte und Theorie der Komparatistik / ed. by Hugo Dyserinck together with Manfred S. Fischer. Stuttgart : A. Hiersemann, 1985. 314 p. (Hiersemanns bibliographische Handbücher, Bd. 5). **BE18**
An international bibliography tracing the theory, methodology, and history of comparative literature, 1800 through 1982, emphasizing the development of the discipline worldwide. Principally directed toward scholars in comparative literature. Covers a wide range of materials: collections, conferences, festschriften, newspapers, and scholarly journals. Entries for 1800–99 are by author. Beginning with 1900, entries are listed for each year, again by author. For each discrete time period entries are divided into three categories: general works on theo-

ry; specialized studies of issues in theory and methodology (e.g., the relations between comparative literature and other disciplines); and finally, works that chart the history and development of the discipline. Indexes of subjects and proper names, and of authors.

Kiell, Norman. Psychoanalysis, psychology, and literature : a bibliography. 2nd ed. Metuchen, N.J. : Scarecrow, 1982. 2 v. (1269 p.). **BE19**
1st ed., 1963.

Lists articles, monographs, and books that deal with literary writing from a psychological point of view. Classed arrangement with sections for various types of literary works (fiction, drama, autobiography, diaries, poetry, criticism, film, etc.). About 20,000 items in this edition, including many foreign-language entries. Author, title, and subject indexes in v. 2.

————. ————. *Supplement to the second edition* (Metuchen, N.J. : Scarecrow, 1990. 587 p.). Adds 7,754 new citations to works published for the most part 1980–87. Z6514.P78K53

Kohl, Benjamin G. Renaissance humanism, 1300–1550 : a bibliography of materials in English. N.Y. : Garland, 1985. 354 p. (Garland reference library of the humanities, v. 570). **BE20**

Developed for undergraduates and beginning graduate students in various disciplines: art history, English, Romance languages, classics, history, and philosophy. The 19 chapters fall in two fairly distinct halves. Chapters 1–8 list reference works, journals, bibliographies, guides, and seminal studies. Chapters 9–19 cover specific humanists, (e.g., Boccaccio) or geographic locations (e.g., Great Britain) in approximate chronological sequence. Chapters subdivide by topic and/or by type of publication. Lists English translations of works by humanists, other source material, and secondary texts, with a few foreign language bibliographies. Most items were published prior to 1983. Author/editor/translator and subject indexes. Z7128.H9K64

Livingston College. A syllabus of comparative literature / comp. by the faculty of comparative literature, Livingston College, Rutgers Univ. ; ed., John O. McCormick. 2nd ed. Metuchen, N.J. : Scarecrow, 1972. 220 p. **BE21**
Previous ed., 1964.

A series of reading lists arranged by period for Western literature, plus brief sections for Indian, Chinese, and Japanese literatures.
Z6511.L57

Magill, Frank Northen. Magill's bibliography of literary criticism : selected sources for the study of more than 2,500 outstanding works of Western literature / ed. by Frank N. Magill ; assoc. eds., Stephen L. Hanson, Patricia King Hanson. Englewood Cliffs, N.J. : Salem Pr., 1979. 4 v. **BE22**
A listing of studies—published as books, parts of books, and periodical articles—of works of fiction, drama, and poetry. Arrangement is by literary author, then by individual work, with studies listed alphabetically by author. "There are 613 authors represented, 2,546 literary works covered, and 36,137 individual citations listed. Major novels and plays usually have about 25 sources listed, while minor works average about a dozen."—*Pref.* Includes literary works of all periods, and foreign works available in English translation. Emphasizes publications from the 1960s and 1970s. Sources were selected with the undergraduate student and general reader in mind. Title index in v. 4.
Z6511.M25

Marshall, Donald G. Contemporary critical theory : a selective bibliography. N.Y. : Modern Language Assoc. of America, 1993. 201 p. **BE23**
Designed for advanced undergraduates, graduate students, and others surveying the field of critical theory. Only books are listed, and works in foreign languages are excluded, since the bibliography focuses on the effect of critical theory on American literary study. Sections (e.g. structuralism and semiotics, poststructuralism and deconstruction) may be subdivided and may include listings for introductory anthologies and surveys, other books and collections, and bibliographies of

works by and about individual critics. Titles may be cross-listed in more than one section; many of the 1,690 entries are annotated briefly. Indexed. Z6514.C97M37

Meurs, Jos van. Jungian literary criticism, 1920–1980 : an annotated, critical bibliography of works in English (with a selection of titles after 1980) / by Jos van Meurs with John Kidd. Metuchen, N.J. : Scarecrow, 1988. 353 p. **BE24**

Aims to offer "a complete bibliography of all secondary works (books and articles, critical and scholarly), written in English, that apply the psychology of C.G. Jung to the interpretation of literary texts written in English."—*Introd.* Comprehensive 1920–80, with some citations to works published in the early 1980s. In two main sections: (1) a survey of the history and development of Jungian criticism in narrative form; (2) the bibliography of 902 items arranged alphabetically by critic, with author and subject indexes. Z6514.P78M48

Natoli, Joseph P. Psychocriticism : an annotated bibliography / comp. by Joseph P. Natoli and Frederik L. Rusch. Westport, Conn. : Greenwood, 1984. 267 p. (Bibliographies and indexes in world literature, 1). **BE25**

Unlike Norman Kiell's *Psychoanalysis, psychology, and literature* (BE19) coverage is limited "... to articles and books in which a fairly recognizable school or method of psychology is applied to literature."—*Pref.* Includes critical and scholarly secondary works published 1969–82, grouped by literary period from ancient and classical times to the 20th century, with subdivisions for individual authors. A separate chapter lists general studies and essay collections. Subject and author indexes. Z6514.P78N38

Pfeiffer, Joachim. Literaturpsychologie, 1945–1987 : eine systematische und annotierte Bibliographie / Joachim Pfeiffer ; hrsg. in Verbindung mit Wolfram Mauser und Bernd Urban und mit Unterstützung der Breuninger-Stiftung. Würzburg : Königshausen & Neumann, c1989. 516 p. **BE26**

Lists 2,411 books, articles, dissertations, and conference proceedings in a classified arrangement. Some overlap with Norman Kiell's *Psychoanalysis, psychology, and literature* (BE19) but contains many more citations to German-language publications. Interdisciplinary in focus, the bibliography includes many items not strictly pertinent to literature. Nearly half the entries are for individual authors. Author and subject indexes.

Supplemented by "Literaturpsychologie 1987–1990 ... erste Fortsetzung und Nachträge" by Pfeiffer, in *Literatur und Sexualität*, ed. by Johannes Cremerius ... [et al] (Würzburg : Königshausen & Neumann, 1991), p. 221–308. Adds 515 items. Z6514.P78P47

Pownall, David E. Articles on twentieth century literature : an annotated bibliography, 1954 to 1970. N.Y. : Kraus-Thomson, 1973–1980. 7 v. **BE27**

"An expanded cumulation of 'Current bibliography' in the journal *Twentieth century literature*. Volume one to volume sixteen, 1955 to 1970."—*t.p.*

Arranged by name of literary author (the proposed section on general literary topics has not appeared); substantially expanded from the quarterly bibliographies on which it is based. "Current bibliography" continued to be a regular feature of *Twentieth century literature* through v. 25, no. 1 (Spring 1979), then appeared sporadically through v. 27, no. 2 (Summer 1981). Z6519.P66

Progress of medieval and Renaissance studies in the United States and Canada. Bulletin no. 1 (Mar. 1923)–no. 25 (1960). Boulder, Colo. : Univ. of Colorado, 1923–1960. Irregular. **BE28**

Title varies.

Renaissance studies added with no. 15. Each number contains lists of papers, publications, projects, doctoral dissertations, and a list of medieval and Renaissance scholars, with their publications. Z6203.P96

Recent studies in myths and literature, 1970–1990 : an annotated bibliography / comp. by Bernard Accardi... [et al.]. N.Y. : Greenwood, 1991. 251 p. (Bibliographies and indexes in world literature, no. 29). **BE29**

A selective annotated bibliography for teachers and scholars of British and American literature that traces the 20-year period of scholarship on myth in literature as influenced by structuralism, semiotics, anthropology, narratology, neo-Freudianism, history of conciousness, and genre studies. Includes sections on theory and themes, on classical, English, and American literature, from their beginnings into the 20th century. For sections on periods, general studies precede those on individual authors. Limits studies on science fiction and children's literature while excluding altogether dissertations, book reviews, and most work on English-speaking authors outside Britain and the U.S. Studies on influential authors such as Dante, Kafka, and Mann appear among the general studies. Annotations are generally descriptive and often extensive. Author and subject indexes. PR149.M95

The relations of literature and science : an annotated bibliography of scholarship, 1880–1980 / ed. by Walter Schatzberg, Ronald A. Waite, Jonathan K. Johnson. N.Y. : Modern Language Assoc. of America, 1987. 458 p. **BE30**

Incorporates the annual bibliographies produced by the Division on Literature and Science of the Modern Language Association, 1939–80, with significant additions and deletions, and extends the work back to 1880. Excludes historical background studies on general issues, focusing instead on scholarly works on specific aspects. Some 2,500 carefully selected entries are organized from general to particular topics, covering classical antiquity to the 20th century, with concise informative annotations and excellent subject and personal name indexing.

§ Schatzberg also edited *Relations of literature and science : a bibliography of scholarship* ([Worcester, Mass.] : Clark Univ. Pr., [1979/80–1983]. 4 v.), listing items by period. Z6511.R44

Reuss, Jeremias David. Repertorium commentationum a societatibus litterariis editarum / secundum disciplinarum ordinem digessit I. D. Reuss .... Gottingae : apud Henricum Dieterich, 1801–21. 16 v. **BE31**

Contents: T.8, Historia ... Historia litteraria; T.9, Philologia, Linguae, Scriptores graeci, Scriptores latini, Litterae elegantiores, Poesis, Rhetorica, Ars antiqua, Pictura, Musica. For full description, *see* EA21. Z5051.R44

Revue des revues. 1974–1988. (*In* Canadian review of comparative literature : v. 1 [1974]–v. 15 [1988]). Annual. **BE32**

An annotated bibliography of periodical articles on comparative literature, noted for lengthy, detailed abstracts. In three sections: literary history and relations; literary theory and methods of literary study; and literature and the other arts. In each section, studies are listed alphabetically by author. Indexes of authors and subjects.

Thompson, George A. Key sources in comparative and world literature : an annotated guide to reference materials. N.Y. : Ungar, 1982. 383 p. **BE33**

A bibliographic guide intended for graduate students. Chapters for general and comparative literatures, classical, Romance, French, Italian, Hispanic, and German literatures, literature in English, other European literatures, Oriental literatures, and related fields. Lists many specialized bibliographies (e.g., of specific themes, genres, movements) and bibliographies and concordances for individual authors. Descriptive and evaluative annotations; citations to reviews. Classed arrangement within chapters (an outline preceding each chapter); index of editors, compilers, etc.; selective index of titles; subject index. Z6511.T47

Wortman, William A. A guide to serial bibliographies for modern literatures. N.Y. : Modern Language Assoc. of America, 1982. 124 p. **BE34**

Lists and annotates about 950 "current serial bibliographies in modern literatures of use to students of literature."—*Pref.* Classed arrangement; author/title/subject index. Z6519.W67

Current

Annual review. (*In* : Journal of modern literature 1 [1970]–). Annual. **BE35**

Initially publ. as a supplement; with v. 5 (1976), appeared as one of the quarterly issues.

An important serial bibliography of scholarship in English on the modernist period. Divided into sections for general studies and individual writers. The former covers reference and bibliography; themes and movements; regional, national and ethnic literature; comparative studies of two or more authors; criticism of modern literature in general, and of fiction, poetry, drama, and film as literature. Includes monographs, critical editions of literary works, dissertations, symposia, articles in books and journals, and other miscellaneous materials. Many entries are annotated, some extensively.

The eighteenth century : a current bibliography. n.s. 1 (1975)– . Philadelphia : American Society for Eighteenth-Century Studies, 1978– . Annual. **BE36**

"A current bibliography incorporating English literature 1660–1800."—*verso of t.p.*

The successor to "English literature 1660–1800" which appeared in *Philological quarterly* 1926–70 (repr. in 6 v., Princeton Univ. Pr., 1950–72) and in a new series of annual volumes 1971–75 that became international and interdisciplinary in coverage. "The purpose of this bibliography is annually to record and evaluate the year's significant scholarship concerning the Enlightenment in Europe and the New World."—*Foreword.* Z5579.6.E36

Essay and general literature index. v. [1] (1900/33)– . N.Y. : H.W. Wilson, 1934– . Frequency varies. **BE37**

For annotation, *see* BA4. AI3.E752

FRANCIS. Bulletin signalétique. v. 1 (1947)– . Paris : Centre de Documentation du C.N.R.S. [Centre National de la Recherche Scientifique], 1947– . Quarterly. **BE38**

Includes Sec. 523, *Histoire et science de la littérature. Arts du spectacle* (title varies). Covers generalities (bibliographies, congresses, etc.), literary theory (including comparative literature), and the history of literature, with numerous subdivisions. Since 1988, scope has narrowed to French and English literatures, Middle Ages to the 20th century, including French and English literatures of Africa and the Antilles. For full description, *see* AD254.

Modern Language Association of America. MLA international bibliography of books and articles on the modern languages and literatures. 1921– . [N.Y.] : Modern Language Assoc. of America, [1921]– . Annual. **BE39**

Title varies.

Publ. as supplements to *PMLA*, v. 37–1980?

1921–1954/55 repr. as *MLA American bibliography*; 1956–68 repr. (N.Y. : Kraus).

From 1921 to 1955 entitled *American bibliography* and limited to writings by Americans on the literatures of various countries; coverage varied. 1956–62, title changed to *Annual bibliography* and coverage extended to include writers in other languages. 1963, title changed to *MLA international bibliography* (this title used in reprint edition). Selections are made from various book sources and from a basic master list of several hundred periodicals in modern languages and literatures. By 1963, listed books and articles in English, French, German, Spanish, Italian, Portuguese, Rumanian, the Scandinavian languages, Netherlandic, Celtic, and a selection of East European languages. Beginning with the issue covering publications of 1969, the longer title cited here has been used and coverage further extended.

National literature sections are subdivided by literary periods; names of authors treated are printed in boldface. Some volumes have author indexes. No cumulations.

Beginning with the volumes covering 1981, publ. in 5 v.: (1) British, American, Australian, English-Canadian, New Zealand, and English-Caribbean literatures; (2) European, Asian, African, and South American literatures; (3) Linguistics; (4) General literature and related topics; (5) Folklore. Subscriptions are available for individual volumes or various combinations as well as for the entire set. Author and subject indexes are available for the entire set and for certain other combinations.

Although computer-produced, the subject indexes are not merely keyword-in-context; "the indexers use terms that describe [an item's] content. These descriptors, based on the document author's own wording, are assigned to facets [of the structured index] pertinent to that item ... ."—*Guide for users 1981*. Regarding scope, there are now no restrictions as to place of origin or of publication or the original language of the works cited, nor is there a restriction as to the physical type or medium of works. "Works limited to pedagogy, even as it relates to the teaching of language, literature, composition, and related subjects, are excluded ... . There are no historical-period restrictions on language coverage; for literature, works exclusively on classical Greek and Latin literatures are excluded since those literatures are covered in *L'année philologique* [BE990]."

The version found in most research collections will be the full set with author and subject indexes. Entries in the subject index refer to volume and item numbers.

•Machine-readable versions are called *MLA international bibliography* [database] (N.Y. : MLA). An online version offers some one million records, covers 1963– , and is updated monthly Dec.–June and again in Oct. Versions are available online through OCLC FirstSearch and on CD-ROM from SilverPlatter. FirstSearch begins coverage with 1963 and is updated 10 times a year. The CD-ROM begins coverage with 1981, and is updated quarterly. Z7006.M64

The Romantic movement bibliography, 1936–1970 : a master cumulation from ELH, Philological quarterly and English language notes / ed. and with a pref. by A. C. Elkins, Jr. and L. J. Forstner; with a foreword by David V. Erdman. [Ann Arbor, Mich.] : Pierian Pr., 1973. 7 v. (3289 p.). (Cumulated bibliography series, no. 3). **BE40**

A photo-reproduction of annual bibliographies originally published in *ELH, a journal of English literary history*, 1937–49; in *Philological quarterly*, 1950–64; in *English language notes*, 1965–79.

The bibliography focuses on the movement in Great Britain and Western Europe. Initially a checklist, it evolved into a more selective and critical bibliography. David V. Erdman outlines these changes in the Foreword, which warrants careful study. Vol. 7 is devoted to a series of indexes by author/main entry/reviewer and by subject for personal names and categories. Subject access is limited due to insufficient detail.

A continuation, ed. by Erdman, is published annually as *The Romantic movement : a selective and critical bibliography for 1979–* (N.Y. : Garland, 1980–). Like its predecessors, it emphasizes the literary movement in England and on the Continent. Z6514.R6R65

Yearbook of comparative and general literature. v. 1 (1952)– . Bloomington : Indiana Univ., 1952– . Annual. **BE41**

Published in collaboration with the Comparative Literature Committee of the National Council of Teachers of English; the American Comparative Literature Association; and the Comparative Literature Section of the Modern Language Association.

Includes literary research studies, among them intercultural and interdisciplinary articles, and studies of genres, themes, motifs, and movements. Vols. 1–19 (1952–70) contained an "Annual bibliography" for the period 1949–69, intended to supplement Fernand Baldensperger and Werner P. Friederich's *Bibliography of comparative literature* (BE12). An important contribution for the period 1960–78/79 was the "List of Translations" from foreign languages into English published in v. 10–29 (1961–80).

A more recent feature reflecting the intercultural emphasis is "Bibliography on the Relations of Literature and Other Arts for ..." which began appearing in v. 34 (1985). The bibliography for 1989 was not published in v. 38, but appeared in v. 39 as a combined bibliography for 1989 and 1990. PN851.Y4

Periodicals

Modern Language Association of America. MLA directory of periodicals : a guide to journals and series in languages and literatures. 1978/79– . [N.Y.] : Modern Language Assoc. of America, 1979– . Biennial.   **BE42**
Provides as full information as available on all journals and series included in the master list of the *MLA international bibliography* (BE39). Listing is by title, with indexes of editorial personnel, languages, sponsoring organizations, and subjects. With the 1990–91 ed., the directory also included an index of periodicals with an author-anonymous submission policy. In addition to address, name of editor, first date of publication, ISSN and MLA acronym, information is given on subscriptions, editorial content, and submission requirements.
P1.A1M62a

Patterson, Margaret C. Author newsletters and journals : an international annotated bibliography of serial publications concerned with the life and works of individual authors. Detroit : Gale, 1979. 497 p. (American literature, English literature, and world literatures in English, 19).   **BE43**
Lists and annotates 1,129 titles of serial publications devoted to the life and work of a single author. Includes both current and defunct publications covering 435 authors, representing 28 countries, ranging from antiquity to the 20th century. Numerous appendixes; title index.
Patterson published three supplements in *Serials review* 8, no. 4 (Winter 1982): 61–72; 10, no. 1 (Spring 1984): 51–59; 11, no. 3 (Fall 1985): 31–44.
§ Another source for locating author newsletters is *Oxbridge directory of newsletters* (AE37).   Z6513.P37

Dissertations

See also *Dissertation abstracts international* (AG13).

Naaman, Antoine. Répertoire des thèses littéraires canadiennes de 1921 à 1976 / Antoine Naaman, avec la collab. de Léo A. Brodeur. Sherbrooke, Québec : Éditions Naaman, [1978?]. 453 p.   **BE44**
Lists some 5,600 doctoral dissertations and master's theses (in English as well as French) on literature and language completed at Canadian universities 1921–76. The first part is a classed arrangement within seven broad categories: (1) Civilisation, folklore et mouvement des idées; (2) Genres littéraires; (3) Histoire littéraire; (4) Écriture française dans le monde (hors de la France et du Québec); (5) Études comparées; (6) Traduction; (7) Sciences du langage. The second part is an alphabetical listing of the authors who are the subject of the study. Indexed by authors; by authors studied; by subject—in French, English, and other languages; and by title of work studied.   Z6511.N26

Translations

For translations from specific languages, consult the regional and country sections below. See also: *Yearbook of comparative and general literature* (BE41), which included a list of translations from foreign languages into English in v. 10–29 (1961–80).

Farrar, Clarissa Palmer. Bibliography of English translations from medieval sources / Clarissa Palmer Farrar, Austin Patterson Evans. N.Y. : Columbia Univ. Pr., 1946. 534 p. (Records of civilization; sources and studies, no. 39).   **BE45**
"Aims to include English translations of important literary sources produced during the period from Constantine the Great to the year 1500 within an area roughly inclusive of Europe, northern Africa and western Asia."—*Pref.* Lists works published through 1942, with a few items published later which were inserted in proof.

An outstanding work including almost 4,000 entries arranged alphabetically by author, with many annotations describing content, translator's comment, editions or reprints of a given translation, adequacy of translation, etc. Extensive index to authors, translators, editors, titles, subjects, etc.
§ Supplemented by: Mary Anne Heyward Ferguson, *Bibliography of English translations from medieval sources, 1943–1967* (N.Y. : Columbia Univ. Pr., 1974. 274 p. [Records of civilization; sources and studies, no. 88]).   Z6517.F3

Criticism

Classical and medieval literature criticism. v. 1– . Detroit : Gale, 1988– . Annual.   **BE46**
Subtitle: Excerpts from criticism of the works of world authors from classical antiquity through the fourteenth century, from the first appraisals to current evaluations.
Presents "significant passages from the most important criticism published in English to aid students in the location and selection of commentaries on the authors of this period …. Each entry in CMLC provides an overview of major criticism on an author or literary work … four to six authors in each 500 page volume."—*Pref.* Each entry includes a historical and critical introduction, a list of principal translations, criticism, and additional bibliography. Various indexes.
PN681.5.C57

Contemporary literary criticism. v. 1 ([1973])– . Detroit : Gale, 1973– .   **BE47**
Subtitle varies; editors vary. Also called *CLC*.
An ongoing series of selected excerpts from critical writings on contemporary authors. Writers treated are "those who are either now living or who have died since January 1, 1960."—*Pref.* Critiques are drawn mainly from writings of the past 25 years. About 175 authors are treated in each volume (fewer in recent volumes), with an average of five excerpts (from books, reviews and periodical articles) about each. Full citations to source follow the excerpts. In addition to well-established authors, consideration is given to writers of current interest and authors of mystery and science fiction writings. By mid-1993 series numbered 75 volumes. Various indexes throughout series.
PN771.C59

Critical survey of literary theory / ed. by Frank N. Magill. Pasadena, Calif. : Salem Pr., c1987. 4 v. (1833, 47 p.).   **BE48**
For each of 257 Western and non-Western theorists, lists principal critical works, indicates the subject's influence as a theorist, provides biographical information and explication of theories and criticism, and cites several secondary critical works. Vol. 4 includes a glossary, 12 essays surveying historical and national trends in literary theory, and an index. Especially useful for undergraduates.
PN45.C74

Humm, Maggie. An annotated critical bibliography of feminist criticism. Boston : G.K. Hall, 1987. 240 p.   **BE49**
Treats "contemporary feminist criticism: its theories, techniques, debates, and development in America and England."—*Introd.* Covers not only literary criticism, but also psychology, sociology, anthropology, and allied fields. Citations to books are arranged alphabetically by author in chapters on broad subject areas, with subject and author indexes.
§ See also: Wendy Frost, *Feminist literary criticism : a bibliography of journal articles, 1975–1981* (N.Y. : Garland, 1988).
Z7963.F44H85

Literature criticism from 1400 to 1800. v. 1– . Detroit : Gale, c1984– . Irregular.   **BE50**
Subtitle: Excerpts from criticism of the works of fifteenth, sixteenth, seventeenth, and eighteenth-century novelists, poets, playwrights, philosophers, and other creative writers, from the first published critical appraisals to current evaluations.

Similar to the publisher's other series of excerpts from literary criticism (e.g., *Contemporary literary criticism*, BE47). International coverage, with considerable emphasis on English authors; excludes Shakespeare. PN86.L53

Modern black writers / comp. and ed. by Michael Popkin. N.Y. : Ungar, c1978. 519 p. **BE51**

Like other volumes in the "Library of literary criticism" series, this is a compilation of excerpts from critical appraisals (originally published in books or periodicals) of the writers included. "The eighty writers discussed in this volume are all noted primarily for their work in either fiction, poetry, or drama."—*Introd.* Authors from some 23 countries (writing in English, French, and several African languages) are included. Index of critics, and a list of literary works mentioned. PN841.M58

Orr, Leonard. Research in critical theory since 1965 : a classified bibliography. N.Y. : Greenwood, 1989. 465 p. (Bibliographies and indexes in world literature, no. 21). **BE52**

About 5,500 books, articles, and dissertations in English, French, and German are arranged by school of criticism (e.g., structuralist, reception aesthetics). Index by author and by type of criticism, but not by a specific literary work on which the article may be based. Z6514.C97O77

Selden, Raman. A reader's guide to contemporary literary theory. 3rd ed. / Raman Selden and Peter Widdowson. Lexington : Univ. Pr. of Kentucky, c1993. 244 p. **BE53**

1st ed., 1985; 2nd ed., 1989, by Raman Selden.

Lucid chapters explain the antecedents, development, and recent trends of critical theory. In eight main sections: (1) New Criticism, moral formalism and F. R. Leavis; (2) Russian formalism; (3) Reader-oriented theories; (4) Marxist theories; (5) Structuralist theories; (6) Poststructuralist theories; (7) Postmodernist and postcolonialist theories; (8) Feminist theories. Sections conclude with bibliographies of selected works. Index. PN94.S45

Twentieth-century literary criticism. v. 1 (1978)– . Detroit : Gale, [1978]– . Irregular. **BE54**

Subtitle (varies): Excerpts from criticism of the works of novelists, poets, playwrights, short story writers, and other creative writers who died between 1900 and 1960, from the first published critical appraisals to current evaluations.

Annual, 1978–1980; irregular since 1981.

A companion to *Contemporary literary criticism* (BE47), but limited to deceased writers as indicated in the subtitle. For each author there is an identifying paragraph and a list of principal works followed by excerpts from criticism (with citations to sources). International in coverage, with all critical excerpts in English. Various indexes in each volume. Indexes frequently cross-reference entries in other Gale series.

Beginning with v. 34, every fourth volume is devoted to topics rather than individual authors (e.g., German Expressionism, psychoanalysis and literature, Czechoslovakian literature).

§ *Nineteenth-century literature criticism* (Detroit : Gale, 1981–) follows the same model, but is limited to writers who lived between 1800 and 1900. PN771.G27

Twentieth-century literary movements index / Laurie Lanzen Harris, ed., Helene Henderson, assoc. ed. Detroit : Omnigraphics, c1991. 419 p. **BE55**

Subtitle: A guide to 500 literary movements, groups, schools, tendencies, and trends of the twentieth century, covering more than 3,000 novelists, poets, dramatists, essayists, artists, and other seminal thinkers from 80 countries as found in standard literary reference works.

An index to 28 reference sources published 1959–88. The first part indexes literary movements of the 20th century, including significant schools of literary criticism; the second part is an index of individuals. Z6514.L57T9

Weiner, Alan R. Literary criticism index / by Alan R. Weiner, Spencer Means. 2nd ed. Metuchen, N.J. : Scarecrow, 1994. 559 p. **BE56**

1st ed., 1984.

An index to bibliographies of literary criticism, giving references to the bibliographies and checklists, not direct citations to the critical studies. This edition supersedes and updates the 1st ed., adding titles published since 1984 and titles inadvertently omitted from the previous edition. Indexes 146 bibliographies and guides to criticism. Arranged by literary author with subdivisions for individual works. Z6511.W44

Wellek, René. A history of modern criticism : 1750–1950. New Haven, Conn. : Yale Univ. Pr., 1955–1992. v. 1–8. (In progress?). **BE57**

Contents: v. 1, The later eighteenth century; v. 2, The romantic age; v. 3, The age of transition; v. 4, The later nineteenth century; v. 5, English criticism, 1900–1950; v. 6, American criticism, 1900–1950; v. 7, German, Russian and Eastern European criticism, 1900–1950; v. 8, French, Italian and Spanish criticism, 1900–1950.

A magisterial work in the history of literary criticism for the period indicated. Interprets "criticism" in broad terms, encompassing the common meaning of the term, but focusing on "mainly what has been thought about the principles and theory of literature, its nature, its creation, its function, its effects, its relations to other activities of man, its kinds, devices, and techniques, its origins and history."—*Pref. v. 1.*

Although the history follows a more or less chronological sequence, individual chapters concentrate on overviews of criticism in particular countries, or on significant literary figures or movements within them. Where appropriate to the text each volume has a chronological table of works. Chapters have substantive, detailed notes, and selective bibliographies with critical comments. Each volume is indexed by name, and by topics and terms. PN86.W4

Encyclopedias

Benét's reader's encyclopedia. 3rd ed. N.Y. : Harper & Row, c1987. 1091 p. **BE58**

1st ed., 1948; 2nd ed., 1965.

Many of the older entries have been revised or dropped, and a substantial number of new entries added "with an eye to expanding the book's international scope."—*Introd.* Compiled by many hands, the 3rd ed. emphasizes 20th-century and non-Western literatures, with the result that some of the more obscure classical and European authors, characters, works, and motifs have been excluded. PN41.B4

Cassell's encyclopaedia of world literature. 2nd rev. and enl. ed. / gen. ed., J. Buchanan-Brown. London : Cassell ; N.Y. : Morrow, 1973. 3 v. (585, 836, 791 p.). **BE59**

1st ed., 1953, in 2 v., ed. by S. H. Steinberg, had title: *Cassell's encyclopaedia of literature.*

Contents: v. 1, Histories and general articles; v. 2–3, Biographies, A–Z.

The first volume includes entries for histories of national literatures, literary genres, literary movements, schools, and themes, and specific literary terms. Vols. 2–3 contain brief biographical sketches of literary figures, plus occasional entries for individual literary works. All biographical articles are signed with initials of the contributor, as are all but the briefest entries in v. 1. There are selective bibliographies for a very high percentage of articles. PN41.C3

Columbia dictionary of modern European literature. 2nd ed., fully rev. & enl. / Jean-Albert Bédé and William B. Edgerton, gen. editors. N.Y. : Columbia Univ. Pr., 1980. 895 p. **BE60**

The 1st ed., 1947, was a scholarly dictionary offering biographical sketches, with critical evaluations of modern European authors, together with articles on the many national literatures.

This is a thorough revision incorporating the contributions of some 500 scholars from the U.S., Canada, and several European countries. Takes as its starting point "the period toward the end of the 19th century when Europe was swept by a wave of new literary movements," although writers were selected for inclusion "on the basis of their relevance to 20th-century literature."—*Pref.* Survey articles on the various national literatures are again included along with articles on individual writers (which now total 1,853). Articles are signed with the initials of the contributors; many articles were newly prepared, and revisions by different hands of articles from the first edition are so indicated. Some entries from the earlier edition were dropped. The brief bibliographies appended to the articles were compiled "especially with a view to meeting the needs of readers who may not be specialists in the literature to which the writer belongs."   PN771.C575

Critical terms for literary study / ed. by Frank Lentricchia and Thomas McLaughlin. Chicago : Univ. of Chicago Pr., 1990. 369 p.   **BE61**

A collection of 22 substantial essays by prominent scholars discussing key concepts for the understanding of contemporary literary theory. Includes topics such as Discourse, Narrative, Canon, Gender, and Ethnicity, each followed by a list of suggested readings. Concludes with a lengthy set of references.   PN81.C84

Dictionnaire historique, thématique et technique des littératures : littératures française et étrangères, anciennes et modernes / sous la direction de Jacques Demougin. Paris : Larousse, c1985–c1986. 2 v. : ill. (some col.).   **BE62**

A work of wide coverage, with entries for authors, titles, and terms from all literatures and periods. Each volume concludes with bibliographies for selected entries.   PN41.D487

Dizionario letterario Bompiani delle opere e dei personaggi di tutti i tempi e di tutte le letterature. Milan : Bompiani, 1947–50. 9 v. : ill.   **BE63**

Repr. with rev. introductory matter: Milan : Bompiani, 1963–64.

Contents: v. 1–7, A–Z; v. 8, a dictionary of literary characters; v. 9, indexes.

An encyclopedia, listing and describing the works of all times and all countries in literature, art, and music. Although the emphasis is on literature, musical works and many famous pictures are described. Lavishly illustrated with many colored plates and black-and-white illustrations. The first half of v. 1 is devoted to 58 *movimenti spirituali,* arranged alphabetically, e.g., Dadaism, euphuism, mysticism. The main part of the work consists of signed articles, arranged alphabetically by the Italian form of the title of the work, followed by the original title in brackets. Brief biographical notes are usually included in the articles, but there are no author entries.

Vol. 8 is a dictionary of literary characters alphabetized according to the Italian form of the name. The scope is broad, ranging from Adam to Superman. Vol. 9 includes synoptic tables showing literary development in all parts of the world; a list of titles in the original languages with their Italian equivalents; an index of authors; and an index of illustrations by artist.

An *Appendice* (Milan : Bompiani, 1964–79. 3 v.) supplements the original volumes with additional information; v. 3 is an index to this appendix.

Dizionario letterario Bompiani degli autori di tutti i tempi e di tutte le letterature (Milano : Bompiani, 1987. 4 v.) contains biographical and critical sketches of approximately 9,000 authors, with listings of their important works but not works about them. Covers the classical period up to the late 1980s. An earlier edition, profusely illustrated, appeared in 1956–57 (Milano : Bompiani. 3 v.).

An abridged French edition of Bompiani was published in 4 v. as *Dictionnaire des oeuvres de tous les temps et de tous les pays : littérature, philosophie, musique, sciences par Laffont-Bompiani* ([4. éd.]. Paris : Soc. d'Édit. de Dictionnaires et Encyclopedies, [1962]). A fifth volume appeared as *Dictionnaire des oeuvres contemporaines de tous les pays : littérature, philosophie, musique, sciences* (Paris : Soc. d'Édit. de Dictionnaires et Encyclopedies, [1968]). The companion volume to these five is *Dictionnaire des personnages littéraires et dramatiques de tous les temps et de tous les pays : poésie, théâtre, roman, musique* (ed. in chief, Jacques Brosse. Paris : Soc. d'Édit. de Dictionnaires et Encyclopedies, 1960. Various reprints.).

Dizionario universale della letteratura contemporanea / [Direttore : Alberto Mondadori]. Milano : Mondadori, [1959–1963]. 5 v. : ill.   **BE64**

An encyclopedia of world literature covering 1870–1960 and supplementing *Dizionario letterario Bompiani ...* (BE63) Arranged alphabetically, it includes authors ("non-literary" as well as literary), literary movements, periodicals, national literatures, etc. Bibliographies are generally substantial and include works by and about an author. Extensively illustrated in black-and-white and in color. Vol. 5 includes chronological tables, 1870–1961, and various indexes: authors, titles both in Italian and in the original language; works not translated; illustrations, etc.   PN41.D53

Encyclopedia of literature and criticism / ed. by Martin Coyle ... [et al.]. London : Routledge, 1990. 1299 p.   **BE65**

A collection of signed substantive essays on English literature and critical debate about it. Major sections cover literary periods from medieval to postmodern; the genres of poetry, drama, and the novel; literary criticism, ranging from biblical hermeneutics to deconstruction and the new historicism; the production and reception of literature, including such topics as: the printed book, publishing, libraries, and censorship; the relation of literature to the history of ideas, the visual arts, music, science, culture and popular culture; and finally, literature in English from countries and traditions other than British and American. Essays conclude with suggested scholarly readings and a bibliography of additional works cited. Detailed index.   PN81

Encyclopedia of world literature in the 20th century : based on the first edition edited by Wolfgang Bernard Fleischmann / Leonard S. Klein, gen. ed. Rev. ed. N.Y. : Ungar, c1981–c1993. 5 v. in 6 : ports.   **BE66**

Includes separate volume for index.

The previous edition was published in 3 v., 1967–71, with a supplement in 1975; Fleischman's edition, in turn, was based on the *Lexikon der Weltliteratur im 20. Jahrhundert* (Freiburg : Herder, 1960–61. 2 v.). This edition represents a thorough revision with a special effort to achieve uniformity and truly international coverage throughout the set. Articles are either revised and updated or completely new; none of those derived from the Herder work were retained; all articles are signed, and there is a list of contributors in each volume.

Biographical/critical articles predominate and include bibliographies of works by and about an author; there are topical articles on national literatures and literary movements; entries for literary genres have been excluded. Vol. 5 provides a complete index of personal names and some subject access.   PN771.E5

Le grand atlas des littératures / [réalisé par Encyclopædie Universalis]. [Paris] : Encyclopædia Universalis, c1990. 435 p. : ill. (some col.).   **BE67**

Presents signed articles on the history, genres, political and social contexts and influences of world literature. Useful for its extensive color illustrations. Selected scholarly works included in brief bibliographies. Glossary of terms functions as partial index.   PN41.G7

The Johns Hopkins guide to literary theory and criticism / ed. by Michael Groden and Martin Kreiswirth. Baltimore : Johns Hopkins Univ. Pr., c1994. 775 p.   **BE68**

A compilation of 236 signed articles on critics and theorists, countries, schools and movements, and historical periods. Includes entries for persons from other disciplines who influenced theory and criticism, or who were themselves influenced by it. Entries are followed by selective bibliographies of primary and secondary works. Cross-references both within and at the ends of articles; indexes of names and of topics.   Z6514.C97J64

Kindlers neues Literatur Lexikon / hrsg. von Walter Jens. München : Kindler, c1988–1992. 20 v.   **BE69**

Rudolf Radler, ed. in chief, v. 5–20.

A reworking of *Kindlers Literatur Lexikon* (Zurich : Kindler Verlag, 1965–74. 7 v.), arranged in alphabetical order by author, rather than title of work. While some articles are reprinted verbatim from the earlier set, a great many 20th-century authors have been added—

especially poets, women and Third World authors. Entries include birth and death dates and places, synopses of works, and bibliographical information on selected editions, translations, and criticism. Shorter genres, such as lyric poetry and short stories are discussed in collective genres. Literature is here interpreted in the broadest sense—history, journalism, and folklore—and includes philosophical and scholarly works as well. Vols. 19–20 contain essays on more than 130 national literatures, in addition to the index in v. 20. A major work, *Kindlers* is international in scope and comprehensive in coverage of literary periods. PN44.K54

Sáinz de Robles, Federico Carlos. Ensayo de un diccionario de la literatura. [4th ed.]. Madrid : Aguilar, [c1973–] . 3 v. (In progress). **BE70**
1st ed., 1949–50; 3rd ed., 1964–67.
Contents: v. 1, Términos y conceptos, literarios; v. 2, Escritores españoles e hispanoamericanos; v. 3, Escritores extranjeros.
The entries in v. 1 range from definitions of terms to extensive articles on literary concepts with bibliographies. The biobibliographical articles in v. 2–3 include sketches of authors of all periods. PN41.S2

Schneider, Georg. Die Schlüsselliteratur. Stuttgart : Hiersemann, 1951–53. 3 v. **BE71**
Contents: v. 1, Das literarische Gesamtbild; v. 2, Entschlüsselung deutscher Romane und Dramen; v. 3, Entschlüsselung ausländischer Romane und Dramen.
A key to the identities of real characters and events appearing in literature under fictitious names. Not all-inclusive, but treats the significant works of many literatures. Vol. 1 gives general explanations and definitions, history, and discussion, with indexes of authors and prototypes. Vol. 2 is devoted to German fiction and drama; v. 3, to non-German literature. Z1026.S4

Die Weltliteratur : biographisches, literarhistorisches und bibliographisches Lexikon in Übersichtern and Stichwörten / hrsg. von Erich Frauwallner, Hans Giebisch und E. Heinzel. Wien : Hollinek, [1951–54]. 3 v. **BE72**
A scholarly German encyclopedia of world literature from the earliest times to 1951, giving concise information about national literatures, literary forms, and outstanding authors, alphabetically arranged with many cross-references. Articles include bibliographies; for personal names, these include both works by and about. Vol. 3 includes an appendix and an index.
———. *Ergänzungsband* (Wien : Hollinek, 1968–70. 2 v.).
Contents: v. 1–2, A–O.
In addition to articles on authors not previously covered, additional information and new bibliographical citations are given for many writers previously treated. No more published.
§ Can be supplemented by Gero von Wilpert's *Lexikon der Weltliteratur* (3., neubearb. Aufl. Stuttgart : A. Korner, c1988. v. 1 [In progress]).
1st ed., c1963–68; 2nd ed., c1975–80 (2 v.).
Bd. 1 is a biobibliographical dictionary of authors and anonymous works, with comprehensive coverage of all time periods and literatures. Brief entries, including some for contemporary writers, list primary and secondary bibliographies. PN41.W4

Dictionaries

Abrams, M. H. A glossary of literary terms. 6th ed. Fort Worth, Tex. : Holt, Rinehart, and Winston, c1993. 301 p. **BE73**
1st ed., 1941; 5th ed., c1988.
Defines "terms, critical theories, and points of view that are commonly applied to the classification, analysis, interpretation, and history of works of literature"—*Pref.* A collection of succinct essays, newly revised for this edition, arranged alphabetically by term or phrase, with subsidiary topics and related terminology discussed in context. In two sections: Literary terms; Modern theories of literature and criticism. Many entries incorporate bibliographic references.

§ Another recent glossary, *The concise Oxford dictionary of literary terms* (N.Y. : Oxford Univ. Pr., 1990), provides short definitions and illustrative examples. Less comprehensive is *Dictionary of modern critical terms* (Rev. and enl. ed. London ; N.Y. : Routledge & K. Paul, 1987), ed. by Roger Fowler, in which some 150 terms covering such topics as "farce," "feminist criticism," and "foregrounding" are discussed in signed essays by scholars, many with additional references. PN41.A184

Allusions—cultural, literary, biblical, and historical : a thematic dictionary / Laurence Urdang and Frederick G. Ruffner, Jr., editors, David M. Glixon, assoc. ed. 2nd ed. Detroit : Gale, c1986. 634 p. **BE74**
1st ed., 1982.
Lists and explains 8,700 allusions under 712 themes (e.g., Virility, Joviality). Themes are arranged alphabetically, with a general index. Bibliography of works cited. PN43.A4

Ayuso de Vicente, María Victoria. Diccionario de términos literarios / María Victoria Ayuso de Vicente, Consuelo García Gallarín, Sagrario Solano Santos. Madrid : Akal, c1990. 420 p. : ill. **BE75**
A Spanish-language dictionary of terms found in literature, including poetry, theater, mythology, and literary theory and movements. Provides linguistic and historical context, often with quotations (in Spanish) from literary works. Bibliographical references. PN44.5.A97

Beckson, Karl E. Literary terms : a dictionary / Karl Beckson and Arthur Ganz. 3rd ed., rev. and enl. N.Y. : Noonday Pr., 1989. 308 p. **BE76**
2nd ed., 1975, was a rev. and enl. ed. of the same authors' *Reader's guide to literary terms*, 1960.
Gives definitions, adding new critical terms, updating older entries, and revising bibliographic citations. Not as detailed or extensive as C. Hugh Holman's *Handbook to literature* (BE84), but useful for examples and historical notes. Adds a selected list of entries arranged by subject; for example, critical terms, literary movements and groups, and prosodic forms. PN44.5.B334

Cuddon, John A. A dictionary of literary terms and literary theory. 3rd ed. Oxford [Eng.] ; Cambridge, Mass. : Blackwell Reference, 1991. 1051 p. **BE77**
Rev. ed. of: *A dictionary of literary terms* (1st ed., 1977; rev. (i.e., 2nd) ed., 1979).
Comprehensive dictionary covering all literatures and time periods with basic definitions as currently used. Categories include technical terms, forms, genres, groups, movements, -isms, character types, phrases, motifs or themes, concepts, objects, and styles. Entries often indicate origin and cite examples. Numerous *see* and *see also* references. PN41.C83

Dupriez, Bernard Marie. Dictionary of literary devices : gradus, A–Z / Bernard Dupriez ; tr. and adapted by Albert W. Halsall. Toronto ; Buffalo : Univ. of Toronto Pr., c1991. 545 p. **BE78**
A guide to rhetorical devices derived from many fields: linguistics, poetics, semiotics, socio-criticism, rhetoric, pragmatics, and psychology. Definitions are illustrated with examples from modern literary texts, followed by alternative definitions and/or analagous terms, and remarks on usage. Minor terms can be identified through the index. An extensive bibliography lists critical works and literary and other noncritical sources. The translator has adapted many of the original literary examples to accommodate English readers. PN172.D813

Encyclopedia of contemporary literary theory : approaches, scholars, terms / Irena R. Makaryk, gen. ed. and comp. Toronto : Univ. of Toronto Pr., 1993. 656 p. **BE79**
A scholarly encyclopedic dictionary surveying the field of literary theory, its varied approaches, trends, and chief proponents since the introduction of the New Criticism 50 years ago. Some earlier theorists and schools are included since they laid the groundwork for contempo-

rary theory. Divided into three sections: Approaches, evaluative essays on schools and theories; Scholars, critcs and others who have influenced literature, including historians, philosophers, linguists, social scientists, theologians, polemicists, authors, as well as literary theorists; and Terms, a compilation of the vocabulary of literary theory. Most entries in all three sections conclude with bibliographies of primary and of secondary sources.   PN81.E43

Frenzel, Elisabeth. Motive der Weltliteratur : ein Lexikon dichtungsgeschichtlicher Längsschnitte. 3., überarbeitete und erw. Aufl. Stuttgart : A. Kröner, c1988. 907 p.   **BE80**
1st ed., 1976; 2nd ed., 1980.
Extended discussion of themes and motifs throughout world literature, with bibliographies of relevant scholarly studies updated for this edition. Cross-references and index.   PN43.F7

Grote, David. Common knowledge : a reader's guide to literary allusions. N.Y. : Greenwood, 1987. 437 p.   **BE81**
Attempts "to present in one place the fundamental names in mythology, theater, literature, religion, history, and popular culture that reasonably educated persons might be expected to know in order to understand most general literature."—*Introd.* Alphabetically arranged.
§ While Grote briefly identifies some 4,000 names likely to be encountered by the general reader, Elizabeth Webber's *Grand allusions* (Wash. : Farragut Publ. Co., 1990) offers "an eclectic collection of those allusions, figures of speech, terms of art, terms of the trade, foreign language phrases and jargon that appear in our daily reading" and "add color and vigor to language."—*Pref.* Intended for a popular audience, it provides pronunciations for foreign words and examples of contemporary usage for most allusions. No index.   PN43.G68

Harris, Wendell V. Dictionary of concepts in literary criticism and theory. N.Y. : Greenwood, 1992. 444 p. (Reference sources for the social sciences and humanities, no. 12). **BE82**
This unusual dictionary defines and discusses 70 concepts relevant to literary theory and criticism—e.g., hermeneutics, myth criticism, semiotics. The etymology of each term is traced to its current meaning, emphasizing bibliographic sources. Entries conclude with a section of additionaly information which may include extensive critical reviews, encyclopedic articles, and similar materials.   PN41.H36

Hawthorn, Jeremy. A glossary of contemporary literary theory. London ; N.Y. : E. Arnold ; N.Y. : distr. by Routledge, Chapman & Hall, 1992. 282 p.   **BE83**
A dictionary primarily of terms used by literary critics and theorists. Although most of the terms have come into usage since 1970, some older terms ("New criticism") are also included. Hawthorn's intent is to interpret specialist terms not found in other dictionaries, either general or literary. The introduction includes a list of terms "grouped according to their intellectual associations or origins"; for example, Bakhtin group, deconstruction, linguistics, narratology, and semiotics and information theory. A bibliography identifies works quoted in the text.
§ Hawthorn's glossary is a useful adjunct to M. H. Abrams' *A glossary of literary terms,* (BE73) and to C. Hugh Holman and William Harmon's *A handbook to literature* (BE84).   PN44.5.H37

Holman, C. Hugh. A handbook to literature. 6th ed. / C. Hugh Holman, William Harmon. N.Y. : Macmillan ; London : Collier Macmillan, c1992. 615 p.   **BE84**
Original ed. by William Flint Thrall and Addison Hibbard, 1936; rev. and enl. by Holman, 1960, 1972 and 1980; and in 1986, by William Harmon.
This classic work, one of the most useful of its kind, offers clear, concise explanations of terms, concepts, schools, and movements in literature. Alphabetical arrangement with numerous cross-references as well as bibliographical references for some entries. Appendixes include an outline of British and American literaary history, lists of Nobel prizes for literature and Pulitzer prizes for fiction, poetry, and drama through 1991.

§ Also useful, though less detailed, is *The Harper handbook to literature,* by Northrop Frye, Sheridan Baker and George Perkins (N.Y. : Harper & Row, 1985). Includes a chronology of literature and world events.   PN41.H6

Orr, Leonard. A dictionary of critical theory. N.Y. : Greenwood, 1991. 464 p.   **BE85**
Defines terms from their literary critical use. In addition to English, includes key terms from other languages, among them Chinese, French, German, Greek, Japanese, Latin, Russian, and Sanskrit. Excludes terms from other disciplines unless they have a literary critical focus. Entries vary from a single sentence to several pages, and related articles are noted. The longer essays conclude with source bibliographies, citing English-language titles where available. Separate appendix for foreign terms arranged by language; index of theorists.

Rees, Nigel. Bloomsbury dictionary of phrase & allusion. London : Bloomsbury, c1991. 358 p.   **BE86**
Gives the meaning and origin of approximately 5,000 words, names and phrases requiring some explanation for understanding their use "in literature, the Bible, politics, historical writing, and the popular arts."—*Introd.* Some 2,000 main entries here complement Rees's *Dictionary of popular phrases* (London : Bloomsbury, 1990. 277 p.). The latter "is a selective examination of 1,500 contemporary catch phrases, cliches, idioms, popular sayings and slogans."—*Introd.*
§ Also useful are: *The Facts on File dictionary of twentieth-century allusions : from atom bomb to Ziegfeld girls* by Sylvia Cole and Abraham Harold Lass (N.Y. : Facts on File, c1991. 287 p.) and their *The Facts on File dictionary of classical, biblical, and literary allusions* (N.Y. : Facts on File, c1987. 240 p.).   PN43.R43

Room, Adrian. Dictionary of translated names and titles. London ; Boston : Routledge & Kegan Paul, 1986. 460 p. **BE87**
Lists primarily literary names, titles, terms, and places in French, German, Italian, Spanish, and Russian. Titles here include novels, musical works, films, plays, fairy tales, and books of the Bible, with a few short stories or poems. Arranged alphabetically in English, with separate language cross-indexes.   NX80.R66

Ruttkowski, W. V. Nomenclator litterarius. Bern ; München : Francke, 1980. 548 p.   **BE88**
Foreword in German, English, Dutch, French, Spanish, Italian, and Russian.
A multilingual dictionary of literary terms in seven languages. In the body of the work terms are usually entered under the German word, followed by equivalents in the other languages (although terms more or less universally used in the language of origin are entered under the well-known form), but there is an index in which terms in all languages are interfiled. About 2,600 entries. Bibliography of literary dictionaries arranged by language.
§ See also: Saad Elkhadem's *The York dictionary of English-French-German-Spanish literary terms and their origin* (Fredericton, N.B., Canada : York Pr., [1976]. 154 p.). This English-language dictionary of terms gives equivalents in the other languages and definitions in English. Especially useful are indexes from the other languages.
More comprehensive than either is *Dictionnaire international des termes littéraires* by Robert Escarpit, appearing in fascicle form (The Hague : Mouton, 1973–1989. v. 1–6. In progress). Provides etymologies, semantic analyses, equivalent terms in foreign languages, historical overviews, and bibliographies for each word. A fascicle containing introductory matter was published in 1973.

Similes dictionary / Elyse Sommer, editorial dir. ; Mike Sommer, ed. Detroit : Gale, c1988. 950 p.   **BE89**
Subtitle: A collection of more than 16,000 comparison phrases from ancient times to the present, compiled from books, folklore, magazines, newspapers, plays, politics, stage, screen, and television and arranged under more than 500 thematic categories.   PN6084.S5S55

Quotations

Boller, Paul F. They never said it : a book of fake quotes, misquotes, and misleading attributions / Paul F. Boller, Jr., and John George. N.Y. : Oxford Univ. Pr., 1989. 159 p.   **BE90**
Two historians discuss and clarify misquotes credited to historical personages, literary authors, and the Bible. Arranged alphabetically by attributed source. Footnotes and author/title index.   PN6081.B635

Collison, Robert Lewis. Dictionary of foreign quotations / comp. by Robert and Mary Collison. N.Y. : Everest House, [1982], c1980. 406 p.   **BE91**
First publ. N.Y. : Facts on File, 1980.
A compilation of some 6,000 foreign quotations, arranged alphabetically by language under English subjects. Covers many languages: Arabic, Danish, French, German, Greek, Italian, Latin, etc. Quotations from languages in nonroman alphabets are transliterated. Provides good English translations with occasional notes to clarify meaning; but sources identify only author and title. Supplemented by list of headwords, and index of authors and their works. No keyword or opening line indexes.   PN6080.C54

Encyclopédie des citations / [par] Paul Dupré ; Comité de rédaction sous la présidence de Fernand Keller. Paris : Éd. de Trévise, [1959]. 701 p.   **BE92**
Includes quotations from many languages and periods, all translated to French. Sections on French authors are arranged chronologically. Other chapters cover ancient Greek and Latin, German, English, Spanish, Italian, Russian, and Scandinavian authors. A separate chapter is devoted to miscellaneous quotations; for example, Arabic, Chinese, Gaelic, Japanese, Portuguese and Tibetan. This is followed by a section on sacred writings (the Bible, the sacred books of India, the Talmud, and the Koran). A final chapter lists French and foreign proverbs. References are usually to exact sources. Indexed by personal names, by keywords, and by ideas.

King, William Francis Henry. Classical and foreign quotations : a polyglot manual of historical and literary sayings, noted passages in poetry and prose, phrases, proverbs, and bons mots. 3rd ed., rev. and rewritten.... London : J. Whitaker & sons, limited, 1904. 412 p.   **BE93**
Repr. : Detroit, Gale, 1968.
An excellent collection of more than 3,000 quotations from Latin, Greek, French, German, Italian, and others. Interfiled alphabetically by the beginning word. Quotations are followed by an English translation, often poetical, and an explanatory note usually about origin, meaning, and/or usage. Indexes: (1) authors, authorities, and editions; (2) by subject, in English; (3) other quotations and parts of quotations that are not printed in the main alphabetical sequence; (4) Greek quotations in the original.   PN6080.K5

Mottoes : a compilation of more than 9,000 mottoes from around the world and throughout history / Laurence Urdang, ed. dir. ; Ceila Dame Robbins, ed. ; Frank R. Abate, assoc. ed. Detroit : Gale, c1986. 1162 p.   **BE94**
Subtitle: A compilation of more than 9,000 mottoes from around the world and throughout history, with foreign examples identified and translated into English, the entries arranged in the text under thematic categories, supplemented by alphabetic indexes of all mottoes and of the families, institutions, individuals, etc., to which they are attributed.
Identifies mottoes appearing on coats of arms, emblems, and seals.
§ In conjunction with Urdang's work, see also L. G. Pine's A dictionary of mottos (London : Routledge & Kegan Paul, 1983) which notes the origin of some entries.   PN6309.M68

Tripp, Rhoda Thomas. The international thesaurus of quotations. N.Y. : Crowell, [1970]. 1088 p.   **BE95**
An attempt to adapt the basic principles of Roget's Thesaurus to the classification of quotations. The volume "is primarily intended for those who want to use quotations, rather than simply to read them or recall them to mind."—Pref. Arrangement, however, is not greatly different from that found in Burton Egbert Stevenson's Home book of quotations, classical and modern (BE120), since entries are grouped under "idea categories" arranged alphabetically—though Tripp includes various terms and concepts (some of them more precise), as well as numerous quotations, not found in Stevenson. Thorough cross-referencing. Index of authors and sources, and of keywords.   PN6081.T77

Vega, Vicente. Diccionario ilustrado de frases célebres y citas literarias. 4. ed. Barcelona : Gustavo Gili, 1966. 939 p. : ill.   **BE96**
1st ed., 1952.
Quotations, in various languages, arranged alphabetically under subjects, with indexes by topic, first word of quotation, and author. When phrases are given in other languages, Spanish translations are included. In some cases quotations are translated into Spanish and are not given in the original. Citations to exact sources are given irregularly.   PN6095.S5V4

English

Andrews, Robert. The Columbia dictionary of quotations. N.Y. : Columbia Univ. Pr., 1993. 1092 p.   **BE97**
Focuses on quotations chosen for their appropriateness to contemporary life, featuring established writers as well as lesser-known figures, and groups underrepresented in other quotation collections (women, minorities, homosexuals and lesbians, etc.). In addition to the usual categories adds subjects such as The consumer society, Getting ahead, and Talk shows. Includes contemporary quotes, as well as older quotations, where these are apt, but eliminates those which have become hackneyed through overuse. Identifies authors together with birth and death dates, and exact sources, often adding brief notes to provide context. The "Index of sources" lists authors and the subjects under which their quotations are entered.
•Available in machine-readable form as part of Microsoft bookshelf '94 [database] (AB27).   PN6081.A652

———— The concise Columbia dictionary of quotations. N.Y. : Columbia Univ. Pr., c1989. 343 p.   **BE98**
Also published as The Routledge dictionary of quotations (London: Routledge, c1987).
Witty or provocative quotations, many of recent vintage, arranged by topic from "Absence" or "Absurdity" to "Writing" or "Youth." Gives author of each quote and his or her dates, but not the title of the specific work. Index of subjects.   PN6081.A653

Bartlett, John. Familiar quotations : a collection of passages, phrases and proverbs traced to their sources in ancient and modern literature / John Bartlett ; Justin Kaplan, gen. ed. 16th ed. Boston : Little, Brown, 1992. lvi, 1405 p.   **BE99**
1st ed., 1855; 15th (125th anniversary) ed., rev. and enl. by Emily Morison Beck.
A standard collection, comprehensive and well selected. Arranged chronologically by author, with exact references. Includes many interesting footnotes, tracing history or usage of analogous thoughts, the circumstances under which a particular remark was made, etc. Author and keyword indexes.
One of the best books of quotations with a long history. The 11th ed. almost doubled the size of the 10th; the 12th ed. is the same as the 11th to p. 787, but after that is re-edited to include new authors, particularly contemporary authors, and additional quotations. The miscellaneous section, Addenda, is also enlarged by the inclusion of both old and new quotations. The 13th, or Centennial, edition was thoroughly revised by the staff of the publishing firm. The chronological arrangement by author was maintained, and all quotations integrated into one listing except for quotations from anonymous works, the Bible, the Book of Common Prayer, and the Koran. The 14th ed. again showed extensive revision, adding quotations from both old and new sources and with additional subject indexing; it follows a single chronological sequence (the Book of Common Prayer being inserted after the Bible).

The 15th ed., following the arrangement of its predecessor, added 400 new authors, and increased the number of quotations from the Bible, the Koran, ancient Buddhist and Sanskrit writings, and the section of anonymous quotations. Revisions included new translations of older quotations.

The 16th ed. departs from earlier editions by extending the scope to nonliterary sources. Some 50 quotations from the movies are included. Other nontraditional sources are television, rock and pop lyrics, business, sports, politics and public affairs. Of 2,550 authors, 340 are new to this edition; 245 older authors have been deleted. Review: *Smithsonian*, v. 22 no. 5 (Aug. 1991): 68 ff.

Because recent editions omit quotations previously included and add new ones, earlier editions should be retained.   PN6801.B27

Benham, William Gurney. Benham's book of quotations, proverbs, and household words. New and rev. ed. with suppl. and full indexes. N.Y. : Putnam, [1949]. 1384 p.   **BE100**
1st ed., 1907; 2nd rev. ed., 1936.

Contains: (1) Quotations, British and American, p. 1–440; (2) Bible and Book of Common Prayer, p. 441–65; (3) "Waifs and strays," e.g., political phrases, epitaphs, London street sayings, bell inscriptions, etc., p. 466–512; (4) Foreign (Greek, Latin, German, Italian, Spanish, Dutch), p. 513–764; (5) Proverbs, p. 765–928; and (6) Index, p. 929–1259.

Includes about 30,000 quotations. Frequently reprinted with little change. In the 1949 ed., the main part of the work is substantially the same as in the 1936 ed., with some errors corrected and dates of death added. A supplement with its own index has been added. The supplement includes a few recent quotations by modern authors, but is largely devoted to additional quotations of authors included in the main work.   PN6080.B35

Bloomsbury dictionary of quotations / ed. John Daintith … [et al.]. 2nd ed. London : Bloomsbury, 1991. 586 p.   **BE101**
1st ed., 1987.

Attempts to include "both familiar quotations and perceptive or witty sayings that are less well known … especially … quotations that reflect contemporary issues as well as those from literature and the Bible."—*Introd.* Arranged alphabetically by author, with brief notes on the author's works or importance. Does not provide exact references, in most instances furnishing only the title of the quoted work. Keyword index.   PN6081

Colombo, John Robert. Colombo's Canadian quotations. Edmonton, Alta. : Hurtig Publishers, c1974. 735 p.   **BE102**
A compilation of 6,000 quotations, arranged alphabetically by author, covering the period 400 BCE through 1973, by persons who have some connection with Canada. Quotations by non-Canadians are about Canada or its peoples; those from Canadians are on any topic. According to the editor, more than half the quotes are from the modern period and more than a quarter "have to do with the contemporary scene."—*Pref., p. viii.* Section under "Anonymous" is divided into: Eskimo, Indian, lore, mottos, select epitaphs, one dozen limericks, R.C.M.P., some documents, martial airs, songs, verses and rhymes. Where possible, passages of prose and poetry have been traced to their first recorded use. Occasional notes are added to bibliographical references for clarification. Extensive index by keyword and subject.

§ See also: *New Canadian quotations*, comp. by Colombo (Edmonton, Alta. : Hurtig, c1987) which emphasizes quotations of contemporary interest, 1967–87.   PN6081.C58

The dictionary of biographical quotation of British and American subjects / ed. by Richard Kenin and Justin Wintle. N.Y. : Knopf ; distr. by Random House, 1978. 860 p.   **BE103**
Intended "to give an impression of the rich diversity of the things people have written and said about one another."—*Introd.* Quotations have been drawn from a wide range of sources and are arranged under name of the person who is the subject of the quotation. Index of persons quoted. Sources are identified for each quote, but exact references are not.   CT773.D38

The dictionary of Canadian quotations and phrases / comp. by Robert M. Hamilton and Dorothy Shields. Rev. & enl. ed. Toronto : McClelland & Stewart, c1979. 1063 p.   **BE104**
1952 ed. (repr. 1965) had title *Canadian quotations and phrases.*

A topically arranged collection (with topics in alphabetical sequence) of "quotations and phrases selected from predominantly Canadian sources," but including "those which originated with outside observers of the Canadian scene—British, American, French—from the beginnings of our [i.e., Canadian] history up to the present."—*Pref.* Index of authors and anonymous titles, but no keyword indexing.

PN6081.H24

Hoyt, Jehiel Keeler. Hoyt's new cyclopedia of practical quotations / completely rev. and greatly enl. by Kate Louise Roberts. N.Y. ; London : Funk & Wagnalls, 1922. 1343 p.   **BE105**
Subtitle: Drawn from the speech and literature of all nations, ancient and modern, classic and popular, in English and foreign text. With the names, dates, and nationality of quoted authors, and copious indexes.

1st ed., 1882; 2nd ed. enl., 1896. Reissued in 1940 with a few corrections and the addition of death dates for some authors in the author list. The "New 1947 Edition" published by Somerset Books, N.Y., is practically unchanged.

Contents: (1) Quotations, arranged alphabetically by general subjects; (2) Index of quoted authors, with brief biographical data; (3) Concordance of quotations.

A very comprehensive collection of some 21,000 quotations given with exact references. Omits quotations from the Bible. The indexes are excellent. Although now more than 70 years old, still useful except for contemporary writers.   PN6081.H7

Keyes, Ralph. "Nice guys finish seventh" : false phrases, spurious sayings, and familiar misquotations. N.Y. : HarperCollins, c1992. 273 p.   **BE106**
Not a collection of quotations but a study that examines familiar quotations and sayings to determine what was said, who actually said them, the context in which they were said, and whether the source is original or secondhand. Extensive section of notes follows a bibliography. Keyword and name indexes.

The Macmillan dictionary of quotations. N.Y. : Macmillan, c1989. 790 p.   **BE107**
More than 20,000 quotations arranged thematically and biographically, with sections for biblical quotations, proverbs, and nursery rhymes. When known, the source is provided for author, title, and chapter. Keyword index.   PN6081.M27

Magill, Frank Northen. Magill's quotations in context. N.Y. : Harper, [1965]. 1230 p.   **BE108**
An attempt to go beyond identification of the source of a quotation and elucidate the meaning by providing background remarks or summary of the original context. Some 2,000 quotations are included in alphabetical arrangement, with keyword and author indexes. Sources, author, date of first appearance, and type of work are indicated for each. Owing to the comparatively limited number of quotations dealt with, the work is chiefly useful as a supplement to the standard books of quotations.

———. ———. 2nd series. (N.Y. : Harper, [1969]. 1350 p.). An extension rather than a revision of the earlier volume. Contains an additional 1,500 quotations.   PN6081.M29

Mencken, Henry Louis. A new dictionary of quotations on historical principles from ancient and modern sources. N.Y. : Knopf, 1942. 1347 p.   **BE109**
A comprehensive collection with emphasis on lesser-known quotations. Includes many proverbs and some foreign quotations, mainly in English translation. Arranged by category with many cross-references to allied headings. Quotations are dated whenever possible and arranged chronologically under topic. An attempt has been made to trace each quotation to its earliest usage. No index. Gives name of author and title of work, but not exact reference.   PN6081.M49

The new Penguin dictionary of quotations / J.M. and M.J. Cohen. Rev. and expanded ed. London : Viking, 1992. 726 p. **BE110**

First publ. as: *Penguin dictionary of quotations.*

Universal in coverage, emphasizing traditional quotations—the Bible, Shakespeare, established authors like Tennyson—with a sprinkling of foreign and classical quotations accompanied by English translations. Arranged alphabetically by author, indexed by keywords. Sources are identified. Adds to the 1st ed. some quotations from contemporary figures, but readers will find more satisfactory *The Penguin dictionary of twentieth-century quotations*, also ed. by the Cohens (Rev., expanded ed. London; N.Y. : Viking, c1993).

The new quotable woman : the definitive treasury of notable words by women from Eve to the present / comp. and ed. by Elaine Partnow. N.Y. : Facts on File : Meridian, 1993. 714 p. **BE111**

A completely revised and updated edition of two works by Partnow: *The quotable woman from Eve to 1799* (N.Y. : Facts on File, c1985) and *The quotable woman, 1800–1981* (N.Y. : Facts on File, c1982), which was a reprint of *The quotable woman, 1800–1975* (Los Angeles : Corwin Books, c1977) with a supplement (p. 473–520) and an updated index.

A collection of some 15,000 quotations by approximately 2,500 women covering 4,000 years of women in history; broad coverage of countries and professions. This new edition drops about one-third the quotations previously included, updates items on some 150 more contemporary women, and adds about 450 new contributors. About 2,000 quotations are completely new, as are many quotes.

Arrangement is chronological by birth date, then alphabetical. Sources are cited, but not always with chapter and page references. The subject index, substantially revised and augmented, is content-oriented rather than strictly keyword, and uses nonsexist terminology. This index is supplemented by a biographical index, a career and occupation index, and an ethnicity and nationality index.

§ *The Beacon book of quotations by women*, comp. by Rosalie Maggio (Boston : Beacon Pr., c1992) follows a subject arrangement. Like Partnow, Maggio's selection is subjective. While there is some overlap in the women quoted, the quotations chosen for inclusion are different. Maggio includes suggestions for using quotes whose language "is today considered sexist and inaccurate."—*Note to the reader.* Separate name and subject indexes. PN6081.5.N49

The New York Public Library book of twentieth-century American quotations / ed. by Stephen Donadio ... [et al.]. N.Y. : Warner Books, c1992. 622 p. **BE112**

A collection of quotations limited exclusively to 20th century Americans, arranged by thematic categories such as Dreams and ideals, Popular culture, Religion and spirituality, and Social issues, all subdivided. Emphasizes diversity of persons, comments, and points of view—scholarly statement to colloquial quip—in their historical context, the whole reflecting American life in the 20th century. Quotations identify either a primary or secondary source, including the date of publication or of broadcast. Cross-references listed after major topics complement an extensive subject index. Indexed by author and source. PN6081.N53

The Oxford dictionary of quotations / ed. by Angela Partington. 4th ed. Oxford ; N.Y. : Oxford Univ. Pr., 1992. 1061 p. **BE113**

1st ed., 1941; 3rd ed., 1979.

A thorough revision with numerous deletions, substitutions, and additions, especially of non-English authors and other prominent persons, and of nonliterary areas such as philosophy, psychology, economics, and the sciences. Hymns and songs, omitted in the 3rd ed., are again included. Proverbs and nursery rhymes are excluded because they are covered elsewhere. Some 17,500 quotations are arranged in one alphabetical sequence of 2,500 English and foreign authors, the Bible, the Book of Common Prayer, and anonymous works. Most quotations from foreign literatures are given both in their original language as well as in an English translation. Exact bibliographical references are provided for known printed sources. Indexed by keyword.

§ A related title with some overlap in coverage is *The Oxford dictionary of modern quotations*, ed. by Tony Augarde (Oxford ; N.Y. : Oxford Univ. Pr., 1991), similar in arrangement and features. Some of its 5,000 quotations are repeated in the more comprehensive source above, but other authors are included only here. "Modern" means twentieth-century. PN6081.O9

Powell, David. The wisdom of the novel : a dictionary of quotations. N.Y. : Garland, 1985. 729 p. (Garland reference library of the humanities, v. 459). **BE114**

Hoping to rectify the scant attention paid to novelists in most quotations collections, this work draws maxims and sayings from "all of the major British and American novels, and hundreds of the lesser ones, from 1470 through 1900."—*Pref.* Arranged in an alphabetical list of subject headings with author/novel and keyword indexes. PN6083.P58

Quotations in black / Anita King, comp. and ed. Westport, Conn. : Greenwood, c1981. 344 p. **BE115**

Quotations by black persons are arranged by author in chronological sequence of date of birth, and there is a separate section of proverbs arranged by country. Author and subject/key word indexes. The review in *Booklist* 78 (1 May 1982) : 1189 notes inconsistencies in the keyword indexing. PN6081.3.O67

Respectfully quoted : a dictionary of quotations requested from the Congressional Research Service / ed. by Suzy Platt. Wash. : Library of Congress : for sale by U.S. Govt. Print. Off., 1989. 520 p. **BE116**

Superintendent of Documents classification: LC 14.2:D56.

Repr. as *Respectfully quoted : a dictionary of quotations requested from the Library of Congress* (Wash. : Congressional Quarterly, 1992).

Scrupulously researched and satisfyingly thorough, this volume presents 2,100 quotations from the Congressional Reading Room Quotations File developed as result of trying to identify or verify quotations for more than 50 years. Topical arrangement, with author and subject indexes. Sources are given in most instances, with untraceable quotations so marked. PN6081.R435

Shipps, Anthony W. The quote sleuth : a manual for the tracer of lost quotations. Urbana : Univ. of Illinois Pr., c1990. 194 p. **BE117**

An excellent, unique source that functions as a handbook, a bibliography, and a scholarly tool for serious researchers of quotations. Organized by type of resource: general dictionaries; single subject and special category; single author; dictionaries of the English language; concordances and word indexes to works in English and American literature; and indexes to first lines, last lines, opening words, and keywords. Chapters compare and evaluate sources, and suggest how they can best be used in searching. One chapter focuses solely on tracing classical and foreign quotations. The final chapter entitled "Some axioms of a quote sleuth" offers practical advice for tracking quotes. The last third of the book is an annotated bibliography organized by categories discussed in the text. PN6081.S44

Simpson, James Beasley. Simpson's contemporary quotations. Boston : Houghton Mifflin, 1988. 495 p. **BE118**

An earlier version was published as *Contemporary quotations* (New York : Crowell, c1964).

"Contemporary" is here defined as the latter half of the 20th century. Arranged in three main categories (The world, Humankind, and Communications and the arts), with subcategories such as sports, travel, or medicine. Exact source citations, in many cases including page numbers, are given for each quote. Source and subject/keyword indexes. PN6083.S53

Stephens, Meic. A dictionary of literary quotations. London ; N.Y. : Routledge, c1990. 193 p. **BE119**

Collects some 3,250 quotations which refer to "literature, writers, writing, books and reading, defined in a fairly broad way and taking in a number of contiguous areas such as journalism and the book trade."—*Pref.* Does not include quotes about specific authors. Arranged in 180 topical areas, such as Best-seller, Editor, etc. Citations are to author and title of work; author and subject indexes.

PN6081.S728

Stevenson, Burton Egbert. The home book of quotations, classical and modern. 10th ed. rev. N.Y. : Dodd, 1967. 2816 p. **BE120**

1st ed., 1934.

A comprehensive and well-chosen collection of more than 50,000 quotations, arranged alphabetically by subject with subarrangement by smaller topics. Usually gives exact citation. Includes an index of authors, giving full name, identifying phrase, and dates of birth and death, with references to all quotations cited, and an index of quotations by leading words (usually nouns, but sometimes verbs and adjectives). For some smaller subjects, the word index prints entries in boldface without indexing the quotations individually, requiring one to turn to the subject and scan the entries.

The 10th ed. includes two appendixes: (1) p. 2273–98j (for the most part, added in the 5th ed.); and (2) p. 2298k–z, p. 2299a–z (added in later editions). The quotations on these pages are indexed in a separate section at the end of the main index, p. 2811–16.

The 3rd ed. (1937) was a thorough revision of the first two editions, with the addition of more than 1,000 quotations, revisions of notes, etc., and a much enlarged index.

Of other editions, the 5th (1947) and the 9th include the most revision. The 9th adds more than 500 new entries, with clarification of others. The changes are in the appendixes and the separate index.

§ A useful addition to Stevenson is Bergen Evans, *Dictionary of quotations* (N.Y. : Delacorte, [1968]. 1029 p.) which follows a similar topical arrangement. The "subject index" in Evans is basically a keyword index with the addition of references to names or terms that occur in the explanatory notes rather than in the actual quotations. Indexed by author.   PN6081.S73

A treasury of Jewish quotations / ed. by Joseph L. Baron. New rev. ed. N.Y. : J. Aronson, 1985. 623 p. **BE121**

1st ed., 1956.

An extensive collection of quotations in English, including aphorisms, maxims, and proverbs, of Jewish authorship or Jewish themes covering the whole range of Jewish history. Authorship is interpreted in the broadest sense, incorporating cultural affiliation as well as ethnic background. Arranged alphabetically by topic, and within topics alphabetically by author. Identifies sources by date or edition, often with exact pages, sometimes with notes. Additional features include a glossary of Jewish terms, a bibliography, and subject and author indexes.

§ *Leo Rosten's treasury of Jewish quotations* (N.Y. : McGraw-Hill, [1972]) has a somewhat lighter focus. Rosten includes only humorous sayings, but, like Baron, covers a broad range of proverbs, folk sayings, and maxims. Rosten gives an overview of the genre and provides extensive notes throughout, designed for a popular audience. Saying are arranged by subject with references to related topics. Indexed by author but not by subject.   PN6095.J4T74

Webster's new World dictionary of quotable definitions / ed. by Eugene E. Brussell. 2nd ed. Englewood Cliffs, N.J. : Prentice Hall, c1988. 674 p. **BE122**

1st ed., 1970, had title: *Dictionary of quotable definitions.*

Adds some 5,000 new entries and some new subject areas. Arranged alphabetically by subject, with an author index. No sources provided.   PN6081.B77

What they said. 1969– . [Beverly Hills, Calif.] : Monitor Book Co., 1970– . Annual. **BE123**

Subtitle: The yearbook of spoken opinion.

1979–80 not issued; publisher intends to issue retrospectively.

Presents the statements, ideas, and opinions of persons prominent in the news during the year in question. Quotations are grouped in subject categories within three main sections: (1) National affairs; (2) International affairs; and (3) General. Indexes of speakers and of detailed subjects. For each quotation the speaker is briefly identified, the cir-

cumstances of the quotation are indicated, and (with a few exceptions) reference is given to the published appearance of the statement in the newspaper or periodical press of the nation.   D410.W46

Arabic

Field, Claud. A learner's dictionary of Arabic and Persian quotations : transliterated with English translation. Beirut : Librairie du Liban, 1974. 351 p. **BE124**

Previous editions publ. as: *A dictionary of Oriental quotations (Arabic and Persian)* (1911 ed. repr. Detroit : Gale, 1969).

Gives quotations in transliteration, arranged alphabetically by first word, with translations. Index of authors and index of subjects and catchwords, the latter not very full. Includes more than 80 authors.

§ See also: *Arabic proverbs : or, The manners and customs of the modern Egyptians ...* , tr. by Johann Lewis Burckhardt (London : J. Murray, 1830; 2nd ed., London : B. Quaritch, 1875, repr. London : Curzon, 1984). Although this collection has no index it offers almost 800 sayings in Arabic followed by an English translation and notes explaining the saying in its linguistic and cultural context.

PN6095.O7F6

Dutch

Groot literair citatenboek van Nederlandse en Vlaamse auteurs uit de 19e en 20e eeuw : samengesteld door Gerd de Ley. Amsterdam : Loeb, [1982?]. 205 p. **BE125**

Arranged by author of the quotation, with only a very brief keyword index. Sources are given in a separate author listing at the back of the book rather than immediately following the quotation.

PN6095.D8G76

Flemish

Ley, Gerd de. Modern citatenboek : meer dan 10,000 citaten en definities. Antwerpen : Standaard, 1990. 787 p. **BE126**

A collection of quotations arranged by catchword, the greater portion given to contemporary topics and persons. About a third of the quotations are from Dutch authors and persons who have gained prominence recently, though other 20th-century figures are also represented. Contains an extensive glossary, with definitions of words as used in the quotations. Indexed by author, but no sources are identified.

§ *See also* Ley's *Standaard modern citatenboek : citaten, aforismen en boutades van de 20ste eeuw, gerangschikt naar trefwoorden en met uitgebreide auteursnota's en bronvermelding* (Antwerpen : Standaard, [1973]) which also emphasizes 20th-century Dutch authors and other less-often quoted personages. Unlike the newer collection this one provides bibliographic references for the quotations. Indexed by author. Ley's collections complement the classic work of S. W. F. Margadant, *Twintigduizend citaten, aforismen en spreekwoorden* ([2. druk]. 's-Gravenhage : Leopold, 1952), which includes some 20,000 quotations in Dutch, many of them translations from other languages for which the original is usually given. Sources include ancient and modern literatures, proverbs, and maxims. Arranged by topic with some cross-references. No word index.   PN6277.N4L4

French

The Anchor book of French quotations : with English translations / comp. by Norbert Guterman. N.Y. : Anchor Books, 1990. 474 p. **BE127**

Originally publ. as *A book of French quotations*, 1963.

Arranged chronologically by author, with French quotations and English translations on facing pages. Brief descriptive notes in English are given for the authors. Indexes of authors, of first lines in French, and of first lines in English. PN6086.G85

Bologne, Jean-Claude. Les grandes allusions : dictionnaire comment e des expressions d'origine littéraire. Paris : Larousse, c1989. 335 p. : ill. **BE128**

A compilation of well-known quotations and expressions derived from French and other literature, tracing their meaning and usage. Arranged alphabetically by the most significant word. An appendix lists less-well-known experssions alluded to in 19th-century songs. Indexed by French keyword.

Dictionnaire des citations françaises et étrangères / [publíe sons la direction de Robert Carlier ... et al.]. Paris : Larousse, 1980. 896 p. **BE129**

Publ. 1976 as: *Larousse des citations françaises et étrangères* (Paris : Larousse, 1976).

Almost half the quotations collected here are from French authors; the two remaining sections include Latin and ancient Greek, sacred writings (the Bible, the Koran and the Talmud), historical quotations, with a final selection of quotations from Procençal and other "foreign" languages. Arrangement in each section is alphabetical by author, but there is no cumulative author list. Non-French quotations are generally given in French translation followed by the original language. Sources are cited for many quotes, but vary in completeness. Subject index lists keyword in context. PN6086.D451

Dournon, Jean-Yves. Le grand dictionnaire des citations françaises. Paris : Acropole, c1982. 906 p. **BE130**

A general collection of about 10,000 French quotations, about half representing modern or contemporary authors and about 4,500 representing classical writers. Arranged by keyword, with references to authors cited and a separate list of keywords.

§ Dournon has also published *Le dictionnaire des proverbes et dictons de France* (Paris : Hachette, c1986), a compilation of well-known sayings, in French and translated into French from other languages, arranged by keyword. Forms a useful complement to *Le grand dictionnaire*. Many entries are followed with brief notes of explication. Dournon frequently cites authors who have used the proverb or a variant. No indexes. PN6086.D68

Guerlac, Othon Goepp. Les citations françaises : recueil de passages célèbres, phrases familières, mots historiques, avec l'indication exacte de la source, suivi d'un index alphabétique par auteurs et par sujets. 7. éd. Paris : Colin, 1961, [c1931]. 458 p. **BE131**

May be a reprint of an earlier edition.

Organizes quotations in four parts: literary quotations, exact sources cited; various nonliterary quotations whose sources cannot be identified precisely; well-known French and foreign historical expressions whose authenticity is verified, where possible, from other specialized sources; and a section of biblical quotations. Arranged in main by authors, chronologically, with two alphabetical indexes: authors and catchwords. Includes modern as well as older quotations, with many footnotes giving additional facts; for example, parallel passages in other writers. PN6086.G8

Harbottle, Thomas Benfield. Dictionary of quotations (French and Italian) / Thomas Benfield Harbottle, P. H. Dalbiac. London : Sonnenschein ; N.Y. : Macmillan, 1901. 565 p. **BE132**

Repr.: N.Y. : Ungar, 1958.

Divided into two sections by language, each arranged alphabetically by first word of quotation. An English translation is supplied for each quote. Identifies exact source of reference. Indexed by author, with separate indexes for French, Italian and English subjects. PN6086.H3

Oster Soussouev, Pierre. Dictionnaire des citations françaises / Pierre Oster ; avec le concours de Elisabeth Hollier ... [et al.]. Ed. 1992. Paris : Dictionnaires Le Robert, [1992]. 934 p. **BE133**

Previous ed., 1978.

Some 16,591 French quotations arranged by century (preceded by a section of the Middle Ages), then alphabetically by author. Source of the quotation is indicated, sometimes citing chapter, or act or scene of a play, but reference is often only to the title of the source. Separate list of authors; index by subject. Most useful when author of quote is known. PN6086.D455

German

Dalbiac, Lilian. Dictionary of quotations (German) : with authors' and subjects' indexes. London : Swan Sonnenschein ; N.Y. : Macmillan, 1906. 485 p. **BE134**

Repr.: N.Y. : Ungar, 1958.

German quotations, followed by an English translation, arranged alphabetically by opening word. Exact sources are cited. Separate subject indexes in English and in German list terms in context. Indexed by author. PN6090.D3

Geflügelte Worte : der Zitatenschatz des deutschen Volkes / gesammelt und erläutert von Georg Büchmann ; fortgesetzt von Walter Robert-Tornow ... [et al.]. 34. Aufl. / bearb. von Winfried Hofmann. Frankfurt am Main ; Berlin ; Wien : Ullstein, 1981. 543 p. : port. **BE135**

1st ed., 1866.

A collection in German of quotations from many languages, including German, arranged by country of origin. Cites sources, with explanatory notes in German. Indexed by personal name, with separate index by opening words of quotations. PN6090.B8

Geflügelte Worte : Zitate, Sentenzen und Begriffe in ihrem geschichtlichen Zusammenhang / Kurt Böttcher ... [et al.]. [5. unveränd. Aufl.?]. Leipzig : Bibliographisches Institut, 1988. 778 p **BE136**

1st ed., 1981; 4th ed., 1985.

Arranged by historical period, then by country and author. Notes characterizing the author precede the quotation, and notes on context, meaning, etc., follow. Non-German quotations are given in the original language with German translation; sources are cited. Includes many coined and compound words, familiar phrases, book titles, etc. Index of personal names and a German keyword index. PN6090.G4

Zitatenlexikon / [hrsg. von] Ursula Eichelberger. [Leipzig] : Bibliographisches Institut Leipzig, 1981. 920 p. **BE137**

A topical arrangement of some 12,500 German-language citations, giving for each quotation the author, title, chapter, and page. List of authors with full bibliographic citation to text used. International in coverage; text in German. PN6092.Z55

Greek

Ramage, Craufurd Tait. Beautiful thoughts from Greek authors : with English translations. London ; N.Y. : Routledge, 1895. 589 p. **BE138**

Also published under title: *Familiar quotations from Greek authors* (Repr. : Detroit : Gale, 1968).

Arranged alphabetically by author, with quotations in Greek and in English translation. Exact citations to sources. English index. PN6080.R33

Italian

Fumagalli, Giuseppe. Chi l'ha detto? : tesoro di citazioni italiane e straniere, di origine letteraria e storica, ordinate e annotate. 10th ed., riveduta ed aumenta. Milan : Hoepli, c1980. 848 p.   **BE139**

    1st ed., 1894.

    Covers quotations as late as about 1933 in different languages arranged by subject, with references to exact sources and some explanatory notes. Includes a special section on quotations from World War I (1914–1918). Indexes of authors and quotations.   PN6080.F8

Palazzi, Fernando. Il libro dei mille savi : massime, pensieri, aforismi, paradossi di tutti i tempi e di tutti i paesi, accompagnati dal testo originale e dalle citazione delle fonti / F. Palazzi e S. Spaventa Filippi. 5. ristampa della 2. ed. con l'aggiunta di circa altri mille aforismi. Milan : U. Hoepli, 1967. 1095 p.   **BE140**

    Repr. : Milan : Cisalpino-Goliardica, [1983].

    A compilation of quotations from many languages rendered into Italian, the original text given in footnotes at the bottom of the page. Quotations from Russian are given only in Italian translation. Arranged by subject, the collection covers many countries and time periods. Sources are identified, but references are often incomplete. Indexed by author; the 1983 reprint also indexes by subject.

                         PN6095.I7P353

Spagnol, Elena. Il libro delle citazioni. [Milan] : A. Vallardi, c1983. 1153 p.   **BE141**

    1st ed., 1971, had title: *Dizionario di citazioni.*

    Topically arranged quotations from Italian and other western languages, many given in the original as well as Italian translation. Cites author and title of source, but frequently omits precise reference. Indexed by keyword and by author.   PN6095.I7S64

Latin

Finzi, Giuseppe. Dizionario di citazioni latine ed italiane. Milano : Sandron, [1902]. 967 p.   **BE142**

    Repr. : Sala Bolognese : Forni, 1979.

    Contents: Citazioni latine; Detti proverbiali; Frasi e versi curiosi; Versi leonini e salernitani; Detti e motti storici e allegorici; Massime di diritto romano; Citazioni italiane.

    8,560 entries arranged by rubric. Keyword index. References are usually to exact sources.   PN6080.F5

Guterman, Norbert. A book of Latin quotations : with English translations. Garden City, N.Y. : Anchor Books, [1966]. 433 p.   **BE143**

    Arranged by author with Latin and English on facing pages, this small but select list cites sources exactly. Indexed by author, with an English subject index, and a Latin index by keyword and opening words.   PN6080.G8

Harbottle, Thomas Benfield. Dictionary of quotations (classical). 2nd ed. London : S. Sonnenschein, 1902. 678 p.   **BE144**

    Repr.: San Antonio, Tex. : Scylax Pr., c1984 as *Anthology of classical quotations.*

    An excellent dictionary of Latin and Greek quotations, each section arranged alphabetically by opening word. Lists each quotation in the original, with exact reference to source, and an English translation with name of the translator. Indexed by author, with separate subject indexes in Latin, Greek and English.   PN6080.H2

Ramage, Craufurd Tait. Beautiful thoughts from Latin authors : with English translations. London : Routledge, 1895. 855 p.   **BE145**

Various editions; also published under title: *Familiar quotations from Latin authors* (Repr. : Detroit : Gale, 1968).

    Arranged alphabetically by author, with quotations in Latin and in English translation. Exact citations to sources. Latin and English indexes.   PN6080.R35

Norwegian

Norsk sitatleksikon : 6000 bevingede ord. 2. revid. utg. ved Fridtjof Voss. Stavanger : Stabenfeldt, [1955]. 678 col.   **BE146**

    A general quotation book including not only Norwegian quotations, but many from various languages translated into Norwegian, followed by the original. Alphabetical by catchword subject. First-line indexes in Norwegian and in each of the other languages. Author index.   PN6095.N6N67

Spanish

Borras y Bemejo, Tomás. Diccionario de sabiduría : frases y conceptos / Tomás Borras y Federico Carlos Sáinz de Robles. [2a. ed.]. Madrid : Aguilar, 1956. 1369 p.   **BE147**

    1st ed., 1953.

    A collection of quotations in Spanish, international in scope, arranged by subject. Identifies authors, but not their works. Indexed by author and by subject.

Clarasó Daudí, Noel. Antología de textos, citas, frases, modismos, y decires. Barcelona : Acervo, [1970]. 1082 p.   **BE148**

    In three main sections: (1) "Antología de textos" (arranged by author, then topically within each author section); (2) "Antología de citas" (topically arranged, with indication of author, but not specific work); (3) "Antología de modismos, frases hechas y cedires." Except for a separate section of Latin phrases, all quotations are given in Spanish. Author index, but no overall subject index.   PN6095.S5C6

Martínez Kleiser, Luis. Refranero general, ideológico español. Madrid : Real Academia Española, 1953. 783 p.   **BE149**

    More than 65,000 entries arranged under concepts, gathered from other collections of proverbs with references to the collections.

    § Martínez Kleiser is one of the sources used by Luis Iscla Rovira's *Spanish proverbs : a survey of Spanish culture and civilization* (Lanham, N.Y. ; London : Univ. Pr. of America, 1984). Designed as a work for students of Spanish language and culture, it groups Spanish proverbs thematically under broad topics such as time, family, animals, love, and the human condition. English translations are provided in a separate section followed by a glossary of words used in the proverbs and an index of subjects. While limited in content the work is creative in its approach and helpful for those less skilled in the language.   PN6491.M25

Mir y Noguera, Juan. Diccionario de frases de los autores clásicos españoles. 1. ed. argentina, con mas de 70.000 locuciones. Buenos Aires : Gil, 1942. 1328 p.   **BE150**

    This Argentinian edition of a work previously published in Madrid in 1899 was revised and an index of authors and works from which the phrases were taken was added. Arranged by rubric. Gives exact references to sources.   PC4650.M5

Proverbs

Apperson, George Latimer. English proverbs and proverbial phrases : a historical dictionary. London : Dent ; N.Y. : Dutton, [1929]. 721 p.   **BE151**

Traces the history of English proverbs and proverbial phrases, through references to the literature. In one alphabetical arrangement, but in a twofold manner: (1) all proverbs which classify naturally under such headings as months and seasons, animals, birds, God, the Devil, sun, moon, rain, time, war, etc., are listed under these headings; (2) all other proverbs are alphabetical under their first main word. Examples are listed in chronological order from the earliest date.

PN6421.A7

Buchanan, Daniel Crump. Japanese proverbs and sayings. Norman : Univ. of Oklahoma Pr., [1965]. 280 p. **BE152**

Proverbs are grouped under what are termed "Japanese characteristics" ("Aesthetics" through "Women"), with a subject index. The quotation is given in romanized Japanese, followed by a translation and explanation of its meaning and usage. PN6519.J3B8

Champion, Selwyn Gurney. Racial proverbs : a selection of the world's proverbs arranged linguistically, with authoritative introductions to the proverbs of 27 countries and races. 2nd ed. N.Y. : Barnes & Noble, 1950. cxxix, 767 p. **BE153**

1st ed., 1938.

A sampling of proverbs in English translation from the nations and languages of the world. In addition to more familiar languages there are large sections on African and Asian languages (74 for Africa, and 18 for India and Ceylon among the Asian languages). The introductory section features scholarly articles on 27 major languages and their proverbs by leading folklorists as well as an extensive bibliography of national proverb collections (p. cix-cxxix). Proverbs are arranged by country with indexes by language and geography, subject matter, nationality, and alternative keyword. PN6405.C37

A dictionary of American proverbs / Wolfgang Mieder, ed. in chief ; Stewart A. Kingsbury and Kelsie B. Harder, editors. N.Y. : Oxford Univ. Pr., 1992. 710 p. **BE154**

Described as the first major proverb collection in English based on actual field research in the contiguous U.S. and parts of Canada. Includes about 15,000 proverbs and their variants as actually used in American speech, some recorded for the first time in this collection. Entries are arranged alphabetically under their most significant word, followed by any variants, with occasional short comments to clarify the meaning. Notes the recorded distribution of proverbs and their variants based on oral tradition rather than from written sources alone. Also cites, when possible, the date, author and title of the earliest known British and/or American written source, as well as other standard Anglo-American proverb collections. Concludes with a 20-page scholarly bibliography. PN6426.D53

Gluski, Jerzy. Proverbs = Proverbes = Sprichwörter = Proverbi = Proverbios = Poslovitsi. Amsterdam [etc.] : Elsevier, 1971. 448 p. **BE155**

Subtitle: A comparative book of English, French, German, Italian, Spanish and Russian proverbs with a Latin appendix.

About 1,100 proverbs are grouped in 48 topical sections. Proverbs are listed first in English, followed by equivalent forms in other languages. Indexed separately in each language by keyword. PN6404.G6

Mieder, Wolfgang. International proverb scholarship : an annotated bibliography. N.Y. : Garland, 1982. 613 p. (Garland folklore bibliographies, 3). **BE156**

An author listing of 2,142 scholarly book and periodical citations, with name, subject, and proverb indexes. Focuses on scholarship rather than collections of proverbs. Annotations are full, and often evaluative as well as descriptive. Mieder's work complements Otto Moll's *Sprichworter-Bibliographie* (BE158), a major bibliography of proverb collections.

————. *International proverb scholarship : an annotated bibliography. Supplement I (1800–1981)* (1990), continues its numbering, adding 1,881 new entries.

§ More narrowly focused is Mieder's *Proverbs in literature : an international bibliography* (Berne : P. Land, [1978]). Approximately 1,200 entries—books, articles, and theses—are organized in two sections: general studies of proverbs in literature (including relevant dic-

tionaries of proverbs and works dealing with more than one author) and studies of individual literary authors arranged alphabetically by author. Covers Anglo-American, German and Romance languages; also Classical, Germanic, Slavic, African, and Near and Far Eastern literatures. Index of scholars' names.

Mieder has also compiled *Investigations of proverbs, proverbial expressions, quotations and cliches : a bibliography of explanatory essays which appeared in Notes and Queries (1849–1983)* (Bern ; N.Y. : P. Lang, c1984). Z7191.M543

———— The Prentice-Hall encyclopedia of world proverbs : a treasury of wit and wisdom through the ages. Englewood Cliffs, N.J. : Prentice-Hall, c1986. 582 p. **BE157**

A collection assembled by a folklorist that presents proverbs from peoples and languages throughout the world. Arranged by keyword; all proverbs are given in English, with language of origin indicated. About 18,500 entries. Select bibliography. PN6405.M54

Moll, Otto E. Sprichwörter-Bibliographie. Frankfurt am Main : Klostermann, [1957–58]. 630 p. **BE158**

A landmark work in the study of proverbs. Lists more than 9,000 items focusing primarily on proverb collections. Arranged by language groups (Romance, Germanic, Asiatic, Slavic, Turkish, etc.), then subdivided into national languages and dialects, with entries arranged chronologically within localities. One section deals with collections in all languages, arranged by categories such as nature, plants, medicine, eating and drinking, weather, women, religion, etc. Lists editions for collections, and adds brief notes for some entries. Includes dialect dictionaries. Indexed by author but not by subject.

§ See also Wolfgang Mieder's *International proverb scholarship : an annotated bibliography* (BE156).

Oxford dictionary of English proverbs. 3rd ed. / rev. by F. P. Wilson. Oxford : Clarendon Pr., 1970. 930 p. **BE159**

1st–2nd eds. (1935–48) by W. G. Smith.

The 1st ed. (1935) contained about 10,000 proverbs, arranged alphabetically by first word, including "a," "an," "the." Successive editions have been somewhat enlarged and some earlier sources noted. Proverbs are now alphabetized under significant words (usually the first), with the preceding words, if any, transferred to the end or, occasionally, to an intermediate point. Liberal cross-references are included from all other significant words, usually with enough of the phrase so that it is readily identifiable. Many proverbs and examples from Morris Palmer Tilley's *A dictionary of the proverbs in England in the sixteenth and seventeenth centuries* (see BE166 note) have been incorporated into the 3rd ed.

Dated references are given for each proverb to the earliest uses and sources found, with variant usages at succeeding times, shown by examples from the literature in the manner of the *Oxford English dictionary.*

Although billed as an abridged version, J.A. Simpson's *The concise Oxford dictionary of proverbs* (Oxford ; N.Y. : Oxford Univ. Pr., c1982) emphasizes 20th century proverbs from Britain and America, and is limited to about 1,000 items. Like its parent volume it attempts to record and illustrate the earliest known use of each saying. A 2nd ed., comp. by Simpson with the assistance of Jennifer Speake (c1992) has been revised and the scope "has been broadened to include for the first time a number of proverbs which are known principally in North America, resulting in a more international coverage than was possible in the first edition." —*Pref.* Adds 90 proverbs new to this edition, all of recent origin. Updates illustrative quotations, and in some instances cites new evidence for the historical development of proverbs. This edition adds a thematic index. PN6421.O9

Scarborough, William. Collection of Chinese proverbs / rev. and enl. by the addition of some six hundred proverbs, by C. Wilfrid Allan. Shanghai : Presbyterian Mission Pr., 1926. 381 p. **BE160**

Classified arrangement. Subject index. PN6519.C5S4

Schwamenthal, Riccardo. Dizionario dei proverbi italiani : 6.000 voci e 10.000 varianti dialettalli / Riccardo Schwamenthal, Michele L. Straniero. Milano : Rizzoli, 1991. 563 p.
     BE161

An alphabetical listing of Italian proverbs, noting where appropriate the Latin source and any dialectal variants. Numerous cross-references to related proverbs. Thematic index and bibliography.

Stephens, Thomas Arthur. Proverb literature : a bibliography of works relating to proverbs / ed. by Wilfrid Bonser ; comp. from materials left by the late T. A. Stephens. London : W. Glaisher, 1930. 496 p. (Folk-lore Society. Publications, 89).
     BE162

First publ. 1930; frequently reprinted.

A major research bibliography, annotated in English, identifying collections of proverbs. Organizes by language more than 4,000 works on the proverbs of all nations, including collections of particular localities and special subjects. Major languages are subdivided into dialects. Section on nonregional proverbs covers topics such as animals; the human body; calendar, weather, agriculture; clothes; women and children; food; fools and jesting; hunting; law and crime; medicine and hygiene; moon and stars; music; pictorial proverbs; plants; politics; the sea, sailors and fishermen; wine, beer and taverns. Annotations are critical as well as descriptive. Extensive author/subject index.
     Z7191.S83

Stevenson, Burton Egbert. The home book of proverbs, maxims and familiar phrases. N.Y. : Macmillan, 1948. 2957 p.
     BE163

Repr. 1965, 1987 with title: *The Macmillan book of proverbs, maxims and famous phrases.*

Attempts to trace back to their sources, proverbs, maxims, and familiar phrases in ordinary English and American use and to show their development.

Follows the pattern of the author's *Home book of quotations, classical and modern* (BE120), with subject arrangement and detailed word index. Very comprehensive, including more than 73,000 expressions from many languages and periods; many of them might be considered quotations, as the interpretation of proverb and maxim is very broad. Dates for proverbs are noted, and those from foreign sources are given in English translation followed by the original language (except for the oriental). Indexes at least one and sometimes more keywords.
     PN6405.S8

Taylor, Archer. The proverb. Cambridge : Harvard Univ. Pr., 1931. 223 p.
     BE164

Repr. with index in 1 v.: Hatboro, Pa : Folklore Associates; Copenhagen : Rosenkilde & Bagger, 1962. 223 p., 105 p.

A classic study in proverb scholarship. The main volume discusses the origin, content and style of proverbs citing numerous examples from English, Bohemian, Danish, Dutch, French, German, Greek, Icelandic, Italian, Latin, Norwegian, Polish, Spanish, and Swedish. Although there is no separate bibliography, there are bibliographical references in the footnotes. The index (Helsinki : Suomalainen tiedakatemia, Academia scientiarum fennica, c1934. Repr. with text, Hatboro, Penn. : Folklore Assoc., 1962) arranges the proverbs by language (Arabic and modern Greek under English because they are quoted only in translation). Taylor also supplies references to important collections of proverbs that appear in the List of books cited.

Whiting, Bartlett Jere. Modern proverbs and proverbial sayings. Cambridge, Mass. : Harvard Univ. Pr., 1989. 709 p.
     BE165

Presents more than 5,500 proverbs, mostly American and English, collected from writings published primarily from 1930 to the early 1980s. Listed by keyword, with source citations providing page numbers and dates of publication, as well as references to earlier compilations. Not indexed.

§ The chronological predecessor is Archer Taylor and Whiting's *A dictionary of American proverbs and proverbial phrases, 1820–1880* (Cambridge, Mass. : Belknap Pr. of Harvard Univ. Pr., 1958), which established the format used in later works—keyword arrangement with source citations, illustrated with many examples from American literature, 1820–80.

The period from the first decades of the 17th century to 1820 is covered by Whiting's *Early American proverbs and proverbial phrases* (Cambridge, Mass. : Belknap Pr. of Harvard Univ. Pr., 1977). Although entries are derived from American sources, the compiler points out that prior to 1820, American proverbs were basically English and states that "It is not to oversimplify to say that the contents of this book are English proverbs used by writers who happened to be in North America at the time."—*Introd.* Again, arrangement is by keyword, with examples from a 32-page list of sources. A separate index of important words facilitates subject searching. Also indexed by proper nouns.
     PN6403.W48

———————— Proverbs, sentences, and proverbial phrases : from English writings mainly before 1500. Cambridge, Mass. : Belknap Pr. of Harvard Univ. Pr., 1968. li, 733 p.   **BE166**

Similar to other collections by Whiting, this compilation draws largely from sources written before 1500. A common form of the proverb or saying, entered alphabetically by keyword, is followed by variants arranged in chronological order, with reference to printed sources and date of usage. Index of significant words, and a 31-page bibliography.

§ For the 16th and 17th centuries consult: Morris Palmer Tilley, *A dictionary of the proverbs in England in the sixteenth and seventeenth centuries : a collection of the proverbs found in English literature and the dictionaries of the period* (Ann Arbor : Univ. of Mich. Pr., 1950. 854 p. Repr.: N.Y. : AMS Pr., 1983). Contains some 11,780 proverbs arranged by catchword. Each proverb is followed by citations arranged chronologically. Includes a bibliography of the works cited, an index of Shakespearean quotations appearing in the text, and an index of significant words in the proverbs.
     PN6083.W45

Wintle, Justin. The dragon's almanac : Chinese, Japanese and other Far Eastern proverbs. London : Routledge & Kegan Paul, 1983. 226 p. : ill.
     BE167

An eclectic collection of oriental sayings, numbered and arranged in calendar form, with four selected for each day of the year (February 29th has only one for its posititon in leap year). A section of notes adds brief explanatory comments for some of the 1,461 proverbs. The majority are Chinese, followed by Japanese, with a sprinkling of Malay, Thai, Korean and others. Indexed by broad categories, e.g., Thematic references, and by keywords and phrases.

Periodicals

ANQ. v. 1, no. 1, new ser. (Jan. 1988)– . Lexington, Ky. : [Univ. Pr. of Kentucky for the Dept. of English, Univ. of Kentucky], c1988– . Quarterly.
     BE168

Subtitle: A quarterly journal of short articles, notes and reviews.

Continues: *American notes and queries* (v. 1–24. New Haven, Conn. ; Lexington ; Owingsville, Ky., 1962–1986). Neither title is related to an earlier *American notes and queries* ed. by Walter Pilkington and B. Asterlund (North Bennington, Vt., 1941–50. 8 v.).

Includes questions and answers, book reviews, bibliographical essays, and short articles, primarily about English and American language and literature, film, and linguistics, but excludes textual explication. The previous title was somewhat broader in scope, and included notes on work in progress, resources and collections, and recent foreign reference books.

Notes and queries. v. 1 (1849)– . London : Oxford Univ. Pr., 1850– . Monthly.
     BE169

Subtitle (varies): For readers and writers, collectors and librarians. Earlier subtitle: A medium of communication for literary men, artists, antiquarians and genealogists.

Imprint, title, and frequency vary.

Formerly grouped in a series of 12 v. each, but numbered continuously beginning with the second volume of the 13th series (v. 146 [1924]). An index to each volume, and a general index at six-year intervals until 1935. The index for July 1935–Dec. 1947 was published in 1 v. in 1955.

Contains interesting and often very valuable information on out-of-the-way questions—usually small points in general and local history and literature, bibliography, manners, customs, folklore, local observances, quotations, proverbs, etc. Much of the information is in the form of signed answers to questions from readers; sources of information are given. Indexes are well-made and detailed, and should be used as supplements to handbooks of allusions, quotations, proverbs, etc. AG305.N7

Directories

Barlow, Richard G. The fifth directory of periodicals publishing articles on American and English language and literature, criticism and theory, film, American studies, poetry and fiction. Athens : Swallow Pr./Ohio Univ. Pr., c1992. 349 p. **BE170**

1st ed., 1959. Rev. and expanded ed. of *Fourth directory of periodicals publishing articles on English and American literature and language*, comp. by Donna Lorine Gerstenberger and George Hendrick (Chicago : Swallow Pr., 1974).

A guide for scholars placing manuscripts for publication. Indicates editorial policy and fields of interest of journals, with information on submitting manuscripts, format, etc. Z2015.P4G4

The guide to writers conferences. 1st ed. (1988)– . Coral Gables, Fla. : Shaw Associates, c1988– . Irregular. **BE171**
4th ed. publ. 1992.

Describes and lists alphabetically conferences, retreats, residency programs, and organizations. Appendixes include a conference calendar; geographical, specialty, and organization indexes; lists of events for special interest groups, such as women or students; and a list of those organizations that sponsor prizes or scholarships.

Literary market place : LMP. 1989– . New Providence, N.J. : Bowker, c1988– . Annual. **BE172**
For annotation, *see* AA282. PN161.L5

MLA directory of scholarly presses in language and literature. 1991– . N.Y. : Modern Language Assoc. of America, 1991– **BE173**
Ed. by James L. Harner.
Announced as annual; noted by editor as triennial.

A companion to *MLA directory of periodicals* (BE42), this directory "describes the fields of interest, submission requirements, contract provisions, and editorial procedures of scholarly publishers of book-length literary and linguistic studies."—*Introd.* Data in the 1st ed. was current for 1989, with some dating from late 1990. Includes separate indexes to publishing interests, imprints and subsidiary firms, series titles, editorial personnel, and languages of publication. Z286.P46M4

Writers' and artists' year book. v. 1 (1906)– . London : Black ; N.Y. : Macmillan, 1906– . Annual. **BE174**
Subtitle: A directory for writers, artists, playwrights, writers for film, radio and television, photographers and composers (varies slightly).

Contains lists of British, Commonwealth, Irish, African and U.S. journals and magazines, with statement of kind of material accepted by each and rate of payment. Includes lists of publishers and literary agents; describes markets for writers, plays, films, broadcasting artists, photographers, musicians, etc. PN12.W8

Writer's handbook. 1936– . Boston : Writer, inc., 1936– . Annual. **BE175**
A collection of articles, most of which appeared originally in *The writer*, on various phases of professional writing, including fiction, nonfiction, and specialties. Some articles are carried over from earlier editions, some are new, none are dated. The specialties section is a market guide, mainly to the periodical field, giving for each title: address, editor, and type of material accepted with indication of rate of payment. Also has sections for greeting card and drama markets, including regional and university theaters, television, and for book publishers. Revised annually. PN137.W73

The writer's market. 1922– . Cincinnati : Writer's Digest, 1922– . Annual. **BE176**
Subtitle: Where & how to sell what you write.

A guide for freelance writers, covering the practical side of writing for publication, including information about book publishers; consumer magazines; trade, technical and a few professional journals; scriptwriting; syndicates; greeting card and gift markets. Provides extensive lists of contests and awards and of relevant organizations and publications. Subject index of book publishers. PN161.W83

Literary awards

Labes, Bertrand. Guide Mont Blanc des prix et concours littéraires. Paris : Le Cherche midi, 1992. 332 p. **BE177**
A directory of prizes and competitions in French literature awarded in France and in French-speaking countries, divided into three parts: literary prizes, prose competitions, and poetry competitions. Identifies awarding body, particular genre (short story, novel, science fiction, etc.), kind of prize (monetary, publication, medal, etc.), and regulations governing entries. Selectively lists winners of some awards. Indexed alphabetically, by category, by kind of award, by names of judges, and by geographic site (France, Martinique, Canada, Sweden, etc.).

§ Also still useful is E. C. Bufkin's *Foreign literary prizes : Romance and Germanic languages* (N.Y. : Bowker, 1980), which selectively lists prizes with descriptive notes and full lists of recipients. Prizes included are meant to be "representative of the famous and the obscure, the old and the recent, the discontinued and the continuing."—*Pref.* Arranged by country; indexed. PQ150.L5L33

Literary and library prizes. 1935– . N.Y. : Bowker, 1935– . Irregular. **BE178**
Title varies.

Lists literary and library awards, grants, etc., of the U.S., Canada, and Great Britain, giving some explanation and background of the award and a record of the recipients for each since its establishment. Library awards first appeared in the 4th ed., 1959. PN171.P75L5

Strachan, Anne. Prizewinning literature : UK literary award winners. London : Library Assoc., 1989. 267 p. **BE179**
Provides author/title and publication information for winners of 58 different literary prizes through June 1989. Excludes juvenile or specialized literary awards. Z2013.3.S77

World dictionary of awards and prizes. London : Europa, [1979]. 386 p. **BE180**
For annotation, *see* AL162. Also useful for its listings of awards in literature is *Awards, honors, and prizes* (AL161). AS911.A2W58

Handbooks

Brewer, Ebenezer Cobham. Brewer's dictionary of phrase and fable. 14th ed. / by Ivor H. Evans. N.Y. : Harper & Row, c1989. 1220 p. : ill. **BE181**
1st ed., 1870; "Centenary ed.," 1970, rev. 1981.

A useful and fascinating collection of brief entries for colloquial and proverbial phrases, biographical and mythological references, fictitious characters, titles, etc., giving origin, derivation, or meaning, as appropriate. Much revised over the years by various editors. The 14th ed. adds about 300 new entries; other entries have been revised and updated. Older editions of this indispensable source will prove useful since much material has been dropped in the course of numerous revisions.

§ Also still useful is Brewer's *Reader's handbook of famous names in fiction, allusions, references, proverbs, plots, stories, and poems* (New ed. rev. and greatly enl. London : Chatto ; Philadelphia : Lippincott, 1899. 1243 p. Repr. : Detroit : Gale, 1966. 2 v.).

PN43.B65

Daemmrich, Horst S. Themes & motifs in western literature : a handbook / Horst S. and Ingrid Daemmrich. Tübingen : Francke, c1987. 255 p.   **BE182**

A scholarly dictionary listing such literary motifs and themes as City, Love, Paradise, and Suicide. Each entry defines a concept and then details its significance, function, and historical development, citing representative literature. Includes bibliographies, with most works cited in their original language. Translations into English, if available, are noted.   PN43.D34

Dictionary of literary themes and motifs / Jean-Charles Seigneuret, ed. ... [et al.]. N.Y. : Greenwood, 1988. 2 v. (1507 p.).   **BE183**

Some 600 scholars examined more than 5,000 works of literature to determine the 143 themes discussed in these volumes. The themes, which range from "utopia" to "grotesque" to "marriage," are explored in alphabetically-arranged, signed essays, which include brief bibliographies. Cross-index of related themes and general index of authors, works, and topics.   PN43.D48

Harris, Laurie Lanzen. Characters in 20th-century literature. Detroit : Gale, c1990. 480 p.   **BE184**

§ Companion work: Kelly King Howes, *Characters in 19th-century literature* (Detroit : Gale, c1993. 597 p.).

Similar in approach, these titles summarize representative works of major novelists, dramatists, and short story writers of the 19th and 20th centuries. Some authors appear in both volumes, depending on birth-death dates and their period of greatest creative productivity. The majority are from Western Europe and North America, but some effort was made to include lesser-known women writers and writers from other cultures. Characters are identified in context (usually plot summary); some critical commentary is provided. Howes's discussions of plots and characters are somewhat fuller than Harris's. Both works are arranged alphabetically by author and include short bibliographies. Indexed by character and title.   PN56.4.H37

L'intermédiaire des chercheurs et curieux : mensuel de questions et réponses historiques, littéraires, artistiques et sur toutes autres curiosités. Année 1 (1951)– . Paris : Chercheurs et Curieux, 1951– . Monthly.   **BE185**

Title varies: 1951–55, *Chercheurs et curieux.*

Modeled on *L'intermédiaire des chercheurs et curieux : correspondance littéraire, historique et artistique, questions et réponses, lettres et documents inédits* ... (v. 1–103. Paris, 1864–1940).

Designed to print answers to questions asked by readers. The December issue includes an annual index by keywords.

Cumulative index: *L'intermédiaire des chercheurs et curieux ... Supplément 1960 : table décennal I (1951–1960)*, ed. by Joseph Valynseele (Paris, 1965).   AG305.I64

Magill, Frank Northen. Cyclopedia of literary characters. N.Y. : Harper, [1963]. 1280, xiv, 50 p.   **BE186**

Also publ. as: *Masterplots cyclopedia of literary characters* (N.Y. : Salem Pr., [1963]).

Based on the original *Masterplots* series (*see* text for *Digests and collections* section), which included books of all periods, ancient Greeks to 20th century.

————. *Cyclopedia of literary characters II* (Pasadena, Calif. : Salem Pr., c1990. 4 v.; 1775, lxxxi p.).

Based on the *Masterplots II* series for American, British, Commonwealth, and world fiction, and drama.

Entries for works are arranged alphabetically by title, listing the characters with a brief description and analysis of each. In *Cyclopedia II* entries are signed, and genre and setting described. Indexed by characters and authors, and in *Cyclopedia II* by titles.   PN44.M3

Meyers Handbuch über die Literatur : ein Lexikon der Dichter und Schriftsteller aller Literaturen / hrsg. von der Lexikonredaktion des Bibliographischen Instituts, redaktionelle Leitung, Ingrid Adam und Gisela Preuss. 2., neubearb. Aufl. Mannheim : Bibliographisches Institut, [1970]. 987 p. : ill.   **BE187**

1st ed., 1964.

Devoted to brief biobibliographical sketches of major (and some relatively minor) literary figures of all periods and from all countries. Includes entries for important anonymous works of literature. Good coverage for contemporary writers. An appendix provides bibliographical references to histories of national literatures.   PN41.M45

Pringle, David. Imaginary people : a who's who of modern fictional characters. N.Y. : World Almanac, [1988], c1987. 518 p. : ill.   **BE188**

An alphabetical listing of information on more than 1,300 modern fictional characters beginning with Daniel Defoe's Robinson Crusoe (1719). Characters are not limited to literary works but may have appeared in opera, ballet, comic strips, songs, films, or radio and television. Emphasizes characters from or familiar to the English-speaking world who "have been perpetuated by the original author from work to work, or ... by other authors and by adaptations to different media"— *Introd.* In this respect Pringle's work differs from William Freeman's *Dictionary of fictional characters* (*see*: Martin Seymour-Smith, *Dictionary of fictional characters*, BE189).   PN56.4.P75

Seymour-Smith, Martin. Dictionary of fictional characters. Completely rev. ed. Boston : The Writer, 1992. 598 p. **BE189**

"1st U.S. edition"—verso of t.p. Originally publ. as: *The Dent dictionary of fictional characters.*

Lists more than 50,000 characters from fiction, poetry, drama, and opera by British and American authors. Characters are identified by single words or brief phrases, followed by the title of the work in which they appear, its date, author, and literary genre. A "Glossary of authors and titles" is appended.

§ A completely revised edition of William Freeman's *Dictionary of fictional characters* (1st ed., London : Dent ; Boston : The Writer, 1963; rev. ed. by Fred Urquhart with indexes of authors and titles by E. N. Pennell, London : Dent, 1973; Boston : The Writer, [1974]). The 1974 revision listed some 20,000 fictitious characters. Older editions are still useful for characters omitted from the revisions.   PR19.F7

Shankle, George Earlie. American nicknames : their origin and significance. 2nd ed. N.Y. : H.W. Wilson, 1955. 524 p.   **BE190**

1st ed., 1937.

Not limited to nicknames of persons, but includes also those applied to places, institutions, or objects, arranged by real names with cross-references from nicknames. Information under the real names includes some explanation of the nicknames and their origin, and gives references to sources of information in footnotes.   E179.S545

Thomas, Edmund J. Writers and philosophers : a sourcebook of philosophical influences on literature / Edmund J. Thomas and Eugene G. Miller. N.Y. : Greenwood, 1990. 269 p.   **BE191**

Intended for the beginning researcher; describes the philosophical influences on 123 Western European and American authors. Entries are arranged alphabetically and contain basic biographical and critical information, with brief bibliographies. A second section profiles 77 philosophers whose work is discussed in the author entries. Appendixes include a glossary of philosophical terms and a selected bibliography; general index.   PN49.T447

Chronologies

Rogal, Samuel J. Calendar of literary facts : a daily and yearly guide to noteworthy events in world literature from 1450 to the present. Detroit : Gale, c1991. 877 p.   **BE192**

A literary chronology of more than 2,000 writers and their works, representing all nationalities and literary periods, 1450–1989. The day-by-day calendar lists birth and death dates of important literary figures. Beginning with 1450, the year-by-year calendar notes births, deaths, significant literary events, and major publications, including newspapers, periodicals, journals, translations, and important editions. Representative rather than comprehensive; most entries, either of authors or of literary works, are briefly annotated. Indexed by author and title and by subject.   PN6075.R64

Digests and collections

Various handbooks and compilations that give plot summaries of novels or other fiction, and synopses or digests of well-known books, are often found in reference collections. Synopses may also be found in many author dictionaries and handbooks, in such works as the Oxford "Companion" series, and in some encyclopedias (e.g., Pierre Larousse, *Grand dictionnaire universel du XIXe siècle*, AB46).

The best-known of the synopsis sets are those edited by Frank Northen Magill, whose "Masterplots" series have appeared in many editions. The revised edition, *Masterplots : 2,010 plot stories & essay reviews from the world's finest literature; including the four series and further critical evaluations*, ed. by Frank N. Magill; story editor, Dayton Kohler (Rev. ed. Englewood Cliffs, N.J. : Salem Pr., c1976. 12 v.) combines and supersedes all prior editions.

A second set was published under the series title "Masterplots II," with separate series for American fiction, British and Commonwealth fiction, drama, nonfiction, short stories, and world fiction. For both sets of "Masterplots" and several other Magill titles, see: *Magill index to Masterplots : cumulative indexes, 1963–1990* (Pasadena, Calif. ; Englewood Cliffs, N.J. : Salem Pr., c1990).

Like "Masterplots II," a "Critical survey" series appeared in multivolume sets for drama, long fiction, short fiction, poetry, mystery and detective fiction, and literary theory. In some categories, separate sets were published for works in English and for works in other languages. For a combined index, see: *Magill index to Critical surveys : cumulative indexes, 1981–1988* (Pasadena, Calif. : Salem Pr., c1990).

Besides these series, Magill also issued prior to 1980 other sets for literature, philosophy, religion, cinema, and history. For access to these titles, consult: *Magill books index : all authorized editions, 1949–1980, by title and by author*, comp. by Salem Pr. staff (Englewood Cliffs, N.J. : Salem Pr., c1980).

All the Salem series are intended for beginning students. None can be regarded as a substitute for the original work or for more thorough works of reference prepared by specialists.

Haydn, Hiram. Thesaurus of book digests : digests of the world's permanent writings from the ancient classics to current literature / comp. under the editorial supervision of Hiram Haydn & Edmund Fuller. N.Y. : Crown, [1949]. 831 p.   **BE193**

Repr. : N.Y. : Avenel Books ; distr. by Crown, c1977.

Very concise digests arranged by title, with an author index and an index to characters. In some cases, when authors are remembered for the body of their work rather than for a particular title, discussion is given under the author's name.

§ *Thesaurus of book digests, 1950–1980* by Irving and Anne Weiss (N.Y. : Crown, [1981]. 531 p.) supplements Haydn and Fuller's work, covering important books for the 30-year period indicated. For older works consult Helen Rex Keller's *Reader's digest of books* (New and greatly enl. ed. N.Y. : Macmillan, 1929. 1447 p.) a standard title

appearing in several editions and frequently reprinted. Summarizes outstanding works, fiction and nonfiction, of many countries and periods.   PN44.H38

Plot locator : an index to summaries of fiction and nonfiction / Reference Department, John Davis Williams Library, Univ. of Mississippi. N.Y. : Garland, 1991. 704 p.   **BE194**

Indexes 82 plot summary sources covering novels, plays, short stories, and poems, as well as nonfiction sources in other subjects, such as philosophy, history, biography, and political science. Entries for individual titles are listed under the author's name, with cross-references for second authors and pseudonyms. Foreign titles are given in English translation, and popular variant titles to classical works are cross-referenced. Plot summaries identified in the index are generally one page or more in length; brief summaries are excluded. Selective entries for Shakespeare. Separate author-title and title-author indexes.

Der Romanführer. Stuttgart : Hiersemann, 1950–92. Bd. 1–26. (In progress).   **BE195**

Editors vary; originally ed. by Wilhelm Olbrich.

Vols. 1–2 of 2nd ed. publ. 1960.

Digests of novels and short fiction from world literature with individual volumes treating authors of countries or regions during a particular period. Emphasizes German novels, but coverage of Romance, Scandinavian, Slavic, and English-language works is extensive. Entries list the author's place and date of birth, bibliographic information for each title, its type, and a plot summary. Bd. 15 indexes v. 1–14 by author's name, language and nationality, and chronologically by birth date; by title, including the original title of non-German language works; and by type. Later volumes in the set add newer authors and extend coverage to non-Western literatures. Bds. 25–26 (1992), for example, cover works of the German Democratic Republic spanning the period 1945/49 to the end of 1990. Bds. 27–28 will cover German fiction from 1986 to 1990 with the exception of East German authors covered in the two pervious volumes.   PN3326.R6

Biography

Author biographies master index / Barbara McNeil, ed. 4th ed. Detroit : Gale, c1994. 2 v. (1662 p.). (Gale biographical index series, no. 3).   **BE196**

1st ed., 1978; 3rd ed., 1989.

Subtitle: A consolidated index to more than 1,030,000 biographical sketches concerning authors living and dead as they appear in a selection of the principal biographical dictionaries devoted to authors, poets, journalists, and other literary figures.

A specialized index to some 1,100 volumes and editions of more than 365 biographical dictionaries of authors, significantly increasing the number of entries from previous editions. These multiple biographical works, both current and retrospective, include living and deceased persons from all time periods, nationalities, and subject areas. Sketches from periodicals and books on single authors are excluded as are the names of literary characters and those from myth or legend.

Names are spelled as they are entered in particular sources; variant forms of names should be searched, especially in the case of compound surnames, oriental names, differing transliterations, pseudonyms and stage names, and names entered in full or with initials.   Z5304.A8A88

Combs, Richard E. Authors: critical & biographical references / Richard E. Combs, Nancy R. Owen. 2nd ed. Metuchen N.J. : Scarecrow, 1993. 478 p.   **BE197**

1st ed., 1971.

Greatly expanded in coverage, this edition supersedes the first and reflects changes in critical and popular taste. It analyzes more than 1,100 books of English-language literary criticism and biography for critical materials on the works and lives of more than 3,300 writers of fiction, nonfiction, prose, and poetry. Excludes reference sources such as literary encyclopedias and works on a single author; only cites passages six or more pages in length.   PN524.C57

Contemporary authors : a bio-bibliographical guide to current authors and their works. v. 1– . Detroit : Gale, 1962– . Annual.　　**BE198**

Gives biobibliographical sketches of living authors of fiction, poetry, drama, etc., as well as general nonfiction. For complete information, *see* AH42.　　Z1224.C6

Contemporary world writers / ed., Tracy Chevalier. 2nd ed. Detroit : St. James, c1993. 686 p.　　**BE199**

1st ed., publ. 1984 as: *Contemporary foreign language writers*.

A biobibliography of approximately 340 living authors from 60 countries, whose works have been translated in whole or in part into English. For each writer, a biographical sketch is followed by a bibliography of works (with translated English language titles or publications), a section of secondary studies in English if available, and a signed critical essay reviewing the author's work. Index by title and by nationality, both current and previous. Includes current address for author or literary agent.　　PN51.C6235

Dictionary of literary biography. Detroit : Gale, 1978–1994. v. 1–135. (In progress).　　**BE200**

A series of separately edited volumes, each a collection of biographical, bibliographical, and critical essays on authors. Initially limited to North American literature, the scope has been expanded to include British, Commonwealth, and modern European literatures, as well as those of areas such as Latin America, Africa, and the Caribbean. Authors include novelists, dramatists, poets, essayists, critics, historians, journalists, publishers, screen writers, scholars and biographers. A list of volumes in the set is printed in the endpapers of each volume.

Each volume of collected essays is devoted to a single type, genre, geographic area or time period; e.g., *Victorian novelists before 1885*, ed. by Ira B. Nadel and William E. Fredeman, 1983; *Twentieth-century Caribbean and black African writers*, 1st ser., ed. by Bernth Lindfors and Reinhard Sander, 1992; *American humorists, 1800–1950*, 2 pts. ed. by Stanley Trachtenberg, 1982. Because each volume has a single focus an author may appear in more than one volume; the approach in each will be different.

The signed essays are substantial, and generally combine biographical and critical aspects with synopses of works and their bibliographical details, emphasizing in varying degrees the writer's historical importance and influence. Many list substantial primary bibliographies and selected secondary criticism. Many give locations of manuscripts, papers, and archival collections. Entries are usually illustrated with black-and-white photographs or line drawings, and often reproduce facsimiles of an author's manuscript.

Companion works are: *Dictionary of literary biography yearbook* (1980–); *Dictionary of literary biography documentary series* (1982–). Initially the *Yearbook* published updated articles on authors already in *DLB* and articles on new authors, but beginning with 1987 (publ. 1988) articles covering major literary events, prizes and awards, reviews of the year's publications, and obituaries were added. The *Documentary series* supplements *DLB* by publishing documents of major writers from particular periods; e.g., letters, interviews, notes and diary entries, and book reviews.

Cumulative indexes to the three series appear in each volume.

European writers / William T. H. Jackson, ed., George Stade, ed. in chief. N.Y. : Scribner, 1983–91. 14 v.　　**BE201**

A collection of 261 signed essays on continental authors and their works, chronologically arranged: Middle Ages and Renaissance (v. 1–2); Age of reason and the enlightenment (v. 3–4); The romantic century (v. 5–7); The twentieth century (v. 8–13): Index (v. 14).

Most of the essays cover individual authors, and are substantial enough to detail an author's life in historical context, and to critique the literary output. A few essays are devoted to themes and genres (e.g., The Arthurian legend, Troubadours and trouvères). The work addresses general readers from high school onward. Select bibliographies include editions, translations, background studies, and critical work. Detailed indexing links related articles and topics.

§ A companion series to *Ancient writers : Greece and Rome*, ed. by T. James Luce (BE1012), *British writers*, Ian Scott-Kilvert, gen. ed. (BE622), and *American writers*, ed. by Leonard Unger (BE444).　　PN501.E9

Hargreaves-Mawdsley, William Norman. Everyman's dictionary of European writers. London : Dent ; N.Y. : Dutton, [1968]. 561 p.　　**BE202**

Offers brief biographical sketches of European writers of all periods (including some living authors). Influential writers on fields other than literature are also included.　　PN451.H3

Index to the Wilson authors series. Rev. 1991 ed. N.Y. : H.W. Wilson, c1991. 108 p.　　**BE203**

1st ed., 1976.

Indexes articles on approximately 9,000 authors from *American authors, 1600–1900* (N.Y. : Wilson, 1938), *British authors before 1800* (BE624), *British authors of the 19th century* (BE625), *European authors 1000–1900* (BE204), *Greek and Latin authors 800 B.C.–A.D. 1000* (BE1025), *Twentieth-century authors* and its *First supplement*, *World authors, 1950–1970, 1970–1975, 1975–1980*, and *1980-1985* (BE205).　　PN451.I5

Kunitz, Stanley Jasspon. European authors, 1000–1900 : a biographical dictionary of European literature / Stanley J. Kunitz, Vineta Colby. N.Y. : H.W. Wilson, 1967. 1016 p. : ill.　　**BE204**

Part of the "Wilson author series," these biographies profile 967 European writers, representing 31 different literatures, who lived between 1000 and 1925. Bibliographies, although brief, list the author's works and any translations into English as well as articles about the author.　　PN451.K8

———— Twentieth century authors : a biographical dictionary of modern literature; complete in one volume with 1850 biographies and 1700 portraits / Stanley J. Kunitz, Howard Haycraft. N.Y. : H.W. Wilson, 1942. 1577 p. : ill.　**BE205**

Profiles world writers of the period whose translated works are familiar to readers in England and the U.S. Biographical details are often complemented with statements from the author as well as a photograph. Entries include bibliographies by and about the author.

Kunitz and Vineta Colby collaborated on the *First supplement* (N.Y. : Wilson, 1955), which added 700 new biographees and updated the biographies and bibliographies in the original volume.

Following the pattern established by Kunitz, John Wakeman produced *World authors, 1950-1970 : a companion to Twentieth century authors* (N.Y. : Wilson, 1975), but Wakeman treated 959 new authors who achieved literary prominence during this period as well as some who had not been included in the two original volumes. Like its predecessor, *World authors* provided biographical sketches and authors' statements, but critical comment was generally fuller than in the earlier works. Bibliographies again list principal works and a selection of writings about each author.

The series continued with *World authors, 1970-1975*, ed. by John Wakeman (N.Y. : Wilson, 1980.). The 348 authors here were mostly imaginative writers—poets, novelists, and dramatists—but included philosophers, historians, biographers, critics, scientists, journalists and others who gained prominence and popularity during the five-year period. Fewer entries contained autobiographical statements, and bibliographies listed works by and about the author, the former in English translation.

Two more works, both ed. by Vineta Colby, *World authors, 1975-1980* (N.Y. : Wilson, 1985) and *World authors, 1980-1985* (N.Y. : Wilson, 1991) follow the criteria established in the earlier volumes.

For a review of the series, see: *RSR : reference services review*, 16, no. 3 (1988): 31-44.　　PN771.K86

Literary criticism and authors' biographies : an annotated index / comp. by Alison P. Seidel. Metuchen, N.J. : Scarecrow, 1978. 209 p.　　**BE206**

Provides references to biographical and critical materials appearing in collective works, volumes of literary history and criticism, etc. "Most entries refer to a chapter or discrete subchapter at least two pages long."—*Introd.* Aims not to duplicate indexing of volumes treated in Irving Adelman and Rita Dworkin, *The contemporary novel : a checklist of critical literature on the British and American novel since 1945* (Metuchen, N.J.: Scarecrow, 1972); Inglis Freeman Bell and Donald Baird, *The English novel, 1578–1956* (BE671); Richard E. Combs and Nancy R. Owen, *Authors : critical and biographical references* (see BE197); etc. Z6511.L56

Literary exile in the twentieth century : an analysis and biographical dictionary / ed. by Martin Tucker. N.Y. : Greenwood, 1991. 854 p. **BE207**

A biobibliography of 20th-century writers who have experienced exile from their native land. "Exile" is broadly interpreted in both its physical and psychological meanings. Group entries following the introduction discuss topics such as American expatriates in Europe, Holocaust writing, Iranian writers in exile, and gay and lesbian writers. Signed biographical entries on some 550 writers analyze and assess their work in light of an exile's experience, concluding with a list of selected titles and some critical references. Useful appendixes identify the countries of flight and expulsion and those of refuge and haven. Another appendix lists writers by category of exile (expatriate, legal, political, social, etc.). Complemented by a substantive general bibliography and an index. PN495.L43

Magill, Frank Northen. Cyclopedia of world authors II. Pasadena, Calif. : Salem Pr., c1989. 4 v. **BE208**

Similar in format to the first *Cyclopedia of world authors*, ed. by Magill (N.Y. : Harper, c[1958]) this biobibliography continues rather than supersedes the revised edition (Englewood Cliffs, N.J. : Salem Pr., c[1974]). In addition to updating some previous entries it adds a significant number of new writers (about 80%). The 705 entries concentrate on modern writers of fiction, poetry, drama, literary criticism, science fiction, and mystery/detective fiction, but the set includes a few nonliterary authors from other disciplines as well. Emphasizes English-language authors but includes important writers from throughout the world.

Signed articles give place and date of birth and death (when appropriate), a list of principal works, and a biographical sketch, followed by a narrative bibliography of biographical/critical references. PN41.M26

New Century cyclopedia of names / ed. by Clarence L. Barnhart with the assistance of William D. Halsey ... [et al.]. N.Y. : Appleton, 1954. 3 v. **BE209**

For annotation, *see* AH29. PE1625.C43

Nobel laureates in literature : a biographical dictionary / ed. by Rado Pribic. N.Y. : Garland, 1990. 473 p. (Garland reference library of the humanities, vol. 849). **BE210**

For annotation, *see* AL168. PN452.N6

Who was who among English and European authors, 1931–1949. Detroit : Gale, [1978]. 3 v. (Gale composite biographical dictionary series, 2). **BE211**

"Based on entries which first appeared in 'The author's and writer's who's who & reference guide,' originally compiled by Edward Martell and E. G. Pine, and in 'Who's who among living authors of older nations,' originally compiled by Alberta Lawrence."—*t.p.*

The latest entry for each of the writers represented in the various volumes of *The author's & writer's who's who* has been reproduced here, together with the entries from the 1931 Lawrence compilation. No attempt was made to establish death dates. Especially useful for information about minor writers, including journalists, who flourished during this period. PN451.W5

The writers directory. [Ed. 1] (1971/73)– . London : St. James ; N.Y. : St. Martin's, [1970]– . Biennial. **BE212**

The 10th ed. (1992/94) of this biographical directory features 17,000 living authors from Australia, Canada, Ireland, New Zealand, South Africa, the U.K., and the U.S., and other authors writing in English. Includes fiction and nonfiction authors who have published at least one full-length book in English.

Factual biographical information is solicited from the writers themselves. In addition to personal data, entry includes subject categories, a complete bibliography and, with some exceptions, an address. Separate index to writing categories.

§ Some 6,000 entrants are writers featured in other works published by St. James Press: *Contemporary poets*, ed. by Tracy Chevalier (BE334); *Contemporary novelists*, ed. by Lesley Henderson (BE252); *Contemporary dramatists*, ed. by D. L. Kirkpatrick (BE223); *Contemporary literary critics*, ed. by Elmer Borklund (BE426); *Twentieth-century children's writers*, ed. by D. L. Kirkpatrick (BE391), *Twentieth-century crime and mystery writers*, ed. by John M. Reilly (BE275); *Twentieth-century science-fiction writers*, ed. by Noelle Watson and Paul E. Schellinger (BE306); *Twentieth-century romance and historical writers*, ed. by Lesley Henderson (BE249); *Twentieth-century western writers*, ed. by Geoff Sadler (BE579). PS1.W73

GENRES

Biography

Biography. v. 1 (winter 1978)– . [Honolulu : Univ. Pr. of Hawaii for the Biographical Research Center]. Quarterly. **BE213**

Subtitle (varies): an interdisciplinary journal.

"Current bibliography on life-writing," publ. in Fall issue, v. 1–6 (1978–83). Continued by: "Bibliography of works about life-writing...," v. 8 (1985)– .

Annotated entries for books and articles about biography, autobiography, and life-writing from British and American publications. Beginning with v. 9 (1976) the bibliography included dissertations, periodicals, articles, reviews, and books. The bibliographers often prefix the list with a brief account of trends in the genre.

Beginning with v. 10, no. 3 (Summer 1987) the journal initiated a section in each issue entitled "Reviewed elsewhere," which lists biographies and books about life-writing that have been reviewed in other journals. Each entry contains a brief selected passage from the review.

Garraty, John Arthur. The nature of biography. N.Y. : Knopf, c1957. 289 p. **BE214**

Repr.: N.Y. : Garland, 1985.

A guide to the nature, history, and method of biography as a literary form. A detailed "Essay on sources," although dating from the 1950s, provides excellent bibliographical coverage of the subject to that time. CT21.G3

Rollyson, Carl E. Biography : an annotated bibliography. Pasadena, Calif. : Salem Pr., c1992. 215 p. **BE215**

Rollyson notes that this is the first bibliography "to organize and to annotate the literature on biography."—*Introd.* Entries consist of English-language titles published in the U.S. with broad coverage of the genre, excluding specialized works. Generally excludes book reviews of biographies unless the reviewer raises issues related to the genre. Chapters include such topics as biographers on biography; historical and critical studies ; psychobiography; feminist biography; biography in fiction; Johnson and Boswell; and Leon Edel. Descriptive annotations; general index, complemented by an index of biographical subjects.

St. James guide to biography / ed., Paul E. Schellinger. Chicago : St. James, 1991. 870 p. **BE216**

For annotation, *see* AH7. CT21.S68

Winslow, Donald J. Life-writing : a glossary of terms in biography, autobiography, and related forms. Honolulu : Publ. for the Biographical Research Center by the Univ. Pr. of Hawaii, c1980. 51 p. **BE217**

Initially published as : "Glossary of terms in life-writing," *Biography: an interdisciplinary journal*, 1, no. 1 (Winter 1978) : 61–68; 1, no. 2 (Spring 1978) : 61–85 (*see* BE213).

A list of terms comprising the critical vocabulary of biography as a literary form. Based largely on *Oxford English dictionary*. Select bibliography of works cited, and of related titles.

Drama

Boyer, Robert D. Realism in European theatre and drama, 1870–1920 : a bibliography. Westport, Conn. : Greenwood, 1979. 236 p.   **BE218**

Includes 62 dramatists of Austria, Belgium and Holland, England, France, Germany, Ireland, Italy, Norway and Sweden, Russia, and Spain. Entries list an author's plays, together with books, articles, and dissertations concerning those works. Index to authors cited.

Z5784.R27B69

Breed, Paul Francis. Dramatic criticism index : a bibliography of commentaries on playwrights from Ibsen to the avant-garde / comp. and ed. by Paul F. Breed and Florence M. Sniderman. Detroit : Gale, [1972]. 1022 p.   **BE219**

Includes some 12,000 entries in English on about 300 American and foreign playwrights, most from the 20th century, and drawn from more than 600 books and 200 periodicals. Some play reviews are included, especially for foreign playwrights. Arrangement is alphabetical by name of the playwright; title and critic indexes.

§ *See also* Irving Adelman and Rita Dworkin, *Modern drama : a checklist of critical literature on 20th century plays* (Metuchen, N.J. : Scarecrow, 1967), which also stresses critical articles rather than reviews of productions. Includes parts of books as well as periodical articles.   Z5781.B8

Carpenter, Charles A. Modern drama scholarship and criticism, 1966–1980 : an international bibliography. Toronto ; Buffalo : Univ. of Toronto Pr., c1986. 587 p.   **BE220**

"A classified, selective list of publications on world drama since Ibsen."—*Introd.* International in scope, but limited to publications in Roman-alphabet languages. About 27,300 items in classed arrangement. Index of playwrights at front; index of names (i.e., authors of critical writings) at back. Table of contents, but no subject approach other than through playwrights' names.   Z5781.C37

Coleman, Arthur. Drama criticism / Arthur Coleman and Gary R. Tyler. Denver : Alan Swallow, [1966–71]. 2 v.   **BE221**

Contents: v. 1, A checklist of interpretation since 1940 of English and American plays; v. 2, A checklist of interpretation since 1940 of classical and continental plays.

Another in the publisher's series of bibliographies of criticism and interpretation. Lists book and periodical materials. Vol. 1 covers publications of 1940–64; v. 2, 1950 to about 1968.   Z1231.D7C6

A companion to the medieval theatre / ed. by Ronald W. Vince. N.Y. : Greenwood, 1989. 420 p.   **BE222**

A dictionary arrangement of authors, anonymous works, literary styles and forms, regions, and symbols, covering roughly 900–1550. Brief bibliographies at the end of most entries; chronology, name, title, and subject indexes.   PN2152.C66

Contemporary dramatists / ed., K.A. Berney. 5th ed. London ; Wash. ; Detroit : St. James, c1993. 843 p.   **BE223**

1st ed., 1972; 4th ed., 1988.

Offers biographical and critical notes on more than 300 living playwrights writing in English. Entries give a short biography, a list of works produced and/or published, and a signed essay. Some also include comments from the playwright. Indexed by title. American and British dramatists predominate.   PR737.C57

Drama criticism. v. 1– . Detroit : Gale, c1991– . Irregular.   **BE224**

A biobibliography of major playwrights from all time periods and countries intended for beginning students in literature and drama and for general readers. Each volume contains lengthy articles on 12–15

dramatists focusing on major dramatic works. Each entry gives a biography and critical introduction to the author, followed by a list of dramatic works and of works in other genres. If available, the entry includes a commentary by the author on his/her work, complemented by an overview of the playwright's literary career and by studies on individual plays. The latter two sections consist of excerpts from critical articles placed in chronological order. Studies on specific works focus first on performance aspects and then on literary merits. Like other Gale publications the cumulative index includes other literary criticism series.

Drury, Francis K. W. Drury's guide to best plays / James M. Salem. 4th ed. Metuchen, N.J. : Scarecrow, 1987. 480 p.   **BE225**

1st ed., 1953; 3rd ed., 1978.

Lists about 1,500 nonmusical full-length plays in English, covering the period 400 BCE to 1985. Intended as a guide for those producing plays (for example, amateur groups) as well as a selection guide for libraries. Gives dates of first production or printing, editions (including anthologies or collections), description, plot, number of characters, and information on royalties. Includes various indexes and special lists.   Z5781.D8

Firkins, Ina Ten Eyck. Index to plays, 1800–1926. N.Y. : Wilson, 1927. 307 p.   **BE226**

Repr. : N.Y. : AMS Pr., 1971.

A comprehensive index of 7,872 plays by 2,203 authors, showing where the text of each can be found in collections or other publications. Indexes only plays in English but includes translations of foreign plays. In two parts: (1) author index, giving full bibliographical information about each play, and, in many cases, number of acts and brief characterizations, as comedy, tragedy, social, domestic, etc.; (2) title and subject index, referring to the author list.

——. *Supplement* (N.Y. : Wilson, 1935) continues the coverage from 1927 focusing on the work of new writers, but including some omitted from the earlier volume, and adding further references to titles in the first work.

Keller, Dean H. Index to plays in periodicals. Rev. and expanded ed. Metuchen, N.J. : Scarecrow, 1979. 824 p.   **BE227**

1st ed., 1971.

A finding aid for plays published in periodicals. Indexes 267 periodicals, usually from the beginning through 1976. Author listing with title index.

§ Supplemented by the compiler's *Index to plays in periodicals, 1977–1987* (Metuchen, N.J. : Scarecrow, 1990) which indexes about 4,600 plays in those periodicals from the earlier list which continued to publish plays and that are still in existence, plus several new titles.

Z5781.K43

Logasa, Hannah. An index to one-act plays / comp. by Hannah Logasa and Winifred Ver Nooy. Boston : Faxon, 1924. 327 p. (Useful reference series, no. 30).   **BE228**

Title, author, and subject indexes to one-act plays in collections, and also to separately published pamphlets. Indexes plays written in or translated into English, 1900–24.

Five supplements have been published, covering: 1924–31 (publ. 1932); 1932–40 (1941); 1941–48 (1949); 1948–57 (1958); 1956–64 (1966). (Useful reference series, no. 46, 68, 78, 87, 94). The 3rd supplement includes radio plays; the 4th and 5th, radio and television plays.

Major modern dramatists / comp. and ed. by Rita Stein, Friedhelm Rickert. N.Y. : Ungar, c1984–c1986. 2 v.   **BE229**

Contents: v. 1, American, British, Irish, German, Austrian, and Swiss dramatists; v. 2 (ed. by Blandine M. Rickert [et al.]), Norwegian, Swedish, French, Belgian, Italian, Spanish, Russian, Czech, Hungarian, and Polish dramatists.

A collection of excerpts from critical writings similar to those found in other volumes of the "Library of literary criticism" series, the difference here being that genre rather than nationality or language is the focal point. All excerpts are in English, some translated specifically for this compilation.   PN1861.M27

Matlaw, Myron. Modern world drama : an encyclopedia. N.Y. : Dutton, 1972. 960 p. : ill.   **BE230**

Includes four types of articles in a single alphabetical sequence: (1) summary articles on the modern drama of individual countries; (2) biographical entries for playwrights who lived in the 20th century; (3) entries for specific dramatic works, including notes on publication, first production, and a synopsis; and (4) technical terms.

§ See also: *McGraw-Hill encyclopedia of world drama* (BH72) for more extensive treatments and excellent bibliographies of editions and/or critical works. Another guide to post-World War II drama in Europe and the Americas is *Crowell's handbook of contemporary drama*, by Michael Anderson [et al.] (N.Y. : Crowell, [1971]). Includes entries for playwrights, individual plays, national developments in specific countries, and some terms. Precise bibliographic information is sparse.   PN1851.M36

Ottemiller, John H. Ottemiller's index to plays in collections : an author and title index to plays appearing in collections published between 1900 and 1985. 7th ed. / rev. and enl. by Billie M. Connor, Helene G. Mochedlover. Metuchen, N.J. : Scarecrow, 1988. 564 p.   **BE231**

1st ed., 1943; 6th ed., 1976.

Contents: (1) Author index, giving name and dates, title of play, date of first production (or of first publication if never performed), references from original titles and variant translated titles, references from joint authors and translators; (2) List of collections analyzed and key to symbols; and (3) Title index, referring from all forms of titles, translated titles, and subtitles.

Indexes some 6,548 plays by 2,555 different authors in 1,350 collections published 1900–75 in England and America, and 1975–85 in the English-speaking world. All editions of the same collection have been included when the contents of successive editions vary. Generally excludes collections of children's plays, one-act plays, radio and television plays, and holiday and anniversary plays, unless they appear in one of the collections. Includes plays in languages other than English if they appear in collections published in the English-speaking world.   Z5781.O8

Palmer, Helen H. European drama criticism, 1900–1975. 2nd ed. Hamden, Conn. : Shoe String Pr., 1977. 653 p.   **BE232**

1st ed. (1968) and its supplements 1–2 (1970–74) by H. H. Palmer and A. J. Dyson.

Cumulates the entries from the earlier edition and its supplements, and adds new material through 1975.

§ A companion to Floyd Eugene Eddleman's *American drama criticism* (BE457). Lists English and foreign-language criticisms with heavy emphasis on English-language materials.   Z5781.P2

Patterson, Charlotte A. Plays in periodicals : an index to English language scripts in twentieth century journals. Boston : G. K. Hall, 1970. 240 p.   **BE233**

Indexes more than 4,000 plays appearing in 97 periodicals during the period 1900–68. Title listing with author index.   Z5781.P3

Play index. v. 1 (1949–52)– . N.Y. : Wilson, 1953– .   **BE234**

1949–52, an index to 2,616 plays in 1,138 volumes, ed. by Dorothy H. West and Dorothy M. Peake; 1953–60, an index to 4,952 plays in 1,735 volumes, ed. by Estelle A. Fidell and Dorothy M. Peake; 1961–67, an index to 4,793 plays, ed. by Estelle A. Fidell; 1968–72, an index to 3,848 plays, ed. by Estelle A. Fidell; 1973–77, an index to 3,878 plays, ed. by Estelle A. Fidell; 1978–82, an index to 3,429 plays, ed. by Juliette Yaakov; 1983–87, an index to 3,964 plays, ed. by Juliette Yaakov and John Greenfieldt; 1988–92, an index to 4,397 plays, ed. by Juliette Yaakov and John Greenfieldt.

Each volume in four parts: (1) the main list, arranged by author, title, and subject; (2) a list of the collections indexed; (3) cast analysis, listing each play under type of cast (male, female, mixed, puppet) and

further by number of characters; (4) directory of publishers. All types of plays are indexed, including translations into English. The dictionary catalog arrangement and the large amounts of subject indexing are particularly helpful.   Z5781.P53

Schwanbeck, Gisela. Bibliographie der deutschsprachigen Hochschulschriften zur Theaterwissenschaft von 1885 bis 1952. Berlin : Gesellschaft für Theatergeschichte, 1956. 563 p. (Schriften der Gesellschaft für Theatergeschichte, Bd. 58).   **BE235**

A classified list of 3,309 German dissertations on the drama and theater from antiquity to the present. Author and catchword index.   Z5781.S4

Shipley, Joseph Twadell. The Crown guide to the world's great plays, from ancient Greece to modern times. Rev., updated ed. N.Y. : Crown, c1984. 866 p.   **BE236**

1st ed., 1956, had title: *Guide to great plays*.

A listing, by author, of several hundred "great" plays of all periods. For each a plot synopsis is given, with additional information on the play's history and production, excerpts from reviews, notes on famous casts, etc. In this edition numerous older plays were dropped and newer ones added (along with a number of older plays previously omitted); new critical notes and information on recent revivals have been added to many of the earlier entries.   PN6112.5.S45

Stratman, Carl Joseph. Bibliography of medieval drama. 2nd ed., rev. and enl. N.Y. : Ungar, [1972]. 2 v. (1035 p.).   **BE237**

1st ed., 1954.

Covers early liturgical forms, mystery and miracle plays, moralities, interludes, etc. Lists manuscripts, published texts, and various editions of individual plays, with critical studies of them, including academic dissertations. Sections on general works and festschriften are followed by chapters devoted to liturgical Latin drama, English, Byzantine, French, German, Italian, Low Countries, and Spanish drama. The sections on Continental medieval drama "have been included on a selective basis, as the material is intended primarily as an aid for students of the English drama."—*Pref.* Library locations are given for manuscripts and for most of the book materials. More than 9,000 entries; indexed.   Z5782.A2S8

Thomson, Ruth Gibbons. Index to full length plays, 1895 to 1925. Boston : Faxon, 1956. 172 p. (Useful reference series., no. 85).   **BE238**

Continues Thomson's *Index to full length plays, 1926 to 1944* (1946). These volumes include a title index—giving author, translator, number of acts, number of characters, subject, and scene—followed by author and subject indexes referring to the title index and a bibliography giving publisher and date.

§ Coverage continues with Norma Olin Ireland's *Index to full length plays, 1944 to 1964* (Boston : Faxon, 1965) which combines author, subject, and title indexes in a single alphabetical list, and adds numerous new subject headings.

Essays

The A.L.A. index : an index to general literature, biographical, historical, and literary essays and sketches, reports and publications of boards and societies dealing with education, health, labor, charities and corrections, etc., etc / by William I. Fletcher ... with the cooperation of many librarians. 2nd ed., greatly enl. and brought down to January 1, 1900 / issued by the Publishing Board of the American Library Association. Boston ; N.Y. : Houghton, Mifflin, 1901. 679 p.   **BE239**

Repr.: Ann Arbor, Mich. : Pierian Pr., 1970.

A subject index that attempts to do for books of essays and general literature what *Poole's index* (AD282) does for periodicals. Indexes books belonging to the following classes: (1) Essays and similar collections of critical, biographical, and other monographs; (2) Books of travel and general history whose chapters or parts are worthy of separate reference; (3) Reports and publications of boards and associations

dealing with sociological matters, and of historical and literary societies; and (4) Miscellaneous books and some public documents. Includes only books in English. Indexing is by catchword subject, not by
modern catalog subject headings.

———. *Supplement*, covering 1900–1910, was issued in 1914
(223 p.).

Continued by: *Essay and general literature index* (BA4), which
indexes collections published since 1900. Some of the books indexed
in the *Supplement* have been taken over by the *Essay and general literature index*, but others, particularly those on travel, have not been rein-
dexed; therefore, the *Supplement* has not been entirely superseded. For
a more detailed discussion of the relationship of the two indexes, *see*
the preface to the *Essay and general literature index*.   AI3.A32

Fiction

Baker, Ernest Albert. Guide to the best fiction, English and
American : including translations from foreign languages / by
Ernest A. Baker and James Packman. New and enl. ed. Lon-
don : Routledge ; N.Y. : Macmillan, 1932. 634 p.   **BE240**
    Repr.: N.Y. : Barnes and Noble, [1967].

1st ed., 1903; 2nd ed., 1913. This 3rd ed. is much enlarged from
the 2nd by the addition of material from 1911 through 1930, and differs from the 2nd ed. in arrangement, i.e., has one alphabetical list instead of national lists with chronological subdivisions.

An older but still useful work, with good annotations and a detailed general index of authors, titles, subjects, historical names, allusions, places, and characters.   Z5916.B18

Critical survey of long fiction : English language series / ed.
by Frank N. Magill. 2nd ed. Pasadena, Calif. : Salem Pr.,
c1991. 8 v. (3892, lii p.).   **BE241**
    1st ed., 1983.

A revision and expansion of the original edition; offers signed
critical articles on 332 novelists (v. 1–7), plus 14 overview essays on
the development and subgenres of the novel, a glossary of terms and
techniques, and a subject index of literary terms and concepts (v. 8). It
includes, as well, updated entries on the English-language novelists
from the *Supplement* (c1987). Secondary bibliographies from the original edition have been augmented, updated, and annotated.

§ For a similar compilation on foreign language novelists *see* Magill's *Critical survey of long fiction : foreign language series* (Englewood Cliffs, N.J. : Salem Pr., c1984. 5 v.).   PR821.C7

Cumulated fiction index. 1945/60– . London : Assoc. of Assistant Librarians, [1960]– . Irregular.   **BE242**
    Individual volumes have title: *Fiction index : a guide to works of
fiction available during the year and not previously indexed in the Fiction Index Series.*

The 1945/60 volume, also called "Fiction index three," superseded a 1953 volume entitled *Fiction index*, covering 1945/53, and its
1957 supplement. The subtitle to that volume reads: "A guide to more
than 25,000 works of fiction, including short story collections, anthologies, omnibus volumes, extracts and condensed books, mainly available between January 1945 and February 1960, arranged under 3,000
subject headings with numerous references, and intended for use in
public and circulating libraries, schools and bookshops and by the general reader." Excludes "formula" novels and most children's books. Includes folklore, myths, legends, autobiographies and quasi-autobiogra-
phies when they have a substantial element of fiction. Listings are limited to author and title, without publication information. Each of the
supplementary volumes adds some older titles not previously listed
along with thousands of new titles from their respective periods.
                                                          Z5916.F52

Eastman, Mary Huse. Index to fairy tales, myths and legends. 2nd ed., rev. and enl. Boston : Faxon, 1926. 610 p. (Useful reference series, no. 28).   **BE243**

A title index—with entry under best-known title and cross-
references from variant titles—to the fairy tales and legends included
in a large number of collections. Useful to children's librarians as well
as students of folklore.

———. ———. *Supplement* (Boston : Faxon, c1937–52. 2 v.
[Useful reference series, no. 61, 82]).

Additional supplements by Norma Olin Ireland: *Index to fairy
tales, 1949–1972, including folklore, legends & myths, in collections*
(Westwood, Mass. : Faxon, 1973. [Useful reference series, 101]); 4th
suppl. (1979); 5th suppl. comp. by Ireland and Joseph W. Sprug
(Metuchen, N.J. : Scarecrow, 1989).

Fiction, 1876–1983 : a bibliography of United States editions.
N.Y. : Bowker, c1983. 2 v. (2328 p.).   **BE244**
    Contents: v. 1, Classified author index; Main author index; v. 2,
Title index; Key to publishers and distributors abbreviations; Directory
of publishers and distributors.

Derived from the Bowker databases for *Books in print* and *American book publishing record*. Lists about 170,000 titles of novels, novellas, short stories, and anthologies of fiction. The classified author
index lists authors by country and period; full publication information
appears in both the main author and title sections, though the amount
of bibliographic detail varies considerably from entry to entry.
                                                          Z5916.F49

Fiction catalog / ed. by Juliette Yaakov and John Greenfieldt.
12th ed. N.Y. : H.W. Wilson, 1991. 943 p.   **BE245**
    1st ed., 1908.
    Kept up-to-date by annual supplements; new editions are now is-
sued quinquennially.

A standard work that lists and annotates a selection of the best
fiction in English, along with a generous representation of foreign fiction that has been translated into English. The 12th ed. includes 5,159
titles with an additional 1,948 analytical entries for novelettes and
composite works. Early editions were in dictionary form. Now in two
sections: an author alphabet with full bibliographical information and
annotations, and a title and subject index. Annotations include notes on
plot or content, along with excerpts from critical reviews. Availability
of large-type editions is noted; out-of-print titles are included as well
as prices.

§ Together with its companion *Public library catalog* (AA328),
which includes works of fiction criticism, it forms a comprehensive
bibliography of recommended fiction and nonfiction for adults.
                                                          Z5916.F5

Hicken, Marilyn E. Sequels. 10th ed. London : Assoc. of Assistant Librarians, 1991. v. 1. (In progress).   **BE246**
    Contents: v. 1. Adult books, comp. by Marilyn E. Hicken.
    1st ed., 1922, by T. Aldred; 2nd ed., 1928, by W. H. Parker; 3rd–
6th eds., 1947–74, by F. M. Gardner; 7th–9th eds., 1982–89.

Includes (a) novels and stories in which the same character appears; (b) novels with a connected narrative or theme; (c) nonfiction,
especially autobiography, where the connection between titles is not
readily apparent; and (d) series of novels with a connection that is
mainly historical or geographical. Listing is by author, with indication
of series title or name of principal character, followed by individual titles; nonfiction is noted. Paperbacks in series are included. Index of series titles and characters.

§ For children's and young adult literature, *see also*: Susan
Roman, *Sequences : an annotated guide to children's fiction in series*
(Chicago : Amer. Libr. Assoc., 1985) and Vicki Anderson, *Fiction sequels for readers 10–16 : an annotated bibliography of books in succession* (Jefferson, N.C. ; London : McFarland, 1990).   Z6514.S4H52

Postmodern fiction : a bio-bibliographical guide / ed. by Larry McCaffery. N.Y. : Greenwood, 1986. 604 p. (Movements in
the arts, no. 2).   **BE247**
    Provides "biographical and bibliographical information, as well as
critical assessments, about many of the important figures in the field of
post-modern literature."—*Introd.* In two main sections: (1) Overview
articles, which contains 15 chapters by contributing scholars on topics
such as realism, journalism, feminist fiction, or Latin American litera-

ture; and (2) Authors and critics, signed biographical and critical sketches of more than 100 individual writers. Both sections include bibliographies at the end of each chapter or sketch; citations are for the most part to English-language works. General index.   PN3503.P594

Rosenberg, Betty. Genreflecting : a guide to reading interests in genre fiction. 2nd ed. Littleton, Colo. : Libraries Unlimited, 1986. 298 p.   **BE248**
1st ed., 1982.
Focuses on original genre publications in hardback editions and publications of older genre authors republished in paperback; also notes current trends especially the blending of genres. Genres include western, thriller, romance, science fiction, fantasy, and horror. Each category is divided into subgenres, generally by themes and types, followed by topics such as reviews or review journals, associations and conventions, awards, book clubs, and others. Originally written as a textbook for library school; especially useful to book selectors and reader's advisors. Indexed by genre author and by theme with an index to secondary materials.   PS374.P63R67

Twentieth-century romance and historical writers. 2nd ed. / ed., Lesley Henderson ; consulting ed., D. L. Kirkpatrick. Chicago ; London : St. James, 1990. 856 p.   **BE249**
1st ed., 1982, had title: *Twentieth-century romance and Gothic writers.*
A biobibliography of more than 400 authors, from popular romance novelists (e.g., Barbara Cartland and Victoria Holt) to Pulitzer Prize winners (Robert Penn Warren) and Poets Laureate (John Masefield) who have employed historical settings in their work. The signed entries are arranged alphabetically and include exhaustive bibliographies. Title index.   PR888.L69T87

Novels

Baker, Ernest Albert. Guide to historical fiction. London : Routledge ; N.Y. : Macmillan, 1914. 565 p.   **BE250**
Repr. : N.Y. : Argosy-Antiquarian, 1968.
Lists about 5,000 novels that portray the life of the past (including medieval romances and novels of manners), as well as avowedly historical novels. Emphasizes British, American, and French history. Arrangement is first by country then chronologically by historical period. Descriptive notes indicate briefly the plot and scene of each story, and its historical characters. Full index of authors, titles, historical names, places, events, and allusions. Especially useful for its subject index.
§ Standard but now dated: Jonathan Nield, *Guide to the best historical novels and tales* [5th ed. rev., enl., rearranged, and mostly rewritten] (London : Mathews ; N.Y. : Macmillan, [1929]. Repr. : N.Y. : B. Franklin, 1968). This old but comprehensive list features mainly works in English but includes some foreign material in English translation or in the original. The 4th (1911) and 5th editions differ substantially in deletions and additions. Indexed by author and title; and, like Bakers's *Guide,* useful for its subject index.
See also Daniel D. McGarry and Sarah Harriman White, *World historical fiction guide : an annotated, chronological, geographical, and topical list of selected historical novels* (2nd ed. Metuchen, N.J. : Scarecrow, 1973) which is more up-to-date. Its annotations, however, are so brief as to be negligible, and it lacks any subject indexing.   Z5917.H6B2

Bold, Alan Norman. Who was really who in fiction / Alan Bold and Robert Giddings. Burnt Mill, Harlow, Essex, Eng. : Longman, 1987. 383 p.   **BE251**
Arranged by character. Reveals the real person on whom a fictional character is based, as well as actual events in the person's life that find their way into fiction. Entries recount plot summaries and biographical details, and provide one or two references to biographical and critical works. General index. Some of the entries appeared earlier in *True characters : real people in fiction : pocket companion,* by Bold and Giddings (Harlow, Essex, Eng. : Longman, 1984).

§ Less detailed is William Amos' *The originals : an A–Z of fiction's real-life characters* (Boston : Little, Brown, c1985) which includes characters from essays and poems as well as novels and plays. Emphasizes English and American literature, but includes some French, German, Italian, and Russian. Index of persons.   PN41.B57

Contemporary novelists / ed., Lesley Henderson ; assoc. ed., Noelle Watson. 5th ed. Chicago ; London : St. James, 1991. 1053 p.   **BE252**
1st ed., 1972; 4th ed., 1986.
For each writer there is a brief biographical sketch (including an address), a bibliography of published works, a comment by writers who chose to make one, and a critical essay by a contemporary scholar. References to other critical studies are limited to those suggested by the biographee. Limited to living authors. Although American and British writers predominate, many Commonwealth novelists and Africans writing in English are included.   PR883.C64

Hartman, Donald K. Themes and settings in fiction : a bibliography of bibliographies / comp. by Donald K. Hartman and Jerome Drost. N.Y. : Greenwood, 1988. 223 p. (Bibliographies and indexes in world literature, no. 14).   **BE253**
Lists bibliographies, bibliographic essays, review articles, and literary surveys of novels and short stories. Covers publications of 1900–85 in English. One-sentence annotations; joint author and subject indexes.   Z5916.H28

Hicken, Mandy. Now read on : a guide to contemporary popular fiction / Mandy Hicken, Ray Prytherch. Aldershot, England ; Brookfield, Vt. : Gower, c1990. 328 p.   **BE254**
A selective bibliography of contemporary fiction in 19 different genres: e.g., adventure stories; country life; humorous novels; spy stories. Intended not simply to list authors and their works, but to suggest other authors and their works written in a similar vein. Focuses primarily on British authors, but includes American, Australian, and African novelists as well. Generally excludes westerns, light romance, and literary novels. Entries give brief biographical details on the author, followed by a list of publications and other recommended authors. Indexed by author, including pseudonyms, and by series title and names of recurring characters. Appendix lists genre literary prizes and awards.   PR881.H53

Husband, Janet. Sequels : an annotated guide to novels in series / Janet Husband and Jonathan F. Husband. 2nd ed. Chicago : Amer. Libr. Assoc., 1990. 576 p.   **BE255**
1st ed., 1982.
A bibliography of sequence novels with brief commentary. A criterion for selection was probable availability in medium-sized public libraries; therefore, incorporates popular works as well as those of literary merit. This edition retains listings from the 1st ed. with the exception of two paperback series, expands coverage of genre fiction to include detective series, and adds new series published through 1989. Arranged by author with title and subject indexes.
§ Older but still useful is Elizabeth Margaret Kerr's *Bibliography of the sequence novel* (Minneapolis : Univ. of Minnesota Pr., [1950]). It attempts to list all the novels in series in which the sequence of the volumes depends upon the development of characters and themes. Divided into language groups: British-American, Romance, Teutonic, and Slavic. The foreign sections of the bibliography are more selective than complete. For the 20th century, entries are current through 1948. *See also* Marilyn E. Hicken, *Sequels* (BE246).   Z5917.S44H87

Irwin, Leonard Bertram. A guide to historical fiction for the use of schools, libraries, and the general reader. 10th ed., new and rev. Brooklawn, N.J. : McKinley, 1971. 255 p.   **BE256**
1st-9th eds., 1930–68, by Hannah Logasa had title: *Historical fiction.*
In general, limited to books published since 1940, and to those that were favorably reviewed. Geographical/chronological arrangement; author and title indexes. Very brief annotations. 1st–6th eds. included some nonfiction titles, the latter now listed in a separate publication, Fred R. Czarra, *A guide to historical reading : nonfiction for schools, libraries, and the general reader* (11th rev. ed. Wash. : Heldref Publ., c1983).

§ Lynda G. Adamson, *A reference guide to historical fiction for children and young adults* (N.Y. : Greenwood, c1987) concentrates on historical novels written since 1940 by authors of recognized excellence. Major entries are by author, with brief entries interspersed alphabetically for titles of works, protagonists, historical personages, places, and other relevant terms. Entries for authors give some biographical details, a short synopsis for each novel, and comments on style and themes. Appendixes classify works by setting and locale, and by age level of readability. Also appended is a bibliography of works about writing historical fiction, and a secondary bibliography of writings about the authors and novels discussed in the guide.

Z5917.H6I7

Kearney, E. I. The Continental novel : a checklist of criticism in English, 1900–1960 / [by] E. I. Kearney and L. S. Fitzgerald. Metuchen, N.J. : Scarecrow, 1968. 460 p.   **BE257**

A bibliography of criticism published since 1900 in books and periodicals. Includes English-language criticism of the French, Spanish and Portuguese, Italian, German, Scandinavian, Russian and East European novel of all periods. Arrangement is by national/regional grouping, then by author and individual novel.

Updated by Kearney and Fitzgerald's *The Continental novel : a checklist of criticism in English, 1967–1980* (Metuchen, N.J. : Scarecrow, 1983).   Z5916.K4

Menendez, Albert J. The Catholic novel : an annotated bibliography. N.Y. : Garland, 1988. 323 p. (Garland reference library of the humanities, v. 690).   **BE258**

A list of 490 critical works on religious fiction, Catholic novels, and individual authors, followed by an author list of 1,703 representative Catholic novels. Covers English-language works almost exclusively. Title index.   Z5917.C47M46

What do I read next? 1990– . Detroit : Gale, c1991– . Annual.   **BE259**

An annual reference guide to approximately 1,500 recommended titles, classic and contemporary, in six genres—mystery, romance, western, fantasy, horror, and science fiction—published within the previous months. Written by an expert in the genre, each section opens with an overview of the year's developments, followed by a selection of titles. In addition to bibliographic information, each entry provides a brief plot summary, names of major characters, time period, and locale, followed by citations to reviews of the book, titles of other works by the author, and titles of other works of similar style or theme. Eight indexes—series, time period, geographic, genre, character name, character description, author, and title.   PN3427.W43

Short stories

Cook, Dorothy Elizabeth. Short story index : an index to 60,000 stories in 4,320 collections / comp. by Dorothy E. Cook [and] Isabel S. Monro. N.Y. : H.W. Wilson, 1953. 1553 p.   **BE260**

"Supersedes the *Index to short stories* compiled by Ina Ten Eyck Firkins ([2nd and enl. ed.] 1923) and its Supplements (1929 and 1936)."—Pref.

Supplements to the Cook and Monro index were issued to cover 1950–54, 1955–58, 1959–63, 1964–68, and 1969–73. The annual *Short story index* began publication in 1974; quinquennial cumulations to date cover 1974–78, 1979–83, and 1984–88.

Indexes by author, title, and, in many cases, subject some 178,200 stories in more than 11,200 collections. Beginning 1974, coverage was extended to include stories in approximately 60–80 selected periodicals also indexed in *Readers' guide to periodical literature* (AD285) and *Humanities index* (BA5). Pt. 2 of each volume lists the collections indexed.

Short story index : collections indexed 1900–1978, ed. by Juliette Yaakov (N.Y. : Wilson, 1979) lists 8,355 collections indexed to that date. Main entry listing with *see* references from titles and joint authors. Serves as a useful bibliography of short stories in English and English translation.   Z5917.S5C6

Critical survey of short fiction / ed. by Frank N. Magill. Rev. ed. Pasadena, Calif. : Salem Pr., 1993. 7 v. (2819, lxvi p.).   **BE261**

Original edition, 1981; Supplement, 1987.

This updated and expanded edition incorporates the 1987 supplement. Includes articles on 348 individual authors, some new to this edition, which now covers authors of detective and science fiction stories. In addition to updated biographical details and bibliographical information, entries now provide expanded analysis, and an annotated secondary bibliography. Vol. 7 contains 12 articles surveying the historical development of the short story, an annotated bibliography of short story criticism, a chronology, and a glossary of terms and techniques. Comprehensive subject index.   PN3321.C7

Hannigan, Francis J. Standard index of short stories, 1900–1914. Boston : Small, [c1918]. 334 p.   **BE262**

An author and title index to stories published in 24 American magazines, 1900–14. Contains some 35,000 entries for stories by about 3,000 authors. Although there is much duplication, it does include titles not found in Dorothy E. Cook and Isabel S. Monro's *Short story index* (BE260) or in *Readers' guide* (AD285).   Z5917.S5H2

Short story criticism. SSC 1– . Detroit : Gale, 1988– . Annual.   **BE263**

A compilation of passages from criticism of short story writers representing all countries and all periods, combined with biographical and bibliographical information. Eight to 20 authors are included in each volume, with excerpts of criticism ranging from four to ten paragraphs drawn from books, articles, and reviews. Criticism is presented in chronological order to reflect the historic critical response to an author's work. The number of excerpts is intended to reflect the relative importance of the writer. Cumulative author and title indexes in successive volumes.   PN3373.S386

Walker, Warren S. Twentieth-century short story explication : interpretations, 1900–1975, of short fiction since 1800. 3rd. ed. Hamden, Conn. : Shoe String Pr., 1977. 880 p.   **BE264**

1st ed., 1961; supplements 1963, 1965; 2nd ed., 1967, supplements 1970, 1973.

A bibliography of interpretations which have appeared since 1900 in books, monographs and periodicals, of short stories published after 1800. Coverage of this edition and its five supplements (publ. 1980–91) is current through 1988. Arranged by author, then by individual story, with checklist of books and journals used at the end of each volume. List of journals and abbreviations for the main volume appear in the 1st supplement. This edition and supplements treat almost 16,700 stories and more than 2,300 authors, including Hispanic, Japanese and Latin American. The explications, regardless of the original language of the stories, are limited to those in the major West European languages. Incorporates the "Annual bibliography of short story explication" from *Studies in short fiction* (v. 1– . Newberry, S.C. : Newberry College. 1963–).

Cumulated index: Warren S. and Barbara K. Walker, *Twentieth-century short story explication : an index to the third edition and its five supplements 1961–1991* (Hamden, Conn. : Shoe String Pr., 1992).

Continued by: Warren S. Walker, *Twentieth-century short story explication: new series* (v. 1 [1989–90]. Hamden, Conn. : Shoe String Pr., 1993), which continues the original series, extending coverage through 1990.   PN3373

Detective and mystery fiction

Albert, Walter. Detective and mystery fiction : an international bibliography of secondary sources. Madison, Ind. : Brownstone Books, 1985. 781 p.   **BE265**

Covering crime, detective, mystery, suspense, and espionage fiction, this international annotated bibliography includes sections on: bibliographies, dictionaries, encyclopedias, and checklists; historical and critical reference works; dime novels, juvenile series and pulps; and a section on authors. Excludes Sherlockiana and materials relating to films, radio, television, and the theater unless these touch on written fiction. Foreign-language works are cited with translated titles. Annotations vary, but are often critical as well as descriptive. Indexed by authors of primary and secondary works, speciality magazines and publishing houses, and series characters, the latter listed by first name. Extensive cross-references to other sources.

Continued in "Murder once removed : a continuing supplement to *Detective and mystery fiction*," *Armchair detective* 20–24 (1987–91). See also *Crime fiction criticism : an annotated bibliography*, ed. by Timothy W. Johnson and Julia Johnson (N.Y. : Garland, 1981). Covers literary criticism on all types of mystery and detective fiction, and on writers of the genre. Annotations for the more than 2,000 entries are descriptive only. PN3448.D4A36

Barzun, Jacques. A catalogue of crime / Jacques Barzun & Wendell Hertig Taylor. Rev. and enl. ed. N.Y. : Harper & Row, c1989. 952 p. **BE266**
1st ed., 1971.

A guide for readers of crime fiction and the literature of true crime, this annotated bibliography lists more than 5,000 entries in the genre, offering critical comments and biographical notes on many authors. Sections include: novels of detection, crime, mystery, and espionage; short stories, collections, anthologies, magazines, pastiches, and plays; studies and histories of the genre, lives of writers, and the literature of the unfinished novel; true crime, covering trials, narratives of cases, criminology and police science, espionage, and cryptography; and the literature of Sherlock Holmes. This edition differs from the first by including more works by established authors, fuller treatment of subgenres, notable single works, and works by Japanese and Continental writers. Unlike the 1st ed., excludes ghost stories and supernatural fiction.

§ A similar work, Susan Oleksiw's *A reader's guide to the classic British mystery* (Boston : G.K. Hall, c1988. Rcpr.: N.Y. : Mysterious Pr., 1989), provides synopses for novels and novellas by 121 British authors published 1900–85. Arranged by author, with works in series listed chronologically by period in which the story is laid. Indexed by character, occupations of series characters, time period, locations outside England, and setting, among others. Z5917.D5B37

Conquest, John. Trouble is their business : private eyes in fiction, film, and television, 1927–1988. N.Y. : Garland, 1990. 497 p. (Garland reference library of the humanities, v. 1151). **BE267**

Lists alphabetically authors and characters in private eye fiction, with cross-references and brief descriptions of characters. A "yellow pages" section lists fictional private eyes by geographical location. Title index.

§ More detailed information may be found in *Encyclopedia of mystery and detection*, Chris Steinbrunner and Otto Penzler, editors in chief (N.Y. : McGraw-Hill, c1976), which includes some 600 articles, primarily on authors but covering a broad range of topics related to mystery fiction and films. The genre is broadly interpreted to include Gothic romance.

See also: *Detectionary : a biographical dictionary of leading characters in detective and mystery fiction, including famous and little-known sleuths, their helpers, rogues, both heroic and sinister, and some of their most memorable adventures, as recounted in novels, short stories, and films*, comp. by Otto Penzler; ed. by Otto Penzler, Chris Steinbrunner and Marvin Lachman (Woodstock, N.Y. : Overlook Pr., 1977). A revised edition of an earlier work by the same title, privately printed in 1972. P96.D4C66

Contento, William. Index to crime and mystery anthologies / William G. Contento with Martin H. Greenberg. Boston : G.K. Hall, c1991. 736 p. **BE268**
A convenient index to crime and mystery stories contained in more than 1,000 anthologies published 1875–1990. Books are listed first by author or editor with full publication information, then by title; stories listed by author, then by title. Complete contents of anthologies are listed under the name of the book author or editor. Publication information for books includes ISBN and price; for stories, length and original publication information. Z2014.F4C58

Cook, Michael L. Mystery, detective, and espionage fiction : a checklist of fiction in U.S. pulp magazines, 1915–1974 / Michael L. Cook and Stephen T. Miller. N.Y. : Garland, 1988. 2 v. (Fiction in the pulp magazines, v. 1 ; Garland reference library of the humanities, v. 838). **BE269**

An index to fiction published in U.S. pulp magazines, as well as a bibliography of the magazines themselves compiled from a survey of collections. Vol. 1 identifies more than 300 magazines alphabetically by title, with a chronological listing of contents, and summary publication information; v. 2 lists stories alphabetically by author.

§ See also: *Monthly murders : a checklist and chronological listing of fiction in the digest-size mystery magazines in the United States and England*, comp. by Michael Cook (Westport, Conn. : Greenwood, 1982). Indexes digest-size mystery magazines, 1941–80. Like the companion work above, it lists magazines and their contents, along with details of publication, followed by an author index. Z1231.D47C66

———— Mystery, detective, and espionage magazines. Westport, Conn. : Greenwood, 1983. 795 p. **BE270**
Intended as a source for the serious study of popular culture. Magazines are presented alphabetically; for each there is a profile giving brief history, characteristics, and content, plus indication of indexing and location sources, bibliographic references to additional information on publication history, and notes on editors, title changes, and physical description. Includes sections of notes on foreign magazines and on book clubs, as well as numerous appendixes. PN3448.D4C56

Hubin, Allen J. Crime fiction II : a comprehensive bibliography, 1749–1990. N.Y. : Garland, 1994. 1568 p. (Garland reference library of the humanities, v. 1353). **BE271**
Cumulates, revises, and supersedes the author's *Crime fiction, 1749–1980: a comprehensive bibliography* (1984) and *1981–1985 supplement to Crime fiction, 1749–1980* (1988).

This edition, which extends coverage through 1990, includes mystery, detective, suspense, thriller, Gothic, police, and spy fiction and films for adults. Limited to English-language works published in book format. Author listing, with title, setting, and series indexes, a series character chronology, and film title, screenwriter, and director indexes. Cites some 81,000 book titles, individual story titles in more than 4,500 collections, and more than 4,500 film titles.

§ Narrower in scope, covering 1841–1969, Ordean Hagen's *Who done it? A guide to detective, mystery and suspense fiction* (N.Y. ; London : Bowker, 1969) complements Hubin. Besides a bibliography of mystery fiction (pt. 1), Hagen includes a bibliographic guide to mystery fiction (pt. 2), consisting of a subject guide, film versions of mystery novels, mystery plays, settings, characters, anthologies and collections, award-winning titles, a bibliography on the mystery novel, and a "murder misellany"—bits of information on organizations and societies, collaborations, pseudonyms, title changes, best sellers, and other details. Spy fiction is dealt with more fully in Myron J. Smith's *Cloak and dagger fiction : an annotated guide to spy thrillers* (Santa Barbara, Calif. : ABC-Clio, 1982). Z2014.F4H83

McCormick, Donald. Spy fiction : a connoisseur's guide / Donald McCormick & Katy Fletcher. N.Y. : Facts on File, c1990. 346 p. **BE272**
1st ed. had title: *Who's who in spy fiction* (London: Elm Tree Books, 1977).

Approximately 200 American and British authors are profiled in articles that include pseudonyms, names of major characters, brief biographical sketches, critical analyses, bibliographies, and filmographies. In two sections: alphabetically-arranged entries and eight essays on the history and critical reception of espionage literature. A glossary, general bibliography, and index conclude the volume.

PN3448.S66M3

Menendez, Albert J. The subject is murder : a selective subject guide to mystery fiction. N.Y. : Garland, 1986–90. 2 v. (Garland reference library of the humanities, v. 627, 1060).   **BE273**

A bibliography of mystery novels published, for the most part, 1950– . Arranged by subject (e.g., Gardening, Academia, Theater, Amnesia). Vol. 2 lists works published since 1985 and adds sections on several new subjects. An appendix to v. 1 lists specialty bookshops. Author index; v. 2 also has a title index.

§ See also: *Murder ... by category : a subject guide to mystery fiction*, by Tasha Mackler (Metuchen, N.J. : Scarecrow, 1991). Organized by subject, most entries are briefly annotated, indicating basic plot and theme. Covers works in print or readily available in libraries, 1985–91. Includes convenient lists of British women mystery writers, female detectives, and a short bibliography. Indexed by author.

           Z1231.D47M46

Niebuhr, Gary Warren. A reader's guide to the private eye novel. N.Y. : G.K. Hall ; N.Y. : Maxwell Macmillan International, c1993. 323 p.   **BE274**

A bibliography of novels, novellas, and collections of short stories and novellas in which the main character is a private detective. 90 authors are listed with descriptions of their works up to and including some from 1992, arranged chronologically by series character; works without a series character follow. Annotations are brief plot summaries rather than reviews. Additional features include lists of pseudonyms; series characters and their creators and vice versa; time periods, by decade, beginning with 1920; locations, settings, and other miscellaneous subjects; and finally, a listing of "One hundred classics and highly recommended titles."   PN3448.D4N54

Twentieth-century crime and mystery writers / ed. by Lesley Henderson. 3rd ed. Chicago : St. James, c1991. 1294 p.   **BE275**

1st ed., 1980; 2nd ed., 1985.

Like other volumes in the "Twentieth-century writers series," this biobibliography offers biographical information, lists of writings, and signed critical assessments; and, for some living writers, personal comments. Covers English-language authors published from the time of Sir Arthur Conan Doyle (roughly the late 1800s) to the present. Bibliographies include works published under pseudonyms, and identify series characters for novels and short story collections. Entries also note available bibliographies, the location of the author's manuscripts, and book-length critical studies. Entries from previous editions have been updated. Appendixes list representative 19th-century writers preceding Doyle, and popular foreign-language writers whose works have appeared in English translation.

§ See also: *Critical survey of mystery and detective fiction : authors*, ed. by Frank N. Magill (Pasadena, Calif. : Salem Pr., 1988. 4 v.) which surveys 270 authors of the genre, expanded to include espionage, police procedurals, psychological thrillers, hard-boiled detective novels, and romantic suspense. Signed entries list biographical details, outline principal series and characters, pinpoint the author's importance to the genre, and analyze the works. Bibliographies identify the author's works in the genre as well as other nonmystery writings, followed by a bibliography of selected critical studies.   PR888.D4T8

Science fiction, fantasy, the Gothic

Anatomy of wonder : a critical guide to science fiction / ed. by Neil Barron. 3rd ed. N.Y. : Bowker, 1987. 874 p.   **BE276**
     1st ed., 1976; 2nd ed., 1981.   Z5917.S36A52

Fantasy literature : a reader's guide / ed. by Neil Barron. N.Y. : Garland, 1990. 586 p. (Garland reference library of the humanities, v.874).   **BE277**
           Z5917.F3F36

Horror literature : a reader's guide / ed. by Neil Barron. N.Y. : Garland, 1990. 596 p. (Garland reference library of the humanities, v.1220).   **BE278**

Three companion guides, similar in format. Signed chapters cover historical periods, research sources, and special topics such as film and television, art and illustration, and magazines. Most chapters include annotated bibliographies and references to other biographical dictionaries and encyclopedias. Each volue concludes with a section listing a recommended core collection, award-winning works, organizations, and works publisherd in series. Author, title, and subject or theme indexes.

The three editions of *Anatomy of wonder* should be retained, since the bibliographic essays are by different contributors. The 3rd ed. enlarges coverage of foreign-language science fiction, including German, French, Russian, Japanese, Italian, Danish, Swedish, Norwegian, Dutch, Belgian, Romanian, Yugoslav, and Hebrew.

§ Still useful but somewhat dated is *The science fiction reference guide : a comprehensive handbook and guide to the history, literature, scholarship, and related activities of the science fiction and fantasy fields*, ed. by Marshall B. Tymn (Mercer Island, Wash. : Starmont House, 1981).   Z5917.H65H67

Bleiler, Everett Franklin. The guide to supernatural fiction. Kent, Ohio : Kent State Univ. Pr., 1983. 723 p.   **BE279**

Subtitle: A full description of 1,775 books from 1750 to 1960, including ghost stories, weird fiction, stories of supernatural horror, fantasy, Gothic novels, occult fiction, and similar literature. With author, title, and motif indexes.

A comprehensive bibliography identifying authors, providing detailed bibliographic information, and giving full plot summaries for books and for stories in collections, with judicious critical comments. Includes both rare and well-known titles. Especially valuable is the index of motifs and story types, each item entered in as many categories as are applicable. Indexed by author and title, including those of individual stories in collections.   PN56.S8B57

———————— Science-fiction, the early years. Kent, Ohio : Kent State Univ. Pr., c1990. 998 p.   **BE280**

Subtitle: A full description of more than 3,000 science-fiction stories from earliest times to the appearance of the genre magazines in 1930. With author, title, and motif indexes.

A major bibliography documenting the literature of science fiction, both books and periodicals. Follows the arrangement of Bleiler's *The guide to supernatural fiction* (BE279); identifies authors, provides detailed bibliographic information, gives full plot summaries with evaluative comments for each title. Bleiler includes extensive annotations for "Background books" which contributed to the rise of science fiction as a genre. Individual titles appear in the motif and theme index under as many catagories as apply. A date index enters first publication dates for books and stories; and for foreign titles, original publication date and the date of translation. Magazine story entries are also indexed by magazine title and year of publication. These latter indexes graphically illustrate publishing trends in the development of the genre.   Z5917.S36B62

Burgess, Michael. Reference guide to science fiction, fantasy, and horror. Englewood, Colo. : Libraries Unlimited, 1992. 403 p.   **BE281**

An annotated bibliography that is among the best and most current. Covers a wide range of reference sources, including encyclopedias and dictionaries, atlases and gazetteers, yearbooks, directories (biographical and literary), guides to criticism, magazine and anthology indexes, numerous bibliographies (general, national, subject, publisher, author, artist), film and television catalogs, calendars and chronologies, price guides, fan guides, professional organizations, key periodicals, and listings of core collections for academic, public, and personal research libraries. Also includes statistical sources, awards, and pseudonym lists. Annotations are full, descriptive, and evaluative. Author, title, and subject indexes.

§ Older but still useful: *A research guide to science fiction studies*, comp. and ed. by Marshall B. Tymn, Roger C. Scholobin, L. W. Currey, with a bibliography of doctoral dissertations by Douglas R.

Justus (N.Y. : Garland, 1977), a selective annotated bibliography of more than 400 sources, including surveys, bibliographies, indexes, subject and author studies and bibliographies, periodicals, and directories. Z5917.S36B87

Clarke, Ignatius Frederick. Tale of the future : from the beginning to the present day. 3rd ed. London : Libr. Assoc., 1978. 357 p. **BE282**

1st ed., 1961; 2nd ed., 1972.

Subtitle: An annotated bibliography of those satires, ideal states, imaginary wars and invasions, coming catastrophes and end-of-the-world stories, political warnings and forecasts, inter-planetary voyages and scientific romances—all located in an imaginary future period—that have been published in the United Kingdom between 1644 and 1976.

A chronological listing with brief annotations. Short-title and author indexes. Scope limited to U.K. publications. Z5917.S36C56

Contento, William. Index to science fiction anthologies and collections. Boston : G.K. Hall, [1978]. 608 p. **BE283**

Covers English-language science fiction anthologies and collections published through 1977. Indexes more than 2,000 book titles with full contents listings for some 1,900 books containing about 12,000 stories by 2,500 authors. In limiting the index to science fiction, Contento excludes works that deal exclusively with horror, the supernatural, or fantasy. Main sections include a list of abbreviations, checklist of books indexed, author and story indexes, and a list of book contents.

Approximately 1,000 additional collections were indexed in: *Index to science fiction anthologies and collections, 1977–1983* (Boston : G.K. Hall, [1984]). The contents listings for anthologies continue in *Science fiction, fantasy & horror* (BE300). Z1231.F4C65

Cottrill, Tim. Science fiction and fantasy series and sequels : a bibliography / Tim Cottrill, Martin H. Greenberg, Charles G. Waugh. N.Y. : Garland, 1986. v. 1. (Garland reference library of the humanities, v. 611). (In progress). **BE284**

Contents: v. 1, Books.

A "comprehensive checklist of publications comprising extended series, two-volume sequences, sequels to an author's original work by other authors, and other multi-volume book formats ... published between 1700 and 1985."—*Foreword.* Arranged alphabetically by author, with a separate section for anthologies. Series title index. Z5917.S36C67

Currey, L. W. Science fiction and fantasy authors : a bibliography of first printings of their fiction and selected nonfiction. Boston : G. K. Hall, c1979. 571 p. **BE285**

For the scholar and the collector of first editions this bibliographic checklist is a standard in the field of science fiction and fantasy. Covers 215 major or important authors from the late 19th century through 1977. Under each author's name are listed all fiction and selected nonfiction with detailed bibliographical descriptions of first editions, first printings, and other significant editions and printings. Where applicable other titles are added for some authors. These include edited books of fiction; translated books of fiction; books by others based on an author's fictional work; nonfiction works on science fiction and fantasy; and bibliographical, biographical, and critical works on the author. Z1231.F5C87

The encyclopedia of science fiction / ed. by John Clute and Peter Nicholls ; contributing ed., Brian Stableford ; technical ed., John Grant. N.Y. : St. Martin's, 1993. 1370 p. **BE286**

1st ed. publ. as *The science fiction encyclopedia* (Garden City, N.Y. : Doubleday, 1979).

Revised and updated, this standard source has grown from 2,800 entries to more than 4,360. Signed entries, contributed by science fiction specialists, cover numerous aspects of the genre, including authors, themes, terminology, films, television, magazines, comics, illustrators, book publishers, original anthologies, awards. Extensive cross-references.

§ See also: *The new encyclopedia of science fiction*, ed. by James Gunn (N.Y. : Viking, 1988) which covers some of the same topics, but far fewer. Gunn specifically excludes fantasy. Categories include personal names (for authors, artists and illustrators, actors, and others); film titles; and essays on selected topics. Lacks cross-references and index.

An important older work is Donald H. Tuck's *The encyclopedia of science fiction and fantasy through 1968 : a bibliographic survey of the fields of science fiction, fantasy, and weird fiction through 1968* (Chicago : Advent Publ., 1974–82? 3 v.). In the "Who's who and works" section (v. 1–2) Tuck identifies the different forms of an author's novels, collections, and anthologies. Vol. 3 gives detailed information on magazines, paperbacks and their publishers, lists of pseudonyms and of connected stories, series, and sequels. PN3433.4E53

Fisher, Benjamin Franklin. The Gothic's Gothic : study aids to the tradition of the tale of terror. N. Y. : Garland, 1988. 485 p. (Garland reference library of the humanities, v. 567). **BE287**

Provides 2,614 citations, some with brief annotations, to biographical and critical books and articles published from the late 18th century until the early 1980s. Includes some material on art. In two sections: (1) Authors, which covers more than 100 British, American, and Canadian authors in alphabetical order; (2) Subjects, which lists citations to topics such as "orientalism" or "vampires." Author/artist/subject, title, and critic indexes. Z5917.G66F57

Frank, Frederick S. The first Gothics : a critical guide to the English Gothic novel. N.Y. : Garland, 1987. 496 p., 14 leaves of plates : ill. (Garland reference library of the humanities, v. 710). **BE288**

A selective primary bibliography of the English Gothic novel from its beginnings in 1764 through its decline in the late 1820s. For 500 titles, alphabetically arranged by author, provides bibliographic information, including modern editions; classification according to type of Gothic; selected references to secondary sources of biographical and critical data; and a detailed critical synopsis. Appendixes: Gothic glossary, selected bibliography of critical sources, and annual chronology for the titles in the bibliography. Indexes of authors, titles, and critics.

§ For the American Gothic, *see* Frank's *Through the pale door : a guide to and through the American Gothic* (Westport, Conn. : Greenwood, 1990), a selective primary bibliography of 509 titles, covering 1786–1988. Follows the arrangement and format of the English Gothic work (above). Appendixes, annual chronology; critical sources on American Gothicism. Indexes: authors and critics; titles; and Gothic themes, motifs, events, character names and settings. Z2014.H67F7

———— Guide to the Gothic : an annotated bibliography of criticism. Metuchen, N.J. : Scarecrow, 1984. 421 p. **BE289**

Includes sections for English, Canadian, American, French, and German Gothic literature, with subdivisions for individual writers. Most entries have descriptive annotations. Also includes a section for various subjects; e.g., Demonological roots of the Gothic, The vampire and vampirism. Index of critics and of authors, artists, and actors.

§ Although the arrangement is different and the entries are not annotated, many of the same items are repeated in Frank's later work *Gothic fiction : a master list of twentieth century criticism and research* (Westport, Conn. : Meckler, c1988). The latter title, however, covers fewer individual English and American Gothic writers, and has no separate listings for individual writers under the French, German, and other national Gothic sections. Z5917.G66F7

Hall, Halbert W. Science fiction book review index : 1923–1973. Detroit : Gale, [1975]. 438 p. **BE290**

This title and its continuations represent cumulations of Hall's *Science fiction book review index: SFBRI* (Bryan, Tex. : H. W. Hall, 1970–1983. 14 v.) and its continuation, *Science fiction and fantasy book review index: SFFBRI* (Bryan, Tex. : SFBRI, 1985– . Annual).

An important reference source that indexes all books reviewed in selected science fiction magazines 1923–73, whether or not they are works of science fiction. For 1970–73, reviews of science fiction books appearing in a selection of non-science fiction magazines are also included. Full information appears in an author listing. Indexed by title. A "Directory of magazines indexed" gives complete bibliographic information on the science fiction magazines, including editors, and changes of title, and tables of issue numbers and dates.

Continued by: *Science fiction book review index, 1974–1979* c1981 and *Science fiction and fantasy book review index, 1980–1984* c1985. The revised and corrected citations originally published in "Science fiction and fantasy research index" in the 1980–84 cumulation now appear in Hall's *Science fiction and fantasy reference index, 1878–1985* (Detroit : Gale, c1987. 2 v.).   Z5917.S36H35

Justice, Keith L. Science fiction, fantasy, and horror reference : an annotated bibliography of works about literature and film. Jefferson, N.C. : McFarland, c1989. 226 p.   **BE291**

Compiled "to help librarians, collectors, researchers, and others with an interest in SF/fantasy/horror reference materials determine what books might be of use or interest to them or their library's patrons."—*Introd.* Provides bibliographic, critical, and evaluative information concerning 304 titles, which are arranged alphabetically by author in topical chapters (e.g., Author studies and bibliographies, Encyclopedias, Comics, or Television, film, and radio). Appendixes cover publications in series and provide a list of suggested core materials. Title and author/editor indexes.

§ In *Reference guide to science fiction, fantasy and horror* (BE281), Michael Burgess comments on significant omissions and on structural problems in Justice's bibliography while noting the length and quality of some of the annotations (p. 75–76).   Z5917.S36J86

McNutt, Dan J. The eighteenth-century Gothic novel : an annotated bibliography of criticism and selected texts. N.Y. : Garland, 1975. 330 p. (Garland reference library of the humanities, 4).   **BE292**

Includes sections on the aesthetic, the literary, and the psychological, social, and scientific background; general history and influence; and specific aspects of the genre. Following these are sections on Horace Walpole, Clara Reeve, Charlotte Turner Smith, Ann Ward Radcliffe, and Matthew Gregory Lewis. Almost 1,200 entries cover scholarly monographs, reviews, and selected dissertations, as well as essays, and important editions of original works.

§ *The English Gothic : a bibliographic guide to writers from Horace Walpole to Mary Shelley* by Robert Donald Spector (Westport, Conn. : Greenwood, 1984) provides bibliographic essays on the genre and the writers treated by McNutt, adding sections on Charles Robert Maturin and Mary Shelley.   Z2014.F5M3

Modern mystery, fantasy, and science fiction writers / comp. and ed. by Bruce Cassiday. N.Y. : Continuum, 1993. 673 p.   **BE293**

A survey of more than 85 major authors of mystery, fantasy, and science fiction, with mostly verbatim excerpts from critiques and reviews of their work. Some excerpts have been edited slightly and some have been shortened. In some cases, excerpts are absent because of failure to obtain copyright clearance. Authors are confined to the 20th century except for a few from the 19th century included because of their importance to the genres. Addressed primarily to schools and the general public. Bibliography of works mentioned in the text, and an index to critics.   PN3503.M526

The N.E.S.F.A. index to short science fiction. 1987– . Cambridge, Mass. : NESFA Pr., c1989– . Annual.   **BE294**

Alternate title: New England Science Fiction Association index to short science fiction.

Continues: *Index to the science fiction magazines, 1926–1950*, ed. by Donald B. Day (Portland, Or. : Perri Pr., [1952]. Rev. ed., Boston : G.K. Hall, 1982); *The MIT Science Fiction Society's index to the s-f magazines, 1951–1965*, comp. by Erwin S. Strauss (Cambridge, Mass. : Erwin S. Strauss, 1965); *Index to the science fiction magazines, 1966–1970* ([Cambridge, Mass.] : New England Science Fiction Assoc., 1971); *The N.E.S.F.A. index to the science fiction magazines and original anthologies* (1971/72–1986 [1984–85 omitted]. Cambridge, Mass. : New England Science Fiction Assoc., 1983–88. 6 v.).

Beginning with Day's index, these titles provide continuous, if somewhat disparate, indexing for science fiction periodicals. The scope of materials included has changed over the years; beginning 1971/72, "original anthologies" were indexed. A note in the 1989 annual (publ. 1992) promises an index for the missing years 1984–85.   Z5917.S36I55

Reader's guide to twentieth-century science fiction / comp. and ed. by Marilyn P. Fletcher ; James L. Thorson, consulting ed. Chicago : Amer. Libr. Assoc., 1989. 673 p.   **BE295**

Concentrates on science fiction writers, giving for each a biographical sketch combined with a discussion of works, themes, and styles, and plot summaries of major works. Each of the more than 125 entries concludes with a section of biographical/bibliographical readings. Appendixes list science fiction magazines and critical journals, and Nebula and Hugo award winners. Indexed by title.

PN3433.8.R44

Reginald, Robert. Science fiction and fantasy literature : a checklist, 1700–1974, with Contemporary science fiction authors II. Detroit : Gale, c1979. 2 v.   **BE296**

An earlier edition of v. 2 was publ. 1974 under title: *Contemporary science fiction authors.*

An important bibliography listing by author almost 16,000 English-language titles in the genres, including weird supernatural fiction. In v. 1, the bibliography proper serves as the author index, and provides complete bibliographical information. Other indexes of the checklist are by title, and by series, with additional indexes of awards and of the Ace and Belmont doubles. Vol. 2 is a biographical directory of science fiction and fantasy writers of the 20th century, similar in format to *Contemporary authors* (AH42), listing name, education, career, awards, memberships, and interests, occasionally with comments supplied by the writer.

For a continuation of the bibliographic checklist *see* Reginald's *Science fiction and fantasy literature, 1975–1991: a bibliography of science fiction, fantasy, and horror fiction books and nonfiction monographs* (Detroit : Gale, c1992). Continues the numbering of the original list, and documents the enormous output of science fiction, fantasy, and horror literature during the 17-year period. The two editions together cover 2,000 authors and some 38,000 unique monographs—15,000 in the first edition and 22,000 in the second.   Z5917.S36R42

Schlobin, Roger C. The literature of fantasy : a comprehensive, annotated bibliography of modern fantasy fiction. N.Y. : Garland, 1979. 425 p. (Garland reference library of the humanities, v. 176).   **BE297**

For this bibliography, "modern" spans the period from the mid-1850s through mid-1979, and is limited to adult fantasy fiction or to juvenile fantasy fiction that appeals to adults. Only prose titles originally published in English in book form are included, except for a few major foreign-language authors who contributed to the Anglo-American literary tradition. In the first section novels and collections are arranged by author, followed by series information with title listings in reading order, and concluding with author bibliographies. The second section identifies anthologies and their contents. Annotations for novels are descriptive with occasional critical comments. Annotations for collections and anthologies are generally limited to a listing of contents. Indexed by author, compiler, editor, and translator, and by title.   Z2014.F4S33

Science fiction & fantasy book review annual. 1988– . N.Y. : Greenwood, 1988– . Annual.   **BE298**

Publisher varies: 1988–89, Westport, Conn. : Meckler.

Directed toward literary historians rather than book collectors. Intended to give a critical overview of science fiction, fantasy, and horror. Approximately 600 short signed reviews of books published in the previous year are arranged alphabetically by author in three sections: fiction, young adult fiction, and nonfiction. Lengthy profiles of specific authors, surveys of publishing trends in the three genres, articles on major trends, recommended reading lists, and lists of award winners precede the general review sections. Title index.

PN3433.8.S35

Science fiction and fantasy reference index, 1878–1985 : an international author and subject index to history and criticism / ed. by H. W. Hall. Detroit : Gale, c1987. 2 v. (1460 p.). **BE299**

Contents: v. 1, Author entries; v. 2, Subject entries.

Draws together and adds to material from previous bibliographies by the same editor, including *Science fiction and fantasy book review index* (1923–1973; 1974–1979; 1980–1984) and *Science fiction and fantasy research index* (Bryan, Tex. : SFBRI, 1980–84). Has become the standard guide to the secondary literature in science fiction, fantasy, and horror. Indexes some 19,000 books, articles, news reports and audiovisual works by author and subject. Although the material dates from 1878, the primary emphasis is on the period from 1945 through 1985. English-language materials predominate but other non-English criticism is represented, notably French, German, and Italian.

§ There is some overlap with *The year's scholarship in science fiction and fantasy* (BE310). Hall's work, however, is considerably more comprehensive, and has been extended by his *Science fiction and fantasy reference index, 1985–1991: an international author and subject index to history and criticism* (Englewood, Colo. : Libraries Unlimited, 1993). Z5917.S36S297

Science fiction, fantasy & horror. 1986– . Oakland, Calif. : Locus Pr. ; Westport, Conn. : Meckler Corp., c1987– . Annual. **BE300**

Editors: Charles N. Brown and William G. Contento.

Vol. for 1984 published 1990; vol. for 1985 had title *Science fiction in print: 1985* by Charles N. Brown (Oakland, Calif.: Locus Pr., 1986).

Intended to supplement Contento's *Index to science fiction anthologies and collections* (BE283). Based on a monthly column in *Locus* magazine, this index lists American and British books and short stories in seven sections: books arranged by author and title; new publications in all formats, by author; subjects/formats, by author; short stories, by author and title; and contents lists for anthologies and individual magazine issues. Appendixes include statistical summaries of science fiction publishing, recommended reading, awards, necrology, and a directory of publishers. Z131.F4 C65

Science fiction in America, 1870s–1930s : an annotated bibliography of primary sources / comp. by Thomas D. Clareson. Westport, Conn. : Greenwood, c1984. 305 p. (Bibliographies and indexes in American literature, no. 1). **BE301**

A compilation of more than 800 extensively annotated entries for works that marked the emergence of modern science fiction. Emphasizes American editions, but includes British and continental writers. Clareson attempts "to show in some detail the variety of responses to science between the 1870s and 1930s made by writers who used some aspect of the new sciences as a basis for their fantasy or extrapolations."—*Introd.*

§ Earlier, Clareson produced *Science fiction criticism : an annotated checklist* ([Kent, Ohio] : Kent State Univ. Pr., [1972]), listing both books and periodical articles, the latter excluding materials from science fiction "fanzines" unless the article appeared later in book form. Now dated, the checklist documents the critical reception of the genre for the period. Z1231.F4S38

Summers, Montague. A Gothic bibliography. London : Fortune Pr. ; N.Y. : Columbia Univ. Pr., 1941. 621 p. : ill. **BE302**

Repr. : N.Y. : Russell & Russell, 1964.

Contents: Index of authors, p. 1–219; Title index, p. 220–568; Addenda, p. 569–620.

One of the first major primary bibliographies of the Gothic novel, 1728–1916. Usually omits well-known writers for whom there are already standard bibliographies. Often includes titles other than Gothics. There are some peculiarities of arrangement, inclusion and exclusion, and questionable attributions of anonymous works. Some works listed have not survived, and the bibliographic information may be incomplete. In addition to English Gothics, Summers includes French, German, and other foreign Gothics, some in English translation. Nevertheless, an important bibliography for researchers. Z2014.F4S9

Supernatural fiction writers : fantasy and horror / E.F. Bleiler, ed. N.Y. : Scribner, c1985. 2 v. (1169 p.). **BE303**

Similar in scope and authoritativeness to Bleiler's *Science fiction writers: critical studies of the major authors from the early nineteenth century to the present day* (N.Y. : Scribner, c1982). Presents signed chapters on some 150 authors, mostly British, American, French, and German, beginning in the earliest times with Apuleius and continuing into the modern period. Includes authors not primarily known for this genre; for example, James Thurber and Edith Wharton. Chapters include biographical and critical information, as well as selected primary and secondary bibliographies. General index.

Science fiction writers spans a shorter time period and covers only about half the number of authors. But Bleiler, who established a high level of critical content in the earlier title, maintains it in the second. Although most of the writers are British and American (grouped by period), three Continental authors are also included. Indexed by author and title.

§ For biographical information on artists of the genres, *see* Robert E. Weinberg's *A biographical dictionary of science fiction and fantasy artists* (N.Y. : Greenwood, 1988). PN3435.S96

Survey of modern fantasy literature / ed. by Frank N. Magill. Englewood Cliffs, N.J. : Salem Pr., c1983. 5 v. (2538, li p.). **BE304**

Defines the genre broadly to include "high fantasy, low fantasy, horror, Gothic fantasy, science fantasy, psychological fantasy, avant-garde experiments, and various unclassified fantastic works."—*Pref.* Offers about 500 signed essay reviews comprised of synopses, background notes, and critical commentary, arranged by title of the work. Vol. 4 contains essays on the short fiction of 33 individual authors; v. 5 concludes with a list of essays on various topics, including one on contemporary theories of fantasy. A chronology of modern fantasy literature extends from 1764 through 1981. Other features include annotated bibliographies of general and specific books on the genre, and of fantasy anthologies.

§ Diana Waggoner's *The hills of faraway : a guide to fantasy* (N.Y. : Atheneum, 1978. 326 p.) offers chapters on the theory of fantasy and trends in fantasy literature, followed by a bibliographic guide to the genre. PN56.F34S97

Survey of science fiction literature / ed. by Frank N. Magill. Englewood Cliffs, N.J. : Salem Pr., c1979. 5 v. **BE305**

Subtitle: Five hundred 2,000-word essay reviews of world-famous science fiction novels with 2,500 bibliographical references.

A compilation of signed review articles arranged by title covering more than 500 titles by 280 authors, including about 90 foreign-language works representing some 20 countries. Follows the format of other titles by Magill; entries combine plot summary with commentary and a brief bibliography.

———. *Bibliographical supplement* (1982), ed. by Magill, bibliographies comp. by Marshall B. Tymn. Keyed to articles in the basic work. PN3448.S45S88

Twentieth-century science-fiction writers / ed., Curtis C. Smith. 2nd ed. Chicago : St. James Pr., 1986. 933 p. **BE306**

1st ed., 1981.

A biobibliography featuring 20th-century English-language writers of science fiction, with a few major writers from earlier periods. A separate appendix treats 32 representative foreign-language authors whose works have also appeared in English translation.

Entries consist of a biographical sketch, noting pseudonyms; a bibliography of science fiction works and of other publications, with separate listings for works written under pseudonym; and a signed critical essay. Some authors have added their own comments. Bibliographies identify series characters for novels and short story collections. Entries note secondary bibliographies and other critical studies, and the location of manuscript collections. PS374.S35T89

Tymn, Marshall B. Science fiction, fantasy, and weird fiction magazines / ed. by Marshall B. Tymn and Mike Ashley. Westport, Conn. : Greenwood, 1985. 970 p. **BE307**

The main section, English-language magazines, offers signed profiles of the magazines with publication history and references to additional sources of information (including index sources, reprints, and library locations). Additional sections for: Associational English-language anthologies, Academic periodicals and major fanzines, and Non-English language magazines, by country. Chronology; bibliography; index.

§ An earlier title, Halbert W. Hall's *Science fiction magazines* (San Bernardino, Calif. : Borgo Pr., 1984), based on the collection at Texas A&M, provides publication, volumes and numbering, and indexing information for English and American magazines, with an editor index and an appendix of non-English language titles. PN3433.T9

Versins, Pierre. Encyclopédie de l'utopie, des voyages extraordinaires, et de la science fiction. [2nd ed.]. [Lausanne] : L'Age d'Homme, 1984. 1037 p. : ill.   **BE308**
Spine title: *Encyclopédie de l'utopie et de la science fiction.*
1st ed., 1972.
This illustrated French-language encyclopedia provides the most complete coverage of European science fiction and fantasy. Entries, arranged alphabetically, include numerous biographies of writers and illustrators, both American and European, characters, terms, topics, and themes in Utopian and science fiction. Articles on writers in these genres concentrate on their contributions and influence in the field. Writers' works with initial publication date are cited, with most titles translated into French, but there is no bibliography other than the table of sources of illustrations which gives citations to several hundred publications.   PN3448.S45V4

Wolfe, Gary K. Critical terms for science fiction and fantasy : a glossary and guide to scholarship. N.Y. : Greenwood, 1986. 162 p.   **BE309**
The first literary glossary specific to the critical study of science fiction and fantasy. An introduction, Fantastic literature and literary discourse, provides an insightful and lengthy overview of the discipline and its historical evolution. The glossary consists of some 500 terms drawn from the writings of critics and of science fiction writers, and from the scholarly vocabulary of literature and related disciplines. Definitions vary in length from several sentences to a page or more and are well documented from 218 scholarly resources, as well as with citations from other titles. Numerous cross-references. Indexed by the names of authors whose works are used as examples in the text.
PN3435.W64

The year's scholarship in science fiction and fantasy. Kent, Ohio : Kent State Univ. Pr., c1979–c1982. 2 v. (Serif series, bibliographies and checklists, 36, 41).   **BE310**
Editors: Marshall B. Tymn and Roger C. Schlobin.
Contents: [v. 1], 1972–75; [v. 2], 1976–79.
Cumulations and revisions of annual annotated bibliographies of secondary literature in science fiction and fantasy published in the journal *Extrapolation.* These bibliographies were intended to supplement Thomas D. Clareson's *Science fiction criticism : an annotated checklist* (BE301 *note*). Scope is meant to be comprehensive for American scholarship, selective for British. Includes books, dissertations, articles, scholarly reprints, and instructional audivisual materials; book reviews are excluded. Indexed.
Continued by an annual bibliography, *The year's scholarship in science fiction, fantasy and horror literature*, ed. by Tymn (1980–82. Kent, Ohio, [1983–84]. 3 v.). Publication was then assumed by *Extrapolation*, which published annual bibliographies as "The year's scholarship in science fiction, fantasy, and horror literature" for 1983–84 (v. 26, no. 2 [Summer 1985]: 85–142 and no. 4 [Winter 1985]: 316–380) and for 1985–87 (Fall issues, v. 27 [1986]–v. 29 [1988]). Subsequent bibliographies have been published as "The year's scholarship in fantastic literature and the arts," 1988– , in *Journal of the fantastic in the arts* (1990–).

Poetry

Bibliography

Brogan, Terry V. F. Verseform : a comparative bibliography. Baltimore : Johns Hopkins Univ. Pr., 1989. 122 p.   **BE311**
Updates the author's *English versification, 1570–1980* (BE696), by expanding coverage internationally. Whereas the earlier work provided evaluative annotations and attempted to be comprehensive for studies of English versification, the new is an unannotated bibliography that lists "the standard and best studies of poetic form in all the major languages of the world ...."—*Pref.* In two parts: (1) structures, devices, forms (e.g., sound patterning, stanza forms, rhythm, and visual prosody); (2) verse system (e.g., Greek and Latin, English, African, etc.). Numerous cross-references. Index of scholars. Review: *English studies* 73:4 (August 1992): 354.   Z7156.V6B76

Critical survey of poetry : English language series / ed. by Frank N. Magill. Rev. ed. Pasadena, Calif. : Salem Pr., c1992. 8 v. (4090, xcv p.).   **BE312**
1st ed., 1982.
Arranged alphabetically by author. Provides biocritical essays for 368 English-language poets from the time of Beowulf to the present. Essays list principal poetry and work in other genres, include sections for achievements, biography, and analysis, and provide highly selective secondary bibliographies. Vol. 8 contains 22 overview essays (including essays on the oral tradition, various periods and critical schools, the poetry of various minority traditions, and approaches to explication). Also in v. 8: glossary of poetic terminology, an index for stanza poems, and a detailed index for the set.
Companion series: *Critical survey of poetry : Foreign language series*, ed. Frank N. Magill (c1984. 5 v.). Biocritical essays for "197 poets whose works have had an important influence on the literature of their native language."—*Pref.* International in scope, including poets from all periods. Vol. 5 contains background essays and an index for the set.   PR502.C85

McCullough, Kathleen. Concrete poetry : an annotated international bibliography, with an index of poets and poems. Troy, N.Y. : Whitston Publ. Co., 1989. 1010 p.   **BE313**
Arranged by main entry. Covers primary and secondary materials drawn from monographic works published from the mid-1950s through the first half of 1985, including "anthologies, collections, conference papers, criticism, dissertations, exhibition catalogs, history, and independent publication of individual poems"—*Introd.* Analyzed entries are provided for anthologies. Separate indexes for titles and subjects, poem titles, books, and independently published poems by language and by date. "The most comprehensive bibliography of concrete poetry to date."—*Choice* 27:4 (Dec. 1989): 613.
Z7156.C64M33

Indexes

Guy, Patricia A. Women's poetry index. Phoenix : Oryx, 1985. 174 p.   **BE314**
Compiled because standard indexes such as *Columbia Granger's index to poetry* (BE315) offer limited access to poems by women. Indexes poems written in English or translated into English in 51 anthologies which are either in print or available in many libraries. In three main parts: (1) Author index; (2) Title index, (3) First line index.
PN1024.G89

Hazen, Edith P. The Columbia Granger's index to poetry. 10th ed., completely rev., indexing anthologies published through June 3, 1993. N.Y. : Columbia Univ. Pr., c1994. 2150 p.   **BE315**
1st ed., 1904; 9th ed., 1990. Supplements issued periodically.

Early editions ed. by Edith Granger.

A very useful index, important in public, college, and school libraries since it indexes a large number of standard and popular collections of poetry (the 1st–3rd editions also indexed prose selections). Beginning with the 4th ed., title and first-line indexes are combined, followed by author and subject indexes. The 7th ed. departed from the cumulative pattern of the 2nd–6th eds., indexing only anthologies of the 1970–81 period.

New to this edition is the inclusion of dates for authors and the indexing of the last lines (designated "LL") of "the 12,500 poems that have been anthologized most frequently"—*Pref*. In total, this edition indexes 79,000 poems by some 11,000 authors collected in 400 anthologies. As with earlier editions, 150 anthologies have been dropped and 150 new anthologies have been added. The 10th ed. includes fewer collections translated from languages other than English than did the 9th.

§ A companion volume to the 10th ed., *The Columbia Granger's guide to poetry anthologies*, ed. by William Katz, Linda Sternberg Katz and Esther Crain (2nd ed. N.Y. : Columbia Univ. Pr., 1994) groups collections in chapters devoted to particular topics or regions. Entries are annotated. Appendixes list recommended titles; general index.

•Available in machine-readable form as: *Columbia Granger's world of poetry on CD-ROM* [database] (N.Y. : Columbia Univ. Pr.). Incorporates the 8th and 9th eds. of the printed index, the *Guide to poetry anthologies* (above), and *The Columbia Granger's dictionary of poetry quotations*, ed. by Edith P. Hazen (N.Y. : Columbia Univ. Pr., 1992. 1132 p.). The CD-ROM also reproduces the complete text of some 8,500 well-known poems. A new edition of the CD-ROM is scheduled for spring 1995. PN1022.H39

Hoffman, Herbert H. Hoffman's index to poetry : European and Latin American poetry in anthologies. Metuchen, N.J. : Scarecrow, 1985. 672 p. **BE316**

Intended to serve as a non-English language supplement to *Granger's index to poetry* (now *Columbia Granger's index to poetry*, BE315). Indexes 110 anthologies by author, title, and first line (the latter subdivided by language: French, German, Italian, Polish, Portuguese, Russian, and Spanish). Citations to anthologies appear in the author section. PN1022.H627

Kline, Victoria. Last lines : an index to the last lines of poetry. N.Y. : Facts on File, 1991. 2 v. (2829 p.). **BE317**

Contents: v. 1, Last line index and title index; v. 2 Author index and keyword index.

A useful reference source intended to serve as a companion to *The Columbia Granger's index to poetry* (BE315). Indexes the last lines of approximately 171,000 poems published in anthologies, 1900–87 (including the same 405 anthologies of *Granger's* 8th ed., 74 "classic" anthologies from *Granger's* 6th ed., and 18 significant anthologies published 1985–87). The keyword index is a list of important words in the titles and last lines of the poems indexed. Review: *Choice* 29 : 7 (March 1992) : 1209. PN1022.K55

Marcan, Peter. Poetry themes : a bibliographical index to subject anthologies and related criticism in the English language, 1875–1975. London : Clive Bingley ; Hamden, Conn. : Linnet Books, 1977. 301 p. **BE318**

Intends to index "subject anthologies which bring together poetry on one subject or a group of related subjects."—*Introd*. Includes some anthologies of poetry and prose. Critical literature (books, periodical articles, academic theses) is also listed as being useful for bibliographies and footnote references providing sources for thematic and comparative studies. Arranged according to a classification scheme outlined on p. x–xvi, but there is no alphabetical subject index. Brief notes regarding coverage, period, emphasis, etc., frequently follow the bibliographic citations; studies and criticism are separately listed within each subject category. Index of authors and compilers. Anthologies indexed are mainly British imprints. PN1022.M3

Master index to poetry / prep. by the Editorial Board, Roth Publishing, Inc. 2nd ed., enl. & rev. Great Neck, N.Y. : Roth Publ., c1992. 1939 p. **BE319**

1st ed., 1988.

Subtitle: A companion index to poetry in anthologies and collections for CoreFiche, anthologies listed in "Granger's index to poetry" plus, phases I–III : an access by author and translator, title, and first line to poems in 1,360 volumes.

Indexes approximately 140,000 poems by more than 20,000 poets, drawn from some 1,300 anthologies and single-author collections that are reproduced in *CoreFiche : poetry in Granger* [microform] ([Great Neck, N.Y. : Core Collection Micropublications], 1985–). Provides index files by author, translator, poem title, and first line, and a cumulative index by title and author of works reproduced in *CoreFiche*. Poems appearing in more than one anthology are now indexed only once.

Although intended as an index to the microfiche set, *Master index* is useful as a poetry index in its own right; besides indexing poems in the collections indexed by *Columbia Granger's index to poetry* (BE315), it indexes collections from other standard poetry indexes—e.g., Roth's own *Poetry index annual* (BE321). Review of the 1st ed.: *American reference books annual* 21 (1990): 475.

•Machine-readable version: *CD CoreWorks* [database] (Great Neck, N.Y. : Roth Publ., 1990). Available in CD-ROM. Includes, besides *Master index to poetry*, the following indexes publ. by Roth: *Roth's essay index; Roth's index to short stories*; and *World's best drama index*. The initial release of this CD-ROM has been faulted as cumbersome and confusing (*CD-ROM professional*, 4:6 [Nov. 1991]: 121). *See also* Roth's *Poem finder on disc* (BE320). PN1022.M37

•**Poem finder on disc** [database]. Great Neck, N.Y. : Roth Publ., 1992– . **BE320**

Available on CD-ROM.

A machine-readable index of more than 360,000 poems in English or in English translation dating from antiquity to the present. Indexes 1,600 anthologies, 2,100 single-author collections, and more than 100 periodical titles. The 1994 release features new software that permits Boolean and combined set searching, "... including searches by subject, author, translator, poem title, book or periodical title, and first line or last line."—*Publisher's brochure*.

Poetry index annual. 1982–93– . Great Neck, N.Y. : Granger Book Co., c1982–93. Annual. **BE321**

Subtitle: A title, author, and subject index to poetry in anthologies.

Each volume systematically indexed anthologies of poetry in English or translated into English published during the preceding year. The main index included authors, titles, first lines, and translators. Beginning with 1988, a separate keyword subject index listed significant title words; prior to that date, the more inclusive subject indexing was incorporated into the main index. The volume for 1992 provides a cumulative list of the 511 anthologies indexed 1982–91. PN1022.P63

Subject index to poetry for children and young people / comp. by Violet Sell ... [et al.]. Chicago : Amer. Libr. Assoc., 1957. 582 p. **BE322**

Repr. : Great Neck, N.Y. : Core Collection Books, 1982.

Indexes 157 collections and anthologies. Subject headings were "chosen on the basis of children's and young people's needs and interests...."—*Pref*.

Supplemented by: Dorothy B. Frizzell Smith and Eva L. Andrews, *Subject index to poetry for children and young people : 1957–1975* (Chicago : Amer. Libr. Assoc., 1977. 1035 p.). Indexes an additional 263 anthologies. PN1023.A5

Sound recordings

Hoffman, Herbert H. International index to recorded poetry / comp. by Herbert H. Hoffman, Rita Ludwig Hoffman. N.Y. : H.W. Wilson Co., 1983. xlvi, 529 p. **BE323**

The work "identifies and indexes—by author, title, first line, and reader—the contents of more than 1,700 recordings issued up through 1981 in the United States and abroad: some 15,000 poems by approximately 2,300 authors, read in upwards of twenty languages on phonodiscs, tapes, audio cassettes, film strips, and video cassettes."—*Pref.*

§ Still valuable for evaluative discussions of selected recordings is: Helen Pauline Roach, *Spoken records* (3rd ed. Metuchen, N.J. : Scarecrow, 1970).   PN1022.H63

Library of Congress. Poetry Office. Literary recordings : a checklist of the Archive of Recorded Poetry and Literature in the Library of Congress / comp. by Jennifer Whittington. Rev., enl. ed. Wash. : The Library : for sale by the U.S. Govt. Print. Off., 1981. 299 p.   **BE324**
    Previous ed., 1966.
    An inventory of the Archive's holdings through May 1975, listing recordings of nearly a thousand poets reading their own work. "It includes recordings of poetry readings and other literary events held in the Library's Coolidge Auditorium or the Whittall Pavilion, tapes of poets reading their poems in the Recording Laboratory or elsewhere for the archive, and recordings received through occasional gifts, exchanges, or purchases."—*Pref.*   PS306.5.Z9U53

Criticism

Poetry criticism : excerpts from criticism of the works of the most significant and widely studied poets of world literature. v. 1– . Detroit : Gale, c1991– .   **BE325**
    Similar in format to Gale's other genre-oriented series, *Short story criticism* (BE263) and *Drama criticism* (BE224). Designed to provide "...substantial critical excerpts and biographical information on the world's most frequently discussed poets...."—*Pref.* Each author entry includes a biographical and critical introduction, a portrait (when available), a list of principal works, critical excerpts (arranged chronologically to emphasize critical reception), and a list of suggested readings. Excerpts are prefaced with an explanatory note to provide critical context. Each volume contains a cumulative author index (with cross-references to the various Gale series), a cumulative nationality index for poets featured in *PC*, and a cumulative title index of individual poems, book-length poems, and collection titles. Approximately 250 poets are projected to be included.   PN1010.P499

Encyclopedias; Dictionaries

Deutsch, Babette. Poetry handbook : a dictionary of terms. 4th ed. N.Y. : Funk & Wagnalls, [1974]. 203 p.   **BE326**
    1st ed., 1957.
    A useful handbook for the student and practitioner.
    § Also helpful for providing numerous examples of stanza patterns and poetic forms are the following: Lewis Turco, *The new book of forms : a handbook of poetics* (Hanover, N.H. : Univ. Pr. of New England, 1986. 280 p.); Miller Williams, *Patterns of poetry : an encyclopedia of forms* (Baton Rouge : Louisiana State Univ. Pr., c1986. 203 p.).   PN44.5.D4

Morier, Henri. Dictionnaire de poétique et de rhétorique. 4e éd. rev. et augm. Paris : Presses Universitaires de France, 1989. 1320 p. ; [4] folded leaves of plates : ill.   **BE327**
    1st ed., 1961; 3rd ed., 1981.
    A dictionary of terms in modern poetry and rhetoric. Runs heavily to long, detailed articles, with numerous examples of use, and charts, diagrams, etc. to illustrate specific points. Particular attention is given to phonetics.   PN1021.M6

Myers, Jack Elliott. The Longman dictionary of poetic terms / Jack Myers, Michael Simms. N.Y. : Longman, c1989. 366 p.
                                                        BE328

An unacknowledged reprint of *Longman dictionary and handbook of poetry* (N.Y. : Longman, 1985). A review of the latter in *Review of English studies* n.s. 40, no. 159 (Aug. 1989): 398–99 notes its limitations. Errors in the original are repeated in the reprint.
    Attempts "to define a critical vocabulary for the poet and the student of poetry," and claims to be "the most comprehensive list of poetic terms that has yet been compiled."—*Pref.* Includes a number of essays of substantial length. Excerpts from poems illustrate many of the terms defined. The appendixes group the terms topically or according to type of rhetorical or poetical device.   PN1042.M94

The new Princeton encyclopedia of poetry and poetics / Alex Preminger and T. V. F. Brogan, co-editors. Rev. ed. Princeton, N.J. : Princeton Univ. Pr., 1993. 1383 p.   **BE329**
    1st ed., 1965 (*Encyclopedia of poetry and poetics*); enl. ed., 1974 (*Princeton encyclopedia of poetry and poetics*).
    Represents a thorough revision of this standard, authoritative encyclopedia. "It provides surveys of 106 national poetries; descriptions of poetic forms and genres major and minor, traditional and emergent; detailed explanations of the devices of prosody and rhetoric; ... overviews of all major schools of poetry ancient and modern, Western and Eastern ... accounts of the major movements and issues in criticism and literary theory, and discussion of the manifold relations of poetry to the other fields of human thought and activity."—*Pref.*
    Entries have been revised, and 162 added to encompass recent theoretical movements and emergent and non-Western poetries. Bibliographies have been revised and expanded, and the number of cross-references expanded. One review points out that a personal name index would help locate specific poets and critics.—*Choice* 31:2 (Oct. 1993): 271. Nonetheless, an indispensable reference work.
    § *The Princeton handbook of poetic terms*, ed. Alex Preminger, Frank J. Warnke, and O. B. Hardison, Jr. (1986) provides a selection of entries from the rev. ed. of the *Encyclopedia* (1974), some of which are revised, and is intended to be a compact and affordable handbook of poetic terminology.   PN1021.N39

Packard, William. The poet's dictionary : a handbook of prosody and poetic devices. N.Y. : Harper & Row, c1989. 221 p.   **BE330**
    Intended for the practicing writer, this handbook describes and gives examples of various meters, techniques, and forms. An appendix lists guidelines for submitting manuscript copy for publication; selected bibliography.   PN44.5.P3

Handbooks

Poet's market. 1986– . Cincinnati, Ohio : Writer's Digest Books, c1985– . Annual.   **BE331**
    Useful for those aspiring to publish their poems in literary journals and magazines. The 1992 issue lists more than 1,700 publishers of poetry. Entries include a brief journal profile, submission requirements, and contact information. Offers advice to beginning poets on getting published, brief articles by working poets/editors, grant information, contests and awards, poetry readings, writing colonies, organizations and publications useful to poets. Indexes for chapbook publishers, publishers by subject, publishers by state, and a general index.
                                                        PN1059.M3P59

Anthologies

The Norton anthology of modern poetry / ed. by Richard Ellmann and Robert O'Clair. 2nd ed. N.Y. : Norton, c1988. 1865 p.   **BE332**
    1st ed., 1973.
    A critical anthology of 180 poets (predominately English and American) and of 1580 poems. Coverage begins with poets writing in the second part of the 19th century. Provides substantial introductions and critical notes; includes a selective bibliography. Title index.

§ *The Heath anthology of American literature* (BE441) and *The Norton anthology of American literature* (BE442) cover other periods of American poetry. See also *The Norton anthology of English literature* (BE619) and *The Oxford anthology of English literature* (BE618).

PS613.N67

Biography

Bold, Alan Norman. Longman dictionary of poets : the lives and works of 1001 poets in the English language. Burnt Mill, England : Longman, 1985. 314 p. **BE333**
Brief entries include nationality, birthplace, dates, biographical details, and an illustrative quotation from the poetry. PR106.B65

Contemporary poets / ed., Tracy Chevalier. 5th ed. Chicago : St. James Pr., c1991. 1179 p. **BE334**
1st ed., 1970, had title: *Contemporary poets of the English language*; 4th ed., 1985.
Provides biobibliographical information on more than 1,000 poets currently writing in the English language, chosen by their peers and editors. The signed entries, arranged alphabetically, include biographical sketches, addresses, bibliographies of first editions, sound recordings, other publications (e.g., novels or essays), and lists of critical studies. Some entries give locations of manuscript collections. Title index. PR603.C6

Romances, Epics, etc.

Bibliography

British Museum. Dept. of Manuscripts. Catalogue of romances in the Department of Manuscripts in the British Museum. London : Trustees, 1883–1910. 3 v. **BE335**
Repr., 1961–62.
v. 1–2, by H. L. D. Ward; v. 3, by J. A. Herbert.
Vol. 1 treats classical romances (the cycles of Troy and Alexander, along with other classical subjects), British and English traditions (Arthurian cycles, etc.), French traditions (Charlemagne, etc.), miscellaneous romances, and allegorical and didactic romances. Vol. 2 covers Northern legends and tales, Eastern legends and tales, Aesopic fables, Reynard the Fox, visions of heaven and hell, Les Trois Pèlerinages, and miracles of the Virgin. Vol. 3 includes exempla and moralized tales in prose, exempla in verse, and collected tales. Entries provide, in addition to a description of the manuscript, a summary account of the tale, reference to variants, description of its authorship, history, etc., references to printed texts, and critical commentary.
Z6621.B87R7

Coleman, Arthur. Epic and romance criticism. N.Y. : Watermill, 1973–1974. 2 v. **BE336**
Contents: v. 1, A checklist of interpretations, 1940–72, of English and American epics and metrical romances; v. 2, A checklist of interpretations, 1940–73, of classical and continental epics and metrical romances.
A selective, unannotated bibliography of approximately 20,000 English-language books, pamphlets, festschriften, and articles; arranged by title of the work. "Epic" is defined broadly to include modern works like Pound's *Cantos* and Ginsberg's *Howl*. Lacks an index of scholars. A useful compilation, although numerous errors and omissions have been noted. Review: *Literary research newsletter* 1:3 (July 1976): 117–121. Z7156.E6C64

Esdaile, Arundell James Kennedy. List of English tales and prose romances printed before 1740. London : pr. for the Bibliographical Society by Blades, East and Blades, 1912. 329 p. **BE337**

Repr.: [Folcroft, Pa.] : Folcroft Pr., 1974.
Contents: pt. 1, 1475–1642; pt. 2, 1643–1739.
Each part is arranged alphabetically by author and title, with plentiful cross-references. Gives full title and imprint, list of editions, libraries in which copies were seen, and bibliographies in which the work is described. Scope of list includes both English tales and English translations of foreign works. Notes are bibliographical, not critical. Of value to the specialist, the bibliographer, and the cataloger.
Z6511.E83

International Arthurian Society. Bulletin bibliographique de la Société internationale arthurienne = Bibliographical bulletin of the International Arthurian Society. v. 1 (1949)– . Paris : the Society, 1949– . Annual. **BE338**
An annual international bibliography arranged in sections by nationality, with the sections subdivided as follows: 1, texts, translations, and adaptations; 2, critical and historical studies; 3, reviews; 4, reprints; and 5, theses. Many entries are descriptively annotated. Index of scholars and of subjects. For a cumulation see Cedric E. Pickford, *The Arthurian bibliography* (BE339). Z8045.I5

Pickford, Cedric Edward. The Arthurian bibliography / ed. by Cedric E. Pickford and Rex Last ; assistant ed., Christine R. Barker. Cambridge, Eng. : D.S. Brewer ; Totowa, N.J. : Biblio, 1981–83. 2 v. **BE339**
Contents: v. 1, Author listing; v. 2, Subject index.
A cumulative bibliography that merges a number of separate Arthurian bibliographies (cf. p. xiv–xvi for a complete listing), among them the annual bibliographies appearing in *Modern language quarterly* (1940–63, v. 1 [1940] cumulating 1936–39) and in *Bulletin bibliographique de la Société Internationale Arthurienne* (1949–79; BE338), and the following separately published bibliographies: John J. Parry, *A bibliography of critical Arthurian literature for the years 1922–1929* (N.Y. : Modern Language Assoc., 1929), and John J. Parry and Margaret A. Schlauch, *A bibliography of critical Arthurian literature for the years 1930–1935* (N.Y. : Modern Language Assoc. of America, 1936). Z8045.P53

Reiss, Edmund. Arthurian legend and literature : an annotated bibliography / Edmund Reiss, Louis Horner Reiss, Beverly Taylor. N.Y. : Garland, 1984. v. 1. (Garland reference library of the humanities, v. 415). (In progress). **BE340**
Contents: v. 1, The middle ages.
An international, selective, annotated bibliography of editions, English-language translations, and critical scholarship. Covers early 19th century to 1982, and includes "...Arthurian works from the sixth through the fifteenth century, noting sixteenth-century (and later) versions of earlier works when they are not significantly different from their medieval source."—*Pref.* In a classified arrangement with appendixes for chivalry and courtly love, and a listing of Arthurian works by language. Indexes: Arthurian writers/works; subjects; scholars. Reviews: *Speculum* 61:4 (Oct. 1986): 991–92; *Romance philology* 40:1 (Aug. 1986): 123–26.
A second volume covering Renaissance to the present is in progress.
§ For an annotated bibliography of editions and scholarship limited to Malory and *Morte Darthur* see Page West Life, *Sir Thomas Malory and the Morte Darthur : a survey of scholarship and annotated bibliography* (Charlottesville : publ. for the Bibliographical Soc. of the Univ. of Virginia by the Univ. Pr. of Virginia, 1980. 297 p.).
Z8045.R45

Encyclopedias; Dictionaries

Guerber, H.A. The book of the epic : the world's great epics told in story. Philadelphia ; London : Lippincott, 1913. 493 p. : ill. **BE341**
Repr.: N.Y. : Biblo & Tannen, 1966.
Gives synopses of the stories of the great Greek, Latin, French, Spanish, Portuguese, Italian, British, German, Dutch, Scandinavian,

Russian and Finnish, Balkan, Hebrew and Early Christian, Arabian and Persian, Indian, Chinese and Japanese, and American epics.

PN683.G8

Lacy, Norris J. The Arthurian handbook / Norris J. Lacy, Geoffrey Ashe. N.Y. : Garland, 1988. 455 p. : ill. (Garland reference library of the humanities, v. 765). **BE342**

A survey of the Arthurian legend, treating "all periods, from the fifth and sixth centuries through the Middle Ages, and to the present, examining Arthurian origins, the development of the legend in chronicles and other sources, the interpretation of Arthurian themes in literature, and their treatment in the other arts."—*Pref.* In chapters by period, with a glossary, chronology, bibliography, and index. PN685.L3

The new Arthurian encyclopedia / ed. by Norris J. Lacy ... [et al.]. N.Y. : Garland, 1991. 577 p. : ill. (Garland reference library of the humanities, v. 931). **BE343**

1st ed. had title: *The Arthurian encyclopedia* (N.Y. : Garland, 1986).

A substantially enlarged and revised edition offering "...a comprehensive and critical treatment of Arthurian subjects, artists, and works, both medieval and modern, in all languages."—*Pref.* Signed articles in dictionary arrangement; selected bibliographic references. This edition provides expanded coverage of modern Arthurian texts (and of film versions). Includes a classified list of entries, a selective bibliography, and a chronology. Many fine black-and-white illustrations; general index. Review: *American reference books annual* 23 (1992): 481–2. DA152.5.A7N48

Spence, Lewis. A dictionary of medieval romance and romance writers. London : Routledge ; N.Y. : Dutton, [1913]. 395 p. **BE344**

Repr. : N.Y. : Humanities Pr., 1962; Boston : Longwood, 1977.

A list, in one alphabet, of the titles and characters of the principal British, Celtic, French, Italian, Scandinavian, Spanish, and Teutonic romances from the 11th to the 14th centuries. Gives: (1) under title, a fairly detailed synopsis of the story of the romance with some bibliographical references but no full list of editions, and (2) under character, a brief description of the character, and the title of the romance in which it appears.

§ *An Arthurian dictionary*, by Ruth Minary and Charles Moorman (Rev. ed. Chicago : Academy Chicago Publ., c1987. 117 p.) is a student's handbook to characters, places, and topics connected with the Arthur legend. PN669.S6

SPEECH AND RHETORIC

Abstracts of theses in the field of speech. (*In* Speech monographs : v. 13–36, 1946–69). **BE345**

An annual listing giving abstracts of doctoral dissertations and master's essays.

American orators before 1900 : critical studies and sources / ed. by Bernard K. Duffy and Halford R. Ryan. N.Y. : Greenwood, 1987. 481 p. **BE346**

Companion title: *American orators of the twentieth century : critical studies and sources*, ed. by Bernard K. Duffy and Halford R. Ryan (c1987. 468 p.).

Each volume presents more than 50 signed essays on individual speakers, providing for each a biographical sketch, a discussion of speaking style with illustrative quotations from the speeches, an evaluation of the person's contribution, a bibliography of information sources, and a chronology of major speeches. Both volumes contain bibliographies of basic research sources, glossaries of rhetorical terms, and general indexes. PN4055.U5A4

Brewer, David Josiah. World's best orations : from the earliest period to the present time. St. Louis, Mo. : Kaiser, [1901]. 10 v. : ill. **BE347**

Arranged alphabetically by author. Gives for each a brief biographical sketch and selected orations. Indexes: (1) orators; (2) subjects; (3) chronological index of orators; (4) chronological index of periods and events; (5) chronological indexes of law, government, and politics, of religion and philosophy, of literature; (6) general index of orators, subjects, events. PN6121.B85

CCCC bibliography of composition and rhetoric. 1987– . Carbondale, Ill. : Southern Illinois Univ. Pr., c1990– . Annual. **BE348**

Sponsored by the Conference on College Composition and Communication. Continues: *Longman bibliography of composition and rhetoric*, by Erika Lindemann, and retains its arrangement.

Each annual volume lists and briefly annotates citations to books, articles, and dissertations drawn from sources such as *Dissertation abstracts international* (AG13), *Resources in education* (CB61), and *Current index to journals in education* (CB54). Arranged in classified chapters devoted to topics such as: writing theory; teacher education; curricula; and testing, measurement, and evaluation. The section on textbooks and other instructional materials which appeared in the Longman bibliography was dropped when the title changed with the 1987 annual volume. PE1404.L66

Cleary, James W. Rhetoric and public address : a bibliography, 1947–1961 / James W. Cleary, Frederick W. Haberman. Madison : Univ. of Wisconsin Pr., 1964. 487 p. **BE349**

Based on annual bibliographies published in the *Quarterly journal of speech*, 1947–51, and in *Speech monographs*, 1952–61, but not merely a cumulation of these. The entries were reviewed, some corrected, some dropped, and about 1,500 items added. An alphabetically arranged list of 8,035 items with subject index. Also a list of practitioners and theorists, and an index of reviewers.

§ Continued by: "Bibliography of rhetoric and public address" appearing annually in *Speech monographs* through 1969 (covering 1968 publications). Z6514.S7C5

Doctoral dissertations in speech : work in progress, 1951–68. (*In* Speech monographs : v. 18 [1951]–35[1968]). **BE350**

Lists dissertations in progress, arranged by subject. Appeared annually.

Donker, Marjorie. Dictionary of literary-rhetorical conventions of the English Renaissance / Marjorie Donker and George M. Muldrow. Westport, Conn. : Greenwood, 1982. 268 p. **BE351**

A dictionary of rhetorical terms and the vocabulary of poetics based on Elizabethan and Jacobean usage with illustrations drawn from literature of the period. Entries take literary perspective, excluding any mention of politics, religion, philosophy, and biography. A scholarly selective bibliography following each entry is arranged in chronological order, suggesting "the main direction of modern scholarship on the topic in question through 1979."—*Pref.* Bibliographies exclude foreign-language titles, dissertations, bibliographies, and works predating 1900. One appendix lists modern literary terms with their relevant counterparts, another assigns the Renaissance terms to appropriate literary categories.

§ Another dictionary useful in this context is Lee A. Sonnino's *A handbook to sixteenth-century rhetoric* (London : Routledge & Kegan Paul; N.Y. : Barnes & Noble, 1968), which uses definitions selected from classical and 16th-century sources with examples from literary texts. Sections cover Latin rhetorical terms, Greek figures of speech, and terms relevant to style and genre. Other sections include major systems for the division of rhetoric, a descriptive index of tropes and schemes, and separate indexes of Greek and Latin terms.

Glenn, Robert W. Black rhetoric : a guide to Afro-American communication. Metuchen, N.J. : Scarecrow, 1976. 376 p. **BE352**

Intended as "a guide to available sources that would simplify the work of an instructor or a student interested in the content and communication of speeches and essays by Afro-Americans" (*Pref.*) from early to contemporary times. In four sections: (1) Bibliographies; (2) Anthologies; (3) History and criticism; (4) Speeches and essays. Not annotated. Z1361.N39G55

Graduate theses : an index of graduate work in speech. (*In* Speech monographs : v. 2–36, 1935–69). **BE353**

The first installment covers 1902–34; annual thereafter. Includes both doctoral and master's theses completed.

Continued by *Bibliographic annual in speech communication* ([Falls Church, Va.] : Speech Communication Assoc., 1970– . Ceased publication?).

Historical rhetoric : an annotated bibliography of selected sources in English / ed. by Winifred Bryan Horner. Boston : G. K. Hall, c1980. 294 p. **BE354**

A selective annotated bibliography tracing the history of rhetoric from classical times through the 19th century. Focuses on materials in English, and for later periods, on the rhetoric of English literature. Divided into five sections by historical period: classical period, Middle Ages, Renaissance, 18th and 19th centuries. A short introduction to each section outlines the context for the period, and is followed by separate lists of primary and secondary sources. Primary sources are entered in chronological order by publication date; secondary sources, alphabetically by author. Useful for identifying reliable translations of classical texts. Z7004.R5H57

Houlette, Forrest. Nineteenth-century rhetoric : an enumerative bibliography. N.Y. : Garland, 1989. 308 p. (Garland reference library of the humanities, v. 787). **BE355**

Lists almost 4,000 primary and secondary sources, primarily American, published between 1800 and 1920 on rhetoric, grammar, composition, and the teaching of English. Includes articles in books and periodicals. Entries are not annotated, but are identified with a one- or two-word descriptor, the latter forming the subject index; but these categories are so broad they are of little use. Z2015.R5H68

Lanham, Richard A. A handlist of rhetorical terms. 2nd ed. Berkeley : Univ. of California Pr., c1991. 205 p. : ill. **BE356**

1st ed., 1968

An alphabetical list of terms with definitions, followed by a number of classified lists of the terms. Designed as a guide to specialized terminology, this edition has been redesigned typographically, key terms are defined in greater detail; and more modern examples have been used as illustrations.

§ See also: *Dictionary of literary devices : gradus, A–Z*, by Bernard Marie Dupriez, adapted by Albert W. Halsall (BE78).

PE1445.A2L3

Lyle, Guy Redvers. I am happy to present : a book of introductions / comp. by Guy Redvers Lyle and Kevin Guinagh. 2nd ed. N.Y. : H.W. Wilson, 1968. 251p. **BE357**

1st ed. 1953.

A brief essay on the art of introducing speakers precedes a selection of more than a hundred examples of introductory speeches made by well-known persons; introductions are grouped in broad professional categories. PN4305.I7L9

Manning, Beverley. Index to American women speakers, 1828–1978. Metuchen, N.J. : Scarecrow, 1980. 672 p. **BE358**

Indexes by author, subject, and title the speeches by women appearing in more than 200 publications, including collected works, proceedings of conferences and conventions, congressional committee hearings, and documentary histories. Speeches under variant titles are cross-referenced.

§ Manning updated the work with *We shall be heard : an index to speeches by American women, 1978 to 1985* (Metuchen, N.J. : Scarecrow, 1988). Covers many of the same issues as the initial work, but surveys other issues germane to the more recent period. Also indexes newly published collections on some of the historical figures appearing in the previous volume. Represents about 2,500 women, including all

women senators and representatives, 1828–1978. Title and subject indexes refer to author index, which provides full citations.

Z1231.O7M36

Murphy, James Jerome. Medieval rhetoric : a select bibliography. 2nd ed. Toronto ; Buffalo : Univ. of Toronto Pr., 1989. 198 p. (Toronto medieval bibliographies, 3). **BE359**

1st ed., 1971.

Designed to "facilitate the study of the perceptive arts of discourse in Europe from the time of Saint Augustine ... to the rediscovery of complete major classical rhetorical texts in the early fifteenth century."—*Pref.* Lists editions and translations of primary sources and key secondary works in chapters devoted to particular time periods or topics, with some annotations. Name index.

Z7004.R5M87

——————— Renaissance rhetoric : a short-title catalogue of works on rhetorical theory from the beginning of printing to A.D. 1700, with special attention to the holdings of the Bodleian Library, Oxford : with a select basic bibliography of secondary works on Renaissance rhetoric / comp. by James J. Murphy ; produced with the technical assistance of Kevin P. Roddy. N.Y. : Garland, 1981. 353 p. (Garland reference library of the humanities, v. 237). **BE360**

A scholarly bibliography arranged into two parts as stated in the subtitle. At least one holding library or secondary source citing the edition is identified for each primary source in the catalogue section. The select list of secondary works which comprises the second part serves as a guide to the basic issues and authors of the Renaissance period.

PN185

The present state of scholarship in historical and contemporary rhetoric / ed. by Winifred Bryan Horner. Rev. ed. Columbia : Univ. of Missouri Pr., 1990. 260 p. **BE361**

1st ed., 1983.

A collection of bibliographic essays outlining current scholarship and trends. Like Horner's *Historical rhetoric* (BE354), which is intended for students rather than scholars, it is divided into sections by chronological period, each contributed by one or more scholars. Essays review primary texts and translations, noting surveys, general studies, journals, and series. An important feature is a summary identifying areas for future scholarship. A bibliography of sources mentioned in the essay completes each section. PN183.P7

Prochnow, Herbert V. Speaker's & toastmaster's handbook. Rocklin, Calif. : Prima Pub. & Communications, c1990. 357 p. **BE362**

A collection of more than 2,000 humorous stories, definitions, epigrams and quips, stories and comments from unusual or famous people, and pithy quotations. Designed as an aid to public speakers. Focuses on humor.

§ See also: *The toastmaster's treasure chest* comp. by Herbert V. Prochnow and Herbert V. Prochnow, Jr. (2nd ed. N.Y. : Harper & Row, c1988), a collection of quotations from famous persons and from sacred writings and miscellaneous periodicals, as well as proverbs and anonymous epigrams. PN4193.I5P67

Representative American speeches. 1937/38– . N.Y. : H.W. Wilson, 1938– . Annual. **BE363**

Representative speeches of the year. Issued each year as a number of *The reference shelf* (BE373). PS668.B3

Research in composition and rhetoric : a bibliographic sourcebook / ed. by Michael G. Moran and Ronald F. Lunsford. Westport, Conn. : Greenwood, 1984. 506 p. **BE364**

Contains 17 bibliographical essays on research in aspects of college-level composition instruction, including psychology, philosophy, sociology, and literary theory, as well as more practical skill-specific topics such as orthography, punctuation, and usage. Appendixes include chapters on evaluating textbooks and usage handbooks. Author and subject indexes. Z5818.E5R47

Speech Association of America. A history and criticism of American public address. N.Y. : McGraw-Hill, 1943–55. 3 v. **BE365**

Vols. 1–2, ed. by W. N. Brigance; v. 3, ed. by M. K. Hochmuth and associates : W. N. Brigance and D. Bryant.

Chapters written by specialists treat the great speakers of America, from Jonathan Edwards to Franklin Delano Roosevelt, with extensive footnotes and bibliographies. PS400.S66

Sutton, Roberta Briggs. Speech index : an index to 259 collections of world famous orations and speeches for various occasions. 4th ed., rev. and enl. N.Y. : Scarecrow, 1966. 947 p. **BE366**

A dictionary catalog with entries for each speech under author, subject, and type of speech. The 4th ed. includes all the material from the three previous volumes (published 1935–62), and incorporates new materials and some older items previously overlooked. Covers through 1965.

§ Quinquennial supplements published 1972 and 1977 have been superseded by Charity Mitchell's *Speech index : an index to collections of world famous orations and speeches for various occasions. Fourth edition supplement, 1966–1980* (Metuchen, N.J. : Scarecrow, 1982), which also adds indexing of speeches published in books 1975–80.

Vital speeches of the day. v. 1 (Oct. 8, 1934)– . N.Y. : City News Pub. Co., 1934– . Two issues monthly. **BE367**

Prints in full the important addresses of contemporary leaders of public opinion in the fields of economics, politics, education, sociology, business, labor; heavy representation from government and big business.

———. *25 year index, Oct. 8, 1934–Oct. 1, 1959* (Pelham, N.Y. : City News Pub. Co., 1963. 137 p.). PN6121.V52

Debating

Debate index / comp. by Edith M. Phelps. New ed. rev. N.Y. : H.W. Wilson, 1939. 130 p. (The reference shelf, v. 12, no. 9). **BE368**

A subject index of debates, briefs, bibliographies, and collections of articles on public questions. Many of the topics mirror an age, and the index now has greater historical interest than as a source for present-day current opinion.

Debate index supplement, comp. by Julia E. Johnsen (1941. 90 p. [The reference shelf, v. 14, no. 9]).

Debate index : second supplement, comp. by Joseph R. Dunlap and Martin A. Kuhn (1964. 176 p. [The reference shelf, v. 36 no. 3]).

§ *See* BE373 for *The reference shelf.*

Eisenberg, Abné M. Argument : a guide to formal and informal debate / Abné M. Eisenberg, Joseph A. Ilardo. 2nd ed. Englewood Cliffs, N.J. : Prentice-Hall, c1980. 230 p. : ill. **BE369**

1st ed., 1972.

Developed initially during the turbulent 1960s, this guide "presents a plan for disciplined disagreement, rational rebuttal, and calm confrontation…a manual for social transformation."—*Prologue.* Divided into two main sections: rhetorical aspects of argument, and interpersonal aspects of argument. Substantial bibliography; index. PN4181.E49

Ericson, Jon M. The debater's guide / Jon M. Ericson & James J. Murphy, with Raymond Bud Zeuschner. Rev. ed. Carbondale : Southern Illinois Univ. Pr., c1987. 146 p. **BE370**

1st ed., 1961.

A manual for both beginning and experienced debaters, outlining the process— preparation of the argument, analysis of the propositions, sections on the rules of debate, and actual presentation. Appendixes: stock cases, glossary. Bibliography.

Freeley, Austin J. Argumentation and debate : critical thinking for reasoned decision making. 8th ed. Belmont, Calif. : Wadsworth Pub. Co., c1993. 478 p. : ill. **BE371**

1st ed., 1961.

A standard text for a beginning course in argumentation and debate. Presents clear explanations with many up-to-date examples (Operation Desert Storm, Senate hearings on Justice Thomas, dissolution of the Soviet Union). Begins with chapters on critical thinking, and applied and academic debate; and concludes with chapters on modern procedures for academic debate and on parliamentary debate. Includes a glossary of terms in argumentation and debate. Indexed.

§ Another helpful text is George Ziegelmueller, Jack Kay, and Charles Dause, *Argumentation : inquiry and advocacy.* (2nd ed. Englewood Cliffs, N.J. : Prentice Hall, 1990. 1st ed., 1975). Provides basic information on the theory of argumentation and the practices of academic debate. Clear definitions and illustrations are complemented by selective bibliographies in each chapter, the chapters arranged in the logical sequence of the process. PN4181.F68

Kruger, Arthur N. Argumentation and debate : a classified bibliography. 2nd ed. Metuchen, N.J. : Scarecrow, 1975. 520 p. **BE372**

1st ed., 1964.

A comprehensive, classified bibliography of books and articles in English, covering all aspects of debating and argument. About 6,000 entries in this edition, including doctoral dissertations and master's theses. Detailed subject index.

§ *Rhetorik, Topik, Argumentation: Bibliographie zur Redelehre und Rhetorikforschung im deutschsprachigen Raum 1945–1979/80* by Robert Jamison and Joachim Dyck (Stuttgart-Bad Cannstatt : Frommann-Holzboog, c1983. 349 p.) provides a listing of German publications. Z7161.5.K75

The reference shelf. v. 1– . N.Y. : H.W. Wilson, 1922– . 6 no. a year. **BE373**

Some numbers issued in revised editions.

Each number is devoted to a timely controversial question, with reprints of selected articles from books and periodicals giving background information and pro and con arguments, followed by a comprehensive bibliography. PN4181.R33

STYLISTICS

Bailey, Richard W. English stylistics : a bibliography / [by] Richard W. Bailey and Dolores M. Burton. Cambridge : M.I.T. Pr., [1968]. 198 p. **BE374**

A classed bibliography of writings, including dissertations, relating to the linguistic study of literary texts, chiefly English and American but including more important stylistic studies of other literatures. Covers the classical and medieval periods; and, for English texts, the period from 1500 to about 1966. Some annotations; indexed.

§ *See also*: Louis Milic's *Style and stylistics : an analytical bibliography* (N.Y. : Free Press, [1967]), a more selective classified bibliography of books and articles on literary style in its various aspects. Most items are in English, although some are in French on French literature, and some in Italian and German. Rather than conventional annotations Milic assigns descriptors to each of the more than 800 entries. The introduction has a glossary of key terms. Cross-references, and detailed indexing. Although Milic and Bailey/Burton overlap, each contains citations not found in the other.

These bibliographies were extended by James R. Bennett in *A bibliography of stylistics and related criticism, 1967–83* (N.Y. : Modern Language Assoc. of America, 1986). Z2015.S7B2

Wales, Katie. A dictionary of stylistics. London ; N.Y. : Longman, 1989. 504 p. **BE375**

Designed for undergraduate or beginning graduate students "both as a dictionary and as a guide-book: not only to explain the meanings of terms, but also overall to give a general picture of the nature and aims of stylistics, its approaches, methodologies and insights, its historical origins and potential developments."—*Introd.*   P301.W35

CHILDREN'S LITERATURE

Brewton, John Edmund. Index to children's poetry : a title, subject, author, and first line index to poetry in collections for children and youth / comp. by John E. and Sara W. Brewton. N.Y. : Wilson, 1942. 965 p.   **BE376**

Indexes 15,000 poems in 130 collections. Together, this volumes with its supplements (below) index approximately 36,500 poems in 446 collections.

————. ————. *First supplement* (1954. 405 p.) indexes 7,000 poems in 66 collections publ. 1938–51; *Second supplement* (1965. 453 p.), indexes 8,000 poems in 85 collections publ. 1949–63.

Continued by: *Index to poetry for children and young people, 1964–1969: a title, subject, author, and first line index to poetry in collections for children and young people*, comp. by the Brewtons and G. Meredith Blackburn (N.Y. : H.W. Wilson, 1972. 575 p.), which indexes more than 11,000 poems in 117 collections and is "in effect a supplement to *Index to Children's Poetry* but because of the larger number of books at the 7–12 grade level, it seemed appropriate to give the present volume a new, more inclusive title."—*Introd.* Supplements have been issued comp. by John Edmund Brewton, G. Meredith Blackburn, and Lorraine A. Blackburn covering 1970–75 (1978. 472 p.), indexing 10,000 poems in 110 collections; for 1976–81 (1984. 320 p.), indexing 7,000 poems in 110 collections; and for 1982–87, ed. by G. Meredith Blackburn alone (1989. 408 p.).   PN1023.B7

Carpenter, Humphrey. The Oxford companion to children's literature / Humphrey Carpenter and Mari Prichard. Oxford ; N.Y. : Oxford Univ. Pr., 1984. 586 p. : ill.   **BE377**

Offers articles on authors and illustrators of children's books, genres of children's literature, characters, and individual titles, together with "very brief summaries of the state of children's literature in all languages, countries and continents" *(Pref.)*, as well as accounts of early school books and entries for recurring subjects of children's reading matter. Emphasis is on English and American materials, with those of Asia and Africa least thoroughly covered. Occasional references to scholarly work in the field, but no bibliography as such.   PN1008.5.C37

Children's literature review. [v. 1]– . Detroit : Gale, 1976– . Irregular.   **BE378**

"Excerpts from reviews, criticism, and commentary on books for children and young people."—*t.p.*

Editors vary.

Each volume offers excerpts from reviews and criticism (from both books and periodicals) of some 20–40 authors. International in scope. Cumulative indexes to authors and titles in successive volumes.   PN1009.A1C5139

Doyle, Brian. The who's who of children's literature. London : Evelyn ; N.Y. : Schocken, [1968]. 380 p. : ill.   **BE379**

300 biographical sketches of the most notable authors and illustrators of children's books, from the early 19th century to the present day, with a few earlier writers included. Authors and illustrators in separate sections.   PN452.D6

Dunhouse, Mary Beth. International directory of children's literature. N.Y. : Facts on File : c1986. 128 p.   **BE380**

Gives addresses and other information for publishers, magazines, organizations, fairs and conferences, prizes, libraries and special collections, with statistics for 1979–81.   PN1008.4.D86

Fisher, Margery Turner. Who's who in children's books : a treasury of the familiar characters of childhood. N.Y. : Holt, Rinehart and Winston, [1975]. 399 p. : ill.   **BE381**

An avowedly personal selection of memorable characters from children's literature, "not intended primarily as a reference book."— *Pref.* Includes "as many as possible of the characters who have now become household names, together with others less familiar" whom the compiler found particularly interesting. Entries usually run to half a column or more in length, placing the character in setting and circumstances of the story, with comment on the author's technique or approach to the character.   PN1009.A1F575

Helbig, Alethea. Dictionary of American children's fiction, 1859–1959 : books of recognized merit / Alethea K. Helbig and Agnes Regan Perkins. Westport, Conn. : Greenwood, 1985. 666 p.   **BE382**

————. *Dictionary of American children's fiction, 1960–1984 : recent books of recognized merit*, by Alethea K. Helbig and Agnes Regan Perkins (N.Y. : Greenwood, 1986. 914 p.).

Taken together, these two volumes provide almost 9,000 sketches on characters, authors, and individual works, with detailed general indexes which include subject entries for topics such as Old persons, Nieces, Fires, or Eighteenth century.   PS374.C454H45

———————— Dictionary of British children's fiction : books of recognized merit / Alethea K. Helbig and Agnes Regan Perkins. N.Y. : Greenwood, 1989. 2 v. (1632 p.).   **BE383**

Contains "1,626 entries on such elements as titles, authors, characters, and settings based on 387 books published from 1678 to 1985."—*Pref.* General index.   PR830.C513H4

Kunitz, Stanley Jasspon. The junior book of authors / ed. by Stanley J. Kunitz and Howard Haycraft. 2nd ed. rev. N.Y. : Wilson, 1951. 309 p. : ill.   **BE384**

The 1st ed., 1934, included biographical or autobiographical sketches of some 268 writers and illustrators (living and deceased) for younger readers. The 2nd ed. contains 289 sketches, of which 160 are repeated with revisions; the remaining 129 are new writers who came into prominence after 1934. The 108 names dropped are largely classics, (e.g., Louisa M. Alcott), and the borderline group of books between adult and juvenile. All these names are to be found in other Wilson biographical dictionaries, but libraries may wish to keep both editions on their shelves.

Continued by Muriel Fuller, *More junior authors* (N.Y. : Wilson, 1963), then by the following works:

Doris de Montreville and Donna Hill, *Third book of junior authors* (1972).

Doris de Montreville and Elizabeth D. Crawford, *Fourth book of junior authors & illustrators* (1978).

Sally Holmes Holtze, *Fifth book of junior authors & illustrators* (1983).

————. *Sixth book of junior authors & illustrators* (1989).

Each volume in the series focuses on authors and illustrators who have come to prominence since the previous volume. The *Third book* contains the first cumulative index to the series. Beginning with the *Fourth book*, artists as well as writers were included in the series.   PN1009.A1K8

Lexikon der Kinder- und Jugendliteratur : Personen-, Länder- und Sachartikel zu Geschichte und Gegenwart der Kinder- und Jugendliteratur / Hrsg. von Klaus Doderer. Weinheim ; Basel : Beltz, 1975–82. 4 v. : ill.   **BE385**

"Erarbeitet im Institut für Jugendbuchforschung der Johann Wolfgang Goethe-Universität in Frankfurt/Main. Bibliographische Angaben unter Mitwirkung der Internationalen Jugendbibliothek in München."—*t.p.*

Contents: v. 1–3, A–Z; [v. 4], Ergänzungs- und Registerband.

An international encyclopedia of the history of children's literature with articles on individual authors, types of children's literature (including comics), publishers, specific topics, and children's literature in countries throughout the world. Signed articles; bibliographies.   PN1009.A1L49

Lynn, Ruth Nadelman. Fantasy literature for children and young adults : an annotated bibliography. 3rd ed. N.Y. : Bowker, c1989. 771 p.   **BE386**

1st ed., 1979; 2nd ed., 1983, had title: *Fantasy for children.*

Provides extremely brief annotations to "over 3,300 fantasy novels and story collections for children and young adults in grades 3 through 12, as well as a research guide on the authors who write fantasy for children and young adults."—*Pref.* In two main parts: (1) Annotated bibliography, which presents material in a classified arrangement under topics or themes such as Talking animal fantasy or Travel to other worlds; (2) Research guide, which lists materials on history and criticism, teaching aids and bibliographies. Author/illustrator, title, and subject indexes.   Z1037.L97

Nakamura, Joyce. Children's authors and illustrators : an index to biographical dictionaries. 4th ed. Detroit : Gale, c1987. lxvi, 799 p. (Gale biographical index series, no. 2).   **BE387**

1st ed., 1976; 3rd ed., 1981.

Retains all material from previous editions. The 4th ed. indexes biographical sketches of writers and illustrators of children's books in more than 450 reference books. Seeks comprehensive coverage of writers and artists whose work is available in English, including those who produced works specifically for children and those whose works appeal to younger readers.

Many of the same sources are also indexed in the 2nd ed. of *Author biographies master index* (*see* BE196).   Z1037.A1N18

The Phoenix Award of the Children's Literature Association, 1985–1989 / ed. by Alethea Helbig and Agnes Perkins. Metuchen, N.J. : Scarecrow, 1993. 166 p.   **BE388**

This collection honors the first five winners of the Phoenix Award, a prize bestowed on the author, or the estate of an author, recognizing the literary merit of a book which was not recognized at the time of its initial publication 20 years earlier. The work is made up of the acceptance speeches given at the annual conference of the Children's Literature Association when the prize was awarded. For each writer the acceptance speech is followed by a biographical sketch, a bibliography of the author's works, and three to five critical essays on the work of the author. In 1989, two additional authors received honor book awards; for each, a biographical sketch is followed by a bibliography and a single critical essay.   PS490.P48

Something about the author. v. 1 (1971)– . Detroit : Gale, [1971]– . Irregular.   **BE389**

An ongoing series providing biographical information about authors and illustrators of books for young people. Emphasizes authors from English-speaking countries, but includes authors from around the world whose works are available in English translation. "Children's literature" here covers picture books, humor, folk and fairy tales, animal stories, mystery and adventure, science fiction and fantasy, historical fiction, poetry and nonsense verse, drama, biography, and nonfiction. In addition to directory information most entries include a title-by-title chronological bibliography of the author's or illustrator's work. Illustrated with photographs, manuscript samples, book covers, movie stills, etc.   PN451.S6

Trefny, Beverly Robin. Index to children's plays in collections, 1975–1984 / by Beverly Robin Trefny and Eileen C. Palmer. Metuchen, N.J. : Scarecrow, 1986. 108 p.   **BE390**

1st ed., 1972; 2nd ed., 1977, by Barbara A. Kreider.

This 3rd ed. indexes 48 play collections with copyright dates 1975–84. The 1st–2nd eds. indexed collections with copyright dates 1965–69 and 1965–74. The three editions together index almost 2,000 plays, including skits, monologs, pantomimes, puppetry, and variety programs when in play form. Indexes by authors, titles, and subjects. "Subjects" includes theme, type of play, occasion, period, setting, legendary or historical persons, and genre. Provides separate "cast analysis" section.   PN1627.T73

Twentieth-century children's writers / ed., Tracy Chevalier ; consulting ed., D. L. Kirkpatrick. 3rd ed. Chicago : St. James, 1989. 1288 p.   **BE391**

1st ed., 1978; 2nd ed., 1983.

Provides brief biographical notes, bibliographies of published writings, references to critical studies (if any), locations of manuscript collections, and a signed critical evaluation of English-language authors of fiction, poetry and drama for children and young people, most of whose work was published after 1900. The 3rd ed. contains approximately 800 entries, about 100 new to this edition. Most other biographical sketches and bibliographies have been updated.

PN1009.A1T9

Writers for children : critical studies of major authors since the seventeenth century / Jane M. Bingham, ed. N.Y. : Scribner, c1988. 661 p.   **BE392**

Signed essays, each with a selected bibliography, profile 84 authors who have either written specifically for children or whose works have a largely juvenile audience. All are deceased and continue "to hold either popular or scholarly status."—*Introd.* General index.

PN1009.A1W73

LITERATURES OF THE ENGLISH-SPEAKING COUNTRIES

United States

General works

Guides

Bracken, James K. Reference works in British and American literature. Englewood, Colo. : Libraries Unlimited, 1990-91. 2 v.   **BE393**

Contents: v. 1, English and American literature; v. 2, English and American writers.

Narrower in scope and providing less ancillary material than either James L. Harner's *Literary research guide* (BE396) or Michael J. Marcuse's *A reference guide for English studies* (BE398), v. 1 is intended to serve "the basic needs of literary researchers of all degrees of sophistication."—*Introd.* Provides critical annotations for 512 entries, including listings for core journals and principal research centers and associations. The second volume (995 entries) provides critical annotations to book-length works (including some unpublished dissertations) for approximately 600 individual English and American writers. Included (when available) are primary and secondary bibliographies; dictionaries, encyclopedias, and handbooks; indexes and concordances; and currently published journals.

A review in *Analytical & enumerative bibliography*, n.s. 4:4 (1990): 171–83, comparing Bracken (v. 1 only), Harner, and Marcuse suggests that Bracken's annotations, though full, are sometimes less critical than they should be of seriously flawed works.   Z2011.B74

Fenster, Valmai Kirkham. Guide to American literature. Littleton, Colo. : Libraries Unlimited, 1983. 243 p.   **BE394**

Intended for students at both the graduate and undergraduate level. Pt. 1 consists of chapters dealing with research methodology, general reference tools, literary surveys, criticism, political and social history, language studies and dictionaries, and anthologies and series used in teaching. Pt. 2 is devoted to 100 individual American authors, providing primary and secondary bibliographies. Includes an author/title/subject index to pt. 1 and subject index to pt. 2. For a qualified recommendation see *Choice* 21 (Nov. 1983): 400.   Z1225.F46

Gohdes, Clarence Louis Frank. Bibliographical guide to the study of the literature of the U.S.A. / Clarence Louis Frank Gohdes, Sanford E. Marovitz. 5th ed., completely rev. and enl. Durham, N.C. : Duke Univ. Pr., 1984. 256 p.   **BE395**
    1st–4th eds. (1959–76) by C. L. F. Gohdes.

    A standard guide for the student of American literature, with sections on such closely related topics as the book trade and publishing, the American language, literary relations with other countries, and literary aspects of women's studies and racial and minority studies. Classed arrangement; concise annotations; separate author and subject indexes.

    § Long a standard aid for students, *Guide to American literature and its backgrounds since 1890* by Howard Mumford Jones and Richard M. Ludwig (4th ed., rev. and enl. Cambridge : Harvard Univ. Pr., 1972. 264 p.) is now somewhat out of date.   Z1225.G6

Harner, James L. Literary research guide : a guide to reference sources for the study of literatures in English and related topics. 2nd ed. N.Y. : Modern Language Association of America, 1993. 766 p.   **BE396**
    1st ed., 1989.

    An indispensable guide for the study of British literature (including Irish, Scottish and Welsh literatures) and literatures of the U.S., this volume supersedes Margaret C. Patterson's *Literary research guide* (2nd ed. N.Y. : Modern Language Assoc., 1983). Also included are brief chapters for other literatures in English, foreign-language literatures, comparative literature, and related topics such as art and literature, bibliography and textual criticism, and scholarly writing and publishing. Provides extensive critical annotation for reference sources, gives suggestions for further reading, lists core journals, provides numerous cross-references, and cites 745 review articles. Name, title, and subject indexes. Entries are current through April 1992, although provisional annotations are given for significant works in progress or in press. "Intended as a vademecum for researchers—from advanced undergraduates to experienced scholars" (*Introd.*), this volume excludes collections of plot synopses as well as excerpts of criticism. A model of its kind, Harner's work is especially valuable for the candor of its critical evaluations.

    A review in *Analytical & enumerative bibliography*, n.s 4:4 (1990): 171–83, comparing the relative merits of Harner (1st ed.), James K. Bracken's *Reference works in British and American literature* (BE393, v. 1 only), and Michael J. Marcuse's *A reference guide for English studies* (BE398) suggests that Harner and Marcuse have produced reference guides of a very high order.

    § Undergraduates needing an introductory research guide should consult Nancy L. Baker's *A research guide for undergraduate students : English and American literature* (3rd ed. N.Y. : Modern Lanuage Assoc., 1989).   Z2011.H34

Leary, Lewis Gaston. American literature : a study and research guide / Lewis Leary, with the collaboration of John Auchard. N.Y. : St. Martin's, [1976]. 185 p.   **BE397**

    A series of bibliographic essays covering the history of the study and teaching of American literature, literary histories, genre studies, foreign influences and influences abroad, schools of criticism, language, periodicals, and bibliographic and biographical resources. One chapter is devoted to 28 American authors. Includes a chapter on planning and writing the research paper. Author index. Although somewhat dated, still valuable for its evaluative comments.

    § A review in *Criticism* 19 (Fall 1977): 378 points out various inaccuracies and suggests that Clarence Gohdes's *Bibliographical guide to the study of the literature of the U.S.A.* (*see* BE395) is superior. Harold H. Kolb's *A field guide to the study of American literature* (Charlottesville : Univ. Pr. of Virginia, 1976) consists of 373 annotated entries arranged alphabetically within broad chapter headings (e.g., Bibliographies, Reference works). There is no further subject organization; annotations are principally quoted from prefatory matter.   Z1225.L47

Marcuse, Michael J. A reference guide for English studies. Berkeley : Univ. of California Pr., c1990. lxxii, 790 p. **BE398**

    An ambitious, impressive guide to English and American literature including much ancillary material. Entries are arranged in 24 variously divided sections: general reference works; libraries (including union catalogs and major library catalogs and guides for North American, British, and continental libraries); retrospective and current national bibliography; serial publications; miscellany (including dissertations, microforms, and reviews); history and historical ancillae (including chronological and topographical ancillae); biography; archives and manuscripts; language, linguistics, and philology; literary materials (including folklore, mythology, the Bible, and proverbs); literature (including classical studies, foreign languages and literatures, children's literature and women's studies); English literature (including various literatures in English); medieval literature; Renaissance and early 17th century; Restoration and 18th century; 19th century; 20th century; American literature; poetry and versification; the performing arts (theater, drama, and film); prose fiction and nonfictional prose; theory, rhetoric, and composition; bibliography; and the profession of English. Entries are generally current only through 1985 though some are as late as 1989. Critical annotations for reference sources are very full, usually giving publication history, organization, and scope, and listing contents. Many sections provide selected reviews of research, and list scholarly journals and recommended works in the field. Individual author bibliographies for 25 American and 42 British authors. The subject index should be used for comprehensive searching.

    § Broader in scope than James L. Harner's *Literary research guide* (BE396), it is an extremely valuable complement to that work.   PR56.M37

Bibliography

See also v. 2, Bibliography, at *Literary history of the United States* (BE440).

American women writers : bibliographical essays / ed. by Maurice Duke, Jackson R. Bryer and M. Thomas Inge. Westport, Conn. : Greenwood, c1983. 434 p.   **BE399**

    Patterned after *Eight American authors* (BE403), presents bibliographical essays evaluating scholarship "current through the fall of 1981" (*Pref.*) on 24 writers: Bradstreet, Rowlandson, Knight, Jewett, Freeman, Murfree, Chopin, Wharton, Stein, Barnes, Nin, Glasgow, Porter, Welty, O'Connor, McCullers, Hurston, Rourke, Buck, Rawlings, Mitchell, Moore, Sexton, and Plath. Each essay describes bibliographies, editions, manuscripts and letters (citing locations of collections and discussing scholarship relating to manuscripts and correspondence), biographies, and criticism. Suggests topics needing further investigation. Personal name index.

    § Research reviews for Emily Dickinson will be found in *Fifteen American authors before 1900* (BE404) and for Willa Cather in *Sixteen modern American authors* (BE413).   Z1229.W8A44

Blanck, Jacob Nathaniel. Bibliography of American literature / comp. by Jacob Blanck for the Bibliographical Society of America. New Haven : Yale Univ. Pr., 1955–91. 9 v.   **BE400**

    Vol. 7 ed. and completed by Virginia L. Smyers and Michael Winship; v. 8–9 ed. and completed by Michael Winship.

    Contents: v. 1–9, Henry Adams–Elinor Wylie.

    A major descriptive bibliography of the works of 281 American authors from the Federal period through 1930. Authors included are those who were known and read in their own time and who published primarily belles lettres. Description is for separate publications (including books, broadsides, anthologies, pamphlets, and ephemera), with emphasis on first editions and "the first appearance of any prose (except letters) or poetry" (*Pref.*) for the authors included. Full description is given for first American editions (including variant issues or states) and for European editions in English when they precede, or possibly precede, the American. Brief description is provided for works containing the initial printing of a prose work or poem. Excluded are periodical and newspaper publications, later editions (universal reprints), translations into other languages, and volumes containing isolated correspondence.

    Arranged alphabetically by author and then by date of publication in three parts. Listed first are books and pamphlets written wholly or substantially by the author; broadsides, leaflets, etc. containing first publication; first separate publication (poem or story) reprinted from a book by the author; revised editions; books reissued under changed titles; books containing first appearances by the author. Second are reprints followed by selected bibliographical and biographical references. Locations are provided for most copies. Careful attention should be given to Blanck's preface for inclusions and exclusions, as well as to the headnotes for individual authors. *BAL* therefore does not provide a complete primary bibliography for the authors included nor is it a census of copies. According to James L. Harner, *Literary research guide* (BE396, p. 368), a short-title list of each author's separately published works and a title, publisher, and chronology index are planned for future publication.

A work of meticulous scholarship benefitting from close examination of copies in private as well as institutional collections. For a review (through v. 7), see *Papers of the Bibliographical Society of America* 78:1 (1984): 45–56. Z1225.B55

Boos, Florence Saunders. Bibliography of women & literature / ed. by Florence Boos with Lynn Miller. N.Y. : Holmes & Meier, c1989. 2 v. **BE401**

Contents: v. 1, Articles and books (1974–1978) by and about women from 600 to 1975; v. 2, Supplement, articles and books (1979–1981).

A selective, predominantly unannotated bibliography of some 10,000 entries (books, articles, dissertations, and reviews) on literature by and about women. Vol. 1 is drawn from the annual bibliographies in the journal *Women and literature* (1976–78), entries for the supplemental volume from *MLA international bibliography* (BE39) and *Annual bibliography of English language and literature*, 1979–81 (BE588), though in fact there are few entries later than 1979. Arranged by a classification divided by nationality, period, and genre for Great Britain and America (with additional chapters for Canada, Australia, New Zealand, other English-speaking countries, and for languages other than English). Separate indexes for subject authors and scholars; index of generic categories. No subject access apart from the classified arrangement. A third volume (1981–85) is expected. Although coverage is for a limited time span, and ease of use is hindered by awkward indexing, still useful for the sheer amount of material covered.

A review in *Review of English studies*, ns 42:166 (May 1991): 235–6, points out various inaccuracies and inconsistencies and offers a qualified recommendation as to its usefulness. Z2014.W65B66

Contemporary lesbian writers of the United States : a bio-bibliographical critical sourcebook / ed. by Sandra Pollack and Denise D. Knight. Westport, Conn. : Greenwood, 1993. 640 p. **BE402**

A companion volume to Emmanuel S. Nelson's *Contemporary gay American novelists* (BE469), this provides signed essays on 100 contemporary writers "who, at some point during the 1970–1992 period, had written as self-identified lesbians."—*Pref.* Some prominent names are conspicuously absent, because those writers wished not to be included. Each essay includes a biographical sketch, a discussion of major works and themes, an overview of critical studies, and primary and secondary bibliographies. Appendixes: publishers of lesbian writers; selected periodicals and journals of interest to readers of lesbian writings. Bibliography of nonfiction writings on lesbian issues. Index of authors, titles, and broad subject headings.

§ Forthcoming is David William Foster, *Latin American gay and lesbian narrative : a bio-bibliographical critical sourcebook.* PS153.L46C65

Eight American authors : a review of research and criticism / ed. by James Woodress. Rev. ed. N.Y. : Norton, [c1971]. 392 p. **BE403**

"Sponsored by the American Literature Section of the Modern Language Association."—*t.p.*

Floyd Stovall edited the 1st ed., which appeared in 1956; a bibliographical suppl. by J. Chesley Mathews was publ. in 1963.

Bibliographic essays by eight scholars are devoted to discussion of published bibliographies, editions, biographies, and criticism (variously subdivided) of the following authors: Poe, Emerson, Hawthorne, Thoreau, Melville, Whitman, Twain, and James. Necessarily selective

in regard to periodical articles. Bibliographic detail is minimal; cutoff is generally 1969. Personal name index. Although dated, still valuable for its evaluations of criticism prior to 1970.

§ *American literary scholarship* (BE418) provides more recent evaluative surveys of criticism of these authors. PS201.E4

Fifteen American authors before 1900 : bibliographical essays on research and criticism / ed. by Earl N. Harbert and Robert A. Rees. Rev. ed. Madison, Wis. : Univ. of Wisconsin Pr., 1984. 531 p. **BE404**

1st ed., 1971.

Similar in plan and purpose to *Eight American authors* (BE403) and *Sixteen modern American authors* (BE413). Scholars have contributed bibliographic essays on Henry Adams, William Cullen Bryant, James Fenimore Cooper, Stephen Crane, Emily Dickinson, Jonathan Edwards, Benjamin Franklin, Oliver Wendell Holmes, William Dean Howells, Washington Irving, Henry Wadsworth Longfellow, James Russell Lowell, Frank Norris, Edward Taylor, and John Greenleaf Whittier. Two survey essays from the 1st ed. on the literature of the Old South and the New South have been deleted because "these subjects have simply grown too large for inclusion here."—*Pref.* All chapters include sections for bibliographies, editions, manuscripts and letters, biographies, and criticism. Suggestions for further research are included. Personal name index.

§ Consult the annual volumes of *American literary scholarship* (BE418) to update these surveys of the scholarly literature. PS55.F53

First printings of American authors : contributions toward descriptive checklists / Matthew J. Bruccoli, series ed. Detroit : Gale, 1977–87. 5 v. **BE405**

An ambitious descriptive bibliography for 336 American authors ranging from the 17th century through the 1970s. Description is given for first English and American printings of all separate publications wholly or substantially by the authors, though with far less detail than is found in Jacob Blanck's *Bibliography of American literature* (BE400). Arranged in separate alphabets for each volume; v. 5 covers 53 authors and provides a cumulative index for the set.

A review, "American Literary Bibliography—FPAA Style," *Review* 1 (1979): 173–81, points out various inconsistencies and inaccuracies and lists desiderata for future editions. Also still of interest to the collector is *Merle Johnson's American first editions*, 4th ed., rev. and enl. by Jacob Blanck (AA242). Z1231.F5F57

Harvard University. Library. American literature. Cambridge : Harvard Univ. Libr., 1970. 2 v. (Widener Library shelflist, v. 26–27). **BE406**

For a note on the series, *see* AA115.

Contents: v. 1, Classification schedule, classified listing by call number, chronological listing; v. 2, Author and title listing.

"The 50,000 books and periodicals in the AL, ALA, and ALB classes include literary histories, anthologies, and works by and about individual literary authors. To ensure full coverage of American authors, 8000 works of British and American fiction comprising the PZ and PZB classes have been added to the chronological and alphabetical lists. Since PZ and PZB represent strictly alphabetical arrangements, classified listings have not been included for them."—*Pref.*

Z1225.H35

Koster, Donald Nelson. American literature and language : a guide to information sources. Detroit : Gale, c1982. 396 p. (Gale information guide library. American studies information guide series, v. 13). **BE407**

A selective guide consisting of 1,885 brief, descriptive (occasionally critical) annotations to books in English. Criticism since 1950 predominates. Pt. 1 is devoted to general reference aids includings bibliographies, checklists, biographical resources, general and literary histories, and general critical studies. Following this are secondary bibliographies for approximately 140 American authors. Pt. 2 consists of 31 entries dealing with American usage, idioms, and linguistic history. Author/title/subject indexes. Subject index includes titles mentioned in annotations. Review: *American reference books annual* 14 (1983): 548. Z1225.K68

Leary, Lewis Gaston. Articles on American literature, 1900–1950. Durham, N.C. : Duke Univ. Pr., 1954. 437 p.   **BE408**

A very useful bibliography—a revision and extension of the author's earlier work which covered 1920–45 (publ. 1947)—based on the bibliographies published quarterly in *American literature* since 1929, and annually in *PMLA* since 1922. The coverage has been broadened as well as extended backward to 1900 by the examination of periodicals and other bibliographies.

Continued by:

Articles on American literature, 1950–1967, comp. with the assistance of Carolyn Bartholet and Catharine Roth (Durham, N.C. : Duke Univ. Pr., 1970. 751 p.).

Compiled on the same basic principles as the earlier volume and employing the same arrangement, this work is both "more inclusive (principally of articles appearing in foreign periodicals) and more selective (in assumptions by the compiler of the value or usefulness of some articles)."—*Introd.*

Articles on American literature, 1968–1975, comp. by Lewis Leary and John Auchard (Durham, N.C. : Duke Univ. Pr., 1979. 745 p.). Follows the plan of the earlier volumes, including additions and corrections to them. Bibliographical essays are marked with an asterisk.   Z1225.L49

Literary writings in America : a bibliography. Millwood, N.Y. : KTO Pr., 1977. 8 v.   **BE409**

Photoreproduction of a card file prepared at the University of Pennsylvania under the auspices of the Works Progress Administration during 1938–42. "The primary purpose of the project was to establish bibliographical controls for materials hitherto inaccessible to researchers; specifically, to construct a complete listing of creative American literature written between 1850 and 1940."—*Pref.*

Arranged alphabetically by literary author, with sections for separate works, periodical publications, biography, and criticism as applicable. "The principal sources of material used in compiling *Literary Writings* are over 2,000 volumes of magazines, more than 500 volumes of literary history and criticism, and more than 100 bibliographics."—*Pref.* Signed book reviews are entered under the name of the reviewer as well as under the name of the author of the book reviewed.

A review in *Booklist* 74 (1 June 1978): 1571 notes various inconsistencies, but recommends the set as a complement to *Poole's index to periodical literature* (AD282), early volumes of *Readers' guide* (AD285), etc.   Z1225.L58

Nilon, Charles H. Bibliography of bibliographies in American literature. N.Y. : Bowker, 1970. 483 p.   **BE410**

A predominantly unannotated bibliography of books, portions of books, and articles compiled primarily from secondary sources. Entries are arranged in four sections: (1) bibliographies (general, national, union catalogs), (2) authors (chronologically, by century), (3) genres, and (4) ancillary subjects including a variety of topics such as humor, satire, presses, and travels. Includes a detailed personal name/title index. Reviewed in *Times literary supplement* (2 July 1971): 788.   Z1225.A1N5

Nilsen, Don Lee Fred. Humor in American literature : a selected annotated bibliography. N.Y. : Garland, 1992. 580 p. (Garland reference library of the humanities, v. 1049).   **BE411**

A selective bibliography of criticism and commentary, including books, book chapters, and articles, most written after 1970 and current through 1988/89. Entries for individual authors range from the 17th century through the 20th. Useful for its inclusion of criticism discussing humor in authors not recognized solely or primarily as "humorists." Individual chapters for thematic or topical aspects of humor in American literature: gallows or black humor, regional humor, political humor, satire and parody, sex-role humor, and humor theory. Index includes personal names and a few broad subject headings. Individual authors are arranged in a somewhat confusing graduated chronology that often requires the use of the index to locate them. Review: *Choice* 30:2 (Oct. 1992): 277.

§ See also: *Encyclopedia of American humorists,* ed. by Steven H. Gale (N.Y. : Garland, 1988–); *Dictionary of literary biography* (BE200), v. 11, *American humorists, 1800–1950,* 2 parts, ed. by Stanley Trachtenberg (Detroit : Gale, 1982).   Z1231.W8N55

Schwartz, Narda Lacey. Articles on women writers : a bibliography. Santa Barbara, Calif. : ABC-Clio, c1977–1986. 2 v.   **BE412**

A bibliography of articles and dissertations on women writers writing in English from the Middle Ages to the present. Articles are drawn from popular publications as well as scholarly journals. Vol. 1 lists secondary sources published 1960–75 for approximately 600 authors; v. 2, sources published 1976–84, covering approximately 1,000 women writers predominantly but not exclusively British and American. Index of scholars.   Z2013.5.W6S37

Sixteen modern American authors : a survey of research and criticism / ed. by Jackson R. Bryer. Durham, N.C. : Duke Univ. Pr., 1974. 673 p.   **BE413**

A revision of *Fifteen modern American authors* (1969).

Patterned after *Eight American authors* (BE403), this volume presents similar survey chapters by specialists, each discussing bibliographies, editions, manuscripts and letters, biography, and critical studies of the individual author. Authors treated: Sherwood Anderson, Cather, Hart Crane, Dreiser, Eliot, Faulkner, Fitzgerald, Frost, Hemingway, O'Neill, Pound, Edwin Arlington Robinson, Steinbeck, Wallace Stevens, Wolfe, William Carlos Williams. Indexed.

Supplemented by: *Sixteen modern American authors : volume 2, a survey of research and criticism since 1972 /* ed. by Jackson R. Bryer (Durham, N.C. : Duke Univ. Pr., 1990. 810 p.).

Because of the sheer volume of material published since the original volume, "it seemed best simply to ask each contributor to prepare a new essay, updating the version in the 1973 edition and incorporating material inadvertently omitted earlier."—*Pref.* As a result, this volume supplements the original work rather than replacing it, listing for the most part material published 1972–85, with some supplements through mid-1988. General index.   PS221.F45

Somer, John L. American and British literature, 1945–1975 : an annotated bibliography of contemporary scholarship / John Somer and Barbara Eck Cooper. Lawrence : Regents Pr. of Kansas, 1980. 326 p.   **BE414**

A valuable selective, annotated bibliography of more than 1,000 book-length studies intended as a guide to the issues, debates, patterns, trends, and backgrounds of contemporary British and American literature. Annotated entries list principal authors treated, are descriptive rather than evaluative, and are arranged in five broad categories: general studies, drama, fiction and prose, poetry, critical theory. Following this are unannotated entries for 162 studies published after 1975. Single-author studies are excluded. Works included must be in English and deal with authors who either began their careers after 1944 or wrote important work before and after 1944. Pt. 2 lists study guides for: abstract, summary, and excerpt collections; general, genre, and topical bibliographies; biographical guides and directories; handbooks. Index includes personal names and subjects.   Z1227.S65

Thompson, Ralph. American literary annuals & gift books, 1825–1865. N.Y. : Wilson, 1936. 183 p.   **BE415**

Contains a history and discussion of representative American annuals and gift books, and a catalog describing some 230 titles, with detailed information as to the different editions of each, location of copies, indication as to whether the annual is for juvenile or adult readers, and many notes concerning reprints under changed titles. Contains much antebellum material as well as the first printings of authors such as Hawthorne, Emerson, and Poe.

§ Should be used in conjunction with: *Indices to American literary annuals and gift books, 1825–1865 /* comp. by E. Bruce Kirkham and John W. Fink (New Haven, Conn. : Research Publications, 1975. 627 p.), which is a reel guide to the microfilm set, *American literary annuals & gift books, 1825–1865* [microform] (Woodbridge, Conn. : Research Publications, 1966) based on Thompson's work. Pt. 1 of the reel guide reproduces the "title page, publishing information, table of contents, and list of illustrations with painters and engravers for each of Thompson's 469 main entries."—*Introd.* Pt. 2 provides indexes for editors, publishers, cities, stereotypers, printers, titles, authors, engraving titles, painters and engravers.   AY10.T5

The Transcendentalists : a review of research and criticism / ed. by Joel Myerson. N.Y. : Modern Language Association of America, 1984. 534 p.   **BE416**

Part of the Modern Language Association's "Reviews of Research" series, this is an invaluable guide to the transcendentalist movement and its members. Five introductory bibliographic essays cover the history of the movement, its historical context, its relationship to Unitarianism, transcendentalist communities, and transcendentalist periodicals. The second section is devoted to 28 individual authors, many not found in other bibliographies of the period. Discussion of Emerson and Thoreau emphasizes their transcendentalist phase. A third section details the response of 11 "major contemporaries who influenced, were influenced by, or reacted against the Transcendentalists".—*Pref.* Research extends from the 19th century through the end of 1981. Extensive bibliography; indexes of persons, titles, with some subject access. For a detailed review, see: *Analytical and enumerative bibliography* n.s. 1:2 (1987): 92–97.   Z7128.T7T7

Wittman, Sandra M. Writing about Vietnam : a bibliography of the literature of the Vietnam Conflict. Boston : G.K. Hall, c1989. 385 p. : ill.   **BE417**

An annotated bibliography of more than 1,700 predominantly literary works on Vietnam, 1954–88, although some notable works published earlier are included. Lists works reflecting "the French period just prior to American involvement, the antiwar activities in the United States during the war, Vietnam after the fall of Saigon, the plight of refugees, and the readjustment of American soldiers returning home as well as ... American involvement in the actual fighting."—*Pref.* Arranged by literary genre with chapters as well for anthologies, adventure novels (unannotated entries), and personal narratives/biographies. Secondary bibliography of literary criticism, bibliographies (books and articles), dissertations and theses, teaching materials, and periodicals with a Vietnam emphasis. Histories, purely historical bibliographies, documents, and political science treatises are excluded. Author and title indexes. A lack of subject indexing and cross-references hinders its ease of use.

Reviewed (with Butler, below) in *The journal of American history*, 77:4 (March 1991): 1483–84.

§ See also: Deborah A. Butler's *American women writers on Vietnam: unheard voices. A select annotated bibliography* (N. Y. : Garland, 1990); Philip K. Jason's *The Vietnam War in literature : an annotated bibliography of criticism* (Pasadena, Calif. : Salem Pr., c1992); and John Newman, *Vietnam literature : an annotated bibliography of imaginative works about Americans fighting in Vietnam* (2nd ed. Metuchen, N. J. : Scarecrow, 1988).   Z3226.W58

Current

See also *MLA international bibliography* (BE39), *Annual bibliography of English language and literature* (BE588), and the two chapters on American literature in *The year's work in English studies* (BE589). Consult *Bibliographic index* (AA15) for bibliographies in books and journals, and William A. Wortman's *A guide to serial bibliographies for modern literatures* (BE34) to identify serially published bibliographies.

American literary scholarship. 1963– . Durham, N.C. : Duke Univ. Pr., 1965– . Annual.   **BE418**

Patterned after *The year's work in English studies* (BE589), *ALS* provides a series of bibliographic essays by scholars reviewing the state of literary scholarship for major individual American authors, American period and genre studies, thematic studies, foreign scholarship, and general reference works. Individual chapters for: Emerson, Thoreau, and transcendentalism; Hawthorne; Poe; Melville; Whitman and Dickinson; Mark Twain; Henry James; Pound and Eliot; Faulkner;

Fitzgerald and Hemingway. Includes an index of scholars and subject authors. An invaluable source for updating and assessing the state of scholarship for American literature.   PS3.A47

English and American studies in German : summaries of theses and monographs. 1968– . Tübingen : M. Niemeyer, 1969– . Annual.   **BE419**

Issued as a supplement to *Anglia*.

Provides English-language abstracts of studies completed in German-speaking countries. Included are treatises and dissertations (most of which are available in book form), annuals, anthologies, casebooks, Festschriften, manuals, conference proceedings, seminars, societies, and symposia. Arranged in four sections: (1) language; (2) English literature (including summaries of theoretical and comparative studies and works on non-British literature in English); (3) American literature (including Canadian literature); and (4) teaching of English. Provides a limited number of summaries, but useful for indexing and summarizing works often omitted from standard bibliographies. Indexes: scholars and editors; contributors to collectanea; authors and subjects.

PE3.A6

Periodicals

See also *Index to little magazines* [1900–67] (AD276) and Frank Luther Mott's *A history of American magazines* [1741–1930] (AD40).

American literary magazines : the eighteenth and nineteenth centuries / ed. by Edward E. Chielens. Westport, Conn. : Greenwood, 1986. 503 p.   **BE420**

Signed essays profile and provide short bibliographies for 92 magazines. Each essay discusses publishing history, editorial personnel and policies, and influence. Appendixes list and briefly describe minor literary magazines or nonliterary magazines which published fiction or belles lettres, and a chronology of publishing and social or literary events. General index.

§ For 19th century indexes see *Poole's index to periodical literature* (AD282), and Daniel A. Wells, *The literary index to American magazines, 1815–1865* (Metuchen, N.J. : Scarecrow, 1980).

American literary magazines : the twentieth century, also ed. by Chielens (Westport, Conn. : Greenwood, 1992), follows the same plan as his earlier work. It profiles 76 magazines, including the most famous little magazines. Two appendixes cover the same material as the 1986 work; a third gives information on 28 repositories of little magazines in the U.S. and Canada.

See also Chielens's bibliography, *The literary journal in America to 1900* (BE421) and Marion Sader, *Comprehensive index to English-language little magazines, 1890–1970* (AD287).   Z1231.P45A43

Chielens, Edward E. The literary journal in America to 1900 : a guide to information sources. Detroit : Gale, [1975]. 197 p. (American literature, English literature, and world literatures in English, v. 3).   **BE421**

A selective annotated bibliography of books, articles, book chapters, and dissertations (in English). An introductory essay is followed by sections for: general studies and contemporary views; literary periodicals by region (including studies of individual periodicals); bibliographies and checklists; and background studies. Includes appendixes for literary material in nonliterary periodicals and for "Poe and the American literary periodical." Excludes dailies and annuals.

———. *The literary journal in America, 1900–1950 : a guide to information sources* (1977. 186 p.) includes chapters on general literary periodicals, little magazines, regional literary periodicals, politically radical literary periodicals, and academic quarterlies of scholarship and criticism. Indexed.   Z6951.C57

Kribbs, Jayne K. An annotated bibliography of American literary periodicals, 1741–1850. Boston : G.K. Hall, c1977. 285 p.   **BE422**

An alphabetical listing of 940 American literary periodicals published during the period. Periodicals included contain a "significant amount of literature" or "are of distinctly literary interest."—*Explanatory notes*. Excluded are dailies, almanacs, gift or emblem books and, for the most part, annuals. Periodicals are indexed by their first title (with title changes noted). The amount of detail varies, but fully annotated entries include: title(s), place of publication, dates of first and last issue, frequency, editor, holdings, and a summary of contents with names of contributors. Indexes: chronological index of periodicals; geographical index; editors and publishers; literary authors; index of tales, novels and drama (approximately 5,000 titles).

Z1219.K75

Dissertations

See also *Comprehensive dissertation index* (AG12) and Michael M. Reynolds, *A guide to theses and dissertations* (1985 ed., AG7).

Gabel, Gernot U. Dissertations in English and American literature : theses accepted by Austrian, French, and Swiss universities, 1875–1970 / comp. by Gernot U. Gabel and Gisela R. Gabel. Hamburg : Gabel, 1977. 198 p. **BE423**
2,169 entries. Arranged by period, general studies being followed by sections for individual literary authors; American literature is treated separately. Author and subject indexes.

————. ————. *Supplement 1971–1975 and additions* (Koln : Edition Gemini, 1982. 56 p.) lists an additional 418 titles.

Z2011.G25

McNamee, Lawrence F. Dissertations in English and American literature : theses accepted by American, British and German universities, 1865–1964. N.Y. : Bowker, 1968. 1124 p. **BE424**
With its two supplements (below), provides a subject bibliography of approximately 26,000 dissertations in a classified arrangement of 35 chapters, variously subdivided. Dissertations are listed chronologically within subdivisions, and are limited to those written in departments of English. Institutions and subjects are coded; an index of major authors is linked to the subject coding. Dissertations that treat several authors are indexed under the first author only, requiring use of a cross-index of authors to locate entries concerned with other authors. Index of dissertation writers. An awkward index, perhaps now most useful as a supplement to more comprehensive sources such as *Comprehensive dissertation index* (AG12) or *Dissertation abstracts international* (AG13).

————. ————. *Supplement 1* (1969. 450 p.); *Supplement 2* (1974. 690 p.). Z5053.M32

Woodress, James Leslie. Dissertations in American literature, 1891–1966. Newly rev. and enl. ed., with the assistance of Marian Koritz. Durham, N.C. : Duke Univ. Pr., 1968. 185 p. **BE425**
1st ed., 1957 (covering 1891–1955); 2nd ed., 1962 (repr. with a suppl. covering 1956–61).
A classified bibliography of almost 4,700 dissertations on American literature, including a number from foreign institutions. In addition to entries for individual authors and genres (further classified), there are topical sections for, e.g., almanacs, gift books, and annuals; Civil War; fine arts; folklore; foreign relationships; periodicals and journalism; philosophy and intellectual history; regionalism; and religion. Includes dissertations in progress at the time of publication. Index of dissertation authors; cross-references at the end of sections. Useful for its inclusion of dissertations from departments other than English. Updated by *Comprehensive dissertation index* (AG12) and *Dissertation abstracts international* (AG13).

§ See also: Patsy C. Howard, *Theses in American literature, 1896–1971* (Ann Arbor, Mich. : Pierian Pr., 1973) for a listing of approximately 7,000 baccalaureate and master's theses from American and foreign universities. Z1225.W8

Criticism

Borklund, Elmer. Contemporary literary critics. 2nd ed. Detroit : Gale, 1982. 600 p. **BE426**
1st ed., 1977.
Intended as a guide to the work of about 125 modern British and American critics. For each, gives a brief biographical sketch, a bibliography of works by and about the critic, and a description of the writer's critical theories and position, together with representative quotations from his works.
§ See also: *Critical survey of literary theory*, ed. by Frank Northen Magill (BE48); René Wellek's *A history of modern criticism : 1750–1950* (BE57); and volumes of the *Dictionary of literary biography* (BE200) that deal with American literary critics, scholars, and literary biographers. PS78.B56

Curley, Dorothy Nyren. Modern American literature / comp. and ed. by Dorothy Nyren Curley, Maurice Kramer [and] Elaine Fialka Kramer. 4th enl. ed. N.Y. : Ungar, [1969–85]. 5 v. **BE427**
1st ed., 1960.
An enlargement and updating of Dorothy Nyren's 1964 volume (3rd ed.) of this title, which was designed as a successor, for American literature, to Charles Wells Moulton's *Library of literary criticism of English and American authors* (BE598). Gives excerpts from critical material found in popular and scholarly journals and in books, on American authors who wrote or became prominent after the turn of the century. Definite citation is given for each excerpt. "One hundred and fifteen authors have been added [in the 4th ed.] … , while more recent excerpts have also been added on two-thirds of the authors in the third edition; none of the excerpts previously included has been omitted."—*Foreword*. Additions include both older and newly established authors; this edition treats nearly 300 authors. Vol. 3 (publ. 1976) includes an index of critics. Vol. 4 is a supplement bringing up to date the criticism on about half the authors represented in vols. 1–3, and treating 49 additional writers. Vol. 5, comp. and ed. by Paul Schleuter and June Schlueter, provides updated brief critical excerpts on 143 authors from the previous editions and criticism on 31 new authors, particularly women authors. Writers whose careers extended from the late nineteenth century have been excluded, and there are fewer critical excerpts for major figures like Eliot.
§ For earlier American writers, see: *The critical temper* (BE597), Charles Wells Moulton's *Library of literary criticism of English and American authors*, and *The new Moulton's library of literary criticism* (BE599). PS221.C8

Twentieth-century American literature / gen. ed., Harold Bloom. N.Y. : Chelsea House Publ., 1985–1988. 8 v. (4747 p., [80] p. of plates) : ports. **BE428**
Attempts to provide for 20th-century American and Canadian authors "the most representative essays and reviews of the modern era."—*Pref*. Excerpts are drawn from newspapers, magazines, journals, and book-length studies. Most author entries are comprised of two sections: (1) extracts (including material from memoirs, interviews, and biographies, as well as short theoretical statements and reviews of individual works); and (2) essays providing more extensive critical analysis. A brief biography is provided for each author; each volume concludes with suggestions for further reading. In addition to a few late 19th-century writers, includes some "mystery, science fiction, fantasy, and non-fiction authors whose works have inspired substantial critical examination." Vol. 8 is a bibliographical supplement and index. PS221.T834

Manuscripts; Archives

See also: *National union catalog of manuscript collections* (DB34), *Directory of archives and manuscript repositories in the United States* (DB30), and Philip M. Hamer, *A guide to archives and manuscripts in the United States* (New Haven, Conn. : Yale Univ. Pr., 1961. 751 p.).

Henry E. Huntington Library and Art Gallery. Guide to literary manuscripts in the Huntington Library. San Marino, Calif. : Huntington Libr., 1979. 539 p.   **BE429**
Sue Hodson, comp.
"The two primary criteria for including an author in the guide are common identification as a literary figure and the appearance of his name in at least one standard biographical dictionary."—*Pref*. Reflects the library's strengths in British and American literature, but includes a few Canadian and European authors. (Manuscripts of authors who died before 1600 will be included in a separate volume devoted to medieval and renaissance manuscripts.) Arrangement is alphabetical by author, with type and extent of the manuscripts indicated; a few of the larger collections are described in some detail.   Z6621.H527H46

Robbins, John Albert. American literary manuscripts : a checklist of holdings in academic, historical, and public libraries, museums, and authors' homes in the United States. 2nd ed. Athens : Univ. of Georgia Pr., c1977. 387 p.   **BE430**
1st ed., 1960.
Sponsored by the American Literature Section of the Modern Language Association.
Lists about 2,800 American writers indicating, by Library of Congress symbol for nearly 600 participating libraries, the holdings of manuscripts of creative works, journals or diaries, letters to and from the author, documents, memorabilia, etc. Type and extent of holdings are shown by "category-symbols," with, when possible, indications of the number of pieces. There is a separate list of authors for whom no holdings were reported.   Z6620.U5M6

Encyclopedias; Dictionaries

Benét's reader's encyclopedia of American literature / ed. by George Perkins, Barbara Perkins, and Phillip Leininger. N.Y. : HarperCollins, c1991. 1176 p.   **BE431**
"Portions of this book appeared in a somewhat modified form in *The reader's encyclopedia of American literature*, published by T.Y. Crowell in 1962, and in *Benét's readers's encyclopedia*, third edition [BE58], published by Harper & Row in 1987"—*t.p. verso*.
Based on Max. J. Herzberg's *The reader's encyclopedia of American literature* (N.Y. : Crowell, [1962]), this volume now includes entries for Canada and Latin America. Interspersed among entries for individual authors and works are longer essays dealing with literary history, literary criticism, genre, period, and ethnic studies, feminism, newspapers and magazines, motion pictures, science fiction and fantasy, humor, and the South. A useful complement to James David Hart, *Oxford companion to American literature* (BE435). Reviewed in *Booklist* 88 (15 Dec. 1991): 781.
§ Less ambitious and covering predominantly major authors and works is *The Cambridge handbook of American literature*, Jack Salzman, ed. (Cambridge : Cambridge Univ. Pr., 1986).   PS21.B46

Burke, William Jeremiah. American authors and books, 1640 to the present day / William Jeremiah Burke, Will D. Howe ; rev. by Irving Weiss and Anne Weiss. 3rd rev. ed. N.Y. : Crown, [c1972]. 719 p.   **BE432**
1st ed., 1943; 2nd ed., 1962.
Provides brief entries for authors and works, literary characters, scholars, societies and associations, literary awards, publishers, literary terms, libraries, magazines and newspapers, and a wealth of related

material. Useful for its breadth and number of entries. Updates but does not supersede the first edition, *American books, 1640–1940*.
Z1224.B87

Duyckinck, Evert Augustus. Cyclopaedia of American literature / Evert Augustus Duyckinck, G. L. Duyckinck ; ed. to date by M. L. Simons. Philadelphia : Baxter, 1875. 2 v. : ill.   **BE433**
Repr. : Detroit : Gale, 1965.
1st ed., 1855. Various printings.
Subtitle: Embracing personal and critical notices of authors, and selections of their writings, from the earliest period to the present day, with portraits, autographs, and other illustrations.
Arranged chronologically, 1626–1875. Still useful for minor earlier writers.   PS85.D7

Handbook of American popular literature / ed. by M. Thomas Inge. N.Y. : Greenwood, 1988. 408 p.   **BE434**
Provides 15 signed bibliographic essays treating categories of popular literature: best sellers, big little books, children's literature, comic books, detective and mystery novels, fantasy, Gothic novels, historical fiction, popular history and biography, pulps and dime novels, romantic fiction, verse and popular poetry, westerns, and young adult fiction. Chapters include sections on research collections and reference tools and provide a historical overview and summary of critical reception for each popular form. Each essay concludes with a secondary bibliography of books and articles; some list relevant indexes and periodicals. Index of personal names.
Ten of the essays were taken from *Handbook of American popular culture* (CF78) and have been revised and updated for this book.
Z1231.P74H36

Handbooks

Hart, James David. The Oxford companion to American literature. 5th ed. N.Y. : Oxford Univ. Pr., 1983. 896 p.   **BE435**
1st ed., 1941; 4th ed., 1965.
A standard reference work for the student of American literature. Although the bulk of entries are for individual authors (including brief biographies and bibliographies) and individual works, there are also entries for literary schools and movements, literary awards, literary societies, scholarly organizations, anthologies, cooperative publications, newspapers and magazines, book collectors, printers, etc. The scope of Hart's volume is more inclusive than belles lettres and "treats major nonliterary aspects of the American mind and the American scene as these are reflected in and influenced by American literature."—*Pref*. Includes a useful chronological index of literary and social history.
A 6th ed. is expected in 1995.   PS21.H3

Chronologies

Ludwig, Richard M. Annals of American literature, 1602–1983 / ed. by Richard M. Ludwig and Clifford A. Nault, Jr. N.Y. : Oxford Univ. Pr., 1986. 342 p.   **BE436**
Patterned after *Annals of English literature, 1475–1950* (BE612). Provides a chronological listing of significant American books, with a side column mentioning new journals, important events of social and political history, and outstanding foreign literary publications. Detailed index.   PS94.L83

Rogal, Samuel J. A chronological outline of American literature. N.Y. : Greenwood, 1987. 446 p. (Bibliographies and indexes in American literature, no. 8).   **BE437**
Covers from the 16th century through 1986. For each year gives names of literary authors and editors who were born or died in that year, two or three political and literary events, and a list of literary works published. Emphasis is on "variety and representation, as well as literary diversity."—*Introd*. Index of authors and events.

§ See also Rogal's *Calendar of literary facts* (BE192). Of interest as well but more topical and anecdotal is Karen L. Rood, *American literary almanac : from 1608 to the present : an original compendium of facts and anecdotes about literary life in the United States of America* (N.Y. : Facts on File, c1988). PS92.R67

Guidebooks

Ehrlich, Eugene H. The Oxford illustrated literary guide to the United States / Eugene H. Ehrlich, Gorton Carruth. N.Y. : Oxford Univ. Pr., 1982. 464 p. : ill. **BE438**

Intended "to help travelers find places associated with the lives and works of writers."—*Pref.* Arranged by state within regions, then by city or town. Includes brief comment on the site or the literary figure associated with it. Index of authors.

§ See also: Emille C. Harting, *A literary tour guide to the United States : Northeast* (N.Y. : Morrow, 1978); Rita Stein, *A literary tour guide to the United States : South and Southwest* (N.Y. : Morrow, 1979); and Rita Stein, *A literary tour guide to the United States : West and Midwest* (N.Y. : Morrow, 1979). PS141.E74

Histories

Columbia literary history of the United States / Emory Elliott, gen. ed. N.Y. : Columbia Univ. Pr., 1988. 1263 p. **BE439**

A worthwhile successor to Robert E. Spiller, *Literary history of the United States* (BE440). Arranged in five sections: from the beginnings (including Native American cave narratives) to 1810; 1810–1865; 1865–1910; 1910–1945; 1945 to the present. Within each section, experts provide essays on genres, schools, major figures, and social, political, and historical developments. The editors have "sought to represent the variety of viewpoints that enliven current scholarship."—*Pref.* A conscious effort has been made not to exclude authors on the basis of gender, race, or ethnic or cultural background; the work "acknowledges diversity, complexity, and contradiction by making them structural principles, and it forgoes closure as well as consensus." The detailed index is necessary to locate all references to a particular author or subject. No bibliography or suggested readings.

§ In progress: *The Cambridge history of American literature* / ed. by Sacvan Bercovitch, assoc. ed., Cyrus R. K. Patell (Cambridge ; N.Y. : Cambridge Univ. Pr., 1994. v. 1). Contents: v. 1, 1590–1820. Planned for 5 v. Now outdated is the earlier *Cambridge history of American literature* / ed. by William Peterfield Trent ... [et al.] (N.Y. : Putnam, 1917–21. 4 v.). PS92.C64

Literary history of the United States / eds.: Robert E. Spiller [et al]. 4th ed., rev. N.Y. : Macmillan, [1974]. 2 v. **BE440**

1st ed., 1948 in 3 v.; various reprintings; bibliography supplements issued 1959 and 1972.

Contents: v. 1, History; v. 2, Bibliography.

The first comprehensive history since the *Cambridge history of American literature* (*see* BE439). Vol. 1 (originally published in 2 v.) presents a survey from colonial times to the present in a series of chapters written by authorities and integrated into a whole by a board of editors. The chapters are not signed, but a list of them with the author of each is given on p. 1476–79. No footnotes. In the 4th ed., the main text remains the same except for minor corrections, but "new scholarship has made imperative ... a wholly new chapter on Emily Dickinson. The chapter on the 'End of an Era,' dealing with the writers who survived World War II, has also been virtually rewritten as time has cleared perspective."—*Pref.* A final section entitled "Mid-century and after" includes new subsections for poetry, drama, and fiction. The Reader's bibliography in v. 1 (p. 1480–1520) has been updated, and the history volume has its own index.

Vol. 2, Bibliography, is a reprinting, with corrections, of the 1963 edition and the bibliography supplements of 1959 and 1972. Tables of contents of the three volumes have been combined, and a new consolidated index is supplied. The volume consists of bibliographical essays

organized to develop the treatment of the text. Divided into four main sections: (1) Guide to resources; (2) Literature and culture; (3) Movements and influences; and (4) Individual authors. This fourth section furnishes information on about 240 authors, usually listing separate and collected works, edited texts and reprints, biography and criticism, primary sources (including location of manuscripts), and bibliographies. Gives valuable critical and evaluative comments on editions, biographies, etc. The index lists names of literary authors treated, titles of periodicals, and some subject and form headings, e.g., Anthologies, Negro writers and writing, Regionalism and local color, etc.; authors of periodical articles are specifically omitted. PS88.L522

Anthologies

The Heath anthology of American literature / Paul Lauter, gen. ed. ; Juan Bruce-Novoa ... [et al.]. 2nd ed. Lexington, Mass. : D.C. Heath, c1994. 2 v. : ill. **BE441**

Contents: v. 1, The colonial period to 1700; 18th century; early 19th century, 1800–1865; v. 2, Late 19th century, 1865–1910; modern period, 1910–1945; contemporary period, 1945 to present.

An anthology of American literature that attempts to be representative of the cultural diversity of the country in which the literature was produced. Includes works by Native Americans, the literature of discovery and exploration (including that of Spanish Americans), and writers formerly ignored or considered undervalued (including many women and minority authors), as well as figures in the traditional literary canon. "It is not that heretofore non-canonical texts provide, so to speak, the landscape of 'minor' writing from which the great monuments of American literature rise. Rather, studying and comparing these differing works will enlarge our understanding of—even help us fundamentally redefine—the literature that has in fact been produced in the United States."—*To the reader.* Introductory essays and critical notes. Each volume includes an index of authors, title, and first lines of poems.

For differing reactions to the 1st ed., see: *Times literary supplement* (19 Oct. 1990): 1133; *Women's review of books* 8 (Sept. 1991): 15. PS507.H35

The Norton anthology of American literature / [ed. by] Nina Baym ... [et al.]. 4th ed. N.Y. : Norton, c1994. 2 v. **BE442**

1st ed., 1979; 3rd ed., 1989.

Contents: v. 1, Literature to 1620; Native American literatures; early American literature 1620–1820; American literature 1820–1865; v. 2, American literature 1865–1914; American literature between the wars 1914–1945; American prose since 1945; American poetry since 1945.

A standard anthology of American poetry and prose. This edition adds a section for literature to 1620, gathering "the writings of encounter—the journals and letters of the first European explorers" (*Pref.*), gives more attention to Native American oral and written traditions, and is generally more inclusive of women and minority authors. Provides reliable introductions to periods and individual authors as well as critical notes for the texts. Each volume includes a selective bibliography and author/title index. PS507.N65

Biography

American women writers : a critical reference guide from colonial times to the present / ed. by Lina Mainiero. N.Y. : Ungar, [1979–94]. 5 v. **BE443**

An abridged edition was edited by Langdon Lynne Faust (N.Y. : Ungar, 1983. 2 v.).

Vol. 5 (1994) is a supplement.

Offers biobibliographical essays (with some critical comment) on a wide range of American women writers of all periods. Articles are signed by the contributors and carry lists of works by and about the authors treated. Aims to include all women writers of established literary reputation; a representative selection of popular writers, "nontraditional" writers (of diaries, letters, etc.), and children's writers; and a number of writers "best known for extraliterary achievements who have had wide general readership."—*Foreword.* Includes living authors.

§ See also: *Notable American women* (AH66).   PS147.A4

American writers : a collection of literary biographies / Leonard Unger, ed. in chief. N.Y. : Scribner, 1974–1991. 7 v. in 10.
BE444

Each suppl. publ. in two parts.

Signed essays on the life and works of selected American authors; selective bibliographies by and about each author. The basic set (1974. 4 v.) contains 97 essays originally published in the University of Minnesota pamphlets on American writers series; some have been revised and updated. Each of the 2-v. supplements covers 29 writers not included in the parent series; the supplements give greater attention to women and minorities. Alphabetic arrangement. Index in each volume; cumulative index in Suppl. 3.

§ See also: *Modern American women writers* (BE448).

PS129.A55

American writers before 1800 : a biographical and critical dictionary / ed. by James A. Levernier and Douglas R. Wilmes. Westport, Conn. : Greenwood, [1983]. 3 v. (1764 p.).
BE445

A significant reference work offering biographical/critical sketches of 786 writers by some 250 scholars. "Writers" is defined broadly to include many lesser known figures of interest to students of American culture, as well as some non-Americans "whose writings concern America and influenced, in some significant way, the development of an American literary heritage and cultural self-identity."—*Pref.* Each entry contains four sections: a chronological list of the writer's major works; a biographical sketch; a critical appraisal; and a selective bibliography of suggested readings. Appendixes list writers by date of birth, place of birth (state), and place of principal residence (state). Chronology (1492–1800); index.   PS185.A4

Biographical dictionary of contemporary Catholic American writing / ed. by Daniel J. Tynan. N.Y. : Greenwood, 1989. 341 p.   **BE446**

Presents "135 biographical-critical essays on a representative group of contemporary Catholic American poets, dramatists and fiction writers."—*Pref.* Signed articles of evaluation for each author are followed by a bibliography. Indexed.   PS153.C3B5

A dictionary of British and American women writers, 1660–1800 / ed. by Janet Todd. Totowa, N.J. : Rowman & Allanheld, 1985. 344 p.   **BE447**

This biographical dictionary of some 450 writers aims "to stimulate research into female literary history and to indicate the wealth and abundance of female writing."—*Pref.* The introductory essay addresses women's writing, discussing class, education, politics, marriage, motives, genres, and themes. Signed, well-written essays range in length from one column (Ann Chandler) to six (Maria Edgeworth) and nearly all the writers profiled receive more extensive treatment here than in other biographical dictionaries. There are no bibliographies of primary or secondary works, although major works are discussed within each essay. Writers are listed alphabetically by their most commonly known name, with cross-references only in the table of contents. Brief subject index.   PR113.D5

Modern American women writers / Elaine Showalter, consulting ed., Lea Baechler, A. Walton Litz, gen. editors. N.Y. : Scribner : Maxwell Macmillan International, c1991. 583 p.
BE448

Also publ. Toronto : Collier Macmillan Canada.

Patterned after the *American writers* (BE444) and *British writers* (BE622) sets. Provides biographical and critical essays on 41 "representative women writers who have published in the United States since the 1870s."—*Introd.* Selective primary and secondary bibliographies. Includes an American feminist chronology (1640–1990) and a detailed index.   PS151.M54

Reference guide to American literature / ed. by D. L. Kirkpatrick. 2nd ed. Chicago : St. James, 1987. 816 p.   **BE449**

A combined and updated edition of *American writers to 1900*, *American writers since 1900*, both ed. by James Vinson, and the chronology portion of *History of American literature* by Walker Marshall (all three publ. Chicago : St. James, 1983).

In three main parts: Writers, Works, and Chronology. Entries for writers provide a biographical sketch, a complete short-title bibliography of the writer's books, a selected bibliography of critical studies, and a signed critical essay. Entries for works consist of short signed essays on particular novels, short stories, poems, or plays. Introductions by Lewis Leary (to 1900) and Warren French (since 1900) summarize American literary history. Title index.

§ See also: Stanley J. Kunitz and Howard Haycraft, *American authors, 1600–1900 : a biographical dictionary of American literature* (N.Y. : H.W. Wilson, 1938. 846 p.) which gives 1,300 biographies, with brief bibliographies by and about the authors.   PS129.R44

Vrana, Stan A. Interviews and conversations with 20th-century authors writing in English : an index. Metuchen, N.J. : Scarecrow, 1982–1990. 3 v.   **BE450**

Vol. 2 called Series II; v. 3 called Series III.

Interviews are drawn from magazines, scholarly journals, newspapers, and books, mostly 1900–85, and mostly with American authors. Index of interviewers and editors. By no means comprehensive, but a useful guide.   Z2013.V73

Who's who in writers, editors & poets, United States & Canada. 3rd ed. (1989/1990)– . Highland Park, Ill. : December Pr., c1989– . Biennial.   **BE451**

1st ed., 1986–87, publ. 1987.

The 4th ed. (1992/93) "contains the biographies of just over 9,000 poets, novelists, nonfiction writers, translators, critics, playwrights, scriptwriters, and biographers from the United States and Canada."—*Pref.* Included are biographical data (date and place of birth, spouse and children, education, awards, memberships, grants, and special achievements), current addresses, and a full publishing and/or editing history. Geographical index.

§ See also: *The writers directory* (BE212) and *Directory of American poets and fiction writers* (N.Y. : Poets & Writers, Inc., 1976–).
PS129.W47

Genres

Drama

See also Section BH, Theater and Performing Arts, for sources for American theater.

Bibliography

American playwrights since 1945 : a guide to scholarship, criticism, and performance / ed. by Philip C. Kolin. N.Y. : Greenwood, c1989. 595 p.   **BE452**

A collection of signed biobibliographic essays on "forty representative, influential playwrights whose works have unquestionably shaped the course of American theatre since World War II."—*Pref.* The essays have six sections: an assessment of achievement and reputation; primary bibliography (including nondramatic production); production history; an evaluative survey of secondary sources (including bibliographies, biographies, influence studies, general studies, and analyses of individual plays); suggested future research opportunities; and a bibliography of sources cited parenthetically throughout the essays. Index of names; index of plays and screenplays.

§ See also: *Dictionary of literary biography* (BE200), v. 7, *Twentieth-century American dramatists* (ed. by John MacNicholas, 1981) for additional biobibliographic essays on American dramatists.
Z1231.D7A53

Bergquist, G. William. Three centuries of English and American plays, a checklist : England: 1500–1800; United States: 1714–1830. N.Y. : Hafner, 1963. 281 p.　　**BE453**

For annotation, *see* BE636.　　Z2014.D7B45

The best plays of [...]. 1992–1993– . N.Y. : Limelight Editions : Proscenium Publishers, Inc., c1993– . Annual. **BE454**

Editors: Otis L. Guernsey, Jr., Jeffrey Sweet; illustrations by Al Hirschfeld.

Continues: *Best plays of [1894/99–] and year book of the drama in America* and *The Applause/best plays theater yearbook.* Publisher and title vary; some annual issues called *Best plays of* [date]; some, *Burns Mantle best plays; The Burns Mantle theater yearbook of* [date]; and *Otis Guernsey Burns Mantle theater yearbook.*

Contents of the annual volumes vary somewhat but include such sections as: (1) Digests with critical comment on selected plays of the year; (2) Title list of plays produced in New York during the year, giving for each: title, author, number of performances, theater, cast of characters, and brief outline of plot; (3) Plays produced outside of New York; (4) Shakespeare festivals; (5) Statistics of runs; (6) List of actors with place and date of birth of each; (7) Prizes and awards; and (8) Index of authors, Index of plays and casts, Index of producers, directors, designers.

Index, 1899–1950 (N.Y. : Dodd, 1950. 147 p.); *Index, 1949–60* (N.Y. : Dodd, 1961. 46 p.).

Include indexes, by title, to the plays appearing in the annual volumes, and indexes to authors, adapters, composers, and lyricists. Symbols indicate one of the "ten best," a Pulitzer-prize play, and a New York Drama Critics Circle award play. A cumulative index was published as: Otis L. Guernsey, *Directory of the American theater, 1894–1971* (BE463).　　PN6112.B45

Bzowski, Frances Diodato. American women playwrights, 1900–1930 : a checklist. Westport, Conn. : Greenwood, 1992. 420 p. (Bibliographies and indexes in women's studies, no. 15).　　**BE455**

A checklist of more than 12,000 plays by American women during the first three decades of the 20th century. "Play" is defined "to include all kinds of dramatic presentations—plays, pageants, stunts, exercises, musical comedies, masques, operas, cantatas and dialogues."—*Pref.* Plays written by women for children and for holiday celebrations are also included. Location codes are provided when available, and the absence of a location code indicates that the play was "probably published" but has not been located. Plays appearing in periodicals and unpublished plays existing in typescript in library collections are also cited. The presence of a playwright in a major biographical source is noted. Concludes with a selective bibliography for American women dramatists. Review: *American reference books annual,* 24 (1993): 495.　　Z1231.D7B95

Davis, Gwenn. Drama by women to 1900 : a bibliography of American and British writers / comp. by Gwenn Davis and Beverly A. Joyce. Toronto ; Buffalo : Univ. of Toronto Pr. ; London : Mansell, 1992. 189 p. (Bibliographies of writings by American and British women to 1900, v. 3).　　**BE456**

A bibliography of 2,828 English-language plays, dramatic poems, and poems for recitation written by English and American women to 1900. Includes published and unpublished plays, as well as plays no longer extant. The entries are drawn principally from *National union catalog, pre-1956 imprints* (AA113) and British Museum, *General catalogue of printed books* (AA103), supplemented by records from OCLC. Appendixes include a chronological listing and a list of actresses. Indexes of translations and adaptations, and of subjects (which includes only very general headings, e.g., "domestic drama," "farce," etc.).　　Z1231.D7D38

Eddleman, Floyd Eugene. American drama criticism : interpretations, 1890–1977. 2nd ed. Hamden, Conn. : Shoe String Pr., 1979. 488 p.　　**BE457**

1st ed. and supplements (1967–76) by Helen H. Palmer and Anne Jane Dyson.

A selective bibliography of critical "interpretations of American plays published primarily between 1890 and 1977 in books, periodicals, and monographs."—*Pref.* Excluded are interviews, biographical studies, and primary bibliographies. Includes some plays by Canadian and Caribbean dramatists whose works have been performed in the U.S. The year is given for the first production of a play. Indexes: books indexed; journals indexed; critics; adapted authors and works (changed titles); titles; and playwrights.

Supplements:

————. ————. *Supplement I* (1984) includes citations through 1982. For many playwrights a general section is included preceding entries for individual plays.

————. ————. *Supplement II* (1989) includes citations through 1987. Includes some European dramatists who live and work in the U.S. or Canada. Greater attention is given to plays by women and minorities. The general section is continued.

————. ————. *Supplement III* (1992) includes citations through 1990 and continues the arrangement of the preceding volumes.

　　Z1231.D7P3

Furtado, Ken. Gay and lesbian American plays : an annotated bibliography / by Ken Furtado and Nancy Hellner. Metuchen, NJ : Scarecrow, 1993. 217 p.　　**BE458**

An annotated bibliography of approximately 700 plays "containing major characters whose gay or lesbian sexuality is integral to the play's message, and plays whose primary themes are gay or lesbian."—*Introd.* Annotations include publication and production information, a plot synopsis, the number or acts, and the number of male and female characters. Also includes a title index of plays, an index of approximately 150 additional plays for which full information could not be obtained, an index of agents, an index of theaters, and a directory of 75 contemporary playwrights. Bibliography of primary and secondary sources for gay and lesbian drama.　　Z1229.G25F87

Gavin, Christy. American women playwrights, 1964–1989 : a research guide and annotated bibliography. N.Y. : Garland, 1993. 493 p. (Garland reference library of the humanities, v. 879).　　**BE459**

Arranged in three sections: (1) a bibliographic essay that assesses the principal studies relating to contemporary women playwrights and feminist theater; (2) a critically evaluative listing of general discussions of American women dramatists and feminist theater; (3) a section for individual playwrights (including bibliographies of selected plays, biographical profiles and interviews, production reviews, and critical studies). Many entries for individual authors are extensively annotated. Books, book chapters, dissertations, periodical and newspaper articles are cited. Included are "American women writers of full-length plays who have demonstrated a sustained record of achievement and who have produced at least one play on Broadway, Off Broadway, or Off-Off Broadway from the early 1960s through 1989."—*Pref.* Lacks a complete index of playwrights; includes indexes for scholars/reviewers and for multicultural playwrights.

§ Broader in scope but less satisfactory is Brenda Coven's *American women dramatists of the twentieth century : a bibliography* (Metuchen, N.J. : Scarecrow, 1982), which lists predominantly unannotated entries for 133 playwrights.　　Z1231.D7G38

Harris, Richard Hough. Modern drama in America and England, 1950–1970 : a guide to information sources. Detroit : Gale, c1982. 606 p. (American literature, English literature, and world literatures in English, v. 34).　　**BE460**

Lists of bibliographies for drama and theater and a section of selected critical writings are followed by writings by and about 255 individual American and English playwrights. Brief annotations (occasionally evaluative) accompany most entries. "The listing of plays extends through 1975 although the reader will find citations or critical essays on only those works published from 1950 through 1970."—*Introd.* Plays performed prior to 1950 but published between 1950 and 1970 are included; plays performed between 1950 and 1975 but not published until after 1975 are excluded. Indexes for personal names, titles, and subjects.　　Z1231.D7H36

Library of Congress. Copyright Office. Dramatic compositions copyrighted in the United States : 1870 to 1916. Wash. : U.S. Govt. Print. Off., 1918. 2 v. (3547 p.).   **BE461**
Repr. : N.Y. : Johnson Reprint Corp., 1968.
Prepared by the Catalogue and index division of the Copyright office under the supervision of Henry S. Parsons, chief of the division.
A list of about 60,000 plays registered for copyright July 21, 1870–Dec. 31, 1916. The main list is arranged alphabetically by title and gives, for each title, author's name, number of acts, number of pages, place published and date of a published play (or the word "typewritten" to indicate the typed manuscript of an unpublished play), date of copyright, holder of copyright, number of copies deposited, etc. Cross-references from alternate, secondary, and translated titles are given in the main alphabet. Also includes a supplementary alphabet of recent titles (1915–16), and a detailed author index containing names of authors, joint authors, editors, translators, and copyright proprietors, pseudonyms, etc.
§ For titles of plays copyrighted later than 1916, the *Catalog of copyright entries* (AA433) should be consulted.   Z5781.U55

Meserve, Walter J. American drama to 1900 : a guide to information sources. Detroit : Gale, c1980. 254 p. (American literature, English literature, and world literatures in English, 28).   **BE462**
A bibliography of American drama, not American theater. Thus, "the entries deal with dramatists and their plays plus discussions of dramatic theory, dramatic criticism, and the critics themselves."— *Introd.* A section dealing with "Critical, historical, and reference resources" is followed by a section devoted to individual dramatists. Author, title, and subject indexes.   Z1231.D7M45

Indexes

Guernsey, Otis L. Directory of the American theater, 1894–1971 : indexed to the complete series of *Best plays* theater yearbooks. N.Y. : Dodd, Mead, [1971]. 343 p.   **BE463**
Subtitle: Titles, authors, and composers of Broadway, off-Broadway, and off-off-Broadway shows and their sources.
An author, title, composer index to the Otis Guernsey/Burns Mantle *Best plays* series (BE454 *note*) rather than a directory in its own right.   PN6112.B4524

Hixon, Donald L. Nineteenth-century American drama : a finding guide / Donald L. Hixon, Don A. Hennessee. Metuchen, N.J. : Scarecrow, 1977. 579 p.   **BE464**
Essentially a finding list to the "American plays, 1831–1900" portion of the Readex Corporation's microprint collection *English and American plays of the nineteenth century*. Lists about 4,500 plays, including plays of British and continental authors adapted or translated for the American stage. Author listing with three appendixes: (1) Series (which lists the contents of the many series analyzed in the main work); (2) Ethnic/racial (which lists those plays which include characters of a particular racial or ethnic origin); and (3) Subject/form (which "groups those plays dealing with particular broad subject areas, or representing specific literary and dramatic forms, into a variety of appropriate categories."—*Pref.*).
§ *See also:* Robert F. Roden, *Later American plays, 1831–1900 : being a compilation of the titles of plays by American authors published and performed in America since 1831* (N.Y. : Dunlap Soc., 1900. Repr. : N.Y. : B. Franklin, 1964).   PS632.H57

Marks, Patricia. American literary and drama reviews : an index to late nineteenth century periodicals. Boston : G.K. Hall, c1984. 313 p.   **BE465**
Cites reviews published in some thirteen periodicals during the period 1880–1900. Drama reviews and literary reviews are listed in separate sections, the first by title of the drama reviewed, the second by author of the book reviewed. Only "domestic presentations by American and foreign playwrights" (*Pref.*) are indexed in the drama section; U.S. publications predominate in the literary reviews section, but other works are not excluded. Indexed.   PN2256.M37

Histories

Meserve, Walter J. An emerging entertainment : the drama of the American people to 1828. Bloomington : Indiana Univ. Pr., c1977. 342 p.   **BE466**
————. *Heralds of promise : the drama of the American people during the age of Jackson, 1829–1849* (N.Y. : Greenwood, 1986. [Contributions in American studies, 86]).
The first two of a projected six-volume history of American drama, from its beginnings to the present, in which a critical assessment of American drama is seen in relation to the cultural and social history of the nation. Both volumes conclude with a selected bibliography and an index of American playwrights and plays, 1829–49. Reviews: for *An emerging entertainment: American literature* 50 (Nov. 1978): 519; for *Heralds of Promise: American literature* 59 (May 1987): 292 and *Journal of American history* 73 (Mar. 1987): 1028.
§ Does not supersede Arthur Hobson Quinn's *A history of the American drama from the beginning to the Civil War* (2nd ed. N.Y. : Crofts, 1943) or *A history of the American drama from the Civil War to the present day* ([Rev. ed.]. N.Y. : Crofts, 1937. 2 v. in 1). *See also* two recent volumes in "Twayne's critical history of American drama" series: Jordan Yale Miller's *American drama between the wars : a critical history* (Boston : Twayne, c1991) and Gary A. Richardson's *American drama from the Colonial period through World War I : a critical history* (N.Y. : Twayne, c1993).   PS332.M39

The Revels history of drama in English / gen. editors, Clifford Leech and T. W. Craik. London : Methuen ; N.Y. : Barnes and Noble Import Div., 1976–1983. 8 v. : ill.   **BE467**
In v. 8, *American drama*, by Travis Bogard, Richard Moody, and Walter J. Meserve (1977), a chronological table of historical and theatrical events, 1492–1975, precedes the history proper. Bibliographic essay, p. 297–310. Indexed. For complete annotation, *see* BE667.   PR625.R44

Fiction

Bibliography

Bibliography of American fiction, 1919–1988 / ed. by Matthew J. Bruccoli and Judith S. Baughman. N.Y. : Facts On File, 1991. 2 v. (648 p.).   **BE468**
Gives bibliographies for 219 American fiction writers born before 1941 whose "earliest significant volume of fiction" was published after 1918 (an author is characterized as a fiction writer if "fiction represents a principal aspect of his [*sic*] career."—*Introd.*). Publications included are current through 1988. In addition to established literary authors, the work includes a number of popular writers of science fiction, mystery, westerns, and children's literature. For each author, includes: a brief headnote intended to establish the author's reputation; a primary bibliography (including a list of the first American editions of the author's books in all genres; standard editions and collections; letters, diaries and notebooks; and major institutional repositories for manuscripts); a selective secondary bibliography that includes biographies, concordances, interviews, and critical studies from books, articles, and theses. A brief bibliography intended as a vade mecum for students of American literature and a more general bibliography of reference and research works precede the individual author entries. Includes a chronology of American fiction (1919–88) and an index of scholars and critics.
Part of an ambitious series from Facts on File under Bruccoli's general editorship which will attempt to provide a selective bibliography of American literature from 1588 through 1988. Arrangement is to be by genre and by period within genre. Although considered by some to be eclectic in its coverage of authors, this series promises to fill a genuine need for a bibliography of American literature. Reviews: *Booklist* 88:9 (1 Jan. 1993): 845; *Choice* 29 (Feb. 1992): 873.

§ For updates, consult the fiction sections of *American literary scholarship* (BE418) and *MLA international bibliography* (BE39); *see also* individual author bibliographies in Twayne's United States authors series. Z1231.F4B47

Contemporary gay American novelists : a bio-bibliographical critical sourcebook / ed. by Emmanuel S. Nelson. Westport, Conn. : Greenwood, 1993. 421 p. **BE469**

Provides signed essays on 57 contemporary gay American novelists following an introductory essay on gay literature. Each author essay includes a biographical sketch, a statement of major themes and works, a discussion of the author's critical reception, and a bibliography of primary and secondary works. Includes a directory of small presses that regularly publish works of gay fiction and a list of selected journals of interest to the student of gay literature. Index of authors and titles.

§ *See also*: Sandra Pollack and Denise D. Knight, *Contemporary lesbian writers of the United States : a bio-bibliographical critical sourcebook* (BE402). PS374.H63C66

Dickinson, A. T. Dickinson's American historical fiction. 5th ed. / Virginia Brokaw Gerhardstein. Metuchen, N.J. : Scarecrow, 1986. 352 p. **BE470**

1st ed., 1958; 4th ed., 1981.

"A total of 3,048 novels casting light on some aspect of American history are classified into natural chronological periods from Colonial days to the 1970's."—*Pref.* Annotations; author/title and subject indexes. Mainly publications of 1917-84, with some earlier standard works.

§ *See also*: Otis Welton Coan and Robert Gordon Lillard, *America in fiction : an annotated list of novels that interpret aspects of life in the United States, Canada, and Mexico* (5th ed. : Palo Alto, Calif. : Pacific Books, 1967); and Jack Warner Van Derhoof, *A bibliography of novels related to American frontier and colonial history* (Troy, N.Y. : Whitston, 1971). Z1231.F4D47

Eichelberger, Clayton L. A guide to critical reviews of United States fiction, 1870-1910. Metuchen, N.J. : Scarecrow, 1971-74. 2 v. **BE471**

Vol. 1 provides critical reviews for both major and minor fiction authors, drawn from approximately 30 periodicals of the period (e.g., *Athenaeum, Atlantic monthly*); v. 2 provides reviews from an additional ten periodicals. Although plagued by inaccuracies, these volumes are useful for the number of lesser figures included. For a review of its shortcomings see: *Nineteenth-century fiction* 27:2 (Sept. 1972): 245-7. Z1225.E35

Facts on File bibliography of American fiction, 1866-1918 / ed. by James Nagel and Gwen L. Nagel. N.Y. : Facts on File, c1993. 412 p. **BE472**

Following the plan of the *Bibliography of American fiction, 1919-1988* (BE468), this work provides bibliographies for 149 American fiction writers who published their significant fiction between 1866 and 1918. This work also includes a brief bibliography for students of American literature and a general bibliography of reference and research sources for the period covered. Z1231.F4B46

Gerstenberger, Donna Lorine. The American novel : a checklist of twentieth-century criticism / by Donna Gerstenberger and George Hendrick. Denver : A. Swallow, [1961-70]. 2 v. **BE473**

Contents: [v. 1] The American novel, 1789-1959; v. 2, Criticism written 1960-1968.

A selective, unannotated bibliography of books, book chapters, and articles published 1900-68. Arranged in two sections: (1) individual authors (including criticism of individual novels, general studies of the author, and bibliographies); (2) general studies of American fiction (by century). Cites a number of standard works.

§ See Lewis Gaston Leary's *Articles on American literature, 1900-1950* and its continuations (BE408) for additional articles written during roughly the same time period. Z1231.F4G4

Grimes, Janet. Novels in English by women, 1891-1920 : a preliminary checklist / Janet Grimes, Diva Daims. N.Y. : Garland, 1981. 805 p. (Garland reference library of the humanities, v. 202). **BE474**

Lists some 15,000 novels by more than 5,000 authors published in England and the U.S. In three sections: (1) alphabetical listing of authors with their novels, verified; (2) anonymous and pseudonymous works, also verified; (3) citations to books not seen. Most entries are annotated. Title index.

§ See also the authors' *Toward a feminist tradition : an annotated bibliography of novels in English by women, 1891-1920* (N.Y. : Garland, c1982). Selected from their earlier work, provides descriptive annotations for 3,407 titles that focus on the "efforts of women to control their lives or on social attitudes and conditions functioning as counterforces to that achievement."—*Introd.* Z2013.5.W6G75

Hanna, Archibald. A mirror for the nation : an annotated bibliography of American social fiction, 1901-1950. N.Y. : Garland, 1985. 472 p. (Garland reference library of the humanities, v. 595). **BE475**

Aims "to provide an annotated guide to the large body of fiction published between 1901 and 1950, which is useful as source material for the economic, political and social history of the United States during that period."—*Introd.* Arrangement is alphabetical by author; covers nearly 4,000 works. Because of the importance of popular fiction to this kind of study, literary quality was not a criterion for inclusion. By far the largest group of novels deal with the literature of place (specific regions, cities, etc.); also includes works dealing with trades and occupations, social institutions, political activities, etc. Generally excludes detective stories and the classic Western fiction. Detailed subject index, title index, index of illustrators. Z1231.F4H32

McPheron, William. The bibliography of contemporary American fiction, 1945-1988 : an annotated checklist / William McPheron and Jocelyn Sheppard. Westport, Conn. : Meckler, c1989. 190 p. **BE476**

A useful guide to multi-author and single author bibliographies. Emphasizes "writers of adult fiction whose reputations have been established since 1945."—*Pref.* Provides more than 550 single-author bibliographies for approximately 125 authors. Cites bibliographies in journals and dissertations as well as book-length studies.

§ See also: *Bibliographic index* (AA15) for more recent works. Now largely out of date is Patricia Pate Havlice, *Index to American author bibliographies* (Metuchen, N.J. : Scarecrow, 1971).

Z1231.F4M36

Menendez, Albert J. Civil War novels : an annotated bibliography. N.Y. : Garland, 1986. 174 p. (Garland reference library of the humanities, v. 700). **BE477**

Lists some 1,000 novels depicting the Civil War, the South during Reconstruction, and novels of the pre-war period that deal with slave or plantation life. Arranged alphabetically by author; short annotations. Title index; subject index intended to identify books for younger readers. Z1231.F4M46

Parker, Patricia L. Early American fiction : a reference guide. Boston : G.K. Hall, c1984. 197 p. **BE478**

Provides descriptive annotations of book-length studies, articles, and dissertations on American fiction to 1800. Includes general and thematic studies as well as studies of 28 individual authors. Excludes Charles Brockden Brown, who is covered by the author's *Charles Brockden Brown : a reference guide* (Boston : G.K. Hall, 1981).

§ Somewhat dated but covering 19th- as well as 18th-century fiction is David K. Kirby's *American fiction to 1900 : a guide to information sources* (Detroit : Gale, [1975]). Z1231.F4P25

Weixlmann, Joseph. American short fiction criticism and scholarship, 1959-1977 : a checklist. Chicago : Swallow Pr. ; Athens, Ohio : Ohio Univ. Pr., c1982. 625 p. **BE479**

Covers more than 500 authors, 18th-20th centuries, and provides a checklist of English-language articles, portions of books, interviews, and bibliographies drawn from approximately 5,000 books and more than 325 serial titles. Entries cover both general studies of short fiction

and individual authors. The author entries include criticism of individual short stories, general studies, interviews, and bibliographies. Extensive cross-referencing. The lack of an index hinders use. A valuable
guide to short-fiction scholarship and criticism for the period.

§ For multinational coverage of authors of short fiction, *see*:
Frank N. Magill, *Critical survey of short fiction* (BE261) and Warren
S. Walker, *Twentieth-century short story explication* (BE264).

Z1231.F4W43

White, Barbara Anne. American women's fiction, 1790–
1870 : a reference guide. N.Y. : Garland, 1990. 294 p. (Garland reference library of the humanities, v. 1110).   **BE480**
  Provides critical or biographical information on American women
fiction writers born before 1841 who published a significant amount of
their fiction before 1870. Pt. 1 contains annotated entries for books,
book chapters, and articles that discuss American women's fiction (not
single authors), 1790–1870. Also included in pt. 1 are more general
works that "emphasize either literature or women and discuss three or
more women who wrote fiction" (*Pref.*) for that same period, such as
Notable American women : a biographical dictionary (AH66). Each
entry lists women authors covered in the cited work. Pt. 2 is an author
list of 328 women fiction writers discussed in the sources represented
in pt. 1, cross-referenced to those entries. Indexes: pt. 1, authors and
editors, subjects; pt. 2, pseudonyms and alternative names. Reviewed:
Choice 27 : 11/12 (July/Aug. 1990): 1811.
  § For more recent works, see: *Novels in English by women,
1891–1920* (BE474).   Z1231.F4W49

Woodress, James Leslie. American fiction, 1900–1950 : a
guide to information sources. Detroit : Gale, [1974]. 260 p.
(American literature, English literature, and world literatures
in English, v. 1).   **BE481**
  Pt. 1, General bibliography, contains four brief sections: one lists
general background source material; the others, specialized source materials on the novel, the short story, and interviews with authors. Pt. 2
comprises 44 individual bibliographical essays on those writers "who
seem in 1973 to be the most significant producers of fiction during the
first half of the twentieth century. They have been selected on the basis
of the critical esteem accorded them during the 23 years that have
passed since 1950."—*Introd.* The bibliographical essays include notes
on bibliography and manuscripts, editions and reprints, biography, and
criticism. Indexed.   Z1231.F4W64

Wright, Lyle Henry. American fiction, 1774–1850 : a contribution toward a bibliography. 2nd rev. ed. San Marino, Calif. :
Huntington Libr., 1969. 411 p.   **BE482**
  1st ed., 1939; rev. ed., 1948.
  This work and its like-named companion volumes (below) constitute the most complete primary bibliography of American fiction
through 1900. They include novels, romances, tales, short stories, fictitious biographies, travels, sketches, allegories, tractlike tales, and
other writings of a similar nature. The three works exclude "annuals
and gift books, publications of the American Tract Society and the
Sunday School Union, juveniles, Indian captivities, jestbooks, folklore,
anthologies, collections of anecdotes, periodicals, and extra numbers
of periodicals."—*Introd.* Intended to serve as a guide to American fiction rather than as a complete descriptive bibliography. This volume
attempts to list all American editions, whereas the subsequent volumes
list only the first or earliest located edition of a title. Lists approximately 3,500 items and locates copies in 22 libraries.
  Continued by:
  (1) *American fiction, 1851–1875 : a contribution toward a bibliography.* Additions and corrections appended (San Marino, Calif. :
Huntington Libr., 1965. 438 p.).
  First publ. 1957; this is a reprint with additions and corrections, p.
417–38.
  Lists more than 2,800 titles. Locates copies in 18 libraries and one
private collection.
  (2) *American fiction, 1876–1900 : a contribution toward a bibliography* (San Marino, Calif. : Huntington Libr., 1966. 683 p.).
  Lists 6,175 items, with locations (representing 15 libraries) given
for most.

§ Almost all the works cited in Wright have been microfilmed
and are part of the research collection *American fiction, 1774–1910*
(New Haven, Conn. : Research Publ., [1984]. 1328 reels). Editions
after 1900 were based on the Library of Congress shelflist of American adult fiction.   Z1231.F4W9

Indexes

White, Ray Lewis. Index to *Best American short stories* and
O. Henry prize stories. Boston : G.K. Hall, c1988. 183 p.
    BE483
  Provides author and title indexes for *Best American short stories*
(1915–86) and *Prize stories : the O. Henry awards* (1919–87), as well
as descriptive essays on the history of those two publications. Also
lists O. Henry prizewinners by year.   Z1231.F4W52

Encyclopedias; Dictionaries

Dictionary of American literary characters / ed. by Benjamin Franklin V ; associate editors, Gary Geer and Judith Haig.
N.Y. : Facts on File, 1990. 542 p.   **BE484**
  A dictionary of "major characters in significant American novels—in addition to those in some uncelebrated novels and in a sampling of bestsellers" published 1789–1979. The brief entries identify
and describe a character and the novel in which the character appears.
Some historical figures (e.g., Babe Ruth, George Washington) are included as well as purely fictional characters. Includes an index of authors and novels, with characters listed for the novels included. "Because a novelist is included does not mean that characters from all his
or her novels are described."—*Pref.* A convenient quick reference
source.
  § See also: *Cyclopedia of literary characters* (BE186) and *Dictionary of British literary characters : 18th- and 19th-century novels*
(BE688).   PS374.C43D5

Histories

The Columbia history of the American novel / Emory Elliott, general ed. ; associate editors, Cathy N. Davidson ... [et
al.]. N.Y. : Columbia Univ. Pr., c1991. 905 p.   **BE485**
  Essays attempt to present a history of the American novel more
inclusive of women and minorities. Arrangement is by period (beginnings to the mid-19th century; the late 19th century; the early 20th century; the late 20th century). The approach is thematic rather than strictly chronological and reflects a concern for issues of race, gender, and
class. Traces the development of the novel in Canada, the Caribbean,
and Latin America, as well as the U.S. Includes biographical sketches
for approximately 200 writers, and a selective critical bibliography (for
which there is no thematic arrangement).
  This volume is not without its critics. For a balanced review, *see*:
American book review 14, no. 3 (Aug/Sep. 1992): 24–25.
  § Still of value: Alexander Cowie, *The rise of the American novel*
(N.Y. : American Book, 1948); and Arthur Hobson Quinn, *American
fiction : an historical and critical survey* (N.Y. : Appleton-Century-
Crofts, 1936).   PS371.C7

Anthologies

The best American short stories. 1978– . Boston : Houghton
Mifflin, 1978– . Annual.   **BE486**
  Title varies: 1915–41, *Best short stories and the Yearbook of the
American short story*; 1942–77, *The best American short stories and
the Yearbook of the American short story.*
  The stories selected for this anthology must have been published
in the preceding calendar year and meet the following criteria: "(1)

original publication in nationally distributed American or Canadian periodicals; (2) publication in English by writers who are American or Canadian, or who have made the United States or Canada their home; (3) publication as short stories (novel excerpts are not knowingly considered)."—*Foreword.* A distinguished writer serves as each volume's guest editor. The volume for 1992 includes 20 short stories from 1991, a list of 100 other distinguished stories for the same year, and a directory of American and Canadian magazines that publish short stories.
PZ1.B446235

Poetry

Davis, Lloyd M. Contemporary American poetry : a checklist / by Lloyd Davis and Robert Irwin. Metuchen, N.J. : Scarecrow, 1975. 179 p. **BE487**
Primarily a guide to separately-published volumes of American poetry of the 1950s and 1960s, though some earlier works by poets born after 1900 who continued to be productive after 1950 are included. Entries current through 1973. Generally excludes vanity press publications; collaborations; translations; greeting cards and light verse; children's books; broadsides; reprints (except when incorporating substantial revision or enlargement); and books that are predominately illustrative. Title index. Necessarily selective, but a useful checklist for the period.
A volume called *Second series, 1973–1983,* ed. by Davis, was publ. 1985. Patterned after the earlier work, it identifies about 5,000 titles for the decade. Title index. Z1231.P7D38

Bibliography

Alexander, Harriet Semmes. American and British poetry : a guide to the criticism, 1925–1978. Athens, Ohio : Swallow Pr., c1984. 486 p. **BE488**
Identifies explications of poems of a thousand lines or less. Citations are drawn from books and articles, although books on single poets are excluded. Because of the number of poets included, this work complements *Guide to American poetry explication* (BE491) and *Guide to British poetry explication* (BE710). Z1231.P7A44

Davis, Gwenn. Poetry by women to 1900 : a bibliography of American and British writers / comp. by Gwenn Davis and Beverly A. Joyce. Toronto ; Buffalo : Univ. of Toronto Pr., 1991. 340 p. (Bibliographies of writings by American and British women to 1900, v. 2). **BE489**
Second "in a series designed to make accessible literary works by well known and neglected writers in order to re-establish the range and variety of books published by women from 1475-1900."—*Introd.* Some 6,000 entries, arranged by author. Entries include author's name; the author's husband's name (when applicable); nationality; birth and death dates; alternative forms of her legal name; and pseudonyms. Includes a bibliography of general sources and of sources of poetry. Subject index.
§ For other volumes in this series, see: *Personal writings by women to 1900* (BE508) and *Drama by women to 1900* (BE456). Volumes are planned for short fiction, long fiction, and juvenile literature. Z2013.5.W6D38

Gingerich, Martin E. Contemporary poetry in America and England, 1950–1975 : a guide to information sources. Detroit : Gale, c1983. 453 p. (Gale information guide library. American literature, English literature, and world literatures in English information guide series, v. 41). **BE490**
Seven chapters are devoted to general studies: (1) bibliographies and reference works; (2) contemporary culture and sociology; (3) general aesthetics and poetic theory; (4) studies of poetry and poets; (5) American poets and literature; (6) English poets and literature; (7) studies of two or more poets. Sections for approximately 130 individual poets list primary bibliographies and secondary bibliographies (including biographies, bibliographies, critical books, and articles). Criticism is generally current through 1978, though some articles are as late

as 1981. Indexes of authors (scholars and subject authors) and of titles. It is necessary to use the author index to identify all references to a specific poet.
§ More selective is Charles F. Altieri, *Modern poetry* (Arlington Heights, Ill. : AHM Publishing, c1979). Z1231.P7G56

Guide to American poetry explication. Boston : G.K. Hall, c1989. 2 v. **BE491**
Contents: v. 1, Colonial and nineteenth century, ed. by James Ruppert; v. 2, Modern and contemporary, ed. by John R. Leo.
With the *Guide to British poetry explication* (BE710), effectively supersedes Joseph M. Kuntz and Nancy C. Martinez's *Poetry explication* (3rd ed. Boston : G.K. Hall, 1980), extending coverage of that work through December 1987 and maintaining that volume's arrangement. Unlike the earlier work, includes explications from books devoted to single authors, explications of poems of more than 500 lines, and adds many poets formerly excluded from the literary canon. "American" has been expanded to include Canadian poets; Canadian journals are cited as well. An indispensable reference tool. Z1231.P7G85

Jantz, Harold Stein. The first century of New England verse. N.Y. : Russell & Russell, 1962. 292 p. **BE492**
Provides an anthology, historical survey, and bibliography of early New England verse. Includes fragments, epitaphs, and lists of all known verse (both manuscript and published) by New England writers up to those born in the 1670s. Cites approximately 180 writers. Entries for anonymous writings follow the author entries. Gives locations Still useful for identification. PS312.J3

Jason, Philip K. Nineteenth century American poetry : an annotated bibliography. Pasadena, Calif. : Salem Pr., c1989. 257 p. **BE493**
Treats 16 poets, citing both general studies and books or articles devoted to specific poems. Highly selective; annotations are descriptive rather than evaluative. Author index; index of scholars. Z1231.P7J37

John Carter Brown Library. Dictionary catalog of the Harris collection of American poetry and plays, Brown University Library, Providence, Rhode Island. Boston : G.K. Hall, 1972. 13 v. **BE494**
An earlier catalog of the collection was published by the Brown University Library as *The Anthony memorial : a catalogue of the Harris collection of American poetry with biographical and bibliographical notes,* by John C. Stockbridge (Providence, R.I. : Providence Press Printers, 1886. 320 p. Repr. 1972, 1978).
Reproduction of the catalog cards for more than 150,000 printed books and pamphlets by American and Canadian authors. The library attempts to acquire every volume of American and Canadian verse and every play of similar origin. (Latin American poetry and plays were collected up to the 1950s, but since that time only Mexican authors are collected.) The catalog does not include the extensive collections of broadsides, manuscripts, and sheet music in the library.
§ Many of the titles listed in the Harris Collection have been microfilmed and are available as part of the research collection *American poetry 1609–1870* (Woodbridge, Conn. : Research Publ., [c1975]–). Z1231.P7B72

McPheron, William. The bibliography of contemporary American poetry, 1945–1985 : an annotated checklist. Westport, Conn. : Meckler Publ., c1986. 72 p. **BE495**
Emphasis is on poets "whose reputations have been established since 1945."—*Pref.* Excludes writers whose poetry is incidental to their literary output. Concentrates on works providing significant coverage of individual poets or of the small presses responsible for publication of much of their poetry. Annotations are succinctly evaluative. Highly selective checklists are generally excluded. An extremely useful source for author bibliographies.
§ Now somewhat dated is Patricia Pate Havlice, *Index to American author bibliographies* (Metuchen, N.J. : Scarecrow, 1971). Z1231.P7.M37

Reardon, Joan. Poetry by American women, 1900–1975 : a bibliography / by Joan Reardon and Kristine A. Thorsen. Metuchen, N.J. : Scarecrow, 1979. 674 p.   **BE496**

Identifies "separately published volumes of poetry by women who are United States citizens whose major works have appeared during the period 1900–1975."—*Introd.* Lists approximately 9,500 volumes of poetry by more than 5,500 American women poets. Excludes audiovisual works, collaborative works, mixed genre works, foreign language editions, reprints, broadsides, and testimonials. Includes an index of titles. An extremely useful checklist!

A supplement ed. by Reardon covering 1975–89 (publ. 1990) follows the arrangement of the earlier volume, and identifies 2,880 titles by 1,565 authors; unlike the other work, includes collaborative works and reprints.   Z1229.W8R4

Scheick, William J. Seventeenth-century American poetry : a reference guide / William J. Scheick and JoElla Doggett. Boston : G. K. Hall, c1977. 188 p. (Reference guides in literature, no. 14.).   **BE497**

Provides an annotated bibliography of criticism for "all identifiable colonial poets (including immigrants and transients) born in the 1670's or before, even if their poetry was not published until later."—*Pref.* Sections for approximately 60 individual poets; general and thematic studies, literary influences and aesthetics; almanacs; Bay Psalm Book, psalm-singing, and other church music; broadsides, ballads, and anonymous verse; and elegies. Within sections, criticism is arranged chronologically and further divided into books, shorter writings, and dissertations. Excludes bibliographies and checklists. Index of scholars, poets, and selected subjects. Although the arrangement is somewhat awkward, this is a useful bibliography of secondary scholarship for the period.   Z1227.S3

Wegelin, Oscar. Early American poetry : a compilation of the titles and volumes of verse and broadsides by writers born or residing in North America, north of the Mexican border. 2nd ed. rev. and enl. N.Y. : Peter Smith, 1930. 2 v. in 1. : ill.   **BE498**

Covers 1650–1820, listing 1,379 titles of British and American eiditons of poetry by Americans. Arranged by author within each volume, with the author's works listed chronologically. Earliest identified editions generally include descriptive annotations. Gives some locations. Title index, vol. 2.

Supplemented by Roger Stoddard's *A catalogue of books and pamphlets unrecorded in Oscar Wegelin's Early American poetry, 1650–1820* (Providence, R.I. : Friends of the Library of Brown Univ., 1969. 84 p.).

Reprinted from *Books at Brown*, v. 23 (1969).

Describes and locates more than 250 books and pamphlets not recorded in Wegelin's bibliography, or not fully described therein.

§ Most of the titles in these two works are part of the microfilm collection *American poetry 1609–1870* (Woodbridge, Conn. : Research Publ., [1975]–).   Z1231.P7W4

Indexes

Index of American periodical verse. 1971– . Metuchen, N.J. : Scarecrow, 1973– . Annual.   **BE499**

Covers poems "published in a broad cross-section of poetry, literary, scholarly, popular, general, and 'little' magazines, journals and reviews published in the United States, Canada, and the Caribbean."—*Introd.* The volume for 1991 indexes 287 periodicals, citing more than 18,000 poems by approximately 7,000 poets and translators. Translations are indexed by both poet and translator. For periodicals indexed, gives publisher, address, editor, frequency, and subscription information. Also includes separate listings for periodicals added and periodicals deleted. Publishing lag, one to two years.

§ *Roth's American poetry annual* (BE502) provides additional indexing of individual poems. *The American humanities index* (BA2), *Humanities index* (BA5), and *Readers' guide to periodical literature* (AD285) also provide access, under the subject heading Poems.

Two works by Jefferson D. Caskey index poems in popular magazines: *Index to poetry in popular periodicals, 1955–1959* (Westport, Conn. : Greenwood, 1984), and *Index to poetry in popular periodicals, 1960–1964* (N.Y. : Greenwood, 1988).   Z1231.P7I47

Index to poetry in periodicals, American poetic renaissance, 1915–1919 : an index of poets and poems published in American magazines and newspapers / prep. by the Editorial Board, Granger Book Co., Inc. Great Neck, N.Y. : Granger Book Co., c1981. 221 p.   **BE500**

Indexes 122 American magazines and newspapers. No title index. Two later volumes, *Index to poetry in periodicals, 1920–1924* (publ. 1983) and *Index to poetry in periodicals, 1925–1929* (1984) index more than 300 and 400 works respectively. Both also lack a title index.

§ Another source is Marion Sader's *Comprehensive index to English-language little magazines, 1890–1970* (AD287).   Z1231.P7I48

Lemay, J. A. Leo. A calendar of American poetry in the colonial newspapers and magazines and in the major English magazines through 1765. Worcester, [Mass.] : American Antiquarian Soc., [c1970]. 353 p.   **BE501**

Originally published in parts in the *Proceedings* of the American Antiquarian Society, Worcester, Mass.

Lists chronologically more than 2,000 poems of five or more lines, published in 53 periodicals, 1705–1765. For each poem is given: date and place of publication; first line; title; number of lines; author or pseudonym; and a note on the poem (including reprintings, accounts of the author, or other useful information). Indexes of first lines; names, pseudonyms, and titles; and subjects and genres. An essential guide to individual poems of the period.   Z1231.P7L44

Roth's American poetry annual. 1988– . Great Neck, N.Y. : Roth Pub., 1989– . Annual.   **BE502**

Continues three separate Roth publications: *American poetry index* (1981–86), *Annual index to poetry in periodicals* (1984–86), and *Annual survey of American poetry* (1985–86).

Indexes selected U.S. literary periodicals and single-author collections (104 periodicals and 199 collections in the 1990 volume). Surveys activity for the preceding year (events, awards, obituaries, etc.); includes an anthology of poems and a bibliography of books and articles about poets/poetry. Lists grants, fellowships, writing colonies, and schools. The Unified index includes poets, translators, titles, and first lines. Also includes a cumulative author index. Publishing lags two to three years.   PS580.R68

Histories

The Columbia history of American poetry / ed. by Jay Parini. N.Y. : Columbia Univ. Pr., 1993. 894 p.   **BE503**

A collection of 31 signed essays treat major poets, movements, and themes. In addition to chapters on major poets, there are essays on early African-American poetry, the epic in the 19th century, the Transcendentalists, women poets and the emergence of modernism, poetry of the Harlem Renaissance, the Agrarian poets, the 20th-century long poem, the Beats and the San Francisco poetry renaissance, confessional poetry, the postconfessional lyric, nature's refrain in American poetry, and Native American poetry. Helps fill a pressing need for a fuller history of American poetry. Essays include suggestions for further reading. Detailed author/title/subject index.   PS303.C64

Pearce, Roy Harvey. The continuity of American poetry. Princeton, N.J. : Princeton Univ. Pr., 1961. 442 p.   **BE504**

Repr. with a new introduction: Middletown, Conn. : Wesleyan Univ. Pr., 1987.

Provides a critical survey of American poetry from the 17th century through the poetry of Wallace Stevens. Pearce's graceful study is "of necessity a study in cultural history" (*Chap. 1, Argument*), concentrating on major poets, periods, and modes of poetic expression.

§ Also of interest is Hyatt H. Waggoner, *American poets, from the Puritans to the present* (Rev. ed. Baton Rouge : LSU Pr., 1984), which discusses more individual poets as well as more contemporary figures.   PS303.P4

Anthologies

The best American poetry. 1988– . N.Y. : Collier Books, c1988– . Annual.   **BE505**

Each volume is guest edited by a distinguished poet. Consists of 60–75 poems published in American periodicals during the preceding calendar year. Excludes translations. Includes a section for contributors' notes and comments, and a listing of periodicals where the poems were first published.   PS615.B474

The Norton anthology of modern poetry / ed. by Richard Ellmann and Robert O'Clair. 2nd ed. N.Y. : Norton, c1988. 1865 p.   **BE506**

For annotation, *see* BE332.   PS613.N67

Diaries, letters, autobiography

Arksey, Laura. American diaries : an annotated bibliography of published American diaries and journals / Laura Arksey, Nancy Pries, and Marcia Reed. Detroit : Gale, c1983–87. 2 v.   **BE507**

Contents: v. 1, Diaries written from 1492 to 1844; v. 2, Diaries written from 1845 to 1980.

A revised and greatly expanded edition of William Matthews' *American diaries : an annotated bibliography of American diaries written prior to the year 1861* (Los Angeles : Univ. of Calif. Pr., 1945. 383 p.).

Arranged by beginning date of the diary, then by diarist; publication information is given in full, including references to extracts published in periodicals, etc. Annotations indicate period of coverage, content, special events described, or field of particular interest. Includes all diaries listed in Matthews "with the exception of a few Canadian diaries containing no evidence of any American content" (*Introd.*), a few foreign diaries for which no English translation could be found, and a few items cited in Harriette M. Forbes's *New England diaries, 1602–1800* (1923) for which no copies could be located. The definition of "American" now includes Alaskan, Hawaiian, and much Spanish-American material previously omitted. Detailed subject and geographic indexes.

§ *See also*: Patricia Pate Havlice, *And so to bed : a bibliography of diaries published in English* (BE726); Louis Kaplan, *A bibliography of American autobiographies* (AH89); and Mary Louise Briscoe, *American autobiography, 1945–1980 : a bibliography* (AH89, *note*).   Z5305.U5A74

Davis, Gwenn. Personal writings by women to 1900 : a bibliography of American and British writers / comp. by Gwenn Davis and Beverly A. Joyce. Norman : Univ. of Oklahoma Pr., 1989. 294 p.   **BE508**

Called the "1st University of Oklahoma Press ed." 1st publ. London : Mansell.

Provides a checklist of more than 4,900 personal writings by women; includes autobiographies, letters, diaries, and travel literature. "The main criteria [for inclusion] are that these works represent women's accounts of their feelings and pursuits in their own words that they appeared in printed books."—*Introd.* Arranged alphabetically by author. Includes a chronological grouping of authors and a subject index (broad headings only).

§ *See also*: Patricia K. Addis, *Through a woman's I* (CC485); Cheryl Cline, *Women's diaries, journals, and letters* (BE725); and Carolyn H. Rhodes, ed., *First person female American: a selected and annotated bibliography of autobiographies of American women living after 1950* (Troy, N.Y. : Whitston, 1980).   Z1229.W8D38

Goodfriend, Joyce D. The published diaries and letters of American women : an annotated bibliography. Boston : G.K. Hall, c1987. 230 p.   **BE509**

Published collections of letters and diaries by American women written in the U.S., arranged by year of first entry. Most of the diaries are listed in *American diaries* (BE507) but the inclusion of letters and identification of materials by women make this bibliography worthwhile. Annotations; author and subject indexes.   Z5305.U5G66

Matthews, William. American diaries in manuscript, 1580–1954 : a descriptive bibliography. Athens : Univ. of Georgia Pr., [1974]. 176 p.   **BE510**

A chronological listing of more than 5,000 unpublished diaries (including those published only in part). Gives name, date of diary, brief statement of contents if known, and location. Author index.

§ *See also*: *National union catalog of manuscript collections* (DB34).   Z5305.U5M32

Literature of ethnic groups

Peck, David R. American ethnic literatures : native American, African American, Chicano/Latino, and Asian American writers and their backgrounds : an annotated bibliography. Pasadena, Calif. : Salem Pr., c1992. 218 p.   **BE511**

Brings together in one source many disparate resources for the study of various American ethnic literatures. Provides chapters for the following: general bibliographies, reference works, and journals; the social and historical record; the teaching of ethnic literature (including comparative ethnic literature collections); general studies of American ethnic literature (including literary history, genre studies, autobiography, and women and literature); and separate chapters for Native American literature, African American literature, Chicano/Latino literature, and Asian American literature. Individual ethnic literature chapters include a brief narrative history, a listing of primary works (anthologies and primary bibliographies for individual writers) and a listing of secondary bibliographies (general studies, interviews, genre studies, etc.). A useful, timely bibliography. Review: *Choice* 30:10 (June 1993): 1608.   Z1229.E87P43

African-American literature

Bibliography

Afro-American poetry and drama, 1760–1975 : a guide to information sources. Detroit : Gale, 1979. 493 p. (American literature, English literature, and world literatures in English, v. 17).   **BE512**

Contents: Afro-American poetry, 1760–1975, by W. P. French, M. J. Fabre, A. Singh; Afro-American drama, 1850–1975, by G. E. Fabre.

In each section a listing of general studies is followed by bibliographies of writings by and about individual authors.

§ Recently published, with biobibliographic essays: *Black American poets and dramatists : before the Harlem Renaissance*, ed. by Harold Bloom (N.Y. : Chelsea House, 1994).   Z1229.N39A37

Arata, Esther Spring. Black American playwrights, 1800 to the present : a bibliography / by Esther Spring Arata and Nicholas John Rotoli. Metuchen, N.J. : Scarecrow, 1976. 295 p.   **BE513**

Arranged alphabetically by name of playwright. Lists published and unpublished works (including filmscripts, musicals, theater criticism, etc.), together with references to reviews and criticism of the writers' works. Contributions to anthologies and periodicals are noted. Title index.

§ Arata also compiled a supplement, *More black American playwrights : a bibliography* (1978). "Approximately 490 playwrights appear in this bibliography, of which 190 appeared in the 1976 edition."—*Pref.*

In lieu of an adequate bibliography of criticism of African-American drama, consult the *MLA international bibliography* (BE39) and the *Annual bibliography of English language and literature* (BE588). For a bibliographic essay, see the annual *American literary scholarship* drama chapter, "African-American and Hispanic theater."

Z1229.N39A7

Bassett, John Earl. Harlem in review : critical reactions to Black American writers, 1917–1939. Selinsgrove : Susquehanna Univ. Pr. ; London ; Cranbury, N.J. : Associated Univ. Pr., c1992. 232 p.   **BE514**

A bibliography of book reviews and criticism of Harlem Renaissance authors, 1917–39, with selected entries for 1940–44. Arranged in five chapters by period. Each chapter lists books by black authors, followed by book reviews (arranged by reviewer), then general criticism and scholarship. Many entries include excerpts from reviews. Index of authors; index of critics. Valuable for tracing the critical reception of Harlem Renaissance writers. Review: *Choice* 30, no. 5 (Jan. 1993) : 762.   PS153.N5

Black American writers : bibliographical essays / ed. by M. Thomas Inge, Maurice Duke, Jackson R. Bryer. N.Y. : St. Martin's Pr., c1978. 2 v.   **BE515**

Contents: v.1, The beginnings through the Harlem renaissance and Langston Hughes; v.2, Richard Wright, Ralph Ellison, James Baldwin, and Amiri Baraka.

"Intended as an appraisal of the best biographical and critical writings about America's seminal black writers, as well as identification of manuscript and special resources for continued study."—*Pref.* Essays by contributing scholars deal with an individual writer, a group of writers, or a specific genre. Name index.   PS153.N5B55

Clark, Edward. Black writers in New England : a bibliography, with biographical notes, of books by and about Afro-American writers associated with New England in the collection of Afro-American literature, Suffolk University, Museum of Afro-American History, Boston African American National Historic Site. Boston : National Park Service, 1985. 76 p. : ill., ports.   **BE516**

Superintendent of Documents classification: I 29.82:B56.

Pt. 1 identifies approximately 625 titles by roughly 200 authors of separately published volumes (including sermons, addresses, lectures, tracts, treatises, etc.) who were either born in New England or who lived, studied, or worked there. Each entry includes a brief biographical note, a primary bibliography, and when available, a secondary bibliography. Pt. 2 identifies and provides biographical notes for an additional 80 black authors associated with New England but not represented in the collection at Suffolk University.   Z1229.N39C57

Fairbanks, Carol. Black American fiction : a bibliography / by Carol Fairbanks and Eugene A. Engeldinger. Metuchen, N.J. : Scarecrow, 1978. 351 p.   **BE517**

Includes citations to short fiction appearing in periodicals and collections as well as separately published works; citations to reviews, biography, and criticism are also given. Does not include non-fiction or works for children and young people. General bibliography of the subject, p.327–51.   Z1229.N39F34

Foster, Mamie Marie Booth. Southern black creative writers, 1829–1953 : biobibliographies. N.Y. : Greenwood, 1988. 113 p. (Bibliographies and indexes in Afro-American and African studies, no. 22).   **BE518**

Offers brief biographical notes for some 200 African-American writers who were born or spent time in the South. Each entry includes a primary bibliography drawn from peridicals and anthologies as well as separately published volumes. Appendixes provide author listings by state and by period. Includes a bibliography of reference sources.   Z1229.N39F67

Glikin, Ronda. Black American women in literature : a bibliography, 1976 through 1987. Jefferson, N.C. : McFarland, c1989. 251 p.   **BE519**

Lists "the poetry, short fiction, novels, essays, and plays by, and criticism on, approximately 300 women whose work has been published in periodicals and anthologies between 1976 and 87."—*Introd.* Also cites full-length studies or published books. Arranged by literary author, with appendixes listing general works of criticism and authors by genre. Author/title index.

§ *See also* Ann Allen Shockley, *Afro-American women writers, 1746–1933 : an anthology and critical guide* (Boston : G.K. Hall, c1988. 465 p.).   Z1229.N39G57

Hatch, James Vernon. Black image on the American stage : a bibliography of plays and musicals, 1770–1970. N.Y. : DBS Publ., [1970]. 162 p.   **BE520**

Lists full-length and one-act plays, musicals, revues, and operas written or produced in America between 1767 and 1970; each work contains at least one black character or was written by a black playwright or on a black theme. Listing is by period, then alphabetically by author. Author index. Locates copies of many works, but there is no documentation for unlocated unpublished works.   Z5784.N4H35

—————— Black playwrights, 1823–1977 : an annotated bibliography of plays / comp. and ed. by James V. Hatch and Omanii Abdullah. N.Y. : Bowker, 1977. 319 p.   **BE521**

An author listing of some 2,700 plays by approximately 900 African-American writers. Entries include author, title, date of composition or copyright, genre, a brief summary, cast (by race and gender), length, production information, publication information, a single holding location (when known), and permission information. Includes a bibliography of reference sources on black drama and theater artists, and a bibliography of dissertations and theses. Appendixes: (1) taped interviews in the Hatch-Billops Archives; (2) awards to black theater artists; (3) addresses of playwrights, agents, and agencies, ca.1977. An indispensable guide.

§ To update, *see* Bernard L. Peterson, *Contemporary black American playwrights and their plays* (BE530). See also *Afro-American poetry and drama, 1760–1975* (BE512).   Z1231.D7H37

Houston, Helen Ruth. The Afro-American novel, 1965–1975 : a descriptive bibliography of primary and secondary material. Troy, N.Y. : Whitston, 1977. 214 p.   **BE522**

Treats some 56 African Americans who have published novels since 1964. A brief biographical note is followed by a listing of the writer's recent novels, a section of critical books by and about the author, and a listing of reviews of the post-1964 novels.

Z1229.N39H68

Howard University. Library. Dictionary catalog of the Arthur B. Spingarn collection of Negro authors. Boston : G.K. Hall, 1970. 2 v.   **BE523**

For annotation, *see* BE1504.   Z1361.N39H78

Jordan, Casper LeRoy. A bibliographical guide to African-American women writers. Westport, Conn. : Greenwood, 1993. 387 p. (Bibliographies and indexes in Afro-American and African studies, no. 31).   **BE524**

Provides primary and secondary bibliographies for approximately 900 African-American women writers from Lucy Terry (1730–1821) to the present (a supplement covers 1988–91 for additional sources). Cited are books, articles, book chapters, and anthologies, including many works published privately or by small presses. Authors are arranged alphabetically, with primary works listed first (by title), followed by secondary works (by author). Also includes separate bibliographies for anthologies and general works. Index of primary and secondary authors. Review: *Choice* 31 : 3 (Nov. 1993) : 423.

Z1229.N39J67

Margolies, Edward. Afro-American fiction, 1853–1976 : a guide to information sources / Edward Margolies, David Bakish. Detroit : Gale, c1979. 161 p. (American literature, English literature, and world literatures in English, v. 25).   **BE525**

In four sections: (1) Checklist of novels; (2) Short story collections; (3) Major authors—secondary sources; (4) Bibliographies and general studies. Author, title, and subject indexes.   Z1229.N39M37

Matthews, Geraldine O. Black American writers, 1773–1949 : a bibliography and union list / comp. by Geraldine O. Matthews & the African-American Materials Project staff. Boston : G. K. Hall, 1975. 221 p.   **BE526**

A classed bibliography listing monographic publications by more than 1,600 black authors; does not include journal articles and unpublished theses. In addition to literature, there are chapters for general works, philosophy, religion, social science, language, science, technbology, fine arts, history, and bibliography. Approximately 60% of the entries provide locations in libraries in the South. Author index.   Z1361.N39M35

Newby, James Edward. Black authors : a selected annotated bibliography. N.Y. : Garland, 1991. 720 p. (Garland reference library of the humanities, v. 1260).   **BE527**

A classified, selective bibliography of book-length works, monographs, and separately published essays "written, coauthored, or edited by black Americans."—*Pref.* Includes some works by African or Caribbean authors living or publishing in the U.S. Lists more than 3,200 titles in all subject areas, published 1733–1990; of this number, over 800 are language and literature titles. Author and title indexes. Review: *Choice* 28 (June 1991): 1620.

§ *See also* Elsie Burnett, et al., *Bibliography of contemporary African-American literature : 1940–1989* (Dallas, Tex. : E. Burnett [et al.], c1990) for a checklist of African-American poetry, drama, and fiction.   Z1215.N57

Peavy, Charles D. Afro-American literature and culture since World War II : a guide to information sources. Detroit : Gale, 1979. 302 p. (American studies information guide series, v. 6).   **BE528**

In two parts: (1) Subjects (including general materials, literary genres, aspects of culture, sections for Black Muslims, Black Panthers, Civil Rights movement, etc.) and (2) Individual authors. Indexed.   Z1229.N39P4

Perry, Margaret. The Harlem Renaissance : an annotated bibliography and commentary. N.Y. : Garland, 1982. 272 p. (Critical studies on black life and culture, v. 2 ; Garland reference library of the humanities, vol. 278).   **BE529**

An annotated bibliography of books, articles, reviews, portions of books, and dissertations. Consists of chapters for general reference materials, literary histories, general and multiauthor studies, studies of individual authors, miscellaneous articles, anthologies, libraries and special collections, and dissertations. Selective primary and secondary bibliographies for the following authors: Arna Bontemps, Sterling Brown, Countee Cullen, W.E.B. Du Bois, Jessie Fauset, Rudolph Fisher, Angelina Grimke, Langston Hughes, Zora Hurston, James Weldon Johnson, Nella Larsen, Claude McKay, Willis Richardson, George Schuyler, Anne Spencer, Wallace Thurman, Jean Toomer, Eric Walrond, and Walter White. Author and title indexes.

§ *See also* Lorraine Elena Roses, *Harlem Renaissance and beyond* (BE545), and Bruce Kellner, *The Harlem Renaissance : a historical dictionary for the era* (DB130).   Z5956.A47P47

Peterson, Bernard L. Contemporary black American playwrights and their plays : a biographical directory and dramatic index. N.Y. : Greenwood, 1988. 625 p.   **BE530**

Similar in format to James Vernon Hatch, *Black playwrights, 1823–1977* (BE521), this volume provides biobibliographic information on more than 700 contemporary black American playwrights (including "U.S. resident dramatists, screenwriters, radio and television scriptwriters, musical theatre collaborators, and other originators of theatrical and dramatic works, written, produced, and/or published between 1950 and the present."—*Pref.*). Appendixes: (A) more than 100 additional playwrights whose scripts are located in special repositories; (B) approximately 75 additional contemporary black American playwrights. Includes a bibliography of information sources (including libraries and repositories, a list of anthologies, reference books and critical studies, dissertations and theses, and periodicals). Title index and general index.   PS153.N5P43

————————— Early black American playwrights and dramatic writers : a biographical directory and catalog of plays, films, and broadcasting scripts. N.Y. : Greenwood, 1990. 298 p.   **BE531**

A companion volume to *Contemporary black American playwrights and their plays* (BE530). Provides biobibliographic information "on approximately 218 pioneer playwrights, screenwriters, and other originators of dramatic works written and/or produced in the United States and in Europe during the nineteenth century and the first half of the twentieth century."—*Pref.* Entries in the main directory include biographical information (when available), a listing of published or unpublished collections, an annotated index of individual works, and other pertinent writings by the author. Includes an introduction concerning the origin and development of the black American playwright. Appendixes: other early black American playwrights and their plays; additional musical librettists and brief descriptions of their shows; a chronology of plays and dramatic works classified by genre. Bibliography of information sources; title index, index of early black American theater organizations and producing groups, and general index.

§ By the same author: *A century of musicals in black and white : an encyclopedia of musical stage works by, about, or involving African Americans* (Westport, Conn. : Greenwood, 1993).   PS153.N5P44

Rush, Theressa Gunnels. Black American writers : past and present: a biographical and bibliographical dictionary / by Theressa Gunnels Rush, Carol Fairbanks Myers, Esther Spring Arata. Metuchen, N.J. : Scarecrow, 1975. 2 v. (865 p.).   **BE532**

Aims to present biographical, bibliographical and critical information on about 2,000 black writers. (In some instances only a record of publications is available.) In general, a biographical sketch is followed by a list of published books, representative references to contributions to periodicals and anthologies, and references to biographical and critical studies on the writer.   Z1229.N39R87

Sherman, Joan R. Invisible poets : Afro-Americans of the nineteenth century. 2nd ed. Urbana : Univ. of Illinois Pr., c1989. 288, [216] p. of plates : ill.   **BE533**

1st ed., 1974.

Biobibliographic essays for 26 representative poets born between 1796 and 1883 who have been omitted from traditional bibliographies and literary histories. Each entry includes a documented biography and a critical evaluation of the poet's work. Introductory essays attempt to place the poets in their historical and cultural setting. Includes bibliographies (with copy locations) and a bibliographic essay that describes research materials available for the study of African American literature (a second essay updates the research since the 1974 edition). Appendixes: 35 additional 19th-century poets (biographical notes, publications, locations); 68 occasional poets; anonymous poets and Ada (whose poems appeared in Garrison's *The Liberator*); turn-of-the-century poets; poets erroneously identified as African-Americans; Creole poets of *Les Cenelles*; and bibliographies of Phillis Wheatley and Jupiter Hammon. Index.

§ For a history *see* Blyden Jackson's *A history of Afro-American literature* (BE540) and Jean Wagner's *Black poets of the United States from Paul Laurence Dunbar to Langston Hughes* (tr. of *Les poètes nègres des États-Unis*, tr. by Kenneth Douglas. Urbana : Univ. of Illinois Pr., c1973).   PS153.N5S48

Yellin, Jean Fagan. The pen is ours : a listing of writings by and about African-American women before 1910 with secondary bibliography to the present / comp. by Jean Fagan Yellin [and] Cynthia D. Bond. N.Y. : Oxford Univ. Pr., 1991. 349 p. : ill.   **BE534**

Part of "Schomburg library of nineteenth-century black women writers" series (gen. ed., Henry Louis Gates, Jr.), this volume is a valuable contribution to the bibliography of early African-American women writers. In five parts: (1) writings by and about African-American women who produced separately published writings before the end of 1910; (2) writings by and about African-American women who had been held in slavery and whose dictated narratives or biographies were published before the end of 1910; (3) writings by and about African-American women whose works appeared in periodicals and collections and whose earliest publications appeared before the end of 1910; (4) notable African-American women who were not writers but who were the subjects of published writings before the end of 1910; (5) selected contemporary writings about but not by African-American women (to the end of 1910). Includes a bibliography of sources consulted, a listing of newspapers and periodicals searched (including dates searched), and an index of all African-American women listed in Pts. 1–4.   Z1229.N39Y44

Indexes

Black literature, 1827–1940. Alexandria, Va. : Chadwyck-Healey Inc., 1990. 1 v. (In progress).   **BE535**

Ed. by Henry Louis Gates, Jr., dir. of the Black Periodical Literature Project.

An author/title to the microfiche collection of the same name, produced by the Black Periodical Literature Project. When completed, the microfiche collection will consolidate more than 150,000 pieces of fiction, poetry, book reviews, and literary notices appearing in 900 black periodicals for the period 1827–1940. Of inestimable value to the task of reassessing the early contributions of African Americans to U.S. literature.

•Machine-readable version: *Black literature, 1827–1940 index on CD-ROM* [database] (Alexandria, Va. : Chadwyck-Healey, [1994]–).

Chapman, Dorothy Hilton. Index to black poetry. Boston : G. K. Hall, 1974. 541 p.   **BE536**

Largely an expansion of Dorothy Burnett Porter, *North American negro poets : a bibliographical checklist of their writings, 1760–1944* (Hattiesburg, Miss. : The Book Farm, 1945).

"Black poetry is here defined in the broadest manner … . References are included for the work not only of black poets but also of those poets who have in some way dealt with the black experience or written within the black tradition, regardless of their racial origins."— *Foreword*. Indexes about 125 collections. A title and first line index is followed by separate author and subject indexes.

§ In part superseded by Chapman's *Index to poetry by black American women* (N.Y. : Greenwood, 1986. 424 p. [Bibliographies and indexes in Afro-American and African studies, no. 15]).

Indexes 120 books by individual women poets, and 83 anthologies of African-American poetry—in total, more than 4,000 poems by more than 400 black poets. Also includes 185 anonymous poems. Title and first line index; author and subject indexes.

Forthcoming from the same author is a companion volume indexing male African-American poets.   PS153.N5C45

Kallenbach, Jessamine S. Index to black American literary anthologies / comp. under the direction of Jessamine S. Kallenbach ; sponsored by the Center of Educational Resources, Eastern Michigan University. Boston : G. K. Hall, c1979. 219 p.   **BE537**

An author index to 142 literary anthologies, including autobiographies, plays, essays, fiction, narratives, poetry, short stories, and speeches. The most recent anthologies date from the mid-1970s. Under an author's name, titles are listed alphabetically within the genre(s) represented. Author entries include birth and death dates when known. Title index, but no subject index.

§ *See also* two works by Dorothy Hilton Chapman, *Index to black poetry* and *Index to poetry by black American women* (both BE536).
   Z1229.N39K34

Yancy, Preston M. The Afro-American short story : a comprehensive, annotated index with selected commentaries. Westport, Conn. : Greenwood, 1986. 171 p. (Bibliographies and indexes in Afro-American and African studies, no. 10).   **BE538**

Indexes more than 850 stories by more than 300 authors published in anthologies, 1950–82. In three main parts: (1) a chronology; (2) an alphabetical list of collections and their contents; (3) commentaries on particular stories. Author and title indexes.   Z1229.N39Y36

Handbooks

Southgate, Robert L. Black plots & black characters : a handbook for Afro-American literature. Syracuse, N.Y. : Gaylord Professional Publications, 1979. 456 p.   **BE539**

Provides summaries and commentaries for approximately 100 works by African-American authors (including speeches, novels, plays, and long poems). For literary works lists genre, time and setting, first publication date, and important characters. Includes an encyclopedic companion for the study of African-American literature and culture, primary and (when available) secondary bibliographies for approximately 100 writers, a general bibliography for the study of black literature and culture, a chronological index (1619–1978), and an author index. Although somewhat dated, still useful.   PS153.N5S65

Histories

Jackson, Blyden. A history of Afro-American literature. Baton Rouge : Louisiana State Univ. Pr., c1989. v. 1. (In progress).   **BE540**

Contents: v. l, The long beginning, 1746–1895.

The first of four volumes in a history of African-American literature, 1746 to the present. Not confined to a discussion of belles lettres, it also concerns itself with slave narratives, histories, folk literature, sermons, spirituals, and journalism. Attempts to define authors in terms of their historical, social, and cultural milieus and to evaluate their work. Vol. 1 concludes with a bibliographic essay that evaluates literary scholarship and histories. Subject/author index. Promises to provide the most complete history of African-American literature to date. Review: *Mississippi quarterly* 45, no. 1 (Winter 1991–92) : 105–110.   PS153.N5J33

Anthologies

The new cavalcade : African American writing from 1760 to the present / ed. by Arthur P. Davis, J. Saunders Redding, and Joyce Ann Joyce. Wash. : Howard Univ. Pr., 1991–92. 2 v.   **BE541**

Rev. ed. of *Cavalcade*, 1971.

Contents: v. 1, pt. 1, Pioneer writers: 1760–1830; pt. 2, Freedom fighters: 1830–1865; pt. 3, Accommodation and protest: 1865–1910; pt. 4, The new Negro renaissance and beyond: 1910–1954; v. 2, pt. 1, Integration versus black nationalism: 1954 to ca.1970; pt. 2, The African American literary revival: the 1970s to the present.

An anthology of approximately 150 African-American writers, Phillis Wheatley to Rita Dove. The purpose is "to provide a representative selection of as much as possible of the best prose and poetry written by African Americans since 1776."—*Pref*. Periods are prefaced by critical introductions, and there is a brief biobibliographical headnote for each author. Each volume includes a selective bibliography and index. Review: *American visions* 7:2 (April–May 1992): 35.
   PS508.N3N48

Biography

See also *Contemporary authors* (AH42) and *Black biography 1790–1950* (*note*, AH59). For bio-critical essays, see the *Dictionary of literary biography* (BE200), vols. 38, 41, 50, 51, and 76.

African American writers / Valerie Smith, consulting ed. ; Lea Baechler, A. Walton Litz, gen. editors. N.Y. : C. Scribner's Sons ; N.Y. : Maxwell Macmillan International, c1991. 544 p. **BE542**

Designed to complement *American writers* (BE444), this volume consists of biographical/critical essays for 34 African-American authors. The essays provide selective primary and secondary bibliographies. Also included is a chronology (1441–1990) and an author/title/subject index. PS153.N5A344

Campbell, Dorothy W. Index to black American writers in collective biographies. Littleton, Colo. : Libraries Unlimited, 1983. 162 p. **BE543**

Provides references to biographical information on approximately 1,900 African-American writers appearing in 267 collective biographies published 1837–1982. In addition to literary authors, also includes biographers, autobiographers, historians, journalists, literary critics, book illustrators, and scholars/bibliographers. Z1229.N39C35

Page, James A. Selected black American, African, and Caribbean authors : a bio-bibliography / comp. by James A. Page and Jae Min Roh. Littleton, Colo. : Libraries Unlimited, 1985. 388 p. **BE544**

Represents a revised and enlarged edition of Page's *Selected black American authors* (Boston: G.K. Hall, 1977). Provides biobibliographical information on 632 authors, both literary and nonliterary. Emphasizes African-American literature of the U.S.; non-U.S. writers included are those who "have either lived, studied, or been published in the United States."—*Pref.* Bibliography of sources. Nationality, occupational, and title indexes. Z1229.N39P34

Roses, Lorraine Elena. Harlem Renaissance and beyond : literary biographies of 100 black women writers, 1900–1945 / Lorraine Elena Roses, Ruth Elizabeth Randolph. Boston : G.K. Hall, c1990. 413 p. **BE545**

"It is the purpose of this book to focus attention on black women writers whose work belongs primarily to the early half of the twentieth century and whose achievements or very existence has been little recognized, even within specialized circles."—*Pref.* Profiles of poets, journalists, novelists, essayists, playwrights, scholars, critics, and biographers are arranged alphabetically and include primary and secondary bibliographies. Appendixes list writers by genre, geographical locations, and date; a title index and a general bibliography conclude the volume. PS153.N5R65

Asian-American literature

Cheung, King-Kok. Asian American literature : an annotated bibliography / King-Kok Cheung, Stan Yogi. N.Y. : Modern Language Association of America, 1988. 276 p. **BE546**

A "reference guide to literature written by Asian American writers in the United States and Canada."—*Pref.* Includes "works by writers of Asian descent who have made the United States or Canada their home, regardless of where they were born, when they settled in North America, and how they interpret their experience … writers of mixed descent who have one Asian parent … as well as authors who may not be permanent North American residents but who have written specifically on the experiences of Asians in the United States or Canada." Includes primary and secondary sources, selected background studies, fiction and poetry collections. Arranged by ethnic group (e.g., Chinese Americans), then by format. Brief annotations; index of names.

§ See also: David Peck, *American ethnic literatures* (BE511); Hyung-chan Kim, ed., *Asian American studies* (CC407); and W. C. Miller, *Comprehensive bibliography for the study of American minorities* (N.Y. : New York Univ. Pr., 1976. 2 v. [1380 p.]). Z1229.A75C47

Kim, Elaine H. Asian American literature : an introduction to the writings and their social context. Philadelphia : Temple Univ. Pr., 1982. 363 p. **BE547**

Focusing "on the evolution of Asian American consciousness and self-image as expressed in the literature", this volume attempts "to trace the topography and rich textures of the Asian American experience as it is expressed in Asian American literature from the late nineteenth century to the present day [ca. early 1980s]."—*Pref.* Provides an overview and history and includes a bibliography of primary and secondary sources.

§ The following collection of 20 essays also provides broad overviews as well as readings of specific works: *Reading the literatures of Asian America*, ed. Shirley Geok-lin Lim and Amy Ling (Philadelphia : Temple Univ. Pr., 1992). Favorably reviewed in *American literature* 65:3 (September 1993): 602. PS153.A84K55 1982

Native American literature

Bibliography

Beidler, Peter G. The American Indian in short fiction : an annotated bibliography / Peter G. Beidler and Marion F. Egge. Metuchen, N.J. : Scarecrow, 1979. 203 p. **BE548**

Provides brief plot summaries for 880 short stories about Native American characters appearing in books and periodicals. The majority of stories are by non-Native American authors writing after 1890. Excluded are oral tales, myths, and legends recorded by anthropologists. Includes a useful Indian tribes index and keyword subject index.

§ *See also*: Joseph Weixlmann, *American short fiction criticism and scholarship, 1959–1977* (BE479). Z1231.F4B44

Brumble, H. David. An annotated bibliography of American Indian and Eskimo autobiographies. Lincoln : Univ. of Nebraska Pr., c1981. 177 p. **BE549**

A bibliography of more than 500 autobiographies. Annotations provide biographical information and a synopsis. Includes a bibliography of references and indexes of: editors, anthropologists, ghosts, and amanuenses; tribes; and subjects. Z1209.B78

Colonnese, Tom. American Indian novelists : an annotated critical bibliography / Tom Colonnese, Louis Owens. N.Y. : Garland, 1985. 161 p. (Garland reference library of the humanities, v. 384). **BE550**

Biographical notes and annotated primary and secondary bibliographies for 21 Native American novelists. Primary bibliographies include nonfiction works; secondary bibliographies include criticism, book reviews, and biographical sources. Highly selective and at best a starting point for research. Z1229.I52C65

Littlefield, Daniel F. A biobibliography of native American writers, 1772–1924 / by Daniel F. Littlefield and James W. Parins. Metuchen, N.J. : Scarecrow, 1981. 343 p. (Native American bibliography series, no. 2). **BE551**

Provides an author checklist of more than 4,300 English-language publications written by 250 Native Americans (excluding those from Canada) from Colonial times to 1924 (when Congress granted citizenship to all native-born Native Americans). Excluded is material by Native Americans but written down by non-Native Americans. Not strictly literary, this volume also indexes political essays and addresses, published letters, historical works, memoirs, etc. Includes a separate bibliography of Native American writers known only by pen names, biographical notes, and an index of writers by tribal affiliation. Subject index but no title index. An essential bibliography for early publications.

———. *Supplement* / by Daniel F. Littlefield and James W. Parins (Metuchen, N.J. : Scarecrow, 1985. 339 p. [Native American bibliography series, no. 5]). Similar in plan to the base volume. Identifies publications of an additional 942 Native American writers. Many entries in the supplement are annotated, and biographical notes include source materials.

§ Not entirely superseded by Littlefield and Parins is Angeline Jacobsen, *Contemporary Native American literature : a selected & partially annotated bibliography* (Metuchen, N.J. : Scarecrow, 1977. 262 p.). For additional authors see also: Arlene B. Hirschfelder, *American Indian and Eskimo authors : a comprehensive bibliography* (N.Y. : Assoc. of American Indian Affairs [distr. by Interbook, Inc., c1973]. 99 p.).   Z1209.2.U5L57

Rock, Roger O. The Native American in American literature : a selectively annotated bibliography. Westport, Conn. : Greenwood, 1985. 211 p. (Bibliographies and indexes in American literature, no. 3).   **BE552**

A selectively annotated bibliography of books, scholarly and popular magazine articles, pamphlets, catalogs, theses, dissertations, and microforms. Arranged in three sections, including a bibliography of bibliographies, a bibliography of criticism that focuses on the Native American as a character in American literature, and a bibliography of works by and about Native Americans (including works edited, translated, or retold by non-Native Americans). Author and subject indexes.   Z1229.I52R64

Handbooks

Ruoff, A. LaVonne Brown. American Indian literatures : an introduction, bibliographic review, and selected bibliography. N. Y. : Modern Language Assoc. of America, 1990. 200 p.   **BE553**

An introduction and guide to Native American literatures arranged in three sections. Pt. 1, an introductory essay, discusses backgrounds and oral traditions, oral and written autobiographies, and provides a history of the written literature. Pt. 2 is a bibliographic essay that includes sections for bibliographies and research guides; anthologies, collections, and recreations; and scholarship and criticism (further divided into sections for oral literatures, autobiographies, studies of individual authors, and teaching of American Indian literatures, and backgrounds). Pt. 3 provides an unannotated, classified bibliography that includes, in addition to the categories in pt. 2, listings for films and videotapes, and journals and small presses. Includes a chronology of important dates in American Indian history 1500–1989. Index to only pts. 1 and 2.   PM155.R86

Histories

Wiget, Andrew. Native American literature. Boston : Twayne Publ., c1985. 147 p. : ill. (Twayne's United States authors series, TUSAS 467).   **BE554**

A survey and critical history of Native American literature that includes oral traditions, the beginnings of a written literature, modern fiction, contemporary poetry, and new directions in Native American writing. Chronology, selected primary and secondary bibliography, and index.

§ See also: *Columbia literary history of the United States* (BE439).   PM155.W54

Anthologies

American Indian literature : an anthology / ed. and with an introduction by Alan R. Velie. Rev. ed. Norman : Univ. of Oklahoma Pr., 1991. 373 p.   **BE555**

1st ed., 1979.

An anthology of Native American literature, both traditional (including tales, songs, and oratory) and mainstream (including the standard genres of fiction, poetry, biography, and history). Provides critical introductions. Indexed.

See also *Heath anthology of American literature* (BE441).   PM197.E1A4

Latino literature

See also: Donald W. Bleznick, *A sourcebook for Hispanic literature and language* (BE1426); David R. Peck, *American ethnic literatures* (BE511); and Barbara J. Robinson, *The Mexican American : a critical guide to research aids* (Greenwich, Conn. : JAI Pr., [1980]. 287 p.).

Bibliography

Chicano literature : a reference guide / ed. by Julio A. Martínez and Francisco A. Lomelí. Westport, Conn. : Greenwood, 1985. 492 p.   **BE556**

Signed articles cover individual authors as well as topics (e.g., Chicano theater, Contemporary Chicano novel), providing literary and historical significance, critical evaluations, and bibliographies of primary and secondary works. Appendixes include information on nonliterary Chicanos, (e.g., Anthony Quinn), a chronology, a glossary, and a general bibliography. General index.   PS153.M4C46

Eger, Ernestina N. A bibliography of criticism of contemporary Chicano literature. Berkeley, Calif. : Chicano Studies Library Publications, Univ. of California, 1982. 295 p. (Chicano Studies Library publication series, no. 5).   **BE557**

A classified bibliography of books, journal and magazine articles, newspaper articles, commercially distributed audio and video tapes, dissertations, theses, published and unpublished conference papers, and works in progress. The bibliography covers the critical literature, 1960 through mid-1979. Appendixes: articles written prior to 1960; Chicano literary journals. The 2,181 entries are arranged in 12 sections: analyzed collections; bibliographies; miscellaneous articles; studies of the Chicana; criticism (critical theory); linguistic studies; poetry; prose fiction; theater; literature festivals; individual authors; and anthologies. Author and title indexes.   Z1229.M48E36

Trujillo, Roberto G. Literatura Chicana : creative and critical writings through 1984 / comp. by Roberto G. Trujillo and Andrés Rodríguez. Oakland, Calif. : Floricanto Pr., c1985. 95 p.   **BE558**

A bibliography of approximately 800 primary and secondary publications, arranged by genre or form (e.g., unpublished dissertations, video and sound recordings), then by scholar or literary author. Author and title indexes. Within genre/form classifications primary and secondary works are not separated, and this makes for a somewhat awkward arrangement.

§ *See also*: Francisco A. Lomeli and Donaldo Urioste, *Chicano perspectives in literature : a critical and annotated bibliography* (Albuquerque, N.M. : Pajarito Publ., 1976).   Z1229.M48T78

Zimmerman, Marc. U.S. Latino literature : an essay and annotated bibliography. Chicago : MARCH/Abrazo Pr., c1992. 156 p.   **BE559**

1st ed., 1990.

An introductory essay discusses Latino literature in the cultural process, Latinos and their culture, the history and development of U.S. Latino literature, and postmodern perspectives. Includes annotated primary and secondary bibliographies for Chicano literature, U.S. Puerto Rican literature, and U.S. Cuban literature. No index.

Z1229.H57Z55

Histories

Tatum, Charles M. Chicano literature. Boston : Twayne Publ., c1982. 214 p. (Twayne's United States authors series, TUSAS 433). **BE560**

A historical survey and overview of Chicano literature, with discussion of its historical background, its origins and evolution, genres, and past achievements and future promise. Chronology, selective bibliography, and index.

§ For theater history *see*: Nicolas Kanellos, *A history of Hispanic theatre in the United States : origins to 1940* (Austin, Tex. : Univ. of Texas Pr., c1990. 240 p.). PS173.M39T36

Biography

See also: Bryan Ryan, ed., *Hispanic writers : a selection of sketches from contemporary authors* (BE890); Diane Telegen and Jim Kamp, editors, *Notable hispanic American women* (AH78); and Nicolas Kanellos, *The Hispanic-American almanac* (BE562). For biocritical essays, *see* the following volumes of the *Dictionary of literary biography* (BE200), both edited by Francisco A. Lomelí: *Chicano writers* 1st series (v. 82); *Chicano writers* 2nd series (v. 122).

Bruce-Novoa, Juan D. Chicano authors : inquiry by interview. Austin : Univ. of Texas Pr., c1980. 292 p. : ill. **BE561**

Interviews (with photographs) of 14 authors. Includes a critical introduction and selective bibliography. PS153.M4B7

Kanellos, Nicolás. Biographical dictionary of Hispanic literature in the United States : the literature of Puerto Ricans, Cuban Americans, and other Hispanic writers. N.Y. : Greenwood, 1989. 357 p. **BE562**

For each of the 50 authors covered, a signed essay points up literary significance, then gives a biographical statement, a survey of criticism, and a bibliography of works by and about the biographee. General bibliography and index.

§ See also: Julio A. Martínez, *Chicano scholars and writers: a bio-bibliographical directory* (Metuchen, N.J. : Scarecrow, 1979. 579 p.). Provides biographical information and lists of publications for more than 500 scholars and writers in the humanities, social sciences, and education. Critical works on the biographies are also noted. Subject index by field of interest. PQ7420.2.K3

Partial autobiographies : interviews with twenty Chicano poets / ed., with an introduction, a glossary, and bibliographies by Wolfgang Binder. Erlangen : Palm & Enke, 1985. 263 p. (Erlanger Studien, Bd. 65/1). **BE563**

Provides interviews for 20 Chicano poets. Introduction, glossary, primary and secondary bibliographies, index. PS153.M4P37

Jewish-American literature

Cronin, Gloria L. Jewish American fiction writers : an annotated bibliography / Gloria L. Cronin, Blaine H. Hall, Connie Lamb. N.Y. : Garland, 1991. 1233 p. (Garland reference library of the humanities, v. 972). **BE564**

Provides primary and secondary bibliographies for 62 Jewish American fiction writers. Major figures (e.g., Bellow, Malamud), for whom bibliographic material is readily available, are excluded. The primary bibliographies cite works of short fiction appearing in anthologies and periodicals as well as editions of novels and collected works. Excludes non-fiction. Secondary bibliographies, current through 1988, cite English-language books, book chapters, articles, book reviews, interviews, standard biographical sources, and dissertations. Descriptive annotations are provided for articles, chapters, book reviews, and interviews, but not for book-length studies or dissertations. No index.

§ *See also*: Murray Blackman, *A guide to Jewish themes in American fiction, 1940–1980* (Metuchen, N.J. : Scarecrow, 1981). Z1229.J4C76

Handbook of American-Jewish literature : an analytical guide to topics, themes, and sources / Lewis Fried, ed. in chief ; Gene Brown, Jules Chametzky, and Louis Harap, advisory editors. N.Y. : Greenwood, 1988. 539 p. **BE565**

In 18 chapters, specialists discuss English-language, German-language, and Yiddish fiction, poetry, drama, and criticism, as well as nonliterary forms such as theology, autobiography, history, and philosophy. Includes chapters on Zionist ideology, the fiction of the Holocaust, and the portrayal of Eastern Europe. Selected bibliographies follow each chapter; chapter 18 comprises a bibliography of European writings on American-Jewish literature. General index.

PS153.J4H365

Nadel, Ira Bruce. Jewish writers of North America : a guide to information sources. Detroit : Gale, c1981. 493 p. (Gale information guide library. American studies information guide series, v. 8). **BE566**

A select, annotated bibliography of books and articles concerning American and Canadian Jewish literary authors. General reference guides include: bibliographies, biographical sources, periodical indexes and source materials, research catalogs and manuscript collections, literary history, literary criticism, and anthologies. Primary and secondary bibliographies for 118 individual authors chosen for their "literary excellence, cultural significance, and historical importance."—*Introd.* Arrangement for author bibliographies is first by genre and then by nationality (e.g., American-Jewish poets). Some authors appear in multiple genre classifications. Appendixes: Yiddish literature and checklists of additional American and Canadian Jewish authors. Author, title, and subject indexes.

§ For additional information on Jewish American fiction writers consult: Gloria L. Cronin, *Jewish American fiction writers* (BE564) and *Dictionary of literary biography* (BE200), v. 28, *Twentieth-century American Jewish fiction writers*. Z1229.J4N32

Regional literature

Bibliography

A bibliographical guide to Midwestern literature / Gerald Nemanic, gen. ed. Iowa City : Univ. of Iowa Pr., c1981. 380 p. **BE567**

A selective guide to the culture and literature of the Midwest. Pt. 1 is composed of nine classified, topical bibliographies covering literature and language, history and society, folklore, personal narratives, architecture and graphics, Chicago, black literature, Indians, and literary periodicals; each is preceded by an evaluative overview of the literature. Citations in this section are principally to book-length studies; most entries have brief, critical annotations. Pt. 2 consists of bibliographies for 120 individual authors, each listing primary works and selective, unannotated secondary scholarship. Two appendixes list (1) brief entries for an additional 101 writers and (2) an additional 101 fictional narratives on the Midwest. The lack of an index and cross-referencing aids hinders its ease of use. Valuable especially for its topical bibliographies and bibliographies of minor figures. Review: *Analytical & enumerative bibliography* 6:2 (1982): 135–37.

Z1251.W5B52

Contemporary fiction writers of the South : a bio-bibliographical sourcebook / ed. by Joseph M. Flora and Robert Bain. Westport, Conn. : Greenwood, 1993. 571 p. **BE568**

Patterned after *Fifty Southern writers before 1900* and *Fifty Southern writers after 1900* (both BE571), this volume provides substantive signed essays for 49 contemporary southern fiction writers. Each essay consists of an overview of a writer's life and work, a biographical sketch, discusses major themes, provides a survey of criticism, and concludes with a primary and secondary bibliography. Criteria for an author's inclusion: each author must have written four novels (with a few exceptions); been reviewed widely; and received critical attention outside the South. Appendixes: supplementary material on nine contemporary novelists included in *Fifty Southern writers after 1900*; and contents for a forthcoming companion volume, *Contemporary poets, dramatists, essayists, and novelists of the South*. Indexed.

PS261.C565

Emerson, O. B. Southern literary culture : a bibliography of masters' and doctors' theses / comp. and ed. by O. B. Emerson and Marion C. Michael. Rev. & enl. ed. University : Univ. of Alabama Pr., c1979. 400 p. **BE569**

1st ed. (1955) by C. H. Cantrell and W. R. Patrick.

A checklist of some 8,000 theses and dissertations granted through 1969 (with some listings for 1970) on Southern literature and authors (defined as those who flourished in the South). Includes some foreign theses and dissertations, as well as some completed in academic departments other than English. Arranged by degree recipient in three sections: (1) individual authors; (2) cultural, historical, and social backgrounds, including folklore, education, libraries and lyceums, southern speech and oratory; (3) literature, including studies that treat the South in general or more than one southern writer. No index of cross-references.

§ Supplemented by: *Southern literary culture, 1969–1975 : [checklist of theses and dissertations : a supplement]* / comp. by Jack D. Wages and William L. Andrews (Mississippi State : Mississippi State Univ., c1979). A special issue of *Mississippi quarterly* 32 no. 1 (Winter 1978–79) lists an additional 2,982 theses and dissertations completed at U.S. universities. Index of degree recipients.

Z1251.S7C3

Etulain, Richard W. A bibliographical guide to the study of Western American literature. Lincoln : Univ. of Nebraska Pr., 1982. 317 p. **BE570**

A selective, predominantly unannotated bibliography for authors "who were born and reared in the trans-Mississippi West or who spent large portions of their lives in the West"—*Pref.* Limited primarily to literary authors, but includes authors whose work has influenced western literature as well as some notable western historians and nonfiction writers. Sections for bibliographies, anthologies, general works (books, dissertations, and theses), topical articles (e.g., local color and regionalism, dime novels and the western, Western films as literature), and select secondary bibliographies (articles, dissertations, and books) for approximately 375 individual authors. Entries for major figures like Twain and Cather are very selective. Recent criticism is stressed and current through 1981. No cross-references; indexing of scholars only. Valuable for the number of authors covered. Complemented by: *Fifty Western writers* (BE572).

Updated by: "Annual bibliography of studies in western American literature" and "Research in western American literature ..." (the latter including Masters' theses and Ph.D. dissertations), both appearing in *Western American literature* (1966–).

§ Narrower in focus is John Q. Anderson ... [et al.], *Southwestern American literature : a bibliography* (Chicago : Swallow Pr., c1980). For additional background, *see* Jon Tuska, *The frontier experience : a reader's guide to the life and literature of the American west* (Jefferson, N.C. : McFarland, 1984). Z1251.W5E8

Fifty Southern writers before 1900 : a bio-bibliographical sourcebook / ed. by Robert Bain and Joseph M. Flora. N.Y. : Greenwood, c1987. 601 p. **BE571**

Companion work: *Fifty Southern writers after 1900 : a bio-bibliographical sourcebook* / ed. by Joseph M. Flora and Robert Bain (N.Y. : Greenwood, 1987. 628 p.).

These two substantial volumes provide signed essays which present an overview of each writer's life and works; a biographical sketch, discussion of the author's major themes, assessment of scholarship, chronological list of the author's works, and bibliography of criti-

cism. Arranged alphabetically within each volume, with general indexes. A few nonliterary authors, such as Thomas Jefferson, are included.

PS261.F543

Fifty Western writers : a bio-bibliographical sourcebook / ed. by Fred Erisman and Richard W. Etulain. Westport, Conn. : Greenwood, 1982. 562 p. **BE572**

Patterned after *Eight American authors* (BE403). Provides signed essays by specialists presenting an overview of the author's life and works, a biographical sketch, a discussion of predominant themes, an evaluation of scholarship, a chronological listing of works, and a select bibliography of criticism. Index of titles and personal names with some subject access. Complements Richard W. Etulain's *A bibliographical guide to the study of Western American literature* (BE570).

§ Updated by: "Annual bibliography of studies in Western American literature" and "Research in Western American literature ..." (the latter including Masters' theses and Ph.D. dissertations), both appearing in *Western American literature* (1966–). PS271.F5

Gohdes, Clarence Louis Frank. Literature and theater of the states and regions of the U.S.A : an historical bibliography. Durham, N.C. : Duke Univ. Pr., 1967. 276 p. **BE573**

Lists "monographs, anthologies, pamphlets, chapters of books, and periodical articles which will provide materials for the study of the local belles-lettres and theater of the United States, from earliest times to the present."—*Pref.* Arrangement is by state or region, with literature and theater treated in separate listings. Works on individual writers are generally excluded. Not indexed. Z1225.G63

Rubin, Louis Decimus. A bibliographical guide to the study of Southern literature / ed. by Louis D. Rubin, Jr., with an appendix containing sixty-eight additional writers of the colonial South by J. A. Leo Lemay. Baton Rouge : Louisiana State Univ. Pr., [1969]. 368 p. **BE574**

Attempts "to bring together, within the covers of a single book, a compilation of some of the most useful material available for the student who would begin work in the field of Southern literary study."—*Introd.* A section of more than 20 bibliographical surveys of general topics (literary periods, genres, etc.) is followed by checklists of biographical and critical writings on about 135 individual authors. About 100 scholars contributed to the volume.

§ Continued by: Society for the Study of Southern Literature. Committee on Bibliography. *Southern literature, 1968–1975* / conflated, ed., and supplemented by Jerry T. Williams (Boston : G.K. Hall, [1978]. 271 p.). Cumulates the annotated entries from the Spring issues of the *Mississippi quarterly* and adds new citations, cross-references, and a name index. Z1225.R8

Histories

The history of Southern literature / general ed., Louis D. Rubin, Jr. ... [et al.]. Baton Rouge : Louisiana State Univ. Pr., c1985. 626 p. **BE575**

Provides signed essays on major literary figures, movements, genres, as well the historical and social backgrounds of Southern literature. In four parts: Colonial and Antebellum Southern literature, 1607-1860; the war and after, 1861–1920; the Southern Renaissance, 1920–50; the recent South, 1951–82. Two appendixes: a bibliographic essay for the study of Southern literature, and an essay, "The black academy and Southern literature." Indexed.

§ Still of value is Jay B. Hubbell's *The South in American literature, 1607–1900* ([Durham], N.C. : Duke Univ. Pr., 1954). PS261.H53

A literary history of the American West / sponsored by the Western Literature Association. Fort Worth, Tex. : Texas Christian Univ. Pr., c1987. xliii, 1353 p. : ill. **BE576**

Provides signed essays (most with bibliographies) on individual writers, regions, periods, genres and a variety of topics, including oral traditions, folklore, literary scholarship and historiography, ethnic expression, women's writing, nature writing, and western movies. Historical chronology of the frontier and the American West; epilogue on western literary criticism; bibliography of major reference sources on the West. Indexed.   PS271.L58

Westbrook, Perry D. A literary history of New England. Bethlehem, Penn. : Lehigh Univ. Pr. ; London ; Cranbury, N.J. : Associated Univ. Pr., c1988. 362 p.   **BE577**

A history of the literary expression of New England covering the major figures, schools, and movements from 1620–1950. An epilogue includes discussion of some authors after 1950. Selective bibliography; index.

§ See also: *Dictionary of literary biography* (BE200), especially v. 1, Joel Myerson, *The American Renaissance in New England* (Detroit : Gale, 1978. 224 p.).   PS243.W42

Biography

Southern writers : a biographical dictionary / ed. by Robert Bain, Joseph M. Flora and Louis D. Rubin, Jr. Baton Rouge : Louisiana State Univ. Pr., c1979. 515 p.   **BE578**

Published under the auspices of the Society for the Study of Southern Literature, this volume provides brief biographical sketches and primary bibliographies for 379 southern authors. Useful for its inclusion of a number of lesser known writers.

§ See also: *Fifty Southern writers before 1900* and *Fifty Southern writers after 1900* (both BE571) for more detailed treatment of better known southern authors.   PS261.S59

Twentieth century western writers / ed., Geoff Sadler. 2nd ed. Chicago : St. James, c1991. 848 p.   **BE579**

1st ed., 1982.

Provides biobibliographies for approximately 450 western fiction writers. Poets, dramatists, and authors of nonfiction are excluded unless they wrote fiction as well. The introduction includes a reading list of books and articles on western literature. Title index.   PS271.T84

Great Britain

General works

Guides

For classified guides to English and American literature, *see also*: James L. Harner, *Literary research guide* (BE396) and Michael J. Marcuse, *A reference guide for English studies* (BE398). Harner and Marcuse have largely superseded the longtime standard *Selective bibliography for the study of English and American literature*, by Richard D. Altick and Andrew Wright (6th ed. N.Y. : Macmillan, c1979). For discussion of research methodology, *see*: Richard D. Altick and John J. Fenstermaker, *The art of literary research* (BE1), and Jacques Barzun and Henry F. Graff, *The modern researcher* (DA3).

Bateson, Frederick Wilse. A guide to English and American literature / F. W. Bateson and Harrison T. Meserole. 3rd ed. N.Y. : Gordian Pr., 1976. 334 p.   **BE580**

Previous editions (1965–67) had title: *A guide to English literature*.

Provides an evaluative guide to reliable editions and significant criticism of principal writers in addition to surveying bibliographies, anthologies, and literary histories for various periods of English literature. Includes a chapter on literary criticism, a chapter on literary research methodology, and a chapter on American literature (by Harrison T. Meserole). Although dated, still worthwhile.   Z2011.B32

Bibliography

Allibone, Samuel Austin. A critical dictionary of English literature and British and American authors, living and deceased : from the earliest accounts to the latter half of the nineteenth century, containing over 46,000 articles (authors), with forty indexes of subjects. Philadelphia : Lippincott, 1858. 3 v. (3140 p.).   **BE581**

Repr. : Detroit : Gale, 1965, with suppl.

A standard, older work very useful in spite of the fact that it is not entirely accurate and so must often be checked for important points. Based in part upon Robert Watt's *Bibliotheca Britannica* (AA664) and reflects Watt's inaccuracies. Arranged alphabetically by authors, giving for each: brief biographical sketch, list of works with dates, and references to critical comments or reviews.

Supplement … containing over 37,000 articles (authors), and enumerating over 93,000 titles by John Foster Kirk (Philadelphia : Lippincott, 1891. 2 v. [1562 p.]).   Z2010.A44

Cambridge bibliography of English literature / ed. by F. W. Bateson. …. Cambridge : Univ. Pr., 1940–57 ; N.Y. : Macmillan, 1941–57. 5 v.   **BE582**

Contents: v. 1–3, 600–1900; v. 4, Index; v. 5, Supplement.

Covers with fullness and considerable detail, though avowedly not with actual comleteness, the Old English, Middle English, modern English, and Latin literature of the British Isles, with comparatively brief treatment of the English literature of the Dominions and India; does not include American literature or the French literature of Canada, and gives only incidental inclusion of Welsh, Gaelic, or Celtic material.

Arranged chronologically, and under periods by literary forms, e.g., Poetry, Drama, Periodicals, etc., and large class groups, such as History, Philosophy, etc., with further subdivision under forms and groups by special topics and by the individual authors treated. References given under each author vary according to his importance or to the amount of material available, but generally include: bibliographies of that author, either separately published or included in some periodical or other work; collected editions of his works; separate works, with date of first edition and of subsequent editions within the next 50 years, with references to later editions having special features or editing; and a selection of biographical and critical works about the author.

Within the Drama sections, a useful reference feature is the analytical reference to texts of separate plays as printed in the standard collections of plays, such as Dodsley, Bell, French, Lacy, etc. The *Supplement* lists publications on the study of English language and literature, down to 1900, which appeared approximately from 1940 to 1955; it has no index, but sections are roughly keyed to comparable sections in v. 1–3.

Now largely superseded by the revised edition (*The new Cambridge bibliography of English literature*, BE585), but some of the background chapters not carried forward to the new work will continue to be useful.   Z2011.B28

Harvard University. Library. English literature. Cambridge, Mass. : distr. by Harvard Univ. Pr., 1971. 4 v. (Widener Library shelflist, 35–38).   **BE583**

For a note on the Widener shelflist series, *see* AA115.

Contents: v. 1, Classification schedule; Classified listing by call number; v. 2, Chronological listing; v. 3–4, Author and title listing.

"The 112,000 books, pamphlets, and periodicals in the *10441–23899* and *ELB* classes include literary histories, anthologies, and works by and about individual literary authors. To ensure more complete coverage of British authors, 8000 works of American and British fiction comprising the *PZ* and *PZB* classes have been added to the chronological and alphabetical lists."—*Pref.*   Z2011.H36

Myers, Robin. A dictionary of literature in the English language, from Chaucer to 1940. Oxford ; N.Y. : Pergamon, [1970]. 2 v. (1497 p.) : ill., facsim.   **BE584**

Comp. for the National Book League.

Offers biographical and bibliographical information concerning some 3,500 authors writing in English. Biographical information is sketchy, and the bulk of v. 1 is made up of lists of the individual writers' works, with publication dates. Vol. 2 provides a title-author index—possibly the most useful aspect of the work.

Continued by: ———. *A dictionary of literature in the English language from 1940–1970 : complete with alphabetical title-author index and a geographical-chronological index to authors* (Oxford ; N.Y. : Pergamon, 1978. 519 p.).   Z2010.M9

The new Cambridge bibliography of English literature. Cambridge : Univ. Pr., 1969–77. 5 v.   **BE585**

Contents: v. 1, 600–1660, ed. by George Watson; v. 2, 1660–1800, ed. by George Watson; v. 3, 1800–1900, ed. by George Watson; v. 4, 1900–1950, ed. by I. R. Willison; v. 5, Index, comp. by J. D. Pickles.

An extensive though necessarily selective bibliography intended to replace *Cambridge bibliography of English literature* (BE582). Coverage is "confined to literary authors native to or mainly resident in the British Isles" (*Introd., v. 1*), with no restriction of nationality or language for secondary materials. Excluded from secondary materials are unpublished dissertations, reviews of secondary works, encyclopedia articles, and ephemeral works. Within period divisions there are subdivisions for subjects, forms, genres, and authors (further subdivided into major and minor authors). Individual author entries include bibliographies, collections, primary works, and criticism. Headnotes for selected authors locate manuscript collections. Within divisions entries are listed by date of publication (except when a list of secondary materials includes multiple studies by an individual scholar, in which case the studies are grouped together under the earliest published piece). Entries are not always cross-referenced and therefore the index must be consulted for comprehensive searching. Vols. 1–4 are individually indexed. No index of scholars. The *CBEL* is not entirely superseded by the newer edition, since it contains sections on Commonwealth literatures and social and political backgrounds that were excluded from the *NCBEL*.

An indispensable reference source and often the best place for beginning research. A new edition is planned. For updating see: *MLA international bibliography* (BE39) and *Annual bibliography of English language and literature* (BE588).   Z2011.N45

The shorter new Cambridge bibliography of English literature / ed. by George Watson. Cambridge ; N.Y. : Cambridge Univ. Pr., 1981. 1622 p.   **BE586**

Essentially an abridgment of the *New CBEL* (BE585), but with some additions (mainly newly published items) and corrections. "All the major authors in *New CBEL*, and many minor ones, have been included. ... In each case the primary section, or the canon of an author's works, has been wholly or largely kept; the secondary section, however, which consists of books and articles concerning that author, has usually been reduced substantially . ..."—*Pref.*

A review in *The library* ser. 6, v. 4, no. 2 (June 1982): 188–89 terms this "an unimagnative scissors-and-paste job which shows little thought for the needs of the student and private person." Z2011.S417

Bibliography of bibliography

Howard-Hill, Trevor Howard. Index to British literary bibliography. Oxford : Clarendon Pr. ; N.Y. : Oxford Univ. Pr., 1969–92. v. 1–8. (In progress).   **BE587**

Contents: v. 1, Bibliography of British literary bibliographies (2nd ed., rev. and enl., c1987); v. 2, Shakespearian bibliography and textual criticism : a bibliography (c1971); v. 3, British literary bibliography to 1890 : a bibliography (In progress); v. 4, British bibliography and textual criticism : a bibliography (c1979); v. 5, British bibliography and textual criticism : a bibliography (authors) (c1979); v. 6, British literary bibliography and textual criticism, 1890–1969: an index (c1980); v. 7, British literary bibliography, 1970–1979 : a bibliography (c1992); v. 8, Dissertations on British literary bibliography to 1980 (In progress).

An annotated bibliography of books, substantial portions of books, and articles that attempts to record "all publications in English [and some foreign language publications] which list the printed works of British writers, which list and describe the works published in Britain from 1475 to the present day, whether generally or classified by period, or literary form or genre, or which describe English works dealing with particular subjects."—*Introd., v. 1, 2nd ed.* Annotations are descriptive and often cite reviews. Arrangement within sections and subsections is chronological by date of publication. Vol. 1 lists bibliographies published in Britain 1890–1969 on writers active since 1475 and includes sections for general and period bibliographies, regional bibliographies, book production and distribution, forms and genres (e.g., ballads, copybooks, playbills), subjects (e.g., angling, heraldry, railways), and bibliographies for approximately 1,500 authors. The revised edition adds 1,860 new entries to v. 1 (1st ed. 1969, 5,219 entries), but does not extend coverage beyond 1969. Index includes authors, editors, compilers, publishers, titles, and subjects. Vol. 2 lists critical and textual Shakespearean studies published 1890–1969 and includes a (now superseded) supplement to v. 1. Indexed. Vols. 4 and 5 provide bibliographies of textual studies published 1890–1969 and include general, period, and regional bibliographies, book production and distribution, forms, genres, and subjects, and authors (v. 5) and are indexed by v. 6. Vol. 6 provides an interim cumulative index to volumes 1 (1st ed.), 2, 4, and 5. Vol. 7 provides a decennial supplement for 1970–79. Further updates and revisions are planned. This ongoing project represents the most complete bibliography of British literary bibliography. Review: Peter Davison, *The review of English studies*, n.s. 41 (Feb. 1990): 104–105. For updating see: *Bibliographic index* (AA15).   Z2011.A1H68

Current

Annual bibliography of English language and literature. Vol. 4 (1923)– . Cambridge : Bowes & Bowes, 1924– . Annual.   **BE588**

Continues: *Bibliography of English language and literature* (v. 1 [1920]–3 [1922]).

Edited for the Modern Humanities Research Association. Often referred to as *ABELL*. Publisher varies.

An international, classified bibliography of scholarship for literatures in English. Includes books, portions of books, articles, and dissertations, and cites reviews for some books listed. In addition to literature, there are sections for the following: festschriften and other collections; bibliography (general bibliography, book production, etc.); scholarly method; language, literature, and the computer; newspapers and other periodicals; the English language (general studies, phonetics and phonology, grammar, etc.); and traditional culture, folklore and folklife. Sections for literature include divisions for general studies and periods, with further subdivisions for genres, related studies, literary theory, and individual authors. Index of subject authors and subjects (broad form divisions rather than thematic indexing, e.g., biography—17th century); index of scholars. Generally superior to *MLA international bibliography* (BE39) in its coverage of British items and should be used in conjunction with *MLA* for reasonably comprehensive searching. Lag time for publication is approximately three years. A standard, important serial bibliography that would be greatly enhanced by thematic access in an online environment.

Some reservations about the arrangement, indexing, and general editing are expressed in *English studies* 55 (Apr. 1974) : 152–54.   Z2011.M69

The year's work in English studies. v. 1 (1919/20)– . London : publ. for the English Association by John Murray, 1921– . Annual.   **BE589**

Often referred to as *YWES*.

An annual collection of signed bibliographic essays surveying the year's scholarship in English literature. Includes essays for: periods and genres; reference materials, literary history, and bibliography; the English language; literary theory; American literature (to 1900 and for the 20th century); and new literatures in English. Separate chapters for

Chaucer, Shakespeare, and Milton. Includes a list of books received. Indexed. Lag time for publication is approximately three years. An important evaluative reference source.

§ See also: *American literary scholarship* (BE418) for evaluative surveys of scholarship in American literature. PE58.E6

Periodicals

British literary magazines / ed. by Alvin Sullivan. Westport, Conn. : Greenwood, 1983–1986. 4 v. **BE590**

Contents: v. 1, The Augustan Age and the Age of Johnson, 1698–1788; v. 2, The Romantic Age, 1789–1836; v. 3, The Victorian and Edwardian Age, 1837–1913; v. 4, The Modern Age, 1914–1984.

Utilizing the same format as Edward E. Chielens' *The literary journal in America to 1900* (BE421), this collection provides profiles of 369 British literary magazines. Each volume contains an introductory essay, profiles of approximately 90 magazines (arranged by title), a chronology of social and literary events, and an index. Selection of titles is meant to reflect the range and variety of reviews, journals, essay periodicals, and illustrated magazines for the period. Signed essays offer information on the history, content, contributors, and significance of each title. Bibliographic references to information sources, notes on indexes, reprints, library locations, and details of publishing history are given for each title. Various other appendixes list additional titles with descriptive annotations. PN5124.L6.B74

Stanton, Michael N. English literary journals, 1900–1950 : a guide to information sources. Detroit : Gale, 1982. 119 p. (American literature, English literature, and world literatures in English, v. 32). **BE591**

About 135 literary journals of the period are listed with publication dates, frequency, and names of editors, plus an annotation characterizing the publication and listing notable contributors. A bibliography lists background readings, general works, and studies of individual journals. Indexed. Z2005.S73

White, Robert B. The English literary journal to 1900 : a guide to information sources. Detroit : Gale, c1977. 311 p. (American literature, English literature, and world literatures in English, v. 8). **BE592**

Aims to present "a bibliography of what has been written since about 1890 and what is now accessible to the general reader concerning pre-1900 British literary periodicals."—*Pref.* Sections for bibliographies and general studies are followed by sections for specific periodicals, persons, and places. Indexed. Z6956.G6W47

Dissertations

Howard, Patsy C. Theses in English literature, 1894–1970. Ann Arbor, Mich. : Pierian Pr., 1973. 387 p. **BE593**

Lists some 9,000 unpublished baccalaureate and master's theses from a wide range of American and foreign universities. Listing is by literary author treated, then alphabetically by author of the thesis. Index of authors of theses, and a brief subject index. Coverage is admittedly incomplete, and precise coverage for individual institutions is not indicated but appears to be spotty in various instances. Z2011.H63

Mummendey, Richard. Language and literature of the Anglo-Saxon nations as presented in German doctoral dissertations, 1885–1950 : a bibliography. Bonn : H. Bouvier ; Charlottesville : Bibliographical Society of the Univ. of Virginia, 1954. 200 p. **BE594**

Added t.p. in German; prefatory matter and captions in English and German.

Provides a classified list of approximately 3,000 dissertations on English language and literature accepted by German universities 1885–1950. Also includes very brief sections for Commonwealth and

American literature. Index includes subject authors, dissertation writers, and subjects. Subject indexing is inadequate and coverage is not complete.

§ See also: *Jahresverzeichnis der deutschen Hochschulschriften 1885–1969*, bearb. von der Deutschen Bücherei (Jahrg. 1–85. Leipzig : VEB Verlag für Buch– und Bibliothekswesen, 1887–1973). Z2011.M8

Criticism

Borklund, Elmer. Contemporary literary critics. 2nd ed. Detroit : Gale, 1982. 600 p. **BE595**

For annotation, *see* BE426. PS78.B56

The critical perspective / gen. ed., Harold Bloom. N.Y. : Chelsea House Publishers, 1985–89. 11 v. **BE596**

Contents: v. 1, Medieval–early Renaissance; v. 2, Renaissance; v. 3, Elizabethan–Caroline; v. 4, Restoration–early Georgian; v. 5, Georgian; v. 6, Late Georgian–Romantic; v. 7, Early Victorian; v. 8, Mid-Victorian; v. 9, Late Victorian; v. 10, Edwardian; v. 11, Bibliographical supplement and index.

Part of "The Chelsea House library of literary criticism" series, ed. by Harold Bloom, this is a companion set to *The new Moulton's library of literary criticism* (BE599), offering a compilation of 20th-century criticism of 296 English-language authors whose principal works predate 1904. The editors "have sought to provide the essays most representative of the modern era, as well as interesting critical experiments by current scholars."—*Pref.* Entries include biographical sketches as well as criticism, and each volume concludes with suggested readings. The final volume provides primary bibliographies for all authors in the set. Indexes: author bibliographies; series contents; authors and critics. PR85.C76

The critical temper : a survey of modern criticism on English and American literature from the beginnings to the twentieth century / Martin Tucker, gen. ed. N.Y. : Ungar, [1969–89]. 5 v. **BE597**

Contents: v. 1, From Old English to Shakespeare; v. 2, From Milton to Romantic literature; v. 3, Victorian literature and American literature; v. 4, Suppl. (1979); v. 5, 2nd. Suppl. (1989).

Supplements Charles Wells Moulton's *Library of literary criticism of English and American authors* (BE598) with excerpts of 20th-century literary criticism for approximately 220 English and American authors writing prior to 1900. Entries include a biographical sketch, and list standard editions and biographical studies. Vol. 3 includes a cross-reference index to authors and an index of critics. Vols. 4 and 5 update the criticism and incorporate some authors previously excluded. PR83.C77

Moulton, Charles Wells. The library of literary criticism of English and American authors. Buffalo, N.Y. : Moulton Publ. Co., 1901–05. 8 v. : ill. **BE598**

Repr.: Gloucester, Mass. : Peter Smith, 1959.

A compilation of quoted material, not an encyclopedia of original articles. Covers the years 680–1904. For each author treated gives brief biographical data, then selected quotations from criticisms of his work, grouped as: (1) personal, (2) individual works, (3) general. Extracts are of some length and are given with exact references, so that the work serves both as an encyclopedia of critical comment and as an index of literary criticism.

Dorothy N. Curley's *Modern American literature* (BE427) and Ruth Z. Temple and Martin Tucker's *Modern British literature* (BE600) serve as continuations.

Abridged version: ———. *Library of literary criticism of English and American authors through the beginning of the twentieth century* (Abr., rev. and with additions by Martin Tucker. N.Y. : Ungar, [1966]. 4 v.).

Contents: v. 1, The beginnings to the seventeenth century; v. 2, Neo-classicism to the romantic period; v. 3, The romantic period to the Victorian age; v. 4, The mid-nineteenth century to Edwardianism.

Both abridges and updates the earlier compilation but the coverage differs—some authors not previously treated are added and some of only marginal literary interest have been dropped. Excerpts from critical appraisals are drawn from publications through 1964. Index of critics in the final volume.

The new Moulton's library of literary criticism, gen. ed., Harold Bloom (BE599), provides a more recent update.   PR83.M73

The new Moulton's library of literary criticism / gen. ed., Harold Bloom. N.Y. : Chelsea House Publishers, 1985–1990. 11 v. : 29 cm.   **BE599**

Contents: v. 1, Medieval–Early Renaissance; v. 2, William Shakespeare; v. 3, Elizabethan–Caroline; v. 4, Restoration–Early Georgian; v. 5, Georgian; v. 6, Late Georgian–Romantic; v. 7, Early Victorian; v. 8, Mid-Victorian; v. 9, Late Victorian; v. 10, Late Victorian–Edwardian; v. 11, Bibliographical supplement and index.

Designed "to present a concise portrait of the critical heritage of every crucial British and American author."—*Pref.* Provides excerpts from criticism written before the 20th century concerning 532 authors and anonymous works written from the 8th century up to 1904. Entries, which include biographies as well as critical information, are arranged chronologically by death date within each volume. Figures covered include nonliterary authors (e.g., Thomas Jefferson, Charles Darwin). Vol. 11 contains bibliographical references and author and critic indexes for the entire set.

Abridges and updates Charles Wells Moulton's *Library of literary criticism of English and American authors* (BE598).   PR85.N39

Temple, Ruth Zabriskie. Modern British literature / Ruth Z. Temple, Martin Tucker. N.Y. : Ungar, [1966–1985]. 5 v.   **BE600**

Contents: v. 1–3, (comp. & ed. Ruth Z. Temple and Martin Tucker, 1966); v. 4, Suppl. (comp. & ed. Martin Tucker and Rita Stein, 1975); v. 5, 2nd Suppl. (comp. & ed. Denis Lane and Rita Stein, 1985).

Like Dorothy Nyren Curley's *Modern American literature* (BE427), this serves to continue Charles Wells Moulton's *Library of literary criticism* (BE598). Vols. 1–3 offer brief critical excerpts of authors (including some nonliterary figures) who lived in the 20th century or who gained recognition after 1900 (e.g., Gerard Manley Hopkins). Each volume contains primary bibliographies of the authors' separately published works. Indexes (v. 3): cross-reference index to authors; critics. Vol. 4 selectively updates the criticism for approximately one-third of the authors previously treated and adds 49 new writers. Vol. 5 updates the criticism for 175 modern writers.

§ *The new Moulton's library of literary criticism*, gen. ed., Harold Bloom (BE599), provides a more recent update.   PR473.T4

Twentieth-century British literature / gen. ed., Harold Bloom. N.Y. : Chelsea House Publishers, 1985–1987. 6 v. : ports.   **BE601**

Covers modern authors from the U.K. and its former colonies. Authors are listed alphabetically; each brief biographical sketch is followed by excerpts from criticism and evaluations by various writers which appeared in journal articles, memoirs, reviews of individual works, and book-length studies. Some of the longer, essay-like pieces include footnote references. Lists of additional readings appear at the end of v. 1–5. Vol.6 includes full lists (with publication dates) of all titles of each author treated; a "Series contents" section that lists the authors and sources of extracts concerning each writer; and an alphabetical index to critics represented in the full set.   PR473.T84

Manuscripts; Archives

Early English manuscripts in facsimile. Copenhagen : Rosenkilde and Bagger ; Baltimore : Johns Hopkins Pr., 1951–93. v. 1–25. (In progress).   **BE602**

An ongoing project, now under the chief editorship of Geoffrey Harlow, that makes more generally accessible the great English and Latin manuscripts of the medieval period in England. The editions are accompanied by detailed introductions by well-known scholars that are intended to serve as guides to the facsimiles.

Index of English literary manuscripts / editorial board, P.J. Croft, Theodore Hofmann, and John Horden ; editorial advisors, Rodney G. Dennis and Stephen Parks. London : Mansell ; N.Y. : Bowker, 1980–1993. . (In progress).   **BE603**

Imprint varies; some have imprint London ; New York : Mansell.

Contents: v. 1, 1450–1625 (2 pts. Comp. by Peter Beal); v. 2, 1625–1700 (2 pts. Comp. by Peter Beal); v. 3, 1700–1800, (3 pts.; to be complete in 4 pts. Comp. by Margaret M. Smith); v. 4, 1800–1900 (4 pts.; in progress. Pt. 1 comp. by Barbara Rosenbaum and Pamela White; pts. 2–3 comp. by Barbara Rosenbaum); v. 5, Indexes of titles, first lines, names, repositories (forthcoming).

An index that describes and locates extant manuscripts of some 300 English, Irish, Scots, and Welsh authors who flourished between 1450 and 1900. Selection of authors to be included was originally based on those chosen for the *Concise Cambridge bibliography of English literature, 600–1950*, ed. George Watson (2nd ed. Cambridge : Cambridge Univ. Pr., 1965), but is is not confined to that list and fairly radical departures from it will be noted in later volumes. "Coverage is not restricted to authors' manuscripts and typescripts, but also includes authors' corrected proof-sheets, diaries and notebooks, their marginal notes in printed books, and especially for the period to c.1700, scribal copies."—*Gen. introd.* Generally excluded are letters, business documents, nonliterary autograph manuscripts, prompt-copies of plays, and contemporary annotated printed exempla of an author's works. These exclusions are briefly discussed in an introduction to each author's entry, which also serves to draw attention to the extent and importance of surviving manuscripts. Typical entries include a physical description of the manuscript, date and provenance, editions and facsimiles, germane scholarship, and location. Additions and corrections are to be included in v. 5. An essential source for British literary scholarship.   Z6611.L7I5

Ker, Neil Ripley. Catalogue of manuscripts containing Anglo-Saxon. Oxford : Clarendon Pr. ; N.Y. : Oxford Univ. Pr., 1990. 579 p. : ill.   **BE604**

First publ. 1957.

Describes and locates more than 400 Old English manuscripts dating before ca.1200. The catalog is arranged alphabetically by collector or by the city in which the collection resides, then by collection and surname of the collector (e.g., London. British Museum, Cotton Vitellius A. xv). A detailed introduction includes notes on the paleography and history of the principal manuscripts. Bibliography of printed books and manuscripts. Includes tables of first and second series of homilies. Indexes: contents of manuscripts; paleographical and historical index; index of owners. Facsimiles.

This reissue of the 1957 ed. includes Ker's "Supplement to *Catalogue of Manuscripts Containing Anglo-Saxon*," originally in *Anglo-Saxon England* 5 (1976) : 121–131. *See also* Mary Blockey, "Addenda and Corrigenda to N.R. Ker's 'A Supplement to *Catalogue of Manuscripts Containing Anglo-Saxon*,' " *Notes and Queries* n.s. 29 (1982) : 1–3.   Z6605.A56K4

Location register of twentieth-century English literary manuscripts and letters : a union list of papers of modern English, Irish, Scottish, and Welsh authors in the British Isles. Boston : G.K. Hall, 1988. 2 v.   **BE605**

" 'British' includes not only English, Irish, Scottish, and Welsh writers who used the English language, but also immigrants, refugees and others who spent a considerable part of their life in the British Isles … . 'Literary' includes poets, novelists, dramatists and men and women of letters of all styles and qualities … . [and] 'Twentieth-century' has … been interpreted to include anyone who lived beyond the year 1899."—*Introd.* Not limited to literary manuscripts and letters, the *Register* also refers to "photographs, tape recordings and floppy diskettes, as well as to proofs of published works. Entries have been made for photostat, xerographic, and microfilm copies of literary papers, whether or not the originals remain in the British Isles." Microfilm copies which are published commercially have also been noted." Within the alphabetical arrangement of authors' names, manuscripts are listed alphabetically, followed by a miscellaneous list of letters in chronological sequence. "For many authors … the first entry is a note which may explain omissions from the entries which follow. The note may outline holdings of papers by repositories overseas [sometimes including *NUCMC* references] … but may also describe authors' policies for retention or destruction of their papers and even mishaps and disasters which have befallen them." Appendix giving full addresses of institutions at the end of v. 2. Z6611.L7L63

Storey, Richard. Primary sources for Victorian studies : a guide to the location and use of unpublished materials / by Richard Storey and Lionel Madden. London : Phillimore, 1977. 81 p. **BE606**

"Concentrates on collections within Britain, but a short section is included as an introduction to the problems of discovering collections of relevant materials outside Britain."—*Pref.* Bibliographic references; index.

Updated by Storey's *Primary sources for Victorian studies : an updating* (Leicester : Victorian Studies Centre, Univ. of Leicester, 1987. 38 p.). Z2019.S86

Handbooks

Blain, Virginia. The feminist companion to literature in English : women writers from the Middle Ages to the present / Virginia Blain, Patricia Clements, Isobel Grundy. New Haven, Conn. : Yale Univ. Pr., 1990. 1231 p. **BE607**

Includes "women writing in English in several national traditions, including African, American, Asian, Australian, Canadian, Caribbean, New Zealand, South Pacific, the British Isles; not only works issuing from and reflecting the dominant ideologies of race, class, sexual practice; not only the canonized genres, but also diaries, letters, writing for children, and popular forms"—*Introd.* More than 2,700 brief biological entries (500 word maximum) and approximately 60 topical entries (abolition of slavery, bluestockings, feminist theory, spiritualism and theosophy, etc.). Includes a bibliography of frequently cited works, an index of topics, a chronological index of names, and an index of cross-references (including many women for whom there are no individual entries). Although there are inevitable omissions and exclusions, this is the fullest biographical guide to date for women writing in English. Review: *Times literary supplement* (18 Jan. 1991): 8. PR111.B57

The Cambridge guide to literature in English / ed. by Ian Ousby. Rev. ed. Cambridge ; N. Y. : Cambridge Univ. Pr., 1993. 1054 p. : ill. **BE608**

A handbook to the literature in English produced by all English-speaking cultures. The earlier edition by this title (1988) virtually replaces *Cambridge guide to English literature*, comp. by Michael Stapleton ([Cambridge : N. Y.] : Cambridge Univ. Pr., c1983), although this volume makes no mention of that work. Includes entries for authors, major individual works, and genres, movements, groups, critical concepts, etc. Attempts to be very current and includes a number of living authors. Also has black-and-white illustrations. "…in general the standard of information is extremely reliable."—*English studies* 74 : 6 (Dec. 1993) : 540. PR85.C29

A dictionary of biblical tradition in English literature / David Lyle Jeffrey, gen. ed. Grand Rapids, Mich. : W.B. Eerdmans, c1992. 960 p. **BE609**

An important reference work that focuses "on literature of the English-speaking world and the exegetical tradition most pertinent to it."—*Pref.* Longer entries typically describe a word or phrase or motif as it has been used: (1) in the Bible; (2) in the exegetical tradition (including Jewish commentators, the church fathers, and exegetical writings by period); and (3) in English literature (tracing "significant strands in literary development through exemplary representations from the Middle ages to the twentieth century"). Provides more than 750 entries, the more substantial being signed and including bibliographies. Numerous cross-references. Bibliographies in the following categories: (1) Biblical studies; (2) History of biblical interpretation; (3) Biblical tradition in English literature. Review: *Choice* 30 : 11 (July–August 1993) : 1748. PR149.B5D53

Drabble, Margaret. The Oxford companion to English literature. 5th ed. Oxford ; N.Y. : Oxford Univ. Pr., 1985. 1155 p. **BE610**

1st ed., 1932–4th ed., 1967, ed. by Paul Harvey.

The 5th ed. represents a thorough revision. Entries for literary authors, works, critics, terminology, nonliterary figures, and important periodicals. Now includes authors born through 1939, with many author entries providing a brief bibliography. Foreign authors important to English literature are also included. Three appendixes: (1) Censorship and the law of the press; (2) Notes on the history of English and copyright; (3) The calendar (including tables for Julian and Gregorian calendars, saints' days and feasts, and movable feasts. Reviews: *New York times book review* (July 14, 1985) :1 ff. ; *The American scholar* 55 (Summer 1986) :410–418.

§ An abridgment is publ. as *The concise Oxford companion to English literature*, ed. Margaret Drabble and Jenny Stringer (Oxford : Oxford Univ. Press, 1990. 631 p.). PR19.D73

Prentice Hall guide to English literature : the new authority on English literature / ed. by Marion Wynne-Davies. N.Y. : Prentice Hall, c1990. 1066 p. **BE611**

Published in U.K. as *Bloomsbury guide to English literature* (London : Bloomsbury, 1989).

Represents a reworking of Christopher Gillie's *Longman companion to English literature* (1977). In three parts: an essay section (12 chapters on political, social, and historical topics); an alphabetical dictionary of authors, works, themes, historical and literary figures, places, and events; and a chronology.

§ Deriving from the *Prentice Hall guide*, and following its format, several compact period/genre guides have been published in London by Bloomsbury in the "Bloomsbury guide to English literature" series: *A guide to English Renaissance literature, 1500–1600*, ed. Marion Wynne-Davies (c1992); *A guide to romantic literature, 1780–1830*, ed. Geoff Ward (c1993); *The twentieth century: a guide to literature from 1900 to the present day*, ed. Linda R. Williams (c1992); *The novel: a guide to the novel from its origins to the present day*, ed. Andrew Michael Roberts (c1993). Forthcoming is *A guide to Restoration and Augustan literature*, ed. Eva Simmonds. PR19.B5

Chronologies

Annals of English literature, 1475–1950 : the principal publications of each year together with an alphabetical index of authors and their works. 2nd ed. Oxford : Clarendon Pr., 1961. 380 p. **BE612**

1st ed., 1935, comp. by J. G. Ghosh and E. G. Withycombe; 2nd ed. rev. and brought up to date by R. W. Chapman.

A chronological list giving, under each year, authors and brief titles of outstanding books published that year, and, in parallel columns, important literary or historical events of the same year. Detailed author index, p. 296–380.

§ *See also*: Frederick Maurice Powicke and E. B. Fryde's *Handbook of British chronology* (DC295). Z2011.A5

Rogal, Samuel J. A chronological outline of British literature. Westport, Conn. : Greenwood, 1980. 341 p. **BE613**

A chronology of literary births, deaths, events, and works from 516 through 1979 designed to aid "in determining the extent of literary activity and literary related events in England, Scotland, Ireland, and Wales during a specific year, decade, or century."—*Introd.* Indexed. PR87.R57

Guidebooks

Eagle, Dorothy. The Oxford illustrated literary guide to Great Britain and Ireland / comp. and ed. by Dorothy Eagle and Hilary Carnell. 2nd ed. / ed. by Dorothy Eagle and Meic Stephens. Oxford ; N.Y. : Oxford Univ. Pr., 1992. 322 p. : ill. (some col.), 13 maps. **BE614**

1st ed., 1977, had title: *The Oxford literary guide to the British Isles*; a 1981 ed., also called 2nd ed., used the current title.

Alphabetical entries for 1,337 place-names in England, Ireland, Scotland, and Wales (keyed to grid maps at the end of the volume). Fictitious place-names are cross-referenced to actual places and, whenever possible, directions to extant literary sites are provided. Following the geographical section is an index of 1,050 authors (deceased); entries give biographical and bibliographic details, and are cross-referenced to geographical entries. Includes many fine illustrations.

§ Oxford has also issued in a smaller format and without illustrations: *The Oxford literary guide to Great Britain and Ireland*, comp. and ed. by Eagle and Stephens (2nd ed. Oxford ; N.Y. : Oxford Univ. Press, 1993. 468 p.).   PR109.E18

Histories

Baugh, Albert Croll. A literary history of England. 2nd ed. London : Routledge & K. Paul ; N.Y. : Appleton-Century-Crofts, [1967]. 1605, [190], 1xxx p.   **BE615**
1st ed., 1948.
Also issued in a 4-v. ed.
Contents: v. 1, The Middle Ages: the Old English period (to 1100) by K. Malone; The Middle English period (1100–1500) by A. C. Baugh; v. 2, The Renaissance (1500–1660) by T. Brooke and M. A. Shaaber; v. 3, The Restoration and eighteenth century (1660–1789) by G. Sherburne and D. F. Bond; v. 4, The nineteenth century and after (1789–1939) by S. C. Chew and R. D. Altick; Bibliographical supplement; Index.
A scholarly history, with bibliographical footnotes in the text. The "Bibliographical supplement" (unpaged) of the new edition provides extensive listings of books and periodical articles extending the scope of the footnote references and bringing the record up to date. Written by distinguished scholars and still considered one of the finest one-volume histories of English literature. Index of authors and titles.
PR83.B3

The new Pelican guide to English literature / ed. by Boris Ford. Rev. and expanded ed. Harmondsworth, Eng. ; N.Y. : Penguin Books, 1982–1988. 9 v.   **BE616**
Rev. ed. of *The Pelican guide to English literature*, 3rd ed., 1973.
Contents: v. 1, pt. 1, Medieval literature : Chaucer and the alliterative tradition; v. 1, pt. 2, Medieval literature : the European inheritance; v. 2, The age of Shakespeare; v. 3, From Donne to Marvell; v. 4, From Dryden to Johnson; v. 5, From Blake to Byron; v. 6, From Dickens to Hardy; v. 7, From James to Eliot; v. 8, The present; v. 9, American literature.
These volumes present a series of essays by well known critics rather than a unified history. Characteristically they include overview essays for the social setting as well as the literary scene, and essays for authors, movements, genres, etc. Individual volumes are indexed and include appendixes of classified bibliographies of suggested readings and primary bibliographies for authors. These appendixes have been publ. in a separate volume: *A guide for readers to the new Pelican guide to English literature*, ed. Boris Ford (N.Y. : Penguin, c1984).
PR83.N49

The Oxford history of English literature / ed., Frank Percy Wilson and Bonamy Dobrée. Oxford : Clarendon Pr., 1945–90. v. 1–13 in 16 v.   **BE617**
Repr. : Oxford : Clarendon Pr., 1990. With publ. of v. 13, volumes in this standard history have been renumbered, and many are being reissued with new titles.
Contents [original titles, with renumbered vols. in parentheses]: v. 1, pt. 2 (v. 1), Middle English literature, J. A. W. Bennett, ed. and comp. by Douglas Gray (c1986); v. 2, pt. 1 (v. 2), Chaucer and the fifteenth century, Henry Stanley Bennet (1947); v. 2, pt. 2 (v. 3), English literature at the close of the middle ages, E. K. Chambers (1947); v. 3 (v. 4), English literature in the sixteenth century excluding drama, C. S. Lewis (c1954); v. 4, pt. 1 (v. 5), The English drama, 1485–1585, F. P. Wilson (c1969); v. 4, pt. 2, (In progress, will be v. 6), English drama 1586–1642 : Shakespeare and his Age; v. 5 (v. 7), English literature in the earlier seventeenth century, 1600–1660, Douglas Bush

(2nd ed. rev., c1962); v. 6 (v. 8), English literature of the late seventeenth century, James Runcieman Sutherland (c1969); v. 7 (v. 9), English literature in the early eighteenth century, 1700–1740, Bonamy Dobrée (c1959); v. 8 (v. 10), The mid-eighteenth century, John Butt, ed. and comp. by Geoffrey Carnall (c1979); v. 9 (v. 11), English literature, 1789–1815, W. L. Renwich (c1963); v. 10 (v. 12), English literature, 1815–1832, Ian Jack (c1963); v. 11, pt. 1 (v. 14), English literature, 1832–1890, Paul Turner (c1989); v. 11, pt. 2 (publ. only as v. 13), The victorian novel, E. A. Horsman (c1990); v. 12 (v. 15), Eight modern writers, J. I. M. Stewart (c1963); v. 13 (In progress), English literature, 1890–1945.
An ongoing, standard history of English literature from ca.1100 CE through the mid-20th century. Volumes by eminent scholars typically provide an overview and discussion of background issues, a discussion of major and minor literary figures, movements and genres. Most volumes include chronological tables (identifying social and political as well as literary events), a selective, classified bibliography, and are individually indexed.
§ Dated but not entirely superseded is *Cambridge history of English literature*, ed. A. W. Ward and A. R. Waller (Cambridge : Univ. Press, 1907–27. 15 v.). See also: *The concise Cambridge history of English literature*, George Sampson (3rd ed., rev. by R. C. Churchill. London : Cambridge Univ. Pr., 1970), a revision which extends coverage to American literature and other literatures in English.

Anthologies

Kermode, Frank. The Oxford anthology of English literature / gen. editors: Frank Kermode and John Hollander. N.Y. : Oxford Univ. Pr., 1973. 2 v. : ill.   **BE618**
Contents: v. 1, The Middle Ages through the eighteenth century; v. 2, 1800 to present.
Like *Norton anthology of English literature* (BE619), selections are made by established scholars, with introductions provided for periods and authors, and critical annotations for the prose and poetry. Includes a glossary, suggestions for further reading (by period), and indexes for authors and titles, and for first lines of poems. Also has many fine illustrations. For a comparison of the Norton (2nd ed.) and Oxford, and a humorous discussion of the marketability of literary anthologies generally, see *New York Times book review* (Dec. 30, 1973) : 6.
§ A more recent multivolume anthology is *St. Martin's anthologies of English literature*, Norman Jeffares and Michael Alexander, gen. editors, (N.Y. : St. Martin's Pr., c1990. 5 v.).   PR1105.K4

The Norton anthology of English literature / M.H. Abrams, gen. ed. ... [et al.]. 6th ed. N.Y. : Norton, c1993. 2 v. : maps in color.   **BE619**
Contents: v. 1, The Middle Ages–The Restoration and the eighteenth century; v. 2, The Romantic period–The twentieth century.
A standard anthology, the aim of which is "to make available, for the indispensable courses that introduce students to the excellence and variety of English literature, the major works in prose and verse from *Beowulf* to the present, in accurate and readable texts, edited so as to make them readily accessible to students."—*Pref., 5th ed.* Provides introductions for periods and individual authors, and explanatory notes for the prose and poetry. Each volume has selected bibliographies (by period) and an index of authors and titles. Appendixes: British money; the British baronage; religious sects in England; and poetic forms and literary terminology.
§ Less favorably received: Sandra M. Gilbert and Susan Gubar, *The Norton anthology of literature by women : the tradition in English* (N. Y. : Norton, c1985). Reviews: *Atlantic* 256 (August 1985) : 88; *New York times book review* (April 28, 1985) : 13.   PR1109.N6

Biography

Biographical sketches for major English authors can often be found in *Dictionary of national biography* (AH226) and in other works in the Biography section (AH) for Great Britain. *See also* relevant volumes of *Dictionary of literary biography* (BE200). Also consult section for American literature (above) for biographical sources dealing with American and English authors.

A biographical dictionary of English women writers, 1580–1720 / [ed. by] Maureen Bell, George Parfitt, Simon Shepherd. Boston : G.K. Hall, c1990. 298 p.   **BE620**

Aims to include every woman writing in English in the British Isles whose work was published betweed 1580 and 1700, whether during her lifetime or posthumously; and a selection of 17th-century women whose writing is unpublished or was published after 1700. Writers are listed alphabetically; each entry includes brief biographical facts (patronym, places of birth and residence, social status or occupation, religion, husband's name, and husband's social status or occupation) and a paragraph concerning the subject's writings. Entries do not cite secondary sources, but a selection is included in a general bibliography at the beginning of the volume. Appendixes list anonymous and pseudonymous texts and false ascriptions. The volume ends with an essay discussing women's writing before and after 1640, Quaker writers, writers of petitions and letters, and the role of women in the book trade.   PR113.B46

British women writers : a critical reference guide / ed. by Janet Todd. N.Y. : Continuum, 1989. 762 p.   **BE621**

Publ. in U.K. as: *Dictionary of British women writers* (London : Routledge, c1989).

Provides signed biographical sketches for approximately 450 women writers, Middle Ages to the present, including writers on nonliterary subjects such as cookery, religion, history, and travel. Entries include primary bibliographies and cite secondary references. Index of authors and subjects. There is considerable overlap in coverage and similarity of style between Todd and the Schlueters' *An encyclopedia of British women writers* (BE623); 273 authors are common to both sources.

§ *See also* Todd's earlier *A dictionary of British and American women writers 1660–1800* (BE447), which includes American women and provides an introductory essay on aspects of women's writing for the Restoration and 18th century.   PR111.B75

British writers / ed. under the auspices of the British Council; Ian Scott-Kilvert, gen. ed. N.Y. : Scribner, [1979–84]. 8 v.   **BE622**

Contents: v.1, William Langland to the English Bible; v.2, Thomas Middleton to George Farquhar; v.3, Daniel Defoe to the Gothic novel; v.4, William Wordsworth to Robert Browning; v.5, Elizabeth Gaskell to Francis Thompson; v.6, Thomas Hardy to Wilfred Owen; v.7, Sean O'Casey to poets of World War II; v.8, Index.

A companion set to the same publisher's *American writers* (BE444), "the British collection originates from a series of separate articles entitled *Writers and their work*" (*Introd.*) initiated by the British Council in 1950. Offers signed essays with bibliographies of works by and about the writers. "The articles are intended to appeal to a wide readership, including students in secondary and advanced education, teachers, librarians, scholars, editors, and critics, as well as the general public."

————. ————. *Supplement I, Graham Greene to Tom Stoppard* (c1987. 465 p.). 23 additional authors. Like the parent set, includes a chronology (1904–84) and index.

————. *Supplement II, Kingsley Amis to J.R.R. Tolkien*, George Stade, gen. ed. (c1992. 626 p.). 26 additional authors. Includes a chronology (1835–1991) and a cumulative index for v. 1–8 and Suppl. I–II.   PR85.B688

An encyclopedia of British women writers / ed. by Paul Schlueter and June Schlueter. N.Y. : Garland, 1988. 516 p. (Garland reference library of the humanities, v. 818).   **BE623**

Intended as a companion to *American women writers* (BE443). Provides biographical sketches for nearly 400 British women writers ranging chronologically from Marie de France (born ca.1160) to present day writers like Fay Weldon, P. D. James, and Margaret Drabble. Entries (500–1500 words) cite primary bibliographies, some secondary materials, and other biographical sources. Index of authors and subjects.

§ Less favorably received but providing biographical and bibliographic entries for more than 400 British women is Joanne Shattocks, *The Oxford guide to British women writers* (Oxford : Oxford Univ. Pr., c1993); faulted primarily for the arbitrariness of women included and its author's failure to make explicit her selection criteria. Review: *Times literary supplement* (16 July 1993): 26. *See also* Virginia Blain's more inclusive *The feminist companion to literature in English* (BE607).   PR111.E54

Kunitz, Stanley Jasspon. British authors before 1800 : a biographical dictionary / ed. by Stanley J. Kunitz and Howard Haycraft. N.Y. : Wilson, 1952. 584 p. : ill.   **BE624**

Complete in one volume with 650 biographies and 220 portraits.   PR105.K9

———————— British authors of the 19th century / ed. by Stanley J. Kunitz ; associate ed., Howard Haycraft. Complete in one volume with 1000 biographies and 350 portraits. N.Y. : Wilson, 1936. 677 p. : ill.   **BE625**

Both this and its companion volume covering authors "before 1800" (above) contain sketches which are informal and popular in nature, the length of the articles ranging from 300 to 1,500 words, depending on the importance of the writer. Bibliographies of principal works are included with brief citations for works about the author.

§ *See also*: Samuel Austin Allibone's *Critical dictionary of English literature and British and American authors, living and deceased* (BE581) and David Clayton Browning's *Everyman's dictionary of literary biography : English and American, compiled after John W. Cousin* (Rev. ed. London : Dent ; N.Y. : Dutton, [1960]).   PR451.K8

Reference guide to English literature. 2nd ed. / ed. D. L. Kirkpatrick. Chicago ; London : St. James, 1991. 3 v.   **BE626**

1st ed, 1985, had title: *St. James reference guide to English literature*, ed. James Vinson (8 v.).

Contents: v. 1, Introductions; writers A–G; v. 2, Writers H–Z; v. 3, Works; Title index.

Unlike the 1st ed., this set excludes 20th-century American authors and focuses on English-language writers of Great Britain, Ireland, Canada, Australia, New Zealand, Africa, Asia, and the Caribbean. Includes introductory essays and suggested readings for periods and genres. Entries for 894 individual authors include brief biographical data, a list of publications, a bibliography of book-length critical studies (expanded and updated through 1990), and a succinct critical essay (300–500 words). Also new to this edition are signed critical essays on almost 600 "best-known" English novels, short stories, plays, and poems; cross-references to these essays appear at the end of author entries. Includes: alphabetical and chronological lists of authors; alphabetical and chronological lists of titles; and an index of titles cited in primary bibliographies. Review: *American reference books annual* 23 (1992): 482–83.

§ An earlier series, *Great writers of the English language* (N.Y. : St. Martin's, [1979]. 3 v.), does not include introductory essays, suggested readings, or critiques of individual works.   PR106.S7

Atlases

Goode, Clement Tyson. An atlas of English literature / by Clement Tyson Goode and Edgar Finley Shannon. N.Y. ; London : Century, 1925. 136 p. : ill.   **BE627**

Repr. : Norwood, Pa. : Norwood Eds., 1976.

Provides historical maps by period (499–1900) for England and Wales, each with a list of associated authors and places. Single maps and lists for Scotland, Ireland, London and Italy. Index of places (with associated authors) and authors.   PR109.G6

Hardwick, Michael. A literary atlas & gazetteer of the British Isles / Michael Hardwick ; cartography by Alan G. Hodgkiss. Newton Abbot : David & Charles ; Detroit : Gale, 1973. 216 p. : maps ; 26 cm.   **BE628**

Offers a series of county maps with sites and literary landmarks numbered thereon, each map preceded by a page or more of gazetteer entries keyed to the maps; there is a separate map for London. Alphabetical index of people and an index of people grouped by county.

§ Frank Morley's *Literary Britain : a reader's guide to its writers and landmarks* (N.Y. : Harper & Row, 1980. 510 p.) takes the form of a tour guide with background information and commentary on literary associations of various places.   PR109.H25

Gazetteers

Fisher, Lois H. A literary gazetteer of England. N.Y. : McGraw-Hill, [1980]. 740 p. : ill.   **BE629**

Intends to provide "a comprehensive survey of the 'literary associations' of more than 500 English (and occasionally foreign) authors with more than 1,200 English localities."—*Pref.* Arranged alphabetically by place-name, with entries for towns, villages, rivers, mountains, etc. Includes relevant information on the history, geography, and archaeology of the place; many quotations from literary works are included. The London entry, p. 322–477, consists mainly of entries for individual writers (arranged by birth date) detailing their association with the city. Index of personal names and a few titles.   PR109.F5

Genres

Ballads

Coffin, Tristram Potter. The British traditional ballad in North America. Rev. ed. / with a supplement by Roger deV. Renwick. Austin : Univ. of Texas Pr., c1977. 297 p.   **BE630**

1st ed., 1950.

"Presents the published scholarship on the Child ballad in the New World and centers it around the central theme of story variation."—*Introd.* In four parts: a descriptive essay on ballad variation; the bibliographic guide to story variation; treatment of the evolutions of the ballad into an art from; and a bibliography of titles abbreviated in the guide. Entries in the bibliography are by Child number and include citations to texts, local or variant titles, synopses of the story types, and discussion of variations. Title index of ballads. This edition adds a supplement of scholarship from 1963 to the spring of 1975.   ML3553.C6

Crawford, James Ludovic Lindsay. Bibliotheca Lindesiana : catalogue of a collection of English ballads of the XVIIth and XVIIIth centuries, printed for the most part in black letter. [Aberdeen : Aberdeen Univ. Pr.], 1890. 686 p.   **BE631**

Repr.: N.Y. : Burt Franklin, [1961].

An alphabetical listing of 1,466 ballads by first lines. Entries include title, tune (when applicable), imprint, and descriptive information (e.g., woodcuts, column arrangement). Index of printers, publishers, and booksellers, and a general index (including titles). Appendixes: first lines and titles of ballads printed in Thackeray's list (1685); ballads in the Huth and Euing collections.   Z2014.B2L7

The English and Scottish popular ballads / ed. by Francis James Child. Boston : Houghton, 1883–98. 5 v.   **BE632**

Repr.: N.Y. : Dover, 1965.

The standard scholarly collection of English ballads. Contains the text of 305 distinct ballads, each given in its extant versions. For each ballad a historical and bibliographic introduction is provided, with an

account of parallels in other languages, the diffusion of the story, etc. Vol. 5 includes a glossary, sources of the texts, an index of published airs, ballad airs from manuscript, an index of ballad titles (by nationality), books of ballads, a general index, and an extensive bibliography.

§ Complemented by Bertrand Harris Bronson, *The traditional tunes of the Child ballads : with their texts, according to the extant records of Great Britain and America* (BJ314). *See also* the abridgment (necessarily lacking much of the critical apparatus), *English and Scottish popular ballads*, ed. from the collection of Francis James Child by Helen Child Sargent and George Lyman Kittredge (Boston : Houghton Mifflin, c1904) and *The Oxford book of ballads*, ed. James Kinsley (Oxford ; N.Y. : Oxford Univ. Pr., c1982).   PR1181.C5

Richmond, W. Edson. Ballad scholarship : an annotated bibliography. N.Y. : Garland, 1989. 356 p. (Garland reference library of the humanities, v. 499 ; Garland folklore bibliographies, v. 4).   **BE633**

Confined largely to studies of ballads (rather than collections) published between 1898 and 1986. Lists and annotates books and articles in 13 chapters devoted to areas of scholarship such as Ballads and history, or Ballad prosody and metrics. Items cited are in all languages although they tend to focus on English and American ballads, and to a lesser extent on Anglo-Saxon, Germanic, and Scandinavian ballads. Author and subject indexes.   Z7156.P7R5

Stationers' Company (London). An analytical index to the ballad-entries (1557–1709) in the Registers of the Company of Stationers of London / comp. by Hyder E. Rollins. Chapel Hill, N.C. : Univ. of North Carolina Pr., 1924. 324 p.   **BE634**

Repr. : Hatboro, Pa. : Tradition Pr., 1967.

The aim of Rollins's index is "to include the title of every ballad entered during the years 1557–1709" (*Introd.*), and therefore it errs on the side of inclusiveness in those cases where determination is difficult. The main body of the work lists 3,081 numbered entries by exact title (modern spelling) and provides date of entry (new style), reference to volume and page (cf. *A transcript of the registers of the Company of Stationers of London, 1554–1640*, ed. Edward Arber [AA674]), and the name of the printer. Many entries are annotated and cross-referenced. Also includes an index of first lines and an index of names and subjects.   Z2014.B2L8

Drama

See also Section BH, Theater and Performing Arts, for additional sources for British theater.

Bibliography

Berger, Sidney E. Medieval English drama : an annotated bibliography of recent criticism. N.Y. : Garland, 1990. 500 p. (Garland medieval bibliographies, v. 2 ; Garland reference library of the humanities, v. 956).   **BE635**

"Focuses only on work which is not already cited in Carl J. Stratman's *Bibliography of Medieval Drama* [BE237]."—*Pref.* In two sections: Editions and collections (87 annotated entries, with citations to reviews and cross-references); and Criticism (1,657 annotated entries citing monographs, articles, and dissertations). The majority of entries cite scholarship published since 1969. Appendixes: (1) the Cycle Plays; (2) plays by known authors and anonymous plays; (3) projected volumes from the Records of Early English Drama (Univ. of Toronto).

Kept up-to-date by "Medieval supplement" in *Research opportunities in Renaissance drama* (v. 8 [1965]– . [New Orleans] : Univ. of New Orleans).   Z2014.D7B43

Bergquist, G. William. Three centuries of English and American plays, a checklist : England: 1500–1800; United States: 1714–1830. N.Y. : Hafner, 1963. 281 p.   **BE636**

"Originally compiled to serve as an index to the contents of the Microprint edition of the *Three Centuries of English and American Plays* ...."—*Foreword*. Arranged alphabetically by author and title; lists about 5,350 British and 250 American titles issued either as separates or in collections, giving the earliest extant edition and later significant editions. Anonymous works are listed by title, and cross-references are provided for alternate titles and variant spellings of authors' names.

§ See also: *The London stage, 1660–1800* (BH101), Oscar Wegelin, *Early American plays, 1714–1830* (2nd ed. rev. N.Y. : Literary Collector Pr., 1905), Frank Pierce Hill, *American plays printed 1714–1830* (Stanford, Calif. : Stanford Univ. Pr., 1934), and v. 6 of *A history of English drama, 1660–1900, A short-title alphabetical catalogue of plays produced or printed in England from 1660 to 1900* (BE666).

Z2014.D7B45

British Museum. Department of Manuscripts. Catalogue of additions to the manuscripts : plays submitted to the Lord Chamberlain, 1824–1851. London : Museum, 1964. 359 p.
BE637

A continuation of the chronological listing of plays contained in *Catalogue of the Larpent plays in the Huntington Library* (BE644). The plays submitted 1824–1900 are in the British Museum, and this is the record of some 4,250 plays submitted to the Lord Chamberlain, 1824–1851. Arranged chronologically; author and title indexes.

Z6621.B87.P53

Carpenter, Charles A. Modern British drama. Arlington Heights, Ill. : AHM Publ. Corp., 1979. 120 p.
BE638

A selective bibliography of scholarship and criticism for British drama from the late 19th century through the early 1970s. Sections for: reference works and collections of essays and reviews; anthologies; modern English drama by period; theater in England since the 1860s; modern Scottish and Welsh drama and theater; modern Irish drama by period; Irish theater since the 1890s; and 54 individual dramatists. Although somewhat dated, still valuable for its judicious selection of criticism.

§ *See also*: Carpenter's *Modern drama scholarship and criticism, 1966–1980* (BE220), and Richard Hough Harris, *Modern drama in America and England, 1950–1970* (BE460). For updating *see* the annual bibliography in *Modern drama* (v. 1– . Toronto : Graduate Centre for Study of Drama, 1958–). Less useful is E. H. Mikail's *English drama, 1900–1950 : a guide to information sources* (Detroit : Gale, c1977), which cites only bibliographies for individual author entries.

Z2014.D7C35

Conolly, Leonard W. English drama and theatre, 1800–1900 / L. W. Conolly, J. P. Wearing. Detroit : Gale, c1978. 508 p. (American literature, English literature, and world literatures in English, 12).
BE639

A selective bibliography of books, book chapters, articles, and dissertations current through 1973. Includes chapters for the following: contemporary history and criticism; modern history and criticism; 110 individual authors; bibliographies and reference works; anthologies of plays; theaters; acting and management; critics; stage design, scenic art and costume; and periodicals. Entries for individual authors include (when appropriate): collected works; acted plays and unacted plays; bibliographies; biography; critical studies; and journals and newsletters. General index of personal names, selected titles, and broad subject headings (e.g., juvenile drama).

§ For checklists of 19th-century English drama *see* James Ellis, *English drama of the nineteenth century* (BE640). For updating, *see Nineteenth century theatre* (v. 15 [1987]– . Amherst, Mass. : J. Donohue).

Z2014.D7C72

Ellis, James. English drama of the nineteenth century : an index and finding guide / comp. and ed. by James Ellis, assisted by Joseph Donohue, with Louise Allen Zak, editorial associate. New Canaan, Conn. : Readex Books, 1985. 345 p.
BE640

Intended primarily "as an index and finding guide to the English plays issued through 1981 in the Readex Microprint Collection *English*

and American Drama of the Nineteenth Century" (*Pref.*), but also useful as a bibliography of about 9,000 English plays (including children's plays, opera libretti, translations of continental dramas, etc.). Various useful appendixes. The American portion of the microform collection is indexed by Donald L. Hixon and Don A. Hennessee's *Nineteenth-century American drama* (BE464). Z2014.D7E42

English drama, excluding Shakespeare : select bibliographical guides / ed. by Stanley Wells. London ; N.Y. : Oxford Univ. Pr., 1975. 303 p.
BE641

Bibliographic essays, current through the early 1970s. Chapters devoted to periods, schools, and major dramatists. Bibliographies at the end of the chapters provide full information on works cited. Index of dramatists and anonymous plays.

§ See *Year's work in English studies* (BE589) for more current scholarship.
Z2014.D7E44

Fordyce, Rachel. Caroline drama : a bibliographic history of criticism. 2nd ed. N.Y. : G.K. Hall : Maxwell Macmillan International, c1992. 332 p.
BE642

1st ed., 1978.

An annotated bibliography of books, articles, dissertations, notes, and prefatory matter that "surveys the major critical and bibliographic issues related to Caroline drama as they have emerged over the last one hundred years."—*Introd.* Coverage includes non-English publications, with sections for the following: general reference sources and bibliographies; textual considerations; Caroline drama (over 1,200 entries); and stage history. Indexes: secondary authors; plays and early sources; and a detailed subject index. The lack of a separate index for dramatists hinders this volume's ease of use. Review: *Choice* 30:7 (March 1993): 1110.
Z2014.D7.F67

Greg, Walter Wilson. A bibliography of the English printed drama to the Restoration. London : pr. for the Bibliographical Society at the Univ. Pr., Oxford, 1939–59. 4 v. (1752 p.). : fronts., facsims. (Illustrated monographs, no. 24).
BE643

Contents: v. 1, Stationers' records. Plays to 1616: no. 1–349; v. 2, Plays, 1617–1689: no. 350–836. Latin plays. Lost plays; v. 3, Collections. Appendix. Reference lists; v. 4, Introduction. Additions. Corrections. Index of titles.

A descriptive bibliography of English printed drama from ca.1512 to the Restoration that "aims at including all editions down to 1700 of all dramatic compositions which were either written before the end of 1642 (the year of the closing of the theatres on 2 September) or printed before the beginning of 1660 (the year of the Restoration on 8 May)."—*Provisional memoranda*. Includes excerpts of the Stationers' Records and a chronological listing of dramatic pieces. Entries are assigned unique numbers (now known as "Greg numbers") and are given full analytical and textual description. A limited number of holdings are given. Vol. 2 also provides description for Latin plays and lost plays. Vol. 3 describes collections, and reprints advertisements, prefaces, actor lists, publication lists, and a wealth of other related material. Includes facsimiles.
Z2014.D7G78

Henry E. Huntington Library and Art Gallery. Catalogue of the Larpent plays in the Huntington Library / comp. by Dougald MacMillan. San Marino, Calif., 1939. 422 p. (Huntington Library lists, no. 4).
BE644

"The licensing act of 1737 required that copies of all plays and other entertainments designed to be performed on the stage in Great Britain be submitted ... for license." John Larpent was appointed Examiner on Nov. 20, 1778, and "died in office on Jan. 18, 1824. The official copies of plays submitted to the Examiner between 1737 and Jan. 1824, in Larpent's possession at the time of his death were bought about 1832 by John Payne Collier and Thomas Amyot."—*Pref. note.* These copies are now in the Huntington Library.

The list is chronological with author and title indexes.

For continuation *see* British Museum. Dept. of Manuscripts, *Catalogue of additions to the manuscripts* (BE637).
Z2014.D7H525

King, Kimball. Twenty modern British playwrights : a bibliography, 1956 to 1976. N.Y. : Garland, 1977. 289 p. (Garland reference library of the humanities, v. 96).   **BE645**

Provides primary and secondary bibliographies for British playwrights active 1956–76. Author entries begin with a biographical and critical précis. Primary bibliographies include sections for stage work, work in other media and genres (radio plays, film adaptations, nonfiction, etc.), and interviews (summarized). Secondary sources include annotated entries for criticism, dissertations, and also cite production reviews. Index of scholars and critics.   Z2014.D7K47

Lidman, Mark J. Studies in Jacobean drama, 1973–1984 : an annotated bibliography. N.Y. : Garland, 1986. 278 p. (Garland reference library of the humanities, v. 597).   **BE646**

Intended to update Terence P. Logan and Denzell S. Smith's four-volume series, "A survey and bibliography of recent studies in English Renaissance drama" (BE648, BE649, BE650, BE651). A general section is followed by sections for individual playwrights (Chapman, Dekker, Heywood, Tourneur, Marston, Middleton, Webster, Massinger, Ford, Brome, and Shirley) each listing editions, followed by critical studies listed alphabetically by author. Indexed by author only.

§ A more useful bibliography for comedy is *An annotated critical bibliography of Jacobean and Caroline comedy (excluding Shakespeare)* by Peter Corbin and Douglas Sedge (N.Y. ; London : Harvester, 1988. 235 p.). Playwrights are treated individually in chapters citing editions, general criticism, and criticism of individual plays. Author index.   Z2014.D7L5

Link, Frederick M. English drama, 1660–1800 : a guide to information sources. Detroit : Gale, c1976. 374 p. (American literature, English literature, and world literatures in English, v. 9).   **BE647**

A survey of research that attempts "to list every substantial book and article dealing with English drama 1660–1800 published through 1973 and most significant material published in 1974."—*Pref.* In two parts, the first dealing with general reference sources, the second covering 155 individual authors, providing minimal biographical information for minor authors, a discussion of editions, biographies, and secondary scholarship. Index of personal names and index of titles. Excludes book reviews, production reviews, theses and dissertations, foreign-language editions, manuscript materials, clearly superseded books and articles, survey treatments of major figures, and student guides. Although some contemporary and 19th-century scholarship is cited, the focus is on that after 1880. Should be supplemented by Carl Joseph Stratman et al., *Restoration and eighteenth century theatre research* (BH47), and updated by *The year's work in English studies* (BE589). Review: *Notes and queries* n.s., 25:1 (Feb. 1978): 82.

§ Designed more for undergraduates, with an introductory essay and bibliography, and annotations for fewer dramatists is Thomas J. Taylor's *Restoration drama : an annotated bibliography* (Pasadena, Calif. : Salem Pr., c1989).   Z2014.D7L55

Logan, Terence P. The predecessors of Shakespeare : a survey and bibliography of recent studies in English Renaissance drama / Terence P. Logan and Denzell S. Smith. Lincoln : Univ. of Nebraska Pr., [1973]. 348 p.   **BE648**

This first volume in Logan and Smith's series, "Recent studies in English Renaissance drama," deals with plays first performed between 1580 and 1593, and provides bibliographic surveys of scholarship for major dramatists (Marlowe, Greene, Kyd, Nashe, Lyly, Peele, and Lodge), followed by essays on anonymous plays and other dramatists. Essays for major dramatists include discussion of editions, biographies, general studies, studies of individual plays, discussion of non-dramatic works (when appropriate), a statement as to the overall state of criticism, and a discussion of the author's canon (further divided into chronology, uncertain ascriptions, apocrypha, etc.). The essays conclude with a classified, enumerative bibliography of suggested readings. Entries for anonymous plays follow the chronological ordering of *Annals of English drama* (BE660) and offer assessment of editions, texts, attributions of authorship, stage history, and other studies. For minor named dramatists of the period an annotated bibliography of

criticism is provided. Indexes: persons, plays. Coverage for this series is generally 1923–68 (consult individual volumes for varying end dates).

§ *See also* Mark J. Lidman's *Studies in Jacobean drama, 1973–1984* (BE646) for an annotated bibliography of criticism 1973–84.
                Z2014.D7L83

———————— The popular school : a survey and bibliography of recent studies in English Renaissance drama / ed. by Terence P. Logan and Denzell S. Smith. Lincoln : Univ. of Nebraska Pr., [1975]. 299 p.   **BE649**

Second in a series on English Renaissance drama, follows the format of the other volumes (major dramatists, anonymous plays, other dramatists), and "includes dramatists who wrote primarily for the open-air public theaters, and anonymous plays first performed in such theaters" (*Pref.*), generally between 1593 and 1616. Bibliographic essays for: Dekker, Middleton, Webster, Heywood, Munday, and Drayton.   Z2014.D7L82

———————— The new intellectuals : a survey and bibliography of recent studies in English Renaissance drama / ed. by Terence P. Logan and Denzell S. Smith. Lincoln : Univ. of Nebraska Pr., c1977. 370 p.   **BE650**

The third volume of a series on English Renaissance drama; together with *The popular school* (BE649) covers the drama 1593–1616. *The new intellectuals* "treats dramatists who either wrote principally for the private theaters or were significantly influenced by them, and the anonymous plays first performed in them."—*Pref.* Bibliographic essays for: Jonson, Chapman, Marston, Tourneur, and Daniel.
                Z2014.D7N29

———————— The later Jacobean and Caroline dramatists : a survey and bibliography of recent studies in English Renaissance drama / ed. by Terence P. Logan and Denzell S. Smith. Lincoln : Univ. of Nebraska Pr., c1978. 279 p.   **BE651**

Includes "plays and playwrights of both popular and private theaters for the period from 1616 to 1642."—*Pref.* There are full bibliographic essays for Beaumont and Fletcher, Massinger, Ford, Shirley, Brome, and Davenant.   Z2014.D7L816

Penninger, Frieda Elaine. English drama to 1660 excluding Shakespeare : a guide to information sources. Detroit : Gale, 1976. 370 p. (American literature, English literature, and world literatures in English, v. 5).   **BE652**

Intended primarily for "undergraduate and graduate students who seek direction towards editions and discussions which will enable them to initiate and pursue a study of a given area of the drama."—*Foreword.* A section of general works (bibliographies, collections and editions, general histories and studies, histories and studies of specific periods, theater and stagecraft, etc.) is followed by sections on individual dramatists. Index of authors, editors, compilers, and anonymous titles.   Z2014.D7P46

Salomon, Brownell. Critical analyses in English renaissance drama : a bibliographic guide. Rev. 3rd ed. N.Y. : Garland, 1991. 262 p. (Garland reference library of the humanities, vol. 1370).   **BE653**

1st ed., 1979.

A selective bibliographic guide, with succinct annotations. Attempts to include every dramatist and dramatic work, 1580–1642, except Shakespeare. Sections for critical theory, concordances, word indexes, and indvdual dramatists. Excludes general studies. Detailed subject index.   Z2014.D7S24

Stratman, Carl Joseph. Bibliography of English printed tragedy, 1565–1900. Carbondale : Southern Illinois Univ. Pr., [1966]. 843 p.   **BE654**

"Restricted to English printed tragedies written in England, Scotland, or Ireland, from the beginnings of formal tragedy in England, to the end of the Nineteenth Century, together with the various adaptations of each work."—*Introd.* (Adaptations of Shakespeare's tragedies are included, but not editions of his works.) Lists 1,483 tragedies in

6,852 entries. Includes a section of anthologies; locates copies. References to standard bibliographies (*STC*, Greg, *CBEL*, etc.) are given, as are notes on production where relevant. There is a chronological table, a title index, and an appendix of manuscript locations.   Z2014.D7S83

Thompson, Lawrence Sidney. Nineteenth and twentieth century drama : a selective bibliography of English language works, numbers 1–3029. Boston : G.K. Hall, c1975. 456 p.   **BE655**

A checklist of 3,209 items of English-language dramatic literature (including monologues, children's plays, puppet plays, vaudeville pieces, temperance plays, etc.) microfilmed by the General Microfilm Co., Cambridge, Mass. Includes some variant editions and English translations of foreign plays. Indexes: titles; subjects; editors; authors and joint authors; translators; pseudonyms; illustrators; and composers.   Z2014.D7T5

White, D. Jerry. Early English drama, Everyman to 1580 : a reference guide. Boston : G.K. Hall, 1986. 289 p.   **BE656**

An annotated bibliography of resources for the study of British drama and dramatists of the period 1495–1580. Sections for bibliographies, collections, and general studies are followed by sections for individual playwrights and plays. Within an author's section entries are subdivided for bibliographies, studies and editions, and specific plays. Covers studies published 1691–1982, together with many unpublished dissertations. Descriptive annotations for most items. Index for specific authors, titles, and subjects.   Z2014.D7W48

Woodward, Gertrude Loop. A check list of English plays, 1641–1700 / by Gertrude Loop Woodward and James Gilmer McManaway. Chicago : Newberry Libr., 1945. 155 p.   **BE657**

Intends " to record the plays and masques, with the variant editions and issues, printed in the English language in the British Isles or in other countries during the years 1641 to 1700, inclusive, and to give the location of copies in [15] American libraries."—*Pref.*

———. ———. *Supplement*, comp. by Fredson Bowers (Charlottesville : Univ. of Virginia, 1949. 22 p.). Locates copies.   Z2014.D7W6

Handbooks

Berger, Thomas L. An index of characters in English printed drama to the Restoration / by Thomas L. Berger and William C. Bradford, Jr. Englewood, Colo. : Microcard Editions Books, 1975. 222 p.   **BE658**

An index to all the characters in the plays listed in Walter W. Greg's *Bibliography of English printed drama to the Restoration* (BE643). Indexing is by name, character types, nationalities, occupations, religious proclivities, psychological states. Reference is to Greg number only; a "Finding list" provides the title, author, dates, and *STC* reference.   PR1265.3.B4

The Cambridge companion to English Renaissance drama / ed. by A. R. Braunmuller and Michael Hattaway. Cambridge [Eng.] ; N.Y. : Cambridge Univ. Pr., 1990. 456 p. : ill., map.   **BE659**

"The predominant organizing principle of this Companion is generic … the essays seek not to be definitive but perhaps to be paradigmatic: to offer the reader examples of recent ways of experiencing texts and performances, to provoke further reading, and above all, to add to the enjoyment of Renaissance dramatic texts in the study and the playhouse."—*Pref.* Ten essays discuss: Playhouses and players; The arts of the dramatist; Drama and society; Private and occasional drama; Political drama; Romance and the heroic play; Pastiche, burlesque, tragicomedy; Comedy; Tragedy; and Caroline drama, with brief bibliographies at the end of each essay. A separate bibliography (p. 381–418) lists reference works, critical studies, biographical sources, and biographies and bibliographies of individual authors. The chronological table lists many (but not all) the plays of the period 1497–1642. Indexed by dramatist, title, and topic (e.g., city comedy); but the bibliographies are not indexed.   PR651.C36

Chronologies

Harbage, Alfred. Annals of English drama, 975–1700 : an analytical record of all plays, extant or lost, chronologically arranged and indexed by authors, titles, dramatic companies & c. / by Alfred Harbage ; rev. by S. Schoenbaum. 3rd ed. / rev. by Sylvia Stoler Wagonheim. London : Rutledge, 1989. 375 p.   **BE660**

1st ed., 1940; 2nd ed., 1964.

A chronology in tabular form of plays, masques, and other forms of dramatic entertainment written in England or by Englishmen abroad, 10th century to 1700. Plays are listed by probable date of first performance, by century to 1495, and by year thereafter. Entries include author, title, "limits" (probable dates), type of production, auspices (including acting company and date), earliest texts, latest texts. Supplementary lists for dramatic pieces of uncertain date and identity. Indexes for playwrights, plays, foreign playwrights, foreign plays translated or adapted, dramatic companies, theaters, and extant play manuscripts (with locations). New to this edition is a selective list of medieval dramatic texts. A detailed review in *Shakespeare quarterly* 42:2 (Summer 1991): 225–230 points out serious inconsistencies, omissions, and errors in this edition and recommends that libraries retain the 2nd ed. and its supplements.   Z2014.D7.H25

Kawachi, Yoshiko. Calendar of English Renaissance drama, 1558–1642. N.Y. : Garland, 1986. 351 p. (Garland reference library of the humanities, v. 661).   **BE661**

Tables of entries arranged by date of eariest performance (when known) include a division code (indicating if a play was performed), company name, place, title, type, author, earliest texts, and a code for the source from which the information was obtained. Patterned after *Annals of English drama* (BE660). Indexes: plays, playwrights, companies.   PN2589.K36

Lancashire, Ian. Dramatic texts and records of Britain : a chronological topography to 1558. Toronto ; Buffalo : Univ. of Toronto Pr., c1984. lxxi, 633 p., [28] p. of plates : ill. (Studies in early English drama, 1).   **BE662**

Spine title: Dramatic texts and records of Britain to 1558.

Chronological list of plays, pageants, and dramatic fragments, published and unpublished, with reference to bibliographical information in standard reference works and to criticism. Includes a listing of doubtful texts and records. Appendixes include indexes of playwrights, of patrons and players, etc., as well as a general index.

§ For primary source material, consult *Records of early English drama* (*REED*), Alexandra F. Johnson, gen. ed. (Toronto : Univ. of Toronto Pr., 1979–).   PN2587.L36

Histories

Bentley, Gerald Eades. The Jacobean and Caroline stage. Oxford : Clarendon Pr., 1941–68. 7 v.   **BE663**

Contents: v. 1–2, Dramatic companies and players; v. 3–5, Plays and playwrights; v. 6, Theatres; v. 7, Appendixes to v. 6, General index.

Intended to follow Edmund K. Chambers' *Elizabethan stage* (BE664), Bently is the standard source for English drama 1616–42. Vol. 1 provides a history of the acting companies (bringing together much primary material such as actor lists, production dates, provincial notices, etc.), while v. 2 is a biographical dictionary of actors, giving a brief career summary for each and quoting "every scrap of biographical evidence … in chronological order."—*Pref., v. 1*. Vols. 3–5 are arranged by playwright (followed in v. 5 by anonymous plays), and typically provide a biographical summary, discussion of editions of the plays, and a discussion of selective scholarship. Vol. 6 provides a history of both public and private theaters, and for theaters at court. Vol. 7 gives appendixes for the foregoing (including annals of theatrical affairs) and a detailed index for v. 1–6. An invaluable source that quotes from or reprints records of the period. For full bibliographic description of the plays *see* Walter W. Greg's *Bibliography of English printed drama to the Restoration* (BE643). PN2592.B4

Chambers, Edmund Kerchever. The mediaeval stage. Oxford : Clarendon Pr., 1903. 2 v. **BE664**
Reissued 1967.
Contents: v. 1, Minstrelsy. Folk drama; v. 2, Religious drama. The interlude. Appendices. Subject index.
Both studies by Chambers, although still valuable, should be supplemented by more recent histories, e.g., the early volumes of *The Revels history of drama in English* (BE667); v. 4 of *The Oxford history of English literature* (BE617); and Glynne William Gladstone Wickham, *Early English stages, 1300–1600* (2nd ed. London : Routledge and Kegan Paul, 1980–). PN2152.C4

——— The Elizabethan stage. Oxford : Clarendon Pr., 1923. 4 v. : ill. **BE665**
Repr. with corrections, 1951.
Partial contents: v. 1, The court. The control of the stage; v. 2, The companies. The play-houses; v. 3, Plays and playwrights; v. 4, Anonymous works. Appendixes. Indexes (by plays, persons, places, subjects).
§ *An index, compiled by Beatrice White, to "The Elizabethan stage" and "William Shakespeare : a study of facts and problems," by Sir Edmund Chambers* (Oxford : Clarendon Pr., 1934. 161 p.). PN2589.C4

Nicoll, Allardyce. A history of English drama, 1660–1900. Cambridge : Univ. Pr., 1952–59. 6 v. **BE666**
Contents: v. 1, Restoration drama, 1660–1700 (4th ed.); v. 2, Early 18th century drama [1700–1750] (3rd ed.); v. 3, Late 18th century drama, 1750–1800 (2nd ed.); v. 4, Early 19th century drama, 1800–1850 [2nd ed.]; v. 5, Late 19th century drama, 1850–1900 [2nd ed.]; v. 6, A short-title alphabetical catalogue of plays produced or printed in England from 1660–1900.
Each historical volume is on the same general plan, giving: (1) history, and (2) appendixes, containing such useful reference material as lists of theaters and handlists of plays produced during the period covered.
Vol. 6 not only serves as a title index to plays recorded in the earlier volumes, but provides additional information on some plays and lists others not previously mentioned; includes numerous cross-references from alternate titles.
§ Continued chronologically by Nicoll's *English drama, 1900–1930 : the beginnings of the modern period* (Cambridge : Univ. Pr., 1973. 1083 p.).
"Both is and is not a continuation of the more extended 'history' concerned with the years 1660–1900. It is a separate volume: yet it could not have come into being if the theatrical activities of the preceding ages had not already been examined."—*Pref.* Includes a "Handlist of plays" for the period, p. 452–1053. Indexed.
See also Nicoll's one-volume survey, *British drama* (6th ed., rev. by J. C. Trewin. N.Y. : Barnes & Noble, c1978). PR625.N52

The Revels history of drama in English / gen. editors, Clifford Leech and T. W. Craik. London : Methuen ; N.Y. : Barnes and Noble Import Div., 1976–1983. 8 v. : ill. **BE667**
Contents: v. 1, Medieval drama, by A. C. Cawley [et al.]; v. 2, 1500–1576, by N. Sanders [et al.]; v. 3, 1576–1613, by J. L. Barroll [et al.]; v. 4, 1613–1660, by P. Edwards [et al.]; v. 5, 1660–1750, by J. Loftis [et al.]; v. 6, 1750–1880, by M. R. Booth [et al.]; v. 7, 1880 to the present day, by H. Hunt [et al.]; v. 8, American drama, by T. Bogard [et al.].
Gives much attention to social background, the theaters, actors and repertory, etc., as well as to the dramatic literature. Each volume has its own bibliography and index. PR625.R44

Fiction

Victorian fiction : a second guide to research / ed. by George H. Ford. N.Y. : Modern Language Assoc. of America, 1978. 401 p. **BE668**
Intended as a companion to Lionel Stevenson's *Victorian fiction* (BE686) which covers publications through 1962. This volume aims "to supply complete coverage from 1963 through 1974" (*Pref.*) with occasional mention of works published 1975 or later, plus chapters on Robert Louis Stevenson and Samuel Butler reviewing the scholarly writing on those two figures from the beginning through 1974. Some pre-1962 items are also mentioned. Chapters are by scholar specialists, and there has been an effort "to provide some fresh emphasis" regarding "the availability of manuscripts and the record of film versions of Victorian novels."—*Pref.* Neglected areas of research are also noted. Fully indexed.
§ More suitable for undergraduate research is Laurence W. Mazzeno, *The Victorian novel : an annotated bibliography* (Pasadena, Calif. : Salem Pr., c1989). PR871.V5

Bibliography

Beasley, Jerry C. A check list of prose fiction published in England, 1740–1749. Charlottesville : publ. for the Bibliographical Society of the Univ. of Virginia by the Univ. Pr. of Virginia, [1972]. 213p. **BE669**
Serves as a continuation of William Harlin McBurney, *A check list of English prose fiction, 1700–1739* (BE678) and attempts to provide as complete a record as possible (338 entries) of English-language novels published in England for the decade 1740–49, including reprinted native works and foreign fiction in translation. Generally omitted are chapbooks, dialogues, jest books, and character sketches. Entries typically provide a short title, bookseller, number of pages or volumes, price (when known), the location of one extant copy, and a brief descriptive annotation. Appendixes: unverified editions of authentic works; unauthenticated titles. Bibliographies and index.
§ For fiction in magazines *see* Robert Donald Mayo, *The English novel in the magazines, 1740-1815 : with a catalogue of 1375 magazine novels and novelettes* (Evanston: Northwestern Univ. Pr., c1962). Z2014.F4B37

——— English fiction, 1660–1800 : a guide to information sources. Detroit : Gale, [1978]. 313 p. (American literature, English literature, and world literatures in English, 14). **BE670**
A selective, annotated bibliography that serves as a guide to Restoration and 18th-century literature. Pt. 1 is a general bibliography that includes sections for background sources, general histories and surveys of the novel, studies in the form and technique of the novel as genre, history and criticism of fiction 1660–1800, checklists and bibliographies, special resources (serials, reprint series, etc.), and selected background readings. Pt. 2 provides selective and primary and secondary bibliographies for 29 authors; included are principal works, collected editions, collections of letters, bibliographies, biographies, and critical studies. Generally well selected, with emphasis on 20th-century criticism. Detailed index. Review: *The yearbook of English studies*, 11 (1981): 268–270.
§ Also of interest is H. George Hahn and Carl Behm III, *The eighteenth century British novel and its background : an annotated bibliography and guide to topics* (Metuchen, N.J. : Scarecrow, c1985). Z2014.F5B42

Bell, Inglis Freeman. The English novel, 1578–1956 : a checklist of twentieth-century criticisms / Inglis Freeman Bell and Donald Baird. [New ed.]. London : Bingley, 1974. 168 p. **BE671**
1st ed., 1958, publ. Denver : A. Swallow. Repr.: Hamden, Conn. : Shoe String Pr., 1974.

A highly selective bibliography of books and articles of 20th-century explication of English novels from Lyly through the mid-20th century. Arranged alphabetically by novelist, then by title. Includes a list of books and periodicals cited.

§ Continued by: *English novel explication : criticisms to 1972*, comp. by Helen H. Palmer and Anne Jane Dyson (BE675).

Z2014.F4B4

Cassis, A. F. The twentieth-century English novel : an annotated bibliography of general criticism. N.Y. : Garland, 1977. 413 p. **BE672**

An annotated bibliography of more than 2,800 entries of general criticism (1900–72) on the English novel of the 20th century. Included are studies of more than one novelist, of narrative technique, and of the novel as genre. Arranged alphabetically by author in the following sections: (1) bibliographies and checklists; (2) criticism (divided into books and articles); and (3) dissertations and theses. Excluded are studies of popular fiction, science fiction, the short story, and Commonwealth literature apart from England. Includes an index of novelists and an index of selected topics and themes. Z2014.F5C35

Dyson, A. E. The English novel. [London ; N.Y.] : Oxford Univ. Pr., 1974. 372 p. **BE673**

Bibliographic essays by specialists for the English novelists Bunyan, Defoe, Swift, Richardson, Fielding, Sterne, Smollett, Scott, Austen, Thackeray, Dickens, Trollope, the Brontes, Eliot, Hardy, James, Conrad, Forster, Lawrence, and Joyce. Provides a survey of editions, biographies, correspondence, bibliographies, and critical studies through the early 1970s. Although the essays vary in quality, this is still a useful guide to the scholarship. Review: *Modern fiction studies* 20:4 (Winter 1974–75): 607–608.

§ For recent surveys of research, see: *The year's work in English studies* (BE589). Z2014.F5D94

The English novel : twentieth century criticism. Chicago : Swallow Pr., [1976–82]. 2 v. **BE674**

Contents: v. 1, Defoe through Hardy, ed. by Richard J. Dunn; v. 2, Twentieth century novelists, ed. by Paul Schlueter and June Schlueter.

Vol. 1 provides a selective bibliography of books, portions of books, and articles (current through 1974) for works by 45 individual novelists and for a section of general studies. Vol. 2 provides entries for 80 20th-century authors and has a section for books cited and a general bibliography (current through 1975). Author entries in v. 2 list interviews, secondary bibliographies, special issues, general studies, and studies of separate novels. Z2014.F4E53

English novel explication : criticisms to 1972 / comp. by Helen H. Palmer and Anne Jane Dyson. [Hamden, Conn.] : Shoe String Pr., 1973. 329 p. **BE675**

A bibliography of criticism in books and periodicals dealing wholly or largely with individual novels. Updates Inglis Freeman Bell and Donald Baird, *The English novel, 1578–1956* (BE671), with criticism from 1958 to 1972, but is more comprehensive in its indexing and not restricted to English-language publications. Includes a list of books and journals indexed. Index includes literary authors and titles but not scholars.

————. *Supplement I*, comp. by Peter L. Abernathy, Christian J. W. Kloesel, and Jeffrey R. Smitten (1976. 305 p.) Updates criticism 1972–74 (with some earlier and later criticisms), incorporating a broader definition of "explication" and thereby omitting only "studies which are ... biography, or bibliography."—*Pref.* "Novel" is broadened to include works such as *Le Morte Darthur*. Includes writers born in England, Scotland, Ireland, and Wales, as well as Commonwealth authors who lived in Great Britain during a significant portion of their creative lives. Excluded are book reviews, dissertations, and reprints of books and articles. Includes anonymous novels, a list of books indexed, and an index of literary authors and titles.

————. *Supplement II*, comp. by Christian J. W. Kloesel and Jeffrey R. Smitten (1980. 326 p.). Updates the criticism from 1975 through 1979 (with some earlier and later items). Due to the publication deadline for this series, coverage is not comprehensive for the specified interim and a later supplement might have to be consulted for an item published 1975–1979.

————. *Supplement III*, comp. by Christian J. W. Kloesel (1986. 506 p.). Updates the criticism from 1980 through 1985.

————. *Supplement IV*, comp. by Christian J. W. Kloesel. Extends coverage from 1986 through the first half of 1989. A fifth supplement is scheduled for 1994 publication. Z2014.F5P26

Harner, James L. English Renaissance prose fiction, 1500–1660 : an annotated bibliography of criticism. Boston : G.K. Hall, c1978. 556 p. **BE676**

An international bibliography of "editions and studies (published between 1800 and 1976) of prose fiction in English—both original works and translations—written or printed in England from 1500 to 1660. Works and translations included are limited to those which may be classified as novelle, romances, histories, anatomies, or jest books (or some combination of these)."—*Introd.* Descriptive annotations are arranged in four main sections: bibliographies; anthologies; general studies; and authors, translators, titles (the latter subdivided for bibliographies, editions, and studies). Indexed by persons, anonymous works, and subjects.

Two supplements list studies published 1976–83 (Boston : G.K. Hall, 1985. 228 p.) and 1984–90 (N.Y. : G.K. Hall : Maxwell Macmillan Internat., c1992. 185 p.). Z2014.F4H37

Leclaire, Lucien. A general analytical bibliography of the regional novelists of the British Isles, 1800–1950. Clermont-Ferrand : Impr. G. de Bussac, [1954]. 399 p. : 2 fold. maps. **BE677**

Arranged chronologically in three major divisions: 1800–1830; 1830–1870; and after 1870 (the latter being further subdivided, e.g., D.H. Lawrence within "Interpretive regionalism, 1920–1939"). Entries for authors include a biographical note, a selective bibliography of biographies, bibliographies, criticism, and a listing of individual works and collected works in various editions (not complete). Indexes for authors, authors by region, and place-names. Includes a map of the British Isles that locates authors and a map that references settings for novels. Z2014.F4L4

McBurney, William Harlin. A check list of English prose fiction, 1700–1739. Cambridge : Harvard Univ. Pr., 1960. 154 p. **BE678**

A chronological checklist of 337 titles (with an additional 54 dubious or unauthenticated titles) "by native authors or translators ... first published in England between 1700 and 1739."—*Introd.* Entries include complete title, printer and bookseller, number of pages, format, price (when available), later editions to 1739, and location of at least one extant copy. Generally excluded are short character sketches, jest books, topical pamphlets, dialogues, chapbooks, and fiction in periodicals. Index of authors, translators, printers, and titles.

§ See also: *Early english fiction : pre–1750.* (Woodbridge, Conn. : Research Publications Inc., 1982), which is the reel guide to titles available in the microfilm collection by the same title.

Z2014.F4M3

Mish, Charles Carroll. English prose fiction, 1600–1700 : a chronological checklist. Charlottesville, Va. : Bibliographical Society of the Univ. of Virginia, 1967. 110 p. **BE679**

A chronological checklist of 17th century fiction with references to the *Short title catalogue* of Wing (AA683) and of Pollard and Redgrave (AA671).

§ Largely supersedes Arundell J. K. Esdaile, *A list of English tales and prose romances printed before 1740* (London : Blades, East & Blades, c1912). *See also* Sterg O'Dell, *A chronological list of prose fiction in English printed in England and other countries, 1475–1640* (BE680) and the bibliography of published English fiction in Paul Salzman, *English prose fiction, 1558–1700 : a critical history* (BE692). Z2014.F4M58

O'Dell, Sterg. A chronological list of prose fiction in English printed in England and other countries, 1475–1640. Cambridge, Mass. : Technology Pr. of M.I.T., 1954. 147 p. **BE680**

Repr.: Norwood, Pa. : Norwood Editions, 1977.

Locates copies in 69 libraries and includes references to Pollard and Redgrave (AA671) and to the Stationers' Registers (*A transcript of the registers of the Company of Stationers of London, 1554–1640*, ed. by Edward Arber [AA674]). Index of authors and anonymous titles. *See also* Charles Carroll Mish, *English prose fiction 1600–1700* (BE679) and the bibliography of published English fiction in Paul Salzman, *English prose fiction 1558-1700* (BE692).   Z2014.F5O33

Raven, James. British fiction, 1750–1770 : a chronological check-list of prose fiction printed in Britain and Ireland. Newark : Univ. of Delaware Pr. ; London : Associated Univ. Pr., c1987. 349 p. : ill.   **BE681**

Continues William Harlin McBurney, *Check list of English prose fiction, 1700–1739* (BE678) and Jerry C. Beasley, *Check list of prose fiction published in England, 1740–1749* (BE669).

Attempts to identify all works of fiction published in the 1750s and 1760s, whether extant or perished, including translations and reprints of early novels. Provides, where possible, number of copies printed, price, printer, bookseller, references to reviews, secondary references, and notes on authorship, translators, and other editions. Entries are arranged chronologically by year and then alphabetically in three sections: anonymous titles, authors, and miscellaneous. Indexed by author, translator, and title.

§ Plagued by errors and omissions are the following checklists: Andrew Block, *The English novel, 1740–1850 : a catalogue including prose romances, short stories, and translations of foreign fiction* (2nd ed. London : Dawsons of Pall Mall, 1961); and Leonard Orr, *A catalogue checklist of English prose fiction, 1750–1800* (Troy, N.Y. : Whitston, 1979).   Z2014.F4R34

Rice, Thomas Jackson. English fiction, 1900–1950 : a guide to information sources. Detroit : Gale, c1979–83. 2 v. (Gale information guide library. American literature, English literature, and world literatures in English information guide series, v. 20–21).   **BE682**

Contents: v. 1, General bibliography and individual authors: Aldington to Huxley; v. 2, Individual authors: Joyce to Woolf.

Vol. 1 lists general sources (bibliographies, histories, genre studies, etc.), and primary and secondary bibliographies for 15 authors, with criticism current through Jan. 1977, and indexes for authors/titles/subjects. Vol. 2 offers bibliographies for 20 additional wroters (current through Dec. 1980); author index only. Entries have annotations and refer almost exclusively to English-language publications. For a qualified recommendation see *Choice* 21:1 (Sep. 1983): 66.

§ Although dated, Paul L. Wiley's *The British novel : Conrad to the present* (Northbrook, Ill. : AHM Publ. Corp., c[1973]), is still useful.   Z2014.F4R5

Sadleir, Michael. XIX century fiction : a bibliographical record based on his own collection. London : Constable ; Berkeley : Univ. of Calif. Press., [1951]. 2 v. : plates.   **BE683**

Repr.: N.Y. : Cooper Square, 1969.

A descriptive bibliography of Sadleir's private collection, with some additions, now held by the Univ. of California, Los Angeles. Includes authors writing during the 19th century, excluding those novelists who published fiction prior to 1800. Valuable for its full description of many rare items.

§ *See also* Robert Lee Wolff, *Nineteenth-century fiction : a bibliographical catalogue based on the collection formed by Robert Lee Wolff* (BE687).   Z2014.F4S16

Sargent, Lyman Tower. British and American utopian literature, 1516–1985 : an annotated, chronological bibliography. N.Y. : Garland, c1988. 559 p. (Garland reference library of the humanities, vol. 831).   **BE684**

1st ed., 1979.

Provides brief descriptive annotations for works judged to be literary utopias, eutopias, dystopias, or utopian satires, and "described [as such] in considerable detail" (*Introd.*) by their authors. Arrangement is chronological by year of publication. Unlike the 1st ed., this volume excludes secondary literature. Index of authors and index of titles. No subject index.   Z2014.U84S28

Stanton, Robert J. A bibliography of modern British novelists. Troy, N.Y. : Whitston, 1978. 2 v. (1123 p.).   **BE685**

Contents: v.1, Kingsley Amis, Elizabeth Bowen, Margaret Drabble, William Golding, L. P. Hartley, Richard Hughes, Rosamond Lehmann, Doris Lessing, Brian Moore; v.2, Iris Murdoch, V. S. Naipaul, Anthony Powell, Jean Rhys, Alan Sillitoe, C. P. Snow, Muriel Spark, Angus Wilson.

For each novelist there is a list of works subdivided by genre (novels, short stories, poems, plays, "other"); a section of general secondary studies, interviews, biographical sketches and other miscellaneous items; and a list of studies and reviews of individual works. A separate section lists works referring to two or more novelists and is subdivided as (1) books and dissertations, and (2) periodical articles; cross-references to this section are provided in the individual author sections. Includes a number of articles and reviews from journalistic publications.   Z2014.F5S72

Stevenson, Lionel. Victorian fiction : a guide to research / by Robert Ashley ... [et al.]. Cambridge : Harvard Univ. Pr., 1964. 440 p.   **BE686**

A companion to Frederic Everett Faverty, *Victorian poets* (BE703) and David J. DeLaura, *Victorian prose* (BE755). Separate chapters on each of the principal novelists provide a survey of research and a critical evaluation of selected writings in the field.

§ Continued by George H. Ford, *Victorian fiction : a second guide to research* (BE668).   PR873.S8

Wolff, Robert Lee. Nineteenth-century fiction : a bibliographical catalogue based on the collection formed by Robert Lee Wolff. N.Y. : Garland, 1981–86. 5 v. : ill. (Garland reference library of the humanities, v. 261, etc.).   **BE687**

A descriptive catalog of Robert Wolff's private collection of novels published during Victoria's reign (1837–1901), as well as some earlier and later novels by authors of this period. Includes nonfiction by novelists, manuscripts of published and unpublished novels, and transcriptions of novelists' letters pertaining to specific novels. Assumes familiarity with Michael Sadleir, *XIX century fiction* (BE683), and where "a title has already been described by Sadleir, mention is made only of significant variants, or of such matters as provenance which are necessarily peculiar to the Wolff copy."—*Publisher's note.* Lists approximately four times the number of entries in Sadleir (almost 8,000 entries, with multiple editions for many); also valuable for the large number of minor works described.

§ *See also* the ongoing *Nineteenth century short-title catalogue* (AA687).   Z2014.F4W64

Dictionaries

Dictionary of British literary characters : 18th- and 19th-century novels / ed. by John R. Greenfield ; associate ed., David Brailow, with the assistance of Arlyn Bruccoli. N.Y. : Facts on File, c1993. 655 p.   **BE688**

A dictionary of 11,663 characters from 486 18th- and 19th-century English novels. A second volume will cover more than 500 novels published 1890–1980s. Besides established novelists, the editors have selected many lesser-known writers, including many women, providing access to characters not found in more general works like Frank Magill's *Cyclopedia of literary characters* (BE186). Attempts to "include all major characters and all other characters who contribute to the plot or themes of the novel in any significant way."—*Pref.* Similar in format to *Dictionary of American literary characters* (BE484); includes an index of authors, with novels listed chronologically by date of first publication. Within the individual novels a listing of characters is provided. Review: *Choice* 31, no. 2 (Oct. 1993): 265.

§ To identify persons who have appeared as fictional characters, consult William Amos, *The originals : an A–Z of fiction's real-life characters* (Boston : Little, Brown ; London : J. Cape, c1985).   PR830.C47D5

Handbooks

Sutherland, John. The Stanford companion to Victorian fiction. Stanford, Calif. : Stanford Univ. Pr., 1989. 696 p.   **BE689**

First published as *The Longman companion to Victorian fiction.* Intended as "a source of ready factual information about Victorian fiction and its immediate context."—*Pref.* Some 1,606 entries in alphabetical arrangement deal with novelists, periodicals, synopses of novels (with indication of serialization), publishers, forms of novels, and major illustrators. Abbreviations at the end of author entries signal lists of works in standard bibliographies (e.g., *NCBEL*, British Museum *Catalogue, Wellesley index*), and biographical entries (*DNB* and *Who's who*). Indexes of proper names and pseudonyms, and of maiden and married names. Review: *The review of English studies* n.s. 42 : 165 (Feb. 1991) : 130–132.   PR871.S87

Vann, J. Don. Victorian novels in serial. N.Y. : Modern Language Association of America, 1985. 181 p.   **BE690**

Provides an index to publication dates and contents of serialized fiction for Ainsworth, Collins, Dickens, Eliot, Gaskell, Hardy, Kingsley, Kipling, Bulwer-Lytton, Marryat, Meredith, Reade, Stevenson, Thackeray, Trollope, and Ward. Since many of the magazines themselves are now difficult to obtain, "this work allows the researcher to know the exact date on which specific parts of the text were available to Victorian readers. "—*Pref.* Includes an introduction on the history and impact of serialized fiction, synopses of periodicals, and a selective bibliography.   Z2014.F4V36

Histories

Baker, Ernest Albert. The history of the English novel. London : Witherby, 1924–39. 10 v.   **BE691**

Repr.: N.Y. : Barnes & Noble, 1950.

Contents: v. 1, The Age of Romance, from the beginnings to the Renaissance (1924); v. 2, The Elizabethan Age and after (1929); v. 3, The later Romances and the establishment of realism (1929); v. 4, Intellectual realism: from Richardson to Sterne (1930); v. 5, The novel of sentiment and the Gothic romance (1929); v. 6, Edgeworth, Austen, Scott (1929); v. 7, The age of Dickens and Thackeray (1936); v. 8, From the Brontes to Meredith: Romanticism in the English novel (1937); v. 9, The day before yesterday [Hardy–James] (1938); v. 10, Yesterday [Conrad–Lawrence] (1939). A work by Lionel Stevenson, *The history of the English novel : yesterday and after [Wells–John Braine] (Barnes & Noble, c[1967]), is designated v. 11 of the set.*

A standard history of the English novel from its beginnings through the 1950s. Emphasis is upon major authors. Each volume is individually indexed.

§ *See also* Lionel Stevenson's one-volume survey, *The English novel, a panorama* (Boston : Houghton Mifflin, c[1960]). For period histories of the novel *see* volumes in "Longman literature in English" series, e.g., Clive T. Probyn, *English fiction of the eighteenth century, 1700–1789* (London : Longman, c1987).   PR821.B3

Salzman, Paul. English prose fiction, 1558–1700 : a critical history. Oxford : Clarendon Pr. ; N.Y. : Oxford Univ. Pr., 1985. 391 p.   **BE692**

A developmental history and survey of English prose fiction during the reign of Elizabeth I and the 17th century. Chapters for genres (political/allegorical romance, picaresque fiction, etc.) and representative authors. Includes a bibliography of "all known extant works of fiction published between 1558 and 1700, including translations" (*Bibliography*), separated into: Elizabethan fiction (alphabetically) and 17th century fiction (a "much more unknown quantity") arranged by categories.   PR836.S24

Poetry

Bibliography

Alexander, Harriet Semmes. American and British poetry : a guide to the criticism, 1925–1978. Athens, Ohio : Swallow Pr., c1984. 486 p.   **BE693**

For annotation, *see* BE488.   Z1231.P7A44

Anderson, Emily Ann. English poetry, 1900–1950 : a guide to information sources. Detroit : Gale, [1982]. 315 p. (American literature, English literature, and world literatures in English, v. 33).   **BE694**

Like other volumes in this series, provides a selective annotated bibliography of general reference sources, background sources, and primary and secondary bibliographies for individual authors. Readers should also consult the *MLA international bibliography* (BE39), the *Annual bibliography of English language and literature* (BE588), and secondary bibliographies of individual poets for this period.

Z2014.P7A54

Beale, Walter H. Old and Middle English poetry to 1500 : a guide to information sources. Detroit : Gale, 1976. 454 p. (American literature, English literature, and world literatures in English, v. 7).   **BE695**

An annotated bibliography of primary texts, translations, general reference sources, and selected critical studies (primarily those of the two decades prior to this publication). A review (*Choice* 14 [May 1977]: 343) points out some inconsistencies and omissions. *See also* v. 1 of Nancy C. Martinez and Joseph G. R. Martinez, *Guide to British poetry explication* (BE710).   Z2014.P7B34

Brogan, Terry V. F. English versification, 1570–1980 : a reference guide with a global appendix. Baltimore : Johns Hopkins Univ. Pr., 1981. 794 p.   **BE696**

A massive annotated bibliography of approximately 6,000 studies that intends "to collect, list, classify by subject, summarize, describe, generally evaluate, cross-reference, and index by poet and author all known printed studies of English versification from ... 1570, up to January 1980."—*Introd.* In two parts: (1) modern English verse (since Wyatt), with classifications for primary references (histories, earlier bibliographies, etc.), general studies, poetic elements and structures (e.g., sound, rhythm, meter, syntax and grammar—all further subdivided), and the poem in performance; and (2) early English verse (to Skelton), with divisions for Old and Middle English. Liberally cross-referenced, with annotations that are detailed and evaluative, serving to place studies in a theoretical context. Appendixes list comparative studies and studies of versification in other languages, including classical Greek and Latin, and medieval Latin. Indexes of poets and authors.

§ *See also:* Alex Preminger and T. V. F. Brogan, *The new Princeton encyclopedia of poetry and poetics* (BE329).   Z2015.V37B76

Brown, Carleton Fairchild. The index of Middle English verse / by Carleton Fairchild Brown and Rossell Hope Robbins. N.Y. : Printed for the Index Soc. by Columbia Univ. Pr., 1943. 785 p.   **BE697**

A scholarly index to all poems published in England before 1500. Designed to complete Brown's *Register of Middle English religious and didactic verse* (BE698). The 2,273 entries in the *Register* (for about 1,100 manuscripts) have been increased in the *Index* to 4,365 entries in more than 2,000 manuscripts. Includes a subject and title index and a list of locations of privately owned manuscripts.

————. ————. *Supplement* ... [by] Rossell Hope Robbins [and] John L. Cutler (Lexington : Univ. of Kentucky Pr., 1965. 551 p.).

"Expands some 2,300 of the 4,365 entries in the original *Index* and adds some 1,500 new entries."—*Introd.* Changes in ownership and location of manuscripts are recorded, and cataloging is completed for manuscripts not available for examination at the time the basic work was published. Editions of poems published since 1943 are also noted.   Z2012.B86

———————— A register of Middle English religious and didactic verse. Oxford : pr. for the Bibliographical Society at the Univ. Pr., 1916–20. 2 v.   **BE698**

Contents: Pt. 1, List of manuscripts; pt. 2, Index of first lines and index of subjects and titles.

Manuscripts are listed according to the library in which they are found. Includes religious and didactic verse written between 1200 and 1500.   Z2012.B87

Case, Arthur Ellicott. A bibliography of English poetical miscellanies, 1521–1750. Oxford : Printed for the Bibliographical Society at the Univ. Pr., 1935 (for 1929). 386 p.   **BE699**

Repr.: Folcroft, Pa. : Folcroft Library Editions, 1970.

A chronological bibliography listing 481 collections of miscellaneous verse—"original or translated verse by British subjects, written in any language and printed in any country."—*Pref.* Excluded are song books containing music and hymn books intended for congregational use. Entries, arranged chronologically by date of earliest publication, with subsequent editions down to 1750 noted, include title, collation, bibliographic notes, and holdings. Based on personal examination of copies in the British Museum, the Bodleian, Harvard, and Yale (but not the Huntington).

§ For additional American holdings *see* Richard C. Boys, *A finding-list of English poetical miscellanies 1700–48 in selected American libraries* (Baltimore, c1940. Repr. from *ELH, a journal of English literary history* 7:2 [June 1940] : 144–162). *See also* Joseph Frank, *Hobbled Pegasus : a descriptive bibliography of minor English poetry, 1641–1660* (Albuquerque : Univ. of New Mexico Pr., [c1968]).   Z2014.P7C3

Donow, Herbert S. The sonnet in England and America : a bibliography of criticism. Westport, Conn. : Greenwood, 1982. 477 p.   **BE700**

"Essentially a bibliography of secondary materials, published prior to mid-1981, on the subject of the sonnet and the sonneteer. Covered in the text are poets of the British Isles and North America who flourished from 1530 ... to the end of the nineteenth century."—*Pref.* An impressive bibliography of some 4,000 entries (most including brief descriptive annotations), with coverage being reasonably comprehensive for English, French, and German materials (less so for Italian, Scandinavian, East European, and Japanese criticism). Arranged in four chapters: (1) general overview (anthologies, general criticism); (2) Renaissance (anthologies, general criticism, individual poets); (3) Shakespeare; and (4) Sonnet revival: 18th and 19th centuries (anthologies, general criticism, poets). Indexes for contributors, poets, and subjects. The poet and subject indexes are highly selective, and it is necessary to consult the table of contents to determine if a specific poet is included. Despite these hindrances, this is a valuable specialized resource. Review: *Choice* 20:4 (Dec. 1982) : 554.   PR509.S7

English poetry : select bibliographical guides / A. E. Dyson, ed. London : Oxford Univ. Pr., 1971. 378 p.   **BE701**

Bibliographic essays surveying editions, biographies, bibliographies, letters, and critical studies for 20 major English poets, Chaucer to Eliot. Although dated, still useful for its generally reliable selection.   Z2014.P7E53

The English romantic poets : a review of research and criticism / John Clubbe ... [et al.] ; ed. by Frank Jordan. 4th ed. N.Y. : Modern Language Association of America, 1985. 765 p.   **BE702**

1st ed., 1950, ed. by Thomas M. Raysor; 3rd rev. ed., 1972.

A standard reference work providing surveys of research for the Romantic movement in England and individually for Blake, Wordsworth, Coleridge, Byron, Shelley, and Keats. Scholarship is generally current through 1982. The essay on English romanticism has sections for bibliographies, histories, guides, and background sources, as well as for the more specifically cultural and historical aspects of romanticism (romanticism, politics, and society; romantic forms and modes; English romanticism abroad, etc.). Essays for individual poets include discussion of editions, biographies, bibliographies, correspondence, critical studies, and of trends and prospects. Detailed index.

§ Now largely dated and in need of revision is Carolyn Washburn Houtchens and Lawrence Huston Houtchens, *The English romantic poets and essayists : a review of research and criticism* (Rev. ed. N.Y. : publ. for the Modern Language Assoc. of America by New York Univ. Pr., c1966), which covers Blake, Lamb, Hazlitt, Scott, Southey, Campbell, Moore, Landor, Hunt, De Quincey, and Carlyle. For annual bibliographies on romanticism see "Current bibliography" in *Keats-Shelley journal* (BE754), and *The romantic movement : a selective and critical bibliography* (*see* BE40).   PR590.E5

Faverty, Frederic Everett. The Victorian poets : a guide to research. 2nd ed. Cambridge : Harvard Univ. Pr., 1968. 433p.   **BE703**

1st ed., 1956.

Serves as a companion to David J. DeLaura, *Victorian prose : a guide to research* (BE755), and to Lionel Stevenson, *Victorian fiction : a guide to research* (BE686). Bibliographic essays for general materials, Tennyson, Robert Browning, Elizabeth Barrett Browning, FitzGerald, Clough, Arnold, Swinburne, the pre-Raphaelites (Dante Gabriel Rossetti, Christina Rossetti, William Morris, and minor poets), Hopkins, and the later Victorians (Patmore, Meredith, Thomson, Hardy, Bridges, Henley, Stevenson, Wilde, Davidson, Thompson, Housman, Kipling, Johnson, and Dowson). Scholarship is current only through 1966. Badly in need of revision.

§ For recent reviews of research, *see* "Guide to the year's work in Victorian poetry" in *Victorian poetry* (BE706).   PR593.F3

First-line index of English poetry, 1500–1800 : in manuscripts of the Bodleian Library, Oxford / ed. by Margaret Crum. Oxford : Clarendon Pr., 1969. 2 v. (1257 p.).   **BE704**

An index to almost 23,000 individual manuscript poems in the Bodleian Library acquired prior to April 1961. Arrangement is alphabetical by first line, and entries include first and last lines of the poem (in modernized spelling except for names), author and title (when known), editorial notes (primarily references to printed versions), and identification of the Bodleian manuscript in which the poem is found. Also includes a list of unidentified poems—"imperfect at beginning" (*Contents*)—that are indexed by last lines. Indexes: (1) Bodleian manuscripts by shelfmark; (2) authors; (3) names mentioned; (4) authors of works translated, paraphrased, or imitated; (5) composers of settings and tunes named or quoted. An indispensable guide to the English poetry of three centuries. For scholars, "the usefulness of this tool can hardly be overestimated"—*Philological quarterly* 49 : 3 (July 1970) : 290–291.   Z2014.P7F5

Foxon, David Fairweather. English verse, 1701–1750 : a catalogue of separately printed poems with notes on contemporary collected editions. London ; N.Y. : Cambridge Univ. Pr., 1975. 2 v.   **BE705**

Contents: v. 1, Catalogue; v. 2, Indexes.

Attempts "to list all separately published verse written in English, as well as works written in other languages and printed in the British Isles, but it omits all works printed in America"—*Introd.* A short-title catalog, it is arranged by author or by first word of anonymous title. Entries for single works include title, imprint collation, first line, notes on authorship and subject, and up to five locations in the British Isles and five in America. Entries for collected editions provide less detail. Generally excluded are: miscellanies (cf. Arthur E. Case, *Bibliography of English poetical miscellanies, 1521–1750*, BE699); popular broadside ballads, slip songs, and chapbooks; engraved sheets or half sheets; oratorios and opera libretti; and works consisting of prose and verse when the prose exceeds the verse. Includes indexes of first lines, chronology, imprints, "bibliographical notabilia," descriptive epithets, and subjects (including proper names, title keywords, verse forms, etc.). According to one reviewer, "the general standard of accuracy is astonishingly high"—*The review of English studies* n.s. 28 (1977) : 473–475.   Z2014.P7F69

Guide to the year's work in Victorian poetry. (*In* Victorian poetry : v. 1 [Jan. 1963]–). Appears annually.   **BE706**

Bibliographic essays by various scholars, intended to update Frederic Everett Faverty, *The Victorian poets : a guide to research* (BE703). PR500.V5

Jackson, James Robert de Jager. Annals of English verse, 1770–1835 : a preliminary survey of the volumes published. N.Y. : Garland, 1985. 709 p. (Garland reference library of the humanities, v. 535). **BE707**

"Based on reports of books rather than on firsthand examination of copies."—*Introd.* Compiled from reviews in periodicals, from the *Cambridge bibliography of English literature* (BE582), and from the British Museum *Catalogue* (AA103). Publications are listed by year, then alphabetically by short title. Hymnals, books of songs, publications of less than eight pages, and titles published outside the U.K. are excluded. Author and anonymous title indexes. Z2039.P6J32

————— Romantic poetry by women : a bibliography, 1770–1835. Oxford : Clarendon Pr. ; N.Y. : Oxford Univ. Pr., 1993. 484 p. **BE708**

A primary bibliography that "attempts to provide a record of all the volumes of verse published by women during the years 1770 to 1835."—*Introd.* Based on the author's *Annals of English verse, 1770–1835 : a preliminary survey of the volumes published* (BE707), but identifies twice the number of women authors (about 900). Includes works in languages other than English (excepting Welsh, Erse, Gaelic, and Asian languages) if written by women whose native language was English, and translations by women from other languages if the translations are in verse. Arranged alphabetically by author, then chronologically. Sections for multiple author and anonymous works. Entries include biographical headnotes (when information is available) and cite source materials. Also provides title in full, editor or translator, place and publisher, page size, pagination, price (when known), author's name as given on the title page, and the library copy on which the description is based. Includes material on the annual rate of publication, an appendix of female pseudonyms, and indexes for authors, titles, publishers (geographically), and publishers outside London (alphabetically). Records more than 2,500 volumes of verse. Review: *Choice* 31:7 (March 1994): 1098. Z2013.5.W6J33

Kallich, Martin. British poetry and the American Revolution : a bibliographical survey of books and pamphlets, journals and magazines, newspapers, and prints, 1755–1800. Troy, N.Y. : Whitston, 1988. 2 v. (1731 p.). **BE709**

Intends "to make readily accessible ... a substantial part of the poetry published in Great Britain between 1763–1783 about its American colonies and about domestic political and social affairs that affected the colonies (including selections from 1755 to 1762 and 1784 to 1800)."—*Introd.* About 5,600 poems are listed by year, then by format (books and pamphlets, serials, and prints), then by author or title. Entries include the verse form, bibliographic data, first lines (and line count), notice of contemporary reviews, references to Evans and Sabin numbers, locations in British and American libraries, and a succinct descriptive annotation setting the poem in historical context. Verse is broadly defined to include songs, ballads, epigrams, fables, etc. Separate indexes for authors (and their poems) and anonymous poems, for topics (including persons, events, themes, etc.), and for verse forms. Review: *American reference books annual* 20 (1989) : 454–455. Z2014.P7K34

Martinez, Nancy C. Guide to British poetry explication / Nancy C. Martinez and Joseph G. R. Martinez. Boston, Mass. : G.K. Hall, 1991–93. v. 1–3. (In progress). **BE710**

Contents: v. 1, Old English–Medieval; v. 2, Renaissance; v. 3, Restoration–Romantic; v. 4 is to cover Victorian–Contemporary.

Like *Guide to American poetry explication* (BE491), these volumes continue and expand, and when completed, the two sets will effectively supersede Joseph M. Kuntz and Nancy C. Martinez, *Poetry explication : a checklist of interpretation since 1925 of British and American poems past and present* (3rd ed. Boston: G.K. Hall, c1980). Unlike Kuntz and Martinez, *GBPE* includes "explications for poems of all lengths...in books about single authors as well as collections surveying periods or several poets."—*Pref.* Within this broadened scope, the coverage (necessarily selective) still dates from 1925. Each volume includes a bibliography of main sources consulted.

§ *See also*: Harriet Semmes Alexander, *American and British poetry : a guide to the criticism, 1925–1978* (BE488); and Gloria Stark Cline, *An index to criticisms of British and American poetry* (Metuchen, N.J. : Scarecrow, c1973). Z2014.P7M34

Mell, Donald C. English poetry, 1660–1800 : a guide to information sources. Detroit : Gale, c1982. 501 p. (American literature, English literature, and world literatures in English, v. 40). **BE711**

A selective annotated bibliography in two parts. Pt. 1 lists general and background sources in four categories: (1) general reference materials; (2) English literature 1660–1800, reference materials (histories, guidebooks, collections, etc.); (3) English literature 1660–1800, background sources (history, political science, religion, aesthetics, etc.); and (4) English poetry for the period (theme, genre, poetic form, versification). Pt. 2 lists selective primary and secondary sources for 31 individual poets. For criticism, emphasis is on 20th-century English-language materials through 1979 (with some later items). Excluded are dissertations and theses, book reviews, untranslated foreign-language materials, and works designed for the classroom. Index includes authors, translators, scholars, and titles.

§ *See also* the highly selective bibliography of major studies: David Nokes, *An annotated critical bibliography of Augustan poetry* (N.Y. : St. Martin's, c1989). Z2014.P7M44

Reilly, Catherine W. English poetry of the First World War : a bibliography. London : G. Prior ; N.Y. : St. Martin's, 1978. 402 p. **BE712**

In two main sections: anthologies and individual poets. English poetry includes poetry by English, Irish, Scottish, and Welsh poets. Title index. Supplementary list of names of war poets of other English-speaking nations.

§ *See also* Reilly's *English poetry of the Second World War: a biobibliography* (London : Mansell, c1986), which follows the same format. Z2014.P7R44

Reiman, Donald H. English romantic poetry, 1800–1835 : a guide to information sources. Detroit : Gale, [1979]. 294 p. (American literature, English literature, and world literatures in English, 27). **BE713**

A selective, evaluatively annotated bibliography with chapters for background studies, the Romantic movement generally, five major poets (Wordsworth, Coleridge, Byron, Shelley, and Keats), and 12 secondary poets (Beddoes, Campbell, Clare, Hogg, Hood, Hunt, Landor, Moore, Peacock, Rogers, Scott, and Southey). Blake and Crabbe are excluded on chronological grounds (a fault of the series). Entries are variously coded to indicate their relative worth (e.g., an asterisk denotes works of "primary" value). Sections for individual authors include primary and secondary works. Primarily English-language criticism, current through the mid-1970s. Separate indexes for authors, titles, and subjects. Generally praised for its selection and for the "forthrightness and judiciousness" of its evaluations (*Keats-Shelley journal* 30 [1981] : 216–8). Z2014.P7R46

Ringler, William A. Bibliography and index of English verse printed 1476–1558. London ; N.Y. : Mansell, 1988. 440 p. **BE714**

Intended to supplement and carry forward to 1558 Carleton F. Brown and Rossell H. Robbins, *Index of Middle English verse* (BE697). In two sections: verse printed 1476–1500, and verse printed 1501–58. Each section has two parts: a bibliography listing indexed books by *STC* number, and a first line index. Entries in the first line index are arranged alphabetically and include author, title, date of composition, number of lines, verse form, and *STC* number of the work containing the verse. Separate indexes for each time period provide access by author, title, subject, and verse form. Review: *The papers of the Bibliographical Society of America* 84, no. 3 (Sep. 1990): 305–8.

§ For manuscript verse *see*: William A. Ringler, *Bibliography and index of English verse in manuscript, 1501–1558* (prep. and completed by Michael Rudick and Susan J. Ringler. London : Mansell, c1992). An additional bibliography and index for manuscript verse 1559–1603 is planned. The usefulness of Nancy A. Gutierrez, *English historical poetry, 1476–1603* (N.Y. : Garland, c1983) is greatly vitiated by the lack of a subject index, since poems are arranged chronologically by dates of the historical topics described. Review: *Analytical & enumerative bibliography* 8, no. 1 (1984) : 32–5.   Z2014.P7R56

Indexes

•**English poetry** : the English poetry full-text database [database]. Cambridge, U.K. ; Alexandria, Va. : Chadwyck-Healey, 1992.   **BE715**

A machine-readable, full-text database incorporating the works of approximately 1,350 poets from the Anglo-Saxon period to 1900. Poets included are primarily those listed in the *New Cambridge bibliography of English literature* (BE585), although future editions are expected to add many others, notably women, that are underrepresented in *NCBEL*. Among the works included are: children's verse; translations into English before 1800; poetry written between 600 and 1900 but not published until after 1900; hymns published before 1800; and verse dramas not intended for the stage. Excluded are poems in languages other than English and unpublished poems or those published only in contemporary newspapers, journals, or miscellanies.

The database makes it possible to search the entire corpus of English poetry 600–1900, search the works of individual or combined poets, search for individual words or phrases, limit searches to structural elements (titles, dedications, prologues, epigraphs, etc.), and to perform Boolean and proximity searches. As such, *English poetry* represents an unprecedented resource for thematic, stylistic and linguistic analysis of the body of English poetry through the end of the 19th century. A printed bibliography of the editions used accompanies the database. Available either on CD-ROM or magnetic tape.

Handbooks

Smith, Eric. A dictionary of classical reference in English poetry. Woodbridge, Suffolk : D.S. Brewer ; Totowa, N.J. : Barnes & Noble, 1984. 308 p.   **BE716**

A dictionary containing "virtually all the Classical allusions in some eighty English poets" (*Pref.*) ranging from Chaucer to the 20th century and including poetic drama. The first section, the dictionary of allusions, arranged alphabetically by classical reference, provides for each allusion a brief account of the classical context, a citation to a classical source, and its occurrence in English poetry. A reverse index lists English poets and poems with the allusions found in each. Verse drama is generally excluded except for Shakespeare and writers who were principally nondramatic poets. A list of classical sources used is provided. Review: *Notes and queries* n.s. 34 (Sept. 1987) : 366.   PR508.C68S63

Histories

The Columbia history of British poetry / Carl Woodring, ed. ; assoc. ed., James Shapiro. N.Y. : Columbia Univ. Pr., 1993. 732 p.   **BE717**

A collective history of the poetry written in England, Ireland, Scotland, and Wales, this volume is made up of 26 essays by various scholars. According to its editors, "the scholarly work of the last twenty years or so has exposed a disturbingly monolithic conception of the canon of English poets, replacing it with a less simple but far richer picture of the accomplishments of British poets over the course of twelve centuries."—*Introd.* As with the other recent histories from Columbia, a conscious effort has been made to make "available voices long suppressed," including many women, and to resituate poets long established within the canon. Essays for major poets, for periods, topics, and regions, with suggestions for further reading. Includes brief

biographies of approximately 120 poets and lists scholarly editions of poetry. Index of subject authors, titles, and broad subject headings.   PR502.C62

Courthope, William John. A history of English poetry. N.Y., London : Macmillan, 1895–1910. 6 v.   **BE718**

Repr.: N.Y. : Russell & Russell, 1962.

A standard work covering from the Middle Ages to the romantic movement. Courthope emphasizes major figures and the impact of social and political history upon poetry. Vol. 6 has a cumulative index.

§ The most encompassing history of English poetry since Courthope will be *The Routledge history of English poetry*, ed. by R. A. Foakes (London : Routledge and Kegan Paul, 1977–). With volumes by specialists, "the aim … is not to provide merely another account of the major figures, but to reassess the development of English poetry."—*General editor's pref.* Published to date: v. 1, *Old English and Middle English poetry*, Derek Albert Pearsall (c1977); v. 3, *Restoration and eighteenth-century poetry, 1660–1780*, Eric Rothstein (c1981); v. 4, *Poetry of the Romantic period*, J. R. de J. Jackson (c1980).   PR502.C8

Perkins, David. A history of modern poetry. Cambridge, Mass. : Belknap Pr. of Harvard Univ. Pr., 1976–1987. 2 v.   **BE719**

Contents: v. 1, from the 1890's to the high modernist mode; v. 2, Modernism and after.

The most comprehensive history of modern British and American poetry. In the course of surveying the major currents of modernism and postmodernism, Perkins discusses almost 300 poets. Predictably controversial, this history has elicited both praise and scorn. Indexed. Reviews: *The Yale review* 77, no. 1 (December 1987) : 103–14; *The Sewanee review* 96, no. 1 (Winter 1988) : 95–105.   PR610.P4

Anthologies

Gardner, Helen Louise. The new Oxford book of English verse, 1250–1950. N.Y. : Oxford Univ. Pr., 1972. 974 p.   **BE720**

Earlier editions (1900, 1939) ed. by Sir Arthur Quiller-Couch had title: *Oxford book of English verse*. The 1st ed. stopped with 1900; the 2nd extended coverage to 1918 and included 966 poems as against 883 in the previous edition, with some changes in the selection from poets previously included as well as the addition of new names. Emphasis was on lyrical verse.

"The present edition is not a revision of Q's revision but a new anthology."—*Pref.* It is not confined to lyric verse, but "attempts to represent the range of English non-dramatic poetry from 1250 to 1950." There are 884 poems, including some excerpts from long poems; some brief notes and references are provided at the back of the book. With the exception of Pound and Eliot, American poets are excluded.

§ See also *The Norton anthology of poetry*, ed. Alexander W. Allison [et al.], (3rd ed. N.Y. : Norton, c1983), which includes poetry by American, Canadian, and English poets, as well as an essay on versification.   PR1174.G3

Opie, Iona Archibald. Oxford dictionary of nursery rhymes / ed. by Iona and Peter Opie. Oxford : Clarendon Pr., 1951. 467 p. : ill.   **BE721**

Repr. with corrections, 1952.

Said to be the most comprehensive and authoritative work ever published on English nursery rhymes; includes 550 rhymes (all current today or until recently), arranged alphabetically by the most prominent word or, in the case of nonsense jingles, by the opening phrase. The standard version of each nursery rhyme is given first, followed by the earliest recorded version (where available), and bibliographical references. Two indexes: (1) "notable figures associated with the invention, diffusion or illustration of nursery rhymes," and (2) first lines of both standard and other versions. Contains many prints of drawings and texts taken from famous old nursery-rhyme books, and a 45-page introduction.   PZ8.3.O6O

Parodies

Hamilton, Walter. Parodies of the works of English and American authors. London : Reeves & Turner, 1884–89. 6 v. : ill.   **BE722**

A very comprehensive collection; many parodies are given in full, some only mentioned. Includes bibliographies. Index in each volume.

PN6110.P3H3

Macdonald, Dwight. Parodies : an anthology from Chaucer to Beerbohm—and after. N.Y. : Random House, [1960]. 574 p.

BE723

In four parts: beginnings; the 19th century; Beerbohm—and after; and specialities (e.g., reviews of unwritten books).

§ See also: *The Faber book of parodies*, ed. Simon Brett (London : Faber and Faber, 1984), and *Twentieth century parody, American and British*, ed. Burling Lowrey (N.Y. : Harcourt, Brace, [1960]).

PN6231.P3M3

Diaries; letters; autobiography

Batts, John Stuart. British manuscript diaries of the nineteenth century : an annotated listing. Totowa, N.J. : Rowman and Littlefield ; Fontwell : Centaur Pr., 1976. 345 p.   **BE724**

Patterned after William Matthews' *British diaries* (BE727) this provides a much fuller listing (with corrections) of unpublished British diaries written during the 19th century. Arrangement is chronological by year of earliest entry, then alphabetically by diarist. Entries include a biographical note, dates, a contents note, and manuscript location. An appendix lists diaries for which no exact dates are known. Indexes for diarists and for broad subject headings.

§ *See also* Cynthia Huff, *British women's diaries : a descriptive bibliography of selected nineteenth-century women's manuscript diaries* (N.Y. : AMS Pr., c1985), which provides detailed descriptions of 59 diaries arranged categorically (aristocracy, gentry, professional commercial, intelligentsia, and religious).   Z6611.B6B38

Cline, Cheryl. Women's diaries, journals, and letters : an annotated bibliography. N.Y. : Garland, 1989. 716 p. (Garland reference library of the humanities, v. 780).   **BE725**

Lists approximately 3,000 "published private writings of appreciable length, including those published as articles or as extracts in larger works."—*Pref.* Works are drawn from all periods and are primarily in English or English translation. Sections for the following: bibliographies; critical works; anthologies; family collections; and diaries, journals and letters (the latter section comprising almost 90% of the entries). Within sections entries are alphabetical by author. Includes an index of authors by profession or significant characteristic, and subject, geographic, and title indexes. Lacks a consolidated author index. Nonetheless, a useful, broad-ranging reference tool. Review: *The sixteenth century journal* 20, no. 2 (Summer 1991): 413.

Z7963.B6C55

Havlice, Patricia Pate. And so to bed : a bibliography of diaries published in English. Metuchen, N.J. : Scarecrow, 1987. 698 p.   **BE726**

Lists chronologically, with brief descriptions, more than 2,500 diaries and journals from 838 to 1983, the majority of which were "written or translated into English and published as books, chapters in books, or journal articles."—*Pref.* Includes an index of diarists and a general index of persons, subjects, and titles. Most usefully, Havlice provides a merged index to William Matthews' three bibliographies, *British diaries* (BE727); *Canadian diaries and autobiographies* (DB185); and *American diaries in manuscript, 1580–1954* (BE510). No selection criteria are given for this highly selective listing.

§ Laura Arksey's *American diaries : an annotated bibliography of published American diaries and journals* (BE507) lists some 6,000 published diaries, including English translations of diaries originally published in other languages.   Z5301.H38

Matthews, William. British diaries : an annotated bibliography of British diaries written between 1442 and 1942. Berkeley : Univ. of California Pr., 1950. 339 p.   **BE727**

Repr. : Gloucester, Mass. : P. Smith, 1967.

Lists diaries, both published and in manuscript, with many of the published diaries being extracts from biographies, histories, and genealogies. Generally, this volume " ... includes diaries written by Englishmen, Scotsmen, Welshmen, and Irishmen in the British Isles, in Europe, and on the high seas, and also the diaries of American and other travellers in the British Isles ... published in England and in English."—*Pref.* Diaries are listed chronologically by date of earliest entry and include a biographical note, dates, and a descriptive annotation suggesting the diary's content. For unpublished items, owner or library location is given. Index of authors and a chronological index of diaries extending over more than ten years.

§ For diaries of British travellers in America, *see*: Laura Arksey, *American diaries : an annotated bibliography of published American diaries and journals* (BE507). For British autobiography, *see*: William Matthews, *British autobiographies : an annotated bibliography of British autobiographies published or written before 1951* (AH236).

Z2014.D5M3

By period

Old English

Greenfield, Stanley B. A bibliography of publications on Old English literature to the end of 1972 : using the collections of E. E. Ericson / Stanley B. Greenfield and Fred C. Robinson. Toronto ; Buffalo : Univ. of Toronto Pr., c1980. 437 p.

BE728

The standard in its field, this classified bibliography lists editions, books, articles, and reviews published from the 15th century through 1972. Arranged in three sections (General works, Poetry, Prose) with numerous classified subdivisions, including sections for individual authors and works. Within subdivisions, listing is chronological by date of publication. Many cross-references, indexes of authors and reviewers and of subjects. Generally excludes studies of Anglo-Latin literature or those treating Anglo-Saxon social, political, or economic history.

§ For dissertations, see: Phillip Pulsiano, *An annotated bibliography of North American doctoral dissertations on Old English language and literature* (BE730), and for recent scholarship see: *Old English newsletter* (BE729).   Z2012.G83

Old English newsletter. v. 1 (Apr. 1967)– . [Binghamton, N.Y., etc.] : Published for the Old English Division of the Modern Language Association of America by the Center for Medieval and Renaissance Studies, SUNY-Binghamton.

BE729

Furnishes two important bibliographies: the annual "Old English bibliography" (including general and miscellaneous subjects, language, syntax and phonology, literature, individual poems, prose, Anglo-Latin and ecclesiastical works, manuscripts and illumination, history and culture, names, archaeology and numismatics, and book reviews); and "The year's work in Old English studies," an evaluative survey of scholarship. Also notes research in progress and publishes abstracts of papers.   PE101.O44

Pulsiano, Phillip. An annotated bibliography of North American doctoral dissertations on Old English language and literature. East Lansing, Mich. : Colleagues Pr., 1988. 317 p. (Medieval texts and studies, no. 3).   **BE730**

Spine title: Bibliography of North American dissertations on Old English.

Includes dissertations completed through 1986 in Canada and the U.S. In two parts: general works, including themes, studies of language and style, and historical and cultural subjects; and poetry, including dissertations on specific Old English poems. Appendix 2 lists homilies that have been edited or translated in dissertations. Author and subject indexes.   Z2012.P85

Quinn, Karen Jane. A manual of Old English prose / Karen J. Quinn, Kenneth P. Quinn. N.Y. : Garland, 1990. 439 p. (Garland reference library of the humanities, v. 453). **BE731**

A bibliography in four main sections: (1) Manuscripts (based on the order established by N.R. Ker); (2) Texts; (3) Editions (a bibliography of all editions but student readers); (4) Criticism (including a bibliography of festschriften and other collections). Indexes: general index (author/translator/subject); modern title index; manuscript title index; first line index. Scholarship is current through 1982, with a few later items.

§ For current scholarship see: Frederick M. Biggs, Thomas D. Hill, and Paul E. Szarmach, *Sources of Anglo-Saxon literary culture: a trial version* (Binghamton, N.Y. : Center for Medieval and Early Renaissance Studies, SUNY-Binghamton, c1990).   PR221.Q5

Middle English

Ackerman, Robert William. An index of the Arthurian names in Middle English. Stanford, Calif. : Stanford Univ. Pr., 1952. 250 p. (Stanford University publications. University series. Language and literature, v. 10). **BE732**

"A register of the personal and place names in all the Middle English versions of the Arthurian legend except the chronicles."—*Introd.* Entries provide a listing of variant spellings with citations to specific editions, comments on scribal blunders (especially those in Old French texts), and selected references to critical commentary. Bibliography of Arthurian texts indexed and selected critical works.   PE1660.A23

The index of Middle English prose / general ed., A. S. G. Edwards ; co-editors, N. F. Blake, L. N. Braswell and R. Hanna III. Cambridge : D.S. Brewer ; Totowa, N.J. : Biblio Distribution Services, 1984–92. Handlist 1–9. (In progress). **BE733**

Contents: Handlist 1: A handlist of manuscripts containing Middle English prose in the Henry E. Huntingdon [sic] Library (Ralph Hanna III, c1984); Handlist 2: A handlist of manuscripts containing Middle English Prose in the John Rylands University Library of Manchester and Chetham's Library, Manchester (G. A. Lester, c1985); Handlist 3: A handlist of manuscripts containing Middle English prose in the Digby Collection, Bodleian Library, Oxford (Patrick J. Horner, c1986); Handlist 4: A handlist of Douce manuscripts containing Middle English prose in the Bodleian Library, Oxford (Laurel Braswell, c1987); Handlist 5: A handlist of manuscripts containing Middle English prose in the Additional Collection (10001–12000), British Library, London and in the Additional Collection (12001–14000), British Library, London (Peter Brown, Elton D. Higgs, c1988); Handlist 6: A handlist of manuscripts containing Middle English prose in Yorkshire Libraries and archives (O. S. Pickering, Susan Powell, c1989); Handlist 7: A handlist of manuscripts containing Middle English prose in Parisian Libraries (James Simpson, c1989); Handlist 8: A handlist of manuscripts containing Middle English prose in Oxford College Libraries (S. J. Ogilvie-Thomson, c1991); Handlist 9: A handlist of manuscripts containing Middle English prose in the Ashmole Collection, Bodleian Library, Oxford (L.M. Eldredge, 1992).

An ongoing project that aims to identify and locate all extant Middle English prose texts, both printed and in manuscript composed between c.1200 and c.1500. Entries are in shelfmark order, include incipits and explicits, and give physical descriptions of manuscripts.

§ For verse, see: *Index of Middle English verse* (BE697) and for printed prose, R. E. Lewis, N. F. Blake, and A. S. G. Edwards, *Index of printed Middle English prose* (N.Y. : Garland, c1985).

A manual of the writings in Middle English, 1050–1500 / by members of the Middle English Group of the Modern Language Association of America. New Haven, Conn. : Connecticut Academy of Arts and Sciences, 1967–93. v. 1–9. (In progress). **BE734**

General ed., v. 1–2, J. B. Severs; v. 3– , A. E. Hartung.

"Based upon *A manual of the writings in Middle English 1050–1400* by John Edwin Wells, New Haven, 1916, and Supplements 1–9, 1919–1951."—*title page.*

Contents: v. 1, Romances (c1967); v. 2, The Pearl poet; Wyclyf and his followers; Translations and paraphrases of the Bible and commentaries; Saints' legends; Instructions for religious (c1970); v. 3, Dialogues, debates and catechisms; Thomas Hoccleve; Malory and Caxton (c1972); v. 4, Middle Scots writers; The Chaucerian apocrypha (c1973); v. 5, Dramatic pieces; Poems dealing with contemporary conditions (c1975); v. 6, Carols; Ballads; John Lydgate (c1980); v. 7, John Gower; *Piers plowman*; Travel and geographical writings; Works of religious and philosophical instruction (c1986); v. 8, Chronicles and other historical writing (c1989); v. 9, Proverbs, precepts, and monitory pieces; English mystical writings; Tales (1993).

Represents an updating and expansion of Wells (above) and now includes the 15th century. Each section of each volume includes: a commentary (discussion of manuscripts, date, dialect, source, form, extent, content, and a summary of scholarship); and a classified bibliography (listing manuscripts and critical studies). Excluded are unpublished papers, research in progress, and unpublished dissertations (with a few exceptions). The early volumes attempt to be complete "for all serious studies down through 1955 and to include selected important studies from 1955 to the date of going to press."—*Pref., v. 3.* Consult individual volumes for cutoff dates and coverage. Future volumes are planned for homilies; science, information and documents; letters; legal writings; Rolle and his followers; lyrics; and undistributed prose. Indispensable for the study of Middle English literature.

§ *See* Joanne A. Rice, *Middle English romance* (BE736) for supplemental scholarship on romances.   PR255.M3

Middle English prose : a critical guide to major authors and genres / ed. by A. S. G. Edwards. New Brunswick, N.J. : Rutgers Univ. Pr., c1984. 452 p. **BE735**

Similar to the M.L.A. reviews of research, this work aims "to provide an authoritative guide to a number of important authors and genres of Middle English prose."—*Pref.* Eighteen scholars have contributed chapters on individual writers and on groups or types of prose writings, each chapter offering "a survey of modern scholarship, a statement of desiderata and suggestions for possible avenues of future inquiry, and a bibliography of primary and secondary sources." Indexed.   PR255.M52

Rice, Joanne A. Middle English romance : an annotated bibliography, 1955–1985. N.Y. : Garland, 1987. 626 p. (Garland reference library of the humanities, v. 545). **BE736**

In two sections, verse and prose, each listing criticism within broad categories and under individual romances by title. "Each romance section has two parts: editions and criticism. The editions, which are not restricted to 1955–1985, as is criticism, are intended to be comprehensive."—*Pref.* Indexed by author and editor. Updates the bibliographies in v. 1 of John Edwin Wells, *A manual of the writings in Middle English, 1050–1400* (1916–51; *see* BE734).

§ *See also*: Jean E. Jost, *Ten Middle English Arthurian romances : a reference guide* (Boston : G.K. Hall, c1986), and Toshio Saito, *A concordance to Middle English metrical romances* (Frankfurt am Main : Verlag Peter Lang, c1988. 2 v.).   Z2014.R6R5

To 1660

Folger Shakespeare Library. Catalog of printed books of the Folger Shakespeare Library, Washington, D.C. Boston : G.K. Hall, 1970. 28 v. **BE737**

In addition to its outstanding collection of materials for Shakespeare studies, the Library has "an exceptional collection of English printed books of the STC period, from 1475 to 1640. Additional holdings of rare books and manuscripts of the Continental Renaissance and the Wing period (1641–1700) make the Library a center not only of Shakespeare studies but also of every aspect of the English and Continental Renaissance."—*Foreword*. A dictionary catalog reproducing the catalog cards for the collection. Vol. 28 includes two appendixes: Periodical collection; Chronological catalog of foreign language pamphlets.

Supplements:

————. ————. *First supplement* (Boston : G.K. Hall, 1976. 3 v.). Represents cataloging and acquisitions from Mar. 1970 through the end of 1975. An additional 12,000 titles are listed; less than a third represent pre-1800 imprints.

————. ————. *Second supplement* (Boston : G.K. Hall, 1981. 2 v.). Represents materials cataloged from Jan. 1976 through the end of 1980.

§ For the Folger's manuscript collections, see: *Catalog of manuscripts of the Folger Shakespeare Library, Washington, D.C.* (Boston : G.K. Hall, 1971. 3 v.) and its *First supplement* (Boston : G.K. Hall, 1988. 338 p.). Z8811.F652

Heninger, S. K. English prose, prose fiction, and criticism to 1660 : a guide to information sources. Detroit : Gale, [1975]. 255 p. (American literature, English literature, and world literatures in English, v. 2). **BE738**

A selective bibliography of editions and criticism, citing books, portions of books, and articles for the following categories of prose: general sources; religious writings; historical writings; travel literature; scientific and technical writings; ephemeral and polemical writings; essays; narrative fiction; literary criticism; writings on education; translations; translations of the Bible. Brief, descriptive annotations. Index of subject authors and scholars. Z2014.P795H45

Ruoff, James E. Crowell's handbook of Elizabethan & Stuart literature. N.Y. : Crowell, [1975]. 468 p. **BE739**

Serves as a companion to the literature for the period 1558–1660, from the accession of Elizabeth I to the Restoration. Includes entries for individuals, literary works, genres, and terminology. Generally, the entries are more extensive than those in *Oxford companion to English literature* (BE610), providing more biographical detail for individuals and more detailed summaries of literary works. Longer entries include bibliographies. Not indexed. PR19.R8

Smith, Hilda L. Women and the literature of the seventeenth century : an annotated bibliography based on Wing's Short title catalogue / comp. by Hilda L. Smith and Susan Cardinale. N.Y. : Greenwood, 1990. 332 p. (Bibliographies and indexes in women's studies, no. 10). **BE740**

An annotated bibliography of more than 600 works by and nearly 1,000 works about women, published 1641–1700. Based on Donald Wing's *Short-title catalogue ...* (AA683), it also cites some works not found in Wing. In two major sections: works by women and works for and about women. Also includes an addendum of 183 works either not read because they were not available or received too late to be included in the numbering sequence. Annotations are succinct and informative, and numerous cross-references in some measure make up for inadequate subject indexing. A chronological index and general index refer to page numbers rather than entry numbers, requiring time-consuming searching. Despite these minor drawbacks, this is a significant reference work that provides subject access to a substantial body of work and "pulls together in one place an amazing amount of information and will certainly facilitate research in women's issues in the seventeenth century for years to come."—*Analytical and enumerative bibliography* 4:4 (1990): 212–16. Pollard and Redgrave's *Short-title catalogue* (AA671) will still need to be consulted for works published prior to 1641. Z2013.5.W6S6

Tannenbaum, Samuel A. Elizabethan bibliographies [concise bibliographies] / by Samuel A. and Dorothy R. Tannenbaum. N.Y. : Author, 1937–50. 41 no. **BE741**

Repr. : Port Washington, N.Y. : Kennikat Pr., 1967. 10 v. (Reprint numbering differs from original).

Contents: no. 1, Christopher Marlowe (1937) and Suppl. 1–2 (1937–47); no. 2, Ben Jonson (1938); no. 3, Beaumont and Fletcher (1938) and Suppl. (1946); no. 4, Philip Massinger (1938); no. 5, George Chapman (1938) and Suppl. (1946); no. 6, Thomas Heywood (1939); no. 7, Thomas Dekker (1939) and Suppl. (1945); no. 8, Robert Greene (1939) and Suppl. (1945); no. 9, Shakespeare's Macbeth (1939); no. 10, Shakespeare's sonnets (1940); no. 11, Thomas Lodge (1940); no. 12, John Lyly (1940); no. 13, Thomas Middleton (1940); no. 14, John Marston (1940); no. 15, George Peele (1940); no. 16, Shakespeare's King Lear (1940); no. 17, Shakespeare's The Merchant of Venice (1941); no. 18, Thomas Kyd (1941); no. 19, John Webster (1941); no. 20, John Ford (1941); no. 21, Thomas Nashe (1941); no. 22, Michael Drayton (1941); no. 23, Sir Philip Sidney (1941); no. 24, Michel Eyquem de Montaigne (1942); no. 25, Samuel Daniel (1942); no. 26, George Gascoigne (1942); no. 27, Anthony Mundy, including the play of "Sir Thomas Moore," (1942); no. 28, Shakespeare's Othello (1943); no. 29, Shakespeare's Troilus and Cressida (1943); no. 30–32, Marie Stuart, Queen of Scots (1944–46. 3 v.); no. 33, Cyril Tourneur (1946); no. 34, James Shirley (1946); no. 35, George Herbert (1946); no. 36, John Heywood (1946); no. 37, Roger Ascham (1946); no. 38, Thomas Randolph (1946); no. 39, Nicholas Breton (1947); no. 40, Robert Herrick (1949); no. 41, Shakespeare's Romeo and Juliet (1950).

Elizabethan bibliographies supplements, no. 1–12, 15, 17–18 (London : Nether Pr., 1967–71).

Contents: no. 1, Thomas Middleton, John Webster, comp. by Dennis Donovan; no. 2, Thomas Dekker, Thomas Heywood, Cyril Tourneur, comp. by Dennis Donovan; no. 3, Robert Herrick, Ben Jonson, Thomas Randolph, comp. by George R. Guffey; no. 4, George Chapman, John Marston, comp. by Charles A. Pennel and William P. Williams; no. 5, Robert Greene, Thomas Lodge, John Lyly, Thomas Nashe, George Peele, comp. by Robert C. Johnson; no. 6, Christopher Marlowe, comp. by Robert C. Johnson; no. 7, Samuel Daniel, Michael Drayton, Sir Philip Sidney, comp. by George R. Guffey; no. 8, Francis Beaumont, John Fletcher, Philip Massinger, John Ford, James Shirley, comp. by Charles A. Pennel and William P. Williams; no. 9, Roger Ascham, George Gascoigne, John Heywood, Thomas Kyd, Anthony Munday, comp. by Robert C. Johnson; no. 10, Sir Thomas Browne, Robert Burton, comp. by Dennis G. Donovan; no. 11, Traherne and the seventeenth-century Platonists, comp. by George R. Guffey; no. 12, Andrew Marvell, comp. by Dennis G. Donovan; no. 15, Francis Bacon, comp. by J. K. Houck; no. 17, Sir Walter Raleigh, comp. by Humphrey Tonkin; no. 18, John Evelyn, Samuel Pepys, comp. by Dennis G. Donovan.

These issues supplement the Tannenbaum bibliographies (above), listing new editions and critical studies, and the series also includes certain Elizabethan authors not covered by Tannenbaum. Nos. 13 14, 16 not published. Z2012.T3

Restoration and 18th century

Bibliography

Duggan, Margaret M. English literature and backgrounds, 1660–1700 : a selective critical guide. N.Y. : Garland, 1990. 2 v. (Garland reference library of the humanities, v. 711). **BE742**

Brings together an impressive amount of background material for the study of Restoration literature. In four sections: (1) General literature (including bibliography, printing and publishing, festschriften, journals and periodicals, etc.); (2) Literary themes and ideas (e.g., literature and philosophy, the hero, the child, madness, women and literature, etc.); (3) Backgrounds (the visual arts, Anglicanism, witchcraft and magic); and (4) Authors and others (including 304 writers and notables of the period). Entries for individuals cite bibliographies, correspondence, and criticism. Index of scholars and subject index.

Only the narrative structure of the entries and the fact that the indexes refer only to page numbers greatly hinder the ease of use of this volume. For a qualified recommendation see *Choice* 28:1 (September 1990) :74. Z2012.D8

English literature, 1660–1800 : a bibliography of modern studies / comp. for *Philological quarterly* by Ronald S. Crane [and others]. Princeton : Princeton Univ. Pr., 1950–72. 6 v.
BE743

Contents: v. 1, 1926–38; v. 2, 1939–50; v. 3, 1951–56; v. 4, 1957–60; v. 5, 1961–65; v. 6, 1966–70.

Reprints, with cumulative indexes in every second volume, the annual bibliographies issued in *Philological quarterly*, 1926–70. Selective, international bibliographies of books, articles, and reviews in a classed arrangement (with one section devoted to individual authors). Excludes dissertations. Annotations for many entries, with significant works receiving lengthy reviews. Index includes scholars and subject authors. A convenient and indispensable resource for the study of 18th-century literature and related subjects.

§ Continued since 1970 by: *The eighteenth century : a current bibliography* (BE36). Shows a considerable time lag; the volume for 1986 publ. 1992.   Z2011.E6

Forster, Antonia. Index to book reviews in England, 1749–1774. Carbondale, Ill. : Southern Illinois Univ. Pr., c1990. 307 p.   **BE744**

Indexes reviews of English-language poetry, drama, and fiction appearing in 16 British periodicals 1749–74, including "all the principal journals doing reviewing and a significant representation of the minor ones available and appropriate."—*Explanatory note*. The 3,023 literary works reviewed are arranged alphabetically by author, translator, or anonymous title, and typically include the format, price, and bookseller. Locations given for reviewed works are for examined copies. Excluded are reviews in newspapers and reviews of dramatic productions. An introductory essay "aims to provide literally an introduction to the scope and methods of reviewing and to its place in literary life."—*Pref*. An excellent source for tracing critical reception. A review index covering the period 1775–1800 is in progress.
Z1035.A1F67

Glock, Waldo Sumner. Eighteenth-century English literary studies : a bibliography. Metuchen, N.J. : Scarecrow Pr., 1984. 847 p.   **BE745**

Aims "to provide the undergraduate and graduate student and the scholar, ... a comprehensive but not exhaustive survey of the critical literature on the most important writers of the eighteenth century."—*Pref*. Arranged by literary author, with subdivisions for individual works. Annotations; index of authors of the studies.   Z2012.G56

Lund, Roger D. Restoration and early eighteenth-century English literature, 1660–1740 : a selected bibliography of resource materials. N.Y. : Modern Language Association of America, 1980. 42 p. (Selected bibliographies in language and literature, 1).   **BE746**

A selective bibliography of important periodicals, bibliographies and concordances, with the following sections: current journals and newsletters; annual bibliographies; general bibliographies; poetry; drama; fiction; literary criticism and language study; translation; publishing and bookselling; newspapers and periodicals; art and music; history, biography, and autobiography; religious literature; miscellaneous bibliographies; and individual authors. Now in need of updating.
Z2012.L88

Spector, Robert Donald. Backgrounds to Restoration and eighteenth-century English literature : an annotated bibliographical guide to modern scholarship. N.Y. : Greenwood, 1989. 553 p. (Bibliographies and indexes in world literature, no. 17).   **BE747**

A bibliography of books and articles arranged by topic for the following categories: bibliographies; publishing, printing, and journalism; history and politics; religion; philosophy; science, medicine, and technology; economics; crime and the law; society, manners, customs, and attitudes; education and scholarship; language and rhetoric; literature and the arts. Studies of individual figures are generally excluded. Index of scholars.   Z2012.S65

Ward, William Smith. Literary reviews in British periodicals, 1789–1797 : a bibliography, with a supplementary list of general (non-review) articles on literary subjects. N.Y. : Garland, 1979. 342 p. (Garland reference library of the humanities, v. 172).   **BE748**

An index to reviews of literary works by British and American authors appearing in British periodicals. Arranged alphabetically by author, then chronologically by publication date of the work under review (with reviews listed alphabetically by periodical title). Anonymous works are grouped by title under "Anonymous." Five appendixes for non-review articles: (1) general articles on contemporary authors; (2) general and genre criticism; (3) reviews of volumes dealing with contemporary authors and their works (Thomas Paine and others); (4) reviews of books and articles dealing with selected authors before 1789 (Shakespeare, Milton, Pope, and Johnson); (5) reviews of operas and musical dramas.

§ Continued for the 19th century by Ward's *Literary reviews in British periodicals, 1798–1820* and *1821–1826* (BE757). For earlier reviews, see: Antonia Forster, *Index to book reviews in England, 1749–1774* (BE744).   Z2013.W36

Encyclopedias

The Blackwell companion to the Enlightenment / John W. Yolton ... [et al.]. Oxford ; Cambridge, Mass. : Blackwell, 1992. 581 p. : ill.   **BE749**

An excellent companion volume that surveys with catholicity the individuals, the social and philosophical issues, and the technological advances that characterized the years 1720–80. Signed entries provide cross-references and include bibliographies. An introductory essay provides an overview of the Enlightenment. Detailed index. Includes many black-and-white illustrations. Review: *European history quarterly* 23:3 (July 1993) : 439–41.   CB411.B57

19th century

Bibliography

Alston, R. C. A checklist of women writers, 1801–1900 : fiction, verse, drama. Boston : G.K. Hall, c1990. 517 p.   **BE750**

Provides a checklist of English-language fiction (14,730 titles), verse (2,079 titles), and drama (298 titles) published in the British Isles or dependent territories by some 2,000 women. With a few exceptions women writing and publishing in America are excluded. Also excluded are: "pre-pubertal" literature, chapbooks, works intended for the nursery, and translations from other languages. Based on the British Library's 19th-century holdings. Bibliographic information is minimal: author, title, date and place of publication, BL pressmark. Appendixes: (1) places of publication other than London and Edinburgh; (2) approximately 50 works held in U.K. libraries other than the BL; (3) a list of approximately 100 Canadian women writers not represented in BL collections. Review: *Choice* 29:1 (September 1991): 51.

§ *See also*: Janet Grimes and Diva Daims, *Novels in English by women, 1891–1920* (BE474).   Z2013.5.W6A48

Altick, Richard Daniel. Guide to doctoral dissertations in Victorian literature, 1886–1958 / comp. by Richard D. Altick and William R. Matthews. Urbana : Univ. of Illinois Pr., 1960. 119 p.   **BE751**

Repr. : Westport, Conn. : Greenwood, 1973.

2,105 dissertations from universities in the U.S., U.K., Germany, France, Austria, and Switzerland. Classifications include generalities, literary forms, literary criticism, and then individual authors. Author index.   Z2013.A4

Annual bibliography of Victorian studies. 1976– . Edmonton, Alberta : LITIR Database, c1980– . Annual.   **BE752**

An annual classified bibliography of principally English-language books, articles, and reviews on Victorian Britain, covering ca.1830–ca.1914. Emphasizes language and literature, with entries arranged alphabetically by author within subdivisions of seven broad categories: general and reference; fine arts; philosophy and religion; history; social sciences; science and technology; language and literature (with subdivisions for general and reference works, genres, and individual authors). "Publications on the British Colonies are included ... if they are on political and administrative matters, or if they have bearing on the cultural relationship between Great Britain and her colonies during the period."—*Pref., 1991.* Authors who are the subject of fewer than three critical articles are grouped under "Other authors," necessitating use of the subject index for comprehensive searching. Indexes: keyword subject, author, title, reviewer. Should be supplemented by the annual bibliographies in *Victorian studies* (BE756) and by general language and literature bibliographies.

The following cumulative indexes have been published by LITIR Database; all are edited by Brahma Chaudhuri. Since the last is a cumulated list of book reviews, in the others reviews are not cumulated.

Cumulative bibliography of Victorian studies, 1976–1980, (c1982). An errata slip points out a computer error that necessitates adjustment of most of the item numbers in the cumulated index.

A comprehensive bibliography of Victorian studies, 1970–1984 (c1984–85. 3 v.).

Cumulative bibliography of Victorian studies, 1970–1984 (c1988. 2 v.). Includes additions and corrections to no. 2.

Cumulative bibliography of Victorian studies, 1985–1989 (c1990).

Cumulated index to reviews of books on Victorian studies, 1975–1989 (c1990).　　　　　Z2019.A64

Bibliographies of studies in Victorian literature for the thirteen years 1932–1944 / ed. by William Darby Templeman. Urbana : Univ. of Illinois Pr., 1945. 450 p.　**BE753**

Repr. : N.Y. : Johnson Reprint, 1971.

A photoprint of bibliographies published originally in the May issues of *Modern philology,* 1933–45, and therefore arranged by year. Includes an index of Victorian authors mentioned in Sec. 4 of each year and in the first three sections of the bibliography for 1932, which was differently arranged.

Continued at ten-year intervals:

　　　—. 1945–54, ed. by Austin Wright (1956. 310 p.).

　　　—. 1955–64, ed. by Robert C. Slack (1967. 461 p.).

　　　—. 1965–74, ed. by Ronald E. Freeman (N.Y. : AMS Pr., [1981]. 876 p.). Reprinted from *Victorian studies.*

　　　—. 1975–84, ed. by Richard C. Tobias (c1991. 1130 p.). Reprinted from *Victorian studies.* "The considerable value of this compilation lies in the author and subject index, a helpful feature absent from the originals."—*American reference books annual* 23 (1992): 481.

Continued by: *Victorian bibliography* (BE756).　　Z2013.B59

Current bibliography. (*In* : Keats-Shelley journal 1 [1952]–). Annual.　　　　　　　　**BE754**

Intended to be a comprehensive "register of literary interest in Byron, Shelley, Keats, Hazlitt, Hunt, and their circles."—*Current bibliography, 1991.* Entries generally include succinct descriptive annotations. Books and articles discussing more than one of the major figures are listed in general section. Index of authors, scholars, and subjects.

§ The following collect but do not cumulate the bibliographies for 1950–74: *Keats, Shelley, Byron, Hunt and their circles : a bibliography, July 1, 1950–December 31, 1962,* ed. by David Bonnell Green and Edwin Graves Wilson (Lincoln : Univ. of Nebraska Pr., [c1964]) and *Keats, Shelley, Byron, Hunt, and their circles : a bibliography, July 1, 1962–December 31, 1974,* ed. by Robert A. Hartley (Lincoln : Univ. of Nebraska, c1978). For earlier materials drawn from *ELH, Philological quarterly,* and *English language notes,* see: A. C. Elkins, Jr. and L. J. Forstner, *The Romantic movement bibliography, 1936–1970* (BE40).　　　　　　　PR4836.A145

DeLaura, David J. Victorian prose : a guide to research. N.Y. : Modern Language Assoc. of America, 1973. 560 p.　**BE755**

A survey of research intended to serve as a companion to Lionel Stevenson's *Victorian fiction* (BE686) and Frederic Everett Faverty's *Victorian poets* (BE703). Coverage is complete through 1971, with a few items from 1972. Bibliographic essays are provided for: general materials; Macaulay; Thomas and Jane Carlyle; Newman; Mill; Ruskin; Arnold (poetry and prose); Pater; the Oxford Movement; Victorian churches; critics (Lewes, Bagehot, Hutton, Dallas, Lee, Swinburne, Symonds, Moore, Saintsbury, Gosse, Wilde, and Symons); and the unbelievers (Harrison, Huxley, Morley, and Stephens). Essays typically include sections for bibliographies, biographies, correspondence, manuscripts, editions, and criticism. Indexed. A reliable guide in need of updating.

§ Supplemented somewhat by Richard C. Tobias, ed., *Guide to the year's work in Victorian poetry and prose* ([Morgantown] : West Virginia Univ., [1974]; issued as *Victorian poetry,* v. 12 suppl. [Spring 1974]). For updating consult the chapter for the Victorian period in annual volumes of *The year's work in English studies* (BE589). Broader in scope but less authoritative than DeLaura is Harris W. Wilson and Diane Long Hoeveler, *English prose and criticism in the nineteenth century : a guide to information sources* (Detroit : Gale, c1979).　　　　　　　　　　　　　　　　　　PR785.D4

Victorian bibliography. (*In* Victorian studies, v. 1 [Sept. 1957]– . [Bloomington] : Indiana Univ., 1957–). Appears annually.　　　　　　　　　　　　　　**BE756**

Publ. under the auspices of the Victorian Division of the Modern Language Association of America.

A selective international bibliography of books, articles, and reviews that continues the bibliographies published 1932–56 in *Modern philology.* Not restricted to literature, the bibliography is currently classed in six sections: (1) bibliography (including printing, publishing, book production, and libraries); (2) history (general histories and historiography); (3) economics, education, religion, politics, science, and social environment; (4) arts (excluding literature); (5) literature (including literary history and the development of literary forms); (6) individual authors. Not indexed. A supplement to v. 20 (1977) offers an annotated checklist of articles and a cumulative index of scholars for v. 1 (1957)–20 (1977).　　　　　　　　　PR1.V5

Ward, William Smith. Literary reviews in British periodicals, 1798–1820 : a bibliography, with a supplementary list of general (non-review) articles on literary subjects. N.Y. : Garland, 1972. 2 v. (633 p.).　　　　　　　　**BE757**

Extends the period covered by Ward's *Literary reviews in British periodicals, 1789–1797* (BE748).

An index to reviews of literary works gleaned from a wide range of British periodicals and two newspapers (*The champion* and *The examiner*). Arrangement is alphabetical by author, then chronological by publication date of the work under review. Appendixes of general (non-review) articles on authors and their works, general and genre criticism, and reviews of operas.

§ Sometimes listed as supplementary to *The Romantics reviewed : contemporary reviews of British Romantic writers,* ed. by Donald H. Reiman (N.Y. : Garland, 1972. 3 v. in 9), which offers photographic reprints of reviews. Continued by: *Literary reviews in British periodicals, 1821–1826 : a bibliography with a supplementary list of general (non-review) articles on literary subjects,* comp. by William S. Ward (N.Y. : Garland, 1977. 301 p. [Garland reference library of the humanities, v. 60]).　　　　　　　　Z2013.W36

Encyclopedias

The 1890s : an encyclopedia of British literature, art, and culture / ed. by G. A. Cevasco. N.Y. : Garland, 1993. 714 p. (Garland reference library of the humanities, vol. 1237).　**BE758**

A broad-ranging encyclopedia covering all aspects of this important transitional decade. The majority of the 800 signed entries are for individuals (including extensive coverage of women authors), but there are also entries for individual works (*À Rebours*), topics (decadence), movements (anarchism), groups (Theosophical Society), continental influences (Nietzsche, Flaubert), periodicals (*The Savoy*), places (Café Royal), and events (the Dreyfus affair). Entries include numerous cross-references and a bibliography. Indexed. Reviews: *Times literary supplement* (September 3, 1993) : 20–21; *Choice* 31, no. 4 (December 1993) : 579.

§ Complemented by Sally Mitchell, *Victorian Britain* (DC337).

DA560.A18

The encyclopedia of romanticism : culture in Britain, 1780s-1830s / Laura Dabundo, ed. N. Y. : Garland, 1992. 662 p. (Garland reference library of social science, v. 1299). **BE759**

Provides 345 signed articles on individuals, ideas, issues, and historical events; intended to survey the "social, cultural, and intellectual climate of English Romanticism."—*Pref.* Entries vary in length from 500 to 2,500 words and include brief bibliographies. Cross-referencing within articles has been minimized, and individuals "identified *Only by last name* in articles on subjects other than themselves have their own separate entries and so are not cross-referenced."—*Pref.* Within the index subjects are most often cross-referenced to full entries rather than to specific pages. For qualified recommendations see: *Choice* 30:2 (Oct. 1992): 271; and *Booklist* 89:5 (Nov. 1, 1992): 545–546.

§ Offering fewer entries than Dabundo's encyclopedia is *A handbook to English romanticism*, ed. by Jean Raimond and J. R. Watson (N. Y. : St. Martin's Pr., c1992). DA529.E53

20th century

Bibliography

Brown, Christopher C. English prose and criticism, 1900–1950 : a guide to information sources / Christopher C. Brown, William B. Thesing. Detroit : Gale, c1983. 553 p. **BE760**

A selective, annotated bibliography of nonfiction by British authors writing in the first half of the 20th century. In two parts: (1) generic and period studies (including bibliographies, literary histories, studies of biography, autobiography, the essay, prose style, literary criticism, and travel writing); (2) 37 individual writers (primary and secondary bibliographies). Criticism is current through the end of 1980 with a few items as late as 1982. Author and title indexes.

Z2014.P795B76

Davies, Alistair. An annotated critical bibliography of modernism. Totowa, N.J. : Barnes & Noble, 1982. 261 p. **BE761**

A guide to literary modernism. Evaluative annotations of books and articles with sections for modernism in relation to theory, its literary context, genre, critical reception, and the other arts. Also cites anthologies of key documents and guides to modernist writing. The general section on modernism is followed by individual primary and secondary bibliographies for Yeats, Wyndham Lewis, Lawrence, and Eliot. Within sections entries are listed chronologically. Index of subjects and index of scholars. Most useful for its evaluation of some of the key discussions of modernism.

§ For postwar literature, *see* John Somer and Barbara Eck Cooper, *American and British literature, 1945–1975* (BE414). For international bibliographies of modernist literature, *see*: (1) the "Annual review" issue of *Journal of modern literature* (v. 1– . Philadelphia : Temple Univ., 1970–), a classified, annotated bibliography; (2) David E. Pownall, *Articles on twentieth century literature : an annotated bibliography, 1954 to 1970* (N.Y. : Kraus Thomson, c1973–80. 7 v.).

Z2014.M6D38

Markert, Lawrence W. The Bloomsbury group : a reference guide. Boston : G.K. Hall, c1990. 325 p. **BE762**

A bibliography of books, portions of books, articles, reviews, and dissertations written 1905–89. Arranged chronologically by year, then by author. In addition to figures central to the Bloomsbury group (including, among others, Virginia and Leonard Woolf, Vanessa and Clive Bell, John Maynard Keynes, Lytton Strachey, E. M. Forster), Markert includes Ottoline Morrell, T. S. Eliot, Bertrand Russell, Vita Sackville-West, Harold Nicolson, the Sitwells, and D. H. Lawrence. "Only material that actually deals with these various figures in relation to Bloomsbury, however, is included and discussed.—*Pref.* Material is chosen to reflect the broad spectrum of activities in which the Bloomsbury figures were engaged. Annotations vary in length and often offer generous quotations from sources. Index of personal names and subjects. Z2013.M37

Mellown, Elgin W. A descriptive catalogue of the bibliographies of 20th century British poets, novelists, and dramatists. 2nd ed., rev. and enl. Troy, N.Y. : Whitston Publ., 1978. 414 p. **BE763**

1st ed., 1972.

Lists bibliographies published through 1977 of works by and about 20th-century British authors. Provides references to bibliographies appearing as parts of books, as periodical articles, and as separate publications, plus indication of bibliographic information appearing in biographical dictionaries and standard reference sources. Numerous annotations.

§ See also: Trevor Howard Howard-Hill, *Index to British literary bibliography* (BE587) and James K. Bracken, *Reference works in British and American literature*, v. 2 (BE393). Z2011.A1M43

Handbooks

Ward, A. C. Longman companion to twentieth century literature. 3rd ed. / rev. by Maurice Hussey. Harlow : Longman, 1981. 598 p. **BE764**

1st ed., 1970.

Provides brief entries for authors, literary works, genres, fictional characters, and terminology. Focuses on English and Scottish writers, but also includes writers of other nationalities with an international reputation whose works have appeared in English. Cross-references.

§ *See also* Harry Blamires, ed., *A guide to twentieth century literature in English* (London : Methuen, [1983], which provides approximately 500 articles on 20th-century authors writing in English.

PN771.W28

Shakespeare

Since identifying reference works dealing with individual authors is a straightforward procedure, Shakespeare alone has been retained by this guide as a literary exemplar. What follows is a highly selective list of reference works chosen to indicate the breadth of materials available for major literary figures.

Editions

Thompson, Ann. Which Shakespeare? : a user's guide to editions / Ann Thompson with Thomas L. Berger ...[et al.]. Milton Keynes [Eng.] ; Philadelphia : Open Univ. Pr., 1992. 197 p. **BE765**

An eminently readable guide to editions of complete works, competing series of editions, and editions of individual plays. Does not aim "simply to identify the 'best' edition of any particular text but acknowledges that different editions will be better or worse according to the user's needs."—*Introd.* Consideration is given to critical apparatus, layout, portability, and cost, among other factors. PR3071.T48

Bibliography

Champion, Larry S. The essential Shakespeare : an annotated bibliography of major modern studies. 2nd ed. N.Y. : G.K. Hall ; Toronto : Maxwell Macmillian International, c1993. 568 p. **BE766**

1st ed., 1986.

An annotated bibliography of more than 1,800 predominantly English-language studies that aims to identify " ... the most significant items of Shakespeare scholarship from 1900 through 1991."—*Pref.* A section for general works is followed by sections for the poems and sonnets, the English history plays, the comedies, the tragedies, and the romances (all subdivided for individual plays). Typically, specific play sections are further divided for reference works, editions, criticism, stage history. Index of authors, titles, and subjects. This edition incorporates more than 650 new entries published 1984–91 (many reflecting new methodologies) and deletes some 350 entries from the 1st ed. Review: *Choice* 31:3 (Nov. 1993): 424. Z8811.C53

The Garland Shakespeare bibliographies / William Godshalk, gen. ed. N.Y. : Garland, 1980–1994. v. 1–18, 20–23. (In progress). **BE767**

Contents: v. 1, *King Lear*, comp. Larry S. Champion (2 v., 1980); v. 2, *Four plays ascribed to Shakespeare : The reign of King Edward III, Sir Thomas More, The history of Cardenio, The two noble kinsmen*, comp. G. Harold Metz (1982); v. 3, *Cymbeline*, comp. Henry E. Jacobs (1982); v. 4, *Henry V*, comp. Joseph Candido (1983); v. 5, *King Henry VI*, comp. Judith Henchcliffe (1984); v. 6, *Love's labor's lost*, comp. Nancy Lenz Harvey and Anna Kirwan Carey (1984); v. 7, *Hamlet in the 1950s*, comp. Randal F. Robinson (1984); v. 8, *As you like it*, comp. Jay L. Halio (1985); v. 9, *Merchant of Venice*, comp. Thomas Wheeler (1985); v. 10, *Timon of Athens*, comp. John J. Ruszkiewicz (1986); v. 11, *Richard III*, comp. James A. Moore (1986); v. 12, *A Midsummer night's dream*, comp. D. Allen Carroll and Gary Jay Williams (1986); v. 13, *Pericles*, comp. Nancy C. Michael (1987); v. 14, *Richard II*, comp. Josephine A. Roberts (1988); v. 15, *Henry VIII*, comp. Linda McJ. Micheli (1988); v. 16, *Two gentlemen of Verona*, comp. D'Orsay W. Pearson (1988); v. 17, *Coriolanus*, comp. Alexander Leggatt and Lois Norem (1989); v. 18, *Hamlet in the 1960s*, comp. Julia Dietrich (1992), v. 20, *Othello*, comp. Margaret Lael Mikesell and Virginia Mason Vaughn (1990); v. 21, *The taming of the shrew*, comp. Nancy Lenz Harvey (1994); v. 22, *Macbeth*, comp. Thomas Wheeler (1990); v. 23, *King John*, comp. Deborah T. Curren-Aquino (1994).

Planned as "a series of annotated bibliographies surveying Shakespeare scholarship published from 1940 until the present. Major contributions published before that period would also be included ... each bibliography would be as comprehensive as possible, fully annotated, cross-referenced, and thoroughly indexed. Each would be divided into major sections that indicate the dominant critical and scholarly concerns of the play being discussed."—*Pref.* A useful series for post-1940 scholarship.

Shakespeare : a bibliographical guide / ed. by Stanley Wells. New ed. Oxford : Clarendon Pr. ; N.Y. : Oxford Univ. Pr., 1990. 431 p. **BE768**

1st ed., 1973.

A series of 19 bibliographic essays by as many scholars. In addition to chapters for individual plays and groupings of plays, there are essays for the study of Shakespeare (including collected editions, bibliographies, biographies, source materials, etc.), for Shakespeare's text, Shakespeare in performance, the nondramatic poems, and new approaches to Shakespeare criticism. Each essay concludes with a bibliography of references. No general index. Praised for its readability, "... this volume constitutes the single best starting point in its field for the student or faculty researcher, as well as for the teacher seeking an overview of approaches and problems relating to a Shakespearean play or genre."—*The sixteenth century journal* 22:4 (Winter 1991): 890–891. For a discussion of strengths and weaknesses of individual essays, see *The review of English studies* n.s., 44: 174 (May 1993) :250–255. Z8811.S5

Criticism

Shakespearean criticism : excerpts from the criticism of William Shakespeare's plays and poetry, from the first published appraisals to current evaluations. v. 1– . Detroit : Gale, 1984– . Annual (irregular). **BE769**

Beginning with v. 13, some issues called *Shakespearean criticism yearbook*.

Ed.: Laurie Lanzen Harris; assoc. ed., Mark W. Scott.

Similar to the publisher's collections of excerpts of criticism of 19th and 20th century literature (e.g., *Poetry criticism*, BE325), this attempts to present a historical overview of the critical response to the plays by identifying "only the major critics and lines of inquiry for each play."—*Pref.* Typically, volumes will reproduce critical excerpts for several plays; some focus on production history for specific plays. Yearbook volumes provide a selection of the previous year's most noteworthy studies of the plays and poetry (printed in their entirety). Cumulative indexes in various volumes for topics, critics, artists. Illustrations; facsimiles. PR2965.S44

Library catalogs

Birmingham Shakespeare Library. A Shakespeare bibliography : the catalogue of the Birmingham Shakespeare Library, Birmingham Public Libraries. [New ed.]. London : Mansell, 1971. 7 v. (1540, 2753 p.). **BE770**

Contents: pt. 1, Accessions pre-1932: v. 1–2, English editions, English Shakespeariana; v. 3, Foreign editions and Shakespeariana, Index of editors, translators, illustrators and series; pt. 2, Accessions post 1931: v. 4–6, English editions, English Shakespeariana; v. 7, Foreign editions and Shakespeariana, Index of editors, translators, illustrators and series.

Reproduces the catalogs of one of the world's major Shakespeare collections. The Shakespeariana sections include vast numbers of analytics for items in periodicals, collections of essays, anthologies, etc. Division of the bibliography into two parts, while unfortunate, results from the decision to avoid the massive expense and the long delay in publication foreseen if the two types of records—the original guard book catalog complete to 1932, and the card catalog which has served to record the Library's accessions since 1932—were to have been combined. Z8813.B5

Folger Shakespeare Library. Catalog of the Shakespeare collection. Boston : G. K. Hall, 1972. 2 v. **BE771**

Contents: v. 1, Works; works in translation; selections; separate plays; v. 2, Shakespeare as subject; titles.

For a note on the complete catalog of the library *see* BE737.

Z8811.F65

Dictionaries

Onions, C. T. A Shakespeare glossary / C. T. Onions ; enl. and rev. throughout by Robert D. Eagleson. Oxford : Clarendon, 1986. 326 p. **BE772**

1st ed., 1911; 2nd ed. rev., 1919.

"The aim of the Shakespeare glossary ... is to supply definitions and illustrations of words or senses of words now obsolete or surviving only in provincial or archaic use, together with explanations of others involving allusions not generally familiar, and of proper names carrying with them some connotative signification or offering special interest or difficulty in the passages in which they occur."—*Original pref.* Also includes obsolete and technical terms occurring only in stage directions. A thorough revision incorporating at least one citation to *The Riverside Shakespeare* (ed. by G. Blakemore Evans [Boston : Houghton Mifflin, 1974]) for each definition. "The general scrupulousness of the book, and good people's adherence to the English of the 1611

Bible, will safeguard our knowledge of the language of this period for years to come."—*The review of English studies* 39:154 (May 1988) : 291–292.

§ More narrowly focused but also of interest is Eric Partridge's *Shakespeare's bawdy : a literary and psychological essay and a comprehensive glossary* (Rev. ed. N.Y. : Dutton, 1969).   PR2892.O6

Schmidt, Alexander. Shakespeare-lexicon : a complete dictionary of all the English words, phrases and constructions in the works of the poet. 4th ed. rev. and enl. by Gregor Sarrazin. Berlin : de Gruyter ; N.Y. : G. E. Stechert & co., 1902. 2 v. (1484 p.).   **BE773**

Reprinted as "6th ed." by de Gruyter, 1971; the 1901 ed. ("3d ed. rev. and enl.") repr.: N.Y. : Arno, 1980.

Attempts "to contain [Shakespeare's] whole vocabulary and subject the sense and use of every word of it to a careful examination."—*Pref., 1st ed.* Not limited to obsolete and obscure words. References are to the Globe edition.

§ More extensive than C. T. Onions' *A Shakespeare glossary* (BE772).   PR2892.S4

Quotations

DeLoach, Charles. The quotable Shakespeare : a topical dictionary. Jefferson, N.C. : McFarland, c1988. 544 p.   **BE774**

Some 6,500 quotations are given under about 1,000 topical headings in alphabetical sequence. Reference is given to the exact line of the source in *The Riverside Shakespeare*, ed. by G. Blakemore Evans (Boston : Houghton Mifflin, 1974). Title, character, and topical indexes.   PR2892.D37

Stevenson, Burton Egbert. Home book of Shakespeare quotations : being also a concordance and a glossary of the unique words and phrases in the plays and poems. N.Y. ; London : Scribner, 1937. 2055 p.   **BE775**

Repr. : N.Y. : Macmillan, 1987.

Arranged alphabetically by topic, this reproduces some 90,000 quotations and is based upon the revised Globe edition (1911). The indexing is very full, with much attention given to variations in minor adjectives.   PR2892.S63

Concordances

Oxford Shakespeare concordances. Oxford : Clarendon Pr., 1969–72. 37 v.   **BE776**

T. H. Howard-Hill, gen. ed.

"In this series ... a separate volume is devoted to each of the plays. The text for each concordance is the one chosen as copy-text by Dr. Alice Walker for the Oxford Old Spelling Shakespeare now in preparation."—*Gen. introd.*

Some problems relating to the choice of text, together with brief comparison to Marvin Spevack's *A complete and systematic concordance to the works of Shakespeare* (BE777) and his *Harvard concordance to Shakespeare* (BE778), are noted in a review in *TLS* (14 Aug. 1969): 903; a further review appears in *TLS* (23 April 1970): 450.

Spevack, Marvin. A complete and systematic concordance to the works of Shakespeare. Hildesheim, Germany : Georg Olms, 1968–80. 9 v.   **BE777**

Contents: v. 1, Drama and character concordances to the folio comedies; v. 2, Drama and character concordances to the folio histories; Concordances to the non-dramatic works; v. 3, Drama and character concordances to the folio tragedies and Pericles, The two noble kinsmen, Sir Thomas More; v. 4–6, "A"–"Zwagger'd"; appendices; v. 7, Concordances to stage directions and speech-prefixes; v. 8, Concordances to the "bad" quartos and The taming of a shrew and The troublesome reign of King John; v. 9, Substantive variants.

Aims to present "a complete and accurate computer-generated concordance to all of Shakespeare."—*Pref.* Text used is that of *The*

Riverside Shakespeare (Boston : Houghton Mifflin, 1974), ed. by G. Blakemore Evans. Appendixes include a word-frequency index, reverse-word index, hyphenated words, homographs, etc.   PR2892.S6

——————   The Harvard concordance to Shakespeare. Cambridge, Mass. : Belknap Pr. of Harvard Univ. Pr., 1973. 1600 p.   **BE778**

A computer-generated concordance covering all the plays and poems. This is a slightly abbreviated version of v. 4–6 of the compiler's *Complete and systematic concordance to the works of Shakespeare* (BE777). Uses the modern-spelling text of *The Riverside Shakespeare*, ed. by G. Blakemore Evans (Boston : Houghton Mifflin, 1974).   PR2892.S62

Periodicals

Shakespeare Jahrbuch. Bd. 61 (N.F. 2. Bd.)–128 (1992). Liepzig : B. Tauchnitz, 1925–1992. Annual.   **BE779**

Continues *Jahrbuch der Deutschen Shakespeare-Gesellschaft* (1865–1924).

The oldest of the Shakespeare journals. Issued 1964/65 and thereafter as two separate publications: *Jahrbuch* (Deutsche Shakespeare-Gesellschaft West, Heidelberg) and *Shakespeare Jahrbuch* (Deutsche Shakespeare-Gesellschaft, Weimar). Traditionally included essays, review articles, and book reviews. *Shakespeare-Bibliographie* has continued as part of the *Jahrbuch*.   PR2889.D4

Shakespeare quarterly. v. 1 (Jan. 1950)– . [Wash., etc.] : Folger Shakespeare Library [etc.]. Five issues a year.   **BE780**

Founded by the Shakespeare Association of America in 1950. Earlier bibliographies for 1925–48 appeared under varying titles in *Shakespeare Association bulletin*, v. 1–24, 1926–49.

A quarterly journal of articles and reviews devoted to Shakespeare scholarship. Issued annually as a supplement is the important "Shakespeare : annotated world bibliography for [year]" (title varies slightly; often cited as the *World Shakespeare bibliography*), a classified, indexed bibliography "that attempts to record annually all important books, articles, reviews of books, dissertations and dissertation abstracts, theatrical productions and reviews of productions, and significant reprints of works related to Shakespeare published during the year.—*Pref. matter, 1989.* Has occasional supplement: *Reviewing Shakespeare* (1985–).   PR2885.S63

Shakespeare studies. v. 1 (1965)– . [Cincinnati, Ohio] : Inaugurated under the sponsorship of the Univ. of Cincinnati, 1965– . Annual.   **BE781**

None publ. for 1971–73.

An annual collection of criticism, research, and reviews.   PR2885.S64

Shakespeare survey. v. 1 (1948)– . Cambridge : New York : Cambridge Univ. Pr., 1948– .   **BE782**

Subtitle: An annual survey of Shakespearian study and production.

Each volume is devoted to a specific theme. International in scope, with information on productions, etc. Includes an annual critical survey of "The year's contributions to Shakespeare studies" (with essays for: critical studies, Shakespeare's life, times, and stage, and editions and textual studies).   PR2888.C3

Handbooks

Boyce, Charles. Shakespeare A to Z : the essential reference to his plays, his poems, his life and times, and more / Charles Boyce ; David White, editorial consultant. N.Y. : Facts on File, c1990. 742 p. : ill.   **BE783**

"This book is not meant as scholarship; my intention has been to assemble conveniently a body of lore for the information and entertainment of the student and general reader."—*Pref.* Entries include synopses of the plays, names of characters, actors, scholars, Shakespeare's contemporaries, place-names, etc. There is a list of suggested readings, but sources of information for the individual articles are not supplied. Cross-references are signalled by use of small capitals in the text of articles. The appendix provides alphabetical lists of names of actors, characters, contemporaries, etc.

§ Still of value: James Oscar Campbell, *The reader's encyclopedia of Shakespeare* (N.Y. : Crowell, [1966]), and Frank Ernest Halliday, *A Shakespeare companion, 1564–1964* (Rev. ed. N.Y. : Schocken Books, [1964]). PR2892.B69

The Cambridge companion to Shakespeare studies / ed. by Stanley Wells. Cambridge ; N.Y. : Cambridge Univ. Pr., 1986. 329 p. **BE784**

Originally publ. as *A companion to Shakespeare studies*, ed. by Harley Granville-Barker and G. B. Harrison (Cambridge, 1934). Publ. in 1971 as *A new companion to Shakespeare studies*, ed. by Kenneth Muir and Samuel Schoenbaum.

Represents a substantial revision of the 1971 ed. with more emphasis on the plays in performance and new critical approaches. Comprised of 17 chapters dealing with Shakespeare's biography, the thought of his time, playhouses and players in Shakespeare's time, theatrical conventions and production history, critical approaches both historically and currently, Shakespeare on film and television, etc. Essays conclude with a list of suggested readings. Index and illustrations. An "excellent, informative compendium." —*Times literary supplement* (Oct. 30–Nov. 5, 1987) :1197. PR2976.C29

William Shakespeare : his world, his work, his influence / John F. Andrews, ed. N.Y. : Scribner, c1985. 3 v. : ill. **BE785**

Contents: v. 1, His world; v. 2, His work; v. 3, His influence.

"Designed to provide a multifaceted twentieth-century view of Shakespeare for the same kind of audience the compilers of the First Folio addressed in 1623 as 'the great variety of readers.' "—*Introd.* Each volume constitutes a series of signed essays (with selective bibliographies) which together explore "virtually every aspect of the phenomenon we refer to as Shakespeare." The first ten essays in v. 1 deal with major institutions and professions (government, religion, law, education, etc.) while the second ten treat subjects such as travel, dress, fine arts, and sports. In v. 2, the first ten essays are meant to provide a broad background (Shakespeare's life, professional career, language, dramatic method, etc.) for the following ten which deal with the works generically and topically, while v. 3 "offers a variety of perspectives on Shakespeare's reception and influence." Contributors (American and British, with two exceptions) are mainly academics but include names from the theater such as John Gielgud, Jonathan Miller and John Simon. Illustrations are fully described in v. 3, which includes a general index to the set. PR2976.W5354

Sources

Bullough, Geoffrey. Narrative and dramatic sources of Shakespeare. London : Routledge and Paul ; N.Y. : Columbia Univ. Pr., 1957–75. 8 v. **BE786**

Contents: v. 1, Early comedies, poems, *Romeo and Juliet* (1957, 1961); v. 2, The comedies, 1597–1603 (1958); v. 3, Earlier English history plays: *Henry VI*, Richard III, *Richard II* (1960); v. 4, Later English history plays: *King John, Henry IV, Henry V, Henry VIII* (1962); v. 5, The Roman plays: *Julius Caesar, Antony and Cleopatra, Coriolanus* (1964); v. 6, Other "classical" plays: *Titus Andronicus, Troilus and Cressida, Timon of Athens, Pericles, Prince of Tyre* (1966); v. 7, Major tragedies: *Hamlet, Othello, King Lear, Macbeth* (1973); v. 8, Romances: *Cymbeline, The Winter's Tale, The Tempest* (1975).

These volumes bring together sources, probable sources, and analogues for the poems and plays. The methodology employed has been "to sketch the conditions in which each of the plays was written, to relate Shakespeare's treatment of plot and character to earlier versions of the same basic material, and to illustrate in some detail ... how he adapted, combined, and transcended his sources."—*Pref., v. 8.* Intro-

ductory essays for individual plays; each volume includes a bibliography (general works, editions, sources and analogues, critical studies of sources). PR2952.5.B8

Muir, Kenneth. The sources of Shakespeare's plays. New Haven, Conn. : Yale Univ. Pr., 1978. 320 p. **BE787**

First publ. 1977 in the U.K.

Provides in one volume succinct discussions of the sources of the plays (but not the poems). Does not reproduce the sources.

PR2952.M84

Characters

McLeish, Kenneth. Longman guide to Shakespeare's characters : a who's who of Shakespeare. Burnt Mill, Eng. : Longman, 1985. 264 p. **BE788**

A dictionary of all Shakespeare's characters. Includes a summary of each of the 38 plays.

§ For historical contemporaries *see*: Alan Warwick Palmer, *Who's who in Shakespeare's England* (N.Y. : St. Martin's, 1981), which covers English men and women of national or local influence for the years 1590–1623. PR2989.M35

Stokes, Francis Griffin. A dictionary of the characters and proper names in the works of Shakespeare : with notes on the sources and dates of the plays and poems. London : Harrap , Boston : Houghton, 1924. 359 p. **BE789**

Repr. : N.Y. : Dover Publ., [1970].

Includes, in one alphabet, titles of Shakespeare's works, with brief account of first editions, sources, etc.; names of all characters—historical, legendary, and fictitious—with brief analysis of the dramatic action of each; names used as allusions; place-names; and miscellaneous names, such as seasons, planets, etc. Gives exact reference to play, act, and line, and some bibliographical references to sources of further information. PR2892.S67

Miscellaneous topics

Hotaling, Edward R. Shakespeare and the musical stage : a guide to sources, studies, and first performances. Boston : G.K. Hall, 1990. 517 p. **BE790**

An alphabetical listing by composer giving, when available, the author of the text; type of composition (e.g., opera, Broadway show, etc.); number of acts; language; place and date of premiere; source of information about the premiere; publisher of earliest published vocal score; sources maintaining that the work was based on a Shakespeare play; comments; and cast. At the end of the volume, the information is sorted into lists by title, city, date of premiere, text, and play. There are also lists, with call numbers, of items held by the Library of Congress and the British Library. ML128.O4H68

Rothwell, Kenneth Sprague. Shakespeare on screen : an international filmography and videography / Kenneth S. Rothwell and Annabelle Henkin Melzer. N.Y. : Neal-Schuman, c1990. 404 p. : ill. **BE791**

Lists and describes more than 750 films and videotapes—including major adaptations, spinoffs, musical and dance versions, abridgments, travesties, and excerpts; documentaries; and television performances in the U.S., Great Britain, Europe, and South America—which were produced or released between 1899 and 1989. Entries, listed alphabetically by the title of the play, and chronologically by date, provide basic factual information (dates, location of first showing, medium, authorship, distribution and availability), and several paragraphs of description and evaluation, with quotations from critics. Documentaries on general topics are listed together at the end of the volumes. Separate indexes list plays; series and genres; dates; actors and speakers; members of the production team; and authors, critics, and editors. PR3093.R68

Shakespeare around the globe : a guide to notable postwar revivals / ed. by Samuel L. Leiter ; assoc. ed., Langdon Brown ... [et al.]. N.Y. : Greenwood, 1986. 972 p.   **BE792**

A detailed guide by various scholars, critics, and artists to 502 notable worldwide postwar productions, arranged alphabetically by play, then chronologically by production. Introductions for individual plays give a historical overview of the play's postwar history, attending primarily to revivals not given their own entries. Entries include (when available) director, designers, composers, translators, company, city, and date; many also give production runs and an abbreviated cast list. Salient features of each production are outlined. A bibliography of sources is provided for each play. Excluded are musical and operatic adaptations (except for the Broadway version of *Two gentlemen of Verona*), television and film productions, and "textually radical or deconstructed versions of the plays, parodistic or serious"—*Pref.* Appendixes: additional revivals; geographical breakdown of productions. Includes a selective bibliography of books dealing with postwar productions. Indexes for artists, critics, and companies.

§ Less useful and faulted for errors and inconsistencies is William Babula's *Shakespeare in production, 1935–1978 : a selective catalogue* (N.Y. : Garland, 1981).   PR3100.S53

Shattuck, Charles Harlen. The Shakespeare promptbooks : a descriptive catalogue. Urbana : Univ. of Illinois Pr., 1965. 553 p.   **BE793**

A catalog of approximately 2,000 promptbooks dating from the early 17th century through 1961. Arrangement is alphabetical by play, then chronological by production. The most complete entries include actor/actress/stage manager, etc., date and place of production, library holding location, a physical description of the promptbook, and a note about its markup. Includes an essay on symbols and abbreviations used in older promptbooks. Detailed index.   PR3091.S4

Sugden, Edward Holdsworth. Topographical dictionary to the works of Shakespeare and his fellow dramatists. Manchester : Univ. Pr. ; London ; N.Y. : Longmans, 1925. 580 p. : ill., maps. (University of Manchester. Publications, 168).   **BE794**

Repr.: Hildesheim ; N.Y. : G. Olms, 1969.

Offers lists of place-names, i.e., countries, towns, rivers, and streets, with a brief article about each and exact reference to the play in which it occurs, and references to sources of further information. Includes also the place-names of Milton and some references to Spenser.   PR2892.S8

Velz, John W. Shakespeare and the classical tradition : a critical guide to commentary, 1660–1960. Minneapolis : Univ. of Minnesota Pr., [1968]. 459 p.   **BE795**

An annotated bibliography of 300 years of scholarship (2,487 entries) dealing with Shakespeare's relationship to the classical tradition. Includes scholarship in English, French, and German excepting "anti-Stratfordian speculations, psychoanalytic studies, most editions of the plays and poems, reviews, and German dissertations and *Schulprogramme.*"—*Pref.* Beginning with the mid-1930s, American dissertations are listed. A classified arrangement, with sections for general works, the comedies, etc. Detailed annotations are critical as well as descriptive.   Z8811.V4

Wells, Stanley W. William Shakespeare, a textual companion / by Stanley Wells and Gary Taylor ... [et al.]. Oxford : Clarendon Pr. ; N.Y. : Oxford Univ. Pr., 1987. 671 p. : ill.   **BE796**

Written in conjunction with editorial work done for the *Complete Oxford Shakespeare*, published in modern spelling and original spelling editions in 1986. Chapters for individual plays include an introductory essay, a series of textual notes, rejected variants, incidentals, and stage directions. Review: *Shakespeare quarterly*, 38:4 (Winter 1987) : 501–519.   PR3071.W44

Ireland

Anglo-Irish literature : a bibliography of dissertations, 1873–1989 / comp. by William T. O'Malley. N.Y. : Greenwood, 1990. 299 p. (Bibliographies and indexes in world literature, no. 26).   **BE797**

Identifies 4,359 dissertations from the U.S., Great Britain, Europe, Commonwealth nations, U.S.S.R., Egypt, Japan, and the Philippines. In two main sections: (1) Author studies, which lists works on 193 Anglo-Irish authors; (2) General and topical studies. Author and subject indexes.   Z2037.A54

Anglo-Irish literature : a review of research / ed. by Richard J. Finneran. N.Y. : Modern Language Association of America, 1976. 596 p.   **BE798**

Provides critical bibliographic "essays on writers of Anglo-Irish background whose careers have been completed and who have been the subject of a substantial body of published research."—*Pref.* Includes chapters (each by a specialist) on general works, 19th-century writers, Oscar Wilde, George Moore, Bernard Shaw, W. B. Yeats, J. M. Synge, James Joyce, "Four Revival Figures" (Lady Gregory, A. E., Gogarty, James Stephens), Sean O'Casey, and modern drama. Indexed.

§ Supplemented by: *Recent research on Anglo-Irish writers : a supplement to Anglo-Irish literature, a review of research* / ed. by Richard J. Finneran (N.Y. : Modern Language Association of America, 1983), which updates the information to 1980 (except for the section on George Moore, which ends with 1979) and adds sections on modern fiction and modern poetry.   PR8712.A5

A biographical dictionary of Irish writers / [ed. by] Anne M. Brady and Brian Cleeve. N.Y. : St. Martin's, 1985. 387 p.   **BE799**

A revised and expanded version of Brian T. Cleeve's *Dictionary of Irish writers* (Cork : Mercier Pr., 1967–1971. 3 v.).

Aims "to offer as much biographical and critical material as possible in the given space, about as many Irish writers as possible, from the time of St. Patrick to the present day."—*Pref.* Separate sections for writers in English and writers in Irish and Latin. Includes nonfiction and academic writers, with particular attention given to contemporary figures.   PR8727.B5

Brown, Stephen James. A guide to books on Ireland. Dublin : Figgis ; London : Longmans, 1912. 371 p.   **BE800**

Repr. : N.Y. : Lemma, 1970.

Pt. 1, Prose literature, poetry, music and plays. Pts. 2 and 3 planned but not published.

Dated but still considered a standard and informative work for earlier bibliography. Most entries are annotated, many extensively, and provide information such as detailed contents notes, plot summaries, quotations from reviews, and cast requirements and production history for drama.

§ Companion work by Brown: *Ireland in fiction : a guide to Irish novels, tales, romances, and folk-lore* (New ed. London ; Dublin : Maunsel, 1919. Various reprints). An author list of 1,713 novels in English with descriptive annotations and some biographical notes. "Includes all works of fiction published in volume form, and dealing with Ireland or with the Irish abroad."—*Pref.* Appendixes include: useful works of reference, publishers and series, classified lists of novels (historical fiction, Catholic clerical life, humorous books, etc.), and periodical fiction. Title and subject index.   Z2031.B86

Cahalan, James M. Modern Irish literature and culture : a chronology. N.Y. : G.K. Hall ; N.Y. : Maxwell Macmillan Internat., c1993. 374 p.   **BE801**

In order by year beginning with 1601, with an entry for every year since 1858. Information for each year is arranged in categories— fiction, drama, poetry, art, prose nonfiction, periodicals, etc.—with historical and political information provided for context at the beginning of a year's entry where the author judged appropriate. There is a section of biographical entries for recurring figures, and a map. Index of persons, titles, and subjects. PR8718.C35

Dictionary of Irish literature / Robert Hogan, ed. in chief. Westport, Conn. : Greenwood, [1979]. 815 p. **BE802**

"The bulk of the dictionary is made up of biographical and critical essays on approximately five hundred Irish authors who wrote mainly in the English language."—*Pref.* A few foreign authors who "have made a rich and lasting contribution to Irish literature" are included; there are "a handful of general articles on topics such as folklore, which have been of major importance to literature"; and a number of entries for literary organizations or publications. Bibliographies of works by and about the authors are included; many of the articles are signed by contributors. A special section on Gaelic literature by Seamus O'Neill, and material on the history of Irish writing in English precede the dictionary proper. There is a chronology, a general bibliography, and an index. PR8706.D5

Hyde, Douglas. A literary history of Ireland from earliest times to the present day / by Douglas Hyde ; new ed. with introd. by Brian Ó Cuív. N.Y. : St. Martin's, [1980]. 654 p. **BE803**

First publ. by T. Fisher Unwin, 1899. This is a reprint, with a revised bibliography, of the 1967 ed. (London : Benn ; N.Y. : Barnes & Noble), which itself was a reprint, with a new introduction, of the 1899 ed.

An important and groundbreaking work which, according to the current editor, has not been superseded (*Introd.*). Extensive notes and many quotations in translation. Index. The reprint has an introduction and bibliography added by Ó Cuív.

§ Sources that supplement and update Hyde include Seamus Deane, *A short history of Irish literature* (London : Hutchinson ; Notre Dame, Ind. : Notre Dame Univ. Pr., 1986) and Patrick C. Power, *A literary history of Ireland* (Cork : Mercier Pr., 1969). Deane is stronger for the 20th century and Power for the earlier periods. A more specialized focus is provided by Maurice Harmon and Roger McHugh, *A short history of Anglo-Irish literature from its origins to the present day* (Totowa, N.J. : Barnes & Noble, 1982.). PB1306.H8

Kersnowski, Frank L. A bibliography of modern Irish and Anglo-Irish literature / by Frank L. Kersnowski, C. W. Spinks, Laird Loomis. San Antonio, Tex. : Trinity Univ. Pr., c1976. 157 p. **BE804**

Lists both primary and secondary material for approximately 60 major writers of fiction, poetry, and drama in Ireland, 1878–1973. Includes "all collected and selected works, first editions, or individual titles, revised and enlarged editions, books edited or translated by the writers, books for which the authors wrote introductory material, and book length critical studies about the writers themselves."—*Pref.* Entries are not annotated. Z2037.K47

Lane, Denis. Modern Irish literature / comp. and ed. by Denis Lane and Carol McCrory Lane. N.Y. : Ungar, 1988. 736 p. **BE805**

Like other volumes in the "Library of literary criticism" series, this is a selection of criticism on the works of individual authors. Covers 87 20th-century authors from both Northern Ireland and the Republic of Ireland. Entries for authors are arranged chronologically; the earliest selections date from the turn of the century. A primary bibliography is provided for each author; index of critics. PR8753.L36

McKenna, Brian. Irish literature, 1800–1875 : a guide to information sources. Detroit : Gale, c1978. 388 p. (Gale information guide library. American literature, English literature, and world literatures in English information guide series, v. 13). **BE806**

An annotated bibliography in two sections: (1) Background and research and (2) Individual authors. Pt. 1 is divided into sections covering anthologies; periodicals; bibliography, biography, and criticism; and supplementary subjects including current awareness and research, Irish literature and Irish antiquities, and Irish history. Pt. 2 lists both primary and secondary works for more than 100 writers. Pt. 1 and lists of secondary criticism in Pt. 2 are selective, but lists of primary works by writers aim to be complete. Author, title, and subject indexes. Z2037.M235

O'Donoghue, David James. The poets of Ireland : a biographical and bibliographical dictionary of Irish writers of English verse. Dublin : Figgis ; London : Frowde, 1912. 504 p. **BE807**

Repr. : N.Y. : Johnson Reprint Corp., [1970, c1968].

Although dated, still invaluable for the many obscure poets O'Donoghue located in newspapers and periodicals and for his extensive detective work to locate biographical and bibliographical information. Z2037.O26

Scotland

Aitken, William Russell. Scottish literature in English and Scots : a guide to information sources. Detroit : Gale, [1982]. 421 p. (American literature, English literature, and world literatures in English, v. 37). **BE808**

A bibliography supporting the study of an independent Scottish literary tradition. A section listing general works is followed by four chronological sections (medieval through 20th century, each subdivided for general works and individual authors), and a final section for popular and folk literature. Author, title, and subject indexes.

§ Beginning in 1969 the *Annual bibliography of Scottish literature*, issued as a supplement to the periodical *The bibliotheck*, and in 1974 *The year's work in Scottish literary and linguistic studies*, published as an additional issue of the *Scottish literary journal* (previously *Scottish literary news*), provide ongoing bibliographic coverage of Scottish literature. Z2057.A35

Bold, Alan Norman. Scotland : a literary guide. London : Routledge, 1989. 327 p. **BE809**

Arranged alphabetically by place, with entries for towns, castles, abbeys, lakes, bridges, etc. Includes information on the history and geography of the place, followed by chronological entries for individual authors with quotations from literary works. Author index. PR8531.D65

Geddie, William. A bibliography of middle Scots poets : with an introduction on the history of their reputations. Edinburgh : print. for the Scottish Text Society by Blackwood, 1912. 364 p. (Scottish Text Society. Publication, 61). **BE810**

A comprehensive and descriptive bibliography of editions and secondary works relating to fourteen middle Scots poets. An extensive introduction followed by a section of general works, then a section for each writer. The lists of secondary works, in chronological order beginning with the earliest available, are particularly strong for biographical information and often include lengthy excerpts and annotations.

§ Complemented and updated for criticism through the 1970s for four of these poets by Walter Scheps and Anna Looney, *Middle Scots poets : a reference guide to James I of Scotland, Robert Henryson, William Dunbar, and Gavin Douglas* (Boston : G.K. Hall, 1986). Titles only for primary works. Annotations for references to criticism. Separate index for each author.

A selective but useful and up-to-date general survey is Duncan Glen, *The poetry of the Scots : an introduction and bibliographical guide to poetry in Gaelic, Scots, Latin, and English* (Edinburgh : Edinburgh Univ. Pr., 1991). Sections for background studies and anthologies and magazines, then arranged by chronological eras, each with an introduction. Lists primary and secondary works, with many lengthy annotations. Index of poets and general index. PR8633.S4

Royle, Trevor. Companion to Scottish literature. Detroit : Gale, 1983. 322 p. **BE811**

British ed. publ. as *The Macmillan companion to Scottish literature* (London : Macmillan, 1983).

Aims "to provide an alphabetical list of references to Scotland's literature from earliest times to the present day. Its backbone is supplied by the biographical essays devoted to the principal poets, novelists, dramatists, critics and men of letters who have written in English, Scots or Gaelic and whose work constitutes the main corpus of Scottish literature."—*Introd.* Also includes entries for individual literary works, periodicals, terms, etc. Bibliographies of authors' works; some references to biographical and critical studies.   PR8511.R67

Wales

Handley-Taylor, Geoffrey. Authors of Wales today. London : Eddison Pr. Ltd., 1972. 76 p.   **BE812**

Subtitle: Being a checklist of authors born in Wales, together with brief particulars of authors born elsewhere who are currently working or residing in Wales ... an assemblage of more than 600 authors together with addresses and (where applicable) their pseudonyms.

Brief biographical information for authors writing in English and in Welsh. Includes novelists, poets, dramatists, journalists, clerics, academics, government officials, business professionals, and others, resident in Wales or abroad. Provides references to inclusion in 63 other standard biographical sources. Dated but still useful for the wide coverage and for references to further sources, which could provide more current information.   Z2077.H35

Jones, Brynmor. A bibliography of Anglo-Welsh literature, 1900–1965. [Swansea] : Wales and Monmouthshire Branch of the Libr. Assoc., 1970. 139 p.   **BE813**

Includes "writers of Welsh birth or extraction who write imaginative literature in English, locating their narratives against a Welsh background and portraying Welsh characters and idiom" and works "set in a Welsh locale, though their authors are not necessarily of Welsh birth."—*Introd.* Separate sections for the literature and for bibliographical and critical materials.   Z2013.3.J64

The Oxford companion to the literature of Wales / comp. and ed. by Meic Stephens. Oxford ; N.Y. : Oxford Univ. Pr., 1986. 682 p.   **BE814**

"This book was commissioned by Yr Academi Gymreig (The Welsh Academy)"—*verso of t.p.*

A new addition to the "Oxford companion" series, covering the literature of Wales from the 6th century to the present. "Some 2,825 entries have been included, of which nearly twelve hundred, the core of the work, deal with authors. Most of the authors listed are writing in the Welsh language, but also included is a selection of those Welsh men and women who have written in English, Latin and, in at least two instances, dialects of Norman French."—*Pref.* Cross-references; some brief bibliographies. Chronology of the history of Wales, p. 675–82.   PB2361.O94

Commonwealth

Modern Commonwealth literature / comp. and ed. by John H. Ferres and Martin Tucker. [N.Y. : Ungar, 1977]. 561 p.   **BE815**

Part of the series, "Library of literary criticism." Offers excerpts from critical writings on authors from Commonwealth countries (including some former Commonwealth nations) throughout the world. Authors are grouped by region: Africa, Australia, Canada, the Caribbean, the Indian subcontinent, New Zealand. Selection was "based on four principal considerations: modernity (writers whose works and influence belong wholly or predominantly to the twentieth century), the author's general reputation at home as well as in Britain and the United States; the existence of worthwhile criticism, particularly in English; and availability of the author's work in the original or in English translation."—*Introd.* Index of critics.   PR9080.M6

New, William H. Critical writings on Commonwealth literatures : a selective bibliography to 1970, with a list of theses and dissertations. University Park : Pennsylvania State Univ. Pr., [1975]. 333 p.   **BE816**

The single most comprehensive bibliography on criticism of Commonwealth literature. A general section is followed by sections for Africa (East and West), Australia, Canada, New Zealand, South Africa and Rhodesia, South Asia, Southeast Asia, and West Indies. A theses and dissertations section is also divided geographically. Includes research aids, general studies, and studies of individual authors. Omits the United Kingdom and the Mediterranean area. Index of critics, editors, translators.

§ Can be updated by the "Annual bibliography of Commonwealth literature" (in the Dec. issue of *Journal of Commonwealth literature*), which usually includes sections for general studies, East and Central Africa, Western Africa, Australia, Canada, India, Malaysia and Singapore, New Zealand, Sri Lanka, the West Indies, Pakistan, and South Africa. A brief essay on significant publications and developments introduces each section.   Z2000.9.N48

Walsh, William. Commonwealth literature. London ; N.Y. : Oxford Univ. Pr., 1973. 150 p.   **BE817**

Signed entries on 120 writers. Each includes biographical information, comprehensive list of book-length works with title and date, selected citations to bibliographical and critical studies, and a critical essay. Introduction and reading list by the editor, notes on contributors. Does not provide criteria for selection.   PR9080.W28

Warwick, Ronald. Commonwealth literature periodicals : a bibliography, including periodicals of former Commonwealth countries, with locations in the United Kingdom. London : Mansell, 1979. 146 p.   **BE818**

At head of title: Working Party on Library Holdings of Commonwealth Literature.

Arranged geographically, with title index. For each title, notes dates, frequency, publisher, editor(s), appropriate cross-references to related titles, and locations. Covers Africa, Australia, Canada, the Caribbean, Hong Kong, Malaysia and Singapore, the Mediterranean, Pacific Islands, South Asia, and former Commonwealth countries.   Z2000.9.W37

Canada

The annotated bibliography of Canada's major authors / ed. by Robert Lecker and Jack David. Downsview, Ont. : ECW Pr. ; Boston : Distr. by G.K. Hall, 1979–1987. v. 1–7. (In progress).   **BE819**

To be in ten volumes, half devoted to prose and half to poetry, each volume covering five writers. Includes French and English-language authors of the the 19th and 20th centuries and aims to provide a comprehensive listing of works by and about each author. Entries for criticism are substantially annotated. Arrangement of authors is alphabetical in each volume but not throughout the series. Index to critics at the end of each bibliography.

§ Two other series, providing biographical and critical information as well as bibliographies of works by and about writers of the last two centuries are: *Canadian writers and their works : poetry series*, ed. Robert Lecker, Jack Davis, and Ellen Quigley, (Toronto : ECW Pr., 1983–1985; vols. 1–3, 5, 6, 9. [In progress]) and the same editors' *Canadian writers and their works : fiction series*, (1983–1989, vols. 1–3, 5–10. [In progress]). Each volume has an introductory essay by George Woodcock and chapters on four or five writers, providing for each a lengthy biographical and critical essay, with extensive quotations from texts, followed by a bibliography. Author and title index in each volume.

Another useful set is *Profiles in Canadian literature*, ed. by Jeffrey Heath (Toronto : Dundurn Pr., 1980–86, 6 series in 3 vols.) which provides signed profiles of 87 English- and French-speaking authors. For each includes a portrait, a critical essay, a chronology, excerpts from the writer's work and from criticism, and a selected bibliography of works by and about the author. Entries are chronological in each volume. No indexes. Z1375.A56

The Brock bibliography of published Canadian plays in English, 1766–1978 / ed. by Anton Wagner ; comp. by Bonita J. Orosz Bryan… [et al.]. [2nd ed.]. Toronto : Playwrights Pr., 1980. 375 p. **BE820**

1st ed., covering 1900–1972, publ. 1972; suppl. publ. 1973.

Lists both Canadian plays in English and French-Canadian plays translated into English. Plays are grouped by century, then listed alphabetically by author. Gives publication data for each play, number of scenes, cast requirements, and a statement of the theme of the play. Short-title index. Z1377.D7B75

Canada's playwrights : a biographical guide / ed. by Don Rubin and Alison Cranmer-Byng. Toronto : Canadian Theatre Review Pubns., 1980. 191 p. : ill. **BE821**

Offers biographical sketches of contemporary playwrights, with lists of stage works (including publication and production data as applicable), other writings, and secondary sources as available. PR9191.5.C3

Canadian literature index. 1985–1988. Toronto : ECW Pr., c1987–1992. **BE822**

Editor, Janet Fraser.

The initial volume was publ. in three quarterly issues, superseded by a cumulative volume. Other volumes covered one year's work.

An extremely useful index to approximately 100 Canadian and international literary journals, popular magazines, and newspapers. A review in *American reference books annual* (19 (1988): 495, calls it "an essential purchase for libraries serving patrons interested in Canadian literature." In two parts: an author index and one by subjects. Includes references to book reviews. Some entries briefly annotated.

§ A new title, *Canadian literary periodicals index*, ed. Gordon Ripley and Jane McQuarrie, has been announced (Teeswater, Ont. : Reference Pr.). Volumes covering 1992 and 1993 are scheduled for publication in 1994. Two older, short-lived indexes were *Canadian essays and collections index*, 1971–72 (Ottawa : Canadian Libr. Assoc., 1976) and *Canadian essay and literature index*, 1973–75 (Toronto : Univ. of Toronto Pr., 1975–77). Z1375.C3

Fee, Margery. Canadian fiction : an annotated bibliography. [Toronto] : Peter Martin Associates, [1976]. 170 p. **BE823**

A bibliography of "Canadian literary prose" for the teacher, student, librarian and general reader. A section on secondary sources is followed by separate sections for "Novel annotations" and "Short story annotations." There is a title index and a "subject guide" to the novels, and separate author and title indexes for the short stories. Z1377.F4F4

——————— Canadian fiction : an annotated bibliography / Margery Fee, Ruth Cawker. [Toronto] : Peter Martin Associates, [1976]. 170 p. **BE824**

A bibliography of "Canadian literary prose" for the teacher, student, librarian and general reader. A section on secondary sources is followed by separate sections for "Novel annotations" and "Short story annotations." There is a title index and a subject guide to the novels, and separate author and title indexes for the short stories. Z1377.F4F4

Harvard University. Library. Canadian history and literature : classification schedule, classified listing by call number, alphabetical listing by author or title, chronological listing. Cambridge : Harvard Univ. Lib. : Distr. by Harvard Univ. Pr., 1968. 411 p. (Widener Library shelflist, 20). **BE825**

For a note on the series, *see* AA115.

More than 10,000 titles. Z1365.H3

Klinck, Carl Frederick. Literary history of Canada : Canadian literature in English. 2nd ed. Toronto : Univ. of Toronto Pr., 1976–1990. 4 v. **BE826**

The 1st ed. (1965. 1 v.) provided the first comprehensive history of Canadian literature in English from the beginning to 1960. The first 3 v. of the new ed. (1976), covered to 1920, 1920–60, and 1960–73. Vol. 4 (1990, ed. by William H. New) covers 1972–84. All volumes consist of chapters contributed by scholars.

Indispensable in a library supporting the study of Canadian literature, although the bibliographic apparatus, at least in the first three volumes, is less than satisfactory. Notes are highly selective and for some chapters are omitted altogether, although those in v. 4 are more comprehensive and thorough. There are extensive bibliographic references in the text, but other sources give more complete bibliographic information.

§ Virtually a companion is: *A checklist of Canadian literature and background materials, 1628–1960* (2nd ed., rev. and enl. Toronto : Univ. of Toronto Press, 1972), by Reginald Eyre Watters. In two parts, the first attempting to be an exhaustive list of poetry, fiction, and drama by English-speaking Canadians, the second, a selective list of works by Canadians on biography, literary criticism, local history, religion, bibliography, etc.

Another companion work, providing information on secondary materials, is by Watters and Inglis Freeman Bell: *On Canadian literature, 1806–1960 : a checklist of articles, books, and theses on English-Canadian literature, its authors, and language* (Toronto : Univ. of Toronto Press, 1966). Modeled roughly on Lewis Leary's *Articles on American literature, 1900–1950* (BE408), it lists biographical, critical, and scholarly writings on English-Canadian literature, both general works and those on individual authors. From 1959 to 1971 (when they ceased), bibliographies published in the spring issue of the journal *Canadian literature* can be used as updates. PR9184.3.K5

McQuarrie, Jane. Index to Canadian poetry in English / comp. and ed. by Jane McQuarrie, Anne Mercer, Gordon Ripley. Toronto : Reference Pr., 1984. 367 p. **BE827**

Modeled on *The Columbia Granger's index to poetry* (BE315). Locates about 7,000 poems in 51 anthologies, providing title and first line, author, and subject indexes. Z1377.P7

Miska, John P. Ethnic and native Canadian literature : a bibliography. Toronto : Univ. of Toronto Pr., 1990. 445 p. **BE828**

Lists 5,497 publications by ethnic immigrants to Canada and by Native Americans in Canada, or about ethnic and native literature in Canada. In three main sections: (1) Reference works; (2) Nationality/language groups, which makes up the main part of the volume; (3) Minorities in Canadian literature, which lists works on the portrayal of immigrants and Native Americans. Name index. Derived in part from the author's *Ethnic and native Canadian literature, 1850–1979* (Lethbridge, Alta. : Microform Biblios, c1980). Z1373.E87M57

Moritz, A. F. The Oxford illustrated literary guide to Canada / Albert and Theresa Moritz. Toronto ; N.Y. : Oxford Univ. Pr., 1987. 246 p. : ill. **BE829**

"More than 500 entries detail the literary associations of cities, towns, villages, hamlets, and even rivers and islands … [or] describe and provide anecdotes about the careers and residences, and moves from place to place" (*Pref.*) of Canadian writers. Geographical arrangement; personal name index. Portraits outnumber literary sites among the illustrations.

§ A comparable source, more generous in the provision of photographs of places, is *Canadian literary landmarks*, by John Robert Colombo (Willowdale, Ont. : Hounslow Pr., 1984). PR9187.M67

Moyles, R. G. English-Canadian literature to 1900 : a guide to information sources. Detroit : Gale, 1976. 346 p. (American literature, English literature, and world literatures in English, v.6). **BE830**

Attempts "to provide a list of all the important primary and secondary sources necessary for a thorough study of this literature."— *Introd.* Includes general reference aids, literary histories and criticism, anthologies, plus sections for individual authors and for the literature of exploration and travel.

§ Continued for the 20th century by *Modern English-Canadian prose : a guide to information sources*, ed. by Helen Hoy (Detroit :

Gale, 1983); and *Modern English-Canadian poetry: a guide to information sources*, ed. by Peter Stevens (Detroit : Gale, 1978). Both follow Moyles in scope and arrangement. The volume for prose contains a section on nonfiction writers. Author, title, and subject indexes.
Z1375.M68

Naaman, Antoine. Guide bibliographique des thèses littéraires canadiennes de 1921 à 1976 / Antoine Naaman, avec la collab. de Léo A. Brodeur. Sherbrooke, Quebec : Éditions Naaman, [1978?]. 453 p.   **BE831**
1st ed., 1970, provided coverage through 1969.

An unannotated bibliography of approximately 5,600 dissertations and master's theses on topics dealing with Canadian and other world literatures, including linguistics and folklore, completed at Canadian universities. The first part is divided into sections on general topics such as literary history, genres, and comparative literature, and the second is devoted to studies of particular authors. There are indexes to authors, to directors of theses, to authors studied, to subjects of theses, and to particular works studied. The first edition also contained a useful bibliography of background works for the study of literature.

§ A less comprehensive source useful for updating the above is *Canadian literature: an index to theses accepted by Canadian universities, 1925–1980*, by Gernot U. Gabel (Cologne : Edition Gemini, 1984). Only lists studies on Canadian literature.   Z6511.N25

National Library of Canada. Literary manuscripts at the National Library of Canada = Les manuscrits littéraires à la Bibliothèque nationale du Canada / by Linda Hoad. 2nd ed., rev. and enl. Ottawa : The Library, 1990. 61 p. : ill.   **BE832**
1st ed., 1984.

Intended "to serve as an introduction to the library's unpublished resources in the field of Canadian literature."—*Introd.* Lists and describes approximately 100 collections, with an index of personal names and a chronological table of collections.   Z6621.N278N37

The Oxford companion to Canadian literature / gen. ed., William Toye. Toronto ; N.Y. : Oxford Univ. Pr., 1983. 843 p.   **BE833**

Based on the literary component of *The Oxford companion to Canadian history and literature*, ed. by Norah Story (Toronto ; N.Y. [etc.] : Oxford Univ. Pr., 1968, c1967. 935 p.), and its *Supplement*, ed. by William Toye (1973. 318 p.), but greatly expanded in range and depth of coverage. Entries for writers and genres predominate, the former including novelists, poets, dramatists, biographers, philosophers, and some authors of children's books; the latter extending to criticism, essays, translations, humor and satire, mystery and crime fiction, science fiction, and travel literature, as well as the expected categories. Includes extensive surveys of novels in English, novels in French, and regional literature. French-Canadian literature and writers are treated at length. Emphasis on modern writing, particularly that of the last forty years. Articles are signed and include bibliographies.

§ See also: *The Oxford companion to Canadian theatre*, ed. by Eugene Benson and Leonard W. Conolly (BH73), for more extensive information on theater and drama.   PS8015.O93

Sylvestre, Guy. Canadian writers = Écrivains canadiens / a biographical dictionary ed. by Guy Sylvestre, Brandon Conron [and] Carl F. Klinck. New [3rd] ed. rev. and enl. Toronto : Ryerson Pr., 1967. 186 p.   **BE834**
1st ed., 1964; 2nd ed. ("new ed."), 1966.

A biographical dictionary containing information on about 350 Canadian authors. Articles appear in English or French according to the language of the biographee's writings. Includes a literary chronology, a brief general bibliography, and a useful index of titles of literary works mentioned in the biographies.   PR9127.S9

Weiss, Allan Barry. A comprehensive bibliography of English-Canadian short stories, 1950–1983. Toronto : ECW Pr., c1988. 973 p.   **BE835**

Records "the appearance of 14,314 short stories in 1,308 different periodicals, anthologies, and radio productions, as well as 391 author collections published in monograph form."—*Introd.* Lists the stories of 4,966 authors alphabetically with a title index.   Z1375.W46

Who's who in Canadian literature. 1983/1984– . Toronto : Reference Pr., 1983– . Biennial.   **BE836**
Publication suspended 1989–91.

Intended as "a general reference work, combining moderately complete bibliographical data with concise biographical information" for "living Canadian poets, playwrights, story writers, novelists, children's writers, critics, editors, or translators who have been active in the field of literature, and who have made some contribution to it."—*Pref.* Entries rely on information submitted by writers in response to questionnaires and provide standard "who's who" information with address, a list of publications including monographs, anthologies, and periodicals in which works have appeared, and work in progress. Entries for French-Canadian writers are in French. Occasional references to criticism. Title index.   PR9189.6.W47

Literature in French

Dictionnaire des oeuvres littéraires du Québec / sous la direction de Maurice Lemire. Montréal : Fides, 1978–1987. 5 v.   **BE837**

Contents: v. 1, Des origines à 1900; v. 2, 1900 à 1939; v. 3, 1940 à 1959; v. 4, 1960–1969; v. 5, 1970–1975. Some volumes in 2nd ed.

A monumental dictionary of signed entries providing plots, critical analyses, and references to criticism for hundreds of literary works by French-Canadian authors of Québec. In addition, biographical information on the author is given when one of this or her works is first included. Each volume begins with a lengthy overview of literature during the period covered, and includes a chronology and a substantial bibliography of primary and secondary works. Many illustrations. Author index in each volume.   PS8015D53

Dionne, René. Bibliographie de la critique de la littérature québecoise et canadienne-française dans les revues canadiennes / René Dionne et Pierre Cantin. [Ottawa] : Presses de l'Université d'Ottawa, c1988–1992. v. 1–3. (In progress).   **BE838**

Contents: v. 1, 1974–78 (publ. 1988); v. 2, 1979–82 (1991); v. 3, 1769–1899 (1992).

The first three volumes of a projected six that will provide comprehensive coverage of criticism on the literature of Quebec published in Canadian journals 1760– . If completed will supersede *Bibliographie de la critique de la littérature québécoise dans les revues des XIXe et XXe siècles*, by Pierre Cantin, Normand Harrington, Jean-Paul Hudon (Ottawa : Centre de recherche en civilization, 1979. 5 v.). Volumes for 1974– based in part on bibliographies appearing in *Revue d'histoire littéraire du Québec et du Canada français*. Volumes published thus far list more than 26,000 entries in a standard arrangement: general studies, genres, authors. Indexes are provided for critics, articles by journal title, and years. All three volumes provide a list of journals examined, and of issues not seen. Vol. 1 and 2 also provide lists of journals omitted.   Z1377.F8.D56

Fraser, Ian Forbes. Bibliography of French-Canadian poetry. N.Y. : Columbia Univ., c1935. 1 v.   **BE839**
Contents: Pt. I: From the beginnings of the litterature through the École littéraire de Montréal. No more published.

Covers general works on French-Canadian literature and poetry as well as providing bibliographies of works by and about individual poets. Also provides listings of general biographical and bibliographical sources and French-Canadian periodicals, and a bibliography of collections and studies of the French-Canadian folk song.

Grandpré, Pierre de. Histoire de la littérature française du Québec. Montréal : Librairie Beauchemin, 1967–69. 4 v.
BE840

Vol. 1 repr. 1971; v. 4 repr. 1973.

A collaborative history consisting largely of biobibliographical sections on authors with extensive selections from their works. Includes historians, journalists, and critics as well as literary figures. Profusely illustrated. Index in each volume.

§ A handier one-volume history is Gerard Tougas' *Histoire de la littérature canadienne-française* (4th ed. Paris : Presses Universitaires de France, 1967), which also appeared in English as *History of French-Canadian literature*, tr. by Alta Lind Cook (2nd ed. Toronto : Ryerson Pr., 1966. Repr.: Westport, Conn. : Greenwood, 1976). A survey arranged by period and genre. Includes sections on individual authors with selections from their works and critical analysis. Bibliographical references in footnotes. Author and title index.   PQ3917.G7

Hamel, Réginald. Dictionnaire des auteurs de langue française en Amérique du Nord / Réginald Hamel, John Hare, Paul Wyczynski. [Montréal] : Fidès, c1989. 1364 p.   **BE841**

Supersedes the same authors' *Dictionnaire pratique des auteurs québécois* (1976) expanded to include some U.S. writers. Provides biography, primary and secondary bibliography, and some photographs for more than 1,600 authors from the late 17th century to the early 1980s. Includes some nonliterary authors.

§ For contemporary writers, *Dictionnaire des écrivains québécois contemporains*, recherche et rédaction Yves Légaré (Montreal : Quebec/Amerique, 1983) provides biography, a list of works, occasionally a reference to criticism, and a photograph for French-Canadian authors who have published at least two books since 1970. The introduction is a useful overview of contemporary French-Canadian literature. §   PQ3900.2.H36

Hayne, David M. Bibliographie critique du roman canadien-français, 1837–1900 / David M. Hayne, Marcel Tirol. Toronto : Univ. of Toronto Pr., 1968. 144 p.   **BE842**

Concerned with the work of Canadian authors writing in French, this bibliography lists the editions (including serializations and published extracts), English translations, and significant studies of French-Canadian prose fiction. Many helpful notes and annotations. Indexed.

§ Continued chronologically by Antonio Drolet, *Bibliographie du roman canadien-français, 1900–1950* (Québec : Presses Universitaires de Laval, 1955). An author listing of 886 titles of French-Canadian novels, preceded by a list of critical studies. Title index.

Z1377.F8II3

Rinfret, Édouard G. Le théâtre canadien d'expression française : répertoire analytique des origines à nos jours. [Montréal] : Leméac, c1975–[c1978]. 4 v.   **BE843**

A solid and substantial dictionary. Vols. 1–3 list plays of all periods by author, giving for each: type of play, number of acts and scenes, cast requirements, plot, date and place of first production, and library locations. Vol. 4 provides a separate list of TV plays, 1952–1973, with a title index to the whole set and a chronological list of the broadcasts of the TV plays.   PQ3911.R5

University of British Columbia. Library. A checklist of printed materials relating to French-Canadian literature, 1763–1968. 2nd ed. Vancouver : Univ. of British Columbia Pr., 1973. 174 p.   **BE844**

Title also in French. Prefatory matter in English and French.

1st ed., 1958.

Gérard Tougas, comp.

Lists belles lettres and selected nonfiction and works on French-Canadian literature by French-Canadian authors writing in both French and English. Alphabetical by author.

§ A more up-to-date and helpfully annotated analytical guide to secondary materials in French and English for the study of French-Canadian literature is: *Guide de la littérature québécoise*, by Marcel Fortin, Yvan Lamonde, and François Richard (Montreal : Boreal, 1988). Covers reference works, histories, works on genres, comparative literature studies, linguistics, literary research, and works for historical and cultural context. Author index.   Z1377.F8B72

Australia

Adelaide, Debra. Australian women writers : a bibliographic guide. London : Pandora, 1988. 208 p.   **BE845**

Provides brief biographical information, a list of monographic publications, mention of other publishing endeavors (e.g., in periodicals), occasional references to secondary sources, and locations of manuscripts. Includes non-fiction writers. No index.

§ A more exhaustive version of this work subsequently appeared as: *Bibliography of Australian women's literature, 1795–1990* (Melbourne : D.W. Thorpe, in assoc. with the National Centre for Australian Studies, [1991]). Includes many more, and more obscure, authors. Biographical information is eliminated; bibliographies still limited largely to monographic publications and other information as noted above. No true index; indexing to names provided by an author checklist, followed by separate checklists for fiction writers, non-fiction authors, writers for children, playwrights, and poets. Both volumes would benefit from a title index.   PR9608.A3

Andrews, Barry G. Australian literature to 1900 : a guide to information sources / Barry G. Andrews, William H. Wilde. Detroit : Gale, [1980]. 472 p. (American literature, English literature, and world literatures in English, 22).   **BE846**

A selective, annotated bibliography, covering bibliographies, reference works, literary histories, periodicals, anthologies, Australian English, selected nonfiction, exploration and travel literature, history, and biography, as well as works by and about 66 individual authors. Provides brief biographical information for each author. Name and title indexes.

§ Supplemented for more recent information by two volumes in the same series:

(1) Arthur Grove Day, *Modern Australian prose, 1901–1975 : a guide to information sources* (Detroit : Gale, [1980]. [American literature, English literature, and world literatures in English, 29]. Similar in arrangement and methodology to Andrews and Wilde above. Covers prose fiction and drama, approximately 50 individual authors, and selected nonfiction including military and naval works, and aboriginal literature. Author, title, and subject indexes.

(2) Herbert C. Jaffa, *Modern Australian poetry, 1920–1970 : a guide to information sources* (Detroit : Gale, c1979. [American literature, English literature, and world literatures in English, 24]). Provides information on general bibliographies and reference materials, but the major focus is on individual poets and schools. For individual "major" and "established" poets, provides substantial analysis of published criticism as well as bibliography. Lengthy annotations for many works listed. For schools and for "other" and "younger" poets, provides an overview, with briefer bibliographical information for individuals. Author, title, and subject index.   Z4021.A54

Annual bibliography of studies in Australian literature. (*In* Australian literary studies : 1964–). Annual.   **BE847**

"Primarily devoted to commentaries useful to criticism and scholarship, the series aims to provide as complete a listing as possible of books and articles on Australian literature."—*Headnote to the 1990 bibliography*. A general section is followed by one on individual authors, arranged by name and including works published, reviews and critiques, and biographies. Valuable for the inclusion of newspaper reviews.

§ Bibliographies on individual authors covering 1963–90 have been cumulated as: *The ALS guide to Australian writers, 1963–1990*, ed. by Martin Duwell and Laurie Hergenhan (Queensland : Queensland Univ. Pr., 1992). Arranged under authors' names. Does not include the general sections.   PR9400.A86

Blake, Leslie James. Australian writers. [Adelaide] : Rigby, [1968]. 268 p.   **BE848**

A survey of Australian authors, 1788–1966, arranged in four categories: historians, biographers, novelists, poets. Offers a critical look at style, works, and where each writer's work fits in the genre. In addition, the many biographical and bibliographical notes and the commentary on Australian literary journals make this a useful reference aid. Includes a selective bibliography. Author and title index.

§ Aimed at a more popular audience, *Australia's writers*, by Graeme Kinross Smith (Melbourne : Nelson, 1980. 342 p.), provides 54 chronologically arranged chapters on the biography and works of individual writers born 1738–1920. Entries vary in length and contain extensive quotes from works or interviews. Many photographs. Brief selective bibliographies. Index to names, titles, and photographs.

Z4021.B55

Cuthbert, Eleanora Isabel. Index of Australian and New Zealand poetry. N.Y. : Scarecrow, 1963. 453 p.   **BE849**

Indexes the contents of 22 older anthologies and collections, published 1888–1960, by author, title, and first line.   Z4024.P7C8

Green, Henry Mackenzie. A history of Australian literature : pure and applied / by Henry Mackenzie Green ; rev. by Dorothy Green. London : Angus & Robertson, c1984. 2 v. (xlviii, 1543 p.).   **BE850**

1st ed., 1961.

A major and comprehensive history, born of "the grave need for serious and systematic criticism, not merely of individual Australian literary works but of Australian literature as a whole: for the presentation of a true picture of it."—*Pref.* Covers 1789–1950, in four time periods (1789–1850, 1850–1890, 1890–1923, 1923–1950); each period contains essays on fiction, verse, magazines, newspapers, and drama. Some chapters on science, the short story, and philosophy are included. Numerous notes and references. Name and title index.

A third volume, planned to cover 1950–1980, has yet to appear.

PR9604.3.G74

Hooton, Joy W. Annals of Australian literature / Joy Hooton & Harry Heseltine. 2nd ed. Melbourne ; N.Y. : Oxford Univ. Pr., c1992. 367 p.   **BE851**

1st ed., 1970, by Grahame Johnston.

Modeled after the *Annals of English literature, 1475–1950* (BE612).

Covers 1789–1988. Lists, by year, noteworthy Australian books, with a parallel column noting births and deaths of authors, and miscellaneous notes such as the founding of newspapers and periodicals. Author and title index.   Z4021.H66

Lock, Fred. Australian literature : a reference guide / Fred Lock and Alan Lawson. 2nd ed. Melbourne ; N.Y. : Oxford Univ. Pr., 1980. 120 p.   **BE852**

1st ed., 1977.

A guide to sources of information for the study of Australian literature. More than 400 annotated entries in seven main sections: (1) Bibliographical aids; (2) Other reference sources (e.g., encyclopedias, dictionaries, biographical dictionaries); (3) Authors (i.e., a listing of bibliographies of individual authors); (4) Periodicals; (5) Library resources; (6) Literary studies; (7) Organizations. Index of authors, and one of titles and subjects.   Z4011.L6

Miller, Edmund Morris. Australian literature : a bibliography to 1938, extended to 1950 / ed., with a historical outline and descriptive commentaries by Frederick T. Macartney. [Rev. ed.]. Sydney : Angus and Robertson, [1956]. 503 p.   **BE853**

An extensive revision of the author's *Australian literature* (1940).

Historical treatment of the writers and literature of Australia, with extensive bibliographies. Arranged alphabetically by author. Contains considerable biographical material. Indexes that were useful because of the chronological arrangement have been omitted from this edition.

Although the rearrangement of contents makes this edition easier to use, the earlier edition remains a standard source and has been reissued in a "facsimile edition with addendum of corrections and additions" (Sydney : Sydney Univ. Pr., 1975. 2 v.).   Z4021.M5

The Oxford history of Australian literature / ed. by Leonie Kramer. Melbourne ; N.Y. : Oxford Univ. Pr., [1981]. 509 p.   **BE854**

Following an introductory essay by the general editor, there are contributed chapters on fiction, drama, and poetry, and a general bibliography in essay form (p. 429–90). Does not include nonfiction prose. Index to the text, but not to the bibliography.

§ *The literature of Australia* ed. by Geoffrey Dutton (Rev. ed. Harmondsworth, Eng. ; Ringwood, Victoria : Penguin Books, 1974) is a convenient one-volume history with chapters by individual scholars, each with notes or references. The first section covers chronological eras, the second is largely devoted to individual authors, the third provides a lengthy bibliography of secondary works, and a biobibliographical listing of authors and works. Name index.

A newer Penguin work, published as a special issue of *Australian literary studies*, v. 13 no. 4 (Oct. 1988) is: *The Penguin new literary history of Australia*, gen. ed. Laurie Hergenham, (Ringwood, Victoria : Penguin Books, 1988). Broader in scope and thematic rather than chronological or biobibliographical in structure. As well as discussion of belles-lettres, includes chapters on "perceptions" of Australian literature, authorship and publishing, journalism, genres, including popular literature such as romance and melodrama, Australian English, humor, nonfiction, and ballads. Bibliographic essay on sources for the study of Australian literature. Author, title, subject index.   PR9604.3.O9

The Oxford literary guide to Australia / gen. ed., Peter Pierce for the Association for the Study of Australian Literature ; assistant ed., Rosemary Hunter ; associate ed., Barry Andrews ... [et al.]. Rev. ed. / assistant ed., Ken Stewart. Melbourne ; Oxford : Oxford Univ. Pr., 1993. 501 p.   **BE855**

Entries are grouped geographically (e.g., Australian territories, New South Wales, Queensland, South Australia, Tasmania, Victoria, and Western Australia), then alphabetically by place. Cities are further subdivided by suburbs, institutions, geographical formations, etc. A history of each place is given, followed by its literary associations. Color and black-and-white illustrations. Entries are keyed to maps in the back of the volume. The author index gives brief biographical facts and lists works mentioned in the text. Unfortunately, there is no geographical index.   PR9607.O94

Ross, Robert L. Australian literary criticism, 1945–1988 : an annotated bibliography. N.Y. : Garland, 1989. 375 p. (Garland reference library of the humanities, v. 1075).   **BE856**

Lists and annotates 1,397 citations to books, articles, and dissertations in a classified arrangement. Includes sections on special topics (e.g., Aborigines, Fiction about the convict period) as well as film, language, multiculturalism, women's studies, fiction, poetry, drama, and 42 individual authors. Index to critics and authors/subjects.

Z4024.C8R67

Stuart, Lurline. Nineteenth century Australian periodicals : an annotated bibliography. Sydney : Hale & Iremonger, 1979. 200 p. : ill.   **BE857**

An alphabetical listing of those periodicals which "contain literary features in the form of essays, articles, fiction, poetry and minor literary items."—*Introd.* Locations are given for most titles, but some titles have been entered and described on the basis of information found in published sources. Indexed.   Z6962.A8S78

Torre, Stephen. The Australian short story, 1940–1980 : a bibliography. Sydney, NSW : Hale & Iremonger, c1984. 367 p.   **BE858**

"An index to short stories by Australian writers in collections, anthologies, miscellanies and a selected number of periodicals published between 1940–1980 inclusive."—*Introd.* Arranged by author; for each includes: collections, publication history of individual stories, anthologies or miscellanies edited by the author, interviews or commentaries by the author, and criticism on the author's work. Lists: periodicals that publish short stories; anthologies and miscellanies; general references. A useful tracking device, although selective.   Z4024.S5T67

Who's who of Australian writers. Port Melbourne, Vic., Australia : Thorpe ; Clayton, Vic., Australia : National Centre for Australian Studies, c1991. 660 p.   **BE859**

Brief career bibliographical, and directory information for more than 5,000 Australian writers of all kinds, among them approximately 2,000 novelists, poets, dramatists, other authors of belles lettres, and film and television writers. Notes birthdate and place, positions held, book-length publications, contributions to periodicals, forthcoming works, awards, memberships, types of writing, recreational activities, availability, and contact (often an agent). Subject index.

PR9606.2.W46

Wilde, William H. The Oxford companion to Australian literature / William H. Wilde, Joy Hooton, Barry Andrews. Melbourne ; N.Y. : Oxford Univ. Pr., 1985. 760 p. **BE860**
Repr., 1991.

Typical of the "Oxford companion" series, with entries for authors, literary works, journals, movements, and a few literary characters. Bibliographical information is limited mainly to lists of author's works (with publication dates), and occasional references to biographies of the writers. PR9600.2.W55

New Zealand

Burns, James. New Zealand novels and novelists, 1861–1979 : an annotated bibliography. [Auckland] : Heinemann, [1981]. 71 p. **BE861**
A chronological listing of authors and works. Brief annotations summarize contents. Author and title indexes.

§ Two complementary works:

Joan Stevens' critical history, *The New Zealand novel, 1860–1965* (Wellington : A.H. & A.W. Reed, [1966]). "The aim has been to give a reasonably comprehensive picture of the topics and the techniques of New Zealand novels from 1860–1965."—*Pref.* Selective; emphasizes individual works and popular literature. Useful for plot information. Intended as a study guide, with suggestions for analysis and discussion. References and index.

New Zealand fiction, by Joseph and Johanna Jones (Boston : Twayne, c1983. [Twayne's world authors series, 643]), is a useful introductory survey with a critically selective bibliography of primary and secondary works. Z4114.F4B83

McNaughton, Howard Douglas. New Zealand drama : a bibliographical guide. Interim ed. [Christchurch] : Univ. of Canterbury Libr., 1974. 112 p. (Reference and bibliographical series, Univ. of Canterbury Library, 5). **BE862**
Attempts to list every New Zealand play which has been published or produced, or which a copy can be traced. Includes radio and television as well as stage productions. Arranged by author, with title index.

§ McNaughton's *New Zealand drama* (Boston : Twayne, 1981. [Twayne's world author series, 26]), an introductory survey, the only full-length study of the whole of New Zealand drama. Includes a chronology, notes and references, and a selective bibliography of primary and secondary sources. Author and title index. Z4114.D7M3

The Oxford history of New Zealand literature in English / ed. by Terry Sturm. Auckland ; N.Y. : Oxford Univ. Pr., 1991. 748 p. **BE863**
An excellent, comprehensive, highly detailed, and much-needed history, covering from colonial times to the late 1980's. Essential in any academic library. According to *American reference books annual* 23 (1992) : 504, this "will remain the essential reference work on New Zealand literature for years to come." In addition to established belletristic authors and genres, includes chapters on Maori, children's and popular literature, nonfiction, and "Publishing, patronage, and literary magazines." Abundant quotes and bibliographical detail throughout, as well as extensive chapter notes and a lengthy bibliographical essay. Author, title, and subject index.

§ Essentially supersedes E. H. McCormick's *New Zealand literature: a survey* (London : Oxford Univ. Pr., 1959), for many years the only work of its kind.

Another recent work, as much a critical analysis as a history, is *Penguin history of New Zealand literature*, by Patrick Evans (Auckland : Penguin Books, 1990). Briefer and less comprehensive, it supplements but does not replace the *Oxford history*. Extensive chapter notes; author and title index. PR9624.3.O94

Thomson, John E. New Zealand literature to 1977 : a guide to information sources. Detroit : Gale, [1980]. 272 p. (American literature, English literature, and world literatures in English, 30). **BE864**
Chapters on bibliographies and reference works, literary history and criticism, and anthologies are followed by sections on individual authors. Indexed. Z4111.T45

LITERATURES OF LATIN AMERICA

See also sections in Literatures of Europe for Spain, Portugal, and Regional literatures—Romance languages.

Anderson Imbert, Enrique. Spanish-American literature : a history. 2nd ed. / rev. and updated by Elaine Malley ; tr. from the Spanish by John V. Falconieri. Detroit : Wayne State Univ. Pr., 1969. 2 v. **BE865**
First English ed., 1963; originally published as: *Historia de la literatura hispanoamericana* (México : Fondo de Cultura Economica, 1954-61).

"Although this general guide is often more a registry of names than an analytical history, it continues to be regarded as indispensable for the vast amount of literary production it surveys."—*Handbook of Latin American literature, p. xv* (BE866). Subdivided chronologically, each section having a general introduction followed by biobibliographical sections on individual authors. Bibliography of general studies; author index in each volume.

§ A more readable English-language history is: *An introduction to Spanish-American literature*, by Jean Franco (Cambridge : Cambridge Univ. Pr., 1969. Spanish translation: *Introduccion a la literatura hispanoamericana* [Caracas : Monte Avila Ed., 1970]). Many quoted passages with English translations. Reading lists; author index.
PQ7081.A56342

General works

Guides

Handbook of Latin American literature / comp. by David William Foster. 2nd ed. N.Y. : Garland, 1992. 799 p. (Garland reference library of the humanities, v. 1459). **BE866**
Aims to provide a "source of information for general readers and non-Hispanists who may require concise information concerning a particular author or work or literary tradition of Latin America … [and is also] intended to meet the needs of students and researchers … seeking reliable and comprehensive information concerning the various national literatures of Latin America and the features that set one national literature off from another."—*Pref.* Signed essays on various national literatures are followed by brief bibliographies of monographic sources, with a name index.

The new edition updates earlier information and adds sections on Hispanic literature in America, film, and paraliterature.
PQ7081.A1H36

Pedraza Jiménez, Felipe B. Manual de literatura española / Felipe B. Pedraza Jiménez, Milagros Rodríguez Cáceres. Pamplona : Cénlit, 1980–1993. v. 1–11. (In progress). **BE867**
For annotation, *see* BE1429. PQ6032.P4

Rela, Walter. A bibliographical guide to Spanish American literature : twentieth-century sources. N.Y. : Greenwood, 1988. 381 p. (Bibliographies and indexes in world literature, no. 13). **BE868**
Does not totally supersede the author's earlier *Guía bibliográfica de la literatura hispanoamericana desde siglo XIX hasta 1970* (Buenos

Aires : Casa Pardo, 1971) and its supplement, *Spanish American literature : a selected bibliography = Literatura hispanoamericana : bibliografía selecta, 1970–1980* (East Lansing : Michigan State Univ., Dept. of Romance and Classical Languages, 1982), but aims to combine them to provide "a single, rigorously selective inventory of sources that must necessarily serve as an initial point of departure for serious scholarship on Latin American literature."—*Foreword*. Lists and annotates 1,884 items in sections devoted to bibliographies, dictionaries, history and criticism, and anthologies. Each section is subdivided by countries and genres. Author index.   Z1609.L7R438

Bibliography

Bibliografía general de la literatura latinoamericana / coordinador, Jorge Carrera Andrade ; revisor, Héctor Luis Arena. Paris : Unesco, 1972. 187 p.   **BE869**

A bibliography of more than 3,100 items in three chronological sections: (1) Periodo colonial; (2) Siglo XIX; (3) Época contemporánea. Each section is subdivided for general works and individual countries. Includes listings of anthologies. Extremely useful for its coverage of all South and Central America and the Caribbean. Author index.   Z1609.L7B5

Fenwick, M. J. Writers of the Caribbean and Central America : a bibliography. N.Y. : Garland, 1992. 2 v. (Garland reference library of the humanities, vol. 1244).   **BE870**

Monumental but bibliographically deficient. Exhaustively covers the belles-lettres literature of all the islands and countries of the Caribbean and Central America. Arranged alphabetical by country, with authors under country of birth and cross-listed under other countries of residence. For each author, provides dates, indication of genre, and individual works listed chronologically, followed by periodicals and anthologies in which the author published. For monographs, including anthologies, gives only title and date, and gives no information on specific works, issue numbers, etc. for periodical publications. A review in *American reference books annual*, 24 (1993): 518–19, praises the book but points out errors and omissions and notes that "This work, while extremely valuable, especially for lesser-known areas, must be used with a degree of caution." Title index.   Z1595.F46 1992

Flores, Angel. Bibliografía de escritores hispanoamericanos, 1609–1974 = A bibliography of Spanish-American writers. N.Y. : Gordian Pr., 1975. 318 p.   **BE871**

In two sections, the first devoted to major writers of all periods, the second to other notable writers 1883–1974. Lists editions of each writer's works and critical/biographical references. Index of authors treated (about 190 in all).   Z1609.L7F55

Forster, Merlin H. Vanguardism in Latin American literature : an annotated bibliographical guide / comp. by Merlin H. Forster and K. David Jackson ... [et al.]. N.Y. : Greenwood, 1990. 214 p. (Bibliographies and indexes in world literature, no. 27).   **BE872**

Aims to provide "an annotated guide to research materials rather then an exhaustive listing of everything ever written by or about Latin American vanguardists."—*Introd.* Covers primary materials published 1920–35 and critical works since 1935 in classed arrangement within both an overview section and sections devoted to particular countries. The country sections include listings for individual writers. General index.

§ For an earlier era, *see*: Robert Roland Anderson, *Spanish American modernism : a selected bibliography* (Tucson : Univ. of Arizona Pr., 1970). A general section on modernism is followed by bibliographies on 18 representative authors. Includes books and articles, but not book reviews. Both works have helpful introductory essays.

Z1609.L7F67

Grismer, Raymond Leonard. A reference index to twelve thousand Spanish American authors : a guide to the literature of Spanish America. N.Y. : Wilson, 1939. 150 p. (Inter-American bibliographical and library association publications. Series 3, v. 1).   **BE873**

An index to more than 125 books of literary history, biography, bibliography, etc., containing material about Spanish-American authors. Arranged alphabetically by author.

§ Grismer's *New bibliography of the literatures of Spain and Spanish America* (Minneapolis : Perine, 1941–46. v. 1–7) remains incomplete, covering only through "Cez".   Z1601.G86

Handbook of Latin American studies. v. 1 (1935)– . Gainesville : Univ. of Florida Pr. ; Austin : Univ. of Texas Pr., 1936– . Annual.   **BE874**

Each volume through 1963 includes a section on literature; beginning with v. 26, literature appears in alternate years in the *Humanities* volume. For full information, *see* DB266.   Z1605.H23

Harvard University. Library. Latin American literature : classification schedule, classified listing by call number; author and title listing; chronological listing. Cambridge : Harvard Univ. Libr., 1969. 498 p. (Widener Library shelflist, 21).   **BE875**

For a note on the series, *see* AA115.

"Briefly, the *SAL* class provides for nearly all literary works—poetry, drama, fiction, essays, etc.—by Latin American authors and for writings about these authors and their work. Literary histories and anthologies are included. ... Approximately 16,500 titles are listed."—*Pref.*   Z1609.L7H33

Hilton, Sylvia L. Bibliografía hispanoamericana y filipina : manual de repertorios bibliográficos para la investigación de la historia y la literatura hispanoamericanas y filipinas / Sylvia-Lyn Hilton, Amancio Labandeira. Madrid : Fundación Universitaria Española, 1983. 411 p. (Publicaciones de la Fundación Universitaria Española. Biblioteca histórica hispanoamericana, 6).   **BE876**

For annotation, *see* DE248.   Z1601.H55

Leguizamón, Julio A. Bibliografía general de la literatura hispanoamericana. Buenos Aires : Ed. Reunidas, [1954]. 213 p.   **BE877**

A much expanded revision of the bibliography which appeared originally in the author's *Historia de la literatura hispanoamericana* (Buenos Aires : Ed. Reunidas, 1945. 2 v.). Classed arrangement with name index.

Simmons, Merle Edwin. A bibliography of the romance and related forms in Spanish America. Bloomington : Indiana Univ. Pr., 1963. 396 p. (Indiana University folklore series, no.18).   **BE878**

Repr.: Westport, Conn. : Greenwood, 1972.

A bibliography of books and articles on the romances, ballads, and folklore of South American countries. Lists more than 2,100 items.   Z1609.P6S5

Wogan, Daniel S. A literatura hispano-americana no Brasil, 1877–1944 : bibliografia de crítica, história literária e traduçoes. Baton Rouge : Louisiana State Univ. Pr., [1948]. 98 p.   **BE879**

An annotated bibliography of 822 items, listing the contributions that Brazilians have made to the history and criticism of the literatures of Spanish America. Arranged by country; includes books and articles published 1877–1945. Portuguese translations of Spanish-American novels, plays, short stories, and poems are included under each country division.   Z1609.L7W6

Yale University. Library. Spanish American literature in the Yale University Library : a bibliography / Frederick Bliss Luquiens. .... New Haven, Conn. : Yale Univ. Pr. ; London : Milford, Oxford Univ. Pr., 1939. 335 p.   **BE880**

Contains 5,668 numbered entries. "The word *literature* … is to be understood in the broad sense of 'good writing.' "—*Introd.* Arranged by the countries of Spanish America, with index to the whole. Although dated, still useful for its thorough bibliographic detail, including extensive contents notes. Z1601.Y1

Zubatsky, David S. Latin American literary authors : an annotated guide to bibliographies. Metuchen, N.J. : Scarecrow, 1986. 332 p. **BE881**

Contains "personal bibliographies of Brazilian and Spanish American writers of novels, drama, poetry, and short stories, as well as essayists, journalists, linguists, and literary critics" (*Pref.*) which have been published in books, journals, dissertations and festschriften. Arranged by author with cross-references from pseudonyms or alternate form of name. A supplement lists bibliographies which treat countries or regions rather than individual authors. No index.

§ For Zubatsky's companion volume, *Spanish, Catalan, and Galician literary authors …* , *see* BE1445. An additional listing of bibliographies of bibliographies is found in Shasta M. Bryant, comp., *A selective bibliography of bibliographies of Hispanic American literature* (2nd ed., greatly expanded and rev. Austin : Inst. of Latin American Studies, Univ. of Texas at Austin, 1976. [Guides and bibliographies series, 8]). A guide for the student. 662 items arranged by author with an index of names and broad topics. Z1609.L7Z82

Periodicals

Carter, Boyd George. Las revistas literarias de Hispanoamérica : breve historia y contenido. México : Ed. de Andrea, 1959. 282 p. (Colleción studium, 24). **BE882**

Contents: pt. 1, A brief history of literary periodicals of Spanish America; pt. 2, Short studies of 50 literary periodicals; pt. 3, A selected bibliography of articles from 125 literary periodicals; pt. 4, General bibliography. Z6954.S8C3

Translations

Corvalán, Graciela N. V. Latin American women writers in English translation : a bibliography. Los Angeles : Latin American Studies Center, California State Univ., c1980. 109 p. (Latin America bibliography series, v. 9). **BE883**

A convenient listing of translated materials by and about Latin American women authors from colonial times to 1979. Particularly useful for locating translations that have appeared in periodicals. The main listing is alphabetical by the names of the authors covered, preceded by listings of reference works, anthologies, and general works on women writers. No index. Z1609.L7C67

Freudenthal, Juan R. Index to anthologies of Latin American literature in English translation / ed. and comp. by Juan R. Freudenthal, Patricia M. Freudenthal. Boston : G.K. Hall, c1977. 199 p. **BE884**

An index to writings in English translation of some 1,122 Spanish-American and Brazilian authors in 116 anthologies. Arranged by author, with translator and geographic indexes. Works are identified as poetry, fiction, drama, or "other." Z1609.T7F74

Hulet, Claude L. Latin American prose in English translation : a bibliography. Wash. : General Secretariat, Organization of American States, [1964?]. 191 p. (Pan American Union. Division of Philosophy and Letters. Basic bibliographies, 1). **BE885**

A substantial bibliography covering "not only imaginative writing but also works relating to anthropology, archaeology, biography, correspondence, history, oratory, philosophy, sociology and wills" (*Introd.*) from the earliest era to the 1960s and including South and Central America and areas of the Caribbean. Arranged alphabetically by genre and then by country, with an author index. Includes both monographs and material from periodicals and provides a separate listing of anthologies. Partly based on but does not supersede Willis Knapp

Jones, *Latin American writers in English translation : a tentative bibliography* (Wash. : Pan American Union, 1944. [Pan American Union. Columbus Memorial Library. Bibliographic ser., 30]), which covers a wider spectrum of belles lettres.

§ Companion title by Hulet: *Latin American poetry in English translation : a bibliography* (Wash. : Pan American Union, 1965. [Pan American Union. Division of Philosophy and Latters. Basic bibliographies, 2]). Arranged alphabetically by country.

Shaw, Bradley A. Latin American literature in English translation : an annotated bibliography. N.Y. : New York Univ. Pr., 1976. 144 p. **BE886**

"A Center for Inter-American Relations book."—*t.p.*

"The scope of the bibliography is limited to published books which include fiction, poetry, drama or the literary essay in English translation. … Periodical literature and literary criticism are not included."—*Pref.* Sections for Spanish American literature, Brazilian literature, and non-Hispanic literature of the Caribbean Islands and Guyanas, each subdivided by genre. Indexes by author, English title, original title, and by country. Z1609.T7S47

Criticism

Foster, David William. Modern Latin American literature / comp. and ed. by David William Foster, Virginia Ramos Foster. N.Y. : Ungar, 1975. 2 v. **BE887**

Like other volumes in the "Library of literary criticism" series (e.g., *Modern German literature*, BE1058), these volumes present critical commentary on 20th-century Latin American authors. Commentary is drawn from book and periodical materials; about half is translated from Spanish and Portuguese sources. 137 writers are treated. Index of critics in v. 2. A review in *Booklist* 73 (1976–77): 275 notes the omission of a number of important authors. PQ7081.F63

Dictionaries

Becco, Horacio Jorge. Diccionario de literatura hispanoamericana : autores. [Buenos Aires] : Huemul, c1984. 313 p. **BE888**

A quick-reference dictionary covering authors from Juan de Castellanos (1522–1607) to those born by 1940, and complete to 1981. For each author, provides a brief biographical and critical statement and a list of monographic works. Many portraits.

§ Providing similar information and covering a broader range of authors geographically but limited to those born 1890–1939 is : *Diccionario de autores iberoamericanos*, ed. by Pedro Shimose (Madrid : Ministerio de Asuntos Exteriores, Direccion General de Relaciones Culturales, Instituto de Cooperacion Iberoamericano, 1982). Covers authors of Spain and Portugal but considerable emphasis is on writers of Latin America and the Caribbean, writing in both Spanish and Portuguese; Latinos are included as well. Z1607.B43

Flores, Angel. Spanish American authors : the twentieth century. N.Y. : Wilson, 1992. 915 p. **BE889**

A monumental and distinguished work covering more than 330 novelists and poets from Central and South America, Puerto Rico, and the Caribbean, some appearing for the first time in a reference source. Essential in any library supporting study of Latin America. Many authors provided autobiographical sketches. Entries are in alphabetical order. For each writer, provides biographical information, critical analysis and summaries of criticism, and a bibliography of primary and secondary works, excluding dissertations. Indicates principal editions. Not indexed. PQ7081.3.F57

Hispanic writers : a selection of sketches from Contemporary authors / Bryan Ryan, ed. Detroit : Gale, c1991. 514 p. **BE890**

Covers "more than 400 authors who are a part of twentieth-century Hispanic literature and culture in the Americas."—*Introd.* Includes writers of diverse genres, not limited to literary figures, from the U.S., Central and South America, and the Caribbean, and a limited number from Spain who have influenced New World literature. 40% of the entries were selected from Gale's *Contemporary authors* (AH42) and revised for this volume. Others are new, and may appear in future volumes of the parent set. Provides current "who's who" information, including addresses, a list of works by the author and mention of works in progress, biographical and critical "Sidelights," (often provided by the author), and selective references to further biographical and critical information. Index by nationality.   PQ7081.3.H58

Latin American writers / Carlos A. Solé, ed. in chief, Maria Isabel Abreu, associate ed. N.Y. : Scribner, c1989. 3 v.   **BE891**

A "comprehensive effort to acquaint the English-speaking world, and other countries where Spanish and Portuguese are not the mother tongue, with the rich and varied literature of Spanish America and Brazil."—*Pref.* A major source, in which 176 writers, 15th–20th centuries, are profiled in signed essays varying in length from 2,500 to 10,000 words. Each essay includes a biographical sketch, a critical appraisal, and a bibliography of primary and secondary works. Arranged chronologically, with a name/subject index and a geographical list of authors. A lengthy introductory essay on the history of Latin American literature and a chronological table of political and cultural events precede the main text.

§ Two older companion bibliographies, both by David William Foster, provide similar information: *A dictionary of contemporary Latin American authors* (1975) and *A dictionary of contemporary Brazilian authors* (1981; both publ. Tempe : Center for Latin American Studies, Arizona State Univ.). Both consist of signed entries by a number of contributors, providing brief biographies and critical analysis.   PQ7081.A1L37

Pan American Union. Division of Philosophy and Letters. Diccionario de la literatura latinoamericana. [Ed. provisional]. Wash. : Unión Panamericana, [1958–63]. 6 v. in 8.   **BE892**

Contents: v. 1, Bolivia; v. 2, Chile; v. 3, Colombia; v. 4, Argentina; v. 5, Ecuador; v. 6, America Central: pt. 1, Costa Rica, El Salvador y Guatemala; pt. 2, Honduras, Nicaragua y Panama. No more published.

Aims to present a comprehensive encyclopedia of Latin American literature with emphasis on the critical evaluation of each writer. Each fascicle is a dictionary of authors, giving for each a biographical sketch, an evaluative critical summary, and a bibliography of works by and about.   PQ7081.P27

Reichardt, Dieter. Lateinamerikanische Autoren : Literaturlexikon und Bibliographie der deutschen Übersetzungen. Tübingen : H. Erdmann, [1972]. 718 p.   **BE893**

Biobibliographies of Spanish and Portuguese-speaking authors, arranged by country and covering South and Central America and the Caribbean. Provides lists of published German translations. A separate section provides selective bibliographies, international in scope, of book-length histories and critical studies, and anthologies, both general works and ones for particular countries. Indexes to authors and translators.   Z1607.R43

Histories

Goić, Cedomil. Historia y crítica de la literatura hispanoamericana. Barcelona : Editorial Crítica, Grupo Editorial Grijalbo, c1988–c1991. 3 v.   **BE894**

Contents: v. 1 Epoca colonial; v. 2, Del romanticismo al modernismo; v. 3, Epoca contemporánea.

A history useful for providing substantial bibliographical information and largely comprising selections reprinted from criticism and analysis by various scholars. Each volume is divided into sections covering chronological or literary eras, genres, movements, or individual writers. Within each section there is a historical, topical, or biobiblio-

graphical introduction and a bibliography of secondary materials, followed by, on the average, six to ten extracts from historical and critical works. Name and title index in each volume.

§ A history on the same model for Spanish literature: Francisco Rico, ed., *Historia y crítica de la literatura española*, (Barcelona : Ed. Crítica, 1980–84. 8 v. Suppl., v. 1–4, 1991–92. In progress).   PQ7081.G54

Grossmann, Rudolf. Historia y problemas de la literatura latinoamericana / traducción del alemán por Juan C. Probst. Madrid : [Rivista de Occidente, 1972]. 758 p.   **BE895**

Translation of *Geschichte und Probleme der lateinamerikanischen Literatur* (Munich : Hueber, 1969).

A well-organized history covering the literature of all Latin America in 25 chapters divided into numerous sections clearly outlined in the table of contents. The first chapters focus on general topics such as the study of literature, the relationship between Latin American and other literatures, and literature and society. Organization is then chronological. An extensive bibliography, including materials on individual countries, is provided. Index to names and titles.

Biography

Spanish American women writers : a bio-bibliographical source book / ed. by Diane E. Marting. N.Y. : Greenwood, 1990. 645 p.   **BE896**

Includes "fifty of the most important women writers of Latin America from the seventeenth century to the present, representing most Spanish-speaking American nations and a variety of literary genres."—*Pref.* Signed entries provide biographical and critical information, discuss major themes and importance, and have bibliographies of primary and secondary works. Two separate chapters discuss Latin American Indian women writers and Latina and genre; title and subject indexes.

§ An earlier work by Marting, *Women writers of Spanish America : an annotated bibliographical guide* (N.Y. : Greenwood, 1987. [Bibliographies and indexes in women's studies, 5]), is an uneven guide to more than 1,000 writers, giving country of origin and dates and listing titles of works, in most instances without other biographical or bibliographical information. Approximately a tenth of the entries include biographical information, full bibliographic references, and analytical annotations.

Two complementary sources are: *Women authors of modern Hispanic South America : a bibliography of literary criticism and interpretation*, by Sandra Messinger Cypess, David R. Kohut, and Rachelle Moore (Metuchen, N.J. : Scarecrow, 1989) and *Spanish-American women writers: a bibliographical research checklist*, Lynn Ellen Rice Cortina (N.Y. : Garland, 1983. [Garland reference library of the humanities, 356]). Cypess covers Spanish-speaking portions of South and Central America, the Caribbean, and the U.S. and lists criticism on 169 writers. Cortina covers almost 2,000 authors from the same geographic areas except for the U.S. and provides dates, in some cases additional biographical information, and lists of primary works with varying degrees of bibliographical detail. Both are arranged by country, with author indexes.   Z1609.L7S6

Genres

Drama

Allen, Richard F. Teatro hispanoamericano : una bibliografía anotada = Spanish American theatre : an annotated bibliography. Boston : G.K. Hall, c1987. 633 p.   **BE897**

Intended to "aid the serious researcher, professor, critic, student, librarian, or play producer in locating and evaluating sufficient primary sources of the Spanish-American Theatre."—*Introd.* Plays published in books or journals are arranged alphabetically by author within chapters devoted to specific countries; 13 general anthologies are listed as well. Each entry gives at least one and up to five library locations in North America, with one-act plays designated by an asterisk. The extensive annotations are in Spanish or Portuguese. Author and title indexes. Z1609.D7A44

Hoffman, Herbert H. Latin American play index. Metuchen, N.J. : Scarecrow, 1983–84. 2 v. **BE898**

Contents: v.1, 1920–1962; v.2, 1962–1980.

Includes references to separately published plays, plays in collections and anthologies, and plays published in periodicals. Arranged by author, with title index. Z1609.D7H63

Lyday, Leon F. A bibliography of Latin American theater criticism, 1940–1974 / Leon F. Lyday and George W. Woodyard. Austin : Inst. of Latin American Studies, Univ. of Texas at Austin, 1976. 243 p. (Univ. of Texas, Austin. Inst. of Latin American Studies. Guides and bibliographies series, 10). **BE899**

The period covered "corresponds to the establishment and development of a truly national theater movement in most areas of Latin America."—*Introd.* Author listing with subject index. 2,360 items. Z1609.D7L9

Toro, Fernando de. Bibliografía del teatro hispanoamericano contemporaneo (1900–1980) / Fernando de Toro, Peter Roster. Frankfurt am Main : Verlag Klaus Dieter Vervuert, 1985. 2 v. (Editionen der Iberoamericana. Reihe II, Bibliographische Reihe, 3). **BE900**

Contents: v. 1, Obras originales; v. 2, Critica.

Probably the most comprehensive bibliography on 20th-century Spanish-American drama. The first volume, with close to 7,000 items, covers primary works in three sections: a list by author for plays published in journals, monographically, and in anthologies; a list of anthologies; and a very selective list of translations. Vol. 2 has 3,132 items of criticism arranged by author including analysis, bibliography, and "miscellaneous." A definite weakness of the work, particularly in the criticism volume, is the lack of any indexing.

§ A more selective listing of primary works, limited to major dramatists, is: *Repertorio selecto del teatro hispanoamericano contemporaneo*, by Giuseppe Erminio Neglia and Luis Ordaz (2nd ed., rev. y ampl. Tempe : Arizona Center for Latin American Studies, Arizona State Univ., 1980). Provides titles of plays, with dates of first performances, and publication information for printed works. List of references; author index. Z1609.D7T67

Fiction

Brower, Keith H. Contemporary Latin American fiction : an annotated bibliography. Pasadena, Calif. : Salem Pr., c1989. 218 p. **BE901**

Similar to other Magill bibliographies. Covers "twenty three contemporary Latin American narrativists and more than one hundred individual works."—*Introd.* Aimed at undergraduates and limited to biography and criticism in English, published (with a few exceptions) 1965–89, and judged to be widely available. Substantial annotations. Index of writers and critics. Z1609.F4B76

Coll, Edna. Indice informativo de la novela hispanoamericana. [Rio Piedras], Editorial Universitaria, Universidad de Puerto Rico, 1974–1992. v.1–5. (In progress). **BE902**

Contents: v. 1, Las Antillas; v. 2, Centroamerica; v. 3, Venezuela; v. 4, Colombia; v. 5, El Altiplano (Bolivia, Ecuador, Peru).

The completed series should offer a comprehensive bibliography of the Spanish American novel. Within each country section the listing is alphabetical by novelist's name. Most entries include a biographical note on the author, together with a list of his novels (often including a note on the character of the work) and bibliographic references to biographical and critical works.

§ A useful comprehensive bibliography covering criticism on 56 novelists, with sections for general studies and specific countries, is: David William Foster, *The 20th century Spanish American novel: a bibliographic guide* (Metuchen, N.J. : Scarecrow, 1975). Listings for authors include books and articles; the general sections list monographs only. Z1609.F4C65

The Latin American short story : an annotated guide to anthologies and criticism / comp. by Daniel Balderston. N.Y. : Greenwood, 1992. 529 p. (Bibliographies and indexes in world literature, no. 34). **BE903**

A substantive and conveniently arranged bibliography that should be welcome in any library supporting an interest in Latin American literature and in the short story as a genre. In two sections, the first listing anthologies and the second criticism on the short story. Anthologies are arranged in sections for general anthologies covering Latin America, general anthologies in English, regional anthologies, and anthologies representing individual countries. Criticism is similarly arranged but without a separate section on work in English. For anthologies gives full contents listing and brief critical statement. Annotations for criticism, when supplied, are brief but useful. Lengthy historical and analytical introduction; indexes to authors, critics, titles, and themes. Z1609.F4B35

Poetry

Sefamí, Jacobo. Contemporary Spanish American poets : a bibliography of primary and secondary sources. N.Y. : Greenwood, 1992. 245 p. (Bibliographies and indexes in world literature, no. 33). **BE904**

A guide to works by and about 86 poets born between 1910 and 1952. Also provides a general section of works on Spanish American poetry and that of particular countries. Lists all works by each poet, including other genres. Criticism includes bibliographies, book-length studies, and essays, reviews, and interviews. Full bibliographical information is provided for all items. A chronological list of poets is included. Index of critics. Z1609.P6S4

LITERATURES OF CENTRAL AMERICA

Guatemala

Albizúrez Palma, Francisco. Historia de la literatura guatemalteca / Francisco Albizúrez Palma, Catalina Barrios y Barrios. Ciudad Universitaria, Guatemala : Editorial Universitaria de Guatemala, c1981–[1987]. 3 v. **BE905**

A panoramic and detailed history covering Guatemalan literature from its beginnings to the present. Vol. 1 covers to the beginning of the 20th century and v. 2 the contemporary era. Much of the discussion is centered on individual writers. No indexes but the detailed tables of contents are adequate to locate specific information. Extensive bibliographies of both primary and secondary works in each volume, including those for individual authors.

§ Albizúrez Palma also is the author of *Diccionario de autores guatemaltecos* (Guatemala : Tip. Nacional, 1984), providing brief bio-bibliographical information and occasional critical comments for selected authors covered more fully in the history. Lists primary works only. PQ7490.A635

Honduras

González, José. Diccionario de autores hondureños / José González. Glosario de términos literarios / S. Turaiev. Tegucigalpa, D.C., Honduras : Editores Unidos, 1987. 120 p.   **BE906**

A dictionary in two parts, the first providing basic biographical information and a list of primary works for authors, the second a dictionary of literary terms, genres, schools, etc.

§ *Diccionario de escritores hondureños*, by Mario R. Argueta ([Tegucigalpa : Centro Tecnico Tipolitografico Nacional?], 1986) has relatively brief entries but often provides critical comments as well as biobibliography.   PQ7500.G66

Mexico

Diccionario de escritores mexicanos, siglo XX : desde las generaciones del Ateneo y novelistas de la Revolución hasta nuestros días / [dirección y asesoría, Aurora M. Ocampo]. México : Universidad Nacional Autónoma de México, Instituto de Investigaciones Filológicas, Centro de Estudios Literarios, 1988. v. 1. (In progress).   **BE907**

Contents: v. 1, A–Ch.

Includes both native-born writers and those born elsewhere who wrote in Mexico. For each author gives a biographical sketch, a critical evaluation, and a very full bibliography of works both by and about. Lengthy list of periodicals indexed; general bibliography.

§ Another recent volume, *Diccionario biobibliográfico de escritores contemporaneos de México*, by Josefina Lara Valdez (Mexico : Instituto Nacional de Bellas Artes ; Brigham Young Univ., 1988), gives short biographical and bibliographical information on writers born for the most part 1930–60.   PQ7106.D53

Dictionary of Mexican literature / ed. by Eladio Cortés. Westport, Conn. : Greenwood, 1992. 768 p.   **BE908**

Contains "approximately 500 entries in English covering the most important writers, literary schools, and cultural movements in Mexican literary history. There is an emphasis on the figures of the twentieth century."—*Pref.* Author entries include comprehensive bibliographies of primary works and selective, but generous, references to criticism. Topical entries also provide references to criticism. A bibliography of general studies is included as well. Author, title, subject index.

A review in *World literature today*, 67 (Summer 1993): 593, notes limitations and exclusions.   PQ7106.D53

Forster, Merlin H. An index to Mexican literary periodicals. N.Y. : Scarecrow, 1966. 276 p.   **BE909**

Indexes 16 Mexican literary periodicals which began and ceased publication during the general period 1920–60, most of them not indexed elsewhere. In two parts: (1) alphabetical author list; (2) index to that list offering a subject approach.   Z1421.F6

Foster, David William. Mexican literature : a bibliography of secondary sources. 2nd ed., enl. and updated. Metuchen, N.J. : Scarecrow, 1992. 686 p.   **BE910**

1st ed., 1981.

In two parts: General references and Authors. Pt. 1 is topically subdivided, with sections for literary genres and periods. "Significant academic literary scholarship has been the guiding criterion in the preparation of this bibliography. By this is meant books and monographs, papers in refereed scholarly journals and similar academic periodicals, and articles and notes in cultural and literary reviews."—*Pref.* The new edition adds 30 authors, updates all sections, and expands the historical chronological range of the 1st ed. Necessary in any library supporting an interest in Mexican and Latin American literature. Index of critics. Review: *American reference books annual* 24 (1993) : 519.   Z1421.F63

González Peña, Carlos. History of Mexican literature / trans. by Gusta Barfield Nance and Florence Johnson Dunstan. 3rd ed. [rev. and enl.]. Dallas : Southern Methodist Univ. Pr., [1968]. 540 p. : port.   **BE911**

Translation of the 9th ed. of *Historia de la literatura mexicana desde los origines hasta nuestros dias* (México : Ed. Porrua, 1966; now available in a 15th ed., 1984).

An authoritative one-volume history covering the literature from its beginnings to World War II, with an appendix covering through the mid-1960s. A list of Mexican literature in translation is included.   PQ7111.G62

Hoffman, Herbert H. Cuento mexicano index. Newport Beach, Calif. : Headway Pubns., 1978. 599 p.   **BE912**

An index to Mexican short stories in some 674 collections (a few of them in English). An "Author & story" section gives reference to the numbered list of anthologies; a listing of titles refers to the "Author & story" section. References to sources providing additional information are provided for some authors.

§ Another work devoted exclusively to the short story is Luis Leal, *Bibliografía del cuento mexicano* (Emory, Ga. : Emory Univ. ; México : Ed. de Andrea, 1958). Indexes short story collections and also lists separately published stories and those published in periodicals.   Z1424.S54H63

Mendoza-López, Margarita. Teatro mexicano del siglo XX, 1900–1986 : catálogo de obras teatrales / Margarita Mendoza López, Daniel Salazar, Tomás Espinosa. México, D.F. : Instituto Mexicano del Seguro Social, c1987–c1989. 4 v. : ill., ports.   **BE913**

Contents: v. 1–2, A–Z; v. 3–4, A–Z.

Provides synopses and production information for plays listed alphabetically by author.   PQ7189.M4

Monterde, Francisco. Bibliografía del teatro en México. Mexico : Impr. de la Secretaría de Relaciones Exteriores, 1933 [i.e., 1934]. lxxx, 649 p. (Monografías mexicanas, 28).   **BE914**

Repr.: N.Y. : B. Franklin, [1970].

A bibliography of works by Mexican authors and by others who lived in Mexico, including original works, translations and adaptations, foreign works printed in Mexico or on Mexican subjects, and works containing studies on the Mexican theater.

§ More current information is available in *Mexican theatre of the twentieth century*, by Ruth S. Lamb (Claremont, Calif. : Ocelot Pr., 1975); publ. earlier as *Bibliografía del teatro mexicano del siglo XX* (Claremont, Calif. : Claremont Colleges ; México : Ed. de Andrea, 1962). The first section is a survey discussing theater through 1975. Following the main listing by author, bibliographies of additional references and theater journals are included.   Z1424.D7M7

Ocampo, Aurora M. Diccionario de escritores mexicanos / Aurora Maura Ocampo de Gómez, Ernesto Prado Velázquez. [México] : Universidad Nacional Autonoma de México, Centro de Estudios Literarios, [1967]. 422 p. : ill.   **BE915**

Treats both living and deceased persons. In addition to writers of belles-lettres, prominent historians, biographers, philosophers, etc., are included, as are writers of other nationalities who have lived in Mexico and contributed significantly to Mexican letters. Biographical sketches are followed by bibliographies of works by and about the authors.   PQ7106.O24

Rutherford, John. An annotated bibliography of the novels of the Mexican Revolution of 1910–1917 : in English and Spanish. Troy, N.Y. : Whitston, 1972. 180 p.   **BE916**

Spine title: *Novels of the Mexican Revolution*.

Supersedes Ernest Moore, *Bibliografia de novelistas de la revolución Mexicana* (México, 1941).

A biobibliographical dictionary arranged by author covering "those wide-ranging prose narratives written by Mexicans which deal in their entirety or in a part of considerable importance with events which took place in Mexico between November 1910 and February

1917."—*Introd*. Each entry provides biographical information and a description of the content and importance of the author's work. Locations in Mexican libraries are indicated for many works, as is the availability of translations. Introduction in English and Spanish. No index.

Z1424.F4R88

Nicaragua

Arellano, Jorge Eduardo. Panorama de la literatura nicaragüense. 5th ed. Managua : Ediciones Nacionales, 1986. 197 p.   **BE917**

4th ed., 1982.

A survey history in five parts, the first devoted to historical eras in chronological order, the others to genres, each section subdivided. Much information centers on individual authors. Extensive notes to each section, as well as a general bibliography. No index.

PQ7510.A7

LITERATURES OF SOUTH AMERICA

Argentina

Arrieta, Rafael Alberto. Historia de la literatura argentina. Buenos Aires : Ed. Peuser, 1958–60. 6 v. : ill.   **BE918**

Contents: v. 1, La literatura colonial: las letras durante la revolucíon y el periodo de la independencia; v. 2, Esteban Echverría y el romanticismo en la Plata: las letras en el destierro; v. 3, Las letras en la segunda mitad del siglo XIX; v. 4, Las letras en la primera mitad del siglo XX; v. 5, Folklore literario y literatura folklórica; Guillermo E. Hudson, escritor Argentino de lengua Inglesa; Índice analítico de folklore; v. 6, Panoramas complementarios; Indice analítico de la obra.

A substantial reference history covering literature through the 1930s, more thinly thereafter. Extensive footnote references throughout. Each volume also has a selective bibliography of general references, the one in v. 5 being more substantial for folklore. That volume has a separate analytical index to folklore as well. Author, title subject index for the set in v. 6. Many illustrations.   PQ7611.A7

Foster, David William. Argentine literature : a research guide. 2nd ed., rev. and expanded. N.Y. : Garland, 1982. 778 p. (Garland reference library of the humanities, v. 338).   **BE919**

1st ed., 1970, by D. W. Foster and V. R. Foster had title: *Research guide to Argentine literature*.

A section of 30 general and special topics is followed by listings for 73 individual authors. "The general criterion has been to list those items considered useful to serious scholarly research and opinion—articles in all types of scholarly journals and the most important cultural ones, and all monographic studies—and those likely to be easily accessible in Latin America and the United States ..."—*Introd*. Also includes review articles and doctoral dissertations. Index of critics.

§ A useful bibliography of bibliographies is *Bibliografía de bibliografías literarias argentinas*, by Horacio Jorge Becco (Wash. : Secretaría General, Organizacíon on de los Estados Americanos, 1972). Includes bibliographies on general topics as well as on individual authors. Author, title, and subject indexes.   Z1621.F66

Orgambide, Pedro G. Enciclopedia de la literatura argentina / Pedro G. Orgambide, Roberto Yahni. Buenos Aires : Editorial Sudamericana, [1970]. 639 p.   **BE920**

Primarily a dictionary of authors, with biographical, critical and bibliographical information, including in some instances references to criticism. Some entries devoted to topics.

§ For 20th century novelists, essayists, and poets active in 1941 a valuable source of information is *Panorama de la literatura argentina contemporanea*, by Juan Pinto (Buenos Aires : Ed. Mundi, 1941). For each writer provides a list of works (including drama if the author wrote that genre as well), references to criticism, a biographical and critical statement, and excerpts from critical evaluations.   PQ7606.O7

Quienes son los escritores argentinos. Buenos Aires : Ediciones Crisol, 1980. 206 p.   **BE921**

Offers biographical sketches of contemporary Argentinian writers.

§ More complete and up-to-date biobibliographical coverage for contemporary dramatists can be found in Perla Zayas de Lima, *Diccionario de autores teatrales argentinos, 1950-1990* (Buenos Aries : Galerna, 1991; 1st ed., 1981). Covers writers active during the period indicated.   Z1620.Q53

Bolivia

Ortega, José. Diccionario de la literatura boliviana / José Ortega, Adolfo Cáceres Romero. La Paz : Editorial Los Amigos del Libro, 1977. 337 p.   **BE922**

A dictionary of Bolivian writers, giving brief biographical information, bibliographies of works by and about the author, and often a brief critical note.

——. ——. *Supplemento 1* ([n.d.]. 12 p.). Adds authors omitted.

§ Fuller critical information on authors is available in two works by Augusto Guzman, publ. 1982 by the same publisher as Ortega: *Biografías de la literatura boliviana : biografia, evaluacion, bibliografia*, covering authors form 1520 to 1925, and *Biografias de la nueva literatura boliviana*, on 20th-century writers. Information on writers of all time periods, including some not in other sources, can be found in *Historia de la literatura boliviana*, by Enrique Finot (5a ed. La Paz : Gisbert, 1981), the standard history. Information centers substantially on individual writers, with bibliographical references throughout and many excerpts. Appendixes provide additional information on the colonial and contemporary eras. Portraits; name index.   Z1650.O77

Brazil

See also *Latin American writers* (BE891), Daniel S. Wogan, *A literatura hispano-americana no Brasil, 1877–1944* (BE879), and the section for Portugal below.

Bibliografia de dramaturgia brasileira. São Paulo : Escola de Comunicações e Artes da USP, Associação Museu Lasar Segall, 1981–83. 2 v.   **BE923**

Vol. 2 has title: Bibliografia da dramaturgia brasileira.

Contents: v. 1, A–M; v. 2, N–Z.

An author listing of dramatic works (more than 3,000 entries) giving publication information, together with indication of library locations and the number of acts and number of performers in each piece. The two volumes have separate title indexes.   Z1684.D7B5

Brasil, Assis. Dicionário prático de literatura brasileira. [Rio de Janeiro] : Edições de Ouro, [1979]. 324 p. : ill.   **BE924**

A brief biographical sketch is followed by a list of each writer's work and a critical note. Entry is under the author's first name.

PQ9527.B7

Carpeaux, Otto Maria. Pequena bibliografía crítica da literatura brasileira. Nova ediç. [i.e., 4. ed.], com um apêndice de Assis Brasil, incluindo 47 novos escritores. [Rio de Janeiro] : Ediçoes de Ouro, [1980?]. 470 p.   **BE925**

1st ed., 1951.

Arranged chronologically by literary periods and movements, with bibliographical listings of works by and about individual authors. Covers from the colonial period to modern times. Apart from the appendix of new writers, the text of this edition is unchanged from the 3rd ed. of 1964.

§ Updated and augmented by David William Foster, *Brazilian literature: a research bibliography* (BE930).   Z1681.C3

Chamberlain, Bobby J. Portuguese language and Luso-Brazilian literature : an annotated guide to selected reference works. N.Y. : Modern Language Association of America, 1989. 95 p. (Selected bibliographies in language and literature, 6).   **BE926**
For annotation, *see* BD163.   Z2725.A2C45

Coutinho, Afrânio. A literatura no Brasil / Afrânio Coutinho, dir. ; Eduardo de Faria Coutinho, co-dir. 3a. ed., rev. e atualizada. Rio de Janeiro : J. Olympio Editora; Niterói : Universidade Federal Fluminense, 1986. 6 v.   **BE927**
1st ed., 1955–59.
Contents: v. 1, Parte I, Preliminares e generalidades; v. 2, Parte II, Estilos de época, era barroca, era neoclassica; v. 3, Parte II, Estilos de época, era romântica; v. 4, Parte II, Estilos de epoca, era realista, era de transição; v. 5, Parte II, Estilos de época, era modernista; v. 6, Parte III, Relações e perspectivas, conclusão, biobibliografia dos colaboradores, índice de nomes títulos e assuntos.
A detailed history with extensive notes and references.   PQ9511.C66

Dictionary of Brazilian literature / Irwin Stern, ed. in chief. N.Y. : Greenwood, 1988. 402 p.   **BE928**
Contains "approximately 300 entries in English covering the most significant writers, literary schools, and selected cultural movements in Brazilian literary history with an emphasis on twentieth-century and very contemporary figures."—*Pref.* The volume is "oriented toward the English-reading public"; essays and bibliographies take particular care to identify English-language translations and criticism. In addition to the alphabetically arranged entries, a map, chronology, glossary, and lengthy introductory essay on Brazilian literature in cultural perspective are included. General index.   PQ9506.D53

Enciclopédia de literatura brasileira / direção, Afrânio Coutinho, J. Galante de Sousa … [et al.]. Rio de Janeiro : Ministério da Educação, Fundação de Assistência ao Estudiante, 1990. 2 v. (1379 p.) : ill.   **BE929**
At head of title: Oficina Literária Afrânio Coutinho, OLAC.
A notable encyclopedia, compiled by a large panel of experts, covering all aspects of Brazilian literature, and essential in research and libraries supporting the study of Latin American and Portuguese literature. Writers covered are from every historical era and include all belles lettres areas as well as essayists, critics, authors of chronicles, historians, philosophers, journalists, and scientists where the style and/or content of their work converges with literature. Entries also are devoted to principal works, themes, genres, literary and rhetorical terms, eras, movements and groups, journals, literary influences, regional literature, folklore, academies, etc. Information provided for authors includes biography and primary and selective secondary bibliographies, and often critical comments. Entries both for writers and for other topics range from a paragraph to lengthy essays. There is no index, but comprehensive cross-references in the main alphabetical sequence serve this purpose.
Introductory material includes a substantial survey discussion of Brazilian literature and generous bibliographies of both general and specialized reference works and studies. The organization and content of the encyclopedia and all abbreviations used also are clearly delineated.   PQ9506.E53

Foster, David William. Brazilian literature : a research bibliography / David William Foster, Walter Rela. N.Y. : Garland, 1990. 426 p. (Garland reference library of the humanities, v. 1162).   **BE930**

Lists books and articles in both a general section, which encompasses anthologies, periods of literary history, and particular literary forms, and an authors section, which includes criticisms on 150 Brazilian authors. Names index.   Z1681.F73

Gomes, Celuta Moreira. O conto brasileiro e sua crítica : bibliografía (1841–1974). Rio de Janeiro : Biblioteca Nacional, 1977. 2 v. (654 p.).   **BE931**
An earlier work by the same author, *Bibliografía do conto brasileiro* (publ. 1968–69 in 2 v.) covered 1841–1967.
A bibliography of the Brazilian short story, together with critical studies of the writers and their works. Arranged by literary author, with listings of their own works followed by references to critical writings. Indexes of titles and of critics.   Z1684.S5G65

Gonçalves, Augusto de Freitas Lopes. Dicionário histórico e literário do teatro no Brasil. Rio de Janeiro : Livraria Editora Cátedra, 1975–82. v. 1–4. (In progress).   **BE932**
Contents: v. 1–4, A–D.
A dictionary of dramatists, actors, actresses and others in various performing arts professions, together with entries for individual theater pieces (comedies, tragedies, operas, zarzuelas, etc.).   PN2471.G6

Igreja, Francisco. Dicionário de poetas contemporâneos. Rio de Janiero : Oficina Letras & Artes, 1988. 148 p.   **BE933**
A dictionary of living poets, with bibliographies of books, anthology contributions, and some secondary literature. Appendixes include lists of periodicals and literary academies with addresses.   PQ9527.I37

Menezes, Raimundo de. Dicionário literário brasileiro. 2. ed., rev., aumentada e atualizada. Rio de Janeiro : Livros Técnicos e Científicos Editora, [1978]. 803 p.   **BE934**
1st ed., *Dicionário literário Brasileiro ilustrado*, 1969. 5 v.
The bulk of the work is devoted to more than 3,000 biographical sketches with bibliographies of works by and about the authors, followed by an alphabetically arranged section of articles on literary terms, schools, and academies. Also includes a dictionary of pseudonyms and a select general bibliography.   PQ9527.M39

Pequeno dicionário de literatura brasileira / organizado e dirigido por José Paulo Paes e Massaud Moisés. 2a. ed. rev. e ampl. São Paulo : Editora Cultrix, [1980]. 462 p.   **BE935**
1st ed., 1967.
Offers brief, signed articles by some 30 scholars. Author entries predominate but literary terms, schools, etc., are included. Entries for authors include biography, some critical information, and lists of works by and about the author. Indexes of authors and titles.   PQ9506.P4

Rela, Walter. Fuentes para el estudio de la nueva literatura brasileña, de las vanguardias a hoy. Montevideo : Instituto de Cultura Uruguayo-Brasileño, [1990]. 193 p.   **BE936**
A bibliography and biobibliographical dictionary focusing on Brazilian literature since 1956 and in particular on writing, most importantly poetry but including other genres, identifiable with the contemporary Vanguardist and experimentalist movement in Brazil. The bibliographies cover general bibliographies and dictionaries, general and regional histories of contemporary Brazilian literature, anthologies, and books and articles specifically on Vanguardism. A brief essay discussing Vanguardist poetry also is provided. Entries for authors include a brief biographical and critical statement, a list of works by the writer with title and date, and occasional references to criticism. Name indexes to critics and to authors.
§ For the earlier Vanguardist era, *see* Merlin H. Foster and K. David Jackson, *Vanguardism in Latin American literature : an annotated bibliographical guide* (BE872).   Z1683.3.R44

Topete, José Manuel. A working bibliography of Brazilian literature. Gainesville : Univ. of Florida Pr., 1957. 114 p.   **BE937**

Arranged by genre, with general works listed first. Includes a section for authors of criticism, essays, journalism, and biography, and one for English and Spanish translations, in addition to those for prose fiction, poetry, and drama. Listings for authors include both primary works and criticism.

§ An older bibliography of primary works still useful for its painstaking bibliographical detail and inclusion of many minor authors is: *A tentative bibliography of Brazilian belles-lettres* (Cambridge, Mass. : Harvard Univ. Pr., 1931) by Jeremiah D. M. Ford, Arthur Whittem, and Maxwell I. Raphael. Alphabetical by author; includes both published and unpublished works. A list of literary periodicals is included.   Z1681.T6

Chile

Castillo, Homero. Historia bibliográfica de la novela chilena / Homero Castillo, Raúl Silva Castro. México : Ed. de Andrea ; Charlottesville : Bibliographical Soc. of the Univ. of Virginia, 1961. 214 p.   **BE938**

Added title page in English: Bibliography of the Chilean novel.

Arranged alphabetically by author; lists more than 4,000 titles, including short stories in collections.   Z1714.F4C33

Durán Cerda, Julio. Repertorio del teatro chileno : bibliografía, obras inéditas y estrenadas. Santiago de Chile : [Ed. Universitaria], 1962. 247 p. (Universidad de Chile. Facultad de Filosofía y Educación. Publicaciones del Instituto de Literatura Chilena. Serie C, no. 1).   **BE939**

The "works" section lists 1,710 items alphabetically by author; a selective list of studies, and author and title indexes are appended.   Z1714.D7D8

Foster, David William. Chilean literature : a working bibliography of secondary sources. Boston : G.K. Hall, [1978]. 236 p.   **BE940**

A section of general references on literary history, genres, etc., is followed by sections on individual Chilean authors. Index to critics.   Z1711.F67

Szmulewicz, Efraín. Diccionario de la literatura chilena. 2a ed. corr. y aum. Santiago de Chile : Editorial Andres Bello, [1984]. 494 p.   **BE941**

1st ed., 1977.

Alphabetical by author. Each entry provides brief biographical information and a list of works giving title and date only. Appendixes include essays on literary topics ("Ruben Dario en Chile") a section of entries for literary groups, one for literary prizes, and a list of general references.   Z1710.S95

University of California, Berkeley. Library. Contemporary Chilean literature in the University Library at Berkeley : a bibliography with introduction, biographical notes, and commentaries / by Gaston Somoshegyi-Szokol. Berkeley : Center for Latin American Studies, Univ. of California, Berkeley, 1975. 161*l*.   **BE942**

In three parts: (1) bibliography of selected 20th-century authors; (2) bibliographical guide to histories of Chilean literature; (3) biographical sketches of "selected contemporary Chilean writers whose works are considered to be the most significant in Chilean letters."—*Introd.* Index of authors.   Z1713.C25

Colombia

Ayala Poveda, Fernando. Manual de literatura colombiana. 3a ed., rev. y actualizada. Bogotá : Educar Editores, 1986. 405 p. : ill., ports.   **BE943**

Treats Colombian literature period-by-period, from earliest to modern times, with attention to individual authors and literary movements. Disappointingly little bibliography. Author index, and a detailed table of contents.   PQ8161.A9

Orjuela, Héctor H. Bibliografía de la poesía colombiana. Bogotá : Instituto Caro y Cuervo, 1971. 486 p. (Instituto Caro y Cuervo. Publicaciones. Serie bibliográfica, 9).   **BE944**

An author listing of the works of Colombian poets published as books, pamphlets, or broadsides. Locates copies in numerous Colombian and foreign libraries.   Z1744.P7

——————— Bibliografía del teatro colombiano. Bogotá : [Instituto Caro y Cuervo], 1974. 312 p. (Instituto Caro y Cuervo. Publicaciones. Serie bibliográfica, 10).   **BE945**

The main section is an author listing of Colombian dramatic literature. The "Secciones complementarias," p. 209–76, offer lists of sources for the study of the Colombian theater, for the study of Latin American theater, and for the study of theater in general. Index of titles of the dramas. Many bibliographical and descriptive notes. Library locations are frequently given, including copies in selected U.S. libraries.   Z1744.D7

——————— Fuentes generales para el studio de la literatura colombiana : guía bibliográfica. Bogotá : [Instituto Caro y Cuervo], 1968. 863 p. (Instituto Caro y Cuervo. Publicaciones. Serie bibliográfica, 7).   **BE946**

A comprehensive bibliographical guide for the study of Colombian literature, with sections for bibliographies, dictionaries and guides, biographical works, anthologies and collections, history and criticism, literary movements and periods, literary genres, translations, etc. Library locations are given. Indexed.   Z1008.C685

Ortega Torres, José Joaquin. Historia de la literatura colombiana. 2. ed. aum. Bogotá : Ed. Cromos, 1935. 1214 p. : ill.   **BE947**

Repr. 1990 in 2 v.

Contains some general literary history, but the greater part of the work consists of biographies and bibliographics, with extracts from the works of some 180 Colombian authors.

§ José Nuñez Segura's *Literatura colombiana : sinopsis y comentarios de autores representativos* (14a ed. Medcllín : Editorial Bedout, 1976. 893 p.) also offers biographical notes on authors, together with excerpts from their writings.   PQ8161.O67

Porras Collantes, Ernesto. Bibliografía de la novela en Colombia : con notas de contenido y crítica de las obras y guías de comentarios sobre los autores. Bogotá : Inst. Caro y Cuervo, 1976. 888 p. (Instituto Caro y Cuervo. Publicaciones. Serie bibliográfica, 11).   **BE948**

Based on the bibliography in A. Curcio Altamar's *Evolución de la novela en Colombia* (Bogotá, 1957). Forms a useful companion to Héctor H. Orjuela's bibliographies (in the same series) covering Colombian poetry and drama (BE944; BE945).

More than 2,300 entries. Arranged alphabetically by author; title and chronological indexes. Bibliographical information is very full, including details of serialization where relevant; reprints and translations are included; library locations are given (including a number of libraries outside Colombia). Numerous notes on contents, and excerpts from critical evaluations; citations to critical studies are frequently given.   Z1008.C685

Sánchez López, Luis María. Diccionario de escritores colombianos. 3a ed., rev. y aum. Bogotá : Plaza & Janés, 1985. 903 p. : ill.   **BE949**

1st ed., 1978.

Offers brief biographical notes and commentary (often no more than an identifying phrase) on Colombian writers both living and deceased, together with lists of their works. Includes a list of pseudonyms with the author's real name given.   Z1740.S26

Ecuador

Barriga López, Franklin. Diccionario de la literatura ecuatoriana / Franklin Barriga López, Leonardo Barriga López. 2a ed., corr. y aum. Quito : Editorial Casa de la Cultura Ecuatoriana, [1980]. 5 v.   **BE950**
  Primarily a dictionary of authors with biography and critical comment but very little bibliography.
  § For a listing of primary works by Ecuadorian authors *see*: Thomas L. Welch and Rene L. Gutierrez, *Bibliografia de la literatura ecuatoriana* (Wash. : Biblioteca Colón, Organizacion de los Estados Americanos, 1989). Title index.   PQ8201.B35

Luzuriaga, Gerardo. Bibliografía del teatro ecuatoriano, 1900–1982. Quito : Casa de la Cultura Ecuatoriana, 1984. 131 p.   **BE951**
  The main portion of the work is an author listing of dramatic works; it is preceded by a list of reference sources and followed by a selection of citations to critical writings.

Rodríguez Castelo, Hernán. Literatura ecuatoriana, 1830–1980. [Otavala] : Instituto Otavaleño de Antropologia, 1980. 171 p. : ill.   **BE952**
  A brief history of Ecuadorian literature for the period indicated, by one who has written extensively on various aspects of the literature.

Paraguay

Welch, Thomas L. Bibliografía de la literatura paraguaya / Thomas L. Welch, Rene L. Gutiérrez. Wash. : Biblioteca Colón, Organizacíon de los Estados Americanos, 1990. 180 p. (Serie bibliografica Hipólito Unanue, 6).   **BE953**
  An unannotated author listing of 1,501 works by Paraguayan authors of novels, poetry, drama, short stories, and essays. Complete bibliographical information is provided and genre is noted if not obvious from the title. Author and title indexes.   Z1831.W45

Peru

Arriola Grande, F. Maurilio. Diccionario literario del Perú : nomenclatura por autores. [2a. ed.]. Lima : Editorial Universo, [1983]. 2 v. : ill.   **BE954**
  Biographical sketches of Peruvian authors and authors who have resided in Peru, most sketches including some critical commentary. Both deceased and living persons are considered.

Foster, David William. Peruvian literature : a bibliography of secondary sources. Westport, Conn. : Greenwood, [1981]. 324 p.   **BE955**
  A comprehensive unannotated bibliography listing general references and criticism followed by materials on individual authors. Includes bibliographies, monographs, dissertations, and critical studies in periodicals and books. Index to critics.
  § For more current information on Spanish-language materials, a useful annotated bibliography is *El Perú y su literatura : guía bibliográfica*, by Miguel Angel Rodríguez Rea (Lima : Pontifica Universidad Católica del Perú, Fondo Editorial, 1992). Does not cover works on individual authors. In sections by type of publication, i.e. histories, anthologies, dictionaries, bibliographies, then by author. Indexes to authors and subjects.   Z1861.F67

Higgins, James. A history of Peruvian literature. Liverpool ; Wolfeboro, N.H. : F. Cairns, 1987. 379 p. (Liverpool monographs in Hispanic studies, 7).   **BE956**
  An inclusive and detailed history covering the literature in chronological order from its native inception to the present. Extensive foot-note references as well as a selective bibliography. Many quoted passages, in their original language with translation. A glossary of literary terms also is provided. Indexes to authors and titles.   PQ8311.H53

Romero de Valle, Emilia. Diccionario manual de literatura peruana y materias afines. Lima : Univ. Nacional Mayor de San Marcos, [1966]. 356 p.   **BE957**
  Covers a much larger number of authors than F. Maurilio Arriola Grande's *Diccionario literario del Perú* (BE954), but provides less extensive information. In addition to authors, includes genres, periodicals, academies.   PQ8306.R6

Uruguay

Diccionario de literatura uruguaya / [direccíon, Alfredo F. Oreggioni ; coordinacíon, Wilfredo Penco]. Montevideo, Uruguay : Arca : Credisol, [1987]. 3 v. : ill., facsims., ports.   **BE958**
  Contents: v. 1–2, A–Z; v. 3, Obras, cenáculos, páginas literarias, revistas, períodos culturales.
  Signed articles provide, for authors, biographical and critical information and primary and secondary bibliographies. Vol. 3 covers representative titles, literary and cultural schools and eras, and literary journals, and also contains a chronological index and a list of references, including bibliographies for individual authors.
  § For additional chronology, *see*: Walter Rela, *Literatura uruguaya : tablas cronologicas, 1835–1985* (Montevideo : Univ. Catolica del Uruguay, [1986]). Presents chronological tables for essays and criticism, drama, poetry, and narratives, and a list of periodicals published 1838–1986. Name index.   PQ8511.D53x

Rela, Walter. Diccionario de escritores uruguayos. Montevideo : Ediciones de la Plaza, [1986]. 397 p.   **BE959**
  Brief biographical and critical articles are followed by listings of primary works with occasional references to book-length criticism. No index.
  § More complete information on playwrights, as well as theater history, is provided by the same author's *Diccionario de autores teatrales uruguayos & breve historia del teatro uruguayo* (Montevideo: Proyeccíon, [1988]. Lists primary works only. For bibliographical information alone, Rela's *Literatura uruguaya: bibliografia selectiva* (Tempe: Center for Latin American Studies, Arizona State Univ., 1986) duplicates much of the information in the *Diccionario*. A weakness of both sources is listing book-length criticism, but not articles, since monographic studies do not exist for many writers. Complements, but does not supersede, the author's earlier *Fuentes para el estudio de la literatura uruguaya, 1835–1968* ([Montevideo] : Ediciones de la Banda Oriental, [1969]), which lists general studies and anthologies as well as works related to individual authors.   PQ8511.R45

Welch, Thomas L. Bibliografía de la literatura uruguaya. Wash. : Biblioteca Colón, Organización de los Estados Americanos, 1985. 502 p.   **BE960**
  Identifies 9,329 volumes of fiction, poetry, plays, criticism, and essays published primarily in the 20th century. Items are arranged alphabetically by author, with name (including editors and personal subjects) and title indexes.   Z1891.W45

Venezuela

Becco, Horacio Jorge. Fuentes para el estudio de la literatura venezolana. Caracas : Ediciones Centauro, 1978. 2 v. **BE961**
  A bibliography of published sources for the study of Venezuelan literature. Includes sections for bibliography, biography, literary history and criticism, theater, anthologies, etc. More than 1,800 items; indexed.

§ For bibliographies of bibliographies, Becco also has edited the more selective *Bibliografía de bibliografías venezolanas : literatura (1968–1978)* (Caracas: Casa de Bello, 1979). Covers general works, those specifically on Venezuelan literature, bibliographies published in periodicals, and reviews of bibliographies. Author index.   Z1921.B4

Diccionario general de la literatura venezolana / Instituto de Investigaciones Literarias "Gonzalo Picón Febres". Ed. no. 2. Mérida, Venezuela : Editorial Venezolana : Consejo de Fomento : Cosejo de Publicaciones, Universidad de los Andes, 1987. 2 v. (568 p.).   **BE962**
1st ed., 1974.
An important biobibliographical dictionary, including foreign-born authors working in or writing about Venezuela. Biographical sketches are followed by bibliographies—frequently extensive—of works by and about the authors. Entries range from a paragraph to several pages. The 2nd ed. updates entries in the 1st and adds writers omitted. At the time of the 1st ed. additional volumes covering important works, and eras, schools, and movements, were planned but have not appeared.   Z1920.D5

Hirshbein, Cesia Ziona. Hemerografía venezolana, 1890–1930. Caracas : Ediciones de la Facultad de Humanidades y Educación, Inst. de Estudios Hispanoamericanos, Univ. Central de Venezuela, 1978. 574 p.   **BE963**
A bibliography of literary writings appearing in Venezuelan periodicals during the period indicated. Entries are grouped by genre, then entered alphabetically by author. Writings of foreign authors are listed in separate sections.   Z1923.H57

Larrazábal Henríquez, Osvaldo. Bibliografía del cuento venezolano / Osvaldo Larrazábal Henríquez, Amaya Llebot, Gustavo Luis Carrera. [Caracas] : Universidad Central de Venezuela, Facultad de Humanidades y Educación, Instituto de Investigaciones Literarias, [1975]. 313 p.   **BE964**
A listing by author of Venezuelan short stories. Includes individual stories published in anthologies and periodicals, and entire collections by one writer with contents noted. Full information on multiauthor anthologies is given in an appendix. Other appendixes list authors represented by only one story, provide a chronology of the short stories, name index, author index, title index of collections, chronology of anthologies and collections, and title index of stories.   Z1924.S5L37

Lovera De-Sola, Roberto J. Bibliografía de la crítica literaria venezolana, 1847–1977. [Caracas] : Instituto Autónomo Biblioteca Nacional y de Servicios de Bibliotecas, [1982]. 489 p.   **BE965**
A bibliography of literary criticism published in Venezuela and therefore not limited to works on Venezuelan literature. Arranged by author, with indexes of authors, editors, etc., and of titles, but not of specific subjects. Brief annotations for most entries; special section on theater criticism.   Z1921.L68

Rojas Uzcátegui, José de la Cruz. Bibliografía del teatro venezolano / José de la Cruz Rojas Uzcátegui and Lubio Cardozo. Mérida : Univ. de Los Andes, Facultad de Humanidades y Educación, Inst. de Investigaciones Literarias "Gonzalo Picón Febres," Consejo de Publicaciones, 1980. 199 p.   **BE966**
An author listing (949 entries) of published dramas is followed by appendixes listing unpublished plays (and those for which only incomplete information was available), of translations, and a chronology. Title index.   Z1924.D7R64

Sambrano Urdaneta, Oscar. Contribución a una bibliografía general de la poesía venezolana en el siglo XX. Caracas : Ediciones de la Facultad de Humanidades y Educación, Escuela de Letras, Univ. Central de Venezuela, 1979. 367 p.   **BE967**
A section listing individual poets and their works is followed by a list of anthologies and a section of critical studies that provides annotations outlining the contents of works listed. Author and title indexes, chronology, and lists of recipients of two major awards are included.   Z1923.S35

LITERATURES OF THE CARIBBEAN

Allis, Jeannette B. West Indian literature : an index to criticism, 1930–1975. Boston : G. K. Hall, [1981]. 353 p.   **BE968**
Indexes relevant materials in selected American and British periodicals as well as in West Indian magazines and newspapers; five collections of literary essays are also indexed. In three sections: (1) Index of authors; (2) Index of general articles; (3) Index of critics and reviewers. Appendix of books on West Indian literature.
§ Can be used with *Caribbean writing: a checklist*, by Roger Hughes (London: Commonwealth Institute Library Services, 1986. [Checklists on Commonwealth literature, no. 4]), which lists works by and about Caribbean writers, including anthologies, collections, and special issues of journals devoted to Caribbean literature. An appendix lists writers by country. Excludes articles, referring readers to Allis.   Z1502.B5A38

Caribbean writers : a bio-bibliographical-critical encyclopedia / ed., Donald E. Herdeck. Wash. : Three Continents Pr., [1979]. 943 p. : ill.   **BE969**
In four main sections: (1) Anglophone literature from the Caribbean; (2) Francophone literature from the Caribbean; (3) Literatures of the Netherlands Antilles and Suriname; (4) Spanish-language literature from the Caribbean. Each section includes one or more introductory essays, biographical/critical entries for individual authors, and supplementary lists of bibliographies, critical studies, selected journals, etc. No general index.   PN849.C3C3

Fifty Caribbean writers : a bio-bibliographical critical sourcebook / ed. by Daryl Cumber Dance. N.Y. : Greenwood, 1986. 530 p.   **BE970**
Essays by contributing scholars treat individual authors according to a uniform pattern: biography, major works and themes, critical reception, honors and awards, and bibliography of editions and studies. Indexed.   PR9205.A52F54

Paravisini-Gebert, Lizabeth. Caribbean women novelists : an annotated critical bibliography / comp. by Lizabeth Paravisini-Gebert and Olga Torres-Seda ; with contributions from the Dutch by Hilda van Neck-Yoder. Westport, Conn. ; London : Greenwood, 1993. 427 p. (Bibliographies and indexes in world literature, no. 36).   **BE971**
Lists primary and secondary works for approximately 150 women fiction writers of the Caribbean and Suriname who have published at least one novel since 1950. Attempts to be comprehensive; many entries are annotated, and biographical information is supplied when available. Includes listings for translations, interviews, recordings, broadcast literature, and reviews. A general section covers sources on Caribbean literature and on individual countries; the main listing is alphabetical by author. Indexes to: authors by country, titles of novels, critics, and themes and key words. An appendix by Hilda van Neck-Yoder covers "Literature in the Netherlands Antilles : a guide to resources."
§ Broader bibliographic coverage for women writers is provided by: *Bibliography of women writers from the Caribbean 1831–1986*, by Brenda F. Berrian (Wash. : Three Continents Pr., 1988). An unannotated bibliography of "creative works—novels, short stories, poetry, folklore, autobiographies, biographies, and children's literature—by women writers of [the] Caribbean...and the Guyanes in English, French, Dutch, Spanish, Creole, Sranen Tongo, and Papiamento."—*Introd.* Includes criticism, cookbooks, book reviews, and broadcast literature. In four sections by language groups, then by genre. Name index in each section.   Z1595.C364

Cuba

Arrom, José Juan. Historia de la literatura dramática cubana. New Haven, Conn. : Yale Univ. Pr., 1944. 132 p. : ill. (Yale Romanic studies, v.23).   **BE972**

Repr.: N.Y. : AMS Pr., 1973.

Bibliografía general, p.93–94; Apéndice bibliográfico de obras dramáticas cubanas, p.95–127. This appendix is a useful bibliography of the Cuban theater. Locates copies in four libraries in the U. S. and five in Cuba.   PQ7381.A7

Diccionario de la literatura cubana / redactora: Marina García. Habana : Editorial Letras Cubanas, 1980–84. 2 v. : ill.   **BE973**

At head of title: Instituto de Literatura y Lingüística de la Academia de Ciencias de Cuba.

Biographical articles predominate, but there are entries for many literary journals, organizations, terms, etc. Bibliographies for authors include works by the writer and generous listings for criticism.   PQ7371.D5

Dictionary of twentieth-century Cuban literature / ed. by Julio A. Martínez. N.Y. : Greenwood, 1990. 537 p.   **BE974**

"Designed to serve as a useful, one volume companion to contemporary Cuban literature, this dictionary produces, in a single alphabetical sequence, ready reference information on contemporary Cuban creative writers on the island and in exile as well as essays on literary genres and movements."—*Pref.* Covers 1900 to mid-1980s. Signed articles on authors, many of some length, include biography, literary analysis, and discussion of criticism. A bibliography of primary works and criticism for each author is included as well. Essays on genres and movements also provide lists of references. An appendix describes nine literary journals. Author/title index.   PQ7378.D53

Foster, David William. Cuban literature : a research guide. N.Y. : Garland, 1985. 522 p. (Garland reference library of the humanities, v.511).   **BE975**

A bibliography of general works, works on special forms and topics, and writings on individual authors; in the latter case "the overriding principle has been to include those authors who have attracted a measurable degree of criticism of interest to research scholars in literature."—*Introd.* Lists books, periodical articles, and dissertations. Index of critics.   Z1521.F694

Maratos, Daniel C. Escritores de la diáspora cubana : manual biobibliográfica = Cuban exile writers : a biobibliographic handbook / by Daniel C. Maratos and Marnesba D. Hill. Metuchen, N.J. : Scarecrow, 1986. 391 p.   **BE976**

In Spanish and English.

Offers biography and bibliography for approximately 420 Cuban literary exiles, 1959 to the present, both living and deceased. Introduction: Exile in the Cuban literary experience. Entries are alphabetical by author, and give basic biographical and career information. Bibliographies attempt to be comprehensive for book-length works, including translations, but do not list articles. Criticism is very selective, and includes monographs and reviews. Title index.   Z1520.M37

Remos y Rubio, Juan Nepomuceno José. Historia de la literatura cubana. [Habana] : Cardenas, 1945. 3 v.   **BE977**

Repr.: Miami, Fla. : Mnemosyne Pub. Co., 1969.

A comprehensive history of Cuban literature from its origin to recent times. Includes biographies and bibliographies.   PQ7371.R4

Puerto Rico

Foster, David William. Puerto Rican literature : a bibliography of secondary sources. Westport, Conn. : Greenwood, [1982]. 232 p.   **BE978**

A section of general references, subdivided topically, is followed by sections on individual authors. Index of authors of critical works.   Z1557.L56F67

González, Nilda. Bibliografía de teatro puertorriqueño : [siglos XIX y XX]. [Río Piedras, P.R.] : Editorial Universitaria, Universidad de Puerto Rico, 1977. 223 p.   **BE979**

A comprehensive listing of Puerto Rican drama, published and unpublished, for the last two centuries. Provides as much information as could be determined for each work: genre, date and location of performance, bibliographical information if published and available, and references to secondary material on the author and on individual plays, including reviews. For unpublished works provides library location or reference to source of information. Bibliography of general criticism is provided, and the introduction is an overview of Puerto Rican theater. Appendixes cover additional topics including operas and musicals, unpublished works in specific collections, theater festivals, theater and drama groups, and pseudonyms. Author and title indexes.   PQ7431

Rivera de Alvarez, Josefina. Diccionario de literatura puertorriqueña. 2. ed. rev. y aumentada y puesta al día hasta 1967. San Juan, P.R. : Instituto de Cultura Puertorriqueña, 1970–74. 2 v. in 3.   **BE980**

1st ed., 1955.

The first volume (578 p.), designated as "Introducción: Panorama histórico de la literatura puertorriqueña," is essentially a literary history of Puerto Rico with a brief general bibliography. Vol. 2 (in 2 v.) is an alphabetically arranged series of articles (with bibliographies) on individual authors, literary terms, movements, etc. Entries for individual writers stress critical evaluation and literary status as much as biographical detail.

§ Considerably less substantive is *Puerto Rican authors: a biobibliographical handbook*, by Marnesba D. Hill and Harold B. Schleifer (Metuchen, N.J. : Scarecrow, 1974), which provides brief biobibliographies in English and Spanish concerning 251 authors from 1493 to the early 1970s, and includes authors living at the time of publication.

Very brief biobibliographical information concerning 2,000 Puerto Rican poets, many not found in other sources, is provided in Salvador Arana Soto, *Catálogo de poetas puertorriqueños* (San Juan : Sociedad de Autores Puertorriqueños, 1968. 257 p. *Suplemento*, 1972. 39 p.). Appendixes lists poets by region, poets born or resident abroad, poets who died abroad, and pseudonyms, and reprint eight critical articles on poetry from periodicals. Bibliography.   PQ7421.R48

Trinidad and Tobago

Wharton-Lake, Beverly D. Creative literature of Trinidad and Tobago : a bibliography. Wash. : Columbus Memorial Library, Organization of American States, 1988. 102 p. (Hipólito Uranue bibliographic series, 4).   **BE981**

Lists 842 works, mostly books, by author, with a title index. Does not include criticism.   PR9272.Z99W53x

LITERATURES OF EUROPE

General works

Bodart, Roger. Guide littéraire de la Belgique, de la Hollande, et du Luxembourg / par Roger Bodart, Marc Galle, et Garmt Stuiveling. [Paris] : Hachette, 1972. 778 p. : maps ; 21 cm.   **BE982**

A detailed, informative, and well-organized guide to literary associations for the Benelux countries, arranged in itineraries outlined in the "Table méthodique." Eight city maps are included, as well as others reflecting particular authors and themes. Indexes of places and names.   DH16.B55

Farrier, Susan E. The medieval Charlemagne legend : an annotated bibliography. N.Y. : Garland, 1993. 646 p. (Garland medieval bibliographies, vol. 15 ; Garland reference library of the humanities, vol. 984).   **BE983**

A classified, annotated, international bibliography, intended for literary scholars but covers comprehensively both the historical and the literary Charlemagne of Europe, and related works and traditions. An important source for all medievalists. More than 2,700 items, including books, articles, dissertations, chapters, focus on, but are not limited to, publications of the last two decades. In three main sections—The historical Charlemagne, Medieval biography and chronicle, and Charlemagne literature—the latter forming by far the bulk of the bibliography. Includes primary works and editions as well as studies. Two appendixes cover "Charlemagne's obscure relatives" and provide a list of Charlemagne texts by language. Indexes of authors, editors, and translators; subjects and works; modern translations; and Festschrift/Denkschrift honorees.   PQ203.5.C45

Fisher, John Hurt. The medieval literature of Western Europe : a review of research, mainly 1930–1960. [N.Y.] : Publ. for the Modern Language Assoc. of America by N.Y. Univ. Pr., 1966. 432 p. (Modern Language Association of America. Revolving fund series, 22).   **BE984**

An MLA-sponsored survey of literary scholarship similar to others sponsored by MLA: *Victorian prose : a guide to research*, ed. by David J. De Laura (BE755); *Victorian fiction : a second guide to research*, ed. by George H. Ford (BE668); *The Victorian poets : a guide to research*, by Frederic Everett Faverty (BE703); *The English Romantic poets and essayists : a review of research and criticism*, ed. by Carolyn Washburn Houtchens and Lawrence Huston Houtchens (see BE702); and *The English Romantic poets : a review of research and criticsm*, by John Clubbe, ed. by Frank Jordan (BE702).

Specialists have contributed chapters (with appropriate subdivisions which make for easy use) on Latin, Old English, Middle English, French, German, Old Norse, Italian, Spanish, Catalan, Portuguese, and Celtic medieval literatures. Chapters are "confined to the tools for research and the most important research produced between about 1930 and 1960" (*Foreword*), with evaluative comments. Indexed.   PN671.F5

Literature of the Renaissance. (*In* Studies in philology : v. 14 [1917]–v. 66 [1969]). Annual.   **BE985**

Title varies; some issues called *Recent literature of the Renaissance*.

Until 1938 covered works on the English Renaissance only. From 1939 covers English, French, Germanic, Italian, Neo-Latin, Spanish, and Portuguese (slight variations). Includes index of proper names.

Ceased publication 1969. "Because of the relatively heavy expense involved in publishing ... and because other bibliographies now duplicate most of the information that has been given in 'Recent Literature of the Renaissance,' the present bibliography [i.e., that covering 1968 publications] will be the last."—*Studies in philology*, May 1969, prelim. note.

May, Charles E. Twentieth century European short story : an annotated bibliography. Pasadena, Calif. : Salem Pr., c1989. 178 p.   **BE986**

Intends to bring together criticism in English, including biography, on 31 authors of short fiction since Chekhov. Includes book-length studies, chapters in books, and articles. Annotations are descriptive. Author index.   Z5917.S5M39 1989

The present state of scholarship in sixteenth-century literature / ed. by William M. Jones. Columbia : Univ. of Missouri Pr., 1978. 257 p.   **BE987**

A series of essays, originally delivered as lectures in 1976–77, giving "a general overview of recent scholarship on the literature of Western Europe in the sixteenth century."—*Pref.* Each essay provides a select bibliography of recent publications, and each makes recommendations concerning areas for future study. No index.   PN731.P7

Reader's encyclopedia of Eastern European literature / ed. by Robert B. Pynsent ; with the assistance of S. I. Kanikova. N.Y. : HarperCollins, c1993. 605 p. : map.   **BE988**

Publ. in the U.K. as *The Everyman companion to East European literature*.

Eastern Europe here refers to those linguistic and political areas which were at one time or another subject to the European continental empires: Austrian, Prussian, Ottoman, and Russian. Limited to fiction, the encyclopedia excludes writers of nonfiction, literary theory, politics, and historiography. Signed entries in alphabetical order give biographical details and comment on the writer's work. Bibliographies for each entry are generally limited to three of the author's works in English translation, and not more than three secondary sources. Other features include historical introduction; a section on anonymous, collective, and oral tradition texts; brief histories of East European literature, alphabetically arranged by language. Separate indexes list authors by language, and anonymous, collective, and oral tradition texts. A general index includes numerous cross-references.   PN849.E9R38

Bibliography

Baltic drama : a handbook and bibliography / ed. by Alfreds Straumanis ; contributing consultants, Joseph Daubenas . [et al.]. Prospect Heights, Ill. : Waveland Pr., c1981. 705 p.   **BE989**

A handbook on Estonian, Latvian, and Lithuanian drama, listing more than 4,600 plays written in the original languages which have been published or produced, with additional historical, biographical, and bibliographical information on the drama and the playwrights. Three main sections, one for each nationality, providing a historical overview, brief biobibliographical essays on individual authors, and a list of plays for each. Most entries are briefly annotated, more important plays at greater length. Chronological table of major dramatists. Subject index to plays dealing with folklore, history, and social change, and to childrens' plays. Bibliography of general historical and critical studies; title and author indexes. Locations in U.S. and Canadian libraries are noted.   PG8103.B34

Regional literatures

Classical literature

General works

Bibliography

L'année philologique : bibliographie critique et analytique de l'antiquité gréco-latine, pub. sous la direction de J. Marouzeau [et al.]. 1924/26– . Paris : Soc. d'Édit. "Les Belles-Lettres,", 28– . Annual.   **BE990**

Continues Jules Marouzeau, *Dix années de bibliographie classique* (BE1003).

A major ongoing international bibliography, in classified arrangement, covering all aspects of classical studies, including authors and texts, literature, linguistics, archaeology, epigraphy and numismatics, history, law, philosophy, and science and technology. Historical coverage ranges from prehistory to the Middle Ages. Each volume includes reference to previous years. Citations are scrupulously detailed and correct. Many entries are annotated and book reviews are noted. Indexes of collections, personal names, geography, and authors.

Beginning with v.36, United States, British, and Commonwealth publications (monographs, reviews, etc.) are reported by a newly established American branch of *L'année philologique* at Chapel Hill, North Carolina. Notes accompanying such entries appear in English. With v.42 (1971), a geographical index was added. Z7016.M35A

Bibliotheca philologica classica. 1874–1938. Leipzig : Reisland, 1875–1941. Annual. **BE991**
"Beiblatt zum Jahresbericht über die Fortschritte der klassischen Altertumswissenschaft."—*t.p.*
An annual survey, wider in scope than Wilhelm Engelmann, *Bibliotheca scriptorum classicorum* and Rudolf Klussmann, *Bibliotheca scriptorum classicorum et graecorum et latinorum* (BE992). No more published. PA3.J3

Engelmann, Wilhelm. Bibliotheca scriptorum classicorum. 8. Aufl. umfassend die Literatur von 1700 bis 1878, neubearb. von E. Preuss. Leipzig : Engelmann, 1880–82. 2 v. **BE992**
Repr. : Hildesheim : G. Olms, 1959.
Contents: v. 1, Greek; v. 2, Latin.
1st ed., 1817; 7th ed., 1858. The 1st–5th eds. were comp. by T. C. F. Enslin (the 5th, ed. by C. W. Löflund, was reissued with a supplement in 1840 by W. Engelmann); 6th–7th eds. comp. by W. Engelmann.
The standard bibliography, useful for information about editions of collected works and separate works, translations, and works about classical authors. Of first importance in the large reference or college library.
§ Continued by: Rudolf Klussmann, *Bibliotheca scriptorum classicorum et graecorum et latinorum. Die Literatur von 1878 bis 1896 einschliesslich umfassend* (Leipzig : Riesland, 1909–13. 2 v. in 4).
Repr. : Hildesheim ; N.Y. : Georg Olms, 1976.
Contents: v. 1, Greek; v. 2, Latin.
Also published as v. 146, 151, 156, and 165 of *Jahresbericht über die Fortschritte der klassischen Altertumswissenschaft* (Berlin : S. Calvary, 1909, 1911–13). Z7016.E58

Fabricius, Johann Albert. Bibliotheca graeca. Editio quarta / variorum curis emendatior atque auctior ; curante Gottlieb Christophoro Harles .... Hamburg : Bohn, 1790–1809. 12 v. **BE993**
Repr.: Hildesheim : G. Olms, 1966–70.
————. ————. Index (Lipsiae : Cnoblock, 1838. 94 p.).
————. *Bibliotheca latina, mediae et infimae aetatis* cum supplemento Christiani Schoettgenii jam a p. Joanne Dominico Mansi ... (Florentiae : Baracchi, 1858–59. 6 v. in 3).
Still useful biobibliographical dictionaries of Greek and Latin authors of the Middle Ages.

Fifty years (and twelve) of classical scholarship : being Fifty years of classical scholarship, rev. with appendices. Oxford : Blackwell ; N.Y. : Barnes & Noble, 1968. 523 p. : ill. **BE994**
A revision and extension of *Fifty years of classical scholarship*, ed. by Maurice Platnauer (1954).
Chapters by contributing scholars survey the advances in various areas of classical scholarship since the founding of the Classical Association. An appendix to each chapter (usually by the original contributor) updates the original edition. Lacks an index. PA3001.F5

Forman, Robert J. Classical Greek and Roman drama : an annotated bibliography. Pasadena, Calif. : Salem Pr., c1989. 239 p. **BE995**
"This volume ... is intended for high school students, college undergraduates, and general readers as a guide to reading and research."—*Introd.* Highly selective. Emphasizes book-length studies and chapters in books providing recommended translations, commentaries, and introductory criticism in English. A section on general studies is followed by individual listings for nine playwrights. Annotations are both descriptive and evaluative. An introduction discusses the evolution of classical drama. Author index. Z7018.D7F67

Gwinup, Thomas. Greek and Roman authors : a checklist of criticism / Thomas Gwinup, Fidelia Dickinson. 2nd ed. Metuchen, N.J. : Scarecrow, 1982. 280 p. **BE996**
1st ed., 1973.
A bibliography of English-language studies intended mainly "for the use of students in the increasingly popular courses in comparative and world literature as well as other courses in the humanities."—*Introd.* A brief section of general works is followed by sections for individual authors. Z7016.G9

Halton, Thomas P. Classical scholarship : an annotated bibliography / Thomas P. Halton and Stella O'Leary. White Plains, N.Y. : Kraus Internat., c1986. 396 p. **BE997**
Updates and reorders Martin McGuire's *Introduction to classical scholarship, a syllabus and bibliographic guide* (Wash. : Catholic Univ. of America Pr., 1961). An annotated bibliography of books, a few essays, serials, and articles divided into 15 subject areas subdivided into smaller topics. Intended for both beginning and advanced researchers. Author and subject indexes. Z6207.C65H34

Harvard University. Library. Classical studies : classification schedules; classified listing by call number; chronological listing; author and title listing. Cambridge : Publ. by Harvard Univ. Libr. ; distr. by Harvard Univ. Pr., 1979. 215 p. (Widener Library shelflist, 57). **BE998**
For a note on the Widener shelflist series, *see* AA115.
Includes about 6,700 shelflist entries for the Widener *Class* class which "provides for much of what is usually thought of as Classical Greek and Roman studies. The class includes works on the history and theory of classical scholarship, the history of classical literature (but not works about individual authors), classical arts and sciences, classical rhetoric, classical prosody, classical inscriptions, and classical mythology and religion."—*p. 3.* Z6207.G7H37

Kristeller, Paul Oskar. Catalogus translationum et commentariorum : Medieval and Renaissance Latin translations and commentaries : annotated lists and guides / ed. in chief, Paul Oskar Kristeller. Wash. : Catholic Univ. of America Pr., 1960–92. v.1–7. (In progress). **BE999**
At head of title: Union Académique Internationale.
Editor in chief varies: later, F. Edward Cranz, Virginia Brown.
This series "will list and describe the Latin translations of ancient Greek authors and the Latin commentaries on ancient Latin (and Greek) authors up to the year 1600 ..."—*Pref.*
This monumental work exemplifies the superb standards of scholarly comprehensiveness and clarity that have come to be expected from projects with which Kristeller is associated. Covers a wide range of authors who wrote prior to 600 CE, not limited to writers of poetry, drama, and literary prose. Vol. 1 contains extensive lists of Greek and Latin authors for whom texts exist (most of whom the series intends to treat) and the first group of biobibliographical chapters. Chapters are published as completed, not in alphabetic or chronological order. Each chapter gives a biographical sketch, then a listing with exhaustive descriptions of manuscript and printed translations and commentaries.
Each volume reprints the preface to v. 1 and includes addenda and corrigenda, an index of manuscripts and of translators and commentators for the volume, a cumulative alphabetic index of ancient authors, and tables of contents for the earlier volumes. Z701.K96

———————— Latin manuscript books before 1600 : a list of the printed catalogues and unpublished inventories of extant collections. 3rd ed. N.Y. : Fordham Univ. Pr., [1965]. 284 p. **BE1000**
For annotation, *see* AA207. Z6601.A1K7

Lambrino, Scarlat. Bibliographie de l'antiquité classique, 1896–1914. Paris : Société d'édition "Les Belles-Lettres", 1951. 1 v. (Collection de bibliographie classique, v. 1). **BE1001**
Contents: pt. 1, Auteurs et textes. No more published.
A valuable work designed to fill the gap in the bibliographical record of classical studies between the works of Wilhelm Engelmann,

Bibliotheca scriptorum classicorum and Rudolf Klussman, *Bibliotheca scriptorum classicorum et graecorum et latinorum* (BE992), which together cover 1700–1896, and the *Dix années de bibliographie classique* of Jules Marouzeau, 1914–24 (BE990 *note*). Following the same plan as the latter, this volume lists editions, translations, and works about classical writers in books and periodicals. The coverage is not limited to literature but includes all phases of Greco-Latin antiquity from prehistory to the Byzantine and Gallo-Roman periods. As in Marouzeau, the second volume was to be concerned with *Matières et disciplines*.   Z7016.L2

Loeb classical library / founded by James Loeb. Cambridge, Mass. : Harvard Univ. Pr., 1912– . v. 1– . (In progress).   **BE1002**

Published in U.K. by Heinemann.

An extensive collection of several hundred volumes in two series, Greek and Latin. Each volume prints parallel texts of the original and an English translation on facing pages, with a brief introduction and a bibliography. The publisher issues periodic catalogs for the set, but there is as yet no general index. Indexes to individual authors, while they vary in kind and value, are frequently useful for locating a subject or specific passage. Some volumes are issued in parts; some have revised editions. Beginning in 1965, the publisher issued reprints of selected volumes.

Marouzeau, Jules. Dix années de bibliographie classique : bibliographie critique et analytique de l'antiquité gréco-latine pour la période 1914–1924. Paris : Société d'Édition "Les Belles-Lettres," 1927–28. 2 v.   **BE1003**

Repr. : N.Y. : B. Franklin, 1969.

Contents: v. 1, Auteurs et textes; v. 2, Matières et disciplines.

Not limited to literature, but covers the whole field of classical studies.

§ Continued by: *L'année philologique* (BE990).   Z7016.M35

Nairn, John Arbuthnot. Classical hand-list / ed. by B. H. Blackwell, Ltd. 3rd ed., rev. and enl. Oxford : Blackwell, 1953. 164 p.   **BE1004**

1st ed., 1931, and 2nd ed., 1939, titled *A hand-list of books relating to the classics and classical antiquity.*

Although dated, still a convenient list of texts and translations of classical authors, with additional sections selectively covering Greek and Roman literary history, philology, history, archaeology and art, religion, philosophy, science, geography, and other areas of classical scholarship. International in scope. Author index.   Z7016.N17

Ooteghem, Jules van. Bibliotheca graeca et latina à l'usage des professeurs des humanités gréco-latines. 3e éd. [Namur : Wesmael-Charlier] : Éd. de la Revue "Les études classiques", [1969]. 387, 107 p.   **BE1005**

The 1st ed. appeared in *Les études classiques* in April and October 1936. This latest ed. updates the 2nd ed. (1946) through 1961 by including a supplementary appendix.

Compiled especially for instructors in the secondary schools and therefore treats mainly authors frequently taught at that level. Nonetheless, the scope is international and scholarly. Both the original edition and the supplement are in three parts: general works, Greek authors, and Latin authors. No author index.   Z7106.O5

Sienkewicz, Thomas J. The classical epic : an annotated bibliography. Pasadena, Calif. : Salem Pr., c1991. 265 p.   **BE1006**

"This bibliography is directed toward the first-time reader of the Classical epics in English translation" and is "designed to help the more advanced high school student and the general college student find a path through the wealth of material which has been written about Homer and Vergil and to discover sources for course papers and projects on the *Iliad*, the *Odyssey*, and the *Aeneid*."—*Introd*. Highly selective. Includes book-length studies and chapters in books. Annotations are descriptive. Author index.   Z7018.E63S55

The year's work in classical studies. v. 1 (1906)–34 (1945/47). London : Arrowsmith, 1907–50. Irregular.   **BE1007**

Repr.: Amsterdam : J. Benjamins, 1969–70.

Ed. for the Council of the Classical Association.

An annual survey in English, not as comprehensive as *Bibliotheca philologica classica* (BE991) or *L'année philologique* (BE990), but international in scope and valuable for providing discussion of the literature as well as bibliography. Chapters often include extensive bibliographic notes and references.   PA11.C7

Bibliography : Periodicals

Southan, Joyce E. A survey of classical periodicals : union catalogue of periodicals relevant to classical studies in certain British libraries. London : Univ. of London, Inst. of Classical Studies, 1962. 181 p. (University of London. Institute of Classical Studies. Bulletin supplement, 13).   **BE1008**

A title list of more than 600 periodicals in some 50 British libraries, providing publishing history and holdings information.

§ Another useful list, covering over 1,800 titles, is Diemut Beck, *Verzeichnis der Zeitschriften in der Bibliothek der Römisch-Germanischen Kommission, bestand am 30. April 1976* (Mainz am Rhein : P. von Zabern, 1977). Arranged by country of publication; gives holdings. Title index.   Z2260.S67

Bibliography : Dissertations

Thompson, Lawrence Sidney. A bibliography of American doctoral dissertations in classical studies and related fields. [Hamden, Conn.] : Shoe String Pr., 1968. 250 p.   **BE1009**

For annotation, *see* DA97.   Z7016.T48

Bibliography : Translations

Parks, George B. The Greek and Latin literatures / George B. Parks, Ruth Z. Temple. N.Y. : Ungar, [1968]. 442 p. (Literatures of the world in English translation, v. 1).   **BE1010**

Separate sections for Greek and for Latin literature, each arranged by chronological period. Within periods translations are listed by author, then by translated title. Scholars specializing in the various periods have assisted in compiling the lists. Publications through 1965 are included. Includes general works as well as Byzantine, neo-Latin, and modern authors translated into English, French, German, and Spanish. Index of authors and anonymous titles, but not of editors and translators.   Z7018.T7E85

Smith, F. Seymour. The classics in translation : an annotated guide to the best translations of the Greek and Latin classics into English. London ; N.Y. : Scribner, 1930. 307 p.   **BE1011**

"No Greek or Latin author has been omitted whose name appears in the standard literary histories and whose works have been translated into English."—*Introd*. The first part of the book contains two essays on the theory of translation, followed by separate sections for Greek and Latin authors, arranged by author. Translations especially recommended are starred. Annotations vary and may include evaluative information, quotations from reviews, and bibliographical information. An appendix deals with the work of the apostolic fathers. List of works consulted and index of translators.   Z7018.T7E87

Criticism

Ancient writers : Greece and Rome / T. James Luce, ed. in chief. N.Y. : Scribner's, [1982]. 2 v. (1148 p.).   **BE1012**

Contents: v. 1, Homer to Caesar; v. 2, Lucretius to Ammianus Marcellinus.

Offers 47 essays by contributing scholars, mainly on individual authors or pairs of authors. Chronologically arranged. Contributors were invited to write "personal, even idiosyncratic, essays in order to show what in their eyes constitute the significant achievements of the writers of the ancient world" (*Introd.*): biographical information and literary background are subordinate features of the essays. Intended for a wide range of readers, "from students in secondary school to advanced classical scholars." Bibliographies of texts and studies. Index in v. 2.   PA3002.A5

Dictionaries

Dizionario degli scrittori greci e latini / diretto da Francesco Della Corte. [Milano] : Marzorati Editore, 1988. 3 v. (2433 p.).   **BE1013**
Contents: v. 1–3, A–V.
Lengthy articles by contributing scholars discuss authors and some literary movements and schools (e.g., Epigrammatici, Peripatetici). Extensive notes and bibliographies of recommended texts, translations, and secondary materials. International in scope. Name index in v. 3.   DE5.D5956

Howatson, M. C. The Oxford companion to classical literature. 2nd ed. Oxford ; N.Y. : Oxford Univ. Pr., 1989. 615 p., [10] p. of plates : ill.   **BE1014**
1st ed., 1937, ed. by Sir Paul Harvey.
Like other Oxford companions, a useful dictionary of concise information on writers, individual works, literary forms and subjects, names and subjects in classical history, institutions, religion, etc. Covers literature from the beginning to 529 CE (the closing of the philosophy academies in Athens). Aims to "pay more attention to the philosophy and political institutions" (*Pref.*) of the ancient world—e.g., Women, position of. Cross-references; some pronunciation information; maps.
§ The same publisher issued *Oxford classical dictionary* (DA103), which provides further information on classical literature and on specific authors.   PA31.H69

Handbooks

Feder, Lillian. The Meridian handbook of classical literature. N.Y. : New American Library, c1986. 448 p., [6] p. of plates : maps.   **BE1015**
A rev. ed. of the same editor's *Crowell's handbook of classical literature* (1964).
An alphabetical dictionary of names, titles, mythological characters, etc. Gives detailed summaries of individual works and supplies references to editions of texts, translations and adaptations, and criticism.   PA31.F4

Harsh, Philip Whaley. A handbook of classical drama. Stanford, Calif. : Stanford Univ. Pr., 1944. 526 p.   **BE1016**
Repr.: Stanford, Calif. : Stanford Univ. Pr., [1970].
Offers discussions of Greek and Roman dramatists and their plays, "designed to be a modern appreciation of the plays as literature and a convenient brief guide to further critical material."—*Pref.* Bibliography lists texts in the original language and English translations with annotations. Recommended translations are starred.   PA3024.H3

Hathorn, Richmond Yancey. Crowell's handbook of classical drama. N.Y. : Crowell, 1967. 350 p.   **BE1017**
In dictionary form. Concentrates on Greek classical drama; includes entries for dramatists, dramatic forms, terms in classical drama, individual plays (with brief background notes and summaries), and characters from extant dramas and from mythology. A more convenient ready-reference tool than Philip Whaley Harsh, *A handbook of classical drama* (BE1016), but without the bibliographic apparatus of that work.   PA3024.H35

Thompson, Edward Maunde. An introduction to Greek and Latin palaeography. Oxford : Clarendon Pr., 1912. 600 p. : 250 facsims.   **BE1018**
For annotation, *see* AA216.   Z114.T472

Wellington, Jean Susorney. Dictionary of bibliographic abbreviations found in the scholarship of classical studies and related disciplines. Westport, Conn. : Greenwood, [1983]. 393 p.   **BE1019**
Aims to bring together the many abbreviations (and their variants) for journals, series, and standard works in the broad range of classical studies, plus some other abbreviations often encountered in scholarly publications in that field. Abbreviations are listed alphabetically with separate sections for Greek and Cyrillic. For abbreviations of journals, serials, etc., reference is given to an item number in the section of bibliographic descriptions where one must turn to find the full form. Includes some abbreviations not found in Otto Leistner's *ITA: Internationale Titelabkürzungen...* (AD22).   PA99.W44

Histories

The Cambridge history of classical literature. Cambridge, Eng. ; N.Y. : Cambridge Univ. Pr., 1982–1985. 2 v.   **BE1020**
Contents: v. 1, Greek literature, ed. by P. E. Easterling and B. M. W. Knox (1985); v. 2, Latin literature, ed. by E. J. Kenney (1982).
A scholarly and critical history. Chapters by specialists discuss authors, genres, and topics, with extensive bibliographical references reflecting recent scholarship. In both volumes material relating to biography, chronology of an author's works, and bibliography of individuals is confined to an Appendix of authors and works. Each also has a Metrical appendix and an index.

Pfeiffer, Rudolf. History of classical scholarship from the beginnings to the end of the Hellenistic age. Oxford : Clarendon Pr., 1968. 311 p.   **BE1021**
For annotation, *see* DA107.   AZ301.P4

Sandys, John Edwin. A history of classical scholarship. Cambridge : Univ. Pr., 1903–08. 3 v. : ill.   **BE1022**
Repr.: N.Y. : Hafner, 1958.
Contents: v. 1, From the sixth century B.C. to the end of the middle ages; v. 2, From the revival of learning to the end of the eighteenth century (in Italy, France, England, and the Netherlands); v. 3, The eighteenth century in Germany, and the nineteenth century in Europe and the United States of America.
Dated but still important for the sheer detail of information. Focus is on the lives and works of individual scholars. Chronological tables of authors and titles are provided throughout. Detailed table of contents in each volume; index.

Biography

Biographisches Jahrbuch für Altertumskunde. v. 1 (1878)–v. 63 (1943). Berlin : Calvary, 1879–1898 ; Leipzig : Reisland, 1899–1944.   **BE1023**
Title varies; 1907–24 called *Biographisches Jahrbuch für die Altertumswissenschaft*.
Issued as a part of *Jahresbericht über die Fortschritte der klassischen Altertumswissenschaft* ("Bursian's Jahrebericht"). No volume published for 1912. No biographical section since 1943.
Contains signed obituaries of classical philologists; articles are of some length, with bibliographies.   PA3.J3

Classical scholarship : a biographical encyclopedia / ed. by Ward W. Briggs and William M. Calder III. N.Y. : Garland, 1990. 396 p. : ports. (Garland reference library of the humanities, vol. 928).   **BE1024**
For annotation, *see* DA113.   PA83.C58

Grant, Michael. Greek and Latin authors, 800 B.C.–A.D. 1000 : a biographical dictionary. N.Y. : Wilson, 1980. 490 p. : ill. **BE1025**

"A volume in the Wilson authors series."—*t.p.*

Includes sketches of some 370 writers. As far as possible, gives an account of the writer's life, a description and critical commentary on the works, and, where relevant, some discussion of the author's influence. Bibliography of useful editions of the works (including translations) and of selected critical studies; chronological list of authors by century. PA31.G7

Tusculum-Lexicon : griechischer und lateinischer Autoren des Altertums und des Mittelalters / von Wolfgang Buchwald, Armin Hohlweg, Otto Prinz. 3., neu bearb. und erw. Aufl. München : Artemis, c1982. 862 p. **BE1026**

Provides brief biographical information and information on texts for authors chronologically, ranging from the early classical era to Christian writers of the Middle Ages. Alphabetically arranged.

Greek

For literature in modern Greek, *see* under Greece below.

Bibliography

The Classical world bibliography of Greek drama and poetry. N.Y. : Garland, 1977. 339 p. (Garland reference library of the humanities, v. 93). **BE1027**

Presents 13 bibliographic essays by different scholars, photographically reproduced, which originally appeared in *Classical world*, 1955–76. Essays focus on recent scholarship on Homer and on various Greek dramatists, as well as on lyric poetry. Format and degree of discussion varies. No index.

§ Companion work: *The Classical world bibliography of Roman drama and poetry and ancient fiction* (BE1038). Z7023.D7C58

Foster, Finley Melville Kendall. English translations from the Greek : a bibliographical survey. N.Y. : Columbia Univ. Pr., 1918. 146 p. (Columbia University studies in English and comparative literature, [62]). **BE1028**

A list of translations from 1476 to 1917. Covers literature to 200 CE. The introduction provides chronological and statistical analyses of translations, and translations by genre.

§ More detailed bibliographic information on a larger number of early translations from both Greek and Latin is provided by *List of English editions and translations of Greek and Latin classics printed before 1641*, by Henrietta R. Palmer (London : Printed for the Bibliographical Society by Blades, East & Blades, 1911). An introduction by Victor Scholderer provides a historical overview and critical analysis. Entries are alphabetical by author, then chronological. Works located in the British Museum, the Bodleian Library, and the University Library, Cambridge, are so noted. Z7018.T7E71

Harvard University. Library. Ancient Greek literature : classification schedules; classified listing by call number; chronological listing; author and title listing. Cambridge : Publ. by Harvard Univ. Libr. ; distr. by Harvard Univ. Pr., 1979. 638 p. (Widener Library shelflist, 58). **BE1029**

For a note on the Widener shelflist series, *see* AA115.

Includes some 19,800 shelf list entries comprising the Widener *G* class. "It includes anthologies of literature and works by and about individual authors. Literary histories are in the *Class* class."—*p. 3.* Z7025.H37

Kessels, A. H. M. A concise bibliography of ancient Greek literature / comp. by A. H. M. Kessels and W. J. Verdenius. 2nd ed., rev. and enl. Apeldoorn : Administratief Centrum, 1982. 145 p. **BE1030**

1st ed., 1979, had title: *A concise bibliography of Greek language and literature.*

A bibliography for students and teachers of the classics. Classed arrangement, with topical sections (e.g., dictionaries, grammar, epigraphy, tragedy) interspersed with sections on individual authors and schools. Lists editions of classical texts together with secondary studies. Brief index.

Riesenfeld, Harald. Repertorium lexicographicum graecum : a catalogue of indexes and dictionaries to Greek authors / Harald and Blenda Riesenfeld. Stockholm : Almqvist and Wiksell, [1954]. 95 p. **BE1031**

A companion volume to Paul Faider's *Répertoire des index et lexiques d'auteurs latins* (BE1044), lists indexes and dictionaries "bearing upon Greek literature from its beginning to the end of the Byzantine epoch," including the Greek Bible. Both separately published works and parts of volumes are listed. Preface and notes are in English. Z7021.R5

Handbooks

Rose, Herbert Jennings. A handbook of Greek literature : from Homer to the age of Lucian. 4th ed., rev., repr. with minor corrections. London : Methuen ; N.Y. : Dutton ; 1956. 458 p. **BE1032**

1st ed., 1934.

A standard, widely available handbook covering all aspects of classical Greek literature, with the exception of Christian and Jewish works in Greek. Very useful for factual information compactly presented. Extensive references in footnotes; brief bibliography. Analytic index with both transliterated and Greek versions of names.

Histories

Croiset, Alfred. Histoire de la littérature grecque / par Alfred Croiset ... [et] Maurice Croiset .... Paris : E. de Boccard, 1914–47. 5 v. **BE1033**

First publ. : Paris : Thoren, 1887–99. Volumes individually revised; edition note varies; t. 1, Homère, La poésie cyclique, Hésiode, 4. éd., 1928; t. 2, Lyrisme, Premiers prosateurs, Hérodote, 3. éd. rev. et augm., 1914; t. 3, Période attique, Tragédie, Comédie, Genres divers, 3. éd. rev. et augm., 1929; t. 4, Période attique; Eloquence, histoire, philosophie, 3. éd. rev. et corr., 1947; t. 5, Période Alexandrine, Période romaine, 3. éd., 1928.

An important reference history; many bibliographies.

PA3055.C8

Lesky, Albin. A history of Greek literature / tr. [from the 2nd German ed.] by James Willis and Cornelis de Heer. London : Methuen, 1966. 921 p. **BE1034**

First published as *Geschichte der Griechischen literatur* (Bern : Franke, 1957/58); 3rd. German ed., 1971.

The standard history, intended to present "knowledge of the subject so as to give a broad outline for the student, initial guidance to the researcher, and to the interested public a speedy but not a superficial approach to the literature of Greece."—*Introd., 1st ed.* Emphasis is on great works having a decisive influence on western civilization. Christian and Jewish Greek literature are excluded. Extensive notes and bibliography. Indexed.

§ Two other widely available histories are Peter Levi, *A history of Greek literature* (N. Y. : Viking, 1985) and Moses Hadas, *A history of Greek literature* (N. Y. : Columbia Univ. Pr., 1950). Levi is aimed at a more general reading public and has minimal references. Hadas is a scholarly work with an extensive bibliography. Both are indexed.

PA3057.L413

Schmid, Wilhelm. Geschichte der griechischen Literatur / von Wilhelm Schmid und Otto Stählin. München : C.H. Beck, 1929–48. 5 v. (Handbuch der Altertumswissenschaft, 7 Abt., T. 1, Bd. 1–5). **BE1035**

An extensive and well-documented work covering the classical period, necessary in research libraries.

§ Replaces v. 1 of Wilhelm von Christ's *Geschichte der griechischen Literatur*, (6. Aufl. München : Beck, 1912–24. 2 v. in 3). Vol. 2 of Christ is still the authoritative work on the postclassical era to 530 CE and functions as pt. 2 of Schmid and Stählin.   PA3057.S3

Texts

●**Thesaurus Linguae Graecae** [database]. [Irvine, Calif.] : Univ. of California, Irvine, 1987.   **BE1036**

A full-text database of Greek literature (in Greek), from Homer through the 10th century CE. The CD-ROM, which can be accessed using several different software packages, can be searched for word or letter strings, phrases, or combinations thereof, making it a vital tool for classical philologists, lexicographers, literary scholars, and historians. For a history of *TLG*, see Theodore F. Brunner, "Databases for the humanities : learning from the *Thesaurus Linguae Graecae*," *Scholarly communication*, no. 7 (Winter 1987): 1, 6–9.

§ *Thesaurus Linguae Graecae canon of Greek authors and works* / Luci Berkowitz, Karl A. Squitier with technical assistance from William A. Johnson (3rd ed. N.Y. : Oxford Univ. Pr., 1990. lx, 471 p.).

Serves as a printed register of the authors, texts, and editions which comprise the *Thesaurus Linguae Graecae* database. Each of almost 3,200 authors is listed alphabetically, followed by an author epithet (e.g., Rhetorician, Historian), date, geographical epithet, and works of that author which have been entered into the *TLG* database, including complete bibliographical information. Indexes by *TLG* author number and work type. Since the *Canon* is included online with the *TLG* itself and can be searched using various software packages, one can identify authors or texts from various geographical areas or time periods in using it.

Latin

Bibliography

Caes, Lucien. Collectio bibliographica operum ad ius romanum pertinentium : Lucien Caes, R. Henrion. Bruxelles : Office Internat. de Librairie, 1949–78. Ser.I, v.1–25; ser.II, v.1–2. (In progress).   **BE1037**

Contents: Ser.I, Opera edita in periodicis miscellaneis encyclopaediisque, v.1–25 (1949–78); Index notarum cumulativus, v.1–20 (called Suppl.I); Index rerum cumulativus, v.11–20 (called Suppl.II); Ser.II, Theses: v.1, Theses Galliae (1800–1848) (publ. 1950); v.2, Theses Germaniae (1885–1958) (publ. 1960).

An extensive listing of scholarly articles in periodicals, collections, miscellanies, festschriften, theses, etc., dating approximately from the mid-19th century. "Law" is broadly interpreted so that a substantial body of classical Latin literature is included. Arrangement of each volume is alphabetical by author, with a subject index.

The Classical world bibliography of Roman drama and poetry and ancient fiction. N.Y. : Garland, 1978. 387 p. (Garland reference library of the humanities, v. 97).   **BE1038**

Photographic reprints of 17 bibliographic essays by different scholars originally published in *Classical world*, 1956–75. Topics include recent work on various authors and on Roman satire, the ancient novel, and prose fiction; Psychoanalytic writings on Greek and Latin authors 1911–1960; and Periodical literature on teaching the classics in translation 1924–1975. Formats and degree of discussion vary. No index.

§ Companion work: *The Classical world bibliography of Greek drama and poetry* (BE1027).   Z7026.C53

Harvard University. Library. Latin literature : classification schedules; classified listing by call number; chronological listing; author and title listing. Cambridge : Publ. by Harvard Univ. Libr. ; distr. by Harvard Univ. Pr., 1979. 610 p. (Widener Library shelflist, 59).   **BE1039**

For a note on the Widener shelflist series, *see* AA115.

Includes some 18,600 shelf list entries comprising the Widener *L* and *ML* classes. The *L* class is for ancient Latin literature, including anthologies of literature and works by and about individual authors. (Literary histories are found in the *Class* class.) Inasmuch as literature is taken in its broadest sense, "writings of all Latin authors of the ancient period are included here regardless of subject. The only major exceptions are the few Latin authors whose works are entirely mathematical in content; they are in the *Math* class. Medieval and modern Latin belles lettres are in the *ML* class."—*p. 3*.   Z7030.H37

Herescu, Niculae I. Bibliographie de la littérature latine. Paris : Soc. d'Édit. "Les Belles-Lettres", 1943. 426 p.   **BE1040**

Collection de bibliographie classique, pub. sous la direction de J. Marouzeau.

An analytical, selective bibliography of materials on Latin subjects. Arranged by period with an alphabetical index to Latin authors. No index to secondary authors. Under each author, material is arranged under such subheadings as manuscripts, editions, extracts, translations, dictionaries and indexes, studies. In works of voluminous authors these may be further subdivided.

Useful because it brings together in a convenient form a large amount of material that is otherwise scattered. Covers to approximately 1940.

———. ———. *Notes additionelles* (Paris : Inst. Roumain d'Etudes Latines, 1951. 15 p.).

IJsewijn, Jozef. Companion to neo-Latin studies. 2nd entirely rewritten ed. Louvain : Louven Univ. Pr. : Peeters Pr, 1990. v. 1. (In progress).   **BE1041**

1st ed. : Amsterdam : North-Holland, 1977.

The first part of a projected two-volume set, this is a reworking of the first ed., which is still needed until publication is complete.

Neo-Latin is defined as covering from approximately 1300 CE to the present. Pt. 1 "encompasses the historical development and geographical diffusion of Neo-Latin and its accompanying bibliographical information. The second will discuss the diverse genres, linguistic, stylistic, metrical, editorial, and bibliographical problems, and the development of Neo-Latin studies. It will contain also the bibliography of individual authors in one continuous alphabetical order."—*Pref.* Indexes: names; places; genres; themes and devices; important subjects; manuscripts.

§ For updated information on genres, language, and authors, IJsewijn recommends the annual *Instrumentum bibliographicum Neolatinum* which appears in the journal *Humanistica Lovaniensia*.   PA8020.I37

Lapidge, Michael. A bibliography of Celtic-Latin literature, 400–1200 / by Michael Lapidge and Richard Sharpe ; with a foreword by Proinsias Mac Cana. Dublin : Royal Irish Academy, 1985. 361 p. (Ancillary publications, 1).   **BE1042**

Attempts "to list all Latin texts which were composed in Celtic-speaking areas or by native speakers of a Celtic language during the period 400–1200," and intends to serve as "the *index fontium* of the Royal Irish Academy's Dictionary of medieval Latin from Celtic sources."—*Introd.* Includes religious literature and historical and political texts. Entries include manuscripts, editions, citations to standard bibliographic listings and catalogs, commentary, and information in general bibliographical studies for individual authors. Index.   Z7028.C44L36

Menéndez y Pelayo, Marcelino. Bibliografía hispano-latina clásica / Marcelino Menéndez Pelayo ; edición prep. por Enrique Sánchez Reyes. Santander : Aldus S. A. de Artes Gráficas, 1950–53. 10 v. (Edición nacional de las obras completas de Menéndez Pelayo, v. 44–53).   **BE1043**

A bibliography listing Spanish editions of Latin classics including: manuscripts, editions, commentaries, translations, critical works, imitations, and works showing the influence of Latin classics on Spanish literature. Comments, extracts, etc., are given throughout. Actual bibliographical information is not always complete. Vol. 10, Miscelánea y notas para una bibliografía Greco-Hispana. Indexes in last volume.

Libraries holding the *Edición nacional* may not list this title separately.

Quellet, Henri. Bibliographia indicum, lexicorum et concordantiarum auctorum Latinorum : Répertoire bibliographique des index, lexiques et concordances des auteurs latins. Hildesheim ; N.Y. : G. Olms, 1980. 262 p. **BE1044**

Also publ. : Neuchâtel : Secrétariat de l'Université, 1980.

More than 1,000 entries for dictionaries, indexes, and concordances relating to the works of Latin authors. Entries are alphabetical by the name of the Latin author, then chronological.

§ Updates, amplifies, and replaces Paul Faider, *Répertoire des index et lexiques d'auteurs latins* (Paris : Soc. d'Édit. "Les Belles-Lettres," 1926). For a similar list of Greek dictionaries, *see* Harald and Blenda Riesenfeld, *Repertorium lexicographicum graecum* (BE1031).

Manuscripts

Munk Olsen, B. L'étude des auteurs classiques latins aux XIe et XIIe siècles. Paris : Editions du Centre national de la Recherche scientifique, 1982–1989. 4 v. in 3. **BE1045**

At head of title: Documents, etudes et repertoires publies par l'Institut de Recherche et d'Histoire des Textes.

Contents: v. 1, Catalogue des manuscrits classiques latins copiés du IXe au XIIe siècles: Apicius–Juvénal; v. 2, Catalogue des manuscrits classiques latins copiés du IXe au XIIe siècle: Livius–Vitruvius, Florilèges; Essais de plume; v. 3, 1re pte., Les classiques dans le bibliothèques médiévales; v. 3, 2e pte., Addenda et corrigenda; Tables.

An aid for the study and location of manucripts and the transmission of texts. Arranged by classical author, then by repository, with description of the manuscripts and some references. Does include information on some manuscripts of the 9th and 10th centuries. Vol. 3, pt. 2, contains indexes by title, geographical and medieval names, classical and medieval authors, editors, and commentators. PA2045.M86

Indexes

Swanson, Donald Carl Eugene. The names in Roman verse : a lexicon and reverse index of all proper names of history, mythology, and geography found in the classical Roman poets. Madison : Univ. of Wisconsin Pr., 1967. 425 p. **BE1046**

A computer-produced index containing "a factual and analytic compilation of all proper names and their meanings found in classical latin verse … The proper names (nouns, adjectives, a few adverbs) include those of persons, animals, places, celestial bodies, personifications, and products, whether real or imaginary …"—*Introd.* A reverse index of the names is also supplied. Appendixes cover dubious readings, the texts used, and name indexes compiled for specific works. PA2379.S9

Dictionaries

Thesaurus linguae latinae : editus autoritatae et consilio academiarum quinque germanicarum Berolinensis, Gottingensis, Lipsiensis, Monacensis, Vidobonensis. Lipsiae : Teubner, 1900–92. v.1–8, v.9², v.10¹⁻⁶. (In progress). **BE1047**

For annotation, *see* AC571.

Handbooks

Rose, Herbert Jennings. A handbook of Latin literature : from the earliest times to the death of St. Augustine / Herbert Jennings Rose, with a supplementary bibliography by E. Courtney. [3rd ed.]. London : Metheun ; N.Y. : Dutton, 1966. 582 p. **BE1048**

First publ. 1936.

A standard widely available handbook covering Latin literature through the early Christian era. Especially useful for succinct factual information and summaries of contents of works. Extensive references in footnotes. Courtney's supplementary bibliography is a solid updating of Rose through the early 1960s. Analytic index.

Histories

See also BE1020.

Bolton, Whitney French. A history of Anglo-Latin literature, 597–1066. Princeton, N.J. : Princeton Univ. Pr., 1967. v. 1. (In progress?). **BE1049**

Contents: v. 1, 597–740. Vol. 2 has not appeared.

A valuable reference and bibliographic history. Covers Anglo-Latin literature from the arrival of Augustine in Britain to the end of the age of Bede. Begins with discussion of British Latin before 597. Provides historical and biographical information but most attention is to the content and context of individual works. Long passages are cited and translated. There is a lengthy bibliography of secondary works. Author, title, and subject index.

§ Continued chronologically by: A. G. Rigg, *A history of Anglo-Latin literature, 1066–1422* (Cambridge : Cambridge Univ. Pr., 1992). Rigg also cites sources covering the gap from 741 to 1066. Similar concentration on individual authors and works but with more focus on genre and style. Extensive notes. An appendix discusses meter. General author, title, and subject index and an index to manuscripts. PA8045.E5B6

Brunholzl, Franz. Geschichte der lateinischen Literatur des Mittelalters. München : Fink, 1975–92. v. 1–2. (In progress). **BE1050**

Contents: v. 1, Von Cassiodor bis zum Ausklang der karolingischen Erneuerung; v. 2, Die Zweischenzeit vom Ausgang des karolingischen Zeitalters bis zur mitte des clftcn Jahrhundcrts.

The first two of four planned volumes that will cover through the middle of the 14th century. When completed will overtake, but not supersede, Maximilianus Manitius, *Geschichte der lateinischen Literatur des Mittelalters* (BE1051). Where appropriate, corrects Manitius and fills in gaps, but is not as exhaustive in detail. Each volume has an index and there are extensive notes and references. An indispensable work for research libraries. Vol. 2, originally planned for 1977, did not appear until 1992. PA8015.B7

Manitius, Maximilianus. Geschichte der lateinischen Literatur des Mittelalters. München : Beck, 1911–31. 3 v. (Handbuch der klassischen Altertumswissenschaft … / hrsg. von I. von Müller., 9. Bd., 2. Abt., 1.–3. t.). **BE1051**

Reissued 1964–65.

Contents: v. 1, Von Justinian bis zur Mitte des 10. Jahrh.; v. 2, Von der Mitte des 10. Jahrh. bis zum Ausbruch des Kampfes zwischen Kirche u. Staat; v. 3, Vom Ausbruch des Kirchenstreites bis zum Ende des 12. Jahrh.

Currently the chief standard history of medieval Latin literature, indispensable in the large research libraries, and likely to remain so. Exhaustive in detail and documentation. Each volume is indexed and the third volume has indexes of geographical names and personal names and subjects. To be overtaken and complemented, but not replaced, by Franz Brunholzl, *Geschichte der lateinischen Literatur des Mittelalters* (BE1050). PA8035.M3

Schanz, Martin. Geschichte der römischen Literatur bis zum Gesetzgebungswerk des Kaisers Justinian. Neubearb. Aufl. / von Carl Hosius. München : Beck, 1914–35. 4 v. in 5. (Handbuch der klassischen Altertumswissenschaft ... / hrsg. von I. von Müller., 8. Bd.).　　　　**BE1052**

Volumes individually revised; edition number and editor vary: v. 1, 4. Aufl., von Carl Hosius, 1927; v. 2, 4. Aufl., von Carl Hosius, 1935; v. 3, 3. Aufl., von Carl Hosius and Gustav Kruger, 1922; v. 4, 1. Halfte, 2. Aufl., 1914; v. 4, 2. Halfte, 1. Aufl., von Martin Schanz, Carl Hosius, und Gustav Kruger, 1920. Of the 4th ed., only v. 1–2 were published. Set reissued, 1966–71.

Contents: v. 1, Die römische Literatur in der Zeit der Republik; v. 2, Die römische Literatur in der Zeit der Monarchie bis auf Hadrian; v. 3, Die Zeit von Hadrian 117 bis auf Constantin 324; v. 4, Von Constantin bis zum Gesetzgebungswerk Justinians: 1. Halfte, Die Literatur des vierten Jahrhunderts; 2. Halfte, Die Literatur des fünften und sechsten Jahrhunderts.

The principal history of Latin literature. Extremely detailed and well-documented. An index to the set is in v. 4.

Continued by: Maximilianus Manitius, *Geschichte der lateinischen Literatur des Mittelalters* (BE1051) and Franz Brunhölzl, *Geschichte der lateinischen Literatur des Mittelalters* (BE1050).

§ In addition to the recent *Cambridge history of classical literature* (BE1020) and Wilhelm Sigismund Teuffel's *History of Roman literature* (BE1053), there are two other standard histories in English: Moses Hadas, *A history of Latin literature* (London ; N.Y. : Cambridge Univ. Pr., 1952) and the dated but still useful J. Wight Duff, *A literary history of Rome from the origins to the close of the golden age* (3rd ed., ed. by A. M. Duff, N.Y. : Barnes & Noble, 1960. Originally publ. 1909).　　　　PA6007.S32

Teuffel, Wilhelm Sigismund. History of Roman literature / rev. and enl. by Ludwig Schwabe. Authorized tr. from the 5th German ed. by George C. W. Warr. London : Bell, 1891–92. 2 v.　　　　**BE1053**

Repr. : N.Y. : B. Franklin, [1967].

Contents: v. 1, The Republican period; v. 2, The Imperial period.

A bibliographical account of Roman history from earliest times to the 16th century A.D.

6th German ed.: *Geschichte der römischen Literatur*, (Leipzig : Teubner, 1910–16. 3 v.).　　　　PA6007.T55

Germanic literature

Autorenlexikon deutschsprachiger Literatur des 20. Jahrhunderts / hrsg. von Manfred Brauneck ; unter Mitarbeit von Wolfgang Beck. Uberarbeitete und erw. Neuausg. Reinbek bei Hamburg : Rowohlt, 1991. 883 p.　　　　**BE1054**

1st ed., 1984.

A dictionary providing biobibliographical sketches of more than 1,000 German writers from Germany, Austria, and Switzerland, representing a wide range of literary endeavors, including belle-lettres, criticism, philosophy and psychology, science fiction, children's literature, and writing for television, radio, and film. For each, provides biographical and critical information, and a list of works by the author. Valuable for an extensive 70-page bibliography of critical works on German literature ranging from general surveys to works on time periods, genres, and specialized studies of children's literature, detective fiction, etc.

§ A comparable older work, still useful for more extensive representation of the earlier 20th century but limited to German-language belles-lettres, is Karl August Kutzbach, *Autorenlexikon der Gegenwart* (Bonn : Bouvier, 1950). Lists primary works and, for some authors, references to criticism. Includes indexes by form of writing, religious outlook, audience, etc. Chronology of literary awards, events, 1945–49, and a bibliography of further references on literature and on publishing and national and trade bibliography. A second volume to cover writers in other fields was planned but has not been published.　　　　Z2230.K95

Blinn, Hansjürgen. Informationshandbuch Deutsche Literaturwissenschaft. Völlig neu bearbeitete Ausg. Frankfurt am Main : Fischer Taschenbuch Verlag, 1990. 434 p. (Informationshandbücher Geistes- und Sozialwissenschaften, 1).　　　　**BE1055**

1st ed., 1982.

A comprehensive guide that, in addition to covering works for the study of literature, provides information on libraries and archives, museums, literary associations and learned societies, and literary prizes in Germany, Austria, and Switzerland. Useful for those planning to do research abroad. Works in German predominate. Author, name, title, subject index.　　　　PT85.Z99B54x

Brinker-Gabler, Gisela. Lexikon deutschsprachiger Schriftstellerinnen, 1800–1945 / Gisela Brinker-Gabler, Karola Ludwig, Angela Wöffen. Originalausg. München : Deutscher Taschenbuch Verlag, 1986. 363 p. : ill., ports.　　　　**BE1056**

Treats 200 women authors from Germany, Austria, and Switzerland, providing biographical and critical sketches, bibliographies of primary and critical works, often locations for manuscripts, and photographs or portraits for most subjects. Index of authors, lists of reference sources and of individuals mentioned in the author entries.　　　　PT167.B75

Brümmer, Franz. Lexikon der deutschen Dichter und Prosaisten vom Beginn des 19. Jahrhunderts bis zur Gegenwart. 6. völlig neubearb. Aufl. Leipzig : Reclam, [1913]. 8 v.　　　　**BE1057**

Repr. : Nendeln, Liechtenstein : Kraus, 1975. 8 v. in 4.

1st ed., 1884; 5th ed., 1901.

A useful handbook containing brief biographical sketches and lists of works of some 9,900 German, Austrian, and Swiss authors. Very strong in pseudonyms. Supplement in v. 8 brings the work down to the end of 1912.　　　　Z2230.B894

Domandi, Agnes Körner. Modern German literature. N.Y. : Ungar, [1972]. 2 v.　　　　**BE1058**

Similar to other titles in the "Library of literary criticism" series.

"For the purposes of these volumes 'modern German literature' includes works written since 1900 by authors from East and West Germany, Austria, and Switzerland."—*Introd.* Includes critical excerpts from literary magazines, newspaper book reviews, academic and scholarly periodicals, and scholarly books. Excerpts from German-language sources are presented in English translation. More than 200 authors are considered. Index of critics.　　　　PT401.D6

Kürschner Nekrolog, 1901–1935 / hrsg. von Gerhard Lüdtke. Berlin : W. de Gruyter, 1936. 976 col.　　　　**BE1059**

Contents: Biographies reprinted from *Kürschners deutscher Literatur-Kalender* (BE1060)—with date and place of death added—of some 3,700 authors who died 1901–35; two chronological lists, arranged by years of (1) births, and (2) deaths.

Continued by: *Kürschner Nekrolog, 1936–1970*, hrsg. von Werner Schuder (Berlin : W. de Gruyter, 1973. 871 p.).

Kürschners deutscher Literatur-Kalender / hrsg. von Gerhard Lüdtke. v. 1– . Berlin : W. de Gruyter, 1879– . Annual.　　　　**BE1060**

Title and imprint vary.

Some years not issued: v. 39, 1917; v. 40, 1922; v. 41, 1924. Beginning with v. 42, 1925, the work is issued in two series, one continuing *Literatur-Kalender*, the other becoming *Kürschners deutscher Gelehrten-Kalender* (AH209).

A useful biographical record of German authors. Includes Austrian and Swiss authors writing in German.　　　　Z2230.K92

Lexikon deutschsprachiger Schriftsteller : von den Anfängen bis zur Gegenwart / von Günter Albrecht ... [et al.] ; Leitung und Gesamtredaktion Kurt Böttcher. Leipzig : VEB Bibliographisches Institut, 1987–93. 2 v. (In progress).　　　　**BE1061**

Contents: Bd. 1, Von den Anfängen bis zum Ausgang des 19. Jahrhunderts; Bd. 2, 20. Jahrhundert.

A new work constituting a revised edition of *Lexikon deutsch-sprachiger Schriftsteller : von den Anfängen bis zur Gegenwart*, [hrsg. von] Günter Albrecht [et al.] (Kronberg Ts. : Scriptor Verlag, 1974. 2 v.). 1st–4th eds., 1960–63, had title: *Deutsches Schriftsteller Lexikon.*

Biographical sketches of German writers of all periods, with bibliographies that include primary works and published editions of letters, journals, etc. Vol. 2 has some information as late as 1991. Includes writers from both the former Germanies, Austria, Switzerland, and other German-speaking regions, as well as medieval Latin authors with connections to Germany.

§ Supplements and updates but does not supersede *Schriftsteller der DDR*, ed. by Albrecht [et al.] (Leipzig : VEB Bibliographisches Institut, 1974), which principally included living authors, but also some deceased who were active in the last quarter century.

PT41.L38

Women writers of Germany, Austria, and Switzerland : an annotated bio-bibliographical guide / ed. by Elke Frederiksen. N.Y. : Greenwood, 1989. 323 p. (Bibliographies and indexes in women's studies, no. 8).   **BE1062**

Covers women writers, 10th–20th centuries, providing for each a short signed biographical sketch and a bibliography of writings. Title index; list of translated titles.   Z2233.5.W6W66

Flemish literature

Arents, Prosper. Flemish writers translated (1830–1931) : bibliographical essay. The Hague : Nijhoff, 1931. 191 p.   **BE1063**

A listing of Flemish works translated into various languages; classified arrangement with indexes of authors, translators, illustrators, etc.   Z2414.T7A6

—————— De Vlaamse schrijvers in het Engels vertaald, 1481–1949. Gent : Erasmus, [1950]. 466 p.   **BE1064**

A bibliography of translations into English from the Flemish, with detailed bibliographical information and location of copies in American and European libraries.

Roemans, Robert. Bibliografie van de Vlaamse tijdschriften. Hasselt : Heideland, 1960–71. Reeks I–III.   **BE1065**

Contents: Reeks I, Vlaamse literaire tijdschriften van 1930 tot en met 1965; Reeks II, Vlaamse niet-literaire tijdschriften van 1886 tot en met 1961; Reeks III, Vlaamse literaire tijdschriften vanaf 1969.

Reeks I indexes literary periodicals, poetry, prose, theater, and critical articles; some issues are devoted to a single periodical, while others index several. Reeks II indexes periodicals in the fields of linguistics, philology, folklore, history, etc. Reeks III indexes literary journals.

Reeks III is continued by *Bibliografie van de tijdschriften in Blaanderen en Nederland* (Antwerp : Roemans, 1974–).   AI5.R6

—————— Bibliographie van de moderne Vlaamsche literatuur, 1893–1930. 1. deel. Kortrijk : Steenlandt, 1930–34. Afl. 1–10.   **BE1066**

For annotation, *see* AD303.   Z2424.F5R7

Friesian literature

Provinciale Bibliotheek van Friesland. Catalogus der Friesche taal- en letterkunde en overige Friesche geschriften. Leeuwarden : Noord-Nederlandsche Boekhandel, 1941. 859 p.   **BE1067**

A comprehensive classified catalog of material in Friesian on Friesian languages and literature. Meticulous bibliographical information. Detailed table of contents and extensive index.   Z2454.F8F7

Wumkes, G. A. Bodders yn de Fryske striid. Boalsert : Osinga, 1926. 751 p.   **BE1068**

A collection of biobibliographic articles, some of considerable length, with extracts from the writings. Index of subjects, names, places.

§ Wumkes also is the author of a history of Friesian literature and culture, *Paden fen Fryslan* (Boalsert : Osinga, 1932–43. 4 v.), of which v. 1, 2, and 4 constitute the historical survey and v. 3 provides a selection of literary and historical texts. Much attention to individual writers and extensive extracts. Index in each volume.

Romance literature

Curley, Dorothy Nyren. Modern Romance literatures / comp. and ed. by Dorothy Nyren Curley [and] Arthur Curley. N.Y. : Ungar, [1967]. 510 p.   **BE1069**

Like D. N. Curley and Maurice and Elaine F. Kramer's *Modern American literature* (BE427) and Ruth Zabrinskie Temple and Martin Tucker's *Modern British literature* (BE600), this consists of excerpts from critical writings appearing in journals and books of both a scholarly and a popular nature. Authors were selected "both because of their intrinsic merit and because of the extent of American interest in them."—*Foreword*. Includes mainly writers of the 20th century. Index to critics.   PN813.C8

Dictionary of the literature of the Iberian peninsula / ed. by Germán Bleiberg, Maureen Ihrie, and Janet Pérez. Westport, Conn. : Greenwood, 1993. 2 v. (1806 p.).   **BE1070**

Includes literature (defined as historical, cultural, and philosophical writings as well as prose, poetry, and drama), authors, and movements, 10th century to the mid-1980s, from the entire Iberian peninsula. Limited to writers born in the Iberian Peninsula and unique in its inclusion of representatives from all major peninsular literatures: Catalan, Galician, Portuguese, and Spanish, as well as some of the the "lesser vernacular languages." Major entries are signed and have bibliographies and references where applicable. Designed to appeal to a range of users, from nonspecialists to scholars. Includes some cross-references. Resembles *Diccionario de literatura Española* by Germán Bleiburg and Julián Marías (BE1451) but excludes Spanish-American authors and foreign-born Hispanists of this country. Many annotations for less important figures are based on former editions of the *Diccionario*. Indexed.   PN849.S6D54

Flasche, Hans. Die Sprachen und Literaturen der Romanen im Spiegel der deutschen Universitätsschriften, 1885–1950 : eine Bibliographie. Bonn : H. Bouvier, 1958. 299 p. (Bonner Beiträge zur Bibliotheks- und Bücherkunde, Bd. 3).   **BE1071**

In German, French, and English.

Publ. also under the title: *Romance languages and literatures as presented in German doctoral dissertations, 1885–1950 : a bibliography* (Charlottesville : Bibliographical Society of the Univ. of Virginia, 1958).

A listing of more than 4,600 German dissertations from the 1885–1950 period. Classified arrangement with author and subject indexes.

§ A companion volume to Richard Mummendey's *Language and literature of the Anglo-Saxon nations as presented in German doctoral dissertations, 1885–1950* (BE594).   Z7031.F55

Hatzfeld, Helmut. Bibliografía crítica de la nueva estilística, aplicada a las literaturas románicas. Madrid : Editorial Gredos, 1955. 660 p. (Biblioteca románica hispánica. I. Tratados y monografías, 6).   **BE1072**

A survey bibliography of style investigation, treating general studies, stylistic comparison, the language of individual authors, history of style, theory of style, and many specialized aspects of stylistics. Two indexes, to style investigators and to proper names, titles, problems, terms, etc.

§ Supplemented by: *Essai de bibliographie critique de stylistique française et romane (1955–1960)*, by Hatzfeld and Yves LeHir (Paris : Presses Universitaires de France, 1961. [Université de Grenoble. Faculté des Lettres et Sciences Humaines, 26]).

The first and less comprehensive edition of Hatzfeld appeared in English as *A critical bibliography of the new stylistics applied to the Romance literatures, 1900–1952* (Chapel Hill : Univ. of North Carolina Pr., 1953. Repr. : N.Y. : Johnson Reprint, 1966. [Univ. of North Carolina studies in comparative literature, 5]). A supplement covering 1953–65 appeared in 1966 (Chapel Hill : Univ. of North Carolina Pr. Repr. : N.Y. : Johnson Reprint, 1972. [Univ. of North Carolina studies in comparative literature, 37]). Both English-language volumes are more selective than the Spanish and French editions, hence cannot fully substitute for them.   Z7031.H379

Palfrey, Thomas Rossman. A bibliographical guide to the Romance languages and literatures / comp. by Thomas R. Palfrey, Joseph G. Fucilla, William C. Holbrook. 8th ed. Evanston, Ill. : Chandler, 1971. 122 p.   **BE1073**

1st ed., 1939.

Contents: (1) General Romance bibliography; (2) French language and literature (including Provençal, French-Swiss, Belgian); (3) Italian; (4) Portuguese and Brazilian; (5) Spanish, Catalan, Spanish-American; (6) Roumanian.

Detailed table of contents and many cross-references but no index.   Z7031.P15

Parks, George B. The Romance literatures / George B. Parks, Ruth Z. Temple. N.Y. : Ungar, [1970]. 1 v. in 2. (Literatures of the world in English translation, v. 3).   **BE1074**

Contents: pt. 1, Catalan, Italian, Portuguese and Brazilian, Provençal, Rumanian, Spanish and Spanish American literatures; pt. 2, French literature.

Separate sections for each country, European sections subdivided chronologically and by individual author. For South American countries lists background works and those of individual authors. Scholars specializing in particular languages and periods have assisted in compiling the lists. Some annotations and references to criticism. Includes entries through 1968. Index of authors and anonymous works, but not editors and translators.   Z7033.T7E56

Slavic literature

Lewanski, Richard Casimir. The Slavic literatures. N.Y. : New York Public Library : Ungar, [1967]. 630 p. (Literatures of the world in English translation: a bibliography, v. 2).   **BE1075**

This volume was in the final stages of publication under the New York Public Library imprint when it was decided to incorporate it into the series in preparation by Ungar. It therefore differs from the overall plan for other volumes of the series (e.g., scope is confined to belles lettres; background materials and bibliographies are not listed, etc.). Arrangement is by language of the original work, then by author. References to translations appearing in periodicals are included. Closing date is 1960. Index of authors and translated titles.   Z7041.L59

Modern Slavic literatures / comp. and ed. by Vasa D. Mihailovich ... [et al.]. N.Y. : Ungar, 1972–76. 2 v.   **BE1076**

Contents: v. 1, Russian literature; v. 2, Bulgarian, Czechoslovak, Polish, Ukrainian, and Yugoslav literatures.

Part of the series, A library of literary criticism.

Vol. 1 presents excerpts from critical writings on 69 of "the most significant authors of the twentieth century" (*Introd.*) writing in Russian. In addition to English-language evaluations, excerpts from Russian critical writings are presented in translation. Similar treatment is accorded 196 writers in v. 2, which is arranged alphabetically by literature, then by author. Index of critics in each volume.   PG501.M518

Universitätsbibliothek Jena. Slavica-Auswahl-Katalog der Universitätsbibliothek Jena : ein Hilfsbuch für Slawisten und Germanoslavica-Forscher. Weimar : H. Böhlaus Nachfolger, 1956–59. 2 v. in 3. (Claves Jenenses, 4–6).   **BE1077**

Contents: v. 1, Allgemeine Literatur, Tschechoslowakei und Polen; v. 2, pt. 1, Russland und Sowjetunion; pt. 2, Jugoslawien und Bulgarien. Hochschul– Gymnasial– und Gelegenheitsschriften der UB Jena vom 16. bis 18. Jahrhundert, mit persönlichem oder sachlichem Bezug auf Südost– und Osteuropa. Nachträge.

A catalog of 7,400 of the Slavic and Germano-Slavic holdings of Jena University Library, particularly strong in 17th- and 18th-century literature. Arrangement is in the form of a bibliographic handbook for Slavic studies. Appendix and author index in v. 3.   Z929.J43

Wytrzens, Günther. Bibliographische Einführung in das Studium der slavischen Literaturen. Frankfurt a. M. : Klostermann, 1972. 348 p. (Zeitschrift für Bibliothekswesen und Bibliographie. Sonderheft, 13).   **BE1078**

A bibliography of more than 5,000 items for the study of the whole range of Slavic literatures. Classified arrangement with name index and detailed table of contents. Includes works in Western European languages as well as those in the Slavic languages.

Supplemented by Wytrzens's *Bibliographie der literarwissenschaftlichen Slawistik, 1970–1980* (Frankfurt am Main : Klostermann, [1982]), which adds 5,000 items with a similar arrangement and scope.

§ The same series includes Wyrtzen's *Bibliographie der russischen Autoren und anonymen Werke* (1975) and a supplement for the period 1975–80 (1982).   Z7041.W9

Yiddish literature

For related works in Hebrew, *see* under Israel, below.

Abramowicz, Dina. Yiddish literature in English translation : books published 1945–1967. N.Y. : Yivo Institute for Jewish Research, 1967. 35*l*.   **BE1079**

A list by author of more than 200 translations, including monographs, anthologies, and collections. For monographs, notes first editions, new editions, reissues, and foreign editions. Not limited to creative literature. Translations published Fall 1966– June 1967 are listed in an appendix. Subject and genre index.

§ Abramowicz has also published a more selective bibliography, *Yiddish literature in English translation : list of books in print* (N.Y. : Yivo Institute for Jewish Research, 1976. 22*l*.), where selection is more limited to belles lettres and to works in print.

Liptzin, Solomon. A history of Yiddish literature. Middle Village, N.Y. : J. David, [1972]. 521 p.   **BE1080**

Repr., 1985.

A comprehensive survey covering Yiddish literature worldwide from its beginnings to the 1960s. Much attention is given to individual writers. A bibliography of general references is included, and a list of English translations of works of major authors. Indexed.   PJ5120.L55

Prager, Leonard. Yiddish literary and linguistic periodicals and miscellanies : a selective annotated bibliography / by Leonard Prager with the help of A. A. Greenbaum. Darby, Pa. : publ. for the Assoc. for the Study of Jewish Languages by Norwood Editions, 1982. 271 p. (Publications of the Association for the Study of Jewish Languages, 1.).   **BE1081**

A bibliography listing, describing, and in most cases locating 386 Yiddish periodicals. Gives Yiddish title, title in English, publishing history and editors, a historical and evaluative annotation, references to additional information, and locations in any of 15 libraries, archives, and private collections. The introduction traces the relationship of periodical publishing to the development of Yiddish literature and the Yiddish language. Exclusions, which include daily and general weekly publications, are clearly noted with reasons for their exclusion. A chronology, "Landmarks in the history of Yiddish literary periodicals," and a list of references are provided. Indexes to titles, editors, contributors, places of publication, and years of publication of miscellanies.   PJ5111

Scandinavian literature

See also under individual countries: Denmark, Finland, Iceland, Norway, Sweden.

Arntz, Helmut. Bibliographie der Runenkunde : mit Unterstützung des Archäologischen Instituts des Deutschen Reiches. Leipzig : Harrassowitz, 1937. 293 p. **BE1082**

An extensive bibliography of materials in various languages on runic antiquities, inscriptions, etc., in Scandinavia, Iceland, England, and elsewhere. The main section, arranged by author, is followed by a title list for anonymous works. Notes reviews. "Zeitschriften und (bio)-bibliographische Hilfsmittel," p. 265–76, is followed by indexes to names of authors and reviewers, to specific inscriptions and sites, and to geographic areas.

§ A standard handbook by the same author, *Handbuch der runenkunde* (2. Aufl. Halle/Saale : Max Niemeyer, 1944), includes a bibliography as well as plates.

A more recent bibliography, more selective in its coverage of European areas, is: *Bibliographie der Runeninschriften nach Fundorten*, hrsg. vom Skandinavischen Seminar der Wissenschaften der Universität Göttingen im Auft. von Wolfgang Krause (Göttingen : Vandenhoeck & Ruprecht, 1961–73. 2 v. [Abhandlungen der Akademie der Wissenschaften in Göttingen, Phil.–Hist. Kl., 3. Folge, Nr. 48, 80]).

Vol. 1, by Hertha Marquardt, covers the British Isles, and v. 2, by Uwe Schnall, both Western and Eastern Europe. The first volume includes the texts of many inscriptions, as well as plates. Z2556.A2A7

Bekker-Nielsen, Hans. Old Norse-Icelandic studies : a select bibliography. [Toronto] : Univ. of Toronto Pr., [1967]. 94 p. **BE1083**

Intended as "an intelligent student's guide to Old Norse-Icelandic studies" and includes "a fairly wide range of different kinds of material relevant for the study of the language, literature, and other aspects of civilization in Norway and Iceland in the Middle Ages."—*Pref.* English- and German-language listings are included for the benefit of students with limited knowledge of modern Scandinavian languages.

§ Can be updated by: *Bibliography of Old Norse-Islandic studies* (v. 1 [1963]– . Copenhagen : Royal Library, 1964– ; vols. covering 1963–68 publ. Copenhagen : Munksgaard). A selective bibliography aimed at the interests of students of "Old Norse language and literature, medieval Norwegian and Icelandic history and related subjects,"—*Pref.* Publication is slow: volume covering 1981–83 appeared in 1988. Z2556.B4

Blankner, Frederika. The history of the Scandinavian literatures. N.Y. : Dial, 1938. 407 p. **BE1084**

Repr. : Westport, Conn. : Greenwood, 1975.

Subtitle: A survey of the literatures of Norway, Sweden, Denmark, Iceland and Finland, from their origins to the present day, including Scandinavian-American authors, and selected bibliographies. Based in part on the work of Giovanni Bach with additional sections by Richard Beck, Adolph B. Benson, Axel Johan Uppvall and others.

The sections on Norwegian, Swedish, and Danish literature are based on the work of Giovanni Bach, translated and enlarged by Frederika Blankner. Other sections are by other specialists. Selected bibliographies of books and articles emphasize works in English. PT7063.B5

Budd, John. Eight Scandinavian novelists : criticism and reviews in English. Westport, Conn. : Greenwood, [1981]. 180 p. **BE1085**

Treats Jonas Lie, Arne Garborg, Selma Lagerlöf, Knut Hamsun, Sigrid Undset, Pär Lagerkvist, Vilhelm Moberg, Halldór Laxness. Indexed. Z2559.F52B82

Dictionary of Scandinavian literature / Virpi Zuck, editor-in-chief ; Niels Ingwersen and Harald S. Naess, advisory editors. N.Y. : Greenwood, 1990. 792 p. **BE1086**

Many years in the making, this first extensive English-language dictionary provides biographical and topical information on the literatures of Denmark, Finland, Greenland, Iceland, Norway, and Sweden for students and scholars of Scandinavian and comparative literature. Only authors who made their literary debut by 1970 are included. There are ca.700 signed entries by 115 contributors. Author entries range in length from 300 to 1,600 words and include: biographical events of importance, analysis of major works, and the writer's influence on society. Following the entries are listings of further works by the author, further translations into English, and references. Topical entries range from 1,000 to 1,500 words. Includes a chronology, 400–1985, and a bibliography of reference sources, journals, histories, anthologies, and biographies for each country and for Scandinavia as a whole in both English and the respective languages. Extensive index. PT7063.D5

Ehrencron-Müller, Holger. Forfatterlexikon omfattende Danmark, Norge og Island indtil 1814. København : Aschehoug, 1924–1939. 13 v. **BE1087**

Contents: v. 1–8, A–Weg; v. 9, Wei–Ø. Supplement; v. 10–12, Bibliografi over Holbergs Skrifter. Supplement 2. Vols. 1–12 publ. 1924–1935; Supplement 2 publ. 1939. The latter includes corrections and additions to all volumes, including the Holberg bibliography.

An authoritative work, giving brief biographical data and full lists of writings for each author.

§ Similar in plan to Thomas Hansen Erslew's *Almindeligt Forfatter-Lexicon for kongeriget Danmark ...* (BE1117) and Jens Braage Halvorsen's *Norsk forfatter-lexikon, 1814–1880* (BE1341), and linked to those two works by cross-references in the case of many authors whose activity extended into the period after 1814. Z2570.E33

Fry, Donald K. Norse sagas translated into English : a bibliography. N.Y. : AMS Pr., c1980. 139 p. (AMS studies in the Middle Ages, no. 3). **BE1088**

An alphabetical listing by saga of all of the translations of Norse sagas located by the author to 1979. Recommended translations are starred and unreliable ones are so noted. Index of translators, editors, and those other than editors and translators. Numerous cross-references within the main list. Appendixes provide a discussion of translation from the Norse, a list of further readings, and a list of sagas needing translation. The review in *Choice* 18 (May 1981): 962 reports: "Because of the ease with which one can work with it, this bibliography will prove to be indispensable." Z2556.F78

Hollander, Lee Milton. A bibliography of skaldic studies. Copenhagen : Munksgaard, [1958]. 117 p. **BE1089**

Lists editions and collections of skaldic verse, as well as books and articles about it. Notes reviews. Index of authors, editors, and translators. Z2555.H6

Kalinke, Marianne E. Bibliography of old Norse-Icelandic romances / comp. by Marianne E. Kalinke and P. M. Mitchell. Ithaca : Cornell Univ. Pr., 1985. 140 p. (Islandica, 44). **BE1090**

A scholarly bibliography which is thorough, informative, and easy to use. The review in *American reference books annual* 17 (1986): 509 notes that "Considerable effort has been made to draw together all relevant material on the romance saga into a single bibliographic resource, with outstanding results." Divided into four sections covering catalogues and bibliography, collections and anthologies, general works on the *riddarasogur*, and the meat of the work, a list by individual saga. For each, identifies all extant manuscripts, editions, translations, and secondary criticism. Reviews are noted. Cross-references are provided between variant titles and spellings. Index of authors, editors, translators, and reviewers. Z2559.R65K34

Nordens litteratur / red. af Mogens Brøndsted. København : Gyldendal, 1972. 2 v. **BE1091**

Contents: v. 1, Før 1860; v. 2, Efter 1860.

Arranged in chronological sections, for early literature and Middle Ages subdivided by genre and from 1500 CE by country. Chapters are signed by the nine scholars who collaborated on the work, and sec-

tions on each country are in the language of that country. There is a bibliography and author index in v. 2, and a chronological chart outlining the political relationships of the Scandinavian countries, 900–1944.
PT7060.N6

Rossel, Sven Hakon. A history of Scandinavian literature, 1870–1980 / Sven Hakon Rossel ; tr. by Anne C. Ulmer in association with the Univ. of Minnesota Pr. Minneapolis : Univ. of Minn. Pr., c1982. 492 p. (The Nordic series, v. 5). **BE1092**
Translation and extension of Rossel's *Skandinavische Literatur, 1870–1970* (Stuttgart : W. Kohlhammer, 1973. 232 p.). Brief bibliography; index of names. PT7078.R6713

Albania

Elsie, Robert. Dictionary of Albanian literature. Westport, Conn. : Greenwood, 1986. 170 p. **BE1093**
Aims "to provide the Western reader with basic information on Albanian literature from its origins to the present day. It contains entries on over five hundred Albanian writers and literature-related topics, including in most cases fundamental biographical and bibliographical data."—*Pref.* Indexed. PG9602.E47

Historia e letërsisë shqiptare : që nga fillimet deri te Lufta Antifashiste Nacionalçlirimtare / hartuar nga Vehbi Bala ... [et al. ; redaktuar nga Dh.S. Shuteriqi (kryeredaktor) ... et al.]. Tiranë : Akademia e Shkencave e RPS të Shqipërisë, Instituti i Gjuhësisë dhe i Letërsisë, 1983. 629 p. : ill. **BE1094**
An important Marxist-Leninist history, spanning old Albanian literature to the Second World War, written by scholars from the Institute of Linguistics and Literature of the National Academy of Sciences. A revision and expansion of an earlier work which first appeared in 1956. Bibliography and index.
§ A briefer survey history from the same Institute available in English translation and covering the literature from its beginnings to the early 1970s is Koço Bihiku's *History of Albanian literature* (Tirana : The "8 Nentori" Publishing House, 1980; first publ. in Albanian, 1978). PG9603.H57 1983

Austria

Giebisch, Hans. Bio-bibliographisches Literaturlexikon Osterreichs : von den Anfängen bis zur Gegenwart / Hans Giebisch, Gustav Gugitz. Wien : Brüder Hollinek, 1964. 516 p. **BE1095**
A dictionary providing information on German-language writers of the Austro-Hungarian Empire and modern Austria up to 1963. For each writer gives dates, pseudonym (if any), brief biographial information, a chronological list of works, and references to criticism. Includes many lesser-known writers. An appendix updates information in the main listing. Index of pseudonyms.
§ A 2nd ed. has appeared (Vienna : Hollinek, 1985). Z2110.G48

Stock, Karl F. Personalbibliographien österreichischer Dichter und Schriftsteller : von den Anfängen bis zur Gegenwart / Karl Franz Stock, Rudolf Heilinger, Marylène Stock. Pullach bei München : Verlag Dokumentation, 1972. 703 p. **BE1096**
Lists general works, works on the literature of specific regions, and works by and about individual authors. When a writer has been included in another standard bibliographical source (e.g., Karl Goedeke, *Grundriss zur Geschichte der deutschen Dichtung aus den Quellen* [BE1218]), a reference to that work is given and the information not repeated. Author and subject index. Z2111.A1S76

Belgium

See also Netherlands.

Charlier, Gustave. Histoire illustrée des lettres françaises de Belgique / Gustave Charlier et Joseph Hanse. Bruxelles : Renaissance du Livre, 1958. 656 p. : ill. **BE1097**
Reissued in two volumes, 1970.
A lavishly illustrated history of the literature of Belgium, in French, from the earliest times to the present day. Chapters are written by specialists and include bibliographies. PQ3814.C5

Coppe, Paul. Dictionnaire bio-bibliographique des littérateurs d'expression wallonne, 1622 à 1950 / Paul Coppe, Léon Pirsoul. Gembloux : Duculot, [1951]. 415 p. **BE1098**
Includes 1,325 sketches and lists some 25,000 titles of works in the Walloon dialect. The sketch of each author indicates place and date of birth and death; pseudonym, if any; profession; and a concise critical note on the value of his contribution and the titles of his works. Bibliographical information is brief, usually consisting of title and date (in some cases dates are omitted). Z2424.W3C6

Culot, Jean-Marie. Bibliographie des écrivains français de Belgique, 1881–1960. Bruxelles : Académie royale de langue et de littérature françaises de Belgique, 1958–88. v. 1–5. (In progress). **BE1099**
Responsibility varies; later volumes produced under the direction of Roger Brucher (v. 2–4) and Jacques Detemmerman (v. 5).
Contents: v. 1, Ouvrages d'histoire littéraire et de critique d'une portée générale ou relatifs à plusieurs écrivains, 1880–1950. Anthologies et ouvrages collectifs; Auteurs, A–Destrée; v. 2–5, Det–Q.
With v. 2 the period of coverage was extended from 1950 to 1960; a section of general works for the period 1950–60 is included in that volume.
Planned to continue the *Bibliographie nationale. Dictionnaire des écrivains belges et catalogue de leurs publications, 1830–80* (AA576) for writers in the field of literature. For each writer gives: dates, works by, and periodicals and collections to which he or she has contributed, with a list of works to consult. Z2413.C8

Frickx, Robert. Lettres françaises de Belgique : dictionnaire des œuvres / Robert Frickx et Raymond Trousson. Paris : Duculot, c1988–c1989. 3 v. **BE1100**
Contents: v. 1, Le roman; v. 2, La poésie; v. 3, Le théâtre.
Covers works published 1830–1980, presenting in chronological sections signed essays on the work, with author indexes. The poetry and essay sections tend to discuss entire volumes, rather than individual works. Name index. PQ3811.Z5

Hanlet, Camille. Les écrivains belges contemporains de langue française, 1800–1946. Liège : Dessain, 1946. 2 v. (1302 p.). : ill. **BE1101**
An extensive survey of all Belgian authors writing in French from the 18th century to 1946. The length of the biography and critical annotation varies from a few lines to several pages. For many writers, bibliographies of works about the person are included. In chronological order with a name index. PQ3814.H3

Seyn, Eugène de. Dictionnaire des écrivains belges, bio-bibliographie. Bruges : Éd. "Excelsior", 1930–31. 2 v. : ill. **BE1102**
Gives biobibliographical sketches of writers regardless of language considered to be Belgian, from early to modern times. Provides brief biography, and a list of works including collaborative works and often the titles of journals to which the writer contributed, few references to secondary material. Z2410.S52

Bulgaria

A biobibliographical handbook of Bulgarian authors / by Mateja Matejic ... [et al.] ; ed. by Karen L. Black ; translated by Predrag Matejic. Columbus, Ohio : Slavica Publishers, c1981. 347 p. : ports. **BE1103**

A dictionary in chronological order providing bliographical, critical, historical, and bibliographical information on approximately 90 authors with birth dates ranging from 827 to 1932. Entries average two to three pages and include a biographical and analytical essay followed by a listing of works, biographical and bibliographical materials, criticism, and materials in English, as available for each writer. The introduction provides a historical survey of the literature. Z2898.L5B56

Czechoslovakia

See also Slovakia.

Balášová, Olga. Bibliografie české literární vědy, 1945–1955 : Práce o české literatuře / Olga Balášová ... [et al.]. Praha : Státní Pedagogické Nakl., [1964]. 693p. **BE1104**

Lists 5,590 items on Czech literature of all periods published 1945–55. Z2138.L5B3

Čeští spisovatelé 19. a počátku 20. století : slovníková příručka / Napsal autorský kolektiv za redakse Květy Homolové, Mojmíra Otruby a Zdeňka Pešata. Vyd. 3. Praha : Československý Spisovatel, [1982]. 371p. **BE1105**

1st ed., 1972.

Offers biographical sketches and brief commentary on the publications of Czech writers of the 19th and first half of the 20th centuries. Index of names and titles cited in the text.

Supplemented by *Čeští spisovatelé 20. století : slovníková příručka* / Napsal authorský kolektiv za red. Milana Blahynky (Praha : Československý spisovatel, 1985), offering sketches of later 20th-century authors with the same format.

§ Two other Czechoslovakian biobibliographical sources are *Slovník českých spisovatelů*, red. Rudolf Havel a Jiří Opelík (Praha : Čeckoslovenský spisovatel, 1964; Ustav pro českou literaturu, Ceskoslovenská akademie v éd) and its sequel, *Slovník české literatury 1970–1981 : basnici, prozaici, dramatici, literarni vedci a kritici publikující v tomto období*, red. Vladimír Forst (Praha : Ceskoslovensky spisovatel, 1985). Both include indexes of pseudonyms. PG5006.C44

Dějiny, české literatury / Hlavní redaktor: Jan Mukařovský. Praha : Nakl. Československé akademie věd, 1959–1961. 3 v. **BE1106**

Half title: Československá akademie věd. Sekce jazyka a literaturyl. Ústav pro českou literaturu. Práce Československá akademie věd.

Contents: v. 1, Starší česká literatura; v. 2, Literatura národního obrození; v. 3, Literatura druhé poloviny devatenáctého století.

The official history, covering 1785–1900. A volume planned to cover the 20th century never appeared. Detailed table of contents and index in each volume. Vol. 1 has extensive footnotes; v. 2–3 contain a section of biobibliographical entries for individual authors. An interesting critique of the Marxist approach based on v. 1–2, by René Wellek, "Recent Czech literary history and criticism," appeared in *The Czechoslovak contribution to world culture*, ed. Miloslan Rechcígl (The Hague : Mouton, 1964) p. 18–28.

§ A recent relatively evenhanded history is *Česká literatura 1785–1985*, by Antonín Měštan (Toronto : Sixty-Eight Publishers, 1987), a revised version of *Geschichte der tschechischen Literatur im 19. und 20. Jahrhundert* (Köln : Böhlau, 1984). The German ed. has sections on Bohemia and Moravia omitted in the Czech.

A history in English is Arne Novak's *Czech literature*, a translation of his *Stručné dejiny literatury české* (1945), ed. with a supplement for 1945–74 by William E. Harkins (Ann Arbor : Michigan Slavic Publications, 1976).

Jelinek, Hanus. Histoire de la littérature tchèque. 3rd–4th éd. Paris : Éd. du Sagittaire, 1930–35. 3 v. **BE1107**

Contents: v. 1, Des origines à 1850 (3rd ed.); v. 2, De 1850 à 1890 (4th ed.); v. 3, De 1890 à nos jours (4th ed.).

Dated but still useful. Some footnote references throughout and a brief bibliography in v. 3. Index in each volume. PG5001.J4

Kovtun, George J. Czech and Slovak literature in English : a bibliography. 2nd ed. Wash. : European Division, Library of Congress; For sale by the U.S. Govt. Print. Off., 1988. 152 p. **BE1108**

1st ed., 1984.

Superintendent of Documents classification: LC1.12/2:C99.

"Bibliography of translations published in monographic form that includes belles-lettres and folklore. Several items dealing with journalism are also listed because of the close relationship between journalism and literary work ... Children's literature is excluded except for works of special importance or works by poets or prose writers known for significant contributions to adult literature."—*Pref.* The 2nd ed. updates to 1986. Z2138.L5K68

Kunc, Jaroslav. Česká literární bibliografie, 1945–1966 : Soupis článků, statí a kritik z knižních publikací a periodického tisku let 1945–1966 o dílech soudobých českých spisovatelů. Praha : Státní Knihovna ČSR Národní Knihovna, 1963–68. 4 v. : ports. **BE1109**

Vols. 1–2 list works by and about Czech literary authors for the period 1945–63; v. 3 continues the listings for 1945–66; v. 4 is an index. Z2138.L5K8

———————— Slovník soudobých českých spisovatelů : krásné písemnictví v letech 1918–45. Praha : Orbis, 1945–46. 2 v. : ill. **BE1110**

A dictionary of Bohemian writers. Restricted to belles lettres.

Continued by the Kunc's *Slovník českých spisovatelů beletristů, 1945–1956* (Praha : Státni Pedagogické Nakl., 1957. 483 p.), a biographical dictionary of 478 Czech literary figures. Z2131.K8

Slovník českých spisovatelů : pokus o rekonstrukci dějin české literatury 1948–1979 / Uspořádali Jiří Brabec [et al.]. [Toronto : Sixty-Eight Publishers Corp., 1982]. 537 p. : ill. **BE1111**

Translated title: A dictionary of Czech writers : an attempt to reconstruct the history of Czech literature 1948–1979.

Provides biography and primary and secondary bibliography for dissident writers both in Czechoslovakia and abroad who at some time were out of favor with the government and barred from publishing and literary recognition. Thus omits some writers who were not dissident, but still of literary merit. Z2138.L5S58

Denmark

Bredsdorff, Elias. Danish literature in English translation : with a special Hans Christian Andersen supplement: a bibliography. Copenhagen : Munksgaard, 1950. 198 p. **BE1112**

Covers translations of Danish literature into English from 1533 to 1949 and also lists materials in English about Danish literature. The supplement, p. 119–98, is "A bibliography of Hans Christian Andersen's works in English translation, and of books and articles relating to H. C. Andersen."

§ Continued by: Carol L. Schroeder, *A bibliography of Danish literature in translation, 1950–1980, with a selection of books about Denmark* (Copenhagen : Det Danske Selskab, 1982). Includes sections for individual authors and genres, and anthologies. "Books about Denmark" is a classed listing of relevant English-language materials in many fields, intended for general readers. Z2574.T7B7

Dansk litteraturhistorie / [forlagsredaktion : Peter Holst]. 2. udg. Copenhagen : Gyldendal, c1990. 9 v. : ill., ports. **BE1113**

First publ. 1983–85.
Contents: Bd. 1, Fra runer til ridderdigtning, o. 800–1480; Bd. 2, Lærdom og magi, 1480–1620; Bd. 3, Stænderkultur og enevælde, 1620–1746; Bd. 4, Patriotismens tid, 1746–1807; Bd. 5, Borgerlig enhedskultur, 1807–48; Bd. 6, Dannelse, folkelighed, individualisme, 1848–1901; Bd. 7, Demokrati og kulturkamp, 1901–45; Bd. 8, Velfærdsstat og kulturkritik, 1945–1980; Bd. 9, Noter og register.
An extensive new history, each volume produced by a different group of scholars. Many illustrations. All references are in v. 9, which also includes name and subject indexes and a list of plates and illustrations.

Dansk skønlitteraert forfatterleksikon, 1900–1950 / Bibliografisk red., Svend Dahl ... [et al.]. København : Grønholt Pedersen, 1959–64. 3 v.   **BE1114**
A biobibliographical dictionary which treats some 3,500 20th-century Danish literary figures. The bibliographies, though presented in abbreviated form, appear to be very comprehensive. Data are meant to be complete through 1950, with some later listings.   Z2573.3.D3

Danske Digtere i det 20. arhundrede / redigeret af Torben Brostrøm og Mette Winge. København : Gad, 1980–1982. 5 v. : ill.   **BE1115**
1st ed., 1951, ed. by Ernst Frandsen; [2nd ed.], 1965–66, ed. by Frederik Nielsen and Ole Restrup.
Contents: v. 1, Fra Johannes V. Jensen til Martin Anderson Nexø; v. 2, Fra Tom Kristensen til H. C. Branner; v. 3, Fra Karen Blixen til Frank Jæger; v. 4, Fra Peter Seeberg til Elsa Gress; v. 5, Fra Anders Bodelsen til Dan Turèll.
A biographical dictionary of Danish poets. Long, signed articles, with a primary bibliography following each article and a bibliography of criticism at the end of each volume. Vol. 5 has an author and title index to the entire set. Many photographs and illustrations.   PT7760.N53

Elkjaer, Kjeld. Skønlitteratur i danske Tidsskrifter, 1913-1942 : en Bibliografi / Kjeld Elkjaer ... [et al.]. København : Folkebibliotekernes Bibliografiske Kontor, 1946. 236 p.   **BE1116**
Largely devoted to Danish literature, but also includes references to articles that have appeared in Danish periodicals on foreign literatures.
A supplement covers the material for 1943–62 (ed. by Alex Eisenberg and Grethe Torfing. Københaven : Bibliotekscentralen, 1970).

Erslew, Thomas Hansen. Almindeligt Forfatter-Lexicon for kongeriget Danmark med tilhørende bilande, fra 1814 til 1840. Kjøbenhavn : Forlagsforeningens Forlag, 1843–53. 3 v.   **BE1117**
An older but still standard biobibliographical dictionary.
———. ———. Supplement : 1841 til efter 1858 (Kjøbenhavn : Rosenkilde og Bagger, 1962–64. 3 v.).
Index: Navneregister (Kjøbenhavn : Rosenkilde og Bagger, 1965. 524 p.). Added t.p.: Alfabetisk register over forfattere og de til disse ved Slægtsabsbaand knyttede personer udarbejdet i aarene 1873–77 / af I. E. Dittmann og A. P. Möller.
An index of all names, both in the original set and the supplement, indicating blood relationships.
§ For earlier periods, see: Holger Ehrencron-Müller, Forfatterlexikon omfattende Danmark, Norge og Island indtil 1814 (BE1087).

A history of Danish literature / ed. by Sven H. Rossel. Lincoln : Univ. of Nebraska Pr. ; [N.Y.] : in cooperation with the American-Scandinavian Foundation, c1992. 709 p. : maps. (A history of Scandinavian literatures, v. 1).   **BE1118**
Covers "Danish literature from its beginnings to 1990, allowing ample space for each literary period and presenting the literary works in their interdependence with various cultural and ideological currents ... separate and extensive discussions have been included on Faroese literature, children's literature, and women's literature."—Introd. The work is aimed at students, comparatists, and general readers. Each chapter is written by a specialist who was responsible for choosing the approach within the chapter. Includes references, chapter bibliographies, and index.
§ An older English-language history is: Phillip M. Mitchell, A history of Danish literature (2nd augm. ed. N.Y. : Kraus-Thompson, 1971).   PT7663.H57

Lindtner, Niels Christian. Danske klassikere : en selektiv bibliografi. Copenhagen : Danmarks Biblioteksskole, 1976. 200 p. (Copenhagen. Danmarks Biblioteksskole. Skrifter, no. 11).   **BE1119**
A selective bibliography of the writings of Denmark's major writers, with detailed bibliographical information. Brief bibliography of critical sources on authors. Name index.
§ 75 yngre danske skonlitter re forfattere : en bibliografisk handbog, ed. by Margit Bryder ... [et al.] (Copenhagen : Danmarks Biblioteksskole, 1981. 183 p.) lists books by and about 20th century writers born after 1925, many not well known outside their geographic area.   Z2571.L45

Mitchell, Phillip Marshall. A bibliographical guide to Danish literature. Copenhagen : Munksgaard, 1951. 62 p.   **BE1120**
A bibliography intended to indicate the most important works of Danish literature, literary history, and criticism, showing standard editions, translations, biographical and critical works, etc. The works considered most significant are starred.   Z2571.M5

Petersen, Carl Sophus. Illustreret dansk Litteraturhistorie / ved Carl S. Petersen of Vilhelm Andersen. Kjøbenhavn : Gyldendal, 1924–34. 4 v. : ill.   **BE1121**
Issued in parts: v. 1, pt. 1, issued 1916, volume completed 1929; v. 2, 1934; v. 3, 1924; v. 4, 1925.
Contents: v. 1, Fra folkevandringstiden indtil Holberg [af] C. S. Peterson; v. 2, Det attende aarhundrede [af] Vilhelm Andersen; v. 3–4, Det nettende aarhundrede [af] V. Andersen.
Planned as a 3rd rev. ed. of Peter Hansen's Illustreret dansk litteraturhistorie (Kjøbenhavn : Det Nordiske forlag, 1902). The standard illustrated history of Danish literature, supplemented but not superseded by Dansk litteraturhistorie (BE1113). Extensive bibliography and index in each volume. Illustrations are numerous and varied and include many facsimiles of pages and manuscripts, some in color and some foldouts.   PT7660.P35

Woel, Cai Mogens. Dansk forfatterleksikon : 338 biografier over nulevende danske forfattere. [København] : Nordiske Landes Bogforlag, 1945. 360 p. : ports.   **BE1122**
Biographical information and bibliographies for authors living at the time the dictionary was published. Bibliographies include works by, translations, and references to biographical information. Photographs. Brief supplement and list of corrections and additions.

Estonia

Eesti kirjanduse biograafiline leksikon / Toimetanud E. Nirk ja E. Sõgel. Tallinn : Eesti Raamat, 1975. 462 p. : ill.   **BE1123**
At head of title: Eesti NSV Teaduste Akadeemia, Keele ja Kirjanduse Instituut.
Offers biobibliographical sketches of Estonian writers of all periods.   PH633.E3

Mauer, Mare. Eesti kirjandus võõrkeeltes : Bibliograafianimestik. Tallinn, 1978. 244 p.   **BE1124**
At head of title: Eesti NSV Kultuuriministeerium. Fr. R. Kreutzwaldi nim. Eesti NSV Riiklik Raamatukogu.
Added title page in English (Estonian literature in foreign languages : a bibliography) and Russian.
A section of collections of folk tales and anthologies in translation is followed by listings of foreign-language translations of works by individual authors. Indexed.

§ Russian translations are listed in Osvald Kivi's five volumes covering 1940–55, 1956–65, 1966–75, 1976–80, and 1981–85, *Estonskaiā khudozhestvennaiā literatura, fol'klor i kritika na russkom i drugikh iazykakh narodov SSSR* (Tallinn : Eesti Raamat, 1956–89. Title varies slightly.). Z2533.M28

Nirk, Endel. Estonian literature : historical survey with biobibliographical appendix / Endel Nirk ; [tr. from Estonian by Arthur Robert Hone and Oleg Mutt]. 2nd ed. Tallinn : Perioodika, 1987. 414 p. : ill. **BE1125**

Translation of *Eesti kirjandus.* 1st ed., 1970.

A survey history for the person unfamiliar with the language, drawn mainly from *Eesti kirjanduse ajalugu,* ed. by Endel Sõgel (Tallinn, 1965–69. 3 v.), but thoroughly updating information for the 2nd ed. Provides a biobibliographical appendix with information on individual writers, and a selected list of Estonian literature in English, French, and German translations. Name index.

§ A brief history in German is Henno Jänes's *Geschichte der estnischen Literatur* (Stockholm : Almqvist & Wiksell, 1965. 188 p.). Endel Mallene's *Estonian literature in the early 1970s : authors, books, and trends of development* (Tallinn : Eesti Raamat, 1978. 115 p.) is primarily a series of biobibliographical sketches.

PH631.N4813

Finland

Ahokas, Jaakko. A history of Finnish literature. [Bloomington] : Publ. for the American-Scandinavian Foundation by Indiana Univ., Research Center for the Language Sciences, [1973]. 568 p. : ports. (Indiana University publications. Uralic and Altaic series, v. 72). **BE1126**

From the beginning to the mid-20th century, with the bulk of the volume devoted to Finnish literature from the beginning of the 19th century. Extensive notes. Index of names and titles. PH301.A35

Suomen kirjailijat 1917-1944 : pienoiselämäkerrat: teosbibliografiat : tutkimusviitteet = Finlands författare 1917–1944 : kortbiografier, verkförteckningar, litteraturhänvisningar = Writers in Finland 1917–1944 : concise biographies : bibliographies : research references / toimitus [editors], Hannu Launonen ... [et al.]. Helsinki : Suomalaisen kiriallisuuden seura, [1981]. 616 p., [40] p. of plates : ill. (Suomalaisen kirjallisuuden seuran toimituksia, 365). **BE1127**

Continued by: *Suomen kirjailijat, 1945–1970 : pienoiselämäkerrat : teosbibliografiat : tutkimusviitteet,* ed. by Hannu Launonen ... [et al.] (Helsinki : Suomalaisen kirjallisuuden seura, 1977. [Suomalaisen kirjallisuuden seuran toimituksia, 332]).

Both are dictionaries of 20th-century Finnish writers, providing brief biographical information and extensive bibliographies of primary and secondary works. Introductions in English, Finnish, and Swedish. Both volumes have general bibliographies and title indexes.

§ Augmented and supplemented by: *Suomen kirjailijat, 1945–1980* ..., ed. by Maija Hirvonen ... [et al.] (Helsinki : Suomalaisen kirjallisuuden seura, 1985. [Suomalaisen kiriallisuuden seuran toimituksia, 402]). Does not supersede the earlier volume covering 1945–70; adds writers omitted from the volume covering 1917–44. Retains the arrangement of the earlier volumes. Z2520.S945

France

See also: Provençal literature (below); Africa—Literature in French; Canada—Literature in French.

General works

Guides

Beugnot, Bernard. Manuel bibliographique des études littéraires : les bases de l'histoire littéraire, les voies nouvelles de l'analyse critique / Bernard Beugnot, J. M. Moureaux. [Paris] : Nathan, c1982. 478 p. **BE1128**

A bibliographic guide for the graduate student of French literature. Treats the basic tools of literary research, the principal areas of research (including the relationships of literature and the arts, psychoanalysis, sociology, etc.), and new trends in literary research (including French literature outside France).

§ A more selective guide that describes 306 reference sources, most of them in French, is Michel Brix, *Guide bibliographique des études d'histoire de la littérature française* (2e éd. rev. et augm. Namur : Bibliothèque universitaire Moretus Plantin : distribué par Presses universitaires de Namur, 1987). Intended as a handbook for the student using the Bibliothèque universitaire Moretus Plantin. Almost a third of the volume is devoted to medieval literature.

Z6511.B48

Osburn, Charles B. Research and reference guide to French studies. 2nd ed. Metuchen, N.J. : Scarecrow, 1981. 532 p. **BE1129**

1st ed., 1968; suppl., 1972.

The earlier edition attempted to cover the whole range of French studies. This revision concentrates on French literature, with limited attention to peripheral fields. About 6,000 citations to "concordances, literary and language dictionaries, iconographies, filmographies, encyclopedias, surveys of scholarship, and especially, bibliographies" (*Introd.*) are grouped in five main sections: French literature (subdivided by period), French language, French language and literature outside France, Romance philology and Occitan studies, general background and related areas. Author and subject indexes. Z2175.A2O8

Bibliography

Bassan, Fernande. French language and literature : an annotated bibliography / Fernande Bassan, Donald C. Spinelli, Howard A. Sullivan. N.Y. : Garland, 1989. 365 p. (Garland reference library of the humanities, v. 954). **BE1130**

For annotation, *see* BD156. Z2175.A2B39

A critical bibliography of French literature. Syracuse, N.Y. : Syracuse Univ. Pr., 1947–85. v. 1–4 and suppl., v. 6, pts. 1–3. (In progress). **BE1131**

David Clark Cabeen was the original editor and the set is often referred to as "Cabeen"; Jules Brody became joint general editor with v. 3; and with v. 6 Richard A. Brooks became general editor.

Contents: v. 1, The mediaeval period, ed. by Urban T. Holmes (1947; enl. ed. 1952); v. 2, The sixteenth century, ed. by Alexander H. Schutz (1956); v. 2, rev., The sixteenth century, ed. by Raymond C. La Charité (1985); v. 3, The seventeenth century, ed. by Nathan Edelman (1961); v. 3A, The seventeenth century; supplement, ed. by H. Gaston Hall (1983); v. 4, The eighteenth century, ed. by George R. Havens and Donald F. Bond (1951); Supplement [to v. 4], ed. by Richard A. Brooks (1968); v. 6, The twentieth century, ed. by Douglas W. Alden and Richard A. Brooks (pt. 1, General subjects and principally the novel before 1940; pt. 2, Principally poetry, theater, and criticism before 1940, and essay; pt. 3, All genres since 1940; index. 1980).

A work of first importance, this is a selective, evaluative, and annotated bibliography compiled by contributing specialists. Arranged by chronological periods; lists books, dissertations, and periodical articles, with references to reviews. Each volume has its own index.

In view of the greatly accelerated scholarly activity in the field of 16th-century French literature since publication of the original v. 2, it was decided to make the new v. 2 a thorough re-examination and re-evaluation. Although designated "revised" on the title page, the introduction to the 1985 volume states that "this volume is neither a revised edition of the 1956 publication nor a mere supplement to it. It is an entirely new and comprehensive work. The 1956 publication is not to be dismissed, however. Numerous entries in this volume refer specifically by number to assessments in the 1956 volume, and readers will no doubt profit from cross-references and comparisons that are both explicit and implicit." There has also been some re-organization of content in the new volume.

Vol. 3A is a supplement to the 1961 volume for the 17th century, extending the listings of editions and critical works through 1979. However, owing to various delays and editorial decisions, "the user may be less assured that exclusions for 1977–78 are deliberate than for the earlier years, while partial coverage of 1979 is offered for future convenience and not for completeness."—*Introd.*

The volume covering the 19th century is still unpublished, and users of v. 6 "should assume that any significant turn-of-the-century author who does not appear in this volume has been relegated to the nineteenth century."—*Introd.*   Z2171.C74

French VII bibliography : critical and biographical references for the study of contemporary French literature. v. [1] (1949)–v. 4 (1968). N.Y. : Stechert-Hafner, 1949–68. Annual.
     BE1132

Vol. 1, numbered in retrospect, consists of five numbers, the last four of which are called "supplements" to the original number. Vol. 1 covered "Books and articles published from 1940 to 1948"; subsequent issues are annual supplements.

Title varies: v. 1, *Bibliography of critical and biographical references for the study of contemporary French literature*, by Douglas W. Alden and others.

Issued by the Bibliography Committee, French VII of the Modern Language Association (with the French Institute).

Indexes: v. 1–2 (whole no. 1–10); v. 3–4 (whole no. 11–20). Indexes are in two parts: (1) Index to author-subjects; (2) Index to authors of books and articles.

A very useful bibliography of material on 20th-century French literature. In two parts: pt. 1, General subjects in a classified arrangement; pt. 2, Author-subjects arranged alphabetically. Includes both books and periodical articles. Items are numbered consecutively throughout, and cross-references by item number link materials under authors' names and those under subject fields.

§ Superseded by: *French XX bibliography : critical and biographical references for French literature since 1885* (v. 5, no. 1 [whole no. 21] [1969]– ; N.Y. : French Inst., 1969– . Annual). Assumes the numbering, scope, and arrangement of its predecessor. Indexes: v. 5 (whole no. 21–25); v. 6 (whole no. 26–30); v. 7 (whole no. 31–35), with "Index to anonymes" for v. 1–7; v. 8 (whole no. 36–40), with "Index to anonymes" for v. 8.

A useful but now defunct companion to *French VII bibliography* was *French VI bibliography : critical and bibliographcal references for the study of nineteenth-century French literature*, 1954/55–1966/67 (N.Y. : publ. by the French Inst. with the cooperation of the Modern Language Assoc., 1956–68). Title and frequency vary; earlier volumes attributed to the French VI Bibliography Committee of the Modern Language Assoc. of America.   Z2173.F7

Gelfand, Elissa D. French feminist criticism : women, language, and literature : an annotated bibliography / Elissa D. Gelfand, Virginia Thorndike Hules. N.Y. : Garland, 1985. lii, 318 p. (Garland reference library of the humanities, v. 351 ; Garland bibliographies of modern critics and critical schools, v. 9).   **BE1133**

Presents 555 items in two main sections: (1) General problematics of feminist criticism, which includes comparative studies and works on feminist criticism in general; (2) French and Francophone voices, which lists works by and about individual critics. An appendix gives contents of special issues of journals; title and subject indexes.
     HQ1386.G44

Griffin, Lloyd W. Modern French literature and language : a bibliography of homage studies / comp. by Lloyd W. Griffin, Jack A. Clarke, and Alexander Y. Kroff. Madison : Univ. of Wisconsin Pr., 1976. 175 p.   **BE1134**

Both supersedes and extends the coverage of the 1953 bibliography of the same title by H. H. Golden and S. O. Simches. Includes references to articles pertinent to French language and literature appearing in some 588 homage volumes; a listing of the festschriften is followed by a classified listing of the relevant contributions. Cutoff date is 1974 with some 1975 items included. Name index with reference both to authors of the articles analyzed and to literary authors as subjects (the latter designated by an asterisk).   Z2175.F45G74

Harvard University. Library. French literature. Cambridge, Mass. : Harvard Univ. Libr., distr. by the Harvard Univ. Pr., 1973. 2 v. (Widener Library shelflist, 47–48).   **BE1135**

For a note on the series, *see* AA115.

Contents: v. 1, Classification schedule; classified listing by call number; chronological listing; v. 2, Author and title listing.

These volumes "list nearly 52,000 titles representing historical and critical works on French literature, anthologies, and individual literary works written in French. Histories and anthologies of global scope appear, but the focus of this collection is on European literature in French."—*Pref.*   Z2189.H3

Kempton, Richard. French literature : an annotated guide to selected bibliographies. N.Y. : Modern Language Assoc. of America, 1981. 42 p. (Selected bibliographies in language and literature, 2).   **BE1136**

Previous ed. (1974) publ. by the Reference Dept. of the University Library at the University of California, Santa Barbara.

An annotated "selected listing of major bibliographies on French literature, most of which can be found in the libraries of institutions where graduate instruction in French is offered."—*Introd.* Indexed.
     Z2171.A1C34

Lanson, Gustave. Manuel bibliographique de la littérature française moderne, XVIe, XVIIe, XVIIIe, et XIXe siècles. Nouv. éd., rev. et augm. Paris : Hachette, 1921. 1820 p.
     BE1137

1st ed. in 5 v., 1909–12; rev. ed. with suppl., 1 v., 1914. The 1921 edition contains a brief section on the beginning of the 20th century and the "littérature de la guerre."

An important bibliography of French literature—selective, not complete—comprising more than 23,000 entries. Indexes a considerable amount of analytical material, including articles from more than 800 periodicals.

Continued by: Jeanne Giraud, *Manuel de bibliographie littéraire pour les XVIe, XVIIe et XVIIIe siècles français, 1921–1935* (2. éd., conforme á la première. Paris : Vrin, 1958. [Publications de la Faculté des Lettres de l'Université de Lille, II]). Repr. from the original ed. (1939). Two supplements also published, covering 1936–45 (Paris : Nizet, 1956) and 1946–55 (Paris : Nizet, 1970). Also serves as a continuation of Hugo Paul Thieme's *Bibliographie de la littérature française de 1800 à 1930* (BE1209).   Z2171.L22

Modern Language Association of America. French III. Bibliography of French seventeenth century studies. no. 1 (1952/53)–25 (1977). Bloomington, Ind. : publ. for the French III Committee, Modern Language Assoc. of America, 1953–77.   **BE1138**

An annotated listing of books and articles on both general topics and individual authors. Annotations become increasingly lengthy through the years. Reviews are noted for books both in the current and in previous volumes and pagination is continuous throughout the series.

§ Continued by: *French 17 : an annual descriptive bibliography*

of French seventeenth century studies (no. 26 [1978]– . Fort Collins, Colo. : publ. for Seventeenth Century French Div. of Modern Language Assoc. of America by Colorado State Univ., 1978– . Annual).
Z2172.M6

Osburn, Charles B. The present state of French studies : a collection of research reviews. Metuchen, N.J. : Scarecrow, 1971. 995 p. **BE1139**
Reprints from various sources bibliographic essays on some 40 topics in French literature from medieval through modern times. Since some of the essays originally appeared as early as the 1950s, the editor has provided an appendix of supplementary bibliographic essays to bring the coverage up through the late 1960s. Index of topics.
PQ51.O8

Current

See also BE1132 and BE1138.

Bibliographie de la littérature française du Moyen Âge à nos jours. Année 1953–80. Paris : A. Colin, 1953–81. Annual. **BE1140**
At head of title: René Rancoeur.
Title varies: 1953–61, *Bibliographie littéraire*; 1962–65, *Bibliographie de la littérature française moderne (XVIᵉ–XXᵉ siècles)*.
1953–61 published as reprints of bibliographies appearing in *Revue d'histoire littéraire de la France*. Indexes: 1953–55 in 1955; 1956–58 in 1958; 1959–61 in 1961.
A general section is followed by period divisions arranged according to author treated. Indexes of author and of topical subjects.
Since 1981 has once again become part of the *Revue*, from 1981–85 appearing in each issue, and then as Issue number 3.   Z2171.B54

Bibliographie der französischen Literaturwissenschaft / hrsg. von Otto Klapp. Bd. 1 (1956/58)– . Frankfurt am Main : Klostermann, 1960– . Annual. **BE1141**
Frequency varies; v. 1–6, biennial.
Editor varies: Bd. 24 (1986)– , hrsg. von Astrid Klapp-Lehrmann.
Added title page in French: Bibliographie d'histoire littéraire française. Introduction and headings in French.
Planned as a companion to *Bibliographie der deutschen Literaturwissenschaft* (*see* BE1235), this work interprets French literature in a broad sense. Lists books, articles, and theses published during the period covered, analyzing in each volume some 400 periodicals and more than 150 collections. Arrangement is chronological, from the Middle Ages to the 20th century, with indexes by name and by subject.
§ *Supplement zu den Bänden I–VI (1956–1968) : Sachregister*, bearb. von Friedrich Albert Klapp (Frankfurt am Main : Klostermann, 1970. 111 p.).   Z2171.B56

Current research in French studies at universities & polytechnics in the United Kingdom & Ireland. v. 19 (1987–1988)– . [Egham, Surrey] : Society for French Studies, 1988– . Biennial. **BE1142**
Continues: *Current research in French studies at universities and polytechnics in the United Kingdom*, which began with v. 1 (1971).
A subject list, in three sections, of theses submitted for a variety of degrees: (1) Linguistic studies and stylistics; (2) Literary, historical, and sociological studies not referring to a specific writer, historical figure, or anonymous work; (3) Alphabetical list of writers, historical figures, and anonymous works.

Periodicals

Admussen, Richard L. Les petites revues littéraires, 1914–1939 : répertoire descriptif. Paris : Nizet ; St. Louis : Washington Univ. Pr., 1970. 158 p. **BE1143**

A title listing of literary "little magazines" appearing between the wars. Gives notes on dates of publication, contents, principal contributors, etc. Index of names cited.   Z2165.A35

Place, Jean-Michel. Bibliographie des revues et journaux littéraires des XIXᵉ et XXᵉ siècles / par Jean-Michel Place et André Vasseur. Paris : Éditions de la Chronique des lettres françaises, 1973–77. 3 v. **BE1144**
For annotation, *see* AD96.   PQ2.P5

Dissertations

Gabel, Gernot U. Répertoire bibliographique des thèses françaises (1885–1975) concernant la littérature française des origines à nos jours. Köln : Gemini, 1984. 336 p. (Bibliographien zur Romanistik, 3). **BE1145**
4,100 entries grouped chronologically by century; within each period a general section is followed by an alphabetical arrangement of authors treated. Indexes of authors of the theses and of subjects.
§ Gabel also is editor with Gisela R. Gabel, of *La litterature française : bibliographie des theses de doctorat soutines devant les universités autrichiennes et suisses, 1885–1975* (Köln : Edition Gemini, 1981; *Supplément 1976–1985 et additions*, Hürth-Efferen : Edition Gemini, 1991), listing dissertations completed in Austrian and Swiss universities.   Z2172.G25

Translations

See also BE1074.

Bowe, Forrest. French literature in early American translation : a bibliographical survey of books and pamphlets printed in the United States from 1668 through 1820 / comp. by Forrest Bowe ; ed. by Mary Daniels. N.Y. : Garland, 1977. lxix, 528 p. (Garland reference library of the humanities, v. 77). **BE1146**
The bibliography is "limited to translations of works written in French which were published in the United States from the colonial period through the year 1820. It includes books and pamphlets, as well as some broadside material. ... In general, unless a printed text in French which served as a basis for an English translation has been located, ... problematical works have been omitted."—*p. xxiii*. Arranged in sections according to the general subject content of the works translated (e.g., philosophy and religion, social sciences, history and biography, fiction and verse, drama, etc.); index of authors, translators and editors, and of French and English titles. Numerous descriptive and explanatory notes. Locates copies (many of the works being in the Bowe collection now at Cornell).   Z1215.B66

Criticism

Modern French literature / comp. and ed. by Debra Popkin and Michael Popkin. N.Y. : Ungar, c1977. 2 v. **BE1147**
Published in the series "A library of literary criticism."
A collection of excerpts from critical writings on 168 modern French authors considered to be "the ones who are most read, taught, and written about today in France, the United States, and Britain."—*Introd.* Excerpts are given in English, many of them translated specifically for this publication. Index to critics in v. 2.   PQ306.M57

Manuscripts; Archives

Gallet-Guerne, Danielle. Les sources de l'histoire littéraire aux Archives Nationales. Paris : Impr. Nationale, 1961. 161 p. : plates. **BE1148**

At head of title: Ministère d'État Chargé des Affaires Culturelles. Direction des Archives de France. Archives Nationales.

A guide to the manuscript materials for literary research to be found in the Archives Nationales in Paris. In the introduction the author also notes other archives, libraries, and collections in France of potential use to literary researchers.

Encyclopedias; Dictionaries

Beaumarchais, Jean-Pierre de. Dictionnaire des littératures de langue française / J. -P. de Beaumarchais, Daniel Couty, Alain Rey. Paris : Bordas, c1987. 4 v. : ill. (some col.).
    BE1149

1st ed., 1984–85.

Adds many new articles, and updates original articles and bibliographies through the 1980s. A comprehensive work, covering: French literature from medieval to contemporary times, with signed entries on authors, terms and themes, titles for anonymous works and literary reviews; other national literatures; and French literatures outside France. Entries for major authors are very full, providing discussion of a writer's life and works, chronological tables, synopses and critiques of important works, and bibliographies of primary and secondary works. Numerous illustrations; v. 4 contains an index of works, a chronological table of literary terms, and lists of literary prizes and winners.
    PQ41.B4

Boisdeffre, Pierre de. Dictionnaire de littérature contemporaine / [par] R. M. Albérès [psued.] … [et al.]. Nouv. éd. mise à jour. Paris : Éd. Universitaires, [1963]. 687 p. **BE1150**

1st ed., 1962.

Covers 20th-century French writers. For each provides brief biographical information, a critical sketch, a bibliography of primary works, highly selective references to book-length critical studies, a photograph, and excerpts from criticism or reviews. Several introductory chapters discuss genres and literary movements. Name index.

§ A more selective work covering fewer writers but with more extensive critical analysis is Bernard Pingaud, *Écrivains d'aujourdui, 1940–1960 : dictionnaire anthologique et critique* (Paris : Grasset, 1960. 539 p.). For each author includes a biographical summary, a list of works by the author, sometimes a few references to secondary works, a critical essay, and illustrative extracts from the writings.
    PQ305.B54

Bonnefoy, Claude. Dictionnaire de littérature française contemporaine / Claude Bonnefoy, Tony Cartano, Daniel Oster … [et al.]. Paris : Delarge, [1977]. 411 p. : ill.   **BE1151**

A dictionary of selected French writers who were alive and still publishing new works as of Jan. 1, 1977. In most cases biographical information is minimal and the bulk of the entry is devoted to critical commentary on the writer's work and place in the contemporary literary scene. A bibliography of works by the author is provided, and a photograph. Appendixes deal with literary movements, regional literatures, literary magazines, and prizes.

§ A more recent work, useful for its inclusion of many young writers born after 1950, is *Le dictionnaire : littérature française contemporaine*, by Jérôme Garcin (Paris : Editions Francois Bourin, 1988). Each entry includes a list of primary works, and a distinctive biographical/critical entry provided by the author. Style and content of the entries vary considerably; some major writers declined to participate, hence are not included.
    PQ305.B584

Bouty, Michel. Dictionnaire des oeuvres et des thèmes de la littérature française. Nouv. ed. [Paris] : Hachette, 1985. 352 p.
    BE1152

1st ed., 1972.

A dictionary in two parts providing plots and thematic analyses of works of French literature from the medieval period on. The first section is alphabetical by title and provides a plot summary and an indication of the themes identified for each work. Pt. 2 is an alphabetical list of the themes referring to the works associated with each. Author index.

Revised editions were issued in 1990 and 1991 (447 p.).

§ A useful related source is *Plots and characters in classic French fiction*, by Benjamin E. Hicks (Hamden, Conn. : Archon Books, 1981. 253 p.), covering 32 French novels ranging chronologically from Mme. de Lafayette's *La princesse de Cleves* (1678) to Zola's *Germinal* (1885). Titles first are listed chronologically, followed by a section alphabetical by title that provides for each work a plot summary and a list of characters. This is followed by a dictionary of characters.

Another work providing plot summaries and a more detailed chronology is *Chronologie de la littérature française*, by Jean-Pierre de Beaumarchais, Daniel Couty, et al. (Paris : Presses Universitaires de France, 1991. 162 p.). Plot summaries are provided for selected works. Title index.

Dictionnaire des lettres françaises / publié sous la direction du Cardinal Georges Grente. Paris : Arthème Fayard, 1951–72. 5 v. in 7.   **BE1153**

Contents: Le Moyen Âge (1964); Le seizième siècle (1951); Le dix-septième siècle (1954); Le dix-huitième siècle (1960); Le dix-neuvième siècle (1972). (v. [4–5] in 2 v. each).

Each period alphabetically arranged. This scholarly dictionary includes articles, varying from a few lines to several pages, on persons, academies, universities, and literary subjects. Articles are signed and contain extensive bibliographies of the works of the authors and of materials to consult concerning persons or subjects.   PQ41.D53

Dizionario critico della letteratura francese / diretto da Franco Simone. Torino : Unione Tipografico-Editrice Torinese, 1972. 2 v. : ill.   **BE1154**

Articles on authors and selected topics by outstanding specialists, with extensive bibliographies.

Dolbow, Sandra W. Dictionary of modern French literature : from the age of reason through realism. N.Y. : Greenwood, 1986. 365 p.   **BE1155**

Aims to provide an "introduction to the major writers, works, and literary movements that flourished during the 180 years from the dawn of eighteenth-century French literature through the age of realism, as well as a starting point for further research."—*Pref.* 1880 is the cutoff date. 300 entries, some quite extensive; short bibliographies conclude each entry, with quite current books and articles cited; cross-references. Appendixes give a chronological list in parallel columns of history and literature, and a list of entries by subject matter or chronological period. General index.   PQ41.D65

Forest, Philippe. Dictionnaire fondamental du français littéraire / Philippe Forest, Gérard Conio. Paris : Editions P. Bordas, 1993. 222 p.   **BE1156**

A clearly presented guide to French literary terminology found in and useful for discussion of literature. For each term provides meaning and etymology with information on source and usage, references to appropriate authors, and often quotations from criticism or literature. Entries range from a paragraph to more than a page.   PQ41.F67

French women writers : a bio-bibliographical source book / ed. by Eva Martin Sartori and Dorothy Wynne Zimmerman. N.Y. : Greenwood, 1991. 632 p.   **BE1157**

A dictionary with chapters by contributing scholars covering 51 "of the most important women writers in the history of French literature" (*Pref.*), with an additional chapter on the "trobairitz," women troubadors of the 12th and 13th centuries. For each author includes a section on biography, with an emphasis on her experience as a writer, a discussion of major themes, a survey of criticism, and a bibliography of primary and secondary works. In the case of prolific authors the bibliographies may be selective, with references to the other published bibliographies when available. Focuses on belles lettres. Two appendixes: "Situating women writers in French history: a chronology," and a list of authors by birthdate. List of contributors with brief biographical information. Title and subject indexes.   PQ149.F73

Harvey, Paul. The Oxford companion to French literature /
Sir Paul Harvey, Janet E. Heseltine. Oxford : Clarendon Pr.,
1959. 771 p.   **BE1158**
     Repr. with corrections, 1961.
     Covers French literature from medieval times to approximately
1939, in the manner of other Oxford "companions." Includes: (1) articles on authors, critics, historians, religious writers, savants, scientists,
etc.; (2) articles on individual works, allusions, places, and institutions;
and (3) general survey articles on phases or aspects of French literary
life, movements, etc.
     Updated and revised by: *The concise Oxford dictionary of French
literature*, ed. by Joyce M. H. Reid (Oxford : Clarendon Pr., 1976.
669 p.).
     "Abridgement has been effected by condensation and amalgama-
tion rather than omission … . Many new articles have been added, and
a great many existing articles revised or expanded, in an attempt to
bring the whole work more nearly up to date … ; a few articles have
also been added to fill gaps in the coverage of earlier periods."—*Pref.*
                                                           PQ41.H3

Le Sage, Laurent. Dictionnaire des critiques littéraires : guide
de la critique française du XXe siècle / par Laurent LeSage et
André Yon. University Park : Pennsylvania State Univ. Pr.,
[c1969]. 218 p.   **BE1159**
     Offers biographical sketches of French literary critics of this cen-
tury, together with notes on the critical theories and concepts of each.
Each sketch is followed by a bibliography of works by and about the
critic.   PQ67.A2L4

Lemáitre, Henri. Dictionnaire Bordas de littérature française
et francophone. Paris : Bordas, c1985. 850 p.   **BE1160**
     An alphabetical list covering French literature of all times and ge-
ographical areas, with entries for authors, anonymous works, and literary terms. For authors provides brief biographical information, information on the writer's career, and a complete list of book-length
works. Entries for major authors run for pages and have separate sections discussing individual titles. A bibliography of references, both
general and on selected authors, is provided. Title index.
     § Another convenient general source: *Dictionnaire de la
littérature française et francophone*, ed. Jacques Demougin (Paris :
Larousse, 1987. 3 v.). Entries for authors, titles, terms, literary journals, geographical areas, schools, etc. Libraries should note, however,
that this simply reprints entries for French literature from the more
comprehensive *Dictionnaire historique, thématique, et technique des
littératures: littératures française et étrangéres, anciennes et
modernes*, also ed. by Demougin (BE62).

Levi, Anthony. Guide to French literature. Chicago : St.
James, c1994- . 2 v.   **BE1161**
     Contents: v. 1, Beginnings to 1789; v. 2, 1789 to the present.
     A substantial and impressive work essential for any library sup-
porting French literature. Entries, often lengthy, are devoted to individuals and literary movements. Those for authors include comprehensive bibliographies of works and selective lists of largely book-length
critical studies. The longer essays on authors are divided into sections
on their life and works. Title indexes refer to items in the bibliographies; general analytical indexes also locate entries and information in
them.   PQ226.L48

Malignon, Jean. Dictionnaire des ecrivains français. [Paris] :
Editions du Seuil, [1971]. 552 p. : ill.   **BE1162**
     Covers 281 authors, half from the 20th century. For each pro-
vides a biobibliographical essay, with critical analysis, a bibliography
of works by the author, and very selective references to criticism. Portraits and additional illustrations. A literary/historical chronology also
is provided.   PQ41.M3

Indexes of names

Flutre, Fernand. Table des noms propres avec toutes leurs
variantes : figurant dans les romans du Moyen Âge écrits en
français ou en provençal et actuellement publiés ou analysés.
Poitiers : Centre d'Études Supérieures de Civilisation
Médiévale, 1962. 324 p. (Publications du C.E.S.C.M., 2).
                                                           BE1163
     A listing of proper names, in their variant forms, appearing in me-
dieval romances written in French and Provençal, in two parts: (1) personal names, and (2) geographic, including ethnic, names. Gives citations to texts and a bibliography of the editions used.   PQ155.N2F55

Moisan, André. Répertoire des noms propres de personnes et
de lieux cités dans les chansons de geste françaises et les
oeuvres étrangères dérivées. Genève : Droz, 1986. 2 v. in 5 :
ill. (Publications romanes et françaises, 173).   **BE1164**
     Contents: v. 1, pts. 1–2, Textes français; v. 2, pts. 3–5, Textes
etrangers, textes annexes, suppléments.
     A major handbook and dictionary superseding Ernest Langlois'
*Table des noms propres de toute nature compris dans les chansons de
geste imprimées* (Paris : Bouillon, 1904. Repr. : N.Y. : B. Franklin,
1971 ; Geneva : Slatkine, 1974).
     Covers names of persons, peoples, animals, objects, and geo-
graphical names. In separate sections for names in French texts, foreign texts, and *textes annexes* (historical texts, saints lives, fabliaux,
romances). Each section supplies a bibliography of the texts, followed
by an outline of the cycles, or families, of stories, then the dictionary,
listing geographical names separately. Both the lists of names of persons, etc., and the geographical lists are followed by useful indexes to
groupings, for example horses, magicians, traitors, churches, rivers,
towns, mountains, and countries.
     Vol. 5 contains eight supplements: historical prototypes of char-
acters in chansons; related texts prior to 1100, and references to chansons de geste in works from this period; references to lost epics; allusions to chansons in works after 1100; French prose romances derived
from chansons de geste; a bibliography on the epic credo; genealogical
trees for epics; and the same for relevant historical genealogy.
     For a detailed analytical review see *Speculum*, 63 (1988): 961–66.
                                                           PN689.M65

West, G. D. An index of proper names in French Arthurian
verse romances, 1150–1300. [Toronto] : Univ. of Toronto Pr.,
[1969]. 168 p. (Univ. of Toronto romance series, 15).
                                                           BE1165
     Provides variants, brief descriptions of the contexts in which the
names occur, and exact citations to texts for names of persons, places,
animals, and objects such as swords.
     A companion work by West: *An index of proper names in French
Arthurian prose romances* (Toronto : Univ. of Toronto Pr., 1978), with
the same scope and arrangement.
     § A useful related source is *An index of themes and motifs in
twelfth-century French Arthurian poetry*, by Elaine H. Ruck (Cambridge, Eng.; Rochester, N.Y. : D. S. Brewer, 1991). Divided into 25
broad thematic categories, each further subdivided into more specific
topics. For each, gives references to texts with an explanatory note and
references to additional information.   PQ203.W4

Guidebooks

Guide littéraire de la France / [Etabli par Raymonde Bonnefous, et al. Paris] : Hachette, [1963]. 836, [4] p. : maps, some
in color.   **BE1166**
     An extremely detailed and informative guide to literary associa-
tions for places in France. Arranged in itineraries for six regions, beginning with Paris, which are outlined in the "Table méthodique." Indexes for Paris streets, towns, and names of authors. Maps reflecting
particular authors and regional topics are provided in the text and there
is a foldout road map of France.   DC16.G87

Histories

Adam, Antoine. Littérature française / Antoine Adam, Georges Lerminier et Edouard Morot-Sir. Paris : Larousse, 1967–68. 2 v. : ill.   **BE1167**

1st ed., 1923, had title: *Histoire de la littérature française illustrée.*

Contents: t. 1, Des origines à la fin du XVIIIe siècle; t. 2, XIXe et XXe siècle.

Supersedes the 1948–49 edition of the same title by Joseph Bedier and Paul Hazard, but does not include as many color plates; still richly illustrated. Bibliography and general index in each volume.   PQ101.A3

Boisdeffre, Pierre de. Histoire de la littérature de langue française des années 1930 aux années 1980. Nouv. éd. entièrement ref. Paris : Libr. Academique Perrin, 1985. 2 v.   **BE1168**

1st ed., 1958, had title: *Une histoire vivante de la littérature d'aujourdui : 1938–1958.*

Contents: v. 1, Roman, théâtre; v. 2, Poésie, idées, dictionnaire des auteurs.

A thorough history by a well-established critic covering French and Francophone literature. Especially useful for the 400-page biobibliographical dictionary of authors in v. 2. Each volume has a name index and a detailed table of contents. In addition to the dictionary, v. 2 provides a chronology, lists of literary award winners, and a bibliography. References also are provided in the text.   PQ305.B56

Godefroy, Frédéric Eugène. Histoire de la littérature française depuis le 16ᵉ siècle jusqu'à nos jours. 2. éd. Paris : Gaume, 1878–1881. 10 v.   **BE1169**

Repr.: Nendeln, Liechtenstein : Kraus, 1967.

A standard 19th-century history. Discussion centers almost exclusively on individual writers, with extensive quotations from works. Organized by century, and then divided into prose writers and poets.   PQ231.G7

Histoire de la littérature française / publiée sous la direction de J. Calvet. [Nouvelle éd.]. Paris : de Gigord, 1955–64. 10 v. : ill.   **BE1170**

Contents: v. 1, Le Moyen Âge, par Robert Bossuat (1955); v. 2, La Renaissance, par Raoul Morçay and Armand Müller (1960); v. 3, Le préclassicisme, d'après Raoul Morçay, par Pierre Sage (1962); v. 4, Les écrivains classiques, par H. Gaillard de Champris (1960); v. 5, La littérature religieuse de François de Sales à Fénelon, par J. Calvet (1956); v. 6, De Télémaque à Candide, par Albert Cherel (1958); v. 7, De Candide à Atala, par Henri Berthaut (1958); v. 8, Le romantisme, par Pierre Moreau (1957); v. 9, Le réalisme et le naturalisme, par René Dumesnil (1955); v. 10, Les lettres contemporains, par Louis Chaigne (1964).

Originally published 1931–38; all volumes have been revised, some completely rewritten. A valuable survey from the Catholic point of view, with much bibliography.   PQ101.H47

Histoire littéraire de la France / ouvrage commencé par des religieux bénédictins de la Congrégation de Saint Maur, et continué par des membres de l'Institut (Académie des Inscriptions et Belles Lettres). Paris : Impr. Nationale, 1733–1981. v. 1–41. (In progress).   **BE1171**

Title and imprint vary.

12 v. of this work were publ. by the Maurists, 1733–63. Vols. 11 and 12 were repr. in 1841 and 1830.

Index to v. 9–15 in v. 15; to v. 16–23 in v. 23; to v. 25–32 in v. 32; to v. 33–38 in v. 38.

The most detailed history of French literature, beginning with the earliest period and so full that v. 41 has advanced only through the 14th century. Contains signed contributions by specialists, offering very detailed information and, especially in the later volumes, very full bibliographical references. Includes some articles on literary subjects, forms, movements, etc., but consists in the main of biographical and critical articles on individual authors, including many not treated in other histories.   PQ101.A2H6

Lanson, Gustave. Histoire de la littérature française / remaniée et complétée pour la période 1850–1950 par Paul Tuffrau. [Paris] : Hachette, [1952]. 1441 p.   **BE1172**

The standard one-volume work, frequently reprinted. Extensive references. Includes a literary chronology. Name index and detailed table of contents. A version of this work designed as a school text, co-authored with Paul Tuffrau, appeared as: *Manual illustré de la litterature française* (Paris : Hachette, 1931. Many subsequent editions).

§ Lanson also authored the richly and profusely illustrated *Histoire illustrée de la littérature française* (Paris : Hachette, 1923. 2 v.), intended to celebrate France's literary heritage in the context of victory in World War I and the return to peace and prosperity.   PQ101.L3

A literary history of France / gen. ed., P. E. Charvet. London : Benn ; N.Y. : Barnes & Noble, 1967–74. 6 v.   **BE1173**

Contents: [v. 1], The Middle Ages, J. Fox; [v. 2], Renaissance France, 1470–1589, I. D. McFarlane; v. 2 [i.e., v. 3], The seventeenth century, 1600–1715, P. J. Yarrow; [v. 4], The eighteenth century, 1715–1789, R. Niklaus; v. 4 [i.e., v. 5], The nineteenth century, 1789–1870, P. E. Charvet; v. 5 [i.e., v. 6], The nineteenth and twentieth centuries, 1870–1940, P. E. Charvet.

A standard English language history. Each volume has footnotes, bibliography, and an analytical index.   PQ103.L5

A new history of French literature / ed. by Denis Hollier with R. Howard Bloch ... [et al.]. Cambridge, Mass. : Harvard Univ. Pr., 1989. 1150 p. : ill.   **BE1174**

Presents essays by individual scholars built around a particular date and theme, beginning with Roland's death in 778 and ending Sept. 27, 1985, the 500th broadcast of "Apostrophes" on Antenne 2. Covers French literature outside France (e.g., the Négritude movement in Martinique) and political or social events that influenced literature (e.g., the Dreyfus affair). Each essay includes a short bibliography; a chronology, map, and general index conclude the volume.   PQ119.N48

Petit de Julleville, Louis. Histoire de la langue et de la littérature française des origines à 1900. Paris : Colin, 1896–99. 8 v. : ill.   **BE1175**

Repr. 1922–26.

Contents: T. 1–2, Moyen age (des origines a 1500); T. 3, Seizième siècle; T. 4–5, Dix-septième siècle; T. 6, Dix-huitième siècle; T. 7–8, Dix-neuvième siècle.

A comprehensive history still useful for reference, with chapters written by various authorities. Bibliographies; many illustrations.   PQ101.P5

Pichois, Claude. Littérature française : collection. [Paris] : Arthaud, [1968–79]. 16 v. : ill.   **BE1176**

Contents: v. 1–2, Le Moyen Âge, by J. C. Payen and D. Poiron (1970–71); v. 3–5, La Renaissance, by Y. Giraud [et al.] (1972–74); v. 6–8, L'Age classique, by A. Adam, P. Clarac and R. Pomeau (1968–71); v. 9–11, Le XVIIIᵉ siècle, by Jean Erhard, R. Mauzi and B. Didier (1974–77); v. 12–14, Le romantisme, by M. Milner, C. Pichois and R. Pouilliart (1968–79); v. 15–16, Le XXᵉ siècle, by P. W. Walzer and G. Brée (1975–78).

Each volume includes a "Dictionnaire des auteurs," a bibliography (often very extensive), and a "Tableau synoptique" which lists literary, historical, and cultural events chronologically in parallel columns.   PQ101.P56

Genres

Drama

Brenner, Clarence Dietz. A bibliographical list of plays in the French language, 1700–1789. Berkeley, Calif., 1947. 229 p. **BE1177**

Repr. : N.Y. : AMS Pr., [c1979].

Lists more than 11,000 dramatic compositions by author and title. Analyzes many collections and gives references to other published bibliographies. Provides basic information on each play: date of production, number of acts, tragedy or comedy, verse or prose, publisher if applicable, etc. Z2174.D7B7

Horn-Monval, Madeleine. Répertoire bibliographique des traductions et adaptations françaises du théâtre étranger du XVe siècle à nos jours. Paris : Centre National de la Recherche Scientifique, 1958–67. 8 v. in 7 and index. **BE1178**

Contents: v. 1, Théâtre grec antique; v. 2, Théâtre latin antique. Théâtre latin médiéval et moderne; v. 3, Théâtre italien. Opéras italiens (livrets); v. 4, Théâtre espagnol; Théâtre de l'Amérique latine; Théâtre portugais; v. 5, Théâtre anglais; Théâtre américain; v. 6, Théâtre allemand; Théâtre autrichien; Théâtre suisse; v. 7, Théâtre scandinave (danois, norvégien, suédois). Théâtre flamand; Théâtre hollandais, Pays nordiques (Estonie, Finlande, Islande, Lettonie, Litaunie); v. 8, Théâtres des pays slaves et autres pays européens. Théâtres des pays d'Asie et d'Afrique. Addenda au théâtre américain; [v. 9], Index général des auteurs dramatiques étrangers traduits et cités dans les huit tomes du Répertoire.

The various sections have their own indexes in addition to the general index at the end of the set. Z2174.D7H6

Joannidès, A. La Comédie-Française de 1680 à 1900 : dictionnaire général des pièces et des auteurs / avec une préface de Jules Claretie. Paris : Plon-Nourrit, 1901. 136 p., 274 p. : facsims. **BE1179**

Contents: (1) Alphabetical title list of plays, giving title, author's name, date of first performance; (2) Alphabetical list of authors with short title list of their works; (3) Chronological list, showing plays given each year and number of performances of each; and (4) Appendixes, giving plays of the Comédie Française presented at the Odéon, in the provinces, or in London; list of poems recited at the Comédie, etc.

Continued by:

(1) Annual volumes edited by Joannidès covering 1901–1919, with a final volume covering 1921–25 (Paris : Plon-Nourrit, 1902–26). Contents vary somewhat but each generally provides an alphabetical list of titles, a list by author giving total performances for that year and for all previous years, cast lists, actors and their roles, a chronology of performances, lists of productions outside Paris, and information on the administration and activities of the Comédie Française.

(2) Further continued by La Comédie-Française, 1927–37, ed. Edouard Champion (Nogent-le-Rotrou : Daupeley-Gouveneur, 1934–39.), with five volumes covering 1927–32, 1933–34, 1935, 1936, 1937.

(3) A companion to the volumes by Joannidès is his La Comédie-Française, 1680 à 1920 : tableau des représentations par auteurs et par pièces (Paris : Plon-Nourrit, 1921). An author list, with title index, giving short titles of plays, date of first performance, and total number of times each has been played down to 1920. PN2636.P4C46

Lancaster, Henry Carrington. The Comédie Française, 1680–1701 : plays, actors, spectators, finances. Baltimore : Johns Hopkins Pr. ; London : Milford ; Paris : Les Belles-Lettres, 1941. 210 p. (Johns Hopkins studies in Romance literatures and languages, Extra v. 17). **BE1180**

Arranged chronologically, giving in tabular form the names of the plays, number of spectators, total receipts, and receipts paid to the actors and author. Indexes to plays and persons.

Continued by his article, "The Comédie Française, 1701–74 : plays, actors, spectators, finances," in Transactions of the American Philosophical Society, n.s., v. 41 (1951): 593–849. PN2636.P4C495

——— History of French dramatic literature in the 17th century. Baltimore : Johns Hopkins Pr. ; Paris : Presses Universitaires, 1929–42. 5 v. in 9. **BE1181**

Repr. : N.Y. : Gordian Pr., 1966.

A detailed history with lists of plays, bibliographical footnotes, etc. Vol. 5 includes a subject index, a finding list of plays, and a general index to all five volumes. PQ526.L3

——— Sunset : a history of Parisian drama in the last years of Louis XIV, 1701–1715. Baltimore, Md. : The Johns Hopkins Pr. ; London : H. Milford, Oxford Univ. Pr.; [etc., etc.], 1945. 4 p.l., 365 p. **BE1182**

A sequel to Lancaster's History of French dramatic literature in the 17th century (BE1181), compiled on the same plan, devoted primarily to plays acted or published in or near Paris, and including additions and corrections and a list of plays acted at the Comédie Française, 1701–Sept. 1715. Supplements the author's work on the Comédie Française (BE1180).

Continued by Lancaster's French tragedy in the time of Louis XV and Voltaire, 1715–1774 (1950. 2 v.) and French tragedy in the reign of Louis XVI and the early years of the French Revolution, 1774–1792 (1953. 181 p.). PQ536.L3

Lewicka, Halina. Bibliographie du théâtre profane français des XVe et XVIe siècles / par Halina Lewicka ; [rédacteur, Janina Majerowa]. 2 éd. rev. et augm. Wrocław : Zakład Narodowy im. Ossolínskich ; Paris : Centre National de la Recherche Scientifique, 1980. 181 p. **BE1183**

At head of title: Polska Akademia Nauk, Komitet Neofilologiczny, Institut de recherche et d'histoire des textes.

A well-organized classified bibliography covering all aspects of French secular drama and its relation to society during the period indicated. Some entries are briefly annotated. Indexes to places, to authors and titles of dramatic pieces, and to modern editors and critics. Z2174.D7L43

Soleinne, Martineau de. Bibliothèque dramatique de Monsieur de Soleinne / catalogue rédigé par P. L. Jacob. Paris : Alliance des Arts, 1843–44. 6 v. **BE1184**

Repr. : N.Y. : B. Franklin, 1965.

Contents: t. 1, Théâtre oriental; grec et romain; latin moderne; ancien théâtre français; théâtre français moderne depuis Jodelle jusqu'à Racine. Supplément; t. 2, Théâtre français depuis Racine jusqu'à Victor Hugo; théâtre des provinces; théâtre français à l'étranger; t. 3, Suite du théâtre français; recueils manuscrits; recueils divers; théâtre de la cour; ballets; répertoires des théâtres de Paris; théâtre burlesque; théâtre de société; proverbes dramatiques; théâtre d'éducation; pièces satiriques; pièces en patois; dialogues. Appendice. Autographes; t. 4, Théâtre italien; espagnol et portugais; allemand; anglais; suédois, flamand et hollandais, russe et polonais, turc, grec et valaque; t. 5, 1 pt., Écrits relatifs au théâtre. 2 pt., Estampes et dessins. [3 pt.] Autographes. [4 pt.] Livres doubles et livres omis; [t. 6] Table générale (v. 5, pts. 1–2 and [3–4] publ. in 1 v. in reprint edition; Table called "v. 6" in reprint edition).

An extremely useful catalog of an extensive collection, now dispersed, covering the theater from ancient times through the first part of the 19th century. Particularly strong for all aspects of the French theater, including drama, ballets, burlesque, etc., but includes works dealing with theater in many other countries.

The "Table générale" is an author index to all volumes but a title index only to the "Écrits relatifs au théâtre." A complete title index is provided by Table des pièces de théâtre décrites dans le catalogue de la bibliothèque de M. de Soleinne, par Charles Burnet, pub. par Henri de Rothschild (Paris : D. Morgand, 1914), which gives brief information (author's name, number of acts, verse or prose, drama or comedy, etc.) and provides the entry number for the Soleinne catalog.

§ Two related bibliographies, old but still useful, are: Essai d'une bibliographie générale du théâtre; ou, Catalogue raisonné de la bi-

bliothèque d'un amateur, complétant le catalogue Soleinne, by Joseph de Filippi (Paris : Tresse, 1861. Repr. : N.Y. : B. Franklin, 1967) and *Bibliothèque dramatique de Pont de Vesle. Forniée avec les débris des bibliothèques de Saint-Ange, de Crozat, de Mme. de Pompadour, etc., continuée par Mme. de Montesson, possédée depuis par M. de Soleinne*, by Paul Lacroix (Paris : Administration de l'Alliance des Arts, 1847. Repr. : N.Y. : B. Franklin, 1965). Z2174.D7S62

Thompson, Lawrence Sidney. A bibliography of French plays on microcards. Hamden, Conn. : Shoe String Pr., 1967. 689 p. **BE1185**

About 7,000 items arranged by author or anonymous title. Intended primarily as a guide to the microcard edition of the plays, but useful as a checklist of French plays published prior to about 1910. Z2174.D7T48

Wicks, Charles Beaumont. The Parisian stage : alphabetical indexes of plays and authors. University, Ala. : Univ. of Alabama Pr., 1950–79. 5 pts. (University of Alabama studies, no. 6, 8, 14, 17). **BE1186**

Contents: pt. 1, 1800–1815 (1950); pt. 2, 1816–1830 (1953); pt. 3, 1831–1850 (1961); pt. 4, 1851–1875 (1967); pt. 5, 1876–1900, with cumulative author index 1800–1900 (1979; not designated as part of the series).

Each part is in two sections: (1) an alphabetical list by title, and (2) an author index. Attempts to be a complete list of dramatic productions presented in Paris in the 19th century, giving where possible: title, subtitle, type of play, number of acts, whether in prose or verse, real names of authors, theater and date of first performance in Paris. PN2636.P3W5

Fiction

De Jongh, William Frederick Jekel. A bibliography of the novel and short story in French from the beginning of printing till 1600. Albuquerque : Univ. of New Mexico Pr., 1944. 79 p. (University of New Mexico. Bulletin. Bibliographical series, v.1, no.1). **BE1187**

336 items arranged chronologically, some annotated, with references to library catalogs and bibliographies where entries were located. Includes both original works and translations into French, and what are judged to be short stories a well as works of novel length. Indexes by author and translator and by title for anonymous works.

§ Followed chronologically by Maurice Lever, *La fiction narrative en prose au XVIIème siècle* (BE1190). Z2174.F4D4

Godenne, René. Bibliographie critique de la nouvelle de langue française (1940–1985). Genève : Droz, 1989. 392 p. **BE1188**

A listing, alphabetical by author, of book-length collections of French short stories published in France, Quebec, Switzerland, Belgium, and Africa during the period indicated. Brief annotations provide critical comments. An introduction discusses the literary forms of modern short stories with a statistical analysis of the works listed. Appendixes give lists of collections and anthologies, prizes, periodicals, and festivals; a bibliography of criticism on the short story; and authors' comments on their work. A review in *The French review* 65 (Oct. 1991): 114–15, judges this "an invaluable reference work ... which may serve both as rich bibliographical tool and as a critical appraisal of the French short story of the last half century," but notes it is "far from complete and in need of further development."

Premier supplément à la Bibliographie critique de la nouvelle de langue française (1940–1990) (Genève : Droz, 1992. [Histoire des idées et critique littéraire, 315]). Updates and amplifies the earlier work and includes a bibliography of erotic works. Z2174.S5G63

Jones, Silas Paul. A list of French prose fiction from 1700 to 1750 : with a brief introduction. N.Y. : Wilson, 1939. 150 p. **BE1189**

An annotated, chronological list of French fiction including "imaginary voyages, fictitious memoirs, collections of spurious letters,

fairy tales, etc."—*Introd.* Annotations are bibliographic in nature and often provide extensive information on editions and contents. Locations in the Bibliothèque Nationale and Bibliothéque de l'Arsenal in Paris and the British Museum in London are indicated. Detailed index to authors, titles, and pseudonyms. For 1751–1800 *see* BE1191. Z2174.F4J7

Lever, Maurice. La fiction narrative en prose au XVIIème siècle : répertoire bibliographique du genre romanesque en France (1600–1700). Paris : Éditions du Centre National de la Recherche Scientifique, 1976. 645 p. **BE1190**

At head of title: Centre d'Étude de la Littérature française du XVIIème et du XVIIIème siècle (Paris-Sorbonne).

Interpreting "narrative fiction" as broadly as possible, the compiler aims to transcend the limitations of R. C. Williams' *Bibliography of the seventeenth-century novel in France* (N.Y., 1931) and to overcome the errors and deficiencies of R. W. Baldner's revision of that work (N.Y., 1967). The main listing is by title, and full bibliographic information, library locations, attribution of anonymous works, references to later editions, and the "incipit" of each work are given in that section. An author list (including pseudonyms) provides an author approach. A chronological list is provided as well. Z5918.L47

Martin, Angus. Bibliographie du genre romanesque français, 1751–1800 / Angus Martin, Vivienne G. Mylne, Richard Frautschi. London : Mansell ; Paris : France Expansion, 1977. lxxii, 529 p. : ill. **BE1191**

"Genre romanesque" as defined here includes novels, short stories, and other prose writings (such as dialogues) that embody some element of narrative fiction. In general the plan and scope of the bibliography follow that of Silas Paul Jones, *A list of French prose fiction from 1700 to 1750* (BE1189), except that French translations of works originally published in other languages are included here, as are new editions of older works. Arrangement is chronological, then alphabetical by author, with an index of authors and titles. In addition to information on variant editions, serialization in periodicals, and library locations, there are often useful notes on form and content. About 6,750 entries. Z2174.F5M37

Poetry

Coleman, Kathleen. Guide to French poetry explication. N.Y. : G.K. Hall : Maxwell Macmillan International, 1993. 594 p. **BE1192**

Modeled on Joseph M. Kuntz and Nancy C. Martinez's *Poetry explication : a checklist of interpretation since 1925 of British and American poems past and present* (3rd ed. Boston : G.K. Hall, 1980) and a companion to the two works superseding it, *Guide to American poetry explication* (BE491) and *Guide to British poetry explication* (BE710). Essential in any library supporting the study of French literature.

A selective unannotated bibliography, by author and then title, of explicatory criticism published 1960–90 on French poetry of all periods. Explications are in either English or French and "reflect many schools of critical thought. The traditional scholastic *explication de texte* is well represented in the checklist, as are conventional scholarly studies and newer means of literary analysis, such as close readings following structualist or deconstructionist theories."—*Pref.* Explications come from books covering one or more poets, from edited volumes of essays, and from scholarly journals widely held in the U.S. Bibliography of main sources consulted and index of critics. PQ401.C65

Lachèvre, Frédéric. Bibliographie des recueils collectifs de poésies du XVIe siècle : (du Jardin de plaisance, 1502, aux Recueils de Toussaint du Bray, 1609) .... Paris : Champion, 1922. 613 p. : ill. **BE1193**

Repr.: Geneva : Slatkine, 1967.

Subtitle continues: Donnant: (1) La description et le contenu des recueils; (2) Une table générale des pièces anonymes ou signées d'initiales de ces recueils (titre et premier vers), avec l'indication du nom des auteurs pour celles qui ont pu être attribuées.

A description of the contents of a large number of collections of poetry, with identification of many anonymous items. Due to restrictions on paper following the war, Lachèvre was not able to make this work as substantial and complete as his *Bibliographie des recueils collectifs de poésies publiés de 1597 à 1700* (BE1194) as had been projected.   Z2174.P7L15

——————— Bibliographie des recueils collectifs de poésies publiés de 1597 à 1700 .... Paris : Leclerc, 1901–05. 4 v.   **BE1194**

Repr. : Geneva : Slatkine, 1967.

Subtitle: Donnant: (1) La description et le contenu des recueils; (2) Les pièces de chaque auteur classées dans l'ordre alphabétique de premier vers, precedées d'une notice bio-bibliographique, etc.; (3) Une table générale des pièces anonymes ou signées d'initiales (titre et premier vers) avec l'indication des noms des auteurs pour celles qui ont pu leur être attribuées; (4) La reproduction des pièces qui n'ont pas été relevées par les derniers éditeurs des poètes figurant dans les recueils collectifs; (5) Une table des noms cités dans le texte et le premier vers des pièces des recueils collectifs. Etc., etc.

Vol. 1–3 arranged chronologically, 1597–1700; v. 4, Supplément, additions, corrections, tables générales.

A monumental work describing the collections, giving biobibliographical notices of the authors, with attributions for many anonymous poems, some of which have been disputed.

§ Supplemented by Lachèvre's *Les recueils collectifs de poésies libres et satiriques publiés depuis 1600 jusqu'à la mort de Théophile (1626) : Bibliographie de ces recueils et biobibliographie des auteurs qui y figurant* (Paris : Champion, 1914; Suppl 1922, repr.: Geneva : Statkine, 1968).   Z2174.P7L2

——————— Bibliographie sommaire de l'Almanach des muses (1765–1833). Paris : Giraud-Badin, 1928. 206 p. (Les bibliographies nouvelles. Collection du Bulletin du bibliophile, no.12).   **BE1195**

A chronological list providing contents and often additional information for material published in the periodical *Almanach des muses*. Indexes to French authors, forcign writers translated or imitated, principal names of persons addressed or portrayed, principal subjects addressed, songs, and title and first verse of a selected number of major works.   Z2174.P7L21

Mendès, Catulle. Le mouvement poétique français de 1867 à 1900. Paris : Impr. Nationale, E. Fasquelle, 1903. 218 p., 340 p.   **BE1196**

Repr.: N.Y. : B. Franklin, 1971.

Subtitle: Rapport à M. le ministre de l'instruction publique et des beaux-arts, précédé de réflexions sur la personnalité de l'esprit poétique de France, suivi d'un Dictionnaire bibliographique et critique et d'une nomenclature chronologique de la plupart des poètes français du XIXe siècle.

The survey report is followed by the *Dictionnaire*, arranged alphabetically, listing for each poet the titles of his works and, more important, reprinting extracts from commentary and critical opinions with references to sources, many of them from notable authors of the time period.   Z2174.P7M5

Sabatier, Robert. Histoire de la poésie française. [Paris] : A. Michel, [1975–88]. 6 v. in 9.   **BE1197**

Contents: v. 1, La poésie du Moyen Age; v. 2, La poésie du XVIe siècle; v. 3, La poésie du XVIIe siècle; v. 4, La poésie du XVIIIe siècle; v. 5, La Poésie du XIXe siècle: pt. 1. Les romatismes: pt. 2, Naissance de la poésie moderne; v. 6, La poésie du XXe siècle: pt. 1, Tradition et evolution: pt. 2, Révolutions et conquêtes; pt. 3, Métamorphoses et modernité.

A comprehensive history providing hundreds of sections on individual poets, with lists of works and quoted passages provided in the text. Each volume is indexed and has a detailed table of contents.

§ A useful one-volume source is *Dictionnaire des poètes et de la poésie*, by Jacques Charpentreau and Georges Jean (Paris : Gallimard, 1983). Most entries are for individuals with some on movements. Provides portrait, brief biographical information, selected works, and a short extract.

By period

Medieval

See also Provençal (below).

Bossuat, Robert. Manuel bibliographique de la littérature française du Moyen Âge. Melun : Librairie d'Argences, 1951. 638 p.   **BE1198**

Repr.: Nendeln, Liechtenstein : Kraus, 1971.

A bibliographical manual of the French literature of the Middle Ages, listing material in French and other western European languages. After an introduction giving general works, the book is divided into two sections: L'ancien français and Le moyen français. For each work, the principal editions are listed, followed by translations and adaptations, and critical works. The latter include both books and periodical articles.

Supplements:

——————. ——————. *Supplément, 1949–1953*, avec le concours de Jacques Monfrin (1955. 150 p.).

——————. ——————. *2e. supplément, 1954–1960* (1961. 132 p.).

——————. ——————. *3e. supplément, 1960–1980*, by Françoise Vielliard and Jacques Monfrin (Paris : Editions du Centre national de la recherche scientifique, 1986–91. 2 v.). Contents: v. 1, Les origines; Les légendes épiques; Le roman courtois; v. 2, L'ancien français; Le moyen français.

Gautier, Léon. Les épopées françaises : étude sur les origines et l'histoire de la littérature nationale. 2. éd., entièrement refondue. Paris : [Palme], 1878–97. 5 v.   **BE1199**

Repr. : Osnabrück : Zeller, 1966.

Contents: T. 1–2, 1. pt., Origine et histoire; T. 3–4, 2. pt., Légende et héros. Livre 1, Geste du roi. Livre 2, Geste de Guillaume; T. 5, Bibliographie des chansons de geste.

A well-documented history of French epic and heroic poetry. Vol. 5, *Bibliographie des chansons de geste*, is a valuable comprehensive bibliography in its own right listing both general studies and works on individual *chansons*.   PQ201.G3

Linker, Robert White. A bibliography of old French lyrics. University, Miss. : Romance Monographs, Inc., 1979. 401 p. (Romance monographs, no. 31).   **BE1200**

Constitutes a reworking and updating of the material in Gaston Raynaud's *Bibliographie des chansonniers français* (Paris, 1884) and subsequent corrections and additions to that work.

In two main parts, the first listing bibliographies of manuscripts, descriptions of major manuscripts, a general bibliography of lyrics published in anthologies, periodicals, etc., and works on types of lyrics and on metrics and music of the poems; the second part is the bibliography of the lyrics themselves, arranged by name of the trouvère, then by initial word (anonymous poems are listed separately by first word). There is a cross-index of Raynaud and Linker entry numbers.   Z2174.P7L55

Société Rencesvals. Bulletin bibliographique de la Société Rencesvals. fasc.1– . Paris : A. G. Nizet, 1958– . Irregular.   **BE1201**

A handy, annotated, and analytical bibliography on medieval romances and epics of western Europe and England. More recent volumes divided by country, with a section of general works. Each section includes a list of book reviews. Index of titles and subjects. Each volume also functions as an annual for the society, including such information as membership lists, obituaries, reports of meetings and colloquims, and lists of related societies.   PQ201.S66a

Woledge, Brian. Bibliographie des romans et nouvelles en prose française antérieurs à 1500. Genève : Droz, 1954. 180 p. (Société de Publications romanes et françaises sous la direction de Mario Roques, 42).   **BE1202**

Repr.: Genéve : Droz, 1975.

Lists 190 early French romances, with indication of manuscripts, printings, sources, etc. Supplementary lists of manuscripts are arranged by city, printers, authors, titles, literary themes, etc.

————. ————. *Supplément, 1954–1973* (Genéve : Droz, 1975. 139 p. [Publications romanes et françises, 42]).

Woledge has also compiled *Répertoire des plus anciens texts en prose français, depuis 842 jusqu'aux premières années du XIIIe siècle* (Genéve : Droz, 1964. [Publications romanes et françaises, 79]), which lists more completely prose recorded during this period, including much early religious material (prayers, sermons, saints' lives, etc.). A listing by title provides date, place, manuscripts, incipit, published editions, and secondary sources, and there are indexes of manuscripts, places, dialects, and incipits. Z2174.F4W64

16th–18th centuries

Arbour, Roméo. L'ère baroque en France : répertoire chronologique des éditions de textes littéraires. Genève : Droz, 1977–1985. 4 v. in 5. (Histoire des idées et critique littéraire, v. 165, 178, 191, 229). **BE1203**

Contents: T. 1–2, Première partie, 1585–1615; T. 3, Deuxième partie, 1616–28; T. 4, Troisième partie, 1629–43; T. 5, Quatrième partie: Supplement 1585–1643.

A year-by-year listing of literary texts published in France (whether in French or foreign languages and including translations) and of French literary texts published abroad. Library locations, including many in the U.S. and in Europe outside of France, are given whenever possible. Source of the citation is noted when there is no known location. More than 21,000 entries. Each volume contains indexes to names of persons, editors, and of places of publication. Z2162.A72

Cioranescu, Alexandre. Bibliographie de la littérature française du seizième siècle / Collaboration et préface de V.-L. Saulnier. Paris : Klincksieck, 1959. 745 p. **BE1204**

In two parts: (1) *Généralités*, and (2) individual authors. Pt. 2, the larger section, is arranged alphabetically by 16th-century author, listing works by the author followed by a record of studies about the author, including books and articles published through 1950. The explanation of the coverage of the index should be noted: in general, it includes the names of authors or persons *not* included in alphabetical order in the main work, names of places, anonymous works, literary themes, etc. It does not index the main entries for 16th-century works or the names of the modern authors of books and periodical articles. Z2172.C5

———————— Bibliographie de la littérature française du dix-septième siècle. Paris : Centre National de la Recherche Scientifique, 1965–66. 3 v. (2233 p.). **BE1205**

Similar in plan to the author's bibliography for 16th-century French literature (BE1204), but confining itself more closely to literature alone. Again, a general section—with subdivisions for literary history, social and religious background, literary forms, etc.—is followed by the bibliographies of individual authors. Author and subject indexes. More comprehensive than the corresponding volume of *A critical bibliography of French literature*, (BE1131), but without the annotations found in that work. Z2172.C52

———————— Bibliographie de la littérature française du dix-huitième siècle …. Paris : Éditions du Centre National de la Recherches Scientifique, 1969. 3 v., (2137 p.). **BE1206**

Similar to the compiler's bibliographies for the 16th and 17th centuries (BE1204, BE1205), and following the plan of those works (i.e., a general section followed by bibliographies of 18th-century authors in alphabetical order, plus index). Closing date is 1960 for publications listed. Z2172.C48

Will, Samuel F. A bibliography of American studies on the French Renaissance, (1500–1600). Urbana : Univ. of Illinois Pr., 1940. 151 p. (Illinois studies in language and literature, v. 26, no. 2). **BE1207**

Includes books and periodical articles, published in America or by Americans 1886–1937, on France in the 16th century. 1,895 items, including listings for individual authors, histories of literature, language, theater, literary influences, history and civilization, navigation and discoveries, and religion. Name index. Z2178.W55

19th–20th centuries

Talvart, Hector. Bibliographie des auteurs modernes de langue française (1801–1975) / par Hector Talvart et Joseph Place. Paris : Éd. de la Chronique des lettres françaises, 1928–1976. v. 1–22. (In progress). **BE1208**

Contents: v. 1–22, A–Morgan; Index des illustrateurs des ouvrages décrits, t.I–XXII.

An invaluable bibliography of French authors, planned on a large scale. Arranged alphabetically by author, giving generally for each: (1) a biographical sketch; (2) list of writings and editions; (3) minor literary works, i.e., addresses, prefaces, journals edited, etc.; and (4) lists of biographical and critical works and articles about the author, including a large amount of analytical material.

Each volume comprises material published up to the year of its publication and the dates on the title pages vary accordingly; i.e., v. 1 covers 1801–1927; v. 22, 1801–1975.

Vols. 16–17 comprise a title index to works treated in v. 1–15 (which covered through Mirbeau). Z2171.T16

Thieme, Hugo Paul. Bibliographie de la littérature française de 1800 à 1930. Paris : E. Droz, 1933. 3 v. **BE1209**

Repr. : Geneva : Slatkine, 1983.

1st ed., 1907.

Contents: v. 1–2, A–Z; v. 3, La civilisation.

An important reference bibliography, arranged alphabetically by author, listing both works by an author and extensive bibliographies of biographical and critical material about him. v.3 lists books and articles on the history of the language, literature, and culture of France.

Continued by:

Silpelitt Dreher and Madeline Rolli, *Bibliographie de la littérature française, 1930–1939 … complément à Bibliographie de H. P. Thieme* (Genève : Droz, 1948–49. 438 p.).

Marguerite L. Drevet, *Bibliographie de la littérature française, 1940–1949 … complément à Bibliographie de H. P. Thieme* (Genève : Droz, 1954–55. 644 p.).

§ *See also*: Jeanne Giraud, *Manuel de bibliographie littéraire pour les XVIᵉ, XVIIᵉ et XVIIIᵉ siècles français* (2. éd., conforme à la première. Paris : Vrin, 1958. 304 p.). Z2171.T43

Germany

General works

Guides

Faulhaber, Uwe K. German literature : an annotated reference guide / Uwe K. Faulhaber, Penrith B. Goff. N.Y. : Garland, 1979. 398 p. (Garland reference library of the humanities, v. 108). **BE1210**

An annotated bibliography of the major reference and research tools, works of literary criticism, and periodicals in the field of German literature. Includes a section on related fields, a checklist (without annotations) of information on German art, music, philosophy, history, geography, folklore, philology, and language teaching. Indexed. Z2231.F38

Hansel, Johannes. Bücherkunde für Germanisten : Studienausgabe / von Johannes Hansel ; bearb. von Lydia Tschakert. 9., neubearb. Aufl. Berlin : Erich Schmidt Verlag, 1991. 232 p. **BE1211**

1st ed., 1959; 8th ed., 1983.

A guide to basic works for research in Germanic philology and literature, including guides, bibliographies, general histories, annual surveys, etc.; author/title and subject indexes. German-language works predominate, but a few titles in other languages are cited. The original edition included a section on manuscripts. Z2235.A2H3

Richardson, Larry L. Introduction to library research in German studies : language, literature, and civilization. Boulder, Colo. : Westview Pr., [1984]. 227 p. **BE1212**

A guide for the English-speaking student with considerable emphasis on the use of libraries and bibliographic searching techniques and methods. About 250 reference sources are annotated at some length; many general sources are included, with indication of their relevance to research in German studies. Special section on computerized literature searches which, although dated in terms of databases covered and mode of access, still provides very good practical information on conducting a computer search, doing Boolean combinations, using descriptors and subject headings, etc. Glossary; index. Z2235.A2R5

Bibliography

Albrecht, Gunter. Internationale Bibliographie zur Geschichte der deutschen Literatur : von den Anfängen bis zur Gegenwart, erarbeitet von deutschen, sowjetischen, bulgarischen, jugoslawischen, polnischen, rumänischen, tschechoslowakischen und ungarischen Wissenschaftlern / Günter Albrecht, Günter Dahlke. Berlin : Volk und Wissen, 1969–84. 4 v. in 6. **BE1213**

Preface in German and English.

Contents: v. 1, Von den Anfängen bis 1789; v. 2, Von 1789 bis zur Gegenwart (2 v.); v. 3, Sachregister; Personen-Werk-Register; v. 4, Zehnjahres-Ergängsungsband; Berichtzeitraum: 1965 bis 1974 (2 v.).

Represents "the first effort to systematically bring together the results of Russian and Soviet research in German letters as well as those of the other socialist countries in the same field."—*Pref.* Although the work is necessarily selective, all aspects of literature are represented, and coverage is very broad; books, periodical articles, and dissertations are included. Cutoff date is 1964, with some important later items listed. Vol. 2, pt. 2 includes "Nachträge, Errata und Ergänzungen," p. 857–1109. Vol. 4 brings the record down through 1974; it has its own indexes. Z2231.A4

Arnold, Robert Franz. Allgemeine Bücherkunde zur neueren deutschen Literaturgeschichte. 4. Aufl. neubearb. von Herbert Jacob. Berlin : W. de Gruyter, 1966. 395 p. **BE1214**

1st ed., 1910.

An impressive bibliography almost as valuable for wide-ranging coverage of materials for the study of world history and literature as for the history of German literature as narrowly interpreted. Includes information on general reference works, especially biographical and bibliographical sources, as well. International in scope, although emphasis is on German-language sources. Name and subject indexes. Z2231.A87

Batts, Michael S. The bibliography of German literature : an historical and critical survey. Bern : P. Lang, [1978]. 239 p. (Canadian studies in German language and literature, no. 19). **BE1215**

"The first purpose of the present study is ... to provide a succinct historical survey of the bibliographical sources available to those who study the history of German literature in all its aspects."—*Introd.* Discusses bibliographic sources from the period before printing to the present, offering a critical examination of current bibliographic sources, and suggesting future developments. Now dated for information on electronic resources, but still very valuable for historical discussion and analysis. List of works cited and consulted, p. 201–30. Indexed. Z2231.A1B37

Die Deutsche Literatur : biographisches und bibliographisches Lexikon. Bern : Peter Lang, 1982–1991. Reihe II, Abt. A, Bd. 1$^{1-15}$; Abt. B, Bd. 1$^{1-6}$–2$^{1-2}$; Reihe III, Abt. B, Bd 1$^{1-3}$; Reihe VI, Abt. A, Bd 1$^{1-5}$. (In progress). **BE1216**

Contents: Reihe II, Die Deutschen Literatur zwischen 1450 und 1620, Abt. A: Autorenlexikon, Bd. 1, Lfg. 1–15, A–A1, with register; Abt. B: Forschungsliteratur I, Lfg. 1–6, Forschungsliteratur II (Autoren), Lfg. 1–2; Reihe III, Die Deutsche Literatur zwischen 1620 und 1720, Abt. B : Forschungsliteratur I, Lfg. 1–3; Reihe VI, Die Deutsche Literatur von 1890 bis 1990, Abt. A: Autorenlexikon, Bd. 1, Lfg. 1–5, Aab–Ahlers.

A monumental ongoing work. A review in *Journal of English and Germanic philology* 86 (April 1987): 292–7 notes that the overall plan is to provide "both a primary and a secondary bibliography for the whole of German literature, including Neo-Latin literature written in the German-speaking realm" including "*artes* literature, broadsides, philosophical, theological, medical, historical, and, to a certain extent, technical writings." To be divided into six chronological parts, with these divided into two chief sections, primary and secondary works. Provides biographical information on authors and description and analysis of primary works as well as an exhaustive bibliography. Portraits and reproductions of title pages and illustrations are provided.

§ For a longer description of the project, by its chief editor, *see* Hans-Gert Roloff, "Das biographische und bibliographische Lexikon 'Die Deutsche Literatur' : Intention - Struktur - Realisierung" in *Finhalt in der Vielfalt : Festschrift für Peter Lang zum 60. Geburtstag* (Bern : Peter Lang, 1988), p. 458–479.

Dünnhaupt, Gerhard. Bibliographisches Handbuch der Barockliteratur : hundert Personalbiographien deutscher Autoren des Siebzehnten Jahrhunderts. Stuttgart : Hiersemann, 1980–81. 3 v. (Hiersemanns bibliographische Handbücher, Bd. 2). **BE1217**

A brief biographical sketch is followed by a list of 18th–20th century editions of the author's works and of monographic works about the author. Individual works are then listed chronologically, with full bibliographical information and references to other standard bibliographies and catalogs. Z2232.D85

Goedeke, Karl. Grundriss zur Geschichte der deutschen Dichtung aus den Quellen. 2. ganz neubearb. Aufl. Dresden : Ehlermann, 1884–1989. v. 1–17. (In progress?). **BE1218**

Contents: Bd. 1, Das Mittelalter (1884); Bd. 2, Das Reformationszeitalter (1886); Bd. 3, Vom dreissigjährigen bis zum siebenjährigen Kriege (1887); Bd. 4–5, Vom siebenjährigen bis zum Weltkriege (1891–93); Bd. 6–7, Zeit des Weltkrieges (1898–1900); Bd. 8–17, Vom Weltfrieden, 1815 bis zur französischen Revolution 1830 (1905–89).

The most complete bibliography of German literature, indispensable in the large reference library or for university work, but too exhaustive and special for the small library. Gives some biographical and critical comment on authors; critical and other notes on individual works, sources, etc.; and exhaustive bibliographies of editions, treatises, histories, biographical and critical articles, etc. No cumulated index but detailed index in each volume.

Besides the 2nd ed., which appears to be still in progress, two other editions have made brief appearances:

———. 3. neubearb. Aufl., nach dem Tode des Verfassers in Verbindung mit Fachgelehrten fortgeführt von Edmund Goetze (Dresden : Ehlermann, 1906–60. 1 v. [v. 4] in 5, issued in parts: pts. 1–4, 1906–13; pt. 5, publ. Berlin : Akademie Verlag, 1957–60).

Contents: Bd. 4, Abt. 1, Vom siebenjährigen bis zum Weltkriege: nationale Dichtung; Abt. 2–5, Goethe: Abt. 2, Goethe's Leben, allgemeine Bibliographie; Abt. 3, Bibliographie der Werke Goethe; Abt. 4, Nachträge, Berichtigungen und Register zu Abt. 2–3; Abt. 5, Goethe-Bibliographie, 1912–1950, by Carl Diesch and Paul Schlager. No more published. An extensive bibliography of Goethe's life and works.

————. ————. *Neue Folge* (Fortführung von 1830 bis 1880), hrsg. von der Deutschen Akademie der Wissenschaften zu Berlin unter Leitung von Leopold Magon. Bearb. von Georg Minde-Pouet [und] Eva Rothe (Berlin : Akademie Verlag, 1955–62. 1 v.).

Contents: Bd. 1, Bibliographie der Literatur über die deutsche Dichtung im Zeitraum 1830 bis 1880; Die Schriftsteller in alphabetischer Folge, A–Ays. No more published.

————. ————. *Index*, bearb. von Hartmut Rambaldo (Nendeln, Liechtenstein : Kraus-Thomson, 1975. 393 p. Repr., 1979).

An alphabetical index of the authors treated in Bd. 1–15, 1884–1966 of the 2nd ed., and in Bd. 4 of the 3rd ed.   PT85.G7

Handbuch der deutschen Literaturgeschichte : 2. Abt., Bibliographien / hrsg. von Paul Stapf. Bern : Francke Verlag, [1969–74]. v. 1–6, 8–12.   **BE1219**

No more published?

Contents: v. 1, Frühes Mittelalter, von Henry Kratz; v. 2, Hohes Mittelalter, von Michael Batts; v. 3, Spätes Mittelalter, von G. F. Jones; v. 4, Renaissance, Humanismus, Reformation, von James E. Engel; v. 5, Barock, von Ingrid Merkel; v. 6, Das Zeitalter der Aufklärung, von E. K. Grotegut und G. F. Leneaux; v. 8, Romantik, von John Osborne; v. 9, Neunzehntes Jahrhundert, 1830–1880, von Roy C. Cowen; v. 10, Wilhelminisches Zeitalter, von Penrith Goff; v. 11, Deutsches Schrifttum zwischen den Beiden Weltkriegen (1918–1945), von Gertrud B. Pickar; v. 12, Deutsches Schrifttum der Gegenwart (ab 1945), von Jerry Glenn.

Abt. 1 is "Darstellungen."

Offers selective bibliographies for the individual periods, including bibliographies for individual authors listing both editions and criticism.

Vol. 7, to be "Goethezeit. Sturm und Drang," has never appeared.

Handbuch der Editionen : deutschsprachige Schriftsteller, Ausgang des 15. Jahrhunderts bis zur Gegenwart / bearb. von Waltraud Hagen [et al.]. 2. unveränderte Aufl. München : Beck, 1981. 607 p.   **BE1220**

1st ed., 1979.

For some 240 writers drawn from all periods, identifies and annotates the collected and selected editions of their works, collections of letters, etc., giving contents notes and indicating historical, textual, and comparative commentary, indexes, and other scholarly apparatus.   Z2234.F55H36

Hansel, Johannes. Personalbibliographie zur deutschen Literaturgeschichte / Studienausgabe von Johannes Hansel. Neubearb. und Fortführung von 1966 bis auf den jüngsten Stand von Carl Paschek. 2., neubearb. und erg. Aufl. [Berlin] : E. Schmidt, [1974]. 258 p.   **BE1221**

1st ed., 1967.

A valuable guide to bibliographies for selected German authors of all time periods, including the 20th century. Lists monographic bibliographies and gives references to information to be found in standard bibliographic sources. Provides information on the location of manuscripts and literary remains, and on literary societies. Indexes to the authors covered and to the authors of bibliographies.

§ More extensive information on bibliographies for approximately 500 20th-century authors is provided by: Herbert Wiesner, Irena Zivsa and Christoph Stoll, *Bibliographie der Personalbibliographien zur deutschen Gegenwartsliteratur* (München : Nymphenburger Verlag, 1970. 358 p.). Includes information on criticism and biography. Index of names.   Z1002.H24

Harvard University. Library. German literature. Cambridge, Mass. : Publ. by Harvard Univ. Libr. : distr. by the Harvard Univ. Pr., 1974. 2 v. (Widener library shelflist, 49–50).   **BE1222**

For a note on the series, *see* AA115.

Contents: v. 1, Classification schedule; Classified listing by call number; Chronological listing; v. 2, Author and title listing.

Lists "more than 46,000 titles of works on the history of German language, literature, literary anthologies, and works by and about individual European authors writing in German and its dialects."—*Pref.*   Z2249.H37

Index Expressionismus : Bibliographie der Beiträge in den Zeitschriften und Jahrbüchern des literarischen Expressionismus, 1910–1925 / im Auftrage des Seminars für deutsche Philologie der Universität Göttingen und Zusammenarbeit mit dem Deutschen Rechenzentrum Darmstadt hrsg. von Paul Raabe. Nendeln, Liechtenstein : Kraus-Thomson, 1972. 18 v.   **BE1223**

Contents: v. 1–4, Ser. A, Alphabetischer Index; v. 5–9, Ser. B, Systematischer Index; v. 10–14, Ser. C, Index nach Zeitschriften; v. 15–16, Ser. D, Titelregistr; v. 17–18, Ser. E, Gattungsregister.

A computer-produced index to 100 periodicals and five yearbooks associated with the German expressionist movement and reflecting its influence on the whole range of literature, the arts, and culture. A full citation to each article, poem, etc., is given in Serie A, the alphabetical author index, and in Serie B which offers a subject approach. The indexes by title (Serie D) and by genre (Serie E) give briefer information, and it is necessary to refer to the author index for the full citation. Serie C is arranged by title of the serial and offers a printout of the contents of the full run of each publication indexed, with contributions arranged alphabetically by author; the full citation is given in each entry.   Z5936.E9R3

Jahresberichte für neuere deutsche Literaturgeschichte. v. 1 (1890)–v. 26, pt. 1 (1915). Berlin : Behr, 1892–1919. 1890–1915.   **BE1224**

An important annual survey, including books, pamphlets, theses, and periodical articles. Continued by *Jahresbericht über die wissenschaftlichen Erscheinungen auf dem Gebiete der neueren deutschen Literatur* (BE1225).   Z2231.J25

Jahresbericht über die wissenschaftlichen Erscheinungen auf dem Gebiete der neueren deutschen Literatur / hrsg. von der Literaturarchivgesellschaft in Berlin. n.F., v.1 (1921)–16/19 (1936/39). Berlin : W. de Gruyter, 1924–56.   **BE1225**

Continued by *Jahresbericht für deutsche Sprache und Literatur* (BE1226).   Z2231.J26

Jahresbericht für deutsche Sprache und Literatur / bearb. unter Leitung von Gerhard Marx. 2 v. Berlin : Akademie-Verlag, 1960–66.   **BE1226**

Contents: Bd. 1, 1940–45; Bd. 2, 1946–50.

A continuation in combined form of two bibliographical series: the *Jahresbericht über die Erscheinungen auf dem Gebiete der germanischen Philologie* (BD119) and *Jahresbericht über die wissenschaftlichen Erscheinungen auf dem Gebiete der neueren deutschen Literatur* (BE1225).

A comprehensive bibliography of books and periodical articles on German language and literature of all periods. Includes works in European languages (except Slavic) from European and American periodicals. Classified arrangement with extensive indexes.   Z2235.A2J3

Körner, Josef. Bibliographisches Handbuch des deutschen Schrifttums. 3. völlig umgearb. und wesentlich verm. Aufl. Bern : Francke, 1949. 644 p.   **BE1227**

Reissued 1966.

Previously published as an appendix to Wilhelm Scherer and Oskar Walzel's *Geschichte der deutschen Literatur* (4. Aufl. Berlin : Askanischer Verlag, 1928). Lists books and periodical articles dealing with German literature and authors from ancient times to World War II. Arrangement is chronological by periods, each subdivided by subject. Subject and name indexes, although the latter lists only the names treated, not the authors of critical and biographical studies.

§ In the research library this will not be a substitute for Karl Goedeke's *Grundriss zur Geschichte der deutschen Dichtung aus den*

Quellen (BE1218), but will supplement it for more recent materials. Should be useful in the smaller library not needing the wealth of detail given in Goedeke. Z2231.K6

Köttelwesch, Clemens. Bibliographisches Handbuch der deutschen Literaturwissenschaft, 1945–1969. Frankfurt am Main : V. Klostermann, 1971–79. 3 v. **BE1228**

With v. 2, dates of coverage appear as 1945–1972.

Designed as a select bibliography of works on German literature, including books, articles, contributions to collections, theses, and reprints of books originally published before 1945. In addition to German-language materials, French, English, Russian, Polish, Italian, and Dutch sources are represented. Classed arrangement; v. 3 offers name and subject indexes. Z2231.K63

Melzwig, Brigitte. Deutsche sozialistische Literatur, 1918–1945 : Bibliographie der Buchveröffentlichungen. Berlin : Aufbau-Verlag, 1975. 616 p. **BE1229**

Lists writers' works published 1918–45, and reprints and translations through 1969. Chronological index, title index, and index of names.

§ See also: *Lexikon sozialistischer deutscher Literatur, von den Anfängen bis 1945* (BE1249). Z2233.3.M44

Raabe, Paul. Die Autoren und Bücher des literarischen Expressionismus : ein bibliographisches Handbuch / Paul Raabe, in Zusammenarbeit mit Ingrid Hannich-Bode. 2., verb. und um Ergänzungen und Nachträge 1985–1990 erw. Aufl. Stuttgart : Metzler, c1992. 1049 p. : ill., ports. **BE1230**

1st publ. 1985.

A comprehensive and analytic biobibliographic guide to the authors and works of German literary Expressionism. The first section is a listing by author of primary works, published letters and other biographical material, locations for manuscripts, and, very selectively, criticism. Brief biographical information is provided for each. Additional sections provide a variety of useful listings and rearrangments of the information, such as authors by birth date, illustrators, and books by time period and genre. There is a section of photographs of authors; plates, title pages, etc., are reproduced throughout. The 2nd ed. updates the 1st by means of an appendix with the same arrangement. Name index. Z2234.E93R3

Schmitt, Franz Anselm. Stoff- und Motivgeschichte der deutschen Literatur : eine Bibliographie. 3., völlig neu bearb. und erw. Aufl. Berlin : W. de Gruyter, 1976. 437 p. **BE1231**

1st ed., 1959.

A thorough revision and updating of this useful work, the 1st ed. of which was based on the *Bibliographie der Stoff- und Motivgeschichte der deutschen Literatur* by Kurt Bauerhorst (Berlin : W. de Gruyter, 1932). Lists scholarly studies, mostly in German, on the use of themes and motifs in German literature. Arrangement is alphabetical by *Stoff* or *Motiv*. Includes books, periodical articles, dissertations, chapters in books, and festschriften. Author index. Z2231.S35

Sternfeld, Wilhelm. Deutsche Exil-Literatur, 1933–1945 : eine Bio-bibliographie / Wilhelm Sternfeld, Eva Tiedemann. 2. verb. u. stark erw. Aufl. Heidelberg : Lambert Schneider, 1970. 606 p. (Deutsche Akademie für Sprache und Dichtung. Veröffentlichungen, 29a). **BE1232**

1st ed., 1962.

Very brief biographical sketches of German exiles are followed by lists of books and periodical articles.

§ Another bibliography of German exile literature is: *Exil-Literatur 1933–1945 : Eine Austellung aus Beständen der Deutschen Bibliothek, Frankfurt am Main*, comp. by Werner Berthold (3. erw. und verb. Aufl. Frankfurt am Main : Johannes Weisbecker, 1967. 352 p.). Z2233.S7

Wilpert, Gero von. Erstausgaben deutscher Dichtung : eine Bibliographie zur deutschen Literatur, 1600–1990 / Gero von Wilpert und Adolf Gühring. 2., vollstandig uberarbeitete Aufl. Stuttgart : Alfred Kröner, 1992. 1724 p. **BE1233**

1st ed., 1967, covered 1600–1960.

An extensive listing of approximately 50,000 first editions of some 1,200 German writers. Gives pagination, place, publisher, and date. Z2231.W74

Yale University. Library. Yale Collection of German Literature. German Baroque literature : a catalogue of the collection in the Yale University Library / by Curt von Faber du Faur. New Haven, Conn. : Yale Univ. Pr., 1958–69. 2 v. : ill. **BE1234**

"An attempt to present an outline of literary history based on a catalogue of a collection of books" for the period (*ca.* 1575–1740).—*Pref.* Classified arrangement with detailed bibliographic information. Indexes of authors, composers, and illustrators. Vol. 2 represents additions to the collection since the publication of v. 1.

§ A microform collection, *German Baroque literature* [microform], based on the above ([New Haven, Conn.] : Research Publ., c1970–71. 669 reels), reproduces 2,363 of the 3,087 titles in the catalog (the remainder were not filmed because they were incomplete or in poor condition). *German Baroque literature : bibliography-index to the microfilm edition of the Yale University Library collection* (New Haven, Conn. : Research Publ., 1971. 216 p.) serves as an index to the microfilm set and a partial cumulative index to the 2 v. of the Faber du Faur catalog. Z2232.Y35

Current

Bibliographie der deutschen Sprach- und Literaturwissenschaft. 9. Bd. (1969)– . Frankfurt am Main : V. Klostermann, [c1970]– . **BE1235**

Frequency varies.

Continues: *Bibliographie der deutschen Literaturwissenschaft*, Bd. 1–8 (1953–68).

A comprehensive bibliography of Western-language materials: books, pamphlets, articles, dissertations, reviews, etc. Basic arrangement is by literary period, with author and subject indexes.

§ A complementary work that unfortunately appeared for only three years: *Internationale germanistische Bibliographie*, hrsg. Hans-Albrecht Koch, Uta Koch (München : K.G. Saur, 1980–82). A comprehensive bibliography covering the whole range of German language and literature. Z2231.B5

Germanistik : internationales Referatenorgan mit bibliographischen Hinweisen. Jahrg. 1 (Jan. 1960)– . Tübingen : Niemeyer, 1960– . Quarterly. **BE1236**

An international bibliography of materials, from many countries, on German literature. Lists books, periodical articles, and parts of books. Arranged chronologically by period; some entries carry lengthy annotations. Annual author-subject index. Z2235.A2G4

Dissertations

University of London. Institute of Germanic Studies. Theses in Germanic studies : a catalogue of theses and dissertations in the field of Germanic studies, excluding English, approved for higher degrees in the universities of Great Britain and Ireland between 1903 and 1961 / ed. by F. Norman, director. London : [The Institute], 1962. 46 p. (Institute of Germanic Studies. Publications, 4). **BE1237**

Continued by other Institute publications: *Theses in Germanic studies, 1962–67*, ed. by Siegbert S. Prawer and Victor J. Riley (1968. [Publications, 10]) and *Theses in German studies, 1967–72*, ed. by W. D. Robson Scott and Victor J. Riley (1973. [Publications, 17]). All are author listings with subject indexes.

Further continued by: *Theses in progress at British universities and other institutions of higher education* (1967–80), and then by *Research in progress in German studies* (1980/81– . Annual). The latter contains classified lists. More recent volumes divided into theses completed, theses in progress, works published (i.e., studies other than dissertations), and works due to be published. Includes works on history, society, and institutions as well as languages and literature.

A useful source for French dissertations, covering numerous universities, is *Bibliographie franzosischer Dissertationen zur deutschsprachigen Literatur, 1885–1975*, von Gernot U. Gabel (Koln : Edition Gemini, 1981). Arranged by chronological period covered, with author and title indexes.   Z7036.L58

Translations

Goodnight, Scott Holland. German literature in American magazines prior to 1846. Madison, Wis., 1907. 264 p. (University of Wisconsin. Bulletin, no. 188 ; Philology and literature series, v. 4, no. 1).   **BE1238**
Includes a bibliography, arranged chronologically and by magazines, p. 108–242; and index of (1) authors, and (2) magazines.
Continued by: *German literature in American magazines, 1846–1880*, by Martin Henry Haertel (Madison, Wis., 1908. [Bulletin of the Univ. of Wisconsin, no. 263. Philology and literature series v. 4, no. 2]).

Both are dissertations, with discussion followed by bibliographies arranged chronologically and then by magazine, with indexes by author and magazine.
§ Similar information for British magazines is provided by: Bayard Quincy Morton and A. R. Hohlfeld, *German literature in British magazines, 1750–1810* (BE1240).   PT123.U6G6

Morgan, Bayard Quincy. A critical bibliography of German literature in English translation, 1481–1927. 2nd ed., completely rev. and greatly augm. N.Y. : Scarecrow, 1965. 690 p.   **BE1239**
1st ed., 1922; 2nd ed. with suppl. for 1928–35 (Stanford, Calif. : Stanford Univ. Pr. ; London : Milford, 1938. 773 p.). The basic volume has been reprinted from the 1938 ed., omitting the suppl.
The main list contains 10,797 numbered titles, and is followed by List A, Anonyms (587 titles), List B, Bibliographies (50 titles), List C, Collections (577 titles), and an index of translators.
Supplements:
(1) *Supplement embracing the years 1928–1955* (N.Y. : Scarecrow, 1965. 601 p.). Incorporates the 1928–35 suppl. with new material for the longer period. The list of translators has been dropped, as has the system of rating the quality of translations by diacritical marks.
(2) *A selected bibliography of German literature in English translation, 1956–1960*, by Murray F. Smith (Metuchen, N.J. : Scarecrow, 1972). Broader in scope, including translations from the German in all fields, not only belles lettres.

———— German literature in British magazines, 1750–1860 / ed. by Bayard Quincy Morgan and A. R. Hohlfeld. Madison : Univ. of Wisconsin Pr., 1949. 364 p.   **BE1240**
1750–1810 by Walter Roloff; 1811–35 by Morton E. Mix; 1836–60 by Martha Nicolai.
A chronological list of magazine references with an alphabetical list of the German authors named. Preceded by a historical introduction giving a survey of magazine reflection of the British reception of German literature, 1750–1860.
§ Similar information for American magazines is provided by Scott Holland Goodnight, *German literature in American magazines prior to 1846* and Martin Henry Haertel, *German literature in American magazines, 1846 to 1880* (both at BE1238).   PT123.G7M6

O'Neill, Patrick. German literature in English translation : a select bibliography. Toronto : Univ. of Toronto Pr., [1981]. 242 p.   **BE1241**
Intended "for the teaching scholar in the humanities, the student of comparative literature, and the educated general reader" (*Pref.*), the list reflects the compiler's "personal conception of what the canon of German literature (as available in translation) is at the beginning of the 1980s" and his "impression of what is best, most lasting, and most in-

teresting to the English-speaking reader who has a taste for literature." Arranged by period, then alphabetically by author; introductory section of general collections. Indexes of authors and of translators.
Z2234.T7O5

Manuscripts; Archives

See also: Thomas Dietzel, *Deutsche literarische Zeitschriften, 1880–1945* (AD76) and Alfred Adolph Estermann, *Die deutschen Literatur-Zeitschriften, 1850–1880* (AD77).

Frels, Wilhelm. Deutsche Dichterhandschriften von 1400 bis 1900. Leipzig : Hiersemann, 1934. 382 p. (Modern Language Association of America. Germanic section. Bibliographical publication., v. 2).   **BE1242**
Subtitle: Gesamtkatalog der eigenhändigen Handschriften deutscher Dichter in den Bibliotheken und Archiven Deutschlands, Österreichs, der Schweiz und der ČSR.
In two parts: the first alphabetical by author, the second by location.   Z2231.F86

Dictionaries

Friedrichs, Elisabeth. Literarische Lokalgrössen 1700–1900 : Verzeichnis der in regionalen Lexika und Sammelwerken aufgeführten Schriftsteller. Stuttgart : Metzler, 1967. 439 p. (Repertorien zur deutschen Literaturgeschichte, Bd. 3).   **BE1243**
A guide to biographical information appearing in more than 180 local histories and reference works. Provides places and dates of birth and death, followed by references to other sources. Extremely useful for the large number of relatively obscure writers identified, and for an extensive bibliography of some 600 general, national, and local biographical sources.
§ A similar source by the same author: *Die deutschsprachigen Schriftstellerinnen des 18, und 19. Jahrhunderts : ein Lexikon* (Stuttgart : Metzler, 1981. [Repertorien zur deutschen Literaturgeschichte, Bd. 9]). Covers more than 4,000 women writers, giving brief biographical information and references to further information appearing in approximately 400 biographical and critical sources. Also useful for the extensive bibliography of sources consulted.   PT155.F74

Garland, Henry B. The Oxford companion to German literature / by Henry Garland and Mary Garland. 2nd ed. Oxford ; N.Y. : Oxford Univ. Pr., 1986. 1020 p.   **BE1244**
1st ed., 1976.
Follows the standard dictionary format of other Oxford "companions," with entries for authors, titles, historical figures and events, places, institutions, literary movements and terminology. Covers German literature from about 800 CE to the early 1980s. "Many suggestions from readers have been incorporated [since the 1st ed.], and where necessary entries updated,"—*Pref. to the 2nd ed.* A review in *Modern language review* 83 (July 1988): 777–78 comments on omissions but notes that this work "must by now be regarded as a classic of its kind," and that "admiration for this revised edition of the *Companion* soars."   PT41.G3

Gillespie, George T. A catalogue of persons named in German heroic literature (700–1600), including named animals and objects and ethnic names. Oxford : Clarendon Pr., 1973. 166 p.   **BE1245**
Based on the author's thesis, Univ. of London.
A meticulously detailed and documented directory of names providing "information about the characters in German heroic literature between *c.* 700 and 1600, as it has been set out in manuscripts and prints.... Additional information is also given from the English and Scandinavian analogues as well as from other European literatures."—*Introd.* The introductory bibliography provides a survey of the German, Old English, and Scandinavian sources, a list of the

sources themselves, bibliographic information and abbreviations for other sources frequently mentioned, and a bibliography of books, articles, and editions. For each name gives an account of the activities of the character, references to the character in German heroic literature and other German and European sources, records of the name, and historical information. Extensive notes and references. Index to names found in the catalog, but not listed as entries. PT204.G5

Kosch, Wilhelm. Deutsches Literatur-Lexikon : biographisches und bibliographisches Handbuch. 2., vollständig neubearb. und stark erw. Aufl. Bern : Francke, 1947–58. 4 v.
BE1246
1st ed., 1927–30.
Primarily a dictionary of German authors of all periods. Extensive bibliographies cite both original and critical works. Includes entries on literary forms, titles, allusions, places, etc.
A 3rd ed. is in progress:
Deutsches Literatur-Lexikon : biographisches und bibliographisches Handbuch. 3 völlig neubearb. Aufl. / hrsg. von Bruno Berger und Heinz Rupp (Bern : Francke Verlag, 1966–93. Bd. 1–15. [In progress]).
Contents: Bd. 1–15, A–Schnydrig.
This revision concentrates on authors and anonymous titles, omitting from the previous edition such material as place-names, characters from classical literature, and terms and allusions easily found in other literary encyclopedias. Within the limits established for the new edition, it is very comprehensive as well as reasonably up-to-date (e.g., bibliographies include citations up to press time for successive volumes).
§ A one-volume derivation of the 2nd ed., *Deutsches Literatur-Lexikon : Ausgabe in einem Band* / bearb. von Bruno Berger (Bern ; München : Francke Verlag, 1963. 511 p.) consists almost entirely of sketches of German writers, giving brief biographical information and often extensive bibliographies of primary and secondary works. Most of the subject entries in the larger work are omitted. Z2231.K663

Kritisches Lexikon zur deutschsprachigen Gegenwartsliteratur / hrsg. von Heinz Ludwig Arnold. München : Edition Text + Kritik, 1978– . 4 v. (looseleaf). **BE1247**
At head of title: KLG.
For each author treated there is a brief biographical sketch, followed by a signed critical essay on the writer and his work, plus a bibliography of writings by and about the author. Looseleaf format allows updating of individual entries at irregular intervals.
A lengthy analytical review of this work can be found in *Arbitrium : Zeitschrift fur Rezensionen zur Germanistischen Literaturwissenschaft* 2 (1984): 3–13.

Kunisch, Hermann. Handbuch der deutschen Gegenwartsliteratur. 2., verb. und erw. Aufl. München : Nymphenburger Verlagshandlung, [1968–70]. 3 v. **BE1248**
1st ed., 1965.
A revised and greatly expanded edition of this guide to contemporary German literature and literary criticism. Vol. 1–2 comprise alphabetical author listings, followed by articles on literary movements and genres. Vol. 3 is a "Bibliographie der Personalbibliographien" providing references to author bibliographies in other publications.
Partially superseded by *Neues Handbuch der deutschen Gegenwartsliteratur seit 1945* (BE1250). PT155.K82

Lexikon sozialistischer deutscher Literatur, von den Anfängen bis 1945 : monographisch-biographische Darstellungen. Halle : Verlag Sprache und Literatur, 1963. 592 p.
BE1249
Repr. : Leipzig : Bibliographisches Institut, 1964 (called 2. Aufl.); and S'Gravenhage : van Eversdijck ; Giessen : Prolit-Buchvertrieb, 1973.
An alphabetically arranged dictionary of articles on socialist writers, newspapers, collections, etc. Preface provides historical overview. Articles include bibliographies. Indexes to names and to works based on historical persons and events.

§ See also: Brigitte Melzwig's *Deutsche sozialistische Literatur, 1918–1945* (BE1229). Z2230.L46

Neues Handbuch der deutschen Gegenwartsliteratur seit 1945 / begr. von Hermann Kunisch ; hrsg. von Dietz-Rüdiger Moser ; unter Mitwirkung von Petra Ernst, Thomas Kraft und Heidi Zimmer. München : Nymphenburger, c1990. 687 p.
BE1250
Represents a rev. ed. of *Lexikon der deutschsprachigen Gegenwartsliteratur*, begr. von Hermann Kunisch; neu bearb. und hrsg. von Herbert Weisner (München : Nymphenburger, 1981. 2., erw. und aktualisierte Aufl., ed. Sibylle Cramer, 1987).
Based on Kunisch's *Handbuch der deutschen Gegenwartsliteratur* (BE1248), but does not fully supersede that work, omitting both its articles on movements and genres and its Bibliographie der Personalbibliographien. Biographical articles have been revised and expanded and bibliographies updated; new writers have been added and some dropped. Signed articles range from half a column to several pages. Bibliographies include references to criticism. A standard source.
A lengthy, analytical, comparative review of the 1981 edition of this work and the *Kritishes Lexikon zur deutschsprachigen Gegenwartsliteratur*, (BE1247) appeared in *Arbitrium: Zeitschrift fur Rezensionen zur germanistischen Literaturwissenschaft* 2 (1984) : 3–13.
§ A more selective work covering 47 authors of the post war period in much greater depth is *Deutsche Literatur der Gegenwart in Einzeldarstellungen*, hrsg. von Dietrich Weber (3., uberarb. Aufl. Stuttgart : Kroner, 1976–77). Chapters, many of substantial length, cover individual authors and provide detailed bibliographies of works by the author and criticism. No index. Not as useful for quick reference, but valuable for providing a more substantive analysis of the life and work of authors included. PT401.N48

Reallexikon der deutschen Literaturgeschichte / Begr. von Paul Merker und Wolfgang Stammler. 2 Aufl. Neu bearb. / und unter redaktioneller Mitarbeit von Klaus Kanzog, sowie Mitwirkung zahlreicher Fachgelehrter. Hrsg. von Werner Kohlschmidt und Wolfgang Mohr. Berlin : W. de Gruyter, 1955–1988. 5 v. **BE1251**
1st ed., 1925–31 in 4 v.
Issued in parts. Editors vary.
An alphabetically arranged dictionary with signed articles and extensive bibliographies on periods, types, schools, and kinds of German literature. No entries under personal names. Vol. 5 provides an author, title, and subject index and a list of corrections. PT41.R

Schmitt, Fritz. Deutsche Literaturgeschichte in Tabellen. Bonn : Athenäum-Verlag, 1949–52. 3 v. **BE1252**
Of a 2., durchgesehene und erg. Aufl., 1960– , only v. 2 has appeared.
Contents: v. 1, Die Literatur des Mittelalters, 750–1450; v. 2, Renaissance, Barock, Klassizismus, 1450–1770; v. 3, 1770 bis zur Gegenwart.
A scholarly and detailed chronology of German literature giving brief biographical and bibliographical facts, with references to manuscripts, source materials, and studies. Many fold-out charts and tables. Author and title index in each volume.
§ A much-abbreviated handbook based on this work, by Schmitt and Jörn Göres is *Abriss der deutschen Literaturgeschichte in Tabellen* (5. Aufl. Frankfurt am Main ; Bonn : Athenäum Verlag, 1969).
Another shorter chronology, frequently revised, is *Daten deutscher Dichtung : chronologischer Abriss der deutschen Literaturgeschichte* (27 Aufl. München : DTV, 1993. 2 v.), by Herbert and Elisabeth Frenzel. Arranged under broad period divisions, followed by an alphabetical list of authors of the period, then a chronological list of major works. Brief biographical notes for each author and a summary of each title. Author and title index in v. 2. PT103.S39

Stammler, Wolfgang. Die deutsche Literatur des Mittelalters : Verfasserlexikon, unter Mitarbeit zahlreicher Fachgenossen. Berlin : W. de Gruyter, 1931–1955. 5 v. **BE1253**
Issued in parts. Vols. 3–5 ed. by Karl Langosch.

Long, scholarly articles signed by specialists, with detailed bibliographies of works by and about German medieval authors and writings. Includes works in medieval Latin of significance in German literature, and also anonymous works.

§ A new edition is in progress: *Die deutsche Literatur des Mittelalters : Verfasserlexikon*. 2., völlig neubearb. Aufl. (Berlin ; N.Y. : W. de Gruyter, [1977–92]. Bd. 1–8 [In progress]).

On cover: Lfg. 1, Begründet von Wolfgang Stammler, fortgeführt von Karl Langosch ... hrsg. von Kurt Ruh ... Redaktion, Kurt Illing, Christine Stöllinger.

Contents: Bd. 1–8, A–Sittich.

This edition revised and expanded in the light of recent scholarship. Signed articles with bibliographies. Writers of antiquity and medieval Latin writers continue to be treated if they have had an impact on German literature.   Z2230.S78

History

Bartel, Klaus J. German literary history, 1777–1835 : an annotated bibliography. Berne : Herbert Lang, 1976. 229 p. (German studies in America, no. 22).   **BE1254**

A bibliographic and analytical study of 42 histories of German literature written during the era when "we find the first examples of a literary-historical synthesis."—*Introd.* First is a bibliography of the histories, including later editions, translations, and reprints, by date of first publication. The second part is "an analysis of the works: dependency on earlier publication, either according to the author's statement or as analysis would indicate; the author's outlook on literature and its history; his aims and methods; and the arrangement and presentation of his material." Tables of contents are supplied where they existed, as well as citations to contemporary reviews, library locations in the U.S., and a bibliography of items of further interest.

§ Historical discussion and analysis is continued in *A history of histories of German literature, 1835–1914*, by Michael S. Batts (Montreal ; Kingston : McGill-Queens Univ. Pr., 1993). Includes information on foreign histories. Bibliography of works discussed.   Z2232.B37

Boor, Helmut Anton Wilhelm de. Geschichte der deutschen Literatur von den Anfängen bis zur Gegenwart / Helmut Anton Wilhelm de Boor, Richard Newald. München : Beck, 1949–91. v. 1–2, 3$^{1-2}$, 4$^{1-2}$, 5–6^1, 7$^{1-2}$. (In progress).   **BE1255**

Some volumes have appeared in revised editions.

Contents: Bd. 1, Die deutsche Literatur von Karl dem Grossen zum Beginn der höfischen Dichtung, 770–1170, von H. de Boor; Bd. 2, Die höfische Literatur : Vorbereitung, Blüte, Ausklang, 1170–1250, von U. Henning; Bd. 3, T. 1, Die deutsche Literatur im späten Mittelalter: Zerfall und Neubeginn, 1250–1350, von H. de Boor; Bd. 3, T. 2, Die deutsche Literatur im späten Mittelalter: Reimpaargedichte, Drama, Prosa, 1250–1370, von I. Glier; Bd. 4, T. 1, Die deutsche Literatur vom späten Mittelalter bis zum Barock: Das ausgehende Mittelalter, Humanismus und Renaissance, 1370–1520, von H. Rupprich; Bd. 4, T. 2, Die deutsche Literatur vom späten Mittelalter bis zum Barock: Das Zeitalter der Reformation, 1520–1570, von H. Rupprich; Bd. 5, Die deutsche Literatur vom Späthumanismus zur Empfindsamkeit, 1570–1750, von R. Newald; Bd. 6, Aufklärung, Sturm und Drang, frühe Klassik, 1740–1789, von S. A. Jørgensen, et al. (replaces Bd. 6, T. 1, Von Klopstock bis zu Goethes Tod, 1750–1832, von R. Newald, orig. publ. 1957); Bd. 7, T. 1, Die deutsche Literatur zwischen französischen Revolution und Restauration: Das Zeitalter der französischen Revolution, 1789–1806, von G. Schulz; Bd. 7, T. 2, Die deutsche Literatur zwischen französischer Revolution und Restauration: Das Zeitalter der Napoleonischen Kriege und der Restauration, 1806–1830, v. G. Schulz.

Bd 6, T. 2, Klassik und Romantik, and Bd. 8, Vom jungen Deutschland bis zum Naturalismus, have not appeared.

The standard, scholarly multivolume work in German. Each volume has an author, title and in some cases subject index and extensive references.

§ Not to be confused with another work of the same title edited by K. Gysi [et al.] under the auspices of the Kollectiv für Literatur-

geschichte (Berlin : Volk und Wissen, 1961–89. Bd. 1–2, 4–12. No more published?)—the official East German history, itself a shared scholarly effort important for its political viewpoint.   PT85.B64

Bostock, John Knight. A handbook on Old High German literature. 2d ed, rev. by K. C. King and D. R. McLintock. Oxford : Clarendon Pr., 1976. 344 p., [1] leaf of fold. plates : ill.   **BE1256**

1st ed., 1955.

A historical and philological survey, with extensive notes and references, of German literature in the vernacular, 8th–11th centuries. Includes an appendix on Old Saxon and Old High German meter, a general bibliography, a concordance to major collections cited, genealogical tables and maps, and an index of names and titles.   PT183.B6

Könnecke, Gustav. Bilderatlas zur Geschichte der deutschen Nationallitteratur : Eine Ergänzung zu jeder deutschen Litteraturgeschichte. 2. verb. und verm. Aufl. Marburg : Elwert, [1895]. 423 p. : ill.   **BE1257**

Various printings.

A fascinating work, useful for many purposes, covering German literature from the earliest times to the end of the 19th century, as depicted in book illustrations and manuscript facsimiles. Includes biographical sketches, many with autographs and samples of writing, and pictures of authors. Quality of reproductions is very good; some are in color.   PT43.K7

Lennartz, Franz. Deutsche Schriftsteller der Gegenwart : Einzeldarstellungen zur Schönen Literatur in deutscher Sprache. 11., erw. Aufl. Stuttgart : Kröner, [1978]. 825 p. (Kröners Taschenausgabe, Bd. 151).   **BE1258**

1st ed., 1938; 10th ed., 1974.

1st–5th ed. publ. as *Die Dichter unserer Zeit*; 6th–7th, *Dichter und Schriftsteller unserer Zeit*; 8th–10th, *Deutsche Dichter und Schriftsteller unserer Zeit*.

A dictionary providing biographical and critical sketches, averaging two to three pages in length, with bibliographies largely limited to primary works, for German authors and literary critics, including writers for television, radio, and film.

845 entries chosen from all the editions were published as *Deutsche Schriftsteller des 20. Jahrhunderts im Spiegel der Kritik* (Stuttgart : A. Kroner, 1984. 4 v.), also edited by Lennartz. Vols. 1–3 are alphabetical by author. Vol. 4 provides a title index and an analytical list of authors added and dropped in the 11 editions.   PT155.L4

Robertson, John George. A history of German literature. 6th ed. / by Dorothy Reich ... [et al.]. Edinburgh : Blackwood, 1970. 817 p.   **BE1259**

1st ed., 1902; 5th ed., 1968.

The standard English-language history, covering from the beginnings to the 1950s, with information through the mid-1960s for drama and documentary film. Marginal notations make it easy to locate information in the text. Extensive chronology and bibliography. Author, title, subject index.

§ A newer history, aimed at those with little knowledge of German language and literature, is: *A concise history of German literature to 1900*, ed. by Kim Vivian (Columbia, S.C. : Camden House, 1992). A collective effort by experts in the various eras. A review in *Choice* 30 (Jan. 1993): 800, notes that "Undoubtedly space considerations prevented the authors from continuing through to the present. For the periods covered, however, the book ranks among the very best in English, comparable to John. G. Robinson." Extensive bibliographical references, most to works in English. Author, title, and subject index.

Schnell, Ralf. Geschichte der deutschsprachigen Literatur seit 1945. Stuttgart : Metzler, c1993. 611 p. : ill.   **BE1260**

A clearly presented survey of German literature, 1945–89, covering East and West Germany in separate sections. Opening chapters discuss literature in the cultural and historical setting and discuss the publishing industry, the media, libraries, etc. Many photographs. Provides a dictionary of approximately 250 authors, giving brief biographies and lists of works. Bibliography of works for further reference. Indexes to names and publishers.   PT403.S263

Genres

Drama

Allgayer, Wilhelm. Dramenlexikon : ein Wegweiser zu etwa 10,000 urheberrechtlich geschützten Bühnenwerken der Jahre 1945–1957; 1957–1960 / Wilhelm Allgayer ; begründet von Friedrich Ernst Schulz. Köln ; Berlin : Kiepenheuer und Witsch, [1958–62]. 2 v.   **BE1261**
Original ed., 1942, ed. by F. E. Schulz.
A listing of German plays and plays translated into German, copyrighted between 1945 and 1960. Alphabetical by title, with an author index. Provides various data on publication and production. Vol. 1 also includes an essay on amateur theater, a brief glossary of dramatic terms, and addresses of libraries, publishers, theater organizations, and writers associations.
§ A comparable source for earlier plays is: *The German stage, 1767–1890 : a directory of playwrights and plays*, by Veronica C. Richel (N.Y. : Greenwood, 1988). An author list providing brief biographical information and references to other standard biographical sources, and for each play title, date of publication, city of performance with year. References provided for sources of performance data. Title index.   Z2234.D7S372

Gabel, Gernot U. Drama und Theater des deutschen Barock : eine Handbibliographie d. Sekundärliteratur. Hamburg : [Selbstverlag], 1974. 182 p.   **BE1262**
A classified bibliography of works about the drama and theater of the German Baroque era, 1580–1700. Includes general works on literary history, the relationship of German drama to other European drama of the time, themes and motifs, German literary history, German baroque literature, and European and German theater history, as well as works on specific playwrights. Index of names.   Z2232.G3

Gregor, Joseph. Der Schauspielführer / Joseph Gregor ... [et al.]. Stuttgart : Hiersemann, 1953–1989. v. 1–14. (In progress).   **BE1263**
Contents: Bd. 1, Das deutsche Schauspiel vom Mittelalter bis zum Expressionismus; Bd. 2, Das deutsche Schauspiel der Gegenwart; Das Schauspiel der romanischen Völker, T. 1; Bd. 3, Das Schauspiel der romanischen Völker, T. 2; Das niederländische Schauspiel, Das englische Schauspiel, T. 1–2; Bd. 4, Das englische Schauspiel, T. 3: Nordamerika; Das Schauspiel der nordischen Völker; Das Schauspiel der slavischen Völker: Russland, Ukraine; Bd. 5, Das Schauspiel von slavischen Völker: Polen, Tschechoslowakei, Kroatien, Dalmatien, Slowenien, Serbien; Das Schauspiel Ungarns und Griechenlands, des Nahen und Fernen Ostens; Die antiken dramatischen Kulturen; Bd. 6, Nachträge zu Bd. I–V; vergleichender Abriss der dramatischen Weltliteratur; Gesamtregister zu Bd. I–VI; Bd. 7, Ergänzungen zu Bd. I–VI: Das Schauspiel bis 1956; Bd. 8, Das Schauspiel der Gegenwart von 1956 bis 1965; Bd. 9, Das Schauspiel der Gegenwart von 1966 bis 1970 der Inhalt der Wichtigsten Zeitgenössischen Theaterstücke aus aller Welt; Bd. 10, Das Schauspiel der Gegenwart von 1971 bis 1973; Bd. 11, Das Schauspiel von 1974–1976; Bd. 12, Das Schauspiel von 1977–1979; Bd. 13, Das Schauspiel von 1980 bis 1983; Bd. 14, Das Schauspiel von 1984–1986.
A guide to more than 1,000 years of German drama and German translations of foreign drama, absolutely necessary in research libraries. Provides detailed plot summaries, with critical and historical notes including dates of production, both in Germany and original productions abroad, cast requirements, and references to published editions. Earlier volumes are organized around geographical areas and schools, more recent volumes alphabetical by author. Provides valuable reflection of the popularity of foreign playwrights in Germany. Bd. 14 includes plays from 30 countries aside from the two Germanies, and also provides an author index to all of the previous volumes. Other indexes by geographical area, German title, original title, and for one-act plays.

§ *Kleines deutsches dramalexikon*, hrsg. von Jakob Lehmann (Konigstein/Ts. : Athenaum, 1983. 380 p.) is a convenient one-volume work providing information, including a plot summary, for approximately 90 major plays ranging from the classical drama of Goethe to the present. Includes brief biographical notes on the playwright, information on productions and publications of each play, a critical analysis, and a selective list of editions and of secondary works.
PN6114.G7

Hill, Claude. The drama of German expressionism : a German-English bibliography / by Claude Hill and Ralph Ley. Chapel Hill : Univ. of North Carolina Pr., [1960]. 211 p. (University of North Carolina studies in the Germanic languages and literatures, no. 28).   **BE1264**
Repr.: N.Y. : AMS Pr., 1970.
A comprehensive, classified bibliography of works dealing with Expressionism in general and German Expressionist drama in particular. Includes material by and about 16 major Expressionist dramatists. Work in English is listed separately from that in German within section. Entries for individuals include plays in order of publication, reviews and articles on specific plays, translations into English, nonfictional publications by the dramatist, and books, dissertations, and articles about the life and work. Especially useful for citations to reviews in German newspapers. Play and author indexes.

Lederer, Herbert. Handbook of East German drama, 1945–1985 = DDR drama Handbuch, 1945–1985. N.Y. : P. Lang, c1987. 276 p.   **BE1265**
A biobibliographical guide to more than 700 playwrights and 3,000 plays produced in East Germany, 1945–85. "The purpose of this work is to serve as a reference source on who wrote what when, where and when it was first performed, and whether (and if so where and when) it was published."—*Introd.* Attempts to be exhaustive and covers drama, comedies, one-act plays and a variety of stage productions including pantomimes, operas, and ballets. For each author provides brief biography, a list of works by date of first production, giving place of first production if known, and publication information if applicable. Does not list criticism. Valuable for providing a record of many obscure writers and of works performed but never published, and for reflecting the wide variety and popularity of live theater in the former German Democratic Republic. Title index.   PT3721.L43

Meyer, Reinhart. Bibliographia dramatica et dramaticorum : kommentierte Bibliographie der im ehemaligen deutschen Reichsgebiet gedruckten und gespielten Dramen des 18. Jahrhunderts nebst deren Bearbeitungen und Übersetzungen und ihrer Rezeption bis in die Gegenwart. Tübingen : M. Niemeyer, c1986–1993. v. 1, pt. 1–3, v. 2, pt. 1–3. (In progress).   **BE1266**
Primarily a descriptive bibliography of published plays listed by author, with library locations in Europe, the British Museum, and six libraries in the U.S.   Z5785.M37

Fiction

Luther, Arthur. Land und Leute in deutscher Erzählung : ein bibliographisches Literaturlexikon neubearb.... / Arthur Luther, Heinz Freisenhahn. 3. gänzlich veränd. und erg. Aufl. Stuttgart : Hiersemann, 1954. 555 p.   **BE1267**
A complete revision of Luther's *Deutsches Land in deutscher Erzählung* (1st ed., 1936; 2nd ed., 1937) and his *Deutsche Geschichte in deutscher Erzählung* (1st ed., 1940; 2nd ed., 1943).
In two parts. Pt. 1 lists approximately 8,000 novels under 440 place-names. Pt. 2 lists some 2,200 novels under the names of 680 historical personages. Indexes of places and of authors; chronological list of historical characters.   Z5917.H6L97

O'Pecko, Michael T. The twentieth-century German novel : a bibliography of English language criticism, 1945–1986 / by Michael T. O'Pecko and Eleanore O. Hofstetter. Metuchen, N.J. : Scarecrow, 1989. 810 p.   **BE1268**

Lists 6,417 translations, books, articles, dissertations, and book reviews alphabetically under author and novel or novella studied, with a short section on the German novel in general. No index.

Z2234.F4O63

Schmitt, Franz Anselm. Beruf und Arbeit in deutscher Erzählung : ein literarisches Lexikon. Stuttgart : Hiersemann, 1952. 668 col.   **BE1269**

German novels of the last two centuries arranged according to the protagonist's trade or profession. Within lengthy categories (i.e., Musiker [musician]), entries arranged in reverse chronological order, by decades for the 20th century with one section for the 19th. For some professions, works based on the lives of historical figures are noted under the name of the person. Analytical index of professions; name indexes for authors and historical figures.   Z2234.F4S35

Poetry

Dühmert, Anneliese. Von wem ist das Gedicht? : Eine bibliographische Zusammenstellung aus 50 deutschsprachigen Anthologien. Berlin : Haude u. Spener, [1969]. 564 p.

BE1270

An index to German poetry in 50 anthologies published from the 1850s to the 1960s, by poets with birth dates of 1500–1899. Excludes Goethe, Schiller, dialect poems, riddles, childrens' verse, and poems of fewer than five lines. Indexes to first lines, titles, poets, historical names, and places.

Grosse, Siegfried. Die Rezeption mittelalterlicher deutscher Dichtung : eine Bibliographie ihrer Übersetzungen und Bearbeitungen seit der Mitte des 18. Jahrhunderts / Siegfried Grosse, Ursula Rautenberg. Tübingen : M. Niemeyer, 1989. 459 p.   **BE1271**

Lists translations into modern German and German editions, versions, and adaptations of medieval German poetry, published since the middle of the 18th century. The main section is alphabetical by author or title of the work, as appropriate, and in categories for each title. Includes standard editions and translations, modernized poetic renderings, dramatizations, operas and verse set to music, folklore, children's versions, and parodies and travesties. Sections cover genres of medieval poetry as represented by anthologies (e.g., Minnesang and Heldensagen). Notes reviews. Indexes by editor and translator, illustrator, composer, publisher, and reviewer.   Z2232.G75

Häntzschel, Günter. Bibliographie der deutschsprachigen Lyrikanthologien, 1840–1914 / unter Mitarbeit von Sylvia Kucher und Andreas Schumann ; hrsg. von Günter Häntzschel. Munich ; N.Y. : K.G. Saur, 1991. 2 v. (695 p.).   **BE1272**

A bibliography of anthologies of German lyric poetry. Vol. 1 in three sections: by editor, by title for anthologies with no stated editor, and by title for periodicals which functioned as anthologies. For each work, lists all editions and provides basic bibliographic information, gives library location where possible, and notes the indexing terms assigned to that work. Vol. 2 comprises nine indexes: by subject or theme, by the order in which poems are arranged, by the purpose of the editor, by audience, by title, by publisher, by place of publication, by year for first edition, and by year for all editions. Also includes a biographical section, giving brief information on editors.

§ More recent works are covered by *Bibliographie zur deutschen Lyrik nach 1945*, by Rolf Paulus and Ursula Steuler (2., erganz. u. stark erw. Aufl. Wiesbaden : Athenaion, 1977. 263 p.). A bibliography of post-war lyric poetry of Germany, Austria, and Switzerland, with a classified section for general background and critical studies, followed by sections for the principal poets (giving primary and secondary works), and a section listing anthologies. Index of names.   PT545.H3

Schneider, Max. Deutsches Titelbuch : ein Hilfsmittel zum Nachweis von Verfassern deutscher Literaturwerke. 2., verb. und wesentlich verm. Aufl. Berlin : Haude & Spener, 1927. 798 p.   **BE1273**

1st ed., 1907–09, had title: *Von wem ist das doch?*

German titles and first lines of poems arranged alphabetically with attribution to author. Primarily of the 19th century with occasional 18th- and 20th-century titles. Index of subjects.

§ Continued by: Heinz Jörg Ahnert, *Deutsches Titelbuch 2 : ein Hilfsmittel zum Nachweis von Verfassern deutscher Literaturwerke 1915–1965, mit Nachträgen und Berichtigungen zum Deutschen Titelbuch 1 für die Zeit von 1900–1914* (Berlin : Haude & Spener, [1966]. 636 p.). A keyword-in-title list with a subject index. More limited than Schneider in that it covers book titles only.   Z2231.S37

Greece

See also Europe—Regional literatures—Classical—Greek (above).

Philippides, Dia Mary L. Census of modern Greek literature : check-list of English-language sources useful in the study of modern Greek literature (1824–1987). New Haven, Conn. : Modern Greek Studies Association, 1990. 248 p.   **BE1274**

"The check-list began … with the idea of providing a means by which speakers of English could approach Modern Greek literature through translations and works of criticism."—*Introd.* Arranged in seven parts: Bibliographical sources; Journals; Special issues of journals; Anthologies; Collected essays; Literary history; Authors. These parts are further divided into sections on particular regions, periods, or genres; the anthologies, collected essays, and author chapters have detailed contents notes. Name/title index.   Z2294.C8P46

Hungary

See also BE1378.

Benedek, Marcell. Magyar irodalmi lexikon. Budapest : Akadémiai Kiadó, 1963–65. 3 v. : ill.   **BE1275**

Biographical sketches of Hungarian authors predominate, but there are entries for literary terms, journals, etc. Some of the longer articles are signed; bibliographic references.   PH3007.B4

Czigány, Lóránt. The Oxford history of Hungarian literature from the earliest times to the present. Oxford : Clarendon Pr. ; N.Y. : Oxford Univ. Pr., [1984]. 582 p.   **BE1276**

A solid survey history extending from the origins of the language and literature to the early 1980s. An excellent bibliography is arranged to accompany each chapter. A glossary is included. Name, title, subject index.

§ A recent "official" history available in English translation is *A history of Hungarian literature*, a collaborative work written by Istvan Numeskurty [et al.] and ed. by Tibor Klaniczay (Budapest : Corvina, 1982), Hungarian title: *Magyar irodalom története.* Includes a lengthy bibliography and a section of portraits. Indexed.   PH3012.C94

Harvard University. Library. Hungarian history and literature : classification schedule, classified listing by call number, chronological listing, author and title listing. Cambridge : publ. by Harvard Univ. Lib., distr. by Harvard Univ. Pr., 1974. 186 p. (Widener Library shelflist, 44).   **BE1277**

For a note on the series, *see* AA115.

"This volume … lists 6,550 titles concerning the history and literature of Hungary. The present boundaries of the country define the scope of local history coverage."—*Pref.*   Z2146.H37

A Magyar irodalom és irodalomtudomány bibliográfiája. 1976– . Budapest : Országos Széchényi Könyvtár, 1979– . Annual.   **BE1278**

"Készült a Könyvtár Olvasószolgálati és Tájékoztató Osztályán."—*verso of t.p.*

A bibliography of periodical articles relating to Hungarian literature. Classed arrangement with author index. Includes a section of writings on foreign literatures by Hungarian critics.

§ For information on other serial bibliographies covering Hungarian literature, especially earlier ones, *see* Albert Tezla, *An introductory bibliography to the study of Hungarian literature* (BE1283 note).

A Magyar irodalomtörténet bibliográfiája / Szerk., Vargha Kálmánés V. Windisch Éva. Készült a Magyar Tudományos Akadémia Irodalomtudományi Intézetében. Budapest : Akadémiai Kiadó, 1972–1991. v. 1–3, 6–8. (In progress). **BE1279**

Contents: v. 1, to 1772; v. 2, 1771–1849; v. 3, 1849–1905, pt. 1, A–Gy; v. 6, 1905–1945, pt. 1, A–K; v. 7, 1905–1945, pt. 2, L–Zs; v. 8, 1945–1970.

To be complete in 8 v.

A major bibliography of primary and secondary materials for the history and study of Hungarian literatures. Substantially devoted to entries for individual authors. Each volume has a detailed table of contents and index. Z2148.L5.M35

Magyarországi irodalom idegen nyelven : a hazai szépirodalom fordításainak bibliográfiája 1945–1968 közötti kiadások = Hungary's literature in translation : a bibliography of belles-lettres in foreign languages edited in the years 1945–1968 = [Vengerskaía literatura na inostrannykh íazykakh : bibliografiía perevodov otechestvennoí belletristiki izdannykh v 1945–1968 gg.] / [szerk. Fajcsek Magda és Szilvássy Zoltánne]. Budapest : Országos Széchényi Könyvtar, 1975. 797 p. **BE1280**

Introductory matter in Hungarian, English and Russian.

Anthologies are grouped by genre (poetry, short stories, etc.), then by language of translation; all authors represented in a given work are listed with the title. A section for individual authors is arranged by literary category, then by author's name, followed by titles grouped by foreign languages. Name, language, and publisher indexes.

§ English translations with full bibliographic and contents information and references to reviews are listed in *Hungarian literature in English translation published in Great Britain 1830–1968*, by Magda Czigány (London : Szepsi Csombor Literary Circle, 1969). Also lists generals books and articles on Hungarian literature. Chronological and general indexes. Z2148.T7M34

Pintér, Jenö. Magyar irodalomtörténete : Tudományos rendszerezés. Budapest : [Magyar Irodalomtörténeti Társaság], 1930–41. 8 v. in 13. **BE1281**

A standard history with extensive bibliography—both a general bibliography in v. 1 and special bibliographies at the end of each chapter. Despite few locations in the U.S., a work of importance to experts in the field.

§ The Hungarian Academy's *A Magyar irodalom története* under the general editorship of Istvan Sötér and others (Budapest : Akadémiai Kiadó, 1964–66. 6 v.) is a relatively recent history from the Marxist point of view; it includes bibliographies. PH3012.P55

Szinnyei, József. Magyar írók : élete és munkái a Magyar Tudományos Akadémia megbizásából. Budapest : Hornyánszky V., 1891–1914. 14 v. **BE1282**

For annotation, *see* AH250. Z2141.S9

Tezla, Albert. Hungarian authors : a bibliographical handbook. Cambridge, Mass. : Belknap Pr. of Harvard Univ. Pr., 1970. 792 p. **BE1283**

With Tezla's *Introductory bibliography* (below), forms the best guide in English to Hungarian-language material on Hungarian literature. Research libraries supporting study of the literature of Eastern Europe should have both titles. Treats 162 "representative writers from the beginnings of Hungarian literature to the present."—*Pref.* Aims to give a complete record of first editions, together with citations to important biographical, bibliographical, and critical studies. Most items are annotated and indicate library holdings in Europe and the U.S. Author entries include biographical information. Glossary of Hungarian terms. Appendixes list general treatments of the literature published

1960–65, awards, newspapers, periodicals (including library locations and holdings for those cited in main entries), authors by periods, and libraries. Name index.

———. *An introductory bibliography to the study of Hungarian literature* (Cambridge, Mass : Harvard Univ. Pr., 1964. 290 p.).

Offers 1,295 numbered entries of secondary and primary sources in Hungarian and other languages published through 1960, designed primarily for students in the U.S. Classed arrangement with name index. Titles are annotated, and there are numerous cross-references. Locates copies in American and European libraries. Z2148.L5T39

Iceland

Cornell University. Library. Catalogue of the Icelandic collection bequeathed by Willard Fiske / comp. by Halldór Hermannsson. Ithaca, N.Y. : [The Library], 1914. 755 p. **BE1284**

A major collection originally numbering more than 10,000 items, judged at the time of the bequest to be "the richest in existence, with the exception of the National Library in Reykjavik and the Royal Library in Copenhagen."—*Pref.* Includes editions and translations of Old Icelandic and Old Norse texts, literary history and criticism, and works on the language, religion, history, and customs of the people, as well as works of and about Icelandic literature and Iceland since the 16th century, including works by Icelanders in other languages. An author list with a subject index. Many brief annotations and contents notes and occasional citations to reviews.

Supplemented by:

———. ———. *Additions 1913–1926* (1927) and *Additions 1927–1942* (1943), also ed. by Hermannsson and publ. by the Cornell Univ. Library. Original catalog with *Additions* repr. by the Cornell Univ. Pr., 1960.

Runic materials in the same collection are listed in *Catalogue of Runic literature : forming a part of the Icelandic Collection bequeathed by Willard Fiske*, ed. by Hermannsson (Oxford : Oxford Univ. Pr., 1918). Annotations, citations to reviews, reviewer and subject indexes.

Supplemented on an ongoing basis by *Islandica : an annual relating to Iceland and the Fiske Icelandic Collection in Cornell University Library* (v. 1 [1908]– . Ithaca, N.Y. : Cornell Univ. Pr. for Cornell Univ. Library, 1908– . Annual; later issues irregular. 1908–53 volumes repr.: N.Y. : Kraus, 1966). More recently subtitled "a series relating to Iceland ..."; publication suspended 1959–74.

§ A less extensive working collection held by the University Library, Leeds, is described in: *A catalogue of the Icelandic collection* (Leeds : Univ. Library, 1978).

Einarsson, Stefan. A history of Icelandic literature. N.Y. : Johns Hopkins Pr. for the American-Scandinavian Foundation, 1957. 409 p. **BE1285**

A solid chronological survey covering Icelandic literature from the 12th century to the mid-1950s. Biographical and bibliographical information provided throughout for individual authors. Bibliography, guide to pronunciation, and through analytic index.

§ A more specialized history by the same author: *History of Icelandic prose writers, 1800–1940* (Ithaca, N.Y. : Cornell Univ. Pr., 1948 [*Islandica*, v. 32–33]. Repr. : N.Y. : Kraus, 1966). A companion in the same series is *History of Icelandic poets, 1800–1940*, by Richard Beck (Ithaca, N.Y. : Cornell Univ. Pr., 1950 [*Islandica*, v. 34]. Repr. : N.Y. : Kraus, 1966). PT7150.E4

Kellogg, Robert. A concordance to Eddic poetry. East Lansing, Mich. : Colleagues Pr., 1988. 605 p. (Medieval texts and studies, no. 2). **BE1286**

Originally compiled as a dissertation (Harvard, 1957), using as its text Guðni Jónsson's two-volume edition of *Eddukvæði* (Reykjavik : Íslendingasagnautgafan, 1949) which offers normalized spelling and "follows the best practices of the best editions preceding it."—*Pref.* A review in *Speculum* 65 (July 1990): 711–12 notes it can be used with the standard edition by Gustav Neckel and Hans Kuhn, *Edda* (Heidelberg : C. Winter, 1962–68. 2 v.) "Every word, however humble, that occupies a metrically significant position in its line is given a full reference." For high-frequency words, only metrically significant examples are given. Arrangement is by simple lexical stem with the inflected forms following in order. Separate concordances are given for proper names.

§ A companion to, but does not supplant: Hugo Gering's *Vollständiges Wörterbuch zu den Liedern der Edda* (Halle : Waisenhauses, 1903. Repr. : Hildesheim ; N.Y. : Olms, 1971) and Finnur Jónsson's *Lexicon poeticum antiquæ linguæ septentrionalis* (2. udg. København : Muller, 1931. Repr. : København : Lynge, 1966).   PT7235.K45

Mitchell, Phillip Marshall. Bibliography of modern Icelandic literature in translation : including works written by Icelanders in other languages / comp. by P. M. Mitchell and Kenneth H. Ober. Ithaca, N.Y. : Cornell Univ. Pr., 1975. 317 p. (Islandica, 40).   **BE1287**

In two main sections: (1) Anthologies grouped by language of translation, and (2) Works by individual authors arranged alphabetically by author's name; translations of individual works are entered alphabetically by language of translation. Includes references to translations (including selections from longer works) appearing in periodicals, as parts of books, etc. Index of translators, editors and compilers.

———. ———. *Supplement, 1971–1980*, ed., Kenneth Ober (Ithaca : Cornell Univ. Pr., 1990. [Islandica, 47]). Continues the original arrangement.   Z2551.M57

Italy

See also Europe—Regional literatures—Classical—Latin (above).

General works

Guides

Beccaro, Felice del. Guida allo studio della letteratura italiana. [Milano] : Mursia, [1975]. 350 p.   **BE1288**

A general section is followed by chapters for the literature of each century, with subsections for major writers of each period. Editions and studies are treated in essay form; index of names.   Z2354.C8B4

Mazzoni, Guido. Avviamento allo studio critico delle lettere italiane. 4. ed. riv. e aggiorn. / per cura di Carmine Jannaco, con prefazione di Francesco Maggini e appendici di Pio Rajna e Ernesto Giacomo Parodi. Firenze : Sansoni, [1951]. 238 p. (Manuali di filologia e storia. ser. II, v.3).   **BE1289**

1st ed., 1892.

A bibliographical handbook, still useful primarily for its comments on older materials.   Z2351.M47

Puppo, Mario. Manuale critico-bibliografico per lo studio della letteratura italiana. 14a ed. Torino : Società editrice internazionale, c1987. 462 p.   **BE1290**

1st–2nd ed. publ. under title: *Manuale bibliograficocritico per lo studio della letteratura italiana*. 13th ed., 1980.

A student's manual consisting of surveys of the scholarship on important authors and literary questions, followed by bibliographies of books and important articles.   PQ4037.P8

Bibliography

Contributo a una bibliografia del futurismo letterario italiano / a cura di Anna Baldazzi [et al.]. [Roma : Cooperativa Scrittori, 1977]. 629 p.   **BE1291**

A bibliography of writings on the futurist movement in Italian literature and of writings by authors of the movement. Includes a listing of the contents of the Italian futurist literary magazines. Lacks an index.   Z2354.F87C65

Fucilla, Joseph Guerin. Universal author repertoire of Italian essay literature. N.Y. : Vanni, [1941]. 534 p.   **BE1292**

An index to biographical and critical articles on authors, primarily Italian, but also including non-Italian writers of many countries, contained in 1,697 collections of Italian essays. Arranged alphabetically by subject.

Continued by Fucilla's *Saggistica letteraria italiana : bibliografia per soggetti: 1938–1952* (Firenze : Sansoni, 1956).   Z6511.F8

Golden, Herbert Hershel. Modern Italian language and literature : a bibliography of homage studies / by Herbert Hershel Golden and Seymour O. Simches. Cambridge : Harvard Univ. Pr., 1959. 207 p.   **BE1293**

Repr.: N.Y. : Kraus, 1971.

Indexes 1,966 festschriften, in 474 collections, on modern Italian language and literature from the Renaissance to 1957. Index of authors of the articles and of persons, works, and subjects treated.

   Z2355.A2G6

Harvard University. Library. Italian history and literature : classification schedule, classified listing by call number, chronological listing, author and title listing. Cambridge : publ. by Harvard Univ. Lib., distr. by Harvard Univ. Pr., 1974. 2 v. (Widener Library shelflist, 51–52).   **BE1294**

For a note on the series, *see* AA115.

These volumes "cover Italian history and literature, a collection comprising more than 72,000 titles. Historical topics include the government and administration, religious affairs, civilization, social life and customs, and geography and description of peninsular Italy, Sicily, and Sardinia, as well as Malta, Monaco, and San Marino. Literary histories, anthologies, and works by and about authors writing in Italian from the Duecento to the present are included in the sections for literature."—*Pref.*   Z2341.H37

Prezzolini, Giuseppe. Repertorio bibliografico della storia e della critica della letteratura italiana dal 1902 al 1932 / prep. nella Casa Italiana della Columbia University e con l'aiuto del Council on Research in the Humanities, New York, 1930–1936. Roma : Ed. Roma, [1937–39]. 2 v.   **BE1295**

Arranged alphabetically by names of authors written about or commented on, and by literary forms and subjects, with exact references to an enormous amount of critical and biographical material in books, periodicals, society publications, etc.

Continued by:

Prezzolini's *Repertoria bibliografico della storia e della critica della letteratura italiana dal 1933 al 1942* (N.Y. : Vanni, 1946–48. 2 v.). Follows the plan of the first 2 v., with geographic subdivisions under many form headings.

Repertorio bibliografico della letteratura italiana, 1943–1947, a cura della Facoltá di Magisterio di Roma, sotto la direzione di Umberto Bosco (Firenze : Sansoni, [1969]. 138 p.).

Repertorio bibliografico della letteratura italiana, a cura della Facoltá di Magistero do Roma, sotto la direzione di Umberto Bosco (Firenze : Sansoni, 1953–60. 2 v.). Contents: v. 1, 1948–49; v. 2, 1950–53. Arranged alphabetically by author, with subject indexes; lists books and periodical articles.   Z2341.P93

La Rassegna della letteratura italiana. no. 1 (1893)– . Firenze [etc.] : G.C. Sansoni [etc.].   **BE1296**

Title varies.

Publ. 1893–1987 by Sansoni. Suspended 1949–52.

Numbered by vols. and by "serie," the most recent being vol. 87, serie 8, 1983– .

Each issue of the journal includes a valuable "Rassegna bibliografica" listing books and articles in chronological sections with lengthly, signed, analytical and evaluative annotations, some more than a page long.   PQ4001.R3

Translations

See also BE1178 and BE1450.

Shields, Nancy Catchings. Italian translations in America. N.Y., [1931]. 410 p. **BE1297**

Translations of Italian works arranged chronologically by date of publication, covering the period 1751–1928. Extensive annotations including analysis and history of the works and biographical information on the translator when this could be located. Author/translator index.

§ For earlier translations into English, see: *Elizabethan translations from the Italian*, by Mary Augusta Scott (Boston ; N.Y. : Houghton Mifflin, 1916. Repr.: N.Y. : Burt Franklin, 1969). Arranged by genre, then chronologically, with author and title indexes.

Z2354.T7S51

Encyclopedias

Dictionary of Italian literature / Peter Bondanella and Julia Conway Bondanella, co-eds. Westport, Conn. : Greenwood, [1979]. 621 p. **BE1298**

Also publ. (London : Macmillan) as *The Macmillan dictionary of Italian literature.*

An English-language guide to Italian literature which means to provide "an introduction to major and minor Italian writers from the twelfth century to the present, to Italian metrics and poetic forms or genres, and to literary or critical schools, periods, problems, and movements."—*Pref.* Entries for authors predominate; attention is given to relationships with other national literatures, cultures, and art forms. Many articles are signed; contributors' credentials are given, p.xv–xxi. Bibliographies include English translations of primary texts, as well as critical studies (books and articles) in various languages. Indexed.

PQ4006.D45

Dizionario critico della letteratura italiana / diretto da Vittore Branca ... [et al.]. 2a ed. Torino : Unione tipografico-editrice torinese, c1986. 4 v. : ill., facsims. **BE1299**

1st ed., 1973.

Offers signed articles, most of them several pages in length. A high percentage of articles is biocritical in nature, but there are entries for literary terms, movements, etc. Substantial bibliographies, those for individual authors including both works by and about the writer. Cross-references; index of names in v. 4. PQ4057.D59

Dizionario enciclopedico della letteratura italiana / [Direttore: Giuseppe Petronio]. Laterza : UNEDI, [1966–70]. 6 v. : ill. **BE1300**

Contents: v. 1–5, A–Z; v. 6, Appendice, Indici.

The main part of the dictionary is devoted to entries for: (1) major and minor Italian authors together with classical and foreign authors who have influenced Italian letters; (2) politicians, princes, and popes who have patronized Italian literature; (3) movements, cultural institutions, libraries, journals, and magazines; and (4) the language and terms of literary criticism. Bibliographies; general index.

PQ4006.D5

Dizionario generale degli autori italiani contemporanei / [Coordinamento Enzo Ronconi]. [Firenze] : Vallecchi, 1974. 2 v. (1551 p.) : ill. **BE1301**

Contents: v. 1, Movimenti letterari, Abba-Luzzato Fegiz; v. 2, Maccari-Zumbini, Influenze e corrispondenze.

Primarily a dictionary arrangement of biographical sketches of contemporary Italian authors (with bibliographies) and articles on literary journals; the alphabetical sequence is preceded by an essay on literary movements and followed by essays on relationships of Italian and foreign literatures, philosophy, art, and the cinema. PQ4113.D58

Turri, Vittorio. Dizionario storico della letteratura italiana. Nuova [4 ed.] ed. riv. e aggiorn. sul testo originale di Vittorio Turri [di] Umberto Renda [e] Piero Operti. Torino : Paravia, [1959]. 1241 p. **BE1302**

1st ed., 1900; nuova ed., 1941, by Vittorio Turri and U. Renda.

A biobibliographical dictionary containing some 1,400 entries, many quite extensive, including living Italian writers, as well as articles on literary forms and movements, etc.

§ A similar one-volume dictionary: *Scrittori e idee : dizionario critico della letteratura italiana*, by Enrico M. Fusco (Torino : Società Ed. Internazionale, 1956). Entries and bibliographies are less extensive than in Renda. PQ4006T877

History

Cecchi, Emilio. Storia della letteratura italiana / by Emilio Cecchi and Natalino Sapegno. [Milano] : Garzanti, [1965–69]. 9 v. : ill. **BE1303**

Contents: v. 1, Le origini e il duecento; v. 2, Il trecento; v. 3, Il quattrocento e l'Ariosto; v. 4, Il cinquecento; v. 5, Il seicento; v. 6, Il settecento; v. 7, L'ottocento; v. 8, Dall'ottocento al novecento; v. 9, Il novecento.

Chapters by specialists in each area with extensive notes and bibliographies and quoted passages. Generously illustrated. Index in each volume.

§ A new edition by the same editors began publication in 1987: *Storia della letteratura italiana* (Milano : Garzanti. [In progress]). Contents: [v. 1], Le origini e il duecento; [v. 2], Il trecento; [v. 3], Il quattrocento e l'Ariosto; [v. 4], Il cinquecento; [v. 9], Il novecento (2 v.). Vol. 9 includes a dictionary of authors. PQ4037.C4

De Sanctis, Francesco. History of Italian literature / translated by Joan Redfern. N.Y. : Basic Books, [1960, c1931]. 2 v. (972 p.). **BE1304**

Repr. : N.Y. : Barnes & Noble, 1968.

A translation of a standard narrative history, *Storia della letteratura italiana*, first published 1870–71 and subsequently appearing in many editions, some in one volume, some in two. Name and title index, but no bibliography. PQ4037.D413

Dotti, Ugo. Storia della letteratura italiana. Roma : Laterza, 1991. 1044 p. **BE1305**

A scholarly reference history covering Italian literature from the medieval era to the 1970s. Especially valuable for providing an international and up-to-date 250-page bibliography covering general topics and primary and secondary works for individual authors. Lists works published through the late 1980s. Name and subject index.

PQ4037.D67

Flora, Francesco. Storia della letteratura italiana. [4 ed.]. Verona : Mondadori, 1972. 5 v. **BE1306**

Frequently reprinted. Edition numbers not reliable.

Contents: Dal Medio Evo alla fine del trecento; v. 2, Il quattrocento e il primo cinquecento; v. 3, Il secondo cinquecento e il seicento; v. 4, Il settecento e il primo ottocento; v. 5, Il secondo ottocento e il novecento.

Each volume has a chronology and its own bibliography and index. Illustrated. PQ4037.F63

Momigliano, Attilio. Problemi ed orientamenti critici di lingua e di letteratura italiana. Milano : C. Marzorati, [1948–61]. v. 1–5 in 7. **BE1307**

Some volumes have appeared in revised editions.

Contents: v. 1$^{1-3}$, Notizie introduttive e sussidi bibliografici; v. 2, Tecnica e teoria letteraria; v. 3, Questioni e correnti di storia letteraria; v. 4, Letterature comparate; v. 5, Momenti e problemi di storia dell'estetica.

Articles by specialists, with extensive bibliographies. Generous sections on foreign literatures, literary movements, archives and libraries, as well as Italian literature proper.

Wilkins, Ernest Hatch. A history of Italian literature. [New ed.] / rev. by Thomas G. Bergin. Cambridge, Mass. : Harvard Univ. Pr., 1974. 570 p.   **BE1308**

1st ed., 1954.

Illustrative passages and quotations from the literature are either given in English or accompanied by an English translation. "A list of English translations and books in English dealing with Italian literature," p. 539–48; chronological chart; index.   PQ4038.W5

Biography

Chi scrive : repertorio bio-bibliografico e per specializzazioni degli scrittori italiani. [2. ed.]. Milano : Igap Editrice, [1966]. 699 p.   **BE1309**

1st ed., 1962.

In addition to the biobibliographies (of journalists, academic writers, translators, etc., as well as of writers of belles-lettres) there are lists of publishers, libraries, national and provincial newspapers, etc., plus a grouping of biographees by field of specialization and a list of pseudonyms.

Cosenza, Mario Emilio. Biographical and bibliographical dictionary of the Italian humanists and of the world of classical scholarship in Italy, 1300–1800. [2nd ed., rev. and enl.]. Boston : G. K. Hall, 1962–67. 6 v.   **BE1310**

1st ed., 1954, appeared in microform.

Includes Italian scholars and those who studied in Italy, together with patrons and others concerned with the revival of classical studies. Gives for each humanist, where possible, brief biographical information, a list of variant names, teachers, pupils, works, and occasionally citations to secondary sources. Contains much information not easily available elsewhere, but is difficult to use because of its format—an unedited photoreproduction of Prof. Cosenza's handwitten cards. The 5th volume contains an edited synopsis of the first four and a very selective bibliography of secondary materials on humanism. Vol. 6 is a supplement.   Z7128.H9C6

Dizionario degli scrittori italiani d'oggi. Cosenza : Pellegrini, [1969]. 269 p. : ill.   **BE1311**

Brief biographies of contemporary Italian writers and bibliographies of their works. Some portraits.

Supplemented but not superseded by a 2nd ed. under the same title and from the same publisher (1975). Some of the sketches from the 1st ed. are revised or updated but most of the information is new. More up-to-date for post-World War II writers is *Dizionario autori italiani contemporanei* (Milan : Guido Miano ed., 1991). Provides critical commentary as well as biographical and bibliographical information and consists of signed entries by members of an editorial board.   Z2350.D58

Ferrari, Luigi. Onomasticon : repertorio biobibliografico degli scrittori italiani dal 1501 al 1850. Milano : Hoepli, 1947. 708 p. (Bibliotheca veneta, collana di opere erudite a cura della Scuola Storico-Filologica della Venezie ... della R. Università di Padova, [v.1]).   **BE1312**

Repr.: Nendeln, Liechtenstein : P. Kraus, 1973.

An index to almost 50,000 individual biographies of authors contained in some 375 collections, general and local. The list of these collections, p. xxi–xliv, forms a bibliography of collected works of Italian biography, with indication of location in Italian libraries.   Z2350.F4

Gastaldi, Mario. Dizionario delle scrittrici italiane contemporanee (arte, lettere, scienze) / Mario Gastaldi [e] Carmen Scano. Milano : Gastaldi, [1961?]. 349 p. : ill.   **BE1313**

Previous ed., 1957.

A dictionary of Italian women writers, usually giving place of birth, education, position or occupation, and bibliography of writings. Photographs. Analytical index by type of writing. The 1961 printing appends a supplement covering 1957–60.   CT3450.G3

Genres

Drama

Clubb, Louise George. Italian plays (1500–1700) in the Folger Library : a bibliography. Firenze : Olschki, 1968. 267 p. (Biblioteca di bibliografia italiana, 52).   **BE1314**

890 items. Full collation and numerous descriptive notes are given, including bibliographical information, form, dedication, historical notes on productions, other editions. References are provided to listings in other bibliographies, including catalogs for two other North American collections:

§ Marvin Theodore Herrick, comp. *Italian plays, 1500–1700, in the University of Illinois library* (Urbana : Univ. of Illinois Pr., 1966); and Univ. of Toronto Library, *Catalogue of Italian plays, 1500–1700, in the library of the University of Toronto*, Beatrice Corrigan, comp. (Toronto : Univ. of Toronto Pr., 1961). Two suppls. publ. in *Renaissance news*: 16 (1963) : 298–307 and 19 (1966) : 219–28.

     Z2354.D7C55

Heck, Thomas F. Commedia dell'arte : a guide to the primary and secondary literature. N.Y. : Garland, 1988. 450 p. (Garland reference library of the humanities, vol. 786).   **BE1315**

A classified, extensively annotated bibliography of primary and secondary works, which "assumes an *inclusive* definition of the CdA and its various manifestations throughout Europe: the *Théâtre Italien* in Paris, classic English pantomine, various echoes of the *comici* in central and Eastern Europe, and the 'revivals' of improvisatory theater and the masques in modern times."—*Introd.* Sections are devoted to general studies, sources, historical studies, diffusion of the *commedia dell'arte* outside Italy, actors, masques (stock characters), improvisation, dance and music, modern revivals, iconography, and literature and the CdA. Indexes to authors and works cited, titles of *scenari*, and names.   Z2354.D7H37

Poetry

IUPI : Incipitario unificato della poesia italiana / a cura di Marco Santagata. Modena : Panini, [1988]. 3 v. (1884 p.).   **BE1316**

Vol. 3 ed. by Bruno Bentivogli and Paola Vecchi Galli.

Contents: v. 1–2, A–Z; v. 3, Edizioni di lirica antica.

A monumental index, gathering in one alphabet the contents of approximately 100 published incipit indexes to manuscript poetry produced between the 13th and 17th centuries. In addition, v. 3 is an incipit index to 219 published editions of poetry written between the 13th and the 15th centuries. An extremely valuable source for scholars of medieval and Renaissance literature and for libraries serving this population.

§ A selective index, covering seven major writers, is Maureen E. Buja's *Italian Renaissance poetry : a first-line index to Petrarch, Ariosto, Tasso, and others* (N.Y. : Garland, 1987). The "others" are Bembo, Strozzi, Cassola, and della Casa. Authors were selected because of the frequency with which they were set to music. Each author is indexed separately with the first line, the poem or canto number, and the stanza number, based on the standard edition.   PQ4210.I9

Molinaro, Julius A. American studies and translations of contemporary Italian poetry, 1945–1965 : an historical survey and a bibliography. (*In* N.Y. Public Library bulletin, v. 72 [Oct. 1968]: 522–58. N.Y. : The Library, 1968).   **BE1317**

Bibliography of books, periodical articles, and poems in translation. Numerous annotations and notes on contents.

———. "American studies and translations of contemporary Italian poetry, 1965–1970 : a supplementary survey and bibliography" (*In* New York Public Library bulletin, v. 78 [Spring 1975] : 351–72).

University of Toronto. Library. A bibliography of six-teenth-century Italian verse collections in the University of Toronto Library / comp. by Julius A. Molinaro. [Toronto] : Univ. of Toronto Pr., [1969]. 124 p. : ill., facsims.   **BE1318**

Provides full title and imprint for each collection and the names of the poets represented in each volume. Many reproductions of title pages. Indexes of authors and of first lines of anonymous poems.
Z2354.P7T6

Latvia

Istoriĭa latyshskoi literatury : V 2-kh t / [Red. kollegiĭa ... ĬA. Kalnyn (otv. red.) i dr.]. Riga : "Zinatne", 1971. 2 v. : ill.
BE1319
On leaf preceding t.p.: Akademiĭa Nauk Latviiskoi SSR. Institut ĬAzyka i Literatury.

Contents: v. 1, Do 1917 goda; v. 2, S 1917 goda.
A history of Latvian literature presented mainly in terms of chapters by contributing scholars on individual writers. Bibliography at the end of v. 2.

§ *Latvian literature under the Soviets, 1940–1975*, by Rolfs Ekmanis (Belmont, Mass. : Nordland, 1978. 533 p.) is a study of the effects of Soviet rule on Latvian literature; it includes an extensive classed bibliography, p. 441–515.   PG9005.I8

Latviešu pirmspadomju literatūra : biobibliogrāfisks rāditajs / Sastāditāji: Edgars Timbra [et al.]. Riga, 1980. 744 p.
BE1320
At head of title: Vila Lāča Latvijas PSR Valsts Bibliotēka. Zinātniski Metodiskā un Bibliogrāfiskā Darba Nodala.

Added title page in Russian.
A biobibliography of pre-Soviet literature.
§ For a listing of works by Soviet Latvian authors *see* Valdemars Ancitis, *Piecos gados : bibliogrāfisks pārskats par Padomju Latvijas literatūras darbinieku publikācijām 1966–1970* (Rīgā : Izdevnieciba "Liesma", 1971). Includes works for stage, film, and television, and a section of anthologies.

Lietuvių kalbos ir literatūros institutas (Lietuvos TSR Mokslų akademija). Tarybinis lietuvių literatūros mokslas ir kritika apie literaturini palikimą, 1944–1958 : bibliografinė rodyklė / paruose E. Staniveciene. Vilnius : Valstybin e politinēs mokslin es literatūros leidykla, 1959. 430 p.   **BE1321**
Title in colophon: Sovetskoe litovskoe literaturovedenie i kritika o literaturnom nasledstve, 1944–1958 : bibliograficheskii ukazatel'.
A classified bibliography of critical writings on Lithuanian literature together with Lithuanian writings on foreign literatures. Covers material in Lithuanian and Russian. Indexed.

Continued by:
———. *Tarybinis lietuvių literatūros mokslas ir kritika apie literatūrini palikimą, 1959–1970 : bibliografine rodykle*, sudare Eugenijus Stancikus, red. Jonas Vosylius (Vilnius : Vaga, 1975).
Lietuvių literatūros mokslas ir kritika ... bibliografine rodykle (1971– . Vilnius : Vaga, 1976–).
At head of title: Lietuvos TSR Mokslų Akademija, Lietuvių Kalbos ir Literatūros Institutas.
Editor varies.
Volumes so far publ. cover: 1971–73, 1974–76, 1977–79, 1980–82, 1983–85. Nothing publ. since 1988.   Z2537.S75

Lithuania

Biržiška, Vaclovas. Lietuvių bibliografija [1517–1910]. Kaunas : Švietmo Ministerijos Leidinys, 1924–39. 4 v.   **BE1322**
Contents: pt. 1, 16th-18th centuries; pt. 2, 1800-1864; pt. 3, 1865-1904; pt. 4, v. 1, 1905-1909 (2 pts.), v. 2, 1910-1914, (fasc. 1 [1910] only). No more published. Libraries may bind parts and volumes differently.

A bibliography of Lithuanian literature and related publications. Most parts chronologically arranged, then alphabetical within sections.

Lietuvių rašytojai : biobibliografinis žodynas. Vilnius : Vaga, 1979. 1 v.   **BE1323**
Contents: v. 1, A–L. No more published?
Provides biobibliographical entries for Lithuanian authors, including living authors. Lists periodical contrivutions as well as separately published works and includes biographical writings about the author.
PG8709.L486

Lietuvos TSR Mokslų Akademija. Lietuvių Kalbos ir Literatūros Institutas. Tarybinė lietuvių literatūra ir kritika : bibliografinė rodyklė. 1945/1955–1970. Vilnius : [Lietuvos TSR Mokslų Akademija. Lietuvių Kalbos ir Literatūros Institutas], 1957–1972. Irregular.   **BE1324**
Title and subtitle vary slightly. Vols. publ. so far cover 1945–55, 1961–65, 1966–70. None known for 1956–60.
A classified bibliography of Soviet-Lithuanian literature and literary criticism, in Lithuanian and Russian.   Z2537.L5

Tarybinių lietuvių rašytojų : autobiografijos / [redakcin e komisija: Kazys Ambrasas ... et al. ; sudarė Aldona Mickienė]. Vilnius : Vaga, 1989. 2 v. : ill.   **BE1325**
Title from colophon: Avtobiografii sovetskikh litovskikh pisatelei.
Rev. ed. of *Tarybų Lietuvos rašytojai*, ed. by Juozas Baltŭsis, Jonas Lankutis, Alfonsas Maldonis, 1977.
Provides autobiographical sketches, some lengthy, with portraits and signatures, of contemporary Lithuanian writers. Additional very brief biobibliographical notes are supplied at the end of each volume.
§ A companion of sorts is *Tarybų Lietuvos rašytojai : biobibliografinis žodynas*, 2-as papildytas leidimas, zodyno autores Emilija Dagytė, Danutė Straukaitė (Vilnius : Vaga, 1984; first publ. 1975. Title from colophon: Pisateli Sovetskŏ Litvy). Provides considerably briefer biobibliographical entries with portraits for contemporary writers.   PG8701.T34

Netherlands

Baur, Frank. Geschiedenis van de letterkunde der Nederlanden / onder redactie van prof. dr. F. Baur ... [et al.]. 's Hertogenbosch : Teulings' uitgevers-maatschappij L. C. G. Malmberg, 1939–75. v. 1–7, 9. : ill. (In progress).   **BE1326**
To be in 9 v.
Each volume by a specialist. An illustrated history with bibliographies throughout.   PT5060.B3

Buisman, M. Populaire prozaschrijvers van 1600 tot 1815 : romans, novellen, verhalen, levensbeschrijvingen, arcadia's, sprookjes ; alphabetische naamlijst / Met medewerking van F. J. Dubiez, en een voorwoord van H. de la Fontaine Verwey. Amsterdam : B. M. Israël, [1960]. 508 p.   **BE1327**
A comprehensive bibliography of novels, short stories, biographies, Utopias, and fairy tales, published from 1600 to 1815, in Dutch as well as translations into Dutch.   Z2444.F4B8

Frederiks, Johannes Godefridus. Biographisch woordenboek der Noord– en Zuidnederlandsche letterkunde / Johannes Godefridus Frederiks, F. J. van den Branden. 2. omgew. druk. Amsterdam : Veen, [1888–92]. 918 p.   **BE1328**
A biographical dictionary useful especially for the 18th and 19th centuries and including writers from both Holland and Belgium.
Z2440.F85

Jong, Dirk de. Het vrije boek in onvrije tijd : bibliografie van illegale en clandestiene bellettrie. Leiden : Sijthoff, 1958. 341 p.   **BE1329**

An author listing of more than 1,000 items of belles-lettres published clandestinely in the Netherlands during the German occupation in World War II.　　　　　　　Z6514.U5J63

Knuvelder, Gerard Petrus Maria. Handboek tot de geschiedenis der Nederlandse letterkunde. 6. druk. Den Bosch : Malmberg, [1973–77]. 4 v. (v. 1 publ. 1976).　**BE1330**

1st ed., 1948–53.

Covers Dutch literary history and criticism from the Middle Ages through 1916. Bibliographical footnotes; each volume has its own index.

§ A one-volume condensation is available as *Beknopt handboek tot de geschiedenis der Nederlandse letterkunde* (10. geheel herziene druk. [Nederlands?] : Malmberg, [1982?] 594 p.).　　PT5060.K62

Kritisch lexicon van de Nederlandstalige literatuur na 1945. Brussel, Samsom; Groningen, Wolters-Noordhoff, 1980– . 6 v. (looseleaf).　　**BE1331**

Provides biography, critical analysis, and primary and secondary bibliography for contemporary Dutch authors arranged in alphabetical order. Looseleaf format allows continuous updating.

Lectuur-Repertorium : Auteurslijst bevattende 30,000 biografische notities over auteurs en 100,000 werken in het Nederlands gepubliceerd van 1967 tot 1978. Antwerpen : Katholiek Centrum voor Lectuurinformatie en Bibliotheekvoorziening Antwerpen ; Den Haag : Nederlands Bibliotheek en Lektuur Centrum, 1980–1981. 3 v.　　**BE1332**

Supersedes the 2nd edition (1952–54) and its supplement (1952–66). A detailed biobibliography of major authors writing in or translated into Dutch. Individual titles are keyed to a classification scheme to indicate moral values and literary type.　　Z1010.L43

Lexicon van de moderne Nederlandse literatuur / Samengesteld door J. van Geelen ... [et al.]. [2. herziene en uitgebreide druk]. Amsterdam : Meulenhoff, [1981]. 219 p. : ill.　　**BE1333**

1st printing, 1978.

A biographical dictionary of contemporary writers. Includes a list of literary prizes and their recipients.　　PT5180.L4

Meijer, Reinder P. Literature of the Low Countries : a short history of Dutch literature in the Netherlands and Belgium. New ed. with corrections and additional material. The Hague ; Boston : Nijhoff, 1978. 402 p.　　**BE1334**

A brief history covering from the 12th and 13th centuries to the mid-20th century. Select bibliography.　　PT5061.M4

Petit, Louis David. Bibliographie der Middelnederlandsche taal– en letterkunde. Leiden : Brill, 1888–1910. 2 v.　**BE1335**

Contents: v. 1, Works appearing before 1888; v. 2, Works appearing from 1888–1910.

A bibliography of Middle Dutch language and literature.　　Z2411.P48

Winkel, Jan te. De ontwikkelingsgang der Nederlandsche letterkunde. 2. druk. Haarlem : Bohn, 1922–27. 7 v.　**BE1336**

Repr. : Utrecht : HES Publishers; Leeuwarden : Uitgeverij 'De Tillt', 1973.

1st ed., 1908–21.

Contents: v. 1–2, Geschiedenis der Nederlandsche letterkunde van Middeleeuwen en rederijkerstijd; v. 3–5 Geschiedenis der Nederlandsche letterkunde van de Republiek der Vereenigde Nederlanden; v. 6–7, Geschiedenis der Nederlandsche letterkunde in de eerste eeuw der Europeesche staatsomwentelingen.

An important reference history with extensive footnotes. Index in v. 7.　　PT5060.W5

Norway

Beyer, Edvard. Norges litteratur historie. 4. oppl. Oslo : Cappelen, 1991. 6 v. : ill.　　**BE1337**

1st ed., 1974–75?

Contents: Bd. 1, Fra runene til norske selskab; Bd. 2, Fra Wergeland til Vinje; Bd. 3, Fra Ibsen til Garborg; Bd. 4, Fra Hamsun til Falkberget; Bd. 5, Mellomkrigstid; Bd. 6, Vår egen tid; Literaturveiledning, tidstavle, register.

A well-illustrated, comprehensive history, by Beyer and other specialists. Many quoted passages. Vol. 6 contains an extensive bibliography, a chronology beginning in 400 CE, and a cumulative name and title index.

§An attractively laid out and even more richly illustrated work covering the literature from 1814 to 1972 is *Norges littertur*, by Willy Dahl (Oslo : Aschehoug, 1981–89. 3 v.). Many photographs; students of drama will welcome those depicting productions. Bibliographic references throughout. Vol. 3 has indexes for subjects and for names and titles, making this a convenient reference tool.　　PT8360.B375

Beyer, Harald. A history of Norwegian literature / tr. and ed. by Einar Haugen. [N.Y.] : New York Univ. Pr. for the American-Scandinavian Foundation, [1957]. 370 p. : ill.　**BE1338**

A translation and adaptation for an English-speaking audience of Beyer's *Norsk littertur historie* (Oslo : Aschehoug, 1952), covering Norwegian literature from antiquity to the post-World War II period. Many chapters and sections are devoted to individual authors. Numerous references to translations. There is a list of additional readings, a guide to the pronunciation of Norwegian names, and separate name and title indexes.

The Norwegian version appeared in a 4th ed., 1978, by Harald and Edvard Beyer (Oslo : Aschenhoug).　　PT6360.B42

Bull, Francis. Norsk literaturhistorie. Ny utg. Oslo : H. Aschehoug, 1955–1976. 6 v. : ill.　　**BE1339**

1st ed., 1924–37 (5 v.). The 1st ed. of v. 6 was publ. 1955; this is a reprint.

Contents: v. 1, Norges og Islands litteratur inntil utgangen av middelalderen, by F. Paasche, ed. by A. Holtsmark; v. 2, Norges litteratur fra reformasjonen til 1814, by F. Bull; v. 3, Norges litteratur fra 1814 til 1850–årene, ed. by P. Svendsen; v. 4, Norges litteratur fra Fevruarrevolusjonen til første verdenskrig (2 vols.), by F. Bull; v. 5, Norges litteratur fra 1180–årene til første verdenskrig, by A. H. Winsnes; v. 6, Norges litteratur fra 1914 til 1950–årene, by P. Houm.

A standard history, each volume by a specialist. Chapter bibliographies and name and subject index in each volume.

Dahl, Willy. Nytt norsk forfatterleksikon. Oslo : Gyldendal, 1971 [i.e.1972]. 267 p.　　**BE1340**

Provides brief biographical information, list of titles by the author with dates of publications, and references to biographical and critical information. Not limited to literary writers. No index.

Halvorsen, Jens Braage. Norsk forfatter-lexikon, 1814–1880 : Paa grundlag af J. E. Krafts og Chr. Langes "Norsk forfatter-lexikon 1814–1856" / samlet, redigeret og udgivet med understøttelse af statskassen af J. B. Halvorsen. Kristiania : Norske Forlagsforening, 1885–1908. 6 v.　　**BE1341**

Biographical sketches with bibliographies of Norwegian authors, not limited to bellelettrists. Notes biographies and obituaries.

§ Preceded in time by Holger Ehrencron-Müller, *Forfatterlexikon omfattende Danmark, Norge og Island indtil 1819* (BE1087).　　Z2600.H19

A history of Norwegian literature / ed. by Harald S. Naess. Lincoln : Univ. of Nebraska Pr. in cooperation with the American-Scandinavian Foundation, c1993. 435 p. : map. (A history of Scandinavian literatures, v. 2).　　**BE1342**

Provides a chronological history of Norwegian literature from the older runes to the present with separate chapters for women's and children's literatures. Saami literature has been included where appropriate. Authors were chosen for inclusion by convention, personal taste of the contributor, and literary sociology. Special attention is given to the historical and social context from which literatures emerged, and how this context effected the development of the literature, "making this volume at the same time a handbook of major names and titles in Norwegian letters and a history of the political, social, and cultural conditions that shaped literary currents in Norway. We have emphasized whatever is specific to the Norwegian situation, while trying to show connections to general European trends."—*Pref.* Aimed at students, comparatists, and a general readership. Includes references, chapter bibliographies, and index. PT8363.H57

Øksnevad, Reidar. Norsk litteraturhistorisk bibliografi, 1900–1945. Oslo : Gyldendal Norsk Forlag, 1951. 378 p. **BE1343**

After sections covering bibliography and general history, arranged historically beginning with the 16th century. Author index.

———. ———. *Supplement : 1946–1955* (Oslo, 1958. 139 p.).

§ Continued by Harold S. Næss, *Norwegian literary biography, 1956–1970*, red. Kaare Haukaas (Oslo : Universitetsforlaget, 1975. [Norsk bibliografisk bibliotek, Bd. 50]). A useful compilation of Næss's accumulated entries submitted for the *MLA international bibliography* (BE39), whose arrangement is followed, and *Year's work in modern language studies* (BD28).

Norsk kvinnelitteraturhistorie / redaksjon, Irene Engelstad ... [et al.]. Oslo : Pax, 1988–1990. 3 v. : ill. **BE1344**
Contents: v. 1, 1600–1900; v. 2, 1900–1945; v. 3, 1940–1980.

A well-illustrated and visually appealing history of Norwegian women writers, with chapters by individual scholars, focusing on the lives and works of particular women. Many photographs and portraits. Chapters are broken into sections with headings, making it easy to locate specific information. Each volume contains an author and title index, a bibliography of references for each author discussed and biographical information on the contributors. Vol. 3 provides biobibliographies for all writers covered. PT8397.W6N67

Poland

Bartelski, Lesław M. Polscy pisarze współczesni : informator 1944–1974. Wyd. 3, nowe. poszerzone. Warszawa : Wydawnictwa Artystyczne i Filmowe, 1977. 428 p. **BE1345**
1st ed., 1970.

Offers brief biographical sketches of contemporary Polish writers, with lists of published works. Z2528.L5B37

Bibliografia literatury polskiej : Nowy Korbut / Redaktor naczelny Kazimierz Budzyk ; Komitet redakcyjny Ewa Korzeniewska [et al.]. [Kraków, etc.] : Wydawn. Literackie [etc., 1963–83]. v. 1–9, 12–17. **BE1346**
Issued by Instytut Badan Literackich, Polska Akademia Nauk.

Includes a general bibliography of Polish literature and provides painstakingly comprehensive biobibliographies for Polish writers, listing works by and about the author and including information on unpublished materials. Represents the contributions of many scholars.

A continuation of Gabrjel Korbut, *Literatura polska od początków do wojny światowej* (BE1350). Z2521.B55

Bibliografia literatury tłumaczonej na język polski / [Sanisław Bębenek, redaktor naczelny]. Warszawa : Czytelnik, 1977– . v. **BE1347**
Contents: v. 1, 1945–76: v. 2, 1945–77; v. 3, 1977–80.

A monumental listing of works of all periods translated from other literatures into Polish. Vol. 1 covers works from capitalist countries, the Third World, and ancient literatures; v. 2, literature from the socialist countries together with classics from those areas predating the political changes of 1917–77; v. 3 updates both listings through 1980. Listings are arranged by country, then by author. All volumes have in-

dexes by author and translator. Vol. 3 adds indexes to all three volumes by Polish and original titles. All prefatory matter and indexes in Polish, English, and Russian. Z2521.B56

Coleman, Marion Moore. Polish literature in English translation : a bibliography. Cheshire, Conn. : Cherry Hill Books, 1963. 180 p. **BE1348**
Arranged by author; lists translations of novels, poems, short stories, dramas, etc., dating from the 16th century to 1960. Some references to reviews. Index of translators included. Z2528.T7C6

Czachowski, Kasimierz. Obraz współczesnej literatury polskiej, 1884–[1934]. Lwów : Nakł Państwowego Wydawnictwa Książek Szkolnych, 1934–36. 3 v. **BE1349**
Repr. : Warsaw : Wydawnictwa Artystyczne i Filmowe, 1986.
Contents: v. 1, Naturalizm i neoromantyzm: v. 2, Neoromantyzm i psychologizm; v. 3, Ekspresjonizm i neorealizm.

Includes extensive bibliographies, chronology, and index.

———. *Najnowsza twórczość literacka, 1935–37.* (Lwów, 1938. 273 p.). PG7051.C9

Korbut, Gabrjel. Literatura polska od początków do wojny światowej : książka podręczna informacyjna dla stujujących naukowo dzieje rozwoju piśmiennictwa polskiego … . Wyd. 2., powiększone. Warszawa : Skład Głowny w Kasie Im. Mianowskiego, 1929–31. 4 v. **BE1350**
1st ed., 1917–21, in 3 v.
Contents: v. 1, 10th–17th centuries; v. 2, 18th century–1820; v. 3, 1820–63; v. 4, 1864–1914.

A continuation for the 20th century is provided by Eva Korzeniewska, *Słownik współczesnych pisarzy polskich* (BE1351). A new and expanded edition of the original work is in progress as *Bibliografia literatury polskiej. Nowy Korbut* (BE1346). Z2526.K84

Korzeniewska, Ewa. Słownik współczesnych pisarzy polskich : Opracował zespół. Warszawa : Państwowe Wydawnictwo Naukowe, 1963–66. 4 v. **BE1351**
A continuation of Gabrjel Korbut, *Literatura polska od początków do wojny światowej* (BE1350).

Largely devoted to biobibliographical entries for individual authors, providing brief biographical information and a list of works by and about the author. Vol. 1 contains a section of general sources on Polish literature of the 20th century, including biography and bibliography, history, and works dealing with literary institutions and groups. Vol. 4 provides supplementary information, listings of pseudonyms and cryptograms by pseudonym/crytogram and by author, indexes of titles and names, and errata.

Continued by *Słownik współczesnych pisarzy polskich : seria II*, red. Jadwigi Czachowskiej (Warsaw : Państwowe Wydawn. Naukowe, 1977–80. 3 v.). Covers contemporary writers not treated in the earlier set. Z2528.L5K6

Krzyżanowski, Julian. A history of Polish literature / by Julian Krzyżanowski ; bibliography by Zofia Swidwinska-Krzyżanowska, rev. and enl. by Maria Bokszczanin and Halina Geber ; Polish literature in English translations comp. by Halina Geber. Warszawa : PWN-Polish Scientific Publishers, 1978. 807 p., [34] leaves of plates : ill. **BE1352**
A translation of *Dzieje literatury polskiej od początków do czasów najnowszych* (1972).

A standard chronological survey covering the literature from the medieval period to the era between the World Wars. Contains a lengthy bibliography, including material on individual authors, with a separate section covering Polish literature in English translation. Plates; index.

§ Manfred Kridl, *A survey of Polish literature and culture* (N.Y. : Columbia Univ. Pr.; 's-Gravenhage : Moulton, 1956. Repr., 1967), a translation of the author's *Literatura polska na tle rozwoju kultury* (1945), is a survey covering the same time span with an emphasis on the social background influencing literature. Select bibliography and name index. PG7012.K7713

Literatura polska : przewodnik encyklopedyczny / [komitet redakcyjny, przewodnicz acy Julian Krzyżanowski ... et al.]. Warszawa : Pánstwowe Wydawn. Nauk., 1984. 2 v. **BE1353**

A comprehensive dictionary for Polish literature providing approximately 5,000 signed entries for authors, anonymous works, genres, movements, schools, literary concepts and terms, places, etc. Many entries provide bibliographical references. Ample cross-references; name index.

Lorentowicz, Jan. La Pologne en France : essai d'une bibliographie raisonnée ... / avec la collaboration de A. M. Chmurski. .... Paris : Champion, 1935–41. 3 v. **BE1354**

v. 2, Institut d'Études Slaves de l'Université de Paris. Bibliothèque Polonaise. IV.

Contents: v. 1, Littérature, théâtre, beaux-arts; v. 2, Encyclopédies, langue, voyages, histoire; v. 3, Géographie, sciences, droit; suppléments.

A massive classified bibliography of French writings on all subjects concerning Poland, including both books and periodical articles and material on individuals. Detailed bibliographic information. Author and title indexes.   Z2526.L86

Maciuszko, Jerzy J. The Polish short story in English : a guide and critical bibliography. Detroit : Wayne State Univ. Pr., 1968. 473 p. **BE1355**

A bibliography and guide to Polish short stories translated into English up to 1960, for the most part in books but including some appearing in periodicals. Arranged by author, then Polish title, including all known English editions of a story. Biographical information is given for authors and synopses for selected stories, at least one for most authors. A lengthy introduction discusses the history and theory of literary translation in general and the development of the translation of Polish works into English. A supplementary listing provides selective information on translations of folk tales, legends, fairy tales, fables, and children's stories. Appendixes list anthologies and collections, periodicals cited, translators and their translations, English and Polish titles, and a glossary of Polish given names. Bibliography; author index.   Z2528.T7M33

Miłosz, Czesław. The history of Polish literature. 2nd ed. Berkeley : Univ. of California Pr., 1983. 583 p., [16] p. of plates : ill. **BE1356**

An important history by a Nobel Prize winner. The 2nd ed. reprints the 1st, which covered through the middle of the 1960s, with the addition of an epilogue providing information through the 1970s and an updated bibliography. Name and title index.   PG7012.M48

Polska Akademia Nauk. Instytut Badań Literackich. Bibliografia literatury polskiej okresu odrodzenia : (materiały) / opracowali: Kazimierz Budzyk, Roman Pollak, Stanisław Stupkiewicz. [Warszawa] : Państwowy Inst. Wydawniczy, 1954. 463 p. **BE1357**

A bibliography of Polish literature during the Renaissance and Reformation, and of later studies of the subject in all languages. Biographical articles on the major authors.

Ryll, Ludomira. Polska literatura w przekładac : bibliografia 1945–1970 / Słowo wstepne: Michał Rusinek. Warszawa : Agencja Autorska, 1972. 369 p. **BE1358**

At head of title: Ludomire Ryll, Janina Wilgat.

Lists translations of Polish literary works into various languages. Includes a section of translations in anthologies. Indexes of authors, translators, editors, etc., and an index by country of publication.

§ Supersedes an earlier bibliography by Wilgat, *Literatura polska w świecie* (Warszawa : PEN Club, 1965) which covered translations 1945–61.   Z2528.T7R93

Słownik terminów literackich / Michał Głowiński ... [et al.] ; pod redakcją Janusza Sławińskiego. Wyd. 2., poszerzone i popr. Wrocław : Zakład Narowdowy im. Ossolińskich, 1988. 656 p. **BE1359**

1st ed., 1976.

A dictionary of literary terms, including terms from foreign and classical literatures. Entries provide definition and examples; most give references to sources for more information in European languages and English as well as Polish. A bibliography of additional works on literary terminology, also international, is provided. Indexes give Polish equivalents for English, French, German, and Russian terms.   PN41.S56

Starnawski, Jerzy. Warsztat bibliograficzny historyka literatury polskiej (na tle dyscyplin pokrewnych). [Wyd. 3]. [Warszawa] : Państwowe Wydawnictwo Naukowe, [1982]. 524 p. **BE1360**

A working bibliography of Polish literary history and related fields, including comparative literature.   Z2528.L5S68

Taborski, Boleslaw. Polish plays in English translations : a bibliography. N.Y. : Polish Inst. of Arts and Sciences in America, 1968. 79 p. **BE1361**

Lists translations in manuscript as well as printed translations. Includes a biographical note on the author and gives information on casts, sets, and a brief comment on each play.

§ Updated and augmented by *Polish plays in translation : an annotated bibliography*, ed. Daniel Gerould ... [et al]; prep. under the auspices of the Inst. for Contemporary East European Drama and Theatre of the Center for Advanced Study in Theatre Arts (CASTA) ([New York] : CASTA, The Graduate School and Univ. Center of the City Univ. of New York, 1983). Covers radio and television as well as stage productions. Includes unpublished works. Gives length and casting, fairly detailed plot summaries, first performance in Polish and English, and first publication in each. Includes a bibliography of general works on Polish theater.   Z2528.L5T3

Portugal

See also entries for Spain and Brazil, and BE1519.

Chamberlain, Bobby J. Portuguese language and Luso-Brazilian literature : an annotated guide to selected reference works. N.Y. : Modern Language Association of America, 1989. 95 p. (Selected bibliographies in language and literature, 6). **BE1362**

For annotation, *see* BD163.   Z2725.A2C45

Coelho, Jacinto do Prado. Dicionário de literatura : literatura portuguesa, literatura brasileira, literatura galega, estilística literária / direccão de Jacinto do Prado Coelho. 4. ed. Porto [Portugal] : Figueirinhas, 1989. 5 v. (1526 p.) : ill. **BE1363**

1960 ed. had title: *Dicionário das literaturas portuguesa, galega e brasileira*; 3rd ed., 1978.

Offers entries for authors, terms, movements, genres, etc. Signed articles; bibliographies. Vol. 5 provides indexes of authors and titles.   PQ9006.C65

Dicionário cronológico de autores portugueses / organizado pelo Instituto Português do Livro ; coordenação de Eugénio Lisboa. Mem Martins, Portugal : Publicações Europa-América, c1985–90. v. 1–2. (In progress). **BE1364**

The first two of a projected four-volume set which, when complete, will include authors with birthdates ranging from the 13th century to 1950. The two volumes published thus far present, in chronological order, entries for approximately 1,300 writers of all types. Each entry provides biographical and critical information and a list of principal works. Length varies from a paragraph to several pages. An alphabetical list of authors, and one of pseudonyms, are included in each volume.   PQ9027.D5

Forjaz de Sampaio, Albino. História da literatura portuguesa ilustrada / publicada ... com a colaboração dos senhores Afonso Lopes Vieira, Agostinho de Campos ... [et al.]. Paris : Aillaud, [1929–42]. 4 v. : ill. **BE1365**

A lavishly illustrated history, covering from medieval times to the 19th century with a brief chapter on the 20th century. Each chapter begins with an extensive bibliography. Illustrations include many facsimiles of title pages, manuscripts, etc. PQ9011.F6

Luft, Celso Pedro. Dicionário de literatura portuguêsa e brasileira. 3a ed. Rio de Janeiro : Editora Globo, 1987. 405 p. **BE1366**

1st ed., 1967.

Intended for students and teachers. Runs mainly to entries for individual authors, but includes entries for literary movements and genres. Bibliographies. PQ9006.L8

Moisés, Massaud. Bibliografia da literatura portuguêsa / Massaud Moisés ... [et al.]. São Paulo : Ed. Saraiva, Ed. da Universidade, 1968. 383 p. **BE1367**

A bibliographic guide to Portuguese literature from earliest to modern times. Arranged by period, then by literary genre. The subsections on individual authors include both their own writings and critical works about the authors.

§ Moisés is also compiler of *Literatura portuguesa moderna: guia biográfico, crítico e bibliográfico* (São Paulo : Editora Cultrix, 1973. 202 p.) which presents biobibliographical sketches of contemporary writers. Z2721.M63

Saraiva, António José. História da literatura portuguêsa / António José Saraiva, Óscar Lopes. 16a. éd. corrigida e actualizada. Pôrto : Pôrto Editôra, [1992?]. 1254 p. **BE1368**

1st ed., 1955?

Includes bibliographies and index. A briefer work of the same title by Saraiva alone has also appeared in many editions. PQ9012.S3

Provençal

See also BE1163.

Brunel, Clovis. Bibliographie des manuscrits littéraires en ancien provençal. Paris : Droz, 1935. 146 p. (Société de publications romanes et françaises. [Publications], XIII). **BE1369**

Repr.: Geneva : Slatkine, 1973.

Arranged geographically by depository. For each manuscript gives date, region, a brief description of contents, and editions. Indexes by depository, place of origin, title, and author. Includes a list of works classified by genre. Z6605.P96B8

French XX bibliography : Provençal supplement, no.1. N.Y. : French Institute–Alliance Française and the Camargo Foundation, 1976. 111 p. **BE1370**

Joseph D. Gauthier, comp.

Follows the style of the parent series (see note, BE1132), "but because of the founding of the Félibrige in 1854 and the importance of the second half of the 19th century in the history of Provençal literature" (*Editor's note*), the period of coverage goes back to 1850; as in the main series, publications from 1940 are listed.

§ A series of bibliographies bearing the title *Bibliographie occitane* comp. by Pierre Louis Berthaud and others (Paris : Les Belles Lettres; Montpellier : Centre d'Études Occitanes, Univ. Paul-Valery, etc., 1946–73) lists writings in or treating of the "langue d'Oc"; volumes published to date cover 1919/42, 1943/56, 1957/66 and 1967/71.

Jeanroy, Alfred. Bibliographie sommaire des chansonniers provençaux (manuscrits et éditions) .... Paris : Champion, 1916. 86 p. (Les classiques français du moyen âge. 2. série: Manuels, [16]). **BE1371**

Repr. of 1916 ed.

Lists manuscripts, giving date, provenance, contents, published editions, and citations to fuller descriptions. Z7033.P8J4

———— La poésie lyrique des troubadours. Toulouse : Privat ; Paris : Didier, 1934. 2 v. **BE1372**

Repr.: Geneva : Slatkine, 1973.

Contents: v. 1, Histoire externe. Diffusion à l'étranger. Liste de troubadours classés par régions. Notices bio-bibliographiques; v. 2, Histoire interne. Les genres: leur évolution et leurs plus notables représentants.

A classic study. Vol. 1 contains an alphabetical list of troubadours, giving biographical information, number of compositions, and bibliographical references; v. 2 includes a chronology of the various genres. Bibliographies at the ends of chapters. PC3315.J4

New York Public Library. Provençal literature and language including the local history of southern France : a list of references in the New York Public Library / comp. by Daniel C. Haskell. N.Y. : NYPL, 1925. 885 p. **BE1373**

Repr.: N. Y. : AMS Press, 1973.

"Reprinted with additions October 1925 from the Bulletin of the New York Public Library of June to December 1921, January to April and June to December 1922."—*verso of title page.*

Classified catalog of a collection numbering about 25,000 items. Includes a section on modern Provençal. Z7033.P8N5

Pillet, Alfred. Bibliographie der Troubadours / von Dr. Alfred Pillet ... ergänzt, weitergeführt und hrsg. von Dr. Henry Carstens. Haale (Saale) : M. Niemeyer, 1933. 518 p. (Schriften der Königsberger Gelehrten Gesellschaft. Sonderreihe, Bd. 3). **BE1374**

Repr.: N.Y. : B. Franklin, 1968. Also available in microfilm, Berkeley : University of California.

An author listing giving titles of poems, manuscripts, and editions, with citations to secondary sources. Includes a separate section on manuscripts, giving date, contents, and provenance; a list of anonymous compositions; and a rhyme index.

§ François Zufferey's *Bibliographie des poètes provençaux des XIVᵉ et XVᵉ siècles* (Geneva : Droz, 1981. 91 p.) lists manuscripts, editions, and studies of poets of the period following that dealt with by Pillet. Z7033.P8P6

Taylor, Robert Allen. La littérature occitane du Moyen Age : bibliographic sélective et critique. Toronto ; Buffalo : Univ. of Toronto Pr., c1977. 166 p. (Toronto medieval bibliographies, 7). **BE1375**

A selected, annotated bibliography of the medieval literature of the "langue d'oc." In five main sections: (1) Instruments de travail; (2) Études de critique littéraire; (3) La poésie lyrique des troubadours (with subsections for individual authors); (4) La littérature non-lyrique; (5) Guide d'orientation aux matières contigués. Indexed. Z7033.P8T38

Romania

Academia Republicii Populare Romîne. Biblioteca. Bibliografia literaturii romîne, 1948–1960 / Sub redactis Acad. Tudor Vianu. [Lucrare întocmitade: Sorin Alexandrescu et al.]. Bucuresti : Editura Academiei Republicii Populare Romîne, 1965. 1123 p. **BE1376**

Provides bibliographies of individual authors, listing both separately published works and contributions to periodicals, as well as writings about the author. Includes a section on Romanian folklore. Index of names. Z2921.A17

Adamescu, Gheorghe. Contribuţiune la bibliografia românească. Bucureşti : Cartea Românească, 1921–28. 3 v. **BE1377**

Contents: Fasc. 1–3, Istoria literaturii romăne. Texte şi autori, 1500–1921/25.

An important bibliography of Romanian literature, in chronological order by the birth dates of the writers. Z2921.A19

Biblioteca Centrală Universitară București. Literatura română : ghid bibliografic. București : La Biblioteca, 1979–1982. 2 pts. in 3 vols. **BE1378**

Contents: pt. 1, Surse; pt. 2 (2 vols.), Scriitori A–L, M–Z.

Pt. 1 covers sources for literary research, listing general reference works (encyclopedias, dictionaries, bibliographies, journals, etc.) with sections for aesthetics, literary theory, stylistics, literary history, literary movements, etc. Special sections for German and Hungarian literature in Romania. Includes a dictionary of terms for aesthetics, literary theory, and stylistics, with references to an extensive accompanying bibliography on those topics. Fully indexed.

The two volumes of the second part comprise an author dictionary providing biographical information and primary and secondary bibliography for 669 individual writers. References are given to material in reference works as well as to critical studies.

Călinescu, George. Istoria literaturii române dela origini până in prezent. București : Fundația Regală Pentru Literatură și Artă, 1941. 948 p. : ill. **BE1379**

Frequently reprinted.

A standard comprehensive survey of Romanian literature from the 16th to the early 20th centuries, arranged by periods. Treats many authors at length. Copiously illustrated. Extensive bibliography; alphabetical index of authors.

Dicționarul literaturii române de la origini pînă la 1900. București : Editura Academici Republicii Socialiste România, 1979. 976p. : ill. **BE1380**

At head of title: Academia Republicii Socialiste România. Institutul de Lingvistică, Istorie Literară și Folclor al Universității "Al. I. Cuza" Iași.

Biographical entries predominate, but there is good coverage of individual literary periodicals. Literary societies, types of folklore, etc., are also treated. Extensive bibliographies. PC801.D5

Istoria literaturii romîne. [București] : Editura Academiei Republicii Populare Romîne, [1964]–73. 3 v. : ill. **BE1381**

At head of title: v. 1, Academia Republicii Populare Romîne (2nd ed., 1970); v. 2–3, Academia Republicii Socialiste România.

Vols. 2–3 have title: Istoria literaturii române.

Contents: v. 1, Folclorul. Literatura romînă în perioada feudală (1400–1780); v. 2, De la școala ardeleană la junimea; v. 3, Epica marilor clasici.

An "official" history published under the auspices of the former Communist government. Bibliographies and indexes in each volume. PC801.I8

Russia and the U.S.S.R.

Guides

An introduction to Russian language and literature / ed. by Robert Auty and Dimitri Obolensky. Cambridge ; N.Y. : Cambridge Univ. Pr., [1977]. 300 p. (Companion to Russian studies, 2). **BE1382**

For annotation, see BD186. PG2051.I5

Bibliography

See also BE1078.

Akademiiā Nauk SSSR. Biblioteka. Sovetskiĭ roman, ego teoriiā i istoriiā : bibliograficheskii ukazatel´, 1917–1964 / sost. N. A. Groznova. Leningrad : BAN, 1966. 256 p. **BE1383**

At head of title: Biblioteka Akademii Nauk SSSR. Institut Russkoi Literatury (Pushkinskiĭ Dom) Akademii Nauk SSSR.

A briefly annotated bibliography on the history and theory of Soviet fiction, chronologically arranged. Z2504.F5A52

Akademiiā Nauk SSSR. Fundamental'naiā Biblioteka Obshchestvennykh Nauk. Sovetskoe literaturovedenie i kritika : Russkaiā sovetskaiā literatura (obshchie raboty); knigi i stat'i 1917–1962 godov. Bibliograficheskii ukazatel'. Moskva : Nauka, 1966. 586 p. **BE1384**

An annotated bibliography of critical and historical materials on Soviet literature in general. A separate volume was planned for writings on individual authors.

Continued in three supplements ed. by A. S. Blazer and others, covering 1963–67 (publ. 1970. 180 p.), 1968–70 (publ. 1975. 397 p.), and 1971–73 (publ. 1979. 460 p.). Z2503.A45

Cross, Anthony Glenn. Eighteenth century Russian literature, culture and thought : a bibliography of English-language scholarship and translations / Anthony Glenn Cross, Gerald Stanton Smith. Newtonville : Oriental Research Partners, 1984. 130 p. **BE1385**

"This book brings together and updates the bibliographies that the authors have been publishing together at intervals since 1976, and adds to them a bibliography of translations into English of eighteenth-century Russian literary works."—Introd. Classed arrangement with author and subject indexes, plus chronological lists of scholarly works and translations. Entries for individual authors include both translations and secondary works.

Droblenkova, Nadezhda Feotitovna. Bibliografiiā sovetskikh russkikh rabot po literature XI–XVII vv. za 1917–1957 gg. Moskva, 1961. 434 p. **BE1386**

At head of title: Akademiiā Nauk SSSR. Institut Russkoĭ Literatury.

Chronologically arranged by year of publication. Lists Soviet research published in Russian on the history of Russian literature of the 11th through 17th centuries, and 18th-century manuscript material relevant to the earlier period. Name and subject indexes.

Continued for the 18th century by V. P. Stepanov and ĪU. V. Stennik, Istoriiā russkoĭ literatury XVIII veka (Leningrad : Nauka, 1968). Z2502.D7

Stepanov, V. P. Istoriiā russkoĭ literatury XVIII veka : bibliograficheskiĭ ukazatel' / V. P. Stepanov and ĪU. V. Stennik. Leningrad : Nauka, 1968. 500p. **BE1387**

At head of title: Akademiiā Nauk SSSR. Institut Russkoĭ Literatury.

Fills the gap between the Institute's bibliographies for the 11th–17th centuries (BE1386) and the 19th century (BE1388). Z2502.S76

Akademiiā Nauk SSSR. Institut Russkoĭ Literatury. Istoriiā russkoĭ literatury XIX veka : bibliograficheskiĭ ukazatel' / pod red. K. D. Muratovoi. Leningrad : Izd-vo Akademii Nauk SSSR, 1962. 965 p. **BE1388**

———. Istoriiā russkoĭ literatury kontsa XIX nachala XX veka : bibliograficheskiĭ ukazatel', pod red. K.D. Muratovoi (Leningrad : Izd-vo Akademii Nauk SSSR, 1963. 516 p.).

Two major bibliographies for Russian literature for the 19th and 20th centuries. Introductory sections deal with history of Russian literature and criticism, journalism, censorship, and related themes. Personal bibliographies for more than 450 authors are given, listing editions of complete works and published letters, biographical materials, critical literature, and additional bibliographic and reference materials. Name and subject indexes. Z2503.A47

Fomin, Aleksandr Grigor'evich. Putevoditel' po bibliografii, biobibliografii, istoriografii, khronologii i entsiklopedii literatury : sistematicheskii, annotirovannyi ukazatel' russkikh knig i zhurnal'nykh rabot, napechatannykh v 1736–1932 gg. Leningrad : Goslitizdat, 1934. 335 p. **BE1389**

Repr.: N.Y. : Johnson, 1966.

Still an important guide to Russian bibliographies and reference works in the field of literature for the period indicated. Entries are fully annotated. Name and title indexes. Z2501.F67

Foster, Ludmilla A. Bibliography of Russian émigré literature, 1918–1968. Boston : G. K. Hall, 1970. 2 v. **BE1390**
Added title page in Russian.
Lists "Russian literature written by Russian émigrés and published outside the Soviet Union."—*Pref.* Includes creative literature, memoirs, and literary criticism written in Russian or translated into Russian, whether appearing as separate publications or published in collections or journals. Main entry listing according to the Cyrillic alphabet; index. Library locations indicated. Z2513.F66

Gibian, George. Soviet Russian literature in English : a checklist bibliography. Ithaca, N.Y. : Center for International Studies, Cornell Univ., 1967. 118 p. **BE1391**
"A selective bibliography of Soviet Russian literary works in English and of articles and books in English about Soviet Russian literature."—*t. p.*
Includes sections on 33 individual authors, plus sections on Soviet literature in general and on periodicals. Z2504.T8G5

Gosudarstvennai̐a biblioteka SSSR imeni V.I. Lenina. Russkie pisateli vtoroi poloviny XIX nachala XX vv. (do 1917 goda) : rekomendatel'nyi ukazatel' literatury / [Obshchaia red. R. N. Krendel' i B. A. Peskinoi]. Moskva, 1958–63. 3 v. **BE1392**
A selective, annotated bibliography of writings by and about Russian authors of the second half of the 19th century up to 1917, useful for listing of editions and Soviet criticism. Continues chronologically *Russkie pisateli XVIII veka* (Moskva : Gos. biblioteka SSSR im. V. I. Lenina, 1954) and *Russkie pisateli pervoi poloviny XIX veka* (Mpskva, 1951). Z2503.M7

Gosudarstvennai̐a publichnai̐a biblioteka imeni M.E. Saltykova-Shchedrina. Russkie sovetskie pisateli-prozaiki : bio-bibliograficheskiĭ ukazatel' / [Sost.: V. M. Akimov i dr. Redaktor N. IA. Morachevskiĭ]. Leningrad, 1959–72. 7 v. in 9. **BE1393**
Repr.: Ann Arbor, Mich. : Univ. Microfilms International, 1978.
Offers biography and extensive bibliography for a wide selection of Russian prose writers of the Soviet period. Z2503.L4

Harvard University. Library. The Kilgour collection of Russian literature, 1750–1920 : with notes on early books and manuscripts of the 16th and 17th centuries. Cambridge : Harvard College Libr., 1959. 1 v. (unpaged) : ill. **BE1394**
A catalog of 1,348 first editions "from Lomonosov to Blok ... the holdings of Pushkin being particularly notable."—*Pref.* All title pages are reproduced in facsimile, with translations, collation, and notes to facilitate comparison and identification of editions by persons with limited knowledge of the language. Bookplates, labels, and stamps are also reproduced. Z2491.5.H3

———————— Twentieth century Russian literature : classified listing by call number, alphabetical listing by author or title, chronological listing. Cambridge : Harvard Univ. Library, 1965. 142 p., 139 p., 140 p. (Widener Library shelflist, no. 3). **BE1395**
For a note on the Widener shelflist, *see* AA115.
"This volume, unlike most others in the series, contains only a segment of a classification ... the portion of Twentieth Century Russian Literature that is devoted to individual authors."—*Pref.* Includes 9,430 titles of works by and about Russian literary authors whose main work was done after 1917. Z2503.3.H3

Kandel', Boris L'vovich. Russkai̐a khudozhestvennai̐a literatura i literaturovedenie : ukazatel' spravochno-bibliograficheskikh posobiĭ s kontsa XVIII veka po 1974 god / Boris L'vovich Kandel', L. M. Fediushina, and M. A. Benina. Moskva : Kniga, 1976. 492 p. **BE1396**

At head of title: Gosudarstvennai̐a Publichnai̐a Biblioteka im. M. E. Saltykova-Shchedrina.
A classed bibliography of Russian-language bibliographies of literature and literary criticism from the end of the 18th century to 1974. About 2,500 entries, a substantial proportion devoted to individual authors. Name index.
§ A more selective listing including material in English, *Guide to the bibliographies of Russian literature*, by Serge A. Zenkovsky and Davis L. Armbruster (Nashville : Vanderbilt Univ. Pr., 1970) lists more than 300 items on general topics, periods, and literary forms. Author index. Z2501.A1K36

Matsuev, Nikolai Ivanovich. Khudozhestvennai̐a literatura, russkai̐a i perevodnai̐a : bibliografii̐a 1917/25–1938/53. Moskva : Gos. Izd-vo Khudozh. Lit-ry, 1926–59. 6 v. **BE1397**
The four volumes for the years 1917–37 cover belles-lettres, criticism, and studies in literature written in Russian or translated into Russian from any other language. With the establishment of *Sovetskai̐a khudozhestvennai̐a literatura i kritika* (BE1398), the two volumes continuing the present title are limited to pre-Revolutionary Russian authors in current editions and literary studies, and translations into Russian from foreign literatures. Some volumes have been reprinted. Z2503.M26

Sovetskai̐a khudozhestvennai̐a literatura i kritika, 1938/48, 1949/51–1964/65 : bibliografii̐a. Moskva : Sovetskiĭ Pisatel', 1952–72. Biennial after 1949/51. No more published. **BE1398**
Current bibliography, with reviews, for contemporary Russian literature and criticism, and the literatures of other nationalities of the Soviet Union as translated into Russian.
§ Continues, in part, N. I. Matsuev's *Khudozhestvennai̐a literatura, russkai̐a i perevodnai̐a* (BE1397). Z2503.S6

Gosudarstvennai̐a biblioteka SSSR imeni V.I. Lenina. Velikai̐a Okti̐abr'skai̐a sotsialisticheskai̐a revoli̐utsii̐a v proizvedenii̐akh sovetskikh pisateleĭ : k istoriĭ sovetskoĭ literatury. Bibliograficheskii ukazatel' dli̐a nauchnykh rabotnikov. 1917–1966 / [Sost. : F. E. Ebin i dr.]. Moskva : "Kniga", 1967. 407 p. **BE1399**
A bibliography of belles lettres by Soviet writers on the theme of the Russian Revolution. More than 3,600 items in chronological arrangement. Indexed. Z2503.M72

Proffer, Carl R. Nineteenth-century Russian literature in English : a bibliography of criticism and translations / comp. by Carl R. Proffer and Ronald Meyer. Ann Arbor, Mich. : Ardis, c1990. 188 p. **BE1400**
Covers books, articles, and dissertations published from the 1890s through 1986 on general topics and on 69 individual writers. Arranged alphabetically by writer studied, with a section on general topics. No index. Z2503.P76

Proizvedenii̐a sovetskikh pisatelei v perevodakh na inostrannye iazyki : otdel'nye zarubezhnye izdanii̐a. Bibliograficheskiĭ ukazatel'. 1945/53–1976/-80. Moskva, 1954–81. [v. 1–]. **BE1401**
At head of title: Soiuz Pisatelei SSSR i Vsesoiuznai̐a Gosudarstvennai̐a Biblioteka Inostrannoi Literatury.
Contents: 1945/53, 1954/57, 1958/64, 1965/70, 1971/75, 1976/80.
Bibliography of translations of the works of Soviet Russian and other Soviet writers published abroad as separate books. Does not include translations in anthologies or collections or in periodical literature. Z2504.T8P84

Russkie sovetskie pisateli—poèty : biobibliograficheskiĭ ukazatel' / [sost. I.V. Aleksakhina ... et al.] ; Gos. publ. b-ka im. M.E. Saltykova-Shchedrina. Moskva : Kniga, 1977–91. v. 1–14[1]. (In progress). **BE1402**
Contents: v. 1–14[1], Avramenko–Mayakovsky.

A biographical sketch of each writer is followed by a list of published works (including references for individual poems, etc.) and extensive listings of critical writings about the author.   Z2505.P7R87

Schanzer, George O. Russian literature in the Hispanic world : a bibliography. [Toronto] : Univ. of Toronto Pr., [1972]. 312 p.   **BE1403**
Title also in Spanish.

A bibliography of publications documenting the spread and influence of Russian literature in Spain and Spanish America. The more than 3,700 items include "Spanish collections and anthologies of Russian literature, individual translations, criticisms both general and specific, and sections of semi-literary writings."—*p. xxxiii*. Listing is by author or other main entry, with numerous indexes.   Z2504.T7S3

Smirnov-Sokol'skiĭ, Nikolai Pavlovich. Russkie literaturnye al'manakhi i sborniki XVIII–XIX vv : [bibliografiiā]. Moskva : Kniga, 1965. 590 p.   **BE1404**
A preliminary edition was published 1956.

Lists Russian literary almanacs of the 18th and 19th centuries, including humorous almanacs after 1867 and children's almanacs and collections. Includes 1,607 entries, chronologically arranged, with author and title indexes. Detailed contents notes for many items.

§ For almanacs and related works published in the 20th century see *Literaaturno-khudozhestvennye al'manakhi i sborniki : bibliograficheskiĭ ukazatel'* (BE1406).   Z2504.C6S52

Startsev, Ivan Ivanovich. Khudozhestvennaiā literatura narodov SSSR v perevodakh na russkiĭ iāzyk : bibliografiiā. Moskva : Gos. Izd-vo Khudozh Lit-ry, 1957–64. 2 v.   **BE1405**
Contents: v. 1, 1934–54; v. 2, 1955–59.

A bibliography of the literature of language groups of the USSR as translated into Russian. Arranged by nationality. Name indexes.   Z6514.T7S75

Vsesoiuznaiā Knizhnaiā Palata. Literaaturno-khudozhestvennye al'manakhi i sborniki : bibliograficheskiĭ ukazatel'. Moskva, 1957–60. v. 1–4.   **BE1406**
Contents: v. 1, 1900–11, comp. by O. D. Golubeva; v. 2, 1912–17, and v. 3, 1918–27, comp. by N. P. Rogozhin; v. 4, 1928–37, comp. by O. D. Golubeva.

Analyzes the contents of Russian literary almanacs and related works; chronologically arranged, with various indexes.

§ For earlier almanacs see *Russkie literaturnye al'manakhi i sborniki XVIII-XIX vv.* (BE1404).   Z2504.C6V7

Woll, Josephine. Soviet dissident literature : a critical guide / Josephine Woll, in collaboration with Vladimir G. Treml. Boston : G. K. Hall, c1983. 241 p.   **BE1407**

An author listing of some 1,300 items with broad subject index. Includes "all belletristic samizdat that could be found in Western periodicals or books (poems, songs, stories, novels, novellas, dramas); all nonfiction books; articles and essays, as well as substantial pieces of documentation, which seem to the editor to contribute information, views, insights or analyses of some significance."—*Pref.* Some annotations. A lengthy introduction provides an overview of the history of dissident literature and its authors.

§ *Free voices in Russian literature, 1950s–1980s : a biobibliographical guide*, by Bosiljka Stevanovic and Vladimir Wertsman, ed. by Alexander Sumerkin (N.Y. : Russica Publishers, 1987) covers "over 900 authors who live or lived in the Soviet Union (or who emigrated after 1955) and whose writings, unpublished in the Soviet Union because of censorship, appeared in the Russian emigré press between 1957 and 1985."—*Introd.* Biography is brief but very informative. Bibliography limited to work published outside the Soviet Union. A general bibliography is included, and a list of periodicals, serial editions, and anthologies.   Z2511.U5W64

Dissertations

Magner, Thomas F. Soviet dissertations for advanced degrees in Russian literature and Slavic linguistics, 1934–1962. University Park, Pa., Dept. of Slavic Languages, Pennsylvania State Univ., 1966. 100p.   **BE1408**
1,313 items in classed arrangement. Index of authors as subjects, but none of authors of the dissertations.

§ *See also* Jesse John Dossick, *Doctoral research on Russia and the Soviet Union*, DC554.   Z2505.A2M3

Translations

Bibliography of Russian literature in English translation to 1945. Totowa, N.J. : Rowman and Littlefield, [1972]. 74, 96 p.   **BE1409**

Subtitle: Bringing together: *A bibliography of Russian literature in English translation to 1900*, by Maurice B. Line and *Russian literature, theatre, and art : a bibliography of works in English published between 1900–1945*, by Ameri Ettlinger and Joan M. Gladstone.

Line's book, first published in London, 1963, covers collections, anthologies, and individual authors, and includes a chronological list of translations, with an index of translators.

Ettlinger and Gladstone's work (London, 1947) supplements Philip Grierson's *Books on Soviet Russia, 1917–1924* (London, 1943). It is a classified listing with sections for studies of Russian literature, theater and art, Russian literature in English translation from the 19th century onward, and linguistic sources (including dictionaries, grammars, and bilingual publications). No index.   Z2504.T8B53

Encyclopedias; Dictionaries

Dana, Henry Wadsworth Longfellow. Handbook on Soviet drama : lists of theatres, plays, operas, ballets, films and books and articles about them. N.Y. : The American Russian Institute for Cultural Relations with the Soviet Union, inc., 1938. 258 p.   **BE1410**

Very useful for a contemporary view of theater and other performing arts during the early Soviet era. Provides factual information and bibliography of English-language materials on theaters, plays, Soviet drama in general, operas, ballets, and films. Includes special types of theaters such as peasant theaters, those on collective farms, living newspapers, puppets, and platform entertainment, and on foreign and traditional Russian plays produced in Soviet theaters. Lists plays on various topics reflecting history, the revolution, and the Soviet state. List of plays by author gives a brief statement of plot. Information on ballets, operas, and films includes lists of productions and bibliographies of secondary studies. Index.   Z2504.D8D2

Handbook of Russian literature / ed. by Victor Terras. New Haven : Yale Univ. Pr., [1985]. 558 p.   **BE1411**

A useful handbook for students of Russian literature, scholars in related areas, and general readers. 106 scholar-contributors were asked to write one or two major articles and a number of briefer ones from their general area of specialization. Articles on individual writers (including a few prominent living persons) predominate, but the nearly 1,000 entries encompass literary terms, genres, societies, periodicals, and important anonymous works, together with many useful topical articles. Since it is assumed that many users of the work do not read Russian, names are given in familiar spellings and titles of literary works are given in translation, usually followed by the transliterated Russian title; the bibliographies appended to most articles cite non-English secondary works only when they contain information not available in English. General classed bibliography (p. 535–41); cross-references; detailed index.   PG2940.H29

Kasack, Wolfgang. Dictionary of Russian literature since 1917. N.Y. : Columbia Univ. Pr., 1988. 502 p. **BE1412**

A translation of Kasack's *Lexikon der russischen Literatur ab 1917* (Stuttgart : Kröner, 1976) and its *Ergänzungsband*, by Maria Carolson and Jane T. Hedges; 2nd ed., *Lexikon der russischen Literatur des 20. Jahrhunderts : von Beginn des Jahrhunderts bis zum Ende der Sowjet ara* (München : Verlag Otto Sagner in Kommission, 1992. 1 v.).

"For this translation, all entries were updated and 153 entries were added."—*Pref.* Contains 629 author and 87 subject entries, including coverage of important literary journals, themes, movements, and prizes. Each article includes a selected primary and secondary bibliography; most citations are to German- or Russian-language works. Name and subject indexes. Z2500.K3513

Kratkaiā literaturnaiā entsiklopediiā / Glav. red. A. A. Surkov. Moskva : Sovetskaiā Entsiklopediiā, 1962–78. 9 v. **BE1413**

A general literary encyclopedia, particularly useful for the inclusion of writers of the Soviet period and those of the various national minority groups of the Soviet Union. Vol. 9 contains supplementary articles in alphabetical sequence, plus a name/subject index to the full set. Review: *Slavic and East European journal* 25, no. 2 (Summer 1981) 80–90. PN41.K7

Literaturnaiā entsiklopediiā / Redaktsionnaia kollegiia: P. I. Lebedev-Polianskii, I. M. Nusinov. Moskva : "Khudozhestvennaia Literatura", 1929–39. v. 1–9, 11. : ill. **BE1414**

Repr. 1948: American Council of Learned Societies reprints. Russian ser., no. 20.

An extensive treatment of world literature from a Marxist-Leninist standpoint, with special emphasis on the literatures of Russia and other portions of the USSR. Never completed. PN41.I.46

The modern encyclopedia of Russian and Soviet literature / ed. by Harry B. Weber. [Gulf Breeze, Fla.] : Academic International Pr., 1977–89. v. 1–9. (In progress). **BE1415**

Contents: v. 1–9, Abaginskii–Holovko.

Vol. 9 ed. by George J. Gutsche.

"The coverage envisioned for this series goes beyond writers and their works to include those aspects of Russian and Soviet cultural life which impinge in one way or another on literature in a broad sense: literary criticism, the contributions of past literary scholars (no living scholar is represented), a number of selected linguistic problems, dramatic literature (but not the theater as such), literary genres, literary movements, literary journals, and folklore. ... The encyclopedia strives, ultimately, to arrive at a cultural profile of Russia and the Soviet Union, as revealed in Russian literature, in the many other national Soviet literatures, and in their literary traditions and literary history. This has entailed translating authoritative articles in older reference works, or combining information from many sources into a comprehensive article, or including entries by knowledgeable specialists."—*v. 1, p. vi.* Longer articles are signed; most include bibliographies. Material translated from other sources seems not to be so identified. For a critical review see *Modern Language Review* 84 (Jan. 1989) : 269–70. PG2940.M6

Timofeev, Leonid Ivanovich. Slovar' literaturovedcheskikh terminov / Leonid Ivanovich Timofeev, S. V. Turaev. Moskva : "Prosveshchenie", 1974. 509 p. **BE1416**

A dictionary of general literary terms. Derivation is indicated for terms of Latin, Greek, or other Western-language origin. Entries are signed; many include bibliographies. PN44.5.T5

History

Akademiiā Nauk SSSR. Institut Russkoĭ Literatury. Istoriiā russkoĭ literatury. Moskva : Izd-vo Akademii Nauk SSSR, 1941–56. 10 v. in 13. : ill. **BE1417**

The work of many scholars and the official history of the Soviet Academy, covering from the 11th century to 1917. Bibliographic footnotes but no index or comprehensive bibliography.

Continued by *Istoriiā russkoĭ sovetskoĭ literatury, 1917–1965,* izd. 2, ispr. i dop. red. A. G. Dement'ev (v. 1–3), L. I. Timofeev (v. 4) (Moskva : Akademii "Nauk," 1967–71. 4 v.). Another collaborative effort by many specialists. Many sections are devoted to individual authors. Detailed chronologies are included.

Both histories have many illustrations. PG2950.A47

Brown, William Edward. A history of Russian literature of the romantic period. Ann Arbor : Ardis, c1986. 4 v. : ill. **BE1418**

A monumental and well-written work aimed at graduate nonspecialists and specialists in related areas of Romanticism. Covers the literature from the late 18th century through Gogol. Many excerpts in English. Each volume has extensive notes and an index, and v. 4 provides a selective bibliography. A review in *Choice* 24 (Jan 1987) : 768–9, notes that "Brown tries to include all genres and writers of any stature whatsoever. This is the first discussion in English of many writers ... a mine of interesting information." A review in *TLS* (Dec. 25, 1987) : 1442, points out poor coverage of women writers.

§ Brown is author of two useful histories for the eras preceding this, *A history of seventeenth-century Russian literature* and *A history of eighteenth-century Russian literature*, both published by Ardis in 1980. PG3015.5.R6B76

The Cambridge history of Russian literature / ed. by Charles A. Moser. Rev. ed. Cambridge ; N.Y. : Cambridge Univ. Pr., 1992. 709 p. **BE1419**

1st ed., 1989.

Aims to present "in narrative form a survey of Russian Literature from its beginnings to this decade, in sufficient but not overwhelming detail."—*Pref to 1st ed.* Eleven chapters by specialists cover the history from 988 through the 1980s, with the last chapter on the most recent era being added for the new edition. A lengthy but selective bibliography is provided. General index. PG2951.C36

Mirskii, D. S. A history of Russian literature from the earliest times to the death of Dostoevsky (1881). London : Routledge ; N.Y. : Knopf, 1927. 388 p. **BE1420**

This and its companion, Mirskii's *Contemporary Russian literature, 1881–1925,* comprise a good concise history. A one-volume, abridged edition, *A history of Russian literature : comprising A history of Russian literature and Contemporary Russian literature* ed. by Francis J. Whitfield, (N.Y., Knopf, 1949. 518 p.) is considered inferior to the earlier versions. PG2951.M5

Struve, Gleb. Russian literature under Lenin and Stalin, 1917–1953. Norman : Univ. of Oklahoma Pr., [1971]. 454 p. **BE1421**

A revision of the 1951 edition of the author's *Soviet Russian literature* which, in turn, was based on his 1935 work of that title. A reliable history, with extensive bibliography (p.396–432).

§ Deming Brown's *Soviet Russian literature since Stalin* (Cambridge : Cambridge Univ. Pr., 1978. 394 p.) brings the record nearer the present. PG3022.S82

Biography

Ionov, E. P. Pisateli Moskvy : biobibliograficheskiĭ spravochnik / sostaviteli E.P. Ionov, S.P. Kolov. Moskva : Moskovskiĭ rabochiĭ, 1987. 541 p. **BE1422**

This directory of members of the Moscow writer's organization gives very brief biographical information on authors, critics, translators, and scholars with some selected bibliographies. Arranged alphabetically without index. PG3505.M6I56

Russkie pisateli : biobibliograficheski i slovar / pod red. i P. A. Nikolaeva. Moskva : "Prosveshchenie", 1990. 2 v. : ill.
BE1423

A biobibliographical dictionary covering about 300 authors of the 19th and 20th centuries. Entries range from one to several pages and include a biographical essay and selective bibliography. Each volume has a section of portraits.

§ Updates and augments for the period covered a one-volume dictionary from the same publisher and under the same title published in 1970 and ed. by D. S. Likhachev. The earlier work covered the same number of writers but included writers from the medieval era to the early 20th century.
Z2500.R86

Vengerov, Semen Afanas'evich. Istochniki slovaria russkikh pisatelei. Sanktpeterburg : Tip. Imp. Akademiia Nauk, 1900–1917. 4 v.
BE1424

Repr.: Leipzig : Zentral-Antiquariat der Deutschen Demokratischen Republik, 1965.

Contents: v. 1–4, A–Nekrasov. No more published.

An extremely useful, although incomplete, biobibliographical dictionary including many obscure writers. Biographical information is very brief, often confined to dates of birth and death.
Z2500.V95

Slovakia

See also Czechoslovakia.

Encyklopédia slovenských spisovateľov / [napísal kolektív autorov pod vedením Karola Rosenbauma]. Bratislava : Obzor, 1984. 2 v. : ill., facsims., ports.
BE1425

A major source necessary in research libraries supporting the study of Slavic literatures. In two sections, the first providing biographies and primary and secondary bibliographies for individual authors, the second containing entries for literary journals, academies, movements, some individual traditional works, etc. Criticism noted is in Slovak. Authors out of favors at the time of publication were excluded. Portraits, many in color.
Z2138.L5E53

Spain

See also entries for Latin America and Portugal.

General works

Guides

Bleznick, Donald W. A sourcebook for Hispanic literature and language : a selected, annotated guide to Spanish, Spanish-American, and Chicano bibliography, literature, linguistics, journals, and other source materials. 2nd ed. Metuchen, N.J. : Scarecrow, 1983. 304 p.
BE1426

1st ed., 1974.

More than 1,400 annotated entries in classed arrangement, with author and title indexes. Includes literary history and anthologies, and has directories of publishers and book dealers.
Z2695.A2B55

Foster, David William. Manual of Hispanic bibliography / David William Foster, Virginia Ramos Foster. 2nd ed., rev. and exp. N.Y. : Garland, 1977. 329 p.
BE1427

1st ed., 1970.

"Represents an attempt at providing Spanish and Spanish-American literary scholars with a comprehensive bibliographical guide to primary and important secondary sources of investigation."—*Introd.* Includes annotated listings of both literary and national bibliographies, plus works relating to library resources.
Z2691.A1F68

Jauralde Pou, Pablo. Manual de investigación literaria : guía bibliográfica para el estudio de la literatura española. Madrid : Gredos, 1981. 416 p. : ill. (Biblioteca románica hispánica. III, Manuales, 48).
BE1428

A substantial classified, annotated bibliography, international in scope. Includes useful outlines and charts. No subject index, but the table of contents is very detailed.
Z2691.J38

Pedraza Jiménez, Felipe B. Manual de literatura española / Felipe B. Pedraza Jiménez, Milagros Rodríguez Cáceres. Pamplona : Cénlit, 1980–1993. v. 1–11. (In progress).
BE1429

Contents: v. 1, Edad Media; v. 2, Renacimiento; v. 3–4, Barroco; v. 5, Siglo XVIII; v. 6, Epoca romántica; v. 7, Epoca del realismo; v. 8–9, Generaci on de fin de siglo; v. 10–11, Novecentismo y vanguardia. To be completed in 13 vols.

A monumental guide and history of Spanish literature with a focus on the study and analysis of individual texts. Arranged in numbered sections outlined in a detailed table of contents in each volume. Bibliographies throughout. Author indexes.

§ A companion source for Spanish American literature, *Manual de literatura hispanoamericana*, is appearing from the same publisher, also ed. by Pedraza Jiménez. Since 1991 two volumes of a planned six have appeared, covering the early literature and the 19th century.
PQ6032.P4

Woodbridge, Hensley Charles. Guide to reference works for the study of the Spanish language and literature and Spanish American literature. N.Y. : Modern Language Association of America, 1987. 183 p. (Selected bibliographies in language and literature, 5).
BE1430

A greatly expanded version of the author's *Spanish and Spanish-American literature : an annotated guide to selected bibliographies* (1983). Includes reference books and bibliographies on literature and philology published from 1950 to early 1986. Almost 1,000 citations are listed in a classed arrangement and usually include brief annotations. Indexes to authors/editors/compilers and to individual author bibliographies, glossaries, and concordances.
Z2695.A2W66

Bibliography

Aguilar Piñal, Francisco. Bibliografía de autores españoles del siglo XVIII. Madrid : Consejo Superior de Investigaciones Científicas, Instituto "Miguel de Cervantes", 1981–1993. v. 1–7. (In progress).
BE1431

Contents: v. 1–7, A–S. To be complete in 10 volumes.

Publisher varies.

Covers authors, 1700–1808, writing in Spanish and published in Spain or the Canary or Balearic Islands. For each author, gives biographical sketch, works listed under the categories of letters, manuscripts, printed works, translations, studies. At least one location in a Spanish library is provided. Anonymous works are to be cataloged in v. 9; v. 10 is to provide general studies. Cross-references from variant forms, pseudonyms, or anagrams. Each volume is indexed by name, subject, geographical location, play title, and printer. List of libraries consulted.
Z2682.A64

Bibliographie hispanique. v. 1 (1905)–v. 13 (1917). N.Y. : Hispanic Society of America, [1909–19].
BE1432

Repr. : N.Y. : Kraus, 1962.

Annual bibliography including both books and periodical articles, and covering the languages, literature, and history of the Spanish- and Portuguese-speaking countries, both in Europe and elsewhere.

§ Several journals include ongoing bibliographies. *Revista de filología española* (v. 1 [1914]– . Madrid : Consejo Superior de Investigaciones Científicas. Publisher varies; suspended July 1937–Dec. 1940) provides an annual listing covering language and literature for Spain and Spanish America. Somewhat more thorough for Spanish America is: *Nueva revista de filología hispánica* (v. 1 [1947]– . Mexico : Centro de Estudios Lingüísticos y Literarios, El Colegio de Mexico), which includes a substantial bibliography at regular intervals, most recently five years. (The latter continues *Revista de filología hispánica*, v. 1 [1936]–v. 8 [1946]). Z2685.B61

Bibliography of Old Spanish texts / comp. by Charles B. Faulhaber ... [et al.] (with the assistance of Jean Lentz). 3rd ed. Madison, [Wis.] : Hispanic Seminary of Medieval Studies, 1984. 341 p. (Hispanic Seminary of Medieval Studies. Bibliographic series, 4). **BE1433**

1st ed., 1975; 2nd ed., 1977.

Aims to create "an exhaustive descriptive inventory of the relevant pre-1501 Old Spanish texts" (*Introd.*) from which a selection can be made of the most lexically promising material to use in compiling an Old Spanish dictionary, an ongoing project at the University of Wisconsin—Madison. This edition provides full citations (with indication of present location) for 3,378 items. Indexes of library locations, production dates, authors, titles, production locations, printers or scribes, languages, and bibliographical citations.

§ A companion volume: *Bibliography of old Catalan texts*, comp. Beatrice Jorgensen Concheff (Madison, Wis. : Hispanic Seminary of Medieval Studies, 1985. [Bibliographic series, 5]). Z2682.B52

Cuadernos bibliográficos. v. 1– . Madrid : C.S.I.C., 1961– . Irregular. **BE1434**

Each issue is devoted to a special topic, e.g., no. 1, Cervantes: bibliografía fundamental (1900–1959), by Alberto Sanchez; no. 12, 14, 15, 19, 21, Impresos del siglo XVI, by José Simón Díaz; no. 27, Romancero popular del siglo XVIII, by Francisco Aguilar Piñal; no. 43, Indice de las poesías publicadas en los periódicos españoles del siglo XVIII, by Francisco Aguilar Piñal.

Foulché-Delbosc, Raymond. Manuel de l'hispanisant / Raymond Foulché-Delbosc, Louis Barrau-Dihigo. N.Y. : Putnam, 1920–25. 2 v. **BE1435**

For annotation, *see* AA801. Z2681.A1F7

Golden, Herbert Hershel. Modern Iberian language and literature : a bibliography of homage studies / by Herbert H. Golden and Seymour O. Simches. Cambridge, Mass. : Harvard Univ. Pr., 1958. 184 p. **BE1436**

Repr. : N.Y. : Kraus, 1971.

Indexes articles in festschriften and homage volumes; concerned primarily with Catalan, Portuguese, and Spanish languages and literatures, with some articles relating to Spanish America and Brazil. Indexes 424 books in various languages, published through 1956. Z7031.G6

Moseley, William W. Spanish literature, 1500–1700 : a bibliography of Golden Age studies in Spanish and English, 1925–1980 / comp. by William W. Moseley, Glenroy Emmons, and Marilyn C. Emmons. Westport, Conn. : Greenwood, 1984. lxiii, 765 p. (Bibliographies and indexes in world literature, no. 3). **BE1437**

Intended as "a ready-reference source of books and articles for the generalist and the advanced student rather than the specialist."— *Introd.* Nearly 11,200 entries arranged by literary genre, plus sections for general works, general bibliography, and individual authors. Author and subject indexes. Z2692.M67

Serís, Homero. Manual de bibliografía de la literatura española. Syracuse, N.Y. : Centro de Estudios Hispánicos, 1948–54. 2 v. (Publicaciones del Centro de Estudios Hispánicos, 2). **BE1438**

Pt. 1: fasc. 1, Obras generales (1948. 422 p.); fasc. 2, p. 423–1086 (1954. Repr. : N.Y. : Las Americas, 1968). No more published.

The first volume of what was intended to be a very comprehensive bibliographical manual of Spanish literature. Includes 8,779 numbered items with a full alphabetical index and a general table of contents. Lists both books and periodical articles, some with annotations.

Later parts were to cover: (2) Lengua; (3) Edad media; (4) Siglos XVI y XVII; (5) Siglo XVIII; (6) Siglo XIX; and (7) Siglo XX, suplemento e índices.

§ Serís's *Bibliografía de la lingüística española* (BD169) is not part of this series, but continues the numbering sequence of the *Manual* to emphasize the close relationship between language and literature and to facilitate cross-references from the *Bibliografía* to the *Manual*. Z2691.S47

Simón Díaz, José. Bibliografía de la literatura hispánica. Madrid : Consejo Superior de Investigaciones Científicas, Inst. "Miguel de Cervantes" de Filología Hispánica, 1950–92. v. 1–15 : facsims. (In progress). **BE1439**

Contents: v. 1, General: Literatura castellana; Literatura catalan; Literatura gallega; literatura vasca (3rd ed., 1983); v. 2, Bibliografías de bibliografías; Bio-bibliografías; Índices de publicaciones periódicas; Historia de la imprenta (3rd ed., 1987); v. 3, pts. 1 and 2, Literatura castellana: Edad media. Siglos XI–XV (2nd ed., 1963–65); v. 4, Literatura castellana: Siglos de oro: Fuentes general, Autores A–Agustin (2nd ed., 1972); v. 5–15, Autores, Alaba–Najera (v. 5–6, 2nd ed., 1973; v. 7–15, 1st ed., 1967–92).

An important, comprehensive, and extremely thorough bibliography of all of the Hispanic literatures, including those of pre-independence America. Indispensable in a research library. Books, periodical articles, and unpublished works such as dissertations are included. Book reviews sometimes are noted, as are locations, chiefly in Spanish libraries. Comprehensive indexes in each volume provide multiple access points. Z2691.S5

——————— Manual de bibliografía de la literatura española. 3a ed. refundida, corr. y aum. Madrid : Gredos, [1980]. 1156 p. (Biblioteca románica hispánica. III. Manuales, 47). **BE1440**

1st ed., 1963; *Adiciones 1962–64* (publ. 1966); *Adiciones 1965–70* (publ. 1972). The 1st ed. was reprinted 1966 and 1970 with the 1962–64 suppl. bound at back and designated as a 2nd ed.

A bibliography of nearly 27,000 entries for books and periodical articles covering the whole range of Spanish literature. Not an abridgment of the author's larger work, but highly selective and more limited in scope.

A general section is followed by chronological sections covering one or more centuries. Within period divisions general works are followed by the names of individual authors, arranged alphabetically, with titles of their works and of biographical and critical works about them. Name and subject indexes. Z2691.S54

Simón Palmer, María del Carmen. Escritoras españolas del siglo XIX : manual bio-bibliográfico. Madrid : Castalia, c1991. 834 p., [24] p. of plates : ports. (Nueva biblioteca de erudición y crítica, 3). **BE1441**

A substantial and comprehensive bibliography of works by and about Spanish women writers of all genres, including both belles lettres and nonfiction, published between 1832 and 1900. Covers monographs, material published in perodicals, translations, and collective works. For many authors biographical information (often extensive) and references to criticism are provided. Book reviews are noted, as are locations in Spanish, European, and North American libraries. Indexes to names, subjects, periodicals cited, and collective works. List of works consulted.

§ An older work still important for the earlier periods is *Apuntes para una biblioteca de escritoras españolas : desde al año 1401 al 1833*, by Manuel Serrano y Sanz (Madrid : Establecimiento Tipolitográfico "Sucesores de Rivadeneyra" and Tipografía de la "Revista de Archivos, Bibliotecas y Museos," 1903–1905, 2 v. Repr. : Madrid : Atlas, 1975). Originally published as v. 268–71 of *Biblioteca de autores españoles, desde la formación del lenguaje hasta nuestros días* (Madrid : M. Rivadeneyra, 1846–). In addition to biobibliographical information, quotes extensively from works. Z2693.5.W6S55

Siracusa, Joseph. Relaciones literarias entre España e Italia : ensayo de una bibliografía de literatura comparada. Boston : G.K. Hall, 1972. 252 p. **BE1442**

An author listing of books, articles, and essays. Indexed by name, but not by topic. Z2691.S57

Vera, Francisco. La cultura española medieval : datos bio-bibliográficos para su historia. Madrid : Victoriano Suárez, 1933–34. 2 v.   **BE1443**
A biobibliographical dictionary of the writers of medieval Spain.
DP99.V4

Women writers of Spain : an annotated bio-bibliographical guide / ed. by Carolyn L. Galerstein ; non-Castilian materials ed. by Kathleen McNerney. N.Y. : Greenwood, 1986. 389 p. (Bibliographies and indexes in women's studies, no. 2).
BE1444
Aims "to familiarize readers … with the content and meaning of selected works by 300 women writers of Spain."—*Pref.* Writers are listed alphabetically; a biographical note for each is followed by annotated lists of writings. Title index.   Z2693.5.W6W65

Zubatsky, David S. Spanish, Catalan, and Galician literary authors of the twentieth century : an annotated guide to bibliographies. Metuchen, N.J. : Scarecrow, 1992. 184 p. **BE1445**
Contains "personal bibliographies of twentieth-century Catalan, Galician, and Spanish writers of novels, drama, poetry, and short stories, as well as essayists, journalists, linguists, and literary critics" and "includes citations that appear in periodicals, dissertations, and *festschrift* volumes."—*Pref.* Entries are annotated. A list of references to further information is provided. No index.
§ For Zubatsky's companion volume, *Latin American literary authors,* see BE881.   Z2691.A1Z83

Dissertations

Chatham, James R. Dissertations in Hispanic languages and literatures : an index of dissertations completed in the United States and Canada / James R. Chatham & Enrique Ruiz-Fornells with the collaboration of Sara Matthews Scales. [Lexington] : Univ. Pr. of Kentucky, [1970–1981]. 2 v.   **BE1446**
Contents: v. 1, 1876–1966; v. 2, 1967–1977. Vol. 2 ed. by Chatham and Carmen C. McLendon, with the collaboration of Sara Matthews Scales.
Relevant dissertations completed in departments other than Hispanic languages and literatures are included. Vol. 1 is a classed list with author-subject index and v. 2 alphabetical by author with separate indexes for Catalan, Luso-Brazilian, and Spanish/Spanish-American languages and literatures.
§ Chatham also edited, with Sara Scales et al., *Western European dissertations on the Hispanic and Luso-Brazilian languages and literatures: a retrospective index* (Mississippi State Univ., Dept. of Foreign Languages, 1984), providing information on more than 6,000 dissertations. Author listing with subject index.   Z2695.A2C46

Translations

Pane, Remigio Ugo. English translations from the Spanish, 1484–1943 : a bibliography. New Brunswick, N.J. : Rutgers Univ. Pr., 1944. 218 p. (Rutgers University studies in Spanish, no. 2).   **BE1447**
An unannotated, alphabetical list of 2,682 items of peninsular-Spanish literature and history. A review with corrections and additions by W. K. Jones was published in *Hispanic review* 13 (April 1945): 174–77.   Z2694.T7P2

Rudder, Robert S. The literature of Spain in English translation : a bibliography. N.Y. : F. Ungar, [1975]. 637 p. **BE1448**
Lists translations appearing in periodicals and in collections, as well as separately published works. Listing is by literary period (medieval, Renaissance, etc.), then by author; individual poems and stories are given separate entries. "Literature" is broadly interpreted to include historical writings, etc., of literary merit. "Spain" of the title refers to the country rather than the language, so that translations from Catalan, Basque, etc., are included, as are translations from the Latin of early Spanish writers. Indexes of authors and of anonymous works.

§ For more extensive information on early translations, including those from Portuguese (which Rudder excludes), *see*: Antony Francis Allison, *English translations from the Spanish and Portuguese to the year 1700 : an annotated catalogue of the extant printed adaptations, excluding dramatic adaptations* (London : Dawson of Pall Mall, 1974). Includes biographical information on the authors.   Z2694.T7R83

Criticism

Modern Spanish and Portuguese literatures / comp. and ed. by Marshall J. Schneider, Irwin Stern. N.Y. : Continuum, 1988. 615 p.   **BE1449**
Like other volumes in the "Library of literary criticism" series, presents selected critical commentary, in this case concerning some "eighty twentieth-century authors of the Iberian Peninsula, writing in Spanish, Catalan, Galician, and Portuguese."—*Pref.* Selections, drawn from books and periodicals, in two main sections, Spain and Portugal; many selections have been translated into English by the editors. Index to critics.   PQ6072.M57

Encyclopedias; Dictionaries

Diccionari de la literatura catalana / sota la direcció de Joaquim Molas i Josep Massot i Muntaner. Barcelona : Edicions 62, [1979]. 762 p. (Cultura catalana contemporània, 9).
BE1450
Entries for Catalan authors predominate, but consideration is given to literary forms, terms, and genres, as well as some individual works and literary journals. Bibliographic notes at the end of many articles.   PC3901.D5

Diccionario de literatura española / dirigido por Germán Bleiberg [y] Julián Marías. 4. ed., corr. y aum. Madrid : Ediciones de la Revista de Occidente, [1972]. 1197, [70] p.
BE1451
1st ed., 1949.
An extensive dictionary covering all periods of Spanish literature. Includes biographies (with bibliographies), articles on forms of literature, literary terms, etc. All articles are signed. Provides an index of titles mentioned in the text and a chronological index. This edition adds some new articles (e.g., "lingüística"), new appendixes on Catalan and Gallegan literature, and a lengthy section on paleography.
§ A newer dictionary, similar in scope and scale although limited to Castilian Spanish in coverage of the Iberian peninsula: *Diccionario de literatura española e hispanoamericana*, dirigio por Ricardo Gullón, prólogo de Fernando Lázaro Carreter (Madrid : Quinto Centenario, 1993. 2 v.). Overlaps Bleiberg but each work has many unique entries. Does include information on sephardic literature, some medieval works in Latin, and Philippine and Chicano literature, as well as traditional Spanish and Spanish American literature. Title index.
PQ6006.D5

The Oxford companion to Spanish literature / ed. by Philip Ward. Oxford : Clarendon Pr., 1978. 629 p.   **BE1452**
Publ. in Spanish as *Diccionario Oxford de literatura española e hispanoamericana* / tr. by Gabriela Zayas (Barcelona : Editorial Critica, c1984).
Follows the plan of the publisher's "companions" to other literatures, devoting most space to authors (not only creative writers, but also critics, historians, philosophers, etc.), but including some titles, terms, institutions, and literary movements. An important difference stems from the fact that "a great deal of literature in Spanish has been written beyond the geographical confines of Spain, and this necessitates the inclusion of entries on the more important authors and books, not only of Spain, but also of Argentina, Bolivia, Chile, Colombia, Costa Rica, Cuba, Dominican Republic, Ecuador, El Salvador, Guatemala, Honduras, Mexico, Nicaragua, Panama, Paraguay, Peru, Philippines, Puerto Rico, Uruguay, and Venezuela. The literatures of Portugal and Brazil are excluded, but languages of Spain other than Castil-

ian are represented: Basque, Catalan, and Galician."—*Pref.* Frequently provides bibliographic citations to works offering fuller information. PQ6006.O95

Redfern, James. A glossary of Spanish literary composition. N.Y. : Harcourt Brace Jovanovich, 1972. 224 p.   **BE1453**
Gives Spanish equivalents of English literary terms, with examples. Includes terms derived from persons' names. Bibliography. PC4680.R4

History

Alborg, Juan Luis. Historia de la literatura española. Madrid : Editorial Gredos, [1966–80]. v. 1–4. (In progress?).   **BE1454**
Contents: v. 1, Edad Media y Renacimiento; v. 2, Epoca barroca; v. 3, Siglo XVIII; v. 4, El romanticismo.
A detailed critical history with lengthy bibliographical footnotes and an author and title index in each volume. Vols. 1 and 2 appeared in 1970 in a "2. ed. ampliada" but v. 3–4 are still the 1st ed. All volumes have been reprinted many times.   PQ6032.A45

Cejador y Frauca, Julio. Historia de la lengua y literatura castellana. Madrid : "Revista de Archivos, Bibliotecas y Museos", 1915–22. 14 v. : ill.   **BE1455**
Vols. 1–4 have appeared in a 2nd ed., 1927–35, and v. 1 in a 3rd ed., 1932–33.
1st ed. repr. : Madrid : Ed. Gredos, 1972–74.
A standard history covering the time from Charles V to 1920. Includes bibliographies.   PQ6032.C3

Díaz Plaja, Guillermo. Historia general de las literaturas hispánicas / Guillermo Díaz Plaja ; con una introducción de Ramón Menéndez Pidal. Barcelona : Editorial Barna, [1949–1968, c1967]. 6 v. in 7 : ill.   **BE1456**
Each section written by a specialist, with extensive bibliographies. Covers not only Spanish literature but others, such as Arab, Catalan, Hebrew, and Latin which have flourished in Spain, and the literatures of other Spanish-speaking countries in the Americas, Philippines, etc.
§ Díaz Plaja also is the author of a one-volume work, *Historia de la literatura española*, available in many editions, often jointly with *Historia de la literatura mexicana*, by Francisco Monterde (21a ed. Mexico : Editorial Porrua, 1986) and in an English edition translated by Hugh A. Harter, *A history of Spanish literature* (N.Y. : New York Univ. Pr., 1971), which includes an introductory chapter, a bibliography, and an addendum on contemporary literature.   PQ6032.D5

Valbuena Prat, Angel. Historia de la literatura española. 9a ed. ampliada y puesta al día / por Antonio Prieto. Barcelona : G. Gili, 1981–83. 6 v.   **BE1457**
8th ed., 1968 (4 v.).
Contents: t. 1, Edad media; t. 2, Renacimiento; t. 3, Siglo XVII; t. 4, Siglo XVIII; t. 5, Del realismo al vanguardismo; t. 6, Epoca contemporanea.
An important and useful scholarly history. Extensive bibliographical references in footnotes. Name and title index in each volume. *Literatura hispanoamericana*, by Angel Valbuena Briones (4. ed. ampliada. Barcelona : G. Gili, 1969) served as v. 5 of the 8th ed. and should be used with the 9th ed.   PQ6032.V3

Biography

Instituto Nacional del Libro Español. Quién es quién en las letras españolas. 3. ed. [Madrid] : Instituto Nacional del Libro Español, Ministerio de Cultura, [1979]. 495 p.   **BE1458**
1st ed., 1969.
Biobibliographical sketches of nearly 2,000 writers. Includes journalists, essayists, and critics, as well as poets, novelists, dramatists, etc.   Z2690.I55

Genres

Drama

Bergman, Hannah E. A catalogue of comedias sueltas in The New York Public Library / by Hannah E. Bergman and Szilvia E. Szmuk. [London] : Grant & Cutler, 1980–81. 2 v. (309 p.).   **BE1459**
Provides full bibliographic descriptions of an extensive collection of *sueltas*. Alphabetical title listing.   Z2694.D7B47

Boyer, Mildred Vinson. The Texas collection of *comedias sueltas* : a descriptive bibliography. Boston : G. K. Hall, [1978]. 620 p.   **BE1460**
"This volume has been designed to describe The University of Texas [at Austin] holdings in Spanish dramatic literature in suelta editions prior to 1834."—*Introd.* Arranged by author, with anonymous works listed first. 1,119 items representing some 750 different titles. Indexed.   Z2694.D7B7

Cambridge University Library. *Comedias sueltas* in Cambridge University Library : a descriptive catalog / comp. by A. J. C. Bainton. Cambridge : The Library, 1977. 281 p. (Cambridge University Library. Historical bibliography series, 2).   **BE1461**
Catalog of more than 900 separate editions of single plays, with full bibliographic descriptions.
Supplemented by Bainton's *The Edward M. Wilson collection of comedias sueltas in Cambridge University Library : a descriptive catalogue* (Kassel : Reichenberger, 1987), which follows the same arrangement.   Z2694.D7C35

Coe, Ada May. Catálogo bibliográfico y crítico de las comedias anunciadas en los periódicos de Madrid desde 1661 hasta 1819. Baltimore : Johns Hopkins Pr. ; London : Milford, 1935. 270 p. (Johns Hopkins studies in Romance literatures and languages, extra v.9).   **BE1462**
A list of plays noted in the periodicals of Madrid from 1661 to 1819, arranged alphabetically by title with an author index. Many entries have annotations, some lengthy.   Z2694.D7C6

Cotarelo y Mori, Emilio. Teatro español : catálogo abreviado de una colección dramática española, hasta fines del siglo XIX y de obras relativas al teatro español. Madrid : V. e H. de J. Ratés, 1930. 164 p.   **BE1463**
A listing of more than 1,800 plays and works about the Spanish theater, including theatrical music and acting. Substantial emphasis on collections.
§ Cotarelo y Mori is also the author of *Catálogo descriptivo de la gran colección de comedias escogidas que consta de cuarenta y ocho volúmenes, impresos de 1652 a 1704* (Madrid : Tipografia de Archivos, 1932), which contains full descriptions of each volume of the *Comedias nuevas escogidos de los mejores ingenios de España* (Madrid, 1652–1704).   Z2694.D7T2

Herrera Navarro, Jerónimo. Catálogo de autores teatrales del siglo XVIII. Madrid : Fundación Universitaria Española, 1993. lvii, 728 p. (Publicaciones de la Fundación Universitaria Española. Monografías, 58).   **BE1464**
A scholarly and substantial biobibliographical dictionary covering more than 800 Spanish and Spanish American dramatists of the 18th century, well-known to obscure. Introductory chapters discuss society, literature, and theater in Spain and the Americas at that time, and the methodology, content, and arrangement of the dictionary. For each dramatist provides dates and biographical information and works listed alphabetically, often with performance information. Manuscript locations in Spain, the British Library, or the Bibliothèque Nationale are noted. For most writers gives additional historical and critical informa-

tion. Inclusions in other printed bibliographies, biographical dictionaries, and histories are noted, and occasionally secondary criticism. Bibliography; name and title indexes.   PQ6111.H47

Hispanic Society of America. Library. Spanish drama of the Golden Age : a catalogue of the manuscript collection at the Hispanic Society of America / comp. by J. M. Regueiro, A. G. Reichenberger. N.Y. : Hispanic Soc. of America, 1984. 2 v. (847 p., [67] p. of plates) : ill.   **BE1465**

In three sections: authors, anonymous works, collections. Provides historical information, bibliographical description, and partial transcription for each manuscript. Bibliography of references for further information. Author/title index.

§ For poetry manuscripts in the same collection, *see:* Antonio Rodriguez Moñino and Maria Brey Mariño, *Catálogo de los manuscritos poéticos castellanos existentes en la Biblioteca de The Hispanic Society of America* (BE1478).   Z2694.D7H62

McCready, Warren T. Bibliografía temática de estudios sobre el teatro español antiguo. [Toronto] : Univ. of Toronto Pr., [1966]. 445 p.   **BE1466**

A classified bibliography listing books and articles published 1850–1950 on Spanish drama from the formative period through the mid-18th century. In two chronological sections, each beginning with listings for general works, followed by sections on individual authors. Author index.   Z2694.D7M15

Oberlin College. Library. Spanish drama collection in the Oberlin College Library : a descriptive catalogue / Paul P. Rogers, ed. Oberlin, Ohio : Oberlin College, 1940. 468 p.   **BE1467**

Covers the period from the last quarter of the 17th century to the year 1924. Includes 7,530 numbered items, arranged alphabetically by author.

————. ————. *Supplementary volume, containing reference lists* (1946. 157 p.). Contents: no. 7531–7644; Anonymous plays; Title list; Composers; Printers; List of theaters.

O'Brien, Robert Alfred. Spanish plays in English translation : an annotated bibliography. N.Y. : publ. for the American Educational Theatre Association by Las Américas Pub. Co., 1963. 70 p.   **BE1468**

Annotations for authors and plays. Includes information for producers on number of acts, number of men and women in cast, royalty requirements, etc.   Z2694.D7O3

Reichenberger, Kurt. Das spanische Drama im Goldenen Zeitalter : ein bibliographisches Handbuch = El teatro Español en los siglos de Oro : inventario de bibliografías / Kurt & Roswitha Reichenberger. Kassel : Edition Reichenberger, 1989. 319 p. (Teatro del Siglo de Oro. Bibliografías y catálogos, 2).   **BE1469**

Topical arrangement of books, essays, articles, with special collections in libraries and archives listed by country. Personal subject, subject, modern author, and library location indexes. PQ6105.A1R45

Thompson, Lawrence Sidney. A bibliography of Spanish plays on microcards. Hamden, Conn. : Shoe String Pr., 1968. 490 p.   **BE1470**

An author (or anonymous title) listing of some 6,000 "Spanish, Catalonian, and Spanish-American plays from the 16th century to the present, all published in microcard editions by Falls City Microcards, Louisville, Kentucky, from 1957 through 1966."—*Introd.* Original texts are in the University of Kentucky Library. Spanish plays predominate.

§ Another library collection, of about 3,000 items, which has been microfilmed is itemized in *Spanish drama of the Golden Age : a catalogue of the Comedia collection in the University of Pennsylvania libraries*, by José M. Regueiro (New Haven, Conn. : Research Publications, 1971).   Z2694.D7T48

University of Toronto. Library. A bibliography of *comedias sueltas* in the University of Toronto library / comp. by J. A. Molinaro, J. H. Parker and Evelyn Rugg. [Toronto] : Univ. of Toronto Pr., 1959. 149 p.   **BE1471**

Lists the *sueltas* in a special collection presented to the university; includes principally 18th-century editions of more than 700 Spanish plays, 1703–1825. Arrangement is alphabetical by title, with indexes by authors, and by publishers and booksellers.   Z2694.D7T66

Wayne State University. The Wayne State University collection of comedias sueltas : a descriptive bibliography / comp. by Howard A. Sullivan and Henry N. Bershas. Detroit : Wayne State Univ. Libraries, 1984. 245 p.   **BE1472**

Supersedes: *A descriptive catalogue of the Spanish comedias sueltas in the Wayne State University Library and the private library of Professor B. B. Ashcom*, by Benjamin Bowles Ashcom (Detroit : Wayne State Univ. Pr., 1965. 103 p.).

Lists more than 1,000 titles and refers to entries in several other library catalogs. Arranged by title with author index.   Z2694.D7A8

Fiction

Brown, Reginald F. La novela española, 1700–1850. Madrid : Dirección General de Archivos y Bibliotecas, Servicio de Publicaciones del Ministerio de Educación Nacional, 1953. 221 p.   **BE1473**

Arranged chronologically with an author index. Extensive bibliographical and historical footnotes serve as annotations.

Ferreras, Juan Ignacio. Catálogo de novelas y novelistas españoles del siglo XIX. Madrid : Ediciones Cátedra, [1979]. 454 p.   **BE1474**

Includes some 2,150 entries for authors and anonymous titles. Dates, a brief identifying statement, and notes on the major work or overall achievement are given for most authors, along with a list of novels.   Z2694.F4F47

Laurenti, Joseph L. Bibliografía de la literatura picaresca : desde sus orígenes hasta el presente = A bibliography of picaresque literature : from its origins to the present. Metuchen, N.J. : Scarecrow, 1973. 262p.   **BE1475**

Repr.: N.Y. : AMS Pr., 1981.

A chronological listing of picaresque novels, giving editions, translations, and citations to secondary material. A preliminary section lists works on the picaresque genre in general.

§ *Suplemento* (N.Y. : AMS Pr., [1981]. 163 p.). Cites publications 1973–early 1978, with some omitted from the basic volume.

Z5917.P5L35

Ricapito, J. V. Bibliografía razonada y anotada de las obras maestras de la picaresca española. [Madrid] : Editorial Castalia, [1980]. 613 p.   **BE1476**

A general section of studies of the Spanish picaresque novel is followed by special sections on "La vida de Lazarillo de Tormes," "Guzmán de Alfarache," and "Vida del Buscón." Annotations are of some length. An appendix lists general work on the picaresque genre. Cross-references; index.   Z2694.P5R53

Poetry

El cancionero del siglo XV, c. 1360–1520 / Brian Dutton ; cancioneros al cuidado de Jineen Krogstad. Salamanca : Universidad de Salamanca, 1990–1991. 7 v. : ill. (Biblioteca española del siglo XV. Serie maior, 1–7).   **BE1477**

Old Spanish and Spanish.

1st ed., 1982, publ. Madison, Wis. : Hispanic Seminary of Medieval Studies.

Contents: v. 1–2, Manuscritos. Barcelona, Ateneo (BA)–Madrid, Biblioteca March (MM); v. 3, Manuscritos. Nueva York, Hispanic Society (NH)–Paris Ecole Superieure des Beaux Arts; 4. Manuscritos.

Roma, Casanatense (RC)–Manuscritos Perdidos, etc. (ZZ); v. 5, Impressos. 1474 (74*LV)–1513 (13*TD); v. 6, Impressos. 1474 (74*LV)–1520 (20*YT); v. 7, Indices.

A monumental bibliography and index to *cancioneros* in manuscripts and early printed editions found in libraries and special collections worldwide. Arranged by repository for manuscripts and publisher for editions. Provides full text of most items and first and last stanzas for works of prohibitive length. For each poem gives information on editions, facsimiles, metric form, relationship to other poems, insertions in the manuscripts, textual faults, etc. The last volume provides indexes by author, dedicatee, composer, names (i.e., historical, geographic, etc.), first line, title, genre, lanugage, key words in refrains, manuscript numbers, and an Indice de la Coleccion de Foulche Debosc, as well as by publishers and titles for early printed editions, all keyed to a master index by entry number.

§ A less substantial but still useful work is: *Bibliografia de los cancioneros castellanos del siglo XV y repertorio de sus generos poeticos*, ed. by Jacqueline Steunou and Lothar Knapp (Paris: Centre National de la Recherche Scientifique, 1975–78. 2 v. [France. Institut de Recherche et d'Histoire des Textes. Documents, etudes et repertoires, 22]). A computer-generated index providing an inventory of manuscripts and printed editions with indexes by author and incipit. A third volume planned to provide indexing by genre has never appeared.
PQ6181.C27

Rodriguez Moñino, Antonio R. Catálogo de los manuscritos poéticos castellanos existentes en la Biblioteca de The Hispanic Society of America (siglos XV, XVI y XVII) / Antonio R. Rodriguez Moñino y Maria Brey Mariño. N.Y. : Hispanic Soc. of America, 1965–66. 3 v. : ill.   **BE1478**
Descriptive notes and contents of the collections are given; v. 3 contains detailed indexes.

§ For drama in the same collections, see: *Spanish drama of the Golden Age : a catalogue of the manuscript collection at the Hispanic Society of America*, comp. by J. M. Regueiro and A. G. Reichenberger (BE1465).

Rodrígucs Moñino also edited the more comprehensive *Manual bibliográfico de cancioneros y romanceros*, coor. por Arthur L-F. Haskins, (Madrid : Ed. Castalia, 1973–78. 4 v.), describing manuscripts in libraries worldwide. Vols. 1–2 cover the 16th century, v. 3 the 17th. Vol. 4 provides indexes to authors and titles, libraries, first lines, and manuscript numbers.
Z6621.N5257

Rokiski Lázaro, Gloria. Bibliografía de la poesía española del siglo XIX (1801–1850). Madrid : Consejo Superior de Investigaciones Científicas, 1988. v. 1. (In progress).   **BE1479**
Contents: v. 1, Obras generales; autores y obras anónimas (A–Ch).

Primarily an author listing of Spanish poetry published in books or journals in Spain, although some Latin American imprints do appear. At least one library location in Spain is given for each item cited; contents are given for collections of poems. Author, subject, and first line index.
Z2694.P7R64

Sweden

Åhlén, Bengt. Svenskt författarlexikon, 1900–1940 : biobibliografisk handbok till Sveriges moderna litteratur .... Stockholm : Svenskt Författarlexikons Förlag, [1942]. 3 v.   **BE1480**
Vols. 1–2 are an alphabetical dictionary with brief biographical sketches and lists of works by and about the authors. Vol. 3 is a title index to works mentioned in v. 1–2.

Supplements have been published, initially for the period 1941–50, then quinquennially for 1951–55, 1956–60, 1961–65, 1966–70, and 1971–75 (Stockholm : Rabén & Sjögren, [1953–81]). The suppl. for 1951–55 includes *Register, 1941–1955*.
Z2630.A15

Brandell, Gunnar. Svensk litteratur 1870–1970 / Gunnar Brandell, Jan Stenkvist. [Stockholm : Aldus, 1974–75. 3 v : ports.   **BE1481**

Contents: v. 1, Från 1870 till första världskriget; v. 2, Från första världskriget till 1950; v. 3, Den nyaste litteraturen.

A useful history of the modern era, providing substantial information on individual authors. Many photographs. Vol. 3 contains a dictionary by author, providing biographical information and primary and secondary bibliographies, which also serves as an index.
PT9368.B68

Gustafson, Alrik. A history of Swedish literature. Minneapolis : Publ. for the American-Scandinavian Foundation by Univ. of Minnesota Pr., [1961]. 708 p. : ill.   **BE1482**
A standard, widely available, narrative history ranging from runic literature to the 1950s. Attempts "to trace literary developments and throw light on literary figures in their relation to a dynamic, ever-changing Swedish society, its institutions, its traditions, its way of life."—*Pref.* Contains an excellent and extensive bibliography, a list of translations, and an index to names, titles, places, and subjects.

§ A more recent, but little more up-to-date, English-language work is *A history of Swedish literature*, by Ingemar Algulin ([Stockholm] : The Swedish Inst., 1989). Briefer and aimed at a general reading public. Lacks a substantive bibliography. A more substantial recent work in Swedish is by Algulin with Bernt Olsson, *Litteraturens historia i Sverige* (Stockholm : Norstedts Forlag, 1987). Very well-illustrated and with many author biographies as marginal entries. Extensive bibliography of general works and works dealing with individual authors. Author-title index. Covers through the 1970s and includes information on films.
PT9263.G8

Hagström, Tore. Svensk litteraturhistorisk bibliografi intill år 1900. Uppsala : Svenska litteratursällskapet ; [Stockholm : distr. by Almqvist & Wiksell], 1964–89. 12 v. (Skrifter utgivna av Svenska litteratursällskapet, 34, H. 1–12).   **BE1483**
A retrospective bibliography, arranged chronologically, covering literary history prior to the beginning of *Svensk litteraturhistorisk bibliografi, 1900–35* (BE1487 *note*). As well as books, chapters in books, and articles, includes dissertations and material in newspapers. H. 12 completes the set and provides a general index, title page, and table of contents.
Z2631.H34

Klemming, G. E. Sveriges, dramatiska litteratur till och med 1875 : bibliografi. Stockholm : P.A. Norstedt, 1863–79. 651 p.   **BE1484**
A commendably thorough bibliography covering Swedish drama and theater in the broadest sense from 1400. Arrangement is chronological throughout. The main section covers opera as well as straight drama, and includes foreign works translated into Swedish. Appendixes cover pantomime and ballet, oratorio, quasi-dramatic works, works in foreign languages printed in Sweden, and foreign works reflecting Swedish characters or history. A supplement is included. Author and title index.

§ Overlapped and continued by: G. Wingren, *Svensk dramatisk litteratur under åren 1840–1913 : bibliografisk forteckning* (Uppsala : F.C. Askerberg, 1914), an author list that also includes foreign works published in Sweden. Introductory essay on 19th-century drama. Title index. Wingren in turn continued by: Uppsala. Universitet. Litteraturvetenskapliga institutionen. Avdelningen för dramaforskning. *Dramatik trykt på svenska 1914–1962* (Uppsala : Utgivaren, 1970). Separate sections for foreign drama published in Sweden and Swedish drama. Title index.
Z2634.D7K5

Ny illustrerad svensk litteraturhistoria. [2. bearbetade uppl.]. Stockholm : Natur och kultur, [1965–67]. 5 v. in 6. : ill.   **BE1485**
1st ed., 1955–58 (5 v.), ed. by E. N. Tigerstedt.
Contents: v. 1, Forntiden, medeltiden, vasatiden; v. 2, Karoliska tiden, frihetstiden, gustavianska tiden; v. 3, Romantiken, liberalismen; v. 4, Attiotal, nittiotal; [v. 5], Fem decennier av nittonhundratalet, by E. H. Linder (2 v.).
The standard illustrated history of Swedish literature, superseding *Illustrerad svensk litteraturhistoria*, by Henrik Schuck and Karl Warburg (3 uppl. 1926–32. 7 v.). Each section is by a specialist, with substantial bibliographies at the end of each volume. Covers through the early 1960s and includes information on films.

It is important to note that v. 5, by Erik H. Linder, although is not formally numbered with the set in the 1965–67 edition, is required to complete it, and is a 4th revised, expanded, and updated version of this volume.

Each section is by a specialist, with substantial bibliographies at the end of each volume. PT9260.N9

Runnquist, Åke. Moderna svenska författare : en samblad översikt över svensk litteratur under fyra årtionden. 2. omarb., utökade uppl. Stockholm : Forum, 1967. 255 p. : ill. **BE1486**
1st ed., 1939.
A dictionary arrangement of brief biographical sketches of modern Swedish writers, with an index of names and titles. PT9368.R8

Svensk litteraturhistorisk bibliografi. no. 1 (1880)– . Issued as separately paged supplements to Samlaren : tidskrift för svensk litteraturhistorisk forskning (no. 1 [1880]– . Uppsala [etc.] : Svenska Litteratursällskapet, 1880–). **BE1487**
An annual classified bibliography that in many libraries will be bound with the parent periodical. Publication has been somewhat erratic in recent years.

Several cumulations have appeared:
Svensk litteraturhistorisk bibliografi 1900–1935, ed. by Jonas Samzelius (Uppsala : Svenska Litteratursällskapet, 1939–50. 522 p. [Skrifter utg. av Svenska Litteratursällskapet, 29: 1–6]). Arranged like the original bibliography.
Svensk litteraturhistorisk bibliografi, 1936–1965 (Uppsala : Svenska Litteratursällskapet, 1986–88. [Skrifter utg. av Svenska Litteratursällskapet, 38: 1–3]). Contents: fasc. 1–3, A–Ossiannilsson. No more published? Arranged alphabetically by author.
Svensk litteraturhistorisk bibliografi : teaterhistoria 1936–1960, utarb. vid Litteraturhistoriska Institutionen i Lund (Lund : Lundensiska Litteratursällskapet, 1966). Entries from the annual bibliographies have been clipped and merged. General works arranged chronologically, entries for individual authors alphabetically.
Svensk litteraturhistorisk bibliografi, 1951–1960 : monografier (Lund : Lundensiska Litteratursällskapet, 1965. 243 *l.*). Another cut-and-paste compilation, arranged alphabetically by author. PT9201

Svenskt litteraturlexikon. 2. utvidgáde uppl. Lund : Gleerup, 1970. 643 p. **BE1488**
1st ed., 1964.
An alphabetical handbook offering biographical sketches of Swedish authors together with information on literary terms. Some articles note additional references. The 1st ed. included an index to titles noted in the biographical entries which was eliminated in the 2nd ed. PT9217.S9

Switzerland

Hayoz, Chantal. Bibliographie analytique des revues littéraires de Suisse romande : 1900–1981. Lausanne : Editions Le Front littéraire, c1984. 191 p. **BE1489**
Covers approximately 150 20th-century literary reviews published in French-speaking Switzerland. For each provides subtitle, dates, frequency, format, place of publication, names of founders, chief contributors, information on supplements, special issues and sponsored series, and an indication of the content and *tendences littéraires* of each publication. Also provides a geographical list of titles by canton and list of special issues devoted to authors. Index of founders. Z2775.H39

Lexikon der Schweizer Literaturen : im Rahmen der 700-Jahr-Feier der Schweizerischen Eidgenossenschaft / hrsg. von Pierre-Olivier Walzer. Basel : Lenos Verlag, c1991. 520 p. : ill. **BE1490**
Covers Swiss literature of all time periods in French, German, Italian, and Romansh. While the bulk of the entries are devoted to individual authors, numerous entries treat genres, schools, institutions, etc. Entries in the language appropriate to the topic, with German used for those with a general scope. For authors, provides places and dates of

birth and death, and biographical information focusing on the writer's career and works. Entries range from a paragraph to several pages. Many quoted passages. Generously illustrated. Bibliographies of references for additional information, translations, and works omitted. Indexes to illustrations, subjects, and names.

§ For directory and biobibliographical information specifically on contemporary Swiss authors, see: *Schriftstellerinnen und Schriftsteller der Gegenwart: Schweiz = Écrivaines et écrivains d'aujourdui: Suisse,* ed. by Grégoire Boulanger ... [et al.] (Aarau: Sauerländer, 1988). PN849.S9W35

Turkey

Mitler, Louis. Ottoman Turkish writers : a bibliographical dictionary of significant figures in pre-Republican Turkish literature. N.Y. : P. Lang, c1988. 203 p. : 1 map. (American university studies. Series XIX, General literature, vol. 15). **BE1491**
Provides biographical sketches, a brief sample of the author's work in translation, and primary and some secondary bibliographies, for about 100 Turkish poets, playwrights, and novelists, as well as writers such as historians, journalists, linguists, and theologians, who wrote from c. 1000 CE to the end of World War I. An introduction gives an overview of the history of Turkish literature, and the volume concludes with a literary glossary, a note on pronunciation and transcription of Turkish, and a selected bibliography of criticism by Western writers.

§ Continued by Mitler's *Contemporary Turkish writers : a critical biobibliography of leading writers in the Turkish Republican Period up to 1980* (Bloomington : Indiana Univ., Research Institute for Inner Asian Studies, 1988). Covers a similar scope of authors and provides the same information, and some photographs, for writers 1923–80. An additional appendix lists major Turkish literary awards.
Both volumes provide maps. PL213.M48

Ukraine

Hol'denberh, Lev Izraïlevych. Ukrains'ka radians'ka literaturna bibliohrafiia. Ky'iv : Nauk. dumka, 1971. 177 p. **BE1492**
A bibliographic essay is followed by a bibliography of literary bibliographies for the period 1918–69 (p. 107–70). Indexed. Z2514.U5H62

Istoriia ukraïns'koï literatury / Holova redkolegiï ĨE. P. Kyryliuk. Ky'iv : "Naukova dumka", 1968–71. 8 v. in 9. : ill. **BE1493**
On leaf preceding t.p.: Akademiia Nauk Ukrains'koï RSR. Instytut Literatury im. T. H. Shevchenka.
A work by many contributors, covering from earliest times to 1967. Bibliographical footnotes, but no general bibliography. Each volume has its own index.
§ *A history of Ukrainian literature, from the 11th to the end of the 19th century* (Littleton, Colo. : Ukrainian Academic Pr., 1975. 681 p.) is a translation of Dmytro Chyzhevs'kyj's *Istoriia ukraïns'koï literatury vid pochatkiv do doby realizmu* (1956); it includes a selected bibliography, p. 619–40. PG3905.I8

Piaseckyj, Oksana. Bibliography of Ukrainian literature in English and French : translations and critical works (1950–1986). Ottawa : Univ. of Ottawa Pr., c1989. 386 p. (University of Ottawa Ukrainian studies, no. 10). **BE1494**
Translations and criticism are arranged alphabetically under author or work covered within four major chronological periods. Includes Ukrainian émigré literature. Author index. Z2514.U5P52

Ukrains'ki pys'mennyky : bio-bibliohrafichnyi slovnyk / red. O. I. Bilets'kyi. Ky'iv : Derzh. Vyd-vo Khudozh. Lit-ry, 1960–65. 5 v. **BE1495**

Biobibliography, with a wide range of early texts, source materials, and criticism for Ukrainian and related literature of the 11th–18th centuries cited in the first volume. Vols. 2–3 contain alphabetical lists of authors of the 19th and early 20th centuries. Vols. 4–5 offer similar lists for 20th-century Ukrainian (Soviet) writers.   Z2514.U5U42

Yugoslavia

Adresar pisaca Jugoslavije / [priredili Gordana Granić ... et al.]. Novi Sad : Savez književnika Jugoslavije : Književna zajednica Novog Sada, 1986. 852 p. **BE1496**

For contemporary Yugoslav literary authors gives name, date of birth, profession, list of publications, and address. Includes authors of translations and scenarios as well as poets, novelists, etc. PG564.A37

Barac, Antun. Jugoslavenska književnost. 3. izd. Zagreb : Matica Hrvatska, 1963. 277 p. **BE1497**

The 1st ed., 1954, was translated by Petar Mijušković and published as *A history of Yugoslav literature* (Beograd, 1955).

Includes Serbian, Croatian and Slovenian literature.

A German translation has appeared as *Geschichte der jugoslavischen Literaturen von den Anfängen bis zur Gegenwart*, translated and ed. by Rolf-Dieter Kluge (Wiesbaden : Harrassowitz, 1977).

§ A more comprehensive history covering to 1941 is Anton Slodnjak's *Geschichte der slowenischen Literatur* (Berlin : De Gruyter, 1958).   PG561.B3

Leksikon pisaca Jugoslavije / [Glavni urednik Zivojin Boškov]. Novi sad : Matica Srpska, 1972–87. v. 1–3. : ill. (In progress). **BE1498**

Contents: v. 1–3, A–Lj.

Biobibliographies of Yugoslav writers, including living persons. Some very extensive lists of works by and about the authors. Portraits.

§ A one-volume dictionary providing not only entries for authors but also information on literary journals, academies, movements, etc. is *Jugoslovenski književni leksikon* (red. Zivojin Boškov ... [et al] ; urednik Zivan Milisavac. 2. dop. izd. Novi Sad : Matica Srpska, 1984).   PG564.L4

Mihailovich, Vasa D. A comprehensive bibliography of Yugoslav literature in English, 1593–1980 / Vasa D. Mihailovich, Mateja Matejic. Columbus, Ohio : Slavica Publishers, c1984. 586 p. **BE1499**

Constitues a 2nd enl. ed. of the same compilers' *Yugoslav literature in English : a bibliography of translations and criticism (1821–1975)* (Cambridge, Mass. : Slavica Publishers, [1976]). More than 5,000 entries. Includes translations of anonymous folk literature as well as works of individual authors. Criticism includes entries in reference works, books, articles, reviews, and dissertations. Indexes of English and Yugoslav titles, periodicals and newspapers, and subjects and names.

————. *First supplement ... 1981–1985* (1988) adds more than 3,000 entries, including some items previously omitted.
  Z2958.L5M53

Srpska književna periodika 1768–1941 : popis i drugi prilozi / Dragiša Vitošević ... [et al.]. Beograd : Institut za književnost i umetnost, 1984. 177 p. **BE1500**

The offshoot of a history of literary periodicals, this bibliography lists 1,336 literary periodicals by date of first publication, with a separate listing of 35 almanacs. Title and geographical indexes.
  PN5355.S4S67

LITERATURES OF AFRICA

General works

Klíma, Vladimír. Black Africa : literature and language / Vladimír Klíma, Karel Frantissek Růžička, Petr Zima. Prague : Academia Publishing House of the Czechoslovak Academy of Sciences, 1976. 310 p. **BE1501**

A historical, social, and literary survey for black Africa of languages and literature in African and European languages. Chapters discuss general topics, particular language groups, languages, and geographical areas, and are further divided into subtopics. The section on African languages includes information on scripts. A bibliography of general references; author index and index of African languages and dialects, with a discussion of African dialects and their classification.

§ African-language literatures are covered in *Literatures in African languages : theoretical issues and sample surveys*, ed. B. W. Andrzejewski ... [et al.] (Cambridge ; N.Y. : Cambridge Univ. Pr., 1985. Publ. in Polish, same year), and *African language literatures : an introduction to the literary history of sub-Saharan Africa*, by Albert S. Gérard (Wash. : Three Continents, 1981). The first has chapters by various scholars, largely devoted to language groups, and one on oral literature, with notes and bibliography. Most also have a useful biographical section. Gérard's work is a chronological and critical study, with footnote references. Maps are included. A complementary work ed. by Gérard is: *European-language writing in sub-Saharan Africa* (Budapest : Akademiai Kiado, 1986. 2 v.). 18 chapters by various scholars cover social and political themes, geographic areas, specific languages, eras, and comparative topics. Substantial footnote references and a bibliographical essay on the study of African literature. Indexed.   PL8010.K54

Bibliography

Berrian, Brenda F. Bibliography of African women writers and journalists : ancient Egypt 1984. Wash. : Three Continents Pr., c1985. 279 p. **BE1502**

Authors and their works are listed in chapters devoted to autobiography, biography, fiction, poetry, drama, miscellaneous prose, journalism, and broadcast literature, with separate chapters for interviews, bibliography, and criticism. Lists of authors by country and genre.
  Z3508.L5B47

East, N. B. African theatre : a checklist of critical materials. N.Y. : Africana, [1970]. 47 p. **BE1503**

Lists books and periodical articles. Sections for bibliographies and general works are followed by regional listings. No index. "The bibliography originally appeared in the Spring, 1969, issue of *Afro-Asian Theatre Bulletin* but has been updated since its initial publication."—*Introd.*   Z3508.T4E3

Howard University. Library. Dictionary catalog of the Arthur B. Spingarn collection of Negro authors. Boston : G.K. Hall, 1970. 2 v. **BE1504**

A photographic reproduction of the catalog cards for this major collection of writings by blacks. In addition to African-born and African-American authors, covers works by writers from the Caribbean, Cuba, Brazil, and those writing in European and vernacular languages. A separate section of music listings is included.

§ For more extensive information on writers from Latin America, see *The Afro-Spanish American author: an annotated bibliography of criticism,* by Richard L. Jackson (N.Y.: Garland, 1980. Suppl. covering the 1980s publ. West Cornwall, Conn.: Locust Hill Pr., 1989). Includes both general criticism and primary and secondary works for individual authors. Lists of authors by country and period. Indexed.
  Z1361.N39H78

Jahn, Janheinz. Bibliography of creative African writing / Janheinz Jahn and Claus Peter Dressler. Nendeln, Liechtenstein : Kraus-Thomson, 1971. 446 p.   **BE1505**

Introd. and "Instructions for use" in English, German, and French.

Supersedes the African section of Jahn's *A bibliography of neo-African literature from Africa, America, and the Caribbean* (N.Y. : Praeger, 1965), which did not include secondary literature, and the supplements by Pál Páricsy.

A substantial and valuable bibliography including "all creative literature which has been written in Agisymba—a term which I picked from Ptolemy to be used for 'Black Africa'—as has been published in the form of books and plays which have been performed on the stage."—*Introd.* Manuscripts ready for publication and plays published in periodicals are included. A section on general works is followed by four geographic regions, each divided into works on the region, anthologies, and works about and by individual authors. For authors before 1900 all works are listed, only belles lettres thereafter. A list of forgeries is included. Maps; indexes to books in African languages, translations, books by countries, and authors.   Z3508.L5J28

Lindfors, Bernth. Black African literature in English : a guide to information sources. Detroit : Gale, [1979]. 482 p. (American literature, English literature, and world literatures in English, 23).   **BE1506**

"Attempts to list all the important works produced on black African literature in English up to the end of 1976."—*Introd.* Pt.1, Genre and topical studies and reference sources, is subdivided by genre and special topic (e.g., language and style, audience, publishing, censorship); pt.2 is concerned with individual authors. Brief annotations. Author, title, subject, and geographical indexes.

———.———. Supplements, 1977–81 (N.Y. : Africana Pub. Co., 1986); 1982–86 (London : Zell, 1989).   Z3508.L5L56

Saint-Andre-Utudjian, Eliane. A bibliography of West African life and literature. Waltham, Mass. : African Studies Assoc., Brandeis Univ., [1977]. 146 p.   **BE1507**

Classed arrangement with author index. Concerned with the literary output of English-speaking West Africa, covering "background studies, bibliographies of creative works in English by West Africans, and a wide range of critical writing by either the African writers themselves or by African as well as non-African critics."—*Foreword.*

Zell, Hans M. A new reader's guide to African literature / [by] Hans Zell, Carol Bundy, and Virginia Coulon. 2nd completely rev. and expanded ed. London : Heinemann ; N.Y. : Africana Publ. Co., [1983]. 553 p. : ill.   **BE1508**

1st ed. 1971 by Zell and Helene Silver had title *A reader's guide to African literature.*

"Lists 3091 works by black African authors south of the Sahara writing in English, French and Portuguese. Reference material, critical works and anthologies (many by non-African authors) are also included, as is a section on children's books by African authors."—*Introd.* There are separate sections for the literature of English-speaking Africa, Francophone Africa, and Lusophone Africa; those sections are further subdivided by region and country. Entries are annotated and sometimes include references from reviews. An annotated list of magazines and a section of biographical sketches of about 100 African writers follow the bibliographical sections; and there are directories of publishers and book dealers and of libraries with African literature collections. Indexed.   PN849.A35Z44

Library catalogs

Harvard University. Library. African history and literatures : classification schedule, classified listing by call number, chronological listing, author and title listing. Cambridge : distr. by Harvard Univ. Pr., 1971. 600 p. (Widener Library shelflist, 34).   **BE1509**

For a note on the series *see* AA115.

Supersedes no.2 of the series (*Africa.* 1965).

Lists "works on all the countries of the African continent and some of the neighboring islands" and includes "primarily works on history, civilization and government, general geography and travel, general social and economic conditions ... , religious affairs, and the various races of these countries."—*Note on the classification.* Almost 20,300 titles listed by class, by date of publication, and by author and title.

About 1960 an addition was made at the end of the classification scheme for literature of Africa in both European and indigenous languages (although it does not provide for Afrikaans literature or literatures in the Semitic and Hamitic languages of northern Africa). Generally speaking, only current materials are put into this new part of the "Afr" class.   Z3509.H37

Encyclopedias

African literatures in the 20th century : a guide. N.Y. : Ungar, c1986. 245 p.   **BE1510**

Reprints articles from *Encyclopedia of world literature in the 20th century* (BE66), with a "few minor revisions and corrections."—*Pref.* Includes the African continent, Malagasy Republic, Mauritius, and Reunion.   PL8010.A43

Biography

Herdeck, Donald E. African authors : a companion to black African writing. Wash. : Black Orpheus Pr., 1973. v.1. : ill. (In progress?).   **BE1511**

Contents: v. 1, 1300–1973. 605 p.

2nd ed., publ. 1974, appears not to differ from 1st ed.

Biographical sketches on nearly 600 authors, mainly of sub-Saharan Africa, from all periods, but primarily 20th century. Lists of writings are included (with place and date of separately published works), and sources of biographical and critical information are sometimes given. Writings in 37 African vernacular languages are represented. Appendixes include four critical essays; a chronological list of authors; lists of authors by genre, by country of origin, by African and European languages employed; a list of major publishers of African literature; and bibliographies.   PL8010.H38

Jahn, Janheinz. Who's who in African literature : biographies, works, commentaries / [by] Janheinz Jahn, Ulla Schild, and Almut Nordmann. Tübingen : Horst Erdmann Verlag, 1972. 406 p. : ill.   **BE1512**

Covers sub-Saharan or black African writers (hence excludes North African and Ethiopian authors) writing in European or African languages. Mainly contemporary belles lettres figures, but includes some writers of earlier periods as well as essayists, critics, and political writers. Provides biographical information and discussion of the person's works, often quoting criticism. Full bibliographical information on works and criticism usually are not given, but a cross-reference to Janheinz Jahn's *Bibliography of creative African writing* (BE1505) is provided instead. Indexes by language and country, and a bibliography of general references.   PL8010.J33

Literature in French

Baratte-Eno Belinga, Thérèse. Bibliographie des auteurs africains de langue française / [by] Thérèse Baratte-Eno Belinga, Jacqueline Chauveau-Rabut, and Mukala Kadima-Nzuji. 4ᵉ éd. [Paris] : Fernand Nathan, [1979]. 245 p.   **BE1513**

1st ed., 1965.

Lists French-language writings by African authors, including numerous publications outside the field of literature. Arranged by country, with subdivisions for bibliographies, anthologies, and individual authors. About 2,300 entries; index of authors.

Blair, Dorothy S. African literature in French : a history of creative writing in French from west and equatorial Africa. Cambridge [Eng.] ; N.Y. : Cambridge Univ. Pr., 1976. 348 p. : ill. **BE1514**

A history covering all varieties of French-African literature for the region specified, including folklore, from its beginning. In broad sections by genre, then largely subdivided into sections on specific authors and their major works. The detailed table of contents makes it easy to locate information, and there is an author/title/subject index. A substantial bibliography is provided. PQ3980.B5

Déjeux, Jean. Dictionnaire des auteurs maghrebins de langue française. Paris : Karthala, [1984]. 400 p. **BE1515**

"Algérie: littérature de fiction et d'essais, histoire, sciences humaines, arts (1880–1982); Maroc: littérature de fiction et d'essais (1920–1982); Tunisie: littérature de fiction et d'essais (1900–1982)."—*t.p.*

Offers brief biographical notes with lists of works and an occasional critical comment. Each country is treated separately. Appendixes cover translations, anthologies, periodicals and special numbers, statistics on the publication of fiction, and pseudonyms. Author index.

Dictionnaire des œuvres littéraires négro-africaines de langue française des origines à 1978 / sous la direction de Ambroise Kom. Sherbrooke, Québec : Editions Naaman ; Paris : Agence de coopération culturelle et technique, [1983]. 671 p. (Collection "Dictionnaires", 1). **BE1516**

A dictionary arranged by title offering signed articles by a large group of collaborators, providing bibliographical information, plot summary, and critical analysis for more than 600 African literary works in French by black authors. Entries range from 500 to 2,000 words. Indexes of authors and genres.

§ Brief plot information is provided by *Guide de litterature africaine (de langue francaise)*, by Patrick Merand and Sewanou Dabla (Paris : L'Harmattan, 1979), a bibliography by author of African literature in French. Includes non-belles lettres literature and a section listing English-language African authors who have been translated into French. Another section by country provides brief information on the literature of each nation and a list of its authors. Title index. PQ3980.A52D53

Rouch, Alain. Littératures nationales d'écriture française : Afrique noire, Caraïbes, océan Indien : histoire littéraire et anthologie / Alain Rouch, Gérard Clavreuil. Paris : Bordas, c1987. 511 p. **BE1517**

A survey and introduction to French literature written in Black Africa, the Indian Ocean, and the Caribbean, valuable for historical, biographical, and bibliographical information, and for selections from the literature. Also provides information on many younger writers. Arranged by country, providing for each a brief history of the country, a history of the literature, then sections on authors arranged alphabetically. For each provides biography, critical analysis, a list of works by the writer, and selected works or passages. Bibliography of general references. Some illustrations; index. PQ3809.R75

Waters, Harold A. Théâtre noir : encyclopédie des pièces écrites en français par des auteurs noirs. Wash. : Three Continents Pr., c1988. 214 p. **BE1518**

Covers "the black francophone playwrights of especially Africa, the Indian Ocean, the Caribbean, and French Guiana."—*Introd.* (*version anglaise*). Also includes the Louisianian Sejour, Dumas *père* and *fils*, and some African and Haitian expatriates. In three main parts: (1) Encyclopédie, which is organized by geographical area and lists and briefly describes each author's published plays; (2) Documentation, classements, thématique, etc., which lists critical works, reference

sources, periodicals, anthologies, library collections, and English translations, and provides a selective thematic index to plays; (3) Indexes of names, geographical areas, titles, and playwrights. Z3508.D7W38

Literature in Portuguese

Moser, Gerald M. A new bibliography of the lusophone literatures of Africa = Nova bibliografia das literaturas africanas de expressão portuguesa / Gerald Moser & Manuel Ferreira. 2nd completely rev. and expanded ed. London ; N.Y. : H. Zell Publishers, 1993. 432 p. (Bibliographical research in African literatures, no. 2). **BE1519**

1st ed., 1983, had title: *Bibliografia das literaturas africanas de expressão portuguesa*.

Covers criticism and primary works for Portuguese literature of Africa published as books and parts of books. References to periodicals are made only for creative works; e.g., individual poems. A section of general works, divided into oral literature, creative works, and history and criticism is followed by five national sections so divided. Annotations note contents. Includes early writings and manuscripts, and translations into Romance languages, English, German, and Russian. A section of brief biographical notes is provided. Author and title indexes. Libraries may want to retain the earlier edition for its references to criticism in journals. Z3874.L5M595

Regional literatures

Coptic literature

The future of Coptic studies / ed. by R. McL. Wilson. Leiden : Brill, 1978. 253 p. (Coptic studies, v.1). **BE1520**

A selection of papers presented at the First International Congress of Coptology (Cairo, 1976), surveying numerous aspects of Coptic studies. Articles in English, German, and French. Extensive references. Indexed. PJ2015.F88

Kammerer, Winifred. A Coptic bibliography / comp. ... with the collaboration of Elinor Mullet Husselman and Louise A. Shier. Ann Arbor : Univ. of Michigan Pr., 1950. 205 p. (University of Michigan. General library publ., no. 7). **BE1521**

Contains more than 3,000 references to Coptic texts and to books and periodicals on Coptic philology, literature, history, religion, and art published in all countries through 1948. Early works are included, although most items are from the late-19th and the 20th centuries. Many entries contain brief descriptive annotations, and some references to important reviews. Arrangement is classified, with an author index. Z7061.K3

Algeria

See also BE1515.

Déjeux, Jean. Bibliographie méthodique et critique de la littérature algérienne de langue française, 1945–1977. Alger : Société Nationale d'Édition et de Diffusion, [1979]. 307 p. **BE1522**

In two parts: works published prior to the July 1, 1962 independence, and those published after. An extensive bibliography, partially annotated, covering Algerian literature in French and criticism about it. Covers novels, short stories, poetry, drama, and some cultural essays, and includes monographs, collections, and works published in periodicals. Each part divided into sections for general works, studies on genres, works by authors, and works about them. Listings for novels annotated with plot information. An appendix covers works published 1900 – 1945. Author and title indexes.

§ Another "Algerian" bibliography by Déjeux, with a different focus, is *Bibliographie de la littérature "algérienne" des Français: bibliographie des romans, récits et recueils de nouvelles écrits par des Français inspirés par l'Algérie 1986–1975, précédée de la bibliographie, des études sur la littérature "algérienne" des Français* (Paris: Éditions du Centre National de la Recherche Scientifique, 1978). Lists more than 1,000 items covering Algeria as portrayed in novels, novelettes, and short stories in French by writers from both Algeria and France. Indexed.   Z3684.L5D44

Dictionnaire des oeuvres algériennes en langue française : essais, romans, nouvelles, contes, récits autobiographiques, théâtre, poésie, récits pour enfants / sous la direction de Christiane Achour. Paris : L'Harmattan, c1990. 383 p.   **BE1523**

A dictionary arranged alphabetically by work covering essays, novels, short story and poetry collections, drama, autobiography, and childrens' literature. For each provides bibliographical information, genre, a plot summary, and analysis. Entries range from a short paragraph to more than one page. Author index.   PQ3988.5.A5D53

Benin

Huannou, Adrien. La littérature béninoise de langue française : des origines à nos jours. Paris : A.C.C.T. : Karthala, c1984. 327 p., [4] p. of plates : ill.   **BE1524**

Title on spine: La littérature béninoise.

A substantial survey history covering the literature from the mid-19th century to 1983 with considerable attention to social and political issues. Numerous footnote references and a bibliography are provided. A comparative chronology charts literary and other events in Benin and in Africa. Index.   PQ3988.5.B4H83

Cameroon

Baratte-Eno Belinga, Thérèse. Écrivains, cinéastes et artistes camerounais : bio-bibliographie. Yaoundé, Cameroun : CEPER, 1978. 217 p.   **BE1525**

A dictionary by name providing biographical information, a list of works, performances, exhibits, etc., and references to criticism for writers, artists, performers of various kinds, and filmmakers. More than 60% of the entries are devoted to creative authors, critics, and journalists. A bibliography of general references is included.   CT2556.B37

Zimmer, Wolfgang. Répertoire du théâtre camerounais. Paris : Harmattan, 1986. 119 p. : ill.   **BE1526**

An author listing of some 700 dramatic works of all kinds by about 260 authors. Attempts to be exhaustive, and includes published plays, works in typescript or manuscript, and plays known only from records of performance or mention in the media. Works in French predominate but other Cameroonian languages and English are included. Title index.   PN2989.15.Z55

Côte d'Ivoire

Bonneau, Richard. Écrivains, cinéastes et artistes ivoiriens : aperçu bio-bibliographique. Abidjan : Nouvelles éditions africaines, c1973. 175 p.   **BE1527**

A dictionary providing biography, a picture, a list of works or other accomplishments, and critical references for authors, performers, and filmmakers, although entries for authors predominate. A bibliography of general references is included. Name and title index.   NX589.6.I83B66

Ghana

Ghanaian literatures / ed. by Richard K. Priebe. N.Y. : Greenwood, 1988. 300 p. : map. (Contributions in Afro-American and African studies, no. 120).   **BE1528**

A historical introduction to Ghanaian literature, both in English and native languages, and including oral and popular literatures. Consists of 18 chapters on different topics by various scholars, divided into groups by genre. Much attention is given to individual authors and their works. The introduction provides a useful overview of the literature. Notes or references are provided for each chapter, and a bibliography of general references is included. Indexed.   PL8021.G5G43

Morocco

See also BE1515.

Dugas, Guy. Bibliographie de la littérature "marocaine" des Français, 1875–1983. Paris : Éditions du Centre national de la recherche scientifique, 1986. 121 p. : map. (Cahiers du C.R.E.S.M., 18).   **BE1529**

At head of title: Centre de Recherches et d'Études sur les Sociétés Méditerranéennes.

A bibliography covering French literature, written both in France and in Morocco, inspired by Moroccan settings, themes, and topics. An introduction discusses this literature in both its literary and social/historical contexts. The bibliography lists general works, then is divided into two sections covering travel literature and belles lettres, the latter including novels, short stories, and anthologies, Entries are in chronological order. Author index.   Z2174.P795D82

Nigeria

Baldwin, Claudia. Nigerian literature : a bibliography of criticism, 1952–1976. Boston : G.K. Hall, [1980]. 147 p.   **BE1530**

About 1,500 entries; general criticism is followed by sections for individual authors. Indexes of critics and of titles.   PR9387.B34

Lindfors, Bernth. A bibliography of literary contributions to Nigerian periodicals, 1946–1972. [Ibadan, Nigeria] : Ibadan Univ. Pr., 1975. 231 p.   **BE1531**

A classified bibliography covering primary and secondary works in English published in Nigerian periodicals. Works listed include poetry, fiction, and drama, the latter comprising plays, production reviews, criticism on theater, and radio, television, and film. Commentary includes literary criticism, interviews, and book reviews for titles listed in Janheinz Jahn and Claus P. Dressler, *Bibliography of creative African writing* (BE1505). A miscellaneous section covers conferences and essays on diverse subjects. Author/title index.   Z3597.L55

Senegal

Blair, Dorothy S. Senegalese literature : a critical history. Boston : Twayne, c1984. 176 p. : map. (Twayne's world authors series, TWAS 696).   **BE1532**

An introductory history in four chapters providing basic historical and social background material and a chronological discussion of the literature of Senegal, virtually all in French. The introduction provides a handy brief overview; chronologies of history and of the literature are provided. Notes and a substantial selective bibliography; analytical index.   PQ3988.5.S38B55

South Africa

Companion to South African English literature / comp. by David Adey … [et al.]. Craighall [South Africa] : Ad. Donker, 1986. 220 p. : ports. **BE1533**

A dictionary arrangement of mostly biographical entries that also provide general articles for history, African-language literature, exploration, etc. Treats South Africans by birth or residence, as well as travellers who wrote significantly on South Africa. Short entries, no secondary bibliography. Addendum for writers about whom few details are known. PR9350.2.C66

Dubbeld, Catherine E. Reflecting apartheid : South African short stories in English with socio-political themes, 1960–1987 : a select and annotated bibliography. Johannesburg : South African Inst. of International Affairs, 1990. 337 p. **BE1534**

A chronologically arranged bibliography listing and describing the contents of anthologies of short stories that "will together provide a significant fictional account of the experience of socio-political life under apartheid in South Africa" (*Pref.*) during the years indicated. For background, provides a chronology of political and social events, 1948–59 and a historical and literary overview of the apartheid era. The main part of the bibliography is by year, beginning with a list of events, then anthologies arranged by author. For each, provides bibliographical information, contents, plot summaries, references to other anthologies in which stories also appear, and a list of subject descriptors. Author, title, and subject indexes. Z3608.L5D8

Gorman, G. E. The South African novel in English since 1950 : an information and resource guide. Boston : G.K. Hall, [1978]. 238 p. **BE1535**

The work's approach is "functional" and aims "to assist in the development of that bibliographical expertise which will allow one to answer the basic 'who, what, where' questions arising in the study and provision of South African literary materials."—*Introd.* Pt.1 covers "the literature itself and problems of definition, content and control; the second part, which arises out of this background discussion, presents a critical bibliographical survey of the various types of resource materials available to the investigator or collector of South African fiction." PR9362.5.G6

Senekal, Jan. Bronne by die studie van Afrikaanse prosawerke / Jan Senekal en Elmarie Engelbrecht. Johannesburg : Perskor, 1984. 220 p. **BE1536**

A bibliography by author of Afrikaans prose monographs, largely limited to fiction, providing references to criticism and reviews of particular works. Includes material in books, periodicals, and newspapers. Bibliography of monographs cited. No index, although a list of titles is included without page or author references. PT6525

Strange Library of Africana. Southern African material in anthologies of English literature in the Strange Library of Africana : an index / comp. by Carol Leigh. Johannesburg : City of Johannesburg Public Library, 1988. 330 p. **BE1537**

Provides indexes by author, title, and subject to stories, poems, and essays from approximately 300 anthologies, most of which were published in South Africa. Z965.S77J64

University of South Africa. Library. Subject Reference Dept. A pilot bibliography of South African English literature (from the beginnings to 1971) / comp. by Subject Reference Department of the Library, University of South Africa ; ed. by D. R. Beeton. Pretoria : Univ. of South Africa, c1976. 104 p. **BE1538**

A selective bibliography of primary and secondary materials, covering authors who published at least one volume. The first section lists general works on the literature and on genres, including a list of literary journals, followed by a section on individual authors listing works by and about the writer. For primary works does not, for the most part, list individual works published in periodicals—i.e., poems or short stories. Materials translated from Afrikaans and Bantu are not included. Indexes by chronology and genre. Z3608.L5S68

Tunisia

See also BE1515.

Dugas, Guy. Bibliographie de la littérature "tunisienne" des Français, 1881–1980. Paris : Éds. du Centre national de la recherche scientifique, 1981. 86 p. (Cahiers du C.R.E.S.M., 13). **BE1539**

At head of title: Centre de Recherches et d'Études sur les Sociétés Méditerranéennes.

Includes a section of studies of the literature as well as editions of works of belles lettres and books of travel. Author index. Z2174.P795D83

Zaïre

Kadima-Nzuji Mukala. Bibliographie litteraire de la Republique du Zaïre, 1931–1972. [Lubumbashi] : Centre d'étude des littératures romanes d'inspiration africaine, Université nationale du Zaïre, Campus de Lubumbashi, 1973. 60 p. **BE1540**

A classified bibliography covering French belles lettres literature of Zaïre. Limited to fiction, poetry, drama, and literary essays. The first section lists anthologies. The second is an annotated list of works by author, followed by sections of literary essays and criticism about and by Zaïrian authors. List of works consulted; name index. Z3634.L5K3

Zimbabwe

Pichanick, J. Rhodesian literature in English : a bibliography (1890 1974/5) / comp. by J. Pichanick, A. J. Chennells, and L. B. Rix. Gwelo : Mambo Pr., 1977. 249 p. (Zambeziana, v. 2). **BE1541**

A comprehensive bibliography of Zimbabwean literature in English, 1890 to the mid-1970s, covering novels, short stories, poetry, and drama, published monographically, in anthologies, and in periodicals. Includes material published in the country, works largely set there, and works by writers considered to be native by birth or by virtue of long association. In sections by genre. No index. Z3578.P5

LITERATURES OF ASIA

Anderson, George Lincoln. Asian literature in English : a guide to information sources. Detroit : Gale, [1981]. 336 p. (American literature, English literature, and world literatures in English, v. 31). **BE1542**

A bibliography listing translations into English and major scholarship and criticism in English on the literatures of Asia. India is omitted but is covered in another volume in the series, *Indian literature in English, 1827–1979*, by Amritjit Singh, Rajiva Verma, and Irene M. Joshi (BE1567). Sections are devoted to the Far East, China, Japan, Korea, Southeast Asia, Burma, Cambodia, Indonesia, Laos, Malaysia and Singapore, Thailand, Vietnam, Mongolia, Tibet, and Turkic and other literatures. Some entries have brief annotations. Index.

§ A bibliography of translations narrower in geographical focus but less selective is : *Southeast Asian literatures in translation : a preliminary bibliography*, by Philip N. Jenner (Honolulu : Univ. Pr. of

Hawaii, 1973). Covers Burma, Cambodia, Champa, Indonesia, Laos, Malaysia and Singapore, Philippines, Thailand, Vietnam, and regional and general works. Includes information on inscriptions and chronicles as well as belles lettres.   Z3001.A655

A guide to Oriental classics / prep. by the staff of the Committee on Oriental Studies, Columbia University ; ed. by Wm. Theodore De Bary and Ainslie T. Embree. 3rd ed. / ed. by Amy Vladeck Heinrich. N.Y. : Columbia Univ. Pr., 1989. 324 p.   **BE1543**

    1st ed., 1964; 2nd ed., 1975.

    "Compiled as an aid to students and teachers taking up for the first time the major works of Oriental literature and thought. It is designed especially for general education, which emphasizes a careful reading of single whole works and discussion of them in a group."— *Introd. to 2nd ed.* Sections for the Islamic, Indian, Chinese, and Japanese traditions. For each of the classics considered, provides lists of English translations, selected secondary readings in English, and a list of topics for discussion; brief evaluative notes accompany most citations.   Z7046.C65

Lang, David Marshall. A guide to Eastern literatures. London : Weidenfeld and Nicolson, [1971]. 501 p.   **BE1544**

    Specialists have contributed chapters on Arabic, Jewish, Persian, Turkish, Armenian and Georgian, Ethiopic, Indian and Pakistani, Sinhalese, Indonesian and Malaysian, Chinese, Tibetan, Mongolian, Korean, Burmese, and Japanese literatures. Most chapters include sections on the historical background, main trends in the literature, individual writers, and a bibliography. Indexed.   PJ307.L3

Regional literatures

Arabic language

Altoma, Salih J. Modern Arabic literature : a bibliography of articles, books, dissertations, and translations in English. Bloomington : Indiana Univ., 1975. 73 p. (Asian Studies Research Institute. Occasional papers, no. 3).   **BE1545**

    A guide to materials in English. Classed listing with author index; dissertations appear in a separate listing without subject approach. About 850 items.   Z7052.A58

The Cambridge history of Arabic literature. Cambridge ; N.Y. : Cambridge Univ. Pr., 1983–1992. [v. 1–4]. (In progress).   **BE1546**

    Contents: (volumes are not numbered) : Arabic literature to the end of the Umayyad period, ed. by A. F. L. Beeston ... [et al.] (1983); Religion, learning, and science in the Abbasid period, ed. M.J.L. Young ... [et al.] (1990); Abbasid belles-lettres, ed. Julia Ashtiany (1990); Modern Arabic literature, ed. M.M. Badawī (1992).

    Designed to replace Reynold A. Nicholson's *The literary history of the Arabs* (first publ. 1907), providing more extensive coverage and offering a contemporary survey of scholarship. Despite somewhat mixed reviews sure to become the standard English-language work. Volumes consist of chapters by a roster of international scholars. References, bibliographies, and index in each volume.

    § For a more concise survey, *see* : Muhammad M. Badawī, *A short history of modern Arabic literature* (Oxford : Clarendon Press ; N.Y. : Oxford Univ. Pr., 1993) and two volumes by Badawī covering drama : *Early Arabic drama* (Cambridge ; N.Y. : Cambridge Univ. Pr., 1988) and *Modern Arabic drama in Egypt* (Cambridge ; N.Y. : Cambridge Univ. Pr., 1987).

Chauvin, Victor. Bibliographie des ouvrages arabes ou relatifs aux arabes publiés dans l'Europe chrétienne de 1810 à 1885. Liége : Vaillant-Carmanne, 1892–1922. 12 pts.   **BE1547**

    Contents: (1) Préface. Table de Schnurrer. Les proverbes; (2) Kalilah; (3) Louqmâne et les fabulistes. Barlaam. 'Antar et les romans de chevalerie; (4–7) Les mille et une nuits; (8) Syntipas; (9) Pierre Al-

phonse. Secundus. Recueils orientaux. Tables de Henning et de Mardrus. Contes occidentaux. Les maqâmes; (10) Le Coran et la tradition; (11) Mahomet; (12) Le Mahométisme.

    No general index but some parts have alphabetical or subject indexes, some are arranged alphabetically.   Z7052.C511

Modern Arabic literature / comp. and ed. by Roger Allen. N.Y. : Ungar, 1987. 370 p.   **BE1548**

    A collection of previously published criticism on individual authors typical of other Ungar volumes and particularly useful in that much of the material has been translated from the Arabic by the editor. Covers approximately 70 writers. A list of works discussed, by author, is provided. Index to critics.

Sezgin, Fuat. Geschichte des arabischen Schrifttums. Leiden : Brill, 1967–84. v. 1–9. (In progress).   **BE1549**

    Contents: Bd. 1, Qur Anwissenschaften, Had it Geschichte, Figh, Dogmatik, Mystik, bis ca.430 H.; Bd. 2, Poesie bis ca.430 H.; Bd. 3, Medizin, Pharmazie, Zoologie, Tierheilkunde bis ca.430 H.; Bd. 4, Alchimie, Chemie, Botanik, Agrikultur bis ca.430 H.; Bd. 5, Mathematik bis ca.430 H; Bd. 6, Astronomie bis ca.430 H; Bd. 7, Astrologie, Meteorologie und Verwandtes bis ca.430 H; Bd. 8, Lexikographie bis 430 H; Bd. 9, Grammatik bis ca.430 H.

    A massive work essential for Arabists consisting principally of thematically arranged bibliographies of primary and secondary sources, primarily devoted to individual authors, with textual introductions for sections and for each author. Includes manuscripts as well as published works.

    § Will supersede the earlier standard reference, Carl Brockelmann's *Geschichte der arabischen Literatur* (2. den Supplementbände angepasste Aufl. Leiden : Brill, 1943–49. 2 v.) and its three-volume supplement. Indexes in each volume.   Z7052.S44

Asia, Southeast

South-East Asia : languages and literatures : a select guide / ed. by Patricia Herbert & Anthony Milner. Honolulu : Univ. of Hawaii Pr., c1989. 182 p. : ill.   **BE1550**

    "This Guide was conceived by members of the South-East Asia Library Group ... who felt there was a need for a concise introduction to the history, major languages, scripts, dating systems, manuscripts, printing and publishing histories, and literary genres of South-East Asia."—*Pref.* Chapters, which cover Burma, Thailand, Cambodia, Laos, Vietnam, Malaysia, Indonesia, Philippines, and overseas Chinese, include a historical overview, short essays on the matters mentioned above, and a basic bibliography.   PL3501.S66

Syriac

Wright, William. A short history of Syriac literature. London : Black, 1894. 296 p.   **BE1551**

    Repr. : Folcroft, Pa. : Folcroft Libr. Eds., 1978.

    A brief history with bibliographic footnotes and index.

    PJ5601.W7

China

Davidson, Martha. A list of published translations from Chinese into English, French and German ... . (Tentative edition). Ann Arbor, Mich. : J.W. Edwards for the Amer. Council of Learned Societies, [1952–57]. 2 v.   **BE1552**

    Contents: pt. 1, Literature, exclusive of poetry; pt. 2, Poetry. No more published.

    Arranged by dynasty then in sections for known authors, unidentified authors, and anonymous works. No index.

§ Additional information on translations of poetry into English is provided by *A research guide to English translation of Chinese verse (Han dynasty to T'ang dynasty)*, by Kai-chee Wong, Pung Ho, and Shu-leung Dang (Hong Kong : Chinese Univ. Pr., 1977). Indexes by title and first line of translation, poets in Chinese, poets in English, and translator. More extensive listings for T'ang poets are found in *25 T'ang poets: index to English translations*, by Sydney S. K. Fung and S. T. Lai (Hong Kong : Chinese Univ. Pr., 1984). Arranged by poet and first line. Appendixes list uncertain attributions, wrong attributions, prose and rhymed prose, and unidentified translations. Indexes by first line and translator. Z7059.D38

Gibbs, Donald A. A bibliography of studies and translations of modern Chinese literature, 1918–1942 / Donald A. Gibbs, Yun-chen Li. Cambridge, Mass. : East Asian Research Center, Harvard Univ.; distr. by Harvard Univ. Pr., 1975. 239 p. (Harvard East Asian monographs, 61). **BE1553**

"The subject of this bibliography is the literature of China written during the pivotal era when China sought to convert her institutions from those of an Imperialist China to those of a Socialist China, a highly self-conscious era when literature was written with a consistently close social and political relevance." —*Introd.* In four main sections covering sources, general studies of modern Chinese literature by genre, studies and translations of individual authors, and unidentified authors. Appendixes list conference papers, unpublished works, and Chinese sources. Name index. Z3108.L5G52

The Indiana companion to traditional Chinese literature / William H. Nienhauser, Jr., ed. and comp.; Charles Hartman, assoc. ed. for poetry, Y. W. Ma, assoc. ed. for fiction, Stephen H. West, assoc. ed. for drama. Bloomington : Indiana Univ. Pr., c1986. 1050 p. **BE1554**

An excellent and essential reference compiled by approximately 170 scholars worldwide, covering Chinese literature to 1911. The bulk of the work consists of more than 500 signed entries, some of considerable length, covering authors, works, genres, schools, etc. For each, a bibliography of editions, translations, and criticism is provided. By way of introduction, nearly 200 pages are devoted to ten lengthy signed essays on genres including literary criticism, religiously based literatures, popular literature, and women's literature. A general bibliography is provided, and a chronology of dynasties and historical eras. Name, title, and subject indexes. Z3108.L5I53

Legge, James. Chinese classics : with a translation, critical and exegetical notes, prolegomena and copious indexes. 2nd ed. rev. Oxford : Clarendon Pr., 1893–95. 5 v. in 8. : maps. **BE1555**

Repr.: Hong Kong : Hong Kong Univ. Pr., 1960. 5 v.

Vols. 1–2, 2nd ed., rev., 1893–95, printed at the Clarendon Press, Oxford; v. 3–5—printed at the London Missionary Society's Printing Office, Hong Kong—are a reissue of the older edition with new title page and imprint: London : H. Frowde, [n.d.].

Contents: v. 1, Confucian analects, the Great learning, and the Doctrine of the mean; v. 2, The works of Mencius; v. 3, The Shoo-king, or the Book of historical documents: pt. 1, The first parts of the Shoo-king, or the Books of T'ang, the Books of Yu, the Books of Hea, the Books of Shang, and the Prolegomena; pt. 2, The fifth part of the Shoo-king, or the Books of Chow, and the indexes; v. 4, the She-king, or the Book of poetry: pt. 1, The first part of the She-king, or the Lessons from the states, and the Prolegomena; pt. 2, The second, third, and fourth parts of the She-king, or the Minor odes of the kingdom, the Greater odes of the kingdom, the Sacrificial odes and praise-songs, and the indexes; v. 5, The Ch'un ts'ew, with the Tso chuen: pt. 1, Dukes Yin, Hwan, Chwang, Min, He, Wan, Seuen, and Ch'ing, and the Prolegomena; pt. 2, Dukes Seang, Ch'aou, Ting, and Gae, with Tso's appendix, and the indexes.

The volumes originally planned were "to embrace all the books in 'The thirteen king'," but v. 6–7 were never published. English translations of the *Yih king* and the *Li ki* appeared, respectively, as v. 16 and v. 27–28 of the series *Sacred books of the East* (BC92). A translation of the *Hsiao king* appeared in v. 3 of the same series. PL2948.L5

Li, Tien-Yi. Chinese fiction : a bibliography of books and articles in Chinese and English. New Haven, Conn. : Far Eastern Publ., Yale Univ., 1968. 356 p. **BE1556**

A selective listing "of books and articles in Chinese and English that have been published in the field of Chinese fiction over the past few decades." —*Pref.* Chinese contributions predominate. There is a section for general studies and reference works, and important English translations of Chinese works of fiction are noted. In two main divisions for traditional and contemporary fiction, then by author. Appendixes list periodicals and newspapers, publishers, and pen names. Name index. Z3108.L5L4

Lynn, Richard John. Guide to Chinese poetry and drama. 2nd ed. Boston : G. K. Hall, 1984. 200 p. (Oriental monograph series, 24). **BE1557**

Rev. ed. of: Roger B. Bailey, *Guide to Chinese poetry and drama*, 1973.

A classed bibliography of Western-language studies (monographs and dissertations) on various aspects of Chinese literature, including studies of individual literary figures. Indexed. Z3118.L5L96

Paper, Jordan D. Guide to Chinese prose. 2nd ed. Boston : G. K. Hall, 1984. 149 p. **BE1558**

1st ed., 1973.

Companion volume with Richard John Lynn's *Guide to Chinese poetry and drama* (BE1557) in a series that attempts to fill "the need for intelligent, responsible guides for the nonspecialist to critical studies and translations available in English." —*Series pref.* Entries are listed in classified arrangements with historical and analytic annotations. Coverage of drama is limited to the modern period. Both volumes have introductory essays and name and title indexes. For other volumes in the series, *see* under Japanese literature, below. Z3108.L5P34

Schyns, Joseph. 1500 modern Chinese novels and plays. Peiping : Catholic Univ. Pr., 1948. 484 p. **BE1559**

Subtitle: Present day fiction and drama in China by Su Hsueh-Lin; Short biographies of authors by Chao Yen-Sheng.

A study of contemporary Chinese literature; gives reviews in English of 1,500 novels and plays and about 200 biographies. Names and titles are given in romanized form and in Chinese characters. PL2934.S4

A selective guide to Chinese literature, 1900–1949. Leiden ; N.Y. : Brill, 1988–90. v. 1–4. (In progress). **BE1560**

"This publication is the result of the European Science Foundation project on modern Chinese literature directed by N.G.D. Malmqvist" —*t.p. verso.*

Contents: v. 1, The novel, ed. Milena Doleželová-Velingerová; v. 2, The short story, ed. Zbigniew Slupski; v. 3, The poem, ed. Lloyd Haft; v. 4, The drama, ed. Bernd Eberstein.

A guide prepared by an international group of more than 100 scholars. Each volume has a general introduction and bibliography followed by signed entries for individual works arranged by author providing bibliographical information for first editions, a substantial summary and analysis, and references to criticism and translations. Indexes to authors, journals, publishers, and literary series.

Tsai, Meishi. Contemporary Chinese novels and short stories, 1949–1974 : an annotated bibliography. Cambridge, Mass. : Council on East Asian Studies, Harvard Univ.; distr. by Harvard Univ. Pr., 1979. 408 p. (Harvard East Asia monographs, 78). **BE1561**

An author listing (arranged alphabetically according to Wade-Giles romanization), with titles given in romanization and in Chinese characters, followed by an English translation of the title. Includes publications in book form and in periodicals; English translations of the works are noted. "The rationale for choosing which stories and novels to annotate … is one of informing the reader of the themes and sociopolitical realities reflected in the work." —*Pref.* Biographical notes on the authors are frequently given, as are annotations that include plot summaries. Indexes of titles and of selected topics. Z3108.L5T78

Yang, Winston L. Y. Classical Chinese fiction : a guide to its study and appreciation : essays and bibliographies / Winston L. Y. Yang, Peter Li, Nathan K. Mao. Boston : G. K. Hall, [1978]. 302 p.   **BE1562**

A guide for the student, teacher, scholar, or general reader. "The term 'classical Chinese fiction' is used to refer to traditional or pre-modern works ranging from the fictional writings of the Chou and the Han periods to novels of the late Ch'ing period. The emphasis, however, is on the major novels and short stories of the Ming and Ch'ing dynasties."—*Pref.* In two parts: (1) Essays (providing an introduction to the major classical Chinese novels and short stories) and (2) Bibliographies (which offer additional guidance through the annotated listings of bibliographies and critical studies). The bibliographies are limited to titles in English, French, and German. Glossary; index.

§ A parallel volume by the same authors covering 20th-century literature since 1917 is : *Modern Chinese fiction : a guide to its study and appreciation : essays and bibliographies*, (Boston: G.K. Hall, 1981). Follows the same format but more limited to material in English. Essays and bibliographies are divided into sections covering 1917–49 and Chinese Communist fiction since 1949. Both volumes provide chronologies and are indexed.

More selective, but providing comparable information on six classic novels is : *The Chinese classic novels : an annotated bibliography of chiefly English-language studies*, by Margaret Berry (N.Y. : Garland, 1988). A general introduction and bibliography of general sources are included.   Z3108.L5Y29

India

Central Institute of English and Foreign Languages, Hyderabad. A bibliography of Indian English. Hyderabad, 1972. 219 p., 23 p. (2 v. in 1).   **BE1563**

Contents: pt. 1, Indian English literature; pt. 2, Indian English.

Lists publications from 1827 to date and includes literary works as well as critical writings and works on Indian English as a language.   Z3208.L5C36

Emeneau, Murray Barnson. A union list of printed Indic texts and translations in American libraries. New Haven, Conn. : Amer. Oriental Soc., 1935. 540 p. (American Oriental series, v. 7).   **BE1564**

Repr.: N.Y. : Kraus, 1967.

"List includes all books in Sanskrit, Pali, Prakrit, and Apabhraṁśa and most of the books in the older stages of the vernaculars … Translations of the texts are also included."—*Introd.* Does not include secondary works. Locates copies in 15 American libraries.   Z7049.I3E5

Encyclopaedia of Indian literature / chief ed., Amaresh Datta. New Delhi : Sahitya Akademi, c1987–1992. v. 1–5. (In progress).   **BE1565**

Contents: v. 1–5, A–Zorgot. Vol. 6 to be an index volume.

v. 4–5, Monan Lal, chief ed.

Designed "to give a fairly clear and comprehensive idea about the growth and development of Indian literature in 22 languages."—*Editorial.* Signed articles in alphabetical order discuss authors, epic works, styles, influences and terms, with bibliographic references. A review in *Choice* 31 (Oct. 1993): 265, judges this to be "scholarly and authoritative" and "a great contribution to scholarship." A 6th volume, index and cross-references, is planned.

§ Another new multivolume work is *International encyclopaedia of Indian literature*, rev. and enl. ed., by Gaṅgā Rām Garg (Delhi : Mittal Publ., 1987–1991. v. 1, pts. 1–2; v. 2–5, 7–8. [In progress]). A revision of the author's *Encyclopaedia of Indian literature* (Delhi : Mittal, 1982) and *Encyclopaedia of world Hindi literature* (New Delhi : Concept, 1986). Arranged by language. Short, for the most part biographical articles. Criticized and compared unfavorably with Datta in *Choice* 27 (Nov. 1989): 460.   PK2902.E53

A history of Indian literature / ed. by Jan Gonda. Wiesbaden : O. Harrassowitz, 1973–87. v. 1–10². (In progress).   **BE1566**

Contents: v. 1, Veda and Upanishads; v. 2, Epics and Sanskrit religious literature; v. 3, Classical Sanskrit literature; v. 4–6, Scientific and technical literature; v. 7–9, Modern Indo-Aryan literature; v. 10, Dravidian literatures.

A collaborative work of more than 40 scholars. Volumes are made up of individual fascicles, each a monograph devoted to a particular aspect of Indian literature or literature of a specific language; v. 9, for example, covers Sindhi, Assamese, Bengali, Gujerati, Oriya, Marathi, and Maithili literatures. Very valuable for comprehensive coverage. Extensive references. In many libraries fascicles will be separately cataloged.

§ An older work still useful for information on some literatures not well covered elsewhere is *Contemporary Indian literature : a symposium*, issued by the Sahitya Akademi (2nd ed., rev. and enl. New Delhi, 1959). Chapters cover 16 literatures and provide brief bibliographies.

Singh, Amritjit. Indian literature in English, 1827–1979 : a guide to information sources / Amritjit Singh, Rajiva Verma, and Irene M. Joshi. Detroit : Gale, [1981]. 631 p. (American literature, English literature, and world literatures in English information guide ser., v. 36).   **BE1567**

A bibliography of creative writing in English by Indian authors, including works originally written in Indian languages and translated into English by their authors (i.e., Indo-Anglian or Indo-English literature as opposed to Anglo-Indian literature—works with an Indian setting written by Englishmen who lived in India). General sections are followed by sections for individual authors grouped by literary form. Indexed.

§ An older, more specialized work still useful for its introductory material and for the annotations describing plots is : *Indian fiction in English : an annotated bibliography*, by Dorothy Mary Spencer (Philadelphia : Univ. of Pennsylvania Pr., 1960). Lists some 200 works of fiction and about 45 autobiographies, written by Indians in English or translated into English.   Z3208.L5S56

Singh, Bhupal. Survey of Anglo-Indian fiction. Oxford : Univ. Pr., 1934. 344 p.   **BE1568**

Repr.: London : Curzon Pr.; Totowa, N.J. : Rowman and Littlefield, 1974.

A survey and criticism of the Anglo-Indian novel is followed by a bibliography in three parts: (1) Anglo-Indian novels; (2) criticism and biography; and (3) articles and reviews.

§ A useful bibliography on the portrayal of India in Indo-English and Anglo-Indian literature is: *India in English fiction, 1800–1970*, by Brijen K. Gupta (Metuchen, N.J. : Scarecrow, 1973). An author list of more than 2,000 works including fiction both originally written in and translated into English, by English and Indian authors. Indexes to authors, titles, and themes, and brief list of sources.   PR830.A5S5

Srinivasa Iyengar, K. R. Indian writing in English. 3rd ed. / with a postscript chapter on the seventies and after, in collaboration with Prema Nandakumar. New Delhi : Sterling Publ., 1983. 838 p.   **BE1569**

1st ed., 1962.

The standard work on the subject by the scholar who pioneered in the field. A review of the 1st ed. in *Modern language review* 58 (July 1963): 424–5, called it a "comprehensive and masterly survey" and said that "English readers must be grateful for this full, rich, stimulating study of a fascinating subject." Most chapters focus on individual authors with several on genres and there are extensive quoted passages. The 3rd ed. updates for the 1970s and early 1980s by an additional chapter coauthored with Prema Nandakumar. Bibliography and index.

§ A more recent and compact introductory survey is *Indian literature in English*, by William Walsh (London ; N.Y. : Longman, 1990). A historical introduction is followed by chapters discussing authors of fiction and poetry, and one on India in English fiction. A chronology and biobibliographical dictionary of authors are included. Select bibliography. Index.   PR9484.3.S7

Who's who of Indian writers, 1983 / comp. and ed. by S. Balu Rao. New Delhi : Sahitya Akademi, 1983. 731 p. **BE1570**

"Contains biographical and bibliographical information about nearly 6,000 living writers in 22 Indian languages including English."—*Half t.p. verso.*

An earlier edition was published 1961; the 1983 edition is essentially a new work, not a revision. Based mainly on information supplied by the biographees; limited to literary authors.

————. *Supplementary volume, 1990*, by K. Satchidanandan (c1993. 249 p.). PK2908.W49

Winternitz, Moriz. A history of Indian literature / Maurice Winternitz ; a new authoritative English translation by V. Srinivasa Sarma. Rev. ed. Dehli : Motilal Banarsidass, 1981–1985. 3 v. **BE1571**

Translated from the author's *Geschichte der indischen Litteratur* (Leipzig : Amelang, 1908–22. Repr.: Stuttgart : K. F. Koehler, 1968). Original translation publ. 1927–67. A "3rd ed." (possibly a reprint) began appearing in 1991.

Contents: v. 1, Introduction, Veda, National epics, Purānas, and Tantras; v. 2, Buddhist literature and Jaina literature (Repr. 1988); v. 3, Sanskrit literature; scientific literature.

A heavily documented history, particularly valuable for its account of classical Sanskrit. PK2903.W62

Iran

Browne, Edward Granville. A literary history of Persia. Cambridge : Cambridge Univ. Pr., 1902–24. 4 v. **BE1572**

Publisher varies; v. 1–2 publ. by T. F. Unwin. Frequently reprinted.

Contents: v. 1, From the earliest times to Firdawsí; v. 2, From Firdawsí to Sa'dí; v. 3, A history of Persian literature under Tartar dominion (1265–1502); v. 4, A history of Persian literature in modern times (1500–1924).

The standard history. Contains extensive quotations with translations, biographical information, illustrations, and detailed footnotes. Each volume has an index. PK6097.B7

Levy, Reuben. An introduction to Persian literature. N.Y. : Columbia Univ. Pr., 1969. 194 p. : map. **BE1573**

A concise introductory history providing many lengthy translated selections. Appendixes provide a discussion of metrical patterns, a short biographical dictionary of authors, and a bibliography of Persian works in English. Indexed.

Storey, Charles Ambrose. Persian literature : a bio-bibliographical survey. London : Luzac, 1927–90. v. 1 in 2 v.; v. 2, pts. 1–3; v. 3 pts. 1–2. (In process). **BE1574**

Contents: v.1, Qur'anic literature. History and biography: pt. 1, General history. The prophets and early Islam. History of India (1927–39; repr. 1970); pt. 2, Biography. Additions and corrections. Indexes; v. 2, pt. 1, Mathematics. Weights and measures. Astronomy and astrology. Geography (1958); v. 2, pt. 2, Medicine (1971); v. 2, pt. 3, Encyclopedias and miscellanies, arts and crafts, science, occult arts (1977); v. 3, pt. 1, Lexicography, grammar, prosody and poetics (1984); v. 3, pt. 2, Rhetoric, riddles and chronograms, ornate prose (1990).

Some volumes publ. by the Royal Asiatic Society of Great Britain and Ireland.

A substantial, meticulous, chronologically arranged bibliography of manuscripts and printed books with biographical and historical annotations. Z7085.S88

Israel

See also Judaism in the Religion section (BC) and Yiddish language under the subject Regional literatures of Europe (above).

Goell, Yohai. Bibliography of modern Hebrew literature in English translation. Jerusalem : Executive of the World Zionist Organization, Youth and Hechalutz Dept. ; Jerusalem ; N. Y. : Israel Universities Pr., 1968. 110 p. **BE1575**

"The present work lists translations of post-*Haskalah* literature only, a period in Hebrew letters dating roughly from the beginning of the penultimate decade of the nineteenth century."—*Introd.* About 7,500 items in classed arrangement with author and translator indexes, and a Hebrew title index of authors and titles. Z7070.G57

———————— Bibliography of modern Hebrew literature in translation. Tel Aviv : Inst. for the Translation of Hebrew Literature, Ltd., 1975. 117 p. **BE1576**

Mainly a listing of translations published separately since 1917, although a few works in special issues or sections of periodicals and anthologies have been included. Covers translations into 26 languages. Listings for English are severely selective in comparison to Goell's 1968 bibliography (BE1575). Arranged by language, subdivided by literary form. Appendix of monographs on modern Hebrew literature. Indexes to Hebrew authors, translators, editors, and authors of monographs.

§ Both works by Goell have been supplemented by *Bibliography of modern Hebrew literature in translation*, ed. by Isaac Goldberg and, for more recent volumes, by Amnon Zipin (v. 1 [1972/76]– ; n.s. v. 1–2 [1985/86]–). Tel Aviv : Inst. for the Translation of Hebrew Literature, 1979–88. No more published?). One issue per year has been devoted to translations into English, the other to translations into other languages. Includes translations appearing in periodicals and anthologies as well as monographs, and English-language reviews and criticism of Hebrew books. Z7070.G58

Waxman, Meyer. A history of Jewish literature. N.Y. : T. Yoseloff, [1960]. 5 v. in 6. : ill. **BE1577**

Contents: v. 1, From the close of the canon to the end of the 12th century; v. 2, From the 12th-century to the middle of the 18th-century; v. 3, From the middle of the 18th-century to 1880; v. 4 (2 pts.), From 1880 to 1935; v. 5, From 1935–1960.

First publ. 1930–41 in 4 v. with title *A history of Jewish literature from the close of the Bible to our own days*; v. 2 and v. 4 appeared in enlarged and corrected eds. 1943–47.

A detailed history of Jewish literature in its various forms and in various countries from about 200 BCE to 1960. Includes bibliography. PJ5008.W323

Zinberg, Israel. A history of Jewish literature / tr. and ed. by Bernard Martin. Cleveland : Pr. of Case Western Reserve Univ., 1972–78. 12 v. **BE1578**

Originally published in Yiddish as *Di Geshikhte fun der literatur bay Yidn* (Vilna, 1929–37. 8 v.).

Covers the literature from the Arabic-Spanish period to Haskalah at its height in the 19th century. Each volume has a detailed table of contents and content notes at the beginning of each chapter. Many translated passages. Handsomely produced and visually pleasing. Extensive footnote references, bibliography, glossary, and index in each volume.

Japan

Biographical dictionary of Japanese literature / [ed. by] Sen'ichi Hisamatsu. Tokyo : International Society for Educational Information, 1982. 437 p. : ill. **BE1579**

In sections by time period; includes authors from all periods and genres beginning with the archaic. Entries range from a paragraph to several pages and include biography, with references to titles of works, and critical comments. Genealogical outlines of literary schools are provided. Glossary. Bibliography of Japanese-language materials on individual authors. Index by title, genre, organization, etc. Notes Japanese character version of proper names and titles.

A 2nd ed. was publ. by the International Soc. for Educational Information in 1982 but was acquired by few U.S. libraries.   PL723.B5

Bonneau, Georges. Bibliographie de la littérature japonaise contemporaine. Paris : Geuthner ; Tôkyô : Mitsukoshi, [1938]. 280 p. (Bulletin de la Maison Franco-Japonaise, t. 9, no.1–4, 1937).   **BE1580**

"5ème supplément à la *Bibliographie des principales publications editées dans l'Empire japonais.*".

Reissued as "2nd. ed." (Tôkyô : Maison Franco-Japonaise, 1938).

A valuable bibliography. Pt. 1, Introduction, gives important sources, Japanese and Western; list of translations from Western works into Japanese; and classification of authors as to type or school. Pt. 2, Bibliographie des oeuvres représentatives originales de la littérature japonaise contemporaine, arranged alphabetically by author, gives transliteration; Japanese characters; date and place of birth and death; subject arrangement of works with title in transliteration, Japanese characters, and translation into French; place and date. Includes magazine articles. Pt. 3, Index to names in the introduction and the bibliography.

§ The series *20–seiki bunken yōran taikei* (Tokyo : Nichigai Asoshietsu, 1976–) offers a variety of bibliographies and indexes on Japanese language, literature, and comparative literature (e.g., no. 16, publ. 1984, *Hikaku bungaku kenkyū bunken yōran, 1945–1980*, is a bibliography of comparative literature in Japan).   Z7072.B72

Gendai Nihon shippitsusha daijiten = Contemporary writers of Japan / [ed. by] Jun'ichiro Kida … [et al.]. Tokyo : Nichigai Asoshietsu, 1984. 5 v.   **BE1581**

1st ed., 1978–79.

Provides biographical information about 13,000 contemporary writers in all fields, including the media, foreign writers active in Japan, and scientists who write for the general public. Gives citations to works by and about the authors. Vol. 5 provides several indexes, including one for pseudonyms and one for names of organizations and associations.

Keene, Donald. Dawn to the west : Japanese literature of the modern era. N.Y. : Holt, Rinehart & Winston, [1984]. 2 v.
                                                              BE1582

Contents: v. 1, Fiction; v. 2, Poetry, drama, criticism.

Considered to be the standard and definitive study in English. These volumes cover Japanese literature from the Meiji restoration (1868) to the present. Footnotes and bibliography at the end of each chapter. Glossary, selected list of translations into English, and index in each volume. Projected to be in four volumes; no more published?

Translated into Japanese as *Nihon bungakushi, Kindai, gendai hen* (1984–1992).

§ A major Japanese history being translated into English is Jin'ichi Konishi's *History of Japanese literature*, tr. by Aileen Gatten, Nicholas Teele, and Mark Harbison, ed. by Earl Miner (Princeton, N.J. : Princeton Univ. Pr., 1984–1991, v. 1–3 [In progress; projected for 5 v.]; originally publ. Tokyo, 1985–87 as *Nihon bungei shi*). The first three volumes cover the archaic and ancient ages, the early Middle Ages, and the high Middle Ages. Extensive references, chronology, bibliography, and index in each volume. Emphasis on the technical aspects of writing.   PL726.55.K39

Kokubungaku nenkan = Bibliography of research in Japanese literature. 1977– . [Tokyo : Kokubungaku Kenkyū Shiryōkan, 1978–]. Annual.   **BE1583**

Continues: *Kokugo kokubungaku Kenkyu bunken mokuroku* (1963–72), *Kokubungaku Kenkyu bunken mokuroku* (1971–76); publisher varies.

An annual bibliography and yearbook of Japanese literature. The bibliographic section is followed by lists of prizes and grants, and a necrology. Author index.

§ An older yearbook of literature and the arts is *Bungei nenkan* (1929– . Tokyo : Shinchosa. 37th ed., 1984); it includes a who's who section, a chronology, etc., along with the annual bibliographical survey.

Kokusai Bunka Kaikan (Tokyo, Japan). Toshoshitsu. Modern Japanese literature in translation : a bibliography, comp. by the International House of Japan Library. Tokyo : Kodansha Internat. [distr. in U.S. by Harper & Row], [1979]. 311 p.
                                                              BE1584

Arranged alphabetically by authors' names, then by title. Titles appear in Romaji, followed by the title in Japanese characters; translations are given in the language of translation, followed by the translator's name and bibliographic information. Includes references to works published in anthologies, collections, and periodicals. Indexes of titles and of translators.

§ For updated and augmented information see *Japanese literature in foreign languages, 1945–1990*, from the Japan P.E.N. Club ([Tokyo]: Japan Book Publishers Assn., 1990). Covers translations from *The tale of the Genji* to the contemporary era, and also lists foreign-language books, articles, and dissertations on the literature. More than 13,000 items. The P.E.N. Club also produced a bibliography covering pre-1945 translations: *Japanese literature in European languages: a bibliography* (2nd. ed. Tokyo, 1961; suppl. 1964).

Two additional earlier bibliographies are *Modern Japanese literature in western translations* (Tokyo: International House of Japan Library, 1972), covering fiction, poetry, drama, and prose, and Hide Ikehara Inada's *Bibliography of translations from Japanese into western languages: from the 16th century to 1912* (Tokyo : Sophia Univ., 1971), an annotated chronological list of books and articles providing translations of Japanese materials in all subject areas.   Z3308.L5K66

Lewell, John. Modern Japanese novelists : a biographical dictionary. N.Y. ; Tokyo : Kodansha International, 1993. 497 p. : ill.   **BE1585**

A dictionary providing biographical, critical, and bibliographical information concerning 57 20th-century Japanese novelists whose works are available in English translation. Each entry begins with a brief biographical statement followed by a critical and analytical essay discussing the author's life and works. Bibliographies consist of works Lewell considers recommended reading, other works available in English, and a selective list of criticism. A list of general references is provided, and a basic dictionary of Japanese literary terms.

                                                        PL747.55.L48

Mamola, Claire Zebroski. Japanese women writers in English translation : an annotated bibliography. N.Y. : Garland, 1989–1992. 2 v. (Garland reference library of the humanities, vol. 877, 1317).   **BE1586**

The author attempts to list comprehensively works of fiction, biography and autobiography, and nonfiction reflective of the literature, arts, social conditions, politics, and lives of Japanese women, written by native Japanese women and translated into English and in some instances originally written in English. In v. 1, two chronological sections list belles lettres works from 794 to 1987, followed by a section of nonfiction works, all with lengthy annotations. These are followed by unannotated listings of additional specialized nonfiction works and dissertations. Material in collections and periodicals is included. Vol. 2 updates and augments the first, with a similar arrangement but more emphasis on nonfiction. Author indexes.   Z3308.L5M34

Marks, Alfred H. Guide to Japanese prose / Alfred H. Marks, Barry D. Bort. 2nd ed. Boston : G. K. Hall, 1984. 186 p.
                                                              BE1587

1st ed., 1975.

A guide to Japanese literary prose available in English translation. The annotated bibliography is in two sections: (1) Pre-Meiji literature (beginnings to 1867) and (2) Meiji literature and after (1868 to present). An introductory essay places the works in their historical and literary context. Author/title index.   Z3308.L5M37

Miner, Earl Roy. The Princeton companion to classical Japanese literature / by Earl Miner, Hiroko Odagiri, and Robert E. Morrell. Princeton, N.J. : Princeton Univ. Pr., c1985. 570 p. **BE1588**

A major and fascinating guide to Japanese literature from its beginnings to 1868; essential in any library supporting Japanese literature, culture, and history. The first section is a literary history, followed by historical and literary chronologies, and dictionaries of authors and literary terms. Additional sections treat theater, collections, criticism, Buddhism and Confucianism, dictionaries, chronology and yearly celebrations, geography, ranks and offices, architecture, clothing, and armor and arms. Many charts, lists, outlines, and helpful diagrams and illustrations. Index to authors and titles. PL726.1.M495

Nihon kindai bungaku daijiten / [hensha Odagiri Susumu], Nihon Kindai Bungakukan hen. Tōkyō : Kōdansha, Shōwa 52-53 [1977–1978]. 6 v. **BE1589**

The standard encyclopedia for modern Japanese literature. Vols. 1–3 provide a biographical dictionary covering more than 5,000 writers; v. 4 covers historical topics; v. 5 is a dictionary of information on periodicals; v. 6 is the index. Vols. 1–3 have been issued in revised form as *Nihon kindai bungaku daijiten kijoban* (1984).

PL726.55.N485

Nihon kindai bungaku meicho jiten / Nihon Kindai Bungakkan hen. Tokyo : Dō Bungakkan, 1982. 603 p. : ill. **BE1590**

A guide to outstanding works of modern Japanese literature presented in the form of essays by writers and critics. Includes biographical information on the authors, together with background information and critical comment on the works. Z3308.L5N485

Nihon koten bungaku daijiten / [Kanshū Ichiko teiji, Noma Kōshin; henshūsha Nihon Koten Bungaku Daijiten Henshū Iinkai]. Tokyo : Iwanami Shoten, 1983–85. 6 v. **BE1591**

An authoritative dictionary of Japanese literature through the end of the Tokugawa regime. Some 13,000 items incorporate recent research on topics, people, and works in literature and allied fields such as religion, history, and the arts. Signed articles with bibliographies. Vol. 6 is a general index.

Pronko, Leonard Cabell. Guide to Japanese drama. 2nd ed. Boston : G.K. Hall, 1984. 149 p. **BE1592**

1st ed., 1975.

Offers an annotated bibliography of historical and critical works available in English on the Japanese theater, and of texts of the plays available in English translation. Introductory essay on the Japanese theater, its history and traditions, and a brief chronology. Author/title index. Z3308.L5P76

Rimer, J. Thomas. Guide to Japanese poetry / J. Thomas Rimer, Robert E. Morrell. 2nd ed. Boston : G. K. Hall, 1984. 189 p. **BE1593**

1st ed., 1975.

A "Historical sketch and bibliographic outline" is followed by an annotated bibliography of historical and critical works and of Japanese texts available in English translation. Z3308.L5R54

———— A reader's guide to Japanese literature. Tokyo ; N.Y. : Kodansha International : Distr. through Harper and Row, 1988. 208 p. **BE1594**

Descriptions, plot summaries, critical evaluations, and recommended English translations of 20 classics, written from the 10th to 20th centuries. Brief bibliography; general index. PL717.R551

Schierbeck, Sachiko Shibata. Postwar Japanese women writers : an up-to-date bibliography with biographical sketches = Sengo Nihon joryū sakka no rireki / Sachiko Shibata Schierbeck ; ed. by Søren Egerod. Copenhagen s, Denmark : East Asian Institute, Univ. of Copenhagen, 1989. 196 p. (University of Copenhagen. East Asian Institute. Occasional papers, 5). **BE1595**

Covers 53 postwar women writers, most born before the war, who have received or been finalists for Japan's highest literary awards. Entries include a photograph, brief biographical summary, a biographical and critical analysis, an a selective list of works and translations. A brief bibliography of additional references is included, and a list of works by author in Japanese characters. PL723.S38

Yoshizaki, Yasuhiro. Studies in Japanese literature and language : a bibliography of English materials. Tokyo : Nichigai Associates ; distr. by Kinokuniya Book Store, [1979]. 451 p. (Nijisseiki bunken yōran taikei, 8). **BE1596**

Added title page in Japanese.

In three parts: (1) Studies in Japanese literature; (2) Studies in Japanese language; and (3) Materials for further information. Follows a classed arrangement within each section. Aims to cover "most of the studies in Japanese literature and language that have ever been published in the English language."—*Foreword.* Includes books, periodical articles and dissertations. Index of names and titles. Z7072.Y67

Mongolia

Heissig, Walther. Geschichte der mongolischen Literatur. Wiesbaden : Harrassowitz, 1972. 2 v. (969 p.). **BE1597**

Contents: Bd. 1, 19. Jahrhundert bis zum Beginn des 20. Jahrhunderts; Bd. 2, 20. Jahrhundert bis zum Einfluss moderner Ideen.

A substantial scholarly history spanning from the early 19th century to the mid-1930s. Notes are provided at the end of each chapter and an extensive international bibliography in v. 2. Many excerpts in German translation. Illustrations, photographs, and maps are included. Indexes by Mongolian titles, German titles, literary topics, place names, authors' names. PL410.H4

Philippines

Mata, Maria Nena R. Index to Philippine plays, 1923–1983. Metro Manila : National Book Store, 1984. 67 p. **BE1598**

An author and title index to approximately 147 anthologies of plays published both in English and in Philipino. Z7101.T33M38

Philippine literature in English / Esperanza V. Manuel, Resil B. Mojares, editors. Cebu City : E. Q. Cornejo, [1973]. 282 p. **BE1599**

Essentially an anthology of Philippine fiction, poetry, drama, and essays in English, but with useful introductory notes preceding the selections from each genre, biographical notes on the authors represented, and a brief bibliography. PR9550.5.P5

Yabes, Leopoldo Y. Philippine literature in English, 1898–1957 : a bibliographical survey. Quezon City : Univ. of the Philippines, 1958. p. 343–434. **BE1600**

Repr. from *Philippine social sciences and humanities review* 22 (Dec. 1957): 343–434.

Not limited to belles lettres writers. In two parts: (1) a list of periodicals and newspapers published in English; (2) an author list of monographs, with bibliographic information. Both parts arranged alphabetically. An introduction provides the historical context.

§ Complemented and updated to the early 1980s by Francisco G. Tonogbanua, *Philippine literature in English* (Manila : Delna Enterprises, 1984. 71 p.), designed as a reading guide for students and teachers. Divided chronologically into six literary periods, each with an introduction and a list of authors and titles but no bibliographical information. Bibliography of secondary works and anthologies.

Vietnam

Nguyên, Dình Thâm. Studies on Vietnamese language and literature : a preliminary bibliography. Ithaca, N.Y. : Southeast Asia Program, Cornell Univ., 1992. 227 p.   **BE1601**
   For annotation, *see* BD231.   Z3226.N48

BF

Art and Architecture

In order to broaden coverage of non-Western topics in both this section and in Section BG, Design and Applied Arts, some sources covering the art and architecture of European countries and of specific centuries or periods have been omitted. For these topics, readers are encouraged to consult the guides listed below, particularly for collective biographies for individual Western countries outside North America.

GENERAL WORKS

Guides

Arntzen, Etta Mae. Guide to the literature of art history / Etta Mae Arntzen, Robert Rainwater. Chicago : Amer. Libr. Assoc. ; London : Art Book Co., 1980. 616 p.   **BF1**
   Addressed "primarily to persons doing serious subject research" (*Pref.*), this work is a complete revision and updating of Mary Walls Chamberlin's *Guide to art reference books* (Chicago : Amer. Libr. Assoc., 1959). Of the 4,037 reference and research tools cited, about 40% appeared in Chamberlin. New sources are current through 1977 and most titles are in Western languages.
   Arranged in four main sections subdivided by subject or geographical area: (1) General reference sources; (2) General primary and secondary sources; (3) The particular arts (painting, sculpture, architecture, prints, drawings, photography, decorative arts); (4) Serials. Archaeology is treated selectively, as are urban planning, landscape architecture, aesthetics, the philosophy of art, and art criticism. Monographs on individual artists are omitted, but major exhibition catalogs are included. Annotations are descriptive and often give tables of contents. Author/title and subject indexes.
   A supplementary volume has been announced for 1997 publication.   Z5931.A67

Ehresmann, Donald L. Fine arts : a bibliographic guide to basic reference works, histories, and handbooks. 3rd ed. Littleton, Colo. : Libraries Unlimited, 1990. 373 p.   **BF2**
   1st ed., 1975; 2nd ed., 1979.
   With its companion bibliographies, *Architecture* (BF202) and *Applied and decorative arts* (BG2), both edited by Ehresmann, this is "designed to serve two principal users: librarians and college and university students."—*Pref.* In two parts that list major works in Western languages: pt. 1, Reference works (books and periodicals published since 1830) and pt. 2, Histories and handbooks, subdivided by periods and geographic areas (books only published since 1875). Excludes dissertations and exhibition and museum catalogs. The 2,051 annotated citations (with a Sept. 1988 cutoff date) are in 13 chapters (e.g., Bibliographies, Dictionaries and encyclopedias, Iconography, Prehistoric and primitive art, Oriental art, Art of Africa and Oceania). Author/title and subject indexes. The author plans two additional bibliographies, on sculpture and on painting and graphic arts.   Z5931.E47

Goldman, Bernard. The ancient arts of Western and Central Asia : a guide to the literature. Ames : Iowa State Univ. Pr., 1991. 303 p.   **BF3**
   Intended as a compact, selective guide. Annotated entries arranged alphabetically within 26 topical or geographical sections. In addition to the bibliography proper, provides useful bibliographic abbreviations, chronologies and lists by monarch, an essay on researching and writing, and a glossary. Author index; general index.
        Z5961.M58G65

Jones, Lois Swan. Art information : research methods and resources. 3rd ed. Dubuque, Iowa : Kendall/Hunt Publ. Co., c1990. 373 p.   **BF4**
   1st ed., 1978, and 2nd ed., 1984, had title: *Art research methods and resources.*
   Intended for everyone interested in art research, students to specialists, hence includes materials that range from general reference works to specialized sources in foreign languages. In 19,000 citations (most annotated), discusses methodology and bibliography in six parts: Before research begins, Basic research methodology, Beyond the basics, General art research tools, Specialized resources for various media and disciplines, Iconographical resources. Concludes with a section on research centers and appendixes: brief French, German, and Italian dictionaries; a multilingual glossary of pertinent terms in five languages; terminology; databases. General index.   N85.J64

Kleinbauer, W. Eugene. Research guide to the history of Western art / W. Eugene Kleinbauer and Thomas P. Slavens. Chicago : Amer. Lib. Assoc., 1982. 229 p. (Sources of information in the humanities, 2).   **BF5**
   An introduction to methodology, themes and issues. The first and major portion of the book is a series of bibliographic essays on specific aspects of art history grouped under headings such as Art history and its related disciplines, Studying the art object, Psychological approaches. The second section treats reference works and offers annotated listings of selected sources. Indexes: author/title, subject.   N380.K56

Muehsam, Gerd. Guide to basic information sources in the visual arts. Santa Barbara, Calif. : ABC-Clio ; Oxford, Eng. : Jeffrey Norton Publ., 1978. 266 p.   **BF6**
   A series of bibliographical essays followed by an alphabetical list of the 1,045 sources cited. Essays are intended for art and art history students, and discuss research techniques, important general art reference materials, primary sources, and research materials for specific periods and forms in Western art. Brief essays are devoted to individual national schools of art including Asian and non-Western art. Name, title, subject index.   N7425.M88

Van Keuren, Frances Dodds. Guide to research in classical art and mythology. Chicago : Amer. Libr. Assoc., 1991. 307 p.   **BF7**
   In three parts (General research; Mythology; Media studies), covering architecture, sculpture, decorative arts, and literature. Presents major references, related reference books, handbooks, and specialized studies, with thorough explanations about use. Indexes: author-title; subject.   N7760.V3

Woodhead, Peter. Keyguide to information sources in museum studies / Peter Woodhead and Geoffrey Stansfield. London ; N.Y. : Mansell, 1989. 194 p.   **BF8**

"A first source of information about museums" (*Introd.*) in three parts: Overview of museum studies and its literature; Bibliographical listing of sources of information; List of selected organizations (international; arranged by country). Index: authors, titles, subjects, organizations.

§ Two related titles are *The museum : a reference guide* (N.Y. : Greenwood, c1990) and *Museum studies library shelf list*, 2nd ed. (San Francisco : Center for Museum Studies of John F. Kennedy Univ., 1986). See also the author's *Keyguide to information sources in archaeology* (DA61). AM7.W66

Bibliography

Allen, Jelisaveta S. Literature on Byzantine art, 1892–1967. [London] : Mansell for Dumbarton Oaks Center for Byzantine Studies, 1973–76. 2 v. in 3. (Dumbarton Oaks bibliographies, series I). **BF9**

Contents: v. 1, By location: pt. 1, Africa, Asia, Europe (A–Ireland); pt. 2, Europe (Italy–Z), Indices; v. 2, By categories.

Vol. 1 is a topographically arranged cumulation of items pertinent to the history of art of specific places as drawn from the semiannual lists published 1892–1967 in III. Abteilung, "Bibliographische Notizien und Mitteilungen," of *Byzantinische Zeitschrift* (DA163), primarily from the subdivision "Kunstgeschichte : Einzelne Orte." Author and place-name indexes.

In v. 2 the cumulated entries are arranged topically within broad divisions on history of Byzantine art in general, and by art form (the "Iconography" section is by far the largest). For the most part, entries with a purely regional or local orientation have not been repeated in v. 2. Index of topics (including iconographic themes, museums and other owners of collections and manuscripts); index of modern authors.

§ Allen has also edited *Author index of Byzantine studies* [microform] (DA163 *note*). Z5933.3.A45

Art books 1980–1984. N.Y. : Bowker, [1985]. 571 p. **BF10**

Successor to *Art books, 1876–1949* and *Art books, 1950–1979* (N.Y. : Bowker, [1981] and [1979]).

The current volume lists some 9,600 monographs and includes some that are pre-1980 but have been catalogued by the Library of Congress since the previous volume. Format is similar, but has replaced the in-print and museum publication sections with serial indexes for some 2,401 international serial publications. Z5939.A8

Art Institute of Chicago. Ryerson Library. Index to art periodicals. Boston : G.K. Hall, 1962. 11 v. **BF11**

Photographic reproduction of an index of some 353 journals, many foreign, published since 1907. Arranged by subject, alphabeted within the subject by periodical. Material that appears in *Art index* (BF41) is excluded. Also available on microfilm (23 reels).

——. ——. *First supplement* (Boston : G.K. Hall, 1975. 573 p.) covers "indexing activity from 1961 to October, 1974."—*Pref.* Some retrospective indexing was also added. Z5937.C55

Arts in America : a bibliography / Bernard Karpel, ed.; Ruth W. Spiegel, ed. for the publisher. Wash. : Smithsonian Inst. Pr., [1979]. 4 v. **BF12**

At head of title: Archives of American Art, Smithsonian Institution.

Contents: v. 1, Sect. A–G: Art of the Native Americans; architecture; decorative arts; design; sculpture; art of the West; v. 2, Sect. H–M: Painting; graphic arts; v. 3, Sect. N–U: Photography; film; theater; dance; music; serials and periodicals; dissertations and theses; visual resources; v. 4, Index.

About 25,000 entries for various aspects of the arts in America and their relationship to American life and culture. Each of the 21 sections is the work of an individual contributor or team of contributors. The sections considerable variation in selectivity, length, and detail of the annotations. Most sections include entries for individual practitioners of the art in question (i.e., architects, painters, sculptors, photographers, dancers, actors, etc.); the section on periodicals in v. 3 provides

lengthy annotations on 253 individual serials in the visual arts. Bibliographic entries include books, parts of books, periodical articles, and academic theses. Includes publications through 1975. "A survey of pictorial materials on Americana available for study and purchase in institutions in the United States" takes the form of a directory, with notes on special collections, holdings, etc.; it constitutes the Visual resources section in v. 3. Index of authors and subjects. Z5961.U5A77

Bibliografia del libro d'arte italiano. Roma : C. Bestetti, [1952–76]. 3 v. in 5. : ill., facsims., plates. **BF13**

Vol. 1 comp. by Erardo Aeschlimann; v. 2, by C. E. Tanfani.

Contents: v. 1, 1940–52; v. 2, 1952–62 (2 v.); v. 3, 1963–72 e indice generale … (2 v.).

Classified arrangement, with author and subject index in each volume. Includes exhibition catalogs, guidebooks, and proceedings of congresses held in Italy, as well as monographs, in a classified arrangement. Author and subject index.

§ Bibliographies for other countries of Western Europe include: *Bibliografía del arte en España* (Madrid : Consejo Superior de Investigaciones Científicas, Instituto Diego Velázquez, 1976–78. 2 v.); *Bibliographie zu Kunst und Kunstgeschichte* [DDR] (Leipzig : Verlag für Buch- und Bibliothekswesen, [1956–61]. 2 v.); *Bibliography of the history of British art* (Cambridge : Cambridge Univ. Pr., 1936–56. 6 v.). Z5961.I8B5

Borroni Salvadori, Fabia. "Il Cicognara" : bibliografia dell' archeologia classica e dell' arte italiana. Firenze : Sansoni, 1954–67. 2 v. in 12. : ill. (Biblioteca bibliografica italica, 6–7, 10–11, 19, 23, 25, 27, 29, 31–32, 34). **BF14**

A comprehensive, annotated bibliography of classical archaeology and Italian art, arranged under large form categories and then chronologically. Vol. 1 includes: bibliography, catalogs of art libraries and of art books, encyclopedias and dictionaries, aesthetics, academic dissertations and conferences, didactic poems, technical aspects, and conservation, with an analytical index and an index to facsimiles. Vol. 2 has title *Archeologia classica* and includes: treatises and descriptive literature, methods, manuals and general works, congresses and conferences, catalogs, museums, periodicals, travels, topography, numismatics, epigraphy, and costume, with an index. Z2357.B6

Burt, Eugene C. Erotic art : an annotated bibliography with essays. Boston : G.K. Hall, c1989. 396 p. **BF15**

Erotic art is defined as "art that primarily addresses some aspect(s) of the human sexual experience."—*Introd.* Compiled "over fifteen years by scouring a wide range of information sources including published bibliographies … periodical indexes … antiquarian book dealer sales catalogs … and library card catalogs." The 30 chapters are grouped in seven sections, each beginning with an introductory essay: General background; General surveys; Ancient world; Asia; Ethnoart–Africa, Oceania and the Native Americas; Western world; Modern world [20th century]. The latter two sections cite a total of 318 artists, about a third of whom are photographers. Includes entries not only for scholarly titles but for articles from *Penthouse* or *Playgirl*. Most entries have brief annotations or evaluative comments. Author index. Z5956.E7B87

Chiarmonte, Paula L. Women artists in the United States : a selective bibliography and resource guide on the fine and decorative arts, 1750–1986. Boston : G.K. Hall, 1990. 997 p. **BF16**

More substantial than most recent publications on women artists, this work aims "to foster a more critical analysis of the position of women artists in cultural history by examining the modes of production in which they have excelled."—*Pref.* The 16 contributors were chosen "on the basis of their professional expertise and access to special collections representing their media." In two parts: (1) Critics; Organizations; Manuscript repositories and special collections; (2) [Literature]: Biographical reference tools; Documents on women's art (by type or medium) and on women artists. The documents section consists of about 3,900 annotated bibliographic and archival references, constituting two-thirds of the publication. Sections include introductory essays by contributors. Indexes are by author/title and artist; both are further subdivided by folk art and minority art (African American, Latina, Native American, and Asian American categories). The only geographical access in Pt. 1 is by state.

§ Other titles treating women artists include: Sherry Piland's *Women artists : an historical, contemporary, and feminist bibliography* (2nd ed. Metuchen, N.J. : Scarecrow, 1994), Eleanor Tuft's *American women artists, past and present : a selected bibliographic guide* (N.Y. : Garland, 1984–89. 2 v.), and Janet A. Anderson's *Women in the fine arts : a bibliography and illustration guide* (Jefferson, N.C. : McFarland, 1991).   Z7963.A75W65

Creswell, Keppel Archibald Cameron. A bibliography of the architecture, arts, and crafts of Islam to 1st Jan. 1960. [Cairo] : American Univ. at Cairo Pr., 1961. 1330 p.   **BF17**

Contents: Pt. 1, Architecture (divided by country), p. 1–478; pt. 2, Arts and crafts (divided by craft or material, each subdivided by country), p. 479–1330. Index of authors, p. i–xxv.

"Intended to cover every branch of Muslim architecture and art, except numismatics."—*Pref.* Cites 15,850 books and articles and includes an eight-page tabulated list of periodicals examined.

Two supplements have been issued: *Supplement, Jan. 1960 to Jan. 1972* ([Cairo] : American Univ. in Cairo Pr., 1973. 366 p.) and *Second supplement, Jan. 1972 to Dec. 1980 (with omissions from previous years),* by J. D. Pearson, assisted by Michael Meinecke and George T. Scanlon. ([Cairo] : American Univ. in Cairo Pr., 1984, 578 col.). *Suppl. 1* lists 4,000 entries, *Suppl. 2,* 11,000. *Suppl. 2* "includes important *lacunae* from the first two volumes" (*Pref.*), a large number of national, regional, and international exhibitions of Islamic art, and additional dissertations, and incorporates citations for Arabic, Persian, and Turkish publications. Excludes explanatory comments.

Z5961.M6C7

Freitag, Wolfgang M. Art books : a basic bibliography of monographs on artists. N.Y. : Garland, 1985. 351 p. (Garland reference library of the humanities, v. 574).   **BF18**

A listing by artist's name of more than 10,500 monographs on individual artists of all periods. Author index. Includes an 11-page section, Biographical dictionaries and other reference works, arranged by country and region.

Might be considered a new edition of Edna Louise Lucas's *Art books* (Greenwich, Conn. : New York Graphic Soc., 1968) except that Freitag emphasizes individual artists. Lucas's book derives from her *Harvard list of books on art* (Cambridge, Mass. : Harvard Univ. Pr., 1952), which was a revision of her *Books on art* (1936).   Z5938.F73

Frick Art Reference Library. Original index to art periodicals. Boston : G.K. Hall, 1983. 12 v.   **BF19**

Also available on microfilm.

Reproduces a file compiled between 1923 and 1969, indexing 27 French, English and (from 1928 on) Italian journals of the 19th and 20th centuries, some not analyzed elsewhere. Content reflects the Library's concentration at the time on "Western European and American painting, sculpture, and some decorative arts from the fourth century A.D. to 1860."—*Introd.* Imprint dates range from 1850 to 1960. The main strength of the index "is the extremely thorough coverage of individual artists cited in the articles indexed," extending "to individual works of art, ... reproductions, exhibitions, provenance and location at the time of indexing." Entries for authors, artists, galleries, exhibitions, portraits, etc., with complete bibliographical details, in one alphabetical sequence.   Z5937.F74

Goldman, Shifra M. Arte Chicano : a comprehensive annotated bibliography of Chicano art, 1965–1981 / comp. by Shifra M. Goldman and Tomás Ybarra-Frausto. Berkeley : Chicano Studies Libr. Publ. Unit, Univ. of California, 1985. 778 p. (Chicano Studies Library publication series, no. 11.).   **BF20**

Integrates material from alternative and little-known publications and from local and regional newspapers with citations to popular and widely-held publications. The 55-page introduction, with sections on Revealing the image and Outline of a theoretical model for the study of Chicano art (theories, definitions, chronology), has its own index. The body of the bibliography consists of 2,500 annotated citations,

each listed under subject headings (four per citation) taken from *Chicano thesaurus,* 3rd ed. Indexes by author/artist and title. Appendixes: Alphabetical list of Chicano artists (about 2,200 names); Periodical titles cited in bibliography (about 300).   Z5961.U5G64

Gray, John. Action art : a bibliography of artists' performance from futurism to fluxus and beyond. Westport, Conn. : Greenwood, 1993. 343 p. (Art reference collection, no. 16).   **BF21**

In three basic sections, with 3,700 unannotated citations: Action art 1909–1952; Action art 1950s–1970s; Biographical and critical studies. Appendixes: Reference works; Libraries and archives; Addenda; List of artists/artists groups by country; List of artists groups and collectives. Indexes: artists, subject, title, author. Current through 1991; includes cross-references.   Z5936.P47G73

Handbook of Latin American art = Manual de arte latinoamericano : a bibliographic compilation / gen. ed., Joyce Waddell Bailey. Santa Barbara, Calif. : ABC-Clio, [1984–86]. 2 v. in 3.   **BF22**

Regional editors, v. 2: Aracy Abreu Amaral (Brazil), Ramón Gutiérrez and Alberto S. J. de Paula (Southern cone).

Also known as *HLAA.*

Contents: v. 1, General references and art of the nineteenth & twentieth centuries; pt. 1, North America, pt. 2, South America (2 v.); v. 2, Art of the colonial period.

Represents the cooperative efforts of an international group of scholars. Identifies "books, articles, anthologies, exhibition catalogs, and reports (both published and unpublished) written from then nineteenth century through July of 1883 ... in English, Spanish, Portuguese, French, German, Italian, Russian and other languages that cover ancient, colonial and contemporary art."—*Pref.* Format follows that of *Handbook of Latin American studies* (DB266), and relevant citations from the first 44 volumes of that set are interfiled here. In v. 1, the General references section is followed by a geographical arrangement subdivided topically. Indexes: personal and corporate authors, artists. Vol. 2 cites 5,200 titles, has indexes similar to those in v. 1, and also covers architecture. Vol. 3, Art of ancient times, is forthcoming.

§ See also: James A. Findlay, *Modern Latin American art : a bibliography* (Westport, Conn. : Greenwood, 1983) and Robert Chester Smith and Elizabeth Wilder, *A guide to the art of Latin America* (Wash. : U.S. Govt. Print. Off., 1948; repr. : N.Y. : Arno, 1971).

Z5961.L3H36

Heppner, Irene. Bibliography on portraiture : selected writings on portraiture as an art form and as documentation. Boston : G.K. Hall, c1990. 2 v. : ill.   **BF23**

"Covers the portraiture of Western cultures of all times" (*Introd.*), emphasizing American examples, British influences on American trends, and English-language publications. Cites monographs, sections of monographs, periodical articles, museum publications, and theses. The project was undertaken in the library of the National Portrait Gallery in Washington, D.C. The classified arrangement includes such topics as special pose or length, intellectual concepts, and media, and is followed by an index to those topics. The 1,600 pages of the bibliography are photoreproductions of catalog cards.   Z5939.H465

Igoe, Lynn Moody. 250 years of Afro-American art : an annotated bibliography. N.Y. : Bowker, 1981. 1266 p.   **BF24**

A comprehensive bibliography of about 25,000 citations ranging from the popular to the scholarly, and including crafts as well as fine arts. In three main sections: (1) Basic bibliography, arranged by author and including works relating to more than one artist; (2) Subject bibliography, topically arranged; and (3) Artist bibliography, arranged alphabetically by individual artist. Selective brief annotations. Appendixes: artwork by anonymous artists; artwork by groups.

§ There are three older related titles: Lenwood G. Davis and Janet Sim, *Black artists in the United States : an annotated bibliography* (Westport, Conn. : Greenwood [1980]); T. D. Cederholm, *Afro-American artists : a bio-bibliographical directory* (Boston : Boston

Public Library, 1973); and a guidebook by Oakley N. Holmes, *The complete annotated resource guide to black American art* (Spring Valley, N.Y. : Black Artists in America, 1978). Z5956.A47I38

International African Institute. A bibliography of African art / comp. by L. J. P. Gaskin. London : The Institute, 1965. 120 p. **BF25**

Nearly 5,000 entries in geographical arrangement, with subdivisions for the major genres. Includes an extensive listing of published catalogs and guides to museums, exhibitions, and collections, plus a section on bibliographies of Africana. Author, geographical-ethnic, and subject indexes. Lists of periodicals consulted and periodical abbreviations.

§ For newer sources, *see* Janet L. Stanley's *African art : a bibliographic guide* (N.Y. : Africana Publ. Co., 1985; Smithsonian Institution Libraries research guide, 4) and *The arts of Africa : an annotated bibliography* (BG4). Z5938.A3I5

Internationale Bibliographie der Kunstwissenschaft. 1902–1917/18. Berlin : Behr, 1903–20. Annual. **BF26**

Classified bibliography of books and periodical articles published in Europe. Topics: reference, aesthetics, art history, iconography, building, sculpture, painting, graphic arts, decorative arts, heraldry, preservation, topography, museums and collections, exhibitions, biography and necrology, auctions. Author and subject indexes for each year. Z5931.I61

Jagdish Chandra. Bibliography of Indian art, history & archaeology. Delhi : Delhi Printers Prakashan, 1978– . v. 1. **BF27**

Contents: v. 1, Indian art (316 p.). Intended to be in 3 v.

Vol. 1 is a comprehensive bibliography of books, essays, exhibition catalogs, periodical articles, and annual reports on all aspects of Indian art and architecture (including handicrafts). There is a special section on the art of countries composing Greater India from Afghanistan to Borneo and Sarawak. Most publications cited are in Hindi or English. Lacks an index.

§ The author also compiled *Bibliography of Nepalese art* (1980). See also *Bibliography of modern Indian art* by D. C. Ghose (New Delhi : Lalit Kala Akademi [1980]). Z3206.J33

Kendall, Aubyn. The art and archaeology of pre-Columbian Middle America : an annotated bibliography of works in English. Boston : G. K. Hall, 1977. 324 p. **BF28**

An expanded edition of the author's *The art of pre-Columbian Mexico: an annotated bibliography* ... (Austin, Tex. : Institute of Latin American Studies, Univ. of Texas at Austin, 1973).

Presents more than 2,000 annotated entries for books, exhibition catalogs, and periodical articles published through Dec. 1976. Alphabetical author lists within separate sections for books and periodicals. Appendix of selected dissertation titles. Subject index.

Z1208.M4K45

Kiell, Norman. Psychiatry and psychology in the visual arts and aesthetics : a bibliography. Madison : Univ. of Wisconsin Pr., 1965. 250 p. **BF29**

A companion to the author's *Psychoanalysis, psychology, and literature* (BE19), this volume is concerned with the writings of psychologists, psychoanalysts, philosophers, aestheticians, art critics, and educators on their findings and insights relative to the visual arts and aesthetics. Lists 7,208 books and periodical articles. Author index.

§ See also: William Alexander Hammond's *A bibliography of aesthetics and of the philosophy of the fine arts, 1900–1932* (rev. and enl. ed., N.Y. : Longmans Green, 1934; repr. : N.Y. : Russell & Russell, 1967) and Elizabeth J. Sacca and Loren R. Singer's *Visual arts reference and research guide : for artists, educators, curators, historians and therapists* (Montreal : Perspecto Pr., c1983).

Z5931.K5

Koobatian, James. Faking it : an international bibliography of art and literary forgeries, 1949–1986. Wash. : Special Libraries Association, c1987. 240 p. **BF30**

An update and expansion of Robert George Reisner's *Fakes and forgeries in the fine arts : a bibliography* (N.Y. : Special Libraries Assoc., 1950) which covered the period 1848–1948. Cites 1,835 books and articles, sometimes with brief annotations or with reference to citations in five abstracting publications. Arranged by medium and by general, patents, law, and exhibitions. Author index. Z5939.5.K66

Lerner, Loren R. Art and architecture in Canada : a bibliography and guide to the literature to 1981 = Art et architecture au Canada : bibliographie et guide de la documentation jusqu'en 1981 / Loren R. Lerner & Mary F. Williamson. Toronto : Univ. of Toronto Pr., 1991. 2 v. : maps. **BF31**

A bilingual "reference guide to the most significant contributions to the literature of Canadian art and architecture published in Canada and abroad [since 1825]."—*Pref.* The 9,555 bibliographic entries include monographs, exhibition catalogs, some theses, journals and journal articles, and association reports. All entries are annotated, many with abstracts in French and English. Emphasis is on elusive retrospective literature. Vol. 1, the bibliography (organized by topic, geographical area, and chronological period), is preceded by an introduction to Canadian art history. Vol. 2 is a bilingual author and subject index.

Z5961.C3L47

Lietzmann, Hilda. Bibliographie zur Kunstgeschichte des 19. Jahrhunderts : Publikationen der Jahre 1940–1966. München : Prestel-Verlag, 1968. 234 p. (Studien zur Kunst des neunzehnten Jahrhunderts, Bd. 4). **BF32**

A classified bibliography of 4,431 writings on 19th-century art, prefaced by three essays. Author index.

Continued by Marianne Prause's *Bibliographie zur Kunstgeschichte des 19. Jahrhunderts : Publikationen der Jahre 1967–1979 mit Nachtragen zu den Jahren 1940–1966* (München : Prestal-Verlag, 1984 [Materialien zur Kunst des 19. Jahrhunderts, 31]). This continuation is arranged like Lietzmann and adds 29,560 citations. Z5935.L4

Répertoire d'art et d'archéologie : RAA. t. 1 (1910)–t. 67 (1963); Nouv. sér., t. 1 (1965)–t. 25 no. 4 (1989). Paris : Morancé, 1910–89. **BF33**

Frequency varies: annual, 1910–72, except for 1914/19; quarterly (some issues combined) 1973–89.

Subtitle (varies): dépouillement des périodiques et des catalogues de ventes, bibliographie des ouvrages d'art français et étrangers.

Ceased with v. 25 no. 4 (1989). Merged with *Répertoire international de la littérature de l'art (RILA)* (BF34) to form *Bibliography of the history of art* (BF43).

Indexes: for 1910–1914/19, 1925, and 1934–89, each volume has an index of authors, subjects, places; 1926–33 have author index only; for 1920–25, a combined index was published as fasc. 29 (1927).

Publ. under the auspices of the Bibliothèque d'Art et d'Archéologie of the University of Paris and, later, of the Comité International d'Histoire de l'Art; most recently under the direction of the Comité Français d'Histoire de l'Art and Unesco.

A bibliography of periodical articles and, from 1920, books from various countries, classified by large subject (mainly period and country), with indexes of authors and of places. Format changed with 1973; the work continued to be a classified index, but each issue included an index of artists, an author index, and a detailed subject index. Annual cumulated indexes beginning with nouv. sér. v. 10 (1974). Omits Asian and primitive art, which are covered in *Bulletin signalétique 526 : art et archéologie; Proche Orient, Asie, Amérique* (v. 24–44, 1970–90) and by *FRANCIS. Bulletin Signalétique 526 : art et archéologie* (v. 45 [1991]– . AD254, *note*).

•Available in machine-readable form as: *Répertoire d'art et d'archéologie* [database] (Vandoeuvre-lès-Nancy Cedex : Centre National de la Recherche Scientifique [CNRS], 1973–89). Available online. Z5937.R4

Répertoire international de la littérature de l'art : RILA = International repertory of the literature of art. v. 1 (1975)–v. 15 no. 2 (1989). N.Y. : College Art Association of America. **BF34**

Publisher varies; publ. by the Getty Trust, 1982–89.

Volume for 1975 preceded by a number dated 1973 (called "Demonstration issue"). Vol. 1 issued in two parts, Abstracts and Index. Cumulative indexes merging author and subject indexes were publ. for v. 1–5 (1975–79), v. 6–10 (1980–84), v. 11–15 (1985–89).

Ceased; merged with *Répertoire d'art et d'archéologie* (BF33) to form *Bibliography of the history of art (BHA)* (BF43).

A major bibliography and abstract service covering books, dissertations, museum publications, exhibition catalogs, articles and reviews in periodicals, festschriften, and conference proceedings concerned with postclassical European and post-Columbian American art. Abstracts are arranged topically under broad subject headings: Reference works, General works, Medieval art, Renaissance and baroque art, Modern art, Collections and exhibitions. (In the latter section, an "Exhibition list" is a city-by-city listing of exhibits.) Detailed author and subject indexes.

•Available in machine-readable form as the first 15 years of *Art literature international* (Williamstown, Mass. : RILA).   Z5937.R16

Rowland, Benjamin. The Harvard outline and reading lists for Oriental art. 3rd ed. Cambridge : Harvard Univ. Pr., 1967. 77 p.   **BF35**

First published in 1938 under title: *Outline and bibliographies of Oriental art.* Rev. ed., 1958.

Very brief chronological outlines by country are followed by the bibliographical lists.

§ Bibliographies are also incorporated in *Oriental art : a handbook of styles and forms* by Jeannine Auboyer [et al.] (BF126).   N7260.R6

Schimmelman, Janice Gayle. American imprints on art through 1865 : books and pamphlets on drawing, painting, sculpture, aesthetics, art criticism, and instruction : an annotated bibliography. Boston : G.K. Hall, 1990. 419 p.   **BF36**

Identifies "637 titles and covers a broad range of art literature: addresses and essays, biographies of artists, histories of art, descriptions of paintings and sculpture, art journals, trade catalogs of artists' materials, practical handbooks ... and instructional books ... with the exception of exhibition catalogs."—*Pref.* No judgment was made as to quality or content. Arrangement of the main section is alphabetical, first by author, then by artist. In addition to standard bibliographical information, variant titles, and description of contents, gives library locations as identified by the *National union catalog : pre-1956 imprints* (AA113), *Checklist of American imprints for 1830–*, OCLC, and six additional sources. There is a 38-page chronological listing of titles cited, and an index of names and titles.   Z5961.U5S34

Schlosser, Julius, *Ritter von.* La letteratura artistica : manuale delle fonti della storia dell' arte moderna. Trad. di Filippo Rossi. 3. ed. italiana aggiorn. da Otto Kurz. Firenze : Nuova Italia, [1964]. 792 p. (Il pensiero storico, 12).   **BF37**

Repr., 1977 and 1979.

Publ. in French, incorporting corrections and additions to the 3rd Italian ed., as *La littérature artistique* ... (Paris : Flammarion, 1984).

Translation of *Die Kunstliteratur : ein Handbuch zur Quellenkunde der neueren Kunstgeschichte* (Wien : Schroll, 1924; repr., 1985). Originally publ. as *Materialen zur Quellenkunde der Kunstgeschichte* (Wien : 1914–20). An Italian translation with additions by the author was publ. in 1935, and an appendix by Otto Kurz in 1937. A 2nd Italian edition appeared in 1956.

A valuable manual for the literature of art history up to the early 19th century, particularly the Renaissance. Kurz's additions of later material are enclosed in brackets. Indexes of artists and authors.   N5300.S3316

Western, Dominique Coulet. A bibliography of the arts of Africa. Waltham, Mass. : African Studies Assoc., [1975]. 123 p.   **BF38**

Lists books, articles, and exhibition catalogs "on art, architecture, oral literature, music and dance in Sub-Saharan Africa. Each of these major categories has been subdivided into both a general listing ... as

well as broad geographical areas ... further subdivided into ethnic groups and some nations."—*Note.* Some annotations; author index.   Z5961.S85W47

Whittingham, Nik-ki. Arts management in the '90s : the essential annotated bibliography. Chicago : ENAAQ, 1990. 113 p.   **BF39**

A compilation of 419 citations (partly annotated), largely for popular monographs published in the 1980s; appears to have been done as a thesis. Lacks an introduction and a title index. Provides subject index and addresses for arts organizations.

§ Functions as a supplement to Stephen Benedict's *Arts management : an annotated bibliography* (Rev. ed. N.Y. : Center for Arts Administration, 1980). The latter offers arrangement within six broad topics, annotations, author/title index, and a listing of publishers' and distributors' addresses.

In 1986, the Center for Arts Administration published a directory, Henry S. Hample's *For more information : a guide to arts management information centers.* For earlier works, consult Charlotte Georgi's *The arts and the world of business* (2nd ed. Metuchen, N. J. : Scarecrow, 1979. 113 p.).   Z5956.A7W55

Yüan, T'ung-li. The T. L. Yüan bibliography of Western writings on Chinese art and archaeology / Harrie A. Vanderstappen, ed. [London] : Mansell, 1975. 606 p.   **BF40**

A subject listing, with detailed subdivisions. The work was begun by T. L. Yüan and is intended as a companion volume to his *China in Western literature* (DE138); it "now contains over 15,000 items [including reviews] of a variety of materials on Chinese art and archaeology in English, German, Dutch, Scandinavian, Slavic, and French and other Romance languages published between 1920 and 1965."—*Foreword.* Books and articles are listed in separate sections; detailed outline of each section. Author index.   Z5961.C5Y9

Current

See also *Art and archaeology technical abstracts,* (BF198), *Bibliography of American folk art* (BG10), and *Design and applied arts index* (BG11).

Art index. v. 1 (Jan. 1929)– . N.Y. : Wilson, 1930– . Quarterly with annual cumulations.   **BF41**

Subtitle (varies): A quarterly author & subject index to publications in the fields of archaeology, architecture, art history, city planning, crafts, graphic arts, industrial design, interior design, landscape architecture, museology, photography & films, and related subjects.

First permanent cumulation Jan. 1929–Sept. 1932; triennial cumulations, Oct. 1932–Oct. 1950; biennial cumulations Nov. 1950–Oct. 1967; annual cumulations Nov. 1967/Oct. 1968– .

Number of fields covered varies; now indexes 268 American and foreign periodicals in the fields indicated in the subtitle. Method of indexing, which differs somewhat from that followed in the other special indexes issued by this publisher, is as follows: ordinary articles are indexed under author and subject or subjects; book reviews are indexed under the author reviewed and under subject or subjects in a separate section following the main index; exhibitions are indexed under the artist or appropriate form heading; illustrations accompanying an article are listed in the entry for that article but not indexed individually; illustrations without text are indexed under the artist's name.

•Available in machine-readable form as: *Art Index* [database] (Bronx, N.Y. : H.W. Wilson, 1984–). Available online and in CD-ROM; updated quarterly.   Z5937.A78

Artbibliographies modern. v. 4, no. 1 (Spring 1973)– . Oxford : European Bibliographic Center ; Santa Barbara, Calif. : Clio Pr., 1973– . Semiannual.   **BF42**

Supersedes *LOMA: literature of modern art,* 1969–71 (London : Lund Humphries, 1971–73) and assumes its numbering. Outlived *Art, design, photo* (Hemel Hempstead, Eng. : A.Davis Publ., 1972–76/77).

Offers abstracts of books, exhibition catalogs, and periodical articles dealing with art and design throughout the world from about 1900 to the present; before 1989, 19th-century materials were also covered. Coverage began with publications of 1972, and each issue includes any material currently published together with any important items omitted from earlier volumes. Alphabetical listing by topical subjects and artists' names in a single alphabet. English-language translations of foreign titles are given in parentheses following the original titles. Author index and museum/gallery index. Indexes serials listed in *Artbibliographies : current titles* (Santa Barbara, Calif. : ABC-Clio, 1972–).

•Available in machine-readable form as: *Artbibliographies modern* [database] (Santa Barbara, Calif. : ABC-Clio, 1974–). Available online and in CD-ROM; updated semiannually. Z5935.L64

Bibliography of the history of art : BHA = Bibliographie d'histoire de l'art. v. 1/1– . Vandoeuvre-les-Nancy, France : Centre national de la recherche scientifique, Institut de l'information scientifique et technique ; Santa Monica, Calif. : J. Paul Getty Trust, Getty Art History Information Program, 1991– . Quarterly, with annual cumulative indexes. **BF43**

"*BHA* covers the current literature of European art from late Antiquity to the present and American art from the European discoveries to the present."—*Introd.*

Combines the services of *RILA* (*Répertoire international de la littérature de l'art*) (BF34) and *RAA* (*Répertoire d'art et d'archéologie*) (BF33) in a quarterly publication with yearly bilingual cumulative indexes. Coverage includes books, 3,000 periodical titles, conference proceedings, festschriften and other collected essays, exhibition catalogs, selected dealers' catalogs, dissertations, and microform publications. It began with a 1990 volume that in some 22,000 citations covered 1989 imprints and some earlier ones in order to maintain continuous coverage with *RILA* and *RAA*.

•Available in machine-readable form as: *Art literature international* [database] (Williamstown, Mass. : BHA, 1990–). Available online, updated semiannually. Publication in CD-ROM expected in 1996. N1.A1B52

Black arts annual. v. 1 (1987/88)–v. 3 (1989/90). N.Y. : Garland, 1989–92. **BF44**

For annotation, *see* BA1. NX512.3.A35B58

New York Public Library. Art and Architecture Division. Bibliographic guide to art and architecture. 1975– . Boston : G.K. Hall, 1976– . Annual. **BF45**

Serves as a supplement to the Division's *Dictionary catalog* (BF57). In addition to the materials cataloged for the Art and Architecture Division, lists entries from Library of Congress MARC tapes. Z5939.N56a

Periodicals

See also BF49, BF225, BF226.

Lebel, Gustave. Bibliographie des revues et périodiques d'art parus en France de 1746 à 1914 / introd. par Georges Wildenstein. [Paris : Gazette des Beaux-Arts, 1951]. 64 p. : ill. **BF46**

Originally printed in *Gazette des beaux-arts*, 6. période, 93. année, t. 38 (janv.–mars 1951).

Repr. : Nendeln, Liechtenstein : Kraus Reprint, 1968.

Arranged by title; includes date of first issue, frequency, editor, location (Bibliothèque Nationale or Bibliothèque d'Art et d'Archéologie de l'Université de Paris). Many entries have annotations. Chronological index.

§ A similar bibliography for periodicals in architecture: Helene Lipstadt and Bertrand Lemoine, "Les revues d'architecture et de construction en France au XIXe siècle," *Revue de l'art* no. 89 (1990): 65–71.

Robinson, Doris. Fine arts periodicals : an international directory of the visual arts. Voorheesville, N.Y. : Peri Pr., c1991. 570 p. **BF47**

"Contains data in an annotated listing by broad subject areas of more than 2,790 currently published periodicals, newsletters, and newspapers."—*Pref.* International in scope, covers publications issued at least once a year; excludes biographical or membership directories. Sections: Information sources; Visual arts; Museums and art galleries; Decorative arts & crafts; Lettering & fine printing; Commercial art; The arts; Buildings & interiors; Photography; Miscellaneous. Indexes: title, publisher and organization, ISSN, country of publication subject. Z5937.R6

Museum publications

Catalog of museum publications & media : a directory and index of publications and audiovisuals available from United States and Canadian institutions. 2nd ed. / Paul Wasserman, managing ed. Detroit : Gale, 1980. 1044 p. **BF48**

1st ed., 1973 had title: *Museum media.*

Intends "to provide bibliographic control of books, booklets, periodicals, monographs, catalogs, pamphlets and leaflets, films and filmstrips, videotape programs, and other media which are prepared and distributed by museums, art galleries and related institutions in the United States and Canada."—*Pref.* Listing is by museum, with indexes by titles and keywords, periodical titles, subjects, and geographic locations.

§ Related publications include: *World museum publications 1982 : a directory of art and cultural museums, their publications and audiovisual materials* (N.Y. : Bowker, 1982) and Susan P. Besemer's *From museums, galleries, and studios : a guide to artists on film and tape* (Westport, Conn. : Greenwood, c1984). For the U.K., see: *The bibliography of museum and art gallery publications and audiovisual aids in Great Britain and Ireland, 1977–80* (Cambridge : Chadwyck-Healey, [1978]–80). Z5052.M94

Klos, Sheila M. Historical bibliography of art museum serials from the United States and Canada / ed. by Sheila M. Klos and Christine M. Smith ; editorial committee, Alexandra A. de Luise ... [et al.]. Tucson, Ariz. : Art Libraries Society of North America, 1987. 58 p. (Art Libraries Society of North America. Occasional papers, no. 5.). **BF49**

Intends "to provide a reference source for the bibliographic verification of art museum serial titles, including their exact publishing history .... [Cites] frequency changes, suspensions and cessations, irregularities in numbering, merges, and continuations, and [gives] a brief description of the content of the serial."—*Introd.* Covers primarily serials from art museums, noncommercial galleries, college and university art museums and galleries, and art associations with permanent collections. Covers art schools, athenaeums, general museums, and state museums selectively; excludes monographic series. Arrangement is alphabetical by present name of institution. Title index. Z5937.K57

Festschriften

Lincoln, Betty Woelk. Festschriften in art history, 1960–1975 : bibliography and index. N.Y. : Garland, 1988. 220 p. (Garland reference library of the humanities, vol. 745). **BF50**

"Fills the lacuna between [Paul Rave's *Kunstgeschichte in Festschriften*, BF51] and *RILA* [BF34] with a bibliography and analytical index of Festscriften in art history and related fields from the beginning of the Christian era to the present."—*Introd.* Cites 344 festschriften, 1960–75, and lists their 4,676 essays, followed by indexes of subjects, authors, and dedicatees. Z5931.L52

Rave, Paul Ortwin. Kunstgeschichte in Festschriften : allgemeine Bibliographie kunstwissenschaftlicher Abhandlungen in den bis 1960 erschienenen Festschriften / Paul Ortwin Rave, unter Mitarbeit von Barbara Stein. Berlin : Mann, 1962. 314 p.   **BF51**

Contains a list of the festschriften; a list, arranged by subject, of the 5,865 essays on art included in them; and indexes of the titles in the festschriften, of the authors of the art essays, of artists and others, and of places written about.

§ For festschriften after 1960, *see* Betty Woelk Lincoln's *Festschriften in art history, 1960–1975 : bibliography and index* (BF50).
                                                                  Z5931.R35

Library catalogs

See also BF200, BF228, BF229, BF230, BF337, BF338, BF366, BG14, BG15, BG16.

Bibliotheca Hertziana, Max-Planck-Institut. Kataloge der Bibliotheca Hertziana in Rom (Max-Planck-Institut). Wiesbaden : L. Reichert, 1985–1994. v. 1–16, 1–31, 1–8.   **BF52**

Catalog of a unique library of Italian art, housed in the Palazzo Zuccari at Rome, that emphasizes Rome, the Renaissance, architecture, and guidebooks. Current through the end of 1984, when the library held 147,285 volumes. Introductory material, in German, Italian, and English, covers the history of the library, includes a four-page bibliography on the library, and an outline of the classification scheme.

The first 16 v. constitute the systematic shelflist, of which v. 13–15 list catalogs of libraries and museums, arranged alphabetically by city then chronologically, and v. 16 lists 1,500 periodicals. These are followed by some 32 volumes of the alphabetical catalog (in progress, publ. through v. 31, 1994), reproducing only eight cards per page. The final eight volumes are an analytical catalog—i.e., an author list of periodical articles.   Z933.R66

Freer Gallery of Art. Dictionary catalog of the library. Boston : G.K. Hall, 1967. 6 v.   **BF53**

Contents: v. 1–4, Western languages; v. 5–6, Oriental languages.

Photoreproduction of catalog cards for a collection of about 40,000 books, pamphlets, and periodicals. Includes analytics for periodicals pertinent to the collection, which is made up almost exclusively of Asian, West Asian, and 19th-century American art.

2nd enl. ed. : *Dictionary catalog of the library* [microform] (Boston : G.K. Hall, 1991. 252 microfiche).

§ A second library of Asian art has published its catalog: *Catalog of the Rübel Asiatic Research Collection, Harvard University Fine Arts Library* (London : Saur, 1989. 7 v.).

Metropolitan Museum of Art (New York, N.Y.). Library. Library catalog of the Metropolitan Museum of Art. 2nd ed., rev. & enl. Boston : G. K. Hall, 1980. 48 v.   **BF54**

1st ed., 1960; 8 suppls., 1962–80.

A dictionary catalog. Subject entries precede main or added entries, and chronological subdivisions precede other subdivisions. Sales catalogs are cited in v. 46–48, cataloged by subject and by collector or auction house.

For this edition, much of the collection was recataloged to make headings uniform and to update terminology and spelling; new headings have been added to reflect trends and new art movements; explanatory notes and cross-references increased; items from the supplements incorporated; and new materials added.

————. ————. *First supplement* [1979?–80] (1982. 840 p.); *Second supplement, 1980–1982* (1985. 4 v.); *Third supplement, 1983–1986* (1987. 3 v.); *Fourth supplement, 1987–1989* (1990. 3 v.).

The 8th supplement to the 1st ed. (1980. 3 v.) was published more or less simultaneously with the 2nd ed. and is available to libraries owning the earlier edition but not prepared to purchase the new one; cards represented in the 8th supplement are included in the 2nd ed.

§ The library's holdings for primitive art have been separately published as: *Catalog of the Robert Goldwater Library, the Metropolitan Museum of Art* (Boston : G.K. Hall, 1982. 4 v.).   Z881.N6624

Museum of Modern Art (New York, N.Y.). Library. Catalog of the Library. Boston : G.K. Hall, 1976. 14 v.   **BF55**

Photographic reproduction of the dictionary catalog of this library, which is especially strong in the "visual arts from around 1850 to the present."—*Introd.* Includes citations to articles in periodicals not covered by *Art index* (BF41) and the *Répertoire d'art et d'archéologie* (BF33); exhibition catalogs are also represented. "Latin American ephemeral material (exhibition catalogs and artists' files)" are listed separately in v. 7, as are periodical titles.

————. *Annual bibliography of modern art* is based on the museum's acquisitions (Boston : G.K. Hall, 1987–). MOMA has also issued: *The Museum of Modern Art artists scrapbooks* [microform] (Alexandria, Va. : Chadwyck-Healey, 1986. 642 microfiches), which is limited to 44 artists.   Z5939.N557

National Art Library (Great Britain). First proofs of the Universal catalogue of books on art : comp. for the use of the National Art Library and the schools of art in the United Kingdom / by order of the Lords of the Committee of Council on Education. London : Chapman and Hall, 1870. 2 v.   **BF56**

Repr.: N.Y. : Burt Franklin, 1964. 2 v. and suppl.

At head of title: Science and Art Department of the Committee of Council on Education, South Kensington.

John Hungerford Pollen, ed.

"Not only the books in the library, but all books printed and published at the date of the issue of the Catalogue, that could be required to make the library perfect."—*v. 1, p. i.* Alphabetically arranged by author.

————. *Supplement to the Universal catalogue of books on art* (London : Eyre & Spottiswoode, 1877. 654 p.).

New York Public Library. Art and Architecture Division. Dictionary catalog. Boston : G.K. Hall, 1975. 30 v.   **BF57**

Photographic reproduction of cards from the Division catalog; includes materials cataloged through Dec. 1971. Covers "painting, drawing, sculpture, and the history and design aspects of architecture and the applied arts."—*Introd.* Also lists relevant materials in the Cyrillic, Hebrew, and Oriental collections, the Local History and Rare Book divisions, and citations to periodical articles in journals in all parts of the library.

————. ———— *Supplement 1974* (Boston : G.K. Hall, 1976. 556 p.). Covers material added through Sept. 1974.

Continued by: *Bibliographic guide to art and architecture* (BF45).

Archives

Archives of American Art. The card catalog of the manuscript collections of the Archives of American Art. Wilmington, Del. : Scholarly Resources, [1981]. 10 v.   **BF58**

Reproduction of the catalog cards for this extensive collection of papers (18th cent. to the present) of artists, art critics and historians, collectors, galleries and museums, and art societies of the U.S. Holdings of the Archives range from letters, journals and diaries, notebooks, scrapbooks and clippings to business records, photographs, and oral histories. Indexing is primarily by personal name. Each entry includes a statement regarding content and indicates the named collection to which it belongs. Entries are keyed to microfilms of the Archives, sets of which are available at regional centers or through interlibrary loan. Microfilms of papers still in private hands or located at other institutions are available at the Archives of American Art in Washington, D.C.

————. *Supplement 1981–1984* (Wilmington, Del. : Scholarly Resources, 1985. 542 p.), containing descriptions of additions since Oct. 1980 and revisions for more thoroughly processed collections.

§ Related publications include: *Archives of American art : a directory of resources,* by Garnett McCoy (N.Y. : Bowker, 1972); *Inventory of the records of the National Arts Club, 1898–1960,* by Catherine Stover (Wash. : Smithsonian Inst., 1990); and *Guide to archival sources for French-American art history in the Archives of American Art* (Wash. : Archives of American Art, 1992). Z6611.A7A72

————— The card catalog of the oral history collections of the Archives of American Art. Wilmington, Del. : Scholarly Resources, [1984]. 343 p. **BF59**

Reproduces about 2,500 catalog cards for the Archives' collection of tape recordings (both transcribed and untranscribed, restricted and unrestricted materials) of interviews, lectures, panel discussions, symposia, etc., involving 20th-century American artists. N6536.A73

Indexes to art works and reproductions

See also BF231, BF298, BG94.

Illustration index / comp. by Lucile E. Vance. N.Y. : Scarecrow, 1957. **BF60**

A subject index to illustrations in eight to ten popular periodicals and a few selected books.

Continued by:

—————. *First supplement,* comp. by Lucile E. Vance (1961. 230 p.).

—————. 2nd ed., comp. by Lucile E. Vance and Esther M. Tracey (1966. 527 p.). Incorporates the listings from the 1957 ed. and its suppl. with new material, so that the period covered is 1950 through June 1963. Although this and Greer's 1973 work and Appel's 1980 work are called "editions," they actually serve as supplements to the original publication.

—————. 3rd ed., comp. by Roger E. Greer (1973. 164 p.). Covers July 1963–Dec. 1971.

—————. 4th ed., comp. by Marsha C. Appel (1980. 458 p.). Covers 1972–76, with scope widened to include furniture, wildlife, art works, and some personalities.

—————. *V, 1977–1981,* comp. by Marsha C. Appel (1984. 411 p.).

—————. *VI, 1982–1986,* comp. by Marsha C. Appel (1988. 531 p.).

—————. *VII, 1987–1991,* comp. by Marsha C. Appel (1993. 492 p.).

§ Related older titles include three picture indexes by Jessie Crofts Ellis, *Travel through pictures : references to pictures, in books and periodicals, of interesting sites all over the world* (Boston : Faxon, 1935. 699 p.), *Nature and its applications : over 200,000 selected references to nature forms and illustrations of nature as used in every way* (1949. 861 p.), and *Index to illustrations* (1966. 682 p.); and Hewlett-Woodmere Public Library, *Index to art reproductions in books* (Metuchen, N.J. : Scarecrow, 1974. 372 p.). N7525.I558

Monro, Isabel Stevenson. Index to reproductions of American paintings : a guide to pictures occurring in more than eight hundred books / by Isabel Stevenson Monro and Kate M. Monro. N.Y. : Wilson, 1948. 731 p. **BF61**

Lists "the work of artists of the United States occurring in 520 books and in more than 300 catalogues of annual exhibitions held by art museums. The paintings are entered (1) under name of the artist, followed by his [sic] dates when obtainable, by title of the picture, and by an abbreviated entry for the book in which the reproduction may be found; (2) under titles; and (3) in some cases under subjects. Locations of pictures in permanent collections have also been included whenever this information was available."—*Pref.*

—————. —————. *First supplement* (N.Y. : Wilson, 1964. 480 p.); lists paintings in more than 400 books and catalogs, most published between 1948 and 1961. The compilers also published *Index to reproductions of European paintings …* (N.Y. : Wilson, 1956).

Continued by: Lyn Wall Smith and Nancy Dustin Wall Moure, *Index to reproductions of American paintings appearing in more than 400 books, mostly published since 1960* (BF63).

Parry, Pamela Jeffcott. Contemporary art and artists : an index to reproductions. Westport, Conn. : Greenwood, 1978. 327 p. **BF62**

Some 60 major books and exhibition catalogs are indexed for "paintings, sculpture, drawings, prints, happenings, actions, environments, assemblages, conceptual pieces, earthworks, and video art" (*Pref.*) dating from about 1940 to the late 1970s. Complete information (i.e., title of work, date, media, location of work, publication in which reproduction appears) is given under artist's name. Subject and title indexes.

The author later compiled *Photography index* (BF339) and *Print index* (BF367). N6490.P3234

Smith, Lyn Wall. Index to reproductions of American paintings appearing in more than 400 books, mostly published since 1960. Metuchen, N.J. : Scarecrow, 1977. 931 p. **BF63**

Intended as a continuation of Isabel Stevenson Monro and Kate M. Monro's *Index to reproductions of American paintings* (BF61), and similar in arrangement. "Under each artist's name, titles of his [sic] paintings are listed alphabetically and under those are placed abbreviations for books in which a reproduction occurs. Beside or just below the title is an abbreviation signifying the owner of a painting. Only permanent collections—no private owners are cited."—*Pref.* Index of titles arranged by general categories. ND205.S575

Thomison, Dennis. The black artist in America : an index to reproductions. Metuchen, N.J. : Scarecrow, 1991. lx, 396 p. **BF64**

Covers artists from the Colonial period to the present, represented in books, periodicals, and exhibition catalogs published through 1990. The body of the index gives dates, medium, location of a portrait, and biographical sources, along with the list of published reproductions for each artist. A "Source of information" section lists books, articles, bibliographies, dissertations, audiovisual materials and producers, exhibition catalogs. Brief subject index.

§ A related survey is *The image of the black in Western art* (Fribourg : Office du Livre, [1976–89]. 4 v. in 5). N6538.N5T46

Portraits

See also BF23, BF320.

A.L.A. portrait index : index to portraits contained in printed books and periodicals / ed. by W. C. Lane and N. E. Browne. Wash. : Library of Congress, 1906. 1601 p. **BF65**

Repr.: N.Y. : Burt Franklin, 1965.

An index to portraits contained in 1,181 sets (6,216 volumes), including both books and periodicals through the year 1904. Indexes some 120,000 portraits of about 40,000 persons. Information given includes: dates of birth and death, and brief characterization of the sitter and the artist or engraver; and volume and page of the work where the portrait may be found. Does not index portraits in local histories, genealogical works, or collections of engravings as such, or portraits of writers included in sets of their collected works.

§ Three smaller indexes of portraits: v. 1 of Cuthbert Lee's *Portrait register* ([Asheville, N.C.] : Biltmore Pr., [1968]); Hayward and Blanche Cirker's *Dictionary of American portraits …* (N.Y. : Dover, [1967]); and Herbert H. Hoffman's *Faces in the news : an index to photographic portraits, 1987–1991* (Metuchen, N.J. : Scarecrow, 1992). N7620.A2

Dictionary of British portraiture / ed. by Richard Ormond and Malcolm Rogers. London : B.T. Batsford in assoc. with the National Portrait Gallery ; N.Y. : Oxford Univ. Pr., 1979–81. 4 v. **BF66**

Contents: v. 1, The Middle Ages to the early Georgians, by Adriana Davies; v. 2, Later Georgians and early Victorians, by Elaine Kilmurray; v. 3, The Victorians : historical figures born between 1800 and 1860, by Elaine Kilmurray; v. 4, The twentieth century : historical figures born before 1900, by Adriana Davies.

Lists portraits of some 5,000 "famous figures in British history that are either in [British] galleries and institutions or in collections accessible to the public."—*Introd.* Each volume covers a different period, and within volumes arrangement is by name of sitter. Dates and identifying word or phrase are given for the sitter, and information concerning the portraits appears in abbreviated form. Vol. 4 concludes with an index to sitters. Lacks an index of artists.   N7598.D5

Frazier, Patrick. Portrait index of North American Indians in published collections. Wash. : Library of Congress : for sale by the U.S. Govt. Print. Off., 1992. 142 p. : ill.   **BF67**
Superintendent of Documents classification: LC 1.2:P83/3.
The main section is a listing by tribe, within which are given names of subjects, alternate names, sources (from a list of 75 publications, 1835–1987), and pages. A 45-page index lists subjects and cites their tribes.   E89.F725

Singer, Hans Wolfgang. Allgemeiner Bildniskatalog. Leipzig : Hiersemann, 1930–36. 14 v.   **BF68**
Repr. : Stuttgart : A. Hiersemann ; Nendeln : Kraus Reprint, 1967.
An index to about 102,000 engraved portraits of some 35,000 sitters of all periods and nationalities, from 17 German public collections. Vol. 14 provides indexes by occupation and by artist.
Continued by: ———. *Neuer Bildniskatalog* (1937–38. 5 v. Repr. : Stuttgart : A. Hiersemann ; Nendeln : Kraus, 1967), which includes some painted and sculpted likenesses, adding about 40,000 portraits.   N7575.S55

Encyclopedias

Contemporary masterworks / ed., Colin Naylor ; picture ed., Leanda Shrimpton ; advisers, Jean-Christophe Ammann ... [et al.]. Chicago : St. James Pr., 1991. 933 p. : ill.   **BF69**
"Features entries on 450 works of art, architecture, photography and design [which] have made a significant contribution to twentieth century culture"—*Editor's note, p. vii.* Focus is on the period since 1945.   N6490C65675

Enciclopedia del arte en América. [Buenos Aires] : Bibliográfica OMEBA, [1969, c1968]. 5 v. : ill. (part col.), facsims., ports.   **BF70**
Ed. by Vicente Gesualdo.
Contents: v. 1–2, Historia; v. 3–5, Biografías.
Covers North and South America. Vols. 1–2 are arranged by country and then by medium. Name indexes.
§ For Pre-Columbian and American Indian art, see Harmer Johnson's *Guide to the arts of the Americas* (N.Y. : Rizzoli, 1992). For iconography and mythology of the Incas, consult *Iconografía y mitos indígenas en el arte*, by Teresa Gisbert (La Paz, Bolivia : Gisbert, 1980. 250 p., 144 p. of plates).   N6501.E5

Enciclopedia dell'arte antica, classica e orientale. Roma : Istituto della Enciclopedia italiana, 1958–85. 11 v. : ill., col. plates, maps, facsims., plans.   **BF71**
Ed. in chief, Ranuccio Bianchi Bandinelli.
A handsomely illustrated encyclopedia with signed articles and bibliographies, treating the art history and iconography of the countries of classical antiquity, i.e., Asia, Northern Africa, and Europe, from prehistory to about 500 CE. Includes: [v. 8], Supplemento 1970; [v. 9], Atlante dei complessi figurati e degli ordini architettonici.
Volumes for 1981 and 1985 serve as v. 10–11 and are edited by Giovanni Pugliese Carratelli. An index volume, covering v. 1–7 and the supplement, was publ. in 1984 (629 p.).   N31.E48

Enciclopedia dell'arte medievale / [direttore, Angiola Maria Romanini ; redattore capo, Marina Righetti Tosti-Croce]. Roma : Istituto Della Enciclopedia Italiana, c1991–93. v. 1–4 : ill. (In progress).   **BF72**

Contents: v. 1–4, Aaland–Cîteaux.
A major publication, similar to *Enciclopedia dell'arte antica, classica e orientale* (BF71), with excellent color photographs accompanying the scholarly articles and bibliographies.
§ Another vast Italian encyclopedia devoted to book illustration: *IRIDE : Iconografia rinascimentale italiana : dizionario enciclopedico*, ed. by Giuseppina Zappella (Milan : Editrice Bibliografica, c1992–93. [In progress]. v. 1–2, Abaco–Alloggiamento).   N5965.E5

Encyclopedia of world art. N.Y. : McGraw-Hill, [1959–1987]. 17 v. : ill., maps, plans., plates (part col.).   **BF73**
Contents: v. 1–14, A–Z; v. 15, Index; v. 16, Supplement, World art in our time, ed. by Bernard S. Myers; v. 17, Supplement II, New discoveries and perspectives in the world of art, ed. by Giulio Carlo Argan (Palatine, Ill. : J. Heraty, 1987).
Published simultaneously in Italian (*Enciclopedia universale dell'arte.* Firenze : Sansoni, 1958–67) and English; the original articles were written in various languages and translated into English.
The English-language edition corresponds to the Italian, with some minor changes and three major differences: (1) more cross-references; (2) a more extensive article on the art of the Americas; (3) some 300 separate, short biographies added to give more ready access to information about persons treated in longer monographic articles.
The signed articles are by specialists of many nationalities and include extensive bibliographies. The subject matter covers "architecture, sculpture, and painting, and every other man-made object that, regardless of its purpose or technique, enters the field of esthetic judgment because of its form or decoration."—*Pref.* Includes all countries and all periods. Approximately the last half of each volume consists of plates illustrating the articles in the first half.
§ Will be superseded by *The dictionary of art* (N.Y. : Grove's Dictionaries, Inc. Projected for 1996, 34 v.).   N31.E4833

Lexikon der Kunst : Architektur, bildende Kunst, angewandte Kunst, Industrieformgestaltung, Kunsttheorie / [begründet von Gerhard Strauss ; hrsg. von Harald Olbrich ... et al.]. 1. Aufl., Neubearbeitung. Leipzig : E.A. Seemann, 1987–1994. 7 v. : ill. (some col.).   **BF74**
Revision of the 1st ed., 1968–78 (5 v.).
Lengthy entries cover people, places, movements, media, and broad topics such as aesthetics, and are particularly strong on Central and Eastern European art and architecture. Bibliographical references have been updated through the mid-1980s.   N33.L47

Lexikon der Kunst : Malerei, Architektur, Bildhauerkunst / [Gesamtleitung, Wolf Stadler ; Redaktion, Eckhart Bergmann ... et al.]. Freiburg : Herder, c1987–c1990. 12 v. : ill. (chiefly col.).   **BF75**
Similar in format to the somewhat smaller *McGraw-Hill dictionary of art* (BF77). Entries cover artists, concepts, materials, building parts, and are distinguished by color illustrations of reliable quality, particularly in the later volumes. Entries conclude with brief bibliographies, chiefly in German, many current through 1980 or 1985.
          N33.L48

McCulloch, Alan. Encyclopedia of Australian art. Hawthorn, Vic. : Hutchinson of Australia, 1984. 2 v. (1327 p., [180] p. of plates) : ill.   **BF76**
First publ. 1968.
Treats the visual arts in Australia from 1770 to the present. Dictionary arrangement of names of artists, galleries, prizes, societies, and exhibitions. Liberally illustrated.
§ An earlier work is Elizabeth Finn Hanks' *Bibliography of Australian art* (Melbourne : Library Council of Victoria, 1976. 2 v.).   N7400.M27

McGraw-Hill dictionary of art / ed. by Bernard S. Myers. N.Y. : McGraw-Hill, [1969]. 5 v. : ill.   **BF77**
Relatively long articles by more than 125 contributors deal with artists' lives and careers, artistic styles, periods, buildings, museums, and art terms. Bibliographies are included. Special attention is given to non-Western art and to descriptions of important monuments and museums in major cities of the world. Lack of an index is offset by nu-

merous cross-references. A good alternative purchase for the smaller library unable to afford the same publisher's *Encyclopedia of world art* (BF73).

§ *Praeger encyclopedia of art* (N.Y. : Praeger, 1971. 5 v.), which revises and translates *Dictionnaire universel de l'art et des artistes* (Paris : Hazan, 1967), is a comparable source. N33.M23

The Oxford companion to art / Harold Osborne, ed. Oxford : Clarendon Pr., 1970. 1277 p. : ill. **BF78**

A typical addition to the "Oxford companion" series, this volume is "designed as a non-specialist introduction to the fine arts. In planning what to include … the word 'art' has been given the narrower meaning in which it denotes the visual arts generally but excludes the arts of theatre and cinema and the arts of movement such as dance."—*Pref.* Practical arts and handicrafts have also been largely excluded. Individual articles are meant to be merely introductory to the subject under consideration; although contributed by specialists, they are unsigned. A selective bibliography of more than 3,000 numbered items is appended, and references to the bibliography are indicated at the end of each article.

§ Additional one-volume encyclopedias include: *The Thames and Hudson dictionary of art and artists* (Rev. ed. London : Thames and Hudson, 1985); *A visual dictionary of art* (general ed., Ann Hill. Greenwich, Conn. : New York Graphic Soc., [1974]); *The Penguin dictionary of art and artists* (6th ed. London ; N.Y. : Penguin, 1991; based on Peter and Linda Murray, *Dictionary of art and artists* [Rev. ed. London : Thames and Hudson, 1965]). N33.O9

Reallexikon zur deutschen Kunstgeschichte. Stuttgart : J.B. Metzler, 1937–93. Bd. 1–9⁶ (Lfg. 1–102) : ill., ports., diagrams, facsims., plans. (In progress). **BF79**

Ed. by Otto Schmitt and others.

Publisher varies.

Contents: Lfg. 1–102, A–Flammlcistc.

Long, signed articles, with bibliographies and many illustrations, on subjects in art history and on specific works of art. Excludes biographies. Covers countries and regions with predominantly German culture from the early Middle Ages to the mid-19th century. Vol. 3 contains an index of catchwords in German, French, English, and Italian covering the first 3 volumes. Beginning with v. 4, each volume contains such an index covering the single volume. Later volumes contain supplements. N6861.R4

Wessel, Klaus. Reallexikon zur byzantinischen Kunst / hrsg. von Klaus Wessel, unter Mitwirkung von Marcell Restle. Stuttgart : A. Hiersemann, 1963–1994. v. 1–5⁶ (Lfg. 1–38). : ill. (In progress). **BF80**

Contents: v. 1–5⁶, Abendmahl–Madaba.

A scholarly encyclopedia of Byzantine art, with long, signed articles. Bibliographies. N6250.W45

Dictionaries

Adeline, Jules. The Adeline art dictionary : including terms in architecture, heraldry, and archaeology / tr. from the French ; with a supplement of new terms by Hugo G. Beigel. N.Y. : Ungar, [1976]. 459 p. **BF81**

Original French edition published 1884 under title *Lexique des termes d'art.*

A standard work which has appeared in many editions since its first appearance in English in 1891. "A large amount of information has been incorporated from F. W. Fairholt's *Dictionary of terms in art* [London : Virtue, 1854]."—*Introd.* This reprinting has a section of new terms appended, p. 423–59. N33.A223

Baigell, Matthew. Dictionary of American art. N.Y. : Harper & Row, [1979] ; London : John Murray, 1980. 390 p. **BF82**

Repr. with corrections, 1982.

Treats nearly 650 major American painters, sculptors, printmakers, and photographers, together with movements and topics relating to art in the United States from the 16th century to the late 20th century.

Biographical entries emphasize artistic achievement and stylistic development, and usually end with a reference to another printed source. Topical entries tend to be longer.

§ For an illustrated work, with museum information and glossary, see: *The Britannica encyclopedia of American art* (Chicago : Encyclopedia Britannica Educational Corp. [1973]). N6505.B34

Earls, Irene. Renaissance art : a topical dictionary. N.Y. : Greenwood, 1987. 345 p. **BF83**

" … intended to serve as a quick reference source for identifying and understanding Renaissance art of Italy and northern Europe. It contains basic information about topics that were common subjects … entries on characteristic schools, techniques, media, and other terminology have been included as background information."—*Pref.* The 800 entries are alphabetically arranged and include cross-references; those for iconographical topics cite one work depicting the subject. Concludes with a bibliography of about 110 English-language sources and a name and subject index. N6370.E27

Glossarium artis : deutsch-französisches Wörterbuch zur Kunst / Wissenschaftliche Kommission, Hans R. Hahnloser … [et al.]. Tübingen : M. Niemayer Verlag, 1971–1987. 9 v. : ill. **BF84**

Some volumes issued in revised editions.

Sponsored by the International Committee on the History of Art.

A thematically-organized multilingual dictionary that is German-French for v. 1–6 and German-French-English beginning with v. 7 and in the revised edition of earlier volumes. Includes synonyms and homonyms, and a bibliography in each fascicle. N34.G516

Hansford, S. Howard. A glossary of Chinese art and archaeology. [2nd ed., rev.]. London : China Society, 1961. 104 p. : ill. (China Society Sinological series, no. 4). **BF85**

Repr., 1972.

1st ed., 1954.

A small dictionary of technical terms covering a wide variety of fields, including bronzes, gems and gem stones, sculpture in stone, painting, ceramics, lacquer, etc. Words are given in Chinese characters, Chinese transliteration, and English equivalent, with (in many cases) an explanation or definition. Index in Chinese. N7340.H3

Lucie-Smith, Edward. The Thames and Hudson dictionary of art terms. London ; N.Y. : Thames and Hudson, [1984]. 208 p. : ill. **BF86**

"More than 2000 entries … define and explain terms from painting, sculpture, architecture, the decorative and applied arts, and the graphic arts, together with techniques of photography."—*Pref.* Brief definitions; 375 illustrations; cross-references. N33.L75

Mollett, John William. An illustrated dictionary of art and archaeology : including terms used in architecture, jewelry, heraldry, costume, music, ornament, weaving, furniture, pottery, ecclesiastical ritual. N.Y. : American Archives of World Art, [1966]. 350 p. : ill. **BF87**

First published in 1883 under title: *An illustrated dictionary of words used in art and archaeology.* Based upon an amended edition of a dictionary by Ernest Bosc. Includes some non-Western terms. Particularly useful for historical purposes. N33.M6

Munsterberg, Hugo. Dictionary of Chinese and Japanese art. N.Y. : Hacker Art Books, 1981. 354 p. **BF88**

A basic source by the author of several books on Asian art. Includes artists' names; lacks illustrations.

§ For other dictionaries on Japanese art, see also: *A dictionary of Japanese art terms, bilingual* (Tokyo : Tōkyō Bijutsu, 1990) and Shigehisa Yamasaki's *Chronological table of Japanese art* (Tokyo : Geishinsha, 1981). N7340.M78

The Oxford companion to twentieth-century art / ed. by Harold Osborne. Oxford ; N.Y. : Oxford Univ. Pr., 1981. 656 p., [128] p. of plates. : ill. **BF89**

Reprinted in paperback, 1988.

Patterned after *The Oxford companion to art* (BF78), but planned and executed independently. Intended "as a handbook and a guide for students and others who wish to find their way intelligently through the exuberant jungle of contemporary art."—*Pref.* Forerunners of modern art movements are generally excluded except as treated in articles concerning movements which they influenced significantly. "In the case of living artists articles purport to summarize their achievement and to indicate the nature of their performance up to the mid 1970s." Selective bibliography and list of illustrations at end of the volume; cross-references.

§ For an earlier one-volume dictionary, consult *Phaidon dictionary of twentieth-century art* (London ; N.Y. : Phaidon, [1973]).

N6490.O94

The Oxford dictionary of art / ed. by Ian Chilvers and Harold Osborne ; consultant ed., Dennis Farr. Oxford ; N.Y. : Oxford Univ. Pr., 1988. 548 p.   **BF90**

A descendant of *The Oxford companion to art* (BF78), *The Oxford companion to twentieth-century art* (BF89), and *The Oxford companion to the decorative arts* (BG20). Much of the text has been rewritten and incorporates more than 300 new entries, while excluding the long entries on individual countries and those on architecture and Oriental art.   N33.O93

Quick, John. Artists' and illustrators' encyclopedia. 2nd ed. N.Y. : McGraw-Hill, [1977]. 327 p. : ill.   **BF91**

1st ed., 1969.

Describes the wide range of methods and materials used in the arts and graphic arts. Concise technical definitions with numerous line drawings.

§ For more current terminology, consult *The HarperCollins dictionary of art terms and techniques* (2nd ed. N.Y. : HarperPerennial, c1992), ed. by Ralph Mayer.   N33.Q5

Réau, Louis. Dictionnaire polyglotte des termes d'art et d'archéologie. Paris : Presses Universitaires de France, 1953. 247 p.   **BF92**

Repr. : Osnabrück : Zeller, 1977.

At head of title: Comité international d'histoire de l'art.

"Ouvrage publié avec le concours de l'UNESCO."

Unlike the 1928 edition (*Lexique polyglotte des termes d'art et d'archéologie* [Paris : H. Laurens, 1928]), which was grouped by 12 languages with the equivalent French term for each entry, this edition has a single alphabet of common French terms (technical and iconographical) with the equivalent terms for each in Greek, Latin, Italian, Spanish, Portuguese, English, German, Dutch, Danish, Swedish, Czech, Polish, and/or Russian. No definitions are given.   N33.R42

Walker, John Albert. Glossary of art, architecture & design since 1945. 3rd ed., rev., enl., and ill. Boston : G.K. Hall, 1992. 1 v. (unpaged) : ill.   **BF93**

1st ed., 1973; 2nd ed., 1977.

Concerned mainly with Anglo-American terms derived from the published literature on art since 1945. Revision includes updating of articles and of the bibliographies, plus the addition of new entries for terms which gained currency since publication of the earlier edition.

§ Related titles include Doris L. Bell's *Contemporary art trends, 1960–1980 : a guide to sources* (Metuchen, N.J. : Scarecrow, 1981), which has a 30-page annotated bibliography of contemporary art journals; and two works by Robert Atkins, *Artspeak : a guide to contemporary ideas, movements, and buzzwords* (N.Y. : Abbeville Pr., c1990) and *Artspoke* (N.Y. : Abbeville Pr., c1993).   N34.W34

Thesauruses

Art & architecture thesaurus / Toni Petersen, director. 2nd ed. N.Y. : Oxford Univ. Pr., c1994. 5 v.   **BF94**

1st ed., 1990 (3 v.); *Supplement 1*, 1992 (221 p.).

Publ. on behalf of the J. Paul Getty Trust.

A structured set of some 87,500 terms, in 33 hierarchies covering associated concepts, physical attributes, styles and periods, agents, activities, materials, and objects (built environment, furnishings and equipment, and visual and verbal communication). Terms are displayed within context, and the alphabetical list includes synonyms, variants, and some scope notes. Includes a summary of term changes since the 1st ed. and a 141-page bibliography.

•Available in machine-readable form as: *Art and architecture thesaurus* [database] (Mountain View, Calif. : Research Libraries Group, 1993). Available online through RLIN; updated semiannually. Also available in an electronic version as *Art and architecture thesaurus : authority reference tool* (ART), version 2.0 (Oxford Univ. Pr., 1993).

Z695.1.A7A76

Quotations

A dictionary of art quotations / comp. by Ian Crofton. N.Y. : Schirmer Books, 1989. 223 p.   **BF95**

First publ. London : Routledge, 1988.

Quotations are grouped under 182 topics. Author and subject indexes.

§ See also: Donna Ward La Cour's *Artists in quotation : a dictionary of the creative thoughts of painters, sculptors, designers, writers, educators, and others* (Jefferson, N.C. : McFarland, c1989. 196 p.), and *The Faber book of art anecdotes*, ed. by Edward Lucie-Smith (London : Faber, 1992), which is arranged chronologically and is indexed by artist. For architecture, see: *Perspectives : an anthology of 1001 architectural quotations*, ed. by Charles Knevitt (London : L. Humphries, 1986).   PN6084.A8D54

Directories

See also *Directory of museums in Africa* (AL87) and *Directory of museums & living displays* (AL88).

International

Art on screen : a directory of films and videos about the visual arts / Nadine Covert, ed. ; Elizabeth Scheines ... [et al.]. Boston : G.K. Hall, c1991. 283 p. : ill.   **BF96**

Comp. and ed. by the Program for Art on Film, a joint venture of the Metropolitan Museum of Art and the J. Paul Getty Trust.

A directory of some 700 recommended motion pictures compiled from the *Art on film database*, now holding 19,000 entries. Covers productions released since late 1975, continuing *Films on art* (N.Y. : Watson-Guptill for the American Federation of Arts, 1977), compiled by the Canadian Centre for Films on Art. As with the Program's *Films and videos on photography* (BF327), annotated entries provide key data, as well as description, comments and references to reviews. Five signed essays provide an overview; entries are in two sections, Features and Documentaries. Indexes: subject; director; name; series; source (i.e., distributor).

•Available online, and on CD-ROM as *Art on screen on CD-ROM* (N.Y. : Macmillan, 1995).   N366.A78

ARTnews international directory of corporate art collections. 1988– . Largo, Fla. : publ. by ARTnews & International Art Alliance, c1988– . Biennial?   **BF97**

The 1990–91 edition (518 p.) lists 833 American and 337 Canadian and overseas corporate collections. Entries are compiled from information provided by the companies, have explanatory notes covering 17 categories, and include bibliographic references when available. The collections hold paintings, works on paper, prints, photographs, and sculpture. Includes basic information on the Association of Corporate Art Curators (ACAC) and the National Association for Corporate Art Management (NACAM). Appendixes: Group exhibitions of corporate art collections; Collections which have been transferred or dispersed; Other corporate supported art programs. Indexes: state and country; corporate business; status; media and type of collection; personnel.

§ See also: *Directory of fine art representatives & corporations collecting art* (2nd ed. Renaissance, Calif. : Directors Guild, 1990) and Victor J. Danilov, *Corporate museums, galleries, and visitor centers* (BF114).

Hudson, Kenneth. The Cambridge guide to the museums of Europe / Kenneth Hudson and Ann Nicholls. Cambridge ; N.Y. : Cambridge Univ. Pr., 1991. 509 p., [29] p. of plates : ill. (some col.). **BF98**
Covers 20 countries, excluding Eastern Europe, describing 2,000 museums and concentrating "on locations away from capital cities and on museums which illustrate particular aspects of a country's character, history and culture"—*Introd.* Three indexes: subjects, museum names, museums associated with individuals.

§ *The Cambridge guide to the museums of Britain and Ireland*, by Kenneth Hudson and Ann Nicholls (Rev. ed. Cambridge ; N.Y. : Cambridge Univ. Pr., 1989. 452 p.) describes nearly 2,000 museums and historic house museums in a geographical arrangement, giving information on hours, admission fees, handicapped access, tours, public transportation, and refreshments. Unfortunately, "Museums new to this edition" is a separate section rather than being integrated into the main listing. Several regional outline maps show locations of museums. Includes indexes by museum names, subjects, and museums associated with individuals. Broader in scope than Joan Abse's *The art galleries of Britain and Ireland* (London: Sidgwick & Jackson, 1975; Rutherford, N.J.: Fairleigh Dickinson Pr., 1976), which should be consulted for descriptions of major works held by any art museum.
AM40.H83 1991

International directory of arts = Internationales Kunst-Adressbuch = Annuaire international des beaux-arts. v. 1 (1952/53)– . Berlin : Kaupterverlag, [1952]– . Biannual. **BF99**
Absorbed *Deutsches Kunst-Adressbuch* which began publication in autumn of 1949.
Title also in Italian and Spanish. Order and number of languages vary. Prefatory text and table of contents in German, English, French, and variously in Italian or Spanish.
Imprint varies; recent editions in 2 v. Beginning with the 8th ed. (1965/66) the two volumes were sometimes published in alternate years. The 21st ed. (1993–94), the first published by Saur, is current through Fall 1992, and contains 150,000 entries.
Includes lists, with addresses and phone numbers, arranged by country, of: museums (including names of key personnel), art galleries, associations, auctioneers, restorers, dealers, booksellers, numismatists, publishers, and periodicals. Content has varied over the years; earlier volumes listed collectors and universities and art colleges. The most useful of the international directories. N50.I6

Museums of the world. 4th rev. and enl. ed. München ; N.Y. : Saur, 1992. 642 p. : ill. (Handbook of international documentation and information, v. 16). **BF100**
1st ed., 1973; 3rd rev. ed., 1981.
A listing by country and city of some 24,000 museums of all types in 182 countries. Gives address, year of founding, and kinds of collections or strengths. Name and subject indexes. AM1.M76

Year's art : a concise epitome of all matters relating to the arts of painting, sculpture, engraving and architecture, and to schools of design, which have occurred during the year, together with information respecting the events of the year. v. 1 (1880)–64 (1947). London : Macmillan, 1880–1947. Annual. **BF101**
Publisher varies.
Coverage: v. 63, 1942–44; v. 64, 1945–47.
Includes lists of museums, associations, and schools in Great Britain and the major ones in the Dominions and the U.S.; information on sales and exhibitions; a directory of artists and dealers; obituaries; and information on a variety of other pertinent subjects. N9.Y4

United States

American art directory. v. 38 (1952)– . New Providence, N.J. : Bowker, 1952– . **BF102**
Frequency varies.
From v. 1–37, 1898–1945/48, the directory and *Who's who in American art* (BF157) were published as *American art annual*, by or for the American Federation of Arts.
Now in three main sections: (1) Art organizations (national and regional associations, museums, and libraries of the U.S. and Canada); (2) Art schools and college and university departments of art and architecture (U.S. and Canada); (3) Art information (major museums and art schools abroad, state arts councils, art magazines, newspapers carrying art notes and their critics, scholarships and fellowships, open exhibitions and traveling exhibitions, etc.). Indexes of organizations, personnel, and subjects.

§ For additional information, especially about smaller or alternative American art organizations, consult: *Organizing artists : a document and directory of the National Association of Artists' Organizations* (3rd ed., Wash. : The Association, 1992). For Great Britain, see *Arts address book : a classified guide to national (U.K. and Ireland) and international organisations* (3rd ed. High Wycombe : Peter Marcan, 1989). For American feminist organizations, see *Guide to women's art organizations*, ed. by Cynthia Navaretta (N.Y. : Midmarch Associates, 1979). *International contemporary arts directory*, ed. by Ann Lee Morgan; assistant ed., Colin Naylor (N. Y. : St. Martin's, 1985. 393 p.) covers museums, libraries, galleries, periodicals, associations, grants, writers, and bibliographies. N50.A54

Art in America : annual guide to galleries, museums, artists / comp. by the editors of Art in America. 1982– . N.Y. : Neal-Schuman, [1982]– . Annual. **BF103**
A reprinting, without advertisements, of the August issue of *Art in America.*
A geographic listing, by state and city, of some 3,700 exhibition spaces (1993/94 ed.). Three indexes: galleries and museums, private dealers, artists.

Funding for museums, archives, and special collections / ed. by Denise Wallen and Karen Cantrell. Phoenix : Oryx, 1988. 355 p. **BF104**
"Designed to facilitate the search for financial support for museums and museum activities and programs" (*Introd.*), museums being defined as nonprofit institutions whose purpose is educational or aesthetic. Lists more than 500 "sources of support, arranged alphabetically by sponsor, including foundations, corporations, government agencies, associations and organizations, and professional societies." For each program gives location, program description, eligibility or limitations, fiscal information, application information, deadlines. Indexes of subject, geographic restrictions, and sponsor type. List of sponsoring organizations; bibliography. AM122.F86

Money for visual artists / researched by Douglas Oxenhorn. New expanded 2nd ed. N.Y. : American Council for the Arts : Allworth Pr., 1993. 317 p. **BF105**
1st ed., 1991, ed. by Suzanne Niemeyer.
An alphabetical listing of some 235 arts councils, foundations, and related programs within the U.S. Indexes: name, geographic area, and organization type.

§ A successor to Laura R. Green's *Money for artists* (N.Y. : ACA Books, 1987). Two related works: *Money for performing artists* and *Money for film and video artists*, both edited by Niemeyer and produced by the American Council for the Arts, 1991. N347.M59

Money to work II : funding for visual artists / ed. by Helen M. Brunner and Donald H. Russell with Grant E. Samuelson. Wash. : Art Resources International, 1992. 312 p. **BF106**
1st ed., 1988, had title: *Money to work : grants for visual artists.*
The "culmination of an extensive research project conducted by the Center for Arts Information (CAI)" (*About the book*, 1st ed.) to analyze data from a regional perspective. Identifies 340 organizations as

potential sources, based on questionnaires and telephone interviews. Contents: Introduction ("An assessment of visual artists' fellowships"); Profiles of organizations (national, regional, state, and local); Bibliography and resource organizations. Indexes: Geographical eligibility; Media; National grants; Grants available by nomination; Financial need; Emergency grants index; Acronyms of organizations; Common names of awards.   **N347.M6**

Shipley, Lloyd W. Information resources in the arts : a directory / comp. by Lloyd W. Shipley (National Referral Center). Wash. : Library of Congress : For sale by the U.S. Govt. Print. Off., 1986. 161 p.   **BF107**

Superintendent of Documents classification: LC 1.2:In3.

Intended to "enable its user to identify easily ... organizations by most common areas of interest and to compare and contrast groups ...."—*Introd.* Lists federal, state, and local government agencies; national and regional arts service organizations; arts education programs; dance organizations; theater organizations; music organizations; film organizations; television, video, radio, broadcasting, and cable organizations; international arts organizations; and others. Three indexes: geographic, organizations, subjects. Produced by the National Referral Center of the Library of Congress. The printed version is a "preliminary and experimental edition" (*Pref.*), with a new edition intended.
         NX110.S48

Sales

See also different media, e.g., Painting–Sales.

Art prices current. v. [1] (1907/08)–9 (1915/16); n.s., v. 1 (1921/22)–50 (1972/73)– . London : Wm. Dawson & Sons ltd. [etc.], 1908–73. Annual.   **BF108**

Subtitle varies. Publication suspended 1917–20.

Arranged by medium: Pt. A, Paintings, drawings, and miniatures; Pt. B, Engravings and prints. Each part is arranged chronologically by sales, with items within the part consecutively numbered and covering artist, title, size, purchaser, price, sometimes condition. Indexes of artists, engravers, and collectors.

§ *La cote des tableux; ou, Annuaire des ventes de tableaux, dessins, aquarelles, pastels, gouaches, miniatures; guide du marchand, de l'amateur* (Paris : L. Maurice, 1919–31. 11 v.) provides a chronological record of sales for the period Oct. 1918–July 1929. Michèle Bérard's *Encyclopedia of modern art auction prices* (N.Y. : Arco, 1971. 417 p.) records the prices paid for modern paintings, Sep. 1961–July 1969.   **N8670.A7**

International auction records. v. 1 (1967)– . [Zurich, etc. : Edition M, etc.]. Annual.   **BF109**

Comp. by E. Mayer, 1988– .

First publ. N.Y. : Editions Publisol.

Arranged by medium and then by artist. Gives artist's dates, title of work, date, physical description, price, and auction sale number.

§ Other sources: *World collectors annuary* (v. 1 [1946/49]– . Delft : Brouwer [etc.], 1950–); *Art sales index* (v. 1 [1984–85]– . Weybridge, Surrey, England : Art Sales Index Ltd., 1985–); *Annuaire des cotes international = International art price annual* (1988– . Paris : ADEC-Production, 1987–); and *Le semestriel des arts* (1989– . Paris : Van Wilder, 1989–).   **N8640I5**

Lancour, Harold. American art auction catalogues, 1785–1942 : a union list. N.Y. : New York Public Library, 1944. 377 p.   **BF110**

"Reprinted with revisions and additions from the *Bulletin* of the New York Public Library, Jan. 1943–Feb. 1944."—*verso of title page.*

A union checklist of more than 7,000 catalogs of auction sales of art objects including paintings, drawings, statuary, furniture, rugs, jewelry, textiles, musical instruments, curios, etc. Excludes books, maps, bookplates, stamps, and coins. Locates copies in 21 libraries. Includes a list of auction houses and an index of owners.   **Z5939.A1L3**

Leonard's annual price index of art auctions / Auction Index, Inc. West Newton, Mass. : Auction Index, c1982– .   **BF111**

Title varies.

Aims to be "a complete listing of original works of art sold at the major auction houses in the United States."—*Explanatory notes.* Lists roughly 36,000 artworks in the main section under artist's name, giving nationality and dates, title of work, price, indication of signature, medium, dimensions, date and place of sale. Covers painting, sculpture, drawing, and mixed media (but excludes photography and graphic arts) from sales at 36 auction houses, named in a list that cites the date and title of each sale. The 1991 volume covers the 1989–90 auction season and has an introduction summarizing market activity during that year as well as a three-page bibliography.

§ Recommended over the smaller *Jacobsen's ... painting and bronze price guide* (Staten Island, N.Y. : A. Jacobsen, 1975–), which covers catalogs from 24 auction galleries in the eastern U.S.
      N8602.L46

Lugt, Frits. Répertoire des catalogues de ventes publiques : intéressant l'art ou la curiosité, ... The Hague : Nijhoff, 1938–87. 4 v.   **BF112**

Vol. 4 publ. 1987 under the direction of Frits Lugt and the Fondation Custodia in association with the J. Paul Getty Trust.

A publication of Rijksbureau voor Kunsthistorische en Ikonografische Documentatie.

A chronological list of 89,586 catalogs of art sales held throughout Europe, 1600–1925. Information for each entry includes: date and place of sale, provenance, contents, number of items and pages, auctioneers, and location of copies in libraries. Index of names of collections sold.   **N8650.L8**

•**SCIPIO** : Sales Catalog Index Project Input On-line [database]. Mountain View, Calif. : Research Libraries Group, Art and Architecture Program, 1980– .   **BF113**

A union list of sales catalogs, 1599 to the present, from nearly 3,000 auction houses. Contains more than 126,500 records and is updated several times weekly. Founded by the Art Institute of Chicago, the Cleveland Museum of Art, and the Metropolitan Museum of Art (N.Y.), later joined by the Getty Center for the History of Art and the Humanities (Santa Monica, Calif.) and the National Gallery of Art (Wash.). Access points include name of auction house, place of sale, date of sale, a coded name or number for the sale, catalog title, collector's name. Five years of coverage are also available in book form as *Index of art sales catalogs, 1981–1985* (Boston : G.K. Hall, c1987. 2 v. [1253 p.]).

§ An older auction catalog index has recently been published on microfiche by the Frick Art Reference Library, the *Frick Art Reference Library sales catalogue index* [microform] (Boston : G.K. Hall, 1992. 230 microfiches). Accompanied by a 10-p. guide.

Museums

See also Museum publications (above) and BF321.

Danilov, Victor J. Corporate museums, galleries, and visitor centers : a directory. N.Y. : Greenwood, 1991. 211 p. : ill.
      BF114

Within the three categories arrangement is by country, then alphabetically by corporate name. Lacks geographic access. Brief bibliography; index.   **AM5.D36**

Gealt, Adelheid M. Looking at art : a visitor's guide to museum collections. N.Y. : Bowker, 1983. 609 p. : ill.   **BF115**

Intends "to provide basic information that would aid museumgoers ... in understanding what they see."—*Pref.* Not a guide to specific museums as such, but a survey of "the types of art produced by period, outlining the influences that are thought to have informed the artistic production of that age." Chapters on the history of collecting and growth of museums, how museums build collections, and the functions and organization of museums precede the chronological chapters (with subdivisions for the art of individual countries) and chapters for Asian art, pre-Columbian art, and tribal arts. Lists of artists (grouped by genre or medium) and of major representative collections conclude most chapters. Bibliography; index.

§ For the history and collections of the world's major museums, consult Virginia Jackson's *Art museums of the world* (Westport, Conn. : Greenwood, 1987). N5200.G4

The official museum directory. 1971– . Wash. : American Association of Museums, 1971– . Annual since 1980. **BF116**

For annotation, *see* AL90. AM10.A2O4

Rath, Frederick L. A bibliography on historical organization practices / ed. by Frederick L. Rath, Jr. and Merrilyn Rogers O'Connell. Nashville : Amer. Assoc. for State and Local History, [1975–84]. 6 v. **BF117**
Vols. 2–6 comp. by Rosemary S. Reese.
Contents: v. 1, Historic preservation; v. 2, Care and conservation of collections; v. 3, Interpretation; v. 4, Documentation of collections; v. 5, Administration; v. 6, Research.
Represents a new edition of the compilers' *Guide to historic preservation, historical agencies, and museum practices* (1970).
A selective bibliography of books, pamphlets, and periodical articles, most of them published since 1945. Z1251.A2R35

Exhibitions

Archives of American Art. Collection of exhibition catalogs. Boston : G.K. Hall, 1979. 851 p. **BF118**
Photographic reproduction of catalog cards for some 15,000 exhibition catalogs located through a survey in the mid-1960s and microfilmed for use at the Archives or through interlibrary loan. Represents the holdings of major public, museum, and historical society libraries in the U.S., as well as the Archives' own collection. Catalogs are listed under name of gallery or museum and under artist. Covers 19th–20th centuries, but is apparently strongest for the 1900–45 period.
Z5939.A73

The Worldwide bibliography of art exhibition catalogues, 1963 1987. Millwood, N.Y. : Kraus International Publications ; Ithaca, N.Y. : Worldwide Books, c1992. 3 v. (2537 p.). **BF119**
Contents: v. 1, Geographical section : Western art, non Western art; v. 2, Media section; v. 3, Topical section ; Monograph section ; Title index.
Generated from a bibliographical database developed by Worldwide Books.
§ Two other commercial database-generated publications, covering contemporary art exhibitions, appeared in the 1980s: *International directory of exhibiting artists* (1983. 2 v.), and *Guide to exhibited artists* (1985. 5 v.), both from Clio Press (Oxford ; Santa Barbara).
Z5939.W675

Yarnall, James L. The National Museum of American Art's index to American art exhibition catalogues : from the beginning through the 1876 centennial year / comp. by James L. Yarnall and William H. Gerdts. Boston : G.K. Hall, 1986. 6 v. (4944 p.). **BF120**
Took its impetus from a Bicentennial project, the Inventory of American Paintings Executed Before 1914. Intends "not merely to index the publications of specific institutions, but also to provide insight into what artworks Americans in all parts of the country exhibited and viewed ... includes the exhibition name, location, and date; the names of the artists exhibited, with their addresses if known; the titles of the works; the owners of the works, with addresses; narrative excerpts of catalogue commentary ... and subjects of the works."—*Foreword*. Includes works by artists of all nationalities and schools listed in 952 catalogs. Of 118,012 works listed, 843 are American and 16 Canadian. Excludes auction sales catalogs, but photocopies of these are available at NMAA, "including a large number that do not

appear in the standard bibliography of auctions [Harold Lancour's *American art auction catalogues, 1785–1942*; BF110]."—*User's guide*. The subject index in v. 6 includes names of individuals, places, and iconographic objects.
§ See also: Raymond L. Wilson's *Index of American print exhibitions, 1882–1940* (BF368) and indexes specific to particular institutions. N6507.Y363

Handbooks

See also BF304.

Christie's guide to collecting / ed. by Robert Cumming. Oxford : Phaidon ; Englewood Cliffs, N.J. : Prentice-Hall, [1984]. 224 p. : ill. **BF121**
Publ. in French as: *Guide Christie's du collectionneur* (Paris : Gründ, 1986).
Aims "to encourage the spirit and traditions of private collecting and to offer down-to-earth advice on questions which are frequently asked."—*Foreword*. Brief chapters by specialist contributors on individual aspects of collecting are grouped in three sections: Becoming a collector; Looking after a collection; Buying and selling. Appendixes include a select bibliography, a list of professional associations, directories of auction houses and dealers and of museums, galleries, etc. Index. N5200.C48

Feldman, Franklin. Art law : rights and liabilities of creators and collectors / Franklin Feldman, Stephen E. Weil ; with the collaboration of Susan Duke Biederman. Boston : Little, Brown, c1986. 2 v. **BF122**
Successor to the author's *Art works : law, policy, practice* (N.Y. : Practicing Law Institute, c1974).
Kept up to date by supplements (1988, 1993).
Consists of 14 chapters on topics ranging from the right of expression to art as a "collectible" asset that present the text of pertinent cases that are themselves amplified by extensive footnotes. Excludes coverage of tax rules as they relate to artists. Two indexes: table of cases, table of statutes.
§ Less technical is: Ralph Lerner and Judith Bresler's *Art law* (N.Y. : Practicing Law Inst., 1989. 766 p.). Other related titles include Tad Crawford's *Legal guide for the visual artist* (Rev. ed. N.Y. : Allworth Pr. ; Cincinnati : distr. by North Light Books, 1990. 213 p.) and Leonard D. Duboff's *Art law in a nutshell* (2nd ed. St. Paul, Minn. : West Publ., 1993). KF390.A7F45

Goldfinger, Eliot. Human anatomy for artists : the elements of form. N.Y. : Oxford Univ. Pr., 1991. 348 p. : ill. **BF123**
Topics: The skeleton, Joints, Muscles, Muscle action, Surface structures, Proportion, Conceptions of mass. Bibliography; index.
NC760.G67

Goldman, Bernard. Reading and writing in the arts. Rev. ed. Detroit : Wayne State Univ. Pr., 1978. 191 p. **BF124**
1st ed., 1972.
Intended as a bibliographic guide for the undergraduate, but useful for the nonspecialist reading public. Materials chosen for inclusion are, therefore, usually in English, authoritative and not more than 75 years old. Arranged by type of reference source (e.g., bibliographies, dictionaries) with a "Reference key by subject." Annotated. Brief section on writing for art history journals. Index of authors and series.
§ Related titles are Sylvan Barnet's *Short guide to writing about art*, (3rd ed. Glenview, Ill. : Scott Foresman, 1989) and Joshua Charles Taylor's *Learning to look : a handbook for the visual arts*, (2nd ed. Chicago : Univ. of Chicago Pr., 1981). Z5931.G6

Hope, Augustine. The color compendium / Augustine Hope, Margaret Walch. N.Y. : Van Nostrand Reinhold, c1990. 360 p. : ill. (some col.). **BF125**
For annotation, *see* ED59. QC494.2.H67

Oriental art : a handbook of styles and forms / by Jeannine Auboyer ... [et al.]. N.Y. : Rizzoli, 1980. 608 p. : chiefly ill.
BF126
Translation of *La grammaire des formes et des styles*. Also publ. London : Faber and Faber, 1979.
Arranged by region and country. Each chapter includes a brief introduction, list of major museums, and bibliography, as well as numerous small illustrations. Concludes with a modest glossary.
N7260.G6713

Rossol, Monona. The artist's complete health and safety guide : [everything you need to know about art materials to make your workplace safe and comply with United States and Canadian right-to-know laws]. N.Y. : Allworth Pr. ; Cincinnati : Distr. by North Light Books, c1990. 328 p. : ill. **BF127**
Explicit technical information; written by a chemist. Contents: The regulated art world (hazards, etc.); Artists' raw materials; Precautions for individual media; Teaching art. Bibliography; index.
§ For painting, *see also* Ralph Mayer, *The artist's handbook of materials and technicques*, 5th ed. (BF304).   RC963.6.A78R67

Chronologies

Clapp, Jane. Art censorship : a chronology of proscribed and prescribed art. Metuchen, N.J. : Scarecrow, 1972. 582 p. : ill.
BF128
Incidents of art censorship ("artists or art works restricted for economic, social, political, moral or aesthetic reasons by state and church officials, and also by citizen or other groups, individuals, or society as a whole"—*Pref.*) are briefly reported in chronological sequence, with references to each incident keyed to a bibliography of 641 books and periodicals. Indexed.   N8740.C55

History

Gardner, Helen. Gardner's art through the ages / [ed. by] Horst de la Croix, Richard G. Tansey, Diane Kirkpatrick. 9th ed. San Diego, Calif. : Harcourt Brace Jovanovich, c1991. 1135 p. : ill. (some col.).   **BF129**
1st ed., 1926; 8th ed., 1986.
A standard work, intended for students and the general reader; widely used as a basic textbook. This edition has expanded text and images, where warranted by subject matter. Bibliography.
§ Another older standard history is *Art and architecture in the Western world* by D. M. Robb and J. J. Garrison (4th ed. N.Y. : Harper, [1963]), first published in 1935.   N5300.G25

Hauser, Arnold. The social history of art / [tr. in collaboration with the author by Stanley Godman]. N.Y. : Knopf, 1951. 2 v. (1022 p.) : ill.   **BF130**
Repr. : N.Y. : Vintage, 1985. 4 v.
Translation of *Sozialgeschichte der Kunst und Literatur* (München : C. H. Beck, 1953).
Bibliography given in brief form as notes to chapters at the end of each volume, with no systematic arrangement. Indexes of subjects and names at the end of v. 2.   N72.H353

Hunter, Sam. Modern art : painting, sculpture, architecture / Sam Hunter and John Jacobus. 3rd ed. Englewood Cliffs, N.J. : Prentice Hall ; N.Y. : H.N. Abrams, 1992. 440 p. : ill. (some col.).   **BF131**
1st ed., *Modern art from post-impressionism to the present*, 1976; 2nd ed., 1985.
A basic history.
§ Also widely used is H. Harvard Arnason's *History of modern art: painting, sculpture, architecture, photography*, 3rd ed., rev. and

updated by Daniel Wheeler (N.Y. : Abrams, 1986). For the previous century, Robert Rosenblum's *19th century art: 1776–1900* (N.Y. : Abrams, 1984) is recommended.   N6447.H86

Janson, Horst Woldemar. History of art / rev. and expanded by Anthony F. Janson. 4th ed. Englewood Cliffs, N.J. : Prentice Hall ; N.Y. : H.N. Abrams, 1991. 856 p. : ill. (some col.), maps.   **BF132**
1st ed., 1962; 3rd ed., 1986.
A handsomely illustrated summary of Western painting, sculpture, architecture, and photography. The 4th ed. "preserves most of the text of the previous one" (*Pref.*), has three times as many color illustrations, plus new diagrams and architectural drawings. Pt. 4 (The modern world) has been reorganized, with a separate chapter on sculpture since 1900.
§ Similar surveys have also appeared in new editions: Frederick Hartt's *Art : a history of painting, sculpture, architecture* (3rd ed. N.Y. : Prentice Hall & Abrams, 1989), Hugh Honour and John Fleming's *The visual arts : a history* (3rd ed. N.Y. : Abrams, 1991; publ. in Great Britain as *A world history of art*), and *A history of Far Eastern art* by Sherman E. Lee (5th ed. N.Y. : Abrams, 1993). H. W. Janson and Dora Jane Janson also compiled *Key monuments of the history of art : a visual survey* (2nd ed. N.Y. : Abrams, 1964), consisting of 1,200 black-and-white reproductions. Another useful work is *History of art for young people*, by H. W. Janson and Anthony F. Janson (4th ed. N.Y. : Abrams, 1992).   N5300.J3

Pelican history of art / ed. by Nikolaus Pevsner. [Baltimore] : Penguin, 1953–87. v. 1–46. : ill. (In progress).   **BF133**
A series expected to be complete in 50 v., covering world art and architecture of all periods, each written by a specialist and containing substantial bibliographies and many plates. Volumes are not published in chronological or regional sequence of subject matter; after v. 31, volumes do not carry a volume number. Most volumes have been issued in revised editions. Also issued in paperback.
§ A similar set has been published in German: *Propyläen Kunstgeschichte* (Berlin : Propyläen Verlag, 1923–29. 16 v. Rev. ed., Berlin : Propyläen Verlag, 1966–74. 18 v.).

Upjohn, Everard Miller. History of world art / Everard Miller Upjohn, Paul Stover Wingert, Jane Gaston Mahler. 2nd ed., rev. and enl. N.Y. : Oxford, 1958. 876 p. : 671 ill., 17 col. plates, maps (on lining papers).   **BF134**
1st ed., 1949.
Publ. in French as *Histoire mondiale de l'art* (Verviers : Gerard, 1965–66), in Italian as *Storia mondiale dell'arte* (Varese : Dall'Oglio [1966–67]), and in Spanish as *Historia del arte* (Madrid : Ediciones Daimon : M. Tamayo [1984]).
A survey of painting, sculpture, and architecture written for introductory college courses. Suggested readings; glossary; index.
N5300.U6

Biography

See also BF224.

Allgemeines Künstlerlexikon : die bildenden Künstler aller Zeiten und Völker / erarbeitet, redigiert und hrsg. von Günter Meissner und einem Redaktionskollektiv unter internationaler Mitwirkung. München : K.G. Saur, 1983–94. v. 1–9. (In progress).   **BF135**
Publisher varies; v. 1–3 publ. Leipzig : E.A. Seemann, 1983–86.
Contents: v. 1–9, Aa–Berrettini.
Known as *AKL* and likely to equal Ulrich Thieme and Felix Becker's *Allgemeines Lexikon der bildenden Künstler* (BF148) and Hans Vollmer's *Allgemeines Lexikon der bildenden Künstler des XX. Jahrhunderts* (BF149) in thoroughness and quality and to be more than triple their size. Includes painters, graphic artists, sculptors, architects, and decorative artists of all nationalities; excludes photographers. The editorial board for the initial volumes comprises 15 German scholars,

and entries are written by a large international group of scholars. Entries provide biographical data and "creative characteristics" (for persons born up to ca. 1940); locations of the artist's works; references to writings by the artist; listing of exhibitions (solo and group); and bibliography. The entire set is scheduled to be released in CD-ROM.

N40.A63

Artist biographies master index / Barbara McNeil, ed. Detroit : Gale, c1986. 700 p. (Gale biographical index series, no. 9). **BF136**

A listing of sources for more than 275,000 biographical sketches from about 70 English-language reference books. Covers all nationalities and periods. Lists any name or date exactly as found in the source, with no attempt to reconcile variants. "This index is derived from material that has appeared or will appear in the more comprehensive *Biography and genealogy master index* [AH9]."—*Introd.*

§ Two similar earlier indexes are: Daniel Trowbridge Mallett's *Index of artists : international* ... (N.Y. : Bowker, 1935; repr. : N.Y. : Peter Smith, 1948; *Supplement*, 1940); and Patricia Pate Havlice's *Index to artistic biography* (Metuchen, N.J. : Scarecrow, 1973. 2 v.). Havlice also compiled *Earth scale art : bibliography, directory of artists, and index of reproductions* (Jefferson, N.C. : McFarland, 1984).

N40.A78

Bénézit, Emmanuel. Dictionnaire critique et documentaire des peintres, sculpteurs, dessinateurs et graveurs de tous les temps et de tous les pays. Nouv. éd. entièrement refondue, revue et corr. Paris : Gründ, 1976. 10 v. **BF137**

1st ed., 1911–23 (Paris : R. Roger et F. Chernoviz. 3 v.); "Nouvelle éd.," 1948–55 (8 v.).

A comprehensive work, covering artists from the 5th century BCE to the mid-20th century, including many minor names. Includes both Western and Eastern art. Entries, varying in length from a few lines to several columns, usually include a list of chief works, museums where displayed, and (in some instances) prices paid for works. Symbols and signatures are reproduced in facsimile, and at the end of each key letter of the alphabet a list of the signatures used by anonymous artists appears. Brief bibliography of sources at end of v. 10. An unusual feature is the inclusion of tables of 20th-century rates of exchange for pounds, dollars, and francs.

N40.B47

Contemporary artists / ed., Colin Naylor. 3rd ed. Chicago : St. James, c1989. 1059 p. : ill. **BF138**

1st ed., 1977; 2nd ed., 1983, ed. by Muriel Emmanuel [et al.].

While "no rigid criteria were imposed" on the advisory board responsible for the selection of artists treated, guidelines "proposed that all entrants should have worked as professional artists for at least five years, have exhibited their work in several individual important galleries, and have been included in large-scale museum survey shows—and be represented in the permanent collections of major museums throughout the world."—*Introd., 2nd ed.* Entries comprise a brief biography; individual exhibitions; selected group exhibitions; collections in which the artist's work is included; a bibliography by and about the person; and signed commentary.

§ More useful than Claude Marks's *World artists, 1950–1980* (N.Y. : H.W. Wilson, 1984) or *World artists 1980–1990* (N.Y. : H.W. Wilson, 1991). In conjunction with this, *Biographies of creative artists : an annotated bibliography*, by Susan M. Stievater (N.Y. : Garland, 1991), is useful for locating significant and readable biographies. Arrangement is by type (literary, visual artists, composers and musicians, actors and dancers); indexes provide access to women artists and nationalities.

N6490.C6567

Hesse, Gritta. Künstler der jungen Generation : Literaturverzeichnis zur Gegenwartskunst in der Amerika-Gedenkbibliothek, Berliner Zentralbibliothek = Artists of the "young generation" : literature on contemporary art in the American Memorial Library, Berlin Central Library / [comp. by Gritta Hesse and Marie Agnes Bingel]. München ; N.Y. : Saur, 1987. 353 p. **BF139**

Emphasizes European artists, largely because the publications held by the library are primarily from German-speaking countries. For most artists, birth date and city of residence are provided; most were

born in the 1930s and 1940s. Contains 17,000 entries on some 6,500 artists, including illustrators and photographers; entries give bibliographic data but no annotations.

§ For additional information concerning 20th-century artists, see René Édouard-Joseph's *Dictionnaire biographique des artistes contemporains, 1910–1930* ... (Paris : Art & Edition, 1930–34; *Supplement*, 1936) and *Verzeichnis der bildenden Künstler von 1880 bis heute* ... (Darmstadt : Brün, 1988). Z5935.5.H47

McDonald, Jan. Australian artists' index : a biographical index of Australian artists, craft workers, photographers, and architects. Sydney : Arts Libraries Society / Australia and New Zealand, 1986. 432 p. (ARLIS/ANZ publication, no. 1). **BF140**

For more than 10,000 names, cites references from 416 standard sources for Australian art, including exhibition catalogs and the two most essential reference works, Alan McCulloch's *Encyclopedia of Australian art* (BF76) and Max Germaine's *Artists and galleries of Australia*, rev. ed. (Brisbane : Boolarong Publ., 1984).

§ Additional titles include: *Dictionary of Australian artists*, ed. by Joan Kerr (Melbourne : Oxford Univ. Pr., 1992. 900 p.); *A dictionary of women artists of Australia* by Max Germaine (Roseville East, NSW : Craftsman House, 1991); and *Artists in early Australia and their portraits : a guide*, ed. by Eve Buscombe (Sydney : Eureka Research, 1978). N7404.M33

New York Public Library. The artists file [microform]. Alexandria, Va. : Chadwyck-Healey Inc., [1989]. 11,381 microfiches : ill. **BF141**

On header: New York Public Library. Artists file.

Original file compiled by and located in the New York Public Library. Largely a clipping file of 1.5 million items on some 76,000 painters, sculptors and architects taken from 19th- and 20th-century material. The price ($20,000) ensures the file's availability only in research libraries.

The file was begun in 1911. The fiche set includes a printed guide with an index of artists cited. Includes jewelers, furniture and interior designers, handicraft and commercial artists; excludes printmakers, photographers, medalists, and city planners.

Ogilvie, Grania. The dictionary of South African painters and sculptors, including Namibia / Grania Ogilvie, assisted by Carol Graff. Rosebank, Johannesburg, South Africa : Everard Read, 1988. 799 p., [84] p. of plates : ill. (some col.). **BF142**

Lists 1,800 artists from South Africa and Namibia. For each, gives vital dates, media, education, profile of achievements, exhibitions, awards and honors, publications (books), and bibliographic references. Includes a representative selection of color reproductions and a substantial bibliography. The 10-page "Useful addresses" section lists galleries, museums, libraries, associations, art schools, and art centers.

§ A comparable work is Esmé Berman's *Art & artists of South Africa* (New and enl. ed. Cape Town : Balkema, 1983. 545 p.), which also includes entries on genres and survey articles. The newest source for African artists is: Bernice M. Kelly, *Nigerian artists : a who's who & bibliography* (London ; N.Y. : Hans Zell, 1993. 600 p.).

N7395.6.O35

Petteys, Chris. Dictionary of women artists : an international dictionary of women artists born before 1900. Boston : G.K. Hall, [1985]. 851 p. : ill. **BF143**

Includes biographical sketches of "more than 21,000 women painters, sculptors, printmakers, and illustrators born before 1900, regardless of the scarcity of information about them."—*Pref.* Gives references to sources of information at the end of each entry. Bibliography, p. 781–851. N43.P47

Roberts, Laurance P. A dictionary of Japanese artists : painting, sculpture, ceramics, prints, lacquer / Laurance P. Roberts, in collaboration with the International House of Japan. Tokyo ; N.Y. : Weatherhill, [1976]. 299 p. **BF144**

"This dictionary limits itself to artists who were born before 1900, or, if born later, who died before 1972."—*Pref.* Entry is by the most common form of the artist's name, with an index of alternate forms and one of Japanese characters. For each artist is given: all forms of name, dates, education, career, public collections in which represented, references to items in the bibliography (p. 223–32) which provide fuller information. Brief glossary of terms. Appendixes: Collections; Art organizations and institutions; Art periods; Japanese provinces and prefectures.

§ The author also compiled *Roberts' guide to Japanese museums* (Tokyo : Kodansha Internat., 1978). See also: *Biographical dictionary of Japanese art* ed. by Yutaka Tazawa ([Tokyo] : Kodansha International, [1981]) and James Self, *Japanese art signatures* (BF161).   N7358.R6

Robertson, Jack. Twentieth-century artists on art : an index to artists' writings, statements, and interviews. Boston : G.K. Hall, c1985. 488 p.   **BF145**

According to the compiler, two distinct types of primary documents are used in art historical research—works of art and the artists' own words; hence, this index covers "495 published sources ... not otherwise analyzed by individual artist's name."—*Pref.* Entries for some 5,000 artists give dates, nationality, and medium; some figures more prominent in the 19th century are listed to permit inclusion of statements they made in the 20th. 75% of the 14,000 bibliographic citations are in English, the remainder in five Western European languages. They are drawn from anthologies, monographs, group exhibition catalogs, and periodicals, and cite not only statements and interviews but also poems, stories, and group discussions. A bibliography gives full descriptions.

§ For earlier artists, see: *Artists on art : from the 14th to the 20th century*, by Robert Goldwater and Marco Treves (3rd ed. N.Y. : Pantheon, 1958), which has some 160 statements.   NX456.R59

Seymour, Nancy N. An index-dictionary of Chinese artists, collectors, and connoisseurs with character identification by modified stroke count. Metuchen, N.J. : Scarecrow, 1988. 987 p.   **BF146**

Pt. 1, the Master dictionary, "is intended to be a sourcebook for the researcher to use initially for artist information and identification."—*Introd.* The 5,000 name entries provide both Wade-Giles and pinyin romanization, dynasty or period, alternate names or signatures, places and dates for biography, a note of characteristic work and subject matter, strokes in surname, bibliographic sources, and full Chinese characters for the name. Pt. 2 "presents a simple methodology for Western scholars to learn to read Chinese characters in order to identify names." Its sections include: Index of modified stroke count; Index of alternate names; Chronology of Chinese dynasties; pinyin and Wade-Giles romanizations; Selected bibliography; Character index of Chinese names.

§ *See also* James Francis Cahill, *An index of early Chinese painters and paintings* (BF313).   N7348.S48

Spanish artists from the fourth to the twentieth century : a critical dictionary / Frick Art Reference Library. N.Y. : G.K. Hall, 1993. v. 1. (In progress).   **BF147**

Contents: v. 1, A–F.

The first of three volumes, to cover some 7,000 artists. Artist entries provide dates, all known variant forms of the name, statements indicating medium or profession and clarifying relationship with artists with similar names, and 1–20 bibliographic references to sources (Thieme-Becker [BF148], *Ars hispaniae*, monographs, museum and auction catalogs, and journal articles). "Guide to use" in English, Spanish, French, and German. Vol. 3 will include a chronological list of artists' names and dates.

§ Biographical dictionaries of artists are available for many countries. Another example: *Kunstnerleksikon*, ed. by Tove Køie and Ole Malmqvist ([Copenhagen] : AOF, [1985]).   N7112.S67

Thieme, Ulrich. Allgemeines Lexikon der bildenden Künstler : von der Antike bis zur Gegenwart, unter Mitwirkung von etwa 400 Fachgelehrten des In- und Auslandes / Ulrich Thieme, Felix Becker. Leipzig : W. Engelmann : E.A. Seemann, 1907–50. 37 v.   **BF148**

Repr. : München : Deutscher Taschenbuch Verlag, 1992 (37 v. in 19).

Binder's title: *Künstler Lexikon.*

Vol. 16–37 ed. by Hans Vollmer. Statement of contributors varies.

Imprint varies.

Vol. 37 has added title: Meister mit Notnamen und Monogrammisten.

The most complete and authoritative dictionary of painters, sculptors, engravers, etchers, and architects. Frequently gives locations of works of art. Good bibliographies. Longer articles are signed by some 400 contributing specialists. Includes some artists who were living at time of compilation, but Hans Vollmer, *Allgemeines Lexikon der bildenden Künstler des XX. Jahrhunderts* (BF149) is the principal source for 20th-century artists.   N40.T4

Vollmer, Hans. Allgemeines Lexikon der bildenden Künstler des XX. Jahrhunderts / Unter Mitwirkung von Fachgelehrten des In- und Auslandes. Leipzig : Seemann, 1953–62. 6 v.   **BF149**

Repr. : Leipzig : Seemann, [1979?].

Half-title: Künstlerlexikon des XX. Jahrhunderts.

Contents: Bd. 1–5, A–Z. Nachträge, A–G; Bd. 6, Nachträge, H–Z.

A continuation of Ulrich Thieme and Felix Becker, *Allgemeines Lexikon der bildenden Künstler : von der Antike bis zur Gegenwart* (BF148). Includes some overlap from the 19th century. Gives brief biographical notes, lists of works, and bibliographical references.   N40.V6

Who's who in art : biographies of leading men and women in the world of art today. 1st ed. (1927)– . London : Art Trade Pr., 1927– . Biennial.   **BF150**

Frequency of early editions varies: 1st–3rd eds., 1927, 1929, 1934; 4th ed., 1948.

Includes primarily British artists, designers, craftsmen, critics, writers, teachers, collectors, and curators, with appendixes of monograms and signatures, and obituaries, and acronyms. Includes a list of academies, groups, and societies.   N40.W6

United States

See also BF82, BF397, and BF400.

Cummings, Paul. Dictionary of contemporary American artists. 6th ed. N.Y. : St. Martin's, 1993. 1 v.   **BF151**

1st ed., 1966; 5th ed., 1988.

Brief information concerning more than 900 artists, the majority of them still living. Indicates where and with whom artists studied, awards, exhibitions and group shows, collections in which their works are found, and selected bibliographical references. Pronunciation of unusual names is given in the index of artists. Bibliography.

§ Recommended strongly over *Encyclopedia of living artists in America* ... (2nd ed. Renaissance, Calif. : Directors Guild, 1977), a commercial listing of some 330 artists who recommended themselves for inclusion.   N6512.C854

Dunford, Penny. Biographical dictionary of women artists in Europe and America since 1850. Philadelphia : Univ. of Pennsylvania Pr., 1989. 340 p.   **BF152**

For each of approximately 1,700 artists, provides a paragraph summarizing accomplishments, followed by a short list of collections that hold work by the artist and brief citations to monographs. Includes some illustrations and a six-page bibliography (current through 1989), citing monographs, exhibition catalogs, and journal titles.

§ *See also* Chris Petteys's *Dictionary of women artists* (BF143), Paula L. Chiarmonte's *Women artists in the United States* (BF16), Virginia Watson-Jones's *Contemporary American women sculptors*

(BF400), and *Women artists in America : 18th century to the present (1790-1980)*, rev. and enl. (Poughkeepsie, N.Y. : Apollo, 1980).

N6757.D86

Falk, Peter H. Who was who in American art. Madison, Conn. : Sound View Pr., 1985. 707 p. : ill. **BF153**

Compiled by checking more than 120,000 entries in the *American art annual* (BF102 *note*) and adding "many facts and dates … to make this book more useful."—*Acknowledgements*. The resulting 25,000 entries present concise information about education, exhibitions, associations, etc.

§ A companion volume by Falk is: *Dictionary of signatures & monograms of American artists* (Madison, Conn. : Sound View Pr., 1988. 556 p.). Contains approximately 10,000 signatures, based on photocopies taken in galleries by the author. A lengthy introduction discusses forged signatures and the detection of forgeries. Most of the artists were active ca.1860s–1940s. N6512.F26

Fielding, Mantle. Mantle Fielding's dictionary of American painters, sculptors & engravers / ed. by Glenn B. Opitz. 2nd newly-rev., enl., and updated ed. Poughkeepsie, N.Y. : Apollo, c1986. 1081 p. **BF154**

1st ed., 1926; repr. with addenda, 1965. "New" rev. ed., 1983. All publ. by Apollo.

A compendium of biographical sketches ranging from the very briefest information to fairly detailed lists of exhibitions and specific works in the collections of individual museums, etc. About 12,000 entries in this edition, covering major and minor American artists of the 18th–20th centuries. An eight-page bibliography emphasizes mid-19th through early 20th-century publications. N6536.F5

Groce, George C. The New-York Historical Society dictionary of artists in America, 1564–1860 / by George C. Groce and David H. Wallace. New Haven, Conn. : Yale Univ. Pr., 1957. 759 p. **BF155**

"A documented biographical dictionary of painters, draftsmen, sculptors, engravers, lithographers, and allied artists, either amateur or professional, native or foreign-born, who worked within the present continental limits of the United States between the years 1564 and 1860 inclusive."—*Introd.* Based on numerous primary and secondary sources, including city and business directories, census records, and dated works of art. Includes almost 11,000 names. Bibliography, p. 713–59. N6536.N4

Index of twentieth century artists. N.Y. : Arno Pr., [1970]. 4 v. in 1. **BF156**

Reprint of a serial published monthly (except Dec.) in New York by the College Art Association (1933–Feb. 1934 by the Association's Research Institute) and ed. by F. M. Pollack, 1933–Jan. 1937, and G. A. Cornell, Feb.–Apr. 1937. Original coverage: v. 1 (Oct. 1933)–v. 4, no. 7 (April 1937).

Each monthly number contained detailed information about one or more American artists, including for each artist: biographical data, awards and honors, membership in associations, museums containing his or her work, exhibitions, and bibliographical references. The last number (September) of each year was a supplement consisting of additions and revisions of material previously published. The set covers 120 artists. This one-volume edition contains a new cumulative index. N6536.I52

Who's who in American art. v. 1 (1936/37)– . N.Y. [etc.] : R. R. Bowker. Irregular. **BF157**

Volumes for 1936/37–1940/47 (called v. 1–4) publ. by the American Federation of Arts; issued as pt. 2 of the *American art annual* (BF102 *note*). The *Annual* was succeeded by this and the *American art directory*.

Includes painters, sculptors, graphic artists, craftsmen, historians, critics, editors, museum personnel, educators, lecturers, librarians and dealers. Vol. 2 contains a Necrology, Oct. 1927–Oct. 1935, which continues the Necrology, 1897–1927, in v. 25 of the *American art annual*. Necrology is now cumulative; several hundred new entries appear in each new edition. Now includes art personalities of the U.S., Canada,

and Mexico. The 20th ed. (1993–94) had some 11,824 entries, 700 of which were new listings. Arrangement has varied; from 1978, the biographies are in a single alphabet. Indexes : geographic; professional.

N6536.W5

Artists' signatures

See also BG31, BF381.

Caplan, H. H. The classified directory of artists' signatures, symbols & monograms. Enl. and rev. ed. Detroit : Gale, 1982. 873 p. : ill. **BF158**

1st ed., 1976.

Introductory matter in English, French, German, Spanish, Italian.

Intended as a comprehensive dictionary offering: (1) facsimiles of artists' signatures arranged alphabetically by name; (2) facsimiles of monograms arranged alphabetically under first or uppermost letter of monogram, plus an unclassified section of monograms; (3) reproductions of illegible or misleading signatures arranged under the first recognizable letter, again with an unclassified section; and (4) symbols arranged by general shape, with irregular ones entered at the end of the section. Chiefly British and European, with some coverage of North American and Australian artists. Includes a useful list of qualifications and general abbreviations.

§ Not to be confused with the small but more recent *The classified directory of artists' signatures, symbols & monograms : American artists with new U.K. additions* (London : P. Grahame Publ., 1987. 564 p.).

Radway Jackson's *The visual index of artists' signatures and monograms* (New and rev. ed. London : Cromwell Editions, 1991) offers only a sampling (8,000) of artists' marks. N45.C36

Castagno, John. American artists : signatures and monograms, 1800–1989. Metuchen, N.J. : Scarecrow, 1990. 826 p. : ill. **BF159**

Besides signature facsimiles for 5,100 artists, gives dates, nationality (Canadians and Latin Americans are included), and abbreviations for 70 sources used in compilation (e.g., standard reference works, monographs, journals, collectors, galleries).

§ Castagno has also published *European artists : signatures and monograms, 1800–1990, including selected artists from other parts of the world* (Metuchen, N.J. : Scarecrow, c1990. 895 p.) and *Artists' monograms and indiscernible signatures : an international directory, 1800–1991* (Metuchen, N.J. : Scarecrow, 1991 538 p.). N45.C37

Nagler, Georg Kasper. Die Monogrammisten und diejenigen bekannten und unbekannten Künstler aller Schulen : welche sich zur Bezeichnung ihrer Werke eines figürlichen Zeichens, der initialen des Namens, der Abbreviatur desselben, &c., bedient haben … bein für sich bestehendes Werk, aber zugleich auch Ergänzung und Abschluss des Neuen allgemeinen Künstlerlexicons, und Supplement zu den bekannten Werken von A. Bartsch, Robert-Dumesnil, C. Le Blanc, F. Brulliot, J. Heller, u.s.w / bearb. von G. K. Nagler. München : G. Franz, 1858–79. 5 v. : ill., facsims. **BF160**

Vol. 4 continued by A. Andresen; v. 5, by A. Andresen and C. Clauss.

The standard source for artists' monograms of all periods and all nationalities, giving more biographical information than do other monogram directories.

A *General-index zu dr. G. K. Nagler Die monogrammisten* was published in 1920 (München : G. Hirth. Repr. : Nieuwkoop : De Graff, 1966).

§ Nagler's work was complemented by Franz Goldstein's *Monogram-Lexikon* (Berlin : W. de Gruyter, 1964) covering artists since 1850, with a figurative marks section and index. N45.N2

Self, James. Japanese art signatures : a handbook and practical guide / James Self and Nobuko Hirose. Rutland, Vt. : C.E. Tuttle Co., c1987. 399 p. : ill. **BF161**

In eight parts: Introduction on the reading of signatures; Dictionary of *kaisho* characters; Explanation and tables of key characters; Explanation of geographical and place names, and dates; Variant characters, facsimiles, and seals; Catalogue of names (swordsmiths, metal workers, lacquer artists, netsuke carvers); Bibliography; Stroke-count index of *kaisho* characters.   N7358.S45

Wang, Chi-chien. Seals of Chinese painters and collectors of the Ming and Ch'ing periods / reproduced in facsimile size and deciphered, by Victoria Contag and Wang Chi-chien. Rev. ed., with supplement. [Hong Kong] : Hong Kong Univ. Pr., 1966. lxviii, 726 p. : ill.   **BF162**

First published 1940 under title in Chinese.

In Chinese and English. Extensive charts, indexes, and illustrations.   N45.W3

SYMBOLISM AND ICONOGRAPHY

General

Biedermann, Hans. Dictionary of symbolism / Hans Biedermann ; tr. by James Hulbert. N.Y. ; Oxford : Facts on File, c1992. 465 p. : ill.   **BF163**

Repr. : N.Y. : Meridan, 1994.

Translation of: *Knaurs Lexicon der Symbole* (Munich : Droemer Knaur, c1989. 591 p.).

A general source, with some long entries as well as short definitions. Bibliography; index.   AZ108.B5313

Cirlot, Juan Eduardo. A dictionary of symbols. 2nd ed. N.Y. : Philosophical Library, [1971, c1962]. lv, 419 p. : ill.   **BF164**

1st ed., 1962.

Translation of *Diccionario de símbolos tradicionales* (Barcelona : L. Miracle, 1958. Title varies in later editions).

Entries of varying length. Bibliography gives principal and additional sources. Index.   BF1623.S9C513 b

Daniel, Howard. Encyclopedia of themes and subjects in painting : mythological, biblical, literary, allegorical and topical. N.Y. : Abrams, [1971]. 252 p. : ill.   **BF165**

"The largest part of this book comprises a dictionary of the most common recurring subjects to be found in European painting from the early Renaissance to the mid-19th century."—*Introd*. Most of the 300 entries are illustrated in black-and-white reproductions. No artist index, though artists' names accompany the illustrations.   ND1288.D3

Dreyfuss, Henry. Symbol sourcebook : an authoritative guide to international graphic symbols. N.Y. : McGraw-Hill, [1972]. 292 p.   **BF166**

Repr. : N.Y. : Van Nostrand Reinhold, 1984.

Symbols are grouped according to broad subject areas, which are presented in 18 languages in the table of contents. Index by objects and ideas represented. Bibliography.   N7640.D821

Hall, James. Dictionary of subjects and symbols in art. Rev. ed. N.Y. : Harper & Row, 1979. 349 p.   **BF167**

1st ed., 1974.

Also publ. London : Murray, with spine title *Hall's dictionary of subjects and symbols in art*.

A basic dictionary offering entries for persons, picture titles, and objects and attributes in Christian and classical art. Clear definitions; liberal use of cross-references. Except for some additions to the bibliography and a four-page supplementary index, this edition differs little from the first.   N7560.H34

Henkel, Arthur. Emblemata : Handbuch zur Sinnbildkunst des XVI. und XVII. Jahrhunderts / hrsg. von Arthur Henkel und Albrecht Schöne. Im Auftrage der Göttinger Akademie der Wissenschaften. Stuttgart : J. B. Metzler, 1967. lxxxi p., 2196 col. : ill., facsims.   **BF168**

Reproduces emblems, drawn from 45 collections, published 16th–17th centuries. Emblems are grouped by category (e.g., macrocosm, the four elements, plants, animals); reference is given to original source. Indexes of mottoes, illustrations, and meanings.

The supplement (Stuttgart : Metzler, 1976. 217 p.) is primarily a bibliography. Also in 1976, Metzler reissued the two works as one, with the supplement at the front.

Lehner, Ernst. Symbols, signs and signets. Cleveland : World, [1950]. 221 p. : ill.   **BF169**

Repr. : N.Y. : Dover, 1969.

Black-and-white reproductions of signs and symbols from various cultures are given under such headings as Symbolic gods and deities; Astronomy and astrology; Heraldry; Monsters; Japanese crests. No attempt at completeness is claimed. Each section is preceded by a brief introduction. Bibliography. Some sections are indexed, but there is no general index.   AZ108.L4

Liungman, Carl G. Dictionary of symbols. Santa Barbara, Calif. : ABC-Clio, c1991. 596 p. : ill.   **BF170**

Translation of: *Symboler* (Østraby : Fria Akademin, 1974).

Intended to "function both as a reference work in Western cultural history and as a tool for those working with ideograms … "—*Pref*. Contents: Introduction, with useful essays and bibliography; Ideographic dictionary; Word index; Graphic index; Graphic search index.   BL603.L5413

Marle, Raimond van. Iconographie de l'art profane au Moyen-Âge et à la Renaissance, et la décoration des demeures. The Hague : Nijhoff, 1931–32. 2 v. : ill.   **BF171**

Repr.: N.Y. : Hacker, 1971.

The first volume covers daily life of the periods; the second, allegories and symbols. Includes bibliographies and many illustrations. Lacks an index.

§ A related title is Guy de Tevarent's *Attributs et symboles dans l'art profane, 1450–1600 : dictionnaire d'un langage perdu* (Geneva : E. Droz, 1958–64. 3 v., of which v. 3 is a supplement and index).   N5970.M35

Pigler, Andor. Barockthemen : eine Auswahl von Verzeichnissen zur Ikonographie des 17. und 18. Jahrhunderts. 2., erw. Aufl. Budapest : Akadémiai Kiadó, 1974. 3 v. : ill.   **BF172**

1st ed., 1956.

Contents: v.1, religious representations; v. 2, secular representations in Greek and Roman history, legends, and folklore, and in general history, allegories, etc.; v. 3, plates. Index to v. 1–2 in v. 2.

Lists themes represented in the baroque art of the 17th–18th centuries, with references to the artists who have treated them (including artists of the 15th–16th centuries). Includes indication of where the work may be found; and notation where an illustration may be located in book or periodical. Usually includes the artists of Italy, France, Germany, and the Netherlands.   N6410.P5

Seyn, Eugène de. Dictionnaire des attributs, allégories, emblèmes et symboles / [par] Eug. Droulers [pseud.]. Turnhout, Belgium : Brepols, [1949]. 281 p. : ill.   **BF173**

Includes names of people, attributes, allegorical figures, etc. Definitions vary in length from a few sentences to several paragraphs. Alphabetical arrangement. Illustrations in the text and in a section at the end are indexed. Bibliography.   AZ108.S7

Vries, Ad de. Dictionary of symbols and imagery. 2nd rev. ed. Amsterdam : North-Holland Publ. ; N.Y. : Elsevier, 1976. 515 p.   **BF174**

1st ed., 1974. Subsequent editions appear to be reprints.

Publ. in Japanese (Tokyo : Taishūkan, 1984).

Intends to supply "associations which have been evoked by certain words, signs, etc. in Western civilization in the past, and which may float to the surface again tomorrow."—*Pref.* Includes allegories, metaphors, signs, images, etc. Emphasis is on literary, mythological, religious, and proverbial use rather than graphic representation.

BL600.V74

Waal, H. van de. Iconclass : an iconographic classification system / H. van de Waal ; completed and ed. by L. D. Couprie with R. H. Fuchs, E. Tholen. Amsterdam : North-Holland Pub. Co., 1973–1985. 6 v. in 17. **BF175**

At head of title: Koninklijke Nederlandse Akademie van Wetenschappen.

A monumental project whose classification is being adopted by an increasing number of visual resources collections and publications, including *Marburger index : photographic documentation of art in Germany*, Helene Roberts' *Iconographic index[es] to [New Testament and Old Testament] subjects* … (BF298), and *Iconclass indexes : Italian prints* (Doornspijk, Netherlands : Davaco, 1987–90. 4 v.). Begun several decades ago and now totalling 17 v., with system [i.e., classification] volumes accompanied by bibliography volumes. A General introduction in v. 2–3 (System) explains the outline structure of main divisions, and primary, secondary, and tertiary subdivisions. Outline of main divisions: Religion and magic; Nature; Human being, man in general; Society, civilization, culture; Abstract ideas and concepts; History; Bible, Literature, Classical mythology and ancient history. The final 3 v. constitute the index (completed and ed. by L.D. Couprie [et al.]).

Z697.A8W3

Waters, Clara Erskine Clement. Handbook of legendary and mythological art. 10th ed. N.Y. : Hurd and Houghton, 1876. 510 p. : ill. **BF176**

Repr. : Boston : Longwood, 1977.

1st ed., 1871. For several years, new editions were publ. frequently by Hurd and Houghton. Later editions from other publishers did not consistently use sequential edition numbers; several appear to be reprints. The 1876 edition, cited here, is the one generally chosen for reprints.

A widely used 19th-century source. Sections: Symbolism in art; Legends and stories illustrated in art; Legends of place; Ancient myths illustrated in art. Catalogue of pictures.

The first two parts incorporate the text of the author's *Handbook of Christian symbols and stories of the saints as illustrated in art* (Boston : Ticknor and Co., 1886).

N7760.W4

Whittick, Arnold. Symbols, signs and their meaning and uses in design. 2nd ed. Newton, Mass. : C. T. Branford Co., 1971. 383 p., 78 plates : ill. **BF177**

1st ed., 1960, had title: *Symbols, signs and their meaning.*

Also publ. London : L. Hill, 1971.

Introductory discussion of the types and meaning of symbolism is followed by sections: Symbolism in its precise and applied forms, and its practical uses; Individual and collective expression—instinctive, creative and imaginative symbolism; and a dictionary of traditional and familiar symbols. Confined mainly to Western symbols and uses. Indexed.

§ An earlier work by Whittick is *Symbolism for designers : a handbook on the application of symbols and symbolism to design, for the use of architects, sculptors, ecclesiastical and memorial designers, commercial artists, and students of symbolism* (London : Lockwood, 1935. 168 p. Repr.: Detroit : Gale, 1972).

Another work from the same period, but with a more technical emphasis, is *Shepherd's glossary of graphic signs and symbols*, by Walter Shepherd (N.Y. : Dover, 1971. 597 p.).

AZ108.W45

Buddhist

See also BF126.

Bhattacharyya, Benoytosh. The Indian Buddhist iconography : mainly based on the Sādhanamālā and cognate Tāntric texts of rituals. [2nd ed., rev. and enl.]. Calcutta : Mukhopadhyay, 1958. 478 p. : ill. **BF178**

Repr. with minor revisions, 1968.

1st ed., 1924; reissued New Delhi : Cosmo, 1985.

A comprehensive work, illustrated by pictures and line drawings. Appendix: 108 forms of Avalokiteśvara. Glossary. Index of words.

§ Related titles include K. C. Aryan's *Encyclopedia of Indian art, references, symbols, evolution of Devanagari script* (New Delhi : Rekha Prakashan, c1989. 159 p.), a small volume that is less an encyclopedia than a guide, although it fills a gap in the literature on Asian symbolism.

Chinese

Williams, Charles Alfred Speed. Encyclopedia of Chinese symbolism and art motives : an alphabetical compendium of legends and beliefs as reflected in the manners and customs of the Chinese throughout history. N.Y. : Julian, 1960. 468 p. : ill. **BF179**

A re-issue of *Outlines of Chinese symbolism and art motives* (3rd rev. ed. Shanghai : Kelly and Walsh, 1941; repr.: Rutland, Vt. : C. E. Tuttle Co., 1974).

GR335.W53

Christian

See also BF298.

Bles, Arthur de. How to distinguish the saints in art by their costumes, symbols and attributes. N.Y. : Art Culture Publ., 1925. 168 p. : ill. **BF180**

Repr.: Detroit : Gale, 1975.

Covers symbolism in general and for different groups, e.g., Virgin Mary, Evangelists, monastic orders, etc., with illustrations and explanations of pictures showing symbols. Appendixes: Alphabetical table of martyrdoms; Tables of saints classified by habitual costume; Saints classified by categories; Alphabetical table of symbols and attributes with names of those who bear them; Chronological tables of bishops and popes of Rome; List of illustrations. Indexes: general, saints, artists. Brief bibliography.

N8080.B5

Drake, Maurice. Saints and their emblems / by Maurice and Wilfred Drake. London : Laurie ; Philadelphia : Lippincott, 1916. 235 p. : ill. **BF181**

Repr.: Detroit : Gale ; N.Y. : B. Franklin, 1971.

"Illustrated by XII plates from photographs and drawings by Wilford Drake, with a foreword by Aymer Vallance."—*t.p.*

Main sections: Dictionary of saints, Dictionary of emblems. Appendixes: Patriarchs and prophets; Sibyls; Patron saints of arts, trades, and professions; Other patron saints.

N8080.D7

Ferguson, George Wells. Signs & symbols in Christian art : with illustrations from paintings of the Renaissance. 2nd ed. N.Y. : Oxford Univ. Pr., 1955. 346 p. : ill. **BF182**

Also publ. London : Zwemmer, 1955. Frequently republished, sometimes in abridged editions. Pagination varies, especially with plates of the illustrations.

A basic work for quick reference. Uses simple, direct language, line drawings, and reproductions of works of art to explain symbols and illustrate their use. Indexed.

§ Related popular works include: *Christian symbols, ancient & modern : a handbook for students,* by Heather Child and Dorothy Colles (London : Bell, 1971. 270 p.) and *A handbook of symbols in Christian art,* by Gertrude Grace Sill (N.Y. : Collier/Macmillan, 1975. 241 p.). N7830.F37

Kaftal, George. Saints in Italian art / by George Kaftal, with the collaboration of Fabio Bisogni. Firenze : Le lettere, c1952–85. 4 v. : ill. **BF183**

Contents: [v. 1], Iconography of the saints in Tuscan painting; [v. 2], Iconography of the saints in central and south Italian schools of painting; [v. 3], Iconography of the saints in the painting of north east Italy; [v. 4], Iconography of the saints in the painting of north west Italy.

Each volume has two parts: (1) Saints and blessed (alphabetical arrangement, outlining type, images, cycle, scenes, literary sources, bibliography; with illustrations); (2) Indexes (attributes and distinctive signs, painters, topographical index of painting, bibliographical index, index of saints and blessed). ND1432.I8K33 1985

Lexikon der christlichen Ikonographie / hrsg. von Engelbert Kirschbaum, in Zusammenarbeit mit Günter Bandmann [et al.]. Rome : Herder, 1968–76. 8 v. : ill. **BF184**

Repr., 1990.

Contents: v. 1–4, Allgemeine Ikonographie, A–Z (Nachträge in v. 4); v. 5–8, Ikonographie der Heiligen: A–Z, Register.

Vol. 5–8 ed. by Wolfgang Braunfels.

An impressive work in dictionary format, with signed articles and numerous illustrations. Individual entries give description, sources, citations to specific images, and bibliographic references. Vol. 4 concludes with lists of topics covered, in German, English, and French.

§ Hans Aurenhammer's *Lexikon der christlichen Ikonographie,* being published in parts (Vienna : Hollinek, 1959–67), was abandoned after Lfg. 6, which covered through "Christus." BV150.L4

Réau, Louis. Iconographie de l'art chrétien. Paris : Presses Universitaires de France, 1955–59. 3 v. in 6. : plates. **BF185**

Repr. : Nendeln : Kraus, 1974–77; 1988.

Contents: v. 1, Introduction générale; v. 2, Iconographie de la Bible (pt. 1, Ancien Testament; pt. 2, Nouveau Testament); v. 3 (in three volumes), Iconographie des saints.

Classifies iconographic themes, indicates their variations and evolution, and lists principal works of art depicting them. Covers medieval Western and Byzantine art. Includes bibliographies and many illustrations. Vol. 3, pt. 3 includes a substantial repertory of saints that covers names (a multilingual listing), patronages, and attributes. N7830.R37

Schiller, Gertrud. Ikonographie der christlichen Kunst. [Gütersloh] : Gütersloher Verlagshaus G. Mohn, [1966–91]. 5 v. in 7 : plates. (In progress?). **BF186**

Some volumes now in 2nd and 3rd editions.

Contents: Bd. 1, Inkarnation, Kindheit, Taufe, Versuchung, Verklärung, Wirken und Wunder Christi; Bd. 2, Die Passion Jesu Christi; Bd. 3, Die Auferstehung und Erhörung Christi; Bd. 4¹, Die Kirche; Bd. 4², Maria; Bd. 5¹⁻², Die Apokalypse des Johannes.

Text and illustrations (600–700 in each volume) in separate sections. The text of v. 1–2 deals chronologically, and in some detail, with the background and events of the life of Christ, providing references to the biblical sources together with discussion of treatment of the various themes in art. Bibliographical footnotes provide references to specialized studies. The two parts of v. 4 treat the Church and Mary. An index to v. 1–4², ed. by Rupert Schreiner, was published in 1980.

An English translation of v. 1–2 appeared as *Iconography of Christian art,* tr. by Janet Seligman (Greenwich, Conn. : N.Y. Graphic Soc., 1971–72. 2 v.).

§ *Ikonographie der christlichen Kunst* is also the title of an older, two-volume guide by Karl Künstle (Freiburg im Breisgau : Herder, 1926–1928).

Webber, Frederick Roth. Church symbolism : an explanation of the more important symbols of the Old and New Testament, the primitive, the mediaeval and the modern church / [by] Frederick Roth Webber ; introd. by Ralph Adams Cram. 2nd ed., rev. Cleveland : J. H. Jansen, 1938. 413 p. : ill. **BF187**

Repr. : Detroit : Omnigraphics, 1992 (2nd rev. ed.).

1st ed., 1927.

Discussion, with definitions, within 19 chapters. Includes listing of the more important saints and a glossary of the more important symbols. Bibliography. Index. BV150.W4

Classical

See also BF7.

Lexicon iconographicum mythologiae classicae : (LIMC) / [rédaction, Hans Christoph Ackermann, Jean-Robert Gisler]. Zurich : Artemis, [1981–94]. v. 1–7, pt. 2 : ill. (In progress). **BF188**

Contents: v. 1–6, A–Oiax.

To be in 7 v. of two parts each (text and plates) plus a supplement. Known as *LIMC.*

A scholarly, exhaustive, splendidly produced encyclopedia on the iconography of Greek, Etruscan, and Roman mythology from the post-Mycenaean period to the beginning of the early Christian era; includes divinities and heroes of neighboring cultures. An alphabetic arrangement of signed articles in English, German, French, or Italian. Entries comprise: introduction (myth and literary sources); bibliography, catalog (classification, description, date, museum references, etc.); iconographical commentary. Intended to answer the need "for a collective work devoted to the iconography of classical mythology in the widest sense of the term."—*Introd.* Cross-references; excellent plates; line drawings. The final volume is to include an index for the set. N7760.L49

Reid, Jane Davidson. The Oxford guide to classical mythology in the arts, 1300–1990s. N.Y. : Oxford Univ. Pr., 1993. 2 v. (1310 p.). **BF189**

An alphabetical list of subjects, with cross-references. Gives an introductory statement and cites specific classical sources, followed by a chronological list of artists (including literature, music, and dance as well as art) and their individual works (providing genre or medium, date of composition, performance data, locations, and sources). Has 30,000 works of art under some 300 entries and subentries, but does not intend to be exhaustive. A "List of sources," current through 1991, includes reference books, museum publications, and monographs. Index of artists gives nationality, medium, dates, and pertinent mythological subjects.

§ *See also* Percy Preston's *A dictionary of pictorial subjects from classical literature* (N.Y. : Scribner's, 1983). NX650.M9R45

Hindu

Banerjea, Jitendra Nath. The development of Hindu iconography. 2nd rev. and enl. ed. [Calcutta] : Univ. of Calcutta, 1956. 653 p. : ill. **BF190**

1st ed., 1941. The 3rd and 4th editions (New Delhi : Munshiram Manoharlal, 1974 and 1985) are reprints of the 1956 ed.

A comprehensive history dealing with the development and manifestations of Hindu iconography from ancient times. Bibliography. Index.

Gopinātha Rāu, T. A. Elements of Hindu iconography. Madras : Law Printing House, 1914–16. 2 v. in 4. : ill. **BF191**

Repr. : N.Y. : Garland, 1981. A 2nd ed. (Varanasi : Indological Book House, 1971) appears to be a reprint.

Arranged by topic. Includes portions in Sanskrit. Index.
BL1201.G7

Stutley, Margaret. An illustrated dictionary of Hindu iconography. London ; Boston : Routledge & Kegan Paul, 1985. 175 p. : ill. **BF192**
Includes a six-page introduction, a 19-page essay on English subjects and Sanskrit equivalents, and a five-page bibliography. Many entries illustrated with line drawings. N8195.A4S78

Jewish

See also BG113.

Index of Jewish art : iconographical index of Hebrew illuminated manuscripts / Bezalel Narkiss ... [et al.]. Jerusalem : Israel Academy of Sciences and Humanities, 1976–1988. v. 1–4 : ill. (In progress). **BF193**
Running title: *Iconographical index of Hebrew illuminated manuscripts.* Vol. 1 also called *Gross family collection.*
Each volume consists of a box of cards with an introductory booklet.
"Sets out to be complementary to the Princeton Index of Christian Art ...."—*Introd.* This index is being compiled in stages, with annual issues of small groups of manuscripts in card form. Two sections: (1) analytical description; (2) alphabetical list of all subjects. Vol. 4 (1988) includes a 103-page guide to the collection. NK1672.G76

Mayer, Leo Ary. Bibliography of Jewish art / ed. by Otto Kurz. Jerusalem : Magnes Pr. ; London : Oxford Univ. Pr., 1967. 374 p. **BF194**
An author listing of more than 3,000 books and articles on art covering roughly 70 to 1830. Includes publications to Spring 1965. Subject index.
§ For a more recent publication, *see* the historical survey by Michael Kaniel, *A guide to Jewish art* (N.Y. : Philosophical Soc., 1989). *See also* Mayer's *A bibliography of Jewish numismatics* (Jerusalem : Magnes Pr., Hebrew Univ., 1966). Z5956.J4M3

REPRODUCTIONS

Changes in technology in the past decade have greatly diminished interest in publications on art reproductions. Increasingly, many resources are available in new formats, including videodisc, CD-ROM, and digital images, which currently lie beyond the scope of this guide.
See also works in the Indexes portion of this Section, and Ernest H. Robl's *Picture sources 4* (BF347).

Cashman, Norine D. Slide buyers' guide : an international directory of slide sources for art and architecture. 6th ed. Englewood, Colo. : Libraries Unlimited, 1990. 190 p. **BF195**
At head of title: Visual Resources Association.
1st ed. (1970)–4th ed. (1980) ed. by Nancy DeLaurier. 5th ed., 1985.
Lists more than 300 sources compiled from responses to a questionnaire sent to some 450 presumed vendors, of whom roughly half were in the U.S. Entries give location, a profile of offerings, type of photography and production, documentation, purchase, and an evaluation based on guidelines used since 1979. Appendix 1 lists nonrespondents; Appendix 2 is a bibliography of basic art history texts for which slide sets are available, naming vendors. Indexes of names and subjects. N4040.V57C3

New York Graphic Society. Fine art reproductions of old & modern masters : a comprehensive illustrated catalog of art through the ages. Greenwich, Conn. : New York Graphic Society, c1980. 576 p. : chiefly col. ill. **BF196**
1st ed., 1946.
A catalog of color prints published by this company. Arranged by broad group (i.e., Old masters, 20th-century painting, American painting, etc.), with index by artist and selected subject categories for anonymous works. Each entry includes: a small color reproduction, name and dates of the artist, nationality if not indicated by group, title with date and location of the original painting, catalog number, size and price of the print. Indexes: classified subjects, artists.
A 1984 reprint from the Society includes a 17-page supplement with more than 70 new reproductions. NE1860.N4A32

Pierson, William Harvey. Arts of the United States : a pictorial survey / William H. Pierson, Jr. and Martha Davidson, editors. N.Y. : McGraw-Hill, [1960]. 452 p. : ill. **BF197**
Repr. : Athens, Ga. : Univ. of Georgia Pr., 1975.
"Based on a collection of color slides assembled by the University of Georgia under a grant by Carnegie Corporation of New York."—*t.p.*
The Carnegie project undertook: (1) to compile and document material representing the history of American art in most of its phases from the beginning to the mid-20th century; (2) to select from this material some 4,000 works to be reproduced in high-quality color slides, intended for use in schools, museums, and libraries here and abroad. The catalog of these slides—arranged by broad subject and giving identifying information and a small black-and-white reproduction for each entry—is preceded by essays on each subject group written by the specialists who chose the material. Index of artists, titles, and subjects. N6505.P55

RESTORATION AND CONSERVATION

See also works listed under *Architecture—Restoration and conservation* in this Section and BF117.

Art and archaeology technical abstracts. v. 6– . N.Y. [etc.] : Institute of Fine Arts, New York Univ. [etc.], 1966– . Semiannual (irregular). **BF198**
Title varies: *Studies in conservation* (v. 1–2, [1955–57]); *IIC abstracts* (v. 1–5, no. 4) [1958–65]). Known as *AATA*.
Publ. by the Getty Conservation Institute in association with the International Institute of Conservation of Historic and Artistic Works, London.
A classed bibliography, with abstracts in English or language of the original. Author index in each issue; combined subject index in the second issue of the year. Beginning with v. 23 (1986), "compiled and produced through the bibliographic component of the Conservation Information Network, a joint project of the Getty Conservation Institute and the Department of Communications, Canada."—*Acknowledgements, v. 26, no. 1.* Content and arrangement remain the same.
§ Preceded by: *Abstracts of technical studies in art and archaeology, 1943–1952* (Wash. : Smithsonian Institution, 1955) and *Technical studies in the field of the fine arts* (Cambridge, Mass. : Fogg Art Museum, 1932–42; repr. : N.Y. : Garland, 1975, 1932–42. v. 1–10).
•Available in machine-readable form online through the Conservation Information Network. Indexes periodical, monographic, technical report, audiovisual, and machine-readable literature pertaining to the technical aspects of conservation and restoration. Component files include: Bibliographic database (BCIN), Materials database (MCIN), Suppliers database (ACIN). AM1.A7

International index of conservation research = Répertoire international de la recherche en conservation / ICCROM. Wash. : Smithsonian Institution, Conservation Analytical Laboratory, 1988. 142 p. : forms. **BF199**

"The first attempt to summarize the ongoing research that has not yet been published ... [by creating] a directory of professionals who share a concern for the conservation of cultural heritage."—*Pref.* Intended to encourage international collaboration by listing areas of expertise. Provides forms for the submission of information for future editions and for an eventual database. Arranged in 31 categories (media), each subdivided. Lacks name indexes, but includes codes to indicate affiliation with some 170 institutions.   CC135.I57

New York University. Institute of Fine Arts. Conservation Center. Library catalog of the Conservation Center, New York University, Institute of Fine Arts. Boston : G. K. Hall, 1980. 934 p.   **BF200**

Also available from G. K. Hall in microform.

Reproduces catalog cards for the major collection for the study and practice of conservation of works of art.   Z5945.N49

ARCHITECTURE

General works

Guides

Bamford, Lawrence Von. Design resources : a guide to architecture and industrial design information. Jefferson, N.C. : McFarland, 1984. 319 p.   **BF201**

An annotated bibliography of 3,404 sources grouped by: Printed resources, Non-print resources, and Research libraries, all subdivided by topic. Examples: research library catalogs, anthologies, yearbooks, subject bibliographies, films, design information centers, computer data banks, and design competitions and awards. Indexes: subject; author and title.   Z5943.A72B35

Ehresmann, Donald L. Architecture : a bibliographic guide to basic reference works, histories, and handbooks. Littleton, Colo. : Libraries Unlimited, 1984. 338 p.   **BF202**

An annotated bibliography of "books written in English and Western European languages that were published between 1875 and 1980 and are accessible in libraries in the United States. ... Books for the general reader and undergraduate are included together with exhaustive reference works and scholarly histories, handbooks, and special studies."—*Pref.* Sections for reference works and for general histories and handbooks are followed by chronological (primitive and prehistoric through modern) and geographical (European, Oriental, New World, Africa and Oceania) sections. Author/title and subject indexes. Forms a companion to the compiler's *Fine arts* (BF2) and *Applied and decorative arts* (BG2) bibliographies.

§ A related guide emphasizing professional aspects of design: *Information sources in architecture*, ed. by Valerie J. Bradfield (London : Butterworths, [1983]. 419 p.).   Z5941.E38

Kamen, Ruth H. British and Irish architectural history : a bibliography and guide to sources of information. London : Architectural Pr. ; N.Y. : Nichols Publ. Co., 1981. 249 p. **BF203**

Offers "descriptions of books, periodicals and periodical articles, indexes and abstracts, collections, organisations and services ... designed to assist students, scholars, researchers, teachers in schools and universities, librarians, local historians, picture researchers and the general public in identifying and using the sources available when seeking information about British and Irish architecture."—*p. 1*. Topical arrangement, followed by a 60-page selective bibliography. Index of authors, organizations, subjects, and titles.

Wodehouse, Lawrence. American architects from the Civil War to the First World War : a guide to information sources. Detroit : Gale, c1976. 343 p. (Art and architecture information guide series, v. 3).   **BF204**

Spine title: American architects 1.

Intended as a continuation of Frank John Roos's *Bibliography of early American architecture* (BF221). A general section is followed by an annotated listing of books and articles concerning individual architects. Provides a brief biography (with reference to published writings and known repositories of drawings) for each of the 175 architects. A third section is concerned with architects about whom little has been written. Detailed general index; building location index.

Continued by the author's *American architects from the First World War to the present : a guide to information sources* (Detroit : Gale, c1977. 305 p. [Art and architecture information guide series, 4]).

Spine title: American architects 2.

An annotated listing of general reference works on American architects and their architecture is followed by an annotated bibliography for 174 architects. Subject and name index; building location index.

§ Wodehouse also compiled: *Indigenous architecture worldwide : a guide to information sources* (Detroit : Gale, c1980), *British architects, 1840–1976* (Detroit : Gale, 1978), and *The roots of international style architecture* (West Cornwall, Conn. : Locust Hill Pr., 1991).   Z5944.U5W63

Bibliography

American Association of Architectural Bibliographers. Papers. v. 1–13. Charlottesville : Univ. Pr. of Virginia, 1965–79. Annual (irregular).   **BF205**

Publisher varies. Vol. 12–13 issued as Garland reference library of the humanities, v. 115–116.

A bibliographical series superseding the Association's *Publications* (no. 1–27, 1954–64). Presents bibliographies of individual architects and of specific eras and aspects of architecture.

An index to v. 1–10 (1965–73), issued as v. 11 of the series (Charlottesville : Univ. Pr. of Virginia, 1975. 311 p.), mainly covers the authors and titles of works cited in the bibliographies.   Z5941.A5

Archer, John. The literature of British domestic architecture, 1715–1842. Cambridge, Mass. : MIT Pr., c1985. 1078 p., [12] p. of plates : ill.   **BF206**

"Approaches British domestic architecture in the eighteenth and early nineteenth centuries through the literary output of architects and others concerned with domestic design."—*Introd.* A lengthy introductory essay is followed by detailed bibliographic descriptions of the books, with commentary on text and plates. Locates copies. The numerous appendixes include a short-title list of additional publications; list of printers, publishers, and booksellers; chronological list. Indexed.

§ Related works for British research include: John H. Harvey's *Sources for the history of houses* ([London] : British Records Assoc., [1974]. 61 p.), Michael Holmes' *The country house described* (Winchester, U.K. : Saint Paul's Bibliographies in assoc. with Victoria & Albert Museum, 1986. 328 p.), D. J. C. King's *Castellarium Anglicanum* (Millwood, N.Y. : Kraus Internat., 1983. 2 v.), and John F. Smith's *A critical bibliography of building conservation ...* (London : Mansell, 1978. 207 p.).   Z5944.G7A7

Architectural periodicals index. v. 1– . London : British Architectural Library, 1972/73– . Quarterly, with 4th issue being annual cumulation.   **BF207**

Also called *API*.

Vol. 2 appeared quarterly, with a fifth issue as the annual cumulation.

The published version of the British Architectural Library's subject index to periodicals. Subject headings are derived from the controlled vocabulary found in *Architectural keywords* (London : RIBA Publ., 1982) and annual amendments. Fields covered include architecture and allied arts, constructional technology, design and environmental studies, landscape, planning, and relevant research. Indexes some 300 journals, with an emphasis on British topics and work done abroad by British architects. Classed arrangement with alphabetical listing by English-language title within subject categories; foreign-language articles carry a note as to language and presence of English summary. Name index; a topographical and building names index was added beginning with the annual cumulation of v. 6. Concludes with lists of major series and special issues index; list of periodicals indexed; British Architectural Library accessions list.

•Available in machine-readable form as: *Architecture database* [database] (London : British Architectural Library, 1978–). Available online, updated monthly, and on CD-ROM as *Architectural publications index on disc* (London : RIBA Publ., 1978–), updated quarterly. Z5941.A69

Australian architectural periodicals index : APPI / comp. by the staff of the Reference Dept., Stanton Library [microform]. 1910–1983. North Sydney, N.S.W., Australia : Stanton Library, c1986. **BF208**

Photoreproductions, arranged in one alphabet, of 20,000 handwritten index entries covering subjects; building types, materials, and features; architects; and firms. Excludes product or technical material. Covers about 60 journals published in Australia and New Zealand, 1910–83.

§ Related titles: *Australian architectural serials, 1870–1983 : a preliminary list*, by Desley Luscombe and Stanislaus Fung (Kensington : Univ. of New South Wales, School of Architecture, c1985) and *A pictorial guide to identifying Australian architecture : styles and terms from 1788 to the present*, by Richard Apperley, Robert Irving, Peter Reynolds ; photographs by Solomon Mitchell (North Ride, N.S.W., Australia : Angus & Robertson, 1989. 297 p.).

Avery Architectural and Fine Arts Library. Avery index to architectural periodicals. 2nd ed., rev. and enl. Boston : G.K. Hall, 1973. 15 v. **BF209**

1st ed., 1963, in 12 volumes; seven supplements issued 1965–72. Photographic reproduction of the Library's card file. Indexes articles on architecture in its widest sense, including archaeology, decorative arts, interior design, landscape architecture, city planning, and housing. Excludes periodicals in non-Western alphabets. The new edition cumulates material from the supplements, adds corrections and refinements, and provides retrospective indexing of certain periodicals not previously included.

Supplements have been issued since 1975. Early supplements were issued irregularly and covered a multiyear span; since the sixth, 1985, coverage is annual. Published 1975–78 by Columbia University; 1979– by Getty Art History Information Program at Columbia University; since that date, publ. Boston : G.K. Hall. Each supplement includes a list of periodical titles indexed, some 300-500 a year. Suppl. 13 (1992) was publ. 1993. Since 1984, the *Avery index* has been a program of the Getty Art History Information Program.

§ This remains the primary architectural periodical index published in North America, despite the existence of three others with slightly overlapping coverage: *Architectural index* (Boulder, Colo. , 1950– . Annual); *Search : the periodical index for architecture, interior design, housing and construction* (Devon, Pa. : Search Publishing, 1988–); and *Construction index* (Chicago : ArchiText, c1987–). All lack author indexing.

•Since the 4th supplement (1977), available in machine-readable form as *Avery index to architectural periodicals* (N.Y. : Avery Architectural and Fine Arts Library, Columbia Univ.). Available online and on CD-ROM, with coverage beginning 1977 (N.Y. : Macmillan, 1994– . Annual). Z5945.C653

Bergeron, Claude. Index des périodiques d'architecture canadiens, 1940–1980 = Canadian architectural periodicals index, 1940–1980. Québec : Presses de l'Université Laval, 1986. 518 p. **BF210**

In English and French. Provides some 30,000 index entries for articles published 1940–80 in nine journals. The chief section is arranged by 12 broad building categories, gives full bibliographic information for articles cited, and is followed by building type, architect, place name, and author indexes.

§ Related title: Portia Leggat, comp., *A union list of architectural records in Canadian public collections = Catalogue collectif de recherche documentaire sur l'architecture provenant de collections pub-

liques canadiennes (Montréal, Québec : Canadian Centre for Architecture, c1983. 213 p. At head of title: Canadian Architectural Records Survey). NA745.B37

Bibliographie zur Architektur im 19 Jahrhundert : die Aufsätze in den deutschsprachigen Architektur-Zeitschriften 1789–1918 / ed., Stephan Waetzoldt; comp., Verena Haas. Nendeln, Liechtenstein : KTO Pr., 1977. 8 v. **BF211**

"The bibliography lists all contributions on construction projects, reconstruction, renovation, design contests, architectural theory and criticism, as well as the technical aspects of building, which appeared in the 129 most important German-language journals on architecture and the construction industry published between 1789 and 1918 in the German and Austro-Hungarian empires and in Switzerland."—*Pref.* Topically arranged by type of architecture. Table of contents and preface also in English. Vol. 8 is an index by authors, architects, and places.

The Burnham index to architectural literature. N.Y. : Garland, 1989. 10 v. **BF212**

Photoreproductions of some 100,000 cards from an index maintained at the Ryerson and Burnham Libraries of the Art Institute of Chicago. This index was maintained until the mid-1960s and was the only index for architecture from 1919 until the *Avery index to architectural periodicals* (BF209) was begun in 1934. Covers more than 200 serial titles (some retrospectively) and 600 monographs, many from the 19th century. Entries are by architect, firm, place and building name, and author, in one alphabet. Emphasizes Midwestern topics.
Z5944.U5B87

Cuthbert, John A. Vernacular architecture in America : a selective bibliography / John A. Cuthbert, Barry Ward, Magie Keeler. Boston : G. K. Hall, 1985. 145 p. : ill. **BF213**

Focuses on "modern literature pertaining to architecture in the American folk tradition."—*Pref.* An alphabetical author listing of books and periodical articles, with index of authors, abbreviated titles, and subjects.

§*See also* Howard W. Marshall, *American folk architecture* (Wash. : American Folklife Center, Library of Congress, 1981. 79 p.).
Z5944.U5C87

Doumato, Lamia. Architecture and women : a bibliography documenting women architects, landscape architects, designers, architectural critics and writers, and women in related fields working in the United States. N.Y. : Garland, 1988. 269 p., [20] p. of plates : ill. (Garland reference library of the humanities, vol. 886). **BF214**

The main section offers bibliographies of 130 American women architects in one alphabetical sequence, each listing subdivided by primary works (as author) and secondary works (as subject). Begins with a general bibliography listing manuscript and special collections, monographs, dissertations and theses, exhibition catalogs and reviews, and periodical articles published through the mid-1980s. Concludes with an index of topics, personal and institutional names, and places.
Z5944.U5D6886

Hall, Robert de Zouche. A bibliography on vernacular architecture / ed. by Robert de Zouche Hall [for the Vernacular Architecture Group]. Newton Abbot, [Eng.] : David & Charles, 1972. 191 p. **BF215**

An extensive classified bibliography on "the study of houses and other buildings, which, in their form and materials, represent the unselfconscious tradition of a region rather than ideas of architectural style."—*Introd.* Covers the British Isles, with regional and local studies. Arranged by broad topics. Author index.

Regular supplements were intended, but only one was published: *A current bibliography of vernacular architecture* (v. 1 [1970/76]. [York, England] : Vernacular Architecture Group, 1979).
Z5944.G7H3

Harris, Eileen. British architectural books and writers, 1556–1785 / Eileen Harris assisted by Nicholas Savage. Cambridge ; N.Y. : Cambridge Univ. Pr., 1990. 571 p. : ill.   **BF216**

Taking Howard M. Colvin's *Biographical dictionary of British architects, 1600–1840* (BF259) as a model, the compiler treats "authors' books as [Colvin] did architects' buildings. Thus bibliographical descriptions of the works are preceded by an essay, which examines the author's publishing activities as a whole without necessarily discussing every item."—*Pref.* The main section, Writers and their books, is prefaced by introductory essays on books on the orders, books of designs and pattern-books, carpenters' manuals, measuring and price books, books on bridges, archaeological books, publishers and booksellers, and architectural engraving. Excluded are books on garden design and articles in periodicals and encyclopedias. The 950 entries include title, imprint date, collation and contents, editions, locations, and notes. Locates copies in major architectural libraries, including Avery Library (Columbia Univ.), Canadian Centre for Architecture, Royal Institute of British Architects, and Soane Museum. Concludes with a Chronological index of titles and editions and an index of names, subjects, and titles.   NA965.H37

Hitchcock, Henry Russell. American architectural books : a list of books, portfolios, and pamphlets on architecture and related subjects published in America before 1895. New expanded ed. / with a new introd. by Adolf K. Placzek. N.Y. : Da Capo Pr., 1976. 150 p.   **BF217**

1st ed., 1938–39. A 1962 ed. was a reprint of a 3rd rev. edition, 1946, which listed 1,461 items, distinguishing editions and locating copies in more than 130 public and private libraries. It included a new preface offering 30 emendations (eight being new titles or editions, the rest minor corrections of collations and imprints). The 1976 ed. reprints the text of the 1962 ed. with a new introduction and a listing of architectural periodicals before 1895 by Adolf K. Placzek. An appendix, Chronological short-title list of Henry Russell Hitchcock's *American architectural books*, comp. under the direction of William H. Jordy was originally issued as *Publication* no. 4 (Oct. 1955) of the American Association of Architectural Bibliographers.   Z5941.H67

Index to historic preservation periodicals / National Trust for Historic Preservation Library of the University of Maryland, College Park ; gen. ed., Hye Yun Choe. Boston : G.K. Hall, c1988. 354 p.   **BF218**

"A compilation of the monthly listing of articles and ephemera" (*Pref.*) issued by the National Trust for Historic Preservation Library, 1979–87. Articles are from international, national, regional, state, and local historic preservation organizations, as well as from popular and scholarly serials. The topical arrangement includes headings in architecture, law, design review, interiors, real estate, fund raising, and government policy. Contains a limited number of citations (about 5,000). Provides very limited access by subject and geographic location, and none by author.

The *Index to historic preservation periodicals, 1987–1990 : first supplement* (Gen. ed., Allison Smith Mulligan. Boston : G.K. Hall, c1992. 548 p.) reflects increased access by subject headings and geographic headings. It includes a list of periodicals indexed and a thesaurus.   Z1251.A2I54

Massey, James C. Historic American Buildings Survey/Historic American Engineering Record : an annotated bibliography / comp. by James C. Massey, Nancy B. Schwartz, Shirley Maxwell. [Wash.] : HABS/HAER, National Park Service, U.S. Dept. of the Interior, 1992. 170 p.   **BF219**

Spine title: HABS/HAER, an annotated bibliography.
Superintendent of Documents classification: I 29.74:B47 .
Covers works published 1933–91 by HABS and HAER and related publications from the National Park Service and the U.S. Govt. Print. Off. Excludes regional publications which used HABS/HAER records. Annotations. Indexes: authors, organizations, journals, states and subjects (divided by county or city). Appears to be the successor to Donald E. Sackheim, *Historic American Engineering Record catalog* (Wash. : National Park Service, 1976. 193 p.), Ellen Boone and Alice Keys, *HAER checklist, 1969–1985* (Wash. : HABS/HAER, 1985), and *Historic America : buildings, structures, and sites* (comp. by Alice Stamm; ed. by C. Ford Peatross. Wash. : Library of Congress, 1983).

§ Two short bibliographies by coauthor Massey: *Guide to preservation literature* (Rev. ed. Wash. : Historic House Association of America, 1979. 18 p.) and *Readings in historic preservation : an annotated bibliography to key books and periodicals* (Wash. : National Preservation Institute, 1986. 37 p.).   Z5944.U5M39

Parry, Donald W. A bibliography on temples of the ancient Near East and Mediterranean world : arranged by subject and by author / comp. by Donald W. Parry, Stephen D. Ricks, John W. Welch. Lewiston [N.Y.] : E. Mellen Pr., 1991. 311 p. (Ancient Near Eastern texts and studies, v. 9).   **BF220**

Some 2,700 entries arranged by 16 topics under two broad categories: General; Rituals and symbols. Lacks indexing to places, buildings, or subjects.   Z7834.M628P37

Roos, Frank John. Bibliography of early American architecture : writings on architecture constructed before 1860 in eastern and central United States. Urbana : Univ. of Illinois Pr., 1968. 389 p.   **BF221**

A revised and updated edition of the author's *Writings on early American architecture* (Columbus, Ohio : Ohio State Univ. Pr., 1943).
Includes 4,377 items arranged by a general category, by period, and by region; minimal annotations. Bibliographies: general; architects. Index.   Z5944.U5R6

Royal Institute of British Architects. The Royal Institute of British Architects comprehensive index to architectural periodicals, 1956–1970. London : World Microfilms, [1971]. 20 reels.   **BF222**

Photographic reproduction of a card file forming an international index to selected articles from some 200 architecture and planning journals, 1956–70. Topical arrangement, subarranged alphabetically listing by English-language title. The last reel contains the list of subject headings used. Much of the index was published in the quarterly issues of the *RIBA library bulletin* and cumulated in *RIBA annual review of periodical articles*, 1965/66–1971/July 1972 (London : 1967/-73. 7 v.).

Continued by: *Architectural periodicals index* (BF207).

Schimmelman, Janice Gayle. Architectural treatises and building handbooks available in American libraries and bookstores through 1800. Worcester, Mass. : American Antiquarian Soc., 1986. [183 p.].   **BF223**

Identifies 147 books, 65 of which are additions to Helen Park's *A list of architectural books available in America before the Revolution*, first publ. in the Oct. 1961 issue of *Journal of the Society of Architectural Historians* (New ed. Los Angeles : Hennessey & Ingalls, 1973). Titles are available, along with those listed by Henry Russell Hitchcock (BF217), on microfilm.

Schimmelman's purpose "is twofold: to develop a list of European architectural books available in America through 1800, and to identify all eighteenth-century libraries and bookstores that either circulated or sold architectural books ... [with the intention] to enhance, clarify, and expand Park's work by including materials available after the Revolution."—*p. 317*. The body of the work lists each title alphabetically by author and cites references unaltered from the original library or bookseller catalogs, concluding with bibliographic information and numbers from *Early American imprints* (AA410 *note*), Charles Evans's *American bibliography* (AA405), and Robert B. Winans's *A descriptive checklist of book catalogues separately printed in America, 1693–1800* (AA99). Two appendixes: Publication dates and imprints of books cited, in order of number of references; Treatises listed by date of earliest American catalog reference.   Z5941.3.S2

Sharp, Dennis. Sources of modern architecture : a critical bibliography. 2nd ed., rev. and enl. London ; N.Y. : Granada, 1981. 192 p. : ill.   **BF224**

1st ed., 1967.
In three sections: Biographical bibliography, which provides biographical sketches of some 130 architects, with references to writings about them; Subject bibliography, subdivided by period and concerned with general works on modern architecture and theory; and National

bibliography, which lists books about national trends in modern architecture. Select list of architectural periodicals; index of architects and authors.

§ Another of Sharp's numerous books is: *The illustrated encyclopedia of architects and architecture* (N.Y. : Whitney Library of Design, 1991. 256 p.), a popular and smaller alternative to the *Macmillan encyclopedia of architects* (BF262). Z5941.5.S47

Periodicals

Bibliothèque Forney. L'architecture dans les collections de périodiques de la Bibliothèque Forney / Laure Lagardère. Paris : Mairie de Paris, Direction des affaires culturelles, Bibliothèque Forney, c1990. 179 p. : ill. **BF225**

Cover title: Périodiques d'architecture.

Journal descriptions, including older reviews and contemporary reviews, arranged by topics such as construction, urbanism, environment, landscape architecture, architectural history, religious architecture, and preservation. Includes a unique chronological list and synoptic table. Index to titles and subjects.

§ The Architectural Association (Great Britain) produces a similar, but abbreviated, publication: *Periodicals, annuals and government serials held in the Architectural Association Library*, comp. by Elizabeth Underwood (6th ed. London : The Association, 1989. 32 p.) An older but helpful directory for researchers in France is Geneviève Ruyssen, *Les fonds parisiens d'archives de l'architecture : guide d'orientation, octobre 1981* (At head of title: Ministère de la culture. Ecole nationale supérieure des beaux-arts. 2nd ed. rev. et aug. Paris : EBA, 1982. 136 p.). Includes indexes and bibliography. Z5945.B63

Gretes, Frances C. Directory of international periodicals and newsletters on the built environment. 2nd ed. N.Y. : Van Nostrand Reinhold, c1992. 442 p. **BF226**

1st ed., 1985.

Lists and describes some 1,600 periodicals, providing data concerning as many as 20 aspects for each title. Arranged by topics: architecture, office practice, building types, historic preservation, interior design, lighting and signage, fine arts, planning, landscape design, building and construction, building services and systems, engineering, real estate development, jobs. Greatly expanded from the previous edition. Indexes: title, geographic, and subject. NA1.G7

Dissertations

Goode, James M. Bibliography of doctoral dissertations relating to American architectural history, 1897–1991. 1st ed. Philadelphia : Society of Architectural Historians, [1992]. 135 *l.* **BF227**

Although called the 1st ed., this work has been issued in various dated drafts with slightly different dates of coverage: 3rd draft, 3 July 1992 (70 *l*), 1900–1991; September 10, 1992, 1897–1992; September 21, 1992, 1897–1991.

"The principal criteria for inclusion in the list has been those studies dealing with the history of the built environment" (*Introd.*), including the social history of buildings. The primary source used by the compiler was *Dissertation abstracts international* (AG13). Chronological arrangement; entries provide institution, *Dissertation abstracts* number, and availability. Indexes: authors, degree granting institutions, subjects. NA705.A12G6

Library catalogs

Avery Architectural and Fine Arts Library. Catalog of the Avery Memorial Architectural Library of Columbia University. 2nd ed., enl. Boston : G.K. Hall, 1968. 19 v. **BF228**

A printed catalog of the collection first appeared in 1895 (N.Y. : Library of Columbia College). An earlier photoreproduction of the catalog cards was published in 1958 in 6 v.

The Avery Library has long been the outstanding architectural collection in the U.S. This photographic reproduction of all cards in the Library's catalog includes not only Avery Library holdings but most architectural and art books on the Columbia University campus. Multivolume supplements were issued at irregular intervals through 1982.

§ A similar work for the Frances Loeb Library is the *Catalogue of the Library of the Graduate School of Design, Harvard University* (Boston : G.K. Hall, 1968. 44 v.) and its three multivolume supplements, published in 1970, 1974, and 1979. Z5945.C653

Johns Hopkins University. The Fowler architectural collection of the Johns Hopkins University / catalogue comp. by Lawrence Hall Fowler and Elizabeth Baer. Baltimore : Evergreen House Foundation, 1961. 383 p. : 30 plates. **BF229**

Repr. : San Francisco : Alan Wofsy Fine Arts, 1991.

The collection was given to the university in 1945 by Fowler, a practicing architect, and is housed in the John Work Garret Library. This descriptive and analytical catalog includes an index of authors, compilers, editors, illustrators, printers, and publishers.

The Library has expanded the collection since its donation; a microfilm of the entire collection is available for purchase. Fowler and Baer also compiled a guide to the microform collection, which contains a photographically-reduced print of the original catalog and a catalog of more recent accessions (Woodbridge, Conn. : Research Publ., 1982. 152 p.). Z5945.J6

Royal Institute of British Architects. Library. Catalogue of the Royal Institute of British Architects Library. London : Royal Institute of British Architects, 1937–38. 2 v. **BF230**

Contents: v. 1, Authors catalogue; v. 2, Classified index and alphabetical subject index.

The RIBA library was formerly known as the British Architectural Library. It has trebled in size since the publication of its preceding general catalog (London, 1889). In recent years library accessions have been listed in *Architectural periodicals index* (BF207).

§ A related work is *Catalogue of the drawings collection of the Royal Institute of British Architects*, also known as *RIBA drawings collection* (London : Gregg, 1968–89. 19 v.). A *Cumulative index* to names and places was published by Gregg in 1989 as v. 20.

Also of interest: John Harris, *A catalogue of British drawings for architecture, decoration, sculpture and landscape gardening, 1550–1900, in American collections* (Upper Saddle River, N.J. : Gregg, 1971. 355 p.) Z5945.R88

Indexes to illustrations

Teague, Edward H. World architecture index : a guide to illustrations. N.Y. : Greenwood, 1991. 447 p. (Art reference collection, no. 12). **BF231**

Indexes some 7,200 illustrations from more than 100 English-language books published since the 1950s. Primary listing is by site (city, building name). Architect, type, and work (building name) indexes.

§ Teague's *Index to Italian architecture : a guide to key monuments and reproduction sources* (N.Y. : Greenwood, 1992. 278 p.) covers some 1,800 illustrations from about 80 books and overlaps substantially with his earlier work. NA202.T4

Encyclopedias

Architectural Publication Society. Dictionary of architecture. London : Richards, [1892]. 6 v. : ill. **BF232**

Repr. : N.Y. : DaCapo, 1969.

Originally issued in eight volumes, 1852–92.

Remains an important source, necessary for documenting 19th-century usage. Includes terms; architectural forms and subjects; places, with some account of their architectural features; and biographies of architects. Bibliographical references.

§ Another 19th-century source has been reprinted: Joseph Gwilt's *An encyclopedia of architecture, historical, theoretical, and practical* (1st ed. London : Longman, 1842. 1364 p. Repr. of 1867 ed: N.Y. : Bonanza ; Crown, 1982). Also available in microfiche from Chadwyck-Healey.   NA31.A8

Encyclopaedia of 20th-century architecture / general ed., Vittorio Magnago Lampugnani ; [tr. from the German and ed. by Barry Bergdoll]. N.Y. : N.N. Abrams, 1986. 384 p. : ill.
                    BF233

Translation of: *Hatje-Lexikon der Architektur des 20. Jahrhunderts.* Originally publ. 1964 as *Encyclopedia of modern architecture,* which was a translation and adaptation of *Knaurs Lexikon der modernen Architektur,* ed. by Gerd Hatje and Wolfgang Pehnt. Publ. in London as: *The Thames and Hudson encyclopedia of 20th-century architecture.* Also publ. in Spanish (2nd ed., 1970; 3rd ed., 1979) and in French (1964).

Articles, except very brief ones, are signed by the 62 contributors; many include bibliographical references. The articles focus on the architects, schools, styles, associations, countries, construction terms, and materials which, since the mid-19th century, have contributed to the development of modern architecture.   NA680.H3913

Encyclopaedia of architecture : design, engineering & construction / Joseph A. Wilkes, ed. in chief, Robert T. Packard, assoc. ed. N.Y. : Wiley, c1988–c1989. 5 v. : ill.   **BF234**

Substantial (more than 4,000 pages); compiled with the aim of serving "as the first source of information with sufficient coverage to satisfy the needs of the average reader."—*Pref.* Approximately 500 signed articles by some 400 contributors contain bibliographies and emphasize processes and technology but include as well entries on building types, styles, architectural education, and regulations. About 100 biographical entries emphasize 20th-century architects, but overlap somewhat with *Macmillan encyclopedia of architects* (BF262). Illustrations are ample and interesting. Introductory matter includes sections: Conversion factors, abbreviations and unit symbols; Acronyms and abbreviations. Vol. 5 includes a supplement of 23 entries and a 150-page index.

§ An earlier source, still useful, is *Encyclopedia of architectural technology,* ed. by Pedro Guedes (N.Y. : McGraw-Hill, 1979. 313 p.), which was published in London as *The Macmillan encyclopedia of architecture and technological change.*   NA31.E59

Hunt, William Dudley. Encyclopedia of American architecture. N.Y. : McGraw-Hill, c1980. 612 p., [8] leaves of plates : ill.   **BF235**

Offers some 202 articles on major elements in American architecture, from Airport to Zoological garden. Includes entries for 50 of the most important architects and architectural firms. Each term is discussed "in enough depth to explain the general facts and principles ... but not to become so complete or technical that only experts would require or understand so much information."—*Pref.* Short bibliographies; index.   NA705.H86

International dictionary of architects and architecture / ed., Randall Van Vynckt ; European consultant, Doreen Yarwood ; photo and graphic researcher, Suhail Butt. Detroit : St. James, c1993. 2 v. : ill.   **BF236**

A nonessential source, useful for libraries that lack *Macmillan encyclopedia of architects* (BF262) and similar to *International dictionary of art and artists* (Chicago : St. James, 1990. 2 v.). Emphasis is on Americans and western Europeans.

Vol. 1, Architects, presents basic information on 523 architects, theorists, engineers, landscape designers, and urban planners. Entries are signed (220 contributors) and provide chronology of works, bibliography (including works by and works about), and, typically, one photograph. Geographic index, by country. Vol. 2, Architecture, includes 467 buildings and sites not covered in v. 1, arranged geographically by country, then city, and includes a Classical sites and monuments section.   NA40.I48

Planat, Paul Amédée. Encyclopédie de l'architecture et de la construction. Paris : Dujardin, [1888–92]. 6 v. in 12 : ill.
                    BF237

At head of title: Bibliothèque de la construction moderne, publiée sous la direction de M. P. Planat.

Intended as a summary of the whole of architectural knowledge at the end of the 19th century, covering architectural history, principles, and legislation, and technical phases of construction. Long, signed articles on broad subjects from architectural scholars and practicing architects. Brief biographies of great architects and builders are included.

§ Another 19th-century French dictionary, more specialized, continues to be heavily used: Eugène Emmanuel Viollet-Le-Duc's *Dictionnaire raisonné de l'architecture française du XIᵉ au XVIᵉ siècle* (Paris : Bance, 1854–68. 10 v.). It has been reprinted (Paris : F. de Nobele, 1967) and published in abridged editions in French and in English (*The foundations of architecture : selections from the Dictionnaire raisonné* [N.Y. : Braziller, 1990. 272 p.]).   NA31.P6

Sturgis, Russell. Dictionary of architecture and building : biographical, historical, and descriptive. N.Y. ; London : Macmillan, 1901–02. 3 v. : ill.   **BF238**

Repr.: Detroit : Gale, 1966; and as: *Sturgis' illustrated dictionary of architecture and building* (Mineola, N.Y. : Dover, 1989).

A standard work, in spite of its age. Written in collaboration with many specialists, American and foreign. Longer articles and biographies are signed. Bibliographies at the end of many entries; a bibliography of sources at the end of v. 3.   NA31.S84

Wasmuths Lexikon der Baukunst. Berlin : Wasmuth, [1929–37]. 5 v. : ill.   **BF239**

"Unter Mitwirkung zahlreicher Fachleute hrsg. von Günther Wasmuth; Schriftleitung: dr.-ing. Leo Adler; Bildredaktion: Georg Kowalczyk."—*t.p. verso.*

Covers both practical and artistic aspects of architecture, including terms, encyclopedic articles (often signed, with short bibliographic references), and many biographies.   NA31.W3

Dictionaries

See also BF84, BF277.

Cowan, Henry J. Dictionary of architectural and building technology / Henry J. Cowan and Peter R. Smith ... [et al.]. London ; N.Y. : Elsevier Applied Science Publ, c1986. 287 p. : ill.   **BF240**

1st ed., 1973, had title: *Dictionary of architectural science.*

Aims "to be comprehensive within the field of architectural science ... proper, i.e., structures, materials, acoustics, lighting, thermal environment, sun control, building services, scientific management studies, and architectural computing."—*Pref.* Brief definitions; illustrations are limited to geometry and structural terms. Appendixes in the 1st ed., not continued in the 2nd, included a discussion of information processing, mathematical tables, directory of organizations, and a literature survey.   NA31.C64

Curl, James Stevens. English architecture : an illustrated glossary / James Stevens Curl ; with drawings by John J. Sambrook. 2nd rev. ed. Newton Abbot [Eng.] ; North Pomfret (Vt.) : David & Charles, 1986. 192 p. : ill.   **BF241**

1st ed., 1977.

A heavily illustrated dictionary of English (and some Scottish) terms in historical architecture. Succinct definitions; short bibliography.

§ A more recent work by the same author: *Encyclopedia of architectural terms* (London : Donhead, 1993, c1992. 352 p.), while general, has a British perspective.

Some libraries may hold an earlier work by Arthur Leslie Osborne, *A dictionary of English domestic architecture* (London : Country Life, 1954 ; N.Y. : Philosophical Library, 1956. 111 p.).
                    NA961.C87

Dictionary of architecture & construction / ed. by Cyril M. Harris. 2nd ed. N.Y. : McGraw-Hill, c1993. 924 p. : ill. **BF242**

1st ed., 1975. Translated into Japanese, *Saishin kenchiku ei-wa jiten* (1977).

An essential source for architecture, including terms for building conservation, building trades, materials, products, equipment, and styles. This edition adds 2,300 new terms and updates previous definitions; it reflects new developments in building systems. Contains some 2,000 line drawings. NA31.H32

Dictionnaire illustré multilingue de l'architecture du Proche Orient ancien / sous la direction de Olivier Aurenche ; dessins d'Olivier Callot. Lyon : Maison de l'Orient ; Paris : Diffusion de Boccard, 1977. 391 p. : ill. **BF243**

Part 1 is a dictionary in French, giving definitions of, and usually some commentary on, terms used in describing the technology and archaeology of the Middle East from the Neolithic period to middle of the first millenium. It is heavily illustrated with drawings and photographs. Pt. 2 is a multilingual lexicon, giving French equivalents for terms in German, English, Arabic, Greek, Italian, Persian, Russian, and Turkish.

§ For longer definitions and bibliographical references, consult Gwendolyn Leick, *A dictionary of ancient Near Eastern architecture* (London ; N.Y. : Routledge, 1988. 261 p.). NA31.D524

Fleming, John. The Penguin dictionary of architecture / John Fleming, Hugh Honour, Nikolaus Pevsner ; drawings by David Etherton. 4th ed. London, Eng. ; N.Y. : Penguin, 1991. 497 p. : ill. **BF244**

1st ed., 1966; 3rd ed., 1980.

An essential source. In addition to definitions of terms, includes biographical notes on leading architects. Also published in Spanish and Italian. This edition incorporates more entries for Asia and for contemporary architects.

§ Surpasses two older British dictionaries: *Everyman's concise encyclopedia of architecture* (London : J.M. Dent ; N.Y. : Dutton, 1960, c1959. 372 p.) by Martin Shaw Briggs, and *A short dictionary of architecture, including some common building terms*, by Dora Ware and Betty Beatty (3rd ed., rev. and enl. London : Allen & Unwin, 1953. 135 p.), which has also been published in Spanish. NA31.F55

Historic architecture sourcebook / ed. by Cyril M. Harris. N.Y. : McGraw-Hill, c1977. 581 p. : ill. **BF245**

An "unabridged and unaltered" reprint was issued in paperback with the title *Illustrated dictionary of historic architecture* (N.Y. : Dover, 1983).

Offers brief definitions from ten contributors, covering some 5,000 architectural terms; features more than 2,000 illustrations—mainly line drawings.

§ Some overlap with the 1st ed. of *Dictionary of architecture and construction*, also ed. by Harris (2nd ed., BF242). NA31.H56

Lever, Jill. Illustrated dictionary of architecture, 800–1914 / Jill Lever and John Harris. Expanded and redesigned 2nd ed. London ; Boston : Faber and Faber, 1993. 218 p. : ill. **BF246**

1st ed., 1967, publ. as: *Illustrated glossary of architecture, 850–1830*. The 2nd ed. was first publ. 1989.

Limited to British architecture; excludes archaic terms. Most of the 200 brief definitions have one or more references to a photograph and simple line drawing illustrating the term. NA963.L48

Directories

Architecture on screen : films and videos on architecture, landscape architecture, historic preservation, city and regional planning / Nadine Covert, ed. ; Vivian Wick ... [et al.]. N.Y. : G.K. Hall, c1993. 238 p. : ill. **BF247**

Comp. and ed. by the Program for Art on Film, a joint venture of the Metropolitan Museum of Art and the J. Paul Getty Trust.

"Includes 940 film and video titles on architecture and architects ... landscape architecture, historic preservation, and city and regional planning. These productions originated in thirty-six countries and were produced between 1927 and 1992, with most released since 1980."—*Pref.* Like *Art on screen* (BF96) and *Films and videos on photography* (BF327), this directory is compiled from the Art on Film Database. Annotated entries provide basic data and an evaluation of each film. Includes four introductory signed essays, a resource list, and indexes (subject, geographic, names, series, and sources). NA2588.A73

Catalog of national historic landmarks / comp. by the History Division, National Park Service. Wash. : U.S. Dept. of the Interior, 1987. 290 p. **BF248**

Superintendent of Documents classification: I 29.120.

1st ed., 1985.

Lists 1,811 properties and supplies an introduction that covers the designation process, criteria of national significance, ineligible properties and exceptions to exclusions, recognition and effects of designation, withdrawal of designation, and other regulations. Arranged alphabetically by state, then by building name. Each entry provides address, county, date, architect (if known), a one- or two-sentence description, and date of designation. Lacks an index.

§ Related but more specialized titles include George Cantor, *Historic black landmarks : a travelers' guide* (Detroit : Visible Ink, 1991; also publ. by Gale as *Historic landmarks of black America*), which lists 300 sites; and Eldon Hauck, *American capitols* (Jefferson, N.C. : McFarland, 1991). E159.C33

Greeves, Lydia. The National Trust guide : a complete introduction to the buildings, gardens, coast and country properties owned by the National Trust / Lydia Greeves and Michael Trinick. Rev. [i.e., 4th] ed. N.Y. : Weidenfeld & Nicolson, 1990. 402 p. : col. ill., maps. **BF249**

1st ed., 1973; 3rd ed., 1984, ed. by Robin Fedden and Rosemary Joekes. This ed. first publ. London : National Trust, 1989.

This edition provides "a description of all major holdings in England, Wales, and Northern Ireland" (*p. xxvi*) and mentions two related publications given to members: *Properties of the National Trust* (3rd rev. ed., 1983) and *National Trust handbook for members and visitors* (1987). Arranged alphabetically by site name, descriptions range from a paragraph to a full page, many illustrated in color. A 12-page foreword by John Jules Norwich describes the Trust's goals and activities. Includes maps showing site locations (p. 354–369), a list of Trust properties omitted from the text (by county, p. 370–389), a page of useful addresses, and an index of people and site names. Excludes covenanted properties.

§ Complementary title: *The National Trust atlas : the National Trust and the National Trust for Scotland* (3rd ed., rev. London : National Trust/G. Philip, 1989. 224 p.). Arranged by region and site type, with illustrations, maps, glossary, list of architects and craftsmen. Index. DA60.G746

National register of historic places, 1966–1991. Nashville, Tenn. : American Association for State and Local History ; Wash. : National Park Service ; Wash. : National Conference of State Historic Preservation Officers, 1991. 893 p. : ill. **BF250**

Earlier cumulations published; that for 1966–88 publ. 1989. A new cumulation was publ. 1994.

Lists some 58,000 sites. The *Register*, "the nation's official list of cultural resources worthy of preservation ... is maintained by the National Park Service under the Secretary of the Interior. Expanded from earlier lists of resources of national significance ... now includes properties important in the history of communities and states as well as the nation."—*Introd., 1989 ed.*. Arranged alphabetically by state, then by county and building or site name, providing for each: address, date of designation, codes for four criteria for inclusion and exceptions, identification of National Park Service properties and National Historic Landmarks, and a reference number for the property. Front matter and cumulative list of properties have been compiled and edited by the

American Association for State and Local History. Includes some statistical analysis of the listings as well as listings for state and federal historic preservation officers.

§ Detailed information and photographs from the files amassed for preparation of the serial *National register of historic places* (1969– . Wash. : National Park Service, 1969–) have been reproduced on microfiche by Chadwyck-Healey Inc., Alexandria, Va. Covering material through 1982, the set comprises about 3,200 fiche and carries the title of the serial. E159.N3418

Pro file. 1978– . Wash. : The American Inst. of Architects Pr., 1978– . Irregular. **BF251**
Imprint varies.

Subtitle (varies): The official directory of the American Institute of Architects.

Supersedes *American architects directory*, also produced by the American Institute of Architects (AIA) (ed. 1–3. N.Y. : Bowker, 1955–70).

A directory of members of the AIA and their practices. Principal listing is by name of firm in a geographical arrangement (state, then city). Gives addresses of all offices, type of firm, name of parent organization, principal personnel, work distribution by percentage of gross income (both current and projected), geographical distribution of work, awards. Also includes sections with organizational information, including international groups. Indexes of firms and of principals, plus an alphabetical list of AIA members.

§ In addition to traditional information, *Directory, African American architects* (Biennial. Cincinnati : Univ. of Cincinnati, Center for the Study of the Practice of Architecture, College of Design, Architecture, Art, and Planning, 1991–) includes listings for women, faculty, and states.

Handbooks

Whiffen, Marcus. American architecture since 1780 : a guide to the styles. Cambridge, Mass. : M.I.T. Pr., c1992. 326 p. : ill. **BF252**
1st ed., 1969.

Chronological arrangement (e.g., Styles that reached their zenith in 1780–1820, Styles that have flourished since 1945). For each style, there is a note on its characteristics, a brief history and a few illustrations. Glossary; index.

§ There are three other frequently used guides: Carole Rifkind, *A field guide to American architecture* (N.Y. : New American Library, 1980. Repr.: N.Y. : Bonanza, 1984); Virginia and Lee McAlester, *A field guide to American houses* (N.Y. : Knopf, 1984. Various reprints); and the smaller *Identifying American architecture: a pictorial guide to styles and terms 1600–1945* (2nd ed. rev. and enl. N.Y. : Norton, 1981). NA705.W47

The world atlas of architecture / foreword by John Julius Norwich. Boston, Mass. : G.K. Hall, c1984. 408 p. : ill. (some col.). **BF253**
The English ed. of *Le grand atlas de l'architecture mondiale* (1981); partly based on *Great architecture of the world*, gen. ed., John Julius Norwich (London : Mitchell Beazley ; N.Y. : Random House, 1975. Repr.: N.Y. : Da Capo, 1991).

Repr.: N.Y. : Portland House, 1988.

Intended to counteract the "essentially literary outlook of our culture" by offering "a few guidelines on how to approach and 'read' a building…"—*Introd.* Arranged in six broad periods. Numerous illustrations, diagrams, sections, plans, and photographs. Bibliography; index.

§ Other sources with extensive illustrations include: Henri Steirlin's *Encyclopedia of world architecture* (N.Y. : Van Nostrand Reinhold, 1983, c1977); Richard Reid's *The book of buildings* (Chicago : Rand McNally, 1983, c1980); Doreen Yarwood's *A chronology of western architecture* (London : Batsford, 1987); and *Brian Sachar's An atlas of European architecture* (N.Y. : Van Nostrand Reinhold, 1984). NA200.W67

History

Buildings of the United States. N.Y. : Oxford Univ. Pr., 1993. v. 1–4. (In progress). **BF254**
Contents: Buildings of Iowa, by David Gebhard and Gerald Mansheim (1993. 565 p.); Buildings of Michigan, by Kathryn Bishop Eckert (1993. 603 p.); Buildings of Alaska, by Alison K. Hoagland (1993. 338 p.); Buildings of the District of Columbia, by Pamela Scott and Antoinette J. Lee (1993, 463 p.).

A set, projected for 55 volumes, undertaken by the Society of Architectural Historians; similar to the British *Buildings of England* series (London : Penguin, 1951–74). Each volume includes a substantial introduction to the state's built environment, followed by the guide (arranged by region and city), with entries for individual sites. Includes maps, small photographs, glossary, suggested reading, and index.

Fletcher, Banister. Sir Banister Fletcher's A history of architecture. 19th ed. / ed. by John Musgrove … [et al.]. London ; Boston : Butterworths, 1987. 1621 p. [16] p. of plates : ill. (some col.). **BF255**
A profusely illustrated reference history, first publ. 1896. Beginning with the 17th ed. (1961), an extensive revision and updating offered "a much broader conspectus of the world's architecture" (*Pref.*) while retaining the single-volume format. By eliminating the "comparative analysis" sections which had long been a feature of the work it was possible to cover a good deal of new ground and to rewrite the majority of existing chapters. This edition has four major changes: "extended coverage, new classification of the contents, a new page format, and most important of all—new authorships."—*Introd.* Includes bibliographies, glossary, and index. NA200.F63

Gloag, John. Guide to Western architecture : with over 400 illustrations. 2nd ed., rev. Feltham, Eng. : Spring Books, 1969. 407 p. : ill. **BF256**
1st ed., 1958. (London : Allen and Unwin ; N.Y. : Grove).

A summary outline from the sixth century BCE to the early 20th century. Includes bibliography and index.

§ From the same period: Talbott Faulkner Hamlin, *Architecture through the ages* (Rev. ed. N.Y. : Putnam, 1953), and *Forms and functions of twentieth-century architecture* (N.Y. : Columbia Univ. Pr., 1952. 4 v.). An earlier pictorial history by Hamlin is *The American spirit in architecture* (New Haven, Conn. : Yale Univ. Pr., 1926). NA200.G6

Pevsner, Nikolaus. An outline of European architecture. 7th ed. reprinted (with rev. bibliography). Baltimore : Penguin Books, 1963. 496 p. : ill. **BF257**
1st ed., 1943; 6th ed., 1961. Frequently reprinted.

Treats "the history of European architecture as a history of expression, and primarily of spatial expression."—*Introd.* A standard source, as are Pevsner's *Academies of art past and present* (N.Y. : Macmillan, 1940. Repr.: N.Y. : Da Capo, 1973) and *A history of building types* (Princeton, N.J. : Princeton Univ. Pr., 1976).

§ For additional 20th-century coverage, consult Kenneth Frampton, *Modern architecture : a critical history* (3rd ed., rev. and enl. London : Thames and Hudson, 1992). NA950.P4

Biography

See also BF224.

Avery obituary index of architects / Columbia Univ. 2nd ed. Boston : G.K. Hall, 1980. 530 p. **BF258**
Represents a new edition of *Avery obituary index of architects and artists* (1963); obituaries of artists have not been indexed since 1960, hence the change of title. Begun in 1934, the index cites obituary notices appearing in the approximately 500 periodicals indexed in *Avery index to architectural periodicals* (BF209) and in some newspapers (mainly the *New York times*) through 1978. In addition, there is

back-indexing of obituaries in four leading American architectural periodicals to the dates of their founding and some retrospective indexing of selected English, French, and German periodicals. About 17,000 references.

Since 1979, obituaries have been incorporated in the *Avery index to architectural periodicals*. Z5943.A69A93

Colvin, Howard Montagu. A biographical dictionary of British architects, 1600–1840. [Rev. ed.]. London : J. Murray, 1978 ; N.Y. : Facts on File, 1980. 1080 p. **BF259**

1st ed., 1954, had title: *A biographical dictionary of English architects, 1600–1840.*

A completely revised edition of Colvin's 1954 dictionary which covered about 1,000 architects of the 1660–1840 period. Biographical sketches of approximately 1,400 English and 250 Scottish and Welsh architects of the period. Bibliographical references. Indexes: persons, places.

§ Related titles: *Edwardian architecture : a biographical dictionary*, by Alexander Stuart Gray (Iowa City : Univ. of Iowa Pr., 1986); *British architects, 1840–1976 : a guide to information sources*, by Lawrence Wodehouse (Detroit : Gale, 1978); and Alison Felstead [et al.], *Directory of British architects, 1834–1900*, comp. for the British Architectural Library (N.Y. : Mansell, 1993. 1035 p.). NA996.C6

Contemporary architects / editors, Ann Lee Morgan and Colin Naylor. 2nd ed. Chicago : St. James Pr., 1987. 1038 p. : ill. **BF260**

1st ed., 1980.

Includes some 640 major architects and architectural firms. For each, gives brief biographical details, chronological list of architectural works and publications, secondary works and bibliographies, an architect's statement of purpose, and brief evaluation by an expert. International in scope; most entries are for living architects or those recently deceased, with a few influential figures from the 1940s–1950s.

§ Works in the same format include *Contemporary artists* (BF138), *Contemporary graphic artists* (BF383), and *Contemporary designers* (BG29). Preferred over Sylvia Hart Wright, *Sourcebook of contemporary North American architecture from postwar to postmodern*. (N.Y. : Van Nostrand Reinhold, c1989. 200 p.). NA680.C625

Harvey, John Hooper. English mediaeval architects : a biographical dictionary down to 1550 : including master masons, carpenters, carvers, building contractors, and others responsible for design / by John Harvey ; with contributions by Arthur Oswald. Rev. ed. Gloucester : A. Sutton, 1984. lxi, 479 p. [2] leaves of plates : ports. **BF261**

1st ed., 1954. This ed. reissued 1987.

This edition incorporates corrections and additions; results of searches for more books and papers; a substantial amount of material gathered in newspapers, periodicals, and ephemera; information from archives now available in public repositories. 400 new biographies have been added to the original 1,300. The preface describes at length aspects treated in the course of revision (illustration, the background, foreign influences, evidence, and bibliography). Includes: Key to Christian names ("to assist identification of masters"); Key to occupations; Appendixes (Portraits; Table of remuneration); Indexes (topographical and county); Chronological table (for the commencement of works); Subject index of buildings; General index.

A *Supplement to the revised edition of 1984*, by John Harvey, was publ. in 1987 (Hulverstone Manor, Isle of Wight : Pinhorns. 16 p.). NA963.H37

Macmillan encyclopedia of architects / Adolf K. Placzek, ed. in chief. N.Y. : Free Pr. ; London : Collier Macmillan, [1982]. 4 v. : ill. **BF262**

"Begun in 1979, the encyclopedia includes more than twenty-four hundred biographies of architects from ancient times to the present and from all geographical regions."—*Introd.* Includes only those architects born before the end of 1930 or who are deceased; engineers, bridge builders, landscape architects, town planners, "a few patrons, and a handful of writers, [are included] if their contributions were so influential as to have changed the face of the human environment." Signed articles range from 50 to 10,000 words; lists of works and bibliographies

(some very extensive) conclude most entries. "Chronological table of contents"; glossary; index of names; and index of works in v.4. An important and impressive compilation.

§ For a smaller, one-volume source, use *Who's who in architecture : from 1400 to the present day*, ed. by J. M. Richards ; American consultant: Adolf K. Placzek (London : Weidenfeld and Nicolson ; N.Y. : Holt, Rinehart & Winston, 1977). NA40.M25

Withey, Henry F. Biographical dictionary of American architects (deceased) / by Henry F. Withey & Elsie Rathburn Withey. Los Angeles : New Age Pub. Co., [1956]. 678 p. **BF263**

Brief biographical sketches of nearly 2,000 men and women, working ca.1740–1952, now deceased. Usually indicates best-known works and gives firm names and years of activity. Cites references.

§ Related title: Lamia Doumato, *Architecture and women* (BF214).

Restoration and conservation

See also BF287, BF293.

The historic preservation yearbook. Ed. 1 (1984/85). Bethesda, Md. : Adler & Adler, c1984. **BF264**

No more published?

Publ. in cooperation with National Trust for Historic Preservation.

Documents are interspersed with surveys and summaries of developments on a wide range of preservation issues. Various contributors. Appendixes include a directory of degree programs in preservation. Indexed.

Landmark yellow pages : where to find all the names, addresses, facts, and figures you need / National Trust for Historic Preservation ; Pamela Dwight, gen. ed. [2nd ed.]. Wash. : Preservation Pr., 1993. 395 p. : ill. **BF265**

1st ed., 1990, ed. by Diane Maddex. It was a revision and successor to *The brown book : a directory of preservation information* (Wash. : Preservation Pr., 1983).

Pt. 1, All about preservation, consists of chapters on 26 practical topics. Pt. 2, Products and services, is an advertising supplement. Pt. 3, The preservation network, contains eight chapters on Federal, state, local, and international programs and organizations. Index.

§ Two sources of preservation and restoration information:

Diane Maddex, *All about old buildings : the whole preservation catalog* (Wash. : Preservation Pr., 1985. 433 p.). A useful handbook, prepared for the National Trust for Historic Preservation.

Orin M. Bullock, Jr., *The restoration manual : an illustrated guide to the preservation and restoration of old buildings* (Norwalk, Conn. : Silvermine Publ., 1966. 183 p. Rcpr.: N.Y. : Van Nostrand Reinhold, 1983), which was written for the Committee on Historic Buildings of the American Institute of Architects. E159.L28

Markowitz, Arnold L. Historic preservation : a guide to information sources. Detroit : Gale, [1980]. 279 p. (Art and architecture information guide series, v. 13). **BF266**

An annotated bibliography of books, pamphlets, dissertations, and whole issues of journals. Aims to cite "fairly comprehensively, the classic works and the indispensable works, and, selectively, examples of the wide variety of publications related to the many aspects of the topic."—*Introd.* Primarily English-language publications of the 20th century (to 1978). Author, organization, title, and subject indexes. Z1251.A2M37

Tubesing, Richard L. Architectural preservation in the United States, 1941–1975 : a bibliography of federal, state, and local government publications. N.Y. : Garland, 1978. 452 p. **BF267**

"Developed from a publication of similar title but more limited scope published in 1975 by the Council of Planning Librarians as Exchange bibliography, 811–12."—*Introd.*

"Preservation" is here restricted to "those structures or their ruins which are still standing or which have been at least partially reconstructed." Deals with scholarly works, statistical reports, manuals and guides, tourist brochures published by federal, state, and local governments, Jan. 1, 1941–Dec. 31, 1975. Excludes Congressional publications, which Tubesing covers in a related work, *Architectural preservation and urban renovation : an annotated bibliography of United States Congressional Documents* (N.Y : Garland, 1982). Topical arrangement, usually subdivided geographically. Appendix gives names and addresses of federal and state agencies concerned with historic preservation. Indexed.   Z5942.T82

City planning

For additional sources, *see* Section CC, Sociology, subheading Urbanization.

Guides

Alexander, Ernest R. Urban planning : a guide to information sources / by Ernest R. Alexander, Anthony James Catanese, and David S. Sawicki. Detroit : Gale, [1979]. 165 p. (Urban studies information guide series, v.2).   **BF268**
1st ed., London : Batsford, 1987 (2 v.).
Lists books and articles of "classical or of highest significance" (*Introd.*) in the area of comprehensive urban planning. Topically arranged within three large sections: (1) History and development; (2) Theory and context of planning; (3) Methods and techniques. Only English-language publications are included; all entries are briefly annotated. Author, title, and subject indexes.
§ Two newer guides from the Council of Planning Librarians, "CPL bibliography series": Irwin Weintraub, *Reference sources in urban and regional planning* (Chicago, 1987. 38 p); Marilyn Berger, *Urban planning : a guide to the reference sources*, which describes the reference sources of, and was first published by, the Blackader-Lauterman Library of Architecture and Art, Montreal (Chicago, 1989. 27 p.).   Z5942.A45

Bibliography

Banister, David. Urban transport and planning : a bibliography with abstracts / David Banister and Laurie Pickup. London ; N.Y. : Mansell Pub. Ltd., 1989. 354 p.   **BF269**
Includes indexes.   Z7164.U72B36

Bestor, George Clinton. City planning bibliography : a basic bibliography of sources and trends / by George C. Bester and Holway R. Jones. 3rd ed. N.Y. : American Soc. of Civil Engineers, 1972. 518 p.   **BF270**
1st ed., 1962, and 2nd ed., 1966, publ. under title: *City planning.*
A classified bibliography of 1,837 books, pamphlets, reports, etc., about three-quarters of them annotated. Major sections include the nature and form of cities, history of cities and city planning, contemporary comprehensive planning, and education for planning, plus a list of general bibliographies and one of selected services and periodicals. A "b" following the item number indicates inclusion of a bibliography in that item. Indexes of authors and subjects.
§ Related titles: M. C. Branch, *Comprehensive urban planning* (Beverly Hills., Calif. : Sage, 1970) and *The history of urban and regional planning : an annotated bibliography*, by Anthony Sutcliffe (London : Mansell, 1981. 284 p.).   Z5942.B42

Council of Planning Librarians. Exchange bibliography. no. 1 (1958)–no. 1564/65 (1978). [Monticello, Ill. : The Council], 1959–78.   **BF271**

Issued 1958–60 by the Council under its earlier name, Committee of Planning Librarians.
Place of publication varies.
Each bibliography treats a specific topic touching on some aspect of city planning, urbanization, and related problems. Range of topics is very wide, international in scope, and some deal with historical or background information on urban affairs.
Continued by the Council's *CPL bibliography* (1978–), the first three numbers of which index the entire set of *Exchange bibliographies.*
This work is in turn indexed by *An annotated bibliography and index covering CPL bibliographies 1–253, January 1979–December 1989* by Patricia A. Coatsworth, Mary Ravenhall, and James Hecimovich (Chicago : The Council, 1989. 51 p.).   Z5942.R33C8

Merlin, Pierre. Bibliographie internationale, retrospective (1950–1983) et partiellement commentée sur la planification des transports urbains. Saint-Denis : Presses universitaires de Vincennes, c1984. 206 p. (Institut de recherche des transports (France). Note d'information, no. 31).   **BF272**
Title on added t.p.: Bibliography on urban transport planning.   Z7164.U72M45

—————— Bibliographie sur les villes nouvelles françaises et étrangères = Bibliography on French and foreign new towns. Saint-Denis : Presses universitaires de Vincennes, 1989. 212 p.   **BF273**
Some 2,000 references, a portion of which are annotated. Primary emphasis on France; the fifth chapter covers new towns abroad. Lacks an index.
§ Merlin is co-editor, with Françoise Choay, of *Dictionnaire de l'urbanisme et de l'aménagement* (Paris : Presses universitaires de France, c1988). A related handbook: Gideon Golany, *New-town planning : principles and practice* (N.Y. : Wiley, 1976. Also translated into Spanish).   HT169.57.F8P44x

Schröder, Brigitte. Bibliographie zur deutschen historischen Städteforschung / bearb. von Brigitte Schröder und Heinz Stoob. Köln : Böhlau, 1986. v. 1–2 : ill. (Städteforschung. Reihe B, Handbücher, Bd. 1, etc.). (In progress)   **BF274**
The initial volume contains 8,600 citations extending through the early 1980s, many for 19th-century titles. Front matter includes a list of individual towns named within each region or state, addresses for compilers, an abbreviations list, and list of journals cited. Vol. 1 is in two parts: general city history, subdivided by seven broad topics; bibliography of specific regions (East and West Prussia, Pomerania, Silesia, Saxony, Saxony-Anhalt, Thuringia, Berlin and Brandenburg, Mecklenburg, Hamburg, Schleswig-Holstein and Lübeck, Bremen, and Lower Saxony). Within the region or state, arrangement is alphabetical by city. For each citation in Pt. 1, codes indicate the general geographic area; for those in Pt. 2, codes indicate publication type, such as maps, inventory, or handbook, and citations are alphabetized by author within that category.   DD91.S36

Current

See also BF207, BF209.

Ekistic index of periodicals. v. 18, no. 104 (Jan.–June 1985)– . [Athens, Greece] : Athens Technological Organization, Athens Center of Ekistics, [1985]– . Semiannual.   **BF275**
Continues: *Ekistic index*, 1968–84.
Articles are selected from journals from a wide range of countries, selection being based on their interest to planners, architects, social scientists, and others concerned with ekistics (i.e., with the science of city and area planning in relation to basic needs of the individual and the entire community). The index lists articles by author, broad topic, and country or region.   Z5942.E38

Encyclopedias

See also *Encyclopedia of urban planning*, ed. by Arnold Whittick (N.Y. : McGraw-Hill, 1974. 1218 p. Repr.: Huntington, N.Y : R.E. Krieger, 1980).

Dizionario enciclopedico di architettura e urbanistica / Diretto da Paolo Portoghesi. [Roma] : Ist. editoriale romano, [1968]–1969. 6 v. : ill. ; plates. **BF276**

Signed entries; many are lengthy, and contain bibliographical references and illustrations, including plans and maps. Biographical entries provide a brief list of works.

§ For a German-language encyclopedia published at the same time, see: *Handwörterbuch der Raumforschung und Raumordnung* (2nd ed. Hannover : Jänecke, 1970. 3 v.). NA31.D58

Dictionaries

Logie, Gordon. Elsevier's dictionary of physical planning : in six languages, English, French, Italian, Dutch, German, and Swedish. Amsterdam ; N.Y. : Elsevier, 1989. 468 p. **BF277**

A basic table in English, followed by indexes for the five other languages. Compiled after Logie completed the five-volume *International planning glossaries* (*see* CH653, CG24).

§ From the same publisher: *Elsevier's dictionary of architecture* (1988. 519 p.).

Two other sources of English-language terms: Charles Abrams, *The language of cities : a glossary of terms* (CC293); and *Contemporary subject headings for urban affairs*, compiled for the Urban Documents Program (Westport, Conn. : Greenwood, [1983]). HT166.L62

Vocabulaire international des termes d'urbanisme et d'architecture / présenté par Jean-Henri Calsat et Jean-Pierre Sydler. Paris : Société de Diffusion des Techniques du Bâtiment et des Travaux Publics, 1970. 350 p. : ill. **BF278**

Title also in German and English (*International vocabulary of town planning and architecture*).

In French, German, and English. Words are given in a classed arrangement, with equivalent terms (and definitions) in parallel columns. Alphabetical index from each language.

§ Vol. 9 of *Glossarium artis*, titled *Stadte, Stadtplane, Platze, Strassen, Brucken* ... (BF84) also provides German, French, and English planning terms. Two other polyglot dictionaries: the International Federation for Housing and Planning's *International glossary of technical terms used in housing and town planning* (2nd rev. and enl. ed. by H. J. Spiwak. Amsterdam, 1951. 144 p.), and Marco Venturi, *Town planning glossary* (N.Y. : Saur, 1990. 277 p.), also published in Italian. NA31.V6

Directories

Directory of bodies concerned with urban and regional research / Economic Commission for Europe, Geneva. N.Y. : United Nations, 1990. 444 p. **BF279**

Describes and provides vital information on "government ministries, departments, institutes, specialized agencies and universities" (*Pref.*) of the Economic Commission for Europe countries. Covers 30 countries and 18 international organizations. No index.

§ Related publication: *Directory of human settlements management and development training institutions in developing countries* (Nairobi : United Nations Centre for Human Settlements, 1991). HT165.53.E85D57

Directory of information resources in housing and urban development / HUD USER. 3rd ed. [Rockville, Md.] : HUD USER, 1993. 146 p. **BF280**

Sponsored by the U.S. Dept. of Housing and Urban Development, Office of Policy Development and Research.

Considerable information on 145 national and international groups and on 44 databases. Indexes: names, subjects, and publications.

Directory of planning and urban affairs libraries in the United States and Canada, 1990 / [Patricia Coatsworth, ed.]. [5th ed.]. Chicago : Council of Planning Librarians, c1990. 98 p. **BF281**

4th ed., 1980.

Arranged geographically by state or province and city. Has 261 listings, compared with 291 in the previous edition. Appendixes: Libraries listed in 1980 edition, now merged or defunct; Nonrespondents. Indexes of organizations and library contacts (names). Z675.C55D57

Guide to graduate education in urban and regional planning. 3rd ed.– . Milwaukee, Wis. : Association of Collegiate Schools of Planning, c1978– . Biennial. **BF282**

Place of publication varies.

Frequency varies; irregular, 1978–84.

Issued jointly with American Institute of Certified Planners until 1986.

The 7th ed. (1990. 96 p.) profiles 57 programs offering master's degrees, 30 of which also offer the Ph.D. degree; chiefly U.S. institutions. Introductory matter about career planning. Two appendixes: List of ACSP member schools; Alphabetical list of school faculty. HT165.52.G84

An international directory of building research organizations / Building Research Board, Commission on Engineering and Technical Systems, National Research Council. Wash. : National Academy Pr., 1989. 1 v. **BF283**

In two parts, U.S. and International. The U.S. section includes profiles of associations, corporate bodies, universities, federal laboratories, etc. The International section provides information on some 50 countries. For each organization listed, provides contact, mission, primary work, source of finances, and publications. Indexes: organizations, subjects. TH23.I58

Handbooks

Fortlage, Catharine A. Environmental assessment : a practical guide. Aldershot, Hants, England ; Brookfield, Vt. : Gower, c1990. 152 p. : ill. **BF284**

Intended for architects, planners, landscapers, and other practitioners in the environmental professions in Great Britain. Topics: history and terminology; legislation; schedules; management; program; environmental statement; qualitative assessment techniques. Includes index. TD194.6.F67

Landscape architecture

Bibliography

Desmond, Ray. Bibliography of British gardens. Winchester, Hampshire : St. Paul's Bibliographies, c1984. 318 p., 20 p. of plates : ill. **BF285**

Repr., with corrections, 1988.

The bibliography, called "Catalogue of works," is arranged by site, and lists from one to 30 citations for each site. Includes a preface by John Harvey, a 14-page introduction, a 20-page bibliography of works consulted, 20 plates, a county index (arranged by seven regions, listing each property and its town), and an index to places depicted on Wedgwood dinner service.

§ Complements Desmond's *Dictionary of British and Irish botanists and horticulturists* ... (EG165) and Miles Hadfield, *British gardeners : a biographical dictionary* (London : Zwemmer, 1980).
Z5996.5.G7D47

Ganay, Ernest. Bibliographie de l'art des jardins. [Paris?] : Bibliothèque des Arts Décoratifs, 1989. 169 p., 8 p. of plates : ill.   **BF286**
Covers French publications, chiefly from the 15th century to the early 1940s; chronologically arranged. Includes a bibliography of Ganay's writings. Indexes: authors (prose, poetry), landscape architects, and sites.   SB457.65.G36

Meier, Lauren. Preserving historic landscapes : an annotated bibliography / comp. by Lauren Meier and Betsy Chittenden. Wash. : U.S. Dept. of the Interior, National Park Service, Preservation Assistance Division, 1990. 82 p. : ill.   **BF287**
Superintendent of Documents classification: I 29.82:H 62.
Contents: Landscape history, inventory and evaluation; Preservation approach and treatment; Historic landscape types; Historic landscape features; Reference materials. Appendix: How to find the information. Author index.   Z1231.A2M45

Powell, Antoinette Paris. Bibliography of landscape architecture, environmental design, and planning. Phoenix : Oryx, 1987. 312 p.   **BF288**
"Designed to be enhanced and updated ... by using the MARC Data Base" (*Introd.*) to locate other sources. A brief thesaurus of terms is followed by an unannotated bibliography that is alphabetically arranged and by author and title indexes. To compile the bibliography, subject terms were chosen from *Library of Congress subject headings* for all pertinent English-language titles, without judgment as to value. Theses and dissertations, government publications, and serials are included; books with a geographic focus smaller than the entire U.S. are excluded.   Z5996.A1P67

Indexes; Abstract journals

Garden literature : an index to periodical articles and book reviews. v. 1, no. 1 (Jan.-Mar. 1992)– . Boston : Garden Literature Pr., c1992– . Quarterly.   **BF289**
Fourth quarter issue is annual cumulation.
Indexes some 150 English-language titles, ranging from specialized works such as *Horticulture* and *Places : a quarterly journal of environmental design* to general works (*National geographic*, *New York times*). Entries for authors and subjects; a book review section follows.   Z5996.A1G27

Encyclopedias

The Oxford companion to gardens / consultant editors, Sir Geoffrey Jellicoe, Susan Jellicoe ; executive editors, Patrick Goode, Michael Lancaster. Oxford ; N.Y. : Oxford Univ. Pr., 1986. 635 p.   **BF290**
Primarily concerned with "locating and describing gardens of all kinds ... [and] touches upon the influences such as geography, climate, and ethnic and social factors that have conditioned gardens of all ages."—*Pref.* Includes brief biographies of principal designers and major patrons and excludes gardens which are neither representative of a trend nor outstanding in their design. Topics include places, concepts, influences, plants, countries, garden types, and organizations. The alphabetical entries, by 174 contributors, constitute the body of the work and include illustrations and some color plates. The five-page bibliography is current through 1986.   SB469.25.O95

Dictionaries

Goulty, George A. A dictionary of landscape : a dictionary of terms used in the description of the world's land surface. Aldershot : Avebury Technical ; Brookfield, Vt. : Gower, c1991. 309 p.   **BF291**
"The purpose is to give definitions of terms that are important to all those concerned with the assessment of landscape quality."—*Pref.* Emphasizes technical terms used by landscape architects.
QH75.G645

Morrow, Baker H. A dictionary of landscape architecture. Albuquerque : Univ. of New Mexico Pr., c1987. 378 p. : ill.   **BF292**
International in scope, with entries in one alphabet for people, types of structures, techniques, regions and countries. A straightforward format, illustrated with line drawings and some photographs of landscape architects and sites, and incorporating cross-references for technical terms. "Notes on sources" serves as a bibliography.
§ Related, earlier title: Warner L. Marsh, *Landscape vocabulary* (Los Angeles : Miramar, 1964. 316 p.).   SB469.25.M67

Directories

Historic landscape directory : a source book of agencies, organizations, and institutions providing information on historic landscape preservation / Lauren G. Meier, ed. ; compilers, Sarah S. Boasberg ... [et al.] ; prep. by the Preservation Assistance Division, National Park Service, in collaboration with the Catalog of Landscape Records in the United States, US ICOMOS Historic Landscapes Committee. Wash. : The Division, [1991]. 96 p. : ill.   **BF293**
Superintendent of Documents classification: I 29.126:H 62.
Contents: National and regional organizations; State and local organizations; Educational programs; Resources for historic landscape research; Sources of information on historic plant materials. Index: institutions, associations, states.
§ Serves as a companion to *Preserving historic landscapes*, comp. by Lauren Meier and Betsy Chittenden (BF287).   E159.H7135

Handbooks

See also BF390.

American landscape architecture : designers and places / [ed. by William H. Tishler]. Wash. : Preservation Pr., c1989. 244 p. : ill.   **BF294**
The fifth volume in the "Building watchers series," intended to provide "an introduction to several centuries of the landscape tradition in America" (*Introd.*) by highlighting accomplishments. The 21 essays on designers are in chronological order ranging from Thomas Jefferson to those active until about 1960, while the 21 essays on topics include campuses, historic landscapes, national forests, parkways, and waterfronts. The 43 contributors are landscape architects. Bibliography; index; and small, though numerous, illustrations.   SB470.53.A44

Brookes, John. The book of garden design. N.Y. : Macmillan : Maxwell Macmillan International, c1991. 352 p. : ill. (some col.).   **BF295**
Originally publ.: London : Dorling Kindersley, 1991.
The author has produced many popular books on gardens. Other frequently used titles: *The garden book* (N.Y. : Crown, 1984) and *Garden styles : an illustrated history of design and tradition* (London : Pyramid Books, c1989).

§ For additional information on European garden history, consult Virgilio Vercelloni, *European gardens : an historical atlas* (N.Y. : Rizzoli, [1990]. Trans. of *Atlante storico dell'idea di giardino Europeo*). SB473.B723

The traveler's guide to American gardens / ed. by Mary Helen Ray and Robert P. Nicholls. Chapel Hill : Univ. of North Carolina Pr., c1988. 375 p. : ill. **BF296**

A revision and expansion of the same editors' *A guide to historic & significant gardens of America* (Athens, Ga. : AGEE Publishers, [1982]). Provides concise information and directions for visitors. Arrangement by state and city. Index. SB466.U6T7

PAINTING

Guides

Keaveney, Sydney Starr. American painting : a guide to information sources. Detroit : Gale, [1974]. 260 p. (Art and architecture information guide series, v.1). **BF297**

A selective bibliography of books, exhibition catalogs, and journal articles, published post-World War II through July 1973. Topical arrangement; brief annotations. Includes a directory of periodical publications, publishers, research libraries, national art organizations, and museums of importance to the researcher in the field of American painting. Index.

§ In the same series: *American drawing : a guide to information sources* by Lamia Doumato (Detroit : Gale, [1979]). Keaveney later wrote *Contemporary art documentation and fine arts libraries* (Metuchen, N.J. : Scarecrow, 1986). Z5949.A45K4

Indexes to art works and reproductions

Roberts, Helene E. Iconographic index to New Testament subjects represented in photographs and slides of paintings in the visual collections, Fine Arts Library, Harvard University / Helene E. Roberts, Rachel Hall. N.Y. : Garland, 1992. v. 1 : ill. (Garland reference library of the humanities, vol. 1154). (In progress). **BF298**

Contents: v. 1, Narrative paintings of the Italian School.

Begins with an index of concepts, terms, and proper names, followed by Paintings in the collection, an outline of seven broad topics, subdivided by more specific subjects. A second volume is intended to cover Christian devotional paintings of the Italian school.

§ *See also* Robert's companion work, *Iconographic index to Old Testament subjects represented in photographs and slides of paintings in the visual collections, Fine Arts Library, Harvard University* (N.Y. : Garland, 1987. 197 p.). ND1430.R6

Encyclopedias

See also BF165.

Champlin, John Denison. Cyclopedia of painters and paintings / John Denison Champlin, Charles C. Perkins. N.Y. : Scribner, 1892 [c1885–87]. 4 v. : ill. **BF299**

Repr.: N.Y. : Empire State Book Co., 1927.

Gives, in one alphabet, biographical articles on painters and descriptive articles on famous paintings. The biographies give main facts of the artist's life; list of his paintings, with reference to the museums or collections where they are located; and some bibliography. Articles on paintings give brief description, some facts of history, museum, a

statement of whether engraved and by whom, and some bibliographical references. Illustrated by outline drawings and plates. Includes numerous facsimiles of monograms and signatures. ND30.C4

Dictionaries

Dictionary of modern painting / gen. editors: Carlton Lake and Robert Maillard. [3rd ed. rev. and enl.]. N.Y. : Tudor, [1964]. 416 p. : ill. **BF300**

1st American ed., 1955; 2nd ed., 1958.

Original French edition: *Dictionnaire de la peinture moderne* (Paris : Hazan, 1954), German translation: *Knaurs Lexikon moderner Kunst* (Münich : Knaur, 1955).

Includes, in alphabetical order, articles on persons, schools of painting, art movements, places, etc. The English version has some additional entries and illustrations. Covers the period from the Impressionists to approximately World War II; i.e., the only living painters to be included are those who had made their mark before the outbreak of the second World War.

§ Related title: Ferdinand Louis Berckelaers (pseudonym, Michel Seuphor), *A dictionary of abstract painting* (N.Y. : Tudor, 1957). ND30.D515

Gaunt, William. Everyman's dictionary of pictorial art. London : Dent ; N.Y. : Dutton, [1962]. 2 v. : ill. **BF301**

"The aim is to provide in concise form and within the limits of 250,000 words and 1,000 illustrations a handy reference to painters and periods, forms and techniques of pictorial art in all parts of the world ... from the earliest times to the present."—*Introd.*

Includes biographical sketches of some 1,200 artists; descriptions of the main periods and schools of art; galleries; definitions of terms; descriptions of some famous paintings, etc. Supplementary lists of British and American artists are included in vol. 2. N31.G3

Sales

The index of paintings sold in the British Isles during the nineteenth century / ed. by Burton B. Fredericksen ; assisted by Julia I. Armstrong and Doris A. Mendenhall. Santa Barbara, Calif. : ABC-Clio, c1988–1993. v. 1–3. (In progress). **BF302**

Contents: v. 1, 1801–1805; v. 2, 1806–1810 (2 pts.); v. 3, 1811–1815 (2 pts.).

A monumental index to catalogs of sales of paintings, produced by the Provenance Index of the Getty Art History Information Program, based on its growing computerized database. Each volume covers a five-year period and is in three sections: a chronological index of sales, an alphabetic index of paintings (under the name of the painter, subdivided by sale date and giving specifics of each painting), and an alphabetic index of owners. Catalog citations note known sellers' and buyers' names and prices, and offer comments on the sale and on annotated copies of the catalog. Incorporates nearly 30% more catalogs than Frits Lugt's *Répertoire des catalogues de ventes publiques* (BF112) and goes beyond Algernon Graves's *Art sales from early in the eighteenth century to early in the twentieth century* (London : A. Graves, 1918–21. 3 v. Repr. : N.Y. : B. Franklin, 1970). 20 volumes are projected. ND47.I5

Handbooks

Foskett, Daphne. Miniatures : dictionary and guide. Woodbridge, Suffolk : Antique Collectors' Club, c1987. 702 p. : ill. (some col.). **BF303**

Comprises, with revisions, the author's *Collecting miniatures* (Woodbridge, Eng. : Antique Collectors' Club, 1979) and *Dictionary of British miniature painters* (N.Y. : Praeger, 1972).

Chapters from *Collecting miniatures* treat: Forming the collection; The early masters; Nine periods; Fakes, forgeries and facts. The index covers those chapters but omits material from the *Dictionary*. The bibliography is current only through the 1970s.

ND1337.G7F465

Mayer, Ralph. The artist's handbook of materials and techniques. 5th ed., rev. and updated / by Steven Sheehan. N.Y. : Viking, 1991. 761 p. : ill.   **BF304**

1st ed., 1940; 4th ed., 1985.

Aims to give the artist "a complete and up-to-date account of the materials and methods of his craft."—*Pref.* Chapters on pigments, oil painting, tempera painting, watercolor and gouache, pastel, mural painting, solvents and thinners, new materials, conservation of pictures, etc. This edition includes new information, such as changes concerning pigments, and excludes that which is no longer relevant. Miscellaneous notes; bibliographies; appendix; index.

§ Supersedes Frederic Taubes, *The painter's dictionary of materials and methods* (N.Y. : Watson-Guptill, 1971). A more recent related source is Frederick Palmer's *Encyclopaedia of oil painting : materials and techniques* (London : Batsford ; Cincinnati : North Light, 1984). For safety-related information, *see* Monona Rossol, *The artist's complete health and safety guide* (BF127).   ND1500.M3

Guidebooks

Morse, John D. Old master paintings in North America : over 3000 masterpieces by 50 great artists. N.Y. : Abbeville Pr., 1979. 309 p. : ill. (some col.).   **BF305**

1st ed., 1955, had title: *Old masters in America : a comprehensive guide : more than two-thousand paintings in United States and Canada by forty famous artists.*

Arranged by artist. Under each a biographical sketch, brief comment on the work, and a list of the artist's paintings, arranged by state or province, city and museum. Includes a geographical index to the museums.   ND1242.M6

Wright, Christopher. The world's master paintings : from the early Renaissance to the present day : a comprehensive listing of works by 1,300 painters and a complete guide to their locations worldwide. London ; N.Y. : Routledge, 1992. 2 v.

BF306

Contents: v. 1, Index of painters; Painters and paintings (biography, bibliography, important collections and complete list of paintings) [arranged by century]; v. 2, Locations and institutions; Index of titles [in English, arranged by century].

A massive, but selective, compilation that covers the Western tradition only. The thousands of bibliographical references are cited under either painter or location.   ND40.W75

History

Haftmann, Werner. Painting in the twentieth century / [tr. by Ralph Manheim]. [Newly designed and expanded ed.]. N.Y. : Praeger, [1965]. 2 v. : ill.   **BF307**

Translation of *Malerei im 20. Jahrhundert* (1954–55); 1st English ed., 1961.

Contents: v. 1, An analysis of the artists and their work; v. 2, [A pictorial survey with 1011 reproductions].

A good general survey. Vol. 1 includes a section of short biographies of the artists discussed. Indexes: names, subjects.

§ Similar work: Herbert Edward Read, *A concise history of modern painting* (3rd ed. N.Y. : Praeger, [1975]). Among the histories use in recent decades: Robert Rosenblum, *Cubism and twentieth-century art* (N.Y. : Abrams, 1960, 1976); and Udo Kultermann, *The new paintings* (Boulder, Colo. : Westview, [1977]; tr. from the 2nd German ed.).

ND195.H323

Mather, Frank Jewett. Western European painting of the Renaissance. N.Y. : Holt, [1939]. 873 p. : ill.   **BF308**

Repr.: N.Y. : Cooper Square, 1966.

A comprehensive survey. Bibliography and notes; index.

There is no single-volume survey in recent years that covers painting alone.   ND170.M3

Richardson, Edgar Preston. Painting in America, from 1502 to the present. [Rev. ed.]. N.Y. : Crowell, [1965]. 456 p. : ill.

BF309

Previous ed., 1956.

A historical survey from the time of the artist-explorer to modern times, including a good deal of biographical information and critical comment. Select bibliography; index.

§ Two older histories much used in the past are Samuel Isham, *The history of American painting* (New ed. N.Y. : Macmillan, 1927. Reissued, 1942), and Virgil Barker, *American painting, history and interpretation* (N.Y. : Macmillan, 1950; N.Y. : Bonanza, 1960). For additional, newer sources, *see* Barbara Novak, *American painting of the nineteenth century* (2nd ed. N.Y. : Harper & Row, [1979]).

ND205.R53

Biography

Aeschlimann, Erardo. Dictionnaire des miniaturistes du Moyen Âge et de la Renaissance dans les différentes contrées de l'Europe / [par] Paolo d'Ancona [et] Erhard Aeschlimann. 2. éd. rev. et augm. Milan : Hoepli, 1949. 239 p. : 155 pl. (some in color).   **BF310**

Repr.: Nedeln, Liechtenstein : Kraus, 1969; Millwood, N.Y. : Kraus, 1982.

1st ed., 1940.

Brief biographical notes with bibliographical references. The 2nd ed. adds some names and additional references. 13 new plates have been added, but the plates in the 1st ed. seem superior to those in the 2nd. An index, arranged by epochs subdivided by country, is new in the 2nd ed.   N7616.A4

Bradley, John William. A dictionary of miniaturists, illuminators, calligraphers, and copyists : with references to their works, and notices of their patrons, from the establishment of Christianity to the eighteenth century / comp. from various sources, many hitherto unedited. London : Quaritch, 1887–89. 3 v.   **BF311**

Repr.: N.Y. : B. Franklin, 1958.

Entries include: name of artist, century, designation (whether miniaturist or other), and brief comment on work, with sources. Appendix lists supplementary names.

§ Also recommended: *Bibliografia della miniatura*, by Lamberto Donati (Florence : Olschki, 1972. 2 v.); and the more recent Harry Blättel, *International dictionary miniature painters, porcelain painters, silhouettists* (Munich : Arts & Antiques Edition Munich, 1992. 1422 p.).   ND2890.B8

Bryan, Michael. Bryan's dictionary of painters and engravers. [4th ed.] / rev. and enl. under the supervision of George C. Williamson. London : Bell ; N.Y. : Macmillan, 1903–1905. 5 v. : ill.   **BF312**

Repr: London : Bell, 1926–34 (v. 1, 1930); Port Washington, N.Y. : Kennikat, 1964.

1st ed., 1816; new ed. rev. 1884–89.

A standard biographical dictionary which usually lists works and frequently indicates location. Monograms of painters and engravers, v. 5, p. 421–25.

§ A similar source: *Cyclopedia of painters and paintings* (BF299).   N40.B94

Cahill, James Francis. An index of early Chinese painters and paintings : T'ang, Sung, and Yüan / by James Cahill, incorporating the work of Osvald Sirén and Ellen Johnston Laing. Berkeley : Univ. of California Pr., 1980. 391 p. **BF313**

Originally planned for three volumes, the next two to cover Ming and Ch'ing periods.

Artists are grouped by dynasty; entries give brief biographical information (with references to published sources) and a listing of every known extant painting, together with indication of present location of the work and source of any reproductions. An asterisk indicates a painting of special importance, and a brief note tries to assess the genuineness of the painting. At the end of each dynasty section there is a list of anonymous paintings. Includes bibliography.

§ The "incorporated" works referred to in the title are Osvald Sirén, *Chinese painting* (N.Y. ; London, 1956–58. 7 v.) and Ellen Johnston Laing, *Chinese paintings in Chinese publications* (Ann Arbor, 1969). Laing compiled a related index, *An index to reproductions of paintings by twentieth century Chinese artists* (Eugene : Univ. of Oregon, 1984). Related work: Victoria Contag and Wang Chi-chien, *Seals of Chinese painters and collectors of the Ming and Ch'ing periods* (BF162). ND1043.3.C3

Harper, J. Russell. Early painters and engravers in Canada. [Toronto] : Univ. of Toronto Pr., [1970]. 376 p. **BF314**

Offers such biographical data as are available for artists who worked in Canada, whose birth dates were before 1867. Includes artists who visited Canada and painted Canadian subject matter during the early period. For each artist gives date and place of birth and death, known details of the artist's life, list of public exhibitions where works have appeared, collections in which the artist is represented, and reference to biographical sources. Bibliography, p. 343–76.

§ Harper is also the author of a standard history, *Painting in Canada : a history* (2nd ed. Toronto ; Buffalo : Univ. of Toronto Pr., 1977). Related collective biographies: *A dictionary of Canadian artists*, comp. by Colin S. McDonald (Ottawa : Canadian Paperbacks Publ., 1967–1990. v. 1–7. In progress); David Karel, *Dictionnaire des artistes de langue française en Amérique du nord* (Quebec : Musée du Québec, 1992) Blake McKendry, *A dictionary of folk artists in Canada from the 17th century to the present* (BG33). N6548.H37

Jakovsky, Anatole. Peintres naïfs : lexicon of the world's naive painters = Lexikon der Laienmaler aus aller Welt = Dictionnaire des peintres naifs du monde entier / Anatole Jakovsky ; [transl. into English and German by Ruth A. Marsden]. [2e éd. rev. et augm.]. Basel : Basilius-Presse, 1976. 649 p. : numerous ill. (some col.). **BF315**

1st ed., 1967.

Includes vital information, list of exhibitions, bibliography, and, for most painters, a portrait.

§ Related title: *World encyclopedia of naive art*, by Oto Bihalji-Merin and Nebojša-Bato Tomašević (London : F. Muller, 1984). ND196.P7J34

Johnson, Jane. The dictionary of British artists, 1880–1940 : an Antique Collectors' Club research project listing 41,000 artists / comp. by J. Johnson and A. Greutzner. [Suffolk, Eng.] : Antique Collectors' Club, [1976]. 567 p. **BF316**

An extension and updating of A. Graves's *Dictionary of British artists, 1760–1893* (London, 1901).

A listing of every artist (including architects and foreigners) who exhibited in any of 47 selected galleries (the selection intended to provide a representative view of art in London and across Great Britain) during 1880–1940. Gives for each: birth and/or death dates (if unknown, first and last exhibition years); towns of residence; memberships and honors; places exhibited and number of times; and, occasionally, art schools attended.

§ Related titles: Stanley W. Fisher, *A dictionary of watercolour painters, 1750–1900* (London ; N.Y. : Foulsham, 1972) and Grant M. Waters, *Dictionary of British artists, working 1900–1950* (Eastbourne : Eastbourne Fine Art, 1975). N6767.J63

Kindlers Malerei Lexikon / hrsg.: Germain Bazin ... [et al.]. Zürich : Kindler Verlag, [1964–71]. 6 v. : ill. **BF317**

Repr.: Munich : Deutscher Taschenbuch, 1982 (15 v.).

The first five volumes are devoted to biographies of individual artists, with lists of their works and selective bibliographies of works about them; v. 6 includes essays on various periods and styles, etc., together with indexes of places and names. Scope is international and covers all periods. Lavishly illustrated. ND35.K5

King, Jeanne Snodgrass. American Indian painters : a biographical directory. N.Y. : Museum of the American Indian, Heye Foundation, 1968. 269 p. (Museum of the American Indian, Heye Foundation. Contributions, v. 21, pt. 1). **BF318**

Entries for some 1,100 artists provide dates, biographical and career information, awards, collections, and address. Includes a tribal index, bibliography, and lists of exhibitions, public collections, and private collectors.

The information from this work was later incorporated within the *Native American artists directory*, which is part of an ongoing database at the Resource Collection of the Heard Museum Library.

§ Related North American source: *Biographies of Inuit artists* (3rd ed. [Mississauga, Ont.] : Published by Tuttavik for Arctic Cooperatives, Fédération des coopératives du Nouveau-Québec, Indian and Northern Affairs Canada, 1988. 4 v.). E51.N42 vol. 21, pt. 1

Norman, Geraldine. Nineteenth century painters and painting : a dictionary. Berkeley : Univ. of California Pr. ; London : Thames & Hudson, [1977]. 240 p. : ill. **BF319**

A brief discussion of various art movements (with colored illustrations) is followed by an alphabetical arrangement of some 700 biographies. For each artist is given a note on historical context and type of work, information on influences, career, honors received, prominence during lifetime, and location of representative works in public museums. References to standard works on the artist are provided, and there are often black-and-white reproductions of a typical painting by the artist. Entries for prominent schools and art movements are also included in the dictionary. Bibliography.

§ Related title: *Dictionary of nineteenth-century American artists in Italy, 1760–1914*, by Regina Soria (Rutherford, N.J. : Fairleigh Dickinson Univ. Pr. ; London : Associated Univ. Presses, 1982). ND190.N57

Simon, Robin. The portrait in Britain and America : with a biographical dictionary of portrait painters 1680–1914. Boston : G.K. Hall ; Oxford : Phaidon Pr., 1987. 255 p. : ports. (some col.). **BF320**

Equally divided between a critical history and biographical entries. The latter are selective, limited to 626 portraitists who worked in oils or crayons (pastel) and were primarily specialists, and give key biographical information and locations of some of the work. Bibliography current through the mid-1980s. Index of names, techniques, and portrait titles. ND1314.S46

Subject catalogue of paintings in public collections. London : Visual Arts, c1989–1990. 2 v. **BF321**

Contents: v. 1, London : The National Gallery, the Wallace Collection, the Wellington Museum; v. 2, London : The Tate Gallery, Old Masters Collection.

A catalog of paintings in British collections open to the public. Neither of the first two volumes contains an explanation of the project's scope and timetable. In each, paintings are listed in a "Descriptive listing by artist," although in v. 1, descriptions are strictly textual, while in v. 2, briefer descriptions are accompanied by small black-and-white photographs of the paintings. Entries provide artist's name, dates, title of the work, medium and dimensions, and accession number. Both volumes have a subject index, based on nearly identical lists of some 60 headings, with centuries as subheadings. Vol.1 has an index of artists by alternate names, an index of persons in the paintings, and a topographical index.

§ From the same publisher: *Museum of Fine Arts, Budapest*, that catalogs works in that collection (v. 1 [1991]– . In progress). ND45.S94

Witt Library. A checklist of painters, c.1200–1976, represented in the Witt Library, Courtauld Institute of Art, London. London : Mansell, 1978. 337 p.   **BF322**

A listing of some 50,000 names of artists, European or European inspired, active since 1200. Nationality and dates are given for each name. Although the library concentrates on painting and drawing, many decorative artists and engravers are included, as are a few sculptors and architects. Includes cross-references from variant forms of the names. Choice of nationality is somewhat arbitrary: care is taken to distinguish between Flemish and Dutch, but not between German and Austrian.   ND35.W5

Wood, Christopher. Dictionary of Victorian painters / Christopher Wood ; research by Christopher Newell. 2nd ed., rev. and enl. Woodbridge, Eng. : Antique Collectors' Club, [1978]. 764 p. : ill.   **BF323**

1st ed., 1971.

Aims to list every British artist from the 1837–1901 period, with biographical information (although, in many instances, little more is known than the date and place of a single exhibited painting). About 500 illustrations in a separate section of plates.

§ This is but one example of the many biographical dictionaries of British genre artists. Similar works include: *The dictionary of British book illustrators and caricaturists, 1800–1914,* by Simon Houfe (Rev. ed., 1981); *The dictionary of British 18th century painters in oils and crayons,* by Ellis K. Waterhouse (1981); *A dictionary of British equestrian artists,* by Sally Mitchell (1984); *A dictionary of British flower, fruit, and still life painters,* by Robert B. Burbidge (1974); *Dictionary of British landscape painters,* by Maurice H. Grant (1952); *A dictionary of British marine painters,* by Arnold Wilson (1967); *A dictionary of British military painters,* by Arnold Wilson (1972); *A dictionary of British sporting painters,* by Sidney H. Pavière (1980); *Dictionary of Victorian engravers, print publishers and their works,* by Rodney K. Engen (1979) and its companion volume by the same compiler, *Dictionary of Victorian wood engravers* (1985); *Dictionary of 16th and 17th century British painters,* by Ellis Waterhouse (1988); and *Dictionary of sea painters,* by E. H. H. Archibald (2nd ed. 1989).   ND467.W65

Catalogs

Beazley, John Davidson. Attic red-figure vase-painters. 2nd ed. Oxford : Clarendon Pr., 1963. 3 v. (lvi, 2036 p.).   **BF324**

Translated from German (Tübingen : Mohr, 1925). Repr.: N.Y. : Hacker Art Books, 1984. 1st English ed., 1942.

A definitive source for the study of ancient art, along with subsequent titles (listed below). Arrangement is chronological, then by painter. Entries provide detailed descriptions of individual vases, with bibliographical references. Appendixes cover names and signatures. Indexes: Proveniences; Mythological subjects; Collections; Publications; Artists.

Continued by:

Beazley's *Attic black-figure vase-painters* (Oxford : Clarendon Pr., 1956. Repr.: N.Y. : Hacker Art Books, 1978).

Paralipomena : additions to Attic black-figure vase-painters and to Attic red-figure vase-painters (second edition) (Oxford : Clarendon Pr., 1971).

Lucilla Burn, *Beazley addenda* (Oxford ; N.Y. : Publ. for the British Academy by Oxford Univ. Pr., 1982).

Thomas H. Carpenter, with Thomas Mannack and Melanie Mendonça, at the Beazley Archive, *Beazley addenda : additional references* (Oxford : Publ. for the British Academy by Oxford Univ. Pr., 1989).

A related Beazley Archive database project is sponsored by the British Academy.   NK4649.B44

Fredericksen, Burton B. Census of pre-nineteenth-century Italian paintings in North American public collections / by Burton B. Fredericksen and Federico Zeri. Cambridge : Harvard Univ. Pr., 1972. 678 p.   **BF325**

A listing by artist gives title or subject of the painting and its location. This is followed by a classified "Index of subjects" in which the principal divisions are religious subjects, secular subjects, portraits and donors, unidentified subjects, and fragments. Appendixes. Index of collections.   ND611.F73

PHOTOGRAPHY

Bibliography

Boni, Albert. Photographic literature : an international bibliographic guide to general and specialized literature on photographic processes; techniques; theory; chemistry; physics; apparatus; materials and applications; industry; history, biography; aesthetics / Albert Boni ; associate ed., Hubbard Ballou … [et al.]. N.Y. : Morgan and Morgan, [1962]. 335 p.   **BF326**

Covers some 12,000 books, pamphlets, and periodical articles on the many technical aspects of photography noted in the title. Works are listed under personal names and subject headings, with numerous cross-references. Author index. Includes abbreviations list of journals and monographs. Material is mainly in English, German, and French.

A supplementary volume, covering 1960–70, follows the earlier pattern and encompasses many new developments and additional subject headings (N.Y. : Morgan and Morgan, 1972. 535 p.).   Z7134.B6

Films and videos on photography / comp. by Program for Art on Film, Direction des Musées de France. [N.Y.] : The Program, c1990. 114 p.   **BF327**

More than 500 entries bring together records from *Art on film database* (formerly *Critical inventory of films on art*), compiled by the Program for Art on Film, a joint venture of The Metropolitan Museum of Art and the J. Paul Getty Trust, and from *Base audiart,* a database compiled by the Audiovisual Department of the Direction des Musées de France, Ministry of Culture and Communication, Paris.

Arranged by title; annotated entries provide information on series titles, length, black-and-white or color, date, country, language, distributors, production agency, and reviews and awards where pertinent. Names index lists film or video titles under filmmaker's name. Source index is international.   TR147.F55

Gernsheim, Helmut. Incunabula of British photographic literature : a bibliography of British photographic literature, 1839–75, and British books illustrated with original photographs. London ; Berkeley, Calif. : Scolar Pr. in association with Derbyshire College of Higher Education, 1984. 159 p. : ill.   **BF328**

Serves as a catalogue raisonné or checklist restricted to the early period and to the 638 titles that have original photographs. The preface provides a thorough explanation of technological changes and publishing characteristics during the four decades. Pt. 1 is the bibliography, chronologically arranged. Pt. 2 is a bibliography of early British photographic literature. Pt. 3 lists photographic journals, almanacs, annuals, nonphotographic journals, and important essays. Appendix includes an outline of the historical use of three photography terms. Indexes: photographers; authors and artists.

§ A welcome complement to: *The origins of photography,* by Helmut and Alison Gernsheim (3rd. ed., rev. N.Y. : Thames and Hudson, 1982) and to Helmut Gernsheim's *The rise of photography : 1850–1880, the age of collodion* (Rev. 3rd ed. London ; N.Y. : Thames and Hudson, 1988). Both are revised portions of the Gernsheims' *The history of photography : from the camera obscura to the beginning of the modern era* (Rev. and enl. ed. London : Thames and Hudson, 1969. 1st ed., 1955).   Z7134.G47

Heidtmann, Frank. Bibliographie der Photographie deutschsprachige Publikationen der Jahre 1839–1984 : Technik — Theorie — Bild = Bibliography of German-language photographic publications, 1839–1984 : technology — theory — visual. 2nd rev. and enl. ed. München : Saur, 1989. 2 v. (Schriftenreche der Deutschen Gesellschaft für Photographie, Bd. 3). **BF329**

First published as *Die deutsche Photoliteratur 1839–1978* (Münich : Saur, 1980).

Approaches the subject from a broad perspective, serving as a "national bibliography of photographic literature" and taking into account "the important technical aspects of photography, the social sciences side and above all the pictorial aspect of photography … ."—*Pref.* Prefatory material in German and English. Vol. 1 contains a classified arrangement by subject (history, bibliography, practice, technology, techniques, genres, theory, etc.); v. 2 is a name and subject index. This edition, with 24,347 titles, is nearly 50% larger than the 1st, is current through 1984, and includes some new sections (e.g., illustrated children's books). Z7134.H44

International photography index. 1979–1981. Boston : G.K. Hall, 1983–1984. **BF330**

Ed. by William S. Johnson.

Intended to be an annual publication. Suspended 1985.

Continues: *Index to articles on photography, 1977–78* (2 v.).

Offers in subject arrangement a listing of articles "that focus on photography as a medium of creative expression, or a vehicle for communication, or that deal with the history of photography and its practitioners."—*Pref. 1979*. How-to articles are excluded. The 1981 volume (publ. 1984) indexes about 100 periodicals, American and foreign, and contains 6,910 entries; about two thirds are in the "By artist" (i.e., photographer) section. Indexes: authors of articles; authors of book reviews; institutions. Z134.I53

Johnson, William S. Nineteenth-century photography : an annotated bibliography, 1839–1879. Boston : G.K. Hall, 1990. 962 p. : port. **BF331**

A current bibliography of some 21,000 annotated references to English-language books and articles from 60 periodicals—general interest as well as specialized—with a list of journals indexed. "In addition to articles about photography … contains examples of photographic practice during the period."—*Introd.* The compiler chose "broad and simple" subject headings such as "History : country" and "Exhibitions : country," subdivided by artist or author. The first 720 pages are the artist or author section, alphabetically arranged and providing substantial biographical information in some cases and simply dates and nationality in others. The following 220 pages are the topics section: Bibliography; Prehistory; History; Country; Apparatus or equipment [five categories]; Application or usage [nine categories]. Includes an author index, but lacks a title index. A second volume is planned to cover the period from 1880 through World War I. Z7134.J64

Photographic abstracts. 1921–87. London : Royal Photographic Society of Great Britain, 1921–87. **BF332**

Issued six times a year, 1979–87.

Indexes issued annually and to cover every ten-year period.

Abstracts in English on technical aspects of photography. Includes above 4,500 abstracts a year "from both technical journals and patent specifications."—*Aims and scope*.

§ Continued by: *Imaging abstracts* (Elmsford, N.Y. : Pergamon, 1988–). For other abstracts consult *Abstracts of photographic science and engineering literature* (Albion, N.Y. : Graphic Arts Research Center, Rochester Inst. of Technology, 1962–72. 11 v. in 18) and *Photohistorica : literature index of the European Society for the History of Photography* (Antwerpen : The Society, 1978–).

Photography and literature : an international bibliography of monographs / Eric Lambrechts and Luc Salu. London ; N.Y. : Mansell, 1991. 296 p. **BF333**

An unannotated, alphabetical listing by author/photographer of some 3,900 titles in numerous languages. Includes monographs, exhibition catalogs, dissertations, and special issues of magazines in seven categories, (anthologies, studies on the relationship of photography and literature, and on art movements such as surrealism, books with portraits of writers, and other categories that include credited photographs). Subject index. Z1023.L33

Roosens, Laurent. History of photography : a bibliography of books / Laurent Roosens and Luc Salu. London ; N.Y. : Mansell, 1989. 446 p. **BF334**

Lists some 11,000 citations, current through the mid-1980s, in a dozen languages, including not only monographs but also company literature, dissertations, and exhibition catalogs, while excluding juvenile literature. Arrangement follows a structured format that includes topics, photographers, and types of publications in a single alphabet. Broad subjects or categories (e.g., History, Manuals) are subdivided by language. Listings for photographers give nationality and dates of birth and death, and are limited to photographers born before 1914. Citations list all editions of a title, including reprints. Although otherwise selective, the work aims to be comprehensive for pre-1914 publications. Name index for photographers and authors. Z7134.R66

Sennett, Robert S. The nineteenth-century photographic press : a study guide. N.Y. : Garland, 1987. 97 p. (Garland reference library of the humanities, v. 694). **BF335**

Primarily a bibliography of 88 journals published between 1840 and the end of the century. Citations give pertinent dates and usually a one-line annotation. This is introduced by a seven-page overview of the birth and development of the press. Appendix: a geographic listing of journals by country. Index to names, subjects, book reviews, and exhibitions.

§ Recommended for use in conjunction with the author's *Photography and photographers to 1900 : an annotated bibliography* (N.Y. : Garland, 1985), which treats only books. Z7134.S45

Library catalogs

Columbia University. Libraries. A catalogue of the Epstean collection on the history and science of photography and its applications especially to the graphic arts. N.Y. : Columbia Univ. Pr., 1937. 109 p. : ill. **BF336**

The catalog of a comprehensive collection of scientific and applied photography. 1,418 citations are arranged by topic within 11 broad subjects.

Augmented by: *Author and short title index. Corrected, with additions, to May 1, 1938* (31 p.) and *Accessions, May 1938–Dec. 1941 with addenda 1942* (29 p.) All three titles, together with a bibliography of Edward Epstean by Beaumont Newhall, were reprinted in one volume (Pawlet, Vt. : Helios, 1972).

International Museum of Photography at George Eastman House. Library. Library catalog of the International Museum of Photography at George Eastman House. Boston : G.K. Hall, 1982. 4 v. **BF337**

Contents: v. 1–2, Author/title; v. 3–4, Subject.

Also issued by G.K. Hall in 66 microfiche or four microfilm reels.

Reproduces catalog cards of the 30,000-volume reference library. Rich in the "history, aesthetics, and technology of photography and cinematography from its earliest developments to the present day."—*Introd.* Two sequences: author/title, and subject. Includes many rarities; excludes manuscripts and periodicals. Z7134.I58

New York Public Library. Research Libraries. Photographica : a subject catalog of books on photography. Boston : G.K. Hall, 1984. 380 p. **BF338**

"Includes books, pamphlets, and selected periodical articles on still photography and allied topics drawn from the holdings of the Research Libraries of the New York Public Libraries, Astor, Lenox, and Tilden Foundations."—*t.p.*

A subject catalog only, reproducing catalog cards with nearly 8,000 entries under some 120 subject headings. Excludes individual photographs or collections of individual photographers, cinematography and television.　　　　　Z7137.N48

Indexes to photographs

Parry, Pamela Jeffcott. Photography index : a guide to reproductions. Westport, Conn. : Greenwood, 1979. 372 p.　**BF339**

Indexes some 80 English-language books and exhibition catalogs, most published 1960–1976, dealing with artistic, journalistic, and documentary photography. Major listing is by name of photographer or firm (or, if photographer is unknown, by title); subject and title indexes.

§ Related titles: Martha Moss, *Photography books index : a subject guide to photo anthologies* (Metuchen, N.J. : Scarecrow, 1980) and *Photography books index II* (1985), which index 22 and 28 anthologies, respectively.　　　　　TR199.P37

Encyclopedias

Focal encyclopedia of photography / ed. by Leslie Stroebel and Richard Zakia. 3rd ed. Boston : Focal Pr., c1993. 914 p. : ill.　　　　　**BF340**

1st ed., 1956; rev. ed., 1965 (2 v.).

A combination dictionary and encyclopedia, bringing together definitions of terms and articles on the history, techniques, art, and application of photography. "This third edition updates material from the previous edition that is still relevant and includes numerous new topics related to changes and advances"—*Pref.* Only about one in four of the terms appeared in the previous edition. Although the work was British in origin, most of the 90 contributors are American. Illustrated with line drawings. Excludes motion picture photography, video, and electronic still photography.

§ The same publisher later produced *The Focal dictionary of photographic technologies*, by Douglas Arthur Spencer (London ; Englewood Cliffs, N.J. : Prentice Hall, 1973).

For historical information, *The encyclopaedic dictionary of photography* by Walter E. Woodbury (N.Y. : Scovill & Adams, 1898. Repr.: N.Y. : Arno, 1979), provides definitions of technical terms with simple illustrations.　　　　　TR9.F6

ICP encyclopedia of photography. N.Y. : Crown, [1984]. 607 p. : ill.　　　　　**BF341**

At head of title: International Center of Photography.

A handsomely produced work which "is intended to give the general reader a comprehensive view of the medium in a single volume. The view provided by some 1,300 entries describes the current state of the aesthetic, communicative, scientific, technical, and commercial applications of photography; it describes how the medium developed; and it identifies the photographers, scientists, and inventors who have been and are responsible for this development."—*Pref.* Articles are unsigned, although there is a list of contributors (without credentials) and an international board of advisers for photographer inclusion. Photographs appear in close proximity to the pertinent articles; line drawings illustrate various processes and devices. A biographical supplement of photographers briefly identifies some 2,000 photographers not accorded articles in the main text. Classified bibliography.　TR9.I24

Dictionaries

Elsevier's dictionary of photography in three languages : English, French, and German / comp. and arr. by A. S. H. Craeybeckx. Amsterdam ; N.Y. : Elsevier, 1965. 600 p.

　　　　　BF342

English base with German and French indexes.　　　TR9.E46

Stroebel, Leslie D. Dictionary of contemporary photography / Leslie D. Stroebel, Hollis N. Todd. Dobbs Ferry, N.Y. : Morgan & Morgan ; London : Fountain Pr., [1974]. 217 p. : ill.

　　　　　BF343

Intended as "a record of current usage in professional and illustrative photography, cinematography (including animation), and photographic engineering and science. In addition, terms have been included from disciplines that relate to photography, such as art, electronics, photomechanical reproduction, physics, psychology, television, and applied statistics."—*Pref.* Illustrated with line drawings and photographs.　　　　　TR9.S88

Directories

See also BF327.

Index to American photographic collections / Andrew H. Eskind and Greg Drake, editors ; comp. at the International Museum of Photography at George Eastman House. 2nd enlarged ed. Boston : G.K. Hall, 1990. 1 v. (various paging).

　　　　　BF344

First ed., 1982, comp. by James McQuaid.

Gives information on 540 collections, arranged by state, then city and institution. Provides cross-references and date(s) and/or nationality for a large number of the names. Some name listings show no holdings in the collections, forming what amounts to a "not-collected" index within the index to collections. Collection entries give name of contact person. Drawn from the museum's database.

§ The National Photographic Record's *Directory of British photographic collections*, comp. by John Wall (London : Heinemann, 1977) describes some 1,600 collections.　　　　　N4010.A1I5

Photographers : a sourcebook for historical research / Richard Rudisill ... [et al.] ; [ed. by Peter E. Palmquist]. Brownsville, Calif. : Carl Mautz Pub., 1991. 103 p. : ill.

　　　　　BF345

Contains six essays on the experience of regional directory research, and "Directories of photographers : an annotated world bibliography," comp. by Richard Rudisill. Index of authors.　TR15.P477

Photographer's market. 1978– . Cincinnati : [Writer's Digest Books], 1978– . Annual.　　　　　**BF346**

Subtitle: Where and how to sell your photographs.

Michael Willins, ed.

The 1994 edition lists "2,500 places to sell your news, publicity, product, scenic, portrait, fashion, wildlife, audiovisual, sports, and travel photos."—*cover*. Includes directories of many types of business firms (e.g., advertising agencies, galleries, book and periodical publishers, record companies, stock photo agencies) with their photographic requirements and name of contact person. Data on contests and workshops, plus feature articles on the profession and the business of freelancing. Bibliography; glossary; indexes (first markets, subjects, general).

§ From the same publisher: *Artist's market* (1974–) and *Writer's market* (BE176).　　　　　TR12.P515

Robl, Ernest H. Picture sources 4. [4th ed.]. N.Y. : Special Libraries Assoc., 1983. 180 p. : il.　　　　　**BF347**

Earlier editions issued 1959, 1964, 1975, as *Picture sources*.

A directory for picture researchers, librarians, editors, artists, and other professional users of pictures. Lists some 900 collections, with entries giving name of collection, location, contact person, contents, subject and chronological coverage, and terms of access. Collections, geographic, and subject indexes.

§ Also beneficial is *Stock photo deskbook* (4th ed. N.Y. : Photographic Arts Center, 1992. 1st ed., 1977, had title *Stock photo and assignment source book : where to find photos instantly*). David N. Bradshaw, *World photography sources* (N.Y. : Directories, 1982) is less useful.

Another work by Robl is *Organizing your photographs* (N.Y. : Amphoto, [1986]).   N4000.N68

Sales

See also BF356.

The Artronix index : photographs at auction, 1952–1984 / ed. by Bhupendra Karia. N.Y. : Artronix, 1986. 1507 p. **BF348**
A massive and unique compilation that is priced outside the reach of most libraries. Arrangement is alphabetical by photographer, preceded by a listing of photographers' names that is useful in verification. Includes a user's guide, list of photographic auctions, statistical overview of selected sales, and a chronology of photochemical and photomechanical processes and photosensitive materials.   TR6.5.A77

Handbooks

Picture researcher's handbook : an international guide to picture sources and how to use them / comp. by Hilary and Mary Evans. 5th ed. N.Y. : Van Nostrand Reinhold, 1992. 516 p. : ill.   **BF349**
1st ed., 1975; 4th ed., 1989.
Also publ. London : Blueprint.
A directory of libraries, museums, government agencies, commercial firms, and studios, providing brief descriptions of picture collections, scope, address, hours, availability, etc. Information is based on replies to questionnaires. Covers over 1,000 sources. In four divisions: general; regional; national; specialist (including topics such as art, entertainment, natural history, religion, and an interesting "Various"). Indexes of subjects and sources.
§ For a directory of picture sources in Britain, see *Picture sources UK* (London : Macdonald, 1985), and for Mexico, *Picture collections, Mexico* (Metuchen, N.J. : Scarecrow, 1988).   N4000

Schultz, John. Picture research : a practical guide / John Schultz and Barbara Schultz. N.Y. : Van Nostrand Reinhold, c1991. 326 p. : ill.   **BF350**
The authors' purpose is "to define the profession of picture research for picture professionals and for all those in the graphic arts who use pictures in their work"—*Pref.* Chapters cover the visual heritage, production and reproduction of photographs, types of professional positions, researchers and buyers, public sources (museums and archives), commercial agencies, legal issues, electronic picture transmission and research. Appendixes: Handling and storage; Professional organizations worldwide; Glossary. Annotated bibliography and indexes of names, topics, and periodical titles.
§An earlier handbook by Hilary Evans, *The art of picture research : a guide to current practice, procedure, techniques and resources* (Newton Abbott : David & Charles, 1979) has been revised under the title *Practical picture research* (London : Blueprint, 1992).
                                                        TR147.S38

Wilhelm, Henry Gilmer. The permanence and care of color photographs : traditional and digital color prints, color negatives, slides, and motion pictures / by Henry Wilhelm with contributing author, Carol Brower. Grinnell, Iowa : Preservation Publ. Co., c1993. 744 p. : ill. (some col.).   **BF351**
A practical manual with 20 chapters on various technical topics. Numerous charts and appendixes. Index.   TR465.W55

Witkin, Lee D. The photograph collector's guide / Lee D. Witkin, Barbara London. Boston : New York Graphic Society, [1979]. 438 p. : ill.   **BF352**
Aims to provide "concise biographies of the most important figures in photographic history, lucid discussions of the major questions about collecting, conservation, and value, and explanations of the many historical photographic processes."—*Foreword.* Major sections

include: the art of collecting; a collector's chronology; a collector's glossary; the care and restoration of photographs; selected photographers; limited-edition portfolios; contemporary group exhibitions and catalogues. Appendix of "museums, galleries, auction houses, exhibition spaces." Bibliography; index.
§ For practical guides, consult: *Photographs : a collector's guide* by Richard E. Blodgett (N.Y. : Ballantine, 1979), and *The photograph collectors' resource directory* (3rd ed. N.Y. : Photographic Arts Center, 1983). See also: *Collectors' guide to nineteenth-century photographs*, by William Welling (N.Y. : Macmillan, 1976).   TR6.5.W47

Biography

See also BF331.

Auer, Michèle. Encyclopédie internationale des photographes de 1839 à nos jours = Photographers encyclopaedia international 1839 to the present / Michèle Auer, Michel Auer. Hermance, Switzerland : Editions Camera obscura, c1985. 2 v. : ill.   **BF353**
Provides more than 1,600 biographies in English and French. Entries cite key biographical information; most have a portrait of the photographer and/or example of the work, list of exhibitions, and bibliography. Includes a two-page list of abbreviations (many specific to photography) and a 14 page chronology of the history of photography through 1985. Indexes of photographers (by country) and other names.
§ A more recent work by the same authors: *Encyclopédie internationale des photographes = Photographers encyclopaedia international* (Paris : Maison Européenne de la Photographie ; Hermance, Switzerland : Camera Obscura, 1992).
An alphabetical list of some 25,000 names that overlaps and supplements the photographers covered in the original encyclopedia. Gives for each known nationality, birth and death dates, period of activity, processes used, genres, and countries travelled to. Appears to have been generated from a database associated with the Maison Européene de la Photographie or the authors in Hermance, Switzerland.
                                                        TR139.A94

Browne, Turner. Macmillan biographical encyclopedia of photographic artists & innovators / Turner Browne, Elaine Partnow. N.Y. : Macmillan ; London : Collier Macmillan, [1983]. 722, [104] p. of plates.   **BF354**
Inasmuch as the work "strives to inform the reader about the world of photography as well as the photographers," it includes "persons, other than photographers, whose contributions to the field have proved vital to its growth and advancement."—*Pref.* Thus, there are entries for photographic curators, inventors, photography critics, etc., as well as for photographers living and deceased. The 144 plates appear in roughly chronological sequence. Lists of museums and photographic galleries appended.   TR139.B767

Contemporary photographers / ed., Colin Naylor ; advisers, Ryszard Bobrowski ... [et al.]. 2nd ed. Chicago : St. James Pr. ; Detroit : Distr. by Gale, 1988. 1145 p., [1] p. of plates : ill., ports.   **BF355**
1st ed., 1982.
"The choice of 750 entrants is intended to reflect the best and most prominent of contemporary photographers (those who are living and those who have died in the recent past); photographers from earlier generations whose reputations are essentially contemporary; and photographers from the inter-war years and after who continue to be important influences."—*Editor's note.* Entries include a biographical sketch, list of exhibitions, listing of galleries and museums holding the entrant's work, bibliography, personal statement, and signed critical essay. Some color photographs.   TR139.C663

Edwards, Gary. International guide to nineteenth-century photographers and their works : based on catalogues of auction houses and dealers. Boston : G.K. Hall, c1988. 591 p. **BF356**

An alphabetical listing by photographer, preceded by a list of the 50 auction catalogs from which the listings are derived, with auction location and date. For each photographer, cites nationality, birth and death dates, inclusive dates of activity, processes used, formats (portraiture, genre, topography, documentary), geographic range (for topographic and documentary photographers), and location of studio. Attempts to distinguish different people with the same name; this is in keeping with the compiler's statement that he was "more interested in uncovering basic information on obscure figures than obscure information on well-known figures."—*Pref.*   TR15.E48

Willis-Thomas, Deborah. An illustrated bio-bibliography of black photographers, 1940–1988. N.Y. : Garland, 1989. 483 p. : ill. (Garland reference library of the humanities, vol. 760).   **BF357**

A companion to the author's *Black photographers, 1840–1940 : an illustrated biobibliography* (N.Y. : Garland, 1985). Arranged alphabetically, with entries for some 400 persons and studios. For half the photographers, gives only region and/or decade of activity; for others, provides birth date, a paragraph or two describing activity, a list of collections holding their work, a selected exhibitions list and bibliography, and one or more photographs. A general bibliography includes books, articles, and exhibitions. No index.

§ Makes a greater contribution to photography reference than *American photographers : an illustrated who's who among leading contemporary Americans* (N.Y. : Facts on File, 1989), and is useful in conjunction with Jeanne Moutoussamy-Ashe's *Viewfinders : black women photographers* (N.Y. : Dodd, Mead, 1986).   TR139.W55

GRAPHIC ARTS

Bibliography

Abrams, Leslie E. The history and practice of Japanese printmaking : a selectively annotated bibliography of English language materials. Westport, Conn. : Greenwood, 1984. 197 p. (Art reference collection, no. 5).   **BF358**

Lists 1,231 citations, 1861–1980, many giving descriptive annotations or citing reviews. Section headings: General work by period; Subjects depicted in prints; Types of prints; Techniques; Printmakers. Several other sections are devoted to Eastern and Western influences and collections. Concludes with a glossary of about 100 Japanese terms and author and subject indexes.

§ Related title; *Who's who in modern Japanese prints* by Frances Blakemore (N.Y. : Weatherhill, [1975], a small but well-illustrated work, with index.   Z5947.3.J30.A27

Bridson, Gavin D. R. Printmaking & picture printing : a bibliographical guide to artistic & industrial techniques in Britain, 1750–1900 / Gavin Bridson and Geoffrey Wakeman. Oxford : Plough Pr. ;.Williamsburg, Va. : Bookpress, 1984. 250 p.   **BF359**

Arranged by broad topics (general, historical, various processes), then by narrower subject areas. List of periodicals consulted; bibliography; subject and name indexes.

§ Additional sources of information on British prints: Merlyn Holloway, *Steel engravings in nineteenth century British topographical books* (London : Holland Pr., 1977); Basil Hunnisett, *A dictionary of British steel engravers* (Leigh-on-Sea, Eng. : F. Lewis, 1980); Rodney K. Engen, *Dictionary of Victorian wood engravers* (Cambridge, Eng. ; Teaneck, N.J. : Chadwyck-Healey, 1985); Raymond Lister, *Prints and printmaking : a dictionary and handbook of the art in nineteenth-century Britain* (London : Methuen, 1984).   Z117.B84

Held, John. Mail art : an annotated bibliography. Metuchen, N.J. : Scarecrow, 1991. xlviii, 534 p.   **BF360**

A unique bibliography, with 2,200 entries covering 1955–89, compiled with the assistance of contributors from around the world. Sections by format (books, magazines, etc.); also includes essays and appendixes. Indexes: author, title, subject.   Z5936.M33H45

Levis, Howard Coppuck. A descriptive bibliography of the most important books in the English language relating to the art & history of engraving and the collecting of prints, with supplement and index. London : Chiswick Pr., 1912–1913. 2 v. : ill., facsims.   **BF361**

Repr.: Folkestone : Dawsons, 1974, in one volume.
Works listed in 26 chapters on broad topics, further subdivided.   Z5947.A3L62

Ludman, Joan. Fine print references : a selected bibliography of print-related literature / by Joan Ludman and Lauris Mason. Millwood, N.Y. : Kraus Internat., [1982]. 227 p.   **BF362**

A classed bibliography of "the published writings on prints from all historical periods and every part of the world. All possible references are cited on the history and technique of fine and historic prints. Entries on photographs, posters, bookplates, illustrations or ephemera are not included. ... "—*p.xv.* 3,215 entries. Author and museum/gallery indexes. Detailed table of contents, but a good subject index would have been helpful.   Z5947.A3L82

Mason, Lauris. Old master print references : a selected bibliography / comp. by Lauris Mason, Joan Ludman, Harriet P. Krauss. White Plains, N.Y. : Kraus Internat., c1986. 279 p.   **BF363**

Similar in format to the authors' *Print reference sources*, (2nd ed. Millwood, N.Y. : KTO Pr., 1979). References are to the work of some 900 artists, in 3,000 citations which "include catalogues raisonnés, checklists, articles in periodicals, listings in multi-volume indices and ... museum, exhibition and dealer catalogues."—*Introd.* Appears to be current through 1980 or 1982.   Z5947.3.E85M37

Riggs, Timothy A. The Print Council index to oeuvre-catalogues of prints by European and American artists. Millwood, N.Y. : Kraus Internat., [1983]. 834 p.   **BF364**

Comp. under the sponsorship of the Print Council of America.

An "oeuvre-catalogue" is here defined as "any listing of the artist's total output in prints or some clearly defined section of that output" (*Note to user*); bibliographies of books illustrated by a given artist are also included. Arranged by artist, with catalogs listed chronologically thereunder. Cutoff date is 1972. Locates copies of hard-to-find items in 50 collections worldwide and provides "List of abbreviations for [85] frequently cited books and periodicals."   Z5947.A3R53

Library catalogs

Library of Congress. Prints and Photographs Division. American prints in the Library of Congress : a catalog of the collection / comp. by Karen F. Beall .... Baltimore : publ. for the Library of Congress by Johns Hopkins Pr., [1970]. 568 p. : ill.   **BF365**

"The book, with entries for about 1,250 artists, includes approximately 12,000 prints, arranged alphabetically by artist's name, and if an artist is represented by more than one print, by title of the print."—*Introd.* Current through 1966; provides brief facts on the artist's life when available. Includes selected bibliography and geographical and name indexes.

§ Related titles: *Guide to the special collections of prints and photographs in the Library of Congress* (Wash., 1955); *Finder's guide to prints and drawings in the Smithsonian Institution* by Lynda Corey Classen (Wash. : Smithsonian Institution Pr., 1981); and *Guide to photographic collections at the Smithsonian Institution* (Wash. : Smithsonian Institution Pr., 1989– . [In progress]).   NE505.A47

New York Public Library. Prints Division. Dictionary catalog of the Prints Division. Boston : G.K. Hall, 1975. 5 v. **BF366**

Photographic reproduction of "entries for book and book-like materials, including pamphlets, clipping files, and other items of an ephemeral nature, that have been added to the collection through July 1975. Cataloging for individual prints does not appear."—*Foreword.* However, the catalog does analyze some collections of prints, scrapbooks of cartoonists, and periodicals (for biographical articles and reproductions).

§ The library has also published *The print file* [microform] (Alexandria, Va. : Chadwyck-Healey, 1989–1990), a collection of 4,461 microfiches reproducing visual and textual material in the clippings and ephemera file, with an index of some 16,000 names. Price: ca.$15,000. Z5950.N562

Indexes to prints

See also BF386.

Parry, Pamela Jeffcott. Print index : a guide to reproductions / Pamela Jeffcott Parry, Kathe Chipman. Westport, Conn. : Greenwood, [1983]. 310 p. (Art reference collection, 4). **BF367**

Intended as an aid for "locating illustrations of prints dating from the early eighteenth century through the mid-1970s."—*Pref.* Lists references to prints in 100 English-language monographs, exhibition catalogs, and collection catalogs. Main listing is by artist, with subject and title index.

§ Similar publications for other media: *Photography index*, also by Parry (BF339), and Jane Clapp's *Sculpture index* (BF388). NE90.P17

Wilson, Raymond L. Index of American print exhibitions, 1882–1940. Metuchen, N.J. : Scarecrow, 1988. 906 p. **BF368**

"The aim ... is to make available a reference to individual prints and printmakers represented at the annual salons of the leading [print] societies."—*Pref.* Arrangement is chronological under the following societies: New York Etching Club, Chicago Society of Etchers, California Society of Etchers, Printmakers Society of California, Brooklyn Society of Etchers, Fine Prints of the Year, Fifty Prints of the Year, Panama-Pacific International Exposition, Victoria and Albert Museum, New York World's Fair [1939]. Artists index lists individual print titles under each name. NE507.W55

Encyclopedias

Stevenson, George A. Graphic arts encyclopedia / George A. Stevenson ; rev. by William A. Pakan. 3rd ed. N.Y. : Design Pr., 1992. 582 p. : ill. **BF369**

1st ed., 1968; 2nd ed., 1979.

A one-volume dictionary, with excellent diagrams and illustrations. Various appendixes; bibliography.

§ Related titles: *Graphics, design and printing terms : an international dictionary* (N.Y. : Design Pr. ; London : Lund Humphries, 1989) and *The Thames and Hudson encyclopaedia of graphic design and designers*, by Alan and Isabella Livingston (N.Y. : Thames and Hudson, 1992). A bibliographic guide: *American graphic design : a guide to the literature*, by Ellen Mazur Thomson (Westport, Conn. : Greenwood, c1992). Z118.S82

Dictionaries

Folsom, Rose. The calligraphers' dictionary. N.Y. : Thames and Hudson, 1990. 144 p. : ill. (some col.). **BF370**

The dictionary itself contains ample illustrations and cross-references. A "Guide to further information" section contains listings for important collections, societies and their publications, suppliers, and a bibliography; the appendix includes parts of the letter, timeline, and maps. Z43.F67

Sales

Gordon's print price annual. 1978– . N.Y. : M. Gordon Inc., 1978– . Annual. **BF371**

13th ed., 1990, ed. by Albert Wehmer.

The oldest of several current indexes for print prices. *Gordon's* 1991 volume has some 37,221 entries.

§ For earlier 20th-century prices, use *Print prices current* (v. 1 [Oct. 1918]–21 [Aug. 1939]. London : F. L. Wilder, 1919–1940).

§ The past decade has seen the appearance of four other price indexes: *Printworld directory of contemporary prints and prices* (Annual. [Bala-Cynwyd, Pa.] : Printworld, [1982]–); *Print price index*, ed. by Peter Hastings Falk (Annual. Madison, Conn. : Sound View Pr., 1991–); *Leonard's annual price index of prints, posters & photographs* (Newton, Mass. : Auction Index, Inc., 1992–); and *Lawrence's dealer print prices 1992* (Phoenix : Long & Strider Pr., 1992). Thorough reviews of these sources essential to their evaluation include two by Marcia Reed in *Art documentation* 11, no. 4 (Winter 1992): 198–199; 12, no. 2 (Summer 1993): 88; and one by Laura Suffield in *Print quarterly*, 9, no. 3 (Sept. 1992): 310–311. NE85.G67

Handbooks

Best, James J. American popular illustration : a reference guide. Westport, Conn. : Greenwood, [1984]. 171 p. **BF372**

A guide to "sources that are reasonably accessible, dealing with American illustrators who have made a significant contribution to the body of American illustration."—*Pref.* Books and articles are cited in six major sections: Historical overview; History and aesthetics; Most noteworthy books on American illustrators; Biographical materials on major illustrators; Social and artistic context; Book illustration techniques. Each section takes the form of a bibliographical essay, followed by a list of works cited. The three short appendixes include one on research collections. Name index.

§ Other titles concerned with illustrators include: James Castagno's *Artists as illustrators : an international directory with signatures and monograms, 1800–the present* (Metuchen, N.J. : Scarecrow, 1989) and Robert E. Weinberg's *A biographical dictionary of science fiction and fantasy artists* (N.Y. : Greenwood, 1988). NC975.B45

Gascoigne, Bamber. How to identify prints : a complete guide to manual and mechanical processes from woodcut to ink jet. [London] : Thames and Hudson, c1986. 1 v. (various pagings) : ill. (some col.). **BF373**

Repr.: N.Y. : Thames and Hudson, 1991.

A handbook that was begun in order to answer the author's own needs as a print collector, and is "not concerned with artistic merit."—*Foreword.* Three main sections: The prints (manual prints, process prints, screenprints); Keys to identification; Reference (vocabulary, brief bibliography, "The Sherlock-Holmes approach," a sequence of questions). Glossary-index.

§ Related titles: William Mills Ivins, *How prints look : photographs with commentary* (Rev. and expanded ed. Boston : Beacon Pr., 1987) and Paul Goldman, *Looking at prints, drawings, and watercolours : a guide to technical terms* (London : British Museum Publications ; Malibu, Calif. : J. Paul Getty Museum, c1988). NE850.G37

Schwartz, Lillian. The computer artist's handbook : concepts, techniques, and applications / Lillian F. Schwartz with Laurens R. Schwartz. N.Y. : Norton, 1992. 317 p. **BF374**

Contents: Developing an approach; Drawing; Proportion and perspective; Color; Animation; Sound and music; Video and film; Computer-controlled art; Analysis with computers. Bibliography and index.   N7433.8.S39

Shapiro, Cecile. Fine prints : collecting, buying, and selling / by Cecile Shapiro and Lauris Mason, with glossaries of French and German terms by Joan Ludman. N.Y. : Cornerstone Library, 1978. 256 p. : ill.   **BF375**

Originally publ. N.Y. : Harper & Row, 1976.

A good general handbook for the amateur or beginning collector of prints. Covers all aspects of the subject from how to buy and sell, to how to catalog a collection and build a reference library. The glossaries define French and German terms most often encountered in the field. Includes a directory of museums, clubs, and dealers.

§ Comparable title: *Prints and the print market: a handbook for buyers, collectors, and connoisseurs* (N.Y. : Crowell, 1977), by Theodore B. Donson.   NE885.S42

History

Castleman, Riva. Prints of the twentieth century. Rev. and enl. ed. N.Y. : Thames and Hudson, 1988. 240 p. : ill. (some col.).   **BF376**

1st ed., 1976, publ. by the Museum of Modern Art.

A historical survey with many illustrations, a brief bibliography, and index. Revisions are chiefly in final chapters, notes, and bibliography.

§Castleman's *Contemporary prints* (N.Y. : Viking, 1973) features works by 40 artists, with brief biographies and photographic portraits.
                                                            NE490.C39

Delteil, Löys. Manuel de l'amateur d'estampes au XVIIIe siècle. Paris : Dorbon-Aîné, [1910]. 447 p. : 106 plates.
                                                            BF377

A detailed history of 18th-century engraving, chiefly in France but including other European work. Prints cited in the text are noted at the bottom of the page, often with information on sales and prices. Includes a "Table alphabétique" of works mentioned in the text, and a detailed index of artists and prints cited.

———. *Manuel de l'amateur d'estampes des XIXe et XXe siècles (1801–1924)* (2 v.).

———. *700 reproductions d'estampes des XIXe et XXe siècles pour servir de complément au 'Manuel'* ... (2 v.). Both publ. in 1925.

Delteil also compiled a set of catalogues raisonnés, *Le Peintre-graveur illustré (XIXe et XXe siècles* (Paris : Chez l'auteur, 1906–1930. 31 v. Repr.: N.Y. : Collectors editions, Da Capo, 1969–70). An *Appendix and glossary*, prepared under the supervision of Herman J. Wechsler, was publ. as v. 32 of the reprint edition.

§ Related titles: Henri Beraldi, *Les graveurs de XIXe siècle : guide de l'amateur d'estampes modernes* (Paris : Conquet, 1885–92. 12 v.); A. P. F. Robert-Dumesnil's *Le peintre-graveur français, ou catalogue raisonné des estampes gravées* (Paris : Warée et Huzard, 1835–71. 11 v. Repr.: Paris : Nobele, 1967; Hildesheim : Olms, 1978), supplemented by Prosper de Baudicour's *Le peintre-graveur français continué* (Paris : Bouchard-Huzard; Leipzig : Weigel, 1859–61. 2 v. Repr., 1967, 1978); and the series of catalogs of the collection of the Bibliothèque Nationale in Paris, *Inventaire du fonds français*.
                                                            NE885.D4

Eichenberg, Fritz. The art of the print : art, masterpieces, history, techniques. N.Y. : Abrams, London; Thames and Hudson, [1976]. 611 p. : ill.   **BF378**

A history and survey with chapters by various contributors. Numerous illustrations; glossary; select bibliography; index.

§ Six chapters were reprinted as *Lithography and silkscreen : art and technique* (N.Y. : Abrams, 1978).   NE400.E32

Zigrosser, Carl. Prints and their creators : a world history : an anthology of printed pictures and introduction to the study of graphic art in the West and the East. 2nd rev. ed. N.Y. : Crown Publishers, [1974]. 136 p., [159] leaves of plates : 738 ill.
                                                            BF379

Published in 1937 under title: *Six centuries of fine prints*; in 1948 and 1956 under title: *The book of fine prints*.

A well-illustrated survey.

§ Zigrosser's other widely-used work is *A guide to the collecting and care of original prints* (Christa M. Gaehde, co-author. N.Y. : Crown, [1965]). Contemporaries of Zigrosser whose publications have been widely read for decades include A. Hyatt Mayor, William Mills Ivins, and Arthur Mayger Hind.   NE430.Z5

Biography

See also BF314.

Bailly-Herzberg, Janine. Dictionnaire de l'estampe en France, 1830–1950. [Paris] : Arts et métiers graphiques : distr. by Flammarion, c1985. 384 p. : ill.   **BF380**

Biographies, arranged alphabetically. Concludes with a section of bibliography, as well as sections on associations and societies and on techniques. Index.   NE647.3.B34

Bartsch, Adam von. The illustrated Bartsch / [gen. ed., Walter L. Strauss]. N.Y. : Abaris Books, 1978– . [80] v. : ill. (In progress).   **BF381**

An initial volume was publ. in 1971 (University Park : Pennsylvania State Univ. Pr.).

An ambitious publication program that not only illustrates all 20,000 European prints described in *Le peintre graveur* (BF382), but also provides supplementary "picture atlases" and commentary volumes. Some 80 of a projected 100 volumes have appeared. Captions in English and French.   NE90.B213

——————— Le peintre graveur. Nouv. éd. Leipzig : J. A. Barth, 1854–76. 21 v. in 19 : ill.   **BF382**

1st (Vienna) ed., 1808 [?]–1821. Various reprints.

Contents: v. 1–5, [Dutch and Flemish engravers]; v. 6–11, Les vieux maîtres allemands; v. 12, Les clair-obscurs des maîtres italiens; v. 13, Les vieux maîtres italiens; v. 14, Oeuvres de Marc-Antoine et de ses deux principaux élèves Augustin de Venise et Marc de Ravenne; v. 15, Les graveurs de l'école de Marc-Antoine Raimondi; v. 16–18, Peintres ou dessinateurs italiens: Maîtres du seizième siècle; v. 19–20, Peintres ou dessinateurs italiens: Maîtres du dix-septième siècle.

§ The important basic compilation is complemented and supplemented by the following works: *Der deutsche Peintre-graveur : oder Die deutschen Maler als Kupferstecher nach ihrem Leben und ihren Werken, von dem letzten Drittel des 16. Jahrhunderts bis zum Schluss des 18. Jahrhunderts*, by Andreas Andresen (v. 1–3, Leipzig : Weigel, 1864–66; v. 4–5, Leipzig : Danz, 1874–1878. Repr.: N.Y. : Olms, 1973); *Dutch and Flemish etchings, engravings and woodcuts, ca.1450–1700*, by F. W. H. Hollstein (Amsterdam : M. Hertzberger, 1949–93. v. 1–43. [In progress]). Place of publication and publisher vary. Supplemented by *The new Hollstein Dutch & Flemish etchings* ... [1993. In progress]) and *German engravings, etchings and woodcuts, ca.1400–1700* (Amsterdam : Van Gendt & Co., 1954–1994. v. 1–36 [In progress]. Publisher varies), both by F. W. H. Hollstein; and *Aide-mémoire de l'amateur et du professional : le prix des estampes, anciennes et modernes*, by Lucien Monod (Paris : Morancé, 1920–1931. 9 v. Repr.: Nendeln : Kraus, 1976).

Contemporary graphic artists. v. 1–3. Detroit : Gale, c1986–88.   **BF383**

Title page note: "a biographical, bibliographical, and critical guide to current illustrators, animators, cartoonists, designers, and other graphic artists."

Editor: Maurice Horn.

Ceased with v. 3, published in 1988.

Each volume of *CGA* included entries for 100 artists (primarily American), citing personal data and information on career, awards and honors, writings, films, exhibitions, and work in progress. Complements the editor's *World encyclopedia of cartoons* (1979–83).

§ Preferred over *Who's who in graphic art : an illustrated world review* ([2nd ed.] Dübendorf, Switzerland ; De Clivo, 1982).

NC999.2.C65

Osterwalder, Marcus. Dictionnaire des illustrateurs. Paris : Hubschmid & Bouret, [1983–92]. v. [2–3]. (In progress).
BF384

Contents: [v. 2], 1800–1914: illustrateurs, caricaturistes et affichistes, avec la collaboration de Gérard Pussey et Boris Moissard; [v. 3], 1890–1945: XXᵉ siècle, première génération, illustrateurs du monde entier nés avant 1885 (artistes du livre, dessinateurs de la presse et de la mode, caricaturistes, bédéistes et affichistes). Vol. 3 publ. Neuchâtel : Ides et Calendes.

For each artist, provides a biographical sketch, list of works, and representative illustration. Index of literary works cited, with names of illustrators. A forthcoming volume is planned to cover 1500–1800.

NC961.6.O88

Prein, Wolfgang. Handbuch der Monogramme in der europäischen Graphik vom 15. bis zum 18. Jahrhundert = Manual of monograms in European graphic arts from the 15th to the 18th centuries. Munich : Deutscher Kunstverlag, [1989–1991]. 2 v. : ill. **BF385**

Spine title: Monogramme.

Introduction also in English.

The main section in both volumes is a "register" in alphabetical order of 2,482 monograms; this includes brief biographical and bibliographical data. Concludes with a name index, including monogrammists.

N45.P74

Stauffer, David McNeely. American engravers upon copper and steel. N.Y. : Grolier Club, 1907. 2 v. : ill. **BF386**

Repr.: N.Y. : B. Franklin, 1964.

A pioneer work on engravers working in America before 1825. Vol. 1 includes some 700 biographical sketches, a brief introduction on copperplate engraving in the U.S., a short section of advertisements about prints from early American newspapers, and an index of the engravings described. Vol. 2 is a checklist of 3,438 works, arranged by engraver.

Two related works:

An artist's index to Stauffer's "American engravers," by Thomas Hovey Gage (Worcester, Mass. : American Antiquarian Society, 1921. 49 p. Repr. from the Society's *Proceedings*, Oct. 1920).

Mantle Fielding, *American engravers upon copper and steel: biographical sketches and check lists of engravings, a supplement to David McNeely Stauffer's American engravers* (Philadelphia : privately printed, 1917. 365 p. Repr.: N.Y. : B. Franklin, 1964), which expands the earlier work with checklists of 1,932 additional engravings, with biographical information. Includes an index by subject of engraving.

SCULPTURE

Guides

Ekdahl, Janis. American sculpture : a guide to information sources. Detroit : Gale, 1977. 260 p. (Art and architecture information guide series, v. 5). **BF387**

A section of general research materials is followed by chronological sections and one for individual sculptors. Annotated. "American" is taken to mean artists "who have lived and worked in the United States for a significant portion of their careers and have contributed substan-

tially to the art of America."—*Introd.* A brief directory of major sculpture collections in public institutions, arranged by state, is appended. Author, title, and subject indexes. Z5954.U5E37

Indexes to illustrations

Clapp, Jane. Sculpture index. Metuchen, N.J. : Scarecrow, [c1970–71]. 2 v. in 3. **BF388**

Contents: v. 1, Sculpture of Europe and the contemporary Middle East; v. 2, Sculpture of the Americas, the Orient, Africa, the Pacific area, and the classical world (2 v.).

Offers "a guide to pictures of sculptures in a selected number of around 950 publications that may be found in public, college, school and special libraries."—*Pref.* Works indexed are mainly in English. Indexed by artist's name, by distinctive title, and by selected subjects.

NB36.C55

Dictionaries

Dictionnaire de la sculpture : la sculpture occidentale du Moyen Age à nos jours / sous la direction de Jean-Philippe Breuille. Paris : Larousse, c1992. 605 p. : ill. (some col.).
BF389

Signed entries by some 60 art historians and conservators, chiefly French. Excellent color illustrations, brief glossary, and selective bibliography.

NB185.D53

Guidebooks

American battle monuments : a guide to military cemeteries and monuments maintained by the American Battle Monuments Commission / Elizabeth Nishiura, ed. Detroit : Omnigraphics, c1989. 469 p. : ill. **BF390**

Based on information gathered by the Commission over a period of 65 years, and compiled from a series of pamphlets describing the sites. The monuments span "four continents, five wars and nearly 150 years of American military history ... ."—*Pref.* Sections: Introduction; American memorials and overseas military cemeteries; World War I cemeteries and memorials; World War II cemeteries and memorials (both World War sections arranged by country); Cemeteries and memorials of other American military efforts. Most entries include location, directions, hours, brief history, a photograph of the site, and a simple map. Index: artists and architects, battles, historical figures, and locations.

§ See also *American military cemeteries : a comprehensive illustrated guide to the hallowed grounds of the United States, including cemeteries overseas*, by Dean W. Holt (CJ632). UB393.A45

Bober, Phyllis Pray. Renaissance artists & antique sculpture : a handbook of sources / by Phyllis Pray Bober and Ruth Rubinstein ; with contributions by Susan Woodford. London : H. Miller ; Oxford : Oxford Univ. Pr., c1986. 522 p. : ill. **BF391**

"Intended as a reference guide to the ancient monuments which served Renaissance artists as a visual reservoir of sculptural styles, iconographic types, and expressive poses ..."—*Pref.* A catalog of 200 works, based on the Census of Antique Works of Art Known to Renaissance Artists at the Warburg Inst. of the Univ. of London. Extensive illustrations. Includes catalog sections on Greek and Roman gods and myths, and on Roman history and life. Appendixes: annotated lists of Renaissance artists and sketchbooks, and of Renaissance collections. Bibliography; index. NB85.B63

History

Bazin, Germain. The history of world sculpture / [Tr. from the French by Madeline Jay]. Greenwich, Conn. : New York Graphic Soc., [1968]. 459 p. : ill.   **BF392**

Repr. : Secaucus, N.J. : Chartwell Books, c1976.

Chronological arrangement. The historical essay, p. 7–87, is followed by a section of color illustrations, p. 89–448, for more than a 1,000 works. Signed descriptive notes by 16 contributors accompany the illustrations for each work. Index of artists and museums.

§ A survey by Bazin, *A concise history of world sculpture*, was published in 1981 (N.Y. : Alpine Fine Arts Collection ; Newton Abbot, Devon : David & Charles. 317 p.).   NB60.B3813

Post, Chandler Rathfon. History of European and American sculpture from the early Christian period to the present day. Cambridge, Mass. : Harvard Univ. Pr., 1921. 2 v. : plates.   **BF393**

Repr.: N.Y. : Cooper Square, 1969.

Remains a standard work. Vol. 2 concludes with a bibliography and index.

§ For more recent histories, consult the following:

A history of Western sculpture, ed. by John Pope-Hennessy (Greenwich, Conn. : New York Graphic Soc., 1967–69. 4 v.). Contents: [v. 1], *Classical sculpture*, by George M. A. Hanfmann; [v. 2], *Medieval sculpture*, by Roberta Salvini; [v. 3], *Sculpture : Renaissance to rococo*, by Herbert Keutner; [v. 4], *Sculpture, 19th & 20th centuries*, by Fred Licht.

Maurice Rheims, *19th century sculpture* (N.Y. : Abrams, 1977. 430 p.). Tr. by Robert Wolf; originally publ. 1972 as *La sculpture au XIXe siècle*.

H. W. Janson, *19th century sculpture* (N.Y. : Abrams, 1985. 288 p.), ed. by Phyllis Freeman.

A. M. Hammacher, *Modern sculpture : tradition and innovation* (Enl. ed. N.Y. : Abrams, 1988. 447 p.), originally publ. as *The evolution of modern sculpture* (1969).   NB60.P6

Biography

Gunnis, Rupert. Dictionary of British sculptors, 1660–1851. New rev. ed. London : [Abbey Libr.], 1968. 515 p. : 32 plates, ill., ports.   **BF394**

1st ed., 1953, London : Odhams; 1954, Cambridge : Harvard Univ. Pr.

Gives the lives and known work of more than 1,700 sculptors. Provides more attention, when possible, to lesser-known sculptors than to those for whom biographies already exist. Indexes: places, names.   NB496.G85

Lami, Stanislas. Dictionnaire des sculpteurs de l'école française . . . . Paris : Champion, 1898–1921. 8 v.   **BF395**

Repr.: Nendeln : Kraus, 1970.

Contents (not volumed as a set): Du moyen âge au règne de Louis XIV (1898. 581 p.); Sous le règne de Louis XIV (1906. 504 p.); Au 18e siècle (1910–11. 2 v.); Au 19e siècle (1914–21. 4 v.).

Each period arranged alphabetically by artist, giving biographical sketch, list of works, and bibliography. The volumes for the 19th century include only artists deceased before 1914.

§ *An iconographic index to Stanislas Lami's Dictionnaire des sculpteurs de l'Ecole française au dix-neuvième siècle*, comp. by H. W. Janson, with the editorial assistance of Judith Herschman (N.Y. : Garland, 1983. 218 p.) covers all italicized entries from Lami's dictionary. Page numbers refer to a list of works in the *Dictionnaire*.

An earlier work by Lami: *Dictionnaire des sculpteurs de l'antiquité* (Paris : Librarie Academique Didier, 1884).

Mackay, James A. The dictionary of Western sculptors in bronze. [Woodbridge, Eng.] : Antique Collectors' Club, c1977. 414 p. : geneal. tables.   **BF396**

Repr., 1992, under title: *The dictionary of sculptors in bronze*.

Designed "to enable the collector, dealer and student to identify bronzes that bear a signature."—*Author's pref.* Includes eight family trees and a select bibliography.

§ Related titles: *A concise history of bronzes*, by George Savage (N.Y. : Praeger, 1969; London : Thames and Hudson, 1968) and *A biographical dictionary of wax modellers*, by E. J. Pyke (Oxford : Clarendon Pr., 1973. Supplements, 1981, 1983, 1986).   NB1115.M27

Maillard, Robert. New dictionary of modern sculpture. N.Y. : Tudor Pub. Co., [1971]. 328 p. : illus.   **BF397**

Translation of *Nouveau dictionnaire de la sculpture moderne* (Paris : Hazan, 1970). Publ. 1960 under title: *Dictionnaire de la sculpture moderne*; previous translation, 1962: *Dictionary of modern sculpture*.

Biographical and critical sketches of some 600 sculptors. Signed entries from 34 contributors. Index of photographers.   NB50.N6813

Opitz, Glenn B. Dictionary of American sculptors : 18th century to the present. Poughkeepsie, N.Y. : Apollo, 1984. 656 p. : ill.   **BF398**

"Illustrated with over 200 photographs."—*t.p.*

Offers biographical sketches of more than 5,000 American sculptors, both living and deceased. "Selection criteria included the presence of the artist's work in exhibitions or collections in major cultural centers of the U.S. Artists of strictly local significance have generally been omitted."—*Pref.*   NB236.O64

Souchal, François. French sculptors of the 17th and 18th centuries : the reign of Louis XIV : illustrated catalogue / [by] François Souchal, with the collaboration of Françoise de la Moureyre, Henriette Dumuis. Oxford : Cassirer ; London : distr. by Faber, 1977–1993. 4 v. : ill., geneal. tables (on lining papers), ports.   **BF399**

Translated from the French by Elsie and George Hill (v. 1–3) and by Augusta Audubert (v. 4). Vol. 4 publ. London : Faber and Faber.

Entries, arranged alphabetically, give a short biography and bibliography, then list the sculptor's works in chronological order with full data, but exclude extensive discussion of attribution or style. All volumes list bibliographic sources and have an index of names, sites (numerous references for the palace and gardens of Versailles), and subjects. Vols. 1–2 include several pages of errata and addenda; v. 4, is a supplement, with a separate alphabetical arrangement.   NB546.S6813

Watson-Jones, Virginia. Contemporary American women sculptors. Phoenix : Oryx, 1986. 665 p. : ill.   **BF400**

"This book is about artists whose work is strong, vital, and often innovative."—*Introd.* For some 300 artists, gives basic information on education, individual and group exhibitions, public collections, awards, select bibliography, gallery affiliations, artist's statement, artist's signature, and photograph of one work. The artists range in age from 27 to 89. Two indexes are provided: geographic (by state) and media (30 categories).

§ Related title: Charlotte Streifer Rubenstein, *American women sculptors : a history of women working in three dimensions* (Boston : G.K. Hall, 1990).   NB212.W37

BG

Design and Applied Arts

GENERAL WORKS

Guides

American folk art : a guide to sources / ed. by Simon J. Bronner. N.Y. : Garland, 1984. 313 p. : ill. (Garland reference library of the humanities, v. 464).   **BG1**

Aims to guide the student and scholar through the field of folk art study "identifying the basic sources and the common topics" and "probing the relation of sources to topics of current concern, thus placing folk art study in the context of broader cultural studies."—*Introd.* Essays by specialists give an overview of the field and a sampling of its subfields. Annotated bibliographies for each chapter include books, articles, museum catalogs, dissertations, and films. Author and subject indexes.   Z5956.F6A53

Ehresmann, Donald L. Applied and decorative arts : a bibliographic guide to basic reference works, histories, and handbooks. 2nd ed. Englewood, Colo. : Libraries Unlimited, 1993. 629 p.   **BG2**

1st ed., 1977.

A classified, annotated bibliography of books in Western European languages, primarily publications from the period since 1875. General sections on applied and decorative arts and on ornament are followed by sections for folk art, arms and armor, ceramics, clocks, watches and automata, costume, enamels, furniture, glass, ivory, jewelry, lacquer, leather and bookbinding, medals and seals, metalwork, musical instruments, textiles, toys, and dolls. This edition includes more entries on regional literature and adds works on major artist-designers, in addition to doubling the size of the 1st ed. Author and subject indexes.   Z5956.A68E47

Material culture : a research guide / Kenneth L. Ames ... [et al.] ; ed. by Thomas J. Schlereth. Lawrence, Kan. : Univ. Pr. of Kansas, c1985. 224 p.   **BG3**

Provides an overview of American material culture studies, with essays by six contributors on topics such as landscape, vernacular architecture, household furnishings, technology and material culture, American folkloristics, social history, and general reference sources for material culture. Index.   E161.M35

Bibliography

The arts of Africa : an annotated bibliography. v. 1 (1986/87)– . Atlanta : Crossroads Pr., [1986]– . Biennial.   **BG4**

Derives from the acquisitions lists of the National Museum of African Art Branch Library, Washington. States as its purpose to cover "significant publications" (*Introd.*) and as its criteria substance and originality. In two main sections: General studies (grouped by 21 subjects) and Country and regional studies (Western, Central, Southern, Eastern, Northern Africa and African islands). Entries, including mon-

ographic and serial literature, are intended to be descriptive and informative. The main sections are followed by four others: Recommended titles on African art; OCLC numbers for serials cited in the bibliography; Author index; Subject index.

§ Related titles: *Catalog of the Library of the National Museum of African Art branch of the Smithsonian Institution Libraries* (Boston : G.K. Hall, 1991. 2 v.). See also the International African Institute's *A bibliography of African art*, comp. by L.J.P. Gaskin (BF25) and *A bibliography of the arts of africa*, by Dominique Coulet Western (BF38).

Biebuyck, Daniel P. The arts of Central Africa : an annotated bibliography. Boston : G.K. Hall, c1987. 300 p. (Reference publications in art history, [3]).   **BG5**

The third volume in a series intended to fill the gap in non-Western arts by reviewing both anthropological and art historical scholarship. Each volume cites books, periodical articles, dissertations, exhibition and sales catalogs. All will have indexes for authors, titles, and subjects (e.g., ethnic groups, media). Includes 1,920 citations, most with brief annotations, from publications in all languages. Covers overlapping ethnic units in neighboring countries.

§ Related titles: *An annotated bibliography of the visual arts of East Africa* by Eugene C. Burt (Bloomington : Indiana Univ. Pr., 1980); and *The arts of Zaire* by Biebuyck (Berkeley : Univ. of California Pr., 1985– . 2 v. [In progress]).   Z5961.Z28B53

Coulson, Anthony J. A bibliography of design in Britain, 1851–1970. London : Design Council, [1979]. 290 p.   **BG6**

Intended as an introductory bibliography of relatively accessible works, but embracing "a very wide range of books and articles on many different subjects, including a lot that have scarcely been studied hitherto."—*Introd.* Topical arrangement within three main sections: Fostering design; Design and designers; Areas of design activity. Includes a brief list of journals, and another of "Bibliographies, indexes, abstracts and catalogues." A "Subject finder" indexes the sections and major subjects of the bibliography. Lacks an author/title or detailed subject index.   Z5956.D5C68

De Winter, Patrick M. European decorative arts, 1400–1600 : an annotated bibliography. Boston : G.K. Hall, c1988. 543 p. : ill.   **BG7**

Intends "to select and call attention to a specialized body of literature ... [and to present it] in such a manner that [it] will also be a useful tool for collectors."—*Introd.* Prefatory material offers an overview of the topic and of the various terms for "decorative arts." The 2,200 annotated references are arranged in a topical outline that provides great detail. Subjects are subdivided by form of publication and for geographical and media groupings. Emphasizes titles published 1960–86, including regional publications, most in Western languages, and cites English versions or translations.   Z5956.D3D38

Hanson, Louise. The art of Oceania : a bibliography / Louise Hanson and F. Allan Hanson. Boston : G.K. Hall, [1984]. 539 p. (Reference publications in art history, [1]).   **BG8**

The first bibliography in a series described by the editor as reflecting increased interest in non-Western arts. Incorporates monographs, catalogs, theses and dissertations, and periodical literature in five sections (Cross-region, Polynesia, Micronesia, Melanesia, Australia) which are then subdivided alphabetically by author. Entries include very short annotations. A sixth section lists sales catalogs alphabetically by city and gallery name. Indexes: personal names; titles; subjects.   Z5961.A84H36

Parezo, Nancy J. Southwest Native American arts and material culture : a guide to research / Nancy J. Parezo, Ruth M. Perry, Rebecca Allen. N.Y. : Garland, 1991. 2 v. (1506 p.). (Garland reference library of the humanities, vol. 1337 ; Garland reference library of the humanities. Studies in ethnic art, vol. 1).   **BG9**

Pt. 1, Resource guide, offers informative sections: A beginner's guide to southwest Native American material culture; Sources for researching; Journals and series containing numerous articles; Glossary of cultures; Key-words and their definitions. The major part, pt. 2, is a bibliography of 8,363 references to books, periodical articles, dissertations and theses, exhibition catalogs, directories, and government documents, published between the mid-19th century and 1988. Indexes by culture and subject in pt. 3.   Z1209.2.U52S686

Current

Bibliography of American folk art for the year / comp. by Eugene P. Sheehy, Rita G. Keckeissen, Edith C. Wise. [1987]– . N.Y. : Museum of American Folk Art, [1988?]– . Annual.   **BG10**

"Intended as an aid to scholars, collectors, students, and folk art enthusiasts at many levels of interest ... is limited to separately-published works—books, pamphlets, and exhibition catalogues, plus a reasonably comprehensive listing of relevant auction catalogues."—*Introd.* Each issue covers imprints for only that year and does not repeat the date of publication. "American" refers only to North America north of Mexico. Categories covered include folk art of ethnic groups and religious sects as well as the various media. Author-editor, title, and subject indexes.   NK805.A1.B5

Design & applied arts index. v. 1, pt. 1 (1988?)– . Burwash, England : Design Documentation, c1988– . Semiannual, cumulated triennially.   **BG11**

Entries are annotated, include book and video reviews, and are arranged by topics and designers' names in one alphabet; there is no access by author. As of 1992, indexes more than 310 current journals and about ten retrospective titles. Also known as *daai*. Beginning 1992, the publishers distributed to subscribers *Design and applied arts periodicals*, a guide to materials indexed in *daai*.

§ Not to be confused with *Design index* (Evanston, Ill. : Design Information, 1982–83) or with *Designers international index* (BG32).

•Available in CD-ROM.   NK1160.D45

Ethnoarts index. v. 5, no. 1 (Jan.–Mar. 1987)– . [Seattle, Wash.] : Data Arts, c1987– . Quarterly.   **BG12**

Continues: *Tribal arts review* (v. 1 [Jan. 1984]–v. 4 [Dec. 1986]. Seattle : s.n., c1984–86).

Covers "indigenous peoples of Africa, Oceania, and the Americas ... [and] endeavors to locate all publications relevant to the study of ethnoart published since July 1983 ... [including] books, periodical articles, catalogs, book reviews, exhibition reviews, conference papers, theses and dissertations ... ."—*Using the Ethnoarts index.* Each issue includes an abbreviations list for journal titles, the bibliography (arranged by general subject and by region or hemisphere), and subject and author indexes. Entries are coded by region, include title translation if not in English, and may include a descriptive statement. A series of bibliographies derived from *Ethnoarts index* is called *Ethnoarts index supplemental publication.* The first six titles (1988–91) treated Oceanic, African, Native American, and Latin American art.

Serials guide to ethnoart : a guide to serial publications on visual arts of Africa, Oceania, and the Americas (N.Y. : Greenwood, 1990) was developed from the database for *Ethnoarts index.* The main section cites 682 titles. Useful appendixes.

•Machine-readable version: *Ethnoarts index* [database] (Seattle : Data Arts, 1983–). Available online.

§ See also: *Tribal and ethnic art* (Santa Barbara, Calif. : ABC-Clio, [1982]).   N5310.7.T74

Dissertations

Burt, Eugene C. Ethnoart : Africa, Oceania, and the Americas : a bibliography of theses and dissertations. N.Y. : Garland, 1988. 191 p. (Garland reference library of the humanities, vol. 840).   **BG13**

Compiled by consulting some 30 published sources, most of which are listed in the preface. Also encompasses "a few bachelor degree honors theses from British or Commonwealth universities."—*Pref.* Each title had to indicate that the topic related to the indigenous peoples of the regions covered and that it "was primarily concerned with the visual arts, architecture, material culture, or archaeology ... ." Covers late 19th century through April 1987, with a total of 1,022 citations. Arrangement of the five chapters follows that of *Ethnoarts index* (BG12), and is hierarchical within the chapters, based on geography, culture groupings, historical periods, and other factors. Four indexes: author, year of completion (in chronological order), institution granting the degree, and subject (including places).

§ Burt also compiled *Serials guide to ethnoart : a guide to serial publications on visual arts of Africa, Oceania, and the Americas* (see BG12, *note*).   Z5956.P68B88

Library catalogs

See also BG81, BG93, BG177, BG200.

Bibliothèque Forney. Catalogue matières : arts-décoratifs, beaux-arts, métiers, techniques. Paris : Société des Amis de la Bibliothèque Forney, 1970–75. 4 v.   **BG14**

Reproduction of the subject catalog cards for the Library's collection of some 100,000 books and more than 1,300 periodical titles.

———. ——— *Index alphabétique des auteurs* (1974–75. 4 pts. in 1 v. [367 p.]).

———. ——— *Supplément au Catalogue matières, arts-décoratifs, beaux-arts, métiers, techniques* (1979–80. 2 v.). Adds ten years of acquisitions, some 12,563 volumes, in dictionary arrangement.

In 1972, the library published an index to periodical articles, covering primarily 1919–1950, *Catalogue d'articles périodiques, arts décoratifs et beaux-arts* (Paris; Boston : G.K. Hall, 1972).

Cooper-Hewitt Museum. Library. Catalog of the Cooper-Hewitt Museum of Design Library of the Smithsonian Institution Libraries. [Boston] : G. K. Hall, 1993. 6 v. (Smithsonian Institution Libraries research guide, 8).   **BG15**

Catalog of more than "37,000 cataloged items including some 1,500 rare books dating from the late 1600s. European and American decorative arts from the Renaissance to the present, textiles broadly defined, European and American wallpaper, architecture and all aspects of design, including interior, industrial, landscape, theatrical, and graphic design are emphasized."—*Foreword.* Includes trade catalogs and descriptive materials of the world's fairs. Holdings are online at the Smithsonian Institution and on OCLC.   Z5939.C7

Henry Francis du Pont Winterthur Museum. Libraries. The Winterthur Museum Libraries collection of printed books and periodicals. Wilmington, Del. : Scholarly Resources, c1974. 9 v.   **BG16**

Contents: v. 1-7, General catalog (authors, titles, subjects, including periodical articles); v. 8–9, Rare books, auction catalogs, Shaker collection.

The library collection covers the period 1600–1913.   Z5939.H46

Catalogs

The consolidated catalog to the Index of American design / ed. by Sandra Shaffer Tinkham. Cambridge [Eng.] : Chadwyck-Healey ; Teaneck, N.J. : Somerset House, 1980. ca.600 p.   **BG17**

Index to *Index of American design* [microform] (1979. 303 microfiches).

Lists and gives key data on each object included in *Index of American design*, which was part of the Federal Art Project of the WPA in the 1930s. Arranged by medium. Indexes: renderers; owners; craftsmen, designers and manufacturers; subjects.   NK805.I5

Hornung, Clarence Pearson. Treasury of American design : a pictorial survey of popular folk arts based upon watercolor renderings in the Index of American Design, at the National Gallery of Art. N.Y. : Abrams, [1972]. 2 v. : ill. **BG18**
Repr.: N.Y. : Harrison House / H. N. Abrams, 1986, with title *Treasury of American design and antiques* (846 p.).
"The collection in the Index of American Design contains over 17,000 renderings of American decorative arts ranging from before 1700 to about 1900. The selections in this book have been carefully made to show the most representative specimens of these works from various regions and cultures of our country. The watercolors here reproduced were rendered ... by American artists in many states during the years 1935–41 under grants from the Federal and State governments."—*Foreword.*
Illustrations are grouped by type of object (furniture, glassware, ships' figureheads, toys, dolls, harness pieces, etc.). Index of artists and general index. NK805.H67

Encyclopedias

The encyclopedia of arts and crafts : the international arts movement, 1850–1920 / Gillian Naylor ... [et al.] ; Wendy Kaplan, consulting ed. N.Y. : E.P. Dutton, c1989. 192 p. : ill. **BG19**
A handbook featuring eight chapters by specialists on interiors, architecture, furniture, textiles and wallpaper, glass, pottery, graphics, and metalwork. The introduction surveys the movement; an afterword reviews Arts and Crafts influences through the 20th century. Includes ample illustrations, a skeletal chronology, 53 biographies (each a paragraph long), and index. NK1140.E54

The Oxford companion to the decorative arts / ed. by Harold Osborne. Oxford : Clarendon Pr., 1975. 865 p. : ill. **BG20**
Reissued in 1985 : Oxford ; N.Y. : Oxford Univ. Pr.
Aims to provide an introduction "to those arts which are made to serve a practical purpose but are nevertheless prized for the quality of their workmanship and the beauty of their appearance. The Companion includes...leather-working, ceramics, textiles, costume, wood working, metal-working, glass-making...bell-founding, paper-making, clock-making, typography, landscape gardening, photography; ... arms and armour, enamels, lacquer, jewellery, toys, lace-making and embroidery."—*Pref.* Unsigned articles, some of considerable length. Bibliography; references to the bibliography are indicated by numbers at the end of an article. NK30.O93

Dictionaries

Fleming, John. The Penguin dictionary of decorative arts / John Fleming and Hugh Honour. New ed. London : Viking, 1989. 935 p., : ill. **BG21**
1st ed., 1977.
Planned as a companion to the *Penguin dictionary of architecture* (BF244), the work is "concerned with furniture and furnishings—i.e. movable objects other than paintings and sculpture—in Europe from the Middle Ages onwards and in North America from the colonial Period to the present day." —*Foreword, 1st ed.* Excludes articles of personal adornment, musical and scientific instruments, clocks (but not their cases), and printed books (although their bindings are considered). Cross-references; bibliographic notes. Concludes with small sections on ceramic marks, and silver- and pewter-makers' marks. NK28

Jervis, Simon. The Facts on File dictionary of design and designers. N.Y. : Facts on File, [1984]. 533 p. **BG22**
Published in U.K. as *Penguin dictionary of design and designers* (London : A. Lane, 1984).

Aims "to provide brief biographies of leading designers, mainly from about 1450 to the present day, and briefer accounts of some minor and a few insignificant figures."—*Pref.* Includes figures from the fields of ceramics, furniture, glass, interior decoration, ornament and textile, with little or no attention given to graphic design, heavy industrial design, theater and dress design. Concentrates on figures from Europe and North America. Includes definitions of terms and entries for styles and a few important periodicals and other publications in the field. NK1165.J47

Lewis, Philippa. Dictionary of ornament / Philippa Lewis & Gillian Darley. N.Y. : Pantheon Books ; London : Macmillan, c1986. 319 p. : ill. **BG23**
"A survey of ornament, pattern and motifs in the applied arts and architecture .... The coverage is mainly of European and North American buildings and objects from the Renaissance to the present day, with reference, where relevant, to ancient and oriental sources and precedents."—*p. 5.* In one alphabet, the 1,020 entries include styles and personal names, with cross-references and small illustrations. Front matter includes a long, unannotated bibliography, and a ten-page "visual key" that groups motifs by type (plant, animal, human, linear and surface, architectural and decorative). NK1165.L48

Stafford, Maureen. An illustrated dictionary of ornament / Maureen Stafford and Dora Ware. N.Y. : St. Martin's Pr., [1975, c1974]. 246 p. : ill. **BG24**
Repr.: N.Y. : St. Martin's Pr., 1984.
A dictionary of terms used in architecture, the decorative arts, coins, games, heraldry, etc. "Ornament" is defined as "an accessory to, but not the substitute of the useful ... a decoration or adornment."—*Introd.* Profusely illustrated with line drawings. Includes a select bibliography and short index of names and places. NK1165.S72

Studio dictionary of design and decoration / ed., Robert Harling. Rev. and enl. ed. N.Y. : Viking Pr., [1973]. 538 p. : ill. **BG25**
British ed. had title *House and garden dictionary* ... (London : Collins, 1973).
Based on a series by Robert Harling published in *House and garden* over a period of years.
A copiously illustrated work with entries for terms, styles, architects, and designers, etc. Articles are generally brief; no bibliography. NK1165.S78

Directories

See also BG130.

Burnette, Charles. Directory to industrial design in the United States : a comprehensive guide to people, capabilities, and information. N.Y. : Van Nostrand Reinhold, c1992. 289 p. **BG26**
Contents: Consulting firms, Design departments, Schools, Institutions, Organizations, Resources (books, indexes, etc.). TS23.B84

Sellen, Betty-Carol. 20th century American folk, self-taught, and outsider art / by Betty-Carol Sellen with Cynthia J. Johanson. N.Y. : Neal-Schuman, c1993. 462 p., [16] p. of plates : ill. (some col.). **BG27**
An impressive compilation, current through 1992, with sections on galleries, art centers, museums, exhibitions, organizations, publications, educational opportunities, books and exhibition catalogs (459, annotated), periodical articles (645, annotated), newspaper articles (362, annotated), audiovisual materials, artists (brief biographies). Appendix: Art environments by states. Index. NK805.S46

Smithsonian Institution. Finders' guide to decorative arts in the Smithsonian Institution / Christine Minter-Dowd. Wash. : Smithsonian Institution Pr., 1984. 213 p. : ill. **BG28**

For 13 museums and sites (and their individual departments, divisions, collections, and galleries), provides a brief description of holdings, notes finding aids and selected publications, lending and photo-duplication policies, and public access information. Indexed. Concludes with a location guide to artists, designers, makers, manufacturers, production centers, and retailers.　　　　NK460.W3S67

Biography

Contemporary designers / ed., Colin Naylor. 2nd ed. Chicago : St. James Pr., 1990. 641 p. : ill.　　　　**BG29**
　　1st ed., 1984 (London : Macmillan ; Detroit : Gale).
　　This edition covers 600 entrants currently active and "many who have died since 1970 but whose reputations remained essentially contemporary." —*Editor's note*. Entries are by 123 design critics and historians, and include lists of exhibitions and publications along with the biographical information, for graphic, industrial, fashion, textile, interior, and stage designers. A 3rd ed. was scheduled for publication in 1993.　　　　NK1166.C66

Folk artists biographical index / George H. Meyer, ed., George H. Meyer, Jr. and Katherine P. White, assoc. editors. Detroit : Gale, c1987. 496 p.　　　　**BG30**
　　Subtitle: A guide to over 200 published sources of information on approximately 9,000 American folk artists from the seventeenth century to the present, including brief biographical information; a full bibliography of sources cited; art locator, ethnicity, geographic, media, and type of work indexes; and a directory of nearly 300 institutions where the works of the artists are located.
　　Published in association with the Museum of American Folk Art.
　　Uses a broad definition of folk art, with entries for craftsmen, businesses, or manufacturers. For each, provides artist's name; nickname, pseudonym, or variant spelling as pertinent; birth and death dates; period and place where the artist flourished; ethnicity; media; museums holding the artist's work (coded); reference to the published source of this information. Format is similar to that of *Artist biographies master index* (BF136). Indexes: Museums and collections, with list of artists represented; Ethnicity; Geography (by state and city); Media; Type of work (subjects).
　　§ Related title: *A dictionary of folk artists in Canada* (BG33).
　　　　　　NK805.F63

Haslam, Malcolm. Marks and monograms of the modern movement, 1875–1930 : a guide to the marks of artists, designers, retailers, and manufacturers from the period of the Aesthetic Movement to Art Deco and Style Moderne. Guildford, Eng. : Butterworth ; N.Y. : Scribner, 1977. 192 p. : ill.　**BG31**
　　Marks are geographically arranged under five major headings: ceramics; glass; metalwork and jewelry; graphics; furniture and textiles. A brief paragraph adjacent to each mark identifies the artist or workshop. Name index.　　　　N45.H37

Jagger, Janette. Designers international index / comp. at Leicester Polytechnic Library by Janette Jagger and Roger Towe. London ; N.Y. : Bowker-Saur, 1991. 3 v. (1977 p.).
　　　　　　BG32
　　Rev. ed. of: *Design international* [microform].
　　An extensive and expensive source that provides biographical and bibliographical information concerning 30,000 designers. Compiled from a machine-readable database. Also known as *dii*. For a comparison of this work and *Design & applied arts index* (BG11), *see* reviews in *Art documentation*, 11 no. 1 (Spring 1992): 33–34 and *Journal of design history*, 5 no. 3 (1992): 237–239.　　　　NK1390.J35

McKendry, Blake. A dictionary of folk artists in Canada from the 17th century to the present : with inclusions of popular portrait, topographical, genre, religious, and decorative artists of the 17th, 18th, and 19th centuries. Elginburg, Ont. : B. McKendry, c1988. 287 p.　　　　**BG33**

For some 3,000 artists, entries provide dates or period of activity, place of activity, medium, a brief discussion, and references to bibliographic sources (current through 1987).
　　§ McKendry also is author of a survey, *Folk art: primitive and native art in Canada* (Toronto : Methuen ; N.Y. : Facts on File, [1983]).　　　　N6540.5.P7M38

Prather-Moses, Alice Irma. The international dictionary of women workers in the decorative arts : a historical survey from the distant past to the early decades of the twentieth century. Metuchen, N. J. : Scarecrow, 1981. 200 p.　　**BG34**
　　Brief biographies based on some 95 published sources. Concludes with an index listing artists within some 55 categories of activity or medium.　　　　HD6069.P7

Rosenak, Chuck. Museum of American Folk Art encyclopedia of twentieth-century American folk art and artists / Chuck and Jan Rosenak. N.Y. : Abbeville Pr., c1990. 416 p. : ill.
　　　　　　BG35
　　Provides information, much of it obtained during extensive interviews, concerning 257 artists working in various media. Entries cite biographical data, background on the artist's life, subjects and sources for images, materials and techniques, recognition or reputation, and footnotes. Each entry has a color photograph of the artist's work, augmented in the appendix by black-and-white portraits of many of the artists. Includes a listing of public collections in the U.S. holding folk art, a chronological list of major exhibitions, and a bibliography. Index of names, works of art, galleries and museums, organizations, and exhibition titles.　　　　NK808.R6

ANTIQUES

Bibliography

Franklin, Linda Campbell. Antiques and collectibles : a bibliography of works in English, 16th century to 1976. Metuchen, N.J. : Scarecrow, 1978. 1091 p. : ill.　　　**BG36**
　　Aims "to provide the researcher, the serious collector and the librarian with a comprehensive listing of English language books and exhibition catalogues dealing with objects now considered 'antiques' or 'collectibles.' "—*Pref.* More than 10,000 items (books, pamphlets, dissertations, periodicals) in classified order. For books published before 1925, library locations are given for over 50 collections, chiefly in the U.S. Indexes: subject, author.　　　　Z5956.A68F7

Encyclopedias

The complete color encyclopedia of antiques / comp. by the Connoisseur, London ; ed. by L. G. G. Ramsey. 2nd ed. N.Y. : Hawthorn Books, 1975. 704 p. : ill.　　　　**BG37**
　　Publ. in London as: *The Connoisseur complete color encyclopedia of antiques*.
　　1st ed., 1962.
　　The 1st ed. was adapted from Connoisseur's *Concise encyclopaedia of antiques* (5 v., 1954–61) and *The concise encyclopaedia of American antiques*, by Helen Comstock (2 v., 1958). The random grouping of chapters by some 100 contributors in those volumes was changed to bring like subject material together under 17 headings, an arrangement followed in this edition. Many chapters contain glossaries. Includes a list of major museums in Great Britain, Europe, and the U.S. arranged under the 17 subjects represented. Incorporates articles on Art Nouveau and Art Deco, "the two collecting subjects which succeeded Victoriana as the avant-garde in collecting during the 1960s."—*Pref.* Bibliography.　　　　NK1125.R343

Phillips, Phoebe. The collectors' encyclopedia of antiques. London : The Connoisseur ; N.Y. : Crown, 1973. 704 p. : ill. (some col.). **BG38**

Repr. : London : Bloomsbury, 1988.

Topical arrangement; includes essays by 35 contributors, numerous illustrations and examples, short glossaries and bibliographies, and lists of museum collections. Entries are by large categories such as: arms and armor, bottles and boxes, carpets and rugs, ceramics, clocks, furniture, glass, metalwork, etc. Bibliographic references and brief glossaries at ends of sections. Brief index. NK28.P494

Phipps, Frances. The collector's complete dictionary of American antiques. Garden City, N.Y. : Doubleday, 1974. 640 p. : ill. **BG39**

Employs a dictionary arrangement within topical sections such as: Historic periods and styles; Rooms—their placement and use; Crafts, trades, and useful professions; Weights and measures; Terms used by joiners and cabinetmakers; Woods and their preferred uses; Paints, dyes, finishes, varnishes, etc. Lacks an index. NK805.P52

The Random House collector's encyclopedia : Victoriana to Art Deco. N.Y. : Random House, [1974]. 302 p. : ill. **BG40**

Published in London by Collins, 1974, with title *The collector's encyclopedia.*

A companion to *Random House encyclopedia of antiques* (N.Y., [1973], publ. in U.K. as *Collins encyclopedia of antiques*) which covers to 1875. This volume is concerned with the period 1851 to 1939, treating decorative arts of the time and "items which are collected in the same way as antiques."—*p. 9.* Aims "to compress the maximum amount of information into the available space, employing a highly condensed style to avoid relying on abbreviations." Cross-references are indicated by asterisks; numerous illustrations, many in color. Appendix of ceramic marks and silver date letters. Brief bibliography.

§ A similar source: *The encyclopedia of Victoriana* (London : Hamlyn; N.Y. : Macmillan, [1975]). NK775.R36

Wills, Geoffrey. A concise encyclopedia of antiques. N.Y. : Van Nostrand, [1976] ; Reading, U.K. : Osprey, 1975. 304 p. : ill. **BG41**

"The subjects discussed and illustrated are furniture, pottery and porcelain, glass, silver, and pewter and other metals, made between 1500 and 1890."—*Foreword.* Deals almost exclusively with English antiques. A 5-v. (but unrelated) work with the same title, publ. in 1954–61, was later issued as *The connoisseur's complete period guide to houses* ... (London : Connoisseur, 1968).

§ For American coverage, *see*: Helen Comstock's *The concise encyclopedia of American antiques* (N.Y. : Hawthorn Books, [1965]. 848 p.), which has chapters by specialists, bibliographies, and glossaries. NK928.W53

Dictionaries

Boger, Louise Ade. The dictionary of antiques and the decorative arts : a book of reference for glass, furniture, ceramics, silver, periods, styles, technical terms, etc / comp. and ed. by Louise Ade Boger and H. Batterson Boger. N.Y. : Scribner, [1967]. 662 p. : ill. **BG42**

An earlier ed. was published 1957 (566 p.).

Publ. in Italian as *Enciclopedia dell'antiquariato* (Firenze : Sansoni, 1966).

Includes a classified list of subjects and terms and a bibliography. A supplement lists 700 new terms (related primarily to 20th-century topics). NK30.B57

Das grosse Fachwörterbuch für Kunst und Antiquitäten / hrsg. von Christian Müller. München : Weltkunst Verlag, [1982]. v. 1. (In progress?). **BG43**

Added title pages in English *(The art and antiques dictionary)* and in French.

A dictionary of technical terms "used in the art and antiques trade in English, French and German to meet the needs ... of scientists, collectors ... dealers ... specialized experts and translators."—*Pref.* Terms are drawn from Eastern and Western art, architecture, textiles, book illustration, medals, heraldry, etc. Arranged on an English base with French and German equivalents, but without definitions. Appendix: Essential terms of heraldic terminology. N33.G76

Savage, George. Dictionary of antiques. 2nd ed. London : Barrie & Jenkins ; N.Y. : Mayflower, 1978. 534 p. : ill. **BG44**

1st ed., 1970.

"Devised primarily to help both collectors and dealers in antiques of one kind or another to date and attribute those specimens which come their way. To this end considerable emphasis has been laid on styles or fashions in art at various periods because these are of great assistance in dating."—*Pref.* Covers from the Renaissance to the 20th century. Includes "Select bibliography and reading list."

§ The author's *Dictionary of 19th century antiques and later objets d'art* (N.Y. : Putnam, 1979) provides fuller treatment of that period. NK30.S27

Handbooks

Jackson, Albert. The antiques care & repair handbook / Albert Jackson & David Day. N.Y. : Knopf ; London : Dorling Kindersley, 1984. 255 p. : ill. **BG45**

Publ. in Spanish as: *Manual para la restauración de antigüedades* (2nd ed. Madrid : Editorial Ráices, 1988).

Describes and illustrates processes of repair and restoration for many categories of antiques. Addressed chiefly to beginners, with difficulty of procedure indicated. Classified arrangement. Index, glossary, and several useful appendixes. NK1127.5.J32

Ketchum, William C. The catalog of world antiques : a fully illustrated collector's guide to styles and prices. [London] : Windward ; N.Y. : Rutledge Pr., c1981. 320 p. : ill. **BG46**

Aims "to provide ... collectors with a general price and identification guide to the major areas of world antiques and collectibles."—*Introd.* Emphasizes "those items that collectors can actually find" rather than museum examples. Arranged in 14 chapters, each comprising a short introductory historical survey with a note on the current market, and a selection of good, detailed photographs with description and price range. Includes the major subjects of furniture, pottery, glass, textiles, etc., and the newer interests such as primitive and folk art, toys, woodenware. Glossary; bibliography; index.

§ Ketchum also wrote: *The catalog of American antiques* (N.Y. : Rutledge, [1977] ; 2nd ed., rev. [1980]) and *All-American folk arts and crafts* (N.Y. : Rizzoli, 1986), a well-illustrated survey. NK1125.K47

Kovel, Ralph M. The Kovels' antiques & collectibles price list / by Ralph and Terry Kovel. 15th ed. (1982–83)– . N.Y. : Crown, c1982– . Annual. **BG47**

26th ed., 1993.

Continues the authors' *Kovels' antiques price list, Kovels' complete antiques price list,* etc.

Lists alphabetically by category or object the antique or collectible, giving a one-line description and price asked by seller as reported from American sales and shows of the preceding 12-month period. About 50,000 entries. Paragraph headings provide some background information. Paintings, books, stamps and coins are excluded. NK1125.A39

Miller, Judith. Miller's international antiques price guide / comp. and ed. by Judith and Martin Miller. American ed. 1985– . N.Y. : Viking Penguin, 1985– . Annual. **BG48**

Eds.1–5 publ. in Britain 1979–84.

Offers the collector and professional "a guide to the market, not just a theoretical survey."—*Introd., 1985 ed.* In the 1993 edition, more than 10,000 objects are listed, each with photographic illustration, description, and price range based on previous year's sales. Arranged by category of antique (furniture, pottery, silver, toys, etc.). Directory of auctioneers; index.

§ Another guide, geared to dealers, lists some 5,000 objects per year: *The Lyle official antiques review* (N.Y. : Putnam, 1971/72–).

NK1133.M53

Warman's Americana & collectibles. 1st ed.– . Elkins Park, Pa. : Warman, c1984– . Biennial.   **BG49**

Subtitle: A price guide devoted to today's collectibles, with collecting hints, histories, references, clubs, museums.

Harry L. Rinker, ed.

5th ed., 1991.

Lists, describes, and prices "collectibles," which are defined as 20th century, mass-produced items made or heavily collected in America and selling for a few cents up to one hundred dollars. Arranged by categories (baseball cards, dolls, newspapers, watch fobs, etc.) with prices in the low to middle range. "Emphasis [is] on those items which are actively being sold in the marketplace."—*Introd.*

§ A few of the same categories are included in *Warman's antiques and their prices* (1976– ; 27th ed., 1993). Another handbook, ed. by Rinker and Dana G. Morykan, is *Warman's country antiques & collectibles* (2nd ed. Radnor, Pa. : Wallace-Homestead Book Co., c1994).   AM303.9.W37

Biography

Coysh, Arthur Wilfred. The antique buyer's dictionary of names. Newton Abbot : David & Charles ; N.Y. : Praeger, [1970]. 278 p. : 16 plates, ill.   **BG50**

A biographical dictionary intended for quick reference over a wide range of fields. "It lists many craftsmen, decorators, and designers who worked in America, Britain, Europe and Japan, and special care has been taken to include names that appear frequently in auction sale catalogues and dealers' advertisements."—*Pref.* Entries are grouped in 17 sections. Not indexed.

§ For a dictionary with British emphasis, consult David Benedictus's *The antique collector's guide* (London : Macmillan, 1980 ; N.Y. : Antheneum, 1981).   N40.C67

CERAMICS AND GLASS

Guides

Campbell, James Edward. Pottery and ceramics : a guide to information sources. Detroit : Gale, c1978. 241 p. (Art and architecture information guide series, v. 7).   **BG51**

An annotated bibliography of specialized works, mainly in English, dealing with ceramic techniques or historical periods. Includes lists of ceramic organizations and societies and museum collections. Intended for the artist, collector, or ceramic historian. Indexed.

§ In the same series: *Stained glass : a guide to information sources*, by Darlene Brady and William Serban (1980). Also on stained glass is David Evans, *A bibliography of stained glass* ([Cambridge, Eng.] : D. S. Brewer, [1982]).   Z7179.C35

Bibliography

Caviness, Madeline Harrison. Stained glass before 1540 : an annotated bibliography / Madeline Harrison Caviness ; with the assistance of Evelyn Ruth Staudinger. Boston : G.K. Hall, c1983. 304 p. : ill.   **BG52**

Sections on general works, techniques, collections and sales, and exhibitions are followed by sections on countries. Indexes: authors, glass painters and designers, topographical names.

§ Caviness also is an author of four volumes in *Stained glass before 1700 in American collections : Corpus vitrearum checklist* (Wash. : National Gallery of Art, 1985–), published as "Studies in the history of art," v. 15, 23, 28, and 39.   Z5956.G5C38

Corning Museum of Glass. The history and art of glass : index of periodical articles, 1956–1979 / comp. by Louise K. Bush and Paul N. Perrot ; ed. by Gail P. Bardhan. Boston : G.K. Hall, 1982. 876 p.   **BG53**

Lists more than 10,000 articles in many languages drawn from periodicals, conference proceedings, annuals and yearbooks. Arranged in three sections: (1) General publications; (2) Technological publications (including preservation); (3) Historical publications; each section is appropriately subdivided. Compiled from the annual checklists published in the Museum's *Journal of glass studies.* Author index.

A supplement, *The history and art of glass : index of periodical articles, 1980–1982,* comp. by Louise K. Bush ; ed. by Gail P. Bardhan (Boston : G.K. Hall, 1984. 298 p.) adds almost 4,000 articles in similar arrangement.

§ The Museum has also published *Guide to trade catalogs from the Corning Museum of Glass* (N.Y. : Clearwater Publ. Co., 1987. 500 p.).

Oppelt, Norman T. Southwestern pottery : an annotated bibliography and list of types and wares. 2nd ed., rev. and exp. Metuchen, N.J. : Scarecrow, 1988. 325 p. : ill.   **BG54**

1st ed. published as *Occasional publications in anthropology. Archaeology series,* no. 7 (Greeley : Museum of Anthropology, University of Northern Colorado, 1976).

Similar in format to Susan R. Strong's *History of American ceramics : an annotated bibliography* (BG56). Pt. 1, the annotated bibliography, is arranged alphabetically and chronologically by author and includes books, theses, obscure journals such as *Highway salvage archaeology,* and regional series such as *Utah anthropological papers.* Pt. 2 is a "List of Southwestern pottery types and wares," which cites both published and unpublished examples, with dates, synonyms, illustrations, and references to descriptions. Index to site names and subjects. This edition incorporates revisions suggested by Southwesternists and adds 300 citations (and additional dates) for a total of 965, as well as some 1,240 type, ware, and variety names.

§ Oppelt also wrote *Guide to prehistoric ruins of the Southwest* (Boulder, Colo. : Pruett Publ. Co., 1981. 208 p.).   Z1208.S68O66

Solon, Louis Marc Emmanuel. Ceramic literature. London : Griffin ; Philadelphia : Lippincott, 1910. 660 p.   **BG55**

Subtitle: An analytical index to the works published in all languages on the history and the technology of the ceramic art; also to the catalogues of public museums, private collections, and of auction sales in which the description of ceramic objects occupy an important place; and to the most important price-lists of the ancient and modern manufactories of pottery and porcelain.

Repr.: Leipzig : Zentralantiquariat der Deutschen Demokratischen Republik, 1985.

Pt. 1, Author list, annotated; pt. 2, Classified list (20 topics, including technology, history, classical, oriental, European, decorative tiles, stoves, biographics, collections, exhibitions).   Z7179.S68

Strong, Susan R. History of American ceramics : an annotated bibliography. Metuchen, N.J. : Scarecrow, 1983. 184 p.   **BG56**

A classified, annotated bibliography of more than 600 items. A section for regional and local history lists accounts of potteries and related developments in specific states and regions; there are also sections for individual potteries and potters. Indexed.   Z7179.S85

Weidner, Ruth Irwin. American ceramics before 1930 : a bibliography. Westport, Conn. : Greenwood, 1982. 279 p. (Art reference collection, no. 2).   **BG57**

Covers " … from the earliest colonial manufacture through about

1930, when styles, production methods and terminology changed … ."—*Pref.* Lists 2,921 unannotated citations—about 90% of the nontechnical literature published through 1980. Arranged by seven types of publications: Books and pamphlets; Conference proceedings and chapters from books; Catalogs from exhibitions, collections, and sales; Theses and dissertations; Federal, state, and municipal publications; Trade publications; Periodical articles. Includes a section of "Suggestions for additional research." Appendix: Guide to selected American clayworking, ceramics, china painting, and crockery journals before 1930. Indexes: author, subject.   Z7179.W43

Encyclopedias

Cameron, Elisabeth. Encyclopedia of pottery & porcelain, 1800–1960. N.Y. : Facts on File, c1986. 366, [18] p. : ill.   **BG58**

Publ. in U.K. as: *Encyclopedia of pottery & porcelain : the 19th & 20th centuries* (London ; Boston : Faber and Faber, 1986).

Covers materials, techniques, styles, and movements of all nations. "Modern makers have been included only if they have produced work, other than as students, before 1960."—*About this book.* Entries range in length from a short paragraph to several pages (e.g., Doulton & Co.); many have bibliographical references. Includes numerous small illustrations, some cross-references between firm and personal names, and asterisks within entries to refer the reader to other personal name entries. Concludes with an 11-page abbreviations list that also serves as a partial, unannotated bibliography.   NK3920.C36

The encyclopedia of glass / ed. by Phoebe Phillips. N.Y. : Crown, [1981]. 320 p. : ill.   **BG59**

In two main sections: (1) History (offering historical overviews by country or region, plus sections on ancient glass and stained glass); (2) Techniques (with sections on glass melting, flat glass, paperweights, bottles, tableware, etc.). Glossary; bibliography; index. Heavily illustrated.   NK5104.E5

Godden, Geoffrey A. Encyclopaedia of British porcelain manufacturers. London : Barrie & Jenkins, 1988. 855 p. : ill.   **BG60**

Arranged alphabetically by maker's name. Provides photographs of representative objects and drawings of marks, along with biographical and production information. Introductory chapters cover basic types, characteristics of makers' marks and pattern numbers, and a list of manufacturers' names by decade of activity. Includes a list of identifying initials, an eight-page bibliography, and an index to names and terms.

§ *See also* the author's *Encyclopedia of British pottery and porcelain marks* (London : Jenkins ; N.Y. : Crown [1964]) and *Godden's guide to European porcelain* (London : Barrie & Jenkins, 1993).

Sotheby's concise encyclopedia of glass / gen. editors, David Battie, Simon Cottle. London : Conran Octopus ; Boston : Little, Brown, c1991. 208 p. : col. ill.   **BG61**

Chapters by 16 contributors, complemented by information on care and conservation, paperweights, and canes; bibliography; glossary; glasshouses and biographies; index. Excellent color illustrations.   NK5104.S66

Sotheby's concise encyclopedia of porcelain / gen. ed., David Battie. London : Conran Octopus, 1990. 208 p. : ill. (some col.).   **BG62**

Chapters by 15 contributors; bibliography, glossary, biographies, index.   NK4370.S67

Dictionaries

Barber, Edwin Atlee. Ceramic collectors' glossary. N.Y. : Walpole Soc., 1914. 119 p. : ill.   **BG63**

Repr.: N.Y. : DaCapo Pr., 1967; with *The furniture collectors' glossary* by L. V. Lockwood (1913) and *A silver collectors' glossary* … by H. French (1917) as: *The ceramic, furniture, and silver collectors' glossary* (1976).

A dictionary of terms only, frequently with small line drawings.   NK3370.B3

Fournier, Robert L. Illustrated dictionary of pottery form. N.Y. : Van Nostrand Reinhold, [1981]. 256 p. : ill.   **BG64**

1st ed., 1973; rev., 1977.

"The prime objective … is to be a source of ideas, inspiration, and interest to the craftsman."—*Introd.* Employs a dictionary arrangement (name of the artifact, feature or shape of the vessel, etc.). Numerous photographs and line drawings. Includes a "Booklist."

§ Fournier has also published *Illustrated dictionary of practical pottery* (1st ed. N.Y. : Van Nostrand Reinhold, 1981. 256 p. ; 3rd ed. Radnor, Pa. : Chilton, 1992), which has been translated into Spanish as *Diccionario illustrado de alfarería práctica* (Barcelona : Omega, 1981).   TT919.5.F67

Hamer, Frank. The potter's dictionary of materials and techniques / Frank and Janet Hamer. 3rd ed. Philadelphia : Univ. of Pennsylvania Pr. ; London : A. & C. Black, 1991. 384 p. : ill.   **BG65**

1st ed., 1975; 2nd ed., 1986.

A practical work for potters, teachers, and students. Articles are in dictionary arrangement according to key words and phrases, with cross-references to related terms. Generously illustrated with line drawings and photographs. Appendixes: 42 tables; list of suppliers; recipes; brief bibliography.

§ Other practical sources: David Hamilton's *The Thames and Hudson manual of pottery and ceramics* (N.Y., 1982. 188 p.) and Glenn C. Nelson's *Ceramics : a potter's handbook* (5th ed. N.Y. : Holt, Rinehart, and Winston, c1984. 350 p.).   TT919.5.H35

Newman, Harold. An illustrated dictionary of glass. London : Thames & Hudson, c1977. 351 p., [8] leaves of plates : ill.   **BG66**

Subtitle: 2,442 entries, including definitions of wares, materials, processes, forms, and decorative styles, and entries on principal glassmakers, decorators, and designers, from antiquity to the present; with an introductory survey on the history of glass-making by Robert J. Charleston.

Issued in paperback (N.Y., 1987).

The work is "intended primarily to define terms relating to glass and glassware, such as the constituent elements, the methods of production and decoration, and the styles in various regions and periods, and also to describe some pieces that bear recognized names."—*Pref.* Cross-references; occasional bibliographic references.   TP788.N48

Savage, George. An illustrated dictionary of ceramics : defining 3,054 terms relating to wares, materials, processes, styles, patterns, and shapes from antiquity to the present day / George Savage, Harold Newman. London : Thames & Hudson ; N.Y. : Van Nostrand, [1974]. 319 p. : ill.   **BG67**

A dictionary of terms, with many illustrations (some in color). Includes a chart of "Principal European factories and their marks."   NK3770.S38

Directories

Glass collections in museums in the United States and Canada / the Corning Museum of Glass and the American National Committee of the International Association for the History of Glass. Corning, N.Y. : The Museum, 1982. 224 p. : ill.   **BG68**

Arranged by country and city, providing essential information, bibliographic sources, and a description for each collection. Indexes: museum names; places.   NK5101.8.G54

Handbooks

Ceramics and glass. 1990– . Lausanne, Switzerland : Éditions Vie Art Cité, 1990– .   **BG69**

Editor: 1990– Sylvio Acatos.

Covers archeology, faience, glass, porcelain, pottery, stoneware, and terra cotta. Arranged in seven sections: Oriental; Occidental, ancient and medieval; Occidental, Renaissance and modern (subdivided by country); Near and Middle Eastern; Pre-Columbian American; African; 19th and 20th centuries. Entries provide name and description of each object, dimensions, maker when applicable, place and date of the sale, and sale price in three currencies. Includes some illustrations.

Cushion, John Patrick. Handbook of pottery and porcelain marks / comp. by J. P. Cushion in collaboration with W. B. Honey. 4th ed., rev. and exp. London : Faber, 1980. 272 p. : ill.   **BG70**

1st ed., 1956; 3rd ed., 1976.

An aid to the identification of pottery and porcelain. "Marks recorded here are restricted to true factory marks and those others which … are of actual use in identifying the place of manufacture of a piece."—*Introd.* This edition expanded to include more than 3,850 marks. Especially strong in British marks, but includes marks of China and Japan; coverage of European countries is considerably enlarged over previous editions. Indexed.

§ The author's *Pocket book of British ceramic marks* (3rd ed. London : Faber, 1976. 431 p.) is a similar work limited to ceramic marks of Great Britain and Ireland.   NK4215.C80

Lehner, Lois. Lehner's encyclopedia of U.S. marks on pottery, porcelain & clay. Paducah, Ky. : Collector Books, c1988. 634 p. : ill.   **BG71**

Chiefly an alphabetical listing of factories, with detailed information and dates and samples of marks. Also includes a listing of companies by location, nine other miscellaneous lists of types of manufactures, railroad symbols, Syracuse National winners, and electrical porcelain insulator markings. Bibliography; index.

§ Additional pottery source: *Kovel's new dictionary of marks*, by Ralph and Terry Kovel (N.Y. : Crown, [1986]), 290 p. ; 1st ed., 1953).   NK4215.L36

Rice, Prudence M. Pottery analysis : a sourcebook. Chicago : Univ. of Chicago Pr., c1987. 559 p. : ill.   **BG72**

This substantial survey of the technical aspects of pottery addresses the subject "as a source of insights into people and cultures, and it is directed toward those with such interests : primarily to social scientists such as anthropologists, archaeologists, and ethnoarchaeologists."—*Pref.* Provides numerous diagrams and tables to illustrate chapters on history, raw materials used, properties of clays and their firing behavior, pottery manufacture and use, production and distribution, vessel functions, decoration and stylistic analysis, archaeological and ethnographic studies, description and characterization of pottery (color, mineralogical, chemical, and physical properties), special topics, and social topics. Bibliographic references are abundant. Concludes with a 15-page glossary, 55-page bibliography, and subject index.   NK3780.R53

History

The history of porcelain / gen. ed., Paul Atterbury. London : Orbis ; N.Y. : Morrow, 1982. 256 p. : ill. (some col.).   **BG73**

Thirteen chapters by specialists, with excellent illustrations. Includes an appendix on forgeries and deceptions, a glossary, bibliography, and index.

§ Atterbury has since written *The dictionary of Minton* (Woodbridge, Eng. : Antique Collectors' Club, 1990).   NK4370.H5

Honey, William Bowyer. European ceramic art, from the end of the Middle Ages to about 1815. London : Faber and Faber, [1949–52]. 2 v. : ill.   **BG74**

Contents: [v. 1], Illustrated historical survey, rev. by A. Lane (1963); [v. 2], A dictionary of factories, artists, technical terms, etc.; bibliography.

A comprehensive work by the author of numerous works on specific aspects of ceramics.   NK4083.H62

Kämpfer, Fritz. Glass : a world history; the story of 4000 years of fine glass-making / by Fritz Kämpfer and Klaus G. Beyer. Tr. and rev. by Edmund Launert. Greenwich, Conn. : New York Graphic Soc., [c1966]. 314 p. : ill.   **BG75**

A revised translation of *Viertausend Jahre Glas* (Dresden, 1966).

Chronological presentation of photographs (many in color) and text representing various periods and techniques in the history of glass-making. A glossary also includes brief notes on outstanding glass artists and engravers. Lacks an index.

§ For a similar but newer work, see: *The history of glass*, ed. by Dan Klein and Ward Lloyd (London : Orbis, [1984]).   NK5106.K313

McKearin, George S. American glass / George S. and Helen McKearin ; 2000 photographs, 1000 drawings by James L. McCreery. N.Y. : Crown, c1941. 622 p., 262 p. of plates : ill.   **BG76**

Repr. : N.Y. : Bonanza Books : distr. by Crown, 1989.

A comprehensive survey.   NK5112.M26

Biography

Chaffers, William. Marks & monograms on European and Oriental pottery and porcelain : the British section / ed. by Geoffrey A. Godden. The European and Oriental sections ed. by Frederick Litchfield & R. L. Hobson. 15th rev. ed. London : Reeves, [1965]. 2 v. : ill.   **BG77**

1st ed., 1863?

The standard work in English, identifying more than 5,000 potter's marks. In this edition the British section has been completely revised; the others have been corrected, but are substantially unchanged.

§ Also by Chaffers: *The new keramic gallery* … (3rd ed., 1926. 2 v.) and *Collector's handbook of marks and monograms on pottery and porcelain* (4th ed., rev. by Frederick Litchfield. 1968. 367 p.).   NK4215.C46

Catalogs

See also BF324.

Carpenter, Thomas H. Summary guide to Corpus vasorum antiquorum. Oxford ; N.Y. : publ. for the British Academy by Oxford Univ. Pr., 1984. 77 p.   **BG78**

Begun in 1922, the *Corpus vasorum antiquorum (CVA)* is an extensive effort by the Union Académique Internationale to publish country-by-country and collection-by-collection more than 200 catalogs of photographs of ancient vases.

§ A similar undertaking, begun in 1949 with cooperation of the Comité Internationale d'Historie de l'Art, is *Corpus Vitrearum Medii Aevi (CVMA)*, which has been publishing catalogs of stained glass since 1956. NK4640.C6Z9

Valenstein, Suzanne G. A handbook of Chinese ceramics. Rev. and enl. ed. N.Y. : Metropolitan Museum of Art : distr. by H.N. Abrams, c1989. 331 p., [32] p. of plates : ill. (some col.). **BG79**

First publ. 1975.

Although this survey is based on objects in the collection of one museum (the Metropolitan Museum of Art, New York), it is an excellent introduction to the topic. Includes glossary and bibliography. NK4165.V34

CLOCKS, WATCHES, AND JEWELRY

Bibliography

Baillie, Granville Hugh. Clocks and watches : an historical bibliography. London : N.A.G. Pr., [1951]. 414 p. : ill. **BG80**

Repr.: London : Holland Pr., 1978.

Comprehensive chronological list of books, pamphlets, manuscripts, and periodical articles—published up to 1800—on mechanical timepieces only. Preface gives a brief history of horology, with a list of earlier bibliographies on the subject and indications of London libraries rich in the field. Annotations are exceptionally full, with biographical notes on authors, locations of copies, outlines of contents, and quotations and illustrations from many items listed. Indexes: names, subjects. Z7876.B33

Library Catalogs

Worshipful Company of Clockmakers (London). The clockmakers' library : the catalogue of the books and manuscripts in the library of the Worshipful Company of Clockmakers / comp. by John Bromley. [London] : Sotheby Parke Bernet Publ., [1977]. 136 p. : ill. **BG81**

A revised version of the catalog of the Company's library produced by G. H. Baillie in 1951.

"Today the library comprises more than one thousand printed items, mainly in the field of historical horology; unique manuscript material, including the records of the Company from its incorporation in 1631; and a small collection of prints, portraits and photographs."—*Pref.* Separate sections for printed books, for manuscripts, for portraits, and for prints, drawings, etc. Includes accessions through Sept. 1975.

§ Related catalog: *Clocks and watches : the collection of the Worshipful Company of Clockmakers*, by Cecil Clutton and George Daniels ([London] : Sotheby Parke Bernet [1975]). Z7876.L85

Dictionaries

Mason, Anita. An illustrated dictionary of jewellery. N.Y. : Harper & Row, [1974]. 389 p. : ill. **BG82**

First publ. Reading, England : Osprey, 1973.

Intended "both for those involved in the jewellery trade and for those with a less specialized interest in jewellery."—*Pref.* Attempts to cover the whole field concisely, dealing with "gemstones and their identification, with the techniques of jewellery-manufacture, with the history of jewellery, and with subjects of interest to the retail jeweller such as hallmarking." Cross-references; brief bibliography.

§ For terms in other languages, see: *Elsevier's dictionary of jewellery and watchmaking in five languages, English, French, German, Italian, and Spanish*, comp. by Carl Forget. NK7304.M37

Newman, Harold. An illustrated dictionary of jewelry : 2,530 entries, including definitions of jewels, gemstones, materials, processes, and styles, and entries on principal designers and makers from antiquity to the present day. N.Y. : Thames and Hudson, [1981]. 334 p. : ill. **BG83**

Paperback ed., 1987.

Encompasses the types of entries indicated in the subtitle, jewelry defined as "any decorative article that is made of metal, gemstones and/or hard organic material of high quality, contrived with artistry or superior craftsmanship, and intended to be worn on a person (such as a necklace, bracelet, earrings or brooch), including such articles that are functional as well as decorative (e.g. cuff links, buckles, tie clips)."—*Pref.* Numerous illustrations; cross-references. No bibliography. NK7304.N43

Handbooks

Distin, William H. The American clock : a comprehensive pictorial survey 1723–1900, with a listing of 6153 clockmakers / William H. Distin and Robert Bishop. N.Y. : E. P. Dutton, 1976. 359 p. : ill. **BG84**

Repr. : N.Y. : Bonanza Books, 1983.

About 700 photographs of American clocks arranged chronologically within sections for types of clocks (e.g., tower clocks, tall case clocks, shelf clocks, novelty clocks), with indication of kind of movement, maker (if known), place and approximate date made. The "List of clockmakers" (64 p.) gives location and working dates for each. Index to illustrations. Brief glossary, bibliography, and name index.

§ Related work: Carl William Drepperd's *American clocks and clockmakers* (Enl. [2nd] ed. Boston : Branford, 1958 [1947]). TS543.U6D57

History

Britten, Frederick James. Britten's old clocks and watches and their makers : a historical and descriptive account of the different styles of clocks and watches of the past in England and abroad, containing a list of nearly fourteen thousand makers. 8th ed. / by Cecil Clutton … [et al.]. London : Methuen ; N.Y. : Dutton, 1973. 532 p. : ill. **BG85**

1st ed., 1899; 7th ed., 1956. A 9th ed. was publ. 1982.

The standard work in this field. A chronological history of the measurement of time to 1830, with a final brief chapter bringing the record forward to 1970, and an extensive list of clock and watch makers (with dates and places of work). Appendixes: glossary of technical terms; hall marks; bibliography. There is also a list of 25,000 former clock and watch makers and an index. TS542.B8

Bruton, Eric. The history of clocks and watches. London : Orbis Publ., c1979. 288 p. : ill. (some col.). **BG86**

Repr. : N.Y. : Crescent Books, 1982; 1989.

A general survey, with color illustrations, glossary, bibliography and index.

§ Bruton's earlier books include *Clocks and watches, 1400–1900* (London : Barker, [1967]) and *Dictionary of clocks and watches* (N.Y. : Bonanza, [1963]). The latter "covers the subject of timekeeping in all its aspects" (*Introd.*), some of which is technical and includes line drawings, diagrams, and photos. Index. TS542.B845

The Country life international dictionary of clocks / consultant ed., Alan Smith. N.Y. : Putnam, [1979]. 350 p. : ill. **BG87**

Repr. with title *International dictionary of clocks* : N.Y. : Exeter Books, 1984.

In five main sections: The history and styles of clocks; The mechanical parts of clocks; Tools, materials, and workshop methods; International clockmaking, with a selection of important makers (arranged by country); and Sundials and astronomical instruments. Articles are signed; there are 18 contributors. Bibliography; index.
TS540.7.C68

Biography

Baillie, Granville Hugh. Watchmakers and clockmakers of the world. [3rd ed.]. [London] : N.A.G Pr., [1951]. 388 p. : maps.   **BG88**

Repr.: 1966.

1st ed., 1929.

An alphabetical directory giving name, place, dates, type of clock or watch, and sometimes other brief information. Lists makers to 1825 with a few outstanding later names. The 2nd ed. included some 35,000 names—10,000 more than the 1st ed. The 3rd ed. reproduces this text with an "Addenda" of some 600 new entries in a separate section.

In 1976 a supplement by Brian Loomes appeared as "volume 2" of this title (London : N.A.G. Pr. 263 p.).   NK7486.B26

Sposato, Kenneth A. The dictionary of American clock & watch makers. White Plains, N.Y. : K.A. Sposato, c1983. 190 p.   **BG89**

Includes vital information on clock-related people (extended to cover clock peddlers, case makers, label printers, dial makers, and inventors) and cites references to text and images in 34 sources.

§ Highly recommended: Dorothy T. Rainwater, *American jewelry manufacturers* (West Chester, Pa. : Schiffer Publ., 1988. 296 p.).
TS543.U6S68

COSTUME AND FASHION

Bibliography

African dress II : a selected and annotated bibliography / Ila M. Pokornowski ... [et al.]. East Lansing : African Studies Center, Michigan State Univ., c1985. 316 p. : map.   **BG90**

Lists 1,260 citations for books and articles that supplement those in Joanne Bubolz Eicher's *African dress : a select and annotated bibliography of Subsaharan countries* (East Lansing : African Studies Center, Michigan State Univ., 1970). Sections: The study of African dress; Resource materials for the study of African dress; Bibliography by six regions; Author index. Lacks a subject index.   Z5694.A4A47

Colas, René. Bibliographie générale du costume et de la mode : description des suites, recueils, séries, revues et livres français et étrangers relatifs au costume civil, militaire et religieux, aux modes, aux coiffures et aux divers accessoires de l'habillement. Avec une table méthodique et un index alphabétique. Paris : Colas, 1933. 2 v.   **BG91**

Repr.: N.Y. : Hacker Art Books, 1963, 1969; Genève : Slatkine; Paris : Libr. Gaspa, 1991.

The 3,121 entries are listed by author. Bibliographical information for each item includes references to important bibliographies in which it appears. Indexes.   Z5691.C68

Hiler, Hilaire. Bibliography of costume : a dictionary catalog of about eight thousand books and periodicals / comp. by Hilaire and Meyer Hiler, ed. by Helen Grant Cushing, assisted by Adah V. Morris. N.Y. : Wilson, 1939. 911 p.   **BG92**

Repr.: N.Y. : Blom, 1967.

Lists "approximately eighty-four hundred works on costume and adornment, including books in all languages."—*Pref.*   Z5691.H64

Library catalogs

Kunstbibliothek (Berlin, Germany). Katalog der Lipperheideschen Kostümbibliothek / neubearb. von Eva Neinholdt und Gretel Wagner-Neumann. 2., völlig neubearb. u. verm. Aufl. Berlin : Mann, 1965. 2 v. (1166 p.) : ill.   **BG93**

1st ed., 1896–1905, had title: *Katalog der Freiherrlich von Lipperheide'schen Kostümbibliothek.* Repr.: N.Y. : Hacker Art Books, 1963.

At head of title: Stiftung Preussischer Kulturbesitz, Staatliche Museen Berlin. Kunstbibliothek.

Classed catalog of an important collection which became the property of the Staatliche Kunstbibliothek, Berlin. Index.   Z5691.L76

Indexes

Monro, Isabel Stevenson. Costume index : a subject index to plates and to illustrated texts / ed. by Isabel Stevenson Monro and Dorothy E. Cook. N.Y. : Wilson, 1937. 338 p.   **BG94**

An index to more than 600 works either wholly on costume or containing much material on the subject. Indexing is specific and detailed: under countries and localities, under classes of persons having special types of costume, and under details of costume—e.g., shoes, hats, etc.—with chronological subdivisions under important or large classes. The list of books indexed marks location of copies in some 33 libraries.

——. —— *Supplement*, ed. by I. S. Monro and K. M. Monro (1957. 210 p.). Indexes 347 books.

Encyclopedias

Harrold, Robert. Folk costumes of the world in colour. Poole [Eng.] : Blandford Pr., [1978]. 255 p. : ill.   **BG95**

Reissued, 1988.

A country-by-country description of folk costumes, with regional subdivisions for many countries. Line drawings illustrate various accessories and details of costume; 80 color plates. Indexed.
GT511.H38

Racinet, A. The historical encyclopedia of costumes. N.Y. : Facts on File, 1988. 320 p. : col. ill.   **BG96**

Based on Racinet's *Le costume historique* (Paris : Firmin-Didot, 1888. 6 v.). An edition with a selection of 92 plates was published N.Y. : Dover, 1987.

The earlier work "has been translated, re-organized, edited and re-designed to produce this book" (*Publisher's note*), removing material on furniture and ornaments and including a chronology. Quality of the color plates is excellent.

§ Another standard 19th-century source is J. R. Planché's *A cyclopaedia of costume; or, Dictionary of dress* (London : Chatto and Windus, 1876–79. 2 v.).   GT510.R3313

Schoeffler, O. E. Esquire's encyclopedia of 20th century men's fashions / O. E. Schoeffler, William Gale. N.Y. : McGraw-Hill, [1973]. 709 p. : ill.   **BG97**

"A lavishly illustrated encyclopedia that, in seminarrative style, covers in detail every item of apparel worn by the American man of this century while exploring the society of which his clothes are a reflection."—*Introd.* Items of apparel are treated in categories and chronologically within categories. Includes a section of brief biographies of designers. Glossary; detailed index.   TT617.S36

Dictionaries

Calasibetta, Charlotte Mankey. Fairchild's dictionary of fashion. 2nd ed. N.Y. : Fairchild, 1988. 749 p.　**BG98**
1st ed., 1975.
　Aims to present "clothing terminology from both historical and contemporary viewpoints"—IPref and is meant to be used with *Fairchild's dictionary of textiles*, ed. by I. B. Wingate (N.Y., 1967). Concise definitions; words or terms from the same basic category are grouped together and cross-references made from the individual terms. Numerous line drawings and a few plates in color. Following the main alphabetic arrangement, a section on fashion designers gives brief biographical sketches; portraits and photographs of typical "designer styles" are included.
　§ *See also*: Georgina O'Hara, *The encyclopedia of fashion* (N.Y. : Abrams, [1986]). For additional information on designers, see: *The fashion guide : international designer directory* (N.Y. : Fashion Guide International, 1991).　TT503.C34

Cunnington, Cecil Willett. A dictionary of English costume [900–1900] / by Cecil Willett Cunnington, Phillis Cunnington, and Charles Beard. London : A. & C. Black ; Philadelphia : Dufour, [1960]. 281 p. : ill.　**BG99**
Repr., 1976.
　Has a separate "Glossary of materials" and one page of "Obsolete colour names (prior to 1800)." The 1976 reprint adds a "Glossary of laces."
　§ The author's publications on costume are numerous and include a series of handbooks covering the medieval period through the 20th century (all publ. London : Faber) as well as *Occupational costume in England* ... (N. Y. : Barnes & Noble, [1967]), *Children's costume in England* ... (London : Adam & Charles Black, 1972, c1965), and *Costume for births, marriages & deaths* (N. Y. : Barnes & Noble, [1972]).　GT507.C8

Picken, Mary (Brooks). The fashion dictionary : fabric, sewing, and apparel as expressed in the language of fashion. Rev. and enl. N.Y. : Funk & Wagnalls, [1973]. 434 p. : ill.　**BG100**
　Based on the author's *Language of fashion* (1939). Includes more than 10,000 terms and names associated with wearing apparel, with small line drawings and photographic illustrations. Indicates pronunciation. Index of illustrations.　TT503.P5

Wilcox, Ruth Turner. The dictionary of costume. N.Y. : Scribner, [1969] ; London : Batsford, 1970. 406 p. : ill.　**BG101**
Repr. : N.Y. : Macmillan, 1986 ; London : Batsford, 1989.
　Attempts to describe all facets of costume and fashion, from names of garments, fabrics, and designs, to fashion fads and personal names associated with specific articles of clothing or styles. Especially useful are the line drawings accompanying many of the definitions.
　§ Also by Wilcox: *Folk and festival costume of the world* (N. Y. : Scribner, [1965]. 1 v.).　GT507.W5

Yarwood, Doreen. Encyclopaedia of world costume. London : Batsford ; N.Y. : Scribner, c1978. 471 p. : ill.　**BG102**
Repr. : N.Y. : Bonanza, 1986.
　Articles are presented in a dictionary arrangement, with closely related topics considered together in a single, longer article. Discusses history and development of individual garments, fabrics, accessories, etc. The volume "is intended for use in the English-speaking world so is geared primarily to those needs, though the coverage of other regions is fairly wide."—*Pref.* Bibliography; index.
　§ Other works by Yarwood include *Costume of the western world : pictorial guide and glossary* (N.Y. : St. Martin's, [1980]) and *Fashion in the western world, 1500–1900* (N.Y. : Drama Book Publishers, c1992).　GT507.Y37

Directories

Huenefeld, Irene Pennington. International directory of historical clothing. Metuchen, N.J. : Scarecrow, 1967. 175 p.　**BG103**
　Contents: North America; Europe; Institutions (by title); Institutions (by clothing and clothing accessory); Clothing terms (by category, century and institutions).
　Lists collections of clothing.　NK4700.H8

Handbooks

Arnold, Janet. A handbook of costume. [London] : Macmillan, [1973]. 336 p. : ill.　**BG104**
　Contents: Primary sources (sections on 12 topics and media); Dating costume from construction techniques; Costume conservation, storage and display; Costume for children and students; The stage; Bibliography; Collections.　GT510.A75

Hughes, Elizabeth. The big book of buttons / Elizabeth Hughes, Marion Lester. Sedgwick, Me. : New Leaf Publishers, c1991. 813 p. : ill. (some col.).　**BG105**
1st ed., 1981.
　Contents: pt. 1, Materials (more than 50 categories); pt. 2, Topics (some 50 categories); pt. 3, Uniform buttons.
　Aims "to summarize in one volume as much as possible of the information about buttons ... [and is] written with general regard to the classification guidelines proposed by the National Button Society"—*Introd.* Appendix: American and British makers and marks. Bibliography. Index.　NK3668.5.H8

History and illustration

Boucher, François. 20,000 years of fashion : the history of costume and personal adornment / by François Boucher ; with a new chapter by Yvonne Deslandres. Expanded ed. N.Y. : H.N. Abrams, 1987. 459 p. : ill.　**BG106**
　1st ed. was a translation of *Histoire du costume en Occident, de l'antiquité à nos jours* [Paris] : Flammarion, [1965].
　Published in Great Britain under the title: *A history of costume in the West* (London : Thames & Hudson, 1967).
　Both men's and women's garments and accessories are illustrated and described, and the historical, political, and social background of each era is sketched. Some attention is given to children's clothing. Indexed.
　In addition to the new chapter on recent fashion, a general bibliography and glossary are included.　GT510.B6713

Brooke, Iris. Western European costume and its relation to the theatre. London : Harrap, [1939–40]. 2 v. : ill., col. plates.　**BG107**
Repr. : N.Y. : Theatre Arts Books, 1964–66.
　Contents: v. 1, 13th to 17th century; v. 2, 17th to mid-19th century.
　By the author of numerous popular books on costume. "The aim and scope of this book is to point out differences in costume, and the manner in which those costumes were worn at corresponding dates in the more important countries of Western Europe ... also to give their connexions in relations to the theatre and dramatists contemporary with them."—*v. 1, p. 17.*
　In 1993, a "revised-third edition" by Brooke appeared under the title *Western European costume, 13th to 17th century, and its relation to the theatre*, with additional material by William-Alan Landes (Studio City, Calif. : Players Pr.).　GT720.B73

Davenport, Millia. The book of costume. N.Y. : Crown, [1948]. 2 v. (958 p.) : ill.   **BG108**

Repr., 1979.

A chronological survey from early times to the end of the American Civil War. The almost 3,000 illustrations (partly in color) are mainly from contemporary paintings, engravings, sculpture, etc. Location of the originals is usually given. Index.

§ For a recent chronological survey, see Phyllis G. Tortora's *A survey of historic costume* (N. Y. : Fairchild, 1989).   GT513.D38

Laver, James. Costume and fashion : a concise history / James Laver ; concluding chapter by Christina Probert. New ed. London : Thames and Hudson, [1982] ; N.Y. : Oxford Univ. Pr., 1983. 288 p. : ill.   **BG109**

1st ed., 1969, had title: *A concise history of costume.*

A basic survey of fashion and social change from earliest times through the 1970s by the author of numerous costume books. Illustrations are placed close to pertinent text and their sources are identified. Select bibliography. Index.   GT511.L39

Lester, Katherine Morris. An illustrated history of those frills and furbelows of fashion which have come to be known as: accessories of dress / by Katherine Morris Lester and Bess Oerke. Peoria, Ill. : Manual Arts, [c1940]. 587 p. : ill.   **BG110**

Cover title: Accessories of dress.

Treats in groups the accessories worn or carried in connection with the costume: hats, veils, earrings, combs, fans, bracelets, walking sticks, muffs, buttons, buckles, etc. Bibliography; index to illustrations.

§ For a chronological survey, consult Margot Lister's *Costume : an illustrated survey from ancient times to the twentieth century* (London : Jenkins, 1967 ; Boston : Plays, [1968]).   GT2050.L4

McClellan, Elisabeth. History of American costume, 1607–1870. N.Y. : Tudor, 1937. 661 p. : ill.   **BG111**

Repr. with a new introd. : N.Y. : Tudor, 1969.

First published as *Historic dress in America 1607–1800* (Philadelphia : Jacobs, [1904]) and *Historic dress in America 1800–1870* (Philadelphia : Jacobs, [1910]). Arranged by century and then by women's and men's categories. Includes glossary and index.   GT607.M22

Payne, Blanche. The history of costume : from ancient Mesopotamia through the twentieth century / Blanche Payne, Geitel Winakor, Jane Farrell-Beck. 2nd ed. N.Y. : HarperCollins, c1992. 659 p. : ill., maps.   **BG112**

1st ed., [1965].

For each period there is brief consideration of the historical background, followed by descriptions—with many photographs and line drawings—of both men's and women's costumes. Some attention is given to footwear, hair styles, and accessories. Bibliography; index.   GT510.P36

Rubens, Alfred. A history of Jewish costume. New and enl. ed. London : Weidenfeld and Nicolson ; N.Y. : Crown, [1973]. 221 p. : ill.   **BG113**

1st ed., 1967.

The traditional dress of Jewish peoples from biblical times to the present is discussed and illustrated, with attention given to costumes of Jews in individual countries of the Western world. This edition in larger format, with additions and corrections and many color illustrations.

§ Rubens' other works include one based upon his own prints and drawings collection, *A Jewish iconography* (Rev. ed. London : Nonpareil, 1981. 277 p.) and its *Supplementary volume* (1982. 128 p., chiefly plates). For illustrations, *see also*: Thérèse and Mendel Metzger's *Jewish life in the Middle Ages* (N. Y. : Alpine Fine Arts Collection Ltd., [1982]).   GT540.R73

Tilke, Max. National costumes from East Europe, Africa and Asia. N.Y. : Hastings House, 1978. 38 p. : 128 leaves of colored plates.   **BG114**

British ed. (London : A. Zwemmer, 1978) has title *Folk costumes from East Europe, Africa, and Asia.*

Translation of *Trachten und Kostüme aus Europa, Afrika und Asien in Form, Schnitt und Farbe* (Tübingen, 1978) which, in turn, is based on Tilke's *Orientalische Kostüme* (1923) and *Osteuropäische Volkstrachten* (1925). Incorporates the plates from those volumes with some previously unpublished costume illustrations.

128 pages of colored plates are preceded by descriptive text concerning each of the costumes and individual garments illustrated. Lacks an index.   GT513T5

Biography

McDowell, Colin. McDowell's directory of twentieth century fashion. London : F. Muller, 1984. 320 p. : ill. (some col.).   **BG115**

Alphabetical entries for fashion designers of all nationalities, many with a photograph of the designer, and most illustrating the designer's work. Begins with five essays on 20th-century fashion, and concludes with: an essay on "The image makers"; a listing of autobiographies; information on fashion education, organizations, and awards; a 12-page glossary; and an index of personal names.

§ For a chronological discussion, *see* Prudence Glynn's *In fashion: dress in the twentieth century* (N. Y. : Oxford Univ. Pr., 1978). For men's costume, *see* O.E. Schoeffler and William Gale, *Esquire's encyclopedia of 20th century men's fashions* (BG97).   TT505.A1M37

Stegemeyer, Anne. Who's who in fashion. 2nd ed. N.Y. : Fairchild Publications, c1988. 243 p. : ill. (some col.).   **BG116**

1st ed., 1980; repr., 1984.

"Emphasis here is on designers with an established track record."—*Pref.* Includes portraits and examples of work. Unlike the previous edition, lists Americans and other nationalities in one alphabet.

A *Supplement* to the 2nd ed. appeared in 1992.

§ Not to be confused with *Who's who in fashion* (ed. 1– . Zurich : Who's who, the International Red Series Verlag, 1982–).   TT505.A1S74

FURNITURE AND INTERIOR DESIGN

Bibliography

Decorative arts and household furnishings in America, 1650–1920 : an annotated bibliography / ed. by Kenneth L. Ames and Gerald W. R. Ward. Winterthur, Del. : Henry Francis du Pont Winterthur Museum ; Charlottesville : distr. by the Univ. Pr. of Virginia, 1989. 392 p.   **BG117**

"Records the current state of scholarship in the field of historic furnishings."—*Introd.* Provides useful coverage of the material culture of domestic life. Chapters, compiled by 20 contributors, treat references and surveys, architecture, furniture, metals, ceramics and glass, textiles, timepieces, household activities and systems, and artisans and culture. Chapters begin with essays introducing the selective bibliographies (current through 1986) and have annotations that are for the most part not evaluative. An introduction covers previous bibliographies and the state of current scholarship, and highlights ten significant changes in recent decades. Index to authors and titles.   Z5956.D3D43

Viaux, Jacqueline. Bibliographie du meuble (mobilier civil français). Paris : Société des Amis de la Bibliothèque Forney, 1966. 589 p.   **BG118**

A classed bibliography, mainly periodical articles, on French furniture and furnishings. More than 5,000 items. Indexed.

———. —— *Supplément 1965–1985* (Paris : Agence culturelle de Paris, 1988) includes holdings for French libraries.

Z5995.3.F7V5

Catalogs

Nutting, Wallace. Furniture treasury (mostly of American origin) : all periods of American furniture with some foreign examples in America, also American hardware and household utensils. Framingham, Mass. : Old America, [1928–33]. 3 v. : ill. **BG119**

Vols. 1–2 reissued: N.Y. : Macmillan, 1948 (2 v.); also reissued as 2 v. in 1: N.Y. : Macmillan, 1954, 1968.

Vols. 1–2 include 5,000 plates, arranged by type with descriptions and often dimensions and owners, covering styles to the end of the Empire period; index in v. 2. Vol. 3 has subtitle: Being a record of designers, details of designs and structure, with lists of clock makers in America, and a glossary of furniture terms, richly illustrated. It is intended to supplement the first two volumes by supplying fuller details.

NK2406.N73

Pictorial dictionary of British 19th century furniture design : an Antique Collectors' Club research project. Woodbridge, Eng. : Antique Collectors' Club, [1977]. 583 p. : ill. **BG120**

Aims "to show the complete range of Victorian furniture in illustrations drawn from contemporary sources."—*Introd.* Also includes antecedents of the Victorian era and examples of very early "modern" furniture, so that coverage ranges from 1800 to 1914. The bulk of the work is made up of small black-and-white illustrations of furniture arranged according to broad categories, appropriately subdivided. Illustrations are dated and name of designer or firm is indicated. A section on "The designers and design books" provides background notes on individual designers, firms, and styles. Chronology and list of contemporary sources quoted.

§ Related title: *Pictorial dictionary of British 18th century furniture design : the printed sources* (Woodbridge, Eng. : Antique Collectors' Club, 1990).

NK2530.P5

Encyclopedias

Aronson, Joseph. The encyclopedia of furniture. 3rd ed., completely rev. N.Y. : Crown, [1965]. 484 p. : ill. **BG121**

Repr., 1967, with new title page, as: *The new encyclopedia of furniture.*

Repr: London : Batsford, 1989.

1st ed., 1938.

Alphabetical arrangement of short articles, illustrated with about 1,400 photographs and numerous line drawings. Increased coverage for the 19th century in this edition.

NK2205.A7

Bajot, Édouard. Encyclopédie du meuble du XVᵉ siècle jusqu'à nos jours : Recueil de planches contenant des meubles de style de toutes les époques et de tous les pays, depuis le XVᵉ siècle … classées par ordre alphabétique … 2000 meubles de style reproduits à grande échelle. Paris : C. Schmid, [1901–09]. 20 pts. in 8 v. : 600 plates. **BG122**

A rare source that is useful for the many plates grouped by furniture type. Text is limited to very brief captions on the plates—identifying material, country, and period—and a "Table analytique des planches" and a "Notice" in v. 1. Both list the 54 types of furniture alphabetically, the "Notice" giving a short historical paragraph for each type.

NK2260.B3

Macquoid, Percy. Dictionary of English furniture, from the Middle Ages to the late Georgian period / Percy Macquoid, Ralph Edwards. [2nd ed.] / rev. and enl. by Ralph Edwards. London : Country Life, [1954]. 3 v. : ill. **BG123**

1st ed., London : Offices of Country Life ; N.Y. : Scribner's Sons, 1924–27.

Reissued : Woodbridge, Suffolk : Antique Collectors' Club, 1986.

Of first importance. "A drastic revision of the former text, [1924–27. 3 v.] with the addition of numerous sections and a very large *corpus* of illustrations."—*Foreword.*

An abridged edition "concerned only with domestic furniture" (*Foreword*) and omitting minor accessories was published as *The shorter dictionary of English furniture,* by Ralph Edwards (London : Country Life, 1964. 684 p. Repr., 1972).

NK2529.M32

Viollet-Le-Duc, Eugène Emmanuel. Dictionnaire raisonné du mobilier français de l'époque carlovingienne à la Renaissance. Paris : Morel, 1858–75. 6 v. : ill. **BG124**

Repr. : Paris : Grund, 1914.

Issued in parts. Imprint varies.

Contents: v. 1, pt. 1, Meubles; v. 2, pt. 2, Ustensiles; pt. 3, Orfèvrerie; pt. 4, Instruments de musique; pt. 5, Jeux, passetemps; pt. 6, Outils, outillages; v. 3–4, pt. 7, Vêtements, bijoux de corps, objets de toilette; v. 5–6, pt. 8, Armes de guerre offensives et défensives.

Index in each volume, with one for the whole work in v. 6. A rare and important source.

NK30.V7

Dictionaries

Dictionary of furniture / [ed. by] Charles Boyce. N.Y. : Facts on File, c1985. 331 p. : ill. **BG125**

Repr. : N.Y. : Holt, 1988. Portions have been reprinted in Li Chung, *An English-Chinese dictionary of furniture industry* (Beijing, 1989).

A straightforward work that overstates its usefulness as "the most comprehensive listing in a single volume of terms … in all countries and cultures" (*Foreword*), although it does incorporate a noticeable number of entries on Asian furniture. Entries for persons, styles, objects, and parts of furniture, in one alphabet with some cross-references, range in length from a few words to two pages, and have simple line drawings. Biographical entries cover persons born up to the early 1930s. Lacks an index, any bibliography, or bibliographic references.

NK2205.D5

Gloag, John. John Gloag's dictionary of furniture. Rev. and enl. ed. / rev. by Clive D. Edwards. London : Unwin Hyman, 1990. 828 p. : ill. **BG126**

1st ed., 1952. Previous ed. had title: *Short dictionary of furniture* (London : Allen & Unwin, 1969).

Reissued in 1991 as: *A complete dictionary of furniture* (Woodstock, N.Y. : Overlook Pr.).

Brief but clear definitions and descriptions, with many line drawings. Preliminary sections cover: (1) description and (2) design of furniture. The dictionary is followed by lists of British and American furniture makers and designers, and British clockmakers; books and periodicals; and tabulated lists of periods, types of furniture, materials, and craftsmen from 1100 to 1950. Emphasis is mainly British. The Appendix (p. 814–828) supplies some 85 additional terms ranging from adhesives to water beds and xylonite.

NK2270

Pegler, Martin. The dictionary of interior design. N.Y. : Crown, [1966]. 500 p. : ill. **BG127**

Repr. in a changed format and with a reduction in the number of illustrations (N.Y. : Fairchild, 1983. 217 p.).

Includes terms relating to furniture and period styles, architecture, woods, fabrics, ornament, etc., plus biographical notes on famous designers and architects. Illustrations are numerous, but very small.

NK1165.P4

Salaman, R. A. Dictionary of tools used in the woodworking and allied trades, c. 1700–1970. London : Allen & Unwin, [1975] ; N.Y. : Scribner, 1976. 545 p. : ill.   **BG128**

Tools and trades are entered alphabetically, with "families" of tools and tools of a particular trade grouped together; cross-references are provided from the name of the specific tool when it is treated with tools of a trade. Many illustrations; bibliography.

Rev. ed., revised by Philip Walker, under the title: *Dictionary of woodworking tools c. 1700–1970, and tools of allied trades* (Newtown, Conn. : Taunton Pr., 1990).   TT186.S24

Sotheby's concise encyclopedia of furniture / gen. ed., Christopher Payne. London : Conran Octopus ; N.Y. : Harper & Row, c1989. 208 p. : ill. (some col.).   **BG129**

A chronological treatment that concludes with a chapter on "Modern times" and benefits from good color illustrations. Includes an index to names and styles; a one-page bibliography; a two-page "Anatomy of furniture," highlighting key terms for beds, chairs, and tables; and a six-page glossary.   NK2235.S68

Directories

The Conran directory of design / ed. by Stephen Bayley. London : Octopus Conran ; N.Y. : Villard Books, 1985. 255 p. : ill. (some col.).   **BG130**

Thematic chapters emphasize product design, followed by 180 pages of alphabetical entries for persons and firms, terms, and events (e.g., major exhibitions). Biographical entries give dates and brief descriptions of the designer's work. Provides bibliographical information within the entries, a short general bibliography, and a list of design museums and organizations. Concludes with an index of products and designs.

§ A related title is John F. Pile's *Dictionary of 20th-century design* (N.Y. : Facts on File, 1990). A. Allen Dizik's *Concise encyclopedia of interior design* (2nd ed. N.Y. : Van Nostrand Reinhold, 1988) is very general and somewhat uneven.   NK1165.C6

History

Boger, Louise Ade. The complete guide to furniture styles. Enl. ed. N.Y. : Scribner, [1969]. 500 p. : ill.   **BG131**

Previous edition, 1959.

For the student and general reader. " ... material was selected to provide the practical knowledge for following the development of the styles of furniture in Italy, France, The Netherlands, Spain, England and America. Chinese furniture of the Ming dynasty has also been included."—*Foreword.* Four new chapters on cabinetwork of the 19th and 20th centuries were added in the new edition. Bibliography and indexes.   NK2270.B63

Kovel, Ralph M. American country furniture, 1780–1875 / Ralph M. Kovel, Terry H. Kovel. N.Y. : Crown, [1965]. 248 p. : ill.   **BG132**

Repr., 1987.

About 700 items are illustrated and briefly described.

§ Related title: Marjorie Filbee's *Dictionary of country furniture* (N.Y. : Hearst ; London : Connoisseur, [1977]).   NK2406.K6

Thornton, Peter. Authentic decor : the domestic interior, 1620–1920. N.Y. : Viking, [1984]. 408 p. : ill.   **BG133**

Publ. in Great Britain by Weidenfeld & Nicolson.

Offers a survey, through illustrations and descriptive text, of how people in Europe and North America arranged and decorated their rooms through the centuries. In general, the numerous illustrations (many in color, and including paintings, drawings, floor plans, details of decoration, etc.) were made when the decoration was new; restorations were avoided as misleading. Arranged in six 50-year periods with background notes to each. Illustrations are described in considerable detail, with attention given to materials and fabrics. International in scope; interiors range from the homes of aristocrats to those of the middle classes. Bibliographic notes; index.   NK1860.T49

Biography

Bjerkoe, Ethel Hall. The cabinetmakers of America / by Ethel Hall Bjerkoe ; assisted by John Arthur Bjerkoe. Rev. and corrected ed. Exton, Pa. : Schiffer Ltd., c1978. 272 p. : ill.   **BG134**

1st ed., 1957.

A basic biographical dictionary for furniture makers and designers active through the 19th century. Photographs and line drawings. Glossary; bibliography; index.   NK2406.B55

Dictionary of English furniture makers, 1660–1840 / ed. by Geoffrey Beard and Christopher Gilbert. [London] : Furniture History Society, 1986. 1046 p., [16] p. of plates : ill., facsims.   **BG135**

Covers all principal furniture trades and specialist branches, while ignoring fringe trades such as trunkmakers or coach builders, resulting in a much more comprehensive listing than Ambrose Heal's *The London furniture makers from the Restoration to the Victorian era, 1660–1840* (London : Batsford, 1953. 276 p. Repr.: London : Portman, 1988). Several hundred members of the Furniture History Society working in 25 regional groups contributed to this work by evaluating listings in trade directories, insurance registers, and newspapers, and periodicals. The several thousand entries give dates, places of apprenticeship and later activity. Brief bibliography. Index.   TS810.G7

METAL ARTS

General Works

Dictionaries

Clayton, Michael. The collector's dictionary of the silver and gold of Great Britain and North America. 2nd ed. [Woodbridge, Suffolk] : Antique Collectors' Club, 1985. 481 p. : ill. (some col.).   **BG136**

1st ed., 1971 (Feltham : Country Life ; N.Y. : World).

Entries for makers, materials and processes, objects, and subjects, many with short bibliographies. Numerous photographs. Bibliography, current through 1983.   NK7143.C55

General works

Directories

Culme, John. The directory of gold & silversmiths, jewellers, and allied traders, 1838–1914 : from the London Assay Office registers. Woodbridge, Suffolk : Antique Collectors' Club, 1987. 2 v.   **BG137**

Contents: v. 1, The biographies; v. 2, The marks.

Based upon information from the Makers' Marks Registers, Goldsmiths' Hall, London. Introductory material includes an essay, "Attitudes to old plate 1750–1900," a list of terms to describe trades, and an abbreviations list that has bibliographic references. The actual biographies (individuals and companies interfiled) are thorough in documentation; many are footnoted. The marks are photographs of 16,127 marks, which are accompanied by a name index. NK7143.C924

Jackson's silver & gold marks of England, Scotland & Ireland / ed. by Ian Pickford ; with contributions from Timothy Kent ... [et al.]. 3rd ed. rev. Woodbridge, Suffolk : Antique Collectors' Club, c1989. 766 p. : ill. **BG138**

"A third revised and enlarged edition of Sir Charles Jackson's classic work 'English goldsmiths and their marks'."—*t.p.*

1st ed., 1905; 2nd ed., 1921.

A standard source. This edition has 21 chapters by various contributors, an appendix, a brief bibliography, and indexes of initials and signatures. NK7143.J15

Biography

Chaffers, William. Hall marks on gold and silver plate : illustrated with revised tables of annual date letters employed in the assay offices of England, Scotland and Ireland. 10th ed. extended and enl. and with the addition of new date letters and marks, and a bibliography, also incorporating makers' marks from the "*Gilda aurifabrorum*," ed. by C. A. Markham. London : Reeves and Turner, 1922. 395 p. : ill. **BG139**

1st ed., 1863.

Title varies slightly.

Includes also material on English gold- and silversmiths, tables of statutes and ordinances, chronological list of English plate, etc., bibliography, and a general index. NK7210.C45

Grimwade, Arthur. London goldsmiths 1697–1837 : their marks and lives from the original registers at Goldsmiths' Hall and other sources. 3rd rev. and enl. ed. London : Faber and Faber, 1990. 773 p. **BG140**

First publ., 1976; 2nd rev. ed., 1982.

A solid contribution, with two sections: "Marks" provides many subsections (derived from categories found in goldsmiths' lists, the largest being the Goldsmiths' Hall registers) and small images; entries in "Lives" cite evidence of work, apprenticeships, addresses, existence of marks, and documentation. "Lives" refers to pertinent marks by number and uses asterisks to denote additional information in the addenda. An introduction describes the origins of the project, the plan, and the registers, with reference to Sir Ambrose Heal's *The London goldsmiths, 1200–1800* (Repr.: Newton Abbott : David & Charles, 1972). "Addenda to biographical dictionary" (p. 734–772) contains new material and concludes with a list of some 70 names found in John Culme's *The directory of gold & silversmiths, jewellers, and allied traders, 1838–1914* (BG137). NK7144.L66G74

Nocq, Henry. Le poinçon de Paris : répertoire des maîtres-orfèvres de la juridiction de Paris depuis le Moyen-Âge jusqu'à la fin du XVIIIe siècle. Paris : H. Floury, 1926–31. 5 v. : ill., plates (part col.). **BG141**

Repr. : Paris : L. Laget, 1968.

Arranged alphabetically by name of the gold- or silversmith, giving brief information and mark. Vols. 1–4, A–Z; v. 4 includes a "*Résumé chronologique*" and other historical lists and notes; v. 5 contains "Errata et addenda" and three indexes. NK7210.N6

Rosenberg, Marc. Der goldschmiede Merkzeichen. 3. erweit. und ill. Aufl. Frankfurt am Main : Frankfurter Verlags-Anstalt, 1922–28. 4 v. : ill. **BG142**

Repr. : Hofheim am Taunus : Schmidt und Günther, between 1980 and 1984.

1st ed., 1890 (Frankfurt am Main : Keller).

Vols. 1–3, *Deutsches Reich*, are arranged by city with its goldsmiths chronologically listed. Vol. 4, *Das europäische Ausland*, is arranged by country, then city. It includes Byzantine goldsmiths. Index of marks and names in each volume. NK7210.R6

Silver

Brett, Vanessa. The Sotheby's directory of silver, 1600–1940. [London] : Sotheby's Publications ; N.Y. : distr. by Harper & Row, 1986. 432 p. : ill. **BG143**

Arranged by seven countries or regions of Europe and North America, within which some 2,000 objects are described and illustrated under makers' names. Includes appendixes; bibliography (current through 1985); and indexes of objects; goldsmiths, designers and engravers; heraldry and inscriptions.

§ The same firm recently brought out *Sotheby's concise encyclopedia of silver*, ed. by Charles Truman (London : Conran Octopus, 1993). NK7142.B74

Ensko, Stephen Guernsey Cook. American silversmiths and their marks IV. 1st ed., a rev. and enl. ed. / comp. by Dorothea Ensko Wyle. Boston : D.R. Godine, 1989. 477 p. **BG144**

The "final, revised edition is a compilation of the 1915 book ... and the 1927, 1937, 1948 books."—*Dedication*. Contents: Names of early American silversmiths; Marks of early American silversmiths; Locations of silversmiths' shops (New York, Boston, and Philadelphia); Facsimile pages. Bibliography.

§ Related sources: Hollis French, *A silver collectors' glossary and a list of early American silversmiths and their marks* (N.Y. : Da Capo, 1967; [Repr. of the 1917 ed.]); Martha Gandy Fales, *Early American silver* (Rev. and enl. ed. N.Y. : Dutton, 1973. 336 p. 1st ed., 1970). NK7112.E66

Kovel, Ralph M. Kovels' American silver marks / Ralph and Terry Kovel. N.Y. : Crown, c1989. 421 p. : ill. **BG145**

Portions of this book originally appeared in Kovel's *A directory of American silver, pewter, and silver plate* (N.Y. : Crown, [1961]).

The introduction gives a brief history for 1640–1850 and 1850–1980. The extensive entries interfile initials with full personal and company names, making ample use of cross-references. Each entry gives dates of activity, city, bibliographic sources, and mark or monogram when pertinent. Closes with a bibliography of 160 books published through the mid-1980s. NK7210.K68

Newman, Harold. An illustrated dictionary of silverware : 2,373 entries relating to British and North American wares, decorative techniques and styles, and leading designers and makers, principally from c1500 to the present. N.Y. : Thames and Hudson, 1987. 366 p., [16] p. of plates : ill. (some col.). **BG146**

Includes "the many types of articles for domestic use ... and the highly important fields of ware made for religious use."—*Pref.* Excludes silver jewelry, which is treated in the author's *An illustrated dictionary of jewelry* (BG83) and "many other small portable objects of vertu." Emphasizes 17th–19th centuries. Alphabetical entries treat objects, styles, subjects depicted in silver, makers, and techniques. Entries range in length from one sentence to half a page, with a single bibliographic reference. Numerous small photographs and 16 color plates. NK7104.N49

Okie, Howard Pitcher. Old silver and old Sheffield plate. Garden City, N.Y. : Doubleday, 1928. 420 p. : ill. **BG147**

Reissued in 1944 and 1952.

Subtitle: A history of the silversmith's art in Great Britain and Ireland, with reproductions in facsimile of about thirteen thousand marks. Tables of date letters and other marks. American silversmiths and their marks. Paris marks and Paris date letters with a description of the methods of marking employed by the Paris Guild of Silversmiths. Hallmarks, and date letters when used, of nearly all the countries of continental Europe, reproduced in facsimile. A history of Old Sheffield plate and a description of the method of its production, with the names and marks in facsimile of every known maker. NK7143.O4

Rainwater, Dorothy T. Encyclopedia of American silver manufacturers. 3rd ed. rev. West Chester, Penn. : Schiffer Publ., c1986. 266 p. : ill. **BG148**

1st ed., 1966; 2nd ed., 1975.

Entries, alphabetical by manufacturer's name, give location, diagram of the mark, a list of variants of the manufacturer's name or trademark (when pertinent), and one or more paragraphs describing the firm's activity. Sources for trademarks and dates include trade journals and related directories and indexes. Concludes with illustrations of nine unascribed marks, an alphabetical list of trade names and their companies, a key to unlettered marks, and a four-page glossary. Bibliography is current only to the mid-1970s. Lacks an index.

NK7112.R3

Pewter

Brett, Vanessa. Phaidon guide to pewter. Englewood Cliffs, N.J. : Prentice-Hall, c1983 ; Oxford : Phaidon, c1981. 256 p. : ill. (some col.).   **BG149**

A working guide with information on processes, guilds, and styles, followed by ten sections on pewter of various European areas and American periods. Concludes with representative marks, brief bibliography, and glossary. Index.   NK8404.B74

Cotterell, Howard Herschel. Old pewter : its makers and marks in England, Scotland and Ireland. London : Batsford ; N.Y. : Scribner, 1929. 432 p. : ill.   **BG150**

Repr. : London : Batsford ; Rutland, Vt. : Tuttle, 1963.

Subtitle : An account of the old pewterer and his craft, illustrating all known marks and secondary marks of the old pewterers with a series of plates showing the chief types of their wares.

Begins with five chapters on history, but is primarily an alphabetical list of pewterers with illustrations of their marks where known, p. 145–344. Also includes: Initialled marks; Alphabetical list; Illustrations of those marks which bear neither their owner's names nor initials; Index to the devices; Index to the "Hallmarks"; Bibliography; General index.

§ Cotterell also wrote a general history, *Pewter down the ages* (London : Hutchinson & Co. ; Boston : Houghton Mifflin, 1932). Related title: John Hatcher's *A history of British pewter* (London : Longman, 1974).   NK8415.G7C6

Laughlin, Ledlie Irwin. Pewter in America : its makers and their marks. Barre, Mass. : Barre Publ., 1969–71. 3 v. : ill., 115 plates.   **BG151**

First publ. 1940 in 2 v. In the 1969–71 ed. v. 1–2 are reprinted unchanged; v. 3 corrects and supplements those volumes, following the same format and chapter headings, adding "all pertinent available material" (*Pref., v. 3*) which has accumulated in the 30 years following 1940. This ed. reprinted, 3 v. in 1, by American Legacy Pr., N.Y., 1981 (687 p.).

A standard work, giving history, problems for the collector, and biographical sketches of pewterers working in America prior to 1850, grouped geographically, then chronologically. Contains a "Check list of American makers of pewter, britannia or block tin … prior to 1850"; a list of "Dethroned pewterers" (names from previous lists omitted for cause). Index and bibliography in v. 2 and v. 3.

§ Related titles: Katherine Ebert's *Collecting American pewter* (N.Y. : Scribner's, [1973]) and Charles F. Montgomery's *A history of American pewter* (rev. and enl. ed. N.Y. : Dutton, 1978). NK8412.L3

TEXTILES

General

Abegg, Margaret. Apropos patterns for embroidery, lace and woven textiles. Bern : Stämpfli, 1978. 210 p. : 234 ill. (some col.). (Schriften der Abegg-Stiftung Bern, Bd. 4.).   **BG152**

A scholarly history that begins with 16th-century Europe. Includes English, French, and German summaries; index.   TT771.A23

Arthur D. Jenkins Library. Rug and textile arts : a periodical index, 1890–1982 / the Textile Museum, Arthur D. Jenkins Library. Boston : G.K. Hall, 1983. 472 p.   **BG153**

"Represents the selective indexing of textile and rug articles found in over 300 periodical titles owned by the Museum [in Washington, D.C.]."—*Pref.* While the earliest articles date from 1890, the majority were published from 1920 to the early 1980s. Reproduces the catalog cards arranged in two sections: (1) author and (2) subject/title. Bibliographical information is complete for each entry.

§ Related title: *Textile arts index, 1950–1987 : selecting weaving, spinning, dyeing, knitting, fiber periodicals*, comp. by S. T. Wilson and R. D. Jackson (Nashville : Tunstede, 1988), an imperfect but useful index to 16 periodicals.   Z7914.T3A77

Burnham, Dorothy K. Warp & weft : a dictionary of textile terms. N.Y. : Scribner, 1981. 216 p. : ill.   **BG154**

First publ. in Canada as *Warp and weft : a textile terminology* (Toronto : Royal Ontario Museum, c1980).

Adapted and expanded from *Vocabulary of technical terms*, 1964, with permission of the Centre International d'Étude des Textiles Anciens (CIETA).

"The word *textile* is taken in its narrow sense of a *woven* fabric."—*Introd.* Provides terms in English, French, German, Italian, Portuguese, Spanish, and Swedish, with definitions and explanations in English, accompanied by excellent line drawings and photographs. Appendixes. Bibliography.   TS1309.B87

Jerde, Judith. Encyclopedia of textiles. N.Y. : Facts on File, 1992. 260 p. : ill. (some col.).   **BG155**

A general source, that emphasizes manufactured textiles and is illustrated with line drawings and photographs. Index.

§ Two additional, fairly technical sources with titles very similar to Jerde's *Encyclopedia*: *Encyclopedia of textiles, fibers, and nonwoven fabrics*, ed. by Martin Grayson (N.Y. : Wiley, 1984) and *Encyclopedia of textiles* (3rd ed. Englewood Cliffs, N.J. : Prentice-Hall, 1980), also known as *AF encyclopedia of textiles*.   TS1309.J47

Montgomery, Florence M. Textiles in America, 1650–1870. N.Y. : Norton, c1984. 412 p., [32] leaves of plates : ill.   **BG156**

Subtitle: A dictionary based on original documents, prints and paintings, commercial records, American merchants' papers, shopkeepers' advertisements, and pattern books with original swatches of cloth.

In addition to the dictionary proper (p. 141–377), there are explanatory sections on furnishing practices in England and America, bed hangings, window curtains, upholstery, and textiles for the period room in America. Numerous illustrations, many in color; bibliography.

§ Related surveys: Frederick J. Dockstader's *Weaving arts of the North American Indian* (N.Y. : Crowell, 1978) and *Labors of love : America's textiles and needlework, 1650–1930* (N.Y. : Knopf, 1987).   TS1767.M66

United States & Canada : an illustrated guide to the textile collections in United States and Canadian museums / ed., Cecil Lubell ; with essays on the traditions of North American textile design by Andrew Hunter Whiteford (North American Indians), Robert Riley (United States), Dorothy K. Burnham (Canada). N.Y. : Van Nostrand Reinhold Co., c1976. 336 p. : ill. (some col.). (Textile collections of the world, v. 1).   **BG157**

Arranged by topic (e.g., color, traditions, and fabrics) with numerous illustrations. Index.

Subsequent volumes in the series are: v. 2, *United Kingdom and Ireland* (1976) and v. 3, *France* (1977).   NK8812.U54

Hand weaving

Buschman, Isabel. Handweaving : an annotated bibliography. Metuchen, N.J. : Scarecrow, 1991. 250 p. **BG158**

"Coverage is limited to printed works in the English language … and … those which have been written or reprinted during the past 50 years."—*Introd.* Has sections for: Handweaving processes and projects; History and artistry; Weaving of the Native Americans; Reference works; Periodicals. Has 553 entries, current through the late 1980s. Indexes: author, title, subject.

§ Related titles: Sylvia Fraser-Lu, *Handwoven textiles of South-East Asia* (Singapore ; N.Y. : Oxford Univ. Pr., 1988); Nicholas Barnard, *Living with decorative textiles : tribal art from Africa, Asia, and the Americas* (N.Y. : Doubleday, 1989). Z6153.T4B87

Porter, Frank W. Native American basketry : an annotated bibliography. N.Y. : Greenwood, 1988. 249 p. (Art reference collection, no. 10). **BG159**

Organized under the ten major culture areas. The 1,128 entries are for books, dissertations and theses, and journal and newspaper articles. Current through 1985. Indexes: author and subject. Z1209.2.N67P67

Lace

Jackson, Emily. A history of hand-made lace : dealing with the origin of lace, the growth of the great lace centres, the mode of manufacture, the methods of distinguishing and the care of various kinds of lace / with suppl. information by Ernesto Jesurum. London : Gill ; N.Y. : Scribner, 1900. 245 p. : ill. **BG160**

Repr. : Detroit : Tower Books, 1971. Repr. in 1987 as: *Old handmade lace : with a dictionary of lace.*

A standard source. Includes: Bibliography, p. 98–105; "Dictionary of lace," p. [107]–206; "Glossary relating to hand-made lace," p. 207–19.

§ Another standard work, dating from the 19th century, is Bury Palliser's *A history of lace*, most recently publ. as a reprint of the 4th ed. (N.Y. : Dover, 1984). NK9406.J3

Powys, Marian. Lace and lace-making. Boston : Branford, 1953. 219 p. : ill. **BG161**

Repr. : Detroit : Gale, 1981.

A practical handbook, giving descriptions of various types of lace with methods of identification; also directions for making, mending, and cleaning lace.

§ For a newer source, *see:* Ernst Erik Pfannschmidt's *Twentieth-century lace* (London : Mills and Boon ; N.Y. : Scribner, [1975]). NK9404.P75

Whiting, Gertrude. Lace guide for makers and collectors : with a bibliography and five-language nomenclature, profusely illustrated with halftone plates and key designs. N.Y. : Dutton, [c1920]. 415 p. : ill. **BG162**

Nomenclature in English, French, Italian, Spanish, and German, p. 38–68. Bibliography, p. 243–401. Illustrations and instructions for making various types of lace. TT800.W5

Quilts

Houck, Carter. The quilt encyclopedia illustrated. N.Y. : H. N. Abrams in association with the Museum of American Folk Art, 1991. 192 p. : col. ill. **BG163**

Abundant color photographs accompany entries on all aspects of quilting and quilt history. Index.

§ Another recent quilt source is Barbara Brackman's *Encyclopedia of pieced quilt patterns* (Paducah, Ky. : American Quilter's Soc., 1993). NK9104.H68

Makowski, Colleen Lahan. Quilting, 1915–1983 : an annotated bibliography. Metuchen, N.J. : Scarecrow, 1985. 157 p. : 1 ill. **BG164**

Cites 733 books, exhibition catalogs, periodical articles, nonprint media, and museum catalogs published through 1983 on American quilts. Entries are annotated. Index to titles, places, names, styles, and themes. Z6153.Q54M34

Rugs

See also BG153.

Eiland, Murray L. Oriental rugs : a new comprehensive guide. 3rd ed. Boston : Little, Brown, c1981. 294 p., [48] p. of plates : ill. **BG165**

1st ed., 1973.

Concentrates "on presenting and evaluating the findings of recent scholarship and at the same time on providing a foundation for the beginner in rug studies."—*Pref.* Chapters deal with history and development of rugs and carpets, elements of design, dyes, construction, rugs of Persia, Turkish rugs, Turkoman rugs, and rugs of the Caucasus. Numerous illustrations (many in color); brief notes on sources; index.

§ Other well-illustrated sources include E. Gans-Ruedin's *The great book of Oriental carpets* (N.Y. : Harper & Row, [1983], tr. from the French *Beauté du tapis d'Orient*) and Jon Thompson's *Oriental carpets : from the tents, cottages and workshops of Asia*, (N.Y. : Dutton, 1988), rev. ed. of *Carpet magic* (London : Barbican Art Gallery, 1983). NK2808.E44

Erdmann, Kurt. Seven hundred years of oriental carpets / ed. by Hanna Erdmann and tr. from the German by May H. Beattie and Hildegard Herzog. London : Faber ; Berkeley, Calif. : Univ. of California Pr., 1970. 238 p. : ill. **BG166**

Translation of: *Siebenhundert Jahre Orientteppich* (Herford : Busse, 1966).

An illustrated historical survey treating the various types of oriental carpets by country and period. Index.

§ Erdmann also wrote: *Oriental carpets : an essay on their history* (2nd ed. London : Zwemmer ; N.Y. : Universe Books, [1962], a translation of *Der orientalische Knüpfteppich* (2nd ed. Tübingen : Wasmuth, 1960). NK2808.E7513

Faraday, Cornelia Bateman. European and American carpets and rugs : with more than 400 illustrations of antique and modern European and American carpets and rugs, with 32 plates in full color. Grand Rapids, Mich. : Dean-Hicks Co., 1929. 382 p. : ill. **BG167**

Repr.: Suffolk, Eng. : Antique Collectors' Club, 1990.

Subtitle: A history of the hand-woven decorative floor coverings of Spain, France, Great Britain, Scandinavia, Belgium, Holland, Italy, the Balkans, Germany, Austria, and early America; and of the machine-made carpets and rugs of modern Europe and of the United States.

A standard work on carpets other than Oriental. NK2795.F3

Lewis, George Griffin. The practical book of Oriental rugs. [6th] rev. ed., with 32 color plates, 80 halftones and numerous line designs. Philadelphia : Lippincott, c1945. 317 p., 112 p. of plates : ill. **BG168**

1st ed., 1911.

A useful handbook on the classification of Oriental rugs and their identification, materials, dyes, weaving, designs and their symbolism, etc. Glossary; bibliography; index. NK2808.L65

The Macmillan atlas of rugs & carpets / ed. by David Black. N.Y. : Macmillan, c1985. 255 p. : ill. (some col.), maps ; 30 cm. **BG169**

The body of the work is a gazetteer, arranged geographically with large sections on Turkey, the Caucasus, Persia, Turkoman tribes, and East Turkestan, and smaller sections on areas of Asia, Morocco, Europe, and North America. All include a simple outline map, and one or more color illustrations and description of a characteristic rug, along with text. Concludes with information on the buying and care of carpets, a four-page glossary of techniques and designs, a select bibliography, and an index.   NK2795.M25

COINS, NUMISMATICS, AND CURRENCY

Bibliography

Clain-Stefanelli, Elvira Eliza. Numismatic bibliography. München : Battenberg ; N.Y. : K.G. Saur, c1985. 1848 p. **BG170**

1st ed., 1967, had title: *Select numismatic bibliography.*
Preface in English, German, and French.

A classed, international bibliography of more than 18,300 entries covering books, periodical articles, conference proceedings, etc. Includes works on monetary theory and evolution of money, as well as coinages (by period and country/region), collections and collecting, tokens, medals, and many special topics. Indexes: authors, collectors, personal names, geographical terms.   Z6866.C44

Coole, Arthur Braddan. A bibliography on Far Eastern numismatology and a coin index / by Arthur Braddan Coole, assisted by Hitoshi Kozono [and] Howard F. Bowker. [Denver : s.n., 1967]. 581 p. : ports. (Encyclopedia of Chinese coins, v. 1). **BG171**

An extensive bibliography in three sections: works in Chinese, in Japanese, and in Western languages; the first and second parts are alphabetical by romanized title. Western language materials are listed alphabetically by author (the latter part incorporating Bowker's *A numismatic bibliography of the Far East*, 1943).

§ Coole is also the author of *An encyclopedia of Chinese coins* (Denver : A. B. Coole, 1967–81. v. 1–7. [In progress]).

Grierson, Philip. Bibliographie numismatique. 2ᵉ ed. rev. et aug. Bruxelles, 1979. 359 p. (Cercle d'Études Numismatiques. Travaux, 9.). **BG172**

1st ed., 1954, had title *Coins and medals : a short bibliography.*

Within period divisions, listings are by country and by peoples. Various sections and subsections have introductory notes. Bibliographies include essential reference works and selected monographs and articles illustrating research trends. There is also a section on auction catalogs. Indexed.

§ Among Grierson's numerous other works are a handbook, *Byzantine coins* (London : Methuen; Berkeley : Univ. of California Pr., [1982]) and a history, *Numismatics* (London; N.Y. : Oxford Univ. Pr., 1975).

Related title: Ivo Suetens, *Bibliographie numismatique : supplément : ordres et decorations* (Bruxelles, 1969–77. 2 v.).

Lipsius, Johann Gottfried. A bibliography of numismatic books printed before 1800 / by J. G. Lipsius. With a supplement to 1866 by Johan Jakob Leitzmann. Colchester, Eng. : J. Drury, 1977. 558, 189 p. **BG173**

Reprints, unchanged, Lipsius' *Bibliotheca numaria* (1801), the standard pre-1800 numismatic bibliography (an author list with subject index) together with Leitzmann's *Schriften über Münzkunde* (1867), which added works of 1801 to 1866.

Mayer, Leo Ary. Bibliography of Moslem numismatics, India excepted. 2nd, considerably enl. ed. London : Royal Asiatic Soc., 1954. 283 p. (Oriental Translation Fund [London. Publications, new series], v. 35). **BG174**

Lists more than 2,000 titles arranged alphabetically. The annotation after each title gives names of dynasties mentioned in the relevant book or article. In many cases references are given to reviews.

§ Mayer is also author of *A bibliography of Jewish numismatics* (Jerusalem : Magnes Pr., Hebrew Univ., 1966. 78 p.).

Numismatic literature. no. 1 (Oct. 1947)– . N.Y. : American Numismatic Soc., 1947– . Semiannual. **BG175**

Frequency varies.

A classified listing of book and periodical publications with abstracts; separate sections of reviews and obituaries; hoard list. Commences with an excellent periodicals and abbreviations list. Author and subject indexes.   Z6866.A53

Vermeule, Cornelius Clarkson. A bibliography of applied numismatics in the fields of Greek and Roman archaeology and the fine arts. London : Spink, 1956. 172 p. **BG176**

1,309 numbered items, both books and periodical articles, some annotated. Contents: Archaeology and art history; Iconography; Geography, topography, and architecture; Related works … ; Index.   Z6869.G8V4

Library catalogs

American Numismatic Society. Library. Dictionary catalogue. Boston : G. K. Hall, 1962. 7 v. (5920 p.). **BG177**

[Vol. 7], unnumbered, has title *Auction catalogue.*

Reproduces the catalog cards of "the most comprehensive numismatic library in America"—*(Pref.)*, encompassing every branch of the subject. Includes books, periodical articles, pamphlets, microforms and manuscripts in one alphabetic sequence. More than 70,000 items in all.

Auction catalogs, both American and foreign, are listed in the last volume of the basic set, appearing under dealer and under owner; in the supplements they are in a separate section, listed by dealer.

————. ———— *Supplements 1–3* (Boston : G.K. Hall, 1967–78. 4 v.). List acquisitions 1962–77.

§ Another large collection (20,000 items) is that of the American Numismatic Assoc., which published its *Library catalogue* (2nd ed. Colorado Springs, Colo., 1977. 768 p.) as a classified list of books, periodicals, and auction catalogs, with an author index.

Dictionaries

Doty, Richard G. The Macmillan encyclopedic dictionary of numismatics. N.Y. : Macmillan ; London : Collier Macmillan, [1982]. 355 p. : ill. **BG178**

A "general dictionary of numismatic terms, ranging from the basic to the specialized" (*Introd.*) and intended for use by hobbyists and specialists alike. Each entry offers a brief definition of the term, followed by an account of its history, purpose, physical appearance, etc., as applicable. Cross-references; bibliography.

§ Related encyclopedias: Ewald Junge's *World coin encyclopedia* (London : Barrie & Jenkins ; N.Y. : Morrow, 1984) and B. Hobson and R. Obojski's *Illustrated encyclopedia of world coins*, rev. and expanded ed. (Garden City, N.Y. : Doubleday, [1983] ; London : Hale, [1984]).   CJ69.D67

Frey, Albert Romer. Dictionary of numismatic names : with Glossary of numismatic terms in English, French, German, Italian, Swedish / by Mark M. Salton. [N.Y.] : Barnes & Noble, [1947]. 311, 94 p. **BG179**

Repr. : London : Spink, 1973.

A reprint of a work originally published in 1917 as v. 50 of *American journal of numismatics*; gives information about terms used in numismatic works in English and foreign languages. Includes a list of principal authorities cited; a geographical index; and a paper money index. The Glossary lists numismatic terms alphabetically in each of the five languages, with equivalents in the other four, but without definitions. CJ67.F7

Room, Adrian. Dictionary of coin names. London ; N.Y. : Routledge & K. Paul, 1987. 250 p. : ill. **BG180**
The introduction offers an explanation of "numismonymics," together with discussions of the use of multiple and/or colloquial names, the presence of portraits, geographical and historical links to monarchs, and values. Entries give a skeletal history of each named coin. A majority of the entries are for foreign names. A "glossary" precedes the dictionary and functions as a small dictionary of technical terms. CJ69.R66

Schrötter, Friedrich. Wörterbuch der Münzkunde / hrsg. von Friedrich Frhr V. Schrötter ; in Verbindung mit N. Bauer ... [et al.]. Berlin : W. de Gruyter, 1930. 777 p., [14] leaves of plates : ill. **BG181**
Repr., 1970.
An encyclopedia of numismatics from ancient to modern times.
§ Related title: Tyll Kroha's *Lexikon der Numismatik* ([Gütersloh] : Bertelsmann Lexikon-Verlag, [1977]). CJ67.S3

Handbooks

Cribb, Joe. The coin atlas : the world of coinage from its origins to the present day / Joe Cribb, Barrie Cook, Ian Carradice. N.Y. : Facts on File, c1990. 337 p. : ill. (some col.). **BG182**
With an introduction by the American Numismatic Association.
Arranged by continent, then by country, providing an overview of the history of each nation's coinage. Maps are plentiful (totaling 100) and illustrations assist in identification of coins discussed. Glossary and bibliography are brief.
§ An earlier work with excellent chronologies is *All the monies of the world : a chronicle of currency values*, by Franz Pick and René Sédillot (CH286). CJ59.C75

Holtz, Walter. Lexikon der Münzabkürzungen mit geschlichtlich-geographischen Erläuterungen. München : Klinkhardt & Biermann, 1981. 606 p. : ill. **BG183**
Provides coin collectors and historians with a key to abbreviated Latin inscriptions of medieval and modern European coins. In three alphabetical lists: Neuzeit [since c1500]; Religiös-kirchliche Abkürzungen [medieval and modern]; Mittelalter [c800 to c1500]. A three-column page gives abbreviation, expanded Latin term, and German translation. Includes a section of background notes of historical and geographical information; list of Latin place names with modern German equivalents. Bibliography. CJ2455.H64

Schlickeysen, F. W. A. Erklärung der Abkürzungen auf Münzen der neueren Zeit, des Mittelalters und des Altertums, sowie auf Denkmünzen und münzartigen Zeichen / [von] F. W. A. Schjlickeysen, R. Pallmann. 4. Aufl. Graz : Akademische Druck-u. Verlagsanstalt, 1961. 511 p. : ill. **BG184**
Reprint of 3. verb. und verm. Aufl. bearb. von Reinhold Pallmann (Berlin : Spemann, 1896). 1st ed., 1855; 2nd ed., 1882.
The section on medieval and modern coins includes information on marks on Russian coins. The section on antiquity concerns Greek and Roman coins. CJ71.S3

History

Coins : an illustrated survey, 650 BC to the present day / Martin J. Price, gen. ed. N.Y. : Methuen ; London : Hamlyn/Country Life, [1980]. 320 p. : ill. **BG185**
Without pretending to be a complete history of coinage "this volume sets out to illustrate through more than 2000 photographs the main trends of coinage in its many different facets; and the accompanying essays [by various authors] show how the coins relate to their cultural and historical background."—*Foreword*. Short essays treat the nature of coinage, money before coinage, many periods of Western history, paper money, ancient Near East, Islam, India, and the Far East. Size of coin is indicated in the "List of illustrations." Brief bibliography and an index, chiefly of names and places. CJ59.C64

Biography

Forrer, Leonard. Biographical dictionary of medallists : coin, gem, and seal-engravers, mint-masters, etc., ancient and modern, with references to their works B.C.500–A.D.1900. London : Spink, 1902–30. 8 v. : ill. **BG186**
Repr.: London : Baldwin, 1979–80.
Contents: v. 1–6, A–Z; v. 7–8, Suppl. A–Z. Vol. 8 contains a 2nd suppl. and an index of illustrations.
Serves as a corpus that lists and attributes known medals prior to the 20th century.
See also J.S. Martin, *Biographical dictionary of medallists by L. Forrer : index* (London : Numismatic Soc., 1987), also known as *Index to the Biographical dictionary of medallists*. Appendixes: Society medals; Schools and institutions; Exhibition medals. CJ5535.F7

Catalogs

Friedberg, Robert. Gold coins of the world : from ancient times to the present : an illustrated standard catalogue with valuations. 6th ed. / rev. and ed. by Arthur L. Friedberg and Ira S. Friedberg. Clifton, N.J. : Coin and Currency Inst., c1992. 723 p. : ill. **BG187**
Subtitle: Complete from 600 A.D. to the present. An illustrated standard catalogue with valuations.
1st ed., 1958; 5th ed., 1980.
Preface in English, French, German, Italian, and Spanish.
"The aim has been to start the coin issues of each place with the first distinctive coins that positively identify the place as we know its name today."—*Pref., 5th ed.* In two parts, each alphabetical by country, then chronological by issue: pt. 1, from earliest date to 1960; pt. 2, recent issues beginning 1960. Geographical index. CJ1545.F74

Krause, Chester L. Standard catalog of world coins / by Chester L. Krause and Clifford Mishler ; Colin R. Bruce II, ed. 21st ed. [Iola, Wis. : Krause Publications, 1994]. 2128 p. : ill. **BG188**
1st ed. 1972.
A popular catalog of national coin issues. Arranged geographically, with more than 1,300 coin-issuing countries, states, provinces, and cities, and some 51,000 coin photographs. Glossary; index of coin denominations; mint index; legend index; illustrated guide to mint names for Arabic, Persian, and Turkish coinage.
§ Another Krause catalog, similar in format, is *Standard catalog of world gold coins* ([1985]. 640 p.). CJ1755.K72

Pick, Albert. Standard catalog of world paper money / by Albert Pick ; ed. by Neil Shafer and Colin R. Bruce II. 6th ed. Iola, Wis. : Krause Publications, c1990. 2 v. : ill. **BG189**
1st ed., 1975; 5th ed., 1986.

Contents: v. 1, Specialized issues; v. 2, General issues.
Includes bibliographical references (v. 2, p. 34–35) and indexes.

HG353.P543

Rayner, P. Alan. English silver coinage from 1649. 5th rev. ed. London : Seaby, 1992. 254 p. : ill.   **BG190**

1st ed., 1949; 4th ed., 1974, ed. by Herbert Allen Seaby.

Contents: Pt. 1, Pre-decimal currency, 1649–1971; pt. 2, Decimal currency; pt. 3, Nickel-brass high-value coins. Appendixes: Coinage tables, select bibliography.

Aims "to provide collectors with a standard work of reference ... giving details of dates, varieties, comparative rarity, patterns and proofs, etc."—*Introd.*

§ *Coins of England and the United Kingdom*, ed. by P. Frank Purvey (20th ed. London : Seaby, 1984. 320 p. [Standard catalogue of British coins, v. 1]), is an illustrated catalog for both collectors and historians, covering coins from Celtic and Roman eras to the present. Values given represent the retail scale at Seaby's. Issued annually.

CJ2485.S4

Reinfeld, Fred. Catalogue of the world's most popular coins / by Fred Reinfeld and Burton Hobson. 12th ed. / ed. by Robert Obojski. N.Y. : Sterling, c1986. 580 p. : ill.   **BG191**

1st ed., 1956.

Coins are listed by country or issuing region, with illustrations of both obverse and reverse sides and price quotes.

CJ63.R4

Yeoman, Richard S. A catalog of modern world coins, 1850–1964 / rev. and ed. by Arthur L. Friedberg and Ira S. Friedberg. 13th ed. Fort Lee, N.J. : Coin & Currency Inst., [1983]. 507 p.   **BG192**

1st ed., 1957.

Includes coins of all countries, in all metals, issued from 1850 to 1964. Gives estimated values in multiple conditions; Yeoman and Friedberg numbers.

§ A companion series, *Current coins of the world* (ed.1 [1966]–7 [1976]) served as a reference for coins currently in circulation (i.e., from about 1955).

CJ1753.Y4

United States

Breen, Walter H. Walter Breen's complete encyclopedia of U.S. and colonial coins. Garden City, N.Y. : Doubleday, c1988. 754 p. : ill.   **BG193**

Describes in 8,035 entries (and 4,000 photographs) "historical circumstances of issue, physical characteristics, designer, engraver, mint of issue, quantity minted, and level of rarity."—*How to use this book.* Provides four metrology tables, bibliography, abbreviations, typographical conventions, glossary, and indexes (names, subjects).

§ Supersedes the author's and Anthony Swiatek's *The encyclopedia of United States silver & gold commemorative coins, 1892–1954* (N.Y. : Arco Publ./F.C.I. Pr., [1981]).

CJ1830.B69

Friedberg, Robert. Paper money of the United States : a complete illustrated guide with valuations. 13th ed. / with additions and revisions by Ira S. and Arthur L. Friedberg. Fort Lee, N.J. : Coin and Currency Institute, [1992]. 284 p. : ill.   **BG194**

"Large size notes, fractional currency, small size notes, encased postage stamps from the first year of paper money, 1861, to the present."—*t.p.*

1st ed., 1953.

A complete listing of colonial and Continental currency, 1690–1788.

§ Useful for illustrations is Eric P. Newman, *The early paper money of America* ([Racine, Wis. : Whitman Publ. Co., 1967]).

HG591.F7

A guide book of United States coins : fully illustrated catalog and valuation list, 1616 to date. Ed. 1 (1947)– . Racine, Wis. : Western Publ. Co., [1946?]– . Annual.   **BG195**

47th ed., 1993.

Subtitle varies slightly.

At head of title: The official red book of United States coins.

By Richard S. Yeoman; ed. by Kenneth Bressett.   CJ1826.G785

Hessler, Gene. The comprehensive catalog of U.S. paper money : all United States federal currency since 1812. 5th ed. Port Clinton, Ohio : BNR Pr., 1992. 518 p. : ill.   **BG196**

1st ed., 1974; 4th ed., 1983.

Includes both large- and small-sized notes, U.S. military payment certificates, and "all the notes circulated under U.S. authority in the districts, territories, and possessions outside the continental United States."—*Pref., 1st ed.*

HG591.H47

Krause, Chester L. Standard catalog of U.S. paper money / Chester L. Krause and Robert F. Lemke. 12th ed. [Iola, Wis. : Krause Publ., 1993]. 206 p. : ill.   **BG197**

1st ed., 1981.

Intended as "a guide to those paper money issues since 1812 of the Government of the United States of America, along with several related currency issues which are traditionally collected by paper money hobbyists...."—*Introd.* Gives brief background information on large size notes, national bank notes, small size notes, etc., selected illustrations, and lists of notes and their current values.   HG591.K7

POSTAGE STAMPS

Guides

Lehnus, Donald J. Angels to zeppelins : a guide to the persons, objects, topics, and themes on United States postage stamps, 1847–1980. Westport, Conn. : Greenwood Pr., 1982. 279 p. : ill.   **BG198**

Analyzes U.S. postage issues for the "persons, objects, topics, and themes" of the subtitle and presents the data in lists and tables, accompanied by text. Discusses such topics as nationality and birthplace, professions, persons honored while alive, etc., incorporating brief identification of person or theme, but information on categories and statistics predominates. Scott and Minkus numbers given in an appendix. Bibliography; index.   HE6185.U5L34

Bibliography

Smith, Chester M. American philatelic periodicals. State College, Pa. : Amer. Philatelic Research Lib., 1978. 79 p.   **BG199**

A title listing of American philatelic journals, giving where possible: title (with cross-references for changes, variants, etc.), publisher, dates, and number of volumes or issues published. Index of publishers, and a state-by-state geographic index. Does not locate holdings.

Z7164.P85S63

Library catalogs

Collectors Club (New York, N.Y.). Library. Philately : a catalog of the Collectors Club Library, New York City. Boston : G.K. Hall, 1974. 682 p.   **BG200**

Contents: Author catalog; Subject catalog; Title catalog; Periodicals catalog.

Reproduction of the catalog cards for one of the world's largest philatelic collections.   Z7164.P85C64

Crawford, James Ludovic Lindsay. Catalogue of the philatelic library of the Earl of Crawford / by E. D. Bacon. London : Philatelic Literature Soc., 1911. 924 col. **BG201**

Repr., with Suppl. and Addenda: N.Y. : B. Franklin, 1969.

Originally publ. for private distribution as: J. L. L. Crawford, *Bibliotheca Lindesiana*, v. 7: *A bibliography of the writings, general, special and periodical, forming the literature of philately* (Aberdeen : Univ. Pr., 1911. 924 col.).

———. ——— *Supplement* (1926. 136 col.). Contains corrections and additions of separate works published to the end of 1908, and of periodicals to the end of 1906.

———. ——— *Addenda to the supplement* (1938. 8 p.). Issued as a supplement to the March 1938 issue of *London philatelist*, official journal of the Philatelic Literature Soc.

Revised ed.: British Library. *Catalogue of the Crawford library of philatelic literature at the British Library* (Fishkill, N.Y. : Printer's Stone in assoc. with the British Library, 1991. 923, 136, 8 p.).

Dictionaries

Konwiser, Harry Myron. American philatelic dictionary and Colonial and Revolutionary posts. N.Y. : Minkus, 1947. 152 p., 56 p. : ill. **BG202**

Defines the "words and phrases that carry a definite meaning to the philatelist."—*Foreword. Colonial and Revolutionary posts : a history of the American postal systems* (at end) is a partial reprint of a work published in 1931 (Richmond, Va. : Dietz Printing Co.).

HE6196.K6

Handbooks

Cabeen, Richard McP. Standard handbook of stamp collecting. New rev. ed. N.Y. : Crowell, [1979]. 630 p. : ill. **BG203**

Repr. : N.Y. : Harper & Row ; Toronto : Fitzhenry & Whiteside, 1986.

Rev. by the Committee on Publications, Collectors Club of Chicago.

1st ed., 1957.

A thorough and wide-ranging guide in five main sections: Introduction to stamp collecting; Postal history and cover collecting; Miscellaneous subjects; Technical matters; Classification and identification. Glossary. Index.

§ Related guide: Richard H. Rosichan, *Stamps and coins* (Littleton, Colo. : Libraries Unlimited, 1974). HE6215.C2

History

Brookman, Lester G. The United States postage stamps of the 19th century. North Miami, Fla. : D.G. Phillips Publ. Co., [c1989]. 3 v. : ill. **BG204**

Provides historical and technical information. First published as *The 19th century postage stamps of the United States* (N.Y. : Lindquist, 1947). The current edition is a reprint of the 1966–67 ed. and has some 450 new illustrations and additional material. Useful for historical and technical information. HE6185.U5B752

Catalogs

Partington, Paul G. Who's who on the postage stamps of Eastern Europe. Metuchen, N.J. : Scarecrow, 1979. 498 p. : ill. **BG205**

In two sections: Native personalities and Foreign personalities. Full biographical sketches are provided in the first category; dates and brief identification in the second. References to *Scott standard postage stamp catalogue* (BG206) are given, as are sources of biographical information. Useful to the general reader as well as to the philatelist. Includes a topical index, by profession. CT759.P37

Scott standard postage stamp catalogue. 129th ed.– . N.Y. : Scott Publ. Co., 1973– . Annual. **BG206**

150th ed., 1994.

Title and publisher's name vary.

Continuously published since 1867(?).

Recent editions published in 5 v. Contents: v. 1, United States and affiliated territories, United Nations, British Commonwealth of Nations, v. 2–5, European countries and colonies, independent nations of Africa, Asia, Latin America [arranged alphabetically].

Gives illustrations, description, denominations, and value of the principal stamps, used and unused, of all countries.

§ Related title: *Specialized catalogue of United States stamps* (51st ed. [1973]– . Annual). 72nd ed. (1994) publ. Sidney, Ohio : Scott Publ. Co., 1993. HE6226.S48

BH

Theater and Performing Arts

Although live performances of plays, dance, and music (all among the earliest forms of cultural expression) continue to attract interest and support, the scope of the performing arts has been greatly expanded by the newer media of radio, television, film, and video. This section lists reference works that treat (1) performing arts in general, including popular entertainment such as the circus; (2) performance aspects of live theater; (3) dance; (4) film; (5) performance and entertainment aspects of television and radio. Works dealing with plays and history of the drama will be found in section BE, Literature; with music, including opera and musical drama in BJ, Music; with economic and social aspects of broadcast media in Mass media under CH, Economics; and with technical aspects of broadcast media in EJ, Engineering.

Interest in film as an art form, together with easy access to films by way of television and video, has led to a remarkable proliferation of reference works on film. Although some of these are of indifferent quality, many provide information not found readily elsewhere. The selection of film resources given here is therefore generous.

PERFORMING ARTS (GENERAL)

Guides

Pruett, Barbara J. Popular entertainment research : how to do it and how to use it. Metuchen, N.J. : Scarecrow, 1992. 581 p.   **BH1**

A wide-ranging guide to information on the entertainment industries, featuring full annotations of resources and extensive practical advice on search strategies. Emphasis lies on the mainstream forms of theater, popular music, film, and broadcasting (television, radio, video), as well as on commercial entertainment in general. Each of these areas is covered in a separate chapter, which describes: the research context; reference works (in a single alphabetical sequence); periodicals; libraries, research centers, and archives; and organizations.

Preliminary chapters examine the research process in general, interviewing techniques, computers and databases, and "small town research" (for relevant general reference works), while two concluding chapters detail sources for collectors and research resources in Great Britain. Cross-references; index of authors, titles, and organizations. Limited to English-language sources.

§ An older guide, Marion K. Whalon, *Performing arts research : a guide to information sources* (Detroit : Gale, 1976. 280 p.) has a somewhat more historical orientation, provides coverage of dance and classical music, and describes important foreign language sources. Arranged by type of source (dictionaries, directories, bibliographies, etc.); author-title-subject index.   PN1576.P78

Wilmeth, Don B. American and English popular entertainment : a guide to information sources. Detroit : Gale, [1980]. 465 p. (Performing arts information guide series, v. 7).   **BH2**

"In general, popular entertainment in the context of this guide refers to live amusements created by professional showmen for profit and aimed at broad, relatively unsophisticated audiences. A small section is devoted to precinematic optical entertainments. ... "—*Pref.* Includes fairs, circuses, carnivals, minstrel shows, dime museums, burlesque, lyceum and chautauqua, stage magic, puppetry, popular theater, etc. Topical arrangement, with author, title, and subject indexes. Nearly 2,500 items (books, periodical articles, and dissertations) with brief annotations.

§ Wilmeth covers many of the same forms in his collection of bibliographic essays on American popular culture, *Variety entertainment and outdoor amusements : a reference guide* (Westport, Conn. : Greenwood, 1982. 242 p.).   Z7511.W53

Bibliography

Performing arts books, 1876–1981 : including an international index of current serial publications. N.Y. : Bowker, c1981. 1656 p.   **BH3**

Derived from Bowker's American Book Publishing Record database, "a comprehensive bibliography of over a hundred years of United States publishing in the performing arts as catalogued by the Library of Congress."—*Pref.* About 50,000 book entries, with full bibliographic information, listed under 12,000 Library of Congress subject headings for topics and names. Includes author and title indexes.   Z6935.P43

Toole-Stott, Raymond. Circus and allied arts : a world bibliography, 1500–1957: based mainly on circus literature in the British Museum, the Library of Congress, the Bibliothèque Nationale and on his own collection. Derby, Eng. : Harpur & Sons, [1958–71]. 4 v. : ill., facsims.   **BH4**

Title page of v. 4 gives the dates of coverage as "1500–1970" and includes the Universiteitsbibliotheek van Amsterdam among the basic collections.

Lists books and pamphlets in various languages dealing with circus history and biography; technical aspects of performances; and the circus in drama, literature, art, and fiction. Vol. 3 has an index to v. 1–3; v. 4 has its own index.   Z7514.C6S7

Library resources

Bibliothèques et musées des arts du spectacle dans le monde = Performing arts libraries and museums of the world / publ. sous la dir. de André Veinstein et Alfred S. Golding. 4e éd. Paris : Ed. du Centre National de la Recherche Scientifique, 1992. 740 p.   **BH5**

French and English text in parallel columns; separate title pages in French and English.

1st ed., 1960; 3rd ed., 1984.

Describes performing arts collections in public and private repositories in 44 countries. Indicates size and nature of holdings, regulations for use, hours, catalogs, etc.; level of detail varies, depending on questionnaire responses. Broad scope, encompassing legitimate theater, opera and musical theater, film, radio, television, puppetry, circus, and other forms. Index of cited names and special collections.   Z675.P45B53

Performing arts resources. v. 1 (1974)– . N.Y. : Theatre Library Assoc., [1975]– . Annual.   **BH6**

Publisher varies: v. 1–3 publ. for Theatre Library Assoc. by Drama Book Specialists, N.Y.; v. 4– publ. by Theatre Library Assoc.

According to prefatory note in v. 16, "designed to gather and disseminate scholarly articles dealing with location of resource materials relating to theatre, film, television, radio, video and popular entertainments; descriptions, listings, or evaluations of the contents of such collections, whether public or private; and monographs of previously unpublished original source material." Most of the early volumes were devoted to descriptions of specific U.S. collections (e.g., Folger Shakespeare Library, Vanderbilt Television News Archives) and served to update and expand listings in William C. Young's *American theatrical arts* (BH7). In recent years, coverage has shifted somewhat toward articles on archival practice and translations or reproductions of historical materials. Useful as an overview of performing arts documentation. Z6935.P46

Young, William C. American theatrical arts : a guide to manuscripts and special collections in the United States and Canada. Chicago : Amer. Libr. Assoc., 1971. 166 p. **BH7**
Designed "to help scholars and students to locate manuscripts and other primary materials relating to the American and Canadian theatrical arts in the possession of institutions in the United States and Canada."—*Introd.* Manuscripts and special collections are briefly described under repository arranged according to National Union Catalog symbol. Index of persons and subjects. Z6935.Y68

Indexes

Guide to the performing arts. 1957–68. N.Y. : Scarecrow, 1960–72. **BH8**
1957–67 comp. by Sara Yancey Belknap; 1968 by Louis Rachow and Katherine Hartley.
Indexes articles and illustrations in 40–50 primarily U.S. and Canadian periodicals. Began as a supplement to *Guide to the musical arts* (N.Y. : Scarecrow, 1957); partially absorbed *Guide to dance periodicals* (BH136) in 1962. Despite variations in coverage and sources indexed from year to year, provides access to many articles not indexed elsewhere during its decade-plus of publication. ML118.G8

Reviews and criticism

Performing arts [microform]. v. 9, card 61 (Mar. 1983)– . [Greenwich, Conn.] : NewsBank, 1983– . Monthly. **BH9**
Continues *Newsbank performing arts*, 1975–83.
A clipping service on microfiche, reproducing reviews, interviews, and news articles on theater, music, dance, and recordings drawn from newspapers published in more than 450 U.S. cities. Indexed by the printed *Review of the arts : performing arts* (Greenwich, Conn. : NewsBank, 1975– . Monthly). Index entries for reviews include title, author(s), performing company or group, and category (e.g., theater, dance, opera); entries refer to year, fiche number, and fiche row and column. Theatrical performers and directors are indexed for interviews and articles but not for reviews. A valuable source for reviews of regional productions and performances.
•In machine-readable form as part of *NewsBank reference service plus* [database] (AE111 *note*).

Encyclopedias

Enciclopedia dello spettacolo. Roma : Casa Ed. le Maschere, [1954–62]. 9 v. : ill. **BH10**
Similar in format and in profusion of illustration to the *Enciclopedia italiana* (AB66), and designed to cover the "grand spectacle" from antiquity to the present. Includes the theater, opera, ballet, motion pictures, vaudeville, the circus, etc. Treats performers, authors, composers, directors, designers, etc.; types of entertainment; dramatic themes; historical and technical subjects; organizations and acting companies; and pertinent place-names. International roster of contributors; good bibliographies.

————. *Appendice di aggiornamento. Cinema* ([Venezia : Istit. per Collaborazione Culturale, 1963]. 178 col. ; ill.).
————. *Aggiornamento 1955–1965* (Roma : Unione Editoriale, [1966]. 1292 col. ; ill.). Mainly devoted to biographical sketches of contemporary figures not found in the basic set.
———— *Indice repertorio* (Roma : Unione Editoriale, [1968]. 1024 p.). An index of titles of works mentioned in the main set and in the *Aggiornamento*, referring to the article in which the work is mentioned but not to volume or page. PN1625.E7

Ogden, Tom. Two hundred years of the American circus : from Aba-Daba to the Zoppe-Zavatta Troupe. N.Y. : Facts on File, c1993. 402 p. : ill. **BH11**
Contains entries for terms, troupes, acts, animals, individuals, films, and stage productions associated with circus history in the U.S. Extensively cross-referenced. Bibliography; general index. GV1815.O33

Dictionaries

Wilmeth, Don B. The language of American popular entertainment : a glossary of argot, slang, and terminology. Westport, Conn. : Greenwood, c1981. 305 p. **BH12**
Attempts "to collect in one source the special language of the principal forms of American popular entertainment: circus, carnival, vaudeville, burlesque, tent shows, popular theatre, magic shows, medicine shows, early optical entertainments, and fairs."—*Introd.* Select bibliography. PN1579.W5

Directories

Handel's national directory for the performing arts. 4th ed. (1988)– . New Providence, N.J. : R.R. Bowker, c1988– . Irregular. **BH13**
Publisher varies; prior to 5th ed. (1992), publ. Dallas : NDPA, Inc.
Formed by the merger of *National directory for the performing arts and civic centers* and *National directory for the performing arts/educational*.
Contents: v. 1, Organizations and facilities; v. 2, Educational institutions.
Vol. 1 lists and describes performing arts groups and venues by state and city, with city subdivisions for dance, instrumental music, vocal music, theater, performing series (e.g., festivals, historical dramas) and local facilities. Organizational data include addresses, telephone and fax numbers, founding date, purpose, management, number of staff (paid and volunteer), budget, income sources, attendance, and facilities used. Facility descriptions give type of stage and dimensions, seating capacity, year built, architect, rental contact, resident groups, etc. Separate indexes for groups by performance categories and for facility names; combined alphabetical index of all organizations and facilities.
Vol. 2 lists, by state, colleges and schools offering programs in dance, music, and theater. Directory information for each school is followed by descriptions of individual departments, showing department heads, courses, degrees, number of faculty and students, technical training, financial assistance, resident artists, performing groups, workshops and festivals, etc. Indexes by performance areas and institutional names. PN2289.H34

The lively arts information directory / Steven R. Wasserman and Jacqueline Wasserman O'Brien, editors. 2nd ed. Detroit : Gale, c1985. 1040 p. **BH14**
1st ed., 1982.
Subtitle: A guide to the fields of music, dance, theater, film, radio, and television in the United States and Canada, covering professional and trade organizations, arts agencies, government grant

sources, foundations, educational programs, journals and periodicals, consultants, special libraries, research and information centers, festivals, awards, and book and media publishers.

In 13 directory sections, by category of information, each with its own indexes (e.g., alphabetical, geographic, subject).   PN2289.L55

The nostalgia entertainment sourcebook : the complete resource guide to classic movies, vintage music, old-time radio and theatre / comp. by Randy Skretvedt and Jordan R. Young. Beverly Hills, Calif. : Moonstone Pr., c1991. 158 p. : ill.
                                                        BH15

Intended to "cover roughly the period 1920–1950" (*Pref.*) for popular forms of entertainment, this collector's and enthusiast's guide has broader value for performing arts research. In four sections (movies, music, radio, theater), each with its own categories, depending on the medium (film and video dealers, record companies, rental libraries, memorabilia and book dealers, fan clubs, periodicals, festivals, cable TV networks, radio stations, etc.), each identifying archives, libraries, special collections, and museums of interest. Appendixes for publishers and reference books; bibliography; index. Entries include capsule descriptions.   PN1577.N67

Performing arts yearbook for Europe : PAYE. 1st ed. (1991)– . London : Arts Publ. International, 1990– . Annual.
                                                        BH16

A classified directory, listing: ministries of culture and funding agencies; national organizations; supranational organizations; opera companies; orchestras; theater companies; puppet companies; ballet and dance companies; festivals; venues; promoters; agents and producers; radio and television stations; recorded media companies; competitions; publications; courses; and products and services. Subarranged by country. Index of organizations, companies, and facilities.

PN2570.P44

Slide, Anthony. Sourcebook for the performing arts : a directory of collections, resources, scholars, and critics in theatre, film, and television / comp. by Anthony Slide, Patricia King Hanson, and Stephen L. Hanson. N.Y. : Greenwood, 1988. 227 p.   **BH17**

In three parts: (1) a listing by state of colleges and universities, libraries, and historical societies that have research collections in theatre, film, radio, and television, with brief notes on their holdings; (2) a who's who of 200 leading academics, critics, archivists, historians, librarians, and scholars; (3) addresses of bookshops, journals, organizations, studios and production companies, networks, etc. Name and topical index to the first two parts.   PN2289.S55

Stern's performing arts directory. 1989– . [New York?] : DM, Inc., c1988– . Annual.   **BH18**

Continues: *Dance magazine annual*, 1973–84; *Performing arts directory*, 1985–87.

In three parts: Dance, Music, Resources. Lists U.S. and Canadian dancers, singers, musicians, companies and other groups, professionals (e.g., composers, conductors, choreographers), schools, services, organizations, merchandisers, festivals, presenters, etc. Includes international listings for dance companies (ballet, ethnic, folk, national, modern), opera companies, symphony orchestras, and festivals. The section on resources has categories relating to the performing arts in general, such as artists' representatives, costume and set designers, theater design consultants, and make-up suppliers.   GV1580.D247

Handbooks

Kaplan, Mike. Variety's directory of major U.S. show business awards. N.Y. : Bowker, 1989. 750 p.   **BH19**

Has separate chronological rosters for the Oscars, Emmys, Tonys, and Grammys through 1988, with both winners and nominees listed. Also notes Pulitzer Prize-winning plays. Name and title index.

PN2270.A93K36

Leonard, William Torbert. Theatre : stage to screen to television. Metuchen, N.J. : Scarecrow, 1981. 2 v. (1804 p.).   **BH20**

Documents productions of those works that have been presented in all three media. Entry is by title of the play; a synopsis is followed by a section giving comments on the original and subsequent productions and notes on critical reception. Stage, screen, and television credits are given for each, including revivals, remakes under variant titles, etc. Limited to American and British stage productions; excludes Greek classics, Gilbert and Sullivan, and Shakespearean plays.

Alvin H. Marill's *More theatre : stage to screen to television* (Metuchen, N.J. : Scarecrow, 1993. 2 v.) is an updated supplement, which also includes additions and corrections to the 1981 set.

PN2189.L44

Sharp, Harold S. Index to characters in the performing arts / comp. by Harold S. Sharp and Marjorie Z. Sharp. N.Y. : Scarecrow, 1966–73. 4 v. in 6.   **BH21**

Imprint varies.

Contents: pt. 1, Non-musical plays (2 v.); pt. 2, Operas and musical productions (2 v.); pt. 3, Ballets; pt. 4, Radio and television.

A dictionary of major and minor characters (about 73,000 in all) from works of all periods.   PN1579.S45

Biography

Contemporary theatre, film, and television. v. 1– . Detroit : Gale, [1984]– . Annual.   **BH22**

Subtitle: A biographical guide featuring performers, directors, writers, producers, designers, managers, choreographers, technicians, composers, executives, dancers, and critics in the United States and Great Britain.

Intended as a successor to *Who's who in the theatre* (BH122), extending its scope to film and television and expanding the categories of individuals selected for inclusion. Modeled on *Contemporary authors* (AH42), each volume includes biographies of new and established talents, as well as revised sketches and obituaries of persons profiled in earlier volumes of this series or its predecessor; emphasizes currently active American personalities. Entry data has varied; v. 11 (1994) includes personal information (e.g., birth place and date, family, colleges attended, professional training), contact addresses, career capsules, memberships, awards and honors, full credits, recordings, writings, adaptations, and other sources (usually newspaper and magazine articles). Selective inclusion of photographs discontinued after v. 8 (1990). Cumulative index in each volume refers to all sketches in the series, plus v. 16–17 (the final two volumes) of *Who's who in the theatre*, and the cumulation of the latter's first 15 volumes, *Who was who in the theatre* (see BH122).   PN2285.C58

Mapp, Edward. Directory of blacks in the performing arts. 2nd ed. Metuchen, N.J. : Scarecrow, 1990. 594 p.   **BH23**

1st ed., 1978.

Provides information on "black performing artists in film, television, radio, theatre, dance and musical performance."—*Pref.* Although most listings are for contemporary Americans, also includes important nonliving personalities (e.g., Bill Robinson, Josephine Baker). Alphabetical by name, entries give profession(s), birth (and death) date, place of birth, education, address, special interests, honors, career data, memberships, and credits by medium. Bibliography; classified index by profession.   PN1590.B53M3

Smith, Ronald L. Who's who in comedy : comedians, comics, and clowns from vaudeville to today's stand-ups. N.Y. : Facts on File, c1992. 528 p. : ill.   **BH24**

Affectionate narrative profiles containing personal details and critical commentary, as well as career highlights and a list of major credits. Not limited to living entertainers (many silent film stars are profiled) but, with a few exceptions (e.g., Cary Grant, Claudette Col-bert), omits "straight" actors who sometimes worked in comedy. Nickname/character name, catch phrase, and categorical indexes.

PN1583.S6

Variety obituaries : including a comprehensive index. v. 1– . N.Y. : Garland, 1988– . Biennial. **BH25**

Project editors: Chuck Bartelt and Barbara Bergeron.

Contents: v. 1–10, 1905/28–1984/86; v. 11, Index [1905–86]; v. 12, 1987–88; v. 13, 1989–90; v. 14, 1991–92.

Reprints from *Variety* news stories, editorials, and obituary columns covering the deaths of individuals connected with show business. Arranged chronologically by date of publication. Vols. 12– have their own indexes. PN1583.V35

Variety's who's who in show business / Mike Kaplan, ed. Rev. [i.e., 3rd] ed. N.Y. : Bowker, 1989. 412 p. **BH26**

1st ed., 1983; rev. ed., 1985.

6,500 entries for "major talents and executives in film, television, music and the legitimate theatre."—*Pref.* Emphasizes career data and professional credits. International in scope. PN1583.V37

Who's who in entertainment. 1989-90– . Wilmette, Ill. : Marquis Who's Who, c1988– . Irregular. **BH27**

The 2nd ed. (1992–93) contains "over 18,000 biographical sketches of the most prominent individuals in the entertainment industry, as well as those people who work behind the scenes."—*Pref.* Biographical/career data, most of it supplied by the biographees, is presented in standard Marquis format modeled on the publisher's *Who's who in America*. Ceased? PN1583.W47

Indexes

McNeil, Barbara. Performing arts biography master index : a consolidated index to over 270,000 biographical sketches of persons living and dead, as they appear in over 100 of the principal biographical dictionaries devoted to the performing arts / ed. by Barbara McNeil and Miranda C. Herbert. 2nd ed. Detroit : Gale, [1982], c1981. 701 p. (Gale biographical index series, no. 5). **BH28**

Rev. ed. of· *Theatre, film, and television biographies master index*, ed. by Dennis La Beau (Gale, 1979).

Doubles the number of entries in the first 1st ed. and expands coverage to reference works on music, dance, puppetry, and magic. Listings by name, as used in the cited source, with no standardization of variant forms and spellings. PN1583.M37

Perry, Jeb H. Variety obits : an index to obituaries in Variety, 1905–1978. Metuchen, N.J. : Scarecrow, 1980. 311 p. **BH29**

Unrelated to *Variety obituaries* (BH25), this is a selective index of the trade journal's death notices for "those people who worked in the production-related areas of motion pictures, television, radio, the legitimate stage, minstrelsy and vaudeville."—*Foreword.* Entries include age at death, date of death, profession, and issue/column of *Variety*. Individuals associated exclusively with the business side or with dance, music, cabaret, etc. are not covered. PN1583.P4

THEATER

Guides

Bailey, Claudia Jean. A guide to reference and bibliography for theatre research. 2nd ed., rev. and exp. Columbus : Ohio State Univ. Libr., Publ. Comm., 1983. 149 p. **BH30**

1st ed., 1971.

An annotated guide for the student and research worker. In two main sections: (1) General reference, and (2) Theatre and drama. The first part is very wide-ranging, covering national bibliography, library catalogs, general periodical and newspaper indexes, dissertation lists, etc.; the second deals with more specialized materials. Emphasis is on American and British theater. Author-title index. Z5781.B15

Bibliography

Asian theatre : a study guide and annotated bibliography / James R. Brandon, ed. Wash. : Univ. and College Theatre Assoc., 1979. 197 p. (Theatre perspectives, no. 1). **BH31**

A briefly annotated bibliography of 1,348 items for the English-language reader. Arranged by country, with subdivisions for (1) history, theory, practice; (2) plays; (3) audiovisual materials; (4) reference works. Country overviews are included, and additional subdivisions for genres, time periods, etc., used as required. No index.

Z3008.D7A84

Gray, John. Black theatre and performance : a pan-African bibliography. N.Y. : Greenwood, 1990. 414 p. (Bibliographies and indexes in Afro-American and African studies, no. 25). **BH32**

Attempts to "provide as comprehensive a record as possible of the wealth of performance/theatre genres to be found among the Black communities of sub-saharan Africa, the Caribbean, Latin America, Europe and Canada."—*Introd.* Cites 4,141 books, dissertations, archival materials, periodical and newspaper articles, and media in a variety of languages, arranged by regions, countries, and individual dramatists. Appendixes: reference works; regional list of playwrights and theatre companies. Artist, play title, subject, and author indexes.

Z5784.B56G7

New York Public Library. Research Libraries. Catalog of the theatre and drama collections. Boston : G.K. Hall, 1967–76. 51 v. **BH33**

Contents: pt. 1 [A], Drama collection: author listing (1967. 6 v.); pt. 1 [B], Drama collection: listing by cultural origin (1967. 6 v.); pt. 2, Theatre collection: books on the theatre (1967. 9 v.); pt. 3, Theatre collection: nonbook collection (1976. 30 v.).

Photoreproduction of card files of collections at the library. Pt. 1 has entries for editions of some 120,000 printed plays in Western languages, including translations from works written in Cyrillic, Hebrew, and Asian alphabets, and indexes some playscripts in anthologies and periodicals. Pt. 2 contains about 121,000 entries representing more than 23,500 volumes, including typescript plays and promptbooks, as well as selected periodical articles. Treats all aspects of theater (history, production techniques, acting, biography, etc.), encompassing film, television, circus, vaudeville, etc., but excluding dance, which is covered by *Dictionary catalog of the Dance Collection* (BH135). Pt. 3 reproduces about 744,000 cards for such archival and ephemeral materials as playbills, programs, production photographs, portraits of theater personalitites, reviews, and press clippings.

In 1973, supplements to Pt. 1 (548 p.) and Pt. 2 (2 v.) were published, covering cataloged additions through 1971. A second supplement, *Dictionary catalog of the theatre and drama collections, 1974* (1976. 276 p.) recorded items cataloged from 1972 through Sept. 1974.

———. *Bibliographic guide to theatre arts* (1975– . Boston : G.K. Hall, 1976– . Annual) lists materials newly cataloged by NYPL with additional entries from Library of Congress MARC tapes. Authors, titles, and subjects in a single alphabet. Z5785.N56

Steadman, Susan M. Dramatic re-visions : an annotated bibliography of feminism and theatre, 1972–1988. Chicago : Amer. Libr. Assoc., 1991. 367 p. **BH34**

A bibliography of English-language publications, dealing not only with the drama as literature but with performance aspects of the theater and with the work of feminist theater groups. Includes academic publications in theater and in feminism, other scholarly journals, and non-scholarly feminist publications. Emphasizes American publications, with secondary emphasis on British and Canadian criticism. Separate appendixes identify bibliographies and directories; special issues of journals and periodicals; and selected works published after 1988. Indexed by name, title, category (usually geographic place and time period), and subject. PN1590.W64

Stoddard, Richard. Theatre and cinema architecture : a guide to information sources. Detroit : Gale, c1978. 368 p. (Performing arts information guide series, v. 5). **BH35**

Cites more than 1,800 English-language and heavily illustrated foreign-language writings that emphasize architectural history of U.S. and European theaters, with some coverage of Canada, Australia, and other countries. Basic arrangement is by country and time period. Indexes for authors; architects, designers, consultants, and decorators; theater buildings and cinemas; and subjects. Z5784.S8S82

Periodicals

Stratman, Carl Joseph. American theatrical periodicals, 1789–1967 : a bibliographical guide. Durham, N.C. : Duke Univ. Pr., 1970. 133 p. **BH36**

Lists 685 magazines, newspapers, annuals, and other serials by year of first issue. Indicates U.S. library locations, including partial holdings, where these have been determined. Index of titles, editors, cities of publication, etc.

§ Stratman also compiled *Britain's theatrical periodicals, 1720–1967 : a bibliography* (N.Y. : New York Public Library, 1972. 160 p.), which lists 1,235 publications in chronological sequence and locates files in American, Canadian, and British libraries. Z6935.S75

Dissertations

Litto, Fredric M. American dissertations on the drama and the theatre : a bibliography. [Kent, Ohio] : Kent State Univ. Pr., [1969]. 519 p. **BH37**

Attempts to list "references to all doctoral dissertations on subjects related to theatre and drama completed in *all* academic departments of American (the United States and Canada) universities."—*Pref.* Computer-produced; the arrangement is by "reference code," with author, keyword-in-context, and subject indexes. Cutoff date is 1965.

§ Although there is no comparable bibliography for post-1965 dissertations, an annual feature, "Doctoral Projects in Progress in Theatre Arts," has appeared regularly in *Theatre journal* and its predecessor, *Educational theatre journal*, since 1950. Lists only dissertation work undertaken at U.S. institutions. Z5781.L56

Stage history

Arnott, James Fullarton. English theatrical literature, 1559–1900 : a bibliography, incorporating Robert W. Lowe's A bibliographical account of English theatrical literature published in 1888 / James Fullarton Arnott and John William Robinson. London : Society for Theatre Research, 1970. 486 p. **BH38**

Expands and revises Lowe's founding work. A scholarly, classified listing of pre-1901 imprints dealing with British theater. Areas covered include arts of the theater, the London theater, the theater out of London, biography, theory and criticism, and periodicals. Includes opera and music hall but excludes circus, ballet, dramatic texts, and (for the most part) textual criticism of plays. American and other overseas editions are noted, and holdings in major British and U.S. libraries are indicated. Indexes by author, short title, and place of publications.

Continued by: John Cavanagh's *British theatre : a bibliography, 1901–1985* (BH40). Z2014.D7A74

Ball, John. Bibliography of theatre history in Canada : the beginnings through 1984 = Bibliographie d'histoire du théâtre au Canada : des débuts-fin 1984 / ed. by John Ball and Richard Plant. Toronto : ECW Pr., 1992. 445 p. **BH39**

A revision and continuation of *A bibliography of Canadian theatre history, 1583–1975* (Toronto : Playwrights Co-op, 1976) and its *Supplement 1975–1976* (1979).

Classed bibliography of about 10,800 books and periodical articles on Canadian stage history and related topics (e.g., radio and television drama, set design, drama in education). Covers both English-Canadian and French-Canadian theater. Index of subjects, theaters, associations, and personal names. PN2301.B28

Cavanagh, John. British theatre : a bibliography, 1901 to 1985. Mottisfont, Hampshire, Eng. : Motley Pr., 1989. 510 p. (The Motley bibliographies, 1). **BH40**

Planned as a sequel to James Fullarton Arnott and John William Robinson's *English theatrical literature, 1559–1900* (BH38).

More than 9,300 20th-century books and pamphlets, dealing with all periods, are listed topically within "three major divisions: A. Theatre, B. Drama, C. Music. Division A emphasizes performance, describes theatres, stage conditions and the lives and work of those actually engaged in production. Division B, while excluding the more literary aspects of the play, covers the history of dramatic genres and influences, and the lives and work of dramatists. Division C deals with music as an adjunct to dramatic theatre, and with musical theatre, covering opera, operetta, and musical comedy."—*Pref.* Author and subject indexes. Z2014.D7C38

Duffy, Susan. The political left in the American theatre of the 1930's : a bibliographic sourcebook. Metuchen, N.J. : Scarecrow, 1992. 213 p. **BH41**

Contains nearly 1,300 entries for works on a vital period of U.S. theater history. Divided into publication categories: books (annotated); book chapters; periodical and newspaper articles (arranged by publication name); plays; and dissertations. Also identifies relevant archival collections and funding sources. Index. Z1231.D7D84

Langhans, Edward A. Eighteenth century British and Irish promptbooks : a descriptive bibliography. N.Y. : Greenwood, 1987. 268 p. : ill. (Bibliographies and indexes in the performing arts, no. 6). **BH42**

Describes in detail more than 380 promptbooks (production scripts annotated for stage directions, technical cues, etc.) located in U.S. and British libraries. Arranged by author, then by title. Appendix of prompters and annotators; bibliography. The topically arranged index includes such headings as "People named in annotated copies" and "Play titles, subtitles, and alternate titles."

§ Some 2,000 items from the Nisbet-Snyder Collection, Northern Illinois University Libraries, are listed in William R. Dubois, *English and American stage productions : an annotated checklist of prompt books 1800-1900* (Boston : G.K. Hall, 1973. 524 p.). PN2593.L36

Larson, Carl F. W. American regional theatre history to 1900 : a bibliography. Metuchen, N.J. : Scarecrow, 1979. 187 p. **BH43**

Arranged by state, then by city (exclusive of New York City). Nearly 1,500 items, including books, parts of books, theses, periodical and newspaper articles, and some manuscript sources. Indexed. Less inclusive than Carl Joseph Stratman's *Bibliography of the American theatre ...* (BH46), although it corrects errors in the earlier work and adds more recent materials. Z5781.L34

Silvester, Robert. United States theatre : a bibliography : from the beginning to 1990. N.Y. : G.K. Hall ; Romsey, Eng. : Motley Pr., 1993. 400 p. (The Motley bibliographies, 2). **BH44**

Organized like John Cavanagh's *British theatre* (BH40), lists 7,464 books, pamphlets, and theses on various aspects of the American stage. In three main divisions: (1) Theater, encompassing general reference, governmental and religious influences, technical production, acting, regional and local history, collective and individual biography, criticism, community and educational theater, and other topics; (2) Drama, for historical, critical, and biographical studies; and (3) Music (i.e., the stage musical and its creators). Reflects English and Native American cultural traditions, excluding most ethnic theater (to be treated in planned volumes on other cultures). Dance, mime, circus, puppetry, and opera are also excluded. Location in a major U.S. or British library is indicated for most items, with short descriptive annotations provided for some. Arrangement within subsections is chronological by imprint date. Subject and author indexes.

Stevens, David. English Renaissance theatre history : a reference guide. Boston : G.K. Hall, [1982]. 342 p.   **BH45**

An annotated bibliography of scholarship, arranged chronologically, 1664 through 1979. Generally omits items whose scope is purely literary. Index of authors and subjects.   Z2014.D7S78

Stratman, Carl Joseph. Bibliography of the American theatre, excluding New York City. [Chicago] : Loyola Univ. Pr., [1965]. 397 p.   **BH46**

Lists 3,856 books, periodical articles, theses, and dissertations on all phases of the American regional theater outside New York. Includes ballet, opera, children's theater, community theater, repertory theater, vaudeville, scenery, etc. Arranged by state, then city, with author-subject index. At least one location is indicated for each book.   Z1231.D7S8

——————— Restoration and eighteenth century theatre research : a bibliographical guide, 1900–1968 / Carl Joseph Stratman, David G. Spencer, and Mary Elizabeth Devine. Carbondale, Ill. : Southern Illinois Univ. Pr., [1971]. 811 p.   **BH47**

An alphabetical subject arrangement of more than 6,500 20th-century writings on Restoration and 18th-century theater research. Brief annotations for most entries. Indexed.   Z2014.D7S85

Taylor, Thomas J. American theatre history : an annotated bibliography. Pasadena, Calif. : Salem Pr., c1992. 162 p.   **BH48**

A selective bibliography (about 600 items) of books and dissertations, grouped as follows: The beginnings to 1914; 1914–1945; New York, 1945 to the present; Regional theatre; Experimental, ethnic, community, academic, and children's theatre. Also describes important periodicals. Emphasizes histories, critical studies, reference works, biographies, and memoirs published in the U.S. during the 20th century. Lively annotations. Index of names and a few topics.   Z5781.T25

Wilmeth, Don B. The American stage to World War I : a guide to information sources. Detroit : Gale, [1978]. 269 p. (Performing arts information guide series, v. 4).   **BH49**

Concerned with aspects of the American theater "other than the literature of the stage. Thus, the major thrust of this collection of sources is the legitimate stage as a purveyor of entertainment, a business, and a producer of drama."—*Pref.* Includes sections for general reference sources, bibliographies, indexes, histories, individual theater personalities, stagecraft, theater collections, etc. Brief annotations; author, title, and subject indexes.   Z1231.D7W55

Stagecraft

Howard, John T. A bibliography of theatre technology : acoustics and sound, lighting, properties, and scenery. Westport, Conn. : Greenwood, 1982. 345 p.   **BH50**

Lists some 5,700 items—books, periodical articles, theses—arranged by title within the categories noted in the subtitle (plus a brief section on research materials and collections). Subject and author indexes. Derived from an ongoing computer database at the University of Massachusetts Computing Center.   Z5784.S8H68

Kesler, Jackson. Theatrical costume : a guide to information sources. Detroit : Gale, c1979. 308 p. (Performing arts information guide series, v. 6).   **BH51**

Compiled primarily for costume designers as "a practical, utilitarian listing, mostly of English-title books in the field."—*Pref.* Since most publications included were issued after 1957, serves as a partial update of Isabel Stevensen Monro and Dorothy E. Cook's *Costume index* and its supplement (BG94). Classed arrangement of the more than 1,700 items, about half of which are concerned with historical costume of various cultures and "accoutrements and special categories of costume." Short annotations. Author, title, and subject indexes.   Z5691.K47

Stoddard, Richard. Stage scenery, machinery, and lighting : a guide to information sources. Detroit : Gale, c1977. 274 p. (Performing arts information guide series, v. 2).   **BH52**

Lists and briefly describes some 1,600 articles, pamphlets exhibition catalogs, and doctoral dissertations, for the most part written in English. Emphasizes historical aspects of scenic design and practice throughout the world. Scenery and lighting for opera and dance, as well as drama, are covered. Classified arrangement, with author, subject, and person as subject indexes.   Z5784.S8S79

Library resources

Howard, Diana. Directory of theatre resources : a guide to research collections and information services. 2nd ed. [London] : Library Assoc. Information Services Group and the Soc. for Theatre Research, 1986. 144 p.   **BH53**

1st ed., 1980.

In two sections: Pt. 1, Collections of theater material in libraries, museums and record offices (alphabetically arranged by city and collection); pt. 2, Theater societies and associations providing information services (by organization name). Brief descriptions of collections and services. Indexes to collection names and subjects.   PN2598.5.H68

McCallum, Heather. Directory of Canadian theatre archives / comp. by Heather McCallum and Ruth Pincoe. Halifax, N.S. : Dalhousie Univ., School of Library and Information Studies, 1992. 217 p. (Dalhousie University. School of Library and Information Studies. Occasional papers series, 53).   **BH54**

Rev. ed. of McCallum's *Theatre resources in Canadian collections* (Ottawa : National Library of Canada, 1973).

Identifies and briefly describes materials (principally nonbook and visual items) in government archives, public and academic libraries, drama departments, theater companies, schools, associations, museums, and private collections. Basic arrangement by province and city. Bibliography; general index.   Z5785.M29

Indexes

Dramatic index for 1909–49 : covering articles and illustrations concerning the stage and its players in the periodicals of America and England and including the dramatic books of the year. Boston : Faxon, 1910–52. Annual.   **BH55**

Issued separately, and also as pt. 2 of the *Annual magazine subject index, 1907–49* (AD262). Contains the cumulation of the *Dramatic index* published in the quarterly numbers of the *Bulletin of bibliography* (AA89). Vols. 1–8, 11–41 have appendix *Dramatic books and plays (in English)* published 1912–16, 1919–49.

An important index to materials on theatrical production and dramatic texts during the first half of the 20th century. Covering general and specialized English-language periodicals, serves as: a subject index to articles on theater, drama, opera, ballet, film, actors and actresses, opera singers, playwrights, producers, etc.; a locator for reviews of stage performances and films; an index to stage and dramatic portraits, scenes from plays, and other theatrical illustrations; and a record of play texts published either as books or in magazines. Articles are entered under subject only; reviews of plays are found under title, with cross-references from authors; costume portraits are indexed by performer name and cross-referenced by character name. While the index nominally begins with 1909, some retrospective indexing is included. The appendix, *Dramatic books and plays*, consists of (1) author list of books about the theater, (2) author list of play texts, and (3) title list of texts.

A consolidation of entries from the 41 volumes has been published as *Cumulated dramatic index, 1909–1949 : a cumulation of the F. W. Faxon company's Dramatic index* (Boston : G. K. Hall, 1965. 2 v.).   AI3.M26

Hoffman, Herbert H. Recorded plays : indexes to dramatists, plays, and actors. Chicago : Amer. Libr. Assoc., 1985. 139 p.
                                                        BH56

An index to "performances and readings of plays that have been recorded on phonodiscs, audio cassettes or tapes, video cassettes, and 16mm film"—*Pref.* 1,844 entries for some 700 plays (or excerpts) by 284 playwrights in 15 languages. Full information appears in the alphabetical author list, with title and actor indexes. List of anthology recordings analyzed and directory of recording companies.

                                                PN1701.5.H64

International bibliography of theatre. 1982– . [Brooklyn, N.Y.] : Theatre Research Data Center, Brooklyn College, City Univ. of New York ; N.Y. : distr. by the Publishing Center for Cultural Resources, [1985]– . Annual.   **BH57**
On cover: IBT.

"Sponsored by the American Society for Theatre Research and the International Association of Libraries and Museums of the Performing Arts in cooperation with the International Federation for Theatre Research."—*t.p.*

A major ongoing attempt to document theater materials published throughout the world. Lists books, book sections, dissertations, journal articles, and miscellaneous publications, classed as follows: theater in general; dance; dance-drama; drama; media; mime; mixed entertainment (e.g., circus, variety acts); music-drama; and puppetry. Full information and brief annotation are given in the numerical "Classed entry" section, with three indexes keyed to entry numbers: subject; geographical/chronological; and document authors. List of periodicals indexed in full or scanned. Time lag, although a 1988–89 double volume, publ. 1993, announces plans to publish additional multiyear volumes in an effort to lessen the gap. 1990–91 volume publ. 1994.

                                                    Z6935.I53

Reviews

New York theatre critics' reviews. 1943– . N.Y. : Critics' Theatre Reviews, Inc., 1943– . Irregular.   **BH58**
Vols. for 1940–42 had title *Critics' theatre reviews.*

Reproduces the original reviews from the New York press and other media. Issues are distributed throughout the year and filed in special binders, each issue typically containing reviews of two to three productions, usually within a couple of months of opening, and a cumulative title index. The last issue of each year contains annual indexes by category of contribution (actors, playwrights, directors, set designers, etc.). Cumulative title indexes: 1940–60; 1961–72; 1973–86.

As the series has evolved, coverage has changed. Originally, reprinted only reviews from the New York dailies; currently draws from a mix of newspaper, television, and national magazine critics. Off-Broadway productions were not included until 1968, when separate supplements for selected shows began to appear; current practice is to ignore the distinction, although off-Broadway coverage remains selective.   PN2000.N76

The New York times theater reviews. 1870–1919 ; 1920– 1970 ; 1971/72– . N.Y. : New York Times, 1971– . Biennial.
                                                        BH59
A reprinting in chronological sequence of reviews of theater productions as they appeared in the *Times*. Consists of: (1) 1870–1919 (1976. 6 v.); (2) 1920–70 (1971. 10 v.); and (3) a biennial series commencing with 1971–72. The two historical sets, as well as the biennial

volumes, have indexes of titles, production companies, and personal names. Appendixes of awards and prizes and of productions and runs by season.   PN2266.N48

Theatre record. v. 11, issue 1 (Jan. 1991)– . Middlesex, Eng. : I. Herbert, c1991– . Biweekly.   **BH60**
Continues: *London theatre record*, v. 1–10, 1981–90.

Functions both as a current awareness service for British theatergoers and a source of reprinted newspaper and magazine reviews. Biweekly issues contain full reviews of 20–35 London and regional productions, lists of currently running productions and future openings, production photographs, and a cumulative title index to reviews in recent numbers. Most reviews are reprinted within four to six weeks of their original publication. The annual *Theatre index* (formerly *London theatre index*) has a variety of title, personal name, and playhouse indexes keyed to *Theatre record*, in addition to awards listings and major critic's overviews of the year's activity.   PN2596.L6L66

Indexes

Salem, James M. A guide to critical reviews. 3rd ed. Metuchen, N.J. : Scarecrow, 1984–91. pt. 1–2. (In progress).
                                                        BH61
Contents: pt. 1, American drama, 1909–1982 (657 p.); pt. 2, The musical, 1909–1989 (820 p.).

Originally published in 4 pts., 1966–71. Pts. 1–3 were issued in a 2nd ed. (1973–79) with the following contents: pt. 1, American drama, 1909–1969; pt. 2, The musical, 1909–1974; pt. 3, Foreign drama, 1909–1977. No 2nd ed. of pt. 4 ("The screenplay from *The jazz singer* to *Dr. Strangelove*") was published, but a supplementary volume designated as "The screenplay, supplement 1, 1963–1980" was published 1982 (698 p.).

For plays and musicals, provides citations to reviews of staged productions, not to scholarly studies of the works. Reviews cited are from popular and generally available American and Canadian periodicals and include those appearing in the *New York times*. Listing for plays is by playwright, with title and coauthor indexes. Musicals and screenplays are entered by title. The musicals volume has indexes for authors, composers, lyricists, directors, designers, choreographers, and sources. No indexes in the screenplays volumes.   Z5781.S16

Encyclopedias

The Back Stage theater guide : a theatergoer's companion to the world's best plays and playwrights / [ed. by] Trevor R. Griffiths and Carole Woddis. N.Y. : Back Stage Books, 1991. 466 p. : ill.   **BH62**
Rev. ed. of *Bloomsbury theatre guide* (London : Bloomsbury, 1988).

Although it contains a smattering of topical entries (e.g., off- and off-off-Broadway, women in theater), most of the content is devoted to individual playwrights and their plays. Emphasizes modern British and American stagings of contemporary dramatists and classic playwrights whose works are currently in vogue. Notes on contributors; general index. Special feature: "try these" cross-references, linking the reader to playwrights and works that have common or contrasting elements.   PN1625.B3

Bloom, Ken. Broadway : an encyclopedic guide to the history, people, and places of Times Square. N.Y. : Facts on File, c1991. 442 p. : ill.   **BH63**
Consists of long, anecdotal articles on major entertainers, playwrights, composers, lyricists, producers, columnists, critics, theaters, restaurants, nightclubs, etc. associated with New York's theater district. Although generously illustrated, most of the photographs lack dates. General index includes show and song titles mentioned in the entries.   F128.65.T5B56

BH73

Bordman, Gerald Martin. The Oxford companion to American theatre. 2nd ed. N.Y. : Oxford Univ. Pr., 1992. 735 p. **BH64**

1st ed., 1984.

In addition to entries for actors, directors, playwrights, theater companies, etc., and a few selected topics (e.g., censorship), about half the space is allotted to individual plays or musicals of merit or popularity. Some foreign works are also included, as are a number of non-American figures whose careers had an impact on theatre in the U.S. Emphasis is on Broadway and the New York stage. No index, but numerous cross-references within the articles.

————. *The concise Oxford companion to the American theatre* (N.Y. : Oxford Univ. Pr., 1987. 451 p.), based on the 1st ed., retains about 60% of the content and incorporates some updated and new material. PN2220.B6

Cambridge guide to American theatre / ed. by Don B. Wilmeth and Tice L. Miller. Cambridge ; N.Y. : Cambridge Univ. Pr., 1993. 547 p. : ill. **BH65**

Aims "to offer scholars, students, and general readers a comprehensive view of the history and present practice of the theatre in the United States."—*Pref.* Essentially a reworking of material on the American stage from *The Cambridge guide to world theatre* (BH67), with considerable expansion and additional information. Consists of signed articles (many by contributors to the parent work) on performers, dramatists, directors, set designers, plays, companies, theatrical forms and movements, etc. Complements Gerald Bordman's *The Oxford companion to American theatre* (BH64) by including more topical entries (about 80), more bibliographic references, and more extensive coverage of popular forms of entertainment and ethnic and alternative theater, although it has fewer entries and less detail on specific plays. Illustrations; cross-references; "biographical index" of individuals who are mentioned in the text of articles but do not have their own entries. PN2220.C35

Cambridge guide to Asian theatre / ed. by James R. Brandon, advisory ed., Martin Banham. Cambridge ; N.Y. : Cambridge Univ. Pr., 1993. 253 p. : ill. **BH66**

Consolidates and expands on entries from *The Cambridge guide to world theatre* (BH67) dealing with theater in Asian nations. Consists of 19 country surveys (and an overview of Oceania), arranged alphabetically from Bangladesh to Vietnam and covering historical development, current status, performance genres, and artists. Signed articles include bibliographies of English-language sources. Index of artists and genres. PN2860.C35

The Cambridge guide to world theatre / ed. by Martin Banham. Cambridge ; N.Y. : Cambridge Univ. Pr., 1988. 1104 p. : ill. **BH67**

A broad-ranging source of information on individuals, organizations, theatrical forms and movements, individual countries, and a variety of specific topics. Articles are signed; some longer articles have bibliographies. Covers popular theater and entertainments, as well as the legitimate stage. Because of global perspective, especially useful for country surveys of cultures outside the U.S. and Western Europe and entries for forms and individuals associated with those cultures.

§ Revised paperback edition issued as *The Cambridge guide to theatre* (Cambridge ; N.Y. : Cambridge Univ. Pr., 1992. 1104 p.). PN2035.C27

The encyclopedia of world theater : with 420 illustrations and an index of play titles / [ed. with an] introd. by Martin Esslin. N.Y. : Scribner, [1977]. 320 p. : ill. **BH68**

"Based on *Friedrichs Theaterlexikon* [Hanover : Friedrich, 1969] by Karl Gröning and Werner Kliess ... this English-language edition has been translated by Estella Schmid, and adapted and amplified under the general editorship of Martin Esslin."—*verso of t.p.*

Brief entries for actors and actresses, playwrights, directors, designers, types of drama, theatrical institutions, awards, etc. PN2035.E52

The Facts on File dictionary of the theatre / ed. by William Packard, David Pickering, Charlotte Savidge. N.Y. : Facts on File, c1988. 556 p. **BH69**

Contains nearly 5,000 brief articles on "actors, actresses, playwrights, directors and producers, plays, venues, genres, technical terms, organizations, and other related topics."—*Pref.* Focus is on British and American theatre, with selective coverage of continental European figures and topics. The numerous play entries include concise summaries and data on first performances. PN2035.F27

Gassner, John. The reader's encyclopedia of world drama / John Gassner and Edward Quinn. N.Y. : Crowell, [1969]. 1030 p. : ill. **BH70**

In addition to entries for playwrights, selected titles, and types of drama, includes articles giving brief historical surveys of the development of the theater in individual countries. Articles are signed with the initials of the contributor, and there are some bibliographic references. Appendix of "Basic documents in dramatic theory." PN1625.G3

International dictionary of theatre / ed., Mark Hawkins-Dady. Chicago ; London : St. James Pr., c1992. v. 1–2 : ill. (In progress). **BH71**

Contents: v. 1, Plays; v. 2, Playwrights.

Selection of plays and people covered in this set is based on recommendations of an advisory panel of theater and drama scholars; individual articles are signed by one of more than 200 scholarly contributors.

Vol. 1 contains entries for 620 plays that have become world classics, are of historical importance (even if rarely performed), or represent the work of notable contemporary playwrights. Plays written in languages other than English are "those works which, through study, performance, or reputation, have become highly regarded and well known in the English-speaking world."–*Editor's note.* Alphabetical by title in English, entries include: dramatist; dates of first publication and production; editions; translations into English; a selected bibliography of critical books and articles in major European languages (usually published since the mid-1960s); and a critical essay that also provides a plot summary and may comment on stage history or specific productions of the play. List of plays by author; numerous black-and-white illustrations, often photographs of productions.

Vol. 2 profiles 485 dramatists of all periods and many nationalities. For each, gives: biographical sketch; lists of collected and individual works, published bibliographies (where available), and recent studies; contributor's critical overview; and, as applicable, reference to individual plays in v. 1. Includes portraits, engravings, photographs, etc. Play title index refers to entry for playwright.

Each volume includes notes on the advisers and the various contributors to the volume. When published, v. 3 will cover actors, directors, and designers. PN2035.I58

McGraw-Hill encyclopedia of world drama : an international reference work / Stanley Hochman, ed. in chief. [2nd ed.]. N.Y. : McGraw-Hill, [1984]. 5 v. : ill. **BH72**

1st ed., 1972.

Concerned mostly with dramatists and dramatic literature but also offers extensive articles on national and ethnic theater traditions in individual countries or areas, as well as entries for theater companies, major directors, and selected performance topics.

For each major dramatist there is a biographical sketch, a brief critique of the playwright's work, synopses of selected plays, a bibliography of editions, and a list of critical and biographical studies. For lesser dramatists, provides a brief account of their careers, achievements, and dramatic output and, occasionally, a synopsis of one or more plays. Signed articles by contributing scholars. Indexes (in v. 5): play title list (of all plays listed at the end of major articles); and general index (including all play titles mentioned in the texts of articles). Includes hundreds of good-quality illustrations. PN1625.M3

The Oxford companion to Canadian theatre / ed. by Eugene Benson and Leonard W. Conolly. Toronto ; N.Y. : Oxford Univ. Pr., 1989. 662 p. : ill. **BH73**

Covers genres, plays, playwrights, theaters, criticism. Scholarly articles, signed. Topical index.   PN2300.O94

The Oxford companion to the theatre / ed. by Phyllis Hartnoll. 4th ed. Oxford : Oxford Univ. Pr., 1983. 934 p. : ill.
                                        BH74

1st ed., 1951.

Offers definitions of terms, sketches of theater personalities of all periods, articles on specific theater companies and buildings, and historical profiles of theater in individual countries and cities. Scope is international, although emphasis is on British and American theater. In general, concentrates on "what is known as 'legitimate' theatre throughout its history" (*Pref.*), with ballet and opera excluded and with limited coverage of popular genres such as vaudeville. Articles are unsigned, but a panel of 87 specialist contributors is listed. Cross-references; 96 thematically grouped plates. "A guide to further reading" identifies standard English-language works.

§ *The concise Oxford companion to the theatre*, ed. by Phyllis Hartnoll and Peter Found (2nd ed. Oxford ; N.Y. : Oxford Univ. Pr., 1992. 568 p.) functions both as a reworking of material from the 1st ed. (1972) of the concise version and an updated reduction of the full *Oxford companion*, 4th ed. Except for the elimination of articles on countries, most categories of entries have been retained.   PN2035.H3

Taylor, John Russell. Penguin dictionary of the theatre. 3rd ed. London : Penguin, 1993. 349 p.   **BH75**

1st ed., 1966; rev. ed., 1974.

Plays, players, playwrights, theater terms, etc., are included in this handy pocket encyclopedia. About 1,500 entries, most quite brief, although some notable individuals and important topics receive fuller treatment. Anglo-American orientation.   PN2035.T3

Dictionaries

Boulanger, Norman. Theatre lighting from A to Z / Norman C. Boulanger, Warren C. Lounsbury. Seattle : Univ. of Washington Pr., c1992. 197 p. : ill.   **BH76**

An extraction and expansion of lighting term definitions from the authors' *Theatre backstage from A to Z* (BH80), with additional new terms and definitions. Like the related work, has elements of a manual, with practical advice offered in many of the entries. Numerous illustrations and cross-references. List of manufacturers and distributors; bibliography.

§ Francis Reid's *The ABC of stage lighting* (London : A & C Black; N.Y. : Drama Book Publ., 1992. 129 p.) has concise definitions of terms currently in use, as well as "references to types of equipment which, although no longer in use, still influence today's techniques through their operational philosophy."—*Prologue.* Illustrated.
                                        PN2091.E4B59

Bowman, Walter Parker. Theatre language : a dictionary of terms in English of the drama and stage from medieval to modern times / Walter Parker Bowman, Robert Hamilton Ball. N.Y. : Theatre Arts, [1961]. 428 p.   **BH77**

Contains more than 3,500 definitions of words and phrases. For the most part, excludes terms peculiar to grand opera and ballet.

§ Similar in intent, Wilfred Granville's *A dictionary of theatrical terms* (London : A. Deutsch, 1952. 206 p.) defines many terms having particular application to the British stage.   PN2035.B6

Hodgson, Terry. The drama dictionary. N.Y. : New Amsterdam, c1988. 432 p. : ill.   **BH78**

British title: *The Batsford dictionary of drama* (London : Batsford).

Offers full working definitions of terms used in the theater and by theater critics. Includes some illustrations and bibliographic references. Extensively cross-referenced.   PN1625.H64

An international dictionary of theatre language / Joel Trapido, gen. ed. ; Edward A. Langhans, ed. for Western theatre ; James R. Brandon, ed. for Asian theatre. Westport, Conn. : Greenwood, 1985. 1032 p.   **BH79**

Defines 10,000 English and 5,000 foreign-language terms used in the English-speaking world. Among exclusions are trade names, standard implements and materials, and terms from the mass media and popular entertainment (circus, nightclubs, magic acts). Entries include language (if not English), definition, and references to sources cited in the bibliography. Contains a brief historical essay on theater glossaries and dictionaries.   PN2035.I5

Lounsbury, Warren C. Theatre backstage from A to Z / Warren C. Lounsbury, Norman Boulanger. 3rd ed., rev. and expanded. Seattle : Univ. of Washington Pr., c1989. 213 p. : ill.
                                        BH80

1st ed., 1967; rev. ed., 1972.

A manual in dictionary form of the technical aspects of theatrical production. This edition has new material on sound, electronic control, and equipment, but retains many terms relating to older technologies. Useful illustrations; historical essay on scenery and lighting practices in the U.S; selected list of manufacturers and distributors.
                                        PN2091.M3L68

Rae, Kenneth. An international vocabulary of technical theatre terms in eight languages : (American, Dutch, English, French, German, Italian, Spanish, Swedish) / Kenneth Rae, Richard Southern. Bruxelles : Elsevier ; N.Y. : Theatre Arts Books, [1959]. 139 p.   **BH81**

Added title page in French: Lexique international de termes techniques de théâtre en huit langues.

In two parts: pt. 1, numbered list of terms in English, alphabetically arranged, with equivalent terms in other languages; pt. 2, indexes in the other languages. U.S. index lists only those terms that differ from British usage.   PN2035.R3

Vaughn, Jack A. Drama A to Z : a handbook. N.Y. : Ungar, [1978]. 239 p.   **BH82**

Defines and discusses "approximately 500 words and phrases commonly found in writings on the drama, from Aristotle to the present."—*Pref.* Includes bibliographic chronology of dramatic theory and criticism and suggestions for further reading.   PN1625.V3

Directories

Black theatre directory / comp. and ed. by Addell Austin Anderson. 3rd ed. Detroit : Black Theatre Network, 1993. 52 p.
                                        BH83

Also called *BTN black theatre directory.*

1st ed., 1988; 2nd ed., 1990.

In five sections: Individuals (primarily educators, playwrights, critics, directors, and producers); Theater companies; Colleges/universities; Black theater organizations; Theater related arts organizations. Name indexes to the first three sections, which are arranged by state.   PN2270.A35B59

Charles, Jill. Directory of theatre training programs : profiles of college and conservatory programs throughout the United States : information on admissions, degrees offered, faculties, courses, facilities, productions, and philosophy of training / comp. and ed. by Jill Charles ... [et al.]. 3rd ed. Dorset, Vt. : Theatre Directories, c1991. 176 p.   **BH84**

1st ed., 1987; 2nd ed., 1989.

Gives data on 333 graduate and undergraduate programs, arranged by state and school. Alphabetical index of institutions also tabulates areas of program concentration (e.g., acting, design) and level of degree offered for each area.

§ The 1992 edition of *Directory of doctoral programs in theatre studies in the U.S.A. and Canada* (Philadelphia : American Soc. for Theatre Research, 1992– . Biennial.) offers detailed profiles of 43 schools that grant a PhD or Doctor of Fine Arts in theater studies. Includes information on library holdings and a list of recent dissertations completed. PN2078.U6C48

Dramatists sourcebook. 1981/82– . N.Y. : Theatre Communications Group, 1981– . Annual. **BH85**

Guide to opportunities for aspiring playwrights, translators, and musical theater writers. More than 850 listings (1993–94 ed.) for: U.S. nonprofit professional theaters; playwriting contests; play publishers, magazines, and small presses; festivals, conferences, and workshops; agents; fellowships and grants; emergency funds; state art agencies; colonies and residences; and membership and service organizations. Also describes publications that list opportunities. Submission calendar; special interests and name indexes.

§ Similar in focus and coverage: *The playwright's companion* (N.Y. : Feedback Theatrebooks, 1985– . Annual.) has more listings in some categories, especially theater companies, but no index of names included. Both directories offer practical advice on submissions and contacts. PN2289.D73

The New York theatrical sourcebook / comp. and ed. by Association of Theatrical Artists and Craftsmen. Shelter Island, N.Y. : Broadway Pr., c1990. 561 p. : ill. **BH86**

Classified list of theater-related products and services (e.g., artificial flowers and plants, clocks, costume rental and construction, fog machines, police equipment) available in the New York area. Company name and subject indexes. Appendixes include list of organizations, unions, and support services.

§ *TCI* [Theatre crafts international] (v. 26– . N.Y. : Theatre Crafts Assoc., 1992– . Formerly *Theatre crafts*, 1967–92) publishes an annual directory issue, "Industry resources" (June/July) that lists American firms and has indexes of products and services.

The original British theatre directory. 1986– . London : Richmond House Pub. Co., c1986– . Annual. **BH87**

Publ. 1972–85 as *British theatre directory*.

Contains listings for venues (theaters, concert halls, and other spaces), municipal agencies, producing managements, performing arts companies, festivals, agents, publishers and booksellers, arts councils, organizations, suppliers, and services.

§ *McGillivray's theatre guide* (Cardiff : Rebecca Books, 1994– . Annual) duplicates many of these categories and listings but focuses more on alternative (or fringe) companies and venues and less on services and suppliers. Continues *The British alternative theatre directory* (1979–93. Annual).

Theatre profiles. v. 1 (1973)– . [N.Y.] : Theatre Communications Group, 1973– . Biennial. **BH88**

Subtitle: The illustrated reference guide to America's nonprofit professional theatre.

In addition to address, telephone number, administrative directors, founding date, finances, and union contracts, includes a statement of purpose and a list of recent productions (with credits for writers, directors, and designers, but not performers) for more than 200 companies. Regional index; name and play title indexes.

§ The annual *TCG theatre directory* (N.Y. : Theatre Communications Group, 1980/81–) gives the most essential directory information for these companies and about 70 associated theater groups, and has capsule descriptions of relevant organizations and associations. Index of companies by state.

Other U.S. directories : *Regional theatre directory* (Dorset, Vt. : Theatre Directories, 1985/86– . Annual) and *Summer theatre directory* (Dorset, Vt. : Theatre Directories, 1984– . Annual), both of which serve as employment guides and include profiles of the companies listed. Each is arranged geographically, with theater name index. Addresses and telephone numbers of more than 3,500 theaters of all kinds, listed by name, are given in *Playhouse America!: a directory of theatres and theatre companies in the U.S.A.* (N.Y. : Feedback Theatrebooks; Hollywood, Calif. : Distr. by Samuel French Trade, 1991. 308 p.) No geographical index, but has index of specialties (e.g., ethnic, Shakespeare). PN2266.T48

Handbooks

Carter, Paul. Backstage handbook : an illustrated almanac of technical information. Shelter Island, N.Y. : Broadway Pr., 1988. 253 p. : ill. **BH89**

A practical manual that describes a wide range of tools, hardware, materials, electrical devices, mathematical formulas, architectural elements, and stage machinery likely to be encountered by those involved in technical theater. Consists mostly of tables, charts, and clear line drawings. Separate table of standard conversions; bibliography (manuals, codes, etc.); index.

Cassin-Scott, Jack. Costumes and settings for staging historical plays. Boston : Plays Inc., [1979]. 4 v. : ill. **BH90**

British ed. (London : Batsford, 1979–80) has title: *Costumes and settings for historical plays*.

Contents: v. 1, The classical period; v. 2, Medieval; v. 3, The Elizabethan and Restoration periods; v. 4, The Georgian period. (British ed. has v. 5, The nineteenth century.).

Each volume includes a general introduction to the period, followed by illustrated descriptions of the costume of specific cultures and smaller time divisions, discussion and illustrations of stage properties, and basic stage setting and lighting considerations. Volume indexes.

§ Also oriented to theatrical production: Shirley Miles O'Donnol, *American costume, 1915-1970 : a source book for the stage costumer* (Bloomington : Indiana Univ. Pr., 1982. 270 p.), a chronological presentation with narrative descriptions and illustrations (photographs and line drawings) of clothing worn by the general public during this period.

For other costume reference works, *see* Section BG, Decorative and Applied Arts, Costume and Fashion. PN2067.C33

Herman, Lewis. Foreign dialects : a manual for actors, directors and writers / Lewis Herman, Marguerite Shalett Herman. N.Y. : Theatre Arts Books, [1959]. 415 p. : ill. **BH91**

First published in 1943 as: *Manual of foreign dialects for radio, stage and screen*.

This and the Hermans' companion volume, *American dialects : a manual for actors, directors and writers* (N.Y. : Theater Arts Books, [1959, c1947]. 328 p.), are standard texts for accent acquisition and practice. Several audio recordings accompanied by manuals (such as those of Evangeline Machlin, Jerry Blunt, and David A. Stern) are also available. PN2071.F6H4

James, Thurston. The what, where, when of theater props : an illustrated chronology from arrowheads to video games. Cincinnati, Ohio : Betterway Books, c1992. 222 p. : ill. **BH92**

Attempts to assist those who assemble or build stage properties by "describing and picturing a wide variety of obscure to pretty common items and placing them in a historical context."—*Introd.* In five parts: (1) Daily living (eating, furniture, writing tools, etc.); (2) Civil authority (e.g., scepters, crowns, flags); (3) Warfare; (4) Science and technology (Stone Age tools, alchemy, telephones); and (5) Religion (for ceremonial objects). Entries give a description of the object, its size or dimension, and the time and place of its introduction into use; about half the objects are accompanied by line drawings. List of sources; index. Because of its scope and the inclusion of chronological tables for many classes of objects (e.g. eyeglasses, toys), also useful for general historical and cultural reference. PN2091.S8J35

Stevenson, Isabelle. The Tony Award : a complete listing, with a history of the American Theatre Wing / ed. by Isabelle Stevenson ; research consultant, Sonia Ediff. N.Y. : Crown, c1987. 197 p. : ill. **BH93**

1st issued 1980; updated 1984.

A year-by-year listing of all Tony Award nominees and winners. Index of winners.

New edition publ. 1994. PN2270.A93S8

Chronologies

Meserve, Walter J. A chronological outline of world theatre / Walter J. Meserve and Mollie Anne Meserve. N.Y. : Feedback Theatrebooks & Prospero Pr., c1992. 143 p. : ill.   **BH94**

Through the use of time lines and brief notes, shows developments in various cultures and countries. Arranged by large time periods, from 3000 BCE in Egypt to the early 1980s. Indexed.

PN2101.M47

History

American theatre companies / ed. by Weldon B. Durham. N.Y. : Greenwood, c1986–89. 3 v.   **BH95**

Contents: v. 1, 1749–1887; v. 2, 1888–1930; v. 3, 1931–86.

Provides summaries of stock and resident acting companies founded during the periods covered by each of the volumes. Entry for each company gives: a brief history, including date of founding, location(s), season highlights, policies, and critical assessment; rosters of administrative and creative personnel; complete or representative repertory, arranged chronologically; and a bibliography of published and archival sources. Each volume has index of play titles and personal names mentioned in the narrative profiles and two appendixes: chronology of companies, and listing of companies by state. PN2237.A43

Blum, Daniel C. A pictorial history of the American theatre, 1860–1985 / by Daniel Blum; enlarged by John Willis. New 6th ed. N.Y. : Crown Publishers, 1986. 496 p. : ill.   **BH96**

1st ed., 1950.

A year-by-year narrative chronicle (decade-by-decade for 1860–1900) of successes and failures, accompanied by a generous selection of production and performer photographs. Deals almost exclusively with the New York stage. Title and name index.   PN2266.B585

Bordman, Gerald Martin. American theatre : a chronicle of comedy and drama, 1869–1914. N.Y. : Oxford Univ. Pr., 1994. 793 p.   **BH97**

Conceived as "the first of several projected volumes in which we hope to do for America's non-musical theatre what we did for song-and-dance entertainments in our earlier *American Musical Theatre : a Chronicle*."—*Pref.* For each theater season, in chronological order, provides an overview and traces nonmusical productions, highlighting successes and failures. Each of the plays (including many of foreign origin) is described in some detail, often incorporating contemporary commentary on the production and individual performances. Indexes of plays, play sources, and people.   PN2256.B6

Bronner, Edwin. The encyclopedia of the American theatre, 1900–1975. San Diego, Calif. : A.S. Barnes, c1980. 659 p. : ill.   **BH98**

Less an encyclopedia than an alphabetical chronicle of individual plays "written (or adapted) by American or Anglo-American authors" (*Introd.*) and produced on or off-Broadway during the period. Entries vary but typically include date of opening, theater, number of performances in the original run, brief plot summary, critical comment (often with quotations from contemporary reviews), principal players, author, producer, director, and (as relevant) revivals, musical versions, and screen adaptations. Appendixes include a calendar of notable premieres, Broadway debuts of actors and playwrights, longest-running shows, statistical record of Broadway productions by season, and awards. Personal name index.

§ The various decade compilations of Samuel Leiter's *The encyclopedia of the New York stage* (BH100) offer fuller, more systematic coverage of New York productions for the 1920–50 period, but Bronner's is a convenient one-volume source.   PN2266.B68

Howard, Diana. London theatres and music halls, 1850–1950. London : Libr. Assoc., 1970. 291 p. : ill.   **BH99**

Pt. 1, "A–Z directory of theatres, music halls, and pleasure gardens, with bibliographies," attempts to document every commercial stage (910 theatres) in London for this hundred-year period. Each entry includes name, address, dates, building details, management, contemporary accounts, historical accounts, and location of other pertinent material. Pts. 2–3 list general records and publications, newspapers, periodicals, and collections. Building name index.

§ Raymond Mander and Joe Mitchenson, *The theatres of London* (New ed., rev. and enl. London : New English Library, 1975. 344 p.), offers descriptions and brief stage histories of 63 major theaters extant at the time of publication.   PN2596.L6H595

Leiter, Samuel L. The encyclopedia of the New York stage, 1920–1930 / Samuel L. Leiter, ed. in chief ; Holly Hill, associate ed. Westport, Conn. : Greenwood, 1985. 2 v. (1331 p.).   **BH100**

Aims "to provide a description of every legitimate theatre production—play, musical, revue, revival—given in the New York professional theatre" (*Pref.*) during the period June 16, 1920–June 15, 1930. Restricted to works produced in Manhattan (Broadway and off-Broadway equivalents), but includes visiting foreign-language productions reviewed in the English-language press. Entries, by show title, cite categories (such as type of play or general subject content), author(s), source, director, designer, producer, theater, opening date, length of run, etc., followed by brief plot summary (with cast members noted), critical reception (often with quotations from reviews), and commentary. Appendixes include a calendar of productions by opening date, listings of plays by categories, awards, productions of theater companies, longest-running shows, seasonal statistics, and theaters. Selected bibliography; index of proper names.

Leiter continues his decade surveys with: *The encyclopedia of the New York stage, 1930–1940* (1989. 1299 p.); *The encyclopedia of the New York stage, 1940–1950* (1992. 946 p.).   PN2277.N5L36

The London stage, 1660–1800 : a calendar of plays, entertainments and afterpieces, together with casts, box-receipts and contemporary comment, comp. from the playbills, newspapers and theatrical diaries of the period. Carbondale, Ill. : Southern Illinois Univ. Pr., 1960–68. 5 pts. in 11 v. : ill.   **BH101**

Contents: pt. 1, 1660–1700, ed. by William Van Lennep; pt. 2, 1700–1729, ed. by E. L. Avery (2 v.); pt. 3, 1729–1747, ed. by A. H. Scouten (2 v.); pt. 4, 1747–1776, ed. by G. W. Stone (3 v.); pt. 5, 1776–1800, ed. by C. B. Hogan (3 v.).

An important scholarly work, which provides a vast amount of information on stage productions of the period. Arranged chronologically by season, then by date, entries include title, theater, performers, historical notes, etc. Lengthy introductions to each of the five parts; season overviews; volume indexes.

§ Ben Ross Schneider's *Index to the London stage, 1660–1800* (Carbondale : Southern Illinois Univ. Pr., [1979]. 939 p.) contains all titles and names appearing in the calendars of the above set and refers to its entries by performance date and theater. Profession or performing specialty noted for individuals.

Other calendars for this period, both modeled on *The London stage, 1660–1800*: William J. Burling's *A checklist of new plays and entertainments on the London stage, 1700–1737* (Rutherford, N.J. : Fairleigh Dickinson Univ. Pr., 1993. 235 p.); and John C. Greene and Gladys L. H. Clark's *The Dublin stage, 1720–1745 : a calendar of plays, entertainments, and afterpieces* (Bethlehem, Pa. : Lehigh Univ. Pr., 1993. 473 p.). Burling complements the earlier work by incorporating additional titles, notes, and attributions.   PN2592.L6

Loney, Glenn Meredith. 20th century theatre. N.Y. : Facts on File, [1983]. 2 v. : ill.   **BH102**

Presented as a chronological record, the work intends "to offer an overview of theatre activity in North America and the British Isles since 1900, and to provide a 'date-finder' for those who want to obtain capsule information about a particular theatre event, production, personality, or playhouse."—*Pref.* Each year includes sections for: American premieres, British premieres, revivals/repertories, births/deaths/debuts, and theaters/productions. Index of names, titles, theater companies.   PN2189.L65

Mullin, Donald C. Victorian plays : a record of significant productions on the London stage, 1837–1901. N.Y. : Greenwood, 1987. 444 p. (Bibliographies and indexes in the performing arts, no. 4).   **BH103**

For each play included, provides production records taken from original playbills, giving playwright, first (or earliest known) production date, revivals, names of principal players and characters, and set design and music credits, where applicable. Alphabetical by play title. Index of playwrights, adapters, translators. A companion volume for performers is projected.   PN2596.L6M85

Mullin, Michael. Theatre at Stratford-upon-Avon : a catalogue-index to productions of the Shakespeare Memorial/ Royal Shakespeare Theatre, 1879–1978 / by Michael Mullin and Karen Morris Muriello. Westport, Conn. : Greenwood, [1980]. 2 v. (1038 p.).   **BH104**

Contents: v. 1, Catalogue of productions; v. 2, Indexes and calendar.

Provides details of virtually all Stratford productions (including non-Shakespearean plays) of the first 100 years, based on the archives of the Shakespeare Centre Library. Vol. 1 lists the plays by title, then chronologically by production, giving playwright, director, set designer, lighting designer, theater where performed, cast, and references to reviews (as available). Vol. 2 has indexes to playwrights; directors, designers, actors; reviewers; and contains a year-by-year calendar of productions.   PN2596.S82S86

Odell, George Clinton Densmore. Annals of the New York stage. N.Y. : Columbia Univ Pr., 1927–49. 15 v. : ill. **BH105**

A very full narrative account of theatrical activity in New York City from about 1699 through the 1893–94 season. Drawing from contemporary newspapers, diaries, playbills, account-books, and other primary sources, covers actors, producers, theaters, plays, operas, ballets, etc. Detailed index in each volume.

Access to the numerous illustrations is aided by: *Index to the portraits in Odell's Annals of the New York stage, transcribed from the file in the Theatre Collection at Princeton University* ([N.Y.?] : Amer. Soc. for Theatre Research, [1963]. 179 p.).

Theatre companies of the world / ed. by Colby H. Kullman and William C. Young. Westport, Conn. : Greenwood, 1986. 2 v. (979 p.).   **BH106**

Contents: v. 1, Africa, Asia, Australia and New Zealand, Canada, Eastern Europe, Latin America, the Middle East, Scandinavia; v. 2, United States of America, Western Europe (excluding Scandinavia).

Nine area editors with "specialized knowledge of the theatrical tradition of a specific geographical area" (*Pref.*) have selected the companies to be included and with other contributors have written narrative essays giving: name and address; significance, brief history; philosophy; seating facilities; and future plans. Within a region, companies are listed by country, then entered alphabetically by English form of name, with no cross-reference from name in the original language. Vol. 2 concludes with "Suggestions for additional readings" and a name index.   PN2052.T48

Theatre world annual (London) : a pictorial review of West End productions with a record of plays and players. no. 1 (1949/50)–no. 16 (1964/65). London : Rockliff ; N.Y. : Macmillan, 1950–65. Annual.   **BH107**

Subtitle varies.

Almanac for each season includes: review of the year's offerings; profiles of leading performers; play runs; production credits (alphabetical by play title); obituary notes; and narrative accounts of productions (by opening date). Heavily illustrated.   PN2596.L6T542

Wearing, J. P. The London stage, 1890–1899 : a calendar of plays and players. Metuchen, N.J. : Scarecrow, 1976. 2 v. (1229 p.).   **BH108**

Contents: v. 1, 1890–1896; v. 2, 1897–1899, Index.

First of a series of volumes that aim "to furnish a daily listing of the plays and players on the London stage" (*Introd.*) decade by decade from 1890. Arrangement is chronological by date of opening, then by theater for multiple openings on the same date. Drawn from newspapers, archives, and other sources, entries include: full title, author (including details of adaptation or translation where applicable); genre and number of acts or scenes; playhouse; opening date, length of run, and number of performances; cast (including changes); production staff, and references to reviews of first performance. Index of titles, authors, performers, theaters, managers, etc.

Other volumes, all publ. by Scarecrow: 1900–1909 (1981. 2 v.); 1910–1919 (1982. 2 v); 1920–1929 (1984. 3 v); 1930–1939 (1990. 3 v.); 1940–1949 (1991. 2 v.); 1950–1959 (1993. 2 v.).

PN2596.L6W37

Woll, Allen L. Dictionary of the black theatre : Broadway, off-Broadway, and selected Harlem theatre. Westport, Conn. : Greenwood, [1983]. 359 p.   **BH109**

In two main sections: (1) The shows, a dictionary arrangement of plays, musicals, and revues "by, about, with, for and related to blacks" (*Pref.*) 1898–1981, covering opening date and theater, number of performances, author, producer, cast, and notes on content and reception; (2) Personalities and organizations, for biographical and historical sketches. Chronology; discography; selected bibliography; index of names, play and film titles, and song titles.

§ Other handbooks of African-American theater history: Henry T. Sampson, *The ghost walks : a chronological history of blacks in show business, 1865–1910* (Metuchen, N.J. : Scarecrow, 1988. 570 p.), an illustrated documentary chronicle of shows, events, personalities, etc., which "attempts to trace the development of black entertainment in the United States from its beginning, just at the end of the Civil War, to 1910" (*Pref*); and James Vernon Hatch, *Black image on the American stage : a bibliography of plays and musicals, 1770–1970* (BE520).

PN2270.A35W64

Young, William C. Famous American playhouses. Chicago : Amer. Libr. Assoc., 1973. 2 v. (327, 297 p.) : ill. (Documents of American theater history, v. 1–2).   **BH110**

Contents: v. 1, 1716–1899; v. 2, 1900–1971.

Concerned with the physical structure of 199 American theaters of historical, architectural, and social/cultural importance, these volumes comprise a sourcebook of primary and secondary readings. Types of documents extracted include diaries, letters, journals, autobiographies, newspaper articles and reviews, magazine articles, playbills, publicity materials, and architectural descriptions. Most documents are contemporary with the matter being discussed, but later sources (especially comments of architects and historians) are sometimes quoted. Illustrations include architects' drawings, etchings, and photographs.

Within each volume, arrangement is by area or category (e.g., New York, regional, college and university), then chronological by date of opening. Indexes for each volume: theater names; geographical locations; personal names and special topics.

§ A survey of about 900 extant theatres built before 1915 and featuring live entertainment: *Directory of historic American theatres*, ed. by John W. Frick and Carlton Ward for the League of Historic American Theatres (N.Y. : Greenwood, 1987. 347 p.). By state and city; theater name and subject indexes.   NA6830.Y67

Annuals

Theatre world. v. 1 (1944/45)– . N.Y. : Theatre World, 1945– . Annual.   **BH111**

Publisher and title vary. Editors: Daniel Blum, 1945–65; John Willis, 1966– . Currently published by Applause.

Illustrated yearbook of the American theater. Emphasis is on theater in New York City, but also records productions of national touring companies, professional regional companies, and Shakespeare festivals. Gives casts, production credits, dates of run or season, etc. Includes brief performer biographies, obituaries, lists of awards, and name/title index.   PN2277.N5A17

Biography

Highfill, Philip H. A biographical dictionary of actors, actresses, musicians, dancers, managers & other stage personnel in London, 1660–1800 / by Philip H. Highfill, Kalman A. Burnim, and Edward A. Langhans. Carbondale : Southern Illinois Univ. Pr., [1973–93]. 16 v. : ill.   **BH112**

"The purpose of these volumes is to provide brief biographical notices of all persons who were members of theatrical companies or occasional performers or were patentees or servants of the patent theatres, opera houses, amphitheatres, pleasure gardens, theatrical taverns, music rooms, fair booths, and other places of public entertainment in London and its immediate environs from the Restoration of Charles II in 1660 until the end of the season 1799–1800."—*Pref.*

A monumental undertaking. Sketches vary in length from a few lines to many pages and often include an impressive amount of detail. Information has been culled from a wide range of printed and manuscript sources, as summarized in the preface; although entries lack bibliographies and there is no general list of references, sources are sometimes cited within the text. Cross-references from variant forms of names. Amply illustrated with portraits and engravings of performers and theaters, as well as reproductions of contemporary documents (e.g., playbills, letters, financial accounts).   PN2597.H5

Kosch, Wilhelm. Deutsches Theater-Lexikon : biographisches und bibliographisches Handbuch. Klagenfurt : Kleinmayr, 1951–94. Lfg. 1–24. (In progress).   **BH113**

Contents: Lfg. 1–24, A–Stix. (v. 1–3 complete in 23 Lfg.).

Compilation continued by Ingrid Bigler-Marschall. Vol. 3– publ. by Francke Verlag, Bern.

An encyclopedia of the German-speaking theater, focusing on individual actors, singers, playwrights, composers, etc. Also has articles on dramatic theory, history, and themes. Bibliographic notes (books, periodical and newspaper articles) for most entries.   PN2035.K6

Lacy, Robin Thurlow. A biographical dictionary of scenographers, 500 B.C. to 1900 A.D. N.Y. : Greenwood, 1990. 762 p. : port.   **BH114**

Scholarly, thoroughly researched sketches of pre-20th century scene designers and scene painters, described as "the makers of pictures to represent the intended or actual visual appearance of the stage for a performance."—*Description of the format.* Alphabetical by scenographer, includes individuals whose careers were predominantly theatrical, as well as painters, architects, and other artists (e.g., Leonardo da Vinci, Raphael) who created designs for theatrical presentations (plays, operas, pageants, ceremonial occasions, etc.). Entries focus on contributions to the theater and give dates of major activity, notable credits and achievements, and references to a 435-item bibliography of published sources and archives. Appendix: Geographical-chronological list. Cross-references; no index.

§ Complements *Theatrical designers* (BH120), which is concerned primarily with stage designers of the modern period.   PN2096.A1L33

Lyonnet, Henry. Dictionnaire des comédiens français (ceux d'hier) : biographie, bibliographie, iconographie. Genève : Bibliothèque de la Revue Universelle Internationale Illustrée, [1911–12]. 2 v. : ill.   **BH115**

At head of title: Histoire du théâtre.

Issued in parts, 1902–12.

Provides sketches of French actors no longer living at the time of compilation. Portraits; entry bibliographies.

§ Georges Mongrédien, *Dictionnaire biographique des comédiens français du XVIIᵉ siècle : suivi d'un inventaire des troupes (1590–1710), d'après des documents inédits* (Paris : Centre National de la Recherche Scientifique, 1961. 239 p.) and *Supplément* (Paris : CNRS,

1971. 62 p.) have brief listings for 17th-century stage performers, keyed to numbered references in an extensive bibliography of source documents, as well as information on acting companies of the period.   PN2637.L8

Morley, Sheridan. The great stage stars : distinguished theatrical careers of the past and present. N.Y. : Facts on File, 1986. 425 p., [44] p. of plates : ports.   **BH116**

Provides 200 biographies, ranging from half a page to a page and a half, of performers whose announced appearance in a play or musical guaranteed immediate activity at the box office. Mostly 20th-century British and American players, although some continental and 19th-century actors are included.   PN2597.M64

Notable names in the American theatre. [New and rev. ed.]. Clifton, N.J. : James T. White & Co., 1976. 1250 p.   **BH117**

Represents a 2nd ed. of Walter Rigdon's *Biographical encyclopaedia and who's who of the American theatre* (N.Y. : James H. Heineman, 1966. 1101 p.).

Main section offers detailed biographical/career sketches of performers, directors, playwrights, critics, etc., of importance to the American stage and living at the time of publication. As in the earlier edition, includes a necrology, listings of productions, premieres, awards, published biographies, and profiles of theater groups and buildings.   PN2285.N6

Notable women in the American theatre : a biographical dictionary / ed. by Alice M. Robinson, Vera Mowry Roberts, and Milly S. Barranger. N.Y. : Greenwood, 1989. 993 p.   **BH118**

Lengthy, signed articles on about 350 influential actresses, directors, scholars, designers, etc. Bibliographies and notes on archival sources are attached to the entries. Appendixes list individuals by place of birth and professional category. Cross-references; topical index.   PN2285.N65

Nungezer, Edwin. Dictionary of actors and of other persons associated with the public representation of plays in England before 1642. New Haven, Conn. : Yale Univ. Pr. ; London : Milford, 1929. 438 p. (Cornell studies in English, 13).   **BH119**

Brings together information on early players, with references to sources.   PN2597.N8

Theatrical designers : an international biographical dictionary / ed. by Thomas J. Mikotowicz. N.Y. : Greenwood, 1992. 365 p.   **BH120**

Offers signed articles on "approximately 270 set, costume, and lighting designers of drama, opera, dance, and film productions, as well as theatre architects and theoreticians." —*Pref.* International and historical in scope, with emphasis on 20th-century American and European designers. Entries include biographical data, extensive credits, discussion of career highlights, awards received, and suggestions for further reading. Appendixes list designers by date and country of birth. Selected bibliography; index of personal names and titles of stage works.

§ Bobbi Owen's *Scenic design on Broadway : designers and their credits, 1915–1990* (N.Y.: Greenwood, 1991, 286 p.) has brief biographical sketches and comprehensive Broadway credits (based on playbills, interviews, etc.) for about 1,000 set designers. Appendixes of theater award winners for scenic design; bibliography; index of show titles, giving year of production and designer's name. Owen's companion volumes follow the same basic plan: *Costume design on Broadway : designers and their credits, 1915–1985* (N.Y.: Greenwood, 1987. 254 p.); and *Lighting design on Broadway : designers and their credits, 1915–1990* (N.Y.: Greenwood, 1991. 159 p.).   PN2096.A1T48

Theatrical directors : a biographical dictionary / ed. by John W. Frick & Stephen M. Vallillo. Westport, Conn. : Greenwood, 1994. 567 p.   **BH121**

Signed, critical articles on some 300 prominent 19th- and 20th-century directors. For each, includes a biographical sketch with comments on major professional contributions, a listing of additional productions directed by the individual, and a selected bibliography. Appendixes list directors by birth date and by country of principal activity. Name index; play, film, and television title index. PN2205.T54

Who's who in the theatre : a biographical record of the contemporary stage. Ed. 1–17. London : Pitman, 1912–81. **BH122**

Originally comp. by John Parker.

Publisher varies; ed. 17 publ. Detroit : Gale.

Presents fairly detailed biographies of persons connected with the English-speaking theater, including actors, actresses, directors, dramatists, composers, scenic designers, critics, and theater historians. Emphasis in early editions was on London stage personalities, but more recent editions cover the New York stage as well. Also includes playbills for London and New York productions, listings of long-running shows, etc. *Contemporary theatre, film, and television* (BH22) is intended as a continuation of the series.

§ *Who was who in the theatre, 1912–1976* (Detroit : Gale, [1978]. 4 v.) reproduces the most recent sketches from the first 15 editions of *Who's who in the theatre* for those personalities whose listings were dropped "because of death or inactivity in the theatre."—*Foreword.* Death dates through 1976 have been added for individuals known to be deceased, although this aspect of the publication appears not to have been thoroughly researched. About 4,100 entries. PN2012.W5

Young, William C. Famous actors and actresses on the American stage. N.Y. : Bowker, 1975. 2 v. (1298 p.) : ill. **BH123**

Intended as a companion to the same author's *Famous American playhouses* (BH110).

Aims "(1) to present contemporary evaluations of the abilities of a certain actor or actress; and (2) to relate a performer's philosophy of acting and approach to certain roles."—*Pref.* 225 actors and actresses (not necessarily Americans) are treated. For each performer there is a portrait, brief biographical data, and a number of extracts from contemporary criticism (reviews of plays, interviews, memoirs of fellow actors, etc.). Index of persons, plays, and characters mentioned in the extracts. PN2285.Y6

Indexes

Archer, Stephen M. American actors and actresses : a guide to information sources. Detroit : Gale, [1983]. 710 p. (Performing arts information guide series, v. 8). **BH124**

Concerned with actors and actresses in the professional legitimate theater. General and reference works are cited first, followed by writings on performers (from earliest times but limited to those whose careers were established before World War II). Performer citations are mostly to books and periodical articles; reviews of specific performances are not included. Cross-references. Author, title, and subject indexes. Z5784.M9A7

Johnson, Claudia D. Nineteenth-century theatrical memoirs / Claudia D. Johnson and Vernon E. Johnson. Westport, Conn. : Greenwood, [1982]. 269 p. **BH125**

Lists autobiographies, many published in the 20th century, of "those individuals of every nationality who performed in England and America for all or much of their careers."—*Introd.* Descriptive annotations also serve as career summaries. Index to theaters mentioned prominently in the memoirs, as well as an author-subject index. Z6935.J63

Moyer, Ronald L. American actors, 1861–1910 : an annotated bibliography of books published in the United States in English from 1861 through 1976. Troy, N.Y. : Whitston, 1979. 268 p. **BH126**

Cites memoirs, biographies, and compendia that contain substantial information on U.S. performers active 1861–1910 (including some

whose major period of theatrical activity was outside this time span). 363 annotated entries, arranged by principal author or title, with indexes to actors, titles, and authors. Z5784.A27M65

Stage deaths : a biographical guide to international theatrical obituaries, 1850 to 1990 / comp. by George B. Bryan. N.Y. : Greenwood, 1991. 2 v. (1354 p.). (Bibliographies and indexes in the performing arts, no. 9). **BH127**

Aims to provide basic biographical information and citations to printed English-language sources (obituaries and books) for theatrical personalities who died between 1850 and 1990. Includes major figures, but gives extensive coverage to little-known or forgotten individuals, in keeping with the work's "conception of obscure lives as necessary, colorful complements to the more celebrated ones."—*Introd..* Arranged alphabetically by professional name, entries vary greatly in detail and may include: real name; parents; spouse(s); date and place of birth and death; profession(s); references to obituary notices in nine Anglo-American publications (e.g., *New York times, The clipper*); and a list of books on the person. In some cases obituaries are not cited for individuals, because none were found in the sources consulted. Name cross-references. Z5781.S76

Stage lives : a bibliography and index to theatrical biographies in English / comp. by George B. Bryan. Westport, Conn. : Greenwood, 1985. 368 p. (Bibliographies and indexes in the performing arts, no. 2). **BH128**

Pt. 1, Bibliography of biographies, has annotated lists of collective biographical books that include sketches of theater personalities and an unannotated author listing of individual biographies and autobiographies. All cited sources (about 2,750) are in English, but persons of various nationalities and time periods are represented. Pt. 2, Index of biographees, is keyed to entries in the bibliography and, in addition, usually includes brief data, such as birth and death dates, real name, and identifying phrase (e.g., "Irish actor") for the biographees. Necrological annals list individuals by date of death. Z5781.S78

Wearing, J. P. American and British theatrical biography : a directory. Metuchen, N.J. : Scarecrow, 1979. 1007 p. **BH129**

A guide to biographical information appearing in works of collective biography, theater yearbooks, encyclopedias of the theater, etc. For each person listed gives "name (with cross-references to stage names, pseudonyms, etc.), dates of birth and death, nationality, theatrical occupation(s), and a code to the source(s) containing fuller biographical information."—*Introd.* Focuses on American and British personalities, but others are included if "the sources surveyed make some mention of their contribution to the American or British theatre." PN2285.W42

DANCE

Guides

Bopp, Mary S. Research in dance : a guide to resources. N.Y. : G.K. Hall : Maxwell Macmillan, c1994. 296 p. **BH130**

Dedicated "to fostering and encouraging study and research in all areas of dance."—*Introd.* In two major sections: (1) Sources for dance research materials, which has descriptive listings of U.S. and international dance library collections and archives, as well as directories of specialized publishers, book dealers, bookstores, associations, and organizations; (2) The reference literature of dance, which includes an annotated list of reference sources by type (dictionaries, handbooks, bibliographies, etc.), identifies relevant serial publications, and describes available indexes and abstracts. Index of collections, authors, titles, and organizations. Z5514.D2B6

Bibliography

Adamczyk, Alice J. Black dance : an annotated bibliography. N.Y. : Garland, 1989. 213 p. : ports. (Garland reference library of the humanities, v. 558).   **BH131**
　　Cites 1,392 books, journal articles, and newspaper articles published in the Western hemisphere. Main listing is by author or title, with subject index of people, dance companies, places (e.g., Haiti) and topics (e.g., slave dancing, cakewalk). Based on collections of the New York Public Library, principally the Schomburg Center for Research in Black Culture and the Dance Collection.   Z7514.D2A33

Forbes, Fred R. Dance : an annotated bibliography, 1965–1982. N.Y. : Garland, 1986. 261 p. (Garland reference library of the humanities, v. 606).   **BH132**
　　Arranged by broad topic, identifies and describes 1,166 English-language writings on aesthetics, anthropology, education, history, relationships with literature, physiology, and sociology of all forms of dance. Includes books, articles, chapters, and dissertations. Author and subject indexes.   Z7514.D2F58

Leslie, Serge. A bibliography of the dance collection of Doris Niles and Serge Leslie / annotated by Serge Leslie, ed. by Cyril Beaumont. London : C.W. Beaumont [distr. by "Dancing Times"], 1966–81. 4 v.   **BH133**
　　v. 4 publ. by Dance Books Ltd., London.
　　Contents: pt. 1–2, A–Z; pt. 3–4, A–Z, mainly 20th-century publications.
　　Catalog of about 4,000 books and ephemera, arranged by author or title, based on a distinguished private collection. Emphasis is on ballet. Each volume has its own index of broad subject categories.
　　§ Cyril William Beaumont's *A bibliography of dancing* (London : Dancing Times, 1929. 228 p. Repr. : N.Y. : Blom, 1963) is an established source for important early works, fully described and indexed.   Z7514.D2L4

Magriel, Paul David. A bibliography of dancing : a list of books and articles on the dance and related subjects. N.Y. : Wilson, 1936. 228 p. : ill.   **BH134**
　　Repr.: N.Y. : Blom, 1966.
　　Classified, partially annotated list of international writings on all aspects of the dance. Cites many older periodical articles. Author-subject index.
　　———. ———. *4th cumulated supplement, 1936–40* (1941. 104 p.).

New York Public Library. Dance Collection. Dictionary catalog of the Dance Collection : a list of authors, titles, and subjects of multi-media materials in the Dance Collection of the Performing Arts Research Center of the New York Public Library. Boston : New York Public Libr. and G.K. Hall, 1974. 10 v.   **BH135**
　　Incorporates, in book form, 300,000 entries representing 96,000 items cataloged for the Dance Collection as of Oct. 1, 1973, plus entries for relevant materials in other divisions of the Research Libraries of the New York Public Library. Coverage is comprehensive and international; materials include not only books and pamphlets, but "microfilms, periodicals, music scores, dance notation scores, ballet libretti, manuscripts, photographs, slides, lithographs and engravings, original decor and costume designs, drawings, recordings, and other memorabilia."—*Introd.* Has numerous analytics for book and periodical articles.
　　———. *Bibliographic guide to dance* (1st– . Boston : G.K. Hall, 1976– . Annual). Represents an ongoing supplement to the above, listing materials (including older ones) newly cataloged for the collection.
　　•The original *Dictionary catalog* and the *Bibliographic guide to dance* series have been cumulated and made available for searching in CD-ROM format: *Dance on disc* [database] (Boston : G.K. Hall, 1993–). Updated annually.   Z7514.D2N462

Indexes

Guide to dance periodicals. v. 1 (1931/35)–v. 10 (1961/62). Gainesville : Univ. of Florida Pr., 1948–63.   **BH136**
　　Frequency varies: quinquennial, 1931/35–1946/50; biennial, 1951/52–1961/62.
　　Comp. by S. Y. Belknap.
　　Publisher varies.
　　Subject and author index to journals devoted to the dance, with some coverage of dance-related articles in other performing arts periodicals. Detailed illustration notes. Partially absorbed by *Guide to the performing arts* (BH8).   Z7514.D2G8

Index to dance periodicals / Dance Collection, the New York Public Library for the Performing Arts. 1990– . Boston : G.K. Hall, 1992– . Annual.   **BH137**
　　Indexes about 60 journals concerned with dance or allied arts (e.g., opera, theater) for articles, reviews, obituaries, etc. Broad topical coverage includes performance, history, therapy, choreographic technique, education, and various dance genres.   Z7514.D2I53

Studwell, William E. Ballet plot index : a guide to locating plots and descriptions of ballets and associated material / William E. Studwell and David A. Hamilton. N.Y. : Garland, 1987. 249 p. (Garland reference library of the humanities, v. 756).   **BH138**
　　Index to 54 ballet handbooks and monographs for plot summaries, illustrations, criticism, analysis, etc. of about 1,600 ballets of all periods. Listing by title of the ballet, with composer index.
　　　　　　GV1790.A1S77

Encyclopedias

Chujoy, Anatole. The dance encyclopedia / comp. and ed. by Anatole Chujoy and P. W. Manchester. Rev. and enl. ed. N.Y. : Simon & Schuster, [1967]. 992 p. : ill., facsims., ports.   **BH139**
　　1st ed., 1949.
　　Combines long articles on various aspects of the dance (including contributions by specialists) with briefer entries for people, types of dances, individual works, and dance terms. Illustrated.   GV1585.C5

Dictionary of modern ballet / gen. editors, Francis Gadan and Robert Maillard; American ed., Selma Jeanne Cohen. N.Y. : Tudor, [1959]. 360 p. : ill.   **BH140**
　　Originally published as: *Dictionnaire du ballet moderne* (Paris, 1957). Translated from the French by John Montague and Peggie Cochrane.
　　Has short articles on individual ballets, dancers, choreographers, composers, ballet companies, etc. Includes portraits of performers and excellent color renderings of set and costume designs.   GV1787.D513

The encyclopedia of dance & ballet / ed. by Mary Clarke & David Vaughan. London : Pitman ; N.Y. : Putnam's, 1977. 376 p. : ill.   **BH141**
　　The title is meant "to indicate that the entries are not confined to classical ballet but record also activity in contemporary dance styles."—*Introd.* The work is, however, concerned "only with dance raised to a theatrical level as a performing art in any of the media of the twentieth century." Entries for dancers, companies, choreographers, individual ballets, and types of dances. Well-illustrated, with many colored plates.   GV1585.E53

International dictionary of ballet / ed., Martha Bremser ; assistant ed., Larraine Nicholas ; picture ed., Leanda Shrimpton. Detroit : St. James, c1993. 2 v. (1600 p.) : ill.   **BH142**
　　This impressive international encyclopedia offers, in one alphabet, 750 signed articles on: (1) major artists of all periods (dancers,

choreographers, designers, composers, librettists, and teachers), with biographical sketch, listings of roles, works, etc., and a critical essay; (2) ballets, giving data on first performance and other major productions, plot summary, reception, and analysis; and (3) dance companies, providing historical background and commentary on selected companies of international renown. All entries include bibliographic references. Country index of persons and companies; professions and institutions index; notes on the 160 contributors. Attractively illustrated with black-and-white photographs, lithographs, etc., a large number of which are full-page. GV1585.I57

Koegler, Horst. The concise Oxford dictionary of ballet. 2nd ed., updated. Oxford ; N.Y. : Oxford Univ. Pr., 1987. 458 p. : ill. **BH143**

Original German edition, 1972 had title: *Friedrichs Ballettlexikon von A–Z.* First English edition, 1977; 2nd ed., 1982.

Although based on a German work, focus has been shifted to matters of Anglo-American interest, with much new material added. Attempts "to cover the whole ballet scene, past and present, its personalities, works, companies, places of performance, and technical terms, with some consideration of modern dance, ethnic dance, and ballroom dance."—*Foreword.* GV1585.K6313

Wilson, George Buckley. A dictionary of ballet. 3rd ed. London : Black ; N.Y. : Theatre Arts Books, 1974. 539 p. : ill. **BH144**

1st ed., 1957.

Consists of entries for terms, historical topics, individual ballets, companies, and brief biographies of leading dancers, choreographers, composers, and designers. Concerned chiefly with classical ballet, but also covers modern dance and other forms "which a serious lover of the dance is likely to encounter in the course of his ballet-going or his reading and writing."—*Pref.* GV1585.W5

Dictionaries

Grant, Gail. Technical manual and dictionary of classical ballet. 3rd rev. ed. N.Y. : Dover, 1982. 139 p. : ill. **BH145**
1st ed., 1950.
Gives brief definitions and pronunciation of dance terms, with small line drawings of main positions. GV1787.G68

Kersley, Leo. A dictionary of ballet terms / Leo Kersley, Janet Sinclair. [3rd rev. ed.]. London : Black, [1977]. 112 p. : ill. **BH146**
1st ed., 1952.
A glossary of technical terminology. Some definitions are of considerable length, with related terms often treated under a single heading. Many cross-references; helpful line drawings. Pronunciation is not indicated. GV1585.K45

Raffé, Walter George. Dictionary of the dance / comp., written, and ed. by W. G. Raffé ; assisted by M. E. Purdon. N.Y. : A.S. Barnes, [c1964]. 583 p. : ill. **BH147**
Repr.: N.Y. : A.S. Barnes ; London : T. Yoseloff, 1975.
Defines dance-related terms representing all countries, cultures, and time periods. Describes in some detail specific dances and types of dances. A geographical index lists dances and other terms by country or culture of origin. Also includes some topical entries (e.g., fable in dance, masks) but none for individual dancers, choreographers, or companies. GV1585.R3

Directories

Dance directory. [v. 1] (1956/57)– . Wash. : National Dance Association. **BH148**

Cover subtitle: "Programs of professional preparation in colleges, universities, and performing arts schools in the United States and Canada."

Issuing body varies; formerly, Dance Division, American Alliance for Health, Physical Education, Recreation and Dance.

Separate sections for colleges and secondary schools, each arranged by state and institutional name. Gives address, telephone number, admission requirements, etc., but emphasizes curriculum (degrees, faculty roster, course titles).

§ *Dance magazine college guide* (N.Y. : Dance Magazine, Inc., 1978– . Irregular.) is intended for high school juniors and seniors and has detailed narrative descriptions of about 120 programs, by name of college, plus capsule listings or addresses and telephone numbers of more than 400 other schools. Name and geographical indexes for all institutions included. GV1754.A1D3

Dance film and video guide / Dance Films Association ; comp. by Deirdre Towers. Princeton, N.J. : Dance Horizons/ Princeton Book Co., c1991. 233 p. : ill. **BH149**

Annotated listing of more than 2,000 films and videos available for rent or sale, ranging from filmed ballets to ballroom instruction videos. Entries include format, date, length, distributor, dancing and production credits, and statement of content. Indexes of choreographers, composers, dance companies, dancers, directors, and subjects. Directory of distributors and institutional resources.

§ David L. Parker and Esther Siegel, *Guide to dance in film : a catalog of U.S. productions including dance sequences, with names of dancers, choreographers, directors, and other details* (Detroit : Gale, 1978. 220 p.). Identifies 1,750 films, primarily produced for commercial exhibition, that have substantial dance content. Name index. GV1595.D32

Handbooks

Balanchine, George. Balanchine's complete stories of the great ballets / by George Balanchine and Francis Mason. Rev. and enl. ed. Garden City, N.Y. : Doubleday, 1977. 838 p. : ill. **BH150**

1954 ed. entitled: *Complete stories of the great ballets*; 1968 ed. called *Balanchine's new complete stories of the great ballets.*

Provides summaries of 404 ballets, both those "of lasting importance in the history of the art" (*Pref.*) and significant newer works. In addition to the stories, includes notes on first productions and notable revivals, quotations from critics, and Balanchine's observations. Also contains a brief history of the ballet, a chronology of significant events, and a glossary. Index of personal names, company names, and titles. MT95.B3

Beaumont, Cyril William. Complete book of ballets : a guide to the principal ballets of the nineteenth and twentieth centuries. [Rev.]. London : Putnam, [1951]. 1106 p. : ill. **BH151**
1st ed., 1937; 1st American ed., 1938.
Arranged by choreographer, entries on ballets give story, information on first production, historical notes, and excerpts from reviews. Black-and-white plates. Index.

§ In addition to *Supplement to Complete book of ballets* (London : C. W. Beaumont, 1945. Repr.: Putnam, 1952. 212 p.), two other supplements by Beaumont include works not in the main volume:

(1) *Ballets of today ... 2nd supplement* (London : Putnam, [1954]. 250 p.).

(2) *Ballets past and present ... 3rd supplement* (London : Putnam, [1955]. 259 p.).

McDonagh, Don. The complete guide to modern dance. Garden City, N.Y. : Doubleday, 1976. 534 p. : ill. **BH152**
A survey of modern dance works, arranged by choreographer within historical groupings (forerunners, founders, and contemporary practitioners). Entries for choreographers include a brief biographical

sketch, full descriptions of representative works, and a "choreochroni-cle," which lists titles and dates of all known works. Bibliography; chronology of significant dates and events; index.   GV1783.M26

Robertson, Allen. The dance handbook / Allen Robertson, Donald Hutera. Boston : G.K. Hall, [1990]. 278 p. : ill.   **BH153**

A selective guide to 200 key choreographers, companies, dancers, and dance works, arranged in historical groupings (e.g., origins, romantic ballet, classical ballet, birth of modern dance, the dance explosion, alternatives). Entries, geared to the nonspecialist, note essential achievements and emphasize linkages and influences. Country directories of periodicals, companies, organizations, festivals, archives, etc.; name and title index.   GV1601.R63

Terry, Walter. Ballet guide : background, listings, credits, and descriptions of more than five hundred of the world's major ballets. N.Y. : Dodd, Mead, c1976. 388 p., [16] leaves of plates : ill.   **BH154**

Based in part on Terry's *Ballet : a new guide to the liveliest art* (N.Y. : Dell, 1959).

Listed alphabetically by title of the ballet. Gives choreographer, composer, scenery and costume designers, company and date of first performance, principal dancers in first performance and important recreations of the roles. Descriptions are provided for most ballets. Glossary. Index of dancers, choreographers, companies, etc.

GV1790.A1T47

Annuals

Ballet annual : a record and year book of the ballet. 1st (1947)–18th (1963). N.Y. : Macmillan ; London : A. & C. Black, 1947–63. Annual.   **BH155**

Contains a list of outstanding events of the year; articles on various aspects of the ballet by well-known authorities and critics; and a checklist of ballet performances in European centers and America (chiefly New York).   GV1787.B25

Dance world. v.1–14. N.Y. : Crown, 1966–79. Annual.   **BH156**

John Willis, ed.

Similar to *Theatre world* (BH111), offering a pictorial survey of the New York dance season and the year's activity of regional American dance companies. Lists administrative and creative personnel, company dancers and guest artists, repertoires, etc. Includes section of brief biographies of dancers and choreographers. Indexed.

GV1580.D335

World ballet and dance. 1989/90– . London : Dance Books, c1989– . Annual.   **BH157**

An international yearbook, with two principal sections: The dancing world, for country-by-country critical overviews of dance activity; and The statistics of dance companies, also arranged by country, for data on the personnel, repertory, premieres, number of performances, etc., of companies and dance festivals.   GV1787.W67

Biography

Cohen-Stratyner, Barbara N. Biographical dictionary of dance. N.Y. : Schirmer Books ; London : Collier Macmillan, c1982. 970 p.   **BH158**

Offers biographical, sometimes critical, sketches of more than 2,900 figures from "the last four centuries of dance history in Europe and the Americas, embracing a wide range of theatrical genres, from the *Opéra-ballet* to the Broadway musical, from the burlesque striptease to the television variety show."—*Pref.* Includes impresarios,

composers, and artists associated with dance, as well as performers and choreographers. Entries emphasize individuals' professional contributions.   GV1785.A1C58

FILM

Reference sources on film have grown from the modest number available in 1970 to today's almost unmanageable wealth and variety. The listing here does not attempt to be inclusive, but only suggestive; titles included are those that have been found especially useful. Excluded are the numerous biobibliographies of film personalities and filmographies of individual studios. Only a handful of works on films of particular genres is included under Filmography—Themes and genres.

Guides

Armour, Robert A. Film : a reference guide. Westport, Conn. : Greenwood, 1980. 251 p.   **BH159**

Provides bibliographic essays, citing English-language books on various aspects of film (history, criticism, film and society, major actors and directors, international influences, reference works and periodicals, etc.). Appendix on research collections. Subject and author indexes. A useful guide for its time, now dated.

§ Eileen Sheahan's *Moving pictures : an annotated guide to selected film literature, with suggestions for the study of film* (South Brunswick, N.J. : A. S. Barnes, 1979. 146 p.) describes reference sources and film histories, including major foreign-language works. By type of source, with subject and author/title indexes.

PN1993.45.A75

Fisher, Kim N. On the screen : a film, television, and video research guide. Littleton, Colo. : Libraries Unlimited, 1986. 209 p.   **BH160**

Describes about 600 English-language reference sources for film and television, listed by type of source (e.g., bibliographic guides, dictionaries and encyclopedias, indexes, biographies, directories, bibliographies). Concluding chapters note core periodicals, research centers and archives, societies, and associations. Full, evaluative annotations. Author/title and subject indexes.   Z5784.M9F535

Hoffer, Thomas W. Animation : a reference guide. Westport, Conn. : Greenwood, 1981. 385 p.   **BH161**

A thorough guide to animation literature and resources through 1979. Offers bibliographic essays on the history, development, and production of animated films; a chronology of animation; descriptions of major research centers; sources of collectibles, films, and videos; and data on relevant periodicals. Includes a section on personalities in animation, which identifies writings on animators, background artists, and directors. Indexed.   TR897.5.H63

Bibliography

Austin, Bruce A. The film audience : an international bibliography of research with annotations and an essay. Metuchen, N.J. : Scarecrow, 1983. 179 p.   **BH162**

Lists articles, theses, and conference papers of theoretical or historical value for analyzing the relationship of the commercial film to its audience. By author, with subject and title indexes.

Z5784.M9A87

British Film Institute. Library. Catalogue of the book library of the British Film Institute. Boston : G. K. Hall, 1975. 3 v.   **BH163**

Reproduction of the Library's card catalog of more than 20,000 titles, including books, pamphlets, and some 4,000 film scripts. Scope is international and encompasses television and mass media, as well as film. Numerous analytics for book chapters and sections. Although periodicals are excluded, a fair number of extracted articles have been cataloged as pamphlets.

———. ———. *First supplement* (1983. 2 v.).
Adds about 10,000 titles. Z5784.M9B85

Gebauer, Dorothea. Bibliography of national filmographies / comp. by Dorothea Gebauer with the assistance of the members of the Cataloguing Commission of the International Federation of Film Archives ; ed. by Harriet W. Harrison. Bruxelles : FIAF, c1985. 80 p. **BH164**
Compiled as an aid to film catalogers, a country-by-country listing of national lists, reference works, serial publications, monographs, etc., that provide film and credit information on the country's output. Annotations for most items, describing organization and types of data included. Some unpublished sources are noted. Z5784.M9G42

Gray, John. Blacks in film and television : a Pan-African bibliography of films, filmmakers, and performers. N.Y. : Greenwood, 1990. 496 p. (Bibliographies and indexes in Afro-American and African studies, no. 27). **BH165**
Lists about 6,000 sources, more than half concerned with individual American filmmakers, actors, and actresses. Includes books, dissertations, periodical and newspaper articles, films, videotapes, audiotapes, and archival material relating to Africa, Europe, the Caribbean, and Latin America, in addition to the U.S. For Africa, identifies material on "colonial and ethnographic film activity as well as works on indigenous African films and filmmaking" (*Introd*), but excludes television. U.S. section also cites references on the image of African Americans in film and television. Appendix for film resources (archives and research centers, societies and associations, production companies, distributors, and festivals). Artist, film/series title, subject, and author indexes. Based largely on research collections of the New York Public Library. Z5784.M9G72

Hecht, Hermann. Pre-cinema history : an encyclopaedia and annotated bibliography of the moving image before 1896 / Hermann Hecht ; ed. by Ann Hecht. London : Bowker Saur, c1993. 476 p. : ill. **BH166**
A scholarly survey of the literature on precursors of modern film projection. Cites more than 1,000 books, scientific monographs, journal articles, manuscripts, etc., arranged by date from the 14th century to 1986. Covers camera obscura, magic lanterns, stereoscopic projection, and other forms of optical entertainment. Detailed bibliographic data for each item, with exceptionally full critical abstracts for most. Name and subject indexes. TR848.H38

Manchel, Frank. Film study : an analytical bibliography. Rutherford, [N.J.] : Fairleigh Dickinson Univ. Pr. ; London : Associated Univ. Pr., c1990. 4 v. **BH167**
A revision and reworking of the author's *Film study : a resource guide* (Rutherford, N.J. : Fairleigh Dickinson Univ. Pr., 1973).
A complex set, combining elements of a research guide, textbook, and bibliographic handbook. Organized around broad concepts (e.g., film technique and criticism, genre study, stereotyping in film, themes, film history), with many subsections, the first three volumes consist of extensively footnoted essays accompanied by annotated lists of English-language books and representative films. In all, provides critical analyses of about 2,000 books, often at review length. Vol. 4 contains: glossary; appendixes of periodicals, distributors, production codes, archives and libraries, bookstores, publishers, etc.; and indexes of authors, titles, personalities, subjects, and films. Despite the intricate arrangement and a small, poorly registered typeface, a useful survey of film literature in English. Z5784.M9M34

McCarty, Clifford. Published screenplays : a checklist. [Kent, Ohio] : Kent State Univ. Pr., [1971]. 127 p. **BH168**
Identifies 388 separately published scripts, as well as full and excerpted screenplays appearing in anthologies or writers' manuals. Alphabetical title listing, with index of names and source titles.

§ G. Howard Poteet's *Published radio, television, and film scripts : a bibliography* (Troy, N.Y. : Whitston Pub. Co., 1975. 245 p.) performs a similar function for television and radio shows and adds some film materials (mostly excerpts) not covered by McCarty. Separate title listing for each medium.
See also Gordon Samples, *The drama scholars' index to plays and filmscripts : a guide to plays and filmscripts in selected anthologies, series, and periodicals* (Metuchen, N.J. : Scarecrow, 1974–86. 3 v.). Z5784.M9M3

Prichard, Susan Perez. Film costume : an annotated bibliography. Metuchen, N.J. : Scarecrow, 1981. 563 p. **BH169**
More than 3,600 entries for "literally any literature relevant to film costume … even the most trivial."—*Introd*. Entry is by author or anonymous title. Includes references to biographical sketches of costume designers. Annotations not only indicate content but mention illustrations of costumes worn in specific films. An index provides access by subject, designer, film title, and performer. Z5691.P75

Rehrauer, George. The Macmillan film bibliography. N.Y. : Macmillan, [1982]. 2 v. **BH170**
Vol. 1 contains 6,762 "reviews" of English-language books, mostly from 1950–80 but including some earlier works. Alphabetical by title; covers critical studies, biographies and memoirs, published filmscripts, histories, handbooks, reference works, etc., with annotations ranging from a brief note on content to a lengthy evaluative assessment. Vol. 2 has an author index and an extensive analytic subject index of topics, films, and individuals.
§ Supersedes Rehrauer's *Cinema booklist* (Metuchen, N.J. : Scarecrow Pr., 1972) and supplements (1974, 1977). Somewhat complementary for the period is *The film book bibliography, 1940–1975* by Jack C. Ellis, Charles Derry, and Sharon Kern (Metuchen, N.J. : Scarecrow Pr., 1979. 752 p.) a sparsely annotated classified listing. Z5784.M9R423

Schmidt, Nancy J. Sub-Saharan African films and filmmakers : an annotated bibliography = Films et cinéastes africains de la région Subsaharienne : une bibliographie commentée. London ; N.Y. : Zell, 1988. 401 p. **BH171**
Preliminary ed.: Bloomington : African Studies Program, Indiana Univ., 1986.
A listing by author in two parts: Books, monographs, and theses (77 items); and Articles, reviews, and pamphlets (nearly 4,000). References are to materials in European languages, predominantly French-language periodicals and newspapers. Short annotations for about half the entries. Generally excludes South African films and filmmakers, as well as films about Africa by non-African directors. Indexes: actors and actresses; film festivals; film titles; filmmakers; countries; and broad subjects. Z5784.M9S3

Writers' Program (New York, N.Y.). The film index : a bibliography. N.Y. : Museum of Modern Art Film Lib. and the Wilson Co., 1941–1985. 3 v. : front., ill., plates. **BH172**
Contents: v. 1, The film as art; v. 2, The film as industry; v. 3, The film in society.
"Compiled by the Workers of the Writers' Program of the Work Projects Administration in the city of New York, 1935–1940, with the cooperation of the Museum of Modern Art, New York"—*t.p. of v. 2–3*.
Vols. 2–3 have imprint: White Plains, N.Y. : Kraus International Publications.
Under the editorship of Harold Leonard, this extensive, annotated, classified bibliography was compiled under the auspices of the Work Projects Administration. After the appearance of v. 1 in 1941, publication of the remaining two volumes was abandoned when the WPA went out of existence; a card file of entries for v. 2–3, housed in the Museum of Modern Art, was used to assemble these volumes when they were eventually published in 1985.
The set contains more than 20,000 entries for English-language books, pamphlets, book chapters, and periodical articles through December 31, 1935. The bulk of the entries are for periodical articles and reviews, with most book references confined to v. 1; newspaper cita-

tions are omitted. Within each volume, arrangement is by broad subject (history and technique, types of film, advertising, distribution, finance, labor relations, production, censorship, moral and religious aspects, social and political aspects, etc.), with numerous topical subdivisions. Nonevaluative annotations (referred to as "digests") describe content in detail. Index of names and titles in v. 1; combined name index for v. 2–3 in v. 3. A landmark undertaking of lasting historical value.   Z5784.M9W75

Wulff, Hans Jürgen. Bibliographie der Filmbibliographien = Bibliography of film bibliographies / comp. and ed. by Hans Jürgen Wulff ; including a bibliography of Slavic language film bibliographies, comp.by Andrzej Gwóźdź and Anna Wastkowska. München : New York : K.G. Saur, 1987. 326 p.   **BH173**

Lists more than 1,000 bibliographies published as books, catalogs of individual library collections, pamphlets, articles and essays (and also parts of articles and essays) in English and in European languages, through 1985. Excludes almost all filmographies. Classified arrangement; *see also* references; author and subject indexes. "Retrospective, cumulative indexes to individual film journals," p. 64–70.
                                                    Z5784.M9W84

Periodicals

Brady, Anna. Union list of film periodicals : holdings of selected American collections / Anna Brady, comp. and ed., Richard Wall, assistant ed., Carolyn Newitt Weiner, computer ed. Westport, Conn. : Greenwood, 1984. 316 p.   **BH174**

Intends "to facilitate serious film scholarship."—*Pref.* Locates holdings for about 1,300 international journals in 35 U.S. libraries. Alphabetical title listing, with title change and geographical (i.e., country of publication) indexes.   Z5784.M9B76

International film, radio, and television journals / ed. by Anthony Slide. Westport, Conn. : Greenwood, 1985. 428 p.
                                                    BH175

For some 200 major periodicals of all periods, offers: a lengthy critical/historical profile; sources of indexing; reprint editions; selected U.S. locations of files; and a detailed publication history. Titles included are predominantly American or British. Appendixes discuss fan magazines and in-house journals and list entries by country and type or subject.

§ Similarly titled, Katharine Loughney's *Film, television, and video periodicals : a comprehensive annotated list* (N.Y.; London : Garland, 1991. 431 p.) has succinct descriptions but covers more than 1,000 English-language and foreign publications in current distribution. Indexes by country of origin, medium, and general type (popular, scholarly, technical, annual).   Z5784.M9I485

Dissertations

Fielding, Raymond. A bibliography of theses and dissertations on the subject of film, 1916–1979. Houston, Tex. : Univ. Film Assoc., School of Communication, Univ. of Houston, 1979. 72 p. (University Film Association. Monograph, no. 3).
                                                    BH176

An author listing of 1,420 master's theses and doctoral dissertations, with subject index of broad terms (e.g., social aspects of film, general film history). References to individuals' names are found under the subject category "Critical and biographical studies...," but there are no index entries for specific films.

§ Fielding's bibliography builds on periodic lists that appeared in issues of *The journal of the University Film Association*. Additional listings by Fielding of 770 theses and dissertations through 1984 (including some older studies) were published in the *Journal*'s successors, *The journal of the University Film and Video Association* (v. 24 [Winter 1982] : 41–54) and *The journal of film and video* (v. 27 [Fall 1985] : 37–52), without accompanying subject indexing. Beginning

with v. 7, 1987, *Historical journal of film, radio, and television* has included an annual computer-produced author list of dissertations and some master's theses, derived from the *Dissertation abstracts international* and *Masters abstracts* databases.

Adaptations

Ross, Harris. Film as literature, literature as film : an introduction to and bibliography of film's relationship to literature. N.Y. ; London : Greenwood, 1987. 346 p. (Bibliographies and indexes in world literature, no. 10).   **BH177**

Lists 2,495 articles and books published 1908–85, classified by topic (general relationships; relationships to specific literary genres; adaptation in general; adaptations or contributions of individual literary figures throughout the world, etc.). Omits reviews, newspaper articles, and foreign-language materials. Annotations are provided only to clarify content or identify films discussed. Author index; subject index to writers, film and literary titles, and topics.

§ Jeffrey Egan Welch's *Literature and film : an annotated bibliography* (N.Y. : Garland, 1981. 315 p.) is arranged by year and indexed by names and subjects. Useful annotations. A supplement covers 1978–88 (1993. 341 p.).   Z5784.M9

Library resources

Footage 89 : North American film and video sources / ed. by Richard Prelinger and Celeste R. Hoffnar. N.Y. : Prelinger Associates, c1989. 83, 795 p. : ill.   **BH178**

Aims to "facilitate access to moving image materials (film, videotape, and computer graphics) for all potential users, whether their interests are academic, artistic, commercial, documentary, educational, historical, newsworthy or scientific."—*Pref.* Following some articles on practical matters (e.g., investigating copyright status, using consultants), lists 1,635 academic institutions, corporations, stock footage libraries, associations, etc., that house collections. Entries, arranged geographically, include address, telephone and fax numbers, services, access, restrictions, and a lengthy description of holdings (sometimes running to a page or more). Source/collection name index. Directory of researchers and research organizations. Extensive subject index, including persons and places.

Supplemented by *Footage 91 : North American film and video sources*, ed. by Prelinger (N.Y. : Prelinger Assoc., 1991. 246 p.). By name of repository, gives changes, corrections, and additions to earlier listings, plus descriptions of 150 new sources.   PN1993.4.F69

International directory of film and TV documentation centres / ed. by Frances Thorpe. [3rd ed.]. Chicago : St. James Pr., c1988. 140 p.   **BH179**

Published for the International Federation of Film Archives (FIAF); updates a work originally issued in 1976 and revised in 1980.

Lists 104 collections from 40 countries. For each gives name and address, staff contact, hours of service, reproduction services, date of founding, and description of collection (books, periodicals, clippings, scripts, stills, posters, special collections, etc., but not films and videos). Topical index to special collections.   PN1993.4.I57

Mehr, Linda Harris. Motion pictures, television and radio : a union catalogue of manuscript and special collections in the western United States. Boston : G. K. Hall, [1977]. 201 p.
                                                    BH180

Sponsored by The Film and Television Study Center, Inc.

Locates and describes research collections (libraries, museums, historical societies, etc.) in 11 western states. Collections include production and personal papers of individuals, scripts, promotional materials, photographs, stills, clipping files, scrapbooks, etc. Collections of films, videos, and recordings are generally excluded. By repository, with name and topic index of individuals by occupation.
                                                    PN1993.4.M37

Researcher's guide to British film & television collections / ed., Elizabeth Oliver. 2nd rev. ed. London : British Universities Film & Video Council, [1985]. 176 p. : ill. **BH181**

1st ed., 1981.

In six sections: national archives; regional collections; television company archives; newsreel, production, and stock shot libraries; specialized collections; and associated information and documentation sources. Entries give history, holdings, cataloging, access to facilities, etc. Collection and subject indexes.

4th rev. ed. (1993. 226 p.); James Ballantyne, ed.

PN1993.4.R47

Rowan, Bonnie G. Scholars' guide to Washington, D.C. : film and video collections. Wash. : Smithsonian Inst. Pr., 1980. 282 p. (Scholars' guide to Washington D.C., no. 6). **BH182**

Published for the Woodrow Wilson International Center for Scholars.

The main section lists collections, referral services, and academic programs in the Washington area, arranged alphabetically by institution or agency. Descriptions of collections or programs; notes on services, access, etc. Numerous appendixes and indexes. PN1998.A1R68

Film catalogs

Listed here are catalogs of some of the more important film archives, as well as broad-based published lists of films and catalogs of films produced in a particular country.

American Film Institute. The American Film Institute catalog of motion pictures produced in the United States. N.Y. : Bowker, 1971–93. [9 v.]. (In progress). **BH183**

Publisher varies.

Contents: F1, Feature films, 1911–1920 (Berkeley : Univ. of California Pr. 2 v.); F2, Feature films, 1921–1930 (2 v.); F3, Feature films, 1931–1940 (Berkeley : Univ. of California Pr. 3 v.); F6, Feature films, 1961–1970 (2 v.).

This monumental set aims to "provide complete cataloging of every feature, short, and newsreel produced by the American film community since 1893."—*Pref.*, v. F3. To date, four decades of feature-length films, covering 1911–40 and 1961–70, have been documented, based on viewed prints, production records, copyright entries, censorship records, contemporary news items and reviews, trade annuals, critical studies, memoirs and biographies, interviews, etc.

Films are listed alphabetically by title. For each is given, as applicable: (1) production company, copyright and release dates, physical description, running time; (2) production credits; (3) source; (4) cast credits; (5) genre designation and plot summary; (6) notes on the production's history. Extent of information varies; for the 1931–40 series (publ. 1993), story details and historical notes have been greatly expanded.

Each series has name and subject indexes. Indexing varies in depth, as the set progresses. Currently provided are: chronology of film titles; personal names; corporate names; subjects; genres; series; geographic shooting locations; productions filmed in foreign languages; songwriters and composers; literary and dramatic source credits.

PN1998.A57

Chirat, Raymond. Catalogue des films français de long métrage : films de fiction, 1919–1929. [Toulouse] : Cinémathèque de Toulouse, [1984]. Unpaged. **BH184**

"Avec la collaboration de Roger Icart."—*t.p.*

A title listing of 1,055 feature-length films (excluding documentaries) with production and actor credits, synopsis, and notes. Chronological and name indexes.

Supplemented for feature films of the sound period by:

———. ———. *Films sonores de fiction, 1929–1939* (2ᵉ éd. Bruxelles : Cinémathèque Royale, 1981. 319 p.).

———. ———. *Films de fiction, 1940–1950* (Luxemborg : Impr. Saint-Paul, S.A., 1981. Unpaged). PN1998.C453

•**Film index international** [database]. London : British Film Inst. **BH185**

Available on CD-ROM, updated annually.

Based on SIFT (Summary of Information on Film and Television), a database compiled by the British Film Institute since 1934. Initial disk contains two linked files: (1) details of 90,000 entertainment, mostly feature, films of the sound era (and silent pictures of major filmmakers), including title, director, production company, country, release year, main credits, cast, running time, color/black-and-white, footage, genre, and plot synopsis; (2) biographical information and filmographies for 30,000 personalities. Both files include references to periodical reviews and articles, about 250,000 in all.

Gifford, Denis. The British film catalogue, 1895–1985 : a reference guide. N.Y. : Facts on File, c1986. ca. 1000 p. **BH186**

British ed. publ. Newton Abbott: David & Charles.

A revision and expansion of the 1973 edition, which covered 1895–1970. Intended as a comprehensive record of the British "entertainment film," includes some films never released but excludes newsreels, documentaries, and films made for television. The listing is chronological in two sections, 1895–1970 and 1971–85, with separate film title indexes for each period. Information given includes, as available, length in footage or running time, color system employed, producer, director, distributor, story source, cast and characters played, subject descriptor, and brief plot summary. Details are understandably minimal for many early films.

§ David Quinlan's *British sound films : the studio years, 1928–1959* (London : Batsford, 1984; Totowa, N.J. : Barnes & Noble, 1985. 406 p.) offers, in addition to credits and running time, plot details and critical evaluations for feature films of the period. Arranged by decade, then by title, with introductory overviews for each decade. Not indexed. PN1998.G543

Helt, Richard C. West German cinema since 1945 : a reference handbook / by Richard C. Helt and Marie E. Helt. Metuchen, N.J. : Scarecrow, 1987. 736 p., : ill. **BH187**

Covers "feature-length, commercial films produced between 1945 and early 1986" (*Pref.*), including coproductions with directors from other countries. Alphabetical by title, gives year, synopsis, production credits, principal performers, length in minutes. Short biographies of major directors. Indexes: directors; actors and actresses; English title equivalents referring to the German original.

Supplemented by the authors' *West German cinema, 1985–1990 : a reference handbook* (Metuchen, N.J. : Scarecrow, 1992. 259 p.). PN1993.5.G3H435

The international film index, 1895–1990 / ed. by Alan Goble. London ; [New Providence], N.J. : Bowker-Saur, c1991. 2 v. (1687 p.). **BH188**

Prefatory matter in English, French, German, and Italian.

Contents: v. 1, Film titles; v. 2, Directors' filmography and indexes.

Attempts to provide "a comprehensive index to films by title and director on a worldwide basis."—*Pref.* Vol. 1 lists some 232,000 "master" titles and alternate titles representing 177,000 films of all types—full-length, short, documentary, animated, serial, made for television—of the silent and sound eras. Master title entries give year of release, director(s), other credits (where director has not been established), type of film, country of origin, and alternative titles. Filmographies for 25,000 directors in v. 2 show directing credits chronologically (codirecting and uncredited contributions are usually omitted here, although they are noted under film titles in v. 1). Type of film is indicated, as are the director's nationality and (where determined) dates. Indexes of directors by country and animated film directors. Select bibliography of sources consulted.

§Includes more films than Brooks Bushnell's *Directors and their films: a comprehensive reference, 1895–1990* (BH204). Despite likelihood of errors in projects of this magnitude, both works are useful in themselves and serve as broad-based platforms for further research.

PN1998.I52

Lauritzen, Einar. American film-index, 1908–1915 : motion pictures, July 1908–December 1915 / by Einar Lauritzen and Gunnar Lundquist. Stockholm : Film-Index : distr. by Akademibokhandeln, [1976]. 704 p. : ill.   **BH189**

A title listing of some 23,000 American films, supplying date, producer, director, author, cast, etc., as available.

Lauritzen and Lundquist's *American film-index, 1916–1920 : motion pictures, January 1916–December 1920* (Stockholm : Film-Index, 1984. 612 p.) has about 12,000 listings. Credits are generally fuller. Includes additions and corrections to the earlier volume.

PN1998.L26

Library of Congress. Motion Picture, Broadcasting, and Recorded Sound Division. Early motion pictures : the paper print collection in the Library of Congress / by Kemp R. Niver ; ed. by Bebe Bergsten. Wash. : Motion Picture, Broadcasting, and Recorded Sound Div., Library of Congress : for sale by U.S. Govt. Print. Off., 1985. 509 p. : ill.   **BH190**

Superintendent of Documents classification: LC 40.9:Ea7.

A revision, expansion, and updating of Niver's *Motion pictures from the Library of Congress paper print collection, 1894–1912* (Berkeley : Univ. of California Pr., 1967).

Serves as a guide to the more than 3,000 American and foreign films restored from paper-positive prints deposited with the Library of Congress under early copyright arrangements. Films are listed by title. Information given includes producer/distributor, copyright number and date, production credits, location and date of production, alternate titles, length, summary, and notes. Index of names and subjects, keyed to film titles; separate "credits" index identifies individuals by category (actors and actresses, cameramen, directors, scriptwriters and authors). This edition adds 50 films and expands coverage to 1915.

§ Also of importance is another catalog issued by the Division, *The George Kleine collection of early motion pictures in the Library of Congress* (Wash. : The Library, 1980. 270 p.), based on a private collection of films acquired by the Library of Congress in 1947. Contains full descriptions of some 450 films, 1898–1926, a chronological index, and a detailed name/subject index.   Z5784.M9L5

Museum of Modern Art (New York, N.Y.). The film catalog : a list of holdings in the Museum of Modern Art / general ed., Jon Gartenberg with Lee Amazonas ... [et al.]. Boston : G.K. Hall, 1985. 443 p., : ill.   **BH191**

Provides basic data concerning 5,500 titles in the Museum's collections, which contain "nearly all types of films, including fiction and documentary, animation and avant-garde, and other classifications, as well as some television and video, from all countries and every period, from the 1890s to the present."—*Introd.* Title listing, with producer/director index. Cross-references from alternate titles.   PN1993.4.M8

Turner, D. John. Canadian feature film index, 1913–1985 = Index des films canadiens de long métrage, 1913–1985 / D. J. Turner ; French text, Micheline Morisset. [Ottawa] : Public Archives Canada : National Film, Television, and Sound Archives, c1987. 816 p.   **BH192**

An "attempt to compile the principal credits of every Canadian feature film from 1913, when the first known feature was produced, to 1985."—*Introd.* The films are chronologically arranged by the date the film was shot. For each, gives: " ... technical information related to the making of the film (film stock, laboratory, dialogue), then the principal participants (producers, directors, technicians, actors), the cost and running time followed by distribution and release information and lastly the Archives' holdings."—*User's guide.* Includes 1,222 films. Indexed by title, personal name, production company, etc.

PN1998.T83

Walls, Howard Lamarr. Motion pictures 1894–1912 identified from the records of the United States Copyright Office. Wash. : Copyright Off., Lib. of Congress, 1953. 92 p.   **BH193**

Lists "8,506 works, representing approximately 6,000 titles, which were registered in the Copyright Office as photographs" (*Foreword*) and were later identified as films by the compiler. In two parts: (1) a title list, with copyright claimant, date, and registration number shown; (2) an index of claimant names (e.g., Biograph Company, Thomas A. Edison), with sublisting by year and film title.

§ A retrospective extension of Copyright Office listings of film registrations, four of which were issued in the Office's *Catalog of copyright entries, cumulative series: Motion pictures, 1912–1939* (publ. 1951); *Motion pictures, 1940–1949* (publ. 1953); *Motion pictures, 1950–1959* (Publ. 1960); and *Motion pictures, 1960–1969* (publ. 1971). These lists also supply physical description and production and script/source credits. For post-1969 listings of film registrations, see Library of Congress. Copyright Office, *Catalog of copyright entries* (AA433).   PN1998.W25

Film guides

Noted here are evaluative handbooks that provide brief critical appraisals designed to guide viewers of films in movie houses or on video. Systems of rating notations are often used.

Bergan, Ronald. The Holt foreign film guide / Ronald Bergan and Robyn Karney. N.Y. : Holt, 1989. 638 p.   **BH194**

Publ. in U.K. as: *Bloomsbury foreign film guide* (London : Bloomsbury, 1988).

Profiles more than 2,000 non-English-language motion pictures seen in the U.S. or Great Britain, including acknowledged classics, box-office successes, and films that represent significant trends and styles. Listed by British title, with cross-references from original and American alternate titles. Gives for each: country of origin, date of first release, running time, production company, credits, summary and critical comment, major awards received. No index.

PN1995.9.F67B4

A guide to world cinema : covering 7,200 films of 1950–84 including capsule reviews and stills from the programmes of the National Film Theatre, London / ed. by Elkan Allan. London : Whittet Books in association with the British Film Institute ; Detroit : distr. by Gale, 1985. 682 p. : ill.   **BH195**

Reprints critical notes originally prepared for the National Film Theatre's series of film programs, accompanied in most cases by a small black-and-white still. The guide reflects the eclectic and international character of NFT screenings, as well as their retrospective nature (numerous pre-1950 productions are included). Country of origin, date, director, and major players are given in addition to succinct critical commentary. By title, with director index.   PN1995.G84

Halliwell's film guide. [1st ed.] (1977)– . N.Y. : Harper-perennial, 1977– . Irregular.   **BH196**

Ed. by Leslie Halliwell, 1st–6th ed.; John Walker, 7th ed. (1989)– .

Publisher varies. Published also in a British ed.

Arranged by title, currently includes about 18,000 English-language and selected foreign-language feature films, and gives: rating of quality, from zero to four stars; country of origin; year; running time; studio; producer; one-line indication of contents or story; brief, pointed critical note; production credits; cast; awards. Promotional taglines and short excerpts from critics accompany many of the entries. Notes availability in video format. No illustrations or index. Especially useful for inclusion of British films seldom or never seen in the U.S.

Kael, Pauline. 5001 nights at the movies. N.Y. : H. Holt, c1991. 945 p.   **BH197**

Earlier ed., 1982, had title: *5001 nights at the movies : a guide from A to Z.*

A collection of brief film notices that originally appeared in the "Goings on about town" section of *The New Yorker.* Written in Kael's distinctive style, entries give year, studio (for American productions), and color and lensing process indications, with credits incorporated in the body of the notice rather than listed systematically. Refers to anthologies of Kael's criticism that contain full reviews, where applicable. Name index.   PN1995.K19

Maltin, Leonard. Leonard Maltin's movie and video guide / ed. by Leonard Maltin ; assoc. ed., Luke Sader ... [et al.]. 1995 ed. N.Y. : Penguin Groups, 1994. 1580 p.　**BH198**

New editions publ. annually, under similar titles (e.g., *Leonard Maltin's TV movies and video guide*. First issued in 1969 as *TV movies.*

A standard guide for armchair viewers and a useful film reference source in its own right. Currently includes more than 19,000 entries for televised theatrical films and made-for-television movies, with symbols indicating availability in video format. Gives year of release, original running time, director, and performers (often through the full supporting cast). Evaluations have minimal notes on plot, short narrative assessments, and a one- to four-star ranking system (with "Bomb" reserved for the truly execrable). Recent editions include indexes of major players and directors.

§ A competitive guide that first appeared in 1958, *Movies on TV and videocassette*, ed. by Steven Scheuer, (17th rev. ed. [1993–1994]. N.Y. : Bantam Books, 1992. 1326 p.), covers about the same number of films and has a similar format. Cast listings are generally less full than in Maltin's guide.

Nash, Jay Robert. The motion picture guide / Jay Robert Nash, Stanley Ralph Ross. Chicago : Cinebooks, 1985–1987. 12 v.　**BH199**

Contents: v. 1–9, 1927–84, comp. by Nash and Ross (4181 p.); v. 10, Silent film, 1910–36, comp. by Robert Connelly (439 p.); v. 11–12, Index, comp. by Nash and Ross (3170 p.).

Offers data on more than 40,000 films released in the U.S. through 1984, together with evaluations for most. In general, gives title (with variants noted), rating (0 to 5 stars), year of release, country of origin for foreign films, running time, producing and distributing companies, color or black-and-white indication, cast (including character names), synopsis and critical commentary, production credits, genre note, Motion Picture Academy of America rating. For especially noteworthy or popular films, may include extensive critical or anecdotal material on the production. Vol. 9 includes 1984 releases and a listing of additional sound films considered to be of minor significance. Vols. 11–12 have variant title and series indexes, in addition to a name index.

Useful for the amount of information contained and the considerable detail in many of the entries. Although generally lauded in reviews, the work's claims to authority, comprehensiveness, accuracy, and consistency have been seriously challenged in some quarters, notably in *Film quarterly* 41, no. 2 (Winter 1987–88): 59–63 and *Journal of film and video* 40, no. 4 (Fall 1988): 58–62.

Kept up-to-date by *The motion picture guide annual*, beginning in 1986 (for films of 1985); some additional features and indexes are provided (e.g., obituaries, "people to watch," stills, list of films by genre).

•Available on CD-ROM, 1992– . Called a "2nd ed." of the *Guide*; incorporates the basic set and the first six annuals, with revisions.
PN1995.N346

Sadoul, Georges. Dictionary of films / Georges Sadoul ; tr., ed., and updated by Peter Morris. Berkeley : Univ. of California Pr., [1972]. 432 p.　**BH200**

A translation, revision, and expansion of *Dictionnaire des films* (Paris, 1965).

Lists about 1,100 films by original title, indicating country of origin, date, principal credits and cast, together with a plot summary and critical note. International in scope, selectively surveying artistically important films from the silent era through the 1960s. Cross-references from all known release titles.

§ The original French work has subsequently been revised, most recently as *Dictionnaire des films* (Nouv. éd. rev. et augm. par Émile Breton. Paris : Seuil, 1990. 383 p.).　PN1993.45.S3213

The Time out film guide / ed. by Tom Milne. 3rd ed. London ; N.Y. : Penguin Books, 1993. 949 p.　**BH201**

1st ed., 1989; 2nd ed., 1991.

Gathers about 10,000 capsule reviews from *Time out*, a weekly British guide to cultural events. Entries include basic data (year, length, director, cast) and succinct critical comment. Appendixes of film categories and country listings; actor, director, and general subject indexes. Useful for British perspective on American productions and inclusion of numerous films made outside Britain and the U.S.
PN1998.T46

VideoHound's golden movie retriever. 1991– . Detroit : Visible Ink, c1991– . Annual.　**BH202**

Cover subtitle: The complete guide to movies on video cassette and laserdisc.

Editors: Martin Connors, Julia Furtaw ... [et al.].

Frequency varies; biennial, 1991.

A relative newcomer to the crowded field of film guides. Covers some 22,000 feature film video releases. By title, entries give short plot/critical summary, year, MPAA rating, running time, color indication, country, director, cast, format, price, distributor, and a one- to four-bone rating of quality (with negative "woofs" also indicated). May also list songwriters, songs, and major award winners and nominations. Various indexes, including: foreign films by country; alternative titles; categories (subjects and genres); series; cast; directors. Directory of distributors. Films not released in video format are excluded. Multimedia CD-ROM and personal computer versions are available.

§ Some 13,000 feature films on video are briefly described and evaluated in Mick Martin and Marsha Porter's annual *Video movie guide* (N.Y. : Ballantine Books, 1985–). Arrangement is by category (e.g., drama, horror, musical), then title. Cast, director, and title indexes. Entries do not list distributors or prices.　PN1992.95.V554

Filmography

Besides lists of credits for performers, directors, etc., two other types of filmographies are cited here: those that match screenplay adaptations with their original source materials, and those that identify films dealing with specific themes, genres, or groups.

Annual index to motion picture credits. 1978– . Westport, Conn. : Greenwood, 1979– . Annual.　**BH203**

Compiled by the Academy of Motion Picture Arts and Sciences. Continues *Screen achievement records bulletin* (1976–77) and earlier publications with similar titles issued by the Academy.

Recent volumes have six sections: (1) Film titles (alphabetical catalog of films with full list of credits); (2) Credits by category (actors, art direction, cinematography, costume designers, directors, film editors, makeup, music, producers, sound, writers); (3) Releasing companies; (4) Alphabetical index of individual credits; (5) Casting (for films assigning casting credit); (5) Cumulative film titles (for all volumes to date). Based on data collected to determine eligibility for Academy Award consideration.　PN1993.A48a

Bushnell, Brooks. Directors and their films : a comprehensive reference, 1895–1990. Jefferson, NC : McFarland & Company, c1993. 1035 p.　**BH204**

An "international listing of director credits for more than 108,000 film titles."—*Introd.* In two parts: (1) Directors, showing films; (2) Films, showing directors. Director entries in pt. 1 list films chronologically and give original and alternate titles; movies made for television are excluded unless also released in theaters. Codirecting credits (including contributions not credited on-screen) are indicated by an asterisk. Nationality of directors (or other biographical data) not supplied. Index to films in pt. 2 includes all forms of title cited in the filmographies, noting date and director's name. Bushnell's listings appear to be reasonably complete and accurate, but authority is difficult to assess, since criteria and a bibliography of sources are lacking.

§ Bears more than a passing resemblance to *The international film index, 1895–1990* (BH188). Also related: Alison J. Filmer and Andre Golay, *Harrap's book of film directors and their films : a comprehensive guide from 1924 to the present day* (London : Harrap,

1989. 491 p.), which has filmographies of all feature film directors in the U.K. and the U.S. and foreign directors with at least one English-language film credit. Title index.   PN1998.B85

Corey, Melinda. A cast of thousands : a compendium of who played what in film / comp. by Melinda Corey and George Ochoa. N.Y. : Facts On File, c1992. 3 v. (2462 p.).   **BH205**
  Contents: v. 1, The casts, A–L; v. 2, The casts, M–Z. Index of directors; v. 3, Index of actors.
  Lists performers and their character names for about 10,000 selected films (classics, award winners, financial successes, representative silent and foreign films, etc.) released 1912–91. Films are entered alphabetically in v. 1–2, giving year, studio, director, and cast (generally limited to 15 players). Director and actor indexes show film titles and dates. Full coverage of films of some major stars and directors; for others, because of the selective nature of the compendium, filmographies may not be complete.
  § Similar in purpose and more comprehensive for the 1949–74 period: Richard Bertrand Dimmitt, *An actor guide to the talkies* (Metuchen, N.J. : Scarecrow, 1967–68. 2 v.), covering 8,000 feature-length films 1949–64; and the continuation volume by Andrew A. Aros, *An actor guide to the talkies, 1965 through 1974* (1977. 771 p.). Cast and role lists, with performer indexes; director credits are not included.
                    PN1998.C65

Darby, William. Masters of lens and light : a checklist of major cinematographers and their feature films. Metuchen, N.J. : Scarecrow, 1991. 1043 p. : ports.   **BH206**
  Documents the film contributions of more than 700 individuals "who are credited as principal or co-principal photographer on at least five works."—*Pref.* Entrants are primarily American but include important British, German, Italian, Swedish, and Russian cinematographers as well. By name, then alphabetically by film title, showing release date and studio or country. Also has separate section for miscellaneous films of interest not included in the filmographies, with camera credits. Appendix of awards; film title index.   PN1998.D285

Film directors : a complete guide. [Ed. 1]– . [Beverly Hills, Calif.] : Lone Eagle, [1983?]– . Annual.   **BH207**
  Michael Singer, comp. and ed.
  Title varies.
  Provides filmographies of American and foreign directors currently active (in some cases, alive but inactive), including theatrical features, television films, and miniseries. Entries also give, as available, birth date, addresses, and agent. Director interviews, Academy Awards, film title index, lists of agents and managers, etc. Beginning with the 6th ed. (1988), includes section of filmographies, "Notable directors of the past."
  § Other directories published by Lone Eagle, annually or every two to three years: *Film actors guide* (ed. 1 [1991]–) *Film writers guide* (ed. 1 [1988]–); *Film producers, studios, agents, and casting directors guide* (ed. 1 [1989]–); *Cinematographers, production designers, costume designers and film editors guide* (ed. 1 [1988]–); *Film composers guide* (ed. 1 [1990]–); and *Special effects and stunts guide* (ed. 1 [1989]–). These sometimes include special listings and features, but focus on film credits of individuals currently active in the American film industry.   PN1998.A2D568

International directory of cinematographers, set- and costume designers in film / International Federation of Film Archives (FIAF). München ; N.Y. : K. G. Saur, 1981–92. v. 1–12. (In progress).   **BH208**
  Alfred Krautz, ed.
  Contents: v. 1, German Democratic Republic (1946–1978), Poland (from the beginnings to 1978); v. 2, France (from the beginnings to 1980); v. 3, Albania, Bulgaria, Greece, Rumania, Yugoslavia (from the beginnings to 1980); v. 4, Germany (from the beginnings to 1945); v. 5, Denmark, Finland, Norway, Sweden (from the beginnings to 1984); v. 6, Supplementary volume: new entries, additions, corrections, 1978–1984; v. 7, Italy (from the beginnings to 1986); v. 8, Portugal, Spain (from the beginnings to 1988); v. 9, Hungary (from the beginnings to 1989); v. 11, General index vols. 1–10 (Pt. A, Film titles; Pt. B, Film directors); v. 12, Cuba (from the beginnings to 1990).

For each person, provides identifying word or phrase and a chronological list of film credits. Entries may also include brief biographical information (e.g., dates, schooling, professional employment). Film title and director indexes in v. 11 cumulate separate indexes in v. 1–10.   PN1998.A1I55

Langman, Larry. A guide to American film directors : the sound era, 1929–1979. Metuchen, N.J. : Scarecrow, 1981. 2 v.   **BH209**
  Vol. 1 is alphabetically arranged by director, with feature films listed by date; v. 2 is a title index. Excludes television and silent films. Includes non-U.S. films of American directors but lists only American films of foreign directors.   PN1998.A2L34

———————— A guide to American screenwriters : the sound era, 1929–1982. N.Y. : Garland, 1984. 2 v.   **BH210**
  Contents: v. 1, Screenwriters; v. 2, Films.
  Vol. 1 is an alphabetical list of about 5,000 screenwriters, with names of films in chronological order; coauthors are noted. Vol. 2 lists films by title and gives date and writers' names for each. Attempts to deal with uncredited and misattributed contributions.
  § Essentially replaces The Academy of Motion Pictures Arts and Sciences and Writers Guild of America's *Who wrote the movie and what else did he write? : an index of screen writers and their film works, 1936–1969* (Los Angeles : The Academy, 1970. 491 p.), although the earlier work credits individual responsibility for original story, additional dialogue, etc., and source material, features lacking in Langman's guide.   PN1998.L24

Palmer, Scott. British film actors' credits, 1895–1987. Jefferson, N.C. : McFarland, c1988. 917 p.   **BH211**
  An expansion and reworking of Palmer's *A who's who of British film actors* (Metuchen, N.J. : Scarecrow, 1981).
  Lists about 5,000 performers alphabetically in two sections (the sound era, the silent era) and provides birth/death dates (where determined), a brief statement on types of roles or films, and a chronology of films (including some made for television). Includes actors born in the U.K. or the Commonwealth, as well as non-British players who worked in British films. Not indexed.
  § Denis Gifford's *The illustrated who's who in British films* (London, Batsford, 1978. 334 p.) contains some biographical data, but focuses on credits (British productions only) of some 1,000 important actors and directors of all periods. Photograph or poster illustration for about a fourth of the entries.   PN1998.2.P3

Shiri, Keith. Directory of African film-makers and films. Westport, Conn. : Greenwood, 1992. 194 p.   **BH212**
  Publ. in the U.K. by Flicks Books, Trowbridge, Wiltshire, Eng.
  Provides brief biographical data and complete filmographies for "the most important and active directors who have been involved in feature, documentary and animation film production in 29 countries and states from the whole of the African continent over the last 60 years."—*Introd.* Country, film title, and general indexes.
  § Also available: *Directory of Eastern European film-makers and films 1945–1991*, comp. and ed. by Grzegorz Balski (Westport, Conn. : Greenwood, 1992. 546 p.). Other Flicks/Greenwood volumes for Indian and Spanish/Portuguese directors forthcoming. PN1993.5.A35S48

Truitt, Evelyn Mack. Who was who on screen. 3rd ed. N.Y. : Bowker, 1983. 788 p.   **BH213**
  1st ed., 1974.
  About 13,000 entries for screen personalities (mainly American, British, French, and German) who died 1905–82. Entries are primarily devoted to a full list of screen appearances, with dates. Biographical information is generally limited to birth and death dates (and places, when known) and statement of profession; industry-related family relationships and cause of death are sometimes indicated. Includes animals and nonactors who were seen in films, but directors, writers, etc., are included only if they appeared in front of the camera.
                    PN1998.A2T73

Weaver, John T. Forty years of screen credits, 1929–1969. Metuchen, N.J. : Scarecrow, 1970. 2 v. (1458 p.).   **BH214**

Films of stars and featured players, listed by name, then date. Birth/death dates sometimes included.

§ The author's *Twenty years of silents, 1908–1928* (Metuchen, N.J. : Scarecrow, 1971. 514 p.) covers actors of the silent film era and includes a section on directors and their credits.   PN1998.A2W37

Adaptations

Baskin, Ellen. Enser's filmed books and plays : a list of books and plays from which films have been made, 1928–1991 / comp. by Ellen Baskin and Mandy Hicken. Aldershot, England ; Brookfield, Vt. : Ashgate, c1993. 970 p.   **BH215**

Original list, *Filmed book and plays*, comp. by A. G. S. Enser (London : Grafton, 1951), followed by a number of supplements and cumulative editions.

A thorough reworking of a standard source. Offers approaches from the film title, author's name, and original title when it differs from the screen version. Film company or distributor, country or origin, year released, and director's name are indicated, as are (where applicable) title variations, made-for-television versions, and availability on video. Indexes to musicals, televisions films and series, and animated features; list of studios and distributors. Most of the 6,000 films are English-language, but some major foreign releases are also included.

§ More limited in focus, Larry Langman's *Writers on the American screen: a guide to film adaptations of American and foreign literary works* (N.Y. : Garland, 1986. 329 p.) has some titles not found in *Enser's*, mostly for silent films and adapted short stories and poems. Author list, with title index. For identification of more than 2,200 English-language feature films and television movies inspired by women's writings, see *Women writers, from page to screen* by Jill Rubinson Fenton [et al.] (N.Y. : Garland, 1990. 483 p.). Covers 1913–88 releases. By author, with essential details provided; indexes of film titles and literary sources.   Z5784.M9B385

Daisne, Johan. Dictionnaire filmographique de la littérature mondiale = Filmographic dictionary of world literature / Johan Daisne [i.e., H. Thiery]. Gand : E. Storyscientia, 1971–75. 2 v. : ill.   **DH216**

Title also in German and Flemish; introduction in French, English, German, and Flemish.

Identifies the works of world literature, major and minor, with the films derived from them. Each volume is in three parts: (1) a filmography arranged by writer's name and giving film title, original title if different from that of the film, country and year of production, director, and principal cast members (usually shown with character names); (2) an extensive section of stills from selected films; and (3) a title index of films and literary works, cross-referenced to authors. Details on remakes and other versions are also included, with alternate titles noted. International in coverage.

———. ———. *Suppl. (A–Z).* (1977. 638 p.). In French; preliminary matter in French, English, German, and Dutch. Indexed.   PN1997.85.T5

Dimmitt, Richard Bertrand. A title guide to the talkies : a comprehensive listing of 16,000 feature-length films from October, 1927 until December, 1963. N.Y. : Scarecrow, 1965. 2 v.   **BH217**

Conceived as an aid to identifying the source material used as the basis for American (and some foreign) feature films. Arranged by film title; lists source (published novel, play, short story, etc.), unpublished work, original screen story) but does not give screenplay credits. Bibliographic data supplied for published sources. Also gives production company, date, and producer. Author index.

Two supplementary volumes compiled by Andrew A. Aros, *A title guide to the talkies, 1964 through 1974* (Metuchen, N.J. : Scarecrow, 1977. 336 p.) and *A title guide to the talkies, 1975 through 1984*

(1986. 347 p.) list the director's name in lieu of the producer, provide broader coverage of foreign films, and give screenplay (as well as source) credits.   PN1998.D55

Emmens, Carol A. Short stories on film and video. 2nd ed. Littleton, Colo. : Libraries Unlimited, 1985. 337 p. : ill.   **BH218**

1st ed., 1978, had title: *Short stories on film*.

Identifies about 1,375 motion picture and television adaptations, 1920–84, of stories "by American authors or outstanding international authors well known in America."—*p. vii.* Arranged by author, gives story and film titles, running time, year, production and cast information, and (as applicable) source(s) for distribution on film or videotape. Short story and film title indexes; directory of distributors.   PN1997.85.E45

Gifford, Denis. Books and plays in films, 1896–1915 : literary, theatrical, and artistic sources of the first twenty years of motion pictures. Jefferson, N.C. : McFarland ; London : N.Y. : Mansell, 1991. 206 p.   **BH219**

Alphabetical by author, then chronological by date of film. Entry gives film title, original title if different, month and year of release, production company, length in reels, and genre of source. Index of film and source titles.   PN1997.85.G54

Themes and genres

Armstrong, Richard B. The movie list book : a reference guide to film themes, settings, and series / by Richard B. Armstrong and Mary Willems Armstrong. Jefferson, N.C. : McFarland, 1990. 377 p.   **BH220**

Includes 450 topics (e.g., amnesia, butlers, football, look-alikes) and major series, with a narrative discussion of each and a list of films (selective for subjects, complete for series) by date. Primarily English-language sound films and television movies. No index.

A 2nd ed. in paperback (Cincinnati : Betterway Books, 1994. 413 p.) adds about 100 thematic categories.

§ In a similar vein: *Dictionnaire des personnages du cinéma*, sous la direction de Gilles Horvilleur (Paris : Bordas, 1988. 559 p.), presents signed essay-filmographies on named characters (e.g., Tarzan, Pancho Villa), types of characters (e.g., hypochondriacs, inventors, peasants), and places or concepts that have figured prominently in films (e.g., New York, nature). Some essays include bibliographic references. Performer and title indexes.

See also *Halliwell's filmgoer's and video viewer's companion* (BH249) for useful surveys of films dealing with various themes (jewel thieves, staircases, etc.).   PN1997.8.A76

Cyr, Helen W. A filmography of the Third World : an annotated list of 16mm films. Metuchen, N.J. : Scarecrow, 1976. 319 p.   **BH221**

Intended for teachers and students. Lists films dealing with the cultures of developing countries, broadly defined as "all non-Western nations—that is, all except the United States, Europe and the Soviet Union—and ethnic minorities of North America and Europe."— *Foreword.* By region and country, gives title, producer, date, length, distributor, and note on content. Title index.

Continued by Cyr's *A filmography of the Third World, 1976–1983 : an annotated list of 16mm films* (1985. 275 p.) and *The Third World in film and video, 1984–1990* (1991. 246 p.).   HC59.7.C97

Drew, Bernard A. Motion picture series and sequels : a reference guide. N.Y. : Garland, 1990. 412 p. : ill. (Garland reference library of the humanities, vol. 1186).   **BH222**

For about 900 English-language film series (e.g., Abbott and Costello, James Bond) and films that inspired one or more sequels (e.g., *Rocky*), lists the individual titles and gives their dates, studios, directors, and stars. Short subjects and films made for television are included, but remakes, television miniseries, and animated features are not. Title index.

§ Robert A. Nowlan and Gwendolyn Wright Nowlan's *Cinema sequels and remakes, 1903–1987* (Jefferson, N.C. : McFarland, 1989. 954 p.) includes "all films, silent or sound, from the genres of drama, action-adventure, romance, comedy or thriller, which have at least one English-speaking sound remake or sequel."—*Introd.* For each entry, gives source and synopsis of the original, production data (year, production company, director, screenwriter, leading performers) for each version, and a comparative commentary. Series are excluded. Index of names, source titles, etc.   PN1995.9.S29D66

Handbook of American film genres / ed. by Wes D. Gehring. N.Y. : Greenwood, 1988. 405 p.   **BH223**

Essays by scholars on 18 individual genres (e.g., screwball, comedy, Western, film noir), covering development of the genre, themes, notable films, influential directors and stars, etc., and including bibliographic overview, checklist of readings, and a selected filmography. Index of names and titles.   PN1993.5.U6H335

Hardy, Phil. The Western. 2nd rev., updated ed. London : Aurum, 1991. 416 p. : ill.   **BH224**

Prev. ed., 1983, publ. as v. 1 of *The Aurum film encyclopedia*.

One of several available filmographic guides to the Western film. Arranged by decade (beginning with the 1930s), then year and title, gives for each film: studio; length; color/black-and-white; production credits; cast; and critical synopsis. Appendixes list rental champions, critics' top tens, Academy Awards in the genre, etc. Select bibliography; index. Well illustrated.

§ Companion filmographies in this series: *Science fiction*, ed. by Hardy (Rev. updated ed. London : Aurum Pr., 1991. 478 p.); and *Horror*, ed. by Hardy (2nd ed. London : Aurum Pr., 1993. 496 p.).

Another useful genre filmography: *Film noir : an encyclopedic reference to the American style*, ed. by Alain Silver and Elizabeth Ward (3rd ed., rev. and expanded. Woodstock, N.Y. : Overlook Pr., 1992. 479 p.). In addition to the titles noted here, numerous filmographic guides that cover these and other major genres (war, gangsters, musicals, etc.) and specialized themes and subgenres (e.g., ghosts and angels, the Vietnam War) are also available.   PN1995.9.W4H37

Jewish film directory : a guide to more than 1200 films of Jewish interest from 32 countries over 85 years / [ed. by Matthew Stevens]. Westport, Conn. : Greenwood, 1992. 298 p.   **BH225**

British ed. publ. by Flicks Books, Trowbridge, Wiltshire, Eng.

Includes feature films, documentaries, made-for-television movies, Yiddish cinema, etc., with emphasis on "major films released theatrically, screened at film festivals or on television, or available on video or for hire."—*Pref.* Arranged by English-language title, entries include original/alternative titles, country of origin, date, length, color, production and acting credits, references to reviews in *Variety* and *Monthly film bulletin*, and a short description. Indexes of directors, countries of production, subjects, and source material. List of Jewish film festivals; bibliography.   PN1995.9.J46J48

Karsten, Eileen. From real life to reel life : a filmography of biographical films / by Eileen Karsten with the assistance of Dorothy-Ellen Gross. Metuchen, N.J. : Scarecrow, 1993. 475 p.   **BH226**

Lists more than 1,000 commercial, noneducational films about famous people. Arranged alphabetically by name of the individual (with dates and identifying phrase); entries give theatrical and television film features that deal primarily with the person, the performer playing the role, supporting cast, year, length, studio, and director. Performer, title, subject, and date of release indexes.   PN1995.9.B55K37

Klotman, Phyllis Rauch. Frame by frame : a black filmography. Bloomington : Indiana Univ. Pr., [1979]. 700 p. **BH227**

Provides information on more than 3,000 films "with black themes or subject matter ... ; films that have substantial participation by Blacks as writers, actors, producers, directors, musicians, animators, or consultants; and films in which Blacks appeared in ancillary or walk-on roles."—*p. xiii.* As far as possible, each entry indicates: film title/series title; narrator/cast; writer; producer; director; studio/company; technical information; date/country of origin; type; distribu-

tor/archive; annotation. Annotations emphasize the participation or presence of blacks in the film. Arranged by film title; index of names of black actors, authors, directors, etc., but no subject index.

§ *See also* Donald Bogel's *Blacks in American films and television : an encyclopedia* (BH270).   PN1995.9.N4K57

López, Daniel. Films by genre : 775 categories, styles, trends, and movements defined, with a filmography for each. Jefferson, N.C. : McFarland & Co., c1993. 495 p.   **BH228**

Covers all standard film genres (science fiction, Western, musical, etc.), plus subgenres (e.g., time travel, spaghetti Western, aquamusical) and miscellaneous subjects (e.g., old age, small towns). Alphabetical by category, entries provide definitions of terms and a list of representative American, British, and foreign language films that exemplify the category. Title, country (other than the U.S.), date, director, and alternative titles are given for cited films, but not detailed credits or summaries. Extensive use of cross-references; bibliographic notes; name and film title indexes. Many films are listed in multiple categories.   PN1998.L6

Parish, James Robert. Gays and lesbians in mainstream cinema : plots, critiques, casts and credits for 272 theatrical and made-for-television Hollywood releases. Jefferson, N.C. : McFarland & Co., c1993. 496 p. : ill.   **BH229**

A filmography that also functions as a specialized guide to American films and network movies with homosexual characters or plot elements. For each film, provides studio, length, rating, complete production and cast credits, synopsis, analysis, and quotations from critics. Film chronology, 1914–92; brief history of regulatory codes; name and title index. British and other foreign films are excluded, as are documentaries and short subjects.

Richard, Alfred Charles. The Hispanic image on the silver screen : an interpretive filmography from silents into sound, 1898–1935. N.Y. : Greenwood, 1992. 571 p. (Bibliographies and indexes in the performing arts, no. 12).   **BH230**

A record of more than 1,800 feature films that potentially influenced U.S. audience perceptions of "accepted stereotypes, those associated with Hispanics living anywhere, but especially in the United States, Mexico, the Caribbean, all areas south, and also in Spain and the Philippines."—*Pref.* By year, then title, gives production company, a summary and analysis of images portrayed (often with reference to censorship issues), and published reviews. Performers and directors are not separately identified, although their names are often noted in the summary. Indexes: titles; actors and actresses; countries/place names; subjects (including stereotypical labels, e.g., cantina girl).

———. *Censorship and Hollywood's Hispanic image : an interpretive filmography, 1936–1955* (Westport, Conn. : Greenwood, 1993. 588 p.) continues the work, discussing an additional 2,100 films. A third volume is projected.   PN1995.9.L37R55

Indexes

Batty, Linda. Retrospective index to film periodicals, 1930–1971. N.Y. : Bowker, 1975. 425 p.   **BH231**

Indexes 14 English-language film journals plus relevant articles and reviews in *Village voice*. Only two of the periodicals covered predate 1950. In three sections: reviews of individual films; subjects, including directors and other film personalities; and book reviews.   Z5784.M9B39

Film literature index. v. 1 (1973)– . Albany, N.Y. : Film and Television Documentation Center, State Univ. of New York at Albany, 1974– . Quarterly, with annual cumulation. **BH232**

Subtitle: A quarterly author-subject index to the international periodical literature of film and television/video.

Publisher varies; v. 1–20, 1973–92, publ. Albany, N.Y. : Filmdex.

Some 300 periodicals are scanned, with full coverage of established film journals and specialized publications and selective indexing of English-language general magazines and scholarly journals. In two sections beginning with v. 14, 1986: Film, incorporating entries for individual film titles, personal names, and subjects in one alphabet; and Television/video, similarly arranged. Expanded coverage of television actually began in 1977. Z5784.M9F45

Gerlach, John C. The critical index : a bibliography of articles on film in English, 1946–1973, arranged by names and topics / John C. Gerlach, Lana Gerlach. N.Y. : Teachers College Pr., [1974]. 726 p. **BH233**

Indexes articles from 22 American, British, and Canadian film periodicals on directors, producers, actors, critics, screenwriters, cinematographers, films, and on the history, aesthetics, influence, and economics of the film industry. In two main sections: names alphabetically; and topics in classified order. Reviews of individual films are listed under director in the name section; separate film title index keyed to directors' names. About 5,000 items. Z5784.M9G47

International index to film periodicals. 1972– . London : International Federation of Film Archives (FIAF), [1973]– . Annual. **BH234**

A cooperative effort of indexers in film archives throughout Europe and the Americas. Annual volumes cumulate entries distributed to subscribers of a microfiche service offered by FIAF. Indexes 60–85 periodicals, selected to reflect international periodical literature of lasting aesthetic or critical value. Originally a classed listing in many parts; beginning 1985 has been divided into three alphabetical sections: general subjects; individual films; biography. Author index; director index, referring to works listed in the "individual films" section. Citations include brief, informative annotations.

•Machine-readable version : International filmarchive CD-ROM [database] (London : FIAF, 1993?–). Updated semiannually. Also includes material from International index to television periodicals (BH297). Publisher plans to extend coverage back to 1972. Z5784.M9I49

MacCann, Richard Dyer. The new film index : a bibliography of magazine articles in English, 1930–1970 / by Richard Dyer MacCann and Edward S. Perry. N.Y. : Dutton, 1975. 522 p. **BH235**

Intended as a supplement to The film index (BH172), for periodical literature through 1970. Indexes some 12,000 articles from film periodicals and general circulation magazines, classified in 278 subject categories, with author index. Brief annotations for many items. Does not attempt to index film reviews or book reviews. Z5784.M9M29

Reviews and criticism

Film and television / NewsBank, inc. [microform]. v. 9, card 82 (Mar. 1983)– . [New Canaan, Conn.] : NewsBank, inc., 1983– . Monthly. **BH236**

Title varies; issued as NewsBank. Film and television, 1975–Feb. 1983. Issued bimonthly, 1975–81.

A clipping service on microfiche, covering moving-image media, as reported in newspapers from 450 U.S. cities. Reviews, interviews, and news articles on motion pictures, broadcast and cable television, and film festivals are "clipped" and reproduced on microfiche sheets, distributed to subscribers on a monthly basis. Index access is provided by Review of the arts : film and television, issued monthly, with four-month and annual cumulations. Index entries for reviews include titles of films and programs, directors, leading players, and country of production, with reference made to the year, fiche number, and row/column on the microfiche set.

•In machine-readable form as part of NewsBank reference service plus [database] (AE111 note). Coverage of film and television begins July 1980.

Film review annual. 1981– . [Englewood, N.J.] : J. S. Ozer, [1982]– . Annual. **BH237**

Reprints in their entirety reviews "of full-length films released in major markets in the United States during the course of the year."—

Pref. Reviews (citing date and page) are drawn from a wide range of newspapers, magazines, and scholarly journals; citations only are given to some additional reviews in publications (e.g., New York times, Variety) for which reprint rights were not available. Arranged by title of film, with production and cast credits, running time, etc. Awards listing; addendum for additional reviews of films included in earlier volumes. Indexes: cast; producers; directors; screenwriters; cinematographers; editors; music; production crew. PN1995.F465

Magill's cinema annual. 1981– . Englewood Cliffs, N.J. : Salem Pr., [1982]– . Annual. **BH238**
Ed. by Frank N. Magill.

Serves as a continuation of Magill's survey of cinema (BH239), covering American films and foreign releases in the U.S. Each volume has a section of signed essay-reviews on about 100 films of the previous year, with production credits, principal characters/players, length, review citations, etc.; another 200–300 productions are listed with basic credits and brief comment. 1982–88 vols. also cover retrospective films not previously reviewed in a Magill series. Selected film books; major awards; obituaries. Title, director, screenwriter, cinematographer, editor, art director, music, performer, and subject indexes; separate cumulative index to 1982–86 annuals. PN1993.3.M34

Magill's survey of cinema : English language films, first series / ed. by Frank N. Magill; assoc. eds., Patricia King Hanson, Stephen L. Hanson. Englewood Cliffs, N.J. : Salem Pr., [1980]. 4 v. **BH239**
———. English language films, second series (Englewood Cliffs, N.J., Salem Pr., 1981. 6 v.). Also edited by Magill, Hanson, and Hanson.

The two series cover 1,266 American, British, Canadian, Australian, and other English-language films of the sound era, 1927–81. Focus is on major genres, directors, and performers, although representative minor works are also included. Entries for individual films (alphabetical by title within each set) give release date, producer and studio, production credits, running time, and principal character/cast, followed by a signed essay of 1,000–2,500 words, which includes a plot summary and critical evaluation. Series indexes of titles, directors, screenwriters, cinematographers, editors, and performers, as well as a chronological listing, are cumulated in the final volume of the second series.

§ Related sets edited by Magill: Magill's survey of cinema : silent films (1982. 3 v.), which profiles 308 movies, 1902–36, and has introductory essays on important people and trends; and Magill's survey of cinema : foreign language films (1985. 8 v.), an examination of 700 outstanding films from around the world produced in languages other than English. Multiple indexes (including country and subject indexes in the foreign language series).

•**Magill's survey of cinema** [database]. Pasadena, Calif. : Salem Pr. **BH240**
Available online, updated every two weeks, and on CD ROM, updated annually.
Coverage: 1902– .
Machine-readable version of Magill's cinema annual (BH238) and the Magill's survey of cinema titles (BH239), augmented by abstracts and credits for additional films.

The New York times film reviews. 1913/-68– . N.Y. : New York Times, 1970– . Biennial. **BH241**
Publisher varies. Currently publ. by Garland.
Offers photographic reprints of film reviews as they appeared in the Times. The original 1913/68 set reprints about 16,000 reviews, chronologically arranged in 5 v., and a separate volume with an appendix (for corrections and inadvertent omissions) and indexes by title, personal name, and corporate name. Continued on a biennial basis, beginning with the 1969/70 vol., publ. 1971. PN1995.N4

Variety film reviews. v. 1 (1907–1920)– . N.Y. : Bowker, c1983– . Biennial. **BH242**
Publisher varies; v. 1–16, N.Y. : Garland.
Frequency varies; v. 1–16, irregular.

Vols. 1–15 reproduce about 40,000 reviews in chronological sequence as they appeared in *Variety*, 1907–80. Vol. 16 is a title index to v. 1–15. Continued by biennial volumes with title indexes, 1981–82– . Includes many obscure U.S. films, but is especially useful for its strong coverage of international film festivals and markets. There are no reviews for Mar. 1911–Dec. 1912; short subjects were reviewed until July 1927.   PN1993.V36

Indexes

Bowles, Stephen E. Index to critical film reviews in British and American film periodicals : together with: Index to critical reviews of books about film. N.Y. : Burt Franklin, [1974–75]. 3 v. in 2.   **BH243**

Contents: v. 1–2, Critical film reviews, A–Z; v. 3, Critical reviews of books about film, A–Z, and indexes.

Indexes "all articles designated as 'reviews,' and includes, as well, those articles which deal with the entirety of a film (rather than a restricted aspect)" (*Introd.*) appearing in some 31 British and American film journals. In general, a full run of the journal is indexed through 1971; 1939 is the earliest publication date. Entry is by title of the film, with indexes by directors and film reviewers. The separate section of "Critical reviews of books about film" is arranged by book title, with author, reviewer, and subject indexes.   Z5784.M9B64

Film review index / ed. by Patricia King Hanson, Stephen L. Hanson. Phoenix : Oryx, 1986–1987. 2 v.   **BH244**

Contents: v. 1, 1882–1949; v. 2, 1950–85.

Provides citations to criticism of "those pictures that have established themselves as being of continuing importance to film researchers" (*Introd.*), as well as lesser works that attained great popularity or reflect sociological trends. Rather than indexing a stated group of sources, attempts to identify substantive, fairly accessible materials in English-language periodicals (general, trade, and some scholarly), newspapers, and selected film books, on a film-by-film basis. List of books consulted and director, chronological, and country indexes in each volume.   Z5784.M9F513

Encyclopedias

The BFI companion to the Western / ed. by Edward Buscombe. N.Y. : Atheneum, 1988. 432 p. : ill.   **BH245**

Repr.: N.Y. : DaCapo, 1991.

Encyclopedic handbook of a major genre. Has separate alphabetically arranged sections dealing with selected Western films, filmmakers (character actors and cinematographers as well as stars and directors), and television programs; also includes a short history of the Western and an extensive section of articles on cultural and historical topics (e.g., fur trade, Gatling gun, Crazy Horse), with examples of relevant films. Copiously illustrated with portraits, stills, engravings, maps, and charts. Bibliography; no index.   PN1995.9.W4B45

Cinema : a critical dictionary : the major film-makers / ed. by Richard Roud. N.Y. : Viking Pr., c1980. 2 v. (1121 p.) : ill.   **BH246**

A collection of signed articles by an international roster of film critics. Most of the articles are devoted to directors, but there are some entries for individual actors, and a few topical entries such as "American film noir" and "Polish cinema since the War." Although the articles are signed by the contributors, the editor appends his own comments (sometimes in disagreement with the contributor) at the end of each article: suggestions for further reading are often included. Index of names, film titles, and illustrations.   PN1993.45.C5

Dictionnaire du cinéma / sous la direction de Jean Loup Passek ... [et al.]. Paris : Larousse, c1986. 888 p. : ill. **BH247**

International and historical in scope, offers brief articles on individuals, studios, genres, film technology, developments in various countries, etc., in one alphabetical sequence. Complete filmographies

for major stars and filmmakers, partial for others. Nearly 100 pages of black-and-white and color plates. Separate section for production information and credits for 2,001 important films. Bibliography; glossary of technical terms.

§ Other French sources with international coverage: Maurice Bessy and Jean-Louis Chardans, *Dictionnaire du cinéma et de la télévision* (Paris : Jean-Jacques Pauvert, 1965–71. 4 v.); and Roger Boussinot, *L'encyclopédie du cinéma* (2e éd. Paris : Bordas, 1980. 2 v.).   PN1993.45.D53

Filmlexicon degli autori e delle opere. Roma : Bianco e Nero, 1958–74. 9 v. : ill.   **BH248**

Introduction in Italian, French, English, German, and Spanish. Text in Italian.

Contents: v. 1–7, Autori, A–Z; v. 8–9, Aggiornamenti (1958–71).

International in scope. Planned to be in two sections, Authors and Works; the latter section has not been published. The term "authors" includes directors, story and scriptwriters, producers, actors, cameramen, composers, art directors and costume designers of both silent and sound cinematography of the world. Entries contain biographical sketches, filmographies (which list film titles, principals, and dates), and, for the most important names, bibliographies.

Halliwell, Leslie. Halliwell's filmgoer's and video viewer's companion / ed. by John Walker. 10th ed. N.Y. : HarperPerennial, 1993. 834 p.   **BH249**

1st ed., 1965; 9th ed., 1990. Title varies.

A standard work, intended for general viewers rather than specialists or film students. Presents concise entries on: actors, directors, and other filmmakers; terms; fictional characters; series; and studios. Also includes articles on selected themes, with examples of their use in specific films. Entries for personalities have filmographies, with the most important titles shown in italics, and frequently include famous lines from films and quotes by or about the individual. In this edition, entries for notable films have been dropped, but they may be found in *Halliwell's film guide* (BH196).   PN1993.45.H3

International dictionary of films and filmmakers / ed., Nicholas Thomas; consulting ed., James Vinson. 2nd ed. Chicago : St. James Pr., c1990–1994. 5 v. : ill.   **BH250**

Vols. 3–5 ed. by Samantha Cook.

1st ed., publ. 1984–87.

Contents: v. 1, Films; v. 2, Directors; v. 3, Actors and actresses; v. 4, Writers and production artists; v. 5, title index.

Retains and updates most entries from the 1st ed. and adds several hundred new ones. International and historical in scope, includes films and personalities of all periods from Asia, South America, and Australia, as well as North America and Europe. Inclusion is based on recommendations of a panel of advisors. Vol. 1 profiles about 600 major or representative films, and gives country, year, director, running time, full production and cast credits, filming location, awards, bibliographies of books and articles, and a signed critical essay. Vols. 2–4 provide short biographical sketches, complete filmographies, bibliographies, and evaluative essays for the more than 1,600 directors, performers, screenwriters, producers, cinematographers, art directors, designers, composers, etc., selected for treatment. The title index lists all films in v. 1–4 and provides cross-references for alternative titles. Attractive format and illustrations.   PN1997.8.I58

Katz, Ephraim. The film encyclopedia. 2nd ed. N.Y. : HarperPerennial, 1994. 1496 p.   **BH251**

1st ed., 1979.

Definitions of terms, historical articles on countries, profiles of studios and other organizations, etc., are in evidence, but the large majority of entries are devoted to international players and filmmakers. Fairly lengthy biographical sketches of directors, producers, screenwriters, cinematographers, art directors, composers, editors, actors, and actresses, each accompanied by a complete or selective filmography. Cross-references; no index.   PN1993.45.K34

Langman, Larry. Encyclopedia of American film comedy. N.Y. : Garland, 1987. 639 p. : ports. (Garland reference library of the humanities, vol. 744).   **BH252**

Combines articles on comedy genres (e.g., screwball comedy, war humor), themes (e.g., child comedy stars), representative films, series, characters, and notable personalities (comedians, comedy teams, light actors and actresses, directors, and screenwriters). Selective filmographies; cross-references. Not indexed.   PN1995.9.C55L34

The Oxford companion to film / ed. by Liz-Anne Bawden. N.Y. : Oxford Univ. Pr., 1976. 767 p. : ill.   **BH253**

Aims "to answer any query which may occur to the amateur of film in the course of reading or film-going."—*Pref.* Entries for individual films, actors and actresses, directors and other production personnel, film genres, and selected technical terms, as well as brief surveys of film activity and accomplishment in individual countries. No index, but extensive use of cross-references.   PN1993.45.O9

Slide, Anthony. The American film industry : a historical dictionary. N.Y. : Greenwood, 1986. 431 p.   **BH254**

More than 600 entries for "American producing and releasing companies, technological innovations, film series, industry terms, studios, genres, and organizations."—*Pref.* Cross-references; some bibliographic citations; index.

§ Slide's companion volume, *The international film industry : a historical dictionary* (N.Y. : Greenwood, 1989. 423 p.) is similar in arrangement and topical coverage. Also provides "brief historical essays on the cinema in virtually every country of the world, certainly all countries that have any pretense at a film industry."—*Introd.*   PN1993.5.U6S539

Women in film : an international guide / ed. by Annette Kuhn with Susannah Radstone. N.Y. : Fawcett Columbine, 1991. 500 p. : ill.   **BH255**

Originally publ. as *The women's companion to international film* (London : Virago Pr., 1990).

Signed articles, written from a feminist perspective, on film personalities, movements, theory and criticism, genres, etc., around the world. Entries for individuals concentrate on women directors, producers, and screenwriters, although high-profile women stars (e.g., Greta Garbo) and male directors whose work is associated with women's themes (e.g., George Cukor) are included. Bibliographies; filmographies; index of films directed, written, or produced by women. American ed. has general index (not included in British ed.).   PN1995.9.W6W657

Dictionaries

Beaver, Frank E. Dictionary of film terms. N.Y. : McGraw-Hill, c1983. 392 p. : ill.   **BH256**

Defines and discusses a variety of technical, critical, and historical terms, often with specific examples of relevant films. Also contains a chronology of film history. Index of terms and film titles; topical index of broad concepts (e.g., editing). Illustrated.   TR847.B43

Gartenberg, Jon. Glossary of filmographic terms. 2nd ed., enl. Brussels, Belgium : Fédération internationale des archives du film, 1989. 149 p.   **BH257**

1st ed., 1985.

A multilingual handbook of terms encountered in film credits, designed for use by archive catalogers. Terms are in a classed arrangement, by function. Each term is given and defined (in parallel columns) in each of the five languages—English, French, German, Spanish, and Russian. In this edition, equivalent terms, without definitions, are also supplied for seven additional languages (Bulgarian, Czech, Dutch, Hungarian, Italian, Portuguese, and Swedish). Two separate indexes for entries in the Roman and Cyrillic alphabets.

§ An older multilingual source covering a much broader range of terms is *Elsevier's dictionary of cinema, sound, and music, in six languages : English/American, French, Spanish, Italian, Dutch, and Ger-* *man*, comp. and arr. on an English alphabetical base by W. E. Clason (Amsterdam ; N.Y. : Elsevier, 1956). 3,213 terms, with equivalents in each language and separate language indexes.   PN1993.45.G36

Konigsberg, Ira. The complete film dictionary. N.Y. : New American Library, c1987. 420 p. : ill.   **BH258**

Offers "a comprehensive lexicon of the motion picture as art, technology, and industry."—*Pref.* Includes practical, technical, and business terms, as well as selected terms relating to film history and criticism. Numerous line drawings and production stills.   PN1993.45.K66

McAlister, Micheal J. The language of visual effects. Los Angeles : Lone Eagle, c1993. 160 p. : ill.   **BH259**

Practical glossary of some 1,500 special effects terms used by film professionals. Concise, clear definitions, with numerous cross-references. Indexes identify terms relating to computer graphics and bluescreen processes.   TR858.M325

Penney, Edmund F. The Facts on File dictionary of film and broadcast terms. N.Y. : Facts on File, c1991. 251 p. : forms.   **BH260**

Contains about 3,000 short definitions intended for "those who, for whatever reason, have an active interest in the performing arts in mass media and the adjuncts of those arts: hardware, advertising, publicity, to give a few examples."—*p.xiii.* Mix of general and specialized vocabulary.   P87.5.P43

Singleton, Ralph S. Filmmakers dictionary. Beverly Hills, Calif. : Lone Eagle, c1986. 188 p.   **BH261**

According to the cover, includes "over 1,500 motion picture and television terms from technical to slang." Brief definitions; many cross-references. Useful for media jargon and specialized commercial terms.   PN1993.45.S56

Quotations

The movie quote book / comp. by Harry Haun. N.Y. : Lippincott & Crowell, c1980. 415 p.   **BH262**

Collection of memorable lines from films, classified by topics (e.g., eyes, drunken rantings, Paris), with category cross-references. List of source films gives studio, year, writing credits, director, and references to quoted dialogue.   PN6083.M75

Directories and annuals

The American Film Institute guide to college courses in film and television. 8th ed./ William Horrigan; ed., Greg Beal, ed.; Emily J. Laskin, editorial director... [et al.]. N.Y. : Arco : Distr. by Prentice Hall Trade Sales, c1990. 286 p.   **BH263**

1st ed., 1969/70, called *Guide to college film courses.*

Intended for "students, teachers, counselors, parents, and others interested in post-secondary film and television education" (*p.xvi*); lists programs (2-year through doctorate) by state, then school. Gives institutional data, department or program, degrees offered, admission requirements, curricular emphasis, faculty, financial aid, etc. Separate section for Canadian institutions; listing of foreign school names and addresses. Index of degrees offered, by state; college name index.   PN1993.8.U5A453

BFI film and television handbook / British Film Institute. 1990– . London : British Film Institute, 1990– . Annual.   **BH264**

Continues *BFI film and television yearbook*, 1983–1988/89.

Consists mostly of a series of directories for the U.K. film, television, and video industries, including: archives and film libraries; awards; bookshops; cable and satellite franchises; cinemas; courses; distributors; facilities; film societies; international sales offices; organizations; press contacts; production companies; releases; studios; and workshops. Introductory statistical overview has tables, charts, box office grosses and audience ratings, commentary on trends, etc. General index.

Bowser, Kathryn. The guide to international film and video festivals. 3rd ed. N.Y. : Foundation for Independent Video and Film, Inc., c1992. 238 p.   **BH265**
Earlier eds. (1986–88) publ. as *AIVF guide to international film and video festivals.*

Aims to provide "an overview of a majority of the world's festivals, from small local showcases to major international events" (*Introd.*), as an aid to independent film/video makers. More than 500 festivals, markets, and award competitions, listed by name in separate sections for domestic and foreign events. Gives address, telephone and fax numbers, description, fees, requirements, formats accepted, festival and deadline dates, category, and contact person for each. Date, deadline, category, and country indexes.

International motion picture almanac. 1929– . N.Y. : Quigley, 1929– . Annual.   **BH266**
Title varies: 1929–1935/36, *The motion picture almanac;* 1952/53–55, *Motion picture and television almanac.*

Most information relates to the U.S. film industry, including: the year in review; industry statistics; awards and polls; who's who in the entertainment world; obituaries; directory of services; state and city film commissions; distributors; credits for recent feature films; brief data on features of the last several years; corporate histories of major studios; corporations and personnel; theater circuits; independent theaters; buying and booking services; organizations (e.g., associations, unions); and trade publications. Also has sections for international film festivals and markets, the British and Canadian motion picture industries, and summaries of activity in other foreign countries. The extensive "who's who" section makes up half the volume.   PN1993.3.I55

Screen international : international film & television directory. 1993– . London : EMAP Media Information, 1993– . Annual.   **BH267**
Title varies.

Currently issued in 3 pts: pt. 1, Europe; pt. 2, America/Rest of world; pt. 3, Who's who.

Pts. 1–2 contain, for each country, general and industry statistics and a classified directory of agents, distributors, laboratories, organizations, production companies, studios, etc. Pt. 3 has useful biographical/career sketches of individuals currently working in the world's motion picture and television industries.

§ See also *Kemps film, TV & video yearbook* (East Grinstead, West Sussex, Eng. : Read Information Services, 1956– . Annual), which bears the subtitle: A comprehensive, international production guide to the film, television, and video industries. Title varies.

Screen world. v. 1 (1949)– . N.Y. : Greenberg, 1950– . Annual.   **BH268**
Publisher varies; currently published by Applause.

Editors: Daniel Blum, 1949–65; John Willis, 1966– . Also titled *Daniel Blum's screen world* and *John Willis' screen world.*

Heavily illustrated survey of the year's films, including foreign pictures released in the U.S., with cast and production credits. Lists Academy Award winners, top box office stars, and promising new actors. Also has sections for biographical data on performers (birth place and date, schooling) and obituaries. Name and title index.

PN1993.3.D3

Variety international film guide. 1990– . London : Andre Deutsch ; Hollywood : Samuel French, c1989– . Annual.   **BH269**
Peter Cowie, ed.

Continues *International film guide,* 1964–89.

Country-by-country survey of current film activity. In addition to discussion of highlights and trends in each country, may include details of recent and forthcoming films, lists of top grossing movies and national awards, and addresses of producers, distributors, and organi-

zations. Includes separate listings of film festivals, schools, archives, bookshops, etc., in various countries. Profiles and filmographies of five "directors of the year" in each volume.

Handbooks

Bogle, Donald. Blacks in American films and television : an encyclopedia. N.Y. : Garland, 1988. 510 p. : ill. (Garland reference library of the humanities, v. 604).   **BH270**
Repr.: N.Y. : Simon & Schuster, 1989.

In three main sections: (1) Movies, which concentrates on mainstream American films featuring black performers, but also provides information on selected "race movies" of the 1919–49 period and more recent black-oriented films; (2) Television, which covers major series, television movies, miniseries, and specials; and (3) Profiles, for biographical/career articles on black performers and directors in the two media. In addition to credits and synopses, entries for individual films and programs offer extensive critical commentary. Name and title index.   PN1995.9.N4B58

Handbook of Soviet and East European films and filmmakers / ed. by Thomas J. Slater. N.Y. : Greenwood, 1992. 443 p.   **BH271**
Signed contributions on the history and development of the motion picture in the Soviet Union, Poland, Czechoslovakia, Yugoslavia, Hungary, East Germany, Romania, and Bulgaria. Chapter for each country includes: historical/bibliographical essay; bibliography (mostly English-language sources); biographical sketches of important directors, cinematographers, performers, etc.; and chronological list of selected films, with major credits. Appendix: A chronology of major historical, cultural and film events in the Soviet Union and Eastern Europe, 1890–1990. Indexes of subjects and film titles (in English translation).

Sackett, Susan. The Hollywood reporter book of box office hits. N.Y. : Billboard Books, 1990. 365 p. : ill.   **BH272**
Based on domestic (U.S. and Canada) film rentals paid to distributors by exhibitors, ranks the top five money-makers of each year from 1939 through 1988. Each film is given a one- to two- page treatment, which includes studio, rentals in dollars, screenwriter, producer, director, principal cast, Academy Award nominees and winners, production history and influence of the film, and illustration(s). Appendixes list films by year, title, and studio. Name and title index.

PN1993.5.U6S18

Prizes and awards

Hammer, Tad Bentley. International film prizes : an encyclopedia. N.Y. : Garland, 1991. 901 p. (Garland reference library of the humanities, vol. 1333).   **BH273**
Provides "a survey of forty-two film-producing nations and the prizes given within their respective industries."—*Introd.* Arranged by country, prize name, and year, shows films and individuals honored in each category of award presented. Film titles are given in the original, with English-language release title or translation. Has brief historical summaries of countries and specific awards. Bibliography; title index (including variants); name index. Excludes prizes awarded at major international film festivals, such as Cannes, Venice, and Berlin.

PN1993.4.H28

Mowrey, Peter C. Award winning films : a viewer's reference to 2700 acclaimed motion pictures. Jefferson, N.C. : McFarland, c1994. 544 p.   **BH274**
To qualify for inclusion, each film must have won at least one prize in a major competition (e.g., Oscar, British Film Academy, Cannes, Golden Globe) or been named on any one of several "best" lists (e.g., *New York times* annual ten best films), as of 1990. Alphabetical by film, includes country of origin, running time, studio, direc-

tor, screenwriter, featured players, subject, evaluative note, sequels/ remakes, and prize(s) awarded. Index of actors, writers and directors; subject index of broad topics.

§ Roy Pickard's *The award movies : a complete guide from A to Z* (N.Y. : Schocken Books, 1981. 294 p.) offers similar coverage for "best picture" winners of the major American, British, and international festival prizes. Films are listed by title, followed by a section arranged by granting organization, festival, etc., listing awards in various categories by year. Index of all films mentioned. PN1993.9.M68

Shale, Richard. The Academy Awards index : the complete categorical and chronological record. Westport, Conn. : Greenwood, 1993. 785 p. : ill. **BH275**

Constitutes a revision of Shale's *Academy Awards : an Ungar reference index* (N.Y. : Ungar, 1978; 2nd ed. updated, 1982).

Pt. 1, Listing by Academy Award categories, gives brief histories of each category (including honorary, technical, and discontinued) and rosters of nominees and winners, by category, 1927–92. Pt. 2, Chronological index of Academy Awards, has year-by-year listings in all categories. Annotated bibliography of books and articles. Index of names and film titles.

§ A fully illustrated chronological listing of honorees and nominees, Robert A. Osborne's *60 years of the Oscar : the official history of the Academy Awards* (N.Y. : Abbeville Pr., 1989. 319p.), features decade and annual overviews, quotations from winners, Academy facts and records. Indexed.

All films with a winner in any category are listed by title alphabetically in Roy Pickard's *The Oscar movies* (N.Y. : Facts on File, 1993. 292p.), with entries giving award(s) won, comment on film, studio, major credits, and length. Earlier ed. publ. as *The Oscar movies from A–Z* (London : Muller, 1977). PN1993.92.S53

Screen characters

Lieberman, Susan. Memorable film characters : an index to roles and performers, 1915–1983 / comp. by Susan Lieberman and Frances Cable. Westport, Conn. : Greenwood, 1984. 291 p. (Bibliographies and indexes in the performing arts, no. 1). **BH276**

A dictionary of more than 1,500 character names, drawn primarily from films and players nominated for major awards (U.S., British and Cannes), plus others readily recalled by American filmgoers. Gives brief character description, followed by film title, year, and player for each depiction. Film and actor indexes.

§ Also arranged by character name, Roy Pickard's *Who played who on the screen* (N.Y. : Hippocrene Books, 1989. 351 p.) identifies sound films featuring some 800 well-known historical or fictional characters, with performer, country, and release date of each treatment. Index of performers. British ed., 1988, publ. by Batsford, London. A revision of Pickard's *Who played who in the movies : an A–Z* (London : F. Muller, 1979). PN1995.9.C36L5

Nowlan, Robert A. Movie characters of leading performers of the sound era / Robert A. Nowlan and Gwendolyn Wright Nowlan. Chicago : Amer. Libr. Assoc., 1990. 396 p. **BH277**

Identifies "key roles" played by some 450 actors and actresses "who, for most of their careers, have played an important part in carrying the story of the movies in which they appeared."—*Pref.* Arranged by performer, then role, gives name of the film, year, studio, director, and description of the character. Also has brief career sketches and film/character name listings for other parts played by the performer. No indexes.

§ Tom Scott Caden's *What a bunch of characters! : an entertaining guide to who played what in the movies* (Englewood Cliffs, N.J. : Prentice-Hall, 1984. 326 p.) takes a similar approach for 50 major stars but describes virtually all roles played and notes co-players and credits for each film. Title index. PN1995.9.C36N69

———— The name is familiar : who played who in the movies? a directory of title characters / Robert Anthony Nowlan and Gwendolyn Wright Nowlan. N.Y. : Neal-Schuman, c1993. 1014 p. **BH278**

Limited to characters in the titles of English-language feature films, but very broadly interpreted to encompass individual's names (e.g., Oliver Twist), collective names (e.g., the various characters who make up *The dirty dozen*), inferred names (e.g., Barbara Graham, as the "I" in *I want to live!*), etc. In three alphabetical sections: (1) The performers, listing films (with date and studio) and title character names; (2) The title characters, giving film title, studio/year, player, and character description; and (3) The films, with release date, title character and performer names, director, and other leading players. Approximately 9,000 characters included. PN1995.9.C36N696

Biography

Acker, Ally. Reel women : pioneers of the cinema, 1896 to the present. N.Y. : Continuum, 1991. 374 p. : ill. **BH279**

A celebration of women's behind-the-scenes contributions to film. Divided into 13 main sections relating to directors, producers, writers, film editors, animators, stunt women, foreign notables, etc. Sketches contain filmographies and emphasize career accomplishments (and sometimes hurdles). Select bibliography; index of names, titles, and topics. PN1998.2.A24

American screenwriters / ed. by Robert E. Morsberger, Stephen O. Lesser, and Randall Clark. Detroit : Gale, c1984. 382 p. : ill. (Dictionary of literary biography, v. 26). **BH280**

Following the format of the series (BE200), contains "studies of the careers of sixty-five significant motion-picture writers" (*Foreword*), accompanied by lists of screenplays and other writings, photographs, bibliographic references, and locations of papers. In general, writers in other media who wrote for the screen only occasionally (e.g., F. Scott Fitzgerald) and those whose film careers consisted mostly of adapting their own works (e.g., Tennessee Williams) are omitted.

§ An additional 64 scenarists are profiled in *American screenwriters : second series*, ed. by Randall Clark (Detroit : Gale, 1986. 464 p. [Dictionary of literary biography, v. 44]). PN1998.A2A585

Cinegraph : Lexikon zum deutschsprachigen Film / hrsg. von Hans-Michael Bock ; [Redaktion, Frank Arnold ... et al.]. München : Edition Text + Kritik, 1984– . **BH281**

Prefatory matter in German, English, and French.

Biographical encyclopedia of the German-speaking cinema, covering all categories of filmmakers (actors, directors, technicians, etc.), including notable immigrants and emigrés, from the beginnings to the present. Arranged alphabetically, provides two-to-three page articles with bibliographies and detailed filmographies. Published in 2 v. in looseleaf format, with new and revised pages issued on an irregular basis. PN1993.45.C455

The illustrated who's who of the cinema / ed. by Ann Lloyd and Graham Fuller. London : Orbis ; N.Y. : Macmillan, [1983]. 480 p. : ill. **BH282**

A selective dictionary of film personalities (actors, directors, screenwriters, etc.) of all periods, with emphasis on mainstream cinema of the 1920s, '30s, and '40s. Brief biographical/critical sketches are followed by lists of representative films. Black-and-white and color photographs (average of three per page). PN1998.A2I48

Monaco, James. The encyclopedia of film / James Monaco and the editors of Baseline ; James Pallot, senior ed. N.Y. : Perigee Books, c1991. 596 p. **BH283**

Biographical data and filmographies derived from Baseline's online database services to the film and television industries. Covers about 3,000 international performers, directors, and other filmmakers past and present, with some emphasis on contemporary personalities.

Most of the sketches are brief, although those for highly regarded or influential individuals often run to several columns. Filmographies note Academy Award nominations and wins. PN1993.45.M638

Quinlan, David. Quinlan's illustrated registry of film stars. N.Y. : Henry Holt, 1991. 495 p. : ill. **BH284**

British ed. publ. as *Quinlan's illustrated directory of film stars* (London : Batsford, 1991). Updated ed. of a work first published in 1981 and revised in 1986.

Contains brief biographical and career sketches, each with a comprehensive filmography (including television films) and a small black-and-white photograph. About 1,800 personalities of all periods, predominantly British, American, and famous international stars.

§ Complemented by Quinlan's *The illustrated encyclopedia of film character actors* (N.Y. : Harmony Books, 1986), which provides similar treatment for 850 memorable supporting or featured players. Originally publ. as *The illustrated directory of film character actors* (Batsford, 1985).

For longer profiles of about 300 stars and character performers who excelled in comedy (most of whom are included in the above titles), see *Quinlan's illustrated directory of film comedy actors* (N.Y. : Holt, 1992), publ. in the U.K. by Batsford. PN1998.2.Q56

Sadoul, Georges. Dictionary of film makers / tr., ed., and updated by Peter Morris. Berkeley : Univ. of California Pr., [1972]. 288 p. **BH285**

A translation, revision, and expansion of *Dictionnaire du cinéastes* (Paris, 1965).

A biographical dictionary of selected producers, directors, scenarists, cinematographers, designers, etc., but excluding performers. International in scope, surveys the work of artistically important filmmakers of 60 nations, from the beginnings through the 1960s.

§ The original French work has been revised three times, most recently by Émile Breton as *Dictionnaire des cinéastes* (Nouv. éd. rev. et augm. Paris : Sueil, 1990. 347 p.). Includes bibliographies. PN1993.45.S313

Shipman, David. The great movie stars. 2nd rev. ed. London : Mcdonald, 1989–91. 3 v. : ill. **BH286**

1st ed. 1970–72 (2 v.); new rev. ed., 1979–80 (3 v.).

Contents: v. 1, The golden years; v. 2, The international years v. 3, The independent years.

Presents generally lengthy profiles, incorporating biographical data and critical comment on the films, performances, etc. Choices for inclusion were "guided by the box-office figures, by popularity polls and by the reputation that remains."—*Introd., v. 1*. Vol. 3 is devoted to 100 stars of the 1980s and 1990s. PN1998.A2S54

Thomson, David. A biographical dictionary of film. 2nd ed., rev. N.Y. : Morrow, c1981. 682 p. **BH287**

First published with title: *A biographical dictionary of the cinema* (London : Secker & Warburg, 1975); American ed. with new title, 1976.

Self-described as "a Personal, Opinionated and Obsessive Biographical Dictionary of the Cinema."—*Introd.* Has critical profiles of some 900 international actors, directors, etc., accompanied by good filmographies. Biographical data is sparse.

A 3rd ed. (834 p.) was publ. 1994, with updated information and 200 new profiles. PN1998.A2T55

Tulard, Jean. Dictionnaire du cinéma. Nouv. éd. rev. et actualisée. Paris : Laffont, c[1991]–1992. 2 v. **BH288**

1st ed., 1982–84.

Contents: v. 1, Les realisateurs; v. 2, Les acteurs.

International dictionary of directors (v. 1) and performers (v. 2), giving basic biographical information, a full list of films, and a short assessment of career. Index in v. 2. PN1998.A2T84

Who's who in Hollywood : the actors and directors in today's Hollywood / ed. by Robyn Karney. N.Y. : Continuum, c1993. 499 p. **BH289**

Informal profiles of some 600 actors and directors currently or recently active in U.S. films. For each, gives birth date and place, real name (if different), a fairly long discussion of life and career, and a list of theatrical films. Foreign personalities working in American films are included. PN1998.2.W46

World film directors / ed., John Wakeman. N.Y. : H.W. Wilson, 1987–1988. 2 v. : ports. **BH290**

Contents: v. 1, 1890–1945; v. 2, 1945–88.

Similar in orientation and presentation to Wakeman's *World authors* (BE205 *note*), provides "introductions to the work and lives of about four hundred of the world's best-known film directors, from the beginning of cinema to the present."—*Pref.* Vol. 1 covers directors whose careers were established by 1945, while v. 2 deals with those who emerged after World War II. Lengthy, clearly written articles include biographical information, discussion of popular and critical reputation (often with quotations from critics or the director), a filmography, and a bibliography. Not indexed.

§ David Quinlan's *The illustrated guide to film directors* (London : Batsford; Totowa, N.J. : Barnes & Noble, 1983. 335 p.) has briefer sketches, focusing on the careers and achievements of some 570 (mostly British and American) directors of commercial features. Geoff Andrew's *The film handbook* (Boston : G.K. Hall, 1990. 362 p.), which aims to be of use to both film students and general moviegoers, covers more than 200 world-famous directors, with emphasis on major films and influences.

Also of interest: Jean-Pierre Coursodon and Pierre Sauvage's, *American directors* (N.Y. : McGraw-Hill, 1983. 2 v.), which offers 118 critical essays "on virtually every American film director of recognized (and, in quite a few instances, underrecognized) stature."—*(Pref.)*; and Dennis Fischer's *Horror film directors, 1931–1990* (Jefferson, N.C. McFarland, 1991. 877 p.), for extended treatment of directors whose careers are largely associated with the horror genre. PN1998.2.W67

Indexes

Schuster, Mel. Motion picture directors : a bibliography of magazine and periodical articles, 1900–1972. Metuchen, N.J. : Scarecrow, 1973. 418 p. **BH291**

Lists English-language articles of a biographical or career-oriented nature that appeared in general and specialized periodicals. Reviews of films are generally excluded. Alphabetical by name, then chronological by article date.

§ Citations to articles on actors and actresses is provided in Schuster's *Motion picture performers : a bibliography of magazine and periodical articles, 1900–1969* (Metuchen, N.J. : Scarecrow, 1971. 702 p.) and its *Supplement no. 1, 1970–1974* (1976. 783 p.). Includes selective indexing of fan magazines. Z5784.M9S34

TELEVISION AND RADIO

Guides

Cassata, Mary B. Television : a guide to the literature / by Mary Cassata and Thomas Skill. Phoenix : Oryx, 1985. 148 p. **BH292**

Bibliographic essays, in three sections: (1) Test patterns (overview of mass communication processes, historical development of television, reference sources); (2) The environment (television processes and effects in general and with regard to children, news, and politics); (3) Directions (the industry, criticism, collected works). Author, title, and subject indexes. Z7711.C37

TV genres : a handbook and reference guide / ed. by Brian G. Rose ; Robert S. Alley, advisory ed. Westport, Conn. : Greenwood, 1985. 453 p. **BH293**

Central elements of 19 various formats or styles of television programming (documentary, game show, science fiction and fantasy) are each discussed in a chapter ending with a bibliographical survey, a short list of books and articles, and a videography. Chapters by specialists present a historical survey and an analysis of themes and issues. The vidoegraphy cites about 10–15 shows of special interest in studying that genre.

Bibliography

Hill, George H. Blacks on television : a selectively annotated bibliography / by George H. Hill and Sylvia Saverson Hill. Metuchen, N.J. : Scarecrow, 1985. 223 p.   **BH294**

Consists of 156 entries for books, dissertations and theses, and scholarly articles, in addition to about 2,700 unannotated citations to articles in the African-American and general press. The newspaper and magazine section is subdivided by topic (e.g., news, ownership, sports) but lacks a detailed contents listing of topics included. Program index; author, personal name, and organization index. Appendixes include list of Emmy winners by category.

§ George Hill, Lorraine Raglin, and Chas Floyd Johnson's *Black women in television : an illustrated history and bibliography* (N.Y. : Garland, 1990. 168 p.) provides, in similar fashion, expanded coverage of African-American women's contributions.   Z1361.N39H53

Dissertations

Kittross, John M. A bibliography of theses & dissertations in broadcasting, 1920–1973. Wash. : Broadcast Education Assoc., 1978. [238] p.   **BH295**

An author listing of some 4,300 dissertations and master's theses completed at American universities, with keyword-in-title index plus an index by year of completion and another by broad topics.

Sparks, Kenneth R. A bibliography of doctoral dissertations in television and radio. [3rd ed.]. Syracuse, N.Y. : School of Journalism, Syracuse Univ., [1971]. 119 p.   **BH296**

A classified listing of some 900 dissertations completed through June 1970. Author index.   Z7221.S65

Indexes

International index to television periodicals : an annotated guide. 1979/80– . London : Internat. Federation of Film Archives, [1983]– . Biennial.   **BH297**

Michael Moulds, ed.

Cumulates entries from a microfiche service with the same title offered by the International Federation of Film Archives (FIAF). Indexes about 100 media periodicals, selected to reflect international periodical literature of lasting critical or aesthetic value. In four sections: (1) General subjects; (2) Individual programmes and TV films; (3) Biography; (4) Author index. Brief annotations indicate scope or content of each article.

• Machine-readable version: *International filmarchive CD-ROM* [database] (London : FIAF, 1993?–). Updated semiannually. Contains the present index, *International index to film periodicals* (BH234), and other FIAF publications. Publisher plans to extend coverage back to 1972.

Reviews and criticism

Variety television reviews, 1923–1988 : the first fifteen volumes of the series including a comprehensive index / ed. by Howard H. Prouty. N.Y. : Garland, 1989–1991. 15 v. **BH298**

Reprints all reviews in chronological order by issue date. Title, subject, name, local programming, and international programming indexes.

Continued by: *Variety and Daily variety television reviews* (v. 16 [1989/90]– . N.Y. : Garland, 1992– . Biennial).   PN1992.3.U5V36

Program catalogs

Television

Brooks, Tim. The complete directory to prime time network TV shows, 1946–present / Tim Brooks and Earle Marsh. 5th ed., completely rev. and updated. N.Y. : Ballantine Books, c1992. 1207 p. : ill.   **BH299**

1st ed., 1979; 4th ed., 1988.

Provides information on "every regular series ever carried on the commercial broadcast networks during 'prime time'—roughly 7:30–11:00 P.M., E.S.T." (Introd.), as well as late night network shows and top syndicated programs aired primarily during the evening. Entry is by title of series and gives inclusive dates of telecasting, broadcast history, cast (regulars and notable guests), notes on the story line, memorable episodes, etc. Numerous appendixes, including prime time schedules 1946–91, Emmy Award winners, top-rated programs by season, spin-offs, hit theme songs from series. Name index.

§ Similar in concept and format is: Alex McNeil, *Total television : a comprehensive guide to programming from 1948 to the present* (3rd ed. N.Y. : Penguin Books, 1991. 1142 p.). Gives less detail for most shows, but includes daytime and public television series and has broader coverage of syndicated programs. *See also* Vincent Terrace's *Fifty years of television : a guide to series and pilots, 1937–1988* (N.Y. : Cornwall Books, 1991. 864 p.) for data on early programs and series pilots.

Einstein, Daniel. Special edition : a guide to network television documentary series and special news reports, 1955–1979. Metuchen, N.J. : Scarecrow, 1987. 1051 p.   **BH300**

Lists and describes content of: commercial television documentary series, by series title and date; documentaries produced by David L. Wolper, by year; and network news specials and special reports, by program date. Indexes of personalities (e.g., interviewees, subjects of profiles) and production and technical personnel (e.g., producers, journalists, narrators).   PN1992.8.D6E56

Erickson, Hal. Syndicated television : the first forty years, 1947–1987. Jefferson, N.C. : McFarland, c1989. 418 p.   **BH301**

Describes "programs either made exclusively for non-network play, or ... programs perhaps intended for network telecasts but ultimately making their debuts in syndication."—*Introd.* By decade, then program type (e.g., adventure/mystery, game/quiz, religious, sports, talk/interview). Annotated bibliography; individual and program name index. Useful for details on a sometimes elusive body of programs.   PN1992.55.E67

Gianakos, Larry James. Television drama series programming : a comprehensive chronicle, 1947–1959. Metuchen, N.J. : Scarecrow, 1980. 565 p.   **BH302**

The first volume, chronologically, of a complex but useful series. Preliminary sections offer a season-by-season overview of programs and schedules for prime-time drama shows on ABC, CBS, and NBC during the 12-year period. The main section, arranged by season, chronicles drama series introduced during each season and lists episodes for that year (and for subsequent seasons for continuing series). Episode data include title, date shown, principal cast, and source (for adaptations). Index of series titles.

Continued by:

———. ———. 1959–1975 (1978. 794 p.).
———. ———. 1975–1980 (1981. 457 p.).
———. ———. 1980–1982 (1983. 678 p.).
———. ———. 1982–1984 (1987. 830 p.).
———. ———. 1984–1986 (1992. 705 p.).

Over the years, the basic format has been retained, but a number of changes have been instituted. New volumes list series from earlier seasons that were omitted and provide corrections and expansion of material in earlier volumes. Recent volumes add credits for writers and directors and contain useful appendixes (e.g., teleplays adapted from Pulitzer Prize-winning works, from Greek drama, or from Shakespeare). Cumulative index of series titles, beginning with volume for 1982–84.   PN1992.3.U5G48

Marill, Alvin H. Movies made for television : the telefeature and the mini-series, 1964–1986. N.Y. : New York Zoetrope, c1987. 576 p. : ill.   **BH303**

Previous editions cover 1964–79 (publ. 1980) and 1964–84 (publ. 1984).

Offers details on "nearly 2,100 films and mini-series made expressly for television" (*Introd.*), excluding episodes of continuing series. In alphabetical order by title, entries give: network; date(s) shown; production company; length; characters and cast; credits for director, producer, teleplay author, photographer, etc.; and plot summary, with comment. Indexes of producers, directors, writers, and performers. Chronological list of titles.   PN1992.8.F5M35

Shapiro, Mitchell E. Television network prime-time programming, 1948–1988. Jefferson, N.C. : McFarland & Company, c1989. 743 p. : ill.   **BH304**

Provides "month-by-month prime-time schedules for all national broadcasting networks; a detailed listing of all network programming moves, including series premieres, cancellations, and time slot moves; and a yearly recap of key programming moves."—*Introd.* In seven sections, by night of the week. For each network (ABC, CBS, NBC, DuMont, and Fox) shows, in grid fashion, which program(s) occupied a particular time slot during a given month in the 7–11 p.m. Eastern Standard Time period. Details and hightlights of the networks' programming changes are given in the chronological summaries. Show title index.

§ Companion sources by Shapiro: *Television network daytime and late-night programming, 1959–1989* (1990. 264 p.); *Television network weekend programming, 1959–1990* (1992. 464 p.).
                                                          PN1992.3.U5S54

Television directors guide. 1st ed.– . Beverly Hills, Calif. : Lone Eagle, c1990– . Annual.   **BH305**

Lynne Naylor, comp. and ed.

Provides directors' credits for post-1979 comedy series, drama series, variety series, specials, and pilots produced primarily for prime time. Arranged by director, includes credits for network, cable, and syndicated programs, but not for television movies and mini-series, which are included in the companion series *Film directors : a complete guide* (BH207). Director entries give contact name and telephone number. Includes Emmy Awards and nominations; genre listing of shows; film title index; directory of agents and managers.

§ Also published by Lone Eagle and ed. by Naylor: *Television writers guide* (ed. 1 [1989]–).   PN1992.T42

Terrace, Vincent. Encyclopedia of television : series, pilots, and specials. N.Y. : New York Zoetrope, c1985–c1986. 3 v. : ill.   **BH306**

Contents: v. 1, 1937–73; v. 2, 1974–84; v. 3, Index: Who's who in television, 1937–84.

Vols. 1–2 consist of title listings of more than 7,000 series, pilots, specials, and experimental programs, alphabetically arranged in each volume. For each program, gives genre, story line or content, cast and

production credits, network, show length, dates. Vol. 3 has separate indexes for performers, producers, directors, and writers; lists of credits are keyed to entry numbers in v. 1–2.   PN1992.9.T47

Woolery, George W. Animated TV specials : the complete directory to the first twenty-five years, 1962–1987. Metuchen, N.J. : Scarecrow, 1989. 542 p. : ill.   **BH307**

Covers "all special animated television presentations aired on the various networks or syndicated exclusively in the United States."—*Pref.* By title, gives broadcast history, production credits, principal characters and voices, and plot summary. Appendixes include listings of holiday and topical specials. Name indexes: producers, directors, filmmakers; writers, musicians and lyricists; voices. Also has studio/production company and distributor indexes.

§ For coverage of animated cartoon series, as well as live, film, and tape series produced for children, *see* Woolery's *Children's television : the first thirty-five years, 1946–1981* (Metuchen, N.J. : Scarecrow, 1983–1985. 2 v.).   PN1992.8.S64W66

Radio

Dunning, John. Tune in yesterday : the ultimate encyclopedia of old-time radio, 1925–1976. Englewood Cliffs, N.J. : Prentice-Hall, c1976. 703 p., [16] leaves of plates : ill.   **BH308**

Narrative articles, often lengthy, concerning some 1,000 entertainment shows, emphasizing history, memorable features, and notable cast members. Indexed.   PN1991.3.U6D8

Pitts, Michael R. Radio soundtracks : a reference guide. 2nd ed. Metuchen, N.J. : Scarecrow, 1986. 337 p.   **BH309**

1st ed., 1976.

Catalog of "programs from the golden age of radio (from the late 1920s to the early 1960s) that are available on both tape recordings and records"—*Introd.* Index of personalities and show titles.
                                                          PN1991.9.P58

Swartz, Jon David. Handbook of old-time radio : a comprehensive guide to golden age radio listening and collecting / by Jon D. Swartz and Robert C. Reinehr. Metuchen, N.J. : Scarecrow, 1993. 806 p.   **BH310**

The main section, "Program descriptive log," is arranged by title and has brief profiles of some 2,000 selected programs of all kinds. These and an additional 2,500 shows are included in "Program category logs," arranged by category (e.g., music and variety, comedy, soap operas, drama), with information as to network, inclusive years of broadcast, and number of episodes available. An appendix lists sources of radio programs (public collections, organizations and fan clubs, dealers and distributors). Annotated bibliography; name and program title indexes.   PN1991.3.U6S93

Terrace, Vincent. Radio's golden years : encyclopedia of radio programs, 1930–1960. San Diego : A. S. Barnes ; London : Tantivy Pr., [1981]. 308 p. : ill.   **BH311**

About 1,500 nationally broadcast network and syndicated entertainment programs are listed by title, with information on program type, format (story line or general content), cast, announcer, sponsor, length, network, date of first broadcast, etc. Index of names.

§ Frank Buxton and Bill Owen's *The big broadcast, 1920–1950...* (N.Y. : Viking Pr., 1972. 301 p.) is less systematic in presenting information but provides details on theme music, openings and closes, comedy routines, etc., for many shows. Survey articles on 21 selected topics (e.g., commercials, singers, sports and sportscasters). Name index.   PN1991.3.U6T47

Program credits

Parish, James Robert. The complete actors' television credits, 1948–1988 / by James Robert Parish and Vincent Terrace. 2nd ed. Metuchen, N.J. : Scarecrow, 1989–90. 2 v. : ill. **BH312**

Rev. ed. of: *Actors' television credits 1950–1972* (1973) and three supplements.

Contents: v. 1, Actors; v. 2, Actresses.

Listed by name of performer. Covers "all network, cable, and syndicated entertainment programs, including cartoons, aired and unaired pilot films, experimental TV (1931–1947), variety series (appearances as a host or regular only), and variety specials (as host or guest)."—*Foreword, v. 2.* PN1992.4.A2P3

Encyclopedias

Brown, Les. Les Brown's encyclopedia of television. 3rd ed. Detroit : Gale, c1992. 723 p. : ill. **BH313**

1st ed., 1977, publ. as *The New York times encyclopedia of television*; 2nd ed., 1982.

An established source for concise articles on a broad range of topics. This edition includes "3,000 entries on notable people, programs, and companies as well as legal, regulatory, and technical issues."—*p.xiii.* Useful surveys of television genres (e.g., game shows, news) and developments in various countries. Numerous appendixes (e.g., top-rated network sports events, worldwide TV advertising expenditures). Bibliography; general index. PN1992.18.B7

Halliwell, Leslie. Halliwell's television companion / Leslie Halliwell with Philip Purser. 3rd ed. London : Grafton, 1986. 941 p. : ill. **BH314**

1st ed., 1979, had title: *Halliwell's teleguide*; 2nd. ed., 1982.

Covering U.S. and British television, focuses on entertainment programs but also has articles on individuals, companies, networks, technical and trade terms, and general subjects (e.g., doctors, lookalikes). Entries for programs (series, television movies, televised plays, selected documentaries) include a rating of quality (zero–4 stars), year(s), producer, company/network, one-sentence summary, brief critical comment, and acting and production credits. Listing of episodes for some well-known series (e.g., *Alfred Hitchcock presents*). PN1992.3.G7

Reed, Robert M. The encyclopedia of television, cable, and video / by Robert M. and Maxine K. Reed. N.Y. : Van Nostrand Reinhold, c1992. 622 p. **BH315**

Contains 3,100 entries in 14 topical areas: advertising; agencies, associations, companies, and unions; awards; educational/corporate communications; engineering; events; general terms and processes; government/legal; home video; people; personnel; production; programming; and programs. Fairly long entries, especially for important individuals, shows, and technologies. Initials and acronyms index; bibliography; cross-references. P87.5.R44

Slide, Anthony. The television industry : a historical dictionary. N.Y. : Greenwood, 1991. 374 p. **BH316**

Patterned after Slide's *The American film industry : a historical dictionary* (BH254) and its companion volume on the international film industry. Provides "more than 1,000 entries on production companies, distributors, organizations, genres, technical terms"—IPref ., as well as on such topics as animals, cigarette advertising, and nudity. Does not cover programs or individuals, except for an appendix of sketches on the major network figures, Leonard H. Goldenson, William S. Paley, and David Sarnoff. In addition to bibliographic references for many of the entries, has a separate bibliography of television reference sources. Indexes of names (personal, companies, organizations, and stations) and program titles. PN1992.3.U5S57

Dictionaries

Ensign, Lynne Naylor. The complete dictionary of television and film / Lynne Naylor Ensign and Robyn Eileen Knapton. N.Y. : Stein and Day, 1985. 256 p. **BH317**

Attempts to bring some standardization to the language—particularly the slang and jargon—of the film and television industries. Includes terms from silent film days as well as current terminology. Cross-references. PN1992.18.E57

McDonald, James R. The broadcaster's dictionary : dictionary of terms, directory of associations and government agencies, broadcasting techniques, solutions, and circuits. Broomfield, Colo. : Wind River Books, 1986. 198 p. : ill. **BH318**

Briefly defines terms used in broadcast engineering, operations, and production. Appendixes contain directories of key associations and government agencies as well as a series of "tutorials" (e.g., schematic abbreviations, introduction to digital audio) aimed at nonengineering station personnel. Includes a short bibliography. TK6544.M37

Directories

International television & video almanac. 32nd. ed. (1987)– . N.Y. : Quigley Publ. Co., 1987– . Annual. **BH319**

Continues: *International television almanac* ([1st ed., 1956]-31st ed. [1986]).

Most information relates to the U.S. television industry, including: the year in review; industry statistics; awards; who's who in the entertainment world; obituaries; directory of services; histories of networks; companies and personnel; producers and distributors; network programs; syndicated programs; stations, cable television; organizations; and the press. Brief coverage of British and world markets. Separate section on home video lists companies, services, and markets. The extensive "who's who" section makes up half the volume. HE8698.I55

Biography

Brooks, Tim. The complete directory to prime time TV stars, 1946–present. N.Y. : Ballantine Books, 1987. 1086 p. **BH320**

Regular performers on nighttime (6 p.m. to midnight) series are listed, giving date and place of birth, television credits and awards, with biographical/career sketches provided for the best-known players. Appendixes include lists by birthday and birthplace. Index of production titles.

BJ

Music

For specialized collections, the standard guide continues to be *Music reference and research materials : an annotated bibliography*, by Duckles and Keller (BJ4), which should be consulted for extensive and detailed information.

For general libraries, an attempt has been made to list here a substantial selection of works from which information may be sought, e.g., *The new Grove dictionary of music and musicians* (BJ141), long the standard work in English; *Baker's biographical dictionary of musicians* (BJ203); and *The new Oxford companion to music* (BJ142). Most libraries will need at least one or two books on the opera and opera plots, e.g., Ewen's *The new encyclopedia of the opera* (BJ248); Rosenthal's *Concise Oxford dictionary of opera* (BJ253); or *Kobbé's complete opera book* (BJ237). Sears's *Song index* (BJ289) is essential. For recorded music, catalogs of historical interest as well as those with current listings, will probably be needed.

All libraries will need to include titles from the growing, and in many cases, extensive literature on nonclassical music.

GENERAL WORKS

Guides

Brockman, William S. Music : a guide to the reference literature. Littleton, Colo. : Libraries Unlimited, 1987. 254 p.   **BJ1**
A guide to "the important current and retrospective sources of information on music [that] emphasizes, but is not restricted to, works in English."—*Pref.* Contains 841 annotated entries for general reference sources, general bibliographical sources, bibliographies of music literature, bibliographies of music, discographies, key journals, associations, and research centers. A very good overview of the literature. Author/title and subject indexes.   ML113.B85

Crabtree, Phillip. Sourcebook for research in music / Phillip D. Crabtree and Donald H. Foster. Bloomington : Indiana Univ. Pr., c1993. 236 p.   **BJ2**
Intended as "an introductory reference source of varied information, largely bibliographical, pertaining to research in the field of music."—*Pref.* Consists of an introductory chapter followed by seven chapters of bibliographies: basic tools, area bibliographies, dictionaries and encyclopedias, sources treating the history of music, current research journals, editions of music, and miscellaneous sources. A brief overview precedes each bibliography, and many entries have annotations. Emphasis is on more recent materials in English. Author and title indexes.   ML113.C68

Druesedow, John E. Library research guide to music : illustrated search strategy and sources. Ann Arbor, Mich. : Pierian Pr., [1982]. 86 p. : ill. (Library research guide series, 6).   **BJ3**

A brief guide intended "primarily for the undergraduate music student who is preparing to write on the subject of music, perhaps for the first time."—*Pref.*   ML111.D78

Duckles, Vincent Harris. Music reference and research materials : an annotated bibliography / Vincent H. Duckles, Michael A. Keller. 4th ed. N.Y. : Schirmer ; London : Collier Macmillan, c1988. 714 p.   **BJ4**
1st ed., 1964; 3rd ed., 1974.
Lists (with annotations) more than 3,000 items in the following principal categories: Dictionaries and encyclopedias; Histories and chronologies; Guides to systematic and historical musicology; Bibliographies of music literature; Bibliographies of music; Catalogs of music libraries and collections; Catalogs of musical instrument collections; Histories and bibliographies of music printing and publishing; Discographies; Yearbooks and directories; Women in music; Miscellaneous and bibliographical tools. Appropriate subdivisions within most sections; useful headnotes to the sections. This ed. marred by somewhat haphazard editing. Indexes of authors, editors, and reviewers; of subjects; and of titles.   ML113.D83

Marco, Guy A. Information on music : a handbook of reference sources in European languages. Littleton, Colo. : Libraries Unlimited, 1975–84. v. 1–3.   **BJ5**
Contents: v. 1, Basic and universal sources; v. 2, The Americas; v. 3, Europe.
An annotated listing of books considered to be the most useful to students of music. Designed to supplement and extend Vincent H. Duckles and Michael A. Keller's *Music reference and research materials* (BJ4) rather than supersede that work. In addition to the listing of sources relevant to the study of European music, v. 3 offers an update to v. 2, and there is an appendix of revisions to v. 1–2. Each volume has its own index.   ML113.M33

Phelps, Roger P. A guide to research in music education / by Roger P. Phelps, Lawrence Ferrara, Thomas W. Goolsby. 4th ed. Metuchen, N.J. : Scarecrow, 1993. 367 p. : ill.   **BJ6**
1st ed., 1969; 3rd ed., 1986.
A bibliographic and procedural guide prepared with needs of the graduate music student particularly in mind. Organized in 4 parts: Research problem identification; Writing the research proposal and the research document; The research methodologies; Music education research.
§ Covering the same area is *Research in music education : an introduction to systematic inquiry*, by Edward L. Rainbow and Hildegard C. Froehlich (N.Y. : Schirmer, 1987).   MT1.P5

Pruett, James W. Research guide to musicology / James W. Pruett and Thomas P. Slavens. Chicago : Amer. Libr. Assoc., 1985. 175 p. (Sources of information in the humanities, no. 4).   **BJ7**
Organized in two sections: the first an essay on the history and development of research in the field, and the second an annotated list of approximately 125 reference books and 16 periodicals.   ML3797.P78

Bibliography : Books, 1851–1980

Bibliographia musicologica = A bibliography of musical literature. v. 1 (1968)–v. 9 (1976). Utrecht [Netherlands] : Joachimsthal, 1970–80.   **BJ8**
An annual alphabetical author listing of books (and some dissertations) from an international group of publishers. Name/subject index.   ML113.B52

Blum, Fred. Music monographs in series. N.Y. : Scarecrow, 1964. 197 p.   **BJ9**
Subtitle: A bibliography of numbered monograph series in the field of music current since 1945.

Lists more than 250 series from some 30 countries, arranged alphabetically by title of series or issuing organization. Entries for each volume give author, title, and date. Includes list of publishers and their agents; alphabetical list of series and issuing organizations; index of names. Superseded for German titles by Hermann Walther, *Bibliographie der Musikbuchreihen 1886–1990* (BJ45).   ML113.B63

Charles, Sydney Robinson. A handbook of music and music literature in sets and series. N.Y. : Free Pr., [1972]. 497 p.
                                        BJ10

Intended to complement rather than duplicate Fred Blum, *Music monographs in series* (BJ9) and Anna Harriet Heyer, *Historical sets, collected editions, and monuments of music* (BJ58). In four sections: (1) sets and series containing music of several composers and sets and series containing both music and music literature; (2) sets and series devoted to one composer; (3) music literature monograph and facsimile series; (4) music periodicals and yearbooks. Indexed.   ML113.C45

Chase, Gilbert. A guide to the music of Latin America. 2nd ed., rev. and enl. Wash. : Pan American Union, 1962. 411 p.
                                        BJ11

Repr. : N.Y. : AMS Pr., 1972.

A joint publication of the Pan American Union and the Library of Congress.

1st ed., 1945, had title: *Guide to Latin American music.*

Still a very valuable annotated bibliography with introductory comments for each country. Subheadings for each country vary somewhat but usually include: Introduction, General and miscellaneous; Biography and criticism; National anthems; Folk and primitive music.
                                   ML120.S7C47

Coover, James B. Music lexicography : including a study of lacunae in music lexicography and a bibliography of music dictionaries. 3rd ed., rev. and enl. Carlisle, Pa. : Carlisle Books, [1971]. 175 p.   **BJ12**

1st ed., 1952, had title: *A bibliography of music dictionaries.*

Lists biographical as well as terminological works. Includes an essay on lacunae in music bibliography between 1500 and 1700, and has been enlarged to include about 1,800 "lexicographic works," including autonomous works as well as portions and appendixes of larger works and some periodical articles. Indexes of personal names and of "topics and types of dictionaries."   ML128.D5C6

Gerboth, Walter. An index to musical festschriften and similar publications. N.Y. : Norton, [1969]. 188 p.   **BJ13**

Based on an earlier version appearing in a commemorative volume, *Aspects of medieval and renaissance music* (N.Y. : Norton, 1966), the work has been expanded to include festschriften published through 1967, earlier volumes previously overlooked, and works published in the Slavic languages. In three parts: (1) a list of the festschriften; (2) a subject listing of the articles appearing in those volumes; and (3) an index by author and specific subject.   ML128.M8G4

Horn, David. The literature of American music in books and folk music collections : a fully annotated bibliography. Metuchen, N.J. : Scarecrow, 1977. 556 p.   **BJ14**

Nearly 1,500 books relating to any aspect of American musical life are cited and carefully annotated. Arranged chronologically, then by type or form. Indexed. Both this volume and the supplement (below) devote more than two-thirds of the entries to folk and popular music.

————.————. *Supplement 1*, by David Horn with Richard Jackson (Metuchen, N.J. : Scarecrow, 1988. 570 p.). Follows the same format with annotations for books published from mid-1975 to the end of 1980, as well as for a number of books overlooked in the original edition or included without annotations. Contains 996 annotated and 323 unannotated pre-1981 entries.   ML120.U5H7

Jackson, Irene V. Afro-American religious music : a bibliography and catalogue of gospel music. Westport, Conn. : Greenwood, [1979]. 210 p.   **BJ15**

In two parts, the first offering a bibliography of books, essays, magazine and newspaper articles, and dissertations on "the music of the established Black churches or denominations in the United States and the Caribbean as well as African-American cults in the Caribbean and South America" (*Pref.*) also including entries on West African music, particularly in the area of religious ritual. The second part is a catalog, by composer, of the compositions of African Americans (1938–65) based on the collection at the Library of Congress. Subject index to the bibliography; list of composers.   ML128.S4J3

Jahresverzeichnis der deutschen Musikalien und Musikschriften. v. 1–117. Leipzig : Hofmeister, 1852–1968. Annual.   **BJ16**

Title varies: 1852–53, *Kurzes Verzeichnis sämmtlicher in Deutschland und den angrenzenden Ländern gedruckter Musikalien* ... ; 1854–1928, *Verzeichnis der im Jahre ... erschienen Musikalien*; 1929–42, *Hofmeisters Jahresverzeichnis.*

In three sections: (1) Musikalien, Musikschriften, Zeitschriften und Jahrbücher in one alphabet; (2) Systematischer und Register-Teil; (3) Titel und Textregister.

§ Superseded by: *Jahresverzeichnis der Musikalien und Musikschriften* (BJ49).   ML113.H715

Kahl, Willi. Repertorium der Musikwissenschaft : Musikschrifttum, Denkmäler und Gesamtausgaben in Auswahl (1800–1950) mit Besitzvermerken deutscher Bibliotheken und Musikwissenschaftlicher Institute / Im Auftr. der Gesellschaft für Musikforschung bearb. von Willi Kahl und Wilhelm Martin Luther Kassel : Bärenreiter, 1953. 271 p.   **BJ17**

A list of 2,795 titles of literature on music and scores, in classified arrangement, representing holdings of German libraries. Includes name and subject indexes, and an index to national and folk music.

Lieberman, Fredric. Chinese music : an annotated bibliography. 2nd ed., rev. and enl. N.Y. : Garland, 1979. 257 p. (Garland reference library of the humanities, v. 75).   **BJ18**

1st ed., 1970.

Provides exhaustive coverage of some 2,441 books and articles in Western-language publications containing critical commentary on Chinese music, dance, and drama. Arrangement is by author in a single alphabet. Index of serial titles; index of names. A topical outline of Chinese music serves as a kind of subject index since item numbers of relevant entries are given under each heading in the outline.
                                     ML120.C5L5

Sendrey, Alfred. Bibliography of Jewish music. N.Y. : Columbia Univ. Pr., 1951. 404 p.   **BJ19**

Repr. : N.Y. : Kraus, 1969.

This comprehensive bibliography of almost 10,000 items is in two separate listings: (1) literature on the subject, and (2) the music itself, including recordings. Author indexes for both sections.   ML113.S5

Tyrrell, John. A guide to international music congress reports in musicology, 1900–1975 / John Tyrrell, Rosemary Wisc. N.Y. : Garland, 1979. 353 p. (Garland reference library of the humanities, v. 118).   **BJ20**

A chronological listing of general congresses of music, anthropology, poetry, etc., but not specialized congresses such as those concerned with music education, music therapy, dance, or music copyright. For each congress gives the name in the language of its publications, place, date, published proceedings, and a listing of the papers relating specifically to music. There are a number of useful indexes: places; titles, series, and sponsors; authors and editors; subjects.

§ Covering music papers read at congresses during part of the same period is Marie Briquet, *La musique dans les congrès internationaux, 1835–1939* (Paris : Société Française de Musicologie, 1961).   ML128.M8T9

Warfield, Gerald. Writings on contemporary music notation : an annotated bibliography. [Ann Arbor, Mich.] : Music Libr. Assoc., 1976. 93 p. (MLA index and bibliography series, no. 16).   **BJ21**

Aims to be comprehensive in citing books and articles on new notation published 1950–75, but is selective in coverage of writings on music notation generally, new performance techniques, music copying, autographing and printing, ethnomusicology, and writings published 1900–50. Author arrangement, with subject index. Brief annotations.

ML128.N7W37

Bibliography : Books, 1981–

Antônio, Irati. Bibliografia da música brasileira : 1977–1984 / [projeto e organização, Irati Antonio, Rita de Cássia Rodriques, Heloísa Helena Bauab]. São Paulo : Universidade de São Paulo, Escola de Comunicações e Artes, Serviço de Biblioteca e Documentação : Centro Cultural São Paulo, Divisão de Pesquisas, 1988. 275 p.   **BJ22**

A bibliography of books, chapters from books, pamphlets, dissertations, theses, and articles on Brazilian music, published both in Brazil and abroad, 1977–84. Includes 2,239 author entries with bibliographies along with locations in seven Brazilian libraries. Subject and name indexes. Projected future volumes are to provide retrospective coverage up to 1976, as well as an ongoing bibliography of works published since 1985.   ML120.B7A57

Baily, Dee. A checklist of music bibliographies and indexes in progress and unpublished. 4th ed. Philadelphia : Music Library Association, c1982. 104 p. (Music Library Association index and bibliography series, no. 3).   **BJ23**

1st ed., 1963; 3rd ed. comp. by Linda Solow, 1974.

Lists 533 items by author (personal or institution). Entries based on questionnaires, and all unpublished as of July, 1981. Subject index of names and topics.   ML113.B28

A basic music library : essential scores and books / comp. by the Music Library Association Committee on Basic Music Collection under the direction of Pauline S. Bayne ; ed. by Robert Michael Fling. 2nd ed. Chicago : Amer. Libr. Assoc., 1983. 357 p.   **BJ24**

1st ed., 1978.

A thorough revision of a work "designed as a buying guide or selection tool for those who have responsibility for collecting music materials in small and medium-sized libraries, whether public or academic."—Pref. Principal sections: Score anthologies; Study scores; Performing editions; Vocal scores; Instrumental methods and studies; Music literature. Appendix of selected music dealers. Indexed. A 3rd ed. is in progress.   ML113.B3

British catalogue of music, 1957–1985 / [editors, Michael D. Chapman, Elizabeth Robinson]. London ; N.Y. : K.G. Saur, 1988. 10 v.   **BJ25**

Contains bibliographic records of U.K. and foreign publications for post-1980 and additional pre-1981 imprints cataloged since the publication of the British Library's The catalogue of printed music in the British Library to 1980 (BJ53).   ML120.G7B72

Brookhart, Edward. Music in American higher education : an annotated bibliography. Warren, Mich. : Harmonie Park Pr., 1988. 245 p. : ill. (Bibliographies in American music, no. 10).   **BJ26**

An author bibliography of 1,300 items with brief, descriptive annotations on the history of music in American higher education. Entries are alphabetically arranged within general categories and cover publications from ca. 1830 to 1985. Author and subject indexes.   ML120.U5B77

Coover, James. Antiquarian catalogues of musical interest. London ; N.Y. : Mansell, 1988. 372 p.   **BJ27**

A listing of 5,531 catalogs, bulletins, and lists from 640 antiquarian dealers arranged alphabetically by firm. For each catalog, includes date of issue, form of publication if other than a catalog, specific title

of the catalog, dealer's number, and the number of lots or pages. Informative introductory essay by Albi Rosenthal. Subject and place indexes.   ML152.C65

Crisp, Deborah. Bibliography of Australian music : an index to monographs, journal articles, and theses. Armidale [N.S.W.] : Australian Music Studies Project, 1982. 260 p. (Australian music studies, 1).   **BJ28**

Contains 2,218 entries for published journal articles, monographs, and theses relating to Australian music and musicians, including aboriginal music and culture, which have "informative value to the scholar."—Introd. Covers works published by the end of 1981, with the earliest entry dating from 1790. Organized in two parts: Pt. 1, subject index, and Pt. 2, bibliographic listing by author.   ML120.A86C74

Damschroder, David. Music theory from Zarlino to Schenker : a bibliography and guide / by David Damschroder and David Russell Williams. Stuyvesant, N.Y. : Pendragon Pr., 1990. 522 p. : ill. (Harmonologia series, no. 4).   **BJ29**

An alphabetical listing of approximately 200 theorists with introductory summary of their work, a bibliography of their published and unpublished treatises (with notes on the sources and available facsimiles and translations), and a bibliography of secondary literature. Coverage spans the history of Western music, from Glarean's Isagoge in musicen (1516) through Schoenberg's Fundamentals of musical composition (1967). A Literature supplement includes secondary works on more than one theorist. Topical, chronological, title, and name indexes.   ML128.T5D27

Davis, Deta S. Computer applications in music : a bibliography. Madison, Wis. : A-R Editions, c1988. 537 p. (The computer music and digital audio series, v. 4).   **BJ30**

International in scope. Lists 4,585 items alphabetically by author, or title if author is lacking, in 25 categories. Covers works published prior to mid-1986. English translations are provided for titles not in English, German, or French. Includes review citations and abstract citations when available. Index by author, with title entries for articles having no author.

———. ———. Supplement 1 (Madison, Wis. : A-R Editions, 1992. 597 p.) lists 4,287 items in 36 categories and updates the entries through 1989. Brief annotations are given if the content is not clear from the title. Adds a subject index.   ML128.C62D4

De Lerma, Dominique-René. Bibliography of black music. Westport, Conn. : Greenwood, 1981–84. 4 v.   **BJ31**

Contents: v. 1, Reference materials; v. 2, Afro-American idioms; v. 3, Geographical studies; v. 4, Theory, education, and related studies.

An extensive, international bibliography of many areas of African-American musical culture. "The arrangement ... is patterned after that of RILM abstracts [BJ108], with changes made to satisfy the specific needs of the subject and breaks in the numerical sequence to permit the inclusion of new subject areas at a later date."—Introd. Rather than using cross-references, items are repeated in all relevant sections. Includes "articles, graduate papers, journals, and monographs." Indexes in v. 3 and 4 only.   ML128.B45D44

Duggan, Mary Kay Conyers. Italian music incunabula : printers and type. Berkeley : Univ. of California Pr., c1992. 323 p. : ill.   **BJ32**

A descriptive bibliography of 152 books containing printed music or space for manuscript music. Arrangement is alphabetical by short title and chronological within that title. Preceding the bibliography is a discussion of Italian music type, typefounders, and specimens, as well as chapters organized by city on individual printers. Several indexes (chronological, printers by location, etc.) and appendixes.   ML112.D8

Floyd, Samuel A. Black music in the United States : an annotated bibliography of selected reference and research materials / Samuel A. Floyd, Marsha J. Reisser. Millwood, N.Y. : Kraus Internat., 1983. 234 p.   **BJ33**

Offers a survey of all types of reference materials— bibliographies and indexes, catalogs, discographies, biographical dictionaries, and anthologies—pertinent to the study of African-American music. Also includes a directory of relevant archives. Indexes of titles, names, and subjects. ML128.B45F6

Folter, Siegrun H. Private libraries of musicians and musicologists : a bibliography of catalogs : with introduction and notes. Buren [The Netherlands] : F. Knuf, 1987. 261 p. : ill. (Auction catalogues of music, v. 7). **BJ34**

Lists 392 catalogs arranged by name of collector. Each entry includes title and publication information, libraries holding the catalog, contents, and annotations. Entries are limited to published catalogs from auction houses, dealers, exhibitions, privately printed and institutional catalogs, together with those published in monographs or articles. Chronological and dealer indexes. ML111.F64

Harvey, D. R. A bibliography of writings about New Zealand music published to the end of 1983. [Wellington, N.Z.] : Victoria Univ. Pr., 1985. 222 p. : ill. **BJ35**

Contains "a comprehensive listing of all material pertaining to music and music-making in New Zealand, published in periodicals, or as monographs, or produced as dissertations."—*Introd.* Excludes material published in newspapers, reviews and notices of performances, and articles on recent popular music and Maori music. Entries are arranged alphabetically by author or title within larger subject categories, all of which are listed in the table of contents. Author and subject indexes. ML120.N53H3

Heintze, James R. Early American music : a research and information guide. N.Y. : Garland, c1990. 511 p. (Music research and information guides, vol. 13 ; Garland reference library of the humanities, vol. 1007). **BJ36**

An annotated bibliography of 1,959 books, articles, dissertations, papers, published sermons and discourses, catalogs, lists, directories, and other materials available for research on American music from its beginning to 1820. Within two large categories, General reference works and Historical studies, the listing is broken down into systematically arranged sections. Each section contains entries listed alphabetically by author; many are preceded by brief but bibliographically useful introductions. Author-title and subject indexes.

§ A related work is the author's *American music studies : a classified bibliography of master's theses* (Detroit : Information Coordinators, 1984), which contains 2,370 entries organized by topic. ML120.U5H46

Heskes, Irene. The resource book of Jewish music : a bibliographical and topical guide to the book and journal literature and program materials. Westport, Conn. : Greenwood, 1985. 302 p. (Music reference collection, no. 3). **BJ37**

An annotated bibliography of 1,200 items intended to provide a "tool for the examination of Jewish music."—*Pref.* Entries consist of English-language books, periodicals, instruction manuals, music collections, and dance materials, and are arranged alphabetically by author under 16 categories. Cutoff date for inclusion is 1984. Author and topical indexes. ML128.J4H48

Krüger-Wust, Wilhelm J. Arabische Musik in europäischen Sprachen : eine Bibliographie. Wiesbaden : Harrassowitz, 1983. 124 p. **BJ38**

Primarily an author listing of 2,100 books and articles published from the mid-19th century through the 1970s, with a few subject categories (e.g., recordings with European commentary listed under *Schallplatten*, subdivided by country). Contains an index by 30 broad subject terms. ML120.A7K8

Krummel, Donald William. Bibliographical handbook of American music. Urbana : Univ. of Illinois Pr., c1987. 269 p. **BJ39**

An annotated bibliographical guide to literature on many aspects of American music. The sources are systematically arranged in four broad categories: Chronological perspectives; Contextual perspective;

Musical medium and genres; and Bibliographical forms. Critical, informative essays introduce each broad category which is then further subdivided systematically. Name and subject index. ML120.U5K78

———————— The literature of music bibliography : an account of the writings on the history of music printing & publishing. Berkeley, Calif. : Fallen Leaf Pr., c1992. 447 p. : ill. (Fallen Leaf reference books in music, no. 21). **BJ40**

An annotated bibliography of 976 items organized in nine chapters covering the field systematically, chronologically, and geographically. Interspersed are the author's informative and incisive prose commentaries. Author and subject indexes. ML112.K765

Répertoire bibliographique de textes de présentation générale et d'analyse d'oeuvres musicales canadiennes (1900–1980) = Canadian musical works 1900–1980 : a bibliography of general and analytical sources / comp. by Chantal Bergeron ... [et al.] ; under the direction of Lucien Poirier. [Ottawa] : Canadian Association of Music Libraries, c1983. 96 p. (Canadian Association of Music Libraries. Publications, 3). **BJ41**

"This checklist consists of nearly 2,000 references from 82 secondary sources which mention close to 1,500 serious works which over 165 Canadian composers have created between 1900 and 1980."–*Pref.* Listing is alphabetical by composer, subarranged by title. Bibliographical references are listed under each title alphabetically by author or, lacking an author, by appropriate source reference. Author index. ML120.C2R46

Smialek, William. Polish music : a research and information guide. N.Y. : Garland, 1989. 260 p. (Music research and information guides, vol. 12 ; Garland reference library of the humanities, vol. 1093). **BJ42**

An annotated bibliography of 600 books and articles published through 1987, organized roughly by RILM classification (*see* BJ108). The author chose the "most useful and important Polish writings in Western publications" (*Foreword*) and focused on the most readily available materials. Excludes Chopin for space reasons. Notes Western-language summaries of Polish works. Traces an item's publication if published both in the East and West. Discography, arranged by composer, for over 400 sound recordings. Index. ML120.P6S6

Thompson, Donald. Music and dance in Puerto Rico from the age of Columbus to modern times : an annotated bibliography / by Donald Thompson and Annie F. Thompson. Metuchen, N.J. : Scarecrow, 1991. 339 p. (Studies in Latin American music, no. 1). **BJ43**

Contains an annotated bibliography of 995 books and periodicals intended to provide bibliographic groundwork for further study. Entries are organized alphabetically by author within larger, systematically organized chapters. Subject and personal name indexes. "First in a series conceived to expand the range of scholarly resources available in English for the study of Latin American Music."—*Pref.* ML125.P8T55

Tsuge, Gen'ichi. Japanese music : an annotated bibliography. N.Y. : Garland, 1986. 161 p. (Garland bibliographies in ethnomusicology, 2 ; Garland reference library of the humanities, vol. 472). **BJ44**

An annotated bibliography of 881 items in Western languages which appeared through 1983. Includes scholarly books, articles, review essays, bibliographies, discographies, as well as translations of song texts, libretti, and synopses of dance-drama productions. Subject, name, and format indexes. ML120.J3T8

Walther, Hermann. Bibliographie der Musikbuchreihen 1886–1990. Kassel ; N.Y. : Bärenreiter, c1991. 352 p. (Catalogus musicus, 12). **BJ45**

A bibliography of music-related monographs published in series. Limited to numbered series from German-speaking countries. Excludes series of facsimiles. Organized alphabetically by series title with monographs listed in numerical order. Includes series editor(s) and/or sponsoring agency. Indexes by name and place/subject provide access to the content of the individual monographs. Supersedes Fred Blum, *Music monographs in series* (BJ9) and Sydney Robinson Charles, *A handbook of music and music literature in sets and series* (BJ10) for this literature.   ML113.C35 vol. 12

Warner, Thomas E. Periodical literature on American music, 1620–1920 : a classified bibliography with annotations. Warren, Mich. : Harmonie Park Pr., 1988. 644 p. (Bibliographies in American music, no. 11).   **BJ46**
    Contains 5,348 entries drawn from over 600 periodicals, many with brief descriptive annotations. Organized by topics: research and reference materials; historical studies; theory and composition; ethnomusicology; organology; and special topics. Excludes Eskimo, American Indian, and folk music. Author and subject indexes.
     ML120.U5W18

Bibliography : Books, Current

Bibliographie des Musikschrifttums. 1936– . Frankfurt am Main : Hofmeister, 1936– . Annual.   **BJ47**
    Frequency varies; publication runs well behind date of coverage. Not published 1940–49.
    Vols. for 1936–39 called "1–4. Jahrg."
    A classified bibliography of books and "serious" periodical articles. Author and subject indexes. Emphasizes German publications, but coverage is international.   ML113.B54

Deutsche Nationalbibliographie und Bibliographie der im Ausland erschienenen deutschsprachigen Veröffentlichungen : Reihe M, Musikalien und Musikschriften. Monatliches Verzeichnis / Bearbeiter und Herausgeber, Die Deutsche Bibliothek. Jan. 1991– . Frankfurt am Main : Buchhändler-Vereinigung, 1991– . Monthly.   **BJ48**
    Monthly.
    Presents new publications of printed music and literature about music in separate sections. The printed music is arranged in approximately 10 sections by genre or performing force, subarranged by author or title, and concludes with publisher and name/title indexes. The literature section includes works culled from Reihe A, B or H, and concludes with one index of name, title, subject, and keyword entries.
    Sound recordings are listed in a separate series, Reihe T. Included are music and spoken word recordings, systematically arranged, with subarrangement by composer or title. Publisher and author/title indexes.   ML5.D43

Jahresverzeichnis der Musikalien und Musikschriften. Jahrg. 118 (1969)– . Leipzig : VEF Friedrich Hofmeister Musikverlag, 1969– . Annual.   **BJ49**
    "Veröffentlichungen der DDR, der BRD und Westberlins sowie der deutschsprachigen Werke anderer Länder."—*t.p.*
    Continues *Jahresverzeichnis der deutschen Musikalien und Musikschriften* (BJ16). Issued in two parts: Alphabetischer Teil, and Systematischer und Register-Teil.

New York Public Library. Music Division. Bibliographic guide to music. 1975– . Boston : G.K. Hall, 1976– . Annual.
     BJ50
    Serves as an ongoing supplement to the *Dictionary catalog of the music collection* (BJ88) in that it includes all publications cataloged by the Research Libraries of the New York Public Library in the field of music, but also includes additional entries from Library of Congress MARC tapes in "such areas as literature of music (bibliography, history and criticism, philosophy of music), and music instruction and study (composition, orchestration, singing and voice culture)."—*Introd., 1975.*   ML136.N5N5732

Bibliography : Scores

1845–1980

Albrecht, Otto Edwin. A census of autograph music manuscripts of European composers in American libraries. Philadelphia : Univ. of Pennsylvania Pr., 1953. 331 p.   **BJ51**
    Lists 2,017 manuscripts by more than 500 European composers. Gives full bibliographical information. Includes list of owners.
     ML135.A2A4

American Society of Composers, Authors and Publishers. ASCAP index of performed compositions. N.Y. : ASCAP, 1978. 1423 p.   **BJ52**
    "The material in this volume is an unedited alphabetical listing of compositions in the ASCAP repertory which have appeared in the Society's survey of radio, television and wired music performances [through March 1977]."—*Pref.* Listing is by title, with name of performer and publisher.
    A 99-p. supplement was published 1981.   ML120.U5A53

British Library. Music Library. The catalogue of printed music in the British Library to 1980 / [Laureen Baillie, ed.]. London ; N.Y. : K. G. Saur, 1981–87. 62 v.   **BJ53**
    Often called *CPM*.
    "Unites in a single sequence the various music catalogues maintained for the use of readers in the British Library reading rooms, and for the first time makes the full range of the collection accessible to an international public."—*Pref.* A main entry listing with cross-references from various alternative entry points.
    Supplemented by: *British catalogue of music, 1957–1985* (BJ25).
    For current listings of printed music, see *British catalogue of music* (BJ79).
    •Machine-readable version: *CPM plus : catalogue of printed music in the British Library to 1990* [database] (London : Bowker-Saur, 1993). Available in CD-ROM, not updated. Includes both the basic catalogue to 1980 and its 1957–85 supplement (above), and additional pre-1981 imprints that do not appear in the printed catalogs.
     ML136.L8B62

British union-catalogue of early music printed before the year 1801 : a record of the holdings of over one hundred libraries throughout the British Isles / Edith B. Schnapper, ed. London : Butterworth, 1957. 2 v.   **BJ54**
    A scholarly bibliography drawn from the British Museum, Dept. of Printed Books, *Catalogue of printed music published between 1487 and 1800 now in the British Museum*, by W. Barclay Squire (London, 1912 and 2nd suppl., Cambridge, 1940), but is essentially an entirely new work. Listing is generally by composer or anonymous title; periodicals are grouped under "Periodical publications." Extensive index of song titles.   ML116.B7

Corbin, Solange. Répertoire de manuscrits mediévaux contenant des notations musicales. Paris : Éditions du Centre national de la Recherche scientifique, 1965–74. 3 v.   **BJ55**
    At head of title: École pratique des hautes-études, Sorbonne. 4. section: Sciences historiques et philologiques.
    Madeleine Bernard, ed.
    Contents: v. 1, Bibliothèque Sainte-Geneviève, Paris; v. 2, Bibliothèque Mazarine, Paris; v. 3, Bibliothèques parisiennes: Arsenal, Nationale (Musique), Universitaire, École des Beaux Arts et fonds privés.
    A listing and description of each medieval manuscript containing chant notation. Arrangement within volumes is by type of notation (e.g., neume, square note, etc.). Indexes by manuscript numbers, by original owner of manuscript, by form of manuscript (hymnal, the offices), by type of lines on the page, and by neume. Vols. 1–2 include a listing of manuscripts with pictures of musical instruments, though only the folio number is listed, not the name of the instrument pictured. Indexes of repositories and of incipits in v. 3.   M135.A2C67

Dichter, Harry. Handbook of early American sheet music, 1768–1889 / Harry Dichter, Elliott Shapiro. N.Y. : Dover, 1977. 287 p. : ill. **BJ56**

A reprint, with corrections, of the 1941 edition published under title: *Early American sheet music : its lure and its lore.*

Arranged by class in chronological periods. Each piece is described with bibliographical details, illustrations, etc. Includes "Famous American musical firsts," p. xxv–xxvii; and pt. 3, "Lithographers and artists working on American sheet music before 1870," by Edith A. Wright and Josephine A. McDevitt, p. 249–57.

§ A complementary work is Dichter's *Handbook of American sheet music : a catalog of sheet music for sale by the compiler* (Philadelphia : Dichter, 1947. 100 p.), a catalog of about 2,000 items in classified arrangement without index; although designated as "First annual issue," nothing further was published. ML112.D53

Eitner, Robert. Biographisch-bibliographisches Quellen-Lexikon der Musiker und Musikgelehrten der christlichen Zeitrechnung bis zur Mitte des neunzehnten Jahrhunderts. Leipzig : Breitkopf, 1900–04. 10 v. **BJ57**

Repr. : N.Y. : Musurgia, 1947.

Gives brief biographies and full bibliographies of music; the first systematic attempt to provide bibliographies of manuscripts, early editions, etc., of authors and composers. In many cases indicates location of the items in European libraries. A criticism by Michel Brenet (Marie Bobillier) in *La revue musicale* (1905): 480–89, contains various corrections. Corrections and additions are also included in the *Miscellanea musicae bio-bibliographica* ... by Hermann Springer and others (published quarterly, 1912–16. Repr. : N.Y. : Musurgia, 1947. 435 p.). The latter volume is also reprinted along with Giuseppe Radiciotti's "Aggiunte e correzioni ai Dizionari biografici dei musicisti" (first published in *Sammelbände der Internationalen Musikgesellschaft* v. 14–15) as the final volume of the 11 v. reprint edition (termed "2. verb. Aufl.") published by Akademische Druck– und Verlagsanstalt, Graz, 1959.

The bibliographies and locations will be superseded by *Répertoire international des sources musicales* (BJ77) when that work is completed. Z6811.E363

Hoyer, Anna Harriet. Historical sets, collected editions, and monuments of music : a guide to their contents. 3rd ed. Chicago : Amer. Libr. Assoc., 1980. 2 v. (1105 p.). **BJ58**

1st ed., 1957; 2nd ed., 1969.

Contents: v. 1, Text; v. 2, Index.

Vol. 1 lists, with contents and bibliographical information, "the complete editions of the music of individual composers and the major collections of music that have been published or are in the process of publication."—*Pref.* Encompasses "collections, anthologies, or monumental sets of music considered by the author to have historical value, musical worth, reliable editing, or significance to music research"; aims to be as complete as possible for the 19th and 20th centuries, with some emphasis on current publications (through June 1979). About 1,300 entries in this edition. Index lists entries by composers, compilers, editors, and by titles for title entries.

§ To be superseded by: George R. Hill and Norris L. Stephens, *Collected editions, historical sets, and monuments of music : a bibliography* (Berkeley, Calif. : Fallen Leaf Pr., 1996. [Fallen Leaf Reference Books in Music, no. 14]). Forthcoming indexes to be published on CD-ROM. ML113.H52

Hixon, Donald L. Music in early America : a bibliography of music in Evans. Metuchen, N.J. : Scarecrow, 1970. 607 p. **BJ59**

Provides an index to "the music published in seventeenth and eighteenth century America as represented by Charles Evans' *American bibliography* [AA405] and the Readex Corporation's microprint edition of *Early American imprints, 1639–1800* [AA410 note]."—*Pref.* ML120.U5H6

Hofmeisters Handbuch der Musikliteratur : oder, Allgemeines systematisch-geordnetes Verzeichniss der in Deutschland und in den angrenzenden Ländern gedruckten Musikalien auch musikalischen Schriften und Abbildungen, mit Anzeige der Verleger und Preise. 3., bis zum Anfang des Jahres 1884 ergänzte Aufl. / bearb. und hrsg. von Adolf Hofmeister. Leipzig : Hofmeister, [1844–45]. 3 v. **BJ60**

First published in Leipzig by Anton Meysel, 1817, covering music and music literature to 1815, with ten supplements to 1827 (Repr. : N.Y. : Garland, 1975). Karl Friedrich Whistling issued a revised 2nd ed. in 1828 with three supplements: 1829, 1834, and 1839 (Repr. : Hildesheim : Olms, 1975. 2 v.).

Adolf Hofmeister edited this 3rd ed., called *C. F. Whistling's Handbuch* (varies), with supplementary volumes, as follows: *Handbuch der musikalischen Literatur: oder, Verzeichnis der im Deutschen Reiche, in den Ländern deutschen Sprachgebietes, sowie der für den Vertrieb im Deutschen Reiche wichtigen, im Auslande erschienenen Musikalien auch musikalischen Schriften, Abbildungen und plastichen Darstellungen, mit Anzeige der Verleger und Preise.* Bd. 4–19 (incompl.), 1844–1940 (Leipzig : Hofmeister, 1852–1943). (Bd. 19, Lfg. 1–8 includes only A–L; no more published.). ML113.H71

Library of Congress. Library of Congress catalog : music and phonorecords. 1953–1972. Wash. : Library of Congress, 1953–72. **BJ61**

Subtitle: A cumulative list of works represented by Library of Congress printed cards.

Issued semiannually with annual and quinquennial cumulations, the latter now forming part of the *National union catalog* cumulation, but independently numbered and available separately.

"*Music and Phonorecords* contains entries for music in the broadest sense. It includes music, phonorecords (i.e., sound recordings, musical and nonmusical), libretti, and books about music and musicians."—*Introd., 1963–67 cumulation.*

§ Superseded by: *National union catalog. Music, books on music, and sound recordings* (BJ62). Z881.A1C328

National union catalog. Music, books on music, and sound recordings. Jan./June 1973–1989. Wash. : Library of Congress, 1973–89. **BJ62**

At head of title: Library of Congress catalogs.

Supersedes the Library's *Music and phonorecords* (BJ61).

"Music in the broadest sense, including music scores, sheet music, libretti, and books about music and musicians, is covered in this catalog. It also contains entries for sound recordings of all kinds, whether these are musical, educational, literary, or political."—*Foreword.* In addition to Library of Congress printed cards, cards supplied by nine cooperating libraries with extensive music collections are reproduced in the catalog, although all these libraries did not contribute throughout.

Cumulations have been published for 1973–77 (8 v.) and 1979–80 (7 v.). Published in paper annually from 1981–89.

§ Continued by: *The music catalog* (BJ82). Z881.A1C328

Olmsted, Elizabeth H. Music Library Association catalog of cards for printed music, 1953–1972 : a supplement to the Library of Congress catalogs. Totowa, N.J. : Rowman & Littlefield, 1974. 2 v. **BJ63**

Includes entries for printed music reported to the National Union Catalog for the period 1956–72, thus supplementing *Library of Congress catalog : music and phonorecords* (BJ61). Much editing was done for this publication, but cards were not retyped and a considerable number are virtually unreadable. Name of the library supplying the card was not included, therefore the catalog cannot be used as a tool for locating copies. ML113.O42

Sonneck, Oscar George Theodore. Bibliography of early secular American music (18th century). Rev. and enl. by William Treat Upton. Wash. : Library of Congress, Music Div., 1945. 616 p. : ill. **BJ64**

Repr. : N.Y. : Da Capo Pr., 1964.

1st ed., 1905.

Revised edition adds much new material. Lists by title—with complete bibliographical information, including first lines—secular music issued by the American press prior to the 19th century. Also contains a list of articles and essays relating to music, and a list of composers, with their works. Locates copies.   ML120.U5S6

Tischler, Alice. A descriptive bibliography of art music by Israeli composers. Warren, Mich. : Harmonie Park Pr., 1988. 424 p. (Detroit studies in music bibliography, no. 62).   **BJ65**

Covers 63 composers selected according to the following criteria: "(1) the date of 1910 as a starting-point, i.e., the beginning of organized musical activity in the newly-founded city of Tel Aviv; (2) composers who have won recognition in the musical life of Israel by having their works performed and/or published; and (3) those who have matured and are settled in their profession in Israel."—*Introd.* Excludes composers born after 1947. For each, gives brief overview of career, addresses, sources, and full information on individual compositions (including performance medium, first performances, etc.).

ML120.I75T57

Wolfe, Richard J. Secular music in America, 1801–1825 : a bibliography. N.Y. : New York Public Library, 1964. 3 v.

BJ66

Lists approximately 10,000 titles and editions of secular music published in America, although not confined to American composers. Includes sacred music when printed in secular collections or in series, and religious pieces written by American composers and published in sheet-music form. Arranged alphabetically by composer or anonymous title with detailed bibliographical information. Gives short biographical sketches of lesser-known composers. Indexes of titles, first lines, publishers, etc., and a general index. Locates copies.

A scholarly work useful to research workers and students of American history, as well as to music scholars.   ML120.U5W57

1981–

The Boston composers project : a bibliography of contemporary music / Boston Area Music Libraries ; Linda I. Solow, ed. Cambridge, Mass. : MIT Pr., [1983]. 775 p.   **BJ67**

Aims "to list every composition, published or unpublished, by every art music and jazz composer resident in the greater Boston area during the latter half of the 1970s" (*Pref.*), thus serving as a prototype work to meet the needs of music researchers and cultural historians and to encourage similar work in other geographical areas. Listing is by composer, with index of names and titles.   ML125.B66B67

Britton, Allen Perdue. American sacred music imprints, 1698–1810 : a bibliography / by Allen Perdue Britton and Irving Lowens, and completed by Richard Crawford. Worcester, Mass. : American Antiquarian Society, 1990. 798 p.   **BJ68**

An annotated bibliography of some 500 collections of sacred music, intended as a complement to Oscar George Theodore Sonneck, *Bibliography of early secular American music (18th century)* (BJ64). Alphabetically-arranged headings consisting of the name of the compiler, or if none, the agency that issued the work, or, lacking an agency, the formal title, or, if none, a uniform title, are used to organize the works. Appendixes include a chronological list of imprints; a listing of sacred sheet music; a list of composers and sources; the core repertory; and a geographical directory of engravers, printers, publishers, and booksellers.   ML128.H8B68

Census-catalogue of manuscript sources of polyphonic music, 1400–1550 / comp. by the University of Illinois, Musicological Archives for Renaissance Manuscript Studies. [Rome] : American Institute of Musicology ; Neuhausen-Stuttgart : Hänssler-Verlag, 1979–1988. 5 v. (Renaissance Manuscript Studies, 1).   **BJ69**

Contents: v. 1–3, A–U; v. 4, V–Z and supplement; v. 5, Cumulative bibliography and indexes.

Aims to list "all known manuscripts containing polyphonic music composed between 1400 and 1550."—*Introd., v. 4.* Excludes tablatures, manuscripts containing only anonymous "primitive" polyphony contained in *RISM*, BIV³⁻⁴ (BJ77), and most sources copied later than 1700. For each entry, includes siglum, manuscript designation, contents, composers, physical description, other historical information, and bibliography. Vol. 4 contains a supplement of additional and revised entries; v. 5, composer, geographical/institutional, geographical/chronological, and general indexes.   ML169.8.R46

Fitch, Donald. Blake set to music : a bibliography of musical settings of the poems and prose of William Blake. Berkeley : Univ. of California Pr., c1990. 281 p. (University of California publications. Catalogs and bibliographies, v. 5).   **BJ70**

Bibliography of solo songs, choral works, chamber and orchestral works with vocal parts, and other works without voice, either set to or manifestly inspired by the works of Blake. Contains 1,412 entries listed alphabetically by composer; each entry contains title of composition, performing forces, publisher if applicable, duration, performance information, contents notes, and other notes. Indexes of Blake titles, performing combinations, translated texts, and names.

ML134.5.B6F6

Gooch, Bryan N. S. A Shakespeare music catalogue / Bryan N.S. Gooch, David Thatcher ; Odean Long, associate ed. ; incorporating material collected and contributed by Charles Haywood. Oxford : Clarendon Pr., 1991. 5 v. (xcv, 2847 p.).

BJ71

Contents: v. 1–3, the plays listed alphabetically followed by other literary works (v. 3); v. 4, indexes; v. 5, bibliography.

A comprehensive listing of more than 20,000 published and unpublished musical compositions related to Shakespeare's works, composed from his day through 1987. In addition to works expressly composed with a specific Shakespeare association in mind, covers incidental music for productions in major cities, by major companies, by Shakespearean companies, or by university or college groups. Also included are projected and unfinished works, misattributions, or works which might misleadingly be associated with Shakespeare. Numerous indexes and extensive bibliography.   ML134.5.S52G6

Guillo, Laurent. Catalogue de la musique imprimée avant 1801 : conservée dans les bibliothèques de Lyon, Grenoble et la région. Grenoble : Agence de coopération régionale pour la documentation, 1986. 156 p. : ill.   **BJ72**

Contains bibliographical records for works by individual authors, collections from the 16th through 18th centuries, psalters, and other psalm collections held by 21 institutions in 11 cities outside Paris. Index of names includes composers, publishers, printers, engravers, and donors.

§ Complements François Lesure's *Catalogue de la musique imprimée avant 1800 : conservée dans les bibliothèques publiques de Paris* (BJ73).   ML120.F7G84

Lesure, François. Catalogue de la musique imprimée avant 1800 : conservée dans les bibliothèques publiques de Paris. Paris : Bibliothèque nationale, 1981. 708 p.   **BJ73**

An author catalog (with a separate section for anonymous works, p. 657–708) of early printed music in the Bibliothèque Nationale and other public libraries of Paris. Gives full bibliographic information, library location, and shelfmark.   ML125.P27L5

Matsushita, Hitoshi. A checklist of published instrumental music by Japanese composers. Tokyo : Academia Music, c1989. 181 p.   **BJ74**

A checklist of published instrumental music written in Western notation by Japanese composers from the mid-19th century to the present. Includes 2,271 works by more than 350 composers published by 80 Japanese publishers. Each entry contains Japanese and English title with publication information. Genre index.   ML128.I65M38

Metzner, Günter. Heine in der Musik : Bibliographie der Heine-Vertonungen. Tutzing : H. Schneider, 1989–94. 12 v.
BJ75

An index to musical settings of Heine's text compiled from a large number of standard reference works. Vols. 1–8 contain an alphabetical listing by composer, and under each composer her or his musical works with bibliographical references and listing of performances; v. 9–10 contain an alphabetical list of Heine's works, and under each, a listing by genre of the musical settings of that text with a reference to its entry in the composer vols. Vol. 11 is a Register, v. 12 Literaturverzeichnis. ML134.5.H43M47

Pierreuse, Bernard. Catalogue général de l'édition musicale en France : livres, méthodes et partitions de musique sérieuse en vente = General catalog of music publishing in France : books, methods, and scores of serious music on sale. Paris : Editions Jobert : Distribution, Editions musicales transatlantiques, 1984. 476 p. : ill. **BJ76**

A listing of books, methods, and scores of serious music published in France and in print and available for sale as of 1982. Entries are arranged by subject and performance medium; a full list of subject headings appears at the front. Within each entry, listing is by composer, with title and publication information. Contains composer index, addresses of publishers, and list of exclusive agents in other countries. ML120.F7P5

Répertoire international des sources musicales = International inventory of musical sources. Munich : G. Henle, 1960– . v. (In progress). **BJ77**

"Publié par la Société Internationale de Musicologie et l'Association Internationale des Bibliothèques Musicales."—*half title page.*

Title and introductory matter also in German and in English.

Often referred to as *RISM.*

Contents: *Série alphabetique*, AI[1-10], Einzeldrucke vor 1800, Redaktion: Karlheinz Schlager (v. 1–9, Aarts–Zwingmann; Anhang 1–2; [v. 10], Text– und Musikincipit-Register zu den Anhängen 1 und 2 in RISM AI[9]); AI[11-12], Addenda et corrigenda, A–L, Redaktion: Ilse und Jürgen Kindermann; AII, Music manuscripts, 1600–1800; 2 microfiches.

Série systématique [BI[1]], Recueils imprimés, XVIe–XVIIe siècles, liste chronologique ... sous la direction de François Lesure; DII, Recueils imprimés, XVIIIe siècle; ... sous la direction de François Lesure; BIII[1], The theory of music from the Carolingian era up to 1400; a descriptive catalogue of manuscripts ... ed. by Joseph Smits van Waesberghe [and others]; BIII[2], The theory of music from the Carolingian era up to 1400 ... Italy, ed. by Pieter Fischer; BIII[3], The theory of music manuscripts from the Carolingian era up to ca.1500 in the Federal Republic of Germany (D-brd), by Michel Huglo and Christian Meyer; BIII[4], The theory of music manuscripts from the Carolingian era up to ca.1500 in Great Britain and in the United States of America, by Christian Meyer (Great Britain), and Michel Huglo and Nancy C. Phillips (U.S.); BIV[1], Manuscripts of polyphonic music, 11th–early 14th century, ed. by Gilbert Reaney; BIV[2], Manuscripts of polyphonic music, ca.1320–1400, by Gilbert Reaney; BIV[1-2] Suppl. 1, Manuscripts of polyphonic music, The British Isles, 1100–1400, by Andrew Wathey; BIV[3-4], Handschriften mit Mehrstimmiger Musik des 14., 15. und 16. Jahrhunderts, hrsg. Max Lütolf, 2 v.; BIV[5], Manuscrits de musique polyphonique: XVe et XVIe siècles: catalogue, Nanie Bridgman; BV[1], Tropen– und Sequenzenhandschriften, von Heinrich Husmann; BVI[1-2], Écrits imprimés concernant la musique; ... sous la direction de François Lesure, 2 v.; BVII, Handschriftlichen überlieferte Lauten– und Gitarrentabulauturen des 15. bis 18. Jahrhunderts, by Wolfgang Boetticher; BVIII[1-2], Das deutsche Kirchenlied, DKL: krit. Gesamtausg. der Melodien, hrsg. Konrad Ameln, Marcus Jenny, Walther Lipphardt; BIX[1], Hebrew notated manuscript sources up to circa 1840, by Israel Adler; BIX[2], Hebrew writings concerning music, its manuscripts and printed books from Geonic times up to 1800, by I. Adler; BX, The theory of music in Arabic writings (ca.900–1900): descriptive catalogue of manuscripts in libraries of Europe and the U.S.A., by Amnon Shiloah; BXI, Ancient Greek music theory: a catalogue raisonné of manuscripts, by Thomas J. Mathiesen.

An ongoing major bibliographic series for pre-1900 (and selected 19th-century) source materials in music. Intended "to provide a catalogue of all available bibliographical musical works, writings about music and textbooks on music from all countries of the world."— *Foreword, v. BI[1].*

The first two volumes to be published were unnumbered. It was announced in BII that the volumes of the general alphabetical series would be denoted by the symbol A, followed by the number of the volume in Roman figures. The volumes of the classified series would bear the symbol B, followed by the number of the volume in Roman figures.

Bibliographical descriptions are full; copies are located. Indexes are included with each volume or group of volumes.

§ For Series C, *Directory of music research libraries*, see: BJ169.

Current

Bibliographie nationale française. Musique : bibliographie établie par la Bibliothèque nationale à partir des documents déposés au titre du dépôt légal. 1992, no. 1/3–. Paris : La Bibliothèque, 1992– . Three times a year. **BJ78**

Subset of the French national bibliography for the printed music collections of the Bibliothèque Nationale, Département de la Musique; the Bibliothèque du Conservatoire; and the Bibliothèque de l'Opéra. The listing is classified with subarrangement by composer/author and title. Indexes of authors, titles, uniform titles, and genres.

For full information concerning the *Bibliographie nationale française*, see AA627. Z2165.B5725

The British catalogue of music. Jan./March 1957– . London : British Library Bibliographic Services Div., 1957– . Semiannual, with an annual cumulation in December. **BJ79**

Lists new music published in Great Britain, or new music available in Great Britain through a sole agent, based on the Legal Deposit records at the British Library. In addition, includes new music acquired by the Music Library from foreign publishers who do not have an agent in Great Britain. (Based on *Pref.*, 1992 annual volume.) Classified arrangement, with composer/title and subject indexes.

§ For cumulated lists of printed music, see the *British catalogue of music, 1957–1985* (BJ25). For records of books about music, see *The British national bibliography* (AA689). ML120.G7B7

Deutsche Musikbibliographie. Jahrg. 1– . Leipzig : Hofmeister, 1829– . Monthly. **BJ80**

Supersedes: *Handbuch der musikalischen Literatur*, 1817–29.

Title varies: 1829–1907, *Musikalisch-literarischer Monatsbericht*; 1908–42, *Hofmeisters Musikalisch-literarischer Monatsbericht*.

Now an alphabetical list, by composer or author, of music and musical writings published in German. Gives place of publication, publisher, and price. Indexed by subject and by publisher. Cumulated in *Jahresverzeichnis der deutschen Musikalien und Musikschriften* (BJ16). 19th-century issues were generally organized systematically by musical genre with little indexing, making them difficult to use. ML113.H72

Library of Congress. Copyright Office. Catalog of copyright entries : part 3 : Musical compositions. n.s. v. 1 (July 1906)–v. 41 (1946). [Wash.] : Library of Congress, Copyright Office, 1906–46. **BJ81**

Through 1945, all musical compositions (published and unpublished) were entered by title in one alphabet in each monthly issue, followed by the list of renewals, with an annual index. In 1946 the *Catalog* was divided into four groups: (1) Unpublished music; (2) Published music; (3) Renewals; (4) Title index to groups 1 and 2.

Superseded by: ———— *Catalog of copyright entries : third series, part 5 : Music* (v. 1 [Jan./June 1947]–v. 31 [July/Dec. 1977]. Wash. : Library of Congress, Copyright Office : for sale by U.S. Govt. Print. Off., 1947–77).

Issued in three parts, 1947–56: pt. 5A, Published music; pt. 5B, Unpublished music; pt. 5C, Renewal registrations. (Pt. C issued as pt. 14B, 1947–50.) Each part published in two numbers per year: (1) Jan./June, and (2) July/Dec.

Beginning with Jan./June 1957 (3rd ser., v. 11, pt. 5, no. 1), the three parts are combined and issued as pt. 5, in three groupings: (1) current registrations, (2) renewal registrations, and (3) name index.

Lists all music published in the U. S. and foreign countries deposited for copyright registration during the period covered. Arrangement is by title. The index to names lists names of composers, authors of words, editors, compilers, arrangers, tc. as given in the main entry.

The most comprehensive bibliography of music available for the period of coverage.

A 4th series includes pt. 3, Performing Arts, and pt. 7, Sound recordings.   Z642.A2

The music catalog [microform]. 1981–90– . Wash. : Library of Congress, Cataloging Distribution Service, c1991– . Quarterly.   **BJ82**

Issued in two parts: Register and Index.

The Register contains selected fields from bibliographic records presented in a card-like format. The indexes include name, publisher number, series, subject, and title indexes.

The first set in this title is a 10-year retrospective cumulation, 1981–90, drawn from online cataloging records, which not only supersedes the cumulated volumes of *National union catalog. Music, books on music* … (BJ62) for these years, but also includes material from all formats and classes of materials outside the scope of *Music, books on music*, if the material has a subject heading that contains the word "music." Because of its online source, this publication provides indexing, not only for LC's bibliographic records, but also for contributing members' cataloging records. Omitted from this cumulation are score and sound recordings catalog records created by LC 1981–83, as these were not available online.

Subsequent volumes issued are quarterly and cumulate annually. Additionally, as a result of its online downloading source, these volumes contain records for sound recordings from libraries outside the regular contributing libraries.   ML136.U5N9

Music-in-print series. 1974– . Philadelphia : Musicdata, Inc., 1974– . Irregular.   **BJ83**

Contents: v. 1, Sacred choral music in print, by Gary S. Eslinger (2nd ed., 1985) and Arranger index (1987), Master index (1992), and Supplements (1988, 1992); v. 2, Secular choral music in print, by F. Mark Daugherty (2nd ed., 1987), Supplements (1991, 1993), and Arranger index (1987); v. 3. Organ music in print, by Walter A. Frankel (2nd ed., 1984) and Supplement (1990); v. 4, Classical vocal music in print, by Thomas R. Nardone (1976) and Supplement (1985), by Gary S. Eslinger and F. Mark Daugherty; v. 5, Orchestral music in print, by Margaret K. Farish (1979) and Supplement (1983); v. 6, String music in print, by Margaret K. Farish (2nd ed., 1980) and Supplement (1984); v. 7, Classical guitar music in print, ed. by Mijndert Jape (1989); Master composer index (1989), a composer and title index to the entire set.

Compiled from publishers' catalogs with the aim of providing an ongoing record of music in print. Revised editions and interim supplements for individual volumes are published from time to time.

The full series is kept up-to-date on an annual basis by: *Music in print annual supplement* (Philadelphia : Musicdata, 1979– . Annual).

"Each year's Supplement contains a separate section updating each volume already published in the … series. The updates are cumulative, so that only the latest Supplement is needed, in addition to the base volumes of the series. … When special supplements or revised editions of the base volumes are published, the listings from the Annual Supplement are incorporated in them and dropped from the Supplement."—*Guide to use.*

Library catalogs : Books

Boston Public Library. Dictionary catalog of the music collection. Boston : G.K. Hall, 1972. 20 v.   **BJ84**

Reproduction of the catalog cards (author, title, subject, and added entries) for the collection. Includes the Allen A. Brown collection, but not sheet music, recordings in the Sound Archives, or the Koussevitsky Archives.

§ *1st supplement* (Boston : G.K. Hall, 1976. 4 v.) lists the musical scores, books, pamphlets, and periodicals cataloged since Jan. 1972, together with corrections to the basic catalog.   ML136.B7B73

British Museum. Department of Printed Books. Hirsch Library. Books in the Hirsch Library, with supplementary list of music. London : Trustees of the British Museum, 1959. 542 p. (Catalogue of printed books in the British Museum. Accessions, 3rd ser., pt. 291B).   **BJ85**

A catalog of more than 12,000 books, forming part of the Hirsch Library acquired in 1946. Entries are brief but generally adequate, with German titles most strongly represented. For the German catalog *see* BJ87, *Katalog der Musikbibliothek Paul Hirsch.*

A catalog of the music in the collection was issued in 1951 (BJ94). A supplement to that catalog is included as an appendix in the present volume.

Detroit Public Library. Catalog of the E. Azalia Hackley memorial collection of Negro music, dance, and drama. Boston : G.K. Hall, 1979. 510 p.   **BJ86**

Reproduction of the catalog cards representing books, scores, sheet music, broadsides, posters, and photographs in this noted collection.   ML136.D48D4

Hirsch, Paul. Katalog der Musikbibliothek Paul Hirsch, Frankfurt am Main / hrsg. von Kathi Meyer und Paul Hirsch. Berlin : M. Breslauer, 1928–47. 4 v.   **BJ87**

Vol. 4 has imprint: Cambridge Univ. Pr.

Contents: Bd. 1, Theoretische Drucke bis 1800; Bd. 2, Opern-Partituren; Bd. 3, Instrumental– und Vokalmusik bis etwa 1830; Bd. 4, Erstausgaben, Chorwerke in Partitur, Gesamtausgaben, Nachschlagewerke, etc. Ergänzungen zu Bd. 1–3.

A catalog of one of the largest and finest libraries of music of Europe, acquired by the British Museum in 1946 (see: *Books in the Hirsch Library*, BJ85, and *Music in the Hirsch Library*, BJ94). For description see: P. H. Muir, "The Hirsch catalogue," in *Music review* 9 (1948): 102–107.   ML138.H64

New York Public Library. Research Libraries. Dictionary catalog of the Music Collection. 2nd ed. Boston : G.K. Hall, 1982. 45 v.   **BJ88**

1st ed., 1964, with supplements 1973 and 1976, issued by the Reference Dept.

Photographic reproduction of the catalog cards for one of the great music collections, one particularly strong in folk song, 18th- and 19th-century librettos, full scores of operas, complete works, historical editions, Beethoven materials, Americana, music periodicals, vocal music, literature on the voice, programs, record catalogs, and manuscripts. Offers detailed cataloging for books, pamphlets, essays, periodical articles, microforms, scores and librettos; recordings are not included. More than 3,500,000 items are represented, including imprints through 1971.

Supplemented by the Library's *Bibliographic guide to music* (BJ50).

Pierpont Morgan Library. The Mary Flagler Cary music collection : printed books and music, manuscripts, autograph letters, documents, portraits. N.Y. : [The Library], [1970]. 108 p. : ill.   **BJ89**

A descriptive catalog of one of the important music collections in the United States. Complemented by *Nineteenth-century autograph music manuscripts in the Pierpont Morgan Library*, ed. by J. Rigbie Turner (N.Y. : The Library, 1982. 53 p.).   ML136.N52P5

Wood, David A. Music in Harvard libraries : a catalogue of early printed music and books on music in the Houghton Library and the Eda Kuhn Loeb Music Library. Cambridge, Mass. : Houghton Library of the Harvard College Library; Harvard Univ. Dept. of Music; distr. by Harvard Univ. Pr., 1980. 306 p. : ill. **BJ90**

Repr. as: *History of music : a guide to the microfilm edition : based on Music in Harvard libraries ...* (Woodbridge, Conn. : Research Publ., 1985).

A descriptive bibliography of the music and books on music printed before 1801 which had been cataloged for the Harvard libraries by Jan. 1967. Includes scores, sets of parts, part-books, songbooks with music, monographs, treatises and pamphlets on music, music periodicals, dance manuals with music. Listing is alphabetical by author or composer; name index.

§ Complemented by: Barbara Mahrenholz Wolff, *Music manuscripts at Harvard: a catalogue of music manuscripts from the 14th to the 20th centuries in the Houghton Library and the Eda Kuhn Loeb Music Library* (Cambridge : Harvard Library, 1992. 245 p.).

ML136.C23H33

Library catalogs : Scores

Bayerische Staatsbibliothek. Katalog der Musikdrucke : BSB-Musik. München ; N.Y. : K.G. Saur, 1988–1990. 17 v. **DJ91**

An author-title catalog of printed music from the earliest publications through approximately 1974. In dictionary format, with main entries, added entries, and cross-references interfiled. Composer entries are subarranged by title; series title entries are further subarranged by titles of individual works. ML136.M92B42

British Broadcasting Corporation. Central Music Library. [Catalogues]. [London] : British Broadcasting Corp., 1965–82. [13 v.]. **BJ92**

An unnumbered series of catalogs listing printed and manuscript materials in the BBC's vast collection. The published volumes include: *Chamber music catalogue* (1965. 1 v.); *Choral and opera catalogue* (1967. 2 v.), *Piano and organ catalogue* (1965. 2 v.); *Song catalogue* (1966. 4 v.); *Orchestral catalogue* (1982. 4 v.).

British Museum. Department of Manuscripts. Catalogue of manuscript music in the British Museum / by Augustus Hughes-Hughes. London : Printed by order of the Trustees, 1906–09. 3 v. **BJ93**

Repr.: London : British Museum, 1964.

Contents: v. 1, Sacred vocal music; v. 2, Secular vocal music; v. 3, Instrumental music, treatises, etc.

Classified list, with author, subject, and title indexes in each volume.

§ Continued by: British Museum. Department of Manuscripts, *Handlist of music manuscripts acquired 1908–67*, prep. by Pamela J. Willetts (London : British Museum, 1970). Covers accessions of manuscript music to the end of 1967. ML136.L8B72

British Museum. Department of Printed Books. Hirsch Library. Music in the Hirsch Library. London : Trustees of the British Museum, 1951. 438 p. (Catalogue of printed music in the British Museum. Accessions, pt. 53). **BJ94**

Lists vocal scores, operas, orchestral scores, chamber music, and collections of early editions, totaling nearly 9,000 entries, many of which are not included in *Katalog der Musikbibliothek Paul Hirsch* (BJ87).

Brown, Rae Linda. Music, printed and manuscript, in the James Weldon Johnson Memorial Collection of Negro Arts and Letters : an annotated catalog. N.Y. : Garland, 1982. 322 p. (Critical studies on black life and culture, v. 23 ; Garland reference library of the humanities, vol. 277). **BJ95**

A catalog of more than 1,000 musical works now in the collection of the Beinecke Rare Book and Manuscript Library, Yale University.

ML136.N48Y33

Newberry Library. Bibliographical inventory of the early music in the Newberry Library, Chicago, Illinois / ed. by D. W. Krummel. Boston : G. K. Hall, 1977. 587 p. **BJ96**

Reproduction of the relevant catalog cards from this library which is particularly strong in medieval, Renaissance, and American music. Sections for manuscripts and for printed music and treatises are followed by eight geographical sections (with subdivisions, usually chronologically arranged). Index of composers, editors, and musical subjects; index of printers, engravers, artists, copyists, and publishers.

ML136.C5N43

———————— The Newberry Library catalog of early American printed sheet music / comp. by Bernard E. Wilson. Boston : G. K. Hall, 1983. 3 v. **BJ97**

Contents: v. 1, Main entries; Added entries, A–G; v. 2, Added entries, H–Z; Chronology; v. 3, Places; Title index.

Reproduces the catalog cards for the Library's Driscoll collection and other early American sheet music at Newberry—about 9,450 main entry cards and 11,550 added entries. The chronology runs to about 9,150 cards; the Places index to 9,500; and the title index to 4,800.

ML136.C5N434

Philadelphia Free Library. The Edwin A. Fleischer Collection of Orchestral Music : a cumulative catalog, 1929–1977. Boston : G. K. Hall, 1979. 956 p. **BJ98**

1st ed., 1933–45; Suppl., 1966.

The collection has been completely recataloged since 1975 and new materials integrated to form this catalog of a major collection containing more than 13,000 scores (including about 2,500 scores for orchestra and solo instrument or voice). Arranged alphabetically by composer, each entry giving brief information about instrumentation, publisher, performing time, dates, pagination, incipit, and commentary. Three indexes: (1) ensembles other than standard orchestra (e.g., brass ensemble, string orchestra); (2) works requiring one or more solo or featured instrument; (3) works requiring voice. The scores in the public domain are available for loan to recognized organizations.

ML136.P4F68

Periodicals

Basart, Ann Phillips. Writing about music : a guide to publishing opportunities for authors and reviewers. Berkeley, Calif. : Fallen Leaf Pr., c1989. 588 p. (Fallen Leaf reference books in music, no. 11). **BJ99**

Contains detailed information on editorial policies and publishing requirements of more than 430 current periodicals from 21 countries "that publish serious, informative, music-related articles and/or reviews in English."—*Pref.* Titles are listed alphabetically, with four indexes: Titles & organizations; Subject; Geographical; Type of materials reviewed. Concludes with list of titles considered but not included.

ML128.P24B37

Bayerische Staatsbibliothek. Katalog der Musikzeitschriften : BSB-MuZ = Catalogue of music periodicals. München ; N.Y. : K.G. Saur, 1990. 242 p. **BJ100**

A list of the 2,621 music periodicals in the collections of the Bavarian State Library in Munich. Entries are listed alphabetically under both corporate author and title, giving holdings information and call number. Indexed systematically in ten broad categories.

ML136.M92B46

Fellinger, Imogen. Verzeichnis der Musikzeitschriften des 19. Jahrhunderts. Regensburg : Bosse, 1968. 557 p. (Studien zur Musikgeschichte des 19. Jahrhunderts, 10). **BJ101**

A chronological listing of 19th-century music periodicals, with indexes by title, editor, and subject. ML117.F44

International music journals / ed. by Linda M. Fidler and Richard S. James. N.Y. : Greenwood, c1990. 544 p. **BJ102**

A selective, alphabetical listing of over 160 journal titles, both ongoing and ceased, chosen as the profession's leading journals on the basis of their historical and contemporary significance. Annotations cover the physical properties of the journals, historical development, content profiles, critical assessment, and bibliography. Appendixes include similar descriptions for nine recent journals from the 1980s, and periodical indexes, as well as chronological, geographical, and subject listings. Index; cross-references.   ML128.P24I6

Meggett, Joan M. Music periodical literature : an annotated bibliography of indexes and bibliographies. Metuchen, N.J. : Scarecrow, 1978. 116 p.   **BJ103**

"Intended primarily for college and university music students as an aid to their research through music periodical literature ... ."—*Pref.* An annotated listing of periodical indexes and bibliographies (the latter appearing in book form or as an essay or periodical article which includes references to periodical literature) on music and music-related topics. Indexes of authors/editors/compilers, subjects, and titles.
                                                         ML128.P24M43

Robinson, Doris. Music and dance periodicals : an international directory & guidebook. Voorheesville, N.Y. : Peri Pr., c1989. 382 p.   **BJ104**

Provides comprehensive and international coverage of music and dance periodicals. Lists 1,867 currently published periodicals with descriptive annotations in 19 categories: Reference; Musicology and ethnomusicology; Music industry; Musical instruments; Regional; Education; Classical; Religious and choral; Opera, theater, show music; Band; Composers and songwriters; Computer and electronic; Popular; Jazz and blues; Folk music; Dance; Sound; Miscellaneous; Unclassified. Five indexes: Title; Publisher & organization; Subject; Country of publication; ISSN.   ML128.P24R58

Thoumin, Jean-Adrien. Bibliographie rétrospective des périodiques français de littérature musicale, 1870–1954. Paris : Éd. Documentaires Industrielles et Techniques, 1957. 179 p.
                                                              BJ105

On cover: Union Française des Organismes de Documentation.
A list of 600 titles with locations indicated. Indexes by date and by editors.

Indexes; Abstract journals

Diamond, Harold J. Music analyses : an annotated guide to the literature. N.Y. : Schirmer : Maxwell Macmillan International ; Toronto : Collier Macmillan Canada, c1991. 716 p.
                                                              BJ106

An index to 4,655 analyses in books, periodicals, dissertations, and theses, of compositions by major composers. Entry is by commonly-known name of the composer, subarranged by title, with entries under "Anonymous" for medieval works. Most entries have brief descriptive annotations. Index of distinctive titles.   ML128.A7D5

——————————— Music criticism : an annotated guide to the literature. Metuchen, N.J. : Scarecrow, 1979. 316 p.   **BJ107**

Index to writings about music in readily-available periodicals and books. Organized into seven musical forms and subarranged alphabetically by composer, with further subheadings for prolific composers. Includes bibliography of works indexed. Indexes by composer and composition titles.   ML113.D5

International Repertory of Music Literature. RILM abstracts of music literature. v. 1 (Jan./Apr. 1967)– . [N.Y. : RILM], 1967– . Quarterly.   **BJ108**

"*RILM Abstracts* ... published abstracts indexed by computer of all significant literature in music that has appeared since 1 January 1967."—*v. 1, no. 2.* Includes abstracts of books, articles (in periodicals or as parts of books), reviews, dissertations, iconographies, catalogs, etc. Classed arrangement with annual author-subject index and quinquennial cumulated indexes.

A useful complement is *RILM abstracts of music literature: English-language thesaurus for volumes XXI-1987–* , (c1992. 1 loose-leaf) containing all the indexing terms applicable to RILM from vol. 21 (1987) onwards. A translation of this thesaurus into about 10 foreign languages is reprinted in the back of the latest (4th) cumulative index, covering 1982–1986 (1990).

•Machine-readable form: *MUSE* [database]. 1989– . Includes records from the RILM database supplemented by records from the Music Catalog of the Library of Congress. Vols. 1–2 not yet available on CD-ROM.   ML1.I83

Krohn, Ernst Christopher. The history of music : an index to the literature available in a selected group of musicological publications. St. Louis : Washington Univ., 1952. 463 p. (Washington University. Library studies, no. 3).   **BJ109**

Repr. : St. Louis : Baton Music Co., 1958.

An index to material on the history of music appearing in some 40 periodicals, mainly German and English. Arrangement is by broad period divisions, further subdivided under such headings as General studies, Composers, and the various musical forms. Includes book reviews. Indexes by authors and composers. The material was collected in card-index form by the compiler over 25 years, but the periodicals covered are not confined to that period.

§ Overlapping chronologically, but covering a larger number of music and nonmusic periodicals is *A bibliography of periodical literature in musicology and allied fields, October 1938–September 1940,* assembled for the Committee on Musicology of the American Council of Learned Societies by D. H. Daugherty, Leonard Ellinwood, and Richard S. Hill (Wash. : ACLS, 1940–43. [Repr. : N.Y. : Da Capo, 1972]).   ML113.K77

Music article guide. v. [1] (Winter 1966)– . Philadelphia : Information Services, Inc., 1966– . Quarterly.   **BJ110**

Subtitle varies; 1983: The nation's only annotated quarterly reference guide to selected, significant signed feature articles in American music periodicals geared exclusively to the special needs of school and college music educators.

Arrangement has varied; currently offers subject and author approaches, with full information appearing under the subject entry.

§ The short-lived *Popular music periodicals index* (Metuchen, N.J. : Scarecrow, 1973–76. 4 v.) indexed relevant articles in 65 to 70 publications.   ML1.M22795

Music index : the key to current music periodical literature. v. 1 (1949)– . Detroit : Information Service, 1949– . Monthly with annual cumulations.   **BJ111**

Indexes by author and subject about 350 periodicals, some selectively, representing various aspects of the field, ranging from musicology to the retailing of music. Indexes musical periodicals completely and indexes articles pertinent to music in some more general publications. Includes obituaries, book reviews, and reviews of music performances and recordings.

•Machine-readable form: *The music index on CD-ROM* [database] (Alexandria, Va. : Harmonie Park Pr. : Chadwyck-Healey, 1981–90). Updated annually.   ML118.M84

Répertoire international de la presse musicale. Ann Arbor, Mich. : Univ. Microfilms Internat., c1988– . v. (In progress).
                                                              BJ112

Alternate title: *RIPM.*

Published under the auspices of the International Musicological Society and the International Association of Music Libraries, Archives and Documentation Centres; in conjunction with the Center for Studies in Nineteenth-Century Music, University of Maryland, College Park.

When complete, will provide indexing for approximately 60 music periodicals from Western Europe and the U.S. published during the 18th, 19th, and early 20th centuries. For each periodical, the index has two sections: a calendar or annotated listing of article titles for each issue, and a keyword-author index generated by computer from the calendar.

Wenk, Arthur B. Analyses of nineteenth- and twentieth-century music, 1940–1985. Boston : Music Library Association, c1987. 370 p. (Music Library Association index and bibliography series, 25). **BJ113**
"Cumulates and updates the indexes originally published as numbers 13, 14, and 15 in this series"—*Ser. t.p.*
Indexes periodicals, monographs, festschriften, and dissertations for articles containing discussions incorporating the technical materials of "analysis." Contains 5,664 entries organized alphabetically by composer, and subarranged by genre or by the works, if more than ten entries; if fewer than ten, by author or title. Author index.   ML113.W45

Indexes to scores

Fellinger, Imogen. Periodica musicalia (1789–1830) / im Auftrag des Staatlichen Instituts für Musikforschung Preussischer Kulturbesitz. Regensburg : G. Bosse, 1986. 1259 p. (Studien zur Musikgeschichte des 19. Jahrhunderts, Bd. 55). **BJ114**
A companion to Fellinger's *Verzeichnis der Musikzeitschriften des 19. Jahrhunderts* (BJ101). Contains a chronologically-arranged index to music in periodicals published 1789–1830. Includes some 250 titles, with each entry containing publication information, library repositories, and a listing by issue of the titles and page numbers for the compositions. Numerous indexes for text and music.   ML117.F43

Hilton, Ruth B. An index to early music in selected anthologies. Clifton, N.J. : European American Music Corp., [1978]. 127 p. (Music indexes and bibliographies, no. 13).   **BJ115**
The anthologies indexed were selected because they were available in most music libraries and are not devoted to a particular period, form, country, etc. "Early music" is defined as music "from antiquity to the end of the Baroque."—*Introd.* Main listing is under composer, anonymous title, or first line of an untitled text, and includes date and country of origin, type of work, performing medium, thematic-catalog number, and anthology citation; there are cross-references from titles as added entries. Index by genre or medium.   ML116.H54

Murray, Sterling E. Anthologies of music : an annotated index. 2nd ed. Warren, Mich. : Harmonie Park Pr., 1992. 215 p. (Detroit studies in music bibliography, no. 68).   **BJ116**
1st ed., 1987.
Indexes 66 anthologies, most published 1961–91. Includes anthologies that are arranged historically and contain complete movements or compositions, with special consideration given to readily accessible works. Contains 4,670 entries by more than 600 composers, arranged by composer. Genre locator index.   ML128.A7M87

Encyclopedias, 1945–75

Encyclopédie de la musique / [publié sous la direction de François Michel en collaboration avec François Lesure et Vladimir Féderov et un comité de rédaction composé de Nadia Boulanger et al.]. Paris : Fasquelle, 1958–61. 3 v. : ill. **BJ117**
A general music encyclopedia particularly strong in biography, including contemporary Europeans. The biographical articles are not only more numerous but are usually longer than in *Larousse de la musique* (BJ120). Illustrations in black-and-white and in color include facsimiles of music and manuscripts. Bibliographies are included with the articles; longer articles are signed. Vol. 1 includes much "preliminary matter" (e.g., sections on the work of contemporary composers, discography, music libraries, institutions, organizations, chronologies, etc.).   ML100.E48

Encyclopédie des musiques sacrées / publiée sous la direction de Jacques Porte. Paris : Éditions Labergerie, [1968–70]. 4 v. : ill.   **BJ118**

Contents: v. 1, L'expression du sacré en Orient, Afrique, Amérique du Sud; v. 2–3, Traditions chrétiennes; v. 4, Documents sonores [avec] commentaires.
Chapters on the sacred music of individual countries and various religious groups have been contributed by specialists; many include bibliographies or bibliographical footnotes. Vol. 4 consists of eight recordings.   ML102.E53

Entsiklopedicheskiĭ muzykal'nyĭ slovar' / Avtory-sostaviteli B. S. Shteĭnpress i I. M. IAmpol'skiĭ. Izd. 2. ispr. i dop. Moskva : Sovetskaiā Entsiklopediiā, 1966. 631 p. : ill., ports., music.   **BJ119**
1st ed., 1959.
Brief articles on musical terms, forms, and instruments, and numerous biographical sketches. Many entries include bibliographies.   ML100.E58

Larousse de la musique / publié sous la direction de Norbert Dufourcq avec la collaboration de Félix Raugel et Armand Machabey. Paris : Larousse, [1957]. 2 v. : ill. **BJ120**
An international encyclopedia with articles on musical terminology, subjects, places, performing groups (such as orchestras), etc. Primarily a dictionary of subjects rather than of persons, although there are many biographical sketches, usually brief. Little on contemporary musicians or artists; for these *Encyclopédie de la musique* (BJ117) is much fuller. Articles are well-balanced in length, and some are signed. Illustrations in black-and-white and in color are numerous and well reproduced. Lists of works with composers are given; other bibliographic references are at the end of each volume.   ML100.L28

Mayer-Serra, Otto. Música y músicos de Latinoamérica. México : Ed. Atlante ; N.Y. : W.M. Jackson, 1947. 2 v. (1134 p.) : ill., ports., music.   **BJ121**
An alphabetical encyclopedia covering history, biography, folklore, religious music, musical instruments, terminology, legislation, etc., of all the countries of Latin America. In some cases full bibliographies are given for composers. Includes portraits; musical examples; words and music of the national hymns of the various countries, etc. "Still the only biographical and terminological source for the entire region."—*Fontes artis musicae* v. 3., no. 4 (Sept.–Dec. 1984): 217.   ML199.M3

Die Musik in Geschichte und Gegenwart : allgemeine Enzyklopädie der Musik / Unter Mitarbeit zahlreicher Musikforscher des In– und Auslandes, hrsg. von Friedrich Blume. Kassel : Bärenreiter-Verlag, 1949–1986. 17 v. : ill., ports., facsims, music.   **BJ122**
Contents: v. 1–14, A–Z; v. 15–16, Suppl., A–Z; v. 17, Register.
A scholarly, comprehensive work, international in scope, with long, signed articles by specialists. Includes extensive bibliographical notes. Profusely illustrated. The index (v. 17) contains a single alphabetical listing of approximately 330,000 names and terms, with a visual key further identifying major articles and headings in text illustrations, plates, musical examples, and errata. An indispensable reference work for research in the field. Revision in progress.   ML100.M92

Muzykal'naiā entsiklopediiā / Gl. red. IUriĭ Vsevolodovich Keldysh. Moskva : "Sov. entsiklopediiā"–"Sov. kompozitor", 1973–1982. 6 v. : ill.   **BJ123**
Offers extensive, signed articles with bibliographies and work lists. Includes much biographical material.   ML100.M97

Pena, Joaquín. Diccionario de la música Labor / iniciado por Joaquín Pena, continuado por Higinio Anglés, con la colaboración de Miguel Querol .... Barcelona : Labor, 1954. 2 v. (2318 p.) : ill., ports., facsims., music.   **BJ124**
Biobibliographical dictionary, covering all periods, places and persons, but especially strong on Spanish and Latin American musical life. Articles are fairly extensive, including lists of works and bibliographies. Contains numerous portraits.   ML105.P4

Riemann, Hugo. Riemann musik Lexikon. 12. völlig neubearb. Aufl., hrsg. von Wilibald Gurlitt. Mainz : B. Schott's
Söhne ; N.Y. : Schott Music Corp., 1959–67. 3 v. : ill. **BJ125**
   1st ed., 1882.
   Contents: v. 1–2, Personenteil, A–Z; [v. 3], Sachteil.
   A considerably revised edition of a standard work, with text and
bibliographies brought up to date. The first 2 v. include articles on persons only; v. 3 is devoted to musical subjects. Covers all periods and
places with strong emphasis on German music. Includes lists of works
throughout the text, and also bibliographies.
   ———. ——— *Ergänzungsband, Personenteil*, hrsg. von Carl
Dahlhaus (Mainz ; N.Y. : B. Schott, 1972–75. 2 v). Includes new articles and additions and corrections to articles in the 12th edition.
                                                      ML100.R52

Sohlmans Musiklexikon / [huvudred.: Hans Åstrand]. 2 revid.
o. utvidgade uppl. Stockholm : Sohlman, [1975–79]. 5 v. : ill.
                                                      BJ126
   1st ed., 1948–52.
   A revised edition of this major Scandinavian music encyclopedia,
offering signed articles on composers, performers, institutions, works,
and movements of Scandinavian music. Many bibliographies. Vol. 5
includes a list, arranged by broad topics, of articles in the encyclopedia
(e.g., Popmusik, Scenisk Musik).
   § *Cappelens Musikkleksikon*, ed. by Kari Michelsen ... [et al.], is
a Norwegian encyclopedia based on the Sohlmans work (Oslo : Cappelen, 1978–80). Entries revised for the Norwegian publication are
noted, and new entries pertinent to Norway are included. It concludes
with a discography of Norwegian recordings from the acoustic era
throught the 1970s, arranged by performer.   ML100.S66

Encyclopedias, 1976–85

Algemene muziek encyclopedie / hoofdred., J. Robijns en
Miep Zijlstra. Haarlem : De Haan, [1979–1984]. 10 v. : ill.
                                                      BJ127
   1st ed., 1957–72 had title: *Algemene muziekencyclopedie*.
   A dictionary of terms, musical forms, musicians, instruments,
etc., covering all types of music from all periods and countries. Most
of the entries are short and unsigned, an exception being coverage of
the musical life of an individual country (e.g., 8½ columns are devoted
to Belgium) and the history of a type of music (e.g., ballet music) or a
musical style (e.g., baroque). These more extensive articles are signed
and a brief bibliography is often appended. Handsomely and profusely
illustrated. Vol. 10 includes lists of musical terms and instruments with
equivalents in several languages, and a section of corrections.
                                                      ML100.A4

Brockhaus Riemann Musiklexikon / hrsg. von Carl
Dahlhaus und Hans Heinrich Eggebrecht. Wiesbaden : Brock-
haus ; Mainz : B. Schott's Söhne, 1978–79. 2 v. : ill., music.
                                                      BJ128
   Repr. : Erw. Taschenbuchausgabe. Mainz : Schott ; München :
Piper, c1989. 5 v. ; ill. Contents: v. 1–4, A–Z; v. 5, Ergänzungsband,
A–Z.
   Offers short articles with brief bibliographies on people, terms,
instruments, types of music (e.g., Arbeiterlied), etc. Especially useful
for questions relating to German music. The supplementary volume in
the reprint edition incorporates new entries: popular, rock, and jazz
composers and performers; timely topics (e.g., Frau und Musik); and
revised entries for more recent developments.   ML100.B85

Dictionnaire de la musique / publié sous la direction de Marc
Honegger. [Paris] : Bordas, [1970–76]. 4 v. : ill.   **BJ129**
   Contents: v. 1–2, Les hommes et leurs oeuvres; v. 3–4, Science de
la musique: techniques, formes, instruments.
   Vols. 1–2 form an alphabetical biographical dictionary of composers and others associated with music (e.g., music publishers, instrument makers, librettists, conductors, musicologists), both living and
dead. Longer articles are signed; bibliographies are included. Vols.

3–4 comprise an alphabetical arrangement of survey articles on the
music of individual countries, specific instruments and their development, forms of music, problems of acoustics, definitions of terms.
Signed articles with bibliographies.   ML100.D65

**Dizionario enciclopedico universale della musica e dei
musicisti : il lessico** / diretto da Alberto Basso. Torino :
UTET, c1983–c1984. 4 v. : ill. (some col.).   **BJ130**
                                                      ML100.D63

**Dizionario enciclopedico universale della musica e dei
musicisti : le biografie** / diretto da Alberto Basso. Torino :
UTET, c1985–1988. 8 v. : geneal. tables.   **BJ131**
   Successors to *La musica* ([Torino] : Unione Tipografico-Editrice
Torinese, [1966–71]).
   Together, these titles constitute the most important Italian encyclopedia of music. The dictionary portion contains terms arranged alphabetically, with extensive signed articles and bibliographies. The biographical portion offers signed articles on composers, arranged alphabetically, with worklists and bibliographies. Both parts have illustrations and cross-references.
   Accompanied by *Appendice* (1990. 1 v.) that contains both names
and terms, and is meant to supplement both parts of the main set.
                                                      ML105.D65

Enciclopédia da música brasileira : erudita, folclórica, popu-
la. São Paulo : Art Editora, 1977. 2 v. (1190 p.) and 2 records.
                                                      BJ132
   A dictionary devoted primarily to people involved with Brazilian
music—popular, folkloric, or scholarly—but including entries for instruments, terms, etc. Most articles include a bibliography and/or a discography. Appendixes: discography of long-playing classical recordings by Brazilians; list of symphony orchestras in Brazil; music periodicals; list of Brazilian theaters (with a brief history). Title index; bibliography.   ML106.B7E5

Enciclopedia della musica. Milano : Rizzoli, 1972–74. 6 v. :
ill.   **BJ133**
   At head of title: Rizzoli Ricordi.
   A short-entry dictionary giving definitions, biographies, histories,
etc., of music and musicians of all countries and periods, but strongest
for European-based music. Each volume has an appendix giving for
selected major composers a complete listing of all works (e.g., v. 4
contains listings of the works of Liszt, Mozart, and Palestrina).
   Another work of the same title under the editorial direction of
Claudio Sartori was published by Ricordi, 1963–64 in 4 v.

Encyclopedia of music in Canada / ed. by Helmut Kallmann
and Gilles Potvin. 2nd ed. Toronto ; Buffalo : Univ. of Toronto
Pr., c1992. 1524 p. : ill.   **BJ134**
   1st ed., 1981.
   Contains an alphabetical listing of approximately 3,800 articles,
with 300 cross-references, covering all aspects of music in Canada, as
well as general topics in their Canadian aspects. Articles are signed,
and most have bibliographies and discographies. The discographies
have been expanded from the 1st ed., and articles on recorded sound in
general arc increased. Events up to 1991 arc reported. As in the previous edition, the method of preparation and criteria for inclusion are
carefully set forth in the introduction.   ML106.C3E5

Griffiths, Paul. The Thames and Hudson encyclopaedia of
20th-century music. London ; N.Y. : Thames and Hudson,
1986. 207 p.   **BJ135**
   A dictionary arrangement of entries, mostly brief, for names,
terms, institutions, and trends in 20th-century music. A list of headings
precedes the dictionary. Composer entries predominate (over 500), and
generally contain a catalog of works (limited to those composed in the
20th century), principal publishers and/or record companies, and bibliographies. Cross-references, general bibliography, and chronology.
                                                      ML100.G85

Das Grosse Lexikon der Musik / hrsg. von Marc Honegger und Günther Massenkeil. Freiburg i. Br. ; Basel [etc.] : Herder, c1978–83. v. 1–10 : ill. (some col.). (In progress). **BJ136**

Revised translation of *Dictionnaire de la musique* (BJ129). Articles from the French edition have been translated, revised, and in some cases expanded (e.g., articles on harmony and music theory). Bibliographies at the ends of articles have been revised and updated, with more current citations given.

A German translation of Gerald Abraham's *Concise Oxford history of music* (BJ197) has been published as v. 9–10 of the set, with title *Geschichte der Musik*. ML105.D5515

The international cyclopedia of music and musicians. 11th ed. N.Y. : Dodd, Mead, 1985. 2609 p. : ill. **BJ137**

"Editor in chief, Oscar Thompson; editor, fifth–eighth editions, Nicolas Slonimsky; editor, ninth edition, Robert Sabin; editor, tenth and eleventh editions, Bruce Bohle."—*t.p.*

1st ed., 1939.

Later editions show spotty revision, adding dates of death, making some corrections, and sometimes offering additional material in the appendixes. The 11th ed. represents a reprinting of the previous edition (2511 p.), with the addition of an addenda section (p. 2513–2609) consisting of about a thousand entries which revise and extend the articles in the earlier pages or add new entries for items not previously treated. ML100.I57

Kennedy, Michael. The Oxford dictionary of music. Oxford ; N.Y. : Oxford Univ. Pr., 1985. 810 p. **BJ138**

Revised and enlarged edition of Kennedy's *Concise Oxford dictionary of music* (1980), which was in turn a third edition of Percy A. Scholes' first and second editions of that title (1952–64). It is the work of a single compiler, not a condensed version of the *New Oxford companion to music* (BJ142). Includes entries for composers and musicians (including living persons), individual compositions, musical instruments, terms, firms and organizations, etc. ML100.K35

Michaelides, Solon. The music of ancient Greece : an encyclopedia. London : Faber, 1978. 365 p. : ill., music. **BJ139**

A dictionary of musical terms, instruments, dances, composers, critics, theorists, and poets and philosophers of classical Greek music. Bibliographies for most articles give both classical Greek sources and modern studies. Alphabetical index of entries in Greek characters. ML107.M5

The new Grove dictionary of American music / ed. by H. Wiley Hitchcock and Stanley Sadie. N.Y. : Grove's Dictionaries of Music, 1986. 4 v. : ill. **BJ140**

An important new work. Includes names and terms germane to the musical tradition of the U.S. Expands articles from *The new Grove dictionary of music and musicians* (BJ141) where appropriate, but adds many more on art music, varieties of popular music, the political and patriotic repertories, specifically American genres, music of the present day, etc. Standard music topics are treated in the American context. Signed articles, many with bibliographies, lists of works, and discographies. Many useful illustrations. List of contributors in v. 4. ML101.U6N48

The new Grove dictionary of music and musicians / ed. by Stanley Sadie. London : Macmillan ; Wash. : Grove's Dictionaries of Music, 1980. 20 v. : ill. **BJ141**

Originally issued in parts as: *A dictionary of music and musicians.* ed. by George Grove (London ; N.Y. : Macmillan, 1878–89); 5th ed., 1954 (10 v.). 2nd (1904–20) and subsequent eds. called: *Grove's dictionary of music and musicians.* Editor varies.

Based on Grove's *Dictionary*, but virtually a new work retaining only about 3% of the material from earlier editions. No longer emphasizing the 19th century, *The new Grove* "seeks to discuss everything that can be reckoned to bear on music in history and on present-day musical life."—*Pref.* More than half of the entries are for composers, but performers, scholars, theorists, patrons and publishers of music, and people in other arts whose work was important to music are included. Terminology, musical genres, and forms are fully treated; and there are entries for institutions, orchestras, and societies, as well as

for cities and towns with significant musical traditions. "The biggest departure [from previous editions] ... lies in the dictionary's treatment of non-Western and folk music, far more extensive and more methodical than anything of the kind attempted before."

Most articles are signed (the approximately 2,500 contributors are listed in v. 20); longer articles generally follow a uniform structure; and bibliographies include both studies used as source materials and recommended readings. Both older and fairly recent publications are listed in the bibliographies. The "work lists" for individual composers "are designed not only to show a composer's output ..., but also to serve as a starting-point for its study."—*Introd.* British terminological usage may present occasional difficulty for the American user. There is adequate cross-referencing for most entries, and Appendix A (in v. 20) provides an "Index of terms used in articles on Non-Western music, folk music and kindred topics." Lacks general index.

A series of reviews of individual volumes of *The new Grove* appeared in *Musical times*, v. 122 (Mar.–June 1981). ML100.N48

The new Oxford companion to music / gen. ed., Denis Arnold. Oxford : Oxford Univ. Pr., 1983. 2 v. : ill. **BJ142**

Reprint with corrections and some revisions: 1990.

Although based on *The Oxford companion to music* originally edited by Percy Scholes and published in ten editions 1938–70, this is essentially a new work. Both broader in scope and more comprehensive in coverage than its predecessor, it is truly international without pretending to offer exhaustive treatment of non-Western music. Intended for the general reader; frequent suggestions for further reading are given. Articles, often many pages in length, concern the people who make music (mainly composers, including living persons), their careers and achievements; the musical environment or history of music in individual countries or geographic areas; and the music itself—individual works, instruments, forms, scales and modal patterns, music theory, etc. Many articles are signed; numerous cross-references; illustrations appear in proximity to relevant text.

A review in *TLS* (30 Dec. 1983): p. 1451 asserts that "although the balance of entries is not yet right, and the quality of the material is disconcertingly variable, the framework has nevertheless been established for a small, modern encyclopedia, suitable for all those who have an essentially academic interest in music, and whose resources do not stretch to *The New Grove*." ML100.N5

The Norton/Grove concise encyclopedia of music / ed. by Stanley Sadie ; assistant ed., Alison Latham. N.Y. : W.W. Norton, 1988. 850 p. : ill. **BJ143**

A ready-reference work intended for general readers. Uses *The new Grove dictionary of music and musicians* (BJ141) as its primary source, with expanded coverage of more recent events, and names or nicknames of individual works. Cross-references. ML100.N88

South African music encyclopedia / gen. ed., Jacques P. Malan. Cape Town : Oxford Univ. Pr., 1979–1986. 4 v. : maps. **BJ144**

An effort to provide a comprehensive, scholarly account of music in South Africa from 1652 to 1960, with some later information supplied. Offers signed articles on music, both European and native (although coverage of the latter is admittedly not as full as could be desired), musicians, "accounts of music in cities and towns, church music, theatres and concert halls, music education, musical instruments, Afrikaans folk music, visiting artists from overseas, the early years of the gramophone industry and musical societies."—*Introd.* Bibliographies; cross-references. ML106.S66S7

Vinton, John. Dictionary of contemporary music. N.Y. : Dutton, [1974]. 834 p. **BJ145**

British ed. has title: *Dictionary of twentieth-century music* (London : Thames and Hudson, 1974).

The work is "confined to [contemporary] concert music in the Western tradition" (*Pref.*) with jazz and popular music limited to general articles under those entries, and Asian music and folk music also limited to general surveys. Biographical entries are limited to composers. Many of the articles are signed; many include bibliographic references. ML100.V55

Dictionaries

Bobillier, Marie. Diccionario de la música, histórico y técnico. Barcelona : J. Gil, [c1946]. 548 p. : ill., music, fac-sims.   **BJ146**

Translation of the author's *Dictionnaire pratique et historique de la musique*, par Michel Brenet [pseud.] (Paris : Colin, 1926).

This profusely illustrated edition includes many terms not in the French edition.

Dictionary of terms in music : English-German, German-English / [ed. by] Horst Leuchtmann. 4th rev. and enl. ed. München ; N.Y. : K.G. Saur, 1992. 411 p.   **BJ147**

1st ed., 1964; 2nd ed., 1977.

A specialized dictionary of equivalent terms with separate sections for English-German and German-English. Diagrams of musical instruments called for in the preface are not present.   ML108.W73

Eggebrecht, Hans Heinrich. Handwörterbuch der musikalischen Terminologie : Im Auftrag der Kommission für Musikwissenschaft der Akademie der Wissenschaften und der Literatur zu Mainz. Wiesbaden : F. Steiner, [c1972–]. v. (In progress).   **BJ148**

Ongoing German-language dictionary of specialized musical terms defined by extensive, scholarly, and heavily-documented essays. Each entry is by an individual contributor, and all entries are signed. New terms are issued in fascicles to be kept in the binders provided by the publisher. A list of the terms currently defined is published with each new addition and provided for all the fascicle binders.

ML108.E29

Fink, Robert. The language of twentieth century music : a dictionary of terms / by Robert Fink and Robert Ricci. N.Y. : Schirmer Books, 1975. 125 p. : ill.   **BJ149**

Offers brief definitions of "the basic terminologies of chance music, computer music, electronic music, film music, jazz, musique concrète, multimedia, rock, twelve-tone music and other more traditional styles of music composition … , as well as … a number of instruments and performance practices that have developed as composers have searched for new means of expression. Also, new tools for musical analysis have been included along with many of the important movements in contemporary plastic and graphic arts which employ techniques and aesthetic points of view similar to those found in twentieth century music."—*Pref.* Appendix: "A topical listing of terms included." Brief bibliography.   ML100.F55

Katayen, Lelia. Russian-English dictionary of musical terms / by Lelia Katayen and Val Telberg. N.Y. : Telberg Book Corp., [1965]. 125*l.*   **BJ150**

Russian-English only.   ML108.K33

Leksikon jugoslavenske muzike / [glavni urednik Krešimir Kovačević]. Zagreb : Jugoslavenski Leksikografski Zavod "Miroslav Krleža", 1984. 2 v. : ill. (some col.), music. **BJ151**

Offers short articles on Serbio-Croatian people, terms, and instruments found in Serbia, Croatia, or elsewhere. Contains lists of works or bibliographies for major composers, or for performers, lists of works performed.

§ Another work by the same author is *Muzicka enciklopedija* (2. izd. Zagreb : Jugoslavenski Leksikografiski Zavod, 1971–77). While it includes figures relevant to the Serbo-Croatian region, it encompasses people and terms within the entire sphere of Western classical music.

ML100.L54

Levarie, Siegmund. Musical morphology : a discourse and a dictionary / Siegmund Levarie, Ernst Levy. Kent, Ohio : Kent State Univ. Pr., [1983]. 344 p. : ill.   **BJ152**

"An earlier edition of this work was published by the Institute of Mediaeval Music, Binningen, Switzerland, [1980] despite the objections of the authors, who took the position that it was unauthorized, incorrect, and not truly representative of their work. The present edition is fully authorized."—*Verso of t.p.*

The dictionary portion consists of long, discursive entries and constitutes p. 49–305. Appendixes of illustrations and quotations. Bibliography; index of composers and compositions cited.   ML108.L48

The new Harvard dictionary of music / ed. by Don Michael Randel. Cambridge, Mass. : Belknap Pr. of Harvard Univ. Pr., 1986. 942 p. : ill., music.   **BJ153**

2nd ed., 1969, ed. by Willi Apel, had title: *Harvard dictionary of music.*

A new edition of this standard work, listing terms with definitions and language of origin. Continues to emphasize Western art music, with expanded coverage of non-Western music, popular music, and instruments from all cultures. Signed articles with bibliographies. Contributors are listed; cross-references.   ML100.N485

Orovio, Helio. Diccionario de la música cubana : biográfico y técnico. Havana : Editorial Letras Cubanas, 1981. 442 p. : ill.   **BJ154**

Biographical sketches predominate, but there are entries for music organizations, instruments, and terms in Cuban music. ML106.C8O7

Poultney, David. Dictionary of Western church music. Chicago : Amer. Libr. Assoc., 1991. 234 p. : ill.   **BJ155**

Intends to provide concise information regarding all aspects of sacred music in the Christian tradition. Contains approximately 400 entries, alphabetically arranged with cross-references. Definitions are short; few have bibliographical references. Appendixes include a list of music publishers, societies and organizations, and a selected list of sacred music periodicals. Composer/title index.

§ James Davidson's *A dictionary of Protestant church music* (Metuchen, N.J. : Scarecrow, 1975) contains definitions of terms evaluated as relevant to Protestant church music, historically treated, and with bibliographies.   ML102.C5P77

Ranade, Ashok D. Keywords and concepts : Hindustani classical music. New Delhi : Promilla, 1990. 160 p. : ill.   **BJ156**

Uses a thesaurus format to provide a conceptual overview to the subject. Arrangement is by systematic category in three major subdivisions: Music making; Technical and qualitative terms; and Musical instruments. All headwords are listed within their category at the head of the dictionary. Alphabetic index; bibliography.   ML338.R257

Roche, Jerome. A dictionary of early music : from the troubadours to Monteverdi / Jerome Roche, Elizabeth Roche. N.Y. : Oxford Univ. Pr., 1981. 208 p. : ill.   **BJ157**

Concerned with music of the Middle Ages, Renaissance and early Baroque period. "The aim … is to deal, as fully as possible within a compact format, with the instruments, musical forms, technical terms and composers" (*Introd.*) of the designated periods. Some brief bibliographical notes; cross-references.   ML100.R695

Slonimsky, Nicolas. Lectionary of music. N.Y. : McGraw-Hill, c1989. 521 p.   **BJ158**

A dictionary of music terms and phrases, composers, compositions, etc., with pithy, germane, and idiosyncratic definitions from a major writer on music.   ML100.S637

Terminorum musicae index septem lingus redactus = Polyglot dictionary of musical terms. Budapest : Akadémiai Kiadó ; London : Bärenreiter, 1978. 798 p.   **BJ159**

Horst Leuchtmann, ed. in chief.

Terms in English, German, French, Italian, Spanish, Hungarian, and Russian are given in a single alphabetical sequence, with equivalents in each of the other languages. The base word is in the language from which the word originated or, if not in one of the seven languages of the dictionary, in German; cross-references are given from terms in the other languages to the base word. Separate Cyrillic alphabet section. An appendix gives equivalents in all seven languages for music notation terms and a large range of instruments through drawings and diagrams.   ML108.T4

Thomsett, Michael C. Musical terms, symbols, and theory : an illustrated dictionary. Jefferson, N.C. : McFarland, c1989. 277 p. : music. **BJ160**

Contains an alphabetical listing of terms with brief, elementary definitions. Also includes a list of instruments in five languages and an illustrated guide to musical notation. ML108.T46

Vannes, René. Essai de terminologie musicale : dictionnaire universel comprenant plus de 15,000 termes de musique en italien, espagnol, portugais, français, anglais, allemand, latin et grec, disposés en un alphabet unique. Thann : "Alsatia", 1925. 230 p. **BJ161**

Terms arranged in one alphabet by original language, with brief definitions and equivalents in the other languages. ML108.V18

Quotations

Crofton, Ian. A dictionary of musical quotations / comp. by Ian Crofton and Donald Fraser. N.Y. : Schirmer, 1985. 191 p. **BJ162**

Brief quotations from literary works, composers' writings, newspaper articles, books on music, etc., organized under 291 headings, alphabetically arranged, with appropriate cross-references. Headings include composers and topics, and are listed in table of contents. Quotations, varying in number from one to more than 50, are arranged chronologically under each heading. Author and subject indexes. ML66.C86

An encyclopedia of quotations about music / comp. and ed. by Nat Shapiro. Garden City, N.Y. : Doubleday, 1978. 418 p. **BJ163**

Repr. : N.Y. : Da Capo, 1981.

A topical arrangement of more than 2,000 "wise, witty, and beautiful quotations about music."—*Introd.* Index of names and sources; index of keywords and phrases. ML66.E6

Dissertations

Adkins, Cecil. Doctoral dissertations in musicology / Cecil Adkins and Alis Dickinson. 7th North American ed., 2nd Internat. ed. Philadelphia : Amer. Musicological Soc. ; Basel : Internat. Musicological Soc., 1984. 545 p. **BJ164**

"The second combined publication of the American-Canadian *Doctoral Dissertations in Musicology* (seventh cumulative edition) and the *International Doctoral Dissertations in Musicology* (second cumulative edition)."—*Pref.*

Doctoral dissertations in musicology was separately published in five editions 1952–71. The previous edition of this work was published 1977 as *International index of dissertations and musicological works in progress.*

About 6,500 titles in this edition, approximately 63% of which are American-Canadian works, the remainder being from universities in 30 other countries (non-American dissertations having been included only since 1972). Following a General-miscellaneous section, dissertations are listed by period with topical subdivisions. References to abstracts in *Dissertation abstracts international* (AG13) and in *RILM abstracts of music literature* (BJ108) follow the bibliographic citations; an asterisk preceding the classification number indicates that the work is still in progress. Separate author and subject indexes. Nonstudent works are no longer listed, but are to appear from time to time in *Acta musicologica.*

Updated by: *Doctoral dissertations in musicology. Second series*, ed. by Cecil Adkins and Alis Dickinson (1st cumulative ed. Philadelphia : American Musicological Soc. ; [s.l.] : International Musicological Soc., 1990. 177 p.). Cumulations of interim editions were publ. annually beginning 1985. Lists 2,230 titles; does not supersede the 1984 ed. Updated by annual Interim lists.

§ An older list, more limited in scope, is W. S. Larson, *Bibliography of research studies in music education, 1932–1948* (Rev. ed. Chicago : Music Educators' Nat. Conference, 1949). It was continued on an irregular basis by lists of "Doctoral dissertations in music and music education," first compiled by Larson (later by Roderick D. Gordon) and appearing in the *Journal of research in music education:* 1949–56 (Fall 1957), 1957–63 (Spr. 1964), 1963–67 (Sum. 1968), 1968–71 (Spr. 1972), 1972 (Sum. 1974), 1972–77 (Fall 1978). ML128.M8A43

Schaal, Richard. Verzeichnis deutschsprachiger musikwissenschaftlicher Dissertationen 1861–1960. Kassel : Bärenreiter, 1963. 167 p. (Musikwissenschaftliche Arbeiten, no. 19). **BJ165**

Cites 2,819 dissertations in German, listed alphabetically by author. Subject index.

§ Continued by: Schaal's *Verzeichnis deutschsprachiger musikwissenschaftlicher Dissertationen 1961–1970 : mit Ergänzungen zum Verzeichnis 1861–1960* (Kassel : Bärenreiter, 1974. 91 p. [Musikwissenschaftliche Arbeiten, no. 25]). 1,271 dissertations, most written between 1961 and 1970, listed alphabetically by author, with subject index. ML128.M8S3

Thèses de doctorat en langue française relatives à la musique : bibliographie commentée = French language dissertations in music : a bibliography / collected and annotated by Jean Gribenski. N.Y. : Pendragon Pr., c1979. 270 p. (RILM retrospectives, no. 2). **BJ166**

Lists some 438 dissertations at the doctoral level written in French and accepted by universities in Belgium, Switzerland, Canada, and France, 1883–1976. Brief annotations frequently point out chapters in which music is discussed. Classed arrangement based on the RILM scheme (BJ108), with indexes by author, subject, date of degree, and university. ML128.L3G7

Directories

Computing in musicology : a directory of research. Oct. 1989– . Menlo Park, Calif. . Center for Computer Assisted Research in the Humanities, 1989– . Annual. **BJ167**

Continues: *Directory of computer assisted research in musicology* (Menlo Park, Calif. : Center for Computer Assisted Research in the Humanities, 1985–88).

Addressed "principally to musicologists seeking current information about research in progress, discussion of that research, and practical examples of applications."—*Pref.* (1989). Based on reports by readers, each issue covers current events, special topics, music printing, software, and other topics. ML73.D57

Directory of music faculties in colleges and universities, U.S. and Canada. [Ed. 4] 1972/74– . [Binghamton, N.Y.] : College Music Society, [1974]– . Irregular. **BJ168**

Comp. and ed. by Craig R. Short.

[15th] ed., 1993/–95, publ. 1993.

Ed. 1–3 entitled: *Directory of music faculties in American colleges and universities* (publ. 1967–70).

Lists music faculty members at institutions of higher learning. In four sections: (1) alphabetical listing by state of names and addresses of colleges and universities, with list of faculty members and area of teaching interest; (2) list of faculty members by area of interest; (3) alphabetical listing by name of faculty member; (4) listing of schools by type of degree offered (e.g., M.A. in ethnomusicology). ML13.D57

Directory of music research libraries / Rita Benton, gen. ed. Kassel ; N.Y. : Bärenreiter, 1967–85. 5 v. : maps. (In progress). **BJ169**

At head of title: International Association of Music Libraries. Commission of Research Libraries.

Constitutes Series C of the *International inventory of musical sources (RISM)*; see BJ77.

Contents: v. 1, Canada, Marian Kahn and Helmut Kallmann; United States, Charles Lindahl (2nd rev. ed., 1983); v. 2, Thirteen European countries, Rita Benton, ed. (prelim. ed., Iowa City : Univ. of Iowa, 1970); v. 3, Spain, France, Italy, Portugal, Rita Benton, ed. (prelim. ed., Iowa City : Univ. of Iowa, 1972); v. 4, Australia, Cecil Hill; Israel, Katya Manor; Japan, James Siddons; New Zealand, Dorothy Freed; v. 5, Czechoslovakia, Hungary, Poland, James B. Moldovan; Yugoslavia, Lilian Pruett.

The European countries covered in v. 2 are: Austria, Belgium, Denmark, Finland, Germany (East and West), Great Britain, Ireland, Luxemburg, Netherlands, Norway, Sweden, Switzerland.

Vols. 2–3 are in revision.   ML12.D615

Resources of American music history : a directory of source materials from Colonial times to World War II / D. W. Krummel ... [et al.]. Urbana : Univ. of Illinois Pr., c1981. 463 p.
                                                          BJ170
Offers a survey of the evidence of American musical life and activity "as recorded in documents located in 3000 repositories in the United States and abroad."—*Introd.* In soliciting information from repositories, ten general types of documents were mentioned: sheet music; songbooks; other printed music (opera scores, band or orchestra music, etc.); manuscript music; programs for concerts, etc.; catalogs of music publishers and dealers; organizational papers and archives of music groups, clubs, orchestras, opera houses, commercial firms, etc.; personal papers; pictures; sound recordings (including oral history tapes). Entries give name and address of the repository, with notes on types of collections and extent of holdings; criteria for the descriptive notes are carefully set out, and names of respondents to the editorial inquiries are given. Geographical arrangement (i.e., by states of the U.S., U.S. territories, Canada, other countries). Index of personal and institutional names and subjects.   ML120.U5R47

Thorin, Suzanne E. International directory of braille music collections / comp. and ed. by Suzanne E. Thorin ; rev. and updated by Shirley Piper Emanuel. Wash. : National Library Service for the Blind and Physically Handicapped, Library of Congress, 1987. 41 p.   **BJ171**
Superintendent of Documents classification: LC 19.2:IN8/3.

Lists more than 40 institutions, with entries arranged alphabetically by country, city, and organization. For each, gives description of the collection, institutional collecting and lending policies, and any products for the blind created by the institution.   ML12.T5

Uscher, Nancy. The Schirmer guide to schools of music and conservatories throughout the world. N.Y. : Schirmer ; London : Collier Macmillan, c1988. 635 p.   **BJ172**
Lists the histories, curricula, special programs, tuition, admission requirements, and other information on some 750 music institutions with programs for training professional musicians. In two sections: U.S., arranged alphabetically by state; International, arranged alphabetically by country. Indexes of institutions, program areas, and instruments taught.   ML12.U8

Handbooks

Berkowitz, Freda Pastor. Popular titles and subtitles of musical compositions. 2nd ed. Metuchen, N.J. : Scarecrow, 1975. 209 p.   **BJ173**
A listing of titles associated with works of serious music from 1600 to the present, with notes as to origin of name. Arranged alphabetically in English except where the foreign-language title is well known. Includes bibliography and list of composers.   ML113.B39

Hodgson, Julian. Music titles in translation : a checklist of musical compositions. London : Bingley ; Hamden, Conn. : Linnet Books, 1976. 370 p.   **BJ174**
"The list gives in one alphabetical sequence the original or English language translation followed by the translation or original as the case may be."—*Pref.* No index.   ML111.H7

Johnson, Harold Earle. First performances in America to 1900 : works with orchestra. Detroit : Publ. for the College Music Soc. by Information Coordinators, 1979. 446 p. (Bibliographies in American music, no. 4).   **BJ175**
Under name of composer works are listed by type (overture, incidental music, etc.), with place and date of first performance of each work anywhere in the United States; also given are performing organization and conductor or soloist, together with extracts from contemporary reviews. Form and media indexes. An appendix gives a list of leading music critics prior to 1900 with name of newspaper and dates of affiliation; there is also a list of major auditoriums, theaters, and concert halls arranged by city.   ML120.U5J6

Kupferberg, Herbert. The book of classical music lists. N.Y. : Penguin Books, c1988. 244 p.   **BJ176**
Originally publ. : N.Y. : Facts on File, 1985.

Intends to present " ... a book of musical lists consisting entirely of trivia and oddities."—*Pref.* Off-beat, but potentially useful. Numerous lists, including Metropolitan Opera ticket prices, musicians who left the Soviet Union, one-opera composers, etc. Indexes to composers and compositions.   ML63.K88

The musical woman : an international perspective. Westport, Conn. : Greenwood, 1984–[1990?].   **BJ177**
Judith Lang Zaimont, ed. in chief; Catherine Overhauser and Jane Gottlieb, assoc. editors.

Contents: v. 1, 1983; v. 2, 1984–85; v. 3, 1986–90.

Planned as an ongoing series devoted to the achievements of women in music. Each volume has two parts: a gazette of performances, festivals, commissions, films, new books, and other summary information; and a series of individual essays on various topics.
                                                          ML82.M8

Pallay, Steven G. Cross index title guide to classical music. N.Y. : Greenwood, 1987. 206 p. (Music reference collection, no. 12).   **BJ178**
Contains more than 6,000 titles for vocal and instrumental compositions by 220 composers. Titles are listed under multiple and variant names (including the title under which the piece is most likely to be found in reference sources or catalogs), cross-indexed titles, and composer's name. Concludes with a list of composers, common thematic catalog numbers, and principal sources.

§ A companion, the author's *Cross index title guide to opera and operetta* (N.Y. : Greenwood, 1989; Music reference collection, no. 19), contains more than 5,500 titles of vocal and instrumental excerpts from approximately 1,400 operas and operettas by 535 composers.
                                                          ML113.P34

Music business

Baskerville, David. Music business handbook & career guide. 5th ed. Los Angeles : Sherwood Pub. Co., c1990. 541 p. : ill.
                                                          BJ179
1st ed., 1979; 4th ed., 1985.

Presents a discussion of music as a profession; in six sections (1) overview; (2) songwriting, publishing copyright; (3) business affairs (including agents, licensing, concert promotion); (4) the record industry (contracts, distribution, etc.); (5) music in broadcasting and film (including music for advertising); (6) career planning and development. The appendix reprints forms used by the Copyright Office and ASCAP, and there is a brief directory of professional organizations and trade associations. Indexed.   ML3795.B33

Devriès, Anik. Dictionnaire des éditeurs de musique française / Anik Devriès, François Lesure. Genève : Minkoff, 1979–1988. v. 1–2 in 3 v. : ill. (Archives de l'édition musicale française, t. 4). (In progress).   **BJ180**
Contents: v. 1, Des origines à environ 1820 (2 v.); v. 2, De 1820 à 1914.

Contains names of publishers, printers, and dealers responsible for French music publications from the early 16th century. Entries are arranged alphabetically by French city, with the bulk of the entries under Paris. Where available, each entry contains brief biographical information, successive addresses, plate numbers, and bibliographical information. ML112.D45

Humphries, Charles. Music publishing in the British Isles from the beginning until the middle of the nineteenth century : a dictionary of engravers, printers, publishers and music sellers, with a historical introduction / by Charles Humphries and William C. Smith. 2nd ed., with suppl. Oxford : Blackwell, 1970. 392 p. : facsims., music. **BJ181**

A reprinting of the 1st ed. (1954) with the addition of a supplement of addenda and errata, p. 357–90.

§ There are similar compilations for Paris and Vienna: *A dictionary of Parisian music publishers, 1700–1950,* by Cecil Hopkinson (London : Author, 1954. 131 p.); and *Der Wiener Musikaleinhandel von 1700 bis 1778,* by Hannelore Gericke (Graz : Böhlaus, 1960. 150 p.). ML112.H8

Music industry directory. 7th ed. (1983). Chicago : Marquis Professional Publ., 1983. **BJ182**

Continues: *The musician's guide,* 1st–6th eds., 1954–80. Ceased with 7th ed.

Provides directory information on many aspects of the music profession and industry. The 7th ed. is in seven sections: (1) Organizations and councils, (2) Competitions, awards and grants, (3) Education; (4) Resources (including publications, reference works, etc.); (5) Performance (orchestras, opera companies, etc.); (6) Profession; (7) Trade and industry. Sections are separately indexed. ML13.M505

Music printing and publishing / ed. by D. W. Krummel and Stanley Sadie. N.Y. : W.W. Norton, 1990. 615 p. : ill. **BJ183**

Based on the article "Printing and publishing" in *The new Grove dictionary of music and musicians* (BJ141). The first section, "Music printing" by H. Edmund Poole, contains specialized text excised from the original article, as well as revisions and additions that treat recent developments. The second section consists of a dictionary of music publishers and printers, including those in *The new Grove,* supplemented by more than 150 additional entries. The final section is a glossary contributed by Stanley Boorman. ML112.M86

Parkinson, John A. Victorian music publishers : an annotated list. Warren, Mich. : Harmonie Park Pr., 1990. 315 p., [1] leaf of plates : ill. (some col.). (Detroit studies in music bibliography, no. 64). **BJ184**

A comprehensive list of British music publishers, 1830–1900. Includes roughly 750 firms, continuing Charles Humphries and William C. Smith's *Music publishing in the British Isles from the beginning until the middle of the nineteenth century* (BJ181), whose cutoff date was 1850. Lists more than 500 publishers alphabetically by firm name with known addresses, for each citing a representative example of the publisher's work. Annotations included for many entries. ML21.G7P3

Shemel, Sidney. This business of music / by Sidney Shemel and M. William Krasilovsky. Rev. and enl. 6th ed. N.Y. : Billboard Books, 1990. 688 p. : ill. **BJ185**

3rd ed., 1982 ; 5th ed., 1985.

A compendium of useful information on contracts, copyrights, record production, music videos, agents and managers, performing-rights organizations, and other business practices specific to music. ML3790.S5

Chronologies, outlines, tables

Burbank, Richard. Twentieth century music. N.Y. : Facts on File, 1984. 485 p. : ill. **BJ186**

A chronology of musical events from Jan. 1900 through Dec. 1979, tracing "evolutionary changes that have taken place in twentieth century music."—*Author's pref.* Includes opera, dance, instrumental and vocal musical events; births, deaths, debuts, etc., of relevant figures; and selected statements and quotations about music. Indexed. ML197.B85

Hall, Charles J. An eighteenth-century musical chronicle : events, 1750–1799. N.Y. : Greenwood, 1990. 177 p. (Music reference collection, no. 25). **BJ187**

A year-by-year chronology of political and social events, cultural history, musical events, biographical highlights, musical literature and compositions, etc. General musical index.

§ Similarly organized are the author's two additional volumes: *A nineteenth-century musical chronicle : events, 1800–1899* (N.Y. : Greenwood, 1989. 374 p.) and *A twentieth-century musical chronicle : events, 1900–1988* (N.Y. : Greenwood, 1989. 347 p.). ML195.H28

Slonimsky, Nicolas. Music since 1900. 4th ed. N.Y. : Scribner's, [1971]. 1595 p. **BJ188**

1st ed., 1938; 3rd ed., 1949.

Partial contents: Descriptive chronology, 1900–1969; Letters and documents; Dictionary of terms.

A chronology of musical events (with commentary on the events listed) makes up the bulk of the volume. Fully indexed.

———. ———. *Supplement* (1986) updates the chronology to 1985 and includes additions, amplifications, and corrections. ML197.S634

Style manuals

Writing about music : a style sheet from the editors of *19th-century music* / D. Kern Holoman. Berkeley : Univ. of California Pr., c1988. 61 p. : music. **BJ189**

A style manual intended for publications in music, used by the editors and staff of the journal *19th-century music,* with examples from journal issues. Deviations from *The Chicago manual of style,* 13th ed. (AA319) are noted. ML63.W68

Guidebooks

Brody, Elaine. The music guide to Austria and Germany / Elaine Brody and Claire Brook. N.Y. : Dodd, Mead & Co., 1975. 271 p. **BJ190**

Companion works by the same compilers: *The music guide to Belgium, Luxembourg, Holland and Switzerland* (1977. 156 p.); *The music guide to Great Britain : England, Scotland, Wales, Ireland* ([1975]. 240 p.); *The music guide to Italy* (1978. 233 p.).

All four volumes follow a similar plan. A summary discussion of music developments in each country is followed by notes for each major city, indicating guides and services available, opera houses and concert halls, libraries and museums, conservatories and schools, and musical organizations. Musical festivals and competitions are also noted. Volumes are separately indexed. ML21.B77

Gusikoff, Lynne. Guide to musical America. N.Y. : Facts on File, 1984. 347 p. : ill., maps. **BJ191**

Aims "to present historic highlights of different styles of music as they developed in particular regions of the United States at various times; and to specify certain geographic locations where one may hear different styles of music today."—*Introd.* Arranged by region, with brief introductory notes on types and development of music therein, and state/city directories of performing arts centers, festivals, etc. Indexed. ML200.G95

International music guide. 1977–1985. London : Tantivy Pr. ; Cranbury, N.J. : A. S. Barnes, [1976]–1985. **BJ192**

Ceased with 1985.

Similar to, and produced by the same group as, the *International film guide* (*see* BH269), "surveying internationally all points of interest to the modern concertgoer and general music-lover."—*Introd.* Includes a survey of music of the year in various countries, a review of recordings, directories of festivals, music magazines, music shops, and music schools.

§ Superseded by *International music & opera guide*, publ. 1986–87 (London : Tantivy Pr. ; N.Y. : New York Zoetrope).

The music lover's guide to Europe : a compendium of festivals, concerts, and opera / Roberta Gottesman, editor ; Catherine Sentman, associate editor. N.Y. : Wiley, c1992. 434 p. : ill.   **BJ193**

Informative compendium organized by country and subarranged by city or region. Contains brief notes, many having local addresses and phone numbers for organizations and concert halls. Covers Western and Eastern Europe, as well as the former Soviet Union. Appendixes of U.S. addresses of national tourist bureaus and major European opera festivals.

§ Covering the same geographical territory is Kenneth Bernstein, *Music lover's Europe* (N.Y. : Scribner's, 1983), but with a descriptive, narrative presentation of historically and architecturally related items of musical interest.   ML12.M87

Norris, Gerald. A musical gazetteer of Great Britain & Ireland. Newton Abbot, Eng. ; North Pomfret, Vt. : David & Charles, c1981. 352 p. : ill.   **BJ194**

Similar in concept to literary gazetteers, but concerned with the places where composers, conductors, singers, pianists, etc., lived, stayed, worked or performed. Arranged by region, then by county and place. Indexed.   ML285.N67

Rabin, Carol Price. Music festivals in America : classical, opera, jazz, pops, country, old-time fiddlers, folk, bluegrass, Cajun. 4th ed. Great Barrington, Mass. : Berkshire Traveller Pr., c1990. 271 p. : ill., maps.   **BJ195**

Revised ed., 1983, had title: *A guide to music festivals in America.*

Describes more than 160 festivals in 40 states, arranged under the categories of classical, opera, jazz, pops, folk, bluegrass, old-time fiddlers, and country and Cajun. Excludes rock festivals. Entries mention where to write for tickets and for accommodations. Indexed by name of festival.   ML19.R3

——————————— Music festivals in Europe and Britain. Rev. and enl. ed. Stockbridge, Mass. : Berkshire Traveller, c1984. 190 p. : ill.   **BJ196**

A listing by country of the major European music festivals. Includes Israel, Russia, Turkey and Japan. Entries are similar to those for the compiler's book on music festivals in America (BJ195).

ML35.R23

History

Abraham, Gerald. The concise Oxford history of music. London ; N.Y. : Oxford Univ. Pr., 1979. 968 p. : ill., music.

BJ197

Not a condensation of *New Oxford history of music* (BJ200), but an attempt to present in one volume a history of the "main stream of Western music" (*Pref.*) from the music of Mesopotamia to "crosscurrents after 1945." Except for the 19th century, there is some emphasis on less familiar compositions. The "Suggestions for further reading" section is arranged according to the chapter divisions, and is the work of specialist scholars.   ML160.A27

Collaer, Paul. Historical atlas of music : a comprehensive study of the world's music—past and present / [by] Paul Collaer [and] Albert Vander Linden, with the collaboration of F. van den Bremt; preface by Charles Van den Borren, translated [from the French] by Allan Miller. London ; Toronto [etc.] : Harrap, 1968. 176 p. : plates, illus., facsims., col. maps, music, ports.   **BJ198**

Translation of: *Atlas historique de la musique*, (1960).

Maps and plates, with accompanying text, to illustrate the history of music from primitive times to the present.   ML160.C6813

Kinsky, Georg. A history of music in pictures / ed. by Georg Kinsky with the co-operation of Robert Haas, Hans Schnoor and other experts. N.Y. : Dover Publications, [c1951]. 363 p. : ill., ports., music.   **BJ199**

A collection of approximately 1,500 illustrations—portraits, instruments, facsimiles, etc.—forming a pictorial history of music from the earliest times to the present. The pictures constitute the main part of the work, the brief text consisting merely of: (1) explanatory notes on each plate of illustrations, (2) indexes and contents, and (3) introduction and foreword. Issued in three editions: (1) original German edition, *Geschichte der Musik in Bildern* (Leipzig : Breitkopf, 1930); (2) French edition, *Album musical* (Paris : Delagrave, 1930), printed from the same plates of pictures with notes, indexes, etc., translated into French and a new French introduction; and (3) the English edition originally published in London (Dent, 1930), also printed from the original German plates with translation of text.   ML89.K55

New Oxford history of music. Oxford ; N.Y. : Oxford Univ. Pr., 1954–1990. 10 v. : music.   **BJ200**

Contents: v. 1, Ancient and oriental music, ed. by Egon Wellesz (1957); v. 2, Early medieval music up to 1300, ed. by Richard Crocker and David Hiley (2nd ed., 1990); v. 3, Ars nova and the Renaissance, 1300–1540, ed. by Dom Anselm Hughes and Gerald Abraham (1960; repr. with corrections, 1986); v. 4, The age of humanism, 1540–1630, ed. by Gerald Abraham (1968); v. 5, Opera and church music 1630–1750, ed. by Nigel Fortune and Anthony Lewis (1975; repr. with corrections and rev. bibliography, 1986); v. 6, Concert music (1630–1750), ed. by Gerald Abraham (1986); v. 7, The age of enlightenment, 1745–1790, ed. by Egon Wellesz and Frederick Sterfeld (1973); v. 8, The age of Beethoven, 1790–1830, ed. by Gerald Abraham (1982; repr. with corrections, 1985); v. 9, Romanticism (1830–1890), ed. by Gerald Abraham (1990); v. 10, The modern age, ed. by Martin Cooper (1974).

An entirely new edition of *Oxford history of music* (1929–38), surveying music from the earliest times to the present, written by outstanding authorities.   ML160.N44

Biography

American Society of Composers, Authors and Publishers. ASCAP biographical dictionary / comp. for the American Society of Composers, Authors, and Publishers by Jaques Cattell Press. 4th ed. N.Y. : Bowker, 1980. 589 p.   **BJ201**

1st ed., 1948.

More than 8,000 biographical sketches of individual ASCAP members (both living and deceased). List of publisher members, p. 563–89.   ML106.U3A5

Anderson, E. Ruth. Contemporary American composers : a biographical dictionary. 2nd ed. Boston : G.K. Hall, 1982. 578 p.   **BJ202**

1st ed., 1976.

Offers biographical sketches with information derived from questionnaires. Criteria for inclusion were "Birth date no earlier than 1870 and American citizenship or extended residence in the United States."—*Pref.* Those who have written only one or two pieces or those who write only teaching pieces, jazz, popular, rock, or folk music are omitted.   ML390.A54

Baker, Theodore. Baker's biographical dictionary of musicians. 8th ed. / rev. by Nicolas Slonimsky. N.Y. : Schirmer Books : Maxwell Macmillan International, c1992. 2115 p. : ports. **BJ203**

The standard and most authoritative single-volume biographical dictionary. This revision includes many substantial rewrites for major figures, as well as increased coverage of non-Europeans, women, ethnomusicologists, and other groups overlooked in previous editions. For most entries, includes biographical information, work lists, and brief bibliographies. Written in the reviser's enjoyable and idiosyncratic style. ML105.B16

Biographical dictionary of Russian/Soviet composers / editors in chief, Allan Ho and Dmitry Feofanov. N.Y. : Greenwood, 1989. 739 p. **BJ204**

An alphabetical listing of over 2,000 composers and others associated with music who were born in Russia or the U.S.S.R., were noteworthy émigrés, or were foreigners who settled and were influential in Russia. Each entry contains biographical information, work lists, bibliographies, discographies, and comments on style. Appendixes include a supplementary list of persons not included in the main listing and a discography for recordings cited. Name index and list of contributors. ML106.S68B56

Blackmore, A. S. G. An index of composers. Winsley : Saracen, 1993. 319 p. **BJ205**

Four separate indexes give names, dates, and country of origin for more than 4,600 composers, with each index subarranged by one of these elements. The first lists composers in alphabetical order, the second composers listed in chronological order by year of birth (992–1967), the third in chronological order by year of death (1050–1992), and the fourth by country of origin (72 countries represented). The appendix contains a list of composers known to have lived only during specific centuries.

Butterworth, Neil. A dictionary of American composers. N.Y. : Garland, 1984. 523 p. (Garland reference library of the humanities, v. 296). **BJ206**

Offers biographical sketches of American composers who "have their music performed widely beyond their own immediate circle."—*Introd.* Does not include composers of light music and jazz unless they have produced music in other media. Foreign-born composers who have become American citizens are included. Biographies of living composers were submitted to the biographees for correction whenever possible. Appendix lists teachers and their pupils. ML106.U3B87

Claghorn, Charles Eugene. Women composers & hymnists : a concise biographical dictionary. Metuchen, N.J. : Scarecrow, 1984. 272 p. **BJ207**

Aims to be a "comprehensive biographical dictionary of women hymnists and composers of church and sacred music covering all leading Protestant denominations, many Roman Catholics and a few Jewish hymnists."—*Introd.* About 755 entries.

§ See also Jane Weiner LePage, *Women composers, conductors, and musicians of the twentieth century* (BJ215). BV325.C58

Cohen, Aaron I. International encyclopedia of women composers. 2nd ed., rev. and enl. N.Y. : Books & Music USA, c1987. 2 v. (1151 p., [48] p. of plates) : ports. **BJ208**

1st ed., 1984.

Includes 6,196 historical and contemporary composers from all nationalities. Annotations focus on the composer's musical education, achievements, and works. Addendum at beginning of v. 1 lists names inadvertently omitted; v. 2 includes bibliography, photographs, appendixes, and discography. ML105.C7

Contemporary composers / editors, Brian Morton, Pamela Collins. Chicago : St. James Pr., c1992. 1019 p. **BJ209**

Covers approximately 500 living composers (or composers who died while the project was in progress) by some 200 contributors. Entries are signed, and each includes: biographical details; a list of works, usually comprehensive; and a short evaluative article, many of which

include statements by the composer. An appendix listing the names and addresses of major music publishers and one listing the names and addresses of contemporary music information centers conclude the work. ML105.C75

Ewen, David. American composers : a biographical dictionary. N.Y. : G.P. Putnam's Sons, c1982. 793 p. **BJ210**

Treats 300 composers from Colonial times to the present. Aims to provide in-depth treatment (especially of living composers), with greater biographical detail than is usually found in other dictionaries and encyclopedias, plus "a succinct description of each composer's musical style" (*Foreword*) and notes on its development. Often includes a statement of the composer's artistic creed. Lists of principal works and brief bibliography for each composer. Index of programmatic titles. ML390.E815

——————— Composers since 1900 : a biographical and critical guide. N.Y. : Wilson, 1969. 639p. : ill. **BJ211**

Designed to serve as a replacement for three of the compiler's earlier publications: *Composers of today, American composers today,* and *European composers today* (originally published 1934, 1949, and 1954, respectively). Covers 220 composers, living and deceased, who have been writing music since the beginning of this century.

——————. ———————. *First supplement* (1981. 328 p.) covers 1970–85, corrects the basic chronology and adds new composers and several new documents. Index of names and subjects. ML390.E833

Gray, John. Blacks in classical music : a bibliographical guide to composers, performers, and ensembles. N.Y. : Greenwood, c1988. 280 p. (Music reference collection, no. 15). **BJ212**

An author listing of books, articles, unpublished papers, recordings, and media performances documenting the "full range of black activity in classical music."—*Introd.* Organized topically with subdivisions under: general; composers; symphony and concert artists; concert and opera singers; reference works; and research centers. Artist and author indexes. ML128.B45G7

International who's who in music and musicians' directory. 7th ed. (1975)– Cambridge, Eng. : [Melrose Pr.], 1975 . Irregular. **BJ213**

Publisher varies.

Represents a change of title for *Who's who in music and musicians' international directory* (eds. 1–6, 1935–72). The 12th ed. (1990) includes 7,500 biographical sketches, more than 3,000 listed for the first time, and many previous sketches updated. Scope is international. No selection criteria are indicated, and most entries are compiled from questionnaires. Appendixes contain lists of organizations and competitions. ML106.G7W4

Kutsch, K. J. Grosses Sängerlexikon / K. J. Kutsch, Leo Riemens. Bern : Francke, c1987. 2 v. (3452 columns) : geneal. table. **BJ214**

Builds on and supersedes *Unvergängliche Stimmen* (2. Aufl. Bern : Francke, 1966; 2., neu bearb. u. erw. Aufl., 1982) and its English translation, *A concise biographical dictionary of singers* (Philadelphia : Chilton, 1969. 487 p.).

Contains biographies of singers from the last decades of the 16th century to the present. Some entries include a bibliography and, if applicable, the singer's recording company. Appendix contains an alphabetical listing of operas and operettas with information on their first performance. Composer index.

Two *Ergänzungsbände* (1991–94. 2 v.) contain additional entries, as well as an extensive list of additions and corrections to the original volumes. ML105.K83

LePage, Jane Weiner. Women composers, conductors, and musicians of the twentieth century : selected biographies. Metuchen, N.J. : Scarecrow, 1980–1988. 3 v. : ill. **BJ215**

Each volume contains entries for approximately 17 composers. Quotations from personal interviews are interwoven with biographical information. Entries conclude with lists of compositions, works in progress, discographies, and publisher addresses.   ML82.L46

Musicos españoles de todos los tiempos : diccionario biográfico / [recopilado y compuesto por Juan Piñero García]. Madrid : Tres, 1984. 465 p. : ill., ports.   **BJ216**

A biographical dictionary of Spanish musicians, including personal names and names of places as they relate to performers. Performers are listed only by performance names. Lacks cross-references.   ML106.S7M9

Southern, Eileen. Biographical dictionary of Afro-American and African musicians. Westport, Conn. : Greenwood, [1982]. 478 p.   **BJ217**

"Draws together widely dispersed and, in many instances, heretofore unpublished information on more than 1500 musicians of African descent, including living persons as well as figures of the past."—*Pref.* Bibliographical sources are cited at the end of each article; much information was derived from questionnaires. References to discographies appearing in works cited in the select bibliography (p. 447–52) are also given.   ML105.S67

Who's who in American music : classical / ed. by Jaques Cattell Pr. 2nd ed. N.Y. : Bowker, c1985. 783 p.   **BJ218**
1st ed., 1983.

Provides biographical data on 9,038 members of the music community, including 2,433 names new to this edition. Biographees include educators, librarians, writers, editors, organization administrators and executives, directors, patrons, etc., as well as composers and performers. Information was obtained mainly from questionnaires and concentrates on career and achievements, with current position and address. Geographic and professional classification indexes.

Bibliography

Cowden, Robert H. Concert and opera singers : a bibliography of biographical materials. Westport, Conn. : Greenwood, 1985. 278 p. (Music reference collection, no. 5).   **BJ219**

Contains information on 708 concert and opera singers who are the subject of an autobiography or biography, and who have entries or articles in one or more of ten major reference works or nine periodicals. In three sections: a bibliography, with annotations, of collective works; a bibliography of related works; and the bibliography arranged by individual singers. Additional reference sources are listed in Appendix I, while a very useful index to concert singers in *The new Grove dictionary of music and musicians* (BJ141) constitutes Appendix II. Overlaps considerably with Andrew Farkas's *Opera and concert singers : an annotated bibliography* (N.Y. : Garland, 1985).

§ A related work is the author's *Concert and opera conductors : a bibliography of biographical materials* (N.Y. : Greenwood, 1987), organized in the same manner as the above work, but with an appendix to conductors drawn from *Baker's biographical dictionary of musicians*, 7th ed. (N.Y. : Schirmer, 1984).   ML128.B3C7

Floyd, Samuel A. Black music biography : an annotated bibliography / Samuel A. Floyd, Jr., Marsha J. Reisser. White Plains, N.Y. : Kraus Internat., c1987. 302 p.   **BJ220**

Entries for 87 individuals include for each a "brief career vignette" followed by summaries of biographical books about the artists, including 147 monographs and 32 autobiographies. Some entries contain review citations culled from general indexes and selective discographies.   ML128.B3F6

Garland composer resource manuals. v. 1– . N.Y. : Garland, 1981– . Irregular.   **BJ221**

A series on the most important composers from the Renaissance to the present day. Each volume contains annotated lists of writings in all major European languages about one or more composers, as well as lists of works, biographical sketches, guides to library resources, etc.

To date, some 34 volumes have appeared. Each is individually authored, resulting in variation in quality among volumes. On the whole, a valuable resource.

§ A similar series is: *Bio-bibliographies in music* (Westport, Conn. : Greenwood, 1984–); approximately 40 volumes have appeared.

Hixon, Donald L. Women in music : an encyclopedic biobibliography / by Don L. Hixon and Don A. Hennessee. 2nd ed. Metuchen, N.J. : Scarecrow, 1993. 2 v. (1824 p.).   **BJ222**
1st ed., 1975.

Indexes 157 music and nonmusic encyclopedias, including many multiple editions, and general biographical sets. Obituary information from significant newspapers and trade publications is included. Each entry consists of the musician's name, place and date of birth, death dates, source, and one or more fields of specialization. An asterisk indicates the presence of an illustration. Concludes with a detailed index by specialization.   ML105.H6

Skowronski, JoAnn. Women in American music : a bibliography. Metuchen, N.J. : Scarecrow, 1978. 183 p.   **BJ223**

Lists 1,305 books and periodical articles which treat any aspect of women as composers or musicians. Topical arrangement with name index. Most entries are briefly annotated.   ML128.W7S6

Indexes

Bull, Storm. Index to biographies of contemporary composers. N.Y. : Scarecrow, 1964–87. v. 1–3. (In progress).   **BJ224**

Concerned with composers who were "alive or born 1900, or later, or died in 1950 or later."—*v. 1.* Information is given in columns: name, country with which the composer is identified, year of birth, country of birth (if different from the previous listing), date of death if known, indication (by abbreviation) of sources of further biographical information. About 4,000 composers listed in v. 1; the second volume adds some 4,000 more names, plus further information on some of those included in v. 1. The third volume lists more than 13,500 composers, including 7,600 from v. 1–2 with additional information, and 5,900 new names. It contains indexing for 98 reference works, half of them in English and almost all published after 1974.   ML105.B9

De Lerma, Dominique-René. Black music and musicians in The new Grove dictionary of American music and The new Harvard dictionary of music / Dominique-René de Lerma and Marsha J. Reisser. Chicago : Center for Black Music Research, Columbia College, c1989. 56 p.   **BJ225**

A useful index of entries related to African-American music and musicians found in *The new Grove dictionary of American music* (BJ140) and *The new Harvard dictionary of music* (BJ153). Entries are arranged alphabetically within three sections: individuals and ensembles; subjects (taken directly from the dictionaries); and authors of the articles. Each entry is coded for the presence of a bibliography, discography, musical example, or illustrations; length of the article is given in centimeters.   ML128.B45D445

Green, Richard D. Index to composer bibliographies. Detroit : Information Coordinators, 1985. 76 p.   **BJ226**

A selective list of separately published bibliographies or bibliographical essays on 74 composers or 20th-century popular performing groups (e.g. the Beatles). Entries are drawn from monographs and serial publications, and each entry is annotated. Particularly useful for pre-1949 coverage of major composers.   ML113.G793

Greene, Frank. Composers on record : an index to biographical information on 14,000 composers whose music has been recorded. Metuchen, N.J. : Scarecrow, 1985. 604 p.   **BJ227**

An index to 14,000 composers of "serious" music drawn from 66 discographies and record catalogs, and from the record collection at the University of Toronto. Each citation includes the composer's dates, national origin, and two types of indexing: to biographical information in basic reference books, and to discographies. Entries without indexing indicate composers found only in the collection at the University of Toronto. ML105.G78

MUSICAL FORMS

Themes

Barlow, Harold. A dictionary of musical themes / Harold Barlow, Sam Morgenstern. Rev. ed. N.Y. : Crown, [1975]. 642 p. **BJ228**

1st ed., 1948.

The "Bartlett" for musical themes; contains some 10,000 themes of instrumental music arranged by composers, with a notation index arranged alphabetically by the first notes of the themes. Index of titles. ML128.I65B3

——————— A dictionary of opera and song themes : including cantatas, oratorios, lieder, and art songs / Harold Barlow, Sam Morgenstern. N.Y. : Crown, [1966]. 547 p. **BJ229**

A reprint of the work originally published under the title: A dictionary of vocal themes (1950). 1976 issue called "Rev. ed." (547 p.).

Companion volume to the authors' A dictionary of musical themes (BJ228). Contains themes from operas, oratorios, cantatas, art songs, and miscellaneous vocal works. Includes index to songs and first lines. ML128.V7B3

Brook, Barry S. Thematic catalogues in music. Hillsdale, N.Y. : Pendragon Pr., [1972]. 347 p. (RILM retrospectives, no. 1). **BJ230**

Subtitle: An annotated bibliography including printed, manuscript and in-preparation catalogues; related literature and reviews; an essay on the definitions, history, functions, historiography, and future of the thematic catalogue.

More than 1,400 items arranged by individual composer, compiler, publisher, or library collection. Index of names and subjects. ML113.B86

Fuld, James J. The book of world-famous music : classical, popular, and folk. 3rd ed., rev. and enl. N.Y. : Dover, 1985. 714 p., [8] p. of plates : ill., music. **BJ231**

1st ed., 1966; rev. ed., 1971.

Attempts to "trace each of the well-known melodies back to its original printed source"—Introd. With each entry, a good deal of historical information is briefly presented, including biographical notes on the composers and lyricists, many of whom are little known. Arrangement is by title, with the opening bars of the music given. This edition reprints the text of the revised ed., adding a supplement section (25 p.) with new information and corrections. ML113.F8

Wettstein, Hermann. Bibliographie musikalischer thematischer Werkverzeichnisse. [Laaber] : Laaber-Verlag, 1978. 408 p. **BJ232**

An alphabetical composer listing. Contains bibliographical citation for the thematic catalog, along with a descriptive annotation. ML113.W48

——————— Thematische Sammelverzeichnisse der Musik : ein bibliographischer Führer durch Musikbibliotheken und -archive. [Laaber] : Laaber-Verlag, c1982. 268 p. **BJ233**

Indexes publications about library collections which contain thematic catalogs. Entries are arranged geographically by country and library. Citations include bibliographical information, a brief annotation, and a list of composers for whom incipits are present. Name index for authors and composers, and listing of institutions. ML128.T48W47

Opera

Borroff, Edith. American operas : a checklist / by Edith Borroff ; ed. by J. Bunker Clark. Warren, Mich. : Harmonie Park Pr., 1992. 334 p. : ill. (Detroit studies in music bibliography, no. 69). **BJ234**

Contains a listing of operas by U.S. composers. Includes more than 4,000 titles by some 2,000 composers from the 18th century through 1991. Listing is alphabetical by composer, with operas sublisted chronologically. For each opera, may include (where known), date, title, length, librettist, or performance information. ML128.O4B58

Eaton, Quaintance. Opera production : a handbook. Minneapolis : Univ. of Minnesota Pr., [1961–74]. 2 v. **BJ235**

Vol. 1 gives information on the production of 259 contemporary and standard operas, with brief information on some 260 in the supplementary list. The second volume treats about 350 more operas. Each volume is divided as to "Long operas" and "Short operas" (90 minutes or less), and arrangement is alphabetical by title within each section. Includes synopsis, time, requirements of roles, chorus, orchestra, sources of scores, list of performing companies, etc. MT955.E25

Ewen, David. The book of European light opera. N.Y. : Holt, Rinehart and Winston, [1962]. 297 p. : ill. **BJ236**

Repr. : Westport, Conn. : Greenwood, 1977.

"A guide to 167 European comic operas, light operas, operettas, opéra comiques, opéra-bouffes, and opera buffas from The Beggar's opera (1728) ... to Ivor Novello's King's rhapsody (1949), by 81 composers, with plot, production history, musical highlights, critical evaluations, and other relevant information"—Pref. MT95.E9

Kobbé, Gustav. Kobbé's complete opera book / ed. and rev. by the Earl of Harewood. 10th ed. London : Bodley Head, 1987. 1404 p., [32] p. of plates : ill. **BJ237**

1st ed., 1919, entitled: The complete opera book; rev. 1954, with later printings showing minor revisions. 1972 ed. entitled: Kobbé's complete opera book. 1976 ed., called The new Kobbé's complete opera book (variously referred to as "4th rev. ed." and "9th ed."), reset and considerably expanded.

The most complete general opera guide available. Discusses the development of opera, giving the stories of more than 320 operas, brief notes on the composers, illustrative musical phrases, dates of first performances, important revivals (with names of principal singers), etc. Includes older operas which are still being performed and modern works by contemporary composers. Indexed. MT95.K52

Kornick, Rebecca Hodell. Recent American opera : a production guide. N.Y. : Columbia Univ. Pr., c1991. 352 p. **BJ238**

Contains information on 213 American opera/musical-theater works by approximately 120 composers. Most had their premières after 1972 and were reviewed by major publications. Entries are organized by composer, and for each work provide brief assessment, summary of plot, production requirements, and citations to reviews. MT955.K82

Library of Congress. Music Division. Catalogue of opera librettos printed before 1800 / prep. by O. G. T. Sonneck. Wash. : U.S. Govt. Print. Off., 1914. 2 v. **BJ239**

Repr.: N.Y. : B. Franklin, 1967; N.Y. : Johnson, 1968.

Contents: v. 1, Title catalogue; v. 2, Author list, composer list, and aria index.

A detailed catalog giving for each libretto: full cataloging information, date and place of first performance, and valuable bibliographical and historical notes. Entry is first by original title, and then by replicas and translations, with reference from alternate, later, and translated titles. ML136.U55C45

——————— Dramatic music (class M 1500, 1510, 1520) : catalogue of full scores / comp. by Oscar George Theodore Sonneck, Chief of the Division of Music. Wash. : U.S. Govt. Print. Off., 1908. 170 p. **BJ240**

Repr. (N.Y. : Da Capo Pr., 1969) as *Dramatic music : catalgoue of full scores in the collection of the Library of Congress.*
Arrangement is alphabetical by composer.   ML136.U55D7

Lubbock, Mark Hugh. The complete book of light opera / with an American section by David Ewen. London : Putnam, [1962] ; N.Y. : Appleton-Century-Crofts, [c1963]. 953 p. : ill., ports., facsims., music.   **BJ241**

Intended to serve as a companion volume to *Kobbé's complete opera book* (BJ237). Selection is limited to lightest genre of light opera, dating from mid-19th century to 1961. Contains some 300 "musicals" which "the visitor is likely to encounter" in Paris, Vienna, Berlin, London, and New York. Arranged by these places. Gives title, composer, story, source, and first-production information.   MT95.L85

Marco, Guy A. Opera : a research and information guide. N.Y. : Garland, 1984. 373 p. (Garland reference library of the humanities, vol. 468).   **BJ242**

A useful bibliography of 704 annotated entries dealing with the music and general literature. Most entries cite studies of individual composers, but other topics include reference works, historical studies, opera houses, international directories, production, specific countries, etc. Author-title and subject indexes.   ML128.O4M28

Sartori, Claudio. I libretti italiani a stampa dalle origini al 1800 : catalogo analitico con 16 indici. Cuneo : Bertola & Locatelli, c1990–93. v. 1–6. (In progress).   **BJ243**

Contents: v. 1–5, A–Z, v. [6]– , Indexes.

An extensive work which when complete will contain over 25,000 entries, with librettos listed by title. Entries vary in length depending on available information, but may include place of performance, librettist, composer, other personnel associated with the opera (impresarios, designers, choreographers, etc.), conductor, performers, singers, etc., and conclude with repositories identified by RISM institution codes.   ML136.A1S27

The Viking opera guide / ed. by Amanda Holden with Nicholas Kenyon and Stephen Walsh. London ; N.Y. : Viking, 1993. 1305 p. : ill.   **BJ244**

Aims to provide a ready-reference guide to the standard opera repertory. Entry is alphabetical by composer with brief biographical information. Further subarrangement is chronological by opera. For important operas, score and recording publication information and brief bibliography are provided. Title and librettist indexes.   ML102.06V45

Indexes; Abstract journals

Drone, Jeanette Marie. Index to opera, operetta and musical comedy synopses in collections and periodicals. Metuchen, N.J. : Scarecrow, 1978. 171 p.   **BJ245**

Indexes plot synopses appearing in 74 collections and four periodical series. In four sections: (1) collections indexed; (2) title index, with indication of collection or periodical in which a synopsis may be found; (3) composer index, with reference to the title section; (4) bibliography of additional sources.   ML128.O4D76

Studwell, William E. Opera plot index / William E. Studwell, David A. Hamilton. N.Y. : Garland, 1989. 466 p. (Garland reference library of the humanities, vol. 1099).   **BJ246**

Indexes plots, descriptions, illustrations, historical background, criticism and analysis, musical themes, and bibliographical references for 2,900 operas and other works of musical theater from 169 books in 10 languages. Each entry gives the title of the work, the composer and date of first performance (if known), followed by codes giving the source indexed. Composer index.   ML128.O4S8

Encyclopedias; Dictionaries

Anderson, James. The Harper dictionary of opera and operetta. N.Y. : Harper & Row, 1990. 691 p.   **BJ247**

Publ. in U.K. as: *Bloomsbury dictionary of opera and operetta* (London : Bloomsbury Publ. Ltd., 1989).

A general guide to opera and operetta repertory, national aspects, audience practice, geographical considerations, etc., intended for general readers. Dictionary arrangement of name, title, and subject entries, with brief definitions and cross-references. Aims at currency, focusing on composers, opera titles, and contemporary performances rather than historical singers.

§ Another general guide on a smaller scale is Mary Hamilton's *A–Z of opera* (N.Y. : Facts on File, 1990), with approximately 850 entries and numerous illustrations. Plot summaries, historical overview, and recording information for 200 regularly-performed operas are provided in John Lazarus's *The opera handbook* (Boston : G.K. Hall, 1987).   ML102.O6A6

Ewen, David. The new encyclopedia of the opera. N.Y. : Hill and Wang, [1971]. 759 p.   **BJ248**

Prev. eds., 1955 and 1963, had title: *Encyclopedia of the opera.*

Aims to satisfy the basic needs and curiosity of the opera public. A resetting and enlargement of the previous editions, with approximately 5,000 entries in one alphabetical listing. Includes entries for the stories of operas, their major characters, selected excerpts, biographies of important figures, historical topics, performance aspects, literary sources, technical terms, and many special articles.   ML102.O6E9

International dictionary of opera / ed., C. Steven LaRue ; picture ed., Leanda Shrimpton. Detroit : St. James Pr., c1993. 2 v. (1543 p.) : ill.   **BJ249**

Aims to provide "a comprehensive source of biographical, bibliographical, and musicological information on people and works important to the history and development of opera."—*Introd.* All 1,100 entries are listed at the beginning of v. 1 in the following categories: composers; conductors; librettists; performers; producers, directors, and designers; and operas. The entries in the body of the work are listed alphabetically, and each contains biographical or other historical information, publication and publisher information if relevant, and bibliography. Many entries are lengthy, and all are signed. Notes on the advisers and contributors are provided. Both volumes are heavily illustrated. Title and nationality indexes in v. 2.   ML102.O6I6

The Metropolitan Opera encyclopedia : a comprehensive guide to the world of opera / ed. by David Hamilton ; contributors, Aliki Andris-Michalaros ... [et al.]. N.Y. : Simon and Schuster, c1987. 415 p. : ill. (some col.).   **BJ250**

A "guide to the world of opera, prepared under the auspices of the Metropolitan Opera Guild ... and a compendium of information specifically related to the Metropolitan Opera, its history, repertory, and performers."—*Pref.* Alphabetical listing of operas, composers, librettists, performers, places, and terms. Includes 24 guest essays by prominent artists.   ML102.O6M47

The new Grove dictionary of opera / ed. by Stanley Sadie. N.Y. : Grove's Dictionaries of Music , 1992. 4 v. : ill. **BJ251**

Latest of the dictionaries to be developed from *The new Grove dictionary of music and musicians* (BJ141); however, most articles are newly written. Signed articles, with bibliographies and work lists, cover all aspects of Western opera, including people, opera houses, traditions, terminology, liberettos, etc., as well as most opera-related genres. Individual operas are listed under their titles, rather than their composers. Non-Western musical drama is not included. Indexes to role names and to the first lines of arias, ensembles, etc., a list of contributors, and illustration acknowledgements comprise the appendixes.   ML102.O6N5

Pipers Enzyklopädie des Musiktheaters : Oper, Operette, Musical, Ballet / hrsg. von Carl Dahlhaus und dem Forschungsinstitut für Musiktheater der Universität Bayreuth unter Leitung von Sieghart Döhring. München : Piper, c1986-91. v. 1-4 : ill. (In progress).   **BJ252**

Contents: v. 1. Abbatini–Donizetti; v. 2. Donizetti–Henze; v. 3. Henze–Massine; v. 4, Massine–Piccine.

German-language encyclopedia of operas, operettas, musicals, and ballets focusing on works in the European tradition from its beginnings to the 20th century. To be complete in 8 volumes: v. 1–5, main listing of works; v. 6, Register/Nachträge; v. 7–8, Sachteil. Vols. 1–5 will contain an alphabetical listing of composers or choreographers with their works subarranged chronologically. Vol. 1 contains more than 1,000 titles for roughly 115 composers or choreographers. Each entry contains: birth and death information for the composer/choreographer, title of the work with its German translation if necessary, its text sources, librettists, first performance information, characters, orchestration, performance timings and stagings, background on the composition of the work, summary of contents, descriptive commentary, performance history, autograph and printed sources, and bibliography. Entries are signed; numerous illustrations (many in color).

ML102.O6P5

Rosenthal, Harold D. The concise Oxford dictionary of opera / by Harold Rosenthal and John Warrack. 2nd ed. London ; N.Y. : Oxford Univ. Pr., 1979. 561 p.   **BJ253**

1st ed., 1964; 2nd ed., with corrections, frequently reprinted.

Includes entries for terms and characters in opera; brief synopses of operas; and biographical notes on composers, conductors, directors, producers, and singers.

Intended as a "concise but comprehensive work of reference—and perhaps also one of some entertainment."—*Foreword.* A thorough revision and updating, with facts rechecked and errors corrected. Coverage of operatic activities is extended to all countries; more biographies of singers and composers are included; and the number of literary references has been expanded. Articles often cite standard works on the subject.   ML102.O6R67

Chronologies

Annals of the Metropolitan Opera Guild : the complete chronicle of performances and artists : chronology 1883–1985. N.Y. : Metropolitan Opera Guild ; Boston : G.K. Hall, 1989. 1000 p. : ill.   **BJ254**

Gerald Fitzgerald, ed. in chief.

Contains the "complete record of all performances by the company from October 1883 through June 1985."—*Pref.* 21,872 performances are grouped by their 100 seasons, including performances in New York and elsewhere. Vol. 1 contains the chronology of performance information; v. 2, indexes of performances, composers and librettists, production artists, performing artists, locations, broadcast performances, and translations. Supersedes William Seltsam's *Metropolitan Opera annals* (N.Y. : H.W. Wilson, 1947) and its supplements.

ML1711.8.N3M38

Loewenberg, Alfred. Annals of opera, 1597–1940 / comp. from the original sources by Alfred Loewenbert. 3rd ed. rev. & corr. Totowa, N.J. : Roman & Littlefield, 1978. 1756 col.   **BJ255**

1st ed., 1943; 2nd ed., 1955 (2 v.) repr. 1970.

Lists nearly 4,000 operas, arranged chronologically according to dates of first performance, followed by the name of the composer and title of the opera (titles are given in the form in which they first appeared and in the original language; except for Italian, French, and German titles, a translation has been included), name of town where first performed, sometimes name of theater, and a history of performances. References to translations, revivals, etc.

Indexes: (1) Operas; (2) Composers, with dates of birth and death, giving the names of operas by each and dates; (3) Librettists; and (4) General index.

The review in *Booklist* 77 (1 Apr. 1981): 119–20 notes that this is "scarcely more than a reprint of the 1970 volume," and concludes that "those having the 1955 edition would do well to wait for the promised supplement, which will list premieres and revivals from 1940 to date. But libraries not having an earlier edition might wish to acquire this ... and add the supplement when it appears." Unfortunately the supplement has yet to appear.   ML102.O6L6

Mattfeld, Julius. A handbook of American operatic premières, 1731–1962. [Detroit : Information Service], 1963. 142 p. (Detroit studies in music bibliography, no. 5).   **BJ256**

Listing is alphabetical by title; gives dates of U.S. premières of nearly 2,000 operas. Index of composers.   ML128.O4M3

Pitou, Spire. The Paris Opéra : an encyclopedia of operas, ballets, composers, and performers. Westport, Conn. : Greenwood, c1983–90. v. 1–3, in 4 v. (In progress).   **BJ257**

Contents: v. 1, Genesis and glory, 1671–1715; v. 2, Rococo and romantic, 1715–1815; v. 3, Growth and grandeur, 1815–1914 (2 v.).

An alphabetical listing of operas, ballets, singers, dancers, composers, choreographers, librettists, and scenarists connected with the Paris Opéra. Informative entries contain biographical information, synopses of dramatic action, asterisked cross-references to other articles, and bibliographies.   ML1727.8.P2P5

Musical theater

Bloom, Ken. American song : the complete musical theatre companion. N.Y. : Facts on File, c1985. 2 v.   **BJ258**

A compilation of information on nearly 3,300 American musicals, 1900–84. Vol. 1 contains an alphabetical listing by title with performance information, composers, lyricists, song titles, casts, etc.; v. 2 contains indexes by songs and personal names, as well as a chronological list. Covers the same subject as David Hummel's *The collector's guide to the American musical theatre* (Metuchen, N.J. : Scarecrow, 1984), but expands coverage to include non-New York performances, omits recordings, and offers more personal annotations.   ML128.M78B6

Bordman, Gerald Martin. American musical theatre : a chronicle. 2nd ed. N.Y. : Oxford Univ. Pr., 1992. 821 p.   **BJ259**

1st. ed., 1978. Expanded ed., with corrections, 1986.

Describes in lively, narrative style almost every musical to appear on Broadway through the 1989/90 season; for the period before World War I, coverage includes the musical theater in Boston, Philadelphia, and Chicago. The pre-1866 period is summarized, but the arrangement thereafter is by theater season. Following an overview of the season, musicals are presented by date of opening, with plot synopsis, performers' names, principal songs, and some estimate of the work's place in the history of the musical. Interspersed are brief biographical sketches of composers, playwrights, lyricists, actors, producers, and directors. New to this edition is an appendix incorporating information on a few dozen late 19th-century "farces" newly identified as musical comedies. An index of "shows and sources" lists the musicals with the titles of works on which they are based and gives a separate list of sources and the musicals based on them. Index of songs; index of personal names.   ML1711.B67

Diccionario de la zarzuela : biografias de compositores, argumentos y comentarios musicales sobre las principales zarzuelas del repertorio actual / R. Alier, X. Aviñoa, F. X. Mata. Madrid : Daimon, 1986. 386 p. : ill., ports.   **BJ260**

Focuses on some 100 composers of zarzuelas, primarily Spanish, as well as other individuals associated with the genre. Entries include biographical information, together with lengthy discussions of individual works for many composers. Concludes with a discography.

ML102.Z3D53

Ewen, David. New complete book of the American musical theater. N.Y. : Holt, Rinehart, and Winston, [1970]. 800 p. : ill., ports. **BJ261**

Earlier ed., 1958, publ. under title: *Complete book of the American musical theater.*

Covers almost 500 musicals, 1866–1970, in two sections. The first contains an alphabetical listing of musicals by title, with plot and production history, the second, biographies of the people involved with them, including librettists, lyricists, composers, etc. Concludes with two appendixes, a chronology of the musical theater, 1866–1970, and a list of outstanding songs with their shows and performers. Excludes most operas; includes some notable failures, e.g., *Allegro* and *Paint Your Wagon.* Name/title index. ML1711.E9

Gänzl, Kurt. Gänzl's book of the musical theatre / Kurt Gänzl and Andrew Lamb. N.Y. : Schirmer, 1989. 1353 p., [4] p. of plates : ill. **BJ262**

Publ. in U.K. : London : Bodley Head, 1988.

A companion to *Kobbé's complete opera book,* (BJ237) for the light musical theater. Contains production and performance information, characters, and plot summaries for more than 300 musicals organized by country, then chronologically. Selection based on current performance availability, artistic or historic significance, and the authors' preferences. Includes discography and two indexes: Titles, authors, composers, and lyricists; and Song titles. MT95.G2

Green, Stanley. Encyclopaedia of the musical theatre. N.Y. : Dodd, Mead, c1976. 488 p. **BJ263**

Repr. : N.Y. : Da Capo, 1984.

Offers "succinct information regarding the most prominent people, productions, and songs of the musical theater, both in New York (incl. off-Bway) and London."—*Pref.* Includes a list of awards and prizes (with recipients), a table of "long runs," a brief bibliography, and a discography. ML102.M88G7

———— Broadway musicals, show by show. 3rd ed. Milwaukee, Wis. : H. Leonard Books, 1990. 372 p. : ill. **BJ264**

1st ed., 1985; 2nd ed., 1987.

Contains information on approximately 300 shows presented both on and off Broadway, 1866–1975, arranged chronologically. For each, includes credits, brief description and history of the show, theater where it was performed, and photographs from the production. Criteria for inclusion were "length of run … seminal importance, people involved, uniqueness of approach or subject matter, quality of score, and general acceptance as a significant work in the field."—*Pref.* ML1711.G735

———— The world of musical comedy : the story of the American musical stage as told through the careers of its foremost composers and lyricists. 4th ed., rev. & enl. San Diego : A.S. Barnes, 1980. 480 p. : ill. **BJ265**

Repr. : N.Y. : Da Capo, 1984. "Supplemented with author's corrections."—*t.p. verso.*

1st ed., 1960.

Each chapter is devoted to one or more composers and lyricists, with detailed record of productions of works. Appendixes include a list of shows with data on production, casts, and discography. Index of names and titles.

Principal changes in this edition involve chapters 22–31, and reflect the rise of composers and lyricists who have made significant contributions since the previous revision. The appendix has been extensively revised and updated to include new shows and important new recordings of scores. ML1711.G74

Iglesias de Souza, Luis. El teatro lírico español. La Coruña, España : Excma. Diputación Provincial, 1991. v. 1 : ill. (In progress). **BJ266**

Contents: v. 1, A–E.

Comprehensive title listing of Spanish lyric theater works, 17th through 20th centuries. For each title, identifies specific genre, length, librettist, composer, theater, city, date of first performance, and printed or manuscript source. Performers are listed if known. Projected for three volumes.

Lewine, Richard. Songs of the theater / Richard Lewine, Alfred Simon. N.Y. : H.W. Wilson, 1984. 897 p. **BJ267**

Effectively supersedes the compilers' *Encyclopedia of theater music* (1961) and *Songs of the American theater* (1973). Covers songs, both published and unpublished, from 1891 through 1983. "In the early period … lists all the important shows and scores of the era, the balance of our musical stage at the time still being devoted to vaudeville and imported operetta. Beginning with the mid-teens the book includes the songs from virtually every theater piece seen on Broadway" (*Pref.*), plus songs from Off-Broadway shows that ran 15 or more performances, or that were of unusual interest. Title listing with name of composer and lyricist, plus name and date of the show in which the song appeared. Index of composers, lyricists and authors; alphabetical list of shows, with dates and musical numbers; chronology of shows; index of films and television productions. ML128.S3L55

Wildbihler, Hubert. The musical : an international annotated bibliography = eine internationale annotierte Bibliographie / by Hubert Wildbihler and Sonja Völklein. München ; N.Y. : Saur, 1986. 320 p. **BJ268**

Aims to present the "entire theoretical literature on the stage and film musical from its beginnings to 1986."—*Foreword.* Although international in scope, most citations follow the development of the genre, and are from Anglo-American sources. Entries number 3,629 items in five categories: General reference works, Stage musical, Stage musical outside North America, Film musical, and People. List of sources consulted; author and subject indexes.

§ An earlier version: *Internationale Musical-Bibliographie*, by Hubert Wildbihler and Gerhard Tischler (Landshut : Country Pr., 1981. [Musical-Dokumentation, 1]), has t.p. verso statement: "Das Bühnenmusical in den Vereinigten Staaten, Grossbritannien und Deutschland. Das Film-Musikal in den Vereinigten Staaten. Internationales, systematisches Auswahlverzeichnis selbständiger Literatur von den Anfängen bis zur Gegenwart." ML128.M78W56

Chamber music

Baron, John H. Chamber music : a research and information guide. N.Y. : Garland, 1987. 500 p. (Music research and information guides, vol. 8 ; Garland reference library of the humanities, vol. 704). **BJ269**

An annotated bibliography of 1,600 items, most written after 1950. Entries are listed under six broad subjects, many with subdivisions. The most important works are listed first in each category; the remainder appear to be in random order. Helpful cross-references. Contains indexes by subjects, persons, authors, and chamber groups. ML128.C4B37

Cobbett, Walter Wilson. Cyclopedic survey of chamber music / comp. and ed. by Walter Willson Cobbet with supplementary material ed. by Colin Mason. 2nd ed. N.Y. ; London : Oxford Univ. Pr., 1963. 3v. **BJ270**

1st ed., 1929–30 (2 v.).

Vols. 1–2 of the 2nd ed. are reissues of the 1929–30 edition except for a few amendments to the text, and the insertion of symbols in the margin to indicate a further reference in v. 3.

The first two volumes contain signed articles (in alphabetical arrangement) on subjects concerned with chamber music: topics, persons, instruments, organizations, etc.; biographies, with lists of composers' works, are included. Vol. 3 is a selective survey of chamber music since 1929, with a bibliography, additions and corrections to the original edition, and an index of composers. ML1100.C7

Songs

Ewen, David. American songwriters. N.Y. : H.W. Wilson, 1987. 489 p. : ports. **BJ271**

Replaces the author's *Popular American composers from revolutionary times to the present* (N.Y. : H.W. Wilson, 1962) and its 1st suppl. (1972). Contains lengthy biographies of 90 composers and 50 lyricists or composer/lyricists, along with the performance history of some individual songs. Index to the 5,600 compositions mentioned. Bibliographical references.   ML390.E825

Hovland, Michael A. Musical settings of American poetry : a bibliography. Westport, Conn. : Greenwood, 1986. 531 p. (Music reference collection, no. 8).   **BJ272**

Contains 5,800 settings by 2,100 composers of the poems of 99 prominent American authors. Selective coverage of collections and hymns; some discographies are listed. Composer and literary title index.   ML128.V7H67

Seaton, Douglass. The art song : a research and information guide. N.Y. : Garland, 1987. 273 p. (Music research and information guides, vol. 6 ; Garland reference library of the humanities, vol. 673).   **BJ273**

An annotated bibliography of 970 items, including monographs, journal articles, and dissertations published during the 20th century. Annotations are brief and summary; entries are organized in eight useful categories: General studies, Individual composers, Individual poets, Aesthetics and analysis, Texts and translations, Performance, Bibliographies, and Sources. A brief historical overview of the art song precedes the bibliography. Name and subject indexes.   ML128.S3S33

Studwell, William E. Christmas carols : a reference guide. N.Y. : Garland, 1985. 278 p.   **BJ274**

Approximately 800 carols pertaining to Christmas and adjacent events from 171 anthologies are indexed. Each entry contains brief information on creator, place, and date for both text and music, along with pertinent supplementary notes. Title, person, and group indexes.   ML102.C3S9

Bibliography

Day, Cyrus Lawrence. English song-books, 1651–1702 : a bibliography with a first-line index of songs / by Cyrus Lawrence Day and Eleanore Boswell Murrie. London : pr. for the Bibliographical Society at the Univ. Pr., Oxford, 1940. 439 p. : ill.   **BJ275**

"The aim of this volume is to list, describe and index all the secular song-books published in England and Scotland between 1651 and 1702. The term secular song-book, as it is here somewhat arbitrarily used, means any publication containing the words and music of two or more secular songs."—*Introd.*

A detailed chronological bibliography of 252 numbered items, with indexes by first lines and by composers, authors, singers and actors, tunes and airs, sources, songbooks, printers, publishers, and booksellers.

§ Overlapping chronologically, but with emphasis on a particular genre is Joan Swanekamp's *English ayres : a selectively annotated bibliography and discography* (Westport, Conn. : Greenwood, 1984. 141 p.).   ML120.G7D31

Edwards, J. Michele. Literature for voices in combination with electronic and tape music : an annotated bibliography. Ann Arbor : Music Libr. Assoc., 1977. 194 p. (MLA index and bibliography series, no. 17).   **BJ276**

A listing of 400 compositions for at least three live performers who sing or speak "in combination with electronic and tape music ... from the earliest known works through 1975 .... Second, the bibliography is a finding list of compositions currently available to performers."—*Pref.* Arranged by composer, with "Index by medium" (e.g., mixed choir, mixed choir and keyboard, etc.). Directory of addresses for publishers, non-score sources, foreign and hard-to-find record labels, studios. Selected bibliography of sources.   ML128.E4E37

Ewen, David. American popular songs from the Revolutionary War to the present. N.Y. : Random House, [1966]. 507 p.   **BJ277**

A title listing of more than 3,600 popular songs, with indication of composer, lyricist, date, and films or musical productions in which the song may have been featured. A list of American performers and some of the songs associated with them is appended.   ML128.N3E9

Gooch, Bryan N. S. Musical settings of early and mid-Victorian literature : a catalogue / Bryan N. S. Gooch, David S. Thatcher. N.Y. : Garland, 1979. 946 p. (Garland reference library of the humanities, v. 149).   **BJ278**

A companion to the same compilers' *Musical settings of late Victorian and modern British literature* (BJ279), but covering "published and unpublished settings of texts by prominent British authors who were, for the most part, born after 1800 and who lived to 1850 or later."—*Pref.* Follows the plan of the companion volume; cutoff date for published settings is 1977. Index of composers and one of titles and first lines.   ML128.V7G58

——————— Musical settings of late Victorian and modern British literature : a catalogue / Bryan N. S. Gooch, David S. Thatcher. N.Y. : Garland, 1976. 1112 p. (Garland reference library of the humanities, v. 31).   **BJ279**

A companion to the same compilers' *Musical settings of early and mid-Victorian literature* (BJ278).

A listing of texts set to music (both published and unpublished) up to July 1975. All authors included are British or "sufficiently identified with the English literary tradition" (*Pref.*), and all were "born after 1840 and lived to 1900 or later." Arranged by literary author, with each text identified by title, first line or literary form, and date of first publication; this is followed by the composer's name, the setting and publication information thereof, vocal specifications, and accompaniment. Indexes of authors and composers.   ML120.G7G66

Lowens, Irving. A bibliography of songsters printed in America before 1821. Worcester, Mass. : American Antiquarian Society, 1976. 229 p.   **BJ280**

A songster is defined as "a collection of three or more secular poems intended to be sung."—*Introd.* These 650 collections are listed chronologically by title, alphabetically within each year. Geographical directory of printers, publishers, booksellers, engravers; index of compilers, authors, proprietors, and editors; title index. Locations are indicated for each collection.   ML128.S3L7

Discography

Stahl, Dorothy. A selected discography of solo song : a cumulation through 1971. Detroit : Information Coordinators, 1972. 137 p. (Detroit studies in music bibliography, 24).   **BJ281**

1st ed., 1968.

Provides a listing by composer, title, and first line, of recordings featuring classical songs for the solo voice.

Supplements cover 1971–74 (1976. 99 p. [Detroit studies in music bibliography, 34]) and 1975–82 (1984. 236 p. [Detroit studies in music bibliography, 52]).

Indexes

Chipman, John H. Index to top-hit tunes, 1900–1950. Boston : B. Humphries, [1962]. 249 p.   **BJ282**

Contains 3,000 titles of American popular songs which have sold at least 100,000 copies of sheet music or 100,000 records. Listed by title alphabetically, and chronologically. Gives composer, publisher, and date; also indicates if featured in a film or musical.

     ML128.V7C54

Cushing, Helen Grant. Children's song index : an index to more than 22,000 songs in 189 collections comprising 222 volumes. N.Y. : H.W. Wilson, 1936. 798 p.   **BJ283**

Repr.: St. Clair Shores, Mich. : Scholarly Pr., 1977.

In general, similar in plan to Minnie Earl Sears's *Song index* (BJ289), except that subject entries are added. Main entry, with full information, is under title, with cross-references from alternate titles, different titles in different collections, translated titles, and original titles in certain languages (e.g., Russian), and from first lines and sometimes first line of chorus; and with added entries under composer of music, author of words, and subject.   ML128.S3C9

DeCharms, Désirée. Songs in collections : an index / Désirée DeCharms, Paul F. Breed. [Detroit] : Information Service, 1966. 588 p.   **BJ284**

Indexes 9,493 songs in 411 collections, with separate sections for composed songs, anonymous and folk songs, carols, and sea chanteys. Index to all titles and first lines, and an author index. A useful complement to Sears's *Song index* (BJ289).   ML128.S3D37

Havlice, Patricia Pate. Popular song index. Metuchen, N.J. : Scarecrow, 1975. 933 p.   **BJ285**

301 song books published between 1940 and 1972 are here indexed as an aid to finding both the words and music of folk songs, popular tunes, spirituals, hymns, children's songs, sea chanteys, and blues. Index by title, first line of song, and first line of chorus; index of composers and lyricists.

Three supplements (1978, 368 p.; 1984, 530 p.; 1989, 875 p.) follow the plan of the basic volume, covering song books published to 1987, while picking up a few titles published earlier.   ML128.S3H4

Lax, Roger. The great song thesaurus / Roger Lax, Frederick Smith. 2nd ed., updated and expanded. N.Y. : Oxford Univ. Pr., 1989. 774 p.   **BJ286**

1st ed., 1984.

A compendium of various lists (e.g., a chronology of "greatest" songs from the 16th century to the present; award winners; lyricists and composers with titles of their songs), the most extensive being of song titles (with a separate section for British titles). The "thesaurus" aspect of the work is provided by section IX, Thesaurus of song titles by subject, key word, and category, which permits finding the full title, date, and composer of a song of which only a portion of the title or the subject is known. This edition contains an additional section listing key lines of many popular song lyrics with their titles.   ML128.S3L4

Leigh, Robert. Index to song books. Stockton, Calif., 1964. 237 p.   **BJ287**

Repr. : N.Y. : Da Capo Pr., 1973.

Subtitle: A title index to over 11,000 copies of almost 6,800 songs in 111 song books published [in the United States] between 1933 and 1962.

A title index to songs in books containing words and music. No entries for authors or composers. Serves as a partial continuation of Minnie Earl Sears's *Song index* (BJ289).   ML128.S3L45

Rabson, Carolyn. National tune index microfiche : 18th-century secular music / by Carolyn Rabson and Kate Van Winkle Keller [microform]. N.Y. : Univ. Music Editions, 1980. 80 microfiche.   **BJ288**

Includes a user's guide.

Almost 40,000 examples of British and American secular tunes gathered from 500 18th-century sources have been indexed by computer to "help identify the tunes and song texts, to suggest their relationship to one another, and to lead the researcher directly to the original sources."—*Pref.* The index is arranged as follows: (1) text index (title, first line, indicated tune name, burden index—usually the first line of the refrain or chorus); (2) music index (scale degrees, stressed notes, interval sequence); (3) source index (ballad operas, dance collections, instrumental collections, manuscripts, Playford's *Dancing master* 1651–1728, song collections, song sheets, theater works).

The second phase has been publ. as: Raoul F. Camus, comp., *The national tune index : early American wind and ceremonial music, 1636–1836* [microform] (N.Y. : Univ. Music Editions, 1989. 29 microfiches). Includes a user's guide.   ML120.U5R12

Sears, Minnie Earl. Song index : an index to more than 12,000 songs in 177 song collections comprising 262 volumes / ed. by M. E. Sears, assisted by Phyllis Crawford. N.Y. : Wilson, 1926. 650 p.   **BJ289**

Repr. with suppl. : Hamden, Conn. : Shoe String Pr., 1966.

An important index, useful in public, college, or school libraries, as well as in music libraries. Contains titles, first lines, authors' names, and composers' names in one alphabet. Each song is indexed fully under its title, with added entry under composer and author, and cross-references from first line and from variant or translated titles. Useful for finding: (1) words and music of a wanted song; (2) lists of songs by a given author or composer; (3) authorship of a poem when only its title or first line is known; and (4) whether or not a song has been translated, or is itself a translation, etc. Since many songs were originally poems which have been set to music, this index serves also as an index to poetry, especially for poems and translations not included in *The Columbia Granger's index to poetry* (BE315).

————. ————. *Supplement : an index to more than 7,000 songs in 104 song collections comprising 124 volumes* (N.Y. : Wilson, 1934. 367 p.).

Choral music

Bryden, John Rennie. An index of Gregorian chant / John Rennie Bryden, David G. Hughes. Cambridge : Harvard Univ. Pr., 1969. 2 v.   **BJ290**

Contents: v. 1, Alphabetical index; v. 2, Thematic index.

"The *Index* attempts to cover that portion of the chant that was in general use for a considerable period of time" and "draws its material from the modern printed chant books, from five selected manuscripts, and from certain special studies dealing with specific categories of chant."—*Introd.*   ML102.C45B8

DeVenney, David P. Nineteenth-century American choral music : an annotated guide. Berkeley, Calif. : Fallen Leaf Pr., 1987. 182 p. (Fallen Leaf reference books in music, no. 8).   **BJ291**

"Lists choral music by composers who were active in the United States during the nineteenth century and died or ceased composing after the end of the First World War (ca. 1920)."—*Pref.* The 24 composers are arranged alphabetically, with an alphabetical subarrangement by titles of works. Brief annotations include publisher, repository, and other information. Contains an annotated bibliography of 134 items and several indexes by author, genre, etc.

§ A companion is the author's *Early American choral music : an annotated guide* (Berkeley, Calif. : Fallen Leaf Press, 1988), which lists choral music by 32 composers active from about 1670 to 1825.   ML128.C48D48

May, James D. Avant-garde choral music : an annotated selected bibliography. Metuchen, N.J. : Scarecrow, 1977. 258 p.   **BJ292**

An "annotated bibliography of avant-garde choral compositions readily available from the music publishers of the United States" (*Pref.*) intended for use of high school, church, college and university choral directors. Gives full publishing information, voice requirements, accompaniment, supplementary requirements. Indexed.   ML128.V7M43

Orchestral music

Goodenberger, Jennifer. Subject guide to classical instrumental music. Metuchen, N.J. : Scarecrow, 1989. 163 p.
BJ293

Guide to nonmusical subjects represented in the standard concert repertory, primarily from the 19th century. Musical compositions are listed under 208 subject categories, many of which are further subdivided.   ML128.I65G59

Rehrig, William H. The heritage encyclopedia of band music : composers and their music / by William H. Rehrig ; ed. by Paul E. Bierley. Westerville, Ohio : Integrity Pr., c1991. 2 v.   **BJ294**

"An attempt to document all editions of all music ever published (and some unpublished) for concert and military bands."—*Publisher's Introd.* Includes music composed expressly for band, as well as music adapted for band use. Not included are "British-style brass band works," works of anonymous composers, medleys of songs arranged for special events, works of composers who did not respond to queries, or football marching band shows. Entries organized alphabetically by composer, with brief biographies, references, and lists of works. The authors acknowledge that non-Western composers are underrepresented. The authors claim little overlap with entries in other music encyclopedias and dictionaries.   ML102.B35R4

Stedman, Preston. The symphony : a research and information guide. N.Y. : Garland, 1990. v. 1. (In progress).   **BJ295**

A projected three-volume set. Vol. 1, an annotated bibliography of 931 books, articles, and dissertations on the 18th-century symphony, offers entries with brief, summary annotations, divided into three section: general resources; the symphony; and national activities, including individual countries and composers. Future volumes are to cover the 19th and 20th centuries.   ML128.S9S7

Symphony orchestras of the United States : selected profiles / ed. by Robert R. Craven. N.Y. : Greenwood, c1986. 521 p.
BJ296

Lists approximately 125 leading symphony orchestras in the U.S. geographically by state and city. Signed entries give background information, chronology of music directors, bibliography, and mailing address.

§ A related work is the author's *Symphony orchestras of the world : selected profiles* (N.Y. : Greenwood, 1987. 468 p.), covering 122 orchestras from 44 countries.   ML1211.S95

Jazz

Carl Gregor, *Duke of Mecklenburg.* International jazz bibliography : jazz books from 1919 to 1968. Strasbourg : P.H. Heitz, 1969. 198 p. (Sammlung musikwissenschaftlicher Abhandlungen (Valentin Koerner GmbH), v. 49.).   **BJ297**

Intended for "the serious friend of Jazz, the Jazz musician and the musicologist."—*Introd.* An author listing of more than 1,500 items, with indexes of names, countries, and subjects.

Supplements for 1970 and 1971–73 were published as Bd. 3 and Bd. 6, respectively, of *Beiträge zur Jazzforschung = Studies in jazz research* (Graz : Universal Edition, 1971–75).

Revised and expanded by: *International bibliography of jazz books,* by Carl Gregor, Herzog zu Mecklenburg ; comp. with the assistance of Norbert Ruecker (Baden-Baden : Koerner, 1983–88. v. 1–2. [In progress]).

Contents: v. 1, 1921–1949; v. 2, 1950–1959.

Planned to cover 1921–79 in 4 v. Vols. 1–2 contain 823 titles and 55 "phantom" titles. Entries, arranged alphabetically by author, with titles listed chronologically, contain references to *IJB* or its supplements, source of entry, and contributor. Several indexes and chronology.   ML128.J3C4

Carner, Gary. Jazz performers : an annotated bibliography of biographical materials. N.Y. : Greenwood, 1990. 364 p. (Music reference collection, no. 26).   **BJ298**

First publ. as "A bibliography of jazz and blues biographical literature" in *Black American literature forum* 20 (1986) : 161–202.

Attempts to provide biographical information on jazz performers from "all book and scholarly materials related to jazz lives" (*Pref.*), including jazz books, theses, dissertations, and scholarly journal articles, from 1921 to the present. Criteria for inclusion is whether an artist exemplifies the oral tradition of jazz playing and has led a "jazz life"; performers solely from the legitimate concert tradition are not included. The main listing is alphabetical by performer, with bibliographical references subarranged alphabetically by author. The sources used are organized in several lists. Author and subject indexes.

ML128.B3C37

Carr, Ian. Jazz : the essential companion / Ian Carr, Digby Fairweather, Brian Priestley. N.Y. : Prentice Hall, 1988. 562 p. : ports.   **BJ299**

Primarily a biographical dictionary of individuals, but also contains terms relevant to mainstream jazz from its beginnings through 1986. International in scope. Entries generally are brief, with discographies and bibliographical references, and are sometimes uneven, since the entries are written by one of the three author/musicians.

ML102.J3C32

Feather, Leonard G. The encyclopedia of jazz. Rev. and enl. ed. N.Y. : Horizon Pr., c1960. 527 p. : ill.   **BJ300**

Repr. : N.Y. : DaCapo Pr., 1984.

1st ed., 1955; supplementary yearbooks were issued 1956–58, with varying titles.

Contains biographical sketches of more than 2,000 jazz musicians, with a guide to their recordings, history of jazz on records, recommended jazz records, bibliography, and discography.

——— *The encyclopedia of jazz in the sixties* (N.Y. : Horizon Pr., [1966]. 1 v., unpaged. Repr. : N.Y. : Da Capo, 1986). Serves as a companion to Feather's basic encyclopedia, updating many biographies and adding new ones.

——— *The encyclopedia of jazz in the seventies,* with Ira Gitler (N.Y. : Horizon Pr., [1976]. 393 p. Repr. : N.Y. : Da Capo Pr., 1987?). Extends coverage through 1966–75, adding new names and updating earlier sketches. Adds results of polls published in *Down beat* and *Swing journal,* 1966–75; lists of jazz films and recommended recordings; and a brief bibliography.   ML102.J3F4

Gray, John. Fire music : a bibliography of the new jazz, 1959–1990. N.Y. : Greenwood, 1991. 515 p. (Music reference collection, no. 31).   **BJ301**

Presents more than 7,000 references to books, dissertations, periodical and newspaper articles, films, and videos in English and Western European languages. The majority of the citations refer to individual artists. The remainder are organized into the following sections: New jazz chronology, African-American cultural history and the arts, General works and regional studies on the new jazz, Jazz collectives, and the New York loft and club scene. Concludes with four appendixes: Reference works, both general and jazz-related; Archives and research centers, including directory information as well as bibliographical citations; Performers and ensembles by country; and Performers by instrument. Artist, subject, and author indexes.   ML128.J3G7

Hefele, Bernhard. Jazz-bibliography = Jazz-Bibliographie. München ; N.Y. : Saur, 1981. 368 p.   **BJ302**

Subtitle: International literature on jazz, blues, spirituals, gospel and ragtime music with a selected list of works on the social and cultural background from the beginning to the present.

Introductory matter in English and German; section headings in German.

A classed arrangement of about 6,600 items—books and periodical articles, predominantly English and German. Name index.

ML128.J3H43

Jazz index. Jahrg. 1 (1977)–7 (1983). [Frankfurt am Main [etc] : N. Ruecker], 1977–[c1987].   **BJ303**
Frequency varied.
Comp. by Norbert Ruecker and Christa Reggentin-Scheidt.
Introductory matter in English and German; subject headings in English only beginning with v. 2.
Regularly indexed articles and reviews on jazz in more than 50 journals, with selective indexing of other journals carrying occasional articles on jazz. Beginning with v. 2, record reviews were dropped, but book and concert reviews continued to be included. Articles on "blues" are listed in a separate section beginning with v. 2.
ML128.J3J4

Kennington, Donald. The literature of jazz : a critical guide / Donald Kennington, Danny L. Read. 2nd ed., rev. Chicago : Amer. Libr. Assoc., 1980. 236 p.   **BJ304**
1st ed., 1971.
Selective, but aims to list "all the significant material published in English up to the end of 1979."—*Introd.* Periodical articles are not included, but there is a list of jazz periodicals. Chapters are presented in the form of bibliographic essays on specific aspects of the literature, with a full bibliography at the end of each chapter. Name and title indexes. Chapters on blues and on jazz education are new to this edition.
ML128.J3K45

Merriam, Alan P. A bibliography of jazz / by Alan P. Merriam ; with the assistance of Robert J. Brenford. Philadelphia : American Folklore Soc., 1954. 145 p. (Publications of the American Folklore Society. Bibliographical series, v. 4).
BJ305
Repr. : N.Y. : Kraus, 1970.
Contains 3,324 items, arranged alphabetically by author, followed by a list of periodicals devoted to jazz, a subject index, and an index to periodical entries cited. Very useful for literature published to the mid-1950s.   ML128.J3M4

The new Grove dictionary of jazz / ed. by Barry Kernfeld. London : Macmillan ; N.Y. : Grove's Dictionaries of Music, 1988. 2 v. : ill.   **BJ306**
A comprehensive dictionary covering all periods and styles of jazz from many countries. Although it draws on other Grove dictionaries, 90% of the material is newly written. Articles cover individuals, groups and bands, topics and terms, instruments, record companies and labels, and institutions; they are signed, and include bibliographies and selected discographies. Extensive bibliography on jazz and list of contributors in appendixes.   ML102.J3N48

Discography

Bruyninckx, Walter. [Sixty years of recorded jazz]. [s.l. : s.n., 1980?]. v. 4, pts. 7–8. (In progress).   **BJ307**
Originally issued as: *50 years of recorded jazz*, 40 v. (Mechelen, Belgium : the author, 1967–75).
Designed for the collector, but sufficiently comprehensive for the jazz scholar. Entries are arranged by name of performer or group, with brief biographical or historical information, as well as extensive discographies. Artist index.
§ A complementary work by the same author focusing specifically on vocalists: *Jazz : the vocalists, 1917–1986 : the singers and crooners* (Mechelen : Copy Express, 1988? 4 v.). The author's discographies include: *Traditional jazz : origins, New Orleans, Dixieland, Chicago styles* (Mechelen : 60 Years of Recorded Jazz Team, 1986?–88? 6 v.); *Modern jazz : modern big band* (1986? 6 v.); *Progressive jazz : free—third stream fusion* (1984?–87? 5 v.); and *Jazz : modern jazz, be-bop, hard bop, West Coast* (1985?–87? 6 v.).
ML156.4.J3B85

Harrison, Max. The essential jazz records / Max Harrison, Charles Fox, and Eric Thacker. Westport, Conn. : Greenwood, 1984. 1 v. (Discographies, no. 12). (In progress).   **BJ308**

Repr. : N.Y. : Da Capo, 1988.
Contents: v. 1, Ragtime to swing.
The first of two volumes intended to provide a selective, critical guide to recorded jazz. Organized chronologically, v. 1 covers the origins through the 1930s. The 250 signed entries each include recording information, performers, and a critical essay. Indexes of LP titles, tune titles, and musicians.   ML156.4.J3H33

Rust, Brian A. L. Jazz records, 1897–1942. 5th rev. and enl. ed. Chigwell, Essex : Storyville Publ., [1982]. 2 v. (1996 p.).
BJ309
1st ed., 1961; [4th] ed., 1978. Some editions publ. under title *Jazz records, A–Z* as two separate works covering 1897–1931 and 1932–1942.
Contains an alphabetical listing of performers heard on recordings of jazz music, dance music affiliated with jazz, and vocal recordings with jazz groups used as accompaniment made 1917–42, together with some ragtime recordings from 1897. Artist and title indexes.
ML156.4.J3R9

Electronic music

Cary, Tristram. Dictionary of musical technology. N.Y. : Greenwood, 1992. 542 p. : ill.   **BJ310**
A dictionary of terms related to all aspects of music technology, commercial and noncommercial. Definitions are technically focused, but reflect an informed historical perspective. Many are presented in the context of nonelectronic music instruments to provide a frame of reference for musically literate but technically inexpert readers. Many entries contain bibliographical references, as well as extensive illustrations. Excludes audiovisual media.
§ A similar work is Richard Dobson, *A dictionary of electronic and computer music technology : instruments, terms, techniques* (Oxford : Oxford Univ. Pr., 1992). An alphabetical listing of terms, with shorter, primarily technical definitions, focusing exclusively on commercially available instruments. Includes some historical aspects, but lacks bibliographic references.   ML102.E4C37

Davies, Hugh. Répertoire international des musiques électroacoustiques = International electronic music catalog. Cambridge, Mass. : M.I.T. Pr., [1968]. 330 p.   **BJ311**
"A cooperative publication of le Groupe de recherches musicales de l'O. R.T.F., Paris and the Independent Electronic Music Center, New York."—*t.p.*
Intends as far as possible "to document all the electronic music ever composed in the almost twenty years since composers first began to work in this medium."—*Compiler's pref.* Listing is by country, then by city and studio.   ML128.E4D39

Schwartz, Elliott Shelling. Electronic music : a listener's guide. Rev. ed. N.Y. : Praeger, [1975]. 306 p. : ill.   **BJ312**
Repr. : N.Y. : Da Capo, 1989.
1st ed., 1973.
Aims "to make the basic facts of electronic music as clear as possible for the typical 'listener'—the person who cares about music and its development but has little or no background in either the art of music or the science of electronics."—*Pref.* In addition to historical and introductory material includes a section of "Observations by composers," a section on tape composition at home, and a selected bibliography and discography. Indexed.   ML1092.S37

Tomlyn, Bo. Electronic music dictionary : a glossary of the specialized terms relating to the music and sound technology of today / by Bo Tomlyn & Steve Leonard. Milwaukee, Wis. : H. Leonard Books, c1988. 77 p.   **BJ313**
Intended as a "practical, every-day glossary to the basic concepts of synthesizers, amplification, MIDI, computers and the physics of sound."—*Foreword.* Approximately 400 terms are listed alphabetical-

ly with definitions, references to related terms, and the general category or subject to which the term belongs in the context of electronic music. ML102.E4T65

Folk and traditional music

Bronson, Bertrand Harris. The traditional tunes of the Child ballads : with their texts according to the extant records of Great Britain and America. Princeton, N.J. : Princeton Univ. Pr., 1959–72. 4 v. **BJ314**

An exhaustive, scholarly work including all known variants of the texts. Each ballad preceded by historical notes. Vol. 4 includes a section of addenda to v. 1–4 (p. 437–513); a list of printed works and manuscripts referred to in the compilation; and indexes of sources, of tunes and ballads quoted, of singers, of authors and titles cited, and of persons referred to in various other capacities.

§ For Francis James Child's *English and Scottish popular ballads*, see: BE632. ML3650.B82

Brunnings, Florence E. Folk song index : a comprehensive guide to the Florence E. Brunnings collection. N.Y. : Garland, 1981. lxxxi, 357 p. (Garland reference library of the humanities, v. 252). **BJ315**

A title index of some 49,399 songs in the compiler's personal collection of 1,115 books and journals and 695 records. Includes references from variant titles. ML128.F75B83

Cooper, B. Lee. A resource guide to themes in contemporary American song lyrics, 1950–1985. N.Y. : Greenwood, 1986. 458 p. **BJ316**

Lists more than 3,000 popular recordings organized by 15 social, political, and personal themes. A brief essay introducing each general theme is followed by subject subdivisions with record title/performer listings. Song title and recording artist indexes. ML156.4.P6C66

Gray, John. African music : a bibliographical guide to the traditional, popular, art, and liturgical musics of Sub-Saharan Africa. Westport, Conn. : Greenwood, 1991. 499 p. (African special bibliographic series, no. 14). **BJ317**

Contains 5,802 bibliographical entries focusing on ethnographic, anthropological, musicological, and popular studies of sub-Saharan African music from the 1890s to the present. All entries have been verified by the author. Organized into six sections, primarily by genre (popular music, art music, etc.) with some geographical subarrangements. Three appendixes list reference works, archives and research centers, and selected discography. Ethnic group, subject, artist, and author indexes. ML120.A35G7

Kaufmann, Walter. Selected musical terms of non Western cultures : a notebook-glossary. Warren, Mich. : Harmonie Park Pr., 1990. 806 p. (Detroit studies in music bibliography, no. 65). **BJ318**

Terms are listed alphabetically, giving country of origin, brief definitions, and source abbreviations. Sources include 321 items of varying currency, since the glossary was compiled over a 50-year period, albeit by a noted scholar. ML108.K37

Kunst, Jaap. Ethnomusicology : a study of its nature, its problems, methods and representative personalities. 3rd enl. ed. The Hague : Nijhoff, 1959. 303 p. : ill. **BJ319**

Repr. with suppl. 1974.

1st ed., 1950, had title: *Musicologica*.

Contains bibliography (p. 79–215) consisting of books and articles published before Sept. 1958 on music and musical instruments of non-Western people, on ancient and early European music and music instruments, and on Western folk music. Includes some 5,000 entries. Locates copies. Has indexes of subjects; peoples and regions studied; authors; collectors; musicians; and periodicals.

————. ————. *Supplement* (The Hague : Nijhoff, 1960. 45 p.). Adds additional titles to the bibliography, all issued before Sept. 1958.

Lawless, Ray McKinley. Folksingers and folksongs in America : a handbook of biography, bibliography, and discography. New rev. ed with special suppl. N.Y. : Duell, [1965]. 750 p. **BJ320**

Repr. : Westport, Conn. : Greenwood, 1981.

Previous ed., 1960.

The original volume is here reprinted, with a supplement which updates the earlier material and is separately indexed.

Offers a variety of useful material on the subject, including biographical sketches of singers; an annotated bibliography of collections of folk songs; checklists of titles and discography; and chapters on instruments, societies, and festivals. Indexes of names, titles, and subjects. ML3550.L4

Library of Congress. Music Division. Folk music : catalog of folk songs, ballads, dances, instrumental pieces, and folk tales of United States and Latin America on phonograph records. Wash. : Music Div., Recording Laboratory, Ref. Dept., Library of Congress : for sale by U.S. Govt. Print. Off., 1964. 107 p. **BJ321**

Similar catalogs were issued at irregular intervals beginning 1943.

Lists 166 discs containing 1,240 titles, representative of the best of more than 16,000 records in the collection of the Archive of Folk Song. Contains selections from and supplements the Archive's *Checklist of recorded songs in the English language…* (BJ327). ML156.4.F5U5

McLean, Mervyn. An annotated bibliography of Oceanic music and dance. Wellington : Polynesian Soc., 1977. 252 p. (Polynesian Society. Memoir, 41). **BJ322**

Lists nearly 2,200 books, journals, articles, reviews, record notes, theses, and manuscripts relating to music, musical instruments, song texts, and dance in Oceania (i.e., "all islands of the Pacific, together with New Guinea and nearby islands including Torres Strait"—*Introd.*). Excludes Australia, Malaysia, the Philippines, and Indonesia. Materials are in English, French, German, Italian, and Spanish. Arranged alphabetically by author; the annotation includes a geographic or cultural area code based on George Peter Murdock's *Outline of world cultures* (CE59).

§ *Supplement : an annotated bibliography of Oceanic music and dance* (Auckland : Polynesian Soc., 1981. 74 p. [Polynesian Society, Wellington. Memoirs, no. 41, suppl.]). Adds more than 500 citations.

Nettl, Bruno. Reference materials in ethnomusicology : a bibliographic essay. 2nd ed., rev. Detroit : Information Coordinators, 1967. 40 p. (Detroit studies in music bibliography, no.1). **BJ323**

1st ed., 1961.

"Not a survey of research studies but rather a summary of surveys and compendia, and an attempt to provide substitutes where surveys do not exist."—*Pref.* Full citations to the publications mentioned in the essay are listed at the end of the work. ML128.E8N5

Sandberg, Larry. The folk music sourcebook / Larry Sandberg and Dick Weissman. New, updated ed. N.Y. : Da Capo Pr., c1989. 272 p. : ill. **BJ324**

Earlier ed., 1976.

Sponsored by the Denver Folklore Center.

Aims to "provide the reader with information about all aspects of North American folk and folk-based music."—*Pref.* Includes an annotated listing of records, books, and other instructional materials currently in print; information on buying and caring for folk instruments; lists of important folk festivals, archives, periodicals, films, folklore centers; and a glossary. Index of names, with a few topical entries. New material in this edition includes sectional overviews, bibliographies, and guides to resources. ML12.S26

Schuursma, Ann Briegleb. Ethnomusicology research : a select annotated bibliography. N.Y. : Garland, 1992. 173 p. (Garland library of music ethnology, 1 ; Garland reference library of the humanities, v. 1136). **BJ325**

Provides a guide to the "most significant and representative recent literature in the field of ethnomusicology."—*Pref.* Contains 468 citations of books and articles with informative annotations organized in five categories: history of the field; theory and method; fieldwork method and technique; musical analysis; and sources from related fields. Name and subject indexes.   ML128.E8S4

Stambler, Irwin. The encyclopedia of folk, country, & western music / Irwin Stambler, Grelun Landon. 2nd ed. N.Y. : St. Martin's, [1983]. 902 p. : ill.   **BJ326**
> 1st ed., 1969.
> An alphabetical arrangement of articles on individual performers and performing groups is followed by a section listing awards and a selected bibliography.   ML102.F66S7

Discography

Archive of Folk Song (U.S.). Check-list of recorded songs in the English language in the Archive of American Folk Song to July, 1940 : alphabetical list with geographical index. Wash., 1942. 3 v.   **BJ327**
> Repr.: N.Y. : Arno, 1971.
> The alphabetical list, comprising v.1–2, gives title, name of singer, collector, and place and date of recording. Vol. 3 is a geographical index of titles, arranged by state and county.   ML156.U5A72

Indiana University. Archives of Traditional Music. A catalog of phonorecordings of music and oral data held by the Archives of Traditional Music. Boston : G.K. Hall, [1975]. 541 p.   **BJ328**
> Photoreproduction of the classified catalog for a collection of materials "transmitted in the main by performance or word of mouth," which in music features "folk music, music of non-literate societies, non-European classical or art music, and popular music. Among the verbal forms ... are folktales, jokes, proverbs, interviews. ..."—*Pref.* Listing is by code (i.e., classification) number, with a note for each entry indicating geographic area or culture group, name of collector and date, and HRAF number based on George Peter Murdock's *Outline of world cultures* (CE59). Indexes of geographic or cultural areas, subjects, collectors, performers, informants, and recording companies.   ML156.2.I53

Spottswood, Richard K. Ethnic music on records : a discography of ethnic recordings produced in the United States, 1893 to 1942. Urbana : Univ. of Illinois Pr., c1990. 7 v. : ill. **BJ329**
> Contents: v. 1, Western Europe; v. 2, Slavic; v. 3, Eastern Europe; v. 4, Spanish, Portuguese, Philippine, Basque; v. 5, Mid-East, Far East, Scandinavian, English language, American Indian, international; v. 6, Artist and title indexes; v. 7, Record and matrix number indexes.
> A comprehensive discography, produced with cooperation and assistance of the Library of Congress, of all foreign-language recordings produced in the U.S. and its possessions, 1893–1942, with a few exceptions. Over 130 record labels are represented. Entries are arranged by performer within 13 national or language groups. Detailed listing under each performer contains primary and secondary titles, instrumentation, date and place of recordings, master and release numbers.   ML156.4.F5S69

Handbooks

Graham, Ronnie. The Da Capo guide to contemporary African music. N.Y. : Da Capo Pr., 1988. 315 p., 14 p. of plates : ill.   **BJ330**
> Originally publ. as *Stern's guide to contemporary African music* (London : Zwan, 1988). Repr.: London : Off the Record, 1989.
> Country-by-country listing, with an essay and discography on the traditional music of the country, followed by one or more essays on

identifiable modern musical styles. In these essays, individual composers and performers are identified with brief biographies and discographies. Index.   ML3502.5.G7

Popular music

Mattfeld, Julius. Variety music cavalcade, 1620–1969 : a chronology of vocal and instrumental music popular in the United States. 3rd ed. Englewood Cliffs, N.J. : Prentice-Hall, [1971]. 766 p.   **BJ331**
> Rev. ed. 1962.
> Originally published (in a different form) first in *Variety radio directory*, 1938–39, then in weekly issues of *Variety*. Lists popular music chronologically, with a brief account of various events occurring each year. Also includes hymns; secular and sacred songs; choral compositions; and instrumental and orchestral works. Only the musical items are indexed.   ML128.V7M4

Nite, Norm N. Rock on almanac : the first four decades of rock 'n' roll : a chronology. 2nd ed. N.Y. : HarperPerennial, c1992. 581 p. : ill.   **BJ332**
> 1st ed., 1989.
> Compendium of information on rock from the 1940s through 1992. For each year, includes news and music highlights, artists and groups who debuted, monthly listing of popular songs in alphabetical order, top ten singles and albums, Grammy winners, Rock and Roll Hall of Fame inductions (beginning 1986), brief biographical facts on performers, rock movies, and motion picture Academy Awards. Numerous photographs and a glossary; indexes of performers and song titles.   ML3534.N58

Shapiro, Nat. Popular music : an annotated index of American popular songs. N.Y. : Adrian Pr., [1964–73]. 6 v. **BJ333**
> Contents: v. 1, 1950–59; v. 2, 1940–49; v. 3, 1960–64; v. 4, 1930–39; v. 5, 1920–29; v. 6, 1965–69.
> Each volume presents a selective list of popular songs published during the period covered. Arranged by year, then alphabetically by title; gives author, composer, publisher, and first or best-selling record, with indication of performer and recording company.
> Continued by: *Popular music : an annotated index of American popular songs* (Detroit : Gale, c1974–).
> Contents: v. 7, 1970–74; v. 8, 1975–79; v. 9, 1980–84. Annual, beginning with v. 10 (1985).
> A cumulation was published as: *Popular music, 1920–1979 : a revised cumulation*, by Shapiro and Bruce Pollock (Detroit : Gale, 1985. 3 v.).
> § For earlier coverage, Barbara N. Cohen-Stratyner's *Popular music, 1900–1919* (Detroit : Gale, 1988) follows the same format, but includes annotations covering historical data.   ML120.U5S5

Tyler, Don. Hit parade : an encyclopedia of the top songs of the jazz, depression, swing, and sing eras. N.Y. : Quill, c1985. 257 p.   **BJ334**
> Year-by-year chronology of the most popular songs in the U.S., 1920–45. Selection was based on "Your hit parade" radio compilations, weekly charts from *Variety* and *Billboard*, and the "ASCAP all-time hit parade" of 16 songs chosen as the greatest hits, 1914–64. For each song, gives composer, lyricist, and brief annotation. Brief biographies of composers and lyricists are appended. Indexes of names and song titles.   ML102.P66T9

Bibliography

Booth, Mark W. American popular music : a reference guide. Westport, Conn. : Greenwood, [1983]. 212 p.   **BJ335**
> An "inventory of resources for studying American popular music," offering "brief descriptions of books, periodicals, and special library collections" (*Pref.*) concerning various types of music (e.g., Tin

Pan Alley, blues, ragtime, rock) from many periods. A historical sketch precedes sections on popular music in general and popular music before the 20th century; subsequent chapters deal with specific types of music. Bibliography for each chapter; index.

ML102.P66B65

Cooper, B. Lee. Rockabilly : a bibliographic resource guide / by B. Lee Cooper and Wayne S. Haney. Metuchen, N.J. : Scarecrow, 1990. 352 p. **BJ336**

Focuses on a specific style of popular music of the 1950s by providing a bibliography of 1,945 books and periodical articles arranged by performer, with a separate discography of over 200 albums. Includes separate, additional bibliographies of books and periodicals on the genre in general. Author index. ML128.R65C66

Hart, Mary L. The blues : a bibliographical guide / Mary L. Hart, Brenda M. Eagles, Lisa N. Howorth. N.Y. : Garland, 1989. 636 p. (Music research and information guides, v. 7 ; Garland reference library of the humanities, v. 565). **BJ337**

Contains a bibliography of printed items and recordings of approximately 5,000 entries organized systematically into nine chapters by topical heading. Individual editors supplied a core bibliography and introductory remarks for each chapter; additional citations provided by the editors are listed at the end of each chapter. The editors included what they could obtain, and claim neither comprehensiveness nor systematic selectivity. Author and title indexes. ML128.B49H3

Hoffmann, Frank W. The literature of rock, 1954–1978. Metuchen, N.J. : Scarecrow, 1981. 337 p. : ill. **BJ338**

A selective, annotated bibliography of books and periodical articles concerned with rock music arranged in chronological sections to reflect the historical development of the genre. Select discography. Indexed.

Continued by: *The literature of rock II, 1979–1983 : with additional material for the period 1954–1978*, by Frank Hoffmann and B. Lee Cooper, with the assistance of Lee Ann Hoffman (1986. 2 v. [1097 p.]).

Includes some additional entries from the earlier period. Includes a "Related topics" listing with citations related to historical, social, and economic issues. Some brief annotations. Names/titles/subjects index. A compilation covering 1984–90 has been announced. ML128.R6I6

Iwaschkin, Roman. Popular music : a reference guide. N.Y. : Garland, 1986. 658 p. (Garland reference library of the humanities, vol. 642). **BJ339**

Aims to cover literature of the entire popular music field from the "beginnings of the genre to 1984" (*Introd.*), with some titles from 1985. Contains 4,744 entries in several sections: the music, biography, technical aspects, the music business, the product, and literary works. Includes a list of more than 500 periodicals. Many entries have brief annotations. Index. ML128.P63I95

McCoy, Judy. Rap music in the 1980s : a reference guide. Metuchen, N.J. : Scarecrow, 1992. 261 p. **BJ340**

"A guide to the literature documenting the rise of rap as a viable pop music genre."—*Pref.* An annotated bibliography of 1,070 printed items comprises most of the book. The second section contains an annotated discography of 76 items. Concludes with date, subject, artist and personality, and title indexes. ML128.R28M3

Taylor, Paul. Popular music since 1955 : a critical guide to the literature. Boston. : G.K. Hall, 1985. 533 p. **BJ341**

Intends "to provide a critical bibliographical guide to the literature of contemporary music published in English since 1955."—*Pref.* Includes 1,600 entries for monographs covering 1955–82, with some significant works 1983–84, arranged in broad categories for general works, social aspects, artistic aspects, business aspects, musical forms, lives and works, and fiction. Annotations are lengthy and informative. Also lists 200 periodicals. Author, title, and subject indexes.

ML128.P63T39

Discography

Helander, Brock. The rock who's who : a biographical dictionary and critical discography including rhythm-and-blues, soul, rockabilly, folk, country, easy listening, punk, and new wave. N.Y. : Schirmer ; London : Collier Macmillan, c1982. 686 p. **BJ342**

Provides a critical and historical discography of rock and soul recordings released in the U.S. from the mid-1950s through early 1982. Entries are arranged alphabetically by performer and contain a brief annotation concerning the group's or individual artist's career and performance history, followed by discography organized by date of recording. Each item includes the album title, awards it received, label, number, and release date. ML102.R6H5

Rust, Brian A. L. The complete entertainment discography, from 1897 to 1942 / Brian Rust and Allen G. Debus. 2nd ed. N.Y. : Da Capo Pr., c1989. 794 p. **BJ343**

1st ed., 1973.

Entries are organized by artists' names, including minstrel pioneers, vaudevillians, film stars, radio personalities, and actors and actresses, and are limited to artists of American birth or artists as well known in America as their native country. Excludes jazz and blues musicians, commercial dance bands, and selected major artists.

ML156.4.P6R88

Tudor, Dean. Popular music : an annotated guide to recordings. Littleton, Colo. : Libraries Unlimited, 1983. 647 p. **BJ344**

"Represents a thorough updating and revision of the four separate volumes published by Libraries Unlimited in 1979 as *Jazz, Black Music, Grass Roots Music*, and *Contemporary Popular Music*."—*Pref.*

Intended as a survey and buying guide for American popular music available on long-playing records. Arranged by categories, with numerous subdivisions: black music, folk music, jazz music, mainstream music, popular religious music, rock music. Annotations; performing artists index. ML156.4.P6T85

Encyclopedias

Encyclopedia of rock / [ed. by] Phil Hardy, Dave Laing ; additional material, Stephen Barnard, Don Perretta. [2nd ed.]. N.Y. : Schirmer, 1988. 480 p. : ill. (some col.). **BJ345**

Updated and considerably expanded version of 1976 ed.

Contains roughly 2,000 entries for names of rock and rock-related individual and group performers, "backroom figures" (i.e., entrepreneurs and record producers), topics, recording companies, and types of media. Artists were chosen on the basis of chart success in the U.S. or the U.K., or the historical influence and artistic significance accorded them by the editors, who also determined the length of annotations. The latter give general biographic and artistic information, but lack bibliographies and discographies. ML102.R6E5

Gammond, Peter. The Oxford companion to popular music. Oxford [Eng.] ; N.Y. : Oxford Univ. Pr., 1991. 739 p. **BJ346**

Aims to cover "all music that would not normally be found in a reference book on 'classical' or 'serious' music ... and the essential elements and personalities concerned with popular song of all periods."—*Introd.* Dictionary arrangement of entries covers roughly 1850–1985, with emphasis on the English-speaking world. Many entries are lengthy, and some have bibliographies. Indexes: people and groups; shows and films; songs and albums. ML102.P66G35

The Guinness encyclopedia of popular music / comp. and ed. by Colin Larkin. Enfield, Middlesex, Eng. : Guinness Publ. ; Chester, Conn. : New England Publ. Associates, 1992. 4 v. (3295 p.). **BJ347**

Contains approximately 10,000 entries in alphabetical order for individuals and performing groups. The post-1960 period is best represented, with each entry containing background/biographical information and a list of major albums. Covers standard areas such as rock 'n' roll, jazz, blues, soul, country; also attempts to include other genres, such as reggae and Latin and African pop. The editors acknowledge that the Indian subcontinent, the Far East, the Arab states, and the Eastern European bloc are underrepresented, but hope to redress this in future editons. The final volume includes a list of all the entries, an index, and a bibliography.   ML102.P66G84

Hardy, Phil. The Faber companion to 20th-century popular music / Phil Hardy and Dave Laing. London ; Boston : Faber and Faber, 1990. 875 p.   **BJ348**

Contains profiles of nearly 2,000 recording artists who, in the authors' opinion, have contributed to the evolution of popular music in the 20th century, including singers, songwriters, bandleaders, behind-the-scenes technologists, etc. Inclusion based on commercial success, importance in developing a particular stream of popular music (e.g., pioneering recording artists), and artistic excellence. Aims to include all genres of popular music in the Anglo-American tradition. Glossary of these genres is included.   ML105.H37

Kinkle, Roger D. The complete encyclopedia of popular music and jazz, 1900–1950. New Rochelle, N.Y. : Arlington House, [1974]. 4 v. (2644 p.) : ill.   **BJ349**

Contents: v. 1, Music year by year, 1900–1950; v. 2–3, Biographies; v. 4, Indexes and appendixes.

Vol. 1 offers year-by-year listings of Broadway musicals, movie musicals, and representative popular music (the last by year of greatest popularity, not by year of copyright). Vols. 2–3 give brief career sketches (with discographies) of noted performers, lyricists and composers, bandleaders and sidemen, etc., in the field of popular music and jazz, with lesser coverage of light opera, blues, and country and western personalities. Vol. 4 includes indexes of personal names, Broadway musicals, movie musicals, popular songs; appendixes offer lists of important recordings, *Down beat* poll winners, and Academy Award winners and nominees for music, 1934–72.   ML102.P66K55

The Rolling Stone encyclopedia of rock & roll / ed. by Jon Pareles ; consulting ed., Patty Romanowski. N.Y. : Rolling Stone Pr./Summit Books, [1983]. 615 p. : ill.   **BJ350**

Intended as "a guide to the people who have made rock & roll. Each of the alphabetically arranged entries provides basic biographical information and, where appropriate, a selective discography or a discography plus group personnel chronology, followed by an essay that sums up the subject's life and career in music."—*Introd.*   ML102.R6R64

Stambler, Irwin. Encyclopedia of pop, rock & soul. Rev. ed. N.Y. : St. Martin's, c1989. 881 p., [48] p. of plates : ill.   **BJ351**

1st ed., 1975.

Primarily an alphabetical listing of performers, both groups and individuals, with brief biographical information and summary essays on their work. Appendixes include chronological listings of record awards, Grammy winners, and Academy Award nominations and winners in music.   ML102.P66S8

Who's new wave in music : an illustrated encyclopedia, 1976–1982 (the first wave) / comp. and ed. by David Bianco. Ann Arbor, Mich. : Pierian Pr., 1985. 430 p. : ill.   **BJ352**

Pt. I contains a listing of more than 850 bands and artists in the avant-garde of rock music, the primary criteria for inclusion being media recognition. Performers are listed alphabetically with their place and time of formation, style, personnel (if a group), chronology, references, live reviews, and discograpy. Pt. 2 contains a listing of the output by record companies and labels. Various reading lists, discography, necrology, and glossary are among the appendixes. Indexes of personal names, record labels, song and album titles, and geographic locations.

§ The author covers another subset of the rock genre in his *Heat wave : the Motown fact book* (Ann Arbor, Mich. : Pierian Pr., 1988).   ML12.W5

Biography

Gregory, Hugh. Soul music A–Z. London : Blandford ; N.Y. : Sterling Publ. Co., 1991. 266 p. : ill.   **BJ353**

An alphabetical listing of performers, both individuals and groups, as well as producers, businessmen, etc., with some biographical information and listing of recordings. Inclusion is based on the author's admittedly subjective criteria, and includes both African-American and white soul performers from many worlds, including gospel, Motown, and rhythm and blues. Excludes big band vocalists of the 1940s, most disco and sound mixers, hip hop, and rap. Bibliography includes a list of books which influenced the author.

§ Another volume, *Soul music who's who,* by Ralph Tee (Rocklin, Calif. : Prima, 1992) is similarly organized, with very brief biographical information and a brief overview of the artist's career. Lacks bibliography.   ML102.S65G7

Harris, Sheldon. Blues who's who : a biographical dictionary of blues singers. New Rochelle, N.Y. : Arlington House, c1979. 775 p. : ports.   **BJ354**

Repr. : N.Y. : Da Capo Pr., 1981.

Offers some 571 biographies of blues singers active between 1900 and 1977. For each, gives a chronology incorporating personal and career information, a listing of major songs and influences, and brief quotations from articles assessing the singer's style plus references to other biographical sources (usually a periodical article or record jacket). Selected bibliography; film, radio, television, theater, song, names and places indexes.   ML102.B6H3

Jasper, Tony. The international encyclopedia of hard rock & heavy metal / Tony Jasper and Derek Oliver. Fully rev. and updated ed. London : Sidgwick & Jackson, 1991. 448 p.   **BJ355**

1st ed., 1983.

An alphabetical arrangement of almost 1,500 groups and individual musicians. Entries are international in scope, and include biographical information and discography.

Nite, Norm N. Rock on : the illustrated encyclopedia of rock n' roll. Updated ed. N.Y. : Harper & Row, c1982–85. 3 v. : ill.   **BJ356**

1st ed., 1974–78 (2 v.). Original ed. of v. 2 had title: The modern years, 1964–present.

Contents: v. 1, The solid gold years; v. 2, The years of change, 1964–1978; v. 3, The video revolution, 1979–1984.

Each volume comprises biographical sketches (with discographies) of individuals and performing groups. Index of song titles.   ML105.N49

Roxon, Lillian. Lillian Roxon's rock encyclopedia / comp. by Ed Naha. Rev. ed. N.Y. : Grosset & Dunlap, [1978]. 565 p. : ill.   **BJ357**

1st ed., 1969, entitled *Rock encyclopedia.*

An updated edition which tries "to reflect rock and roll as it is today, spotlighting the contemporary artists as well as the prototypical ravers."—*Introd.* Entries are mainly concerned with individuals and performing groups (with lists of recordings), but there are some definitions of terms in rock parlance.   ML102.P66R7

Music in films

Green, Stanley. Encyclopaedia of the musical film. N.Y. : Oxford Univ. Pr., 1981. 344 p.   **BJ358**

Conceived as a companion volume to the author's *Encyclopaedia of the musical theatre* (BJ263), this encyclopedia contains succinct information regarding the musical screen's most prominent individuals, productions, and songs. Emphasizes Hollywood, but some British musical films included. This edition updates the necrology, and provides additional films under existing entries as well as additional Oscar winners. Contains separate lists of Motion Picture Academy nominations and awards, biographical movies of composers and performers, general bibliography, and discography. PN1995.9.M86G7

Harris, Steve. Film, television, and stage music on phonograph records : a discography. Jefferson, N.C. : McFarland, c1988. 445 p. **BJ359**

Lists 11,761 phonograph recordings from the U.S. and Great Britain. Lists recordings from other countries only if they were presented or recorded in the U.S. or Britain. Includes original or adapted music issued through 1986. Tape formats, cylinders, and compact discs are not included. Entries are listed by title, and include date, composer credit, country of pressing, format, and label.

ML156.4.M6H3

Limbacher, James L. Film music : from violins to video. Metuchen, N.J. : Scarecrow, 1974. 835 p. **BJ360**

A section of notes and comment on film music by various composers and writers is followed by an alphabetical list of film titles and dates, a chronological list of films and their composers, an alphabetical list of composers and their films (with dates), and a list of recorded musical scores arranged by film title.

§ Updated by: James L. Limbacher, *Keeping score : film music 1972–1979* (1981. 510 p.), in three main sections: (1) Films and their composers/adaptors; (2) Composers and their films; (3) Recorded musical scores (a discography); and by James L. Limbacher and H. Stephen Wright, *Keeping score : film and television music, 1980–1988, with additional coverage of 1921–1979* (1991. 916 p.), which adds an appendix (film music necrology) and an index of film titles.

ML2075.L54

Lynch, Richard Chigley. Movie musicals on record : a directory of recordings of motion picture musicals, 1927–1987. N.Y. : Greenwood, 1989. 445 p. (Discographies, no. 32).

BJ361

Lists songs (approximately 6,500 titles) and singers on 666 commercial albums. Entries, arranged alphabetically by film title, give the name of the production company, year of first release, original label and reissue information, composer, lyricist, musical conductor, cast members, and all the songs on the album. Concludes with a chronology of films, a performer index, and a technical index to composers, lyricists, and musical directors.

§ Similarly organized is the author's companion volume *Broadway on record*, (N.Y. : Greenwood, 1987. [Discographies, no. 28]), which covers 6,000 songs on 459 albums. ML156.4.M6L9

Meeker, David. Jazz in the movies. [New enl. ed.]. London : Talisman Books, [1981] ; N.Y. : Da Capo Pr., 1982. [336] p. : ill. **BJ362**

1st ed., 1977.

Arranged by film title, with an index of jazz musicians. Notes on each film indicate jazz performers and numbers included. This edition incorporates information on films produced for television.

ML128.M7M38

Sandahl, Linda J. Encyclopedia of rock music on film : a viewer's guide to three decades of musicals, concerts, documentaries and soundtracks 1955–1986. N.Y. : Facts on File, c1987. 239 p. : ill. **BJ363**

Heavily-illustrated listing of films with rock music. Organized in three sections—musicals, concerts and documentaries, and soundtracks—with each section then subarranged alphabetically by film title. Only films at least 50 minutes in length and originally made in English are included. Indexes of film titles, names, and song titles.

PN1995.9.M86S26

Wescott, Steven D. A comprehensive bibliography of music for film and television. Detroit : Information Coordinators, 1985. 432 p. **BJ364**

Contains 6,340 entries, many with brief annotations, in five topical sections: history; individual composers; aesthetics; special topics, including performance on film and television, film music, and animat-

ed sound; and research. An international compilation, representing publications by more than 3,700 authors in 28 countries and 18 languages. Index.

Supplemented by Gillian B. Anderson, "Supplement to Steven D. Westcott's A comprehensive bibliography of music for film and television," *Music reference quarterly*, v. 2, no. 1–2 (1993), p. 105–144.

ML128.M7W47

Woll, Allen L. Songs from Hollywood musical comedies, 1927 to the present : a dictionary. N.Y. : Garland, 1976. 251 p. (Garland reference library in the humanities, v. 44). **BJ365**

"Provides a guide for … nostalgia buffs, allowing them to identify their favorite movie musical show tunes, and, if possible, find soundtrack recordings of them."—*How to use this book.* In four alphabetically arranged sections: (1) title listing of songs (with name of film); (2) title listing of musicals (with date of release, name of principal players, director, song writers, and, when available, recorded songs with name of record company and number); (3) chronological listing of musicals; (4) composers and lyricists. Name index.

ML102.P66W64

INSTRUMENTS

Bowers, Q. David. Encyclopedia of automatic musical instruments. Vestal, N.Y. : Vestal Pr., [1972]. 1008 p. : ill. **BJ366**

Subtitle: Cylinder music boxes, disc music boxes, piano players and player pianos, coin-operated pianos, orchestrions, photoplayers, organettes, fairground organs, calliopes, and other self-playing instruments mainly of the 1750–1940 era; including a dictionary of automatic musical instrument terms.

Arranged by types as mentioned in the subtitle; indexed. Dictionary of terms on p. 947–81. ML1050.B6

Coover, James. Musical instrument collections : catalogs and cognate literature. Detroit : Information Coordinators, 1981. 464 p. (Detroit studies in music bibliography, 47). **BJ367**

In two main sections: (1) Institutions and expositions (arranged by place); and (2) Private collections (arranged by owner). Bibliography with each entry. Appendixes provide a chronological listing of early inventories to 1825, and one of expositions and exhibitions, 1818–1978. The index includes names of auctioneers, antiquarians, and firms. ML155.C63

International directory of musical instrument collections / ed. by Jean Jenkins. Buren (Gld.), Netherlands : Frits Knuf for International Council of Museums (ICOM), 1977. 166 p.

BJ368

A directory of museums, libraries, conservatories, and private collections which contain musical instruments from 163 countries. Arrangement is by country, subarranged by city and institution. The data was gathered by questionnaire. Each entry contains name, address, telephone number, description of the collections, and any publications.

ML12.I57

Lexikon Musikinstrumente / hrsg. von Wolfgang Ruf, unter Mitarbeit von Christian Ahrens … [et al.]. Mannheim : Meyers Lexikonverlag, c1991. 590 p. : ill. (some col.). **BJ369**

An alphabetical listing of terms, as well as names of composers, performers, etc., who played a part in the development of a particular instrument. Many entries are lengthy, and each contains a definition and description, a list of synonyms, date of use, etymological derivations, and a bibliography. Contains numerous illustrations, many in color. ML102.I5L5

Marcuse, Sibyl. Musical instruments : a comprehensive dictionary. Corr. ed. N.Y. : Norton, 1975. 608 p. **BJ370**

1st ed., 1964.

Describes musical instruments used throughout the world from earliest times to the present. Gives names in English with foreign equivalents. Includes numbered list of sources referred to throughout the text. Excellent illustrations, though limited to 24 plates.

ML102.I5M37

The New Grove dictionary of musical instruments / ed. by Stanley Sadie. N.Y. : Grove's Dictionaries of Music, 1984. 3 v. : ill.   **BJ371**

Although this work "takes its title, its method and approach, and some of its material" (*Pref.*) from the *New Grove dictionary of music and musicians* (BJ141), much new material appears here, and there has been substantial revision of many articles derived from the larger work. Five broad categories of articles are included: (1) instruments of classical Western music; (2) makers of those instruments; (3) modern Western instruments (including electronic ones) and their makers; (4) performing practice; and (5) non-Western and folk or traditional instruments—the latter category being particularly well represented. Signed articles, with bibliographies; cross references; numerous illustrations, diagrams, and examples of music. List of contributors in v. 3.

ML102.I5N48

Read, Gardner. Thesaurus of orchestral devices. N.Y. ; London : Pitman, [1953]. 631 p.   **BJ372**

Repr. : N.Y. : Greenwood, [1969].

A lexicon of instrumentation, including index of nomenclature and terminology in English, Italian, French, and German; abbreviations; list of composers and works; and list of music publishers.

MT70.R37

Sachs, Curt. The history of musical instruments. N.Y. : Norton, [1940]. 505 p. : ill.   **BJ373**

Repr., 1968.

A comprehensive historical dictionary of instruments of all countries.   ML460.S2H5

RECORDED MUSIC

Catalogs and discography

All music guide : the best CDs, albums & tapes : the experts' guide to the best releases from thousands of artists in all types of music / ed., Michael Erlewine ; associate ed., Scott Bultman. San Francisco : Miller Freeman, c1992. 1,176 p.   **BJ374**

Contains reviews by approximately 80 editors, most of whom are professional music writers. The more than 23,000 albums listed are culled from a larger database of some 100,000 items which is expected to be made available on CD-ROM.   ML156.9.A38

Clough, Francis F. The world's encyclopaedia of recorded music / by Francis F. Clough and G. J. Cuming. London : Sidgwick and Jackson ; N.Y. : London Gramophone Corp., [1952]. 890 p.   **BJ375**

Based on *The Gramophone Shop encyclopedia of recorded music*, comp. by R. D. Darrell (N.Y. : The Gramophone Shop, 1936). A comprehensive listing of all electrically recorded music of interest to June 1951, and of pre-electrical recordings of unique value. Information is detailed, and the arrangement convenient. An important historical record.

————. ————. *1st supplement* (Apr. 1950–May/June 1951; bound with main vol.).

————. ————. *2nd supplement (1951–1952)* (1953. 262 p.).

————. ————. *3rd supplement (1953–1955)* ([1957]. 564 p.).

Cohen, Aaron I. International discography of women composers. Westport, Conn. : Greenwood, 1984. 254 p. (Discographies, no. 10).   **BJ376**

Lists recordings of compositions by 468 women. Composers are listed alphabetically, with works subarranged alphabetically by title and recording information. Additional lists include record labels and companies, as well as lists of composers by country and instrument. Title index.

§ Similarly organized is Jane Frasier's *Women composers : a discography* (Detroit : Information Coordinators, 1983), which covers the works of 337 women on approximately 1,030 discs.

ML156.4.W6C6

Cohn, Arthur. Recorded classical music : a critical guide to compositions and performances. N.Y. : Schirmer ; London : Collier Macmillan, [1981]. 2164 p.   **BJ377**

Concerned with evaluating classical records, not cassettes and tapes. Presents the compiler's choice of the single best performance of each work (about 12,000 compositions by some 1,600 composers) with critical comment; each piece is judged individually, and not by the overall quality of a collection in the case of several short pieces on a single disc. Covers all periods and performing media. Arranged by composer; no index of performing artists.   ML156.9.C63

Duxbury, Janell R. Rockin' the classics and classicizin' the rock : a selectively annotated discography. Westport, Conn. : Greenwood, c1985. 188 p. (Discographies, no. 14).   **BJ378**

Lists explicit borrowings and associations between rock music and classical music. Entries are listed by performer in several categories: rock versions of classic pieces, classical versions of rock pieces, etc.

————. ————. *First supplement* (N.Y. : Greenwood, 1991. Discographies, no. 43).   ML156.4.R6D9

March, Ivan. The Penguin guide to compact discs and cassettes / Ivan March, Edward Greenfield, Robert Layton ; ed. by Ivan March. London, ; N.Y. : Penguin Books, 1992. 1348 p.   **BJ379**

A distillation of: *The Penguin guide to compact discs* (1990) and *The Penguin guide to compact discs and cassettes yearbook, 1991/92*.

Aims "to give the serious collector a comprehensive survey of the finest recordings of permanent music on CD."—*Introd.* Arranged in two sections: by individual composer, and collections. The composer listing is alphabetical, subarranged by genre, as in *The classical catalogue* (BJ387). Collections are organized in the following categories: orchestral, instrumental and vocal/choral, with subarrangement by performer or performing forces. Each performance is assigned an evaluation, with outstanding discs noted, and every recording is categorized by price. Annotations provide critical comment.   ML156.9.M33

•**Music library** [database]. Dublin, Ohio : OCLC, 1991– .   **BJ380**

Available on CD-ROM, updated annually. Consists of more than 500,000 records extracted from the OCLC database that describe musical sound recordings.

Rosenberg, Kenyon C. A basic classical and operatic recordings collection for libraries. Metuchen, N.J. : Scarecrow, 1987. 255 p.   **BJ381**

Aims to provide librarians with a means for "creating or augmenting a nuclear classical and operatic recordings collection."—*Pref.* Recommends specific performances of the standard repertory, with entries arranged alphabetically by composer, subarranged by title under the author's genre terms. Gives record company, number, and performers, as well as ratings for budgetary considerations, technical recording characteristics, and appropriateness by type of library.

§ Similarly organized is the author's *A basic classical and operatic recordings collection on compact discs for libraries : a buying guide* (Metuchen, N.J. : Scarecrow, 1990), with an additional section containing the author's evaluation of current performing groups.

ML156.2.R7

Rust, Brian A. L. Brian Rust's guide to discography. Westport, Conn. : Greenwood, [1980]. 133 p. (Discographies, no. 4).   **BJ382**

An introduction to the task of compiling a discography. Includes a brief history of major record labels, a bibliography of "booklength" discographies, and a directory of organizations and magazines.

ML111.5.R87

Bibliography

Bibliography of discographies. N.Y. : Bowker, 1977–1983. 3 v. **BJ383**

Contents: v. 1, Classical music, 1925–1975, by Michael H. Gray and Gerald D. Gibson; v. 2, Jazz, by Daniel Allen; v. 3, Popular music, by Michael H. Gray.

Cites discographies appearing in periodicals and as monographs. Each volume has its own index. 5 v. were projected, but v. 4–5 were never published.

§ Michael H. Gray, *Classical music discographies, 1976–1988 : a bibliography* (N.Y. ; London : Greenwood, 1989. [341] p.).

Aims to provide the first cumulative suppl. to v. 1 above. Lists in one alphabetical sequence names and subjects for which discographies have appeared in books, articles, dissertations, and theses, as well as program notes. Considerably expands the entries for record labels and subjects. Index of names. ML156.2.B49

Cooper, David Edwin. International bibliography of discographies : classical music and jazz and blues, 1962–1972 : a reference book for record collectors, dealers, and libraries. Littleton, Colo. : Libraries Unlimited, 1975. 272 p. (Keys to music bibliography, no. 2). **BJ384**

Restricted to Western classical music, jazz and blues. Lists discographies appearing in books and periodical articles. Arranged by period, subject or genre, composer and performer. Includes a "Summary of national discographies, catalogs and major review sources." Index of authors, titles, series, subjects. ML113.C655I6

Current

Artist issue. 17th ed. (1991/92)– . Santa Fe, N.M. : Stereophile, Inc., [1991] . Annual. **BJ385**

Annual cumulation of performing artists of classical music taken from the *Schwann opus* listing (BJ388). Contains an alphabetical arrangement of names of performers with discographies, as well as separate listings by musical forces or function; e.g., conductors, choral groups, etc., with discographies. Contains address/price list.

ML156.2.A75

Bielefelder Katalog Klassik. 1979?– . [Karlsruhe, Germany : G. Braun.], 1979?– . Two no. a year. **BJ386**

Aims to provide a catalog of available compact discs, LPs, and music cassettes for the classical music repertory, as reported by "the German and foreign record industry... [who are] contract partners of the Vereinigte Motor-Verlage Stuttgart."—*Foreword*. The main listing is alphabetical by composer, subarranged by titles, with performers and record labels. Following is a much shorter listing of authors of texts on spoken-word recordings. The final list is organized by record label, with a listing of each record number and its contents. Concludes with a list of publisher addresses. ML156.2.B52

Classical catalogue. 38th yr., no. 150 (Dec. 1990)– . Harrow, Middlesex : General Gramophone Publications Ltd., c1990– . Semiannual. **BJ387**

Formed by the union of *Gramophone compact disc...guide* and *Gramophone classical catalogue.*

Contains currently available recordings in a variety of formats (including compact discs, LPs, cassettes, VHS, laser discs, DCC and Mini-discs) generally available in Great Britain. The "Master" edition, publ. in June and Dec., is updated by monthly cumulative supplements; it contains a composer listing subarranged by title, an artist list-

ing, consisting of the names of artists who appear in most of the other listings, a listing of operas arranged by composer, and a concert index that contains a listing by record company.

Schwann opus. v. 4, no. 1 (Winter 1992/93)– . Santa Fe, N.M. : Stereophile, Inc., [1992]– . Quarterly. **BJ388**

Lists available classical recordings in all popular formats, including compact discs, LPs, cassette tapes, and laser discs (separate section). Primary arrangement is by composer, with a separate listing for collections arranged by instrument or historical period. Contains address/price list. Based on information supplied by manufacturers and distributors. Latest incarnation of the various Schwann titles.

ML156.2.O68

Schwann spectrum. v. 4, no. 1 (Winter 1992/93)– . Santa Fe, N.M. : Stereophile, Inc., [1992]– . Quarterly. **BJ389**

Lists available nonclassical recordings in all popular formats, including compact discs, LPs, and cassette tapes. Sectional arrangement by categories: pop/rock; pop/rock collections; jazz; jazz anthologies; musicals, movies and TV shows; spoken and miscellaneous; international pop and folk; New Age; and CD-videos, with various subarrangements. Based on information supplied by manufacturers and distributors. ML156.2.S69

Reviews

Index to record and tape reviews. 1975–82. San Anselmo, Calif. : Chulainn Pr., [1976]–83. **BJ390**

Continued: *Record and tape reviews index* (1972–74).

Indexed reviews appearing in about 40 of the principal reviewing periodicals of the U.S., England, and Canada. In three sections: (1) Composers; (2) Music in collections; (3) Anonymous works. Each citation gives as full information as is available concerning performers, disc and label number, variant labels, cassette or tape numbers, etc., as well as name of reviewer and location of the review. ML156.9.R32

Index to record reviews / comp. by Kurtz Myers ... [et al.]. (*In* Notes : 2nd ser., v. 5, no. 2 [March 1948]– . Canton, Mass. : Music Library Assoc., 1948–). Quarterly. **BJ391**

Title varies. "Index of record reviews".

Indexes reviews of recordings in some 15–30 American and English periodicals, with indication of the reviewer's opinion of the quality of the performance: excellent, adequate, or inadequate.

Cumulated as : Kurtz Myers, *Index to record reviews* (Boston : G.K. Hall, 1978. 5 v.), a cumulation of the reviews that appeared 1948–early 1977; ———. ——— *1978–1983* (1985. 783 p.); ———. ——— *1984–1987* (1989. 639 p.).

Dictionaries

Encyclopedia of recorded sound in the United States / Guy A. Marco, ed. ; Frank Andrews, contributing ed. N.Y. : Garland, 1993. xlix, 910 p. (Garland reference library of the humanities, v. 936). **BJ392**

An alphabetical listing of more than 2,000 performers, recording labels, individuals, etc., as well as terms related to sound recording in the U.S. up to about 1970. Informative entries; contributors other than the author are identified after their entries. Includes separate bibliography and indexes. ML102.S67E5

White, Glenn D. The audio dictionary. Seattle : Univ. of Washington Pr., c1987. 291 p. : ill. **BJ393**

Terms, definitions and cross-references pertaining to sound recording, sound reinforcement, and musical acoustics. Appendixes contain a mixture of general advice and tabular information.

TK7881.4.W48

BK

Sports and Recreation

SPORTS AND GAMES

General works

Bibliography

Cox, Richard William. Sport in Britain : a bibliography of historical publications, 1800–1987. Manchester [Eng.] ; N.Y. : Manchester Univ. Pr. ; [N.Y.] : St. Martin's, c1991. 285 p. **BK1**

Provides good historical coverage of books and some articles on British sport. Contains some 7,000 entries, without annotations.

Z7515.G7C69

Davis, Lenwood G. Black athletes in the United States : a bibliography of books, articles, autobiographies, and biographies on black professional athletes in the United States, 1800–1981 / comp. by Lenwood G. Davis and Belinda S. Daniels. Westport, Conn. : Greenwood, 1981. 265 p. **BK2**

Focuses on the first, or the major and best-known professional black athletes in baseball, basketball, boxing, football, golf, and tennis. Lists reference books, monographs, and articles by form, subdivided by type of sport and by personality. More than 3,800 entries. Indexed.

Z7515.U5D38

Gratch, Bonnie. Sports and physical education : a guide to the reference resources / comp. by Bonnie Gratch, Betty Chan, and Judith Lingenfelter. Westport, Conn. : Greenwood, 1983. 198 p. **BK3**

Lists English-language monographs published since 1970 and on-going, regularly published reference serials. Classified arrangement in three parts: (1) individual sports; (2) sports and physical education: general and topical; (3) indexes, data bases, and information centers. Personal and corporate author, title, and subject indexes.   Z7511.G7

Jones, Donald G. Sports ethics in America : a bibliography, 1970–1990 / Donald G. Jones with Elaine L. Daly. N.Y. : Greenwood, 1992. 291 p. (Bibliographies and indexes in American history, no. 21). **BK4**

An interdisciplinary work divided into five main sections: general works and philosophy; the team, players, and coaches; the game, competition, and contestants; sports and society; and reference works. Contains 642 book entries and 2,232 article and monograph entries, all annotated with subject headings. Cross-referenced subject index and separate author index.   Z7514.M66J66

The leisure literature : a guide to sources in leisure studies, fitness, sports, and travel / Nancy L. Herron, ed. ; contributing authors, Adele F. Bane ... [et al.]. Englewood, Colo. : Libraries Unlimited, 1992. 181 p. **BK5**

A guide to the interdisciplinary body of literature devoted to aspects of leisure. Describes 283 of the most useful reference sources that support research in leisure, fitness, sport, and travel/tourism. In

four sections representing the four subject areas, each containing an introduction to the discipline and annotated listings of the sources. Appendixes list degree programs, important publishers, and related associations. Author/title and subject indexes.   Z7511.L37

Mallon, Bill. The Olympics : a bibliography. N.Y. : Garland, 1984. 258 p. (Garland reference library of social science, v. 246). **BK6**

Listings of official reports and publications of the various Olympic committees are followed by writings about the Olympics (arranged by country of publication, then by date). Not indexed.   Z7514.O5M35

Remley, Mary L. Women in sport : an annotated bibliography and resource guide, 1900–1990. Boston : G.K. Hall, 1991. 210 p. **BK7**

In four chapters, covers the monographic literature chronologically. Each chapter, covering a 10–30-year period, begins with a brief introductory essay, followed by a bibliography, arranged by year of publication then alphabetically by author's name. Sports are covered in the broadest sense. Includes a list of periodicals that focus on women in sports, a list of national sports organizations that include women, and halls of fame that include women. Author, subject, and title indexes.

Z7963.S6R45

Shoebridge, Michele. Information sources in sport and leisure. London ; N.Y. : Bowker-Saur, c1992. 345 p. **BK8**

Much more than bibliography, this volume employs more than 20 experts in sport and leisure, who offer a descriptive review of major information sources and services in sport and leisure (both general and research levels). Coverage is international, but with a definite U.K. emphasis.   Z7511.S48

Indexes; Abstract journals

Burke, John Gordon. Index to the Sporting news. v. 1 (1975–90)– . Evanston, Ill. : J.G. Burke, c1992– . Triennial. **BK9**

More than 65,000 citations, 1975–90, to this basic source of news about baseball, other major professional and college sports, and the Olympics.   GV583.I53

Physical education index. v. 1 (Mar. 1978)– . Cape Girardeau, Mo. : BenOak Publ. Co., 1978– . Quarterly, the 4th issue being an annual cumulation. **BK10**

Indexes by subject domestic and foreign periodicals published in English or containing English summaries. Covers dance, health, physical education, physical therapy, recreation, sports, sports medicine, kinesiology (including biomechanics), coaching, facilities, measurement and evaluation, motor learning, perception, fitness, sport psychology and sociology, teaching methods, training, and all individual sport activities. A separate section for book reviews, arranged by author, is included in each volume. Preface indicates criteria for inclusion. Includes list of periodicals indexed.   GV201.P534

•**SPORT** [database]. Gloucester, Ont. : Sport Information Resource Centre, c1975– . **BK11**

Coverage: monographs and theses, 1949– ; serials, 1975– . Available online (updated semiannually) and in CD-ROM as *Sport Discus.*

Conflates entries in SIRC's ceased *Sport bibliography* and *Sport bibliography update* sets. Also conflates 20,021 records from the ceased *Sport & leisure* database which was produced by Specialized Information Retrieval and Library Services (SIRLS) at the Univ. of Waterloo, Canada, and was the sole source for the ceased print index, *Sociology of leisure and sport abstracts: a review of social science literature,* and its successor, *Sport & leisure: a journal of social science abstracts.* Also includes the 1990 edition of *Sport thesaurus,* which contains more than 8,000 index terms and 2,000 cross-references.

International in scope, a unique and essential source for searching the practical and research literature for all aspects of sports and fitness. Covers sports medicine, exercise physiology, biomechanics, psychology, training, coaching, physical education, fitness, sport for the disabled, facilities, equipment, and recreation and leisure. Also indexes the microform masters and doctoral theses collection of the International Institute for Sport and Human Performance at the Univ. of Oregon.

Encyclopedias

Ashe, Arthur. A hard road to glory : a history of the African-American athlete. N.Y. : Amistad : distr. by Penguin, 1993. 3 v. : ill. **BK12**
1st ed., 1988.
A comprehensive source that traces the history of African-American athletes. Arranged chronologically by period, each volume contains a reference section with championship statistics and individual athletes' records; each volume is indexed and contains a bibliography. Also available are five separate paperback compendiums on individual sports (basketball, track & field, football, boxing, and baseball), excerpted from the original set. GV583.A74

Biographical dictionary of American sports : 1989–1992 supplement for baseball, football, basketball, and other sports / ed. by David L. Porter. N.Y. : Greenwood, 1992. 752 p. **BK13**
The 5th volume in the "Biographical dictionary of american sports" series: includes baseball, football, and basketball. Preface explains criteria for inclusion. Appendixes include alphabetical listing, entries by major sport, by place of birth, women athletes by sport, cross-references for married women athletes, U.S. sports halls of fame, and sites of Olympic Games.
Supplement to volumes for: baseball (BK52); basketball (BK63); football (BK74); see also outdoor sports (BK14). GV697.A1B494

Biographical dictionary of American sports : outdoor sports / ed. by David L. Porter. N.Y. : Greenwood, c1988. 728 p. **BK14**
Brief, signed articles treat auto racing, communications and promotion, golf, horse racing, lacrosse, miscellaneous sports, skiing, soccer, speed skating, tennis, and track and field. Appendixes provide: an alphabetical list of entries with references to the appropriate sport; lists of entries classed by sport, by state of birth, and of women by sport (with cross-references to married names); major U.S. halls of fame, sports associations and organizations; and sites of Olympic Games. General index. GV697.A1B49

Encyclopedia of physical education, fitness, and sports / Thomas K. Cureton, Jr., series ed. ; sponsored by the American Alliance for Health, Physical Education, and Recreation. Salt Lake City, Utah : Brighton Publ. Co., [1977–85]. 4 v. : ill. **BK15**
Vol. 3 publ. Reading, Mass. : Addison-Wesley; v. 4 publ. Reston, Va. : American Alliance for Health, Physical Education, Recreation, and Dance.
Contents: [v. 1] Philosophy, programs, and history; [v. 2] Training, environment, nutrition, and fitness; [v. 3] Sports, dance, and related activities; [v. 4] Human performance: efficiency and improvements in sports, exercise, and fitness.
Each volume consists of chapters by contributing editors on various aspects of physical education, physical fitness, and sports (including information on the origin and early development of individual sports, etc.). Each volume has its own index. GV567.E49

Hickok, Ralph. The encyclopedia of North American sports history. N.Y. : Facts on File, c1992. 516 p. : ill. **BK16**
With broad but brief coverage of nearly all sports, this source focuses on the growth and development of sports in North America, including general history, biography, sporting events, major awards, cities, stadiums, fields, organizations, and governing bodies. The 1,600 entries are arranged alphabetically with cross-references. Many entries include reference to other works for further reading. Indexed. GV567.H518

Menke, Frank Grant. The encyclopedia of sports. 6th rev. ed. Revisions by Pete Palmer. South Brunswick [N.J.] : A. S. Barnes, 1978. 1132 p. : ill. **BK17**
1st ed., 1939. Title varies slightly.
Covers a wide variety of sports, giving: history, description, basic rules, names and records of champions, and financial statistics, with special attention to the U.S. In general, information has been updated through 1976. GV567.M46

Mohr, Merilyn Simonds. The games treasury : more than 300 indoor and outdoor favorites with strategies, rules, and traditions. Shelburne, Vt. : Chapters Publ., c1993. 351 p. : ill. (some col.). **BK18**
Covers the strategies, rules, and traditions of more than 300 indoor and outdoor games. Organized into five chapters: board games, games with playing pieces, card games, games of guessing and deduction, and outdoor games. Includes lists of manufacturers and organizations. Indexed. GV1201.M67

Norback, Craig T. The New American guide to athletics, sports, & recreation / Craig T. Norback and Peter G. Norback. N.Y. : New American Library, c1979. 659 p. **BK19**
An alphabetical arrangement of entries for some 60 of today's most popular sports, both professional and amateur sports and "recreational sports" such as hiking. Gives general information on the sport itself; background and history; professional and amateur organizations; leagues, clubs, and playing facilities; recent rule changes, etc. GV583.N63

The Oxford companion to world sports and games / ed. by John Arlott. London ; N.Y. : Oxford Univ. Pr., 1975. 1143 p. : ill. **BK20**
Aims to provide an introduction to sports and games "which are the subject of national or international competition" (*Pref.*), but omits blood sports and board and table games. Intends "to help the reader to understand a sport when he watches it for the first time. The descriptive section explains how it is played—as distinct from how to play it." Does not print the rules of each game, but provides digests thereof, together with a diagram of the playing field, etc., as applicable. Entries for individual sports figures and champions, and for specific sporting events and competitions. Articles are unsigned, but a list of contributors is provided. Cross-references; occasional bibliographic citations. GV207.O93

Porter, David L. A cumulative index to the Biographical dictionary of American sports / comp. by David L. Porter. Westport, Conn. : Greenwood, c1993. 325 p. **BK21**
Covers the first 5 v. in the "Biographical dictionary of american sports" series, which together, provide comprehensive biographical information on more than 2,700 of the most exceptional sports figures in America. Includes amateur and professional athletes, as well as club and league administrators, referees, broadcasters, writers, etc.
Volumes in the series: baseball (BK52); basketball (BK63); football (BK74); outdoor sports (BK14); supplement, 1989–92 (BK13). GV697.A1P576

Rooney, John F. Atlas of American sport / John F. Rooney, Jr., Richard Pillsbury ; cartographic supervisor, Jeffrey McMichael. N.Y. : Macmillan : Maxwell Macmillan International, c1992. 198 p. : col. ill., col. maps ; 29 x 45 cm. **BK22**
Explores the geographical elements of American sport by mapping the distributions of facilities, players, and activities. Maps include descriptive text. 25 major sports are examined in detail and more than 45 additional sports briefly. Appendixes contain a list of associations with addresses, a select bibliography, general index, and geographical index. G1201.E63R6

Sports encyclopedia North America / ed. by John D. Windhausen. Gulf Breeze, Fla. : Academic International Pr., 1987–93. v. 1–5 : ill. (In progress). **BK23**
Contents: v. 1–5, Aaron–Berg.
Proposes to be the "most complete reference guide to American

and Canadian sports, present and past ... both in the breadth of its subject entries and its insistence upon depth of coverage, including statistical information and reference aids."—*From the editor.* To be complete in 50 v. Relies heavily on information reprinted verbatim from various sports organizations. Entries include bibliographic references. Despite its promise of completeness, early volumes have no entries for, e.g., anabolic steroids, American College of Sports Medicine, attribution, attention, anxiety.   GV581.S65

Dictionaries

Considine, Tim. The language of sport. N.Y. : Facts on File : World Almanac Publ., 1982. 355 p.   **BK24**
   Terms and phrases are grouped by sport (baseball, basketball, bowling, boxing, football, golf, ice hockey, soccer, and tennis) with a historical sketch of the sport at the beginning of each section. Includes entries for associations, tournaments, etc. Indexed.   GV567.C59

Dictionary of the sport and exercise sciences / Mark H. Anshel, editor ; Patty Freedson ... [et al]. Champaign, Ill. : Human Kinetics Books, c1991. 163 p. : ill.   **BK25**
   Written by authors who are experts in the growing disciplines of sport and exercise sciences, this work includes terms from nine subdisciplines: adapted physical education, biomechanics, exercise physiology (including body compositon and cardiac rehabilitation), motor control, motor development, motor learning, sport pedagogy, sport psychology, and sport sociology. Not included are terms from physical education, dance, sports medicine, or specific sports. Approximately 3,000 terms are concisely defined; diagrams are occasionally used for illustration.   GV558.D53

Matz, David. Greek and Roman sport : a dictionary of athletes and events from the eighth century B.C. to the third century A.D. Jefferson, N.C. : McFarland, c1991. 169 p.   **BK26**
   Contains a wealth of information about sports and games in ancient Greece and Rome. Events, individuals, terms, etc. are arranged alphabetically. Also includes seven special essays on such topics as gladiatorial combat, chariot races, etc., and a brief history of Greek and Roman sport. Includes lists of athletes and horses, a glossary of places, and a list of classical texts cited in the work. Indexed.   GV17.M38

The Oxford companion to Australian sport / ed. by Wray Vamplew ... [et al.]. Melbourne ; N.Y. : Oxford Univ. Pr., 1992. 430 p. : ill.   **BK27**
   "The first comprehensive presentation of sport in Australia."—*Foreword.* Alphabetical entries describe people, events, teams, sports, historical developments, and significant themes such as violence and nationalism. Illustrations; bibliography of Australian sports history.   GV675.O93

Palmatier, Robert A. Sports talk : a dictionary of sports metaphors / Robert A. Palmatier and Harold L. Ray. N.Y. : Greenwood, 1989. 227 p.   **BK28**
   More than 1,700 sports metaphors, giving for each: full, popular form of the expression; an illustration of correct grammatical usage; definition; the earliest date used, with probable source; the definition of the original sports term; a coded source of other works recognizing the source of the metaphor; and comparative and contrastive cross-references to other entries. Index is arranged by sport.   PE1689.P27

Wörterbuch der Sportwissenschaft : Deutsch, Englisch, Französisch = Dictionary of sport science : German, English, French / ed., Erich Beyer. Schorndorf : K. Hofmann, c1987. 770 p. : ill.   **BK29**
   A polyglot dictionary on a German base that gives English and French equivalents in parallel columns, with indexes of French and English terms. The detailed entries discuss terms thoroughly and employ many synonyms for characteristics and attributes. Some cross-references embedded in the entries; extensive bibliography, chiefly of German-language sources.   GV567.W62

Quotations

Dictionary of sports quotations / comp. by Barry Liddle. London ; N.Y. : Routledge & K. Paul, 1987. 210 p.   **BK30**
   Arranged by sport. Cites sources of quotations. Author index.   GV706.8.D53

Maikovich, Andrew J. Sports quotations : maxims, quips and pronouncements for writers and fans. Jefferson, N.C. : McFarland, c1984. 168 p.   **BK31**
   Entries are arranged alphabetically by author within sections by sport. Profession is given for the author of each quotation. Name and subject indexes.   GV706.8.M34

Directories

The big book of halls of fame in the United States and Canada : sports / comp. and ed. by Paul Soderberg, Helen Washington, Jaques Cattell Press. N.Y. : Bowker, 1977. 1042 p.   **BK32**
   Cover title: Halls of fame.
   Arranged alphabetically by particular fields of sport (Angling through Wrestling, plus a separate section for Special fields). Entries include directory and general information about each hall of fame, followed by a list of members with a biographical sketch of each intended to give enough information to indicate why the biographee was worthy of inclusion in the hall of fame. Indexed.   CT215.B53

The blue book of college athletics for senior, junior & community colleges. 61st (1991–92)– . Montgomery, Ala. : Athletic Publ., c1991– . Annual.   **BK33**
   Title varies: *Blue book of college athletics*; *Blue book of senior college, university and junior & community college athletics*; *Blue book of college, university and junior & community college athletics*.
   A comprehensive directory of information on college programs in the U.S. and Canada. Contains listings for senior colleges, junior and community colleges, and their conferences and related associations. Lists addresses, phone numbers, names of coaches and other administrators, and adds limited but useful information on the colleges themselves and athletic facilities. Indexed by state, as well as by type of college or organization; cross-references of college names.
          GV351.B58

Event line. 1990– . Amsterdam ; N.Y. : Elsevier, 1989– .   **BK34**
   For annotation, *see* AL28.   AS8.E94

Gelbert, Doug. Sports halls of fame : a directory of over 100 sports museums in the United States. Jefferson, N.C. : McFarland & Co., c1992. 176 p. : ill.   **BK35**
   In three sections: national sports museums, multisport museums and those devoted to the achievements of individual sports figures, and local sports museums. Listings include address, phone number, days of operation, fees, and directions. Each entry contains historical information about the museum and includes special features and a section on other historical attractions in the vicinity.   GV583.G45

Sport on film and video : the North American Society for Sport History guide / Judith A. Davidson, ed. and comp., and Daryl Alder, comp. Metuchen, N.J. : Scarecrow, 1993. 194 p.   **BK36**
   A filmography of productions appropriate for educational use (e.g., in a sport history course). Topics range from general to historical, sociological, and psychological coverage of sports. Does not in-

clude "how-to" or commercial films. Entries describe the film and list release date, length, format, age, appeal, and chronological placement of the subject. With distributor index, name index, and a very useful topic index.   GV576.S578

Sports fan's connection : an all-sports-in-one-directory to profesional, collegiate, and Olympic organizations, events, and information sources / Bradley J. Morgan, ed. ; Peg Bessette, associate ed. 1st ed.– . Detroit : Gale, c1992– . Biennial.   **BK37**

Provides coverage of approximately 50 competitive spectator sports played at the professional, collegiate, and Olympic levels. Includes full descriptive and contact information for professional teams and leagues, college and university athletics programs and conferences, organizations, associations, fan clubs, halls of fame, radio and TV stations, and other sources of information. Includes master name and keyword indexes.   GV583.S6853

Sports market place. 1984– . Princeton, N.J. : Sportsguide, c1984– . Annual.   **BK38**

Published annually in Jan., with supplement in July and optional quarterly updates.

A useful directory, listing organizations, suppliers of sports products, media personnel, sports officials, arenas and other facilities, and marketing and other services. Geographic, keyword, and specific sport indexes.

§ Continues: *Sportsguide master reference* (Princeton, N.J. : Sportsguide, 1981–83. Annual.) An abridgment, *Sports market place register* (1992– . Semiannual) contains directorial information similar to that in the parent work, but omits organization descriptions, marketing data, and the keyword index.   HD9992.U5S667

Handbooks

Kirby, Ronald F. Kirby's guide to fitness and motor performance tests. Cape Girardeau, Mo. : BenOak Publ. Co., 1991. 458 p. : ill.   **BK39**

Contains comprehensive information on tests that measure physical fitness and motor performance. Tests relate to 11 performance components, such as balance, agility, muscular endurance. Describes and evaluates 193 tests; reviewing was done by a group of 124 authorities in the field (who are listed with affiliations). Appendixes list relevant books published since 1980, and references from the evaluative text describing tests.   QP301.K55

Paciorek, Michael J. Sports and recreation for the disabled : a resource handbook / Michael J. Paciorek, Jeffery A. Jones. Indianapolis : Benchmark Pr., c1989. 396 p. : ill.   **BK40**

Describes more than 200 national and regional organizations that offer information on sport and recreation opportunities for individuals with disabilities. In 53 chapters, each covering a different activity. For each, the manual includes an overview of the activity, appropriate governing bodies for the sport or activity, an indication of which disabilities it is best suited for, a list of adapted equipment available, equipment suppliers and manufacturers, additional resources, references, and bibliography.   GV709.3.P33

Woolum, Janet. Outstanding women athletes : who they are and how they influenced sports in America / by Janet Woolum ; forewords by Billie Jean King, Anita DeFrantz, Deborah Slaner Anderson. Phoenix : Oryx, 1992. 279 p. : ill.   **BK41**

Contains biographies of 60 women athletes, a brief essay on the history of American women's sports and women in the Olympics, a bibliography, list of organizations, and list of female Olympic medalists arranged by sport.   GV697.A1W69

Almanacs; Compendiums

The Guinness book of sports records. 1991– . N.Y. : Facts On File, c1991– . Annual.   **BK42**

Organized by specific sport, each entry includes a note on origins of the sport. Covers approximately 70 sports, including all major U.S. sports, plus others such as rodeo, frisbee, trampolining, snooker, orienteering. Gives basic records, such as most points, wins, medals, titles; fastest speed; highest scoring game. Includes previous year's season in review and results of recent Olympic contests; indexed.

GV741.G843

The Information please sports almanac. 1990– . Boston : Houghton Mifflin Co., c1989– . Annual.   **BK43**

Date in title.

Begins with information on the previous year: top personalities (with photographs) and a month-by-month review of major sports happenings. A unique feature is the year in review essays written by top U.S. sportswriters on major sports and topics (ballparks, business and media, international sports, etc.). A basic reference for major sports facts and records of the past 125 years.   GV741.I58

The Sports Illustrated sports almanac. 1992– . Boston : Little, Brown, c1991– . Annual.   **BK44**

Date appears in title.

This all-in-one-volume source of sports records provides team and individual records for major sports as well as the less popular, such as swimming, figure skating, bowling, tennis, horse racing, motor sports, boxing, archery, cycling, etc. Each sport is covered separately, with a brief descriptive essay, then the statistics.

• Machine-readable version: *Sports Illustrated CD-ROM sports almanac* [database] (Burbank, Calif. : Warner New Media, 1992–). Available on CD-ROM, updated annually.   GV741.S768

Rules

Official rules of sports & games. 1949– . London : Nicholas Kaye, [1954]– . Biennial.   **BK45**

Publisher varies: some issues publ. London : Kingswood Pr. Publ. in U.S. : New Rochelle, N.Y. : Kaye & Ward Ltd., 1968– .

Covers 31 sports played competitively in Great Britain. Included for the first time in the 18th ed. are curling, handball, korfball, and softball. Rules are adapted from the official sporting bodies in Great Britain. For most entries, only the playing field or court is illustrated.

GV731.O27

Rules of the game : the complete illustrated encyclopedia of all the sports of the world / by the Diagram Group. N.Y. : St. Martin's, 1990. 320 p. : col. ill.   **BK46**

Earlier versions had title: *The rules of the game* (N.Y. : Paddington Pr., 1974); *The way to play : the illustrated encyclopedia of the games of the world* (N.Y. : Paddington Pr., 1975); *The rule book : the authoritative, up-to-date, illustrated guide to the regulations, history, and object of all major sports* (N.Y. : St. Martin's, 1983).

Covers some 150 international sports, including those more recently popular, such as hang gliding, freestyle skiing, running game target shooting, windsurfing, and jiu jitsu. Uses a visual presentation, with more than 2,000 illustrations, to explain features and rules. Official international sports governing bodies are listed with addresses. Indexed by type of sport activity group (combat, target, court, water, team, stick and ball, etc.) and alphabetically by name of sport; also includes a general index, with terms.   GV731.D52

Sports rules encyclopedia / Jess R. White [ed.]. 2nd ed. Champaign, Ill. : Leisure Pr., c1990. 732 p. : ill.   **BK47**

1st ed., Palo Alto, Calif. : National Pr., [1961].

Provides rules for 52 sports, excluding "activities that involve animals or mechanical devices as primary elements in the performance."—*Pref.* Each entry includes a description of the U.S. group that governs the sport, the rules, and two periodicals concerned with the sport. Most rules are taken verbatim from the published official rules. Rules for some wheelchair sports are given. Appendixes list other sport organizations, including those concerned with sports for persons with disabilities. Very useful.   GV731.S75

Individual sports

Baseball

The ballplayers : baseball's ultimate biographical reference / ed. by Mike Shatzkin ; managing ed., Stephen Holtje ; created and developed by Mike Shatzkin & Jim Charlton. N.Y. : Arbor House/William Morrow, c1990. 1230 p. : ill.   **BK48**

Includes about 6,000 20th-century players through 1989 and 1,000 19th-century players; special attention is given to the Negro League. Compiled from *The baseball encyclopedia* (N.Y. : Macmillan, 1988), *The sports encyclopedia : baseball* (BK58), and *Total baseball* (BK62). Entries include biographical and statistical information, stadiums, and descriptions of awards. Black-and-white photographs.   GV865.A1B323

The baseball encyclopedia : the complete and definitive record of major league baseball. 9th ed., rev., updated, and exp. N.Y. : Macmillan : Maxwell Macmillan International, 1993. 2857 p.   **BK49**

Subtitle varies.

1st ed., 1969; 8th ed., 1990.

An exhaustive record of individual player, team, and league statistics, lists, rosters, etc., derived from a computerized databank. Updated through the 1992 World Series. Not indexed.   GV877.B27

Baseball's greatest quotations / [comp. by] Paul Dickson. N.Y. : Edward Burlingame Books, c1991. 524 p. : ill.   **BK50**

An indexed compendium of quotations from the early years of America's favorite game through 1990.   GV867.3.B366

Benson, Michael. Ballparks of North America : a comprehensive historical reference to baseball grounds, yards, and stadiums, 1845 to present. Jefferson, N.C. : McFarland, c1989. 475 p. : ill.   **BK51**

Arranged alphabetically by city, then chronologically. Entries include league, first team to play in park, location, dimensions, seating capacity, attendance records. Extensive bibliography and good name index. Includes parks not covered in Philip J. Lowry's *Green cathedrals* (BK57).   GV879.5.B46

Biographical dictionary of American sports : baseball / ed. by David L. Porter. N.Y. : Greenwood, 1987. 713 p.   **BK52**

Brief signed articles with short bibliographies treat 423 players, 27 managers, 6 umpires, and 61 executives. Appendixes list professional major leagues, Negro leagues, Hall of Fame members, and contributors. Special indexes by types, position, place of birth by state, and Negro League entries. Coverage not as extensive as *The ballplayers* (BK48).

For a supplement, *see* BK13; for the cumulative index, *see* BK21.   GV865.A1B55

Daguerreotypes / ed., Craig Carter. 8th ed. St. Louis : Sporting News, c1990. 320 p. : ports.   **BK53**

Rev. ed. of: *Daguerreotypes of great stars of baseball*, ed. by Paul MacFarlane ([3rd ed.], 1981).

Presents lifetime records, other notable facts, and photographs of 397 of baseball's greatest players, managers, umpires, and executives. Introduction notes criteria for inclusion. Includes all Baseball Hall of Fame members.   GV877.M25

Dewey, Donald. Encyclopedia of major league baseball teams / Donald Dewey & Nick Acocella. N.Y. : HarperCollins, c1994. 594 p. : ill.   **BK54**

Covers the six major leagues which have been officially acknowledged by the Office of the Baseball Commissioner. Separate entries for teams that have moved from one city to another. Arranged alphabetically, the entries include the team's ballpark, other names the team has used, its overall record, a historical essay, and annual standings and managers of the team from the earliest known time to 1992.   GV875.A1D48

Dickson, Paul. The Dickson baseball dictionary. N.Y. : Facts on File, c1989. 438 p. : ill.   **BK55**

Offers very readable definitions of nearly 5,000 baseball terms. Entries include origin and etymology, first usage with citations. Usage outside baseball, historic background, and cross-references included as applicable. Black-and-white photographs; bibliography.   GV862.3.D53

——————— The Worth book of softball : a celebration of America's true national pastime. N.Y. : Facts on File, c1994. 276 p. : ill.   **BK56**

An illustrated history and record of softball. Contains a year-by-year chronology, appendix of organizations, bibliography, index, and glossary.   GV863.A1D53

Lowry, Philip J. Green cathedrals. Cooperstown : Society for American Baseball Research, 1986. 157 p. : ill.   **BK57**

A roster of baseball stadiums, giving name, style of park, nickname or alternate name, occupants in chronological order, location, surface, dimensions, fences, former and current use, and phenomena of historical importance. Arranged by league; covers major and minor leagues, Negro League, home and neutral parks. Black-and-white photographs; bibliography. Lack of an index requires users to know the league associated with a particular ballpark.   GV879.5.L69

Neft, David S. The sports encyclopedia : baseball / David S. Neft, Richard M. Cohen. 13th ed. N.Y. : St. Martin's, c1993. 670 p.   **BK58**

1st ed., 1976; 12th ed., 1992.

Team statistics for each league, as well as data for individual batters and pitchers. Pennant, championship, and World Series statistics provided, as are those for both annual and lifetime batting and pitching leaders. Arranged chronologically by season, and also divided into broader categories spanning ten to 30 years.   GV877.N43

Reichler, Joseph L. The great all-time baseball record book. Rev. and updated / by Ken Samelson. N.Y. : Macmillan : Maxwell Macmillan International, c1993. 592 p.   **BK59**

A well-organized compendium of baseball statistics from the earliest period through 1992. Major sections for individual batting, pitching, and fielding records, rookie records, and team records. Player index.   GV877.R39

Smith, Myron J. Baseball : a comprehensive bibliography. Jefferson, N.C. : McFarland, 1986. 915 p. : port.   **BK60**

Lists monographs, government publications, theses and dissertations, yearbooks, some fiction and poetry, and articles from 365 journals. Sections, which begin with brief introductions, cover reference works, general works, history, special studies; professional leagues and teams; youth leagues, college, and amateur/semiprofessional play; rules and techniques; collective bibliography; and individual biography. Author and subject indexes.

———. ———. *Supplement 1 (1985–May 1992)* (Jefferson, N.C. : McFarland, 1993. 422 p.).

8,000 citations. Criteria for inclusion are broad and basically the same as for the main volume; represented are books, monographs, articles from more than 450 periodicals, and other documents. Arranged like the main volume, so lengthy section introductions are omitted. Author and subject indexes.   Z7514.B3S64

The Sporting news baseball guide. 1990– . St. Louis, Mo. : Sporting News, 1990– . Annual. **BK61**

Title varies: *Baseball guide.*

Supersedes: *Baseball guide and record book*, 1943–48; *Baseball official guide*, 1949–62; *Official baseball guide*, 1963–89.

The bible for information on the teams and players of professional baseball. Issued annually, it contains every conceivable statistic for the previous season, with retrospective information also included. Team stories are arranged according to finishing order in the previous season. GV877.B324

Total baseball / ed. by John Thorn and Pete Palmer with Michael Gershman. 3rd ed. N.Y. : HarperPerennial, c1993. 2362 p. **BK62**

Purports to correct omissions and errors in *The baseball encyclopedia* (7th ed., 1988). Includes an extensive introductory history of major league baseball by David Q. Voigt; team histories and listing of defunct clubs and leagues; post-season play, World Series, and All-Star games; 400 biographical sketches; chronology of major events; mascots; scandals; umpires; awards and honors; black players. Other leagues, business, law, and the farm system are covered as well as Japanese, Caribbean, armed services, and women's baseball. Includes a large statistical compilation of players, umpires, coaches, and home-road statistics, and a chronology of rule changes, 1859–1992. Extensive, briefly-annotated bibliography. GV863.A1T68

Basketball

Biographical dictionary of American sports : basketball and other indoor sports / ed. by David L. Porter. N.Y. : Greenwood, 1989. 801 p. **BK63**

More than half the 558 entries describe basketball figures, but people from bowling, boxing, diving, figure skating, gymnastics, ice hockey, swimming, weightlifting, wrestling, and miscellaneous sports are also included. Each entry is followed by a brief bibliography. Appendixes list players by category, position played, and state of birth; hall of fame members; conferences; women by sport; and ring names and real names of boxers. Index and list of contributors.

For a supplement, *see* BK13; for the cumulative index, *see* BK21. GV697.A1B494

Krause, Jerry V. Basketball resource guide / Jerry V. Krause, Stephen J. Brennan. 2nd ed. Champaign, Ill. : Leisure Pr., c1990. 238 p. **BK64**

1st ed., 1982, had title: *The basketball bible.*

A comprehensive bibliography of books, articles, and other sources of basketball literature, including theses and dissertations. Extensive coverage of *Athletic journal* and *Scholastic coach*. Indexed. Z7514.B34K7

Neft, David S. The sports encyclopedia : pro basketball / David S. Neft & Richard M. Cohen. 5th ed, rev. and updated with assistance from John Hogrogian, Bob Gill and Doug Feinberg. N.Y. : St. Martin's, 1992. 624 p. **BK65**

1st ed., 1975.

Arranged chronologically by periods; presents a historical summary of the game, as well as a complete statistical record from 1938 through the 1991–92 season. Includes yearly individual and team, lifetime, and single season leaders. Extensive table of contents, but no index. GV885.5.N44

The Sporting news official NBA guide. 1993–94 ed.– . St. Louis : Sporting News, c1993– . Annual. **BK66**

Title varies: some issues called *Official NBA guide.*

With its companion work, *NBA register* (1982/83–), contains year-by-year statistics, 1946 to the present, top performers, career statistics, etc. Extensive coverage of the previous season, team office/administration information, schedule for the upcoming season. Brief topical index. GV885.N26

Taragano, Martin. Basketball biographies : 434 U.S. players, coaches, and contributors to the game, 1891–1990. Jefferson, N.C. : McFarland & Co., c1991. 318 p. : ports. **BK67**

Contains brief biographies of 434 players, coaches, and others who have been important to the game. Arranged alphabetically, entries provide career statistics and other information explaining the person's major contributions. Criteria for inclusion can be found in the introduction, but include career scores, top ten leader status, longevity, etc. Indexed. GV884.A1T37

Billiards

Shamos, Michael Ian. The illustrated encyclopedia of billiards. N.Y. : Lyons & Burford, c1993. 308 p. : ill. **BK68**

In more than 2,000 entries and 200 illustrations, covers billiards, pool, snooker, and other cue sports. Defines the terminology in a historical context. Includes a list of organizations, bibliography, and index. GV891.S53

Boxing

Fleischer, Nat. A pictorial history of boxing / by Nat Fleischer and Sam Andre. New rev. and updated ed. / by Peter Arnold. N.Y. : Carol Publ. Group, 1993. 416 p. : ill. **BK69**

1st ed., 1959; 1st. rev. ed., 1975.

"Emphasis has been laid on picturing as many of the champions and the top contenders as possible in every division"—*Pref*. Profusely illustrated. Documents the beginnings of boxing in 1719 through events of 1993. Indexed. GV1121.F63

Odd, Gilbert E. Encyclopedia of boxing. Secaucus, N.J. : Chartwell Books, 1989. 244 p. : ill. (some col.). **BK70**

1st ed., 1983.

Arranged alphabetically by boxers' names, presents biographies of the world's greatest boxers of all time, and then a "facts and figures" section that lists world championships and winners by year in each division. Glossary of boxing terms. Index of illustrations. GV1118.O33

Cricket

Padwick, E. W. A bibliography of cricket. 2nd ed., rev. and enl. to the end of 1979. London : Libr. Assoc. in assoc. with J. W. McKenzie (bookseller) on behalf of the Cricket Society, 1984. 877 p. **BK71**

1st ed., 1977.

Supplemented by: *Padwick's bibliography of cricket*, comp. by Stephen Eley and Peter Griffiths, 1991. Called v. 2.

An international bibliography of books and periodicals related to cricket. General sources are listed first, then sources by country. The 2nd ed. cites materials published through 1979, the supplement those published 1980–89; the supplement includes more than 800 items prior to 1980 that were not in the previous editions. Title/keyword and author/title index. Z7514.C7.P3

Cycling

Leccese, Michael. The bicyclist's sourcebook / Michael Leccese & Arlene Plevin. Rockville, Md. : Woodbine House, 1991. 355 p. : ill. **BK72**

Throughout the work, names and addresses of more than 1,000 bicycling sources are listed. All types of cycling are included. Contains articles written by cycling experts on a number of relevant topics. Indexed. GV1043.7.L43

Football

Baldwin, Robert. College football records : Division I-A and the Ivy League, 1869–1984. Jefferson, N.C. : McFarland, c1987. 198 p. **BK73**

Provides statistics for 111 college and university Division I-A teams still active; arranged by conference, with a separate section for independent schools. Lists wins, losses, and ties against Division I and other opponents, total overall record, and total conference and bowl record. Entries give nickname, colors, location, stadium capacity, first year of football, year entered conference, number of conference championships. Appendixes give ranked summaries of various conference and bowl records. Index of nondivision and other opponents. Finding the entry for a Division I-A team requires knowledge of the conference in which it plays. GV950.B35

Biographical dictionary of American sports : football / ed. by David L. Porter. N.Y. : Greenwood, 1987. 763 p. **BK74**

Brief, signed biographies of 520 notable football figures, including players, coaches, executives, league administrators, rules developers, and promoters, arranged alphabetically. Each entry concludes with a brief bibliography. Appendixes list entries by category, position played, state of birth, collegiate and Professional Hall of Fame members, and conferences or leagues. Index and list of contributors.

For a supplement, *see* BK13; for the cumulative index, *see* BK21.
GV939.A1B56

The college football bibliography / comp. by Myron J. Smith, Jr. Westport, Conn. : Greenwood, 1994. 951 p. (Bibliographies and indexes on sports history, no. 2). **BK75**

Covers the literature of college football from the 1880s through Jan. 1993. A comprehensive bibliography of 12,100 entries, many briefly annotated. Five major sections: Reference works; General works, history, and special studies; Associations, conferences, and teams; Rivalries, big games, and post-season play; and Biography. Includes a list of journals, author and subject indexes. Z7514.F7C65

Harrington, Denis J. The Pro Football Hall of Fame : players, coaches, team owners, and league officials, 1963–1991. Jefferson, N.C. : McFarland, c1991. 354 p. : port. **BK76**

Provides brief profiles of 150 inductees, including career records and other major accomplishments. GV959.5.U6H37

National Football League. Official National Football League record & fact book. 1984– . N.Y. : Workman Publishing Co., c1984– . Annual. **BK77**

Year of coverage appears in title.

Continues the official record manual and the media information book published by the NFL.

Authorized by the NFL. Contains all-time NFL individual and team records. Includes a digest of rules, coaching records, and a chronological history of professional football since 1869. Lists extensive statistics for the previous year and the complete schedule for the current year. GV955.N334b

Ours, Robert M. College football encyclopedia : the authoritative guide to 124 years of college football. Rocklin, Calif. : Prima Pub., c1994. 501 p. : ill. **BK78**

Contains all statistics for 86 NCAA division I-A teams. Includes histories of teams, as well as individual players' records and awards. Arranged by conference, with appendixes for team national champions, coaching records, and top ten team and individual statistics. GV956.8.O87

Pro football guide / ed., Craig Carter. 1993 ed. St. Louis : The Sporting News, c1993. 327 p. : ill. **BK79**

Provides comprehensive coverage of teams and players, present and past seasons, championship games, etc. Arranged in four sections: present season, past season review, past season statistics, and miscellaneous. Not indexed.

Smith, Myron J. Professional football : the official Pro Football Hall of Fame bibliography. Westport, Conn. : Greenwood, 1993. 414 p. (Bibliographies and indexes on sports history, no. 1). **BK80**

An authoritative bibliography containing more than 15,000 entries, covering comprehensive sources published from the early 1900s through mid-June 1991. Arranged in four major sections: Reference works; General works, history, and special studies; Professional leagues, teams, and games; Biography. Author/subject index. Z7514.F7S64

Golf

Campbell, Malcolm. The Random House international encyclopedia of golf : the definitive guide to the game. N.Y. : Random House, c1991. 336 p. : ill. (some col.). **BK81**

Traces the early development of golf, and describes the game as it is today. Includes information on equipment and golf course architects. Describes in detail 50 of the world's most famous golf courses, including history, layout (with photographs). Briefly describes an additional 50 courses worldwide. Includes biographies of the 100 most important people in golf. Championship statistics are included through 1991. Glossary. GV965.C32

Golf magazine's encyclopedia of golf : the complete reference / the editors of Golf magazine. 2nd ed. N.Y. : HarperCollins, c1993. 517 p. : ill. **BK82**

1st ed., 1970; updated and rev., 1979.

Covers the history of the game and of courses around the world, tournament and championship records, equipment, rules, terms, and biographies of golfers. Includes a section on golf architecture, with biographies of influential golf architects and ranked listings of best courses worldwide. Glossary and index. GV965.G5455

Marrandette, David G. Golf playoffs : a sourcebook of major championship men's and women's amateur and professional playoffs, 1876–1990. Jefferson, N.C. : McFarland, c1991. 157 p. : ill. **BK83**

In separate sections for men's and women's events, provides brief descriptions of each tournament playoff, arranged chronologically. Records are listed in appendixes. Includes a brief bibliography. Indexed. GV970.M36

Morrison, Ian. The Hamlyn encyclopedia of golf. Twickenham : Hamlyn, 1986. 176 p. **BK84**

Includes the language of golf, records and statistics, histories of major tournaments around the world, rule summaries, and major courses. Illustrated with many color photographs. GV965

The official United States golf course directory and guide. Chicago : Kayar Co., Inc. Annual. **BK85**

Title varies. Date appears in title.

Includes all full courses in the U.S., arranged alphabetically by state and city. With orientation maps for each state. GV981.O36

Hockey

The complete encyclopedia of hockey / ed. by Zander Hollander. 4th ed. expanded & updated. Detroit : Gale, c1993. 604 p. : ill. **BK86**

Begins with essays that document important events in the history of hockey, 1917–92. Includes biographies of the 35 greatest players, as well as brief entries for Hockey Hall of Fame members. Contains NHL individual and team records, trophy winners, all-star teams, as well as information on the World Hockey Association, collegiate programs, Olympic Games, and world championships. An all-time hockey player register, coach directory, glossary, official rules and signals, and index are included. GV847.8.N3C64

Fischler, Stan. The hockey encyclopedia : the complete record of professional ice hockey / Stan Fischler and Shirley Walton Fischler. N.Y. : Macmillan, [1983]. 720 p. **BK87**

A compendium of registers of players and teams, giving year-by-year statistics from 1917/18 through the 1982/83 season.

§ A 1975 publication entitled *Fischler's hockey encyclopedia* (N.Y. : Crowell, 628 p.) runs heavily to entries for individual players, but includes terms, teams, equipment, etc. GV847.5.F57

The National Hockey League official guide & record book. [1985–86?]– . Toronto : National Hockey League ; Chicago : Triumph Books, c[1985?]– . Annual. **BK88**

Provides complete team and individual records. Includes player registers, lifetime statistics for retired players, and the coming year's schedule. A comprehensive source of information on hockey.

Martial arts

Frederic, Louis. A dictionary of the martial arts / Louis Frederic ; translator and editor, Paul Crompton. Rutland, Vt. : Charles E. Tuttle Co., 1991. 276 p. : ill. **BK89**

Covers approximately 40 martial arts. Because some entries are quite detailed, this is more encyclopedia than dictionary. Arranged alphabetically by name of martial art; illustrated with useful drawings and photographs. GV1101.L68

Martial arts encyclopedia / ed. by Larry Winderbaum. Wash. : Inscape, [1977]. 215 p. : ill. **BK90**

"This ... is neither a how-to book nor a detailed history. It attempts to present both the rich cultural heritage of the arts and to survey their contemporary impact ... , but nowhere in the book is there a guide to practicing any single art presented."—*Introd.* Includes general information "on all of the martial arts, including aikido, iaido, judo, jujutsu, karate, kendo, kung fu, kyudo, sumo, tae kwon do, t'ai chi ch'uan, bando, jodo, and pentjak-silat." Dictionary arrangement of terms, names, places, etc. Lists of relevant books and magazines. GV1112.M34

Nelson, Randy F. The martial arts : an annotated bibliography / Randy F. Nelson with Katherine C. Whitaker ; illus. by Forrest Williams and Jerry Lilly. N.Y. : Garland, 1988. 436 p. : ill. (Garland reference library of social science, v. 451.). **BK91**

Covers journal literature and monographs; some entries are annotated. Arranged by sections: general topics, specific forms of martial arts, other arts, weapons, and works prior to 1920. Z7514.M37N44

Olympic Games

The Olympics factbook : a spectator's guide to the winter and summer Games / Martin Connors, Diane L. Dupuis, Brad Morgan, [editors]. Detroit : Visible Ink, c1992. 613 p. : ill. **BK92**

For each Olympic sport, includes a brief history of the game, past Olympic highlights, a review of important rules, techniques, equipment, and profiles of potential medalists. Lists part winners of each event and includes a television schedule for events in the 1992 Albertville and Barcelona Games. Contains a chronology of the Olympics from ancient history to the present. GV721.5.O393

Page, James A. Black Olympian medalists. Englewood, Colo. : Libraries Unlimited, 1991. 190 p. : ill. **BK93**

Contains brief biographies of 465 African-American Olympians. Each entry lists major achievements and other sources to consult (full information on sources is found in the bibliography at the end of the book). Includes statistics by event. GV697.A1P284

Wallechinsky, David. The complete book of the Olympics. 1992 ed. Boston : Little, Brown, 1992. 763 p. : ill. **BK94**

1st ed., 1984. Rev. ed., 1988, 1991.

Summer and Winter Games are treated in separate sections. Within those sections, sports are considered individually, with complete information on each event, lists of winners (with times, scores, etc) by year, often with commentary on specific contests and notes on the contestants. Includes discontinued events. Gives overall results of each Olympiad and presents a brief history of the Games. Covers every Olympiad from 1896 through the 1988 Summer Games in Seoul. Detailed table of contents, but no index. GV721.5.W25

———— The complete book of the Winter Olympics. 1994 ed. Boston : Little, Brown, c1993. 205 p. : ill. **BK95**

1st ed., 1984.

Contains national medal totals in each Olympics, and a brief history of the Winter Games. Sports are considered in separate sections, with full information on each event, lists winners (with times, scores, etc.) by year, usually with commentary on specific contests and notes on the contestants. Some sections include a glossary of terms for the particular sport. Includes discontinued events. Covers through the 1992 Winter Games in Albertville, France. Illustrated; not indexed. GV841.5.W26

Skiing

Gamma, Karl. The handbook of skiing. Rev. and updated. N.Y. : Knopf, 1992. 320 p. : ill. (some col.), maps. **BK96**

1st ed., 1981.

Covers the equipment of the sport, ski techniques, and mechanics. Many drawings throughout the volume illustrate different types of skiing and other aspects of the sport. Includes a gazetteer of international ski resorts. GV854.G28

Ski magazine's encyclopedia of skiing / ed. by Richard Needham. Rev. and updated. N.Y. : Harper & Row, c1979. 452 p. : ill. **BK97**

1st ed., 1970, by R. Scharff.

In six sections: (1) The history of skiing; (2) Ski equipment; (3) Principles of skiing, (4) Ski competition; (5) Where to ski; (6) Glossary, lexicon, and ski associations. Indexed. GV854.E53

Soccer

LaBlanc, Michael L. The world encyclopedia of soccer / Michael L. LaBlanc and Richard Henshaw. Detroit : Gale, 1994. 430 p. : ill. **BK98**

This comprehensive source opens with a spectator's guide to the 1994 World Cup competition. Included are a history of the game, complete rules, tactics, biographies of the world's greatest players, profiles of the world's teams, international and U.S. soccer associations, leagues and teams, and sections on women's soccer and Olympic soccer. Contains a historical timeline, glossary, and index.

Rollin, Jack. The World Cup, 1930–1990 : sixty glorious years of soccer's premier event. N.Y. : Facts on File, c1990. 191 p., [16] p. of plates : ill. (some col.). **BK99**

Includes history of the World Cup and detailed information on each competition. Profiles 21 World Cup all-time heroes, and the historical achievements of each national team that qualified in 1990. Includes records and trivia; indexed. GV943.49.R65

Swimming

Besford, Pat. Encyclopedia of swimming. 2nd ed. London : R. Hale ; N.Y. : St. Martin's, 1976. 302 p., [8] leaves of plates : ill. **BK100**

1st ed., 1971.

An alphabetical arrangement of entries for persons and topics associated with the sport. Includes numerous lists of champions, trophy winners, world records, etc.   GV837.B44

Tennis

Bud Collins' modern encyclopedia of tennis / ed. by Bud Collins and Zander Hollander. 2nd ed. Detroit : Visible Ink Pr., 1994. 666 p. : ill.   **BK101**

1st ed., 1980.

Chapters by Collins and other contributors cover the history of tennis, the 1919–45 era and the 25 greatest players of those years, the 1946–67 and 1968–79 periods and their greatest players, the officials, equipment, International Tennis Hall of Fame, and "tennis lingo." Appendixes of rules and records. Indexed.   GV993.C6

Lumpkin, Angela. A guide to the literature of tennis. Westport, Conn. : Greenwood, c1985. 235 p.   **BK102**

Bibliographic essays on the history of the sport; history of championship players and performance; rules and administration; equipment, facilities, and travel; technique; players and teaching professionals; health and fitness; psychology; biography; children's books, humor, films; general works; periodicals; and promotional organizations. Appendixes list organizations, halls of fame, champions in various competitions. Subject and author indexes.   GV991.2.L85

Phillips, Dennis J. Teaching, coaching, and learning tennis : an annotated bibliography. Metuchen, N.J. : Scarecrow, 1989. 178 p.   **BK103**

Contains approximately 500 citations to books, theses, and other materials published in the U.S., 1968–88. Briefly annotated entries are arranged alphabetically, and cross-references are given where appropriate. Separate subject and title indexes.   Z7514.T3P47

United States Tennis Association. The official United States Tennis Association yearbook and tennis guide with the official rules. Lynn, Mass. : H.O. Zimman, [1976]– .   **BK104**

Continues *Official United States Lawn Tennis Association yearbook and tennis guide with the official rules.*

Contains USTA's top ten rankings for men and women, 1885–1992, with biographical information and photographs included for the current year's top ten. Includes U.S. national rankings in all categories from the 1880s to 1992; also covers cup matches, international championships and the Pan American and Olympic Games. Extensive coverage for the previous year's season.

Wrestling

Chapman, Mike. Encyclopedia of American wrestling. Champaign, Ill. : Leisure Pr., c1990. 533 p. : ill.   **BK105**

Traces the history of wrestling in America and provides statistics on Olympic wrestling, world championships and other major world meets, AAU National Freestyle, U.S. Freestyle Senior Open, Greco-Roman Nationals, Collegiate Nationals, Midlands Championships, Junior Nationals, and Junior World Tournaments. Lists special honors and awards, halls of fame and biographical sketches of 78 members of the National Wrestling Hall of Fame through 1988. Brief bibliography. No index.   GV1198.12.C43

Clayton, Thompson. A handbook of wrestling terms and holds / comp. by Thompson Clayton with the help of Doug Parker [and others]. New and rev. ed. South Brunswick [N.J.] : A.S. Barnes, [1974]. 192 p. : ill.   **BK106**

1st ed., 1968.

Aims to provide a common language for wrestling coaches. Lists and illustrates 445 maneuvers, with alternate terms given for each; illustrations are captioned with the most popular name of the maneuver. Indexed.   GV1195.C55

Other outdoor sports and recreation

General works

Landi, Val. The Bantam great outdoors guide to the United States and Canada : the complete travel encyclopedia and wilderness guide. Toronto ; N.Y. : Bantam, 1978. 854 p., [8] leaves of plates : ill.   **BK107**

Arranged by region, then by state or province. A map and an introduction for each region are followed by an "encyclopedia" section (giving information on accommodations for tourists, fishing and hunting, camping, canoeing, highways, etc.) and a "travel and recreation guide" for each state and province. Indexed.   GV191.4.L36

Recreation and outdoor life directory : a guide to national and international organizations / Steven R. Wasserman, ed. 2nd ed. Detroit : Gale, c1983. 1020 p.   **BK108**

1st ed., 1979.

In two main parts, the first covering general sources such as organizations, state and federal agencies, consultants, special libraries and information centers. The second part provides information concerning parks, scenic trails, shorelines, fish and game reserves, and similar outdoor recreational facilities under federal and state auspices. Indexed.   GV191.35.R4

Smith, Stephen L. J. Dictionary of concepts in recreation and leisure studies. N.Y. : Greenwood, 1990. 372 p. (Reference sources for the social sciences and humanities, no. 9).   **BK109**

Provides brief (one- to eight-page) authoritative discussions of major concepts in recreation and leisure studies (e.g., play, conservation, sport, therapeutic recreation, environment, volunteerism). Entries consist of four parts: current meaning, historical development, list of sources cited in the discussion, and sources of additional information. Entries contain cross-references. Subject and name indexes.

GV11.S57

Camping

Guide to accredited camps. 1989– . [Martinsville, Ind.] : American Camping Assoc., c1989– . Annual.   **BK110**

Continues: *Parents' guide to accredited camps* (1982–88).

Supersedes directories for 1977–81 issued in four regional editions, which superseded the Association's *National directory of accredited camps for boys and girls* (1971–76), which superseded *Directory of accredited camps ...* (1961–70).

Lists and provides information on camps accredited by the American Camping Association. Arranged by state. Tabular guide to activities; a separate section lists camps serving groups with special needs.   GV193.P37

Woodall's campground directory. North American ed. Ed.11 (1977)– . Highland Park, Ill. : Woodall, 1977– . Annual.   **BK111**

Continues *Woodall's trailering parks and campgrounds* (varies; 1967–76); also issued in regional editions.

Includes facilities in the U.S. and Canada.   GV198.56.W66

Hiking

Cook, Charles. The essential guide to hiking in the United States. N.Y. : M. Kesend Publ., 1991. 228 p. : ill., maps. **BK112**

Provides general information on hiking, including equipment, clothing, food, types of terrain, weather, and safety. Offers a state-by-state review of hiking areas, major trails, and a list of resources available. GV199.4.C66

Fletcher, Colin. The complete walker III : the joys and techniques of hiking and backpacking. 3rd ed., rev., enl., and updated. N.Y. : Knopf, 1984. 668 p. : ill. **BK113**
Rev. ed. of: *The new complete walker*, 1974.

A practical backpacking and hiking guide with extensive coverage of the required techniques and equipment for a successful trek. Appendixes list retailers, organizations, and a checklist of equipment, with the approximate weight of a load of gear recommended for a typical trip. GV199.6.F53

Hunting and fishing

Calabi, Silvio. The illustrated encyclopedia of fly-fishing : a complete A–Z of terminology, tackle & techniques. N.Y. : Holt, 1993. 336 p. : ill. (some col.). **BK114**
More than 500 entries detail the terminology and history of angling techniques and equipment. Arranged alphabetically; some long entries are subdivided (e.g., Knots). Color photographs and illustrations. SH456.C28

Elman, Robert. The hunter's field guide to the game birds and animals of North America. Rev. ed. N.Y. : Knopf, 1982. 655 p. : ill. **BK115**
1st ed., 1974.

Gives information about the life, habitat, and behavior of all North American game species. Sections for upland birds, ducks, geese, swans, shore and marsh birds, small game, deer, medium game, and big game. Many illustrations. Indexed. SK40.E45

Gartner, Robert. The national parks fishing guide. Chester, Conn. : Globe Pequot Pr., c1990. 445 p. : ill., maps. **BK116**
Arranged by state, describes fishing conditions in 125 national parks. Also notes availability of camping and lists other sources of information. SH463.G37

Schuh, Dwight R. Bowhunter's encyclopedia : practical, easy-to-find answers to your bowhunting questions. Harrisburg, Pa. : Stackpole Books, c1987. 574 p. : ill. **BK117**
Arranged alphabetically by broad subject category. Provides comprehensive coverage of the sport of bowhunting, and has geographic listings (for U.S. states and Canadian regions) that describe hunting conditions, type of game found, and contact point/office, with especially strong detail on Western states. Covers equipment, archery manufacturers, shooting techniques and hunting methods. Indexed, and illustrated with many photographs. SK36.S37

Mountaineering

Cleare, John. The world guide to mountains and mountaineering. N.Y. : Mayflower Books, 1979. 208 p. : ill. **BK118**
A practical guide to the most accessible mountain ranges of the world. Illustrated with photographs and detailed maps of the ranges themselves, with peaks, passes, cites, roads and other landmarks clearly labeled by symbols. Arranged by geographic area; includes entertaining text, a section on equipment, glossary of terms, bibliography, and index. GV200.C58

Noyce, Wilfrid. World atlas of mountaineering / ed. by Wilfrid Noyce and Ian McMorrin. N.Y. : Macmillan, [1970]. 224 p. : ill. **BK119**
Intended as a concise summary of mountaineering activity, and meant to be read through as well as to serve as a reference book. "The main concern throughout has been wih general tendencies, with the result that some peaks and some personalities are not mentioned."— *Pref.* Signed contributions offer descriptive, factual accounts of specific peaks, ranges, and geographical regions, followed by highlights of mountaineering activity in the area. Indexed. GB511.N67

Unsworth, Walter. Encyclopedia of mountaineering. [Rev. ed.]. Harmondsworth ; N.Y : Penguin, 1977. 398 p., 16 p. of plates : ill., maps, ports. **BK120**
1st ed., 1972.

An alphabetical arrangement of entries for places (i.e., "all the important mountain areas of the world and most of the lesser ones"— *Pref.*), people (about 400 climbers from various countries and periods), techniques and equipment, terms, and topics from other fields which have some bearing on mountain climbing. Indexed. GV199.85.U57

Sailing and water sports

An A–Z of sailing terms / ed. by Ian Dear and Peter Kemp. [2nd ed.]. Oxford [Eng.] ; N.Y. : Oxford Univ. Pr., 1992. 216 p. **BK121**
1st ed., 1987, had title: *Pocket Oxford guide to sailing terms*.

An abridged version of the classic *Oxford companion to ships and the sea* (1976), this work contains complete definitions of approximately 1,500 sailing terms. Some entries are extensive, others brief, some illustrated with diagrams. A small and inexpensive volume with good coverage. GV811.P63

Encyclopedia of sailing / rev. and updated by the editors of Yacht racing/cruising, with Robert Scharff and Richard Henderson. N.Y. : Harper & Row, c1978. 468 p. : ill. **BK122**
1st ed., 1971.

Information is presented in eight topical sections: (1) The history of sailing; (2) Sailboats and sailing gear; (3) Catalog of one-design and offshore sailboats; (4) The art of sailing; (5) Sailing is fun [concerned with cruising]; (6) The lure of racing; (7) Sailing competition; (8) Glossary of sailing terms. Detailed table of contents, but no index. GV811.E52

Schult, Joachim. The sailing dictionary / Joachim Schult ; tr. and extensively rev. by Barbara Webb. 2nd ed. / rev. by Jeremy Howard-Williams. Dobbs Ferry, N.Y. : Sheridan House, 1992. 331 p. : ill. (some col.). **BK123**
1st ed., 1981.

Defines some 4,000 technical terms of the sailing language briefly and concisely; many definitions are illustrated with clear drawings. Includes modern navigation electronics, grand prix racing, and new classes. GV811.S36613

Parks and protected areas

The complete guide to America's national parks : the official visitor's guide of the National Park Foundation. [1st ed.] (1979)– . Wash. : National Park Foundation, c1979– . Biennial? **BK124**
1979 issue lacks numerical designation but constitutes 1st ed.; 1981 issue called rev. ed.; later editions identified by two-year designation (e.g., 1992–1993 ed. publ. 1991).

Later issues lack subtitle.

A guide to national parks, monuments, historic sites, preserves, etc., arranged by state. For each park gives name, address, telephone, name of superintendent, directions, visitor activities, any interesting features such as proximity to other parks, and reference to a "Climatable." The latter are graphs and charts for each park, showing temperature, precipitation, sunshine/cloudiness, and temperature means and extremes. Name index.   E158.C78

International handbook of national parks and nature reserves / ed. by Craig W. Allin. N.Y. : Greenwood, 1990. 539 p. : ill., maps.   **BK125**

National parks and nature reserves are described for 25 nations and one regional cluster (Argentina, Australia, Canada, Chile, Republic of China, Colombia, Federal Republic of Germany, Great Britain, Greece, Honduras, India, Indonesia, Japan, Kenya, Malaysia, New Zealand, Norway, Papua New Guinea, Peru, South Africa, Uganda, Union of Soviet Socialist Republics, United States, Venezuela, West Africa, and Zimbabwe). "Each of the chapters is written to a common outline. Each author addresses the history of park preservation, the natural values associated with parks and reserves, and the legal and administrative structures charged with park protection and management."—*Pref.* Bibliographies at the end of each chapter. Indexed.   SB481.I565

O'Brien, Tim. The amusement park guide : fun for the whole family at more than 250 amusement parks from coast to coast. Chester, Conn. : Globe Pequot Pr., c1991. 220 p. : ill. **BK126**

Covers more than 250 parks in the U.S. and Canada, arranged by state or province. Entries include size and scope of park, food service, entertainment, other attractions, season dates, hours, admission policy, prices, directions, and advice on how to maximize one's visit.
                                                          GV1853.2.O25

Board and card games

Markey, Kay. The Neal-Schuman index to card games. N.Y. : Neal-Schuman Publishers, c1990. 153 p.   **BK127**

Indexes more than 30 reference sources for information on some 2,000 card games. Arranged by card game name or its variants, and by broad game category (bridge, cribbage, children's games, etc.). *See* and *see also* references account for overlapping rules, games, and categories.   GV1243.M37

The new complete Hoyle : the authoritative guide to the official rules of all popular games of skill and chance / by Alfred H. Morehead, Richard L. Frey, Geoffrey Mott-Smith. Rev, rev. by Richard L. Frey ... [et al.]. N.Y. : Doubleday, c1991. 692 p. : ill.   **BK128**

Rev ed. of Morehead's *Hoyle's rules of games* (2nd rev. ed. N.Y. : New American Library, 1983).

A new version of the classic source offering rules to board and card games.   GV1243.H88

Parlett, David Sidney. The Oxford guide to card games. Oxford ; N.Y. : Oxford Univ. Pr., 1990. 361 p., [24] p. of plates : ill. (some col.).   **BK129**

Not a rules book, this work emphasizes historical and social information about card games of the Western world. Illustrated with color and black-and-white plates. Appendixes include general rules of play, national suit systems, a glossary, notes for each chapter, a general index, and an index of card games.   GV1233.P37

Bridge

The official encyclopedia of bridge / Henry G. Francis, ed. in chief ... [et al.]. Newly rev., 4th ed. / Diane Hayward, ed. N.Y. : Crown, c1984. 922 p. : ill.   **BK130**

"Authorized by the American Contract Bridge League and prepared by its staff."—*t.p.*

1st ed., 1964.

A general information section offers an alphabetical arrangement of entries for technical, historical, procedural, and terminological information. There are separate sections for biographies, tournament results, and bibliography.   GV1282.22.O35

Chess

Divinsky, N. J. The chess encyclopedia. N.Y. : Facts on File, 1991. 247 p. : ill.   **BK131**

Originally published: London : Batsford, 1990.

Provides brief profiles of grand masters and others who have made significant contributions in the world of chess, information on important tournaments and games in history, and definitions of terms. Indexed, but no bibliography.   GV1314.5.D58

Graham, John. The literature of chess. Jefferson, N.C. : McFarland, c1984. 250 p. : ill.   **BK132**

"This book surveys the literature in a number of areas, reviews recommended books and provides a basis for choice" (*Pref.*) among the hundreds of titles available. Chapters deal with introductory works, works on openings, middle game, endings, chess lore, etc., each chapter preceded by a list of titles surveyed (136 in all, with bibliographic information). Indexed.   GV1445.G74

Hooper, David. The Oxford companion to chess / David Hooper and Kenneth Whyld. N.Y. : Oxford Univ. Pr., 1984. 407 p. : ill.   **BK133**

"Embraces all branches of chess including its history and gives recommended books for further reading. All terms commonly used by players are explained, about 570 biographies are given, and there are entries for about 650 names representing some 700 openings or variations."—*Pref.* Includes more than 220 games and more than 190 compositions. Index of named openings; multilingual glossary of chess terminology.   GV1445.H616

Lusis, Andy. Chess : an annotated bibliography, 1969–1988. London ; N.Y. : Mansell, 1991. 320 p.   **BK134**

Continues: *Chess : an annotated bibliography of works published in the English language, 1850–1968*, by Douglas A. Betts (1974).

Contains more than 3,200 entries, some dated beyond 1988. The table of contents specifies the subject classification scheme; under specific subjects, works are arranged chronologically, and within each year, alphabetically. Cross-references are made to Betts's earlier work. Also contains an extensive list of chess serials. Indexed separately by title, name, subject and series.   Z5541.L87

Sunnucks, Anne. The encyclopaedia of chess. 2nd ed. London : Hale ; N.Y. : St. Martin's, 1976. 619 p., [16] p. of plates : ill., facsims., ports.   **BK135**

1st ed., 1970.

Provides information on chess as played throughout the world, lists of national champions, results of major international tournaments, biographies of leading players, etc. A Subscription Books Committee review in the *Booklist* 74 (1 June, 1978): 1573 terms the work "an excellent informational source ... appropriate for all types of libraries." Some information in the 1st ed. was not carried over into the new work.   GV1314.5.S93

Gambling

Clark, Thomas L. The dictionary of gambling & gaming. Cold Spring, N.Y. : Lexik House, c1987. 263 p.   **BK136**

Provides concise explanations for the unique language of games and the gambling world. Entries include the source (written, oral, or fugitive) from which the author gleaned the definition, as well as cross-references, illustrative quotations, and etymological references.
                                                          GV1301.C58

Sifakis, Carl. Encyclopedia of gambling. N.Y. : Facts on File, c1990. 340 p. : ill.   **BK137**

Describes hundreds of gambling games and their variations, the history, customs and rules of gambling (including cheating), and information on casinos, famous gamblers throughout history, and the terminology and slang used in the gambling world. Nicely illustrated with drawings and photographs. Includes cross-references, a glossary, an index, and a bibliography.   HV671OC.S54

CRAFTS

Encyclopedias

The encyclopedia of crafts / Laura Torbet, ed. N.Y. : Scribner, c1980. 3 v. : ill.   **BK138**

A dictionary arrangement of entries for individual crafts and the terms, materials, tools, etc., relevant to those crafts. About 50 crafts are accorded lengthy articles and there are about 12,000 entries for specific terms identified with those crafts. Definitions and explanations are clear and concise, and the numerous diagrams and line drawings are effectively used. There are many *see* and *see also* references, and use of boldface type for terms within an article indicates that the word or phrase in boldface has its own individual entry.   TT9.S37

Pilger, Mary Anne. Crafts index for young people. Englewood, Colo. : Libraries Unlimited, 1992. 286 p.   **BK139**

Indexes more than 1,000 books for a broad array of educational craft projects that children can do. Projects are arranged alphabetically by subject.   TT157.P533

Directories

Boyd, Margaret Ann. The crafts supply sourcebook : a comprehensive shop-by-mail guide. Rev. 2nd ed. Cincinnati, Ohio : Betterway Books, 1992. 286 p. : ill.   **BK140**

1st ed., 1989.

Provides names and addresses of craft supply dealers.   TT12.B683 1992

C

Social and Behavioral Sciences

CA

General Works

GUIDES

Encyclopedia of public affairs information sources : a bibliographic guide to approximately 8,000 citations for publications, organizations, and other sources of information on nearly 300 subjects relating to public affairs / Paul Wasserman, James R. Kelly, and Desider L. Vikor, editors. Detroit : Gale, c1988. 303 p.   **CA1**

Designed for professionals, researchers, and librarians seeking factual information in the interdisciplinary field of public affairs. Its title notwithstanding, *EPAIS* is not an encyclopedia, since it contains no articles. The body of the work consists of alphabetically arranged subject headings (e.g., Acid rain, Child abuse, Hospices, Zoos), under which are listed sources by type (e.g., Abstract services, Indexes, Information systems; Associations and professional societies; Online databases; Research centers, institutes, clearinghouses). An alphabetical outline of contents lists topical headings with cross-references.

       Z7165.U5E53

Handbook for research students in the social sciences / ed. by Graham Allan and Chris Skinner. London ; N.Y. : Falmer Pr., 1991. 283 p.   **CA2**

Chapters, most with bibliographies, in three sections. Pt. 1 includes "Personal views" from doctoral candidates regarding development of research strategies, and from dissertation advisors discussing their roles. Pt. 2 is devoted to pragmatic concerns: negotiating with agencies for access to data, using computer-based library resources, presentation skills, etc. Pt. 3 covers research methodologies: e.g., qualitative research, statistical analysis, and case studies. Index.

       H62.H24526

Inter-university Consortium for Political and Social Research. Guide to resources and services. 1976/77– . Ann Arbor, Mich. : ICPSR,[1977]– . Annual.   **CA3**

The ICPSR is a repository and dissemination center for machine-readable social science data from over 130 countries. Prefatory chapters provide information about membership in ICPSR, its services and training programs, and ways of accessing its archives. Descriptions of data files are organized under such headings as Census enumerations, Elites and leadership, Legal systems, and Mass political behavior and attitudes. Indexed by ICPSR study number, title of research study, and principle investigator.   H61.3.I56a

Li, Tze-chung. Social science reference sources : a practical guide. Rev. and enl. 2nd ed. N.Y. : Greenwood, 1990. 590 p. (Contributions in librarianship and information science, no. 68).   **CA4**

1st ed., 1980.

In two parts: (1) the social sciences in general, dealing with their nature, bibliographic structure, and research resources; (2) detailed, critical and comparative descriptions of major reference sources and periodicals of each discipline. Contains 2,200 entries (the 1st ed. had 800) and discusses CD-ROM and other electronic resources. Comparable in content and organization to Nancy L. Herron's *The social sciences* (CA7) and William H. Webb's *Sources of information in the social sciences* (CA8). Name, title and subject indexes.   Z7161.A1L5

Oakes, Elizabeth H. Guide to social science resources in women's studies / Elizabeth H. Oakes and Kathleen E. Sheldon ; under the auspices of the Women's Studies Program, University of California, Los Angeles. Santa Barbara, Calif. : ABC-Clio, 1978. 162 p.   **CA5**

An annotated bibliography of books and special collections of articles in journals and books which are current, readily available, interdisciplinary and international in scope. Materials have been included which would be useful as readings for undergraduate women's studies courses. Organized by academic discipline—anthropology, economics, history, psychology, sociology, feminist thought—with appropriate subdivisions. Lists of bibliographies, journals, and other resources. Author and subject indexes.   Z7961.O23

Rama Reddy, E. Social science information : some Indian sources. New Delhi : Affiliated East-West Pr., 1985. 169 p.   **CA6**

Begins with a survey of the development of the social science disciplines in India in the mid-20th century, followed by ten bibliographic chapters devoted to categories of publication: books, Indian newspapers, periodicals, dissertations, government publications, etc. A separate chapter describes the mission, activities, publications, and library collections of the Social Science Documentation Centre (founded by the Indian Council of Social Science). Defines the social sciences in the broadest possible terms; "Books," for example, describes the tools providing bibliographic access to India's publishing output, as well as statistics on production, language, and subject matter. Intended for Indian social scientists, but helpful to researchers from other countries interested in Indian scholarship and culture. A brief index is of limited use.   Z7161.A1R35

The social sciences : a cross-disciplinary guide to selected sources / gen. ed., Nancy L. Herron ; contributing authors, Cynthia Faries … [et al.]. Englewood, Colo. : Libraries Unlimited, 1989. 287 p.   **CA7**

An annotated bibliography of reference sources in the social sciences and related subjects. Arranged by discipline; each section opens with an introduction that defines its scope and bibliographic structure and suggests appropriate search strategies. Comparable to *Sources of information in the social sciences*, ed. by William H. Webb (CA8) but Herron treats the online databases Webb neglects. Author, title, subject index.   Z7161.S648

Sources of information in the social sciences : a guide to the literature / William H. Webb … [et al.]. 3rd ed. Chicago : Amer. Libr. Assoc., 1986. 777 p.   **CA8**

1st ed. (1964) and 2nd ed. (1973) by Carl M. White and associates.

Designed for librarians and researchers in the social sciences. Nine principal chapters treat, respectively: social science in general, history, geography, economics and business administration, sociology, anthropology, psychology, education, and political science. Each consists of two main sections: (1) a bibliographic essay written by a specialist that explains the history and methodology of the discipline, and cites, as applicable, a substantial number of significant monographs; (2) annotated lists of reference sources, grouped by form, type, or specialized aspect: e.g., guides to the literature, abstracts, bibliographies, encyclopedias, handbooks, etc. Periodicals are listed in each category. Detailed table of contents and index of authors, titles and subjects. Little coverage of social sciences databases.   Z7161.S666

BIBLIOGRAPHY

American Behavioral Scientist. The ABS guide to recent publications in the social and behavioral sciences. N.Y. : [ABS], 1965. 781 p.   **CA9**

An older bibliography of historical value. Cumulates the monthly bibliography section, "New studies," as it appeared in the *American behavioral scientist* from 1957 to late 1964. This is, therefore, a selective bibliography of books and periodical articles in the whole range of the social and behavioral sciences. Most entries are annotated. Arranged by author or other main entry, with indexes by title, by proper name, and by a broad topical classification according to the system devised by Alfred de Grazia for the social and behavioral sciences.

Supplemented by: *Recent publications in the social and behavioral sciences* (N.Y. : ABS, 1966–75. 10 v.).   Z7161.A4

Caton, Hiram. The bibliography of human behavior / Hiram Caton, ed. in chief ; Frank K. Salter and J. M. G. van der Dennen, associate editors. Westport, Conn. : Greenwood, 1993. 575 p. (Bibliographies and indexes in anthropology, no. 7).   **CA10**

Multidisciplinary approach. Citations, without annotations, are grouped alphabetically by scholar's name in such categories as human evolution, prehistory, cultural evolution, sexuality, altered consciousness, and politics. Most articles publ. after 1979; includes classic earlier studies. Author and subject indexes.   Z7201.C37

Goehlert, Robert. Policy analysis and management : a bibliography / Robert U. Goehlert, Fenton S. Martin. Santa Barbara, Calif. : ABC-Clio, [1985]. 398 p.   **CA11**

A detailed classed bibliography of almost 10,000 English-language journal articles, books, research reports, and selected essays; author and subject indexes. Complemented by John S. Robey's *Analysis of public policy : a bibliography of dissertations, 1977–1982* (Westport, Conn. : Greenwood, 1984).   Z7161.G587

Guide to the Bureau of Applied Social Research / ed. by Judith S. Barton. N.Y. : Clearwater Publ. Co., c1984. 222 p.   **CA12**

A bibliography of the Bureau's publications, arranged chronologically under the following headings: Reports, Monographs, Books, Articles, Masters Essays, Doctoral Dissertations, Audio-Visual Materials, and Foreign Publications. Includes a list of data sets available from the Roper Center for Public Opinion at the University of Connecticut. Project number, title and author indexes.   Z7161.G83

London bibliography of the social sciences. London : Mansell Information/Publishing Ltd., 1929–1989. 47 v.   **CA13**

Subtitle (v. 1–4): Being the subject catalogue of the British Library of Political and Economic Science at the School of Economics, the Goldsmiths' Library of Economic Literature at the University of London, the libraries of the Royal Statistical Society and the Royal Anthropological Institute, and certain special collections at University College, London, and elsewhere, compiled under the direction of B. M. Headicar … and C. Fuller, … with an introduction by Sidney Webb (Lord Passfield) … .

Issued under the auspices of the British Library of Political and Economic Science; v. 1–5 issued by the London School of Economics.

Vols. 1–4 include material to June 1, 1929 (v. 1–3, A–Z; v. 4, Author index, Periodicals list, Tables of subject divisions and subject headings). Vol. 5–47 also numbered as Supplement 1–23, with some supplements having multiple volumes (e.g., 7th supplement, 1969–72, is also v. 22–28).

Vols. 1–14 issued as no. 8 of the series Studies in economics & political science.

The most extensive subject bibliography in its field, important to all large libraries and researchers. International in scope, recording books, pamphlets, and documents in many languages. Arranged alphabetically by subject, with brief information: author, title (often abbreviated), pagination, date, location, and indication as to whether the work contains a bibliography. Many cross-references.

Coverage varies. Vols. 1–4 and v. 5 (1st suppl.) include holdings of nine London libraries and special collections. Vol. 6 (2nd suppl.) includes holdings of Goldsmiths' Library of Economic Literature, British Library of Political and Economic Science, and Edward Fry Library of International Law. Vol. 7 (3rd suppl.) and subsequent volumes include holdings of the British Library and the Fry Library only. Vol. 38 and following use Library of Congress subject headings.

From 1990 onward, the bulk of the data that would previously have been published as *London bibliographies* appear in the four parts of *International bibliography of the social sciences*: economics (CH43), political science (CJ15), social and cultural anthropology (CE24), and sociology (CC8).   Z7161.L84

Maunier, René. Manuel bibliographique des sciences sociales et économiques. Paris : Sirey, 1920. 228 p.   **CA14**
Repr.: N.Y. : Burt Franklin, 1968.

This older bibliography of bibliographies is useful for historical purposes, as it includes many 18th- and 19th-century publications. Includes works in French, English, German, and Italian. Section 1 concerns interdisciplinary approaches to the social sciences, including bibliographies, periodicals, guides to organizations, biographical information, etc. Section 2 consists of chapters of bibliographies on sociology and related disciplines: philosophy, political science, and folklore. Section 3 treats the subdivisions of economics: political economics, industrial economics, transportation, etc. Appendix: bibliography of bibliographies on war and peace. Indexes of authors and of persons and places.

Mayne, Alan J. Resources for the future : an international annotated bibliography for the 21st century. Westport, Conn. : Greenwood, 1993. 351 p.   **CA15**

Designed to provide policymakers and researchers with resources that will help them anticipate future economic, environmental, political, social, scientific, and technological developments. Initial chapters list and annotate 1,000 books, 200 periodicals, and 50 newsletters. Subsequent sections are devoted to nonprint media (e.g., microfiche, CD-ROMs, databases) and to organizations (e.g., learned societies, global and grassroots movements, trusts). Detailed subject index. Index of publishers of works cited.   Z5990.M39

Social sciences in the USSR / Academy of Sciences of the USSR, Institute of Scientific Information on Social Sciences. 1979–1990. Moscow : The Institute, 1982–1991.   **CA16**
Title also in Russian.

A selective bibliography of monographs written by Soviet social scientists, defined broadly to include history, philosophy, linguistics, and literary criticism. Bibliographic descriptions in the vernacular, with English-language titles and abstracts. Arranged by discipline. No index.

§ Superseded by: *Social sciences and humanities in Russia* / Russian Academy of Sciences, Institute of Scientific Information on Social Sciences (Moscow : The Institute, 1992– . Annual. 1991–).
                                                Z7165.R9S6

Current

Current contents. 1961– . Philadelphia : Inst. for Scientific Information, 1961– . Weekly.   **CA17**

The *Social and behavioral sciences* issues reproduce tables of contents, grouped in 13 broad subject categories, of about 1,350 international journals, as well as articles from multiauthored books. For information on other sections and machine-readable files, *see* EA68.

Periodicals

Liste mondiale des périodiques spécialisés dans les sciences sociales = World list of social science periodicals. 1st ed. (1953)– . [Paris] : UNESCO, 1953– . Irregular.   **CA18**
Prepared by the Unesco Social and Human Sciences Documentation Centre.

None published 1967–75.

The 8th ed., 1991, lists 4,459 social science periodicals, 1,450 new to this edition. Five sections: (1) alphabetical list of titles; (2) full entry for each periodical, alphabetized under country of publication; (3) subject index; (4) bibliographic and abstracting periodicals, ar-

ranged by subject discipline and geographical area covered; (5) abbreviation for each abstracting or indexing service. Title, prefatory matter, and headings in English, French, and Spanish.   Z7163.L523

Wepsiec, Jan. Social sciences : an international bibliography of serial literature, 1830–1985. London ; N.Y. : Mansell, 1992. 486 p.   **CA19**

Lists alphabetically 5,254 periodicals dating from 1830, the year the first journal in a social science discipline (economics) was published, to the mid-1980s. Entries include bibliographic information and representation in an index or abstract journal. An appendix provides a historical overview of each discipline. Key to abbreviations; subject index.   Z7161.A15W38

Dissertations

Ilsar, Nira. Bibliyografyah shel 'alvodot doktor be-mada'e ha-ruaḥ yeha-ḥevrah she-nikhtevu be-universiṭa'ot Yiśra'el. Yerushalayim : Bet ha-sefarim ha-le'umi yeha-universiṭa'i, 1992. 284 p. (Pirsume Bet ha-sefarim, mis. 8).   **CA20**
For annotation, *see* AG53.   Z5055.I753I45

Indian dissertation abstracts. v. 1, no. 1 (Jan./Mar. 1973)– . Bombay : Popular Prakashan, 1973– . Quarterly.   **CA21**
Issued by the Indian Council of Social Science Research and the Association of Indian Universities.

Lists doctoral dissertations in the social sciences as approved by Indian universities. Entries include name of scholar, dissertation title, university, year degree was awarded, and name of supervisor. Substantial abstracts summarize problem addressed, methodology, and major research findings. Arranged by candidate's name within discipline: economics, education, management, political science, psychology, and the social science aspects of anthropology, demography, geography, history, law and linguistics.

————. *Index.* Covers v. 1–10, 1973–81. Issued as NASSDOC research information series no. 25.

Two additional sources for doctoral dissertations from India in the social sciences:

Bibliography of doctoral dissertations: social sciences and humanities (New Delhi : Assoc. of Indian Universities, 1975/76).

Social science research index (New Delhi : National Social Science Documentation Centre, Indian Council of Social Science Research, c1986–), a listing of Indian doctoral, postdoctoral, and other funded social science research projects. Indexed by subject, author, institution, and title. Includes bibliography of National Social Science Documentation Centre (NASSDOC) publications.

Zubatsky, David S. Doctoral dissertations in history and the social sciences on Latin America and the Caribbean accepted by universities in the United Kingdom, 1920–1972. London : Univ. of London, Institute of Latin American Studies, [1973]. 16 p.   **CA22**

Arranged by country or region, entries include author's name, title of dissertation, university, degree received, and year conferred. Bibliography.   Z1601.Z8

INDEXES; ABSTRACT JOURNALS

APAIS, Australian public affairs information service : a subject index to current literature. no.1 (July 1945)– . Canberra : National Library of Australia, 1945– . Monthly (except Dec.).   **CA23**
Vols. for 1955– , cumulated annually; vols. for 1945–60, issued by the library under its earlier name: Commonwealth National Library.

Subject index to articles on Australian political, economic, social, and cultural affairs. Indexes comprehensively 200 Australian scholarly journals in the social sciences and humanities, and provides selective coverage of a broad range of Australian books, periodicals, and newspapers. *APAIS* also indexes books, pamphlets and conference proceedings on Australian subjects published outside Australia that do not qualify for *Australian national bibliography* (AA944). Separate author index.   Z7165.A8A8

Applied social sciences index & abstracts : ASSIA. v. 1, no. 1– . London : Library Association, 1987– . Bimonthly, with an annual cumulation.   **CA24**

Intended for service professionals in such fields as youth work, race relations, and employment. Citations (with abstracts of 150 words or less) appear in alphabetical arrangement by topic. More than 500 English-language journals from 16 countries are indexed. A review in *Choice* 26 (Apr. 1989): 1299 finds little overlap with *PAIS* (CA25) and *Social sciences index* (CA29) and praises especially the coverage of women's studies and anthropology.   Z7163.A66

PAIS international in print. v. 1, no. 1 (Jan. 1991)– . N.Y. : Public Affairs Information Service, Inc., 1991– . Monthly, every fourth issue being cumulative.   **CA25**

Merges and continues *Public Affairs Information Service bulletin*, v. 1–77 (1915–90) and *Public Affairs Information Service foreign language index*, v. 1–14 (1972–90).

An interdisciplinary subject index to current periodical articles, books, government publications, pamphlets, and reports relating to public issues and policy. Includes publications in English, French, German, Italian, Portuguese, and Spanish issued throughout the world. Useful to researchers in economics, political science, public administration, international law, etc.

•Available in machine-readable form as: *PAIS international* [database] (N.Y. : PAIS, 1972–), available online, updated monthly; and on CD-ROM as: *PAIS on CD-ROM* [database] (N.Y. : PAIS, 1972–).

§ Thesaurus published as: *PAIS subject headings*, eds., Alice Picon and Gwen Sloan (2nd ed. N.Y. : PAIS, 1990. 536 p.). Intended for use with both the printed and machine-readable versions above. An alphabetical listing of authorized headings, subheadings, main and subheading combinations, cross-references, and scope notes. Includes only terms in use since 1974. Two appendixes: list of subheadings with instructions for use; and rotated authorized main headings, a permuted list in which each word in a heading is listed alphabetically as an object word.   A13.P85

Rand Corporation. Selected Rand abstracts. v. 1 (1963)– . Santa Monica, Calif. : Rand, 1963– . Issued quarterly.   **CA26**

Each issue is cumulative within the calendar year.

Includes publications previously listed in the supplements to the *Index of selected publications of the Rand Corporation* (Oct. 1962–Feb. 1963).

Rand studies appear as articles in professional journals, books by commercial and university presses, and as three numbered series: "Reports" (documentation of Rand research findings); "Notes" (reports on other sponsored research); and "Papers" (personal views of Rand staff on a variety of subjects).

Each issue of *Selected Rand abstracts* consists of subject and author indexes, abstracts, and a bibliography of published Rand books.   AS36R284

Social sciences citation index. 1972– . Philadelphia : Institute for Scientific Information, 1973– .   **CA27**

"An international interdisciplinary index to the literature of the social, behavioral and related sciences"—*t.p.*

Issued three times a year, the third issue being the annual bound cumulation. Began publication with the issue covering [Jan.–Apr.] 1973; a cumulated issue giving retrospective coverage for 1972 was published 1974. Five-year cumulations have been published for 1966–70, 1971–75, and 1976–80; they offer expanded journal coverage beyond the annual volumes.

Annual volumes are in four parts. The Citation index is arranged alphabetically by cited author, with references to articles in which a work is cited. Separate sections list corporate and anonymous authors. The Sources index is arranged alphabetically by author with full bibliographic citations for publications. It contains a Corporate index in

two sections, place and organization, with names of primary author and abbreviated bibliographic citation. The Permuterm subject index provides access through key title words. The fourth section, Guide and list of source publications, started in 1979.

Patterned after the same publisher's *Science citation index* (EA75), this service enables the user to identify related writings (periodical articles, reviews, etc.) by indicating sources in which a known work by a given author has been cited. Covers about 4,700 journals, many of them selectively (i.e., relevant articles from journals in the physical, chemical and life sciences are included since the index draws on material in the total Institute for Scientific Information database).

•Available on CD-ROM as *Social sciences citation index : compact disc edition* [database]. (Philadelphia : ISI, 1986–). Also available online as *Social SciSearch*, covering 1972 and after, updated biweekly.   Z7161.S65

Social sciences in modern India / ed. by Suresh K. Sharma and Sartaj A. Abidi. New Delhi : Deep & Deep Publications, 1990. 3 v.   **CA28**

Subject index to two prestigious, long-running Indian social science journals: *Indian review*, founded by G. A. Natesan (Madras, 1900–) and *Modern review*, founded by Ramanand Chatterjee (Calcutta, 1907–). Though both journals are still published, a spot check revealed no citations to articles published since the mid–1970s. List of libraries throughout India, with specific holdings of each title. Author and subject indexes.

Social sciences index. v. 1, no. 1 (June 1974)– . N.Y. : H.W. Wilson, 1974– . Quarterly, with annual cumulations.   **CA29**

Continues in part *Social sciences and humanities index* (AD288).

Author and subject index to English-language "periodicals in the fields of anthropology, area studies, community health and medical care, economics, family studies, geography, gerontology, international relations, law and criminology, minority studies, planning and public administration, police science and corrections, policy sciences, political science, psychiatry, psychology, social work and public welfare, sociology, urban studies, and related subjects."—*Prefatory note, v. 20, n. 3*. As in *Humanities index* (BA5), a separate section of book reviews appears at the end of each issue. Originally indexed 77 periodical titles from *Social sciences and humanities index* (AD288) plus 186 titles selected by subscribers to the index; as of June 1994 issue, will index 415 titles.

•Machine-readable version. *Social sciences index* [database] (Bronx, N.Y. : H.W. Wilson, 1983–). Available online, updated twice weekly, and on CD-ROM, updated quarterly.   AI3.S62

ENCYCLOPEDIAS

The Blackwell dictionary of twentieth-century social thought / ed. by William Outhwaite, Tom Bottomore. Oxford ; Cambridge, Mass. : Blackwell, 1993. 864 p.   **CA30**

Signed scholarly articles with bibliographies. Entries of one to five pages provide a historical perspective on social concepts (Consensus, Social mobility), as well as institutions, schools, or movements (Confucianism, Durkheim school). Biographies do not appear in the dictionary proper but in a biographical appendix with brief notes on persons who influenced social thought (e.g., Antonio Gramsci, Margaret Mead). Citations from individual entries are brought together in a bibliography at the end. Index.   H41.B53

Dictionary of theories / Jennifer Bothamley. London ; Detroit : Gale, c1993. 637 p.   **CA31**

More than 4,000 brief definitions of theories: e.g., penis envy, Peter Principle. Includes theories from all periods, accepted and discredited, from science, linguistics, psychology, sociology, economics, anthropology, philosophy, law, art, and religion; however, social and behavioral science theories are most heavily represented. Each entry includes relevant academic disciplines, when and by whom the theory was first proposed, description, validity, and reference to a source providing a fuller explanation. Lists sources by subject in a bibliography at the end. People and subject indexes.   AG5.D537

Dictionnaire de sociologie : familiale, politique, économique, spirituelle, générale / publié sous la direction de G. Jacquemet ... avec le concours de nombreux collaborateurs. Paris : Letouzey, 1931–39. v. 1–4.   **CA32**

Contents: v. 1–4, A–Cercles. Published in fascicles. No more published.

A scholarly encyclopedia with long, signed articles, often with bibliographies. Contains biographies, and many short articles on tribes, clans, etc. Written from the Catholic point of view.   HM17.D5

Encyclopaedia of the social sciences / ed. in chief, Edwin R. A. Seligman; assoc. ed., Alvin Johnson. N.Y. : Macmillan, 1930–35. 15 v.   **CA33**

Vol. 1 includes Introductions: I, Development of social thought and institutions (12 articles), p. 3–228; II, The social sciences as disciplines by country (11 articles), p. 231–49. Index in v. 15.

The first comprehensive encyclopedia of the whole field of the social sciences, projected and prepared under the auspices of ten learned societies. Aims to cover all important topics in the fields of political science, economics, law, anthropology, sociology, penology, and social work, and the social aspects of ethics, education, philosophy, psychology, biology, geography, medicine, art, etc. International in scope and treatment, but fuller for the English-speaking world and western Europe than for other regions or interests. Articles are by specialists, are signed, and have bibliographies. About 50 percent of the articles are biographical.

The *International encyclopedia of the social sciences* (CA36) complements but does not supersede this work.   H41.E6

Encyclopedia of policy studies / ed. by Stuart S. Nagel. 2nd ed., rev. and expanded. N.Y. ; Basel : Dekker, c1994. 956 p.   **CA34**

1st ed., 1983.

Defines "policy studies" as "the study of the nature, causes, and effects of alternative public policies."—*Introd.* Consists of survey chapters with bibliographies by scholars (all but one from U.S. universities) in two sections: General approaches to policy studies and Specific policy problems. Chapters in the latter are arranged by discipline: political science, economics, sociology/psychology, urban planning, natural science/engineering. Indexed by author and subject.   H97.E6

Filler, Louis. A dictionary of American social change. Malabar, Fla. : Krieger Pub. Co., 1982. 256 p.   **CA35**

1st ed., 1963, had title: *A dictionary of American social reform.*

Presents brief articles on issues, persons, court decisions, slogans, and cultural phenomena (e.g., Abrams *vs.* United States; Federal Theatre Project; Mailer, Norman; "Malefactors of great wealth"; Post-Watergate morality; Sacco-Vanzetti case). Witty and insightful, the entries do not claim objectivity. Articles added to this edition encompass the early years of the Reagan presidency, while those pertaining to earlier periods have been reprinted unchanged from the previous edition (although bibliographies have been updated). There are cross-references in the text (e.g., ABSCAM *see* Corruption) but no index. Set in very small type.   H41.F5

International encyclopedia of the social sciences / David L. Sills, ed. [N.Y.] : Macmillan, [1968–91]. v. 1–19. (In progress?).   **CA36**

"Designed to complement, not to supplant" (*Introd.*) its predecessor, *Encyclopaedia of the social sciences* (CA33). Reflects the rapid expansion of the social sciences in the 1960s. Signed articles with bibliographies by scholars from more than 30 countries treat concepts, principles, theories, and methods in the disciplines of anthropology, economics, geography, history, law, political science, psychiatry, psychology, sociology, and statistics. Vol. 18, Biographical supplement, provides signed sketches, with bibliographies, of 215 social scientists

either deceased or born no later than Dec. 31, 1908. Vol. 19 (subtitled "Social science quotations") is also published separately as the *Macmillan book of social science quotations.*   H40.A2I5

The social science encyclopedia / ed. by Adam Kuper and Jessica Kuper. Rev. and repr. London ; N.Y. : Routledge, 1989. 916 p. : ill.   **CA37**

1st ed., 1985. Although this is called a revised edition, it appears to be a reprint of the 1985 version.

Contains over 700 essays on the major social science disciplines; applied social sciences (market research crimnology); and related areas (demographics, semiotics). Entries on theories (Say's law of markets), issues (welfare state), and the life and work of individual scholars (Levi-Strauss, Machiavelli). Signed articles are alphabetically arranged with cross-references and bibliographies. Lists of entries and of contributors. No indexes.   H41.S63

DICTIONARIES

Koschnick, Wolfgang J. Standard dictionary of the social sciences = Standardwörterbuch für die Sozialwissenschaften. München ; N.Y. : K.G. Saur, 1984–1993. v. 1, v. 2 pt. 1–2 : ill. (In progress?).   **CA38**

Contents: v. 1, English-German; v. 2, pt. 1–2, German-English. Preface in German and English.

A word book for the translation of English to German and vice versa. Provides brief definitions of terms common to all social science disciplines. Names of persons associated with particular concepts in parentheses. Double-column pages; cross-references.   H41.K68

Miller, P. McC. A dictionary of social science methods / P. McC. Miller and M. J. Wilson. Chichester, [West Sussex] ; N.Y. : Wiley, 1983. 124 p. : ill.   **CA39**

Defines terms used in research in the empirical social sciences; includes many statistical models and terms.   H41.M54

Rodionova, Z. V. Russko-angliĭskiĭ slovar' obshchestvenno-politicheskoĭ leksiki : okolo 9,000 slov / Z. V. Rodionova, V. P. Filatov ; pod red. V. P. Filatova. Moskva : "Russkiĭ îazyk", 1987. 543 p.   **CA40**

Title on added t.p.: Russian-English dictionary of socio-political terms. Preface in Russian and English.

Aimed at English-speaking readers of Russian newspapers, social science and political writings. Approximately 9,000 entries provide modern Russian terms and related idioms in politics, international relations, philosophy, economics, law, diplomacy, history, and military science. Includes new words and phrases coined by the press. Supplement lists the Russian names, with English translations, of ministries and departments of the Soviet government, as well as parties, agencies, and movements.   H40.R63

Smith, R. E. F. A Russian-English social science dictionary. Rev. and enl. ed. Birmingham : Institute for Advanced Research in the Humanities, Univ. of Birmingham, c1990. 595 p.   **CA41**

Title on added t.p.: Russko-angliĭskiĭ slovar' obshchestvennykh nauk.

1st ed., 1962, had title: *A Russian-English dictionary of social science.*

Terms, including abbreviations, taken from sociology, politics, economics, law, accounting, public administration, welfare and education. Appendixes provide conversion tables of weights and measures, as well as information on Soviet culture and finance.   H49.S55

Thinès, Georges. Dictionnaire général des sciences humaines / Georges Thinès et Agnès Lempereur. Paris : Éditions Universitaires, [1975]. 1033 p.   **CA42**

"Sciences humaines" is broadly interpreted to include, among other fields, anthropology, biology, criminology, demography, esthetics, linguistics, literature, mathematics, pedagogy, physiology, political science, psychiatry, psychology, sociology, statistics, etc. Field of usage is indicated for each term defined, with two or more definitions given for terms having specialized meanings in different fields. *See* and *see also* references; occasional bibliographic citations; charts and diagrams. Includes some name entries, mainly for psychologists and sociologists.   BF31.T47

THESAURUSES

Knapp, Sara D. The contemporary thesaurus of social science terms and synonyms : a guide for natural language computer searching. Phoenix : Oryx, 1993. 400 p.   **CA43**

Lists alphabetically more than 6,000 concepts (e.g., Male nurses, Professional ethics, Spirit possession, Teamwork) from a wide range of social science disciplines. Terms were derived from newspapers, specialized thesauruses, actual search requests, and subject dictionaries. Entries include synonyms, related terms, alternative endings, and *see also* references. Appendixes and introductory chapters, aimed at persons new to electronic databases, provide information on the logic and strategies of natural language searching.   Z699.5.S65K57

QUOTATIONS

International encyclopedia of the social sciences / David L. Sills, ed. [N.Y.] : Macmillan, [1968–91]. v. 1–19. (In progress?).   **CA44**

Vol. 19, "Social science quotations," contains substantial passages with complete citations, arranged alphabetically by name. Includes social scientists and public figures whose social commentary is widely quoted. Published separately as *Macmillan book of social science quotations*. For annotation of the complete set, *see* CA36.   H40.A2I5

DIRECTORIES

Annual report—Indian Council of Social Science Research. New Delhi : [ICSSR].   **CA45**

ICSSR is an autonomous organization established by the Indian government in 1969 to promote social science research. Its *Annual report* lists research projects sanctioned, cancelled, and completed; fellowships awarded; scholars engaged in travel and exchange programs; and reports on workshops sponsored, data sets acquired by its archives, and services provided by its documentation center. A substantial portion of each *Report* is devoted to the status of affiliated regional research institutes.   H62.5.I5I515

Current research in Britain : social sciences : CRB. Boston Spa, Wetherby, West Yorkshire : British Library Lending Division, 1985– . Annual.   **CA46**

Each edition is in four parts: *Physical sciences* (EA138); *Biological sciences* (EG47); *Social sciences*; *The humanities* (BA8).

Continues v. 3 of *Research in British universities, polytechnics and colleges.*

Provides information on research in the social sciences at British educational institutions. Institutions and, within them, departments (with address and name of chairperson) are arranged in the body of the volume by an alphanumeric code. Under department, research topics are listed in alphabetical order by the name of the principal investigator and include project descriptions, names of all researchers, project dates, sponsors, and publications. Institution/department, name and subject indexes.   H62.5.G7C87

ICSSR research projects, 1969–1987 : a list of research projects sanctioned since the inception of the ICSSR to March 1987. New Delhi : Indian Council of Social Science Research, c1988. 200 p.   **CA47**

1st ed., 1976; 2nd ed., 1986.

Lists 1,742 research projects sanctioned by the Indian Council of Social Science Research from its establishment in 1969 through March 1987. Arranged by time period, then by discipline. Entries include name of chief investigator and project title and indicate whether research was complete and/or published. Tables show distribution of research projects by region and by state. Indexed by author/project director and subject.   Z3206.I28

Répertoire mondial des institutions de sciences sociales = World directory of social science institutions / prep. by the Unesco Social Science Documentation Centre. Paris : UNESCO, 1977– .   **CA48**

An earlier version had title: *World index of social science institutions : research, advanced training, documentation and professional bodies* (Paris : UNESCO, 1971).

Preface, contents, and section heads in English, French, and Spanish.

Arranged by country. The 5th ed. (1990) provides descriptions of 2,088 institutions in 199 countries. Includes national, regional and international social science research and advanced training institutions and professional societies. Among other information, entries supply address, name of head, activities, publications, and research areas. Indexed by country, name and acronym of institution, head of institution, and subject.

§ For information about organizations concerned with peace or human rights research, see Unesco's companion publications *World directory of peace research and training institutions* (CJ696) and *World directory of human rights teaching and research institutions* (note, CJ696).   H62.A1R46

Selective inventory of social science information and documentation services = Inventaire sélectif des services d'information et de documentation en sciences sociales / prepared by the Unesco Social and Human Sciences Documentation Centre. 4th ed. Oxford, UK ; Cambridge, Mass. : Blackwell, 1993. 388 p.   **CA49**

1st ed., 1981, and 2nd ed., 1985, had title: *Selective inventory of information services*; 3rd ed., 1988.

Title page, contents, and preface in English, French, and Spanish.

Descriptions, arranged alphabetically under host country, of 1,199 organizations that provide information to social science professionals. Indexed by name and acronym of information service, personal name, subject, geographical area, and database.   H61.9.S45

Smallwood, Carol. Current issues resource builder : free and inexpensive materials for librarians and teachers. Jefferson, N.C. : McFarland, c1989. 402 p.   **CA50**

Designed to help teachers and librarians locate free or inexpensive resources (under $16.00). Section 1 combines issues (AIDS, smoking, terrorism) and formats (abstracts, large print, newsletters) in one alphabetical list, listing under each heading public and private agencies willing to provide material. Section 2 is an alphabetical list of organizations, with profiles that indicate purpose, examples of material provided, prices, and ordering aids. The review in *ARBA* 20 (1990): 39, notes that this compilation differs from the *Educators guide to free [materials]* series (CB13) in that it lists types, rather than specific titles of materials.

§ A similar work, the author's *Free resource builder for librarians and teachers* (2nd ed. Jefferson, N.C. : McFarland, c1992. 313 p.), is limited to free materials, chiefly from state and federal government agencies. Has ten chapters devoted to broad topical areas (e.g., Education, Environment, Health), in which agency and directory information are listed directly rather than in a separate section, as in *Current issues*. Index to subjects and a few larger agencies.   Z692.F73S6

Steinmetzarchief. Steinmetz archive data catalogue and guide : Dutch social science data, 1962–1992. [7th ed.]. Amsterdam : Steinmetz Archive/SWIDOC, 1993. 481 p. + 1 computer disk. **CA51**

1st ed., 1972; 6th ed., 1986.

Includes descriptions of of some 1,100 Dutch social science research projects, giving for each: alphanumeric code, title in English and Dutch, years, discipline, keywords, themes (descriptive phrases in English), kind of data, sampled universe, number of cases, number of variables, investigator, depository, restrictions on accessibility of data, and mode of storage. Accompanying computer disk contains a KWIC index; the printed version is indexed by keyword, keyword for population studied (e.g., immigrants), title in English, title in Dutch or original language, depository, and investigator. Z7165.N4S75

FINANCIAL AIDS; GRANTS

Guide to federal funding for social scientists / prep. by the American Political Science Association ; Anne G. Mantegna, ed. 2nd ed. Wash. : The Association, 1990. 368 p. **CA52**

1st ed., 1986.

Designed to introduce scholars in the social sciences to more than 300 federal programs that provide research funding. Entries include application and review procedures, examples of funded projects, and indication of future directions. The handbook includes valuable discussions of ongoing cooperation with federal agencies, winning research proposals, and dissemination of results. Indexed by research topics and sources of fellowships and dissertation support. H62.5.U5G85

HANDBOOKS

Asia, case studies in the social sciences : a guide for teaching / ed. by Myron L. Cohen. Armonk, N.Y. : M.E. Sharpe, c1992. 626 p. : ill. **CA53**

Intended to provide social science teachers with multicultural comparisons. Three tables of contents: (1) discipline (Anthropology, Economics, Political Science, and Sociology); (2) discipline and sub-discipline (e.g., Gender relations, Religion); (3) country. Includes some 40 essays by specialists on such topics as Family organization in China, The new religions in Japan, and Political transition on Taiwan. Each chapter contains an outline of contents, summary of central points, discussion of major topics, list of issues for discussion, and selected bibliography. Index.

§ One of the series published by the Columbia Project on Asia in the Core Curriculum, to help teachers of undergraduates introduce Asian material into courses. Two companion works: *Asia in Western and world history* (forthcoming) and *Masterworks of Asian literature in comparative perspective : a guide for teaching*, ed. by Barbara Stoler Miller (1994). H62.5.U5A83

Maier, Mark. The data game : controversies in social science statistics. Armonk, N.Y. : M.E. Sharpe, 1991. 245 p. **CA54**

Written for researchers who utilize social statistics and general readers. Chapters on demography, housing, health, education, crime, the national economy, wealth and poverty, labor, business, and government. Each chapter begins with a bibliography assessing primary data sources, followed by discussion of the most controversial and commonly cited statistical conclusions. Chapters end with case study questions. Index. HA29.M236

Runkel, Philip Julian. A guide to usage for writers and students in the social sciences / Philip Runkel and Margaret Runkel. Totowa, N.J. : Rowman & Allanheld, 1984. 155 p. **CA55**

The Runkels' witty, dogmatic tone, as well as their insistence on simplicity and precision in professional writing, recall William Strunk and E. B. White's *The elements of style* (3rd ed. N.Y. : MacMillan, 1979). The authors advocate returning to the original meaning of words that have become "too handy" (e.g., "exotic," "inroad," "input"), eliminating excess words, and avoiding euphemisms. Headwords (e.g., "Apostrophe," "Believe, feel, think," "Overused words") are arranged alphabetically with numerous cross-references. PE1479.S62R86

RESEARCH METHODS

Directory of social research organisations in the United Kingdom / ed. by Wendy Sykes, Martin Bulmer, and Marleen Schwerzel. London : Mansell, 1993. 1 v. **CA56**

Describes 1,050 organizations that conduct empirical social research, including government, health, higher education, market research, charities, trade unions, and public companies. Arranged alphabetically by name or acronym, entries include directory information, description of organization, fields of research, recent projects, training opportunities, and research services offered. Begins with essays on aspects of social research in the U.K. Addenda include lists of freelance researchers, professional associations, and training courses. Six indexes, including research fields, research services, and subcontracting research organizations.

Miller, Delbert Charles. Handbook of research design and social measurement. 5th ed. Newbury Park, Calif. : Sage Publications, c1991. 704 p. : ill. **CA57**

1st ed., 1964; 4th ed., 1983.

Aimed at researchers in the pure and applied social sciences. Serves three functions: (1) professional sourcebook, with lists of core journals, reviews of computer resources, etc.; (2) guide to professional organizations, research institutes, etc.; (3) step-by-step review of the research process and research methodologies. Consists of seven substantial chapters, divided into sections and subsections. Many bibliographical references. Personal name index. H62.M44

Rea, Louis M. Designing and conducting survey research : a comprehensive guide / Louis M. Rea, Richard A. Parker. San Francisco : Jossey-Bass, 1992. 254 p. : ill. **CA58**

Traces sample survey projects from the conceptualization of a research problem to the final report. Chapters detail the major types of surveys, development and administration of the questionnaire, statistical analysis (including major compuuter software programs), scientific accuracy, use of tables and graphs, and presentation of findings. Table of areas of a standard normal distribution. Glossary; bibliography; index. HA31.2.R43

Research methodology in social science in India / editors, L.P. Vidyarthi and A.K. Haldar. New Delhi : Today & Tomorrow's Printers and Publishers, 1985. 246 p. **CA59**

Seminar papers describe methods used by Indian social scientists, most notably anthropologists, and explore their use in other branches of the social sciences. Essays with bibliographies in six sections: scientific methods in social investigation, psychological and statistical methods, tribal and folk culture, study of complex societies, time perspective in culture study, and methodological problems in applied and action research. Author index. H62.5.I5R48

Young, Copeland H. Inventory of longitudinal studies in the social sciences / Copeland H. Young, Kristen L. Savola, Erin Phelps. Newbury Park, Calif. : Sage Publ., c1991. 568 p. **CA60**

Revises and continues two earlier studies: *Inventory of longitudinal studies of middle and old age*, ed. by Susan Migdall ... [et al.] (N.Y. : Social Sciences Research Council, 1981) and *Inventory of longitudinal research on childhood and adolescence*, ed. by Frederick Verdonik ... [et al.] (N.Y. : Social Science Research Council, 1984).

Describes approximately 200 currently active U.S. research studies on such subjects as the psychosocial effects of disaster, acquisition of literacy skills, crime causation, and life patterns of college-educated women. Descriptions of data sets include the name and address of contact, topics covered, characteristics of original sample, years of completed "waves," instruments used, bibliography, and current status of study. To qualify for inclusion, investigators must have collected information during at least two time points during a span of at least a year. Arranged alphabetically by the name of researcher. Author and subject indexes.   H62.Y667

BIOGRAPHY

American men & women of science. 17th ed. (1989/90)– . N.Y. : Bowker, 1989– . Irregular.   **CA61**

Separate coverage of the social and behavioral sciences began with the 9th ed. *Social and behavioral sciences* constitutes a separate two-volume publication within the set in the 13th ed. It contains biographical sketches of some 24,000 figures prominent in the fields of administration and management, area studies, business, communications and information science, community and urban studies, economics, environmental studies, futuristics, international studies, political sciences, psychology, and sociology. The social and behavioral sciences were dropped from the 14th ed. (1979), although *American men and women of science* still includes psychiatry, public health, and statistics, formerly considered social sciences. For complete information on the parent set, *see* EA170.   H50.A47

Contemporary issues criticism / Dedria Bryfonski, ed. ; Robert L. Brubaker, project ed. Detroit : Gale, c1982–84. 2 v. : ill.   **CA62**

Modeled on Gale's literary criticism series (e.g., *Contemporary literary criticism*, BE47). Each volume treats the nonfiction work of an unrelated group of figures either living or deceased since 1 Jan. 1960: e.g., Rachel Carson, Shirley Chisholm, Carl Sagan. Arranged alphabetically, entries include a photograph, a brief biographical/critical introduction, excerpts from the most prestigious works, and chronologically arranged extracts from scholarly commentaries, popular articles, and book reviews. Vol. 2 includes cumulative indexes to authors, critics, and subjects.   H31.C755

Internationales Soziologenlexikon / hrsg. von Wilhelm Bernsdorf und Horst Knospe. 2., neubearb. Aufl. Stuttgart : Enke, 1980–198? 2 v.   **CA63**

1st ed., 1959.

Contents: Bd.1, Beiträge über bis Ende 1969 verstorbene Soziologen; Bd. 2, Beitrage über lebende oder nach 1969 verstorbene Soziologen.

Provides biographies of sociologists, here defined to include economists, ethnosociologists, social anthropologists, social geographers, political scientists, social historians, and social psychologists. Signed entries, alphabetically arranged, include date and place of birth, education, career, achievements, overview and evaluation of major theories, and bibliographies of primary and secondary sources. International in scope; however, sociologists from Western Europe, most notably Austria, predominate.   HM19.I6

McGuire, William. American social leaders / William McGuire and Leslie Wheeler ... [et al.]. Santa Barbara, Calif. : ABC-Clio, c1993. 500 p.   **CA64**

Profiles 350 individuals, living and dead, including social movements leaders, influential intellectuals, journalists, publishers, inventors, and philanthropists. Civil Rights leaders are especially well-represented. Entries include life dates, occupation/activities, cross-references, and a brief bibliography, and range in length from two to four columns each. Many photographs. Alphabetical list of persons, but no general index.   HN65.M38

CB

Education

In past editions of the *Guide*, most entries in the Education section were found in a General Works subsection. For this edition, it has seemed suitable to establish a number of topical subsections—e.g., Tests and Measurements, Educational Law and Legislation, Teachers and Teacher Education. Form subdivisions are more numerous, and there are subsections for junior colleges, religious and ethnic education, etc., under bibliographies and directories within the General Works and Higher Education divisions. Some divisions have been dropped, including Associations, Current Works (since it was found difficult to draw a line between current and historical treatments), and Elementary and secondary education (now found under General subdivisions because elementary and secondary levels tend to be the focus of general works).

This edition also departs from its predecessors in providing Ratings subsections under General Works and under Higher Education, where works that attempt to rank institutions according to the quality of education they provide will be found. Because such works are frequently requested, they are listed here; but readers should be aware that ratings are usually based on the opinions of educators, so are by definition subjective and hence neither authoritative nor completely reliable.

GENERAL WORKS

Guides

ARBA guide to education / comp. and ed. by Deborah J. Brewer. Littleton, Colo. : Libraries Unlimited, 1985. 232 p.   **CB1**

Reprints 453 substantial critical annotations (many of them signed) selected from the more than 1,200 reviews of works in education published in *American reference books annual* 1970–85. Arranged in chapters citing specific kinds of reference works (e.g., indexes) or materials on special topics such as reading and special education. Coverage of database resources is incomplete: online versions of *Education index* and *Resources in education* are omitted (although *Current index to journals in education* is mentioned), and CD-ROM products are not discussed. Author, title, and subject indexes.   Z5811.A59

Berry, Dorothea M. A bibliographic guide to educational research. 3rd ed. Metuchen, N.J. : Scarecrow, 1990. 500 p.   **CB2**

1st ed., 1975; 2nd ed., 1980.

Provides descriptive (but not evaluative) annotations for 1,050 reference sources. Arranged by type of work. In addition to resources on scholarly works, includes sources on instructional materials used in public school classrooms. Author, editor, compiler, title, and subject indexes.   Z5811.B39

Buttlar, Lois. Education : a guide to reference and information sources. Englewood, Colo. : Libraries Unlimited, 1989. 258 p. (Reference sources in the social sciences series, no. 2).
CB3

Describes more than 900 titles, including databases as well as printed sources. Almost all are in English and were published after 1980, with the exception of a few important works, such as unique bibliographies. Entries contain substantial annotations, some evaluative. Arranged in 20 chapters, most of which treat specific areas of the field (e.g., special education, educational administration, evaluation in education). Other chapters cover education periodicals, research centers and organizations, social science reference sources, and general reference works related to education. General index.   Z5811.B89

Freed, Melvyn N. The educator's desk reference (EDR) : a sourcebook of educational information and research / Melvyn N. Freed, author and ed. ; Robert K. Hess and Joseph M. Ryan, authors. N.Y. : American Council on Education, c1989. 536 p. : ill.   **CB4**

A guide designed to assist professional educators in conducting research. Includes an annotated bibliography of 134 reference works; directories of journals, book publishers, and microcomputer software publishers, giving their specialties and guidelines for manuscript submission; lists of microcomputer software; reviews of standardized tests; guidelines for selection of appropriate research design, sampling techniques, and statistical procedures; and descriptions of national and regional organizations. Because emphasis is "less on 'how to' and more on 'information lookup' " (*Pref.*), readers are referred to further sources of information. Cross-references; general index.

LB1028.27.U6F74

Woodbury, Marda. A guide to sources of educational information. Completely rev. 2nd ed. Arlington, Va. : Information Resources Pr., 1982. 430 p.   **CB5**
1st ed., 1976.

Describes and often evaluates more than 700 print, non-print, and organizational sources for educational research. Arrangement is basically by form (dictionaries, directories, bibliography, nonprint, etc.) with other sections on finance and government, special education, and writing style. General index includes cross-references. No longer up to date, but still directs researchers toward useful sources.

Z5811.W65

Bibliography

Columbia University. Teachers College. Library. Dictionary catalog of the Teachers College Library. Boston : G.K. Hall, 1970. 36 v.   **CB6**

A photoreproduction of the catalog cards for this collection of more than 400,000 items. Author, title, and subject cards in one alphabetic arrangement.

Three *Supplements* covered material added to the Library, 1970–76 (1st, 1971, 5 v.; 2nd, 1973, 2 v.; 3rd, 1977, 10 v.).

Supplemented by: *Bibliographic guide to education* (CB9).

Z5819.C73

Grambs, Jean Dresden. Sex differences and learning : an annotated bibliography of educational research, 1979–1989 / Jean Dresden Grambs, John C. Carr. N.Y. : Garland, 1991. 280 p. (Garland reference library of social science, v. 418 ; Garland bibliographies in contemporary education, v. 11).
CB7

Contains 795 entries briefly describing research articles one could "reasonably expect to find ... in a [university] library...."—*Introd.* In 23 chapters with such titles as Cognitive styles/cognitive structures, Mathematics, and School attendance/ dropouts. Author and subject indexes.   Z5815.U5G73

General

Aby, Stephen H. The IQ debate : a selective guide to the literature / comp. by Stephen H. Aby, with the assistance of Martha J. McNamara. N.Y. : Greenwood, 1990. 228 p. (Bibliographies and indexes in psychology, no. 8).   **CB8**

A selective annotated bibliography of 408 English-language works, most of which were published after Arthur Jensen's 1969 article suggesting that American blacks might be less intelligent than whites. Most of the cited works relate to the subsequent debate, representing a cross-section of positions taken. In two parts, the first a list of 25 reference books. The second is arranged by format: books, book chapters, journal articles, popular magazine articles, newspaper articles, education documents, and nonprint media. Annotations are 100–300 words long and nonevaluative. Name and subject indexes.

Z7204.I5A29

Bibliographic guide to education. 1978– . Boston : G. K. Hall, 1979– . Annual.   **CB9**

Serves as a supplement to the *Dictionary catalog* of the Teachers College Library, Columbia University (CB6).

Lists, in dictionary arrangement, materials cataloged by the Teachers College Library during the year of coverage, together with selected publications in the field of education cataloged by the Research Libraries of the New York Public Library.   Z5813.B4

Blyth, Dale A. Philosophy, policies and programs for early adolescent education : an annotated bibliography / Dale A. Blyth, Elizabeth Leuder Karnes. Westport, Conn. : Greenwood, 1981. 689 p.   **CB10**

Cites 1,600 books, journal articles, ERIC documents, dissertations, and other materials. Intended as a comprehensive source for researchers and practitioners; hence, unpublished materials were included if they could be obtained. Annotations are "longer than usual for a book of this type" (*Introd.*) because the compilers wanted readers to "learn from the annotations themselves" the nature of the work and the authors' conclusions. In 12 sections on topics such as curriculum, internal organization of schools, discipline and problem behavior, etc. Author and subject indexes. No longer up to date, but a prolific source of meaty annotations.   LB1623.B49

Cooperative learning : a guide to research / Samuel Totten ... [et al.]. N.Y. : Garland, 1991. 390 p. (Garland bibliographies in contemporary education, v. 12 ; Garland reference library of social science, v. 674).   **CB11**

An annotated bibliography of 818 works on the application of the various teaching strategies that fall under the rubric "cooperative learning." Cites items, dating from Dewey's writing in the early 1900s to the present, on uses at grade levels ranging from kindergarten through higher education. Describes books, essays, articles, dissertations, book reviews, nonprint media, reports and curricula. Topically arranged, with chapters on specific teaching strategies, instruction in individual subject areas, organizations, educational media, classroom environment, etc. Author and title indexes.   Z5814.G84C66

Education literature, 1907–1932. N.Y. : Garland, 1979. 25 v. in 12.   **CB12**

A reproduction of the 117 published indexes to periodical articles, books, conference proceedings, government publications, pamphlets, and other material received by the U.S. Office of Education Library, 1907–32. Vol. 12 is a cumulative index expanded by entries for the previously unindexed v. 15–16 and edited to eliminate inconsistencies.

Z5811.E415

Educators guide to free [materials]. Randolph, Wis. : Educators Progress Service.   **CB13**

This service issues: *Educators guide to free films* (1941– . Annual); *Educators guide to free filmstrips* (1949– . Annual); *Educators guide to free audio and video materials* (1977– . Annual).

All are annotated lists giving source, availability, terms of loan, etc., arranged by subject with subject and title indexes.

The same publisher offers other annual guides to free materials in special areas and on special subjects, including: *Educators guide to free guidance materials* (1962–); *Educators guide to free social studies materials* (1960–); *Educators guide to free health, physical education and recreation materials* (1968–); *Elementary teachers guide to free curriculum materials* (1944–). AG600.E3

Hoffman, Andrea C. Kits, games, and manipulatives for the elementary school classroom : a source book / Andrea C. Hoffman and Ann M. Glannon. N.Y. : Garland, 1993. 605 p. (Garland reference library of social science, v. 892 ; Source books on education, vol. 36). **CB14**

Entries for some 1,500 items are organized in chapters by broad subject area (e.g., social studies). Information on the materials and their uses, including the learning goals for which they were designed, appropriate grade levels, prices, and sources. Subject (discipline) index. LB1043.H63

Leming, James S. Contemporary approaches to moral education : an annotated bibliography and guide to research. N.Y. : Garland, 1983. 451 p. (Garland bibliographies in contemporary education, v. 2 ; Garland reference library of social science, v. 117). **CB15**

Presents citations to material on "the important thinking and research surrounding the practical side of the moral education movement of the 60's and 70's."—*Introd.* Classed arrangement of more than 1,850 entries, most annotated, for journal articles, ERIC documents, books, dissertations, bibliographies, collections of readings, and sections of journals. Omits curriculum materials and unpublished works. Covers publications of the mid-1960s–1981. Author and subject indexes.

§ *See also* the author's *Foundations of moral education : an annotated bibliography* (Westport, Conn. : Greenwood, 1983. 325 p.), which contains nearly 1,500 entries in classed arrangement within two main sections: (1) Reflections on the domain of moral education and (2) Moralization : the learning of morality. Author and subject indexes. Z5814.M7L45

O'Brien, Nancy P. Core list of books and journals in education / by Nancy Patricia O'Brien and Emily Fabiano. Phoenix : Oryx, 1991. 125 p. **CB16**

Assembles a selected group of approximately 1,000 monographs, journals, U.S. and Unesco documents, reference works, conference papers, and handbooks, most published in the late 1980s, although a few important or classic works are included. Organized around 18 categories representing broad areas of education, such as educational technology and media and educational administration and law. Entries for books are annotated. Author/editor, title, and subject indexes. Z5811.C798

•**OCLC education library** [database]. Dublin, Ohio : OCLC, Inc., 1600–[19??]. **CB17**

Available on CD-ROM. Ceased publication.

A compilation of records pertaining to education drawn from the OCLC database. Provides full bibliographic and cataloging information for 500,000 books, serials, audio and video recordings, dissertations, software files, and other materials.

Resources for educational equity : a guide for grades pre-kindergarten–12 / [ed. by] Merle Froschl, Barbara Sprung. N.Y. : Garland, 1988. 266 p. (Garland reference library of social science, v. 444 ; Source books on education, vol. 17). **CB18**

A guide to materials used to educate students in attitudes of equality toward all races, sexes, and people with disabilities. Eleven chapters treat such topics as Early childhood education, Language arts and literature, and Teenage childbearing. Each chapter is written by an expert and contains a short essay followed by bibliographic entries with evaluative annotations. Author and subject indexes. LC213.2.R47

Woodward, Arthur. Textbooks in school and society : an annotated bibliography and guide to research / Arthur Woodward, David L. Elliott, Kathleen Carter Nagel. N.Y. : Garland, 1988. 176 p. (Garland bibliographies in contemporary education, v. 6 ; Garland reference library of social science, v. 405). **CB19**

Arranges 471 citations in two topical sections, Textbook producers and consumers and Evaluation and criticism of textbooks, preceded by introductions that provide an overview of the topics. Most of the citations were published 1975–87, but selected items from earlier years are included if they "made a lasting contribution to our knowledge of the area."—*Introd.* Subject and author indexes. Z5817.W64

Periodicals

Cabell's directory of publishing opportunities in education. 1st ed. (1984)– . Beaumont, Tex. : Cabell Pub. Co., [1984]– . **CB20**

Provides information about the characteristics, requirements, and procedures for potentional authors for more than 400 journals, including topics published, readership, fees charged authors, length of manuscripts accepted and guidelines on style and format, acceptance rates, review procedures, etc. Table of contents lists journals alphabetically; subject index classifies them according to topics.

Collins, Mary Ellen. Education journals and serials : an analytical guide. N.Y. : Greenwood, 1988. 355 p. (Annotated bibliographies of serials, no. 12). **CB21**

Intended for professionals submitting manuscripts for publication or librarians developing collections. Attempts comprehensive coverage of journals in English, omitting only periodicals of marginal quality or limited interest. Includes newsletters, state and regional publications, and some titles from related disciplines. The 803 entries provide publishers' addresses and information on subscription costs, number of subscribers, availability of reprints, microform editions, coverage by print indexes and databases, target audiences, and type of manuscript selection (e.g., whether refereed, etc.). Most include descriptive, evaluative, or comparative annotations. In 39 chapters, most treating publications for specific education levels, curricular areas or topical areas (e.g., educational administration). Publisher, title, geographical, and subject indexes. Z5813.C64

Loke, Wing Hong. A guide to journals in psychology and education. Metuchen, N.J. : Scarecrow, 1990. 410 p. **CB22**

A valuable complement to *Journals in psychology* (CD13). Lists more than 350 journals, including many published outside the U.S. Entries are balanced between psychology and education journals. Detailed information on manuscript submission and publishing policies are provided in the main alphabetical list; indexes for journal titles and editors. BF76.8.L65

Dissertations and theses

Master's theses directories. 1993– . Cedar Falls, Iowa : H. M. Silvey, c1993– . Annual. **CB23**

Formed by the union of *Master's theses directories. Education*; *Master's theses directories. Arts and social sciences*; and *Master's theses directories. Natural and technical sciences*.

In recent years has listed approximately 4,000 theses per year from more than 900 American and Canadian universities. Not a complete listing; includes only theses which circulate on interlibrary loan. For each thesis gives author, title, institution and date. Arranged into 75 sections and subsections treating broad subject areas (e.g., home economics curriculum, achievement). Author, subject, and institutional indexes. Z5055.U5M46

Parker, Franklin. American dissertations on foreign education : a bibliography with abstracts. Troy, N.Y. : Whitston, 1971–1988. v. 1–20. (In progress). **CB24**

Editors: v. 1–4, F. Parker; v. 5– , F. Parker and B. J. Parker.

Contents: v. 1, Canada; v. 2, India; v. 3, Japan; v. 4, Africa; v. 5, Scandinavia; v. 6, China (in 2 vols.); v. 7, Korea; v. 8, Mexico; v. 9, South America; v. 10, Central America; v. 11, Pakistan and Bangladesh; v. 12, Iran and Iraq; v. 13, Israel; v. 14, Middle East; v. 15, Thailand; v. 16, Asia, South and Southeast (general); v. 17, Pacific Islands; v. 18, Philippines; v. 19, Australia and New Zealand; v. 20, Britain.

In addition to U.S. dissertations, includes Canadian and some European works. Each volume is an author listing, with subject index. Not all indexes include abstracts. Further volumes are planned for additional European countries.   Z5815.C3P28

Research studies in education : a subject and author index of doctoral dissertations, reports and field studies; and a research methods bibliography, 1941/51–70. 1952–70. Bloomington, Ind. : Phi Delta Kappa, 1953–72. Annual.   **CB25**

Subtitle varies.

1953/63 cumulation publ. 1965.

Includes doctoral dissertations completed and under way.

Z5811.R4

Young, Arthur P. Higher education in American life, 1636–1986 : a bibliography of dissertations and theses. N.Y. : Greenwood, 1988. 431 p. (Bibliographies and indexes in education, no. 5).   **CB26**

For annotation, *see* CB233.   Z5814.U7Y69

By country or region

International

Kelly, David H. Women's education in the Third World : an annotated bibliography / David H. Kelly, Gail P. Kelly. N.Y. : Garland, 1989. 478 p. (Reference books in international education, vol. 5 ; Garland reference library of social science, v. 544).   **CB27**

Describes 1,188 journals, monographs, and books, including "many individual chapters hidden in books that didn't have women or education as their central concern."—*Introd.* Omits dissertations, unpublished reports, and conference papers. Further limited to "substantial research studies" on developing (rather than industrialized) countries, and to works in five languages: English (in which it attempts to be comprehensive), Portuguese, Spanish, French, and German. Most items were published in the 1970s and 1980s, though a few appeared earlier. Grouped into 15 topics, each subdivided by region and country, that relate to access to education, educational processes, and societal outcomes. Author and geographical indexes.   Z5815.D44K44

United States

●**A-V online** [database]. Boston : SilverPlatter, c1986– .

CB28

Also known as the National Information Center for Educational Media (NICEM) database. Corresponds in part to NICEM's *Audiocassette & compact disc finder* (formerly *Audiocassette finder*), *Filmstrip & slide set finder*, *Index to AV producers & distributors*, *Vocational & technical audiovisuals*, *Wellness media*, *Science & computer literacy audiovisuals*, and *Film and video finder*. Has more than 330,000 citations and abstracts for 16mm films, 35mm filmstrips, 8mm movie cartridges, slides, overhead transparencies, audio and video tapes, phonograph records, CD-ROMs, and software. Available online, updated quarterly, and in CD-ROM, coverage 1913– , updated annually.

A bibliography of American educational history : an annotated and classified guide / [ed.] by Francesco Cordasco, William W. Brickman … [et al.]. N.Y. : AMS Pr., [1975]. 394 p.

CB29

Sections contributed by various scholars cover the breadth of the field. In three parts: (1) listings of general bibliographies, encyclopedic works, collections of source materials, and comprehensive histories; (2) sections on specific topics such as the teaching profession and biographies of American educators; (3) sections for specific periods in American educational history. Author index.   Z5815.U5B5

Bilingual education and English as a second language : a research handbook, 1988–1990 / [ed. by] Alba N. Ambert. N.Y. : Garland, 1991. 379 p. (Garland reference library of social science, v. 634).   **CB30**

Describes and analyzes 1988–90 research. Ten chapters (e.g., The acculturation of ethnolinguistic minorities, Early childhood education: the effects of language on learning) are each written by an expert and contain a general analysis of the topic, recommendatations for future research, and an annotated bibliography listing both 1988–90 and earlier works. Appendixes list multifunctional resource centers, organizations, and journals and newsletters. Author and subject indexes.

An earlier version covering 1986–87 research (N.Y. : Garland, 1988) is similarly organized, but pays less attention to social variables.

LC3731.B5468

Educational film & video locator of the Consortium of College and University Media Centers and R. R. Bowker. 4th ed. (1990/91)– . N.Y. : Bowker, c1990– .   **CB31**

1st ed., 1978. Title varies.

A union list of educational and feature films held by the 46 member libraries of the Consortium; the 1990/91 ed. indexes 52,000 video and film titles. Annotated entries indicate running time, format, color or black-and-white, production date, subjects, audience level, rental sources, and lending terms. Subject, title and audience level indexes.

LB1044.Z9E37

Jones, Leon. From Brown to Boston : desegregation in education, 1954–1974. Metuchen, N.J. : Scarecrow, 1979. 2 v. (2175 p.).   **CB32**

A bibliography of desegregation in education from the period of the 1954 case of *Brown v. Board of Education of Topeka* to the 1974 *Miliken v. Bradley* case and the Boston school crisis which followed. In v. 1, books and articles are treated in separate sections; items are grouped by year within sections, then listed alphabetically by author or other main entry. Legal cases are summarized in v.2, arranged chronologically. Substantial annotations. Indexes of authors/titles, cases/legal issues, and subjects.   Z5814.D5J65

Sedlak, Michael W. American educational history : a guide to information sources / Michael W. Sedlak, Timothy Walch. Detroit : Gale, [1981]. 265 p. (American government and history information guide series, v.10).   **CB33**

An annotated, selective bibliography of books and periodical titles, with preference given "to those items which … have enduring value; to items which have not appeared previously in other bibliographies, to periodical literature which has not appeared in other bibliographies; and to periodical literature which is not ordinarily found in library card catalogs. We have also emphasized materials published since 1965."—*Pref.* "Guides to further research" (p.227–39) lists general histories of American education, historiographical studies, and reference bibliographies and guides. Broad subject arrangement; author and subject indexes.   LA205.S42

Songe, Alice H. Private school education in the U.S : an annotated bibliography, 1950–1980. Jefferson, N.C. : McFarland, 1982. 89 p.   **CB34**

A selective annotated bibliography treating all aspects of independent and church-related schools, their aims and objects, history, administration, financing, and social and racial problems. Pays special attention to four controversial aspects: the consitutionality of providing public funds and services for church-related and other private schools; the impact of private schools on the public school system; the rights of parents in choosing types of schooling for their children; objectives of private schools in relation to the goals of a democratic society. Separate sections for types of publications: books, monographs, and serials; federal and state government publications; periodical articles; dissertations. Author and subject indexes.   Z5814.P65S58

United States. Department of Health, Education, and Welfare. Library. Author-title catalog of the Department Library. Boston : G. K. Hall, 1965–67. 29 v.   **CB35**
    ————. ————. *Supplement* (1973. 7 v.).
    ————. *Subject catalog of the Department library* (Boston : G. K. Hall, 1965. 20 v.; Suppl., 1973. 4 v.).

Both the author/title and subject sets offer photoreproduction of the cards from the Library's catalogs. The collection of more than 500,000 volumes is strong in the fields of education and the social sciences, and is particularly notable as having "the most complete set of the Departmental and operating agencies' publications."—*Foreword*. The subject catalog reproduces 350,000 cards with another 109,000 in the supplements; the author/title catalog has 540,000 entries with 61,700 added in the supplement.

Religious and ethnic education

Grant, Mary A. Catholic school education in the United States : development and current concerns / by Mary A. Grant and Thomas C. Hunt. N.Y. : Garland, c1992. 296 p. (Garland reference library of social science, v. 474 ; Source books on education, vol. 31).   **CB36**

An annotated bibliography organized into chapters by historical periods. Each chapter consists of several pages of text, followed by the bibliography covering that period. Substantial annotations. Author and subject indexes.   LC501.G65

Hunt, Thomas C. Religious schools in America : a selected bibliography / [comp. by] Thomas C. Hunt, James C. Carper, Charles R. Kniker. N.Y. : Garland, 1986. 391 p. (Garland reference library of social science, v. 338.).   **CB37**

Contains 1,181 entries on religiously affiliated elementary and secondary schools. Cites journal articles, books, dissertations and theses, reports and other works. Of 24 chapters, 17 deal with the schools of 17 individual religious groups. Other chapters treat such topics as court decisions on government aid to religious schools, state regulation of these schools, and statements about the schools by their supporters and public school educators. Author and subject indexes.
    Z5814.C57I186

McGee, Leo. Education of the black adult in the United States : an annotated bibliography / comp. by Leo McGee and Harvey G. Neufeldt. Westport, Conn. : Greenwood, 1985. 108 p. (Bibliographies and indexes in Afro-American and African studies, no. 4).   **CB38**

Spans the entire period from the arrival of blacks in 1619 to the present, divided into four eras, each covered by a chapter. A fifth chapter, General resources, treats sources not restricted to one of these periods. Annotations are nonevaluative and vary in length. Author and subject indexes.   LC2801.M27

Menendez, Albert J. School prayer and other religious issues in American public education : a bibliography. N.Y. : Garland, 1985. 168 p. (Garland reference library of social science, v. 291).   **CB39**

Arranged in 21 chapters; cites 1,566 unannotated references to books, journal and newspaper articles, dissertations, and theses. Provides historical perspective on such issues as bible reading, teaching religion, religious elements in textbooks, grades in school. Author index; a subject index lists only states.   Z5815.U5M46

•**NCBE bibliographic database** [database]. Wash. : National Clearinghouse for Bilingual Education, 1978– .   **CB40**

Available online, updated monthly.

Has 16,000 citations and abstracts of journal articles, reviews of the literature, conference papers, reports, bibliographies, and classroom materials on bilingual education. Includes unpublished as well as published works, many issued by associations, school districts, universities, foundations, and government funded programs.

•**NCBE resources database** [database]. Wash. : National Clearinghouse for Bilingual Education.   **CB41**

An online directory of American (and some international) organizations concerned with bilingual education, including associations and advocacy groups. Entries include contact information and describe the organizations' purposes and activities.

Canada

Finley, E. Gault. Education in Canada : a bibliography = L'éducation au Canada : une bibliographie. Toronto : Dundurn Pr., 1989. 2 v.   **CB42**

Publ. in cooperation with the National Library of Canada and the Canadian Government Publishing Centre, Supply and Services Canada.

"Comprises a comprehensive, computerized database of selected items in relation to the development of Canadian education from the 17th Century to the early 1980s."—*Introd*. Treats the pre-primary through postsecondary levels, "with both academic and technical/vocational streams, as well as the informal system and its life long dimension." Contains entries for more than 14,000 published and unpublished books, theses reports, research studies, government documents, etc., in English or French. Omits curriculum guides, directories, almanacs, statutes, nonprint items, pedagogical treatises, textbooks, proceedings, and yearbooks. Entries are generally in the original language; the bibliography's introductory sections and headings are in both languages. Author, title, imprint, and subject indexes.
    Z5815.C3F56

Latin America

Lauerhass, Ludwig. Education in Latin America : a bibliography / Ludwig Lauerhass, Jr. and Vera Lucia Oliveira de Araujo Haugse. [Los Angeles] : UCLA Latin American Center Pubns., Univ. of Calif., Los Angeles ; Boston : G. K. Hall, [1980]. 431 p. : ill. (UCLA Latin American Center Publications reference series, v. 9).   **CB43**

"Designed as an introductory reference volume for research on education in Latin America in all its formal and nonformal aspects from its beginning in pre-Columbian times to the mid-1970s in all areas of Latin America and the Caribbean."—*Introd*. Emphasis is on formal, in-school aspects of education from the period 1945–75.

§ A companion volume for nonformal education is Susan L. Poston's *Nonformal education in Latin America*, published by the Center in 1976.   Z5815.L3L46

Great Britain

Parker, Franklin. Education in England and Wales : an annotated bibliography / Franklin Parker, Betty June Parker. N.Y. : Garland, 1991. 531 p. (Reference books in international education, vol. 19 ; Garland reference library of social science, v. 581).   **CB44**

Contains more than 2,000 briefly annotated entries for books, articles, and ERIC documents; excludes dissertations. Arranged into 13 chapters on subjects such as administration and higher education, but also on topics unique to the U.K. (e.g., Wales and Welsh language, Education Reform Act of 1988). Introductory chapters on the history and structure of English and Welsh educational systems. Author and subject indexes.   Z5815.G5P37

Russia and the U.S.S.R.

Brickman, William W. Russian and Soviet education, 1731–1989 : a multilingual annotated bibliography / William W. Brickman, John T. Zepper. N.Y. : Garland, 1992. 538 p. (Garland reference library of social science, v. 200 ; Reference books in international education, vol. 9).   **CB45**

Lists 1,755 items "intended to aid mature Russian-Soviet scholars, and ... students in Russian-Soviet studies and allied fields."—*Pref.* Many entries result from the authors' visits to libraries in the former Soviet Union, its satellites, and nine other countries. The main section lists books, periodical articles, association reports, and government publications, and is arranged alphabetically by main entry. A separate section cites dissertations. Works cited are in 21 languages, and there is a language as well as a subject index, but all annotations are in English.

§ More comprehensive than Yushin Yoo's *Soviet education : an annotated bibliography and readers' guide to works in English, 1893–1978* (Westport, Conn. : Greenwood, [1980]), which omits foreign titles, covers a briefer period, and is largely drawn from *Soviet education*, which is itself abstracted in *Current index to journals in education*.   Z5815.S66B75

Africa

Urch, George E. F. Education in Sub-Saharan Africa : a source book. N.Y. : Garland, 1992. 192 p. (Garland reference library of social science, v. 576 ; Reference books in international education, vol. 11).   **CB46**

A briefly annotated selective bibliography of journal articles, books, book chapters, and published reports of governmental and international organizations. The 443 articles appeared 1970–80; other materials, 1970–90. Includes only works written in English, so useful sources in other languages may have been omitted. Arranged in chapters on major areas (e.g., Southern Africa, Africa–General), each divided into subsections (History and philosophy, Curriculum and methods, etc.) Index.   LA1501.U73 1992

China

Parker, Franklin. Education in the People's Republic of China, past and present : an annotated bibliography / Franklin Parker, Betty June Parker. N.Y. : Garland, 1986. 845 p. (Reference books in international education, vol. 2 ; Garland reference library of social science, v. 281).   **CB47**

Cites over 3,000 books, journal and newspaper articles, and other works covering both the Communist period and earlier years. Lists publications in several languages, but all annotations are in English. Arranged by subject, with some chronological subdivisions. Author and subject indexes.   Z5815.C54P37

Reading and literacy

Hladczuk, John. Comparative reading : an international bibliography / comp. by John Hladczuk and William Eller. N.Y. : Greenwood, 1987. 174 p. (Bibliographies and indexes in education, no. 4).   **CB48**

Cites 1,947 sources, including periodical articles, books, government publications, dissertations, conference proceedings, and reports. Interdisciplinary in scope, containing entries related to psychological, sociological, historical, philosophical, and economic aspects of reading. In two parts: (1) International research, with sections treating national, world, regional, and cross-cultural research, and (2) Correlates of reading, with chapters on such subjects as Correlates of learning to read, Correlates of language, and Correlates of the psychology of comparative reading. Author and subject indexes.   Z5818.L3H58

————————— General issues in literacy/illiteracy : a bibliography / comp. by John Hladczuk, William Eller, and Sharon Hladczuk. N.Y. : Greenwood, 1990. 420 p. (Bibliographies and indexes in education, no. 8).   **CB49**

Cites 4,085 journal articles, ERIC documents, books, dissertations, unpublished papers, proceedings, government documents and other materials. Attempts to be comprehensive but not exhaustive. Arranged topically in 37 chapters on subjects such as: Mathematical literacy, Economics of illiteracy, and Technology and literacy. Author and subject indexes. Emphasizes international and national research.

————————. *Literacy/illiteracy in the world : a bibliography* / comp. by John Hladczuk, William Eller, and Sharon Hladczuk. (N.Y. : Greenwood, 1989. 201 p. [Bibliographies and indexes in education, no. 6]).

Lists works on 126 specific countries, states of the U.S., world regions, and literacy worldwide. Author and subject indexes. Although the two titles cite many of the same works, each lists works not treated by the other, so both should be consulted.   Z5814.I3H56

Indexes; Abstract journals

British education index. v. 1 (1954/58)– . London : Libr. Assoc., 1961– . Quarterly, with annual cumulations.   **CB50**

Comp. by the Librarians of Institutes of Education, volumes for 1954–1982; issued by British Library Bibliographic Services Division since that volume.

Frequency of cumulation varies: v. 1, Aug. 1954–Nov. 1958; v. 2, Dec. 1958–Dec. 1961; v. 3–7, 1962/63–1970/71, biennial; v. 8, 1972– , annual.

"Aims to list and analyze the subject content of all articles of permanent educational interest appearing in a wide range of English language periodicals published in the British isles, together with certain internationally published periodicals."—*Pref.* In two sequences, an author list and a subject list, both with full citations.

•Available online (1976–), with 60,000 citations to articles plus 12,000 *British education theses index* (*BETI*) citations, 1950– ; both updated quarterly. Also available on CD-ROM as one of the three separate databases of *International ERIC* (also known as *DIALOG On-Disc international ERIC*; see CB57), the British portion of which also contains *BETI* and *British education thesaurus* (CB81).   Z5813.B7

Business education index. 1940– . [Little Rock, Ark.] : Delta Pi Epsilon Fraternity, [1940]– . Annual.   **CB51**

Indexes approximately 50 journals, 2 yearbooks, the proceedings of Delta Pi Epsilon, dissertations, and other works. Covers the broad spectrum of business education, "with an emphasis on information systems (including business communications), business teacher education, and vocational education (primarily marketing education)."—*Editorial policy.* In two parts, an alphabetical author index and a topical subject index, both providing complete citations. The latter is preceded by an alphabetical table of topics and subtopics.   Z5814.C7B85

Canadian education index = Répertoire canadien sur l'éducation. v. [1] (Jan./Mar. 1965)– . Toronto : Canadian Education Assoc., 1965– . Three issues a year, including the annual cumulation.   **CB52**

Frequency varies; period of cumulation varies; publisher varies (1965–72 issued by Canadian Council for Research in Education, 1973–75 by the Canadian Education Association).

In 1988 absorbed *Directory of education studies in Canada.*

Indexes "the principal education literature published in Canada" (*Introd.*), including articles from more than 200 Canadian periodicals; monographs; "all significant reports and publications" of federal, provincial, and territorial government departments, faculties of education, teacher's associations, large school boards, and educational organizations; graduate theses and dissertations; forthcoming books from Canadian publishers; book, media, and software reviews; and provinciallyapproved curriculum documents. In several sections, including abstracts of reports, monographs, theses, and dissertations (but not of periodical articles); short citations arranged by subject; and short citations arranged by personal or corporate name, including corporate proceedings. Provides accession numbers through which items may be found in the *MICROLOG education collection*, a monthly microfiche publication analogous to *ERIC*. Many of these items are also available in microfiche or paper from the publisher.

•Available online from Info Globe Online, 1976– . Updated every four months. Also available on CD-ROM (1976–) as one of the three separate databases of *International ERIC* (also titled *DIALOG OnDisc international ERIC*, CB57), the Canadian portion of which supersedes *CD: Education* (produced by Micromedia).   Z5813.C3

Contents pages in education. v. 1, no. 1 (July 1986)– . [Abingdon, Oxfordshire] : Carfax Pub. Co., 1986– . Monthly.
CB53
Reprints the tables of contents of more than 600 journals; each monthly issue treats approximately 175 journals. Monthly issues also contain author and subject indexes and lists of journals cited in that issue and during the year. Cumulative indexes appear in the June and December issues and triennially.   Z5813.C66

Current index to journals in education : (CIJE). v. 1, no. 1/2 (Jan./Feb. 1969)– . Phoenix : Oryx, 1969– . Monthly, with semiannual cumulations.   **CB54**
Publisher varies.
Annual cumulations, v. 1 6, 1969 74; semiannual v. 7 (1975)– .
The most widely-used print index to journals in the field. Contains both citations and short abstracts. Published as part of the U.S. Office of Education's Educational Resources Information Center (ERIC) program, this service provides detailed indexing for articles in more than 800 education and education-related journals. Currency of coverage is an important feature, though there are inevitable delays of many months in the case of some journals. Classed arrangement, with subject and author indexes which cumulate semiannually and annually. Serves as a companion to ERIC's monthly *Resources in education* (CB61), which indexes and abstracts non-journal materials. Indexes: subject, author, and journal contents. Semiannual cumulative indexes.
CIJE : cumulated author index, 1969–1984 (Phoenix : Oryx, 1985. 2218 p.) is a cumulated author index to all entries of the first 16 years of *Current index to journals in education*. Like the author indexes of *CIJE*'s monthly issues, provides only titles and entry numbers.
•Available in machine readable form: *CIJE OnDisc*, updated quarterly. *ERIC* [database] is a machine-readable version of *Resources in education* and *CIJE*. For more information, *see* CB56.

Education index. v. 1 (Jan. 1929)– . N.Y. : H.W. Wilson, 1932– . Monthly (except July and Aug.).   **CB55**
Subtitle (varies): a cumulative author subject index to a selected list of educational periodicals and yearbooks.
Cumulates throughout the year, with annual bound cumulations: v. 1–8, 1929–May 1953, issued with triennial cumulations; v. 9–13, June 1953–June 1963, biennial cumulations.
Now indexes by author and subject some 450 periodicals and six yearbooks treating the breadth of the field. Until June 1961, included many references to books, pamphlets, and analytics in books and society transactions; thereafter, non-periodical material is omitted. From July 1961–June 1969 (v. 13–19), indexing was by subject only. Utilizes many subject and geographical subheadings. Separate book review section.
•Available online (June 1983–), on CD-ROM, and on magnetic tape. Producers and frequency vary.   Z5813.E23

•**ERIC** [database]. Rockville, Md. : ERIC Processing and Reference Facility.   **CB56**
Contains more than 800,000 citations, with abstracts, to journal and report literature in the field of education and related fields, including early childhood education and development, interpersonal and social skills, perception and cognition, and tests and measurements. The machine-readable counterpart to the two major print indexes in education, *Current index to journals in education* (CIJE. CB54) and *Re-*

sources in education (*RIE*. CB61). Emphasizes English-language materials. Available both online (updated monthly) and in CD-ROM (updated quarterly).
Thesaurus of ERIC descriptors lists standard ERIC subject headings. *See* CB83 for complete information.

•**International ERIC** [database]. [Palo Alto, Calif.] : Dialog Information Services.   **CB57**
Part of *DIALOG OnDisc*; also called *DIALOG OnDisc international ERIC*.
A CD-ROM file containing machine-readable versions of three indexes:
British education index (CB50), 1976– , with 75,000 records, including *British education theses index* (*BETI*) entries.
Canadian education index (CB52), 1976– , with 115,000 records, including the ONTERIS collection of provincial curriculum documents.
Australian education index, 1978– , with 54,000 records.
Each database is presented separately with its own thesaurus (*see* CB81 for the *British education thesaurus*) and is updated quarterly.

Language teaching. [v. 15, no. 1] (Jan. 1982)– . Cambridge : Cambridge Univ. Pr., 1982– . Quarterly.   **CB58**
Subtitle: The international abstracting journal for language teachers and applied linguists.
Supersedes *Language teaching & linguistics* (1975–81) and assumes its numbering. Also continues *Language-teaching abstracts*, v. 1 (1968)–v. 7 (1974).
Highly selective; for each year, abstracts only 500 of "the most useful and significant articles" in some 400 journals from many countries. Four main subject areas: Language learning and teaching— theory and practices; Teaching particular languages; Research in relevant related sciences; and Language development and use. Subject and author indexes in each issue, cumulated annually.   PB35.L32

Multicultural education abstracts. v. 1, no. 1– . [Abingdon, England] : Carfax Pub. Co., 1982– . Quarterly.   **CB59**
International in scope, annually presenting nonevaluative abstracts of articles from 500 journals, of books and book chapters, and of materials not always easy to locate, such as conference reports and theses. Quarterly author and subject indexes, cumulating annually. Most elusive items are available in microfiche from CORE (Collected Original Resources in Education; Abingdon, England: Carfax, 1977–).

Reading abstracts. v. 1 (Apr. 1975)– . [La Jolla, Calif. : Essay Pr., 1974]– .   **CB60**
Frequency varies; annual since v. 10, 1984.
Contains abstracts of "scholarly articles that are selected from the world's serial literature regardless of publication or country or provenance."—*t.p.* Arranged by subject, subdivided into narrower topics. Includes works in related areas such as psycholinguistics. Author and subject indexes.   LB1050.R352

Resources in education / Educational Resources Information Center. v. 10, no. 1 (Jan. 1975)– . Wash. : Office of Educational Research and Improvement : distr. by U.S. Govt. Print. Off., [1975]– . Monthly.   **CB61**
Superintendent of Documents classification: HE 19.210: ; ED 1.310: .
At head of title: RIE.
Issuing agency varies.
Supersedes *Research in education* and continues its numbering.
Contains abstracts of items in the ERIC microfiche collection of some 400,000 research reports, papers from professional meetings, government documents, pamphlets, and related materials. Also abstracts books and cites dissertations, neither of which are on the microfiche. Does not index journal articles, which are abstracted in the companion work, *Current index to journals in education* (CIJE. CB54). Indexes: subject, author, institutional, and publication types.
A subscription includes monthly issues and semiannual cumulations. Oryx Press has issued annual cumulations since 1979.

•*ERIC* [database] is a machine-readable version of *RIE* and *CIJE*. For more information, *see* CB56.   Z5813.R4

Second language instruction/acquisition abstracts. v. 1, no. 1 (July 1991)– . San Diego : Sociological Abstracts, Inc., c1991– . Two no. a year.   **CB62**

Provides some 2,000 entries per year "which reflect the world's literature in language instruction and areas of related interest."—*What SLIA Offers*. Includes nonevaluative abstracts of books and journal articles, and enhanced citations for dissertations. Describes works on child and adult language development, native and non-native language instruction, bilingual education, language testing, reading instruction, literacy, and writing. Not comprehensive; does not screen every journal issue. Arranged under 37 topics such as sociolinguistics, syntactic processing, and reading testing. Bibliography of book reviews. Author, title, and subject indexes.   P51.S336

Sociology of education abstracts. v. 1 (1965)– . Abingdon, U.K. [etc.] : Carfax Publ. Co., [1965]– .   **CB63**

Publisher and sponsoring agency vary.

Abstracts some 600 journal articles and books per year. Scope is international and broad, with articles selected from some 350 journals representing several disciplines. Abstracts of articles and books appear in separate sections, with articles arranged by journal title and books by author. Subject and author indexes; annual cumulative index.   Z5813.S67

State education journal index. v. 1 (Sept./Dec. 1963)– . Westminster, Colo. : [s.n.], 1964– . Semiannual.   **CB64**

Title varies: State education journal index and educator's guide to periodicals research strategies (1985).

Subtitle (varies): An annotated index of state education journals.

Indexes 45–50 state and association publications. Arranged alphabetically by subject.   Z5811.S845

Encyclopedias

Dejnozka, Edward L. American educators' encyclopedia / Edward L. Dejnozka and David E. Kapel. Rev. ed. / by David E. Kapel, Charles S. Gifford, and Marilyn B. Kapel. N.Y. : Greenwood, c1991. 716 p. : ill.   **CB65**

1st ed., 1982.

Contains more than 2,000 alphabetically arranged short entries (with references) for concepts, individuals, organizations, programs, methods, publications, and laws. Extensive cross-referencing. Appendixes list codes of ethics, award winners, addresses of organizations, and past presidents of associations. General index.   LB15.D37

Encyclopedia of early childhood education / ed. by Leslie R. Williams, Doris Pronin Fromberg. N.Y. : Garland, 1992. 518 p. : ill. (Garland reference library of the social sciences, vol. 504).   **CB66**

Reflects a "crosscut view of the field today by the 25 scholars on the Editorial Board and ... the 200 scholars who authored articles."—*Introd*. Five main sections: Historical and philosophical roots; Sociocultural, political and economic contexts; Perspectives on children; Early childhood curricula and programs; and Perspectives on educators. Each has a classified arrangement and detailed table of contents. Bibliographies. Index.   LB1139.25.E53

Encyclopedia of education / ed. by Edward Blishen. N.Y. : Philosophical Library, [1970]. 882 p. : illus.   **CB67**

First publ. 1969 under title: Blond's encyclopaedia of education.

Short signed articles by British contributors. Now out of date.   LB15.B56

Encyclopedia of education / Lee C. Deighton, ed. in chief. [N.Y.] : Macmillan, [1971]. 10 v.   **CB68**

When written offered "a view of the institutions and people, of the processes and products, found in educational practice. The articles deal with history, theory, research, and philosophy, as well as with the structure and fabric of education."—*Pref*. Now dated and lacking treatment of the scholarship and practices developed during the last two decades, but still useful, especially for historical perspective. Limited to slightly more than 1,000 signed articles, most several pages in length, including bibliographies. Closely related articles are often grouped under a broad heading. Separate index volume offers a directory of contributors, a detailed subject index, and a guide to articles, listing each entry in alphabetical sequence, followed by a list of *see* and *see also* references.   LB15.E47

Encyclopedia of educational research / ed. in chief, Marvin C. Alkin ; sponsored by the American Educational Research Association. 6th ed. N.Y. : Macmillan : Maxwell Macmillan Internat., c1992. 4 v. : ill.   **CB69**

1st ed., 1941; 5th ed., 1982.

A synthesis of research written for college students, researchers, practitioners, policymakers, and general readers. Consists of 257 alphabetically arranged, signed articles by 325 contributors asked to develop general integrative statements summarizing "what is known in the field and to ... restrict references to landmark books and to general review articles"—*Pref*. Among the criteria for inclusion of topics were the availability and accessibility of research, hence some subjects about which there was considerable interest were not treated. This edition includes many new topics discussing societal issues—e.g., Pregnant and parenting teenagers, AIDS education. Articles vary in length, averaging six pages and including substantial bibliographies. Use is facilitated by a category listing at the beginning of the work and the employment of many cross-references within the text, at the ends of articles, and within the general index.   LB15.E48

The international encyclopedia of education : research and studies / editors in chief, Torsten Husén, T. Neville Postlethwaite. Oxford ; N.Y. : Pergamon, 1985. 10 v. : ill.   **CB70**

An impressive work which surveys the state of the art in the various branches of education, including theory, practice, and research, plus suggestions for future research. Signed, alphabetically arranged articles by leading scholars from many countries. Most entries are several pages in length and include bibliographies. Many outline the systems of education of individual nations.

Vol. 10 offers a classified list of entries, grouping the article titles according to broad subject fields. It also has a detailed subject index, an author index for works cited in the text and the bibliographies, and a list of contributors.

•Available in CD-ROM from the publisher.

———. Supplementary volumes 1–2 (1989, 1991) contain additional articles by experts charged to revise portions that "either needed expansion from the parent work or in which major new research or information was available."—*Pref., v. 1*. Cross-references, both within the supplements and to articles in the basic set, are extensive. Name, subject, and contributor indexes.

A second edition of the *Encyclopedia* is scheduled for publication in 1994. It will have been expanded and its scope broadened, giving move coverage of the sociology of education, females in education, instructional psychology, and the history, anthropology, and philosophy of education. In addition, more attention will be paid to developing countries.

§ Several titles published by Pergamon are based on chapters from the *Encyclopedia*, to which new articles have been added. Included are: *The international encyclopedia of teaching and teacher education*, ed. by Michael J. Dunkin (1987. 878 p.); *Economics of education : research and studies*, ed. by George Psacharopoulos (1987. 482 p.); *Educational research, methodology, and measurement : an international handbook*, ed. by John P. Keeves (1988. 832 p.); *The encyclopedia of comparative education and national systems of education*, ed. by T. Neville Postlethwaite (1988. 777 p.); *Lifelong education for adults : an international handbook*, ed. by Colin J. Titmus (1989. 590 p.); *The international encyclopedia of educational technology*, ed. by Michael Eraut (1989. 654 p.); *The encyclopedia of human development and education : theory, research, and studies*, ed. by R. Murray Thomas (1989. 519 p.); *The international encyclopedia of educational evaluation*, ed. by Herbert J. Walberg and Geneva D. Haertel (1990. 796 p.); *The foundations of students' learning*, ed. by Kevin Marjoribanks (1991. 349 p.); *The international encyclopedia of curriculum*, ed. by Arieh Lewy (1991. 1064 p.).   LB15.I569

Monroe, Paul. A cyclopedia of education / ed. by Paul Monroe, with the assistance of departmental editors and more than 1000 individual contributors. N.Y. : Macmillan, 1911–13. 5 v. : ill.   **CB71**

A reprint (Detroit : Gale, 1968) includes "a new introductory essay by William W. Brickman, Francesco Cordasco, [and] Thomas H. Richardson."

Excellent when issued; now out-of-date, but still useful, particularly for historical and biographical entries. Signed articles by specialists, with good bibliographies and excellent illustrations, some in color. The scope of the work is general, including education in all countries and all periods, but American subjects receive somewhat fuller treatment than foreign topics. Analytical index in v. 5 groups articles by larger subjects than those used in the main alphabet.   LB15.M6

Dictionaries

Barrow, Robin. A critical dictionary of educational concepts : an appraisal of selected ideas and issues in educational theory and practice / Robin Barrow, Geoffrey Milburn. 2nd ed. N.Y. : Teachers College Pr., Teachers College, Columbia Univ., 1990. 370 p.   **CB72**

Unlike dictionaries designed to be exhaustive or free of specific points of view, this work selects entries by "what we think important ... so as to constitute a dictionary of ideas worth contemplating and examining ... to explore and make sense of conflicting and sometimes confused or obscure ideas."—*Pref.* Contains 160 entries, typically one-half to three pages long, usually with references. Words in the text that have their own entries are printed in boldface; cross-references.   LB15.B29

A dictionary of education / ed. by P. J. Hills. London ; Boston : Routledge & Kegan Paul, 1982. 284 p.   **CB73**

Rather than the short definitions frequently found in one-volume dictionaries, provides substantial entries with extensive cross referencing and citations to key references. "... does not set out to be totally comprehensive ... nor adopt a neutral view .... It is intended to give the reader an entry into the subject, so that by subsequent exploration he can come to his own conclusions about the shades of meaning within the subject."—*Introd.* Alphabetically arranged definitions are preceded by brief essays on 15 areas of education. British emphasis.   LB15.D48

A dictionary of reading and related terms / Theodore L. Harris and Richard E. Hodges, coeditors. Newark, Del. : International Reading Association, c1981. 382 p. : ill.   **CB74**

Defines a 5,400-term specialized vocabulary of reading instruction. Terms were drawn from scholarly and technical journals, specialized dictionaries, and glossaries. Some multiple definition entries are preceded by brief introductory essays. Appendix of equivalents for ambiguous or confused English words as they are translated into French, Spanish, German, Danish, and Swedish.   LB1049.98.D53

Good, Carter V. Dictionary of education. 3rd ed. N.Y. : McGraw-Hill, [1973]. 681 p.   **CB75**

Prep. under the auspices of Phi Delta Kappa.

1st ed., 1945.

A scholarly dictionary of 33,000 definitions and cross-references representing the work of nearly 200 coordinators, associates, and reviewers. Educational terms used in Canada and in England and Wales are defined in separate sections following the main body. Similar sections for France, Germany, and Italy, previously included, have been omitted from this edition. No longer up to date, but useful because of the number of definitions and extensive cross-references.   LB15.G6

Gordon, Peter. A guide to English educational terms / Peter Gordon & Denis Lawton. N.Y. : Schocken Books, 1984. 220 p.   **CB76**

A glossary intended to make the educational system of England (and Wales) "more comprehensible to students ... from overseas."— *Introd.* Some entries give historical background or bibliographic references. Contains an introduction to education in England and Wales and appendixes that include a list of acronyms, a short bibliography, and a list of Ministers of Education.   LB15.G62

Page, G. Terry. International dictionary of education / G. Terry Page, John Bernard Thomas, and Alan R. Marshall. London : Kogan Page ; N.Y. : Nichols, [1977]. 381 p. : ill.   **CB77**

More than 10,000 entries covering expressions and terms, international organizations, major national institutions and associations, educators, etc. Appendixes list abbreviations for associations and organizations, as well as United States honor societies, fraternities and sororities.   LB15.P34

Palmer, James C. Dictionary of educational acronyms, abbreviations, and initialisms / comp. and ed. by James C. Palmer and Anita Y. Colby ; ERIC Clearinghouse for Junior Colleges. 2nd ed. Phoenix : Oryx, 1985. 97 p.   **CB78**

1st ed., 1983.

Includes 4,011 acronyms and other short forms. In two sections, the first arranged alphabetically by acronym, the second a "reverse" list, alphabetical by unabbreviated form. Contains 1,995 terms not found in the 1st ed., but omits many of its terms, hence the 1st ed. must be consulted for short forms used prior to 1983.   LB15.P35

Rowntree, Derek. A dictionary of education. Hagerstown [Md.] : Harper & Row, 1981. 354 p.   **CB79**

Presents short definitions of English-language terms in alphabetical order. Includes some names of prominent educators and educational theorists, as well as entries for organizations, laws, certificates, etc. Its British origin makes this less useful in the United States than in the Commonwealth.   LB15.R64

Shafritz, Jay M. The Facts on File dictionary of education / Jay M. Shafritz, Richard P. Koeppe, Elizabeth W. Soper. N.Y. : Facts on File, c1988. 503 p.   **CB80**

Entries are of two basic types: "brief glossary descriptions," and "those that are given more comprehensive coverage, occasionally in the form of authors' comments and interpretations."—*Pref.* Besides entries that define terms, concepts, and practices, some identify individuals, court cases, publications, laws, organizations, and tests.   LB15.S43

Thesauruses

British education thesaurus / ed., Joan V. Marder ; technical ed., Philip Sheffield. 2nd ed. [Leeds, England] : Leeds Univ. Pr., 1991. 427 p.   **CB81**

1st ed., 1988.

The source of the controlled vocabulary of subject terms used by *British education index* (CB50) since 1986 and by the British section of *International ERIC* (CB57). Contains more than 8,200 terms.

ERIC identifier authority list. 1992– . Phoenix : Oryx, c1992– . Irregular.   **CB82**

A one-volume compilation of: *ERIC identifier list : alphabetical display* (1980– . Rockville, Md. : ERIC Processing and Reference Facility) and *ERIC identifier list : category display* (1991–).

Identifiers are semi-controlled retrieval terms, usually specific entities or new concepts not yet chosen as ERIC descriptors; this list indicates the preferred form. In two sections: an alphabetical display of the terms indicating the number of their postings in the ERIC database; and an Identifier category display, placing the 45,000 identifiers in 20 categories.   Z695.1.E3E738

Thesaurus of ERIC descriptors / comp. by the Educational Research Information Center, Bureau of Research. 1st ed. (Dec. 1967)– . Phoenix : Oryx, 1968– . Irregular.   **CB83**

Lists standard subject headings used by the ERIC system, including *Resources in education* (CB61), *Current index to journals in education* (CB54), CD-ROMS, and databases. The main section is an alphabetical display of descriptors with entries that list related terms and, where necessary, scope notes. Includes a rotated display of descriptors, an alphabetical index to all significant words that form descriptors; and a hierarchical term display showing the broader-narrower relationships of all main terms.   Z695.1.E3T49

Quotations

Dale, Edgar. The educator's quotebook. Bloomington, Ind. : Phi Delta Kappa Educational Foundation, c1984. 107 p.
   CB84

Quotations are arranged under 51 alphabetical topics (e.g., Teaching, Potential, Democracy) two to 50 quotations per topic. No index or thesaurus, but a table of contents lists the 51 topics.   PN6081.D23

A teacher's treasury of quotations / comp. by Bernard E. Farber. Jefferson, N.C. : McFarland, c1985. 370 p.   **CB85**

Arranged alphabetically by topic, the quotations represent many countries, cultures, and periods and portray differing points of view. Author and subject indexes.   PN6081.T4

Directories

Long, Kim. Directory of educational contests for students K–12 / Kim Long. Santa Barbara, Calif. : ABC-Clio, c1991. 257 p.   **CB86**

Describes nearly 200 national and international competitions designed to foster skill development and intellectual growth. Excludes athletic contests, local and regional competitions, and awards not based on merit. Entries provide: purpose of the competition; how it is run; entry process and requirements; eligibility; deadlines; and awards, prizes, and scholarships. Three indexes: organizations and sponsors, subjects, grade and age category.

§ Contests organized "just for fun" (i.e., for which no awards are given) are described in *Contests for students* (Detroit : Gale, 1991).
   LB3068.L66

By country or region

International

Directory of educational documentation and information services = Répertoire des services de documentation et d'information pédagogiques. 1975– . Paris : UNESCO, 1975– .   **CB87**

Prepared by the International Bureau of Education, Geneva.

Has separate sections for national, regional (e.g., Arab countries), and international agencies. Entries are arranged alphabetically within sections and list address, type of activities, population served, services given, collection size, publications, studies conducted, etc. Separate section gives addresses of member institutions of the International Bureau of Education. New with the 5th ed. (1988) is a section listing databases by country, with entries outlining the scope, time span, size, etc., of each. Available in English, French, or Spanish versions.
   LB1028.D484

Directory of educational research institutions = Répertoire des institutions de recherche en éducation / prepared by the International Bureau of Education. 2nd ed. Paris : UNESCO, 1986. 428 p.   **CB88**

1st ed., 1980.

Designed to facilitate direct contact with these organizations for researchers, administrators, and teacher trainers wanting to obtain documents which are not commercially available or are not yet published. Arranged in sections of national, regional (e.g., Latin America), and international institutions. Entries may be in English, French, or Spanish, and introductory material, directions for use, and indexes are in all three languages. Entries for institutions include address, year of creation, parent organization, staff size, type and functional objectives of research, monographic and periodical publications, study names, and surveys in preparation. A keyword index gives only entry numbers.
   LB1028.D54

Foreign study

Advisory list of international educational travel and exchange programs. 1985/86– . Reston, Va. : Council on Standards for International Educational Travel, 1985– . Annual.
   CB89

Covers more than 60 high school travel and exchange programs, giving addresses and information on countries served, sponsoring organization's philosophy and goals, program descriptions, age ranges, number of participants, application procedures, and selection criteria for participants and host families.

Blum, Laurie. Free money for foreign study : a guide to more than 1,000 grants and scholarships for study abroad. N.Y. : Facts on File, c1991. 262 p.   **CB90**

For annotation, *see* CB373.   LB2337.2.B575

ISS directory of overseas schools. [1st ed.] (1981/82)– . Princeton, N.J. : International Schools Services, 1981– . Annual.   **CB91**

Includes only those private schools using English as the major language of instruction or adhering to an American curriculum, either alone or combined with a national or British curriculum. Entries for more than 400 schools in some 130 nations are arranged alphabetically by country, then by city or town. For each school, provides information on costs, faculty, special programs and curricula, student body composition, grade levels, boarding and other academic facilities, languages offered, and names, addresses, and phone numbers.   L900.I83

Schools abroad of interest to Americans. Boston : Sargent, [1959?]– . Irregular.   **CB92**

7th ed. (1988) describes more than 800 elementary and secondary schools in 130 countries. Short entries are arranged geographically and include information on enrollment, faculty, accreditation, facilities, tuition, curriculum, language of instruction, and age and grade levels, plus a paragraph describing the school's goals, administrative structure, special programs, extracurricular activities, etc. Separate sections include a group of longer, illustrated advertisements for some schools; descriptions of post-secondary schools offering degree programs or preparation for transfer to American institutions; entries for travel, study, or year-abroad programs; and summer sessions. Index of names of schools.   L900.S33

Work, study, travel abroad : the whole world handbook. N.Y. : St. Martin's, 1972– . Biennial.   **CB93**

Editions prior to 1984 had title: *Whole world handbook.*

Publ. for the Council on International Educational Exchange.

Provides introductory sections of general advice on some 1,200 work, study, and travel programs in 79 countries, followed by chapters on 11 regions of the world, including discussions of individual countries and brief descriptions of specific programs. Beginning with the 10th ed. (1990), also includes comments by travelers. An appendix lists addresses of organizations offering high school programs. General index.   LB2376.W48

United States

Christo, Doris H. National directory of education libraries and collections. Westport, Conn. : Meckler, c1990. 269 p.
CB94

An alphabetical listing by state and city. Entries include information on size and scope of holdings, special collections, personnel, and budget. A personal name list indicates title and institutional affiliation of staff members. Index includes library names, parent institutions, subject specializations, and names of special collections.
Z675.P3C48

•**Educational directory online** : (EDOL) [database]. Shelton, Conn. : Market Data Retrieval, Inc., [c1989]– .   **CB95**

Available online; current file, updated semiannually.

Title varies; earlier versions called *Dun's electronic directory of education; Electronic directory of education; Educational database.*

Provides information concerning U.S. institutions at all levels of education. Includes 3,500 colleges and universities, 110,000 schools, school districts and dioceses in all states, and 15,000 public libraries, including branches.

General

Curriculum Information Center. CIC's school directory. [State edition]. [1978/79–1993/94]. Westport, Conn. : Curriculum Information Center. Annual.   **CB96**

Formerly the "Marketing edition" of *School universe data book* (Denver : Curriculum Information Center. Annual).

Published in 51 v., each covering one of the states or the District of Columbia; each may be purchased individually.

Lists public and parochial school districts giving chief administrative officers and key personnel, and listing individual schools with their addresses and phone numbers, grade ranges, and enrollment.

Continued by: *MDR's school directory* [State] (Shelton, Conn. : Market Data Retrieval, 1995–).

MDR's sales manager's guide to the U.S. school market (1994/95. Shelton, Conn. : Market Data Retrieval, 1995– . Annual) provides a national summary of selected information from the directories.
L901.S473u

Directory of public elementary and secondary education agencies. Fall 1986– . Wash. : U.S. Office of Educational Research and Improvement, Center for Education Statistics, [and] Information Services, [1987]– . Annual.   **CB97**

Superintendent of Documents classification: ED 1.111/2: ; for ERIC version: ED1.310/2: .

Continues *Education directory : public school systems*, 1969/70–1985. Available in microfiche.

Issuing agency varies. Issued by National Center for Education Statistics since 1988.

Lists "all reported public elementary/secondary agencies" (*Introd.*) in the 50 states, District of Columbia, and outlying areas, including school districts, state and federally operated agencies, supervisory administrative centers, and regular education service agencies. One-line entries contain addresses and phone numbers, metropolitan status codes; grade spans; and number of schools, teachers, and graduates.
L901.E35

Directory of state education agencies. 1982/1983– . [Wash.] : Council [of] Chief State School Officers, [1983]– . Annual.   **CB98**

Recent volumes have title: *Directory, state education agencies.*

Provides information for states and possessions of the U.S., including: addresses of state education agencies; addresses and telephone numbers of selected education associations and organizations; and names, addresses, and telephone numbers of selected personnel of the U.S. Dept. of Education and of the Council of Chief State School Officers.

ERIC directory of education-related information centers / ed. by Andrew M. Silver, Kristine Kaplan, Paula Seidman. Wash. : Educational Resources Information Center (ERIC), [1992]. 274 p.   **CB99**

On cover: ACCESS ERIC.

1st ed., 1990.

Lists 400 federally- and privately-funded organizations providing services and products such as reference and referral, online searches, publications, information dissemination, technical assistance, outreach, and audiovisual materials. Includes such groups as Access Clearinghouse of the National Committee for Citizens in Education, Buros Institute of Mental Measurement, and Federal Student Aid Information Center. Entries include contact information and brief descriptions of the organizations, their audiences, services, publications, and access procedures. Organization name, geographic, and subject indexes.
L901.E74

•**FEDIX** : Federal information exchange [database]. Wash. : Federal Information Exchange, Inc.   **CB100**

Available online through Internet.

A full-text bulletin board that lists federal government research related to education. Includes research opportunities, scholarships, fellowships, and grants; minority opportunities; and government agency activities.

Guide to American educational directories. 1st ed. (1963)– . Rye, N.Y. : Todd Publications, 1963– . Irregular.
CB101

6th ed., 1990.

Publisher varies.

Limited neither to directories in the traditional sense nor to the discipline of education. Includes a variety of reference sources— yearbooks, biographical dictionaries and registers, bibliographies, and fact books, as well as standard general and special directories, membership lists, etc. Some can be considered educational (e.g., *Who's who of American women* [AH88] or *Moody's bank and finance manual* [CH309 *note*]) only if the term is broadly interpreted. Arranged by subject (e.g., Accounting, Colleges and universities) with annotations. Alphabetical list of publications.   Z5813.G8

Guide to international education in the United States. 2nd ed. (1991)– . Detroit : Gale, c1991– . Biennial.   **CB102**

1st ed., 1984 had title: *Global guide to international education.*

For educators, students (elementary through postgraduate), researchers, and librarians, describes programs and resources concerned with other countries, cultures, and languages. Three sections: Topics in international, intercultural, and global education (e.g., educational exchange, language instruction, peace and conflict resolution studies, international affairs); Area studies by region; Area studies by country. Lists programs, organizations, research centers, grants and awards, reference sources, periodicals, and publishers. General index.

The Macmillan guide to correspondence study / comp. and ed. by Modoc Press, Inc. 4th ed. N.Y. : Macmillan ; Toronto : Collier Macmillan Canada, 1990. 676 p.   **CB103**

1st ed., 1983; 3rd ed., 1988.

Describes courses offered by accredited schools; gives information on admission requirements and procedures and tuition and fees. In three parts: (1) Colleges offering courses for which credit earned can be transferred to a formal degree program, noncredit professional courses, or courses for career enrichment; (2) privately owned and operated home study schools offering vocational, high school, college, or professional programs; (3) schools operated by private foundations, nonprofit organizations, federal agencies, and the military. Subject index.   L901.M26

Patterson's American education. v. [1] (1904)– . Mount Prospect, Ill. : Educ. Directories, 1904– . Annual.   **CB104**

Coverage and arrangement vary. Title varies.

Beginning with 1993 volume, publ. in two parts: Secondary schools and Patterson's schools classified. The former corresponds to earlier editions of *Patterson's American education*, the latter to *Patterson's schools classified* (CB282), which this title absorbs.

The first part lists public, private, and Catholic junior high school and high school districts, and combined elementary and secondary districts. Arranged by state, beginning with addresses of officials of state departments of education; then by community; then by district, with names of top officials; then by individual schools, giving names, addresses, and phone numbers of principals. Has separate listings of schools in U.S. territories; Catholic, Seventh-day Adventist, and Lutheran school superintendents; and educational associations and societies. The second part consists of a directory of schools classified by specialty.   L901.P3

Patterson's elementary education. v. 1 (1989)– . Mount Prospect, Ill. : Educational Directories Inc., c1989– . Annual.
            CB105

Attempts to list all public elementary schools in the U.S., with the exception of kindergarten-only and special needs schools. Includes primary and middle schools and schools enrolling grades 1–12. Arranged by state, city, then district, listing chief state and district officers and their addresses and phone numbers; individual schools, their addresses, principals, and phones; and private and church-affiliated schools with 100 or more students.

§ Complements *Patterson's American education* (CB104), which lists secondary and postsecondary institutions.   L901.P33

State education documents : a state-by-state directory for their acquisition and use / Education-related Government Publications Subcommittee, Curriculum Materials Committee, and Problems of Access and Control of Educational· Materials Committee, Education and Behavioral Sciences Section, Association of College and Research Libraries, American Library Association. Chicago : Association of College and Research Libraries, c1989. 45 p.   **CB106**

Publications subcommittee chaired by Eileen E. Schroeder.

Designed to help librarians acquire these documents, but also useful to researchers, practitioners, and general readers. Arranged alphabetically by state; entries are typically less than a page in length. For each state, tells where to write for information, types of materials published (e.g., directories), availability, depository programs, checklists of state documents, indexing, availability in microform, and whether the state collects or distributes municipal documents.   Z688.G6S73

Private schools

Handbook of private schools. Ed. 1– . Boston : Sargent, 1915– . Annual.   **CB107**

Title varies. Popularly known as "Porter Sargent."

Subtitle: An annual descriptive survey of independent education.

Describes more than 1,700 boarding and day schools, providing information on age and grade ranges, whether co-educational or for boys or girls, enrollment, faculty size and background, academic orientation and curriculum, and where graduates attend college. "Features classified" section lists institutions offering military programs, elementary boarding divisions, programs for students with learning differences, international and bilingual schools, and schools with more than 500 or fewer than 100 students. Index of institutions.   L901.H3

The Harvard independent insider's guide to prep schools / ed. by Christopher J. Georges and James A. Messina, with members of the staff of the Harvard independent. N.Y. : New American Library, c1987. 453 p.   **CB108**

Describes not so much the best schools as those with "interesting" programs where current Harvard undergraduates attended, some of whom either wrote school descriptions or provided information. The main body consists of two-page entries on 200 schools, most private, but a few public. Provides information on enrollment, selectivity, students' SAT scores, colleges attended by graduates, academic programs, social atmosphere, and dress code. Arrangement is alphabetical by state. Additional schools are briefly described in chapters on "Big preps," "New York preps," etc. There are also ranked listings of largest schools, most expensive and inexpensive, highest and lowest student SAT scores, etc. Not indexed.   L901.H364

Peterson's guide to private secondary schools. 14th ed. (1993–94)– . Princeton, N.J. : Peterson's Guides, c1993– . Annual.   **CB109**

Continues *Peterson's annual guide to independent secondary schools*, 1980–92.

Describes more than 1,600 American and foreign boarding and day schools including schools that serve children with special needs. Outlines each institution's setting; enrollment by sex, race, grade, and geographic origin; faculty size and educational background; facilities; subjects offered; special programs; graduation requirements; tuition; admissions procedures; and where the graduates go to college. 28 specialized indexes list military schools, schools with programs for the gifted, institutions with tuition installment plans, etc.   L900.P48

Private independent schools. Ed. 1– . Wallingford, Conn. : Bunting and Lyon, 1943– . Annual.   **CB110**

Title varies: 1943, *Independent schools, a directory*.

Subtitle varies.

Describes some 1,000 American and 100 foreign boarding and day schools, from kindergarten through high school, plus one-year post-high school programs. Roughly a quarter of the entries are descriptive; the remainder give the school's size, age range, application procedures, administrative control, cost, and special programs, plus a brief statement of its philosophy. A classification grid, arranged by state, identifies institutions with specific characteristics, such as military programs, church affiliation, and restriction to one sex. Separate section on summer programs emphasizing academics, recreation, or travel.

Handbooks

Chismore, W. Dale. A classification of educational subject matter / by W. Dale Chismore and Quentin M. Hill. Wash. : National Center for Education Statistics : For sale by U.S. Govt. Print. Off., 1978. 223 p.   **CB111**

Offers a classification intended to provide educational agencies, institutions, and administrators with a single, standardized scheme to facilitate the recording, reporting, and exchange of data about subject matter. Employs a hierarchical array employing code numbers. General index.

Handbook of educational ideas and practices / gen. ed., Noel Entwistle. London ; N.Y. : Routledge, 1990. 1140 p. : ill.
           CB112

A summary of recent thinking, research findings, and innovative practices for practitioners. Not an encyclopedia; "rather, it samples a restricted number of topics and deals with them in more depth."—*Pref.* In four topical sections (Nature and function of education, Management and content of education, Learning environment, and Individual development) containing 101 chapters, most written by British experts with British orientations. Name and subject indexes.   LB17.H267

The handbook of qualitative research in education / ed. by Margaret D. LeCompte, Wendy L. Millroy, Judith Preissle. San Diego : Academic Pr., c1992. 881 p. : ill.   **CB113**

Contributions from leading researchers in education and related disciplines in 18 chapters, containing sections on the field's current boundaries and future directions, issues relating to execution, and research applications. Extensive bibliography. Index.   H62.H2456

Handbook of reading research / ed., P. David Pearson; section editors, Rebecca Barr ... [et al.]. N.Y. : Longman, c1984–c1991. 2 v. : ill.   **CB114**

A summary of key research, each volume offering chapters by experts. Vol. 1 provides comprehensive coverage of both reading processes and instructional practices, and practices and issues in reading research. Vol. 2, although published seven years later, is "not a second edition of the same book, but another volume in a continuing effort" (*Pref.*), emphasizing societal variables. Extensive bibliographies. Author and subject indexes.   LB1050.H278

Handbook of research on curriculum : a project of the American Educational Research Association / Philip W. Jackson, ed. N.Y. : Macmillan Pub. Co. : Maxwell Macmillan International, c1992. 1088 p.   **CB115**

A review of the field's literature, in which the "needs of graduate students in education were … uppermost."—*Pref.* 34 chapters written by leading researchers and scholars, in four sections: Conceptual and methodological perspecitves, How the curriculum is shaped, The curriculum as a shaping force, and Topics and issues within curriculum categories. Includes suggestions for future areas of research. Extensive bibliographies; name and subject indexes.   LB1570.H264

Handbook of research on social studies teaching and learning / James P. Shaver, ed. N.Y. : Macmillan ; Toronto : Collier Macmillan ; N.Y. : Macmillan International, c1991. 661 p.   **CB116**

The "first handbook on social studies education [attempting] to provide a comprehensive view and analysis of research in the field."—*Pref.* Designed primarily for researchers, curriculum developers, and school administrators, and only secondarily for teachers. In eight sections (e.g., Issues of epistemology and methodology, The student in social studies education, Components of instruction), each containing several chapters written by experts. Name and subject indexes.

§ Similar works from the same publishers:

Handbook of research on mathematics teaching and learning (Douglas A. Grouws, ed. 1992. 771 p.) Consists of 29 chapters arranged in five parts: Overview, Mathematics teaching, Learning from instruction, Critical issues, and Perspectives. Published in conjunction with the National Council of Teachers of Mathematics.

Handbook of research on music teaching and learning (Richard Colwell, ed. 1992. 832 p.) A project of the Music Educators National Conference. Its 55 chapters are in eight sections, covering such broad areas as teaching and learning strategies, teaching specific musical skills and knowledge in different instructional settings, and school curricula.   LB1584.H275

Handbook of research on teaching / ed. by Merlin C. Wittrock. 3rd ed. N.Y. : Macmillan ; London : Collier Macmillan, 1986. 1037 p.   **CB117**

A project of the American Educational Research Association.

2nd ed., 1973, had title: *Second handbook of research on teaching.*

A summary and critical analysis of research; consists of 35 lengthy chapters, written by experts, treating all major aspects of teaching. Five sections: Theory and methods of research in teaching; Research on teaching and teachers (with chapters on such topics as Teachers' thought processes, and Media in teaching); Social and institutional context of teaching; Adapting teaching to differences among learners; and Research on the teaching of subjects and grade levels (with individual chapters on the teaching of reading, of social studies, etc.). Extensive bibliographies. Subject and name indexes.   LB1028.H315

Handbook of research on teaching the English language arts / ed. by James Flood … [et al.]. N.Y. : Macmillan : Maxwell Macmillan, c1991. 888 p. : ill.   **CB118**

Sponsored by the International Reading Association and the National Council of Teachers of English.

A review of research for which prominent scholars and professional leaders were asked "to assess the significance of research, evaluate new developments, find relationships to scholarship in related fields, examine current conflicts, controversies, and issues, and identify tomorrow's priorities."—*Pref.* Consists of 39 chapters in five groups: Theoretical bases, Methods of research on English language arts teaching, Research on language learners, Environments, and Research on teaching specific aspects (e.g., reading, writing). Extensive bibliographies; author and subject indexes.   LB1576.H234

International handbook of early childhood education / ed. by Gary A. Woodill, Judith Bernhard, Lawrence Prochner. N.Y. : Garland, 1992. 562 p. (Garland reference library of social science, vol. 598).   **CB119**

Describes history and current programs of early childhood education in 45 countries. Articles on individual nations written by authors with both knowledge of and experience with early childhood education in their countries. Alphabetically arranged by nation. Index.   LB1139.23.I68

International handbook of reading education / ed. by John Hladczuk and William Eller. Westport, Conn. : Greenwood, 1992. 510 p. : ill.   **CB120**

Investigates the state of the teaching of reading in a broad cross-section of the world, as represented by 26 widely-varying nations. A chapter summarizes each country's programs, including sections on each of 10 factors: the country's language(s), reading policy, goals, illiteracy, questions pertaining to rate and diagnosis of reading disabilities, reading readiness programs, teacher qualification procedure, sources and availability of materials, financing of reading education, and research thrusts. Substantial bibliography.   LB1050.2.I58

Review of research in education. 1 (1973)– . Itasca, Ill. : F. E. Peacock Publishers, 1973– .   **CB121**

Published for the American Educational Research Association.

Articles review research in specific areas of education, with no attempt to cover the entire discipline. Areas reviewed vary with each annual issue; some treat broad fields such as music education, while others cover more focused topics such as teacher participation in school decision-making. Produced by leading scholars in the field. Lacks a cumulative index.   LB1028.R43

Standard education almanac. 1st ed. (1968)–17th ed. (1984/85). Chicago : Marquis Academic Media, Marquis Who's Who, 1968–85.   **CB122**

Subtitle: A comprehensive, up-to-date guide to educational facts and statistics.

Publisher varies.

Brings together discussions of current issues, statistics, specially selected articles and reports, directories, and lists of resources relating to all levels and aspects of education in the U.S. and Canada. General index.

Van Scotter, Richard D. Public schooling in America : a reference handbook. Santa Barbara, Calif. : ABC-CLIO, c1991. 240 p. : ill.   **CB123**

Useful as a source of information on current issues, especially those pertaining to educational reform; includes such topics as school choice, desegregation, equality vs. excellence. Begins with a discussion of the issues, followed by a chronology. Also contains biographical sketches of 19 educational leaders; synopses of 13 key reports such as "A nation at risk;" a chapter of statistics; a directory of national associations, organizations, and agencies; and bibliographies of reference materials and journals. General index.   LA217.2.V36

World survey of education. Paris : UNESCO, 1955–71. 5 v.   **CB124**

Supersedes *World handbook of educational organization and statistics* (1951).

Contents: v. 1, Handbook of educational organization and statistics (1955); v. 2, Primary education (1958); v. 3, Secondary education (1961); v. 4, Higher education (1966); v. 5, Educational policy, legislation and administration (1971).

Covers some 200 countries, including states not members of Unesco. Each volume arranged by country. Includes surveys, statistics, bibliographies, etc. Vol. 1 has a glossary of terms in various languages. Useful for historical research.   L900.W56

National systems of education

International handbook of education systems / ed. by J. Cameron ... [et al.]. Chichester, [Eng.] ; N.Y. : Wiley, 1983–84. 3 v. : ill.   **CB125**

Contents: v. 1, Europe and Canada, ed. by Brian Holmes; v. 2, Sub-Saharan Africa, ed. by John Cameron; North Africa and the Middle East, ed. by Paul Hurst; v. 3, Asia, Australasia and Latin America, ed. by Robert Cowen and Martin McLean.

Offers profiles of educational systems worldwide, except the U.S., U.S.S.R., and the U.K. Entries include information on geography, population, society and culture, history and politics, the economy, the education system, educational administration, educational finance, and development and planning of the education system.   LB15.I58

International handbook of women's education / ed. by Gail P. Kelly. N.Y. : Greenwood, 1989. 657 p. : ill.   **CB126**

Summarizes the history, current status, and outcomes of women's education and its degree of equality to education for men. Focuses on the situations in 23 countries representing a range of social, political, and economic systems, industrial development, and wealth. In sections for major regions (e.g., Middle East), with individual chapters on each country by experts and a summary chapter by the editor. Contains statistical tables, extensive bibliography, and general index.

World education encyclopedia / ed. by George Thomas Kurian. N.Y. : Facts on File, c1988. 3 v. (1720 p.) : ill.   **CB127**

Describes the national education systems of 181 countries. Unusual organization groups nations into "major," "middle," or "minor" sections, based on how much information about their system was obtainable. Articles on individual countries range in length from one paragraph (Andorra) to 42 pages (the U.S.) At the ends of most articles are bibliographies. Appendixes contain 1984 Unesco statistics on national literacy rates, numbers of schools, expenditures per capita, etc. General index.   LB15.W87

Yearbooks

International yearbook of education. [10th] (1948)– . Paris : UNESCO ; Geneva : International Bureau of Education, 1948– . Annual.   **CB128**

Assumes the numbering of the *Annuaire international de l'éducation et de l'enseignement*, 1933–47 (suspended publication, 1940–45). Publication suspended 1970–79.

Each year's volume is a factual, conceptual, theoretical, and practical overview of the state of a particular facet of education throughout the world (literacy, secondary education, etc.). The content originates in the sessions of the International Conference on Education. Includes statistical tables.   L101.A2A63

The world year book of education. 1965– . London ; Philadelphia : Kogan Page, c1965– . Annual.   **CB129**

Title varies slightly. Publisher varies.

Continues *The year book of education*. Publication suspended 1940–45 and 1975–79.

Contains many articles on education in specific countries or regions. Since 1953, each volume follows a central theme (e.g., the status and position of teachers), with the articles focusing on that topic as it pertains to the specific countries.   L101.G8Y4

Biography

Biographical dictionary of American educators / ed. by John F. Ohles. Westport, Conn. : Greenwood, [1978]. 3 v. (1666 p.).   **CB130**

Aims "to provide a ready source of biographical information about those people who have shaped American education from colonial times to the American bicentennial of 1976. Because education in the United States developed on the state level, leaders in education in the states have been included, as well as national figures and those who have been leaders in subject matter fields. Basic criteria for selection were persons who had been engaged in education, were eminent, and had reached the age of sixty, had retired, or had died by January 1, 1975."—*Pref.* Signed articles, averaging about a page in length, are mainly by educators and concentrate on the biographee's education, employment, contributions to the field of education, and participation in professional associations and activities. Bibliographic sources are cited. General index in v. 3. Appendixes include lists of biographees by place of birth, by state of major service, by field of work, and by year of birth.   LA2311.B54

Leaders in education. 5th ed. N.Y. ; London : Jaques Cattell Pr. ; Bowker, 1974. 1309 p.   **CB131**

1st ed., 1932.

Basic biographical information on 17,000 educators, nearly all Americans or Canadians, including "officers and deans of accredited institutions of higher learning, professors of education, directors and staff of educational research institutes, state and provincial commissioners of education and certain members of their staffs, leading figures in the public and private school fields, officers of foundations concerned with education, officials of the Office of Education and major educational associations, and authors of important pedagogical books."—*Pref.* Emphasizes research, publications and administrative positions. Includes specialty and geographic indexes. Although not up to date, may be the only biographical source for many educators.
LA2311.L4

Nauman, Ann Keith. A biographical handbook of education : five hundred contributors to the field. N.Y. : Irvington Publishers, c1985. 237 p.   **CB132**

Alphabetically arranged entries include dates of birth and death, nationality, profession, a short paragraph summarizing contributions and significance, and bibliography. Intended as "a jumping off point or ready reference" (*Introd.*) for those beginning research. Worldwide in scope.   LA2301.N38

Who's who in American education : an illustrated biographical dictionary of eminent living educators of the United States and Canada. Ed. 1–23. Nashville, Tenn. : Who's Who in American Education, 1928–68. Biennial.   **CB133**

Contains sketches of faculty and administrators in higher education, primary and secondary school administrators, and some persons peripherally connected with education, such as public librarians. Does not include college presidents, and many distinguished faculty are also absent, but may be the only source of biographical information on many of those included. Contains photographs of most biographees.
LA2311.W45

Who's who in American education. 1988/89– . New Providence, N.J. : Marquis Who's Who, c1988– . Irregular.   **CB134**

Publisher varies; previously publ. by the National Reference Institute.

Biographical data for some 27,000 public and private school principals; local, state, and federal agency heads; researchers; school district administrators; heads of educational associations and other national organizations and programs; winners of teaching awards; college professors and administrative officers, and other leaders. Alphabetically arranged entries include addresses, education, current and former positions, professional activities, honors, research and publications, etc. Indexed.

§ Not to be confused with *Who's who in American education*, publ. 1928–68 (CB133).   LA2311.W47

Statistics

120 years of American education : a statistical portrait / ed., Thomas D. Snyder. Wash. : U.S. National Center for Education Statistics, [1993]. 107 p. : ill. **CB135**

Superintendent of Documents classification: ED 1.302: ED 8/12.

A compilation of longitudinal data drawn from a number of sources. In three chapters: Education characteristics of the population, Elementary education, Higher education. Provides information on demographics, enrollment, attendance, educational attainment, expenditures, sources of revenue, etc. Narrative accounts of trends. Tables and graphs. LA209.A16

Benson, Peter L. Private schools in the United States : a statistical profile, with comparisons to public schools / Peter Benson, Marilyn Miles McMillen. Wash. : U.S. National Center for Education Statistics ; For sale by the U.S. Govt. Print. Off., [1991]. 162 p. : ill. **CB136**

Superintendent of Documents classification: ED1.102:P 93/2.

Based largely on data from the 1980s, with different variables measured in different years. In five chapters: Schools, Students, Teachers, School resources and student outcomes, and Parental choice. Each chapter begins with a discussion of findings followed by the tables on which the discussion is based. Lists sources of data. LC49.B46

Bugher, Wilmer. The Phi Delta Kappa Gallup polls of attitudes toward education, 1969–1988 : a topical summary. Bloomington, Ind. : Phi Delta Kappa, c1990. 84 p. **CB137**

Rev. ed. of: *Gallup polls of attitudes toward education, 1969–1984* (1984). An earlier version was publ. 1978 as *A decade of Gallup polls of attitudes toward education, 1969–1978*, ed. by Stanley M. Elam.

Presents results of the annual Gallup polls of attitudes toward U.S. public schools (regularly published in the journal *Phi Delta Kappan*) and includes responses to several other Gallup polls. Responses to more than 400 questions, noting years in which they were asked, are arranged in 38 categories such as Discipline, Perceived importance of education/schools, and Testing and promotion. For questions asked in more than one poll, results are displayed side by side, permitting comparisions. No index; a table of contents lists the categories. LA217.B84

The condition of education. 1975– . Wash. : U.S. National Center for Education Statistics : U.S. Govt. Print. Off., 1975– . Annual. **CB138**

Superintendent of Documents classifications numbers: HE 19.314; ED 1.310/2; ED 1.109.

Issuing agency varies. 1988–90, issued in two volumes, *Elementary and secondary education* and *Postsecondary education*, with a companion work, *Education indicators*.

A well-known source providing statistics on "indicators"—key data that measure the health of education, monitor important developments, and show trends in major aspects of education. In six areas: (1) access, participation, and progress; (2) achievement, attainment, and curriculum; (3) economic and other outcomes of education; (4) size, growth, and output of educational institutions; (5) climate, classrooms, and diversity in educational institutions; (6) human and financial resources of educational institutions. Covers all levels, elementary through postsecondary. Reports on 60 indicators, such as college costs and SAT scores. Includes tables, graphs, and textual commentary. Appendixes include more than 250 pages of supplementary tables and notes, bibliography of the sources of data, glossary, and general index. L112.N377a

Digest of education statistics. 1975– . Wash. : U.S. National Center for Education Statistics : For sale by the U.S. Govt. Print. Off., 1976– . Annual. **CB139**

Superintendent of Documents classification (ERIC version): ED 1.310/2: .

ERIC version issued to depository libraries in microfiche.

Issuing agency varies. Volumes for 1977–8, 1983–4 and 1985–6 issued together.

Supersedes *Digest of educational statistics*, 1962–74.

Probably the most frequently used source for statistics of American education; contains a selection of nationwide data from many public and private sources, including many important surveys by the National Center for Education Statistics. In seven chapters: All levels of education; Elementary and secondary education; Postsecondary education; Federal programs for education and related activities; Outcomes of education, International comparisons of education; and Learning resources and technology. Extensive tables of data. Subject index.

•Available on CD-ROM as part of *National economic, social and environmental data bank* (*NESE-DB*), from the U.S. Office of Business Analysis, 1992– . L11.D48

Educational Testing Service. Trends in academic progress : achievement of U.S. students in science, 1969–70 to 1990, mathematics, 1973 to 1990, reading, 1971 to 1990, writing, 1984 to 1990 / by Ina V.S. Mullis ... [et al.] ; prep. by Educational Testing Service under contract with the National Center for Education Statistics. Wash. : The Center : For sale by the U.S. Govt. Print. Off., [1991]. 373 p. : ill. (National Assessment of Educational Progress (Project). Report, no. 21–T–01). **CB140**

Superintendent of Documents classification: ED 1.102:T 72/3.

Reports trends in the findings of the National Assessment of Educational Progress (NAEP), which monitors the scholastic achievement of the nation's 9- , 13- , and 17-year-olds. Provides data for the demographic subpopulations (e.g., Hispanics, extreme rural) as well as for the whole country. In four parts, one for each of the school subjects treated. An introductory chapter describes overall trends. Contains many tables and graphs and extensive discussion of the findings. Appendixes presenting detailed tables for each NAEP item occupy nearly half the volume. LA209.2.E35

Kindergarten programs and practices in public schools. Arlington, Va. : Educational Research Service, c1986. 123 p. : ill. **CB141**

Presents the results of a 1985 nationwide survey of a random sample of public school kindergarten teachers and principals, providing statistics on such topics as enrollment; number and characteristics of teachers; programs and practices; teachers and principals' opinions on goals, priorities, and other aspects of programs; etc. Findings are topically arranged in six categories: Demographics, The kindergarten pupil, Schedule of day, The kindergarten program, Kindergarten schedule of personnel, and Administrative concerns. No index, but the table of contents locates results for each question. LB1205.K56

Morgan, Frank. State profiles of public elementary and secondary education, 1987–88. Wash. : U.S. Office of Educational Research and Improvement : For sale by the U.S. Govt. Print. Off., [1990]. 477 p. : ill. **CB142**

Superintendent of Documents classification: ED 1.328:E1 2.

National Center for Education Statistics survey report.

Designed to permit comparisons between states. The main section consists of six pages for each state, providing for each approximately 40 basic statistics, in tabular and graphic form that comprise a "thumbnail sketch of the resources, needs, organization, and special characteristics of education within a state."—*Introd.* Presents fiscal data, institutional statistics (e.g., number of schools by grade span), and student and staff characteristics (e.g., number of Hispanic students, number of administrative workers). Also has a section ranking states on key considerations such as number of teachers. Includes statistics for outlying territories (e.g., Guam, Puerto Rico). LA210.M62

National School Boards Association. Survey of public education in the nation's urban school districts. [Wash. : National School Boards Association], 1979– . **CB143**

Spine title: *Triennial report—Council of Urban Boards of Education*.

Designed for school leaders, this work presents data on the finances, staffing, programs, etc., of 52 school districts, and on the educational, political, and social conditions and issues that affect them. Each of the nine sections (which have such titles as School district finances, The school board, and Federal issues) opens with a narrative description of current facts, statistics, and trends, followed by information in tabular form on individual school districts. A rich source of data not easily found elsewhere (e.g., districts using television programming technology, desegregation strategies, districts covered by bargaining laws, methods of debt financing). Detailed table of contents, but no index.   LB2817.N33a

Projections of educational statistics to [...]. 1975–76– . Wash. : U.S. Office of Education : For sale by the U.S. Govt. Print. Off., 1966– . Annual.   **CB144**
> Superintendent of Documents classification: HE 19.320: .
> ERIC version distributed to depository libraries in microfiche.
> Title varies.
> Provides ten-year projections of statistics for elementary and secondary schools and institutions of higher education; includes enrollment, graduates, teachers, and expenditures. Most projections give three estimates: low, middle or "best" projection, and high. For many tables, statistics are retrospective to 1978.   LA210.A28

Statistical yearbook = Annuaire statistique / Unesco. 1963– . [Paris : UNESCO], 1964– . Annual.   **CB145**
> "Reference tables, education, science and technology, and culture and communication."
> Supersedes United Nations Educational, Scientific and Cultural Organization's *Basic facts and figures.*
> Presents not only educational statistics, but data on other concerns as well. For some 200 countries and territories, contains statistics "gathered mainly from official reports and publications supplemented by information available to the Secretariat from other national and international sources."—*Introd.* In 11 chapters. The first, Reference tables, deals largely with population; this is followed by three chapters on education, which stress enrollment, staff and public expenditures, and also include statistics by educational level. Other chapters cover science and technology; culture and communication (e.g., books published); printed matter (e.g., libraries, newspapers); film and cinema; broadcasting; international trade in printed matter; and cultural heritage (e.g., museums). In English; general introduction, table of contents, introductory text to chapters, and individual tables also in French and Spanish. Appendixes providing introductions to chapters in Russian and Arabic.

United States. Office of Education. Biennial survey of education. 1916/18–1956/58. Wash. : U.S. Govt. Print. Off., 1921–63.   **CB146**
> Ceased publication; superseded by *Statistics of education in the U.S.* (1958/59) and a variety of statistical publications covering special subject fields.
> Contains basic data and statistics on education in the U.S. from kindergarten through graduate school.   L111.A6

United States. Office of Educational Research and Improvement. OERI directory of computer tapes. [Wash.] : The Office, [1987]– . Annual.   **CB147**
> Superintendent of Documents classification: ED 1.24/2: .
> Gives brief, nontechnical synopses of the major files of education survey data, describing content (e.g., average daily attendance), years covered, and subjects. All files are available for purchase on either tape or disk; price and ordering information is included.

Ratings

Harrison, Charles Hampton. Public schools USA : a comparative guide to school districts / by Charles Harrison. 2nd ed. Princeton, N.J. : Peterson's Guides, c1991. 483 p.   **CB148**
> Cover title: Peterson's public schools USA.

1st ed., 1988.
> Evaluates more than 400 school districts in 41 major metropolitan areas. Among the 27 factors considered are expense per pupil, SAT scores, experience level of teachers, student-teacher ratio, and age of school buildings. Ten statistics are combined into an Effective schools index, permitting educators, parents, and researchers to compare districts with state and national averages. Not comprehensive; only districts within 25 miles of their core cities having grades K-12 and 2,500 students are included. Arranged alphabetically by metropolitan area, then by school district. Statistical tables supplemented by brief comments by local district officials or local expert observers. Appendixes give state average daily attendance percentages, expenses per pupil, SAT and ACT scores, average teacher salaries, and addresses and phone numbers of individual schools.   LA217.2.H37

National Education Association. Research Division. Rankings of the states. 1973– . [Washington] : National Education Association, 1973– . Annual.   **CB149**
> Continues an annual of the same title, publ. 1959–72, which replaced the N.E.A.'s *Educational differences among the states* (1948, 1954).
> Provides tabular rankings, highest to lowest, of educational statistics by state in eight categories: Population, Enrollment and attendance, Faculty, General financial resources, Government revenue, School revenue, Governmental expenses, and School expenses. Some of the information was drawn from other National Education Association studies, U.S. government publications, and the "Survey of buying power" issues of *Sales and marketing management.*   LA212.N36a

TESTS AND MEASUREMENTS

Educational measurement / ed. by Robert L. Linn ; sponsored jointly by National Council on Measurement in Education and American Council on Education. 3rd ed. N.Y. : American Council on Education : Macmillan Pub. Co., c1989. 610 p. : ill.   **CB150**
> 1st ed., 1951; 2nd ed., 1971.
> A comprehensive evaluation of the current state of the field. Contains 17 chapters in three sections: Theory and general principles (including reliability, bias in test use, etc.); Construction, administration and scoring; Applications (e.g., administrative use of school testing, testing of linguistic minorities). An introductory chapter examines the effects of recent changes in technology, in demand for and expectations of testing, and the social and legal contexts of educational measurements. Extensive bibliography. Index.   LB3051.E266

The ETS Test Collection catalog / comp. by Test Collection, Educational Testing Service. 2nd ed. Phoenix : Oryx, 1993. v. 1. (In progress).   **CB151**
> For annotation, *see* CD68.   LB3051.E79

Fabiano, Emily. Index to tests used in educational dissertations. Phoenix : Oryx, 1989. 371 p.   **CB152**
> Indexes references to some 35,000 published and unpublished tests occurring in the 1938–80 volumes of *Dissertation abstracts international* and its predecessors. Index entries are drawn both from dissertation titles and from the abstracts. Access to the tests (sometimes difficult in the case of unpublished instruments) is facilitated by a section of the Preface that suggests ways of acquiring them. Indexes only *DAI*'s A section (Humanities and social sciences), hence dissertations in some related fields (e.g., psychology) are not covered. In two parts: (1) Test title index, which lists instruments alphabetically and refers to *DAI* volume and page; (2) Keyword/names index, which contains three kinds of terms (topic keywords, author names, and test title acronyms) and refers to entries in the test title index.   LB3051.F3

Index to ETS research series, 1948–1991 [microform]. 10th ed. Princeton, N.J. : ETS Archives, Educational Testing Service, 1992. 10 microfiches.   **CB153**

Provides citations for more than 4,000 ETS publications, with abstracts. Indexes by report number, author, title, and subject. Includes a guide, *Index to ETS research report series, 1948–1991*, by Gary D. Saretsky, that explains how to obtain copies of reports. LB3051.I484

EDUCATIONAL LAW AND LEGISLATION

Deskbook encyclopedia of American school law. 1980/81– . Rosemount, Minn. : Data Research, Inc., 1981– . Annual. **CB154**

Publisher varies: 1981–84, Informational Research Systems.

Designed to provide educators and lawyers with a compilation of recent state and federal appellate court decisions. Topically arranged, with chapters on subjects such as Freedom of speech; Accidents, injuries and deaths; and Employment discrimination; subdivided into narrower topics. Contains appendixes citing recent Supreme Court cases and recently published law review articles, and presenting portions of the Constitution most frequently cited in education cases. Subject index. KF4114.D46

Gatti, Daniel Jon. The educator's encyclopedia of school law / Daniel J. Gatti, Richard D. Gatti. Englewood Cliffs, N.J. : Prentice Hall, c1990. 1 v. **CB155**

Intended for both professionals and general readers. Contains 244 articles on topics such as free speech, accountability, and Equity Pay Act. Entries vary from short paragraphs to several pages long. Cross-references. General index and a "Categorical index" that lists broad subject areas and the terms defined within the subjects.

KF4114.5.G37

Lantzy, M. Louise. The Individuals with Disabilities Education Act : an annotated guide to its literature and resources, 1980–1991. Littleton, Colo. : F.B. Rothman & Co., 1992. 148 p. (loose-leaf). **CB156**

Permits tracing evolution of the act (a legal keystone of American special education) and lists sources relating to it. The latter are divided into primary sources (e.g., federal statutes and regulations; selected case law), secondary sources (e.g., books, journal articles), and tertiary sources (e.g., governmental organizations, information clearinghouses). Entries for primary sources provide chronologically arranged references to legal publications and legislative history. Includes table of cases and subject index. KF4210.A1L36

The yearbook of education law. 1988– . Topeka, Kan. : National Organization on Legal Problems of Education, c1988– . Annual. **CB157**

Stephen B. Thomas, ed.

Continues *Yearbook of school law* (1950–87).

Also available in microfiche.

Contains digests and analyses of court decisions affecting education. Chapters on employees, bargaining, pupils, persons with disabilities, torts, sports, finance, and higher education. Table of cases, detailed table of contents, and subject index; also indexed by *Education index* (CB55).

TEACHERS AND TEACHER EDUCATION

Bibliography

Ayers, Jerry B. Teacher education program evaluation : an annotated bibliography and guide to research / Jerry B. Ayers, Mary F. Berney. N.Y. : Garland, 1990. 274 p. (Garland bibliographies in contemporary education, v. 10 ; Garland reference library of social science, v. 619). **CB158**

Intended for those planning the evaluation and subsequent redesign of teacher education programs, attempting to meet evaluation requirements, or seeking accreditation from official agencies. Cites with brief descriptive annotations 941 books, research reports, journal articles, dissertations, reviews of research, and essays. Nearly all were published 1976–March 1989, and were drawn from *Resources in education* (CB61), *Cumulative index to journals in education* (CB54), *Dissertation abstracts international* (AG13), or *Books in print* (AA425). Entries are grouped in seven chapters, each of which treats a major component of teacher education programs (e.g., Management and governance, Follow-up evaluation). Indexes of authors, titles, and subjects, and an index that relates citations to specific standards of the National Council for Accreditation of Teacher Education (NCATE).

Z5814.T3A97

Powell, Marjorie. Teacher attitudes : an annotated bibliography and guide to research / Marjorie Powell, Joseph W. Beard. N.Y. : Garland, 1986. 457 p. (Garland bibliographies in contemporary education, v. 4 ; Garland reference library of social science, v. 199). **CB159**

Contains more than 1,900 entries for journal articles, ERIC documents, and dissertations published from 1965 through June 1984. Arranged in seven topical sections, including Attitudes toward students, Attitudes toward teaching, Effects of teaching attitudes, and Reviews of research on teacher attitudes. Author, title, and subject indexes.

Z5815.U5P68

——————— Teacher effectiveness : an annotated bibliography and guide to research / Marjorie Powell, Joseph W. Beard. N.Y. : Garland, 1984. 730 p. (Garland reference library of social science, v. 116 ; Garland bibliographies in contemporary education, v. 3). **CB160**

Provides brief annotations for more than 3,000 books, journal articles, research reports, conference papers, and dissertations. Divided into sections on teacher characteristics, teacher expectations, teacher perceptions, teacher behavior, the influence of teacher behavior, teacher-student relations, student perceptions and behavior, and methodology. Covers preschool through secondary schools, 1965–80. Author, title, and subject indexes. Z5814.T3P68

Directories

English language and orientation programs in the United States. 1964– . [New York] : Institute of International Education, 1964– . Triennial. **CB161**

Separate sections describe intensive English as a Second Language (ESL) programs at colleges and language schools and ESL courses at colleges and universities. Entries give information on dates, eligibility, tests for which students are trained, costs, admission requirements, and orientation period. Also lists programs at private secondary schools, and summer teacher training programs for ESL teachers from other nations. Indexes of sponsoring institutions, beginning dates, and programs on English for specific purposes.

PE1068.U5E53

Handbooks

Handbook of research on teacher education / W. Robert Houston, ed. ; Martin Haberman, John Sikula, assoc. editors. N.Y. : Macmillan ; London : Collier Macmillan, c1990. 925 p. **CB162**

A review of the literature in which experts "were asked not only to synthesize the most important research in their areas, but also to place it in a conceptual framework, to analyze trends, to summarize new directions, and to evaluate the potential for future research."— *Pref.* In 48 chapters divided among nine sections on major areas such as Participants in teacher education, Curriculum of teacher education, and Teacher education in the curriculum areas. Extensive bibliography; name and subject indexes.   LB1715.H274

The NASDTEC manual. 1984– . Dubuque, Iowa : Kendall/
Hunt Publ. Co., 1984– .   **CB163**
     Cover title, 1991: Manual on certification and preparation of educational personnel in the United States.
     Issued by the National Association of State Directors of Teacher Education and Certification.
     An impressively comprehensive publication. Individual chapters outline each state's requirements for specific kinds of certification, including initial certification, administration/supervision certificates, special education certificates for teaching persons with specific disabilities, emergency certificates, etc. Other chapters are devoted to considerations such as reciprocity, discipline of certificate holders, and examination and assessment.
     •*NASDTEC information system* [database]. Corresponds to the *NASDTEC manual*. Available from NASDTEC Information Network (NIN), Woodinville, Wash. Updated annually on 3.5" disks.
     LB1771.N37

Requirements for certification of teachers, counselors, librarians, administrators for elementary and secondary schools. 54th ed. (1989–90)– . Chicago : Univ. of Chicago Pr., 1989– . Annual.   **CB164**
     Title varies.
     Comp. by John Tryneski, 57th ed.– .
     Outlines initial certification requirements for each state. Gives requirements for specialized certificates for related personnel (e.g., school nurses).

Statistics

The condition of teaching : a state-by-state analysis. 1983– . Princeton, N.J. : Carnegie Foundation for the Advancement of Teaching : Available from Princeton Univ. Pr. Irregular.   **CB165**
     A survey of the opinions of 21,000 elementary and secondary school teachers on a wide range of topics relating to the teaching profession. In two parts, National profile and State-by-state comparisons, each divided into eight sections that treat such subjects as teachers' attitudes and values, working conditions, and judgments concerning students and academic programs. The 1990 ed. was based on responses to the 203 questions in the Carnegie Foundation for the Advancement of Teaching's National Survey of Public School Teachers. Data are presented primarily in tabular form, with results of the previous National Survey adjacent to the current survey results. Brief narrative summaries highlight the findings. Index of tables.   LB2832.2.C66

Feistritzer, C. Emily. Profile of teachers in the U.S.—1990 / C. Emily Feistritzer, author and survey director ; Fred Quelle, computer data analysis ; David T. Chester, ed. Wash. : National Center for Education Information, c1990. 83 p. **CB166**
     Provides information on teacher training, attitudes about various educational issues, job satisfaction, etc., through a summary of responses to a nationwide survey of 3,000 public and private elementary and secondary school teachers. Four main sections: Demographics; Teacher preparation (including opinions about factors that contribute to success); Attitudes about learning and reform proposals; Attitudes and future plans.
     A 1986 study of the same title used some of the same survey questions, permitting comparisons over time.   LB2832.2.F45

Status of the American public-school teacher. [Wash.] : National Education Association of the United States, Research Division, [1971?]– . Quinquennial.   **CB167**
     Based on a National Education Association survey of a sample of teachers. The 1990–91 questionnaire had sections on respondents' professional preparation, teaching experience, teaching assignment staffing patterns, pupils, hours teaching, available instructional resources, professional development, attitudes toward the profession, economic status, personal characteristics such as gender and ethnic background, and community and civil life (including political views). Many tables with longitudinal data.   LB2832.N3

EDUCATIONAL TECHNOLOGY

Bibliography

Tennyson, Robert D. Evaluation and educational technology : a selected bibliography / Robert D. Tennyson and Ronald O. Anderson. Englewood Cliffs, N.J. : Educational Technology Publ., 1990. 65 *l*. (Educational technology selected bibliography series, v. 3).   **CB168**
     Contains nearly 700 entries on articles, books, book chapters, and government documents published 1980–88. In two main categories: Methodology, subdivided into Evaluation methods and models and Measurement; and Applications, divided into Computer-based software and programs, Curricular programs, and Instructional materials. No index. Intended for instructional designers, but also potentially useful for other professionals attempting evaluations.   Z5814.E34T46

Indexes; Abstract journals

Educational technology abstracts. v. 1, no. 1– . [Abington, England] : Carfax Pub. Co., c1985– .   **CB169**
     Frequency varies: v. 1–4 (1985–88), quarterly; v. 5 (1989)– , bimonthly.
     Annually provides 850–950 signed abstracts, without evaluation, of books, book chapters, and articles drawn from 300 journals. Has six topical subdivisions: Design and planning, Teaching methods, Instructional media, Instructional resources, Learning, and Assessment and evaluation. Bimonthly author and subject indexes cumulate annually.

Encyclopedias

The encyclopaedia of educational media communications and technology / ed. by Derick Unwin and Ray McAleese. 2nd ed. N.Y. : Greenwood, 1988. 568 p. : ill.   **CB170**
     1st ed., 1978.
     Combines elements of an encyclopedia and a dictionary, with 1,800 short definitions and 62 signed, extended entries. The longer entries range from a page to a chapter in length and include bibliographies. Arranged alphabetically. Subject index.   LB1042.5.E52

Dictionaries

AECT Task Force on Definition and Terminology. Educational technology : a glossary of terms. Wash. : Association for Educational Communications and Technology, c1979. 371 p.   **CB171**
     An expansion of the 1977 ed., which focused on the instructional development process. This edition includes a section of definitions relating to media management. Each of the work's 14 chapters discusses a broad concept, treated in terms of its relevant functions and learning resources, to place the concept in the context of the field as a whole.   LB1028.3.A767

Brisebois, Madeleine. Vocabulaire de technologie éducative et de formation = Vocabulary of educational technology and training / Madeleine Brisebois, Mariette Grandchamp-Tupula, with the collaboration of Françoise Parc. [Ottawa, Canada] : Secrétariat d'Etat du Canada, c1991. 1005 p.   **CB172**

An English/French–French/English dictionary in which 6,400 expressions are arranged in parallel columns of English and French. Provides definitions for most words. In addition to concepts of educational technology and training, also translates some adult education and psychological terms.   LB15.B7

Ellington, Henry. Dictionary of instructional technology / comp. by Henry Ellington and Duncan Harris. London : Kogan Page ; N.Y. : Nichols Publ. Co., 1986. 189 p. : ill.   **CB173**

Defines 2,800 terms drawn from instructional technology, and from fields that "impinge upon or overlap" (*Introd.*) with it. Includes British and U.S. terms and those used in other English-speaking countries. Many clear, simple diagrams.   LB15.E42

Glossary of educational technology terms = Glosario de términos de tecnología de la educación. Paris : UNESCO, c1986. 243 p.   **CB174**

One of three versions, the others being for French, *Glossaire des termes de technologie éducative* (2nd ed., rev. and enl., Paris : UNESCO, 1987. 263 p.) and Russian, *Glossariĭ terminov po tekhnologii obrazovaniĭa* (Paris : UNESCO, 1986. 239 p.).

"Prepared by the Methods, Materials, and Techniques of Education Section, Unesco, for the International Bureau of Education."—*t.p.*

Each version lists some 1,650 terms in two glossaries, one for each language, giving equivalent or correlative terms in the other.   LB15.G555

Directories

International yearbook of educational and training technology / Association for Educational and Training Technology. 1989– . London : Kogan Page, [c1989]– . Annual.   **CB175**

Former title, 1976–88: *International yearbook of educational and instructional technology.* Formerly biennial.

A directory of centers for instructional technology, including universities, associations, foundations, research organizations consortia, etc. In four parts arranged by location: (1) international and regional (e.g., Middle East); (2) United Kingdom, (3) U.S. (arranged by state), and (4) other countries (by country). Entries give addresses and list areas of interest, services, publications, and related information.

Only the best. 1985 ed.– . N.Y. : R. R. Bowker, c1985– . Annual.   **CB176**

Subtitle: The discriminating software guide for preschool–grade 12 : a special report from the editors of SchoolTechNews.

Publisher varies.

Describes software previously evaluated by others, selecting the products with the most favorable ratings. Descriptions generally include subject, grade levels, hardware requirements, costs, and references to reviews, evaluation, and criticism. A cumulative edition for 1985–89 was published in 1989.

•Machine-readable versions for DOS, Windows, and Macintosh were produced on disk in 1993 by the Education and Technology Resources Center of the Association for Supervision and Curriculum Development, Alexandria, Va. Plans are to produce annual updates for each version.   LB1028.7.O54

Yearbooks

Educational media and technology yearbook. v. 11 (1985)– . Littleton, Colo. : Libraries Unlimited, Inc., 1985– . Annual.   **CB177**

Continues *Educational media yearbook.*

Sponsored by the Association for Educational Communications and Technology.

Summarizes important developments and indicates current sources of information in educational technology and educational media. Recent volumes in six to eight main sections; 18th ed. (1992) had: Trends and issues; The profession; Current developments; Professional literature; Leadership profiles; Organizations and associations in North America; Graduate programs; and Mediagraphy, print and nonprint resources.   LB1028.3.E37

EDUCATIONAL ADMINISTRATION

Bibliography

Richardson, Michael D. Publication sources in educational leadership : a compilation of publication outlets for the creative exchange of information in educational administration and supervision / Michael D. Richardson, Robert L. Prickett. Lancaster, Pa. : Technomic Pub. Co., c1991. 116 p.   **CB178**

Broader in scope than its title would suggest. Contains entries for more than 300 international journals that cover virtually the breadth of the field, but contain articles on leadership. Brief entries provide editors' names and addresses, information on the periodical's purpose or content, and tell whether it is refereed. Alphabetically arranged by periodical title, with index by subject.   Z286.E3R53

Indexes; Abstract journals

Educational administration abstracts. v. 1 (Spring 1966)– . [College Station, Tex., etc. : Univ. Council for Educational Administration], 1966– . Quarterly, Jan. 1983–.   **CB179**

Frequency varies: 1966–82, three numbers per year; 1983– , quarterly. Publisher varies; currently Corwin Pr., Thousand Oaks, Calif.

Abstracts 1,000 works per year, including books, articles from 120 journals, and other materials. International in scope; organized by broad subject areas (e.g., Administrative structure and processes, Student personnel), which are further subdivided. Quarterly author and subject indexes cumulate annually.   LB2805.E32

Encyclopedias

Encyclopedia of school administration & supervision / ed. by Richard A. Gorton, Gail T. Schneider, James C. Fisher. Phoenix : Oryx, 1988. 321 p.   **CB180**

Contains nearly 300 articles written by more than 200 specialists. Entries are arranged alphabetically and are short, typically one page, followed by bibliographies of three citations. A "Guide to related topics" groups article titles under such broad rubrics as School facilities, Community-school relations, and Curriculum areas and issues. In addition, each article contains three or four cross-references. A subject index also includes cross-references.   LB2805.E53

Dictionaries

Dejnozka, Edward L. Educational administration glossary. Westport, Conn. : Greenwood, [1983]. 247 p.   **CB181**

Offers short definitions of 1,400 terms that are used in administration of elementary and secondary schools. Contains a bibliography and several appendixes, including names and addresses of organizations and associations, pertinent periodicals, and accredited education programs for training administrators.   LB15.D373

Handbooks

Handbook of research on educational administration : a project of the American Educational Research Association / Norman J. Boyan, ed. N.Y. : Longman, c1988. 767 p. **CB182**

Summarizes 30 years of research. 33 chapters, each written by an expert, are arranged in five sections: The administrator; Organizations; Economics and finance; Politics and policy; and Special topics. Substantial bibliographies. Name and subject indexes.   LB2805.H2864

Biography

American Association of School Administrators. Who's who in educational administration. 1976/77– . Arlington, Va. : American Association of School Administrators, [1977]– .   **CB183**

"Roster of members, American Association of School Administrators."—*t.p.* For each person, gives current position, business address, and highest degree earned and institution. Arranged alphabetically by state, with a separate section listing foreign members. Alphabetical index of names that gives the state under which the member's entry is found.   L13.A366

EDUCATION OF THE GIFTED

Anthony, John B. The gifted and talented : a bibliography and resource guide / John B. Anthony, Margaret M. Anthony. Pittsfield, Mass. : Berkshire Community Pr., 1981. 200 p.   **CB184**

A bibliography and resource directory of approximately 3,200 items (books, articles, dissertations, etc.), arranged in six broad categories (e.g., identification, characteristics, special issues). The resources section lists diagnostic instruments, media aids, relevant organizations, etc. No index.

Greenlaw, M. Jean. Educating the gifted : a sourcebook / M. Jean Greenlaw, Margaret E. McIntosh. Chicago : Amer. Libr. Assoc., 1988. 468 p.   **CB185**

An overview, particularly valuable for its annotated bibliography of more than 200 pages that treats the breadth of the field.   LC3993.9.G74

Karnes, Frances A. Handbook of instructional resources and references for teaching the gifted / Frances A. Karnes, Emily C. Collins. 2nd ed. Boston : Allyn and Bacon, c1984. 196 p.   **CB186**

1st ed., 1980.

Lists commercially produced materials, most described in tables outlining the skills they develop, their formats and components, educational levels, and costs and producers. Includes not only academic materials, but also games, puzzles, and brain teasers. Substantial annotated bibliography on educating the gifted and on teaching methods for specific subjects.   Z5814.G5K37

Stein, Morris Isaac. Gifted, talented, and creative young people : a guide to theory, teaching, and research. N.Y. : Garland, 1986. 465 p. (Garland reference library of social science, v. 120).   **CB187**

An annotated bibliography of books, book chapters, articles, and conference and symposium papers, most published 1970–80 but including older classics and later works, representing the "major issues, orientations, research results, [and] curricular and instructional programs."—*Pref.* Intended to give graduate students and professional researchers a rapid survey of the field. Organized in chapters covering broad areas (e.g., Evaluation, Stimulating creativity); within chapters the arrangement varies, some alphabetical by author, some chronological, some thematic. Annotations contain "Suggestions for further reading"; some annotations are detailed summaries as long as two pages. Author and subject indexes.   Z5815.U5S73

Wicker, Gerald L. Gifted & talented information resources : a comprehensive guide for parents and educators of gifted and talented children. Snellville, Ga. : Cardinal Publ., 1991. 95 p.   **CB188**

Lists organizations, publications, publishers and distributors, teacher training and consultant services, private schools and summer programs, competitions, scholarships and grants, government and private information sources, and colleges training teachers of the gifted. Brief entries, with addresses, for most sources.   LC3993.9.W42

SPECIAL EDUCATION

Bibliography

Compton, Carolyn. A guide to 85 tests for special education. New ed. Belmont, Calif. : Fearon Education, c1990. 336 p. : ill.   **CB189**

Prior eds.: *Guide to 65 tests for special education*, 1980; *Guide to 75 tests for special education*, 1984.

Describes psychological and educational tests used to assess students for special education programs. Arranged by type of test in six sections: (1) Academic; (2) Perceptual, memory, and visual-motor skills; (3) Speech and language; (4) Bilingual (Spanish-English) language; (5) Gross and fine motor skills; (6) General intelligence tests and developmental scales. Entries describe test purpose, major areas tested, age or grade range, scoring, time involved, format, subtests, strengths, and limiting factors. Appendixes include: a glossary of testing terms and lists of tests for academic skills, cognitive processes, and reading, and of tests for preschool children. No index, but an alphabetical list of the tests follows the table of contents.   LB1131.C5416

High/low handbook : encouraging literacy in the 1900s / comp. and ed. by Ellen V. LiBretto. 3rd ed. N.Y. : Bowker, c1990. 290 p. : ill.   **CB190**

1st ed., 1981; 2nd ed., 1985.

For "teachers, librarians, and others who provide easy reading materials for disabled or reluctant teenage readers."—*Introd.* Has annotated citations for 412 "Core collection" books, divided into works for the disabled reader (giving grade and interest levels) and books for reluctant readers. Other sections outline ways of serving high/low readers and selecting materials for them, the latter listing titles and addresses of magazines and educational software. An appendix lists sources of book reviews. Author, title, and subject indexes.   Z1039.S5H54

National Council of Teachers of English. Committee to Revise High Interest-Easy Reading. High interest easy reading : a booklist for junior and senior high students / William G. McBride, ed., and the Committee to Revise High Interest-Easy Reading. 6th ed. Urbana, Ill. : National Council of Teachers of English, c1990. 133 p.   **CB191**

2nd ed., 1972; 5th ed., 1988.

Suggests 436 fiction and non-fiction books for students whose reading levels are significantly lower than their age levels. Primarily for the " 'reluctant' student who can read—but often does not" (*Note to the Reader*), but also may be useful to teachers and librarians. Annotations do not indicate grade, sophistication, or reading levels because "interest will be the most significant factor." Avoids books with formats suggesting an elementary level, or content that seems too complex. Arranged by type (e.g., science, adventure).   Z1039.S5N4

Sternlicht, Manny. Special education : a source book. N.Y. : Garland, 1987. 431 p. (Garland reference library of social science, v. 375 ; Garland reference library of social science. Source books on education, vol. 7).   **CB192**

An annotated bibliography of 1,001 sources, mostly journal articles. Organized by type of disability, with an additional chapter on mainstreaming. Author and subject indexes.   Z5814.S73S74

White, James P. Materials and strategies for the education of trainable mentally retarded learners. N.Y. : Garland, 1990. 348 p. (Garland reference library of social science, v. 476 ; Garland reference library of social science. Source books on education, vol. 24).   **CB193**

Essentially an annotated bibliography of articles, books, assessment instruments, and instructional materials. 15 chapters, each beginning with a brief outline, treat either the teaching of specific subjects or topics such as Assessment or Working with parents. Appendixes include an extensive list of relevant state-level public and private agencies, publishers, and suppliers, and microcomputer resources. General index.   LC4601.W52

Indexes; Abstract journals

Exceptional child education resources. v. 9 (Spring 1977)– . Reston, Va. : Council for Exceptional Children, 1977– . Quarterly.   **CB194**

Continues: *Exceptional child education abstracts*, v. 1 (Apr. 1969)–v. 8 (Winter 1977).

Indexes more than 200 journals as well as books, reports, government publications, and dissertations in education and psychology. Emphasizes the education and development of children and infants who are gifted or are physically, mentally, or learning disabled. Until v. 24 (1992–93), overlapped with *Resources in education* (CB61) and *Current index to journals in education* (CB54) but provided supplementary material to both indexes; Thereafter, continues full coverage of *CIJE* but contains only selected entries from *RIE*. Resembles both in format, descriptor structure, and indexes. Six-year cumulative indexes are in production, in microfiche and disk formats.

•Available in machine-readable form as: *Exceptional child education resources (ECER)* [database] (Reston, Va. : Council for Exceptional Children, 1966–). Available online, updated monthly.   Z5814.C52E9

Encyclopedias

Concise encyclopedia of special education / ed., Cecil R. Reynolds, Elaine Fletcher-Janzen. N.Y. : Wiley, c1990. 1215 p. : ill.   **CB195**

Essentially a condensation of Reynolds and Lester Mann's three-volume *Encyclopedia of special education* (CB196) intended to provide professionals and parents with a less expensive and less bulky desk book. Some 90% of the parent work's articles have been condensed and streamlined, others have been updated or completely rewritten, and new articles have been added. Nearly all entries on living persons have been deleted. Articles are alphabetically arranged and typically vary from a paragraph to two pages in length, followed by brief bibliographies and cross-references. General index.   LC4007.E53

Encyclopedia of special education : a reference for the education of the handicapped and other exceptional children and adults / editors, Cecil R. Reynolds, Lester Mann. N.Y. : Wiley, c1987. 3 v. : ill.   **CB196**

Articles by more than 400 experts on some 2,000 topics. Entries describe handicapping conditions, intervention and service delivery, educational and psychological tests, prominent workers in the field, laws and legislation, etc. Cross-references; name and subject indexes. Intended for intelligent general readers as well as professionals. A condensation, *Concise encyclopedia of special education* (CB195) is a less expensive, updated one-volume desk version for professionals and parents.   LC4007.E53

Dictionaries

A glossary of special education / ed. by Phillip Williams. Milton Keynes, England ; Philadelphia : Open Univ. Pr., 1988. 222 p. : ill.   **CB197**

Attempts to provide "reasonably simple explanations of terms ... for teachers and parents ... and also for administrators. But it is not intended to offer detailed explanations for experts."—*Introd.* British emphasis. Diagrams and photographs.   LC3986.G7

Terminology of special education = Terminologie de l'éducation spéciale. Rev. ed. Paris, France : UNESCO, 1983. 167 p.   **CB198**

1st ed., 1977, had title *Terminology : special education.*

Separate English, French, Spanish, and Russian glossaries which define terms and give their equivalents in the other three languages. For some terms also serves as a thesaurus, listing related and narrower terms. A "Term cluster" section groups concepts into six broad fields (e.g., prevention and identification) with subdivisions (e.g., etiology, hearing tests).   LC4007.T47

Vergason, Glenn A. Dictionary of special education and rehabilitation. 3rd ed. Denver, Colo. : Love, 1990. 207 p.   **CB199**

2nd ed., 1985, by Vergason and Leo J. Kelly.

Short entries, with important terms in italics to provide cross-references. Pronunciation keys included where needed. Appendixes: associations and national centers, periodicals in English, sources of legal assistance.   LC3957.K445

Directories

The complete directory for people with learning disabilities : products, resources, books, services. 1993/94– . Lakeville, Conn. : Grey House Publ. ; Detroit : Gale, c1993– . Annual.   **CB200**

In addition to entries for schools, learning centers, vocational training programs, associations and organizations, and government agencies, this impressive work has "comprehensive chapters on teaching methods, assistive devices, technological resources, magazines, newsletters, and workshops that are specifically designed to meet the needs of individuals with learning disabilities as well as those who work with them ... including parents and siblings and the wide range of supportive services available to that group."—*Introd.* Approximately 5,900 resources are arranged in sections on organizations, specialized media, programs, and materials, each subdivided. Short entries provide addresses, phone numbers, and brief annotations. Entry and subject indexes.   LC4818.3.C65

Directory for exceptional children. [1st] ed. (1954)– . Boston : Sargent, 1954– .   **CB201**
   Subtitle: A listing of educational and training facilities.
   13th ed., 1994.
   More than 2,500 entries describe facilities and organizations "encompassing the entire range of developmental, organic, and emotional handicaps."—*Pref.* Contains 14 sections on facilities for specific handicaps (residential facilities for mentally retarded persons, speech and hearing clinics, etc.); within each section, entries are arranged geographically. Each entry includes names of directors, medical directors, and admissions officers, as well as information on which handicaps are targeted; grades served; academic orientation and curriculum; therapy offerings; enrollment; staff; fees and financial aid; summer programs; and organizational structure; plus descriptive text. List of associations, foundations, and societies for specific disabilities; directory of state agency personnel. Institutional index.   LC4007.D5

The FCLD learning disabilities resource guide : a state-by-state directory of special programs, schools, and services. N.Y. : Publ. for the Foundation for Children with Learning Disabilities by Education Systems, Inc., c1985. 409 p.   **CB202**
   1st ed. (1984) had title: *The FCLD guide for parents of children with learning disabilities.*
   Lists organizations concerned with learning disabilities, relevant state department of education personnel, private and day schools, summer camps and programs, postsecondary special programs and services, and hospital clinics and services. Short entries give contact information and describe the organization's function, its programs, grades served, enrollment, full-time staff, and available financial aid. Also includes short dictionary of learning-disability terms; general index.
                                        LC4704.6.F35

Handbooks

Davis, William Edmund. Resource guide to special education : terms, laws, assessment procedures, organizations. 2nd ed. Boston : Allyn and Bacon, c1986. 317 p.   **CB203**
   1st ed., 1980, had title: *Educator's resource guide to special education.*
   A practical, basic guide arranged in five sections, the first and most extensive of which provides definitions of terms in special education. Other sections include: acronyms; tests, surveys, and inventories; federal legislation and litigation; and organizations concerned with exceptional persons.
   Features new to this edition include: a section explaining word roots, stems, prefixes, and suffixes used in special education; an extensive listing of computer terminology related to the field; substantially expanded treatment of terminology in other areas of special education; expanded and updated listing of organizations and agencies; expansion and updating of the section on legislation and litigation. LC4007.D38

Handbook of special education : research and practice / ed. by Margaret C. Wang, Maynard C. Reynolds, Herbert J. Walberg. Oxford ; N.Y. : Pergamon, c1987–1991. 4 v. : ill.
                                        CB204
   Contents: v. 1, Learner characteristics and adaptive education; v. 2, Mildly handicapped conditions; v. 3, Low incidence conditions; v. 4, Emerging programs.
   Consists of 59 chapters that summarize the "well-confirmed knowledge" for the topic treated, covering first the research literature, then the "tested experience and practices of leading professionals," and finally recommending "improvements for effectively linking practice with the state of the art."—*Pref.* Vols. 2–4 contain sections of several chapters each on specific disabilities, e.g., severe handicaps, learning disabilities, and behavioral disorders. Extensive bibliographies; author and subject indexes in each volume.

§ A synopsis of the first three volumes, *Special education : research and practice : synthesis of findings* (Oxford ; N.Y. : Pergamon, 1990. 223 p.) summarizes findings and contains an epilogue offering impressions, observations, and suggestions for future practice and research. Substantial bibliographies; author and subject indexes.
                                        LC3965.H263

Weller, Carol. Educators' desk reference for special learning problems / Carol Weller, Mary Buchanan. Boston : Allyn and Bacon, c1988. 373 p.   **CB205**
   Describes 229 educational methods, including techniques for each exceptionality and severity level, briefly outlining each method and its uses and referring to published sources for more detailed descriptions. Methods are indexed by title, author, source publications describing the method, intervention areas (e.g., mathematics, sensory disorders, therapy), and ages for which the method is appropriate.
                                        LC4704.W45

Statistics

Ficke, Robert C. Digest of data on persons with disabilities / prep. by Robert C. Ficke (Science Management Corporation). Wash. : National Institute on Disability and Rehabilitation Research, 1992. 179 p. : ill.   **CB206**
   For annotation, *see* CC198.   HV1553.F53

To assure the free appropriate public education of all children with disabilities : annual report to Congress on the implementation of the Individuals with Disabilities Education Act / prep. by the Division of Innovation and Development, Office of Special Education Programs, U.S. Office of Special Education and Rehabilitative Services. 13th (1991)– . Wash. : U.S. Dept. of Education, 1991– . Annual.   **CB207**
   Superintendent of Documents classification: ED 1.310/2: .
   Issued also to depository libraries in microfiche.
   A key source of national and state-by-state statistics on students with disabilities and educational provisions for them. Has four chapters of text with many tables and graphs, followed by several hundred pages of appendixes consisting mostly of tables. The chapters are: Students with disabilities served, placement and exiting patterns, and special education personnel; Meeting the needs of infants, toddlers, and preschool children with disabilities; Dropouts with disabilities ... ; and Assisting states and localities in educating all children with disabilities.   LC4031.T6

GUIDANCE

Bibliography

Professional careers sourcebook : an information guide for career planning. 1st ed.– . Detroit : Gale, c1990– . Biennial.
                                        CB208
   For annotation, *see* CH707.   HF5382.5.U5P76

Encyclopedia

The encyclopedia of careers and vocational guidance / William E. Hopke, ed. in chief. 9th ed. Chicago : J.G. Ferguson Pub. Co., c1993. 4 v. : ill.   **CB209**
   1st ed., 1967; 8th ed., 1990.
   Contents: v. 1, Industry profiles; v. 2, Professional careers; v. 3, General and special careers; v. 4, Technicians' careers.

Vol. 1 describes 74 industries, their historical backgrounds, employment statistics, products, structure, and career patterns and outlooks. Vols. 2–4 discuss 540 jobs arranged in 14 broad categories (e.g., professional, clerical, machine trades). Entries describe educational and training requirements, duties, salaries, and prospects. Each volume contains a complete index of the job titles in all four volumes; v. 4 has an index of jobs by *Dictionary of occupational titles* number (CH693). Appendixes list organizations that assist in training and job placement for disabled and other special groups and provide information on internships, apprenticeships, and special training programs.

HF5381.E52

Directories

•**The guidance information system** : GIS [database]. Cambridge, Mass. : Houghton Mifflin, Educational Software Div.
CB210

Updated biennially.

An online service of several separate files: "Occupational information," describing the characteristics, requirements, and outlook for 1,025 occupations; "Armed services," with information on 215 jobs for which training is available in the armed forces, with cross-references to related civilian occupations; "Two-year college" and "Four-year college" files, providing information on admissions, costs, campus life, financial aid, enrollment, etc., for 1,800 two-year colleges and technical institutes and 1,750 four-year colleges and universities; a file of similar information for 1,550 graduate and professional schools; a file on financial aids from federal, state, and private sources, with the standard contacts, eligibility, and deadline information; and "The career decision-making system," designed to facilitate occupational choice by weighing such factors as school subject preference, future educational plans, and abilities, and suggesting possible careers.

Handbooks

Career information center. 4th ed. Mission Hills, Calif. : Glencoe ; [N.Y.] : Macmillan, c1990. 13 v.
CB211

For use "by anyone seeking career information for people of all ages at all stages of career development." *Foreword.* The 13 relatively thin volumes present 648 occupational profiles and more than 3,000 jobs. Each volume covers a broad field (e.g., health, construction), with an overview of its job market followed by entries for individual careers that describe work characteristics, entry procedures, advancement possibilities and employment outlook, working conditions, earnings, and benefits. Appendixes in each volume list further reading and offer a directory of institutions offering training and an index by occupation. The last volume has an index covering the entire work.

HF5382.5.U5C32

Cohen, Jeffrey J. Handbook of school-based interventions : resolving student problems and promoting healthy educational environments / Jeffrey J. Cohen, Marian C. Fish. San Francisco : Jossey-Bass Publishers, c1993. 512 p.
CB212

Provides one- to two-page outlines of published articles on techniques for alleviating behavioral problems in elementary and secondary schools. In seven sections by type of problem, further arranged by specific behavior; examples: Classroom management (dishonesty, annoying others); Cognitive and social competence (substance abuse); Relationships with adults (running away). Name and subject indexes.

LB1027.55.C64

•**Peterson's career options** [database]. Princeton, N.J. : Peterson's Guides, Inc., 1991– .
CB213

Produced 1986–87 as *Peterson's career planning service.*

Consists of four diskettes and a student workbook.

Derived in part from the online *Peterson's college database* (CB283).

Contains information on occupations, related jobs, and training requirements. Software provides exercises utilizing users' interests, abilities, educational background, and similar considerations.

Vocational careers sourcebook. 1st ed.– . Detroit : Gale, c1992– . Biennial.
CB214

1st ed. has subtitle: Where to find help planning careers in skilled, trade, and nontechnical vocations.

Compiled in cooperation with InfoPLACE career information center.

Profiles 135 vocational occupations such as aircraft mechanic, correction officer, and hotel clerk, providing concise job descriptions and sources for further information. Entries are arranged by occupation and divided into 11 categories, including Job description, Career guides, Associations, Standards/certification agencies, Educational directories and programs, Periodicals. Each entry includes, as appropriate and available, organization or publication name; contact information; bibliographic information; a brief description of purpose, services, or content; and toll-free and fax numbers. The table of contents lists individual occupations, and an index of information sources refers to publications and organizations cited. May be used in conjunction with *Occupational outlook handbook* (CH704), which gives more detailed job descriptions.
Z7164.V6V62

HIGHER EDUCATION

Guides

Olevnik, Peter P. American higher education : a guide to reference sources / Peter P. Olevnik ... [et al.]. Westport, Conn. : Greenwood, 1993. 211 p. (Bibliographies and indexes in education, no. 12).
CB215

The only up-to-date guide to the literature. 790 annotated entries in chapters by type of work (bibliographies, etc.), including a chapter on computer files. Excludes: periodicals; pamphlets; unpublished materials; and works on single institutions, states, or regions, or on single fields of study. Author, title, and subject indexes.
Z5815.U5O44

Quay, Richard H. Research in higher education : a guide to source bibliographies. 2nd ed. [Phoenix] : Oryx, 1985. 133 p.
CB216

1st ed., 1976

Citations for 932 works, mostly journal articles, ERIC documents, and books, in 15 chapters on subjects such as two-year institutions, faculty, and financial management. Some entries have brief annotations. Also contains a bibliography of works on higher education as a field of study and a directory of research centers and advanced programs. Author and title indexes.
Z5814.U7Q39

Bibliography

Altbach, Philip G. American students : a selected bibliography on student activism and related topics / Philip G. Altbach and David H. Kelly. Lexington, Mass. : Lexington Books, [1973]. 537 p.
CB217

A revised and greatly expanded version of Altbach's *Student politics and higher education in the United States* (1968). Lists books, periodical articles, and doctoral dissertations in classed arrangement. Detailed table of contents, but no index. Items of special importance are starred.
Z5814.S86A55

Anson, Christopher M. Writing across the curriculum : an annotated bibliography / comp. by Chris M. Anson, John E. Schwiebert, and Michael M. Williamson. Westport, Conn. : Greenwood, 1993. 187 p. (Bibliographies and indexes in education, no. 13).   **CB218**

Provides 1,067 entries with unevaluative annotations for books, journal articles, government documents, ERIC documents, book chapters, and conference papers. In two parts: Scholarship, with sections for Bibliographies and literature, Collections and special issues, History and implementation, Research studies, and Theory and rationale; and Pedagogy, with sections for school subjects (e.g., Social and behavioral sciences). Author and subject indexes.   Z5818.E5W75

Beach, Mark. A bibliographic guide to American colleges and universities : from colonial times to the present. Westport, Conn. : Greenwood, 1975. 314 p.   **CB219**

"An effort to bring together in one source citations to major books, articles and dissertations relating to the history of specific institutions of higher learning."—*Introd.* Listing is by state, with general works followed by histories of specific institutions. Subject index. 2,806 entries.   Z5815.U5B4

Herring, Mark Youngblood. Ethics and the professor : an annotated bibliography, 1970–1985. N.Y. : Garland, 1988. 605 p. (Garland reference library of the humanities, v. 742).   **CB220**

Cites books and articles on moral law and the "action of that law in our educational realm."—*Pref.* Excludes reference and non-English language materials. Humorously worded table of contents and subdivisions. Author, title, and subject key word indexes.   Z5814.P73H47

Higher education : a bibliographic handbook / ed. by D. Kent Halstead. Wash. : U.S. National Institute of Education, 1981–84. 2 v.   **CB221**

Vol. 2 publ. 1981. A prototype of v. 1 was publ. 1979 with the title *Higher education planning: a bibliographic handbook.*

"The purpose of this bibliography and future editions is to identify and publicize on a continuing basis high-quality references in higher education."—*Introd.*

Vol. 1 approaches subjects from an aggregate state or national perspective; v. 2 deals with topics usually approached at the individual institutional level. Covers mainly the period 1968–81. Arranged by 38 topical categories, with lengthy annotations (some evaluative); author and title indexes.   Z5814.U7H63

Hines, Edward R. Higher education finance : an annotated bibliography and guide to research / Edward R. Hines, John R. McCarthy. N.Y. : Garland, 1985. 357 p. (Garland bibliographies in contemporary education, v. 4 ; Garland reference library of social science, v. 198).   **CB222**

Covers 1970–83. Includes books, reports, studies, and articles from a list of core journals. Entries are numerically arranged, with full citations and annotations, in topical chapters on financing and fiscal support, general trends and economics, government support, external funding, student aid, institutional financial management, planning and budgeting, and reduction and retrenchment. Topic and author indexes; list of acronyms.   Z5815.U5H56

Hunt, Thomas C. Religious colleges and universities in America : a selected bibliography / Thomas C. Hunt and James C. Carper. N.Y. : Garland, 1988. 374 p. (Garland reference library of social science, v. 422).   **CB223**

Contains 26 chapters that deal with colleges and universities affiliated with specific denominations. Other chapters treat major works on religion and American colleges and universities, and government aid to and regulation of church-affiliated institutions. Author and subject indexes.   Z5814.R34H86

Menges, Robert J. Key resources on teaching, learning, curriculum, and faculty development : a guide to the higher education literature / Robert J. Menges, B. Claude Mathis. San Francisco : Jossey-Bass Publishers, 1988. 406 p.   **CB224**

An annotated bibliography of 686 books, journal articles, periodicals, reference tools, ERIC documents, book chapters, and UNESCO documents. Arranged in chapters on teaching, learning, curriculum, faculty development, and periodicals and reference books. Name and subject indexes.

§ One of five Jossey-Bass annotated bibliographies on higher education. The others:

Marvin W. Patterson and Lisa A. Mets, *Key resources on higher education governance, management, and leadership* (1987).

Arthur M. Cohen, James C. Palmer, and Diane K. Zwemer, *Key resources on community colleges* (1986).

A. Westley Rowland, *Key resources on institutional advancement* (CB227).

Albert B. Hood and Cathann Arceneaux, *Key resources on student services* (1990).   Z5814.U7M45

Parker, Franklin. U.S. higher education : a guide to information sources / Franklin Parker, Betty June Parker. Detroit : Gale, 1980. 675 p. (Education information guide series, v.9).   **CB225**

An annotated bibliography of 3,194 entries for books and reports on the breadth of the field. Attempts to "include the most important 19th Century works and to approach comprehensive inclusion" of 20th century writings (*Pref.*). Although years have passed since its publication, it may still prove a guide to useful sources.   LA227.3.P35

Quay, Richard H. The financing of American higher education : a bibliographic handbook. Phoenix : Oryx, 1984. 142 p.   **CB226**

Offers annotated entries for works on principal issues and trends in financing higher education for the period 1960–81. More than 1,100 briefly-annotated entries describe books, journal articles, ERIC documents and dissertations. Most entries are arranged in four chapters: The political economy of American higher education; Institutions, programs, and coalitions; Human resources; and Research, planning and policy management. Appendixes include related bibliographic sources and financial data sources for higher education. Author and subject indexes.   Z5814.U7Q382

Rowland, A. Westley. Key resources on institutional advancement. San Francisco : Jossey-Bass Publishers, 1986. 251 p.   **CB227**

An annotated bibliography of important items that "significantly contributed to the basic foundation of the advancement field and to its growth and development."—*p. x.* Classic works are starred. Arranged in 13 topical chapters, including public relations, fund raising, institutional relations, government relations, and enrollment management. Indexes of subjects and names. Appendixes: statement of ethics for advancement professionals; annotated, alphabetical list of pertinent periodicals with addresses.   Z5815.U5R69

Sontz, Ann H. L. The American college president, 1636–1989 : a critical review and bibliography. N.Y. : Greenwood, c1991. 176 p. (Bibliographies and indexes in education, no. 10).   **CB228**

Updates Walter C. Eells and Ernest V. Hollis's *The college presidency, 1900–1960* ([Wash.] : Office of Education, [1961]). Includes materials relevant to early academic presidencies as well as those since the 1960s to mirror "concerns of both historic and modern academic leaders."—*p.xxii.* Lists publications in four chapters: (1) Bibliographies; (2) Background sources (general treatises, alphabetical by author in broad subject categories); (3) Biographies (alphabetical by institution, then by president) and (4) Presidential works—the bulk of the citations. Introductory material includes a short review essay, "Guide to the study of the academic presidency," and seven tables of statistical data. Author and subject indexes.   Z5814.U7S66

Sparks, Linda. Institutions of higher education : an international bibliography. N.Y. : Greenwood, c1990. 478 p. (Bibliographies and indexes in education, no. 9).   **CB229**

Attempts "to bring together in one comprehensive source citations of books, dissertations, theses, and ERIC microfiche relating to the history of specific institutions of higher education worldwide."—*Pref.* Treats all types of postsecondary education, including two-year colleges and specialized institutions as well as colleges and universities, but omits works on individual academic departments. Entries for 85 countries are alphabetically arranged, as are those for individual states of the U.S. Author and subject indexes.   Z5814.U7S69

——————————— College admissions : a selected, annotated bibliography. Westport, Conn. : Greenwood, 1993. 187 p. (Bibliographies and indexes in education, no. 11).   **CB230**

Cites 906 titles on "all aspects of undergraduate admission in the United States."—*Pref.* Entries for books, book chapters, journal articles, dissertations, and ERIC documents; most include short annotations. Omits "popular handbooks on how to get into college." In four sections: General admissions, Marketing and recruitment, Offices and officers, and Foreign admissions. Subject index (with cross-references); author and title indexes.   Z5814.U7S685

Swanson, Kathryn. Affirmative action and preferential admissions in higher education : an annotated bibliography. Metuchen, N.J. : Scarecrow, 1981. 336 p.   **CB231**

Spine title: Affirmative action in higher education.

In three parts: (1) The law and the courts (containing government and legal sources); (2) The academic community response; (3) The philosophical debate. Pts. 2 and 3 are arranged by author, with no detailed subject access. Concentrates on the literature from 1970 "primarily because it was not until the early 1970's that application of federal … guidelines … became more stringent, resulting in more opposition to them within the academic community."—*Introd.* Name and title indexes.   Z5814.U7S93

White, Jane N. Higher education literature : an annotated bibliography / ed. by Jane N. White and Collins W. Burnett. Phoenix : Oryx, 1981. 177 p.   **CB232**

A classified bibliography of more than 1,600 citations to monograph and report literature on two- and four-year accredited degree-granting colleges and universities in the U.S. Arranged in chapters on such subjects as Organization and administration, further divided by subtopics. Appendixes list reference sources, professional journals, important legislation, etc. Author and subject indexes.   Z5814.U7W53

Young, Arthur P. Higher education in American life, 1636–1986 : a bibliography of dissertations and theses. N.Y. : Greenwood, 1988. 431 p. (Bibliographies and indexes in education, no. 5).   **CB233**

In two parts: By states and territories and Topical studies; each contains sections on specific subjects such as federal aid, athletics, and student life. Entries list author, title, degree, lcoation, date, and number of pages. Author and subject indexes.   Z5814.U7Y69

Indexes; Abstract journals

Higher education abstracts. v. 20, no. 1 (Fall 1984)– . Claremont, Calif. : Claremont Graduate School, c1984– . Quarterly.   **CB234**

Contains abstracts derived from some 120 scholarly journals, plus conference papers and published and unpublished monographs. Omits articles treating only one institution or state, dissertations, book reviews, news items, program descriptions, and case studies. Arranged in sections on topics such as faculty attitudes, admissions, student health, and legal issues. Quarterly issues contain author, title, and subject indexes, which cumulate in the fourth issue of each volume.

Supersedes *College student personnel abstracts* (v. 1 [Oct. 1965]–19 [Summer 1984]), which focused on college student development and behavior. With the title change, the scope has broadened to include all issues relating to higher education.   Z5814.P8C66

Research into higher education abstracts. v. 1 (June 1967)– . Guildford, [Eng.] [etc.] : Society for Research into Higher Education, [1967]– .   **CB235**

Vol. 1, no. 1 preceded by two trial issues.

Attempts comprehensive coverage of British higher education, plus selective treatment of sources relating to higher education elsewhere. Abstracts more than 600 works per year, mostly articles, with selective attention to books and other monographs. Arranged topically in eight sections: General (philosophy, research, etc.), Systems and institutions, Teaching and learning, Students, Staff, Student assessment and course evaluation, Continuing education, and Information technology and networks. Author and subject indexes in each issue, with cumulative indexes bound into the final issue of the year.   LB2331.R47

Encyclopedias

The encyclopedia of higher education / editors-in-chief, Burton R. Clark and Guy R. Neave. Oxford ; N.Y. : Pergamon, 1992. 4 v.   **CB236**

Contents: v. 1, National systems of higher education; v. 2–3, Analytical perspectives; v. 4, Academic disciplines and indexes.

Vol. 1 describes the national systems of 138 countries. Vols. 2–3 contain articles arranged in five sections: Higher education and society; Institutional fabric of higher education, with articles on such topics as adult education and agricultural universities; Governance, administration and finance; Faculty and students; Teaching, learning, and research; and Disciplinary perspectives, which examines higher education from the views of several academic disciplines. The final volume contains chapters on most major arts and sciences and medical science disciplines. Contributor, name, and subject indexes.   LB15.E49

The international encyclopedia of higher education / Asa S. Knowles, ed. in chief. San Francisco : Jossey-Bass, 1977. 10 v.   **CB237**

Contents: v. 1, Contents, contributors, acronyms, glossary; v. 2–9, [Entries] A–Z; v. 10, Indexes.

Represents the contributions of an international roster of scholars (listed with their positions in v. 1). Entries are presented in an alphabetical arrangement, but with some grouping of materials in order to "reduce duplication of data and give readers easier access to related subjects."—*Pref.* Types of entries may be broadly categorized as: (1) national systems of higher education; (2) topical essays; (3) fields of study; (4) educational associations; (5) research centers and institutes; (6) reports on higher education; (7) documentation centers. No biographical entries are included. Articles are signed and bibliographies are appended. Intended for the layman as well as the specialist, with basic information in each article meant to be understandable to the non-specialist. *See* and *see also* references in addition to the name and subject indexes in v. 10.   LB15.I57

International higher education : an encyclopedia / ed. by Philip G. Altbach. N.Y. : Garland, 1991. 2 v. (1165 p.) : ill. (Garland reference library of social science, v. 506).   **CB238**

Contents: v. 1, Topics; Regions and countries: Africa and Asia; v. 2, Regions and countries: Australia, Europe, Latin America, Middle East, and North America.

In two parts: a section of 15 essays on selected topics, and 52 chapters on higher education in individual countries or regions. Not comprehensive; countries treated include "the world's major nations and in some instances smaller countries that have seen some particularly significant developments in higher education." Similarly, the substantive essays are limited to "some of the more important topics relevant … everywhere." Authors are leading scholars who were given "considerable latitude to express their own views and interpretations."—*Introd.* Extensive bibliography.   LB15.I59

Directories

By country or region

International

Directory of higher education institutions / Commission of the European Communities. 1984– . Luxembourg : Office for Official Publications of the European Communities, 1984– .
                                                    CB239

At head of title: Higher education in the European Community.

Issued in cooperation with the Office for Cooperation in Education of the European Institute of Education and Social Policy.

Issued also in Danish, Dutch, French, German, Greek, and Italian.

Chapters for each country contain sections on the organization of education in that nation, admissions and registration, requirements for language of instruction, language courses, other courses, financial assistance and scholarships, entrance and residence regulations, and social aspects (e.g., advisory services, student employment, cost of living). Appendixes provide addresses of government agencies and universities, surveys of courses of study at specific universities, student statistics, bibliography of university publications, and a glossary.
                                                    L914.5.D58

International handbook of universities and other institutions of higher education. 2nd ed. (1962)– . Paris : International Assoc. of Universities, 1963– . Triennial.   **CB240**

Entries contain a basic description of each institution, as well as information about degrees offered; admissions; costs; names of high-ranking administrative officers and heads of major academic components; languages of instruction; academic year; and university publications. Arranged by country. Index of institutions.

§ Omits coverage of institutions in the U.S. and the Commonwealth, which are found in what can be considered its companion publications, *American universities and colleges* (CB248) and *Commonwealth universities yearbook* (CB319).   L900.I58

World list of universities = Liste mondiale des universités. 1st ed. (1974)– . Paris : International Association of Universities ; N.Y. : Stockton Press. Biennial.   **CB241**

In two parts: (1) a list, by country, of universities and other institutions of higher education, including, for some countries, national academic and student associations; (2) descriptions of international and regional organizations concerned with higher education. For universities and some organizations, entries have only addresses and phone numbers; some entries include fax, telex, or Easy Link numbers, plus lists of the institution's colleges. For other organizations substantial entries outline their history, aims, structure, and activities. Addresses are in the native language, explanatory text and descriptive materials in English and French.   L900.I57

Foreign study

Academic year abroad. 15th ed. (1986–87)– . N.Y. : Institute of International Education, c1986– . Annual.   **CB242**

Continues *The learning traveler* : v. 1, *U.S. college-sponsored programs abroad*.

Lists more than 2,000 programs, of which 75% are sponsored by accredited U.S. universities and colleges, the remainder by foreign universities, adult education centers, language schools, and other U.S. and foreign organizations. Arranged alphabetically by continent or region, then country. Five indexes: sponsoring institutions, consortia, fields of study, special options (such as courses for professionals), cost ranges.
                                                    LB2376.U46

Judkins, David. Study abroad : the astute student's guide. Charlotte, Vt. : Williamson Pub., c1989. 301 p. : ill.   **CB243**

Both a source of practical general advice and a guide to specific programs. The guide is arranged alphabetically by country or region, with information on passport and visa requirements, currency rates, degrees granted, accreditation, the kinds of credit available, class locations, language of instruction, whether foreign students take classes with nationals, subjects taught, housing, costs, financial aid, course loads, and facilities. An unusual section, Major players in study abroad, describes the programs of a small number of colleges and universities, consortia, and other organizations, such as the American Institute for Foreign Study. Index.   LB2376.J83

Vacation study abroad. 38th ed. (1988)– . N.Y. : Institute of International Education, c1987– . Annual.   **CB244**

Vol. 2 of the "Learning traveler" series. Subtitle (varies): the complete guide to summer and short-term study.

Continues: *The learning traveler. Vol. 2, Vacation study abroad* (34th ed. [1983]–37th ed. [1987]); *The learning traveler : vacation study abroad* (31st ed. [1980]–33rd ed. [1982]).

Describes summer programs lasting from one week to several months and short courses during the rest of the year, approximately 60% of which are sponsored by accredited U.S. colleges and universities, the rest by foreign universities, language schools, and other organizations. Includes programs that combine study with travel. Entries are brief, listing sponsoring organization, site, dates, subjects, eligibility, credit, language of instruction, format (lecture, field study, etc.), costs, housing, deadlines, contacts. Six indexes: sponsor, consortium, field of study, cost, duration, special options (e.g., adult courses, independent study).   LB2375.S8

United States

300 most selective colleges / College Research Group of Concord, Massachusetts. N.Y. : Arco : Distr. by Prentice Hall Trade, c1989. 499 p.   **CB245**

Provides the usual fare found in guides for prospective undergraduates (costs, school enrollment, programs of study, student life, and financial aid), but highlights data on selectivity by placing such considerations as percentage of applicants accepted, average SAT scores, and the institution's basis for selection (e.g., class rank, school recommendation, extracurricular activities) at the top of each entry.   L901.A12

Accredited institutions of postsecondary education, programs, candidates / publ. for the Council on Postsecondary Accreditation. 1976–77– . Wash. : American Council on Education, [1977]– . Annual.   **CB246**

Lists institutions accredited by the various national and regional accrediting agencies recognized by the Council on Postsecondary Accreditation. Includes more than 5,500 public and private two- and four-year colleges and vocational schools, including U.S.-sponsored institutions in 14 countries. Entries include date of first accreditation, accrediting agency, degrees offered, enrollment, branch campuses, etc.
                                                    L901.A48

Adler, Joe anne. Women's colleges / Joe anne Adler, Jennifer Adler Friedman. N.Y. : Prentice Hall : Arco, c1994. 299 p.
                                                    CB247

Describes "the 82 women's colleges in this nation" (*Foreword*), including junior colleges. Entries are several pages long, each with separate sections on Academics, Students and student life, Campus and community, and Admissions statement (which covers philosophies and acceptance criteria), plus a list of academic programs offered. An appendix lists required entrance examinations, application deadlines, costs, and percent of freshmen receiving financial aid.   LC1756.A17

American universities and colleges / produced in collaboration with the American Council on Education. N.Y. : W. deGruyter, 1928– .   **CB248**

Publ. quadrennially since 1928 (except 1944). Publisher varies.

The preeminent directory of American institutions of higher education. The 14th ed. (1992) describes more than 1,900 accredited schools offering baccalaureate or higher degrees. Its main section, arranged by state, presents narrative data for each college, covering its history, institutional structure and control, admissions and degree requirements, enrollment and degrees conferred, fees and financial arrangements, numbers of teachers in specific departments and degrees they hold, library collections, and student life (dormitories, intercollegiate athletics, car regulations, surrounding communities). Another section lists institutions offering professional degrees at baccalaureate, masters, and doctoral levels, arranged alphabetically by course of study. A beginning section presents survey articles on higher education in the U.S. Appendixes outline academic customs and ceremonies, list colleges with ROTC units, and provide statistical data on degrees conferred by American colleges, 1861–1986. Institutional index.

§ Companion publication: *American community, technical, and junior colleges* (N.Y.: American Council on Education/Macmillan; London : Collier Macmillan, 1984–).   LA226.A65

America's best colleges. 1989– . Wash.: U.S. News & World Report, c1988– . Annual.   **CB249**
1st ed., 1987.

Rates colleges in several categories: (1) the top 25 national universities; (2) the top 25 liberal arts colleges; (3) the best of the remaining national universities and liberal arts colleges; (4) the top regional liberal arts colleges; (5) the top three specialized schools in several fields (e.g., arts, engineering). Ratings are based on academic reputation, student selectivity, faculty, financial resources, and student satisfaction. Gives statistics for SAT/ACT scores, acceptance rates, faculty with doctorates, student-faculty ratio, spending per student, and graduation and student retention rates. Provides a directory of rated colleges that describes the undergraduate student body, degrees offered, most popular majors, faculty, admissions selectivity, expenses and percent receiving financial aid, and percent of graduates entering graduate or professional study. Index of colleges.   LB2331.63.A46

Barron's profiles of American colleges : descriptions of the colleges / comp. and ed. by the College Division of Barron's Educational Series. 18th ed. (1991)– . Hauppauge, N.Y. : Barron's Educational Series, Inc., 1991– . Annual.   **CB250**
1st ed., 1964. Publishing pattern varies.

A comprehensive guide to more than 1,550 American colleges and universities, including some Canadian and Mexican institutions and American-operated schools abroad. Substantial entries highlight data on enrollment, faculty, costs, curriculum, student activities, etc. One section, Index of college majors, was published separately as v. 2 from 1982–92. Arranged alphabetically by state; index of colleges.   L901.F5

Barron's top 50 : an inside look at America's best colleges / Tom Fischgrund, ed. 2nd ed. Hauppauge, N.Y. : Barron's, c1993. 682 p.   **CB251**
Attempts to show "what it is really like" (*Introd*) to attend each college, rather than focus on academic considerations. Recent graduates contribute profiles providing insider views of each school's philosophy of education, academic environment, and social activities and interaction. Schools selected for inclusion often differ from those selected by other listings of top institutions, the major criteria for inclusion being percent accepted, percent accepted who enroll, and SAT scores. Describes a larger proportion of small colleges than comparable lists.   L901.B34

Bear, John. College degrees by mail : 100 good schools that offer bachelor's, master's, doctorates, and law degrees by home study. Berkeley, Calif. : Ten Speed Pr., c1991. 212 p. : ill.   **CB252**
One-page entries provide information on degree levels available, accreditation, residency requirements, costs, fields of study, and specific characteristics of the program, such as materials used (e.g., videocassettes, syllabi), when students must be in residence, and time requirements. Introductory chapters cover topics such as how credits are awarded and how to investigate schools. An appendix lists 50 schools not included in this book, and why. General index and an index to *Bear's guide to earning degrees non-traditionally* (CB253).   L901.B35

———— Bear's guide to earning college degrees non-traditionally. 11th ed. [updated and corr.]. Benicia, Calif. : C & B Pub., c1993. 304 p.   **CB253**
1st ed., 1980. Title of other editions varied.

Entries cover a wide variety of programs offering credit and degrees for work and experiences outside a traditional classroom-based program. International in scope, although most institutions are in the U.S. or Canada. In 25 chapters, the largest containing brief entries for schools offering degrees, in sections for accredited and non-accredited institutions. Many of the chapters focus on specific forms of nontraditional education, such as correspondence study. Lists institutions omitted from this edition, with rationale for exclusion. Indexes of schools and of colleges with no or limited residency requirements.   L901.B37

Birnbach, Lisa. Lisa Birnbach's new and improved college book / Lisa Birnbach with Annette Geldzahler. Rev. and updated ed. N.Y. : Simon & Schuster, c1992. 681 p.   **CB254**
Emphasizes the social side of student life in a light, informal, entertaining vein. Describes only 210 institutions, including some small specialized colleges. Entries are several pages long and include students' ratings of the schools on such factors as food quality, interest in sex/dating/marriage, residence halls, etc.   L901.B53

Byrne, John A. A Business week guide : the best business schools / John A. Byrne with a team of Business week editors. 3rd ed. N.Y. : McGraw-Hill, c1993. 355 p. : ill.   **CB255**
For annotation, *see* CH76.   HF1131.B95

Campus-free college degrees. 5th ed. 1989– . Tulsa, Okla. : Thorson Guides, c1989– . Irregular.   **CB256**
Continues *Thorson's guide to campus-free college degrees.*

Information concerning bachelor, master, or doctorate degrees that can be earned with little or no time on campus. Lists schools offering college credit for correspondence study, life experiences, examination scores, military service, work-study experiences, and certificates or diplomas. One- or two-page entries describe degrees offered; residency requirements, if any; options for earning credit (e.g., on-campus classes, telenet courses, correspondence work from other intstitutions); how long programs take; etc. Additional sections on high school diploma programs and tests for credit by examination. Directory of colleges by state.   LC6251.C33

•**CASPAR** : Computer Aided Science Policy & Research Database System / developed by Quantum Research Corp [database]. [Bethesda, Md. : Quantum Research Corporation, 1993].   **CB257**
Developed for the National Science Foundation.
On CD-ROM.

Contains data collected by several federal agencies on American colleges and universities, 1966–91. In nine files pertaining primarily to resources and expenditures for science and engineering, but including data for other fields as well. Individual files cover development expenditures, federal support for higher education, demographics of graduate students in science and engineering, full-time workers in those fields, earned degrees, institutional enrollment, faculty salaries and benefits, financial statistics of institutions, and doctorate program ratings.

College blue book. N.Y. : Macmillan, 1972– .   **CB258**
A leading directory of American and Canadian colleges. In five volumes. Vol. 1, Narrative descriptions, provides information for some 3,000 institutions, with entries arranged by state or province. Vol. 2, Tabular data, outlines information such as costs, accreditation, enrollment, and faculty characteristics; it also gives the names of college presidents, registrars, and admissions officers. Vol. 3 is in two parts: Degrees offered by college, which lists for each school the majors it offers; Degrees offered by subject provides a list of all majors offered, showing which schools offer each major. All three volumes have indexes by institution; v. 2 also includes indexes of intercollegiate athletics and of professional accreditation.

See separate entries for v. 4, *Occupational education* (CB297) and v. 5, *Scholarships, fellowships, grants, and loans* (CB393).
                                                                    LA226.C685

College Entrance Examination Board. College Scholarship Service. The college cost book. 1980/81–1993. N.Y. : College Entrance Examination Board, College Scholarship Service. Annual.   **CB259**

Issues for 1982/83–1993 also called 3rd–13th ed.

Continues *Student expenses at postsecondary institutions*, 1974/75–1979/80.

Estimates costs and describes availability of financial aid at 2,800 colleges, junior colleges, and technical schools. Lists, for each institution, cost of tuition, books and supplies, room and board, transportation, etc. Also lists colleges offering scholarships, with separate sections for assistance to music and drama majors, art students, and athletes (by sport). Another section lists schools offering fee waiver, deferred payments, or credit card payments, and special plans for adult students, minority students, and children of alumni. Alphabetical index of colleges.

Continued by the College Scholarship Service's *College costs and financial aid handbook* (14th ed. [1994]– . N.Y., 1993– . Annual).
                                                                    LB2342.C633a

•**College explorer** [database]. N.Y. : College Entrance Examination Board, 1990– .   **CB260**

Available on diskettes in MS-DOS and Apple II versions. Updated annually.

A college guide describing two- and four-year American institutions.

The college handbook. 1941– . N.Y. : College Entrance Examination Board. Annual.   **CB261**

Some annuals called *Annual handbook : terms of admission to the colleges.*

Subtitle from cover: The College Board's official guide to 3,200 two- and four-year colleges, including campus setting, majors and academic programs, admissions requirements and selection criteria, tuition and fees, financial aid, student life, athletics.

Frequency varies; biennial prior to 1980.

In two main sections: (1) College indexes, which list schools by type, including junior and community colleges, bible colleges, historically black institutions, schools with military programs, small urban colleges, institutions with special admissions programs, etc.; (2) College descriptions, with detailed entries describing the characteristics of individual institutions. Index of institutions.   LB2351.A1C6

The college handbook for transfer students. 1990– . N.Y. : College Entrance Examination Board, 1990– . Annual.
                                                                    CB262

Designed to provide information needed by students planning to transfer from, as well as into, specific two-year and four-year colleges. Among considerations treated are whether the school has a two-year transfer program, at which levels transfers are accepted (e.g., first semester sophomores), whether one has to have been in good standing at the first institution to be accepted at the second, and the percentage of a two-year college's graduates who enter four-year programs. A separate section gives tips and general information about transferring.
                                                                    L901.C7438

The college media directory. 7th ed. (1989)– . [New York] : Oxbridge Communications, Inc., c1989– .   **CB263**

Vol. 1 (1967)–6 (1986) had title: *Directory of the college student press in America.*

Lists student and alumni publications at North American colleges, including newspapers, newsletters, yearbooks, alumni magazines, and literary magazines. Entries give type of publication (e.g., newspaper), circulation, kinds of articles, advertising rates, and the availability of colored ads. Identifies college radio stations, law journals, college advertising, alumni associations, and alumni and college publications that accept advertising.   Z6944.S8D57

The common-sense guide to American colleges. 1991/1992– . Lanham [Md.] : Madison Books, c1991– . Biennial.
                                                                    CB264

Surveys 60 widely varied institutions–large and small, public and private, religious and secular. Expresses judgments based on the editors' stated bias toward traditional American values, such as "excellence" and "achievement," rather than "left of center politically correct attitutdes"—*Introd.* Focuses on undergraduate liberal arts education; evaluates the institutions' social and ethical climate.   L901.C8124

Comparative guide to American colleges for students, parents, and counselors. 1st ed.– . N.Y. : Harper & Row, c1964– . Biennial (1973–).   **CB265**

J. Cass and M. Birnbaum, editors.

Emphasizes career-oriented considerations of college selection, with special attention to career counseling and job placement programs, and a Selectivity index categorizing colleges according to their students' academic potential as suggested by SAT and ACT scores, ranks in high school classes, etc. A Graduate career data section tells percentages of institutions' graduates going immediately to graduate and professional schools, and which of these they attend most frequently, plus the percentages of graduates pursuing business careers. Also lists each college conferring degrees in a given field and the number of its students majoring in that field. The 1,500 schools described are all regionally accredited institutions conferring the baccalaureate degree.   L901.C819

Consortium directory. [1st ed.] (1967)– . [University, Ala., etc.] : Council for Interinstitutional Leadership [etc.], [1973?]– . Annual.   **CB266**

Until 1973, issued by American Association for Higher Education.

Describes academic consortia of 1,400 institutions. Alphabetically arranged entries give addresses, names of member institutions, descriptions of purposes, major activities, governance, funding, and operating budgets. Three indexes: (1) Topical index, listing consortia by type of activity (e.g., fund-raising, film library, government liaison), (2) College and university index, (3) Geographic index.   L901.C83

Directory of curriculum materials centers. 2nd ed. (1981)– . Chicago : A.C.R.L., E.B.S.S., 1981– . Irregular.
                                                                    CB267

Publisher varies. 1st issue publ. by A.C.R.L. (1985) also called 2nd ed.

Three major parts: centers in the U.S., centers in Canada, and centers incorporated into main library collections. Main section, arranged by state, lists only names and addresses, hours, and centers' purposes, with more detailed data on holdings, finances, etc., in foldout tables at the end of the book. Not comprehensive, with responses from 272 of 725 institutions surveyed. Name and institution indexes.
                                                                    LB3044.72.D57

Directory of postsecondary institutions / [Center for Education Statistics]. 1986– . Wash. : Office of Education Research and Improvement : for sale by the U.S. Govt. Print. Off., [1987]– . Biennial.   **CB268**

Superintendent of Documents classification: ED 1.310/2: .

Continues *Education directory : colleges & universities.*

Distributed to depository libraries in microfiche. Issued since 1988 by the National Center for Educational Statistics.

In two volumes: v. 1 covers two- and four-year institutions; v. 2, institutions less than two-year.

"A comprehensive listing of the 10,144 postsecondary institutions known to be in operation in the United States, the District of Columbia, and the outlying areas …."—*Foreword, 1991–92.* Skeletal entries, arranged by state, give addresses, enrollment, programs, highest offerings, availability of dormitories, room costs, tuition, accreditation, and control. Appendixes list institutional changes since the previous edition: additions and deletions, schools no longer accredited, new names, and mergers.   L901.E34

English language and orientation programs in the United States. 1964– . [New York] : Institute of International Education, 1964– . Triennial.   **CB269**
For annotation, *see* CB161.   PE1068.U5E53

The Fiske guide to colleges / by Edward B. Fiske …[et al.]. 1989– . N.Y. : Times Books, c1988– . Annual.   **CB270**
Continues as an expanded and updated version of: *Selective guide to colleges* (1983–88).
Selective, describing 317 schools which are "the best and most interesting… the ones that students want to know about."—*Introd.* Ratings, which are "obviously general in nature and inherently subjective," on Academics, Social life, and Quality of life. Also ventures judgments on institutions' academic climates and their stronger and weaker programs. A special section, "quality liberal arts at a public school price," describes 14 colleges considered to provide this in a "manageable setting."   L901.N48

The GIS guide to four-year colleges / by the editors of the Guidance Information System. 1989– . Boston : Houghton Mifflin Co., 1988– . Annual.   **CB271**
For more than 1,500 colleges, gives the usual information on programs of study, admissions, campus life, etc., but adds three unusual features: (1) comments by students of some colleges (2) "Express access," which permits tabular comparison of colleges by setting, size, type, cost, selectivity, etc.; (3) lists that rank institutions by various criteria ("most intense academics," "most underrated," "most politically active." etc.). Includes list of majors.   L901.G5

HEP higher education directory. 1983– . Wash. : Higher Education Publishers, 1983– . Annual.   **CB272**
Lists accredited institutions of postsecondary education, Entries are arranged alphabetically by state and include address, phone number, date established, affiliation, highest degree offered, program, undergraduate tuition and fees, calendar system, accreditation, and administrative officers. Provides lists of agencies, associations and consortia of higher education. Includes junior and community colleges and technical institutes as well as four-year colleges. Separate listings of U.S. service schools, colleges in the territories, institutions by religious affiliation, consortia, and schools recognized by various accrediting groups. Indexes to key administrators and to institutions according to accrediting body.   L901.E34

Index of majors and graduate degrees. 15th ed. (1993) . N.Y. : College Entrance Examination Board, c1992– . Annual.   **CB273**
Supersedes *Index of majors*, publ. 1979–92.
Directory of colleges offering specific majors at bachelors, master, doctoral, professional, associate, and certificate levels. Lists of institutions and the degree levels offered for each major are arranged alphabetically by major, then by state. A section on specialized academic programs lists schools that offer cooperative education, dual majors, independent study, study abroad, etc. Index of colleges.   L901.C744

The insiders' guide to the colleges. [1st] (1970)– . [New York] : St. Martin's Pr., 1970– . Annual.   **CB274**
Title varies slightly.
"Attempts to provide a snapshot of life at more than 300 colleges and universities in the U.S. and Canada, relying on the opinions of students."—*Pref.* Emphasizes the institutions's ambience (e.g., academic atmosphere, interaction with professors, social life, etc.), relegating the usual information on tuition, enrollment, etc., to less prominence. Selection was based primarily on the quality of curricula or students; includes a broad range of large universities (mostly state-affiliated) and small colleges, and some technical isntitutes and specialty schools. Entries are arranged by state and typically contain two or three pages of text.   L901.I54

Lederman, Ellen. College majors : a complete guide from accounting to zoology. Jefferson, N.C. : McFarland, c1990. 122 p.   **CB275**
Describes college-level majors based on the Taxonomy and Clas-

sification of Instructional Programs in Higher Education of the Higher Education General Information Survey. Each major includes definition, degree levels offered, typical courses, related or complementary majors, needed abilities, and career possibilities.   LB2390.L43

Lovejoy's college guide. 1940– . N.Y. : Simon & Schuster, 1940– . Irregular.   **CB276**
Title varies: 1940–41, *So you're going to college*; 1948–50/51, *Complete guide to American colleges and universities*.
Publisher varies; editor varies.
Presents concise, but substantial, information on four-year colleges and two-year institutions (those having residential facilities) in the U.S., its territories, and several foreign countries. For nonresidential two-year schools and technical institutes, provides addresses and phone numbers only. The main section, with entries for colleges arranged by state, lists all majors offered by each school, each college's most popular majors, information on freshman admissions and transfer requirements, percent accepted and average SAT scores, specialized facilities such as museums and computer labs, and such indexes of student life as student organizations, percent of students that are natives of other countries, and percent receiving financial aid. Other lists include Curricula (specific majors and special programs such as dual majors and early admissions) and colleges offering specific intercollegiate sports or athletic scholarships. Index of college names.
                    LA226.L6

The Macmillan guide to correspondence study / comp. and ed. by Modoc Press, Inc. 4th ed. N.Y. : Macmillan ; Toronto : Collier Macmillan Canada, 1990. 676 p.   **CB277**
For annotation, *see* CB103.   L901.M26

Moll, Richard. The public ivys : a guide to America's best public undergraduate colleges and universities. N.Y. : Viking, 1985. 289 p. : ill.   **CB278**
Detailed information on fifteen of what the author considers the nation's best public colleges, plus nine of "the best of the rest," with each institution described in a separate chapter.   L901.M63 1985

The National review college guide : America's top liberal arts schools / ed. by Charles J. Sykes and Brad Miner ; introduction by William F. Buckley, Jr. Rev. and updated. N.Y. : Simon & Schuster, c1993. 270 p. : ill.   **CB279**
Decrying the "lowering of admission standards" and "debasing of curricula," the editors find 58 "fine schools (big and small, urban and rural, religious and secular) that still educate students in the liberal arts tradition … designed to graduate well-rounded scholar citizens."—*Pref.* Describes less-well-known colleges such as Asbury and Millsaps while not recommending highly-rated institutions such as Harvard, Duke, and Smith. Criteria for approval are quality and accessibility of faculty, quality of curriculum, "with special regard for schools with a liberal arts 'core' that respects the tradition of the West," and quality of intellectual environment.
The main section consists of entries several pages in length that emphasize academic atmospheres and philosophies (sometimes including detailed descriptions of core curricula), with only brief outlines of such considerations as costs, enrollment, and application deadlines. A section called "The academic gulag" criticizes a small number of famous but not recommended institutions.   L901.N3485

Ohles, John F. Private colleges and universities / John F. Ohles and Shirley M. Ohles. Westport, Conn. : Greenwood, [1982]. 2 v. (1619 p.). (Greenwood encyclopedia of American institutions, 6).   **CB280**
Offers "institutional sketches of 1,291 American private colleges and universities listed in 1977–78 directories published through the U.S. Department of Education and Marquis Educational Media."—*Introd.* Gives historical information and institutional profile. Bibliographical references at the end of many articles; indexed.   L901.O33

—————— Public colleges and universities / John F. Ohles and Shirley M. Ohles. N.Y. : Greenwood, c1986. 1014 p. (The Greenwood encyclopedia of American institutions , 9). **CB281**

A companion to the compilers' *Private colleges and universities* (CB280). Provides sketches of 547 public colleges and universities and 31 state systems of higher education, based on information gleaned from a survey. Alphabetical arrangement by institution with cross-references. References follow each entry. Appendixes: Years founded, Location by states, Land-grant institutions, Specialized institutions. Indexes of personal and institutional names.   L901.O333

Patterson's schools classified. 1951–1993. North Chicago, Ill. : Educational Directories, 1951–1993.   **CB282**

Imprint varies.

Lists some 7,000 accredited postsecondary schools, including colleges and universities, junior colleges, career schools, teaching hospitals, preparatory schools, schools for persons with handicaps, and home study institutions. Entries give addresses and names of contacts; some contain brief descriptions. Arranged by academic classifications, including majors offered and such broader categories as women's colleges. Index arranged by type of institution.

Absorbed by *Patterson's American education*, CB104.

L901.P35

●**Peterson's college database** [database]. Princeton, N.J. : Peterson's Guides.   **CB283**

Online version of *Peterson's guide to four-year colleges* (CB286) and *Peterson's guide to two-year colleges* (CB298). Updated annually.

Also called *Peterson's undergraduate database*.

Describes some 3,400 U.S. and Canadian undergraduate institutions, providing complete statistical information on costs, financial aid, student enrollment, etc., as well as detailed directory information. Information available for each institution varies somewhat.

Peterson's college selection service [database] (1986– . Annual) is a distilled version of the larger database. Its purpose is to assist in college selection, using various parameters such as cost, majors offered, etc. Available in DOS and MacIntosh versions, updated annually.

Peterson's competitive colleges. 3rd ed. (1984)– . Princeton, N.J. : Peterson's Guides, c1984– . Annual.   **CB284**

Continues *Competitive colleges*.

Describes "the 359 colleges and universities with the highest proportion of incoming freshmen who come from the high achieving group … ."—*What is a Competitive College?* One-page entries include sections on applying, academic programs (including unusual curricula), college life, housing, career planning (including the number of corporations recruiting on campus). Provides data on the school's latest freshman class, including percent of applicants accepted, percent from the top tenth of their high school classes, average high school grade point average. Index of majors; specialized lists of colleges costing $7,000 per year or less, reporting 50% or more need-based financial aid recipients, accepting fewer than half of their applicants, and graduating more than 70% of their students.   LB2351.2.C663

Peterson's guide to certificate programs at American colleges and universities / editors, George J. Lopos … [et al.]. Princeton, N.J. : Peterson's Guides, c1988. 343 p.   **CB285**

Developed in cooperation with the National University Continuing Education Association (NUCEA).

Describes specialized programs at four-year institutions of higher education, leading to professional and occupational certificates. Arranged alphabetically by state, with programs listed by institution, giving for each entry: contact personnel, costs, program, and enrollment requirements. Institutional index; index by program classification (e.g., management science).   L901.P4577

Peterson's guide to four-year colleges. 19th ed. (1989)– . Princeton, N.J. : Peterson's Guides, c1988– . Annual. **CB286**

Formerly issued as *Peterson's annual guide to undergraduate study*.

In two major sections: (1) half-page entries for some 2,000 institutions, with details of enrollment, admission requirements, expenses, housing, student aid, and programs offered; (2) two-page in-depth descriptions of more than 800 institutions, prepared by their officials, which emphasize campus environment, student activities, and lifestyle. Indexes: major, entrance difficulty, cost, and name of institution.

●Available online as part of *Peterson's college database* (CB283), which also contains its companion, *Peterson's guide to two-year colleges* (CB298). Selected information also available through *Peterson's college selection service* (CB283 note).   L901.P447

Peterson's national college databank : the college book of lists. 6th ed. Princeton, N.J. : Peterson's Guides, c1993. 520 p. **CB287**

1st ed., 1979; 5th ed., 1990.

Lists of colleges and universities, arranged in broad sections by specific characteristics such as campus life, expenses, and entrance difficulty. Each section contains a number of lists on narrower topics (e.g., colleges with tuition prepayment plans, colleges requiring chapel attendance). The appendix provides a geographical list (by state) of colleges offering work opportunities to undergraduates.   L901.N295

Peterson's register of higher education. 3rd ed. (1990)– . Princeton, N.J. : Peterson's Guides, c1989– . Annual. **CB288**

"Covers all institutions of higher education in the United States… and U.S. territories… accredited to grant postsecondary degrees."—*Introd*. Arranged alphabetically by institution; brief entries provide not only the usual data on tuition, enrollment, and similar concerns, but also, e.g., information on computer facilities and names of affiliated research organizations and of such personnel as deans and development officers. Appendixes list major government higher education agencies, accrediting bodies, associations, and consortia, and another section lists recent institutional changes such as newly-adopted college names and school closings. Indexes of major academic units and their parent institutions (e.g., Medill School of Journalism, Northwestern University), personal names, specialized and professional accreditation (by subject), and institutions, arranged by state.   L901.P47

The right college. [1st ed.] (1988)– . N.Y. : Arco/Prentice Hall Pr., c1987– . Annual.   **CB289**

Comp. by College Research Group of Concord, Massachusetts.

Entries for 1,500 schools contain information on: costs; enrollment; selectivity; faculty; religious orientation; library, museum, athletic, and computer facilities; student body composition; undergraduate achievement; study programs; most popular majors. A special section lists minors offered, experimental programs, dual degrees, double majors, programs conducted in conjunction with other universities, exchange programs, and accelerated study. A Student life section treats student organizations, percentage of students joining fraternities, handicapped student services, etc. Excludes: colleges with fewer than 1,000 students; vocational and technical schools; business schools; religious colleges and seminaries.

The compact right college (1990/91–) "distills the most pertinent and essential information available on 350 of the nation's most recognizable and prestigious undergraduate colleges and universities."—*Introd*.   L901.R535

Sherrill, Jan-Mitchell. The gay, lesbian, and bisexual students' guide to colleges, universities, and graduate schools / Jan-Mitchell Sherrill and Craig A. Hardesty. N.Y. : N.Y.U. Pr., c1994. 279 p.   **CB290**

Based on descriptions and evaluations by 1,464 gay, lesbian, and bisexual undergraduate, graduate, and professional school students at 189 American colleges and universities. Considers only the campus's social climate with regard to this population; does not provide information on majors, admissions, fees, and other traditional college guide topics. Institutional entries estimate the number of homosexuals enrolled, describe administration positions on gays and responses to incidents involving them, and assesses attitudes and beliefs of heterosexual students. Also describes campus committees handling gay issues, homosexual groups on campus, courses pertaining to gays, and the availability of counseling for homosexuals. Arranged by institution name; index of colleges.   LC192.6.S54

Solórzano, Lucia. Barron's 300 best buys in college education. N.Y. : Barron's, c1990. 658 p.   **CB291**

Describes "schools that breach the supposed link between college price and college quality" that "run the gamut from sprawling state universities of more than 20,000 undergraduates to private colleges whose enrollments seem more like extended families."—*Introd.* Includes colleges sufficiently expensive to "stretch the definition of a 'best buy' " until one looks at what others of similar quality are charging. Two-page entries are arranged by state; alphabetical index of colleges.   L901.S567

Songe, Alice H. American universities and colleges : a dictionary of name changes. Metuchen, N.J. : Scarecrow, 1978. 264 p.   **CB292**

Records name changes undergone by 1,120 four-year colleges and universities, listed alphabetically. Includes colleges that have closed; an appendix gives locations of defunct institutions' records. Useful despite its publication date, which precludes inclusion of recent changes.   L901.S57

The student access guide to the best ... colleges / The Princeton Review. 1992 ed.– . N.Y. : Villard Books, 1992– .   **CB293**

Number of colleges described is included in title; i.e., 286 colleges for 1994 ed., 306 colleges for 1995 ed.

Frequency varies.

Provides qualitative information on such considerations as quality of life (represented by a numerical rating), number of hours per day the average student studies, and whether professors are interesting and accessible. Much of this information came from consultation with 55 independent counselors nationwide. Entries, organized by college name, are systematically arranged on facing pages containing sections on academics, college life, students, admissions, costs, and financial aid. Also has statistics for male/female ratios, academic ratings, most popular majors, and competitiveness of admissions. Index of schools by state.   LB2350.5sS8

Wilcha, Jennifer. The college student's guide to transferring schools : the hows, whens, and whys of switching colleges / Jennifer Wilcha & David A. Smith. N.Y. : Avon Books, c1990. 229 p. : ill.   **CB294**

Mostly a book of practical advice, but an appendix provides college profiles with names, addresses, and phone numbers of admissions directors and transfer coordinators, statistics on transfer applications and acceptances, and number of articulation agreements with other colleges. Also provides information on required residency, whether mid-year transfers are permitted, minimum grade point averages required, and application deadlines. General index.   LB2360.W55

Junior and community colleges; Technical schools

American trade schools directory. 1st ed. (1953)– . Queens Village, N.Y. : Croner Publications, 1953– .   **CB295**

Looseleaf; updated monthly.

A directory of trade, technical, and vocational schools, designed for use by guidance counselors and training advisors, as well as prospective students. Comprehensive, with brief entries for thousands of public and private institutions that provide training in more than 300 occupational categories. Includes nonacademic programs at two- and four-year colleges, business schools, and a number of apprenticeship programs. Entries give contact information, accreditation, and occupational codes. Organized alphabetically by state, with an index by occupational code.   T73.A78

A directory of public vocational-technical schools and institutes in the U.S.A. 2nd ed. (1984–85)– . Mankato, Minn. : Minnesota Scholarly Pr., c1984– . Biennial.   **CB296**

Editor: 1984–85– , M. Johnston.

Arranged by state; entries for institutions list majors offered (e.g., photography, construction technology, real estate). Includes junior and community colleges. Indexes by school and by major.   T73.D58

Occupational education. 1972– . N.Y. : Macmillan, 1972– . Irregular.   **CB297**

Issued as the fourth volume of *The college blue book* (CB258).

Lists some 8,000 business, trade, and technical schools. Short entries provide addresses and information on entrance requirements, tuition, enrollment, accreditation, availability of financial aid, placement services, curricula, and program length. A Curricula and programs of instruction section lists institutions by majors offered.   L901.O3

Peterson's guide to two-year colleges. 19th ed. (1989)– . Princeton, N.J. : Peterson's Guides, 1988– . Annual.   **CB298**

Cover title: *Peterson's two-year colleges.*

Previous editions (with its companion guide to four-year colleges) had title: *Peterson's annual guide to undergraduate study.*

Describes 1,400 accredited institutions in the U.S. and its territories awarding the associate degree as their most popular undergraduate offering, plus some non-degree-granting schools. The latter are usually branch campuses of multi-campus systems that offer the first two years of college, transferrable to degree-granting institutions. In addition to the usual information on admission and graduation requirements, programs, costs, etc., treats considerations peculiar to junior colleges, giving advice on profiting from two-year colleges and transferring to four-year schools, statistics on students transferring from individual colleges, and a list by major of colleges offering associate degree programs.

•Available online as part of *Peterson's college database* (CB283), which also contains its companion, *Peterson's guide to four-year colleges* (CB286). Selected information also available through *Peterson's college selection service* (CB283 note).   L901.P448

Graduate schools

Doughty, Harold R. Guide to American graduate schools. 6th ed., completely rev. N.Y. : Penguin Books, 1990. 624 p.   **CB299**

1st ed. 1967; 5th ed., 1986. Compiler varies.

Entries for more than 1,100 institutions providing graduate and professional study in liberal arts and sciences, education, medicine, dentistry, pharmacy, nursing, law, social work, agriculture, theology, applied arts, engineering, and business. Gives information on admission and degree standards and requirements, number of faculty and students, tuition, financial aid, and housing facilities. Indexes of institutions by state and by field of study.   L901.D65

Innovative graduate programs directory. Aug. 1975– . [Saratoga Springs, N.Y.] : Empire State College, [1975]– .   **CB300**

Developed for adult learners who seek full- or part-time nontraditional education. Programs typically feature: student participation in curriculum planning, time flexibility, or emphasis on independent, individualized, or experiential learning. Most are offered by traditional campus-based institutions, but noncollegiate organizations are also listed. Entries describe majors, accreditation, residency requirements, work assignments, philosophical bases, and unique characteristics.   L901.I53

The official GRE/CGS directory of graduate programs. 13th ed.– . Princeton, N.J. : Educational Testing Service, 1991– . Biennial.   **CB301**

Title varies.

Issued in four volumes: A, Natural sciences; B, Engineering, business; C, Social sciences, education; D, Arts, humanities, other fields.

Contains not only the usual fare on admissions, costs, programs, enrollment, and degree requirements, but also information on research affiliates and cooperative programs, students' average GRE scores, and scientific research and computer facilities. Each volume in four main sections: Program information and Institution information, both consisting of charts outlining basic data on the individual colleges; Narratives, with more detailed descriptions; and Addresses, which includes contact information for assistantships, housing, etc. L901.G72

Peterson's annual guides to graduate study. 1984– . Princeton, N.J. : Peterson's Guides, 1983– . Annual. **CB302**
   Continues *The annual guides to graduate study* (title varies).
   Issued in six books (titles vary slightly): v. 1, Peterson's guide to graduate and professional programs: an overview; v. 2, graduate programs in the humanities and social sciences; v. 3, graduate programs in the biological and agricultural sciences; v. 4, graduate programs in the physical sciences and mathematics; v. 5, graduate programs in engineering and applied sciences; v. 6, graduate programs in business, education, health, and law.
   The institutional profiles appearing in the first volume provide basic information about colleges and universities in the United States, Canada, and American territories offering graduate work; that volume serves both as a basic reference source and as foundation for the other volumes in the series. Its Essays section provides in-depth description of the programs, including such details as names and phone numbers of department heads. The other volumes describe programs of institutions offering degrees in each field, as well as listing faculty members and their research interests. Describes some 300 disciplines at 1,500 accredited institutions.
   •Available in machine readable form: *Peterson's gradline* [database] (1990– . Annual). L901.P46

Religious and ethnic education

The black student's guide to college success / ed. by Ruby D. Higgins ... [et al.]. Westport, Conn. : Greenwood, 1993. 357 p. **CB303**
   Both a directory of colleges and a source of advice aimed specifically at African-American students. In three parts: "How to succeed in college" (with chapters such as "Getting along with non-blacks on campus," and "Should I choose a black college or an integrated college?"); a section of autobiographical success stories; and the directory, which has sections for the top ten historically and predominantly black institutions, for other black schools, for the most prestigious undergraduate institutions, for major universities and colleges in the U.S., and for universities in Africa, Central America, and the Caribbean. Index of institutions. LC2781.B4656

Bowman, J. Wilson. America's black colleges. South Pasadena, Calif. : Sandcastle Pub., c1992. 242 p. **CB304**
   Describes the nation's 100 four-year colleges and universities that are historically or predominantly black. Two-page entries, arranged alphabetically by state, give the schools' addresses and telephone numbers, and profile their histories and purposes, locations and available transportation, fees, degrees and majors offered, enrollment, housing, and student/faculty ratios. Appendixes list institutions supported by the United Negro College Fund, schools conferring doctorates, and church-related colleges. Index by name of institution. L901.B73

Directory of Catholic colleges and universities. 1991– . Decatur, Ga. : Kilkenny Pr., 1992– . **CB305**
   Publisher varies.
   Two-page entries for two- and four-year American Catholic schools are arranged alphabetically by state, then by college. Entries include the usual information on tuition, room and board, application deadlines and fees, and admission requirements; for each institution a paragraph describes its history, major goals, and academic programs. Other data provided include percentages of out-of-state students, non-Catholics, and male students; availability of student loans, employment, and scholarships, and percent of the student body receiving such aid; grade point averages and SAT and ACT scores of enrollees; percentage of applicants accepted and of acceptees enrolling; activities; and housing. Index of majors. LC501.D57

Goldberg, Lee. The Jewish student's guide to American colleges / by Lee and Lana Goldberg. N.Y. : Shapolsky Publ., 1989. 221 p. : ill. **CB306**
   Designed to meet the needs of Jewish students, emphasizing such concerns as how many Jewish students attend, the availability of kosher food, nearby synagogues, and social and religious programs for such students. Describes only 93 secular colleges with superior reputations. Entries are alphabetically arranged by institution and are typically two pages in length. LB2350.5.G65

Historically black colleges and universities fact book / Division of Black American Affairs, U.S. Dept. of Health and Human Services. Wash. : The Division, 1983. 3 v. **CB307**
   Superintendent of Documents classification: HE 1.2:B 56/v.– .
   Contents: v. 1, Junior and community colleges; v. 2, Private colleges/graduate schools; v. 3, Public colleges/graduate schools.
   Based on Department of Health and Human Services data on 107 institutions, supplemented by a questionnaire. Separate sections on each college outline its history, mission, curricula, degrees conferred, faculty, facilities, community involvement, and plans for the future, including new courses and research. L901.H557 1983

•**Minority on-line information service** : [MOLIS] [database]. Gaithersburg, Md. : Federal Information Exchange. **CB308**
   Provides full-text information on minority colleges and universities, describing their academic programs, faculty, student bodies, and research and other facilities.
   User's guide available (Gaithersburg, Md. : Federal Information Exchange, 1993. 34 p.).

Mitchell, Robert. The multicultural student's guide to colleges : what every African-American, Asian-American, Hispanic, and Native-American applicant needs to know about America's top schools. N.Y. : Farrar, Straus & Giroux, 1993. 839 p. : ill. **CB309**
   Multipage essays examine 200 colleges, describing the degree to which each is socially segregated, how administrations respond to incidents of racism, political activism, and level of interaction between different cultural groups. Includes statistics on student enrollment by race, retention rates of nonwhite students, ethnic studies programs and courses, and organizations for nonwhites. L901.M58

Wilson, Erlene B. The 100 best colleges for African-American students. N.Y. : Plume, c1993. 326 p. **CB310**
   Assesses campus social environments and academic resources for African-American students, based on a detailed survey of student representatives assigned by each college. Multi-page entries report on such considerations as race relations on and off campus, including racially motivated incidents and the way the administration handled them, cultural resources in the community for African-American students, campus programs, African-American fraternities and sororities, and percentages of students and faculty that are African-American. L901.W58

Education for persons with disabilities

Directory of college facilities and services for people with disabilities / ed. by Carol H. Thomas and James L. Thomas. 3rd ed. Phoenix : Oryx, 1991. 361 p. **CB311**
   1st ed., 1983, called *Directory of college facilities and services for the handicapped*.
   Compiled "to serve as a basic guide for disabled individuals and for high school and college counselors who seek to assist the population in locating postsecondary educational opportunities."—*Introd., 1983 ed.*. Provides an overview of more than 1,600 programs and services in the U.S. and Canada. Includes information on special services, auxiliary aids, and access, plus demographic data on the institutions, degree or certificate granted, information on the physical terrain and names of resource persons. Includes an alphabetical list of colleges and

universities, an index of disabilities, and lists of organizations, clearinghouses and databases, printed sources, and grant programs. Indexed.   LC4812.6.D57

A guide to colleges for learning disabled students / [ed. by] Mary Ann Liscio. Rev. ed. Orlando : Academic Pr., 1986. 423 p.   **CB312**

  1st ed., 1980.

  Gives information on special testing requirements for admission; special services offered, such as diagnostic testing; remedial and tutorial help available; reader services; learning laboratories; and availability of learning disabilities specialists. Also lists modifications to the traditional learning environment, such as oral presentations instead of written examinations, permission to use calculators, adaptive physical education, use of tapes to record lectures, and longer time allowed to complete examinations.   L901.G843

Kravets, Marybeth. The K & W guide to colleges for the learning disabled : a resource book for students, parents, and professionals / Marybeth Kravets, Imy F. Wax. 2nd ed. N. Y. : HarperPerennial, 1993. 459 p.   **CB313**

  1st ed., 1991, was a rev. ed. of *The K & W guide, colleges and the learning disabled student.*

  Describes 150 American universities, junior colleges, and community colleges of special importance to students with learning disabilities. Allots two pages per institution in uniform format of 66 brief items covering, e.g., special programs and services, special preadmission testing required, tutorial help given, and whether oral examinations are permitted. Not comprehensive; colleges offering only minimal services and those not providing room and board are excluded, hence some with exemplary programs are omitted, but these are represented in a Quick reference list of one-line entries giving names of contacts, phone numbers, and program titles. School name index.
                                              L901.K73

Lovejoy's college guide for the learning disabled. 1st ed.– . N.Y. : Prentice-Hall, 1985– .   **CB314**

  Publ. by Monarch Pr., 1985–93.

  In addition to the usual information found in college guides, contains materials of special interest to persons with learning disabilities, such as special admission criteria, remedial and tutorial services, learning centers, permission to use tape recorders in the classroom, and the possibility of lighter course loads. Several chapters of special advice for learning-disabled students and their parents.   L901.L69

Peterson's guide to colleges with programs for learning-disabled students / Charles T. Mangrum II and Stephen S. Strichart, editors. 2nd ed. Princeton, N.J. : Peterson's Guides, c1988. 398 p. : ill.   **CB315**

  "Differentiates between colleges with specially designed programs for learning-disabled students and colleges that offer services that are available to LD students but that are not specifically designed for them."—*Foreword.* Includes two-year and four-year colleges in one alphabetical list of "Colleges with comprehensive programs." Contains a step-by-step guide to selecting a college for a learning-disabled student. Has a geographical index to listed colleges and a directory of organizations with additional information on programs and services for learning-disabled students.   L901.P458

Education for foreign nationals

The college handbook. Foreign student supplement. 1987–88– . N.Y. : College Entrance Examination Board, c1987– . Annual.   **CB316**

  Intended for foreign students considering higher education in the U.S. In separate sections for undergraduate and graduate education, each of 3,100 accredited institutions (including junior colleges) occupies a single line of data that gives information on degrees, enrollment, tests and scores required for admission, application deadlines and fees, student services, tuition, and financial aid. Other sections list colleges offering conditional admission and telephone numbers of admission offices. An introductory section gives general information and advice.
                                              LB2376.4.C65

Howard, Edrice. Specialized study options U.S.A. 2nd ed. N.Y. : Inst. of International Education, c1986. 2 v. : map.
                                              CB317

  Contents: v. 1, Technical Education; v. 2, Professional development.

  Rev. ed. of: *Specialized study options U.S.A.*, ed. by Barbara Cahn Connotillo, 1986.

  Lists two-week to one-year courses either intended for or open to non-American students. Includes programs in nearly every field of study, with business and technical subjects most heavily represented. Within each volume arranged by subject, subdivided by institution. Entries provide information on specializations; dates; locations; instruction methods; eligibility, including language requirements; costs; housing; application deadlines; contact persons; and program hightlights. Each volume has indexes of sponsoring institutions, entries by state, and fields of study.   L901.C825

Europe

Boswick, Storm. Guide to the universities of Europe. N.Y. : Facts on File, c1991. 296 p.   **CB318**

  Arranged by country, with separate sections for western and eastern Europe. Provides information for foreign students on admission requirements, procedures, and deadlines; academic and degree requirements; accreditation; registration requirements; visa requirements and residence regulations; tuition and fees; living expenses; scholarships; and university calendars. Brief entries for individual colleges; for many countries, entries are preceded by a section on education for foreign students in that nation. Index.   L914.5.B67

Commonwealth universities yearbook. 1958– . London : Assoc. of Commonwealth Universities, 1958– . Annual.
                                              CB319

  "A directory of the universities of the Commonwealth and the handbook of their association"—*t. p.*

  Continues *Yearbook of the universities of the Empire* (1914–47) and *Yearbook of the universities of the Commonwealth* (1948–57).

  Issued in 4 pts., 1977/78– .

  Publication suspended 1941–46.

  Extensive information on individual universities, including names of faculty members, arranged alphabetically by country. For some nations, prefatory articles give information on admissions, programs, the academic calendar, etc. General, personal name, institution, and subject of study indexes; glossary of abbreviations of degrees.

                                              LB2310.Y5

European faculty directory. 1st ed. (1991)– . London : Gale Research International, 1991– . Annual.   **CB320**

  A listing of approximately 300,000 faculty in nearly 1,400 institutions of postsecondary education in Europe. Vol.1 contains a geographical arrangement of the colleges and universities, with addresses and phone numbers, and an alphabetical list of faculty with addresses; v. 2 arranges faculty according to 96 academic disciplines. Does not include the former Soviet Union, Bulgaria, Albania, and certain very small countries.   L914.5.E95

The students' guide to graduate studies in the UK / CRAC [Careers Research and Advisory Centre]. 1985– . Cambridge : CRAC, c1984– . Annual.   **CB321**

  A comprehensive work, with a main section in four parts: (1) Humanities and social sciences; (2) Biological, health, and agricultural sciences; (3) Physical sciences; and (4) Engineering and applied sciences. Within these sections are separate chapters for individual curricula, subdivided into higher degrees by research, higher degrees by instruction, and certificates and diplomas. Under these are listed institutions offering programs. Advertisements more fully describe the programs of some institutions. List of institutional addresses; index of subject headings.   L915.S73

Handbooks

A classification of institutions of higher education. 1987 ed. Princeton, N.J. : Carnegie Foundation for the Advancement of Teaching, c1987. 148 p.   **CB322**

     1st ed., 1973; rev. ed., 1976.

     Classes 3,388 institutions and 128 central offices in one of ten categories: Research institutions I or II; Doctorate granting universities I or II; Comprehensive universities I or II; Liberal arts colleges I or II; Two-year community, junior, or technical colleges; and Professional schools or other specialized institutions. Criteria for categorization include range of baccalaureate and graduate programs, priority given to research, amount of federal support received, number of Ph.D.s awarded, enrollment, and degree of selectivity. The first part lists colleges by classification and gives their average enrollment, the second lists them alphabetically and gives their classifications.   LA227.3.C5

Fonseca, James W. The atlas of American higher education / James W. Fonseca and Alice C. Andrews. N.Y. : New York Univ. Pr., c1993. 257 p. : maps ; 27 cm.   **CB323**

     Uses maps to present statistics which "need to be viewed spatially" because "not only does public education differ from state to state, but there is an amazing diversity of private institutions in American higher education that differ from place to place."—*Introd.* 86 maps with interpretive text accompany ten chapters on, e.g., Students and faculty, Cultural diversity, Specialized institutions, Outcomes of higher education, Financing of higher education. Supplemented by an appendix of statistical tables. Index.   G1201.E68F6

International guide to qualifications in education / The British Council, National Academic Recognition Information Centre. 3rd ed. London ; N.Y. : Mansell Pub., 1991. 1 v.   **CB324**

     1st ed., 1984; 2nd ed., 1987.

     Designed to aid educators and others who evaluate the educational background of applicants in terms of their equivalence to British credentials. Outlines the structure of the educational systems of some 150 countries, including types of institutions, training offered, and marking systems. Briefly describes the degrees to which a country's various certificates and diplomas are accorded credit by British institutions (e.g., satisfies entrance requirements of higher education).   LB2376.6.G7I58

The national guide to educational credit for training programs. Wash. : American Council on Education, [1980?]– . Irregular.   **CB325**

     Intended to assist educational institutions in granting credit for courses offered by private industry and government agencies. Course entries are arranged alphabetically by the sponsoring organization and include location, length, dates, objective, learning outcomes, instruction outline, and credit recommendations. Appendixes: alphabetical list of evaluators and their institutional affiliations; index by subject to programs and sponsoring units.

Student political activism : an international reference handbook / ed. by Philip G. Altbach. N.Y. : Greenwood, 1989. 505 p.   **CB326**

     Gives the recent history of "virtually all kinds of political involvement" (*Introd.*) of postsecondary students in 29 countries, including revolutionary movements, political parties and cultural organizations, campus politics concerning student government or university governance, ad hoc activism relating to campus or societal issues, and political attitudes in general. Chapters on individual nations, each with a selective short bibliography. Index.   LB3610.S79

National systems of education

Handbook of world education : a comparative guide to higher education & educational systems of the world / Walter Wickremasinghe, ed. in chief. Houston, Tex. : American Collegiate Service, c1991. 898 p.   **CB327**

     Describes the educational systems of 101 countries. A chapter for each nation outlines the structure of the system, from preschool through higher education, briefly recounting its history, aims and objectives, and current issues and trends.   LB43.H36

World guide to higher education : a comparative survey of systems, degrees, and qualifications / Unesco. 2nd ed. Epping, Essex : Bowker ; N.Y. : Unipub, 1982. 369 p.   **CB328**

     1st English ed., 1976. Also available in French and Spanish eds.

     Prep. by the International Association of Universities.

     Describes the higher education systems of 142 nations. Individual chapters for each country describe its system's governance, curricula, access to postsecondary education, etc. Each chapter also contains a glossary of the nation's degrees, titles, and certificates, with the amount and kind of education each requires.

Yearbooks

The NEA almanac of higher education. 1984– . Wash. : NEA Communications Services, c1984– . Annual.   **CB329**

     In four major sections: (1) NEA faculty salary report, providing data for specific academic ranks for schools offering different degree levels, by sex, by state, etc.; (2) Review of the year, including a chronology, reports of trends, legislation, court decisions, new books; (3) Resources and references, listing forthcoming academic meetings, higher education journals and reference aids, and fellowship sources for faculty; and (4) The NEA and higher education, with various NEA policy statements, resolutions, descriptions of NEA legislative advocacy programs, etc.   LA227.3.N37

Biography

Faculty white pages. 1989–1991. Detroit : Gale, c1989–c1991. Annual.   **CB330**

     1st ed. had title *Faculty directory of higher education.*

     Lists more than 500,000 faculty by 41 subject disciplines, giving departments, addresses, and phone numbers. Covers more than 3,000 American institutions of higher education. A "Guide to subjects covered" refers the user from a specialized area to the subject under which it is assigned (e.g., Calculus–Mathematics).   L901.F27

National faculty directory. 1970– . Detroit : Gale, [1970]– .   **CB331**

     Issued in two volumes, 1971–82; beginning in 1983, issued in three volumes.

     Lists 600,000 members of teaching faculties at 3,430 two- and four-year American colleges and universities and 240 Canadian institutions. Entries, arranged alphabetically, contain name of academic department, name of college or university, and home address. Includes only those with classroom teaching responsibilities. Kept up to date by supplements.   L901.N34

Who's who among students in American universities and colleges. [1956/57]– . Tuscaloosa, Ala. [etc] : Randall Publ. Co., [1957]– . Annual.   **CB332**

     Published 1935–56 as: *Official who's who among students in American universities and colleges.*

Lists undergraduate and graduate "students who have compiled an exceptional record of achievement ..."—*Pref.* Typical who's who entries list hometowns, degrees, majors, memberships and activities, honors, and employment history. Not comprehensive; a number of prestigious colleges are not represented.

Statistics

The American freshman, national norms / prep. by the staff of the Cooperative Institutional Research Program. 1971– . Los Angeles : The Program, Univ. of California, Los Angeles, 1971– . Annual. **CB333**

Title incorporates year of coverage.

Vols. for 1971–72 issued by American Council on Education.

Continues *National norms for entering college freshmen*, 1966–70 (annual).

Reports data concerning entering freshmen collected by the Cooperative Institutional Research Program (a continuing longitudinal study of the effects of college on students, sponsored by the American Council on Education). The 1990 sample of 194,000 students was drawn from 382 institutions. The main body of data consists of tables presented separately for men and women attending 35 kinds of institutions classed according to racial composition, institutional control, type (e.g., university), and selectivity. Statistics pertain to students' ages and races, parental income and education, student lifestyles, plans and objectives, political views, etc.

§ A companion title by Eric L. Dey, Alexander W. Astin, and William S. Korn, *The American freshman : twenty-five year trends, 1966–1990* (Los Angeles : Higher Education Research Inst., Univ. of California, 1991. 192 p.) treats the 1966–90 entering classes.

LA227.3.A444

Annual survey of colleges : summary statistics / the College Board. N.Y. : College Entrance Examination Board, [1982?]. Annual. **CB334**

Statistical tables, arranged by type of institution, present aggregate data for some 3,700 two- and four-year institutions. Emphasizes enrollment (with separate numbers for part-time and transfer students) and admissions (including selectivity). Includes data on financial aid and student progress (e.g., retention, percent graduating). In three parts: National profiles, National trends, and Regional undergraduate and freshmen enrollment. LA227.3.A56

Astin, Alexander W. The American college teacher : national norms for 1989–90 HERI faculty survey / by Alexander W. Astin, William S. Korn, Eric L. Dey. Los Angeles : Higher Education Research Institute, Graduate School of Education, Univ. of California, Los Angeles, 1991. 102 p. : ill., forms. **CB335**

Summarizes findings of a national survey of 35,478 full-time faculty at 392 universities and two- and four-year colleges. Focuses on such issues as: how faculty spend their time, interaction with students, how students are taught and tested, perceptions of institutional climate, primary sources of stress or satisfaction, and demographic and biographical characteristics. Presents separate data for male, female, and all faculty at 12 types of institutions (e.g., two-year colleges, public universities). Two main parts: interpretations of the findings illustrated by tables, and tabular presentation of responses to each question.

LB2331.72.A88x

The chronicle of higher education almanac. Sept. 1, 1988–Sept. 5, 1990; v. 38, no. 1 (Aug. 28, 1991)– . [Wash.] : The Chronicle, [c1988]– . Annual. **CB336**

Beginning 1991, has the volume numbering of the *Chronicle of higher education*.

An annual paperbound issue of *Chronicle of higher education* that provides national and state-by-state statistics or rankings on all major aspects of higher education. Includes data such as library holdings, administrators' salaries, enrollment, federal spending, and tuition. In two parts: The nation, with separate sections on students, faculty and staff,

resources, and institutions; and The states, with sections on demographics, universities, faculties, and money. Additional data is found in *Almanac of higher education*, which is essentially a modified reprint of articles from the *Chronicle of higher education almanac*. It too contains a section providing statistics on enrollment by race for each of more than 3,000 institutions. LA226.C55

Community college fact book / comp. by Elaine El-Khawas, Deborah J. Carter, and Cecilia A. Ottinger. N.Y. : American Association of Community and Junior Colleges : American Council on Education : Macmillan Pub. Co. ; London : Collier Macmillan Publishers, c1988. 167 p. : ill. **CB337**

Sponsored by the American Association of Community and Junior Colleges and the American Council on Education.

A compendium of data from government and private sources which "besides providing a descriptive analysis of community, technical, and junior colleges ... portray the larger social environment in which they operate."—*Introd.* Pt. 1, General information, summarizes trends in enrollment, student characteristics and achievement, and institutional finances and administration. Pt. 2, Planning information, details social and economic indicators bearing on the future, including trends in educational attainment, ethnic and age-related changes in the population and shifts in the labor force. The appendix contains detailed tables of educational and demographic data. Subject index.

LB2328.E47

Community, technical, and junior college statistical yearbook. 1987/88 ed.– . Wash. : American Association of Community and Junior Colleges, c1987– . Annual. **CB338**

Some years have title: *Statistical yearbook of community, technical, and junior colleges.*

In two parts: (1) Data on individual colleges, by state, including enrollment (full-time, part-time, noncredit, and minority); full-time and part-time faculty; number of professional staff and administrators; and tuition and fees; (2) State data, with totals for full- and part-time faculty and students, by private or public institutions; for public schools, gives minority enrollment. Index. LB2328.C694

Fact book on higher education. 1984-85– . N.Y. : American Council on Education : Macmillan, c1984– . Biennial. **CB339**

Title varies: *Fact book for academic administrators*; *Fact book for academic administration*; *Fact book for higher education*; *F B : a fact book on higher education*.

A compendium of statistics from more than 40 U.S. government and private sources. Separate sections on demographic and economic data, enrollment, finances, faculty and staff, students, institutions, earned degrees, and student aid. Much of the data is displayed in tables and graphs illustrating trends. Subject index. LA227.3.A44a

Harris, Seymour Edwin. A statistical portrait of higher education. N.Y. : McGraw-Hill, [1972]. 978 p. : ill. **CB340**

"A report for the Carnegie Commission on Higher Education."—*t.p.*

Has 700 tables with explanatory text representing all aspects of higher education. Includes "not only data available from official sources, but ... tables drawn from a wide variety of private surveys and research projects as well."—*Foreword.* A prolific source of historical statistics. Detailed table of contents, but no index. LA227.3.H25

Hill, Susan. Profile of education doctorates : 1976 to 1986 / Susan T. Hill, P. Elaine Kroe, Summer D. Whitener. Wash. : Center for Education Statistics : For sale by the U.S. Govt. Print. Office, [1987?]. 30 p. : ill. **CB341**

Superintendent of Documents classification: ED 1.102:P 94.

Provides trend data on number, demographic characteristics, and field of specialization of education doctorate recipients. Most data is presented in tables and graphs, some including statistics for as early as 1966. LB2386.H55

National Research Council. Board on Human-Resource Data and Analysis. A century of doctorates : data analyses of growth and change. Wash. : Nat. Academy of Sciences, 1978. 173 p. : ill. **CB342**

Subtitle: U.S. PhD's—their numbers, origins, characteristics, and the institutions from which they come : a report to the National Science Foundation, to the National Endowment for the Humanities, and to the United States Office of Education from the Board on Human Resource Data and Analyses, Commission on Human Resources, National Research Council. Lindsey R. Harmon, project director.

Offers statistical data showing production of "third-level research degrees such as PhD, ScD, EngD, and EdD; professional degrees such as MD, DDS and DVM are not included."—*Pref.* Tabular arrangement by field, institution, etc. This extensive analysis also contains statistics on parents' education, recipients' employment after graduation, doctorates in specific disciplines, and degrees awarded by specific universities. LB2386.N32

State higher education profiles. 1985– . Wash. : Center for Education Statistics : For sale by the U.S. Govt. Print. Off, 1987– . Annual. **CB343**

Superintendent of Documents classification (ERIC version) : ED 1.310/2: .

Volumes for 1991– called: 3rd ed.– and cover FY 1987– .
ERIC version distributed to depository libraries in microfiche.
Issuing agency varies.

In three chapters: National data, with national statistics on enrollment, faculty, revenues, and expenditures; State rankings tables, with information on sources of income (e.g., endowment, gifts), research expenditures, etc.; and State profiles. Most data given in tables; in the National data chapter, the tables are supplemented by interpretive text. Many statistics are presented as ratios (e.g., upper undergraduates to first time students); other statistics given by control (e.g., private) and level (e.g., two-year vs. four-year colleges). An appendix lists institutions by state. LB2342.S74

Touchton, Judith G. Fact book on women in higher education / comp. by Judith G. Touchton and Lynne Davis. N.Y. : American Council on Education : Macmillan ; : Maxwell Macmillan International, c1991. 289 p. : ill. **CB344**

A compendium of statistics from nine sources—government agencies, associations, private organizations—that provides information concerning the status of women (including minority women) in higher education. In two sections: (1) graphs and brief observations on highlights and trends in: demographic and economic factors; transition from high school to college; enrollment; earned degrees; faculty; administrators, trustees, and staff; and student financial aid; (2) statistical tables on which the graphs and observations are based. Cites sources for graphs and tables. General index. LC1756.T68

Ratings

Educational rankings annual. 1991– . Detroit : Gale, c1991– . Annual. **CB345**

A compendium of lists on many levels and facets of education. Includes not only rankings based on numerical data, but also qualitative considerations such as reputation. Most data is from American sources, although "Canadian and other international studies are included when deemed relevant."—*Introd.* The 1994 volume's 3,000 tables vary widely in scope. Some rankings are for specific states or regions, including many of the tables treating student loan repayment rates. Entries are arranged alphabetically by subject, each containing a short paragraph on the ranking's basis and background, the list itself (usually short, containing 5–15 items), and its source. Extensive cross-references; general index.

§ Although not as comprehensive as the *Gourman report* (CB346), this does include ratings not found there. LB2331.63.E34

Gourman report : a rating of graduate and professional programs in American and international universities. [1st ed.]– . Los Angeles : National Education Standards, 1980– . Biennial. **CB346**

Rates and ranks colleges and universities, their programs in individual disciplines, professional schools, and research libraries. Includes leading foreign institutions. For many areas of study, only schools with very strong programs are mentioned. Lists American teacher education programs, graduate education departments, and criminal justice/criminology programs not on its approved list.

§ Its companion publication, *Gourman report : a rating of undergraduate programs in American and international universities* / Jack Gourman (1980– . Los Angeles : National Education Standards, 1980– . Biennial) is similar in organization. Includes ratings more important to undergraduates, such as counseling centers and academic/athletic balance. Places less emphasis on professional schools, although it does rate undergraduate professional programs and premedical and prelegal curricula. LB2331.63.G67

National Academy of Sciences. An assessment of research doctorate programs in the United States. Wash. : Nat. Acad. of Sci. Pr., 1982. 5 v. **CB347**

Contents: [v.1] Humanities; [v.2] Social & behavioral sciences; [v.3] Biological sciences; [v.4] Engineering; [v.5] Mathematical & physical sciences.

"The present assessment, sponsored by the Conference Board of Associated Research Councils ... , continues a tradition pioneered by the American Council on Education, which in 1966 published *An Assessment of Quality in Graduate Education,* the report of a study conducted by Allan M. Cartter, and in 1970 published *A Rating of Graduate Programs,* by Kenneth D. Roose and Charles J. Andersen [CB348]."—*Pref.*

Offers a comparative study of the quality of programs in 32 disciplines at some 228 doctorate-granting universities. Gives information on program size at each university, characteristics of graduates, reputational survey results, and university library size. The reputational surveys were conducted among faculty members in the various disciplines. H62.A1A8

Roose, Kenneth D. A rating of graduate programs / Kenneth D. Roose, Charles J. Andersen. [Wash.] : American Council on Education, [1970]. 115 p. **CB348**

A follow-up to A. M. Cartter's study, *Assessment of quality in graduate education* (Wash. : American Council on Education, 1966).

A classic accumulation of ratings of graduate faculties in specific disciplines at specific universities and of graduate programs in specific disciplines for the country as a whole. Although dated, provides useful historical data.

§ Continued by: National Academy of Sciences, *An assessment of research doctorate programs in the United States* (CB347).

LA227.3.R65

Rugg, Frederick E. Rugg's recommendations on the colleges. [1st] ([1980])– . East Longmeadow, Mass. : Celecom Corp., c1980– . Annual. **CB349**

Recommends undergraduate majors at 600 "quality institutions of varying sizes. Arranged by major, with listings grouped by "Most selective," "Very selective," and "Selective." For less popular majors a separate "Miscellaneous majors" section lists programs.

ADULT EDUCATION

Guides

Smith, Robert McCaughan. The independent learners' sourcebook : resources and materials for selected topics / Robert M. Smith, Phyllis M. Cunningham. Chicago : Amer. Libr. Assoc., 1987. 306 p. **CB350**

An annotated list of reference sources on 34 subjects, including, for most topics, reference books, introductory works, indexes, government publications, databases, and relevant organizations, with author-title and organization indexes. Written for librarians, teachers, counselors, educational brokers, and others who assist people in finding and using resources for learning. Also designed for their clients and those assuming responsibility for their own continuing education.

Z1035.1.S577

Bibliography

Federally sponsored training materials : a directory and reference guide. Pittsford, N.Y. : Javelin Associates, 1989. 5 v.
CB351

Cover title: 1989 directory of federally sponsored training materials.

Information about training materials available from the National Technical Information Service (NTIS). Approximately 15,000 abstracts of federally sponsored publications, software programs, videos, research papers, and reports. Organized by broad categories and subcategories; keyword index.

Z7164.T7F43

French, Joyce N. Adult literacy : a source book and guide. N.Y. : Garland, c1987. 435 p. (Garland reference library of social science, v. 346 ; Garland reference library of social science. Source books on education, vol. 14).
CB352

In two parts: a short overview of the field, and an annotated bibliography of 591 articles, books, and government documents. Author and subject indexes.

Z5814.I3F73

Greenberg, Reva M. Education for older adult learning : a selected, annotated bibliography. Westport, Conn. : Greenwood, 1993. 219 p. (Bibliographies and indexes in gerontology, no. 20).
CB353

Provides more than 700 entries for books, book chapters, journal articles, videocassettes, papers from proceedings, unpublished manuscripts, ERIC documents, pamphlets, and online databases. In three parts: General issues and key themes (e.g., historical, philosophical, and theoretical perspectives); Specific skills and programs (e.g., instructional techniques, eldercare, retirement); and Resources (e.g., online databases, professional organizations, federal statutes). Author and subject indexes.

Z5814.A24G74

Houle, Cyril Orvin. The literature of adult education : a bibliographic essay. San Francisco : Jossey-Bass, c1992. 441 p.
CB354

A comprehensive treatment of English-language books on American adult and lifelong education published from World War I to the present. Arranged in 12 chapters on topics such as Adult learners, their nature and needs; Goals related to aspects of adult life; and Theory and program design. Only authors' names appear in the text, so users must consult the work's 1,241-item bibliography for complete citations. Name and subject indexes.

LC5251.H69

•Training media database : TMD [database]. Albuquerque, N.M. : National Information Center for Educational Media (NICEM), 1975– .
CB355

Available online, updated biennially, and as part of *A-V online* (CB28).

Primarily for workplace training and personnel programs. Offers 136,000 citations with abstracts for audiovisual materials, such as video and audio tapes and films, on management and supervision techniques, leadership, drugs, safety on the job, and similar topics.

Dictionaries

Jarvis, Peter. An international dictionary of adult and continuing education. London ; N.Y. : Routledge, 1990. 372 p.
CB356

Contains entries not only for concepts, but for personal names, programs, schools, associations, etc., including some terms in foreign languages and some from social science disciplines other than education. Definitions range from several words to substantial paragraphs; some entries are merely names and addresses of organizations. Many cross-references.

LC5211.J37

Directories

•EDVENT : educational and training courses [database]. Waltham, Mass. : Timeplace, Inc.
CB357

Available online; updated weekly. Current coverage.

Formerly *Educational events : educational and training courses*. Sometimes called *T.R.A.I.N.*

Describes more than 100,000 continuing education courses and materials—seminars, conferences, workshops, and other training programs sponsored by 6,000 organizations, and 25,000 training materials such as manuals, video and audio tapes, films, and software. Used by corporations and other organizations interested in human resource development.

Independent study catalog : NUCEA's guide to independent study through correspondence instruction. 1983/1985– . Princeton, N.J. : publ. for the National Univ. Continuing Education Assoc. by Peterson Guides, 1983– . Biennial.
CB358

Lists approximately 12,000 correspondence courses in 1,000 subject areas at 71 colleges and universities in the U.S. and Canada. Includes courses for high school, college, and graduate credit, as well as noncredit courses. Arranged by institution. Entries include course title, department offering the course, course number, number of credits, and level. Also includes some general information on each program, such as degree offered, availability of telecourses, time requirements, etc. Index of subjects offered.

LC5951.N34a

Sullivan, Eugene J. The adult learner's guide to alternative and external degree programs. Phoenix : Oryx, 1993. 227 p.
CB359

The "programs listed are the result of an extensive and thorough survey of all accredited colleges and universities in the United States ... conducted by the American Council on Education."—*Introd.* In two parts: Alternative programs, or evening, weekend, or other programs for adults who need to earn at least 25% of their credits on campus; and External programs, which require less than 25% on campus and generally provide distance education options. Entries include degrees offered, program descriptions, accreditation, admission requirements, credit awards for prior learning and the limits to these awards, credit awards for examinations, estimated completion time, credit hour requirements, distance learning options, and student support services.

L901.S84

Handbooks

Costa, Marie. Adult literacy/illiteracy in the United States : a handbook for reference and research. Santa Barbara, Calif. : ABC-Clio, 1989. 167 p.
CB360

A compendium of information including a chronology; biographical sketches; statistics; directory of organizations, associations, and government agencies; bibliography of reference materials; and lists of computer networks, databases, and nonprint media. Glossary; index.

LC151.C64

A guide to the evaluation of educational experiences in the armed services / Commission on Accreditation of Service Experiences. Wash. : American Council on Education, 1944– . Biennial.   **CB361**

Superintendent of Documents classification: D 1.6/2-3: .

Biennial since 1974; irregular publication prior to that date. Earlier editions kept up to date with supplements.

Since 1986, issued by: American Council on Education and prepared under contract with Defense Activity for Non-Traditional Education Support on behalf of the Dept. of Defense. Depository copies in microfiche since that date.

In four volumes: (1) Army courses; (2) Army MOSs (military occupational specialties); (3) Navy; (4) Air Force, Coast Guard, Department of Defense, Marine Corps.

Used for determining the credit to be awarded for coursework provided by the military. Describes more than 10,000 courses offered by all service branches and the Department of Defense; includes ACE identification number, program title, military course number, location, course evaluation date, learning outcomes, instructional method, length, credit recommendation, and related occupational codes.

U408.3.G77

Handbook of adult and continuing education / Sharan B. Merriam, Phyllis M. Cunningham, editors. 6th ed. San Francisco : Jossey-Bass Publ., 1989. 718 p.   **CB362**

5th ed., 1970, had title *Handbook of adult education.*

Unlike its predecessors, this edition is a review of the literature only and does not include directories or lists of information sources. Includes 48 chapters, written by experts, in five sections: Adult education as a field of professional practice (with chapters on its purpose, history, social context, etc.); Adult learners and educational practice; Major providers of educational programs for adults (with chapters on public schools, the armed forces, colleges, etc.); Adult education and special clienteles (with chapters on adult basic education, older adults, etc.).; and Adult education in the future. Name and subject indexes.

LC5215.H25

Biography

International biography of adult education / ed. by J. E. Thomas and Barry Elsey. Nottingham : Dept. of Adult Education, Univ. of Nottingham, c1985. 709 p.   **CB363**

Provides signed biographies of 200 18th–20th century figures who contributed to the field, some as professional adult educators, others as public leaders, writers, or scholars. International in scope, although there are more entries from the Commonwealth than the U.S. The biographies, alphabetically arranged, are typically one to three pages long and are followed by brief bibliographies. A "Thematic index" lists biographees arranged by areas of adult education, and a subject index locates articles on specific individuals.   LA2303.I615

FELLOWSHIPS AND SCHOLARSHIPS

Directory of internships, work experience programs, and on-the-job training opportunities / ed., Alvin Renetsky ; assistant ed., Rebekah Berger ; indexer, Robin Mayper Balaban. 2nd ed. Santa Monica, Calif. : Ready Reference Pr., 1986. 2 v. in 1 (600 p.).   **CB364**

1st ed., 1976, with a 1977 supplement. A "three-ring binder ed." was produced in 1990.

Includes programs in virtually every field, from the arts to engineering. Also describes summer internship opportunities, work/study programs, and specialized opportunities for high school and undergraduate students. Arranged by sponsoring organization, describing backgrounds and characteristics of programs (including recipients' duties), stipends, and eligibility requirements and providing contact information. Appendixes list federal job information and testing services,

state and local job information sources, state apprenticeship agencies, and apprenticeship information centers. Has geographical and subject field indexes.   HD5715.2.D57

National guide to foundation funding in higher education / ed. by Stan Olson & Ruth Kovacs. [N.Y.] : Foundation Center, 1989. 692 p.   **CB365**

Lists the awards granted by 2,900 organizations providing funding to individuals and institutions. Arranged by state, then awarding organization. Entries give contact information, financial data of the foundation, fund purposes and activities, limitations (e.g., California only), application deadlines and notification dates, and type of support (e.g., scholarship funds). Bibliography of state and local foundation directories. Four indexes: geographic; type of award; foundation name; and donors, officers, and trustees.   LB2336.N37

By country or region

International

Financial aid for research and creative activities abroad. 1st ed. (1992–1994)– . San Carlos, Calif. : Reference Service Pr., 1992– . Biennial.   **CB366**

Title page note: A list of scholarships, fellowships, loans, grants, awards, and internships for research and creative activities abroad; an annotated bibliography of financial aid directories; and a set of five indexes: title, organization, geographic, subject, and deadline.

Issues for 1992–94– ed. by Gail Ann Schlachter, R. David Weber.

With its companion volume (below), succeeds the same publisher's *Financial aid for research, study, travel and other activities abroad* (San Carlos, Calif., 1990). Brief entries are arranged by educational level: High school/undergraduate students, Graduate students, Postdoctorates, Professionals and other individuals. Information given includes address, purpose, eligibility, amount of award, duration, and deadlines.

§ Companion volume: *Financial aid for study and training abroad.* 1st ed. (1992–94)– . San Carlos, Calif. : Reference Service Press, 1992– . Biennial.

Title page note: A list of scholarships, fellowships, loans, grants, awards, and internships for study and training abroad; an annotated bibliography of financial aid directories; and a set of five indexes: title, organization, geographic, subject, and deadline.

Issues for 1992– ed. by Gail Ann Schlachter, R. David Weber.

Arranged like *Financial aid for research and creative activities abroad,* with entries providing similar information.   LB2337.2.F572

Grants register. 1969/70– . Chicago : St. James, c1969– . Biennial.   **CB367**

Frequency varies; biennial since 1971/73.

Imprint varies.

An international directory of financial aids available to graduate students and "for all who require professional or advanced vocational training" (*Editor's note*) throughout the English-speaking world. Grant-giving foundations, institutions, etc., are listed alphabetically with brief information on type of assistance offered. Includes scholarships, fellowships, and research grants; exchange opportunities; vacation study and travel awards; grants for equipment, publication, translation, artistic or scientific projects, competitions, and honoraria; professional and vocational awards, etc. Index by subject, award, and awarding body.   LB2338.G7

Internships. 1981– . Princeton, N.J. : Peterson's Guides, c1981– . Annual.   **CB368**

For annotation, *see* CH697.   L901.I66

Scholarships, fellowships & grants for programs abroad : a handbook of awards for US nationals for study or research abroad / [consulting ed., W. Wickremasinghe]. Houston, Tex. : American Collegiate Service, c1989. 299 p.   **CB369**

The main section has 374 entries on specific awards, arranged alphabetically by name of granting institution. Data provided includes person to contact; number, value, and duration of awards; fields of study; closing dates for applications; where tenable; and eligibility requirements. Another section briefly profiles host countries, giving their languages, religions, currency rates, academic years, required skills for awardees (such as knowledge of French), and sources of information in the host country. Appendixes provide information on various Fulbright awards. Four indexes: general, by country or region, by subject, and by level of studies.   LB2338.S36

Study abroad = Études à l'étranger = Estudios en la extranjero. v. 1 (1948)– . Paris : UNESCO, 1948– . Triennial.   **CB370**

Subtitle varies. Title and introductory matter also in French and Spanish; text in English, French, or Spanish.

Frequency varies: originally annual; biennial until 1981.

Beginning with issue for 1968/70, continues *Vacations abroad*, which was issued as a separate publication 1948–66.

Lists, for 124 countries, financial aid and courses for foreign students, with information on scholarships, fellowships, and other assistance for study, teaching, research, training, and observation; university-level and short courses; continuing education and training programs; and student employment opportunities. In two parts: International scholarships and courses, arranged by sponsoring organization; and National scholarships and courses, with course descriptions listed by individual university. Three indexes: international organization, national organization, and subject of study.   LB2338.S86

United States

The A's and B's of academic scholarships. 1st ed. (1978/ 1979)– . Alexandria, Va. : Octameron Associates, 1978– . Annual.   **CB371**

Title varies: *The A's & B's*, 1985–86.

Data on scholarships at 1,200 colleges, arranged in tables outlining number and value ranges of awards, class standing and SAT/ACT requirements, permissible study fields, renewability, restrictions, and application dates. Identifies need-based scholarships and awards for transfer students.

Bauer, David G. The complete grants sourcebook for higher education. 2nd ed. N.Y. : American Council on Education : Macmillan, 1985. 465 p.   **CB372**

1st ed., 1980.

Pt. 1 provides information on successful grantsmanship; pt. 2 is a directory of more than 500 federal, foundation, and corporate sources of support. Entries include the funding source's area of interest, financial data, eligibility requirements, application information, policy, and sample grants.   LB2336.P8

Blum, Laurie. Free money for foreign study : a guide to more than 1,000 grants and scholarships for study abroad. N.Y. : Facts on File, c1991. 262 p.   **CB373**

In two sections, by country and by subject of study. Short entries, arranged alphabetically within each section, include addresses and phone nubmers of awarding organizations, eligibility requirements, amounts given, grant durations, and application deadlines. General index.

§ One of a number of "Free money" works by the same author: *Free money for graduate school* (2nd ed. N.Y. : Henry Holt, 1993).

Free money from colleges and universities (N.Y. : Henry Holt, 1993).

Free money for athletic scholarships (N.Y. : Henry Holt, 1993).

Free dollars from the federal government (N.Y. : John Wiley, 1993).

Free money for college (3rd ed. N.Y. : Facts on File, 1994).

Free money for college from the government (N.Y. : Henry Holt, 1993).

Laurie Blum's free money for private schools (N.Y. : Simon and Schuster, 1992).

Free money for science students (N.Y. : Barnes and Noble, 1985).

Free money for professional students (2nd ed. N.Y. : Paragon House, 1987).

Free money for humanities and social sciences (2nd ed. N.Y. : Paragon House, 1987).

Free money for mathematics and natural sciences (2nd ed. N.Y. : Paragon House, 1987).   LB2337.2.B575

Cassidy, Daniel J. Graduate scholarship directory : the complete guide to scholarships, fellowships, grants and loans for graudate and professional study. 3rd ed. Hawthorne, N.J. : Career Pr., 1993. 369 p.   **CB374**

Rev. ed. of *Graduate scholarship book* (1990).

Main section is arranged by areas of study, then awarding organization. Brief entries provide limited information on award types (e.g., post-doctoral fellowship), their number and amount, eligibility, and application requirements and deadlines. Preceding these is a "Quick find index," with entry numbers for awards relevant to specific considerations: current grade point average, country of residence, occupational goals, ethnic groups, and physical handicaps. Alphabetical index of organization and program names.

§ Companion volumes: *The scholarship book : the complete guide to private scholarships, grants and loans for undergraduates* (4th ed. Englewood Cliffs, N.J. : Prentice-Hall, 1993) and *The international scholarship directory : the complete guide for study abroad* (3rd ed. Hawthorne, N.J. : Career Pr., 1993).   LB2337.2.C36

College Entrance Examination Board. College Scholarship Service. The college cost book. 1980/81–1993. N.Y. : College Entrance Examination Board, College Scholarship Service. Annual.   **CB375**

For annotation, *see* CB259.   LB2342.C633a

Dennis, Marguerite J. Dollars for scholars : Barron's complete college financing guide. N.Y. : Barron's, c1989. 248 p. : ill., forms.   **CB376**

A guide to sources of financial aid at state, federal, and international levels, giving addresses of institutions, organizations, and government offices, together with descriptions of assistance programs.   LB2337.4.D455

Directory of financial aids for minorities. 1984/85– . Santa Barbara, Calif. : ABC-Clio, [1984]– . Irregular?   **CB377**

Gail A. Schlachter, ed.

Chapters by type of award (scholarships, loans, grants, internships, etc.) are divided into sections: minorities in general, Asian Americans, Black Americans, Hispanic Americans, and Native Americans. Organized alphabetically by name of sponsoring agency within each section. Additional chapters provide information on state sources of information on educational benefits and list reference sources on financial aid. Entries include address and phone numbers for sponsoring organizations, purpose of the awards, eligibility requirements, number and dollar amounts of awards, special features, and application deadlines. Indexes: program title, sponsoring organization, geographical area, subject, and application deadline.   LB2338.D56

Directory of financial aids for women. 1st ed. (1978)– . Santa Barbara, Calif. : Reference Service Pr., 1978– . Biennial.   **CB378**

For annotation, *see* CC546.   LB2338.D564

Funding for U.S. study. 1st ed.– . N.Y., NY : Institute of International Education, c1989– .   **CB379**

Provides information on agencies that offer awards for foreign nationals to study, teach, perform research, or pursue other educational objectives in the U.S. Describes 600 fellowships, grants, travel grants, scholarships, and paid internships geared to all levels of postsecondary education and research. Entries, arranged by administrative agency, contain information on contacts, fields of study, award purposes, amount given, duration of support, restrictions, eligibility, application procedures, and deadlines. Four indexes: organizations, nationality, educational level, and fields of study.   LB2337.2.F86

Guide to federal funding for education. 1981– . Arlington, Va. : Education Funding Research Council, c1981– . Annual.   **CB380**

Imprint varies. Recently issued in two volumes.

Kept up to date by monthly supplements since 1988: Grant update! for Guide to federal funding for education.

Detailed descriptions of more than 400 federal programs offering financial assistance to state and local education agencies, postsecondary institutions, and other public and private organizations working in the field of education. In two looseleaf volumes arranged by type of program served (drug abuse, science education, etc.). Lengthy entries on the purpose of each program, eligibility requirements, application procedures, allocation of funds, allowable activities, and selection criteria. Indexes by "fundable activity" and by title.   LB2805.F29

Higher education opportunities for minorities and women, annotated selections. 1982 ed.– . Wash. : U.S. Dept. of Education, Assistant Secretary for Postsecondary Education : distr. by U.S. Govt. Print. Off., 1983– . Annual.   **CB381**

Superintendent of Documents classification (ERIC version): ED 1.310/2: .

ERIC version issued to depository libraries in microfiche.

Name of issuing agency varies.

Lists government agencies, foundations, corporations, associations, etc., providing financial help for women and minority students. In six sections: general undergraduate opportunities, undergraduate opportunities by academic area, general graduate opportunities, graduate by academic area, postdoctoral, and sources describing opportunities. Entries give addresses, purposes of the award, requirements (e.g., SAT scores), number and amount of awards, and deadlines.   LB2338.H48

Keeslar, Oreon. Financial aids for higher education. 1974/75– . Dubuque, Iowa : Wm. C. Brown, 1975– . Biennial.   **CB382**

Title varies: 1st–2nd eds. called *National catalog of scholarships and other financial aid for students entering college*; 3rd–5th eds. called *National catalog of financial aids for students entering college*; Vols. for 1974/75–82 have title: *Financial aids for higher education, catalog*.

Contains information on more than 3,500 programs, listed alphabetically. Entries are typically half a page long and list the program's sponsoring organization and contact address and describe its basis, subject areas, eligibility and other requirements, number and value of awards, and application process and deadlines. Includes a general index and a "Program finder" index that lists programs for specific groups (e.g., war orphans).   LB2338.K39

Kirby, Debra M. Fund your way through college : uncovering 1,000 great opportunities in undergraduate financial aid / Debra M. Kirby with Christa Brelin. Detroit : Visible Ink Pr., c1992. 454 p.   **CB383**

Lists scholarships, grants, loans, internships, and work-study programs, most of which are sponsored by associations, corporations, religious groups, fraternal organizations, foundations, and other private organizations. Also includes a "broad representation" (*Pref.*) of state and national government awards. Main section arranged by name of awarding organization. Short entries provide information on the program's purpose and its types and amounts of awards, eligibility requirements and selection criteria, and application procedures and deadlines. A "Vocational pathfinder," listing awards in specific fields, precedes the main section. Index of sponsoring organizations and awards.   LB2337.2.K57

McKee, Cynthia Ruiz. Cash for college / Cynthia Ruiz McKee and Philip C. McKee, Jr. N.Y. : Hearst Books, c1993. 510 p.   **CB384**

Has separate sections for awards by public and private organizations within which brief entries describing 4,000 scholarships are listed alphabetically by program or sponsor. Entries give contact information and data on number and amount of scholarships, application deadlines, and requirements for eligibility. An "At-a-glance scholarship index" lists awards by subject of study and qualifications such as native ancestry, parental membership in specific organizations, and place of residence.   LB2337.4.M285

The national directory of internships. 1984– . Raleigh, N.C. : National Society for Internships and Experiential Education, 1984– . Irregular.   **CB385**

Lists internships in chapters by broad subject areas (e.g., social sciences, museums and history). Within chapters, arranged by sponsoring organization. Entries contain descriptions of sponsors; a paragraph outlining duties, pay, and schedules; eligibility requirements; and application procedures. Alphabetical, geographical, and field indexes.

Paying less for college. 10th ed. (1993)– . Princeton, N.J. : Peterson's Guides, c1992– . Annual.   **CB386**

11th ed. has title: *Peterson's paying less for college*.

Continues *Peterson's college money handbook*, 1988–91.

The main section, College financial programs, outlines, for individual schools: expenses; kinds and numbers of scholarships available and average stipends; kinds and amounts of loans; part-time jobs; average percentage of need met; options available (e.g., ROTC, waivers for children of employees); information on contacts. The first section, Freshman year costs : reducing the sticker price, provides a chart that lists, for individual colleges: percent of freshmen applying for aid; percent judged needing aid; average gift; tuition and fees; average cost after gift; and average loan and work-study packages. Other sections describe top sources of federal aid, and list the largest state and private aid providers. Indexes: non-need scholarships, athletic grants, cooperative programs, ROTC, tuition waivers, and tuition payment alternatives.

•For machine-readable counterparts, see *Peterson's freshman financial aid database* (CB388), *Peterson's noninstitutional aid database* (CB390), and *Peterson's financial aid service* (CB387).   LB2337.2.C65

•**Peterson's financial aid service** [database]. Princeton, N.J. : Peterson's Guides, 1986– .   **CB387**

Available in machine-readable form from producer; updated annually.

Includes information from *Peterson's noninstitutional aid database* (CB390) and *Peterson's freshmen financial aid database* (CB388). Derived in part from *Peterson's college database* (CB283).

Among sources of aid described are need-based scholarships at specific colleges, Pell grants and Stafford student loans, and 470 private programs.

•**Peterson's freshman financial aid database** [database]. Princeton, N.J. : Peterson's Guides.   **CB388**

Available in machine-readable form from producer; updated annually.

Describes need-based and non-need-based scholarships and grants administered and funded by the 1,750 institutions listed. Entries for need-based awards contain information on numbers of freshmen applying for aid and percent of need met, sources of aid, whether aid is available to foreign students, and average number of hours worked weekly by freshmen. For non-need-based aid, data are divided into awards for academic interests and achievements, creative arts and performance, athletics, special achievements and activities, and special characteristics, and include number and total dollar value of awards.

§ Information from this database contributes to *Peterson's financial aid service* database (CB387) and to *Paying less for college* (CB386).

Peterson's grants for graduate study / [comp. by the University of Massachusetts at Amherst]. 3rd ed.– . Princeton, N.J. : Peterson's Guides, c1992– . Biennial. **CB389**

Continues *Peterson's grants for graduate students*.

Detailed listings of some 700 sources for financial aid: grant and fellowship programs; internships and traineeships; prizes; awards for travel, summer study, or research; awards for study and research abroad. Brief entries present contact information; program descriptions (including number, value, and duration of awards); names of funding organizations; eligibility requirements; and application procedures. Also includes directories of fields of study and special eligibility requirements, an annotated bibliography of books and pamphlets related to searching for funds and to proposal writing, and an index of administering agencies. LB2337.2.P46

•**Peterson's noninstitutional aid database** [database]. Princeton, N.J. : Peterson's Guides. **CB390**

Formerly *Peterson's private aid file*.

Available in machine-readable form from producer; updated annually.

Contains information on scholarships and loans for American college students awarded by foundations, corporations, and other private organizations. Entries provide names of programs and their sponsors and contact personnel, descriptions of programs, and information on number and types of awards, eligibility, application procedures and deadlines, and percentage of applicants receiving awards.

§ Information from this database contributes to *Peterson's financial aid service* database (CB387) and to *Paying less for college* (CB386).

Peterson's sports scholarships and college athletic programs / Ron Walker, ed. Princeton, N.J. : Peterson's Guides, c1994. 818 p. : ill. **CB391**

Outlines the availability of athletic scholarships at specific colleges; describes the athletic programs at each. Reports numbers of full and partial scholarships and whether they are need-based, as well as contact information and estimates of the difficulty of entrance requirements for each school. Information on athletic programs includes conference memberships, program budgets, facilities, names of sports administrators, names and phone numbers of coaches, and won-lost records in intercollegiate sports for previous years. Arranged by intercollegiate sports division membership (e.g., NCAA Division I). Alphabetical index of institutions.

Scholarships, fellowships, and loans. 1st ed.– . Detroit : Gale, 1949– . Biennial. **CB392**

Editor varies: v. 1–5, S. Norman Feingold; v. 6–8, S. Norman Feingold and Marie Feingold.

Publisher varies: v. 1–8, Bellman Publishing Co.

Frequency varies: irregular, 1949–87.

The "most comprehensive single directory of education-related financial aid available…provides descriptions of more than 2,600 awards available to U.S. and Canadian students for study throughout the world."—*Introd.* In addition to scholarships, fellowships, and loans, includes internships, work-study programs, and prizes and other awards of private organizations and state and federal government agencies. Does not include awards of individual educational institutions. The main section consists of descriptive entries arranged alphabetically by administering organization, giving contact information and detailed descriptive material including qualifications, selection criteria, funds available, application procedures, and deadlines. Six indexes: Vocational goals, Field of study, Legal residence, Special recipient (e.g., Asian-American, Fraternal), Place of study, and Organization and award. LB2338.S46

Scholarships, fellowships, grants, and loans. N.Y. : Macmillan Information, 1975– . Irregular. **CB393**

M. Lorraine Mathies, ed.

Arranged by broad study area, with sections on area studies, environmental studies, humanities, life sciences, physical sciences, social sciences, and technology, with each section divided into individual disciplines. Separate chapter on financial aid for minorities. Within subsections, entries are arranged by awarding agency, providing informa-

tion on the agency and its purpose; names of awards; areas, fields, or subjects of study; number, amount, and types of awards; eligibility requirements; application deadlines; and addresses. Indexes by subject, level of education, sponsoring organization, and award title.

Issued as the fifth volume of *The college blue book* (CB258). LB2338.S36

ACADEMIC CUSTOMS

Costume and protocol

Gunn, Mary Kemper. A guide to academic protocol. N.Y. : Columbia Univ. Pr., 1969. 112 p. **CB394**

Concerned with entertainment and social occasions on campus as well as with academic ceremonies. LB2379.G8

Sheard, Kevin. Academic heraldry in America. Marquette, Mich. : Northern Michigan College Pr., [1962]. 78 p. : ill. **CB395**

Gives descriptions of hoods worn at colleges and universities in the United States. Arranged first by institution, then by color. Includes brief information on academic ceremonies, seals, and flags. Not a complete listing and not always accurate, but useful, as it brings together information in convenient form for ready reference. LB2389.S5

Smith, Hugh. Academic dress and insignia of the world : gowns, hats, chains of office, hoods, rings, medals and other degree insignia of universities and other institutions of learning. Cape Town, South Africa : A.A. Balkema, 1970. 3 v. : ill. **CB396**

Contents: v. 1, British Commonwealth, Irish Republic, and Republic of South Africa; v. 2, Europe, Africa, Asia, United States of America, Central and South America; v. 3, Glossary and definitions; Hood identification tables; U.S.A. Inter Collegiate code; Abbreviations; Index.

Detailed descriptions and illustrations of academic costume of individual institutions throughout the world. LB2389.S6

College colors, songs, nicknames

Sparks, Linda. American college regalia : a handbook / comp. by Linda Sparks and Bruce Emerton. N.Y. : Greenwood, 1988. 380 p. **CB397**

For American colleges and universities with enrollment of 2,500 or more, indicates nickname, mascot, name of newspaper, colors, title of yearbook, fight song, and alma mater. LB3630.S64

Fraternities

Baird's manual of American college fraternities. Ed. 1 (1879)– . Menasha, Wis. : George Banta, 1879– . **CB398**

Title and publisher vary.

The standard manual of American college social and professional fraternities. Includes for each its history, traditions, and organization and lists individual chapters. A separate section lists organizations by college; another analyzes college fraternal organizations as an institution, treating their history and prospects. Also includes honor and recognition societies. LJ31.B2

CC

Sociology

GENERAL WORKS

Guides

Aby, Stephen H. Sociology : a guide to reference and information sources. Littleton, Colo. : Libraries Unlimited, 1987. 231 p. (Reference sources in the social sciences series, [no. 1]). **CC1**

In three sections: (1) works of use to all social sciences; (2) individual social science resources of use to sociologists; (3) sociological sources, including general works and a section on resources especially useful in 22 subdivisions of sociology. Author-title index and cross-referenced subject index. Z7164.S68A24

Selth, Jefferson P. Alternative lifestyles : a guide to research collections on intentional communities, nudism, and sexual freedom. Westport, Conn. : Greenwood, c1985. 133 p. (Bibliographies and indexes in sociology, no. 6). **CC2**

Describes 36 collections in the U.S. which total 120,000 volumes, 15,000 periodicals, 125,000 audiovisual items, over 3 million photographs, and many ephemeral materials. Introductory pages to the three sections noted in the subtitle provide definitions and scope. Entries, which vary in length from two to ten pages and are arranged alphabetically by title, include address, phone, contact name, hours, general description, holdings, and bibliographic access. Alphabetical index of collections and institutions; geographical index of collections; and separate indexes for periodicals, names, and subjects. HQ971.S45

Bibliography

Barkas, J. L. Friendship : a selected, annotated bibliography. N.Y. ; London : Garland, 1985. 134 p. : ill. (Garland bibliographies in sociology, v. 4 ; Garland reference library of social science, v. 244). **CC3**

Groups 693 entries by type of material: books, dissertations, reports; articles and chapters; unpublished material; and organizational resources. Most entries have annotations, and are arranged alphabetically by author. Author/editor and subject indexes. Z5873

Berndt, Judy. Rural sociology : a bibliography of bibliographies. Metuchen, N.J. : Scarecrow, 1986. 177 p. **CC4**

Contains annotated entries for 434 English-language bibliographies published since 1970, arranged alphabetically by author in 16 chapters covering topics such as rural development, irrigation, overview studies, women, land tenure, and nomadism. Chapter headings provide the only subject access. Personal and corporate name, title, and geographic indexes. Z7164.S688B47

Brown, Samuel R. Finding the source in sociology and anthropology : a thesaurus-index to the reference collection. N.Y. : Greenwood, 1987. 269 p. (Finding the source, no. 1). **CC5**

An attempt to provide a quicker means of finding specific information than the usual annotated guide to reference sources. In two sections: (1) citations listed by broad subjects, then titles, with author and title/subtitle indexes following; and (2) the "thesaurus-index," which gives related terms and also refers users back to citations in section one. No annotations. Z7164.S68B75

Bruhn, John G. Medical sociology : an annotated bibliography, 1972–1982 / John G. Bruhn, Billy U. Philips, Paula L. Levine. N.Y. : Garland, 1985. 779 p. (Garland bibliographies in sociology, v. 6 ; Garland reference library of social science, v. 243). **CC6**

Serves to update Theodor J. Litman's bibliography *The sociology of medicine and health care* (San Francisco : Boyd & Fraser, 1976) which cited literature published through 1971. Contains 1,949 annotated entries for books, articles, and government documents in 14 topical sections. Author and subject indexes. Z6675.S53B78

Ghorayshi, Parvin. The sociology of work : a critical annotated bibliography. N.Y. : Garland, 1990. 214 p. (Garland library of sociology, v. 17 ; Garland reference library of social science, v. 591). **CC7**

An interdisciplinary and international bibliography of 405 selected books, articles, and reports, intended for students, academics, professionals, and general readers. In six subject chapters (e.g., Division of labor; Hazards of work; The trade union, Industrial conflict, and The strike), divided into sections such as Union's power and Experience of unemployment. Author and subject indexes. Z7164.I45G46

International bibliography of sociology = Bibliographie internationale de sociologie / prep. by the International Committee for Social Sciences Documentation in co-operation with the International Sociological Association. v. 5 (1955)– . London ; N.Y. : Tavistock, 1955– . Annual. **CC8**

Publisher varies; originally publ. by Unesco.

Titles appear in English. Preface in eight languages; text headings in English and French.

Compiled from published literature (mostly periodicals), and contributions from worldwide correspondents. Omits previously published material, most translations, textbooks, newspapers, and work from the popular press. Includes material from some 25 languages, cited in the original form. Groups entries within classification scheme, alphabetical by title. Author, placename, and subject indexes. Additional subject index in French.

§ Complemented by the monthly *International current awareness services : sociology and related disciplines* (v. 1 [1990]– . London : Routledge, 1990–). Z7161.I594

Kinloch, Graham Charles. Social stratification : an annotated bibliography. N.Y. : Garland, 1987. 357 p. (Garland library of sociology, v. 11 ; Garland reference library of social science, v. 393). **CC9**

Emphasizes social science literature published 1960s–1980s. 1,744 numbered entries in six chapters cover general bibliographies and research trends, theoretical and conceptual issues, methodological issues, historical studies, the U.S., and societies outside the U.S. Entries are alphabetical by author within subtopics. List of journals; author and subject indexes. Z7164.S64K56

Wepsiec, Jan. Sociology : an international bibliography of serial publications, 1880–1980. London : Mansell ; Bronx, N.Y. : distr. by H.W. Wilson, 1983. 183 p. **CC10**

An alphabetical listing of 2,311 journals, monograph series, transactions and numbered reports from institutions, and directories; full bibliographic reference includes abstracting or indexing source. Indexed by subject and form (e.g., abstracts, bibliographies, indexes). Z7164.S68W46

Periodicals

Current sociology = La sociologie contemporaine. v. 1 (1952)– . Beverly Hills, Calif. : Sage Publ., [1952]– . 3 no. a year. **CC11**

Editors vary; publishers vary.

Each issue is a monograph on a special topic, surveying recent research and including a bibliography. Z7161.C8

Indexes; Abstract journals

C.R.I.S : combined retrospective index set to journals in sociology, 1895–1974 / with an introd. and user's guide by Evan I. Farber ; Annadel N. Wile, exec. ed. Wash. : Carrollton Pr., 1978. 6 v. **CC12**

Contents: v. 1, Anthropology, applied sociology, culture, death and death rates, differentiation and stratification, group interactions; v. 2–3, Institutions: in general; bureaucratic structures; family; formal voluntary organizations; health; medical systems and structures; industrial systems and structures; law and legal systems; military (personnel) systems and structures; political institutions; religion; v. 4, Knowledge, research in sociology, rural systems and structures, sex roles, social change and economic development; v. 5, Social disorganization, social ecology, sociology as a profession, theorists, theory of sociology, urban systems and structures; v. 6, Authors.

About 85,000 articles from 118 English-language sociology journals are arranged in 137 subject categories, each with date and keyword indexes. Each entry provides keyword, brief title, author's name, year, volume and code number for journal title, and beginning page number.

Sociological abstracts. v. 1 (Jan./Oct. 1952/53)– . [San Diego, etc. : Sociological Abstracts, inc.], 1953– . 6 issues yearly. **CC13**

Cosponsored by the International Sociological Association.

Frequency varies: quarterly, Jan./Oct. 1953–Oct. 1957; five issues per year, 1958–1989.

Provides indexing and nonevaluative abstracts for sociology and related disciplines. International in scope. Each issue contains user's guide; abstracts arranged by subject classification; subject, author, and source indexes; and a supplement called *International review of publications in sociology (IRPS)* that includes book abstracts and a bibliography of book reviews. Descriptors are drawn from *Thesaurus of sociological indexing terms* (CC20).

Beginning with v.37 (1989), proceedings of association meetings are no longer published as "Conference abstracts supplement" sections within regular issues; they have the same title, but comprise the sixth issue of each volume, which formerly contained the annual cumulative indexes. The latter are still published separately, but without an issue number.

•Machine-readable versions: *Sociological abstracts* [database] (San Diego, Calif. : Sociological Abstracts, 1963–). Available online (updated bimonthly) and on CD-ROM (quarterly). Provides citations with abstracts to articles in more than 1,900 serials in sociology and related disciplines. HM1.S67

Encyclopedias

Encyclopedia of sociology. New and updated. Guilford, Conn. : DPG Reference Publ., c1981. 317 p. : ill. **CC14**

1st ed., 1974.

Brief definitions or descriptions (some signed) of "the language of sociology, the full range of its theories, the institutions of society, and the leading figures in both historical and contemporary sociolo-

gy."—*Pref*. More than 1,300 articles, ranging in length from 25 to 2,500 words. Classified bibliography of approximately 700 recent publications for "nonprofessionals in the field." HM17.E5

Encyclopedia of sociology / Edgar F. Borgatta, ed. in chief, Marie L. Borgatta, managing ed. N.Y. : Macmillan : Maxwell Macmillan International, c1992. 4 v. (xlvii, 2359 p.) : ill. **CC15**

The first comprehensive encyclopedia for general sociology, intended for a broad audience. 370 lengthy, signed articles, two to 18 pages in length, concluding with bibliographies, and written by 339 national and international sociologists. Includes classic topics, as well as those reflecting emerging fields. Omits biographical entries. Sample entries: Social problems, Homelessness, Family violence, Feminist theory. Entries are cross-referenced and arranged alphabetically. Lists of articles, authors, institutions. Most references from 1970–90. Detailed cross-referenced subject index. HM17.E5

International encyclopedia of sociology / ed. by Michael Mann. N.Y. : Continuum, [1984]. 434 p. **CC16**

Also publ. under title: *The Macmillan student encyclopedia of sociology*.

About 750 short, signed entries for terms, phrases, persons, and schools of thought; some bibliographic references. Editors and contributors are affiliated with the London School of Economics, resulting in some British emphasis. HM17.I53

Dictionaries

Boudon, Raymond. A critical dictionary of sociology / Raymond Boudon and François Bourricaud. Chicago : Univ. of Chicago Pr., 1989. 438 p. : ill. **CC17**

Translation of: *Dictionnaire critique de la sociologie* (Paris : Presses universitaires de France; 1st ed., 1982; 2nd ed., 1986).

A foreword describes the abridgment adopted for the English edition and lists excluded entries. The thematic index in the English edition gives page references omitted from the French edition. Includes introductions to the 1st and 2nd eds. Provides lengthy essays on subjects such as beliefs, Comte, ideologies, Marx, minorities, prophetism, and social control. Bibliographies follow each essay. HM17.B6813

The encyclopedic dictionary of sociology / Richard Lachmann, editorial advisor. 4th ed. Guilford, Conn. : Dushkin, c1991. 321 p. **CC18**

1st ed., 1974.

More than 1,350 entries by 120 contributors. For nonprofessional readers, designed to answer specific questions and illustrate interrelationships among sociological elements. Includes *see* and *see also* references, and references linking simple definitions with other related articles. Alphabetical arrangement of entries; longer articles are signed. Includes illustrations, subject maps, and topic guides, each with separate table of contents. HM17.E529

Jary, David. HarperCollins dictionary of sociology / David Jary and Julia Jary. N.Y. : HarperPerennial, c1991. 601 p. : ill. **CC19**

"Its main aim is to function as a study aid."—*Introd*. Includes terms of central importance; terms from other disciplines widely used in sociology; influential sociologists; major social theorists and philosophers; main research methods; statistical terminology; and frequently used common terms that present problems for sociology students. More than 1,200 entries provide brief definitions, some followed by longer entries. Includes cross-references. Some British emphasis. 40 p. bibliography. HM17.J37

Terminology

Booth, Barbara. Thesaurus of sociological indexing terms / Barbara Booth, principal lexicographer, and Michael Blair, thesaurus development & indexing manager. 3rd ed. San Diego, Calif. : Sociological Abstracts, 1992. 330 p.   **CC20**
1st ed., 1986.
Used in creation and searching of *Sociological abstracts* (CC13). Introductory material describes use and publishing history. Lists descriptors added with 3rd edition. Main section lists terms alphabetically. Entries may include history note, used for, scope notes, and broader, narrower, and related terms. Includes rotated descriptor display, classification scheme, bibliography.   Z695.1.S63B66

Thematic list of descriptors—sociology = Liste thématique des descripteurs—sociologie / prepared on behalf of UNESCO by the International Committee for Social Science Information and Documentation. London ; N.Y. : Routledge, 1989. 475 p.   **CC21**
Companion to *International bibliography of sociology* (CC8). For full description, see CE52.   Z695.1.S63T48

Quotations

Bardis, Panos Demetrios. Dictionary of quotations in sociology. Westport, Conn. : Greenwood, 1985. 356 p.   **CC22**
Intends "to present the nature, origin, development, and current status of general sociological concepts through direct quotation."—*Pref.* Cross-cultural, interdisciplinary, and historical in coverage, entries appear in chronological order under alphabetically arranged subject headings such as alienation, class struggle, ideology, methodology, power, division of labor, and violence. Each entry provides author, book title, and date of first publication. Bibliography; name and subject indexes.   HM17.B37

Handbooks

Bart, Pauline. The student sociologist's handbook / Pauline Bart, Linda Frankel. 4th ed. N.Y. : Random House, c1986. 291 p.   **CC23**
1st ed., 1971; 3rd ed., 1981.
"A survival kit for sociology students."—*Pref.* In seven subject chapters, describes more than 500 reference sources and journals. Unlike earlier editions, sections on sex roles and women's studies journals have been greatly expanded. Adds chapter on computers in sociology. Appendixes include Dewey Decimal and Library of Congress classifications. Index.   HM68.B37

Fredericks, Marcel A. Second steps in sociology : use and misuse of sociological concepts / Marcel Fredericks and Steven I. Miller. N.Y. : P. Lang, c1990. 261 p. : ill.   **CC24**
Introduces the student to conceptual analysis, focusing upon basic sociological terms. Chapters cover the classifying and defining of terms; approaches for analyzing sociological definitions; deductive logic; inductive logic; and descriptive models of analysis. Study questions follow each chapter; a final set of questions is organized by topic. Appendixes notable for reference use, as they describe contributions of influential sociologists (p. 175–98); provide 14-page glossary of selected concepts; and list references, grouped by subject and alphabetically by author (p. 213–50). Subject and author indexes.   HM24.F733 1990

Handbook of clinical sociology / ed. by Howard M. Rebach and John G. Bruhn. N.Y. : Plenum Pr., c1991. 410 p. : ill.   **CC25**

Intended for students, sociologists, instructors, and those in clinical disciplines. 22 essays each in four parts: covers definition and history; the common concerns of practitioners; practice in several settings; mental health settings and work with ethnic minorities, women, elderly, and substance abusers. General index.   HM73.H315

Handbook of contemporary developments in world sociology / ed. by Raj P. Mohan and Don Martindale. Westport, Conn. : Greenwood, 1975. 493 p. (Contributions in sociology, 17).   **CC26**
Analyzes, on a regional and an individual country basis, the status of post-World War II sociology. Each article, written by a scholar in the field, discusses historical and intellectual background of the discipline, teaching and research, methodology, and fields of specialization; some articles also treat organizations, research centers, and periodicals in the field. Bibliographical notes.   HM19.H23

Handbook of sociology / Neil J. Smelser, ed. Newbury Park, Calif. : Sage, c1988. 824 p.   **CC27**
The first general handbook of sociology since Robert E. L. Faris's *Handbook of modern sociology* (Chicago : Rand McNally, 1964). Individual chapters by experts treat nearly all the discipline's major fields, discuss "problems and issues that have persisted in the field" (*Introd.*), and summarize recent trends in empirical research. Substantial bibliographies.   HM51.H249

Krathwohl, David R. Methods of educational and social science research : an integrated approach. N.Y. ; London : Longman, 1993. 789 p. : ill.   **CC28**
Designed to introduce research methodology to advanced students. Chapters begin with an overview and outline of contents, and conclude with a summary, definitions of terms, suggested readings, and application problems. Section 1, The nature of research, analyzes the components of the research process, with copies of actual research studies. Subsequent sections deal with research skills (e.g., literature review, statistics), causal inference, research methods (e.g., historical methods, longitudinal studies); and the social context in which research takes place. Glossary. Substantial bibliography. Name and subject indexes.
————. *Social and behavioral science research : a new framework for conceptualizing, implementing, and evaluating research studies* (San Francisco : Jossey-Bass, 1985. 324 p.). Describes and evaluates current social science research methodology. Although this earlier work covers similar ground, it is not superseded by the more recent and more ambitious publication.   H62.K6793

SOCIAL CONDITIONS AND SOCIAL WELFARE

General Works

Bibliography

Biegel, David E. Social networks and mental health : an annotated bibliography / David E. Biegel, Ellen McCardle, Susan Mendelson. Beverly Hills, Calif. : Sage, [1985]. 391 p. **CC29**
Lists 1,340 citations, mostly to journal articles, 1950–82, under five major headings: Overview and theory; Research—physical health; Research—mental health; Intervention; and Professional roles and policy. Entries are consecutively numbered and alphabetically arranged by author under various chapter subtopics. Author and subject indexes.
Continued by: *Social support networks : a bibliography, 1983–1987*, comp. by David E. Biegel (N.Y. : Greenwood, 1989. 334 p.).

Updates Biegel's earlier bibliography with 2,693 entries covering 1983–87. Similar arrangement; each entry includes several keywords.
Z6664.N5B54

Discrimination and prejudice : an annotated bibliography / comp. and ed. by Halford H. Fairchild ... [et al.]. 2nd ed. San Diego, Calif. : Westerfield Enterprises, c1992. 312 p. **CC30**
1st ed., 1991.
Covers social science material pertaining to economic, employment, health, housing, criminal justice, and political discrimination. 1,568 entries include articles, books, and dissertations, most from 1960–80. Four parts: African Americans, Native Americans, Asian Americans, Hispanic Americans. A fifth part treats research on two or more groups. Each part is divided by subtopic, within which entries are arranged alphabetically by author. Entries include annotations. Each bibliography includes subject index.
Z1361.E4D57

Social support and health : an annotated bibliography / John G. Bruhn ... [et al.]. N.Y. : Garland, 1987. 504 p. (Garland library of sociology, vol. 13 ; Garland reference library of social science, v. 412). **CC31**
Presents 1,247 entries in seven chapters covering social networks, physical health and rehabilitation, mental health, the life cycle, social and cultural factors, and applications. Entries, arranged alphabetically under subdivisions, provide brief summary, suggested audience, and type of material (literature review, research, case report, etc.) Emphasizes English-language publications of the 1980s; omits popular literature. Author and subject indexes.
RA418.S6495

Social welfare in America : an annotated bibliography / ed. by Walter I. Trattner and W. Andrew Achenbaum. Westport, Conn. : Greenwood, 1983. 324 p. **CC32**
Provides 1,410 citations to "general surveys, major monographs, scholarly articles, and dissertations written since 1945, as well as some documentaries and a number of older works ... concerning social welfare ... from the early 1600s to the early 1980s."—*Introd.* Topical arrangement by age group, further subdivided chronologically and topically. Author and subject indexes.
Z7164.C4S6

Encyclopedias

DiCanio, Margaret. The encyclopedia of violence : origins, attitudes, consequences. N.Y. : Facts on File, c1993. 404 p.
CC33
"An album of snapshots of the places violence enters everyday life in late 20th century America."—*Introd.* Cross-referenced entries range in length from several lines to several pages. Sample entries: hate groups, arson, illiteracy in prisons, riots, satanic cult rituals, serial killers. Appendixes include 36-page article on organized crime; shorter article on behavioral sciences' limitations in studying violence; list of resources, grouped by subject. 15-page bibliography; general index.
HM291.D4857

Directories

Schorr, Alan Edward. Refugee and immigrant resource directory. 3rd ed. Juneau, Alaska : Denali Pr., c1994. 255 p. : ill.
CC34
1st ed., 1987, had title: *Directory of services for refugees and immigrants*; 2nd ed., 1990/91.
Entries are arranged by state and city, then by name of group. Includes names, address, phone, fax, contact, services offered, year established, staff, budget, Board of Immigration Appeals (BIA) status, religious affiliation, clientele, narrative, publications. Appendixes include relevant documents and statistical data, directory of INS and U.N. offices. Indexes for organizational names, contact persons, services, clientele, religious affiliation, and BIA appeals status.
HV640.4.U54S365

Volunteerism : the directory of organizations, training, programs, and publications. 1991– . New Providence, N.J. : Bowker, c1991– . Irregular. **CC35**
1st ed., 1980, had title: *Community resource tie line*; 2nd ed., 1984, had title: *Community resources directory*.
"Who is doing what for whom across the country?"—*Introd.* Includes organizations that assist local volunteer program leaders for free or at nominal costs. Administrative/organizational resource section covers business/industry, self-help, information and referral, training, fundraising, communications, community services, etc. Entries provide name, address, objectives, sponsor, contact, services, publications, etc. Section 2 arranges entries by subject (e.g., AIDS, day care, drug abuse, health, literacy, welfare reform). Chapters divided into national/state, training, and individual program profiles. Annotated bibliography (Section 3) lists and describes some 2,000 resources, grouped alphabetically under subject. Organization name and geographic indexes.
HN90.V64C65

Webster, Linda. Sexual assault and child sexual abuse : a national directory of victim/survivor services and prevention programs. Phoenix : Oryx, 1989. 353 p. **CC36**
The foreword includes statistics on sexual assault and describes the history of rape and rape crisis centers. The directory proper includes rape crisis centers; domestic violence shelters; victim assistance programs; mental health services for child victims, their families, and adult survivors; prevention programs; self-defense classes; and offender treatment programs. Arranges entries by state, then city, then alphabetically. Appendixes state agencies; national organizations with descriptions and publications; facilities alphabetically by name. Index of specialized services and clientele.
HV6561.W45

Handbooks

Female criminality : the state of the art / ed. by Concetta C. Culliver. N.Y. : Garland, 1993. 549 p. (Garland library of sociology, v. 22 ; Garland reference library of social science, v. 796). **CC37**
Chapters in Pt. 1 review the problems, changes, and trends; in Pt. 2 they analyze new developments, e.g., gender issues, white collar crime, drug dealing, intrasexual homicide, serial killing. Pt. 3 examines the justice system's responses and treatment of female offenders. All chapters conclude with reference lists; many provide statistical tables. Epilogue estimates research and program needs by year 2000. No indexes.
HV6046.F363

Biography

American reformers / ed., Alden Whitman. N.Y. : H.W. Wilson, 1985. 930 p. : ports. **CC38**
A work for students and general readers, giving "brief but incisive biographical sketches of the principal reformers in America from the seventeenth century to modern times."—*Pref.* Includes both moderate and radical reformers ("disturbers of the social peace") in 61 categories (e.g., abolition, anarchism, black rights, libraries, food reform/vegetarianism, women's rights, temperance). 508 signed entries, alphabetically arranged, include a photograph, biographical sketch, detailed endnotes, and location of the subject's papers, if known. CT215.A67

Biographical dictionary of social welfare in America / Walter I. Trattner, ed. N.Y. : Greenwood, 1986. 897 p. **CC39**
Emphasizes the doers and activists, not the philosophers or givers. More than 300 signed articles, each three to four pages in length and alphabetically arranged, provide birth and death dates; a summary of life, career, and contributions; and a selected bibliography of sources by and about the subject. Indicates location of the subject's papers, if known. Useful appendixes offer a chronology of significant events and a list of subjects by year and place of birth. General index.
HV27.B57

Statistics

Wood, Elizabeth J. She said, he said : what men and women really think about money, sex, politics, and other issues of essence / Elizabeth J. Wood, Floris W. Wood. Detroit : Visible Ink Pr., c1992. 284 p. : ill.   **CC40**

In question and answer format. Compares responses of women and men to questions regarding politics, family, money, drugs, crime, religion, death, etc. Table of contents provides the only subject access. Data derived from Floris Wood's *American profile : opinions and behavior 1972–1989* (CJ484) and *General social survey (GSS)* conducted by National Opinion Research Center (NORC). No indexes.

HN90.P8W66

Social work

Guides

Mendelsohn, Henry N. An author's guide to social work journals. 3rd ed. Wash. : NASW Pr., National Association of Social Workers, c1992. 282 p.   **CC41**

1st ed., 1983; 2nd ed., 1987.

Entries for the 138 journals include journal affiliation, editorial focus, where indexed/abstracted, circulation, special issues, formats required, style guidelines, acceptance rates, publication lag, reprint policies, subscription costs, etc. Information gleaned from current journal issues, questionnaires sent to journal editors, and periodical directories. Appendix lists publication information and brief descriptions for 15 style manuals.

HV85.M46

Bibliography

Li, Hong-Chan. Social work education : a bibliography. Metuchen, N.J. : Scarecrow, 1978–89. 2 v.   **CC42**

Contents: v. 1, 1960–76; v. 2, 1977–87.

Classed bibliography of some 5,800 entries. Includes books, periodicals, government documents. International in scope, but limited to English-language materials. Sample headings include radical social work, private practice, off-campus programs, homosexuality. Author index in each volume; cumulative subject index in v. 2.

Z7164.C4L49

Parham, Iris A. Gerontological social work : an annotated bibliography. Westport, Conn. : Greenwood, 1993. 207 p. (Bibliographies and indexes in gerontology, no. 19).   **CC43**

Groups entries into chapters compiled by leaders in the field, covering topics of general works, clinical practice issues, educational issues, geriatric and health services in social work, and resource materials. Entries are arranged alphabetically by author within chapters. Lists and describes journals, audiovisuals, organizations, media resource guides. Author and subject indexes.

Z7164.O4G44

Indexes; Abstract journals

Kendall, Katherine A. Social casework. Cumulative index, 1920–1989 / comp. by Katherine A. Kendall ; rev. and updated by Janice T. Paine. Greenwich, Conn. : JAI Pr., c1992. 673 p.   **CC44**

1st ed., 1982, was cumulative index for 1920–79.

Revises and updates 1982 edition, adding entries for 1980–89. Citations grouped under 272 subject areas. Includes 168 separate *see*

references. Covers 70 years of *Social casework* and its predecessor journals. Most articles appear under more than one classification. Consists of subject, author, title, and book review indexes.   HV1.K45

Social work research & abstracts. v. 13, no. 2 (Summer 1977)– . [N.Y.] : National Assoc. of Social Workers, 1977– . Quarterly.   **CC45**

Supersedes *Abstracts for social workers* which ceased with v. 13, no. 1 (Spring 1977), and continues its numbering.

Each issue presents five or six research papers, followed by abstracts of articles grouped within four main sections: (1) social work profession; (2) theory and practice; (3) areas of service; (4) social issues/social problems. Quarterly author and subject indexes cumulate annually.

•Machine-readable version: *Social work abstracts* [database] (Wash. : National Assoc. of Social Workers, 1977–). Available online and on CD-ROM, updated quarterly. Citations with abstracts to literature of social work and related disciplines. International in scope; cites English-language journal articles and dissertations.   HV1.A2

Encyclopedias

Encyclopedia of social work / Anne Minahan, ed. in chief. 18th ed. Silver Spring, Md. : National Association of Social Workers, 1987. 2 v.   **CC46**

1st ed., 1929. 1st–14th ed. called *Social work yearbook*. 17th ed., 1977.

Offers 225 topical articles, alphabetically arranged, that reflect the increasingly interdisciplinary nature of social work. Highlights implications "for social work practice, for ethnic, racial, and cultural minorities, and for women."—*Pref.* The Preface explains eight content areas, and a how-to-use section lists article titles, names of those in the biography section, and contributors. Approximately a third of the articles retain their titles from the 1977 edition, but new titles treat such topics as adolescent pregnancy, divorce and separation, homelessness, homosexuality, immigrants, purchasing social services, and workfare. The lengthy, signed articles conclude with source bibliographies and cross-references to other articles, and many provide reading lists. Each volume contains a general index to both volumes. Appendixes: (1) Code of ethics of the National Association of Social Workers; (2) Curriculum policy for the Master's degree and Baccalaureate degree programs in social work education; (3) NASW standards for the practice of clinical social work; and (4) Guide to sources of information on social welfare agencies.

————. *1990 supplement*, Encyclopedia Supplement Committee, Leon Ginsberg ... [et al.] (Silver Spring, Md. : National Association of Social Workers, 1990. 348 p.). Extends and updates topics from the 18th edition. 21 signed articles address such issues as AIDS-HIV, homelessness, home care, youth gangs. One chapter reviews statistics in social work education, employment, social welfare expenditures, demographics. Reference lists for each chapter. Index.

§ The statistics were updated by: *Face of the nation, 1987 : statistical supplement to the 18th edition of the Encyclopedia of social work* / Sumner M. Rosen, David Fanshel, and Mary E. Lutz, editors (Silver Spring, Md. : National Association of Social Workers, c1987. 124 p.) Presents data on various subjects covered in the 18th ed. For teachers, students, and practitioners. 11 sections provide text, tables, and charts on demographics, employment, social indicators, child welfare, social welfare expenditures, and other topics. Sources of data are cited. Table of contents indicates section topic and lists tables and graphics. No index.   HV35.E6

Dictionaries

Barker, Robert L. The social work dictionary. 2nd ed. Silver Spring, Md. : National Assoc. of Social Workers, NASW Pr., c1991. 287 p.   **CC47**

1st ed., 1987.

Contains brief entries for some 3,000 terms selected from major social work journals, textbooks, and the literature of related disciplines, reflecting various social work orientations and philosophy. Includes a chronology of significant social welfare events, 1750 BCE to the present, and National Association of Social Workers' code of ethics. Cross-references.   HV12.B37

Directories

National directory of children, youth & families services. 7th ed. (1991–92)– . Longmont, Colo. : Marion L. Peterson, c1991– . Biennial.   **CC48**

Supersedes *National directory of children & youth services* and continues its numbering.

For the human services professional, student, or practitioner. Pt. 1 (p. 1–724) includes entries for state, county, and city agancies, first listing statewide agencies, then alphabetically by county. Includes social, health, juvenile justice, special service agencies. Includes personnel, addresses, phone, fax, etc. Pt. 2 includes directory information for federal level programming, including executive branch, senate, house, national organizations. Pt. 3 groups resources, services, and products by subject. Introductory material instructs on best use of directory, also lists community names alphabetically by state. Lists health and welfare hotline numbers.   HV741.N3157

Rao, Vijaya. World guide to social work education / comp. by Vijaya Rao ; ed. by Katherine A. Kendall. 2nd ed. N.Y. : Publ. by the Council on Social Work Education for the International Association of Schools of Social Work, c1984. 223 p.   **CC49**

Previous ed., 1974, by Patricia J. Stickney and Rosa Perla Resnick.

Aims to assist schools of social work, employers of social workers, and interested readers in assessing "the approximate comparability of social work qualifications"—*(Pref.)* among countries. Describes 74 schools in 61 countries, 24 national and regional associations, and the International Association of Schools of Social Work. Countries and regions are listed alphabetically in each of the three sections: Schools, National associations, and Regional associations. No indexes.

HV11.R3125

Who's who among human services professionals. 1986/ 1987– . Owings Mills, Md. : National Reference Institute, c1986– . Biennial.   **CC50**

Includes such occupations as social worker, nurse, counselor, psychiatrist, psychologist, health administrator, school administrator, family therapist. Entries provide name, occupation, vital statistics, parent, marriage, children, education, professional certifications, career, writings, civic or political activities, military, awards and fellowships, professional and association memberships, political affiliation, religion, home and office addresses. Entries listed alphabetically by name. Abbreviations list.   HV40.3.W48

Handbooks

Blackburn, Clare. Improving health and welfare work with families in poverty : a handbook. Buckingham ; Philadelphia : Open Univ. Pr., 1992. 119 p. : ill.   **CC51**

Designed for social services and health care professionals. Eight sections, each with introduction, aims, activities, facilitator's notes, etc. Sections address: defining and understanding poverty, critical thinking, family health and well-being, experience of poverty, planning for change, and evaluation. U.K. orientation, but useful for U.S. readers. Distills information; provides guidelines, questions, and activities for team training.   RA418.5.P6B52

Ginsberg, Leon H. Social work almanac. Wash. : NASW Pr., c1992. 215 p. : ill., maps.   **CC52**

Intended as a single compendium of relevant data for social workers and other interested readers. Tables and figures with explanatory text arranged in nine topical chapters covering U.S. demographics, children, crime and delinquency, education, health and mortality, mental illness, older adults, social welfare, and professional issues. Data sources provided, most from U.S. census, state and federal agencies, and voluntary social organizations. Four-page reference list; general index.   HV90.G53

Mental health and social work career directory / Bradley J. Morgan and Joseph M. Palmisano, editors ; Diane M. Sawinski, associate ed. Detroit : Visible Ink Pr., c1993. 357 p.   **CC53**

In four sections: (1) Advice from the pros, with 25 chapters written by practitioners, describing specific careers (e.g., family psychologist, school social worker, community organizer); (2) Job search process, treating evaluation of strengths, networking, targeting employers, résumé and letter writing, interview questions; (3) Job opportunities databank, describing some 350 facilities offering entry-level jobs or internships, including their benefits and application procedures; (4) Career resources, listing professional associations, employment agencies, sources for job ads, career guides, periodicals, reference sources. General index.

Professional writing for the human services / ed. by Linda Beebe. Wash. : National Association of Social Workers, NASW Pr., 1993. 325 p. : ill.   **CC54**

Practical information organized in four parts. Pt. 1 covers basic writing techniques, qualitative and quantitative research, and graphics, and offers a very thorough overview of library research and tools. Pt. 2 addresses peer review, journal submissions, book proposals, and production. Pt. 3 covers frequently-seen problems and offers tips from the NASW Press's internal style guide. Pt. 4 includes sample contracts and permission statements, submission guidelines for NASW Press books and journals, lists ethical responsibilities, and gives editors and addresses for 34 core journals. General index.   HV41.P759

Aging

Bibliography

Abuse of the elderly : issues and annotated bibliography / comp. and ed. by Benjamin Schlesinger and Rachel Schlesinger. Toronto ; Buffalo : Univ. of Toronto Pr., [1988?]. 188 p.
CC55

Includes social and health sciences materials, 1978–87, for U.S. and Canada. Ten introductory essays with reference lists; 267-item bibliography in 43 subject categories. Entries are alphabetical by author; author index.   HV6626.3.A28

Aday, Ron H. Crime and the elderly : an annotated bibliography. N.Y. : Greenwood, 1988. 118 p. (Bibliographies and indexes in gerontology, no. 8).   **CC56**

A bibliography of 361 entries in two main units: the first details crimes against the elderly and has chapters dealing with criminal justice, victims, abuse and neglect, etc.; the second treats the elderly as criminals, and has chapters dealing with old age, crime patterns, prisoners, etc. Pt. 3 lists other resources and information such as crime prevention programs for older persons. Includes sources published, for the most part, in the U.S. since 1970. Author and subject indexes.

Z5703.4.A35A33

Aging : a guide to resources / ed. by John B. Balkema. N.Y. : Gaylord Professional Publ. in assoc. with Neal-Schuman, 1983. 232 p.   **CC57**

An annotated bibliography of reference sources and "working tools" for professionals in social gerontology. Emphasizes bibliographies, directories, statistics, periodicals, guides, handbooks and manuals; English-language books, pamphlets, periodicals. Broad subject arrangement; each chapter is further subdivided by topics and formats. Name and subject indexes. Z7164.O4A33

An annotated bibliography on adult day programs and dementia care / National Council on the Aging, Alzheimer's Association, Dementia Care & Respite Services Program. Winston-Salem, N.C. : Bowman Gray School of Medicine of Wake Forest Univ., Dementia Care and Respite Services Program, 1992. 141 p. **CC58**

For caregivers, experts, and day center staff in the field of aging. Section 1 describes 214 articles and books for adult day programs, alphabetically by author. Section 2 contains three separate listings: references on Alzheimer's, dementia care, and respite services, including articles, catalogs, manuals, books, periodicals, audiovisuals. Combined author/title index; subject "guide" (index). Lists addresses of indexed periodicals. Z6665.7.A45A54

Anthropology of aging : a partially annotated bibliography / Marjorie M. Schweitzer, gen. ed. N.Y. : Greenwood, 1991. 338 p. (Bibliographies and indexes in gerontology, no. 13). **CC59**

Prep. under the auspices of the Association for Anthropology and Gerontology (AAGE); updates its *Topical bibliography* and the *Supplement to the topical bibliography on the anthropology of aging* (Chicago, 1982).

Includes books, book chapters, and articles, primarily from the 1980s. Annotates entries considered important. Organized into 14 chapters by two types of topics: (1) subjects; (2) regional or cultural groups. Entries arranged by author within chapters or chapter subtopics. Final chapter lists bibliographies. General index. Z7164.O4A55

Bailey, William G. Human longevity from antiquity to the modern lab : a selected, annotated bibliography. N.Y. : Greenwood, 1987. 208 p. (Bibliographies and indexes in gerontology, no. 4). **CC60**

A unique work that lists books and journal articles in 15 chapters covering topics such as health planning, rejuvenation, and biomedical research. Three appendixes include addresses of health centers and descriptions of research; addresses of U.S. health resorts, spas, and mineral baths; and science fiction novels and plays. Author and subject indexes. Z6663.A3B28

Borenstein, Audrey. Older women in 20th-century America : a selected annotated bibliography. N.Y. : Garland, 1982. 351 p. (Women's studies, v. 3 ; Garland reference library of social science, v. 122). **CC61**

Provides lengthy annotations for more than 800 books, essays, journal articles and dissertations concerned with women over 40. Includes literary works, oral histories, and published personal documents as well as social science materials and bibliographies. Subject arrangement; name index.

§ *The mature woman in America : a selected annotated bibliography, 1979–1982*, by Eleanor F. Dolan and Dorothy M. Gropp (Wash. : Nat. Council on the Aging, 1984. 122 p.) is intended to include nonliterary works not listed in the Borenstein bibliography for the 1979–82 period; 423 citations are entered under author, with subject index. Z7164.O4B67

Brazil, Mary Jo. Building library collections on aging : a selection guide and core list. Santa Barbara, Calif. : ABC-Clio, c1990. 174 p. **CC62**

In two main sections. The first, focusing on policy statements, selection criteria, and building a collection, lists book publishers, associations, federal offices, and other resources. The second, the "core list," occupying most of the book, contains bibliographies on 27 topics (e.g., alcohol and drug abuse, Alzheimer's disease, elder abuse, ethics and legal issues), subarranged by format (books, periodicals, videocassettes, etc.). Entries are annotated and listed alphabetically. General index. Z688.A58B7

Bull, C. Neil. The older volunteer : an annotated bibliography / comp. by C. Neil Bull and Nancy D. Levine. Westport, Conn. : Greenwood, 1993. 111 p. (Bibliographies and indexes in gerontology, no. 21). **CC63**

Covers North American material, 1980–91. Nearly 400 entries in seven chapters cover statistics, national databases, empirical studies, characteristics, barriers, settings, programs, special populations. Numbered entries, alphabetical by author, include citations and descriptive abstracts. Omits material on general volunteerism and related topics. Separate author and subject indexes. Z7164.V65B85

Coyle, Jean M. Families and aging : a selected, annotated bibliography. N.Y. : Greenwood, 1991. 208 p. (Bibliographies and indexes in gerontology, no. 14). **CC64**

Organizes 778 numbered entries into 11 subject chapters, e.g., grandparents, adult children, racial and ethnic minority groups, living arrangements, widowhood. Entries arranged by author under headings for formats: articles/chapters, books, audiovisuals, documents, dissertations. Covers 1980–90. Author and subject indexes. Z7164.O4C67

Davis, Lenwood G. The black aged in the United States : a selectively annotated bibliography. Rev. and updated, 2nd ed. N.Y. : Greenwood, 1989. 277 p. (Bibliographies and indexes in Afro-American and African studies, no. 23). **CC65**

1st ed., 1980.

Lists 633 titles published through 1987, grouped by subject and format. Includes books, dissertations, theses, articles, government publications. Topics include aged abuse, alcoholism, crime, hypertension, mental health, legal services. Provides directory of homes for the black aged, current as of 1988. Z1361.N39D354

Donavin, Denise Perry. Aging with style and savvy. Chicago : Amer. Libr. Assoc., 1990. 163 p. : ill. **CC66**

Includes nonfiction, plays, film/videos, and fiction, most published after 1983. Ten chapters list nonfiction entries by topic (e.g., Family relations; Health, fitness and sex; Travel and recreation; Retirement; Humor and reflections; Poetry). Chapters on plays, films, and fiction follow. Some 280 annotated entries appear alphabetically by author under each subtopic. Lists 22 organizations and associations. General index. HQ1064.U5D665

Edwards, Willie M. Gerontology : a cross-national core list of significant works / Willie M. Edwards and Frances Flynn. Ann Arbor, Mich. : Institute of Gerontology, Univ. of Michigan, c1982. 365 p. **CC67**

Prior ed., 1978, had title: *Gerontology : a core list of significant works*.

Classed bibliography of social gerontology, international in scope but emphasizing U.S., Canada, U.K., and eight other developed nations. Includes articles and books. Author and title indexes. Expands coverage of 1978 edition. Z7164.O4E39

Ethnicity and aging : a bibliography / comp. by Edward Murguia … [et al.]. San Antonio, Tex. : Trinity Univ. Pr., c1984. 132 p. (Checklists in the humanities and education, 8). **CC68**

Organizes 1,432 entries in six sections covering Multiethnic and general studies, Black Americans, Hispanic Americans, Native Americans, Asian and Pacific Americans, and European origin ethnic groups. Subarranged by topic with entries listed alphabetically by author. Most publications date from the 1970s and early 1980s. Includes only readily available materials; omits unpublished material and ephemera. No annotations; author indexes. Z7164.O4E85

Guttmann, David. European American elderly : an annotated bibliography. N.Y. : Greenwood, 1987. 122 p. (Bibliographies and indexes in gerontology, no. 6). **CC69**

Consists of 310 entries—books, articles, and government publications in English—arranged alphabetically by author under 24 topical sections included in six chapters. Publication dates range from the early 1970s to 1986. A seventh chapter contains a short list of other bibliographies; an appendix provides a list of related journal titles. Author and subject indexes. Z7165.U5G92

Harris, Diana K. Sociology of aging. 2nd ed. N.Y. : Harper & Row, c1990. 510 p. : ill. **CC70**

1st ed., 1985, covered 1960–80.

Topically arranged, English-language titles. Subjects include the older criminal, elder abuse, Alzheimer's, cryonics, shopping bag women, emergency response systems. Includes cross-cultural materials. Author index. HQ1064.U5H27

Johnson, Tanya F. Elder neglect and abuse : an annotated bibliography / comp. by Tanya F. Johnson, James G. O'Brien, and Margaret F. Hudson. Westport, Conn. : Greenwood, 1985. 223 p. (Bibliographies and indexes in gerontology, no. 1). **CC71**

For each of 144 annotated entries, provides topics, methods, and conclusions, also giving profession of the first author, type of exposition, and issues addressed. An unannotated list of 144 entries follows, divided into sections for periodical articles, state publications, and federal publications. Entries arranged by author within each list. Coverage: 1975–85. Lists state agencies, offices, and organizations. Appendix includes Model Adult Protective Services Act. List of journal abbreviations; author index. Z7164.O4J56

Nordquist, Joan. The elderly in America : a bibliography. Santa Cruz, Calif. : Reference and Research Services, 1991. 64 p. **CC72**

Arranges entries alphabetically by author within topical chapters, some with subtopics. Includes books, journals, book chapters, pamphlets, documents, directories, bibliographies. Seeks to represent a variety of viewpoints, and includes scholarly, general, and activist literatures. Topics include long-term and health care, abuse, minorities, women, ageism, law, statistics. Resources chapter lists bibliographies, directories, and organizations. No indexes. Z7164.04N57

Nuessel, Frank H. The image of older adults in the media : an annotated bibliography. Westport, Conn. : Greenwood, c1992. 181 p. **CC73**

558 annotated entries, arranged alphabetically by author in 21 topical chapters, which include ageism, attitudes and stereotypes, children's literature, art, humor, cartoons, greeting cards, advice, film, newspapers, oral history, television, etc. Author and cross-referenced subject indexes. Z5633.A39B5824

Oriol, William E. Federal public policy on aging since 1960 : an annotated bibliography. N.Y. : Greenwood, 1987. 127 p. (Bibliographies and indexes in gerontology, no. 5). **CC74**

Covers 1960–86. Pt. 1 (162 entries) covers general critiques and major themes. Pt. 2 (589 entries) covers issues and programs (e.g., income and retirement, health and long term care, Older Americans Act, discrimination, minorities, consumer issues, women). Entries are arranged alphabetically by author under each heading. An appendix describes relevant congressional committees and lists national organizations. Author and subject indexes. Z7164.O4O74

Strange, Heather. Aging & cultural diversity : new directions and annotated bibliography / Heather Strange, Michele Teitelbaum & contributors. South Hadley, Mass. : Bergin & Garvey Publ., 1987. 350 p. **CC75**

Eight essays in Pt. 1 treat inter- and intra-cultural diversity. The annotated bibliography of Pt. 2 is in five chapters covering: General works; Ethnic, national, racial, or regional studies; Comparative studies; Cross-cultural studies; and Bibliographies. Arranges entries alphabetically by author within each subtopic. Author and subject indexes. GN485.S77

Topics in gerontology : selected annotated bibliographies / ed. by Thomas O. Blank. Westport, Conn. : Greenwood, c1993. 212 p. (Bibliographies and indexes in gerontology, no. 22). **CC76**

For students and professionals. Includes social, behavioral, and biological perspectives. Arranged in an 11-chapter sequence which runs from macro- to micro-level; chapter essays introduce and define topics (e.g., history, health care, nursing, sleep, Alzheimer's, growth hormone). Alphabetically arranged entries include citations and evaluative abstracts. Separate author and subject indexes. Z7164.O4T66

Wharton, George F. Sexuality and aging : an annotated bibliography. Metuchen, N.J. : Scarecrow, 1981. 251 p. **CC77**

A 1978 ed. without annotations had title: *A bibliography of sexuality and aging.*

1,106 citations to a wide variety of literature are grouped in broad subject classifications, with author and title indexes. Some foreign language titles are included. Z7164.S42W48

Indexes; Abstract journals

Abstracts in social gerontology. v. 33, no. 1 (Mar. 1990)– . Newbury Park, Calif. : Sage Publications, c1990– . Quarterly. **CC78**

Continues *Current literature on aging* (Wash. : National Council on Aging) which ceased with v. 32, no. 4 (1989). Continues its volume numbering.

Abstracts about 250 journal articles per issue, including biological, medical, psychological, demographic, societal, economic, governmental, theoretical and other aspects. "Related citations" section follows abstracts, indexing books, articles, government publications, pamphlets, other fugitive material. Published in cooperation with the National Council on the Aging, Inc. Author and subject indexes cumulate annually.

•**AgeLine** [database]. Wash. : Amer. Assoc. of Retired Persons, National Gerontology Research Center, 1978– . **CC79**

Available online and on CD-ROM. Updated bimonthly.

Contains citations with abstracts to the journal, monograph, and report literature of social gerontology, focusing on social, psychological, and economic aspects of aging. Primarily U.S. coverage in English. Documents indexed using *Thesaurus of aging terminology* (CC84).

Encyclopedias

The encyclopedia of aging / George L. Maddox, ed. in chief. N.Y. : Springer Publ., c1987. 890 p. : ill. **CC80**

Signed articles, alphabetically arranged, treat key topics regarding aging, legislation, government agencies, foundations, and membership organizations. Entries (typically two to three columns, some as long as 16—e.g., Social security) include Asian-American aged, Cell morphology, Demography, Congressional committees, Gray Panthers, Health care policy, Sexuality, and World Assembly on Aging. Separate list of headwords; tables, diagrams, and figures; list of 224 contributors. 128 pages of references; detailed general index. HQ1061.E53

Roy, Frederick Hampton. The encyclopedia of aging and the elderly / F. Hampton Roy and Charles Russell. N.Y. : Facts on File, c1992. 308 p. : ill. **CC81**

Cross-referenced entries, most ½–2 columns in length, arranged alphabetically; some entries include short reference lists. Multidisciplinary in coverage; useful for general readers and specialists alike. Appendixes: tables and graphs; addresses for national and state organizations. Bibliography; detailed general index. HQ1061.R69

Dictionaries

Harris, Diana K. Dictionary of gerontology. N.Y. : Greenwood, 1988. 201 p. **CC82**

Contains statistical and research terms used in gerontology. Entries include bibliographies, cross-references, origin, and first usage. Name index. HQ1061.H338

International glossary of social gerontology = Glosario internacional de gerontología social = Glossaire international de gérontologie sociale = Internationales Wörterverzeichnis für Sozialgerontologie / editors, Mary Jo Storey Gibson, Charlotte Nusberg. N.Y. : Van Nostrand Reinhold Co., c1985. lxx, 96 p.
CC83

Defines 287 terms in English, Spanish, French, and German (across four columns per page), arranged alphabetically by the English version. Introductory materials and the subject index are presented in all four languages.   HQ1061.I5348

Thesaurus of aging terminology : AgeLine database on middle age and aging / produced by the American Association of Retired Persons. 4th ed. Wash. : National Gerontology Resource Center, American Association of Retired Persons, 1991. 202 p.   **CC84**

Contains 1,788 main descriptors and 347 additional terms used as cross-references. Three sections: Relational terms, Rotated terms, and Geographical terms. Entries provide date term first included, scope notes, and used for (UT), broader term (BT), narrower term (NT), and related term (RT) references. Lists descriptors new to this edition. Used to produce *AgeLine* database (CC79).   Z695.1.A376T48

Directories

Congregate care by county. Jan. 1989– . Phoenix : Oryx, c1989– . Semiannual.   **CC85**

A directory of more than 6,800 continuing care retirement communities in the U.S. Arranged geographically by state and county, each entry contains the name of the institution, address and telephone, contact person, average monthly fees, type and number of nursing beds, etc. Indexed by type of facility and by type of ownership.   HD7287.92.U54C67

National directory of educational programs in gerontology and geriatrics / members of the Association for Gerontology in Higher Education. 5th ed. (1991)– . Wash. : Association for Gerontology in Higher Education, 1991– . Every three years.   **CC86**

Continues *National directory of educational programs in gerontology* (1976–1987).

Presents results of a survey by the Association to determine the extent of training in the field offered by American and Canadian institutions. In two main sections: (1) a brief tabular listing of all institutions surveyed providing little more than the number of courses and units each offers and of faculty involved; (2) one-page descriptions of each program including degrees offered, areas of specialty, course requirements, etc. In alphabetical order by state.   HQ1060.N35

Older Americans information directory / John Krol, ed. ; Jolen Marya Gedridge and Sara Tal Waldorf, assoc. editors. Detroit : Gale, 1994. 648 p.   **CC87**

Subtitle: Guide to organizations, agencies, institutions, programs, publications, services, and other resources concerned with older Americans in the United States.

Organizes more than 5,500 entries in 20 chapters by type of resource. Includes organizations, research centers, legal aid resources, discount programs, hotlines, awards and prizes, education programs, libraries, agencies, publications, videos, and electronic resources. Entries provide name, address, phone, most with description. Brief chapter introductions. 106-p. name and subject index.   HV1450.O43

Post, Joyce A. Gerontology and geriatrics libraries and collections in the United States and Canada : a history, description, and directory. Westport, Conn. : Greenwood, 1992. 196 p.   **CC88**

Following a description of history and bibliographic activities, including federal government involvement, the directory section describes collections: geographic location; types; hours, space, and seating; staffing; equipment; collection information (special, serials, sub-

ject strength); cataloging and classification; services (reference, circulation, interlibrary loans, database searching); public relations; automation; users; networking and resource sharing. The directory is arranged geographically, then alphabetically by name. Five appendixes provide: survey questionnaire; indexes for type of library or collection; serial holdings; collection strengths; and hardware or software used. 9-page bibliography; general index.   Z688.A58P67

Resource directory for older people / National Institute on Aging. [Bethesda, Md.] : U.S. National Institutes of Health, 1993. 240 p. (United States. National Institutes of Health. NIH publication, no. 93-738).   **CC89**

Superintendent of Documents classification: HE 20.3868:R 31.
Previous ed., 1989.

Lists and describes only 227 national associations, institutes, and foundations which offer health, legal, self-help, educational, social services, or consumer assistance. Includes federal, professional, private, and voluntary groups. Arranges entries alphabetically by name, one per page, leaving much blank space on bottom of many pages. Entries provide address, phone, mission, services, publications. Subject index.   HV1450.R47

Senior citizen services : how to find and contact 15,000 providers. 1st ed.– . Detroit : Gale, c1993– . Biennial.   **CC90**

In four regional volumes covering Northeastern, Southern and Mid-Atlantic, Midwestern, and Western states. In each volume, separate sections for each state begin with a useful geographic/service index for cities, counties, and types of services. Numbered entries are listed geographically by state, then alphabetically by name. Entries provide name, address, phone, contact person, areas served, days/hours, and services. Includes government agencies, nonprofit organizations, and companies that offer free or low-cost services. A cumulative organization/agency index covers all states in each regional volume.

U.S. aging policy interest groups : institutional profiles / ed. by David D. Van Tassel and Jimmy Elaine Wilkinson Meyer. N.Y. : Greenwood, 1992. 258 p. : ill.   **CC91**

Describes 83 organizations that attempt to influence U.S. public policy on the aging. Omits official government groups, and groups less focused on advocacy, e.g., recreation or service groups. An introductory essay, providing subject background and including references, is followed by a 2 p. chronological list of enacted federal legislation. Signed entries list interest groups alphabetically, providing address, phone, fax, description, origins and development, funding, policy concerns and tactics, publications, and further information list. Appendixes list additional organizations, with addresses and phones, and organizational members of aging coalitions for 1991. 4 p. selected bibliography. General index.   HQ1064.U5U22

Handbooks

Abuse of the elderly : a guide to resources and services / [ed. by] Joseph J. Costa. Lexington, Mass. : Lexington Books, [1984]. 289 p.   **CC92**

Pt. 1 (p. 3–95) consists of essays on physical abuse and crimes against the aged in the United States; pt. 2 (p. 99–289) provides directory information and a partially annotated bibliography (arranged alphabetically by main entry, with no subject access).   HV1461.A28

America's elderly : a sourcebook / ed. by Edward E. Duensing. New Brunswick, N.J. : Center for Urban Policy Research, c1988. 190 p. : ill.   **CC93**

More than 200 graphs and tables in seven chapters that cover demographics, income and expenditures, employment and unemployment, health and health care, housing and homeownership, federal programs and expenditures, and social characteristics. Tables and figures indicate sources of data. No indexes.   HQ1064.U5A646

Developments and research on aging : an international handbook / ed. by Erdman B. Palmore. [Rev. ed.]. Westport, Conn. : Greenwood, 1993. 429 p. : ill. **CC94**

1st. ed., 1980, had title: *International handbook on aging : contemporary developments and research.*

Surveys programs and research in 25 countries or regions; those included tend to have higher proportions of industrialization, urbanization, and aged population. Chapters describe unique features, roles and status of aged, growth of discipline, information sources. Includes tabular data. Appendix lists gerontological and geriatric associations by region. Brief bibliography; general index. HQ1061.D48

Doress-Worters, Paula Brown. Ourselves, growing older : women aging with knowledge and power / Paula Brown Doress and Diana Laskin Siegal and the Midlife and Older Women Book Project ; in cooperation with the Boston Women's Health Book Collective. N.Y. : Simon and Schuster, c1987. 511 p. : ill. **CC95**

Addresses specific concerns of older women, in style and format similar to *New our bodies, ourselves* (CC564). In three parts: aging well; living with ourselves and others; and understanding, preventing, and managing medical problems. Chapters address changing habits, appearances, nutrition, movement, sexuality, birth control, menopause, living arrangements, caregiving, osteoporosis, memory loss, hysterectomy, and much more. Includes high quality illustrations and photographs, detailed end notes, statistics, demographic data, social and feminist analysis, poetry, personal stories. Resources chapter (p. 417–79) lists and describes organizations, books, periodicals, older women's presses, catalogs, audiovisuals, etc. for each of the 30 chapters. HQ1064.U5D67

Encyclopedia of senior citizens information sources : a bibliographic guide to approximately 13,500 citations for publications, organizations, and other sources of information on nearly 300 subjects / Paul Wasserman, Barbara Koehler, and Yvonne Lev, editors. Detroit : Gale, c1987. 492 p. **CC96**

Includes English-language sources, most published after 1980, organized by topic (e.g., alcoholism, counseling, day care, poverty, senility). Entries are arranged alphabetically by title within subcategories such as abstract services and indexes, associations and professional societies, bibliographies, directories, handbooks, online databases, and statistical sources. Cross-references; detailed table of contents. Z7164.O4E53

Handbook of aging and the social sciences / editors, Robert H. Binstock and Linda K. George ... [et al.]. 3rd ed. San Diego, Calif. : Academic Pr., c1990. 489 p. : ill. **CC97**

1st ed., 1976; 2nd ed., 1985.

Reviews research; chapters written by specialists. Topics include diversity and heterogeneity, old age pensions, leisure and time use, geographic distribution and migration, illness, social structure, etc. Exhaustive bibliographies for each chapter. Author and subject indexes.

§ Other titles in the "Handbooks of aging" series are *Handbooks of the biology of aging*, ed. by Edward L. Schneider and John W. Rowe (3rd ed., 1990), and *Handbook of the psychology of aging*, ed. by James E. Birren and K. Warner Schaie (3rd ed., 1990). HQ1061.H336

Kouri, Mary K. Volunteerism and older adults. Santa Barbara, Calif. : ABC-Clio, c1990. 197 p. **CC98**

Pt. 1 includes chapters on types of volunteerism, opportunities, locations, and keys to success. Pt. 2 describes organizations, professional societies, volunteer networks, books, bibliographies, directories, periodicals, newsletters, pamphlets, films, videos, and databases. Entries are alphabetical by name or author in each category. General index. HN90.V64K68

Millman, Linda Josephson. Legal issues and older adults. Santa Barbara, Calif. : ABC-Clio, c1992. 273 p. **CC99**

Pt. 1, in eight chapters, addresses such issues as legal services, income security, health care, housing, estate planning, and family law. Following the same topics, Pt. 2 lists corresponding government, pri-

vate, nonprofit, and community organizations; many entries include descriptions. The final chapter summarizes resources for these topics, including books, articles, pamphlets, looseleaf services, audiovisuals, databases, and software. Eight-page glossary; general index.
KF390.A4M55

Pritchard, Jacki. The abuse of elderly people : a handbook for professionals. London ; Philadelphia : J. Kingsley Publ., 1992. 174 p. **CC100**

For all professionals who work with older people, and for students. Defines abuse and neglect, outlines basic rights, and provides guidelines and many cases. Includes statistical data and background. Suggested reading list. Slight British emphasis. HV6626.3.P75

Rix, Sara E. Older workers. Santa Barbara, Calif. : ABC-Clio, c1990. 243 p. **CC101**

Narrative section consists of topical chapters, each starting with a list of facts and addressing subjects such as trends, age discrimination, social security, training, opportunities, and older women. Resources section lists and describes, with full citation or address, organizations, publications, computerized sources, videos, and films. Glossary, list of references, general index. HD6280.R57

Wallace, Steven P. The senior movement : references and resources / Steven P. Wallace, John B. Williamson with Rita Gaston Lung. N.Y. : G.K. Hall : Macmillan International, c1992. 204 p. **CC102**

Includes books, research articles, and policy, advocacy, and popular literature. Original abstracts written by the editors. Omits unpublished interviews and hard-to-find material. 863 numbered entries are arranged alphabetically by author within chapters covering leaders, political strategies, public policies, social security, intergenerational conflict, legal system, and pensions. Resources section lists only six reference books; however, an introductory chapter includes a reference list, and provides overview, scope, definitions, and background. Appendix provides addresses and missions of advocacy organizations. Author and subject indexes. Z7164.O4W38

Zito, Dorothea R. A guide to research in gerontology : strategies and resources / Dorothea R. Zito and George V. Zito. N.Y. : Greenwood, 1988. 130 p. **CC103**

A guide to resources and research in eight chapters, the first three providing an introduction to the field, research strategies, and an overview of the organization of information. The remaining five chapters give general discussions of handbooks, directories and encyclopedias, indexes and abstracts, agencies, computerized systems, and community resources. Appendixes include a reading list on aging, and lists of indexes and abstracts, journals, and selected databases. Subject index.
Z7164.O4Z57

Statistics

Statistical handbook on aging Americans / Frank L. Schick and Renee Schick, editors. 1994 ed. / comp. by Renee Schick. Phoenix : Oryx, 1994. 360 p. : ill. (Statistical handbook series, no. 5). **CC104**

1st ed., 1986.

Features 378 charts, tables, and graphs as they originally appeared, most from the 1990 census and other government sources. Omits tables based entirely on pre-1985 data. Data arranged by specific topics within six broad subject chapters. Separate list of table and chart titles. Includes three-page glossary, list of table and chart sources, copy of "Telephone contacts for data users" for the Census. General index. HQ1064.U5S695

Statistical record of older Americans / Arsen J. Darnay. Detroit : Gale, c1994. **CC105**

Covers a wide variety of topics—e.g., opinions, crime, health, housing, employment, social security, income, families, demographics, education. Offers more than 900 tables from 143 governmental, academic, association, technical, trade, and journal sources. Includes some comparative data on countries outside the U.S. Detailed table of contents includes table names and numbers for all 16 chapters. Lists sources by main entry; includes corresponding table numbers. Keyword index; abbreviations and acronyms list. **HQ1064.U5S697**

Vierck, Elizabeth. Fact book on aging. Santa Barbara, Calif. : ABC-Clio, c1990. 199 p. **CC106**
"Over 1,500 statistical 'one liners.' "—*Pref.* 20 chapters cover geographic distribution, money, living arrangement, recreation, world records, native languages, crime, the senior market, etc. 13-page bibliography; general index. **HQ1064.U5V494**

Alcoholism and drug abuse

Bibliography

Barnes, Grace M. Alcohol and the elderly : a comprehensive bibliography / comp. by Grace M. Barnes, Ernest L. Abel, and Charles A. S. Ernst. Westport, Conn. : Greenwood, 1980. 138 p. **CC107**
An international selection of more than 1,200 citations to articles, books, reports, and monographs, the majority covering 1970–80. Subject index. **Z7721.B36**

——————— Alcohol and the family : a comprehensive bibliography / comp. by Grace M. Barnes and Diane K. Augustino. N.Y. : Greenwood, 1987. 461 p. (Bibliographies and indexes in sociology, no. 9). **CC108**
Includes more than 6,000 books, book chapters, and journal articles from the social sciences and human services arranged alphabetically by author. Non-English entries include English translations of titles. Subject index. **Z7721.B364**

——————— Alcohol and youth : a comprehensive bibliography / comp. by Grace M. Barnes with special assistance from Robert J. Brown. Westport, Conn. : Greenwood, 1982. 452 p. **CC109**
An international bibliography of books, articles, theses, reports, and government documents; English translations have been provided for foreign titles. Author arrangement of 4,666 entries. Subject index. **Z7721.B37**

Berg, Steven L. Jewish alcoholism and drug addiction : an annotated bibliography. Westport, Conn. : Greenwood, 1993. 160 p. **CC110**
Includes 583 numbered entries, arranged alphabetically by author within subject chapters. Brief descriptive annotations. Chapters present general, scholarly, and theoretical studies; compare cultural groups; and cover first person stories and case studies. Also addresses Alcoholics Anonymous (AA) and Jewish Alcoholics, Chemically Dependent Persons, and Significant Others (JACS), rabbis, and alcoholism in Israel. Final chapters describe minority groups within the Jewish community and the portrayal of Jewish alcoholics in literature. Author, title, and subject indexes. **Z7721.B45**

Chalfant, H. Paul. Social and behavioral aspects of female alcoholism : an annotated bibliography / comp. by H. Paul Chalfant and Brent S. Roper, with Carmen Rivera-Worley. Westport, Conn. : Greenwood, 1980. 145 p. **CC111**
A listing of 488 periodical articles covering 1970–80 and arranged by broad topics, such as rates, psychological aspects, social and cultural aspects, death, deviant behavior, the family, and treatment. Author index. **HV5824.W6C46**

Derivan, William J. Prevention education : a guide to research / William J. Derivan, Natalie Anne Silverstein. N.Y. : Garland, 1990. 282 p. (Garland bibliographies in contemporary education, v. 9 ; Garland reference library of social science, v. 524). **CC112**
An annotated bibliography of 611 works on prevention of drug and alcohol abuse, including books, articles, curriculum guides, teacher training materials, government publications, project evaluation guides, research reports, and other sources. In seven main categories (e.g., Prevention programs—school based, Curricula/material, Family systems). Appendixes list sources of information and resources and periodicals on drug and alcohol abuse. Author, title, and subject indexes. **Z7164.N17D44**

Heath, Dwight B. Alcohol use and world cultures / Dwight B. Heath and A. M. Cooper. Toronto : Addiction Research Foundation, 1981. 248 p. (Addiction Research Foundation bibliography series, 15). **CC113**
Subtitle: A comprehensive bibliography of anthropological sources.
Aims to provide "easier and more comprehensive access to the large, diverse and widely scattered literature that deals with alcoholic beverages in relation to human behavior among various populations throughout the world."—*Introd.* Covers prehistoric times to mid-1978. Appendix of research in progress. Indexed by author and subject, including concept, theory, nation, and tribe or other special population. **Z7721.H4**

Lobb, Michael L. Native American youth and alcohol : an annotated bibliography / Michael L. Lobb and Thomas D. Watts. N.Y. : Greenwood, 1989. 165 p. (Bibliographies and indexes in sociology, no. 16). **CC114**
A 37-page introduction and review of the literature is followed by ten broad subject sections (e.g., accidental death, biomedical factors, gender, policy and prevention, urban vs. rural). Entries arranged by author in each chapter. Lengthy, descriptive abstracts; subject and author indexes. **Z1209.2.U5L6**

Miletich, John J. Treatment of cocaine abuse : an annotated bibliography. N.Y. : Greenwood, 1992. 234 p. (Bibliographies and indexes in medical studies, no. 9). **CC115**
Preface provides brief historical overview of cocaine use. Organizes more than 600 entries into four subject chapters, the largest covering definitions, identification, and diagnosis (386 entries). Other chapters cover treatment, occupations, and women and children. Separate chapter numbering of entries. Includes books, articles, conference proceedings, dissertations, government publications. Brief appendixes list common names for cocaine; videocassettes; and a cocaine "time-line" (1500 BCE–1990). Author and subject indexes. **RC568.C6M55**

——————— Work and alcohol abuse : an annotated bibliography. N.Y. : Greenwood, 1987. 263 p. (Bibliographies and indexes in sociology, no. 12). **CC116**
More than 1,000 entries, numbered and arranged alphabetically by author in seven subject chapters: Definitions, identification, and diagnosis; Companies and management; Unions, safety, and employee dismissal; Government; Occupations; Women; and Counseling and treatment. Includes English-language books, articles, government publications, theses, dissertations, and conference proceedings, 1972–86. Separate author, subject, and company name indexes. **Z7164.C81M619**

Nordquist, Joan. Substance abuse I : drug abuse : a bibliography. Santa Cruz, Calif. : Reference and Research Services, 1989. 68 p. (Contemporary social issues, no. 16). **CC117**
Nine sections drawn from recent legal, psychological, business, and social literatures. Citations pertain to specific populations, crime, the workplace, AIDS, treatment, legal aspects, and the drug war. Sections divided by format: books, pamphlets, and documents, or articles in periodicals and books. Entries are alphabetical by author in each

subsection. A final section lists resources: bibliographies, guides, directories, statistical sources, and organizations. No indexes.
Z7164.N17N67

——————— Substance abuse II : alcohol abuse : a bibliography. Santa Cruz, Calif. : Reference and Research Services, 1990. 68 p. (Contemporary social issues, no. 17). **CC118**

In ten sections, drawing from the last five years of the legal, social, political, and psychological literatures. Citations pertain to genetic, biological, and familial explanations for abuse; specific populations; violence and crime; the workplace; prevention and regulation; drunk driving; and treatment. Sections list books followed by articles; entries are alphabetical by author within subsections. The final section lists resources: bibliographies, directories, organizations, and statistical sources. No indexes.

Page, Penny Booth. Alcohol use and alcoholism : a guide to the literature. N.Y. : Garland, 1986. 164 p. **CC119**

Intended for general readers or professionals. Includes English-language books, pamphlets, leaflets, and government publications, most from the mid-1970s to 1985; omits journal articles and audiovisual materials. Offers 405 consecutively numbered entries, arranged alphabetically by author, in 16 subject chapters that include: Effects on body; Treatment; Use among women; Alcohol and the fetus; and Traffic safety. Each chapter begins with an introductory paragraph and ends with cross-references. Two appendixes include alcohol-related periodicals and resource organizations; author and title indexes.
Z7721.P33

——————— Children of alcoholics : a sourcebook. N.Y. : Garland, 1991. 249 p. (Garland reference library of social science, v. 461). **CC120**

Includes popular, professional, and research literature; covers English-language books, journal articles, and pamphlets, 1969–90 (journal coverage, 1985–90). Excludes inspirational books of poetry or affirmations; fetal alcohol syndrome; audiovisuals; games. Pt. 1 focuses on minor children; pt. 2, adult children. Chapters within each part cover research, family issues, treatment, recovery, fiction, and general reference. Annotated, numbered entries arranged by format within each chapter, then alphabetically by author or title. Appendixes list or describe organizations, audiovisual resources, and periodicals. Author, title, and subject indexes. List of publishers' addresses.
Z7721.P334

Ruben, Douglas H. Drug abuse and the elderly : an annotated bibliography. Metuchen, N.J. : Scarecrow, 1984. 247 p.
CC121

An international, topically arranged bibliography of 787 annotated citations to books, articles, and government documents; indexed by journal, author, and subject.
Z7164.N17R82

Substance abuse among ethnic minorities in America : a critical annotated bibliography / Howard Rebach ... [et al.]. N.Y. : Garland, 1992. 469 p. (Garland library of sociology, vol. 20 ; Garland reference library of social science, v. 737).
CC122

Contains 168 numbered entries, arranged alphabetically by author, describing literature from the 1980s (mostly the later 1980s). Each entry provides citation, type of article, purpose, methodology, results, discussion, and a useful evaluation. A unique chart indicates ethnic group, age group, topic, and substance covered by every article. Entries average two to four pages in length. Bibliography; list of 65 journal titles; 22-page reference list. Author index.
Z7164.D78S8

Watts, Thomas D. Black alcohol abuse and alcoholism : an annotated bibliography / Thomas D. Watts, Roosevelt Wright, Jr. N.Y. : Praeger, 1986. 265 p. **CC123**

Intended for students, practitioners, and professionals. Draws from social, economic, medical, and historical literature, 1943–85. 533 entries are arranged chronologically and include detailed informative annotations. Includes a list of social service and information organizations. Author and subject indexes.
Z7721.W37

Encyclopedias

Evans, Glen. The encyclopedia of drug abuse / Glen Evans, Robert O'Brien, and Sidney Cohen. 2nd ed., rev. and expanded. N.Y. : Facts on File, c1991. 1 v. **CC124**
1st ed., 1984.

For general readers and professionals; international in scope. 13-page introductory essay on history of drug use. Cross-referenced entries cover physical, medical, legal, political aspects and range in length from two to three lines to several columns. Occasional short reference lists. Four appendixes include: street language; drug slang; tables and figures; and information sources: state, federal, Canadian, and international associations; 81 periodical addresses. 25-page bibliography. Detailed index.

§ Designed as a companion to *Encyclopedia of alcoholism* (CC125), by Evans, O'Brien, and Morris Chafetz. HV5804.E94

O'Brien, Robert. The encyclopedia of alcoholism / Robert O'Brien and Morris Chafetz ; ed. by Glen Evans. 2nd ed. N.Y. : Facts on File, 1991. 346 p. : ill. **CC125**
1st ed., 1982.

For students, professionals, or general readers. Dictionary arrangement of more than 600 terms that relate to alcoholism. *See* references; some reference lists and tabular data. Entries cover health and medical aspects, specific populations, terms specific to the experience (e.g. antabuse, near beer, relapse, detoxification). The first appendix provides statistical data; the second lists national, state, Canadian, foreign organizations; self-help groups; addresses for 33 periodicals. 31-page bibliography. General index. HV5035.O27

Dictionaries

Abel, Ernest L. A dictionary of drug abuse terms and terminology. Westport, Conn. : Greenwood, 1984. 187 p. **CC126**

Emphasizes slang words and expressions; a glossary offers a thesaurus approach. Omits alcohol- and tobacco-related terms. Bibliography. HV5804.A23

——————— A marijuana dictionary : words, terms, events, and persons relating to cannabis. Westport, Conn. : Greenwood, 1982. 136 p. **CC127**

Definitions of slang terms are accompanied by illustrative quotations, chronologically arranged. Also includes terms referring to the use of the plant as a source of the fiber, hemp. Appendix lists foreign words and expressions about marijuana. Bibliography of about 150 titles. Cross references; index. HV5822.M3A2

Fay, John. The alcohol/drug abuse dictionary and encyclopedia. Springfield, Ill. : Thomas, c1988. 167 p. **CC128**

Includes "language that extends from the coarse jargon of the illicit drug subculture to the complex dialect of pharmacology."—*Pref.* Headwords (130 p.) include: "anabolic steroid," "deterrence theory," "Mexican brown," "meprobamate," "nutmeg," "PCP." Appendix includes additional jargon arranged alphabetically under drug name or type; matched lists of generic and brand names; state agencies, drug poison information centers, and resource agencies; and six toll-free helplines. Three-page bibliography. RC564.F39

Keller, Mark. A dictionary of words about alcohol / by Mark Keller, Mairi McCormich and Vera Efron. 2nd ed. New Brunswick, N.J. : Publications Div., Rutgers Center of Alcohol Studies, 1982. 291 p. **CC129**
1st ed., 1968.

International in scope; cross-referenced entries provide some etymologies. Bibliographic references; 12-page bibliography.
HV5017.K42

Directories

Drug, alcohol, and other addictions : a directory of treatment centers and prevention programs nationwide. 2nd ed. Phoenix : Oryx, 1993. 646 p.   **CC130**

    1st ed., 1989.

    Includes more than 12,000 programs and facilities involved in prevention and treatment, from responses to a 1992 questionnaire. Entries provide name, address, phone/fax, hotline number, addictions treated, treatments, type of program, statistics, special programs, payment methods, accomodations, and parent organization. Alphabetical by state, then city, then by name of facility. Table of contents provides access by states. No index.   RC564.73.D78

Substance abuse & kids : a directory of education, information, prevention, and early intervention programs. Phoenix : Oxyx, 1989. 466 p. : ill.   **CC131**

    Includes services for children to age 18. Omits Alcoholics Anonymous and similar groups. Arranges entries alphabetically by state, then by city. Program profiles are descriptive, not evaluative, and provide service name, address, phone, contact, and may include date established, affiliations, age/grade level served, special groups served, addictions/disorders, programs/services, staff ratio, setting, number of clients, evaluation/effectiveness, ownership, follow-up services. Indexes for age/grade level, addictions/disorders, programs/services.   RJ501.A2S83

Substance abuse residential treatment centers for teens. Phoenix : Oryx, 1990. 286 p.   **CC132**

    Includes more than 1,000 residential and inpatient programs treating alcohol, drug, or behavioral disorders in teenagers, ages 9–19. Arranges entries by state and city, then alphabetically by name. Entries include organization name, address, contact, and phone number; and may include hotline, fax, date established, parent organization, affiliations, licensure, evaluation, addictions/disorders treated, treatment methods, setting, services offered, staffing, groups served, ownership, referral policies, fees, follow-up. Indexes for organization name, addiction/disorder, and treatment method. Brief glossary.   RC564.73.S93

Women's recovery programs : a directory of residential addiction treatment centers. Phoenix : Oryx, 1990. 339 p.   **CC133**

    Profiles some 1,200 residential and inpatient programs in the U.S. that treat drug, alcohol, and behavioral disorders in women. After two essays on women and addiction, the directory listings are arranged alphabetically by state and geographically within each state. Separate indexes for organization names, addictions/disorders, and treatment methods. List of abbreviations; one-page glossary of terms.   RC564.73.W66

Handbooks

Blum, Kenneth. Handbook of abusable drugs. N.Y. : Gardner Pr., c1984. 721 p. : ill.   **CC134**

    Written for general readers and professionals. Liberal use of tables and figures. The first four chapters review basic pharmacology and human drug use. Chapters 5–18 cover narcotics, narcotic antagonists, methadone, internal opiods, CNS depressants, solvent and aerosol inhalants, alcohol, stimulants, tranquilizers, antidepressants, tobacco, OTC drugs, marijuana, psychedelics, and psychotropics. Additional chapters group drugs into legal schedules I–V, and address drugs and sexual functioning. Glossary in Appendix 1 lists street and scientific terms; Appendix 2 classifies substances. Separate author, subject, and drug name indexes.   RC564.B58

Handbook for assessing and treating addictive disorders / ed. by Chris E. Stout, John L. Levitt, and Douglas H. Ruben. N.Y. : Greenwood, 1992. 371 p. : ill.   **CC135**

    Provides signed chapters with bibliographies in five sections: Behavioral, family systems, and psychoanalytic approaches; Assesment; Treatment; Minorities and special groups; and Clinical issues. Appendixes briefly describe types of resources that may be available and lists a sampling of groups, including only city in address; and credentialing organizations by state. Reading lists; general index.   RC564.H355

Stimmel, Barry. The facts about drug use : coping with drugs and alcohol in your family, at work, in your community / Barry Stimmel and the editors of Consumer Reports Books. N.Y. : Haworth Pr., c1993. 374 p. : ill.   **CC136**

    First publ. by Consumer Reports Books, 1991.

    Written in non-technical language. 20 chapters in three parts. Pt. 1 classifies drugs and discusses dependency, symptoms, tolerance, effects. Pt. 2 provides use patterns, preparations, dependency, withdrawal, effects, treatment for various mood-altering drugs. Pt. 3 covers issues such as multiple drug use, AIDS, pregnancy, sports, and the "war against drugs." Three appendixes: drug use reporting sources, drug-testing technology, and common street names. References list grouped by chapter; general index.   RM315.S8919

Woods, Geraldine. Drug abuse in society : a reference handbook. Santa Barbara, Calif. : ABC-Clio, c1993. 269 p. : ill.   **CC137**

    Seven chapters provide an overview of the problem; precolonial–1993 chronology of events, discoveries, legal decisions; biographical summaries; and a variety of charts and tabular data, primarily from 1980s and early 1990s. Describes helplines, computer bulletin boards, public agencies, and private organizations. Two final chapters describe print and nonprint resources. Glossary; general index.   HV5825.W5746

Biography

Lender, Mark Edward. Dictionary of American temperance biography : from temperance reform to alcohol research, the 1600s to the 1980s. Westport, Conn. : Greenwood, 1984. 572 p.   **CC138**

    Provides brief narrative biographies of about 2,000 figures; bibliographic references include primary and secondary sources, and citations to standard biographical reference works. Indexed.   HV5239.A2L46

Childhood and adolescence

Guides

Haag, Enid E. Research guide for studies in infancy and childhood. N.Y. : Greenwood, 1988. 430 p. (Reference sources for the social sciences and humanities, no. 8).   **CC139**

    Section 1 reviews research strategy, describes 25 databases, and provides a brief bibliography of online searching materials, with 50 pages devoted to reference works, grouped by subject area. Section 2 offers subject bibliographies, with names of related databases, in broad categories (e.g., families, communication, social/cultural development), further subdivided by subject. Entries are alphabetical by title within each subtopic. Includes books, articles, and reports from psychology, social work, education, sociology, medicine, law, home economics, and the arts. Approximately 1,400 annotated entries. Separate author, title, and subject indexes. In conjunction with Marda Woodbury's *Childhood information resources* (CD80) offers a comprehensive guide to the research literature on developmental stages from birth to age 13.   Z7164.C5H3

Washington, Valora. Black children and American institutions : an ecological review and resource guide / Valora Washington, Velma La Point. N.Y. : Garland, 1988. 432 p. (Garland reference library of social science, v. 382 ; Garland source books on education, vol. 16). **CC140**

An essay that examines African-American children in relation to schools, family, criminal justice, social services, and physical and mental health is followed by a bibliography, arranged by author with descriptive annotations. One section lists organizations with their activities and contact names, and describes seven organizations at greater length (e.g., Children's Defense Fund, National Urban League). Author/name and subject indexes.   Z1361.N39W34

Woodbury, Marda. Youth information resources : an annotated guide for parents, professionals, students, researchers, and concerned citizens / comp. by Marda Woodbury ; with a chapter on data bases, comp. by Donna L. Richardson. N.Y. : Greenwood, 1987. 357 p. (Bibliographies and indexes in sociology, no. 10). **CC141**

Examines U.S. and Canadian English-language literature on adolescents (ages 13–19), focusing on in-print or widely available sources. More than 1,000 entries into chapters, providing helpful introductory material and guidance on research and library use. Research and Access chapter provides checklist of research questions, hints on terminology, definitions of types of resources, etc. Includes chapters, each with introduction, for dictionaries, encyclopedias, thesauri, guides, library catalogs, bibliographies, directories, abstracting and indexing services, periodicals, statistics, and surveys. Provides detailed descriptions and tips for use. Nonprint section describes online databases. Appendix lists clearinghouses and organizations. Author/title/organization and subject/format indexes.

§ For sources of information about younger children, *see* Woodbury's *Childhood information resources* (CD80), which covers from conception to age 12.   Z7164.Y8W66

Bibliography

Alali, A. Odasuo. Mass media sex and adolescent values : an annotated bibliography and directory of organizations. Jefferson, N.C. : McFarland & Co., c1991. 138 p. **CC142**

Offers 285 numbered entries organized into subject chapters: sex-role portrayals; sexual curricula and media use; adolescents' attitudes and values; contraception, pregnancy, and health issues. Final 58 entries comprise the directory of organizations. Includes journal articles, reports, documents, dissertations. Further readings list; general index.   Z7164.Y8A4

Black adolescence : current issues and annotated bibliography / by The Consortium for Research on Black Adolescence with Velma McBride Murry and assistance from Georgie Winter. Boston : G.K. Hall, 1990. 160 p. **CC143**

Consists of 11 chapters, each in three parts: a literature review, a list of annotated references, and a list of additional references. Topics covered include psychosocial development, psychological and physical health, drug abuse, education, employment, sexuality, and family relationships. No index.   Z1361.N39B495

De Young, Mary. Child molestation : an annotated bibliography. Jefferson, N.C. : McFarland, c1987. 176 p. **CC144**

An introduction that defines child molestation is followed by 557 numbered entries from journals and books, listed alphabetically by author under topical sections (e.g., effects on children, prevention, treatment, sex rings, child pornography, legal issues). Also has sections for statistical studies, literature reviews, and historical works. Each section is prefaced with a scope note. Covers early 1960s through 1986; draws from psychology, sociology, medicine, law, and other disciplines. Author, title, and subject indexes.   Z7164.S42D39

Gouke, Mary Noel. One-parent children, the growing minority : a research guide / Mary Noel Gouke, Arline McClarty Rollins. N.Y. : Garland, 1990. 494 p. (Reference books on family issues, v. 14 ; Garland reference library of social science, v. 344). **CC145**

Includes 1,142 abstracts of English-language scholarly books, journal articles, essays, and conference papers; also lists dissertations, but without abstracts. Covers research from the U.S. and many other countries, 1970–89. In 15 chapters, arranged by four major sections: types of families (e.g., fatherless, lesbian or gay, adoptive); circumstances of loss or absence (e.g., single-parenthood, employment, divorce); general aspects; and schools. Separate geographic, programs/projects/associations/institutions, author, and subject indexes.

            Z7164.C5G68

Hirsch, Elisabeth S. Problems of early childhood : an annotated bibliography and guide. N.Y. : Garland, 1983. 253 p. (Garland reference library of social science, v. 124). **CC146**

A series of topical bibliographic essays are followed by briefly annotated entries subdivided by form and audience level: books and pamphlets for adults, studies and articles (including essays and ERIC reports), and books for children. Topics include: separation, illness, death, divorce, single-parent families, working mothers, siblings, discipline, social relations, etc.; handicapping problems are excluded. Author and subject indexes.   Z5814.C5H57

Honig, Alice S. Prosocial development in children : caring, helping, and cooperating: a bibliographic resource guide / Alice Sterling Honig, Donna Sasse Wittmer. N.Y. : Garland, 1992. 384 p. (Reference books on family issues, v. 19 ; Garland reference library of social science, v. 538). **CC147**

In two sections, theoretical and applied. Covers 1970–91 and includes journals, books, book chapters, articles, newsletters, monographs, dissertations, periodicals, and audiovisuals. The 584 entries have detailed descriptive annotations. Subject index.   Z7164.C5H66

Scheffler, Hannah Nuba. Infancy : a guide to research and resources / Hannah Nuba Scheffler, Deborah Lovitky Sheiman, Kathleen Pullan Watkins. N.Y. : Garland, 1986. 182 p. (Garland reference library of social science, v. 324). **CC148**

Addresses development from prenatal period to two years. Compiled for students, parents, and teachers. In 11 chapters (e.g., Physical, cognitive, and language development; Nutrition and health; Infant-family interaction; Exceptional infant; Play). Chapter 10 lists books for babies, chapter 11 includes an alphabetized list of organizations and publications. Chapters begin with introductory essays and conclude with annotated bibliographies, alphabetically arranged by author. Author and title indexes.   HQ774.N83

——————— Resources for early childhood : an annotated bibliography and guide for educators, librarians, health care professionals, and parents. N.Y. : Garland, 1983. 584 p. (Garland reference library of social science, v.118). **CC149**

Topically organized into 16 chapters, each preceded by an essay and concluded with an evaluative bibliography, based on the collection at the New York Public Library Early Childhood Resource and Information Center. Author and title indexes.   HQ767.9.S3

Sheiman, Deborah Lovitky. Resources for middle childhood : a source book / Deborah Lovitky Sheiman, Maureen Slonim. N.Y. : Garland, 1988. 138 p. (Reference books on family issues, v. 12 ; Garland reference library of social science, v. 433). **CC150**

Annotated bibliographies follow the six to eight pages of text in each chapter, covering various topics: physical, psychosocial, and cognitive development; family interactions; peer relationships; etc. A practical treatment of the subject for undergraduates, parents, and teachers. Focuses upon the six- to 12-year old child (the elementary school years). Author and title indexes only.   HQ767.9.S48

Slonim, Maureen. Children, culture, and ethnicity : evaluating and understanding the impact. N.Y. : Garland, 1991. 275 p. (Reference books on family issues, v. 18 ; Garland reference library of social science, v. 470).   **CC151**
For general readers, students, and professionals. Intends to provide a multidisciplinary overview of how children are affected by culture and ethnicity. The first five chapters address personality development, family systems, understanding one's culture, framework for assessment, and implications for services; the last four address Asian, Hispanic American, African American and European cultures. All chapters include an introductory essay, notes, and annotated bibliographies. Author, title, and subject indexes.   HQ767.9.S55

Sutherland, Neil. Contemporary Canadian childhood and youth : a bibliography / comp. by Neil Sutherland, Jean Barman, and Linda L. Hale ... [et al.]. Westport, Conn. : Greenwood, 1992. 492 p. (Bibliographies and indexes in world history, no. 29).   **CC152**
Includes books, monographs, government reports, scholarly and professional articles, magistral and doctoral theses, published through 1990. Subdivides 7,328 entries by region under geographic headings, then alphabetically by author. No annotations. Sections: General (Canada), British Columbia, The Prairies, Central Canada, Atlantic Canada, and Northern Canada. Lists journals indexed. Subject and name indexes.   Z7164.C5S94

———— History of Canadian childhood and youth : a bibliography / comp. by Neil Sutherland, Jean Barman, and Linda L. Hale ... [et al.]. Westport, Conn. : Greenwood, 1992. 486 p. (Bibliographies and indexes in world history, no. 28).   **CC153**
Includes books, monographs, government reports, scholarly and professional articles, magistral and doctoral theses. Covers material through 1990. Subdivides 7,998 entries by region under geographic headings, listed alphabetically by author within. No annotations. Sections for General (Canada), British Columbia, The Prairies, Central Canada, Atlantic Canada, and Northern Canada. Lists journals indexed. Subject and name indexes.   Z7164.C5S942

Watkins, Kathleen Pullan. Day care : a source book / Kathleen Pullan Watkins, Lucius Durant, Jr. N.Y. : Garland, 1987. 207 p. (Garland reference library of social science, v. 360).   **CC154**
Compiled for day care workers, faculty and students, parents, and community and business leaders. Consists of topical essays followed by annotated bibliographies; entries arranged alphabetically by author. Brief glossary. Four-page list of journals and addresses; author index.   HQ778.7.U6W38

———— Parent-child attachment : a guide to research. N.Y. : Garland, 1987. 190 p. (Reference books on family issues, v. 11 ; Garland reference library of social science, v. 388).   **CC155**
Written for professionals, parents, and general readers. Emphasizes attachment in infancy and early childhood; includes only English-language works. In 11 chapters, each beginning with a topical essay on subjects such as theory, the adoptive family, prematurity, chronic illness, parents with disabilities, and single parenthood, followed by an annotated bibliography. Essays and bibliographies average eight pages each. Author and subject indexes.   BF723.A75W38

Indexes; Abstract journals

•**Child abuse and neglect and family violence** [database]. [Wash.] : National Center on Child Abuse and Neglect, Clearinghouse on Child Abuse and Neglect Information, [1967]– .   **CC156**
Title varies: *Child abuse and neglect.*
Available online; updated twice yearly.

Contains citations with abstracts to materials on the definition, identification, prevention, and treatment of child abuse and neglect, and family violence. English-language materials; U.S. focus.
Child abuse and neglect and family violence thesaurus (CC161) is used in constructing and searching this database.

Child development abstracts and bibliography. v. 2 (Feb. 1928)– . Chicago : Publ. by the Univ. of Chicago Pr. for the Society for Research in Child Development, 1928– . 3 no. a year.   **CC157**
For annotation, *see* CD81.   HQ750.A1C47

Encyclopedias

Clark, Robin E. The encyclopedia of child abuse / Robin E. Clark and Judith Freeman Clark. N.Y. : Facts on File, c1989. 328 p. : ill.   **CC158**
For general readers and professionals. Draws from various disciplines (e.g., law, medicine, sociology, psychology, economics, and education); international in scope, although U.S. information predominates. Omits biographical information. A 17-page overview is followed by 200 pages of entries, alphabetically arranged and written by the compilers. Cross-references; some entries conclude with suggested readings. 15 appendixes include organizations, agencies, reporting procedures and statutes by state, types of immunity, and statistics. Bibliography; general index.   HV6626.5.C57

Encyclopedia of adolescence / ed. by Richard Lerner, Anne C. Petersen, Jeanne Brooks-Gunn. N.Y. : Garland, 1991. 2 v. : ill. (Garland reference library of social science, v. 495).   **CC159**
More than 200 signed entries by 233 specialists in the social sciences, sciences, and humanities, alphabetically arranged, each concluding with a bibliography and cross-references. Addresses subjects such as eating disorders, friendship, Hispanic adolescents, adolescent fathers, chronic illness, gay and lesbian youth, and suicide. Subject index.   HQ796.E58

Dictionaries

Interdisciplinary glossary on child abuse and neglect : legal, medical, social work terms. Rev. April 1980. Wash. : National Center on Child Abuse and Neglect : For sale by the U.S. Govt. Print. Off., [1980]. 45 p. : ill.   **CC160**
DHHS publication no. (OHDS) 80–30137.
Revises and updates 1978 issue of the same name.
Created to facilitate communication among disciplines; also useful for researchers, students, general readers. Terms arranged alphabetically with definitions from a few lines to a column in length. Examples: affadavit, central register, custody, Head Start, involuntary placement, parens patriae, passive abuser, trauma X. Group addresses or phone may be outdated, but definitions useful for present day as well as historical research. Three-page bibliography; list of acronyms.   HV711.I57

Thesauruses

Child abuse and neglect and family violence thesaurus / National Center on Child Abuse and Neglect. [Wash.] : The Center, [1976?]– .   **CC161**
Title varies: *Child abuse and neglect thesaurus.*
Alphabetical display of terms includes descriptor group codes for computerized searching, as well as "used for," "broader," "narrower," and "related" terms. Groups descriptors in a permuted display and by descriptor group. Used in constructing and searching *Child abuse and neglect and family violence* [database] (CC156).   HV741.C458

Quotations

Reflections on childhood : a quotations dictionary / [comp. by] Irving Weiss & Anne D. Weiss. Santa Barbara, Calif. : ABC-Clio, c1991. 398 p. **CC162**

"A historical collection of observances, opinions, and reminiscences about childhood and children ... "—*Pref.* Quotations range in length from 1 line to ½ page, listed alphabetically by author under 160 subjects such as adoption, night, pets, talking back, and credulity. Contents list includes cross-references. Index by author and subject. Some authors: Lorraine Hansberry, Abbie Hoffman, John Muir, Leo Tolstoy, Fran Lebowitz, Bruno Bettelheim. PN6084.C49R44

Directories

Caring for kids with special needs : residential treatment programs for children and adolescents. Princeton, N.J. : Peterson's Guides, c1993. 481 p. : ill. **CC163**

A unique source, compiled for human services or health care professionals and parents. Describes U.S. and Canadian facilities that address a variety of problems including behavior disorders, learning disabilities, substance abuse, depression, schizophrenia, developmental disorders, eating disorders, and more—for ages 8–18. Data current as of 1992. Provides a quick reference chart for all 817 facilities listed. A section of program profiles includes descriptions of treatment programs, staff, facilities, costs, and contact information. Facilities listed alphabetically. A detailed announcements section covers 35 selected facilities. A glossary of illness terms and types of mental health professionals is particulary helpful for parents or the general reader. Descriptions of eight national associations; facility index. HV863.C35

International directory of youth bodies = Répertoire international des organismes de jeunesse = Repertorio internacional de organismos de juventud. 1990– . Paris : UNESCO, c1990– . **CC164**

Describes 559 nonprofit governmental and private organizations in 123 countries. In two parts: (1) international, regional, and nongovernmental organizations, arranged alphabetically by organization; (2) national organizations, arranged alphabetically by country, subarranged by Governmental coordinating bodies and Governmental and non-governmental youth organizations, research centres, training centres, and information centres. Entries give address, short description of purpose, programs and activities, relationships to other organizations. Includes alphabetical list of countries; list of organizations; index of interests coordinated by government bodies (e.g., Cultural activities) that lists countries that sponsor programs; and similar index for programs of youth organizations and of centers for training, research, or information. In English, with French and Spanish prefaces.

Sherman, Barbara Smiley. Directory of residential treatment facilities for emotionally handicapped children and youth. Phoenix : Oryx, 1988. 231 p. **CC165**

1st ed., 1985, had title: *Directory of residential treatment facilities for emotionally disturbed children.*

Lists facilities by state, within which the arrangement is alphabetical by name. Entries give addresses, types of placement, children served (ages, diagnoses, etc.), tuition, setting (e.g., cottages in the country), social and rehabilitation services, educational and vocational services, and referral requirements. Indexes of institutions by type of placement, type of funding, and characteristics exhibited by children (e.g., autistic, drug abuse, hearing impaired). RJ504.5.S54

Handbooks

Children in historical and comparative perspective : an international handbook and research guide / ed. by Joseph M. Hawes and N. Ray Hinter. N.Y. : Greenwood, 1991. 571 p. **CC166**

Pt. 1 treats the premodern world, with signed chapters on childhood in antiquity, medieval and early modern Europe, and premodern China. Pt. 2 covers the modern world, including signed chapters on Australia and New Zealand, Brazil, Canada, East Africa, England, France, Germany, Israel, Italy, Japan, Mexico, Muslim Middle East, Russia and the U.S.S.R., and the U.S. All chapters include extensive notes and references. Topics include ceremonies and rituals, juvenile delinquency, youth movements, sexism, legal status, expectations, mortality and neglect, and illegitimacy. Detailed general index. HQ767.87.C48

Finkelhor, David. A sourcebook on child sexual abuse / David Finkelhor with Sharon Araji ... [et al.]. Beverly Hills, Calif. : Sage Publications, c1986. 276 p. **CC167**

A review of research that summarizes findings on five topics: prevalence, high risk children, abusers, effects of abuse, and prevention. Bibliography; subject index. HQ71.F52

Handbook of adolescent sexuality and pregnancy : research and evaluation instruments / ed. by Josefina J. Card. Newbury Park, Calif. : Sage Publications, c1993. 280 p. **CC168**

Simplifies any investigation on this subject by offering the evaluator or researcher pretested and validated instruments. Pt. 1 provides actual items and scales taken from leading national surveys. Variables include: sexual activity, contraceptive use, demographics, family and social contexts, beliefs and attitudes, drug use, work status, etc. Parts 2 and 3 provide instruments for evaluation and data collection; pt. 4 provides order information and detailed abstracts for 64 research and evaluation instruments in the public domain. General index. HQ759.4.H367

International handbook of adolescence / ed. by Klaus Hurrelmann. Westport, Conn. : Greenwood, 1994. 470 p. : ill. **CC169**

Systematically surveys and compares national policies and adolescent life in various countries. Preface describes the countries surveyed. Each signed chapter is devoted to a particular country and presents historical developments, 1945–90; demographic data; education, family building, cultural and political participation; psychological and social problem behaviors; policy issues. Defines adolescence as 10–25 years of age. Appendix lists experts in youth research by region and country. Selected bibliography organized geographically. General index. List of contributors and affiliations. HQ796.I513

International handbook of child care policies and programs / ed. by Moncrieff Cochran. Westport, Conn. : Greenwood, 1993. 688 p. : ill. **CC170**

Examines the "public face of child care."—*Introd.* Signed chapters, most written by native scholars, cover 29 countries. Chapters describe existing policies and programs within the cultural and historical context, including strengths and shortcomings. Chapters are alphabetical by country, with bibliographies. Appendixes compare maternal and paternal leave policies, and demographics. Three-page selected bibliography; index. HQ778.5.I58

Layman, Richard. Child abuse. Detroit : Omnigraphics, c1990. 122 p. **CC171**

In 11 chapters, provides definitions and statistics, reviews characteristics of abused children, and covers treatment of victims and families, operation of child protective agencies and the courts, and state reporting procedures. Lists interest group publications, organizations, and books for further reading. Several chapters report interviews of two lawyers and a child therapist. General index. HV6626.5.L39

The new child protection team handbook / editors, Donald C. Bross ... [et al.]. N.Y. : Garland, 1988. 636 p. : ill., forms. (Garland reference library of social science, v. 380).   **CC172**
Revises and updates Barton D. Schmitt, *The child protection team handbook*, (N.Y. : Garland STPM Pr., 1978).
Written for the various professionals who could comprise a child protection team: social workers, nurses, pediatricians, psychologists, lawyers, welfare workers, etc.; as well as students and parents. Chapters cover: organizing teams in various settings, diagnostic tasks, case conferences, legal system, specialized teams, team development, trends, funding. Each of the seven chapters includes reference or further readings lists. General index.   HV741.N397

Reeves, Diane Lindsey. Child care crisis : a reference handbook. Santa Barbara, Calif. : ABC-Clio, c1992. 173 p.   **CC173**
Provides overview, chronology (1828–1991), and biographical sketches of significant contributors. Provides definitions, statistics, survey results, employer and government policies, recent legislation, and a sources list. Describes major child care support organizations, reference materials, and nonprint resources. Includes regulatory information by state: agencies, networks, and regulatory features, e.g., number of inspections per year, training requirements. U.S. focus. Glossary; general index.   HQ778.7.U6R44

Sander, Daryl. Focus on teens in trouble : a reference handbook. Santa Barbara, Calif. : ABC-Clio, c1991. 182 p.   **CC174**
Examines various kinds of youth offenses or experiences, e.g., gangs and violence, substance abuse, runaways, crimes, the juvenile justice system. Each of the seven topical chapters includes references, resources lists. Includes fiction, nonfiction books and articles, nonprint materials, organizations, and hotlines. Text runs to short paragraphs throughout, interspersed with statistics, definitions, and quotations. For students, adult youth workers, and general readers. General index.   HV9104.S315

Atlases

International Bank for Reconstruction and Development. World atlas of the child / prep. by the World Bank in recognition of the International Year of the Child. Wash. : The Bank, 1979. 39 p. : some maps in color.   **CC175**
Contains "a country locator map and nine choropleth maps of child-related indicators." — Notes on the maps. Introductory text in English, French, and Spanish. Maps cover social and economic indicators such as population, gross national product, birth rates, infant mortality, children in the labor force, and pupil-teacher ratios. Statistical data provided in appendix.   HQ781.I57

Statistics

The state of the world's children. 1980– . Oxford ; N.Y. : Oxford Univ. Pr. for UNICEF, 1980– . Annual.   **CC176**
Pt. 1 summarizes problems of child protection, malnutrition, immunization, AIDS, death, sanitation, education, health knowledge, clean water, decline in breast feeding, etc. Reprints *World declaration on the survival, protection, and development of children* and the *Convention on the rights of the child*. Pt. 2 provides nine detailed statistical tables comparing countries of the world. Covers basic, demographic, and economic indicators; nutrition; health; education; women; and progress. Contrasting colors facilitate use of tables. Lists table footnotes, definitions, sources by subject.   HQ792.2.S73

Death and dying

Bibliography

Basford, Terry K. Near-death experiences : an annotated bibliography. N.Y. : Garland, 1990. 182 p. (Garland reference library of social science, v. 481).   **CC177**
A selective list, chronologically arranged, of 759 titles of books, articles, and dissertations published 1847–1975. In three sections: (1) Near-death experiences; (2) Death visions; (3) Analogues of near-death experiences. Author index.   Z6878.P8B37

Benson, Hazel B. The dying child : an annotated bibliography. N.Y. : Greenwood, 1988. 270 p. (Contemporary problems of childhood, no. 6).   **CC178**
In six main sections (General aspects, The young child, The adolescent, The family, Caregivers, and Physical care) with numerous subdivisions. 743 entries are arranged alphabetically by author within subchapters. Includes popular and professional journals, books, book chapters, conference reports, government publications, pamphlets, and dissertations, 1960–87. Omits foreign languages, speeches, and unpublished papers. All entries except dissertations have descriptive annotations. Six appendixes list children's books, audiovisuals, support organizations, wish-granting organizations, hospices, and reference tools. Author index; selective keyword subject index.   Z6671.52.T47B46

Death education : an annotated resource guide / Hannelore Wass ... [et al.]. Wash. : Hemisphere Pub. Corp., 1980–85. 2 v. (467 p.).   **CC179**
For the general reader or professional. Organized into parts covering printed, audiovisual, organizational, and community (v. 1 only) resources. Appendixes to v. 2 include 19 documents: medical oaths and principles, declarations, legislation, living wills. Each volume has an audiovisual topics index and a general index; v. 1 has a topical index for organizations.   HQ1073.D42

Simpson, Michael A. Dying, death, and grief : a critical bibliography. Pittsburgh : Univ. of Pittsburgh Pr., c1987. 259 p.   **CC180**
1979 ed. had title: *Dying, death, and grief : a critically annotated bibliography and source book of thanatology and terminal care.*
Lists, alphabetically by title, more than 1,700 books published 1979–87 and rates them by a five-star system. Provides for some titles critical annotations that vary in length. Two "stop press" sections (books identified after the main section was written) follow the main book list, as do three additional unannotated bibliographies of books on murder, terrorism and the political uses of death, and nuclear holocaust and megadeath. A useful subject index arranges the main list and "stop press" entries into subject categories where they are listed in order of their rating. Author index.   Z5725.S55

Southard, Samuel. Death and dying : a bibliographical survey / comp. by Samuel Southard ; G. E. Gorman, advisory ed. N.Y. : Greenwood, 1991. 514 p. (Bibliographies and indexes in religious studies, no. 19).   **CC181**
Compiled by a member of the clergy involved in hospice care. Cites more than 2,200 English-language books, chapters, articles, and reports, covering many disciplines and reflecting Western philosophies. Omits technical material in medicine, pharmacology, and mortuary science. Numbered entries grouped in topical chapters: general works, philosophical theology, counseling terminally ill, grief, caretaking professions, death education, research and evaluation, bibliographies. Author, title, and subject indexes.   Z5725.S67 1991

Encyclopedias

Encyclopedia of death / ed. by Robert Kastenbaum and Beatrice Kastenbaum. Phoenix : Oryx, 1989. 295 p. : ill. **CC182**

Contains 131 lengthy, signed articles, aimed at students, academics, and general readers, on such topics as Rigor mortis, Grief counseling, and National Funeral Directors Association. Contributors are academicians from many disciplines, theologians, physicians, hospice directors, officials of associations, etc., who attempt to write "well-balanced entries with an objective tone," but have also been "invited to share their own experiences, beliefs, and suggestions."—*Introd.* Many articles are followed by lists of suggested readings and cross-references. Subject index.   HQ1073.E54

Evans, Glen. The encyclopedia of suicide / Glen Evans and Norman L. Farberow. N.Y. : Facts on File, c1988. 434 p. **CC183**

Intended for both professionals and general readers; multidisciplinary in coverage. Consists of more than 500 entries, alphabetically arranged, on such topics as black Americans, college students, myths, and John Lennon. A third of the book is devoted to appendixes of detailed tabular data on U.S. suicide rates by sex, age, race, geographic area, marital status, month of occurrence, and method. An introductory essay reviews the history of suicide. Lists U.S. organizations specializing in suicide prevention and crisis, and a smaller number of Canadian, U.N., and international organizations. List of English-language periodicals; 14-page bibliography. Cross-references; general index.   HV6545.E87

Handbooks

Norrgard, Lee E. Final choices : making end-of-life decisions / Lee E. Norrgard, Jo DeMars. Santa Barbara, Calif. : ABC-Clio, c1992. 258 p. : ill. **CC184**

A prescriptive and practical source, geared towards older adults and their children. Useful for those in the helping professions. Five narrative chapters in pt 1 cover right-to-die, coping with death, funerals, financial details. Pt. 2 describes national, state, and local organizations. Appendix A includes detailed letter of instruction form. Appendix B includes funeral and cemetery regulations, right-to-die laws, and schools that accept body donations. Seven-page glossary; general index.   HQ1073.5.U6N67

Disabilities and the disabled

Bibliography

Disability, sexuality, and abuse : annotated bibliography / by Dick Sobsey ... [et al.]. Baltimore : P.H. Brookes Pub. Co., c1991. 185 p. **CC185**

Developed by the University of Alberta Sexual Abuse and Disabilities Project.

Contains 1,123 multidisciplinary entries, arranged alphabetically by author. Includes research studies, position papers, program descriptors, clinical reports, and media accounts. Provides English-language abstracts, although some source materials are in other languages. Covers material on adults and children. Name and subject indexes.   HV6626.7.D57

Physical disability : an annotated literature guide / ed. by Phyllis C. Self. N.Y. : Dekker, 1984. 474 p. **CC186**

Twelve chapters on varying aspects of disability and rehabilitation (blindness, deafness, communication, legal rights, etc.) begin with bibliographic review essays and conclude with annotated monograph entries; three chapters deal with federal government publications, journals, and audiovisual reference services. Author and title indexes.   RD797.P483

Ritter, Audrey L. A deafness collection : selected and annotated / comp. by Audrey L. Ritter and Karen A. Hopkins. Chicago : Assoc. of Specialized & Cooperative Library Agencies, 1985. 186 p. **CC187**

Claimed by the compilers to be the most comprehensive bibliography on deafness to date. Cites books, periodical articles, government publications, reports, and other materials, excluding dissertations. Annotations are "written in a generally descriptive and occasionally critical manner."—*Pref.* Arranged topically in 19 chapters on such subjects as Audiology, Multiply-handicapped, and Sign language. General index.

Encyclopedias

Gallaudet encyclopedia of deaf people and deafness / John V. Van Cleve, ed. in chief. N.Y. : McGraw-Hill, c1987. 3 v. : ill. **CC188**

Contains 273 alphabetically arranged signed articles treating characteristics of the deaf, educational practices, specific individuals, organizations, periodicals, etc. Many entries are divided into sections and subsections ("Sign language" has 41 of them), and most include cross-references and bibliographies. General index.   HV2365.G35

Turkington, Carol. The encyclopedia of deafness and hearing disorders / Carol Turkington and Allen E. Sussman. N.Y. : Facts on File, c1992. 278 p. : ill. **CC189**

Topics encompass physiology of the ear, famous deaf persons, organizations, deaf culture in foreign countries, various technologies and techniques, and information about related experts in science, education, linguistics, and communication. Some illustrations and tabular material. 13 useful appendixes list community programs, organizations, manufacturers and distributors of devices, housing, performance groups, periodicals, ministries, residential programs, summer camps, training centers for hearing ear dogs, schools for communication skills. 16-page bibliography; detailed index.

§ For a similar treatment of blindness, *see* Jill Sardegna and T. Otis Paul, *Encyclopedia of blindness and vision impairment* (EH90).   RF290.T93

Dictionaries

Lindsey, Mary P. Dictionary of mental handicap. London ; N.Y. : Routledge, 1989. 345 p **CC190**

For general readers, and readers from various disciplines. Includes historical terms; medical conditions; organizations; acronyms; psychological, educational, sociological, and psychiatric terms. Includes cross-references, reference list. British emphasis.   RC569.95.L56

Directories

AFB directory of services for blind and visually impaired persons in the United States and Canada. 24th ed.– . N.Y. : American Foundation for the Blind, c1993– . Biennial. **CC191**

Continues *Directory of services for blind and visually impaired persons in the United States and Canada.*

Includes schools, organizations, agencies, and programs in governmental and private nonprofit sectors that provide services or information for blind or visually impaired children, adults, their families, and helping professionals. Sections cover U.S., then Canada, for federal programs; state and provincial listings; federal agencies and national organizations; producers and publishers of alternate media; product manufacturers and distributors. Subject index on yellow pages. Organization index is divided by country.   HV1790.A4

The complete directory for people with disabilities : products, resources, books, services : a one-stop sourcebook for individuals and professionals, 1993. [2nd ed.]. Lakeville, Conn. : Grey House Publ. ; Detroit : Gale, c1993. 784 p.   **CC192**
     1st ed., 1991.
     This edition, larger by a third with eight new chapters, (e.g., law, support groups and hotlines, veterans) has 8,034 entries in 27 chapters. Entries provide name, address, phone, fax, sometimes a brief description and fees. Institutions section, grouped by type of disability, includes construction/design, government agencies, independent living centers, libraries. Media section includes books, films, videos, periodicals, conferences. Products directory covers assistive devices, clothing, computers, toys/games. Programs section includes arts, camps, educational, consultants, rehabilitation, sports, employments, travel. Separate indexes for entry name, geographic area, and disability/need. Many non-U.S. entries.   HV1559.U6C65

The complete directory for people with learning disabilities : products, resources, books, services. 1993/94– . Lakeville, Conn. : Grey House Publ. ; Detroit : Gale, c1993– . Annual.   **CC193**
     For annotation, *see* CB200.   LC4818.3.C65

Directory of grants for organizations serving people with disabilities. 8th ed. (1993)– . Loxahatchee, Fla. : Research Grant Guides, c1993– .   **CC194**
     Editor: Richard M. Eckstein.
     Supersedes *Handicapped funding directory* and continues its numbering.
     Includes blindness; deafness; developmental, emotional, learning, mental, and physical disabilities; independent living programs; eye research; mental health; rehabilitation; and speech impairment. Introductory material provides suggestions and strategies for obtaining funding. Directory section lists and describes foundations by state, then alphabetically by name. Detailed list of federal programs outlines eligibility and application process for each. Lists publishing organizations with addresses. Appendixes define types of federal assistance, list Foundation Center Cooperating Collections by state, and describe the Grantsmanship Center. Foundation name and subject indexes.   HV1553.H35

Directory of national information sources on disabilities. [5th ed.]. [Wash.] : National Institute on Disability and Rehabilitation Research, [1991]. 555 p.   **CC195**
     1st ed., 1976. 4th ed., 1986, had title: *Directory of national information sources on handicapping conditions and related services.*
     Revises organizational format of earlier editions. Describes organizations providing disability information, referral, or direct services on a nationwide basis (readers are advised to consult phone directories for local branch information). Entries provide name, address, phone; indicate disabilities and users served; describe organization and services. Sample entries: National Institute for Burn Medicine, Courage Center, American Pain Society, National AIDS Hotline, Guide Dog Foundation for the Blind, Inc. Lists and describes 57 relevant databases. 14-page list of directories, arranged by subject. Lists hotlines; religious and sports organizations. Detailed subject index.   HV1553.D544

Library resources for the blind & physically handicapped : a directory with FY 1992 statistics on readership, circulation, budget, staff, and collection / National Library Service for the Blind and Physically Handicapped. Wash. : Library of Congress, [1977?]– . Annual.   **CC196**
     Continues *Directory of library resources for the blind and physically handicapped*; title varies slightly.
     Organizes National Library Service network libraries by state, with regional library first, then subregional libraries alphabetically by city. Entries indicate whether library lends machines or braille materials, and provide library name, address, telephone, in-WATS, TDD,

and fax numbers. Also includes service area, librarian's name, hours, and brief descriptions of collections, assistive devices, special services, and publications. Appendix includes comparison tables for readership, circulation, budget, staff, and collections.   Z675.B6L52

Shrout, R. N. Resource directory for the disabled. N.Y. : Facts on File, c1991. 392 p.   **CC197**
     Groups entries into sections for general resources, as well as resources for mobility, visually, and hearing impaired. Sections include categories for appliances and devices, using computers, travel helps, recreation, organizations and groups, employment and training, education, and publications. Entries provide names, address, phone, and description. General index.   HV1569.5.S57

Statistics

Ficke, Robert C. Digest of data on persons with disabilities / prep. by Robert C. Ficke (Science Management Corporation). Wash. : National Institute on Disability and Rehabilitation Research, 1992. 179 p. : ill.   **CC198**
     1st ed., 1979; 2nd ed., 1984.
     "Includes only data and explanations issued by federal statistical agencies."—*Introd.* In seven sections. Table of contents does not match actual section arrangement; see p. 53, List of detailed tables, for accurate representation. Sections cover prevalence, characteristics, chronic conditions and impairments, health status and care utilization, work disability, prevalence in institutions, federal programs, and state level data. Appendix provides overview of Americans with Disabilities Act of 1990. No indexes. Omits index matrix included in the 1984 edition.   HV1553.F53

The state of the states in developmental disabilities / by David Braddock ... [et al.]. Baltimore : P.H. Brookes Pub. Co., c1990. 527 p. : ill.   **CC199**
     Pt. 1 provides a statistical overview of U.S. public spending for mental retardation and developmental disabilities. Includes many figures, tables, and a list of references. Pt. 2 includes alphabetical listing of state profiles, with pie charts, bar graphs, and other figures, along with technical notes for each state. Aggregate data for U.S. follows. Pt. 3 provides supplementary financial and program data in the form of tables and technical notes, comparing all states. Covers 1977–1988.   HV1570.5.U65S74

Homelessness and the homeless

Burt, Martha R. America's homeless : numbers, characteristics, and programs that serve them / Martha R. Burt, Barbara E. Cohen. Wash. : Urban Inst. Pr. ; Lanham, Md. : Distr. by Univ. Pr. of America, c1989. 176 p. (Urban Institute report, 89-3).   **CC200**
     From three Urban Institute research projects, brings together findings on the homeless, presenting statistics on their number, location, racial characteristics, nutrition, etc., and a summary of state and national programs intended for their assistance. Verbal descriptions are supplemented by numerous tables. No index, but a detailed table of contents includes a complete list of statistical tables.   HV4505.B89

Henslin, James M. Homelessness : an annotated bibliography. N.Y. : Garland, 1993. 2 v. (Garland reference library of social science, v. 534).   **CC201**
     Includes books, book chapters, journal articles, and newspapers. Vol. 1, the main bibliography, presents annotated entries alphabetically arranged by author. Many anonymous entries follow, in a separate category. Vol. 2 groups the same entries under 41 subtopics, omitting the annotations. Author index.   Z7164.H72H46

Hombs, Mary Ellen. American homelessness : a reference handbook. Santa Barbara, Calif. : ABC-Clio, c1990. 193 p. **CC202**

Presents an "organized overview of the wide variety of ... resources and tools" (*Pref.*) for understanding the causes and characteristics of homelessness. In nine chapters, including a chronology, biographical sketches of advocates for the homeless, summaries of legislation and court cases, a directory of organizations, and an annotated bibliography of reference materials. Glossary; general index.

HV4505.H647

Homelessness in the United States / ed. by Jamshid A. Momeni. N.Y. : Greenwood, 1989–1990. 2 v. : ill. (Contributions in sociology, no. 73, 87). **CC203**

Presents national, state, and local statistical data on the homeless, plus discussions and analyses of the problem. Vol. 1 contains 14 chapters, each by an expert, concerning homeless distributions, variations, trends, and characteristics in individual states and cities. Vol. 2 offers 11 chapters on varied topics such as drug abuse among the homeless, public policies for reducing homelessness, and a national overview of the problem. Many statistical tables. Both volumes have general indexes.

HV4505.H656

Nordquist, Joan. The homeless in America : a bibliography. Santa Cruz, Calif. : Reference and Research Services, 1988. 64 p. (Contemporary social issues, no. 12). **CC204**

Contains approximately 500 entries from scholarly, technical, and popular sources, including recent books, journals, conference papers, and government publications. Arranged in topical categories (e.g., families, women, children, drugs, federal policies, mental health, legal issues), subdivided by format; entries in sections are alphabetical by author. Includes list of bibliographies, directories, and organization names. No indexes.

Z7164.H72N67

Marriage and the family

Bibliography

Acock, Alan C. The influence of the family : a review and annotated bibliography of socialization, ethnicity, and delinquency, 1975–1986 / Alan C. Acock, Jeffrey M. Clair. N.Y. : Garland, 1986. 315 p. : ill. (Garland library of sociology, v. 9 ; Garland reference library of social science, v. 353). **CC205**

Focuses on families and their adolescent or young adult children, with the theme of intergenerational influences. Nearly 800 entries for articles, conference papers, books, and book chapters, published in the U.S. Includes sections on family influence, ethnicity, and delinquency, each with an introductory essay. Lists references alphabetically by author within each section. Provides keywords for each entry. Author and subject indexes.

Z7164.Y8A26

Black American families, 1965–1984 : a classified, selectively annotated bibliography / Walter R. Allen, ed. in chief ; Richard A. English and Jo Anne Hall, associate editors. N.Y. : Greenwood, 1986. 480 p. (Bibliographies and indexes in Afro-American and African studies, no. 16). **CC206**

Lists 1,153 entries, arranged alphabetically by author. Provides subject descriptors for each reference; some include annotations and notes. Indexes: classified, keyword, co-author/co-editor. List of periodical titles and publishers. Lack of variation in typeface or size makes text difficult to use.

Z1361.N39B5

De Young, Mary. Incest : an annotated bibliography. Jefferson, N.C. : McFarland, c1985. 161 p. **CC207**

Focuses on professional journals and books, most from the last ten years, in 13 chapters covering the forms, effects, and treatment of incest. Includes statistical studies, book reviews, and a useful chapter on definitions. Entries are arranged alphabetically by author under chapter subheadings. Author and subject indexes.   Z7164.S42D4

Dixon, Penelope. Mothers and mothering : an annotated feminist bibliography. N.Y. : Garland, 1991. 219 p. (Women's history and culture, 3 ; Garland reference library of social science, v. 646). **CC208**

Eleven topical chapters treating mothering and daughters, sons, family, children, feminism, psychoanalysis, and reproductive issues; also covers single, working, lesbian, and black mothers. Includes 351 annotated entries for articles and books, 1970–90. Omits theses, how-to books, historical, fictional, and cross-cultural material. Author index.

Z7963.M67D59

Engeldinger, Eugene A. Spouse abuse : an annotated bibliography of violence between mates. Metuchen, N.J. : Scarecrow, 1986. 317 p. **CC209**

Lists scholarly and popular English-language books, articles, government publications, theses, dissertations, conference papers, directories, pamphlets, and handbooks through 1983; omits newspaper articles, films, and recordings. 1,783 entries, alphabetically arranged by author in a single listing. Name and subject indexes.

Z5703.4.W53E53

Family therapy : a bibliography, 1937–1986 / comp. by Bernard Lubin ... [et al.]. N.Y. : Greenwood, 1988. 470 p. (Bibliographies and indexes in psychology, no. 4). **CC210**

A comprehensive work, intended for undergraduates and graduate students. Includes 6,167 cross-referenced entries, primarily journal articles, with some books and dissertations, arranged alphabetically by author. Author and subject indexes.   Z6665.7.F35F36

Gondolf, Edward W. Research on men who batter : an overview, bibliography and resource guide. Bradenton, Fla. : Human Services Institute, c1988. 93 p. **CC211**

For social workers, therapists, researchers working with men who batter. Provides 14-page critical overview of research, and nearly 1,000 non-annotated entries organized by subtopic under six major categories: research on wife battering, roots of wife battering, research on batterers, intervention with batterers, and program resources (books, manuals, films, periodicals, reference books). Author index.

Z5703.4.W53G66

Gruber, Ellen J. Stepfamilies : a guide to the sources and resources. N.Y. : Garland, 1986. 122 p. (Garland reference library of social science, v. 317). **CC212**

Includes books and periodical articles, 1980–84. Sections for professionals who work with parents or children, for parents, and for children and young adults. Entries are alphabetical by author. Separate, brief list of audiovisual materials, organizations, and newsletters. Index of names and some broad subjects.   Z7164.M2G78

History of the family and kinship : a select international bibliography / ed. by Gerald L. Soliday ... [et al.]. Millwood, N.Y. : Kraus Internat. Publ., c1980. 410 p. **CC213**

"A project of the *Journal of Family History* [and] the National Council on Family Relations."—*t.p.*

About 6,200 entries, representing Western-language sources published through 1976. Arrangement is by region; further subdivisions are usually based on form of material (general surveys and bibliographies), individual country, or historic period. Chapters on classical antiquity and the Middle East and North Africa offer broad subject approach. Index of names.   Z7164.M2H57

Kemmer, Elizabeth Jane. Violence in the family : an annotated bibliography. N.Y. : Garland, 1984. 192 p. (Garland reference library of social science, v. 182). **CC214**

Covers periodical articles and books published in English, 1960–82, and includes contributions from many fields: psychology, social work, medicine, women's studies, law, criminology, nursing, and the popular press. 1,055 consecutively numbered entries are arranged alphabetically by author. Author and subject indexes.

Z7164.C5K46

Melina, Lois Ruskai. Adoption : an annotated bibliography and guide. N.Y. : Garland, 1987. 292 p. (Garland reference library of social science, v. 374).   **CC215**

   Includes English-language books and journals published after 1973 in sociology, social work, psychology, anthropology, education, psychiatry, child development, medicine, and law. Lists works readily available; intended for a wide audience. 845 cross-referenced entries are listed alphabetically by author in 13 topical chapters (e.g., Infant, special needs, intercountry, and minority adoption; Sealed records, proadoption issues, and termination of parent rights). Lists children's resources, education and training materials, and audiovisuals. Author and subject indexes.   Z7164.A23M44

Nofsinger, Mary M. Children and adjustment to divorce : an annotated bibliography. N.Y. : Garland, 1989. 282 p. (Reference books on family issues, 13 ; Garland reference library of the humanities, vol. 554).   **CC216**

   Contains three bibliographies, an audiovisual resource list, and an organizational resources list, each with an introduction. In the main bibliography of books and articles, arranged by author, entries indicate categories of professionals to whom the items would be of interest. Separate bibliographies for parents, children and young adults follow. The audiovisual resources list, alphabetical by title, includes the audience level for each entry, from preschool to adult. Organizational resources listed alphabetically by name. Author, book title, user category, and subject indexes.   Z7164.C5N66

Nordquist, Joan. Domestic violence : spouse abuse, marital rape. Santa Cruz, Calif. : Reference and Research Services, 1986. 64 p. (Contemporary social issues, no. 4).   **CC217**

   A slim volume with very recent English-language, multidisciplinary coverage. Includes scholarly and general interest books, articles, pamphlets, and advocacy group publications. Section I covers domestic violence and spouse abuse; Section II, marital rape. Entries are grouped by format and listed alphabetically by author. Section III lists bibliographies, directories, organizations, and periodical titles. No indexes.   HQ809.3.U6N67

Rubin, Richard. Incest, the last taboo : an annotated bibliography / Rick Rubin, Greg Byerly. N.Y. : Garland, 1983. 169 p. (Garland reference library of social science, v. 143).   **CC218**

   Contains 419 citations grouped by form, including books, dissertations, articles, and audiovisual materials. Emphasis is on English-language titles published since 1970. Indexed by periodical title, author, and subject.   HQ72.U53R8

Sadler, Judith DeBoard. Families in transition : an annotated bibliography. Hamden, Conn. : Archon Books, 1988. 251 p.   **CC219**

   Intended for a wide audience. An introduction provides statistical information and an overview. The bibliography lists 970 books, articles, and audiovisual materials, late 1970s–mid-1980s; a late additions list includes items as recent as 1987. Except for chapter 15 (audiovisuals), entries are grouped in 14 topical chapters, including Single parents, Adoptive and foster families, Parental kidnapping, Working parents and latchkey children, Works for children and youth, and Homosexual relationships. Entries are alphabetical by author within each chapter. Appendix lists addresses for associations and organizations. Separate indexes for subjects, authors, book titles, and article titles.   Z5118.F2S23

Zollar, Ann Creighton. Adolescent pregnancy and parenthood : an annotated guide. N.Y. : Garland, 1990. 244 p. (Reference books on family issues, v. 16 ; Garland reference library of social science, v. 523).   **CC220**

   A bibliography of 700 articles, book chapters, and books from the sociological and psychological literatures, plus an additional 87 references to holdings of the Data Archive on Adolescent Pregnancy and Pregnancy Prevention (DAAPPP). Arranged by 12 broad topical areas (e.g., Contraception, Sex education, Adolescent fathers, Legal issues), with no other subject access and no cross-references. Author index.   Z7164.Y8Z64

Indexes; Abstract journals

Inventory of marriage and family literature. v. 3 (1973/74)– . St. Paul, Minn. : National Council on Family Relations, 1974– . Annual.   **CC221**

   Continues *International bibliography of research in marriage and the family* (v. 1 [1900–64]–2 [1965–72]. Minneapolis : Univ. of Minnesota Pr. in assoc. with the Inst. of Life Insurance for the Minnesota Family Study Center, 1964–72) and assumes its numbering.

   Publisher varies.

   Indexes several hundred leading professional journals, adding books with v. 17. Comprised of subject, author, and Key Word in Title (KWIT) indexes. Brief bibliographic citations; no abstracts. Entries in very small print. One–two year publication lag.

   •Machine-readable version: *Inventory of marriage and family literature* [database] (Minneapolis : National Council on Family Relations, 1970–). Available online. Updated monthly. Also called *IMPL online*. Continues *Family resources database*.   Z7164.M2I57

Sage family studies abstracts. v. 1, no. 1 (Feb. 1979)– . Beverly Hills, Calif : Sage Publ., 1979– . Quarterly.   **CC222**

   Each issue abstracts about 250 articles, books, and some government publications, pamphlets, etc. Abstracts are grouped by broad topic; e.g., gender roles, life cycles, reproductive issues, minority and cross-cultural relations. Author and subject indexes in each issue.   HQ536.S23

Encyclopedias

Adamec, Christine A. The encyclopedia of adoption / Christine Adamec, William L. Pierce. N.Y. : Facts on File, c1991. 382 p.   **CC223**

   A multidisciplinary text for general readers and adoption experts. 17-page introductory essay on adoption history, with references. Alphabetical arrangement of cross-referenced entries, each 1–8 columns in length, some with brief reference lists. Appendixes include tabular data on birth and adoptions; U.S. and Canadian social service offices, adoption agencies, related organizations, parent groups; 11 international agencies in the U.S.; addresses for periodicals, newspapers, and newsletters. 12-page bibliography; detailed index.   HV875.55.A28

DiCanio, Margaret. The encyclopedia of marriage, divorce, and the family. N.Y. : Facts on File, c1989. 607 p.   **CC224**

   A comprehensive treatment of present-day family life in North America, presented through more than 500 entries on such subjects as living wills, throwaway children, bisexual spouses, and homeless families. Entries are alphabetically arranged, vary in length from a few lines to several pages, and include cross-references. Detailed index of authors, titles, and subjects; 32-page bibliography. Nine appendixes include: How to choose therapists, mental health agencies, and divorce attorneys; Sample antenuptial and living-together agreements; Directories of state child-care licensing and child-support enforcement agencies.   HQ9.D38

Encyclopedia of childbearing : critical perspectives / ed. by Barbara Katz Rothman. Phoenix : Oryx, 1993. 446 p. : ill.   **CC225**

   Multidisciplinary treatment; includes about 250 entries. Groups related subject headings together into a two-page list for cross-referencing. Signed articles, most two or more columns in length, include cross-references and resource lists. Sample topics: amniocentesis; anti-abortion movement; cesarean birth: history and legend; creation stories in Western culture; imaging techniques; midwife-attended birth; Norplant. Also includes entries for various countries. Tables, photographs, illustrations, figures. Brief biographical sketches for the 206 contributors; alphabetical list of article titles. Appendix lists organizations and resources by topic. General index.   RG525.E52

Dictionaries

Family therapy glossary / Craig A. Everett, ed. ; Candice S. Russell, James Keller, associate editors. [Rev. ed.]. Wash. : American Assoc. for Marriage and Family Therapy, c1992. 40 p. : ill.   **CC226**

1st ed., 1982.

Alphabetical arrangement of terms, with three- to six-sentence definitions. Includes *see* references and entry references. Sample terms: collusion, emotional divorce, gender roles, perturbation, zero-sum game. Six-page bibliography.   RC488.5.F3395

Sauber, S. Richard. Family therapy : basic concepts and terms / S. Richard Sauber, Luciano L'Abate, Gerald R. Weeks. Rockville, Md. : Aspen Systems Corp., 1985. 181 p.   **CC227**

An encyclopedic dictionary whose entries provide definitions, examples, sources, and references to uses of the term. A brief appendix describes professional organizations and publications.   RC488.5.S27

Directories

The adoption directory / Ellen Paul, ed. Detroit : Gale, c1989. 515 p.   **CC228**

Subtitle: The most comprehensive guide to family-building options, including state statutes on adoption, public and private adoption agencies, adoption exchanges, foreign requirements and adoption agencies, independent adoption services, foster parenting, biological alternatives, and support groups.

A comprehensive work, covering official policies, statutes, and agencies by state. Describes organizations that match children with families, foster care agencies and groups, support groups, and facilities providing biological alternatives such as in vitro fertilization and artificial insemination. Describes agencies and adoption criteria for Colombia, Guatemala, India, Korea, Philippines, and Taiwan. Includes glossary and list of suggested readings. Geographic, name, and subject indexes.   HV875.55.A364

Partridge-Brown, Mary. In-vitro fertilization clinics : a North American directory of programs and services. Jefferson, N.C. : McFarland & Co., c1993. 234 p.   **CC229**

Parts 1 and 2 describe process of fertilization and three methods of assisted reproduction. Pt. 3 (p. 23–224) contains profiles of programs by state, followed by those for Canada. Within each state, entries are arranged alphabetically by program name and provide address, phone, description of services, detailed costs, requirements/restrictions, and staff names and years of experience. Appendix describes eight related organizations, with directory information. Index.   RG133.5.P37

Paul, Ellen. Adoption choices : a guidebook to national and international adoption resources. Detroit : Visible Ink Pr., c1991. 590 p.   **CC230**

Written for prospective parents. Describes public, private, and independent agencies, private facilitators, support groups, and adoption laws. Four main sections: U.S. agencies and support groups; Adoption exchanges; Canada (organized by territory); and Foreign (seven countries). Brief section on foster care. Each entry provides address, phone, contact, profile, procedures and fees, home study details, and branches of the organization. Index of agency and facilitator names.   HV875.55.P38

Posner, Julia L. CWLA's guide to adoption agencies : a national directory of adoption agencies and adoption resources. Wash. : Child Welfare League of America, c1989. 668 p.   **CC231**

Sections, arranged by state, list the following: public adoption programs/community resources; out-of-state agencies; and licensed private adoption agencies. Entries listed alphabetically in each category. Private agency entries provide information on cost, waiting period,

requirements, and the children. An appendix lists agencies providing nationwide services. Based on data collected 1987–88.   HV875.55.P67

Handbooks

Alexander-Roberts, Colleen. The essential adoption handbook. Dallas : Taylor Publ. Co., c1993. 242 p. : ill.   **CC232**

Written for prospective adoptive parents. Discusses the adoption process; organizing the search for a child; preparing for agency adoptions; adoptive parent support groups; the home study process; and intercounty, single parent, and independent adoptions. Includes instructions, suggestions from more than 100 adoptive parents, sample forms, and checklists. Lists books by type of adoption. Nine-page bibliography organized by subject. Appendixes list adoption attorneys by state; publishers; parent support organizations by state; governmental, national, and international organizations; periodicals; private agencies by state; and state public agencies. Index.   HV875.55.A44

American Association for Marriage and Family Therapy ethics casebook / George W. Brock, ed. Wash. : American Assoc. for Marriage and Family Therapy, c1994. 292 p. : diagrams, forms.   **CC233**

Useful for therapists, students, and consumers. In five chapters; discusses background and evolution of the code of ethics, results of a national survey of therapists, each of the eight principles, and special topics such as dual relations, impaired therapists, and client confidentiality. References and suggested reading list. Appendixes include past and present AAMFT codes of ethics, list of procedures, sample complaint form, decision tree, and questionnaires. 16-p. bibliography.   RC488.5.A51

American families : a research guide and historical handbook / ed. by Joseph M. Hawes and Elizabeth I. Nybakken. N.Y. : Greenwood, 1991. 435 p.   **CC234**

Presented as an introductory guide emphasizing recent work. Organized into chronological and topical chapters, two introductory, five addressing various time periods, 1600 to the present, and four dealing with specific topics, e.g., women, Native Americans, working class, and African Americans. Chapters are signed and include notes and references. 45 page selected bibliography; detailed general index.   HQ535.A585

Bennett, Tess. Developing individualized family support plans : a training manual / by Tess Bennett, Barbara V. Lingerfelt, and Donna E. Nelson. Cambridge, Mass. : Brookline Books, c1990. 232 p. : ill.   **CC235**

For group training or self-study. Assists families and professionals in developing the Individualized Family Support Plan (IFSP), using PL99-457 as a guideline. Glossary; list of references.

§ Designed for use with *Enabling and empowering families : principles and guidelines for practice*, ed. by Carl J. Dunst, Carol M. Trivette, and Angela G. Deal [et al.] (1988).   HV888.5.B46

Cline, Ruth K. J. Focus on families : a reference handbook. Santa Barbara, Calif. : ABC-Clio, c1990. 233 p.   **CC236**

For undergraduate or high school students and teachers. Introductory essays to each of the nine topical chapters provide background, statistics, definitions, and quotations. Half of each chapter is devoted to annotated lists of fiction, nonfiction, and nonprint materials, and organizations. Chapter topics include stepfamilies, single-parent families, grandparents, one-child families, adoptions, child abuse, etc. General index.   HQ535.C55

Family research : a sixty-year review, 1930–1990 / ed. by Stephen J. Bahr. Lexington, Mass. : Lexington Books, 1991–1992. 2 v.   **CC237**

For researchers, teachers, students, policymakers, and practitioners. Ten signed chapters review research on various topics, e.g., marital and extramarital sexuality, violence, recreation, gender roles, etc.

Chapters organized by decade and by subtopic; lengthy reference lists. Tables compare research studies, showing dates, author, topic, sample size, methods, etc. General index.   HQ518.F3428

Franck, Irene M. The parent's desk reference / Irene Franck and David Brownstone. N.Y. : Prentice Hall, c1991. 615 p. : ill.   **CC238**

Some 2,500 cross-referenced entries, alphabetically arranged, ranging in length from one line to six columns. Many include background works, reference list, and descriptions of relevant organizations. Sidebar information includes checklists, tips, guidelines. Sample entries: cesarean section, early screening inventory, MMPI, mumps, family shelter, Parent Locator Service (PLS), status offense, vitamin E. 129-page Special help section addresses topics such as pregnancy, baby safety, school curricula, books for children and parents, hotlines, helplines.   HQ769.F717

Handbook of family measurement techniques / John Touliatos, Barry F. Perlmutter, Murray A. Straus, editors. Newbury Park, Calif. : Sage, 1990. 797 p.   **CC239**

Describes 976 instruments organized in five categories—(1) Dimensions of interaction; (2) Intimacy and family values; (3) Parenthood; (4) Roles and power; (5) Adjustment—and 16 subcategories. Entries are typically a page or less in length and provide brief descriptions of the variables measured, the instrument's content and procedures, reliability and validity, availability, and one to four references. Author and title indexes, and a Classification index, arranging entries by subcategories and by "primary interactants" (e.g., husband-wife, parent-child). For clinicians and researchers.   HQ728.T68

Handbook of family violence / ed. by Vincent B. Van Hasselt … [et al.]. N.Y. : Plenum Pr., c1988. 500 p.   **CC240**

A useful, thorough source for practitioners and students of law, education, human services, and others. Groups 19 chapters in four parts. Pt. 1 is an overview. Pt. 2 describes psychoanalytic, social learning, and sociological theoretical models. Pt. 3 covers forms of family violence: wife battering, physical abuse of children, child sexual abuse, incest, marital rape, husband battering, elder abuse, family homicide, and murders committed by victimized women. Pt. 4 addresses epidemiology, neurological factors, alcohol use, legal issues, cross-cultural perspectives, and research issues. Separate author and subject indexes.   HQ809.3.U5H35

Handbook of marriage and the family / ed. by Marvin B. Sussman and Suzanne K. Steinmetz. N.Y. : Plenum Pr., c1987. 915 p. : ill.   **CC241**

Offers 30 signed articles by specialists in sociology, demography, history, social work, and psychology. Articles include many charts, tables, and figures and conclude with lengthy bibliographies. Topics include comparative perspectives, family theory, methodology, ethnicity, nontraditional family forms, gender roles, therapy, and voluntary childlessness. List of contributors; subject index.   HQ518.H154

Klinman, Debra G. Fatherhood U.S.A : the first national guide to programs, services, and resources for and about fathers / Debra G. Klinman, Rhiana Kohl. N.Y. : Garland, 1984. 321 p. : ill.   **CC242**

Five broad subject chapters cover health care, education, law, social and supportive services, and the workplace, and are divided into subchapters on, for example, programs for expectant and new fathers, services for teen fathers, the gay fathers network, fathers' rights organizations, and parental leave policies. A sixth chapter lists books, films, videocassettes, and newsletters. Alphabetical and state indexes of programs and organizations; brief subject index.   HQ756.K55

Samuelson, Elliot D. Unmarried couples : a guide to your legal rights and obligations. N.Y. : Insight Books, c1992. 295 p.   **CC243**

For the general reader and the specialist. Addresses issues faced by unmarried domestic partners, e.g., living-together and prenuptial agreements; support and property division; adoption; custody; housing; inheritance; pensions; etc. In 14 topical chapters, the last listing rele-

vant organizations, with basic directory information. Appendixes list common law marriage states, term life insurance rates for nonsmokers, state provisions to enact living wills, medicare eligibility, and states legally requiring support from nonparents. Appendixes also provide sample living-together and prenuptial agreements, health care proxy, living will, financial disclosure affadavit, retainer letter. Brief bibliography organized by subject; general index.   KF538.S26

Statistics

The new American family : significant and diversified lifestyles. N.Y. : Simmons Market Research Bureau, [c1992]. 64 p. : ill.   **CC244**

Draws on data from government sources and from the same publisher's *Simmons study of media and markets*. Provides tables, charts, figures on income, shopping habits, marital status, mobility, etc. for groups such as new mothers, singles, baby boomers, empty nesters, teens, etc. Most data are from late 1980s and 1990. No indexes.

HQ536.N493

Population planning

Abortion : choice & conflict / ed., Oliver Trager. N.Y. : Facts on File, c1993. 208 p. : ill.   **CC245**

Provides full text of editorials and cartoons from leading U.S. newspapers. Two-page overview introduces each of the four parts: Abortion and the courts; Politics and abortion; Pro-life v. Pro-choice; and Health, youth, and abortion. Newspaper entries include newspaper name, city, and date. General index: names, subjects, states, and newspapers.   HQ767.5.N7A26

Abortion and family planning bibliography for [...]. 1987– . Troy, N.Y. : Whitston, c1990– . Annual.   **CC246**

Continues: *Abortion bibliography* (Troy, N.Y. : Whitston, 1970–86) and *Population bibliography* (Troy, N.Y. : Whitston, 1970–76).

Covers abortion, family planning, and related topics such as birth control, contraceptives, fertility, and sterilization, citing 711 journals. Multidisciplinary and international in scope. Separate brief lists for books and dissertations, arranged by author; section for periodical literature (p. 7–172) arranged by subject. Author and subject indexes.

Z6671.2.A2F57

Abortion factbook : readings, trends, and state and local data to [...] / the Alan Guttmacher Institute. 1992 ed.– . N.Y. : The Institute, c1992– .   **CC247**

Continues *Abortion services in the United States, each state & metropolitan area*, publ. 1980–85.

Contains readings published in *Family planning perspectives* (N.Y. : Alan Guttmacher Inst.), 1988–92, and detailed abortion statistics, including comparative data, starting as early as 1973. Topics include world review, abortion accessibility, U.S. consumer characteristics, why women have abortions, politics, public opinion, state laws, effects of abortion, etc. Readings include reference lists. Includes copy of Abortion Provider Survey.

Adolescent reproductive behaviour : an annotated bibliography. [N.Y.] : Population Division, Dept. of International Economic and Social Affairs, United Nations, 1988. 284 p.   **CC248**

Organizes entries, mostly of materials published 1973–87, alphabetically by country under regional headings. Includes references to programs for adolescents, socioeconomic and health studies, and prenatal care and services. Entries include detailed abstracts; many from *POPLINE* database (CC257). No indexes. Print quality varies.

HQ27.A363

Costa, Marie. Abortion : a reference handbook. Santa Barbara, Calif. : ABC-Clio, c1991. 258 p.   **CC249**

Presents historical and factual background and resources for further exploration into the social, psychological, legal, medical, and moral aspects. Six chapters deal with the history of abortion, biographical sketches of some personalities involved, facts and statistics, directory of organizations and organized groups, and annotated selective bibliographies of print and nonprint resources. Glossary of terms; index.

§ Provides more detailed biographical data than Carl N. Flanders, *Abortion* (CC252).   HQ767.5.U5C67

Family planning and child survival programs as assessed in 1991 / John A. Ross ... [et al.]. N.Y. : Population Council, 1992. 182 p. : ill.   **CC250**

Provides 39 tables of statistics for most developing countries, for middle to late 1980s, with some 1990 data. In addition to demographics and vital statistics, addresses contraceptive use, family planning programs, maternal care, government policies, and child survival programs.

§ See *Family planning and child survival : 100 developing countries* (N.Y. : Center for Population and Family Health, Columbia Univ., 1988) for historical data and patterns.

Fitzsimmons, Richard. Pro-choice/pro-life : an annotated, selected bibliography (1972–1989) / comp. by Richard Fitzsimmons and Joan P. Diana. N.Y. : Greenwood, 1991. 251 p. (Bibliographies and indexes in sociology, no. 20).   **CC251**

Compiled for theologians, researchers, general readers, and lawyers to provide access to U.S. periodical and monographic works including legal, ethical, social, moral/religious, and medical material. 1,660 consecutively numbered entries alphabetically arranged by author, or by title when no author listed. At least one LC subject heading per entry; subject index. Offset from typescript.   Z6671.2.A2F48

Flanders, Carl N. Abortion / Carl N. Flanders ; bibliographic materials prep. by Caroline M. Brown. N.Y. : Facts on File, c1991. 246 p. : maps.   **CC252**

Pt. 1 includes an introductory chapter, a 25-year chronology, court cases (1965–89), and 39 brief biographical sketches of figures considered significant in recent abortion history. Pt. 2 describes research tools such as card catalogs, automated systems, and indexes; provides a bibliography of sources grouped by type; and lists national, state, and local organizations. In the introduction to Chapter 7, NARAL, the national abortion rights group, is mistakenly referred to as "pro-life." Appendixes list acronyms; show state public funding and consent/notification laws on U.S. maps. General index.   HQ767.5.U5F62

International handbook on abortion / ed. by Paul Sachdev. N.Y. : Greenwood, 1988. 520 p.   **CC253**

Presents data on laws and policies for regions or individual countries. Written for educators, administrators, public health officials, human service providers, students. Avoids arguments concerning moral or religious aspects. 33 chapters, written by acknowledged authorities, cover policy history, medical and public attitudes, demographic data, fertility trends, illegal abortion, roles of various groups and players, profiles of contracepting and aborting women. General index with some cross-references.   HQ767.I668

Lucas, Caroline. Population/family planning thesaurus : an alphabetical and hierarchical display of terms drawn from population-related literature in the social sciences / Caroline Lucas and Margaret Osburn. 2nd ed. / rev. by Karen Long and Carann Turner. Chapel Hill : Library, Carolina Population Center, Univ. of North Carolina, 1978. 286 p.   **CC254**

1st ed., 1975.

Lists and indicates relationships among 3,900 terms in population literature, including equivalent terms in the National Library of Medicine's *Medical subject headings* (MeSH) (EH143) and the International Institute for the Study of Human Reproduction's *Fertility modification thesaurus*.   Z695.1.B55L83

Moore, Gloria. Margaret Sanger and the birth control movement : a bibliography, 1911–1984 / by Gloria Moore and Ronald Moore. Metuchen, N.J. : Scarecrow, 1986. 211 p.   **CC255**

Arranges an initial 1,160 entries, covering 1911–66 (Sanger's year of death), in chronological order. Within each year, lists items written by Sanger followed by items written by others. Sections for obituaries, major biographies, and the years 1967–1984 follow, encompassing entries 1161–1300 which are listed alphabetically by author within each section. Includes annotations, some very brief. Index for titles written by Sanger; also author and subject indexes.   Z7164.B5M66

Muldoon, Maureen. The abortion debate in the United States and Canada : a source book. N.Y. : Garland, 1991. 238 p. (Garland reference library of social science, v. 648).   **CC256**

Organized into chapters concerned with demographics, sociological research, opinions, philosophical perspectives, religious positions, advocacy groups, politics, and law. Chapters include bibliographies and notes; some provide statistical data, official statements, article abstracts, or legislative summaries. General index.   HQ767.5.U5M85

•**POPLINE** [database]. Bethesda, Md. : National Library of Medicine, 1970– .   **CC257**

Alternate title: *Population information online.* Former title: *Population information (POPINFORM).*

Available online (updated monthly) and on CD-ROM (updated semiannually).

Provides bibliographic citations to international English-language published and unpublished social science and biomedical literature on population research and demography, including family planning, human fertility, maternal and child health, overpopulation, and many related topics.

§ *A user's guide to POPLINE keywords* (formerly *POPLINE thesaurus*) is produced by the Johns Hopkins University Population Information Program (3rd ed. Baltimore : Johns Hopkins, 1991. 195 p.).

Reynolds, Moira Davison. Women advocates of reproductive rights : eleven who led the struggle in the United States and Great Britain. Jefferson, N.C. : McFarland & Co., c1994. 169 p. : ill.   **CC258**

For general readers. Each chapter profiles one woman, and ranges in length from five to 22 pages. Ten illustrations; eight-page bibliography organized by chapter. General index.   HQ766.5.G7R48

Winter, Eugenia B. Psychological and medical aspects of induced abortion : a selective, annotated bibliography, 1970–1986. N.Y. : Greenwood, 1988. 162 p. (Bibliographies and indexes in women's studies, no. 7).   **CC259**

Describes 500 works that are "either classics in the field or representational of the kind of writing being published ... ."—*Pref.* Besides books and research articles, includes a number of films and audio and video recordings. Author, title, and subject indexes.   Z6671.2.A2W56

Poverty and the poor

Chalfant, H. Paul. Sociology of poverty in the United States : an annotated bibliography. Westport, Conn. : Greenwood, 1985. 187 p. (Bibliographies and indexes in sociology, no. 3).   **CC260**

Cites 621 selected books, book chapters, and articles, most published 1970–early 1984. Entries are arranged in broad topical sections. Annotations are of substantial length. Author index.   Z7164.C4C44

Feinberg, Renee. The feminization of poverty in the United States : a selected, annotated bibliography of the issues, 1978–1989 / Renee Feinberg, Kathleen E. Knox. N.Y. : Garland, 1990. 317 p. (Garland reference library of social science, v. 530).   **CC261**

Contains 18 chapters that treat such topics as families headed by women, children of poverty, comparable worth and pay equity, older women and poverty, women of color and poverty, and housing and homelessness. Each chapter includes several introductory paragraphs, usually with references to other sources.   Z7164.C4F45

Flynt, J. Wayne. Southern poor whites : a selected annotated bibliography of published sources / J. Wayne Flynt, Dorothy S. Flynt. N.Y. : Garland, c1981. 320 p. (Garland reference library of social science, v. 88).   **CC262**

Interprets subject primarily in an economic sense, and emphasizes general materials, economics, and folk culture rather than politics. Omits unpublished material. Groups 1,455 numbered references into subject chapters, each with an introductory defining statement. Topics include economics, occupations, folk culture, health, migration, race relations, women, religion. Author and subject indexes.   Z1251.S7F6

Nordquist, Joan. The feminization of poverty. Santa Cruz, Calif. : Reference and Research Services, 1987. 64 p. **CC263**

Three sections draw from the last ten years of feminist, economic, political, and activist literatures. Section I focuses on the labor force, comparable worth, sex discrimination in employment, poverty, and the family, Section II on the feminization of poverty, subdivided by topic. Entries are grouped by format and alphabetically arranged by author. Section III lists 15 bibliographies and 33 organizations. No indexes.   HQ1381.N67

Poverty in developing countries : a bibliography of publications by the ILO's World Employment Programme, 1975–91. Geneva : International Labour Office, 1992. 152 p. (International labour bibliography, no. 12).   **CC264**

Covers ILO publications and documents, addressing poverty, rural poverty, and trends and measurement. Lists 350 entries with abstracts alphabetically by author. Entries indicate text language(s) and provide report or document numbers. Author, corporate author, subject, and geographical indexes.   Z7164.U5P68

Sex and sexual behavior

Lambda book report. v. 2, no. 3 (Feb./Mar. 1990)– . Wash. : Lambda Rising, Inc., 1990– . Bimonthly.   **CC265**

Title page note: A review of contemporary gay and lesbian literature.

Continues: *Lambda Rising book report* (Dec. 1989–Jan. 1990).

Includes many reviews, some lengthy, as well as bestseller and award lists, letters, interviews with authors, and essays on literary topics. Impressive array of contributors, excellent writing, visually appealing arrangement. Each issue 50 pages in length.   PN56.H57L36

Bibliography

An annotated bibliography of homosexuality / Vern L. Bullough … [et al.]. N.Y. : Garland, 1976. 2 v.   **CC266**

Sponsored by the Institute for the Study of Human Resources, Los Angeles.

"The … aim has been to bring together representative entries from a multidisciplinary point of view."—*p.xv*. More than 12,700 citations are classed under broad subject headings, e.g., behavioral sciences, education and children, law and its enforcement, novels, the homophile movement, transvestism and transsexualism. Author index and index of pseudonyms for each volume, but no detailed subject approach. Despite the title, annotations are few and exceedingly brief.   Z7164.S42A66

August, Eugene R. Men's studies : a selected and annotated interdisciplinary bibliography. Littleton, Colo. : Libraries Unlimited, 1985. 215 p.   **CC267**

Cites 591 English-language books "about males as males" (*Introd.*), exploring topics such as men's rights, divorce and custody, masculine gender role, men in families, literary works, autobiographies and biographies, etc. Subject arrangement; author and title indexes.   Z7164.M49A84

Dynes, Wayne R. Homosexuality : a research guide. N.Y. : Garland, 1987. 853 p. (Garland reference library of social science, v. 313).   **CC268**

Lists 4,858 annotated entries alphabetically by author under 24 main and 176 subtopics. Brief introductions provide useful context for the subtopics. International in scope; includes many materials in European languages. Emphasizes books and journal articles from major disciplines in the social sciences and humanities; omits fiction, poetry, drama, and most unpublished dissertations. Coverage from the 19th century to 1986. Subject and names index.   Z7164.S42D96

Frayser, Suzanne G. Studies in human sexuality : a selected guide / Suzanne G. Frayser, Thomas J. Whitby. Littleton, Colo. : Libraries Unlimited, 1987. 442 p.   **CC269**

Provides citations, informative abstracts, and brief descriptions of content for 627 monographic works. Entries grouped by subject; anthropology, biology, history, law, literature, arts, medicine, politics, psychology, and sociology. Most titles were published in the last two decades, but early landmark works are also included. Indicates suggested reading level. The introduction includes an overview of the literature.   Z7164.S42F73

Friedman, Leslie. Sex role stereotyping in the mass media : an annotated bibliography. N.Y. : Garland, 1977. 324 p. (Garland library of social science, v. 47).   **CC270**

Concerns sex role stereotyping in the American mass media. Arranged by broad topic, with more detailed subdivisions. Covers the mass media in general, advertising, broadcast media, film, print media, popular culture (music, humor, comic strips and books, science fiction, pornography), media image of minority group women, media image of men, children's media, impact of media stereotypes on occupational choices. Author and subject indexes.   Z7164.S42F74

Garber, Linda. Lesbian sources : a bibliography of periodical articles, 1970–1990. N.Y. : Garland, 1993. 680 p. (Garland reference library of the humanities, v. 1557).   **CC271**

Entries provide full citations and are arranged alphabetically by author under topical sections, also alphabetically arranged. Sample topics: abuse, Asian/Pacifica Lesbians, censorship, detective novels, lesbians around the world, parenting, political organizing, racism, separatism, etc. Covers articles written by or about lesbians, and focuses upon readily available materials. Omits archival material and most newspapers; does not overlap with Clare Potter's *The lesbian periodicals index* (CC286). Includes addresses for the 65 periodicals indexed, and for U.S. and international archives.   Z5866.L44G37

Lesbian studies : present and future / ed. by Margaret Cruikshank. Old Westbury, N.Y. : Feminist Pr., c1982. 286 p.   **CC272**

Essays on lesbian studies in the curriculum; numerous bibliographic references. Also provides resource directory, sample syllabi, and 275-page annotated bibliography.   HQ75.3.L48

Maggiore, Dolores J. Lesbianism : an annotated bibliography and guide to the literature, 1976–1986. Metuchen, N.J. : Scarecrow, 1988. 150 p.   **CC273**

Includes entries for some 350 books, articles, and resources from fields such as social work, sociology, law, and women's studies. Excludes items that contain erroneous information or negative views of lesbians. In five topical sections: The individual lesbian; Minorities within a minority; Lesbian families; Oppression; Health issues; and Resources. Entries are arranged alphabetically by author within each section; exemplary works are starred. Each section concludes with a list of related organizations. Section VI lists bookstores and publications. Separate author and title indexes.

—. —— *1976–1991* (Metuchen, N.J. : Scarecrow, 1992).
A supplement that adds 200 references. Z7164.S42M33

Ridinger, Robert B. Marks. The homosexual and society : an annotated bibliography. N.Y. : Greenwood, c1990. 444 p. (Bibliographies and indexes in sociology, no. 18). **CC274**

Entries treating homophobia (discrimination against, and irrational fear of, homosexual men and women) are arranged chronologically in seven categories: Adoption and foster care; Child custody; The military establishment; Employment discrimination; Censorship; Religion; and Police attitudes and actions. "The time span covered comprises some two thousand years of time."—*Pref.* Omits literature dealing with AIDSphobia and items issued after December 1987. General index. Z7164.S42R5

Sahli, Nancy Ann. Women and sexuality in America : a bibliography. Boston : G.K. Hall, 1984. 404 p. **CC275**

Contains 1,684 annotated references to 19th–20th century English-language literature, arranged chronologically and by topic. Includes books, articles, pamphlets; omits biography, popular press. Author/title and subject indexes. Z7964.U49S26

Sellen, Betty-Carol. Feminists, pornography & the law : an annotated bibliography of conflict, 1970–1986 / Betty-Carol Sellen, Patricia A. Young. Hamden, Conn. : Library Professional Publ., 1987. 204 p. **CC276**

Contains six sections by type of resource: books, periodical articles, newspapers, nonprint media, unpublished material, and organizations. An introductory essay summarizes the conflict and provides a chronology. Each section contains an introductory scope note and lists entries alphabetically by author. Appendixes list publications which contain frequent references to the feminist antipornography movement and a chronology of newspaper articles. General index.

Z7164.P84S45

Encyclopedias

Encyclopedia of homosexuality / ed. by Wayne Dynes ; associate editors, Warren Johansson, William A. Percy. N.Y. : Garland, 1990. 2 v. (1484 p.). (Garland reference library of social science, v. 492). **CC277**

A pioneering work written for a broad audience that offers more than 770 signed articles arranged alphabetically. A useful 22-page reader's guide provides an outline of major topics and disciplines, with relevant article titles. The preface explains the work's scope and structure and the difficulties inherent in defining homosexuality. List of contributors; detailed 66-page index of subjects and names; cross-references in the text. HQ76.25.E53

Human sexuality : an encyclopedia / ed. by Vern L. Bullough and Bonnie Bullough. N.Y. : Garland, 1994. 643 p. : ill. (Garland reference library of social science, v. 685). **CC278**

Some 200 signed articles by 100 experts, representing a range of ages, viewpoints, and disciplines. Entries range from expected topics such as impotence, oral-genital sex, and psychoanalytic theories; to broader, multidisciplinary, and very timely issues, e.g., body imagery and guided imagery; the double standard and sex; sexuality and disabilities. Entries include reference lists. Appendix is a signed article on research stategies and information sources. Detailed index, main entries indicated in bold. HQ9.H846

Dictionaries

Camphausen, Rufus C. The encyclopedic dictionary of erotic wisdom : a reference guide to the symbolism, techniques, rituals, sacred texts, psychology, anatomy, and history of sexuality. Rochester, Vt. : Inner Traditions International ; [s.l.] : distr. by American International Distribution Corp., c1991. 269 p. : ill. **CC279**

A dictionary of sacred and erotic terms, aphrodisiacs, festivals, rituals, customs, biochemistry, etc., pertaining to heterosexuality. Entries are arranged alphabetically and range in length from several lines to several pages. Asterisks within text indicate separate entries. Includes and labels multiple meanings. Ten-page bibliography. Appendix includes 27 index lists that group entry terms by topic.

HQ12.C32

Carrera, Michael. The language of sex : an A to Z guide. N.Y. : Facts on File, c1992. 180 p. : ill. **CC280**

Covers topics in sexual practice and expression, health issues, physiology, medical procedures, pregnancy, childbirth, and social problems. Clearly defines technical terms; includes 11 detailed line drawings. Special sections on subjects of current or wide interest, e.g., rape myths, mammogram safety, how to use condoms. Alphabetically arranged entries, cross-references. Separate resources list; bibliography arranged by subject; cross-referenced index. HQ9.C35

A descriptive dictionary and atlas of sexology / Robert T. Francoeur, ed. in chief ... [et al.]. N.Y. : Greenwood, 1991. 768 p. : ill. **CC281**

"Brings together terms and definitions from all the disciplines."—*Introd.* Omits slang, jargon, and pronunciations. Entries range in length from a short sentence to many pages. Subjects include: birthing chair, degeneracy theory, dominatrix, feminization of poverty, herpes genitalis, lust. Appendixes: philias and paraphilias; phobias and sexual anxieties; individuals (biographical sketches); Supreme Court decisions on sexual behaviors; 19-page atlas of human sexuality.

HQ9.D34

Kahn, Ada P. The A–Z of women's sexuality : a concise encyclopedia / Ada P. Kahn and Linda Hughey Holt. Rev. and expanded ed. Alameda, Calif. : Hunter House, c1992. 362 p. : ill. **CC282**

Spine title: The new A–Z of women's sexuality.
1st ed., 1990.

Presents more than 2,000 alphabetically arranged definitions of terms pertaining to sexual behavior, reproduction, obstetrics, and gynecology. Includes many terms relating to male physiology and behavior. 24-page bibliography of books and articles alphabetically arranged by author within 47 subject categories. No statement of criteria for inclusion, preface, introduction, or table of contents. Duplicates the 1990 ed. except it adds or adds to seven entries, which are placed at the ends of chapters. No changes made to original index or bibliography. References to the seven items are found within square brackets, added to the original text. Although this makes the few additions easy to identify, it hardly warrants purchase of the "revised and expanded" edition if a library already owns the first. HQ30.K34

Richter, Alan. Dictionary of sexual slang : words, phrases, and idioms from AC/DC to zig-zig. N.Y. : Wiley, c1993. 250 p. : maps. **CC283**

"Focused exclusively on the words and phrases that have come to have sexual meanings in English over the past 500 years or so."—*Introd.* Entries include various meanings, cross-references. Omits pronunciations. Four-page bibliography. HQ9.R53

Rodgers, Bruce. The queens' vernacular : a gay lexicon. [San Francisco, Calif.] : Straight Arrow Books, [1972]. 265 p. **CC284**

More than 12,000 entries reflecting gay male slang and culture. Locates words by region and historical period; includes pronunciation keys, derivations, etymologies. Abundant examples and cross-references. Index; bibliography.   HQ9.R63

Periodicals

Malinowsky, H. Robert. International directory of gay and lesbian periodicals. Phoenix : Oryx, 1987. 226 p.   **CC285**

Lists 1,924 periodicals by title. Full entries provide detailed publication and circulation information, advertising rates, subject index terms, and a descriptive paragraph. There are also brief entries for titles that have ceased, are non-deliverable, or for which only name and address were available. Cross-references; separate subject/geographic and publisher/editor indexes.   HQ76.25.M35

Potter, Clare. The lesbian periodicals index. Tallahassee, Fla. : Naiad Pr., 1986. 413 p.   **CC286**

Indexes 42 lesbian periodicals selected to reflect the political, cultural, racial, and class diversity within the lesbian community. Serves as a retrospective index, since all titles have ceased. In four sections: (1) Authors and subjects; (2) Lesbian writings (diary and journal entries, humor, satire, stories, poems); (3) Book reviews; and (4) Visual arts (cartoons, drawings, photographs, miscellaneous).   HQ75.6.U5P68

Handbooks

The Alyson almanac. 1st ed. (1989)– . Boston : Alyson Publications, Inc., c1989– . Biennial.   **CC287**

Some editions have subtitle: A treasury of information for the gay and lesbian community.

Contains 24 chapters that describe: studies involving homosexuality; historical highlights; gay symbols; noteworthy people; everyday advice; best and worst books, plays, films; openly gay elected officials; publications, organizations, hotlines; and much more. Includes cartoons, photographs, illustrations. Detailed index facilitates quick reference use; also useful for browsing.

Curry, Hayden. A legal guide for lesbian and gay couples / by Hayden Curry, Denis Clifford, and Robin Leonard. 7th national ed. Berkeley : Nolo Pr., 1993. 1 v. (various pagings) : ill.   **CC288**

1st ed., 1980; 6th ed., 1991.

For general readers. Explains legal alternatives and shows applications. In 10 chapters, treats contracts, housing, investments, marriage, children, divorce, medical emergencies, estate planning, etc. Text and appendixes include many sample forms and documents. Introduction includes chart of sodomy laws by state. Table of contents lists chapter headings and subtopics; separate table of contents for appendix. General index.   KF538.C87

International handbook on gender roles / ed. by Leonore Loeb Adler. Westport, Conn. : Greenwood, 1993. 525 p.   **CC289**

Signed chapters briefly describe the founding, history, geography, and population of 31 countries. Each compares male and female gender roles during school years, young adulthood, adulthood, and old age; and provides reference lists. Examines educational and day care systems, socialization, heterosexism, economy, class structure, etc. 27-page bibliography; general index.   HQ1075.I58

Osanka, Franklin Mark. Sourcebook on pornography / Franklin Mark Osanka, Sara Lee Johann. Lexington, Mass. : Lexington Books, c1989. 627 p.   **CC290**

Presents different positions and philosophies; compiled for general readers and professionals. In 14 chapters, examines definitions, public opinion, the industry, victims and perpetrators, influence on behav-

ior, morality, feminist perspectives, laws and regulations, child pornography, etc. Chapters include end notes. Appendixes include model state obscenity statute; cliche arguments and responses; organization addresses and phone; reprinted article on antipornography crusaders; overview of state laws on child pornography; etc. Extensive 95-page bibliography organized by chapter plus additional resources. General index.   HQ471.O83

Prostitution : an international handbook on trends, problems, and policies / ed. by Nanette J. Davis. Westport, Conn. : Greenwood, 1993. 403 p. : ill.   **CC291**

Contains 16 signed articles by scholars, each representing a different country (African countries and the Middle East are not included). Articles address social and legal definitions, trends and history, laws/legal status, politics, theories, interventions, classifications, and research; some include tabular data or figures. All chapters list references. Six-page bibliography; name and subject indexes.   HQ117.P767

Sexuality-related measures : a compendium / ed. and publ. by Clive M. Davis, William L. Yarber, Sandra L. Davis. Syracuse, N.Y. : C.M. Davis, c1988. 270 p. : ill.   **CC292**

Designed for researchers and practitioners. Groups more than 100 measures by subject categories (e.g., abortion, aging, contraception, education, homosexuality, rape), subarranged by author. Most entries indicate instrument or scale, reliability, validity, scoring, and references; some include only a brief description of the measure. No indexes, but the table of contents includes cross-references.   HQ60.S53

Urbanization

Abrams, Charles. The language of cities : a glossary of terms. N.Y. : Viking, 1971. 365 p.   **CC293**

Also publ. N.Y. : Equinox Books, 1972, c1971.

An attempt to identify and define terms used in the various disciplines concerned with urban affairs. Includes terms from the fields of housing, city planning, land economics, real estate, public administration, architecture, social welfare, transportation, public law, government, and race relations.   HT108.5.A24

Bryfogle, R. Charles. City in print : a bibliography. Agincourt, Ont. : General Learning Pr., c1974. 324 p.   **CC294**

A comprehensive, multidisciplinary, classed bibliography that includes books, articles, pamphlets, reprints, technical reports, maps, and audiovisual materials. Entries are arranged alphabetically by author under chapter subtopics. Includes evaluative abstracts and codes that indicate whether works are suited for personal use, as significant reference titles, for academic use only, or are not recommended.

———. ———. *Supplements 1–4/5* (1975, 1977, 1979, 1987). Imprint varies.   Z7164.U7B75

Casper, Dale E. Urban America examined : a bibliography. N.Y. : Garland, 1985. 212 p. (Garland reference library of social science, v. 269).   **CC295**

A topical arrangement of 2,070 entries on urban environment, ethnicity, socialism, politics, religion, transportation, and education. Entries are alphabetical by author within subsections. Includes scholarly books and journal articles, 1973–83. Geographic index; brief subject index.   Z7164.U7C375

Chandler, Tertius. Four thousand years of urban growth : an historical census. Lewiston, N.Y. : St. David's Univ. Pr., c1987. 656 p. : maps.   **CC296**

Fully updates and revises *Three thousand years of urban growth*, by Chandler and Gerald Fox (N.Y. : Academic Pr., 1974).

Based on measured and inferred population figures for major cities of the world. Provides tables and maps which show population for cities of certain sizes, measured at intervals between the years 800 and 1850. "Data sheets" give available details, e.g., land mass, number of households, number of temples, battle casualties, plague victims, number of public baths, etc. Tables for world's largest cities, by time period. Provides data and maps for the top six cities of every continent. Indicates year in which the cities first passed 100,000 population. Also provides "whereabouts of unfamiliar cities," giving locations based on nearest urban area. Introductory material provides purpose, scope, and methodology. Includes some data to 1975. 63-page bibliography; city name index.   HB2161.C46

Clapp, James A. The city : a dictionary of quotable thought on cities and urban life. New Brunswick, N.J. : Center for Urban Policy Research, 1984. 288 p. : ill.   **CC297**
Drawn from a wide variety of writers and speakers. Contains historical observations, scriptual references, lyrics, epigrams, epithets, proverbs, literary references, etc. Quotations are listed alphabetically by author, then alphabetically by source. Provides life dates for many authors, but no additional information beyond author and title of source; there is no list of references. Indexes: cities and subject.   HT111.C576

Diner, Hasia R. Women and urban society : a guide to information sources. Detroit : Gale, 1979. 138 p. (Urban studies information guide series, v. 7).   **CC298**
Most of the literature listed here dates from the 1940s to the late 1970s and concerns women in Africa, Asia, and Latin America. Issues include urban family structure, fertility, women's employment, social interaction among urban women, etc. Appendixes present a core collection, list of abstracts and indexes, and periodical titles. Author, title, and subject indexes.   Z7961.D55

Modern urban history research in Europe, USA, and Japan : a handbook / ed. by Christian Engeli and Horst Matzerath. Oxford ; N.Y. : Berg ; N.Y. : Distr. by St. Martin's, 1989. 575 p.   **CC299**
Pt. 1 is a survey of the development of the discipline and a state-of-the-art report on the research in each country, written by scholars of the country. Pt. 2 presents selective bibliographies of relevant works published in each country. Not indexed.   HT113.M63

O'Connor, Anthony M. Urbanization in tropical Africa : an annotated bibliography. Boston : G. K. Hall, 1981. 381 p.   **CC300**
Focuses on English- or French-language publications and doctoral dissertations produced since 1960 on the urbanization process, excluding public administration and labor relations. Geographical arrangement; only the general African items are subdivided by topic. Indexed by place names and authors.   Z7165.A47O26

Sage urban studies abstracts. v. 1, no. 1 (Feb. 1973)– . Newbury Park, Calif. : Sage Publ., 1973– . Quarterly.   **CC301**
Each issue offers abstracts of English-language books, periodical articles, reports, and documents. A section for "related citations" includes similar materials (some in foreign languages) without annotations. Author and subject indexes.   HT51.S24

Schultz, Marilyn Spigel. Encyclopedia of community planning and environmental management / Marilyn Spigel Schultz, Vivian Loeb Kasen. N.Y. : Facts on File, 1984. 475 p. : ill., maps.   **CC302**
About 2,000 articles, including biographies, entries for legislation, governmental and private agencies, etc., concerned with planning and the environment in the U.S., Canada, and Western Europe. Thematic index.   HD108.6.S38

Sutcliffe, Anthony. The history of urban and regional planning : an annotated bibliography. N.Y : Facts on File, 1981. 284 p.   **CC303**
About 1,400 citations to secondary materials are grouped into eight major subject chapters, subdivided by detailed topics. General sections on planning and pertinent reference titles are followed by

chapters on planning in individual countries and in towns and cities, individual planners, 19th-century antecedents, and various aspects, such as new towns. Indexed by names and authors.   Z5942.S93

Urban affairs abstracts. Aug. 1971– . Wash. : National League of Cities : United States Conference of Mayors, 1971– . Monthly with annual cumulations.   **CC304**
Each issue abstracts about 70 periodicals, newsletters, and journals. Entries organized alphabetically by title within 43 subject categories, which are listed in table of contents. Lists journals indexed, with addresses. No index in monthly issues; annual cumulation provides author, geographic, and descriptor indexes.   HT123.U7

Van Willigen, John. The Indian city : a bibliographic guide to the literature on urban India. New Haven, Conn. : Human Relations Area Files, 1979. 2 v.   **CC305**
A list of more than 3,800 books, essays, periodical articles, conference papers, theses and dissertations published between the mid-19th century and 1973. Arranged by name of geographic entity (city, state, region), then by broad subject area. No author index.
§ For a more topical (though chronologically more limited) approach, the user is referred to Ashish Bose's *Bibliography on urbanization in India, 1947–1976* (New Delhi : Tata McGraw-Hill, 1976).   Z5942.V36

White, Paul M. Soviet urban and regional planning : a bibliography with abstracts. N.Y. : St. Martin's, 1980. 276 p.   **CC306**
A topically arranged bibliography of 370 citations, fully annotated, to English- , French- , and German-language sources and translations of Soviet works. Author and subject indexes.   Z5942.W48

Zikmund, Joseph. Suburbia : a guide to information sources / Joseph Zikmund II, Deborah Ellis Dennis. Detroit : Gale, 1979. 142 p. (Urban studies information guide series, v.9).   **CC307**
An annotated, topically arranged bibliography of 392 references covering 1965–78. Popular periodical articles, doctoral dissertations, and government documents have been excluded. Chapters on demography, education, politics, economics, sociology, and minorities. Author, title, and subject indexes.   Z7164.U7Z54

ETHNIC GROUPS

General works

Bibliography

Allworth, Edward. Soviet Asia, bibliographies. N.Y. : Praeger, 1975. 686 p.   **CC308**
Subtitle: a compilation of social science and humanities sources on the Iranian, Mongolian, and Turkic nationalities, with an essay on the Soviet-Asian controversy.
Lists about 5,200 bibliographies, in book and periodical format, published in Czarist Russia and the Soviet Union between 1850 and 1970. Classified by five geographical divisions, and further subdivided into national groups, entries are listed under broad subject categories. Annotations indicate: language of the book, main languages of the entries and number of entries, period covered and dates within which the entries were published, and pagination.   Z3414.M54A44

Bailey, J. P. Intercontinental migration to Latin America : a select bibliography / J. P. Bailey and Freya Headlam. London : Inst. of Latin American Studies, 1980. 62 p.   **CC309**
Covers the 1830–1950 migration of about 50–70 million Europeans and Asians to Latin America. Section A, Latin America in general,

and Section B, Individual countries of settlement, are further subdivided for general migration, and migration from specific regions and ethnic groups. 570 citations. Author index.   Z7164.I3B433

Bentley, G. Carter. Ethnicity and nationality : a bibliographic guide. Seattle : Univ. of Washington Pr., [1981]. 381, [53] p. (Publications on ethnicity and nationality of the School of International Studies, Univ. of Washington, 3).   **CC310**

A selective, partially annotated bibliography of more than 2,300 English-language items published through 1979; excludes "ethnic studies" literature (e.g., biographies, literature, folklore, music, dance and drama, newspapers and periodicals, and histories), as well as ethnographies of individual groups. The first 308 entries are annotated; all entries are coded as to content, geographical area covered, and group under study. Alphabetical author arrangement; indexed by geographical area and content.   Z5118.E84B46

Black immigration and ethnicity in the United States : an annotated bibliography / Center for Afroamerican and African Studies, the University of Michigan. Westport, Conn. : Greenwood, 1985. 170 p. (Bibliographies and indexes in Afro-American and African studies, no. 2).   **CC311**

Consists of 1,049 annotated entries alphabetically arranged in six sections: (1) Bibliographies and general surveys of literature, (2) General literature on immigration and ethnicity, (3) U.S. immigration legislation and policies, (4) Aspects of black immigration, (5) Studies of black immigrant groups, (6) Selected works on black immigration to Canada and Great Britain. Books, articles, dissertations, and government publications are included. Author and subject indexes.

Z1361.N39B553

Blessing, Patrick J. The Irish in America : a guide to the literature and the manuscript collections. Wash. : Catholic Univ. of America Pr., 1992. 347 p.   **CC312**

Covers Irish-born (including the Scotch-Irish) and their descendents. In four sections: (1) bibliography of books, articles, and dissertations, arranged under broad topics (e.g., social adjustment, war and the military) and by geographic area; (2) descriptions of manuscript collections based on results of questionnaires, phone calls and visits; (3) lists of government manuscripts and publications with concentration on the National Archives and Congressional documents; and (4) a statistical overview featuring 30 tables, with cautionary notes and sources, which focus on census, migration and labor (including Ireland's population by county 1841–1914). Index for manuscript collections and government publications.

§ *See also* DeeGee Lester, *Irish research : a guide to collections in North America, Ireland, and Great Britain* (DC402), for additional descriptions of archival collections in the U.S., Canada, Ireland, and Great Britain, and Susan Elueterio-Comer, *Irish American material culture*, (DC402 *note*) for a list of festivals, National Register sites and descriptions of 90 collections.   Z1361.I7B54

Buenker, John D. Immigration and ethnicity : a guide to information sources / John D. Buenker, Nicholas C. Burckel. Detroit : Gale, 1977. 305 p. (American government and history information guide series, v. 1).   **CC313**

A selected, annotated bibliography of more than 1,400 English-language books, periodical articles, and doctoral dissertations, emphasizing post-1945 imprints. Excludes African Americans and Native Americans, fiction, autobiographical and audiovisual material. Topical arrangement includes general accounts, "old" and "new" immigration, Asians, "recent" ethnics after the 1920s, acculturation and restriction, private centers and federal government information sources. Author and subject indexes.   Z7165.U5B83

Center for Minority Group Mental Health Programs (U.S.). Bibliography on racism. Rockville, Md. : the Center : for sale by Govt. Print. Off., 1972–78. 2 v.   **CC314**

Contents: v. 1, Bibliography on racism; v. 2, Bibliography on racism, 1972–75.

Each volume contains a listing of all abstracts available at time of publication from the database of the National Clearinghouse for Mental Health Information. The second volume is organized by ethnic group, then by broad subject, and includes books, periodical articles, reports, and doctoral dissertations. Author and keyword subject indexes.   Z7164.R12U52

Centro Paraguayo de Documentación Social. Las migraciones en America Latina : bibliografía / Centro Paraguayo de Estudios Sociológicos, Centro Paraguayo de Documentación Social, Grupo de Trabajo de Migraciones Internas, Comisión de Población y Desarrollo, Consejo Latinoamericano de Ciencias Sociales. Buenos Aires : El Consejo, 1976. 76 p.   **CC315**

Contains 1,556 entries arranged by author or main entry; indexed by topical subject, country, and chronological period. Lists other relevant bibliographies.   Z7165.L3C44

Choice ethnic studies reviews / comp. by the Choice editorial staff. Middletown, Conn. : Choice, 1992–1993. [v. 1–4].   **CC316**

Editor and publisher: Patricia E. Sabosik.

Contents: *African and African American studies* (1992. 152 p.); *Asian and Asian American studies* (1993. 113 p.); *Latino studies* (1992. 112 p.); *Native American studies* (1992. 60 p.).

Full text reviews published by *Choice* magazine. Most reviews originally published Sept. 1989–July 1992 (v. 27–29), although *Asian and Asian American studies* provides coverage through July 1993 (v. 30). Entries arranged in topical sections: reference, humanities, science and technology, and social sciences. Author and title indexes.

Cordasco, Francesco. Italian Americans : a guide to information sources. Detroit : Gale, [1978]. 222 p. (Ethnic studies information guide series, 2).   **CC317**

Some 2,000 English- and Italian-language sources are grouped under five main headings: (1) General reference works; (2) Social sciences; (3) History and regional studies; (4) Applied sciences; (5) Humanities. Two separate chapters deal with newspapers and periodicals, and fraternal, professional, and religious organizations. A very brief appendix treats audiovisual materials. Locations are indicated for rare items.

§ Cordasco is the author of two earlier, related publications: *Italians in the United States : a bibliography* (N.Y. : Oriole, 1972) and *The Italian American experience : an annotated and classified bibliographical guide* (N.Y. : B. Franklin, 1974).   Z1361.I8C659

————— The Italian emigration to the United States, 1880–1930 : a bibliographic register of Italian views, including selected numbers from the Italian Commissariat of Emigration, Bollettino dell'emigrazione / Francesco Cordasco and Michael Vaughn Cordasco. Fairview, N.J. : Junius-Vaughn Pr., 1990. 187 p. : facsims.   **CC318**

Consists of two main parts: a bibliography, arranged alphabetically by author, of 607 firsthand accounts of the immigrant experience, and 114 pages of reprints from the *Bollettino dell'emigrazione*, published by the Italian Commissariat of Emigration. Italian-language materials predominate. Includes a nine-page bibliography of publications, containing both English- and Italian-language materials on Italian emigration. Subject index for the bibliography of firsthand accounts.

Z1361.I8C6594

————— The new American immigration : evolving patterns of legal and illegal emigration : a bibliography of selected references. N.Y. : Garland, 1987. 418 p. (Garland reference library of social science, v. 376).   **CC319**

Contains 2,328 entries, alphabetically arranged and some annotated, in four parts: (1) American immigration before 1865; (2) American immigration after 1865; (3) Illegal immigrants in the United States; (4) Miscellanea. Books (general interest and scholarly) and law journal and law review articles are included. The appendix reprints the introduction and recommendations of the report of the U.S. Select Commission on Immigration and Refugee Policy (*U.S. immigration policy and the national interest*, Wash. : The Select Commission, 1981). Authors and organizations index.   Z7164.I3C58

Doezema, Linda Pegman. Dutch Americans : a guide to information sources. Detroit : Gale, 1979. 314 p. (Ethnic studies information guide series, v. 3). **CC320**

An annotated bibliography of about 800 English- and Dutch-language sources in four main sections: (1) reference works; (2) general works on the Dutch in America; (3) the Colonial period; (4) the new immigration, from 1846 to the present. Appendixes list archives and libraries, newspapers and periodicals, and audiovisual materials and curriculum aids. Author, title, and subject indexes. Z1361.D8D64

Gakovich, Robert P. Serbs in the United States and Canada : a comprehensive bibliography / Robert P. Gakovich, Milan M. Radovich. [Minneapolis] : Immigration History Research Center, Univ. of Minnesota, 1976. 129 p. : ill. (IHRC ethnic bibliography, no.1). **CC321**

A bibliography and partial union catalog for nearly 800 archival collections, books, pamphlets, and articles; also lists current and historical newspapers and periodicals. Author index.

Other titles in the series include: no.2, *Hungarians in the United States and Canada,* comp. and ed. by Joseph Szeplaki (1977. 113p.); and no.3, *Slovenes in the United States and Canada,* by Joseph D. Dwyer (1981. 196p.). Z1361.S4G34

Haines, David W. Refugee resettlement in the United States : an annotated bibliography on the adjustment of Cuban, Soviet and Southeast Asian refugees. Wash. : Office of Refugee Resettlement, Dept. of Health and Human Services, 1981. 104 p. **CC322**

Superintendent of Documents classification: HE 1.18:R 25.

Cites 304 titles relevant to refugee resettlement. Includes printed materials, and unpublished papers and reports. Author listing; subject index. HV640.4.U54H15

Jerabek, Esther. Czechs and Slovaks in North America : a bibliography. N.Y. : Czechoslovak Society of Arts & Sciences in America, 1976. 448 p. **CC323**

A classed bibliography of more than 7,600 items relating to Czechs and Slovaks in North America. Useful list of periodicals and newspapers, p. 314–64. Fully indexed.

Keresztesi, Michael. German-American history and life : a guide to information sources / Michael Keresztesi, Gary R. Cocozzoli. Detroit : Gale, 1980. 372 p. (Ethnic studies information guide ser., v. 4). **CC324**

About 1,000 English-language monographs are grouped by broad subjects. Notes biographies, scholarly series titles, and journals. Directory of archival and literary resources. Author, title, and subject indexes. Z1361.G37K47

Kittelson, David J. The Hawaiians : an annotated bibliography. Honolulu : Social Science Research Inst., Univ. of Hawaii, 1985. 384 p. (Hawaii series, no. 7). **CC325**

2,712 alphabetically arranged annotated entries. Includes books, government publications, journal articles, and dissertations. All entries are in English. Glossary; subject index. Z4708.E85K57

Madan, Raj. Colored minorities in Great Britain : a comprehensive bibliography, 1970–1977. Westport, Conn. : Greenwood, 1979. 199 p. **CC326**

A subject arrangement of more than 1,800 English-language titles on the peoples of Asia, Africa, and the West Indies, both immigrants and citizens, living in Great Britain. Includes books, government publications, theses and dissertations, pamphlets, and periodical articles. Author, title, and subject indexes.

§ For retrospective coverage, *see* Ambalavaner Sivanandan, *Coloured minorities in Britain* (3rd ed. London : Institute of Race Relations, 1969). Z2027.N4M3

Metress, Seamus P. The Irish-American experience : a guide to the literature. Wash. : Univ. Pr. of America, 1981. 220 p. **CC327**

A topically arranged bibliography of social science literature on the Irish in the United States and Canada. Z1361.I7M47

Miller, Joseph Calder. Slavery and slaving in world history : a bibliography, 1900–1991. Millwood, N.Y. : Kraus International Publ., c1993. 556 p. **CC328**

Title varied in earlier versions: *Slavery : a comparative teaching bibliography* (1977); *Slavery : a worldwide bibliography 1900–1982* (1985).

Consists of 10,000 entries grouped by topic or region (e.g., North America, Spain, The Caribbean, Medieval and Modern Europe, The slave trade). Entries are not annotated, and are listed alphabetically in each section. Most citations are to English-language books, but some journal articles are included. All titles from the earlier versions have been carried forward. Author and subject indexes. Z7164.S6M544

Pochmann, Henry August. Bibliography of German culture in America to 1940 / Henry August Pochmann, comp. ; Arthur R. Schultz, ed. Rev. and corrected by Arthur R. Schultz with addenda, errata, and expanded index. Millwood, N.Y. : Kraus Internat., 1982. cclxxxvi, 489 p. **CC329**

1st ed., 1953.

The approximately 13,400 entries of the first edition are reprinted and an additional 4,900 entries are collected in the addenda section of this edition; corrections and changes to the old material are presented in the errata section. New materials are strongest in the fields of Pennsylvania German culture, emigration, World War I, and genealogies. Author arrangement; the index includes entries in both the bibliography and addenda. Z1361.G37P6

Schultz, Arthur R. German-American relations and German culture in America : a subject bibliography, 1941–1980. Millwood, N.Y. : Kraus Internat., 1984. 2 v. **CC330**

Forms a supplement to Henry August Pochmann, *Bibliography of German culture in America to 1940* (CC329), listing "works on German ethnic culture and history in America, as well as sources dealing with German-American literary, philosophical, and cultural relations. Included here are books, monographs, articles, and dissertations from the past forty years, and the reviews thereof."—*Pref.* Some annotations; index. Appendix of academic programs, festivals, historic sites, museums, etc.

§ Emil Meynen's *Bibliographie des Deutschtums der kolonialzeitlichen Einwanderung in Nordamerika ... 1683 1933* (Leipzig : Harrassowitz, 1937) has been reprinted under an English title, *Bibliography on the colonial Germans of North America, especially the Pennsylvania Germans and their descendants* (Baltimore : Genealogical Pub. Co., 1982. 636 p.). Z1361.G37S38

Tatla, Darshan Singh. Sikhs in North America : an annotated bibliography. N.Y. : Greenwood, 1991. 180 p. (Bibliographies and indexes in sociology, no. 19). **CC331**

Annotated entries, alphabetically arranged in eight chapters, cover general sources, migration and settlement, employment, education, family and social life, language, literature, media, politics and religions. Books, government publications, dissertations, journal and newspaper articles, films and videos are included. Lists primarily English-language materials, although some references are in Panjabi. The appendix lists current and discontinued North American Panjabi- and English-language newspapers, magazines and journals. Author index. Z1361.S47T37

Weaver, Jack W. Immigrants from Great Britain and Ireland : a guide to archival and manuscript sources in North America / comp. by Jack W. Weaver and DeeGee Lester. Westport, Conn. : Greenwood, 1986. 129 p. (Reference guides to archives and manuscript collections on immigrant culture, no. 1). **CC332**

A companion to DeeGee Lester's *Irish research* (DC402). A directory of 389 repositories in the U.S. and Canada holding relevant unpublished materials; based on responses to questionnaires. For the few archives or manuscript repositories not answering, information was supplied from U.S. National Historical Publications Commission, *A guide to archives and manuscripts in the United States*, ed. by Philip M. Hamer (New Haven, Conn. : Yale Univ. Pr., c1961. 775 p.) Arrangement is geographical, each entry giving name, address, telephone, hours of access, copying facilities, description, published finding aids. Index for names of collections and ethnic groups.   Z1361.B74W43

Weinberg, Meyer. World racism and related inhumanities : a country-by-country bibliography. N.Y. : Greenwood, 1992. 1048 p. (Bibliographies and indexes in world history, no. 26).
                                                        CC333
Contains 12,123 entries covering 135 countries, from ancient times through the late 1980s. 10,028 entries are arranged by country, continent, and region, the remainder in three topical sections: Elsewhere; Ancient history; Bibliography. Topics include: racism, slavery, class domination, sexism, national oppression, imperialism, colonialism, and anti-Semitism. More than 90% of the entries are in English; no annotations. Author and subject indexes.   Z7164.R12W5

Woll, Allen L. Ethnic and racial images in American film and television : historical essays and bibliography / Allen L. Woll, Randall M. Miller. N.Y. : Garland, 1987. 408 p. (Garland reference library of social science, v. 308).   **CC334**
Ten of the 12 chapters cover specific groups, an eleventh is devoted to a number of groups, and one is an introduction. Groups receiving major coverage: African Americans, Arabs, Asians, East Europeans and Russians, Germans, Hispanic Americans, Irish, Italians, Jews, and Native Americans. Gives lesser coverage to Africans, Armenians, Dutch, East Indians, Greeks, Hawaiians, Cajuns, Norwegians, Swedes, and Turks. Also covers media stereotyping of national characteristics (e.g., militaristic depiction of Germans). Each chapter includes an overview of issues and review of existing literature; a list of major films and television programs discussed in the studies, with reference to the bibliography; and an unannotated bibliography of books, theses, articles, government reports, etc. Lists books, general and scholarly articles, dissertations, and filmographies. Indexes of authors, films and television shows, and subjects.
§ Bibliographies dealing with specific ethnic groups include Marshall Hyatt, *The Afro-American cinematic experience* (Wilmington, Del. : Scholarly Resources, 1987. 260 p.) and Gretchen M. Bataille and Charles L. P. Silet, *Images of American Indians on film* (N.Y. : Garland, 1985. 216 p.). Each provides an author listing of books and articles from the general and ethnic press, with lists of representative films and an index.   Z5784.M9W65

Zurawski, Joseph W. Polish American history and culture : a classified bibliography. Chicago : Polish Museum of America, 1975. 218 p.   **CC335**
About 1,700 English-language sources, organized within a detailed subject classification. Includes citations on American-Polish foreign relations. Indexed by organization and personal name.
                                                        Z1361.P6Z87

Periodicals

The Oxbridge directory of ethnic periodicals. N.Y. : Oxbridge Communications, [1979]. 247 p.   **CC336**
A directory of some 3,500 ethnic periodicals, newspapers, newsletters, directories, etc. Arranged according to about 70 ethnic groups; title index. Information was derived from the Standard Periodical Data Base augmented by data from questionnaires.   Z6953.5.A1O9

Dissertations

Gilbert, Victor Francis. Immigrants, minorities and race relations : a bibliography of theses and dissertations presented at British and Irish universities, 1900–1981 / Victor Francis Gilbert and Darshan Singh Tatla. London ; N.Y. : Mansell, 1984. 153 p.   **CC337**

In two main sections: general studies, subdivided by topic; national and regional studies, subdivided by country and subject as appropriate. Subject and author indexes.   Z7164.I3G5

Manuscripts; Archives

Guide to Swedish-American archival and manuscript sources in the United States. Chicago : Swedish-American Historical Society, [1983]. 600 p.   **CC338**
A survey of 3,090 collections of personal and private papers, records of businesses, churches and fraternal organizations relating to Swedish immigration to, as well as life in, the United States. Arranged by state and city; collections are briefly described. Indexed.
                                                        Z1361.S9G8

Indexes; Abstract journals

•**Ethnic newswatch** [database]. Stamford, Conn. : Softline Information, Inc., Aug. 1991– .   **CC339**
For annotation, *see* AE107.

Sage race relations abstracts. v.1, no.1 (Nov. 1975)– . London ; Beverly Hills, Calif. : Sage, 1976– . Quarterly.   **CC340**
Published on behalf of the Institute of Race Relations, London.
Abstracts European and American periodical literature on immigration and race relations, with some books, essays, and "grass-roots and other fugitive literature" included. Some British emphasis. Each issue contains a bibliographical essay, e.g., "The Netherlands as a multi-racial society." Author and subject, but no geographical, indexes.
§ Continues *Race relations abstracts* (v. 1–2, no. 2. London : Institute of Race Relations, 1968–1970), which also maintained a British emphasis, but included some material from Europe, the U.S., Australia, and New Zealand.   HT1521.S15

Encyclopedias

Cashmore, Ernest Ellis. Dictionary of race and ethnic relations / E. Ellis Cashmore ; with Michael Banton ... [et al.]. 3rd ed. London : Routledge & Kegan Paul, 1994. 370 p.   **CC341**
1st ed., 1984.
Offers essay-length articles on schools of thought, major persons, theories, concepts, and empirical studies, with emphasis on the U.K. and the U.S. Bibliographical references; index.   DA125.A1C35

Harvard encyclopedia of American ethnic groups / Stephan Thernstrom, ed. Cambridge, Mass. : Belknap Pr. of Harvard Univ., 1980. 1076 p. : maps.   **CC342**
The core of this encyclopedia consists of 106 signed essays on ethnic groups, ranging in length from 3,000 to 40,000 words, "based on the estimated size of the group, the length and complexity of its history in the United States, and the availability and nature of source material."—*Introd.* "Ethnic" should not be interpreted as "foreign," since there are essays on Mormons, Appalachians, Amish, Hutterites, Southerners, and Yankees. Each essay touches on origins, migration, arrival, settlement, economic and social life, religion, culture, education, politics, maintenance of ethnicity; bibliographies are brief and stress readily available works. In addition to the group essays, there are 29 thematic essays on such topics as federal policy toward American Indians, concepts of ethnicity, folklore, health beliefs and practices, politics, prejudice, etc. A series of 87 maps and numerous statistical tables complete the work.   E184.A1H35

Directories

Directory of special programs for minority group members : career information services, employment skills banks, financial aid. 1974–. Garrett Park, Md. : Garrett Park Pr., 1973– . Irregular.   **CC343**

Subtitle varies.

Ed. by Willis L. Johnson.

Defines minorities as Native Americans, African Americans, Hispanic Americans, and Asian Americans. Lists alphabetically 2,940 organizations, including colleges and universities, government and social service agencies, service clubs and programs, churches, etc. Addresses and annotations are provided for most entries. Includes a bibliography, a glossary of terms, and a general subject index.   HD5724.D56

Minority organizations : a national directory. 1st ed. (1978)– . Garrett Park, Md. : Garrett Park Pr., c1978– .   **CC344**

The 4th ed. (1992) provides names, addresses, and telephone numbers, plus brief descriptions, of some 9,700 organizations established by and for Native Americans, African Americans, Latinos, and Asian Americans. Entries are alphabetically arranged. Organizations listed include schools and colleges, migrant worker and Native American service centers, community development and civil rights agencies, businesses and chambers of commerce, fraternities and sororities, etc. Omits list of lost organizations featured in earlier editions. Three indexes: (1) geographical (arranged by states and regions within large states), (2) program or service areas, (3) membership organizations.   E184.A1M544

World directory of minorities / ed. by the Minority Rights Group ; regional introductions by Patrick Thornberry ; main compilers Miranda Bruce-Mitford ... [et al.]. Chicago : St. James Pr., [1990]. 427 p. : maps.   **CC345**

Describes 160 groups "numerically inferior to the rest of the population of a state," non-dominant, possessing "ethnic, religious or linguistic characteristics,"and showing "a sense of solidarity towards preserving their culture, traditions, religion or language."—*Pref.* Entries, arranged alphabetically in 11 sections that reflect regions of the world, give alternative names, location, population, percentage of total population, religion, and language, and conclude with references for further reading. Information was gathered from Minority Rights Group Reports, nongovernmental research organizations, and human rights groups. Appendixes of extracts of international documents on human rights. Maps accompany some entries. Subject index; cross-references.   HM131

Handbooks

Akiner, Shirin. Islamic peoples of the Soviet Union : with an appendix on the non-Muslim Turkic peoples of the Soviet Union : an historical and statistical handbook. 2nd ed. London ; N.Y. : KPI : Distr. by Routledge & Kegan Paul, 1986. 462 p. : maps.   **CC346**

1st ed., 1983.

For each ethnic group, provides historical background, population data, and information on educational levels, language, religion, and distribution outside the Soviet Union. Chronology; bibliography; index.   DK34.M8A35

Arab American almanac. 3rd ed.– . Glendale, Calif. : News Circle Publ. Co., c1984– . Irregular.   **CC347**

Continues *American Arabic speaking community almanac,* 1974–1983.

The only publication of its kind. Three chapters list names and addresses of organizations, the press and other media, and religious institutions; a fourth, "Who's who," provides biographical information

otherwise available only in a number of specialized sources. The remaining six chapters contain information found in basic encyclopedias. Detailed table of contents and index of names.   E184.A65A45

Armenian American almanac / Hamo B. Vassilian, ed. 2nd ed., completely rev. Glendale, Calif. : Armenian Reference Books Co., c1990. 402 p.   **CC348**

Subtitle: a guide to organizations, churches, print and non-print media, libraries, Armenian studies, bookstores, Armenian schools, etc., and who is who in the medical, dental, health, and legal professions in the U.S.A. and Canada.

1st ed., 1985.

In three parts: (1) a directory, subdivided into nine topical sections, of 1,305 organizations, institutions, and cultural agencies, giving addresses and telephone numbers, and, for many, annotations; (2) two alphabetical lists, the first of professionals by category (e.g., physicians, dentists, lawyers), the second an index to the names in the first, both giving addresses and telephone numbers; (3) an index to the entries in the first part, and two geographical indexes to the entire directory, one for the U.S., the other for Canada.   E184.A7A76

Handbook of major Soviet nationalities / Zev Katz, ed. ; Rosemarie Rogers, assoc. ed., ; Frederick Harned, assist. ed. N.Y. : Free Pr., [1975]. 481 p.   **CC349**

Groups 17 nationalities by geographical and/or cultural area: the Slavs, the Baltics, the Transcaucasus, Central Asia, and other nationalities (Jews, Tatars, and Moldavians). The chapter on each nationality includes general information (territory, economy, history, demography, culture, external relations), media (language, media, and educational institutions), and national attitudes. Each chapter is written by a specialist and includes bibliography. Appendix of comparative tables for the nationalities. Subject index.   DK33.H35

Handbook on international migration / ed. by William J. Serow ... [et al.]. N.Y. : Greenwood, 1990. 385 p.   **CC350**

Offers essays, accompanied by references, on 19 countries, including those with significant immigration (the U.S., Canada, Israel, Australia), sending countries (Jordan, Mexico, the Philippines, Turkey), and refugee havens (Pakistan, Nigeria). The Soviet Union and Eastern Europe are omitted. Although each essay is written by a specialist, all cover legal and public policy issues, analyze the demographic, social, and economic effects of international migration, and evaluate all data presented. Tables, charts, and graphs accompany the essays. List of selected references; subject index.   JV6035.H36

Hobbie, Margaret. Italian American material culture : a directory of collections, sites, and festivals in the United States and Canada. N.Y. : Greenwood, 1992. 173 p. (Material culture directories, no. 4).   **CC351**

Presents 252 entries in three topical chapters: (1) collections, (2) historical sites, (3) feasts and festivals. Entries include descriptive materials, along with addresses, and cross-references. Data collected by questionnaire. Entries are proceeded by an essay on the demographics of Italian immigration. Bibliography. Name and subject indexes.   E184.I8H64

————— Museums, sites, and collections of Germanic culture in North America : an annotated directory of German immigrant culture in the United States and Canada. Westport, Conn. : Greenwood, [1980]. 155 p.   **CC352**

Focuses on the material culture and non-bibliographic resources for German-American and German-Canadian history through descriptive listings of repositories where such material can be found: museums, historical societies, libraries and archives; historic houses and sites; European collections. Bibliography; name and general indexes.   E184.G3H58

Multiculturalism in the United States : a comparative guide to acculturation and ethnicity / ed. by John D. Buenker and Lorman A. Ratner. N.Y. : Greenwood, c1992. 271 p.   **CC353**

Consists of 12 essays; eleven of which are devoted to one ethnic group each, the twelfth, a bibliographic essay. Groups covered: African Americans, American Indians, German Americans, Irish Americans, Scandinavian Americans, Polish Americans, Jewish Americans, Italian Americans, Chinese Americans, Mexican Americans. Essays accompanied by notes and a bibliography. Subject index.

E184.A1M85

Refugees in the United States : a reference handbook / ed. by David W. Haines. Westport, Conn. : Greenwood, 1985. 243 p. **CC354**

In two parts: (1) Context and overview, consisting of three essays with accompanying bibliographies, on general issues; (2) The refugees, containing nine essays with accompanying bibliographies, covering the Chinese from Southeast Asia, Cubans, Haitians, Hmong, Khmer, Lao, Salvadoreans and Guatamalans, Soviet Jews, and the Vietnamese. Some survey data and demographic information in tables. 19-page annotated bibliography of books, articles, and government information, 1968–83. Subject index.

E184.A1R43

Schoenburg, Nancy. Lithuanian Jewish communities / Nancy Schoenburg, Stuart Schoenburg. N.Y. : Garland, 1991. 502 p. : maps. (Garland reference library of the humanities, vol. 1321). **CC355**

Chapter 1 consists of a history of Lithuania and Lithuanian Jewry, and a selected bibliography. Chapter 2 lists nearly 400 entries arranged alphabetically by Yiddish name, describing a location and a reference number to the maps in Appendix 1; others contain four to five pages of historical information. Bibliographic references accompany many entries. Three appendixes: (1) the communities, along with their current names and alternative names, including maps indicating community locations; (2) information compiled by the American Federation of Lithuanian Jews listing individuals, their towns, and fates; (3) resources for Lithuanian Jewish genealogy. Glossary.   DS135.R93L556

University of Minnesota. Immigration History Research Center. The Immigration History Research Center : a guide to collections / comp. and ed. by Suzanna Moody and Joel Wurl ... [et al.]. N.Y. : Greenwood, 1991. 446 p. : ill. (Bibliographies and indexes in American history, no. 20).   **CC356**

In 24 sections, each describing a single collection. Collections cover Americans of these antecedents: Albanian, Armenian, Bulgarian and Macedonian, Byleorussian, Carpatho-Rusin, Croatian, Czech, Estonian, Finnish, Greek, Hungarian, Italian, Jewish, Latvian, Lithuanian, Near Eastern (includes Turks, Arabs, Syrians, Lebanese), Polish, Russian, Romanian, Serbian, Slovak, Slovenian, and Ukrainian. One section describes the general collection. Sections consist of: an annotated list of manuscript holdings, a one-to-two page description of monographs held, list of newspapers and serial publications held. Includes a history of the Center. Two appendixes (1) Information about the services provided by the center (2) Publications of the center. Subject index.   Z1361.E4U58

Chronologies

Newton, Michael. Racial & religious violence in America : a chronology / by Michael Newton and Judy Ann Newton. N.Y. : Garland, 1991. 728 p. (Garland reference library of social science, v. 501).   **CC357**

Consists of more than 8,000 entries, arranged by year and by date. Describes events occuring 1501–1989. Includes a list of abbreviations, a selected bibliography, and index.   HN90.V5R33

Atlases

Allen, James Paul. We the people : an atlas of America's ethnic diversity / James Paul Allen, Eugene James Turner. N.Y. : Macmillan, c1988. 315 p. : maps in color ; 29 x 43 cm.
CC358

Graphically depicts, in 111 full-color maps, data from the 1980 census on ancestral origins. Text accompanying the maps presents historical perspective, including comparison with 1920 data but no analysis of current data. Three introductory chapters provide essential documentation and explain data and methodology. 66 possible ethnic origins are shown in nine broad categories: early North American, western European, northern European, eastern European, southern European, Middle Eastern, African, Middle and South American, and Asian and Pacific island. A final chapter presents general patterns. Extensive list of references. Appendixes provide tables of ethnic population data at state and county levels and reference maps of U.S. counties. Indexes to place names and ethnic populations.   G1201.E1A4

Segal, Aaron. An atlas of international migration / cartography by Patricia M. Chalk and J. Gordon Shields. London ; New Providence, N.J. : Hans Zell Publ., 1993. 233 p. : maps ; 31 cm. ; scales differ.   **CC359**

Consists of five sections: Human migrations, Voluntary migrations, Involuntary migrations, World's major diasporas, Global migrations. Information presented by means of maps, tables (with sources cited), and text. Coverage begins with prehistory, but about 80% of the material is concerned with migrations of the past 25 years. Topics include: sending and receiving countries, freedom to travel, brain drain, study abroad, zones of conflict. Glossary; bibliography; index.

G1046.E27S4

United States

African Americans

Bibliography

Abajian, James de T. Blacks and their contributions to the American West : a bibliography and union list of library holdings through 1970 / comp. by James de T. Abajian for the Friends of the San Francisco Public Library. Boston : G.K. Hall, 1974. 487 p.   **CC360**

Publ. in cooperation with the American Library Association.

A classed list of some 4,300 items with detailed author/subject index.   Z1361.N39A27

Aby, Stephen H. The IQ debate : a selective guide to the literature / comp. by Stephen H. Aby, with the assistance of Martha J. McNamara. N.Y. : Greenwood, 1990. 228 p. (Bibliographies and indexes in psychology, no. 8).   **CC361**

For annotation, see CB8.   Z7204.I5A29

Amistad Research Center. Author and added entry catalog of the American Missionary Association Archives : with references to schools and mission stations. Westport, Conn. : Greenwood, [1970]. 3 v.   **CC362**

For annotation, see BC302.   Z7817.A45

Brignano, Russell Carl. Black Americans in autobiography : an annotated bibliography of autobiographies and autobiographical books written since the Civil War. Rev. and expanded ed. Durham, N.C. : Duke Univ. Pr., 1984. 193 p.   **CC363**

1st ed., 1974.

In two main sections: (1) Autobiographies ("volumes describing appreciable spans of the authors' lives") and (2) Autobiographical books (diaries, journals, collections of essays, eyewitness accounts of important events, etc.). Locates copies. Occupational, institutional, organizational, geographical, chronological and title indexes.

Z1361.N39B67

Davis, Lenwood G. A bibliographical guide to black studies programs in the United States : an annotated bibliography / comp. by Lenwood G. Davis and George Hill, with the assistance of Janie Miller Harris. Westport, Conn. : Greenwood, 1985. 120 p. (Bibliographies and indexes in Afro-American and African studies, no. 6). **CC364**

Contains 725 annotated entries, alphabetically arranged in four chapters: 79 major books and pamphlets providing a history and overview of the topic, 72 general works including titles on the development of black studies at large traditionally white universities, 68 dissertations, and 500 articles published in scholarly and general interest periodicals. Author index. Z1361.N39D353

———————— The black family in the United States : a revised, updated, selectively annotated bibliography. N.Y. : Greenwood, 1986. 234 p. (Bibliographies and indexes in Afro-American and African studies, no. 14). **CC365**

1st ed., 1978.

722 annotated entries grouped by type (books, articles, dissertations), and subdivided by subject (slavery, poverty, economic status, religion, education, health, sex, etc.) Separate section lists major books. Index. Z1361.N39D355

———————— Black-Jewish relations in the United States, 1752–1984 : a selected bibliography. Westport, Conn. : Greenwood, 1984. 130 p. (Bibliographies and indexes in Afro-American and African studies, no. 1). **CC366**

Lists 1,241 annotated entries, alphabetically arranged in four sections: major books and pamphlets, general works, dissertations and theses, and articles. Sections are subdivided by topic, including: black anti-Semitism, Jews as slave owners, various African American leaders' opinions of Jews, black-Jewish relations in the civil rights movement, and black-Jewish relations in N.Y., California, Atlanta, Philadelphia, and New Jersey. The introduction provides a brief history of the topic. Author index. Z1361.N39D357

Herod, Agustina. Afro-American nationalism : an annotated bibliography of militant separatist and nationalist literature / Agustina and Charles C. Herod. N.Y. : Garland, 1986. 272 p. (Canadian review of studies in nationalism, v. 6 ; Garland reference library of social science, v. 336). **CC367**

In ten sections, with 620 annotated entries for works published since 1945, alphabetically arranged. Eight of the sections cover historical periods, the ninth treats definitions of black nationalism, and the tenth lists bibliographies. Among the viewpoints represented are Christian, Muslim, Marxist, integrationist, and separatist. Cross-references at the end of each chapter. A table of contents provides the only subject access; author index. Z1361.N39H47

Miller, Elizabeth W. The Negro in America : a bibliography. 2nd ed., rev. and enl. / comp. by Mary L. Fisher. Cambridge : Harvard Univ. Pr., 1970. 351 p. **CC368**

1st ed., 1966.

A listing of books and periodical articles grouped under such headings as History, Intergroup relations, Urban problems, Employment, Education, Political rights and suffrage, with new sections added in the revised edition to cover music, literature and the arts. Emphasis is on materials published since 1954. Author index. A useful and thorough compilation.

§ A needed complement to Monroe Nathan Work, *Bibliography of the Negro in Africa and America* (N.Y. : Wilson, 1928. 698 p. Repr.: N.Y. : Octagon, 1965). Z1361.N39M5

Myers, Hector F. Black child development in America, 1927–1977 : an annotated bibliography / comp. by Hector F Myers, Phyllis G. Rana, Marcia Harris. Westport, Conn. : Greenwood, 1979. 470 p. **CC369**

More than 1,200 citations from social sciences monographic and professional journal literature are grouped in five areas: language development, physical development, cognitive development, personality development, and social development. Most abstracts are quoted directly from the eight original abstract sources surveyed for this bibliography. Author and subject indexes. Z1361.N39M94

The Negro in print. v. 1 (May 1965)–7, no. 2 (Sept. 1971). Wash. : Negro Bibliographic and Research Center, 1965–71. Bimonthly. **CC370**

At head of title: Bibliographic survey.

Listings, with annotations, of publications on African Americans and, to a lesser extent, other minority groups. Most issues have sections for nonfiction, fiction, paperbacks, books for young readers, and periodical articles. Some issues are devoted to a specific topic (e.g., Jan. 1966 is a "Negro history issue") or stress a particular feature. Individual issues not indexed; a 5-year subject index, 1965–70, was published 1971. Z1361.N39N39

Newman, Richard. Black access : a bibliography of Afro-American bibliographies. Westport, Conn. : Greenwood, 1984. 249 p. **CC371**

Lists bibliographies which have "an independent existence as a book, pamphlet, article, or chapter in a book."—*Pref.* Covers a broad range of topics relating to African Americans; includes Canadian material. Main-entry listing with subject and chronological indexes. Z1361.N39N578

Obudho, Constance E. Black-white racial attitudes : an annotated bibliography. Westport, Conn. : Greenwood, 1976. 180 p. **CC372**

An annotated, classified bibliography of books and periodical articles published 1950–74 on attitude formation and change and associated factors in the U.S. Articles include doctoral dissertation abstracts in *Dissertation abstracts international*. Author and subject indexes. Z1361.N39O28

Obudho, Robert A. Afro-American demography and urban issues : a bibliography / comp. by R.A. Obudho and Jeannine B. Scott. Westport, Conn. : Greenwood, 1985. 433 p. (Bibliographies and indexes in Afro-American and African studies, no. 8). **CC373**

Consists of 5,234 entries, alphabetically arranged by author in eight chapters. Topics covered include bibliography, demography, urbanization, housing patterns, ghettoization, suburbanization, rural studies, and planning. Books, articles, dissertations, and government publications are listed. Libraries in the U.S. holding major collections in African-American studies are noted, and there is a list of periodicals consulted by the compilers. Author index. Z1361.N39O29

Porter, Dorothy Burnett. The Negro in the United States : a selected bibliography. Wash. : Libr. of Congress, 1970. 313 p. **CC374**

A selective bibliography (1,781 entries) "designed to meet the current needs of students, teachers, librarians, researchers, and the general public for introductory guidance to the study of the Negro in the United States."—*Pref.* Although slightly more selective than the same author's *Working bibliography on the Negro* (CC375), it includes numerous items not found in that work; it also has the advantage of a more detailed subject approach through the author-subject index. Some brief descriptive notes. Z1361.N39P59

———————— A working bibliography on the Negro in the United States. Ann Arbor, Mich. : Univ. Microfilms, 1969. 202 p. **CC375**

A classed list of nearly 2,000 items (mainly books, with a few periodical citations) intended to facilitate book selection "for public, private and university collections of Afro-Americana."—*Introd.* Some brief annotations. Author index. Z1361.N39P62

Sims, Janet L. The progress of Afro-American women : a selected bibliography and resource guide. Westport, Conn. : Greenwood, 1980. 378 p. **CC376**

A classed bibliography of 19th and 20th century materials on all aspects of the life of the African-American woman, from slavery to participation in the women's rights movement. Author index. About 4,000 items.   Z1361.N39S52

Smith, John David. Black slavery in the Americas : an interdisciplinary bibliography, 1865–1980. Westport, Conn. : Greenwood, 1982. 2 v. (1847 p.).   **CC377**

A classed bibliography with author and subject indexes; 15,667 citations in 25 chapters (both topical and geographical) with many subdivisions. Limited to English-language materials: books, articles, theses and dissertations, review articles. Covers all aspects of slavery, except that political aspects (including antislavery and abolition movements) are largely omitted. Citations are reproduced from computer printout.   Z7164.S6S63

Stevenson, Rosemary M. Index to Afro-American reference resources. N.Y. : Greenwood, 1988. 315 p. (Bibliographies and indexes in Afro-American and African studies, no. 20).   **CC378**

In two main parts: a list of nearly 180 reference books, alphabetically arranged by title, and a classed index to the contents of the reference books. Covers the arts, social sciences, and humanities. Author and title index.   Z1361.N39S77

Library catalogs

Howard University. Libraries. Moorland Foundation. Dictionary catalog of the Jesse E. Moorland Collection of Negro Life and History, Howard University Library, Washington, D.C. Boston : G.K. Hall, 1970. 9 v.   **CC379**

An earlier, classified catalog ed. by Dorothy B. Porter was published 1958.

Reproduction of the catalog cards for a collection of more than 100,000 books, pamphlets, periodical titles, master's theses, manuscripts, music, newspaper clippings and pictures. Particularly strong in publications relating to American Colonization Society, African slave trade and its suppression, and abolition of slavery.

§ Supplemented by: Moorland-Spingarn Research Center, *Dictionary catalog of the Jesse E. Moorland Collection of Negro Life and History, Moorland Collection Research Center, Howard University, Washington, D.C. Supplement* (1st [1976]– . Boston : G.K. Hall, 1976–). Lists additions to the book collection since 1970, but excludes manuscript, photographic, music, and oral history resources since the Library's Manuscript Division plans to issue a separate catalog of those additions.

Schomburg Center for Research in Black Culture. Bibliographic guide to black studies. 1975– . Boston : G. K. Hall, [1975]– . Annual.   **CC380**

The volume for 1975 covers materials acquired by the Center Sept. 1974–Sept. 1975; later volumes add some entries from Library of Congress MARC tapes. Dictionary arrangement; employs some subject headings developed especially for the Center's collections.   Z1361.N39S373a

Schomburg Collection of Negro Literature and History. Dictionary catalog. Boston : G.K. Hall, 1962. 9 v.   **CC381**

Photographic reproduction of the cards for the dictionary catalog of the New York Public Library's "library and archive of materials devoted to Negro life and history ... international in scope ... includes books by authors of African descent, regardless of subject matter or language ... and all significant materials about peoples of African descent."—*Pref.* Catalogs more than 36,000 bound volumes.

Three supplements were published: 1967 (2 v.), 1972 (4 v.), 1976 (5 v.). The supplements include all acquisitions, old and new, for which cards were printed after publication of the basic set. Many major microform holdings are not yet represented. Materials processed after 1974 appear in: *Bibliographic guide to black studies* (CC380).   Z881.N592S35

Manuscripts; Archives

Plunkett, Michael. Afro-American sources in Virginia : a guide to manuscripts. Charlottesville : Univ. Pr. of Virginia, 1990. 323 p.   **CC382**

Consists of 1,038 annotated entries alphabetically arranged in 22 sections, each covering a single repository. Collections of historical societies and of college and university libraries are described. Materials cited include plantation and church records, the archives of traditionally black colleges and universities, diaries, photographs, and the papers of politicians, businesses, and civil rights groups. Subject index.   Z1361.N39P496

Indexes; Abstract journals

The Kaiser index to black resources, 1948–1986 / from the Schomburg Center for Research in Black Culture of the New York Public Library. Brooklyn, N.Y. : Carlson Pub., 1992. 5 v.   **CC383**

Consists of 174,000 references to articles, reviews, and obituaries published in 150 African-American scholarly and general interest periodicals, general interest periodicals, and publications covering the Caribbean. Entries are arranged chronologically (newest items first) in 15,000 subject headings. Subject headings were derived from headings used by the New York Public Library, along with additional headings developed for this publication. Notes, photographs, and illustrations that accompany articles indexed. Annotations accompany some entries. Scattered cross-references. No index.   Z1361.N39K34

Newman, Richard. Black index : Afro-Americana in selected periodicals, 1907–1949. N.Y. : Garland, 1981. 266 p. (Garland reference library of social science, v.65 ; Critical studies on black life and culture, v. 4).   **CC384**

An author and subject guide in dictionary arrangement to more than 1,000 articles from some 350 periodicals published in the United States, Canada, and Great Britain. Articles are drawn from the *Annual magazine subject index, 1907–49* (AD262) and new indexing is provided by author and book reviewer, plus expanded subject access. Does not include citations from the *Journal of negro history*, for which a separate index is available.   Z1361.N39N58

Encyclopedias

The African American encyclopedia / Michael W. Williams, ed. N.Y. : Marshall Cavendish Corp., 1993. 6 v.   **CC385**

Consists of long topical entries (usually one to three pages), and shorter entries, of one to three paragraphs, primarily devoted to personalities. Covers a wide variety of individuals, including politicians, sports figures, entertainers, military, and civil rights leaders, as well as historical persons. Suggested readings accompany many of the longer entries. Photographs with approximately one-half the entries. Five lists: (1) the 100 most profitable black-owned businesses; (2) research centers and libraries; (3) periodicals; (4) radio and television stations; (5) people profiled, organized by profession; bibliography; index.   E185.A253

Dictionary of Afro-American slavery / ed. by Randall M. Miller and John David Smith. N.Y. : Greenwood, 1988. 866 p. : ill.   **CC386**

A short-entry encyclopedia of 297 signed articles and accompanying bibliographies that attempts to cover the "diverse aspects of the slavery experience in North America."—*Introd.* Designed both to be a comprehensive reference book, and to provide a synthesis of the scholarship of African-American slavery. Includes a chronology of slavery and a list of editors and contributors with institutional affiliations. Subject index.   E441.D53

Nuñez, Benjamin. Dictionary of Afro-Latin American civilization / Benjamin Nuñez, with the assistance of the African Bibliographic Center. Westport, Conn. : Greenwood, 1980. 525 p. : ill., maps. **CC387**

Offers more than 4,500 multilingual entries for words and phrases, biographies, and historical events; sources are given for some entries. Focus is on the Caribbean, with lesser attention to Latin America. Selected bibliography; subject index and name index organized by country or region. F1408.3.N86

Directories

Black Americans information directory. 1st ed. (1990– 91)– . Detroit : Gale, c1990– . Biennial. **CC388**

Contains 17 chapters that cover a variety of topics (e.g., awards, prizes, and honors; local, state, regional and national associations; governmental agencies and programs; the print and broadcast media; universities, libraries and research centers; videos). Scope notes describe the contents and arrangement of individual chapters. Addresses are included for all entries; contact persons and telephone numbers are supplied if available, and annotations accompany some entries. The information was compiled from other Gale directories, government publications, unnamed directories and lists, questionnaire responses, or telephone inquiries. Combined name and keyword index. E185.5.B513

The black resource guide. 1981– . Wash. : Ben Johnson, 1981– . Annual. **CC389**

Lists names, addresses and some telephone numbers for 35 categories of individuals and organizations. Includes federal, state, and local officials, sports agents, consultants, information processing companies, religious and civil rights organizations, studies and scholarship programs, and alumni associations. Also includes statistical material based on the 1990 census. No index. E185.5.B565

Handbooks

The African-American almanac. 6th ed.– . Detroit : Gale, c1994 . Every three years. **CC390**

1st ed., 1967–5th ed., 1989, had title, *The Negro almanac.*

Editor: 1994, Kenneth Estell.

Consists of topical chapters that cover significant documents in African American history, civil rights, elected officials, demography, employment, historic landmarks, income and earnings, education, the military, sports, artists, writers and academics, music, media, religion, biography, slavery, and blacks in Africa and the Western hemisphere. Includes photographs, tables, charts chronology, selected bibliography. Appendixes consist of indexes to the tables and charts. Subject index. E185.5.N34

Cantor, George. Historic landmarks of Black America. Detroit : Gale, c1991. 372 p. : ill., maps. **CC391**

A guide to more than 300 sites in 46 states and Ontario. Entries, alphabetical by state, are arranged by region: Midwest, Northeast, South Central, Southeast, West, and Ontario. Includes monuments, parks, archives, colleges, museums, churches, libraries, theaters, birthplaces, grave sites, battlefields and forts. All entries include an address, and telephone numbers, hours, fees, and information on programs and accessibility are noted where appropriate. Includes a chronology and bibliography. Subject index. E185.53.A1C36

Documentary history of the modern civil rights movement / ed. by Peter B. Levy. N.Y. : Greenwood, 1992. 275 p. **CC392**

Consists of articles, essays, interviews, Supreme Court opinions, speeches, and chapters of books arranged in twelve topical chapters. Materials were published 1944–93. Topics covered include: school desegregation, the Montgomery bus boycott, freedom rides and sit-ins, marches, white resistance to civil rights, and the black power movement. Notes accompany each piece. Appendix, A statistical profile of black America, consists of maps, charts, and graphs. Bibliography. Index. E185.61.D64

Chronologies

Hornsby, Alton. Chronology of African-American history : significant events and people from 1619 to the present. Detroit : Gale, c1991. 526 p. : ill. **CC393**

A chronology, with entries presented in 11 topical chapters. Covers through 1990. An appendix contains reprints of laws and constitutional amendments relating to slavery and civil rights, texts of speeches, statistical materials on business, demography, and salaries of sports figures. Selected bibliography linked to topics covered in each chapter. Index. E185.H64

Annuals

National Urban League. The state of black America. 1976– . [N.Y.] : The League, 1976– . Annual. **CC394**

Consists of essays, statistics, and yearly chronology.

E185.5.N317

Biography

Black leaders of the nineteenth century / ed. by Leon Litwack and August Meier. Urbana : Univ. of Illinois Pr., c1988. 344 p. : ports. **CC395**

Arranged in 16 chapters that consist of biographies, 16–28 pages in length, treating such persons as: Nat Turner, Harriet Tubman, Blanche K. Bruce, and Robert Brown Elliot. A bibliographic essay provides references for further reading. Subject index.

E185.96.B535

Contemporary black biography. v. 1– . Detroit : Gale, c1992– . Twice a year. **CC396**

For annotation, see AH43. E185.96.C66

Hawkins, Walter L. African American biographies : profiles of 558 current men and women. Jefferson, N.C. : McFarland, c1992. 490 p. : ill. **CC397**

An alphabetically arranged collective biography. The short entries consist of approximately 150–750 words. Individuals included must have been living in 1969. Photographs accompany many entries. No notes or bibliographies to indicate the sources of information. Occupational and geographic indexes.

§ See also *Who's who among black Americans* (AH73).

E185.96.H38

Hill, George H. Black media in America : a resource guide. Boston : G.K. Hall, c1984. 333 p. **CC398**

Contains 4,049 entries divided by format: 317 monographs, theses, and dissertations; 342 journal articles; and 3,388 newspaper and magazine articles. Within each format, entries are subdivided by topic and arranged alphabetically by author. Topics include advertising, public relations, marketing, book and magazine publishing, and newspaper, radio, and television journalism. Three indexes: author/subject, radio stations, and television stations. Z5633.A37H55

Atlases

Asante, Molefi K. The historical and cultural atlas of African Americans / Molefi K. Asante, Mark T. Mattson. N.Y. : Macmillan : Maxwell Macmillan International, c1991. 198 p. : ill. (some col.), some maps in color, ports. ; 32 cm. **CC399**

Roughly chronological arrangement of narrative, illustrations and maps, covering prehistoric African origins to contemporary (1990) social and economic issues. While most textual information can be found elsewhere in more depth and accuracy, the maps are clear and informative, and represent a different approach to this type of information. Appended chronology of African American history. Selected references grouped by format; general index.   E185.A8

Statistics

Statistical record of black America. 1st ed.– . Detroit : Gale, c1990– . Biennial.   **CC400**

Comp. and ed. by Carrell Peterson Horton and Jessie Carney Smith.

A compendium of data, presented in tables and graphs, that illustrate aspects of African-American life: attitudes and values, business and economics, crime, law enforcement and justice, education, family, health and medical care, income, labor and employment, military affairs, politics, and elections, population, professions, sports and leisure, vital statistics. Data were originally published by agencies of the U.S. government or resulted from surveys conducted by academic researchers, public opinion polling organizations, or private research firms. Bibliography of sources; subject index.

Asian Americans

Asian Americans information directory. 1st ed.– . Detroit : Gale, c1992– .   **CC401**

Contains 5,211 entries, organized by topic in 20 sections. 19 sections each cover one ethnic group from east or southeast Asia which has significant representation in the U.S. The remaining section covers general resources. Groups include: Bangladeshi, Burmese, Cambodian, Chinese (including Hong Kong, Manchurian, Mongolian, Taiwanese, and Tibetan), East Indian, Filipino, Hmong, Indonesian, Japanese, Laotian, Malaysian, Nepalese, Pacific Islanders, Pakistani, Singaporean, Sri Lankan, Thai, and Vietnamese. Lists national, regional, and state organizations, museum collections, state and local government agencies, embassies, and consulates, Asian Studies Programs, library collections, publications, broadcast media, sources of videos. Addresses and telephone numbers are provided for all entries. Most entries annotated. Combined name and keyword index.   E184.O6A844

Dictionary of Asian American history / ed. by Hyung-Chan Kim. N.Y. : Greenwood, [1986]. 627 p.   **CC402**

In two sections: 15 essays (114 p.) by various authors and an encyclopedia containing 800 brief entries, all written by the editor. Seven of the essays treat the historical experience of Asian Americans and Pacific Islanders; the remainder deal with the place of Asian Americans in the "American social order."—*Pref.* The encyclopedia entries are accompanied by bibliographies and concentrate on the historical experiences of persons of Chinese, Japanese, Korean, Asian Indian, and Filipino ancestry, give some attention to refugees from Vietnam, Kampuchea, and Laos, and mention Pacific Islanders. Three appendixes: Select bibliography, Chronology of Asian American history, and 1980 Census data. Subject index.   E184.O6D53

Doi, Mary L. Pacific/Asian American research : an annotated bibliography / by Mary L. Doi, Chien Lin, and Indu Vohra-Sahu. Chicago : Pacific/Asian American Mental Health Research Ctr., c1981. 269 p. (Pacific/Asian American Mental Health Research Center. Bibliography series, no. 3).   **CC403**

Cites 556 journal articles, essays, etc., mostly published since 1969; dissertations are excluded. Alphabetical main-entry arrangement; indexed by 19 ethnic groups, geographic regions, and subjects.   Z1361.O7D64

Handbook of social services for Asian and Pacific islanders / ed. by Noreen Mokuau. N.Y. : Greenwood, 1991. 254 p.   **CC404**

Consists of 14 essays in three main sections: (1) Social services for Asian and Pacific Islander populations; (2) Asian and Pacific Islander populations; (3) Contemporary problems and issues. Seven of the essays cover ethnic groups: Japanese-Americans, Chinese-Americans, Filipino-Americans, Vietnamese-Americans, Indigenous Hawaiians, Samoans, and Chamorros. Seven topical essays cover the aged, and youth, family violence, and history, nature and scope of current and future developments in social services. References accompany each essay. Index.   HV3186.A2H36

Hansen, Gladys C. The Chinese in California : a brief bibliographic history / selected by Gladys C. Hansen, annotated by William F. Heintz. [Portland, Ore.] : Abel, 1970. 140 p.   **CC405**

Based on material in the Californiana Collection, Dept. of Rare Books and Special Collections, San Francisco Public Library.

Represents a sampling of books from the period 1850–1968, largely historical in content. Author listing with subject index.

     Z1361.C4H36

Haseltine, Patricia. East and Southeast Asian material culture in North America : collections, historical sites, and festivals. N.Y. : Greenwood, 1989. 163 p. (Material culture directories, no. 3).   **CC406**

Describes 191 American and Canadian museums, historic sites, and cultural festivals of Chinese, Japanese, Korean, Hmong, Indonesian, Malaysian, Thai, and Vietnamese immigrant cultures. Arranged alphabetically by state or province, then by name of institution. Includes a list of material culture museums in east and southeast Asia, a glossary, and a bibliography. Index of institutions, general index.

     E184.O6H37

Kim, Hyung-chan. Asian American studies : an annotated bibliography and research guide. N.Y. : Greenwood, 1989. 504 p. (Bibliographies and indexes in American history, no. 11).   **CC407**

Lists 3,396 books, periodical articles, theses, and dissertations in the social and behavioral sciences and the humanities relating to 22 ethnic groups in two broad sections: historical perspectives and contemporary perspectives, with appropriate subdivisions. Also included are three essays that attempt to place the Asian-American experience "within the context of American scholarship on immigration and emigration."—*Pref.* Author and subject indexes.   Z1361.O7K56

Matsuda, Mitsugu. The Japanese in Hawaii : an annotated bibliography of Japanese Americans / by Mitsugu Matsuda ; rev. by Dennis M. Ogawa with Jerry Y. Fujioka ; supported by the Japanese American Research Center (JARC). Honolulu : Social Sciences and Linguistics Inst., Univ. of Hawaii, 1975. 304 p. (Hawaii series, no. 5).   **CC408**

Matsuda's original bibliography covering 1868–1967 was published 1968.

An author listing of more than 750 published English-language items, plus a list of newspapers and periodicals and a separate section of Japanese materials. Subject index to the English-language materials. Intended for undergraduate student use.   Z4708.J3M3

Saito, Shiro. Filipinos overseas : a bibliography. N.Y. : Center for Migration Studies, 1977. 156p.   **CC409**

An updating and expansion of the author's "Bibliographic considerations and research status of the overseas Filipinos," a working paper submitted at the first Conference on International Migration from the Philippines, June 10–14, 1974. Entries are arranged according to the conference agenda: Demographic overview of migration; U.S. immigration policy; Views from the barrios; The brain drain; and Destinations of migration, with a section on each area. Includes published and unpublished English-language materials. Appendixes list papers presented at the first and second Conferences on International Migration from the Philippines, relevant dissertations and theses done at the University of Hawaii, and a list of Filipino newspapers and periodicals published in Hawaii and located in the University of Hawaii Library. Author index.   Z3298.I3S24

Statistical record of Asian Americans / Susan B. Gall and Timothy L. Gall, editors. Detroit : Gale, c1993. 796 p.   **CC410**

Consists of some 900 statistical tables and graphs describing people of Chinese, Japanese, Korean, Vietnamese, Cambodian, Filipino, and Hawaiian descent residing in the U.S. and Canada. Topics covered: attitudes, business and economics, crime and civil rights, domestic life, education, employment, health, housing, immigration, income, military life, population, public life, religion, demographics, the family, education, culture and tradition. U.S. and Canadian government publications were the sources of most data; some data derived from publications of Asian groups. Provides comparative data for Asians, blacks, whites, and Latinos. Appendix explains terminology use and scope of information. Bibliography. Keyword index includes subjects, nationalities, and geographic locations.   E184.O6S73

Yu, Elena S. H. Bibliography of Pacific/Asian American materials in the Library of Congress / Elena S. H. Yu, Alice K. Murata, Chien Lin. Chicago : Pacific/Asian American Mental Health Research Center, c1982. 254 p. (Pacific/Asian American Mental Health Research Center. Bibliography series, no. 3).   **CC411**

In two parts, roman and nonroman alphabet materials; each part is subdivided by ethnic groups. Lacks a detailed subject index.

Z1361.O7Y8

Native Americans

Bibliography

•**Bibliography of native North Americans on disc** [database]. Santa Barbara, Calif. : ABC-Clio, 1992– .   **CC412**
Available on diskettes.

Consists of 49,000 citations drawn from *Ethnographic bibliography of North America*, by George Peter Murdock and Timothy J. O'Leary, and its *Supplement 1973–1987* (CC419), with an additional 10,000 unique records. Covers 290 groups from the Arctic coast, Canada, parts of Central America, northern Mexico, and the U.S. Indexes books, conference papers, dissertations, essays, journal articles, and U.S. government publications. Fields indexed: descriptor, identifier, ethnic group, region, title, author, publication date, format (article, book, or dissertation), series.

Haas, Marilyn L. Indians of North America : methods and sources for library research. Hamden, Conn. : Library Professional Publ., 1983. 163 p. : ill.   **CC413**

In three parts: (1) a guide to library methodology and relevant reference works; (2) an annotated, topical bibliography of standard monographs, subject bibliographies, and journal titles; (3) an unannotated list of books on individual tribes. Most titles published in English since 1960. For the beginning researcher.   Z1209.H22

Hippler, Arthur E. The Alaska Eskimos : a selected, annotated bibliography / Arthur E. Hippler and John R. Wood. Fairbanks : Inst. of Social and Economic Research, Univ. of Alaska, 1977. 334 p. in various pagings. (ISER report series, 45).
                                                      CC414

Pt. 1 lists materials by author; full bibliographic information, including annotation, is provided in pt. 2. Entries are arranged by linguistic groups in pt. 3, and by time of observation in pt. 4.

§ The Institute has also issued: *Eskimo acculturation : a selected annotated bibliography of Alaskan and other Eskimo acculturation studies*, by Arthur E. Hippler (1970. 209 p.); *The subarctic Athabas-*

cans : a selected annotated bibliography, by Hippler and John R. Wood (1974. 331 p.); and *An Aleut bibliography*, by Dorothy M. Jones and John R. Wood (CC418).   Z1210.E8H49

Hoxie, Frederick E. Native Americans : an annotated bibliography / Frederick E. Hoxie and Harvey Markowitz. Pasadena, Calif. : Salem Pr., c1991. 325 p.   **CC415**

In four sections (General studies and reference, History, Culture areas, Contemporary life), with annotated entries listed alphabetically in each section. Contains books and articles, 75% published since 1970. Omits government publications. Topics include folklore, land use, material culture, family and tribal life, law and government, images and self-identity, urban life, and contemporary art and literature. Covers the U.S. and Canada, including materials on Arctic peoples. Author index.   Z1209.2.N67H68

Index to literature on the American Indian. [San Francisco] : Indian Historian Pr., 1970–73. 4 v.   **CC416**
Sponsored by the American Indian Historical Society.

An alphabetical author and subject index of book and periodical materials, both popular and scholarly. Drawn from 300 periodicals (mainly from the U.S. and Canada).

Johnson, Steven L. Guide to American Indian documents in the Congressional serial set, 1817–1899. N.Y. : Clearwater Publ. Co., c1977. 503 p.   **CC417**
"A project of the Institute for the Development of Indian Law."—*t.p.*

Lists some 10,649 documents relating to Indian affairs "which were located in the Serial Set volumes from 1817 through 1899."—*p. xv.* A chronological section lists the documents sequentially, giving title and date, citation to the Serial Set, and a brief description of the contents of the document. A subject index, organized mainly by tribal headings, is intended as "an index to the listings and not to the contents of the documents."   KF8201.A1J63

Jones, Dorothy Miriam. An Aleut bibliography / Dorothy M. Jones and John R. Wood. Fairbanks : Inst. of Social, Economic and Govt. Research, Univ. of Alaska, 1975. 195 p. in various pagings. : maps. (ISEGR report series, 44).   **CC418**

A selective, annotated survey of English-language materials on Aleut cultural and social life. In four sections: (1) alphabetical list of Aleut literature by author; (2) complete bibliographic information, including annotation; (3) list of literature arranged by time of observation (precontact and aboriginal period, Russian administration to 1867, American administration, 1867 to 1940, contemporary); (4) list organized by broad subject and type of publication.   Z1210.A4J6

Murdock, George Peter. Ethnographic bibliography of North America / George Peter Murdock and Timothy J. O'Leary ... [et al.]. 4th ed. New Haven, Conn. : Human Relations Area Files Pr., 1975. 5 v. : maps.   **CC419**

Contents: v. 1, General North America; v. 2, Arctic and subarctic; v. 3, Far West and Pacific coast; v. 4, Eastern United States; v. 5, Plains and Southwest.

1st ed., 1941.

Contains about 40,000 entries for books and articles on the native ethnic groups of North America. This edition shows an expanded number of ethnic group bibliographies (especially for the North Mexican area) which have been added to correspond to the Smithsonian's *Handbook of North American Indians*, ed. by William C. Sturtevant (CC432). New bibliographies on Pan-Indianism, urban Indians, Canadian Indians, and U.S. and Canadian government relations with the native peoples. The general introduction supplies excellent discussion of sources of materials not included: government publications, ERIC documents, theses and dissertations, manuscripts and archives, nonprint materials and maps, and general bibliographic sources.

——. —— *Supplement 1973–1987*, by M. Marlene Martin and Timothy J. O'Leary (1990. 3 v.).

Contents: v. 1, Indexes; v. 2–3, Citations.

Contains 25,058 alphabetically arranged entries published 1973–87. Includes books, journal articles, ERIC documents, theses and dissertations, and U.S. and Canadian government publications. Subject, ethnic group, and author indexes.   Z1209.2.N67M87

Native American bibliography series. No. 1– . Metuchen, N.J. : Scarecrow, 1980– . Irregular.   **CC420**
Contents: v. 1, Bibliography of the Sioux, by Jack W. Marken and Herbert T. Hoover (1980. 370 p.); v. 3, Bibliography of the languages of native California, including closely related languages of adjacent areas, by William Bright (1982. 234 p.); v. 4, A guide to Cherokee documents in foreign archives, by William L. Anderson and James A. Lewis (1983. 768 p.); v. 5, A biobibliography of Native American writers, 1772–1924 : a supplement, by Daniel F. Littlefield, Jr. and James W. Parins (1985. 350 p.); v. 6, Bibliography of the Osage, by Terry P. Wilson (1985. 172 p.); v. 7, A guide to Cherokee documents in the northeastern United States, by Paul Kutsche (1986. 541 p.); v. 8, In pursuit of the past : an anthropological and bibliographic guide to Maryland and Delaware, by Frank W. Porter III (1986. 268 p.); v. 9, The Indians of Texas : an annotated research bibliography, by Michael L. Tate (1986. 514 p.); v. 10, Bibliography of the Catawba, by Thomas J. Blumer (1987. 575 p.); v. 11, Bibliography of the Chickasaw, by Anne Kelley Hoyt (1987. 230 p.); v. 12, Kinsmen through time : an annotated bibliography of Potawatomi history, by R. David Edmunds (1987. 237 p.); v. 13, Bibliography of the Blackfoot, by Hugh A. Dempsey and Lindsay Moir (1989. 255 p.); v. 14, The upstream people : an annotated research bibliography of the Omaha tribe, by Michael L. Tate (1991. 522 p.); v. 15, Languages of the aboriginal southeast, by Karen M. Booker (1991. 265 p.); v. 16, Yakima, Palouse, Cayuse, Umatilla, Walla Walla, and Wanapum Indians : an historical bibliography by Clifford Trafzer (1992. 253 p.).
A series consisting of bibliographies of individual Native American tribes of North America and of general topics concerning Native Americans. The number of entries varies from about 1,500 to more than 6,000; some entries have annotations.

Newberry Library. Center for the History of the American Indian. The Newberry Library Center for the History of the American Indian bibliographical series. Chicago, 1976–1983. 30 v.   **CC421**
Contents: Native American historical demography, by Henry F. Dobyns (95 p.); The Indians of California, by Robert F. Heizer (68 p.); The Indians of the Subarctic, by June Helm (91 p.); The Plains Indians, by E. Adamson Hoebel (75 p.); The Navajos, by Peter Iverson (64 p.); The Ojibwas, by Helen Hornbeck Tanner (78 p.); The Apaches, by Michael E. Melody (86 p.); United States Indian policy, by Francis Paul Prucha (54 p.); The Cherokees, by R. D. Fogelson (98 p.); Indian missions, by J. P. Ronda and J. L. Axtell (85 p.); The Indians of the Northeast, by E. Tooker (77 p.); The Delawares, by C. A. Weslager (84 p.); The Creeks, by M. D. Green (114 p.); Native Americans of the Northwest coast, by R. S. Grumet (108 p.); The Sioux, by H. T. Hoover (78 p.); Indians in Maryland and Delaware, by F. W. Porter III (107 p.); Native American prehistory, by D. R. Snow (75 p.); The emigrant Indians of Kansas, by W. E. Unrau (78 p.); The Pawnees, by M. R. Blaine (96 p.); The Indians of the Southwest, by H. B. Dobyns and R. C. Euler (192 p.); The Choctaws, by C. S. Kidwell and C. Roberts (96 p.); The Cheyennes, Maheoo's people, by P. J. Powell (128 p.); Sociology of American Indians, by R. Thornton and M. K. Grasmick (96 p.); Southeastern frontiers: Europeans, Africans, and American Indians, 1513–1840, by J. H. O'Donnell (118 p.); The Indians of New England, by N. Salisbury (109 p.); The Yakimas, by H. H. Schuster (158 p.); Indians of the Great Basin, by O. C. Stewart (138 p.); Canadian Indian policy, by R. J. Surtees (107 p.); The urbanization of American Indians, by R. Thornton, G. D. Sandefur and H. G. Grasmick (87 p.); Native American women: a contextual bibliography, by R. Green (120 p.).
Each volume has two main parts: a bibliographical essay and an alphabetical list of all works cited. There are also two sets of recommended titles: (1) books for beginners; (2) books for a basic library collection. The alphabetical list of all works cited is keyed as to level of suitability, and includes books and periodical articles.

Parezo, Nancy J. Southwest Native American arts and material culture : a guide to research / Nancy J. Parezo, Ruth M. Perry, Rebecca Allen. N.Y. : Garland, 1991. 2 v. (1506 p.). (Garland reference library of the humanities, vol. 1337 ; Garland reference library of the humanities. Studies in ethnic art, vol. 1).   **CC422**
For annotation, *see* BG9.   Z1209.2.U52S686

Prucha, Francis Paul. A bibliographical guide to the history of Indian-white relations in the United States. Chicago : Univ. of Chicago Pr., 1977. 454 p.   **CC423**
"A publication of the Center for the History of the American Indian of the Newberry Library."—*t.p.*
A classed bibliography of about 9,700 items. "Emphasis is on United States history, but British colonial Indian affairs have been included."—*Pref.* In two parts: (1) Guides to sources (i.e., reference works on archives, government documents, manuscripts, and similar materials); (2) Classified bibliography of published works through 1974. Author/subject index.
§ Continued by Prucha's *Indian-white relations in the United States : a bibliography of works published 1975–1980* (Lincoln : Univ. of Nebraska Pr., c1982. 179 p.). Follows the plan of his earlier volume. While British colonial Indian affairs have been included, Canadian items have been excluded, and no attempt has been made to provide materials on Spanish-Indian relations. Author/subject index.
          Z1209.2.U5P67

Periodicals

Littlefield, Daniel F. American Indian and Alaska native newspapers and periodicals / Daniel F. Littlefield, Jr., and James W. Parins. Westport, Conn. : Greenwood, 1984–1986. 3 v.   **CC424**
Contents: v. 1, approx. 200 titles publ. 1826–1924; v. 2, approx. 500 titles publ. 1925–70; v. 3, approx. 1,000 titles publ. 1971–85.
Lists 1,700 titles, published 1826–1985, "by American Indians or Alaskan natives and those whose primary purpose was to publish information about *contemporary* Indians or Alaska Natives."—*v. 1, p. 7.* Excludes Canadian and Mexican titles as well as those focusing on archaeological, ethnological, and historical topics. Alphabetically arranged entries provide description, publication, history, bibliographic information, bibliography, and selected locations. Appendixes list titles chronologically, by location, and by tribal interest or affiliation. Subject index.   PN4883.L57

Dissertations

Dockstader, Frederick J. The American Indian in graduate studies : a bibliography of theses and dissertations / comp. by Frederick J. Dockstader, Alice Dockstader. N.Y. : Museum of the American Indian, Heye Foundation, 1973–74. 2 v. (Museum of the American Indian, Heye Foundation. Contributions, v. 25).   **CC425**
Pt. 1 of the bibliography, covering theses of 1890–1955, was originally published 1957. It was reprinted 1973 in a 2nd ed. omitting the "Addenda," p. 362–64 and the index. Pt. 2 covers the period 1955–70; it continues the item numbering from the main section of pt. 1 (i.e., beginning with item 3660) and incorporates the addenda from the original volume into the alphabetical author sequence of pt. 2. A new index to both volumes is provided. The total number of entries is now 7,446. Dissertations known to be available from University Microfilms are marked with an *M* following the citation.   Z1209.D62

Manuscripts; Archives

American Indian resource materials in the Western History Collections, University of Oklahoma / Donald L. DeWitt, ed. Norman, Okla. : Univ. of Oklahoma Pr., c1990. 272 p. **CC426**

Consists of 1,056 entries that describe 269 manuscript collections, 96 collections of photographs, 20 oral histories, 165 microform sets, and 506 newspapers and periodicals, all held by the Western History Collections. In four sections: primary documentation, photography, oral histories, and holdings of the Library Division of the Collections. The preface provides a history of the Collections, and each section begins with a summary essay. Emphasizes history of the Western U.S., but includes materials on other regions and on Canada. Subject index. E78.O45A69

Chepesiuk, Ronald. American Indian archival material : a guide to holdings in the Southeast / comp. by Ronald Chepesiuk and Arnold Shankman. Westport, Conn. : Greenwood, 1982. 325 p. **CC427**

A guide to materials held by 174 repositories in Alabama, Florida, Georgia, Kentucky, Louisiana, Mississippi, the Carolinas, Tennessee, Virginia, and West Virginia, principally on the Creek, Seminole, Cherokee, Chickasaw, Choctaw, and Lumbee tribes. List of repositories reporting no holdings or not responding, p. 171–265. Index. Z1209.2.U52S663

Encyclopedias

Klein, Barry T. Reference encyclopedia of the American Indian. 6th ed. West Nyack, N.Y. : Todd Publications, c1993. 679 p. **CC428**

1st ed., 1967, 5th ed., 1990.

Consists of four sections: a directory with separate listings for the U.S. and Canada, a bibliography of about 4,000 in-print books, and a collective bibliography of some 2,000 Native Americans. E76.2.K5

Directories

Eagle Walking Turtle. Indian America : a traveler's companion. 3rd ed. Santa Fe, N.M. : John Muir Publications ; N.Y. : Norton, 1993. 460 p. : ill., maps. **CC429**

1st ed., 1989; 2nd ed., 1991.

Lists reservations in 36 states, alphabetically by state, grouped by region. Addresses, telephone numbers, and descriptions accompany all entries. Approximately half the entries list dates of public ceremonies, provide information about tribal arts, and give a history of the group. The appendix provides a list of native moons, addresses for Alaska bands, an events calendar, and a chart comparing 1980 and 1990 Native American population in every state. Some cross-references; subject index. E77.E117

Frazier, Gregory W. The American Indian index : a directory of Indian country, USA / by Gregory W. Frazier ; ed. by Randolph J. Punley. Denver, Colo. : Arrowstar Publ., c1985. 320 p. **CC430**

A directory listing interest groups, state and federal agencies, social service agencies, reservations, health and housing programs, festivals, arts and crafts sources, and publications. In 17 topical chapters, each subarranged by state or region with the entries alphabetically arranged. No index. E76.2.F7

Indian reservations : a state and federal handbook / comp. by the Confederation of American Indians. Jefferson, N.C. : McFarland, c1986. 329 p. **CC431**

Provides descriptions of 278 reservations located in 31 states. Organized by state, with entries listed alphabetically in each state. Each entry includes the location of the reservation, notes its relationship with the federal and state governments, the location of the tribal headquarters, and the names of the tribes residing on the reservation. Additional information is provided on the land area, history, culture, government, population, economy, climate, availability of transportation, and recreation on each reservation. Name index. E93.I3828

Handbooks

Handbook of North American Indians / William C. Sturtevant, gen. ed. Wash. : Smithsonian Institution : for sale by the U.S. Govt. Print. Off., 1978–1990. v. 4–11, 15 : ill. (In progress). **CC432**

Contents: v. 4, History of Indian-white relations, ed. by Wilcomb E. Washburn; v. 5, Arctic, ed. by D. Damas; v. 6, Subarctic, ed. by J. Helm; v. 7, Northwest Coast, ed. by Wayne Suttles; v. 8, California, ed. by R. F. Heizer; v. 9–10, Southwest, ed. by A. Ortiz; v. 11, Great Basin, ed. by Warren L. D'Azevedo; v. 15, Northeast, ed. by B. G. Trigger.

These are the first published parts of a 20-volume set planned to give "an encyclopedic summary of what is known about the prehistory, history, and cultures of the aboriginal peoples of North America who lived to the north of the urban civilizations of central Mexico."—*Pref.* Each volume comprises essays by specialists on specific aspects of Indian life, with extensive bibliography and detailed index.

Other volumes are to cover: [1] Introduction, methodology, sources, and continental summaries; [2] Indian and Eskimo communities in the twentieth century; [3] Environmental and biological backgrounds, physical anthropology, and earliest prehistoric cultures; [12–14] will deal with major culture areas other than California; [16] Technology and the visual arts; [17] Native languages; [18–19] Biographical dictionary; [20] Cumulated index. E77.H25

Heard, J. Norman. Handbook of the American frontier : four centuries of Indian-white relationships. Metuchen, N.J. : Scarecrow, 1987–1991. v. 1–3. (Native American resources series, 1). (In progress). **CC433**

Contents: v. 1: The southeastern woodlands; v. 2, The northeastern woodlands; v. 3, Plains Tribes.

The first published parts of five-volume set designed to "provide a series of brief articles in dictionary arrangement about American Indian tribes and leaders, explorers, traders, frontier settlers, soldiers, missionaries, mountain men, captives, battles, massacres, forts, treaties, and other topics of importance or interest in the history of the first forty eight states…"—*Pref.* References accompany entries. Entries derived from primary and secondary published sources. Forthcoming volumes: (4) Rocky Mountains, southwestern deserts, and Pacific Coast, (5) index, chronology, bibliography. E76.2.H43

The Native North American almanac : a reference work on native North Americans in the United States and Canada / Duane Champagne, ed. Detroit : Gale, c1994. 1275 p. **CC434**

In 17 topical chapters, including chronology, demography, major culture areas, languages, laws and legislation, activism, the environment, urbanization and nonreservation populations, religion, arts, literature, media, health, education, economy, biography. Bibliographies or directories accompany some chapters. Glossary; general bibliography; index of occupations organized by tribe; subject index. E77.N37

Biography

Frazier, Patrick. Portrait index of North American Indians in published collections. Wash. : Library of Congress : for sale by the U.S. Govt. Print. Off., 1992. 142 p. : ill. **CC435**

For annotation, *see* BF67. E89.F725

United States. Department of the Interior. Library. Biographical and historical index of American Indians and persons involved in Indian affairs. Boston : G.K. Hall, 1966. 8 v.   **CC436**

Developed by Anita S. Tilden; continued by Eugenia Langford.

A reproduction of the card file developed in the Bureau of Indian Affairs and now incorporated into the library of the Dept. of the Interior. It is a subject catalog only and, having been reproduced without editing, exhibits numerous irregularities in filing, forms of names, subject headings, etc. Includes references to some materials not in the Departmental collections.   Z1209.U494

Waldman, Carl. Who was who in Native American history : Indians and non-Indians from early contacts through 1900. N.Y. : Facts on File, c1990. 410 p. : ill.   **CC437**

An alphabetically arranged short-entry collective biography. Entries include birth and death dates, if available, and alternative names, if appropriate. Illustrations and cross-references are provided. The appendix consists of an alphabetical list of tribes which lists the Native Americans, and a list of occupations, which notes the non-Indians. Sources are not noted and bibliographies or reading lists are omitted. No index.   E89.W35

Atlases

Atlas of Great Lakes Indian history / ed. by Helen Hornbeck Tanner ... [et al.] ; cartography by Miklos Pinther. Norman : Publ. for the Newberry Library by the Univ. of Oklahoma Pr., c1987. 224 p. : ill., maps in color ; 32 cm. (The civilization of the American Indian series, v. 174).   **CC438**

Contains 182 pages of text, 30 maps (many of which are two-page spreads), and 86 illustrations, covering the years 1400–1880. The maps illustrate such topics as vegetation, wars of the 17th–19th centuries, locations of native villages at various periods, and location of reservations in the late 19th century. Includes a bibliographic essay and a select bibliography arranged alphabetically by author. Subject index.   E78.G7A87

Ferguson, T. J. A Zuni atlas / by T. J. Ferguson and E. Richard Hart ; new cartography by Ronald Stauber and Troy Lucio. Norman : Univ. of Oklahoma Pr., c1985. 154 p. : ill. ; 32 cm. (The civilization of the American Indian series, v. 172).   **CC439**

Contains 44 maps showing landforms, geologic features, natural and mineral resources, climate, 16th-century villages, 19th-century areas of Zuni sovereignty, traditional hunting and grazing lands, religious sites, historical and current locations of reservations. All maps are accompanied by text, many by black-and-white photographs. There is a nine-page bibliography, arranged by topic. Two appendixes: Zuni land use sites and Summary of land use by site. Subject index.   G1496.E1F4

Prucha, Francis Paul. Atlas of American Indian affairs. Lincoln : Univ. of Nebraska Pr., c1990. 191 p. : ill., maps ; 31 cm.   **CC440**

Thorough coverage in maps, text, and statistical tables of historical and contemporary issues concerning Native Americans. Some 100 black-and-white maps are arranged topically in ten sections that include cultural and tribal areas, census enumerations, land cessions, reservations, and agencies. U.S. maps supplemented by more detailed regional maps as appropriate. Notes on individual maps listed separately. General index of subjects, tribal names, and geographic names.   G1201.E1P7

Waldman, Carl. Atlas of the North American Indian / Carl Waldman ; maps and ill. by Molly Braun. N.Y. : Facts on File, c1985. 276 p. : ill. (some col.).   **CC441**

In eight topical chapters (e.g., Ancient civilizations, Indian culture, The Indians and the explorers, The Indian wars, Indian land cessions, and Contemporary Indians). The 246 maps are surrounded by text and cover quarter- or half-pages. Includes reproductions of histori-

cal maps and maps produced for this volume. Illustrated with historical drawings and contemporary photographs. A chronology of explorers' contacts with the Indians, and an Indian language classification table are provided in the relevant chapters. Six appendixes: (1) a chronology of Indian history; (2) a list of tribes with their historical and contemporary locations; (3) federal and state reservations; (4) Indian bands in Canada; (5) major Indian place names; (6) a list of museums, historical and archaeological sites. Bibliography; subject index.   E77.W195

Statistics

Statistical record of Native North Americans / Marlita A. Reddy, ed. Detroit : Gale, c1993. lxvi, 1661 p.   **CC442**

Consists of 1,007 statistical tables, graphs, and charts arranged in 12 topical chapters. Eleven cover for the U.S.: history, demographics, the family, education, culture and tradition, health, social and economic conditions, business and industry, land and water management, government relations, and law enforcement. The twelfth chapter covers the same topics for Canada. Publications of the U.S. and Canadian governments were the source for most data, although state agency and tribal government publications and newspapers are also cited. Figures from the 1990 census are not included. Bibliography of sources; keyword index.   E98.P76S73

Stuart, Paul. Nations within a nation : historical statistics of American Indians. N.Y. : Greenwood, 1987. 251 p.   **CC443**

Consists of statistical tables organized in eight topical chapters: land base and climate, population, removal, relocation and urbanization, vital statistics and health, government activities, health care and education, employment, earnings and income, and economic development. Introductory notes accompany each chapter. Statistics are derived from government publications. Bibliography; subject index.   E77 b .S924

Latinos

Bibliography

Cabello-Argandoña, Roberto. The Chicana : a comprehensive bibliographic study / comp. and ed. by Roberto Cabello-Argandoña, Juan Gómez-Quiñones, Patricia Herrera Durán. Los Angeles : Aztlán Publ., c1976, 1975. 308 p. : ill.   **CC444**

For annotation, *see* CC596.   Z1361.M4C245

Camarillo, Albert. Mexican Americans in urban society : a selected bibliography. Oakland, Calif. : Floricanto Pr., c1986. 296 p.   **CC445**

Offers 2,133 entries arranged alphabetically by author in topical chapters on art and theater, Chicana studies, culture and identity, employment, family, history, immigration, language, law and criminal justice, literature, mass media, politics, religion, social stratification, education, and general reference. Contains books, articles, dissertations and government publications published through 1983. Author index.   Z1361.M4C38

Herrera, Diane. Puerto Ricans and other minority groups in the continental United States : an annotated bibliography, with a new foreword and supplemental bibliography by Francesco Cordasco. Detroit : Blaine Ethridge Books, c1979. 397 p.   **CC446**

Earlier ed. had title: *Puerto Ricans in the United States : a review of the literature.*

Focuses on bilingual and bicultural education of Puerto Rican and other non-English-speaking students; also includes sociological, psychological, and literary studies of the Puerto Rican experience. More than 2,500 citations arranged by subject; author index.   Z1361.E4H47

MacCorkle, Lyn. Cubans in the United States : a bibliography for research in the social and behavioral sciences, 1960–1983. Westport, Conn. : Greenwood, 1984. 227 p. (Bibliographies and indexes in sociology, no. 1).   **CC447**

Approximately 1,600 citations, alphabetically arranged by author in eight topical sections: economics, education, public administration, psychology, health, politics, sociology, and demography. Books, scholarly articles, dissertations, government reports, conference papers, and unpublished papers are listed. Author index.   Z1361.C85M32

Meier, Matt S. Bibliography of Mexican American history. Westport, Conn. : Greenwood, 1984. 500 p.   **CC448**

Organizes 4,372 citations within broad categories. Six chapters follow chronological periods from colonial times to the present; three chapters treat topics of labor, politics, and culture; and the concluding three chapters list reference works, libraries and archives, and journals. Within the chronological/topical chapters works are grouped by form—books, dissertations, articles—with many contents notes. Author and subject indexes.   Z1361.M4M414

Pino, Frank. Mexican Americans : a research bibliography. East Lansing : Latin American Studies Center, Michigan State Univ., 1974. 2 v. (Latin American Studies Center. Research report, 11).   **CC449**

The work "is intended as an interdisciplinary guide to the study of the Mexican American" and "includes materials ranging from the early Spanish settlements to the present day activities of the Hispano, Mexican-American and Chicano."—p. ix. Lists books, monographs, master's theses, doctoral dissertations, articles in journals, and government publications. Arranged in 35 subject categories, with extensive cross-referencing. Author index, but no detailed subject index.

Z1361.M4P55

Puerto Rican Research and Resources Center. The Puerto Ricans : an annotated bibliography / ed. by Paquita Vivó. N.Y. : Bowker, 1973. 299 p.   **CC450**

A selective bibliography on all aspects of Puerto Rican history, life, and culture. In four main sections: (1) Books, pamphlets, and dissertations; (2) Government documents; (3) Periodical literature (i.e., a list of periodicals, plus a selection of periodical articles); (4) Audiovisual materials. The first three sections are subdivided by subject field; there are author, subject, and title indexes. Emphasizes recent materials, and English-language publication is given preference where both English and Spanish versions exist.   Z1551.P84

Sable, Martin Howard. Mexican and Mexican-American agricultural labor in the United States : an international bibliography. N.Y. : Haworth Pr., c1987. 429 p.   **CC451**

3,224 entries, chronologically arranged in two sections—popular and scholarly specialized materials—and in three appendixes: audiovisual materials, archives and manuscript materials, and directories. Dissertations, conference papers, and government publications are included in the scholarly materials sections. 150 entries in Spanish, the remainder in English. Five indexes: authors, books, periodicals, audiovisual materials, archival and manuscript materials.   Z7164.L1S2

Valk, Barbara G. BorderLine : a bibliography of the United States-Mexico borderlands. Los Angeles : UCLA Latin American Center Publications ; Riverside : UC MEXUS, Univ. of California Consortium on Mexico and the United States, c1988. 711 p. (UCLA Latin American Center Publications. Reference series, v. 12).   **CC452**

For annotation, *see* DB167.   Z1251.M44V35

Woods, Richard D. Reference materials on Mexican Americans : an annotated bibliography. Metuchen, N.J. : Scarecrow, 1976. 190 p.   **CC453**

Lists separately published bibliographies and reference-type works (dictionaries, collective biographies, etc.) on Mexican Americans in the United States. 387 entries in classed arrangement, with author, subject, and title indexes.   E184.M5W66

Indexes

The Chicana studies index : twenty years of gender research, 1971–1991 / comp. and ed. by Lillian Castillo-Speed. Berkeley, Calif. : Chicano Studies Library Publications Unit, Univ. of California at Berkeley, 1992. 427 p. (Chicano Studies Library publication series, no. 18).   **CC454**

For annotation, *see* CC528.   Z1361.M4C457

•**Chicano database** [database]. Berkeley, Calif. : Chicano Studies Library Publications, Univ. of California, 1990– .   **CC455**

Updated semiannually on CD-ROM.

Entries derived from *Arte Chicano*, comp. by Shifra M. Goldman and Tomás Ybarra-Frausto, (BF20) the *Chicano anthology index* (CC457), *Chicano periodical index* (1967–1988), and *Chicano index* (*see* CC456). Also includes some 200 references from the Latinos and AIDS databases produced by the Chicano Research Center, University of California, Los Angeles.

Chicano periodical index : a cumulative index to selected Chicano periodicals published between 1967 and 1978 / produced by the Committee for the Development of Subject Access to Chicano Literatures ; dir., Richard Chabrán, associate dir., Francisco García. Boston : G.K. Hall, 1981. 972 p.   **CC456**

A subject index to more than 4,900 articles appearing in some 18 Chicano academic journals, literary publications, popular magazines, and special interest periodicals. Author/title index.

———. *A cumulative index to selected periodicals, 1979–81 (with selected serials indexed retrospectively)* / ed. by Francisco García-Ayvens, Richard Chabrán ; comp. by the Chicano Periodical Indexing Project (1983. 648 p.). Adds about 4,500 citations to articles from 23 periodicals.

§ The *Chicano periodical index*, publ. 1981–89, is continued by *Chicano index* (v. 7 [Jan.–Mar. 1989]– . Berkeley, Calif. : Chicano Studies Library Publ. Unit, Univ. of California at Berkeley, 1989–). Both are included in the *Chicano database*, CC455.   Z1361.M4C47

García-Ayvens, Francisco. Chicano anthology index : a comprehensive author, title, and subject index to Chicano anthologies, 1965–1987. Berkeley : Chicano Studies Library Publications Unit, Univ. of California, 1990. 704 p. (Chicano Studies Library publication series, no. 13).   **CC457**

Consists of 15,577 subject entries that index approximately 5,000 analytical and critical articles and creative writing in 280 anthologies published 1965–87. Entries are arranged alphabetically by author under each subject entry. Covers topics in the social sciences and the humanities, as well as poetry, song lyrics, short stories, and plays. English-language materials predominate. List of the anthologies indexed; notes on the compilation of the work; author and title index.

Z1361.M4G37

Varona, Esperanza Bravo de. Cuban exile periodicals at the University of Miami Library : an annotated bibliography. Madison : Secretariat, Seminar on the Acquisition of Latin American Library Materials, Memorial Library, Univ. of Wisconsin-Madison, c1987. 203 p. (Seminar on the Acquisition of Latin American Library Materials bibliography and reference series, 19).   **CC458**

For annotation, *see* AD47.   Z1361.C85D4

Dictionaries

Glazer, Mark. A dictionary of Mexican American proverbs. N.Y. : Greenwood, 1987. 347 p.   **CC459**

Lists 986 proverbs alphabetically by Spanish keyword, accompanied by translations and explanatory material in English. Material compiled from published sources, and by surveying residents of the lower Rio Grande Valley (Texas). Notes identifying the sources of information accompnay each entry. Appendix contains the questionnaire and summary data about those surveyed. Spanish and English keyword indexes.   PN6426.3.T4G5

Stephens, Thomas M. Dictionary of Latin American racial and ethnic terminology. Gainesville : Univ. of Florida Pr., c1989. 401 p.   **CC460**

In two sections: Spanish American terms and Brazilian Portuguese terms. Entries consist of four components: (1) the term; (2) a definition; (3) racial or ethnic definitions, including related definitions, country or region of use, source of the information, historical period of use; (4) explanatory commentary. Definitions and commentary in English. Bibliography. Index.   GN564.L29S84

Directories

Carrasquillo, Angela. Hispanic children and youth in the United States : a resource guide. N.Y. : Garland, 1991. 321 p. (Reference books on family issues, v. 20 ; Garland reference library of social science, v. 608).   **CC461**

In 12 chapters, 11 of which are essays on history, diversity, family, education, language issues, health, the criminal justice system, and labor force participation. Chapter 12 consists of two parts: profiles of Hispanic childrens' advocacy groups, and a directory of social welfare and immigration agencies and organizations. Addresses and telephone numbers are supplied. Selected references, annotated bibliography. Author and subject indexes.   E184.S75C37

Gonzales, Sylvia Alicia. Hispanic American voluntary organizations. Westport, Conn. : Greenwood, 1985. 267 p.   **CC462**

Contains approximately 200 entries, alphabetically arranged, listing Mexican-American, Puerto Rican, and Cuban-American associations and groups. Entries include history, goals, structure, activities, and sources consulted. Information included was gathered by questionnaire. Three appendixes: (1) entries grouped by geographic location; (2) entries grouped by function or activity; (3) a chronology of general events, and events directly related to the organizations covered. Author and subject index.   E184.S75G65

Hispanic resource directory. [1988]– . Juneau, Alaska : Denali Pr., c1988– . Triennial.   **CC463**

Editor: Alan Edward Schorr.

Approximately 6,200 entries alphabetically arranged in 16 topical chapters. In some chapters, entries further arranged by state. Entries contain locations, contact persons, telephone, and fax numbers. Annotations provided for some entries. Topics covered: national, regional, and state associations, libraries, research centers, and museums, studies programs, colleges, university, and secondary schools with significant Latino enrollment, education programs, human rights, health, business, and economics media, Latin American, and Spanish diplomatic offices. The appendix consists of four tables of census information. Three indexes: Organization, geographic, and names of contact persons.   E184.S75H584

Handbooks

Fernández-Shaw, Carlos M. The Hispanic presence in North America from 1492 to today / Carlos M. Fernández-Shaw ; tr. by Alfonso Bertodano Stourton ... [et al.]. N.Y. : Facts on File, c1991. 375 p. : ill., maps.   **CC464**

Translation of: *Presencia española en los Estados Unidos.*

Chapter 1 is a general history; each of the remaining seven chapters covers a region of the U.S. Three appendixes: (1) History, listing the colonial Spanish governors, misssions, forts, historical societies, and historic sites; (2) Language and culture, listing associations of Spanish teachers and students, Hispanic associations, and holidays and festivals; (3) Media, including Spanish language periodicals, periodi-

cals highlighting Hispanic history and culture, and Spanish radio and television stations. Selective bibliography; subject index.
    E169.1.F375

Graham, Joe Stanley. Hispanic-American material culture : an annotated directory of collections, sites, archives, and festivals in the United States. N.Y. : Greenwood, 1989. 257 p. (Material culture directories, no. 2).   **CC465**

"Describes collections of artifacts, structures, and other aspects of the built environment, where Hispanics in the United States and its territories demonstrate components of material culture distinctive to Hispanics."—*Pref.* Includes descriptions of museum collections, holdings of historical societies and other public agencies, and sites listed on the National Register of Historical Places. Includes material on the Basques, but acknowledges that Basques are not Hispanics. A bibliography emphasizes titles in arts and crafts. Indexed only by name or type of artifact.   E184.S75G69

The Hispanic almanac. 2nd ed. N.Y. : Hispanic Policy Development Project, c1990. 203 p. : ill. (some col.).   **CC466**

1st ed., 1984.

In three sections: (1) brief narrative histories of Hispanic groups in the Western Hemisphere who have emigrated to the U.S.; (2) socio-economic, demographic, and linguistic data for the entire Hispanic population in the U.S., with detailed and comparative analyses of four subgroups (Mexican Americans, Puerto Ricans, Cuban Americans, and other Hispanics); (3) detailed descriptive analysis of the 20 Standard Metropolitan Statistical Areas with the largest Hispanic populations. There is also a description of the voting behavior of Hispanic electorates. Information is presented in maps, tables, graphs, and text. Data was drawn from the U.S. census, and references are included in the text. Includes a spotty list of cultural organizations, communications and media organizations, and research institutes. The technical appendix describes preparation of the data. No index.   E184.S75H47

The Hispanic-American almanac : a reference work on Hispanics in the United States / Nicolás Kanellos [ed.]. Detroit : Gale, c1993. 780 p. : ill., map.   **CC467**

In 25 topical chapters, covers both people who emigrated from, and descendents of people who emigrated from, Spain, Mexico, Puerto Rico, Cuba, and the Spanish-speaking countries of Central and South America and islands of the Caribbean. Subjects included: history, including Spanish explorers and historical documents, landmarks, relations with Spain, family, population growth and distribution, language, law, politics, business, labor, and employment, women, religion, organizations, scholarship, literature, the arts and theater, media science, sports, and prominent Hispanics. Chronology; bibliography. Subject index.   E184.S75H557

Meier, Matt S. Dictionary of Mexican American history / Matt S. Meier and Feliciano Rivera. Westport, Conn. : Greenwood, 1981. 498 p. : ill.   **CC468**

An alphabetically arranged dictionary of Chicano culture, covering 1519–1980. Brief entries sometimes include suggestions for further reading. Appendixes offer general bibliography, chronology, glossary of Chicano terms, list of Mexican American journals, statistical tables, and maps. Indexed.   E184.M5M453

Biography

Meier, Matt S. Mexican American biographies : a historical dictionary, 1836–1987. N.Y. : Greenwood, 1988. 270 p.   **CC469**

A compilation of 270 biographical sketches, 200 of which treat living individuals. Sources of additional information are included with each entry. Appendixes list the biographees by field of endeavor and by state of residence. Index of names and organizations included in the entries.   E184.M5M454

Who's who among Hispanic Americans. 1st ed. (1991–92)– . Detroit : Gale, 1991– . Biennial.   **CC470**

For annotation, *see* AH81.

Statistics

Statistical record of Hispanic Americans / Marlita A. Reddy, ed. Detroit : Gale, c1993. xlvi, 1173 p. : ill.   **CC471**
Consists of 922 statistical tables and graphs arranged in topical chapters, describing peoples of Hispanic, Mexican, Cuban, and Puerto Rican descent residing in the U.S. and Canada. Topics covered: demography, family, education, culture, health and health care, social and economic conditions, business and industry, government and politics, law and law enforcement. U.S. government publications were the sources of most data; other data derived from newspapers, trade press, and religious organizations. Provides comparative data for Asians, blacks, whites, and Latinos. Appendix; bibliography; keyword index.
§ *See also* Frank Leopold Schick and Renee Schick's *Statistical handbook on U.S. Hispanics* (Phoenix : Oryx, 1991. 225 p.).
E184.S75S74

Canada

Abler, Thomas S. A Canadian Indian bibliography, 1960–1970 / Thomas S. Abler, Sally M. Weaver, with Claire C. Veillitte ... [et al.]. Toronto : Univ. of Toronto Pr., 1974. 732 p., [2] leaves of plates : maps.   **CC472**
An annotated listing of material "of scholarly interest published between 1960 and 1970 on the Canadian Indian and Metis."—*Introd.* More than 3,000 entries (for books, periodical articles, reports, theses) in classed arrangement. A "case law digest" section (p. 306–62) attempts "to bring together all case law relating to Indian legal questions decided since 1 July 1867."   Z1209.2.C2A24

Gakovich, Robert P. Serbs in the United States and Canada : a comprehensive bibliography / Robert P. Gakovich, Milan M. Radovich. [Minneapolis] : Immigration History Research Center, Univ. of Minnesota, 1976. 129 p. : ill. (IHRC ethnic bibliography, no.1).   **CC473**
For annotation, *see* CC321.   Z1361.S4G34

Gregorovich, Andrew. Canadian ethnic groups bibliography : a selected bibliography of ethno-cultural groups in Canada and the province of Ontario. Toronto : Dept. of the Provincial Secretary and Citizenship of Ontario, 1972. 208 p.   **CC474**
More than 2,100 items arranged by ethnic group considered. Some annotations.   Z1395.E4G74

South America

Porter, Dorothy Burnett. Afro-Braziliana : a working bibliography. Boston : G. K. Hall, [1978]. 294 p.   **CC475**
A selective bibliography which intends "to make known a selection of published works written by Afro-Brazilians and their contribution to the life and history of Brazil ... . Works listed are those to be found in American repositories ... ."—*Pref.* In two parts: (1) a classified section; (2) writings of selected authors, with critical and biographical references. More than 5,200 items; some annotations. Indexed.
§ *See also* Henrique L. Alves, *Bibliografía afro-brasileira : estudios sobre o negro* (2nd ed. Rio de Janeiro : Cátedra, 1979. 181 p.).
"Em convênio com o Instituto Nacional do Libro."—*t.p.*
1st ed., 1976.
Lists 2,283 works (books, periodical and newspaper articles, essays, reports, government documents) by author; no subject approach.
Z1697.N4P67

Ramos Guédez, José Marcial. Bibliografía Afrovenezolana. Caracas : Instituto Autónomo Biblioteca Nacional y de Servicios de Bibliotecas, 1980. 125 p. (Colección bibliográfica y documental venezolana, 1 ; Instituto Autónomo Biblioteca Nacional y de Servicios de Bibliotecas. Serie Bibliográfica, 2).   **CC476**
A classed bibliography of nearly 1,000 titles, with some contents notes. Name index.   Z1937.N4R35

Welch, Thomas L. The Aztecs : a bibliography of books and periodical articles / comp. by Thomas L. Welch and René L. Gutiérrez. Wash. : Columbus Memorial Library, Organization of American States, 1987. 169 p. (Hipólito Unanue bibliographic series, 3).   **CC477**
Lists 778 books and 438 articles in Spanish or English, arranged alphabetically by author. Covers Aztec culture, including much on language. Title and subject indexes.   Z1210.A9W45

——————— The Incas : a bibliography of books and periodical articles / comp. by Thomas L. Welch and René L. Gutiérrez. Wash. : Columbus Memorial Library, Organization of American States, 1987. 145 p. (Hipólito Unanue bibliographic series, 1).   **CC478**
Includes 401 articles and 715 books in Spanish or English, arranged by author. Title and subject indexes.   Z1210.I53W45

International ethnic groups

Brotherton Library. Catalogue of the Romany collection : formed by D. U. McGrigor Phillips and presented to the University of Leeds. Edinburgh : publ. for the Brotherton Collection by Nelson, 1962. 227 p. : port.   **CC479**
Spine title: Leeds University Romany catalogue.
A classified bibliography of more than 1,200 items, including books and pamphlets, manuscripts, music, letters, playbills, pictures, engravings, etc., relating to Gypsies in many countries. Author and title index.

WOMEN

General works

Guides

Carter, Sarah. Women's studies : a guide to information sources / Sarah Carter and Maureen Ritchie. London : Mansell ; Jefferson, N.C. : McFarland, 1990. 278 p.   **CC480**
A highly useful sourcebook that includes "all major woman-centered English-language reference works, monographic and serial."—*Introd.* 1,076 annotated entries with cross-references are arranged in three sections: General material (reference works, biographical dictionaries, women's sources); Women in the world (i.e., works relating to women of specific geographic areas); and Special subjects (e.g., Black women, Law and politics, Lesbians, Spirituality). Omits sources on children's literature and individual women writers. Detailed general index.   Z7961.C37

Chapman, Anne. Feminist resources for schools and colleges : a guide to curricular materials. 3rd ed. N.Y. : Feminist Pr. at The City Univ. of New York, 1986. 190 p.   **CC481**
1st ed., 1973, ed. by Merle Froschl and Jane Williamson; 2nd ed., 1977.
Includes 445 annotated entries, 1975–84, alphabetically arranged by author or title within the major disciplines covered in the high

school and undergraduate college curriculum. The first section lists 310 print resources, the second 135 audiovisual resources. Annotations are descriptive and evaluative. Omits biographies, novels, poetry, and drama. Eight-page directory of publishers and distributors; separate author/title indexes for print and audiovisual resources; combined subject index.   Z5817.C48

Schuster, Marilyn R. Selected bibliography for integrating research on women's experience in the liberal arts curriculum / comp. by Marilyn Schuster and Susan Van Dyne. 6th ed. Northampton, Mass. : Smith College, 1988. 101 p.   **CC482**
1st ed., 1983; 5th ed., 1986.
Compiled for teachers for instructional and research purposes. Multidisciplinary; organized by academic field, Afro-American studies to theater. In each section, lists citations alphabetically by author under two categories, Classroom use and Teacher preparation. Offset from typescript; some running heads obscured by spiral binding. No indexes.   HQ1181.U5OCS38

Searing, Susan E. Introduction to library research in women's studies. Boulder, Colo. : Westview Pr., 1985. 257 p.   **CC483**
Pt. 1 describes the nature of women's studies, reviews basic research strategy, and explains use of card catalogs, periodical indexes, and interlibrary loan. Pt. 2 provides annotated lists of specific research tools, including: guides to research, bibliographies, indexes, library catalogs, guides to special collections, biographical sources, directories, microform sources, online sources, periodicals, guides, and handbooks. Three appendixes contain the Dewey Decimal and Library of Congress classification systems, and review essays from *Signs*, 1975–Summer 1984.   Z7961.S42

Tingley, Elizabeth. Women and feminism in American history : a guide to information sources / Elizabeth Tingley, Donald F. Tingley. Detroit : Gale, c1981. 289 p. (American government and history information guide series, v. 12).   **CC484**
An annotated bibliography of English-language works on suffragism, equal rights, and "any activity or analysis which concerns itself with women and the action necessary for women to obtain their rightful status as full human beings, including ... the creation of a women's culture ...."—*Pref.* Eleven chapters provide reference sources and a historical approach; the remaining 22 chapters deal with topics such as antifeminist writing since 1940. Author, title, and subject indexes.
Z7964.U49T52

Bibliography

Addis, Patricia K. Through a woman's I : an annotated bibliography of American women's autobiographical writings, 1946–1976. Metuchen, N.J. : Scarecrow, 1983. 607 p.
CC485
An author listing of more than 2,200 autobiographies, diaries, published collections of letters, travel narratives, etc. Indexed by profession, subject or narrative type, and title.
§ Supplements Louis Kaplan, *Bibliography of American autobiographies* (AH89).   Z7963.B6A32

Blair, Karen J. The history of American women's voluntary organizations, 1810–1960 : a guide to sources. Boston : G.K. Hall, c1989. 363 p.   **CC486**
An introduction gives inclusion criteria for more than 670 entries, listed alphabetically by author with detailed descriptive annotations. Entries include full bibliographic citation and code(s) indicating type of organization. Excludes unpublished dissertations or masters theses and works of fiction that deal with club life. 54 p. index.
Z7964.U49B53

Buhle, Mari Jo. Women and the American left : a guide to sources. Boston : G.K. Hall, 1983. 281 p.   **CC487**

An annotated bibliography of 595 items arranged by historical periods from 1871 to 1981, subdivided by form (histories, biographies, books and pamphlets on "the woman question," periodicals, fiction and poetry). General index.   Z7964.U49B84

Conway, Jill K. The female experience in eighteenth- and nineteenth-century America : a guide to the history of American women / Jill K. Conway, with the assistance of Linda Kealey, Janet E. Schulte. N.Y. : Garland, 1982. 290 p. (Garland reference library of social science, v. 35).   **CC488**
Repr.: Princeton, N.J. : Princeton Univ. Pr., 1985.
Bibliographical citations to primary and secondary works are preceded by introductory review essays in more than 40 subject chapters. Arranged in six principal sections: culture and society, work, education, religion, politics, health. Author index.   HQ1410.C66

Coyle, Jean M. Women and aging : a selected, annotated bibliography. N.Y. : Greenwood, 1989. 135 p. (Bibliographies and indexes in gerontology, no. 9).   **CC489**
Intended for practitioners, researchers, and older women. 622 numbered entries appear in 13 topical sections (e.g., Employment, Health, Retirement, Racial and ethnic groups, Policy issues, Housing). Subarranged by type of material, then alphabetically by author. Includes books, articles, films, documents, and dissertations. Subject and author indexes.   Z7164.O4C68

Davis, Nanette J. Women and deviance : issues in social conflict and change: an annotated bibliography / Nanette J. Davis, Jone M. Keith; compilers, Melody Hedrick ... [et al.]. N.Y. : Garland, 1984. 236 p. (Garland reference library of social science, vol. 157 ; Applied social science bibliographies, v. 1; Garland reference library of social science, v. 157).   **CC490**
A selection of 516 titles on crimes by and crimes against women in the United States, as well as such "social control" topics as abortion, substance abuse, lesbianism, poverty, suicide, teenage pregnancy, etc. Subject and name indexes.   Z7964.U49D38

Feinberg, Renee. The Equal Rights Amendment : an annotated bibliography of the issues, 1976–1985. N.Y. : Greenwood, 1986. 151 p. (Bibliographies and indexes in women's studies, no. 3).   **CC491**
Documents the struggle for ERA ratification. Designed as sequel to Equal Rights Amendment Project's *The equal rights amendment* (Westport, Conn. : Greenwood, [1976]. 367 p.) expanding coverage to include TV news and selective annotations. Includes over 700 entries from books, articles, government publications, and television news programs in 11 chapters covering public opinion, federal and state interpretations, employment, education, family and religion, military, ratification efforts, and more. Lists of organizations; subject and author indexes.   KF4758.A1F45

Franzosa, Susan Douglas. Integrating women's studies into the curriculum : an annotated bibliography / comp. by Susan Douglas Franzosa and Karen A. Mazza. Westport, Conn. : Greenwood, 1984. 100 p. (Bibliographies and indexes in education, no. 1).   **CC492**
Nine subject chapters corresponding to academic disciplines (literature, science, fine arts, etc.) are subdivided for sections on women in the field, reconceptualizing the discipline, thematic guides, and curriculum strategies. Author index.   Z7964.U49F73

Haber, Barbara. Women in America : a guide to books, 1963–1975; with an appendix on books published 1976–1979. Urbana, Ill. : Univ. of Illinois Pr., 1981. 262 p.   **CC493**
Updates 1978 ed. publ. by G.K. Hall.
Lists nonfiction works, grouped by broad subject, with full annotations. A 56-page appendix is a subject listing of references cited in bibliographic essays. General index.   Z7964.U49H3

Huls, Mary Ellen. United States government documents on women, 1800–1990 : a comprehensive bibliography. Westport, Conn. : Greenwood, 1993. 2 v. (Bibliographies and indexes in women's studies, no. 17–18).   **CC494**

Contents: v. 1, Social issues; v. 2, Labor.

More than 7,000 numbered entries, most with short descriptions, in subject chapters (each with an introductory essay) representing "most of the published reports of agencies, commissions, and Congress on women or on topics directly affecting women's health and welfare."—*Introd.* Entries provide full citation, including SuDoc or report numbers. Vol. 1 covers issues such as discrimination, abortion, poverty programs, violence against women, retirement and survivor benefits. Vol. 2 addresses paid employment, affirmative action, day care, protective legislation, vocational assistance, etc. In small type. List of abbreviations. Personal author and subject indexes.

Z7964.U49H85

Jarrard, Mary E. W. Women speaking : an annotated bibliography of verbal and nonverbal communication, 1970–1980 / Mary E. W. Jarrard, Phyllis R. Randall. N.Y. : Garland, 1982. 478 p. (Garland reference library of social science, v. 108).   **CC495**

Contains 1,327 entries for English-language publications (excluding theses and dissertations), classed according to subject in three broad areas—settings, characteristics, and means (verbal, nonverbal) of communication, then further subdivided by topic. A fourth section gives comprehensive references. Subject index; the lack of an author index somewhat hampers use.

For additional references, see also *Language, gender, and society*, ed. by Barrie Thorne, Cheris Kramarae, and Nancy Henley (Rowley, Mass. ; Newbury House, 1983).   HQ1426.J37

Kennedy, Susan E. America's white working-class women : a historical bibliography. N.Y. : Garland, 1981. 253 p. (Women's studies: facts and issues, v. 2 ; Garland reference library of the humanities, v. 260).   **CC496**

An annotated bibliography of more than 1,000 citations to English-language materials, including dissertations and government documents. General works are followed by sections organized by historical period, subdivided by topic. Author and subject indexes.

Z7903.E7K45

Kinnard, Cynthia D. Antifeminism in American thought : an annotated bibliography. Boston : G.K. Hall, c1986. 321 p.   **CC497**

Examines the opposition to the women's rights struggle, "the essential negative side to understanding feminism as it developed in the first women's movement."—*Introd.* Numbered entries with annotations are arranged chronologically within subject chapters. Includes more than 900 periodical articles and 400 books and pamphlets published in the U.S. from colonial times through the period of suffrage. Foreign material included if reprinted in the U.S. Excludes newspaper articles. Names index.   Z7964.U49K56

Krichmar, Albert. The women's movement in the seventies : an international English-language bibliography / Albert Krichmar, assisted by Virginia Carlson Smith and Ann E. Wiederrecht. Metuchen, N.J. : Scarecrow, 1977. 875 p.   **CC498**

Lists some 8,600 "English-language publications concerning the status of women in nearly 100 countries. ... The emphasis is on change, attempted change, and continuing problems confronting women in the countries in which they live."—*Introd.* Includes doctoral dissertations, books, pamphlets, research reports, periodical articles, and government documents published or reprinted 1970–75, plus some 1976 publications. Geographical arrangement, with topical subdivisions under those countries or areas about which there is a considerable quantity of literature. Author and subject indexes; numerous annotations.   Z7961.K74

———— The women's rights movement in the United States, 1848–1970 : a bibliography and sourcebook / Albert Krichmar ... [et al.]. Metuchen, N.J. : Scarecrow, 1972. 436 p.   **CC499**

A topically arranged bibliography on "the legal, political, economic, religious, educational, and professional status of women since 1848."—*Introd.* In addition to the more than 5,100 references to book, periodical, and pamphlet materials, there are sections on manuscript sources and women's liberation serial publications. Some annotations; indexed.   Z7964.U49K75

Lent, John A. Women and mass communications : an international annotated bibliography. N.Y. ; Westport, Conn. : Greenwood, c1991. 481 p. (Bibliographies and indexes in women's studies, no. 11).   **CC500**

Includes mass media (publishing, radio, magazines, television, newspapers, film, and video) as well as wire services, public relations, and advertising. Omits speeches and interpersonal communications. 3,235 entries represent published and unpublished literature, 1960–90. A preface provides a history of the literature, databases searched, and a detailed review of chapter content and background. The first chapter treats global and comparative perspectives, and the five remaining chapters focus on different regions of the world. Entries are alphabetically arranged by author. An appendix gives alphabetical lists of organizations and periodicals. Author and subject indexes.

Z5633.W65L45

Loeb, Catherine. Women's studies : a recommended core bibliography, 1980–1985 / Catherine R. Loeb, Susan E. Searing, Esther F. Stineman ... [et al.]. Littleton, Colo. : Libraries Unlimited, 1987. 538 p.   **CC501**

Continues *Women's studies : a recommended core bibliography*, by Esther Stineman (Littleton, Colo. : Libraries Unlimited, 1979).

Includes 1,211 English-language or translated works from women's small presses and university and trade publishers. Lists annotated entries alphabetically by author within 17 subject chapters, and in a chapter on reference sources and one on periodicals (the latter describing nearly 60 feminist serials). Includes addresses of publishers not listed in *Books in print* or *Ulrich's international periodicals directory*. Author, title, and subject indexes.

An abridged version with the same title (1987. 222 p.), intended for smaller libraries, focuses on items that are in print, from well known publishers, of general subject interest, and lower priced. 645 entries.   Z7963.F44L63

McCullough, Rita I. Sources : an annotated bibliography of women's issues. Manchester, Conn. : KIT, 1991. 320 p.   **CC502**

Annotates 1,500 books, most from late 80s–1990. Entries are arranged alphabetically by title under broad topics such as history, humor, feminism, education, women and the arts. No other subject access. Surprisingly, lists only 10 items in the journals/periodicals section, omitting many core titles. One title misspelled: *off our backs*. Lists publishers with addresses and phone. Title and author indexes.

Z7961.M4

McFeely, Mary Drake. Women's work in Britain and America from the nineties to World War I : an annotated bibliography. Boston : G.K. Hall, 1982. 140 p.   **CC503**

In two sections, Women's work in Great Britain and Women's work in America, with more than 500 entries for books (including fiction), pamphlets, and articles written between 1890 and 1914, plus later material dealing with that period. Includes both paid employment and voluntary work in social welfare, etc.

§ For historical material on American women and trade unions, see *American women and the labor movement* by M. J. Soltow and M. K. Wery (CC511).   Z7963.E7M43

Miller, Connie. Feminist research methods : an annotated bibliography / Connie Miller, with Corinna Treitel. N.Y. : Greenwood, 1991. 279 p. (Bibliographies and indexes in women's studies, no. 13).   **CC504**

Groups 416 annotated entries into 11 subject chapters, each with an introductory bibliographic essay; within each chapter, entries are arranged alphabetically by author. Represents feminist methodology in disciplines of history, science, psychology, anthropology, sociology, communications, political science, economics, geography, architecture, and urban planning. Covers English-language works, 1920s–1990. Omits feminist literary criticism, philosophy, education, nursing, and medicine. Subject and author indexes.   Z7963.F44M54

Mumford, Laura Stempel. Women's issues : an annotated bibliography. Pasadena, Calif. : Salem Pr., c1989. 163 p.   **CC505**

Intended for high school and college students. An introduction provides context, background, definitions, and an annotated list of 12 general reference sources. The bibliography is divided into sections that include: History, politics, and education; Women's movement; Economics; Health issues and sexuality; Family, home, and relationships; Violence against women; and Religion and spirituality. Index of names.   Z7961.M85

Nelson, Barbara J. American women and politics : a selected bibliography and resource guide. N.Y. : Garland, 1984. 255 p. (Garland reference library of social science, v. 174).   **CC506**

A topically arranged list of about 1,600 citations, emphasizing work published 1970–82. "Politics" has been broadly interpreted to include social movements, political socialization, women's role in the welfare state, and feminist/political theory. Author and subject indexes.   Z7964.U49N38

Nordquist, Joan. The feminist movement : a bibliography. Santa Cruz, Calif. : Reference and Research Services, 1992. 68 p. (Contemporary social issues, no. 24).   **CC507**

Entries arranged by format (books or articles) under such topics as sexuality debates, developing countries, issues of race, and history. Lists 15 other bibliographies, seven directories, and 73 organizations; no annotations.   Z7963.F44N67

Papachristou, Judith. Bibliography in the history of women in the progressive era. [Bronxville, N.Y.] : Sarah Lawrence College, c1985. 70 p.   **CC508**

Covers 1890–1930, depending on subject. Organizes numbered entries into nine chapters with some subtopics; entries arranged alphabetically by author within these sections. Omits dissertations, most primary sources, much of the arts and humanities. Includes material on work, sex roles, sexual preference, community activism, feminism, suffrage, biography, autobiography, etc. No annotations. General index.   Z7964.U49P36

Ritchie, Maureen. Women's studies : a checklist of bibliographies. London : Mansell, 1980. 107 p.   **CC509**

A bibliography of 489 English-language bibliographies published as books, articles, or pamphlets. 19 broad subject groups are usually further subdivided. Author and keyword indexes.   Z7961.A1R58

Rosenberg-Dishman, Marie Barovic. Women and society : a critical review of the literature with a selected annotated bibliography / comp. and ed. by Marie Barovic Rosenberg, Len V. Bergstrom. Beverly Hills, Calif. : Sage, 1975. 345 p.   **CC510**

The "Introduction: a selective review of the literature" is a 20-page survey of classic books on women in history, women at work, and women in politics; the remainder of the volume cites 3,600 books, articles, documents, periodicals and newspapers, and women's collections and libraries grouped into large subject areas; most chapters have more detailed subject breakdowns. Brief annotations. Indexed by authors, journal issues devoted to women, persons, places, subjects.

§ Continued by JoAnn Delores Een and Rosenberg-Dishman, *Women and society : citations 3601 to 6000* (1978. 275 p.). Retains the basic organization of the preceding work while adding sections on the political status of women and women's handbooks and almanacs, and omitting sections on women's collections and libraries and women's

periodicals and newspapers. Indexed by authors, places and topics, with a special index of journal issues or sections devoted to women.   Z7961.R67

Soltow, Martha Jane. American women and the labor movement, 1825–1974 : an annotated bibliography / Martha Jane Soltow and Mary K. Wery. [2nd ed.]. Metuchen, N.J. : Scarecrow, 1976. 247 p.   **CC511**

A revised edition of *Women in American labor history* (East Lansing, Mich., 1972).

Classed arrangement under the following main headings: (1) Employment; (2) Trade unions; (3) Working conditions; (4) Strikes; (5) Legislation; (6) Worker education; (7) Labor leaders; (8) Supportive efforts. Author and subject indexes.   Z7963.E7S635

Stanwick, Kathy. The political participation of women in the United States : a selected bibliography, 1950–1976 / Center for the American Woman and Politics, Eagleton Institute of Politics, Rutgers University ; Kathy Stanwick and Christine Li. Metuchen, N.J. : Scarecrow, 1977. 160 p.   **CC512**

Expansion and updating of the Center's *Women and American politics : a selected bibliography, 1965–1974* (New Brunswick, N.J., 1974).

Groups more than 1,500 entries by type, with biographical and author indexes, but no topical subject approach. Includes substantial amounts of unpublished material and research in progress at the time of publication.   Z7961.S74

Sullivan, Kaye. Films for, by, and about women. Metuchen, N.J. : Scarecrow, 1980. 552 p.   **CC513**

An international, annotated title listing of about 4,000 films—feature, documentary, educational, etc. The synopsis for each film includes credits, citation to a script or filmbook if available, whether the film is based on a book, and whether the film is sexually explicit. Directory of film sources, with addresses. Indexed by women filmmakers and subject.

Continued by: *Films for, by, and about women. Series II* (1985. 780 p.) Lists some 3,200 films alphabetically by title. Follows the format of the 1980 volume, except the subject index includes the names of women and many new headings (e.g., Child custody, Children's rights, Adoption).   PN1995.9.W6S95

Watson, G. Llewellyn. Feminism and women's issues : an annotated bibliography and research guide / G. Llewellyn Watson with the assistance of Janet P. Sentner. N.Y. : Garland, 1990. 2 v. (1710 p.). (Garland reference library of social science, v. 599).   **CC514**

Groups 7,364 citations, many without annotations, alphabetically by author into subject categories outlined in the table of contents, the only source of subject access. Journal articles from the 1960s and 1970s predominate.   Z7961.W37

Wilkinson, Carroll Wetzel. Women working in nontraditional fields : references and resources, 1963–1988. Boston : G.K. Hall, 1991. 213 p.   **CC515**

Groups 737 numbered entries, 590 with annotations, in topical chapters, each with introductory text. Covers mostly print sources: journals, magazines, books, book chapters, dissertations, government documents. Attempts to include small press and nonacademic sources. Includes the trades, certain professions, and technological fields, e.g., carpentry, fire fighting, surgery, piloting, rabbinical work, and farming. References for broader issues also, e.g., change, sex segregation, career education. Author, subject, and title indexes.   Z7963.E7W53

Williamson, Jane. New feminist scholarship : a guide to bibliographies. Old Westbury, N.Y. : Feminist Pr., 1979. 139 p.   **CC516**

A bibliography of 391 English-language bibliographies, resource lists, and literature reviews in monograph or article form, arranged in 30 subject sections. Literary bibliographies of individual women writers are excluded, as are lists of non-sexist books for children and young adults. About half of the entries are annotated. Author and title indexes.   Z7161.A1W54

Wilson, Carolyn F. Violence against women : an annotated bibliography. Boston : G.K. Hall, 1981. 111 p.   **CC517**

A selection of 213 books and articles, most from 1975–80, on battered women, rape, sexual abuse of children, and pornography. Topical arrangement; author/title and subject indexes.   HV6250.4.W65W54

Current

Feminist bookstore news. 1976– . San Francisco, Calif. : Feminist Bookstore News. Bimonthly (6 times/year).   **CC518**

For booksellers, librarians, students, teachers, book reviewers, publishers, and women's studies faculty. Describes and reviews newly published materials from small and university presses. Includes bibliographic essays on special topics and regular sections for Canadian, art, music, gay men's materials, etc. Announces new and ceased titles, press or store relocations, etc. Many illustrations and photographs.
                                          WMLC 93/2679

Feminist collections. Madison, Wis. : [Women's Studies Librarian-at-Large for The Univ. of Wisconsin System]. Quarterly.   **CC519**

A quarterly survey of publications in women's studies. Regular sections include book reviews; essays on feminism and publishing; research exchange information; new periodicals, title changes, or cessations; and a list of books recently received. The last issue in each volume contains combined author and title index for entire volume.

New books on women and feminism. [No. 1] (June 1979)– . Madison, Wis. : Memorial Library, Univ. of Wisconsin System, 1979– . Irregular.   **CC520**

A bibliography of books and periodicals listed alphabetically by title within broad subject areas (e.g., anthropology, literature: poetry, religion/spirituality). Each issue provides author and subject indexes and an abbreviations list.

Periodicals

Doughan, David. Feminist periodicals, 1855–1984 : an annotated critical bibliography of British, Irish, Commonwealth, and international titles / David Doughan, Denise Sanchez. N.Y. : New York Univ. Pr., 1987. 316 p.   **CC521**

A chronological listing of 920 primarily British journals 1855–1984, which "define themselves ... as committed to improving the social, legal and economic position of women in relation to men," although many of the pre-1960 titles are "far more philanthropic than feminist in intention."—*Foreword.* Lists a few titles explicitly opposed to feminism, and some that appear to be feminist but are not. Entries include, when available, title, variant titles, editor, publisher, frequency, dates, locations, availability on microfilm. Has a brief introduction, list of abbreviations, explanation of entry format, and short bibliography. Name/title, subject, and chronological indexes.   Z7963.F44D68

Humphreys, Nancy K. American women's magazines : an annotated historical guide. N.Y. : Garland, 1989. 303 p. (Garland reference library of the humanities, vol. 789).   **CC522**

"Women from three centuries, every geographical region, age, racial and class background, sexual preference, and ideology are represented by these periodicals."—*Introd.* In sections for alternative publications and mainstream publications. Pt. 1 covers 19th and early 20th century women's rights, as well as the feminist movement from the 1960s to present. Pt. II emphasizes mass market periodicals, covering 19th century ladies' magazines, 20th century women's magazines, women's pages in newspapers, and confession/romance magazines. 888 entries, alphabetically arranged by author in each subsection. Subject index.   Z6944.W6H85

Zuckerman, Mary Ellen. Sources on the history of women's magazines, 1792–1960 : an annotated bibliography. N.Y. : Greenwood, 1991. 297 p. (Bibliographies and indexes in women's studies, no. 12).   **CC523**

Introduction provides historical background and instructions for use. 11 chapters cover topics such as portrayal of women, content studies, employees of women's magazines, advertising and ad agencies, market research, selected archives. The final chapter covers individual titles or publishers. Author and subject indexes.
                                          Z6944.W6Z83

Manuscripts; Archives

Barrow, Margaret. Women, 1870–1928 : a select guide to printed and archival sources in the United Kingdom. London : Mansell ; N.Y. : Garland, 1981. 249 p.   **CC524**

In four parts: (1) archives, arranged by subject and then by holding institution; (2) printed works, divided by type of publication and then by subject; (3) non-book materials, such as films, photographs, newspaper clippings, and oral history; (4) directory of libraries and record offices. Indexed.   HQ1595.B37

The Canadian women's movement, 1960–1990 : a guide to archival resources / ed. by Margaret Fulford [for] Canadian Women's Movement Archives. Toronto : ECW Pr., c1992. 380 p.   **CC525**

Title page also in French. Text in English and French.

Includes "any organization having as one of its principal goals the improvement of women's social, economic, or political condition."—*Introd.* Omits charities run by women, government departments, royal commissions, and advisory councils. Pt. 1, Records held by archives; pt. 2, Records held by groups. Entries describe archive/group, records held, size and condition, and nature of access. Address and phone included. Appendix includes addresses and entry numbers for archives. List of illustrations; name and subject indexes.

Women's history sources : a guide to archives and manuscript collections in the United States / ed. by Andrea Hinding. N.Y. : Bowker, 1979. 2 v.   **CC526**

For annotation, *see* DB39.   Z7964.U49W64

Indexes; Abstract journals

The Canadian feminist periodical index = Index des périodiques féministes canadiens / comp. by the Canadian Women's Indexing Group (CWIG). 1972–1985– . Toronto, Ont. : OISE Pr., 1991– .   **CC527**

Interfiles French and English subjects and entries, but items printed in English are listed only under English subjects, French under French. Entries give: subject term, accession number, geographic area, author, title, descriptive notes, source. Indexes for authors, titles, and separate French and English subjects follow the main list. Concludes with an address list for the 15 periodicals indexed. Provides helpful how-to-use material in both languages. Uses terms from *Canadian feminist thesaurus* (CC541).

The Chicana studies index : twenty years of gender research, 1971–1991 / comp. and ed. by Lillian Castillo-Speed. Berkeley, Calif. : Chicano Studies Library Publications Unit, Univ. of California at Berkeley, 1992. 427 p. (Chicano Studies Library publication series, no. 18).   **CC528**

Expands and updates the author's bibliography, "Chicana studies : a selected list of materials since 1980," publ. in *Frontiers : a journal of women's studies* (Albuquerque, N.M. : Frontiers Editorial Collective, 1990).

Focuses upon women of Mexican heritage living in the U.S. Main sections lists approximately 1,150 entries by subject descriptor. Entries provide full citation, language, and index terminology, indicating major descriptor terms. Each entry located under an average of three descriptors in the index. Covers journal articles, books, book chapters, dissertations, and reports. Excludes most poems, short stories, biographical articles. Lists periodicals indexed. Author and title indexes.   Z1361.M4C457

Fischer, Gayle V. Journal of women's history guide to periodical literature. Bloomington : Indiana Univ. Pr., c1992. 501 p.   **CC529**

Compiled because "women's history is the fastest growing field in the profession."—*Foreword*. Covers 1980–90, indexing more than 700 journals. Some 5,500 cross-listed entries are alphabetically arranged by author within 40 subtopics. Samples: agriculture, feminism, ethnicity, material and popular culture, biography, and work. 23% of the entries concern countries other than the U.S.. Countries or regions are included as subtopics. List of journal titles. No index.

Z7962.F57 1992

Manning, Beverley. Index to American women speakers, 1828–1978. Metuchen, N.J. : Scarecrow, 1980. 672 p.   **CC530**

For annotation, *see* BE358.   Z1231.O7M36

Studies on women abstracts. v.1, no.1– . [Abingdon, Oxfordshire] : Carfax, [1983]– . Quarterly.   **CC531**

Each issue provides about 150–200 numbered nonevaluative abstracts, first for journals, then books. Scans about 500 journals. International coverage; some British emphasis. Includes education, employment, family, community, medicine, health, sex-role socialization, social policy, social psychology, female culture, media treatment, biography, literary criticism, historical studies. Author and subject indexes; annual cumulations.

Women studies abstracts. v.1, no.1 (Winter 1972)– . [Rush, N.Y. : Rush Publ. Co.], 1972– . Quarterly, with annual index.   **CC532**

Each issue abstracts 400–500 articles from about 35 journals, followed by additional non-annotated listing of biography and criticism, media reviews, resources, and book reviews. Includes wide range of subjects, e.g. education, sexuality, family, society, religion, sports, history, art, theatre, abortion, language. Lists journals abstracted and indexed, with addresses; indicates specific issues covered. General index includes *see* and *see also* references; indicates citations that include abstracts. Index cumulates annually.   Z7962.W65

Women's studies index. 1989– . Boston : G.K. Hall, c1991– . Annual.   **CC533**

A selective author/subject index to relevant articles in a wide range of scholarly and popular periodicals, mainly American in origin. Includes concise instructions on use of the index, cross-references, and addresses of the approximately 80 periodicals scanned. Two-year publication lag.

Book reviews

The women's review of books. v. 1 (Oct. 1983)– . Wellesley, Mass. : Wellesley College Center for Research on Women, [c1983]– . Monthly.   **CC534**

Newspaper format. Seeks to "represent the widest possible range of feminist perspectives both in the books reviewed and in the content of the reviews."—*Masthead*. Includes lengthy reviews, often by academic faculty; classifieds; list of recently published nonfiction titles. September issue includes volume indexing for author/title and reviewer.

§ For reviews of fiction and popular titles, consult *Belles lettres : a review of books by women*, ed. by Janet Palmer Mullaney (v. 12 [Sept./Oct. 1985]– . Arlington, Va. : Belles Lettres, 1985–).

HQ1101.W768

Encyclopedias

Tuttle, Lisa. Encyclopedia of feminism. N.Y. : Facts on File, 1986. 399 p.   **CC535**

Intended for both readers new to and those familiar with feminism, this alphabetically arranged work covers "individuals, organizations, classic works, and specialized terminology."—*Introd*. Sample entries include: Bambara, Toni Cade; COYOTE; Seneca Falls; Gynarchy; Muslim feminists; Publishing; Separatism. Cross-references; 21-page bibliography.   HQ1115.T87

Warren, Mary Anne. The nature of woman : an encyclopedia & guide to the literature. Inverness, Calif. : Edgepress, 1980. 708 p.   **CC536**

Offers a series of author and topical entries concerned with the following issues: "(1) moral, psychological, theological and other 'intrinsic' differences between women and men (apart from the obvious biological ones); (2) causal explanations of sex dominance, where it occurs; (3) the moral implications of sex roles, and the moral aspects of other issues of special relevance to women, e.g. abortion; and (4) possible means of engineering social change with respect to sex roles."—*p. i*. Cross-references are provided from the topical articles to the author entries. Bibliography; glossary; index.   HQ1115.W37

Women's studies encyclopedia / ed. by Helen Tierney. N.Y. : Greenwood, 1989–1991. 3 v.   **CC537**

Contents: v. 1, Views from the sciences; v. 2, Literature, arts, and learning; v. 3, History, religion, and philosophy.

Signed articles reflect a variety of feminist viewpoints and average 1,000–1,500 words. Intended for general readers, emphasizes U.S. experience with more attention to non-Western women in vols. 2 and 3. Some articles contain cross-references and many end with brief bibliographies. All volumes have lists of consultants and contributors, general indexes, and select bibliographies. Sample entries: v. 1, Differential socialization, Osteoporosis, Rape; v. 2 Chicana writers, Fiber arts, Hagiography, Women's colleges; v. 3, Witch craze, Dowry in India, Abolitionism, Settlement house movement.   HQ1115.W645

Dictionaries

Humm, Maggie. The dictionary of feminist theory. Columbus : Ohio State Univ. Pr., c1990. 278 p.   **CC538**

Cross-cultural and international in scope, although focus is on Anglo-American and French theory. Each entry provides definitions, commentary, and references to the 28-page bibliography which follows. Preface includes sections on aims, definitions, issues, criteria, and design.   HQ1115.H86

Kramarae, Cheris. A feminist dictionary / Cheris Kramarae and Paula A. Treichler. London ; Boston : Pandora Pr., 1985. 587 p.   **CC539**

Repr. : Chicago : Univ. of Illinois Pr., 1991, entitled *Amazons, bluestockings, and crones: a feminist dictionary*.

"Places women at the center and rethinks language from that crucially different perspective."—*p. 15*. A 22-page introduction, "Words on a feminist dictionary," provides useful background, rationale, and editorial information. Cross-referenced, English-language entries range in length from a few lines to several columns. Extensive 73-page bibliography.   HQ1115.K73

Mills, Jane. Womanwords : a dictionary of words about women. N.Y. : Free Pr. : Maxwell Macmillan International, 1992. 291 p.   **CC540**

Provides various meanings, historical background, cross-references, and related terms for over 300 words. Some entries a short paragraph or two; others four or five pages long. 21-page bibliography.   HQ1115.M546

Terminology

The Canadian feminist thesaurus = Le thésaurus féministe du Canada / comp. by the Canadian Women's Indexing Group (CWIG). Toronto, Ont. : Ontario Institute for Studies in Education, c1990. 683 p.   **CC541**

Compiled to help locate or organize written material on Canadian women and women's studies. Cross-disciplinary in emphasis; accessible to both generalists and specialists. Separate sections for English terms (3,321 terms) and French (3,192). Based on feminist literature 1972–82. Provides some scope notes, and includes "BT," "NT," "RT," and "UF" references. Advice to users precedes each section; a rotated index of terms follows the thesaurus. Supplementary lists of Canadian political parties, Native peoples' cultural and language groups, major legislation, and a combined list of countries with corresponding nationality names and adjectives. Brief 23-item bibliography. Used in preparing *Canadian feminist periodical index* (CC527).   Z695.1.W65C36

Dickstein, Ruth. Women in LC's terms : a thesaurus of Library of Congress subject headings relating to women / ed. by Ruth Dickstein, Victoria A. Mills, and Ellen J. Waite. Phoenix : Oryx, 1988. 221 p.   **CC542**

Lists more than 3,500 subject headings and cross-references pertaining to women, derived from a review of all the headings in the Dec. 1983 printing of *Library of Congress subject headings* (AK220 note). Terms are arranged in a main alphabetical list, then under the 11 sections prescribed in *A women's thesaurus* (CC543). Five appendixes: Free-floating subdivisions; Free-floating subdivisions used under classes of persons; Subdivision pattern headings for names of individual authors; Free-floating subdivisions used under names of persons; Library of Congress call numbers assigned to women and topics relating to women.   Z695.1.W65D53

A women's thesaurus : an index of language used to describe and locate information by and about women / ed. by Mary Ellen S. Capek. N.Y. : Harper & Row, c1987. 1052 p.   **CC543**

Repr. : N.Y. : Perennial Library, 1989.

"A project of the National Council for Research on Women and the Business and Professional Women's Foundation."

A much-needed compilation, containing more than 5,000 terms recommended for indexing and subject cataloging of works relating to women. Terms are arranged in alphabetical, rotated, and hierarchical displays, and under 11 broad subject groups (e.g., History and social change; International women). Entries include references to broader, narrower, and related terms; variant forms; and scope notes. There are separate lists of "use/do not use" terms and of delimiters (generic search terms or proper nouns—e.g., historical periods, national and regional descriptors). An introductory section describes thesaurus construction and applications, form of entry, guidelines, etc. Provides rosters of contributors and members of the Thesaurus Task Force, cites the lists that were combined to form the thesaurus, and lists test sites. Brief bibliography.   Z695.1.W65W65

Quotations

The last word : a treasury of women's quotes / [comp. by] Carolyn Warner ; foreword by Erma Bombeck. Englewood Cliffs, N.J. : Prentice Hall, c1992. 363 p.   **CC544**

In 40 broad subject chapters, each with an introduction. Sample authors include: Rosa Parks, Rita Mae Brown, Sally Ride, Muriel Rukeyser, Marian Wright Edelman. Biographical index, alphabetical by name, provides birth and death dates and brief identification (country, occupation). Name index.   PN6084.W6W37

Directories

Burnham, Linda. Women of color : organizations & projects : a national directory. Berkeley, Calif. : Women of Color Resource Center, c1991. 100 p.   **CC545**

Includes organizations which are "founded by, are led by, and whose staff, membership, or constituency is predominantly women of color."—*Introd.* Covers national organizations but excludes individual chapters. Uses terminology and language of the organizations themselves. Entries (by group name) include address, phone, contact name, goals, purpose, publications, activities, etc. Indexes for race/ethnicity/nationality and issue (e.g., domestic violence, health).   HQ1904.B87

Directory of financial aids for women. 1st ed. (1978)– . Santa Barbara, Calif. : Reference Service Pr., 1978– . Biennial.   **CC546**

Prepared by Gail Ann Schlachter, 1978– . Frequency varies; biennial since 1985/86 ed.

Describes 1,901 (1993–95 ed.) scholarships, grants, loans, fellowships, internships, and awards, for women at high school and higher education levels. Arranged by award type (e.g., scholarships), then by award name. Entries provide address, phone, purpose, eligibility, financial data, duration, number awarded, deadline. Lists address and phone for state sources of educational benefits. Program title, sponsoring organization, geographic, subject, and calendar indexes.   LB2338.D564

Directory of Third World women's publications. Santiago, Chile : Isis International, [1990?]. 197 p. : ill.   **CC547**

This illustrated directory, organized alphabetically by title within country or region, includes periodicals, pamphlets, papers, bulletins, reports, directories, and catalogs. There are sections for Africa, Asia, Caribbean, Central America, South America, Middle East, Pacific, International. Entries provide title, publishing group, acronym, address, subjects and issues, objectives, language, frequency, level of action (local, national, international), type of organization, and activities. No indexes.   HQ1870.9.Z99D57

Directory of women's studies programs & library resources / ed. by Beth Stafford. Phoenix : Oryx, 1990. 154 p.   **CC548**

Reflects data collected 1987–88 from U.S. colleges and universities. More than 400 entries, arranged by state and city, provide name, address, coordinator, descriptions of courses, degrees, library resources, names of women's studies faculty. Indexes by institution, degree offered, library collections, and subject area.   HQ1181.U5D57

DWM : a directory of women's media. 1988– . N.Y. : National Council for Research on Women, 1988– . Annual.   **CC549**

Title varies: 1988–91, *Directory of women's media*. Publisher varies: 1988–91 publ. by Women's Institute for Freedom of the Press, Wash., D.C. 1992 ed. (16th ed.) comp. by Dawn Henry and ed. by Susan A. Hallgarth.

Numbering continues that of *Index/directory of women's media* (1972–87), publ. by Women's Institute for Freedom of the Press.

Arranged by topic (e.g., periodicals, news services, film/video/cable, art, bookstores, libraries/archives/museums, music). Entries provide name, address, phone, contact, description, services, programs, publications. Separate indexes for publications and organizations, individuals, and states/countries. Use both the main listings and the 32-page additional resource list in the appendix.   RA644.A25G843

The guide to resources on women and AIDS. May 1990– . Wash. : Center for Women Policy Studies, c1989– . Annual.   **CC550**

Entries arranged alphabetically by program name within each state. Describes program, staff, age of program, geographic area served, services, women served, budget, key issues, and materials. Introductory material summarizes background, problems, and issues. Appendix includes questionnaire.   RA644.A25G843

International centers for research on women. 1985– .
N.Y. : National Council for Research on Women, 1985– . Annual.   **CC551**
  Alphabetical by country. Entries provide name, address, and contact. U.S. centers follow, alphabetical by state, with phone and fax numbers added.   HQ1180.I57

Women scholars in women's studies / comp. by Women's
Studies Progam, University of Illinois at Urbana-Champaign.
Rev. ed. Champaign, Ill. : Committee on Institutional Cooperation, 1987. 173 p.   **CC552**
  "Expands and updates the 1982 listing of women scholars active in women's studies at institutions affiliated with the Committee on Institutional Cooperation (CIC)."—*Introd.* Includes degrees, employment history, research interests, subjects taught, publications, and community involvement (the latter new to this edition). Entries are alphabetical and reflect data collected in 1985. Separate institution, disciplines and fields, and subject indexes.   HQ1181.U5W55

Women's information directory. 1st ed.– . Detroit : Gale,
c1993– . Biennial.   **CC553**
  Comprehensive source covering regional, state, local, and national organizations; battered women services; displaced homemakers services; libraries; museums and galleries; scholarships; awards; research centers; top women-owned businesses; journals; newsletters; videos; electronic resources; and much more. Typical entry provides name, address, phone, contact, description. Chapters organized alphabetically by state, then by city or town. Master name and subject index.
                                                          HV1445.W67

Women's movements of the world : an international directory and reference guide / ed. by Sally Shreir. Phoenix : Oryx, 1988. 384 p.   **CC554**
  "A guide to the current status of women's issues and organizations throughout the world."—*Pref.* For each of 184 countries arranged in alphabetical order, provides an introductory section (including statistics) on key topics (e.g., political participation, education, marital and divorce rights, the workforce, contraception, and abortion), followed by an alphabetized list of "all major nationally-operating organizations and a selection of lesser groups."—*Introd.* Separate annotated list of 81 international organizations. Brief bibliography; no index.
                                                          HQ1883.W63

Handbooks

Aaron, Titus E. Sexual harassment in the workplace : a guide
to the law and a research overview for employers and employees / by Titus E. Aaron, with Judith A. Isaksen. Jefferson, N.C. : McFarland, 1993. 215 p.   **CC555**
  18 chapters discuss background, the rising awareness of the issue, element of power, litigation process, curbing false accusations, theories of liability, etc. Appendix A describes legal procedures and results for a particular order case. Appendix B is a brief glossary of terms. 13-p. bibliography. General index.   KF3467.A915

Beere, Carole A. Gender roles : a handbook of tests and
measures. N.Y. : Greenwood, c1990. 575 p.   **CC556**
                                                          HM253.B43

——————— Sex and gender issues : a handbook of tests
and measures. N.Y. : Greenwood, 1990. 605 p.   **CC557**
  These titles jointly constitute a revision of Beere's *Women and women's issues : a handbook of tests and measures*, 1979. *Gender roles* lists 211 titles in 11 chapters, updating for the period 1979–88 information concerning tests and measures related to gender roles (e.g., stereotypes, marital and parental roles, attitudes toward gender roles). *Sex and gender issues* lists 197 titles in nine chapters, updating for 1979–88 information concerning tests and measures related to sex and gender issues (e.g., heterosexuality, contraception, abortion, pregnancy). Both volumes are indexed.   BF692.B38

Brennan, Shawn. Resourceful woman / Shawn Brennan, Julie
Winklepleck; with Gina Renée Misiroglu and Marie J. MacNee. Detroit : Visible Ink, c1994. 833 p. : ill.   **CC558**
  Combines annotated directory entries with additional offerings in the margins: quotations, poetry, photographs, article reprints, essays, short fiction. Covers organizations, publications, institutions, print and nonprint resources, etc. under broad subject chapters, which begin with 2–3 introductions. The table of contents provides the only subject access. Some of the sidebar offerings are indexed. Sample chapters: politics, youth, kinship, global issues, work. The unusual organization could make specific subject searching difficult; for example, the education chapter lists fellowships, newsletters, archives, colleges, associations, publishers, awards, etc. in a single alphabet. Name index.
                                                          HQ1115.B83

Clardy, Andrea. Words to the wise : a writer's guide to feminist and lesbian periodicals & publishers. 4th rev. ed., updated and expanded. Ithaca, N.Y. : Firebrand Books, 1993. 52 p. : ill. (Firebrand sparks pamphlet, no. 1).   **CC559**
  1st ed., 1986; 3rd ed., 1990.
  Covers some 165 presses, periodicals, and resources. Focuses upon explicitly feminist and lesbian publishers and material, specifically upon material useful to a writer. Alphabetically lists and describes presses; provides chart indicating relevant data by press, e.g., year started, numbers of books in print, if unsolicited manuscripts accepted, if royalties paid, etc. Also lists academic and trade presses, then periodical titles. Relevant information for periodicals also presented in handy chart format. Resources list describes various organizations, centers, and projects.   Z286.F45C55

Eichler, Margrit. Nonsexist research methods : a practical
guide. Boston : Allen & Unwin, c1988. 183 p.   **CC560**
  For researchers, teachers, and college level students. Attempts to order the diverse materials which critique sexism, breaking the topic into seven problems intended to serve as tools in recognizing and correcting sexism in research. Seven chapters cover sexism in general, delineate the seven problems and provide examples, and provide guidelines for nonsexist research. Appendix includes problem checklist with references to specific sections of text providing descriptions, examples, identification, and resolution. Index.   H62.E453

Eisaguirre, Lynne. Sexual harassment : a reference handbook. Santa Barbara, Calif. : ABC-Clio, c1993. 217 p. : ill.
                                                          CC561
  Briefly summarizes four perspectives: feminist, legal, management, and male. Provides chronology of events, landmark publications, legal decisions, and 29 biographical sketches. Includes data on state laws, prevalence, costs, harasser profiles. Descriptive directory entries for organizations. Includes print and nonprint sources. Glossary; general index.   KF4758.E36

Franck, Irene M. The women's desk reference / by Irene
Franck & David Brownstone. N.Y. : Viking, 1993. 840 p. : ill.
                                                          CC562
  Alphabetically arranged entries, some several pages in length, provide definitions and descriptions. Covers individuals, organizations, social issues, medical conditions. Includes diagrams, guidelines, and many boxed "Help, information, and action guides." Appendix includes several women's rights documents, dates for international voting rights, U.S. and U.N. data, list of 75 books by women, and a chronology of women's rights (1701–1992).   HQ1236.5.U6F73

Nelson, Carol. Women's market handbook : understanding
and reaching today's most powerful consumer group. Detroit : Gale, c1994. 366 p. : ill.   **CC563**
  Guides students and professionals in targeting women as a consumer market. Utilizes specific cases and examples, based on the author's experience as advertising consultant and copywriter. 15 chapters, each with a sequence of short paragraphs interspersed with photos of ads, tables and charts, quotations, checklists, questions to the reader. Topics include: specific audiences (e.g., feminists, grandmothers, executives), use of humor, shopping patterns, most effective media, etc.

Useful "mini sourcebook" provides description, address, phone for consultants, directories, electronic resources, periodicals, organizations, newsletters, research centers, top 25 women-owned businesses, and videos. Statistical section provides tables for education, income level, child care, leisure activities, etc. Bibliography; general index.
HF5415.N3495

The new our bodies, ourselves : a book by and for women / Boston Women's Health Book Collective. Updated and expanded for the 1990s. N.Y. : Simon & Schuster, c1992. 751 p. : ill. **CC564**

First published, 1969; previous ed., 1984.

Comprehensive and thorough, useful for self-help, research purposes, and as resource for training. Provides social and political analyses and practical information. Lists many references for articles, books, audiovisuals, organizations, newsletters, bookstores, archives, and presses and publishers. Organizes material into 27 broad topical chapters. Sample topics include body image, relationships, sexuality, AIDS/HIV, reproductive technologies, politics of health care, violence against women, childbirth, and environmental and occupational health. Includes charts, photographs, detailed illustrations. General index.

§ Also from the Collective: *Ourselves, growing older* (CC95).
RA778.N67

The rights of women : the basic ACLU guide to a woman's rights / Susan Deller Ross ... [et al.]. 3rd ed., completely rev. and up-to-date. Carbondale : Southern Illinois Univ. Pr., c1993. 317 p. **CC565**

1st ed., 1973; 2nd ed., 1983.

Written for nonspecialists, and in a question and answer format, this manual addresses employment, reproductive freedom, the military, parenting and work, pregnancy, homelessness, and other topics. In 13 chapters, each with extensive endnotes. KF478.Z9R67

Schneider, Dorothy. The ABC-CLIO companion to women in the workplace / Dorothy Schneider and Carl J. Schneider. Santa Barbara, Calif. : ABC-Clio, c1993. 371 p. : ill. **CC566**

Addresses history of paid employment of any form; covers colonial period to present. 17-page introductory essay with endnotes. Entries, arranged alphabetically, describe individuals, events, concepts, organizations, and court cases. *See* and *see also* references. References provided for each entry, corresponding to full bibliography which preceeds the index. Many photographs. Separate chronology of events (1714–1993). General index. HD6095.S34

Segrave, Kerry. Women serial and mass murderers : a worldwide reference, 1580 through 1990. Jefferson, N.C. : McFarland & Co., c1992. 327 p. **CC567**

For general readers. Profiles 87 women, over 45 from the U.S., who have killed at least three people, not including themselves if suicide was involved. Each entry begins with birth and death dates, place of birth, her age and the year(s) of the killings, number of victims, and method. The story follows, as do sources lists, which include mostly newspaper and magazine articles, some monographs, and reference books. Index. HV6515.S44

Sisterhood is global : the international women's movement anthology / comp., ed., and with an introduction by Robin Morgan. Garden City, N.Y. : Anchor Press/Doubleday, 1984. 815 p. **CC568**

Reprint: N.Y. : Anchor Books, 1990.

Although dated, this source remains very useful, providing data and policies not easily found elsewhere, and illustrating needed elements in future research. Chapters for 70 countries and the U.N. provide comprehensive demographic data, including such elements as women's wages as a percentage of men's; women in government; women percentages in labor force (by sector, occupation), etc. Describes policies on marriage, divorce, contraception, illegitimacy, incest, rape, prostitution, sexual harassment, etc. Chapters also include sections on herstory (legends, folktales) and mythography; followed by

an essay by a native feminist and a further readings list. Brief author biographies; glossary; detailed index. Bibliography, alphabetical by country, then by author. HQ1154.S54

Snyder, Paula. The European women's almanac. N.Y. : Columbia Univ. Pr., c1992. 399 p. : ill. **CC569**

Chapters for 26 countries include map; data on vital statistics, lesbian rights, child care, abortion, parental leave, state benefits, employment, unions, politics, education, etc. Omits Baltic states and the former Soviet Union. Chapters provide addresses, sources. 24 comparative tables rank countries on population; spending; birth, death, marriage, and divorce rates; political offices, etc. HQ1587.S69

Women and HIV/AIDS : an international resource book : information, action, and resources on women and HIV/AIDS, reproductive health and sexual relations / written and ed. by Marge Berer and Sunanda Ray. London : Pandora Pr., 1993. 383 p. : ill. **CC570**

Publ. in association with Appropriate Health Resources and Technologies Action Group (AHRTAG).

An illustrated handbook for general readers, professionals, activists. The first 11 chapters summarize medical and social issues (gender differences, transmission, prevention, perceptions and attitudes, testing, counseling, etc.). Chapter 12 contains nine personal histories; Chapter 13 describes 15 women-centered projects or services around the world; Chapter 14 describes networks and organizations, grouped by region and country. Bibliography is grouped by chapter; general index. RA644.A25W6

Women online : research in women's studies using online databases / Steven D. Atkinson, Judith Hudson, editors. N.Y. : Haworth Pr., c1990. 420 p. (Haworth series on library and information science, 3). **CC571**

Includes 17 signed chapters, each with bibliographies, that address the challenges involved in locating feminist scholarship online. Covers searching in broad disciplines (e.g., social sciences, law, biomedical, humanities); in various database types (e.g., bibliographic, cited reference); and on specific groups (lesbians, women of color, women in developing countries). Chapters address database coverage, terminology, comparisons, and indexing consistency; many examples included. Appendix lists and describes 78 databases and database vendors. No indexes. HQ1180.W675b

Chronologies

Carabillo, Toni. Feminist chronicles, 1953–1993 / Toni Carabillo, Judith Meuli, June Bundy Csida. Los Angeles : Women's Graphic, c1993. 306 p. : ill. **CC572**

An excerpt from a larger work in progress, *Feminist chronicles of the 20th century.* Pt. 1 consists of a narrative chronology, illustrated with pictures of political buttons. Pt. 2 provides a year-by-year chronological chart, including U.S. and NOW presidents; major events; lifestyle, economic, religious, media, and political issues; and a unique section on backlash. Includes many photographs. A seven-page epilogue covers 1993. Pt. 3 consists of documents: e.g., NOW's statement of purpose, ERA position paper (1967), Homemakers' bill of rights (1979), Lesbian rights (1917), etc. Brief bibliography. Full-page author biographies include photographs. Detailed general index.
HQ1420.C33

Clark, Judith Freeman. Almanac of American women in the 20th century. N.Y. : Prentice Hall, c1987. 274 p. : ill. **CC573**

Each of nine chapters covers one decade in this overview of U.S. women's history, 1900–87. Chronologies of events, brief biographies, and topic essays are interspersed. Events are categorized by topics such as education, reform, military, arts and culture, politics, and labor. Photographs; general index. HQ1420.C55

Guidebooks

Tinling, Marion. Women remembered : a guide to landmarks of women's history in the United States. N.Y. : Greenwood, 1986. 796 p. : ill.   **CC574**

Indexes the commemorations to women throughout the U.S., such as monuments; park, school, building, or street names; historical markers; birthplaces and homes. Omits living women or women described primarily in relation to famous men, as well as generic statues to nameless heroines or occupations, e.g., nurses, nuns, pioneers. Attempts to include sites that can still be viewed. Organized by geographic region: New England, South, Mid-Atlantic, Midwest, and West. Entries arranged by state within each region, within each state by city or town, and within the city in alphabetical order by woman's name. Entries include birth and death dates, historical dates, alternate names, cross-references, and descriptions of the woman's life and the commemoration. Chapters conclude with reference notes. Appendixes list women by occupation or activity and provide chronology of significant dates. Four-page bibliographic essay; general index.   E159.T56

Biography

Echols, Anne. An annotated index of medieval women / by Anne Echols and Marty Williams. N.Y. : M. Wiener Publ., c1992. 635 p.   **CC575**

Brief biographies for some 1,500 medieval women living between 800–1500, arranged alphabetically by first name. Covers some 30 countries and a variety of social classes and activities. Instructions for use, p. xiii–xxiv. The main index, listing women alphabetically by name, provides life dates; countries; characteristics, accomplishments; up to ten subject descriptors; and references. Separate indexes for dates, countries, biographical categories, names/titles/estates/regions/cities. Lists of sources, alphabetical by author; shorter list of sources without authors, alphabetical by title.   CT3220.A56

Famous American women : a biographical dictionary from colonial times to the present / ed. by Robert McHenry. N.Y. : Dover, 1993. 482 p.   **CC576**

Reprint of *Liberty's women* (Springfield, Mass. : Merriam, 1980), adding death dates up to 1993.

Alphabetically arranged biographical sketches describe the lives of 1,035 women: "artists and astronomers, church leaders and criminals, feminists and frontier heroines, poets and politicians."—*Introd.* Entries, in small, dense text, average 400 words and include data, place of birth (if known), education, special circumstances, career, accomplishments, death date or current activities if living. Careers index groups names under various occupations, except for the heading of "Indians," under which seven women are listed. Proper names index.   HQ1412.F35

Hardy, Gayle J. American women civil rights activists : biobibliographies of 68 leaders, 1825–1992. Jefferson, N.C. : McFarland, c1993. 479 p.   **CC577**

Interpreting civil rights broadly, this impressive work profiles those working on behalf of African Americans, Latinos, Native Americans, homosexuals, children, adoptees, older adults, women, people with disabilities, prisoners, and others. Alphabetical arrangement by activist's name. Entries provide place of birth, education, chronology of events and achievements, family, pseudonyms or alternate names, ethnicity, and influences. Separate bibliographies of materials by and about the activists, organized by type of material (books, films, theses, plays, etc.) Omits foreign language works, newspaper articles, book reviews. Contributions by 13 scholars. Preface includes chronological chart including activists' birth and death dates. Separate appendixes list women by birthplace, date of birth, ethnicity, field of activity, geographic location, occupation, religion, schools attended, tribal membership. Cross-references for alternate names. Detailed general index.   JC599.U5H273

Jackson, Guida. Women who ruled. Santa Barbara, Calif. : ABC-Clio, c1990. 190 p. : ill.   **CC578**

An illustrated encyclopedia covering "all women rulers, de facto rulers, and constitutional monarchs, living or deceased, of the world's kingdoms, islands, empires, nations, and tribes since the beginning of recorded history."—*Pref.* An eight-page introduction provides historical context for regions of Africa, India and the Middle East, Central Asia, China and the Far East, Polynesia and the Western Hemisphere, and Europe. Includes a useful chronology of rulers by century. Entries, arranged alphabetically by ruler, begin with name, title, place of rule, and years of rule and vary in length from a short paragraph to several columns. Separate list of illustrations; six-page bibliography.

                                    D107.J33

Read, Phyllis J. The book of women's firsts : break-through achievements of almost 1,000 American women / Phyllis J. Read, Bernard L. Witlieb. N.Y. : Random House, c1992. 511 p. : ill.   **CC579**

Arranged alphabetically by personal name. Includes entries for relevant organizations and some events not particular to an individual; e.g., the first sexually integrated jury. Entries average a half page, describing the "first" and summarizing the subject women's life. Topical index.   CT3260.R428

Women in North America : summaries of biographical articles in history journals / Pamela R. Byrne and Susan K. Kinnell, editors. Santa Barbara, Calif. : ABC-Clio, c1988. 146 p.   **CC580**

Includes U.S. and Canadian women, famous and unknown. Covers English-language works, 17th century to mid-1980s, providing 241 numbered entries from journals indexed by *America : history and life* (DB24). Entries provide name, bibliographic citation, and descriptive abstract, and are listed alphabetically by biographee. Detailed subject index includes regions, occupations, and terms for ethnic origin. Author index; list of periodical titles.   CT3260.W664

Atlases

Gibson, Anne. The women's atlas of the United States / Anne Gibson and Timothy Fast. N.Y. : Facts on File, c1986. 248 p. : maps in color ; 24 x 30 cm.   **CC581**

National level maps present statistical information on American women in seven categories: demographics, education, employment, family, health, crime, and politics. Comprehensive seven-page introduction explains the types of maps and how to read them, the data and its sources, and a caution about census statistics. Although most information is from the 1980s, some historical data is included. Notes to text listed separately. Includes bibliography for maps, suggestions for further reading, and general index.   G1201.E1G5

Seager, Joni. Women in the world : an international atlas / Joni Seager & Ann Olson ; ed. by Michael Kidron. N.Y. : Simon and Schuster, c1986. 128 p. : col. ill., maps in color ; 26 cm.   **CC582**

Unique compilation of maps dealing with information on women on a worldwide level. Arranged in ten chapters with 40 topics; each topic is covered by text, colored maps, and graphs or charts. Sample subjects: marriage and motherhood; work and resources; politics and protest. A country table provides statistical background for the maps; background notes list sources. Extensive bibliography; subject index.

                                    G1046.E1S4

Statistics

Statistical record of women worldwide / comp. and ed. by Linda Schmittroth. Detroit : Gale, c1991. 763 p. : ill.   **CC583**

Draws data from government documents, periodical literature, reports and studies, research centers, companies, organizations, etc. "Coverage is approximately 50% U.S. and 50% international."—*Pref.*

Organized in topical sections; entries give titles, brief explanatory notes, sources. Depending on availability of data, geographic scope ranges from city or state level to major world areas. List of sources; subject and geographic index.

§ *See also* Cynthia Taeuber's *Statistical handbook on women in America* (CG108). HQ1150.S73

WAC stats : the facts about women / ed. by Women's Action Coalition. 2nd updated and rev. ed. N.Y. : New Pr. : distr. by W.W. Norton, c1993. 64 p. **CC584**

A slim volume presenting statistics on abortion, AIDS, breast cancer, cosmetic surgery, eating disorders, homelessness, hysterectomy, menopause, osteoporosis, prison, rape, sex industry, sexual harassment, etc. Presents data in the form of statements, listed under alphabetically arranged topics. Lists sources for every topic. Index.
HQ1421.W33

The world's women, 1970–1990 : trends and statistics. N.Y. : United Nations, 1991. 120 p. : col. ill. (Social statistics and indicators. Series K, no. 8). **CC585**

Covers 178 countries. Eight-page overview precedes sections on families, households, education and training, health, childbearing, housing, settlements, environment, workforce, and the economy. Includes sidebar and boxed data, in addition to various graphs, tables, and charts. Provides aggregate numbers for regional and subregional levels. HQ1154.W95

Women in specific countries, regions, or ethnic groups

Annotated bibliography on women in development in Asia and the Pacific. Bangkok, Thailand : United Nations, Economic and Social Commission for Asia and the Pacific, 1988–89. 2 v. **CC586**

Contents: v. 1 covers up to 1986; v. 2, covers 1988–89.

Addresses development at national, sub-regional, regional, and international levels. Includes government publications and reports, monographs, research papers, training manuals, journal articles, and meeting reports. 249 entries, many with abstracts, arranged alphabetically by title. Includes keywords. Author/corporate body, country/subregion/region/area, and subject indexes. Z7964.A78A55

Bailey, Susan F. Women and the British empire : an annotated guide to sources. N.Y. : Garland, 1983. 185 p. (Themes in European expansion, v. 3 ; Garland reference library of social science, v. 159). **CC587**

In four main sections: wives of administrators; settlers; missionaries; native women. Each section begins with a lengthy bibliographic essay, concludes with critically annotated citations to primary and secondary sources, including unpublished materials. General index.
Z7964.G7B34

Bataille, Gretchen M. American Indian women : a guide to research / Gretchen M. Bataille, Kathleen M. Sands ; editorial assistant, Catherine Udall. N.Y. : Garland, 1991. 423 p.
CC588

Covers bibliographies and reference works in eight chapters: ethnography, cultural history, and social roles; politics and law; health, education, and employment; arts; literature; autobiography, biography, and interviews; and film and video. Offers 573 annotated references to English-language material about Native American women in the U.S. and Canada. Omits unpublished and hard to find material, as well as book reviews and most popular fiction. General index.
Z1209.2.N67B36

Bibliographic guide to studies on the status of women : development and population trends / Unesco. [Essex, Eng.] : Bowker ; N.Y. : UNIPUB, 1983. 292 p. **CC589**

A general introduction dealing with women's labor force participation, education, and demographics in Africa, the Arab states, Asia, Eastern Europe, Latin America, North America and western Europe is followed by annotated bibliographies on each region; these are subdivided by topic and include special journal issues and research institutes. Indexed by country, subject, and author. Z7963.E7B5

Bodman, Herbert L. Women in the Muslim world : a bibliography of books and articles primarily in the English language. Providence, R.I. : Assoc. for Middle East Women's Studies, 1991. 162 p. **CC590**

The first two chapters cover women and Islam and Arab women; the remainder are organized geographically by region. Entries are alphabetical by author, without annotations. Author and subject indexes.
Z7964.I74B63

Brady, Anna. Women in Ireland : an annotated bibliography. N.Y. : Greenwood, 1988. 478 p. (Bibliographies and indexes in women's studies, no. 6). **CC591**

Restricted to women of Irish ancestry whose lives were spent primarily in Ireland, those strongly connected to Irish affairs, or well-known figures. Includes 2,312 books, book chapters, articles, theses, memoirs, travel accounts, pamphlets, and correspondence; excludes fiction, poetry, and most literary criticism and newspaper items. Covers from the early Celtic period to the present. Entries arranged by author under subject categories (e.g., biography and autobiography; religion and witchcraft; revolutionary movements). English-language entries are annotated; author and subject indexes. Z7964.I73B7

Bullwinkle, Davis. African women : a general bibliography, 1976–1985. N.Y. : Greenwood, 1989. 334 p. (African special bibliographic series, no. 9). **CC592**

Entries are alphabetically arranged by author under 32 subject headings (e.g., Abortion, Education and training, Sexual mutilation/circumcision). Includes references not specific to a region or nation. No annotations. Appendixes include organizations, official names and capitals, and geographic and historical names. Author index.
Z7964.A3B84

———————— Women of eastern and southern Africa : a bibliography, 1976–1985. N.Y. : Greenwood, 1989. 545 p. (African special bibliographic series, no. 11). **CC593**

Lists entries by subject under regional and national headings; nations with a small number of entries are not divided by subject. Utilizes 34 subject headings (e.g., Apartheid and race relations, Sex roles, Status of women). Lists entries alphabetically by author within each category. No annotations; author index. Z7964.A337B84

———————— Women of northern, western, and central Africa : a bibliography, 1976–1985. N.Y. : Greenwood, 1989. 601 p. (African special bibliographic series, no. 10). **CC594**

Arranged by subject under regions or nations, using 33 subject subdivisions (e.g., Divorce, Equality and liberation, Slavery). Nations with a small number of entries are not subdivided. Lists entries alphabetically by author within categories; no annotations. Author index.
Z7964.A3B85

Byrne, Pamela R. Women in the Third World : a historical bibliography / Pamela R. Byrne, Suzanne R. Ontiveros, editors. Santa Barbara, Calif. : ABC-Clio Information Services, c1986. 152 p. (ABC-Clio research guides, 15). **CC595**

Organizes 601 citations with abstracts into six chapters covering general topics and specific regions of the world (Africa, Asia, Middle East, Pacific Region, Latin America, and the West Indies). Entries, arranged alphabetically by author within chapters, include articles from ABC-Clio's database, 1970–85. A rotated subject index provides a descriptor profile for each entry, including subject, geographic, and biographical terms and dates. Includes cross-references. Separate author index. Z7964.D44B96

Cabello-Argandoña, Roberto. The Chicana : a comprehensive bibliographic study / comp. and ed. by Roberto Cabello-Argandoña, Juan Gómez-Quiñones, Patricia Herrera Durán. Los Angeles : Aztlán Publ., c1976, 1975. 308 p. : ill. **CC596**

Lists 491 citations, some with evaluative or descriptive annotations, by format within 17 subject chapters. Covers books, periodical articles, journals, government publications, films, and serials. Brief introductions for each chapter. All entries are in English; some Spanish-language source material is included. Sample topics: women's movement, folk culture, discrimination in employment. Author and title indexes. Z1361.M4C245

Cantor, Aviva. The Jewish woman, 1900–1985 : a bibliography / partially annotated by Aviva Cantor with 1983–1986 citations comp. by Ora Hamelsdorf. [2nd ed.]. Fresh Meadows, N.Y. : Biblio Pr., 1987. 193 p. **CC597**

First publ. 1972.

Organized into two parts. Pt. 1 is comprised of a reprint of a 1979 edition, which covered 1900–1978, along with eight pages of corrections and additions, which were issued as supplements in 1981 and 1982. Pt. 2 contains the 2nd ed., which includes materials published 1980–85 and provides 11 pages of selected 1986 titles. Includes English-language books, articles, reference sources, poetry, anthologies, children's books, etc. International treatment of the Jewish woman as subject, including the Holocaust and resistance movements. Personal names index. Z7963.J4C36

Coles, Catherine M. Nigerian women in development : a research bibliography / by Catherine M. Coles and Barbara Entwisle, with the assistance of Margaret Hardner. Los Angeles : Crossroads Pr., c1986. 170 p. **CC598**

Covers social science literature, e.g., demography, anthropology, sociology, economics, and women's studies. Includes books, articles, book chapters, conference papers, theses, unpublished material, and reports, 1968–85. Organizes some 2,000 unannotated entries into 12 topical chapters, some on women's roles, others on development issues such as health and nutrition. Entries alphabetical by author within chapters. No indexes. Z7964.N6C65

Fan, Kok-sim. Women in Southeast Asia : a bibliography. Boston : G. K. Hall, 1982. 415 p. **CC599**

Groups 3,865 entries by broad subject and subdivided by country—Brunei, Burma, Indochina, Indonesia, Malaysia, Philippines, Singapore, and Thailand. Includes published and unpublished materials in English, Malay, Indonesian, Dutch, and French. Author index. Z7961.F35

Fenton, Thomas P. Women in the Third World : a directory of resources / comp. and ed. by Thomas P. Fenton and Mary J. Heffron. Maryknoll, N.Y. : Orbis Books, c1987. 141 p. : ill. **CC600**

Five chapters cover organizations, books, periodicals, pamphlets and articles, and audiovisual materials. In each chapter, annotated entries are followed by brief entry lists and lists of information sources. Organization, individuals, title, geographical area, and subject indexes. Z7964.D44F46

Gabaccia, Donna R. Immigrant women in the United States : a selectively annotated multidisciplinary bibliography. N.Y. : Greenwood, 1989. 325 p. (Bibliographies and indexes in women's studies, no. 9). **CC601**

Cites books, articles, and dissertations in English concerning immigrants of all periods and geographic origins. Entries are arranged alphabetically by author within 12 chapters: Bibliography, General works, Migration, Family, Work, Working together, Body, Mind, Cultural change, Biography, Autobiography, Fiction. Each chapter begins with a page of introductory comment. Separate author, person, group, and subject indexes. Z7164.I3G33

Green, Rayna. Native American women : a contextual bibliography. Bloomington : Indiana Univ. Pr., c1983. 120 p. **CC602**

Contains 672 annotated entries, arranged alphabetically by author. A 20-page introduction surveys the topics. Although the earliest entry appeared in 1620, most titles listed were published since the 1920s. Books, periodicals, firms, audio recordings, dissertations and government publications are included. Chronological and subject indexes. Z1209.2.N67G75

Hauck, Philomena. Sourcebook on Canadian women. Ottawa : Canadian Library Association, c1979. 111 p. : ill. **CC603**

Includes English-language books, periodicals, pamphlets, and audiovisuals published or produced in Canada. Organizes entries into chapters covering women's rights, law, day care, work, health, biography, literature, children's books, periodicals, audiovisuals, poetry, and bibliographies. Many illustrations and graphics. Most material published in the 1970s. Includes publisher addresses. Author and title index. Z7964.C36H38

Huber, Kristina R. Women in Japanese society : an annotated bibliography of selected English language materials. Westport, Conn. : Greenwood, 1992. 484 p. (Bibliographies and indexes in women's studies, no. 16). **CC604**

Attempts comprehensive coverage, including translations of original and 19th- and 20-century sources, addressing all aspects of the lives of Japanese women. Includes books, book chapters, scholarly journal articles, published conference papers, and popular magazine articles published between 1841–1990. Excludes newspapers, unpublished manuscripts, juvenile literature audiovisuals, dissertations. 2,311 numbered entries, with brief annotations, arranged alphabetically by author, then chronologically within chapters or chapter subtopics. Chronology of historical periods (552–present). Indexes. Z7964.J3H82

Joel, Susan. Women factory workers in less developed countries : an annotated bibliography. [East Lansing, Mich.] : Michigan State Univ., c1990. 83 p. (Working papers/Women in International Development, 214). **CC605**

Covers 1967–89. Lists about 600 citations in three sections covering women in transnational employment, transnational corporations, and Third World women and work. Emphasizes processing areas such as Southeast and East Asia, Latin America, and Mexico. Arranges entries alphabetically by author or title; some include annotations. No indexes. Z7963.E7J64

Joint Bank-Fund Library. Women and development : articles, books, and research papers / indexed in the Joint World Bank-International Monetary Fund Library, Washington, D.C. Boston : G.K. Hall, 1987. 181 p. **CC606**

"An earlier version of this bibliography was distributed at the World Conference on the United Nations Decade for Women, Nairobi, Kenya, in 1985"—Introd.

Entries for subjects, titles, and names in a single alphabetical arrangement. Many entries have brief descriptions in addition to bibliographic citations. Covers 1977–86. Z7963.E18J65

Kanner, Barbara. Women in English social history, 1800–1914 : a guide to research. N.Y. : Garland, 1987–1990. 3 v. (Garland reference library of social science, v. 155, 408–409). **CC607**

Vols. 1 (6,000 entries) and 2 (5,000 entries) list books, periodical articles, critical reviews, theses, and dissertations on broad topics such as marriage and the family, sickness and health care, law, religion and spiritualism, and education (v. 1); and employment, philanthropy, crime and deviance, sexual issues, natural and social sciences, and women's rights (v. 2). In each section, entries are arranged chronologically, some with annotations. A 62-page general index is printed in both volumes. Vol. 3 contains 776 annotated entries in two sections, Introduction and Autobiographical writings. No subject or title indexes. Z7964.G7K36

Knaster, Meri. Women in Spanish America : an annotated bibliography from pre-conquest to contemporary times. Boston : G.K. Hall, c1977. 696 p. **CC608**

More than 2,500 items in classed arrangement, with author and subject indexes. Unpublished doctoral dissertations and master's theses are separately listed without annotations. A geographic index would have been helpful. Z7964.L3K525

Koh, Hesung Chun. Korean and Japanese women : an analytic bibliographical guide / ed. by Hesung Chun Koh with contributions from Maureen Donovan, Kathleen Molony, and the HRAF Korea Project staff. Westport, Conn. : Greenwood, 1982. 903 p. ; maps. **CC609**

Some 600 items in a wide variety of formats, issued between 1789 and 1979 in the Korean, Japanese, and English languages, are listed first by historical period and then by subject. Annotated entries. Coverage for Japan is selective. Indexed. Z7964.K6K63

Meghdessian, Samira Rafidi. The status of the Arab woman : a select bibliography / comp. ... under the auspices of the Institute for Women's Studies in the Arab World, Beirut University College, Lebanon. Westport, Conn. : Greenwood, 1980. 176 p. **CC610**

A bibliography of more than 1,600 entries, primarily English- and French-language books, articles, conference proceedings, master's theses, doctoral dissertations, and bibliographies, most published 1950–79. Arrangement is by general subjects and individual countries, with no subject subdivision under country. Author and broad subject index. Z7964.A7M43

Oshana, Maryann. Women of color : a filmography of minority and Third World women. N.Y. : Garland, 1985. 338 p. : ill. (Garland reference library of social science, v. 173). **CC611**

Covers English-language films, 1930–83, whose characters include a woman of color. Titles selected to show variety and types of roles. Omits silent films. Entries, alphabetical by film title, provide, when available, production company, running time,year of release, producer, director, screenwriter, cameraperson, editor, music director, principal cast members, and ethnic classification. Indexes for actress, director, and minority/Third World classification. Photographs. Z5784.M9O84

Pandit, Harshida. Women of India : an annotated bibliography. N.Y. : Garland, 1985. 278 p. (Garland reference library of social science, v. 152). **CC612**

An introductory essay reviews demographics and legal rights. 1,119 numbered entries are grouped by subject or format (legal status, social problems, art and culture, films, etc.) and arranged within categories alphabetically by author. Gives scope notes for each category. Author index. Z7964.I5P36

Raccagni, Michelle. The modern Arab woman : a bibliography. Metuchen, N.J. : Scarecrow, 1978. 262 p. **CC613**

Nearly 3,000 books, articles, reports, and dissertations in Western languages and Arabic are grouped in general or country sections, then subdivided by more detailed subject areas. Some titles are briefly annotated. Author and broad subject index. Z7964.A7R32

Redfern, Bernice. Women of color in the United States : a guide to the literature. N.Y. : Garland, 1989. 156 p. (Garland reference library of social science, v. 469). **CC614**

A classed list of 636 annotated entries covering African Americans, Asian Americans, Hispanics, and Native Americans. Entries are arranged alphabetically by author within topics, which include biography, autobiography, education, employment, literature and the arts, history and politics. Includes books, essays, indexes, articles, and dissertations, most published since 1975. Author and subject indexes. Z7964.U49R4

Sakala, Carol. Women of South Asia : a guide to resources. Millwood, N.Y. : Kraus Internat., 1980. 517 p. **CC615**

In two parts: pt. 1, Published resources, is a classified, annotated bibliography of about 4,600 Western-language books, essays, articles, serials, dissertations, and audiovisual materials for the areas of India, Pakistan, Bangladesh, Sri Lanka, and Nepal; pt. 2, Libraries, archives, and other local resources, is a series of reports by individual scholars on libraries, government archives, and records of women's organizations in India, Pakistan, Bangladesh, and Sri Lanka. Author and subject indexes. Z7964.S65S23

Simmons, Donita Vasiti. Women in the South Pacific : a bibliography / comp. and ed. by Donita Vasiti Simmons, Sin Joan Yee. Suva : Univ. of the South Pacific, Library, 1982. 124 p. (University of the South Pacific. Library. Selected publication, no. 10). **CC616**

Includes monographs, serials, theses, reprints, photocopies, some newspapers, and unpublished papers. Organizes entries into 14 subject areas, divided geographically by country, alphabetically arranged. Topics include roles, sociology, anthropology, economics, law, health, religion, education, literature and the arts, sports, biography, communications, appropriate technology, associations. Covers through 1981. No annotations. Three "annexes" include bibliographies and handbooks; periodical titles and addresses; periodicals cited. Name index. Z7964.O25S55

Stoner, K. Lynn. Latinas of the Americas : a source book. N.Y. : Garland, 1989. 692 p. (Garland reference library of social science, v. 363). **CC617**

"Includes both published and unpublished research on women in Spanish-, Portuguese-, and French-speaking Latin America, as well as on Hispanic American women in the United States."—*Pref.* 15 topical chapters, each consisting of an essay in English followed by a bibliography alphabetically arranged by author. Bibliographies cover 1977–86 and include works in English, Spanish, Portuguese, French, and other languages. Chapters include such topics as biography, feminist studies, religion, development, law. Author, country/region, and subject indexes. Z7964.L3S76

Vyas, Anju. Women's studies in India : information sources, services, and programmes / comp. by Anju Vyas, Sunita Singh. Newbury Park, [Calif.] : Sage Publications, 1993. 257 p. **CC618**

Includes a wide variety of resources—reference sources such as bibliographies, directories, handbooks, indexes, and statistical and biographical sources; periodical titles published by women in India; scholarly and popular titles; and newsletters. Represents a variety of languages, including English. Lists 20 years of Indian women's studies conferences and seminars. Includes doctoral dissertations, government documents, government programs, women's studies courses, women's organizations, research centers, networks, and publishers. Lists sources of funding for women's projects, domestic and foreign and audiovisual and popular art materials that represent women's issues. Index. HQ1181.I4V93

Wei, Karen T. Women in China : a selected and annotated bibliography. Westport, Conn. : Greenwood, 1984. 250 p. (Bibliographies and indexes in women's studies, no. 1). **CC619**

More than 1,100 citations to Western-language sources are presented in topical arrangement. Focuses on China and Taiwan from the mid-19th century to 1984. Separate chapters on bibliographies and special journal issues. Author and title indexes. Z7964.C5W44

Weitz, Margaret Collins. Femmes : recent writings on French women. Boston : G.K. Hall, 1985. 245 p. **CC620**

Annotated entries focus on French monographs of 1970–79 and are arranged by subject; earlier works (1830–1969) are listed by author without annotations. Lengthy chapter introductions and annotations; subject, author, and title indexes. Z7964.F8W44

Women and development : an annotated bibliography, 1990–1992. Amsterdam : Royal Tropical Institute, Dept. of Information and Documentation, 1992. 206 p. **CC621**

Based on *Abstracts on rural development in the tropics*, 5 no. 1–7 no. 4. Contains 539 references for Jan. 1990–Aug. 1992, arranged in 19 subject categories concerning human resources, education, employment, division of labor, demography, health, environment, conservation. Numbered entries provide citation, language, subject headings, and descriptive abstract. Subject, geographical, project name, and author indexes.

A 1988 volume covered Oct. 1985–Oct. 1987.

HQ1240.5.D44W63

Women in development : a resource guide for organization and action / ISIS Women's International Information and Communication Service. Philadelphia : New Society Publishers, c1984. 225 p. : ill. **CC622**

Essays focus on five issues: multinationals, rural development, health, education and communication, and migration and tourism. Subtopics include food production and appropriate technology. Resource lists follow each chapter and include organizations, reference tools, research centers, periodicals, and bibliographies. Numerous graphics and photographs, but no indexes. HQ1240.5.D44W663

Women of color and Southern women : a bibliography of social science research 1975 to 1988. Memphis, Tenn. : Center for Research on Women, Memphis State Univ., c1988. **CC623**

Andrea Timberlake, ed.

Includes articles, books, newsletters, working papers, dissertations, and conference proceedings. Six main sections: culture, education, employment, family, health, and political activism/social movements, subarranged by ethnic group (African American, Asian American, Latina, Native American) with added categories for women of color and southern women. Entries are listed alphabetically by author within subgroups. Relevant keywords from Mary Ellen Capek, *A women's thesaurus* (CC543) appear with every entry. Author index; keyword index.

————. *Annual supplement* (1989– , publ. 1988– .) Each follow the same format as the original work, adding some 900 new entries. Nos. 1–2, 1989–90, ed. by Andrea Timberlake; 1991/92 ed. by Lynn Weber [et al.].

The women of England from Anglo-Saxon times to the present : interpretive bibliographical essays / ed. with an introd. by Barbara Kanner. Hamden, Conn. : Archon Books, 1979. 429 p. **CC624**

Bibliographic essays by contributing scholars on women in specific periods of English history (e.g., Anglo-Saxon, Norman, Plantagenet, 18th century) or specific aspects of English women's studies (e.g., Women under the law in medieval England, Demographic contributions to the history of Victorian women, Using novels to study Victorian women). Includes references to both primary and secondary sources. Subject index; bibliographies at the end of each chapter are arranged alphabetically. HQ1599.E5W65

Women, race, and ethnicity : a bibliography / project directors: Susan Searing, Linda Shult; eds.: Linda Shult, Susan Searing, Elli Lester-Massman ... [et al.]. Madison : Univ. of Wisconsin System Women's Studies Librarian, 1991. 202 p. **CC625**

Offers nearly 2,500 entries, most from the 1980s, "on women of non-WASP background in the United States.—*Introd.* Organized by topic with subsections for: Asian and Pacific American, Black, Euro-American, Indian, Jewish, and Latina women. Introductory pages discuss terminology. Excludes critical articles on individual authors. Includes print and audiovisual materials. Lists nonprint distributors, address, and phone. Detailed subject index. HQ1233.W65

Women's studies in Western Europe : a resource guide / ed. by Stephen Lehmann and Eva Sartori. Chicago : Assoc. of College and Research Libraries, 1986. 129 p. (WESS occasional publication, no. 2). **CC626**

Contains three essays: (1) Women's publishing in Europe, which includes lists of organizations, archives, databases, directories, publishers, journals, and bookstores for Europe as a whole and for 27 countries and geographic areas; (2) Women's studies education and research, including a list of related agencies by country; (3) The Fawcett Library and collection development issues, which includes a list of British libraries devoted exclusively to women's collections. Essays range in length from 10–15 pages and include resource lists. An appendix includes an alphabetical list of North American periodicals relevant to European women's studies. No indexes. HQ1181.E85W66

World survey on the role of women in development / Department of International Economic and Social Affairs. N.Y. : United Nations, 1986. 238 p. **CC627**

The introduction describes the mandate for this publication and indicates those responsible for each section. In eight parts, providing textual and tabular information and reference lists. Covers the role of women in development; agriculture; industrial development; money and finance; science and technology; trade; and the development, use, and conservation of energy resources. A final chapter covers self-reliance and integration of women into development. No indexes.

HQ1240.W676

CD

Psychology

Psychology is a highly diversified field in which researchers often require very specialized and technical texts primarily found in special libraries. This section identifies some of the more general bibliographies and indexes used in general libraries, as well as some of the more general works used in specialized areas of the field.

GENERAL WORKS

Guides

Baxter, Pam M. Psychology : a guide to reference and information sources. Englewood, Colo. : Libraries Unlimited, 1993. 219 p. (Reference sources in the social sciences series, no. 6). **CD1**

An annotated guide for both beginning and advanced students. Presents a wide range of general and specialized resources covering all major psychological disciplines, emphasizing works published after 1970. In four general sections; the largest, Specialized topics in psychology, follows the classification used in *Psychological abstracts* (CD17). Author/title and subject indexes. Z7201.B39

Borchardt, D. H. How to find out in psychology : a guide to the literature and methods of research / by D. H. Borchardt and R. D. Francis. Oxford ; N.Y. : Pergamon, c1984. 189 p. : ill. **CD2**

While emphasizing British works, this guide stands as a fine introduction to reference sources, the organization of information, and research methodology. Its 11 chapters cover: Overviews of the field;

Historical and theoretical works; Reference sources; Indexes; Databases; Surveys of specialized fields in psychology; Conducting a literature search; Maintaining a citation file; Quanitative methods; Presentation of results; and The psychology profession. Appendixes treat such topics as the components of a sample empirical paper and guidelines for evaluating published research and include a directory of major psychological societies. Bibliography; subject index. BF76.8.B67

Klein, Barry T. Reference encyclopedia of American psychology and psychiatry. 2nd ed. N.Y. : Irvington, 1982. 450 p. **CD3**

Covers a broad range of information sources—e.g., professional organizations, research centers, special library collections, training programs, print resources, audiovisual materials. Most entries are briefly annotated; purchase and contact information is provided where applicable. A "subject/category" index is arranged under broad topical headings. RC437.K55

McInnis, Raymond G. Research guide for psychology. Westport, Conn. : Greenwood, 1982. 604 p. : ill. (Reference sources for the social sciences and humanities, no. 1). **CD4**

A critical guide to more than 1,200 information sources, this work holds a place as a major resource for the literature against more recent publications. 16 topical chapters and a general psychology chapter are based on the subject arrangement of *Psychological abstracts* (CD17), with most chapters subdivided. Covers books, serials, government publications, journal and review sources, and other research tools; a key retrospective guide for advanced students and researchers. Index of authors, titles, and subjects. Z7201.M35

Reed, Jeffrey G. Library use : a handbook for psychology / Jeffrey G. Reed, Pam M. Baxter. 2nd ed. Wash. : Amer. Psychological Assoc., 1992. 179 p. : ill. **CD5**

Particularly useful for beginning students, this volume reviews the search process: where to begin, topic selection, definition, and refinement. Most of the text is devoted to using a relatively small number of psychology sources, with additional chapters outlining computer searching, interlibrary loan, and related general reference sources. Appendixes present more specialized resources, review the basics of the research process, and provide some sample research topics. Author, title, and subject index. BF76.8.R43

Bibliography

L'année psychologique. 1894– . Paris : Presses Universitaires de France, 1895– . Semiannual. **CD6**

Presents signed abstracts of original research, periodical articles, bibliographic analyses, and critical book reviews, with excellent international coverage. Text in French, with summaries in English and French. Provides a fine historical and contemporary review of the literature. Periodical articles were discontinued after v. 65 (1965). BF2.A6

Bibliographic guide to psychology. 1975– . Boston : G.K. Hall, 1976– . Annual. **CD7**

Based on selected publications cataloged by the Research Libraries of the New York Public Library and entries taken from the BF classification of the Library of Congress MARC tapes. The limited MARC coverage often excludes materials in both applied and clinical psychology, which fall into other LC classes, but this work still provides extensive international and multilingual coverage of print and other formats in most areas of psychology. Dictionary arrangement; author and main entries provide full bibliographic data, while title and subject entries are in shortened form. Z7203.N47a

Caton, Hiram. The bibliography of human behavior / Hiram Caton, ed. in chief ; Frank K. Salter and J. M. G. van der Dennen, associate editors. Westport, Conn. : Greenwood, 1993. 575 p. (Bibliographies and indexes in anthropology, no. 7). **CD8**

For annotation, *see* CA10. Z7201.C37

Grinstein, Alexander. The index of psychoanalytic writings. N.Y. : International Universities Pr., [1956–71]. 14 v. **CD9**

A comprehensive international bibliography of psychoanalytic literature, covering the period 1900–69, issued in three large sets. Includes more than 200,000 references to books, articles, reviews, and pamphlets, providing an exhaustive record on the origins and development of psychoanalytical theory and practice. Continues John Rickman's *Index psychoanalyticus 1893–1926* (London : publ. by L. & V. Woolf at the Hogarth Press and the Institute of Psychoanalysis, 1928.). Z7204.P8G7

Harvard University. The Harvard list of books in psychology / comp. and annotated by the psychologists in Harvard University. 4th ed. Cambridge, Mass. : Harvard Univ. Pr., [1971]. 108 p. **CD10**

First published in 1938 as *Books in psychology* and intended as a guide to authoritative books in the discipline; subsequent editions (1949, 1964) have expanded the original list, the 4th ed. including 744 books. While outdated, it serves as a useful historical guide to the literature of psychology with virtually none of the coverage of interdisciplinary areas or related fields that fills many later bibliographies. Works are listed under 31 topical categories; author index. Z7201.H28

Harvard University. Library. Philosophy and psychology. Cambridge, Mass. : Harvard Univ. Lib., distr. by Harvard Univ. Pr., 1973. 2 v. (Widener Library shelflist, 42–43). **CD11**

For annotation, *see* BB6. Z7130.H3

Osier, Donald V. A century of serial publications in psychology, 1850–1950 : an international bibliography / Donald V. Osier, Robert H. Wozniak. Millwood, N.Y. : Kraus Internat., 1984. 805 p. (Bibliographies in the history of psychology and psychiatry, v. 2). **CD12**

An exhaustive international list that presents an excellent historical overview of publishing in psychology. Although the focus is 1850–1950, many titles as early as 1783 are included, and a lengthy prefatory essay provides a useful summary of psychological research during this formative period. Each entry includes all known title variations and a publishing history. An appendix lists more than 700 additional titles of related interest, grouped by subject. Title and editor/author name indexes for both the main section and the appendix. Z7203.O8

Periodicals

Journals in psychology : a resource listing for authors. 4th ed. Wash. : Amer. Psychological Assoc., c1993. 195 p. **CD13**

1st ed., 1988; 3rd ed., 1990.

Lists more than 250 U.S. professional and research journals, providing detailed information on possible sources for publication. Covering both mainstream and specialized interdisciplinary titles, entries are arranged both by title and by broad subject. BF76.8.J68

Wang, Alvin Yafu. Author's guide to journals in the behavioral sciences. Hillsdale, N.J. : L. Erlbaum Associates, c1989. 481 p. **CD14**

Updates Allen Markle and Roger C. Rinn's *Author's guide to journals in psychology, psychiatry and social work* (N.Y. : Haworth Pr., 1977).

Presents entries for 460 journals, alphabetically arranged by title, with detailed information on publication, scope, and editorial policies. Its broader coverage of the behavioral sciences includes many interdisciplinary publications missed by other journal lists focusing narrowly on psychology. BF76.8.W36

Indexes; Abstract journals

A history of American psychology in notes and news, 1883–1945 : an index to journal sources / Ludy T. Benjamin, Jr. [et al.]. Millwood, N.Y. : Kraus, c1989. 591 p. (Bibliographies in the history of psychology and psychiatry, 5).   **CD15**

Provides access to nonarticle information published in the journals *Science* (1883–1945); *American journal of psychology* (1887–1945); *Psychological review* (1894–1903); *Psychological bulletin* (1904–45); *Journal of philosophy, psychology and scientific method* (1904–45); and *Journal of applied psychology* (1917–45). Valuable for historical studies.   Z7201.H52

PsycBOOKS : books & chapters in psychology. 1987–1990. Arlington, Va. : Amer. Psychological Assoc., c1987–91.   **CD16**

An index to English-language books and chapters in psychology and related fields that helped fill the gap when *Psychological abstracts* (CD17) discontinued book indexing in 1980. Annual sets consisted of four volumes covering experimental psychology, basic and applied psychology, developmental psychology, professional psychology, and educational psychology. A fifth volume provided an author/title/subject and a publisher's index.

•The complete retrospective contents of this index are included in *PsycLIT* [database] (Wash. : Amer. Psychological Assoc., 1974–). Available in CD-ROM, updated quarterly.   Z7201.P76

Psychological abstracts. v. 1 (1927)– . Lancaster, Pa. : Amer. Psychological Assoc., 1927– . Monthly.   **CD17**

The most comprehensive index to the literature of psychology, indexing more than 1,200 English-language journals and reports and providing descriptive, nonevaluative abstracts. Coverage has varied widely over the history of the title. Abstracts are now arranged under 17 subject categories using terminology from *Thesaurus of psychological index terms* (CD34). Coverage of books and dissertations, dropped in 1980, was resumed in 1992. Coverage of foreign-language materials was dropped in 1988; these materials are now covered by the *PsycINFO* database (below). Provides excellent coverage of abnormal and clinical psychology, experimental psychology, human and animal development, and social psychology. Applied areas (e.g., educational psychology, neurosciences) are better served by specialized subject indexes.

Index: *Cumulative author index to Psychological abstracts, 1959/63–1981/83* (Wash. : Amer. Psychological Assoc., 1965–84). See also: *Author index to Psychological index, 1894–1935, and Psychological abstracts, 1927–1958* (CD18 *note*).

•Available in machine-readable form as: *PsycINFO* [database] (Arlington, Va. : Amer. Psychological Assoc., 1967–). Available online (updated monthly) and in CD-ROM as *PsycLIT* (updated quarterly). Some versions of the machine-readable file were included in *PsycBOOKS* (CD16).   BF1.P65

Psychological index 1894–1935 : an annual bibliography of the literature of psychology and cognate subjects. Wash. : Amer. Psychological Assoc., 1894–1935. 42 v.   **CD18**

Continued by: *Psychological abstracts* (CD17).

Now primarily of historical interest, originally published as an annual bibliographic supplement to the journal *Psychological review*. Lists books and periodical articles in all languages, together with translations and new editions in English, French, German, and Italian. A classified subject list with an author index, but no subject index.

Index: Columbia University. Libraries. Psychology Library. *Author index to Psychological index, 1894–1935, and Psychological abstracts, 1927–1958* (Boston : G.K. Hall, 1960. 5 v.).

Reproduced from cards without editing. Consists of a cumulation of author entries in both journals, combined with an earlier file that precedes *Psychological index*. Provides a historically valuable index to psychological books and articles in many languages, 1890–1958.   Z7203.P97

Encyclopedias

Baker encyclopedia of psychology / ed. by David G. Benner. Grand Rapids, Mich. : Baker Book House, c1985. 1223 p. (Baker reference library, 2).   **CD19**

Covers many specialized areas not included in other general psychology encyclopedias, e.g., psychology of religion. Some 500 signed articles cover topics such as mental disorders and assessment instruments. About 100 biographical entries are also included. Most articles are neutral and factual, with cross-references and brief bibliographies included for most entries.   BF31.B25

Encyclopedia of human behavior / ed. by V. S. Ramachandran. San Diego : Academic Pr., 1994. 4 v. (2400 p.).   **CD20**

Presents 250 signed articles on "human action and reaction" (*Pref.*), focusing primarily on physiological, abnormal, and clinical psychology and cognition. Each entry provides a glossary, table of contents, and bibliography of sources, as well as ample cross-references to related materials. Author, title, subject index.   BF31.E5

Encyclopedia of psychology : Raymond J. Corsini, ed. [et al.]. 2nd ed. N.Y. : Wiley, c1994. 2016 p.   **CD21**

1st ed., 1984 (4 v.).

A significant revision, presenting more than 2,100 signed articles on topics and persons (living and dead) in all areas of psychology. Full citations for references are provided in a general bibliography. An excellent general resource for beginning and advanced students.   BF31.E52

The encyclopedic dictionary of psychology / ed. by Rom Harré and Roger Lamb. Cambridge, Mass. : MIT Pr., 1983. 718 p. : ill.   **CD22**

Offers definitions of terms, explanations of theories, processes, etc., in the areas of cognitive psychology, psycholinguistics, and neuropsychology, including entries for key personalities in the field. Signed articles; bibliographies; cross-references; index.

§ From this work, the editors have selected materials which they have updated and supplemented and have reissued as four independent titles, all published by MIT Pr. in 1986: *Dictionary of developmental and educational psychology* (CD82); *Dictionary of physiological and clinical psychology* (CD99); *Dictionary of personality and social psychology* (CD95); and *Dictionary of ethnology and animal learning*.   BF31.E555

International encyclopedia of psychiatry, psychology, psychoanalysis, and neurology / ed. by Benjamin B. Wolman. N.Y. : Aesculapius Publ., 1977. 12 v. : ill.   **CD23**

An unparalleled source whose more than 1,800 signed articles provide authoritative and comprehensive information in most areas of psychology and in many related fields. Emphasizes theoretical, experimental, and therapeutic approaches. Although coverage of applied psychology and neurosciences is limited, the *Progress volume* provides slightly better, updated, coverage of neuropsychology.

————. *Progress volume 1* (N. Y. : Aesculapius Publ., c1983) provides lengthy articles with bibliographies covering theory, historical development, and recent interpretations. Includes biographies and cross-references to articles in the parent work. Name and subject indexes.   RC334.I57

A lexicon of psychology, psychiatry, and psychoanalysis / ed. by Jessica Kuper. London ; N.Y. : Routledge, 1988. 471 p.   **CD24**

An encyclopedia with more than 100 essays on significant issues or individuals in the development of theory and research in psychology. Topical essays focus on recent research more than concepts, and coverage can be somewhat uneven. Ample cross-references help compensate for the lack of any index, but reference lists with each entry are helpful guides to key psychological literature. Useful for beginning students.   BF31.L48

The Oxford companion to the mind / ed. by Richard L. Gregory, with the assistance of O. L. Zangwill. Oxford ; N.Y. : Oxford Univ. Pr., 1987. 856 p. : ill.   **CD25**
　　Arranged alphabetically, covering a wide range of topics, persons, and theories in psychology and related fields including art, language, and mythology. Many of the signed entries have brief bibliographies. Use of cross-references is limited; subject index. Numerous illustrations.   BF31.O94

Popplestone, John A. Dictionary of concepts in general psychology / John A. Popplestone and Marion White McPherson. Westport, Conn. : Greenwood, 1988. 380 p. (Reference sources for the social sciences and humanities, no. 7).   **CD26**
　　Presents lengthy articles on broad concepts such as aggression, curiosity, and Gestalt, rather than defining specific subjects or terms. Emphasizes experimental psychology, cognition, and learning; social, developmental, clinical, and applied psychology receive less emphasis. Cross-references link most essays, but subject indexing is minimal.   BF31.P665

Dictionaries

Bruno, Frank Joe. Dictionary of key words in psychology. London ; Boston : Routledge & K. Paul, 1986. 275 p.   **CD27**
　　A selective list of key terms frequently used. Intends to define and provide a contextual placement for the discipline's vocabulary. Entries consist of a working definition and an explanation of the concept's place in psychological thought. Selective bibliography of readings, broad topical index, name and subject indexes.   BF31.B78

Chaplin, James Patrick. Dictionary of psychology. 2nd rev. ed. N.Y. : Laurel, [c1985]. 499 p. : ill.   **CD28**
　　1st ed., 1968; new rev. ed., 1975.
　　Listed as 3rd ed. on cover.
　　Provides concise and accurate definitions of technical terms and concepts, and strong coverage of related areas such as psychiatry and biology. A standard dictionary, useful for students.   BF31.C45

Dictionary of behavioral science / comp. and ed. by Benjamin B. Wolman. 2nd ed. San Diego : Academic Pr., c1989. 370 p. : ill.   **CD29**
　　1st ed., 1973.
　　Provides brief definitions of some 20,000 terms in psychology and related fields. Brief biographical entries are provided for important figures (living or dead) in the history and development of the field. Extensive cross-references are provided, but no bibliographies. A good source for quick definitions of concepts and terms covering all aspects of psychology.   BF31.D48

Psychoanalytic terms and concepts / ed. by Burness E. Moore and Bernard D. Fine. New Haven, Conn. : Yale Univ. Pr., c1990. 240 p.   **CD30**
　　A revised version of the compilers' *Glossary of psychoanalytic terms and concepts* (2nd ed. N.Y. : American Psychoanalytic Assoc., [1968]). About 1,000 terms are defined, accompanied by relevant references both to Freud and more modern interpreters of psychoanalysis. Clear definitions explain or avoid technical terms, providing for general readers an excellent presentation of often ambiguous and misused concepts.   RC501.4.P79

Stratton, Peter. A student's dictionary of psychology / Peter Stratton and Nicky Hayes. 2nd ed. London ; N.Y. : E. Arnold ; N.Y. : Routledge, Chapman, and Hall, c1993. 223 p. : ill.   **CD31**
　　Focuses on the vocabulary of psychology and excludes terms more commonly associated with other fields such as medicine. Definitions are brief, examples are provided where possible, and extensive illustrations and cross-references are provided. No biographical entries; brief bibliography of readings. A good source for concise and informative definitions.   BF31.S69

Sutherland, N. S. The international dictionary of psychology. N.Y. : Continuum, c1989. 491 p. : ill.   **CD32**
　　Similar to Peter Stratton and Nicky Hayes's *A student's dictionary of psychology* (CD31). Lists terms used in psychology but not those associated more commonly with other fields. Contains eponyms, abbreviations, and ample cross-references, but no biographical entries; greatest emphasis lies on experimental and neuropsychophysiology. Five appendixes of anatomical drawings of the brain.   BF31.S83

Zusne, Leonard. Eponyms in psychology : a dictionary and biographical sourcebook. N.Y. : Greenwood, 1987. 339 p.   **CD33**
　　Lists numerous complexes, measures, syndromes, theorems, and other phenomena in psychological literature named after people or places. More than 850 terms are covered, alphabetically listed by concept, test, or syndrome (e.g., Jocasta complex), providing information on the person or place and usually citing the first appearance of the eponym. Index by eponym; references to other biographical works.   BF31.Z87

Thesauruses

Thesaurus of psychological index terms. 6th ed. / Alvin Walker, Jr., ed. Arlington, Va. : Amer. Psychological Assoc., c1991. 332 p.   **CD34**
　　1st ed., 1974; 5th ed., 1988.
　　A controlled vocabulary designed to provide structured access to the subject matter indexed by *Psychological abstracts* (CD17), both in print and online. Nearly 7,000 terms include scope notes, posting notes, term clusters, cross-references, hierarchical relationships, and related terms.   Z695.1.P7T48

Directories

American Psychological Association. APA membership register. 1982– . [Wash.] : Amer. Psychological Assoc., c1982– . Irregular.   **CD35**
　　Supersedes the Association's *Membership register* (1967–81); issued between editions of the Association's more comprehensive *Directory* (CD46). Provides names and locational information only, no biographical data.   BF30.A49

American Psychological Association's guide to research support / Kenneth Lee Herring, ed. 3rd ed. Wash. : The Association, c1987. 276 p.   **CD36**
　　1st ed., 1981.
　　Provides a useful overview of private and public research grants, federal aid, and other funding available to students and scholars in psychology. Entries include names and addresses for contact persons, areas of research supported, types of awards and eligibility requirements, and information on the application and review process. Bibliography of additional guides to funding.   BF76.5.A64

Graduate study in psychology. 25th ed. (1992)– . Wash. : Amer. Psychological Assoc., c1992– . Annual.   **CD37**
　　Continues the Association's *Graduate study in psychology and associated fields* (1971–1991) and *Graduate study in psychology* (1968–1970).
　　New ed. publ. biennially, the same ed. with addendum publ. the following year.
　　More than 600 entries based on questionnaires completed by academic departments (not all of them psychology departments) who are therefore totally self-reporting. Programs are arranged in four sections: APA accredited doctoral programs; other doctoral programs; psychology programs offering less than a doctorate; related departments awarding degrees less than a doctorate.   BF77.G73

Keith-Spiegel, Patricia. The complete guide to graduate school admission : psychology and related programs. Hillsdale, N.J. : L. Erlbaum Associates, 1990. 373 p.   **CD38**

A useful companion to *Graduate study in psychology* (CD37). Presents practical information covering five major perspectives (e.g., factors and activities that enhance an applicant's chances; the actual application process). Most of the text is in question-and-answer format and there is no index. Includes supplementary reading lists and a list of references.   BF77.K35

Wolman, Benjamin B. International directory of psychology : a guide to people, places, and policies. N.Y. : Plenum Pr., c1979. 279 p.   **CD39**

Compiled from questionnaires completed by national associations of psychologists and other sources. 64 countries are presented, along with general surveys for sub-Saharan Africa and Ukraine. Entries vary in scope but most include names and descriptions of major associations, memberships of psychologists, research facilities, institutes, and educational and training programs, primary journal publications, and research opportunities open to foreign visitors.   BF30.W64

Handbooks

Krug, Samuel E. Psychware sourcebook. 3rd ed. Kansas City, Mo. : Test Corp. of America, c1988. 613 p.   **CD40**

1st ed., 1984, had title: *Psychware : a reference guide to computer-based products for behavioral assessment in psychology, education, and business.* 2nd ed., 1987.

Describes many computer-based products applicable to the assessment or modification of human behavior. Most products are interpretive instruments, not simple scoring devices. Listings are alphabetical by title and include information on supplier, applications, sale restrictions, and cost. Indexed by title, category, application, service, and supplier.   BF176.2.K78

Wolman, Benjamin B. Handbook of general psychology. Englewood Cliffs, N.J. : Prentice-Hall, [1973]. 1006 p. : ill.   **CD41**

Although somewhat dated, this handbook still serves as a useful historical and survey resource on all aspects of psychology, from theory and methodology to experimental and physiological research. Organized under eight broad areas, chapter contributors represent some of the most distinguished names in the field.   BF121.W63

Style manuals

Publication manual of the American Psychological Association. 3rd ed. Wash. : The Association, c1983. 208 p.   **CD42**

Rev. ed. of *Publication manual* (2nd ed., 1974).

"This Publication Manual draws its rules from a large body of psychological literature, from editors and authors experienced in psychological practices. Writers who employ this Manual conscientiously will express their ideas in a form and style both accepted by and familiar to a broad readership in psychology."—*Introd.*   BF76.7.P83

Sternberg, Robert J. The psychologist's companion : a guide to scientific writing for students and researchers. 3rd ed. Cambridge ; N.Y. : Cambridge Univ. Pr., 1993. 226 p. : ill. **CD43**

1st ed., 1977, had title: *Writing the psychology paper* (Woodbury, N.Y. : Barron's Education Series, Inc.); 2nd ed., 1988.

"Chapter 7 and appendix B were contributed by Chris Leach."—*t.p.*

For undergraduates, this guide provides a step-by-step approach to contructing a research paper. Chapters cover the style and mechanics of preparing, writing, and evaluating reports and research papers. Includes sample papers and information on submitting papers for publication. General index.   BF76.8.S73

Reviews of research

Annual review of psychology. v. 1 (1950)– . Palo Alto, Calif. : Annual Reviews, 1950– .   **CD44**

Editor: v. 1– C. P. Stone.

One of the most frequently cited sources in the discipline. Approximately 20 review articles written by experts appear in each issue, covering the most influential current research and providing extensive reference lists. Each volume has its own author and subject index.   BF30.A56

International handbook of psychology / ed. by Albert R. Gilgen and Carol K. Gilgen. Westport, Conn. : Greenwood, 1987. 629 p. : ill.   **CD45**

With so much of psychological practice and theory dominated by English-language publications, this work provides a useful view of recent worldwide research. Essays survey the development of the profession and the discipline in 29 countries, providing more in-depth coverage for each than Benjamin B. Wolman's *International directory of psychology* (CD39). Name and subject indexes.   BF77.I62

Biography

American Psychological Association. Directory of the American Psychological Association. Wash. : The Association, 1978– . Quadrennial.   **CD46**

Supersedes the Association's *Biographical directory* (1970–75), which superseded its *Directory* (1948–68) and *Yearbook* (1916–47).

The 1993 edition lists more than 73,000 names of Association members and gives brief biographical data. Contains a geographical index and a divisional membership roster, as well as a newly revised statement of ethical standards. Also includes nonmember international affiliates of the Association.   BF11.A67

A history of psychology in autobiography. v. 1 (1930)– . Stanford, Calif. : Stanford Univ. Pr., 1930– .   **CD47**

Vols. 1–4 (publ. as International university series in psychology) ed. by Carl Murchison and Edwin G. Boring; v. 5–6 (Century psychology series) ed. by Boring and Gardner Lindzey; v. 7 (Series of books in psychology) ed. by Lindzey.

A key source for the history of psychology, each volume profiling more than a dozen researchers from all areas of the field. Subjects discuss how their work has evolved over the years, influences on their work, and how they perceive their contributions to psychology. Each essays ends with a list of selected publications.   BF105.H5

International directory of psychologists, exclusive of the U.S.A : a publication of the International Union of Psychological Science / ed., Kurt Pawlik. 4th ed. Amsterdam ; N.Y. : North-Holland : distr. by Elsevier, 1985. 1181 p.   **CD48**

1st ed., 1958; 3rd ed., 1980.

This edition offers biographies of some 36,000 psychologists from 48 countries in the Union and eight countries affiliated with the International Association for Cross-Cultural Psychology. Alphabetically arranged by country. Also includes a section on the history and programs of the Union and the current status of the field in each country.   BF30.I52

Krawiec, T. S. The psychologists. N.Y. : Oxford Univ. Pr., 1972–74. 2 v. : ill.   **CD49**

Containing autobiographical essays by 35 significant contributors to psychology, this volume makes up in depth what it lacks in breadth. It presents lengthier, more detailed accounts than essays in *History of psychology in autobiography* (CD47) and includes longer, more comprehensive bibliographies.   BF109.A1K7

Portraits of pioneers in psychology / ed. by Gregory A. Kimble, Michael Wertheimer, Charlotte White. Wash. : Amer. Psychological Assoc. ; Hillsdale, N.J. : L. Erlbaum Associates, 1991. 368 p. : ill. **CD50**

Presents lengthy essays on 22 pioneers and founders in the budding field of psychology (all but one born in the 19th century). Written by descendants, colleagues, or students, these informal essays vary widely in format and organization, but in every instance the personal approach presents these major figures of psychology in a light unlike any other standard biographical source. Subject and name index; each essay contains a list of references. BF109.A1P67

Stevens, Gwendolyn. The women of psychology / by Gwendolyn Stevens and Sheldon Gardner. Cambridge, Mass. : Schenkman Publ., 1982. 2 v. : ports. **CD51**

Since earlier biographical sources afforded limited coverage of women, this useful set presents sketches of some key figures in psychology who otherwise might prove difficult to locate. Vol. 1, Pioneers and innovators, contains an introductory essay on the roles of women in the early days of psychology and provides 37 essays that vary widely in length. Vol. 2, Expansion and refinement, presents 100 considerably shorter entries on more recent women in the field. Entries are grouped under thematic headings such as "The Researchers." BF95.S73 1982

Women in psychology : a bio bibliographic sourcebook / ed. by Agnes N. O'Connell and Nancy Felipe Russo. N.Y. : Greenwood, 1990. 441 p. **CD52**

A nice complement to Gwendolyn Stevens and Sheldon Gardner's *The women of psychology* (CD51). Provides biographies of 36 women prominent in psychology. Arranged in five sections: (1) Overview of selection process; (2) The women and their contributions, including a bibliography; (3) Awards and recognition; (4) Bibliographic resources; (5) Appendixes, grouping subjects by year of birth, birthplace, and major fields of study. General index. BF109.A1W65

HISTORY AND THEORY

Brennan, James F. History and systems of psychology. 4th ed. Englewood Cliffs, N.J. : Prentice-Hall, 1994. 1 v. **CD53**
1st ed., 1982; 3rd ed., 1991.

Covering more than 2,500 years of psychology's development, provides a good introduction to Eastern and Western psychological traditions. Topical chapters include primary and secondary resource listings for further study. Brief glossary; name and subject index. A good introductory resource for students. BF81.B67

Hillner, Kenneth P. History and systems of modern psychology : a conceptual approach. N.Y. : Gardner Pr., c1984. 348 p. : ill. **CD54**

Dividing entries into "systems" of classical (pre-1930) and contemporary thought, chapters cover topics such as behaviorism, structuralism, gestalt, and psychoanalysis. Each chapter is organized similarly, making it easy to compare origins and premises. Bibliography of key sources; subject index. BF95.H54

Lawry, John D. Guide to the history of psychology. Totowa, N.J. : Littlefield, Adams, 1981. 114 p. **CD55**
Repr. : Lanham, Md. : Univ. Pr. of America, 1990.

Provides a brief but helpful overview to the history and philosophical basis of psychology. It focuses on biographical sketches of 118 major contributors to the science of psychology from antiquity to the present; an Innovations section lists significant events in psychology. Glossary; name and subject indexes. BF81.L38

Guides

Gottsegen, Gloria Behar. Humanistic psychology : a guide to information sources / Gloria B. Gottsegen, Abby J. Gottsegen. Detroit : Gale, c1980. 185 p. (Psychology information guide series, v. 6). **CD56**

An alternative guide to the classical historical approach to psychology; focuses on self-awareness, interpersonal relations, and social interactions. Provides some 500 annotated citations to works in the history and theory of psychology, encounter and sensitivity groups, nontraditional and experimental therapies, applied settings, reference sources, periodicals, and organizations. Author, title, and subject indexes. Z7204.H85G67

Viney, Wayne. History of psychology : a guide to information sources / Wayne Viney, Michael Wertheimer, Marilyn Lou Wertheimer. Detroit : Gale, c1979. 502 p. (Psychology information guide series, v. 1). **CD57**

Covers some 3,000 references to the history of psychology gleaned from books and articles published mostly after 1940. A chapter on reference works and general works in psychology is followed by specialized chapters on topics such as schools and systems of psychological thought and histories of related fields such as psychiatry and biology. Does not include foreign-language materials. Z7204.H57V56

Bibliography

Sokal, Michael M. A guide to manuscript collections in the history of psychology and related areas / comp. by Michael M. Sokal and Patrice A. Rafial. Millwood, N.Y. : Kraus Internat., c1982. 212 p. (Bibliographies in the history of psychology and psychiatry, 1). **CD58**

Includes personal papers and correspondence of individuals, professional associations, organizations, and journals influential in the history of psychology. Listings provide information on collection scope and size, and related information on literary rights and repository access. Covering both original and microform materials, and focused primarily on the U.S., its coverage is somewhat uneven. Indexes by name, institution, repository, and subject are provided, as well as a list of sources consulted. BF81.S58

Vande Kemp, Hendrika. Psychology and theology in Western thought, 1672–1965 : a historical and annotated bibliography / Hendrika Vande Kemp and H. Newton Malony. Millwood, N.Y. : Kraus Internat., [1984]. 367 p. **CD59**
For annotation, *see* BC20. Z7204.R4V36

Watson, Robert Irving. The history of psychology and the behavioral sciences : a bibliographic guide. N.Y. : Springer, [1978]. 241 p. **CD60**

Nearly 800 works on the history and philosophy of psychology are listed under 45 broad categories (e.g., reference tools; historical accounts). No name, author, or subject indexes are included, but extensive cross-references are provided. Most references are to books published since 1900, and English-language materials predominate.
Z7201.W373

Handbooks

Neel, Ann. Theories of psychology : a handbook. Rev. and enl. ed. Cambridge, Mass. : Schenkman Publ. ; N.Y. : Halsted Pr., c1977. 699 p. **CD61**
1st ed., 1969.

Focus is on "matured theories" the author has selected; the resulting coverage is sometimes uneven, but, within the topics included, a thorough analysis of schools of thought and their contributions is presented. Includes classified reading and reference lists and a subject index. BF38.N38

Biography

Watson, Robert Irving. The great psychologists : a history of psychological thought / Robert I. Watson, Sr., Rand B. Evans. 5th ed. N.Y. : HarperCollins Publishers, c1991. 658 p. : ports. **CD62**.

1st ed., 1963. Subtitle varies in earlier editions.

A useful and well-written summary of the development and impact of psychological philosophies and methodologies through the lives and works of more than 50 great psychologists. Other chapters focus on recent national and international developments in the field. Includes name and subject indexes. BF81.W35

RESEARCH METHODOLOGY AND STATISTICS

Handbooks

Handbook of survey research / ed. by Peter H. Rossi, James D. Wright, Andy B. Anderson. N.Y. : Academic Pr., c1983. 755 p. : ill. **CD63**

Provides a good introduction to constructing, administering, and analyzing surveys and questionnaires. Chapters focus on topics such as defining population, sampling, measurement, and scaling techniques. Covers a variety of social survey methods. Includes sample case studies and a subject index. HN29.H294

Reference handbook of research and statistical methods in psychology : for students and professionals / R. M. Yaremko ... [et al.]. N.Y. : Harper & Row, c1982. 335 p. : ill. **CD64**

Republished 1986 as *Handbook of research and quantitative methods in psychology* (Hillsdale, N.J. : Lawrence Erlbaum).

A handy guide, part handbook and part dictionary, to terms and concepts frequently used in behavioral research. As a handbook it provides statistical charts and tables including random number tables, frequently used symbols, and conversion values. As a dictionary it provides brief, clear definitions of terms used in design, statistical methods, and psychometrics. BF76.5.R43

Udinsky, B. Flavian. Evaluation resource handbook : gathering, analyzing, reporting data / by B. Flavian Udinsky, Steven J. Osterlind, Samuel W. Lynch. San Diego, Calif. : EdITS Publishers, 1981. 250 p. : ill. **CD65**

A general introduction that discusses approaches and techniques frequently used in behavioral sciences. Chapters cover topics such as issues and ethics, problem-solving and data classification, and reporting results. Brief selective bibliographies accompany each topical chapter, and a larger cumulative bibliography to additional materials is included. Name and subject indexes. Ample charts and graphs illustrate applications. H62.U3

Wilkening, H. The psychology almanac : a handbook for students / [by] Howard E. Wilkening, in collaboration with Gregory Wilkening and Peter Wilkening. Monterey, Calif. : Brooks/Cole Pub. Co., [1973]. 241 p. : ill. **CD66**

A good general introduction to statistics, with brief listings of individuals, concepts, and symbols and terms used in psychology. A valuable statistical reference work despite its age. BF31.W49

TESTS AND MEASUREMENTS

Bibliography

Chun, Ki-Taek. Measures for psychological assessment : a guide to 3,000 original sources and their applications / Ki-Taek Chun, Sidney Cobb, John R. P. French, Jr. Ann Arbor, Mich. : Survey Research Center, Institute for Social Research, 1975. 664 p. **CD67**

A comprehensive bibliography primarily of unpublished mental health measures that appeared in major journals in psychology and sociology, 1960–70. Each citation includes the author, test title, and basic bibliographic information; many also include descriptive test data. Author and subject indexes. BF698.5.C45

The ETS Test Collection catalog / comp. by Test Collection, Educational Testing Service. 2nd ed. Phoenix : Oryx, 1993. v. 1. (In progress). **CD68**

1st ed., 1986–92. 6 v.

Contents: v. 1, Achievement tests and measurement devices.

Lists a wide range of educational tests and measurement devices. Each volume provides brief annotations for more than 1,000 tests, including for each test its scope, target audience, and availability. Includes difficult-to-locate research instruments as well as commercially available standardized tests. Serves as an index to the ETS collection, *Tests in microfiche* [microform] (Princeton, N.J. : ETS, 1975– . [In progress]). Author, title, and subject indexes. Later volumes will cover vocational, aptitude, attitude, and personality tests.

•Was once available in machine-readable form as: *ETS Test Collection* [database] (Princeton, N.J. : ETS), with coverage from 1950. No longer published. LB3051.E79

The mental measurements yearbook. 9th ed. (1985)– . Lincoln, Nebr. : Buros Inst. of Mental Measurements, Univ. of Nebraska, 1985– . Irregular. **CD69**

[1st ed.], 1938.

Publisher varies.

Editor varies: 1940–78, Oscar Krisen Buros; 1985– , James V. Mitchell, Jr.

A monumental collection of standardized measurements, now in its 11th ed. Each edition follows much the same pattern and is intended to supplement rather than supersede earlier volumes. References are numbered consecutively and each has cross-references to reviews, excerpts, and bibliographic references in earlier volumes. Information for each test includes: title; intended population; author and publisher; acronym; scoring; availability of forms, parts, levels, and computer-assisted scoring; cost; time to administer; and a statement concerning validity and reliability. Test bibliographies cover English-language materials.

An index to the first six yearbooks is provided in Oscar Buros, *Personality tests and reviews* (Highland Park, N.J. : Gryphon Pr., [1970–75]. 2 v.).

•Available in machine-readable form as: *Mental measurements yearbook* [database] (Lincoln, Nebr. : Buros Inst. of Mental Measurements, Univ. of Nebraska, 1977–). Available online; updated monthly. Z5814.P8B932

O'Brien, Nancy P. Test construction : a bibliography of selected resources. N.Y. : Greenwood, 1988. 299 p. **CD70**

Cites more than 2,700 books, reports, journal articles, dissertations and ERIC documents published from 1900 through 1986. Very few of the works cited appear in other bibliographies. Citations are arranged by test type, following the classification scheme of the early *Mental measurements yearbook* (CD69). No annotations; author and subject indexes. Z5814.E9O18

Test critiques / Daniel J. Keyser. Richard C. Sweetland, gen. editors. v. 8 (1991)– . Austin, Tex. : Pro-Ed, c1991– . Annual. **CD71**

Vol. 1–7 publ.: Kansas City. Mo. : Test Corp. of America, 1984–90.

Each volume contains approximately 100 critical reviews of commercial tests most frequently used in psychological assessment, business, and education. Arrangement is by title, and beginning with v. 3, test title, publisher, author/reviewer, and subject indexes cumulate. Review essays include a description of the development and applications of the test, technical data, a lengthy critique, and list of references. Since it often duplicates entries in *Mental measurements yearbook* (CD69), this title is best used as a supplement to that work.

BF176.T418

Tests : a comprehensive reference for assessments in psychology, education, and business / Richard C. Sweetland, Daniel J. Keyser, general editors. 3rd ed. Austin, Tex. : Pro-Ed, c1991. 1250 p.   **CD72**

1st ed., 1983; 2nd ed., 1986.

More than 3,000 published English-language instruments are listed under three broad subject headings, with numerous specialty subdivisions. Designed for quick identification of tests, each entry gives the purpose and a brief description of the measure, intended population, administrating and assessing the results, and cost and availability. Critical evaluations are not included. Indexes include test publisher, availability of computer scoring, tests for special populations (e.g., non-English speakers), title, and author.

BF176.T43

Tests in print III : an index to tests, test reviews, and the literature on specific tests / ed. by James V. Mitchell, Jr. Lincoln, Nebr. : Buros Institute of Mental Measurements, Univ. of Nebraska-Lincoln, 1983. 714 p.   **CD73**

Original issue, 1961, had title: *Tests in print* (479 p.); 1974 issue had title: *Tests in print II* (1107 p.).

Considerably larger than the original issue. A "comprehensive bibliography of commercially available tests for use with English-speaking subjects" (*Pref.*), it also serves as a cumulative retrospective index to the reference lists and reviews of tests included through the 8th ed. of *Mental measurements yearbook* (CD69). More than 2,600 test entries are arranged alphabetically, with a supplemental title, subject, and author/name index.

Z5814.E9T47

Directories

Directory of selected national testing programs / comp. by Test Collection, Educational Testing Service. Phoenix : Oryx, 1987. 280 p.   **CD74**

Describes 220 programs conducted mainly for educational purposes in areas such as admissions, licensing, certification, academic credit. Entries provide information on each test's content, purpose, and cost, plus dates given, registration, and agencies to contact. Arranged by test type.

LB3051.D56

Goldman, Bert A. Directory of unpublished experimental mental measures. v. 1 (1974)– . N.Y. : Human Sciences Pr., 1974– . Irregular.   **CD75**

Publisher varies; v. 5 (1990) publ. Dubuque, Iowa : Wm. C. Brown.

Vols. 1–4 (1974–85) prep. with J. L. Saunders; v. 5 (1990) prep. with David F. Mitchell.

Serves "as a supplement to the *Mental measurements yearbooks* [CD69] by publishing periodic surveys of tests not available commercially, using as sources those journals that carry studies and reports employing experimental instruments. Its orientation is predominantly educational, but it includes material related to psychology, sociology, and personnel work as well."—*Foreword.* Under a broad subject arrangement, each entry gives test name, purpose, author, article, and journal. Author and subject indexes.

BF431.G625

Standards

American Psychological Association. Standards for educational and psychological testing / American Educational Research Association, American Psychological Association, National Council on Measurement in Education. Wash. : Amer. Psychological Assoc., c1985. 100 p.   **CD76**

Supersedes: *Standards for educational and psychological tests* (rev. ed., 1974).

Intends to provide "criteria for the evaluation of tests, testing practices, and the effects of test use."—*Introd.* Addresses professionals' needs for ethically, scientifically, and clinically sound procedures. In four sections: (1) Technical standards for test construction and evaluation; (2) Professional standards for test use; (3) Standards for particular applications; and (4) Standards for administration. Each is divided into subsections that begin with textual explanations and definitions followed by individually numbered statements of standards. Includes a glossary of technical terms and a subject index referring to specific standards.

LB3051.A693

DEVELOPMENTAL PSYCHOLOGY

Guides

Haag, Enid E. Research guide for studies in infancy and childhood. N.Y. : Greenwood, 1988. 430 p. (Reference sources for the social sciences and humanities, no. 8).   **CD77**

For annotation, *see* CC139.   Z7164.C5H3

Scheffler, Hannah Nuba. Infancy : a guide to research and resources / Hannah Nuba Scheffler, Deborah Lovitky Sheiman, Kathleen Pullan Watkins. N.Y. : Garland, 1986. 182 p. (Garland reference library of social science, v. 324).   **CD78**

For annotation, *see* CC148.   HQ774.N83

Sheiman, Deborah Lovitky. Resources for middle childhood : a source book / Deborah Lovitky Sheiman, Maureen Slonim. N.Y. : Garland, 1988. 138 p. (Reference books on family issues, v. 12 ; Garland reference library of social science, v. 433).   **CD79**

For annotation, *see* CC150.   HQ767.9.S48

Woodbury, Marda. Childhood information resources. Arlington, Va. : Information Resources, 1985. 593 p.   **CD80**

Used in conjunction with Enid E. Haag's *Research guide for studies in infancy and childhood* (CC139), offers a comprehensive guide to the interdisciplinary research literature on childhood. Pt. 1 addresses research methods and skills; pt. 2 covers more than 500 specific resources, with critical annotations, arranged under nine broad topical headings; pt. 3 covers more than 300 electronic and other nonprint resources and organizations focused on children; pt. 4 covers statistics and testing resources and parent education. An appendix provides a classified list of multidisciplinary works used by professionals in the field. Author, title, and subject indexes.

§ *See also* Woodbury's *Youth information resources* (CC141).

Z5814.C5W6

Indexes; Abstract journals

Child development abstracts and bibliography. v. 2 (Feb. 1928)– . Chicago : Publ. by the Univ. of Chicago Pr. for the Society for Research in Child Development, 1928– . 3 no. a year.   **CD81**

Vol. 1 (1927) had title: *Selected child development abstracts.* Title, frequency, and publisher have varied.

Indexes more than 200 major journals in the fields of education, psychology, sociology, and pediatrics. Abstracts are organized under broad topical headings such as biomedicine and health, social psychology and personality, and historical and methodological issues. A separate section includes lengthy reviews of recent books. Author and subject indexes cumulate annually.   HQ750.A1C47

Encyclopedias

The dictionary of developmental and educational psychology / ed. by Rom Harré and Roger Lamb. Cambridge, Mass. : MIT Pr., 1986. 271 p.   **CD82**

Derived from the authors' *Encyclopedic dictionary of psychology* (CD22), with many entries and reference lists updated to provide tighter focus on the main theories and issues of development. The extensive use of cross-references helps supplement the somewhat uneven subject index.   BF712.7.D53

Encyclopedia of adolescence / ed. by Richard Lerner, Anne C. Petersen, Jeanne Brooks-Gunn. N.Y. : Garland, 1991. 2 v. : ill. (Garland reference library of social science, v. 495).   **CD83**

For annotation, *see* CC159.   HQ796.E58

Handbooks

Handbook of adolescent psychology / Vincent B. Van Hasselt, Michel Hersen. N.Y. : Pergamon, c1987. 508 p. : ill. (Pergamon general psychology series, v. 142).   **CD84**

Chapters written by experts are arranged under five broad categories: a brief history of the study of adolescent human development; theoretical perpectives on adolescence; topical issues such as sexuality and social adjustment; psychological disorders common to adolescence; and recent issues in adolescent development and behavior. Author and detailed subject indexes.   BF724.H333

Handbook of child psychology : formerly Carmichael's Manual of child psychology / Paul H. Mussen, ed. 4th ed. N.Y. : Wiley, [1983]. 4 v. : ill.   **CD85**

Originally publ. as: *Manual of child psychology*, ed. by Leonard Carmichael (N.Y. : Wiley ; London : Chapman & Hall, [1946]. 1068 p.).

Contents: v. 1, History, theory, and methods, ed. by William Kessen; v. 2, Infancy and developmental psychobiology, ed. by Marshall M. Haith and Joseph J. Campos; v. 3, Cognitive development, ed. by John H. Flavell and Ellen M. Markman; v. 4, Socialization, personality, and social development, ed. by E. Mavis Hetherington.

This edition combines older material of historical value with more recent developments in theory and applied research to provide one of the most important handbooks in study of the child. Each volume can stand alone as a major specialized work, with chapters prepared by recognized leaders in their field; each volume has separate author and subject indexes.   BF721.H242

Handbook of developmental psychology / Benjamin B. Wolman, ed. ; George Stricker, associate ed. Englewood Cliffs, N.J. : Prentice-Hall, c1982. 960 p.   **CD86**

The 50 essays in this handbook cover the full range of human development, from research methodologies and theories to adolescence and old age. Physical growth, perceptual skills, and cognitive development are closely linked in each topical essay, and some areas such as socialization and the family receive more extensive coverage than other topics. An author index, broad subject index and a table of contents arranged roughly by age group provide somewhat limited access to the extensive time span covered.   BF713.H363

Handbook of infant development / ed. by Joy Doniger Osofsky. 2nd ed. N.Y. : Wiley, c1987. 1391 p. : ill.   **CD87**

Focusing on the first two years of life, the chapters in this work are arranged under five broad subject categories: Physiological, cognitive, and perceptual aspects of development; Social and interpersonal aspects; Methodological approaches to research; Identification of "at-risk" infants and treatment strategies; and a review of recent developments in research. The focus emphasizes mental health issues, but also contains more general topics of interest to researchers. An author and subject index is included.   BF719.H36

EDUCATIONAL PSYCHOLOGY

Bibliography

Baatz, Olga K. The psychological foundations of education : a guide to information sources / Olga K. Baatz, Charles Albert Baatz. Detroit : Gale, c1981. 441 p. (Gale information guide library. Education information guide series, v. 10).   **CD88**

Focusing on the relationship between education and psychology, this work provides a useful bibliography of primarily English-language books published before 1975. Most chapters are arranged thematically, with extensive subject subdivision under general headings (e.g., "Intellectual and moral education"). About half the entries include annotations, and there are author, title, and subject indexes.   Z5811.B2

A bibliographic guide to the literature of professional school psychology (1890–1985) / Thomas K. Fagan ... [et al.]. Stratford, Conn. : National Association of School Psychologists, 1986. 339 p.   **CD89**

A useful historical guide to the literature of school psychology, its nearly 5,000 citations include journals, books, newsletters, conference papers, reports and proceedings, and selected government publications. Emphasizes English-language materials. Entries are arranged under four broad headings (e.g., Assessment techniques) with topical subdivisions. Additional sections focus on formats, presenting lists of special journal issues, dissertations, and related nonjournal publications.   LB1027.55.A1B5

Indexes; Abstract journals

Current index to journals in education : (CIJE). v. 1, no. 1/2 (Jan./Feb. 1969)– . Phoenix : Oryx, 1969– . Monthly, with semiannual cumulations.   **CD90**

For annotation, *see* CB54.

●**ERIC** [database]. Rockville, Md. : ERIC Processing and Reference Facility.   **CD91**

For annotation, *see* CB56.

Exceptional child education resources. v. 9 (Spring 1977)– . Reston, Va. : Council for Exceptional Children, 1977– . Quarterly.   **CD92**

For annotation, *see* CB194.   Z5814.C52E9

Handbooks

See also section Tests and measurements (above).

Handbook of psychological and educational assessment of children / ed. by Cecil R. Reynolds, Randy W. Kamphaus. N.Y. : Guilford Pr., c1990. 2 v. : ill.   **CD93**

A directory of tests that provides a balanced review of a wide range of assessment instruments. Vol. 1 covers intelligence and achievement tests, v. 2 personality, behavior, and social skills. General essays cover issues such as test development and administration, but the majority of both volumes address specific instruments drawn from a wide range of specialized fields of study. Strengths and weaknesses are examined fully, and detailed reference lists are provided for each instrument.   BF722.H33

The handbook of school psychology / editors, Terry B. Gutkin, Cecil R. Reynolds. 2nd ed. N.Y. : Wiley, 1990. 1056 p. : ill.   **CD94**
1st ed., 1982.
Covers the broad topic of educational psychology under sections headed: History of school psychology; Current and future research issues; Related issues in theory and practice; Special topics in educational psychology including testing, legal, and ethical issues. Appendixes include a reprint of the American Psychological Association and National Association of School Psychologists' codes of ethics, and recent federal legislative regulations relevant to educators. Author and subject indexes.   LB1051.H2356

SOCIAL PSYCHOLOGY

Encyclopedias

The dictionary of personality and social psychology / ed. by Rom Harré and Roger Lamb. Cambridge, Mass. : MIT Pr., 1986. 402 p.   **CD95**
Derived from the authors' *Encyclopedic dictionary of psychology* (CD22), with many entries and reference lists updated to provide tighter focus on the main theories and issues of personality and social psychology. Extensive cross-references are provided, as is a modest subject index.   BF698.D527

Handbooks

Handbook of personality : theory and research / ed. by Lawrence A. Pervin. N.Y. : Guilford Pr., c1990. 738 p. : ill.
CD96
Essays by specialists cover both historical and recent developments in personality theory. In four sections, covers the development of personality theories, major theoretical approaches, the influence of other disciplines on the psychological study of personality, and environmental and interpersonal influences on personality, including sex roles. Extensive bibliographies with each chapter; subject index.
BF698.H335

Handbook of social psychology / Gardner Lindzey, Elliot Aronson. 3rd ed. N.Y. : Random House ; Hillsdale, N.J. : L. Erlbaum Associates, c1985. 2 v. : ill.   **CD97**
1st ed., Cambridge, Mass. : Addison-Wesley, 1954.
Contents: v. 1, Theory and method; v. 2, Special fields and applications.
A standard work since its first appearance, providing comprehensive and authoritative coverage both for theory and practical applications. Vol. 1 includes learning and cognitive theory, experimental method, and surveys, and v. 2 topics such as sex roles, mass communication, and socialization. Provides literature reviews for most topics. Author and subject indexes in each volume.   HM251.H224

Testing and measurement

Measures of personality and social psychological attitudes / ed. by John P. Robinson, Phillip R. Shaver, Lawrence S. Wrightsman. San Diego : Academic Pr., c1991. 753 p. (Measures of social psychological attitudes, v. 1).   **CD98**
Title varies; rev. ed., 1973, had title: *Measures of social psychological attitudes*, ed. by Robinson and Shaver (Ann Arbor, Mich. : Survey Research Center, Inst. for Social Research, 1973. 750 p.).
Focuses on effective instruments for measuring attitudes and opinions. A sample, and in some cases the entire instrument, is reproduced, accompanied by an evaluative essay describing the intent, reliability, and validity of the test. Most instruments were previously published in journals, books, or research reports.   BF698.4.M38

CLINICAL PSYCHOLOGY

See also section Psychiatry under EH, Medical and Health Sciences.

Encyclopedias

The dictionary of physiological and clinical psychology / ed. by Rom Harré and Roger Lamb. Cambridge, Mass. : MIT Pr., 1986. 314 p. : ill.   **CD99**
Derived from the authors' *Encyclopedic dictionary of psychology* (CD22), with many entries added and reference lists updated. Contains some 250 lengthy entries covering all aspects of abnormal behavior, including the chemistry and neurophysiology of the brain and nervous system. Subject index.   RC467.D48

Doctor, Ronald M. The encyclopedia of phobias, fears, and anxieties / Ronald M. Doctor and Ada P. Kahn. N.Y. : Facts on File, c1989. 487 p.   **CD100**
Entries include the clinical names of phobias, their causes, and various treatment options. Entries vary greatly in size and scope, and some include bibliographies. Aimed at students rather than practitioners, this work makes use of extensive cross-references and has a subject index.   RC535.D63

Howells, John G. A reference companion to the history of abnormal psychology / John G. Howells and M. Livia Osborn. Westport, Conn. : Greenwood, 1984. 2 v. (1141 p.) : ill.
CD101
More than 4,200 entries broadly cover the field of abnormal and clinical psychology, including some psychic and paranormal phenomena. Most entries focus on theories, individuals, and institutions central to the history, diagnosis, and treatment of the mentally ill. Coverage is international and most entries include additional references. An appendix classifies the entries under 40 broad subject categories, and there is an author/subject index.   RC454.4.H68

Dictionaries

Goodwin, Diana M. A dictionary of neuropsychology. N.Y. : Springer-Verlag, c1989. 325 p.   **CD102**
A concise and useful work for students, providing definitions of syndromes, symptoms, and terminology used widely in physiology, as well as descriptions of methodologies, instrumentation, and treatments used in this area of psychology. Cross-references are provided as well as an appendix of cited references.   QP360.G66

Handbooks

The clinical psychology handbook / ed. by Michel Hersen, Alan E. Kazdin, Alan S. Bellack. 2nd ed. N.Y. : Pergamon, c1991. 846 p. : ill. (Pergamon general psychology series, 120).
CD103

Topical essays on major themes in clinical psychology, from its theoretical foundations to personality models and treatments, including behavior modification and group therapy. Written by experts, the essays present a good balance of historical information and current research. Extensive bibliographies accompany each essay; author and subject indexes.   RC467.2.C55

The handbook of clinical psychology : theory, research, and practice / ed. by C. Eugene Walker. Homewood, Ill. : Dow Jones-Irwin, c1983. 2 v. (1439 p.) : ill.   **CD104**

Provides detailed, extensive coverage of all aspects of clinical psychology, from theoretical and experimental foundations to research, diagnosis, and treatment. Vol. 2 focuses on recent developments in treatment methods, e.g., substance abuse, stress management, family therapy, biofeedback. Selected reading lists accompany each essay, and there is a subject index.   RC467.H27

Handbook of counseling psychology / ed. by Steven D. Brown, Robert W. Lent. 2nd ed. N.Y. : Wiley, c1992. 861 p. : ill.   **CD105**

More than 20 essays, arranged in six broad categories covering ethical, historical, and legal issues in psychotherapeutic counseling. Each chapter contains lengthy bibliographies that list both historical and contemporary resources, making this a useful work for both practitioners and students. Subject index.   BF637.C6H315

Meyer, Robert G. The clinician's handbook : the psychopathology of adulthood and adolescence. 2nd ed. Boston : Allyn and Bacon, c1989. 419 p. : ill.   **CD106**

Provides an integrated overview of personality styles, symptoms, tests, and treatment recommendations. Designed primarily for practitioners, but students will find the review of a wide range of behavior disorders valuable, presenting a brief description and methods for assessment. An extensive bibliography reflects recent research in the field. Author and subject indexes.   RC469.M46

COGNITION AND INTELLIGENCE

Bibliography

Emmett, Kathleen. Perception : an annotated bibliography / Kathleen Emmett and Peter Machamer. N.Y. : Garland, 1976. 177 p. (Garland reference library of the humanities, v. 39).
CD107

More than 1,400 citations to works published 1935–74 in books and journals, with an emphasis on English-language materials. Arrangement is by author with a brief subject index. Some entries are annotated. Although the work focuses mostly on philosophical approaches to perception, it provides a valuable unified historical and contextual view of a topic that is often the focus of many disparate fields of study.   Z7204.P45E45

Miletich, John J. States of awareness : an annotated bibliography. N.Y. : Greenwood, 1988. 292 p. (Bibliographies and indexes in psychology, no. 5).   **CD108**

Covers English-language publications from the late 1800s to the 1980s. More than 1,100 citations focus on the theme of altered states. Works are organized under nine topical headings such as amnesia, out-of-body experiences, and sleepwalking, with lengthy annotations for each entry. Personal name, author, subject, and acronym indexes.
Z7204.C64M54

Parsifal-Charles, Nancy. The dream : 4,000 years of theory and practice : a critical, descriptive, and encyclopedic bibliography. West Cornwall, Conn. : Locust Hill Pr., 1986. 2 v. (576 p.).   **CD109**

An annotated, evaluative bibliography of more than 700 books on dreams, dream theory, and interpretation, arranged alphabetically by author and focusing primarily on 20th-century works. Journal articles are excluded. International in scope, it covers classical and modern theories and figures. Detailed subject and personal name indexes.
BF1078.P33

Encyclopedias

Encyclopedia of learning and memory / Larry R. Squire, ed. in chief. N.Y. : Macmillan : Maxwell Macmillan International, c1992. 678 p. : ill.   **CD110**

The 189 essays in this work cover all aspects of learning and memory, with an emphasis on the human experience. Written by specialists in psychology and neuroscience, most entries have bibliographies. Entries are alphabetically arranged with numerous cross-references to related materials. General overview essays also have been provided for some broad subjects (e.g., learning).   BF318.E53

Encyclopedia of sleep and dreaming / Mary A. Carskadon, ed. in chief. N.Y. : Macmillan : Maxwell Macmillan International, c1993. 703 p. : ill.   **CD111**

More than 400 signed articles on all aspects of sleep, sleep disorders, and dreams. Ample cross-references and extensive illustrations, as well as a detailed author/title/subject index make this a useful resource for all levels of students and researchers. Each entry provides at least one reference for further reading.   BF1078.E63

Handbooks

Handbook of human intelligence / ed. by Robert J. Sternberg. Cambridge ; N.Y. : Cambridge Univ. Pr., 1982. 1031 p. : ill.   **CD112**

Drawing on all areas of psychology, this work provides an advanced review of all aspects of intelligence. Chapters are grouped under four categories: Nature and measurement of intelligence; Learning and memory; Reasoning, perception, and artificial intelligence; and The effects of environment, evolution, and genetics on intelligence. Name and subject indexes.   BF431.H3186

Handbook of perception and human performance / editors, Kenneth R. Boff, Lloyd Kaufman, James P. Thomas. N.Y. : Wiley, c1986. 2 v. : ill.   **CD113**

Contents: v. 1, Sensory processes and perception; v. 2, Cognitive processes and performance.

A comprehensive review intended for both students and researchers. Vol. 1 includes sections on theory and methods, the senses, and space and motor perception; v. 2, sections on cognition, information processing, and performance. Detailed subject index.   BF311.H3345

Stevens' handbook of experimental psychology. 2nd ed. / ed. by Richard C. Atkinson ... [et al.]. N.Y. : Wiley, c1988. 2 v. : ill.   **CD114**

1st. ed., 1951, had title: *Handbook of experimental psychology*, ed. by S. S. Stevens.

Contents: v. 1, Perception and motivation; v. 2, Learning and cognition.

Treats all aspects of human cognition, learning, and perception. Vol. 1 includes other aspects of sensation, v. 2 includes memory and problem solving. Each volume has author and subject indexes.
BF181.H336

PHYSIOLOGICAL AND COMPARATIVE PSYCHOLOGY

See also section Clinical psychology (above).

Bibliography

Butler, Francine. Biofeedback : a survey of the literature. N.Y. : IFI/Plenum, c1978. 340 p. **CD115**
An overview of virtually every aspect of biofeedback as a physiological and therapeutic process, covering the period 1950–70, although a few earlier works are included. English-language materials from a wide range of subject fields are represented. Entries are by author, with keyword title index. Z7204.B56B87

Davis, Martha. Understanding body movement : an annotated bibliography. N.Y. : Arno Pr., 1972. 190 p. **CD116**
————. *Body movement and nonverbal communication : an annotated bibliography, 1971–1981*, ed. by Martha Davis and Janet Skupien (Bloomington : Indiana Univ. Pr., c1982. 294 p.).
Together, these bibliographies present a fine overview of the anthropological and psychological aspects of body movement and nonverbal communication, including motor learning and physiology. More than 2,300 works are cited, with annotations. The 1972 title lists works published in English since 1900; the later volume includes some foreign-language materials. Entries are arranged by author, with a subject index. An appendix lists journals relevant to human movement research. Z7201.D3

Dingwall, William Orr. Language and the brain : a bibliography and guide. N.Y. : Garland, 1981. 2 v. (1017 p.). **CD117**
More than 5,700 entries covering the international literature about language development and the brain, arranged under five broad headings: General works and philosophy; Language functions; Neurological disorders; Development of language; and The evolution of communication and the brain. Each section is preceded by an introductory essay, and is subdivided by topic, thus providing structured access to the field. Most entries were published after 1960 although a few earlier works are included. An appendix lists journals, series, and societies. Intended for students or active researchers. Author and subject indexes. Z6663.B8D56

Indexes; Abstract journals

Animal behavior abstracts. v. 2 (Feb. 1974)– . London : Information Retrieval Limited, 1974– . Quarterly. **CD118**
Publisher varies; v. 10 (Mar. 1982)– publ.: Bethesda, Md. : Cambridge Scientific Abstracts.
Vol. 1 (Feb.–Nov. 1973) publ. as: *Behavioural biology abstracts. Section A : Animal behaviour*.
Citations are topically arranged. Gives extensive coverage to such subjects as migration, evolution, innate behavior, learning and memory, and behavioral ecology. Annual index. QL750.B54

Encyclopedias

The dictionary of ethology and animal learning / ed. by Rom Harré and Roger Lamb. Cambridge, Mass. : MIT Pr., 1986. 171 p. : ill. **CD119**
Derived from the authors' *Encyclopedic dictionary of psychology* (CD22), the lengthy entries covering all aspects of animal behavior reflect the greatest amount of revision and updating from the original work. Cross-references are used extensively and a detailed subject index is provided. QL750.3.D53

The Oxford companion to animal behaviour / ed. by David McFarland. Oxford ; N.Y. : Oxford Univ. Pr., 1987. 685 p. : ill. **CD120**
Originally publ. 1981; 1987 printing incorporates corrections and a new index.
A basic encyclopedia covering animal behavior, physiology, and psychology. Most entries contain bibliographies and many have cross-references. An appendix provides a cumulative reference list and an index to common and scientific names. QL750.3.O94

Dictionaries

Immelmann, Klaus. A dictionary of ethology / Klaus Immelmann, Colin Beer. Cambridge, Mass. : Harvard Univ. Pr., 1989. 336 p. : ill. **CD121**
Translation of: *Wörterbuch der Verhaltensforschung* (Berlin : Parey, 1982).
Defines key terms and concepts in psychology and biology related to animal studies. Entries include the historical significance and provide examples of research relevant to the term defined. Cross-references; list of cited works. QL750.3.I4513

Handbooks

Gazzaniga, Michael S. Handbook of psychobiology / ed. by Michael S. Gazzaniga, Colin Blakemore. N.Y. : Academic Pr., 1975. 639 p. : ill. **CD122**
Covering psychology, biochemistry, and neurology, this work despite its age provides an excellent overview of the field. Essays are arranged in four areas: Elementary processes and foundations; Neurochemical behaviors (emphasizing nonhuman species); Sensory and motor functions; and Integrative functions (e.g., learning, communication, and dreaming, emphasizing primates). Subject index.
QP360.G38

Lehner, Philip N. Handbook of ethological methods. N.Y. : Garland STPM Pr., c1979. 403 p. : ill. **CD123**
A fine introduction to the purpose of ethology and the methods used to study nonhuman species. Appendixes of statistical tables; a valuable bibliography; subject index. QL751.L398

INDUSTRIAL AND ORGANIZATIONAL PSYCHOLOGY

Bibliography

Riggar, T. F. Stress burnout : an annotated bibliography. Carbondale : Southern Illinois Univ., c1985. 299 p. **CD124**

Provides references to English-language books and journal articles on job stress, with emphasis on the period 1976–82. Arranged by author, each entry gives bibliographical information and lengthy annotations. Three topical indexes class the citations by signs and symptoms, causes and sources of burnout, and coping strategies.

BF481.R53

Walsh, Ruth M. Job satisfaction and motivation : an annotated bibliography / comp. and ed. by Ruth M. Walsh and Stanley J. Birkin. Westport, Conn. : Greenwood, 1979. 643 p. **CD125**

Some 1,000 citations, covering primarily 1970–78, including books, journals, research reports, and government publications. Covering the literatures of psychology, sociology, personnel administration and management, and related fields, the annotated entries are searchable through author and keyword indexes. Z7164.C81W25

Handbooks

Bass, Bernard M. Bass & Stogdill's handbook of leadership : theory, research, and managerial applications. 3rd ed. N.Y. : Free Pr. ; London : Collier Macmillan, c1990. 1182 p. : ill. **CD126**

1st ed. (1974), ed. by Ralph Melvin Stogdill, had title: *Handbook of leadership*; rev. and expanded ed. (1981), also ed. by Stogdill, had title: *Stogdill's handbook of leadership*.

One of the most important works in the field, reviewing more than 5,000 works on leadership theory and research, management styles, and training. Includes many unpublished or limited circulation reports. Glossary; author and subject indexes. HM141.S83

Handbook of industrial and organizational psychology / Marvin D. Dunnette and Leaetta M. Hough, editors. 2nd ed. Palo Alto, Calif. : Consulting Psychologists Pr., c1990–92. v. 1–3. (In progress). **CD127**

1st ed., 1976.

Vol. 1 covers theory in industrial psychology, v. 2 individual and organizational behaviors, and v. 3 covers organizational conflict and stress and consumer psychology. A final volume will focus on cross-cultural issues. Reference lists accompany each chapter; name and subject indexes in each volume. HF5548.8.H265

Handbook of organizational behavior / Jay W. Lorsch, ed. Englewood Cliffs, N.J. : Prentice-Hall, c1987. 430 p. : ill. **CD128**

More than 20 essays are arranged under six broad headings covering all aspects of industrial and organizational psychology. Emphasizes the influence of other disciplines, including other areas of psychology. A valuable work for beginning students, but the lack of any indexes makes identifying specific topics difficult. HD58.7.H355

Handbook of vocational psychology / ed. by W. Bruce Walsh and Samuel H. Osipow. Hillsdale, N.J. : Lawrence Erlbaum Associates, 1983. 2 v. : ill. **CD129**

Aimed at advanced students and researchers; covers many of psychology's specialized subfields with an emphasis on historical and theoretical issues. Vol. 1 treats history, theory, and current issues in vocational psychology; v. 2 covers issues and methods in career counseling and vocational rehabilitation. Each volume has its own author and subject index. HF5381.H1335

PARAPSYCHOLOGY

Bibliography

Kies, Cosette N. The occult in the western world : an annotated bibliography. Hamden, Conn. : Library Professional Publications, 1986. 233 p. **CD130**

Lists works on traditional and modern witchcraft, magic, secret societies, psychics, ghosts, UFOs, astrology, and related topics. Each chapter begins with introductory essay; annotations vary greatly in length. Brief glossary; name and title indexes. Z6876.K53

White, Rhea A. Parapsychology : sources of information / comp. under the auspices of the American Society for Psychical Research by Rhea A. White and Laura A. Dale. Metuchen, N.J. : Scarecrow, 1973. 302 p. **CD131**

Supplemented and updated by: *Parapsychology : new sources of information, 1973–1989* by Rhea A. White (Metuchen, N.J. : Scarecrow, 1990. 699 p.).

Together, these works provide a comprehensive guide to parapsychology, with citations to nearly 1,000 English-language books classified under 24 broad headings. Evaluative annotations, cross-references, and a useful glossary and chronology are provided, as are name, title, and subject indexes. Topics such as as astrology, the occult, and witchcraft are excluded. Z6878.P8W47

Indexes; Abstract journals

Exceptional human experience. v. 8 (1990)– . Dix Hills, N.Y. : Parapsychology Sources of Information Ctr., 1990– . Semiannual. **CD132**

Subtitle: Summaries of the literature of parapsychology from earliest times to date.

Rhea A. White, ed.

Continues *Parapsychology abstracts international* (v. 1–7, 1983–90).

Covers some 100 journals, books, and conference proceedings representing anthropology, philosophy, psychology, sociology, and related disciplines. Abstracts are arranged by broad format. (Parapsychology journals, General interest works, Nonperiodical formats) and focus on current research, experiences, and methodologies. Author and title indexes in each issue, with a cumulative annual subject index. BF1001.P275

Encyclopedias

Berger, Arthur S. The encyclopedia of parapsychology and psychical research / Arthur S. Berger and Joyce Berger. N.Y. : Paragon House, 1991. 554 p. **CD133**

Some 1,400 entries focus on individuals, movements, organizations, phenomena, and research techniques. Some longer entries have brief bibliographies, and coverage of recent publications and non-Western beliefs is especially good. Numerous cross-references. Appendixes provide access to the entries by country and outline the history and state of current research in 18 countries. BF1025.B47

Encyclopedia of occultism & parapsychology / ed. by Leslie Shepard. 3rd ed. Detroit : Gale, c1991. 2 v. (2008 p.). **CD134**

2nd ed., 1984.

Subtitle: A compendium of information on the occult sciences, magic, demonology, superstitions, spiritism, mysticism, metaphysics, psychical science, and parapsychology, with biographical notes and comprehensive indexes.

An update and revision of two classic resources, *Encyclopaedia of occultism* by Lewis Spence (London : G. Routledge, 1920) and Nandor Fodor's *Encyclopedia of psychic science* (London : Arthurs Pr., 1934), this comprehensive work covers concepts, real and fictional individuals, organizations, and influential publications. Emphasizes 19th- and early 20th-century works, although some entries have been substantially updated. Most entries contain bibliographic references. General and topical indexes lists articles under nine broad subjects (e.g., demons, gods, paranormal phenomena).   BF1407E56

CE

Anthropology and Ethnology

GENERAL WORKS

Dictionaries

The Donning international encyclopedic psychic dictionary / June G. Bletzer. Norfolk, Va. : Donning, c1986. 875 p.
CD135
Provides definitions for some 8,000 terms used in psychic and paranormal research, including biofeedback and altered states. Presents balanced and comprehensive coverage between Eastern and Western cultures. Appendixes include a lengthy bibliography of parapsychological works as well as a classified list of all entries under four broad subject categories.   BF1025.D66

Riland, George. The new Steinerbooks dictionary of the paranormal. N.Y. : Steinerbooks, c1980. 358 p. (Spiritual science library, v. 5).   **CD136**
Nearly 2,800 brief alphabetical entries cover traditions and terms from different ages, countries, cultures and religions. Entries define terms and outline key concepts and historical impact and importance. A good supplementary dictionary to the larger *Donning international encyclopedic psychic dictionary* (CD135).   BF1025.R5

Handbooks

Guide to the American occult. 1986– . Olathe, Kans. : Laird Wilcox, [1986]– . Annual.   **CD137**
Editor: Laird Wilcox.
Publisher varies.
Alphabetical list of U.S. organizations, coded to indicate involvement with astrology, witchcraft, UFOs, mystical/metaphysical, psychic, holistic health, or related general subjects. Also lists serial publications on the occult, followed by a combined list of publications and organizations arranged by zip code. List of "Counter-Cult organizations" (groups whose mission is to oppose occult thought or particular religions or sects). Glossary; bibliography.   BF1434.U6G85

Handbook of parapsychology / ed. by Benjamin B. Wolman. N.Y. : Van Nostrand Reinhold, [1977]. 967 p., [7] leaves of plates : ill.   **CD138**
Repr. : Jefferson, N.C. : McFarland, 1986.
A solid overview, with chapters arranged under 11 broad headings such as history, theory, and research methods. Signed chapters contain extensive bibliographies covering the international literature, and a separate further reading list is included in a final chapter. Glossary, name, and subject indexes.   BF1031.H254

Guides

Kibbee, Josephine Z. Cultural anthropology : a guide to reference and information sources. Englewood, Colo. : Libraries Unlimited, 1991. 205 p. (Reference sources in the social sciences series, no. 5).   **CE1**
A comprehensive introduction to the field. In sections for general and social science reference, general anthropology reference, bibliographies, 16 traditional subfields, anthropology and the humanities, area studies, periodicals. Entries are annotated and cross-referenced. Subfields covered include: archaeology, linguistics, ethnomusicology, ethnohistory, medical anthropology, and visual anthropology. The last chapter (Supplemental resources) includes lists of organizations, libraries, archives, and publishers. Author/title and subject indexes.
Z5111.K53

Weeks, John M. Introduction to library research in anthropology. Boulder, Colo. : Westview Pr., 1991. 281 p.   **CE2**
Introductory chapters on the nature of the discipline and information on basic library research are followed by 18 chapters detailing sources specific to anthropology. Topics include: specialized library catalogs, archives and manuscripts, bibliographies, dictionaries and encyclopedias, indexes and abstracts, government documents, atlases and maps, online databases, and the Human Relations Area Files. Each section begins with a brief overview; each annotation covers scope, arrangement, and content. Appendixes explain the Library of Congress classification system for anthropology, list U.S. and Canadian library collections, and detail the organization of George Peter Murdock's *Outline of world cultures* (CE59) and Murdock's related work, *Outline of cultural materials* (CE61). Author, ethnic group, and geographic indexes. Has some overlap with Josephine Z. Kibbee's *Cultural anthropology* (CE1), but covers other subdisciplines (e.g., archaeology and physical anthropology) and contains almost twice as many entries.
Z5111.W44

Bibliography

General

Anthropology of aging : a partially annotated bibliography / Marjorie M. Schweitzer, gen. ed. N.Y. : Greenwood, 1991. 338 p. (Bibliographies and indexes in gerontology, no. 13).
CE3
For annotation, *see* CC59.   Z7164.O4A55

Brown, Samuel R. Finding the source in sociology and anthropology : a thesaurus-index to the reference collection. N.Y. : Greenwood, 1987. 269 p. (Finding the source, no. 1). **CE4**

For annotation, *see* CC5. Z7164.S68B75

Bunakova, O. V. Bibliografiĩa trudov Instituta etnografiĩ im. N. N. Miklukho-Maklaĩa, 1900–1962 / sostaviteli: O. V. Bunakova, P. V. Kamenetskaĩa. Leningrad : Nauka, 1967. 281 p. **CE5**

At head of title : Akademiĩa nauk SSSR. Biblioteka Akademii nauk SSR. Institut etnografii im. N.N. Miklukho-Maklaĩa.

Added t.p.: Bibliographie des travaux de l'Institut d'ethnographie Mikloukho-Maclay.

Table of contents in Russian and French.

A classed bibliography of 5,195 items; reviews are noted. Author and subject indexes. Z5111.B8

Comas, Juan. Historia y bibliografía de los congresos internacionales de ciencias antropológicas, 1865–1954. México : Dirección General de Publicaciones, 1956. 490 p. : ill. (University Nacional Autónoma de México. Publicaciones del Instituto de Historia, 1. ser., núm. 37). **CE6**

Covers the activities and publications of four major international organizations in anthropology, plus those of several smaller bodies. Includes a classified subject bibliography of some 3,000 papers which have been published in the reports of the more important congresses. GN17.C6

Conklin, Harold C. Folk classification : a topically arranged bibliography of contemporary and background references through 1971. Rev. reprinting with author index. New Haven, Conn. : Dept. of Anthropology, Yale Univ., 1980. 521 p. **CE7**

1st ed., 1972.

"This 1980 edition differs from the 1972 publication in two respects: a number of corrections have been made and a single Index to all authors, listed together with the Sections in which their works are cited, has been added at the end."—[*p.18*] A classed listing of about 5,000 entries. Includes "references to (1) analyses of specific systems of folk classification, (2) discussions and comparisons of such analyses, and (3) theoretical and practical background literature on classification in general and in various subject fields."—*Introd.* Includes publications only to 1972, as in the earlier edition. Z5118.P5C65

•**Cross-cultural CD** [database]. New Haven, Conn. : Human Relations Area Files, 1991–1993. 4 discs. (In progress). **CE8**

Contents: Disc 1, Human sexuality and marriage (1990); Disc 2, Family, crime and social problems (1991); Disc 3, Old age, death and dying (1992); Disc 4, Childhood and adolescence; Socialization and education (1993).

Available in CD-ROM.

Full-text databases containing information on customs, practices, and traits of 60 selected societies, derived from the original printed Human Relations Area Files (HRAF). Each database contains 6,000–12,000 pages of text, citations to original source documents, and summary information concerning each society. GN345.7.C767

Divale, William Tulio. Warfare in primitive societies : a bibliography. [Rev. ed.]. Santa Barbara, Calif. : ABC-Clio, [c1973]. 123 p. (War/peace bibliography series, 2). **CE9**

1st ed., 1971.

Pt. 1 is divided into sixteen theoretical or topical sections (biological factors, demographic factors, scalping, war ceremonies, etc.); pt. 2 comprises sections on seven major geographical regions (four of which are further subdivided by area), and lists sources on the warfare of the various peoples of these regions. Author and tribal name indexes. Z5118.W3D57

Ferguson, R. Brian. The anthropology of war : a bibliography / R. Brian Ferguson with Leslie E. Farragher. N.Y. : Harry Frank Guggenheim Foundation, 1988. 361 p. (Harry Frank Guggenheim Foundation, no. l). **CE10**

A comprehensive bibliography of "non-modern warfare" (*Introd.*) that excludes warfare as carried on under the influence of the technical and political developments since 15th-century Europe. More than 5,000 citations are divided into 23 topical sections (e.g., Ecology, demography and war; Feud; Magic, religion, ritual and war; Raiding for slaves). No separate author or subject indexes.

§ Complements and updates William T. Divale's *Warfare in primitive societies* (CE9). GN497.F47

Gravel, Pierre Bettez. Anthropological fieldwork : an annotated bibliography / Pierre Bettez Gravel and Robert B. Marks Ridinger. N.Y. : Garland, 1988. 241 p. (Garland reference library of social science, v. 419). **CE11**

An annotated bibliography of 700 entries focusing on "the practical aspects of fieldwork."—*Pref.* Covers journal articles, monographs, and museum literature in English, French, and German. Most citations are from the 20th century, with a few dating as early as 1800 for historical perspective. Entries are alphabetical by author; geographical and subject indexes. Z5118.F44G7

Harrison, Ira E. Traditional medicine / Ira E. Harrison and Sheila Cosminsky. N.Y. : Garland, 1976–84. 2 v. (Garland reference library of social science, v. 19, 147). **CE12**

For annotation, *see* EH185. Z5118.M4H3

Human rights and anthropology / Theodore E. Downing and Gilbert Kushner, editors … [et al.]. Cambridge, Mass : Cultural Survival, c1988. 200 p. (Cultural Survival report, v. 24). **CE13**

In two parts: a collection of conference papers, each with a list of references, and an extensive bibliography with more than 1,000 entries in 20 categories. Topics covered include cultural relativism, racism, genocide and ethnocide, indigenous rights, and the rights of women and children. Entries are not annotated; no index.

International catalogue of scientific literature / publ. for the Internat. Council by the Royal Soc. of London. v. 1 (1901)–v. 14 (1914). London : Harrison, 1902–21. **CE14**

Section P, Anthropology. For full description, *see* EA16.

Kemper, Robert V. The history of anthropology : a research bibliography / Robert V. Kemper and John F. S. Phinney. N.Y. : Garland, 1977. 212 p. (Garland reference library of social science, v. 31). **CE15**

A classed bibliography of more than 2,400 entries arranged in five major sections: (1) general sources; (2) background (largely pre-1900); (3) modern anthropology; (4) related social sciences; (5) bibliographical sources. Each major section is further subdivided by subject, geographic area, and personality. Author index. Z5111.K44

Miller, Mamie Ruth Tanquist. An author, title, and subject check list of Smithsonian Institution publications relating to anthropology / publ. in cooperation with the School of American Research…. Albuquerque : Univ. of New Mexico Pr., 1946. 218 p. (University of New Mexico. Bulletin Bibliographical series, v. 1, no. 2; whole no. 405). **CE16**

For full list of publications of the Bureau of American Ethnology, *see* CE83. Z5111.M5

Rosenstiel, Annette. Education and anthropology : an annotated bibliography. N.Y. : Garland, 1977. 646 p. (Garland reference library of social science, v. 20). **CE17**

An international bibliography of 3,435 books, periodical articles, dissertations, papers, reprints, etc., "reflecting (1) historical influences, (2) current trends, (3) theoretical concerns, and (4) practical methodology at the interfaces of these two disciplines."—*Introd.* Author arrangement, with English translations provided for foreign-language titles. Covers the literature from 1689 to 1976. Two indexes: topical subject and regional, which includes both geographic and cultural group names.   Z5814.E2R67

Van Willigen, John. Anthropology in use : a source book on anthropological practice. Boulder, Colo. : Westview Pr., 1991. 254 p.   **CE18**

1st ed., 1980, had title: *Anthropology in use: a bibliographic chronology of the development of applied anthropology.*

Some 500 case studies topically organized in six chapters: prediscipline activities, early discipline activities, ethics, publications, research and professional organizations, and cases of application and procedure. Entries arranged chronologically within chapters. No cross-references. General index to personal names, institutions, place-names, and some subject terms. Includes only those titles voluntarily submitted to the Applied Anthropology Documentation Project. Does not cover archaeology or physical anthropology, or extensively cover the publications of government, private and academic-sponsored research.   Z5118.A54V37

Bibliography of bibliography

Anthropological bibliographies : a selected guide / comp. by Library-Anthropology Resource Group, Margo L. Smith and Yvonne M. Damien, editors. South Salem, N.Y. : Redgrave Publ. Co., 1981. 307 p.   **CE19**

More than 3,200 bibliographic monographs, periodical articles, essays, filmographies, and discographies are organized geographically, with a separate section for topical bibliographies lacking geographical emphasis. Emphasizes recent publications and updates earlier guides to anthropological bibliographies for Africa, Asia, the Americas, and the Soviet Union. Some brief annotations. Indexed by personal name, geographic area, ethnic group, language, and subject areas.

Titova, Zoia Dmitrievna. Etnografiia : bibliografiia russkikh bibliografii po etnografii narodov SSSR (1851–1969). Moskva : "Kniga", 1970. 141 p.   **CE20**

An annotated listing of 734 items arranged primarily by geographical area. The last chapter lists bibliographies of the works of ethnographers. Indexed by ethnic group, personal name, and subject or geographical name. Also indexes journals, newspapers and collected works, with cumulative indexes included in listing.   Z5117.T53

Current

Annual review of anthropology. v.1 (1972)– . Palo Alto, Calif. : Annual Reviews Inc., 1972– . Annual.   **CE21**

Describes and evaluates recent noteworthy publications in the field. Chapters by specialists on topics of current interest and varying scope in physical, social, and cultural anthropology are followed by extensive bibliographies giving full citations to the writings discussed. International in coverage, but with a high percentage of references in English. Cumulative author and subject indexes.

§ Continues *Biennial review of anthropology* (1958–1971. Stanford, Calif. : Stanford Univ. Pr., 1959–71), which had a similar arrangement and was indexed by subject.   Z5112.A5

Bibliographic guide to anthropology and archaeology. 1987– . Boston : G.K. Hall & Co., c1988– . Annual.   **CE22**

Supplements the Tozzer Library's *Author and subject catalogues of the Tozzer Library* (CE30). "Contains entries for books, serials, microforms, manuscripts, maps and video recordings" (*Introd.*) added to the Library's collections since June 1986. Main entry, title, and subject heading access in one alphabet.   Z5111.B47

FRANCIS. Bulletin signalétique. v. 1 (1947)– . Paris : Centre de Documentation du C.N.R.S. [Centre National de la Recherche Scientifique], 1947– . Quarterly.   **CE23**

Includes Sec. 529, *Ethnologie*, v. 45 (1991)– . International in scope and topically arranged. More than 4,000 articles and chapters indexed annually in quarterly issues. Subject classification scheme explained in introduction. Entries include brief annotations and locations. Subject, geographic (by country), ethnic group (by continent), and author indexes. Annual cumulative index also includes list of journals and collected works indexed. For full description, *see* AD254.

International bibliography of social and cultural anthropology = Bibliographie internationale d'anthropologie sociale et culturelle / prep. by the International Committee for Social Sciences Documentation in cooperation with the International Congress of Anthropological and Ethnological Sciences. v. 1 (1955)– . London : UNESCO ; N.Y. : Tabistock, 1958– . Annual.   **CE24**

Publisher varies: v. 1–5 publ. as part of *Documentation in the social sciences* (Paris : UNESCO); v. 6–32, as a *Publication* of the International Committee for Social Sciences Documentation; v. 33– prep. by the British Library of Political and Economic Sciences.

A companion to the other Unesco annual bibliographies in the social sciences: sociology (CC8), economics (CH43), and political science (CJ15). Broad international coverage of books, periodical articles, and other works. Non-English titles, except for French, are translated. Arranged by a special classification scheme, outlined in the prefatory matter, with author index, place name index, and subject indexes in both English and French. Since 1990, includes information formerly published in the *London bibliography of the social sciences* (CA13).   Z7161.I593

Periodicals

Serial publications in anthropology / comp. by Library-Anthropology Resource Group ; F. X. Grollig and Sol Tax, eds. South Salem, N.Y. : Redgrave, [1982]. 177 p.   **CE25**

1st ed., 1973.

An alphabetical main entry listing of current serial anthropological titles, including publisher's address and frequency. International in coverage. Indexed by topical and geographic subjects, and by corporate author.   Z5112.S47

Williams, John T. Anthropology journals and serials : an analytical guide. N.Y. : Greenwood, 1986. 182 p. (Annotated bibliographies of serials. A subject approach, no. 10).   **CE26**

Lists 404 currently published English-language serials, arranged in five sections: Archaeology, Cultural anthropology, Linguistics, Physical anthropology, and Indexes and abstracts. Each entry has two parts: bibliographic and subscription information, and an annotation that indicates scope, purpose, and format. Title, subject, and geographic indexes. Unique in the discipline for its depth of coverage.   Z5112.W54

Dissertations and theses

McDonald, David Roark. Masters' theses in anthropology : a bibliography of theses from United States colleges and universities. New Haven, Conn. : HRAF Pr., 1977. 453 p.   **CE27**

A list of more than 3,700 titles, arranged by broad subjects— social/cultural anthropology, archaeology, physical anthropology, linguistics. Covers the period 1898–1975. Indexed by subject, ethnic group, geographical area, cross-cultural studies, author, and educational institution.   Z5111.M26

Webber, Jonathan. Research in social anthropology, 1975– 1980 : a register of theses accepted for higher degrees at British universities, 1975–1980. London : Royal Anthropological Institute, c1983. 425 p.   **CE28**

Alphabetical listing, by author, of 404 masters' theses and doctoral dissertations in social anthropology, with abstracts. Five indexes:

author; academic institution; country of research; peoples and cultures; and subject (from words in title). Thorough explanation of conventions used to compile entries; scope defined in preface.   GN316.W42

Library catalogs

Harvard University. Library. Geography and anthropology : classification schedules; classified listing by call number; chronological listing; author and title listing. Cambridge : Publ. by the Harvard Univ. Library; distr. by Harvard Univ. Pr., 1979. 270 p. (Widener Library shelflist, 60).   **CE29**
For a note on the series, *see* AA115.
Includes some "9000 shelf list entries comprising the Widener *Geog* and *An* classes."—*Foreword.* It should be kept in mind that "Harvard's major research collection in anthropology is in the Tozzer Library, whose holdings are represented by the *Catalogue of the Library of the Peabody Museum of Archaeology and Ethnology [Tozzer Library index to anthropological subject headings*, CE53]."
Z6009.H37

Tozzer Library. Author and subject catalogues of the Tozzer Library [microform]. 2nd enl. ed. Boston : G.K. Hall, 1988. 8 v. (1122 microfiches) : negative.   **CE30**
Supersedes: Harvard University. Peabody Museum of Archaeology and Ethnology. Library. *Catalogue : authors* and *Catalogue : subjects* (Boston : G.K. Hall, 1963) and their supplements.
Contains entries for monographs and serials cataloged through 1986 and periodical articles through 1983. Continued, for cataloged entries after 1986, by *Bibliographic guide to anthropology and archaeology* (CE22) and for periodical articles after 1983, by *Anthropological literature* (CE36). Especially useful for its inclusion and indexing of journal articles, festschriften, and conference proceedings. The Author/title catalogue contains approximately 636,000 entries, the Subject catalogue approximately 702,600. The latter uses as headings terms specific to the discipline; a complete list is provided in *Tozzer Library index to anthropological subject headings* (CE53).

Manuscripts; Archives

National Anthropological Archives. Catalog to manuscripts at the National Anthropological Archives, Department of Anthropology, National Museum of Natural History, Smithsonian Institution, Washington, D.C. Boston : G.K. Hall, 1975. 4 v.
CE31
A photographic reproduction of catalog cards representing documents collected by the Bureau of American Ethnology between 1879 and 1965. In three divisions: (1) an alphabetical file on the Indians of North America north of Mexico; (2) a smaller geographical file on peoples of Mexico, Central America, and non-North American areas; (3) a numerical file indicating the subject under which cards have been filed in the other two divisions. Subject approach is by tribe, linguistic group, or name of individual.   Z1209.2.N67N37

——————— Guide to the National Anthropological Archives, Smithsonian Institution / James R. Glenn. [Wash.] : National Anthropological Archives, 1992. 314 p.   **CE32**
First complete listing of the collections of the Archives since 1881. Standard archival elements are used to describe 608 collections; each entry includes a brief description of the materials with provenance, dates, quantity, arrangement, finding aids, and restrictions to access. Index of personal names, place names and subjects. Nine appendixes describe the organization and classification of files.
Z1209.2.U5N38

Filmography

Heider, Karl G. Films for anthropological teaching. 7th ed. Wash. : American Anthropological Assoc., 1983. 312 p. (American Anthropological Association. Special publication, no. 16).   **CE33**
6th ed., 1977.
An annotated guide to 1,575 films, including price and distributor. Arranged by film title; indexed by geographical area, subject, distributor, and persons involved.
An 8th ed. is planned for 1995.   GN42.3.Z9H44

Indexes; Abstract journals

Abstracts in anthropology. v. 1 (Feb. 1970)– . Westport, Conn. : Greenwood, 1970– .   **CE34**
Frequency varies: 1970–86, quarterly; 1987– , 8 issues per year.
Abstracts of books, articles and conference papers are grouped in four sections–Archaeology, Cultural anthropology, Linguistics, and Physical anthropology. Abstracts have been contributed by authors, by journals publishing the original articles, or by the editors. Annual cumulated author and subject indexes.
Several significant changes in format and coverage were introduced with v. 14 (1987). The frequency increased to eight issues in two volumes per year; the number of titles indexed increased by about 25%; the number of citations doubled; and the subject index began to cumulate in each issue. Additionally, Linguistics and Cultural anthropology are now covered only in no. 1 and no. 3 of each volume, and Archaeology and Physical anthropology are covered in no. 2 and no. 4.   GN1.A15

Anthropological index to current periodicals in the Museum of Mankind Library : (incorporating the former Royal Anthropological Institute Library). v. 15 (Jan./Mar. 1977)– . [London] : Royal Anthropological Inst., 1977– . Quarterly.
CE35
Continues the *Index to current periodicals received in the Library of the Royal Anthropological Institute* (1963–76) and assumes its numbering. Title varies.
Maintains the regional, classified approach of the previous title. A revised list of about 650 current periodicals held by the Library was published in 1978, with additions listed in Pt. 1 of each index volume. A cumulative annual author index has been published since 1972. A cumulative author index to v. 1–9 (1963–71) and a subject index to v. 1–5 (1963–67) are available on cards at the Museum of Mankind Library.
Issues since 1992 have supplement : *Reference list of current periodicals*.

Anthropological literature. v. 11, no. 1– . Cambridge, Mass. : Tozzer Library, Harvard Univ., c1989– . Quarterly.
CE36
Vols. 1–5 (1979–83) publ. by Redgrave Publ. Co.; v. 6–10 (1984–88) published in microfiche by Tozzer Library. With v. 11 (1989), publication in printed format resumed.
A broad subject index to articles in about 1,000 serials, as well as colloquia and symposia publications, festschriften, and collections of readings received by the Tozzer Library. Citations are grouped by author in five sections: cultural/social; archaeology; biological/physical; linguistics; general/method/theory. Book review supplement added with v. 14, 1992. Indexes by joint author, archaeological site and culture, ethnic and linguistic group, and geographic area appear in each issue, as well as annually. Subject index added with v. 11, 1989. Includes lists of authors, journals, and edited works and series indexed. International in scope, with primary emphasis on materials published in English, French, German, Spanish, and the Slavic languages.
§ For articles prior to 1983, see *Author and subject catalogues of the Tozzer Library* (CE30).

•Machine-readable versions: *Anthropological literature on disc* [database] (N.Y. : G. K. Hall, 1984/93–), available on CD-ROM, updated annually, and *Anthropological literature* [database] (Cambridge, Mass. : Tozzer Library, Harvard Univ., 1984–), available online through Internet. Z5112.A573

Book reviews

Reviews in anthropology. v. 1, no. 1 (Feb. 1974)– . [Philadelphia, etc. : Gordon & Breach, etc., 1974]– . Quarterly. **CE37**

Frequency varies. Quarterly since 1992.

Publishes long, detailed reviews of books in the field. Reviews frequently cluster books on particular topics and so do not necessarily cover new monographs. Z5111.R47

Encyclopedias

Dictionnaire de l'ethnologie et de l'anthropologie / publié sous la direction de Pierre Bonte, Michel Izard, et Marion Abélès ... [et al.]. 2e éd. revue. Paris : Presses Universitaires de France, 1992. 755 p. **CE38**

1st ed., 1991.

Entries are grouped topically: methodology, concepts, theories, national schools, biography, subfields, techniques, social/cultural, and geographical/cultural. Signed review-length essays are written by 231 contributors from 15 countries. Many English-language sources.

Encyclopedia of anthropology / ed. by David E. Hunter and Phillip Whitten. N.Y. : Harper & Row, [1976]. 411 p. : ill. **CE39**

Intended for the student and instructor in anthropology. About 1,400 entries "ranging in length from 25 to 3,000 words."—*Pref.* Many articles are signed by the contributors; some have brief bibliographies appended. Includes biographies, but no ethnographic articles on cultural groups. Well illustrated. GN11.E52

Encyclopedia of human evolution and prehistory / ed. by Ian Tattersall, Eric Delson and John Van Couvering. N.Y. : Garland, c1988. 603 p. : ill. (Garland reference library of the humanities, 768). **CE40**

First encyclopedia to cover human (i.e., primate) evolution. Some 1,200 signed entries by 40 experts in the field range in length from brief paragraphs to ten-page essays and include many cross-references and brief bibliographies. Illustrated with numerous photographs, diagrams, tables, drawings, and maps. Access provided through Subject list by topic, arranged alphabetically and chronologically, and through heavily cross-referenced prefatory essay "Brief introduction to human evolution and prehistory." Also includes a "Classification of primates" and an evolutionary "Time chart." GN281.E53

Encyclopedia of world cultures / David Levinson, ed. in chief. Boston : G.K. Hall, c1991–1994. v. 1–7. (In progress). **CE41**

Contents: v. 1, North America, ed. by Timothy J. O'Leary and David Levinson; v. 2, Oceania, ed. by Terence E. Hays; v. 3, South Asia, ed. by Paul Hockings; v. 4, Europe, ed. by Linda A. Bennett (rev. ed.); v. 5, East and Southeast Asia, ed. by Paul Hockings; v. 6, Russia and Eurasia-China, ed. by Paul Friedrich and Norma Diamond; v. 7, South America, ec. by Johannes Wilbert.

Prepared under auspices of Human Relations Area Files, Inc., and expected to include more than 1,500 cultural groups. Descriptions of these 20th century cultures vary in length from several paragraphs to several pages. Each signed entry contains the following elements: culture name, ethnonym, history and cultural relations, settlements, economy, kinship, marriage and family, sociopolitical organization, relig-

ion and expressive culture, and bibliography. Each volume will also include: maps indicating current locations of cultures; filmography; list of extinct cultures of the region; ethnonym index; and glossary. To be complete in 10 volumes. GN307.E53

The illustrated encyclopedia of mankind / ed. in chief, Richard Carlisle. New ed. / ed. and comp. by Yvonne Deutch. N.Y. : M. Cavendish, 1990. 22 v. : ill. **CE42**

1st ed., 1978; 2nd ed., 1984.

Profusely illustrated ethnographic encyclopedia aimed at general audiences. The first 15 volumes, arranged alphabetically, profile more than 500 places, nationalities, and cultural groups. Each entry includes a map locating the group under discussion; photographs of daily activities; and discussions of history, language, religion, social organization, and economy. The next five volumes contain essays that present such concepts as "Notion of law" and "Tribal warfare" cross-culturally. Vol. 21, *Origins of mankind : life through the ages*, new to this edition, includes chronologically-arranged essays, beginning with "The stone age" and ending with "Global village." Vol. 22 contains subject, thematic, and regional indexes, population charts, a bibliography and glossary. With the exception of v. 21 and isolated revisions to profiles in v. 1–15, pagination, photographs, and text have been reproduced verbatim from the 1984 edition. GN307.I44

Muslim peoples : a world ethnographic survey / ed. by Richard V. Weekes. 2nd ed., rev. and exp. Westport, Conn. : Greenwood, 1984. 2 v. (953 p.) : maps. **CE43**

1st ed., 1978.

An alphabetical arrangement of brief survey articles on some 190 ethnic groups throughout the world which have been identified as wholly or partly Muslim. Articles are signed, and each carries a bibliography of English-language materials. The work is "designed primarily for the English-speaking nonspecialist, whether academician or layman."—*Introd.* Bibliographic entries are " 'recent,' that is, since 1945," and the bibliographies "concentrate on works related to current patterns of living—the theme of this survey." DS35.625.A1M87

Oxford illustrated encyclopedia of peoples and cultures / volume ed., Richard Hoggart. Oxford ; N.Y. : Oxford Univ. Pr., 1992. 391 p. : ill. (some col), maps, ports. (some col). **CE44**

Some 2,000 entries, arranged alphabetically, cover a wide range of topics: indigenous peoples, religious beliefs, educational systems and political situations. Includes maps, charts and statistical tables. Cross-referenced and well illustrated. Serves as a compendium of information covered more comprehensively in such sources as the *Encyclopedia of world cultures* (CE41). GN11.O94

Stevenson, Joan C. Dictionary of concepts in physical anthropology. N.Y. : Greenwood, 1991. 432 p. (Reference sources for the social sciences and humanities, no. 10). **CE45**

Etymological development, as well as current definitions, for 74 basic concepts in physical anthropology. Each entry includes: a working definition; a history of the term's origin and its application in practice; a comprehensive annotated bibliography; and a list of sources of additional information. Numerous cross-references. Concepts are listed in the table of contents. Subject and personal name indexes.

GN50.3.S74

Winthrop, Robert H. Dictionary of concepts in cultural anthropology. N.Y. : Greenwood, 1991. 347 p. (Reference sources for the social sciences and humanities, no. 11). **CE46**

Thorough treatment of 80 key concepts in the field. Entries of 2,000–6,000 words provide definition and current general usage, philosophical background or historical context, and theoretical developments. Extensive cross-references, briefly annotated references, and sources of additional reading accompany each entry. Includes list of concepts, and name and subject indexes. GN307.W56 1991

. Dictionaries

Caratini, Roger. La force des faibles : encyclopédie mondiale des minorités. Paris : Larousse, c1986. 399 p. : maps.   **CE47**

Other current European dictionaries include: *Diccionario temático de antropología* (Barcelona : PPU, 1988); *Dizionario di sociologia e antropologia culturale* (Assisi : Cittadella, 1984); *Neues Wörterbuch der Völkerkunder* (Berlin : D. Reimer, 1988); *Svod etnograficheskikh poniatiĭ i terminov* (Moskva : Nauka, 1986–91); *Wörterbuch der Ethnologie* (Koln : DuMont, 1987). All provide bibliographical references, and many include additional indexes.

GN307.C26

Dictionary of anthropology / ed. by Charlotte Seymour-Smith. Boston : G.K. Hall, 1986. 305 p.   **CE48**

Contains some 950 entries for terms and concepts used primarily in cultural and social anthropology. Specifically excludes "the fields of linguistics, physical anthropology, archaeology and so on" (*Foreword*) and entries for specific ethnic groups. Includes brief entries for 150 individual anthropologists born before 1920. Entries vary in length from a brief paragraph to several pages. Numerous cross-references to other entries and to the selected bibliography.   GN11.D48

International dictionary of regional European ethnology and folklore / [editorial committee: Sigurd Erixon, chairman, and others. Chief editor : Ake Hultkrantz]. Under the auspices of the International Council for Philosophy and Humanistic Studies and with the support of UNESCO published by CIAP (International Commission of Folk Arts and Folklore). Copenhagen : Rosenkilde & Bagger, 1960–65. 2 v.   **CE49**

Contents: v. 1, General ethnological concepts, by Åke Hultkrantz; v. 2, Folk literature (Germanic), by Laurits Bødker.

Vol. 1 is an alphabetically arranged dictionary designed "to give definitions of ethnological and folkloristic technical terms and concepts."—*Introd.* Arranged by English term with synonyms in French, Spanish, German, and Swedish, and descriptive definitions and references to the literature of the subject. Bibliography, p. 251–52.

Vol. 2 differs in plan, the terms here being entered under the various national denominations rather than grouped under the English equivalent of the term. Entries include bibliographic references. For more information on this volume, *see* CF87.   GN307.I5

Pearson, Roger. Anthropological glossary. Malabar, Fla. : R.E. Krieger Pub. Co., 1985. 282 p.   **CE50**

Defines approximately 4,500 terms used in cultural and physical anthropology, archaeology, and linguistics, including ethnic groups, archaeological sites, and geographical names. Definitions vary in length from two lines to an entire page. Contains more entries than *Encyclopedia of anthropology* (CE39) and a number of terms not included in Charles Winick's *Dictionary of anthropology* (CE51). Lacks illustrations and bibliographical references.   GN11.P43

Winick, Charles. Dictionary of anthropology. N.Y. : Philosophical Lib., 1956. 579 p. (Repr.: Paterson, N.J. : Littlefield, Adams, 1964).   **CE51**

Defines more than 5,000 terms in all subfields of the discipline. Entries are short, most with fewer than 100 words, and include ethnic groups and personal names. Lacks bibliography of sources for additional information.   GN11.W5

Thesauruses

Thematic list of descriptors—anthropology = Liste thématique des descripteurs—anthropologie / prep. on behalf of UNESCO by the International Committee for Social Science Information and Documentation. London ; N.Y. : Routledge, 1989. 522 p.   **CE52**

Presents some 8,000 terms, and includes lists of geographic names, ethnic groups, and languages.

§ One of four similar lists, the others being *Thematic list of descriptors—economics* (CH43 *note*), *Thematic list of descriptors—political science* (CJ43), and *Thematic list of descriptors—sociology* (CE52), each intended to be used with the appropriate section of the "International bibliography of the social sciences" series, for social and cultural anthropology (CE24), economics (CH43), political science (CJ15), and sociology (CC8). Each presents controlled vocabulary terms and cross-references used to index publications listed in the bibliographies in the series and to retrieve information from the parent database maintained by the International Committee for Social Science Information and Documentation. In two sections, alphabetical and thematic. The alphabetical list gives terms in English and French and indicates in which sections of the component bibliographies the terms are used. The thematic list is a coded hierarchical arrangement of English terms with French equivalents. All four thesauruses have lists of geographic terms.   Z5111.A63T47

Tozzer Library. Tozzer Library index to anthropological subject headings. Boston : G.K. Hall, 1981. 177 p.   **CE53**

1971 ed. publ. as *Index to subject headings*, under the Library's earlier name, Harvard University. Peabody Museum of Archaeology and Ethnology. Library.

In the earlier edition, geographic and linguistic headings were given primacy; here emphasis is on ethnic groups, languages, and major archaeological sites. Nine new subfields of anthropology have been added as subject headings, and a list of "floating subheadings" has been provided.   Z695.1.A63T69

Directories

American Anthropological Association. AAA guide. 28th ed. (1989/90)– . Wash. : American Anthropological Association, c1989– . Annual.   **CE54**

Continues *Guide to graduate departments of anthropology* (1962/63–1968/69) and *Guide to departments of anthropology* (1969/70–1988/89).

Describes academic, museum, and research departments and government agencies in the U.S., Canada, and a selected few other countries, and lists the Association's membership in three directories: an alphabetical listing of names and addresses, a listing by Association units of their respective members, and a list of life members. A statistics section is based on numerical data provided in the descriptions. Lists completed doctoral dissertations. Indexed by individuals in departments and by academic departments grouped by state.

Cantrell, Karen. Funding for anthropological research / ed. by Karen Cantrell and Denise Wallen. Phoenix : Oryx, 1986. 308 p.   **CE55**

"Listing more than 700 sponsored research programs alphabetically by program sponsor ... "—*Introd.* Each detailed entry includes: program description, eligibility/limitations, fiscal information, application information, and deadlines. Indexed by subject, sponsor type, and list of sponsors. Bibliography of funding-related publications.

GN42.C36

Handbooks

Bernard, H. Russell. Research methods in cultural anthropology. Newbury Park, Calif. : Sage Publ., c1988. 520 p. : ill.   **CE56**

A comprehensive treatment of research methodology in three sections: preparing for field research, collecting data, and analyzing data. Provides well-illustrated examples of both quantitative and nonquantitative techniques and includes discussion of commonly-used statistical techniques. Index; extensive bibliography.   GN345.B37

Ethnohistory : a researcher's guide / editors, Vinson H. Sutlive ... [et al.] ; [Dennis Wiedman, guest ed.]. Williamsburg, Va. : Dept. of Anthropology, College of William and Mary, [1986]. 438 p. : ill. (Studies in Third World societies, publication no. 35.).   **CE57**

Topically arranged in 15 chapters to cover a broad range of sources: historical and public documents; missionary documents; census materials; maps and remote sensing images; photographs; oral history interviews; artifacts; newspapers; judicial records. Each chapter includes an introductory description of a particular source, an explanation of its application to the discipline, and a case study employing that source, followed by a bibliography.   GN345.E8

Honigmann, John J. Handbook of social and cultural anthropology / ed. by John J. Honigmann ; contributors : Alexander Alland, Jr. ... [et al.]. Chicago : Rand McNally, [c1973]. 1295 p. : ill.   **CE58**

A survey and discussion of the state of knowledge and a review of research in the various branches of anthropology. Each chapter is by a specialist; extensive bibliographies; subject index.   GN315.H642

Murdock, George Peter. Outline of world cultures. 6th rev. ed. New Haven, Conn. : Human Relations Area Files, 1983. 259 p.   **CE59**

1st ed., 1954; 5th rev. ed., 1975.

"An attempt to provide an outline organization and classification of the known cultures of the world."—Pref. Within eight major geographic regions, subdivisions correspond to current political administrations; within these subdivisions, further classifications reflect historical and ethnic groups. Used primarily with a companion volume, *Outline of cultural materials* (CE61), to classify the relatively small subset of identified cultural groups that are included in the Human Relations Area Files (HRAF) database. Extensive combined geographic/ethnic index.   GN345.3.M87

Naroll, Raoul. A handbook of method in cultural anthropology / ed. by Raoul Naroll and Ronald Cohen. Garden City, N.Y. ; publ. for the American Museum of Natural History [by] the Natural History Pr., 1970. 1017 p. : ill.   **CE60**

Chapters by specialists on various aspects of methodology. Principal sections include: General problems; The field work process; Models of ethnographic analysis; Comparative approaches; and Problems of categorization. Extensive references and bibliographies.   GN345.N37

Outline of cultural materials / George P. Murdock...[et al.]. 5th rev. ed, with modifications. New Haven, Conn. : Human Relations Area Files, Inc., 1987. 247 p.   **CE61**

1st ed., 1938; 4th rev. ed., 1961.

"A manual which presents a comprehensive subject classification system pertaining to all aspects of human behavior and related phenomena."—Pref. Used primarily with a companion volume, *Outline of world cultures* (CE59), to classify the economical, social and political traits of the cultural groups included in the Human Relations Area Files (HRAF) database. More than 80 aspects of human behavior are organized and encoded; each trait is further subdivided to provide more detailed analysis. Additional categories contain geographical, historical and bibliographical information. Extensive subject index.

Textor, Robert B. A cross-cultural summary. New Haven, Conn. : HRAF Pr., [1967]. 1 v. (various pagings).   **CE62**

A 400-culture sample derived from G. P. Murdock's *Ethnographic atlas* (CE71 *note*) has been analyzed according to 526 characteristics. Computer-produced, the analysis is set forth in the form of lengthy tables designed to show that for a given cultural characteristic, a series of other characteristics may be expected to occur with a specified degree of probability.   GN307.T4

Yearbooks

Indigenous world. 1993-94– . Copenhagen : International Work Group for Indigenous Affairs, 1994– . Annual.   **CE63**

Continues: *IWGIA yearbook* (1986) and *Yearbook / IWGIA* (1987–92).

Provides illustrated accounts of major events of indigenous peoples of the world. Each issue includes a section on developments in indigenous rights and surveys work of the International Work Group for Indigenous Affairs (IWGIA). The yearbook for 1988 includes an index to articles published in the *IWGIA newsletter* 1976–88.   GN380.I95

Yearbook of physical anthropology. v. [1] (1945)– . N.Y. [etc.] : A.R. Liss [etc.].   **CE64**

Publisher varies. Publication suspended 1953–61 and 1968–71.

Annual supplement to the *American journal of physical anthropology*. "The *Yearbook* provides broad but thorough coverage of developments within the discipline."—Pref. Refereed research reviews averaging 20 pages each. Extensive bibliographies.   GN1.A55

Biography

Biographical directory of anthropologists born before 1920 / gen. ed., Thomas L. Mann ; comp. by Library-Anthropology Resource Group (LARG). N.Y. : Garland, 1988. 245 p. : ill., port. (Garland reference library of the humanities, 439).   **CE65**

"For each person the entries include dates of birth and death, birthplace, profession, major contributions and published sources of biographical information."—Pref. Scope is international, and the discipline of anthropology is broadly defined. Inclusion is based on the identification of a biographical source. Includes tables listing number of entries by country of birth and by career and an index to subject words from the "Statement of contributions" fields.   Z5111.B56

Fifth international directory of anthropologists. Chicago : Univ. of Chicago Pr., 1975. 496 p.   **CE66**

1st–3rd ed. entitled: *International directory of anthropologists*.

Ed. 1–4 publ. 1938–67 with varying issuing bodies: 1938–40 issued by the National Research Council; 1950 by the Committee on International Relations in Anthropology of the Division of Anthropology and Psychology, National Research Council and the American Anthropological Association; 1967 by associates in *Current anthropology*. A "1970 revision" appeared in the periodical *Current anthropology*, 11 (June 1970): 249-400. Place of publication has varied.

Offers biographical data on more than 4,300 scholars in the field. "Other associates of *Current anthropology*" (i.e., those who did not respond to the questionnaire) are listed with name and address only in a separate section. Geographical index; chronological index; subject/methodological index.   GN20.I5

International dictionary of anthropologists / comp. by Library-Anthropology Resource Group (LARG) ; Christopher Winters, gen. ed. ... [et al.]. N.Y. : Garland, 1991. 823 p. (Garland reference library of social science, v. 638).   **CE67**

Biographical entries for 725 anthropologists born before 1920, from more than 50 countries. Includes not only professional anthropologists, but also travellers, museum curators, missionaries and colonial administrators who significantly contributed to the discipline. Each entry contains a brief biography of approximately 500 words, an explanation of the person's significance to the field, a list of major works by, and a list of additional sources about, the person. Detailed 10-page preface provides background, inclusion procedures and format explanations. Brief glossary contains terms not explained in the text. Comprehensive index includes personal names, institutions, place-names, and ethnic groups.   GN20.I5

Kinton, Jack F. Leaders in anthropology : the men and women of the science of man. Aurora, Ill. : Social Science and Sociological Resources, c1974. 113 p. **CE68**
Approximately 400 entries organized broadly by subdiscipline. Each section is preceded by a concise description and history of that subfield. Historical as well as contemporary coverage. Brief entries provide biographical data, education and research interests, and major publications. GN20.K5

Women anthropologists : a biographical dictionary / ed. by Ute Gacs ... [et al.]. N.Y. : Greenwood, 1988. 428 p. **CE69**
Contains four- to six-page signed biographies of 58 anthropologists from the past 100 years. A six-page introduction explains the criteria for selection. Each biography is followed by a list of works about and by the person. Supplementary information includes two appendixes (Fieldwork areas and Chronology of birth dates), an index, and brief biographical entries for contributors. GN20.W63

Atlases

Atlas of mankind. Chicago : Rand McNally, 1982. 191 p. : ill., maps. **CE70**
"A global perspective" (p. 10–55) provides a general, thematic background through world maps, diagrams and photographs on topics such as languages, food production, kinship, and taboo. Each topic is cross-referenced to ethnographic groups described in a section, Peoples of the world (p. 56–191), that divides the world into 11 regions; for each region there are maps of language distribution and land use, diagrams of state populations and religious practices, and a history time bar providing key dates. Some ethnographic groups are described in essays of approximately 500 words. Glossary; index. GN316.A85

Murdock, George Peter. Atlas of world cultures. Pittsburgh : Univ. of Pittsburgh Pr., c1981. 151 p. **CE71**
First publ. as *Ethnographic atlas* (1967).
Identifies 563 societies whose cultures are most fully described in the ethnographic literature, and lists up to two ethnographic sources as a guide to that literature. Presents in coded form data on 76 items of ethnographic information for each society, with a worldwide summary and conclusion. The sample is a significant reduction from the 1,264 cultures coded for the *Ethnographic atlas* and installments appearing in the journal *Ethnology* until 1971. GN345.3.M86

Price, David H. Atlas of world cultures : a geographical guide to ethnographic literature. Newbury Park, Calif. : Sage Publ., c1989. 156 p. : maps, 29 cm. **CE72**
A combined ethnic atlas, bibliography, and guide intended to accompany the Human Relations Area Files (HRAF). The first section consists of 40 numbered maps on which are identifed the geographical locations of 3,500 cultural groups; the second is a 1,237-item bibliography of ethnographic studies concerning the groups. A final section, Culture index, links each culture group to its appropriate map, bibliographic entries, HRAF codes and listing (if any) in George P. Murdock's *Atlas of world cultures* (CE71). G1046.E1P7

Spencer, Robert F. Atlas for anthropology / [by] Robert F. Spencer and Elden Johnson. 2nd ed. Dubuque, Iowa : W. C. Brown, 1968. 61 l. fold. : maps, 29 cm. **CE73**
1st ed., 1960.
This series of maps, intended as a manual for beginning students, covers tribes and ethnic groups, language areas, Old World prehistory, and New World prehistory. G1046.E1S7

THE AMERICAS

Bibliography

Berg, Hans van den. Material bibliográfico para el estudio de las aymaras, callawayas, chipayas, urus. Cochabamba : Facultad de Filosofía y Ciencias Religiosas, Universidad Católica Boliviana, 1980–1988. v. 1–5. (In progress). **CE74**
Vols. 4– have title: *Suplemento* I– .
An annotated bibliography of more than 5,800 entries on these Bolivian and Peruvian ethnic groups. Author listing; the final volume is an index by ethnic group, subject, and author. Z1209.2.B5B47

Bernal, Ignacio. Bibliografía de arqueología y etnografía : Mesoamérica y Norte de México, 1514–1960. México : Inst. Nacional de Antropología e Historia, 1962. 634 p. : maps. (Instituto Nacional de Antropología e Historia. Memorias, 7). **CE75**
More than 13,000 numbered entries, including books, periodical articles, reports, etc., classified by region and then by subject. Author index. Z1209.B45

Boletín bibliográfico de antropología americana / Instituto Panamericano de Geografía e Historia. v. 1, no. 1–2 (Jan.–June 1937)–41 (1979). México : El Instituto, [1937]–79. **CE76**
Frequency varied; annual, 1977–79.
Regularly carried critical reviews of current publications and reports on research activity, as well as many bibliographies of specific topics. Z5112.B33

Brana-Shute, Rosemary. A bibliography of Caribbean migration and Caribbean immigrant communities. Gainesville, Fla. : Reference and Bibliographic Dept., Univ. of Florida Libraries in cooperation with the Center for Latin American Studies, Univ. of Florida, 1983. 339 p. (Univ. of Florida. Libraries. Reference and Bibliographic Dept. Bibliographic ser., no. 9). **CE77**
Almost 2,600 citations on emigration and immigration to the Caribbean islands, Belize, Guyana, Suriname, and French Guiana. International in scope; includes published materials, theses and government reports. Author listing; indexed by location, topic, and names. Z7164.I3B7

Comas, Juan. Bibliografía selectiva de las culturas indígenas de América. México : Instituto Panamericano de Geografía e Historia, Comisión de Historia, 1953. 292 p. : maps. (Instituto Pan-Americano de Geografía e Historia. Comisión de Historia. Publication, 166). **CE78**
Classed arrangement of 2,014 entries, with indexes to indigenous groups and to authors. Lists works in various languages, with a preponderance of English titles. F1401.P153 no.166

Mesoamerica : directorio y bibliografía, 1950–1980 / Alfredo Méndez-Domínguez. Guatemala : Universidad del Valle de Guatemala, 1982. 313 p. **CE79**
Each entry gives information (based on replies to questionnaires received from 700 professionals in Europe, North and South America) concerning education, present position, address, special interests, languages, and, in many cases, an extensive bibliography. Indexed by country of interest, subdivided by broad topic (e.g., cultural and social anthropology, physical anthropology, demography, archeology, ethnohistory and history, folklore, geology, geography, linguistics). Z1209.2.C45M47

Myers, Robert A. Amerindians of the Lesser Antilles : a bibliography. New Haven, Conn. : Human Relations Area Files, 1981. 158 l. : ill., map. **CE80**

A classed bibliography of about 1,300 references to archaeological, historical, and linguistic research on the Ciboney, Arawak, and Carib peoples of the eastern Caribbean. Geographical and author indexes.   Z1209.2.L47M93

O'Leary, Timothy J. Ethnographic bibliography of South America. New Haven, Conn. : Human Relations Area Files, 1963. 387 p. : maps.   **CE81**

Repr. with corrections, 1978.

A listing of books, periodical articles, reports, etc., intended to cover ethnographic literature on continental South America through 1961. No coverage of Panama and the Caribbean Islands except where the latter belong to Colombia or Venezuela. The main part is arranged by areas, and within each area by tribal groups. Includes list of works on general South America and a list of bibliographic aids.   Z5114.O4

Parra, Manuel Germán. Bibliografía indigenista de México y Centroamerica (1850–1950) / por Manuel Germán Parra y Wigberto Jiménez Moreno. México : Inst. Nacional Indigenista, 1954. 342 p. (Memorias del Instituto Nacional Indigenista, v. 4).   **CE82**

A comprehensive bibliography of books and articles, in various languages, covering all aspects of the life of Indians of Mexico and Central America.   Z1029.P3

Smithsonian Institution. Bureau of American Ethnology. Index to Bulletins 1–100 of the Bureau of American Ethnology : with index to Contributions to North American ethnology, introductions, and miscellaneous publications / by Biren Bonnerjea. Wash. : U.S. Govt. Print. Off., 1963. 726 p.   **CE83**

Includes subject, author and title indexes and index to illustrations.

§ *List of publications of the Bureau of American Ethnology, with an index to authors and titles* (Wash. : Smithsonian Inst. Pr., 1971. 134 p.) provides a listing to all the various series published by the Bureau, with indication of "in print" status, and an author-title index.

———. *General index : Annual reports of the Bureau, v. 1–8 (1879–1931)...* , comp. by Biren Bonnerjea (Wash. : U.S. Govt. Prt. Off., 1933. p. 25–1220. [In its 48th Annual report, 1930–31]). Pt. 1, Subject index; pt. 2, List of annual reports ... with an index to authors and titles.   Z1209.U49

Storck, Peter L. A preliminary bibliography of early man in eastern North America, 1839–1973 / comp. by Peter L. Storck, with the assistance of Mima Kapches. Toronto : Royal Ontario Museum, 1975. 110 p. (Archaeology monograph, 4).   **CE84**

"This bibliography contains 1242 ... journal articles, reviews, monographs, and books dealing in whole or in part with the subject of Early Man in eastern North America" (*Introd.*), i.e., early and late Palaeo-Indian and possible antecedent cultures in Canadian provinces east of Manitoba and the U.S. east of the Mississippi River. Author listing, with geographic, subject, and site-locality indexes.   Z1208.N6S77

Sued Badillo, Jalil. Bibliografía antropológica para el estudio de los pueblos indígenas en el Caribe. Santo Domingo : Fundación García-Arévalo, 1977. 579 p. (Serie investigaciones, no. 8).   **CE85**

An international bibliography in two main sections: (1) broad subject arrangement; (2) geographic arrangement. Covers the Caribbean islands and the surrounding countries of Central and South America. No index.   Z1209.2.C27S9

Directories

Díaz Polanco, Héctor. Directorio de antropólogos latinoamericanos, México. México : Instituto Panamericano de Geografía e Historia : Para canje, ventas y distribución de publicaciones se atiende en Secretaría General del IPGH, 1985. 191 p. : ill. (Instituto Pan-Americano de Geografía e Historia. Publication, 410).   **CE86**

First of a projected three-volume series that will cover Mexico, Central America and the Caribbean, and South America and will include professional anthropologists who live in Latin America and whose research is concerned with Latin America. Each entry includes professional affiliation, address, telephone, educational background, subject specialty, list of publications, and description of current research. Indexes by educational degree, subject specialty, research (topical), research (geographical), and research (historical period).   GN41.6.D53

Directory of anthropologists and anthropological research in aging / a publication of [the] Association for Anthropology and Gerontology. Tampa, Fla. : Association for Anthropology and Gerontology, 1971– .   **CE87**

Biennial directory of the international membership of the Association of Anthropology and Gerontology. Editions have some 300 entries; each includes professional affiliation and address, and some include telephone numbers and research and teaching interests. Research index; geographic/societal index.

Hunter, John E. Inventory of ethnological collections in museums of the United States and Canada. 2nd ed., rev. and enl. Wash. : Committee on Anthropological Research in Museums of the American Anthropological Assoc. ; N.Y. : Wenner-Gren Foundation for Anthropological Research, 1968. 120 p.   **CE88**

Repr.: Berkeley, Calif. : California Indian Library Collections, 1992.

1st ed., 1967.

Describes collections and research facilities of 48 museums in the U. S. and four in Canada. Alphabetical arrangement by museum; indexed by culture area.

§ Among the numerous directories in anthropology and ethnology are: *Directory of visual anthropology*, ed. by Thomas D. Blakely and Pamela A. R. Blakely (Wash. : Soc. for Visual Anthropology, c1989); H. Max Drake, Roger D. Karlish, and Ann M. Drake, *Directory of practicing anthropologists* (Wash.? : National Assoc. for the Practice of Anthropology, c1985); *Bibliografía anotada y directorio de antropólogos colombianos*, dir. e introd., Nina S. de Friedemann and Jaime Arocha ([Bogotá] : Soc. Antropológica de Colombia, 1979); Richard H. Osborne and Kenneth A. Bennett, *Centers for training in physical anthropology* (Wash. : American Assoc. of Physical Anthropologists, 1979); Monica Reed, *Directory of anthropological resources in New York City libraries* (N.Y. : Wenner-Gren Foundation for Anthropological Research, c1979); *Teses, pesquisas, antropólogos* (São Paulo : Associação Brasileira de Antropologia, 1990).   GN36.U6H8

Handbooks

Handbook of Middle American Indians / Robert Wauchope, gen. ed. Austin : Univ. of Texas Pr., c1964–1976. 16 v. : ill., maps.   **CE89**

Contents: v. 1, Natural environment and early cultures, ed. by R. C. West; v. 2–3, Archaeology of Southern Mesoamerica, ed. by G. R. Willey; v. 4, Archaeological frontiers and external connections, ed. by G. R. Willey and G. F. Ekholm; v. 5, Linguistics, ed. by N. A. McQuown; v. 6, Social anthropology, ed. by M. Nash; v. 7–8, Ethnology, ed. by E. Z. Vogt; v. 9, Physical anthropology, ed. by T. D. Stewart; v. 10–11, Archaeology of Northern Mesoamerica, ed. by G. F.

Ekholm and I. Bernal; v. 12–15, Guide to ethno-historical sources, ed. by H. F. Cline [and others]; v. 16, Sources cited and artifacts illustrated, ed. by M. A. Harrison.

Each volume or pair of volumes is made up of a series of essays by specialists on specific aspects of the life, customs, arts and culture, environmental influences, etc., of the various groups of Middle American Indians. Each has its own extensive bibliography and detailed index.

———. *Supplement*, Victoria Reifler Bricker, gen. ed. (Austin : Univ. of Texas Pr., c1981–92. v. 1–5. [In progress]).

Contents: v. 1, Archaeology, Jeremy A. Sabloff, ed. (1981. 463 p.); v. 2, Linguistics, Munro S. Edmonson, ed. (1984. 146 p.); v. 3, Literatures, Munro S. Edmonson, ed. (1985. 195 p.); v. 4, Ethnohistory, Ronald Spores, ed. (1986. 232 p.); v. 5, Epigraphy, Victoria Reifler Bricker, ed. (1992. 195 p.).   F1219.A76

McGlynn, Eileen A. Middle American anthropology : directory, bibliography, and guide to the UCLA Library collections. Los Angeles : Latin American Center and Univ. Library, Univ. of Calif., 1975. 131 p. : ill. (Latin American collections in the UCLA Library. Guides, ser. B, no. 1).   **CE90**

In two main sections: (1) international directories of individuals and institutions; (2) bibliography of reference works, serial titles, selected monographs, and rare and non-book materials. Based on, but not limited to, the UCLA library collections. Indexed.   Z1209.2.C45M32

Steward, Julian Haynes. Handbook of South American Indians / prep. in cooperation with the U.S. Dept. of State as a project of the Interdepartmental Committee on Cultural and Scientific Cooperation. Wash. : U.S. Govt. Print. Off., 1946–59. 7 v. : ill. (United States. Bureau of American Ethnology. Bulletin, 143).   **CE91**

Repr.: N.Y. : Cooper Square, 1963.

At head of title: Smithsonian Institution. Bureau of American Ethnology.

Contents: v. 1, The marginal tribes; v. 2, The Andean civilizations; v. 3, The tropical forest tribes; v. 4, The circum-Caribbean tribes; v. 5, The comparative ethnology of South American Indians; v. 6, Physical anthropology, linguistics, and cultural geography of South American Indians; v. 7, Index.

Anthropological descriptions by American specialists of all phases of the life of the tribes considered, with special attention to the time of a tribe's first contact with Europeans. Well illustrated; many ethnographical maps. Extensive bibliographies.

§ For *Handbook of North American Indians*, see CC432.
     F2229.S75

EUROPE

Bibliography

Horak, Stephan M. Eastern European national minorities, 1919–1980 : a handbook / by Stephan M. Horak and Richard Blanke ... [et al.]. Littleton, Colo. : Libraries Unlimited, 1985. 353 p.   **CE92**

A selective, annotated international bibliography of 982 items. Each country chapter includes a historical summary followed by bibliographic citations on minority groups. Includes Slovene and Croat minorities in Italy and Austria, 1945–1980. Statistical data are tabulated, and research centers in Eastern European countries are described. Author/title index.   Z2483.H53

Kuter, Lois. The anthropology of Western Europe : a selected bibliography. [Bloomington, Ind.] : West European Studies, Indiana Univ., 1978. 133 p. (Occasional papers—West European Studies, Indiana University, no. 1).   **CE93**

Based on a broad interdisciplinary definition of anthropology. Geographic arrangement of entries follows introductory chapters that

include a list of major journals in the subfield, general and theoretical issues, and peasant/rural studies. No annotations. Author and subject indexes.   Z2000.K86

O'Leary, Timothy J. Lapps ethnographic bibliography : an HRAF automated bibliographic system product / comp. by Timothy J. O'Leary and Joan Steffens, with the assistance of John Beierle ... [et al.]. New Haven, Conn. : Human Relations Area Files, 1975. 2 v.   **CE94**

A computer-produced list of more than 1,421 books, periodical articles, and chapters from collected works. Each entry is composed of three parts: (1) the standard bibliographic citation; (2) coded descriptive notes on bibliography, cataloging source, format, language; (3) content analysis relative to dates covered, Lapps regional and cultural types discussed, geographic area and site, date of fieldwork, social unit involved, primary or secondary nature of data, author's background, and language used. Indexed by *Outline of cultural materials* (CE61); by author, sub-group, geographic location; by field date and bibliography date.   Z2617.E85O43

Ripley, William Zebina. Selected bibliography of the anthropology and ethnology of Europe. Boston : Public Libr., 1899. 160 p.   **CE95**

Also published as a supplement to the author's *Races of Europe* (N.Y. : Appleton, 1899).

Contains nearly 2,000 entries, arranged by author, including books and serial publications. Subject index with references to main entries.   Z5117.R59

Sanders, Irwin Taylor. East European peasantries : social relations; an annotated bibliography of periodical articles / comp. by Irwin T. Sanders, Roger Whitaker, Walter C. Bisselle. Boston : G.K. Hall, 1976–81. v. 1–2.   **CE96**

No more published?

Each volume represents citations to more than 800 periodical articles added to the 30 volume Collection on East European Peasantries in the Mugar Memorial Library, Boston University, since 1972. Alphabetical arrangement for eight countries of East Europe (Albania is not included); no index.   Z7165.E82S26

Sweet, Louise Elizabeth. Circum-Mediterranean peasantry : introductory bibliographies / Louise E. Sweet, Timothy J. O'Leary, editors. New Haven, Conn. : Human Relations Area Files, 1969. 106 p.   **CE97**

Originally published in five issues of *Behavior science notes*, 1967–68.

Arrangement is by country, and includes North African and Middle Eastern countries as well as European areas. Lacks an index.   Z7165.M38S8

Theodoratus, Robert J. Europe : a selected ethnographic bibliography. New Haven, Conn. : Human Relations Area Files, 1969. 544 p.   **CE98**

Listing is by ethnic groups. Includes all of Europe except "the Caucasus Mountain region and the Finno-Ugric and Turkish peoples of the eastern and northeastern regions of the European part of the Soviet Union."—*Pref.* Lacks an index.   Z5117.T5

Directories

Directorio de instituciones y organismos relacionados con la etnografía. Madrid : Ministerio de Cultura, Dirección General de Bellas Artes y Archivos, Instituto de Conservatión y Restauración de Bienes Culturales, Subdirección General de Informatión e Investigación, 1992. 347 p.   **CE99**

Lists directories of people, institutions, and resources in the discipline.

§ See also *The EASA register*, ed. by Rolf Husmann and Gaby Husmann (Göttingen : European Association of Social Anthropologists, 1990); and *Handbuch der deutschsprachigen Ethnologie = Guide to German-speaking anthrolopology*, ed. by G. Baeck and Rolf Husmann (Göttingen : Edition Re, 1990).   GN307.3.D57

AFRICA

Bibliography

Anthropology of southern Africa in periodicals to 1950 : an analysis and index / comp. under direction of N. J. van Warmelo. Johannesburg : Witwatersrand Univ. Pr., 1977. 1484 p.   **CE100**

A chronological list of periodical articles, 1795–1950; each entry gives bibliographic citation and list of subjects, tribes and ethnic groups, place-names, and persons covered, with coded notation as to fullness of information. Indexed by linguistic group, place-name, and author; the linguistic group index is further subdivided by subject, tribe and group, and person. "The field covered by indices is the history, anthropology, and linguistics of the Bantu ethnic groups of Southern Africa (South Africa, Botswana, Lesotho, and Swaziland), whilst only bibliographies [pt. 4 of the book] cover the adjacent areas."—*Introd.*   Z5113.A56

Armer, Michael. African social psychology : a review and an notated bibliography. N.Y. : Africana Publ. Co., c1975. 321 p. (African bibliography series, v. 2).   **CE101**

Contains 863 abstracts grouped in five broad subject divisions: (1) Attitudes, values, and aspirations (covering such areas as occupation, education, politics, health, the family, religion); (2) Personality types, traits, and abnormalities; (3) Personality development, change, and adjustment (acculturation, modernization, etc.); (4) Psychological structures and processes; (5) Methods, techniques, and bibliographies. Author, country, and cross-classification (i.e., cross-reference) indexes.   Z7165.A4A75

Hambly, Wilfrid Dyson. Source book for African anthropology. Chicago, 1937. 2 v. (953 p.) : ill. (Field Museum of Natural History. Anthropological series, v. 26).   **CE102**

Repr., N.Y. : Kraus, 1968.

Also issued as *Publication* no. 394 and 396 from the Field Museum.

Selective but extensive bibliographies (p. 728–866) listing both books and periodical articles.

Bibliography of African anthropology, 1937–1949 : supplement to Source book of African anthropology, 1937 (Chicago : Natural History Museum, 1952. 155–292 p. [*In* Fieldiana: anthropology, v. 37, no. 2]).

Hertefelt, Marcel d'. African governmental systems in static and changing conditions : a bibliographic contribution to political anthropology. Tervuren, Belgium : Musée Royale de l'Afrique Centrale, 1968. 178 p.   **CE103**

At head of title: Koninklijk Museum voor Midden-Afrika, Tervuren, Belgie.

More than 1,200 items, mainly from the period 1940–66. Arrangement is alphabetical by author, with indexes of peoples and of subjects. Intended for anthropology teachers and students interested in the governmental processes of African peoples.   Z5113.H47

Strohmeyer, Eckhard. Umfassende Bibliographie der Völker namibiens (Südwestafrikas) und Südwestangolas = Comprehensive bibliography of the peoples of Namibia (South West Africa) and Southwestern Angola / von Eckhard Strohmeyer und Walter Moritz. Starnberg : [Max-Planck–Institut zur Erforschung der Lebensbedingungen der Wissenschaftlichtechnischen Welt], 1975–82. 2 v.   **CE104**

Title and subject headings in German and English.

An international bibliography of about 5,000 citations, arranged by ethnic group, subdivided by topic. Some brief contents notes are included. Author-title index.

Wieschhoff, Heinrich Albert. Anthropological bibliography of Negro Africa. New Haven, Conn. : American Oriental Soc., 1948. 461 p. (American Oriental series, v. 23).   **CE105**

Repr. : N.Y. : Kraus, 1970.

Arranged by name of tribe and geographical area, in alphabetical order, with cross-references.   Z5113.W5

Encyclopedias

Dictionary of Black African civilization / gen. editors, Georges Balandier, Jacques Maquet]. N.Y. : L. Amiel, [1974]. 350 p. : ill.   **CE106**

Translation of *Dictionnaire des civilisations africaines* (Paris : Hazan, 1968).

Deals with various aspects of black African culture and civilization. Articles are signed with the initials of contributing scholars but lack bibliographies.   DT352.4.D5213

ASIA

Bibliography

Dessaint, Alain Y. Minorities of Southwest China : an introduction to the Yi (Lolo) and related peoples and an annotated bibliography. New Haven, Conn. : HRAF Pr., 1980. 373 p.   **CE107**

Offers a brief survey (p. 1–34) of the linguistics, history, and ethnography of the Yi (Lolo) people, the fourth largest minority in China, and related tribes of Yunnan, Szechwan, Kweichow, and neighboring North Vietnam, Laos, Thailand, Burma, and India. Author listing of more than 1,000 titles in English, French, German, Russian, Spanish, Portuguese, Chinese, Japanese, and Thai. Annotations. Indexed by ethnic group, periodical title, and classed subject categories derived from George P. Murdock's *Outline of cultural materials* (CE61).

DS730.D45

Fürer-Haimendorf, Elizabeth von. An anthropological bibliography of South Asia : together with a directory of recent anthropological field work. Paris : Mouton, 1958–70. 3 v. (École Pratique des Hautes Études, 6ᵉ sec. ; Le monde d'outre-mer passé et présent. 4. sér.: Bibliographies, III, IV, VIII).   **CE108**

Contents: v. 1 includes a select list of works published prior to 1940 and works issued 1940–54; v. 2, 1955–59; v. 3, 1960–64.

Includes books, periodical articles, and unpublished dissertations in Western languages, dealing mainly with the cultural and social aspects of anthropology. Other fields are covered less completely. The geographic area comprises India, Pakistan, Nepal, Sikkim, Bhutan, and Ceylon. Arranged by regional sections with subject subdivisions, each including a directory of field research and an author index.

Continued by: *An anthropological bibliography of South Asia*, comp. by Helen A. Kanitkar; together with a directory of anthropological field research comp. by Elizabeth von Fürer-Haimendorf (The Hague : Mouton, 1976). Coverage: 1965–69.

Arrangement remains the same, but physical anthropology and prehistoric archaeology have been dropped; tribal welfare and problems, urbanization and industrialization, values and attitudes, political sociology and sociolinguistics have been added. Appendixes on social and cultural anthropology of South Asians overseas, and ethnology of India as depicted in literature to 1750 CE. Author and field research indexes.   Z5115.F83

Kanitkar, J. M. A bibliography of Indology : enumerating basic publications on all aspects of Indian culture / comp. by J. M. Kanitkar ; ed., rev. and enl. by D. L. Banerjee and A. K. Ohdedar. Calcutta : Librarian, National Library, 1960. 290 p.   **CE109**

Vol. 1, *Indian anthropology*, appears to be the only volume published.

More than 2,000 books and articles on Indian anthropology and related subjects: sociology, history, geography, etc. Many annotations, some extensive. Arrangement is by geographical region, with a final section on India as a whole. Author and subject indexes.   Z3201.C3

Ray, Shyamal Kumar. Bibliography of anthropology of India : including index to current literature, 1960–1964 / comp. by Shyamal Kumar Ray ; ed. by N. C. Choudhury. Calcutta : Anthropological Survey of India, 1976. 323 p.   **CE110**

An international classed bibliography of books and articles, largely in the English language, published during the period indicated. Broad subject arrangement, with items listed alphabetically by author within classes. Four indexes: author, ethnic or population group, geographical or Indian state, and regional (pertaining to more than one state).   Z5119.R39

Saito, Shiro. Philippine ethnography : a critically annotated and selected bibliography. Honolulu : Univ. Pr. of Hawaii, [c1972]. 512 p. (East-West bibliographic series, 2).   **CE111**

A classed bibliography of about 4,300 items. Concerned with cultural anthropology as distinct from physical anthropology, but includes items which deal with a specific cultural language group. Indexed.
                                                    Z3296.S23

Strijp, Ruud. Cultural anthropology of the Middle East : a bibliography. Leiden ; N.Y. : Brill, 1992. v. 1. (In progress).
                                                    CE112

Contents: v. 1, 1965–1987.

Extensive survey of social and cultural anthropological research. In four sections: monographs and articles by anthropologists, and books and articles by nonanthropologists. Each section is subdivided alphabetically by country. Entries limited to English, French and German language publications. Many book entries are annotated. Includes list of periodicals, and subject and author indexes.   Z3014.E85S77

AUSTRALIA AND OCEANIA

Bibliography

Greenway, John. Bibliography of the Australian aborigines and the native peoples of Torres Strait to 1959. [Sydney] : Angus & Robertson, [1963]. 420 p.   **CE113**

An alphabetical listing of 10,283 books and periodical articles, primarily in English but with some titles in other European languages. Indexes by subject and by aboriginal tribe.   Z5116.G7

Marshall, Mac. Micronesia, 1944–1974 : a bibliography of anthropological and related source materials / by Mac Marshall and James D. Nason. New Haven, Conn. : HRAF Pr., 1975. 337 p. : ill.   **CE114**

An author listing of book and periodical materials, with a "Guide to topics and areas" serving as a topical index. The Gilbert Islands (because British-controlled rather than part of the Trust Territory administered by the U.S.) are omitted from the compilers' definition of Micronesia. Includes some unpublished papers and doctoral dissertations, but no government documents.

§ *Micronesia, 1975–1987 : a social science bibliography*, comp. by Nicholas J. Goetzfridt and William L. Wuerch (N.Y. Greenwood, 1989. 194 p.), extends the earlier work with a further 1,849 entries.
                                                    Z5116.M37

Library catalogs

Bernice Pauahi Bishop Museum. Library. Dictionary catalog of the Library. Boston : G.K. Hall, 1964. 9 v.   **CE115**
For annotation, *see* DF10.

Handbooks

Oliver, Douglas L. Oceania : the native cultures of Australia and the Pacific Islands. Honolulu : Univ. of Hawaii Pr., c1989. 2 v. (1275 p.) : ill.   **CE116**

A comprehensive collection of ethnographic facts concerning 150 societies. Background information and activities are covered in v. 1, social relations in v. 2. The bibliography includes more than 1,000 books and articles.   GN662.O46

CF

Mythology, Folklore, and Popular Culture

Reference work with folklore and mythology requires a mastery of a wide variety of materials, since the discipline itself has a long history of interdisciplinary interests and connections. Consequently, it is often essential to consult other sections of the present *Guide* depending on the particular research need. The sources listed here, then, are only core titles, most of which have been generated by the discipline of folklore itself.

MYTHOLOGY

International

Hamilton, Edith. Mythology. Boston : Little, 1942. 497 p. : ill.   **CF1**

Repr. : N.Y. : New American Library, 1989.

Includes both classic and Norse myths with comparisons of the original and the later versions. Family charts, p. 457–73.   BL310.H3

Encyclopedias

Ann, Martha. Goddesses in world mythology / Martha Ann, Dorothy Imel. Santa Barbara, Calif. : ABC-Clio, 1993. 655 p.
                                                    CF2

Lists goddesses alphabetically within broad geographic areas. For each, gives description, culture of origin, bibliographic references, and any alternative forms. Indexes by name and attribute.   BL473.5.A66

Companion to literary myths : heroes and archetypes / ed. by Pierre Brunel ; translated from the French by Wendy Allatson, Judith Hayward, Trista Selous. London ; N.Y. : Routledge, 1992. 1223 p.   **CF3**

Translation of *Dictionnaire des mythes littéraires.*

The majority of entries are for the name of a character or hero, though some are thematic or geographically oriented. Suggestions for futher reading and a subject index are included.   PN56.M95D4813

Dictionnaire des symboles : mythes, rêves, coutumes, gestes, formes, figures, couleurs, nombres / sous la direction de Jean Chevalier. Éd. rev. et augm. [Paris] : Robert Laffont, [1982]. 842 p. : ill.   **CF4**

First publ. in 1969. Also publ. in 4 vol., Paris : Seghers, 1975.

About 1,200 entries (most of them signed with the initials of the contributor) with explanation of the symbolism of the term, its mythological, legendary, or religious background, etc. Bibliographies are not included in the articles, but abbreviated references are made to the general bibliography at the end of the volume.   GR931.D52

Mercatante, Anthony S. The Facts on File encyclopedia of world mythology and legend. N.Y. : Facts on File, c1988. 807 p. : ill.   **CF5**

An A–Z listing of about 3,000 entries. Following the "entry name is a concise definition, usually followed by a longer encyclopedic detailed discussion. As an additional reference aid, citations of relevant art, music, films, and literature are provided."—*Author's pref.* Annotated bibliography; key to variant spellings; cultural and ethnic index; general index.   BL303.M45

Mythical and fabulous creatures : a source book and research guide / ed. by Malcolm South. N.Y. : Greenwood, 1987. 393 p. : ill.   **CF6**

"Although this work discusses some creatures invented by individual artists and writers, it mainly deals with creatures that have a place in folklore, myth, or history and have a body of traditional lore connected with them."—*Pref.* Pt. 1 describes 20 fabulous creatures in separate chapters: Birds and beasts, Human-animal composites, Creatures of darkness, and Giants and fairies. Their appearances in literature, history, and art are cited and their functions noted. A bibliography concludes each chapter. Pt. 2, A miscellany and taxonomy, briefly discusses creatures not previously mentioned or given only passing attention earlier, and classifies some 145 creatures in five categories. There is a glossary of the more important creatures, a section of illustrations, a general bibliography, and a selective index.   GR825.M87

Mythologies / comp. by Yves Bonnefoy ; a restructured translation of Dictionnaire des mythologies et des religions des sociétés traditionnelles et du monde antique, prep. under the direction of Wendy Doniger ; trans. by Gerald Honigsblum ... [et al.]. Chicago : Univ. of Chicago Pr., c1991. 2 v. (1267 p.) : ill.   **CF7**

The English edition is considerably reorganized. Geographically arranged in ten parts. Considered idiosyncratic by some critics, but indispensable for its broad scope and depth of coverage. Major figures and themes are discussed. Extensive bibliographies; index.   BL311.D513

New Larousse encyclopedia of mythology / with an introd. by Robert Graves. New ed. [N.Y.] : Putnam, [1968, c1959]. 500 p. : ill.   **CF8**

"Translated by Richard Aldington and Delano Ames, and revised by a panel of editorial advisers from the Larousse mythologie générale edited by Felix Guirand"—*t.p. verso.*

First published in France in 1935; first English edition, 1959. Presents articles on the mythologies of various countries and civilizations from prehistory to present times. Not an encyclopedia in the usual sense of the term, as the material is presented in essay form with no easy approach to specific points. Includes various aspects of folklore, legend, and religious customs.   BL311.N43

Walker, Barbara G. The woman's encyclopedia of myths and secrets. San Francisco : Harper & Row, [1983]. 1124 p. : ill.   **CF9**

A dictionary arrangement of 1,350 entries, ranging in length from 25 words to several pages. Bibliographic notes for each entry refer to citations in the bibliography, p. 1105–18. Textual cross-references and marginalia notes, but no index. The introduction outlines the author's perspective: "Through making God in his own image, man has almost forgotten that woman once made the Goddess in hers. This is the deep secret of all mythologies, and the fundamental secret of this book."   BL458.W34

Wörterbuch der Mythologie : 1 Abteilung, Die alten Kulturvölker / unter Mitarbeit zahlreicher Fachgelehrter hrsg. von H. W. Haussig. Stuttgart : E. Klett, c1961– . Bd. 1–6 (Lfg. 1–24) : ill. (In progress).   **CF10**

Contents: The plan of the work as originally outlined designated the volumes as "Teil l," etc.; but when title pages and prefatory matter were issued, "Teil" was changed to "Band" and some of the parts were retitled. Volumes completed to date consist of the following Lieferungen: Bd. 1, Götter und Mythen im vorderen Orient (Lfg. 1–4); Bd. 2, Götter und Mythen im alten Europa (Lfg. 5–7, 9–10); Bd. 4 (originally designated Teil 3), Götter und Mythen der kaukasischen und iranischen Völker (Lfg. 11–12, 17); Bd. 5, Götter und Mythen des indischen Subkontinents (Lfg. 8, 13–16, 18–19). Lfg. 20 completes Bd. 5 and begins Bd. 6, Götter und Mythen in Zentral-, Ost- und Südostasien; Lfg. 21–24 continue but do not complete Bd. 6. Bd. 3, Götter und Mythen der Antike (dealing with Greek and Roman mythology) is still in preparation. Egidius Schmalzriedt is listed as principal editor beginning with Lfg. 20.

A work treating the mythologies of the world, arranged by geographical area. Each section is written by a specialist and includes a dictionary of names, terms, etc., pertinent to the mythology of the region. Further volumes have been announced to cover East Asia and the early Americas.   BL303.W63

Dictionaries

Bauer, Wolfgang. Lexikon der Symbole : Mythen, Symbole und Zeichen in Kultur, Religion, Kunst und Alltag / Wolfgang Bauer, Irmtraud Dümotz, Sergius Golowin. 3. Aufl. München : Heyne, c1987. 557 p. : ill.   **CF11**

1st ed., 1980.

Symbols are grouped in topical/geographic sections (e.g., Indian, Greek mythology, astrology, tarot), then arranged alphabetically by name of symbol with a line drawing or other illustration. Bibliographic references; index of names.   BF1623.S9B38

Lurker, Manfred. Dictionary of gods and goddesses, devils and demons. London ; N.Y. : Routledge and K. Paul, 1987. 451 p. : ill.   **CF12**

Translation of: *Lexikon der Götter und Dämonen* (Stuttgart : A. Kramer, 1984).

"Offers a conspectus of all the more important beings who have acquired 'personality' [in the sense of having had names bestowed on them] ... both in the pantheons of the classical cultures and in the world religions of today; and the religious systems of the so-called 'primitive' races are also given their due place."—*Pref.* Arranged alphabetically by name; brief entries. Appendixes of functions, etc., and of symbols and motifs. Brief bibliography.   BL303.L8713

Sykes, Egerton. Everyman's dictionary of nonclassical mythology. [4th ed., rev.]. London : Dent ; N.Y. : Dutton, [1968]. 282 p.   **CF13**

1st ed., 1952.

Several thousand personal and place-names, epithets, concepts, etc., are treated briefly but pointedly. Cross-references are indicated, and there is a selective bibliography, arranged by geographical area.
BL303.S9

———————— Who's who in non-classical mythology / Egerton Sykes ; rev. by Alan Kendall. N.Y. : Oxford Univ. Pr., 1993. 235 p.   **CF14**
Rev. ed. of: *Everyman's dictionary of non-classical mythology.*
"Non-classical" is defined broadly to include European groups outside ancient Greece and Rome. Lists more than 2,500 names with extensive cross-references covering variant forms of names. Entries lack bibliographic notes, although an appendix offers an introductory bibliography that is geographically arranged.   BL303.S9

Walker, Barbara G. The woman's dictionary of symbols and sacred objects. San Francisco : Harper & Row, c1988. 563 p. : ill.   **CF15**
Symbols are arranged by shapes (e.g., round and oval, three-way, multipointed) or by types (e.g., birds, rituals). Within each section entries are alphabetically arranged. Indexed by name of symbol and by subject. "It is especially important for women to learn more about the language of symbols, because many common religious symbols were stolen from ancient women-centered systems and reinterpreted in the context of patriarchy."—*Introd.*   CB475.W35

Native American

Gill, Sam D. Dictionary of Native American mythology / Sam D. Gill and Irene F. Sullivan. N.Y. : Oxford Univ. Pr., 1994. 425 p.   **CF16**
Originally published: Santa Barbara : ABC-Clio, 1992.
Covers the region from Northern Mexico to the Arctic Circle. References are included for most entries. Extensive cross-references link entries covering mythical figures, material objects, rituals, and narrative characters. Each entry indicates tribal origin as keyed to introductory regional maps. An index by tribe is also included.
E98.R3G46

Celtic

Ellis, Peter Berresford. Dictionary of Celtic mythology. Santa Barbara, Calif. : ABC-Clio, c1992. 232 p.   **CF17**
"Essentially for the lay reader."—*Pref.* Entries treat not only figures and objects in Celtic mythology but related cultural features. Irish or Welsh origin is indicated. Introductory reading list.   BL900.E45

Green, Miranda J. Dictionary of Celtic myth and legend. N.Y. : Thames and Hudson, 1992. 240 p. : ill.   **CF18**
Broad thematic and geographic scope. Most entries have references. The introduction provides an overview of Celtic culture and religion.   BL900.G73

Greek and Roman

Guides

Van Keuren, Frances Dodds. Guide to research in classicial art and mythology. Chicago : Amer. Libr. Assoc., 1991. 307 p.   **CF19**
For annotation, *see* BF7.   N7760.V3

Bibliography

Peradotto, John Joseph. Classical mythology : an annotated bibliographical survey. Urbana, Ill. : American Philological Assoc., 1973. 76 p.   **CF20**
A "bibliographical survey, which is offered as a set of possible tools—for whatever kind of mythology course (even at the graduate level)."—*Introd.* Presented as a series of brief, evaluative essays on selected works covering various aspects of the study of mythology. Works are rated according to a code indicating suitability for college-level courses.

Encyclopedias

Bell, Robert E. Place-names in classical mythology : Greece. Santa Barbara, Calif. : ABC-Clio, c1989. 350 p.   **CF21**
Intended as a companion to the author's *Dictionary of classical mythology* (CF26). Aims "to organize into one book the geography of classical mythology. For the most part no attention is paid to historical events or individuals unless there are mythological associations (such as religious phenomena, foundation of temples, etc.)."—*Introd.* Articles, in dictionary arrangement, range from a few lines to several pages in length; most include a substantial amount of detail concerning mythological association. Modern names are given in parentheses in many entries, and there is an alphabetical list of modern names and their ancient equivalents. A "Guide to personae" indicates the articles in which various characters are mentioned. Brief bibliography.
DF16.B45

———————— Women of classical mythology : a biographical dictionary. Santa Barbara, Calif. : ABC-Clio, c1991. 462 p.   **CF22**
Repr. : N.Y. : Oxford Univ. Pr., 1993.
Lists more than 2,600 individual women or groups of women. Most entries include citations to classical writers. Many cross-references. Appendix: a table of "The men in their lives."
BL715.B445

Lexicon iconographicum mythologiae classicae : (LIMC) / [rédaction, Hans Christoph Ackermann, Jean-Robert Gisler]. Zurich : Artemis, [1981–94]. v. 1–7, pt. 2 : ill. (In progress).   **CF23**
For annotation, *see* BF188.   N7760.L49

Reid, Jane Davidson. The Oxford guide to classical mythology in the arts, 1300–1990s. N.Y. : Oxford Univ. Pr., 1993. 2 v. (1310 p.).   **CF24**
For annotation *see* BF189.   NX650.M9R45

Tripp, Edward. Crowell's handbook of classical mythology. [N.Y.] : Crowell, [1970]. 631 p.   **CF25**
Primarily a retelling of the classical myths with their variant forms. The alphabetical arrangement (with entries for mythological characters, place names, and some related terms) makes for more convenient reference use than does Charles Mills Gayley's *Classic myths in English literature and in art* (New ed. rev. and enl. Boston : Ginn, 1939. 597 p.). Each story is generally told in full only once, under the name of one of its principal characters; sources are indicated. Treats both Greek and Roman mythology, the former predominating. Numerous cross-references; guide to pronunciation.   BL303.T75

Dictionaries

Bell, Robert E. Dictionary of classical mythology : symbols, attributes & associations. Santa Barbara : ABC-Clio, [1982]. 390 p. : ill.   **CF26**

Offers a topical approach to classical mythology. Arranged according to about a thousand topics, under which mythological characters associated with the term are listed; for each term, summarizes the myth or gives the reason a particular attribute or symbol is associated with the term. Often cites sources in Loeb classical library. A Guide to personae lists topical entries associated with a given character.

BL715.B44

Grimal, Pierre. The dictionary of classical mythology / Pierre Grimal ; translated by A. R. Maxwell-Hyslop. Oxford ; N.Y. : Blackwell, 1985. 603 p. : ill.   **CF27**

Translation of *Dictionnaire de la mythologie grecque et romaine*, (Paris : Presses Universitaires de France, 1951; 4ᵉ éd. rev., 1969).

A dictionary of names in classical mythology, with a summary of associated legends, relationship to other mythological figures, attributes, etc. The Greek form of the name is given in parentheses following the entry as appropriate. Bibliographic references keyed to specific articles appear on p. 471–515. Table of sources, genealogical tables, and a general index.

§ *A concise dictionary of classical mythology*, ed. by Stephen Kershaw (Oxford : Blackwell, 1990. 456 p.) is based on the Maxwell-Hyslop translation of Grimal's work. "Some of the minor supplementary variant myths have been deleted and a number of small extra entries have been added" (*Publisher's note*) and additional cross-references have been introduced, but the bibliographical apparatus, most of the genealogical tables, and the general index do not appear in the concise volume.   BL715.G713

Harnsberger, Caroline Thomas. Gods and heroes : a quick guide to the occupations, associations and experiences of the Greek and Roman gods and heroes. Troy, N.Y. : Whitston, 1977. 396 p.   **CF28**

The main body of the work is arranged alphabetically by terms denoting occupations, characteristics, attributes, etc., together with the names of gods and goddesses associated with the term and a brief explanation of the association. An index of the names of the deities and heroes refers to the term associated with each.   BL715.II29

Room, Adrian. Room's classical dictionary : the origins of the names of characters in classical mythology. London : Routledge & Kegan Paul, [1983]. 343 p. : ill.   **CF29**

Emphasis is on the meaning of the names, but the story or identity of each mythological figure is briefly told. Numerous appendixes; brief bibliography.   BL727.R58

Irish

Ellis, Peter Berresford. A dictionary of Irish mythology. Santa Barbara, Calif. : ABC-Clio, 1989. 240 p.   **CF30**

An A–Z arrangement of personal and place names, together with some terms, in Irish mythology. Cross-references; select bibliography. Covers much of the same ground as Daragh Smyth's *A guide to Irish mythology* (CF31), but each work includes entries not found in the other (and spellings of the same word frequently differ).

BL980.I7E45

Smyth, Daragh. A guide to Irish mythology. Dublin : Irish Academic Pr., c1988. 176 p. : ill.   **CF31**

A dictionary arrangement of personal and place-names and other terms from Irish mythology. An asterisk in the text indicates that the word has its own entry; sources are mentioned, and there is a brief listing of them. Indexed.   BL900.S495

Oceanic

Craig, Robert D. Dictionary of Polynesian mythology. N.Y. : Greenwood, 1989. 409 p. : map.   **CF32**

Gods, goddesses, and ancient heroes are entered alphabetically by name, with occasional entries for objects and places connected with the myths. Cross-references; citations to sources; list of sources, p. xxix–xlvii; an appendix, Categories of gods and goddesses; comprehensive index of all references to mythological characters.

BL2620.P6C7

Scandinavian

Lindow, John. Scandinavian mythology : an annotated bibliography. N.Y. : Garland, 1988. 593 p. (Garland folklore bibliographies, v. 13).   **CF33**

Aims "to offer easy access to the more important parts of the vast amount of scholarship on the subject, most of it in languages other than English."—*Introd.* Owing to the nature of past scholarship, the compiler has felt obliged to include "many works whose emphasis is on religion rather than the mythological corpus." Some 3,059 entries are arranged alphabetically by author with a detailed subject index. Annotations are descriptive, with only occasional value judgments.

Z7836.L58

Slavic

Kulikowski, Mark. A bibliography of Slavic mythology. Columbus, Ohio : Slavica Publ., c1989. 137 p.   **CF34**

"The scope of this bibliography is all written materials (books, dissertations, pamphlets, articles, and selections) from the earliest times up to and including 1981, published in all Slavic and major Western languages."—*Introd.* 805 items are listed alphabetically in sections devoted to primary and secondary sources. These citations, and a supplementary list of journals cited, include library locations. Author/title and subject indexes.   Z7836.K85

Teutonic

Simek, Rudolf. Dictionary of northern mythology. Cambridge, Eng. ; Rochester, N.Y. : D.S. Brewer, 1993. 424 p.   **CF35**

Translation of: *Lexikon der germanischen Mythologie*. Tr. by Angela Hall.

The English edition is augmented from the German original. "The mythology and religion of all Germanic tribes—Scandinavians as well as Goths or Angles and Saxons—have been dealt with insofar as they are Germanic in origin."—*Pref.* Extensive bibliographic references are included with entries, which are usually quite long.   BL850.S5613

FOLKLORE AND POPULAR CULTURE

General works

Guides

Brunvand, Jan Harold. Folklore : a study and research guide. N.Y. : St. Martin's Pr., [1976]. 144 p.   **CF36**

Intended as a guide "for the beginner, chiefly the college undergraduate."—*Introd.* In three main sections: (1) The subject in context; (2) Reference guide; (3) The research paper. The Reference guide is a bibliographic essay on the tools for folklore research. Glossary; index.

Z5981.B78

Bibliography

Bennett, Gillian. Contemporary legend : a folklore bibliography / Gillian Bennett, Paul Smith. N.Y. : Garland, 1993. 340 p. (Garland reference library of the humanities, vol. 1307 ; Garland folklore bibliographies, v. 18.).   **CF37**
In four chapters: Anthologies, Introductions and overviews, Theoretical and technical studies, and Texts and case studies. References are primarily in English. Author and general indexes, mostly subjects, to the 1,116 entries.   Z5981.B46

Carnes, Pack. Fable scholarship : an annotated bibliography. N.Y. : Garland, 1985. 382 p. (Garland reference library of the humanities, vol. 367 ; Garland folklore bibliographies, v. 8).   **CF38**
An author listing of some 1,457 studies of "Aesopic" fables and closely related traditions. Includes books, articles, and dissertations mainly from the 1880–1982 period. Descriptive annotations. Indexes of names and subjects, fables, and tale types (by Perry number).   Z5896.C37

Coleman, Earle Jerome. Magic : a reference guide. N.Y. : Greenwood, 1987. 198 p.   **CF39**
Offers bibliographical essays on the history and psychology of magic, the art of conjuring, etc., as well as pertinent biographies and autobiographies. Appendixes: Selected dates in the history of conjuring; Directory of magic periodicals, research collections, dealers. Author and subject indexes.   GV1547.C595

Steinfirst, Susan. Folklore and folklife : a guide to English-language reference sources. N.Y. : Garland, 1992. 2 v. (1208 p.). (Garland reference library of the humanities, vol. 1429 ; Garland folklore bibliographies, v. 16.).   **CF40**
"The present bibliography is geared toward students and 'beginning' folklorists rather than folklore scholars"—*Pref.* 2,577 titles are listed in seven broad sections each subdivided with useful headnotes and introductions. Author, title, and subject indexes.   Z5981.S74

Current

Abstracts of popular culture. v. 1–3^A-B. Bowling Green, Ohio : Bowling Green Univ. Popular Pr., 1976–82. Biannual.   **CF41**
Subtitle: A bi-annual publication of international popular phenomena.
Frequency has varied.
"By 'Popular Culture' we mean all aspects of life which are not academic or creative in the narrowest and most esoteric sense of the words. ... Important topics such as film, television, radio, popular literature, fairs, parades, theater, amusements, music, circuses, carnivals, urban and rural life, the counter culture, ethnic and women's studies, folklore, the family sports, leisure and work, humor, and all other aspects of the 'New Humanities' " (*Introd., v. 1A*) are included.
Indexes relevant articles from a wide range of periodicals; abstracts are very brief. Full citations appear in an author listing, and there is a subject index. Also aims to provide information on unpublished papers on popular culture and to serve as a clearinghouse for copies of such papers.   Z7164.S66A27

Internationale Volkskundliche Bibliographie = International folklore and folklife bibliography = Bibliographie internationale des arts et traditions populaires. 1939/41– . Bâle : Impr. G. Krebs, 1949– .   **CF42**
Title in German, English, and French; order on title page varies. Language of subtitle varies.
English title varies; also publ. as *International folklore bibliography.*
Publisher varies.

Supersedes *Volkskundliche Bibliographie* (1917–37/38, publ. 1919–57 in 14 v.).
Frequency varies: 1939–54, irregular; 1955– , biennial.
An extensive bibliography covering folklore of all countries and all periods. Classed arrangement with author index. With 1979–80 (publ. 1985), an English-language subject index and complete list of journals scanned for the issue were added. With 1981–82 (publ. 1986), a French preface and index were added. With the *MLA international bibliography* (BE39), the major index to periodicals in folklore.   Z5982.I523

Dissertations

Dundes, Alan. Folklore theses and dissertations in the United States. Austin, Tex. : publ. for the American Folklore Society by the Univ. of Texas Pr., [1976]. 610 p. (Publications of the American Folklore Society. Bibliographical and special series, v. 27).   **CF43**
A chronological listing of doctoral dissertations and master's theses from 1860 through 1968. Indexed by author, subject, and institution.   Z5981.D85

Kerst, Catherine Hiebert. Ethnic folklife dissertations from the United States and Canada, 1960–1980 : a selected annotated bibliography. Wash. : American Folklife Center, Library of Congress, 1986. 69 p. (Publications of the American Folklife Center. Publications, no. 12).   **CF44**
Superintendent of Documents classification: LC 39.9:12.
A selective bibliography of dissertations, arranged by author. The compiler's definition of folklife emphasizes "traditional forms of ethnic folk culture."—*Pref.* Indexed by ethnic group and by state or province.   Z5984.U6K47

Thematic indexes

Aarne, Antti Amatus. The types of the folktale : a classification and bibliography / tr. and enl. by Stith Thompson. 2nd rev. ed. Helsinki : Suomalainen Tiedeakatemia, 1961. 588 p. (FF communications, no. 184).   **CF45**
Original title: *Verzeichnis der Märchentypen* (Helsinki, 1910; FF communications, no. 3).
A catalog of tale plot summaries from Indo-European tradition generically arranged (animal tales, tales of magic, etc.). For each type, references to published versions, other catalogs or archival sources are given. Subject index.   Z5983.F17A27

Ashliman, D. L. A guide to folktales in the English language : based on the Aarne-Thompson classification system. N.Y. : Greenwood, 1987. 368 p. (Bibliographies and indexes in world literature, no. 11).   **CF46**
Intended "to help readers find reliable texts of any given folktale, not only in its best known version, but also in less familiar variants."—*Introd.* Arranged by the Aarne-Thompson tale type numbers, with an alphabetical index "where the titles of the best-known tales and key words from typical plots are located." Each entry gives a brief synopsis and indicates the tale's published title(s) and a published collection in which it can be found. Bibliography of folktale collections.   Z5983.F17A83

Azzolina, David S. Tale type- and motif-indexes : an annotated bibliography. N.Y. : Garland, 1987. 105 p. (Garland reference library of the humanities, vol. 565 ; Garland folklore bibliographies, v. 12).   **CF47**
Designed "to give folklorists and reference librarians access to and background of a genre of a reference tool peculiar to the scholarly discussion of folklore."—*Introd.* 186 entries are arranged alphabetically by author and include books, journal articles, and unpublished dissertations and theses. Annotations are mainly descriptive, but often in-

clude references to related works and citations to reviews. Subject, geographic, and "Additional author" (joint authors, translators, etc.) indexes. Z5983.L5A98

Baughman, Ernest Warren. Type and motif-index of the folktales of England and North America. The Hague : Mouton, 1966. 607 p. (Indiana University. Folklore series, 20). **CF48**

Revision and expansion of a 1953 doctoral dissertation. Employs the motif number system used in Stith Thompson's *Motif-index of folk literature* (CF49); and the alphabetical index for that work also serves for locating motif numbers in the present listing. GR67.B3

Thompson, Stith. Motif-index of folk-literature : a classification of narrative elements in folktales, ballads, myths, fables, mediaeval romances, exempla, fabliaux, jest-books and local legends. Rev. and enl. ed. Bloomington : Indiana Univ. Pr., 1955–58. 6 v. **CF49**

1st ed. 1932–36.

A decimal classification scheme devised to index the motifs found in traditional narrative literature: the folktale, myth, ballad, fable, medieval romance, etc. References are usually furnished to one or more works where material about a motif may be found, but the work is planned primarily as an index and is only incidentally a bibliography. Vol. 6 is a detailed alphabetical index of motifs.

•Machine-readable version: *Motif-index of folk literature* [database] (Bloomington, Ind. : Indiana Univ. Pr., 1993). Available on CD-ROM. GR67.T52

Encyclopedias

Enzyklopädie des Märchens : Handwörterbuch zur histor. u. vergleichenden Erzählforschung / hrsg. von Kurt Ranke zusammen mit Hermann Bausinger … [et al.] ; Red., Lotte Baumann … [et al.]. Berlin ; N.Y. : W. de Gruyter, 1975–1993. v. 1–7. (In progress). **CF50**

Contents: Bd. 1–7, Aarne–Klei.

To be in 12 v., each volume consisting of five *Lieferungen*. Includes material on methodology, types and motifs, figures, regional studies, biographies, seminal works, etc. Lengthy, signed articles with extensive bibliographies. GR72.E58

Funk and Wagnalls standard dictionary of folklore, mythology and legend / Maria Leach, ed. Jerome Fried, assoc. ed. N.Y. : Funk & Wagnalls, [1973]. 1236 p. **CF51**

This is a reissue in 1 v. with minor corrections of the 2-v. ed. publ. 1949–50. A "Key to countries, regions, cultures, culture areas, peoples, tribes, and ethnic groups" (p. 1197–1236) has been added.

A comprehensive encyclopedia and dictionary dealing with the gods, heroes, tales, motifs, customs, beliefs, songs, dances, games, proverbs, etc., of the cultures of the world, including survey articles with bibliographies on regions and on special subjects (ballad, dance, fairy tale, national mythologies, etc.), written and signed by specialists.

A review of the 1-v. edition concludes that the work "remains a standard reference tool for all kinds of libraries. However, since the text of the 1972 edition is basically unchanged and the newly added key is not really an adequate index, this edition is desirable only if the original edition needs replacement or one simply prefers a single-volume edition."—*Booklist* 70 (1 Nov. 1973): 253. GR35.F82

Rinzler, Carol Ann. The dictionary of medical folklore. N.Y. : Crowell, [1979]. 243 p. **CF52**

Attempts to discount or affirm various bits of folk advice, popular beliefs, and "old wives' tales" relating to health, medical problems, nutrition, etc. Entry is under key term, with various beliefs and propositions discussed thereunder. Scientific studies and reports are occasionally referred to within an entry, but bibliographical references or other documentation are not generally given. Indexed. RC81.A2R56

Dictionaries

A dictionary of superstitions / ed. by Iona Opie and Moira Tatem. Oxford ; N.Y. : Oxford Univ. Pr., 1989. 494 p. **CF53**

The superstitions "have been arranged alphabetically according to their central idea or object."—*Pref.* Quotations documenting them are chronological. The analytic index connects the unifying themes of the individual superstitions and most of the cross-references. Definitive for English. BF1775.D53

Unterman, Alan. Dictionary of Jewish lore and legend. N.Y. : Thames and Hudson, 1991. 216 p. : ill. **CF54**

For annotation, *see* BC555. BM50.U58

Directories

American Folklore Society. Membership directory and guide to the field. 1992 ed.– . Wash. : The Society, c1991– . Annual. **CF55**

Describes the organization, purpose, and structure of the American Folklore Society. Includes membership directory with member's interests described, and directory of academic and public programs in folklore. GR1.A572a

Handbooks

Folklore, cultural performances, and popular entertainments : a communications-centered handbook / ed. by Richard Bauman. N.Y. : Oxford Univ. Pr., 1992. 313 p. : ill. **CF56**

Based on *International encyclopedia of communications* (CH482). In three sections: basic concepts and analytical perspectives, communications media and expressive genres, and cultural performances and popular entertainments. Brief bibliographies with each essay. Indexed. GR35.F64

The folklore of world holidays / Margaret Read MacDonald, editor. Detroit : Gale, c1992. 739 p. **CF57**

For annotation, *see* AL145. GT3930.F65

The Americas

Szwed, John F. Afro-American folk culture : an annotated bibliography of materials from North, Central and South America and the West Indies / John F. Szwed and Roger D. Abrahams. Philadelphia : Inst. for the Study of Human Issues, [1978]. 2 v. (Publications of the American Folklore Society, Bibliographical and special series, . 31–32). **CF58**

Contents: pt. 1, North America; pt. 2, The West Indies, Central and South America.

Geographical arrangement; indexed by subject and specific locale. Z5984.A44S95

Bibliography

Bibliografía del folklore de Guatemala, 1892–1980. Guatemala : Dirección General de Antropología e Historia, 1980. 174 p. **CF59**

A classed bibliography of about 700 items on material, social, and intellectual folklore, with many descriptive notes. Author and title indexes. Z5984.G9B52

Bibliografía folclórica. v. 1 (1970)– . [Rio de Janeiro : Ministerio da Educacão e Cultura, Departamento de Assuntos Culturais, Fundacão Nacional de Arte, Campanha de Defesa do Folclore Brasileiro, 1977]– . Annual.   **CF60**

A classed list of materials on Brazilian folklore, with brief descriptive notes.   Z5984.B7B5

Boggs, Ralph Steele. Bibliography of Latin American folklore. N.Y. : Wilson, 1940. 109 p. (Inter-American bibliographical and Library Assoc. Publications. Ser. I, v. 5).   **CF61**

A partially annotated bibliography of 643 titles, classed by subject and further, by country. Includes Central and South America, and the Caribbean islands.

§ Mexican folklore receives a more detailed treatment in the compiler's *Bibliografía del folklore mexicano* (México, D.F. : Instituto Panamericano de Geografía e Historia, 1939).   Z5984.L4B7

Clements, William M. Native American folklore, 1879–1979 : an annotated bibliography / William M. Clements, Frances M. Malpezzi. Athens, Ohio : Swallow Pr., [1984]. 247 p.   **CF62**

Folklore is here viewed as verbal art and its performance, so that the bibliography "includes books and articles which treat oral narratives, songs, chants, prayers, formulas, orations, proverbs, riddles, word play, music, dances, games, and ceremonials."—*Introd*. Entries are arranged by tribal groups within sections for cultural areas. Indexes of subjects and authors/editors/translators. 5,450 entries.   Z1209.C57

Colonelli, Cristina Argenton. Bibliografia do folclore brasileiro. São Paulo : Conselho Estadual de Artes e Ciências Humanas, 1979. 294 p. (Coleção folclore, 20).   **CF63**

An author listing of books and periodical articles, with subject index. 4,919 entries.   Z5984.B7C6

Flanagan, Cathleen C. American folklore : a bibliography, 1950–1974 / Cathleen C. Flanagan and John T. Flanagan. Metuchen, N.J. : Scarecrow, 1977. 406 p.   **CF64**

Concerned "only with verbal folklore: more specifically ballads, folk songs, myths, legends, tales, superstitions, beliefs, cures, proverbs, riddles, and the like."—*Pref*. Sections: Festschriften, symposia, collections; Bibliography, dictionaries, archives; Folklore: study and teaching; and General folklore are followed by sections arranged by type of material treated. Author index, but none of detailed subjects. About 3,600 items. Supplements Charles Haywood's *Bibliography of North American folklore and folksong* (CF67).   Z5984.U6F55

Fowke, Edith F. A bibliography of Canadian folklore in English / Edith F. Fowke, Carole Henderson Carpenter. Toronto : Univ. of Toronto Pr., [1981]. 272 p.   **CF65**

Preliminary ed., 1976.

Basic arrangement is by genre (e.g., folktales, folk music and dance, folk speech and naming, superstitions and popular beliefs, folklife and customs) with subdivisions for major ethnic groups. Separate sections for recordings, films, theses and dissertations. Author index.   Z5984.C33F68

Georges, Robert A. American and Canadian immigrant and ethnic folklore : an annotated bibliography / Robert A. Georges and Stephen Stern. N.Y. : Garland, 1982. 484 p. (Garland folklore bibliographies, v. 2).   **CF66**

A selective bibliography of 1,900 English-language books, essays, and articles published 1888–1980 on the folklore of European and Asian immigrants and their North American descendants. Arrangement is by 56 ethnic groups and a general section; indexed by folklore form and topic, general subject, geographical occurrence, and author.   GR105.G43

Haywood, Charles. A bibliography of North American folklore and folksong. 2nd rev. ed. N.Y. : Dover, [1961]. 2 v. (1301 p.) : maps.   **CF67**

1st ed., 1951.

Contents: v. 1, The American people north of Mexico, including Canada; v. 2, The American Indians north of Mexico, including the Eskimos.

A corrected republication of the 1951 edition, with the addition of a new "Index supplement: composers, arrangers, performers."

A comprehensive, classified bibliography. Covers material on folklore, folksong, legends, dance, etc., as well as music in printed form and on records. Includes some descriptive and evaluative annotations; detailed tables of contents; an author and subject index with title entries for individual songs; and a new index of composers, arrangers, and performers.   Z5984.U5H32

Heisley, Michael. An annotated bibliography of Chicano folklore from the Southwestern United States. Los Angeles : Produced for and distr. by the Center for the Study of Comparative Folklore and Mythology, Univ. of California, 1977. 188 p.   **CF68**

A classed bibliography with author, geographical, and subject indexes. Each subject section is subdivided as (1) published works and (2) theses and dissertations. Slightly more than 1,000 items.   Z5984.U6H45

Niles, Susan A. South American Indian narrative, theoretical and analytical approaches : an annotated bibliography. N.Y. : Garland, 1981. 183 p. (Garland folklore bibliographies, v. 1 ; Garland reference library of the humanities, v. 276).   **CF69**

Includes references to about 600 works which analyze South American Indian narrative folklore or present summaries or collections of tales; excludes "folklorizations" and popular treatments of native beliefs, as well as material from the African-American and Ibero-American traditions. Author arrangement; indexed by tribal group and subject.   Z1209.2.S77N54

Pan American Institute of Geography and History. Comisíon de Historia. Committee on Folklore. Bibliografía del folklore peruano. México ; Lima, 1960. 186 p. (Publicaciones del Comité de Folklore, 2).   **CF70**

Also issued as Publication 92 of Pan American Institute of Geography and History, Commission on History, and as Publication 230 of Pan American Institute of Geography and History.

An annotated bibliography of 1,809 entries in broad subject arrangement, with author and detailed subject indexes.   F1401.P153 no.230

Pereira Salas, Eugenio. Guía bibliográfica para el estudio del folklore chileno. [Santiago] : Instituto de Investigaciones Musicales, Universidad de Chile, [1952]. 112 p.   **CF71**

"Tirada aparte de los *Archivos del folklore chileno, Instituto 'Ramon A. Laval'*, ... Fasciculo 4, 1952."—*t.p*.

A classed bibliography of 1,289 titles.

Continued by Manuel Dannemann Rothstein, *Bibliografía del folklore chileno, 1952–1965* (Austin : Center for Intercultural Studies on Folklore and Oral History, Univ. of Texas, 1970. 60 p. [Latin American folklore ser., 2.]). 425 items, most briefly annotated, in subject arrangement. Author index.   Z5984.C45P4

Scott, Randall W. Comic books and strips : an information sourcebook. Phoenix : Oryx, 1988. 152 p.   **CF72**

Lists and briefly annotates 1,033 books, periodicals, and library collections useful for the study of comics. In five main sections: (1) Core library collection; (2) Books about comics; (3) Books that reprint comics; (4) Periodicals and journals; (5) Library collections. Author, title, and subject indexes.   Z5956.C6S37

Library resources

Directory of popular culture collections / by Christopher D. Geist ... [et al.]. Phoenix : Oryx, 1989. 234 p.   **CF73**

Libraries with relevant collections are arranged by geographical area—state or province, then by city. For each gives address and phone number, names of curators, hours, restrictions and access requirements, and description of collections. Indexed by subject and by name of institution.   E169.1.D54

Thematic indexes

Wilbert, Johannes. Folk literature of South American Indians : general index / Johannes Wilbert and Karin Simoneau. Los Angeles : UCLA Latin American Center Publications, Univ. of California, c1992. 1323 p. : map. (UCLA Latin American studies, v. 80). **CF74**

A cumulative motif index to the 23-v. series, "Folk literature of South American Indians," published by the UCLA Latin American Center—the definitive collection in English. Includes an extensive concordance of new motifs and an encyclopedic introduction and comprehensive bibliography on South American folk literature.

§ *See also* Susan A. Niles, *South American Indian narrative, theoretical and analytical approaches* (CF69). F2230.1.F56W56

Directories

Bartis, Peter. Folklife sourcebook : a directory of folklife resources in the United States and Canada / prepared by Peter T. Bartis and Barbara C. Fertig. Wash. : American Folklife Center, Library of Congress, 1986. 152 p. (Publications of the American Folklife Center, no. 14). **CF75**

Superintendent of Documents classification: LC 39.9:14.

A directory of agencies and programs, organizations and institutions, college and university courses, archival holdings, serials, recording companies, and similar listings. Based on responses to a questionnaire. Not indexed. GR37.B37

Handbooks

The encyclopedia of American comics / ed. by Ron Goulart. N.Y. : Facts on File, 1990. 408 p., [16] p. of plates : ill. (some col.). **CF76**

"The articles in this book are arranged alphabetically and fall into two basic categories: biographical entries on the people of the comics field (artists, creators, packagers, writers) and entries on the comic strips themselves."—*Introd.* Entries are signed and black-and-white illustrations appear throughout. General index. PN6725.E64

Handbook of American folklore / ed. by Richard M. Dorson. Bloomington : Indiana Univ. Pr., [1983]. 584 p. : ill. **CF77**

Provides "an introduction to American folklore as it has been studied in America" and "is intended to show established scholars, students, and the general public what the discipline of folkloristics is all about."—*Introd.* In four main sections: (1) Topics of research; (2) Interpretation of research; (3) Methods of research; (4) Presentation of research. Each section is made up of brief essays by contributing scholars on specific aspects of American folklore research—its content, history, methodology and current state. Bibliographic notes follow each essay and there is a classed bibliography, p. 541–63. Detailed index. GR105.H36

Handbook of American popular culture / ed. by M. Thomas Inge. 2nd ed., rev. and enlarged. N.Y. : Greenwood, 1989. 3 v. **CF78**

1st ed., Westport, Conn. : Greenwood, 1978–81. 3 v.

Offers an impressive body of articles on various aspects of American popular culture, past and present, including various genres of popular literature and arts, film and other mass media, advertising, the circus, games and toys, the occult, pop religion, and self-help theories. Articles, written by specialists, include a chronological survey of the topic, a guide to its literature, a directory of research centers and collections, and a bibliography.

The 2nd ed., basically a revision of the 1st, incorporates "many modifications. New subjects have been added, including chapters on business, catalogs, computers, dance, fashion, gardening, graffiti, musical theater, and the study of popular culture. Some articles have been completely recast; some are contributed by different au-

thors. All others have been extensively revised and updated, with special attention given to recent bibliography."—*Introd.* Articles now appear in a single alphabetical sequence, Advertising to Women, with name and subject indexes at the end of v. 3.

§ The essays on literary aspects of popular culture (e.g., best-sellers, comic books, detective and mystery novels, pulps and dime novels, Westerns) were revised, expanded and separately published as *Handbook of American popular literature* (BE434) which serves as a companion volume. E169.1.H2643

Current surveys

Humor in America : a research guide to genres and topics / ed. by Lawrence E. Mintz. N.Y. : Greenwood, 1988. 241 p. **CF79**

A state-of-the-art review of the various forms of humor (e.g., comic strip, standup comic, film), or topics of humor (e.g., political humor, racial and ethnic humor). Also included in each essay are lists of topics needing research, a checklist, and bibliographical survey. Names/titles index. PS430.H86

Europe

Bibliography

Baer, Florence E. Folklore and literature of the British Isles : an annotated bibliography. N.Y. : Garland, 1986. 335 p. (Garland reference library of the humanities, v. 622 ; Garland folklore bibliographies, v. 11). **CF80**

Concerned with the interrelationship of folklore and literature in the British Isles. Lists more than 1,000 references, mostly in English, in author order with long descriptive annotations. General subject index; indexes by tale type, motif number, Child ballad number. Z2014.F6B34

Danaher, Kevin. A bibliography of Irish ethnology and folk tradition / comp. by Caoimhín O'Danachair. Dublin : Mercier Pr., [1978]. 95 p. **CF81**

In two sections, the first a listing according to the categories of Seán O'Súilleabháin's *Handbook of Irish folklore* (Dublin : Publ. by the Educational company of Ireland Ltd. for the Folklore of Ireland Society, 1942). The second section is a listing by author. Full bibliographical information in both lists. Z5117.D35

Falassi, Alessandro. Italian folklore : an annotated bibliography. N.Y. : Garland, 1985. 438 p. (Garland reference library of the humanities, v. 449 ; Garland folklore bibliographies, v. 6 [i.e., 7]). **CF82**

Lists 3,000 references up to 1983 with brief annotations in English. "The present work is by no means intended as a complete listing but rather as a large and multi-faceted point of entry to key sources as well as an introduction to folklore and folklife of Italy."—*Introd.* Z5984.I8F35

Russkii fol'klor : bibliograficheskii ukazatel'. Leningrad : BAN, 1961–90. v. 1–5; v. 6, pts. 1–2; v. 7; in 8 vol. (In progress). **CF83**

Issued by Institut russkoi literatury (Pushkinskii dom) and Biblioteka of the Akademiia Nauk SSSR.

Contents: v. 1, 1881–1900; v. 2, 1901–1916; v. 3, 1917–1944; v. 4, 1945–1959; v. 5, 1960–1965; v. 6, 1966–1975; v. 7, 1976–1980.

Classed bibliography of folklore and writings on folklore in Russian, published in the Soviet Union, with author index. More than 22,000 items in the series. Z5984.R9R8

Yassif, Eli. Jewish folklore : an annotated bibliography. N.Y. : Garland, 1986. 341 p. (Garland folklore bibliographies, v. 10 ; Garland reference library of the humanities, vol. 450).   **CF84**

Aims to provide "a critical summary of one hundred years of the study of Jewish folklore" (*Introd.*)—i.e., publications of ca. 1872–1980. Concerned with studies of folklore, not collections of tales, etc. Lists and annotates 1,356 items in an author arrangement, with subject index. Does not include the study of East European Jewish culture because it was felt that that extensive area requires a separate bibliography.   Z6374.F6Y37

Library catalogs

Vaughan Williams Memorial Library, London. The Vaughan Williams Memorial Library catalogue of the English Folk Dance and Song Society. [London] : Mansell, 1973. 769 p.   **CF85**

Subtitle: Acquisitions to the library of books, pamphlets, periodicals, sheet music and manuscripts, from its inception to 1971.

"The Library contains 7,000 books, pamphlets and periodicals; 4,000 tape recordings and records; an extensive photograph collection; and a number of archival films dealing with the folk customs and dances of England."—*Introd.* Separate author and subject sections, with a table of subject classes, and an alphabetical index to the subject headings.   ML136.L8V4

Encyclopedias

Bächtold-Stäubli, Hanns. Handwörterbuch des deutschen Aberglaubens / hrsg. unter besonderer Mitwirkung von E. Hoffmann-Krayer .... Berlin : W. de Gruyter, 1927–41. 9 v. (Handwörterbücher zur deutschen Volkskunde, hrsg. vom Verband Deutscher Vereine für Volkskunde, Abt. I).   **CF86**

Nachträge in v. 9.

A scholarly encyclopedia with long, signed articles by specialists, and extensive bibliographies. Treats German superstitions and popular beliefs, covering religious, sociological, and historical aspects.   GR166.H3 Abt.1

Bødker, Laurits. Folk literature (Germanic). Copenhagen : Rosenkilde & Bagger, 1965. 365 p. (International dictionary of regional European ethnology and folklore, 2).   **CF87**

Includes folk literature of the German-speaking parts of Europe, including Scandinavia and Holland. Entries include bibliographies; full bibliography, p. 335–65.

§ For full information on the *Dictionary*, see CE49.

Briggs, Katharine Mary. A dictionary of British folktales in the English language : incorporating the F. J. Norton collection. London : Routledge ; Bloomington : Indiana Univ. Pr., [1970–71]. 2 v. in 4.   **CF88**

Repr.: London : Routledge, 1991.

Contents: pt. A, Folk narratives: v. 1, Fables and exempla; Fairy tales; v. 2, Jocular tales; Novelle; Nursery tales; pt. B, v. 1–2, Folk legends.

"The main distinction between Folk Narratives and Folk Legends is clear enough: Folk Narrative is Folk Fiction, told for edification, delight or amusement, Folk Legend was once believed to be true."—*Introd., pt. A, v. 1.*

Offers a transcription or a summary of each tale or legend. Within each subsection tales are arranged alphabetically by title, admittedly making for some difficulty since many of the tales have no real titles, the titles of others may vary in different collections, and different tales sometimes have the same title. To overcome these difficulties the editor has provided an "Index of tale-types and migratory legends" according to numbers of the Aarne-Thompson tale type index (from *The types of the folktale*, CF45), with some suggested numbers and types

interpolated. An alphabetical index of story titles appears in the first volume of each part; there is an impressive list of books quoted, cited, and consulted.

The F. J. Norton collection is a compilation in manuscript form of tales transcribed from printed sources; it is connected with the Library of the Folklore Society at the University College Library, London.

Selections from the *Dictionary* have been published under various titles, most recently as *British folktales* (N.Y. : Dorset, 1988. 315 p.).   GR141.B69

Ó hÓgáin, Dáithí. Myth, legend & romance : an encyclopaedia of the Irish folk tradition. N.Y. : Prentice Hall, c1991. 453 p. : ill.   **CF89**

An alphabetical encyclopedia of lengthy entries with bibliographic references covering most oral forms of narrative. Indexes by character names, peoples and families, places, and general subjects.   GR153.5.O16

Africa

Coughlan, Margaret N. Folklore from Africa to the United States : an annotated bibliography. Wash. : Library of Congress, 1976. 161 p. : ill.   **CF90**

A selective listing of folklore collections, linguistic, ethnological, and anthropological studies, travel accounts and government reports containing tales. The arrangement is geographical, from general sub-Saharan Africa through regions of Africa to the West Indies and the U.S.; within each region, the material is grouped as studies and collections for adults, and collections for children. Lengthy annotations. Author-title index.   Z5984.A35C68

Görög, Veronika. Littérature annotée littérature orale d'Afrique noire / Veronika Görög-Karady ; avec la participation de Catherine Bouillet, Tal Tamar. Paris : Conseil international de la langue française, 1992. 367 p.   **CF91**

Briefly annotated references to 2,831 titles primarily in the French language. Updates and supplements the author's *Litterature orale d'Afrique Noire : bibliographie analytique* (Paris : G.-P. Maisonneuve et Larose, 1981). In author order with indexes by genre and ethno-linguistic group.   Z5984.A35G67

Scheub, Harold. African oral narratives, proverbs, riddles, poetry, and song. Boston : G.K. Hall, [1977]. 393 p.   **CF92**

An earlier version was published as *Bibliography of African oral narratives* (Madison : [African Studies Program, Univ. of Wis.], 1971).

An international bibliography of more than 5,800 collections appearing either as separate publications or as contributions to periodicals. Listing is by author or other main entry; indexes provide approach by genre, culture, etc. Annotations frequently include quotations from the compiler of the collection.   Z5984.A35S3

Asia

Algarin, Joanne P. Japanese folk literature : a core collection and reference guide. N.Y. : Bowker, 1982. 226 p.   **CF93**

In three main parts: (1) an annotated bibliography of works on Japanese folklore and folktales, arranged by author; (2) an annotated list of Japanese folktale anthologies, with brief descriptions of the stories included; (3) a section of brief synopses of 26 classic Japanese folktales. 138 citations, with detailed annotations. Appendixes list Japanese-language sources and provide a glossary. Indexed.   Z3308.L5A44

Bernardo, Gabriel Adriano. A critical and annotated bibliography of Philippine, Indonesian and other Malayan folk-lore / ed. by Francisco Demetrio y Radaza. Cagayan de Oro City [Philippines] : Xavier Univ., 1972. 150 p. : ill. (Ateneo de Manila University. Dept. of History. Bibliographical series, no. 3). **CF94**

A posthumously published work based on a master's thesis presented in 1923, with some revision and updating. In two parts: (1) Philippine folklore; (2) Indonesian and other Malayan folklore. Each part is subdivided for (1) general and other expository works; (2) myths, legends, fairy tales and other folk stories; and (3) miscellaneous texts. Author and title index.   Z5984.P45B47

Danandjaja, James. An annotated bibliography of Javanese folklore. Berkeley, Calif. : Center for South and Southeast Asia Studies, Univ. of Calif., 1972. 162 p. : maps. (University of California, Berkeley. Center for South and Southeast Asia Studies. Occasional paper, no. 9). **CF95**

Lists nearly 900 monographs and periodical articles arranged by topic, with author index. Descriptive annotations.   DS503.C35

Handoo, Jawaharlal. A bibliography of Indian folk literature. Mysore : Central Institute of Indian Languages, 1977. 421 p. (CIIL folklore ser., 2). **CF96**

An author listing of texts and studies of Indian folk literature, i.e., items "such as myths, tales, legends, fables, ... songs, ballads (or any form of verse), proverbs, riddles, etc."—*Introd.* About 4,250 entries. Lack of a subject index seriously limits the usefulness of the work.   Z5984.I5H36

Kirkland, Edwin Capers. A bibliography of South Asian folklore. Bloomington : Indiana Univ. Research Center in Anthropology, Folklore, and Linguistics, 1966. 291 p. (Indiana Univ. folklore series, 21 ; Asian folklore studies monographs, 4). **CF97**

Concerned with "all types of folklore, not just folk literature."—*Introd.* Citations to texts of songs, tales, legends, etc., are included, as well as writings about the folk literature, customs, dances, festivals, and the like. 6,852 items in an alphabetical author listing with subject index. Most entries are in English.   Z5984.S6K5

The Yanagita Kunio guide to the Japanese folk tale / trans. and ed. by Fanny Hagin Mayer. Bloomington : Indiana Univ. Pr., [1986?]. 363 p. : maps, port. **CF98**

Translation of *Nihon mukashibanashi meii*, comp. under the supervision of Yanagita Kunio and ed. by Nihon Hōsō Kyōkai.

"Yanagita Kunio ... started the movement to collect folk tales in Japan and led it for more than fifty years."—*Pref.* This motif index is in two parts: complete tales and derived or partial stories. Each part contains chapters on various themes (e.g., Marriage, Stepchildren) which in turn have entries for various tale types. Each entry includes a brief summary, geographical locations and variants, and a list of sources. Supplementary material consists of a complete bibliography of sources, a glossary, indexes of English and Japanese tales and titles, and geographical indexes with reference maps.   GR340.N52213

Australia and Oceania

The Oxford companion to Australian folklore / ed. by Gwenda Beed Davey and Graham Seal. Melbourne ; N.Y. : Oxford Univ. Pr., 1993. 381 p. : ill. **CF99**

Alphabetically arranged articles define folklore broadly and include some extensive essays. Articles cover various ethnic groups, major folk figures, folklorists, material culture, and genres. A bibliographic essay is an appendix.   GR365.O94

CG

Statistics and Demography

GENERAL WORKS

Bibliography

Driver, Edwin D. World population policy : an annotated bibliography. Lexington, Mass. : Lexington Books, [1971]. 1280 p. **CG1**

More than 3,500 items, most of them annotated at some length. Restricted to works on general population policy and measures affecting fertility and family size; coverage is for the period 1940–69. Primarily English-language materials.   Z7164.D3D75

Eldridge, Hope T. The materials of demography : a selected and annotated bibliography. N.Y. : International Union for the Scientific Study of Population, 1959. 222 p. **CG2**

Repr. : Westport, Conn. : Greenwood, 1975.

Published by the International Union for the Scientific Study of Population and the Population Association of America (Brown University, Providence, R.I.).

A classified listing of books, articles, and, especially, reports of conferences, special research committees, etc., in English. Many full annotations, and usually listings of individual papers contained in polygraphic works. Author index.   Z7164.D3E4

Gärtner, Karla. Bibliographie deutschsprachiger bevölkerungswissenschaftlicher Literatur, 1978–1984 / Karla Gärtner, Johannes Otto und Manfred Tölle. Wiesbaden : Bundesinstitut für Bevölkerungsforschung, 1986. 802 p. (Materialien zur Bevölkerungswissenschaft, Heft 48). **CG3**

A classified bibliography of materials in German, with exhaustive annotations and author index. Similar compilations covering 1945–80, and 1976–82 were published as Hefte 10, 23, 26 and 31 of the series.   Z7165.G3G37

Golini, Antonio. Bibliografia delle opere demografiche in lingua italiana (1930–1965). Roma : Università di Roma, Istituto di Demografia, 1966. 172 p. **CG4**

A detailed, classed, annotated bibliography of books and periodical articles, with official sources listed separately. Excludes health statistics and studies of socioeconomic problems of population (e.g., labor, housing, and education). No cross references; works are cited under each appropriate subject category with annotations only under the principal category. No index.

Supplemented by Golini and Graziella Caselli's *Bibliografia delle opere demografiche italiane (1966–1972)* (Roma : Facoltà di Scienze Statistiche, Demografiche ed Attuariali, Università di Roma, 1973. 308 p.).

Adds material by Italians published in a foreign language, works on the economically active population, labor force, employment, and health statistics in general. Author index.   Z7164.D3G63

Goode, Stephen H. Population and the population explosion. 1970–1976. Troy, N.Y. : Whitston, 1973–81. Annual. **CG5**

Lists books, periodical articles, and pamphlets that appeared during the year of coverage. Books and pamphlets are listed in a separate author arrangement; periodical articles are arranged alphabetically by subject, then alphabetically by title. Author index.   Z7164.D3G65

Goyer, Doreen S. International population census bibliography : revision and update, 1945–1977. N.Y. : Academic Pr., 1980. 576 p. (Texas bibliography, 2.).   **CG6**

Continues the 1965–68 ed. by the Population Research Center, University of Texas (CG13).

Extends the coverage of the original work to national and territorial population censuses held through 1977, but excludes those taken before 1945. Arrangement is now alphabetical by individual country, rather than by region. Information given includes name of statistical agency and publications distributor, document entries with original and English-language title, and at least one library location. Notes censuses for which no publications are available, administrative changes, and sometimes date of next census.   Z7164.D3G69

——————— National population censuses, 1945–1976 : some holding libraries. Clarion, Pa. : Association for Population/Family Planning Libraries and Information Centers, International (APLIC), 1979. 44 p. (APLIC Special pubn., no.1).   **CG7**

Locates population census reports in 53 U.S. and Canadian libraries. Brief entries give only country, date of census, and library symbols (not those employed in the National Union Catalog).

Z7553.C3G69

Hatten tojō koku no tōkei shiryō mokuroku. 1968–. Tokyo : Ajia Keizai Kenkyūjo. Institute of Economics. [Ajia Keizai Shuppankai hatsubai].   **CG8**

English title: Catalogue of statistical materials of developing countries.

Frequency varies.

Lists statistical materials collected by the Statistics Dept. of the Institute of Economics. Citations are grouped by country in four regions, then by subject within each country. Titles are given in English. The volume for 1989 lists some 9,500 titles from 129 countries. An appendix lists titles from intergovernmental agencies.   Z7164.U5H33

International population census publications : series II, pre-1945: guide to the microfilm edition / ed. by Diane M. Del Cervo. Woodbridge, Conn. : Research Publ., 1984. 454 p.   **CG9**

Based on the *International population census bibliography* (CG13). Provides bibliographic citation and access to the microfilm reels in the publisher's collection of the same title. Arrangement is by country, then date of census. Excludes U.S. censuses, since these have been covered in the publisher's *United States decennial census publications* (CG93).

§ Census publications 1945–67 are listed in Research Publications, inc., *A guide to the microfilm edition of International population census publications, 1945–1967* (CG11).   Z7164.D3I59

Kurian, George Thomas. Sourcebook of global statistics. N.Y. : Facts on File, c1985. 413 p.   **CG10**

A bibliographic guide listing more than 200 sources of statistics whose focus is global. Each entry provides a bibliographic citation, list of contents, and an evaluative annotation. Includes books, annuals, monthlies, and irregular serials issued by official and private sources, national and international. Excludes almanacs, yearbooks, and encyclopedias that use statistical data borrowed from primary sources. Subject index.   Z7551.K46

Research Publications, inc. A guide to the microfilm edition of International population census publications, 1945–1967 : bibliography and reel index. Woodbridge, Conn. : Research Publications, 1979. 595 p.   **CG11**

Based on the *International population census bibliography* and its Supplement (CG13). Accompanies microform collection with title: International population census publications.

Listings are grouped by country within regional sections, then by date of census. Bibliographic description is in modified catalog form.

§ Pre-1945 census publications are listed in *International population census publications: series II, pre-1945* (CG9).   Z7164.D3R47

United Nations. Department of Economic and Social Affairs. Analytical bibliography of international migration statistics : selected countries, 1925–1950. N.Y., 1955. 195 p. (Population studies, no.24).   **CG12**

An analytical bibliography for 24 selected countries, presenting a list of primary sources and other publications containing statistical data, and "within each major category of departures and arrivals the sources and years for which detailed classification and cross-classifications are available."—*Introd.*   Z7164.I3U55

University of Texas at Austin. Population Research Center. International population census bibliography. Austin : Univ. of Texas, Bureau of Business Research, 1965–68. 7 v.   **CG13**

Contents: no. 1, Latin America and the Caribbean; no. 2, Africa; no. 3, Oceania; no. 4, North America; no. 5, Asia; no. 6, Europe; no. 7, Supplement [to v. 1–6].

The series was issued in conjunction with the Center's census acquisition program. It aims to provide a universal bibliography of census reports. Each number consists mainly of listings of separately published population census reports, though other types of series (e.g., housing and agriculture) are sometimes listed if population data are included therein. The entries, arranged alphabetically by area, then chronologically, indicate the contents of multivolume reports. Note is also taken of years in which censuses were known to have been conducted, but for which no published reports were found.

Continued by: *International population census bibliography, revision and update, 1945–1977*, by Doreen S. Goyer (CG6).

Z7164.D3T45

Westfall, Gloria. Bibliography of official statistical yearbooks and bulletins. Alexandria, Va. : Chadwyck-Healey, 1986. 247 p.   **CG14**

Analyzes the contents of recent editions of official yearbooks and bulletins for countries of the world and dependencies; limited to publications wholly or partially in the Roman or Cyrillic alphabet. Gives complete bibliographic description for each title.   Z7551.W47

Indexes; Abstract journals

Current index to statistics, applications, methods and theory. v. 1 (1975)– . Wash. : Amer. Statistical Assoc., [1976]– . Annual.   **CG15**

For annotation, *see* EB22.   QA276.A1

DataMap / Jarol B. Manheim, Allison Ondrasik. 1983–1990. N.Y. ; London : Longman, [1983]–90. Annual.   **CG16**

Publisher varies; publ.: Phoenix : Oryx Pr., 1986–1990.

Ceased with v. 4, June 1990.

The initial volume indexes the tables of 28 statistical sources that "would together provide the most parsimonious coverage of the widest possible variety of social, political, economic, technical, and other data."—*[p.xi]*. The 1984 issue included 29 sources. Most are U.S. government or U.N. publications, as well as the major almanacs.

Z7552.D37

•POPLINE [database]. Bethesda, Md. : National Library of Medicine, 1970– .   **CG17**

For annotation, *see* CC257.

Population index. v. 1 (1935)– . Princeton, N.J. : Office of Population Research, Princeton Univ., and the Population Assoc. of America, 1935– . Quarterly.   **CG18**

Title varies: Jan. 1935–Oct. 1936, *Population literature.* v. 1, no. 1 (rev. May 1, 1935) "replaces 'Review of current research, 1,' including all titles from that publication as well as additional foreign and American citations for 1933. (No 1934 or 1935 titles were added.) The period covered by this number begins Jan. 1, 1933, which terminates the period covered by *Social science abstracts* (1929–1932)."—*Note, v. 1, p. 1.*

Vols. 1–2 were published by the Population Association of America, Wash., D.C.

An annotated bibliography of books and periodical literature on all phases of population problems. Arranged by class, with annual cumulated indexes by author and country. Includes special articles and current items.

Bibliographic entries from issues of the period 1935–81 have been cumulated in two publications. Only basic bibliographic information is provided, so reference to issues of *Population index* is necessary for complete information.

Population index bibliography: cumulated 1935–1968, by authors and geographical areas (Boston : G. K. Hall, 1971. 9 v.).

Contents: Author index, 4 v.; Geographical index, 5 v. (v. 1–3, 1935–1954; v. 4–5, 1954–1968).

Cumulates the bibliographic entries from *Population index*, providing both an author and a geographical approach. In the author part items are cited only once, with no added entries for joint authors or for individuals responsible for publications entered under corporate headings. In the geographical part entries are arranged by continent, then by country or region, with further subdivision by topics if there are more than 100 entries. There are no running heads nor any detailed table of contents to guide the user.

Population index bibliography : cumulated 1969–1981 by authors and geographical areas (Boston : G. K. Hall, 1984. 4 v.).

Contents: v. 1, 1969–1974, Author index; v. 2, 1975–1977, Author, subject and geographical indexes; v. 3, 1978–1981, Author index; v. 4, 1978–1981, Subject and geographical indexes.

Vol. 1 is a photographic reproduction of catalog cards; v. 2–4 are the true index, providing only basic bibliographic data and referring the user to the abstract in the appropriate volume of *Population index.*

Z7164.D3P83

Encyclopedias

International encyclopedia of population. N.Y. : Free Pr., [1982]. 2 v. : ill. **CG19**

John A. Ross, ed. in chief.

Sponsored by the Center for Population and Family Health of the International Institute for the Study of Human Reproduction, Columbia University.

Consists of 129 medium-length, signed articles on the current state of demography and population topics, and serves as a companion to the same publisher's *International encyclopedia of statistics* (CG20) and the *International encyclopedia of the social sciences* (CA36). Alphabetical arrangement by topic and country or geographic area. Limited treatment of historical aspects and specific organizations, with no biographies included. Bibliographies for individual articles are supplemented by articles on directories and publications. Alphabetical and topical lists of contents; indexed.

HB849.2.I55

International encyclopedia of statistics / ed. by William H. Kruskal and Judith M. Tanur. N.Y. : Free Pr., c1978. 2 v. (1350 p.) : ill. **CG20**

This compilation "draws together, expands, and brings up to date the statistics articles of the *International Encyclopedia of the Social Sciences* [CA36]."—*Introd.* In addition to the approximately 70 articles "on statistics proper, numerous articles on social science topics with strong statistical flavor, and about 45 biographies of statisticians and others important in the development of statistics" from the parent work, five new articles and 12 new biographies have been introduced. Nearly all the articles were revised, amended, or have postscripts added. Bibliographies were updated. The detailed index includes references from names of contributors.

HA17.I63

Dictionaries

Hungary. Központi Statisztikai Hivatal. Statisztikai szótár : 1700 statisztikai kifejezés hét nyelven = Statistisches Wörterverzeichnis : 1700 statistische Ausdrücke in sieben Sprachen = Statistical dictionary : 1700 statistical terms in seven languages. [4. kiad.]. Budapest : Statisztikai Kiadó Vállalat, 1964. 171 p. **CG21**

1st published 1960.

Title and introductory material in seven languages: Russian, Hungarian, Bulgarian, Czech, Polish, German, and English. Main listing is in Russian with equivalents in other languages, followed by word indexes of the six non-Russian languages.

HA17.H8

Inter-American Statistical Institute. Statistical vocabulary. 2nd ed. Wash. : Pan American Union, 1960. 83 p. **CG22**

1st ed., 1950.

Title page and text in English, Spanish, Portuguese, and French.

Consists of (1) a main list of more than 1,300 English terms with equivalents in Spanish, Portuguese, and French, and (2) separate Spanish, Portuguese, and French alphabetical indexes, each keyed to the English equivalents.

HA17.I6

Jinkō jiten : yōgo kaisetsu tōkei shiryō / Jinkō Mondai Kyogikai hen. Tōkyō : Tōyō Keizai Shinpōsha, Shōwa 61 [1986]. 302 p. : ill. **CG23**

Detailed explanation of specific demographic terms, arranged by demographic concepts in alphabetical order. Followed by demographic statistics on Japan, and some international statistics. Japanese and English indexes.

HB849.2.J56

Logie, Gordon. Glossary of population and housing : English-French-Italian-Dutch-German-Swedish. Amsterdam : Elsevier Scientific Publ. Co., 1978. 265 p. (International planning glossaries, 1). **CG24**

Terms in the major areas of population, demography, migration, households, housing policy, density, and living climate are given in tabular form with English as the base language and equivalents in each of the other five. Usage of the terms in each section is also given in a paragraph or two in English. Indexes in each of the other languages refer to page numbers in the glossary, making the work somewhat awkward to use.

HD7287.5.L63

Marriott, F. H. C. A dictionary of statistical terms. 5th ed. / prep. for the Internat. Statistical Inst. by F.H.C. Marriott. Burnt Mill, England : Publ. for the Institute by Longman Scientific & Technical ; N.Y. : Wiley, 1990. 223 p. **CG25**

Rev. ed. of *A dictionary of statistical terms* prep. by Sir Maurice G. Kendall and William R. Buckland, 4th ed., rev. and enl., 1982 (1st ed., 1957).

Defines more than 3,000 statistical terms in current use as they appear in books and articles. Many new entries related to medical statistics and statistical computing in this edition. Extensive cross-references and some abbreviated bibliographic references to first use of terms. Omits glossaries of equivalent terms in French, German, Italian, and Spanish, that were part of previous editions.

HA17.K4

Multilingual demographic dictionary. English section. 2nd ed. / adapted by Etienne van de Walle from the French section by Louis Henry. Liège : Ordina, [1982]. 161 p. **CG26**

1st ed., 1958.

Separate volumes (called sections) were also issued for Arabic, Czech, Dutch, Finnish, French, German, Italian, Polish, Portuguese, Serbo-Croatian, Spanish, and Swedish. All volumes are arranged in two parts: (1) Text, in nine topical chapters that define concepts and technical terms used in demography, each entry being assigned an identification number composed of the paragraph number and a sequential number; (2) Index, which lists in alphabetical order terms printed in boldface in the text, and refers to the identification number.

HB849.2.M84

Paenson, Isaac. English-French-Spanish-Russian systematic glossary of the terminology of statistical methods. Oxford : Pergamon, [1970]. 517 p. : ill. **CG27**

Title page and introductory matter in each of the four languages. Spanish translation prep. by J. M. Doblado.

Terms and definitions are grouped in chapters with the aim of placing the various terms in their logical context; full treatment of each term is given in all four languages. Alphabetical index in each language. HA17.P34

Petersen, William. Dictionary of demography : multilingual glossary / William Petersen and Renee Petersen. Westport, Conn. : Greenwood, 1985. 259 p. **CG28**

In two parts: (1) an alphabetic list of English demographic terms, with their equivalents in French, Spanish, Italian, German, Japanese, Chinese, and Russian; and (2) alphabetic lists in the other languages that refer to the English base list. The Japanese and Chinese lists are written in ideograms with romanized transliteration, and the Russian in the Cyrillic alphabet with romanized transliteration; these lists are alphabetized by the transliterated versions. HB849.2.P468

——————— Dictionary of demography : terms, concepts, and institutions / William Petersen and Renee Petersen. N.Y. : Greenwood, 1986. 2 v. (1154 p.) : map. **CG29**

Provides definitions of varying length for more than 1,400 demographic terms. Includes a bibliography of works cited in the definitions; a classified list of institutes, organizations, associations, and agencies concerned with demography; and a long subject index that includes references to the author's *Dictionary of demography: biographies* (CG43). HB849.2.P47

Pressat, Roland. The dictionary of demography / ed. by Christopher Wilson. [Oxford & N.Y.] : Blackwell Reference, [1985]. 243 p. : ill. **CG30**

Originally published in French as *Dictionnaire de démographie* (Paris : Presses universitaires de France, 1979).

The English-language edition differs slightly from the original in that it uses a broader encyclopedic approach, stressing concepts and techniques as they are used in Anglo-American rather than in French demography. Signed definitions, many with bibliographic references. HB849.2.P7413

al-Qāmūs al-dīmūghrāfī al-thulāthī : 'Arabī-Inkilīzī-Faransī : Inkilīzī-Faransī-'Arabī : Faransī-Inkilīzī-'Arabī / i'dād al-Lajnah al-Iqtiṣādīyah wa-al-Ijtimā'īyah li-Gharbī Āsiyā. [Baghdad] : al-Umam al-Muttaḥidah, al-Lajnah ; [S.l.] : al-Ittiḥād al-Dawlī lil-Dirāsāt al-'Ilmīyah lil-Sukkān, 1988. 8, 111, 214 p. **CG31**

Title on added t.p.: Trilingual demographic dictionary = Lexique démographique trilingue.

A thesaurus of terms in demography that complements the English, French, and Arabic sections of *Multilingual demographic dictionary* (CG26). In three parts, each arranged alphabetically, in which one of the three languages is used as the base list and gives equivalent terms in the other two. Terms are provided with reference numbers that point to chapters and paragraphs of the *Multilingual dictionary* where the terms are explained. HB849.2.Q36

Tietjen, Gary L. A topical dictionary of statistics. N.Y. : Chapman and Hall, 1986. 171 p. **CG32**

Attempts "to offer more than the usual string of isolated and independent definitions: it provides also the context, applications, and related terminology."—*Pref.* Intended for statisticans, students, scientists, and other users of statistics. Divided into 15 well-organized topical chapters with references. Index. QA276.14.T54

Vogt, W. Paul. Dictionary of statistics and methodology : a nontechnical guide for the social sciences. Newbury Park, Calif. : Sage Publ., c1993. 253 p. : ill. **CG33**

Intended for specialists in the social and behavioral sciences who are not trained in statistics. Defines statistical and methodological

terms used in the social sciences, but does not explain how to use statistics in research or how to compute, hence definitions tend to be verbal rather than mathematical. Alphabetical arrangement. HA17.V64

Yeh, Hsiu-shu. Jen k'ou hsüeh Ying Han Han Ying fen lei tz'u hui / Yeh Hsiu-shu, Chao Shih-li, ko Su-shan pien. Ch'eng-tu : Ssu-ch'uan ta hsüeh ch'u pan she : Ssu-ch'uan sheng hsin hau shu tien ching hsiao, 1989. 12, 906 p. **CG34**

Cover title also in English: English-Chinese and Chinese-English glossary of demography.

In two sections (English-Chinese, Chinese-English) each of which is divided into subject sections: economic and social aspects, mathematical and statistical methods, family planning, etc. Appendixes with definition of technical terms; acronyms for organizations; English and Chinese names of nationality groups. The Chinese-English section is organized alphabetically by pinyin transliteration. HB849.2.Y43

Directories

American Statistical Association. Directory of members / the American Statistical Association, the Biometric Society, Eastern and Western North American regions. 1981– . Alexandria, Va. : The Association, [1981]– . Every four years. **CG35**

Vol. for 1985 has title: Directory of statisticians.

Imprint varies.

Vols. for 1981– include membership listings of: the American Statistical Association, the Biometric Society, Eastern and Western North American regions; 1985 also includes: the Statistical Society of Canada; 1989– also includes: the Institute of Mathematical Statistics.

A combined membership directory of the American Statistical Association, the Biometric Society, the Institute of Mathematical Statistics, and the Statistical Society of Canada. Arranged alphabetically; provides for each member: position or title, professional affiliation, academic degrees, and professional activities. Includes a geographical index, and appendixes that list sponsoring societies and schools offering degrees in statistics. HA1.D52

Lloyd, Cynthia B. Directory of surveys in developing countries : data on families and households, 1975–92 / Cynthia B. Lloyd, Catherine M. Marquette. N.Y. : The Population Council, c1992. 312 p. **CG36**

Confined to individual surveys and continuing survey programs that were active during 1975–92. Includes 306 surveys from 84 countries. Surveys are arranged by country in alphabetical order, and chronologically within country. Information is presented on up to ten specific aspects of fertility, child welfare, economic role of parents, and household characteristics. Entries include survey name, date, agency, program, sample size, coverage, comments, contact name, address, and telephone number. HB849..L56

Statistical services directory. 1st ed., issue no. 1 (June 1982)– . Detroit : Gale, c1982– . **CG37**

1st ed. publ. in 3 paperbound issues, 1982–83.

A directory of more than 2,000 organizations and agencies that collect and disseminate statistical data for particular topics, industries, or fields. The directory section, with numbered entries in alphabetical order, is followed by four indexes: (1) Geographical, United States first followed by foreign countries, listing organizations alphabetically within each state or country; (2) Contact name, listing key contacts by personal name; (3) Title, an alphabetical listing of publications cited in the entries; (4) Subject, listing organizations according to the subject area in which they collect data. Index entries refer to numbered items in the directory. HA37.U137

Handbooks

Domschke, Eliane. The handbook of national population censuses : Africa and Asia / Eliane Domschke and Doreen S. Goyer. N.Y. : Greenwood, 1986. 1032 p. : ill. **CG38**

Describes censuses of population (most of them taken in the 20th century) for 55 African and 47 Asian countries. Gives for each country its statistical agency, its national repository (if known), and the main U.S. repository. Appendixes contain: (1) international population charts, showing, for example, country and major city population at five-year intervals beginning in 1945, and ranked tables for the latest population figures of major metropolitan areas; and (2) international topic charts, which provide summary census tables by broadly defined topics, also at five-year intervals beginning in 1945. A list of variant country names and capital cities is provided. There is no subject index, but the table of contents gives access by country.

§ One of a series of handbooks covering regions of the world. Others in the series include *The handbook of national population censuses : Europe*, by Doreen S. Goyer and Gera E. Draaijer (N.Y. : Greenwood, 1992. 544 p.); *The handbook of national population censuses : Latin America and the Caribbean, North America, and Oceania*, also by Goyer and Domschke (Westport, Conn. : Greenwood, 1983. 711 p.). HA37.A33D65

Haupt, Arthur. The Population Reference Bureau's population handbook / by Arthur Haupt and Thomas T. Kane. 3rd ed. Wash. : Population Reference Bureau, c1991. 66 p. : ill. **CG39**

1st ed., 1978.

Includes basic concepts of population changes, arranged by topic. Principal demographic variables are explained through examples. Appendix contains glossary of terms and list of information sources. HB871.H357

Müller, Georg P. Comparative world data : a statistical handbook for social science / Georg P. Müller with the collaboration of Volker Bornschier. Baltimore : Johns Hopkins Univ. Pr., c1988. 496 p. : ill. **CG40**

Contains statistical information and rankings for 51 variables for each of 128 countries. Country tables are arranged alphabetically and in a uniform format to allow for comparisons of one country with another on similar time periods, units of measure, decile and percentile rankings, country partners and rankings, and the predecessor nation in an ordered chain of countries. Citations to sources are available only in the footnotes. Includes a statistical table of critical values. "For statistical investigations beyond the exploratory data analysis, the numerical information of this book is also available on PC-diskettes of the DOS-type."—*Appendix.* Suitable for graduate and advanced research. HA155.M85

Social indicators of development. [1987]– . Wash. : World Bank, 1988– . Annual. **CG41**

For annotation, *see* CH159. HC59.69.S63

USA/USSR facts and figures = SShA/SSSR fakty i t͡sifry. [Wash.] : U.S. Bureau of the Census, 1991. 1 v. (various pagings). **CG42**

Presents statistical information from the Bureau of the Census and its Soviet counterpart in eight categories: population, social statistics, labor force and employment, industry, energy, agriculture, transportation, and consumer goods. Covers 1970–89. HA202.U8

Biography

Petersen, William. Dictionary of demography : biographies / William Petersen and Renee Petersen. Westport, Conn. : Greenwood, 1985. 2 v. (1365 p.). **CG43**

An international collective biography of demographers born before 1930 and of those born after that date whose work promises to have lasting significance. Entries average eight to ten lines and include year of birth, affiliation, a brief list of publications, and the source of biographic information. Includes an extensive general index, a list of reference sources, and an index by nationality. HB855.P47

Atlases

McEvedy, Colin. Atlas of world population history / Colin McEvedy and Richard Jones. [Harmondsworth] : Penguin, [1978]. 368 p. : ill., maps. **CG44**

Presents population figures in graph form for most countries of the world from prehistoric times to estimates for the year 2000. Short narrative summaries comment on the historical population changes and include bibliographic guides to primary sources and the most important secondary sources. Geographical arrangement by continent, subdivided by country. General bibliography; index. HB851.M32

COMPENDIUMS

International

ACP basic statistics. [Luxembourg] : Statistical Office of the European Communities, 198?– . Annual. **CG45**

In English and French; title also in French.

Presents statistics on 65 African, Caribbean, and Pacific (ACP) countries. Includes data on population, national accounts, production, foreign trade, prices, finance, aid, and standard of living, presented first for the whole group of countries, followed by selected statistics for individual countries, in alphabetical order. HC59.69.A26

Alderson, Michael Rowland. International mortality statistics. N.Y. : Facts on File, 1981. 524 p. **CG46**

Provides mortality statistics by sex, calendar period, cause of death, and country for the 1901–75 period for 22 European countries, Canada, Chile, the U.S., Japan, Turkey, Australia and New Zealand; the Soviet Union is not included. Data are tabulated for 178 causes of death, including war deaths and immigration statistics; the collection, publication, validity, and uses of these statistics are discussed. Indexed by cause of death. HB1321.A43

Annuaire de statistique internationale des grandes villes = International statistical yearbook of large towns. v. 1 (1961)–6 (1972). La Haye : [Issued by the Permanent Office of the International Statistical Institute and the International Union of Local Authorities], 1961–72. Biennial (irregular). **CG47**

Brings up-to-date the various types of information appearing in separate volumes of the *Statistique internationale des grandes villes* (CG56). HA42.A55

Annuaire international de statistique. The Hague : Institut International de Statistique, Office Permanent, 1916–21. 8 v. : maps. **CG48**

Contents: (1) État de la population (Europe), 1916; (2) Mouvement de la population (Europe), 1917; (3) État de la population (Amérique), 1919; (4) Mouvement de la population (Amérique), 1920; (5) État de la population (Afrique, Asie, Océanie), 1921; (6) Salaires et durée du travail, conventions, collectives, chômage, placement, syndicats ouvriers et patronaux, grèves et lock-outs; (7) Enseignement primaire, agriculture, postes, télégraphie et téléphonie, sociétés anonymes, coopératives, habitations, indices des prix de gros; (8) Finances d'états, production, cours des changes.

No more published.

§ Vol. 1–5 continued by the Institut's *Aperçu de la démographie des divers pays du monde*, 1922–36 (The Hague : Van Stockum, 1923–39. v. 1–[6]). Vol. 6, publ. 1939, covers 1929–36. Contents: (1) État de la population; (2) Mouvement de la population.   HA42.A6

Demographic yearbook = Annuaire démographique. 1948– . N.Y. [etc.] : Dept. of Economic and Social Affairs, Statistical Office, United Nations, [1949]– . Annual.   **CG49**
Prep. by the Statistical Office of the United Nations in collaboration with the Dept. of Economic and Social Affairs (later the Dept. of International Economic and Social Affairs).
A compendium of international demographic statistics based on official data from more than 220 national statistical services and other government offices. It covers populations and their demographic characteristics, natality, mortality, marriages and divorces. Each annual issue presents the general tables, and then in more detail treats a special demographic topic.
The 1978 *Yearbook* is in two volumes: the basic volume presents the general annual tables on basic demographic statistics; the second volume or special issue is a historical supplement presenting time series from 1948 to 1978 on population size, age, sex, urban-rural residence, natality, mortality, and nuptuality. (Similar information from 1936 to 1947 was presented in the 1948 yearbook.) The 1991 yearbook is also in two volumes: the basic volume contains the general tables, while the second volume deals with demographic aging, the special topic for 1991.   HA17.D45

Keyfitz, Nathan. World population growth and aging : demographic trends in the late twentieth century / Nathan Keyfitz and Wilhelm Flieger. Chicago : Univ. of Chicago Pr., 1990. 608 p. : ill.   **CG50**
Sequel to: World population : an analysis of vital data (1968), by Keyfitz and Flieger.
Data, selected from official sources, include estimates for 1950–85 and projections to 2020 for regions and for each of 152 countries with populations over 300,000. Includes population estimates, density, vital rates by sex, infant mortality and life expectancy by sex, general fertility, total fertility, gross reproduction rates, urban population, and age distribution.   HA155.K49

Kurian, George Thomas. The new book of world rankings. 3rd ed. / updated by James Marti. N.Y. : Facts on File, c1991. 324 p.   **CG51**
1st ed. (1979) had title: *The book of world rankings*.
Analyzes and ranks comparatively more than 200 nation-states. Provides brief country profiles. Sources are indicated for most tables. Indexed.   HA155.K87

League of Nations. Economic, Financial, and Transit Department. Annuaire statistique de la Société des Nations = Statistical year-book of the League of Nations. 1926–1942/44. Geneva : [The League], 1927–45. Annual.   **CG52**
Title varies: 1926–1929, *International statistical year-book*.
In French and English.
Annual survey of commerce, finance, and industry in the various countries of the world. Particularly useful for comparative purposes.
Continued by: *Statistical yearbook* of the United Nations (CG57).

Mulhall, Michael George. Dictionary of statistics. 4th ed. rev. London : Routledge, 1899. 853 p.   **CG53**
Repr. : Detroit : Gale, 1969.
Pt. 1, Statistics from the time of Emperor Diocletian to 1890, arranged alphabetically. Pt. 2, 1890–98; List of books of reference; Index to pts. 1–2. Does not give authorities for statistics included.
§ Supplemented by: Augustus Duncan Webb, *New dictionary of statistics* (London : Routledge ; N.Y. : Dutton, 1911. 682 p. Repr. : Detroit : Gale, 1974). Covers the period 1899–1909. Arranged on the same general plan as Mulhall, but superior to that work in that authorities for all statistics are given.   HA17.M8

Population and vital statistics report. Jan. 1949– . N.Y. : United Nations. Quarterly.   **CG54**

Presents estimates of world and continental population, as well as estimates for countries and areas of the world. Also shown are the results of the latest censuses of population, the most recent official estimates of population, and statistics of live births, deaths, and infant deaths for the most recent year available. Countries or areas are arranged in alphabetical order within continents.
———. *Special supplement, 1984*.
Four tables (in 190 pages) of data; in each, countries or areas are arranged alphabetically within continents. Table 1 presents population estimates, birth and death rates, and infant mortality rates for 1974–83. Table 2 gives populations by age, sex, and urban/rural residence, as reported in population censuses taken between 1965 and 1983. In Tables 3 and 4, age-specific birth and death rates are given for the period 1974–82.   HA13.U5

Showers, Victor. World facts and figures. 3rd ed. N.Y. : Wiley, c1989. 721 p. : ill.   **CG55**
Previous ed. (1979) is a revised and enlarged edition of the author's *World in figures* (1973).
This edition, revised and updated, provides information about the world's countries and the largest and best-known cities on a comparable basis. The first four chapters deal with countries and cities. The fifth chapter provides comparisons of cultural features. The last six chapters are devoted to geographic features. Bibliography, arranged by subject; cross-reference index in alphabetical order.   G109.S52

Statistique internationale des grandes villes = International statistics of large towns. [1st] ed. (1927)–[3rd] ed. (1934). La Haye : Institut International de Statistique.   **CG56**
Title varies. Prepared in cooperation with the International Union of Local Authorities.
Sér. A–E. (The Hague : [International Statistical Institute, Committee on Statistics of Large Towns], 1954–65).
In French and English.
A series of volumes as follows: A1, Statistiques démographiques des grandes villes, 1946/51. 1954; A2, Statistiques démographiques des grandes villes, 1946/53. 1957; A3, Statistiques démographiques des grandes villes, 1952/57. 1963; A4, Comments. Including a social economic classification, 1960. 1965; B1, Statistique du logement et de la construction, 1946/53. 1956; B2, Statistique du logement; analyse et tableaux supplémentaires. 1960; C1, Données économiques des grandes villes, 1950/54. 1958; D1, Services publics et transports dans les grandes villes, 1950 et 1955. 1959; E1, Statistique culturelle et des sports, 1951/57. 1961.   HA42.S9

United Nations. Statistical Office. Statistical yearbook = Annuaire statistique. v. 1 (1948)– . N.Y. : United Nations, 1949– . Annual.   **CG57**
A summary of international statistics to continue the *Statistical year-book of the League of Nations* (CG52). Covers population, agriculture, mining, manufacturing, finance, trade, social statistics, education, etc., of the various countries of the world, the tables usually covering a number of years. References are given to sources. A world summary was introduced beginning with v. 15 (1963), summarizing tables appearing in various chapters.
§ Updated by: *Monthly bulletin of statistics* (N.Y. : Statistical Office of the United Nations, 1947–).   HA12.5.U63

World comparisons / editors of the Economist. N.Y. : Times Books, 1990. 254 p. : col. ill., map.   **CG58**
Also published as: *The Economist book of vital world statistics*.
Provides data on 146 countries (those with population greater than 1 million or gross national product greater than $1 billion) in 15 general categories: Demography, Economic strength, Agriculture and food, Industry and energy, Commodities, Transport and communications, Government finance, Inflation and finance, Trade and balance of payments, Debt and aid, Employment, Education, Health, Family life, and Environment. Extensive use of tables, charts, and graphs. "Data are normally shown for the latest year, as indicated in each case."—*Notes*. Sources cited in section-by-section guide. No index.   HC59.W634

World demographic estimates and projections, 1950-2025 : total population, school-age population, economically active population, agricultural and non-agricultural population, urban and rural population : a report / prep. jointly by the United Nations, the International Labour Organisation, and the Food and Agriculture Organization of the United Nations. N.Y. : United Nations, Dept. of International Economic and Social Affairs, 1988. 386 p. **CG59**

Estimates and projections for 191 countries or regions, 1950–2025. Figures for 1950–80 are estimates based on data provided by national statistical authorities. Figures for 1980–2025 are projections based on the median variant. Demographic indicators include birth rates, death rates, fertility rates, life expectancy, and infant mortality rates. Countries are listed in alphabetical order within continents.

HA155.W64

World health statistics annual = Annuaire de statistiques sanitaires mondiales. 1962– . Genève : World Health Organization, 1962– . Annual. **CG60**

Formed by the union of the three sections of *World health statistics annual*: Health personnel and hospital establishments, Infectious diseases, cases, and Vital statistics and causes of death.

Provides statistical overviews, by country and worldwide, of changing trends in health patterns and causes of death. RA651.A485

The world in figures / editorial information comp. by the Economist. [5th ed.]. London : Economist Publications : Hodder & Stoughton ; Boston : G.K. Hall, c1987. 296 p. : ill., maps. **CG61**

Earlier editions appeared in 1976, 1978, 1981, and 1984.

In two parts: (1) general world section which ranks countries according to various subject headings and indicators; (2) a section on regions and countries which provides national data on geography, population, resources, production, finance, and trade. HA155.W66

World population 1983 : recent demographic estimates for the countries and regions of the world. Wash. : U.S. Bureau of the Census : For sale by the U.S. Govt. Print. Off., 1983. 586 p. : ill., maps. **CG62**

Completes and summarizes the series of biennial reports begun in 1973.

Presents final revised estimates of population size, vital statistics, and other demographic indicators for 202 countries for 1950–83. Data used for estimates are from the most recent national sources available, such as population censuses, vital registration systems, and sample surveys. The report has one section for each of six world regions. Each section includes a map, a brief text, and summary tables, followed by data for each country of the region in alphabetical order.

The report series is continued by: *World population profile*, CG63. HB881.U834

World population profile. 1985– . [Wash.] : U.S. Bureau of the Census, 1986– . Biennial. **CG63**

Superintendent of Documents classification: C 3.205/3:WP– .

Supersedes *World population* [year] : *recent demographic estimates for the countries and regions of the world* (Wash. : U.S. Bureau of the Census, 1973–83. Biennial).

"Most of the statistics presented in this report are derived from information in the International Data Base compiled by the Center for International Research, U.S. Bureau of the Census."—*Appendix.* Arranged in broadly defined subject areas, the data represent the most current population estimates and projections the Center prepares on every country of the world and are based on the latest demographic information available for each individual country. Includes tables, a glossary, and an appendix showing the availabilty of demographic data. HA154.W65

World population projections. 1984– . Wash. : World Bank, c1984– . Biennial, 1987/88– . **CG64**

Subtitle varies.

Frequency varies: annual, 1984–1985. Also publ. Baltimore : Johns Hopkins Univ. Pr.

Projections are based on census data and official demographic estimates of each country. The introductory part deals with data and methodology, and describes the results of summarized demographic variables. The main part consists of tables which give detailed projections of population and main demographic variables. World tables, tables for geographical regions, and countries by income level are followed by tables for individual countries in alphabetical order. The 1992–1993 edition introduces a new feature in that it provides demographic estimates and projections separately for each of the fifteen countries of the former Soviet Union. HA154 b .W66

World population prospects / Department of International Economic and Social Affairs. 1982– . N.Y. : United Nations, 1985– . **CG65**

Issuing agency varies: 1992 revision from the U.N. Dept. for Economic and Social Information and Policy Analysis.

Population estimates and projections for the world as a whole, the more developed and less developed regions, seven major areas, and 211 countries, covering population by age and sex, and major demographic indicators. Data presented for each five-year period, 1950–2025, with four alternative projections for 1990–2025.

Supplement: *Sex and age distributions of population* (1990–), formerly *Global estimates and projections of population by sex and age.*

•Data also available on magnetic tape and diskettes.

HA154.W663

World tables. [1st ed.] (1976)– . Baltimore : Publ. for the World Bank by the Johns Hopkins Univ. Pr., c1976– . Annual (1991–). **CG66**

Title varies.

Has semiannual suppl. with title: *World tables update.*

Issued in 2 volumes: (1) Economic data; (2) Social data.

Presents historical time series for individual countries in absolute numbers for the basic economic variables—population, national accounts, prices, balance of payments, external public debt, foreign trade indexes, and central government finance—as well as economic and social indicators in a form suitable for cross-country analysis and comparison.

•Also available on diskette. HC59.W669

Bibliography

Population index. v. 1 (1935)– . Princeton, N.J. : Office of Population Research, Princeton Univ., and the Population Assoc. of America, 1935– . Quarterly. **CG67**

A special bibliography, "Governmental and intergovernmental serial publications containing vital or migration statistics," appeared in the Winter 1980 issue (v. 46, no. 4), p. 617–783, a revised and expanded version of the original bibliographies which appeared in the issues of Oct. 1977 (v. 43, no. 4) and Jan. 1979 (v. 45, no. 1). For complete information, *see* CG18. Z7164.D3P83

Statistics sources. [1st ed.]– . Detroit : Gale, c1962– . Annual. **CG68**

Subtitle: A subject guide to data on industrial, business, social, educational, financial, and other topics for the United States and internationally.

A finding guide to statistics, arranged in dictionary form with topics and countries in alphabetical order. Sources for the U.S. are cited directly under topical headings, whereas sources for other countries are entered under the name of the country with a topical subdivision. With the 10th ed., 1986, appears annually; with the 8th ed. (1983) issued in 2 v.

In the 12th and 13th editions, new helpful sources were added: (1) selected bibliography of key statistical sources; and (2) federal statistical telephone contacts. Z7551.S83

Indexes

Index to international statistics : IIS. v. 1, no. 1 (Jan. 1983)– . Wash. : Congressional Information Service, 1983– . Monthly, with quarterly, annual, and multiple-year cumulations.   **CG69**

"IIS is intended to be a master guide and index to current English language statistical publications of the world's major [intergovernmental organizations]. These 80–90 organizations include the United Nations system, the Organization for Economic Cooperation and Development, the European Community, the Organization of American States...."—*User guide.* Similar in format to the publisher's *American statistics index* (CG96) and *Statistical reference index* (CG99), with abstracts arranged by issuing body and indexed by subject, name, geographic area, category (age, commodity, country, company, industry, sex), issuing source, title, and publication number. Both abstracts and indexes are cumulated on a quarterly and annual basis; a cumulation covering 1983–87 was issued in 4 volumes.

•Also available on CD-ROM as part of *Statistical masterfile.*

The *IIS microfiche library* (Wash. : C.I.S., 1983– . Monthly.) includes about 90% of the titles noted in the *Index.*   Z7552.I53

The Americas

See also CG38.

Mitchell, Brian R. International historical statistics : the Americas 1750–1988. 2nd ed. N.Y. : Stockton Pr., 1993. 817 p.   **CG70**

Rev. ed. of the author's *International historical statistics : the Americas and Australasia* (1983).

A companion to the author's *International historical statistics, Europe* (formerly *European historical statistics,* 2nd ed.; CG189) and *International historical statistics, Africa and Asia* (CG375). Presents comparative statistics for 26 North, Central, and South American countries, mostly from the mid-19th century to the early 1970s. Tables are grouped in 11 broad subject areas; sources are noted. Australasia is to be treated in a forthcoming revision on Africa and Asia.

HA175.M55

Bibliography

Harvey, Joan M. Statistics America : sources for social, economic and market research (North, Central & South America). 2nd ed., rev. and enl. Beckenham, Kent, Eng. : CBD Research ; Detroit : Gale, 1980. 385 p.   **CG71**

For each country, gives description of central statistical office, other major organizations publishing statistics, principal libraries of statistical material, libraries and information services abroad, bibliographies of statistics, and descriptions of major statistical publications arranged in the following groups: general, production, external trade, internal distribution, population, and standard of living. Title, organization, and subject indexes.   Z7554.A5H37

Library of Congress. Census Library Project. General censuses and vital statistics in the Americas / prep. under the supervision of Irene B. Taeuber. Wash. : U. S. Govt. Print. Off., 1943. 151 p.   **CG72**

Superintendent of Documents classification: C 3.2:C 33/10.

Repr. : Detroit : Blaine-Ethridge Books, 1974.

Subtitle: An annotated bibliography of the historical censuses and current vital statistics of the 21 American republics, the American sections of the British Commonwealth of Nations, the American colonies of Denmark, France, and the Netherlands, and the American territories and possessions of the United States.

Also available in microfiche.

In four parts; within parts, arranged in alphabetical order. Each part consists of three sections: a historical note; a list of all national population censuses located; and an annotated list of sources for vital statistics and population estimates.   Z7553.C3U5

North America

See also CG38.

United States

Bogue, Donald J. The population of the United States : historical trends and future projections. N.Y. : Free Pr., [1985]. 728 p. : ill.   **CG73**

Completely new and not a revision of Bogue's *The population of the United States* (Glencoe, Ill. : Free Pr., 1959). "The earlier volume is still useful ... for the years preceding and immediately following World War II. The present book places greatest analytical effort on the years since 1960."—*Pref.* Includes census data available as of July 1, 1984. Provides some comparative international statistics, as well as future estimates. Bibliographies.   HB3505.B63

City government finances. 1964/65– . Wash. : U.S. Bureau of the Census : For sale by the Subscribers Services Section (Publications), Bureau of the Census, 1965– . Annual. **CG74**

Superintendent of Documents classification: C 3.191/2.

Continues: *Financial statistics of cities,* 1909–41; *City finances,* 1942–64.

Includes summary of city government finances, and compendium of city government finances, with figures for the largest cities in some detail.   HJ9011.A4b

County and city data book. [1st ed.] 1949– . Wash. : U.S. Bureau of the Census : For sale by U. S. Govt. Print. Off., 1952– . Irregular.   **CG75**

Superintendent of Documents classification: C 56.243/2:C 83.

A supplement of *Statistical abstract of the United States* (CG81); continues in part *Cities supplement* and also *County data book.*

Issued for 1949, 1952, 1956, 1962, 1967, 1972, 1977, 1983, 1988.

Presents the latest available census figures for each county, and for the larger cities in the United States. Also has summary figures for states, geographical regions, urbanized areas, standard metropolitan areas, and unincorporated places.

•Data issued also in computer file format with title: *County & city data book.*   HA202.A36

Population abstract of the United States / ed. by Donna Andriot. 1993 ed. McLean, Va. : Documents Index, c1993. 1080 p.   **CG76**

Revised ed., 1983, was produced as a companion volume to John L. Andriot, *Township atlas of the United States* (CL297).

Provides all available population totals for states, counties, and cities which had a population of 10,000 or more in the most recent census. "Each state section contains a brief history of the formation of the state; a map and index showing names and locations of counties as of 1980; historical population totals [including urban-rural distribution] for the state, counties, and cities; and the 1980 population for minor civil divisions."—*Foreword.* Indexes and maps to counties and smaller areas are in the *Township atlas.*

Regional differences in America : a statistical sourcebook / Alfred N. Garwood, ed. Seattle, Wash. : Numbers & Concepts, c1988. 590 p.   **CG77**

For annotation, *see* DB150.   HA215.R43

Social indicators III : selected data on social conditions and trends in the United States. Wash. : Bureau of the Census, 1980. 585 p. : col. ill.   **CG78**

Prepared by the Center for Demographic Studies, Bureau of the Census.

Earlier eds. appeared in 1973 and 1977.

Presents maps, charts, and tables illustrating statistical measures of well-being and public perception in eleven major social areas, such as population, the family, social security and welfare, health and nutrition, public safety, etc. Each chapter on these major areas contains introductory text and charts; statistical tables, with source references; and technical notes and definitions, with a brief bibliography. There is also a useful selected bibliography at the end of the introduction.

HN52.S6

State and metropolitan area data book. 1979– . Wash. : U.S. Bureau of the Census : For sale by U.S. Govt. Print. Off., 1980– . Irregular. **CG79**

Superintendent of Documents classification: C 3.134/5: .

A supplement to *Statistical abstract of the United States* (CG81).

In three main parts: (1) statistical data for each state, arranged by census geographic division and region, and for the United States as a whole (2,008 statistical items are presented for each state, including data on population and vital statistics, health, education, employment, income, government, social welfare, crime, construction, housing, banking, elections, energy, transportation, natural resources, trade and services); (2) similar data for metropolitan areas arranged alphabetically; (3) data for metropolitan areas ranked by population-size categories. Five appendixes provide information on standard metropolitan statistical areas ranked by population size, effects of population change, estimates of states and congressional districts population and voting age population, etc. Subject index. HA202.S84

State government finances. 1966– . Wash. : U.S. Bureau of the Census : For sale by U. S. Govt. Print Off., 1966– . Annual. **CG80**

Superintendent of Documents classification: C 3.191/2: .

Previously issued as *Financial statistics of states*, 1915–1941 (publication suspended 1932–36); *State finances*, 1942–65. Title varies slightly.

Issues usually include: individual state reports; topical reports (e.g., budgets, expenditures, debt, tax collections, etc.). HJ275.S7

Statistical abstract of the United States. 1st no. (1878)– . Wash. : U.S. Bureau of the Census, 1879– . Annual. **CG81**

Superintendent of Documents classification: C 56.243, C 3.134.

1st–25 no. (1878–1902), issued by the Bureau of Statistics (Treasury Dept.); 26–34 no. (1903–11), by the Bureau of Statistics (Dept. of Commerce and Labor); 35 no. (1912), by the Bureau of Foreign and Domestic Commerce (Dept. of Commerce and Labor); 36–59 no. (1913–37), by the Bureau of Foreign and Domestic Commerce (Dept. of Commerce); v. 60– (1938–), by the Bureau of the Census. Volumes for 1947– called 68th– ed.

A single-volume work presenting quantitative summary statistics on the political, social, and economic organization of the United States. Statistics given in the tables cover a period of several years, usually about 15 or 20; some tables run back to 1789 or 1800. Indispensable in any library; it serves not only as a first source for statistics of national importance but also as a guide to further information, as references are given to the sources of all tables. Numerous supplements, such as *County and city data book* (CG75), provide additional information. Includes a table of contents arranged by broad subject areas and a detailed alphabetical index. HA202

Statistical record of Asian Americans / Susan B. Gall and Timothy L. Gall, editors. Detroit : Gale, c1993. 796 p. **CG82**

For annotation, *see* CC410. E184.O6S73

Statistical record of black America. 1st ed.– . Detroit : Gale, c1990– . Biennial. **CG83**

For annotation, *see* CC400.

Statistical record of Hispanic Americans / Marlita A. Reddy, ed. Detroit : Gale, c1993. xlvi, 1173 p. : ill. **CG84**

For annotation, *see* CC471. E184.S75S74

Statistical record of Native North Americans / Marlita A. Reddy, ed. Detroit : Gale, c1993. lxvi, 1661 p. **CG85**

For annotation, *see* CC442. E98.P76S73

United States. Bureau of the Census. Census catalog and guide. 1985– . Wash. : the Bureau : For sale by the U.S. Govt. Print. Off., [1985]– . Annual. **CG86**

Superintendent of Documents classification : C 3.163/3.

Title varies; earlier eds. had title: *Census publications, catalog and subject guide*, 1946–51; *Catalog of United States census publications*, 1952–62; *Bureau of the Census catalog of publications*, 1963; *Bureau of the Census catalog*, 1964–84.

First issued quarterly, with annual cumulations; annual beginning 1980. Kept up to date by *Monthly product announcement* and *Data user news* (called *Census and you*). The 1985 issue cumulates the 1980–84 volumes.

Divided into broad subject areas, provides exhaustive abstracts which include information on availability, ordering, and price. Information is also given on available formats such as microfiche or computer tapes. There are four appendixes with yet more information on subscriptions, data files, sources of assistance, and statistical programs. A subject index provides fast access to individual items.

§ A cumulative publication, *Bureau of the Census catalog of publications, 1790–1972* (Wash., 1974) is based primarily on the annual issues for the period 1946–72 together with a reprint of the *Catalog of United States census publications, 1790–1945* (CG90) prepared by Henry J. Dubester; both parts have separate indexes. Z7554.U5U32

———— Historical statistics of the United States : colonial times to 1970. Bicentennial ed. Wash. : U. S. Bureau of the Census : for sale by the U.S. Govt. Print. Off., 1975. 2 v. (1200, 32 p.). **CG87**

House document – 93rd Congress, 1st session, no. 93–78.

A complete revision of the Bureau's *Historical statistics of the United States from colonial times to 1957* and *Continuation* to 1962. Maintains the broad subject arrangements of the previous edition covering all aspects of social, economic, political, and geographic development, 1610–1970. Each chapter offers statistical tables and text; the latter includes definitions of terms, description, and extensive specific source notes.

There are both an excellent detailed table of contents and a detailed subject index. A time series index provides information concerning when statistics for a particular subject begin in the specified 10- or 20-year time segment. HA202.D07

Vital statistics of the United States. 1937– . Wash. : U.S. Bureau of the Census, 1939– . Annual. **CG88**

Imprint and issuing agency vary.

Issued in 2 parts, 1937–49; in 3 parts, 1950–59; in 3 v., 1960– .

Contents: v. 1, Natality; v. 2, Mortality (in 2 pts.); v. 3, Marriage and divorce.

Contains detailed tabulations on natality, mortality, marriages, and divorces in the U.S.

§ Complemented by: U.S. National Office of Vital Statistics, *Vital statistics : Special reports* (v.1 [1934]–54 [1965]. Wash., 1934–65). Individual volumes include selected studies, state or national summaries, life tables, etc. HA203.A22

Guides

Guide to U.S. government statistics. 3rd ed. (1961)– . McLean, Va. : Documents Index, 1961– . Irregular. **CG89**

Editions publ. 1956–58 called *U.S. government statistics*. Later versions drop edition numbering; version publ. 1992 called 1992/93 ed.

Prepared 1961–1987(?) by John L. Andriot; 1988– by Donna Adriot, Jay Andriot, and Laurie Andriot.

Arranged by departments and agencies, listing the various publications containing statistical data according to Superintendent of Documents classification number. Gives information concerning frequency, availability, price, and ordering procedure. Annotations are pertinent and concise. Title and subject indexes.

§ The booklet *Statistical services of the United States government* (Wash. : U.S. Bureau of the Budget, 1968) is reprinted in the 4th ed. (1973), p. 1–44.   Z7554.U5G8

Library of Congress. Census Library Project. Catalog of United States census publications, 1790–1945 / prep. by Henry J. Dubester. Wash. : U.S. Govt. Print. Off., 1950. 320 p.
CG90

Repr. in *Bureau of the Census catalog of publications, 1790–1972* (Wash. : U.S. Govt. Print. Off., 1974. 320, 591 p.).

Designed to serve as a "guide to census statistics and to record the historical development of publication patterns."—*Pref.* Annotated. In two sections: (1) decennial census publications; (2) other publications, arranged by subject, (e.g., agriculture, business, industry, religious bodies). Index to subjects contained in titles and annotations.

§ For brief information, largely supersedes earlier bibliographical surveys and indexes, but the following are sometimes useful for more detailed information: *The history and growth of the United States census*, United States. Bureau of Labor (Wash. : U.S. Govt. Print. Off., 1900. 967 p.); *A century of population growth from the first census of the United States to the twelfth, 1790–1900*, United States. Bureau of the Census. (Wash. : U.S. Govt. Print. Off., 1909. 303 p.); *Circular of information concerning census publications, 1790–1916* (Wash. : U.S. Govt. Print. Off., 1917. 124 p.); *Topical index of population census reports, 1900–1930*, United States. Bureau of the Census (Wash. : U.S. Govt. Print. Off., 1934. 76 p.); *Periodic and special reports on population, 1930–1939*, United States. Bureau of the Census (Wash. : U.S. Govt. Print. Off., 1939. 12 p.).

Supplemented by: Library of Congress. Census Library Project. *State censuses : an annotated bibliography of censuses of population taken after the year 1790 by states and territories of the United States*, prep. by Henry J. Dubester (Wash. : U.S. Govt. Print. Off., 1948. 73 p.). Items from this list are reproduced in *State censuses microfiche collection* [microform] (Millwood, N.Y. : KTO Microform, 1976).
Z7554.U5U62

Bibliography

Balachandran, M. Regional statistics : a guide to information sources. Detroit : Gale, c1980. 257 p.   **CG91**

Socioeconomic data sources in eight chapters, each representing a subject area. Within subject areas, sources are listed in alphabetical order. Short explanatory annotations. Geographical and author indexes.
Z7554.U5B34

Gerhan, David R. A retrospective bibliography of American demographic history from colonial times to 1983 / comp. by David R. Gerhan and Robert V. Wells. N.Y. : Greenwood, [1989]. 474 p. (Bibliographies and indexes in American history, no. 10).   **CG92**

Demographic history is broadly defined to include both quantitative data and "the values people attach to their behavior."—*Pref.* Divided into six sections (subdivided "early," "19th century," and "recent"): General background; Marriage and fertility; Health and death; Migration, pluralism, and local patterns; Family and demographic history; Population, economics, politics, and society. The compilers exclude diaries, letters, and memoirs, and cite 20th-century academic journals sparingly. Each section begins with commentary followed by the bibliography. Indexed by author, geographic area, and major subject grouping (e.g., ethnic, religious, occupation). A second volume is to deal with the post-1983 era.   Z7165.U5G43

Research Publications, inc. Bibliography and reel index : a guide to the microfilm edition of United States decennial census publications, 1790–1970. Woodbridge, Conn. : Research Publ., 1975. 276 p.   **CG93**

Serves both as a bibliography of U.S. decennial census publications and a reel index to the microfilm edition thereof. Final reports are taken from the *Catalog of United States census publications, 1790–1945* (CG90) and the *Bureau of the Census catalog of publications,*

1946–1972 (CG86) and arranged according to the numbering system used in the *International population census bibliography* (CG13).
Z7554.U5R47

State and local statistics sources. 1st ed. (1990–91)– . Detroit : Gale, c1990– . Biennial.   **CG94**

Subtitle: A subject guide to statistical data on states, cities, and locales.

Includes "information on demographic, socioeconomic, and business indicators for the states and local areas of the United States, the District of Columbia, Guam, Puerto Rico, and the Virgin Islands."—*Introd.* Information is arranged in alphabetical order by state, city, and other locations, then by broad subject areas. Appendixes include an annotated bibliography of nonprint sources of statistics and an annotated bibliography of the sources used in compilation.   HA203.S7

Stratford, Juri. Guide to statistical materials produced by governments and associations in the United States / Juri Stratford and Jean Slemmons Stratford. Alexandria, Va. : Chadwyck-Healey, 1987. 279 p.   **CG95**

"An annotated bibliography providing subject access to the statistical contents of over seven hundred publications ... from many federal agencies and the U.S. Congress, state agencies or state funded educational and/or research institutions, and non-profit membership organizations representing a specific industry, profession or sector of the economy."—*Introd.* Arranged alphabetically by sponsoring agency or organization. Includes appendixes and title and subject indexes.
Z7554.U5S8

Indexes

American statistics index. 1973– . Wash. : Congressional Information Service, 1973– . Annual, with monthly supplements.   **CG96**

"A comprehensive guide and index to the statistical publications of the U. S. Government."—*title page.*

Also called ASI.

Contents: pt. 1, Index; pt. 2, Abstracts.

The 1974 "Annual and retrospective edition" covered federal government statistical publications in print, as well as significant publications issued since the early 1960s; in the case of serial publications, only the format and contents of the most recent edition were described, with notes characterizing any major changes throughout the years. The 1974 "Annual" supersedes the initial 1973 edition, which was limited to social statistics. Supplementary "Annual" editions cumulate coverage of publications originally provided by the monthly supplements from 1974 to date.

Attempts to list (with full bibliographical description and price) and index all federal government publications which contain statistical data of probable research significance, whether published periodically, irregularly, or as monographs. Intends to list all relevant publications currently in print, and most publications issued during the ten years prior to 1974.

Monthly supplements, also issued in two parts, report changes on publications included in the preceding annual as well as new publications.

Indexed by: subjects and names; categories (geographic, economic, demographic, and standard classification systems); titles; agency report numbers. Cumulative subject and supplementary indexes issued quinquennially: 1974–79, 4 v.; 1980–1984, 4 v.; 1985–88, 4 v.

•Also available on CD-ROM as part of *Statistical masterfile.*

§ The *ASI microfiche library* (Wash. : C.I.S., 1974– . monthly.) includes almost all publications abstracted and indexed in *American statistics index;* it is available in a variety of purchase possibilities.
Z7554.U5A46

O'Brien, Catherine. Subject index to Current population reports. Wash. : U.S. Bureau of the Census : For sale by U.S. Govt. Print. Off., [1991]. 46 p. (Current population reports, Special studies, Series P-23, no. 174).   **CG97**

Previously publ, in 1981 (Series P-23, no. 109), and 1985 (Series P-23, no. 144).

This index provides access to *Current population reports* and *Household economic studies*. It covers the Bureau's series P-20, P-23, P-60, P-70, P-25, and P-26, and their predecessors, which contain reports on population characteristics, estimates and projections, income, farm population, and special topics of demographic interest. Data cover the period 1940–89. The index is arranged in 27 topical sections. In each section series are listed sequentially, and reports within series by number and title.

Schulze, Suzanne. Population information in twentieth century census volumes, 1950–1980. Phoenix : Oryx, 1988. 317 p. : maps. **CG98**

Provides, on a census-by-census basis, an index to a wide range of population-related information. Numerous social and economic categories are included, as well as the expected demographic and vital statistics. Analyzes printed census reports, with full bibliographical information. Entries are arranged by Dubester number (consecutive numbers assigned to the volumes of the reports). Charts in the endpapers correlate some 40 population characteristics with the Dubester numbers. The entry for each volume gives location of tables in that volume.

§ Information from earlier censuses is similarly analyzed in two volumes by the same author: *Population information in nineteenth century census volumes* (1983. 446 p.), which contains information about microform availability; and *Population information in twentieth century census volumes, 1900 1940* (1985. 274 p.). Z7164.D3S46

Statistical reference index : a selective guide to American statistical publications from sources other than the U.S. government. v. 1, no. 1 (Jan. 1980)– . Wash. : Congressional Information Service, 1980– . **CG99**

Frequency varies: bimonthly, 1984– .

Patterned on the publisher's *American statistics index* (CG96), this service presents abstracting and indexing of national and state data on business, industry, finance, economic and social conditions, government and politics, the environment, and population, derived from publications other than those of the U.S. federal government. Abstracts are grouped by source of information, e.g., associations, business organizations, commercial publishers, independent research organizations, state governments, and universities. Indexed by subject and name; geographic, economic, and demographic categories; issuing source; and title.

•Also available on CD-ROM as part of *Statistical masterfile*.

§ The *SRI microfiche library* (Wash. : C.I.S., 1980–) includes almost all publications abstracted and indexed in the *Statistical reference index* and is available from the same publisher on a monthly or annual subscription basis in a variety of purchase possibilities.

Walsh, Jim. Vital and health statistics series : an annotated checklist and index to the publications of the "rainbow series" / comp. by Jim Walsh and A. James Bothmer. N.Y. : Greenwood, 1991. 388 p. (Bibliographies and indexes in medical studies, no. 7). **CG100**

For annotation, *see* EH406. Z7165.U5W27

Directories

Directory of federal statistical data files / prepared through the coordination of U.S. Dept. of Commerce, National Technical Information Service and the U.S. Dept. of Commerce, Office of Federal Statistical Policy and Standards. March 1981– . [Wash.] : The Department, [1981]– . Annual. **CG101**

Superintendent of Documents classification: C51.15.

Describes publicly accessible data files. Each abstract provides general description, geographical and chronological coverage, accompanying reference materials, related data files, etc. Organized by agency; indexed by title, subject, and agency/subject. Also available in microfiche. HA37.U113

Evinger, William R. Federal statistical data bases : a comprehensive catalog of current machine-readable and online files. Phoenix : Oryx, 1988. 670 p. **CG102**

Complements *Directory of federal statistical data files* (CG101).

Describes with abstracts 2,500 government compiled statistical files, organized by department and agency. Each abstract provides a description of the contents, geographic coverage, date, technical characteristics of the file, accompanying documentation, related reports, an agency contact, and availability information. Title and subject indexes. HA37.U55E84

Handbooks

The complete economic and demographic data source : CEDDS. 1984– . Wash. : Woods & Poole Economics, 1984– . Annual. **CG103**

Issued in three volumes, 1989– .

Based on results of the Woods & Poole regional forecasting model of every county in the United States. Vol. 1 (1992) summarizes the results of the 1992 forecast, points out trends in regional economies, describes the database and methodology, and presents statistical tables that rank states, statistical areas, and counties in terms of population, employment, and income historically and over the forecast period up to 2015. The remainder of v. 1 and the whole of vols. 2 and 3 present detailed statistical tables for counties in each state, in alphabetical order by state. HC101.C616

Kane, Joseph Nathan. Almanac of the 50 states. 1985 ed.– . Burlington, Vt. : Information Publications, c1985– . Annual. **CG104**

Subtitle: basic data profiles with comparative tables.

Editor, 1985– , Alfred N. Garwood.

Place of publication varies.

In two parts: (1) statistical and demographic profiles of each of the 50 states, the District of Columbia, and the entire U.S., with tables of vital statistics, health, education, housing, government finance, etc.; (2) tables that rank the same areas according to 54 selected criteria such as population, households, doctors, hospitals, crime rate, etc. Sources of data are cited.

§ Another resource for information on states: *Facts about the states*, editors, Joseph Nathan Kane, Steven Anzovin, Janet Podell (N.Y. : H.W. Wilson, 1989. 556 p.). HA203.A5

Statistical forecasts of the United States / ed. by James E. Person, Jr. ; Sean R. Pollock, assoc. ed. Detroit : Gale, 1993. 804 p. **CG105**

"A compilation of published information forecasting all aspects of American life through the year 2000 and beyond."—*Introd.* Divided into 14 chapters on specific topics, e.g., Business, banking, finance and economics; Income, prices and spending, and Construction and housing. Information derived from federal and state government publications, corporate sources, private organizations, books and periodicals. Includes a subject index and an index of forecasts by year. HC106.8.S7357

Statistical handbook on aging Americans / Frank L. Schick and Renee Schick, editors. 1994 ed. / comp. by Renee Schick. Phoenix : Oryx, 1994. 360 p. : ill. (Statistical handbook series, no. 5). **CG106**

For annotation, *see* CC104. HQ1064.U5S695

Statistical handbook on the American family / ed. by Bruce A. Chadwick and Tim B. Heaton. Phoenix : Oryx, 1992. 295 p. : ill. (Statistical handbook series, no. 4). **CG107**

Graphs and tables provide detailed information on family life in the U.S. Topical sections deal with marriage, divorce, children, sexual attitudes and contraception, living arrangements, women and the elderly. Data drawn from government documents, Gallup polls, professional journals, research monographs, and surveys. Tables and figures appear as they did in source publications. Most data current as of late 1980s. List of sources; subject index. HQ536.S727

Statistical handbook on women in America / comp. and ed. by Cynthia Taeuber. Phoenix : Oryx, 1991. 385 p. : ill.
CG108

Presents demographic, economic, social, and health status data in more than 400 tables and charts reproduced from federal statistical publications. Many cover the period through 1988, but some tables give projections and forecasts up to the year 2030. The appendix includes a guide to relevant information sources, a list of important telephone numbers at the Bureau of the Census, a glossary of demographic and statistical terms, a list of sources used in the book keyed to table numbers, and a subject index.   HQ1420.T34

Atlases

Mattson, Mark T. Atlas of the 1990 census. N.Y. : Macmillan, c1992. 168 p. : col. ill., maps in color ; 32 x 26 cm.
CG109

For annotation, *see* CL303.   G1201.E2M3

Canada

Canada year book. v.1 (1905)– . Ottawa : Statistics Canada, 1906– . Annual.   **CG110**

Subtitle (varies): Statistical annual of the resources, demography, institutions and social and economic conditions of Canada.

Some volumes cover two years.

Volumes for 1905–71 issued by the agency under its earlier name, Canada. Bureau of Statistics.

Presents official data on the physiography, history, constitution and government, institutions, population, production, industry, trade, transportation, finance, labor, administration, and general social and economic conditions. Includes a useful chapter, Official sources of information and miscellaneous data, containing a directory of sources and a bibliography of special materials published in earlier editions of the yearbook.   HA744.S81

Canadian almanac and directory. 101st (1948)– . Toronto : Copp Clark Co., [1948?]– . Annual.   **CG111**

Continues *Scobie & Balfour's Canadian almanac, and repository of useful knowledge* (1848–1850); *Scobie's Canadian almanac, and repository of useful knowledge* (1851–1854); *The Canadian almanac and repository of useful knowledge* (some called *Maclear & Co.'s Canadian almanac and repository of useful knowledge*) (1857–1894); *Canadian almanac and miscellaneous directory* (1895–1926); *Canadian almanac and legal and court directory* (1927–1947). Also available on microfiche.

Contains reliable legal, commercial, governmental, statistical, astronomical, departmental, ecclesiastical, financial, educational, and general information.   AY414.C2

Canadian statistics index. [v. 1] (1985)– . Toronto : Micromedia, [1985]– . Frequency varies.   **CG112**

Microfiche edition, 1985– .

Includes some text in French.   HA741

Historical statistics of Canada. 2nd ed. / F. H. Leacy, ed. [Ottawa] : Publ. by Statistics Canada in joint sponsorship with the Social Science Federation of Canada, c1983. ca.900 p.
CG113

1st ed., 1965, ed. by M. C. Urquhart and K. A. H. Buckley.

Patterned on *Historical statistics of the United States* (CG87), with some variation in the arrangement of the sections. Most data are for national aggregates, though some are for region or province; the period of coverage is generally 1867 to the mid-1970s. Sources of statistics are indicated, and there are helpful explanatory notes and background information. Detailed index.   HA745.H57

Bibliography

Guide to Statistics Canada data on women : target groups project. Ottawa : Statistics Canada, Housing, Family and Social Statistics, [1987]. 113 p.   **CG114**

An index to statistical data treating women and women's issues that were originally listed separately in Statistics Canada's annual *Catalogue* (CG115) and other of its publications. In three parts: (1) cataloged publications other than census materials, with a subject index; (2) other sources of information, arranged by topic and medium of dissemination (e.g., demographic and census information on computer tape) (3) a select bibliography of related materials (e.g., papers presented at conferences) which are available in the Statistics Canada library.   Z7964.C36G83

Statistics Canada. Library Services Division. Statistics Canada catalogue. 1987/1988– . Ottawa : Statistics Canada, 1988– . Annual.   **CG115**

Publ. in English and French.

1991 never published. Title for 1986, *Current publication index*. From 1972–85 issued under the title *Dominion Bureau of Statistics catalogue*.

A comprehensive guide to print and electronic products available from Statistics Canada. Classed arrangement. Author, title, and subject indexes.

In 1993, the catalog included a special section, Finding and using statistics, to help users find data in the organization's wide range of publications.   Z7554.C2S7c

Stone, Martha. A bibliography of Canadian demography / by Martha B. Stone and George J. V. Kokich. Ottawa : Canada, Census Division, 1966. 147 p. (Canada. Bureau of Statistics. Technical paper, no. 5).   **CG116**

A general and broad treatment, covering early 1900s–1965. Arranged alphabetically by author. Subject index.

Coverage is continued by:

Annotated bibliography of Canadian demography 1966–1982, by Lokky Wai, Suzanne Shiel, T. R. Balakrishnan (London ; Canada : Centre for Canadian Population Studies, Univ. of Western Ontario, c1984. 314 p.). Includes articles, books, dissertations, and official government publications in French and English. Subject and author indexes.

Annotated bibliography of Canadian demography, 1983–1989, comp. by Suzanne Shiel (1990. 237 p.), extends the coverage and adds pertinent and important working papers. Annual updates. Subject and name indexes.

Mexico

Anuario estadístico de los Estados Unidos Mexicanos. 1939– . México : [Dirección General de Estadística], 1941– . Annual.   **CG117**

Continues works of similar titles publ. since 1894. None published 1908–29, 1931–37. Issuing agency varies.

Covers population, education, labor, agriculture, industry, communication, commerce, finance, etc.   HA762.A3

Estadísticas históricas de México. 2a ed. México, D.F. : Instituto Nacional de Estadística, Geografía e Informática : Instituto Nacional de Antropología e Historia, SEP, 1990. 2 v. (910 p.) : ill. (some col.).   **CG118**

In 23 topical chapters with 323 tables, some with data from the beginning of the 19th century. Chapters cover population; education; housing; health; salaries; and employment; agricultural and industrial production; commerce; transportation and communications; investment; public finance; money; prices; water and irrigation; and urbanization.   HA765.E88

Rowe, Patricia M. Detailed statistics on the urban and rural population of Mexico, 1950 to 2010. Wash. : International Demographic Data Center, U.S. Bureau of the Census, 1982. 242 p. ; map.   **CG119**

Superintendent of Documents classification: C 3.2:St 2/16/Mexico.

Presents statistics on population, fertility, mortality, and migration, as well as summary data on family planning, marital status, health, religion, education, literacy, labor force, households, and gross national product. Glossary; bibliographic sources.   HA765.R68

Latin America

See also CG38.

Anuario estadístico de América Latina y el Caribe = Statistical yearbook for Latin America and the Caribbean. 1985– . [Santiago, Chile] : Economic Commission for Latin America and the Caribbean, 1986– . Annual.   **CG120**

Continues *Anuario estadístico de América Latina = Statistical yearbook for Latin America* (1973–84), which in turn superseded *Boletín estadístico de América Latina = Statistical bulletin for Latin America* (1964–72).

In English and Spanish.

Extensive statistical data for the whole region and for individual countries, arranged alphabetically by country. Includes data for population, national accounts, agriculture, industry, import-export, balance of payments, and some social statistics. Indexes; bibliographies.

HA751.A58

Boletín estadístico de la OEA = Statistical bulletin of the OAS. v. 7, no. 1 (1985)– . Wash. : General Secretariat, Organization of American States, 1985– . Quarterly.   **CG121**

Formed by the merger of *Boletín estadístico de la OEA* and *Statistical bulletin of the OAS* (v. 1–6, 1979–1984).

In Spanish and English.

Each quarterly issue in three parts: (1) An analytical article treating a different demographic or economic problem; (2) Regional tables for Latin America and the Caribbean, containing data on regional economic and demographic trends, foreign trade and international reserves; prices, interest and exchange rates; and tourism; (3) Tables for individual countries arranged in alphabetical order.

A guide to Latin American and Caribbean census material : a bibliography and union list / gen. ed., Carole Travis. Boston, Mass. : G.K. Hall, 1990. 739 p.   **CG122**

Also publ. : The British Library, Standing Conference of National and University Libraries, Institute of Latin American Studies, University of London.

A bibliography of the many censuses in the region from the earliest times to 1979 (e.g., major national censuses of population, housing, and agriculture), and some early colonial records that are clearly forerunners of the modern census. Arranged chronologically by country are summaries of each census's general results and supplementary material and data; location of census reports is indicated in U.K. libraries. Index of names of countries, provinces, and towns.

Z7553.C3G85

Resúmenes sobre población en América Latina = Latin American population abstracts. v. 1, no. 1 (June 1977)– . Santiago, Chile : Centro Latinoamericano de Demografía, 1977– . 2 nos. per yr.   **CG123**

Other title: *DOCPAL resúmenes de población en América Latina*.

Vol. for June 1977 also called "Número experimental."

Each issue supplies about 700 Spanish-language abstracts of a wide variety of materials relating to Central and South America and the Caribbean. Detailed subject classification, with subject, geographic, and author indexes. Lists books, conferences, institutional publications, and journals indexed in each issue.

•The Latin American Population Documentation System maintains a computerized database on all Latin American and Caribbean population documents written since 1970; in 1979 the database included 10,000 entries, with 250 added each month. *Resúmenes* includes only the most important titles added since 1975. The entire database is available for searching and document delivery service through the Latin American Population Documentation System.   HB3350.5.R48

Statistical abstract of Latin America / prep. by Committee on Latin American Studies, University of California at Los Angeles. [1st ed.] (1955)– . Los Angeles : The Univ., 1956– . Annual.   **CG124**

Year appears in title.

With edition 17 (1976), several changes in content and format were made: (1) "Non-Latin American countries" (Barbados, Jamaica, Guyana, Trinidad and Tobago) were excluded; (2) a time-series dimension was added, rather than simply presenting material for the most current year; (3) the 20 Latin American countries are presented in alphabetical order in each table; (4) a cartogram series has been added to show the spatial extent of political units in terms of population size; (5) series which have not changed significantly since the previous edition, or which are scheduled for updating in the next edition, are not published. "Beginning with vol. 24 [1986], the editors have included alternative data in the form of partial tables from previous issues going back to vol. 17."—*Pref.* Endpapers give abbreviations, sources of information, and symbols.

Beginning in 1970, a *Supplement* has been issued irregularly. Each covers a specific topic.

Contents: [no. 1], Cuba 1968 (publ. 1970); [no. 2], Latin American political statistics (publ. 1972); [no. 3], Statistics and national policy (publ. 1974); [no. 4], Urbanization in 19th century Latin America: statistics and sources (publ. 1973); [no. 5], Measuring land reform (publ. 1974); [no. 6], Quantitative Latin America studies: methods and findings (publ. 1977); [no. 7], Money and politics in Latin America (publ. 1977); [no. 8], Latin American population and urbanization analysis: maps and statistics, 1950–1982 (publ. 1984); [no. 9], Statistical abstract of the United States–Mexico borderlands (publ. 1984); [no. 10], Society and economy in Mexico (publ. 1990); [no. 11], United States-Mexico border statistics since 1990 (publ. 1990; updated as no. 13, 1993); [no. 12], The rise of professions in twentieth-century Mexico (publ. 1992).   HA935.S8

Central America

Belize

Abstract of statistics. 1982– . Belmopan, Belize : Central Statistical Office, Ministry of Finance, 1983– . Annual.

CG125

Supersedes works published since 1961 as *Abstract of statistics* and *Annual abstract of statistics* for Belize (some under its former name, British Honduras). Issuing agency and frequency vary in earlier publications.

Detailed tables on population and vital statistics, area and climate, trade, finance, and other economic and social topics. Some data presented in time series.   HA791.C46a

Costa Rica

Anuario estadístico de Costa Rica. 1883– . San José : Dirección General de Estadística y Censos, Ministerio de Economía y Comercio, 1884– . Annual.   **CG126**

Title and agency name vary.

Suspended 1894–1906, 1946–47, 1978–1982. The 1982 volume presents data for the 1978–82 period.

Detailed statistical tables with extensive details on population and vital statistics, education, health, and other social topics as well as economic issues including public finance and balance of payments.

HA802.A2

Diez años de estadística vital, 1978–1987 : población, nacimientos, defunciones, contrayentes / República de Costa Rica, Dirección General de Estadística y Censos, Ministerio de Economía, Industria y Comercio. San José, Costa Rica : La Dirección, [1992]. 401 p. **CG127**

Population statistics presented by administrative divisions and by sex; separate sections on births, deaths, and marriages. Detailed tables.

HA805.D54

El Salvador

Anuario estadístico / Ministerio de Economía, Dirección General de Estadística y Censos. 1950–52– . [San Salvador, El Salvador] : La Dirección, 1958– . Annual. **CG128**

Issued in five parts: (1) Comercio exterior (Importación; Exportación); (2) Demografia, Salud; (3) Industria, Comercio, Servicios; (4) Meteorología, Agricultura y ganaderia, Costo de vida y comercio interior, Transporte y communicaciones, Construcciones, Fisco, Banca; (5) Educación, Cultura, Justicia.

Continues a publication of the same title, issued 1911–49.

HA841.A2

Guatemala

Anuario estadístico. 1982– . Guatemala : Instituto Nacional de Estadística, 1982– . Annual. **CG129**

Continues *Guatemala en cifras* (1955–69) and a publication of the same title issued by the Dirección General de Estadística, 1970–1981.

Provides data on geography, demography, social and economic conditions, usually with a 10–year time series. Agencies are listed as sources.

HC144.A1.A58

Arias de Blois, Jorge. Demografía guatemalteca, 1960–1976 : una bibliografía anotada. Guatemala : Univ. del Valle de Guatemala, 1978. 163 p. **CG130**

"2a ed.," 1981; may be a reprint.

Cites 192 books, dissertations, and articles published after 1960. Annotations are often quite long; some include tables. Not indexed.

———. ——— *Primer suplemento, 1977–79* (1983. 99 p.).

Z7164.D3A69

Honduras

Anuario estadístico / Ministerio de Economía y Hacienda, Dirección General de Estadísticas y Censos. 1956– . Tegucigalpa : La Dirección, 1958– . Annual. **CG131**

Continues a similar work publ. 1952–1955.

Offers statistics on climate, population, social security, public health, education, and various aspects of the economy. HA821.A43

Nicaragua

Anuario estadístico de la República de Nicaragua / Dirección General de Estadística. 1938– . Managua : Talleres Nacionales, 1939– . Annual. **CG132**

Title varies; issuing body varies. Publication suspended 1948–68.

Contains detailed statistical data covering geography, climate, population, economy, and social issues at the national and departmental levels. Many tables cover a period of five years.

Panama

Panama. Dirección de Estadística y Censo. Estadística panamena : Situación demografica, sección 221 : Estadísticas vitales. no. 1975– . [Pamaña] : Contraloría General de la República, Dirección de Estadística y Censo, 1975– . Annual. **CG133**

Continuation of *Estadística panameña, ser. B., estadistícas vitales.*

Since 1987, published in three volumes; v. 1, data on marriages and divorces; v. 2, data on births and fetal deaths; v. 3, tables on mortality with details on all important demographic variables. Some tables cover the previous five years; a few are retrospective to 1952.

HA581.A1719

Panama en cifras / Dirección de Estadística y Censos. Años 1955 a 1960– . Panama : La Dirección, 1961– . Annual. **CG134**

Title varies: *Nuestro progreso en cifras* (Ed.1–2, 1953–58).

Most volumes cover a 5–year period.

Contains information on geography and climate, population and vital statistics, agriculture, industry, commerce, and other economic areas including national accounts and social and cultural issues. Some statistical data cover five years. HA852.A57

South America

Argentina

Argentine Republic. Dirección Nacional de Estadística y Censos. Anuario estadístico. 1979–80– . [Buenos Aires? : Instituto Nacional de Estadística y Censos, 1980]– . Annual. **CG135**

Continues *Anuario estadistico de la Republica Argentina* issued by the Institute, 1974–79. Suspended 1958–73; prior to that, issued by different agencies and under slightly different titles since 1895.

Contains basic information on Argentina, its provinces and territories. Presents data on population and employment, social and economic sectors such as education, mass media, justice, housing, social security, health, industry and agriculture, national and international accounts, trade, prices, and salaries. Includes a selection of comparative international statistics. Chronological coverage varies. HA954.A57

Programa nacional de estadísticas de salud : Serie 5, Estadísticas vitales / República Argentina, Dirección de Estadísticas de Salud. No. 23–. Buenos Aires, República Argentina : La Dirección, [1984]– . Annual. **CG136**

Continues: *Estadisticas vitales y de salud. Serie 5.*

Data on mortality and natality for the whole country and for administrative areas. Includes infant mortality, maternal mortality, causes of death, and death rates. HA943.A22

Vázquez-Presedo, Vicente. Estadísticas históricas argentinas (comparadas). Buenos Aires : Ediciones Macchi, [1971]-1988. 3 v. **CG137**

Contents: v. 1, 1875–1914; v. 2, 1914–39; v. 3, Compendio 1873–1973.

Publisher varies; v. 3 publ. by Instituto de Economía Aplicada.

Offers statistical tables for population, immigration and emigration, production, foreign trade, finance, public services, etc. Detailed table of contents in each volume, but no indexes; bibliography in pt. 1.

HA957.V39

Bolivia

Bolivia en cifras. 1972– . [La Paz] : Instituto Nacional de Estadística, [1973–]. Annual.   **CG138**

A statistical compendium of general data and the principal statistical series on demography, economics, and social conditions. No index or detailed list of tables; no bibliographical sources cited.

HA965.B65

Directorio boliviano en población y desarrollo : instituciones, recursos humanos y unidades de información. 2. ed. La Paz : Ministerio de Planeamiento y Coordinacion, Unidad de Politica Social y de Poblacion, Centro de Documentacion en Poblacion y Desarrollo, 1991. 388 p.   **CG139**

1st ed., 1989.

Lists government agencies, institutions, and individuals active in demography, population, and economic development. In three parts: information on institutions, information on individuals, and relevant data about population information centers in Bolivia. Index.

HB850.5.B5D57

Resumen estadístico / República de Bolivia, Ministerio de Planeamiento y Coordinacion, Instituto Nacional de Estadística. La Paz : El Instituto , [1980]– . Annual.   **CG140**

Offers figures on population, education, housing, health, employment, prices, trade, national accounts, etc. The Ministerio is the source for most of the tables provided.   HA961.R47

Brazil

Anuário estatístico do Brasil. v. 32 (1971)– . Rio de Janeiro : Instituto Brasileiro de Estatística, 1971– . Annual.   **CG141**

Continues the publication of the same title issued by the Instituto Brasileiro de Geografia e Estatística, 1908/12–70, and assumes its numbering.

Offers statistical tables (usually with comparative figures for recent years) on physical characteristics, geography, economics, social and cultural conditions, and political and administrative affairs.

HA971.A32

Estatísticas do registro civil / Secretaria de Planejamento da Presidência da República, Fundação Instituto Brasileiro de Geografia e Estatística, Superintendência de Estatísticas Primárias, DEPSO. v. 1 (1974)– . Rio de Janeiro : IBGE, 1979– . Annual.   **CG142**

Continues: Centro Brasileiro de Estudos Demograficos, *Registro civil do Brasil.*

Presented in separate sections on births, marriages, deaths, fetal deaths, separations, and divorces. A final section presents data by municipality.   HA973.E87

Estatísticas históricas do Brasil : séries econômicas, demográficas e sociais de 1550 a 1988. 2a. ed. rev. e atualizada do vol. 3 de Séries estatísticas retrospectivas. Rio de Janeiro : IBGE, 1990. 642 p. (Séries estatísticas retrospectivas, v. 3).   **CG143**

At head of title: Secretaria de Planejamento e Coordenação da Presidência da República, Fundação Instituto Brasileiro de Geografia e Estatística, IBGE.

1st ed., 1987.

Arranged in 13 sections on demography, slave trade, economically active population, agriculture, industry, and other economic fields and indicators. Each section has an introductory text followed by tables. Arranged historically, within each section, but each covers different periods, depending on availability of data.   HA984.E84

Chile

Anuario de demografía / República de Chile, Ministerio de Economia, Fomento y Reconstrucción, Instituto Nacional de Estadísticas. 1983– . Santiago, Chile : Instituto Nacional de Estadísticas, 1983– . Annual.   **CG144**

Continues *Demografía*, publ. by the Instituto 1952–82.

Presents data on population and vital statistics by region and province, and by rural and urban areas. Some retrospective data included for comparative purposes.

Anuario estadístico de Chile. Santiago : Servicio Nacional de Estadística y Censos.   **CG145**

Issuing agency varies. Title varies: some called *Estadística anual*; date appears in title for some years.

The general statistics of Chile first appeared in 1860, the initial volumes covering 1848/58, and ran until 1888/90 (27v). Next published were volumes for 1909 (3v.) and 1910 (3v.). From 1911–51, the statistics have appeared in several subseries, e.g., Demografía, Agricultura, Política y administración, etc., some of them issued without series title. The various subseries are continued after 1951 as independent publications (e.g., *Demografía*, 1952–).   HA991.B2

Chile, series estadísticas. [Santiago de Chile] : Instituto Nacional de Estadísticas, 19??– .   **CG146**

A wide variety of socioeconomic statistics, drawn from other annual statistical publications. Many time series retrospective to 1950. Sources are linked to the agency responsible and not to the printed work.   HA1004.C47

Compendio estadístico. [1971]– . [Santiago] : Instituto Nacional de Estadísticas, [1971]– . Annual.   **CG147**

Issued 1976 as *Anuario estadístico*. Current title resumed in 1977.

Presents information on geography and climate, as well as government and administration. Contains statistical data on demography and a variety of socioeconomic topics. Many maps and graphs in color.

HA991.I58a

Mamalakis, Markos. Historical statistics of Chile. Westport, Conn. : Greenwood, 1978–1989. 6 v.   **CG148**

Contents: v. 1, National accounts; v. 2, Demography and labor force; v. 3, forestry and related activities; v. 4, Money, prices, and credit services, v. 5, Money, banking, and financial services; v, 6, Government services and public sector and a theory of services.

Each volume consists of an introduction, bibliography, and detailed statistical tables. Some statistics date from 1800; coverage varies with the topic.   HA1004.M35

Colombia

Colombia. Departamento Administrativo Nacional de Estadística. Anuario general de estadística. 1905–66/67. Bogotá : Departamento Administrativo Nacional de Estadística, 1905–68. Annual.   **CG149**

Issuing body varies. Title varies.

Supersedes *Anuario estadístico*, 1875/76–1884, issued by Oficina de Estadística Nacional. Publication suspended 1885–1904, 1906–14. 1966/67 last published. Continued in part by *Anuario demográfico*; *Anuario de precio y costos*; and *Anuario de transportes y comunicaciones* (later *Anuario de transporte*).   HA1011.A16

Colombia estadística. 1979– . Bogotá, D.E., Colombia : Departamento Administrativo Nacional de Estadística, 1980– . Annual.   **CG150**

Published in two volumes since 1987. Vol. 1 presents a statistical overview of demographic, economic, political, and social and cultural aspects of the country, with a list of the tables at the beginning of each chapter. Vol. 2 includes municipal statistics and poverty indicators.

HA1011.C64

Urrutia Montoya, Miguel. Compendio de estadísticas históricas de Colombia / Miguel Montoya Urrutia and Mario Arrubla. Bogotá : [Dirección de Divulgación Cultural, Universidad Nacional de Colombia], 1970. 312 p.   **CG151**

Chapters by specialists present and discuss statistics on topics such as wages in Bogotá, censuses, trade, elections, etc.

§ The government of Colombia has also issued tables of historical statistics (mainly 19th century, and on broader areas such as education, health, etc.) in its *Estadísticas históricas* ([Bogotá], Departamento Administrativo Nacional de Estadística, [1975]. 200p.).   HA1016.U76

Ecuador

Banco Central del Ecuador. Boletín anuario – Banco Central del Ecuador. no. 1 (1978)– . [Quito] : Banco Central del Ecuador.   **CG152**

Contains data on population by age and geographic area, agriculture, commerce, industry, public finance and national accounts, and social and cultural affairs. Includes data for provinces.   HA1025.B36a

Delaunay, Daniel. Demografía en el Ecuador : una bibliografía / [Daniel Delaunay]. Poblaciones de las parroquias, Ecuador, 1950–1982 / [Daniel Delaunay, Blanca Carrera, Juan León]. Quito : Centro Ecuatoriano de Investigación Geográfica, 1985. 69 p. (Documentos de investigación [Centro Ecuatoriano de Investigación Geográfica]. Serie Demografía y geografía de la población, no. 1–2.).   **CG153**

Contains two distinct works: *Demografia en el Ecuador, una bibliografia* and *Poblaciones de las Parroquias, Ecuador 1950–1982* (a collection of demographic data). Compiled by the Ecuadorian Center for Geographic Investigation (CEDIG), the Scientific Office of the National Section of the Panamerican Institute of Geography and History (IPGH) as a part of the "Geografia basica del Ecuador." Future volumes in this series are projected for migration, the demographic structure of the Ecuadorian population, and a map showing this geographic distribution.   HA1025.D45

Dirección General de Estadística y Censos (Ecuador). Síntesis estadística del Ecuador. 1955/60– . [Quito : s.n., 1962?]– .   **CG154**

Last known compilation was publ. 1963 for 1955/62, and is also available on microfiche (Cambridge : Chadwyck-Healey, 1978. 2 fiche. [Latin American and Caribbean official statistical serials on microfiche]).   HA1022.A55

Instituto Nacional de Estadística (Ecuador). Anuario de estadística, 1963/68. Quito : [El Instituto], [1968?]. 1 v.? : ill.   **CG155**

Includes data on population, vital statistics, industry, foreign trade, social statistics, etc.

Continued by *Serie estadística* (1967/72– . Quito, [1974?]– . Annual). Annual issues cover overlapping five-year periods. Issuing body later called Instituto Nacional de Estadística y Censos.   HA1025.I55

Paraguay

Anuario estadístico del Paraguay. 1960/65– . Asunción : Dirección General de Estadística y Censos, 1965– . Annual.   **CG156**

Continues *Anuario estadístico de la República del Paraguay* (1886–1954/59).

Contains statistical tables on physical environment, population, vital statistics, agriculture and industry, banking, commerce and transportation, and social affairs. Most tables offer national as well as departmental data.   HA1041.A2

Peru

Anuario estadístico del Perú. 1944/45– . Lima : Oficina Nacional de Estadística y Censos [etc.], 1945– . Annual (irregular).   **CG157**

Supersedes *Extracto estadístico del Peru* (1918–43).

Name of issuing agency varies.

Issued in three volumes.

Detailed tables for a wide range of demographic, economic, and social aspects of the country.

§ See also *Compendio estadístico del Perú, 1900–1990*, by Felipe Portocarrero S., Arlette Beltrán B., María Elena Romero P. (DB389).   HA1052.A452

Perú, las provincias en cifras, 1876–1981 / [compilado por] Héctor Maletta, Aljandro Bardales. [Lima, Peru] : Ediciones AMIDEP : Universidad del Pacífico, [1984?]. 3 v.   **CG158**

Contents: v. 1, Población y migraciones; v. 2, Fuerza laoral y empleo; v. 3, Estructura agraria, comp. by Héctor Maletta, Katia Makhlouf.

Historical statistics on population and migration (including data by age, sex, civil status, rural-urban population, and mortality), the labor force and employment, and agriculture and land utilization.

Uruguay

Anuario estadístico, Uruguay / Presidencia de la República Oriental del Uruguay, Secretaría de Planeamiento, Coordinación y Difusión, Dirección General de Estadística y Censos. 1983– . [Montevideo] : La Dirección, [1984?]– . Annual.   **CG159**

Issuing agency varies.

Continues *Anuario estadístico de la República Oriental del Uruguay* (1884–1944) and *Anuario estadístico* (1949–198?).

Contains information on climate and geography, as well as data on population, vital statistics, economic activities, national accounts and public finance, elections, social and cultural affairs.

    HA1071.A57

Rial Roade, Juan. Estadísticas históricas de Uruguay, 1850–1930 : población, producción agropecuaria, comercio, industria, urbanización, comunicaciones, calidad de vida. Montevideo : Centro de Informaciones y Estudios del Uruguay, 1980. 168p. (Cuaderno [Centro de Informaciones y Estudios del Uruguay], no.40).   **CG160**

Offers statistical tables, graphs, maps, charts describing Uruguay, ranging from population (e.g., age, sex, region) to health and economics (exports, land use, occupations). List of sources at end of volume.   HA1084.R52

Uruguay. Dirección General de Estadística y Censos. Estadísticas vitales. [Montevideo] : Presidencia de la República Oriental del Uruguay, Secretaría de Planeamiento, Corrdinación y Difusión Dirección General de Estadística y Censos, 1961– . Annual.   **CG161**

An initial chapter summarizes time series on births, deaths, infant and perinatal deaths, marriages, and divorces. Each of the following chapters deals with these topics in depth.   HA1073.D57c

Venezuela

Anuario estadístico de Venezuela / República de Venezuela, Presidencia de la República, Oficina Central de Estadística e Informática. 1985– . Caracas : OCEI, 1985– . Annual.   **CG162**

Continues works of similar titles, issued by various agencies since 1878 (except none published 1913–37).

Offers a wide range of detailed statistics. Source of many tables is indicated. HA1091.A4

Caribbean and Islands of the Western Atlantic

See also CG38.

Caribbean year book. [Ed.1] (1926/27)–50 (1979/80). London : Skinner, 1927–1980. **CG163**
Title varies: 1927–76, *West Indies and Caribbean year book.*
Covers: Bermuda, Bahamas, Barbados, Guyana, British Honduras, Jamaica, Cayman, Turks and Caicos Islands, Trinidad and Tobago, Leeward Islands, Windward Islands, Canal Zone (Panama), Colombia, Costa Rica, Cuba, Dominican Republic, El Salvador, French Guiana, French West Indies, Guatemala, Haiti, Honduras, Netherlands Antilles, Nicaragua, Panama, Puerto Rico, Suriname, Venezuela, Virgin Islands. F2131.W47

Antigua and Barbuda

Statistical yearbook. 1975– . St. John's, Antigua : Statistics Division, Ministry of Planning, Development, and External Affairs, 1975– . Annual. **CG164**
Some vols. called *Antigua statistical yearbook.* Issuing agency varies.
Basic statistics on demography, education and health, labor, wages and prices, agriculture and industry, finance and national accounts, arranged in seventeen topical chapters. Some tables contain retrospective data. No index. HA866.A5A75

Bahamas

Bahamas. Department of Statistics. Vital statistics report. Nassau : [s.n.], [197?]– . Annual. **CG165**
A section of summary data for the past ten years is followed by sections with tables on live births, deaths, infant deaths, stillbirths, marriages and divorces. HA861.A33

Statistical abstract / Commonwealth of the Bahamas. 1969– . Nassau : Dept. of Statistics, 1970– . Annual. **CG166**
Offers very detailed statistics on a wide range of socioeconomic topics, usually with a ten-year time series. Special 20-year anniversary edition, covering years 1968–88, published in 1988. HA861.A3

Barbados

Central Bank of Barbados. Annual statistical digest. 1972– . [Bridgetown] : Central Bank of Barbados, 1972– . **CG167**
A companion to the Bank's monthly *Economic and financial statistics* (1973–).
Deals primarily with financial statistics but also presents data on trade, industrial production, and labor. Special section on CARICOM general statistics. Detailed notes explain the tables. No index. HG185.B35C46a

Cuba

Anuario demográfico de Cuba / República de Cuba, Comité Estatal de Estadísticas, Dirección de Demografía. [Havana] : La Dirección, [1961?–1987?]. Annual. **CG168**
Includes data on population by age, sex, province, and rural and urban areas. A vital statistics portion gives fertility and fertility rates, mortality and death rates, marriages, divorces, and migration. Includes a section of comparative international data. HA871.A63

Anuario estadístico de Cuba. 1952– . [La Havana] : Comité Estatal de Estadísticas, 1952– . Annual. **CG169**
Issuing agency varies.
Presents an extensive range of national statistics, with some comparative international statistics. Indexed. HA871.A65

Rowe, Patricia M. Detailed statistics on the urban and rural population of Cuba, 1950 to 2010 / by Patricia M. Rowe and Susan J. O'Connor. Wash. : Center for Internat. Research, U.S. Bureau of the Census, 1984. 297 p. **CG170**
Presents statistics on population, fertility, mortality and migration, with summary data on marital status, foreign birth, health measures, education, literacy, labor force and households. Bibliographic sources cited.

Schroeder, Susan. Cuba : a handbook of historical statistics. Boston : G. K. Hall, 1982. 589 p. : ill., maps. **CG171**
Contains 22 chapters providing figures from the 15th century to the present on climate, demography, education, labor, production, foreign trade, finance, politics, government and the military; introductory texts are followed by statistical tables. Indexed. F1778.S37

Dominican Republic

Dominican Republic. Dirección General de Estadística y Censos. Anuario estadístico. 1936–54. Trujillo . [Dirección General de Estadística y Censos], 1937–57. **CG172**
In topical chapters, with information on geography and climate, demography, public health and social assistance, education and culture, justice, agriculture and fisheries, industry, commerce, finances, transportation and communication. Tables on population and vital statistics for the country and provinces; most tables cover more than one year. HA886.A35

República Dominicana en cifras. v.[1] (1964)– . Santo Domingo : Oficina Nacional de Estadística , [1964?]– . Irregular. **CG173**
Issuing body varies.
Provides statistics on geography, climate, natural resources, population, agriculture, industry, mining, manufacturing, etc. No sources indicated. HA887.A5

Haiti

Bulletin de statistique : Supplément annuel / Institut haitien de statistique et d'informatique. No. I–III (1967-69)– . Port-au-Prince : l'Institut. **CG174**
Supplement to *Bulletin trimestriel de statistique.*
Presents statistics on demography, economics, national accounts and public finance, social topics, and accidents at work. HA881.H35a

Jamaica

Demographic statistics. [Kingston] : Statistical Institute of Jamaica [1971]– . Annual.   **CG175**
    Publisher varies.
    A section on population presents detailed data on population structure and geographical distribution. Sections which follow are concerned with mortality, natality, nuptiality, divorces, migration, and family planning. Includes life tables.   HA891.D46a

Statistical abstract. 1984– . Kingston : Statistical Institute of Jamaica, [1985]– . Annual.   **CG176**
    Continues *Digest of statistics*, 1947–57; *Abstract of statistics*, 1958–71, and *Statistical abstract* (Jamaica Dept. of Statistics), 1972–1984.
    Offers detailed statistics for the latest year and one or two earlier years.   HA891.A27

Statistical yearbook of Jamaica. 1973– . [Kingston : the Section?, 1974]– . Annual.   **CG177**
    Prep. by the Information Section of the Central Planning and Development Division of the Dept. of Statistics.
    Arranged in 20 chapters by subject. Each subject area consists of an introduction and statistical data, some presented in time series.
                                HA891.C45a

St. Lucia

Annual statistical digest. Castries, Saint Lucia : Dept. of Statistics, Ministry of Trade, Industry and Tourism, 197?– . Annual.   **CG178**
    Title and agency name vary.
    Contains statistics on demography, agriculture and industrial production, trade, prices, public finances, and social affairs.
                                HA868.S3A56

St. Vincent and the Grenadines

Digest of statistics. [Kingstown?], Saint Vincent : Statistical Unit, 1968– . Annual.   **CG179**
    Reporting year appears in title.
    Some issues have title: *Digest of statistics for the year...*
    Issuing agency varies.
    Contains data on area and climate, statistical data on demography, economics, finance and banking, and social and cultural issues.
                                HA868.S33A2

Trinidad and Tobago

Annual statistical digest / [issued by the Central Statistical Office]. no. 1 (1935/51)– . [Port of Spain] Trinidad, B.W.I. : G.P.O., 1951– . Annual.   **CG180**
    At head of title: Government of Trinidad and Tobago.
    1951–68 issued by Trinidad Central Statistical Office. No.1 includes data for 1935–51. Sources of statistics indicated.   HA867.A35

Population and vital statistics report / Republic of Trinidad & Tobago, Central Statistical Office. 1988/1989– . Port of Spain, Trinidad and Tobago : The Office, c1991– . Annual.
                                CG181
    Continues works with similar titles, publ. since 1953.
    Presents statistical tables on population at census years by sex and age, on live and still births, and on deaths (including infant deaths, maternal deaths and causes of deaths).   HA867.A372

Europe (by region)

See also CG38.

Basic statistics of the community / Statistical Office of the European Communities. Brussels : The Office, [1961]– . Annual (irregular).   **CG182**
    Title varies: Basic statistics for fifteen European countries.
    Volumes for 1968–69, 1973–74, and 1976–77 issued together.
    Presents general statistics, economy and finance, Population and social conditions, energy and industry, agriculture and forestry, foreign trade, and environment. There are comparative data on some developed countries including the U.S., Canada, and the U.S.S.R.
                                HA1107.5.A12

Befolkningsstatistik = Demographic statistics / [Eurostat]. 1960–1976– . Luxembourg-Kirchberg : De europæiske fællesskabers statistiske kontor, 1978– . Annual.   **CG183**
    In Danish, Dutch, English, French, German, Greek, Italian, Portuguese, and Spanish. Title occasionally varies in each language.
    Population statistics for all member countries and for the whole Community. Covers population by sex and age groups, births, deaths, migration, marriages and divorces, fertility, and life expectancy, along with projections. Both absolute numbers and rates are presented in detail. There is also international comparison of principal demographic indicators from 1960. No index, but a good table of contents and introduction in each of the nine languages.   HA1107.5.B43

Europe in figures. 1988– . Luxembourg : Office for Official Publications of the European Communities, c1987– . **CG184**
    Issues for 1989/90– called also 2nd ed.– .
    Issued by: Statistical Office of the European Communities.
    Current demographic, social, economic, and political aspects of the European Community, presented in diagrams, charts, and tables. Index; list of abbreviations.   HC241.2.E81297

European directory of non-official statistical sources. 1st ed. (1988)– . London : Euromonitor ; Detroit : Gale, c1988– . Annual.   **CG185**
    An index to more than 2,000 key nongovernmental publications (e.g., opinion surveys, forecasts) that provide statistics concerning markets, industries, and products for both individual countries of Europe and the continent as a whole. Stresses pan-European sources and those of the major European Community nations (notably France, West Germany, and the U.K.) but includes selected materials from 12 other European countries. Arranged alphabetically by organization. Subject and geographic indexes, and an organization list arranged geographically.   HA37.E914

Europe, Western

Blake, Judith. Western European censuses, 1960 : an English language guide / Judith Blake, Jerry J. Donovan. Berkeley : Inst. of International Studies, Univ. of California, 1971. 421 p. (Population monograph series, 8).   **CG186**
    Repr.: Westport, Conn. : Greenwood, 1976.
    Furnishes "the titles and page numbers of all statistical tables in every volume of every census ...; a detailed glossary of technical terms that appear in more than one volume of that census ...; [and] a bibliographically correct entry for every volume" (*Introd.*) of the 1960 census publications issued by the governments of western Europe (including Greece, but not the rest of the Balkans).   HA37.E93B5

Harvey, Joan M. Statistics Europe : sources for social, economic, and market research. 5th ed. Beckenham, England : CBD Research, 1987. 320 p.   **CG187**
    1st ed., 1968; 4th ed., rev. and enl., 1981.

Information for each country includes: directory information for the central statistical office and for other major organizations publishing statistical information; principal libraries where statistical materials are available; current bibliographies and sales lists of statistics; list of major statistical publications (arranged as general, production, external trade, internal distribution and service trades, population, social and political, finance, and environment). Topical subdivisions for most groups; organization, title, and subject indexes.

An obvious shrinkage between the 4th and 5th editions has been caused by economic restrictions, affecting both the government documents and the number of non-official statistical publications.

Z7554.E8I135

Library of Congress. Census Library Project. National censuses and vital statistics in Europe, 1918–1939 : an annotated bibliography / prep. by Henry J. Dubester. Wash. : U.S. Govt. Print. Off., 1948. 215 p.   **CG188**

A very useful guide to the national censuses and official statistical publications of the various countries of Europe, for the period between the two World Wars.

A supplement covering 1940–1948 (48 p.) was published the same year. Reprints by Gale, 1967, and B. Franklin, 1969, include both the original work and the supplement.

Mitchell, Brian R. International historical statistics, Europe, 1750–1988. 3rd ed. N.Y. : Stockton Pr., 1992. 942 p.   **CG189**

1st ed., 1975, covered 1750–1970. 2nd ed., 1980, had title *European historical statistics, 1750–1975.*

Official and unofficial statistical sources were used to provide comparative data for 26 European countries. Data for more than two centuries are arranged in ten sections that cover population and vital statistics, labor force, agriculture, industry, external trade, transport and communications, finance, prices, education, and national accounts. Sections include 77 tables; each contains an introduction, notes, and footnotes.   HA1107.M5

Scandinavia

Yearbook of Nordic statistics = Nordisk statistisk årsbok, 1962– . Stockholm : Nordic Council of Ministers and the Nordic Statistical Secretariat [etc.], [1962]– . Annual.   **CG190**

In English and Swedish.

Issuing agency varies.

Provides general statistical information for Scandinavian countries (Denmark, Finland, Iceland, Norway, and Sweden). In 27 chapters covering: area and climate, population and labor, agriculture and forestry, fisheries, industry, trade and transport, finance, and social and political issues. Information is presented in charts, graphs, and tables. Sometimes tables provide retrospective coverage. Subject index.

DL1.N63

Europe (by country)

Albania

40 vjet Shqiperi socialiste = 40 years of socialist Albania. Tiranë : Shtëpia botuese "8 Nëntori", 1984. [160] p. : ill.   **CG191**

Contains charts, tables and graphs that give national statistics, social indicators, industrial and agricultural production, trade, etc. English version; also published in Albanian and French.   DR912.A14

Vjetari statistikor i Shqipërisë = Statistical yearbook of Albania / Republika e Shqipërisë, Ministria e Ekonomise, Drejtoria e Statistikës. 1991– . Tiranë : Drejtoria e Statistikës, 1991– . Annual.   **CG192**

Continues: *Vjetari statistikor i R.P.S. të Shqipërisë*, which was issued irregularly under slightly different title by the same agency since 1958.

Issued irregularly by this agency under slightly varying title since about 1958. Provides statistics of population, employment, agriculture and industry, transportation and communications, trade (including foreign trade), national income, education and health. The 1991 ed. contains a special chapter that includes some important tabulations of the 1989 population and housing census data that have previously been impossible to publish.

Austria

Bibliographie zur Bevölkerungsforschung in Österreich, 1945–1978 / von Karl Husa [et al.]. Wien : A. Schendl, 1980. 167 p. (Abhandlungen zur Humangeographie, Bd. 3).   **CG193**

"Mit einem Beitrag zur Entwicklung der Bevölkerungsforschung in Österreich nach dem Zweiten Weltkrieg von Karl Husa und Christian Vielhaber"—*t.p.*

A classed bibliography of 1,178 items; international in scope, although the great majority are in German. Papers and dissertations are included. Arranged by province, then by subject (e.g., minorities, refugees, guest workers, etc.). Author and subject indexes.

Demographisches Jahrbuch Österreichs. 1975– . Wien : [Öesterreichisches Statistisches Zentralamt], 1976– .   **CG194**

Continues: *Natürliche Bevölkerungsbewegung*, 1956–74.

Text uses graphs and tables to describe the demographic situation and to explain the population forecast. Followed by tables in nine sections of statistics on marriages, births and fertility, deaths and life expectancy, divorces, and migration. Concludes with information on population projections.   HA1173.A27 subser

Gehart, Alois. Statistik in Österreich, 1918–1938 : eine Bibliographie / [Eigentümer, Herausgeber und Hersteller, Republik Österreich, Österreichisches Statistisches Zentralamt]. Wien : Österreichische Staatsdruckerei, 1984. 115 p.   **CG195**

Includes indexes.

Materials published on statistics and publications that contain data on demography, labor, industry, religion, elections, and other social and economic areas. Arranged alphabetically by author or title. Includes materials lost during the war and not available. Lists of institutions, and of laws and regulations. Subject and author indexes.

Z7554.A8G43 1984

Österreichisches Statistisches Zentralamt. Mikrozensus : Jahresergebnisse. Wien : [Kommissionsverlag der Österreichischen Staatsdruckerei]. Annual.   **CG196**

Beginning date unknown.

More than 60 tables grouped in six sections: population, work force, work hours, households, families, and housing. Text at the beginning of each section explains the tables. Some information is presented for provinces. Full data for the current year, and a summary for the preceding three years.   HA1173.A27

———— Sozialstatistische Daten. 1977– . Wien : Österreichisches Statistisches Zentralamt, 1978– .   **CG197**

Irregular; issued approximately every four years.

Covers areas of social studies such as population, family, health, education, income and standard of living, social security, housing, crime, and culture. Lists of sources; keyword index.   HA1171.S73a

Statistisches Jahrbuch für die Republik Österreich / hrsg. vom Österreichischen Statistischen Zentralamt. N.F., 43. Jahrg. (1992)– . Wien : Kommissionsverlag, Österreichische Staatsdruckerei, 1992– . Annual.   **CG198**

Contains detailed tables with data on population and housing, health, education, other social issues, agriculture and industry, trade, finance and insurance, justice and elections. Includes an international section for comparative purposes; subject index.

§ Preceding titles:

(1) *Österreichisches statistisches Handbuch* (Wien : Statistische Zentralkommission, 1882–1916/17). Continued by:

(2) *Statistisches Handbuch für die Republik Österreich* (Jahrg. 1–14, Wien : Bundesamt für Statistik, 1920–33). Continued by:

(3) *Statistisches Handbuch für den Bundesstaat Österreich* (Jahrg. 15–17, Wien : Bundesamt für Statistik, 1935–37). Continued after the annexation of Austria by Germany by:

(4) *Statistisches Handbuch für den Bundesstaat Österreich* (Jahrg. 18, Wien : Statistisches Landesamt, 1938). Publication suspended 1938–49. Resumed as:

(5) *Statistisches Handbuch für die Republik Österreich* (N.F., Jahrg. 1–42, Wien : 1950–91).　　　　HA1171.C3

Belgium

Annuaire statistique de la Belgique. v. 1 (1870)– . Bruxelles : Institut national de statistique, Ministère des affaires économiques, 1870– . Annual.　　　　**CG199**

Issuing body and title vary slightly: v. 1–41 issued by the Ministère de l'interérieur; v. 42–80, 1912–59, called *Annuaire statistique de la Belgique et du Congo belge*. Vol. 1–41 also issued in microfiche by Chadwyck-Healey.

Text in French and Flemish.

Detailed statistics on a wide range of topics, most tables offering comparative figures for a number of years. Fully indexed.

HA1393.A34

National population bibliography of Flanders, 1945–1983 / ed. by M. Devisch & D. Vanderstappen. Brussels : publ. for The International Union for the Scientific Study of Population by the Population and Family Study Centre (CBGS), 1990. 580 p. : ill.　　　　**CG200**

Abstracts for most entries. Author index.　　Hb3603.N3

Bulgaria

Statisticheski godishnik = Statistical yearbook / Republika Bŭlgariĩa, Natsionalen statisticheski institut. 1993– . Sofia : Institut, 1993– . Annual.　　　　**CG201**

Title and agency name vary. Supersedes *Statisticheski godishnik na Tsarstovo Bulgariĩa*, 1909–42; *Statisticheski godishnik na Narodnata Republika Bŭlgariĩa*, 1948–55; *Statisticheski godishnik na Narodna Republika Bŭlgariĩa*, 1956–89; *Statisticheski godishnik na Republika Bŭlgariĩa*, 1990–92).

Detailed tables and graphs offer statistical data on population by census year, region and density, vital statistics, environment, agriculture, commerce, industry, finance, and social affairs.　　HA1621.S45

Commonwealth of Independent States

Demographic yearbook / Statistical Committee of the Commonwealth of Independent States. 1991– . Moscow : Finanstatinform, 1993– . Annual.　　　　**CG202**

Publication "funded by the Netherlands Organization for Scientific Research (NWO) through the Population Research Centre of the University of Groningen."—*t.p.*

Contains statistical information concerning population 1979–90; births, deaths, marriages, and divorces, 1980, 1985, and 1990; and migration, 1989 and 1990. Most of the material is presented at the level of the republics, but some data are given at the level of economic regions and administrative areas.　　HA1444.D3763

Cyprus

Cyprus. Financial Secretary's Office. Statistics Section. Statistical abstract. no. 1 (1955)– . Nicosia : Dept. of Statistics and Research, Ministry of Finance, [1955]– . Annual.　　　　**CG203**

Issuing agency varies.

Offers comprehensive data on geography and climate, population, migration and tourism, education, justice, social welfare, and a variety of economic areas, with comparative international statistics.

HA1950.C9A3

Statistical yearbook = Istatistik yilliği / [Turkish Republic of Northern Cyprus]. 1982– . [s.l.] : Prime Ministry State Planning Organisation, Statistics and Research Department, 1983– . Annual.　　　　**CG204**

Continues *Statistical yearbook* issued by the Turkish Federated State of Cyprus. In Turkish and English.

Arranged in 16 sections, each with a brief introduction. Presents statistical data on various social and economic aspects, and on the national accounts of Northern Cyprus.

Czechoslovakia

Bibliografie československé statistiky a demografie. Praha : Výzkumný ústav statistiky a účetnictví, 1966– . Annual.　　　　**CG205**

Continues *Bibliografie československé statistiky* (1945–65).

Czech and Slovak works on the theory and methodology of statistics and demography. Arranged by subject in three sections: statistics, demography, and publications of the Federal office of statistics. Selective; many items lack annotations. Author index.　　Z7554.C9B52

Historická statistická ročenka ČSSR / odpovědná red. Olga Hebáková. Praha : SNTL, Nakl. technické literatury ; Bratislava : ALFA, Vydavatelstvo technickej a ekonomickej literatúry, 1985. 910 p.　　　　**CG206**

Presents demographic, economic, and social statistics for 1948–83; some tables provide comparisons with the 1918–37 period. Detailed table of contents. Subject index.　　HA1195.H57

National population bibliography of Czechoslovakia, 1945–1977 / ed. by Josef Koubek and Jaroslav Podzimek. Prague : publ. for the International Union for the Scientific Study of Population by the Czechoslovak Demographic Society at the Czechoslovak Academy of Sciences, 1984. 229 p.　　　　**CG207**

Citations in Czech with introduction and abstracts in English.

A selective list, primarily titles of theoretical or methodological value, or otherwise highly informative. Works chosen regardless of the language of publication or nationality of the author. Organized by subject, subdivided by narrower topics. Author and geographical index.

Statistická ročenka České a Slovenské federativní republiky / Federální statistický úřad, Český statistický úřad, Slovenský štatistický úrad. 1990–[1992?]. Praha : SNTL, 1990–[1992?]. Annual.　　　　**CG208**

Continues *Statistická ročenka Československé socialistické republiky* (1960–89); *Statistická ročenka Republiky Československé* (1934–56; suspended 1939–56); and *Statistická prírucka* issued by Státní Urad Statistický (1920, 1925, 1928, 1932).

Contains data on physical environment, demography, economic affairs, national accounts, and public finance. Covers social and cultural topics. In addition to national statistics, includes information for the Republics, regions, and municipalities. Subject index and detailed table of contents.　　HA1191.S73

Denmark

Befolkningens bevægelser = Vital statistics. 1981– . København : Statistiske departement, 1983– . Annual.
CG209
In Danish, with English summaries, table of contents, and table headings.

Vital statistics covering years 1931/33–1980 were published in *Befolkningens bevaegelser*, part of the multivolume series *Statistiske meddelelser* issued by Statistiske departement.

Presents information about events such as births, deaths, marriages, divorces, and migrations, as well as population. Special chapters of data on foreign nationals, Faroe Islands, and Greenland.
HA1473.B43

Statistisk årbog = Statistical yearbook. 1949– . København : [Danmarks Statistik], 1949– . Annual.
CG210
Continues *Statistisk aarbog = Annuaire statistique*, 1896–1948.

Text in Danish and French, 1949–59; Danish and English, beginning 1960.

Includes sections of statistics for Denmark proper, the Faroe Islands, and Greenland, and an international section.
HA1477

Finland

National population bibliography of Finland / [Altti Majava … et al.]. Helsinki : Publ. for the International Union for the Scientific Study of Population by the Finnish Demographic Society, 1984. 296 p.
CG211
Covers publications on vital statistics and population of Finland published in Finland, as well as works on Finland published abroad. Citations are annotated; author index.
HB3608.3N26

Suomen tilastollinen vuosikirja = Statistisk arsbok för Finland = Statistical yearbook of Finland. Ed. 1– . Helsinki : Tilastokeskus, 1903– . Annual.
CG212
Continues a publication of the same title, 1879–1902.

Title and text also in French until 1932; Swedish and French, 1934–52; in Swedish and English, 1953– .

Offers a wide range of detailed statistical tables with indication of sources; includes some comparative statistics for countries other than Finland. Each issue has a retrospective bibliography of Finnish statistical publications.
HA1448.F537c

Väestö = Befolkning = Population. Helsinki : [Tilastokeskus]. Annual.
CG213
English, Finnish, and Swedish.

Beginning date unknown.

For 1978– , issued in three volumes: (1) statistical data on population characteristics, and vital statistics by urban areas and provinces; (2) population characteristics by municipality; (3) vital statistics by municipality.
HA1448.F4

France

Annuaire statistique de l'Union française outre-mer. 1939/46–1947/58. Paris : Impr. Nationale de France, [1951–59]. 3 v.
CG214
1958 volume publ. 1959 with title *Outre-mer*.

An "Édition provisoire" entitled *Annuaire statistique des possessions françaises: années antérieures à la guerre* was publ. 1944.

§ Continued by the Institut national de la statistique et des études économiques, *Annuaire statistique des territoires d'outre-mer* (1959–).
HA1228.A23

Croze, Marcel. Tableaux démographiques : la population en France : histoire et géographie. [Paris] : Institut national d'études demographiques : Institut national de la statistique et des études économiques, 1988. 75 p. : ill.
CG215
Updates his 1976 *Tableaux démographiqes et sociaux* (Paris : INSEE, 1976. 216 p. Supplements, 1979, 1981).

Tables present demographic data on population of France, spatial distribution of population, population by sex, age, marital status, and nationality.
HB3593.C758

Institut national de la statistique et des études économiques (France). Annuaire statistique de la France. v.1 (1878)– . Paris [etc.] : Institut national de la statistique et des études économiques, 1878– . Annual.
CG216
Title varies slightly. Vol. 56 covers 1940/45.

Vol. 59– also called "nouv. sér.", no. 1– .

Vols. 1–56 (1878–1940/45) issued by Statistique générale de la france.

Offers a wide range of statistics for the individual départements as well as for France as a whole. Includes an international section.
HA1213.A4

Lunazzi, Marie-Claude. Bibliographie française de démographie, 1975–1984. Paris : Comité national français de l'Union internationale pour l'étude scientifique de la population, 1985. 119 p.
CG217
Includes about 800 French-language works published in France or by French authors published outside France. Not annotated. Organized by subject. Author index; list of publishers and addresses.
Z7164.D3L86

————— Non-national bibliography of French demographers : 1939–1988 = Bibliografía en extranjero de demógrafos franceses. Paris : French National Committee of the International Union for the Scientific Study of Population, 1989. 103 p.
CG218
Introductory material in English, Spanish, Italian, German, and French.

Entries cover nearly 1,000 works in languages other than French; includes works originally published in French. Not annotated. Citations in English arranged by subject; works in other languages arranged chronologically, then alphabetically by author.

A companion volume to *Bibliographie française de demographie 1975-1984* (CG217) which listed works published by French demographers in French.

La situation démographique. Paris : Ministère de l'économie et des finances, Institut national de la statistique et des études économiques. Annual.
CG219
Title includes year of coverage, i.e., *La Situation démographique en 1990*. Annual for 1990 publ. 1992. Beginning date unknown.

Sections on population, marriages, divorces, births, deaths, abortion, and migration, plus selected data by departments and regions. Appendixes provide information on the French system of vital statistics, and methodology for calculations of vital statistics.
HC271.A218

Germany

Bevölkerung und Erwerbstätigkeit : Reihe 1, Gebiet und Bevölkerung / Hrsg. Statistisches Bundesamt. Stuttgart : Kohlhammer, [1983]– . Quarterly.
CG220
At head of title: Fachserie 1.

Issued also in an annual cumulation.

Formed through the merger of *Bevölkerung und Erwerbstätigkeit*, Reihe 1.3 (Bevölkerung nach Alter und Familienstand, 1975–80) and Reihe 2 (Bevölkerungsbewegung, 1975–80). Before that, statistical data had been published in several separate series of *Bevölkerung und Kultur* issued by Statistisches Bundesamt.

Contains statistics on population, and vital statistics including detailed data on marriages and divorces, births, fertility, deaths, life tables, migration, and population projections.   HA1231.B48

Gärtner, Karla. Bibliographie deutschsprachiger bevölkerungswissenschaftlicher Literatur, 1978–1984 / Karla Gärtner, Johannes Otto und Manfred Tölle. Wiesbaden : Bundesinstitut für Bevölkerungsforschung, 1986. 802 p. (Materialien zur Bevölkerungswissenschaft, Heft 48).   **CG221**

For annotation, *see* CG3.   Z7165.G3G37

Germany (Territory under Allied Occupation, 1945–1955 : U.S. Zone). Statistisches Handbuch von Deutschland, 1928–1944. München : F. Ehrenwirth, 1949. 640 p., 17 p.   **CG222**

Designed to provide some statistical information for the period following the 1938 issue of the *Statistisches Jahrbuch für das Deutsche Reich* (1880–1941/42. 59 v.). 1928 was chosen as a "normal" year to compare with later available statistics.   HA1241.A52

Germany (West). Statistisches Bundesamt. Veröffentlichungsverzeichnis. 1951– . [Mainz : Kohlhammer, 1951?]– . Annual.   **CG223**

Title varies: 1951–82, *Verzeichnis der Veröffentlichungen des Statistischen Bundesamtes.*

Also available in English and French versions.

Lists all sales publications available at the beginning of the calendar year and describes various services of the Federal Statistical Office. New publications are announced weekly in the office's *Bundesanzeiger* and *Statistischer Wochendienst*, and in the monthly *Wirtschaft und Statistik*. Indexed.   Z7554.G3A25

Statistisches Jahrbuch der Deutschen Demokratischen Republik. 1. Jahrg. (1955)–35. Jahrg. ('90). Berlin : Deutscher Zentralverlag, 1956–1990. Annual.   **CG224**

Publisher varies.

Offers a wide range of statistical tables, many with comparative figures for 15 to 20 years. Includes an international section.

Merged with *Statistisches Jahrbuch für die Bundesrepublik Deutschland* in 1991 to form *Statistisches Jahrbuch für das vereinte Deutschland*, which was continued by *Statistisches Jahrbuch für die Bundesrepublik Deutschland* (CG225).   HA1248.A2A33

Statistisches Jahrbuch für die Bundesrepublik Deutschland / Statistisches Bundesamt, Herausgeber. 1992– . [Stuttgart] : Metzler-Poeschel, 1992– . Annual.   **CG225**

Date appears in title.

Continues *Statistisches Jahrbuch für das vereinte Deutschland* (publ. 1991), which was formed by the merger of *Statistisches Jahrbuch der Deutschen Demokratischen Republik* (CG224) and *Statistisches Jahrbuch für die Bundesrepublik Deutschland* (CG226).

Covers the whole territory of united Germany, presenting general statistical data on population and vital statistics, and a wide range of data on social and economic issues. Includes selective data from other countries for comparisons.   HA1231.S73

Statistisches Jahrbuch für die Bundesrepublik Deutschland. 1952–1990. Stuttgart-Mainz : Kohlhammer, 1952–1990. Annual.   **CG226**

Continues the *Statistisches Jahrbuch für das Deutsche Reich*, 1880–1938 (57 v.) for the territory under the Federal Republic of Germany. Contains statistics on population and a wide range of data on economic and social topics. Has an added section for international statistics.

Merged with *Statistisches Jahrbuch der Deutschen Demokratischen Republik* in 1991 to form *Statistisches Jahrbuch für das vereinte Deutschland*, later continued as *Statistisches Jahrbuch für die Bundesrepublik Deutschland* (CG225).   HA1232.A45

Bibliography

Bibliographie bevölkerungswissenschaftlicher Literatur, 1945–1982 : Deutsche Demokratische Republik / Akademie der Wissenschaften der Deutschen Demokratischen Republik, Institut für Soziologie und Sozialpolitik. Berlin : Das Institut, 1984. 511 p.   **CG227**

Contains 1,242 citations to monographs, articles, chapters of books, bibliographies, and dissertations written by German authors or published in Germany, as well as works by foreign authors or published abroad, dealing with German population problems.   Z7164.D3B524

Deutsche Statistische Gesellschaft. Bibliographie der amtlichen westdeutschen Statistik, 1945–1951. München, 1952. 91 p. (Einzelschriften der Deutschen Statistischen Gesellschaft, Hft. Nr. 3).   **CG228**

Thieme, Frank. Bibliographie bevölkerungswissenschaftlicher Aufsätze und Kurzartikel im damaligen Deutschen Reich erschienener sozialwissenschaftlicher und erbbiologischer Fachzeitschriften zwischen 1900 und ca. 1945. Wiesbaden : Bundesinstitut für Bevölkerungsforschung, 1990. 186 p. (Materialien zur Bevölkerungswissenschaft, Hft. 63).   **CG229**

Contains 1,465 unannotated citations to articles in journals and periodicals in the fields of social science, biology, and genetics. Arranged alphabetically by author.   Z7165.G3T45

Gibraltar

Gibraltar abstract of statistics. Gibraltar : Economic Planning & Statistics Office, [1972]– . Annual.   **CG230**

Title and issuing agency vary.

Presents information on physical environment as well as statistical data on population and births, deaths and marriages, economic affairs and finance, and social and cultural topics.

Great Britain

Great Britain. Central Statistical Office. Annual abstract of statistics. v.1 (1840/53)– . London : H.M.S.O., 1840– . Annual.   **CG231**

Vols. 1–83 issued by the Board of Trade as *Statistical abstract for the United Kingdom*. Each of these volumes contained statistics for the preceding 15 years. Coverage varies slightly.

Vol. 83, covering 1924–1938, was published in 1940. No volumes were published during World War II, but v. 84, with a new title and under a new issuing body, appeared in 1948 and covers 1935–46; v. 85, publ. 1949, covers 1938–48; v. 87 (1951)– , published annually, cover the last ten years.

The principal source for general statistical data covering demography, economic affairs, political affairs, and social and cultural topics. Subject index and index of sources.   HA1122.A33

Great Britain. Office of Population Censuses and Surveys. Population trends. 1 (autumn 1975)– . [London] : Govt. Statistical Service, 1975– .   **CG232**

Articles on important demographic and medical topics, and regular series of statistical tables on births, marriages, divorces, migration, deaths, and abortions.   HB3583.G66b

————— The Registrar General's statistical review of England and Wales. 1969–1973. London : H. M. S. O., 1921–1973.   **CG233**

Supplements accompany some issues.

Continues a work issued by the General Register Office, 1921–68.

Discontinued in 1973 and replaced by individual subject volumes published by the Office of Population Censuses and Surveys in following series: FM Family statistics (1–2), DH Deaths (1–5), MB Morbidity (1–2), MN Migration, PP Population estimates and projections (1–3), and VS Local authority vital statistics.

§ Statistical data for Scotland are presented in the Annual report published by the General Register Office (Scotland), and vital statistics for Northern Ireland in the *Annual report of the Registrar General* (CG239). HA1127.A3

Mitchell, Brian R. Abstract of British historical statistics / Brian R. Mitchell, with the collaboration of Phyllis Deane. Cambridge : Univ. Pr., 1962. 513 p. **CG234**

Presents tables of economic statistics of the United Kingdom, with information on sources and coverage and with introduction and bibliographies for each section. In some cases figures go back to the 17th century and earlier, but most series begin with the 18th and 19th centuries and are taken only to 1938.

Continued by: Brian R. Mitchell and H. G. Jones, *Second abstract of British historical statistics* (Cambridge : Univ. Pr., 1971. 227 p.) Primarily a continuation of the earlier abstract, providing tables for 1938 onwards for most series, but adding some series not included in the earlier volume (with pre-1938 figures for these). Cutoff date is usually 1965 or 1966.

Cumulated and expanded by Mitchell's *British historical statistics* (CG235). HA1135.M5

——————— British historical statistics. Cambridge ; N.Y. : Cambridge Univ. Pr., 1988. 886 p. **CG235**

A cumulation and expansion of Mitchell's *Abstract of British historical statistics* and Mitchell and H. G. Jones's *Second abstract of British historical statistics* (CG234).

Emphasizes social and economic history, including population and vital statistics, transportation and communications, public finance and financial institutions. Each of the 16 chapters contains information on sources and coverage. Includes some of the earliest available data; most tables cover to about 1980. Subject index. HA1134.M58

Bibliography

Benjamin, Bernard. Population statistics : a review of UK sources. Aldershot, Eng. ; Brookfield, Vt. : Gower Pub. Co., c1989. 355 p. : ill. **CG236**

A guide to sources of demographical statistics. Arranged by subject in 12 sections. Sources are described in detail, including methodology of collecting data and construction of indexes. Indexed. HA37.G7B445

Great Britain. Central Statistical Office. Guide to official statistics. 1976– . London : H.M.S.O., 1976– . Biennial. **CG237**

Each issue of the guide "tries ... to give a good indication to the user of the likelihood of a particular subject's being included in a given source."—*No. 3, 1980 [p. iv]*. Covers official and significant nonofficial sources of statistics for the United Kingdom published within the last ten years. Classed subject arrangement, with keyword index. Brief introductory remarks for most sections; all sources are abstracted. HA37.G5816

Guide to current official statistics / Permanent Consultative Committee on Official Statistics (Great Britain). 1922–1938. London : H.M.S.O., 1923–1939. Annual. **CG238**

No more published.

A survey of statistics contained in government publications by departments and agencies in the U.K. Consists of a detailed subject index and a list of publications arranged alphabetically by department. A Key to statistical contents links together the two parts by using serial reference numbers of volumes listed in the list of publications, and page numbers in the subject index. Z7554.G7G7

Ireland, Northern

Northern Ireland. General Register Office. Annual report of the Registrar General. 1958– . Belfast : H.M.S.O., 1958– . Annual. **CG239**

Continues *The Registrar-General's annual report*, 1st (1922)–35th (1956).

Includes data on population by age and sex; marriages, divorces, and marriage rates; births and birth rates, including illegitimate births; deaths, death rates, and causes of death; maternal and infant mortality; life tables; and migration. HA1147.N6N66a

Northern Ireland annual abstract of statistics. No. 1 (1982)– . Belfast : H.M.S.O., 1982– . Annual. **CG240**

Continues: *Digest of statistics for Northern Ireland*, 1954–81.

Presents information on physical environment, statistical data on population, vital statistics, statistics on economic affairs (including national accounts and public finance), and social and cultural activities. HA1141.N67

Ulster year book. 1926–1985. Belfast : H.M.S.O., 1926-85. **CG241**

None published 1939–46. Frequency varied.

Prepared by the General Register Office, 1926–62; Northern Ireland Information Service, 1965–85.

The official handbook for Northern Ireland. Presents statistical and other information on social and economic conditions, health, education, etc. HC257.I6A5

Greece

Chouliarakēs, Michaēl G. Statistikē vivliographia peri Hellados, 1821–1971. Athēnai : [Ethnikon Kentron Koinōnikōn Ereunōn], 1971. 78, [108]–118 p. **CG242**

Includes a supplement, Statistikē dēmosieumata kai vivliographia statistikēs en Helladi, 1833–1932, (p. [108]–118) repr. from S. Kladas, *Hē statistikē en Helladi* (Athēnai, 1932).

A classed bibliography of 688 numbered citations, principally in Greek, but with English, French, and Italian-language materials represented. Z7165.G84C46

Statistikē epetēris tēs Hellados = Statistical yearbook of Greece. 1930– . Athens : Ethnikon Typographeion, 1931– . Irregular. **CG243**

Title varies.

Vols. for 1930–39 called v. 1–10. Publication suspended 1940–53. Vols. for 1930–39 in Greek and French; 1954– in Greek and English.

Vols. for 1930–39 issued by Genikē Statistikē Hypēresia; 1954– by Ethnikē Statistikē Hypēresia.

Contains data on geography and environment, demography, public health and other social issues, agriculture, fishing and forestry, money and banking, public finance, national accounts and balance of payments, and all sectors of the economy. A section of international tables is included for comparison. HA1351.S75

Statistikē tēs physikēs kinēseos tou plēthysmou tes Hellados. 1 (1956)– . Athēnai : Ethnikē Statistikē Hypēresia tēs Hellados, 1956– . **CG244**

Volumes for 1956–85 also called A:1–A:56, Population.

Text in French and Greek.

Continues works of similar titles publ. 1860–91 and 1921–39.

Presents detailed statistical data on marriages, births and stillbirths, mortality, infant mortality and causes of death.

Hungary

Demográfiai évkönyv / Központi Statisztikai Hivatal. 1965– . Budapest : A Hivatal, 1966– . Annual.   **CG245**

In Hungarian, with English and Russian explanation of tables.

Continues *Magyarorszag népesedése*, which covered 1955(?)–64.

A general section presents summary data on population, followed by topical sections on vital statistic events such as marriages, divorces, births, mortality and causes of death, infant and perinatal mortality, migration, life tables, and life expectancy.

Volumes issued since 1989 have an English supplement that contains translations of headings by chapters, as well as explanations of terms and methodology.   HA1201.K63a

Fóti, Istvánné. Statisztikai adatforrások : bibliográfia, 1945–1985 = Sources of statistical data : bibliography, 1945–1985. Budapest : Központi Statisztikai Hivatal, Könyvtár és Dokumentációs Szolgálat, 1987. 431 p.   **CG246**

Previous edition covered 1945–74.

A bibliography of sources of statistical data, 1945–85. Entries in Hungarian, English, and Russian.   Z7554.H8F67

Statisztikai évkönyv / Központi Statisztikai Hivatal. [1949/55]–1989. Budapest : Hivatal, [1957]–1989. Annual.   **CG247**

Also published in English and Russian as *Statistical yearbook*; *Statisticheskii ezhegodnik*, which was publ. through 1991, with coverage through 1989.

Supersedes the Office's *Magyar statisztikai évkönyv ... Statistisches Jahrbuch*, 1871–90; *Magyar statisztikai évkönyv. Új folyam*, 1893–1900; and *Annuaire statistique hongrois. Nouv. cours*, 1901–41.

Continued by: *Magyar statisztikai évkönyv* (1990– . Budapest : Hivatal, 1991– . Annual). Issued also in English, in 1990, as *Hungarian statistical yearbook*.   HA1201.A52

Time series of historical statistics 1867–1992 / Klinger András ; Csahók István ... [et al.]. Budapest : Hungarian Central Statistical Office, 1992. v. 1. (In progress).   **CG248**

Translation of *Történeti statisztikai idősorok, 1867–1992*.

Contents: v. 1, Population: vital statistics.

The first of a series of historical statistics, planning to cover different aspects in separate volumes. This first volume contains the most important time series concerning the population as well as the vital events from 1867–1990, taking into consideration the changes in the territory of the country.   HA1205.T63

Iceland

Landshagir = Statistical abstract of Iceland. 1991– . Reykjavík : Hagstofa Íslands, [1991]– . Irregular.   **CG249**

Continues: *Tölfræðihandbók = Statistical abstract of Iceland*, publ. 1967, 1974, 1984.

Contains statistical data on economic affairs including national accounts and public finance, elections, and social and cultural activities.   HA1491.A4

Mannfjöldaskýrslur arin 1971–80 = Population and vital statistics. Reykjavík : Af Hagstofu Íslands, 1988. 301 p. : ill. (Hagskýrslur Íslands = Statistics of Iceland, II, 89).   **CG250**

In Icelandic with captions also in English.

Contains statistics on population, migration, marriages, divorces and separations, births, adoptions, deaths, life tables, and population projections.   HA1491.A4

Ireland

Ireland. Central Statistics Office. Tuarascáil ar staidreamh beatha. 1962– . Dublin : Stationary Off., [1962]– . Annual.   **CG251**

Contains data on marriages, including age at marriage and socioeconomic status, births, including multiple births, deaths and causes of death, and infant and fetal mortality.   HA1141.A36

Ireland statistical abstract. 48th (1982/85)– . Dublin : Stat. Off., 1986– .   **CG252**

Also called *Statistical abstract of Ireland.*

Compiled by the Central Statistics Office.

Continues *Statistical abstract of Ireland* (1949–81), which was a continuation of *Statistical abstract* (Dublin : Dept. of Industry and Commerce, 1931–1947/48).

Contains statistical data on population and migration, vital statistics, statistical tables on economic affairs and finance, national accounts and public finance, elections, and social and cultural activities. Subject index.   HA1141.A35

Irish historical statistics : population, 1821–1971 / ed. by William Edward Vaughan and André Jude Fitzpatrick. Dublin : Royal Irish Academy, 1978. 372 p. (New history of Ireland. Ancillary publications, 2).   **CG253**

Covers statistics on population, age groups, religious denominations, ages and conjugal status, and births, marriages, and deaths for Northern Ireland and the Republic of Ireland, from 1672 to 1971. Sources for all tables are noted. Extensive bibliography.

§ For information on the Ancillary publications series, *see* DC411.   HA1146.I74

Kirwan, Frank. Irish economic statistics / Frank Kirwan and J.W. McGilvray. 2d ed. Dublin : Institute of Public Administration, 1983. 225 p. : il.   **CG254**

1st ed., 1968.

A guide to the sources of Irish economic statistics and their methods of presentation and analysis. Ten chapters discuss population and vital statistics, manpower, agriculture, industry, foreign trade, national income and expenditure, prices and wages, taxation, transport and communication, and regional statistics. Bibliography; index.   HC260.5.K57

Italy

See also CG4.

Annuario statistico italiano. 1878– . Rome : Istituto centrale di statistica, 1878– . Annual (1927–).   **CG255**

1878–1955 called series 1–5. Series 1–2 issued by the Direzione Generale della Statistica.

Includes statistical tables for population, health and social welfare, education, cultural affairs, agriculture, commerce and industry, finance, economics, etc. Numerous supplements cover various specific subject areas.

Compendio statistico italiano (1927– . Roma : Istituto centrale di statistica, 1927– . Annual).

Serves as an abridged edition of the *Annuario statistico italiano*. Publication suspended 1943–45. 1946 issue called ser. 2, v. 1.   HA1367.A3

Sommario di statistiche storiche, 1926–1985. [Roma] : Istituto centrale di statistica, [1986]. 358 p. : col. ill.   **CG256**

Contains statistics covering 60 years, arranged in 19 chapters by subject. Presents detailed data on climate, population (including vital statistics and migration), health and education, cultural and social affairs and elections, labor and economic issues, and national accounts.

§ For coverage of earlier years, see *Sommario di statistiche storiche, 1861–1975* (Rome, 1976), with statistics ranging from 1861 when possible. Same arrangement and subject areas.   HA1374.S65

Sommario storico di statistiche sulla popolazione : anni 1951–87. Rome : Istituto nazionale di statistica, 1990. 503 p., 6 p.   **CG257**

One of numerous supplements to *Annuario statistico italiano* (CG255), covering various subject areas.

Primarily tables on population changes and movements within Italy, based on data from censuses, 1951–81, and general registers. Arranged in three chapters, further divided into 14 topics. Presents detailed information on population by age and sex, civil status, education, and residence, as well as data on births, deaths, and migration by provinces and regions.

Statistiche demografiche. v. 31, t. 2– . Rome : Istituto nazionale di statistica, 1986– . Irregular.   **CG258**

Continues *Annuario di statistiche demografiche*.

Issued in parts; some issues published out of sequence.

Title and issuing agency vary.

Based on general registry data, each part gives detailed information on specific demographic topics. Vol. 1, pt. 1 presents data on population of the preceding year, including natural movement of population and migration. Vol. 1, pt. 2 covers in detail internal migration, emigration, and remigration. Vol. 2, pt. 1 contains comparisons of a five-year period of births and deaths, followed by detailed statistics on births and deaths during the covered year, including causes of deaths. Vol. 2., pt. 2 presents detailed tables on marriages, separations and divorces.

Supplement to *Annuario statistico italiano* (CG255).   HA1363.A36

Liechtenstein

Liechtenstein. Amt für Volkswirtschaft. Statistisches Jahrbuch. 1977– . Vaduz : Amt für Volkswirtschaft, 1977– .   **CG259**

Contains information on geography and climate, and detailed statistical tables on demography, social and cultural affairs, and elections, including popular votes on specific topics.   HA1659.L46A33c

———————— Zivilstandsstatistik. Vaduz : Amt für Volkswirtschaft, 19??– . Annual.   **CG260**

Detailed statistics on marriages, births and deaths. Many tables go as far back as 1950 for purposes of comparison.   HA1659.L46A33d

Luxembourg

Annuaire statistique du Luxembourg. [Luxembourg] : Grand-Duché de Luxembourg, Ministère de l'économie nationale, Service central de la statistique et des études économiques., 1974– . Annual.   **CG261**

Began with 1974 issue.

Before 1940 the annual statistics were published as supplements to the *Annuaire officiel* of the Office de la Statistique Générale, 1925–30, under the title "Note statistique"; 1931–40 as "Aperçu statistique." Publication suspended 1941–45. Publ. as *Annuaire statistique*, 1964–69; as *Annuaire statistique du Luxembourg*, 1969–72; and as *Annuaire statistique rétrospectif du Luxembourg*, 1973.

Contains statistical data on geography and climate, population (including employment and vital statistics), agriculture, industry, banking and money, public finance, and social and cultural affairs. Arranged in topical sections, one of which is devoted to international statistics. Subject index.   HD1413.A55

Luxembourg. Service central de la statistique et des études économiques. Statistiques du mouvement de la population. [Luxembourg] : Le Service, 1966–1984? 2 v.   **CG262**

Kept up to date with replacement volumes, all of which bear the numbering "volume II," and begin coverage with the year 1966.

Consists of statistical tables in two sections: (1) natural movement of population, including births, deaths, marriages, divorces; (2) migration. Detailed description of the methodology and a summary in the introduction.   HB3606.5.L9

Statistiques historiques : 1839–1989. Luxembourg : Grand-Duché de Luxembourg, Ministère de l'économie, Service central de la statistique et des études économiques, [1990]. 616 p., [5] p. of plates : ill.   **CG263**

Issued on the occasion of 150th anniversary of Luxembourg's independence. Depth of retrospective coverage depends on the availability of data. Statistical information in 13 sections on population, national accounts, agriculture and forestry, industry, services, banks and money, prices, foreign economic relations, and various social affairs. Subject index.   HA1415.S73

Malta

Annual abstract of statistics / Central Office of Statistics, Malta. Valetta : The Office, [1961?]– . Annual.   **CG264**

Supersedes *Statistical abstract of the Maltese Islands*, 1947–1960.

Also available in microfiche (Westport, Conn. : Greenwood).

Statistical tables on demographic, economic, and cultural aspects of the area.   HA1117.M3A3

Demographic review of the Maltese Islands / Central Office of Statistics, Malta. 1959–. Valletta, Malta : The Office, 1959– . Annual.   **CG265**

Title varies slightly.

Title contains year of coverage.

Tables of statistical data on population by age, sex, and locale, as well as data on births, deaths, marriages, divorces, and migration. Includes projections for the 21st century.

Netherlands

Jaarcijfers voor Nederlanden = Statistical year book of the Netherlands. 1923/24–1967/68. 'sGravenhage : Centraal Bureau voor de Statistiek, 1924–[1970?].   **CG266**

Supersedes *Jaarcijfers = Annuaire statistique des Pays-Bas* (1885–97) and *Jaarcijfers voor het Koninkrijk der Nederlanden* (1898?–1922). From 1887 to 1921, each volume consisted of two parts: (1) "Rijk in Europa," and (2) "Kolonien"; from 1922 to 1939, the "Kolonien" section was continued as a separate publication by the Dutch East Indies (*Statistisch jaaroverzicht van Nederlandsch-Indie : new ser. of the Statistical annual of the Netherlands (Colonies), 1922/23–39*).

In Dutch. Also issued in French through 1939; in German, 1940–1941/42; and in English, 1943/46–1967/68.

Most tables give comparative figures for a 5-year period or longer.

Superseded by *Statistical yearbook of the Netherlands* (CG267).

Statistical yearbook of the Netherlands. 1969/70– . The Hague : Central Bureau of Statistics, 1971– . Annual.   **CG267**

Supersedes *Jaarcijfers voor Nederlanden* (CG266).

Inasmuch as it was felt that the yearbook was most widely used in foreign countries, the decision was made to publish in English. Includes a bibliography of sources of statistics.   HA1381.S75

Norway

Befolkningsstatistikk = Population statistics. 1986– . Oslo : Statistisk sentralbyrå, 1987– . Annual.   **CG268**

Continues: *Folkemengden etter alder og ekteskapelig status = Population by age and marital status* (ceased with 1984).

In English and Norwegian.

Issued in three parts: (1) population by country/region and municipality; (2) population by sex, age and marital status, with data on foreign population residing in Norway presented separately; (3) survey: births, deaths, marriages, and divorces (including rates), migration, citizenship/country of birth, and families, and tables of population projections.   HA1501

National population bibliography of Norway, 1945–1977 : with an addendum for 1978–1982 / ed. by Bjørn Moen. Oslo : Publ. for the International Union for the Scientific Study of Population by the Central Bureau of Statistics of Norway, 1984. 112 p.   **CG269**

An annotated bibliography covering the period 1945–77; the addendum lacks annotations. Arranged by subject, then alphabetically by author within each subject. Author index.

An identical publication was issued in the official statistical series "Rapporter fra Statistisk sentralbyra."   Z7164.D3N376

Norway. Statistisk sentralbyrå. Historiske tabeller over folkemengde, giftermål og dødsfall 1911–1976 = Historical tables on population, marriages and deaths 1911–1976. Oslo : Statistisk sentralbyrå : [i kommisjon H. Aschehoug], 1978. 135 p. (Norges offisielle statistikk, A 986).   **CG270**

Contains tables with data on the population by sex, age, and marital status. The marriage tables show first marriages as well as marriages of previously married persons. The tables of deaths are arranged by sex, age, and marital status.   HA1501A, nr. 986

Statistisk årbok = Statistical yearbook of Norway. 83. årg. (1964)– . Oslo : Statistisk sentralbyrå, 1964– .   **CG271**

Continues *Statistisk årbok for Kongeriket Norge* (1880–1933) and *Statistisk årbok for Norge*, publ. by the Statistisk Centralbyrå (1934–1963). Title varies; 1946–63: *Norges offisielle statistikk.*

In Norwegian and English.

Issued as part of the official statistical series "Norges offisielle statistikk."

Includes demographic, economic, social, and cultural data. Many tables include comparative figures from earlier years. Includes an international section.

Poland

Bibliografia polskiego piśmiennictwa demograficznego 1945–1975 / opracowała Joanna Górska ; [materiały do bibliografii zbierali Wanda Folman ... et al.]. Warsaw : GUS, 1985. 551 p. : facsims.   **CG272**

At head of title: Centralna Biblioteka Statystyczna.

A bibliography of books, articles, and reports on theoretical issues and formal demography. Works in the first part emphasize Poland; in the second part are works published in Poland but covering the rest of the world. No annotations; subject and author indexes.   Z7164.D3B475

Groblewska, Celina. Bibliografia opracowań demograficznych z lat 1976–1991. Warszawa : Polskie Tow. Demograficzne, 1992. 260 p.   **CG273**

An unannotated bibliography of books, articles, and reports, including unpublished reports for the period 1976–91. Arranged in four parts: (1) population trends, including projections; (2) the demographic situation, and population and social policies; (3) spatial distribution, families and households; (4) list of demographic publications in the official statistical series "Monografie i Opracowania."   Z7164.D3G76

Poland. Główny Urząd Statystyczny. Bibliografia wydawnictw Głownego Urzędu Statystycznego : 1918–1968. Warszawa, 1968. 466 p.   **CG274**

A classified listing, chronological within sections, of Polish statistical publications.

Continued by:

Bibliografia wydawnictw Głównego Urzędu Statystycznego, 1968–1973, opracowała Joanna Górska (1976. 392 p.).

Bibliografia wydawnictw Głównego Urzędu Statystycznego, 1974–1980, opracowała Joanna Górska (1988. 277 p.).

Bibliografia wydawnictw Głównego Urzędu Statystycznego, 1980–1989, opracowała Joanna Górska (1992. 332 p.). At head of title: Centralna Biblioteka Statystyczna im. Stefana Szulca.   Z7554.P6A5

Rocznik statystyczny / Główny Urzad Statystyczny. rok 1 (1920/21)– . Warsaw : Nakadem Głownego Urzadu Statystycznego, 1922– . Annual.   **CG275**

Title varies: 1920/21–38, in Polish and French, *Rocznik statystyki ... Annuaire statistique de la République Polonaise.*

Issued also in English (*Statistical yearbook of the People's Republic of Poland*, now *Polish statistical yearbook*, tr. by U.S. Joint Publications Research Service) and in French and German.

Publication suspended 1939–44.

Offers a wide range of statistical tables, many with comparative figures for recent years. Includes an international section.

    HA1451.A46

Roczniki statystyczne : demografia / Główny Urzad Statystyczny. 1990– . Warszawa : Urzad, 1991– . Annual.   **CG276**

Title from cover.

Continues *Rocznik demograficzny*, publ. annually 1966–89, with the first volume covering 1945–66.

Presents data in tables on the demographic situation and population structure; the natural movement of population, including marriages, divorces, births, and deaths; and migration.   HB3608.7.A33

Portugal

Anuário estatístico = Annuaire statistique. 1974– . Lisboa : Os Serviços, [1975]– . Annual.   **CG277**

Continues a publication with the same title publ. 1962–73 in two parts: (1) Continente e ilhas adjacentes; (2) Provincias ultramarinas.

From 1974 covers only Portugal, the Azores, and Madeira.   HA1575.A58

Estatísticas demográficas / Portugal, Instituto Nacional de Estatística. 1967– . Lisboa : O Instituto, [1967]– . Annual.   **CG278**

Issuing agency varies; Some issues have parallel title and text in French.

Detailed tables contain data on population and population distribution, life expectancy by age, natural movement of population (i.e., statistics on marriages, discontinuation of marriages including divorce, births including stillbirths), deaths, and foreigners living in Portugal.   HA1571.A28

Romania

Anuarul statistic al României. 1904– . Bucureşti : Direcţia Statisticei Generale, 1904– . Annual.   **CG279**

Title varies. Issues since 1990 have title (*Romanian statistical yearbook*) and text in English.

Frequency varies; annual since 1957. Some published 1904–39 cover two years. Publication suspended 1940–56.

In topical chapters covering geography and environment, population and labor force, income and prices, agriculture and industry, transport and trade, social and cultural issues. The last chapter offers comparative international statistics.

A concise version, *Statistical pocket book*, was published in various languages, 1960–71.   HA1641.A2

Spain

Anuario estadístico de España. año. 1 (1912)– . Madrid : Direccíon General de Estadística, 1912– . Annual.   **CG280**

Issuing agency varies.

Known as Series 2; the first work of this title was publ. 1859 1867. Publication suspended, 1953–42.

Arranged in two parts: the first contains data for the whole country; the second, detailed provincial data. Covers territory and climate, population and vital statistics, agriculture and industry, foreign trade, national accounts, public finance, elections, and social and cultural affairs.

A concise version is available as *Avance del anuario estadístico de Espana* (1988– . Madrid : Instituto Nacional de Estadística, 1988–), which replaces *Anuario estadístico de Espana, edicion manual* (1941–88). Both titles were issued for 1988.   HA1543.A5

Estadísticas básicas de España, 1900–1970 / [Amparo Almarcha et al.]. Madrid : Confedericíon Española de Cajas de Ahorros, c1975. 610 p.   **CG281**

Statistical tables for the country as a whole; additionally, some supply data for provinces. Lists sources.   HA1555.E78

Estadísticas históricas de España : siglos XIX-XX / Carlos Barciela ... [et al.] ; coordinación de Albert Carreras. Madrid : Fundación Banco Exterior ; Barcelona : Distribución, Edhasa/ Diagonal, [1989]. 632 p. : ill.   **CG282**

In 13 topical chapters, by various authors, with explanatory text followed by graphs, statistical tables, a bibliography and sources. Most tables represent a time series, some dating since the beginning of the 19th century. Extensive general bibliography; several indexes.   HA1554.E88

Instituto Nacional de Estadística (Spain). Zona de protectorado y de los territorios de soberanía de España en el norte de Africa : Anuario estadístico. Año 1 (1941) 13 (1955). Madrid : [Dirección General de Estadística?], 1942–57.   **CG283**

Comp. with the aid of the Seccretaría General de la Alta Comisaría of Morocco. Issuing agency varies.

Detailed statistical tables for Spanish territories and protectorates.   HA2231.A3

Movimiento natural de la población española / Ministerio de Economía, Instituto Nacional de Estadística. 1975– . Madrid : El Instituto, 1978– . Annual.   **CG284**

Continues: *Movimiento natural de la población de España* (Madrid : Talleres del Instituto Geográfico. Ceased publ. 1974).

Annuals for 1976–86 publ. in 3 v.; 1987– , publ. in 2 v., with v. 2 issued in 18 parts.

Vol. 1 contains vital statistics at the national level and by province, including tables of births, fetal deaths, deaths by age, sex, marital status, and occupation. Several annexes treat summary data, midyear population, trends, etc. The 18 parts of v. 2 (one for each region) have separate sections for births, deaths, fetal deaths, and marriages.   HA1543.A7

Sweden

Befolkningsstatistik. 1991– . [Stockholm] : Statistika Centralbyrån, 1992– . Annual.   **CG285**

Formed by merger of *Befolkningsförändringar* (1967–90) and *Folkmängd* (1968–90).

Issued in four parts: (1) population and vital statistics by municipality and parish; (2) internal and external migration; (3) population distribution by sex, age and citizenship; (4) vital statistics.   HA1523.S94c

Statistisk årsbok för Sverige. årg. 1 (1914)– . Stockholm : [Statistiska Centralbyrån, 1914– . Annual.   **CG286**

Title varies; also called *Statistisk årsbok*. Recent volumes also have title in English: *Statistical yearbook of Sweden*.

Continues *Sveriges officiella statistik i sammandrag*, 1870–1913.

In Swedish and French 1914–51; Swedish and English since 1952.

Contains information on climate and area, and statistical data on population; agriculture and industry; trade; prices and consumption; national accounts and public finance; and social and cultural activities. Includes a section on comparative international statistics. Indexes in Swedish and English.   HA1523.A46

Switzerland

Schweizerische Bibliographie für Statistik und Volkswirtschaft = Bibliographie suisse de statistique et d'économie politique / bearb. vom Eidgenössischen Statistischen Amt, Bern. 1. Jahrg. (1937)– . Bern : Schweizerische Gesellschaft für Statistik und Volkswirtschaft, 1938– . Biennial.   **CG287**

Frequency varies: 1938–74, annual; 1975– , biennial.

Introduction and explanatory materials in German and French.

Classified; beginning with v. 7, has an author index. Includes books, reports, and articles on statistics, primarily by Swiss authors, plus a selection of works by foreign authors.   Z7552.S42

Statistisches Jahrbuch der Schweiz = Annuaire statistique de la Suisse / hrsg. von Statistischen Bureau des Eidg. Departements des Innern. v. 1 (1891)– . Bern : Verlag des Art. Institut Orell Füssli in Zürich, 1891– . Annual.   **CG288**

In place of the yearbook for 1897, the *Graphischstatistischer Atlas der Schweiz, 1897*, was issued.

Some tables give figures for 30 years.   HA1593.A4

Switzerland. Eidgenössisches Statistisches Amt. Bevölkerungsbewegung in der Schweiz = Mouvement de la population en Suisse. Bern : Eidgenössisches Statistisches Amt., [1867]– .   **CG289**

Title varies; issued separately in German and in French, 1867–1929.

In French and German.

Frequency slightly irregular during the 1940s–1950s.

Begins with a section of general data in time series for the past six years, with a summary table from 1871. Separate topical sections deal with marriages and divorces, births, and deaths, including infant mortality. Appendixes offer detailed data on maternal age at birth and age at marriage, as well as life tables.   HA1593.S72a

Turkey

Devlet Istatistik Enstitüsü (Turkey). Türkiye istatistik yilligi = Statistical yearbook of Turkey. 1928– . Ankara : Devlet Istatistik Enstitüsü, 1928– .   **CG290**

Title varies; issuing body varies.

Not published 1954–58; resumed 1959.

Volume for 1928 in French only; to 1968 in Turkish and French; 1968– have title also in English: *Statistical yearbook of Turkey*, with text in Turkish and English.

Provides a statistical summary of various geographical, social, and economic aspects of the country.   HA1911.A3

Spitler, James F. Detailed statistics on the urban and rural population of Turkey, 1950 to 2000 / by James F. Spitler and Michael K. Roof. Wash. : Internat. Demographic Data Center, U.S. Bureau of the Census, 1982. 496 p. : map.   **CG291**

Presents statistics on size of population, and estimates of fertility, mortality, and migration for total, urban, and rural areas, as well as summary information on family planning, marital status, health, religion, education, literacy, labor force, household size, and gross national product. Glossary; bibliographic sources.   HA4556.5.S64

Union of Soviet Socialist Republics

Demograficheskiĭ ėntsiklopedicheskiĭ slovar' / glavnyĭ redaktor D.I. Valenteĭ ; redaktsionnaĭa kollegiĭa E.A. Arab-Ogly ... [et al.]. Moskva : Sov. ėntsiklopediĭa, 1985. 606 p., [4] p. of plates : ill.   **CG292**

At head of title: Nauchno-redaktsionnyĭ sovet Izdatel'stva "Sovetskaĭa ėntsiklopediĭa." Moskovskiĭ gosudarstvennyĭ universitet im. M.V. Lomonosova. Ėkonomicheskiĭ fakul'tet. TSentr po izucheniĭu problem narodonaseleniĭa.

An encyclopedic dictionary of demographic ideas and terminology. Its more than 1,600 alphabetically arranged entries cover not only demography, but also some relevant topics from related disciplines. Very strong Marxist-Leninist bias. Author index.   HB849.2.D46

The first demographic portraits of Russia, 1951–1990. Shady Side, Md. : New World Demographics, L.C., c1993. 129 p. : maps.   **CG293**

Companion to *The FirstBook of demographics for the republics of the former Soviet Union* (CG294), which is organized by topics. The volume for Russia is organized geographically, presenting all demographic and socioeconomic data on a single page for each of Russia's 12 regions and 73 administrative areas. It contains some data (e.g., ownership of cars, televisions, and telephones) which were not available when *The FirstBook* was published. Includes a reference map.

•Available in machine-readable form: *FirstPortraitsPlus*.

HB3607.F46

The FirstBook of demographics for the republics of the former Soviet Union, 1951–1990. Shady Side, Md. : New World Demographics, L.C., c1992. 1 v. (various pagings).   **CG294**

Arranged in 11 topical sections. Section A treats territory and population density and makes comparisons with U.S. areas. Other sections cover rural and urban population, nationalities, family size, education and internal migration, housing, working age, status, employment, and vital statistics. Each section contains statistical tables with data on the republic level, region level, and oblast level. There is no index, but the introduction offers a tabular listing that presents in alphabetical order oblasts and administrative centers with the geographical information needed to locate them quickly without using the enclosed large map.   HB3607.F47

Gel'fand, V. S. Naselenie SSSR za 50 let, 1941–1990 : statisticheskiĭ spravochnik. Perm' : Izd-vo Permskogo universiteta, 1992. 284 p.   **CG295**

Demographic data presented by year. Statistical tables on population distribution by age and sex, birth and death rates, and life expectancy.   HA1444.G38

Narodnoe khozĭaistvo SSSR : statisticheskiĭ ezhegodnik. [1955]– . Moska : Gos. Statisticheskoe Izd-vo, 1956– .   **CG296**

Issued by TSentral'noe Statisticheskoe Upravlenie SSSR.

The official statistical annual, giving data on the area, population, economics, industry, agriculture, health, education, and cultural and social affairs. Most important data include comparative figures for the years 1913, 1928, and 1940, pre-Revolutionary and prewar years.

Several jubilee editions have been published, of which the most recent containing historical statistics is: *Narodnoe khozĭaistvo SSSR za 70 let : ĭubileinyi statisticheskiĭ sbornik* (Moskva : Finansy i statistika, 1987. 765 p.).

§ An abridged version is publ. as: *SSSR v tsifrankh* (1959– . Moskva : Statistika, 1959– . Annual). Includes indicators of economic and social development, territory and population including republics, cities over 500,000, standard of living, radio and television, and institutions of higher education. Detailed table of contents at the end of each volume. Publ. in English, French, German, and Spanish versions. Title in English: *The USSR in figures… : brief statistical handbook.*

HA1432.N3

USSR : facts and figures annual. v. 1 (1977)–v. 17 (1992). Gulf Breeze, Fla. : Academic International Pr., 1977–92. Annual.   **CG297**

Presents statistical and factual data on various areas of Soviet life: government, Communist Party, republics, demography, armed forces, economy, agriculture, foreign trade and aid, health, education and welfare, communications, transportation, institutions, labor, and special topics. Data are derived from Soviet, American, and international sources; bibliographic references are noted for all data. "Future annual editions are planned as revised continuation volumes to UFFA/1977 rather than another year of the same information."—*Introd.,v.1*. A very useful compendium.

Continued by: *Russia & Eurasia facts and figures annual* (v. 18 [1993]–).

Bibliography

Bibliografiĭa po problemam narodonaseleniĭa : sovetskaĭa i perevodnaĭa literatura, 1960–1971 gg / pod red. D. I. Valenteĭa i E. IU. Burnasheva. Moskva : Statistika , 1974. 342 p.   **CG298**

A classed bibliography of 3,299 citations, dealing principally with the demography of the Soviet Union. Supersedes an earlier volume with the same title and by the same editors covering the period 1965–68 (pub. 1971). The same publisher issued *Bibliografiĭa po problemam narodonaseleniĭa, 1972–1975 gg.*, by the same editors, in 1977.

Continued by: *Literatura o naselenii : bibliograficheskii ukazatel, 1975–1978 gg.*, by A. G. Davydova, Valenteĭa, and Burnasheva (*see* CG299).   Z7164.D3B52

Davydova, A. G. Literatura o narodonaselenii : bibliograficheskiĭ ukazatel : 1979–pervaĭa polovina 1983 g.g / [ukazatel literatury o narodonaselenii sostavlen A.G. Davydovoĭ] ; pod redaktsieĭ D.I. Valenteĭa, E.IU. Burnasheva. Moskva : "Mysl", 1987. 286 p.   **CG299**

Continues Valenteĭa and Burnasheva, *Bibliografĭa po problemam narodonaseleniĭa* (CG298). Previous ed., 1981, had title *Literatura o naselenii* and covered 1975–1978.

Presents 2,219 citations arranged in 21 chapters covering a variety of topics (e.g., Theoretical and applied demography, The census, Migration, Marriage and family, Economics, Law). Each chapter is subdivided into narrower topics, with entries alphabetically arranged within sections. Monographs, journal articles, dissertations, conference proceedings are included. Entries are confined to Russian-language publications. Author index.   Z7164.D3D295

Heleniak, Timothy E. Bibliography of Soviet statistical handbooks, 1956 to 1991. Newtonville, Mass. : Oriental Research Partners, 1992. 271 p.   **CG300**

Previous ed., 1988, publ. by the Center for International Research, Bureau of the Census. Editions for 1979, 1980, and 1984 had title: *Bibliography of regional statistical handbooks in the U.S.S.R.*

Lists some 3,000 Soviet statistical handbooks known to have been published 1950–1991. In 18 chapters, for the 15 republics, Central Asia, and international handbooks. Geographical index.

Z7165.S65H47

Mashikhin, Evgeniĭ Aleksandrovich. Statisticheskie publi-katsii v SSSR : bibliogr. ukaz.: [1918–1972] / E. A. Mashi-khin, V. M. Simchera. Moskva : Statistika, 1975. 279 p. **CG301**

Pt. 1 gives a historical survey of statistics in the Soviet Union during the period indicated, the organizations and agencies concerned with their collection, etc. Pt. 2 is a bibliography of monographic and serial statistical sources (with titles of special issues) on the national, republic, autonomous region, oblast, and city level. Pt. 3 lists serial statistical publications by geographic area, on national and republic bases. A final section lists Soviet conferences and symposia proceedings on the subject. Z7554.R9M3

Research guide to the Russian and Soviet censuses / ed. by Ralph S. Clem. Ithaca : Cornell Univ. Pr., 1986. 323 p. **CG302**

In two parts: (1) general and topical essays (accompanied by bibliographies) that analyze data across the five censuses (1897, 1926, 1959, 1970, 1979); (2) Index and guide to the Russian and Soviet census, 1897-1979, which describes briefly each of the five censuses and provides an annotated and translated list of all the tables in each census. Each volume has a table of contents; a keyword index provides detailed cross-references to all five censuses. HB3607.R43

Yugoslavia

Demografska statistika. 1956– . Beograd : Savezni zavod za statistiku, 1956– . Annual. **CG303**

Continues *Vitalna statistika*, publ. 1950–55.

Arranged by topic in seven sections. The first section presents data on population (based on censuses 1921–81) and on population projections. This is followed by a section containing tables on births, deaths, marriages, and divorces, in time series 1979–89 and 1950/52. The remaining sections present detailed statistical tables on births, deaths, marriages, and divorces (all for the current year), and data on births and deaths by districts. HA1631.A334

Statistički godišnjak Jugoslavije / Savezni Zavod za Statistiku. G. 15 (1968)– . Beograd : Zavod, 1968– . Annual. **CG304**

Title varies.

Name of issuing agency varies.

Detailed statistics on a wide range of topics, with comparative figures for recent years.

The Federal Statistical Office of Yugoslavia also issues *Statistical yearbook of the Socialist Federal Republic of Yugoslavia ... English text* (Beograd, 1955–). This is a translation key to be used with original tables in *Statisticki godisnjak*; no figures from the tables are reproduced therein. HA1631.A34

Yugoslavia. Direkcija državne statistike. Statistički godišnjak = Annuaire statistique. knj. 1 (1929)– . Beograd : Opšta državna statistika. **CG305**

In Serbian, Croatian, and French. Some issues cover two years. HA1631.A3

Africa (by region)

African statistical yearbook = Annuaire statistique pour l'Afrique. 1974– . [Addis Ababa] : Economic Commission for Africa, United Nations, [1974]– . Annual. **CG306**

Continues: *Statistical yearbook* issued by the U.N. Economic Commission for Africa.

Contents: v. 1, North Africa; v. 2, West Africa; v. 3, Eastern and Southern Africa; v. 4, Central Africa and others in Africa.

In each volume, countries are arranged in alphabetical order, with tables grouped in nine chapters: population and employment, national

accounts, agriculture and fishing, industry, transport and communications, foreign trade, prices, finance, and social statistics. Statistics frequently cover several years. HA1955.U5

Sahelian countries

M'baye, Saliou. Sources de l'histoire démographique des pays du Sahel conservées dans les archives : 1816–1960. [Ouagadougou, Burkina Faso] : CILSS : Institut du Sahel, 1986. 328 p. **CG307**

For eight Sahelian countries lists statistical and census records, other economic and political records, military and prison documents, and maps. A historical introduction surveys the archives of French West Africa (A.O.F.) in Dakar, those of Sahelian countries not part of the A.O.F. (Cape Verde, The Gambia, and Chad), and of relevant materials published in Paris and now held in France. Z7164.D3M38

La population de la région du Sahel : bibliographie annotée, 1960–86 / préparée par le Réseau sahélien d'information et de documentation scientifiques et techniques, Institut du Sahel. Addis Ababa, Ethiopia : Unité de coordination, Réseau d'information en matière de population pour l'Afrique (PO-PIN-Africa), Division de la population (CEA), 1987. 210 p. (Population in Africa, no. 2). **CG308**

More than 350 annotated citations to literature published 1960–87 concerning population in the Sahel region (including Burkina Faso, Cape Verde, Chad, Gambia, Guinea-Bissau, Mali, Mauretania, Niger, and Senegal), arranged by subject. Indexes by subject, geographic area, institution, and author. Citations are in French or English. Z7165.S23P66

Africa

See also CG38.

Mitchell, Brian R. International historical statistics, Africa and Asia. N.Y. : New York Univ. Pr., 1982. 761 p. **CG309**
For annotation, *see* CG375. HA4675.M55

Bibliography

Gregory, Joel W. African historical demography : a multidisciplinary bibliography / Joel W. Gregory, Dennis D. Cordell, Raymond Gervais. Los Angeles : Crossroads Pr., c1984. 248 p. **CG310**

Cites 2,550 works on pre-1960 African population—age and sex structure, fertility, marriage, divorce, mortality, morbidity, migration, and urbanization; excludes official statistical sources. Arranged by geographical region, then broad topic; indexed by personal and geographical names, and detailed subjects. Z7164.D3G73

Harvey, Joan M. Statistics Africa : sources for social, economic, and market research. 2nd ed., rev. and enl. Beckenham, Kent, Eng. : CBD Research ; [Detroit : Gale], 1978. 374 p. **CG311**

1st ed., 1970.

A section on Africa as a whole precedes sections on individual countries. Each section contains: (1) information on the central statistical office and other organizations collecting or publishing statistical material; (2) principal libraries inside the country with statistical collections open to the public; (3) libraries and information services in other countries (particularly English-speaking countries) where the country's statistical publications are available; (4) statistical bibliographies; (5) the major statistical publications (grouped as general, production, external trade, internal distribution and service trades, population, social, finance, transport and communications). Indexed by organization, title, and subject.   Z7554.A34H37

Library of Congress. Census Library Project. Population censuses and other official demographic statistics of Africa (not including British Africa) : an annotated bibliography / prep. by Henry J. Dubester. Wash. : U.S. Govt. Print. Off., 1950. 53 p.   **CG312**

     Superintendent of Documents classification: C 3.2:P 81/17.

     § A companion volume from the Project is: *Population censuses and other official demographic statistics of British Africa : an annotated bibliography* / prep. by Henry J. Dubester (Wash. : U.S. Govt. Print. Off., 1950. 78 p. Superintendent of Documents classification: C 3.2:P 81/16).   Z7554.A34U5

Pinfold, John R. African population census reports : a bibliography and checklist. München ; N.Y. : H. Zell, 1985. 100 p.   **CG313**

     Lists, by country, the major national census publications, mid-nineteenth century to the present, of continental and island African countries; locations are indicated for major British, Belgian, French, German, Swedish, and Dutch libraries.   HA4672.P5

Algeria

Annuaire statistique de l'Algérie. 1926– . Alger : République Algerienne Démocratique et Populaire, Ministère de la Planification et de l'Amènagement du Territoire, Direction des Statistiques et de la Comptabilité Nationale, 1928– . Annual.   **CG314**

     Issuing body varies.

     Issued in three languages (Arabic, French, and English) beginning 1990.

     In eight parts, further subdivided into 13 chapters by topic. Data for population and housing, employment, economic activities, prices, income, consumption, and finance. A selection of comparative statistics from other countries is included.   HA2071.A32

Angola

Anuário estatístico = Annuaire statistique. 1956–1973. Luanda : O Direcção dos Serviços de Estatística, 1956–73. **CG315**

     Continues: *Anuario estatistico de Angola,* covering 1933–55.

     Issuing agency varies.

     Arranged in chapters by topic, presents basic demographic, social, and economic statistics. Includes a detailed table of contents called "index."

Benin

Annuaire statistique. no. 6 (1980)– . Cotonou : Institut National de la Statistique et de l'Analyse Économiquc, 1980– . Annual.   **CG316**

     Title varies: 1975–79, *Annuaire statistique de la République populaire du Bénin.* Preceded by *Annuaire statistique du Dahomey,* 1965–74.

     Offers detailed statistics on various geographical, demographic, economic, medical, and cultural aspects of the country.

Botswana

Statistical abstract. 1966–76– . Gaberone : Central Statistics Office, 1966–76. Annual.   **CG317**

Prep. by Central Statistics Office, Ministry of Development Planning.

     Also available on microfiche.

     In addition to the usual range of statistical tables, a list of available statistical publications is included in an appendix.

     § Complemented by: *Botswana* (Gaberone : Dept. of Information and Broadcasting, Publications Section, 1982?– . Annual).

     A useful handbook, with text and tables on geography, government, defense, the economy, health, education, transportation, housing and employment.   HA1977.B6A3

Statistical bulletin / Republic of Botswana. Vol. 1, no. 1 (June 1976)– . Gaborone, Botswana : Central Statistics Office, Ministry of Finance and Development Planning, [1976]– . Quarterly.   **CG318**

     Title from cover.

     Contains data on climate and environment, population, agriculture, commerce, industry, finance and national accounts, and social affairs.   HA4706.A26

Burkina Faso

Annuaire statistique du Burkina Faso. 1984– . [Ouagadougou] : Institut national de la statistique et de la démographie, 1984– . Annual.   **CG319**

     Offers statistical data on geography and environment, population and vital statistics, employment, health and education, agriculture, industry and finance, wages and prices.   HA4728.A18

Burundi

Annuaire statistiques / République du Burundi, Ministère du Plan, Service National des Études et Statistiques. 1962/65– . Bujumbura : Le Service, [1966?]– . Annual.   **CG320**

     Title varies slightly: Issuing body varies.

     A source for statistics on population, education, public health, economic conditions, etc.   HA2124.B86A25a

Cameroon

Cameroon. Dept. of Statistics and National Accounts. Note annuelle de statistique / Direction de la Statistique et de la Comptabilité Nationale. 1973/74–. [Yaoundé] : Direction de la Statistique et de la Comptabilité Nationale, Ministère du Plan et de l'Aménagement du Territoire, [1974?]– . Annual.   **CG321**

     General statistical data in sections on agriculture, industry, foreign trade, transportation, and finances, as well as a section of detailed demographic statistics. The latter includes data on age and sex distributions, spatial distribution, fertility, mortality, and migration.

     HA2141.D46a

Central African Republic

Annuaire statistique / République centrafricaine, Ministère du plan, des statistiques et de la coopération économique et financière, Direction de la statistique générale et des études économiques. [Bangui, Central African Republic] : La Direction, [1962]– .   **CG322**

     Published irregularly. Each volume covers several years.

     Presents information on geography and climate, and statistical data on agriculture, production, transportation, finance, and social issues such as health, education, employment, and justice.

     HA4717.A16

Chad

Tchad relance économique en chiffres / République du Tchad, Ministére du plan et de la reconstruction, Direction de la statistique, des études économiques et démographiques. [Chad : La Direction]. Annual. **CG323**

Replaces *Annuaire statistique du Tchad*, 1966–1975/76.

Presents statistics on physical environment, demography and labor force, economic, social, and cultural activities and issues. Also contains a brief description of the national government and territorial divisions.

Congo

Annuaire statistique / Direction du Service national de la statistique, des études démographiques et économiques. [1958/ 1963]– . Brazzaville : la Direction, [1964?]– . Annual. **CG324**

Formerly issued by the Commisariat Général au plan, Direction de la statistique et de la comptabilité économique. Publication suspended 1970–1973.

Data on physical environment, demography (including vital statistics), economic affairs (including public finance), and social and cultural affairs. HA4716.A568

Côte d'Ivoire

La Côte d'Ivoire en chiffres : annuaire statistique de la Côte d'Ivoire. 1975– . [Dakar : Société Africaine d'Édition, 1975?]– . Annual. **CG325**

In four main parts, subdivided by topical chapters: general; agriculture; industry; infrastructure. HC547.I8C63

Djibouti

Annuaire statistique de Djibouti / République de Djibouti, Ministère du commerce, des transports et du tourisme, Direction nationale de la statistique. Résultats de 1981– . [Djibouti] : DI.NA.S., 1981– . Annual. **CG326**

Contains data on environment and demography, economic and social topics (including standard of living), and public finances and national accounts. Detailed table of contents, but no index.

HA4691.A13

Egypt

Annuaire statistique / Gouvernement egyptien, Ministére des finances, Département de la statistique et du rencensement. Cairo : Le Dép., c1927–[1964?]. **CG327**

Continues *Annuaire statistique de l'Egypte*, which began publication as the *Statistical yearbook of Egypt* in 1909.

A wide range of statistical tables, many with comparative figures for five to ten years. HA2042.A5

Statistical yearbook, Arab Republic of Egypt. 1952/73– . Cairo : Central Agency for Public Mobilisation and Statistics, 1973– . Annual. **CG328**

Continues: *Statistical handbook, Arab Republic of Egypt*, for coverage of periods 1952/61–1952/72. Official name of country, 1958–61, United Arab Republic.

Contains information on climate and geography, and statistical data on population and vital statistics, agriculture, industry, commerce,

transportation and communication, education, health, and other social and cultural topics. Most tables offer time series for six or more years, with 1952 as the base year. Explanatory notes and graphs.

HA2041.S85

Ethiopia

Abdulahi Hassen. Annotated bibliography on the population of Ethiopia / prep. by Abdulahi Hasen, Tesfayesus Mahary, Jelaludin Ahmed. Addis Ababa, Ethiopia : Co-ordinating Unit, Population Information Network for Africa (POPIN-AFRICA), Population Division, UNECA, 1990. 207 p. (Population in Africa, no. 4). **CG329**

Contains more than 300 citations for books, articles, and reports publ. 1960–90. Arranged by subject, then author. Author, title, and subject indexes. Z7165.E74A23

'Ityôpyā, ōāmatoawi yastātistiks maṣhét / Yàltyôpyā ne. na. mangést, kaStātistiks [i.e. baStātistiks] ṭaqlāy ṣehfat bét yatazagāja = Ethiopia, statistical abstract / prepared by Imperial Ethiopian Government, Central Statistical Office. 1965–. 'Addis 'Ababa : Ṣehfat bétu, [1965?]– . Biennial. **CG330**

In Amharic and English. Issued by the Central Statistical Authority since 1986.

Frequency varies: annual, 1965–78.

Continues *Statistical abstract* 1963–64.

The first volume offers retrospective information to 1952. Includes an explanation of sources, methodology, limitations of data. Statistical data without methodological explanation is provided in the *Statistical pocket book of Ethiopia* published annually by the Central Statistical Office since 1968, with the initial volume offering retrospective data since 1961. HA1961.A3

Gabon

Annuaire statistique du Gabon / République gabonaise, Ministère de la planification et de l'aménagement du territoire, Direction générale de la statistique et des études économiques. 3. éd. (1976–1980)– . [Libreville] : La Direction, 1980– . Irregular. **CG331**

Previous editions (some without numerical designation) issued to cover 1964, 1968, 1970/75.

Provides general information on the country, including statistics on population, economic and social topics. Extensive explanatory notes. HA4715.A25a

Ghana

Ghana. Central Bureau of Statistics. Statistical hand book of the Republic of Ghana. Ed.1 (1967)– . Accra : [The Bureau], 1967– . Irregular. **CG332**

Statistical tables relative to the social structure and economic trends of the nation. HA1977.G5A23

Population of Ghana : an annotated bibliography, 1980– 1988. Addis Abba, Ethiopia : Coordinating Unit, Population Information Network for Africa (POPIN-AFRICA), Population Division, UNECA, 1988. 322 p. (Population in Africa, no. 3). **CG333**

Prep. by the Regional Institute for Population Studies at the University of Ghana.

Contains some 490 annotated citations for books, articles, and reports dealing with population issues. Organized by subject, then by author. Author, title, and subject indexes. Z7164.D3P833

Statistical year book. 1st ed. (1961)– . Accra : Central Bureau of Statistics, 1962– .   **CG334**
7th issue, 1969/70, published 1973. No more published?
Contains information on geography and climate, and statistical data on population, economic affairs, elections, and social and cultural topics.   HA1977.G6A264

Guinea-Bissau

Anuário estatístico / República da Guiné-Bissau, Secretaria de Estado do Plano e Cooperação International, Direcção-Geral de Estatística. [Bissau] : A Direcção, [1947]– . Annual.   **CG335**
Issuing agency varies.
Contains data on population (based on census returns), agricultural and industrial production, external trade, public finance, education, and health.   HC1080.A1A58

Kenya

Kenya. Central Bureau of Statistics. Statistical abstract. 1972– . [Nairobi] : [The Bureau], 1972– . Annual.   **CG336**
Continues a work by the same title, issued by the Statistics Division, Ministry of Finance and Planning.
Also available in microfiche (Westport, Conn. : Greenwood).
Offers current statistics on a wide range of geographical, social, and economic topics, with the agency usually noted as the source. Updated by the quarterly *Kenya statistical digest*.   HA1977.K4A22

Kenya population : annotated bibliography, 1975–85 / prep. by the Kenya National Library Service, National Reference and Bibliographic Department. Addis Ababa, Ethiopia : Coordinating Unit, Population Information Network for Africa (POPIN-Africa), Population Division, UNECA, 1986. 158 p. (Population in Africa, no. 1).   **CG337**
A broad bibliography with an emphasis on demography, but also including other issues connected with the population of Kenya. Entries for works published 1975–85, arranged by subject then by author. Title, subject, and geographical indexes.   Z7164.D3K47

Lesotho

Lesotho statistical yearbook / comp. by Bureau of Statistics. 1987– . Maseru, Lesotho : Bureau of Statistics, 1987– . Annual.   **CG338**
Title from cover.
Continues *Annual statistical bulletin* publ. 1965–1987 and covering 1963/64–1984.
Contains information on geography and climate, and presents data on population and vital statistics, agriculture and industrial production, national accounts, money and banking, and social affairs.   HA1977.B35A27

Liberia

Statistical bulletin of Liberia / Republic of Liberia, Ministry of Planning and Economic Affairs. v. 1, no. 1 (Jan. 1986)– . Monrovia, Liberia : The Ministry, 1986– . Quarterly. **CG339**
Title varies slightly.
Contains data on demography, economic, social, and cultural affairs. A part of each issue is devoted to detailed information on selected topics.   HC1075.A1S73

Libya

Libya. Maṣlaḥat al-Iḥṣa' wa-al-Ta'dād. Majmu'ah al-iḥṣā'iyah. 1958/62– . Tripoli : al-Maṣlaḥah, 1963– . Annual.   **CG340**
In Arabic and English. Title also in English: *Statistical abstract*.
Strongest in economic statistics, but also includes data on meteorology, demography, health statistics, and education.   HA2167.L5A34

Malawi

Malaŵi statistical yearbook. 1972– . Zomba : National Statistical Office, 1972– . Annual.   **CG341**
Continues *Compendium of statistics for Malawi*, 1966–70.
Also available on microfiche.
Presents statistics provided by government departments, statutory bodies, private firms, and the National Statistical Office. Some printed sources are given, but generally only the agency is listed.   HA1977.M3M33

Mali

Annuaire statistique du Mali / République du Mali, Ministrèere du plan, Direction nationale de la statistique et de l'informatique. 1960?– . [Bamako] : La Direction, 1960?– . Annual.   **CG342**
Issuing agency varies.
Title varies; earlier issues called *Annuaire statistique de la République du Mali*.
Introductory general statistics are followed by data on climate, population, economic resources, transportation and communications, prices, and finances.   HA2096.A15

Imperato, Pascal J. Mali : a handbook of historical statistics / Pascal James Imperato, Eleanor M. Imperato. Boston : G.K. Hall, 1982. 339 p. : maps.   **CG343**
Presents a classed arrangement of statistics, mostly from 1930–73, with introductory essays and bibliographic references. Health statistics are especially comprehensive. Indexed.   HA4727.I56

Mauritania

Annuaire statistique / Direction de la statistique et des études économiques. 1969– . [Noakchott? : La Direction, 1971]– . Annual.   **CG344**
Also available in microfiche (Teaneck, N.J. : Somerset House, 1981–) as part of the African official statistical serials on microfiche series.
Early volumes provided brief chronology as well as statistics on socioeconomic aspects of the country. Emphasizes the current two years, with some ten-year time series.
Supersedes an annual with the same title but different issuing agencies, covering 1963–68.   HA2096.5.A2a

Mauritius

Annual digest of statistics / Mauritius Ministry of Economic Planning and Development, Central Statistical Office. v. 19 (1984)– . Rose Hill, Mauritius : The Office, 1985– . Annual.   **CG345**
Title from cover.

Continues *Bi-annual digest of statistics* (1966–83) and assumes its numbering; this was in turn a continuation of the *Quarterly digest of statistics* (1961–66) and the *Yearbook of statistics* (1946–59).

Contains statistical information on population, including births, deaths and causes of deaths, fertility, and marriages. Also includes data on economic, social, and cultural activities.   HA2305.A15a

Morocco

Annuaire statistique du Maroc / Royaume du Maroc, Ministère du plan, de la formation des cadres et de la formation professionelle. Rabat : Direction de la statistique, [1982]– . Annual.   **CG346**

Issued by: Premier ministre, Ministère du plan, 1985– .

Continues earlier works with similar titles but variant issuing bodies.   HA2181.A3

Atlas démographique du Maroc. [s.1]. : Direction de la Statistique, CERED, 1990. 239 p. : ill., col. maps.   **CG347**

Maps, tables, and descriptive commentaries on population structure by age, population density, growth, vital statistics, education, health, labor, and housing.

Instituto Nacional de Estadística (Spain). Zona de protectorado y de los territorios de soberanía de España en el norte de Africa : Anuario estadístico. Año 1 (1941)–13 (1955). Madrid : [Dirección General de Estadística?], 1942–57.   **CG348**

For annotation, *see* CG283.   HA2231.A3

Niger

Annuaire statistique / [République du Niger, Ministère du Développement et de la Coopération]. 1962– . [Niamey : Ministère du Développement et de la Coopération, 1963?]– . Annual.   **CG349**

Presents data on geography, population, economic activities, finances, relations with foreign countries, planning and national accounts; most statistics have a 10-year time series.   HA2097.A27

Nigeria

Nigeria. Federal Office of Statistics. Annual abstract of statistics - Federation of Nigeria, Federal Office of Statistics. v. 1 (1960)– . Lagos : Federal Govt. Printer, 1960– . Annual.   **CG350**

Statistical tables on area and climate, population, manpower, agriculture, industry, trade, finance, education, etc.   HA1977.N5A22

Rwanda

Bulletin de statistique. Supplément annuel / Direction générale de la statistique. no. 4 (janv. 1977)– . Kigali : [Direction de la Statistique et de la Documentation], [1974]– . Annual.   **CG351**

Issued 1974–77 under similar title. Name of issuing agency varied.

Contains statistical data for the current year and some two years previous; a variety of social and agricultural statistics are unique to the annual supplement, whereas the *Bulletin de statistique* presents primarily economic data.   HA2124.R8A15a

Hategekimana, Grégoire. Bibliographie annotée sur la population du Rwanda / prép. par Grégoire Hategekimana, Alphonse Ngoga. Addis Abéba, Ethiopie : Unité de coordination, Réseau d'information en matiere de population pour l'Afrique (POPIN-AFRICA), Division de la population, CEA, 1991. 272 p. (Population in Africa, no. 5).   **CG352**

Emphasizes demographic issues. Contains books, articles, and official reports, mostly in French. Arranged by subject, and within subject by author in alphabetical order. Provides location for documents. Subject, title, and author indexes.   Z7164.D3H38

Sénégal

Sénégal. Direction de la Statistique. Situation économique du Sénégal. 1962– . [Dakar], République du Sénégal : Ministère des Finances et Affaires Économiques, Direction de la Statistique, [1963]– . Annual.   **CG353**

Offers statistics on demography, education, health, and a variety of economic topics.

§ Supplemented by a series which began publication in 1976 by the Société Africaine d'Édition, *Le Sénégal en chiffre : annuaire statistique du Sénégal.*   HA2099.A262

Sierra Leone

Annual statistical digest. 1968– . [Freetown, Sierra Leone : Central Statistics Office, 1969?]– . Annual.   **CG354**

Published as *Annual digest of statistics* (1980–1984?).

Presents geographical data, social and demographic statistics, and economic/price statistics, all subdivided for detailed topics. Sources indicated are usually an agency or ministry, but some printed sources are cited.

Somalia

Statistical abstract = Koobaha istaatistikada / prepared and printed by the Government of the Democratic Republic of Somalia, Central Statistical Department, Ministry of Planning and Co-ordination. No. 9 (1972)– . Mogadishu : The Department, 1973– . Annual.   **CG355**

In English and Somali.

Title varies.

Offers statistics in meteorology, population, education, foreign trade, agriculture, health, development program, banking, industry, etc.

Continues *Somalia statistical abstract*, nos. 1–7 ([1963–1970]), and *Statistical abstract*, no. 8 (1971) publ. in English and Italian.   HA2167.S6A2

South Africa

Johnson, Peter D. Detailed statistics on the population of South Africa by race and urban/rural residence, 1950 to 2010 / by Peter D. Johnson and Paul R. Campbell. Wash. : Internat. Demographic Data Center, U.S. Bureau of the Census, 1982. 455 p.   **CG356**

Superintendent of Documents classification: C 3.2:St 2/14.

Presents statistics on population, fertility, mortality, and migration, with summary data on family planning, marital status, health, religion, education, literacy, labor force, households, and gross national product. Glossary; bibliographic sources.   HA4701.J64

Official year book of the Union and of Basutoland, Bechuanaland Protectorate and Swaziland. no. 1 (1917)–30 (1960). Pretoria : Govt. Printer, 1918–61.   **CG357**

At head of title, no. 1– : Union of South Africa. Union Office of Census and Statistics.

An important yearbook, giving detailed statistical, descriptive, and historical information, with bibliographies and lists of government publications. Nos. 1–2, 1917–18, do not include Basutoland.

DT752.A3

South Africa. Office of Census and Statistics. Uniestatistieke oor vyftig jaar jubileumuitgawe = Union statistics for fifty years: jubilee issue, 1910–1960. [Pretoria, 1960]. 1 v. (various pagings) : ill., ports., maps, tables. **CG358**

In Afrikaans and English.

Tables for vital statistics, education, labor, agriculture, industry, etc. Table of contents and notes for each section, but no general index.

HA1992.A5

Suid-Afrikaanse statistieke. 1968– . Pretoria : Govt. Printer, 1968– . **CG359**

Continues the Bureau of Statistics' *Statistical yearbook* (1964–66).

In English and Afrikaans.

Includes tables (usually with comparative statistics for recent years) for population, health, education, labor, prices, agriculture, industry, trade, finance, etc. HA1991.A232

Swaziland

Swaziland. Central Statistical Office. Annual statistical bulletin. Mbabane : Central Statistical Office, [1966?]– . Annual. **CG360**

Volume for 1969 not published; 1970 ed. covers 1969 data.

Name of issuing agency varies.

Statistical data for demography, agriculture, foreign trade, industry and other economic activities, national accounts, education, health, and justice. HA1977.S9A24

Tanzania

Selected statistical series, 1951–1990. Dar-es-Salaam : Tanzania, Bureau of Statistics, President's Office, Planning Commission, [1993]. 113 p. **CG361**

Previous ed. publ. 1987, for 1951–85. Issued approximately every five years.

Arranged by topic, with tables for total population, employment and earnings, national accounts, agriculture and industry, transport and communication, some social affairs, and national parks. The only Tanzanian publication which makes possible a time comparison. No index. HA4697.S453

Statistical abstract. 1970– . [Dar es Salaam, Tanzania : Bureau of Statistics, Ministry of Economic Affairs and Development Planning], 1972– . **CG362**

Supersedes: Tanganyika. Central Statistical Bureau. *Statistical abstract* (1961–63), and similar works issued under other agency names.

Includes tables for land and climate, population, trade, transport, agriculture, commerce and industry, finance, employment, public health, education, etc.

Togo

Annuaire statistique / République togolaise, Ministère des finances, de l'Économie et du plan, Direction de la statistique. 1966/69– . Lomé : La Direction, [1971]– . Annual. **CG363**

Presents tables on demography, economic affairs (including national accounts and public finance), social and cultural affairs.

Updated by: *Bulletin mensuel de statistique*, 1952– .

HA4723.A22

Bibliographie sur la population et le développement au Togo : tirée de la base de données POPTOGO / Tilate Agboli ... [et al.]. Lomé : Unité de recherche démographique, 1992. 190 p. : forms. **CG364**

For annotation, *see* DD237.

Tunisia

Annuaire statistique de la Tunisie / Republique Tunisienne Secrétariat d'état au plan et aux finances, Services des statistiques. 1940/46– . Tunis : Le Service, 1946– . Annual. **CG365**

Continues *Statistique générale de la Tunisie*, 1913–39.

Issuing agency varies.

Contains data on population by sex and age, spatial distribution, vital statistics, agriculture and food, commerce and industry, national accounts and public finance, and social and agricultural affairs. Most tables offer time series for six years. There is neither an index nor a detailed list of tables. HA2071.T52

Uganda

Uganda. Office of the President. Statistics Division. Statistical abstract. 1957– . Entebbe : Statistics Division, Office of the President, [1958?]– . Annual. **CG366**

Issuing agency varies.

Offers current figures on population, trade, transport and communications, agriculture, public health, education, justice, and sectors of the economy. HA1977.U35A328

Zambia

Zambia. Central Statistical Office. Statistical yearbook — Central Statistical Office. 1967– . Lusaka : [Central Statistical Office], [1968?]– . Annual. **CG367**

Includes tables on population and housing, health, education, labor, agriculture, transport, commerce and industry, trade, finance, etc. HA1977.R48A33

Zimbabwe

Statistical yearbook of Zimbabwe. 1985– . Harare, Zimbabwe : Central Statistical Office, 1985– . Annual. **CG368**

Presents information on geography and climate, population, health care and education, national income and public finance, industrial production, agriculture, commerce, banking and finance. Many tables offer time series of up to ten years. No index, but each section begins with a list of tables. HA4702.A26

Asia (by region)

Asia yearbook. 1963– . Hong Kong : Far Eastern Economic Review, Ltd., 1963– . Annual. **CG369**

Title varies: 1960–62, *Yearbook*; 1963–72, *Far Eastern economic review yearbook*.

Introductory topical essays with statistics deal with the region as a whole; economic aspects (population, fishing, development banks, energy, investment, etc.) are emphasized. The country profiles which follow deal with political/social affairs, foreign relations, the economy and the infrastructure. There is a summary of the year's events for each country.   HC411.F19

Statistical yearbook for Asia and the Pacific = Annuaire statistique pour l'Asie et le Pacifique / United Nations. 1973– . Bangkok : Economic and Social Commission for Asia and the Pacific, 1973– . Annual.   **CG370**
Continues *Statistical yearbook for Asia and the Far East*, 1968–72.

In English and French.

General statistical tables for the ESCAP (Economic and Social Commission for Asia and the Pacific) region cover the most recent decade. These are followed by detailed country tables, covering from Afghanistan to Vietnam in alphabetical order. Presents data for population, national accounts, agriculture, industry, wages and prices, finance, and for some social issues. Annex I contains data on the Democratic People's Republic of Korea; Annex II lists principal sources of data, and Annex III contains conversion coefficients and factors.   JX1977.A2

Arab states

Bibliography of population literature in the Arab world / United Nations Economic Commission for Western Asia. Beirut : The Commission, 1980. 2 v.   **CG371**
Vol. 1 covers non-Arabic literature relating to population issues of the Arab countries; v. 2 covers sources in Arabic. Contains some 3,500 citations, 1960–1978. Arranged in six topical chapters, and within chapters alphabetically by author. Author index.   Z7164.D3B535

al-Kitāb al-iḥṣā'ī al-sanawī lil-bilād al-'Arabīyah. 1976– . al-'Qāhirah : Majlis al-Wahdah al-Iqtisadiyah al-'Arabīyah, al-Amānah al-'Ammah, al-Maktab al-Markazī al 'Arabī lil-Iḥṣa', [1976]– . Annual.   **CG372**
Added title page. *Statistical yearbook for Arab countries.*
Comp. by the General Secretariat, Council of Arab Economic Unity and Arab Central Statistical Bureau.
Provides data on geography, population, agriculture, industry, economic aggregates, services (health, education, tourism), and the Palestinians, usually with 5- or 10-year time series.   HA1950.5.K56

McCarthy, Justin. The Arab world, Turkey, and the Balkans, (1878–1914) : a handbook of historical statistics. Boston : G. K. Hall, [1982]. 309 p. : maps.   **CG373**
"The statistics in this book are Ottoman, published by the Ottoman government or drawn from the Ottoman Archives. They are intended to give a picture of the Ottoman state and people during the last century of the empire."—*Pref.* Includes tables relating to climate, population, education, justice, manufacturing, transportation, etc. Indexed.   HA4556.M35

Bibliography

'Abbūd, Muḥammad Fatḥi. Dalīl al-maṣādir al-iḥṣā' iyah fī al-bilād al-'Arabīyah. al-Qāhirah : Jumhūrīyat Miṣr al'Arabīyah, Ma'had al-Takhṭīṭ al-Qawmī, 1975. 416 p.   **CG374**
A country-by-country listing of statistical sources of Arab countries, with subject subdivisions. Includes Western-language sources. Index.   Z7554.A6A2

Asia (by country)

See also CG38.

Mitchell, Brian R. International historical statistics, Africa and Asia. N.Y. : New York Univ. Pr., 1982. 761 p.   **CG375**
A companion to the author's *International historical statistics, Europe* (formerly *European historical statistics*, 2nd ed.; CG189) and *International historical statistics, the Americas and Australasia* (CG70).
Presents comparative statistics for 80 African and Asian countries (including Cyprus and the Near East), derived from official governmental and intergovernmental publications, and supplemented by unofficial sources. Dates of coverage vary, but the majority of tables begin during the first half of the 19th century. Topics include climate, population, labor force, agriculture, industry, external trade, transport and communications, finance, prices, education, and national accounts.   HA4675.M55

Bibliography

Harvey, Joan M. Statistics Asia & Australasia : sources for social, economic and market research. 2nd ed. Beckenham, Kent, Eng. : CBD Research, [1983]. 440 p.   **CG376**
Describes the main statistical information sources for each country, including: directory information on the central statistical office and other statistics-gathering organizations; principal libraries with statistical sources open to the public; libraries and information services in other countries (usually English-speaking) where such materials are available; current statistical bibliographies; and major statistical publications. Indexes of titles, organizations and subjects.   HA37.A775H37

Bahrain

Al-Majmuâh al-iḥṣāīyah ul-sunuwīyuh / Dawlat al-Bahrayn, Wizārat al-Dawlah li-Shuūn Majlis al-Wuzarā, Idarat al-Iḥṣā. 1977– . [Manama, Bahrain] : al-Idārah, 1978– . Annual.   **CG377**
Continues: Bahrain. Maktab al-Iḥṣā. *Statistical abstract* (1967–76. 10 v.).
In Arabic and English.
Detailed coverage of climate, population and population projections, labor force, agriculture, industrial production (with a special section on oil production), trade, finance, and social and cultural areas. Some tables arranged in time sequence.   HA1950.B3A34

Bangladesh

Statistical yearbook of Bangladesh = Bāṃlādeśa parisaṃkhyāna barshagrantha. 1975– . Dacca : Bangladesh Bureau of Statistics, Statistics Division, Ministry of Planning, Govt. of the People's Republic of Bangladesh, [1976]– . Annual.   **CG378**
Published 1963–69 as *Statistical digest of East Pakistan*, 1971–74 as *Statistical digest of Bangladesh*.
A detailed presentation of statistics in terms of land and geography, social and economic conditions.
§ A more abbreviated presentation is available in the *Statistical pocket book of Bangladesh* (Bāṃlādeśa parisaṃkhyāna pakeṭa bai. Dacca : the Ministry, 1977– . Annual), in Bengali and English.   HA4590.6.A26

Bhutan

Statistical yearbook of Bhutan. 1987– . Thimphu, Bhutan : Central Statistical Office, Planning Commission, Royal Government of Bhutan, 1987– . Annual.   **CG379**

    Continues: *Statistical handbook of Bhutan*, 1985–86.

    Contains chapters on population (including population projections by region), and data on agriculture, industry, trade, finance, and other economic and social areas. Many tables include time series for five to six years.

Brunei

Brunei Darussalam statistical yearbook / Statistic Div., Economic Planning Unit, Ministry of Finance, Negara Brunei Darussalam. Brunei : The Division, 1988– . Annual. **CG380**

    Continues *Brunei statistical yearbook* (1972/73–86).

    Data in graphs and tables on population and vital statistics, agriculture, commerce, finance, industry, social and cultural affairs, health, education, justice, labor, and salaries and wages.   HA4600.68.A12

China

Chen, Nai-ruenn. Chinese economic statistics : a handbook for mainland China. Chicago : Aldine, [1967]. 539 p. **CG381**

    Official statistics, both national and provincial, relating to the economy of mainland China since 1949 have been compiled from Communist Chinese sources; and whenever possible, statistics for missing years are computed on the basis of the Communist Chinese definitions."—*Pref.* The concept, coverage, and classification of Communist Chinese statistical data are also explained. Indexed.

    HA1706.C48

China facts & figures annual. v.1 (1978)– . [Gulf Breeze, Fla.] : Academic Internat. Pr., [1978]– . Annual.   **CG382**

    Presents statistical and factual data on the People's Republic of China, with sections on: government, foreign affairs, the Chinese Communist Party, armed forces, demography, economy, energy, industries, agriculture, foreign trade and aid, transportation, science, culture and communications, health, education and welfare. Printed sources are indicated for most information, generally official Chinese, Japanese, or American titles. Also offers a chronology of the year, and bibliography of the year's books, articles, government documents, and reports. No index.   DS779.15.C48

China statistical abstract. 1988– . N.Y. : Praeger, 1989– . Irregular.   **CG383**

    Also available in microform (Wash. : Congressional Information Service).

    A revised English language edition of the China statistical abstract published by the Statistical Bureau of the People's Republic of China. Basic information, arranged in topical chapters that cover population and labor force; agriculture; industry; transportation; postal and telecommunications services; finance, trade and price; and some social and cultural activities. The 1st ed. contains data for 1987, with retrospective coverage 1978. Later editions present current data, with a few tables containing retrospective data.

China statistical yearbook / State Statistical Bureau of the People's Republic of China. English ed. Hong Kong : International Centre for the Advancement of Science & Technology ; Beijing : China Statistical Information & Consultancy Service Centre, c1988– .   **CG384**

    Also publ.: N.Y. : Praeger, 1989– .

    The volume for 1989 "contains national and provincial data in social and economic fields for … 1988, as well as major time series of national figures from 1949–1988 … a revised English language volume of the Chinese language edition *Zhongguo Tongji Nianjian 1989*,

published by the State Statistical Bureau of the People's Republic of China."—*Pref.* Arranged in 18 sections covering demographics, finance and economics, industry and commerce, trade and tourism, education, and culture and health. A section of explanatory notes describes concepts, terms, and methodology. Detailed table of contents, but no index.

    § A publisher's brochure adds that this is an improved English-language edition of *Statistical yearbook of China* (publ. 1981–87), which included an appendix for the statistics for Taiwan.

    HA4631.S83

The population atlas of China / comp. and ed. by the Population Census Office of the State Council of the People's Republic of China and the Institute of Geography of the Chinese Academy of Sciences. Hong Kong ; N.Y. : Oxford Univ. Pr., 1987. 217 p. : ill. ; 54 cm.   **CG385**

    Title on added t.p.: Chung-kuo jen k'ou ti t'u chi (in Chinese characters).

    "Published … in association with China Statistics Publishing House"—*t.p. verso.*

    More than 130 full-color maps arranged in sections: background maps, sex and age, population change, educational level, employment, and family, marriage and fertility. Based on 1982 census of China. Three appendixes provide assistance with county level data.

    G2306.E2P6

Hong Kong

Hong Kong annual digest of statistics. 1978– . Hong Kong : Govt. Print., 1978– . Annual.   **CG386**

    Issued by the Census and Statistics Department, Hong Kong.

    Contains statistical data in 20 sections, with emphasis on population and vital statistics, and on economic and social affairs. Includes information on sources and methodology.   HA1950.H6A2

India

Desai, Prasannavadan B. Annotated and classified bibliography of Indian demography / editors, P. B. Desai, R. P. Tyagi. Bombay : Popular Prakashan, 1985. 509 p.   **CG387**

    Sponsored by the Indian Council of Social Science Research, New Delhi.

    A selective bibliography of works published before 1970. 1,853 entries with annotations, organized alphabetically by author in seven topical sections: general demography; population size, growth, policy, projections, and problems; structure and composition of population; marriages, fertility, and family planning; mortality and morbidity; migration, urbanization, density, and distribution of population; methodology of demographic analysis. Subject index.   Z7164.D3D43

India. Office of the Registrar. Vital statistics of India. 1958– . New Delhi : [The Office], [1958]– .   **CG388**

    Arranged in two parts. Pt. 1 contains a review of the civil registration system and steps undertaken for improvement in civil registration. There is also a brief description of the Sample Registration system. Pt. 2 contains tables on births and deaths, infant deaths and maternal deaths, as well as birth and death rates.   HA39.I4A3

Statistical abstract, India. n.s. no. 1 (1949)– . Delhi : Manager of Publications, 1950– . Annual.   **CG389**

    Issuing body varies: n.s. no.1 issued by the Office of Economic Advisers.

    Supersedes *Statistical abstract for British India*, 1911/12–1939/40, issued by the Dept. of Commercial Intelligence and Statistics, and the *Statistical abstract* for 1946/47 issued by the Office of the Economic Adviser. Issued 1963–67 (no. 12–15) as *Statistical abstract of the Indian Union*.

Contains statistics on demographic, economic, social, cultural, and political affairs. Subject index.   HA1713.A732

Bibliography

Guide to official statistics. 3rd ed. New Delhi : Central Statistical Organisation, Dept. of Statistics, Ministry of Planning, Govt. of India ; Delhi : Controller of Publications, 1987 [i.e. 1988]. 156 p.   **CG390**
1st ed., 1979; 2nd ed., 1985.
A comprehensive guide to official statistical publications. Describes publishing agencies, and analyzes contents of their publications. Topical arrangement; title index.   Z7165.I6G78

India. Office of the Registrar General. Bibliography of census publications in India / comp. by C. G. Jadhav ... ; ed. by B. K. Roy Burman. [Delhi : Manager of Publications, 1972]. 520 p. (Census centenary publication, no.5).   **CG391**
On cover: Census of India, 1971.
A chronological listing for India in general is followed by similar lists of publications for the individual states, the union territories, and countries formerly covered by Indian censuses.   Z3205.I85

Indonesia

Heilig, Gerhard. The population of Indonesia : an annotated bibliography with a review of recent demographic trends = Die Bevölkerung Indonesiens : eine kommentierte Bibliographie mit einem Überblick zur jüngsten demographischen Entwicklung. Berlin : Reimer, c1985. 164 p. : ill.   **CG392**
A selective bibliography of some 800 titles, with emphasis on works in English published in the last 20 years. Lists of keywords and of authors; keywords index; index by topics.   Z7164.D3H43

Statistik Indonesia = Statistical yearbook of Indonesia. 1975– . Jakarta : Biro Pusat Statistik, [1975]– . Annual.   **CG393**
In English and Indonesian.
Presents a descriptive analysis of geography and climate, and statistical data on socioeconomic characteristics of population, population distribution, and migration. Other tables contain statistics on economic affairs (including national accounts and public finance), and data on social and cultural affairs.
A condensed version has been published since 1957 by the same agency under the title: *Statistik Indonesia/Statistical pocketbook of Indonesia*.   HA1811.B57c

Statistisch jaaroverzicht van Nederlandsch-Indie : new ser. of the Statistical annual of the Netherlands (Colonies). Batavia : Dutch East Indies. Centraal Kantoor voor de Statistiek., 1924–40. 1922/23–1939.   **CG394**
Title page and text in Dutch and English.
1930–39 issues are pt. 2 of *Indisch verlag*, 1931–40. For additional information, see *Jaarcijfers voor Nederlanden*, CG266.   HA1811.A3

Way, Peter O. Detailed statistics on the urban and rural population of Indonesia, 1950 to 2010. Wash. : Center for International Research, Bureau of the Census, [1984]. 416 p.   **CG395**
Superintendent of Documents classification: C 3.2:St 2/16/Indone.
Contains statistics on the size and geographical distribution of population, estimates of fertility, mortality, and migration for the whole country and rural/urban areas. There is some information on socioeconomic issues.   HA4605.W39

Iran

Sālnāmah-i āmāri-i ... kishvar / Sāzmān-i Bārnāmah va Būdjih, Markaz-i Amār-i Īrān. [Tehran, Iran] : Markaz. Annual.   **CG396**
Description based on: 1351 (i.e., 1972).
In Farsi. English editions published irregularly under title *Statistical yearbook of Iran*.
Contains information on climate and geography, as well as statistics on population, including data on births, deaths, divorces, and marriages. Other tables present data on economic affairs, elections, and social and cultural topics.   HA4570.2.A25

Iraq

Iraq. Jihāz al-Markazī lil-Iḥsā'. Annual abstract of statistics. 1969– . [Baghdad] : Central Statistical Organization, Publications & Public Relations, 1969– . Annual.   **CG397**
Continues *Statistical abstract* (issued until 1966; issuing agency varies) and *Annual statistical abstract* (1967).
Title and text in English and Arabic.
A compendium containing statistical data on demographic, economic, social, and cultural affairs.   HA1950.I75A3

Israel

Israel. ha-Lishkah ha-Merkazit li-Statistiskah. Statistical abstract of Israel. 1949/50– . Jerusalem : Govt. Printer, 1951– . Annual.   **CG398**
Title and text in Hebrew and English.
Offers statistics on population, social and economic aspects of the country.   HA1931.A35

Roof, Michael K. Detailed statistics on the population of Israel by ethnic and religious group and urban and rural residence, 1950 to 2010. Wash. : Center for International Research, U.S. Bureau of the Census, [1984]. 780 p.   **CG399**
Superintendent of Documents classification: C 3.2:St 2/15.
Presents statistical data on rural and urban population including size and distribution, fertility, mortality, and migration. There are also projections by age, sex, and rural/urban residence.   HA4560.R66

Tenu'ah tiv'it shel ha-ukhlosiyah. 1965/1966– . Jerusalem : ha-Lishkah ha-merkazit li-statistikah. Annual.   **CG400**
In Hebrew and English (*Vital statistics* / Central Bureau of Statistics).
Presents detailed statistics on marriages and divorces, births (including illegitimate births), deaths, stillbirths, infant deaths and perinatal mortality, life tables and life expectancy. Includes list of official statistical publications.

Japan

Japan. Kōseishō. Tōkei Jōhōbu. Jinkō dōtai tōkei. 1932– . [Tokyo] : Kōseishō Daijin Kambō Tōkei Jōhōbu.   **CG401**
In Japanese and English. Title also in English : Vital Statistics of Japan (varies slightly).
Publisher varies.
Published in three volumes since 1981. Vols. 1–2 present detailed statistical tables on births and deaths, marriages and divorces. Vol. 3 is concerned with mortality, infant deaths, and perinatal deaths, with a strong emphasis on causes of death.   HA1831.S67a

Nihon tōkei nenkan = Japan statistical yearbook. 1949– . [Tokyo] : Sōrifu, Tōkeikyoku, 1949– . Annual.   **CG402**
In Japanese and English. To replace the *Statistical yearbook of the Empire of Japan,* which ceased with v.59, 1941. The 1949 issue attempts to fill the 8-year gap in statistics; from 1950 on, the issues concentrate on annual figures.   HA1832.J36

Statistical handbook of Japan. [Tokyo] : Statistics Bureau, Management and Coordination Agency, 1964– . Annual.   **CG403**
Earlier volumes issued by the Bureau of Statistics, Office of the Prime Minister.
A brief description, with statistical charts and tables, of modern Japanese economic, social, and cultural activities.   HA1832.S75

Taeuber, Irene B. The population of Japan. Princeton, N.J. : Princeton Univ. Pr., 1958. 461 p. : ill.   **CG404**
Sponsored by Office of Population Research, Princeton University.
A comprehensive work containing statistics from the 12th century to 1950, with projections to 1980. Annotated bibliography, p. 395–461, includes references to statistics for Taiwan, Korea, and Manchoukuo.
§ *See also* Yoshiharu S. Matsumoto's *Demographic research in Japan, 1955–70* (Honolulu : East-West Center, 1974. 78 p. [Papers of the East-West Population Institute, no.30]).   HB3651.T3

Jordan

Jordan. Dā'irat al-Iḥṣa'at al-'Ammah. Statistical yearbook / The Hashemite Kingdom of Jordan, Ministry of National Economy, Department of Statistics. 1958– . [Amman?] : The Department, [1958?]– . Annual.   **CG405**
Issued 1950–57 as *Annual statistical yearbook* and as *Statistical yearbook.*
Text in English and Arabic.
Contains demographic, economic, social, and cultural statistics. Detailed list of tables is followed by explanatory notes and definitions. No index.   HA4561.A22a

Korea, Republic of

Han'guk t'onggye yŏn'gam = Korea statistical yearbook. Che 8-hoe (1961)– . Seoul : Kyŏngje Kihoegwŏn, 1961– . Annual.   **CG406**
Continues *Taehan Min'guk t'onggye yŏn'gam = Statistical yearbook of the Republic of Korea,* publ. 1952–60.
In English and Korean. Also available in microfiche (Westport, Conn. : Greenwood ; Zug, Switzerland : Inter Documentation).
Includes basic statistical data on physical environment, population, economy, social and cultural affairs.   HA4630.5.A34

Han'guk Ūnhaeng. Chosabu. Economic statistics yearbook. Ed. 1– . Seoul : Bank of Korea, 1960– . Annual.   **CG407**
Title also in Korean; text in Korean and English.
Continues *Kyongje yon'gam = Economic review,* which covered 1949–59.
Most recently published by the Bank's Research Department.
Comprehensive statistics on the South Korean economy. Also includes information on the geography of Korea and some population statistics.   HC466.A1B222

Kuwait

al-Majmūʻah al-iḥṣā'īyah al-sanawīyah = Annual statistical abstract / Majlis al-Takhṭīṭ, al-Idārah al-Markazīyah lil-Iḥṣā' (State of Kuwait, the Planning Board, Central Statistical Office). al-Kuwayt : Manshūrāt Majlis al-Takhṭīṭ, [1964]– . Annual.   **CG408**
In Arabic and English.
Statistical data on population (including migrations and vital statistics), economic affairs and national accounts, and social and cultural activities. Detailed list of tables, but no index.

Laos

10 years of socio-economic development in the Lao People's Democratic Republic / State Planning Committee, State Statistical Centre. Vientiane : The Centre, 1985. 196 p. : ill. (some col.), map.   **CG409**
Available in microfiche from the Library of Congress Photoduplication Service.
Contains statistics on geography, agriculture, industry, trade, transportation and communications, population, and social and cultural affairs.

Lebanon

al-Majmūʻah al-iḥṣa'īyah al-Lubnānīyah = Recueil de statistiques libanaises. v.1 (1963)–8 (1972). Beyrouth : Direction Centrale de la Statistique, [1964?–1972?].   **CG410**
Originally biennial; annual, 1968–72.
In Arabic and French.
Offers data on climate, population, housing, agriculture, industry, health, education, and various sectors of the economy, with long time series.   HA1950.L4A35

Maldives

Statistical year book of Maldives. Male', Republic of Maldives : Ministry of Planning and Development, 1981– . Annual.   **CG411**
Title page also in Divehi; text in English and Divehi.
Presents data on population, economics, social and cultural topics. Covers the year preceding the one in the title, but also presents data for selected earlier years on national level and for administrative units. A detailed list of tables, but no index.   HA2300.A34

Malaysia

Buku tahunan perangkaan Malaysia = Yearbook of statistics Malaysia. 1984– . Kuala Lumpur, Malaysia : Jabatan Perangkaan, 1985– . Annual.   **CG412**
Continues *Siaran perangkaan tahunan Malaysia = Annual statistical bulletin, Malaysia.*
Provides detailed and comprehensive information on Malaysia as a whole and on Peninsular Malaysia, Sabah, and Sarawak. Presents data on physical environment, population, agriculture, manufacturing, banking and national accounts, and social topics.   HA1791.D45a

Official year book - Malaysia. v.1 (1961)– . Kuala Lumpur : Printed at the Govt. Pr., [1961?]– . Annual.   **CG413**
Issued in Malay as *Buku rasmi tahunan. Official yearbook,* 1963–69. Currently issued in Malay as *Buku rasmi tahunan Malaysia.* Volumes for 1961–62 issued by the Federation of Malaya.

A handbook with narrative and statistical data on all aspects of Malaysian society, politics, and economic conditions. Chronology; bibliography.   DS591.A27

Nepal

Nepal. Kendrīya Tathyāṅka Vibhāga. Statistical pocket book, Nepal. 1974– . Kathmandu : [The Bureau?], [1974?]– .
CG414

Includes the latest available data on area and population, agriculture, mineral production, education, health, etc., with some international comparative statistics.   HA1950.N5A14a

Pakistan

Finch, Glenda. Detailed statistics on the urban and rural population of Pakistan, 1950 to 2010 / by Glenda S. Finch, Paul R. Campbell, and James F. Spitler. Wash. : Center for International Research, U.S. Bureau of the Census, [1984]. 350 p.
CG415

Superintendent of Documents classification: C 3.2:St 2/16/Pakist. Distributed to depository libraries in microfiche.

For a general annotation for this series see Peter O. Way, *Detailed statistics on the urban and rural population of Indonesia, 1950–2010* (CG395).   HA4590.5.F56

Pakistan demographic survey / Federal Bureau of Statistics, Statistics Division, Government of Pakistan. 1984– . Karachi : Manager of Publications, [1987]– . Annual.   **CG416**

Contains statistical tables which are the result of a series of demographic surveys begun in 1984. Includes data on age, sex, rural-urban distribution, marital status, fertility, and mortality rates.
HA4590.5.A27

Pakistan statistical yearbook. Ed. 1 (1952)– . Karachi : Manager of Publications, 1954– . Irregular.   **CG417**

Issued by the Central Statistical Office of Pakistan, 1952–68; by the Statistics Division, 1974– .

Continues the *Statistical digest of Pakistan*, issued by the Dept. of Commercial Intelligence and Statistics, 1950.

Contains statistical data on demographic, economic, social and cultural affairs. Many tables present ten-year time series. Frequently provides a breakdown by province.

1972 ed. includes comparative statistics for 1947–72; 1982 ed. for 1972–82.   HA1730.5.P33

Philippines

Kinsella, Kevin G. Detailed statistics on the urban and rural population of the Philippines, 1950 to 2010. Wash. : Center for International Research, U.S. Dept. of the Census, [1984]. 492 p.   **CG418**

Superintendent of Documents classification: C 3.2:St 2/16/Philip.

For a general annotation on this series, see Peter O. Way's *Detailed statistics on the urban and rural population of Indonesia* (CG395).   HA4615.K56

Philippine statistical yearbook. 1977– . Manila : Republic of the Philippines, National Economic and Development Authority, 1977– . Annual.   **CG419**

Continues *NEDA statistical yearbook of the Philippines* (1974–1976).

Issuing body varies; 1991– , National Statistical Coordination Board.

Includes statistics on population and housing, vital statistics on births, deaths, infant and maternal mortality, and marriages. Other tables cover agriculture, industry, foreign trade, money and banking, and social issues. Gives data for the country as a whole and for regions and provinces. Most tables are in time series of various lengths.

Philippines. National Statistics Office. Vital statistics report. 1984– . Manila : Republic of the Philippines, National Statistics Office, 1987– . Annual.   **CG420**

Continues annuals of the same title, issued by the Bureau of the Census and Statistics prior to 1972, and by the National Census and Statistics Office, 1972–83.

Data in three sections on marriages, including age at marriage, live births, and deaths (including infant, fetal, and maternal deaths).
HA1821.N36a

Saudi Arabia

Saudi Arabia. Maṣlaḥat al-Iḥṣā'at al-'Āmah. al-Kitāb al-iḥṣā'ī al-sanawī. al-sanah 1 (1965)– . [al-Riyād] : Wizārat al-Mālīyah wa-al– Iqtiṣād al-Waṭanī, Maṣlaḥat al-Iḥṣā'at al-'Ammah, [1965]– .   **CG421**

Added title page: *Statistical yearbook—Central Department of Statistics.*

In Arabic and English.

Provides data for the most recent two years, with occasional 5– and 10–year time series. While most topical areas are covered, demographic statistics are notably absent.   HA1681.M37a

Singapore

Report on registration of births and deaths / by Registrar-General of Births and Deaths. 1980– . Singapore : Republic of Singapore, [1981?]– . Annual.   **CG422**

Continues in part *Report on the registration of births and deaths and marriages* (1966–79).

Provides data on live births, stillbirths, deaths (including causes of death), infant mortality, and neonatal, perinatal, and maternal mortality.

§ Companion publication: *Statistics on marriages and divorces* (Singapore : Dept. of Statistics, 1985– . Annual), which continues *Statistics on marriages* (1980–83. Singapore : Dept. of Statistics, 1981?–84), which itself continued in part the *Report* (above). Contains detailed tables and charts on both marriages and divorces. Pt. 1 deals with marriage trends and the characteristics of grooms and brides; pt. 2 treats problems of divorce.   HA1797.S5A37

Yearbook of statistics: Singapore. 1967– . Singapore : Dept. of Statistics, [1967?]– . Annual.   **CG423**

Presents data on climate and land utilization, demography, labor, agriculture, industry, power, etc., usually with a ten-year time series.
HA1797.S5A35

Sri Lanka

Peebles, Patrick. Sri Lanka : a handbook of historical statistics. Boston : G. K. Hall, [1982]. 357 p.   **CG424**

19th and 20th-century statistics derived from colonial, commercial, and national government sources are grouped in subject chapters with prefatory essays. Subject index.   HA4750.8.P43

Report of the Registrar General on vital statistics, 1981, Sri Lanka. [Colombo] : Dept. of Census and Statistics, Ministry of Plan Implementation, Sri Lanka, [1986]. 178 p. **CG425**

Tables of detailed statistics in four sections: population, marriages, births, and deaths. Tables presenting mid-year population cover 1977–81; all others contain data for 1981 only.   HA4570.8.R47

Srī Laṅkā saṅkhyāta nibandhaya = Ilaṅkaip pulliviparat tokuppu = Statistical abstract of Sri Lanka. 1973– . Kolamba : Janalkhana hā Saṅkhyālēkhana Depārtamēntuva; Rajayē Prakāśana Karyāṃśayen miladī labāgata hăka, 1975– . Annual.   **CG426**

Continues *Statistical abstract of Ceylon* (1949–1970/71).
Vols. for 1977– have English title: Statistical abstract of the Democratic Socialist Republic of Sri Lanka.
In English, Singhalese, and Tamil. Issue for 1982 publ. in English only.
Contains information on climate and area. Statistical data cover population and vital statistics, including life expectancy, agriculture, commerce and industry, national accounts and public finance, and social and cultural issues.   HA1728.C43

Vital statistics, 1967–1980, Sri Lanka. [Colombo] : Dept. of Census & Statistics, 1987. 2 v.   **CG427**
Contents: v. 1, Marriages, births, and deaths; v. 2, Causes of death.
Vol. 1 presents data on registered cases of marriages, births and deaths, including infant deaths. Vol. 2 contains statistical tables with data on causes of deaths according to international classification of diseases. Issued for coverage of a period for which vital statistics were previously unavailable.   HB3636.8.A3V57

Syria

Syria. Wizārat al-Takhtīt al-Qawmī. Mudīrīyat al-Iḥṣā'. al-Majmū al-ihṣāīya. 1948– . Damascus : Govt. Printer, 1948– . Annual.   **CG428**
Issuing agency varies.
In Arabic and English; vol. 1–2 in Arabic only.
Arranged in topical chapters. Information on climate and area is followed by statistical tables—some containing long time series—offering data on demography and on economic, social, and cultural activities.   HA1941.A32

Taiwan

Republic of China yearbook. 1989– . Taipei, Taiwan, R.O.C. : Kwang Hwa Pub. Co., 1989– . Annual.   **CG429**
For annotation, *see* DE265.   DS798.92.R46

Statistical yearbook of the Republic of China. 1975– . [Taipei] : Directorate-General of Budget, Accounting & Statistics, Executive Yuan, Republic of China, [1975]– . Annual.   **CG430**
Pt. 1 consists of statistical tables which are, in numbering and format, identical to those used in the U.N. *Statistical yearbook* (CG57); comparative figures for the period from 1946 are given as appropriate. Pt. 2 contains definitions of terms, sources of data, statistical procedures used in censuses and surveys, etc.   HA1710.5.A183a

Taiwan statistical data book. [1962?]– . [Taipei] : Economic Planning Council, Executive Yuan, Republic of China, [1962?]– . Annual.   **CG431**
Issuing body varies.
"'Taiwan' includes both the municipality of Taipei and the province of Taiwan unless otherwise specified."—*Pref.*   HA1710.5.T35

Thailand

Annotated statistical bibliography. 1984/1986– . Bangkok : National Statistical Office, Office of the Prime Minister, 1986– . Annual?   **CG432**
Supersedes the same office's *Statistical bibliography* (1961–1976–83).
Lists "publications pertaining to statistics printed or published by various functional government agencies, as well as state enterprises … ."—*Pref.* Arranged by agency or ministry. No index, but a lengthy table of contents.

Samoot satidt rai, Bpra tet Thai = Statistical yearbook, Thailand. No. 24 (2506 [1963])– . [Bangkok] : National Statistical Office, Office of the Prime Minister, 1963– .   **CG433**
Publisher varies.
In Thai and English. Volumes cover two to ten years.
Presents statistical tables in the fields of economics, public administration, and social matters.   HA1781.A3

United Arab Republic

Formed by the union of Egypt and Syria, 1958; dissolved 1961. *See* Egypt.

Australia and Oceania

See also CG38.

Statistical yearbook for Asia and the Pacific = Annuaire statistique pour l'Asie et le Pacifique / United Nations. 1973– . Bangkok : Economic and Social Commission for Asia and the Pacific, 1973– . Annual.   **CG434**
For annotation, *see* CG370.   JX1977.A2

Australia

Australia's population trends and prospects. 1984– . Canberra : Australian Govt. Publ. Service, [1984]– . Annual.   **CG435**
Formed by the union of: *Review of Australia's demographic trends* and *Population forecasts*.
Contains chapters on population and growth, population distribution, immigration and emigration, and projections. Bibliography; author and subject indexes.   HB3675.A98

Year book, Australia. no. 62 (1977–1978)– . Canberra : Australian Bureau of Statistics, 1978– . Annual.   **CG436**
Continues *Official yearbook of Australia* (1973–76) and the *Official year book of the Commonwealth of Australia* (1907–72).
Includes chapters on physical geography and climate, general government, defense, population, vital statistics, labor, overseas transactions, transport and communication, public health, public finance, education, industry, etc.   HA3001.B5

Bibliography

Checklist of nineteenth century Australian colonial statistical sources : censuses, blue books, and statistical registers / ed. by Ann E. Miller. [Kensington, N.S.W.] : History Project, Inc., [1982]. 69 p. (Historical bibliography monograph, no. 7).   **CG437**

"Australia 1788–1988 : a Bicentennial History"—*Verso t.p.*
A list of individual parts of the colonial censuses, as well as musters, and statistical registers included in the British Parliamentary papers. Arranged by colony or state, then by format.   Z7554.A77C48

Hagger, A. J. A guide to Australian economic and social statistics. Sydney ; N.Y. : Pergamon, 1983. 116 p.   **CG438**
A guide and bibliography to current statistical publications of the Australian Bureau of Statistics; should be used with that agency's *Catalogue of publications* for complete bibliographic information. The series is designed to extend D. H. Borchardt, *Australian bibliography* ([Rushcutters Bay, N.S.W.] : Pergamon, [1976]. 270 p.). Indexed.

New Zealand

Bloomfield, Gerald T. New Zealand : a handbook of historical statistics. Boston : G.K. Hall, [1984]. 429 p. : maps.   **CG439**
Based on published New Zealand official statistics from 1840 to 1975.
Statistical tables are arranged in chapters by topic. Data are presented for geographical features, population and vital statistics, Maori population, production, trade, transport and communications, finances, banking and national income, and social and cultural issues. Most data are presented in time series. Sources of data are indicated. Indexed.   HA3184.D55

Mortality and demographic data / comp. by National Health Statistics Centre of the Department of Health, Wellington. 1972– . Wellington : The Centre, 1972– . Annual.   **CG440**
Issued as a part of the *Health statistics report*, 1972–82. Continues pt. 1 of *Medical statistics report* (1964–71).
Contains detailed statistical tables on births, deaths (including data for the Maori population), and marriages.   RA407.5.N4N47b

New Zealand official year-book. v. 1 (1892)– . Wellington : Department of Statistics, 1892– . Annual.   **CG441**
Covers a wide range of descriptive as well as statistical information. Recent volumes include a list of special articles appearing in previous issues, and a select bibliography of New Zealand publications.   DU400.A3

Solomon Islands

Statistical year book / Solomon Islands Statistics Office. 1979– . Honiara : Statistics Office, Ministry of Finance, [1979]– . Annual.   **CG442**
Title varies: 1970–73, *Annual abstract of statistics*. Suspended 1974–78.
Presents statistical data on population (including census results and population projections), agriculture, industry, banking and finance, national accounts, and social and cultural issues.   HA4014.A3

Western Samoa

Western Samoa. Department of Statistics. Statistical abstract. 1966– . [Apia] : The Secretary to Government, Western Samoa, 1966– . Annual.   **CG443**
Title varies: *Statistical abstract of Western Samoa* (1966); *Statistical year-book* (1967–73?).
Presents data on physical environment, population by age and sex, external migration, population forecasts, births, deaths, marriages and divorces, economic activities, health, education, justice, and cultural activities.

CH

Economics and Business

In a field as diverse as economics and business, any list of reference sources must be suggestive rather than inclusive. This section therefore attempts to list sources the compilers have found useful, hence it will reflect their experience and preferences.

Because of the proliferation of titles and their increasing cost, guides to the literature of economics and business will be indispensable. Essential for general guidance are Lorna Daniells, *Business information sources* (CH2), Diane Strauss, *Handbook of business information* (CH334), and Michael Lavin, *Business information* (CH4). For access to statistical sources available from governmental and international agencies and from nonprofit and commercial sources, the indexes and microfiche collections *American statistics index* (CG96), *Statistical reference index* (CG99), and *Index to international statistics* (CG69) will be important. To stay aware of the increasing number of databases (online, CD-ROM, magnetic tape, and batch access) in the field, one of the database directories will be needed; perhaps the best is *Gale directory of databases* (AK208).

Since access to the holdings of other libraries becomes steadily easier through bibliographic utilities and through the Internet, the need for lists of the holdings of special collections is declining. Fewer bibliographies are therefore listed in this section than in previous editions of the *Guide*, but reference collections should retain printed sources, especially if they expect to support research use.

GENERAL WORKS

Guides

Ball, Sarah. The directory of international sources of business information. London : Pitman ; Philadelphia : Distr. by Trans-Atlantic Publications, 1989. 698 p.   **CH1**
"Covers business information sources with primary focus on companies, markets, finance, securities and economics"—*Introd.* Separate chapters contain directory listings for European business information brokers and Euro-Info centres, country data sources, industry data sources, online databases–background, and online databases–descriptions. Although print sources are listed, they are not described; the emphasis is on organizations and databases. Appendixes include directories of publishers of market research reports and database hosts and producers, a summary chart showing database country coverage and subject area, and international telephone codes and time differences. No index.   HF54.5.B35

Daniells, Lorna M. Business information sources. 3rd ed. Berkeley : Univ. of California Pr., c1993. 725 p.   **CH2**

1st ed., 1976; 2nd ed., 1985.

Still the classic guide to business information for business persons, students and librarians. "It is a selected, annotated list of business books and reference sources, with an emphasis on recent material in the English language."—*Pref.* Chapters 1–9 discuss basic reference sources; chapters 10–20, more specific areas such as corporate finance and banking. Chapter 21 contains a basic book list for the small office library. Indexed.   Z7164.C81D16

Information sources in economics / ed., John Fletcher. 2nd ed. London : Butterworths, [1984]. 339 p.   **CH3**

1st ed., (1971) had title: *The use of economics literature.*

An attempt by British librarians and economists "jointly to view the literature of economics and provide a guide to it."—*Introd.* Introductory chapters on libraries and literature searches are followed by chapters on types of resources—bibliographies, periodicals, documents of national governments and international organizations, statistics, bibliographic and numeric databases. Contains 13 chapters on various subject areas of economics, written by economists to suggest the most useful sources. Strong British emphasis.   HB71.I53

Lavin, Michael R. Business information : how to find it, how to use it. 2nd ed., new and expanded ed. Phoenix : Oryx, 1992. 499 p. : ill.   **CH4**

1st ed., 1987.

A selective guide, combining descriptions of major business publications and databases with explanations of some relevant business concepts. Detailed coverage of major business information sources, enhanced by the inclusion of sample pages from some sources. Bibliographies; title and subject indexes.   HF5356.L36

Pagell, Ruth A. International business information : how to find it, how to use it / by Ruth A. Pagell and Michael Halperin. Phoenix : Oryx, 1994. 371 p. : ill.   **CH5**

"Describes key international business publications and databases, and provides the subject background needed to understand them."— *Pref.* Most sources are English-language directories, yearbooks, reports, and electronic files that describe companies, industries, markets and international transactions. Extensively illustrated with examples and tables. Appendixes; title and subject index.   HF54.5.P33

Scanlan, Jean M. Business online : the professional's guide to electronic information sources / Jean M. Scanlan, Ulla de Stricker, Anne Conway Fernald. N. Y. : Wiley, c1989. 368 p. : ill.   **CH6**

Combines an introduction to basic online searching and practical information about selecting hardware and vendors with descriptions of selected databases, grouped by subject (Company; News; Management, marketing and industry; Legal and tax; Accounting, economic and demographic; Patent and trademark). Discussion is enhanced by numerous examples, sample searches, and screen prints. CD-ROMs and electronic mail and messaging services receive brief coverage. Also includes a directory of online services, CD-ROM producers and distributors, gateways, and electronic mail services. Indexed.

HF5548.2.S2635

Bibliography

Baker Library. Harvard Business School core collection. 1970/71– . Boston, Mass. : Baker Library, Harvard Business School : distr. by Harvard Business School Pr., 1970– . Annual.   **CH7**

Publ. 1970/71–1987/88 as *Core collection.* None publ. 1988/89.

Baker Library's Core Collection is intended for the student wishing to browse in a small, open-shelf collection of recent books in business and related fields. Based on reading and reserve lists from the School; regularly weeded and updated. Kept up to date by the monthly *Recent additions to Baker Library.*   Z7164.C81H265

The basic business library : core resources / ed. by Bernard S. Schlessinger ; Rashelle S. Karp and Virginia S. Vocelli, associate editors. 2nd ed. Phoenix : Oryx, 1989. 278 p.   **CH8**

1st ed., 1983.

In three parts: (1) updated list of printed business reference sources for small and medium-sized libraries (with critical annotations); (2) bibliography of business reference and business libraries literature, 1976–87; (3) essays on business reference sources and services. Indexed.

A new edition is planned for 1995.   Z675.B8B37

Bibliographie der Wirtschaftswissenschaften. Göttingen : Vandenhoeck & Ruprecht, [1971]–1991.   **CH9**

Began with Jahrg. 60 (N.F., Jahrg. 19).

Superseded the *Bibliographie der Sozialwissenschaften* (Göttingen : Vandenhoeck & Ruprecht, 1906–68) and continued its numbering.

A classified listing of books, parts of books, and periodical articles in many languages. Separate indexes of subjects and of names and titles. Entries drawn from several hundred periodicals and series, which were regularly gleaned for relevant articles. Each annual volume published in two parts, with individual subject and name indexes.

Z7164.E2B5187

Black, Robert Dionysius Collison. A catalogue of pamphlets on economic subjects published between 1750 and 1900 and now housed in Irish libraries. N.Y. : Kelley, 1969. 632 p.

CH10

Comprises a union catalog of "pamphlets of economic interest published anywhere between the 1st January, 1750 and the 31st December, 1900" (*Introd.*) and now housed in one or more of the 17 cooperating libraries. Chronological arrangement with author and title indexes.   Z7164.E2B6

Braeuer, Walter. Handbuch zur Geschichte der Volkswirtschaftslehre : ein bibliographisches Nachschlagewerk. Frankfurt am Main : Klostermann, [1952]. 224 p.   **CH11**

An international biobibliography of the history of political economy from ancient and medieval times to the modern day, with biographical sketches of important economists. Includes books, dissertations, and periodical articles.

Business and economics books, 1876–1983. N.Y. : Bowker, [1983]. 4 v.   **CH12**

Contents: v. 1–3, Subject index; v. 4, Author index, Title index.

More than 143,000 titles published and distributed in the United States are organized by Library of Congress subject headings. Complete bibliographic information appears under subject; author and title indexes provide page references to the main entries in the subject section.   Z7164.C81B927

Business library review. 1990– . N.Y. : Gordon and Breach Science Publ., 1990– . Quarterly.   **CH13**

Continues *The Wall Street review of books* (v. 1–15. Pleasantville, N.Y. : Redgrave Publ. Co., 1973–90) and *Economics and business : an international annotated bibliography* (v. 21–30. N.Y. : Gordon and Breach, 1976–90), adding reviews of monographs, computer software, and audiovisual materials.

The bulk of each issue consists of critical reviews by scholars of about 20–30 titles. The remaining section, Selected titles, lists alphabetically titles from the first section with annotations describing additional works, following the format of *Economics and business.*

Economic books : current selections. v.1 (Mar. 1974)–18 (1991). Clifton, N.J. : Kelley, 1974–1991. Quarterly.   **CH14**

A publication of the Dept. of Economics and the University Libraries of the University of Pittsburgh.

Annotates English-language books, and indicates suitability for libraries of various sizes. Classed subject arrangement; author index.

Z7164.E2E2

Goldsmiths'-Kress Library of Economic Literature : a consolidated guide to Segment I–III of the microform collection. Woodbridge, Conn. : Research Publications, 1976–89. 7 v. **CH15**

Contents: v. 1, Through 1720; v. 2, 1721–76; v. 3, 1777–1800; v. 4, 1801–20; v. 5, 1820–31; v. 6, 1832–50; v. 7, Supplement to monographs through 1800.

An index and guide to the publisher's microform set, *Goldsmiths'-Kress Library of Economic Literature* [microform] (1974–), whose reels cover: Segment 1, Printed books through 1800; Segment 2, Printed books, 1801–50; Segment 3, Serials and periodicals.

Based on two major bibliographies in economics:

(1) *Catalogue of the Goldsmiths' Library of Economic Literature*, comp. by Margaret Canney and David Knott (London : Cambridge Univ. Pr., 1970–83. 4 v.).

Contents: v. 1, Printed books to 1800; v. 2, Printed books 1801–1850; v. 3, Additions to the printed books to 1850. Periodicals. Manuscripts; v. 4, Index, comp. by Margaret Canney and Joan M. Gibbs. Vol. 3–4 publ. by Athlone Pr. for the Univ. of London Library.

The completed set records about 40,000 books printed before 1851, periodicals that began publication before 1851, manuscripts, and autograph letters. The collection is one of the world's finest for early works in economics.

(2) Kress Library of Business and Economics, *Catalogue : with data upon cognate items in other Harvard libraries* (Boston : Baker Library, Harvard Graduate School of Business Administration, [1940]–67. 5 v.).

Contents: [v. 1], Covering material published through 1776; [v. 2], Supplement; covering material through 1776; [v. 3], 1777–1817; [v. 4], 1818–1848; [v. 5], Supplement, 1473–1848.

Arranged chronologically, with alphabetical index of authors and anonymous titles.

The Research Publications guide conflates titles from the Goldsmiths' and Kress catalogs and follows the chronological/subject arrangement of Goldsmiths'. The printed books, manuscripts, and serials are listed (and filmed) in chronological order; subject classifications include agricutlrue, corn laws, population, trades and manufacturers, commerce, colonies, finance, transport, social conditions, slavery, politics, and socialism. Entries give reel numbers.   Z7164.E2G64

Harvard University. Library. Economics and economics periodicals. Cambridge : distr. by Harvard Univ. Pr., 1970. 2 v. (Widener Library shelflist, 23–24). **CH16**

For a note on the series, *see* AA115.

Contents: v. 1, Classification schedule, classified listing by call number, chronological listing; v. 2, Author and title listing

Lists "over 65,000 books and periodicals including works on economic theory, economic history and conditions, transportation and communications, commerce, and finance as well as on more specialized aspects of economics such as demography, corporations, money, taxation, insurance, etc."—*Pref.*   Z7164.E2H37

Hollander, Jacob Harry. The economic library of Jacob H. Hollander / comp. by Elsie A. G. Marsh. Baltimore : [J. H. Furst Co.], 1937. 324 p. **CH17**

3,860 titles, chronologically arranged, 1574–1936. Particularly rich in 18th-century English tracts.   Z997.H73

Hutchinson, William Kenneth. History of economic analysis : a guide to information sources. Detroit : Gale, [1976]. 243 p. (Economics information guide series, 3). **CH18**

A introductory sourcebook on the history of economic analysis, 1600–1940. Each chapter is devoted to a major school of thought: forerunners of classical economics, classical economics, inductivists, marginalists, U.S. economists, and 20th-century British economists. Includes an introduction, annotated major contributions to the field, commentaries on the major contributions, and contributions of lesser importance. Selected list of journals and organizations. Author, title, and subect index.   Z7164.E2H87

Krannert Library. A catalogue of rare books, pamphlets, and journals on business and economics in the Krannert Library special collection, 1500–1870 / comp. by John M. Houkes with Ljudmila T. Mursec. [West Lafayette, In.] : Purdue Univ., 1979. 357 p. **CH19**

Preliminary eds. publ. 1970 and 1974.

A chronologically arranged bibliography of about 5,000 books, pamphlets, and serial titles from the Krannert collection and other Purdue University libraries; government documents have been excluded. Name and title index.   Z7164.C81K75

Schleiffer, Hedwig. Index to economic history essays in festschriften, 1900–1950 / Hedwig Schleiffer, Ruth Crandall. Cambridge, Mass. : publ. by Arthur H. Cole and distr. by Harvard Univ. Pr., 1953. 68 p. **CH20**

Arranged by broad subjects (period and geographical division), followed by history of economic thought and business economics, and economic historiography), with indexes of authors and of proper names.   Z7164.E2S36

Shackelford, Jean A. Urban and regional economics : a guide to information sources. Detroit : Gale, [1980]. 192 p. (Economics information guide series, v. 14). **CH21**

An annotated bibliography of about 600 English-language books dealing with aspects of growth and development, planning and policy, location theory, spatial analysis, regional models and techniques, etc. Indexed.   Z7164.R33S48

Sivolgin, Vladimir Epifanovich. Ekonomika SSSR : annotirovannyi ukazatel' otechestvennykh bibliograficheskikh posobii za 1817–1977 gg. 2e izd., perer. i dop. Moskva : GBL, 1979. 194 p. **CH22**

At head of title: Gosudarstvennaĭa Biblioteka SSSR imeni V. I. Lenina. Informatsionno-bibliograficheskii Otdel.

1st ed., 1965.

An annotated bibliography of bibliographies. 733 entries cover imperial Russia from 1817 through the Soviet period, ending in 1977. Indexed by personal and geographical names and by titles. Cross-references.   Z7164.E2S623

United Nations Library (Geneva). League of Nations & United Nations monthly list of selected articles : cumulative, 1920–1970: economic questions / ed. by Norman S. Field. Dobbs Ferry, N.Y. : Oceana, 1973–75. 6 v. **CH23**

Contents: v. 1, Economic conditions, 1920–1955; v. 2, Economic conditions, 1956–1970, Economic conditions—Food and agriculture, 1920–1955; v. 3, Economic conditions—Food and agriculture, 1956–1970, Economic conditions—Textiles, mining, coal, metals, 1920–1970; v. 4, Economic conditions—Petroleum, 1920–1970, Economic conditions—Miscellaneous industries, 1920–1970; v. 5, Commercial policy, 1920–1970; v. 6, Economic policy, 1920–1970.

Arranged by subject and country in chronological order; compiled from the card file used to issue the Library's *Liste mensuelle d'articles sélectionnés*.   Z7164.E2U445

University of Kansas. Libraries. Descriptive catalog of the history of economics collection, (1850–1930). Boston : G.K. Hall, 1984. 2 v. **CH24**

A dictionary catalog of the collection of some 10,000 titles, described by a former curator of Harvard University's Kress Library of Business and Economics as "unmatched elsewhere" (*Introd.*) for its post-1800 resources. Strong in international materials; about 65% in non-English languages.   HB85.Z99U54x

Periodicals

Business journals of the United States / ed. by William Fisher. N.Y. : Greenwood, 1991. 318 p. **CH25**

Contains descriptions of more than 100 serials, arranged alphabetically by title. The signed entries are in two parts: (1) an essay tracing the history of the publication and describing its current contents and special features; and (2) information such as where indexed, availability of microform copy or reprints, types of libraries where located and bibliographic notes (including title changes, volume and issue data, frequency and place of publication, and editors). Three types of publishers are represented—business school/university presses, professional associations/societies, and commercial publishers. Some government publications are included, but some are omitted (e.g., *Federal Reserve bulletin*, *Survey of current business*); newsletters and house organs are excluded. Three appendixes: a chronology of major U.S. business and economic events, with indication of the years in which specific titles began publication; and lists of journal titles by location and by type of publisher. Indexed.   Z7164.C81B978

Business serials of the U.S. government / Business Reference and Services Section, Reference and Adult Services Division, Amer. Libr. Assoc. ; ed. by Priscilla C. Geahigan, Robert F. Rose. 2nd ed. Chicago : Amer. Libr. Assoc., 1988. 86 p.   **CH26**

1st ed., 1978.

Arranged by broad subject categories: General, Economic conditions, Demographics, International business, Industry, Agriculture, Environment, Labor, Small business, Patents and trademarks, Grants and contracts, Public finance, Taxation, and Consumers. Entries include title, initial date of publication, frequency, previous title(s) and dates of publication, special features, Superintendent of Documents number, where indexed, and a paragraph-long descriptive and evaluative annotation.   Z7165.U5B88

Cabell, David W. E. Cabell's directory of publishing opportunities in business and economics. 5th ed. Beaumont, Tex. : Cabell Pub. Co., c1990. 3 v. (1829 p.).   **CH27**

4th ed., 1988.

Expanded to include more than 550 journals, the increased coverage reflecting growing interest in global issues (with additional new journals from Australia, England, Europe, and other countries) and in quantitative and economic topics. Indexed.

The publisher intends to divide this work into two titles: *Directory of publishing opportunities in accounting, economics and finance; Directory of publishing opportunities in management and marketing.*   H91.C23

Corporate magazines of the United States / ed. by Sam G. Riley. N.Y. : Greenwood, 1992. 281 p.   **CH28**

Describes 324 company magazines or "house organs." Each entry is a "historical essay on the magazine's founding, development, editorial policies and content."—*Introd.* Includes publication history, where indexed, and bibliography. Appendix lists titles by date founded and by location, and 273 other titles not profiled. Name index.   PN4888.E6.C67

Guide to special issues and indexes of periodicals / ed. by Miriam Uhlan and Doris B. Katz. 4th ed. Wash. : Special Libraries Association, c1994. 240 p.   **CH29**

Most titles listed are in the areas of business, commerce and industry. For complete information, *see* AD34.   Z7164.C81G85

Miller, A. Carolyn. Refereed and nonrefereed economic journals : a guide to publishing opportunities / comp. by A. Carolyn Miller and Victoria J. Punsalan ; with the assistance of Kenneth G. Rohm. N.Y. : Greenwood, 1988. 252 p.   **CH30**

"Designed to aid prospective authors seeking publication opportunities in economic journals."—*Pref.* Lists and describes some 200 journals in economics and related disciplines that accept manuscripts in English, presenting bibliographic, review/refereeing, and manuscript submission information for each. Also included are lists of style manual publishers, refereed and nonrefereed journals, and a chart comparing journals' reviewing criteria. Geographic and affiliations/keywords indexes.   HB63.M54

Sichel, Beatrice. Economics journals and serials : an analytical guide / comp. by Beatrice Sichel and Werner Sichel. N.Y. : Greenwood, 1986. 285 p. (Annotated bibliographies of serials, no. 5).   **CH31**

Lists, describes, and evaluates 450 titles drawn from economics and related disciplines. Each entry is in three parts: (1) bibliographic information, also giving databases and indexes in which included; (2) a narrative description discussing scope, content, authority, and when applicable, comparing it to related publications; and (3) a discussion of format, special features, and the like. A brief chapter presents an annotated list of English-language economics indexes and abstracts. Geographical, publisher, and title indexes.   Z7164.E2S49

Indexes; Abstract journals

•**ABI/Inform** [database]. Louisville, Ky. : UMI/Data Courier, [1971]– .   **CH32**

Available online, updated weekly, and on CD-ROM. Available only in machine-readable form.

Abstracts articles selected from an international list of business and management journals; also selects from economics, public administration, and law journals. Informative 150-word abstracts. The online version indexes 1,200 journals, of which about 500, considered core journals, are available in full-text format rather than as abstracts. The CD-ROM version offers three options: *Business periodicals global*, the most comprehensive; *Research edition*, about 800 titles; and *Select edition*, about 350 titles. The current subscription includes the most recent five years, with a backfile to 1971 available.

Abstracts of working papers in economics : the official journal of the AWPE database. v. 1 (1986)– . N.Y. : Cambridge Univ. Pr., c1986– . 8 numbers per year.   **CH33**

Frequency varies: 1986–89, quarterly.

More than 100 series of working papers are listed alphabetically by author with abstracts. Indexes for series, keywords, and permuted titles.

•Machine-readable version: *Abstracts of working papers in economics (AWPE)* [database] (N.Y. : Cambridge Univ. Pr., 1984–). Available on magnetic tape or diskettes, updated monthly. Also included in *Econlit* CD-ROM.   HB1.A27

•**Business dateline** [database]. [Louisville, Ky.] : UMI/Data Courier, 1985– .   **CH34**

Available online, updated weekly, and on CD-ROM, updated monthly.

Contains the full text of articles from more than 180 U.S. and Canadian regional business periodicals, newspapers, and business wire services. Useful for information concerning companies, individuals, and products and services that other databases may not cover.

•**Business index** [database]. Menlo Park, Calif. : Information Access Corp., 1980– .   **CH35**

Available online and on CD-ROM as *Business index on InfoTrac*, both updated monthly.

An index with abstracts to more than 700 business, management, and trade journals, and to *Wall Street journal*, *New York times*, *Asian Wall Street journal*, and *Financial times of Canada*. Began as a computer-output-microfilm index with the same title; now offered in various machine-readable versions. Online versions include *Trade and industry index*, an index with abstracts, and *Trade and industry index ASAP*, with indexing restricted to journals that provide the full text of articles. The CD-ROM version can be linked to *Business ASAP*, a CD-ROM of more than 400 business journals, or *Business collection*, a collection of business journals on microfilm. Magnetic tape versions are available on some OPACs.

•**Business Newsbank plus** [database]. New Canaan, Conn. : NewsBank, 1985– .   **CH36**

Available on CD-ROM, updated monthly.

An index with brief abstracts to more than 600 local and regional newspapers and to business periodicals. Entries refer to the publisher's *Business NewsBank* microfiche collection, which reproduces full text of the articles. Some entries include the full text of articles. Indexed by industry, company name, location, subject, and personal name.

Business periodicals index. v. 1– . N.Y. : Wilson, 1958– . Monthly (except Aug.), with annual cumulation.　　**CH37**

Continues in part *Industrial arts index* (v. 1 [1913]–46 [1957]), which split into this title and *Applied science and technology* (EA67).

Indexes by subject, selected author, and corporate name about 350 journals in business, finance and investment, advertising and public relations, accounting, insurance, labor and management, and economics. Includes book reviews.

•Machine-readable versions: *Business periodicals index* [database] (N.Y. : Wilson, 1982–). Available online, updated twice weekly, and on CD-ROM, updated quarterly. Beginning 1990, abstracts of articles indexed are available on *Wilson business abstracts* [database], available on CD-ROM, updated monthly.　　Z7164.C81B983

Canadian index. v. 1 (1993)– . Toronto : Micromedia, 1993– . Monthly, with semi-annual cumulations.　　**CH38**

Covers some 200 Canadian business periodicals, the weekly *Financial times*, and the dailies *Financial post* and *Toronto globe and mail*. For complete information, *see* AE118.　　AI3C34

Ecodoc : revue bibliographique trimestrielle publiée par le Reseau d'information en économie générale. no. 1 (mai/juin 1981)– . Paris : Centre de Documentation Sciences Humaines, 1981– . Quarterly.　　**CH39**

Issued under the auspices of the Centre National de la Recherche Scientifique.

Continues *Documentation économique*, 1934–Mars/Avril 1981.

A quarterly bibliography of French literature on economics, using the classification system of the *Journal of economic literature*; corresponds to the ECODOC database of the French FRANCIS online system. Offers about 350 French-language abstracts per issue. Indexed by document type, personal and corporate authors, descriptors, and geographic names. Annual index. Subject scope is international. Excludes socioeconomic and health data, employment, energy, agriculture, and transportation (which are covered by other sections of FRANCIS).

Z7163.E27

•**Economic literature index** [database]. Pittsburgh : American Economic Association, 1969– .　　**CH40**

Available online and on CD-ROM as *Econlit*, both updated quarterly.

Compiled since 1969 from the index portion of *Journal of economic literature* and since 1979 from the collective volumes of *Index of economic articles in journals and collective volumes* (CH42). Currently includes articles in more than 340 journals in economics (since 1984, some with abstracts). Beginning 1987, also includes books and dissertations, with abstracts. Beginning 1993, indexes some journals not indexed by the printed counterparts. In the CD-ROM version, coverage begins with 1984.

Economics working papers bibliography. Jan.-June 1987–Jan.-June 1991. Dobbs Ferry, N.Y. : TRANS-Media Publ. Co., 1987–1990. Semiannual.　　**CH41**

Continues *Economics working papers : a bibliography*, 1973–1986.

Publ. in assoc. with the Univ. of Warwick Library and the Center for International Studies, Univ. of Pittsburgh.

Content varies: 1973–76, economics working papers; 1976–80, social science working papers; 1980– , restricted to economics working papers.

International in scope. Author and subject listings with series index. Now indexed on *NetEc* on the Internet.

Selected papers in the series are available in a microform set with the same title, offered by the publisher.

Index of economic articles in journals and collective volumes. v. 1 (1886/1924)– . Homewood, Ill. : R.D. Irwin, 1961– . Annual.　　**CH42**

Title varies: v. 1–7 called *Index of economic journals*.

Frequency varies: v. 20 covering 1978 publ. 1983.

Contents: v. 1, 1886–1924; v. 2, 1925–1939; v. 3, 1940–1949; v. 4, 1950–1954; v. 5, 1954–1959; v. 6, 1960–1963; v. 6A, 1960–1963, Collective volumes; v. 7, 1964–1965; v. 7A, 1964–1965, Collective volumes; v. 8 (1966–), annual.

Lists articles in English from the principal economics journals of various countries—now about 340 titles. Arranged by a detailed classification scheme, with an author index in each volume. Full bibliographic information. Beginning with v. 6A (covering 1960–63), indexes collective works including festschriften, conference reports and papers, collected essays, congressional committee hearings and special committee reports for the U.S. and Canada, collections of English-language translations of foreign articles and essays. Updated by "New books" and "Subject index of articles in current periodicals with selected abstracts" sections of *Journal of economic literature*.

•The *Index* and the updates from the *Journal* are searchable online as *Economic literature index* and on CD-ROM as *EconLit* (CH40).

Z7164.E2I4812

International bibliography of economics = Bibliographie internationale de science économique. v. 1 (1952)– . London : Tavistock ; Chicago : Aldine, 1955– . Annual.　　**CH43**

Publisher varies; v. 1–8, Paris, UNESCO; v. 9, 1960– , issued as *Publications* of the International Committee for Social Sciences Documentation, as one of the series of the *International bibliography of the social sciences* (series title varies slightly). Since 1990, comp. and ed. at the British Library of Political and Economic Science and continues in part the *London bibliography of the social sciences* (CA13).

An extensive, classified list of books, pamphlets, periodical articles, and official government publications, in various languages, including Slavic and Asian. Indexes by author and subject (separate subject indexes in French and English). An associated publication is *Thematic list of descriptors—economics*, prepared on behalf of Unesco by the International Committee for Social Science Information and Documentation (London ; N.Y. : Routledge, 1989; *see* CE52).

Z7164.E2I58

International development abstracts. 1982/1– . Norwich, Eng. : Geo Abstracts, 1982– . Bimonthly.　　**CH44**

Covers the world literature on developing countries contained in more than 500 journals, books, conference proceedings and reports. Surveys agriculture, environment and development, economic conditions, finance and industry, tourism, labor and management, natural resources, and demography. Subject, geographic and author indexes.

•Available online as part of *GEOBASE* (CL30).　　HC59.69.I57

Wall Street journal : index. 1957– . Ann Arbor, Mich. : Univ. Microfilms International under agreement with Dow Jones & Co., c1957– . Monthly with quarterly and annual cumulations.　　**CH45**

Began in 1957; 1st annual cumulation covers 1958.

Includes *Barron's index*.

Each issue is in two parts: corporate news and general news. The annual cumulation is in two volumes: the first indexes corporate news and also contains the green pages, an annual index to articles in *Barron's*. Vol. 2 indexes general news and includes lists of special reports and daily Dow-=Jones averages for the year.

•*Wall Street journal* is available in full text on Dow Jones news/retrieval, and on CD-ROM from UMI.　　HG1.W26

World agricultural economics and rural sociology abstracts. v. 1 (Apr. 1959)– . Wallingford, Oxon [etc.] : CAB International Information Services [etc.]. Monthly.　　**CH46**

Preceded by Preliminary issue dated July 1958 which has title: World agricultural economics abstracts.

Frequency varies; quarterly, 1959–72.

Prepared Sept. 1969– by the Commonwealth Bureau of Agricultural Economics.

Abstracts of articles, documents, and monographs that describe economic aspects of agriculture worldwide. Includes development, environment, and natural resources; employment and income; prices, supply and demand, and marketing; international trade and finance; financial aspects of farm management; rural sociology including demography, migration, and social and cultural aspects of agriculture. Indexed by author and by subjects, which may have geographic subdivisions.

•Available in machine-readable form as part of *CAB abstracts* (EJ18).

Encyclopedias

The Blackwell encyclopedia of industrial archaeology / ed. by Barrie Trinder ... [et al.]. Oxford ; Cambridge, Mass. : Blackwell, 1992. 964 p. : ill., maps. **CH47**
> For annotation, *see* DA178. T37.B55

Block, Walter. Lexicon of economic thought / Walter Block and Michael Walker. Vancouver, B.C., Canada : Fraser Institute, c1989. 390 p. **CH48**
> Contains one- to three-page commentaries, presenting the views of market economists on some 176 economic and social topics, ranging from Aboriginal rights—land claims to Zoning. Examples used in the commentaries are generally drawn from Canada, but the discussion transcends national issues. Indexed, but lacks a bibliography. HB61.B574

Encyclopedia of American economic history : studies of the principal movements and ideas / Glenn Porter, ed. N.Y. : Scribner, [1980]. 3 v. (1286 p.) : ill. **CH49**
> For annotation, *see* DB42. HC103.E52

The Fortune encyclopedia of economics / ed. by David R. Henderson. N.Y. : Warner Books, c1993. 876 p. : ill. **CH50**
> Essays written by economists for informed general readers. Arranged in broad categories: basic concepts, economic systems and schools of economic thought, macroeconomics, economic policy and taxation, money and banking, economic and environmental regulation, finance and markets, and international economics. Appends biographies of Nobel Prize winners and others, excluding those born after 1920. Indexed. HB61.F67

The McGraw-Hill encyclopedia of economics / Douglas Greenwald, ed. in chief. 2nd ed. N.Y. : McGraw-Hill, 1994. 1093 p. : ill. **CH51**
> 1st ed., 1982.
> Written by experts for graduate level students in the fields of economics, econometrics, and statistics. Articles treat concepts (e.g., supply-side economics), institutions (e.g., International Monetary Fund), and historical periods (e.g., the Great Depression); biographical articles are not included. Revised and updated articles, with some new additions and some deletions from the 1st ed. Bibliographies; cross-references. Subject and name indexes. HB61.E55

The new Palgrave : a dictionary of economics / ed. by John Eatwell, Murray Milgate, Peter Newman. London : Macmillan ; N.Y. : Stockton Pr. ; Tokyo : Maruzen, 1987. 4 v. : ill. **CH52**
> Successor to *Palgrave's dictionary of political economy*, first published 1894–96. A sophisticated encyclopedic coverage of modern economic thought, with nearly 2,000 signed entries written by more than 900 prominent economists, historians, philosophers, mathematicians, and statisticians. Articles present diverse philosophies, ideologies, and methodologies and discuss their origin, historical development, and philosophical foundation. The 700 biographical entries exclude living economists born after 1915. Bibliographies accompany most entries. Appendixes list contributors and biographies included in the earlier *Palgrave* but omitted here, and subject entries classified under 53 fields of study. Analytical subject index. HB61.N49

Survey of social science : economics series / ed. by Frank N. Magill ; consulting ed., Demos Vardiabasis. Pasadena, Calif. : Salem Pr., c1991. 5 v. (2494 p.). **CH53**
> 393 articles, written by experts, that provide nonspecialists with essential views of areas that are increasingly important. Each essay defines principal terms, gives an overview, discusses applications, and discusses term in current context; each contains a bibliography. Hb61.S94

Dictionaries

The American dictionary of economics / [ed. by] Douglas A. L. Auld ... [et al.]. N.Y. : Facts on File, [1983]. 342 p. : ill. **CH54**
> A rev. ed. of *The Penguin dictionary of economics* by G. Bannock, R. E. Baxter and R. Rees (2nd ed., 1978).
> Much material from the earlier work has been rewritten to cover American institutions, statistical and illustrative matter. Emphasis on terms, phrases, personalities and organizations important to economic theory and history, econometrics, statistics, and business finance. Public finance, international trade and payments are more selectively covered. HB61.A49

Branciard, Michel. Dictionnaire économique et social : dictionnaire Thomas Suavet. 11. éd., entièrement rev. et corr. Paris : Économie et Humanisme, [1978]. 582, 17p. : ill. **CH55**
> 1st ed., 1962.
> A revision of Suavet's dictionary of economic and sociological terms. Articles group related terms together, giving definitions, bibliographic references, statistical tables, and necessary mathematical formulae; different meanings are numbered separately, and there is an index of about 1,600 words (including personal name references) citing the subject article in which they appear. Chronology; abbreviations. HB61.B73

A concise dictionary of business. Oxford ; N.Y. : Oxford Univ. Pr., 1990. 401 p. **CH56**
> For business students and practitioners, with short definitions of terms and jargon in all fields of business and more selective coverage of economics and law. HF1001.C63

Hanson, John Lloyd. A dictionary of economics and commerce. 5th ed. [Plymouth, Eng.] : Macdonald & Evans, [1977]. 472 p. : ill. **CH57**
> 1st ed., 1965.
> Provides explanations of terms from pure and applied economics and economic history; brief definitions of some of the more important commercial terms are also included. About 5,000 entries; some British emphasis. HB61.H35

Harrap's five language business dictionary : English-French-German-Italian-Spanish. Bromley, Kent : Harrap, 1991. 448 p. **CH58**
> An integrated alphabetical list of 20,000 terms in business and commerce, in five major European languages.

The MIT dictionary of modern economics / ed., David W. Pearce. 4th ed. Cambridge, Mass. : MIT Pr., 1992. 474 p. : ill. **CH59**
> 1st ed., 1981. Prior editions had title: *The dictionary of modern economics.*
> In this edition, about one-sixth of the content has been changed in some way, revisions being the most common form of alteration. Now contains approximately 2,800 entries for terms, organizations, and economists. New to this edition are entries considered important from an East European perspective. HB61.D52

Moffat, Donald W. Economics dictionary. 2nd ed. N.Y. : Elsevier, [1983]. 331 p. : ill. **CH60**

Brief definitions, with extensive cross-references and some repetition of the shorter definitions. Criteria for length of entry are: "for expressions found in the popular and trade press, but not in textbooks, give a full explanation; for expressions involved in controversy, give a summary of what both sides are saying; ordinary economics expressions found in textbooks should be included, but with only a brief explanation."—*Pref.*   HB61.M54

NTC's French and English business dictionary / Michel Marcheteau … [et al.]. Lincolnwood, Ill. : National Textbook Co., 1992. 620 p.   **CH61**

1st publ. 1988 by Presses Poche.

"Designed as a reference for both specialists in the area of business and economics and for nonspecialists who find themselves confronted with the need to use French in business and technical contexts."—*Introd.* Among the most useful appendixes are abbreviations, formulas for correspondence, and common terms in sales contracts.   HF1002.N93

Pass, Christopher. Harper dictionary of economics / Christopher Pass, Bryan Lowes, Leslie Davies. N.Y. : HarperPerennial, 1991. 562 p.   **CH62**

Published in U.K. as: *Collins dictionary of economics* (London : Collins, 1988).

Contains more than 1,700 clearly written definitions of key economic terms, descriptions of organizations, and biographies of major economists. Numerous cross-references; nearly 200 illustrations. Good desk dictionary.   HB61.P39

Presner, Lewis A. The international business dictionary and reference. N.Y. : Wiley, c1991. 486 p.   **CH63**

A vocabulary of international business that includes usage in international marketing, law, economics, banking and finance, and international relations and politics. Supplemented by geographic, topical, and language reference guides and vocabulary lists used in foreign exchange, terms of trade, and international organizations and law. Bibliography and selected information sources.   HF1359.P74

Rutherford, Donald. Dictionary of economics. London ; N.Y. : Routledge, 1992. 539 p. : ill.   **CH64**

Short definitions of words commonly used in economics textbooks, newspapers and journals, including slang and jargon words. British orientation, with entries classified by *Economic journal* system. Includes biographies, cross-references and bibliographies for some entries. Index lists terms by classification numbers.   HB61.R92

Foreign terms

Clifford Vaughan, F. Glossary of economics, including Soviet terminology : in English/American, French, German, Russian / comp. and arranged by F. and M. Clifford Vaughan. Amsterdam ; N.Y. : Elsevier, 1966. 201 p.   **CH65**

The main section gives the English term with French and German equivalents; French, German, and Russian lists are keyed to this section. An appendix of Soviet economic terminology presents the Russian term with English, French, and German equivalents in parallel columns.   HB61.V3

Dictionnaire des sciences économiques / publié sous la direction de Jean Romeuf, avec la collaboration de Gilles Pasqualaggi. Paris : Presses Universitaires de France, 1956–58. 2 v.   **CH66**

A dictionary of terms used in the study of economics. International in scope. Includes biographical sketches of significant figures, excluding living persons. Many articles are signed; some have bibliographies.   HB61.D5

Eichborn, Reinhart von. Cambridge-Eichborn German dictionary : economics, law, administration, business, general. Cambridge : Cambridge Univ. Pr., [1983]. 2 v.   **CH67**

Originally publ. as *Der grosse Eichborn* (Burscheid : Siebenpunkt Verlag, 1981–82).

Contents: v. 1, English-German; v. 2, German-English.

Based on the author's *Spezialwörterbuch für Handel und Wirtschaft* (Stuttgart, 1947–48) and its American edition, *Business dictionary* (Englewood Cliffs, N.J. : Prentice-Hall, 1961–62). About 250,000 entries.   H45.E36

Elster, Ludwig. Wörterbuch der Volkswirtschaft. 4. völlig umgearb. Aufl. Jena : Fischer, 1931–33. 3 v. : ill.   **CH68**

1st ed., 1898, in 2 v.

A standard German encyclopedia of economics, supplementary to the *Handwörterbuch der Staatswissenschaften* which covered political science. Signed articles, bibliographies, and biographies of deceased persons.   HB61.E5

Jong, Frits J. de. Quadrilingual economics dictionary : English/American, French, German, Dutch. The Hague : Nijhoff ; Deventer : Kluwer Technical Books, 1980. 685 p.   **CH69**

Composed of four separate dictionary sections, with English/American, French, German and Dutch alternately serving as the base language, with equivalent terms given in the other three languages.   HB61.J64

McGraw-Hill dictionary of modern economics : a handbook of terms and organizations / Douglas Greenwald, ed. 3rd ed. N.Y. : McGraw-Hill, [1983]. 632 p.   **CH70**

1st ed., 1965.

Pt. 1 lists and defines approximately 1,425 modern economic and related terms. Definitions were written for the nonspecialist and are sometimes supplemented by charts, tables, or diagrams. Pt. 2 alphabetically lists and describes about 235 private and public organizations concerned with economics and marketing. A somewhat abridged paperback version was published as *The concise McGraw-Hill dictionary of modern economics* (N.Y. : McGraw-Hill, [1984]), omitting 250 accounting and insurance terms and the organization list.   HB61.M3

Pozin, Mikhail A. Russian-English/English-Russian dictionary of free market era economics. Jefferson, N.C. : McFarland & Co., c1993. 319 p.   **CH71**

Title on added t.p.: Russko-angliĭskiĭ/anglo-russkiĭ slovar' ėkonomiki svobodnogo rynka.

Reflects usage in books, newspapers and journals within the last five years. Covers accounting, advertising, commerce and trade, corporate law, financial markets, insurance, marketing, licensing and patents. Almost no definitions.   HB61.P68

Quotations

A dictionary of business quotations / comp. by Simon James and Robert Parker. N.Y. : Simon & Schuster, 1990. 172 p.   **CH72**

Quotations are grouped under 215 topics. Entries cite the person being quoted and the publication or other source in which it first appeared. Author/source and keyword indexes.

§ See also: *A treasury of business quotations*, [selected] by Michael C. Thomsett (Jefferson, N.C. : McFarland, c1990. 218 p.). Contains some 2,000 quotations from business leaders, philosophers, writers, and others, grouped under 117 broad subjects. Quotations are numbered in sequence, and source and publication date are given for each. Author and key word indexes.   PN6084.B87D54

A dictionary of economic quotations / comp. by Simon James. 2nd ed. London : C. Helm ; Totowa, N.J. : Barnes & Noble, [1984]. 240 p.   **CH73**

1st ed., 1981.

Quotations are arranged according to more than 130 topics, with indexing by keyword and source.   HB34.D53

The executive's book of quotations / [comp.] by Julia Vitullo-Martin and J. Robert Moskin. N.Y. : Oxford Univ. Pr., 1994. 379 p.   **CH74**

> More than 5,000 quotations are arranged under 500 alphabetical topic headings and cite sources. Indexes of sources, names, and cross-references.   PN6084.B87B93

The Macmillan book of business and economic quotations / ed. by Michael Jackman. N.Y. : Macmillan, [1984]. 302 p.   **CH75**

> Quotations are grouped within about 60 broad subject categories, then arranged chronologically; indexed by person and keyword.   PN6084.B87M33

Directories

Byrne, John A. A Business week guide : the best business schools / John A. Byrne with a team of Business week editors. 3rd ed. N.Y. : McGraw-Hill, c1993. 355 p. : ill.   **CH76**

> Previous ed. published under title: *Business week's guide to the best business schools.*
>
> Ranks business schools, using surveys of recent graduates and of corporate recruiters, coupled with interviews. Names top 20 schools; profiles for those and 40 additional schools. Tables of test scores, employment outcomes, costs, etc.   HF1131.B95

Capie, Forrest. Directory of economic institutions. N.Y. : Stockton Pr., c1990. 472 p.   **CH77**

> Lists by country some 350 economic research organizations. Level of information provided varies, but generally includes: name; address and telephone, telex, and fax numbers; name of parent organization; date founded/incorporated; names of top officials; nature; objectives; type(s) of funding; research interests; publications; and other activities. An Addresses section at the front serves as both directory and index of organizations by name; there is no other index.   HB74.5.C37

The directory of business information resources. 1992– . Lakeville, Conn. : Grey House Publ., 1992– .   **CH78**

> Leslie MacKenzie, ed.
>
> Lists (by industry) associations, newsletters, magazines, and trade shows. Includes short descriptions for each entry, as well as contact persons, editorial and advertising personnel, phone and fax numbers. Includes pricing information. Arrangement is alphabetical by major industry group. Indexed by entry and company name.   HF5035.D464

Guide to graduate study in economics, agricultural economics, public administration, and doctoral programs in business administration in the United States and Canada / ed. by Wyn F. Owen and Douglas A. Ruby. 8th ed. Boulder, Colo. : Economics Institute, c1989. 503 p.   **CH79**

> 7th ed., 1984.
>
> Title has varied: first publ. 1965 as *Graduate studies in economics.*
>
> This edition describes 220 economics programs (including agricultural economics), 29 Ph.D. programs in business administration, and 14 programs in public administration. Also offers general information for prospective graduate students and additional information for foreign graduate students.   HB74.8.G84

Meerhaeghe, Marcel Alfons Gilbert van. International economic institutions. 6th ed. Dordrecht ; Boston : Kluwer Academic, 1992. 398 p. : ill.   **CH80**

> Translation of: *International economische betrekkingen en instellingen*, first publ. 1964 (Leiden : H. E. Stenfert Krose). 1st English language ed., 1966; 5th ed., 1987.
>
> Contains descriptions in three main sections (Introduction, World organizations, European organizations) of U.N., specialized, and regional agencies, of such international organizations as the International Monetary Fund and the World Bank, and of such European organiza-

tions as Benelux and the European Communities. Although descriptions of agencies in the introduction are generally no longer than a paragraph or two, entries in the other sections are considerably longer, usually discussing origins, objectives, organization, functions and operation, and containing an appraisal of the organization, selected statistics, and a bibliography. Appended are lists of articles from legal documents pertaining to each organization, and author and subject indexes.   HF1411.M433

The official guide to MBA programs, admissions, & careers. 1971/72– . [Princeton, N.J.] : Graduate Management Admission Council, [1971]– . Biennial.   **CH81**

> Title varies; since 1986, *The official guide to MBA programs.*
>
> An international directory describing graduate management programs, admissions requirements, expenses, financial assistance, placement activities. Arranged alphabetically by university, with summary tables by country and state.   HF1131.O36

Trade associations and professional bodies of the United Kingdom. Ed. 1 (1962)– . London : Gale, 1962– .   **CH82**

> Subtitle varies. Publisher varies. Revised every two or three years.
>
> Now an alphabetical listing with subject and geographical indexes.   HD2429.G7M5

Trade directories of the world. Queen's Village, N.Y. : Croner Pub., 1952?– . 1 v. (looseleaf).   **CH83**

> Title varies: *Croner's world register of trade directories.*
>
> Lists general, trade, business, and professional directories of the U.S and of more than 60 foreign countries. Most entries are annotated. Kept up-to-date by an amendment service.   Z5771.C7

Handbooks

Berck, Peter. Economists' mathematical manual / Peter Berck, Knut Sydsaeter. 2nd ed. Berlin ; N.Y. : Springer-Verlag, c1993. 166 p.   **CH84**

> 1st ed., 1991.
>
> Offers mathematical formulas useful in: programming and optimization theory; economic theory of the consumer and the firm; risk, finance and growth theory; noncooperative game theory; and elementary statistical theory. Indexed; bibliography.   HB135.B467

Codes of professional responsibility / ed. by Rena A. Gorlin. 2nd ed. Wash. : Bureau of National Affairs, c1990. 555 p.   **CH85**

> For annotation, *see* CK160.   BJ1725.C57

De Vries, Mary Ann. Complete secretary's handbook. 7th ed. Englewood Cliffs, N.J. ; London : Prentice Hall, c1993. 707 p.   **CH86**

> 1st ed., 1951; 6th ed., 1988, ed. by Lillian Doris.
>
> A standard handbook providing a range of practical techniques for general secretarial duties, guides to grammar and letter writing, techniques and forms for records and correspondence, and a collection of quick reference sources and facts. Takes into account modern office equipment and computer technology. Indexed.   HF5547.5.D6

Jaderstrom, Susan. Professional Secretaries International complete office handbook : the secretary's guide to today's electronic office / Susan Jaderstrom, Leonard Kruk, and Joanne Miller ; gen. ed., Susan W. Fenner. N.Y. : Random House, c1992. 573 p. : ill.   **CH87**

> Emphasizes office practices and procedures, selection and maintenance of supplies and equipment; communication and correspondence; brief section on grammar and punctuation. Indexed.   HF5548.J34

Merriam-Webster's secretarial handbook. 3rd ed. Springfield, Mass. : Merriam-Webster, c1993. 590 p.   **CH88**

Rev. ed. of: *Webster's secretarial handbook*, 2nd ed., c1983.

Incorporates electronic office management and procedures into traditional handbook topics (e.g., business etiquette and correspondence). Includes desktop publishing, accounting, and records management. Bibliography and index. HF5547.5.W4

Stuteley, Richard. Economist guide to business numeracy. N.Y. : Wiley, c1993. 237 p. : ill., map. **CH89**

Originally publ. London : Economist Books, 1991 as *The Economist numbers guide : the essentials of business numeracy.*

Introduction to numerical methods and quantitative techniques used in mathematics, statistics, business, accounting and economics. Uses extensive examples, tables, and figures to explain in layman's terms. Appendix is a dictionary, with cross-references to the main section. Indexed. HF5695.S83

Taintor, Sarah Augusta. The secretary's handbook / Sarah Augusta Taintor and Kate M. Monro. 10th ed. / rev. by Margaret D. Shertzer. N.Y. : Macmillan, c1988. 422 p. : ill. **CH90**

1st ed., 1929; 9th ed., 1978.

A standard handbook in two parts, the first treating grammar and good English, the second specific secretarial practices (e.g., filing, word processing, making travel arrangements), business letter writing and forms of address, sources of information for secretaries, and goals and advancement. Appendix of common signs and symbols; index. HF5547.5.T29

Biography

American Economic Association. Survey of members, including classification listings. 1978– . Nashville : Amer. Economic Assoc., 1978– . Irregular. **CH91**

Vols. for 1978– issued as a special number of the *American economic review* (usually in December). Publication lags.

Continues the Association's *Directory* (1974) and the biographical information included in its *Handbook* (publ. irregularly since 1890).

Biographical data gathered by questionnaires distributed to members, plus classification of members by fields of specialization, academic affiliation, etc.

§ The Association's *Telephone directory of members* (1991) contains the names, addresses, and office telephone and fax numbers for most members.

Arestis, Philip. A biographical dictionary of dissenting economists / ed. by Philip Arestis and Malcolm Sawyer. Aldershot, England ; Brookfield, Vt. : E. Edgar Pub. Co.; distr. by Ashgate, 1992. 628 p. **CH92**

"A guide to the significant contribution of a number of important dissenting economists from around the world."—*Pref.* Includes those who are not in the 20th-century neoclassical mainstream, such as institutionalists, post-Keynesians, Kaleckians, Marxians, and neo-Marxians, Sraffians, and radical political economists. Ranges back to the 1870s but the majority are 20th-century economists. Some wrote their own entries. Bibliographies.

Blaug, Mark. Great economists since Keynes : an introduction to the lives & works of one hundred modern economists. Totowa, N.J. : Barnes & Noble, c1985. 267 p. : ports. **CH93**

Repr. : Cambridge ; N.Y. : Cambridge Univ. Pr., 1988.

Describes the careers and contributions of key economists. Entries are arranged alphabetically and include photographs or illustrations as well as biographical and academic information. Index by names (other than main entries) and subjects.

§ For a similar book on earlier economists see Blaug's *Great economists before Keynes : an introduction to the lives & works of one hundred great economists of the past* (Atlantic Highlands, N.J. : Humanities Pr. Internat., c1986. 286 p. Repr.: Cambridge; N.Y. : Cambridge Univ. Pr., 1988). HB76.B55

Business biography master index / Barbara McNeil, ed., Amy L. Unterberger, assoc. ed. Detroit : Gale, c1987. 630 p. (Gale biographical index series, no. 10). **CH94**

Subtitle: A consolidated index to more than 260,000 biographical sketches of business people who appear in a selection of the principal current and retrospective biographical dictionaries and who's who in the field of business and finance.

Derived from material that has appeared or will appear in *Biography and genealogy master index* (AH9). Z7164.C81928

Council of Economic Advisers (U.S.). Biographical directory of the Council of Economic Advisers / ed. by Robert Sobel and Bernard S. Katz. N.Y. : Greenwood, 1988. 301 p. **CH95**

Contains four- to five-page signed biographical essays concerning the 45 economists who have served on the Council of Economic Advisers (CEA) since its beginning in 1946. Arrangement is alphabetical rather than chronological, and the essays, which focus on professional careers prior to and during appointment to the CEA, include bibliographies. An appendix lists membership in the CEA by presidential administration. Indexed. HC102.5.A2C68

Dictionary of business biography : a biographical dictionary of business leaders active in Britain in the period 1860–1980 / ed. by David J. Jeremy. London : Butterworths, 1984. 5 v. : ill. **CH96**

Vol. 5 includes supplement (1986. 120 p.) of indexes, contributors, errata.

Comp. by the Business History Unit, London School of Economics.

Provides entries for more than 1,000 entrepreneurs in Britain— "those who have had real impact, good or bad, whatever their position or title."—*Pref.* Bibliographies accompany each entry; some have photographs or illustrations. HC252.5.A2D53

Dictionary of Scottish business biography, 1860–1960 / editors, Anthony Slaven, Sydney Checkland ; associate editors, Sheila Hamilton ... [et al.]. Aberdeen : Aberdeen Univ. Pr., 1986–1990. 2 v. : ill. **CH97**

Contents: v.1, The staple industries (496 p.); v.2, Processing, distribution, services (447 p.).

Offers signed biographical essays, grouped by industry. Each section begins with an introductory article tracing the history and development of the industry, followed by the biographies, listed alphabetically. Most are two to four pages long, include bibliographies of published and unpublished works, and frequently contain photographs or drawings. Each volume concludes with name and subject indexes. HC252.5.A2D54

Ingham, John N. Biographical dictionary of American business leaders. Westport, Conn. : Greenwood, [1983]. 4 v. (2026 p.). **CH98**

Presents 835 biographical entries, with information on 1,159 "most significant" business leaders of the U.S. from colonial times to the present; entries range in length from 750 to more than 3,000 words and conclude with bibliographic references. Appendixes arrange leaders by industry, company, birthplace and date, ethnic background and religion, place of business activity, and sex. Indexed. HC102.5.A2I53

————— Contemporary American business leaders : a biographical dictionary / John N. Ingham and Lynne B. Feldman. N.Y. : Greenwood, 1990. 788 p. **CH99**

Presents 116 biographies of the historically most significant business leaders, 1945 to the present. Emphasizes important business decisions rather than personal lives. Entries are generally several pages long, each including a bibliography of primary and secondary sources. Appendixes allow access by industry, company, place of business, place of birth, and black and women leaders. Indexed. A useful companion to John N. Ingham's *Biographical dictionary of American business leaders* (CH98). HC102.5.A2I534

———————— African-American business leaders : a biographical dictionary / John N. Ingham and Lynne B. Feldman. Westport, Conn. : Greenwood, c1994. 806 p.   **CH100**

Provides biographies, five to 15 pages in length, concerning 123 African-American business leaders. Includes information on many individuals who do not appear in standard biographical dictionaries. Each biographical essay concludes with a list of references, including some primary sources. Includes bibliographic references and indexes.

HC102.5.A2I52

Leavitt, Judith A. American women managers and administrators : a selective biographical dictionary of twentieth-century leaders in business, education, and government. Westport, Conn. : Greenwood, 1985. 317 p.   **CH101**

Entries treating 226 women are one to two pages long, and generally include bibliographies of works by and about the biographees. Appendix lists women "firsts," founders, presidents of colleges and universities, presidents of businesses, vice presidents of major corporations, and women in positions of national prominence. Indexed.

HC102.5.A2L37

Nobel laureates in economic sciences : a biographical dictionary / ed. by Bernard S. Katz. N.Y. : Garland, 1989. 339 p. (Garland reference library of the humanities, vol. 850).   **CH102**

For annotation, *see* AL167.   HB76.N63

Who's who in British economics : a directory of economists in higher education, business, and government / ed. by Paul Sturges and Claire Sturges. Aldershot, England ; Brookfield, Vt. : Edward Elgar, c1990. 627 p.   **CH103**

Lists address at current position, past positions held, academic training, and list of publications.   HC252.2.W46

Who's who in economics : a biographical dictionary of major economists, 1700–1986 / ed. by Mark Blaug. 2nd ed. Cambridge, Mass. : MIT Pr., 1986. 935 p.   **CH104**

1st ed., 1983.

Lists economists, living and dead, who are most often cited in the journal literature. Entries contain name, year and place of birth, career history, degrees, professional affiliations and awards, major field of interest, brief statements of principal contributions to economics, and selected bibliography. Indexed by place of birth, residence, and major fields of interest.   HB76.W47

Who's who in finance and industry. 17th ed. (1972/73)– . Chicago : Marquis Who's Who.   **CH105**

Continues: 1936–59, *Who's who in commerce and industry*; 1961–68/69, *World who's who in commerce and industry*; 1970/71, *World who's who in finance and industry.*

Gives international coverage of businessmen. Includes index of firms with references to personnel for whom sketches are included.

HF3023.A2W5

Statistics

The economic almanac for … . 1940–1967/1968. N.Y. : National Industrial Conference Board, [1940–67]. Irregular.   **CH106**

Annual, 1940–50. Ceased with 18th ed., 1967/68.

A statistical compendium covering such subjects as: prices, banking, finance, national income, resources, manufacturing, communication and transportation, industries, agriculture, labor, foreign trade, international economic statistics, etc. Includes a glossary of terms used in business and economics. A general index is followed by a separate index for Canada.   HC101.E38

Economic indicators handbook : time series, conversions, documentation / comp. and ed. by Arsen J. Darnay, ed. Detroit : Gale, c1992. 1056 p.   **CH107**

Handy compilation of 805 frequently requested time series of the United States; some begin as early as 1869 and continue to 1991. Includes national income and production accounts, composite indexes of leading, lagging and coincident indicators and their components, other related cyclical indicators and economic series such as consumer price index, producer price index, and selected stock market indexes. Explanations and sources accompany each table.   HC103.E26

Frumkin, Norman. Guide to economic indicators. Armonk, N.Y. : M.E. Sharpe, c1990. 242 p. : ill.   **CH108**

Provides basic descriptions (including where and when available, content, methodology, accuracy, relevance, and recent trends) for more than 50 economic indicators developed by the federal government, private sources, and international organizations. References to primary data sources are also given. Some entries contain charts or tables, but there is no index.   HC103.F9

Moore, Geoffrey Hoyt. International economic indicators : a sourcebook / Geoffrey H. Moore and Melita H. Moore. Westport, Conn. : Greenwood, 1985. 373 p. : ill.   **CH109**

Provides detailed information concerning three categories of international economic indicators—leading, coincident, and lagging—for the seven largest industrial countries (U.S., U.K., Canada, West Germany, France, Italy, and Japan). A discussion of the development of these indicators is followed by country-by-country descriptions of economic indicators, and by monthly and quarterly data (1948–82), for individual countries and for multicountry indexes. Appendixes list current sources of international economic indicators, present chronologies of growth cycles in 13 countries, 1948–83, show the record of leading economic indicators for seven countries, and discuss the method of construction of the composite indexes. An indicator series finding guide lists composite indexes, giving citations to pages on which descriptions and data are included. Statistics in the tables are updated by the monthly *International economic indicators*, published since June 1983 by Columbia University's Center for International Business Cycle Research.   HC59.M62

Statistical forecasts of the United States / ed. by James E. Person, Jr. ; Sean R. Pollock, assoc. ed. Detroit : Gale, 1993. 804 p.   **CH110**

For annotation, *see* CG105.   HC106.8.S7357

The value of a dollar : prices and incomes in the United States, 1860–1989 / ed. by Scott Derks. Detroit : Gale, c1994. 559 p. : ill.   **CH111**

"Records the actual prices of thousands of items that consumers purchased from the Civil War to the present."—*Pref.* In five chapters that cover: the Civil war to 1899, 1900–19, 1920–39, 1940–59 and 1960–89. Each chapter begins with an essay about the social and economic forces of the period, then subsections called: Historical snapshot, Consumer expenditures, Investments, Selected income, Income, Standard jobs, Food basket, Selected prices, and Standard prices.

ECONOMIC CONDITIONS AND WORLD TRADE

General works

Country report : an analysis of economic and political trends every quarter / EIU, the Economist Intelligence Unit. 1988–89– . London : The Unit, 1988– . Quarterly.   **CH112**

Title varies: *Quarterly economic review*; *QER*; *Three-month economic review.*

Provides quarterly information on current political, economic, and business conditions in 165 countries of the world, grouped geographically into 92 regional reports. Typically treats the political scene; economic policy; domestic economy; foreign trade and payments; agriculture, construction, communications, and manufacturing; business news; and prospects. Supplements text with graphs, charts, and statistical appendixes, usually drawn from official national and international statistical sources. Available as a set; regional reports may also be purchased separately.

•Also available in CD-ROM.

§ A companion series, *Country profile* (published annually; included with subscriptions to *Country report* and also available separately) provides more detailed coverage. Profiles are about 50 pages in length, offer background information arranged by such categories as national accounts, employment, tourism, and foreign trade, and include charts, graphs, maps, and select bibliographies.

The development directory : a guide to the international development community in the United States and Canada. 1988/89– . Detroit : Omnigraphics, Inc., c1988– . **CH113**

Imprint varies.

Presents international development directory information in two parts: Organizations and Individuals. The first lists organizations by type, location, sectors (fields of interest), and geographic area, categorizes organizational publications by sector and geographic area, and lists organizational personnel. The second presents biographical entries that include the individual's title, institutional affiliation, degrees, and publications. Indexes to individuals by sector and by geographic area. HC60.D476

Directory of non-governmental environment and develop ment organisations in OECD member countries. [Paris] : Development Centre of the Organisation for Economic Cooperation and Development, [1981]. 2 v. **CH114**

Title, introductory matter, indexes, and some entries also in French.

Lists only development organizations active in environmental activities in OECD or developing countries. Includes voluntary bodies, professional associations, research and educational organizations. Organizations are listed by country, and indexed by name and by environment, education, and development activities, and by geographic area. HC60.D524

Joint Bank-Fund Library. Women and development : articles, books, and research papers / indexed in the Joint World Bank-International Monetary Fund Library, Washington, D.C. Boston : G.K. Hall, 1987. 181 p. **CH115**

For annotation, *see* CC606. Z7963.E18J65

World retail directory and sourcebook. London : Euromonitor PLC, 1991. 770 p. **CH116**

Arranged by major regions of the world. Sec. 1 describes sources of information for retailing in each country; Sec. 2 lists major retailers; Sec. 3 gives statistical data on retail distribution patterns; Sec. 4 describes limitations on trade between countries. HF5429.W672

Bibliography

Transnational business information : a manual of needs and sources / United Nations Centre on Transnational Corporations. N.Y. : United Nations, 1991. 216 p. **CH117**

"The purpose of the manual is to help Governments and local enterprises in developing countries to establish their own collection of information sources."—*Pref.* Lists public and private printed and electronic sources, including international statistics, regional surveys, commercial directories, and databases. Bibliography of sources, directory of information providers, and index to titles, authors, institutions, and subjects. HD2755.5.T673

Indexes; Abstract journals

•**Foreign traders index** [database]. Wash. : U.S. Dept. of Commerce, Office of Commercial Information Management Systems. **CH118**

Available from producer; contains current five years, updated daily.

Contains lists of opportunities for exporters, Directory of U.S. exporters, Army area handbooks.

•**IntlEc CD-ROM** : the index to international economics, development and finance [database]. Wash. : Joint Bank-Fund Library, 1981– . **CH119**

Available on CD-ROM, updated quarterly.

Continues the printed source *Economics and finance : index to periodical articles, 1947–1971, comp. by the staff of the Joint Bank-Fund Library* ... (Boston : G.K. Hall, 1972. 4 v.) and supplements covering 1972–74 and 1975–77 (1976–79. 2 v.).

A selective index to approximately 1,050 periodical titles and more than 700 research papers and series, compiled by the library that serves the World Bank and the International Monetary Fund. Papers indexed emphasize international aid and development, global economic trends, monetary policy, interest rates, and external debt. Approximately 75% of the materials indexed are in English and 20% in French, Spanish, or German.

Encyclopedias

Dictionary of development : Third World economy, environment, society / ed. by Brian W.W. Welsh & Pavel Butorin. N.Y. : Garland, 1990. 2 v. (1194 p.). (Garland reference library of social science, v. 487). **CH120**

Describes major organizations, concepts, and issues relating to Third World development. Entries range from a sentence to a few pages, cross-references are numerous, and most of the longer entries contain brief bibliographies. A preliminary section, "Developing country indicators," presents demographic and economic statistics. Vol. 2 concludes with a list of national and international periodicals and newspapers devoted to development topics. HC59.7.D513

Fry, Gerald. The international development dictionary / Gerald W. Fry, Galen R. Martin. Santa Barbara, Calif. : ABC-Clio, c1991. 445 p. **CH121**

Entries, which combine paragraph-long current definitions and a "Significance" paragraph that discusses historical and current relevance, are arranged in four subject-oriented chapters: Development thinkers/theorists, leaders, and practitioners; Basic development concepts; Analytical concepts; and Development movements, projects, and organizations. Frequent cross-references, with an alphabetic list of terms, glossary of acronyms, bibliography, and detailed index. HF1359.F79

World index of economic forecasts : including industrial tendency surveys and development plans / ed. by Robert Fildes with Thana Chrissanthaki. 3rd ed. N.Y. : Stockton Pr., c1988. 563 p. : ill. **CH122**

1st ed., 1978; 2nd ed., 1981.

Presents profiles of 329 organizations which provide forecasts, plans, and surveys for more than 100 countries; each profile includes a list of publications and descriptions of the coverage of the forecasts, their methodology, techniques, etc. Separate sections treat macroeconomic forecasters, specialist forecasters (commodity, exchange rate, energy, shipping, population, labor force), consumer surveys in 42 countries, and the most recent national development plans. Indexed by organization, geographic focus, and subject. HB3730.W66

Dictionaries

Gipson, Carolyn Renee. The McGraw-Hill dictionary of international trade and finance. N.Y. : McGraw-Hill, c1994. 419 p.   **CH123**
  "Constructed as a broad reference to terms encountered in international trade and finance. It defines banking, customs economics, financial, insurance, regulatory and shipping terms. National currencies are identified. Major international trade agreements, regional trading assocaitons, financial institutions, and stock and commodity exchanges are included."—*Pref.*   HF1373.G57

Rosenberg, Jerry Martin. Dictionary of international trade. N.Y. : J. Wiley, c1994. 314 p.   **CH124**
  More than 4,000 entries define terms, simple to complex, with sometimes more than one definition for an entry—"relatively simple for the layperson, more developed and technical for the specialist."—*Introd.* Contains cross-references. Includes an appendix of currency codes.   HF1373.R67

Foreign terms

IMF glossary : English-French-Spanish. 4th rev. ed. Wash. : International Monetary Fund, 1992. 341 p.   **CH125**
  1st ed., 1980; 3rd ed., 1986.
  Lists English terms frequently found in International Monetary Fund documents, with French and Spanish equivalents; includes words, phrases, and titles of institutions. Indexes by French and Spanish terms refer back to English entry. Appendixes list organizational structure of the IMF and world monetary units in three languages.
                                                   HG3881.5.I58I565

Kohls, Siegfried. Dictionary of international economics : German, Russian, English, French, Spanish. Leiden : Sijthoff ; Berlin : Verlag Die Wirtschaft, 1976. 619 p.   **CH126**
  Prefatory material in the five languages covered.
  Originally published as *Ökonomisches Wörterbuch Aussenwirtschaft.*
  The alphabetically arranged main section gives about 6,500 German terms and phrases with their equivalents in the other four languages; indexes from each of the other languages. Emphasizes terms of commerce, commercial law, payments system, carrying trade, and customs administration; largely exclusive of monetary systems, industrial and trade terminology.   HF1002.K6613

Motta, Giuseppe. Dizionario commerciale : inglese-italiano, italiano-inglese. Economia, legge, finanza (amministrazione, banca, borsa, assicurazione, scambi, commercio estero e marittimo, trasporti, dogane, ecc.). Milano : C. Signorelli, [1966]. 1050 p.   **CH127**
                                                   HF1002.M6

Netto, Modestino Martins. Vocabulário de intercâmbio comercial : português-inglês; inglês-português. Com um apêndice contendo abreviaturas comerciais, pesos e medidas, sistema monetário, modelo de cartas comerciais, etc. Rio de Janeiro : Ed. Civilização Brasileira, [1961]. 251 p.   **CH128**
  A practical glossary of commercial terms.   HF1002.N45

Servotte, Jozef V. Dictionnaire commercial et financier : français, néerlandais, anglais, allemand. 2. éd., rev. et augm. Bruxelles : Éd. Brepols, [1962]. 955 p.   **CH129**
  1st ed., 1956.
  Added title page: Woordenboek voor handel en financien.
                                                   HF1002.S42

Directories

Development aid : a guide to national and international agencies / researched and comp. by Eurofi (UK) Limited. London ; Boston : Butterworths ; Birmingham [England] ; N.Y. : Eurofi (UK), 1988. 587 p. : ill.   **CH130**
  In two main sections: (1) Multilateral aid agencies (e.g., U.N. Development Programme; African Development Bank) and (2) Bilateral aid donors, organized by continent and country. Entries, which may feature statistical tables and flow charts, generally include: origins, objectives, management, nature and scope of operations, methods of operations, funding characteristics, beneficiary countries, and contacts. Nongovernment organizations are excluded. Not indexed.
                                                   HG3881.D43

Directory of foreign trade organizations in Eastern Europe : Bulgaria, Czechoslovakia, East Germany, Hungary, Poland, Romania, and the U.S.S.R. 3rd ed. San Francisco : International Trade Pr., 1990. 488 p.   **CH131**
  Lists and describes import/export organizations and other enterprises engaged in foreign trade activities, including chambers of commerce, banks, state committees, commercial agents, and embassies. Arranged by country. Indexed.   HF3500.7.A48D57

Directory of United States importers. 1967– . N.Y. : Journal of Commerce, 1967– . Biennial.   **CH132**
  Continues: *Directory of United States import concerns* (1948–66).
  A geographical listing of importers is followed by a commodity index.
  § See also: *Directory of United States exporters* (N.Y. : Journal of Commerce, 1992–).   HF3012.D53

World chamber of commerce directory. 1989– . Loveland, Colo. : World Chamber of Commerce Directory, c1989– . Annual.   **CH133**
  Lists U.S. chambers of commerce by state and city, giving mailing address, telephone and telex numbers, name of president, number of members, and local population. Similar information is provided for state boards of tourism, convention and visitors bureaus, economic development organizations, Canadian chambers of commerce, American chambers of commerce abroad, and foreign tourist information bureaus and chambers of commerce in the U.S. and abroad. Also lists members of Congress, key diplomats, U.S. and foreign embassy addresses, and the names and telephone numbers of U.S. Chamber of Commerce executives.   HF294.W75

World development directory / comp. and ed. by Roger East, Miles Smith-Morris and Martin Wright for CIRCA, Cambridge International Reference on Current Affairs, Ltd. Chicago : St. James, c1990. 568 p.   **CH134**
  In three parts: (1) Intergovernmental organizations grouped by category (U.N. bodies; other global organizations; federations of financing institutions; regional intergovernmental organizations for Africa, the Americas, Asia-Pacific, Europe, and the Middle East/Arab world), each entry including: acronym; address, telephone, telex, and cable numbers; founding date; origin and aims; principal officials; structure; areas of operation; sources of finance; publications; and affiliates. (2) Official programs (statistics, distribution of overseas development assistance, and principal government agency/officer) and nongovernmental organizations (NGOs) involved in global development arranged by country. (3) Government agencies handling foreign assistance, branch offices of organizations listed in Pts. 1–2, and locally-based NGOs in developing countries (here called "south countries"). Also includes a list of NGOs classified by type and an index of country profiles and organizations.   HC60.W67

World trade resources guide. 1st ed.– . Detroit : Gale, c1992– . Semiannual.   **CH135**
  A directory of contacts and sources useful in foreign trade: organizations and agencies, banks, companies, government agencies, research centers, and trade associations. Includes publications and other

information sources, such as databases, consultants, and statistical sources. Arranged by country. Name and keyword index.

HF54.U5W67

Handbooks

American export register. 1980– . N.Y. : Thomas Internat. Pub. Co., 1980– . Annual. **CH136**

Continues *American register of exporters and importers*, 1945/ 46–1978.

Lists exporting companies by product line, giving address and telephone information, then lists companies alphabetically with more complete information, such as key executives in export sales, market areas served, fax number, TWX number, cable address, and telex number. A final section contains lists of: embassies, consulates, trade missions, international chambers of commerce, world trade center clubs, banks, freight forwarders, custom house brokers, port authorities, air cargo carriers, railroads, and steamship lines. Includes conversion tables. HF3010.A6

Brooke, Michael. Handbook of international trade / Michael Brooke and Peter Buckley. London : Macmillan, 1988. 460 p. : ill. **CH137**

In eight topical sections: Strategic issues; Export and import; Licensing, franchising, and other contractural arrangements; Foreign investment; Key markets; Special industrial sectors; Influence of treaty organisations; and Sources of information. The sections are divided into chapters, which frequently incorporate charts, statistics, and bibliographies. The emphasis is British. Indexes of: subjects; abbreviations; countries and regions; treaties, companies and other relevant organizations; and publications. HF1008

Croner, U. H. E. Reference book for world traders : a looseleaf handbook covering information required for planning and executing exports and imports to and from all foreign countries. Queens Village, N.Y. : Croner Publications, 1961– . 3 v. (looseleaf). **CH138**

Kept up-to-date with monthly supplements.

Vol. 1 contains condensed tariff, postal, shipping and air freight regulations, and directories of U.S. federal and state agencies, trade associations, transportation and forwarding companies. Vol. 2, is a directory of agencies, private and public, of each country of the world, such as foreign embassies, consulates, banks in the U.S. and U.S. embassies, consulates, banks in that country. Also includes local trade associations, publishers, significant private organizations promoting trade and other pertinent information for doing business in each country.

HF1010.C66

Exporters' encyclopaedia. 1904– . Parsippany, N.J. : Dun's Marketing Services. Annual. **CH139**

Publ. N.Y. : Dun and Bradstreet for 1967–79, under title *Dun & Bradstreet's exporters' encyclopaedia*. Also publ. as *Exporters' encyclopaedia. World marketing guide*, 1980–81.

Incorporates: *Export documentation handbook* (last publ. 1986).

A comprehensive world marketing guide divided into six broad information sections: (1) The export order; (2) Export markets; (3) Export know-how; (4) Communications data; (5) Information sources/ services; (6) Transportation data. Designed as a guide to possible markets and also as an instructional manual for some practicalities, (e.g., shipping and insurance). Section 2, Export markets, the major part of the book divides each market into: country profile; communications; key contracts; trade regulations; documentation; marketing data; transportation and business travel. HF3011.E9

Exporter's guide to federal resources for small business. [3rd rev. ed.]. Wash. : U.S. Small Business Admin., Office of International Trade : U.S. Govt. Print. Off., 1992. 122 p. **CH140**

Superintendent of Documents classification: SBA 1.19:Ex 7/3/ 992.

Summarizes programs of U.S. agencies and provides directory of agency contacts and potential speakers and a bibliography of major agency publications on international trade. HF1455.E935

Foreign commerce handbook. 1922/23– . Wash. : International Division, Chamber of Commerce of the U.S., 1923– . Irregular. **CH141**

A guide to the sources of export and import services and information. HF3011.F6

Handbook of national development plans / Metra Consulting. London : Graham & Trotman, 1983– . 1 v. (looseleaf). **CH142**

The basic volume provides digests of about 50 national development plans; an additional 20 plans are projected for the semiannual supplement service, with annual consolidated editions. Standard format includes comments on previous plans, summary, allocation of funds by sector, expected effect of plan on GDP, and recent performance of plan; summaries range from five to ten pages. Title of each plan is given in English. HC59.7.H297

International business handbook / V.H. (Manek) Kirpalani, ed. N.Y. : Haworth Pr., c1990. 667 p. : ill., map. (Haworth series in international business, #1). **CH143**

"Designed to inform succinctly about global trends, different regions and their consumer cultures and business customs, methods of entry, and global strategies."—*Pref.* Chapters, all by specialists, are signed. The first is a global overview, the last a consideration of the future; the remaining 15 treat specific countries or regions. Although style varies, chapters generally discuss 15 topics, presenting an overview of economic, physical, sociocultural, political, legal, technological, international, and other factors. Sources of information are also discussed, and each chapter concludes with a bibliography. Country/ geographic area and name indexes. HF1379.I567

Investing, licensing & trading conditions abroad / prep. and publ. by Business International Corp. N.Y. : Business International Corp., c1983– . 3 v. (looseleaf). **CH144**

A regularly updated reference service providing detailed information for 60 countries, on operating conditions, controls, and regulations. Information for each country is in sections covering: the operating environment; organizing an investment; incentives; licensing; competition and price policies; exchange and remitting funds; corporate taxes; personal taxes; capital sources; human resources; foreign trade. HG4538.I6543

Price Waterhouse information guide. 1961– . N. Y. : Price, Waterhouse, 1961– . Irregular. **CH145**

A series of guides prepared for the assistance of those doing business in countries outside the U.S. Guides usually include: country profile; business environment; trade opportunities; investment incentives; restrictions on foreign investment; regulatory environment; banking and finance; labor relations; tax system and administration; taxation of corporations, foreign operations, and individuals. General publications in the series include: Individual taxes, a worldwide summary and U. S. citizens abroad. Frequently revised; kept up-to-date with supplements.

U.S. custom house guide. 1988– . [Philadelphia] : North American Publs., c1988– . Annual. **CH146**

Continues: *Custom house guide* (N.Y. : Import Publs., 1862– 1985).

Kept-up-to-date by monthly supplements called *Global trade*.

In nine sections: (1) Import how-to, useful guidelines from industry experts, with a glossary of international trade; (2) Ports, an alphabetical directory that includes addresses, phone, and fax numbers for customs offices, Dept. of Commerce offices, airports, seaports, and foreign trade zones; (3) Shipping services, a directory of international air cargo carriers, ocean carriers, financial institutions, and translators, which also includes information on legal services, automation services, and companies providing hardware, software, and computer services for the international trade industry; (4) Information sources; (5) Tariff, containing the complete Harmonized Tariff Schedule of the United States, Annotated; (6) Binding rulings index; (7) Special and administrative provisions, nontariff provisions of the Tariff Act of 1930; (8) Customs regulations; (9) Import documents, with sample documents. Indexed.

§ Companion title: *Official export guide* (Glen Cove, N.Y. : Budd Publ., 19??– . Annual).

An export handbook for freight forwarders and exporters. Includes requirements for 180 nations.   KF6652.O35

Atlases

The Economist atlas / ed., Ian Castello-Cortes. 1st American ed., fully rev. and updated 2nd ed. N.Y. : Henry Holt, 1992. 384 p. : col. ill., maps in color ; 26 cm.   **CH147**

1st ed., 1989.

Originally publ. : Great Britain : Business Books, Ltd., 1991.

"World maps copyrighted ... by Esselte Map Service ... World comparisons and world encyclopedia maps and diagrams copyright The Economist Books, Ltd."—*Verso of t.p.*

In three main parts: (1) political maps of the world, grouped together by continent and subcontinent; (2) comparative tables, using maps, charts and graphs to depict the political, economic and demographic characteristics of the countries; and (3) a world encyclopedia that presents a brief overview of each country's economy and its economic history, as well as general information (official name, capital city, ethnic composition, religion, language, education, climate, currency, public holidays, and government). Countries are arranged regionally. General and map indexes.   G1046.G1.E26

Freeman, Michael J. Atlas of the world economy / Michael Freeman ; consulting ed., Derek Aldcroft. N.Y. : Simon & Schuster, c1991. 167 p. : ill.   **CH148**

For each of eight broad categories (population, agriculture, energy, industry, national income, transport and trade, labour, and multinationals) and subcategories, contains brief introductory comments accompanied by some 250 maps, charts, tables, and graphs, none in color. Short bibliography.   HC59.F734

Statistics

Direction of trade statistics. Jan. 1981– . Wash. : International Monetary Fund, 1981– . Quarterly.   **CH149**

Presents, for about 135 countries, "current figures on the value of merchandise exports and imports disaggregated according to their most important trading partners. Reported data are supplemented by estimates whenever such data are not current or not available in monthly frequency."—*Introd.* A yearbook of the same title is also available. The latest presents, for 161 countries, figures on the value of merchandise imports and exports for 1986–92.   HF1016.I652a

•**ECONBASE** : time series & forecasts [database]. Bala Cynwyd, Pa. : The WEFA Group, 1948– .   **CH150**

Coverage varies, with earliest time series beginning in 1948. Available online, updated monthly.

Monthly, quarterly, and annual time series, covering such areas as economics, business conditions, finance, manufacturing, income distribution, prices, and national income. Includes international, national, regional, state, Metropolitan Statistical Area (MSA) and Consolidated Metropolitan Statistical Area (CMSA) data. Data is collected from international, federal, and private sources. Two-year forecasts for some 1,100 major economic indicators. *Data directory*, also available from WEFA (1990), is useful for identifying search codes.

FAO yearbook. Trade = FAO annuaire. Commerce = FAO anuario. Comercio. v. 41 (1987)– . Rome : Food and Agriculture Organization of the United Nations, 1988– . Annual.   **CH151**

For annotation, *see* EJ81.   HD9000.4.T7

Foreign commerce yearbook / U.S. Dept. of Commerce, Bureau of Foreign and Domestic Commerce, Office of International Trade. 1933–51. Wash. : U.S. Govt. Print. Off., 1934–53.   **CH152**

Superintendent of Documents classification: C 18:26/2.

Preceded by: U.S. Bureau of Foreign and Domestic Commerce, *Commerce yearbook*, 1922–1932, which included pt. 1, United States, and pt. 2, Foreign countries. Pt. 1 was discontinued in 1932. Pt. 2 was continued by the Office's *Foreign commerce yearbook*, 1933–39; publication suspended 1934, 1940–47.

Gives detailed information on business conditions in the U.S. and foreign countries, summarizing statistical information originally collected by government bureaus, trade associations, and trade journals, with references to sources of information.   HF53.U72

Guide to foreign trade statistics. 1967– . Wash. : U.S. Bureau of the Census : for sale by U.S. Govt. Print. Off., 1967– . Irregular.   **CH153**

Serves as a guide to the various sources of foreign trade statistics and to the content and general arrangement of the data within these publications. Includes information on: CENDATA; Economic bulletin board; Understanding foreign trade data; U.S. foreign trade highlights; etc.   HF105.B73a

Handbook of international economic statistics / Directorate of Intelligence, Central Intelligence Agency. 1992– . Wash. : The Directorate, 1992– . Annual.   **CH154**

Supersedes *Handbook of economic statistics* publ. 1975–91 by the National Foreign Assessment Center.

Provides statistics for selected noncommunist countries and all the communist countries on national accounts, foreign trade, foreign aid, energy, minerals and metals, agriculture, transportation, manufacturing, construction, communications, etc. Tables arranged by topics, with subject indexes.   HA155.H36

Harmonized tariff schedule of the United States / United States International Trade Commission. 1st ed.– . Wash. : The Commission : U.S. Govt. Print. Off., [1987]– . Annual.

     CH155

Superintendent of Documents classification: ITC 1.10: .

Looseleaf; kept up-to-date between editions by supplements.

Approximately 5,000 six- to ten-digit product-based numbers arranged in 96 chapters. The harmonized schedule is the system in use for classifying imported merchandise for rate of duty and for statistical purposes.

§ Exports are regulated according to *U.S. exports: Schedule B commodity by country* (1989– . Annual. Available in machine-readable form as *U.S. exports and imports of merchandise on CD-ROM*, prep. by the Bureau of the Census [Wash. : The Bureau, 1994]).

For an extensive analysis of foreign trade data and its use, see: *Understanding United States foreign trade data*, prep. by Victor B. Bailey and Sara R. Bowden (Wash. : U.S. Dept. of Commerce, International Trade Admin., 1985. 189 p.).   KF6654.599.U55

International trade. 1952– . Geneva : Contracting Parties to the General Agreement on Tariffs and Trade, 1953– . Annual.   **CH156**

1989– also has title: *GATT international trade*. Issued in 2 v., 1987/88– .

Vol. 1 is devoted principally to an analysis of developments in world trade and international commercial relations. Vol. 2 provides statistical tables and charts on trade by country group, region, and products.   HF499.C65

International trade statistics yearbook = Annuaire statistique du commerce international / Department of International Economic and Social Affairs, Statistical Office. 1983– . N.Y. : United Nations, 1983– . Annual.   **CH157**

Supersedes *Yearbook of international trade statistics*, publ. 1950–82, which continued *International trade statistics*, issued by the League of Nations, 1933–39.

In two volumes: v. 1, Trade by country, contains detailed data by countries, with summary tables on trade relations of each with its region and the world; v. 2, Trade by commodity [and] commodity matrix tables, shows the total economic world trade of certain commodities analysed by region and country.

§ Current quarterly statistics are published irregularly in *Commodity trade statistics* (United Nations, *Statistical papers*, series D).
HF91.U473

Liesner, Thelma. One hundred years of economic statistics : United Kingdom, United States of America, Australia, Canada, France, Germany, Italy, Japan, Sweden. Rev. and expanded to 1987. N.Y. : Facts on File, c1989. 344 p. : col. ill.   **CH158**
Rev. ed. of *Economic statistics, 1900–1983* (1985).

A compilation of key economic indicators, drawn primarily from official publications and arranged by country. Also includes analytical tables and charts that present composite data and growth triangles for all nine countries. Indexed.   HC106.L68

Social indicators of development. [1987]– . Wash. : World Bank, 1988– . Annual.   **CH159**
Imprint varies: Baltimore : Publ. for the World Bank by the Johns Hopkins University Press.

Prepared by the Socio-Economic Data Division, International Economics Dept. of the World Bank.

Economic, social, and demographic data compiled by World Bank countries or international agencies specializing in education, health, nutrition, etc. Arranged alphabetically by country with summary tables (for countries with populations greater than 1 million persons) which permit some comparative analysis. Comparisons are made for specific intervals, such as 1965–1975–1985, with projections for the future. 1992 ed. covers 171 countries. Diskette version has time series for all years for which data is available. Data is derived from *World development indicators*. Bibliography.   HC59.69.S63

United Nations Conference on Trade and Development. Handbook of international trade and development statistics. N.Y. : United Nations, 1964– . Irregular.   **CH160**
In English and French.

Offers a basic collection of statistical data on world trade and development. Sources of statistical tables are indicated. Kept up-to-date between editions by annual supplements.   HF1016.U54a

World debt tables. Wash. : World Bank, 1976– . Annual.   **CH161**
Continues *External public debt*.

Each annual issue in 2 v. Vol. 1 contains "analysis and commentary on recent developments in international finance for developing countries, together with summary statistical tables for selected regions, and analytical groups comprising 116 countries that report to the World Bank's Debtor Reporting System."—*Pref.* Incorporates 25 low- and middle-income countries that do not normally report to the System; v. 2 contains statistical tables by country, including former Soviet republics.   HJ8899.W672

World development report. 1978– . [N.Y.] : Oxford Univ. Pr., [1978]– . Annual.   **CH162**
Publ. for the World Bank.

Each volume presents an overview and analysis of a topic currently relevant to international economic development. The statistical portion, *World development indicators*, presents selected social, economic and demographic data on 180 countries (1992 ed.) and is also available on diskette. Bibliography of World Bank background papers and other resources.   HC59.7.W659

World economic outlook : a survey by the staff of the International Monetary Fund. May 1980– . Wash. : The Fund, [1980–]. Semiannual.   **CH163**
Frequency varies: annual, 1980–Apr. 1984. Semiannual since Sept. 1984.

Also called, 1981–1984: *Occasional paper/International Monetary Fund*.

Combines a review of world economic conditions with short- and medium-term (up to five years) economic projections. Slightly more than half the publication consists of expository chapters (supplemented by tables, charts, and notes) that discuss the economy in industrial and developing countries. A lengthy statistical appendix contains 43 tables, showing output, inflation, financial policies, foreign trade, current account transactions, current account financing, external debt and debt service, and flow of funds summary. No index.   HC10.W7979

World economic survey. 1955– . N.Y. : United Nations Dept. of International Economic and Social Affairs, 1956– . Annual.   **CH164**
Succeeds: *Economic report*, 1945/57; *World economic report*, 1948–1953/54. Many issues in 2 pts.

Issued by United Nations Dept. of Economic and Social Affairs, 1955– ; Centre for Development Planning, Projections, and Policies, 1971– ; Dept. of International Economic and Social Affairs, 1977– .

A comprehensive review of world economic conditions and trends, with statistical annex of world economic and financial data. Special supplements issued in some years.   HC59.A169

World trade annual. 1963– . [N.Y. : Walker].   **CH165**
Prep. by the Statistical Office of the United Nations.
1963–68 in 4 v. per year; 1969– in 5 v. per year.

Based on data provided by the 22 principal trading countries of the world, the series is designed to provide both summarized and detailed statistics of trade by commodity by country. Currently arranged by region and country, then by exports and imports according to Standard International Trade Classification number; values shown in U.S. dollars.   HF53.W6

North America

United States

American business climate & economic profiles : a concise compilation of facts, rankings, incentives, and resource listings, for all 319 Metropolitan Statistical Areas (MSAs) and the 50 states / Priscilla Cheng Geahigan, ed. Detroit : Gale, c1994. 1093 p.   **CH166**
In two parts: (1) statistics covering such categories as population, civilian labor force, gross state product, and income, as well as topics such as geographic profile, ranking highlights and quality of life: (2) ranked MSAs (by group) in 22 categories including unemployment rate, labor force size, and violent crime per 1,000 inhabitants. Compiled from a selection of state bureaus, federal and commercial sources. Table of contents lists all MSAs and ranking groups.
HC102.2.A44

Catalog of federal domestic assistance. 1965– . Wash. : U.S. Govt. Print. Off., 1965– . Annual.   **CH167**
Superintendent of Documents classification: PREX 2.20: .
Update publ. 6 mos. after the *Catalog*.
1965–70 issued by U.S. Office of Economic Opportunity.
Title varies: 1965, *Catalog of federal programs for individual and community improvement*; 1967, *Catalog of federal assistance programs*.

"A government-wide compendium of Federal programs, projects and activities which provide assistance or benefits to the American public.—*Introd. 1993*. Describes 1,308 programs administered by 51 Federal agencies. Can be searched online via *Federal assistance programs retrieval system*. Also available on diskette or CD-ROM.
HC110.P63U53a

Economic indicators / prep. for the Joint Economic Committee by the Council of Economic Advisers. May 1948– . Wash. : U.S. Govt. Print. Off. Monthly.   **CH168**
Superintendent of Documents classification: Y4.EC7:EC7/ .

From 1948–56, prep. for the Joint Committee on the Economic Report.

Presents basic statistical series on total output, income, and spending; employment, unemployment, and wages; production and business activity; prices, currency, credit, and security markets; and federal finance.

Supplements, published in 1953 and revised 1955, 1957, 1960, 1962, 1964, and 1967, describe each series and give annual data.

HC101.A186

Government assistance almanac. 1985–86– . Wash. : Foggy Bottom Publications, c1985– . Annual.   **CH169**

Compiled by J. R. Dumouchel, 1985– .

Provides information on federal assistance programs, both financial (direct payments, loans, etc.) and nonfinancial (advisory services, investigation of complaints, etc.), drawn from *Catalog of federal domestic assistance* (CH167). Condenses the profiles of individual programs found in the *Catalog*, adding both an introductory section on application strategies and tables that summarize funding of programs the previous year. Easier to use, but not as comprehensive.

HC110.P63G69

The handbook of economic and financial measures / ed. by Frank J. Fabozzi and Harry I. Greenfield. Homewood, Ill. : Dow Jones-Irwin, [1984]. 517 p. : ill.   **CH170**

In 21 chapters by subject specialists, treats the most commonly used measures of economic activity, explaining their background, construction, uses, and limitations. In six sections: aggregate economic activity; government deficit and trade balance; money supply and capital market conditions; inflation; firms and consumers; forecasting. Bibliographic references; index.   HC106.8.H36

Hoel, Arline Alchian. Economics sourcebook of government statistics / Arline Alchian Hoel, Kenneth W. Clarkson, Roger LeRoy Miller. Lexington, Mass. : Lexington Books, c1983]. 271 p.   **CH171**

Describes more than 50 main statistical series published by the federal government in terms of how they are compiled, strengths and weaknesses, when they become available, primary and secondary sources of current and historical publications, references on the series, and agency to be contacted. In six chapters covering inflation, general business conditions, interest rates, employment and earnings, international finance and trade, the budget. Appendixes; glossary; index.

HC106.8.H63

Hutchinson, William Kenneth. American economic history : a guide to information sources. Detroit : Gale, [1980]. 296 p. (Economics information guide ser., v. 16).   **CH172**

An introductory bibliography for the student of the "new economic history [which] emphasizes the use of statistics, data processing ... and the application of rigorous economic models to the available [historical] data."—*Introd.* Topical arrangement of more than 1,500 books and periodical articles covering the period from the colonial era to 1960; most entries are annotated. Brief appendixes list relevant organizations and journals. Author, title, and subject indexes.

Z7165.U5H89

United States. Bureau of Economic Analysis. Long term economic growth. [Wash. : the Bureau; for sale by the U.S. Govt. Print. Off.].   **CH173**

Superintendent of Documents classification: C56.102: EC7/860– .

Charts, graphs, and statistical tables offer a comprehensive view of the growth of the American economy. Each volume cumulative from 1860.   HA203.A241

United States. President. Economic report of the President transmitted to the Congress. [Dept. ed.]. Jan. 6, 1950– . Wash. : U.S. Govt. Print. Off., 1950– . Annual.   **CH174**

Superintendent of Documents classification: PR 40.9: [etc.].

Reports include the annual report of the Council of Economic Advisers.

Offers a review of the nation's economic condition, documented by statistics.   HC106.5.A272

Canada

Canadian business and economics : a guide to sources of information / Barbara E. Brown, ed. 3rd ed. Ottawa : Canadian Libr. Assoc., c1992. 675 p.   **CH175**

In English and French.

1st ed., 1976.

A comprehensive work, with many annotations, arranged by type of publication (bibliographies, directories, etc.) and by subject. Lists chiefly English-language works with Canadian content published before 1991. Emphasizes currently useful materials; omits trade journals, most annual reports of government agencies, and most publications listed in categories of Statistics Canada. Indexes of authors, titles, corporate authors, and selected series.   Z7165.C2C225

Dick, Trevor J. O. Economic history of Canada : a guide to information sources. Detroit : Gale, [1978]. 174 p. (Economics information guide series, 9).   **CH176**

A classed bibliography of materials grouped in five chapters, with appropriate topical, geographical, and chronological subdivisions: (1) Interpretive and bibliographic sources; (2) From colonial times to the present; (3) The colonial period to 1867; (4) Confederation (1867) to 1920; (5) From 1920 to the present. Brief evaluative comments on the sources precede each subdivision. Author, title, and subject indexes.

Z7165.C2D5

Latin America

Felipe Herrera Library. Index of periodical articles on the economics of Latin America / Inter-American Development Bank, Felipe Herrera Library. Boston : G.K. Hall, 1983. 4 v.   **CH177**

Contents: v. 1, Author index; v. 2, Title index; v. 3–4, Subject index; Geographical index.

Covers articles published 1950–77. The Library receives over 1,200 current periodicals and 70 newspapers and has extensive holdings of official serial publications of international and regional organizations. Covers articles published 1950–77. Uses Spanish-language subject and geographical headings.   Z7165.L3F44

Harvard University. Bureau for Economic Research in Latin America. Economic literature of Latin America : a tentative bibliography. Cambridge : Harvard Univ. Pr., 1935–36. 2 v.   **CH178**

An extensive bibliography of books, pamphlets, and periodical articles listing a total of 12,520 numbered items. Arranged geographically by country or region, with a subject arrangement under each and a general index of authors for each volume. Special features are the introductory notes at the head of important sections; the appendixes on the statistical sources of South America, Mexico, and the Caribbean; and notes on collections of Latin-American economic literature in leading libraries.   Z7164.E2H36

Jones, Tom Bard. A bibliography on South American economic affairs : articles in nineteenth-century periodicals / Tom Bard Jones, Elizabeth Anne Warburton, Anne Kingsley. Minneapolis : Univ. of Minnesota Pr., [1955]. 146 p.   **CH179**

Material from more than 220 sources in English, French, Italian, German and Spanish, arranged by country. Covers agriculture, commerce, communications, finance, immigration, industry, labor, mining, and transportation.   Z7165.S75J6

Latin America : a guide to economic history, 1830–1930 / Roberto Cortés Conde and Stanley J. Stein, editors. Berkeley : Univ. of California Pr., 1977. 685 p.   **CH180**

"Sponsored by the Joint Committee on Latin American Studies of the American Council of Learned Societies and the Social Science Research Council and by the Consejo Latinoamericano de Ciencias Sociales."—*t.p.*

A cooperative effort of an international group of scholars. A section for general bibliography is followed by separate sections for Argentina, Brazil, Chile, Colombia, Mexico, and Peru. Each country section begins with an interpretive essay, and the ensuing bibliography for each is topically subdivided under ten major headings: (1) General and reference works; (2) Demography, manpower, and living conditions; (3) Structures and institutions; (4) Macroeconomic growth and fluctuation; (5) Foreign trade and investment; (6) Regional economy; (7) Agriculture, ranching, forestry; (8) Industry: factory and artisan; (9) Extractive industry; (10) Transport, public utilities and services. Introductory essays and annotations are in the language of the contributor. Indexes of authors and of periodicals.   Z7165.L3L32

Europe

Clarke, Roger A. Soviet economic facts, 1917–81 / Roger A. Clarke, Dubravko J. I. Matko. N.Y. : St. Martin's, [1983]. 228 p.   **CH181**

1st ed., 1972, had title: *Soviet economic facts, 1917–1970.*

"The object of this volume … is to present … complete annual series for the main aggregate economic magnitudes, a list of industrial and agricultural products which is determined basically by availability, and … other more general data related to economic performance."— *Pref.* Compiled from official Soviet sources and Western estimates; sources noted.   HC335.C519

COMECON data / ed. by the Vienna Institute for Comparative Economic Studies. N.Y. : Macmillan, c1980–c1990.   **CH182**

Frequency varied: biennial, 1979–86; annual, 1978–90.

Presents statistical data on economic conditions in the former CMEA (Council of Mutual Economic Assistance)—Bulgaria, Czechoslovakia, German Democratic Republic, Hungary, Poland, Romania, and the U.S.S.R. Includes Yugoslavia as well; earlier editions included Cuba, Mongolia, Vietnam, and Albania. Most tables cover the previous 20 years and incorporate information not previously published. Sources are national statistical yearbooks, periodicals, international organizations, and other Western sources.

§ Published in alternate years: *COMECON foreign trade data* (Westport, Conn. : Greenwood, 1984–88).   HC244.C186

European directory of trade and business associations. 1990– . London : Euromonitor Publications Ltd., 1990– .   **CH183**

Describes about 2,000 major business and trade associations active in Western Europe; covers 17 countries, including the European Community and the European Free Trade Association countries. Emphasizes those that collect statistical data. Directory entries include publications and organizational aims and objectives.   HD2429.E87E875

Panorama of EC industry. 1989– . Luxembourg : Office for Official Publications of the European Communities, 1988– . Biennial (beginning with 1991/1992 volume).   **CH184**

Also available in Spanish, German, French, and Italian.

Describes the current situation for more than 125 European manufacturing and service industries. Major trends are identified, and production, foreign trade, and other statistics are presented. Most analyses include a forecast and outlook section. A macroeconomic outlook for Europe and an index are also included.

A *Short-term supplement* began publication in 1993, issued bimonthly. *Panorama* is also kept up-to-date by a statistical supplement, which began in 1992.   HC241.2.P313

Sources of European economic and business information. 5th ed. Aldershot, Hampshire, England ; Brookfield, Vt. : Ballinger, 1990. 239 p.   **CH185**

1st ed., 1974; 4th ed., 1983, ed. by Euan Blauvelt and Jennifer Durlacher. had title: *Sources of European economic information.*

Lists about 6,000 sources of economic and statistical information for Western and Eastern Europe; includes monographic and serial publications of public and private organizations and publishers. Directory of publications, arranged by country, includes brief annotations. Title and subject indexes, arranged by country.   Z7165.E8B59

A study of the Soviet economy. Wash. : International Monetary Fund, c1991. 3 v. : ill.   **CH186**

A detailed study, undertaken by the International Monetary Fund, Organization for Economic Co-operation and Development, and European Bank for Reconstruction and Development. Vol. 1 covers general economic and reform developments and macroeconomic policies and reform; v. 2 deals with systemic reforms, including prices, enterprises, foreign trade, foreign direct investment, finance, labor, and social policies; and v. 3 focuses on such sectoral issues as the environment, transportation, telecommunications, energy, manufacturing, and housing. A chapter on medium-term economic prospects and an unannotated bibliography are also included. Numerous statistical tables. Not indexed.

§ Related work: *The economy of the U.S.S.R : summary and recommendations* (Wash. : International Monetary Fund, c1990. 51 p.) is a condensed version.   HC336.26.S78

Great Britain

Hanson, Laurence William. Contemporary printed sources for British and Irish economic history, 1701–1750. Cambridge : Univ. Pr., 1963. 978 p.   **CH187**

Includes books, pamphlets, broadsides, etc., totaling more than 6,500 items, published 1701–50 inclusive. Represents the holdings of the principal libraries of Great Britain and eight important libraries of the United States. Locates copies.   Z7165.G8H35

Palmer, Stanley H. Economic arithmetic : a guide to the statistical sources of English commerce, industry, and finance, 1700–1850. N.Y. : Garland, 1977. 207 p. (Garland reference library of social science, v. 26).   **CH188**

A series of essays on the statistics of commerce, prices, the textile industries, mining industries, iron industry, banking and finance; lists statistical sources of the period prior to the appearance of official statistical bureaus and their publications. Notes both primary sources (government documents, books, and pamphlets) and secondary materials. Bibliography; index.   Z7554.G7P34

Africa, North

Blauvelt, Euan. Sources of African and Middle-Eastern economic information / ed. by Euan Blauvelt and Jennifer Durlacher. Westport, Conn. : Greenwood, 1982. 2 v.   **CH189**

A directory of statistical and economic source publications that gives bibliographic data and brief annotations for books, periodicals, government and international documents, reports from public and private organizations and from publishers. Covers countries of West Asia and continental Africa, arranged by country. Indexed by title and subject, subdivided by country. Directory of issuing bodies.

Z7165.A4B55

Asia, West

Khan, Muhammad Akram. Islamic economics : annotated sources in English and Urdu. Leicester, [Eng.], Islamic Foundation, [1983]. 221 p. (Islamic economics series, 7).   **CH190**

A classed bibliography of about 650 entries, with supplement; author and subject indexes.

§ A complementary work is Muhammad Nejatullah Siddiqi's *Muslim economic thinking : a survey of contemporary literature* (Leicester : Islamic Foundation, 1981. 130 p. [Islamic economic series, 1]).   Z7935.M6K48

Middle East review. 1974– . Saffron Walden, Essex, Eng. : Middle East Review Co., Ltd. : Distr. in the U.S. by Rand McNally, 1974– . Annual.   **CH191**

Title varies: 1974–80, *Middle East annual review.*

Also issued in an Arabic ed.

In two main sections: (1) a series of introductory chapters by British and American journalists and researchers on various topics in areas of trade, industry, civil engineering and construction, services, finances, etc.; (2) a country-by-country survey contributed by individual authors; these surveys include politics, foreign relations, social conditions, development plans, budget, foreign investment, balance of payments, etc., and provide factual and analytical information. "Middle East" is defined to include North Africa, Somalia, and the Sudan. Similar volumes cover other geographic regions: *Africa review* (DD61), *Latin America and Caribbean review, Asia & Pacific review.*

HC410.7.A1M517

Nicholas, David. The Middle East, its oil, economics and investment policies : a guide to sources of financial information. Westport, Conn. : Greenwood, 1981. 199 p.   **CH192**

Annotates English-language sources published since 1970 in the following areas: (1) economics and finance (general); (2) petroleum and energy (general); (3) Middle East oil and economics: historical, geographical, and political background; (4) Middle East economies and the petroleum industry; (5) economies of individual Middle Eastern countries; (6) economic relationships between the Middle East and other countries. Within each subject area sources are arranged by form: guides; directories, annuals, reference works; periodicals; books, reports, and pamphlets. Brief discussion of databases and online services. Indexed.   HD9576.N36N52

A selected and annotated bibliography of economic literature on the Arabic speaking countries of the Middle East. 1938/52–1953/65. Beirut : American Univ. of Beirut, Economic Research Institute, 1954–67.   **CH193**

Title varies slightly.

A basic volume covering 1938/52 was publ. 1952 (199 p.), with annual supplements beginning 1953; a second cumulation covering 1953/65 appeared in 1967 (458 p.). A cumulation for the period 1938/60 was publ. Boston : G.K. Hall, 1967 (358 p.); in addition to cumulating the entries from the basic work and the annual supplements, some 800 new entries were added in that volume.

Classified arrangement with author index. Includes works in Arabic, English, and French.   Z7164.E15A6

Asia, South

India

Annotated bibliography on the economic history of India : 1500 A.D. to 1947 A.D. / [chief ed., V. D. Divekar]. Pune : Gokhale Institute of Politics & Economics ; New Delhi : Indian Council of Social Science Research, 1977–80. 4 v. in 5.   **CH194**

Half-title: Economic history of India: a bibliography.

Contents: v. 1, Selections from records; Survey and settlement reports; Gazetteers; Acts and regulations; v. 2, British Parliamentary papers; Reports of committees and commissions; v. 3, Census reports; serials; v. 4A, Books; v. 4B, Articles; theses; addenda.

A classified arrangement of English-language printed sources; each part has an introduction, as well as subject, region, and author indexes. Particular attention has been given to statistical material on economic history. A major bibliography.   Z7165.I6A8

Rath, Vimal. Index of Indian economic journals, 1916–1965. Poona : Gokhale Institute of Politics and Economics; Orient Longman, [1971]. liv, 302 p. (Gokhale Institute studies, no. 57).   **CH195**

Indexes 31 quarterly and monthly English-language journals published in India, plus statistical publications of the government of India and state governments. Uses *Journal of economic literature* classification; author index.

§ For current coverage, see: *Index to Indian economic journals* (1966– . Calcutta : Information Research Academy. Frequency varies).   Z7164.E2R35

Ruokonen, Kyllikki. India information sources, economics and business / Kyllikki Ruokonen, Manohar Lal. New Delhi : Concept Pub. Co., 1992. 232 p. (Concepts in communication, informatics & librarianship, 38).   **CH196**

Lists works by subject, subarranged by format; sources are predominantly Indian, limited to English language. Appendixes include list of recent dissertations published in India.

Expanded version of: *India : sources of economic and business information* (Helsinki : Helsinki School of Economics, 1989).   Z7165.I6R8

Survey of research in economic and social history of India : a project sponsored by Indian Council of Social Science Research / editor, R.S. Sharma. Delhi : Ajanta Publications : Distributors, Ajanta Books International (India), 1986. 283 p.   **CH197**

A collection of bibliographic essays on the economic and social history of ancient (up to 1200 CE), medieval (1250–1750), and modern India. Author and subject index.   HC435.2.S89

TT. Maps & Publications Private Ltd. A social and economic atlas of India. Delhi ; N.Y. : Oxford Univ. Pr., c1987. 254 p. : maps in color ; 37 cm.   **CH198**

Provides an up-to-date picture of India's habitat, society and economy through color maps, significantly enhanced by charts and tables. Supplemented by brief explanatory yet comprehensive text.

Transparent overlay showing boundaries in pocket.   G2281.G1T8

Middle East

See Asia, West.

Pacific Rim

Almanac of China's foreign economic relations and trade / Editorial Board of the Almanac of China's Foreign Economic Relations and Trade. 1984– . Hong Kong : China Resources Trade Consultancy Co. : Joint Pub. Co. (Hong Kong Branch) [distributor], 1984– . Annual.   **CH199**

Published separately in Chinese and in English. Each annual volume reviews China's economy, trade, industry, commerce, and finance. 1992 volume includes official documents, special articles written by officials of the Ministry of Foreign Economic Relations and

Trade, 1991 foreign economic trade laws and regulations, statistics of foreign trade, and directory of leading trade officials and organizations. HF3833.A445

Asia Pacific : an investment guide. London, England : Euromoney Publications, 1990. 282 p. : ill. **CH200**

Presents profiles of 11 countries or territories (Australia, Hong Kong, Indonesia, Republic of Korea, Malaysia, New Zealand, the Philippines, Singapore, Taiwan, Thailand, and China), discussing for each its economy, foreign investment, capital markets, equity market, the corporate sector, regulatory environment, and tax and accounting practices. An introductory chapter considers the development of the Pacific Rim, while the final chapter describes the emerging markets in Laos and Vietnam. Numerous statistics, charts, graphs, photographs and other illustrations. Not indexed. HG5702.A752

Asian-Pacific economic literature. v. 1 (May 1987)– . Canberra : National Centre for Development Studies, Australian National Univ., 1987– . Semiannual. **CH201**

Vols. for 1989–91 published for the Centre by Beech Tree Pub., Guildford, UK.

Contains literature surveys, book reviews, a list of books with shorter annotations, abstracts of journal articles, contents lists of journals, and a list of selected working papers prepared by regional research institutes. Covers all aspects of economic development in the Asian-Pacific region. Author index. HC411.A733

Blauvelt, Euan. Sources of Asian/Pacific economic information / Euan Blauvelt, Jennifer Durlacher. Westport, Conn. : Greenwood, [1981]. 2 v. **CH202**

An annotated bibliography of more than 5,000 entries, providing bibliographic details, language, date or frequency of publication, and summary of contents. Country arrangement. Also lists international organizations which cover more than one country. Includes monographic as well as serial publications. List of publishing bodies includes addresses. Indexed by title, subject, and issuing organization. Z7165.P26B53

China trade and price statistics / State Statistical Bureau, People's Republic of China. 1st ed.– . [Beijing?] : China Statistical Information and Consultancy Service Centre ; Hong Kong : Sole distributor outside the PRC, Oxford Univ. Pr., 1987– . **CH203**

Edition numbering dropped in 1988.

Publ.: N.Y. : Praeger, 1989– .

Tables of statistics in four sections: domestic trade; price indexes and average prices; foreign economic relations; trade and tourism. Generally the statistics begin with the early 1950s. Brief explanatory notes. No index. HF3831.C476

Ruokonen, Kyllikki. Japan, sources of economic and business information / Kyllikki Ruokonen, Takayasu Miyakawa. Helsinki : Helsinki School of Economics and Business Administration, Library, 1991. 100 p. **CH204**

Classified list of briefly annotated reference works about Japan, available in English. Cites general reference works, bibliographies, directories, databases, and provides directory information for publishers, libraries, research institutes, and bookstores. Indexes by author, organization, and subjects. HF5256.R86

FINANCE AND INVESTMENT

General Works

Bibliography

Fisher, William Harvey. Financial journals and serials : an analytical guide to accounting, banking, finance, insurance, and investment periodicals. N.Y. : Greenwood, 1986. 201 p. (Annotated bibliographies of serials, no. 6). **CH205**

Lists more than 500 English-language titles, including scholarly journals, popular periodicals, newsletters, looseleaf services, association publications, and house organs. Entries include an evaluative annotation with publishing particulars; manuscript selection policy; inclusion of book reviews and special issues; where indexed; and target audience. Table of abbreviations and directories of indexes and abstracts, microform and reprint publishers, and databases. Geographic, title, publisher, and subject indexes. Z7164.F5F53

Investigators' guide to sources of information. Wash. : U.S. General Accounting Office, [1992]. 85 p. **CH206**

Superintendent of Documents classification: GA 1.13:OSI-92-1 (microfiche).

1st publ. 1988.

Lists city, county, state, federal, and commercial sources of information about businesses, finances, people, and property. Each chapter has a chart that provides a quick overview, followed by descriptive information. Includes federal and commercial databases. JK468.P76I54

Masui, Mitsuzō. A bibliography of finance. Kobe, Japan : International Finance Seminar in the Kobe Univ. of Commerce ; Tokyo : Keigyosha Pr., 1935. 1614 p., 116 p. **CH207**

(Repr.: N.Y. : B. Franklin, 1969).

Contents: British books and articles; Ouvrages françaises; Deutsche Literatur; American books and articles; Author index.

Lists books, pamphlets, journal articles, and government publications in English, French and German, dating from the 15th century to 1933. Classified by country, with topical subdivisions listed chronologically. Z7164.F5M27

Wilson, Carol R. The World Bank Group : a guide to information sources. N.Y. : Garland, 1991. 322 p. (Research and information guides in business, industry, and economic institutions, 4 ; Garland reference library of social science, v. 572). **CH208**

Lists works published 1944–90 concerning organizations that constitute the World Bank (International Bank for Research and Development, International Development Association, and International Finance Corporation) or were its predecessors (Bretton Woods Conference). Includes International Centre for the Settlement of Investment Disputes (ICSID), Multilateral Investment Guarantee Agency, and Consultative Group on International Agricultural Research. Brief annotations. Indexed by authors, personal names, titles, countries, and subjects. HG3881.5.W57W55

Dictionaries

Downes, John. Dictionary of finance and investment terms / John Downes, Jordan Elliot Goodman. 3rd ed. N.Y. : Barron's, c1991. 537 p. : ill. **CH209**

1st ed., 1985; 2nd ed., 1987.

More than 3,000 terms, which cover current terminology in stocks and bonds, banking, corporate finance, and related operations. HG151.D69

Jarrell, Howard R. Common stock newspaper abbreviations and trading symbols. Metuchen, N.J. : Scarecrow, 1989. 413 p. : ill.   **CH210**

Lists Associated Press abbreviations, primary stock exchange/market on which traded, and ticker symbols for more than 6,300 companies selling common stock on the New York or American Stock Exchanges or traded in the 6,300 companies selling common stock on the New York or American Stock Exchanges or traded in the over-the-counter National Association of Securities Dealers Automated Quotations (NASDAQ) market. Separate sections provide access by company name, AP newspaper abbreviation, and ticker symbol.

————. ————. *Supplement one* (1991), covers some 2,400 changes and new listings that have occurred since the original volume was compiled.   HG4636.J37

Pessin, Allan H. The illustrated encyclopedia of the securities industry. N.Y. : New York Institute of Finance, c1988. 530 p. : ill.   **CH211**

Essentially a dictionary of investment and finance. Definitions range in length from a sentence to a few pages and frequently are supplemented by graphs, charts, or securities tables from newspaper financial pages.   HG4513.P463

———————— The complete words of Wall Street : the professional's guide to investment literacy / Allan H. Pessin, Joseph A. Ross. Homewood, Ill. : Business One Irwin, c1991. 797 p.   **CH212**

Supersedes the authors' *Words of Wall Street* (1983), *More words of Wall Street* (1986), and *Still more words of Wall Street* (1990).

Dictionary of current usage in finance, the securities industry and investments.   HG4513.P46

Siegel, Joel G. Dictionary of personal finance / Joel G. Siegel, Jae K. Shim, Stephen Hartman. N.Y. : Macmillan : Maxwell Macmillan International, c1992. 391 p. : ill.   **CH213**

"For the layperson, consumer, and professional to be able to read and comprehend terms and concepts ... dealing with money management, personal finance, and consumer economics."—*Pref.* Definitions include many practical examples and cross-references.   HG151.S427

Foreign terms

Elsevier's dictionary of financial terms in English, German, Spanish, French, Italian, and Dutch / by Francis J. Thomson. Amsterdam ; N.Y. : Elsevier Scientific Publ. Co., 1979. 496 p.   **CH214**

Originally intended as a revision of S. F. Horn's *Glossary of financial terms* (1965), with the inclusion of two additional languages, Italian and Dutch. For about 2,400 English terms, offers equivalents in the other languages and indexes from those languages.   HG151.E47

Directories

Directory of world stock exchanges / comp. by the Economist Publications. Baltimore : Johns Hopkins Univ. Pr., 1988. 469 p. : ill.   **CH215**

Combines standard directory listings with other useful information (e.g., organization of the exchange, trading hours, types of securities traded and settlement procedures, taxation of income, special rules for foreign investors, technical publications, and information sources). Entries frequently include histories of the exchanges (some with chronologies) and tables that show nominal and market value of shares traded, turnover of the exchange, and share price indexes for 1982–86. Arranged by country, then city. No index.   HG4551.D53

The handbook of world stock and commodity exchanges. 1991– . Oxford ; Cambridge, Mass. : Blackwell Finance, c1991– . Annual.   **CH216**

Year appears in title (*The 1993 handbook ...*).

Pt. 1 reviews the current role of world exchanges, with highlights of new developments and trends in international financial markets. Pt. 2 lists each exchange, arranged by country; includes brief history and structure, officers, trading system, rates and other costs, margins, and other trade contract details. Appendixes: abbreviations and acronyms; glossary; index of personnel and commodities traded.   HG4551.H319

Handbooks

Financing foreign operations : monthly reference service. N.Y. : Business International Corporation, 1966– . 2 v. (loose-leaf).   **CH217**

Provides information on financial opportunities in 45 countries. For each country, has sections for: business overview; currency outlook; foreign exchange regulations; monetary system; sources of capital; short-term financing techniques; medium and long-term financing; equity financing; capital incentives; cash management; short-term investment instruments; trade finance and insurance; tax considerations. Information is also provided concerning financial and technical assistance available through the World Bank, European governments, and U.S. and Canadian governments.

Handbook of financial markets : securities, options, and futures / ed. by Frank J. Fabozzi and Frank G. Zarb. 2nd ed. Homewood, Ill. : Dow Jones-Irwin, c1986. 785 p. : ill.   **CH218**

1st ed., 1981.

Written by subject specialists, organized in three parts: The securities markets: environment, structure, instruments and private financial intermediaries; The options market; and The futures market: commodity and financial. Bibliographic references and index.

HG4527.H25

Marshall, Marion B. Public finance : an information sourcebook. Phoenix : Oryx, 1987. 287 p. (Oryx sourcebook series in business management and management, no. 6).   **CH219**

Intended for those unfamiliar with the basic concepts or literature of public finance in the U.S. Lists and annotates sources, grouped by subject (e.g., theory, state and local fiscal policy, intergovernmental fiscal relations), and identifies and annotates 28 titles for a core library collection. Author, title, and subject indexes.   Z7164.P9555M38

Muksian, Robert. Financial mathematics handbook. Englewood Cliffs, N.J. : Prentice-Hall, c1984. 486 p. : ill.   **CH220**

Demonstrates formulas and tables for the calculation of interest, annuity values, bonds, loan payments, depreciation of assets, etc.; provides general tables of algorithms, exponentials, and compound interest at varying rates.   HF5691.M84

Sources of world financial and banking information / G. R. Dicks, ed. Westport, Conn. : Greenwood, 1981. 720 p.
                                                                  CH221

Brief summaries of about 5,000 sources listed by region and by country. List of publishers, by country. Seven topical indexes, subdivided by country.   Z7164.F5S713

Statistics

Finance, insurance, & real estate USA. 1st ed.– . Detroit : Gale, c1993– . Biennial.   **CH222**

For annotation, *see* CH388.

S & P statistical service. v. 60 no. 6 (June 1994)– . N.Y. : Standard & Poor's Corp. Monthly.   **CH223**

Continues *Standard & Poor's statistical service.*

Three components:

Basic statistics. Records numerous financial and economic time series from commercial and governmental sources.

Current statistics. Updates the Basic statistics, and contains current records of S&P stock price indexes. Industry groups covered are Banking and finance, Production and labor, Price indexes, Income and trade, Building, Electric power and fuels, Metals, Transportation, Textiles-chemicals-paper, and Agricultural products.

Security price index record (biennial). Traces the movement of stock and bond prices by industry groups.   HG4921.S652

Finance

Bibliography

Brealey, Richard A. A bibliography of finance / Richard Brealey, Helen Edwards. Cambridge, Mass. : MIT Pr., c1991. 822 p.   **CH224**

A selective bibliography of English-language works published worldwide, 1750–1989, although more than half were published 1980–89. No annotations. Arranged by 40 main subject areas subdivided into 373 subjects; entries listed in descending chronological order. Index of keywords and authors.   Z7164.F5B76

Indexes

Finance literature index / ed. by Jean Louis Heck. 3rd ed., 50th anniversary ed. N.Y. : McGraw-Hill Book, c1992. 527 p.   **CH225**

1st ed., 1988; 2nd ed., 1989.

Table of contents and author index to about 35 journals in finance, insurance, and real estate. Covers each journal from first issue to 1990.   Z7164.F5F46

Encyclopedias

Fraser, Robert. The world financial system. Burnt Mill, Harlow, Essex, England : Longman ; Phoenix : Oryx, c1987. 582 p.   **CH226**

In three parts. Pt. 1 discusses the evolution of the world financial system, covering such developments as the Marshall Plan, the formation of the International Monetary Fund (IMF), and Third World country indebtedness, providing numerous statistical tables and texts of significant agreements excerpted or printed in their entirety. Pt. 2, International economic organizations, lists some 50 organizations, grouped geographically under four headings (general, monetary, developmental, and trade), giving besides standard directory information, extensive discussion of the organization's background, objectives, membership, and structure. Pt. 3, U.N. declarations, lists, describes, and reprints the text of relevant U.N. declarations. Three appendixes: Independence, U.N. and IMF membership; Country nomenclature; Exchange rate movements 1970–86. Brief bibliography; index.   HG3881.F7118

Dictionaries

Scott, David Logan. Wall Street words. Boston : Houghton Mifflin Co., c1988. 404 p. : ill.   **CH227**

Contains definitions of 3,600 terms, many supplemented by case studies. Also features 87 investment tips from experts, typical examples of technical analysis chart patterns, and a brief bibliography.   HG4513.S37

Directories

The corporate finance bluebook. 1983– . Wilmette, Ill. : National Register Publ. Co., c1983– . Annual.   **CH228**

Publisher varies.

Lists more than 5,000 major public and private U.S. companies. In addition to standard business directory information, entries frequently include: sales estimates, assets and liabilities, net worth, assets of pension/profit sharing fund portfolio, key financial officers, and outside firms providing financial services. Detailed indexes by company name, Standard Industrial Classification (SIC), outside firms providing financial services (grouped by service category), geographical, and personnel.

•Available as part of *Corporate affiliations plus* [database] (CH351 *note*).   HG4057.A15647

The corporate finance sourcebook. 1979– . N.Y. : McGraw-Hill Book Co.   **CH229**

Publisher varies.

A directory of firms (3,719 in 1993) involved in capital investments and financial services (e.g., venture capital, private lenders, commercial and financial factors, business intermediaries, leasing companies and corporate real estate, commercial, U.S.-based foreign, and investments banks and trusts, securities analysts and CPA/auditing firms. Entries include personnel, financial information, and selected clients.   HG4057.A1565

Pratt's guide to venture capital sources. 8th ed. (1984)– . Wellesley Hills, Mass. : Capital Pub., c1984– . Annual.   **CH230**

Overview of the venture capital industry, and directories of U.S. and foreign venture capital companies. Includes names of contacts and project preferences. Indexed by company name, personnel, and project preference.   HG65.G83

Standard & Poor's security dealers of North America. Fall 1975– . N.Y. : Standard and Poor's Corp., 1975– . Semiannual.   **CH231**

Previously issued under variant titles, 1922–1975. Frequency varied.

Aims to provide an up-to-date listing of all stock and bond dealers in the United States and Canada.   HG4907.S4

Handbooks

Berlin, Howard M. The handbook of financial market indexes, averages, and indicators. Homewood, Ill. : Dow Jones-Irwin, c1990. 262 p. : ill.   **CH232**

Covers more than 200 major financial market barometers (averages, indexes, and indicators) in the U.S. and 24 other countries with details of the composition and derivation of each. Selected bibliography and brief directory of stock exchanges, financial publications, and associations. Subject index.   HG4636.B49

Downes, John. Barron's finance & investment handbook / John Downes, Jordan Elliot Goodman. 3rd ed. N.Y. : Barron's, c1990. 1234 p. : ill.   **CH233**

1st ed., 1986; 2nd ed., 1987.

Intended for general readers. In four parts: descriptions of 30 personal investment mediums, giving information on buying/selling/holding and risk, tax, and economic considerations; "how to" sections (e.g., reading annual reports and financial pages); a dictionary of finance and investment; and a ready reference section that lists organizations, companies, publications, and computer software and databases, and contains historical statistical data. Appendixes list titles for further reading, world currencies, and abbreviations and acronyms. All parts except the dictionary are indexed.   HG173.D66

Handbook of financial markets and institutions / ed. by Edward I. Altman ; assoc. ed. Mary Jane McKinney. 6th ed. N.Y. : Wiley, c1987. 1197 p. in various pagings : ill. **CH234**

1st ed. (1925)–5th ed. (1981) had title *Financial handbook.*

Covers domestic and international financial institutions and markets as well as investment theory and practice. Essays written by experts include investment banking, microcomputers and investments, the bond rating process, fixed income portfolios, high yield bonds, asset pricing models, and small business financing. Appendixes on the mathematics of finance and on sources of investment information.

§ No longer covers corporate finance; a companion volume, *The handbook of corporate finance* (N.Y. : Wiley, 1986) continues the treatment of that subject from the previous edition. Both volumes contain signed articles with bibliographies, and are indexed. HG173.H33

Handbook of modern finance / ed., Dennis E. Logue. 2nd ed. Boston : Warren Gorham & Lamont, c1990. 1 v. (various pagings) : ill. **CH235**

1st ed., 1984.

Essays, written by experts, on the technical, analytical, and theoretical aspects of finance. Arranged in seven subject sections: Financial systems and markets; Security analysis, pricing, and portfolio management; Short-term financial management; Long-term financial management; Financial policy; Personal finance; and International dimensions. Each section includes graphs, charts, and bibliographies. Annual updates contain cumulative indexes. HG173.H34

O'Hara, Frederick M. Handbook of United States economic and financial indicators / Frederick M. O'Hara, Jr. and Robert Sicignano. Westport, Conn. : Greenwood, [1985]. 224 p. **CH236**

Explains about 200 economic measures compiled and appearing in some 55 sources. Entry provides brief definition, source, where announced, frequency, historical cumulations. Includes bibliographic references. Alphabetical arrangement with subject index.

HC106.8.O47

Statistics

Statistical information on the financial services industry. 6th ed. Wash. : American Bankers Assoc., c1993. 240 p. **CH237**

1st ed., 1981; 5th ed., 1989.

A compilation of statistics drawn from government agencies, trade groups, and other sources. Tables are arranged in 12 sections describing economic trends and demographics, assets and liabilities of the public sector, consumer attitudes, sources and uses of funds, capital and earnings, bank structure and payment systems, government credit, and international banking. Includes bibliography and subject index.

HG181.S795

Public finance

Balance of payments statistics / International Monetary Fund ; [prep. by Balance of Payments Division of Bureau of Statistics]. v. 32, no. 1 (Jan. 1981)–(Apr. 1991). Wash. : The Fund, 1981–91. Monthly. **CH238**

Continues in part *Balance of payments yearbook* (1947–80).

In two parts: country figures, and world totals for balance of payments components and aggregates. HF1014.I5

Humphreys, Norman K. Historical dictionary of the International Monetary Fund. Metuchen, N.J. : Scarecrow, 1993. 227 p. : ill. **CH239**

Offers a chronology and introduction to the founding and history of the Fund, followed by a dictionary of people, organizations, and activities. Statistical appendix and bibliography of works by and about the IMF. HG3881.I58H86

International financial statistics yearbook. 1979– . Wash. : Internat. Monetary Fund, 1979– . Annual. **CH240**

Issued also in French and Spanish editions.

Contains summary tables by subject—e.g., interest and exchange rates, balance of payments, world trade, money and banking, commodity prices,—followed by detailed tables for each country, describing its financial and monetary conditions. Updated by the monthly *International financial statistics* (1948–).

•Also available on CD-ROM. HG3881.I626

Statistics

Federal reserve bulletin / issued by the Federal Reserve Board at Washington. v. 1 (1915)– . Wash. : [U.S. Govt. Print. Off.], 1915– . Monthly. **CH241**

The most complete current information, including statistics, on financial conditions in the U. S. Also reports on financial developments in foreign countries. HG2401.A5

Government finance statistics yearbook. 1977– . Wash. : Internat. Monetary Fund, [1977]– . Annual. **CH242**

Introduction, Data fund codes, Yearbook line numbers, and Titles of yearbook lines in English, French, and Spanish.

Vols. prepared 1977– by the Government Finance Statistics Division, Bureau of Statistics, of the International Monetary Fund.

Offers detailed tables for each country on central government revenue, expenditure, lending, financing, and debt, plus similar but less detailed data for state and local governments. Comparative statistics are presented in the form of world tables arranged by topic.

HJ101.G68

National accounts statistics. 1982– . N.Y. : United Nations, 1985– . **CH243**

Prepared by: The Statistical Offices of the United Nations Secretariat.

Continues *Yearbook of national accounts statistics* (1957–81) which superseded *Statistics of national income and expenditure* (1952–57).

Detailed national accounts estimates from 170 countries and areas. Data gathered from national statistical services and national and international source publications. Updated by U.N. *Monthly bulletin of statistics*.

Tax Foundation. Facts and figures on government finance. [1st ed.] (1941)– . N.Y. : Tax Foundation, 1941– . Biennial. **CH244**

Title varies. Publisher varies.

Provides data concerning taxes, expenditures, and debt at federal, state, and local levels. Draws data from *Budget of the U.S. government, Treasury bulletin* (1945–), and other federal publications, as well as state and local data from Bureau of the Census. Extracts "the most salient facts and presents them in a reader-friendly way."—*Introd.* Draws historical and geographical comparisons; treats both public and private finance. HJ257.T25

Accounting

Bibliography

Accountants' index : a bibliography of accounting literature to December, 1920. N.Y. : Amer. Inst. of Accountants, 1921. 1578 p. **CH245**

Introductory note signed Louise S. Miltimore, librarian.

———. *Supplement* (1st [Jan. 1921/June 1923]–40th [Jan.–Dec. 1991]. N.Y. : American Inst. of Certified Public Accountants, 1923–92. Quarterly).

Basic volume covers 1912–20.

Frequency of supplement varies; beginning 1973, quarterly, with 4th issue a cumulation for the year. Published 1923–54, American Inst. of Accountants.

A detailed author and subject bibliography of English-language book, pamphlet, and periodical literature. Includes indexing of periodicals, government documents, and references to parts of books dealing with specific subjects.

Continued by: *Accounting & tax index* (CH246).   Z7164.C81A5

Accounting & tax index. v. 1, 1st quarter– . Ann Arbor, Mich. : UMI, c1992– . Quarterly, with 4th issue an annual cumulation. **CH246**

Supersedes: *Accountant's index. Supplement* (CH245).

Provides citations to articles on taxation and accounting. A single alphabetical listing for subjects, authors, corporations, organizations and government agencies. Includes cross-references.

•Machine-readable version: *Accounting & tax database* [database] (Louisville, Ky. : UMI, 1971–), available online, updated weekly; and on CD-ROM.   Z7164.C81A224

Bentley, Harry Clark. Bibliography of works on accounting by American authors / by Harry C. Bentley and Ruth S. Leonard. Boston : H. C. Bentley, 1934–35. 2 v. **CH247**

Repr. in one volume: N.Y. : A. M. Kelley, 1970.

Contents: v. 1, Books published 1796–1900; v. 2, 1901–1934.
   Z7164.C81B5

Institute of Chartered Accountants in England and Wales, London. Library. Historical accounting literature. [London] : Mansell, 1975. 360 p. **CH248**

Subtitle: A catalogue of the collection of early works on bookkeeping and accounting in the Library of the Institute of Chartered Accountants in England and Wales, together with a bibliography of literature on the subject published before 1750 and not in the Institute Library.   Z7164.C81I43

Spiceland, J. David. International guide to accounting journals / by J. David Spiceland and Surendra P. Agrawal. 2nd ed. N.Y. : M. Wiener, 1993. 314 p. **CH249**

1st ed., 1987.

The first section lists journals alphabetically, giving primary readership, review process, subject content, style accepted, and publisher's address. A second section lists journals by country of origin.   HF5657

Indexes; Abstract journals

Commerce Clearing House. Accounting articles. 1963/66– . Chicago : Commerce Clearing House, 1963– . Monthly. **CH250**

"Describing and indexing accounting articles published in accounting and business periodicals, books, and pamphlets"—*t.p.*

Entries, with brief abstracts are grouped by accounting area (e.g., auditing, budgeting, cost accounting). Indexes by topic and by author. Cumulative volumes have been issued for the years 1963–66, 1971–74 and 1975–79.   Z7164.C81C78

Encyclopedias

Encyclopedia of accounting systems / Tom M. Plank and Lois R. Plank, gen. editors. 2nd ed. Englewood Cliffs, N.J. : Prentice-Hall, 1993. 2 v. : ill. **CH251**

1st ed. (1958) and Rev. ed. (1976) ed. by Jerome K. Pescow.

Each chapter covers the accounting system for a particular industry. Typically includes the following topics: the industry in brief; mechanization of the accounting function; account classification; data processing applications; cost systems; time and payroll applications; purchasing and receiving applications; inventory control applications; production control applications; distribution and selling records; receivables and payables applications; depreciation; flow charts; time-saving techniques and the reporting system. Includes growth industries, and a wide spectrum of industries, businesses, professions, farming enterprises and not-for-profit organizations.   HF5635.E54

Dictionaries

Kohler, Eric Louis. Kohler's dictionary for accountants. 6th ed. / ed. by W. W. Cooper, Yuji Ijiri. Englewood Cliffs, N.J. : Prentice-Hall, c1983. 574 p. **CH252**

5th ed., 1975, had title: *A dictionary for accountants.*

1st ed., 1952, was an unofficial revision and expansion of the 1936 *Accounting terminology* of the American Institute of Accountants' Committee on Terminology, of which Kohler was chair. Contains definitions and explanations of about 2,600 terms. The standard dictionary of the subject.   HF5621.K6

Shim, Jae K. Encyclopedic dictionary of accounting and finance / Jae K. Shim and Joel G. Siegel. Englewood Cliffs, N.J. : Prentice Hall, c1989. 504 p. : ill. **CH253**

Contains clear and sometimes lengthy definitions (some more than two pages long), enhanced with formulas, charts, tables, checklists, and practical applications. Covers more than 500 topics in accounting and finance and approximately 100 topics in related fields. Indexed.   HF1001.S525

Siegel, Joel G. Dictionary of accounting terms / by Joel G. Siegel, Jae K. Shim. N.Y. : Barron's, c1987. 472 p. : ill. **CH254**

Briefly defines more than 2,500 words and phrases drawn from all areas of accounting and from related fields of business and economics. Key accounting organizations are also included. Also features a brief list of acronyms and abbreviations, and compounded and present value tables.   HF5621.S54

Directories

Emerson's directory of leading U.S. accounting firms. 1988– . Bellevue, Wash. : Emerson's Professional Services Review, c1988– . Biennial. **CH255**

Spine title: Directory of leading U.S. accounting firms.

Editor, 1988–92, James C. Emerson.

The latest edition (3rd, 1992) lists 6,000 firms with 7,000 offices. In three parts: (1) Key information on nation's largest firms, providing both directory information and approximate U.S. and international revenues; (2) Office listings by state; (3) Alphabetical index to firms.   HF5616.U5E47

Who audits America. Ed. 1 (1976) . Menlo Park, Calif. : Data Financial Pr., 1976– . Semiannual. **CH256**

Subtitle: A directory of publicly traded companies and the accounting firms who audit them.

Listings include; companies, major and minor accounting firms, and a section that matches accounting firms with their clients in each state.   HF5616.U5W5

Handbooks

Accountants' handbook / ed. by D. R. Carmichael, Steven B. Lilien, Martin Mellman. 7th ed. N.Y. : Wiley, c1991. 1 v. (various pagings) : ill. **CH257**

1st ed., 1923; 6th ed., 1981.

An authoritative handbook. Consists of 36 chapters by financial executives, financial analysts, partners in accounting firms, and by faculty, organized in seven sections: (1) Structure of accounting standards and authoritative rule-making organizations; (2) Financial statements—presentation and analysis; (3) Financial statement areas; (4) Specialized industries; (5) Compensation and benefits; (6) Special areas of accounting; (7) Topics in auditing and management information systems. Bibliographies; index. To be kept up-to-date by periodic cumulative supplements, the first of which was issued in 1993 (386 p.).   HF5621.A22

Ameiss, Albert P. Accountant's desk handbook / Albert P. Ameiss and Nicholas A. Kargas. 3rd ed. Englewood Cliffs, N.J. : Prentice Hall, c1988. 724 p. : ill.   **CH258**
1st ed., 1977; 2nd ed., 1981.
Emphasizes trends, techniques, and generally accepted accounting principles currently employed in business operations. Nearly twice the length of the previous edition, but now has only three sections: Financial accounting; Managerial accounting; Standards, procedures, and reporting requirements. Indexed.   HF5635.A474

Cashin's handbook for auditors / James A. Cashin, Paul D. Neuwirth, John F. Levy. 2nd ed. N.Y. : McGraw-Hill, c1986. 1 v. (various pagings).   **CH259**
Rev. ed. of: *Handbook for auditors*, 1971.
Intends to cover all branches of auditing. Updated to conform to current conditions. Chapters by specialists are grouped in seven sections: (1) Principles, standards, and responsibilities; (2) Principal types of auditing; (3) Objectives and audit procedures; (4) Planning, evaluation and administration; (5) Analytical methods; (6) Conclusion, review and reporting; (7) Professional development. Index.
                                                         HF5667.H26

Handbook of accounting and auditing / Robert S. Kay, D. Gerald Searfoss ... [et al.]. 2nd ed. Boston : Warren, Gorham & Lamont, c1989. 1 v. (various pagings) : ill.   **CH260**
This edition adopts "a clean slate approach"—(*Pref.*) to cover the many changes that have deluged the profession. 50 chapters by academics, government personnel, and practitioners are organized in six sections: (1) General financial accounting; (2) General auditing; (3) Major areas of financial accounting, reporting, and auditing; (4) Accounting for specialized industries; (5) Comprehensive coverage of the financial services industry; (6) Major accounting institutions. Index.
Kept up-to-date by cumulative supplements, each containing a cumulative index.   HF5635.H22

International accounting summaries / Coopers & Lybrand (International). 1991– . N.Y. : Wiley, c1991– . Annual.
                                                         CH261
"Provides detailed summaries of accounting standards in 24 countries, plus the International Accounting Standards and European Community Directives."—*Introd.* Includes individual chapters arranged by country and reference matrixes by accounting topic. Includes glossary of accounting terms.   HF5601.I78

Plank, Tom M. Accounting desk book : the accountant's everyday instant answer book / Tom M. Plank, Douglas L. Blensly. 9th ed. Englewood Cliffs, N.J. : Prentice Hall, c1989. 772 p.   **CH262**
1st ed., 1964; 8th ed., 1985.
The three sections of prior editions—accounting, taxes, and management—have been revised and updated, and nine new sections added, reflecting new accounting practices, standards, technology, and technical terminology.
Includes 1990 suppl. (184 p.).   HF5635.B668

Siegel, Joel G. Accounting handbook / Joel G. Siegel, Jae K. Shim. N.Y. : Barron's, c1990. 836 p. : ill.   **CH263**
Arranged in 12 sections by subject (e.g., financial accounting, government and nonprofit accounting) including a dictionary. Indexed, but lacks bibliographies.   HF5635.S586

Money and banking

Indexes

Fed in print : Economics and banking topics. 1990– . Philadelphia : Federal Reserve Bank of Philadelphia, 1990– . Semiannual.   **CH264**
Continues: *Federal Reserve Bank reviews, selected subjects*, which ceased 1976, and *Fed in print : Business and banking topics*, 1977–89.
A subject index to all publications of the Federal Reserve research departments, including periodical articles, regularly occurring series, working papers, annual reports, proceedings, and monographs.
                                                         Z7164.C81F43

Encyclopedias

Banking and finance to 1913 / ed. by Larry E. Schweikart. N.Y. : Facts on File, c1990. 528 p. : ill.   **CH265**
Traces American banking history from colonial times to 1913 through an alphabetic arrangement of more than 100 signed entries that vary in length from one-half to ten or more pages; treats bankers and financiers, key legislation, and financial institutions, associations, and related organizations. Includes brief bibliographies of works issued by, or written about, the person or organization covered, and frequently notes the location of archives. Indexed.
§ A companion work is *Banking and finance, 1913–1989*, also ed. by Schweikart. Both are part of the "Encyclopedia of American business history and biography" series (CH383).   HG2461.B33

The money encyclopedia / ed. by Harvey Rachlin. N.Y. : Harper & Row, [1984]. 669 p. : ill.   **CH266**
Eclectic entries of varying length for the use of consumers and investors; covers banking, financial services, investments, and consumerisim. Signed articles written by scholars and practitioners. Appendix of acronyms and abbreviations.   HG181.M574

Munn, Glenn G. Encyclopedia of banking & finance / Glenn G. Munn, F.L. Garcia, Charles J. Woelfel. 9th ed., rev. and expanded. Chicago : Probus, 1993. 3 v. (lxiv, 1161 p.) : ill.
                                                         CH267
1st ed., 1924; 8th ed., 1983. 9th ed. previous issued (1097 p.) by St. James Pr., 1991.
"Definitions of thousands of basic banking, business and financial terms [and a] wealth of valuable information such as historical background analyses of recent trends, illustrative examples, statistical data and citation of applicable laws and regulations."—*Publisher's foreword*.   HG151.M8

The new Palgrave dictionary of money & finance / ed. by Peter Newman, Murray Milgate, John Eatwell. N.Y. : Stockton Pr., 1992. 3 v.   **CH268**
Companion to *The New Palgrave: a dictionary of economics* (CH52); 20% overlap, although some entries revised for this volume. More than 1,000 essays written by some 800 contributors, reflecting diverse views of the theoretical side of monetary economics and the applications in the business, financial and banking worlds. Some entries are contemporary and explanatory, such as "American banking legislation, recent" and descriptions of the banking system of major countries of the world, as well as the "European monetary system." List of acronyms, cross-references, and some bibliographies.
                                                         HG151.N48

Thorndike, David. The Thorndike encyclopedia of banking and financial tables. 3rd ed. Boston : Warren, Gorham & Lamont, c1987. 1737 p. in various pagings.   **CH269**
1st ed., 1973; 2nd ed., 1980.

Tables for loan payment and amortization, compound interest and annuity, simple interest, savings and withdrawals, installment loans, and investment.

A companion *Yearbook* (1977– . Annual) is prepared in conjunction with the editorial staffs of the *Bankers magazine* and the *Banking law journal*. The *Yearbook* adds tables and narrative materials reflecting new developments in finance, investment, laws and regulations, etc. Index.   HG1626.T49

Dictionaries

Banking terminology. 3rd ed. Wash. : Education Policy & Development, American Bankers Association, c1989. 409 p.   **CH270**

1st ed., 1981; 2nd ed., 1985.

Defines new terms and updates existing terminology in banking and financial services and such related fields as accounting, marketing and sales, and real estate. Numerous cross-references. Five appendixes: acronyms and abbreviations, common bank performance ratios, glossary of economic indicators, the addresses and telephone numbers of Federal Reserve banks by district, and the addresses and telephone numbers of other organizations and agencies useful to bankers.
HG151.B268

Elsevier's banking dictionary in seven languages : English/American, French, Italian, Spanish, Portuguese, Dutch, and German / comp. by Julio Ricci. 3rd rev. and enl. ed. Amsterdam ; N.Y. : Elsevier : distrib. by Elsevier Science Pub., 1990. 360 p.   **CH271**

Rev. ed. of: *Elsevier's banking dictionary in six languages*.

A polyglot dictionary arranged on an English base with equivalent terms in the other languages. More than 2,400 terms; indexed by terms in the other languages.   HG151.E45

Fitch, Thomas P. Dictionary of banking terms / by Thomas P. Fitch ; consulting editors, Irwin Kellner, Donald G. Simonson, Ben Weberman. 2nd ed. N.Y. : Barron's, c1993. 697 p. : ill.
CH272

Concise definitions of key banking terms and descriptions of government agencies and other organizations. Also includes tables and other illustrations and a list of abbreviations and acronyms.
HG151.F57

Rosenberg, Jerry Martin. Dictionary of banking. 3rd ed. N.Y. : Wiley, c1993. 369 p.   **CH273**

1982 ed. had title: *Dictionary of banking and finance*; 2nd ed. (1985) had title *Dictionary of banking and financial services*.

Defines about 7,500 words currently used in banking, finance, investments, and lending. Includes common symbols, acronyms, and abbreviations.   HG151.R67

Terry, John V. Dictionary for business & finance. 2nd ed. Fayetteville : Univ. of Arkansas Pr., 1990. 399 p.   **CH274**

1st ed., 1989.

Includes economic, legal, and statistical terms as well as those from accounting, banking, investment, insurance, management, marketing, and real estate. Definitions vary from brief sentences to a paragraph or more. Appendixes.   HF1001.T43

Directories

The bankers' almanac. Jan. 1993– . West Sussex, Eng. : Reed Information Services, 1993– . Annual.   **CH275**

Volumes for 1919/20–1992 had title: *The banker's almanac and year book*.

Directory of banks by country, with emphasis on British banks.
HG2984.B3

Hay, Tony. A guide to European financial centres. Chicago ; London : St. James Pr., 1990. 289 p.   **CH276**

Provides general information, and discusses background, current trends, and future developments relating to western European financial institutions. Arranged by country. Each country chapter begins with a brief survey of the political structure and economy, followed by separate sections in which banking, insurance, the stock market, and laws and regulations pertaining to them are discussed. Statistics and lists of largest banks are frequently included. Also features lists of information sources, including relevant publications, reference libraries, and the name of the country's central statistics agency. Chapters conclude with a directory of key institutions. List of abbreviations with translations; general index and index of offices.

§ Complements *Directory of European banking and financial associations* (Chicago : St. James Pr. ; London : Woodhead-Faulkner, 1990. 217 p.).   HG3881.H39

Polk financial institutions directory. North American edition. 197th (spring 1993)– . Nashville, Tenn. : R. L. Polk, 1993– . Semiannual.   **CH277**

Previous titles include *Polk's world bank directory* and *Polk bank directory*.

Covers Canada, the U.S., Central America, and Mexico. Entries vary in length from very brief to extensive, the latter providing information about branches and corporate and financial structure. Banks are listed by state, then locality. A separate section lists banks by name and gives ranked lists of banks, commercial banks, savings and loan banks, and credit unions. Includes directories of associations, the Federal Reserve System, pertinent government organizations (e.g., the Secret Service), and a limited directory of the largest international banks.

§ Also publ. as an annual: *Polk bank directory. International edition*, which includes expanded financial data whenever available, as well as information on the 1,000 largest U.S. banks.   HG1536.P635

Thomson bank directory. 230th ed. (July-Dec. 1991)– . Skokie, Ill : Thomson Financial Publ., c1991– . Semiannual.
CH278

Continues and assumes the edition numbering of: *The bankers' directory of the United States and Canada* (Chicago : Rand McNally, 1876–81); *The bankers' directory and list of bank attorneys* (1882–99); *The Rand McNally bankers' directory and list of attorneys* (1899–85th ed., 1918); *Rand McNally bankers directory and the bankers register with list of attorneys* (86th ed., 1919–101st ed., 1926); *Rand McNally bankers directory* (102nd ed., 1927–157th ed., 1954); *Rand McNally international bankers directory* (158th ed., 1955–220th ed., 1986); *The Rand McNally bankers directory* (221st ed., 1986–229th ed., 1990).

Issued in 3 pts.; pts. 1–2 cover U.S. banks; pt. 3 covers international banks.

Provides information concerning U.S. and international banks, including personnel and a financial statement. Also lists government banking agencies and officials.   HG2441.R3

Thomson credit union directory. 1986– . Skokie, Ill. : Thomson Financial Information, c1991– . Annual.   **CH279**

Continues: *The Rand McNally credit union directory* (Chicago : Rand McNally, 1986–90).

Arranged alphabetically by state and city. Entries give address and telephone, managing officer, charter number and year established, number of members, routing number, and a financial summary; and when applicable, primary correspondent, automated clearinghouse code, and wire network participation. Includes an alphabetical list of credit unions; ranks the top 300 credit unions by total assets, shares, and loans; and provides general federal and state industry data.
HG2037.R28

Thomson savings directory. [10th ed.] (1991)– . Skokie, Ill. : Thomson Financial Pub., 1991– . Semiannual.   **CH280**

Vol. 1–7 (also called eds. 1–7) published as: *The U.S. savings and loan directory*. Frequency varies; semiannual since 1992.

Lists savings and loan institutions and savings banks by state and city. Directory includes: legal name, type of charter, type of institution, membership in the U.S. League, location, membership code number, type of insurance for deposits, type of ownership, year established, number of employees, officers, financial data for the past two years, location of branches, routing number, and other operational data. Four preliminary reference sections list the institutions covered, present federal, state, and industry information, and list routing numbers and the savings institutions to which they are assigned. HG2150.U18

Who owns what in world banking. 1975/76– . London : Banker Research Unit, [1975]– . Annual. **CH281**

Subtitle: A guide to the subsidiary and affiliated interests of the world's major banks.

Editors, Philip Thorn and Jean Lack.

An alphabetical list of major individual and consortia banks. For each bank, domestic and international subsidiaries and affiliates are given, with percentage figures for the parent bank holdings. Index for all banks.

§ A companion to *Who is where in world banking* (London : Banker Research Unit, [1975]–).

Handbooks

The bankers' handbook / ed. by William H. Baughn, Thomas I. Storrs, Charls E. Walker. 3rd ed. Homewood, Ill. : Dow Jones-Irwin, c1988. 1347 p. : ill. **CH282**

1st ed., 1966; rev. ed., 1978.

"A basic reference on the subjects that are currently most important to performance in banking."—*Pref*. Contains 85 signed chapters arranged in 16 sections (e.g., financial management; the impact of monetary and fiscal policies on the banking system), enhanced by tables, charts, graphs, and other illustrations. Indexed. HG2491.B25

Deuss, Jean. Banking in the U.S : an annotated bibliography. Metuchen, N.J. : Scarecrow, 1990. 164 p. **CH283**

Lists and annotates "basic books in the history, organization, regulation, and management of U.S. banks and banking."—*Introd*. Citations are arranged by subject in ten chapters; in all but the history chapter, only monographs published since 1984 are included. Two additional chapters list reference sources (bibliographies, dictionaries, and encyclopedias) and serials (indexes; directories, yearbooks, and annual reports; periodicals and newspapers; and services). Appendixes contain acronyms and abbreviations, a chronology of banking landmarks, and brief directory listings of regulatory agencies and trade associations. Author and title indexes. Z7164.F5D48

McCusker, John J. Money and exchange in Europe and America, 1600–1775 : a handbook. Chapel Hill : Univ. of North Carolina Pr. for Inst. of Early Amer. History and Culture, Williamsburg, Va., [1978]. 367 p. : ill. **CH284**

"Aims to provide sufficient information of a technical and statistical nature to allow the reader to convert a sum stated in one money into its equivalent in another."—*p. [3]*. HG219.M33

MRI bankers' guide to foreign currency. v. 1 (Jan.-Mar. 1991)– . Houston, Tex. : Monetary Research International, c1991– . Quarterly. **CH285**

Describes the currency of more than 220 countries. Includes exchange restrictions, current exchange rates and black-and-white pictures of paper notes and traveler's checks. HG353.M75

Pick, Franz. All the monies of the world : a chronicle of currency values / Franz Pick, René Sédillot. N.Y. : Pick, [1971]. 613 p. **CH286**

A translation, enlarged and updated, of Sédillot's *Toutes les monnaies du monde* (Paris, 1954).

Entries for monetary units and for countries issuing currencies appear in a dictionary arrangement. Entries for the moneys include origin of the name, worth, and historical notes; entries for countries provide brief chronologies of events related to monetary systems and changes therein. HG216.P614

Tate, William. Tate's modern cambist. Centenary ed. (28th ed.) / by W. F. Spalding. London : Wilson ; N.Y. : Bankers Publ. Co., 1929. 734 p. **CH287**

Subtitle: A manual of the world's monetary systems, the foreign exchanges, the stamp duties on bills of exchange in foreign countries, the principal rules governing bills of exchange and promissory notes, foreign weights and measures, bullion and exchange operations.

———. *Tate's money manual : being the 1st–2nd annual editions of additions, alterations and amendments to the centenary edition of Tate's modern cambist*, by W. F. Spalding (London : Wilson ; N.Y. : Bankers Publ. Co., [1931–33]. v. 1–2.). HG3863.T2

World currency yearbook. 23rd ed. (1984)– . Brooklyn : International Currency Analysis, Inc., 1985– . Annual. **CH288**

Continues *Pick's currency yearbook*, (ed. 1–22, 1955–77/79) and assumes its numbering.

Forthcoming ed., to cover 1990–92, expected mid-1994.

Extensive descriptions of world currencies, trade areas, restrictions, black markets, Eurocurrency, and directory of central banks. HG219.P5

Biography

Who's who in international banking. 1984– . London : International Insider, 1984– . Annual. **CH289**

Publisher varies: 6th ed., 1992, publ. by Bowker-Saur.

Pt. 1 contains about 4,000 biographies of senior executives of the world's top banks, central banks, and banking institutions. Pt. 2 is a directory of banks of the world, by country, listing senior executives.

Statistics

Balachandran, M. A guide to statistical sources in money, banking, and finance. Phoenix : Oryx, 1988. 119 p. **CH290**

Selected, annotated bibliography of sources of information on capital and credit markets, interest rates, consumer finance, money supply, bank deposits, etc. Sources given for state, regional, national, international and foreign country information. Includes title and subject indexes. Z7164.F5B23

Bank quarterly. 1985– . Austin, Tex. : Sheshunoff Rating Services, Inc., 1985– . Quarterly. **CH291**

A continuously updated evaluative list of FDIC-insured commercial banks, arranged alphabetically by state. Analyzes banks by: size and growth; ratings; loan exposure; capital adequacy; asset quality; earnings and liquidity. Each copy also contains summary industry data.

Companion publication: *S & L quarterly* (Austin, Tex. : Sheshunoff Rating Services Inc., 1985–).

Board of Governors of the Federal Reserve System. All-bank statistics, United States, 1896–1955. [Wash., 1959]. 1229 p. **CH292**

Repr.: N.Y. : Arno Pr., 1976.

A comprehensive revision based on the 1943 ed. of: Board of Governors of the Federal Reserve System (U.S.), *Banking and monetary statistics* (CH293). Gives statistics for all banks by class of bank and by state, with explanatory text. HG2493.A517

——————— Banking and monetary statistics. Wash., [1976]. 2 v. (682, 1168 p.). **CH293**

The 1914–41 volume is a reprint of pt. 1 of the Board's 1943 publication of the same title; it includes "data on the condition and operation of all banks…statistics of bank debits, bank earnings, bank suspensions, branch, group, and chain banking, currency, money rates, security markets, Treasury finance, production and movement of gold, and international financial developments."—*Pref*. Some statistical series predate 1914. Pt. 2 of the 1943 work, giving member bank statistics for each Federal Reserve district, was not reprinted. Vol. 2, 1941–70, amends and updates v. 1, as does the Board's *Annual statisti-*

cal digest (1971–75– ; Wash. : 1976– . Annual), which contains data previously published in *Federal reserve bulletin* (CH241) but which will no longer appear there.

Historical statistics on banking : a statistical history of the United States banking industry, 1934–1991 / Federal Deposit Insurance Corporation, Division of Research and Statistics. Wash. : The Corporation, [1993?]. 592 p. **CH294**

Time series that illustrate major trends in banking, reflected by data on insured commercial and savings banks, at state and national levels. Chiefly tables, with explanatory notes accompanying each.

HG2493.H57

Investment

Bibliography

Gilbert, Victor Francis. Labour and social history theses : American, British and Irish university theses and dissertations in the field of British and Irish labour history, presented between 1900 and 1978. London : Mansell ; N.Y. : H. W. Wilson, 1982. 194 p. **CH295**

A classed bibliography of North American doctoral dissertations, and British and Irish doctoral theses, master's essays, and special studies. Focus on political and trade union movements, together with social history topics such as housing, public health, income, which affected working-class life. Indexes of persons, places, subjects, and authors.

Updated annually in the Autumn issue of the *Bulletin* of the Soc. for the Study of Labour History. Z7164.L1G5

Graham, John W. The U.S. Securities and Exchange Commission : a research and information guide. N.Y. : Garland, 1993. 344 p. (Research and information guides in business, industry, and economic institutions, 8). **CH296**

Annotated bibliography of works by and about the Securities and Exchange Commission, published between 1933 and 1990. Includes books, journals, government publications (including those of the SEC), dissertations, and looseleaf services. Arranged by topic. Appendixes describe the organization of the SEC, biographies of commissioners, various ways to access SEC data, and timeline of SEC events. Author, title, and subject index. Z7164.S37.G73

Hulbert, Mark. The Hulbert guide to financial newsletters. 5th ed. N.Y. : Dearborn Financial Publ., 1993. 574 p. : ill. **CH297**

Title and publisher vary.
1st ed., 1985; 4th ed., 1991.
Evaluates and compares current investment newsletters by giving performance ratings based on methodology developed by Hulbert Financial Digest (HFD). Ranks newsletter recommendations according to total return on investments and risk adjusted performance.

HG4529.H86

The individual investor's guide to investment publications. Chicago : International Pub. Corp., c1988. 269 p. **CH298**

Lists newsletters and other serials "covering mutual funds, stocks, bonds, international investing, collectibles, real estate, financial planning, forecasting, and many other subjects."—*Pref.* Section 1, arranged by investment category, lists and describes (but does not evaluate) 600 titles. Entries include: publisher and address; editor's name, background, and qualifications; editorial philosophy; publication description; format; frequency; average number of pages; subscription prices; circulation; date of first issue; and special publisher's offers. Alphabetical lists of titles and publishers are appended. Section 2 lists and gives addresses for some 800 additional publications, and lists 100 more that the editors were unable to confirm as still being published. Indexed. Z7164.F5I52

Indexes; Abstract journals

•**Investext** [database]. Boston : Thomson Financial Networks, Inc., 1982– . **CH299**

Available online, updated weekly, and on CD-ROM.
Full-text database that supplies financial and market information on approximately 11,000 publicly traded companies and 53 industries. Includes some international information. Coverage includes: stock prices, market forecasts, product information, industry overviews and statistics. Reports are written by financial analysts in investment banking and financial research organizations.

Encyclopedias

Colby, Robert W. The encyclopedia of technical market indicators / Robert W. Colby and Thomas A. Meyers. Homewood, Ill. : Dow Jones-Irwin, c1988. 581 p. : ill. **CH300**

For sophisticated investors or students. In two parts: (1) signed essays focusing on methods of evaluating technical market indicators, and (2) descriptions of more than 100 indicators of stock market performance (e.g., advance/decline divergence oscillator, confidence index, presidential election cycle), arranged alphabetically. Entries vary in length; most occupy at least half a page and frequently contain charts, graphs, and other illustrations. Appendix of indicator interpretation definitions; index. HG4915.C56

Encyclopedia of investments / ed. in chief, Jack P. Friedman. 2nd ed. Boston : Warren, Gorham & Lamont, c1990. 964 p. : ill. **CH301**

1st ed., 1982.
Articles, written by experts, discuss 48 different types of investments, including both traditional investment mediums and nontraditional (e.g., horses, sports memorabilia). Articles follow standard format, covering basic characteristics, attractive features, potential risks, and tax consequences. The types of investors that typically choose the medium are described, and each chapter generally includes a glossary, a suggested reading list, and a directory of dealers and brokers. A separate section, Investment strategy, contains articles intended to provide "a unifying framework for assembling and assessing a portfolio."—*Pref.* Indexed.

Updates with cumulative indexes also issued. HG4527.E5

Dictionaries

Rosenberg, Jerry Martin. Dictionary of investing. N.Y. : Wiley, c1993. 368 p. **CH302**

Rev. ed of: *Investor's dictionary*, 1986.
Briefly defines about 7,500 terms used in securities, commodities, and future exchange systems. Includes symbols, acronyms, and abbreviations. HG4513.R67

Thomsett, Michael C. Investment and securities dictionary. Jefferson, N.C. : McFarland, c1986. 328 p. : ill. **CH303**

Repr. as: *Webster's new World investment and securities dictionary* (N.Y. : Webster's New World ; Dist. by Prentice-Hall Trade, 1988).

Briefly defines or describes more than 2,000 investment terms, associations, government agencies, and key laws and regulations. Includes cross-references, charts and illustrations, a glossary, an abbreviations list, a guide to prospectus and offering documents, and a bond classification list. HG4513.T48

Valentine, Stuart P. International dictionary of the securities industry. 2nd ed. Homewood, Ill. : Dow Jones-Irwin, 1989. 228 p. **CH304**

Focuses on investment terminology used in the overseas markets. About 2,500 words and phrases, with some bibliographic references.
HG4513.V35

Directories

Directory of registered investment advisors. 1987– . Charlottesville, Va. : McGraw-Hill with the Securities and Exchange Commission, 1987– . Annual. **CH305**
Prep. by Money Market Directories, Inc.
Lists, by state and province, investment and mutual fund advisors; describes type of accounts handled, investment style, and strategy. Also ranks advisors by assets managed. Directory of professional and industry associations and of newsletters published by investment advisors.
HG4907.D53

•DISCLOSURE database [database]. Bethesda, Md. : Disclosure, Inc., 1977– . **CH306**
Available online, updated weekly.
Contains financial and management information on some 12,000 publicly held companies, drawn from annual reports to shareholders and various filings with the Securities and Exchange Commission (e.g., registration and proxy statements, 10-K reports).
Disclosure/Worldscope global [database] (Bethesda, Md. : Disclosure, Inc.), available on CD-ROM, updated quarterly, covers companies around the world, principally in OECD countries. Beginning 1994, SEC filings are also available on the Internet via EDGAR.

The guide to world equity markets. 1992– . London : Euromoney Publ., c1992– . Annual. **CH307**
Title varies: 1986–91, called: *The GT guide to world equity markets.*
Provides a "profile of major and developing equity markets" (*Introd.*) through extensive country-by-country analysis. For each country, includes political and economic overview, history of market performance and stock markets, summary of major investors, local taxation and regulation, and reporting requirements. Includes sources of current information for each country.
HG4551.G8

Investment companies yearbook. 53rd ed. (1993)– . Rockville, Md. : CDA/Wiesenberger, c1993– . Annual. **CH308**
Continues: *Investment companies* (N.Y. : Arthur Wiesenberger & Co., 1944–91).
A comprehensive source on mutual funds and investment companies. The first two parts contain general information on the use and selection of mutual funds to meet specific investment objectives. Pt. 3 contains single-page entries for mutual funds, including for each a description of its objective; composition of its portfolio; list of directors, investment manager(s), and other key personnel; a ten-year financial/statistical history, address and telephone; whether or not there is a sales charge, special services offered; and states in which the fund is qualified for sale. Pt. 4 covers closed-end and variable annuity funds. Contains a glossary and index by fund name.
§ *CDA/Wiesenberger mutual funds update* (v. 1– . Rockville, Md. : CDA Investment Technologies, c1992–) provides monthly summary statistics on specific funds and rankings of funds grouped by investment objectives. *Mutual funds panorama*, by CDA/Wiesenberger (Rockville, Md., 1992. 98 p.) is a directory of mutual funds with summary objectives, sales charges, and ten-year performance history.
HG4530.I5

Moody's Investors Service. [Moody's manuals]. N.Y. : Moody's Investors Service, 1909– . Annual. **CH309**
Originally publ. as *Manual of industrial and miscellaneous securities* (1900).
Titles vary.
Also available on microfiche, 1909– .
Now consists of several series that provide extensive and detailed listings of more than 15,000 U.S. publicly traded companies and governmental entities. Titles available 1993:

Moody's bank and finance manual (1928– . Annual), covering bank, insurance companies, investment trusts, and other financial institutions.
Moody's industrial manual (1920– . Annual), covering 2,000 corporations traded on major stock exchanges.
Moody's municipal & government manual (1918– . Annual), covering municipalities and government agencies that issue bonds.
Moody's OTC industrial manual (1970– . Annual), covering 2,000 corporations traded on NASDAQ and regional exchanges.
Moody's OTC unlisted manual (1986– . Annual), covering 2,000 less active corporations.
Moody's public utility manual (1914– . Annual), covering public and private gas, water, telephone, and electric companies.
Moody's transportation manual (1909– . Annual), covering rails, airlines, trucking, bus, vehicle rental, and shipping companies.
Annual volumes are supplemented by weekly or semi-weekly *News reports*. Indexing for all series is provided by *Moody's complete corporate index* (1977– . Three times a year).
Entries typically give company history, describe operations, corporate structure, products and properties, and history of stock and bond activity, and provide summary financial and income statements, balance sheets and cash flow, and debt ratings. Each manual contains a special section on blue pages of statistics and other information pertinent to that business activity.
Related publications: *Moody's international manual* (1981– . Annual), following the same format as other Moody's manuals, covering 7,000 major corporations and institutions in nearly 100 countries. *Moody's handbook of common stocks* (1955– . Quarterly) covers about 950 U.S. firms that are most commonly traded. Issues include summary directory and financial information. *Moody's handbook of NASDAQ stocks* (1991/92– . Quarterly) covers 600 companies.
•Several machine-readable versions are available. Those of widest general interest are: *Moody's corporate profiles* [database], available online, current file updated weekly, covering only companies traded on NYSE, ASE, and selected OTC; and *Moody's company data* [database], available on CD-ROM, updated monthly or quarterly, covering 10,000 companies traded on NYSE, ASE, NASDAQ, OTC, and selected regional exchanges.
HG4905.M85

NASDAQ fact book & company directory. 1991– . Wash. : National Association of Securities Dealers, 1991– . Annual. **CH310**
Formed by merger of *Fact book* and *NASDAQ company directory.*
"Extensive data on the performance of Nasdaq securities and statistics on the Nasdaq market as a whole, as well as information to assist in contacting each company directly."—*Introd.*

Nelson's directory of investment managers. 1st ed. (1988)– . Port Chester, N.Y. : Nelson Publications, c1988– . Annual. **CH311**
Detailed profiles of some 2,000 money management firms listed alphabetically, with up to 18 categories of data (e.g., Investment specialties, Decision-making process, Fees). Separate sections list firms geographically and by total assets managed, organization type, and area of specialization.
§ *America's best money managers* (Port Chester, N.Y. : Nelson Publ., 1992–) provides a ranked list of money managers. Prior to 1991, it was issued as a section of *Nelson's directory.*   HG4907.N44

Nelson's directory of investment research. 13th annual ed. (1988)– . Port Chester, N.Y. : Nelson Publications, c1988– . Annual. **CH312**
Beginning with 16th ed., 1991, published in 2 v. Vol. 1 is a directory of more than 6,000 U.S. corporations, followed by 400 investment research firms. For each corporation, lists summary financial and corporate data and the investment research firms that provide coverage. For research firms, lists key executives and financial data. Vol. 2 provides comparable coverage for approximately 5,500 non-U.S. corporations.
HG4907.N43

Standard & Poor's corporation records. 1940?– . N.Y. : Standard & Poor's Corp., 1940?– . Daily. **CH313**

Vols. 1–6, Standard corporation descriptions; v. 7, Current news edition. Updated daily (except Saturday, Sunday, and holidays).

Beginning with *Poor's manual of railroads* (N.Y. : H.V. and H.W. Poor, 1868/69–1924), Standard & Poor's and its predecessors have issued various titles that describe corporations for the benefit of investors. Titles and coverage have varied.

Currently provides comprehensive financial histories for more than 12,000 publicly held U.S. corporations. Arranged alphabetically by firm. Entries give detailed financial and balance sheet information (drawn from annual and 10K reports), earnings, and dividend history. Available on microfiche. Kept up-to-date with biweekly supplements called *Cumulative news*.

§ Related titles from the same publisher:
Daily stock price record (July/Sep. 1972– . Quarterly). Issued in separate editions for N.Y. Stock Exchange, American Stock Exchange, and Over-the-counter, and beginning 1993 for NASDAQ. Lists trading, earnings, and dividend information for individual stocks.

Stock guide (1971– . Monthly) summarizes investment data for more than 5,400 common and preferred stocks and 700 mutual funds.

Bond guide (1971– . Monthly) covers about 6,000 corporate bonds and convertibles.

Stock reports (1967– . Monthly) covers firms listed on NYSE, ASE, and selected OTC stocks. Summarizes company history, financial record (with stock price range and trading volume over a seven-year period), price/earnings ratio, yield, and S&P ranking.

•Machine-readable versions:
Standard & Poor's corporate descriptions [database] Current file available online, updated biweekly, and on CD-ROM as part of *Standard & Poor's corporations* [database], updated quarterly, which incorporates the printed *Standard & Poor's register of corporations, directors and executives* (CH367).

COMPUSTAT [database]. Current file available online and on CD-ROM, both updated monthly. Provides comprehensive time series information on active and inactive U.S. and Canadian firms over the last 20 years, including ratios, growth rates, daily stock prices, and industry aggregates. HG4501.S76635

Standard & Poor's/Lipper mutual fund profiles. Dec. 1987– . N.Y. : Standard & Poor's Corp., c1987– . Quarterly. **CH314**

Issues for 1988 called v. 1–v. 4. Feb. 1989 (v. 3, no. 1) began current numbering.

Published in cooperation with Lipper Analytical Services, Inc.

Profiles of about 800 equity and long-term fixed income mutual funds. Each half-page entry details prices and assets to assist in evaluating relative fund performance, fund objectives, and summary of asset allocation. Includes Lipper Market Phase Rating and Volatility index. Brief listing of additional 1,800 taxable and 700 municipal bond funds. Directory of fund families gives parent address, types of services, and fund charges. HG4930.S72

Symbol guide. July 1978– . Jersey City, N.J. : ADP Brokerage Information Services Group, 1978– . Irregular. **CH315**

Vol. for Sept. 1983 has ADP at head of title.

Issuing agency varies: 1978–1981, GTE Financial Services Division; 1982–Jan. 1983, GTE Telenet Information Services; Sept. 1983–1987 by: ADP Financial Information Services, Inc.; 1988– by: ADP Brokerage Information Services Group.

Lists standardized symbols used in quotation services, newspapers, and television to report U.S. and Canadian stocks, bonds, mutual and money market funds, and commodities. Includes symbols for standard market indexes compiled by Dow Jones and Standard & Poor's, exchange identifiers, and third party market makers. Updated with supplements.

The Value Line investment survey. N.Y. : Value Line, inc., 1936– . Weekly. **CH316**

Looseleaf. Also available in microfilm, in a Canadian ed., and on diskette.

Covers more than 1,700 companies listed on the major U.S. stock exchanges. "Weekly summary and index" gives key ratios, rankings, and price data in an alphabetical list. Detailed listings for each company are arranged in "Ratings and report" sections, grouped by industry sectors, each introduced with an industry overview. The entry for each company is updated quarterly, giving summary financial information and stock price history, usually for the last 17 years; includes Value Line rating, projections, and betas. "Weekly selection and opinion" contains predictions about economic conditions and outlook, with profiles on recommended investments.

Handbooks

Association for Investment Management and Research. Standards of practice handbook : the code of ethics and the standards of professional conduct, with commentary and interpretation. 6th ed. N.Y. : AIMR, 1992. 225 p. **CH317**

1st ed., 1982; 5th ed., 1990.

Rev. ed. of: *Standards of practice handbook*, Financial Analysts Federation (4th ed., 1988).

Includes a sample ethics examination. HG4921.F38

The Business One Irwin investor's handbook. 1991– . Homewood, Ill. : Business One Irwin, 1991– . Annual. **CH318**

Continues *The Dow Jones investor's handbook*.

Tracks the historical composition of the Dow Jones averages and summarizes the daily averages for the year covered. Directory of stocks currently listed on the New York Stock Exchange, the Amex, selected OTC stocks, bonds, and mutual funds, giving year's highs and lows, earnings per share, yields, and price earnings. HG4921.F3

The financial analyst's handbook / ed. by Sumner N. Levine. 2nd ed. Homewood, Ill. : Dow Jones-Irwin, c1988. 1870 p. : ill. **CH319**

1st ed., 1975.

Updated and revised to reflect the many significant changes in finance, investments and the economy since the publication of the 1st ed. Contains signed chapters, written by experts, in the topics of: economic analysis, company and industry analysis, equity investment analysis, fixed income investing, portfolio theory and practice, quantitative aids, information sources, legal and ethical standards. Indexed. HG4521.F558

Shim, Jae K. Source : the complete guide to investment information : where to find it and how to use it / Jae K. Shim, Joel G. Siegel. Chicago : International Publ. Corp., c1992. 422 p. : ill. **CH320**

Shows "where to find information and advice on different types of investment instruments and how to read and interpret the various sources of data."—*Pref.* Covers general market, company and industry sources, analysis of financial statements, stocks, bonds, mutual funds, options and futures, and real estate and tangibles, with illustrations and documentation. Glossary and index. HG151.7.S55

Standard & Poor's ratings handbook. v. 1 (Apr. 1992)– . N.Y. : Standard & Poor's Corp., c1992– . Monthly. **CH321**

Lists S&P-rated debt by issuer: by corporate issuers, structured transactions, financial institutions and international debt, money market and bond funds, and insurance companies. Excludes tax-free users. Includes latest CreditWatch and International and sovereign ratings, sorted by country. HG4501.S693

Walmsley, Julian. The new financial instruments : an investor's guide. N.Y. : Wiley, c1988. 454 p. : ill. **CH322**

Pts. 1 and 2 discuss the origins and basic concepts of financial futures, swaps and options. Pts. 3 and 4 discuss floating-rate securities, zero coupons and other bond variants, securitization, mortgage-backed, synthetic and index-linked securities, debt-equity hybrids, and option-related instruments. Bibliography. HG4521.W184

Warfield, Gerald. The investor's guide to stock quotations and other financial listings. 3rd ed. N.Y. : Perennial Library, 1990. 254 p.   **CH323**

1st ed., 1983; 2nd ed., 1986.

Overview of investing, brokers, and securities exchanges and the most frequently traded securities (stocks, bonds, mutual funds, options, and futures). Well-explained and illustrated. Includes appendixes (dollar/decimal equivalent of fractions, definitions of ratings by Moody's and Standard & Poor's), a glossary, and an index. Particularly useful for those who are new to investing or who need help in deciphering securities tables in newspapers.   HG4636.W28

Statistics

Chapman, Karen J. Investment statistics locator. Phoenix : Oryx, 1988. 182 p.   **CH324**

Indexes 22 standard sources of investment statistics and gives the frequency of the data. Headings are arranged alphabetically, then in order of information frequency. Includes a sources guide and subject index.   Z7164.C18C47

The Dow Jones averages, 1885–1990 / ed. by Phyllis S. Pierce. Homewood, Ill. : Business One Irwin, c1991. 1 v. (unpaged).   **CH325**

Chronology of the development of the Dow Jones averages. Presents daily figures, beginning with the 14-stock average (combining railroads and industrials) in 1885 and ending with the 1990 daily averages for industrials, transportations, utilities, and bonds. Supersedes earlier volumes.   HG4915.D6433

Morningstar mutual fund sourcebook. 1993– . Chicago : Morningstar, Inc., c1993– . Annual.   **CH326**

Continues: *Mutual fund sourcebook* (Chicago : Morningstar, 1992).

Each annual issue in 2 v. Vol. 1 offers one-page summaries of equity mutual funds, listing for each: investment criteria, performance summary and history, portfolio changes in the last year, personnel, and a biography of the fund manager. Front matter includes a guide to basic terms and tables and charts that rank funds by various criteria. Vol. 2 covers fixed-income mutual funds.

§ Companion publications: *Morningstar closed-end fund sourcebook* (1993–) and *Morningstar variable annuity/life sourcebook* (1993–).

•Machine-readable version: *Morningstar mutual funds ondisc* [database] (Chicago : Morningstar, 1976–). Available on CD-ROM, updated quarterly, monthly, annually.   HG4930.M855

Stock exchange official yearbook. London : London Stock Exchange, 1992– . Annual.   **CH327**

Continues: *The stock exchange official intelligence* (v. 1 [1882]–51 [1933]. London : Spottiswoode, Ballantyne & Co., 1882–1933), called *Burdett's official intelligence*, 1882–98; *The Stock Exchange official year-book* (London : Stock Exchange, 1934–86?); *The International Stock Exchange official yearbook* (London : Macmillan (Journals Div.) under license from the International Stock Exchange, 1987/88–90/91).

Some editions issued in 2 v.

Contains details of securities quoted on the London and other Federated Stock Exchanges, a classified list of quoted securities, particulars relating to stamp duties, scales of minimum stock exchange commissions, charges for stock exchange quotation, trustee investments, and various statistics. Some recent issues include a list of parent companies and their subsidiaries, including dividends, financial data and transfers. Includes selected British, Commonwealth, provincial, and foreign government securities.   HG5431.S82

COMPANY INFORMATION AND INDUSTRY ANALYSIS

Listed here are the most representative sources that treat a broad spectrum of firms and industries. Works concerned with a particular sector (e.g., banking or insurance) will be found in the section for that topic. In this rapidly changing field, reference sources go quickly out of date, so readers must rely on services that specialize in frequent updating. Looseleaf services from suppliers such as Commerce Clearing House provide current information in many business fields and are often the first place legislative and regulatory changes are recorded; unfortunately, their price puts them out of reach for many libraries. Machine-readable databases are also prompt and are heavily used in business libraries. A selection is listed in this section, but more complete listings will be found in guides such as Lorna Daniells, *Business information sources* (CH2), Diane Strauss, *Handbook of business information* (CH334), *Encyclopedia of business information sources* (CH329), or *Gale directory of databases* (AK208).

General works

Guides

Directory of industry data sources. v. 1 (1981)– . [Cambridge, Mass.] : Ballinger, 1981– . Annual.   **CH328**

Contents: v. 1–3, United States of America and Canada; v. 4–5, Western Europe (issued separately, beginning 1983).

An annotated bibliography (more than 22,000 entries in Ed. 2) of sources of marketing, or financial information sources. Each volume in five parts: (1) general secondary reference sources covering more than one industry; (2) data sources for each of 65 industries, arranged by type (e.g., marketing reports, statistical surveys, forecasts, directories, special journal issues, dissertations, numerical and bibliographic databases); (3) publishers, listed alphabetically and by document type; (4) subject indexes, by SIC Code and alphabetical; (5) title index.   Z7165.U5D59

Encyclopedia of business information sources. 1st ed. (1970)– . Detroit : Gale, 1970– . Biennial with periodic supplements.   **CH329**

Subtitle (varies): A bibliographic guide to more than 24,000 citations covering over 1,100 subjects of interest to business personnel.

1970 ed. called 1st ed. An earlier ed., 1969, was published in 2 v.; the second volume later published separately as *Encyclopedia of geographic information sources*. 9th ed., 1993–94.

Editor varies; 1970–80, Paul Wasserman.

Lists primary and secondary sources of information useful to business executives, researchers, students, and librarians. Topical arrangement; cross-references.

§ Complemented by: *Encyclopedia of business information sources : Europe*, ed. by M. Balachandran (Detroit : Gale, 1994. 877 p.).   Z7164.C81E93

Hawbaker, A. Craig. Industry and company information : illustrated search strategy and sources / by A. Craig Hawbaker, Judith M. Nixon. Ann Arbor, Mich. : Pierian Pr., 1991. 172 p. : ill.   **CH330**

A good basic introduction to industry and company research, with several illustrations of key reference sources, a library skills test, bibliography of additional sources, and title index.   HF5365.H38

How to find information about companies / by Washington Researchers. [Ed. 1]– . Wash. : Washington Researchers, c1979– . Annual.   **CH331**

Editions for 1992/1993– in 3 vols.

Vol. 1 combines how-to-do-it instructions for research on U.S. business with directory of sources found in local, state, and federal government agencies, the courts, trade associations and labor unions, credit reporting and bond rating services, databases, and libraries. Vol. 2 concentrates on types of information and v. 3 emphasizes techniques for special situations.   HD2771.H68

Ryans, Cynthia C. Small business : an information source-book. Phoenix : Oryx, 1987. 286 p. (Oryx sourcebook series in business and management, no. 1).   **CH332**

Lists and briefly annotates titles pertaining to small business activities (e.g., strategic planning, marketing). Also included are a core list of 185 key reference sources, a directory of publishers, and several appendixes and indexes.   Z7164.C81R92

Small business sourcebook. 1st ed.– . Detroit : Gale, c1983– .   **CH333**

Biennial, 1983–1991. Annual since 1991. Published in two volumes since 1987.

Vol. 1 gives small business profiles that include sources of information about specific businesses, e.g., start-up information, primary associations, statistical sources, trade periodicals, trade shows and conventions. Vol. 2 contains general small business topics common to the operation of any small business (funding, consultants, sources of supply, etc.). It also contains directories and descriptions of sources of assistance offered by state organizations and federal government agencies, a glossary, and master index. Recent editions contain more non-traditional businesses.

§ Companion publication: *Small business start-up index : a guide to practical information related to starting a small business* (Detroit : Gale, 1990–). Issued three times a year; each issue is cumulative.
                                                         HD2346.U5S66

Strauss, Diane Wheeler. Handbook of business information : a guide for librarians, students, and researchers. Englewood, Colo. : Libraries Unlimited, 1988. 537 p. : ill.   **CH334**

An excellent introduction to basic business concepts and vocabulary as well as to key publications and databases. Chapters 1–8 are format-specific, while the rest focus on fields of business, (e.g., accounting). Generously illustrated, with excerpts from major reference works. 12 appendixes list, for example, business acronyms, free vertical file materials, and relevant government organizations and publications. Extensive index.   Z7164.C81S7796

Bibliography

The European directory of trade and business journals. 1st ed. (1990)– . London : Euromonitor, c1990– .   **CH335**

Lists and describes more than 2,000 major European journals concerned with Western European markets and industries. A pan-European/international section is followed by separate sections for 17 Western European countries. Entries, listed alphabetically in each section, include: address, telephone, telex, and fax numbers; year founded; language; frequency; editorial content (often noting regularly published statistical data, market reports, and company rankings); readership; circulation; editor; and advertising manager. Title and subject indexes.   HF54.E87

Humpert, Magdalene. Bibliographie der Kameralwissenschaften. Köln : Schroeder, 1937. 1184 p. (Kölner bibliographischen Arbeiten, bd. 1).   **CH336**

Repr. : Hildesheim : H.A. Gerstenberg, 1972.

Issued in 12 parts, each with cover title, 1935–37.

Originally planned to include works published 1727–1835, but starting on p. 105, the 16th and 17th centuries are also included, so that the greater part of the work covers 1520–1850.   Z7161.H92

Indexes; Abstract journals

Predicasts F&S index United States. v. 34, no. 5 (May 1993)– . Foster City, Calif. : Information Access Co., 1993– . Monthly, with quarterly cumulations.   **CH337**

Continues *Predicasts F&S index United States* and its annual cumulation (1980–93).

Cumulates annually as *Predicasts F&S index United States annual*, which is issued in parts.

Supplies current information, taken from trade magazines, newspapers, and other financial publications, on companies, products, and industries. In two sections. The product section, arranged by a modified seven-digit SIC code, supplies information on end use, sales, new products, etc. The company section is arranged alphabetically and cites information on management, products, and marketing.

Predicasts F&S index Europe (v. 16, no. 5 [May 1993]–), from the same publisher, is similar in scope, arrangement, and frequency. Issued in 3 pts.: Industries and products, Countries, and Companies. Continues *Predicasts F&S index Europe*. Cumulates annually as *Predicasts F&S index Europe annual*.

Predicasts F&S index international (v. 26, no. 5 [May 1993]–) is issued in the same three sections. It continues *Predicasts F&S index international* and cumulates annually as *Predicasts F&S index international annual*.

•*PTS F&S index* [database] provides online and CD-ROM access to information from the three print titles.

§ *PROMPT : Predicasts overview of markets and technology* (1977– . Monthly, with quarterly and annual cumulations) is a related source for lengthy abstracts about industries. Available on CD-ROM and online as *PTS PROMPT*.   HG4961.F812

•**Trade and industry index** [database]. Foster City, Calif. : Information Access Co., 1981– .   **CH338**

Indexes and selectively abstracts some 300 trade and industry journals, 100 local and regional business publications, and business and trade information from nearly 1,200 additional publications. A companion online database, *Trade and industry ASAP*, contains citations and the full text of articles from more than 200 of the major journals covered in *Trade and industry index*. Also available on CD-ROM as *Business index* (CH35).

Dictionaries

A historical dictionary of American industrial language / ed. by William H. Mulligan, Jr. N.Y. : Greenwood, c1988. 332 p.   **CH339**

Brief definitions, drawn primarily from the period before World War I. An appendix lists terms by industry. Includes a list of contributors, bibliography, and index of institutions and people.   TS9.H57

Hunt, V. Daniel. Dictionary of advanced manufacturing technology. N.Y. : Elsevier, c1987. 431 p. : ill.   **CH340**

For annotation, *see* EK231.   TS155.6.H85

Multinational enterprise : an encyclopedic dictionary of concepts and terms / [comp.] by Ankie Hoogvelt with Anthony G. Puxty ; consultant ed., John M. Stopford. N.Y. : Nichols Publ., c1987. 261 p.   **CH341**

Clearly defines theoretical and technical terms drawn from accounting, economics, finance, law, management, taxation, and related fields; and includes descriptions of key international organizations. Numerous cross-references, three appendixes (references, select list of bibliographies, and brief list of organizations), and an index of terms grouped under 13 broad categories (e.g., industry structure, international marketing).   HD2755.5.M8337

Rice, Michael Downey. Prentice-Hall dictionary of business, finance and law. Englewood Cliffs, N.J. : Prentice-Hall, c1983. 362 p.   **CH342**

Defines about 3,600 words, phrases, and abbreviations, with references to statutory materials and sources of terms, leading cases, and articles in legal and business literature. KF887.R53

Room, Adrian. NTC's dictionary of trade name origins. Rev. ed. Lincolnwood, Ill. : NTC Business Books, 1991. 217 p. **CH343**

1982 ed. had title: *Dictionary of trade name origins.*

A witty examination of the origin of some well-known trade names, with an analysis of the process of choosing a new trade name. T324.R66

Rosenberg, Jerry Martin. Dictionary of business and management. [3rd ed.]. N.Y. : J. Wiley, c1993. 374 p. **CH344**

1st ed., 1978; 2nd ed., 1983.

Offers very brief definitions for terms, phrases, symbols, acronyms, and abbreviations. Appendixes provide tables for various forms of measurement and interest, a list of graduate programs in business and management, quotations, and a chronology of major business and economic events in the U.S. HF1001.R79

Directories

In this volatile field, many directories are published but go out of date quickly. To find those currently available in printed form, consult *Directories in print* (AL3), or for machine-readable directories, *Gale directory of databases* (AK208) or similar lists.

American manufacturers directory. 1992 ed.– . Omaha, Neb. : American Business Directories, c1992– . Annual. **CH345**

First publ. 1990 as *U.S. manufacturers directory.*

A directory of some 125,000 U.S. manufacturing firms with more than 25 employees. Arranged alphabetically by company name; indexed by city and by SIC.

§ A related work, *Big business directory* (Omaha, Neb. : American Business Directories, 1992–), lists 140,000 larger firms with more than 100 employees, giving owners/executives and directors, annual sales volume, and branches/subsidiaries. Firms are listed alphabetically with city, SIC, and name indexes.

•Machine-readable versions: *American business directory* [database] (Omaha, Neb. : American Business Directories). Available online; current coverage with quarterly reloads.

Business America on CD-ROM [database] (Omaha, Neb. : American Business Information). Available on CD-ROM; current coverage, updated twice yearly. HD9723.U27

American wholesalers and distributors directory. 1st ed. (1992)– . Detroit : Gale, c1992– . Biennial. **CH346**

A directory that lists contact name(s), product codes estimated annual sales (when available), and number of employees, listed geographically by state, then city. A separate SIC code list ranks entries by annual sales within each SIC. Available from the publisher on magnetic tape or diskette.

§ Companion title, *European wholesalers and distributors directory* (Detroit : Gale, c1992–), gives similar information concerning more than 5,000 major services in 45 European countries.

HF5421.A615

America's corporate families : the billion dollar directory. 198?– . Parsippany, N.J. : Dun's Marketing Services, c198?– . Annual. **CH347**

Each annual issue publ. in 2 v.

Vol. 1 lists more than 11,000 U.S. parent companies in alphabetical order, together with some 70,000 branches, subsidiaries, and divisions. Each parent entry provides directory information, total number of company locations, total employees, sales and net worth, officers, SIC codes, product line, and D-U-N-S number. For dependent firms, gives directory information, percent of ownership, sales at that location, products, SIC codes, number of local employees, and officers.

Vol. 2 lists all companies in alphabetical order, by state and city, and by SIC code (in numerical order, then by state and city). Includes index of SIC codes.

§ Companion volume, *America's corporate families and international affiliates* (Parsippany, N.J. : Dun's Markerting Services, 1983–), lists approximately 2,400 U.S. parent companies with 19,000 foreign subsidiaries, and 3,000 foreign parent companies with 11,000 U.S. subsidiaries. HG4057.A147

Brands and their companies. 8th ed. (1990)– . Detroit : Gale, c1990– . Annual. **CH348**

1st–7th eds., 1976–89, had title: *Trade names dictionary.*

Editor: 1990– , Donna Wood.

Issued in 2 v.

Alphabetically lists more than 250,000 consumer brand names, giving for each a description of the product, company name, and a code for the source from which the information was taken. Company names (more than 45,000 manufacturers and importers) are listed separately in the yellow pages at the end of v. 2, with entries including address, source code, and telephone number.

Companies and their brands (8th ed. [1990]– . Detroit : Gale, c1990– . Annual). Provides an alphabetical list of the companies and the brand names attributed to them. Each company entry is followed by the firm's address and telephone number and an alphabetical listing of its trade names, collected from printed sources and from information supplied by the company itself.

Brands and their companies. Supplement (8th ed. [1990]– . Detroit : Gale c1990– . Annual). Updates both directories, listing new consumer products introduced since the directories were published. Pt. 1 lists brands alphabetically, with a brief description of the product, manufacturer and importer, and in many instances, a code for the source from which the entry was taken. Pt. 2 lists corresponding company names, addresses, phone numbers, and brand names.

International brands and their companies (2nd ed. [1991–92]– . Detroit : Gale, c1990– . Annual). 1st ed., 1988, had title: *International trade names dictionary. International companies and their brands.* This title and its companion *International companies and their brands* (formerly *international trade names company index*) provide similar information for more than 65,000 international consumer products and the nearly 20,000 manufacturers, importers, and distributors associated with them.

•Machine-readable version: *Trade names database* [database] (Detroit : Gale). Available online. T223.V4A25

Corporate technology directory. U.S. ed. 1986– . Wellesley Hills, Mass. : Corporate Technology Information Services, c1986– . Annual. **CH349**

Contents: v. 1, Indexes; v. 2–4, Corporate profiles, A–Z.

Describes more than 35,000 U.S. companies that manufacture or develop high technology products. Company profiles generally include company name and address; telephone, telex, and fax numbers; executives and their departments (including research and development, marketing, purchasing, and personnel); type of ownership, date established, annual sales, and number of employees; and product codes. Indexed by firm and by product. A table converts SIC codes to CorpTech codes.

•Machine-readable versions: *Corporate technology database* [database] (Woburn, Mass. : Corporate Technology Information Services), available online, updated quarterly; and as part of *SciTech reference plus* [database] (New Providence, N.J. : Bowker Electronic Publ.), available on CD-ROM, updated annually. HG4057.A16

Corporate yellow book : who's who at the leading listed U.S. companies. v. 8, no. 1 (winter 1992)– . N.Y. : Monitor Pub. Co., 1992– . Quarterly. **CH350**

Continues: *The corporate 1000* (Mar. 1985–v. 6, no. 2 [Spring 1990]. Wash. : The Washington Monitor, Inc., 1985–1990).

A directory of 1,000 leading U.S. corporations that includes extensive listings of key executives and directors, with titles and telephone numbers. Includes subsidiaries. Indexed by place, industry, and personal and company name.

§ Companion directories from the same publisher:

For corporations: *Financial yellow book* (v. 5, no. 1 [Winter 1992]–); *NASDAQ yellow book* (v. 4, no. 1 [1992]–); *International corporate yellow book* (1992–).

For governmental agencies: *Congressional yellow book* (CJ216); *State yellow book* (CJ282); *Municipal yellow book* (CJ273); *Federal yellow book* (CJ182); and *Federal regional yellow book* (CJ181).

For professional organizations: *Law firms yellow book* (v. 1 [Summer 1991]–); *News media yellow book of Washington and New York* (1990–1993); *Associations yellow book* (v. 1 [Summer 1991]–).

HG4057.A15646

Directory of corporate affiliations. 1973– . New Providence, N.J. : National Register Publ. Co., 1973– . Annual.   **CH351**

"Who owns whom, the family tree of every major corporation in America."—*t.p.*

Place of publication varies.

Issued in two parts, 1990–92; in four volumes and master index, 1993– .

Absorbed in 1993: *Directory of leading private companies, including corporate affiliations, International directory of corporate affiliations* and *Master index to Directory of corporate affiliations, International directory of corporate affiliations, Leading private companies.*

Offers descriptive information on U.S. and multinational parent companies and their affiliates, divisions, and subsidiaries. Concentrates on those companies listed on the New York Stock Exchange and the American Stock Exchange and traded over the counter, as well as major private companies.

•*Corporate affiliations plus*, available on CD-ROM and online, includes *Directory of corporate affiliations/U.S. public companies, Directory of corporate affiliations/U.S. private companies*, and *Corporate finance bluebook*, covering 16,000 major U.S. companies plus more than 140,000 national and international subsidiaries, divisions, and affiliates.   HG4057.A217

Directory of foreign firms operating in the United States. N.Y. : Simon & Schuster, Technical and Reference Book Division, 1969– .   **CH352**

Most recent edition "lists nearly 1600 foreign firms in 50 countries, and more than 2500 businesses in the U.S. which they own, wholly or in part."—*Introd.* Addresses of both foreign and American firms are given, as are, when available, telephone, telex and fax numbers, number of employees, and primary product or service. Percentage of foreign ownership of the American affiliates is frequently included.   HG4057.A21943

Directory of Japanese-affiliated companies in the USA & Canada. 1989/90– . Tokyo : Japan External Trade Organization, 1988– . Biennial.   **CH353**

Some editions have title: Directory, Japanese-affiliated companies in USA & Canada.

Lists some 9,500 companies with at least 10% Japanese ownership. Includes contacts and trade offices in the U.S. and Canada. Indexed by product and by contact name.   HG4057A18

Directory of multinationals / John M. Stopford. [4th ed.]. N.Y. : Stockton Pr., c1992. 2 v. (1511 p.).   **CH354**

1st ed., 1980, and 2nd ed., 1982–83, had title: *World directory of multinational enterprises*; 3rd ed., 1989.

Lists 428 major multinational industrial enterprises. Articles describe directors, company structure, products, five-year historical and current financial summary, and major shareholders.   HD2755.5.S78

Dun's business rankings. 1982– . Parsippany, N.J. : Dun's Marketing Services, 1982– . Annual.   **CH355**

Ranks leading U.S. public and private businesses by annual sales volume and number of employees, in five separate sections: alphabetically by company name; by state; by industry category (SIC code); public businesses; private businesses. Concluding sections cross-index division names with headquarter companies, and list chief executives and other officers by function.   HG4057.A237

Dun's directory of service companies. 1989– . Parsippany, N.J. : Dun's Marketing Services, c1989– . Annual.   **CH356**

Lists the 50,000 largest U.S. public and private service enterprises—those that employ at least 50 people, have a headquarters or single location, and derive their primary income by providing services in such industries as repair, lodging, amusement and recreation, motion pictures, management consulting, engineering, accounting, and legal, health, and social services. Entries are similar to those in the *Million dollar directory* (CH363), with which the publisher estimates an approximate 10% overlap. Indexed geographically and by SIC code.

HD9981.3.D86

Environmental industries marketplace : guide to U.S. companies providing environmental regulatory compliance products and services. 1st ed. (1992)– . Detroit : Gale, c1992– . Annual.   **CH357**

"Comprehensive guide to manufacturers and providers of environmental regulatory compliance products and services in the United States."—*Introd.* Firms are listed alphabetically; entries give brief descriptions of the business or service, products, and brands. Indexed by places and by environmental topics.   HD9718.U6E58

The Extel Financial Asia Pacific handbook / comp., printed and published by Extel Financial Limited. London ; N.Y. : Extel Financial. Semiannual.   **CH358**

Ranks and describes major companies of Australia, Hong Kong, Japan, Korea, Malaysia, Singapore, and Thailand. Directory, by country, lists company activities, officers, shareholders, and key financial information for last three years.   HG4244.6.A3

Franchise opportunities handbook. [Ed.14]– . Wash. : U.S. Govt. Print. Off., 1980– . Annual.   **CH359**

Superintendent of Documents classification: C 41.6/9:F84/ (etc.).

Title, frequency, and issuing body have varied. Eds.1–6 (1965–70) called *Franchise company data*. Published annually since 1986. Issued since 1991 by Minority Business Development Agency.

Published concurrently as: *Franchise opportunities* (N.Y. : Sterling Pub. Co.).

Identifies about 1,000 franchise operations and provides for each description of operation, number of franchises, founding date, capital needed, financial and managerial assistance available, and training programs. Arranged by type of business, with alphabetical corporate name index. Provides directory of government and private assistance programs, checklist for evaluating a franchise, and bibliography. Date when information was submitted is given in all cases.

§ Peter G. Norback and Craig T. Norback's *The Dow Jones-Irwin guide to franchises* (Rev. ed. Homewood, Ill. : Dow Jones-Irwin, 1982. 308 p.) offers an almost identical subject arrangement and descriptions for about 500 franchises; statistical data appears to date from 1981. This guide does provide telephone numbers, which the handbook does not, and its bibliography, while duplicating many titles from the handbook, appears to have been revised more recently.   HF5429.3.F694

Hoover's handbook of American business. 1992– . Austin, Tex. : The Reference Pr., c1991– . Annual.   **CH360**

Continues *Hoover's handbook : profiles of over 500 major corporations* (Austin, Tex. : The Reference Pr., 1991).

Profiles of more than 500 organizations, including public and private companies, nonprofit and governmental, selected for importance to U.S. and global trade. Includes brief history, summary financial data. Indexed by brands, products, company name and personnel.

§ Companion titles: *Hoover's handbook of world business* (1991– . Annual); *Hoover's masterlist of major U.S. companies* (1993– . Annual); *Hoover's handbook of emerging companies* (1993/94– . Annual).

Japan company handbook. 1986– . [Tokyo : Toyo Keizai Shinposha, etc.]. Quarterly.   **CH361**

Continues *Japan company directory*, Jan. 1974–2nd half 1985.

Frequency varies.

Beginning 1986, published in 2 parts. *First section firms* gives corporate and financial information on companies listed on the Tokyo, Osaka, and Nagoya stock exchanges. Arranged by industry categories;

commentary includes brief description of company, short- and long-term outlook, extract of income and financial statements, sales, exports, stock prices, and major shareholders. *Second section* lists companies traded on the local markets, over-the-counter, and some unlisted companies.

§ The same arrangement is followed in its companion, *Asian company handbook* (Tokyo : Toyo Keizai, Inc., c1990–), which covers corporations from Hong Kong, Malaysia, Republic of Korea, Singapore, Taiwan, and Thailand.   HC461.J35

Major companies of Europe. [1982]– . London : Graham & Trotman, 1982– . Annual.   **CH362**

Issued in 3 v.

Contents: v. 1, Major companies of the continental European Community; v. 2, Major companies of the United Kingdom; v. 3, Major companies of Western Europe outside the European Community.

Covers major companies and related service and professional organizations. Provides directory information, officers, products or services, parent company, number of employees, and summary financial information.

§ Other titles from the same publisher: *Medium companies of Europe* (1990/91–); *Major companies of the Arab world* (CH409); *Major companies of the Far East and Australasia* (1990/91–); *Major business organisations of Eastern Europe and the Soviet Union* (1991–).   HC241.2.P667

Million dollar directory. 1979– . Parsippany, N.J. : Dun's Marketing Services, 1979– . Annual.   **CH363**

Formed by the union of *Dun & Bradstreet million dollar directory* and *Dun & Bradstreet middle market directory* (1959–78).

Annual for 1993 lists about 160,000 American businesses and domestic subsidiaries of foreign companies that meet one of the following criteria: net worth of $750,000, more than 250 employees, or sales greater than $25 million. Reports annual sales, number of employees, division names and functions, etc. Geographic and SIC code indexes.

•Machine-readable versions:

Dun's market identifiers (DMI) [database] (Parsippany, N.J. : Dun's Marketing Services), available online with current coverage, updated quarterly. Provides detailed information concerning 6.7 million business establishments with at least ten employees or $1 million in annual sales. As many as 40 searchable fields (e.g., sales, number of employees, changes over time in sales or size of workforce, net worth, square footage, sales territory, type of ownership).

Similar information can be found in companion databases: *Canadian Dun's market identifiers (CDMI)* (Ottawa : Dun & Bradstreet Canada Ltd.), listing 375,000 Canadian firms; *European Dun's market identifiers (EDMI)* (N.Y. : Dun & Bradstreet International), 1.8 million businesses in some 25 countries; and *International Dun's market identifiers (IDMI)* (N.Y. : Dun & Bradstreet International), 2.4 million firms in 150 African, Asian, European, Central and South American, West Asian, and Pacific Rim countries. All three provide current coverage and are available online, updated quarterly.

Dun's million dollar disc [database] (Parsippany, N.J. : Dun's Marketing Services), available on CD-ROM, updated quarterly. Includes more than 200,000 public and private companies with sales greater than $25 million, more than 250 employees, or net worth greater than $500,000.

Dun's business locator [database] (Parsippany, N.J. : Dun's Marketing Services), available on CD-ROM, updated twice yearly. Lists more than 10 million companies in the U.S., giving simple directory information and SIC code.

National directory of minority-owned business firms. 1986 ed.– . Lombard, Ill. : Business Research Services, c1986– . Annual.   **CH364**

Originally publ. 1985 as: *National directory of minority and women-owned business firms* (1985).

Lists firms (as principal or majority shareholder) by African, Hispanic, or Asian Pacific Americans, as well as by Native Americans, Native Hawaiians, or Hasidic Jews. Directory information in SIC order, then geographical. Company index arranged alphabetically by broad subject categories.

§ A companion volume is: *National directory of women-owned business firms* (1986– . Lombard, Ill. : Business Research Services, Inc., 1986–), which follows the same arrangement, listing some 25,000 firms.   HD2346.U5N332

National directory of nonprofit organizations. 1st ed. (1990)– . Rockville, Md. : The Taft Group, c1990– .   **CH365**

Issued in 2 v. Vol. 1 publ. in two parts, 1992– .

An alphabetical list of more than 256,000 nonprofit organizations. Vol. 1 covers the 175,000 groups which report annual incomes over $100,000; v. 2 includes incomes between $25,000 and $100,000. Includes nonprofit corporations; religious, educational, and charitable organizations; social and recreation clubs; fraternal beneficiary societies; and mutual insurance companies. Each entry includes name, address, and telephone; estimated range of annual income; Internal Revenue Service filing status; and a brief activity/mission description. Also features an IRS filing status table, and activity, income range, and geographic indexes.   AS29.5.N38

Norton, Jane Elizabeth. Guide to the national and provincial directories of England and Wales, excluding London, published before 1856. London : Offices of the Royal Historical Soc., 1950. 241 p. (Royal Historical Society. Guides and handbooks, 5).   **CH366**

For annotation, *see* AL7.   Z2034.N67

Standard & Poor's register of corporations, directors and executives. N.Y. : Standard & Poor's Corp., 1928– . Annual.   **CH367**

Vol. 1, Corporations, lists alphabetically about 55,000 public and private U.S. corporations, with executives, number of employees, subsidiary and parent companies, products or services, number of employees and annual sales volume. Vol. 2, gives biographical profiles of approximately 70,000 executives and corporate directors. Vol. 3 indexes by geography, SIC code, corporate family, with roster of stock exchange personnel, list of S&P 500, new listings, and obituary section of deaths since last edition. Three supplements per year.

•Machine-readable versions: *Standard & Poor's corporate descriptions* [database] (N.Y. : Standard & Poor's), available online, updated biweekly; and *DIALOG OnDisc Standard & Poor's corporations* [database], available on CD-ROM, updated monthly.

HG4057.A4

The states and small business : a directory of programs and activities. 1993 ed. Wash. : Office of Advocacy, U.S. Small Business Admin. : U.S. Govt. Print. Off., 1993. 461 p.   **CH368**

Prior ed., 1989.

Directory of state and local programs, agencies and laws which aid small business. Arranged by state.   HD2346.U5S76

Thomas' register of American manufacturers and Thomas' register catalog file. N.Y. : Thomas Publ. Co., 190?– . Annual.   **CH369**

Title varies.

84th ed., 1994, in 27 v.: v. 1–17, Products and services listed alphabetically; v. 18–19, company names and addresses with zip codes and telephone numbers, listed alphabetically, some with branch offices, capital ratings, and company officials; indexes of trademarks and products and services; v. 20–27, Catalogs of companies appearing alphabetically and cross-indexed in the first 17 volumes.

•Machine-readable versions: *Thomas' register* [database] (N.Y. : Thomas Publ. Co.), available online, current file updated semiannually; and *Thomas' register on CD-ROM* [database], available on CD-ROM, current file updated annually.   T12.T6

Top symbols and trademarks of the world / ed. by Franco Maria Ricci and Corinna Ferrari. [Milan] : Deco Pr., [1973]. 7 v. : ill.   **CH370**

Contents: v.1, United States, pt.1; v.2, United States, pt.2, Canada; v.3, Japan, Spain, Latin America; v.4, Great Britain, Ireland, Benelux; v.5, France, Italy; v.6, Switzerland, West Germany, Austria; v.7, Scandinavia, Socialist countries.

A pictorial dictionary illustrating some 5,500 symbols and trademarks used since 1945 in more than 30 countries. Arranged alphabetically according to firm or organization within country or geographical region. Each entry lists artist, design company, and date of trademark. Volume indexes by designer and studio.

Continued by *Top trademarks annual*, from the same editors (1977 only volume publ.). Recently established trademarks are listed by company within the appropriate country section. Entry gives name of firm, address, type of firm, designer, year trademark was designed, and illustration. Indexed by designer and type of firm.

•**Trademarkscan—federal** [database]. North Quincy, Mass. : Thomson & Thomson, [1984]– . **CH371**

Contains full-text records for all active and pending trademarks filed with the U.S. Patent and Trademark Office, and all inactive trademarks since October 1983. Each record includes the trademark; the serial/registration, U.S., and international classification numbers assigned to it; brief descriptions of the mark and the product or service it represents; and ownership and registration information. Searchers with DIALOGLINK software can also display or type the images of trademarks. Also available on compact disc.

§ A companion database, *Trademarkscan—state* (North Quincy, Mass. : Thomson & Thomson) allows the retrieval of similar information on trademarks filed with all 50 states and Puerto Rico since November 1986. The state file is updated biweekly. European and international files are being added.

Try us : national minority business directory. 1972– . Minneapolis, Minn. : National Minority Business Campaign, 1972– . Annual. **CH372**

Lists firms that are profit-seeking, have either national or regional marketing capability, and at least 51% of whose assets are owned by persons from groups that are historically disadvantaged. Arranged geographically, then by business classification. Entries give business activity, previous customers, length of time in business, and number of employees. HD2346.U5N34

Ward's business directory of U.S. private and public companies. 1990– . Detroit : Gale, c1990– . Annual. **CH373**

Revised, reformatted, and expanded version of *Ward's directory of [number] largest U.S. corporations*.

Vols. 1–3 list alphabetically some 140,000 public and private companies, describing type of company, number of employees, sales, officers, SICs, import/export information, and parent/subsidiary relationship. Vol. 4 lists companies by zip code within states and ranks the 1,000 largest private and 1,000 largest public companies, the 1,000 largest employers, including tabular analyses of companies by state, revenue per employee, and four-digit SICs. Vol. 5 ranks companies by sales within four-digit SICs. Company information in v. 4–5 is abbreviated and limited to address, telephone, type, sales, and number of employees; v. 5 also contains names of chief executive officers. Company name index includes primary SIC and assigned rank number.

•Machine-readable versions: *Ward's business directory of U.S. private and public companies* [database] (Detroit : Gale), available on diskettes and magnetic tape, updated annually; as part of *Company intelligence* [database] (Foster City, Calif. : Information Access co.), available online, updated daily; and as part of *CD/private plus* [database] (Cambridge, Mass. : Lotus Development Corp.), available on CD-ROM, updated quarterly. HG4057

Who owns whom. High Wycombe, U.K. : Dun & Bradstreet Ltd., 1993– . Annual. **CH374**

Issued in 6 v. : v. 1, Australasia and Far East; v. 2, North America; v. 3–4, United Kingdom and Republic of Ireland; v. 5–6, Continental Europe.

Merges: *Who owns whom. Australasia and Far East* (1972–92); *Who owns whom. Continental Europe* (1977–92); *Who owns whom. North America* (1972–92); and *Who owns whom. United Kingdom and Republic of Ireland* (1978–92).

Covers more than 23,500 parent companies and 320,000 subsidiaries. Each section lists (1) parent companies in the region with domestic and foreign subsidiaries and associations; and (2) foreign parent companies with domestic subsidiaries. Gives directory information for all firms. HG4135.Z5W5

Handbooks

European markets / by Washington Researchers. [Ed. 1]– . Wash. : Washington Researchers, c1983– . Triennial (irregular). **CH375**

In three parts: (1) directory of relevant federal, state, international, and private sector organizations; (2) brief bibliography of publications and databases; (3) sources of information listed by individual country, including organizations and published sources. Coverage limited to Western Europe. Combines advice about techniques of research with directory of federal, state, and trade and professional resources relevant to foreign trade. List of databases and published sources; directory of contacts and published works by individual country. Subject and name index.

§ *Asian markets : a guide to company and industry information sources* (3rd ed., 1993) and *Latin American markets : a guide to company and industry information sources* (1993) follow the same format for different world regions. HF3493.E825

Guide to European company information : EC countries. 4th ed. London : London Business School Information Service, 1990. 129 p. **CH376**

1st ed., 1988.

For each of the 12 European Community countries, lists and annotates information sources by format (directories, online databases, CD-ROMs and diskettes, newspapers and magazines, and other services). Preliminary sections list normal business hours, major industrial centers, language, currency, number of public and private companies, number and location of stock exchanges, legal types of companies, and filing requirements and public access to company records. Other sections include a listing of pan-European information sources, a directory and descriptions of company accounts/credit reporting agencies, a brief bibliography, and title and format indexes. HD2844.5.G853

Handbook of small business data / U.S. Small Business Administration, Office of Advocacy. Wash. : The Office : For sale by the U.S. Govt. Print. Off., 1988– . **CH377**

Chapters describe various government and private sources of data on small business; subsequent chapters consist mainly of statistical tables covering employment, income, business failures, new incorporation, growth, financial ratios, and related topics. List of tables and brief glossary. Not indexed. HD2346.U5H37

The Irwin business and investment almanac. 18th (1994)– . Burr Ridge, Ill. : Irwin Professional Pub., c1994– . Annual. **CH378**

Continues: 1991–93, Business One Irwin business and investment almanac; 1982–90, Dow Jones-Irwin business and investment almanac; 1977–81, Dow Jones-Irwin business almanac.

A quick-access source to a variety of current information in business, investment, finance, and economics. Emphasis on American domestic and international business. Indexed. HF5003.D68a

Standard industrial classification manual : 1987 / [prepared by the] Executive Office of the President, Office of Management and Budget. [Wash.] : The Office ; Springfield, Va. : For sale by National Technical Information Service, 1987. 705 p. **CH379**

Superintendent of Documents classification: PrEx 2.6/2:In 27/987.

Supersedes all previous editions and supplements.

Previous ed. prepared by the Statistical Policy Division, United States Office of Management and Budget. Also available from the Government Printing Office.

Developed for use in classifying establishments by type of activity in which they are engaged, for the purposes of facilitating the collection, tabulation, presentation and analysis of data. Titles, numeric codes, and industry descriptions are presented in 11 main divisions and numerous subsections. An alphabetic index lists all manufacturing and non-manufacturing industries and the codes assigned to each; an appendix gives conversion tables between the 1972/77 edition/supplement and the 1987 edition. HF1042.S73

U.S. industrial outlook : prospects for over 350 manufacturing and service industries. 1960– . [Wash.] : U.S. Dept. of Commerce, International Trade Administration : for sale by the U.S. Govt. Print.Off. Annual. **CH380**

Superintendent of Documents classification: C 62.17: ; C 61.34.

Issued 1980–83 as *U.S. industrial outlook for [200] industries with projections for [date]*. Date precedes title in many issues. Issuing agency varies.

An essential reference source containing industry analyses and statistical data for both manufacturing and service industries. Arrangement is by ten broad industry categories (e.g., construction, information, communications), with subsections devoted to specific industries. Entries range from a single page to two or more, and usually include a general description, as well as discussion of U.S. production, foreign trade, the outlook for the current year, and long-term prospects. "Trends and forecasts" tables carry industry, product, and trade data and percent change for the current year and three years preceding. Information is specific to industries, not companies. Entries conclude with the name, office, and telephone number of the government specialist who wrote the report as well as a bibliography of additional references. An industry index lists SIC code(s) and page numbers.

HC101.U55

Histories

Atkins, Peter Joseph. The directories of London, 1677–1977. London ; N.Y. : Mansell, 1990. 732 p. : ill. **CH381**

For annotation, *see* AL1. Z5771.4.G7A85

Dallas Public Library. Business and Technology Division. Business history collection : a checklist. Dallas : The Library, 1974. 236 p. **CH382**

A listing of histories of particular firms, American and foreign, arranged by the name of the firm. No index. Z7165.U5D34

Encyclopedia of American business history and biography. N.Y. : Facts on File, 1988–1993. [v. 1–9]. (In progress). **CH383**

Contents: Railroads in the nineteenth century, ed. by Robert L. Frey (1988); Railroads in the age of regulation, 1900–1980, ed. by Keith L. Bryant, Jr. (1988); The automobile industry, 1920–1980, ed. by George S. May (1989); Iron and steel in the nineteenth century, ed. by Paul F. Paskoff (1989); The automobile industry, 1896–1920, ed. by George S. May (1990); Banking and finance to 1913, ed. by Larry E. Schweikart (1990. CH265); Banking and finance, 1913–1989, ed. by Larry E. Schweikart (1990. CH265 *note*); The airline industry, ed. by William M. Leary (1992); The iron and steel industry in the 20th century, ed. by Bruce E. Seely (1993).

Each volume combines biographical entries with articles discussing major companies, government and labor organizations, inventions, and legislation and legal decisions for the industry and period being covered. The signed entries range in length from one-half to ten or more pages; most include photographs and other illustrations, list publications and references, and note archives and unpublished documents. Indexed.

Annuals

Industry and development / United Nations Industrial Development Organization. 1985– . N.Y. : United Nations, 1985– . Annual. **CH384**

An annual review of the world industrial economy, with an assessment of the current situation and short-term forecasts. Statistics, tables, graphs. HC59.69.I53

Biography

Reference book of corporate managements. Ed. 1– . N.Y. : Dun & Bradstreet, 1967– . Annual. **CH385**

Title varies: Ed. 1–13, *Dun & Bradstreet reference book of corporate managements*.

Brief biographical information on officers and directors of about 12,000 U.S. companies. Companies are listed in alphabetical sequence; indexed by name of principal officers, geographically, and by industry classification. HD2745.D85

Room, Adrian. Corporate eponymy : a biographical dictionary of the persons behind the names of major American, British, European, and Asian businesses. Jefferson, N.C. : McFarland & Co., c1992. 280 p. **CH386**

A biographical dictionary of short entries describing the origin of business names. Emphasizes English-speaking world, with some continental European and Asian names. Strict alphabetical arrangement with cross-references. HC29.R66

•**Standard & Poor's register—biographical** [database]. N.Y. : Standard & Poor's Corp. **CH387**

Machine-readable version of *Standard & Poor's register of corporations, directors, and executives*, v. 2 (CH367).

Brief biographies of more than 70,000 active business executives.

Statistics

Finance, insurance, & real estate USA. 1st ed.– . Detroit : Gale, c1993– . Biennial. **CH388**

Also called *FIRE USA*.

A collection of statistics from a variety of federal, insurance, and association sources. Describes and provides statistical data concerning 36 industries in 50 states and 2,500 counties. Pt. 1, arranged by SIC number, shows national and state industry profiles including: establishments, employment, payroll, inputs and outputs for banking sectors, occupations, and a list of leading companies within each grouping. Pt. 2 is an alphabetical state and county listing, providing information drawn from the federally-produced County Business Patterns. Indexed by SIC, keyword, company and occupation. Includes maps and graphs.

Business history

Baker Library. Studies in enterprise : a selected bibliography of American and Canadian company histories and biographies of businessmen / Lorna M. Daniells, comp. Boston, 1957. 169 p. (Harvard University. Graduate School of Business Administration. Baker Library. Reference list, no.4). **CH389**

An expanded edition of the Library's *Business biographies and company histories* (1948). Updated by Priscilla Geahigan's *U.S. and Canadian businesses, 1955 to 1987* (CH390).

Lists 2,080 items in a classified arrangement, with subject and author indexes. Z7164.C81H26

Geahigan, Priscilla Cheng. U.S. and Canadian businesses, 1955 to 1987 : a bibliography. Metuchen, N.J. : Scarecrow, 1988. 589 p. **CH390**

Lists more than 4,000 titles concerned with business and corporate histories, biographies of business people, and non-profit organizations. Cites primarily books published after 1954, but includes a few reprints from earlier years, some dissertations, company publications, and "substantial" periodical articles. Arranged by two-digit SIC, then by company or individual name. Indexed by company name, personal name, and author.

Supplements *Studies in enterprise* (CH389), which inspired it.

Z7164.C81G32

Goodall, Francis. A bibliography of British business histories. Aldershot, England ; Brookfield, Vt. : Gower, c1987. 638 p.
CH391

The main section lists works alphabetically by author, giving full bibliographic information for each title and noting the presence of indexes or illustrations, the name of the firm described, its primary SIC, and a code for the source library. Preliminary pages include an essay on the nature, new directions, and methodology of business history, the British standard industrial classification, a bibliography of business history bibliographies, libraries with business history collections, and a list of abbreviations. Company name and SIC indexes.

Z7165.G8G59

Hamburgisches Welt-Wirtschafts-Archiv. Verzeichnis der Fest- und Denkschriften von Unternehmungen und Organisationen der Wirtschaft im Hamburgisches Welt-Wirtschafts-Archiv. [Hamburg], 1961. 566 p. **CH392**

A listing of more than 4,000 festschriften and histories of firms and companies. International in scope, but mainly German. Lists works published in this century that are found in the Archiv. In classified arrangement with indexes by: (1) author and personal name; (2) firm; and (3) geographical location. Particularly strong in the histories of individual companies, many of which are not listed in general and national bibliographies.

Z7165.G3H3

Hill, George H. Black business and economics : a selected annotated bibliography. N.Y. : Garland, 1984. 351 p. (Garland reference library of social science, v. 267). **CH393**

Gives citations to 100 books, 180 theses and dissertations, and articles from popular periodicals written since 1885. Book citations, arranged by author, are annotated. Government documents are listed by author, title, or department, and are followed by topically arranged listings of dissertations, theses, journal and newspaper articles. About 2,268 citations in all.

Z7164.C81H47

International directory of company histories / ed., Thomas Derdak ... [et al.]. Chicago : St. James Pr., c1988–93. v. 1–8. (In progress). **CH394**

Contents: v. 1, Advertising—Drugs; v. 2, Electrical and electronics. Food services and retailers; v. 3, Health and personal care products. Materials; v. 4, Mining and metals. Real estate; v. 5, Retail and wholesale. Waste services; v. 6, Advertising and other business services. Utilities; v. 7, and v. 8, without special titles.

A set that aims to provide detailed information on the world's largest companies, each volume containing approximately 250 companies. To be included, a company must have annual sales of at least $500 million or be considered a leading influence in an industry or geographical location. State-owned companies and wholly owned subsidiaries are presented if they meet the requirements for inclusion. Entries, generally two to three pages in length, include the company's logo and legal name, address, telephone number, ownership, date incorporated, employees, assets, and exchange symbol. Lists subsidiaries and further reading. Cumulative alphabetical index in latest volume.

HD2721.I63

Larson, Henrietta Melia. Guide to business history : materials for the study of American business history and suggestions for their use. Cambridge : Harvard Univ. Pr., 1948. 1181 p. (Harvard studies in business history, v. 12). **CH395**

Contents: (1) Introduction; (2) Historical background and setting of American business; (3) Business administrators: Biographical and autobiographical books, pamphlets and articles; (4) The history of individual business units; (5) History of industries; (6) General topics in business history; (7) Research and reference materials. Index.

Has 4,904 annotated entries. Dated, but still a useful guide to historical study.

§ Robert Woodberry Lovett's *American economic business history information sources : an annotated bibliography of recent works pertaining to economic, business, agricultural, and labor history and the history of science and technology for the United States and Canada* (Detroit : Gale, [1971]. 323 p.) is intended in part as a supplement.

HC103.L3

Manufacturing : a historiographical and bibliographical guide / David O. Whitten, ed., Bessie E. Whitten, assistant ed. N.Y. : Greenwood, 1990. 503 p. (Handbook of American business history, v. 1). **CH396**

For each of 23 industries, includes a brief history, bibliographic essay, and bibliography of published and unpublished works. Chapters, written by scholars in business, economics, law, engineering, and social history, are grouped by broad industry category following the Enterprise Standard Industrial Classification (ESIC). More general works on U.S. business history are noted in the introduction. Thoroughly indexed.

HC103.M25

Nasrallah, Wahib. United States corporation histories : a bibliography, 1965–1990. 2nd ed. N.Y. : Garland, 1991. 511 p. **CH397**

1st ed., 1987.

Contains "books, periodical articles, theses, dissertations, pamphlets and other company produced literature, corporate histories embedded in annual reports or fact sheets, and articles from national or regional newspapers."—*Introd.* Arrangement is alphabetical by company name, with *see* references from popular to legal company names, and *see also* references linking corporate name changes. Industry, author, and executive officer indexes.

Z7164.T87N37

Orbell, John. A guide to tracing the history of a business. Aldershot ; Brookfield, [Vt.] : Gower, c1987. 116 p. **CH398**

Outlines the various information sources, including records of government agencies and associations, corporate reports on file, printed indexes, and personal records, for researching the history of British businesses. Includes an unannotated bibliography and the addresses of all record offices, libraries, museums, societies, and other organizations mentioned in the text. Indexed.

HD2321.O7

Robinson, Richard. United States business history, 1602–1988 : a chronology. N.Y. : Greenwood, 1990. 643 p. **CH399**

"Designed to provide a basic calendar of representative events ... in the evolution of U.S. business."—*Pref.* Contains descriptive historical data, arranged by year, then under categories of general news and business news. Significant individuals, specific companies, inventions, trade unions, and key business, economic, and social developments are included. Brief bibliography; detailed index.

§ Complemented by Robinson's *Business history of the world : a chronology* (Westport, Conn. : Greenwood, 1993. 562 p.).

HC103.R595

Romaine, Lawrence B. A guide to American trade catalogs, 1744–1900. N.Y. : Bowker, 1960. 422 p. **CH400**

Repr.: N.Y : Dover, 1990.

An extensive listing of trade catalogs in classified arrangement, indicating location of copies.

Z7164.C8R6

Spear, Dorothea N. Bibliography of American directories through 1860. Worcester, Mass. : Amer. Antiquarian Soc., 1961. 389 p. **CH401**

For annotation, *see* AL8.

Z5771.22b.S68

Company information

United States

Business rankings annual / comp. by Brooklyn Public Library, Business Library Staff. 1989– . Detroit : Gale, c1989– . Annual. **CH402**

Continues: Business Library (Brooklyn Public Library). *Business rankings and salaries index*, 1st ed. (Detroit : Gale, 1988).

A collection of "top ten" lists extracted from newspapers, periodicals, directories, statistical annuals, and other publications, arranged alphabetically by subject. Each subject list describes ranked characteristics and the criteria used, and gives the first ten items in the original list, which is also cited. Index of companies, individuals, organizations, and products.

§ Complemented by: *European business rankings* (1st ed.– . London : Gale Research International, 1992–). HG4050.B88

Foster, Dennis L. The rating guide to franchises. Rev. ed. N.Y. : Facts on File, 1991. 236 p. **CH403**

Combines descriptions and comparative ratings for more than 300 U.S. and Canadian franchises. Arranged by 16 broad industry categories, then alphabetically by name of franchise. Each profile includes: comparative ratings for industry and franchising experience, financial strength, training and services, fees and royalties, and satisfied franchisees; franchise overview and description; franchisee profile; projected earnings; franchisor's services; advertising; disputes and litigation; initial investment; contract highlights; fees and royalties; summary; and franchise highlights. Back matter includes a ranked list of the leading 350 franchise chains and franchisors and category indexes. A useful supplement to *Franchise opportunities handbook* (CH359), which covers more franchises, but in less detail and without the ratings. HF5429.23.F676

Standard & Poor's stock market encyclopedia. Ed. 1– . N.Y. : Standard & Poor's Corp., [1961?]– . Quarterly. **CH404**

Lists S&P 500 plus 250 other leading public corporations. Two pages of information for each firm includes summary of operations, current outlook and S&P forecast, 10 years of per-share data, and three-year balance sheet. HG4921.S68

Multinational

CIFAR's global company handbook : [an analysis of the financial performance of the world's leading 7,500 companies]. 1992 ed.– . Princeton, N.J. : CIFAR, c1992– . Annual. **CH405**

Issued for 1992 in 2 v.; in 4 v., 1993– .

More than 10,000 of the world's leading companies, representing 26 industries in 11 countries, are described using 43 financial and nonfinancial ratios or variables. Vol. 1 analyzes the world's capital markets, with rankings of top performing companies. Vols. 2–4 profile individual firms (including some nontraded companies), giving directory information, most recent five years of financial data and key ratios, per-share data in local currency. Arranged by regions and countries, then by company. HG4009.C54

Principal international businesses. 1974– . N.Y. : Dun & Bradstreet, 1974– . Annual. **CH406**

Subtitle: A world marketing directory.

Introductory matter in English, French, German and Spanish.

Section 1 lists more than 50,000 companies by country, providing for each: sales volume, indication of whether it exports or imports, number of employees, SIC and DUNS numbers, description of field of activity, and name and title of senior operating officer. Section 2 lists businesses by SIC number; Section 3 lists them by name. HF54.U5P74

Worldwide franchise directory. 1st ed.– . Detroit : Gale, c1991– . Irregular. **CH407**

Provides information concerning some 1,574 franchising companies in 16 countries. Arranged by type of business in more than 80 categories, ranging from accounting/tax services to weight control. In addition to standard directory information, entries generally include: date founded and date of first franchise; number of outlets; initial franchise fee and start-up costs; description of the business; type of franchise; equipment needed; support provided; franchise agreement information (terms of contract, renewal terms, sales royalty, selling a franchise, etc.); and source of profile. Also lists U.S. and foreign franchise consulting firms and trade associations. Master name and keyword, geographic, and personal name indexes.

By region

Japan trade directory. 1982– . Tokyo : Japan External Trade Organization, 1982– . **CH408**

Lists Japanese companies involved in international trade. Pt. 1 lists import and export companies by product or services; pt. 2 lists companies, trade and industrial associations and trade names alphabetically, pt. 3 describes business climate in each prefecture. HF3823.J343

Major companies of the Arab world. 1975– . London : Graham & Trotman (distr. in U.S.A. by Franklin Watts), 1976– . Irregular. **CH409**

Title varies: 1975 ed. had title *Major companies of the Arab world and Iran*.

Ed. by Giselle C. Bricault.

A directory of the major commercial and industrial companies (including non-Arab firms), foreign bank branches, shipping agents, etc., providing address, names of principal officers, description of activities, and data concerning agencies, subsidiaries, bankers, ownership, number of employees, and financial information. All information has been derived from questionnaires submitted to the companies. Indexed by company and business activity.

Other titles from the same publisher: *Major companies of Europe* (CH362); *Major companies of the Far East and Australasia* (1990/ 91–); *Major business organisations of Eastern Europe and the Soviet Union* (1991–). HF3866.M332

Europe

Directory of European business. London ; N.Y. : Bowker-Saur, 1992. 366 p. : maps. **CH410**

Details of economic and political operating environment of 35 East and West European countries with details of 4,000 companies. Lists business services and organizations, leading companies, government agencies, and information sources. HF3493.D56

Duns Europa. [1st ed.] (1990)– . High Wycombe, England : D & B Europe, Ltd., c1989– . **CH411**

Issues for 1990– published in 3 vols.

Lists the largest companies in all 12 European Community countries, Austria, and Switzerland. Arrangement in v. 1–2 is by country, then alphabetically (in the language of the country) by company name. Entries include: DUNS number, address, telephone and telex numbers; list of principal directors and executives and numeric codes designating their functions; indication of exporter and/or importer status; name of parent company; nominal capital; number of employees; annual sales and percent of annual sales going to export; and net profit or loss. Vol. 3 contains ranked lists of the 10,000 largest companies and of the top 30% in each main business activity, statistical profiles (sales, SIC) by country and for Europe as a whole, company name and business activity indexes, and SIC and executive function code tables. A supplement indexes companies by principal SIC and country.

•Machine-readable version: *DUNS EUROPA* [database] (High Wycombe : Dun & Bradstreet Ltd.), available online and on diskettes, current coverage.

Eastern European business directory / [ed. by] Frank X. Didik. Detroit : Gale, c1992 [i.e. 1991]. 962 p. **CH412**

Subtitle: A guide to more than 8,000 of the largest business, commercial enterprises, and special interest associations—classified by products and services—in Bulgaria, Czechoslovakia, Hungary, Poland, Romania, the western USSR, and the former East Germany.

Arranged by product or service. Entries include contact person, and telephone, fax, or telex. Geographical and alphabetical indexes.
HF3500.7.A48E23

European business services directory / Michael B. Huellmantel, editor. Detroit : Gale, 1992. 1374 p. **CH413**

Describes more than 20,000 European companies that provide essential business services (finance and accounting, advertising and marketing, engineering services, tourism and support services, law, and transport) to other companies. Arranged by type of service, then geographically by country and by city. Includes number of employees and financial data. Cross-references between parent companies and branches. Geographic and company name index. HF5152.E97

Kelly's. 107th ed. (1994)– . East Grinstead, [Eng.] : Reed Information Services, c1994– . Annual. **CH414**

Continues *Kelly's directory of merchants, manufacturers and shippers of the world*, *Kelly's manufacturers and merchants directory*, *Kelly's business directory*, etc. First publ. 1880.

Alphabetical and classified lists of British manufacturers, merchants, wholesalers, and firms, with a section on brand and trade names. HF54.G7K4

Industry analysis

Mattera, Philip. Inside U.S. business : a concise encyclopedia of leading industries. [2nd] ed. Homewood, Ill. : Business One Irwin, c1991. 568 p. **CH415**

1st ed., 1987.

Contains 25 chapters on specific industries, arranged by broad category (communications, consumer goods and services, electronics, energy, finance, and heavy industry and transportation). Gives industry descriptions and histories, lists and profiles of leading companies, discussion of industry labor relations and a source guide that lists leading stock analysts and experts, trade associations, data sources and directories, online databases, trade publications, and books and reports. Indexed. HC106.8.M337

Service industries USA : industry analysis, statistics, and leading organizations. 1992– . Detroit : Gale, c1992– . Biennial. **CH416**

Combines federal, private, and nonprofit statistics on the U.S. service sector. Arranged by SIC number; 151 industries are covered. Entries are two-thirds of a page in length and include general statistics, indexes of change for seven years, and selected financial and operating ratios. Includes a list of leading companies in each grouping. Summary state and regional data are presented along with profiles of 623 cities or metropolitan areas. Indexed by SIC, services, companies, nonprofits, cities, and occupations. Includes maps.

Standard & Poor's industry surveys. Jan. 1973– . [N.Y.] : Standard & Poor's Corp., 1973– . Quarterly. **CH417**

Detailed analyses of 22 industry categories and the major companies in each category. Contains a basic analysis, a comprensive source of information, updated by a current analysis. Tables, graphs and statistics. Company and industry indexes. HC106.6.S74

Financial and operating ratios

Almanac of business and industrial financial ratios / Leo Troy. Englewood Cliffs, N.J. : Prentice-Hall, 1971– . Annual beginning 1974. **CH418**

For the industry as a whole and for corporations of similar size as measured by assets, gives comparative figures, percentages, and ratios for factors such as net sales, total receipts, cost of operations, compensation of officers, taxes, interest, depreciation, amortization, pensions and benefit plans. 1978 edition is the first to show separate tables for each total industry and for those operating at a profit. Indexed by field of activity. HF5681.R25A45

Statistics

Analyst's handbook. 1964– . N.Y. : Standard & Poor's Corp., 1964– . Annual. **CH419**

Subtitle: Composite corporate per share data—by industries.

Composite corporate per-share data, 1962 to date, for industries represented in the S&P 500 index. Statistics cover sales, profit margin, earnings, dividend yields, book value. HG4905.A66

Business statistics / U.S. Department of Commerce, Office of Business Economics. 1951– . Wash. : The Office : for sale by U.S. Govt. Print. Off., 1951– . Biennial. **CH420**

Title varies: 1932–42 called *Supplement*. Publication suspended 1934, 1942–47.

Tables give monthly and quarterly data for 2,600 statistical series reported in the *Survey of current business* (CH425). HC101.A1322

Industry norms and key business ratios. 1982–83 ed.– . [N.Y.] : Dun & Bradstreet Credit Services, 1983– . Annual. **CH421**

Provides composite financial information and 154 financial and operating ratios for the year of coverage for 800 lines of business arranged by SIC number.

An expanded set is also available in five industry segments: (1) Agriculture/mining/construction/transportation /communication/ utilities, (2) Manufacturing; (3) Wholesaling; (4) Retailing; (5) Finance/real estate/services. HF5681.R25I53

Manufacturing USA : industry analyses, statistics, and leading companies. 1st ed. (1989)– . Detroit : Gale, 1989– . Irregular. **CH422**

Arsen J. Darnay, ed.

Uses data from the U.S. Department of Labor and *Ward's business directory of U.S. private and public companies* (CH373); arranged by four-digit manufacturing SIC codes to show changes, give overview of each industry, and to identify leading companies. Indexed by SIC code, products, company names, and occupations.

Predicasts forecasts. no.1 (Oct. 1960)– . Foster City, Calif. : Information Access, 1960– . Quarterly, the 4th issue being an annual cumulation. **CH423**

Title varies. Formerly publ. Cleveland : Predicasts.

Volumes for 1960–66 publ. by Economic Index & Survey, Inc.

Gives short- and long-term statistical projections for basic U.S. economic indicators and products (by SIC number). For each statistic, gives bibliographic reference to the source, periodical article, government document, or private study.

•Machine-readable version: *PTS U.S. forecasts*. Coverage from July 1971. Updated more frequently than its printed counterpart.
HC101.P7

RMA annual statement studies. 1977– . Philadelphia : Robert Morris Associates, 1977– . Annual. **CH424**

Title formerly: Robert Morris Associates. *Annual statement studies*.

Provides composite financial data (current year plus five preceding years) for some 400 industries, including for each: assets, liabilities, and income data and 16 financial and operating ratios. Arranged by five broad industry categories (manufacturing; wholesaling; retailing; services, and not elsewhere classified; finance), then by industry group and SIC. Preliminary pages explain balance sheet and income data, define the ratios used, list the SICs included, and list and describe industries covered. A bibliography lists sources that publish financial data for industries not covered. Indexed by industry.

Survey of current business. v. 1 (Aug. 1921)– . Wash. : U.S. Govt. Print. Off., 1921– . Monthly.　**CH425**

Superintendent of Documents classification: C 56.109: , C 59.11: .

Issuing agency varies; Bureau of Economic Analysis, Jan. 1972– .

Descriptive and statistical material on basic income and trade developments in the United States. Covers prices, foreign trade, commodities, industries, etc. *Annual review* number issued in Feb., 1939–62; *National income and product accounts* number in July since 1948.

§ Supplemented by: *National income and product accounts of the United States. Statistical tables, Business statistics* (CH420), *Weekly business statistics*, and their predecessor and successor publications.　HC101.A13

Worldcasts. Product. Dec. 15, 1964?– . Cleveland : Predicasts, 1964?– . Quarterly.　**CH426**

Issued in four looseleaf binders called: P-1, Population, labor force, GNP, industrial production, construction, electric power, trade and services, government; P-2, Agricultural products, metal ores, coal and lignite, crude oil and gas, nonmetal mining, food products, textiles and apparel, timber and paper, printing and publishing; P-3, Industrial and agricultural chemicals, plastics, rubber, petroleum and energy products, leather, stone, clay, and glass products; P-4, Metals, electric and nonelectric machinery, transportation, equipment, instruments and related products, manufacturing. Titles vary.

Complementary to *Predicasts forecasts*, which provides short- and long-term projections for basic economic and industrial statistics for countries other than the U.S. Arranged by modified SIC codes. Indicates citation to periodical article, government document, or other source from which the statistics are derived.

Companion work: *Worldcasts. Regional.* (Dec. 15, 1964?– . Cleveland : Predicasts, 1964?– . Quarterly). Also arranged by country.

Issued in four looseleaf binders called: R-1, West Europe; R-2, East Europe, Africa, Middle East; R-3, North America, Latin America; R-4, Asia & Oceania. Titles vary.

• *PTS international forecasts* [database]. (Cleveland : Predicasts, [1971]–). Combines the forecasts contained in the product and regional sections of *Worldcasts*, with the added advantage of regular updates.　HC1040.P74

Yearbook of industrial statistics. 1974–1981. N.Y. : Dept. of Economic and Social Affairs, Statistical Office of the United Nations, 1976–1983. Annual.　**CH427**

Continues *The growth of world industry* (1969–73) issued by the United Nations Statistical Office.

Issued in 2 v. per year: v. 1, General industrial statistics; v. 2, Commodity production data.

Presents (1) national surveys for about 200 countries or areas on various indicators of industrial activity, classified by ISIC code, with a selection of indicators to measure global and regional trends in industrial productivity and employment, and (2) production statistics on more than 527 industrial commodities.　HA40.I6Y4

COMMERCE

General works

Bibliography

Alred, Gerald J. Business and technical writing : an annotated bibliography of books, 1880–1980 / Gerald J. Alred, Diana C. Reep, and Mohan R. Lamaye. Metuchen, N.J. : Scarecrow, 1981. 240 p.　**CH428**

In three main sections: (1) previous bibliographies; (2) the main bibliography, arranged by author, followed by citations to related works (e.g., style guides, works on graphics, oral communication, and publishing); (3) addendum of additional titles. Author, title, and subject indexes.　Z7164.C81A413

Dictionaries

Appleby, Barry Léon. Elsevier's dictionary of commercial terms and phrases : in five languages: English, German, Spanish, French, and Swedish. Amsterdam ; N.Y. : Elsevier, 1984. 1083 p.　**CH429**

Base language is English, with equivalents given in the four other languages. Indexed in all five languages.　HF1002.A66

Commodities

Chapman, Karen J. Commodities price locator. Phoenix : Oryx, 1989. 135 p.　**CH430**

More than 150 government, trade, financial, and other serials that publish commodities price information are listed alphabetically by commodity and briefly annotated. An appendix lists databases (none of which appear in the main list) that contain commodities prices. The emphasis is on cash ("spot") prices paid for commodities received rather than on commodities futures prices, which are not covered.　Z7164.C83C46

Commodity futures trading : bibliography. 1967/73– . [Chicago] : Chicago Board of Trade, 1974– . Annual, with irregular cumulations.　**CH431**

In three sections: (1) books, monographs, and material provided by commodity exchanges; (2) resource material, i.e., scholarly journal articles and government publications; (3) trade, or popular press articles. Each section is subdivided by specific topics or commodity. No index.

§ A "Futures bibliography" appears in each quarterly issue of the *Journal of futures markets*, 1982– .　Z7164.C83C64

Friedman, Catherine. Commodity prices. 2nd ed. Detroit : Gale, c1991. 630 p.　**CH432**

1st ed., 1974, by Paul Wasserman, updated a 1959 work.

Lists sources of prices (spot, cash, retail, and futures) for some 10,400 commodities, drawn from nearly 200 domestic and international trade publications and federal, state, and foreign government publications. Arranged alphabetically by commodity. Index of publishers.　Z7164.P94F74

The Knight-Ridder CRB commodity yearbook / Commodity Research Bureau, Knight-Ridder Financial Publishing. 1993– . N.Y. : Wiley, c1993– . Annual.　**CH433**

Updated quarterly with supplements.

Continues: *CRB commodity year book* (N.Y. : Commodity Research Bureau, 1939–92).

Provides background information and statistical data on agricultural and industrial commodities, and on financial and stock index futures. Organized alphabetically by commodity. Data sources are primarily U.S. official publications, with some from U.N., trade association, and international organization publications. Includes feature articles discussing current issues. HF1041.C56

Labys, Walter C. Primary commodity markets and models : an international bibliography. Aldershot, [England] ; Brookfield, Vt. : Avebury, c1987. 290 p. **CH434**

A guide to the "economics of primary commodity markets, their structure, the various forces influencing their short-term and long-term behavior, and the modeling of these markets for forecasting and policy analysis."—*Foreword*. A 40-page introductory essay on commodity analysis and modeling is followed by the bibliography, which groups entries alphabetically under broad subject categories and subcategories. Not indexed. Z7164.C8L33

Nicholas, David. Commodities futures trading : a guide to information sources and computerized services. London : Mansell, [1985]. 144 p. **CH435**

Sections: market trading and price distribution online systems; computerized news retrieval services from newspapers and newsletters; journals, magazines, and abstracting/indexing services; yearbooks, directories, and reference works; books. Directory of vendors; index. HG6046.N53

Robertson, M. J. M. Directory of world futures and options : a guide to international futures and options exchanges and products. N.Y. : Prentice Hall, 1990. 1 v. (various pagings). **CH436**

Arranged by regions of the world. Each entry contains stock exchange directory information, a brief history of the exchange, a description of what futures and options contracts are available, and details of how each commodity is traded. Includes where trades are quoted, if available. Index by exchange name, category, and product type. Glossary. HG6024.A3R63

Steinbeck, George. The futures markets dictionary / George Steinbeck, Rosemary Erickson. N.Y. : New York Institute of Finance, c1988. 191 p. : ill. **CH437**

Describes key words and phrases used in the commodities, options, forwards, and actuals markets. Explains how to read futures quotations. Many definitions contain examples, illustrations, and cross-references. HG6024.A3S75

UNCTAD commodity yearbook / United Nations Conference on Trade and Development. 1986– . N.Y. : United Nations, 1987– . Annual. **CH438**

Continues: *Yearbook of international commodity statistics*, United Nations Conference on Trade and Development (N.Y. : The Conference, 1984–85).

Intends to provide disaggregated data at regional and country levels for production, trade, and consumption of agriculture commodities, minerals, ores, and metals. HF1040.Y42

Directories

World futures and options directory. 1991–92– . Chicago : Probus, 1991– . Annual. **CH439**

Also published as *St. James world futures and options directory* and as *McGraw-Hill world futures and options directory*; publisher varies.

A directory of more than 600 agricultural, financial, metal, petroleum, equity, and miscellaneous futures contracts and the 48 exchanges on which they are traded. Directory of exchanges includes structure and history, contracts administered, clearing organizations and regulatory authority. Additional sections list contracts available, grouped by commodity type; includes details such as units sold, size and value,

limits, trading hours and days, and sources of quotations. The last section lists members of many of the exchanges. Not indexed. HG6024.A3S7

Handbooks

Commodity trading manual / [prep. by the Education and Marketing Services Department of the Chicago Board of Trade ; project ed., Christine Depp Stebbins]. [Chicago : Board of Trade of the City of Chicago, c1989]. 401 p. : ill. (some col.). **CH440**

"A comprehensive textbook/reference guide on the futures industry covering topics from the historical development of futures markets to nuts-and-bolts description of the day-to-day operations of a futures exchange."—*Foreword*. Each of the major types of futures and options are described in separate chapters in which production, demand, world markets, futures markets, and price considerations are covered; an appendix lists contract specifications for all U.S. exchanges. Includes a bibliography, glossary, and index. HG6049.C65

Statistics

Manthy, Robert S. Natural resource commodities—a century of statistics : prices, output, consumption, foreign trade, and employment in the United States, 1870–1973 / Robert S. Manthy ; [ed. by Joan R. Tron]. Baltimore : Publ. for Resources for the Future by the Johns Hopkins Univ. Pr., 1978. 240 p. : graphs. **CH441**

An update of Resources for the Future's *Trends in natural resource commodities* by Neal Potter and Francis Christy, Jr. (1962).

In five sections: (1) methodology; (2) highlights; (3) detailed agricultural, mineral, and forest commodity summaries, emphasizing the post-1950 period; (4) individual data series for 200 natural resources commodities, from 1870 to 1973; (5) documented sources and explanatory notes for the data tables. HF1052.M35

Transportation

Bibliography

Davis, Bob J. Information sources in transportation, material management, and physical distribution : an annotated bibliography and guide. Westport, Conn. : Greenwood, [1976]. 715 p. **CH442**

Materials are organized under 67 subjects, and within each subject, by type: book and pamphlet (including government publications); periodical titles (including directories, guides, and services); organizations; education (awards, libraries, programs, courses, scholarships, certification); and miscellaneous (analyses and statistics, atlases and maps). Indexed. Z7164.T8D25

Northwestern University. Transportation Center. Library. Catalog of the Transportation Center Library, Northwestern University .... Boston : G.K. Hall, 1972. 12 v. **CH443**

Contents: v. 1–3, Author-title catalog; v. 4–12, Subject catalog.

A photoreproduction of the catalog cards for this library of 80,000 books and reports and 52,000 journal articles on: transportation socioeconomics; highway traffic analysis; and highway police administration. Represents all materials processed since 1960 to time of publication. Author-title section includes books and reports; citations to periodical articles, conference papers, and pamphlets appear in the subject section.

Updated by: *Current literature in traffic and transportation* (v. 1, no. 1 [Jan./Feb. 1960]– . Evanston, Ill. : Library, Transportation Center at Northwestern Univ., 1960– . Monthly.).

A detailed subject-classed list of journal articles, books, conference proceedings, reports, government documents, etc. No index. Supersedes *Current literature in transportation*.   Z7164.T8N75

Sources of information in transportation. 4th ed. Monticello, Ill. : Vance Bibliographies, 1990. 10 v. (Public administration series—bibliography, P 2878–2887).   **CH444**

Daniel C. Krummes, gen. ed.

1st ed., 1964, publ. for the Transportation Center at Northwestern Univ. by Northwestern Univ. Pr.

Contents: (1) General transportation, by Toby Pearlstein and Susan Dresley; (2) Air transportation, by Jane M. Janiak; (3) Shipping, by George J. Billy; (4) Railroads, by Joyce Koeneman and Gilda Martinello; (5) Trucking, by Linda S. Rothbart; (6) Inland water transportation, by Mary L. Roy; (7) Pipelines, by Marie Tilson; (8) Highways, by Daniel C. Krummes; (9) Urban transportation, by Catherine Cortelyou; (10) Intercity bus lines, by Renée E. McHenry.

"One in a series of ten bibliographies prepared by members of the Special Projects Committee of the Transportation Division, Special Libraries Association."—*t.p., each part.*   Z7164.T8S6

Trucksource. Alexandria, Va. : American Trucking Associations, Information Center, c1988– . Annual.   **CH445**

An annotated bibliography in three parts: (1) Trucking fundamentals, containing entries categorized by format (bibliographies, databases, dictionaries, directories, periodicals, statistical sources, videos); (2) Trucking business, with entries grouped by business activity; and (3) Trucking and the law. Also includes a list of industry contacts and an index. A pamphlet listing American Trucking Associations staff specialists and their telephone numbers and areas of expertise is attached to the inside back cover.   HE5623.A45T73

Dictionaries

Logie, Gordon. Glossary of transport : English, French, Italian, Dutch, German, Swedish. Amsterdam ; N.Y. : Elsevier, [1980]. 296 p. (International planning glossaries, 2).   **CH446**

Gives equivalent terms in the broad subject areas of transport and transportation studies, roads and road traffic, parking and road vehicles, railways, waterborne transport, and avaiation. Indexes in all six languages.   HE141.L63

Transportation and distribution dictionary. Neenah, Wis. : J.J. Keller & Assoc., c1987. 294 p.   **CH447**

"Includes terms related to operations, organizations, publications, documents, equipment, transportation modes"—*Introd.* Brief definitions. Appendixes include: abbreviations; title 49 of the Code of Federal Regulations; useful addresses; etc.   HE141.T683

Transportation-logistics dictionary / Joseph L. Cavinato, ed. 3rd ed. Wash. : International Thomson Transport Pr., 1989. 312 p.   **CH448**

1st ed., 1977; 2nd ed., 1982.

More than 4,800 terms relating to systems, operations, equipment, personnel, organizations, and the history of transportation and logistics. A list of acronyms, summary of key legislation and regulations, and standard operational information (metric conversion formulas, state postal abbreviations, and U.S. and foreign time differences) are also included.   HE141.T69

Directories

Directory of transportation libraries and information centers in North America / comp. by Renée E. McHenry and Catherine Cortelyou ; prep. for Special Libraries Association, Transportation Division. 6th ed., June 1993. Evanston, Ill. : Northwestern Univ. Transportation Libr., 1993. 256 p.   **CH449**

1st publ. 1969; 5th ed., 1987.

Arranged alphabetically by library. For each library, describes the collection and services offered, including publications for sale. Subject and geographic indexes.   Z675.T7S5

A directory of urban public transportation service / U.S. Urban Mass Transportation Administration. [Wash.] : UMTA Technical Assistance Program, 19??– . Annual.   **CH450**

Superintendent of Documents classification: TD 7.19:UR 1/ .

Also issued on microfiche.

Lists transit information for 931 conventional and specialized local transit services in 316 urbanized areas with more than 50,000 population. Contains directory information for each service, lists of transit agencies and urbanized areas, vehicle summary counts, and a glossary of terms.   HE4421.D57

Handbooks

Jane's urban transport systems. v. 1 (1982)– . London : Jane's, 1982– . Annual (slightly irregular).   **CH451**

For annotation, *see* EK121.   HE4211.J33

Statistics

National transit summaries and trends for the ... section 15 report year / U.S. Department of Transportation, Federal Transit Administration. 1990– . [Wash.] : Audit Review and Analysis Division, Office of Capital and Formula Assistance, 1992– . Annual.   **CH452**

Continues: *Compendium of national urban mass transportation statistics* (1983–89).

Provides aggregate financial and operational statistics in categories of service consumed, service supplied, operating revenue, operating costs, capital funding, and service reliability and safety.   HE4401.C66

Smith, Frank A. Transportation in America : a statistical analysis of transportation in the United States : historical compendium, 1939–1985. Westport, Conn. : Eno Foundation for Transportation, 1989. 64 p. : ill.   **CH453**

A compendium of historical data, based on annual compilations in *Transportation in America* (1st ed.– . Wash. : Transportation Policy Associates, 1983–88; Westport, Conn. : Eno Foundation, 1989–) and updated by that publication. Tables include: transportation outlays versus gross national product; national economic trends versus transportation trends; intercity travel by mode; employment in transportation. Each table includes brief explanations of its data.   HE203.S55

Transit fact book. [Wash., etc.] : American Public Transit Assoc., 1943– . Annual.   **CH454**

Issued 1943–74 by American Transit Association.

Includes aggregate data for all transit systems in the U.S. and summary data for Canadian transit. Includes an overview of transit facts and issues; a profile of U.S. transit; financial information; ridership and transit usage; and a section on energy and the environment. Glossary and index.   HE4441.A55

Automobiles

Branham automobile reference book : showing in illustrated form the location of motor and serial numbers on all passenger cars and trucks. Santa Monica, Calif. : Branham Publ. Co., [1900]– . Annual.   **CH455**

Provides "The type of body, weight of each type by model and year with actual N.A.C.C. and S.A.E. horsepower rating, cubic inch displacement, bore and stroke in inches, the factory advertised price or list price on passenger cars and factory list price on trucks."—*t.p.* Supplements issued between editions.

World automotive market report. 1990– . Des Plaines, Ill. : Auto & Truck International, 1990– . Annual.   **CH456**

Contents: World motor vehicle production/assembly; World vehicle census summary; Vehicles on the road throughout the world; United States automotive parts trade; World trade in new motor vehicles; World motor vehicle markets. Lists organizations that supply data.

HD9710.A1W665

World motor vehicle data. 1971– . Detroit : Motor Vehicle Manufacturers Assoc. of the United States, 1971– . Annual.   **CH457**

Information on production, exports, imports, registrations, and sales for passenger cars and commercial vehicles. Information derived from government agencies, trade associations, and private sources.

HD9710.A1W67

Railroads

Bureau of Railway Economics. Railway economics : a collective catalogue of books in fourteen American libraries. Chicago : Univ. of Chicago Pr., [1912]. 446 p.   **CH458**

A classified catalog, with index of names.   Z7231.B87

Jane's world railways. Ed. 9 (1965–66)– . N.Y. : Franklin Watts, 1965– . Annual.   **CH459**

Cover title: *Jane's world railways and rapid transit systems.*

1st–8th eds., 1950/51–65/66 called *World railways.*

Contains: alphabetical directories of manufacturers, associations, consultant services; country summaries of railway systems; city reports on rapid transit; tabulated data arranged by country and company.   TF1.J3

Morris, James Oliver. Bibliography of industrial relations in the railroad industry. Ithaca : N.Y. State School of Industrial and Labor Relations, Cornell Univ., [1975]. 153 p. (Cornell industrial and labor relations bibliography ser., 12).   **CH460**

Attempts to identify published source material on the work environment, its influences, and its consequences within the intercity and interstate rail transportation system. Materials are categorized into sections by type, including: bibliographies; manuscripts, books and theses; periodical literature; government serial publications. Books, periodical literature, and government documents are further organized by topic and chronological period. Covers publications 1850 to 1975. No index.   Z7164.T7M67

Ottley, George. A bibliography of British railway history. 2nd ed. London : H.M.S.O., 1983. 683 p.   **CH461**

1st ed., 1965.

A classed bibliography, including books, parts of books, pamphlets, etc., on the history and description of rail transportation in Britain from earliest times through early 1964. Based largely on British Library holdings, but with additional listings for types of materials not regularly deposited there (e.g., unpublished theses). 7,950 items; locates copies. Detailed index.

———. ———. *Supplement, [items] 7951–12956* (1988. 544 p.).

Covers 1964–80, adding some earlier titles. Both works include some historical business information.   Z7235.G7O8

Railroad facts. 1983 ed.– . Wash. : Office of Information and Public Affairs, Assoc. of American Railroads, [1983]– . Annual.   **CH462**

Continues *Yearbook of railroad facts* (1965–82).

Summary of railroad operations throughout the year. Includes statistics on employment, financial results, traffic, etc.   HE2713.Y4

Railway directory : a Railway gazette yearbook. 1990– . London : Reed Business Pub. Ltd., 1990– . Annual.   **CH463**

Continues: *Directory of railway officials & yearbook* (1895–1966); *Railway directory & yearbook* (1968–89).

Provides an international directory and statistical data for railways and rapid transit, associations, trade unions, government departments. Also offers directory information for manufacturers and services. Indexed.   HE1009.U6

Shipping

International shipping and shipbuilding directory. London : Benn ; N.Y. : Nichols, 1883–1981.   **CH464**

Title varies: 1883–1950/51, *Shipping world year book*; 1952–64, *Shipping world year book and who's who.*

Provides directory information for the U.K. and other countries concerning: shipowners, managers, agents, and shipping lines; shipbuilders and repairers; towage and salvage; seaborne containers; maritime organizations; and products and services. Most sections follow a country arrangement; indexed by name of ship and firm.

Continued in part by:

(1) *Lloyd's maritime directory* (1982– . Colchester, Essex : Lloyd's of London, [1982]– . Annual).

An international directory of shipowners, shipbuilders, marine services, marine engine builders, maritime and related organizations. In most sections companies are listed alphabetically, with indexes to country, personnel, subsidiary companies, and vessels.

(2) *Lloyd's ports of the world* (v. 1 [1946]– . London : Shipping World, 1946– . Annual).

Title varies: 1946–81, *Ports of the world.*

Until 1946 issued as a section of *Shipping world year book.*

Arranged by continent, with a separate section for the U.K. Ports are listed alphabetically by country. Usually includes: location, population, accommodations, charges, pilotage, imports, and exports.

Lloyd's register of ships. 1966–67– . London : Lloyd's Register of Shipping, 1966– . Annual.   **CH465**

Published under varying titles since 1760 and by Lloyd's since 1834.

Merged with *Underwriters' registry for iron vessels* in 1885.

Recent issues in four or more volumes, with some variation in contents. The "Register of ships" gives the names, classes, and general information concerning the ships classed by *Lloyd's register*, together with particulars of all known ocean-going merchant ships in the world of 100 tons gross and upwards. It also lists lighters carried on board ship, floating docks, liquefied gas carriers, ships carrying refrigerated cargo, refrigerated cargo containers, refrigerated stores and container terminals, and offshore drilling rigs. The "Register" is updated by means of cumulative monthly supplements containing the latest survey records for all classed ships, and changes of name, ownership, flag, tonnage, etc., for all ships, whether classed or not.

The "Shipowners" section gives a list of owners and managers of the ships recorded in the "Register" with their fleets, as well as lists of former and compound names of ships. An "Appendix" contains a list of shipbuilders with existing ships they have built; marine enginebuilders and boilermakers; dry and wet docks; telegraphic addresses and codes used by shipping firms; marine insurance companies and marine associations.   HE565.A3L7

Maritime affairs—a world handbook : a reference guide for modern ocean policy and management / comp. by the Oceans Institute of Canada ; gen. ed., Edgar Gold. 2nd ed. Harlow, U.K. : Longman ; Detroit : Gale, c1991. 479 p.   **CH466**

1st ed., 1985, by Henry W. Degenhardt.

Intended "to serve as a guide to the present state of international maritime law, sea transport and communications, the exploitation and conservation of the maritime natural resources—*Introd.* Provides textual data on present-day maritime affairs.   JX4408.D44

Maritime services directory. 1989-90– . San Diego, Calif. : Aegis Publications, c1989– . Annual.   **CH467**

Combines directory information with industry analysis and statistics in three main parts. Pt. 1 lists by broad category some 4,000 firms (shipbuilding and repair, marine products, professional service firms, vessel operation and marine services, and cargo handling and management). Entries vary but generally include: address, telephone and fax numbers; key personnel; and a brief description of the business. Some 100 national and regional associations and schools are also listed. Pt. 2 lists relevant regional and federal government agencies and personnel (with organization charts for many of the key federal agencies). Pt. 3, Trends and statistics, contains data on government ship repair and construction programs, labor and materials price trends, ocean-borne trade and container statistics, a vessel inventory report, and U.S. shipbuilding and repair assets. Includes a glossary of maritime terms and company and advertiser indexes.

Sullivan, Eric. The marine encyclopaedic dictionary. 2nd ed. London ; N.Y. : Lloyd's of London Pr., 1988. 470 p. **CH468**

1st ed., Valletta, Malta : Gulf Publ., 1980.

Contains thousands of maritime and technical terms, expressions, and acronyms used by those in the business of shipping, navigation, marine insurance, maritime and commercial law, chartering and operation of ships, and general commerce. Definitions range in length from a phrase to a paragraph. Not illustrated.   HE567.S95

World port index. Wash. : U.S. Defense Mapping Agency, Hydrographic/Topographic Center, 1953– . Biennial. **CH469**

Superintendent of Documents classifications: D 263.22: ; D 5.317:150/ .

Frequency varies; irregular, 1953–71.

Issuing agency varies; originally issued by the Naval Oceanographic Office.

"Gives the location, characteristics, known facilities, and available services of a great many ports and shipping facilities and oil terminals throughout the world."—*Pref.*   HE552.W67

World shipping statistics. 1st ed. (1987)– . London : FISYS Fairplay Information Systems Ltd., 1987– . Annual. **CH470**

Information provided in the form of graphs for: world merchant fleet, new buildings, market prices, freight rates, and port traffic.

HE563.A3W67

Tables of distances

Distances between ports. 5th ed. Wash. : Defense Mapping Agency, Hydrographic/Topographic Center, 1985. 187 p.

   CH471

Superintendent of Documents classification: D5.317:151 .

1st ed., 1964; 4th ed., 1978.

Supersedes U.S. Hydrographic Office, *Table of distances between ports* (1916–43) and an earlier publication with the current title, issued by the U.S. Naval Oceanographic Office.   VK799.D57

Distances between United States ports. 1987 (7th) ed. Wash. : U.S. Dept. of Commerce, National Oceanic and Atmospheric Administration, National Ocean Service, 1987. 59 p.   **CH472**

1st–4th eds., 1929–67, issued by U.S. Coast and Geodetic Survey; 6th ed., 1978.

Nautical mileage charts show distances for Atlantic and Pacific coasts, the Panama Canal, the Great Lakes and New York state waterways; a table for estimating transit time is given. Indexed.

VK799.N35

Airlines

Civil aviation statistics of the world. 1st ed. (1975)– . [Montreal] : International Civil Aviation Organization, 1975– .

   CH473

Summary statistical data selected from detailed Air Transport Reporting forms. "The purpose of this Yearbook is to present in one volume the most widely used statistical information on civil aviation activities."—*Pref.* Appendixes contain a list of all statistical publications currently available for this industry and a glossary of terms.

HE9762.5.C58

Hall, R. J. Dictionary of aviation / R.J. Hall and R.D. Campbell. Chicago : St. James Pr., c1991. 346 p.   **CH474**

In addition to brief definitions of English aeronautical terms, has entries for organizations, including a description of their purpose and activities. Identifies terms used only in the U.S. Cross-references; list of acronyms and abbreviations.   TL509.H25

Miletich, John J. Airline safety : an annotated bibliography. N.Y. : Greenwood, 1990. 222 p. (Bibliographies and indexes in psychology, no. 7).   **CH475**

Lists and briefly describes some 650 books, journal articles, conference proceedings, government documents, and theses published 1960–90. Titles are listed alphabetically in 11 subject-oriented chapters (e.g., Collision avoidance, Airline deregulation). Includes a brief acronyms list and author and subject indexes.   HE9784.M56

Smith, Myron J. The airline bibliography : the Salem College guide to sources on commercial aviation. West Cornwall, Conn. : Locust Hill Pr., 1986–1988. 2 v. : ill.   **CH476**

Vol. 1 is arranged in four parts: (1) Reference works; (2) Historical background of U.S. airlines since 1914; (3) Economic and operational facets of America's airlines and individual passenger airlines; (4) Individual passenger airlines of America 1914– . Includes author and subject indexes and a list of terms. Vol. 2 has five parts: (1) Reference works; (2) Historic, economic and operational facets of foreign air transport; (3) International associations and organizations; (4) Airliners; (5) Airlines of the world outside the United States 1919–1986. Includes author and subject indexes. Both volumes are selectively annotated.   Z5064.C7S54

World air transport statistics. 1957– . Montreal : International Air Transport Association, 1957– . Annual.   **CH477**

Reports data from about 215 member airlines. Information includes number of passengers; number of freight tons; kilometers flown; hours flown; and operating revenues and expenses for the industry.   TL720.A1W6

World aviation directory. v. 1– . Wash. : Ziff-Davis, 1940– . Biennial.   **CH478**

For annotation, *see* EK32.   TL512.A63

Space

Aerospace facts and figures / Aerospace Industries Association of America. Los Angeles : Aero Publishers, 1960– . Annual.   **CH479**

For annotation, *see* EK35.   TL501.A818

D'Angelo, George V. Aerospace agencies and organizations : a guide for business and government. Westport, Conn. : Quorum Books, 1993. 167 p.   **CH480**

"A description of the international framework of public institutions that deal with aerospace activities and help make them possible."—*Introd.* Describes organizations of the major space powers (U.S., Europe, former Soviet Union, China, Japan, Canada, Australia, and India), activities of the U.N. and its specialized agencies, nongovernmental unions and committees, satellite organizations, and other interested foundations and institutes.

Communications

Encyclopedias

The Froehlich/Kent encyclopedia of telecommunications / ed. in chief, Fritz E. Froehlich ; co-ed., Allen Kent. N.Y. : M. Dekker, c1991–94. v. 1–8 : ill. (In progress). **CH481**
Written by experts. Articles are useful to newcomers and informed specialists and include bibliographic references. Principal topics: terminals and interfaces; transmission; switching routing and flow control; network control; communication software and protocols; network and system management, and components and processing. To be complete in 10 v. TK5102.E646

International encyclopedia of communications / Erik Barnouw, ed. in chief … [et al.]. N.Y. ; Oxford : Oxford Univ. Pr., c1989. 4 v. : ill. **CH482**
"Published jointly with the Annenburg School of Communications, University of Pennsylvania."
Attempts to "define, reflect, summarize, and explain" (*Foreword*) the field of communications, interpreted broadly. Coverage extends from cuneiform tablets to communication satellites, and articles examine verbal and nonverbal communication, current communication processes, and the role and influence of the arts, science, commerce, historical events, and social activities in the diffusion of ideas. Signed entries are arranged alphabetically and frequently contain illustrations and brief bibliographies. In some instances, articles on related topics are clustered under a single heading. Directory of contributors, topical guide, and analytical index in v. 4. P87.5.I5

Slide, Anthony. The television industry : a historical dictionary. N.Y. : Greenwood, 1991. 374 p. **CH483**
For annotation, *see* BH316. PN1992.3.U5S57

Dictionaries

The broadcast communications dictionary / Lincoln Diamant, ed. in chief. 3rd ed., rev. and expanded. N.Y. : Greenwood, 1989. 255 p. **CH484**
1st ed., 1974 ; 2nd ed., 1978.
Defines more than 6,000 technical common and slang words used in radio and television broadcasting, programming, and recording. Bibliography lists additional detailed technical works. PN1990.4.D5

Broadcast research definitions / National Association of Broadcasters ; ed. by James E. Fletcher. [3rd ed.]. Wash. : NAB, c1988. 75 p. **CH485**
2nd ed., 1970, had title: *Standard definitions of broadcast research terms.*
Contains brief, clear definitions of broadcasting, statistical, and technical terms, some with illustrations. No cross-references; brief bibliography. PN1992.18.B651

DeVito, Joseph A. The communication handbook : a dictionary. N.Y. : Harper & Row, c1986. 337 p. : ill. **CH486**
Briefly defines more than 2,000 terms, with extended essays on 100 additional terms relating to communication theory and practical communication tasks such as public speaking. Includes graphs, illustrations, and a list of the essays. P87.5.D46

Machovec, George S. Telecommunications and networking glossary. Chicago : Library and Information Technology Association, 1990. 64 p. (LITA guides, 3). **CH487**
Contains brief, nontechnical definitions of key terms and acronyms. Intended for librarians, information managers, and students. Brief, selective bibliography. TK5102.M33x

Weiner, Richard. Webster's new World dictionary of media and communications. N.Y. : Webster's New World : distr. by Prentice Hall Trade Sales, c1990. 533 p. **CH488**
Briefly defines words from a variety of fields, including sales and advertising, broadcasting and publishing, and computers and computer graphics. Also lists and describes leading companies, and trade and professional associations. P87.5.W45

Directories

Broadcasting & cable yearbook. 1993– . New Providence, N.J. : R.R. Bowker, c1993– . Annual. **CH489**
Continues *Broadcasting cablecasting yearbook* (Wash. : Broadcasting Publ., 1982–88); *The broadcasting yearbook* (Wash : Broadcasting Publ., 1990–91); *Broadcasting & cable market place* (New Providence, N.J. : Bowker, 1992).
Issued in two volumes. Vol. 1 covers U.S. federal agencies, laws and regulation, and history and current status of station ownership, and provides a directory of U.S. and Canadian radio and television stations arranged geographically and by type (AM, FM, format). Additional sections treat cable systems, satellite systems, advertising and marketing services, production and programming services, and technological and professional services. Includes directory of trade associations, trade shows, and a bibliography of books and periodicals. Keyword index. Vol. 2 indexes all firms and personnel in v. 1. HE8689.B77

J+W telefax international. 5th ed. (1990)– . Darmstadt, Germany : Telex-Verlag Jaeger + Waldmann, c1989– . Annual. **CH490**
Also called *International facsimile directory, Telefax international, Jaeger + Waldmann telefax international.*
Number of volumes varies; 8th ed. (1993) publ. in 8 v., 9th ed. (1994) in 7.
In 8th ed., v. 1–6 lists telefax subscribers, primarily companies and public organizations, alphabetically, and v. 7–8 list companies by products and services by system. Indexed in English, French, Spanish, and German.
Supplement: *Fax post international.*
•Produced in CD-ROM as *J+W Commdisc.* Semiannual. Current coverage. Disc cases have titles: Commdisc Telex Teletex worldwide; Commdisc Telefax worldwide. TK6710.T43

Marconi's international register. 1944/45– . Larchmont, N.Y. : Telegraphic Cable & Radio Registrations, Inc. Annual. **CH491**
Continues *Marconi's international register of telegraphic and trade addresses.*
Directory of more than 45,000 firms worldwide listed alphabetically and by trade; in addition to address, gives telephone, cable, telex, and fax numbers.

Telecommunications directory. 5th ed. (1992–93)– . Detroit : Gale, c1991– . Biennial. **CH492**
1st ed. (1983)–4th ed. (1989) had title: *Telecommunications systems and services directory.*
John Krol, ed., 1993– .
Lists national and international systems and services: network and teleconferencing facilities; videotext, electronic mail and facsimile services; interactive cable television, satellite and electronic transactional services. Glossary; standards; indexes by function/service, geography, and name. TK5102.5.T3965

Television & cable factbook. no. 12 (1946)– . Wash. : Television Digest, Inc., 1946– . Annual. **CH493**
Subtitle: The authoritative reference for the advertising, television and electronics industries.
Frequency varies.
Title varies; 1946–50 called *TV directory*; 1951–81, *Television factbook.*

Each issue in 3 v.: TV stations, Cable systems, TV and cable services.

Covers the U.S. and Canada. Geographic listings describe basic equipment, services and costs, ownership history and personnel, market rankings, sales and transfers, etc. Services volume includes suppliers, associations, network services, regulations and their agencies, plus advertising and marketing services and statistics.   TK6540.T453

World radio TV handbook. 15th ed. (1961)– . London ; N.Y. : Billboard Publications, 1961– . Annual.   **CH494**
"A complete directory of international radio and television."
Published Copenhagen, Denmark : O. Lund Johansen, 1961–82. Continues *World radio handbook for listeners including world-wide radio who's who*, *World-radio-television handbook*, and *World radio handbook*.

Listing of worldwide radio and TV services; world satellite broadcasts; short, medium, and long wave frequency tables; list of official international broadcasting organizations; and users clubs. Supplementary material varies, but may include equipment reviews, lists of clandestine stations.   TK6540.W67

Handbooks

Internet world's On Internet. 94– . Westport, Conn. : Mecklermedia, c1994– . Annual.   **CH495**
Subtitle: An international guide to electronic journals, newsletters, texts, discussions lists, and other resources on the Internet.
A brief introduction explains Internet protocols. Subject index of Internet files and resources; bibliography of books about Internet.
    TK5105.875.I57I585

Statistics

Sterling, Christopher H. The mass media : Aspen Institute guide to communication industry trends / Christopher H. Sterling, Timothy R. Haight. N.Y. : Praeger, 1978. 457 p.   **CH496**
Published jointly with the Aspen Institute for Humanistic Studies.
A compendium of more than 300 statistical tables describing communication trends in the U.S. since 1900. Organized by broad subject area—growth, ownership, economics, employment, content trends, audiences, and U.S. media abroad—and within these by media categories. Sources of all tables are identified. Extensive, partially annotated bibliography. Subject index.   P92.U5S68

International trade

•**The national trade data bank** : NTDB [database]. [Wash.] : U.S. Dept. of Commerce, Economics and Statistics Administration, Office of Business Analysis, 1990– .   **CH497**
Available on CD-ROM (on two discs beginning Nov. 1992); updated monthly.
A collection of some 90 databases covering the most recent trade promotion, international economics and marketing data from 15 U.S. federal agencies. Some information contained on the two CD-ROM discs includes: consumer price indexes; Business America; Market research reports; distribution licenses; EC directives; EC single market standards; export basics; export tips; GATT standards code; foreign economic trends; NAFTA; *BISNIS bulletin* (newly independent states); *U.S. industrial outlook*; export licensing information. New series and information are introduced regularly. The second disc, called "Foreign traders index," contains lists of opportunities for exporters, the *Export yellow pages*, and the Army Area Handbooks. An indispensable source at a reasonable price.

Insurance

Bibliography

Bibliographie universelle de sécurité sociale = World bibliography of social security = Bibliografía mundial de seguridad social = Weltbibliographie der sozialen sicherheit. v. 1 (1963)– . Genève : [International Social Security Association], 1963– . Quarterly.   **CH498**
Prep. by the Documentation Service of the International Social Security Association.
Supersedes "World bibliography of social security" issued as a special section of the Association's *Bulletin*.
Provides information on social security around the world; includes both periodical and nonperiodical literature. Indexed. Selected listings from this publication are reproduced in *Social security abstracts* 1965– .   Z7164.L1B52

Four decades of international social security research : a bibliography of studies by the Social Security Administration, 1937–80. Wash. : U.S. Dept. of Health and Human Services, Social Security Administration, Office of Policy, Office of Research and Statistics, 1981. 68 p.   **CH499**
Superintendent of Documents classification: HE 3.38:R 31/4/937-80.
A bibliography of articles, research reports, essays and books published by the Social Security Administration. Arranged by country and subject.   Z7164.L1F68

Gunderson, Nels L. Pension funds : an annotated bibliography. Metuchen, N.J. : Scarecrow, 1990. 136 p.   **CH500**
A selective list of books and journal articles published in the last 35–40 years, grouped by subject. Brief list of abbreviations; glossary; and author index.   Z7164.P4G85

Insurance and employee benefits literature. No. 374 (July/Aug. 1981)– . [N.Y.] : Insurance and Employees Division, Special Libraries Association, 1981– . Bimonthly.   **CH501**
Imprint varies.
Continues *Insurance literature* (Nov. 1961–May/June 1981), which superseded *Insurance book reviews* (April 1933–Oct. 1961).
Includes books, pamphlets, reprints, statistical annuals, and association proceedings in all branches of insurance, including economics of aging and social insurance. Author and title index.

Insurance Society of New York. Library. Life insurance catalog of the Library of the Insurance Society of New York. Boston : G. K. Hall, 1960. 352 p.   **CH502**
Subject catalog of a library established in 1901, which in 1960 contained about 80,000 books, pamphlets, and periodicals.
    Z7164.I7I82

Miller, Herbert A. Retirement benefit plans : an information sourcebook. Phoenix : Oryx, 1988. 207 p. (Oryx sourcebook series in business and management, 8).   **CH503**
Lists and sometimes annotates sources (i.e., those in chapters on surveys, promotional literature, periodicals, and miscellaneous sources including databases are annotated, those in the monographs and theses chapters are not). Includes a core library collection of nearly 50 titles and descriptions of relevant organizations. Author, title, and subject indexes.   Z7164.P4M54

Nelli, Humbert O. A bibliography of insurance history / Humbert O. Nelli, Soga Ewedemi. 2nd ed. Atlanta : Publishing Services Division, School of Business Administration, Georgia State Univ., 1976. 115 p. (Georgia State University. School of Business Administration Research monograph, no.70).   **CH504**
1st ed., 1971.

A wide variety of types of material—company histories, periodicals, clippings, photographs, policies, etc.—arranged by broad topic: fire insurance, life insurance, marine insurance, general insurance, friendly societies, guilds, notarial activities. International in scope; no index.

The catalog of the Georgia State Univ. Library catalog, including the Insurance Collection, is available through Internet.   Z7164.I7N37

Soltow, Martha Jane. Worker benefits, industrial welfare in America, 1900–1935 : an annotated bibliography / by Martha Jane Soltow and Susan Gravelle. Metuchen, N.J. : Scarecrow, 1983. 230 p.   **CH505**

A selective bibliography of 712 citations to secondary materials in topical arrangement, with indexing by company, personal, and corporate names.   Z7164.F8S66

Indexes; Abstract journals

Insurance periodicals index. 1963– . [Boston] : Special Libraries Assoc., Insurance Div., 1964– . Annual.   **CH506**

A cumulation of the index published monthly in the periodical *Insurance* through 1968, and thereafter in *Best's review*. Offers a subject index to articles in some 40 insurance periodicals. Author and geographical indexes.

•Machine-readable version: *Insurance periodicals index (IPI)* [database] (Chatsworth, Calif. : NILS Publ. Co., 1984–). Available online, updated monthly.   HG8011.I545

Dictionaries

Employee benefit plans : a glossary of terms / ed. by Mary Jo Brzezinski. 8th ed. Brookfield, Wis. : International Foundation of Employee Benefit Plans, 1993. 202 p.   **CH507**

7th ed., 1990.

Contains definitions, acronyms, and abbreviations derived from U.S. and Canadian sources.   HD4928.N6E46

Lucca, J. L. de. Elsevier's dictionary of insurance and risk prevention : in English, French, Spanish, German, and Portuguese. Amsterdam ; N.Y. : Elsevier, 1992. 429 p.   **CH508**

Contains approximately 4,000 entries and 2,000 abbreviations in five languages. Includes both traditional terms and those reflecting new technologies.   HG8025.L83

Rubin, Harvey W. Dictionary of insurance terms. 2nd ed. N.Y. : Barron's, c1991. 465 p.   **CH509**

1st ed., 1987.

Contains brief definitions of more than 3,000 terms used in life, health, casualty and other types of insurance. Useful for both consumers and practitioners.   HG8025.R83

Thomsett, Michael C. Insurance dictionary. Jefferson, N.C. : McFarland, c1989. 243 p. : ill.   **CH510**

An illustrated nontechnical glossary of insurance terms and phrases, with names and addresses of state insurance commissioners and Canadian provincial agencies. A brief acronyms list is included.   HG151.T48

Directories

Best's key rating guide. Oldwick, N.J. : A.M. Best Co. Annual.   **CH511**

Published in two segments: *Life-health* (1st ed. [1991]–) and *Property-casualty* (70th ed. [1976]– ; continues *Property-liability*).

Provides selected financial data giving the financial condition and operating results of the companies included. Includes ratings and financial size categories. Listed also name changes and retired companies.   HG8945.B483

The Financial times world insurance yearbook. 1976/77– . [London : The Financial Times].   **CH512**

Information on insurance companies arranged alphabetically by country. At the beginning of each country section, general information is given for basic economic and risk statistics, insurance organizations, and the insurance regulatory body. Company information includes: officers, subsidiaries and classes of insurance written. Indexed.   HG8019.F48

Insurance almanac. Ed. 1 (1913)– . Englewood, N.J. : Underwriter Print. and Pub. Co., 1912– . Annual.   **CH513**

Title varies.

Includes directory information for the six principal lines of insurance, insurance agents, brokers, organizations, state officials, insurance groups, etc. Formerly included a section of *Who's who in insurance*, which has been issued as a separate volume since 1948 (CH523).   HG8019.I5

Insurance directory and year book : (Post magazine almanack) containing statistics and facts of ordinary life, industrial life, fire, accident and marine insurance. 1931– . London : Buckley Pr., 1931– . Annual.   **CH514**

Title varies. *Post magazine almanack* established 1840.

Statistical and directory information for the United Kingdom.   HG8596.I53

Society of Actuaries. Year book. [1950]– . Chicago : The Society. Annual.   **CH515**

Formed by the merger of the yearbooks of the Actuarial Society of America and the American Institute of Actuaries.

Lists officers, committees, members, constitution and by-laws. Contains a brief history of the organization.   HG8754.S63

Who writes what in life and health insurance / comp. by Reference Book Department, the National Underwriter Company. 32nd annual ed. (1974)– . Cincinnati, Ohio : The Company, c1973– . Annual.   **CH516**

Continues *Who writes what*, ed. 1 (1942)–31 (1972).

"Comprehensive guide to who's offering new, popular, unusual and hard-to-place, life, health and disability income coverages whether it's on an individual or a group basis."—*Introd.*   HG8861.N3

Handbooks

Best's flitcraft compend : life-health. 81st (1968)– . Oldwick, N.J. : A.M. Best Co. Annual.   **CH517**

Information concerning the policies, rates, values, dividends, ratings, and financials of insurance companies. Includes a section on policy performance and tables on mortality, cash value, and mortgage amortization.

Supplement: *Universal life supplement.*   HG8881.F68

Best's insurance reports. Oldwick, N.J. : A.M. Best Co., c1985– .   **CH518**

Published in three segments: *Life-health* (63rd ed. [1968/69]–); *Property-casualty* (77th ed. [1976]–); and *International edition* (1988–). The first two are published annually; the third, semiannually.

Comprehensive source of financial information on insurers. Primary sources of information used in compilation are the official filings of individual companies. Also includes brief corporate histories, management and operations, new business issues, name changes and Best's ratings.   HG8021.B47

Social security handbook. 4th ed. (Feb. 1969)– . [Baltimore, Md.] : U.S. Dept. of Health, Education, and Welfare, Social Security Administration ; Wash. : U.S. Govt. Print. Off., 1969– . Irregular. **CH519**

Superintendent of Documents classifications: HE 3.6/3:SO 1/3/ ; HE 3.6/8: .

Subtitle: Retirement insurance, survivor's insurance, disability insurance, health insurance, supplemental security income, black lung benefits.

Reflects current provisions of the Social Security Act, its regulations and case decisions in summary form; explains how programs operate, who is entitled to benefits, and how the benefits may be obtained. HD7123.A214

Social security programs throughout the world. 1958– . Wash. : U.S. Dept. of Health, Education and Welfare, Social Security Admin., Div. of Program Research : For sale by U.S. Govt. Print. Off., [1958]– . Biennial. **CH520**

Superintendent of Documents classification: HE 3.49/3 .

Since 1987, available only on microfiche.

Highlights the principal features of social security programs for each country. The current report covers 146 countries and territories. HD7091.U62

Spectator insurance year book. 1874–1962. Philadelphia : Spectator Co., 1874–1962. Annual. **CH521**

Title varies; formerly *Insurance year book.*

Coverage varies; sections on fire, marine, casualty, and surety ceased with 1953/54.

Contains much directory and statistical information, together with some historical data.

Weiner, Alan R. The insurance industry : an information sourcebook. Phoenix : Oryx, 1988. 278 p. (Oryx sourcebook series in business and management, 16). **CH522**

The first of two parts is an annotated bibliographic guide to print and nonprint English-language sources (excluding proceedings), arranged in seven chapters by broad subject areas (e.g., Insurance lines, Legal environment, Consumer guides, Careers), with subdivisions by form (e.g., statistics, handbooks). Annotations are not evaluative, but are "based, for the most part, on author and publisher introductions in the latest editions available."—*Introd.* A core list of titles—some too costly or specialized for general reference collections—concludes the section. The second part is an annotated directory of organizations, including associations, libraries, and database vendors. Author, title, and subject indexes. Z7164.I7W44

Biography

Who's who in insurance. 1948– . Englewood, N.J. : Underwriter Print and Pub. Co., 1948– . **CH523**

Formerly issued as the biographical section of *Insurance almanac* (CH513).

Brief biographical sketches of U.S. insurance executives. HG8523.W5

Statistics

Finance, insurance, & real estate USA. 1st ed.– . Detroit : Gale, c1993– . Biennial. **CH524**

For annotation, *see* CH388.

Life insurance fact book. 1946– . Wash. : American Council of Life Insurance, 1946– . Biennial. **CH525**

Publisher varies. Published annually, 1946–1985.

Offers statistical tables, charts, and interpretive text on the life insurance business in the U.S. Includes some brief historical information on a glossary/index.

§ *Insurance facts* (N.Y. : Insurance Information Inst. Annual) presents similar data of general interest relating to property and liability insurance.

A similar publication for Canada: *Canadian life and health insurance facts* (Toronto : Canadian Life and Health Insurance Assoc., 1986– . Annual). HG8943.L5

Social security bulletin. v. 1, no. 1–3 (Mar. 1938)– . Wash. : Social Security Administration : for sale by the U.S. Govt. Print. Off., 1938– . Quarterly. **CH526**

Frequency varies: monthly, 1938–1991.

Statistical data for each year, 1939–48, were published in the Administration's *Social security yearbooks*, 1940–49. Supplements, with data for each year, 1949–54, were included in the Sept. *Bulletin*, 1950–55.

Beginning with 1955 data, *Supplement* issued separately as *Annual statistical supplement* (1955–). HD7123.S56

Source book of health insurance data. 1st ed. (1959)– . N.Y. : Health Insurance Institute. Annual. **CH527**

Frequency varies: annual, 1959–85; biennial, 1986–88; annual publication resumed 1989.

Issuing agency varies; also prepared by the Health Insurance Association of America.

A statistical report on private health insurance in the U.S. Includes information on: major forms of health coverage; medical care costs, including Medicare, dental, hospital, hospital utilization; physician contacts; government health care programs; etc. Glossary; index.

Some volumes have supplements with title: *Source book of health insurance data. Update.* HG9396.S6

Statistical bulletin : SB. v. 65, no. 1 (Jan.–Mar. 1984)– . N.Y. : Metropolitan Life Insurance Co., c1984– . Quarterly. **CH528**

Continues: Metropolitan Life Insurance Co., *Statistical bulletin - Metropolitan Life* (v. 1 [Jan. 1920]–v. 62 [Oct./Dec. 1981] and *Statistical bulletin*, Metropolitan Life Foundation (v. 63, no. 1 [Jan.–Mar. 1982]–v. 64, no. 1 [Jan.–June 1983]).

Place of publication varies.

Each issue includes three or more statistical reports on selected aspects of morbidity and mortality, disability, birth rates, leading causes of death, etc. Some reports and projections are based on Metropolitan policyholder figures, others are from government or other standard sources. Annual index. HG8963.M5A3

Real estate

Bibliography

Boyce, Byrl N. Minority groups and housing : a bibliography, 1950–1970 / selected and ed. under the direction of Byrl N. Boyce [and] Sidney Turoff. [Morristown, N.J.] : General Learning Pr., [1972]. 202 p. **CH529**

1968 ed. comp. by S. D. Messner.

A topical listing with author and detailed subject indexes. Z7164.H8B73

Harris, Laura A. The real estate industry : an information sourcebook. Phoenix : Oryx, 1987. 170 p. (Oryx sourcebook series in business and management, 5). **CH530**

A select, annotated bibliography of books, journals, reference sources, and other publications. A core library collection of 135 titles, grouped by format (bibliographies, directories, etc.), is followed by a general literature section that contains a list of titles by broad subject categories, descriptions of 158 real estate journals, and "Other sources of information," which describes and provides addresses for associations, government agencies, special libraries, state real estate boards, and other organizations. Brief author, title, subject indexes. Z7164.L3H244

Real estate appraisal bibliography, 1973–1980 / American Institute of Real Estate Appraisers. Chicago : The Institute, [1981]. 146 p.   **CH531**

A detailed classed bibliography emphasizing periodical literature from about ten major real estate appraisal journals, proceedings, and annual publications. Supplements the Institute's *Real estate appraisal bibliography* (Chicago, 1973), which covered works published 1945–72.   Z7164.L3R38

Encyclopedias

Blankenship, Frank J. The Prentice Hall real estate investor's encyclopedia. Englewood Cliffs, N.J. : Prentice Hall, c1989. 539 p. : ill.   **CH532**

Combines definitions of terms with examples of usage and investor advice. Charts, sample forms, and other illustrations are also included.   HD1365.B55

The dictionary of real estate appraisal. 3rd ed. Chicago : Appraisal Institute, c1993. 527 p. : ill.   **CH533**

1st ed., 1984; 2nd ed., 1989.

Combines definitions of terms with examples of usage and investor advice. Contains charts, forms and other illustrations. Additional addenda to this edition include: measures, energy conversion factors, tax information, rural appraisal information and lists of trade symbols. Contains cross-references.   HD1387.D435

Newell, James E. The St. James encyclopedia of mortgage & real estate finance : over 1,000 terms defined, explained and illustrated / James Newell, Albert Santi, Chip Mitchell. Chicago : St. James Pr., c1991. 575 p. : ill.   **CH534**

Repr. under title: *Encyclopedia of mortgage and real estate finance* (Chicago : Probus Publ. Co., c1992. 575p.).

Combines brief definitions and lengthy explanations for more than 2,000 terms, concepts, and organizations. Many cross-references and charts, sample forms, and other illustrations.

Dictionaries

Arnold, Alvin L. The Arnold encyclopedia of real estate / by Alvin L. Arnold ... [et al.]. 2nd ed. N.Y. : J. Wiley, c1993. 610 p.   **CH535**

1st ed., 1978.

Provides basic definitions and explanations of terms and expressions, including legal and banking terms, used in the real estate industry. Includes an abbreviations list.   HD1365.A76

Reilly, John W. The language of real estate. 4th ed. Chicago : Real Estate Education Co., c1993. 456 p. : ill.   **CH536**

1st ed., 1977; 3rd ed., 1989.

Cover title: The ultimate language of real estate.

Contains real estate and building terms. Also includes a classified subject list, an abbreviations list, the realtors' code of ethics, and a sample closing problem.   KF568.5.R44

Thomsett, Michael C. Real estate dictionary. Jefferson, N.C. : McFarland, c1988. 220 p. : ill.   **CH537**

Defines some 1,100 terms pertaining to commercial and residential real estate and investment and briefly describes relevant associations and regulatory agencies. Some charts and statistics, numerous *see also* references. Also includes owner/seller checklists, amortization and remaining balance tables, and a list of abbreviations.   HD1365.T46

Directories

Directory of foreign investment in the U.S. : real estate and business. 1st ed.– . Detroit : Gale, c1991– . Irregular.   **CH538**

In two sections. Section 1 lists some 1,200 real estate properties—office buildings, commercial and industrial developments, apartment complexes, hotels, golf courses, country clubs, farm land—owned in a whole or in part by foreign enterprises. Arrangement is geographical by state and city; most listings are for large urban areas. Besides standard directory information, entries generally include the property's square footage, assessed value, number of stories, purchase date and price, joint owners/ventures, and current or planned use. Section 2 lists more than 10,000 foreign-owned businesses arranged by 3-digit SICs, with directory information for both the U.S. and foreign parent company, annual sales, number of employees, and sometimes purchase date and price, sellers, and joint owners/ventures. In both sections, percentage of foreign ownership is given when available for those properties and businesses that are only partially foreign-owned. Three indexes: foreign owners by country, geographic, alphabetic.   HG4538.D58

Finance, insurance, & real estate USA. 1st ed.– . Detroit : Gale, c1993– . Biennial.   **CH539**

For annotation, *see* CH388.

The real estate directory of major investors, developers and brokers. Wilmette, Ill. : Reed Publ. (USA) Inc., 1992.   **CH540**

Continues: *The directory of real estate investors* (1st ed. [1982]–8th ed. [1989]. Deerfield, Ill. : Whole World Publ., 1982–89); *The real estate sourcebook* (9th ed. [1990]–10th ed. [1991]. Wilmette, Ill. : National Register Publ. Co., Macmillan Directory Div., 1990-91).

A "comprehensive guide to major investors, brokers, syndicators, developers, service firms, international investors, and sources of financial investment."—*Users guide.* Lists approximately 3,000 companies and organizations, grouped by type of business. Entries generally include address; telephone and fax numbers; line of business; key personnel; contact people for acquisitions and depositions; average purchase price/investment range; size of portfolio; investment structure; and geographic preference. Indexed by company name, property preference, investment range, geographical preference, company type, state/city, and personnel.   HD1382.5.D57

U.S. real estate register. v. 17 (1984/85)– . Woburn, Mass. : Barry, Inc., c1984– . Annual.   **CH541**

In four sections: (1) listing of the top 1,000 largest corporations in America with the name of the real estate director, address, telephone number and fax number when available; (2) alphabetical listing of organizations representing all aspects of the real estate industry; (3) list of currently available industrial and commercial properties in the U.S.; (4) listing of companies and organizations classified by type of operation.   HD1394.I45

Handbooks

The McGraw-Hill real estate handbook / Robert Irwin, ed. in chief. 2nd ed. N.Y. : McGraw-Hill, c1993. 641 p : ill.   **CH542**

1st ed., 1984.

Updates and revises the 1st ed. Contains new coverage of current finance, investing, and taxation issues and practices and includes computerized investment analysis. Includes bibliographies and indexes.   HD1375.M17

The real estate handbook / editors in chief, Maury Seldin, James H. Boykin. 2nd ed. Homewood, Ill. : Dow Jones-Irwin, c1990. 1055 p. : ill.   **CH543**

1st ed., 1980.

Contains 58 signed chapters, some illustrated or with bibliographies, organized into sections on real estate transactions, marketing, analysis, financing, and investment. Indexed. HD255.R38

ULI market profiles. 1986– . Wash. : Urban Land Institute, c1986– . Annual. **CH544**

Continues in part: *Development review and outlook* (1983–84).

In two main parts: Market profiles and Market reports. The first contains signed chapters, generally seven to eight pages in length, each dealing in structured format with a specific city or metropolitan area. Discussion of the location's development climate is followed by consideration of real estate development in the residential, retail, office, industrial, and hotel sectors; an area development map; and statistical tables. The second part consists of two-page reports that selectively update information on real estate markets that have been covered in at least one of the previous editions. HD251.U45

Statistics

United States. Bureau of the Census. Housing construction statistics, 1889 to 1964. [Wash. : U.S. Govt. Print. Off., 1966]. 805 p. **CH545**

Repr.: N.Y. : Arno Pr., 1976.

Presents historical statistics consisting mainly of "published data available in some 200 separate reports prepared by the Bureau of the Census, the Bureau of Labor Statistics, the National Bureau of Economic Research, Incorporated, and the Twentieth Century Fund."—*Introd.* Source notes are given for each table.

§ The Bureau's 1970, 1980, and 1990 censuses of housing (subject reports), taken in conjunction with the 19th, 20th, and 21st decennial censuses, offer a wide range of statistical information.

MARKETING AND ADVERTISING

General works

Guides

Marketing information : a professional reference guide / ed. by Jac L. Goldstucker ; comp. by Otto R. Echemendia, with the staff of the Business Publishing Division, Georgia State University. 2nd ed. Atlanta : Business Pub. Division, College of Business Administration, the Univ., 1987. 436 p. **CH546**

1st ed., 1982.

Although originally intended to be a biennial publication, only two editions have so far appeared.

A well-organized guide to marketing associations, agencies, businesses, and organizations. Indexes by subject and geography. Sources of information section lists print, electronic and nonprint sources in advertising, consumer behavior, direct mail, franchising, marketing, public relations, retailing, sales, and statistics. HF5415.124.M37

Pollay, Richard W. Information sources in advertising history. Westport, Conn. : Greenwood, [1979]. 330 p. **CH547**

Three bibliographic essays treating economic data on advertising, commercial and professional sources of data, and the trade press of advertising are followed by a classified, annotated bibliography. Also provides directories of archives, manuscripts and special collections, and professional associations. Indexed. Z7164.C81P66

Indexes; Abstract journals

•**PTS marketing and advertising reference service** [database]. Cleveland, Ohio : Predicasts, 1985– . **CH548**

Available online, updated daily.

Provides abstracts or full-text records drawn from more than 140 trade, research, and consumer periodicals and newsletters dealing with the marketing and advertising of consumer goods and services. No printed counterpart.

Dictionaries

Baker, Michael John. Dictionary of marketing and advertising. 2nd ed. N.Y. : Nichols Pub., 1990. 271 p. **CH549**

1st ed., 1984, had title: *Macmillan dictionary of marketing & advertising*.

Short entries prepared by members of the Department of Marketing, Strathclyde University. Strong British emphasis. HF5415.B273

Imber, Jane. Dictionary of advertising and direct mail terms / by Jane Imber and Betsy-Ann Toffler. N.Y. : Barron's, c1987. 514 p. : ill. **CH550**

Covers 3,000 terms used in broadcasting, print advertising, and direct mail; appendix lists acronyms and abbreviations. HF5803.I46

Jefkins, Frank William. Dictionary of advertising : direct response marketing and sales promotion. London : Pitman, c1990. 236 p. **CH551**

Explains jargon used in British advertising, marketing, and sales promotion. HF5803.J4

Foreign terms

Paetzel, Hans W. Complete multilingual dictionary of advertising, marketing and communications : English, French, German. Lincolnwood, Ill. : Passport Books, [1984]. 606 p. **CH552**

In three sections—German, English, French—which provide the equivalent word or phrase from each of the other two languages. About 8,000 terms.

Directories

European advertising, marketing, and media data. 1st ed. (1990)– . London : Euromonitor, c1990– . **CH553**

Traces advertising expenditure patterns, media patterns, and basic demographics for 16 Western European countries. Includes directories of advertising agencies, major advertisers, media outlets (TV, radio, cable, and satellite), trade associations, market research companies, and publishers. HF5808.E85E92

Event line. 1990– . Amsterdam ; N.Y. : Elsevier, 1989– . **CH554**

For annotation, *see* AL28. AS8.E94

O'Dwyer's directory of corporate communications. 1976– . N.Y. : J. R. O'Dwyer Co., 1976– . **CH555**

Lists public relations and communications personnel at more than 5,000 companies, associations, and government agencies. Indexed by type of industry, geography, by company, and by association.

HD59.O35a

Palder, Edward L. The catalog of catalogs III : the complete mail-order directory. 3rd ed. Rockville, Md. : Woodbine House, 1993. 516 p. **CH556**

1st ed., 1987; 2nd ed., 1990.

Lists about 12,000 retail, wholesale, and manufacturing sources, arranged by broad subject areas. Indexed by company and by product.

HF5466.P35

Trade shows worldwide. 4th ed. (1990)– . Detroit : Gale, c1990– . Annual.   **CH557**

Continues: *Trade shows and professional exhibits directory* (1st–3rd ed., 1985–19??).

An international directory of trade shows, organizers, sponsors, convention centers, exhibit builders, transportation firms, professional associations, consultants, etc. 7th ed. (1992) lists 723 convention centers. Date, location, subject, and master indexes.   T394.T723

Consumerism

Consumer health & nutrition index. v. 1, no. 1 (July 1985)– . Phoenix : Oryx, c1985– . Quarterly.   **CH558**

For annotation, *see* EH57.

Consumer sourcebook. Detroit : Gale, c1974– .   **CH559**

Subtitle: A subject guide to over 10,000 Federal, State and local government agencies and offices, national, regional and grassroots associations and organizations, information centers, clearinghouses, publications, media contracts, and related consumer resources in the fields of general consumerism, automotive matters, credit and personal finance, education, employment, environmental concerns, food and drugs, government performance, health care and promotion, insurance, legal affairs, manufactured goods and product safety, mass communications, real estate and construction, retail and commercial concerns, transportation and travel, and utilities.

8th ed., 1993, covers 1994–95.

Arranged by broad topic, each section introduced by "consumer tips," followed by a directory of federal, state, and local resources, pertinent publications, and corporate publications, and corporate contacts. Appendixes include lists of hotlines and clearinghouses, testing laboratories. Alphabetical and subject index.   IIC110.C63C638

Consumers index to product evaluations and information sources. v. 1, no. 1 (Winter 1974)– . Ann Arbor, Mich. : Pierian Pr., 1973– . Annual.   **CH560**

A broad subject index to the contents of more than 100 consumer, business, health, and general periodicals. Briefly annotated, arranged by topics, (e.g., health food, computers). Indexed by product and company names.   TX335.C676

Consumer's resource handbook Dec. 1979– . [Wash.] : White House Office of the Special Assistant for Consumer Affairs, [1980]– . Biennial.   **CH561**

Superintendent of Documents classification: HE 1.508:C 76/3; HE 1.508/2 .

Issuing agency varies.

Basic consumer tips and directory of consumer assistance numbers, both corporate and governmental.

§ Related titles: *Annual list of consumer information*, and *Consumer information catalog*, a list of free and inexpensive publications aimed at consumers.   HC110.C63C652

The directory of mail order catalogs. 1st ed.– . N.Y. : Grey House Publ. : Facts on File, c1981– .   **CH562**

Vols. for 1991– publ. Lakeville, Conn. : Grey House Publishing.

Lists companies by categories that sell directly to consumers; indexed by product and company name.

§ Companion title: *The directory of business to business catalogs* (1991–).   HF5465.5.D58

Eiler, Andrew. Consumer protection manual. N.Y. : Facts on File, [1984]. 658 p. : ill.   **CH563**

Describes consumer rights under federal and uniform state laws relating to purchasing goods, warranties, methods of payment, consumer credit collection, and small claims court. Appendixes; index.

HC110.C63E38

Encyclopedia of consumer brands / ed. Janice Jorgensen. Detroit : St. James Pr., c1994. 3 v. : ill.   **CH564**

Contents: v. 1, Consumable products; v. 2, Personal products; v. 3, Durable goods.

Provides history of more than 600 well-known brands popular since 1950, including details of origins, marketing strategies, advertising campaigns. Each two- to four-page article includes bibliography. Index to brand names, company and personal names, and advertising agencies.   HF5415.3.E527

Public relations

Bibliography

Ferré, John P. Public relations & ethics : a bibliography / John P. Ferré, Shirley C. Willihnganz. Boston : G.K. Hall, 1991. 127 p.   **CH565**

Bibliography of books and journals articles that focus on morals, values, and ethics; appended is the Public Relations Society of America's *Codes of professional standards*.   Z7164.P957F47

Directories

National directory of corporate public affairs. 1st ed. (1983)– . Wash. : Columbia Books, 1983– . Annual.   **CH566**

Lists more than 1,800 companies that maintain public affairs programs; includes home address and Washington, D.C. address, associated political action committees, corporate foundations and corporate giving programs, publications and lists of contributions. Personnel directory; indexes by geography and by industry.   HD59.N24

O'Dwyer's directory of public relations firms. [1970] . N.Y. : J.R. O'Dwyer Co., 1970– . Annual.   **CH567**

Lists more than 2,000 public relations firms and departments of advertising agencies, including branches in foreign countries. Firms are ranked by city and region, according to income from fees, number of employees, and areas of specialization. Indexed by special skills, geography, and principal clients.   HM263.O37

Handbooks

Lesly's handbook of public relations and communications / ed. by Philip Lesly. 4th ed. Chicago : Probus Pub. Co., c1991. 874 p. : ill.   **CH568**

1st ed. (1950) and 2nd ed. (1967) had title: *Public relations handbook*; 3rd ed. (1983) had title: *Lesly's public relations handbook*.

Defines and describes public relations activities and techniques in short articles. Appendix lists sources of bibliographic and online information, contacts and interest groups, publicity services and clipping bureaus.   HM263.L46

Weiner, Richard. Professional's guide to public relations services. 6th ed. N.Y. : American Management Association, c1988. 483 p.   **CH569**

1st ed., 1968; 5th ed., 1985.

"A compendium of techniques, sources and services which can be helpful to public relations practicioners."—*Introd*. Combines succinct overviews of many public relations techniques with annotated entries describing major services and research sources. Companies and services are grouped under functional categories, such as Clipping bureaus, Media directories, News wire services, Photo and fine art sources, etc. Indexed.   HD59.W38

Advertising

Dictionaries

Sharp, Harold S. Advertising slogans of America. Metuchen, N.J. : Scarecrow, 1984. 543 p.   **CH570**

A dictionary of about 15,000 slogans used by some 6,000 businesses and organizations. Slogans, organizations, and products appear in one alphabetical listing; no keyword or thematic approach.   HF6135.S53

Wiechmann, Jack G. NTC's dictionary of advertising. 2nd ed. Lincolnwood, Ill. : National Textbook Co., c1993. 222 p.   **CH571**

An expanded version of Lawrence Urdang, *Dictionary of advertising terms* (1977).

Offers more than 4,000 headwords that define words, abbreviations, and acronyms in advertising. Covers marketing, media, consumer research, public relations, and graphic arts.   HF5803.W54

Directories

Standard directory of advertisers. 1964– . N.Y. : National Register Pub. Co., 1964– .   **CH572**

Covers more than 25,000 U.S. corporations, listing advertising budgets, key management and marketing directors, and company subsidiaries and divisions, and giving addresses and lists of products. Indexed by type of business, personnel, and product trade name.

———. *Geographical index* ... (Skokie, Ill. : National Register Publ. Co., 19??– . Annual).

•Machine-readable version: *Advertiser & agency red books plus* [database] (New Providence, N.J. : National Register Publ. Co., 1991–). Available on CD-ROM, updated quarterly. Includes data contained in *Standard directory of advertisers*, *Standard directory of advertising agencies* (CH573), and *Standard directory of international advertisers & agencies* (CH574).   HF5805.S7

Standard directory of advertising agencies. 1964– . Skokie, Ill. : National Register Pub. Co., 1964– . Semiannual.   **CH573**

Frequency varies: annual, 1964–78; three times per year, 1979–92; semiannual, 1993– .

Formed by merger of: *Agency list of the Standard advertising register* and *McKittrick agency list*.

Lists approximately 9,700 advertising agencies in the U.S. and other countries. Arranged by type of agency: advertising agencies, house agencies, media buying services, sales promotion firms, and public relations firms. Lists major clients of each agency. Geographic and name indexes.

•Machine-readable version: *Advertiser & agency red books plus* [database]. See CH572 *note* for information.

Standard directory of international advertisers & agencies. 1992– . Wilmette, Ill. : National Register Pub. Co., 1992– . Annual.   **CH574**

Imprint varies; 1993– publ. New Providence, N.J.

Continues: *Standard directory of international advertisers & advertising agencies* (ceased 1986); *Standard directory of worldwide marketing* (1986–90); and *Macmillan directory of international advertisers and agencies* (1991).

Lists more than 4,200 advertisers and advertising agencies (parents and subsidiaries) worldwide. Arranged alphabetically, with indexes by location, trade name, SIC code, and personnel.

•Machine-readable version: *Advertiser & agency red books plus* [database]. *See* CH572 *note* for information.   HF5804.S73

Who's who in advertising. 1st ed. (1990–1991)– . Wilmette, Ill. : Marquis Who's Who, c1989– .   **CH575**

Presents biographical sketches of some 17,500 advertising professionals from a variety of businesses, includng executives, creative directors, photographers, graphic artists, and copywriters, as well as prominent public relations specialists and marketing professionals. Besides standard biographical information, sketches list creative works, honors, and awards. Geographic and professional indexes.   HF6178.W48

Statistics

Ad $ summary. 1973– . N.Y. : Leading National Advertisers, Inc., 1973– . Quarterly, last issues cumulative for the year.   **CH576**

Covers advertising expenditures in magazines, Sunday magazines, newspapers, outdoor advertising, national spot radio, network television, syndicated television, cable TV networks, and network radio. Includes companies spending more than $25,000/year.

§ Related publications: *Company/brand $*, which lists companies alphabetically, and *Class/brand $*, which lists brands and parent companies.

Marketing

Bibliography

Dickinson, John R. The bibliography of marketing research methods. 3rd ed. Lexington, Mass. : Lexington Books, c1990. 1025 p.   **CH577**

1st ed., 1982; 2nd ed., 1986.

Contains 14,000 entries on market research, data collection, and data analysis drawn from marketing journals, handbooks, and conference proceedings, and from related disciplines. Entries are grouped by subject. Not annotated. Author and subject indexes.   Z7164.M18D52

FINDex. 1979– . N.Y. : FIND/SVP, 1979– . Annual.   **CH578**

Subtitle: The directory of market research reports, studies and surveys.

Looseleaf. Updated by semiannual supplement.

Annotated directory of more than 13,000 domestic and international market research reports. Arranged by industry or market segment with subject index and publishers/distributors directory.

•Also available online as *Findex* on Dialog, 1985– .

Encyclopedias

Beacham's marketing reference / ed. by Walton Beacham, Richard T. Hise, Hale N. Tongren. Wash. : Research Pub., c1986. 2 v. (1045 p.).   **CH579**

An alphabetical arrangement of signed articles, written by experts, that treat both the theoretical and practical aspects of 212 marketing topics. Each article follows a standard format in which an overview of the concept is followed by examples, discussion of benefits, implementation, evaluation, and a conclusion. Small business applications are described, and relevant references, software, and databases identified. An index and appendix of software applications are also included.   HF5415.B379

Dictionaries

Clemente, Mark N. The marketing glossary : key terms, concepts, and applications in marketing management, advertising, sales promotion, public relations, direct marketing, market research, sales. N.Y. : American Management Association, c1992. 392 p. : ill. **CH580**

Definitions of 1,400 marketing terms used in theory and in practice with numerous cross-references. Appendix includes a directory of organizations, publications, and a selective bibliography.

HF5415.C5414

Ostrow, Rona. The dictionary of marketing / Rona Ostrow, Sweetman R. Smith. N.Y. : Fairchild Publications, c1988. 258 p. : ill. **CH581**

Contains brief, nontechnical definitions of terms in such fields as marketing research, direct marketing, sales, wholesaling, retailing, and international marketing as well as descriptions of major marketing associations. Features some formulas, graphs, and charts. HF5415.O76

Van Minden, Jack J. R. Dictionary of marketing research. Chicago : St. James, c1987. 200 p. **CH582**

Contains some 2,000 terms in applied and theoretical marketing research and related fields. Definitions are arranged by subject which allows terms to be grouped by concept. Appendixes include a checklist for marketing researchers and the ethical codes of key professional associations. Pt. 1 is an index of terms. HF5415.2.V35

Directories

Bradford's directory of marketing research agencies and management consultants in the United States and the world. 11th ed. (1965–1966)– . Middleburg, Va. : Bradford's Directory of Marketing Research Agencies, 1965-1966 [i.e., 1965]– . Biennial. **CH583**

Previously publ. under various titles: 1944, *Survey and directory, marketing research agencies in New York City*; 1945, *Survey and directory, marketing research agencies in the United States*; 1947–1954/55, *Bradford's survey and directory of marketing research agencies in the United States and the world* (varies).

Lists agencies and individuals engaged in marketing and economic research, etc. HF5415.A2B7

The direct marketing market place. 1980– . Hewlett Harbor, N.Y. : Hilary House Publ., [1979]– . Annual. **CH584**

Some issues have title: *Direct marketing marketplace*. Subtitle: Including a directory of names, addresses and phone numbers.

Publ.: Wilmette, Ill. : National Register Pub. Co., 1992– .

A source similar in purpose and format to *Literary market place* for the direct marketing field. Classified sections list direct marketers of products and services (principally through mail order catalogs), service firms and suppliers, creative and consulting services, associations and events, awards, etc. Primarily U.S. listings, with a chapter on Canadian and foreign firms. Gives names, addresses, and telephone numbers for companies and individuals. Indexes of individuals, companies, and advertisers. HF5415.1.D57

Editor & publisher. Market guide. v.1 (1924)– . N.Y. : The Editor & publisher co., 1924– . Annual. **CH585**

Each recent issue offers individual market surveys of some 1,500 United States and Canadian cities where a daily newspaper is published. Arranged by state and city; gives for each city such information as: population, location, trade area, banks, principal industries, colleges and universities, largest department stores, chain stores, retail outlets and sales, newspapers, etc. HF5905.E38

Greenbook : international directory of marketing research companies and services. 1963– . N.Y. : American Marketing Assoc., 1963– . Annual. **CH586**

29th ed., 1991.

Title varies: some have title *International directory of marketing research companies and services*, and some have title or subtitle *International directory of marketing research houses and services*.

A directory of companies offering market research services. Indexed by types of service offered, market/industry specialties, computer programs used, trademarks, geography, and principal personnel.

Handbooks

ARF guidelines handbook : the Advertising Research Foundation compendium of guidelines to good advertising, marketing and media research practice. N.Y. : Advertising Research Foundation, c1990. 375 p. **CH587**

"A compilation of highly valuable, usable and practical expert advice on what constitutes proper—and improper—advertising, marketing and media research practice."—*Foreword*. Covers marketing and advertising research, audience studies, focus groups, and polls.

HF5801.A74

Crispell, Diane. The insider's guide to demographic know-how : how to find, analyze, and use information about your customers. 3rd ed. Chicago : Probus Publ., 1993. 291 p. : ill. **CH588**

1st ed., 1988; 2nd ed., 1990.

Aimed at those new to demographic research and its business applications. Combines essays, descriptions of sources (some highly specialized), and directories of the organizations issuing them. The essays, reprints of articles from *American demographics*, discuss the uses of demographics, the 1990 census, and Europe in 1992. Descriptions of sources and their publishers are arranged by type of issuing agency (federal government, private, etc.). The most useful parts of the appendix are a glossary, source and subject indexes, a bibliography of reprinted articles, and a list of the contributors and their affiliations; less useful is "Useful publications for additional information," basically a list of *American demographics* publications. HF5415.2.C757

Journal of marketing. v. 1 (July 1936)– . N.Y. : American Marketing Assoc., 1936 . Quarterly. **CH589**

From 1937 through 1984 each issue offered a "Marketing abstracts" section with lengthy abstracts of current periodical articles. In 1985 this became a "Marketing literature review" section offering citations with brief descriptors for articles drawn from about 125 English-language journals. Full abstracts are available from the ABI/INFORM database. Subject arrangement. HF5415.A2J6

Seller's guide to government purchasing. 1st ed. (1991)– . Detroit : Gale, 1991– . Biennial. **CH590**

In three sections. (1) A directory of more than 600 federal civilian and military agency headquarters and regional purchasing centers. (2) A directory of purchasing offices for all 50 states, the District of Columbia, U.S. Trust territories, and the 100 largest cities and the 100 largest counties. Agency entries generally include: address, telephone, and name of contact person; products and services purchases; whether telephone and/or fax bids are accepted; forms required; and the availability of special programs for minority-, women-owned, and small business. (3) A bibliography of more than 600 printed and electronic information sources. Includes products and services index, a master index, "how-to" guidelines, and brief lists of trade and professional associations and of abbreviations.

Statistics

Consumer Europe. [Ed. 1]– . [London : Euromonitor], 1976– . **CH591**

Provides statistical tables covering five years of production, sales, distribution, and consumption for major European countries. Includes comparisons among the European Community, Japan, and the U.S. Lists major sources of statistical offices and trade associations.

Data for the major countries of Eastern Europe, included in the 8th ed. (1991), is now published separately as *Consumer Eastern Europe* (1st ed. London : Euromonitor, 1992–). Similar publications are available for other regions—e.g., *Consumer Spain, Consumer Japan, Consumer Latin America, Consumer Southern Europe.*   HD7022.C68

Demographics USA. 1993– . N.Y. : Market Statistics, 1993– . Annual.   **CH592**

Continues: *Survey of buying power data service* (title varies).

Contains maps and statistics showing state and county current population estimates (with breakdowns by age categories and sex); households (number, size, age of householder); effective buying income distribution; buying power indexes; and retail sales by 12 different store groups (e.g., eating and drinking places, drug stores). Data in most of the 21 sections are arranged geographically, by region, state, metro area and county, and TV market (area of dominant influence). Also includes comparisons with U.S. totals, ranked lists, and projections for metro, county, and TV markets for population, effective buying income, and sales. Similar to, but considerably more detailed than, the "Survey of buying power" issues of *Sales and marketing management magazine.*   HF5415.1.D46

European marketing data and statistics. Ed. 1 (1962)– . London : Euromonitor Pubn. ; distr. in North American by Gale, [1963]– . Annual.   **CH593**

Merges business and marketing information gathered from international and European organizations, national statistics, trade and industry associations, research publications and Euromonitor research. Covers population, employment, production, trade, the economy, standard of living, consumer expenditure, consumption, market size in particular industries, retailing, etc. Also describes governmental and private sources of information and major European business libraries.

§ Companion publication: *International marketing data and statistics* (Ed. 1 [1975/76]– . London : Euromonitor Publ.; distr. by Gale, 1975–), providing similar information for 153 countries in the Americas, Asia, Africa, and Australia.

The lifestyle market analyst. 1989– . Wilmette, Ill. : Standard Rate & Data Service, 1989– . Annual.   **CH594**

Continues: *Lifestyle marketplanner* (ceased 1988).

In four sections: (1) Market profiles, a two-page statistical summary for "designated market areas (DMA)," highlighting demographic characteristics and lifestyle interests for each; (2) Lifestyle profiles, matching broad interest categories (e.g., avid book reading, motorcycles), with demographic characteristics, other lifestyle interests pursued, and DMA locations; (3) Consumer segment profiles, focusing on specific demographic characteristics (e.g., single males) and their DMA concentration; and (4) a list of consumer magazines and direct mail lists targeted to each lifestyle profile.   HF5415.33.U6L54

Market research handbook = Manuel statistique pour études de marché. 1969 ed.– . [Ottawa] : Statistics Canada, 1969– . Annual.   **CH595**

Issuing agencies vary.

An annual summary of Canadian national and international trade statistics. Includes data for national and 25 metropolitan markets, with economic and demographic projections.   HC111.A19

Market share reporter. 1st (1991)– . Detroit : Gale, 1991– . Annual.   **CH596**

Compiles market share statistics drawn from periodicals and brokerage reports, arranged by SIC codes. Covers public and private sector, national and international. Indexed by products, company name, brands, places, sources, and SICs.

§ Following the same format is *European market share reporter* (1993– . Detroit : Gale, c1993– . Ed. by Oksana Newman). Text in English; introduction in English, French, and German.

The marketing fact book. Chicago : Information Resources, [1981?]– . Annual.   **CH597**

Detailed data on household purchases in grocery stores, arranged by food groups and brands. Tracks coupon redemptions.

Markets of the U.S. for business planners : historical and current profiles of 183 U.S. urban economics by major section and industry, with maps, graphics, and commentary / Thomas F. Conroy, ed. Detroit : Omnigraphics, c1992. 2 v. : ill.   **CH598**

Subtitle: Historical and current profiles of 183 U.S. urban economics by major section and industry, with maps, graphics, and commentary.

Data derived from the Bureau of Economic Analysis. Information includes: personal income data for all 183 of the nation's economic regions; population data for each market area; economic profiles for 1969–88 (in 1988 dollars); personal income projections for 1995 and 2000; market area maps and country level growth data. Arranged in chapters by market area.   HC106.8.M333

Simmons study of media and markets. [N.Y.] : Simmons Market Research Bureau, 198?– . Annual.   **CH599**

Date appears in title.

Issued in parts: M-1– [Media Series]; P-1– [Product Series].

Profiles lifestyles of a broad population sample, analyzing products used, TV viewing and radio listening habits, and consumption of newspapers and magazines. Tabulated by sex, age, income, occupations. Data collected by personal interview, self-administered questionnaire, and follow-up telephone interview.

The sourcebook of zip code demographics. 7th ed. (1990)– . [Fairfax, Va.] : CACI, c1990– . Annual.   **CH600**

In two sections: residential and business. The residential section, arranged by state and then by zip code, includes population and age, demographic and buying power, income, and housing and socioeconomic profiles. Statistics are derived from the most recent published decennial census, other Bureau of the Census and Bureau of Economic Analysis data, and CACI projections. A market potential index, based on survey data, compares potential demand for specific consumer products/services in each zip code location to the U.S. average. The business section, extracted from *County business patterns* data files, shows the number of employees and the number of firms of the predominant SIC code for each zip code. Four appendixes: state summary data, SIC codes, county maps, and county FIPS codes.

§ A companion volume from the same publisher, *Sourcebook of county demographics* (formerly *Sourcebook of demographics and buying power for every county in the USA*), contains similar information for each county in the U.S.

•Available on CD-ROM and diskettes.   HA203.S66

Standard rate and data service : [publications]. Skokie, Ill. : Standard Rate and Data Service, 1951– . [various titles].   **CH601**

Continues *Standard rate & data service*, v. 1 (1919)–32 (1950).

Excellent source of information on circulation, advertising rates, and format of advertising media. Published in various sections with varying titles. Includes newspapers, magazines, consumer and community publciations, radio and television, and other media.

Superseded by separate publications, most beginning 1951 and assuming the volume numbering of the *Standard rate and data service;* most are monthly, some quarterly, some semiannual. Titles vary; sections current in 1993 include the following; dates given typically include the earlier titles of the sections.

Business publication rates and data (1951–); *Community publication advertising source* (1978–); *Consumer magazine & agri-media source (1951–); Direct marketing list source* (1967–); *Hispanic media & market sources* (1993–); *Newspaper advertising source* (1951–); *Print media production source* (1968–); *Radio advertising source* (1993–); *Radio local markets source* (1993–); *Spot TV & cable source* (1993–). More recently, titles have changed to include the publisher's name, abbreviated (e.g., *SRDS direct marketing list source*).

ORGANIZATIONAL BEHAVIOR

General works

Handbooks

Bowditch, James L. A primer on organizational behavior / James L. Bowditch, Anthony F. Buono. 3rd ed. N.Y. : Wiley, c1994. 521 p. : ill. **CH602**

1st ed., 1985; 2nd ed., 1990.

Provides an overview of topics and theories in organizational behavior, and serves as an introduction to basic terms and concepts. Includes bibliographical references and indexes. HD58.7.B69

Management

Organization charts : structures of more than 200 businesses and non-profit organizations / ed. by Judith M. Nixon. Detroit : Gale, c1992. 240 p. **CH603**

"*Organization charts* collects more than 200 graphic representations of actual corporate structures of operating companies in one convenient source. Organizations of many types, sizes, and from a variety of industries have been included: large and small, public and private, profit and non-profit, international and local."—*Pref.*

Bibliography

American Management Association. Index to AMA resources of the seventies, 1970–1976. N.Y. : AMACOM, [1977]. 162 p. **CH604**

Elizabeth A. Keegan, comp.

A subject arrangement of all books, periodical articles, reports, studies and services published by the AMA during this period. Title-series and author indexes.

Continued by: *Index to AMA resources, 1977–81* (N.Y.: American Management Association, 1982. 184 p.).

Publications of earlier years found in: ———. *Ten-year index of AMA publications, Jan. 1923/Jan. 1932–1957/66* (N.Y. : AMA, 1932–67. 4 v.). Title varies. Contents: 1923–32, 1932–45, 1954–63, 1957–66. A detailed catalog, arranged by subject with author index. Z7164.O7A49

Balachandran, Sarojini. Decision making : an information sourcebook. Phoenix : Oryx, 1987. 208 p. (Oryx sourcebook series in business and management, 4). **CH605**

Presents "a selective annotated bibliography of books, reports, dissertations and journal articles dealing exclusively with the methodology and applications of managerial decision-making."—*Introd.* Includes journal literature 1971–86 and other literature 1960–86. Author, title, and subject indexes. Z7164.O7B263

Leavitt, Judith A. Women in administration and management : an information sourcebook. Phoenix : Oryx, 1988. 228 p. (Oryx sourcebook series in business and management, 7). **CH606**

Previous editions had title *Women in management* and covered 1970–79 (publ. 1980) and 1970–81 (publ. 1982).

Includes more than 900 citations to books, papers, newspapers and journal articles, and dissertations, 1981–86. Arranged in 23 subject sections with added sections for general literature and a suggested core library. Indexed by author, title, and subject. Z7963.E7L43

The source : a total quality management information guide. 1992 ed. Methuen, Mass. : GOAL/QPC, c1992. 3 v. : loose-leaf. **CH607**

Contents: v. 1, TQM literature, pt. 1; v. 2, TQM literature, pt. 2, TQM service organizations location index, TQM glossary, Publishers; v. 3, Indexes to TQM literature.

Kept up-to-date by supplements, 1993– .

Includes books, periodicals articles, conference proceedings, and research reports. Indexed by subject, author, title, company, and key-word.

Stogdill, Ralph Melvin. Leadership abstracts and bibliography, 1904 to 1974. Columbus : College of Administrative Science, Ohio State Univ., 1977. 829 p. (College of Administrative Science monograph, no. AA10). **CH608**

When the author's *Handbook of leadership* was first published in 1974 (*see* CD126), a review in *Booklist* 71 (1974): 1093 suggested that the most useful section for reference purposes was the bibliography. The abstracts of more than 3,000 books and journal articles from that bibliography are provided here; arrangement is alphabetical by author, with author and subject indexes. Z7164.S68S86

Stout, Russell. Organizations, management, and control : an annotated bibliography. Bloomington : Indiana Univ. Pr., c1980. 189 p. **CH609**

Surveys the monographic and periodical literature produced from 1969 to 1979, grouping it within 11 main subject sections with appropriate subdivisions: accounting and budgeting; analytical methods and quantitative techniques; computers and information; control; decision; developing countries; evaluation; management; organization; planning and policy; and the contributions of R. E. D. Woolsey. Evaluative annotations, with recommended works noted. Author and subject indexes. Z7164.C81S779

Indexes; Abstract journals

•**Management contents** [database]. Foster City, Calif. : Information Access Company, 1979– . **CH610**

Available online and on magnetic tape, updated monthly.

Indexes and abstracts articles related to business and management from more than 120 English-language journals worldwide, together with proceedings, transactions, business course materials, newsletters, and research reports. Also available from the producer on computer tape.

Encyclopedias

The encyclopedia of management / ed. by Carl Heyel. 3rd ed. N.Y. : Van Nostrand Reinhold, [1982]. 1371 p. : ill. **CH611**

1st ed., 1963.

More than 300 signed articles by 203 contributors are alphabetically arranged and range in length from half a page to about 30 pages. 41 articles are new to this edition; they treat such topics as employee privacy, the quality of working life, robots in industry, women in management, and zero-base budgeting. Biographical sketches are included. Bibliographies; cross-references. Appendixes list universities and colleges offering programs in business administration, and provide directory information for organizations and periodicals mentioned in the text. Indexed. HD30.15.E49

Dictionaries

Banki, Ivan S. Dictionary of administration and management : authoritative, comprehensive. Los Angeles : Systems Research Institute, c1986. 1369 p. **CH612**

Previous ed., 1981.

Revised and expanded, with brief definitions for more than 20,000 terms, concepts, and techniques; an extensive list of acronyms and abbreviations, and a bibliography. HD30.15.B36

Hay, Michael. The strategy handbook / Michael Hay and Peter Williamson. Cambridge, Mass. : Blackwell Business, 1991. 284 p. : ill. **CH613**

Detailed definitions and explanations of terms used in business strategy formulation. Arranged in dictionary format with cross-references to other concepts. HD30.15.H39

Johannsen, Hano. International dictionary of management / Hano Johannsen and G.T. Page. 4th ed. N.Y. : Nichols Pub., 1990. 359 p. **CH614**

2nd ed., 1980, had title: *International dictionary of business*; 3rd ed., 1986.

Updated, revised, and expanded to include 6,500 entries, some with charts and diagrams and with numerous cross-references. Also features a directory of banks, trade unions, and professional and employers' associations. Two appendixes: time zones and the world's currencies. HD30.15.J64

Ott, J. Steven. The Facts on File dictionary of nonprofit organization management / J. Steven Ott and Jay M. Shafritz. N.Y. : Facts on File, c1986. 407 p. **CH615**

For annotation, *see* AL10. HD62.6.O88

Statt, David A. The concise dictionary of management. [London] : Routledge, 1991. [192] p. **CH616**

Briefly defines basic management and organization terms from a British perspective. Some charts, numerous cross-references. HD31

Directories

Consultants and consulting organizations directory. 2nd ed.– . Detroit : Gale, c1973– . Annual. **CH617**

Frequency varies: 2nd–7th eds. (1973–1987/88), triennial.

1st ed., 1966, had title: *Consultants and consulting organizations*.

Published in 2 v. Vol. 1 is arranged by broad subject, then alphabetically by firm, with a brief annotation describing the areas covered by the firm. Vol. 2 contains indexes—geographic, consulting activities, personal names, consulting firms.

Kept up-to-date between editions by *New consultants*; with suppl. to 11th ed., 1991, absorbed *New consultants*.

§ Companion volume: *European consultants directory* (1992–). HD69.C6C647

Directory of executive recruiters. [1st ed.] (1988/89)– . Fitzwilliam, N.H. : Consultants News, 1989– . **CH618**

Contains listings in separate sections for retainer- and contingency-based executive recruiting firms. Entries generally include address, minimum salary level handled, names of key contacts, a brief description, codes for the management functions and industries handled, and the professional association affiliations considered by the firm to be important. Each section has its own function and industry indexes. Also has combined (retainer and contigency) geographic and key personnel indexes, appendixes (including a bibliography), and a series of signed essays intended for job candidates or clients of recruiting firms. HF5549.5.R44D58

Dun's consultants directory. 1986– . Parsippany, N.J. : Dun's Marketing Services, 1985– . Annual. **CH619**

Latest edition provides information on more than 30,000 of the largest consulting firms in the U.S. "Complete consultant profiles appear in the consultants alphabetical section. Companies are then cross-referenced two ways: geographically and by consulting activity."—*Introd.*

Handbooks

AMA management handbook / William K. Fallon, ed. 2nd ed. N.Y. : Amer. Management Assoc., c1983. 1 v., various pagings. : ill. **CH620**

1st ed., 1970.

14 sections, with chapters contributed by about 200 specialists, analyze the subdisciplines of management, from finance through public relations. No bibliographic references. Indexed. HD31.A418

Craighead's international business, travel, and relocation guide to ... countries. 6th ed. (1992–93)– . Detroit : Gale, c1993– . Triennial. **CH621**

Continues *International travel, business and relocation directory*.

Number of countries appears in title; e.g., ... *guide to 71 countries* for 6th ed.

6th ed. in five sections: (1–3), general information and useful tips for the international traveler, including subjects such as tipping, beating jet lag, basic medical and insurance information; (4), background information for world regions with lists of contacts and further readings; (5), chapters on individual countries, covering country characteristics, documentation, transportation, hotels, communications, information for a long-term stay. HF5549.5.E45D56

Handbook for professional managers / editors, Lester Robert Bittel and Jackson Eugene Ramsey ; managing ed., Muriel Albers Bittel. N.Y. : McGraw-Hill, c1985. 1000 p. : ill. **CH622**

1978 ed. had title: *Encyclopedia of professional management*.

"In this work there are over 239 comprehensive entries, which contain nearly 17,500 specific definitions. In general, each entry provides: (1) a definition of the underlying principle or concept; (2) application opportunities, techniques, procedures, and examples; (3) an evaluation of the usefulness of the concept or technique; (4) a list of other sources of information. ..."—*Pref.* Signed articles by 229 contributors. No biographical entries. Synoptic and general indexes. HD31.H31245

Production handbook. 4th ed. / [ed. by] John A. White. N.Y. : Wiley, c1987. 1 v. (various pagings) : ill. **CH623**

3rd ed., 1972.

Revised to reflect new approaches and technologies in manufacturing, with more than 60 chapters grouped under the following categories: management, manpower, methods, machines, material, money, space, and systems. Charts, tables, and bibliographies frequently included. Indexed. TS155.P747

Labor and industrial relations

Bibliography

American Federation of Labor. American Federation of Labor records / Randolph Boehm, project ed. ; guide comp. by Martin Schipper. Frederick, Md. : Univ. Publ. of America, 1985. 2 printed guides. **CH624**

Guides to the records filmed from the holdings of the State Historical Society of Wisconsin and AFL-CIO, Washington, D.C. Pt. 1, *Strikes and agreements file, 1893–1953* (55 reels), reflects activities of local unions in the U.S. and Canada. Pt. 2, *President's office files* (38 reels), now includes Series A: *William Green papers, 1934–1952.* The *Minutes of the Executive Council of the American Federation of Labor, 1893–1955,* is available in two sections. Other microfilm sets are available in the series *Research collections in labor studies*, such as *CIO and industrial unionism in America* and *Labor union periodicals*.

Bain, George Sayers. Bibliography of British industrial relations / G. S. Bain and G. B. Woolven. Cambridge ; N.Y. : Cambridge Univ. Pr., [1979]. 665 p.   **CH625**

An impressive attempt to compile "all the secondary source material ... published in English between 1880 and 1970 on British industrial relations. It includes books, pamphlets, articles ... , theses, and government reports. The subject is broadly defined to cover ... the traditional topics of trade unionism and labour-management relations ... and [to include] relevant material from such disciplines as industrial psychology, industrial sociology, labour economics, labour history, labour law, personnel management, and social administration."—*Pref.* Includes material on England, Scotland, Wales, Northern Ireland, and the Republic of Ireland. Arranged by detailed subject classification; indexed by name and title.

Coverage of more recent material is provided by Bain and J. D. Bennett, *Bibliography of British industrial relations, 1971–1979* (1985. 258 p.).   Z7164.L1B26

Bibliographie zur Geschichte der deutschen Arbeiterschaft und Arbeiterbewegung 1863 bis 1914 : Berichtszeitraum 1945 bis 1975, mit einer forschungsgeschichtlichen Einleitung / hrsg. Klaus Tenfelde, Gerhard A. Ritter. Bonn : Verlag Neue Gesellschaft, [1981]. 687 p. (Archiv für Sozialgeschichte, Beiheft 8).   **CH626**

Bibliography of the German working class and worker movement from 1863 to 1914. Offers 7,100 citations to articles, dissertations, monographs and essays in classed arrangement; indexed by place name and author.

Continued by: Kurt Klotzbach, *Bibliographie zur Geschichte der deutschen Arbeiterbewegung, 1914–1945 : Sozialdemokratie, christlich-soziale Bewegungen, kommunistische Bewegung und linke Splittergruppen: mit einer forschungsgeschichtlichen Einleitung* (Bonn : Verlag Neue Gesellschaft, 1981. 394 p.). Includes Social Democrat and Christian-Social movements, as well as communist and leftist splinter groups. An international bibliography of 3,945 citations arranged by chronological period, then topically; author index.

Updated by *Bibliographie zur Geschichte den deutschen Arbeiterbewegung.* Quarterly, 1976–87; annual since 1988.   Z7164.L1B54

Dowe, Dieter. Bibliographie zur Geschichte der deutschen Arbeiterbewegung, sozialistischen und kommunistischen Bewegung von den Anfängen bis 1863 : Unter Berücksichtigung der politischen wirtschaftlichen und sozialen Rahmenbedingungen ; mit einer Einleitung Berichtszeitraum 1945–1975. 3., wesentl. erw. u. verb. Aufl. / bearb. von Volker Mettig. Bonn : Verlag Neue Gesellschaft, 1981. 358 p. (Archiv für Sozialgeschichte, Beiheft 5).   **CH627**

1st ed., 1976.

An international bibliography of the German worker movement up to 1863; 3,286 citations in classed arrangement with author and main-entry title indexes.

§ Continued by: *Bibliographie zur Geschichte der deutschen Arbeiterschaft und Arbeiterbewegung 1863 bis 1914 : Berichtszeitraum 1945 bis 1975 mit einer forschungsgeschichtlichen Einleitung,* hrsg. Klaus Tenfelde, Gerhard A. Ritter (CH626).   Z7164.L1D68

Ente per la Storia del Socialismo e del Movimento Operaio Italiano. Bibliografia del socialismo e del movimento operaio italiano. Rome : Ed. E.S.S.M.O.I., 1956–91. 2 v. in 15.   **CH628**

Contents: v. 1, pts. 1–2, Periodici 1848–1950; v. 2, pts. 1–4, Libri, opuscoli, articoli, almanacchi, numeri unici, 1815–1952 (pts. 1–3, A-Z; pt. 4, Appendix and indexes of names cited and subjects); Aggiornamento: 1953–1967 (pts. 1–2, pt. 3, index); Supplemento: 1968–1977 (pts. 1–2, pt. 3, index); [Aggiornamento:] 1978–1982 (pts. 1–2).

Vol. 1 is a comprehensive listing of the serial publications of Italian socialism, labor parties, workers' movements, unions, etc., issued from 1848 to 1950. Based entirely on the holdings of the Biblioteca Nazionale Centrale di Firenze, it includes 3,866 items with full bibliographic description. Arranged alphabetically with indexes by political party, trade, date of founding, place of publication, personal names, etc. Vol. 2 (with supplements) is an alphabetical list—by author or title—of books, pamphlets, articles, and unique items published from 1815 to 1982, with indexes. Locates copies in 90 Italian libraries.

A projected third volume listing government documents has not been published.   Z7164.S67E5

Ferber, Marianne A. Women and work, paid and unpaid : a selected, annotated bibliography. N.Y. : Garland, 1987. 408 p. (Garland reference library of social science, v. 315).   **CH629**

Lists and critically annotates 1,031 monographs and journal articles, most published since 1960, but with a few classics and curiosities from earlier periods as well. Entries are arranged in nine major chapters—e.g., Economics of the family and Earnings and the female-male pay gap. The annotations are enhanced by codes indicating whether the emphasis is primarily on theory, methodology, empirical evidence, or policy issues, and whether a background in economics or mathematics is required. Author and subject indexes.   Z7963.E7F47

Fink, Gary M. State labor proceedings : a bibliography of the AFL, CIO, and AFL-CIO proceedings, 1885–1974, held in the AFL-CIO Library / Gary M. Fink, ed. ; Mary Mills, comp. Westport, Conn. : Greenwood, [1975]. 291 p.   **CH630**

A guide to the microform collection, *State labor proceedings: AFL, CIO, and AFL-CIO conventions, 1885–1974* [microform] (Bethesda, Md. : Univ. Publications of America, [1975?]– . [In progress]). Pt. 1 of the guide provides brief chronological surveys of each state labor movement, with annotations that describe the types of issues covered in convention proceedings. Pt. 2 is a bibliography of convention proceedings, yearbooks, minutes of executive board meetings, etc., listed alphabetically by state.   HD8055.A6F55

Gulick, Charles Adams. History and theories of working-class movements : a select bibliography / comp. by Charles A. Gulick, Roy A. Ockert [and] Raymond J. Wallace. Berkeley : Bureau of Business and Economic Research, Univ. of California, [1955]. 364 p.   **CH631**

Lists articles, notes, and occasional documents in periodicals culled from the files of the University of California Library, covering 1800–1953. International in coverage, but only articles in English are included. Arrangement is by region and country (with approximately a third of the total devoted to Great Britain), subdivided by subject. No annotations and no indexes.   Z7164.L1G8

Labour information : a guide to selected sources. Geneva : International Labour Office, 1991. 231 p. (International labour bibliography, no. 8).   **CH632**

A core list of reference sources and I.L.O. publications. Pt. 1 lists and selectively annotates reference works by format (book selection, dictionaries and encyclopedias, directories, handbooks and atlases, legislative information and labor standards, and statistics); pt. 2 focuses on current I.L.O. publications categorized by broad subject category (Employment, Training, Labor relations and administration, Working environment, Social security, Promotion of equality, and Workers' education) and subcategories. Nine appendixes list I.L.O. periodicals, serials, databases, and manuals and guides for librarians and documentalists. Index by title.   HD7802.A55

McBrearty, James C. American labor history and comparative labor movements : a selected bibliography. Tucson : Univ. of Arizona Pr., [1973]. 262 p.   **CH633**

Pt. 1, Books, subdivides American labor history by chronological period and by topic, and comparative labor movements by country; pt. 2, Articles, follows the same format. There is a separate section for novels. Limited to English-language materials. Author index.   Z7164.L1M15

Mouvements ouvriers et socialistes : chronologie et bibliographie / Collection dirigée par É. Dolléans et M. Crozier. Paris : Les Éditions Ouvrières, [1950–59]. 5 v. in 6.   **CH634**

Contents: [v. 1], Angleterre, France, Allemagne, États-Unis, 1750–1918, [par] Édouard Dolléans et Michel Crozier (1950); [v. 2], L'Italie, des origines à 1922, [par] Alfonso Leonetti (1952); [v. 3], L'Èspagne, 1750–1936, [par] Renée Lamberet (1953); [v. 4], La Russie, [par] Eugène Zaleski: t. 1, 1725–1907; t. 2, 1908–1917 (1956); [v. 5], L'Amérique latine, 1492–1936, [par] Carlos M. Rama (1959).

Each volume is arranged chronologically by period. Under each period there is a chronology of events important to the labor movement, followed by a bibliography listing documents, newspapers, books, and pamphlets, including official publications. Vols. 1 and 4 have indexes of names cited; the other volumes have no indexes.
Z7161.M64

Naas, Bernard G. American labor union periodicals : a guide to their location / Bernard G. Naas, Carmelita S. Sakr. Ithaca, N.Y. : Cornell Univ., 1956. 175 p.　**CH635**
"Published by the New York State School of Industrial and Labor Relations ... for the Committee of University Industrial Relations Librarians."—*verso of title page.*
A union list of more than 1,700 labor union periodicals to be found in about 20 cooperating libraries.
§ University Press of America is filming periodicals from holdings of the State Historical Society of Wisconsin, Johns Hopkins University library, and the U.S. Department of Labor library. Pt. 1 of the *Labor union periodicals* collection covers *The metal trades*; Pt. 2, *The printing trades.*　Z7164.L1N14

———— American labor unions' constitutions and proceedings : a guide to the microform edition, 1836–1978. Glen Rock, N.J. : Microfilming Corp. of America, 1980. 128 p.　**CH636**
Independently useful as a bibliography of constitutions and proceedings of American labor unions as well as serving as a key to the microform collection with the same title (Glen Rock, N.J. : Microfilming Corp. of America, 1974–). Arranged by broad subject groups (e.g., clothing, transportation, communications, etc.), with keyword index. Updated by annual supplements.　Z7164.L1M62

Neufeld, Maurice F. American working class history : a representative bibliography / Maurice F. Neufeld, Daniel J. Leab, Dorothy Swanson. N.Y. : Bowker, 1983. 356 p.　**CH637**
Rev. ed. of Neufeld's *A representative bibliography of American labor history* (1964).
An international bibliography of 7,261 entries on U.S. labor history. Chapters offer historical, regional, and topical approaches, including sections on 37 specific occupations, trades, and industries. Sources cited include theses, films, and literary works, as well as books, articles, government reports, and union publications. Name index.
Supplemented at irregular intervals by bibliographies of articles and dissertations in the Fall issue of *Labor history.*　Z7164.L1N54

Smith, Harold. The British labour movement to 1970 : a bibliography. [London] : Mansell, [1981]. 250 p.　**CH638**
A subject listing of books, pamphlets, and periodicals published between 1945 and 1970 on British labor history, excluding works on industrial relations (which are covered by George Sayers Bain and Gillian B. Woolven's *Bibliography of British industrial relations* [Cambridge ; N.Y. : Cambridge Univ. Pr., 1979]). Chapters on general works, history and theory of socialism, early radicalism (Luddism, Peterloo, Chartism), the Labour Party and Labour governments, related organizations such as the Fabian Society, trade unionism, cooperative societies. More than 3,800 citations; name index.　Z7164.L1S47

United States. Bureau of Labor Statistics. BLS publications, 1886–1971 / [Rosalie K. Epstein]. Wash. : the Bureau, 1972. 184 p. (United States. Bureau of Labor Statistics. Bulletin, no.1749).　**CH639**
Superintendent of Documents classification: L 2.3.
Contains a numerical listing of all bulletins since 1886 and all reports since 1953, a list of current periodicals, and a subject index of bulletins and reports. The microfilm collection, *Bulletins of the U.S. Bureau of Labor and the U.S. Bureau of Labor Statistics, 1895–1919* (Bethesda, Md. : Univ. Publications of America) reproduces the federal publications.
§ Continued by Bulletin no. 1990, *BLS publications, 1972–1977* (1978), and by Report no. 863, *BLS publications, 1978–93.*
Z7164.L1U6672

Library catalogs

Cornell University. New York State School of Industrial and Labor Relations. Library. Library catalog. Boston : G. K. Hall, 1967. 12 v.　**CH640**
The library's collection included some 78,000 volumes and bound periodicals and 80,000 pamphlets at the time of publication of the catalog. All the books, a selected number of more important pamphlets, and author and subject entries for selected articles from 150 periodicals since 1952 are represented in this photographic reproduction of the catalog cards. Periodical titles and holdings are not included.
Additions for the Aug. 1966/Sept. 1974 period are represented in *Cumulation of the library catalog supplements of the New York State School of Industrial and Labor Relations, Martin P. Catherwood Library, Cornell University* (Boston : G. K. Hall, 1976. 9v.). Annual supplements were published 1977–82.　Z7164.L1C84

State Historical Society of Wisconsin. Library. Subject catalog of the library of the State Historical Society of Wisconsin, Madison, Wisconsin : including the Pamphlet subject catalog beginning in volume 22. Westport, Conn. : Greenwood, [1971]. 23 v.　**CH641**
Half title: Catalogs of the Library of the State Historical Society of Wisconsin.
Reproduces the subject catalog cards for works in the general collection, selected federal and state government publications, Wisconsin obituaries since 1846, biographical sketches in Wisconsin county histories published before 1955, and selected analytics for articles published in Wisconsin periodicals and learned journals; broadsides, street maps, paper manuscripts and photographs were excluded. Pamphlets acquired through 1967 are listed in the Subject catalog; those acquired since 1967 are in the Pamphlet subject catalog. The library has strong collections on the American Indian, the Revolutionary War, the Civil War, the trans-Mississippi West, the old Northwest, denominational and church history, state and local history, radical social movements, blacks, genealogy, labor history, and Mormonism.
The *Author-title catalog*, including City directory catalog, the Atlas catalogs—publishers and geographic, the Newspaper catalog and the Newspaper catalog (Labor), was produced by the same publisher on microfiche (1974. 600 sheets). The pamphlet collection was reproduced on microfiche, with a separate finding aid (see *Pamphlets in American history*, DB20).　Z1236.W57

Tamiment Library. Catalog of the Tamiment Institute Library of New York University. Boston : G. K. Hall, 1980. 4 v.　**CH642**
Reproduction of the catalog cards for a rich collection of materials relating to American labor history, workers' education movements, socialism, communism, anarchism, and American radicalism. Lists books, pamphlets, and periodicals–mainly 19th and 20th century publications acquired by the Rand School during its period of existence, 1906–56. Books are entered by author and in a classified shelflist arrangement; pamphlets are listed in an author/title arrangement and in a separate subject arrangement. There are separate alphabetical listings of periodicals and of manuscript collections, as well as author and subject indexes to the *International socialist review* and *Mother earth.*
For the Library's manuscript collections, see *Guide to the manuscript collection of the Tamiment Library* (N.Y. : Garland, 1977. 82 p.).

Indexes; Abstract journals

Index to labor articles. N.Y. : Rand School of Social Science, 1926–53. Monthly; bimonthly.　**CH643**
Title varies; 1926–27 called *Index to labor periodicals.*
Classified arrangement with no cumulations and no author index. Indexes labor articles in general periodicals and in some labor papers not indexed elsewhere. From the labor point of view.　Z7164.L1I38

United States. Bureau of Labor. Index of all reports issued by bureaus of labor statistics in the United States prior to March 1902 : prep. by Carroll D. Wright. Wash. : U.S. Govt. Print. Off., 1902. 287 p.   **CH644**

Repr.: N.Y. : Johnson, 1970.

Superintendent of Documents classification: L 2.34: 1869–1902.

Indexes the reports of the federal and various state bureaus that published labor statistics. The microfilm collection, *Bulletins of the U.S. Bureau of Labor and the U.S. Bureau of Labor Statistics, 1895–1919* (Bethesda, Md. : University Publications of America), reproduces the federal publications.   Z7164.L1U6

The University of Michigan index to labor union periodicals : a cumulative subject index to materials from a selected list of newspapers and journals published by major labor unions. Jan. 1960–Feb. 1969. Ann Arbor : Univ. of Michigan, Bureau of Industrial Relations, 1960–69. Monthly, with annual cumulation.   **CH645**

An annotated subject index to 50 labor union periodicals.

Z7164.T7U6

Work related abstracts. 1973– . Detroit : Information Coordinators, 1973– . Monthly.   **CH646**

Continues *Labor-personnel index* (Detroit : Information Service, 1950–58) and *Employment relations abstracts* (Detroit : Information Service, 1959–71).

Offers brief abstracts of books and current articles selected from approximately 250 journals in the labor relations field. Arranged under 20 broad categories with a separate detailed subject guide.

Z7164.L1W68

Encyclopedias

Labor conflict in the United States : an encyclopedia / ed. by Ronald L. Filippelli. N.Y. : Garland, 1990. 609 p. (Garland reference library of social science, v. 697).   **CH647**

Intended for students and general readers. Contains 254 alphabetically arranged entries, generally three to five pages long, with brief bibliographies. Covers significant strikes, lockouts, boycotts, and other labor conflicts; also features a chronology of American labor history, a glossary, and a select general bibliography. Entries are unsigned, but a list of contributors is given. Indexed.   HD5324.L32

Labor unions / ed. in chief, Gary M. Fink. Westport, Conn. : Greenwood, [1977]. 520 p. (Greenwood encyclopedia of American institutions, 1).   **CH648**

Offers "historical sketches of more than two hundred national unions and labor federations that have been part of the American labor movement."—*Pref.* Selection criteria included "longevity, historical significance, size and economic power, and the influence a particular union had in the development of organized labor in America. An effort was also made to include unions representative of most minority groups, trades and industries, chronological time periods, and ideological movements." Includes bibliographic references.   HD6508.L234

Marsh, Arthur Ivor. Concise encyclopedia of industrial relations : with bibliography. Farnborough, Eng. : Gower Pr., c1979. 423 p.   **CH649**

First publ. 1973 as *Dictionary of industrial relations.*

A dictionary relating to industrial relations in the U.K. Each entry usually includes a bibliographic reference; the references (about 1,200) are listed in the bibliography (p.355–423), grouped by form.

HD4839.M34

Schneider, Dorothy. The ABC-CLIO companion to women in the workplace / Dorothy Schneider and Carl J. Schneider. Santa Barbara, Calif. : ABC-Clio, c1993. 371 p. : ill.   **CH650**

For annotation, *see* CC566.   HD6095.S34

Taylor, Paul F. The ABC-CLIO companion to the American labor movement. Santa Barbara, Calif. : ABC-CLIO, c1993. 237 p : ill.   **CH651**

"A concise encyclopedia of the American labor movement, [including] information on labor leaders, major unions, landmark court decisions and legislation, key events, and the opposition of American business."—*Pref.* Chronology covers 1828–1981. Bibliography and index.   HD6508.T39

Dictionaries

International Labour Office. ILO thesaurus 1991 : labour, employment, and training terminology = Thesaurus BIT : terminologie du travail, de l'emploi, et de la formation. 4th ed. Geneva : International Labour Office, 1992. 557 p.   **CH652**

3rd ed., 1985.

Alphabetical subject thesaurus designed for online *LABORDOC* database. Also provides hierarchical display of terms with related and narrower terms in English, French, and Spanish.   Z695.1.L12I57

Logie, Gordon. Glossary of employment and industry : English-French-Italian-Dutch-German-Swedish.   Amsterdam [etc.] : Elsevier Scientific Pub. Co., 1982. 290 p. (International planning glossaries, 3).   **CH653**

A glossary of terms relating to employment, minerals, metals, extractive industries, energy resources, marketing, and water supply. Arranged by subject, with brief introductory remarks. Basic table is in English, with equivalents from the other languages. Indexes in all languages.   HD2324.L63

Roberts, Harold Selig. Roberts' dictionary of industrial relations. 4th ed. Wash. : Bureau of National Affairs, c1994. 874 p.   **CH654**

Rev. ed., 1971; 3rd ed., 1986.

Preliminary ed., 1957–63, and 1966 ed. had title: *Dictionary of labor-management relations.*

Prep. by Industrial Relations Center, University of Hawaii at Manoa.

Defines terms used in labor-management relations, with references to sources, bibliographies, and cross-references.   HD4839.R612

Periodicals

Harrison, Royden John. The Warwick guide to British labour periodicals, 1790–1970 : a check list / arranged and comp. by Royden Harrison, Gillian B. Woolven, Robert Duncan. Hassocks, Eng. : Harvester Pr. ; Atlantic Highlands, N.J. : Humanities Pr., 1977. 685 p.   **CH655**

"By a *Labour periodical* we understand one which falls into one or other of the following three categories: First, one which was produced by an organised body consisting wholly or mainly of wage-earners or collective-dependent employees.... Second, ... all periodicals which were produced in the avowed interest of the working class.... Third... those which were produced for wage-earners by members of other social classes who sought to improve them, instruct them, or entertain them."—*Introd.*

An alphabetical listing of some 4,125 titles, giving (as far as the information was available) dates of publication, volumes or issues published, sponsoring body, library locations, a code letter indicating character of the journal, and often, a descriptive or explanatory note. Subject index (which includes names of sponsoring agency or organization) and index of dates.   Z7164.L1H37

Hoerder, Dirk. The immigrant labor press in North America, 1840s–1970s : an annotated bibliography / ed. by Dirk Hoerder ; Christiane Harzig, assistant ed. N.Y. : Greenwood, 1987. 3 v. : ill. (Bibliographies and indexes in American history, no. 4, 7–8).   **CH656**

Contents: v. 1, Migrants from northern Europe; v. 2, Migrants from eastern and southeastern Europe; v. 3, Migrants from southern and western Europe.

Includes about 2,170 titles in the categories of labor unions, radicalism, and reform; "periodicals expressing the radicalism of ethnic groups in agriculture are excluded, whereas papers of farmer-labor alliances are included."—*Chapter 1.* Arranged by ethnic group. Information for each group includes an introductory chapter on its history (concentrating on the working class) with a brief bibliography; an alphabetical listing of labor-related periodicals with detailed descriptions, including selected locations; and title, place, and chronological indexes for the periodicals. Each volume also has a combined title index.   Z6953.5.A1H63

Istituto Giangiacomo Feltrinelli (Milan). Bibliografia della stampa periodica operaia e socialista italiana, 1860–1926 / diretta da Franco Della Perutá. Milan : Feltrinelli, 1956–61. 3 v.   **CH657**

Contents: I periodici di Milano : bibliografia e storia, 1860–1904, 1905–1926 (publ. 1956–61. 2 v., called v. 3, pt. 1–2); I periodici di Messina : bibliografia e storia, a cura di Gino Cerrito (publ. 1961. 1 v., called v. 13. pt. 1). No more published?

Bibliography of worker and socialist press in Italy. Arranged chronologically, with full bibliographic details and a historical description of each title. Indexed by title, personal name, and place of publication.

Reynolds, Lloyd George. Trade union publications : the official journals, convention proceedings, and constitutions of international unions and federations, 1850–1941 / by Lloyd G. Reynolds ... and Charles C. Killingworth .... Baltimore : Johns Hopkins Pr., 1944–45. 3 v.   **CH658**

Contents: v. 1, Description and bibliography; v. 2–3, Subject index, A–Z.

Based on the collections in the U.S. Dept. of Labor Library, the John Crerar Library, and the Johns Hopkins University Library.   Z7164.T7R4

Vocino, Michael C. Labor and industrial relations journals and serials : an analytical guide / comp. by Michael C. Vocino, Jr. and Lucille W. Cameron. N.Y. : Greenwood, 1989. 214 p. (Annotated bibliographies of serials, no. 14).   **CH659**

A selective bibliography of 346 currently published English-language serials, including academic journals, representative trade union newsletters, and state and local government publications. Entries are arranged alphabetically, and contain up to 21 pieces of information including, besides standard serials directory information, the presence of a book review section, where indexed, target audience, special issues, and availability of sample copies. An appendix lists titles not examined and therefore not included in the main section. Indexed geographically and by publisher, title, and subject.   Z7164.L1V6

Directories

American directory of organized labor : unions, locals, agreements, and employers / ed. by Cynthia Russell Spomer ; Judith M. Nixon, contributing researcher. Detroit : Gale, c1992. 1638 p.   **CH660**

"Encompasses the field of organized labor in the United States, providing information on approximately 230 major international unions, the nearly 40,000 local, state and regional unions, nearly 1,500 major collective bargaining agreements, and the hundreds of public and private employers and companies who sign agreements."—*Introd.* Provides current and historical information about major unions, directory information on local, state and regional unions, and available facts on major bargaining agreements in effect. Indexed by: industry, geography, AFL-CIO affiliated union, master name, and keyword.

HD6504.A63

Conditions of work and quality of working life : a directory of institutions / ed. by Linda Stoddart assisted by Kristine Falciola. 2nd rev. ed. Geneva : International Labour Office, 1986. 306 p.   **CH661**

1st ed., 1981.

Lists 288 institutions concerned with the working environment (government agencies, trade unions, employers' organizations, research institutes, university departments) in 56 countries. Arrangement is geographical; regional and international organizations are followed by country listings. Entries generally include: name of the organization in the vernacular with its English translation, acronym, address and telephone, working language(s), date begun, type of organization, subject scope, financial support, budget (local currency and U.S. dollars), total staff, director(s), number of volumes, information services, training audience, training subjects, publications, and research. Personal name and acronym indexes.   HD7260.C64

Directory of labour organizations in Canada = Répertoire des organisations de travailleurs au Canada. 1980– . [Ottawa] : Labour Canada, Labour Data Branch, 1980– . Annual.
                                                   CH662

Imprint varies: 1981– , Labour Canada.
In English and French.

Lists national or international unions and independent local organizations with more than 50 members, as well as central labor congresses. Glossary, list of acronyms, executive index, and English and French subject indexes.   HD6521.A4

Directory of U.S. labor organizations. 1982/83– . Wash. : Bureau of National Affairs, [1982]– . Biennial.   **CH663**

Continues: *Directory of national unions and employee associations,* publ. 1971–79 by the U.S. Bureau of Labor Statistics.

Lists unions affiliated with AFL-CIO and other national, regional, state and local affiliates. Index of unions by common name and by abbreviations; name and index officers.   HD6504.D64

Employers' organizations of the world / ed. by Martin Upham. Burnt Mill, Harlow, Essex, England : Longman ; Chicago : St. James Pr., 1990. 237 p.   **CH664**

Lists key organizations by country with international organizations in a separate section. Each country section begins with a brief overview of pertinent economic, political, and industrial developments. Level of coverage varies, but organization entries generally include: address; telephone, telex and fax numbers; name of the president or director; total membership; aims and objectives; services to members; and publications. A brief list of acronyms and an index of major employers' organizations are also included.   HD6943.E559

European labor unions / ed. by Joan Campbell. Westport, Conn. : Greenwood, 1992. 648 p.   **CH665**

Arranged by country, giving for each a brief essay on the historical background of its union movement and a bibliography. Lists the most important national labor organizations and European regional labor organizations. Chronologies, arranged by country; name and subject indexes.   HD6657.E946

Fenton, Thomas P. Transnational corporations and labor : a directory of resources / comp. and ed. by Thomas P. Fenton and Mary J. Heffron. Maryknoll, N.Y. : Orbis Books, c1989. 166 p. : ill.   **CH666**

Describes organizations, print, and nonprint sources that present progressive labor activist views on transnational corporations and their impact on the economies and people of developing nations. Arranged by format in five chapters (Organizations, Books, Periodicals, Pamphlets and articles, and Audiovisual materials), with supplementary lists of books/periodicals and information sources frequently included at the end of each chapter. Indexed by organization name, individual name, and geographical area.   Z7164.U5F46

Latin American labor organizations / ed. by Gerald Michael Greenfield and Sheldon L. Maram. N.Y. : Greenwood, 1987. 929 p.   **CH667**

Arranged by country; gives basic history of labor movement with brief bibliography; lists most important labor organizations, covering the origin, development, and activities of both active and defunct organizations. Appendixes list international labor organizations, chronologies of labor development by country, and glossary of terms, people, and events. Indexed.   HD6530.5.L38

Marsh, Arthur Ivor. Historical directory of trade unions / Arthur Marsh and Victoria Ryan. Farnborough, Hants., England : Gower, c1980–87. v. 1–3. (In progress).   **CH668**

Contents: v. 1, Non-manual unions; v. 2, Including unions in engineering, shipbuilding, and minor metal trades, coal mining, and iron and steel, agriculture, fishing, and chemicals; v. 3, Building and allied trades, transport, woodworkers and allied trades, leather workers, enginemen and tobacco workers.

So far as possible, the entry for each union includes: name, date of founding (together with name charges, amalgamations, cessations, etc.), characteristics (membership, leadership, policies, outstanding events, etc.), and sources of information (books, articles, minutes, location of documentation). Indexed by name of union.

Vol. 4 intended to include trade unions in textiles, printing and publishing, retail distribution, government and general unions, and miscellaneous industries.   HD6664.M26

————————— Trade union handbook : a guide and directory to the structure, membership, policy, and personnel of the British trade unions. 5th ed. Aldershot, England ; Brookfield, Vt., : Gower, c1991. 424 p. : ill.   **CH669**

1st ed., 1979; 4th ed., 1988.

Contains current and historical overview of British trade union membership and organizations, with a directory of international and British trade unions.   HD6663.M37

National trade and professional associations of the United States. 17th annual ed. (1982)– . Wash. : Columbia Books, [1982]– . Annual.   **CH670**

For annotation, *see* AL45.   HD2425.D53

Trade unions of the world. [1st ed.] ([1987])– . Harlow, U.K. : Longman Group UK Ltd. ; Detroit : Gale, c1987– . Biennial.   **CH671**

Sketches political and economic background for each of 186 countries, with an overview and history of trade union activities. Followed by listing of individual unions, their history, affiliated unions, publications, and international affiliates. Also describes international and regional labor organizations. List of acronyms; organization name index.   HD6483.T675

Handbooks

Kelly, Matthew A. Labor and industrial relations : terms, laws, court decisions, and arbitration standards. Baltimore : Johns Hopkins Univ. Pr., c1987. 200 p.   **CH672**

Intended for students, scholars, and practitioners. In three main parts: a glossary; a compendium of labor legislation, describing and analyzing labor relations and protective labor legislation and pertinent court decisions; and a discussion of arbitration laws, court decisions, and standards. Includes a selective bibliography of reference works and principal texts. Indexed by terms and court decisions.
        KF3369.K45

Labor relations yearbook. 1965–1984. Wash. : Bureau of National Affairs, 1966–84.   **CH673**

Subtitle: Chronology of events, collective bargaining, labor relations conferences, labor organizations, role of federal government, selected analyses, economic data.

In addition to materials mentioned in the subtitle, provides annual coverage of the role of state government, and bibliographic citations to

and summaries of important literature. For subsequent events, see BNA's *Labor relations reporter* (1938– . Three issues weekly), or BNA files available online.   HD8059.L33

Labor Research Association (U.S.). Labor fact book. N.Y. : Internat. Pub., 1931–65. v. 1 (1931)–v.17 (1965).   **CH674**

Repr.: N.Y. : Oriole Eds., 1972–74, accompanied with a combined index to v. 1–17.

Information on political, economic, and social conditions that have affected the labor movement in America, supported by data drawn largely from standard government, business, and labor publications. Some volumes include a chapter on labor abroad. Name and subject index.   HD8072.I253

Histories

Commons, John Rogers. History of labour in the United States. N.Y. : Macmillan, 1935–36. 4 v.   **CH675**

Repr.: N.Y. : Kelley, 1966.

First published 1918–35 in 4 v.

A comprehensive survey of the development of labor organizations and legislation in the U.S., each part by a specialist with introductions by Commons. Based on Commons's *A documentary history of American industrial society* (N.Y. : A. H. Clark, 1910–11. 10 v. in 11. Repr. with new preface to v. 1–2, by Louis Filler: N.Y., Russell & Russell, 1958).   HD8066.C7

First facts of American labor : a comprehensive collection of labor firsts in the United States / arr. by subject, fully indexed, [and comp. by] Philip S. Foner. N.Y. : Holmes & Meier, [1984]. 237 p.   **CH676**

A dictionary of labor "firsts"; no cited sources or bibliographic references.   HD8066.F55

Hepple, B. A. A bibliography of the literature on British and Irish labour law / B. A. Hepple, J. M. Neeson, Paul O'Higgins. [London] : Mansell, 1975. 331 p.   **CH677**

Attempts to cover "all the relevant literature concerned with the legal relationships of people at work" (*Introd.*) in English, Wales, Scotland, Northern Ireland and the Republic of Ireland. Includes "the individual relationship between worker and employer ... the payment of wages, hours, holidays, and other conditions of employment ... protective legislation ... compensation for accidents and diseases ... training and vocational education ... unemployment ... collective bargaining ... industrial conflict ... organization of employers and workers ... and certain international aspects of direct relevance to Great Britain and Ireland." Classed arrangement with author and subject indexes. Mainly English-language materials (books and periodical articles) from the 18th century through the end of 1972. More than 4,500 items; library locations are given for books and pamphlets.

§ A supplement was published as *Labour law in Great Britain and Ireland to 1978*, by B. A. Hepple ... [et al.]. (London : Sweet and Maxwell, 1981. 131 p.).   KD3001.H46

Biography

Biographical dictionary of American labor / ed. in chief, Gary M. Fink. Westport, Conn. : Greenwood, c1984. 767 p.   **CH678**

Rev. ed. of *Biographical dictionary of American labor leaders* (1974).

Includes more than 700 trade union leaders, political radicals, and intellectuals, reflecting the diversity of American working class movements. Entries include references. Appendixes list biographees by union affiliation, religious preferences, place of birth, formal education, political preference, and public offices held. Indexed.
        HD8073.A1B56

Burnett, John. The autobiography of the working class : an annotated, critical bibliography / editors, John Burnett, David Vincent, David Mayall. N.Y. : New York Univ. Pr., 1984–1989. 3 v.   **CH679**

Contents: v. 1, 1790–1900; v. 2, 1900–1945; v. 3, Supplement, 1790–1945.

Abstracts of memoirs and autobiographies from England, Scotland, and Wales, 1790–1945. Additional entries, classed by occupation, appear in the appendixes of each volume and index other miscellaneous works, oral histories, and some political and military history collections and diaries. Indexes by place, occupation, education, and date.   Z7164.L1B95

Statistics

Economically active population estimates and projections, 1950–2025 = Evaluations et projections de la population active, 1950–2025. [3rd ed.]. Geneva : International Labour Office, [1986]–90? 6 v.   **CH680**

Title varies: 1st ed., 1971, had title: *Labour force projections, 1965–1985;* 2nd ed., 1977, had title: *Labour force estimates and projections, 1950–2000.*

Contents: v. 1, Asia; v. 2, Africa; v. 3, Latin America; v. 4, North America, Europe, Oceania, and USSR; v. 5, World summary; v. 6, Methodological supplement.

Presents data on population, labor force, and labor force activity by sex and age group, 1950–2025, plus data on the total labor force in agriculture, industry, and services by age group, 1950–70.

HD5712.I58

Employment, hours and earnings, states and areas / U.S. Bureau of Labor Statistics. 1939/82– . Wash. : The Bureau : For sale by the U.S. Govt. Print. Off., 1984– . Quinquennial.   **CH681**

Superintendent of Documents classification: L2.3 .

Issued in the Bureau's *Bulletin* series.

Groups detailed industry data for states and metropolitan areas. Tables are arranged by state and area, then by industry. Employment data "relate to the nonfarm sector of the economy [and] exclude proprietors, the self-employed, domestic workers in private homes, and unpaid family workers."—*Introd.*

Supplemented by *Bulletin 1320* (Mar. 1989) covering 1972–87 and *Bulletin 2411* (Aug. 1992) covering 1987–92.

Updated by: *Employment and earnings* (v. 16 [1969]– . Wash. : U.S. Bureau of Labor Statistics, 1969–).   HD8051.A62

Employment, hours and earnings, United States. 1909–84– . Wash. : U.S. Bureau of Labor Statistics : For sale by U.S. Govt. Print. Off., 1984– . Irregular.   **CH682**

Superintendent of Documents classification: L 2.3: .

Issued in the Bureau's *Bulletin* series.

A recurring compilation of "historical monthly and annual average data on national establishment-based employment, hours and earnings by detailed industry, classified in accordance with the 1987 Standard Industrial Classification (SIC) manual."—*Bulletin 2370.* Each volume published 1984–90 is cumulative from 1909; volumes 1993– are cumulative from 1981. Data are derived from the Current Employment Statistics program and from payroll records of sample nonfarm establishments. Supplementary *Bulletin 2429* includes benchmark revisions and historical corrections, adjusting to March 1993 benchmarks. Monthly figures are reported in *Employment and earnings* and cumulated annually in *Supplement to employment and earnings.*

HD8051.A62

Great Britain. Department of Employment and Productivity. British labour statistics : historical abstract 1886–1968. London : H.M.S.O., 1971. 436 p.   **CH683**

Provides more than 200 tables drawn from original sources, e.g., *Abstract of labour statistics of the United Kingdom, (1922–1936)* (London : H.M.S.O., 1937), census reports, etc. Sources are indicated for all tables. Glossary; index.   HD8388.A5

International labour statistics : a handbook, guide, and recent trends / ed. by R. Bean. London ; N.Y. : Routledge, 1989. 306 p.   **CH684**

"A tool for assisting and guiding users of international labour statistics."—*Pref.* Specialists explain the relationship between key economic and social indicators, and the interface between data and the interpretation of the results. Accompanied by representative tables and summary labor statistics from OECD and selected developing countries.   HD4826.I636

Labor force statistics derived from the Current population survey : a databook. Wash. : U.S. Dept. of Labor, Bureau of Labor Statistics, 1982–84. 2 v. (United States. Bureau of Labor Statistics. Bulletin, 2096).   **CH685**

Superintendent of Documents classification: L 2.3:2096.

A comprehensive collection of historical monthly, quarterly, and annual data, in many cases retrospective to 1948. Includes data on employment and unemployment classed by occupation, industry, age, sex, race, education, etc.

Updated by: *Labor force statistics derived from the Current population survey, 1948–87* (Aug. 1988. 865 p. [Bulletin 2307]).

§ Supplemented on a current basis by tables in the *MLR, monthly labor review* (CH688) and *Employment and earnings* (CH682 *note*).

HD5724.L19

Professional women and minorities. [1st ed.], 1975– . Wash. : Commission on Professionals in Science and Technology, 1975– . Irregular.   **CH686**

Publisher varies.

Earlier vols. ed. by Betty M. Vetter; some prep. jointly with Eleanor L. Babco. 1st–2nd ed. looseleaf. Vols. for 1975–78 also updated by supplements.

Provides detailed statistical data on the education of women and ethnic minorities and their availability to and participation in the workforce. General data on enrollment, degrees, professions, workforce, and academic workforce are followed by details of subject fields. Bibliography; index.

Updated by: *Scientific, engineering, technical manpower comments* (Wash. : Scientific Manpower Commission, 1964–).

HD6278.U5P76

United States. Bureau of Labor Statistics. Handbook of labor statistics. 1924/26– . Wash. : U.S. Govt. Print. Off., 1927– . Irregular.   **CH687**

Supplement for 1950 published 1951; nothing further published until volume for 1967. Frequency varies.

Summary of statistics covering employment, labor force, occupations, productivity, prices, work stoppages, occupational injuries, employee benefits, etc. Selection of tables varies; 1989 ed. presents data from earliest reliable compilations to 1988, revised and updated.

HD8051.A62

————— MLR, monthly labor review. v. 1 (July 1915)– . Wash. : U.S. Govt. Print. Off., 1915– . Monthly.   **CH688**

Superintendent of Documents classification: L 2.6.

Title varies; 1915–June 1918 called *Monthly review.*

Contains articles, summaries of special reports, and statistics concerning employment, labor turnover, earnings, hours, work stoppages, prices, cost of living, etc. An annual statistical supplement was issued 1956–65.

Subject indexes: v. 1 (1915)–v. 11 (1920) in *Bulletin* 695; v. 12 (1921)–v. 51 (1940) in *Bulletin* 696; v. 52 (1941)–v. 71 (1950) in *Bulletin* 1080; v. 72 (1951)–v. 83 (1960) in *Bulletin 1335; v. 84 (1961)–v. 93 (1970) in Bulletin* 1746; v. 94 (1971)–v. 98 (1975) in *Bulletin* 1922; v. 99 (1976)–v. 114 (1990) in *Bulletin* 2391.   HD8051.A78

United States. Bureau of Statistics. History of wages in the United States from colonial times to 1928 : revision of Bull. no. 499 with suppl., 1929–1933. Wash. : U.S. Govt. Print. Off., 1934. 574 p. : tables. (United States. Bureau of Statistics. Bulletin, no.604). **CH689**

   Repr. : Detroit : Gale, 1966.   HD8051.A62 no.604

World labour report. 1– . Geneva : International Labour Office, 1984– . Annual. **CH690**

   Frequency varies; v. 1–4, biennial.

   Designed to give an overview of recent problems and developments in labor in the contemporary world. Vols. 1–4 each addressed one major theme, reflected in distinctive titles. Vol. 5, the first annual, treats human rights at work, employment, labor relations, social protection, and working conditions. Narratives contain statistical tables and bibliographies. Statistical appendix lists socioeconomic indicators, ratification of ILO conventions, labor forces, employment trends and structure, strikes, and social security.   HD4802.W65

Year-book of labour statistics. 1935/36– . Geneva : International Labour Office, 1936– . Annual. **CH691**

   Title varies; later issues called *Year book of labour statistics.*

   Frequency varies: 1936–42, annual; 1943/44–1951/52, biennial; 1952/53– , annual.

   Preceded by: v. 1, *Annual review,* 1930; v. 2–5, *I.L.O. yearbook,* 1931–1934/35.

   Text in French, Spanish, and English since 1941.

   Summarizes labor statistics on the economically active population of 184 countries and territories. Annual supplements, *Statistical sources and methods* (1984–92), *Sources and methods* (1992–), and *Labour statistics. Vol. 1, Consumer price indices* (1992–), define the method of data collection, coverage, concepts and definitions, classifications, historical changes, with technical references; covers consumer price indices, employment, wages and hours of work, and household income and expenditures. Updated by *Bulletin of labour statistics* (Geneva, 1965– . Quarterly).

   ———. *Retrospective edition on population census, 1945–89 = Édition rétrospective sur les recensements de population, 1945–89* (Geneva, 1990) combines and adjusts data from previous yearbooks with some new data derived from recent or previously unpublished censuses.   HD4826.I63

Occupations

1990 census of population and housing : alphabetical index of industries and occupations. Wash. : U.S. Bureau of the Census : for sale by U.S. Govt. Print. Off., [1992]. 154, 216 p. **CH692**

   Superintendent of Documents classification: C 3.223.22:90-R-3.

   Lists 21,000 industry and 30,000 occupational titles.
             HA201.A566x

Dictionary of occupational titles / U.S. Dept. of Labor, Employment and Training Admin., U.S. Employment Service. 4th ed., rev. 1991. [Wash.] : The Administration, 1991. 2 v. (1404 p.). **CH693**

   Superintendent of Documents classification: L 37.2:Oc 1/2/991/v. 1–2.

   1st ed., 1939–44; 3rd ed., 1973.

   Incorporates 1982 and 1986 supplements to 4th ed., 1977.

   Offers standardized descriptions of job content and structure for about 20,000 occupations. Grouped by occupations to emphasize similarities and variations. Detailed classed arrangement indexed alphabetically by occupation and industry group. Glossary.   HB2595D53

Directories

The career guide : Dun's employment opportunities directory. 1985– . Parsippany, N.J. : Dun's Marketing Services, c1984– . Annual. **CH694**

   The main alphabetical list of employers contains directory information, contact name(s), company history, company job opportunities and hiring practices, career training programs, and benefits. Additional sections list employers geographically and by industry, with indexes of work study and internship opportunities.

Directory of internships, work experience programs, and on-the-job training opportunities / ed., Alvin Renetsky ; assistant ed., Rebekah Berger ; indexer, Robin Mayper Balaban. 2nd ed. Santa Monica, Calif. : Ready Reference Pr., 1986. 2 v. in 1 (600 p.). **CH695**

   For annotation, *see* CB364.   HD5715.2.D57

Federal career directory : the U.S. government, find out why it's becoming the first choice! : career America. Wash. : U.S. Office of Personnel Management : For sale by U.S. Govt. Print. Off., [1990]– . 1 v. (looseleaf) : ill. (some col.), map. **CH696**

   Superintendent of Documents classification: PM 1.2:C 18/8.

   Intended for recent college graduates and others seeking information about federal employment opportunities and benefits. In 14 tabbed sections that include (besides descriptions of major government agencies, their employees, and the address and telephone numbers of their personnel offices) general information about training and development opportunities, special employment programs, employee benefits, federal pay and personnel classification systems, and an index of college majors employed by agencies. Also has a section of instructions on how to apply for federal employment. Photographs, organization charts, and other illustrations.

Internships. 1981– . Princeton, N.J. : Peterson's Guides, c1981– . Annual. **CH697**

   Publ. 1980–91 by Writer's Digest Books, Cincinnati.

   Lists opportunities in the U.S. and abroad, arranged by broad career area and then by type of company or organization. Describes organization, internships available, benefits, eligibility, selection criteria, and application procedures and dates. Geographic and organization indexes.   L901.I66

Job seeker's guide to private and public companies. 1st ed.– . Detroit : Gale, c1992– . Irregular. **CH698**

   In four volumes, divided regionally: West, Midwest, Northeast, and South. Lists more than 16,000 companies geographically (by state, then by city); entries contain directory information, brief financial data and number of employees, and human resource contact names. May also list company goals, hiring practices, benefits, internship opportunities, and other company information. Indexed by corporate name (cumulative in each volume), by industry, and metropolitan statistical area.

Kocher, Eric. International jobs : where they are, how to get them : a handbook for over 500 career opportunities around the world. 3rd ed., rev. and expanded. Reading, Mass. : Addison-Wesley, c1989. 440 p. **CH699**

   Previous ed., 1984.

   In two parts: (1) chapters on career planning, curriculum development, work permits and documentation, and job letters, résumés and interviews; (2) a directory of international career opportunities offered by the federal government, United Nations, nonprofit organizations, international businesses and banks, the communications field, teaching, and international law. Bibliography; index.   HF5382.7.K62

The national job bank. [1st ed.]– . Brighton, Mass. : B. Adams, c1983– . Irregular. **CH700**

   Arranged by state; within state listings, public and private firms are listed by industry. Entries give directory information, contact persons, and brief business descriptions. Entries may indicate typical job classifications, projected hiring activity, and training programs. Regional directories that follow the same format are also available.

HF5382.5.U5N34

U.S. employment opportunities. 1985– . Arlington, Va. : Washington Research Associates. Annual, with quarterly updates. **CH701**

Describes employment prospects in the federal government, telecommunications, education, computer industry, banking and finance, health care, insurance, advertising, law, arts and entertainment, social work, and entrepreneurship. Each section begins with an industry overview, special areas of current hiring, and ends with a list of industry resources. HF5382.5.U5U2

Handbooks

Job hunter's sourcebook. 1st ed.– . Detroit : Gale, 1991– . Biennial. **CH702**

Compiled in cooperation with the Career and Employment Information Center of the Detroit Public Library.

In two main parts: (1) Job-hunting information, organized by profession or occupation, in which 165 occupations are profiled. Descriptions of sources of employment information grouped under six broad categories (Help-wanted ads; Placement/job referral services; Employer directories and networking lists; Handbooks and manuals; Employment agencies and executive search firms; and Other leads). (2) General job-hunting information, containing descriptions of reference works, newspapers, periodicals, audiovisual materials, software and databases. Also includes an essay on library resources and services for job hunters and an index to information sources.

§ A companion to *Professional careers sourcebook* (CH707).

HF5382.7.J62

Krantz, Les. Jobs rated almanac. 2nd ed. N.Y. : World Almanac, c1992. 345 p. : ill. **CH703**

Alternate title: *Jobs rated almanac two*.

1st ed., 1988, had subtitle: 250 jobs!

Ranks some 250 jobs by 12 criteria, including: work environment, income, outlook, stress, travel opportunities, physical demands, extras, security, and where the jobs are. Within each section, jobs are listed alphabetically. A final section, "The big picture," contains an overall ranking of jobs. Not indexed. HF5382.5.U5K7

Occupational outlook handbook / U.S. Dept. of Labor, Bureau of Labor Statistics. 1st ed.– . Wash. : The Bureau, 1949– . Biennial. **CH704**

Superintendent of Documents classification L2.3/4.

Frequency varies; biennial since 1959.

Gives information on employment trends and outlook in more than 800 occupations. Indicates nature of work, qualifications, earnings and working conditions, entry level jobs, where to go for more information, etc.

Updated by *Occupational outlook quarterly*. HF5381.U62

Petras, Kathryn. Jobs '93 / Kathryn and Ross Petras. N.Y. : Simon & Schuster, c1993. 685 p. **CH705**

Section 1 discusses outlook for various careers arranged in broad categories (government employees, scientists, technical careers), with job description and industry trends. Lists major employers, relevant associations, directories, magazines, and hotlines, with special sections on women, minorities, and disabled workers. Section 2 discusses trends in major industries, listing major companies, industry publications, and directories. Section 3 gives regional outlook, listing major employers by state, state business periodical, and employment offices.

HF5382.5.U5P443

Professional and occupational licensing directory. 1st ed.– . Detroit : Gale, c1993– . Biennial. **CH706**

Arranged by occupational title, describes federal and state licensing procedures for about 250 occupations in the U.S. Includes type and duration of license, examinations and procedures required, educational requirements, reciprocity, and special exemptions, waivers, and exclusions. Notes fees and addresses of licensing board. HD3630.U7.P76

Professional careers sourcebook : an information guide for career planning. 1st ed.– . Detroit : Gale, c1990– . Biennial. **CH707**

Compiled in cooperation with InfoPLACE.

An "overview of the literature and professional organizations that aid career planning and related research for 111 careers requiring college degrees or specialized education."—*Introd.* The career profiles, grouped in ten major categories by professional type and then listed alphabetically, generally contain the following information: job descriptions; career guides; professional associations; standards/certification agencies; test guides; educational directories and programs; awards, scholarships, grants, and fellowships; basic reference guides; educational directories and programs; awards, scholarships, grants, and fellowhiips; basic reference guides and handbooks; professional and trade periodicals; professional meetings and conventions; and other sources of information. Also includes a master list of profiled careers, a directory of state occupational and professional licensing agencies, and lists of jobs ranked by employment outlook, security, stress, pay, working environment, and overall job quality. Indexed. Partially drawn from, but complementary to, U.S. Bureau of Labor Statistics, *Occupational outlook handbook* (CH704).

§ Companion volume, *Vocational careers sourcebook* (CB214), follows the same format. HF5382.5.U5P76

Statistics

The American almanac of jobs and salaries. [1982 ed.]– . N.Y. : Avon, c1982– . Irregular. **CH708**

A survey of occupations and their salaries. Sources are indicated for most tables, and some historical data is provided.

HD8038.U5A68

Personnel

Indexes; Abstract journals

Personnel literature / Office of Personnel Management Library. v. 1 (1941)– . Wash. : The Library [for sale by U.S. Govt. Print. Off.], 1941– . Monthly. **CH709**

Issued by U.S. Civil Service Commission. Library, 1941–78.

A detailed subject index of books, reports, periodical articles, government documents, etc., received by the Library. About 250 titles are listed each month. Annual names/subject index.

Z7164.C81U45683

Personnel management abstracts. v. 1 (Jan./Feb. 1955)– . Chelsea, Mich. : Personnel Management Abstracts, 1955– . Quarterly. **CH710**

Publisher varies.

An international bibliography of English-language literature. Currently abstracts articles from more than 80 periodicals, and includes reviews of current books. Broad subject arrangement with author index; no detailed subject approach nor cumulative indexing features. HF5549.P452

Dictionaries

Shafritz, Jay M. The Facts on File dictionary of personnel management and labor relations. 2nd ed., rev. and expanded. N.Y. : Facts on File, c1985. 534 p. : ill. **CH711**
1st ed., 1980, had title: *Dictionary of personnel management and labor relations.*
Revised and expanded, but with the same coverage of court cases, laws, organizations, journals, people, and personnel tests as well as terms. Appendixes list both the official and popular names of national unions with their acronyms and provide the text of the National Labor Relations Board style manual. HF5549.A23S52

Handbooks

The Dartnell personnel administration handbook / [ed.] by Wilbert E. Scheer. 3rd ed. Chicago : Dartnell Corp., 1985. 1124 p. : ill., ports. **CH712**
2nd ed., 1979.
Updated, revised, and expanded, covering more than 500 topics in 13 chapters. Contains illustrations, charts, and sample forms. Indexed, but lacks a bibliography. HF5549.D3392

Human resources

Bibliography

Crimando, William. Staff training : an annotated review of the literature, 1980–1988 / William Crimando, T.F. Riggar. N.Y. : Garland, 1990. 341 p. (Research and information guides in business, industry, and economic institutions, 3 ; Garland reference library of social science, v. 662). **CH713**
An annotated bibliography of scholarly and popular literature, published 1980–88, arranged in 22 chapters under five broad headings (Instructional system, Assessment, Design, Implementation, and Follow-up). Each section begins with a definition, glossary, and brief bibliographic essay discussing the sources and suggesting issues for further consideration. Citations to other works are included. Indexed by title and author. Z5814.T4C75

Dictionaries

Tracey, William R. The human resources glossary : a complete desk reference for HR professionals. N.Y. : American Management Association, 1991. 416 p. **CH714**
"Contains more than 3,000 definitions. Each entry explains the context and application of an acronym, abbreviation, or term, and in the case of terms rooted in federal law, the applicable legislation is cited."—*Pref.* Lists associations and societies. Includes cross-references. HF5549.A23T73

Directories

Personnel executives contactbook. 1st ed.– . Detroit : Gale, c1993– . Annual. **CH715**
Lists the names of personnel executives of about 30,000 public and private companies and organizations, and federal and state agencies. Organizations are listed alphabetically, geographically by city and state, and by industry. Index of personnel names.
HF5549.2.U5P42

Seminars directory. 1st ed. (1989)– . Detroit : Gale, c1988– . **CH716**
Subtitle to 2nd ed.: A descriptive guide to 8,000 public seminars and workshops in 20,000 locations, covering 2,000 subject areas of interest to business, industry, and government.
Lists and describes national and regional public seminars, workshops, and training programs, categorized under 35 major subject sections, such as management and communications. Entries include program title; vendor's name, address, and telephone; a brief description; length, cost, and location(s) of program; and remarks. Geographic and title indexes. HF5549.5.T7S392

The trainer's resource. 1981– . Amherst, Mass. : Human Resource Development Pr., 1981– . Annual, 1986– . **CH717**
1988– issued in 2 v.
A directory of programs for human resource training, education, and development. Arrangement is by broad subject category (e.g., management development, performance appraisal). Entries include: audience for whom intended, program description (outlining objectives and topics covered), delivery system (medium, length of program, recommended participant group size), instructional strategies, date introduced, recent users, cost, and contact organization's name, address, and telephone number. Subject, title, and vendor indexes.
HD30.412.T73

Training and development organizations directory. [1st ed.]– . Detroit : Gale, 1978– . Irregular. **CH718**
Lists training and development companies, with a description of the programs, seminars and workshops offered by them, "in-house, off-site, off-the-shelf or custom design."—*Introd.* Arrangement is within broad subject areas. Includes; geographic, personal name, and subject indexes with a subject index thesaurus.
Beginning with the 2nd ed. (Mar. 1981), kept up-to-date by periodic supplements, *New training organizations.* HD30.42.U5T7

Handbooks

Handbook of human resources administration / [ed. by] Joseph J. Famularo. 2nd ed. N.Y. : McGraw-Hill, c1986. 1 v. (various pagings) : ill., forms. **CH719**
1st ed., 1972, had title : *Handbook of modern personnel management.*
Revised and expanded to reflect changes in the law, attitudes, values, and life-style, with 80 signed chapters grouped by subject. Includes charts, diagrams, bibliographies, and an index. HF5549.H297

Stern's sourcefinder : human resource management. 1991– . Culver City, Calif. : M. Daniels, c1990– . Annual. **CH720**
Compilers: Gerry and Yvette Borcia Stern.
A directory of publications and other information sources. Publications listed are available in various formats, from periodical articles and books to looseleaf services and newsletters. In two parts: (1) indexes of subjects, authors, book titles, periodical titles, associations, government agencies, libraries and information centers/services; (2) information sources by broad subject area. Entries give name, address, telephone, brief description of source, and price. Z7164.C81S7777

CJ

Political Science

Political science may be defined as the study of politics and political behavior, including the principles and conduct of government. Frederick L. Holler's *Information sources of political science* (CJ1) is a classic guide to the field. This section also includes the related topics of public opinion, intelligence and espionage, terrorism, the armed forces, and arms control and peace research. In addition, many interdisciplinary works of interest to those doing research in political science will be found in other sections devoted to social and behavioral sciences, as well as in history and area studies sections.

GENERAL WORKS

Guides

Holler, Frederick L. Information sources of political science. 4th ed. Santa Barbara, Calif. : ABC-Clio, c1986. 417 p.   **CJ1**
    1st ed., 1971; 3rd ed., 1980.
    Offers a section on political reference theory followed by more than 2,400 citations to printed and computerized reference sources. Groups the extensively annotated entries into topical chapters (e.g., international relations and organizations, public administration), each with an introductory discussion. Author, title, subject, and typology indexes.
    § Similar older works that may occasionally be helpful are Robert B. Harmon, *Political science : a bibliographical guide to the literature* (N.Y. : Scarecrow, 1965–74. 3 v.) and Lubomyr Wynar, *Guide to reference materials in political science* (Denver, Colo. : Bibliographic Institute, 1966–68. 2 v.). *See also* Henry York, *Political science: a guide to reference and information sources* (CJ5).   Z7161.H64

Information sources in politics and political science : a survey worldwide / eds., Dermot Englefield and Gavin Drewry. London ; Boston : Butterworths, 1984. 509 p.   **CJ2**
    British academicians, librarians, and specialists present bibliographic review essays on the topical and area studies aspects of politics; p. 135–241 are devoted to the U.K. Includes monographs and periodical titles as well as reference sources. Subject index.
                                                                  Z7161.I544

Kalvelage, Carl. Bridges to knowledge in political science : a handbook for research / Carl Kalvelage, Albert P. Melone, Morley Segal. Pacific Palisades, Calif. : Palisades Publishers, c1984. 153 p.   **CJ3**
    A successor to *Research guide for undergraduates in political science* by Kalvelage, Segal, and Peter J. Anderson ([Morristown, N.J.] : General Learning Pr., [1972]) and *Research guide in political science* by Kalvelage and Segal (2nd ed., 1976).
    Both a practical introduction to research tools and a manual for conceptualizing, researching, and writing a paper. Most appropriate for undergraduates. Consists of chapters that treat steps in developing a re-

search paper; e.g., chapter 1 discusses topic selection. Contains sections on footnotes and bibliographies and on special skills (e.g., interviewing and corresponding with public officials). The general index would be more useful if it included authors and titles for all the sources mentioned.   JA86.K34

Lowery, Roger C. Political science : illustrated search strategy and sources : with an introduction to legal research for undergraduates / by Roger C. Lowery, Sue A. Cody. Ann Arbor, Mich. : Pierian Pr., 1993. 204 p. : ill. (Library research guides series, no.12.).   **CJ4**
    Facilitates the research process for undergraduates by offering a step-by-step introduction to important information sources for political science (most with a U.S. emphasis). Covers choosing and narrowing a topic; books; periodical and newspaper articles; U.S. government documents; legal research; biographies, statistics, and facts; and computer database searching. Uses a sample topic throughout, with illustrations showing actual pages or printouts from the sources being discussed. Appendixes provide a bibliography (arranged in sections corresponding to the chapters in the text) and a reprint of the American Political Science Association's *Style manual for political science* (Wash. : APSA, 1988). Title index to sources cited in the text.   JA88.L69

York, Henry E. Political science : a guide to reference and information sources. Englewood, Colo. : Libraries Unlimited, 1990. 249 p. (Reference sources in the social sciences series, no. 4).   **CJ5**
    Provides annotations for 805 major information sources in political science, its subdivisions, and related social science fields. Groups entries in six chapters: (1) General social science; (2) Social science disciplines; (3) General political science; (4) Political science by geographic area; (5) Political science by topic (e.g., international relations, human rights, peace and conflict); and (6) Public policy. Within chapters, entries are alphabetical under type of publication (e.g., bibliographies, directories, handbooks). Primarily covers English-language publications 1980–87, but serials are included regardless of beginning date. Excludes legal publications, guides to government documents, directories of government officials, texts of laws and treaties, and state publications. Author/title and subject indexes.   Z7161.Y75

Bibliography

Bergerson, Peter J. Ethics and public policy : an annotated bibliography. N.Y. : Garland, 1988. 200 p. (Public affairs and administration series, 20 ; Garland reference library of social science, v. 414).   **CJ6**
    Provides 330 citations to selected books, articles, and dissertations published over the last 25 years on ethics and public policy. An extensive introduction provides an overview of the subject and its literature. Entries are arranged in topical chapters (e.g., Ethics and state and local governments, Health care/medical/bio-scientific) and feature lengthy annotations, some a page long. Author index, but no subject index.   Z7161.A15B47

Black, J. L. Origins, evolution, and nature of the Cold War : an annotated bibliographic guide. Santa Barbara, Calif. : ABC-Clio, c1986. 173 p. (War/peace bibliography series, no. 19).   **CJ7**
    Cites English-language books, articles, and dissertations focusing on the Cold War. Topical chapters (e.g., History, Image of the enemy, American-Soviet relations, Regional influences and developments) are subdivided by topic. Annotations; numerous cross-references. Author index and subject index (divided into sections covering persons, regions, and topics).   Z6465.U5B53

Canadian review of studies in nationalism : bibliography = Revue canadienne des études sur le nationalisme : bibliographie. v. 1 (1974)–14 (1987). Charlottetown, P.E.I. : Univ. of Prince Edward Island, 1974–1987.   **CJ8**

Provides annotated bibliographies for contemporary books and articles. Each bibliography is compiled by an individual scholar and covers a particular region, culture, or topic (e.g., Italy, National Socialism in Germany, Self-determination).

Deutsch, Karl Wolfgang. Nationalism and national development : an interdisciplinary bibliography / Karl W. Deutsch, Richard L. Merritt. Cambridge, Mass. : MIT Pr., [1970]. 519 p.   **CJ9**

Continues: Koppel Pinson, *A bibliographical introduction to nationalism* (N.Y. : Columbia Univ. Pr., 1935), and Karl Deutsch, *An interdisciplinary bibliography on nationalism, 1935–1953* (Cambridge, Mass. : MIT Pr., 1956).

Covers 1935–66 in a classed bibliography of about 5,000 books, pamphlets, and journal articles in the major Western languages, with English-language materials predominating. Author and keyword-in-context indexes.

§ For additional items, *see also* Heinrich Winkler and Thomas Schnabel, *Bibliographie zum Nationalismus* (Gottingen : Vandenhoeck & Ruprecht, 1979) and *Canadian review of studies in nationalism : bibliography* (CJ8).   Z7164.N2D43

International relations : a handbook on current theory / ed. by Margot Light and A.J.R. Groom. Boulder, Colo. : L. Rienner, 1985. 245 p.   **CJ10**

1st ed., 1978, had title: *International relations theory : a bibliography,* ed. by A.J.R. Groom and Christopher Mitchell.

Consists of 15 chapters, each a bibliographic essay by a contributing scholar, in two sections: The paradigmatic debate (e.g., World society and human needs) and Partial theories (e.g., Power, influence and authority). Includes a chapter on textbooks. Each chapter concludes with a bibliography. Author index; notes on contributors. JX1291.I56

Jodice, David A. Political risk assessment : an annotated bibliography. Westport, Conn. : Greenwood, 1985. 279 p. (Bibliographies and indexes in law and political science, no. 3).   **CJ11**

Focuses "on the experience of political risk overseas, e.g., nationalizations, and restrictions on operations, and how American and foreign-based multinational companies and financial institutions have responded to these changes."—*Introd.* Following an essay giving an overview of the field, entries are alphabetically arranged within thematic chapters covering multinational corporations in world politics, sources of political risk, risk management and assessment, and reference sources for risk analysts. Emphasizes books and articles, 1970–83; lengthy annotations. Name index.   Z7164.E17J63

Nagel, Stuart S. Basic literature in policy studies : a comprehensive bibliography. Greenwich, Conn. : Jai Pr., 1984. 453 p.   **CJ12**

Reprints, updates, and supplements bibliographies previously appearing in unspecified issues of *Policy studies journal* and adds several new bibliographies. In three parts: General aspects of policy studies, Specific policy problems, and Bibliographic syllabi for policy studies courses. The first two parts are in topical sections (e.g., social values, economic regulation, labor policy, environmental protection). Bibliographies are signed, generally not annotated, and limited to English-language publications. Index to subjects and authors of the bibliographies.   Z7161.N24

Universal Reference System. Political science, government and public policy series. Princeton, N.J. : Princeton Research, [1965–69]. 10 v.   **CJ13**

Contents: v. 1, International affairs (2nd ed., 1969); v. 2, Legislative process, representation, and decision-making; v. 3, Bibliography of bibliographies in political science, government, and public policy; v. 4, Administrative management; v. 5, Current events and problems of modern society; v. 6, Public opinion, mass behavior, and political psychology; v. 7, Law, jurisprudence, and judicial process; v. 8, Economic regulation: business and government; v. 9, Public policy and the management of science; v. 10, Comparative government and cultures.

The set is a computer-produced bibliography with elaborate indexing for maximum retrievability. Represents a selection of classics and 20th-century writings, with heavy concentration on materials of more recent years. Items are arranged in an arbitrary numerical sequence, with access through the index section of each volume.

§ Continued by: *Political science, government and public policy series. Annual supplement* (1967–79. Princeton, N.J. : Princeton Research Publ. Co., c1969–80) and *Political science abstracts. Annual supplement* (1980– . N.Y. : IFI/Plenum, c1981– .) which are similarly organized and cover contemporary publications.

Bibliography of bibliography

Harmon, Robert B. Political science bibliographies. Metuchen, N.J. : Scarecrow, 1973–1976. v. 1–2. (In progress?).   **CJ14**

Presents classed citations (some briefly annotated) for approximately 1,700 separately published bibliographies. Covers primarily English-language material although a few others (e.g., German, French) are included. Vol. 1 has author and title indexes; v. 2 has an author/title index.   Z7161.A1H35

Current

International bibliography of political science = Bibliographie internationale des sciences sociales / prep. by the International Political Science Association in co-operation with the International Committee for Social Science Documentation, and with the support of the International Studies Conference. v. 1 (1953)– . N.Y. : Tavistock, 1953– . Annual.   **CJ15**

Title page also reads: *International bibliography of the social sciences. Political science.* Absorbed in part *London bibliography of the social sciences* (CA13) in 1989.

Publisher varies. Prefatory matter and headnotes in English and French.

An extensive unannotated listing of books, pamphlets, periodical articles, and official government publications in various languages. Arranged in a detailed classification scheme; includes international relations as well as political science topics. Lists of periodicals consulted and of abbreviations. Indexes by author, place name, and subject (in English and French).

§ Updated by the monthly publication, *International current awareness services : political science and related disciplines* (London : Routledge, 1990–).   Z7163.I64

Periodicals

Martin, Fenton S. Political science journal information / Fenton Martin and Robert Goehlert. 3rd ed. Wash. : American Political Science Assoc., 1990. 111 p.   **CJ16**

1st ed., 1982; 2nd ed., 1984.

Advises political scientists on the submission requirements for 75 journals. Entries, arranged alphabetically by title of journal, include: subscription, frequency, and circulation information; where indexed; types and subjects of articles published; languages; style requirements; length of manuscript, and other submission information; review process; numbers of articles submitted, accepted, and published each year; and publication lag time. Appendixes provide a bibliography on social science publishing, suggestions for evaluating journals and preparing manuscripts, and a list of political science journals. Does not include information on electronic submission. No index.

§ For an older work that covers social science as well as political science journals, see: *Political and social science journals : a handbook for writers and reviewers* (Santa Barbara, Calif. : ABC-Clio, c1983. 236 p.).

Indexes; Abstract journals

ABC pol sci : advance bibliography of contents: political science & government. v. 1 (Mar. 1969)– . [Santa Barbara, Calif. : ABC-Clio], 1969– . 6 no. a year. **CJ17**

Frequency varies.

Lists and indexes the tables of contents of more than 300 international journals in political science, government, law, sociology, and economics. Includes author and subject indexes in each issue, with cumulative annual and five-year indexes.

•Available on CD-ROM as *ABC POL SCI on disc*, 1984– .

Z7161.A214

The combined retrospective index set to journals in political science, 1886–1974 / executive director, Annadel N. Wile, assistant ed., Jeffrey Levi ; with an introduction and user's guide by Evan I. Farber. Wash. : Carrollton Pr., 1977. 8 v. **CJ18**

At head of title: C.R.I.S.

Contents: v. 1, International law, international organizations, international relations, international trade and economics; v. 2, Methodology and theoretical approaches, political behavior and process, political ideologies, political systems, political thought; v. 3, Administration in general, economics in general, financial administration, management in general, organization, departments and functions; v. 4–5, Organization, departments and functions (cont.); v. 6, Organization, departments and functions, personnel, population (cont.); v. 7–8, Author indexes.

More than 115,000 articles from nearly 200 English-language political science journals have been assigned to one or more of 95 subject categories, then computer-sorted by keyword and chronological coverage under each subject category. Each entry provides keyword, brief title, author's name, year, volume and code number for journal title, and beginning page. Endpapers list journal code numbers in numerical sequence and identify the corresponding titles. Z7163.C65

International political science abstracts = Documentation politique internationale. v. 1 (1951)– . Paris : International Political Science Assoc., [1951]– . Bimonthly. **CJ19**

Imprint varies: v. 1 (1951)–22 (1972), Oxford : Basil Blackwell ; Paris : Presses Universitaires de France.

Frequency varies.

Prepared by the International Political Science Association under the auspices of the International Social Science Council, in cooperation with the International Committee for Social Science Information and Documentation and with the financial support of Unesco.

Offers abstracts in English or French to articles selected from more than 1,000 international journals. Entries arranged in six broad areas: political science method and theory, political thinkers and ideas, governmental and administrative institutions, political process, international relations, and national and area studies. Each issue includes a subject index; the last issue of each year contains an author index and a cumulative subject index. JA36.I5

United States political science documents. v. 1 (1975)– . Pittsburgh : Univ. of Pittsburgh, Univ. Center for International Studies, 1976– . Annual. **CJ20**

Issued in two parts: pt. 1, Indexes; pt. 2, Document descriptions.

Publisher varies.

Provides an abstracting service for approximately 150 U.S. journals in the political, social, and policy sciences. Pt. 1 includes five indexes: Author/contributor, Subject, Geographic area, Proper name, and Journal; all give complete bibliographic citations and reference to the abstract printed in pt. 2. Pt. 2 contains paragraph-length abstracts. Subject and geographic area indexes are based on descriptors from the *Political science thesaurus II* (Pittsburgh, Pa. : University Center for International Studies, University of Pittsburgh, c1979).

•A machine-readable version with the same title, covering 1975– , is available online. Also called USPSD. Z7163.U58

Encyclopedias

The Blackwell encyclopaedia of political institutions / ed. by Vernon Bogdanor. Oxford ; N.Y. : Blackwell Reference, 1987. 667 p. **CJ21**

Published (with corrections) in paperback under title: *The Blackwell encyclopedia of political science* (1991).

Identifies and defines key concepts, terms, and individuals related to political institutions. Includes forms of political organization, types of political community, principal parties and movements, political terms, and important political thinkers of the past. Focuses on Western Europe and the U.S. but has a few items relevant to the former Soviet Union (e.g., Nomenklatura, Politburo). Alphabetically arranged entries are signed, contain cross-references, and end with bibliographies. General index.

§ There is some overlap with the companion title, *The Blackwell encyclopaedia of political thought* (CJ22). JA61.B56

The Blackwell encyclopaedia of political thought / ed. by David Miller. Oxford ; N.Y. : Blackwell, 1987. 570 p. **CJ22**

Long entries, alphabetically arranged, provide a comprehensive approach to political ideas, doctrines, and theorists. Discusses ideologies in both historical and contemporary contexts. Emphasizes Western tradition but includes survey articles on Chinese, Hindu, and Islamic political thought. Articles contain cross-references, are signed, and end with bibliographies. General index. JA61.B57

The Cambridge history of medieval political thought c.350–c.1450 / ed. by J. H. Burns. Cambridge ; N.Y. : Cambridge Univ. Pr., 1988. 808 p. **CJ23**

Cambridge history of political thought, 1450–1700 by J. H. Burns with the assistance of Mark Goldie (Cambridge, Eng. ; N.Y. : Cambridge Univ. Pr., 1991. 798 p.).

Companion volumes survey the history of European political thinking in chronologically arranged, signed essays. Each title also includes brief biographies of the writers discussed in the essays, an extensive bibliography, and personal name and subject indexes.

§ Continued chronologically by *The Cambridge history of political thought, 1450–1700* (1991). JA82.C27

A dictionary of conservative and libertarian thought / ed. by Nigel Ashford and Stephen Davies. London ; N.Y. : Routledge, 1991. 288 p. **CJ24**

Treats the ideas and arguments of conservatism and classical liberalism (libertarianism) with emphasis on American and European thought. Lengthy signed entries (two to five pages) are alphabetically arranged and end with brief bibliographies. An alphabetical list of conservatives and liberals cited in the text gives birth and death dates (where applicable), nationality, occupation, and major works. No index.

§ More international in scope than Louis Filler's *Dictionary of American conservatism* (CJ117). JA61.D5

Dictionary of modern political ideologies / M.A. Riff, ed. N.Y. : St. Martin's Pr., 1987. 226 p. **CJ25**

Consists of 42 entries in alphabetic order that treat ideas "since the French and Industrial Revolutions" (*Introd.*) that have shaped and determined political behavior (e.g., the Cold War, the Enlightenment, Islamic fundamentalism, Zionism). The articles are written by specialists, chiefly British, contain cross-references, and end with brief bibliographies. The lack of an index limits its usefulness. JA61.D53

Evans, Graham. The dictionary of world politics : a reference guide to concepts, ideas, and institutions / Graham Evans and Jeffrey Newnham. N.Y. : Simon & Schuster, 1990. 449 p. **CJ26**

Defines the key ideas, concepts, and institutions of world politics (e.g., deterrence, human rights) as well as more specialized terms (e.g., domino theory, no-first-use, SDI). Omits individuals unless they are associated with particular ideas or policies (e.g., Monroe doctrine, Schuman plan) and only includes 20th-century events of continued relevance (e.g., Bay of Pigs, Camp David accords). More than 600 entries, ranging in length from a paragraph to two pages, are alphabetically arranged and contain cross-references. Bibliography; no index.

JA61.E85

Hadjor, Kofi Buenor. Dictionary of Third World terms. London ; N.Y. : I.B. Tauris, c1992. 303 p. **CJ27**

Explains the origins and meaning of key terms, and includes concepts, phrases, events, political parties and movements, organizations, and individuals. Alphabetically arranged, the entries range in length from a paragraph to two pages; they include cross-references and occasionally end with suggestions for further reading. Introduction features a discussion of terminology used to describe the Third World.

D883.H33

Kurian, George Thomas. The encyclopedia of the Third World. 4th ed. N.Y. : Facts on File, c1992. 3 v. (2363 p.) : ill. **CJ28**

1st ed., 1978; 3rd ed., 1987.

In this and its companions, *Encyclopedia of the First World* (1990. 2 v., 1436 p.) and *Encyclopedia of the Second World* (assoc. ed., John J. Karch. 1991. 614 p.), Kurian profiles all independent countries of the world. The divisions, although arbitrary and dated, classify nations as First World (developed or industrialized), Second World (Socialist countries), or Third World (politically nonaligned, economically developing, less industrialized). The works provide information for more than 30 political, economic, and social categories; also included are a post-World War II chronology and a bibliography. The First and Third World titles include descriptions of relevant organizations; each title ends with a general index.

§ See also: *Worldmark encyclopedia of the nations* (CJ35), *The Europa world year book* (CJ94), etc. HC59.7.K87

The Oxford companion to politics of the world / ed. in chief, Joel Krieger ; editors, William A. Joseph ... [et al.]. N.Y. : Oxford Univ. Pr., 1993. 1056 p. : maps. **CJ29**

"Provides a comprehensive guide to international relations and national domestic policies throughout the world."—*Pref.* Offers 650 alphabetically-arranged and signed articles, written by 500 scholars from more than 40 countries. Articles vary in length from short factual entries to major essays. Covers nearly every country, with a focus on the post-World War II period. Includes biographies of major leaders and intellectual figures; 21 interpretive essays analyze significant themes (gender and politics, environmentalism); conventions, treaties, and developments in international law; forms of government and institutions; historical events; international issues; international organizations; and domestic political, economic, and social issues. Cross-references; brief bibliographies. Regional maps. Index. JA61.O95

Plano, Jack C. The international relations dictionary / Jack C. Plano, Roy Olton. 4th ed. Santa Barbara, Calif. : ABC-Clio, c1988. 446 p. **CJ30**

1st ed., 1969; 3rd ed., 1982.

Offers definitions of nearly 600 terms and concepts relating to international relations and foreign policy, together with comments on the significance of each term. Entries are grouped within topical sections rather than being in a single alphabetical sequence; a guide to major concepts provides easy access to terms within these sections. Index of terms. JX1226.P55

Robertson, David. A dictionary of modern politics. 2nd ed. London : Europa Publ., c1991. 495 p. **CJ31**

1st ed., 1985.

Emphasizes key terms and includes concepts (e.g., public interest); political ideologies (e.g., Falangism); influential political thinkers (e.g., Durkheim); organizations (e.g., NATO, PLO); events (e.g., Cuban Missile Crisis); treaties (e.g., SALT); and selected political parties of Western countries (e.g., Parti Socialiste). Alphabetically arranged entries are lengthy (one-half to three pages) and contain cross-references. No index. JA61.R63

Scruton, Roger. A dictionary of political thought. N.Y. : Harper & Row, c1982. 499 p. **CJ32**

"The emphasis ... is conceptual rather than factual, exploring the formulation of doctrines rather than their specific application. Political events are mentioned only when they cast light on intellectual conceptions ... [and] the few proper names ... are those of thinkers rather than those of political figures."—*Pref.* Numerous cross-references. No index. JA61.S37

Shafritz, Jay M. The dictionary of 20th-century world politics / Jay M. Shafritz, Phil Williams, Ronald S. Calinger. N.Y. : H. Holt, 1993. 756 p. ; ill. **CJ33**

Terms, concepts, theories, practices, events, institutions, laws and individuals relevant to contemporary world politics and modern diplomacy appear in more than 4,000 alphabetically-arranged entries. Includes many boxed anecdotes, quotations, chronologies, document excerpts, lists, photographs, and illustrations. Cross-references. An appendix lists key concepts, organized by subject.

§ For fewer but more lengthy entries, see *The Oxford companion to the politics of the world* (CJ29). Other works that are occasionally still useful for historical events and persons include Florence Elliott's *A dictionary of politics* (7th ed. Harmondsworth : Penguin, 1973) and Walter Laqueur's *A dictionary of politics* (Rev. ed. N.Y. : Free Pr., 1974). JA61.S53

Snyder, Louis Leo. Encyclopedia of nationalism. N.Y. : Paragon House, 1990. 445 p. **CJ34**

An introductory essay defining and describing nationalism is followed by alphabetically arranged and cross-referenced entries that range in length from a paragraph to several pages and contain brief bibliographies. Coverage extends to nationalism (e.g., Quebec nationalism), nationalist groups (e.g., Irish Republican Army), concepts and topics (e.g., chauvinism), and individuals (e.g., Yasir Arafat). Bibliography; no index. JC311.S5484

Worldmark encyclopedia of the nations. 7th ed. N.Y. : Worldmark Pr. : J. Wiley, exclusive world distributor, c1988. 5 v. : maps (some col.). **CJ35**

1st ed., 1960; 6th ed., 1984.

Contents: v. 1, United Nations; v. 2, Africa; v. 3, Americas; v. 4, Asia & Oceania; v. 5, Europe.

Provides a wealth of demographic information, plus a bibliography for each country. Vol. 1 also contains information on the polar regions; country comparison tables; glossaries of special terms and religious holidays; a list of abbreviations and acronyms; conversion tables; indexes to countries and territories and to the U.N. and related agencies. Vols. 2–5 are arranged by chapters for each country on the continent covered in the volume.

§ See also George T. Kurian, *Encyclopedia of the Third World* and its companions (CJ28) and *The Europa world year book* (CJ94).

G63.W67

Dictionaries

BBC world service glossary of current affairs / comp. by BBC Monitoring ; ed., Tim Guyse Williams ; contributors, Jackie Bishop ... [et al.]. Chicago : St. James Pr., c1991. 813 p. **CJ36**

Gives brief definitions of terms, including acronyms, political movements and parties, places, events, ethnic groups, organizations, and individuals. Entries arranged alphabetically by country, ending with an international section. Index. D843.B2 1991

Dictionary of international relations terms. [Wash.?] : Dept. of State Library, 1987. 115 p. **CJ37**

Superintendent of Documents classification: S 1.2:In 8/30/987.

1st ed., 1978, and 2nd ed., 1980, both had title: *International relations dictionary.*

Briefly defines or describes terms, phrases, acronyms, abbreviations, organizations, events, treaties, and agreements. Entries are alphabetically arranged and cross-referenced; each has a section that provides bibliographic documentation. List of reference sources.

JX1226.D49

Kruschke, Earl R. The public policy dictionary / Earl R. Kruschke, Byron M. Jackson. Santa Barbara, Calif. : ABC-Clio, c1987. 159 p. (CLIO dictionaries in political science, 15).   **CJ38**

Introduces basic concepts in U.S. public policy and public policy-making. Entries, alphabetically arranged within five broad topical chapters (nature, formulation, implementation, types, and evaluation and impact) include both an up-to-date definition (often ending with cross-references) and a paragraph that describes the term's relevance. Bibliography; general index.   H97.K78

Kurian, George Thomas. Glossary of the Third World : words for understanding Third World peoples & cultures. N.Y. : Facts on File, c1989. 300 p.   **CJ39**

Presents brief, alphabetically-arranged definitions of more than 10,000 words relevant to economic, social, and political aspects of life in the Third World countries. Third World is here defined as all countries of Latin America, Asia (excluding Japan, China, Mongolia, and Israel), and Africa (excluding South Africa). Includes an appendix of language families of the world.

§ Serves as a companion to Kurian's *Encyclopedia of the Third World* (CJ28).   GN307.K87

A new dictionary of political analysis / Geoffrey Roberts and Alistair Edwards. London ; N.Y. : E. Arnold : distr. by Routledge, Chapman and Hall, c1991. 153 p.   **CJ40**

Somewhat misnamed, its broad scope includes not only terms of political analysis (e.g., survey research, game theory) but also political science concepts (e.g., absolutism, privatization, two-party system) typically found in many general political science dictionaries. Entries are alphabetically arranged and cross-referenced.

§ Complements but does not replace *The dictionary of political analysis*, by Jack Plano, Robert E. Riggs, and Helenan S. Robin. (CJ41).   JA61.R625

Plano, Jack C. The dictionary of political analysis / Jack C. Plano, Robert E. Riggs, Helenan S. Robin. 2nd ed. Santa Barbara, Calif. : ABC-Clio, c1982. 197 p. (Clio dictionaries in political science, 3).   **CJ41**

1st ed., 1973.

Focuses on terms used in statistical and behavioral analyses of political data. Alphabetically arranged and cross-referenced entries feature a paragraph of definition followed by one giving the term's significance. Bibliography. Index.   JA61.P57

Smith, John William. The urban politics dictionary / John W. Smith, John S. Klemanski. Santa Barbara, Calif. : ABC-Clio, c1990. 613 p.   **CJ42**

Covers approximately 600 terms relating to 20th-century urban politics and life (e.g., citizen advisory board, enterprise zone, gridlock, sinking fund), primarily in the U.S. and Canada. Alphabetically arranged entries include both a descriptive definition and a paragraph analyzing the term's historical and contemporary significance. Cross-references; suggested readings. General index.   JS48.S65

Terminology

Thematic list of descriptors—political science = Liste thématique des descripteurs—science politique / prepared on behalf of UNESCO by the International Committee for Social Science Information and Documentation. London ; N.Y. : Routledge, 1989. 481 p.   **CJ43**

Companion to *International bibliography of political science* (CJ15). For description, see CE52.   Z695.1.P63T48

Quotations

Eigen, Lewis D. The Macmillan dictionary of political quotations / Lewis D. Eigen and Jonathan P. Siegel. N.Y. : Macmillan, c1993. 785 p.   **CJ44**

Offers more than 12,000 quotations arranged alphabetically by author within 99 topical chapters. Gives citations for quotes and translates any quotes not in English (omitting original language). Author and concept indexes to chapter and quotation numbers.

PN6084.P6E54

Political quotations : a collection of notable sayings on politics from antiquity through 1989 / Daniel B. Baker, ed. Detroit : Gale, c1990. 509 p.   **CJ45**

Some 4,000 quotations on political topics, dating from biblical times to the present, are chronologically arranged under 53 general subject headings (e.g., Democracy, Ethics in politics, War and peace). Each includes the source and the version in the original language if appropriate. Author and keyword indexes cite entry rather than page numbers.

§ *See also* Lewis D. Eigen and Jonathan P. Siegal, *The Macmillan dictionary of political quotations* (CJ44), and Michael C. Thomsett and Jean Freestone Thomsett, *Political quotations* (Jefferson, N.C. : McFarland, c1994. 344 p.). Other useful works include: Robert Stewart, *A dictionary of political quotations* (London : Europa, 1984); Charles Henning, *The wit and wisdom of politics* (Expanded ed. Goldon, Colo. : Fulcrum, 1992).   PN6084.P6P64

Directories

Directory of European political scientists / comp. and ed. by the Central Services, European Consortium for Political Research, University of Essex. 4th fully rev. ed. München ; N.Y. : Zell, 1985. 627 p.   **CJ46**

1st ed., 1972; 3rd fully rev. ed., 1979.

For nearly 2,500 political scientists working in Europe, provides alphabetically arranged entries that include: date of birth, nationality, address, degrees awarded, title of doctoral dissertation, career appointments, selected publications, research interests, and subject specialization. Subject specialization index.   JA84.E9D57

Directory on European training institutions in the fields of bilateral and multilateral diplomacy, public administration and management, economic and social development = Répertoire des institutions européennes de formation, dans les domaines de la diplomatie bilatérale et multilatérale, de l'administration publique et de la gestion, du développement économique et social / United Nations Institute for Training and Research. 1987– . N.Y. : United Nations, 1987– . **CJ47**

Lists institutions alphabetically by English-language name within country groupings. Entries are in English or French, depending on the language the institution used in its response to the questionnaire, and give name, address, telephone number, date of establishment, director, number of staff, objectives, main activities, publications, fields covered, teaching languages, etc. Excludes universities except for those with activities beyond regular academic teaching. Also includes a summary of the activities of the European Office of the United Nations Institute for Training and Research. Institutional name index.

Governmental Research Association (U.S.). Directory of organizations and individuals professionally engaged in governmental research and related activities. 1935– . Ocean Gate, N.J. [etc.] : Governmental Research Assoc., 1935– .   **CJ48**

Supersedes *Directory of organizations engaged in governmental research*, 1935–49. Title varies; cover title frequently begins "G.R.A. directory ... ."

Currently in three sections: (1) Local and state agencies (alphabetical by city within states); (2) National agencies (alphabetical by agency); (3) Members of the Governmental Research Association (alphabetical by name). Entries include address, telephone and fax numbers, and names of professional personnel for the agencies in the first two sections.   JK3.G627

Graduate faculty and programs in political science : a directory to the faculty and graduate degree programs of U.S. and Canadian institutions. Rev. 14th ed. (1992–94)– . Wash. : American Political Science Association, 1992– .   **CJ49**

Continues *Guide to graduate study in political science* (1972–89).

Lists colleges and universities in the U.S. and Canada granting graduate degrees in political science, with descriptions of their master's and doctoral programs. Alphabetical by institution (in two groups—U.S., then Canada), each entry provides address, telephone number, tuition costs, application deadlines, requirements for admission and degrees, financial aid, program description, and faculty list. A separate section provides a statistical summary for each institution (e.g., number of students admitted; women, Latino, African-American students). Faculty and institution indexes.

§The Association's companion volume, *Directory of undergraduate political science faculty* (Wash. : American Political Science Association, 1984–), provides a directory to political science departments and faculty at U.S. colleges with only undergraduate programs.

JA88.U6G8

Financial aids; Grants

Search for security : the Access guide to foundations in peace, security, and international relations / ed. by Anne Allen. Wash. : Access, c1989. 191 p. : ill.   **CJ50**

Designed to assist both those seeking and those awarding grants in peace, security, and international relations. In four parts: (1) an analysis of funding in these fields, including trends and changes in granting agencies; (2) profiles of 158 foundations, describing their priorities and providing guidelines for applicants and selected financial data; (3) information concerning U.S. government and government-funded organizations that award grants in these fields; (4) a list of foundations by activity funded, issues funded, and geographic region of concern. An appendix presents tables on the geographic preferences, amount given, assets, etc., of foundations. Index of foundations.

JX1905.5.S43

Handbooks

Elazar, Daniel Judah. Federal systems of the world : a handbook of federal, confederal, and autonomy arrangements / comp. and ed. by Daniel J. Elazar and the staff of the Jerusalem Center for Public Affairs. Harlow, Essex, U.K. : Longman Current Affairs, c1991. 402 p. : ill.   **CJ51**

Aims "to inventory and describe all known examples of federal and autonomous arrangements, compare their basic features, and classify them by form."—*Introd.* In two alphabetically-arranged sections: (1) Federal, federacy/associated state, home rule arrangements (e.g., Brazil, Liechtenstein, Guam); and (2) Confederal arrangements (e.g., Association of East Asian Nations, European Communities). Entries generally include a descriptive introduction, territorial structure and population, general government structure, constitutional principles and design, political culture, political dynamics, recent constitutional developments, and a bibliography. Appendixes show distribution of functions between general governments and constituent units, shared-rule arrangements; home-rule territories, etc. No index.   JC355.E384

Encyclopedia of government and politics / ed. by Mary Hawkesworth and Maurice Kogan. London ; N.Y. : Routledge, 1992. 2 v.   **CJ52**

Covers twentieth century political studies through 84 signed essays, written by scholars, that give an overview and a critical analysis

of the topic. Arranged in broad categories: introduction, theory, ideologies, institutions, forces and processes, forces in the nation state, policy making and politics, international relations, and major issues in contemporary world politics. Includes bibliographies. Index.

JA61.C66

Greenstein, Fred I. Handbook of political science / Fred I. Greenstein, Nelson W. Polsby. Reading, Mass. : Addison-Wesley, c1975. 9 v.   **CJ53**

Contents: v. 1, Political science: scope and theory; v. 2, Micropolitical theory; v. 3, Macropolitical theory; v. 4, Nongovernmental politics; v. 5, Governmental institutions and processes; v. 6, Policies and policy-making; v. 7, Strategies of inquiry; v. 8, International politics; [v. 9], Cumulative index.

A collection of review articles by scholars representing the major areas of political science, similar in concept to Gardner Lindzey and Elliot Aronson, *Handbook of social psychology* (2nd ed., 1968–69. 5 v.). Each essay concludes with extensive references. Author and subject index in each volume. Extensive review of each volume in *American political science review* 71 (Dec. 1977): 1621–36.   JA71.H35

International handbook of political science / ed. by William G. Andrews. Westport, Conn. : Greenwood, 1982. 464 p.   **CJ54**

A survey of intellectual, institutional, and educational development is followed by alphabetically-arranged country chapters, each surveying the evolution of the field in that country since 1945 (e.g., intellectual structure, teaching, research, associations, relationship with politics). Chapters are written by political scientists, are signed, and end with bibliographies. Appendixes provide information on the International Political Science Association, national associations, etc. Also contains a bibliography of political science works for countries not treated separately. Index.   JA71.I57

International handbook of the ombudsman / ed. by Gerald E. Caiden. Westport, Conn. : Greenwood, 1983. 2 v.   **CJ55**

Contents: v. 1, Evolution and present function; v. 2, Country surveys.

Offers signed essays with notes and bibliographies on the ombudsman's role and function, and on the operations of ombudsman offices in countries around the world. Appendixes include an annotated model ombudsman statute, information on the International Ombudsman Institute, etc. Bibliography. Index in each volume.

JF1525.O45I55

Johnson, Janet Buttolph. Political science research methods / Janet Buttolph Johnson, Richard A. Joslyn. 2nd ed. Wash. : CQ Pr., c1991. 407 p. : ill.   **CJ56**

1st ed., 1986.

Designed for students as an introduction to political science research. Shows how to conduct empirical research projects, evaluate research, and understand statistical calculations through the use of four case studies. Chapters cover different aspects of the research process (e.g., literature review, sampling, data analysis) and include bibliographic notes, definitions of terms, and exercises or suggested readings. Concludes with an annotated example of a research report. Appendix gives table of chi-square values. Index.   JA73.J64

Munro, David. A world record of major conflict areas / David Munro, Alan J. Day. Chicago : St. James Pr., 1990. 373 p. : maps.   **CJ57**

Describes 28 current areas of conflict, with chapters for each, in five sections: Africa, Middle East, Asia/Far East, Americas, and Europe. Includes not only widely known countries such as Afghanistan, but also less familiar regions such as East Timor. Chapters follow a standard format, beginning with a map and an introduction describing the historical background and current status of the conflict, together with a chronology, followed by sections outlining key personalities, important locations, and other ingredients such as organizations, treaties, ethnic groups, etc. Suggestions for further reading at end of each chapter. Brief general bibliography.   D842

Party organisations : a data handbook on party organisations in western democracies, 1960–90 / ed. by Richard S. Katz and Peter Mair. London : Sage, 1992. v. 1 (973 p.). (In progress).   **CJ58**

Provides "long-term, cross-national, and systematically comparable data on the development of party organisations."—*Pref.* The first of 3 v.; presents data on 79 parties in 12 democracies (Austria, Belgium, Denmark, Finland, Germany, Ireland, Italy, Netherlands, Norway, Sweden, U.K., U.S.) since 1960 and three transnational party federations in the European Community. Later volumes will focus on interpretation. Arranged by country, ending with a chapter on the transnational parties, each beginning with an introduction that includes bibliography, sources, glossary, and party codes. Data are given in tables within five major groups: (1) political context; (2) membership; (3) staff; (4) party structure; (5) party finance. Lists parties included in data set and core tables of data included for each country. Introduction explains study, data, and organization of the work. No index.

Political risk yearbook. 1987– . Syracuse, N.Y. : Political Risk Services, 1987– .   **CJ59**
Publisher varies. Publ. 1987–90 by Frost & Sullivan, N.Y.
Published annually in seven volumes.
Contents: v. 1, North and Central America; v. 2, Middle East and North Africa; v. 3, South America; v. 4, Sub-Saharan Africa; v. 5, Asia and the Pacific; v. 6, Europe: countries of the European Community; v. 7, Europe: outside the European Community.
Developed by Political Risk Services for students, faculty, and researchers, this annual publication draws on data gathered from 250 country specialists throughout the world and provides probability forecasts on political and economic matters in addition to political, economic, and social data. Covers 85 countries that are internationally significant, alphabetically dividing each volume into sections by country. Each country report contains: an executive summary; update data (if available before publication); map and list of territorial and maritime disputes; fact sheet; background review; information on politically important individuals and organizations, the regime's stability, level of turmoil, international investment restrictions, trade restrictions, economic policies; and a five-year political and economic forecast projecting three possible scenarios. No index.

Political scandals and causes célèbres since 1945 : an international reference compendium / contributors, Louis Allen ... [et al.]. Chicago : St. James Pr., [1991]. 478 p.   **CJ60**
Brings together information on major political scandals since 1945 (e.g., Waldheim affair, Iran-Contra). Selection was based on the event being political in content or implication and being identifiable as a self-contained episode. Entries examine the evolution and impact of the scandal, provide a summary of the facts and leading interpretations, and put the episode into historical context. Entries are signed, contain cross-references and are arranged chronologically within alphabetically arranged country sections. Personal name index.

Revolutionary and dissident movements : an international guide / contributors, Guy Arnold ... [et al.]. 3rd ed. Burnt Mill, Harlow, England : Longman, 1988. 401 p.   **CJ61**
1st ed., 1983, had title: *Political dissent: an international guide to dissidents, extra-parliamentary, guerilla and illegal political movements.* 2nd ed., 1988, ed. by Henry W. Degenhardt.
Arranged alphabetically by country. Describes the political situation (as of mid-1991) and gives entries for dissident movements that include history, purpose, activities, and leadership. Excludes some historical information found in earlier editions. Information based on the resources of *Keesing's record of world events* (DA187). Select bibliography; index to names of organizations and movements.
§ *See also* Peter Janke and Richard Sim, *Guerrilla and terrorist organisations* (Brighton, Eng. : Harvester Pr., 1983) for its historical information and extensive bibliographies.   JC328.3.D43

Statesman's year-book : statistical and historical annual of the states of the world. v. 1 (1864)– . London ; N.Y. : Macmillan, 1864– . Annual.   **CJ62**
Not an almanac of miscellaneous statistics, but a concise and reliable manual of descriptive and statistical information about the gov-

ernments of the world. Contents vary somewhat but usually cover: (1) British Commonwealth; (2) United States; (3) Other countries, arranged alphabetically. Recent issues have included a section on international organizations. For each country gives: information about its ruler, constitution and government, area, population, religion, social welfare, instruction, justice and crime, state finance, defense, production and industry, agriculture, commerce, navigation, communications, banking and credit, money, weights and measures, diplomatic representatives, etc. A valuable feature is the selected bibliography of statistical and other books of reference given for each country.
The most useful of all the general yearbooks; indispensable in any type of library.   JA51.S7

Chronologies

Jessup, John E. A chronology of conflict and resolution, 1945–1985. N.Y. : Greenwood, 1989. 942 p.   **CJ63**
Briefly describes significant events relating to international and intranational conflicts, beginning with September 2, 1945 (shortly after the end of World War II), giving day, country, and an account of what transpired, typically ranging in length from less than a sentence to several sentences. Glossary of abbreviations. A 96-page general index has few subheadings; some headings are heavily posted.   U42.J47

Yearbooks

Countries of the world and their leaders yearbook. 1980– . Detroit : Gale. Annual.   **CJ64**
1st ed., 1974, had title: *Countries of the world*; 2nd–5th ed., 1975–9, had title: *Countries of the world and their leaders.* Frequency varied.
Subtitle (varies): A compilation of U.S. Department of State reports on contemporary political and economic conditions, governmental personnel and policies, political parties, religions, history, education, press, radio and TV, climate, and other characteristics of selected countries of the world: together with travel alerts, passport and visa information, world health information for travelers, and customs and duty tips for returning residents.
Issued in 2 v., 1984– .
Gathers and reprints current publications, including *Chiefs of state and cabinet members of foreign governments* (CJ83); *Geographic notes*; listings for U.S. embassies, consulates, and foreign service posts; *Background notes* (*see* CJ185); international travel information; and descriptions of international treaty organizations. Updated by a mid-year supplement.   G122.C67

Biography

The Columbia dictionary of political biography / the Economist Books. N.Y. : Columbia Univ. Pr., c1991. 335 p.   **CJ65**
Portrays 2,000 heads of state, top ministers, party leaders, influential politicians, prominent public servants, trade unionists, lobbyists, etc. in alphabetically arranged sketches. International in coverage; includes those who were alive and active as of Dec. 31, 1990. Sketches give brief biographical information (e.g., birth date, education, career) and a summary of the individual's policies, accomplishments, and importance. Has a "Stop press" chronology covering Jan.–March 1991, a glossary, and a list of abbreviations. Personal name index by country.
§ For other current biographies, see also: *Who's who in international affairs* (London : Europa, 1990–), *Current leaders of nations* (Lansdale, Pa. : Current Leaders Publ. Co., 1990–), *International year book and statesmen's who's who* (London : Burke's Peerage Ltd., 1953–), and *Who's who in European institutions and enterprises* (Zu-

rich : Who's Who, 1993–). For those both living and dead who made a lasting contribution to politics, see: *Chambers dictionary of political biography* (Edinburgh : Chambers, c1991).   D108.C65

Kuehl, Warren F. Biographical dictionary of internationalists. Westport, Conn. : Greenwood, 1983. 934 p.   **CJ66**

Offers signed biographical sketches of persons from many countries who "held important or leadership positions in national or international nongovernmental societies or associations to promote the concept of world organization or cooperation"; who "held important posts in functional international bodies"; who "gained public recognition as originators or exponents" of relevant ideas, plans, schemes, etc.; who "sought actively to promote transnationalism in nonpolitical areas" or who "consistently represented by their lifestyle, attitudes, and beliefs an international community idea of transnational cooperation."—*Pref.* Includes only persons now deceased who were still alive after 1800. Bibliographies; chronology; index.

§ Companion volume: *Biographical dictionary of modern peace leaders* (CJ700), ed. by Harold Josephson; the two works cross-reference each other.   JC361.K79

Opfell, Olga S. Women prime ministers and presidents. Jefferson, N.C. : McFarland, c1993. 237 p. : :ill.   **CJ67**

Portrays 21 women, each of whom was the first woman to serve as the head of state in her country. Chronologically arranged essays include photograph or portrait, biographical matter, and details of the individual's political career. Bibliography of books, organized by biographee's name. Index.   D839.5.O64

Rees, Philip. Biographical dictionary of the extreme right since 1890. N.Y. : Simon & Schuster, 1991. 418 p.   **CJ68**

Contains nearly 500 entries, international in scope, alphabetically arranged, sketches typically ranging from one-half to a full page in length followed by several references. Besides political leaders, includes philosophers, novelists, others. The author's intent is to be "critical and evaluative" without "unwarranted judgment and polemic."—*Introd.*   D412.6.R39

The Routledge dictionary of twentieth-century political thinkers / ed. by Robert Benewick and Philip Green. London ; N.Y. : Routledge, 1992. 244 p.   **CJ69**

A guide to individuals closely identified with a political idea, concept, or system of thought. Alphabetically arranged, signed, cross-referenced entries cover political philosophers, writers, and activists (non-Western and Western). Each entry includes biographical data; a narrative describing ideas, activities, and contributions; a list of important writings; and a brief bibliography. No index.   JA83.R725

Statesmen who changed the world : a bio-bibliographical dictionary of diplomacy / ed. by Frank W. Thackeray and John E. Findling. Westport, Conn. : Greenwood, 1993. 669 p.   **CJ70**

Treats 62 statesmen (heads of state, foreign ministers, etc.) of the Western world in essays written by scholars. The essays are arranged alphabetically and contain cross-references; each offers information on the person's life and career, with emphasis on involvement in international affairs; an annotated bibliography that includes archival resources; and a bibliography of signficant works by and about the individual. Appendixes include glossaries of historical names; conferences and treaties; diplomatic, political, and military events; and organizations and terms, as well as a list of heads of state by country. General index.   D108.S73

Who's who of women in world politics. London ; N.Y. : Bowker-Saur, c1990. 311 p. : ill.   **CJ71**

Offers more than 1,500 alphabetically arranged entries for women who are heads of state, members of government or national legislatures, party or trade union leaders, or regional leaders. Each entry covers major aspects of personal life and political and professional career and interests, although some entries contain only name, office held, and address. A statistical survey gives the portion of females in top

government posts by country. Personal name index by country. A review in *RQ* 32 (Fall, 1992) : p. 123–5, notes some shortcomings.   HQ1236.W455

Atlases

Anderson, Ewan W. Atlas of world political flashpoints : a sourcebook of geopolitical crisis / by Ewen W. Anderson ; maps produced by Gareth Owen under the direction of Don Shewan. N.Y. : Facts on File, 1993. 243 p. : maps.   **CJ72**

Focuses on 80 major areas of past, present, or potential conflict. For each area, gives geographic description, history and importance, current status, map, and bibliography. Alphabetically arranged. Index.   G1046.F1A5

Chaliand, Gérard. A strategic atlas : comparative geopolitics of the world's powers / Gérard Chaliand and Jean-Pierre Rageau. 3rd ed. N.Y. : HarperPerennial, 1992. 223 p. : maps in color; 18 x 25 cm.   **CJ73**

1st ed., 1983; 2nd ed., 1985; "1st Perennial Library ed.," 1990.

Translation of: *Atlas stratégique* (Paris : Librairie Arthème Fayard, 1983).

Treats cultural as well as the usual political, military, and economic factors, and pays careful attention to smaller, regional powers. In addition, contains not only maps with the usual Mercator projections, but also polar projections in order to convey the true size of oceans and show why polar regions are not barriers to missiles and nuclear submarines. Arranged topically, with chapters on such considerations as historical context, natural constraints (such as deserts), and security perceptions of individual nations. No index, but has a detailed table of contents.   G1046.F1C513

Wheatcroft, Andrew. The world atlas of revolutions / Andrew Wheatcroft ; [cartography by Malcolm Porter, assisted by Duncan Mackay]. N.Y. : Simon & Schuster, c1983. 208 p. : ill., maps in color ; 29 cm.   **CJ74**

Describes and graphically presents information on revolutions, 1765–1978. Covers each situation with several pages of text, illustrations, and maps. Bibliography; index.   G1035.W5

NATIONAL POLITICS AND GOVERNMENT

General works

Guides

Blackey, Robert. Revolutions and revolutionists : a comprehensive guide to the literature. Santa Barbara, Calif. : ABC-Clio, c1982. 488 p. (War/peace bibliography series, no. 17).   **CJ75**

1976 ed. had title: *Modern revolutions and revolutionists.*

A bibliographic guide to more than 6,200 printed sources in Western languages, on concepts and aspects of revolutions from ancient times through 1979. Also provides a brief chronology and selections of quotations on revolution. Chronological and geographical arrangement; indexed by author and subject.   Z7164.R54B5

Bibliography

Miewald, Robert D. The bureaucratic state : an annotated bibliography. N.Y. : Garland, 1984. 601 p. (Public affairs and administration series, 6 ; Garland reference library of social science, 166). **CJ76**

Lists more than 2,700 English-language books, articles, and pamphlets written since the mid-19th century, arranged in topical chapters (e.g., American bureaucracy, historical bureaucracies, national studies). Author index.   Z7164.A2M53

Encyclopedias

World encyclopedia of political systems & parties / ed. by George E. Delury. 2nd ed. N.Y. : Facts on File, c1987. 2 v. **CJ77**

1st ed., 1983.

Contents: v. 1, Afghanistan–Luxembourg; v. 2. Madagascar–Zimbabwe, smaller countries and microstates, index.

Articles describe each country's executive, legislative, and judicial functions; regional and local structures; electoral system; history, organization, policy, membership, financing, and leadership of individual parties; other political forces; and national prospects. Each article ends with suggestions for further reading. List of acronyms; general index.

§ A similar work, Alan J. Day, *Political parties of the world* (3rd ed. Chicago : St. James Pr., 1988), is useful for its listing of party publications. Both titles are somewhat outdated due to more recent events in the former Soviet Union. For current information, see such works as the *Political handbook of the world* (CJ95).   JF2011.W67

Directories

Morby, John E. Dynasties of the world : a chronological and genealogical handbook. Oxford ; N.Y. : Oxford Univ. Pr., 1989. 254 p.   **CJ78**

A register of major past and present dynasties and their lineage. Arranged by broad geographic area (e.g., Ancient Near East, Europe, Africa), further subdivided by country. For each dynasty, chronological tables list names of rulers, length of reign, relationship to previous rulers, and sobriquets. Also includes supplementary notes and brief bibliographies. Excludes dynasties where no reliable information is available (e.g., kingdom of the Medes, most Hindu Indian royal lines). Geographic and dynasty name index.   CS27.M67

Ó Maoláin, Ciarán. The radical right : a world directory. Burnt Mill, Harlow, Essex, England : Longman ; Santa Barbara, Calif. : Distr. by ABC-Clio, c1987. 500 p.   **CJ79**

Describes 3,000 organizations in 81 countries and four regions or possessions (e.g., Northern Ireland). The groups are as diverse as ultraright death squads and the Republican Party of the U.S. (the latter said to have a "mainstream conservative" orientation), but essentially they represent three overlapping strands: ultraconservative, anticommunist, and right-wing extremist. Each entry is introduced by a brief treatment of the country's political system, recent history, and the evolution of its far right. For most, there follows a list of the country's active organizations, describing their orientation, history, leadership, policies, etc. For some, there are also other sections: Defunct organizations (giving brief descriptions or histories); Other organizations (with brief mention of minor groups); and Individuals, with brief biographical information. Subject index.   HS2303.O18

The right guide : a guide to conservative and right-of-center organizations. 1993– . Ann Arbor, Mich. : Economics America, Inc., c1993– . Annual.   **CJ80**

A guide to right-of-center organizations, excluding racist and hate groups. Alphabetically arranged profiles of U.S. organizations typically give name, address, telephone and fax numbers, contact, officers or principals, publications, mission or interests, number of employees, etc. Lists international organizations (alphabetical by continent, then country), providing name, address, and telephone number. Includes titles and addresses of periodicals and campus newspapers, and essays on selected organizations. Bibliography. Subject index to U.S. profiles; keyword index.

§Focuses more on the U.S. than Ciarán Ó Maoláin's *Radical right* (CJ79), and is more descriptive than Laird M. Wilcox's *Guide to the American right* (see CJ139).   HS2321.R54

The world directory of diplomatic representation. 1st ed.– . London : Europa, 1992– .   **CJ81**

Provides basic directory information for more than 33,000 ambassadors, high commissioners, consuls, and other diplomatic personnel. Organized by country to which the individual is posted. Also gives listings for certain international organizations such as the U.N. and NATO. Personal name index by country of origin.

§ In addition to earlier editions of such works as *The Europa world year book* (CJ94), a number of older titles are suitable for historical research on diplomats. Examples: *Almanach de Gotha* (Gotha : Perthes, 1763–1960); *Repertorium der diplomatischen Vertreter aller Länder seit dem Westfälischen Frieden (1648)* (Zurich : Fretz & Wasmuth, 1936–1965. 3 v.).   JX1625.W67

Worldwide government directory, with international organizations. 1987–88– . Wash. : Belmont Publications, c1987– . Annual.   **CJ82**

Continues *Lambert's worldwide government directory, with inter-governmental organizations* (Wash. : Lambert Publ., 1981–84). Publisher varies.

Pt. 1 serves as a directory, organized alphabetically by country, to government officials in more than 190 countries. Pt. 2 provides alphabetical entries for international organizations. No index.   JF37.L345

Registers

Chiefs of state and cabinet members of foreign governments. [Wash.] : National Foreign Assessment Center, [1966?–]. Monthly.   **CJ83**

Superintendent of Documents classification: PREX 3.11/22.

Issued bimonthly, 1986–mid-1993. Also issued in microform.

Formerly issued by the Central Intelligence Agency.

A country-by-country listing without biographical or other information. Each monthly issue supersedes the previous one. Includes "as many governments of the world as is considered practicable, some of them not yet fully independent and others not officially recognized by the United States."—*Pref.*   JF37.U5

Da Graça, John V. Heads of state and government. N.Y. : New York Univ. Pr., 1985. 265 p.   **CJ84**

A register of leaders of 13 major international organizations and 500 present-day nations, provinces, regions, and territories. Arrangement is alphabetic by country; for each, a short historical note is followed by a list of leaders, chronological under the title of their office, their dates in office, family relationship where appropriate, political party affiliation, how the term of office ended if not by natural cause. The work lists some 10,000 leaders, but the absence of a personal name index limits its usefulness.   JF37.D3

Henige, David P. Colonial governors from the fifteenth century to the present : a comprehensive list. Madison : Univ. of Wisconsin Pr., 1970. 461 p.   **CJ85**

Presents lists of the governors or other colonial administrators "of the European colonies [including American and Australian] from 1415, when the Portuguese occupied Ceuta, to the present time."—*Pref.* Arrangement is by name of the ruling country or "imperial system," with colonies listed alphabetically thereunder. For each colony there is a historical note followed by the chronological list of governors. Both a general index and an index of governors' names.

JV431.H45

Handbooks

Cook, Chris. The Facts on File world political almanac. N.Y. : Facts on File, c1992. 490 p.   **CJ86**

1st ed., 1989.

A concise and convenient assemblage of facts on post-World War II political developments. Divided into sections: International political organizations and movements; Heads of state and government; Legislatures and constitutions; Treaties, alliances, and diplomatic agreements; Political parties; Elections; The violent world; The nuclear age; Population and urbanization; Dictionary of political terms, events and actions, 1943–91; and Biographical dictionary. General index.

D843.C5797

Cossolotto, Matthew. The almanac of transatlantic politics, 1991–92. Wash. : Brassey's (U.S.), c1991. 428 p. : ill.   **CJ87**

A handy compilation of information on 21 countries of Western Europe and North America. In country chapters, covers economics; government; political developments, parties, and leaders; and recent elections. Each chapter also includes key political terms and slogans, a chronology of modern political history, and the English version of part or all of the lyrics of the country's national anthem. Additional chapters treat the European Community, NATO, and six Eastern European countries. Subject index.   JN94.A11C67

Elections since 1945 : a worldwide reference compendium / gen. ed., Ian Gorvin. Burnt Mill, Harlow, Essex, England : Longman ; Chicago : St. James Pr., 1989. 420 p. : ill.   **CJ88**

Describes trends in national presidential and legislative elections for sovereign states, 1945–88 or, in the case of former colonies, from the date of independence. Entries are alphabetical by country (plus a section for the European Parliament), and include electoral system, evolution of suffrage, principal political parties, and an electoral summary. Ranging in length from one to nine pages, entries vary as to completeness of information: some (e.g., U.K., France) contain charts, an electoral map, and many details while others (e.g., Canada, Romania) do not mention political leaders. A brief appendix explains proportional representation electoral systems. No index.

§ More current information can be found in Thomas S. Arms and Eileen Riley, *World elections on file* (CJ92), or other yearbooks and handbooks such as *The Europa world year book* (CJ94) or *Political handbook of the world* (CJ95).   JF1001.E378

Mackie, Thomas T. The international almanac of electoral history / Thomas T. Mackie & Richard Rose. Fully rev. 3rd ed. Wash. : Congressional Quarterly Inc., c1991. 511 p.   **CJ89**

1st ed., 1974; 2nd ed., 1982.

Aims "to provide a complete and accurate compilation of election results in Western nations since the beginning of competitive national elections."—*Introd.* Begins with the first election for each country in which the majority of parliamentary seats were contested, and in which most candidates ran under party labels. Each of the 25 countries is covered in a separate chapter, arranged alphabetically; each chapter includes an introduction with sources, a list of political parties,, and statistical tables of election results (e.g., total votes, votes by party). Covers elections through 1989. Appendix on electoral systems. No index.

§ An older work, covering many of the same countries but still useful for its historical discussions and annotated bibliographies, is *International guide to electoral statistics* (The Hague : Mouton, 1969–).   JF1001.M17

Parliaments of the world : a comparative reference compendium. 2nd ed. N.Y. : Facts on File, c1986. 2 v. (1422 p.).   **CJ90**

1st ed., 1976.

Prepared by the International Centre for Parliamentary Documentation of the Inter-Parliamentary Union.

Covers 83 parliaments, as they existed on June 30, 1985, in a series of comparative tables. Consists of 15 sections (e.g., Parliament and its membership, Parliamentary procedure, Parliament and the media), many subdivided. Within sections, data relating to the parliaments is usually alphabetically arranged by country and presented in tabular form preceded by introductory text. Subject index.   JF501.P36

Truhart, Peter. Regents of nations : systematic chronology of states and their political representatives in past and present : a biographical reference book. Munich ; N.Y. : Saur, 1984–1988. 3 v. (4258 p.).   **CJ91**

Contents: pt.1, Africa/America; pt. 2, Asia/Australia–Oceania; pt. 3/1, Central, Eastern, Northern, Southern, South East Europe; pt. 3/2, Western Europe; addenda-corrigenda; general index.

Title, prefatory matter, and headings also in German.

This impressive compilation lists heads of state, governors of dependent territories and member states of federations, cabinet members, foreign and colonial ministers, heads of counter-governments, and pretenders from the beginning of recorded history (including legendary periods). Entries arranged by continent, region, and country, then chronologically. For each name, gives title, period in office, place and date of birth and death if available, relation to predecessor, and any significant events. General bibliography in pt. 1, plus bibliographies for each region. Pt. 3 has three indexes; (1) Regions, states, confederations; (2) Civilizations, tribes, dynasties; (3) Selected personalities, titles.

§ A similar and still useful work is Martha Ross, *Rulers and governments of the world* (London ; N.Y. : Bowker, 1977–78).   JF37.T78

World elections on file / editors, Thomas S. Arms and Eileen Riley. N.Y. : Facts on File, c1987 . 2 v. (loose-leaf) : ill.   **CJ92**

Updated quarterly.

Compiles articles on every country in the world, giving current heads of state and government, dates of next elections, political outlook, profiles of the major parties and leading political figures, descriptions of the political and electoral system, results of recent elections, and comments on the validity of the elections. Within geographic regions, countries are arranged alphabetically. A supplement in v. 2 relates election results for major democracies since World War II.

JF1001.W6

World government / gen. ed., Peter J. Taylor. N.Y. : Oxford Univ. Pr., 1990. 256 p. : ill. (some col.), maps.   **CJ93**

Surveys the field of political geography, concentrating on the nature of government and governing institutions throughout the world. Concepts treated in three thematic chapters covering sovereignty and territory, power within states, and relations between states are used to explore the history and current roles of governing institutions in chapters on various regions (e.g., Middle East, Southern Africa). Extensively illustrated with photographs and maps. Glossary; bibliography; general index.   JF51.W65

Yearbooks

The Europa world year book. 30th ed. (1989)– . London : Europa Publications Limited, c1989– . Annual.   **CJ94**

Represents a change of title for the *Europa year book*.

History: (1) *Europa year book*, 1926–29; *Europa, the encyclopedia of Europe*, 1930–58. These were looseleaf publications covering: international organizations, including the United Nations and its specialized agencies; world politics, giving the texts of international documents, etc.; and information on each European country. (2) *Orbis, encyclopaedia of extra-European countries*, 1938–59. Also looseleaf; gave the same type of information for the countries of Africa, the Americas, Asia, and Australasia, i.e., surveys and directories of political, industrial, financial, cultural, educational, and scientific organizations. The bound volumes, begun in 1959, supersede the looseleaf series; title changed to *Europa year book* with 1959 volume. 1959 issued in one volume; 1960–88 issued in two volumes: v. 1, covering international organizations and Europe; v. 2, covering Africa, the Americas, Asia, and Australasia. Beginning with 1963, information on educational and learned societies and institutions is omitted and carried only in *World of learning* (AL13). Current title began with 1989 ed. Now issued in two volumes, with v. 1 covering international organizations and the first group of alphabetically arranged country entries and v. 2 the remainder of the country entries.

Covers information on the United Nations, its agencies, and other international organizations followed by detailed information about each country, arranged alphabetically in each volume, giving an introductory survey, a statistical survey, the government, political parties, the constitution, judicial system, diplomatic representation, religion, press, publishers, radio and television, finance, trade and industry, transport, and tourism.

§ Similar Europa publications focusing on a particular geographic area include: *The Far East and Australasia* (1969–), *Middle East and North Africa* (1948–), *The European Communities encyclopedia and directory* (1991–), *Africa South of the Sahara* (DD94), *Western Europe* (1989–), *The USA and Canada* (1990–), *South America, Central America, and the Caribbean* (1986– . DB295), and *Eastern Europe and the Commonwealth of Independent States* (1992–). See also: *Clements' encyclopedia of world government* (Dallas : Political Research, Inc., c1974–).   JN1.E85

Political handbook of the world. 1975– . Binghamton, N.Y. : CSA Publ., 1975– . Annual.   **CJ95**
Publ. for the Center for Social Analysis of the State University of New York at Binghamton and for the Council on Foreign Relations.
Continues *A political handbook of Europe* (1927); *A political handbook of the world* (1928); *Political handbook of the world* (1929–62); *Political handbook and atlas of the world* (1963–70); *The world this year* (1971–73).
Issues combined for 1982–83 and for 1984–85. Publisher varies.
Treats the independent countries of the world in alphabetically-arranged entries that usually give a description of the country and information on its government and politics, heads of state, political parties, legislature, cabinet, news media, and intergovernmental representation. Also contains a section on intergovernmental organizations. Appendixes include chronologies of major international events and conferences. Geographic/organization name and personal name indexes.
          JF3.P6

Atlases

Atlas of the Third World / ed. by George Kurian. 2nd ed. N.Y. : Facts on File, 1992. 384 p. : col. ill., maps in color ; 32 cm.   **CJ96**
1st ed., 1983.
A companion to George Kurian, *Encyclopedia of the Third World* (CJ28). Uses two-color maps, charts, and graphs to illustrate social, economic, and political indicators for the Third World as a whole and for individual countries. In two sections: pt. 1 has thematic profiles for the Third World in 11 categories (e.g., political divisions, industry, environment); pt. 2 is comprised of alphabetically-arranged country profiles. List of sources; general index.   G1046.G1K8

The Americas

Political parties of the Americas : Canada, Latin America, and the West Indies / ed. by Robert J. Alexander. Westport, Conn. : Greenwood, [1982]. 2 v. (864 p.).   **CJ97**
Contents: v. 1, Anguilla–Grenada; v. 2, Guadeloupe–Virgin Islands of the United States.
Each chapter by a specialist briefly describes the political history of a country, each political party which has existed there (with foundation date, orientation, leadership, electoral history), and includes a bibliography. Excludes U.S. parties as they are covered by other titles (e.g., Edward and Frederick Schapsmeier's *Political parties and civic action groups* [CJ266]). Appendixes give political chronology by country, party genealogy by country, and ideological and interest group parties subdivided by country. General index.

§ Continued by: Charles D. Ameringer's *Political parties of the Americas, 1980s to 1990s : Canada, Latin America, and the West Indies* (Westport, Conn. : Greenwood, 1992. 697 p.). Other useful titles in this area include: Ciarán Ó Maoláin's *Latin American political movements* (N.Y. : Facts on File, 1985. 287 p.). and John Coggins and D. S. Lewis, *Political parties of the Americas and the Caribbean : a reference guide* (Harlow, Essex, U.K. : Longman, c1992. 341 p.).
          JL195.P64

North America

United States

Bibliography

Beede, Benjamin R. Military and strategic policy : an annotated bibliography. N.Y. : Greenwood, 1990. 334 p. (Bibliographies and indexes in military studies, no. 2).   **CJ98**
Cites with brief annotations 1,900 works on U.S. policy during the presidencies of Eisenhower through Reagan. In an essentially chronological arrangement, offers chapters on individual administrations and on the Vietnam confrontation, as well as chapters on bibliographies and other reference works and on general and comparative studies. Cites many of the documents reprinted in *U.S. national security policy and strategy : documents and policy proposals*, ed. by Sam C. Sarkesian with Robert A. Vitas (N.Y. : Greenwood, 1988). Author and subject indexes.   Z1361.D4B4

Bowman, James S. Gubernatorial and presidential transitions : an annotated bibliography and resource guide / James S. Bowman and Ronald L. Monet. N.Y. : Garland, 1988. 113 p. (The public affairs and administration series, 19).   **CJ99**
Somewhat misnamed, this brief bibliography (211 entries) actually focuses on several aspects of gubernatorial and presidential government in the U.S. Annotated citations are listed alphabetically in topical chapters that cover: Transitions; Management, leadership, and executive functions; and Executive offices, staffing, and appointments. Includes articles, monographs, and dissertations published in the last 25 years. 16 appendixes, mainly tables, offer a variety of relevant information (e.g., state cabinet systems, the powers and duties of lieutenant governors, dates in gubernatorial transitions). Author index.
          Z1249.P7B68

Dillman, David L. Civil service reform : an annotated bibliography. N.Y. : Garland, 1987. 239 p. (Public affairs and administration series, 18 ; Garland reference library of social science, v. 395).   **CJ100**
Offers 539 annotated citations, emphasizing those that relate to the 1978 Civil Service Reform Act (CSRA). Includes English-language government documents, books, and articles published primarily 1976–86. Within six topical chapters (e.g., Historical perspective, Impetus for reform, State and local reform) entries are arranged alphabetically by author (excepting government documents which are chronological). Appendixes provide excerpts from key provisions of the CSRA and a list of organizations interested in civil service reform. Cross-references; author and subject indexes.   Z7164.C6D54

Directory of political periodicals. 1991– . Topeka, Kan. : Government Research Service, c1991– . Annual.   **CJ101**
Continues: *Directory of political newsletters*, 1990.
Lists newsletters, journals, and newspapers (most available to the general public through commercial subscription) focusing on U.S. national and state politics. Excludes most academic political science journals, legislative reporting/tracking services, and organizational/membership publications. Entries are alphabetical by title and include publisher, address, phone and fax numbers, editor, price, frequency, size, number of pages, year first published, former titles, online availability, inclusion of book reviews, acceptance of advertising, brief de-

scription, and ISSN number. Two appendixes: (1) addresses and telephone numbers for online computer services; (2) periodicals that ceased publication or changed titles since the 1st ed. of this directory. Subject index.   Z7165.U5D597

Johansen, Elaine. Political corruption : scope and resources : an annotated bibliography. N.Y. : Garland, 1990. 241 p. (Public affairs and administration, v. 27 ; Garland reference library of social science, v. 610).   **CJ102**

Contains 914 entries (most annotated) to English-language articles, books, dissertations, government publications, law cases, and statutes, primarily from the last 20 years, on political corruption in the U.S. alone or in comparison with other countries. Excludes material on campaign finance and police corruption. Contains ten topical chapters (e.g., Legal writings, Business-government corruption, Public opinion and corruption) with entries arranged alphabetically. A general introduction explains the scope and framework of the book, and each chapter has its own brief introduction. Author and subject indexes.

Z7164.C94J64

Kaid, Lynda Lee. Political campaign communication : a bibliography and guide to the literature / by Lynda Lee Kaid, Keith R. Sanders, Robert O. Hirsch. Metuchen, N.J. : Scarecrow, 1974. 206 p.   **CJ103**

A listing of more than 1,500 books, articles, pamphlets, federal documents, and unpublished materials on political campaign communication in the United States, 1950–72. Also includes a French- and German-language supplement, an annotated list of fifty "seminal" books on the topic, and a guide to the literature. Subject index. Appendix lists relevant professional and scholarly organizations.

§ Continued by: *Political campaign communication : a bibliography and guide to the literature, 1973–1982*, by Lynda Lee Kaid and Anne Johnston Wadsworth (Metuchen, N.J. : Scarecrow, 1985. 217 p.).

Includes nearly 2,500 entries for items published 1973–82. This volume excludes government documents, unpublished papers presented at meetings and conferences, and articles in popular magazines and newspapers. Omits the French and German supplement, the annotated list of selected books, and the list of professional and scholarly organizations.   Z7165.U5K34

Manheim, Jarol B. Political violence in the United States, 1875–1974 : a bibliography / Jarol B. Manheim, Melanie Wallace. N.Y. : Garland, 1975. 116 p.   **CJ104**

A classed list of over 1,500 entries: books, articles, doctoral dissertations, and government documents covering strikes, race riots, gun control, assassinations, anarchism and terrorism, vigilantism, police violence, etc. Author index but no detailed subject approach.

Z7165.U5M27

Maurer, David J. U.S. politics and elections : a guide to information sources. Detroit : Gale, [1978]. 213p. (American government and history information guide ser., v.2).   **CJ105**

An introductory, annotated bibliography of monographic literature, arranged by historical period from colonial times to 1976. Concluding general section. Each section lists biographies separately. Author, title, and subject indexes.   Z1236.M39

Miles, William. The image makers : a bibliography of American presidential campaign biographies. Metuchen, N.J. : Scarecrow, 1979. 254 p.   **CJ106**

Bibliographic descriptions of 1,283 "books, pamphlets, magazines, almanacs, speeches, [and] political compendia … which are or in which appear … campaign biographies, both favorable and unfavorable, dating from 1796 to 1976."—*Introd.* Arranged chronologically by campaign, then by candidates and those who unsuccessfully sought nomination. Author/candidate and title indexes.   Z7164.R4M63

Plischke, Elmer. U.S. foreign relations : a guide to information sources. Detroit : Gale, 1980. 715 p. (American government and history information guide series, v.6).   **CJ107**

Presents classed, occasionally annotated, citations to monographs,

periodical articles, and documents dealing "with the foreign affairs process, not with diplomatic history, current events, world politics, or substantive foreign policy development and analysis."—*Pref.* In four major segments: (1) diplomacy and diplomats in general (e.g., protocol, privileges and immunities); (2) conduct of U.S. foreign relations (e.g., the President, decision-making); (3) official sources and resources (e.g., executive orders, House documents); and (4) memoirs and biographical literature. No subject index, but a detailed table of contents. Author index.   Z6465.U5P52

Rosenberg, Kenyon C. Watergate : an annotated bibliography / Kenyon C. Rosenberg and Judith K. Rosenberg. Littleton, Colo. : Libraries Unlimited, 1975. 141 p.   **CJ108**

Provides annotated citations, chronologically arranged, to articles, newspaper editorials, and books on Watergate published June 1972–August 1974. Author, title, and subject/personal name indexes.

Z1245.R6

Ross, Lynn C. Career advancement for women in the federal service : an annotated bibliography and resource book. N.Y. : Garland, 1993. 251 p. (Public affairs and administration, v. 28 ; Garland reference library of social science, v. 867).

CJ109

Offers 479 annotated entries for English-language books, articles, and government documents published primarily within the past ten years on women in federal service. Introduction describes historical background, current issues, and the composition of the bibliography. Topical chapters cover career advancement, barriers to advancement, affirmative action and equal employment opportunity, sexual harassment, pay equity, mentors and networking, women and men, training, non-traditional occupations, work and family issues, and bibliographies and general resources. Most chapters also contain additional resources (e.g., lists of organizations offering assistance to victims of sexual harassment, associations and unions, research organizations, excerpts from or summaries of relevant laws and regulations, names of useful publications). Author index.   Z7164.C6R67

Smith, Myron J. Watergate : an annotated bibliography of sources in English, 1972–1982. Metuchen, N.J. : Scarecrow, 1983. 329 p.   **CJ110**

More than 2,500 items listed by main entry, with brief contents notes; reference works are listed separately. Includes a chronology, biographies, a list of audiovisual materials, and a subject index.

Z1245.S64

Unity in diversity : an index to the publications of conservative and libertarian institutions / The New American Foundation ; Carol L. Birch, ed. Metuchen, N.J. : Scarecrow, 1983. 263 p.   **CJ111**

An alphabetically arranged subject index to about 3,000 monographic and article titles published 1970–81 by such organizations as the American Enterprise Institute for Public Policy Research, CATO Institute, Foreign Policy Research Institute, Hudson Institute, Heritage Foundation, Hoover Institution, etc. Author index.   Z7161.U63

University of Iowa. Libraries. The right wing collection of the University of Iowa Libraries, 1918–1977 : a guide to the microfilm collection. Glen Rock, N.J. : Microfilming Corp. of America, 1978. 175 p.   **CJ112**

Designed to accompany the 177-reel microfilm collection published under the same title. Provides access by title or corporate author to the collections of serials and ephemera (e.g., correspondence, pamphlets, cartoons) at the University of Iowa Libraries, the B'nai B'rith Collection at Harvard University's Widener Library, and collections at California State University at Fullerton Library, Northern Arizona University Library, Tulane University Library, and the Kenneth Spencer Research Library of the University of Kansas. Each entry provides description of holdings, type of serial, and general information. Indexed by subject, place of publication, and year of publication.

Z7163.I7

Indexes

Garza, Hedda. The Watergate investigation index : House Judiciary Committee hearings and report on impeachment. Wilmington, Del. : Scholarly Resources, 1985. 261 p.   **CJ113**

————. *The Watergate investigation index : Senate Select Committee hearings and reports on presidential campaign activities* (Wilmington, Del. : Scholarly Resources, 1982. 325 p.).

These volumes provide detailed indexes, respectively, to the 39 volumes of the hearings and report of the House Judiciary Committee on the resolution to impeach President Richard Nixon, and to the 26 volumes of the hearings (including public testimony, Executive Committee testimony, and exhibits) and the final report of the Senate Select Committee on Presidential Campaign Activities (Watergate Committee). The indexes include subjects, personal names, organizations, geographic names, and cross-references. Preceding the House index is a list of indictments brought by the Special Prosecutor; the Senate volume includes a list of Committee members and witnesses. The Senate volume does not cover the two-volume appendix to the hearings.

KF27.J8

Sanchez, James. Index to The Tower Commission report. Jefferson, N.C. : McFarland, c1987. 57 p.   **CJ114**

Facilitates access to government reports regarding the attempt of the Reagan administration to supply arms to Iran and divert the funds to the Nicaraguan Contras. Indexes the popular edition of the *Tower Commission report* (N.Y. : Bantam Books, 1987). Ample cross-references and explanatory notes.

————. *Index to the Iran-Contra hearings summary report* (Jefferson, N.C. : McFarland, 1988. 82 p.) indexes both the U.S. Government Printing Office and the *New York times* versions of the report, as well as four works critical of the investigation.   E876.U55

Encyclopedias

Elliot, Jeffrey M. The presidential-congressional political dictionary / Jeffrey M. Elliot, Sheikh R. Ali. Santa Barbara, Calif. : ABC-Clio, 1984. 365 p. : ill. (Clio dictionaries in political science, 9).   **CJ115**

Covers "concepts, theories, and facts" (*Pref.*) relevant to the presidency and Congress. Entries are arranged alphabetically in 12 topical chapters (e.g., Powers of the President; Agencies, bureaus, and commissions; Congressional leadership), except for Chapter 3, "The Presidents," which is in chronological order. Each entry has a description or definition (often ending with cross-references) and a paragraph describing the item's historical origins and contemporary importance. Appendix includes related information (e.g., Presidential vetoes, Standing committees in Congress). Bibliography; general index.

JK9.E4

Encyclopedia of the American legislative system / Joel H. Silbey, ed. in chief. N.Y. : Scribner, c1994. 1738 p.   **CJ116**

Subtitle: Studies of the principal structures, processes, and policies of Congress and the state legislatures since the Colonial Era.

Covers all major aspects of the American legislative system (national, state, and local) in 91 signed essays written by experts. Groups essays chronologically or topically in six sections: (1) The American legislative system in historical context; (2) Legislative recruitment, personnel, and elections; (3) Legislative structures and processes; (4) Legislative behavior; (5) Legislatures and public policy; and (6) Legislatures within the political system. Each essay ends with an extensive annotated bibliography and cross-references to other essays. Includes many charts and tables and a list of contributors. General index.

JF501.E53

Filler, Louis. Dictionary of American conservatism. N.Y. : Philosophical Library, c1987. 380 p.   **CJ117**

Called by its author the first dictionary of conservatism, this work "defines past and present conservative concepts and illustrates their workings with examples and references" (*Introd.*) and offers entries that describe persons and movements. Explains concepts from a conservative viewpoint (e.g., the entry for World War II says the number of conservatives with fascist tendencies was overestimated by "left-wing propagandists"). Alphabetically arranged.   JA84.U5F55

Findling, John E. Dictionary of American diplomatic history. 2nd ed., rev. and expanded. N.Y. : Greenwood, 1989. 674 p. : ill.   **CJ118**

1st ed., 1980.

Offers biographical sketches of "nearly six hundred persons associated with U.S. foreign policy from the Revolution through 1988, as well as descriptions or definitions of about 600 nonbiographical items connected with American diplomacy, ranging from crises to catch-words."—*Pref.* Biographees were selected mainly from among the roster of U.S. chiefs of mission, though others (e.g., members of Congress, journalists) who had an impact on American diplomacy are included. Alphabetical arrangement; brief bibliographies. Also contains maps and organizational charts. Various useful appendixes (e.g., chronology of American diplomatic history, key diplomatic personnel by presidential administration). General index.   E183.7.F5

Flanders, Stephen A. Dictionary of American foreign affairs / Stephen A. Flanders, Carl N. Flanders ; cartography by Thomas Nast. N.Y. : Macmillan, 1993. 833 p. : ill., maps.

CJ119

Dictionary arrangement of some 1,400 entries covering ideas, events, agreements, organizations, and individuals pertinent to U.S. involvement in foreign relations. The descriptive entries contain background information, assessments of outcome or significance, and usually cross-references. Appendixes: foreign affairs timeline; lists of individuals who held key foreign affairs posts in the executive branch, diplomatic corps, and Congress; major conferences and summits; brief glossary; guide to further sources; and relevant maps (e.g., territorial expansion). No index.

§ John E. Findling's *Dictionary of American diplomatic history* (CJ118) has shorter entries, but does include short bibliographies in most articles.   E183.7.F58

Government agencies / ed. in chief, Donald R. Whitnah. Westport, Conn., Greenwood, 1983. 683 p. (Greenwood encyclopedia of American institutions, 7).   **CJ120**

Over 100 signed articles, alphabetically arranged, for individual federal agencies, departments, bureaus, corporations, commissions, and quasi-agencies. Each entry gives information on the history, functions, structure, and activities of the agency, and includes a bibliography. Appendixes provide a chronology of agency formation, name changes, and lists of umbrella agencies and agencies grouped by broad area of service. List of contributors. General index.   JK421.G65

Renstrom, Peter G. The electoral politics dictionary / Peter G. Renstrom, Chester B. Rogers. Santa Barbara, Calif. : ABC-Clio , c1989. 365 p.   **CJ121**

Contains 404 entries arranged alphabetically within seven topical chapters (e.g., Political parties), each of which begins with an overview of the material covered in the chapter. Focuses on ideas, terms, concepts, organizations, federal statutes, and court decisions relevant to electoral politics in the U.S. Entries feature a lengthy definition and a paragraph called "Significance" that gives historical perspective and puts the entry into a political context. Covers fewer topics, but in more depth, than Michael Young's *The American dictionary of campaigns and elections* (CJ124). Cross-references; name and subject index.

JK1971.R46

Shafritz, Jay M. The HarperCollins dictionary of American government and politics. N.Y. : HarperPerennial, c1992. 661 p. : ill.   **CJ122**

Based on the author's *The Dorsey dictionary of American government and politics* (Chicago : Dorsey Pr., 1988. 661 p.).

Defines more than 5,000 terms, phrases, and processes relevant to U.S. national, state, or local government and politics (e.g., Apportionment, General welfare clause, Primary). Also includes significant Supreme Court cases, laws, federal agencies, biographical sketches, political slang, scholarly journals, and professional associations, with occasional illustrations, sidebars, statistics, or lists. Appendixes include the Declaration of Independence, the U.S. Constitution (with explanatory margin notes), and a list of key concepts organized by subject. Omits the bibliographic sources and three of the appendixes found in the earlier dictionary.

§ Covers more items but in less depth than Jack C. Plano and Milton Greenberg's *American political dictionary* (CJ126).   JK9.S43

Whisker, James B. An American political dictionary. Apollo, Pa. : Closson Pr., [1992?]. 119, [18] p.   **CJ123**

Rev. ed. of the author's *A dictionary of concepts on American politics* (N.Y. : Wiley, 1980).

In twelve topical chapters (e.g., Federalism, Congress, Taxation and fiscal policy), each with two alphabetically arranged sections: (1) ideas, concepts, events, institutions, and acts (e.g., centralization, judicial activism, Watergate, Economic Opportunity Act) and (2) cases (e.g., Roe v. Wade). Entries are generally a paragraph in length and give both a definition and the importance of the item. Includes the Declaration of Independence and the U.S. Constitution. General index.

§ Also publ. as: *A glossary of U.S. government vocabulary* (Lewiston, N.Y. : The Edwin Mellen Pr., 1992) without the inclusion of the Declaration of Independence and the U.S. Constitution.   JK9.W47

Young, Michael L. The American dictionary of campaigns and elections. Lanham, Md. : Hamilton Pr., c1987. 246 p.   **CJ124**

Contains 725 entries that define and describe "the major notions, concepts, tools and terms associated with the contemporary American political campaign" (*Pref.*), arranged alphabetically within seven topical chapters (e.g., Polling and public opinion). Includes a bibliography and a subject index that is awkward to use because it refers to chapters rather than page or entry numbers. Entries end with cross-references. Has more but briefer entries than Peter G. Renstrom's *The electoral politics dictionary* (CJ121).   JK1971.Y68

Dictionaries

Guide to federal government acronyms / ed. by William R. Evinger. Phoenix : Oryx, 1989. 279 p.   **CJ125**

Lists nearly 20,000 acronyms, initialisms, and abbreviations found in federal documents, regulations, publications, news releases, and other materials. In two parts: acronyms, initialisms, and abbreviations followed by their expanded forms; and a reverse list. The first part includes agency, organization, program, and budget names, position titles, laws and the legislative process, budgeting, agency products and services, names of agency computer systems, terms found in regulations, publication titles, names of surveys, and data collections. Also covers international organizations, programs, and activities in which the U.S. participates.   JK464

Plano, Jack C. The American political dictionary / Jack C. Plano, Milton Greenberg. 9th ed. Fort Worth, Tex. : Harcourt Brace Jovanovich, c1993. 672 p.   **CJ126**

1st ed., 1962; 8th ed., 1989.

Presents 14 topical chapters (e.g., political ideas, the legislative process, business and labor), each containing a section of alphabetically grouped terms and most having a section for relevant agencies, cases, and statutes. Approximately 1,300 entries, usually including cross-references. Each has a paragraph of definition or explanation followed by a paragraph detailing the item's historical and current significance and relationship to American government. Appendix contains the U.S. Constitution. General index.   JK9.P55

Safire, William L. Safire's new political dictionary : the definitive guide to the new language of politics. N.Y. : Random House, 1993. 930 p.   **CJ127**

1st ed., 1968, had title: *The new language of politics*; 3rd ed., 1978, had title: *Safire's political dictionary*.

Defines words or phrases of a political nature (e.g., bubba vote, hatchetmen, sound bite), excluding political terms that can be found in other dictionaries. Concerned with language deriving from historical events (e.g., big enchilada, eyeball to eyeball, summitry) rather than the event itself. Entries often include cross-references or quotations for which citations are not always precise. Personal name index.   JK9.S2

Smith, Edward Conrad. Dictionary of American politics / Edward C. Smith and Arnold J. Zurcher. 2nd ed. N.Y. : Barnes & Noble, [1968]. 434 p.   **CJ128**

1949 edition had title: *New dictionary of American politics*. 1955 edition reverted to the earlier title and had no edition number.

1st ed., 1888, by Everit Brown and Albert Strauss; 2nd ed., 1924, by Edward C. Smith; 3rd ed., 1944, by Edward C. Smith and Arnold J. Zurcher.

Still useful, contains brief definitions (with occasional cross-references and illustrations) of words and phrases relevant to comparative government, political theory, constitutional law, public administration, and social welfare. Appendixes include the U.S. Constitution and the nicknames of the states.   JK9.S5

Sperber, Hans. American political terms : an historical dictionary / Hans Sperber and Travis Trittschuh. Detroit : Wayne State Univ. Pr., 1962. 516 p.   **CJ129**

A somewhat dated but still useful work giving origins, meanings, and examples of earliest and developing usage for political terms. Includes many historical words or phrases (e.g., featherhead, Manhattan Club) not found in more contemporary dictionaries. Bibliography.   JK9.S65

Directories

American lobbyists directory. Detroit : Gale, c1990– .   **CJ130**

Subtitle: A guide to the more than 65,000 registered federal and state lobbyists and the businesses, organizations, and other concerns they represent.

Gives the names, addresses, and telephone numbers of businesses/organizations and their lobbyists. Entries are arranged by state (including District of Columbia), then alphabetically by sponsoring body. A section on federal lobbyists, printed on yellow paper for quick reference, precedes the state entries. Includes a list of federal and state disclosure offices. Lobbyists, organizations, and subject/specialty indexes. Excludes laws and rules governing registration of lobbyists but otherwise fills the gap left by the discontinuance with the 2nd ed., 1975, of *Directory of registered lobbyists and lobbyist legislation* (Chicago : Marquis Academic Media). For federal lobbyists, see also *Washington representatives* (CJ144).   JK1118.A65

Beacham's guide to key lobbyists : an analysis of their issues and impact / [executive ed., Walton Beacham ; senior ed., Margaret Roberts ; coordinating ed., C. Peter Kessler]. Wash. : Beacham Publ., 1989. 632 p. : ill.   **CJ131**

Presents information on 125 key lobbyists in Washington—their organizations, issues, and influence. Alphabetically arranged profiles offer a photograph, personal data, organization data, and narrative descriptions of the lobbyist's employment history, lobbying activities, and organization. Three appendixes: Selected PAC contributions for 1987–88, 1987 honoraria paid to members of Congress, and Lobbyists grouped by issue areas. General index.

§ For other directories of lobbyists, consult *Washington representatives* (CJ144) or *American lobbyists directory* (CJ130).   JK1118.B3924

Black elected officials / Joint Center for Political Studies. 1984– . N.Y. : UNIPUB, c1984– . Annual.   **CJ132**

Continues: *National roster of black elected officials* (Wash. : Joint Center for Political Studies, 1971–82).

Provides names, addresses, offices held, and date elected for government officials, including senators, representatives, judges, county and city officers, and members of school boards. Listed by state, then by categories of federal, state, or local offices. Contains a summary, including tables, of the number of African-American officials throughout the U.S. Personal name index.

§ For Hispanic officials, see *National roster of Hispanic elected officials* (Wash. : National Association of Latino Elected and Appointed Officials, Education Fund, 1984–).   E185.615.N29

Clements, John. Taylor's encyclopedia of government officials, federal and state. v. 1 (1967/68)– . Dallas, Tex. : Political Research, Inc., 1968– . Biennial.   **CJ133**

Vol. 1 preceded by a number dated 1776/1966, called v. O.

More a directory than an encyclopedia. The 1993–94 volume lists top officials of the federal executive, legislative, and judicial branches of government; of independent government agencies; and of the 50 states. Also gives U.S. ambassadors and foreign ambassadors to the U.S. Contains no biographical information, but includes descriptive and budgetary information for each state; photographs; color-coded state charts showing political party control; and a wealth of additional information (e.g., delegates to the 1992 Democratic and Republican conventions, inaugural addresses, 1961–93, glossary). Updated by quarterly cumulative supplements. Subscription includes additional supplementary materials (e.g., state leadership chart, summary of current congressional issues and laws, state legislative review) and services (e.g., research assistance). Name index.   JK6.T36

Encyclopedia of governmental advisory organizations. [1st ed.] Issue no. 1 (July 1973)– . Detroit : Gale, 1973– . Irregular.   **CJ134**

Subtitle (varies): A reference guide to over 6,500 permanent, continuing, and ad hoc U.S. presidential advisory committees, congressional advisory committees, public advisory committees, interagency committees and other government-related boards, panels, task forces, commissions, conferences, and other similar bodies serving in a consultative, coordinating, advisory, research, or investigative capacity.

1st ed. issued in 5 no.; 2nd ed.– issued in single vols.

Entries, organized into ten topical chapters (e.g., agriculture, defense and military science, health and medicine), present information on history, members, program, findings or recommendations, publications and reports, meetings, and sponsoring legislation. Appendixes offer a list of committee management officers and the text of the Federal Advisory Committee Act. Five indexes by: (1) personal name, (2) publication or report title, (3) presidential administration, (4) federal department or agency, and (5) organization name and keyword. This last index also refers the user to the *United States government manual* (CJ151) or the *Official congressional directory* (CJ221) for administrative agencies, bureaus, and offices of the federal government and for congressional committees.

§ Updated between editions by: *New governmental advisory organizations* (Detroit : Gale, 1976– . Irregular.).   JK468.C7E52

Federal executive directory annual. 1991/1992– . Wash. : Carroll Publ. Co., [1991]– . Annual.   **CJ135**

Continues in part *Federal/state executive directory*.

Combines listings for the executive and legislative branches in one color-coded directory. Gives name, title, office address, and telephone and fax number for some 35,000 mid- to upper-level officials in the Executive Office of the President, Cabinet departments, major federal administrative agencies, and other organizations (e.g., Corporation for Public Broadcasting, U.S. Postal Service) plus members of Congress (with committee assignments) and their staff. Includes a number of special listings, e.g., federal information centers, libraries, personnel locators. Alphabetical list of executives. Keyword index. Also published in a bimonthly edition, *Federal executive directory*.

§ A companion title, *Federal regional executive directory* is published semiannually and provides listings for executives in Cabinet departments, Congress, federal courts, military bases, and administrative agencies who are not based in Washington, D.C.   JK723.E9F37

Federal regulatory directory. 1979/80– . Wash. : Congressional Quarterly, 1979/80– . Annual.   **CJ136**

The 6th (1990) ed. gives, for 13 of the largest federal regulatory agencies (e.g., Environmental Protection Agency, Federal Reserve System, Interstate Commerce Commission), a profile containing agency address and telephone numbers, history, powers and authority, outlook for future activity, brief biographies and photographs of important

officers, names and telephone numbers of selected personnel by function, organizational structure, relevant congressional committees and legislation, regional offices, information sources, and bibliography. For approximately 100 other regulatory agencies (e.g., Postal Rate Commission, Army Corps of Engineers, Federal Highway Administration), provides briefer profiles with descriptions of responsibilities, names and telephone numbers of selected personnel, information sources, relevant legislation, and regional offices. An introductory essay covers the history of and current issues in regulation. Appendixes explain *Federal register* and *Code of federal regulations* (CK182) and present the texts of relevant acts and executive orders. List of abbreviations. Personal name and subject/agency indexes.

     KF5406.A15F4

Federal staff directory. 1982– . Mt. Vernon, Va. : Congressional Staff Directory, 1982– . 2 no. a year.   **CJ137**

Subtitle (1993): Containing, in convenient arrangement, useful, accurate and timely information concerning the Executive Branch of the U.S. Government and its 32,000 key executives and staff. Carefully indexed by keyword and individual.

Frequency varies: 1982–88, Annual.

Provides biographical and locational information on executive branch staff. 1993 edition lists names, titles, addresses, and phone numbers for 32,000 employees of agencies of the executive office of the president; executive departments; independent agencies (e.g., Federal Election Commission); and selected quasi-official, international, and non-governmental organizations (e.g., American Red Cross, National Research Council). Includes biographies of more than 2,600 key executives. Personal name and keyword subject indexes.

•Machine-readable version: *Staff directories on CD-ROM* [database] (Mt. Vernon, Va. : Staff Directories). Updated biennially. Combines *Judicial staff directory* (CK149), *Congressional staff directory* (CJ215), and *Federal staff directory*.   JK723.E9F44

The government directory of addresses and telephone numbers. 1st ed. (1992)– . Detroit : Omnigraphics, c1992– . Annual.   **CJ138**

A comprehensive compilation of more than 100,000 listings, giving names, mailing addresses, and telephone numbers for key offices and officials at every level of government. Each of the three sections (federal, state, and city and county) begins with quick reference listings of frequently called numbers, abbreviations, area codes, etc. Keyword indexes facilitate access to federal and states offices. While most of this information can be found in other publications (e.g., the "Yellow book" series published by Monitor), this one-volume format proves handy.   JK6.G58

Guide to the American left. Olathe, Kan. : Editorial Research Service, 1984– . Annual.   **CJ139**

Comp. by Laird Wilcox.

Place of publication varies. Title varies: *Directory of the American left*.

The main section is an alphabetically arranged list of organizations and serials representing values, opinions, or beliefs normally identified with the political left. The one-line entries give address, a two-letter code for the organization's chief concern (e.g., AN for antinuclear; MS for Marxist-Socialist), and brief data. A second section contains an extensive bibliography of books, each with a single-sentence annotation. Also provides a lengthy list of appropriate quotations; a list of organizations and serials by zip code or, for Canadian entries, postal code; a variety of reprinted articles, reviews, etc.; and an article on political extremism.

§ Companion publication: *Guide to the American right* (Olathe, Kan. : Editorial Research Service, 1984–).

Official register of the United States : persons in the civil, military, and naval service, exclusive of the Postal service / comp. by the Dept. of Commerce, Bureau of the Census. 1913–59. Wash. : [U.S. Govt. Print. Off.], 1913–59.   **CJ140**

Superintendent of Documents classification: CS 1.31.

Title, subtitle, issuing agency, and frequency vary. Before 1861, publ. by Dept. of State; 1861–1905, by Dept. of the Interior; 1907–32, by Bureau of the Census; 1933–59, by Civil Service Commission. Biennial until 1921; not issued 1922–24; annual, 1925–59.

Also known as *Blue book*, this publication was the official list of government employees. In two main parts: (1) a classified list, arranged by departments, agencies, offices, etc., in Washington, and in the territorial possessions, giving names of the principal officials and assistants, showing, for each, official title, salary, legal residence, and place of employment; (2) alphabetical index of names included in the classified list. Until 1911, included the names of all government employees, including the postal service; from 1913 to 1921, complete except for the postal service. The issues from 1925 to 1959 were much reduced in size and included only principal officials.

§ Earlier, unofficial publications which are occasionally useful are: Charles Lanman, *Biographical annals of the civil government of the United States* (2nd ed. N.Y. : J. M. Morrison, 1887); R. B. Mosher, *Executive register of the United States, 1789–1902* (Baltimore : Fridenwald, 1903); and B. P. Poore, *Political register* (Boston : Houghton, Osgood, 1878).   JK5

Political resource directory. National ed. 1988/89– . Rye, N.Y. : Political Resource Directories, c1987– .   **CJ141**

Covers people and organizations that offer products and services to the political community, primarily in the U.S. The main section lists organizations alphabetically, giving name, address, geographic region, areas of specialization, description of services, percentage of work that is political, and principal contacts. Indexes of organizations by state, specialization (e.g., polling, fundraising, press/public relations), and principal contact. Members of the American Association of Political Consultants are listed in a separate, color-coded section.   JK2283.P65

Public interest profiles. [1st ed.] (1977–1978)– . Wash. : Foundation for Public Affairs, [c1977]– . Biennial, 1988-1989– .   **CJ142**

Issued by Foundation for Public Affairs and Congressional Quarterly, Inc.

Provides information on important public interest organizations (e.g., The Conference Board, Mothers Against Drunk Driving, Greenpeace, League of Women Voters). The 1992–93 ed. contains 251 entries in 12 topical chapters (e.g., Business/economic, Consumer/health, International affairs). Alphabetical entries range from two to five pages in length and offer details such as address, telephone, size of staff, budget, purpose, recent publications, board of directors, and funding sources. Includes assessments of effectiveness and political orientation derived from comments by both supporters and critics in newspapers and magazines. Organization, personal name, and subject indexes.

JK1118.P79

United States. Department of State. The biographic register / Dept. of State, U.S. Foreign Service, International Cooperation Administration, U.S. Information Agency, Foreign Agricultural Service. 1956–1974. Wash. : Office of Special Services, Division of Publishing Services ; for sale by the U.S. Govt. Print. Off., 1956–[1974?]. Annual.   **CJ143**

Superintendent of Documents classification: S1.69 .

Supersedes *Register of the Department of State* (1869–1942). None published for 1943; 1944–55, title and issuing agency vary.

Contents vary. The early *Register* usually contained sections on departmental organization; information about the foreign service of the United States; historical lists; lists of the clerical, administrative, and fiscal service; and a biographical section for administrative and professional employees. Since 1944, the publication has included only the biographical section, and (in later years) provided information on personnel of the State Department and other federal government agencies in the field of foreign affairs. It thus included biographies of ambassadors, ministers, chiefs of missions, foreign service officers, foreign service information officers, foreign service staff officers (classes 1–4) and Civil Service employees of grade GS-12 and above. Also includes personnel from various other agencies: Agency for International Development, U.S. Information Agency, Foreign Agricultural Service, etc.   JK851.A3

Washington representatives. v. 3 (1979)– . Wash. : Columbia Books, 1979– . Annual.   **CJ144**

Subtitle: Who does what for whom in the nation's captial. A compilation of washington representatives of the major national associations, labor unions and U.S. companies, registered foreign agents, lobbyists, lawyers, law firms and special interest groups, together with their clients and areas of legislative and regulatory concern.

Continues *Directory of Washington representatives of American associations and industry* (1977–78) and assumes its numbering.

The 1993 edition is in three sections: (1) alphabetically-arranged entries for more than 14,000 individuals, providing names, addresses, and telephone numbers of their employers, their employment backgrounds, and names of their clients; (2) an alphabetical list of about 17,000 companies and organizations, giving addresses and telephone numbers and listing their representatives, counsel, or consultants; and (3) a list of federal government departments and agencies, with names of personnel responsible for legislative affairs. Includes the text of the Federal Regulation of Lobbying Act. Subject and foreign interests indexes.   JK1112D58

Watson, Cynthia Ann. U.S. national security policy groups : institutional profiles. N.Y. : Greenwood, 1990. 289 p.   **CJ145**

Describes 135 not-for-profit, essentially educational groups that either are interested exclusively in national security or are large organizations with projects on related topics (e.g., disarmament, strategic defense). Entries, alphabetically arranged, vary in length from one to seven pages, and include the group's national headquarters, address, basic orientation or mission, origins, organization and funding, electoral politics (if it is active in this sphere), and policy concerns and tactics. General index.   UA23.W364

Who knows, a guide to Washington experts / by Washington Researchers Publishing. Ed. 8– . Wash. : Washington Researchers, 1986– . Irregular.   **CJ146**

Continues *Researcher's guide to Washington*, 1977–80, and *Researcher's guide to Washington experts, 1981–84(?)*.

Facilitates access to mid- to high-level federal employees with expertise in a specific field. Entries, alphabetically arranged by subject and keyword, list name, title, organization, and telephone number of the expert. 1992–93 edition offers a color-coded section, "Federal fast finder," with: (1) a keyword directory to federal government offices, giving telephone numbers for public information or public affairs offices; (2) telephone numbers for government hotlines; and (3) telephone numbers for recorded messages. Also includes a list of abbreviations and mission descriptions, addresses, and the personnel locator telephone numbers for parent agencies.   JK6W37a

Handbooks

Almanac of federal PACs. 1986– . Wash. : Amward Publications, c1986– . Biennial.   **CJ147**

Editor: 1986– , E. Zuckerman.

Edition for 1992–93 lists every political action committee (PAC) contributing $50,000 or more to candidates for the U.S. Congress in any election since record-keeping began in 1977. PACs are arranged alphabetically in six groups: Business, Labor, Trade association, Special interest group, Leadership, and Ideological. Entries give PAC sponsor; member names, addresses, and telephone numbers; descriptions; Federal Election Commission identification number; and receipts, expenditures, and contributions. Introductory material explains the Federal Election Campaign Act, and includes an essay on the development of PACs. Appendixes offer tables detailing overall PAC contributions (1977–88), and campaign finance histories for every member of the 102nd Congress. Organization name index.

JK1991.A744

Austin, Erik W. Political facts of the United States since 1789 / Erik W. Austin ; with the assistance of Jerome M. Clubb. N.Y. : Columbia Univ. Pr., 1986. 518 p.   **CJ148**

For annotation, *see* DB53.   E183.A97

The lobbying handbook / [collected] by John L. Zorack. Wash. : Professional Lobbying and Consulting Center, c1990. 1118 p., [1] leaf of plates : ill. **CJ149**

Written for the practicing lobbyist, this definitive insider's guide provides advice and pertinent reference sources and documents. In 23 topical chapters (e.g., Getting around Capitol Hill, Lobbying strategy, House legislative procedure, Ethics and the lobbyist), many including essays written by experts. A final chapter offers 80 interviews on lobbying with members of Congress, congressional staff, professional lobbyists, and others. 19 appendixes contain helpful information and relevant documents (e.g., Constitution, Freedom of Information Act, government organization charts, forms of address and salutations). Includes figures and interviews indexes, a general index, and a bibliography. JK1118.L58

Sweeney, Jerry K. A handbook of American diplomacy / Jerry K. Sweeney and Margaret B. Denning. Boulder, Colo. : Westview Pr., 1993. 157 p. **CJ150**

For both students and general readers. In six chronological chapters covering 1686–1900, each with an overview of important themes, a chronology of events, concise summaries of ratified treaties, brief sketches of significant individuals, and an annotated bibliography. Also includes a short diplomatic glossary and a list of treaties, agreements, and organizations with dates.

§ For more extensive works in this area, *see*: John E. Findling, *Dictionary of American diplomatic history* (CJ118) and Stephen and Carl Flanders, *Dictionary of American foreign affairs* (CJ119). E183.7.S97

The United States government manual. 1973/74– . Wash. : Office of the Federal Register : for sale by the U.S. Govt. Print. Off., 1973– . Annual. **CJ151**

Superintendent of Documents classification: GS 4.109: ; AE 2.108/2: .

Title varies: 1949–72, *United States government organization manual*.

Publ. as a special edition of the *Federal register*.

The official organization handbook of the federal government. Gives information on the agencies of the legislative, judicial, and executive branches as well as quasi-official agencies (e.g., United States Institute of Peace), international organizations in which the U.S. participates, and relevant boards, commissions, and committees. Agency entries usually list the chief officials; describe the agency's purpose and role in the federal government, its history and authority, and its programs and services; and give information about the agency's consumer activities, contracts and grants, employment, publications, etc. Also provides organizational charts and several appendixes (e.g., a list of terminated and transferred agencies) and reprints the Declaration of Independence and the U.S. Constitution. Name and agency/subject indexes.

•A machine-readable version, *TAURUSondisc U.S. government organization manual*, is available on CD-ROM. JK421.Un34

Wolfe, Gregory. Right minds : a sourcebook of American conservative thought. Chicago : Regnery Books, c1987. 245 p. **CJ152**

In three parts: (1) a briefly annotated bibliography of American conservative writings; (2) short (typically one paragraph) biographies of American conservative thinkers, organized by historical era; and (3) an annotated guide to sources of information, including periodicals, think tanks and foundations, publishers, and collections of private papers. The bibliography is arranged topically in such categories as: The American conservative tradition, The welfare state, Communism and ideology, and Crime and punishment. Contains a name index and a foreword by William F. Buckley (whose *National review* sponsored the work). Z1249.C74W64

Biography

American leaders, 1789–1991 : a biographical summary. Wash. : Congressional Quarterly, c1991. 534 p. **CJ153**

Lists every American president, vice president, cabinet member, Supreme Court justice, member of Congress, and governor from the first national government through 1991. The six chapters (one for each office) contain short entries listing birth and death dates, incumbency dates, party affiliation, state represented, other offices held, and relatives who held office. For each office, entries are alphabetically arranged (except for governors, for which the entries are chronological by state). Appendixes include: (1) party abbreviations; (2) a chronological list of presidents and vice presidents; (3) a chronological list of cabinet members by administration; (4) a table of political party affiliations in Congress and the presidency; (5) a listing, in chronological order, of the sessions of Congress, their dates, and speakers of the House and presidents pro tempore of the Senate; (6) a chronological list of leaders of the House since 1899 and the Senate since 1911, including floor leaders and whips; and a listing, alphabetical by committee name, of the House and Senate standing committee chairmen since 1947. Index to governors. E176.A495

American Political Science Association. Biographical directory. 1st ed. (1945)– . Wash. : The Association, 1945– . **CJ154**

Title varies.

Serves as a who's who in political science, giving biographical information (i.e., date of birth, education, honors, employment history, professional activities, publications, fields of interest) for members of the Association. The 7th ed., 1988, has field of interest, minority, women, and geographic indexes.

Supplemented at various intervals by the Association's membership directories, containing primarily names, addresses, and telephone numbers, although some include highest degrees obtained and fields of interest. JA28.A56

American political scientists : a dictionary / ed. by Glenn H. Utter and Charles Lockhart ; Aaron Wildavsky, advisory ed. Westport, Conn. : Greenwood, 1993. 374 p. **CJ155**

Portrays "the intellectual development and present state of American political science [by focusing] on the theoretical contributions of 171 political scientists."—*Pref.* Criteria for selection include U.S. citizenship or lengthy U.S. residence, scholarship primarily in political science, activity in the profession prior to 1970, and reputation in the field. Entries, signed and alphabetically arranged, contain: birth date, best known contributions to the field, educational background, career highlights, discussion of scholarly work and writings, and a selected bibliography. Two appendixes list the subjects by degree-granting institution and by specialization (e.g., comparative politics, public administration). List of contributors; bibliography; index. JA61.A525

Biographical dictionary of the American left / ed. by Bernard K. Johnpoll and Harvey Klehr. Westport, Conn. : Greenwood, 1986. 493 p. **CJ156**

Brief biographies of 259 figures, intended to provide a "representative cross-section of the leadership of the American Left which will give scholars and general readers a sense of who was in charge in the various radical parties and from what social or ethnic stratum these parties drew their vitality."—*Introd.* Includes such diverse types as Communists, 1960s radicals, academic labor leaders, civil rights activists, etc. Entries are alphabetically arranged and give birthdate and place, other names used, year of immigration, occupations of the biographee and his or her father, political affiliation, major roles in and contributions to radical movements, and sometimes a bibliography. Appendixes provide a chronology of key events, major radical party affiliation and year of entry, place of birth, birth and death dates, a list of those who abandoned the radical movement, and ethnic origin. General index. HX84.A2B56

Morris, Dan. Who was who in American politics / Dan and Inez Morris. N.Y. : Hawthorn Books, [1974]. 637 p. **CJ157**

Subtitle: A biographical dictionary of over 4,000 men and women who contributed to the United States political scene from colonial days up to and including the immediate past.

The brief, alphabetically arranged entries are useful for historical research. Includes some persons who were living in 1974 but no longer active in politics. E176.M873

O'Brien, Steven. American political leaders : from colonial times to the present / Steven G. O'Brien ; ed., Paula McGuire ; consulting eds., James M. McPherson, Gary Gerstle. Santa Barbara, Calif. : ABC-Clio, c1991. 473 p. : ill. **CJ158**

Profiles more than 400 men and women "elected to or nominated for national office or appointed by the president, as well as some who earned special prominence in other positions."—*Pref.* Includes every president, unsuccessful candidate for president, vice-president, secretary of state, chief justice of the Supreme Court, and Speaker of the House as well as many cabinet members, diplomats, government agency directors, presidential advisors, associate justices, senators, representatives, and others with unusual influence on national affairs. Specifically excludes leaders in social movements, state and local government, the military, education, and cultural affairs. Entries range in length from one half to four pages, are alphabetically arranged, and include birth and death dates; offices held; brief information about the individual's life, accomplishments, and significance; and a short bibliography. Many entries also contain cross-references, anecdotes, quotations, and a portrait or photograph. A timeline of presidential administrations includes all the biographees and notes key events. Name index precedes entries. E176.027

Political profiles / ed., Nelson Lichtenstein; assoc. ed., Eleanora W. Schoenebaum. N.Y. : Facts on File, [1976–79]. 5 v. **CJ159**

Contents: v. 1, The Truman years; v. 2, The Eisenhower years; v. 3, The Kennedy years; v. 4, The Johnson years; v. 5, The Nixon-Ford years.

Although originally intended to be complete in 6 v., with the final volume to cover the Carter years, the set was discontinued after v. 5.

Each volume contains about 500 signed biographies, ranging from 400 to 2,000 words, of the most politically influential persons in each presidential administration. Includes officeholders, journalists, intellectuals, economic leaders, civil rights activists, etc. Figures with long political careers may be found in several volumes, with the text focusing on the person's activity during the period covered. Short bibliographies for some entries. Each volume has a chronology, appendixes of officeholders, general bibliography, and index. E840.6.P64

Stineman, Esther. American political women : contemporary and historical profiles. Littleton, Colo. : Libraries Unlimited, 1980. 228 p. **CJ160**

Presents 60 biographies of congresswomen, ambassadors, special presidential assistants, governors and lieutenant governors, and mayors, emphasizing contemporary women serving in major positions since the late 1970s. Biographies are alphabetically arranged, usually two or three pages in length, and include references to selected speeches and writings, and bibliographies. General bibliography on women and politics, p. 161–89. Appendixes: women in congress, 1917–1980; women chiefs of mission, 1933–1980; and women ambassadors, federal judges, and key government officials as of Spring 1980. Name and subject index. HQ1236.S74

Who's who in American politics. Ed. 1 (1967/68)– . N.Y. : Bowker, 1967– . Biennial. **CJ161**

Issued in two volumes, 1991/92– .

Treats individuals currently or recently participating in politics at the local, state, or national level, from the president to mayors of cities with populations over 50,000. Entries, alphabetically arranged by state (and the District of Columbia and U.S. territories), provide party affiliation; date and place of birth; names of parents, spouse, and children; education; political, governmental, and business positions; military service, honors, and awards; publications; memberships; religion; legal residence; and mailing address. Includes lists of the President and cabinet, state delegations to Congress, members of the U.S. Supreme Court and the U.S. Court of Appeals, governors and lieutenant governors, state chairman for the Democratic and Republican parties, and abbreviations. Name index.

•Available in machine-readable form under the same title (also called *WWAP*). E176.W6424

Who's who in government. Ed. 1 (1972/73)–3 (1977). Chicago : Marquis, [1972–77]. 3 v. **CJ162**

A publication with the same title was issued by the Biographical Research Bureau, 1930–32.

A historically important source of biographical information on individuals who served in federal, local, state, and international government. Alphabetically arranged sketches list position, date and place of birth, parents, education, marital status, children, career, activities, military record, awards, memberships, political affiliation, religion, lodges, clubs, writings, and home and office addresses. Includes table of abbreviations and indexes of biographees by topic (in 1st ed.) and by government department (in all eds.).

§ More current biographical information on key federal employees may be found in the *Federal staff directory* (CJ137). E747.W512

Statistics

Stanley, Harold W. Vital statistics on American politics / Harold W. Stanley, Richard G. Neimi. 4th ed. Wash. : CQ Pr., 1994. 475 p. : ill. **CJ163**

1st ed., 1988; 3rd ed., 1992.

Contains more than 200 statistical tables, lists, and graphs gathered from a variety of sources. Topical chapters (e.g., Elections and campaigns, Congress, Interest groups, Social policy) include brief introductions and questions designed to test the reader's understanding of the statistics. The general introduction has a helpful section on the accuracy of published data. An appendix lists various definitions of U.S. regions and an annotated Guide to references for political statistics describes sources of additional information. Subject index. A teacher's manual is available from the publisher. JK274.S74

Executive branch

Guides

Congressional Quarterly's guide to the presidency / Michael Nelson, ed. Wash. : Congressional Quarterly Inc., c1989. 1521 p. **CJ164**

This massive compendium of information on the origins, evolution, history, and present operation of the presidency also includes facts about the presidents and their families. Has seven sections (e.g., Origins and development of the presidency, Powers of the presidency, The chief executive and the federal government), subdivided into 37 chapters, each ending with footnotes and a selected bibliography. The useful appendix features tables (e.g., a list of cabinet members and officials for each presidential administration, charts (e.g., presidential approval ratings), and documents (e.g., Wilson's "Fourteen Points" speech). General index; cross-references. JK516.C57

Goehlert, Robert. The presidency : a research guide / Robert U. Goehlert, Fenton S. Martin. Santa Barbara, Calif. : ABC-Clio, [1985]. 341 p. **CJ165**

In four main sections: the presidency as an institution, emphasizing official documents and secondary sources; individual presidents, their publications, presidential libraries, and secondary sources; campaigns and elections, with both primary and secondary titles; design and development of a research project and strategy on the presidency. Appendixes (p. 219–98) present research information in tabular format. Bibliography; author and title indexes. Z1249.P7G63

Studying the presidency / ed. by George C. Edwards III and Stephen J. Wayne. Knoxville : Univ. of Tennessee Pr., [1983]. 312 p. **CJ166**

Presents a series of essays (with bibliographic notes) by specialists on the methodology and various other aspects of the study of the

United States presidency. In two sections: (1) "Approaches and analyses" and (2) "Data sources and techniques." The latter includes chapters on information sources (including online databases), use of legal sources, presidential libraries, and interviewing presidential aides. General index.   JK518.S78

Bibliography

Cohen, Norman S. The American presidents : an annotated bibliography. Pasadena, Calif. : Salem Pr., c1989. 202 p.   **CJ167**

Provides annotated citations for selected books. Following an introduction covering general bibliographies and studies are separate chapters on each president, George Washington through George Bush. Within chapters, entries are alphabetical by main entry. Author index. Complements Fenton S. Martin and Robert Goehlert's *American presidents* (CJ173).

§ For more extensive annotated bibliographies on individual presidents, see volumes in *Twentieth-century presidential bibliography series* (Wilmington, Del. : Scholarly Resources, 1984–) and *Bibliographies of the presidents of the United States* series (Westport, Conn. : Meckler, 1988–1991; Greenwood, 1991–1992).   Z1249.P7C63

Davison, Kenneth E. The American presidency : a guide to information sources. Detroit : Gale, 1983. 467p. (American studies information guide ser., v.11).   **CJ168**

Essentially a bibliography in two parts: (1) The presidency (e.g., office, function and powers, problems, documents); and (2) Individual presidents. Chapters composing these parts contain numerous subdivisions within which citations (some annotated) are alphabetically arranged by author. Includes English-language books, articles, and selected government documents published since 1945. Author, title, and subject indexes.   Z1249.P7D38

Goehlert, Robert. The Department of State and American diplomacy : a bibliography / Robert U. Goehlert, Elizabeth R. Hoffmeister. N.Y. : Garland, 1986. 349 p. (Garland reference library of social science, v. 333).   **CJ169**

Presents 3,818 unannotated citations to English-language books, articles, dissertations, research reports, and selected documents (primarily 1945–84) covering the history, functions, organizations, structure, and procedures of the U.S. Department of State. An introduction lists State Department publications, guides to U.S. documents, and relevant bibliographies. In four major sections: (1) Topical (e.g., organization, functions, diplomacy); (2) Conduct of foreign policy; (3) Conduct of diplomacy by geographical area; (4) Biographical. Each section contains numerous subdivisions within which citations are alphabetically arranged by author. Author and subject indexes.   Z6465.U5G63

———————— The executive branch of the U.S. government : a bibliography / comp. by Robert U. Goehlert and Hugh Reynolds. N.Y. : Greenwood, 1989. 380 p. (Bibliographies and indexes in law and political science, no. 11).   **CJ170**

Lists over 4,000 unannotated citations to English-language monographs, articles, dissertations, and selected research reports (but not government publications) on the executive branch of the U.S. federal government, including the history, development, organization, procedures, rulings, and policies of individual departments. Specifically excludes items on the presidency and the executive office of the White House covered in Goehlert and Fenton S. Martin's *The American presidency* (CJ172) A general chapter on the executive branch, public administration, and bureaucracy is followed by chapters for each of the 13 executive departments (e.g., Defense, Education, Treasury) and the U.S. Postal Service. Alphabetically arranged within these chapters, most entries date 1945–85. Author and subject indexes.   Z7165.U5G56

Greenstein, Fred I. Evolution of the modern presidency : a bibliographical survey / Fred I. Greenstein, Larry Berman, Alvin S. Felzenberg. Wash. : American Enterprise Institute for Public Policy Research, c1977. [369] p.   **CJ171**

A classed listing of about 2,500 items; author index. Brief annotations for most entries. Emphasis on developments during the administrations of Franklin D. Roosevelt through Gerald Ford.   Z7165.U5G74

Martin, Fenton S. The American presidency : a bibliography / Fenton S. Martin, Robert U. Goehlert. Wash. : Congressional Quarterly, c1987. 506 p.   **CJ172**

     Z1249.P7M357

———————— American presidents : a bibliography / Fenton S. Martin, Robert U. Goehlert. Wash. : Congressional Quarterly, c1987. 756 p.   **CJ173**

Two complementary works, the first focusing on the history, development, powers and relationships of the office of the presidency, the other on the individual activities, policies, and accomplishments of the presidents themselves, from Washington through Reagan.

Presidency lists 8,567 unannotated citations in 13 topical chapters (e.g., The presidency and the law, The organization of the presidency, The presidency and foreign affairs). *Presidents* arranges 13,150 unannotated citations chronologically by president, then in five general categories: bibliographies, private life, public career, presidential years, and writings. Both titles include English-language books, articles, dissertations, essays, and research reports, 1885–1986, but exclude government publications; *Presidents* excludes the *Public papers of the presidents* series. Sources consulted by the compilers are listed in the introductions to each title; both have author and subject indexes.

     Z1249.P7M36

Library resources

Schick, Frank Leopold. Records of the presidency : presidential papers and libraries from Washington to Reagan / by Frank L. Schick with Renee Schick and Mark Carroll. Phoenix : Oryx, 1989. 309 p.   **CJ174**

Presents "the story of presidential papers from their origin to their place of deposit" and provides "a comprehensive guide to their contents and to bibliographic references to them."—*Introd.* In four parts: (1) agencies responsible for maintenance of presidential papers, legislation relating to presidential libraries, guides to presidential records, and presidential book collections at historic sites; (2) presidential papers in the Manuscript Division of the Library of Congress; (3) presidential papers in historical societies and special libraries; and (4) presidential libraries administered by the National Archives. Appendixes include tabular data on presidential libraries, lists of major presidential records collections and presidential historic sites, and an overview of the White House filing system. Bibliography; general index.   CD3029.82.S35

Veit, Fritz. Presidential libraries and collections. N.Y. : Greenwood, 1987. 152 p.   **CJ175**

Topical chapters discuss the development of presidential libraries; their fiscal impact; the nature of archival collections; the presidential libraries as a group; individually, the repositories of papers of presidents preceding Hoover; and the future of presidential libraries. Information on the libraries and repositories, which includes holdings, policies, services, programs, staff, and budget, was obtained through a questionnaire and from government publications. Appendixes provide statistics on the cost of presidential libraries, 1955–87, a copy of the questionnaire, and a list of organizations supporting presidential libraries. Bibliography; general index.   CD3029.82.V45

Archives

Burton, Dennis A. A guide to manuscripts in the presidential libraries / comp. and ed. by Dennis A. Burton, James B. Rhoads, Raymond W. Smock. College Park, Md. : Research Materials Corp., c1985. 451 p. : ill.　**CJ176**

Describes the holdings of seven presidential libraries (Hoover, Roosevelt, Truman, Eisenhower, Kennedy, Johnson, Ford). Brief data on the institutions themselves (e.g., address, telephone, hours) are followed by entries for manuscript collections, microfilm, and oral histories, arranged alphabetically by the names of individuals, government agencies and offices, countries, and specific subjects. The entries themselves provide a collection reference number, the name and size of the collection, the holding library, a description of the collection, and the *National union catalog of manuscript collections* (DB34) number. General index cites collection reference numbers.
　　CD3029.82.B87

Haines, Gerald K. A reference guide to United States Department of State special files. Westport, Conn. : Greenwood, c1985. 393 p. : ill.　**CJ177**

Describes the special "lot" files of the Department of State, 1940–59—working papers, drafts, notes, annotated memoranda, and other historically valuable documents on foreign policy—an important supplement to the Department's central files. Entries are arranged in 17 topical chapters (e.g., National security, Asia and the Pacific, Congressional relations), generally following State Department organization. Each entry gives title, content description, dates, amount and location of records, lot file and National Archives accession numbers, finding aids available, and access restrictions. Includes a list of abbreviations and three Department of State organization charts. File number and name/subject indexes.　CD3031

Encyclopedias

Encyclopedia of the American presidency / editors, Leonard W. Levy, Louis Fisher. N.Y. : Simon & Schuster, c1994. 4 v. (1827 p.).　**CJ178**

Aims to treat the U.S. presidency comprehensively in more than 1,000 signed articles written by scholars, journalists, and other specialists. Varying in length from 250–8,000 words, entries are alphabetically arranged, cross-referenced, and end with bibliographies. Includes biographies of every president and vice-president, selected first ladies, also-rans, cabinet officers, congressional leaders, and Supreme Court justices. Also treats the powers and prerogatives of the presidency; the multiple roles of the president; the executive branch; relations with Congress and the judiciary; public policies; presidential elections; major wars and treaties; key acts of Congress; important events and concepts in U.S. history; major court cases; and political parties and ideologies. Lists of tables, contributors, entries, and abbreviations. Appendixes: the U.S. Constitution; tables giving personal information on the presidents; lists of presidents, cabinet officers, and other officials; and data on presidential elections. A synoptic outline provides a conceptual overview of the contents. Court cases and general indexes.

§ See also *Congressional Quarterly's guide to the presidency* (CJ164) and Congressional Quarterly's *The presidency A to Z* (CJ179).　JK511.E53

The presidency A to Z : a ready reference encyclopedia / Michael Nelson, advisory ed. Wash. : Congressional Quarterly, c1992. 574 p. : ill. (CQ's encyclopedia of American government, v. 2).　**CJ179**

Presents basic information, alphabetically arranged, on the history, processes, and people relevant to the presidency. Entries are of two types: essays on broad topics (e.g., economic powers); and shorter entries treating narrower topics (e.g., coattail effect). The shorter entries include biographies of presidents, vice-presidents, influential first ladies, selected presidential candidates, presidential advisors, and gov-

ernment officials. Appendixes list presidents and vice-presidents, cabinets, presidential approval ratings, etc. Cross-references within entries; bibliography; general index.

§ Companion publications in this series: *Congress A to Z* (CJ204) and *The Supreme Court A to Z* (CK188).　JK511.P775

Quotations

The bully pulpit : quotations from America's presidents / ed. by Elizabeth Frost. N.Y. : Facts on File, c1988. 282 p.　**CJ180**

Rev. ed. published as: *The world almanac of presidential quotations* (N.Y. : Pharos Books, 1993).

Contains approximately 3,000 quotations by U.S. presidents from George Washington to Ronald Reagan, chosen because of their "historic significance, intrinsic human interest, and colorful or eloquent language."—*Introd.* Quotations are alphabetical by topic (e.g., equality, law, the presidency), then chronological. Each entry includes the name of the president, source of the quote, and date. An appendix lists the presidents, birth and death dates, and dates in office. Bibliography; author and subject indexes.　E176.1.B925

Directories

Federal regional yellow book : who's who in the federal government's departments, agencies, courts, military installations, and service academies outside of Washington, DC. v. 1 (winter 1993)– . N.Y. : Monitor Pub. Co., c1993– . Semiannual.　**CJ181**

Published as a companion to the *Federal yellow book* (below).

Gives names, addresses, and phone numbers for more than 20,000 individuals in some 8,000 regional offices of the federal government. Includes federal departments; independent agencies (e.g., Federal Reserve System); congressional support agencies (e.g., General Accounting Office); and U.S. courts. Geographic, personal name, and subject indexes.　JK6.F425

Federal yellow book. Wash. : Washington Monitor, 1976– . Quarterly.　**CJ182**

A directory of executive departments, administrative agencies, and regional offices, listing more than 35,000 names, addresses, and telephone numbers. Department/agency and personal name indexes.
　JK6.F45

Registers

United States. Department of State. Office of the Historian. Principal officers of the Department of State and United States chiefs of mission, 1778–1990 / United States Department of State. [Wash.] : U.S. Dept. of State, Office of the Historian, Bureau of Public Affairs : For sale by the U.S. Govt. Print. Off., 1991. 219 p. (Department of State publication, 9825.).　**CJ183**

1st ed., 1973, covered 1778–1973; 2nd ed., 1982, covered 1778–1982; new rev. ed., 1986, covered 1778–1986; rev. ed., 1988, covered 1778–1988.

1st and 2nd ed. had title: *United States chiefs of mission*.

Superintendent of Documents classification: S 1.2:Of 2/1778–1990.

Updated through August 31, 1990. Beginning with the 1986 edition, information on major executive officers of the Department of State was rearranged and expanded. The work now features two major parts: (1) Principal officers of the Department of State, and (2) United States chiefs of mission. Appendixes include listings of the heads of the U.S. foreign assistance agencies, U.S. trade representatives, and directors of the U.S. Information Agency and the U.S. Arms Control and Disarmament Agency. Personal name index.　JX1706.A59U54

Handbooks

Almanac of American presidents : from 1789 to the present : an original compendium of facts and anecdotes about politics and the presidency in the United States of America / ed. by Thomas L. Connelly and Michael D. Senecal. N.Y. : Facts on File, c1991. 485 p. : ill.   **CJ184**

Presents little-known information on presidents through George Bush. Chapters, written by scholars in American history, treat personal, political, and historical topics. Bibliography; general index.
E176.1.A626

•**U.S. foreign affairs on CD-ROM** : USFAC / Bureau of Public Affairs, Office of Public Communication, U.S. Department of State [database]. [Wash.] : The Office, 1993– .   **CJ185**

Superintendent of Documents classification: S 1.142/2: .
Began publication with set for Jan. 1990–May 1993. Annual.

Gives "full text access to a selection of official statements, testimony, transcripts, foreign policy fact sheets, and country information which has been printed and released electronically by the U.S. Department of State."—*Introd.* Among the items offered are the Department of State *Dispatch* and *Dispatch supplements*, country *Background notes*, daily press briefings, congressional and special reports, *Patterns of global terrorism* reports, *Key officers at U.S. foreign service posts*, and the Tips for travelers series.

Zink, Steven D. Guide to the presidential advisory commissions, 1973–1984. Alexandria, Va. : Chadwyck-Healey, 1987. 643 p.   **CJ186**

Describes 74 temporary presidential commissions and their work (including task forces, boards, etc.). Arranged by year, entries are systematic and succinct, and for each group list establishment and termination dates, sources of authority (e.g., specific public laws), functions, activities, recommendations, dates and places of meetings, names of members, and publications. For publications, gives title, classification or report number, abstract, and information on availability (the latter useful since nearly half these documents were not distributed through the GPO depository program). Title, subject, and personal name indexes. There are some errors; e.g., the National Commission on Libraries and Information Science is listed in the index but does not appear in the text.   JK468.C7Z56

Sourcebooks

Historic documents on the presidency, 1776–1989 / [ed. by] Michael Nelson. Wash. : Congressional Quarterly, c1989. 528 p.   **CJ187**

Contains selected documents focusing on "the most memorable and significant activities of individual presidents."—*Pref.* Emphasizes the development of the presidency as an institution and the leadership role of the president. Documents are chronologically arranged and introduced by notes that place documents in both their contemporary setting and historical context and provide cross-references to other documents. General index.

§ *See also* the companion volume, *Historic documents on presidential elections* (Wash. : Congressional Quarterly, 1991), which emphasizes documents relevant to presidential elections or the development of the presidential election process (e.g., candidate debates, landmark speeches).   JK511.H57

Speeches of the American presidents / ed. by Janet Podell and Steven Anzovin. N.Y. : H.W. Wilson, 1988. 820 p. : ports.
CJ188

Contains 180 major speeches of U.S. presidents, Washington to Reagan, delivered during their terms of office. Most are complete; a few that are very long are excerpted. Speeches were chosen to show how speechmaking has grown as a political tool or to illustrate each president's character and to cover important issues of his administration. In chronological order, sections on the presidents begin with brief

notes describing the president and his speechmaking style; each speech is preceded by comments on its historical context, composition, and delivery. General index.   J81.C88

Biographical dictionaries

Biographical directory of the United States executive branch, 1774–1989 / Robert Sobel, ed. in chief. N.Y. : Greenwood, 1990. 567 p.   **CJ189**

1971 ed. covered 1771–1971; 1977 ed. covered 1774–1977.

Includes brief, alphabetically-arranged sketches of the careers of all cabinet members, as well as of presidents, vice presidents, and presidents of the Continental Congress. Appendixes provide lists of presidential administrations (chronological), holders of cabinet posts or other political offices (by post), military service (by branch), education (alphabetical), place of birth (alphabetical by state), and marital information (by status). No index.   E176.B578

Kane, Joseph Nathan. Facts about the presidents : a compilation of biographical and historical information. 6th ed. N.Y. : H.W. Wilson, 1993. 433 p. : ill.   **CJ190**

1st ed., 1959; 5th ed., 1989.

In two parts: (1) chapters on each president (through Bill Clinton) in chronological order, with data on family background, political career, and administration; (2) material in tabular form, with collective data and statistics. General index.

§ *See also* William A DeGregorio's *The complete book of U.S. presidents* (3rd ed., rev. N.Y. : Wings Books, 1992) which has biographies in narrative form.   E176.1.K3

The presidents : a reference history / Henry F. Graff, ed. N.Y. : Scribner, 1984. 700 p.   **CJ191**

Offers a chronological history of the presidency through Jimmy Carter, presented in the form of interpretive essays on the individual men who held the office, the events and developments of each administration, and the impact of the man and his policies on the course of American history. The essays (by 35 professional historians and political scientists) follow no rigid pattern, but typically provide an account of the president's early life and pre-presidency years before concentrating on his time in office. Select bibliography for each essay, often with evaluative comment, references to manuscript sources, and citations to editions of the writings of the president. General index.
E176.1.P918

Southwick, Leslie H. Presidential also-rans and running mates, 1788–1980. Jefferson, N.C. : McFarland, [1984]. 722 p.
CJ192

Offers biographical sketches of those "nominated for president or vice president but who failed to achieve that goal."—*Introd.* Chronologically arranged by election year; notes on the election precede the biographies of unsuccessful candidates. Appendixes include a ranking of losing candidates based on their perceived qualifications and prospects for success. Bibliography; general index.   E176.1.S695

Congress

Guides

Congressional Quarterly's guide to Congress. 4th ed. Wash. : Congressional Quarterly Inc., c1991. 836, [348] p. : ill.   **CJ193**

1st ed., 1971; 3rd ed., 1982.

Comprehensive treatment of matters related to the legislative branch. Eight sections: Origins and development of Congress; Powers of Congress; Congressional procedures; Pressures on Congress; Housing and support; Pay and perquisites; Congress and the electorate; Qualifications and conduct. An extensive appendix provides a wealth of information including: rules of the House and Senate; glossary of

Congressional terms; an alphabetical list, with brief biographical data, of all past and present members of Congress. Bibliographies; general index. JK1021.C565

Filson, Lawrence E. The legislative drafter's desk reference. Wash. : Congressional Quarterly, c1992. 450 p. **CJ194**

Intended for those who draft legislation or analyze bills. Shows how to write, analyze, change, and track bills, resolutions, and amendments. Subject index. KF4950.F55

Goehlert, Robert. Congress and law-making : researching the legislative process / Robert U. Goehlert and Fenton S. Martin. 2nd ed. Santa Barbara, Calif. : ABC-Clio ; Oxford : Clio Pr., c1989. 306 p. **CJ195**

1st ed., 1979.

Designed to help users trace congressional legislation and become familiar with basic sources for research on: federal legislation and administrative law; Congress, its budget process, and support agencies; foreign affairs and treaties; campaigns and elections; and secondary sources. Features lengthy annotations and provides illustrations for some sources. Includes section on how to cite government publications, appendixes listing selected depository libraries and research centers, and glossary. Author, title, and subject indexes. KF240.G63

Manion, Judith. A research guide to Congress : how to make Congress work for you / by Judith Manion, Joseph Meringolo, Robert Oaks. 2nd ed. Wash. : Legi-Slate, Inc., c1991. 191 p. **CJ196**

1st ed., 1985.

Designed to facilitate the understanding of federal legislation. In two major sections: (1) the legislative process from the introduction of a bill to its passage as law and the issuance of regulations, and (2) legislative research, the location of information on legislation from bills to laws including using online databases and preparing a legislative history. Includes an annotated bibliography, appendixes (e.g., Statutes at Large and their coverage), and a subject index. KF4950.M36

Bibliography

Baker, Richard A. The United States Senate : a historical bibliography. [Wash. : U.S. Govt. Print. Off.], 1977. 78 p. : ill. **CJ197**

Comp. by the United States Senate Historical Office.

A classed bibliography of approximately 1,000 books, articles, and dissertations on the Senate, its practices, customs, and former members. Includes a reference section for primary materials, directories, indexes, etc. State index of senators for the biographical section; index of authors and editors. Z7165.U5B335

Goehlert, Robert. The United States Congress : a bibliography / Robert U. Goehlert and John R. Sayre. N.Y. : Free Pr. ; London : Collier Macmillan, [1982]. 376 p. **CJ198**

A classed bibliography of more than 5,600 books, essays, articles, government documents, theses and dissertations organized in 14 topical chapters. Focuses on scholarly sources concerning the history, development, and legislative process of Congress published since 1782. Subject and author indexes. Z7165.U5G575

Kennon, Donald R. The speakers of the U.S. House of Representatives : a bibliography, 1789–1984. Baltimore : Johns Hopkins Univ. Pr., c1986. 323 p. (Johns Hopkins University studies in historical and political science, 103d ser., no. 1.). **CJ199**

Lists 4,280 books, articles, dissertations, and manuscripts related to the lives and careers of 46 speakers of the House of Representatives (ending with Tip O'Neill) and to the office itself. A general section of works on the speakership, Congress, congressional history, and congressional research is followed by four chronological sections, each beginning with a brief list of works on the speakership and speakers of that period. The chronological sections are further subdivided into chapters on individual speakers, each including a short biographical

sketch, a list of available manuscript collections of the speaker's papers, and a bibliography. Includes author and subject indexes. Z7165.U5K45

Zwirn, Jerrold. Congressional publications and proceedings : research on legislation, budgets, and treaties. 2nd ed. Englewood, Colo. : Libraries Unlimited, 1988. 299 p. **CJ200**

Rev. ed. of *Congressional publications: a research guide to legislation, budgets, and treaties* (1982).

More than a guide to congressional publications, this work attempts to "explore the relationship between the information environment and the legislative process."—*Pref.* 11 topical chapters (e.g., Legislative history, Committee reports, Federal budget) describe, in essay form, publications rising from the various avenues Congress follows in conducting its business. Appendixes include standing committee jurisdiction charts and a topical annotated list of legislative information sources. Document and subject indexes.

§ *See also* Joe Morehead and Mary Fetzer, *Introduction to United States government information sources* (AF73). JK1067.Z85

Manuscripts; Archives

A guide to research collections of former members of the United States House of Representatives, 1789–1987 / prep. under the direction of the Office for the Bicentennial of the United States, House of Representatives ; Cynthia Pease Miller, ed. in chief. Wash. : The Office, 1988. 504 p. **CJ201**

Superintendent of Documents classification: Y 1.1/7:100-171.

House document (United States. Congress. House), 100–171.

Provides information on historical papers, diaries and/or memoirs, and oral history collections relating to approximately 3,300 former members of the House of Representatives. Arranged alphabetically by name of representative, entries include birth and death dates, an abbreviation for state represented, and names of repositories along with their holdings, document dates, size of collection, and a brief collection description. Includes various supplementary materials: a list of representatives whose papers were not located; documentary publication projects relating to federal government history; addresses of repositories (alphabetical by state); a chronological table of the sessions of Congress; and a copy of the survey form sent to repositories. Lacks a list of collections by repository.

§ A companion to *Guide to research collections of former United States senators, 1789–1982* (CJ202). CD3043.G84

Guide to research collections of former United States senators, 1789–1982 / Kathryn Allamong Jacob, ed. in chief, Elizabeth Ann Hornyak, production ed. Wash. : Historical Office, United States Senate, 1983. 362 p. : ports. (U.S. Senate bicentennial publication, 1). **CJ202**

Superintendent of Documents classification: Y 1.1/3:97–41.

Describes the papers and oral history transcripts pertaining to nearly 1,800 former senators. Arranged alphabetically by senator, entries include the name and location of the repository followed by: for papers, brief descriptions of holdings, giving document dates, number of items, summary of contents, finding aids, and user restrictions; for oral histories, date of the interview, number of transcribed pages, and user restrictions. Entries also note whether the repository has portraits, photographs, or memorabilia. Appendixes list state and party abbreviations; senators by state with information on party affiliation, offices held, and birth and death dates; and collections by repository (arranged by state). CD3043.G85

United States. National Archives and Records Administration. Guide to the records of the United States House of Representatives at the National Archives, 1789–1989 / Charles E. Schamel ... [et al.] ; prep. under the direction of Donald K. Anderson. Bicentennial ed. [Wash. : U.S. Govt. Print. Off., 1989]. 466 p. : ill. **CJ203**

Superintendent of Documents classification: Y 1.1/7:100-245.

§ *Guide to the records of the United States Senate at the National Archives, 1789–1989* / Robert W. Coren ... [et al.] ; prep. under the direction of Walter J. Stewart. Bicentennial ed. ([Wash. : U.S. Govt. Print. Off.], 1989. 356 p.).

Superintendent of Documents classification: Y 1.1/3:100-42.

Two complementary works, focusing on records of the House and Senate that have been transferred to the National Archives. Both offer a chapter on research in the records of Congress, followed by chapters concerning the records of the respective standing, select, and joint committees through 1968; other records through 1968; and recent records, 1969–88. Each work features several appendixes, including lists of congressional leaders, bibliography, glossary, session dates, finding aids, and microfilm publications. Both have a general index.

CD3042.S46U54

Encyclopedias

Congress A to Z : a ready reference encyclopedia / Ann O'Connor, supervisory ed. 2nd ed. Wash. : Congressional Quarterly, c1993. 547 p. : ill., ports. (CQ's encyclopedia of American government, v. 1).   **CJ204**

1st ed., 1988.

Provides comprehensive information on the history, structure, personnel, and operations of the federal government's legislative branch. Written for a wide audience, the entries, alphabetically arranged, are of two types: (1) long essays (three to seven pages) on broad subject areas (e.g., budget process, ethics, lobbying) and (2) briefer entries giving definitions of specific terms, descriptions of congressional committees, and biographies of outstanding members of Congress. An extensive appendix contains factual and statistical data (e.g., historical lists of Speakers of the House of Representatives, Senate and House floor leaders, cases of expulsion), some miscellaneous information (e.g., how to write to a member of Congress). Detailed table of contents, illustrations and photographs, cross-references within entries, and a bibliography. General index.

§ Companion publications in this series: *The presidency A to Z* (CJ179) and *The Supreme Court A to Z* (CK188).   JK1067.C67

Dictionaries

Dickson, Paul. The Congress dictionary : the ways and meanings of Capitol Hill / Paul Dickson, Paul Clancy ; with a special foreword by Thomas P. "Tip" O'Neill, Jr. N.Y. : Wiley, c1993. 400 p. : ill.   **CJ205**

Brings together slang, jargon, and terms used by or in reference to the U.S. Congress. While many of the terms are found in other political dictionaries (e.g., Jay M. Shafritz, *The HarperCollins dictionary of American government and politics*, CJ122), the present work is particularly good for its currency and inclusion of items that may not be found elsewhere (e.g., aardvark politics, Chowder and Marching Society, goo-goos, limousine liberal, talking heads, Tuesday-Thursday Club). Includes cross-references, etymologies or citations to first usage for some words, and many illustrations and sidebars (lists of informal caucuses, Supreme Court nominations rejected or dropped, selected Golden Fleece awards). Bibliography.   JK1067.D5

Kravitz, Walter. Congressional Quarterly's American congressional dictionary. Wash. : Congressional Quarterly Inc., c1993. 305 p.   **CJ206**

Treats nearly 900 alphabetically-arranged terms and expressions (e.g., Dance of the Swans and the Ducks, layover rules) currently in use in Congress, focusing on the legislative process, procedures, organization, staff, and officers. Definitions feature (where applicable) historical origins or examples, cross-references, or explanations of differences in procedure, practice, and terminology between the House and the Senate.   JK9.K73

Periodicals

Congress and the nation. [v. 1] (1945–1964)– . Wash. : Congressional Quarterly Service, 1965– . Quadrennial.   **CJ207**

Offers a survey of United States politics and government based on materials from the *Congressional Quarterly almanac* (CJ208) and information from other sources. Beginning with v. 2, each volume covers one presidential term.

The same agency's publication, *Politics in America, 1945–1964* (CJ214 note), is drawn principally from v. 1 of this work.   KF49C65

Congressional Quarterly almanac. v. 4 (1948)– . Wash. : Congressional Quarterly News Features, c1948– . Annual.   **CJ208**

Continues *Congressional quarterly*, v. 1–3 (1945–47), which was issued quarterly.

Each volume offers a summary of congressional legislation for one session of Congress—e.g., v. 47 (1991) covers the 102nd Congress, 1st session. Divided into sections dealing with categories of legislation (e.g., economics and finance, law and judiciary, defense), each section subdivided by specific topics. Includes voting information on individual measures and several useful appendixes (e.g., vote studies, text of important documents, roll-call votes). Bill number, roll-call vote, and general indexes.

Congressional Quarterly weekly report. v. 14 (1956)– . Wash. : Congressional Quarterly, Inc., 1956– . Weekly.   **CJ209**

Offers an informative weekly summary of congressional action and developments. Most issues include the following sections: Inside Congress; Economics and finance; Government and commerce; Social policy; Defense and foreign policy; Politics; and For the record (e.g., voting charts). Some issues contain special reports or are accompanied by supplements. Quarterly indexes cumulate annually.

•A machine-readable version is available online, with coverage from 1980.   JK1.C15

Directories

The almanac of American politics. Wash. : Barone, 1972– . Biennial.   **CJ210**

Subtitle: *The Senators, the Representatives and the Governors: their records and election results, their states and districts.*

A political overview for each state (with a map of election districts) is followed by information on its governor, senators, and representatives (with district-by-district background and analysis). Includes brief biographies; office addresses and telephone numbers; election results; and (for legislators) committees, interest group ratings, and key votes. Usually offers a variety of additional information (e.g., demographics; campaign finance; Senate, House, and Joint committees and members). General index.

•A machine-readable version with the same title is available online.   JK1012.A44

The almanac of the unelected. 1988– . Wash. : Almanac of the Unelected, Inc., c1988– .   **CJ211**

Contains information on key congressional staff members. The volume for 1993 has two parts: (House and Senate) with profiles arranged alphabetically within leadership and committee sections. Each profile includes a photograph, personal information, professional background, area of expertise, legislative contribution and plans, quotes, and occasionally evaluation by a colleague or observer. Has fewer, but more descriptive, profiles than *Congressional staff directory* (CJ215). Personal name index.   JK1083.A77

•**Biographical directory of the United States Congress, 1774–1989** [database]. Mt. Vernon, Va. : Staff Directories, [1989?].   **CJ212**

Contains machine-readable versions of: *Biographical directory of the United States Congress, 1774–1989* (CJ232); *Guide to research collections of former U.S. senators, 1789–1982* (CJ202); *Guide to research collections of former U.S. representatives, 1789–1982* (CJ201); *Guide to the records of the U.S. Senate at the National Archives, 1789–1989* (CJ203); *Guide to the records of the U.S. House of Representatives at the National Archives, 1789–1989* (CJ203); *Black Americans in Congress, 1870–1989* (CJ231); *Women in Congress, 1870–1989* (CJ233); and *Inaugural addresses of the Presidents of the United States, 1789–1989* (Wash. : U.S. Govt. Print. Off., 1989).

Bosnich, Victor W. Congressional voting guide : a ten year compilation. N.Y. : H.W. Wilson, c1992. 637 p. **CJ213**

1st ed., 1987; 3rd ed., 1991.

Compiles voting records, 1982–92, for members of the 102nd Congress on 144 selected bills chosen by the compilers (e.g., gun control, civil rights). Divided into House and Senate sections, each beginning with a numbered list (in reverse chronological order) that describes the proposed legislation and gives the overall vote, followed by voting records of individual members on the measures. Each record includes a brief biography and presidential support scores for 1990 and 1991. Personal name and subject indexes. JK1051.B67

Congressional Quarterly's politics in America. 1990– . Wash. : CQ Pr., 1989– . Biennial. **CJ214**

Continues *Politics in America* (1982–89).

1st publ. 1965 as *Politics in America 1945–64*, which was drawn from the publisher's *Congress and the nation* (CJ207).

Profile articles summarize members' performances, issues in which they are interested, legislative influence, political alliances, elections, and voting records; statistical data on elections, campaign finances, voting records, interest group ratings, and committee memberships are appended. The politics of states and individual congressional districts are briefly sketched. Geographical arrangement, followed by directories of committee membership and members' offices; name index.

• A machine-readable version, *CQ member profiles*, is available online. Current coverage; updated continuously. JK1012.C63

Congressional staff directory. 1959– . Mt. Vernon, Va. : Staff Directories, Ltd., 1959– . Semiannual. **CJ215**

Publisher varies. Issued annually through 1988.

Useful in locating biographical and locational information for the office staff of members of Congress. Lists in color coded sections, state delegations; mayors of the 65 largest cities; governors; senators and representatives and their staffs; congressional committees and subcommittees and their members and staffs; congressional districts and members of counties and cities with population over 1,500; and biographies of key congressional staff. Personal name and keyword subject indexes.

Between the 1st and 2nd sessions of each Congress, a supplement, *Advance locator for Capitol Hill* (1965–) has been published annually. A biennial companion volume, *Election index*, was published 1966–82.

• Machine-readable version: *Staff directories on CD-ROM* [database] (Mt. Vernon, Va. : Staff Directories). Updated semiannually. Combines *Judicial staff directory* (CK149), *Congressional staff directory*, and *Federal staff directory* (CJ137). Another machine-readable version, *Congressional staff directory on disk*, is available from the same publisher. JK1012.C65

Congressional yellow book. 1976– . Wash. : Washington Monitor. Quarterly. **CJ216**

Subtitle: *Who's who in Congress, including committees and key staff.*

Provides information on senators and representatives and their staffs; congressional committees and subcommittees and their members and staffs; leadership and member organizations (e.g., Senate Anti-Terrorism Caucus, Congressional Aviation Forum); and congressional support agencies (e.g., General Accounting Office, Library of Congress). Includes lists of state delegations with district maps. Staff index. Supplements are issued when November elections warrant supplying updated information between editions. Publication frequency makes it more current than similar directories.

Nelson, Garrison. Committees in the U.S. Congress, 1947–1992 / Garrison Nelson with Clark H. Bensen. Wash. : Congressional Quarterly, c1993. v. 1. (In progress). **CJ217**

"A projected six-volume set documenting all of the assignments to committees in the U.S. Congress from the First Congress in 1789 until the present."—*Acknowledgments*. Draws information from official congressional documents (e.g., *Official congressional directory* [CJ221], *Congressional record* [AF127]), confirmed by nongovernmental sources. Vol. 1 includes listings from January 3, 1947, the opening of the 80th Congress (the first convened after the implementation of the 1946 Legislative Reorganization Act) until January 3, 1993, the closing of the 102nd Congress. Organized in sections covering Senate standing committees, Senate select and special committees, House standing committees, House select and standing committees, and joint committees. Includes historical information on the committee and all members (e.g., rank, party, state, years in Congress). Name index. JK1029.N45

Sharp, J. Michael. The directory of congressional voting scores and interest group ratings. N.Y. : Facts on File, c1988. 2 v. (1204 p.). **CJ218**

Presents ratings of the voting records of members of Congress, 1947–85. Following a helpful introduction explaining the methodology and use of the work, alphabetically arranged entries for each member contain scores on four rating scales compiled by *Congressional Quarterly* (Conservative coalition, Party unity, Presidential support, Voting participation) and ratings by 11 interest groups (e.g., American Civil Liberties Union, National Taxpayers Union). Entries also include biographical data and the percentage of votes received in each election. An appendix lists members of each congress. No index.

JK1051.S555

Stubbs, Walter. Congressional committees, 1789–1982 : a checklist. Westport, Conn. : Greenwood, 1985. 210 p. (Bibliographies and indexes in law and political science, no. 6). **CJ219**

A listing of more than 1,500 committees, including "standing committees, select and special committees, select and special joint committees, and statutory joint committees. Exceptions to this group are honorary, ceremonial, and housekeeping committees. … Also excluded are political committees, committees of the whole, and conference committees."—*Introd.* Arranged alphabetically by keyword in the title of the committee. The entry for each committee includes beginning and ending dates; citations to the resolution or public law creating and terminating it; later names, if any; and the Superintendent of Documents number, if assigned. Contains a chronological list of committees. Subject index. JK1029.S78

Trammell, Jeffrey B. The new members of congress almanac : 103rd Congress / Jeffrey B. Trammell, Gary P. Osifchin. Wash. : The Almanac of the Unelected, [1992]. 134 p. : ill. **CJ220**

Offers descriptive profiles of newly elected members of Congress. Separate sections for House and Senate; within each section, entries are arranged by state. Each profile includes a photograph, personal data, professional background, primary and general election results, analysis of district, campaign issues, and position on key legislative isues. Personal name index. A similar work was publ. 1994 for the 104th Congress (Jeffrey B. Trammell, Stuart D. Serkin).

§ See also *Congressional yellow book* (CJ216). JK1012.T73

United States. Congress. Official congressional directory. 50th Congress, 1st session– . Wash. : U.S. Govt. Print. Off., 1888– . Biennial. **CJ221**

Superintendent of Documents classification: Y 4.P 93/1:1/ .

Publ. 1809–1886 as *Congressional directory*. Some current editions bear that title.

Directories for some sessions issued in revised editions.

Supplements accompany some volumes.

From 1865, printed at the Government Printing Office; before that by private firms. Vols. for 97th Congress- comp. under the direction of the Joint Committee on Printing.

Contains: (1) biographical sketches of members of Congress, arranged by state; (2) state delegations; (3) congressional zip codes; (4) terms of service; (5) committees, membership, and days of meetings; (6) joint committees; (7) committee assignments; (8) boards, commissions, and advisory organizations; (9) statistical information (e.g., sessions of Congress, votes cast for legislators); (10) the Capitol (e.g., officers of the Senate and House, capitol buildings and grounds); (11) executive departments; (12) independent agencies; (13) judiciary; (14) District of Columbia government; (15) international organizations; (16) foreign diplomatic representatives and consular offices in the U.S.; (17) U.S. diplomatic and consular offices; (18) press galleries, rules, representatives entitled to admission; (19) maps of congressional districts. Individual name index.　　　　JK1011

——————— The United States congressional directories, 1789–1840 / ed. by Perry M. Goldman and James S. Young. N.Y. : Columbia Univ. Pr., 1973. 417 p.　　**CJ222**

Collates information provided in the early congressional directories, including names and addresses of state delegations, members of standing and select committees, and the boardinghouse groups (or fraternities) of congressional members. The cutoff date of 1840 was chosen because "most ... libraries possess a complete series of the *Congressional directories* from 1840 on, and ... the earlier directories are rare items." No personal names index or biographical material; the user is referred to the *Biographical directory of the United States Congress* (CJ232) for material on the state delegations.　　JK1011.U53

Handbooks

Congress & defense. 1988– . Palo Alto, Calif. : EW Communications, c1988– .　　**CJ223**

Attempts to indicate by presenting numerical data the relationship between the U.S. defense industry and individual members of Congress. The main section contains profiles of individual senators and representatives, giving for each the leading Department of Defense (DoD) contractors for his or her congressional district, leading weapons systems, leading DoD contractor political action committee donors, and votes on key defense-related issues. Appendixes give such data as state rankings by DoD total contracts, similar rankings for congressional districts and cities, a ranked list of DoD contractor-sponsored political action committees, and Senate and House defense voting records.

•A machine-readable version with the same title, covering the same time period, is available on computer diskettes.　　UC263.C63

Deschler, Lewis. Deschler's precedents of the United States House of Representatives : including references to provisions of the Constitution and laws, and to decisions of the courts. Wash. : U.S. Govt. Print. Off., 1977–1992. 11 v. (House document —94th Congress, 2nd Session, 94–661).　　**CJ224**

Vols. 10–11 have title: *Deschler-Brown precedents of the United States House of Representatives* / by Lewis Deschler, William Holmes Brown.

Continues: *Hinds' precedents* (1907–08), which covered 1789–1907; and *Cannon's precedents* (1935–41), which covered 1908–36.

This extensive compilation reviews precedents from 1936, arranged by topical chapter. Precedents are defined as (1) rulings or decisions of the Speaker or Chairman; (2) expressed or implied decisions or conclusions of the House itself; (3) practice or procedures of the House not specifically ruled on. Precedents serve as the common law of the House and prevent arbitrary rulings. Useful for understanding House procedure and studying its history. Each volume has a table of contents; each chapter begins with an index to precedents.

§ One-volume summary: *Procedure in the U.S. House of Representatives* ... by Deschler and Brown (4th ed. [1982]— . Wash. : U.S. Govt. Print. Off., 1982–). 1st ed. (1975)–3rd ed. (1979) had title: *Deschler's procedure.* Covers the major precedents from 1959 through the end of the 96th Congress. Arranged by topical chapter; subject index. A supplement (1985) covers the 97th and 98th Congresses.　　KF4992.D486

Tiefer, Charles. Congressional practice and procedure : a reference, research, and legislative guide. N.Y. : Greenwood, 1989. 1046 p.　　**CJ225**

An extensive and detailed work that treats both the procedures (i.e., rules and precedents) and practices (e.g., how an agenda is carried out) followed by Congress. Draws heavily on books and articles by members of Congress and political scientists. A lengthy selected bibliography is arranged by topics that correspond to sections of the text—e.g., Agenda setting and structuring House proceedings, Filibuster and cloture, Appropriations. General index. Serves as a valuable companion to the manuals of precedents and procedures published by Congress itself.　　KF4937.T54

United States. Congress. House. Constitution, Jefferson's manual and rules of the House of Representatives of the United States. Wash. : U.S. Govt. Print. Off., [1824]– . Biennial.　　**CJ226**

House document. Y 1.1/7: .

"Contains the fundamental source material for parliamentary procedure used in the House of Representatives ..."—*Pref.* The manual was first prepared by Thomas Jefferson when he was president of the Senate. Although it reflects English parliamentary practice of that time, its provisions still govern House procedures when applicable and when not inconsistent with its standing rules and orders. In addition to the items listed in the title, includes a variety of relevant information (e.g., applicable provisions of legislative reorganization acts; statutes relating to joint and select committees). Subject index.　KF4992.U54

United States. Congress. Senate. Riddick's Senate procedure : precedents and practices / by Floyd M. Riddick and Alan S. Frumin ; with a foreword by Robert C. Byrd ; rev. and ed. by Alan S. Frumin. Wash. : U.S. Govt. Print. Off., 1992. 1608 p. (Senate document, no. 101-28.).　　**CJ227**

Revised editions issued periodically. Previous editions (1958, 1964, 1974, 1981) had title *Senate procedure: precedents and practices.*

"A compilation of the rules of the Senate, portions of laws affecting Senate procedure, rulings by the Presiding Officer, and established practices of the Senate."—*Pref.*

Divided into chapters and arranged alphabetically with a detailed index. Contains much, but not all, of the information included in the *Senate manual* (CJ228) and is arranged differently.　　FK4892.R5

——————— Senate manual : containing the standing rules, orders, laws, and resolutions affecting the business of the United States Senate; Jefferson's Manual; Declaration of Independence; Articles of Confederation; Constitution of the United States, etc. Wash. : U.S. Govt. Print. Off. Biennial.　**CJ228**

Superintendent of Documents classification: Y 1.1/3: .

Title varies. Issued for each session of Congress.

In addition to the items stated in the title, includes various tables (e.g., lists of the presidents pro tempore of the Senate, senators, Supreme Court justices, cabinet officers, electoral votes for president and vice-president). General index.　　JK1151

Vital statistics on Congress. 1980– . Wash. : Congressional Quarterly, Inc., c1980– . Biennial (irregular).　　**CJ229**

Publisher varies.

Presents statistics related to members of Congress and their work. Organizes information in more than 100 tables in eight chapters: members, elections, campaign finance, committees, staff and operating expenses, workload, budgeting, and voting alignments. Each chapter includes a descriptive introduction followed by tables giving both historical and current data (sometimes supplemented by charts or graphs). Appendix (1993–94 ed.) contains facts on individual members of the 103rd and 102nd Congresses (years of service, age, election returns, voting ratings, etc.). List of tables and figures. Index.　JK1041.V58

Biography

Members of Congress since 1789. 3rd ed. Wash. : Congressional Quarterly, c1985. 186 p.   **CJ230**

1st ed., 1977; 2nd ed., 1981.

Contains biographical data on all persons who have served in Congress from 1789 through the first session of the 99th Congress in 1985. In three sections: (1) statistics and summary data on members of Congress (e.g., age, religion); (2) very brief biographies of individual members of Congress; and (3) congressional statistics on sessions, party affiliations, and leaders. Select bibliography.

For more extensive biographies, see *Biographical directory of the United States Congress, 1774–1989* (CJ232).   JK1010.M45

Ragsdale, Bruce A. Black Americans in Congress, 1870–1989 / by Bruce A. Ragsdale and Joel D. Treese (Office of the Historian, U.S. House of Representatives). Wash. : U.S. Govt. Print. Off., 1990. 164 p. : ill.   **CJ231**

Superintendent of Documents classification: Y 1.1/7:101-117.

1977 ed. had title: *Black Americans in Congress, 1870–1977.*

Profiles the 65 African-American men and women who have served in Congress. Arranged alphabetically by name, the lengthy biographical essays (one to two pages each) feature black-and-white photographs. Many also include a brief bibliography. Supplements information found in *Biographical directory of the United States Congress, 1774–1989* (CJ232). No index.   E185.96.R25

United States. Congress. Biographical directory of the United States Congress, 1774–1989 : the Continental Congress, September 5, 1774, to October 21, 1788, and the Congress of the United States, from the First through the One Hundredth Congresses, March 4, 1789, to January 3, 1989, inclusive. Bicentennial ed. Wash. : U.S. Govt. Print. Off., 1989. 2104 p.   **CJ232**

Superintendent of Documents classification: Y 1.1/3:100 34.

1928 ed. had title: *Biographical directory of the American Congress, 1774–1927.* Rev. eds. were publ. 1950, 1961, 1971.

Comp. and ed. under the direction of the Joint Committee on Printing, Congress of the U.S., ed. by Bruce A. Ragsdale and Kathryn Allamong Jacob.

Senate document (United States. Congress. Senate), no. 100–34.

Revised, corrected, and updated through 1989. Presents alphabetically arranged biographies that include date and place of birth; education; profession; military service; public offices held; and death date and burial place (if applicable). Some entries also have short bibliographies. Also features lists of executive officers, 1789–1989 (by administration); the Continental Congress (places and dates of meetings, officers, delegates); representatives under each apportionment; and members of each Congress, 1789–1989 (by Congress, then by state).   JK1010.A5

Women in Congress, 1917–1990 / prep. under the direction of the Commission on the Bicentenary of the U.S. House of Representatives by the Office of the Historian, U.S. House of Representatives. Wash. : U.S. Govt. Print. Off., 1991. 266 p. : ports.   **CJ233**

Superintendent of Documents classification: Y1.1/7:101–238.

1976 ed. had title *Women in Congress, 1917–1976.*

Offers biographical essays on the 129 women who have been elected or appointed to Congress. Arranged alphabetically by name, the essays are generally one page in length and feature a black-and-white photograph. Supplements *Biographical directory of the United States Congress, 1774–1989* (CJ232). No index.   JK1013.W66

Congressional districts

Congressional districts in the 1990s : a portrait of America. Wash. : Congressional Quarterly, [1993]. 1016 p. : ill. **CJ234**

Presents descriptive and statistical profiles of the 435 congressional districts using data from the 1990 census and subsequent reapportionment and redistricting. Arranged alphabetically by state; for each, includes a description of demographic, economic, social, and political changes in the 1980s that led to redistricting; a map illustrating congressional district boundaries; tables giving population, voting age statistics, income and occupation, education, and housing patterns; and individual district profiles containing a textual overview and other data (election returns, universities and colleges, major employers, etc.). Appendixes offer national census tables; House membership in the 100th, 101st, 102nd, and 103rd Congresses; data on the District of Columbia; and zip codes by congressional district. City, county, university and college, cable television company, military installation, and business indexes.

§ For historical coverage, see *Congressional districts in the 1970s* (publ. 1974) and *Congressional districts in the 1980s* (1983).

JK1341.C64

CQ's guide to 1990 congressional redistricting. [Wash.] : Congressional Quarterly, c1993. 2 v. : maps.   **CJ235**

Describes changes in congressional districts due to the 1990 census. Vol. 1 discusses redistricting's effects on the Nov. 1992 general election, featuring 15 state profiles with detailed descriptions of the new districts, district maps, and statistical information about representatives in office during the 102nd Congress and the results of the 1992 election. It also summarizes state redistricting actions and lists 1980 and 1990 census population totals by state and district. Vol. 2 presents similar profiles of the remaining 35 states and gives a redistricting summary. Each volume has a personal name index.   JK1341.C87

Martis, Kenneth C. The historical atlas of state power in Congress, 1790–1990 / Kenneth C. Martis, Gregory A. Elmes. Wash. : Congressional Quarterly, c1993. 190 p. : col. ill., maps in color ; 27 cm.   **CJ236**

Following an introductory essay on apportionment, separate chapters for each decade, 1790–1990, present color-coded maps and tables showing every apportionment change for each state and region along with a brief analysis. A section on major geographical trends gives apportionments for (1) original and new states, 1790–1850; (2) free and slave states, 1790–1860; (3) rural and urban places, 1870–1930; (4) sunbelt and snowbelt, 1970–90. Bibliography. General index.

§ Continues Martis's research on geographical aspects of the U.S. Congress seen in two earlier volumes: *The historical atlas of United States congressional districts, 1789–1983* (CJ237) and *The historical atlas of political parties in the United States Congress, 1789–1989* (CJ258).   G1201.F7M3

——————— The historical atlas of United States congressional districts, 1789–1983. N.Y. : Free Pr. ; London : Collier Macmillan, [1982]. 302 p. : maps; 34 cm.   **CJ237**

Based on *The atlas of congressional roll calls*, prep. by Historical Records Survey, N.Y., 1938–39 ([Cooperstown, N.Y.] : New York State Historical Association, 1943) and by New York Historical Records Survey Project, 1940–42 (Newark, N.J. : The survey, 1943?).

In three parts: (1) Introduction; (2) 97 congressional district maps, one for each Congress, with alphabetical lists of all individuals elected to the Congress and indication of the member's state and district; (3) descriptions of each congressional district's geographic composition, according to law. Bibliography. General index, pt. 1, and personal name index, pt. 2.

§ First in a series on the geographical aspects of the U.S. Congress. *See also* Kenneth C. Martis, *The historical atlas of political parties in the United States Congress, 1789–1989* (CJ258) and *The historical atlas of state power in Congress, 1790–1990*, by Martis and Gregory A. Elmes (CJ236).   G1201.F9M3

United States. Bureau of the Census. Congressional district atlas. Districts of the 89th Congress– . Wash. : U.S. Govt. Print. Off., 1964– . Biennial.   **CJ238**

Superintendent of Documents classification: C3.62/5 .

Continues: *Congressional district atlas of the United States* (Wash. : U.S. Govt. Print. Off., [1960]).

Volumes for the 103rd Congress contain maps of congressional districts, arranged alphabetically by state, including state maps, and a variety of inset maps that show congressional district boundaries that do not follow county boundaries. Also provides five tables: (1) incorporated municipalities, giving countries and congressional districts; (1A) for selected states, county subdivisions, giving countries and congressional districts; (2) counties, giving congressional districts; (3) congressional districts, giving counties; (4) American Indian reservations, county subdivisions, giving congressional districts. Some volumes updated by supplements.   G1201.F7U45

United States congressional districts. Westport, Conn. : Greenwood, 1978–1990. 3 v. (In progress).   **CJ239**
Contents: 1788–1841 (ed. by Stanley B. Parsons, William W. Beach, Dan Hermann, publ. 1978); 1843–1883 (ed. by Stanley B. Parsons, William W. Beach, Michael J. Dubin, publ. 1986); 1883–1913 (ed. by Stanley B. Parsons, Michael J. Dubin, Karen Toombs Parsons, publ. 1990).
Companion volumes provide statistical descriptions of congressional districts by means of tabular data and maps. Information on four to 14 variables (e.g., percentage of African-Americans in the population, value of farm real estate) is generally arranged alphabetically by state within decades. Each volume has an introduction explaining methodology and vols. 2 and 3 have user's guides and tables of congresses. Vol. 1 includes name, party affiliation, number of terms served, and post office/county address for each representative. Vols. 2 and 3 omit material on individual congressmen, since they are treated for these periods in *Biographical directory of the United States Congress* (CJ232).

Elections

America at the polls : a handbook of American presidential election statistics 1920–1964 / comp. and ed. by Richard M. Scammon [for the] Elections Research Center, Governmental Affairs Institute. Pittsburgh : Univ. of Pittsburgh Pr., 1965. 521 p.   **CJ240**
Repr.: N.Y. : Arno, 1976.
Tables, arranged alphabetically by state, analyze by county: (1) total vote, (2) Republican-Democratic-other vote, (3) plurality, and (4) percentages of the total and major party vote for Republican and Democratic candidates. Following the tables are notes giving composition of the "Other" vote in detail and indicating any special circumstances. Also contains the state-by-state presidential vote, 1920–64.
§ Continued by: *America at the polls 2 : a handbook of American presidential election statistics, 1968–1984*, comp. and ed. by Richard M. Scammon and Alice V. McGillivray (Washington : Elections Research Center, Congressional Quarterly, 1988. 594 p. : maps.).
Includes three new features: (1) a national summary of the popular and Electoral College vote for president, 1920–84; (2) population data and county outline maps for each state; and (3) a summary of presidential preference primary elections by state and candidate, 1968–84.   JK524.G6

America votes : a handbook of contemporary American election statistics. v. 1 [1954/55]– . Wash. : Congressional Quarterly, 1956– . Biennial.   **CJ241**
Publisher varies. Ed., v. 1–11, Richard M. Scammon; v. 12– , Richard M. Scammon, Alice V. McGillivray.
Issued by Government Affairs Institute, v. 1–10; Elections Research Center, v. 12– .
Presents statistics, alphabetical by state, for: (1) postwar, statewide vote for president, governor, and senator; (2) vote (by country and/or city/town) in most recent election for president, governor, and senator: (3) vote (by congressional district) in elections for representatives since the last redistricting. Each state entry includes congressional district maps, a political profile, and general election/primary election data for the most recent election. Includes tables of state-by-state presidential votes, 1920– , and information on presidential primaries, postelection changes, and special election results.   JK1967.A8

Blake, Fay M. Verbis non factis : words meant to influence political choices in the United States, 1800–1980 / by Fay M. Blake and H. Morton Newman. Metuchen, N.J. : Scarecrow, 1984. 143 p.   **CJ242**
Presents 1,062 U.S. political slogans (e.g., "Fifty-four forty or fight!", "Win with Willkie") used 1800–1980 on banners, placards, bumper stickers, and buttons, and in campaign songs, speeches, cartoons, advertisements, and commercials. Slogans are listed chronologically and include year, candidate, political party, and at least one book in which the slogan appears. Many entries contain brief explanations of the use or derivation of the slogan. Bibliography; political party, personal name, and keyword indexes.   JK2261.B618

Burnham, Walter Dean. Presidential ballots, 1836–1892. Baltimore : Johns Hopkins Pr., [1955]. 956 p.   **CJ243**
§ Continued by: *The presidential vote, 1896–1932* (Stanford, Calif. : Stanford Univ. Pr., [c1947]) and *They voted for Roosevelt : the presidential vote, 1932–1944* (Stanford, Calif. : Stanford Univ. Pr., [1947]), both by Edgar Eugene Robinson.
Although some of their data (e.g., presidential vote by state) can be found in many recent sources, these titles are still valuable for their historical discussions, for election results by county prior to 1920 (when *America at the polls* [CJ240] began its county coverage), and for election results by nine geographical regions (e.g., New England, Middle Atlantic states).   JK524.B8

Campaign speeches of American presidential candidates, 1948–1984 / ed. & introduced by Gregory Bush. N.Y. : Ungar, c1985. 343 p.   **CJ244**
1st ed., 1976, covered 1928–72.
Presents 44 complete speeches by presidential candidates, 1948–84. Omits speeches 1928–44 that were included in the 1st ed. Includes the nomination acceptance speech and a representative campaign speech for both the Democratic and Republican candidates as well as representative campaign speeches for third-party candidates Henry A. Wallace (1948), J. Strom Thurmond (1948), George C. Wallace (1968), and John B. Anderson (1980). Groups speeches chronologically into election year chapters and begins each with a brief discussion of the major election issues. No index.   E743.C236

Congressional Quarterly's guide to U.S. elections. 3rd ed. Wash. : Congressional Quarterly Inc., c1994. 1543 p.   **CJ245**
1st ed., 1975; 2nd ed., 1985.
An impressive compilation of data on presidential, gubernatorial, and congressional elections drawn from many sources, including "Historical election returns file" of the Inter-University Consortium for Political and Social Research. Divided into sections covering political parties; presidential elections; gubernatorial elections; Senate elections; and House elections. Appendix contains a variety of related information (e.g., methods of electing presidential electors, constitutional provisions on elections). Suggested readings; candidates indexes; general index.   JK1967.C662

The election data book : a statistical portrait of voting in America. 1992– . Lanham, Md. : Bernan Pr., c1993– . Biennial.   **CJ246**
Compiled by: Election Data Services.
Results of the most recent primary, general, and special elections presented through maps, charts, and tables. Chapters for each state (and the District of Columbia) contain ten tables of statistics by county or congressional district: (1) population; (2) voting age population; (3) voter participation; (4) voter registration; (5) vote for president; (6) vote for U.S. senator; (7) vote for governor; (8) vote for U.S. representative; (9) vote for president, Democratic primaries; (10) vote for president, Republican primaries. Other information in each state chapter: information on the state's electoral process; profiles of the candidates; voter registration and turnout statistics from 1948 to the present; and maps showing the geographic area and the percentage vote from various elections. Additional features: essay on using election data; national summary of state data; selected country and congressional district rankings; maps depicting election and demographic data.   JK1967.E4

Fritz, Sara. Handbook of campaign spending : money in the 1990 congressional races / Sara Fritz and Dwight Morris. Wash. : Congressional Quarterly, c1992. 567 p.   **CJ247**

This comprehensive analysis of 1990 congressional campaign spending is based on reports to the Federal Election Commission by 972 candidates. Pt. 1 provides background chapters on relevant issues (e.g., types and purposes of expenditures, role of political consultants, fund raising) and presents data (e.g., top spenders in 18 separate categories, top recipients of PAC donations). Pts. 2–3 contain data on Senate and House races respectively, each arranged alphabetically by state. For each race a narrative describes spending, fund raising, and campaign strategy along with financial tables for each candidate comparing campaign expenditures in 26 categories (e.g., rent, salaries, gifts/entertainment), grouped in seven sections (e.g., overhead, advertising). Tables include total PAC contributions, total individual contributions, and total receipts. Name index.   JK1991.F75

Makinson, Larry. Open secrets : the encyclopedia of congressional money & politics / Larry Makinson, Joshua Goldstein. 3rd ed. Wash. : Congressional Quarterly, c1994. 1362 p. : ill.   **CJ248**

1st ed., 1990, had title: *Open secrets : the dollar power of PACs in Congress*; 2nd ed., 1992.

Identifies and analyzes campaign contributions to all 535 members of Congress from individuals (identified by employer or affiliation, not by personal name), businesses, labor unions, and ideological/single-issue groups. Data (illustrated with charts and graphs) is drawn from Federal Election Commission reports and includes the 1992 elections. An introductory section provides general information. Four profile sections detail contributions: by industry; to members of specific congressional committees; to individual members of Congress; and by individual PACs. Appendixes provide a list of the categories used in classifying the contributions, a breakdown of contributions by industry and interest group sectors, and an index of the members of each state's congressional delegation. General index.   JK1991.M26

———————— The price of admission : campaign spending in the 1992 elections / Larry Makinson. Wash. : Center for Responsive Politics, c1993. 216 p. : ill., maps.   **CJ249**

An earlier ed., *The price of admission : an illustrated atlas of campaign spending in the 1988 congressional elections*, was publ. 1989. A 1991 ed. covered 1990 elections.

Presents findings about campaign spending through graphs and charts illustrating the 1992 U.S. congressional races. Concentrates on the relationship between money and votes, level of competition, advantages of incumbency, role of PACs, and stockpiling funds. An overview of trends, 1974–92, is followed by 1992 data grouped into Senate, House, and state sections. Also includes a section analyzing patterns in PAC giving. Appendixes give the 1992 winners' PAC receipt breakdowns by industry and interest group and provide campaign spending indexes that include amount spent, amount opponent spent, PAC receipts, and cash on hand. Subject and member index.   JK1991.M25

Presidential elections since 1789. 5th ed. Wash. : Congressional Quarterly, c1991. 248 p. : ill.   **CJ250**

1st ed., 1975; 4th ed., 1987.

Presents descriptive and statistical information on: presidential primaries, 1912–88; political party nominees for president and vice-president, 1831–1988; popular vote (by state) for president, 1824–1988; electoral vote (by state) for president, 1789–1988; and electoral vote totals for vice-president, 1804–1988. Appendixes include major election laws and a biographical directory of candidates. Bibliography; general index. Much of this information can also be found in *Congressional Quarterly's guide to U.S. elections* (CJ245).   JK524.P68

Shields-West, Eileen. The World almanac of presidential campaigns / Eileen Shields-West ; illus. by Jeff MacNelly. N.Y. : World Almanac, 1992. 250 p. : ill.   **CJ251**

Portrays presidential campaigns 1789–1988 through facts and interesting details, arranged in chronological chapters by campaigns. Covers major candidates, credentials, campaign tickets, conventions, the campaigns, symbols, slogans, songs, campaign paraphernalia, name-calling, the press, spending, "firsts," trends, the vote, benchmarks, and a relevant quote. Each chapter also gives a two-page narrative that focuses on media coverage and on the tactics, style, and mistakes of the candidates. Bibliography. Personal name index.

JF285.S55

Thomas, G. Scott. The pursuit of the White House : a handbook of presidential election statistics and history. N.Y. : Greenwood, 1987. 485 p.   **CJ252**

In four sections: (1) The elections, which groups presidential elections by period, giving a brief historical account of each followed by statistical tables giving regional results for primaries, conventions, and general elections through 1984; (2) The candidates, which presents brief profiles of presidential candidates and charts of each candidate's presidential election record; (3) The parties, which offers party profiles and charts that provide such information as the number of general elections won by the party's nominee; (4) The role of individual states, which gives brief descriptions of the political role of each state and tables of its voting record. Selected bibliography; general index.

JK524.T44

Statistics

Cox, Edward Franklin. State and national voting in federal elections, 1910–1970. [Hamden, Conn.] : Archon Books, 1972. 280 p.   **CJ253**

Aims to provide voting statistics on a state-by-state basis in all three types of federal elections (presidential, senatorial, representative). In each category figures are given for the Democratic, Republican, and "other" party votes, together with percentages.   JK1965.C59

McGillivray, Alice V. Presidential primaries and caucuses, 1992 : a handbook of election statistics. Wash. : Congressional Quarterly, c1992. 294 p. : maps.   **CJ254**

Designed with its companion title, *Congressional and gubernatorial primaries* (Wash. : Congressional Quarterly, 1993) to complement *America votes* (CJ241). Features data, alphabetical by state, on presidential preference primaries and caucuses in states and other jurisdictions sending delegates to the Republican and Democratic national conventions. The volume for 1992 includes tables of state votes for the 1984, 1988, and 1992 primaries; state roll call votes at the 1992 conventions; and summaries by state of the delegate election process and the pledged delegate count for each candidate, a county outline map, and primary results by county.   JK522.M34

Miller, Warren E. American national election studies data sourcebook, 1952–1986 / Warren E. Miller, Santa Traugott. Cambridge, Mass. : Harvard Univ. Pr., 1989. 375 p.   **CJ255**

Updates a work by the same title, published in 1980, that covered 1952–78. Now includes results of all 18 biennial studies of voter behavior conducted by the Center for Political Studies, Univ. of Michigan, 1952–86. Seven topical chapters (e.g., Social characteristics of the electorate, Positions on public policy issues), each begin with a descriptive introduction and contain tables with data such as age, education, party identification, issue preference. Contains a list of tables and a general introduction explaining the work. Data is also available on tape from the Inter-university Consortium for Political and Social Research.   JK1967.M54

Petersen, Svend. A statistical history of the American presidential elections : with supplementary tables covering 1968–1980. Westport, Conn. : Greenwood, 1981. 250, [25] p.

CJ256

The main section of the work was first publ. 1963. A reprint (1968) included a supplement, "Election of 1968" (1971. 6 p.) inserted in pocket. The 1981 edition is also a reprint with a 25-page supplement covering 1968–80.

Provides tables giving voting results and percentages for: presidential elections 1789–1980, by state and candidate; state results, by date and party; political party, by state and date (Democratic, Republican, and other—e.g., Whig, Greenback, Farmer Labor). Supplementary tables provide a variety of data (e.g., party gains and losses, closest Democratic-Republican presidential races by state).   JK1967.P4

Political parties

In addition to the works listed below, the standard histories of political parties and the campaign textbooks issued by the parties are good sources of information. Contents of the campaign textbooks vary, but normally contain party platforms, statements of the party's stand on important issues, acceptance speeches of candidates, and lists of committee members. Many general statistical sources have sections on elections (e.g., *World almanac and book of facts*, AB110; *Historical statistics of the United States*, CG87; and *Statistical abstract of the United States*, CG81). For state and local elections, *see also* state and local government manuals and legislative handbooks.

Johnson, Donald Bruce. National party platforms. Rev. ed. Urbana : Univ. of Illinois Pr., [1978]. 2 v. (1035 p.).   **CJ257**
An earlier work by Kirk H. Porter, with the same title, was publ. 1924.
1st ed., 1936; 5th ed., 1973; all by Johnson and Porter. Titles include dates of coverage, beginning with 1840.
Contents: v. 1, 1840–1956; v. 2, 1960–1976.
For each campaign, gives a brief history, lists of party candidates, voting totals, and the texts of platforms for all major and principal minor parties. Name and subject indexes in each volume.
§ *National party platforms of 1980 : supplement* ... (Urbana : Univ. of Illinois Pr., [1982]. 233 p.), following the same format, covers the 1980 campaign.   JK2255.J64

Martis, Kenneth C. The historical atlas of political parties in the United States Congress, 1789–1989 / Kenneth C. Martis, author and ed. ; Ruth Anderson Rowles, cartographer ; Gyula Pauer, production cartographer. N.Y. : Macmillan ; London : Collier Macmillan, c1989. 518 p. : maps in color ; 34 x 46 cm.   **CJ258**
Provides political affiliation/party for each district and member of Congress through the 100th Congress (1989). In four parts: (1) a descriptive introduction surveying the history of political parties, congressional elections, and political parties in Congress; (2) national political party maps for each Congress, showing political party affiliation by district and including pie charts of party percentages for House and Senate and lists of members of Congress with their district and party affiliations; (3) and (4) tables showing the sources that were checked to verify party affiliation. Bibliography; general index to Pt. 1 and personal name index to Pt. 2.
§ Second in a series on the geographical aspects of the U.S. Congress. See also Kenneth C. Martis, *The historical atlas of the United States congressional districts, 1789–1983* (CJ237) and Kenneth C. Martis and Gregory A. Elmes, *The historical atlas of state power in Congress, 1790–1990* (CJ236).   G1201.F9M26

Bibliography

Rockwood, D. Stephen. American third parties since the Civil War : an annotated bibliography / D. Stephen Rockwood ... [et al.]. N.Y. : Garland, 1985. 177 p. (Garland reference library of social science, v. 227).   **CJ259**
An introductory bibliography intended to supplement other bibliographic titles on progressivism, socialism, etc. Monographic coverage is stressed, with most periodical titles included in a section on third party movements of the last two decades. In six chapters: General theory and practice; The Populist (People's) party; Parties of the Left; Dixiecrats and American Independents; The Progressive party; Minor third parties. Author and title indexes.   Z7164.P8R63

Wynar, Lubomyr Roman. American political parties : a selective guide to parties and movements of the 20th century. Littleton, Colo. : Libraries Unlimited, 1969. 427 p.   **CJ260**
Lists books, monographs, and unpublished dissertations on American political parties and movements of the 20th century. Includes references to published platforms, proceedings of national conventions, etc., as well as secondary writings about the parties. General index.   Z7165.U5W88

Encyclopedias

Kruschke, Earl R. Encyclopedia of third parties in the United States. Santa Barbara, Calif. : ABC-Clio, c1991. 223 p.   **CJ261**
An overview of third parties is followed by descriptive entries for 81 parties ranging from the significant (e.g., Progressive) to the marginal (e.g., American Vegetarian). The chosen parties "represent ... the ... issues, causes, and personalities that third parties have espoused."—*Pref.* Arranged alphabetically, the entries, varying in length from a few paragraphs to several pages, include origin, objectives, history, notable participants, importance, and short bibliography. An appendix lists the years and places of origin of the 81 parties. General index.   JK2261.K78

Political parties & elections in the United States : an encyclopedia / general ed., L. Sandy Maisel ; associate ed., Charles Bassett. N.Y. : Garland, 1991. 2 v. (1345 p.) : ill. (Garland reference library of social science, v. 498).   **CJ262**
Alphabetically arranged, this comprehensive work treats terms, topics, summary information on elections through 1988, historical and current operations of political parties, other organizations and movements, and individuals. Written by scholars, the signed entries end with cross-references and bibliographies. 18 appendixes (e.g., party switchers in the Congress, Democratic and Republican state committee headquarters). General index.   JK2261.P633

Handbooks

Bain, Richard C. Convention decisions and voting records / Richard C. Bain and Judith H. Parris. 2nd ed. Wash. : Brookings Institution, [1973]. 350 p. : tables.   **CJ263**
1st ed. (1960) by Richard C. Bain.
A handbook of presidential conventions, 1832–1972, with a section on each consisting of the political background, organization of the conventions, platforms adopted, nominations, balloting, etc. Appended are lists of nominees, convention officers, and voting records by state.   JK2255.B3

McKee, Thomas Hudson. National conventions and platforms of all political parties, 1789–1905 : convention, popular and electoral vote. Also the political complexion of both houses of Congress at each biennial period. 6th ed., rev. and enl. Baltimore : Friedenwald, 1906. 418 p., 33 p.   **CJ264**
Repr. : N.Y. : B. Franklin, [1971].
1st ed., 1892; 5th ed., 1904.
Still a useful compilation of information on early political party conventions. Presents, for each convention, a brief history giving date, place, chair, candidates, nominees, platform, and voting totals for major and principal minor parties. General and name indexes; subject indexes to party platforms.   JK2255.M2

National party conventions, 1831–1988. [5th ed.]. Wash. : Congressional Quarterly, c1991. 283 p. : ports.   **CJ265**
1st ed., 1976; 4th ed., 1987.
Provides a brief summary of each party convention, the results of convention ballots, historical profiles of American political parties, lists of nominees, and a bibliographical directory of candidates. Some sections have bibliographies. Name index.   JK2255.N374

Schapsmeier, Edward L. Political parties and civic action groups / Edward L. Schapsmeier and Frederick H. Schapsmeier. Westport, Conn. : Greenwood, [1981]. 554 p.   **CJ266**

Presents profiles of almost 300 national political organizations, about one-third of which are political parties; entries range in length from a brief paragraph to more than 20 pages, with bibliographical references. Alphabetical arrangement; keyword index. Appendixes list organizations by broad functional areas and founding dates. Tables of presidential candidates and votes for major political parties; glossary; index.   JK2260.S36

State and local government

Bibliography

Fisher, Mary L. Guide to state legislative and administrative materials. 4th ed. Littleton, Colo. : F.B. Rothman, 1988– . 1 v. (loose-leaf). (American Association of Law Libraries publications series, no. 15).   **CJ267**

1st ed., 1979–3rd ed., 1983, had title: *Guide to state legislative materials.*

For each state, American Samoa, Guam, Puerto Rico, the U.S. Virgin Islands, and the District of Columbia, gives sources for bills, hearings, legislative digests, committee reports, debates, journals, legislative manuals and directories, slip laws, session laws, codes, attorney general opinions, executive orders, administrative regulations, state law guide, etc. Appendix provides addresses and telephone numbers for publishers, database vendors, and legislative and regulatory service companies.   KF1.G8

Goehlert, Robert. State legislatures : a bibliography / Robert U. Goehlert, Frederick W. Musto. Santa Barbara, Calif. : ABC-Clio, c1985. 229 p.   **CJ268**

Cites more than 2,500 scholarly English-language books, articles, dissertations, reports, and selected documents (excluding state documents) published 1945 through mid-1984 on the history, functions, organization, structure, and procedures of state legislatures. In two sections: (1) theoretical and empirical works arranged alphabetically by main entry within 25 topical chapters (e.g., Committees, Decision making, Reapportionment and redistricting); and (2) studies on individual legislatures grouped alphabetically by state. Author and subject indexes.   Z7164.R4G574

Encyclopedias

Elliot, Jeffrey M. The state and local government political dictionary / Jeffrey M. Elliot, Sheikh R. Ali. Santa Barbara, Calif. : ABC-Clio, c1988. 325 p.   **CJ269**

Defines 290 concepts and terms relevant to the institutions, processes, and policies of state and local government. Entries are arranged alphabetically within 11 topical chapters (e.g., Federal and state constitutions, Intergovernmental relations, Bureaucracy and civil service) and include descriptive definitions, cross-references, and a paragraph explaining the term's historical roots and contemporary importance. General index.   JK2408.E44

Worldmark encyclopedia of the states : a practical guide to the geographic, demographic, historical, political, economic, and social development of the United States. 2nd ed. N.Y. : Worldmark Pr. : Wiley, c1986. 690 p. : maps (some col.).   **CJ270**

1st ed., 1981.

Patterned after the *Worldmark encyclopedia of the nations* (CJ35), this volume offers a wide range of political, social, and economic information on the states of the United States of America. "Every state ... is treated in an individual chapter, within a framework of 50 standard subject headings; generally, the more populous the state, the longer the article. The District of Columbia and the Commonwealth of Puerto Rico each has its own chapter, and two additional articles describe in summary form the other Caribbean and Pacific dependencies. The concluding chapter is a 50-page overview of the nation as a whole."—*Pref.* A headnote for each state gives information on the state name, date of entry into union, state flower, legal holidays, etc.; seals and flags are illustrated and described; a selected bibliography concludes each chapter. List of contributors. Not indexed, but uniform presentation of information in each chapter and use of boldface subheadings make for easy use.   E156.W67

Directories

Election results directory. 1993 ed.– . [Denver, Colo.] : National Conference of State Legislatures, c1993– .   **CJ271**

Subtitle: A complete listing of State and Federal legislative and executive branch officials.

Intends to provide the earliest compilation of state and federal general election results in one volume. Brief articles, reprinted from the National Conference's periodical publication *State legislatures*, analyze changes resulting from the elections. Two listings: (1) the president, vice-president, and members of Congress; (2) governors, lieutenant governors, secretaries of state, state attorneys general, and state legislators (alphabetical by state, followed by the District of Columbia, Guam, Northern Mariana Islands, Puerto Rico, and the U.S. Virgin Islands). Provides party affiliation, district, and gender. Official addresses and telephone numbers are given for executive branch officials; home addresses are given for state legislators. Includes related information (term lengths, telephone numbers to call for bill status, etc.), an appendix giving each state's legislative calendar, and a brief bibliography.

§ See also *State yellow book* (CJ282); *State executive directory annual* (CJ275); and *Book of the states* and its supplements (CJ278).   JK2403.E43

Inside the legislature : the guide to state policymakers. 1993 ed.– . Centerville, Mass. : State Legislative Leaders Foundation, c1993– . Annual.   **CJ272**

Continues *The handbook of state legislative leaders* (Cambridge, Mass. : Ballinger Publ. Co., 1984–1992).

Offers political and biographical information on every House speaker, Senate president, majority and minority leader, and pro tempore in the state legislatures. Each profile contains a photograph, district represented, home address and telephone number, office address and telephone and fax numbers, years in office, party affiliation, staff, other political offices held, legislative priorities, and personal data (e.g., birth date, occupation, family, education, military service). Arranged by state; each state section also includes the state legislative session schedule, terms of office, party composition, names and telephone numbers of standing and joint committee chairs, and names and telephone numbers for major legislative agencies. Name index.

§ A helpful complement is the directory information found in the *State legislative leadership, committees, and staff* supplement to the *Book of the states* (CJ278 note).

Municipal yellow book : who's who in the leading city and county governments and local authorities. v. 1, no. 1 (summer 1991)– . N.Y. : Monitor Pub. Co., c1991– . Semiannual.   **CJ273**

Contains (in three sections, arranged alphabetically) names, titles, addresses, and telephone and fax numbers for key administrative and elective offices and officials in the top cities and counties (based on 1990 census figures) and local authorities (based on revenue and subscriber interest) in the U.S. Includes (Summer 1993 ed.) 130 cities, 115 counties, and 21 operating authorities (e.g, Intermountain Power Agency, New York City Transit Authority). Geographic index gives cities and counties by state; population index provides access to information about top 100 cities and counties; staff index is alphabetical by personal name.

§ Provides names of more executives per city and county but covers fewer cities and counties than the *Municipal/county executive directory annual* (CJ274).   JS39.M79

Municipal/county executive directory annual. 1991/1992– . Wash. : Carroll Pub. Co., 1991– . Annual.   **CJ274**

Formerly *Municipal/county executive directory* (1984–91).

Also published in two separate semiannual editions: *Municipal executive directory* and *County executive directory*.

Covers the administrative and legislative offices of more than 7,000 municipal governments and 3,000 county governments in separate sections. Each section is color-coded and provides organizational listings containing titles, names, addresses, and telephone numbers. Alphabetical index of executives; alphabetical index of municipalities by state or county.   JS363.M85

State executive directory annual. 1991/1992– . Wash. : Carroll Pub. Co., 1991– . Annual.   **CJ275**

Continues in part *Federal/state executive directory*.

In five color-coded sections: (1) state executives, with telephone numbers and state abbreviations; (2) organizational entries (arranged alphabetically by state and also listing U.S. territories), giving addresses of the organizations and directory information for chief state executives; (3) legislative entries (alphabetical by state), with number of legislators by party; name, party affiliation, and phone numbers for officers and members of the legislatures; standing committee chairs and phone numbers; (4) keyword index; (5) list of state agencies by function. Also includes numerous lists, such as governors and state capitals.

Also published yearly in three paperbound editions as *State executive directory*.

State legislative staff directory : key policy and fiscal contacts. Denver, Colo. : National Conference of State Legislatures, 19??– . Annual.   **CJ276**

Identifies key legislative staff with expertise in a particular public policy area. Based on a survey by the National Conference of State Legislatures (NCSL). 1993 issue contains 19 subject chapters (e.g., agriculture, education, fiscal, telecommunications), with listings by state. Each entry gives name, address, telephone number, and area of specialization where applicable. Also includes a topics table, a table listing majority parties for each state legislature, and two appendixes, one listing NCSL policy contacts and the other listing state survey coordinators. No index.   JK2495.S693

State municipal league directory. Wash. : National League of Cities, [1973?]– . Annual.   **CJ277**

Lists, alphabetically by state, the 49 municipal leagues affiliated with the National League of Cities (Hawaii does not have a league). Each entry includes name, address, telephone and fax numbers, name of the executive director, number and type of staff, budget, dues, number of members, and basic information on conventions/conferences (e.g., dates, locations) and principal periodical publication (e.g., frequency, circulation). An alphabetical list of the leagues with addresses and telephone numbers and a chronological list of annual conventions and conferences precede the entries.

Handbooks

The book of the states. v. 1 (1935)– . Lexington, Ky. [etc.] : Council of State Governments, 1935– . Biennial (1948–).   **CJ278**

A valuable compendium. Each volume generally covers the same subjects, with emphasis on developments in the previous two years. The 1992/93 ed. includes: constitutions (e.g., revisions); executive branch (e.g., methods of selection, qualifications for office); legislative branch (e.g., sessions, qualifications and salaries of legislators); judicial branch (e.g., methods of selection, salaries); elections (e.g., legislation, election dates); finances (e.g., trends in taxation); management and administration (e.g., personnel policies and benefits); selected activities, issues, and services (e.g., innovations, the environment); intergovernmental affairs (e.g., federal-state relations) and state pages (general information, officers, statistics). General index.

Three supplements are usually issued in odd-numbered years: *State administrative officials classified by functions* (1967–); *State legislative leadership, committees, and staff* (1979–); and *State elective officials and the legislatures* (1977–).   JK2403.B62

The municipal year book. 1934– . Wash. : International City/County Management Association, 1934– . Annual.   **CJ279**

Subtitle: "The authoritative source book of urban data and developments" (varies).

Formerly publ. in Chicago under the association's previous name, International City Manager's Association.

Succeeds *City manager yearbook* (publ. 1914–1933).

Contents vary. Beginning in 1973 includes data and articles on Canadian municipalities.

Issues for 1964–69 include *The city-manager directory* (also issued separately).

Includes *Salaries of municipal officials* (issued separately, 1971–1985).

Aims to provide local government officials with relevant management information. The 1993 ed. contains essays (written by authors from local, state, and federal government agencies; universities; public interest groups; and staff of the International City/County Management Association) describing data collected by the Association in its yearly survey of local officials and commenting on trends and developments in local government. Following an explanatory introduction and the essays (e.g., management issues, staffing compensation), are directories (e.g., state municipal leagues, state associations of counties); and an extensive bibliography. List of contributors. Subject index in 1993 ed. covers 1989–1993.   JS344.C5A24

State government research directory : a descriptive guide to basic and applied research and data collection programs and activities sponsored and/or conducted by the government agencies of the 50 states, the District of Columbia, and the U.S. territories / Kay Gill and Susan E. Tufts, editors. Detroit : Gale, c1987. 349 p.   **CJ280**

Offers information on research units sponsored by state government agencies. Alphabetically arranged by state names, with separate sections for each of the 50 states and the District of Columbia, followed by the U.S. territories. Within sections, entries are alphabetical and consist of name, address, telephone, date established, size and composition of staff, research descriptions, special facilities, publications and information services, and special remarks. Indexes of names, keywords, and agencies and of subjects.

§ *See also* the companion title: *Government research directory* (AL80).   Q180.U5S78

State legislative sourcebook. 1986– . Topeka, Kan. : Government Research Service, c1985– . Annual.   **CJ281**

Provides basic data and lists sources of information concerning state legislative operations. The 52 chapters (one for each state plus the District of Columbia and Puerto Rico) include such information as: legislative organization and process, legislators, session, interim study period, lobbying, and general state information. Bill status and bill room telephone numbers for each state are given in appendixes. Ends with a 37-page bibliography. Resource guide to influencing state legislatures. No index.   JK2495.S689

State yellow book. v. 1, no. 1 (Winter 1989)– . N.Y. : Monitor Publ. Co., c1989– . Quarterly, beginning Spring 1992.   **CJ282**

Supersedes *State information book* (Washington : Potomac Books ; Rockville, MD : INFAX Corp., 1975–1988).

Offers state profiles and personnel information for all 50 states and the District of Columbia, American Samoa, Guam, Puerto Rico, and the Virgin Islands. The first two sections give the names, titles, telephone numbers, and addresses of some 30,000 key executive and legislative officials. A state profiles section provides a map, brief history, and selected details (e.g., military installations, county data), and an intergovernmental organization section lists national organizations of state officials. Subject index and name index, which groups names alphabetically by state.   JK2403.S77

States in profile : the state policy reference book. 1990– . McConnellsburg, Pa. : Brizius & Foster and State Policy Research, Inc., [1990?]– . Annual.   **CJ283**

Earlier editions, 1984–89, had title: *State policy data book.*

Features four types of current data relating to policy decisions of state governments: (1) State characteristics (e.g., population, age, composition, income); (2) Workloads and tax bases (e.g., number of schoolchildren, cars on the road); (3) Programs (e.g., spending per student); and (4) Program effectiveness (e.g., graduation rate). Compiled from various sources and presented in tabular form, data are grouped into 16 topical chapters (e.g., Education, Health, Transportation). Tables are listed in the table of contents and a cross-reference list compares them with those in the previous edition. Subject index.

Sourcebooks

State legislative manuals on microfiche. [Boulder, Colo.] : Numbers & Concepts, 1990– .   **CJ284**

A convenient collection of current state legislative blue books, rosters, directories, etc.

§ Those institutions not needing such extensive coverage may wish to consult Lynn Hellebust's *State reference publications* (AF146).

Biography

Biographical dictionary of American mayors, 1820–1980 : big city mayors, Baltimore, Boston, Buffalo, Chicago, Cincinnati, Cleveland, Detroit, Los Angeles, Milwaukee, New Orleans, New York, Philadelphia, Pittsburgh, San Francisco, St. Louis / ed. by Melvin G. Holli and Peter d'A. Jones. Westport, Conn. : Greenwood, 1981. 451 p.   **CJ285**

Offers signed biographies with bibliographical sources for 679 mayors of the 15 included cities. Useful appendixes list mayors by city, party affiliation, ethnic background, religious affiliation, and birthplace, and give population data for the cities. Index.
    E176.B5725

Kallenbach, Joseph E. American state governors, 1776–1976. Dobbs Ferry, N.Y. : Oceana, 1977–1982. 3 v.   **CJ286**

Contents: v. 1, Electoral and personal data; v. 2–3, Biographical data.

Vol. 1 offers historical and political data relevant to the office of governor for each state. Following a survey of state practices (e.g., mode of choice, qualifications, removal), alphabetical state listings include the names of all gubernatorial candidates, their party affiliations, and voting results. The biographical sketches in v. 2–3 are arranged chronologically within each state. Bibliography; name index.

§ *See also* Marie Mullaney, *American governors and gubernatorial elections, 1979–1987* (CJ291).   JK2447.K35

McMullin, Thomas A. Biographical directory of American territorial governors / by Thomas A. McMullin and David Walker. Westport, Conn. : Meckler, 1984. 353 p.   **CJ287**

Presents biographies of the governors of American incorporated territories (excluding Puerto Rico, Guam, the Philippines, and Samoa). Articles range from one to two pages in length, and include bibliographies. Arranged by state, with name index and chronology of office.   E176.M17

Raimo, John W. Biographical directory of American colonial and Revolutionary governors, 1607–1789. Westport, Conn. : Meckler, [1980]. 521 p.   **CJ288**

"In this volume the word governor has been interpreted, broadly speaking, to include anyone who held effective executive power in those British colonies which in 1776 became the first thirteen states."—*Introd.*, although exceptions are noted. Arranged by colony and then by chronological date of governorship, the entries provide standard biographical information (e.g., dates of birth and death, parents, family, career), and end with bibliographies. Includes brief general bibliography and a chronology and select bibliography for each colony. Name index.

§ For recent information, consult the following works by the same publisher.

Biographical directory of the governors of the United States, 1789–1978, ed. by Robert Sobel and John Raimo. (1978. 4 v. [1785 p.]).

Biographical directory of the governors of the United States, 1978–1983, ed. by John Raimo. (1985. 352 p.).

Biographical directory of the governors of the United States, 1983–1988, ed. by Marie Marmo Mullaney. (1989. 398 p.).

The set covering 1789–1978 offers short (a page or less) unsigned biographies, usually written by historians or librarians. Entries include dates of birth and death, parents, family, religion, education, political affiliation, electoral results, political and private careers, accomplishments, and a brief bibliography. The introductory essay and a complete index of names of biographees appears in each volume of the set. Reviews in *Library journal* 103 (Oct. 1, 1978): 1968 and *Choice* 15 (Dec. 1978): 1344 point out a few omissions and errors.

All three works are arranged alphabetically by state, then in chronological order of the governorship. The 1789–1978 and 1978–1983 works contain a list of contributors. The 1978–1983 volume has signed biographies. Both of the more recent works give slightly longer entries (two to four pages), each with a photograph; contents are similar to the earlier work.

A volume covering 1988–94 is forthcoming.   E187.5.R34

Ritter, Charles F. American legislative leaders, 1850–1910 / Charles F. Ritter & Jon L. Wakelyn ... [et al.]. N.Y. : Greenwood, 1989. lxvii, 1090 p.   **CJ289**

Profiles the 1,390 men who served as speakers of state or territorial houses of representatives in the U.S., 1850–1910. An introduction describes the shift from agrarian to industrial politics, the political economy and economic issues of the times, the evolution of legislatures, the leadership role of the speakers, and provides a statistical career profile for the speakers. The main body of the work consists of alphabetically arranged biographies containing personal and professional data (e.g., birth and death dates and locations, family, education, offices held), ending with a list of sources. Eight appendixes in tabular form list the speakers alphabetically by state, chronologically by years in office, by party membership, etc. Bibliography; name and subject index.   E663.R57

Elections

Bartley, Numan V. Southern elections : county and precinct data, 1950–1972 / Numan V. Bartley and Hugh D. Graham. Baton Rouge : Louisiana State Univ. Pr., c1978. 407 p. : maps.   **CJ290**

Focuses on major primary elections (gubernatorial and senatorial) and pertinent referenda votes for Alabama, Arkansas, Florida, Georgia, Louisiana, Mississippi, North and South Carolina, Tennessee, Texas, and Virginia; also includes basic demographic and geographic analysis of the votes.

§ Conceived as a continuation of A. Heard and D. S. Strong's *Southern primaries and elections, 1920–1949* (University, Ala. : Univ. of Alabama Pr., 1950. 206 p.).   JK1967.B37

Mullaney, Marie Marmo. American governors and gubernatorial elections, 1979–1987. Westport, Conn. : Meckler, c1988. [103] p.   **CJ291**

A continuation of *American governors and gubernatorial elections, 1775–1978*, comp. by Roy R. Glashan.

Both volumes contain a list by state of (1) governors, providing date and place of birth, party, major occupations, residence, death date, and date at which he or she became governor; (2) gubernatorial elections, giving all significant voting totals by party and candidate. The earlier volume has, scattered throughout, quotes from speeches and writings of selected governors, a bibliography of general and state sources, and a list of quotation sources. The later volume includes a bibliographic note. No indexes.   JK2447.M85

Confederate States of America

Martis, Kenneth C. The historical atlas of the Congresses of the Confederate States of America, 1861–1865 / Kenneth C. Martis ; Gyula Pauer, cartographer. N.Y. : Simon & Schuster, 1994. 157 p.   **CJ292**

Provides maps relating to the Congress of the Confederate States of America, with chapters on the Provisional Confederate Congress, congressional districts, elections, roll-call voting, etc. Includes appendixes (e.g., electoral procedures, candidates, and vote totals), bibliography, and general index.

§ One in a series on geographical aspects of U.S. political history. *See also* Kenneth C. Martis, *The historical atlas of political parties in the United States Congress, 1789–1989* (CJ258), *The historical atlas of state power in Congress, 1790–1990*, by Martis and Gregory A. Elmes (CJ236), and *The historical atlas of United States congressional districts, 1789–1983* by Martis (CJ237).   G1281.F8M3

Canada

The almanac of Canadian politics / D. Munroe Eagles ... [et al.]. Peterborough, Ont., Canada ; Lewiston, N.Y. : Broadview Pr., c1991. 712 p. : ill.   **CJ293**

Complements Frank B. Feigert's *Canada votes, 1935–1988* (CJ298) by providing additional election data at the riding level for the 1984 and 1988 elections. Organized by province, gives a provincial overview followed by riding-by-riding narratives and statistical profiles with political, ethnolinguistic, socioeconomic, industrial, and demographic data. Appendixes give constituency rankings (e.g., 15 best or worst finishes for each party, 15 highest or lowest average family incomes); parliamentary by-election changes to November 1, 1991; definitions of measures used for the statistical profiles; an alphabetical list of candidates in the 1988 general election; and cartograms displaying the spatial distribution of political and socioeconomic characteristics across ridings. No index.   JL167.A56

Campbell, Colin. Canadian political facts, 1945–1976. Toronto ; N.Y. : Methuen, c1977. 151 p.   **CJ294**

A miscellaneous collection of statistical tables, lists of office holders, etc., grouped under such headings as: The executive, Parliament, Elections, Political parties and pressure groups, The Canadian economy, Population and language. No index.   JL65.C35

Canadian parliamentary guide = Guide parlementaire canadien. 1909– . Ottawa : P. G. Normandin.   **CJ295**

In English and in French.

Imprint varies. Succeeds *Canadian parliamentary companion, 1862–1897; Parliamentary guide and work of general reference for Canada, the provinces, Northwest Territories and Newfoundland, 1899–1900; Canadian parliamentary guide and work of general reference for Canada, the provinces, and the Northwest Territories, 1900–1905.*

Lists, and provides biographical sketches for, members of the Governor General's household, the Privy Council, and Canadian legislatures (federal, provincial, and territorial), as well as federal superior court members and senior staff. Also provides descriptions of each of these institutions with historical information and significant facts (e.g., number of members and their salaries). Includes results of all federal general elections since confederation and results of the most recent provincial elections. Personal name index.   JL5.A4

Canadian parliamentary handbook = Repertoire parlementaire canadien. 1982– . Ottawa : Borealis Pr., 1982– . Annual.   **CJ296**

In English and French.

The 1994 ed. provides: an introduction to the Canadian parliamentary process; a biography and description of the role of the Governor General and a list of his staff; and the Senate and House of Commons, their historical background, organization, and principal officers, and biographies of members with photographs. For each member of the House of Commons, gives a description and profile of his or her constituency with results from the past two elections. A separate section covers the Library of Parliament. Includes lists of current Canadian ministry members, parliamentary secretaries, parliamentary fax numbers, and tables of precedence and titles. Constituency and general indexes.   JL131C35

Carrigan, D. Owen. Canadian party platforms, 1867–1968. [Toronto] : Copp Clark ; Urbana : Univ. of Illinois Pr., [1968]. 363 p.   **CJ297**

Gives (in chronological order) historical notes, party platforms or policy statements, and election results for each campaign, 1867–1968. No index.   JL195.C3

Feigert, Frank B. Canada votes, 1935–1988. Durham, N.C. : Duke Univ. Pr., 1989. 351 p.   **CJ298**

Reports results for Canadian national, provincial, and territorial elections, 1935–88. Divided into chapters corresponding to national, regional summary, and regional individual results, each with an introduction providing contextual information. Extensive tables include: numbers and percentages of votes received and seats won by year, province, and party; seats contested, retained, gained, and lost by year, province, and party; seats won by percentage point margins; voter turnout by year and province or territory; national election results by riding; and provincial and territorial election results. A list of tables precedes an introduction that explains the tables and the book's organization. Bibliography.

§ For data on earlier elections, *see* Howard A. Scarrow, *Canada votes* (New Orleans : Hauser Pr., 1962).   JL193.A54

Guide to Canadian ministries since confederation, July 1, 1867–February 1, 1982. [Ottawa] : Govt. of Canada, Privy Council Office, c1982. 326 p.   **CJ299**

1st publ., 1957; supplement, 1966; new ed., 1974.

Also issued in French (332 p.).

A chronological list of ministries, giving names and dates of service together with notes on formation and abolition of offices and departments. Personal name index.   JL97.G84

Heggie, Grace F. Canadian political parties, 1867–1968 : a historical bibliography. [Toronto] : Macmillan, 1977. 603 p.   **CJ300**

An annotated bibliography on federal Canadian politics, with approximately 8,850 entries, including books, essays, historical societies' publications, theses, and journal articles. Pt. 1, The federal political parties of Canada, is arranged by chronological period and individual party; pt. 2, Government and political institutions, lists works on Dominion-Provincial relations, the constitution, government organization and administration, the executive, Parliament, and the judiciary. Appendixes list reference sources and periodicals. Author and subject indexes.   Z7165.C2H43

Lambert, Ronald D. The sociology of contemporary Quebec nationalism : an annotated bibliography and review. N.Y. : Garland, 1981. 148 p. (Canadian review of studies in nationalism, v. 2; Garland reference library of social science, v. 78).   **CJ301**

Contains 586 annotated citations to books and periodical articles in English or French from the post-1945 period (most published since the 1960s). Alphabetically arranged by author, and preceded by a lengthy review of the literature. Subject index.   Z1392.Q3L34

Mahler, Gregory S. Contemporary Canadian politics : an annotated bibliography, 1970–1987. N.Y. : Greenwood, 1988. 400 p. (Bibliographies and indexes in law and political science, no. 10). **CJ302**

Contains 3,738 entries for English and French books and articles published 1970–87 on contemporary Canadian politics. A general sources chapter is followed by 13 topical chapters (e.g., Regionalism and local politics; Political parties, ideology, and elections; The administrative process). Entries in each chapter are alphabetically arranged by author under separate sections for books and articles. Although the subtitle indicates entries are annotated, most are not; when annotations occur, they are brief. Keyword index. Z1385.M35

Maillet, Lise. Provincial royal commissions and commissions of inquiry, 1867–1982 : a selective bibliography = Commissions royales provinciales et commissions d'enquête, 1867–1982 : bibliographie sélective. Ottawa : National Library of Canada, 1986. 254 p. **CJ303**

In English and French.

Facilitates identification and location of reports issued by 767 Canadian provincial royal commissions and commissions of inquiry on political, cultural, economic, or social problems. Unannotated entries are arranged by province, then chronologically. Each entry contains date and name of commission, name and bibliographic data for its report(s), names of chairman and commissioners, and library location symbols. Subject and name (of chairmen and commissioners) indexes. The National Library of Canada's *Symbols of Canadian libraries* (11th ed. Ottawa : National Library of Canada, 1985) is needed to interpret location symbols. Z1373.3.M34

Organization of the government of Canada. 1958– . Ottawa : Information Canada, 1958– . Annual since 1973. **CJ304**

Frequency and issuing agency vary. Issued also in French under title: L'administration federale du canada.

Publication suspended 1981–89.

1990 ed. in four main sections: (1) Crown, (2) Legislature, (3) Judiciary, and (4) Executive. For each department, agency, etc., usually provides head office address, telephone number for inquiries, principal officeholders, historical background, responsibilities, organization and programs, regional offices, parliamentary committees, relevant statutes, and an organization chart. Appendixes furnish the toll-free telephone numbers for the Reference Canada inquiry service; a list of federal organization acronyms; names, addresses, and telephone numbers for Commissions of Inquiry and Royal Commissions; and a glossary of terms. Index of federal organizations. JL5.O7

Mexico

Camp, Roderic Ai. Mexican political biographies, 1884–1935. Austin : Univ. of Texas Pr., 1991. 458 p. **CJ305**

Supplies biographical sketches for leading political figures in Mexico. Includes presidents, cabinet officers, senators, justices, governors, party leaders, ambassadors, military commanders, etc. Alphabetically-arranged entries cover a wealth of information and end with bibliographic sources. Appendixes offer a variety of lists (Supreme Court justices, ambassadors, presidents, etc.); bibliographic essay.

Continued by Camp's *Mexican political biographies, 1935–1981* (2nd ed., rev. and expanded. Tucson : Univ. of Arizona Pr., 1982. 447 p.). A Spanish-language revision, *Biografías politicos Mexicanos, 1935–1988*, was publ. in Mexico City, 1991. F1235.5.A2C35

Latin America

Biographical dictionary of Latin American and Caribbean political leaders / ed. by Robert J. Alexander. N.Y. : Greenwood, 1988. 509 p. **CJ306**

Intended to complement *Political parties of the Americas* (CJ97). Offers 450 sketches of political figures from the 19th and 20th centuries. Entries are lengthy, are signed, and include cross-references and bibliographies. Also included are a chronology of major events in the region, 1804–1985, and a list of biographies by country. Name index.

§ For current political leaders, see also *Who's who in Latin America : government, politics, banking & industry* (CJ310), which has more, but briefer entries. F1414.2.B48

Handbook of political science research on Latin America : trends from the 1960s to the 1990s / ed. by David W. Dent. N.Y. : Greenwood, 1990. 448 p. **CJ307**

Offers a synthesis of political science research on Latin America over the past 30 years. 16 chapters in the form of bibliographic essays by specialists on Latin America focus on a country or region and are grouped in two general sections, comparative politics and international relations. Includes English- and Spanish-language books, articles, government publications, and selected dissertations. Three appendixes: (1) a bibliography of reference works on Latin American politics; (2) data on macrotrends in political science research, 1960–85, from the *Handbook of Latin American studies* (DB266); and (3) a listing of major research centers and institutes in Latin America and the Caribbean. Name and subject indexes. JA84.L3H36

Radu, Michael. Latin American revolutionaries : groups, goals, methods / Michael Radu and Vladimir Tismaneanu. Wash. : Pergamon-Brassey's International Defense Publishers, c1990. 386 p. **CJ308**

Provides comprehensive coverage of leftist groups in Latin America. In two parts: Pt. 1 analyzes violence, ideology, and revolution in Latin America; pt. 2 (the larger) is a handbook of revolutionary organizations in Latin America grouped within chapters arranged alphabetically by country. The entry for each group contains up to 17 categories of information (e.g., origins, membership, leadership, ideology, trends and assessment). Bibliography; name index. JL966.R34

Rossi, Ernest E. Latin America : a political dictionary / Ernest E. Rossi, Jack C. Plano. Santa Barbara, Calif. : ABC-Clio, c1992. 242 p. **CJ309**

1st ed., 1980, had title: *The Latin American political dictionary*.

Covers people, political parties, events, issues, and concepts relevant to Latin American politics in 284 numbered and cross-referenced entries in 11 topical chapters (e.g., Political culture and ideology, The military, International law and organizations). For each entry, gives both a definition and a paragraph describing the term's historical importance and current relevance. Index refers to entry numbers.

F1406.R67

Who's who in Latin America : government, politics, banking & industry. 3rd ed. (1993)– . N.Y. : Norman Ross Publ., 1993– . Annual. **CJ310**

1st ed., 1984, had title: *Who is who in government and politics in Latin America*, with entries in English and Spanish; 2nd ed., 1989, had title: *Who is who [in] government, politics, banking and industry in Latin America*.

Supplies biographical sketches for more than 2,000 leaders in 36 countries. Includes politicians, legislators, diplomats, bankers, economists, trade unionists, lawyers, writers and journalists, engineers, and religious, business, and military leaders. Entries are grouped by country; most include occupation, date and place of birth, education, positions held, and address; some entries list telephone and fax numbers, publications, languages spoken, and recreational interests. Personal name index. Review in *Choice* 31 (Dec. 1993): 1894 notes the lack of diacritics and, in the section on Brazil, the listing of compound surnames under first, rather than last, element.

§ For political figures, see also *Biographical dictionary of Latin American and Caribbean political leaders* (CJ306), which provides fewer but more detailed entries. F1407.W52

Central America

Gunson, Phil. The dictionary of contemporary politics of Central America and the Caribbean / Phil Gunson and Greg Chamberlain, with additional material by Andrew Thompson. N.Y. : Simon & Schuster, 1991. 397 p. : maps.   **CJ311**

Compiled by British journalists, offers alphabetically arranged entries covering people, political parties, events, and terminology of 20th-century Central America and the Caribbean. Headwords are usually in English with the vernacular in parentheses. Cross-references. Maps. List of entries by country.

§*See also* Ernest E. Rossi and Jack C. Plano, *Latin America : a political dictionary* (CJ309).   F2183.G86

South America

Gunson, Phil. The dictionary of contemporary politics of South America / Phil Gunson, Andrew Thompson, and Greg Chamberlain. 1st American ed. N.Y. : Macmillan, 1989. 314 p.   **CJ312**

Written by three British journalists as a guide to themes, events, and personalities in the politics of 20th-century South America. Headwords are usually in English with the vernacular in parentheses. Cross-references in the entries; occasionally, however, important cross-references are omitted (e.g., there is no reference from Malvinas to Falklands). List of entries by country.

§ *See also* Ernest E. Rossi and Jack C. Plano, *Latin America : a political dictionary* (CJ309).   JL1851.A25G86

Europe

Annuaire européen = European yearbook. v.1– . The Hague : Nijhoff, 1955– . Annual.   **CJ313**

Published under the auspices of the Council of Europe.

Aims "to promote the scientific study of a number of international organisations and their work" and "publishes information about European organisations and the OECD to the exclusion of the European organs or Commissions of the United Nations and the Specialised Agencies, information about which is readily available in the [sic] own publications."—*Note, 1991 ed.* In three sections: (1) articles (in French with English summaries or in English with French summaries), (2) documentary (in French and English), and (3) bibliography. The documentary section is comprised of organization entries (e.g., Council of Europe, European Space Agency, Western European Union) giving (as appropriate): description; membership; address; telephone, telex, and fax numbers; organization; officers or representatives; narrative discussion of the year's activities; chronology of major events of the year; list of conferences; and resolutions adopted and texts issued. Cumulative list of articles. Personal name and subject indexes in French and English.   JN3.A5

Babuscio, Jack. European political facts, 1648–1789 / Jack Babuscio, Richard Minta Dunn. N.Y. : Facts on File, 1984. 387 p.   **CJ314**

Designed as a companion work to three earlier works by Chris Cook and John Paxton (below), that cover more recent time periods. Provides chronologies, registers of heads of state and key ministers, and a wealth of information on political systems, parties, and elections; defense, conflicts, and battles; diplomacy and treaties; colonies and dependencies; and other relevant topics. Subject index.

§ Similar coverage and arrangement in the following works by Chris Cook and John Paxton:

European political facts, 1789–1848 (1981. 195 p.).
European political facts, 1848–1918 (1978. 342 p.).

European political facts, 1918–90 (3rd ed. 1992. 322 p. 1st ed., 1975, and 2nd ed., 1986, covered 1918–73 and 1918–84 respectively).   JN9.B3

Europe transformed : documents on the end of the Cold War / ed. by Lawrence Freedman. N. Y. : St. Martin's, 1990. 516 p.   **CJ315**

Presents the texts of treaties, agreements, journalistic accounts, and other statements that document the profound political changes in Eastern Europe that began in 1989. In three chronologically arranged sections: (1) The critical agreements, beginning with a 1945 pact between Poland and the U.S.S.R., that provide the diplomatic framework; (2) Official proposals and draft materials for arms control negotiations; (3) Important proposals and statements by political leaders, including two of Gorbachev's landmark speeches. Detailed table of contents, but no index.   D849.F685

Messick, Frederic M. Primary sources in European diplomacy, 1914–1945 : a bibliography of published memoirs and diaries. N.Y. : Greenwood, [1987]. 221 p. : maps. (Bibliographies and indexes in world history, no. 6).   **CJ316**

Entries, arranged alphabetically by name, include people who held diplomatic or foreign service positions or functioned in that role, or those who witnessed international events or negotiations at first hand and wrote a published memoir or diary in a Western language. For each gives name, dates, a paragraph of explanation, and bibliographic citation. Appendixes provide lists of authors, by nationality, and of selected diplomatic events, 1914–1945, both alphabetically and chronologically. Subject index.   Z2000.M395

New political parties of Eastern Europe and the Soviet Union / ed. by Bogdan Szajkowski ; with contributions by John B. Allcock ... [et al.]. Harlow, Essex, U.K. : Longman Group ; Detroit, Mich. : Gale, c1991. 404 p.   **CJ317**

Covers the development and current state of party politics and political parties in Eastern Europe and the former Soviet Union. Twelve chapters, alphabetically arranged by country and written by scholars, provide a descriptive narrative followed by a political party directory, also arranged alphabetically. For each party gives (if available): address, founding date, membership, leadership, history, organization, program, and affiliations. List of abbreviations. Index.   JN96.A979N49

Opfell, Olga S. Queens, empresses, grand duchesses, and regents : women rulers of Europe, A.D. 1328–1989. Jefferson, N.C. : McFarland, c1989. 282 p. : ports.   **CJ318**

Presents biographies of 39 European royal women, from the 14th century to the present, who were either sitting monarchs or regents with actual power. Entries are chronologically arranged, vary from four to eight pages in length, and include a portrait. Bibliography; name index.   D107.O64

Political and economic encyclopaedia of Western Europe / ed. by Frances Nicholson ... [et al.] for Cambridge International Reference on Current Affairs (CIRCA) Limited. Chicago : St. James Pr., c1990. 411 p. : maps.   **CJ319**

Signed entries treat terms and concepts, political parties, trade unions, organizations, leading politicians, and natural resources. Focuses on the post-World War II period and regards Europe as extending from Iceland to Gibraltar and from Lapland to Cyprus but excludes former Soviet bloc countries, Yugoslavia, and Turkey. Entries are arranged alphabetically and contain cross-references; references to related entries are printed in boldface. General index.   JN94.A2P64

Political parties of Europe / ed. by Vincent E. McHale. Westport, Conn. : Greenwood, 1983. 2 v. (1297 p.).   **CJ320**

Contents: v. 1, Albania–Norway; v. 2, Poland–Yugoslavia, European Parliament.

Country chapters offer introduction, bibliography, alphabetical entries for all parties represented in the national parliments through 1982, and tabular data on electoral history. Includes Eastern Europe countries, the Soviet Union, and historical Germany (pre-1945), Estonia (1917–1940), Latvia (1918–1940), and Lithuania (1918–1940). A separate chapter covers the European Parliament. Appendixes give a chronology of political events by country, a genealogy of parties by country, and parties grouped by ideology and then by country. General index.

§ Other titles useful for historical information on the political parties of European Community countries are Stanley Henig, *Political parties in the European Community* (London : Allen & Unwin, 1979); and Stanley Henig and John Pinder, *European political parties* (London : Allen & Unwin, 1969). JF2011.P595

Rees, Philip. Fascism and pre-fascism in Europe, 1890–1945 : a bibliography of the extreme right. Brighton, Sussex [Eng.] : Harvester ; Totowa, N.J. : Barnes & Noble, 1984. 330 p.
CJ321

A selective bibliography of the "most cited and the most significant writings on the ideology and practice of the extreme right" *(Pref.)*, primarily books, dissertations, and articles of post-1945. After a general chapter (e.g., origins, psychology, racism), citations are grouped by country (and then usually by topic). Country arrangement includes Eastern Europe and the Soviet Union, but excludes Britain (which was covered in Rees's *Fascism in Britain,* CJ339). Also excludes foreign policies of fascist states, anti-fascist resistance movements, the Holocaust and concentration camps. Personal name index.   Z2000.7.R44

Rossi, Ernest E. The European political dictionary / Ernest E. Rossi, Barbara P. McCrea. Santa Barbara, Calif. : ABC-Clio, c1985. 408 p. : maps. (Clio dictionaries in political science, 7).
CJ322

Treats political developments within and among the major European powers (U.K., France, Federal Republic of Germany, and U.S.S.R.); also includes a section on Western European regionalism. For each, includes alphabetically arranged entries on major structures of government, national political parties and interest groups, political culture, recent election summaries, and principal government officials since World War II. Each entry has both a descriptive definition and an analysis of its significance. A geographic index precedes the body of the book, and a general index follows it. Cross-references.
JN12.R65

Western European political parties : a comprehensive guide / ed. and comp. by Francis Jacobs. Burnt Mill, Harlow, Essex, England : Longman ; Detroit : Distr. by Gale, c1989. 730 p. : maps.   **CJ323**

Emphasizes political parties currently represented in national parliaments, providing information (through early 1989) obtained from the parties and through interviews with politicians and party secretariats. In three sections: (1) Countries of the European Community; (2) Other Western European democracies (excluding those with no political party system, such as Monaco, Andorra); (3) Western European political groups (e.g., European Parliament, Nordic Council). Description of the political institutions and systems and recent political history of each country is followed by an alphabetical list of parties, with addresses and telephone numbers of headquarters, party history, support, organization, policies and major personalities. Some countries (e.g., Italy, Spain, U.K.) have regional subsections. Name index.
JN94.A979W475

Who's who in European politics. 1st ed.– . London ; N.Y. : Bowker-Saur, 1990– . Irregular.   **CJ324**

Presents current biographical information for more than 8,000 European political leaders in 43 countries (including the former European Soviet republics) as well as the European Community. In two parts. Pt. 1 consists of alphabetically arranged biographical entries that include (as available) nationality, position, personal data, political and professional careers, memberships, awards and honors, publications, personal and professional interests, personal address, and professional address with telephone, telex, and fax numbers (when available). Pt. 2 is a directory by country that lists the heads of state, government, legislature, political parties, regional government, trade unions, and central bank and gives address, telephone, telex, and fax (if available). Pt. 2

also includes a biographical index to individuals from that country profiled in pt. 1. Glossary of political terms, parties, and institutions. List of abbreviations.   D1070.W49

Albania

Directory of Albanian officials / Directorate of Intelligence, Central Intelligence Agency. 198?– . Wash. : The Agency, 198?– . Irregular.   **CJ325**

Superintendent of Documents classification: PREX 3.10/7: .

Identifies individuals holding positions in selected political party, government, economic, scientific, and public organizations. Personal name index.

§ One of a series of similar directories issued by the CIA. Title and frequency vary. Among the other titles in the series:

Directory of Bulgarian officials (1986–); *Directory of officials of the Republic of Cuba* (1979–); *Directory of Czechoslovak officials* (1985–); *Directory of East German officials* (1987); *Directory of Hungarian officials* (19??–); *Directory of Iranian officials* (19??–); *Directory of Iraqi officials* (1986); *Directory of officials of the Democratic People's Republic of Korea* (197?–); *Directory of the Republic of Nicaragua* (1986–); *Directory of Polish officials* (198?–); *Directory of Romanian officials* (1985–); *Directory of Soviet officials* (Sections for National organizations, Science and education, Republic organizations) (1980–); *Directory of officials of Vietnam* (1983–); *Directory of Yugoslav officials* (1985–).

Austria

Handbuch des politischen Systems Österreichs / hrsg. von Herbert Dachs ... [et al.]. 2., durchgesehene Aufl. Vienna : Manz, 1992. 870 p. : ill.   **CJ326**

1st ed., 1991.

Treats the Austrian political system in signed articles, ten–20 pages in length. Intended for a wide audience; concentrates on the second Austrian Republic from the end of 1970 to the present. Covers political history, constitution, government organization, party system, political parties, relevant organizations, cultural influences, voting behavior, government policy, and local government in chapters grouped within broad topical sections; each chapter ends with a bibliography. Lists of contributors and abbreviations. Keyword index.   JN2012.3.H35

Österreichischer Amtskalender. Jahrg.1 (1922)– . Wien : Österreichische Staatsdruckerei, 1922– . Annual.   **CJ327**

Combines the *Niederösterreichischer Amtskalender* and the *Hof- und Staatshandbuch*. Title pages of each issue carry the volume numbering of each of the earlier series as well as the new series number.

Suspended publication 1938–48, resumed with v. 17, 1949.

A detailed directory of the departments and personnel of the federal, state, and local governments of Austria. Lists of legislative periods and heads of federal and state governments, 1918 to the present. Town and municipality index.   JN1604.A32

France

Biographical dictionary of French political leaders since 1870 / ed. by David S. Bell, Douglas Johnson, Peter Morris. N.Y. : Simon and Schuster, c1990. 463 p.   **CJ328**

Contains some 400 biographies of individuals important in French politics since 1870, featuring political, military, and union leaders, writers, and political philosophers. Varying in length from a few paragraphs to several pages, the entries, alphabetically arranged and signed, include cross-references and short bibliographies (some annotated) of books by or about the individual. Appendixes provide lists of French presidents, prime ministers, postwar union leaders, and Fifth Republic party leaders. General index; notes on contributors (mainly British academicians).

§ Other sources of French political biography include Pierre-Marie Dioudonnat and Sabine Bragadir's *Dictionnaire des 10,000 dirigeants politiques français* (Paris : SEDOPOLS, 1977. 755 p.) and Benoît Yvert's *Dictionnaire des ministres de 1789 à 1989* (DC211).

           DC342.B56

Robert, Adolphe. Dictionnaire des parlementaires français : comprenant tous les membres des assemblées françaises et tous les ministres français depuis le 1ᵉʳ mai 1789 jusqu'au 1ᵉʳ mai 1889, avec leurs noms, état civil, états de services, actes politiques, votes parlementaires, etc / Adolphe Robert, Edgar Bourloton, and Gaston Cougny. Paris : Bourloton, 1891. 5 v. : ill.   **CJ329**

Offers fairly lengthy biographical sketches of French parliamentarians and ministers.

Continued by:

(1) *Dictionnaire des parlementaires français : notices biographiques sur les ministres, sénateurs et députés français de 1889 à 1940*, ed. by Jean Jolly (Paris : Presses Universitaires de France, 1960–77. 8 v.), which superseded *Les parlementaires français, II. 1900–1914. Dictionnaire biographique et bibliographique des sénateurs, députés, ministres ayant siège dans les assemblées législatives*, R. C. L. Samuel and Géo Bonét-Maury (Paris : Roustan, 1914. 479 p.).

(2) *Dictionnaire des parlementaires français : notices biographiques sur les parlementaires français de 1940 à 1958* (Paris : Documentation Française, 1988– . [In progress]).

§ For biographical information on diplomats, see *Annuaire diplomatique et consulaire de la République Française* (Annual. Paris : Imprimerie Nationale, 1858– . Ceased publication?).   JN2771.R7

Germany

DDR Handbuch / wissenschaftliche Leitung, Hartmut Zimmermann, unter Mitarbeit von Horst Ulrich und Michael Fehlauer ; hrsg. vom Bundesministerium für innerdeutsche Beziehungen. 3., überarbeitete und erw. Aufl. Köln : Verlag Wissenschaft und Politik, c1985. 2 v. (xlviii, 1660 p.) : ill.   **CJ330**

2nd ed., 1979.

Now primarily of historical interest. Offers alphabetically arranged lengthy articles as well as short entries on all major aspects of East German society including politics, economy, history, culture, etc. Although entries are written by West German authors, attempts to be an objective account and analysis. Chronology; bibliography. No index.   DD280.6.D37

Kürschners Volkshandbuch Deutscher Bundestag. 1. Wahlperiode (1953/57)– . Darmstadt : Neue Darmstädter Verlagsanstalt, 1954– . Irregular.   **CJ331**

Supersedes: *Kürschners Deutscher Reichstag*, 1890–1933.

Published after each election; gives information on the Bundestag, with biographical sketches and pictures of the members.

           JN3971.A78K8

Osmond, Jonathan. German reunification : a reference guide and commentary / by Jonathan Osmond ; with contributions by Rachel Alsop ... [et al.]. Detroit : distr. by Gale, c1992. 311 p.   **CJ332**

Pt. 1 gives a chronology of events, 1989–92; text focuses on the political, economic, and social conditions in the German Democratic Republic that led to a united Germany. Pt. 2 contains signed essays offering more detailed coverage of aspects of reunification (e.g., trade unions, politicians and parties, women). Pt. 3, the reference section, includes an alphabetical dictionary of people, parties, organizations, institutions, places, and terms; tables of governments, election results, and economic indicators; relevant documents; and a bibliography. Name/subject index.   DD290.25.O85

Schwarz, Max. MdR : biographisches Handbuch der Reichstage. [Hannover] : Verlag für Literatur und Zeitgeschehen GmbH, [1965]. 832 p.   **CJ333**

Lists members of the cabinets and of the parliaments of the First (1848–49), Second (1867–1918), and Third (1919–33) Reich, and gives brief biographical information for each. Includes a short parliamentary history of each period. The appendix offers useful statistics on the political parties. Bibliography.   JN3669.S3

Staatslexikon : Recht, Wirtschaft, Gesellschaft in 7 Bänden / hrsg. von der Görres-Gesellschaft. 7. völlig neubearb. und erw. Aufl. Freiburg : Herder, 1985–1993. 7 v. : ill., maps.   **CJ334**

1st ed. 1889–97; 6th ed. 1957–63.

A standard German work written from the Catholic viewpoint. Focuses on political, economic, social, and cultural developments in West and East Germany, Austria, and Switzerland after 1945. Entries are signed, end with bibliographies listing works primarily in German, and cover a broad range of topics (e.g., government, military, law, religion, education). Includes biographical sketches of politicians, religious leaders, educators, pholosophers, economists, etc. that provide an overview of life and career, major works and ideas, and significant achievements. Each volume has an index listing entries in alphabetical order.   JA63.S82

Wahlhandbuch für die Bundesrepublik Deutschland : Daten zu Bundestags- , Landtags- und Europawahlen in der Bundesrepublik Deutschland, in den Ländern und in den Kreisen, 1946–1989 / Claus A. Fischer (hrsg.). Paderborn : F. Schöningh, 1990. 2 v. (1250 p.). (Studien zur Politik, Bd. 14).   **CJ335**

A massive compilation of election data for West Germany, 1946–89. Covers elections on the federal, state, and county levels for federal parliament, state parliaments, and the European parliament. Organizes entries chronologically by states and type of election. Each volume includes a detailed table of contents listing all tables it contains. Vol. 2 has an index of leading officials of federal and state governments and an index of abbreviations for parties and other political organizations, which refer to the tables of election statistics.

           JN3971.A956W325

Wahlstatistik in Deutschland : Bibliographie der deutschen Wahlstatistik, 1848–1975 / bearb. von Nils Diederich ... [et al.]. München : Verlag Dokumentation, 1976. 206 p. (Berichte und Materialen des Zentralinstituts für sozialwissenschaftliche Forschung (ZI6) der Freien Universität Berlin, Bd. 4).   **CJ336**

Sources in this bibliography of German electoral statistics are arranged geographically by West German state (plus the city of West Berlin), then by type of election—Bundestag, Landtag, municipal, town, etc.—for the period since 1945. A second section treats historical elections before 1945 for the German Empire, Prussia, Bavaria, Hamburg, and other states.   Z7164.R4W33

Great Britain

General works

Bibliography

Britain and Europe since 1945 : a bibliographical guide / comp. by James Hennessy. [Brighton, Eng.] : Harvester Pr., 1973. 98 p.   **CJ337**

Subtitle: An author, title and chronological index to British primary source material on European integration issued since 1945.

A guide to the publisher's microfiche collection of the same title, which reproduces 26,000 pages of literature produced by British pressure groups and other organizations on the topic of British integration into Europe. Participating organizations are briefly described. Includes material produced through 1972. The collection is updated annually and issued with a guide, *Britain and Europe during [year]*.

HC241.25.G7B675

Pidduck, William. The radical right and patriotic movements in Britain : a bibliographical guide: an author, title and chronological index to primary source material on the radical right and patriotic movements in Britain. [Hassocks, Eng.] : Harvester Pr., 1978. 99 p. **CJ338**

A guide to the publisher's microfiche collection of the same title. This first volume indexes the publications of the Bow Group, the Monday Club, Pressure for Economic and Social Toryism, and Aims of Industry, as well as the journal *Solon*. Material published through 1974 is included. Supplementary annual indexes to new materials and materials from other groups have been published through 1979.

Z7165.G8P5

Rees, Philip. Fascism in Britain. Hassocks [Eng.] : Harvester Pr. ; [Atlantic Highlands], N.J. : Humanities Pr., 1979. 243 p. **CJ339**

An annotated bibliography on fascist, pro-Nazi, anti-war, radical right, and anti-Semitic movements in Britain from 1923 to mid-1977. Arranged by historical period, with subject subdivisions; separate sections list writings by and about Sir Oswald Mosley. General index.

Z2021.F2R43

Directories

The civil service year book. 1974– . London : H.M.S.O., 1974– . Annual. **CJ340**

Supersedes the *British imperial calendar and civil service list* (1809–1973). Issuing agency varies; currently issued by the Cabinet Office.

Serves as an up-to-date guide to governmental departments and agencies. Currently consists of six chapters: (1) The royal households; (2) Parliamentary offices; (3) Ministers, departments and executive agencies; (4) Libraries, museums and galleries, research councils, other organizations; (5) Departments and other organisations (separate lists for Northern Ireland, Scotland, and Wales); (6) Salary tables. Entries usually include address, telephone and fax numbers, and a brief description of the department/office/agency's responsibilities. Organization charts. List of abbreviations and acronyms. Subject, personal name, and department/agency/organization indexes.

•A machine-readable version with the same title is available on CD-ROM. JN106.B8

The diplomatic service list. 1966– . London : H.M.S.O., 1966– . Annual. **CJ341**

Issuing agency varies; currently issued by the Foreign and Commonwealth Office.

Continues in part the *Foreign Office list and diplomatic and consular year book* (1806–1965), and *Commonwealth Relations Office year book*.

Describes the organization of the British diplomatic service and the careers of its members. Recent issues in four parts: (1) Home departments; (2) British representation overseas (by country); (3) Chronological lists (e.g., Secretaries of State, Ambassadors); and (4) Biographical notes and list of staff. Entries in pt. 4 include birth date, family, employment grade, and career information. Index to place names in pt. 2. JX1783.A22

International register of research on British politics. [6th ed.] (1985)– . Lewiston, N.Y. : E. Mellen Pr., c1985– . Biennial (irregular). **CJ342**

Studies in public policy, no. 145.

Publisher varies.

1st–5th eds. had title: *British Politics Group research register* (Ames, Iowa : British Politics Group; Glasgow : Univ. of Strathclyde, Center for the Study of Public Policy, 1975–1983).

Supplies entries in alphabetical order for 913 scholars of British politics from around the world (although most are from the U.K. and the U.S.). Entry data, compiled from questionnaires, includes for each respondent: current position, address, education, work/study/research in the U.K., citations to selected publications, relevant courses taught, and research interests/activities (with funding sources, as available). Subject/location, funding, and course indexes, with references to entry numbers. JN101.I57

The Whitehall companion. 1992– . London : Dod's Publishing and Research, c1992– . Annual. **CJ343**

Offers biographies of senior civil servants and descriptions of the structure and functions of government institutions. Arranged alphabetically, the biographies include: name; present job and job grade; career history; personal data (e.g., education, family, recreations); office address with telephone and fax numbers; and often a photograph. Excludes biographies of ministers found in *Dod's parliamentary companion* (CJ357). Divides institutions section into parliamentary offices, government departments (e.g., Education, Health, Treasury), next steps agencies, and regulatory organizations and public bodies (e.g., Civil Aviation Authority, Equal Opportunities Commission, Press Complaints Commission). Provides for each, as appropriate: founding date, organizational structure, responsibilities, officials/ministers, addresses, and telephone and fax numbers. List of abbreviations. Personal name and department or organization name indexes.

Registers

Office-holders in modern Britain. London : Institute of Historical Research, Univ. of London, 1972–1984. 9 v. **CJ344**

Contents: v.1, Treasury officials, 1660–1870, comp. by J. C. Sainty; v.2, Officials of the Secretaries of State, 1660–1782, comp. by J. C. Sainty; v.3, Officials of the Board of Trade, 1660–1870, comp. by J. C. Sainty; v.4, Admiralty officials, 1660–1870, comp. by J. C. Sainty; v.5, Home Office officials, 1782–1870, comp. by J. C. Sainty; v.6, Colonial Office officials, 1794–1870, comp. by J. C. Sainty; v.7, Navy Board officials, 1660–1832, comp. by J. M. Collinge; v.8, Foreign Office officials, 1782–1870, comp. by J. M. Collinge; v.9, Officials of royal commissions of inquiry, 1815–1870, comp. by J. M. Collinge.

"The immediate purpose of the series ... is to provide lists of the officials who served in the departments of the central government between the Restoration and 1870."—*Pref*. The chronological lists of appointments by office are followed by an alphabetical list of officials.

Pickrill, D. A. Ministers of the Crown. London ; Boston : Routledge & Kegan Paul, 1981. 135 p. **CJ345**

Lists holders of ministerial posts in the central government from earliest times (or, in the case of Ireland, from 1801); includes both senior and junior ministers, as well as the Speaker of the House of Commons. A name index to the lists of office-holders would have made the volume more useful. JN401.P5

Handbooks

Britain / prep. by the Central Office of Information. 1949/50– . London : H.M.S.O., [1949?]– . Annual. **CJ346**

Some have subtitle: An official handbook.

Offers, in topical chapters (e.g., Government, Religion, Employment, Overseas trade, The Press), a wealth of information on political, economic, and social matters. Includes maps, graphs, tables, and photographs. General index. DA630.A17

Butler, David. British political facts, 1900–1985 / by David Butler and Gareth Butler. 6th ed. N.Y. : St. Martin's Pr., 1986. 536 p. **CJ347**

For annotation, *see* DC339. JN231.B8

Biography

The Blackwell biographical dictionary of British political life in the twentieth century / ed. by Keith Robbins. Oxford ; Cambridge, Mass. : Blackwell Reference, 1990. 449 p. : ill. **CJ348**
For annotation, *see* DC340.   DA566.9.A1B57

Atlases

Waller, Robert. The atlas of British politics. London ; Dover, N.H. : Croom Helm, c1985. 205 p. ; 21 x 30 cm. **CJ349**
Provides a geographical presentation of the political and social situation in the U.K. Contains 13 sections of maps beginning with a national section followed by regional sections (e.g., Greater London, Yorkshire, Wales). Each section (except Northern Ireland) consists of maps of parliamentary constituencies preceded by explanatory notes, showing election winners, party support, social class, housing, non-white voters, unemployment, car ownership, and educational level. Now somewhat dated, since information is based on the 1981 census and the results of the 1983 general election. No index.
§ Intended as a successor to Michael Kinnear, *The British voter* (CJ369) and a companion to the 1st ed. of Robert Waller, *The almanac of British politics* (CJ361).   G1812.21.F9W3

Political parties

British general election manifestos, 1959–1987 / comp. and ed. by F.W.S. Craig. 3rd ed. Aldershot, England ; Brookfield, Vt. : Dartmouth, 1990. 521 p. **CJ350**
1st ed., 1970, covered 1918–66; 2nd ed., 1975, covered 1900–74.
Contains the texts of election manifestos for the Conservative, Labour, and Liberal parties, 1959–87; omits manifestos 1900–55 that were included in earlier editions. Appendixes provide a copy of the Tamworth Manifesto of 1834 and a list of separate manifestos relating to policy on Scotland and Wales, also for 1959–87.   JN1121.C73

Parliament

Bibliography

Goehlert, Robert. The Parliament of Great Britain : a bibliography / Robert U. Goehlert, Fenton S. Martin. Lexington, Mass. : Lexington Books, 1983. 209 p. **CJ351**
An unannotated bibliography of English-language reference works and secondary literature produced since the late 19th century on the history, development, and legislative process of Parliament, excluding national politics and government policy in general. Subject arrangement. Author and subject indexes.   Z7164.R4G57

Encyclopedias

Abraham, Louis Arnold. Abraham and Hawtrey's parliamentary dictionary. 3rd ed. / by S. C. Hawtrey and H. M. Barclay. London : Butterworths, 1970. 248 p. **CJ352**
1st ed., 1956; 2nd ed., 1964.
A brief encyclopedia of British parliamentary terms and concepts, giving definitions and, in some cases, longer articles, with many cross-references and a subject index.   JN594.A7

Wilding, Norman W. An encyclopaedia of Parliament / Norman Wilding and Philip Laundy. 4th ed., completely rev. N.Y. : St. Martin's, [1971]. 931 p. **CJ353**

1st ed. 1958; 3rd ed., 1968.
A still useful, alphabetically arranged encyclopedia of parliamentary history and procedures. Many brief articles, some long ones. Covers all Commonwealth parliaments, but emphasis is on the Parliament at Westminster. 34 appendixes provide chronological lists of parliaments, ministers, secretaries, etc.; and a bibliography (p. 892–931).   JN555.W5

Registers

Great Britain. Parliament. House of Commons. Members of Parliament ... : [Return of the name of every member of the Lower House of Parliament of England, Scotland and Ireland, with the name of constituency represented and date of return, from 1213 to 1874]. London : Stationery Office, 1878–91. 2 pts. in 4 v. **CJ354**
Repr.: Camden, Me. : Picton Pr., 1989.
Contents: Pt. 1, Parliaments of England, 1213–1702, arranged chronologically. Index to pt. 1, with appendix and corrigenda; pt. 2, Parliaments of Great Britain, 1705–96, Parliaments of the United Kingdom, 1801–74, Parliaments and Conventions of the Estates of Scotland, 1357–1707, Parliaments of Ireland, 1559–1800. Index to pt. 2, with appendix, i.e., names and members 1880–1885, and corrigenda; Parliaments of Great Britain, 1705–1800; Parliaments of the United Kingdom, 1801–85.
An important record.
§ For biographies of members of Parliament, *see*: Josiah Wedgwood, *The history of Parliament, 1439–1509* (CJ355); Romney Sedgwick, *The House of Commons, 1715–1754* (CJ360); Lewis Namier and John Brooke, *The House of Commons, 1754–1790* (N.Y. : Oxford Univ. Pr., 1964); and Michael Stenton, *Who's who of British members of Parliament* (CJ362).
For names and brief biographies of members of the Parliament of Scotland, *see* Joseph Foster, *Members of Parliament, Scotland : including the minor barons, the commissioners for the shires, and the commissioners for the burghs, 1357–1882* (2nd ed., rev. and corr. London : priv. pr. by Hazell, Watson, and Viney, 1882).   JN672.A55

Wedgwood, Josiah Clement. History of Parliament, 1439–1509 / by Colonel the Right Honourable Josiah C. Wedgwood in collaboration with Anne D. Holt. London : H. M. S. O., 1936–38. 2 v. : coats of arms, facsim. **CJ355**
Contents: v. 1, Biographies of the members of the Commons House; v. 2, Register of the ministers and of the members of both houses, 1439–1509. No more published.
Vol. 1 lists 2,600 men, out of a possible total of 3,800 known to have been elected members of 29 Parliaments, 1439–1509, with biographical data about each and many bibliographical footnotes referring to sources. Since only 60 of these subjects are included in *Dictionary of national biography* (AH226), this work is important for British biography as well as Parliamentary history.
Vol. 2 contains introductory chapters on treatment, sources, and analyses; time analysis and lists of parliaments, arranged chronologically; notes on each constituency with alphabetical lists of members; tables and appendixes.   JN505.W4

Handbooks

Craig, Fred W. S. Boundaries of parliamentary constituencies, 1885–1972. Chichester, Eng. : Political Reference Publs., 1972. 212 p. : maps. **CJ356**
Serves as a companion to Craig's five publications entitled *British parliamentary election results*, which cover 1832–1983 (CJ365).   JN561.C7

Dod's parliamentary companion. 33rd ed. (1865)– . Hurst Green, E. Sussex : Dod's Parliamentary Companion, 1865– . Annual.   **CJ357**

First published 1832. Publisher varies. Title varies.

Title varies: *The parliamentary pocket companion*, 1832–46; *Parliamentary companion*, 1847–1864.

Offers a wealth of information relevant to the Parliament of Great Britain including brief biographies of members of the House of Lords and the House of Commons, most with photographs. Also includes a summary of activities of the most recent Parliament; lists of parliamentary committees, officers, and officials; election results; parliamentary terms and proceedings; names of cabinet ministers with descriptions of ministerial responsibilities; listings for government and public offices and organizations of public interest; names of members of the Judiciary and members of the government of London; listings of Commonwealth officials; biographies of U.K. members of the European Parliament; etc. Subject index.   JN500.D7

Guide to the House of Commons. 1970– . London : Times Newspapers Ltd., 1970– .   **CJ358**

At head of title: *The Times*.

Succeeds: *House of Commons* (1880–196?).

Issued following general elections. Gives results of the election, brief biographies of all candidates, photographs of those elected, a statistical analysis of the election results, and a map showing results by constituency. Also includes a variety of related information (e.g., polls, political party manifestos). Candidate name index.   JN956.G9

Norton, Philip. Dissension in the House of Commons : intra-party dissent in the House of Commons' division lobbies, 1945–1974. London : Macmillan, 1975. 643 p.   **CJ359**

Attempts to record all instances in which members of either the Conservative or Labour parties in Parliament voted against the wishes of their party whip or Front bench. Provides name of item being voted on, summary of debate, outcome of the vote, name of dissenting member, and a bibliographic reference to the full Parliamentary debate. Bibliography, subject and personal name indexes.

———. *Dissension in the House of Commons, 1974–1979* serves as a continuation (Oxford : Clarendon Pr., 1980. 524 p.). The compiler's analysis of dissenting actions of the period is presented in a final chapter.   JN675 1975.D57

Sedgwick, Romney. The House of Commons, 1715–1754. N.Y. : publ. for the History of Parliament Trust by Oxford Univ. Pr., 1970. 2 v.   **CJ360**

At head of title: The history of Parliament.

Contents: v. 1, Introductory survey, appendices, constituencies, members, A–D; v. 2, Members, E–Y.

Offers a wealth of historical information on constituencies and members of the House of Commons. Includes background essays, statistical data, and brief biographical sketches that describe each member's parliamentary career and end with bibliographical notes. No index.

§ Continued by: Sir L. B. Namier and John Brooke, *The House of Commons, 1754–1790* (1964. 3 v.). Follows the same general plan; includes references to sources. Contents: v. 1, Introductory survey, constituencies, appendixes; v. 2–3, Members, A–Y.   JN675 1715.S4

Waller, Robert. The almanac of British politics. 4th ed. London ; N.Y. : Routledge, 1991. 717 p. : maps.   **CJ361**

1st ed., 1983; 3rd ed., 1987.

Offers socioeconomic profiles of individual parliamentary constituencies in a manner similar to *The almanac of American politics* (CJ210), but without biographical data on the constituencies' parliamentary representatives. Statistics are provided from the most recent census and general election. Maps. Index of Members of Parliament and index of constituencies.   JN561.W28

Biographical dictionaries

See also Registers, above.

Who's who of British Members of Parliament : a biographical dictionary of the House of Commons based on annual volumes of Dod's Parliamentary companion and other sources / [ed. by] Michael Stenton. [Hassocks, Sussex, Eng.] : Harvester Pr. ; [Atlantic Highlands, N.J.] : Humanities Pr., [1976]–81. 4 v.   **CJ362**

Vols. 2–4 ed. by Michael Stenton and Stephen Lees.

Contents: v. 1, 1832–1885; v. 2, 1886–1918; v. 3, 1919–1945; v. 4, 1945–1979.

The editor has selected "the fullest and most useful entries that Dod [*Dod's parliamentary companion*, CJ357] provides on each MP's parliamentary career" (*Pref.*) and rounded them out with additional information such as the reason for leaving Parliament, highlights of subsequent career, death date. Entries in each volume arranged alphabetically; each volume indexes the Members included in that volume. A review of v. 1 in *TLS* Feb. 18, 1977: 185, notes various shortcomings of the work.   JN672.W47

Elections

British elections and parties yearbook. 1991– . London ; N.Y. : Harvester Wheatsheaf, 1992– . Annual.   **CJ363**

Aims "to present new thinking, original research and cumulative reference material in the field of elections, parties and public opinion in Britain."—*Pref.* In two parts, the first consisting of relevant articles. The second part, the reference section, is a useful assemblage giving a chronology of political events, results of public opinion polls and elections, economic indicators, a bibliography, political party officers and staff, polling companies, mass media organizations, political journals, and other miscellaneous information. No index.

Issued by: Political Studies Association's group on Elections, Public Opinion and Parties in Britain.   JN956.B746

Craig, Fred W. S. British electoral facts, 1832–1987. 5th ed. Aldershot, England : Parliamentary Research Services, Dartmouth ; Brookfield, Vt. : Gower, 1989. 210 p.   **CJ364**

1st ed. (with title *British parliamentary election statistics*), 1968; 4th ed., 1981.

Consists chiefly of tabular information grouped in categories: elections, by-elections, expenses, electorate, forfeited deposits, gains and losses, parties, postal voting, public opinion polls, women, European Parliament, local government, referendums, miscellaneous (e.g., unopposed returns, spoilt ballot papers), and appendixes (e.g., hours of poll, acts of Parliament, void elections). No index.

§ Designed to be used in conjunction with the author's *British parliamentary election results* and *Britain votes* (CJ365 and *note*), each of which contains some unique information (e.g., *Results* gives votes by constituency, *Facts* offers reasons for elections and election timetables).   JN1037.C667

——————— British parliamentary election results, 1832–1885. 2nd ed. Aldershot, England : Parliamentary Research Services, 1989. 746 p.   **CJ365**

1st ed., 1977.

For each constituency, gives date of election; number of electors on the Register; percentage of electors voting; and candidate's name, party, number of votes, and percentage of votes. Its companion volumes (below) are similar; most of the volumes have indexes to candidates, constituencies, and footnotes. For use with the author's *British electoral facts, 1832–1987* (CJ364).

Companion titles:

British parliamentary election results, 1885–1918 (2nd ed. 1977. 1st ed., 1974).

British parliamentary election results, 1918–1949 (3rd ed. 1983. 1st ed., 1969).

British parliamentary election results, 1950–1973 (2nd ed. 1983. 1st ed., 1971, covered 1950–70).

British parliamentary election results, 1974–1983 (1984).

Updated by the interim cumulative supplement, *Britain votes* (Chicester : Parliamentary Research Services, 1977–), new volumes of which are published following each general election.   JN945

——————— Minor parties at British parliamentary elections, 1885–1974. [London : Macmillan, 1975]. 147p. **CJ366**
Serves as a companion to the compiler's several volumes of *British parliamentary election results* (CJ365). Entries are arranged by name of party, outlining history, policy, sources of information, and electoral activity. Statistical summary. Party and personal name indexes.   JN1037.C725

Crewe, Ivor. The British electorate 1963–1987 : a compendium of data from the British election studies / Ivor Crewe, Neil Day, and Anthony Fox. Cambridge ; N.Y. : Cambridge Univ. Pr., 1991. 500 p.   **CJ367**
Data from the British Election Study's sample population questionnaires, 1963–87, presented in tables grouped by topic. 12 chapters: the vote; party identification; party membership; electoral decisions; interest in elections; party image; the economy; business, trade unions, and strikes; nationalization and privatization; the welfare state; issues of citizenship; and newspaper readership. Gives the results by variables such as party affiliation, sex, age, geographic location, and social class. Appendixes provide methodological details of the studies. No index.   JN956.C74

——————— British parliamentary constituencies : a statistical compendium / Ivor Crewe and Anthony D. Fox. London : Faber and Faber, 1984. 397 p. : maps.   **CJ368**
Consists of standardized entries for 650 British election districts, providing electoral, social, and demographic statistics with explanatory text. Appendixes list districts in rank order according to various electoral or socio-demographic characteristics. Usefulness may now be limited, since data is from 1979 and 1983.   JN561.C74

Kinnear, Michael. The British voter : an atlas and survey since 1885. 2nd ed. N.Y. : St. Martin's Pr., 1981. 173 p. : ill.   **CJ369**
1st ed., 1968.
Illustrates social, economic, and organizational factors in British politics and elections from 1885 to 1979, through text, tables, and maps. Bibliography. General index and index of constituencies.   G1811.F9K5

Local government

Municipal year book and public services directory. 1973– . London : Municipal Publications Ltd., 1973– . Annual.   **CJ370**
Supersedes works with similar titles, published since 1897.
Covers all phases of British local government. Features descriptive and directory information on agencies by type of service (e.g., finance, education, power, water); municipal corporations; county and district councils; local government in Wales, Scotland, Northern Ireland, and the Isles; and central government in England. Also lists associations and societies concerned with local government. General index and indexes to local authorities and former local authorities.   JS3003.M8

British Commonwealth

Bloomfield, Valerie. Commonwealth elections, 1945–1970 : a bibliography. Westport, Conn. : Greenwood, 1976. 306 p.   **CJ371**
"This bibliography developed out of the library and research activities of the Institute of Commonwealth Studies, University of Lon-

don."—*Introd.* References to some 760 elections have been provided in some 5,600 citations arranged by geographic region and then by country and form. "Originally it was intended to restrict the survey to elections and referenda at the national level, but in response to suggestions from political scientists coverage has been extended to state and provincial elections as well." Includes unpublished sources, official reports, electoral studies, and political party documents. List of journals cited. Excludes academic theses. Author and name index.
Z7164.R4B55

The Commonwealth yearbook / Foreign and Commonwealth Office. 1987– . London : H.M.S.O., 1987– . Annual. **CJ372**
Title varies: *Commonwealth Office year book* (1967–68), and *A year book of the Commonwealth*, (1969–86).
Gives, for Commonwealth member countries and their dependent territories, a general description (e.g., locations, climate, population, education), history, constitutional development, international organization membership, and current government. Includes information on Commonwealth evolution, structure, organizations, and representation. Statistical tables provide economic, trade, finance, population, and social data. Geographic name/subject index.   JN248.C5912

Cook, Chris. Commonwealth political facts / Chris Cook and John Paxton. N.Y. : Facts on File, 1979. 293 p.   **CJ373**
Follows the format and philosophy of the various editions of David Butler's *British political facts* (DC339), with chapters on: evolution of the Commonwealth; heads of state, governors general, governors and high commissioners; constitutional history and parliamentary organization; ministers; elections; political parties; justice; defense and treaties; population; trade unions. Subject index.   JN248.C63

Ireland, Northern

Flackes, William D. Northern Ireland : a political directory, 1966–88 / W. D. Flackes and Sydney Elliott. Belfast : Blackstaff Pr. ; Chester Springs, Pa. : distr. by Dufour Editions, 1989. 417 p.   **CJ374**
1st ed., 1980; 2nd ed., 1983.
A guide to the politicians, parties, elections, pressure groups, paramilitaries, events, the British role, and international involvement in Northern Ireland. In seven major sections: (1) Chronology of major events, 1921–88; (2) Dictionary of Northern Irish politics; (3) Election results, 1968–88; (4) Systems of government, 1968–88; (5) Officeholders in Northern Ireland, 1968–88; (6) The security system; and (7) Security statistics. List of abbreviations. Review in *Choice* 27 (May 1990): 1472, notes "inconsistencies in the election statistics from the second edition to the third" and "the continued lack of an index and bibliography."   DA990.U46F487

Scotland

Bryan, Gordon. Scottish nationalism and cultural identity in the twentieth century : an annotated bibliography of secondary sources. Westport, Conn. : Greenwood, 1984. 180 p. (Bibliographies and indexes in law and political science, 1).   **CJ375**
A classed bibliography on the political, literary, and linguistic aspects of Scottish nationalism. 894 annotations for articles, pamphlets, books, and chapters of books published in Britain and the U.S., 1900–83, arranged chronologically and topically. Appendix gives addresses for leading journals, and for cultural and political organizations. Chronology; index primarily of authors and titles.
§ Updates Kenneth C. Fraser's *Bibliography of the Scottish national movement (1844–1973)* (Dollar : Douglas S. Mack, 1976. 40 p.).   Z2067.N35B79

Ireland

Ford, Percy. A select list of reports of inquiries of the Irish Dáil and Senate, 1922–72 / P. and G. Ford. [Dublin] : Irish Univ. Pr., [1974]. 64 p.   **CJ376**

Aims "to help students to follow the development of thought on Eire's main lines of domestic policy since the foundation of the State."—*Scope.* Lists reports and papers on policy in constitutional, economic, social and legal matters. Classed arrangement; index based on keywords in title, with addition of names of personal authors and chairmen.   Z7165.I68F67

O'Clery, Conor. The dictionary of political quotations on Ireland, 1886–1987 : phrases make history here. Boston : G.K. Hall, [1987]. 232 p.   **CJ377**

For annotation, *see* DC409.   DA959.O25

A source book of Irish government / ed. by Basil Chubb, assisted by Geraldine O'Dea. Rev. ed. Dublin : Inst. of Public Administration, 1983. 255 p. : ill., map.   **CJ378**

1st ed., 1964.

Describes the functions of the national and local governments, the courts, participation in the European Communities, etc., with excerpts from relevant documents. Bibliography; index.   JN1428.S68

Walker, Brian Mercer. Parliamentary election results in Ireland, 1801–1922. Dublin : Royal Irish Academy, 1978. 438 p. : maps. (New history of Ireland : Ancillary publications, 4).   **CJ379**

Gives results of general and by-elections for the United Kingdom parliament at Westminster, the parliament of Northern Ireland, the Dáil Eireann, and the European Parliament. Provides names of candidates and members elected, political affiliations, number of electors, and votes received. Includes maps of constituencies. Bibliography. Personal name index.

§ Continued by Walker's *Parliamentary election results in Ireland : 1918–92 : Irish elections to parliaments and parliamentary assemblies at Westminster, Belfast, Dublin, Strasbourg* (Dublin : Royal Irish Academy ; Belfast : Queen's University of Belfast, Institute of Irish Studies, 1992. 358 p.). Follows the same format, but includes a list of sources rather than a bibliography.

For information on the Ancillary publications series, *see* DC411.   JN1541.W34

Italy

Bartolotta, Francesco. Governi d'Italia, 1848–1961. [Roma, 1962?]. 330 p.   **CJ380**

Covers the period from Italy's first general election (1848) to 1961. Register of Councils of Ministers (cabinets) and leaders of successive legislatures. Brief explanations of circumstances leading to each change in Italian government. Chronological listing of prime ministers and legislatures. Personal name index.

I deputati e senatori del ... Parlamento republicano. v. 1 (1949)– . Roma : La Navicella, 1949– .   **CJ381**

Numeric designation appears in title, e.g., "undicesimo Parlamento" in 1992 ed.

Contains biographical sketches and photographs of prime minister, council of ministers (cabinet), and members of parliament for each Italian government. Includes statistical information about makeup of parliament: e.g., profession, age, educational credentials. Names cabinet ministers and undersecretaries, as well as members of previous two Italian governments. Information on Italian political parties, including insignia, headquarters, and officials. Lists candidates running for office in regional elections with number of votes received. Acronyms and abbreviations for groups. General index; index of ministers and undersecretaries.

Pallotta, Gino. Dizionario della politica italiana. 1a ed. [rev. ed.]. Roma : Newton Compton, 1985. 442 p. : ill. (Quest'Italia, 81).   **CJ382**

Previous ed., 1976, had title: *Dizionario politico e parlamentare italiano.*

Subtitle: I meccanismi della vita politica con la sua vasta terminologia specifica e quarant'anni di storia in uno strumento di lavoro e di consultazione per il giornalista, il parlamentare, il lettore di prosa politica, il cittadino.

Offers brief definitions of political terms, abbreviations, organizations, and movements, with longer articles on changes in the government and political issues. Includes tables of election statistics. This revised edition includes neologisms coined since earlier publication and updates through 1985 historical articles on such subjects as terrorism, pollution, and Italian political parties.   JN5451.P34

Netherlands

Deth, Jan W. van. Dutch parliamentary election studies data source book, 1971–1989 / Jan W. van Deth, Raymond Horstman. Amsterdam : Steinmetz Archive/SWIDOC, 1993. 219 p. : ill. (Steinmetz Archive codebook, no. P1110).   **CJ383**

1st ed., 1989, covered 1971–86.

Brings together data on electoral behavior and political orientation from the Dutch parliamentary election studies of 1971, 1972, 1977, 1981, 1982, 1986, and 1989. Gives background information, a description of the studies, and a list of variable descriptions. Statistics, in seven sections, cover voting and party identification, political orientation, competence and participation, national problems, political issues, religion in society, and background data (e.g., profession, education, income). Appendixes provide national election statistics, notes on coding schemes used in the studies, and information on the studies' data sets.

●Machine-readable versions of these studies are available as data sets from the Steinmetz Archive of the Social Science Information and Documentation Centre (SWIDOC) of the Royal Netherlands Academy of Arts and Sciences and through the Inter-university Consortium for Political and Social Research (ICPSR).

Staatsalmanak voor het Koninkrijk der Nederlanden 1860– . 'sGravenhage : Statsdrukkerij- en Vitgeverijbedrijf.   **CJ384**

Not published 1940–42, 1945–46, 1959.

The official register of the Netherlands, covering the royal family, States-General, Prime Minister and Council of Ministers, government ministries, government-related organizations, provinces, colonial possessions, municipalities, water districts, etc. Personal name and general indexes.   JN5704

Russia

See also entries for the Union of Soviet Socialist Republics.

Directory of Russian MPs : people's deputies of the Supreme Soviet of Russia-Russian Federation / ed. by Martin McCauley. Harlow, Essex, UK : Longman ; Detroit : distr. by Gale Research, c1992. lii, 326 p. : ill.   **CJ385**

Treats the people's deputies of the Soviet of the Republic and the Soviet of Nationalities (as of April 1992) of the Russia-Russian Federation in alphabetically arranged biographical sketches that include office address and telephone, home town, current parliamentary posts, membership in factions or groups, election details, and a summary of life, career, and voting record. Also includes lists of national territorial subdivisions; deputies by name, nationality, and constituency; Russian

Supreme Soviet committees; Supreme Soviet Presidium; Soviet of the Republic commissions; Soviet of Nationalities commissions; and parliamentary factions and groups. Glossary.   JN6551.D57

Pribylovskiĭ, Vladimir. Dictionary of political parties and organizations in Russia / by Vladimir Pribylovskii ; ed. by Dauphine Sloan and Sarah Helmstadter. Moscow : PostFactum/ Interlegal ; Wash. : Center for Strategic and International Studies, c1992. 129 p. (Significant issues series, v. 14, no. 7).
                                             CJ386
     Serves as a guide to 120 political parties, movements, and parliamentary factions active in Russia since 1987. Alphabetically arranged, the entries include (as available or appropriate): contact, address, telephone number, date and location of founding, size of membership, short biographies of major leaders, and description of its evolution, platforms, and positions. List of acronyms and abbreviations. Name index.   JN6699.A795P75

Russian government today / [editorial content by the International Center]. Spring 1993– . Wash. : Carroll Publ. Co. : International Center, c1993– . Semiannual.   **CJ387**
     Offers a detailed directory of the legislative, executive, and judicial branches of Russian government; federal banks; Russian Academy of Sciences; local governments and business institutions; relevant U.S., international, and Russian organizations, etc. Entries furnish names, job titles, addresses, and telephone numbers. Includes organization charts and maps. Personal name and keyword indexes.
                                           JN6691.A1R87

Switzerland

Gruner, Erich. Die schweizerische Bundesversammlung, 1848–1920. Bern : Francke Verlag, [1966]. 2 v.; portfolio of tables. (Helvetia politica, series A, v. 1–2).   **CJ388**
     Added title page in French: L'Assemblée Fédérale Suisse. Introductory matter in German and French. Vol. 1, text in German, Italian, French; v. 2, text in German and French. Vol. 2 also by Karl Frei.
     The first volume presents biographical information on the 1,467 deputies of the Swiss Federal Assembly from 1848 to 1920, grouped by canton. The second volume is a sociological and statistical study of the professional, educational, etc., backgrounds of the deputies, with illustrative graphs and tables. The portfolio of tables provides a chronological picture of membership by canton.
     ———. *Die schweizerische Bundesversammlung, 1920–1968* (Bern : Francke Verlag, [1970]. 287 p. and portfolio of tables). Extends the coverage of v. 2 of the earlier set, but does not provide biographical sketches.

Ukraine

Liber, George. Nonconformity and dissent in the Ukrainian SSR, 1955–1975 : an annotated bibliography / comp. by George Liber and Anna Mostovych. Cambridge, Mass. : Harvard Ukrainian Research Inst., c1978. 245 p.   **CJ389**
     Contains 1,242 entries pertaining to the Ukrainian national movement, as well as Jewish migration to Israel, religious developments among Catholics, Orthodox, and Protestants, and the Russian civil rights movement in the Ukraine. Includes primary sources published in the Ukraine, as well as *samvydav* and secondary source materials. Name/subject index refers to entry numbers.   Z2514.U5L48

Union of Soviet Socialist Republics

See also entries for Russia.

Handbook of political science research on the USSR and Eastern Europe : trends from the 1950s to the 1990s / ed. by Raymond C. Taras. Westport, Conn. : Greenwood, 1992. 345 p.   **CJ390**
     15 signed bibliographic essays written by specialists review trends in scholarship on the U.S.S.R. and Eastern European communist countries, 1950s–90s. After an introduction on Sovietology, the work's two parts consist of essays on individual countries (Albania, Bulgaria, Czechoslovakia, German Democratic Republic, Hungary, Poland, Romania, and the U.S.S.R.), and essays on international and economic relations. Essays include bibliographies; an appendix lists major research centers, institutes, and programs in Soviet, Russian, and East European studies. List of contributors; author/title and subject indexes.   JN6524.H36

Handbook of reconstruction in Eastern Europe and the Soviet Union / ed. by Stephen White ; contributors John B. Allcock ... [et al.]. Detroit : distr. by Gale, c1991. 407 p. : maps.   **CJ391**
     Concentrates on only two years, 1989 and 1990, in which communist governments were replaced or changed dramatically. Separate chapters treat Albania, Bulgaria, Czechoslovakia, Germany, Hungary, Poland, Romania, Soviet Union, and Yugoslavia, providing for each a chronology, an overview of political and economic developments, details on economic sectors, foreign trade, key personalities, the media, and foreign policy. Two other chapters focus on East-West economic relations, the Council for Mutual Economic Assistance (Comecon), and the Warsaw Treaty Organization. Includes texts of two German reunification treaties and the Soviet constitution. Maps. Name/subject index.
     § *See also* White's *Political and economic encyclopaedia of the Soviet Union and Eastern Europe* (DC52), which covers 1945–90.
                                       HC244.H344

Hodnett, Grey. Leaders of the Soviet Republics, 1955–1972 : a guide to posts and occupants / Grey Hodnett and Val Ogareff. Canberra : Dept. of Pol. Sci., Research School of Social Sciences, Australian Nat. Univ., 1973. 454 p.   **CJ392**
     A listing by republic and office of officials in republic-level party positions, positions in the republic Council of Ministers, and other high-ranking republic-level positions. Names (with service dates) are chronologically arranged within each position category. Personal name index.
     Continued by: Val Ogareff, *Leaders of the Soviet Republics, 1971–1980* (1980. 452 p.).
     Similar format; adds new material on regional leaders of cities, oblasts, autonomous republics, etc.   JN6521.H62

Institut zur Erforschung der UdSSR. Party and government officials of the Soviet Union, 1917–1967 / comp. by the Institute for the Study of the USSR, Munich, Germany ; ed. by Edward L. Crowley, Andrew I. Lebed, Heinrich E. Schulz. Metuchen, N.J. : Scarecrow, [1969]. 214 p.   **CJ393**
     A revised and expanded edition of the Institute's earlier, mimeographed publication, *Key officials of the government of the USSR*.
     The first section, Key officials of the Communist Party of the Soviet Union, lists party officials (congress by congress) for the 1st through 23rd congresses, 1898–1967. The second section lists government officials, 1917–67, arranged by groups of departments and offices. General index and index of names.   JN6598.K7I54

Kraus, Herwig. The composition of leading organs of the CPSU (1952–1982) : CPSU CC Politburo and Secretariat members, CPSU CC full and candidate members, CPSU Central Auditing Commission members (as of May 30, 1982). [Wash.? : s.n., 1982?]. 111 p.   **CJ394**

1st ed., 1976, covered 1952–76.

Supplement to *Radio Liberty research bulletin*.

For each official, provides full name, birth date, present or latest-known position, and major status changes between party congresses, such as appointments, expulsions, deaths, etc. Some sources noted. Lacks a name index.   JN6598.K7K6625

Laird, Roy D. A Soviet lexicon : important concepts, terms, and phrases / Roy D. Laird, Betty A. Laird. Lexington, Mass. : Lexington Books, c1988. 201 p.   **CJ395**

Now primarily of historical interest. Defines words, concepts, and phrases commonly used in Soviet studies (e.g., apparatchik, glasnost, Politburo, revisionism), excluding most geographical and personal names. Begins with an essay describing the Soviet economic, political, and social system. The entries, alphabetically arranged, sometimes include the transliterated Russian equivalents. Three appendixes offer a historical list of full and candidate members of the Politburo, the Soviet constitution, and the rules of the Communist party. Cross-references.   DK266.3.L27

McCrea, Barbara P. The Soviet and East European political dictionary / Barbara P. McCrea, Jack C. Plano, George Klein. Santa Barbara, Calif. : ABC-Clio, 1984. 367 p. (Clio dictionaries in political science, 4).   **CJ396**

Now primarily of historical interest. Groups entries into chapters according to subject matter, with definitions, paragraphs on historical and contemporary significance, and cross references. Comprehensive index and country index.   DJK6.M33

Africa

A bibliography for the study of African politics. [Los Angeles] : Crossroads Pr., 1977–1983. 3 v.   **CJ397**

Vol. 1 previously issued in 1973 by R. B. Shaw and R. L. Sklar. Vol. 2 ed. by Alan C. Soloman; v. 3 ed. by Eric R. Siegel.

Each volume contains a section of general works (subdivided by form and subject), followed by sections for individual regions and countries. Vol. 1 has about 3,900 entries for (primarily) English-language works published through 1970. Vol. 2 is designed as a supplement, covering 1971–75 in more than 3,900 entries. Vol. 3, with 5,720 entries, covers 1976–80, omits items on Egypt, and includes more works in Western languages. Author index in each volume.

§ Still useful for historical research: Harold Alderfer, *A bibliography of African government, 1950–66* (2nd ed. Lincoln University, Pa. : Lincoln University Pr., 1967).   Z3508.P6B52

Bidwell, Robin. Guide to African ministers. London : Collings, 1978. 79p.   **CJ398**

Gives in tabular form the names and dates of heads of state (including colonial governors), prime ministers, and ministers of foreign affairs, defense, interior or local government, and finance serving in African countries, 1950 through 1976. Each of the sections is subdivided into eight parts representing countries grouped together for geographical or historical reasons. Notes. No index.

§ A similar work is the same compiler's *Bidwell's guide to government ministers* ([London] : F. Cass, 1973–74. 3 v.) Contents: v. 1, The major powers and Western Europe, 1900–1971; v. 2, The Arab world, 1900–1972; v. 3, The British Empire and successor states, 1900–1972.   JQ1874.B53

Cook, Chris. African political facts since 1945 / Chris Cook and David Killingray. 2nd ed. N.Y. : Facts on File, c1991. 280 p.   **CJ399**

1st ed., 1983.

Covers the political history of the continent, 1945–1990. Provides a chronology of major events; lists of governors, heads of state, and major ministerial appointments; political data on constitutions, parliaments and parties; brief biographies of important individuals; informa-

tion on conflicts, armed forces, and coups; foreign affairs and treaties; and population and ethnic groups. Bibliography; subject index.

DT30.C594

Drabek, Anne Gordon. The politics of African and Middle Eastern states : an annotated bibliography / comp. by Anne Gordon Drabek and Wilfrid Knapp. Oxford ; N.Y. : Pergamon, 1976. 192 p.   **CJ400**

A geographical listing of principally English-language books on post-independence political development and international politics; within each region, titles are further classed as dealing with: (A) Political history; (B) Political systems, government; (C) Political parties, interest groups and ideologies; (D) Biographies, memoirs, speeches, writings by political leaders; (E) External relations. No index.

Z3508.P6D7

Handbook of political science research on sub-Saharan Africa : trends from the 1960s to the 1990s / ed. by Mark W. DeLancey. Westport, Conn. : Greenwood, 1992. 427 p.   **CJ401**

Presents 13 bibliographic essays, written by specialists, in sections on general, regional, or country surveys. Each essay concludes with notes and an extensive bibliography. Appendix lists social science research centers (including national archives and libraries) by country. Bibliography of bibliographies on African politics; list of contributors; name and subject indexes.   JA84.A337H36

Kirk-Greene, A. H. M. A biographical dictionary of the British colonial governor. Brighton, Eng. : Harvester Pr., 1980. v. 1.   **CJ402**

Contents: v. 1, Africa.

No more published?

Provides brief data (family background, birth and death dates, marriage and children, education, career, governorships, honors, publications, source material) for about 200 governors in Africa between 1875 and 1968. Appendix provides chronological list of governors by country. Reviewed in *African affairs* 81, no. 325 (Oct. 1982): 587–8.

JV1009.A2K57

Phillips, Claude S. The African political dictionary. Santa Barbara, Calif. : ABC-Clio, c1984. 245 p. : maps. (Clio dictionaries in political science, 6).   **CJ403**

Items are arranged alphabetically in ten topical chapters (e.g., Land and people, Political culture and ideology, Governmental institutions and processes). For each entry, provides both a definition and a paragraph describing the term's historical and contemporary relevance. Appendixes contain maps and tables of demographic and political data. Bibliography. List of entries by country. General index.   DT30.5.P47

Political leaders of contemporary Africa south of the Sahara : a biographical dictionary / ed. by Harvey Glickman. N.Y. : Greenwood, c1992. 361 p.   **CJ404**

Presents signed, alphabetically-arranged essays written by specialists on 54 political leaders of sub-Saharan Africa who have helped shape events since 1945. Each essay provides details on personal life; leadership skills; political goals, means, and success; impact on politics (in country of residence, in Africa, and beyond); and a bibliography of works by or about the individual. Also includes a list of biographees by country, a chronology of significant personal or political events for each individual, and a bibliography on political elites and political trends in Africa. List of contributors; personal, corporate, and geographic name index.

§ John A. Wiseman, *Political leaders in Black Africa* (CJ409) and Alan Rake, *Who's who in Africa* (CJ406) include more individuals but give less detail. For leaders from North Africa (including the Sudan), *see* Bernard Reich, *Political leaders of the contemporary Middle East and North Africa* (CJ417).   DT352.8.P63

Political parties of Africa and the Middle East : a reference guide / editors: Roger East and Tanya Joseph. Harlow, U.K. : Longman ; Detroit : Distr. by Gale, c1993. 354 p.   **CJ405**

Concentrates on current recognized and legal political parties in Africa and the Middle East. Alphabetically arranged by country, giving brief political history, constitutional structure, electoral system, recent election data, status of suffrage, and entries for individual political parties. Party entries are generally grouped into sections for major, minor, defunct, and guerrilla groups, as appropriate. Personal name and political party name indexes.

Rake, Alan. Who's who in Africa : leaders for the 1990s. Metuchen, N.J. : Scarecrow, 1992. 448 p.   **CJ406**
    Treats 323 political leaders of sub-Saharan Africa and "concentrates on those in power, those recently in office, and those most likely to succeed ..."—*Pref.* Entries range in length from one-half to three pages and are arranged alphabetically by nation, then by individual. Each provides an assessment of character and career as well as a chronological history of the person's life (focusing on political events). Personal name index.
    § *See also* Harvey Glickman, *Political leaders of contemporary Africa south of the Sahara* (CJ404) and John A. Wiseman, *Political leaders in black Africa* (CJ409).   DT18.R35

Ray, Donald Iain. Dictionary of the African left : parties, movements, and groups. Aldershot, England ; Brookfield, Vt. : Dartmouth, c1989. 273 p.   **CJ407**
    Focuses on groups existing since 1980 and exercising power at the level of the state or beyond. Provides "the most comprehensive survey to date of the various forms of the left in Africa ..."—*p. 3.* Gives "the group's history, orientation, and composition." (*p. 1.*) in dictionary format. Includes a chronology of leftist states in Africa as well as indexes by acronyms and by country.   HX439.R38

Williams, Gwyneth. The dictionary of contemporary politics of southern Africa / Gwyneth Williams and Brian Hackland. London ; N.Y. : Routledge, 1988. 339 p.   **CJ408**
    Includes Angola, Botswana, Lesotho, Malawi, Mozambique, Namibia, South Africa, Swaziland, Tanzania, Zambia, and Zimbabwe. Alphabetically arranged entries cover political figures, political organizations, terms, events, and places. Entries vary in length from one sentence to two pages, have cross-references, and contain the name(s) of the relevant country or countries in parentheses. A list of entries by country and a brief bibliography follow the main body of the work. No index.   JQ2720.A127W55

Wiseman, John A. Political leaders in Black Africa : a biographical dictionary of the major politicians since independence. Aldershot, Hants., England ; Brookfield, Vt. : E. Elgar, c1991. 248 p.   **CJ409**
    1st ed., 1983.
    Brief entries on 485 black and white leaders. Focus on political leaders from about 1960, but also includes others who have had an influence on politics. Includes a chronology of major events since 1960 and a geographic index.
    § *See also* Harvey Glickman, *Political leaders of contemporary African south of the Sahara* (CJ404) and Alan Rake, *Who's who in Africa* (CJ406). An older work, still occasionally useful for historical information on political leaders and parties, is Ronald Segal, *Political Africa* (N.Y. : Praeger, 1961).   DT352.8.W57

South Africa

See also DD185 for a note on *The Namibian issue.*

Bibliographies on South African political history / ed. by O. Geyser, P. W. Coetzer, J. H. Le Roux. Boston : G. K. Hall, 1979–82. 3 v.   **CJ410**
    For annotation, *see* DD213.   Z3608.A5B5

Riley, Eileen. Major political events in South Africa, 1948–1990. Oxford ; N. Y. : Facts on File, c1991. 250 p. : maps.   **CJ411**
    For annotation, *see* DD210.   DT1945.R54

Who's who in South African politics / ed. by Shelagh Gastrow. 4th rev. ed. London ; N.Y. : Zell, 1993. 333 p. : ports.   **CJ412**
    For annotation, *see* DD212.   DT1774.G37

Wynne, Susan G. South African political materials : a catalogue of the Carter-Karis collection. Bloomington, Ind. : Southern African Research Archives Project, 1977. 811 p.   **CJ413**
    A classified catalog of mainly primary material collected in southern Africa by Gwendolen Carter and Thomas Karis and used in preparing *From protest to challenge : a documentary history of African politics in South Africa, 1882–1964* (Stanford : Hoover Inst. Pr., 1977. 4 v.). Also serves as a reel guide to the microfilm copy of the collection in the Melville J. Herskovits Library of African Studies at Northwestern University Library available through the Cooperative Africana Microfilm Project of the Center for Research Libraries. Name index.

Asia (by region)

Political parties of Asia and the Pacific / Haruhiro Fukui, ed. in chief. Westport, Conn. : Greenwood, 1985. 2 v. (1346 p.).   **CJ414**
    Offers information on political parties and party-like organizations for 41 countries or political entities of Asia and the Pacific. Arranged alphabetically by country, each entry containing an essay on the country's political history, a bibliography, and an alphabetical list of political parties with descriptions. The latter are written by specialists, are signed, and often have brief bibliographies and cross-references. Three appendixes: (1) a chronology of political events, (2) a genealogy of parties, and (3) a typology of parties (e.g., listings by ideology, religion). Name index.
    § For more recent information, *see* D. S. Lewis and D. J. Sagar, *Political parties of Asia and the Pacific* (CJ446).   JQ39.A45P64

Who's who in Asian and Australasian politics. London ; N.Y. : Bowker-Saur, c1991. 475 p.   **CJ415**
    For annotation, *see* DE20.   DS35.2.W48

Ziring, Lawrence. The Asian political dictionary / Lawrence Ziring, C.I. Eugene Kim. Santa Barbara, Calif. : ABC-Clio, c1985. 438 p. : maps. (Clio dictionaries in political science, 10).   **CJ416**
    Covers contemporary politics, government, and foreign relations in 27 countries and territories in Asia. Entries are alphabetical within broad categories: Political geography, Political culture and ideology, Political parties and movements, Political institutions and processes, Militarism and the armed forces, Modernization and development, Diplomacy, and International relations and conflict. Each entry includes both a descriptive text, giving historical background (and often ending with cross-references), and a "Significance" section relating the entry to developments, ideologies, or history. Entries are preceded by an Asian countries index and followed by a general index.   DS31.Z57

Asia, West

Political leaders of the contemporary Middle East and North Africa : a biographical dictionary / ed. by Bernard Reich. N.Y. : Greenwood, 1990. 557 p.   **CJ417**
    Profiles 70 individuals who have made substantial contributions to and had lasting effects on the politics of the Middle East and North Africa since World War II. Lengthy entries (from four to twelve pages) are alphabetically arranged and contain essential biographical data (e.g., birth and death dates, education, career); a description and analysis of the person's development, programs, goals, methods, and significant contributions to politics; and a bibliography of books by and about the individual (most in English). Written by specialists, the en-

tries are signed and contain cross-references. Includes a list of the biographees by country, a chronology of important events in the region, and a bibliography of works on the political elite of the region. General index. DS61.5.P65

Political parties of Africa and the Middle East : a reference guide / editors: Roger East and Tanya Joseph. Harlow, U.K. : Longman ; Detroit : Distr. by Gale, c1993. 354 p. **CJ418**
For annotation, *see* CJ405.

Schulz, Ann. International and regional politics in the Middle East and North Africa : a guide to information sources. Detroit : Gale, [1977]. 244p. **CJ419**
Chapters begin with an essay on the literature, then list English-language books, with annotations. Concentrates on post-1945 situation, with chapters on regional issues, foreign policies of individual states, external powers, Arab-Israeli conflict, petroleum. Reference materials are listed in a separate chapter. Author, title, and subject indexes. Z6465.N35S38

Ziring, Lawrence. The Middle East : a political dictionary. Santa Barbara, Calif. : ABC-Clio, c1992. 401 p. **CJ420**
1st ed., 1984, had title: *The Middle East political dictionary.*
Treats terms, events, people, institutions, and movements relevant to the Middle East, primarily since World War II. 271 numbered and cross-referenced entries are arranged in seven broad topical chapters (e.g., Islam, Political parties and movements, Diplomacy). Entries contain both a definition and a section on significance, giving a more interpretative discussion of the term. Index cites entry numbers. DS61.Z58

Asia, Southeast

Sagar, D. J. Major political events in Indo-China, 1945–1990. Oxford ; N. Y. : Facts on File, 1991. 230 p. : maps. **CJ421**
Covers significant political and military events in Cambodia, Laos, and Vietnam from the end of World War II through 1990 in a descriptive and detailed chronology. Includes a section with biographical sketches, a glossary, bibliography, maps, and 28 appendixes. Index. DS550.S34

Asia, East

Nationalism in East Asia : an annotated bibliography of selected works / ed. by F. Gilbert Chan. N.Y. : Garland, 1981. 170 p. (Canadian review of studies in nationalism, v. 1 ; Garland reference library of social science, v. 70). **CJ422**
Contains six chapters covering China, Japan, and Korea. The first three chapters (Chinese nationalism: a bibliographical survey; Communist nationalism in China; Nationalism in China: Chinese and Japanese sources) were compiled by Chan; two chapters on Japan and one on Korea were contributed by other scholars. Subject index. Z3001.N34

Arab states

Mostyn, Trevor. Major political events in Iran, Iraq, and the Arabian Peninsula, 1945–1990. N.Y. : Facts on File, c1991. 308 p. : maps. **CJ423**
For annotation, *see* DE62. DS326.M64

Shimoni, Yaacov. Political dictionary of the Arab world. N.Y. : Macmillan, c1987. 520 p. **CJ424**
Rev. ed. of Shimoni and Evyatar Levine, *Political dictionary of the Middle East in the twentieth century.*

Published in cooperation with the Dayan Center for Middle Eastern and African Studies, Tel Aviv University.
A Hebrew translation has appeared as *Leksikon politi shel ha-olam ha-'Arvi* (Yerushalyim : Keter, [1988]. 434 p.).
Despite its title (and like its companion, *Political dictionary of the state of Israel*, CJ439), more encyclopedia than dictionary (for example, the article "Arab-Israel conflict" is 23 pages long). Covers only the Arab portion of the Middle East; Israel, Iran, Turkey, and Cyprus are included only as they may be linked to Arab affairs. Covers the 20th century to the mid-1980s. Alphabetically arranged; no index. DS37.S53

Middle East

See Asia, West.

Asia (by country)

China

Bartke, Wolfgang. Biographical dictionary and analysis of China's party leadership, 1922–1988. N.Y. : K.G. Saur, 1990. 482 p. : ill. **CJ425**
In two parts, the first consisting of alphabetically arranged biographies of the 1,094 members and alternates of the Central Committees of the Chinese Communist Party (CCP). Entries include photographs where available and such information as date and place of birth, education, military career, party career, visits abroad, posts held. Pt. 2 analyzes (primarily in tabular form) numerous aspects of the membership of both the Politburo (e.g., women members, age at time of election, military leadership, participation in the Long March) and the Central Committee (e.g, women members, purged members, provincial leaders, government cadres, nepotism). Appendixes supply a list of members and alternates organized by Central Committee number and a list of Congresses of the CCP. No index. JQ1519.A5B3

——————— China's new party leadership : biographies and analysis of the Twelfth Central Committee of the Chinese Communist Party / by Wolfgang Bartke and Peter Schier. Armonk, N.Y. : M.E. Sharpe, c1985. 289 p. : ports. **CJ426**
Focuses on the 12th Congress of the Chinese Communist Party and the members of China's 12th Central Committee. In three parts: Pt. 1 in ten descriptive chapters covers the 12th Congress (e.g., political background, composition of the 12th Central Committee and its leading bodies). Pt. 2 contains alphabetically arranged biographies (arranged by pinyin romanization) of the 210 full and 138 alternate members of the 12th Central Committee. Entries feature a photograph where available, brief personal data, and a listing of current and past Party positions. Pt. 3 offers lists of the central leadership of the People's Republic of China as of January 1, 1984, in sections covering the party, the state, and the military. No index.
§ As the cutoff date for biographical data is September 1, 1983, researchers will want to consult sources such as Bartke's *Who's who in the People's Republic of China* (AH344) for more current information. JQ1519.A5B32

China directory in pinyin and Chinese. 1984– . [Tokyo] : Radiopress, [1984]– . Annual. **CJ427**
Title varies: *China directory*, 1971–79; *China directory in pinyin, Wade-Giles*, 1980; *China directory in pinyin and Wade-Giles*, 1981–83.
A comprehensive register of central, provincial, and local officials of agencies and organizations. Includes information on party congresses and conferences. Personal name index.
§ See also: *Directory of Chinese officials and organizations* (CJ428). JQ1507.C5291

Directory of Chinese officials and organizations / Central Intelligence Agency, Directorate of Intelligence. Wash. : The Agency : Document Expediting (DOCEX) Project, Exchange & Gift Division, Library of Congress [distributor] ; Springfield, Va. : National Technical Information Service [distributor], 1986– .　　　　　**CJ428**

Superintendent of Documents classification: PrEx 3.10/7-13.

Merges *Directory of Chinese officials. National level organizations* (Wash. : National Foreign Assessment Center, 1980–[85]); ... *Provincial organizations* (1981–86); and ... *Scientific and educational organizations* (1981–85; 1979 ed. had title *Directory of Chinese scientific and educational officials*).

Essentially a register of officials of the People's Republic of China that draws information primarily from Chinese press releases. In sections (e.g., Judicial system, State bureaus, Military regions) with organization and personal name indexes.

§ For biographical information, consult Wolfgang Bartke, *Who's who in the People's Republic of China* (AH344).　　　JQ1507.D544

Klein, Donald W. Biographic dictionary of Chinese communism, 1921–1965 / Donald W. Klein, Anne B. Clark. Cambridge, Mass. : Harvard Univ. Pr., 1971. 2 v. (1194 p.).　　　　　**CJ429**

Offers "433 biographies of men and women who contributed to the Chinese Communist movement from the establishment of the Chinese Communist Party in 1921 to 1965."—*Introd.* Cross-referenced entries are alphabetically arranged and end with bibliographic notes. Appendixes provide various lists (e.g., participation in important events, travel abroad, fields of work). Bibliography. Personal name index, with names of biographees in italics.　　　DS778.A1K55

Lamb, Malcolm. Directory of officials and organizations in China, 1968–1983. [3rd ed.]. Armonk, N.Y. : M. E. Sharpe, 1984. 717 p.　　　　　**CJ430**

1st ed., 1976; 2nd ed., 1978.

A register of central organizations and officials, with data on key municipal and provincial positions. Personal name index.　　　JQ1507.L36

India

Butler, David. India decides : elections 1952–1991 / David Butler, Ashok Lahiri, Prannoy Roy. 2nd ed. New Delhi : Living Media India, 1991. 380 p. : ill., maps.　　　　　**CJ431**

1st ed., 1989. An earlier version by the same authors had title: *A compendium of Indian elections* (New Delhi : Arnold-Heinemann, 1984).

Summarizes all election statistics through the 1990 by-elections. Pt. 1, Issues, offers five essays on relevant topics (e.g., parties and symbols, polls and forecasting). Pt. 2, Statistics, gives election data for the Presidency, the Rajya Sabha, the Lok Sabha, and the Vidhan Sabhas. It also provides census data by state. Pt. 3, Appendices, includes lists of symbols and parties, an index of constituencies, and a bibliography.　　　JQ292.B89

India. Parliament. Lok Sabha. Who's who / Parliament of India, House of the People. 1st ed. (1952)– . New Delhi : Parliament Secretariat, 1952– .　　　　　**CJ432**

Contains biographical sketches of the members of the current Lok Sabha. Entries usually include photograph; personal data (e.g., date and place of birth, marital status and spouse's name); education; profession; positions held; special interests; pastime or recreation; clubs; countries visited; addresses; etc. Personal name index.

Companion work: India. Parliament. Rajya Sabha. *Who's who* (Biennial. Issued by the Secretariat 1952–).　　　JQ263.A44

Kohli, A. B. Councils of ministers in India, 1947–1982. New Delhi : Gitanjali, 1983. 188 p.　　　　　**CJ433**

In three parts: chronological register; list of "important" ministries and major personnel; biographical sketches of prime ministers. Bibliography. Personal name index.　　　JQ242.K63

Rana, Mahendra Singh. Indian government and politics : a bibliographical study, 1885–1980. New Delhi : Wiley Eastern, [1981]. v. 1.　　　　　**CJ434**

A subject-classed bibliography of English-language books, articles, proceedings, and doctoral theses. Vol. 1 includes historical studies of political thought and institutions, biographies, and ideologies and movements. Includes a separately classified list of doctoral dissertations. Author index. No more published?　　　Z3208.A4R36

Singh, V. B. Elections in India : data handbook on Lok Sabha elections, 1952–85 / V.B. Singh, Shankar Bose. [2nd ed.]. New Delhi ; Beverly Hills, Calif. : Sage Publications, 1986. 784 p.　　　　　**CJ435**

1st ed., 1984.

Provides detailed statistical information on elections to the Lok Sabha, the lower house of the Union Parliament. Data given at three levels: all-India, state, and consitutency.

§ For data on elections to the Vidhan Sabhas, the lower houses of the state legislatures, *see* Singh and Bose, *State elections in India* (New Delhi; Newbury Park, Calif. : Sage Publ., 1987–1988. 5 v.).　　　JQ294.S565

Israel

Benvenisti, Meron. The West Bank handbook : a political lexicon / Meron Benvenisti with Ziad Abu-Zayed and Danny Rubinstein. Jerusalem, Israel : Jerusalem Post, c1986. 228 p., [15] p. of plates : maps.　　　　　**CJ436**

Translation of: *Leksikon Yehudah ve-Shomron*.

Intends "to acquaint those directly involved, namely Jews and Arabs living in the Holy Land, with the facts as well as with the institutions and agencies affecting their daily lives."—*Foreword.* Data are extracted from Benvenisti's *The West Bank data project: a survey of Israel's policies* (Wash. : American Enterprise Institute, 1984) and cover social, economic, institutional, legal, cultural, and political topics relating to the West Bank. Entries are alphabetical, range in length from a paragraph to several pages, and contain cross-references. Includes 15 maps and a detailed table of contents, but no index.　　　DS110.W47B47413

Israel government year-book. [1957]– . [Jerusalem] : Govt. Printer, [1957]– . Annual.　　　　　**CJ437**

Issued also in Hebrew.

Issuing agency varies; title varies slightly.

Published also in Hebrew: *Shenaton ha-memshalah.*

Serves as "an annual survey of the activities of the Government of Israel, its ministries, and major governmental agencies,"—*Pref.* Includes facts and figures; chronologies; chapters on ministries and agencies (with address, telephone and fax numbers, function and structure, activities, and senior officials); and a section on the Knesset. No index.　　　J693.P22213

Mahler, Gregory S. Bibliography of Israeli politics. Boulder, Colo. : Westview Pr., 1985. 133 p.　　　　　**CJ438**

Treats the full breadth of Israeli political life and political culture, including the constitutional system, elections and parties, public opinion, political history, foreign relations, Zionism, the Palestinians, the West Bank and Gaza questions, etc. Contains 1,419 unannotated citations published through 1984, arranged alphabetically. A keyword index to entry numbers only.　　　Z3476.M3

Political dictionary of the state of Israel / Susan Hattis Rolef, ed. 2nd ed. N.Y. : Macmillan, c1993. 417, [2] p. : maps.　　　　　**CJ439**

1st ed., 1987.

More encyclopedia than dictionary; entries range in length from a short paragraph to 17 pages (Arab-Israel conflict). Contains 450 signed articles on all aspects of Israel: politics, including personalities, parties and other groups, political institutions, outstanding events, foreign policy, the media, etc. Some entries give historical background; some contain cross-references. This 2nd ed. reprints the text of the first edition and adds a 68-page supplement that covers 1987–1992 and contains some new articles as well as continuations of entries in the 1st ed. (marked with an asterisk).

§ Supersedes an earlier work, Yaacov Shimoni and Evyatar Levine's *Political dictionary of the Middle East in the twentieth century* (N.Y. : Quadrangle, 1974) and incorporates several articles from that volume. A companion to Shimoni's *Political dictionary of the Arab world* (CJ424). A Hebrew translation of the 1st ed. was publ. 1988. DS126.5.P62

Japan

Who's who in Japanese government. [1st ed.] (1987)– . [Tokyo] : I.C.A. of Japan Co., [1986]– . **CJ440**

Intended to provide "basic and up-to-date information for foreigners who are interested in politics per se or whose work brings them in contact with the Japanese government."—*Foreword*. Begins with a profile of the Japanese political and electoral system, followed by biographical entries for members of the lower and upper houses (House of Representatives and House of Councillors) of the Diet, each containing a photograph, party, number of times elected, constituency, address and telephone number, committee or ministry assignments, posts held, education, and date of birth. Includes a listing of standing, special, and select committees of both houses of the Diet and their membership; political party organization charts; ministry and agency organization charts; lists of ministry and agency officials; and important addresses and telephone numbers. Personal name index. JQ1651.W48

Korea, North

An, Tai Sung. North Korea : a political handbook. Wilmington, Del. : Scholarly Resources, 1983. 294 p. : map. **CJ441**

Aims to offer an "objective, compact description and analysis of North Korea's present political system and the kinds of possible or probable changes that might be expected in the future ... compiled from information available in openly published materials."—*Pref.* Broad topical arrangement. Provides general, statistical, and directory information, with biographies of political leaders and texts of constitution and party rules. Extensive multilingual bibliography.

DS932.A76

Suh, Dae-Sook. Korean Communism, 1945–1980 : a reference guide to the political system. Honolulu : Univ. Pr. of Hawaii, c1981. 592 p. **CJ442**

Provides an annotated bibliography of the writings of Kim Il Sung (with subject and chronological indexes), historical agendas and personnel registers for the Korean Communist party and legislative assemblies, cabinets, and court; also provides translations of constitutions and bylaws, and romanized glossary. Personal name and subject indexes. JQ1729.5.A3.S83

Pakistan

Jones, Garth N. A comprehensive bibliography : Pakistan government and administration / by Garth N. Jones, Shaukat Ali. [Lahore : All Pakistan Public Admin. Research Centre], 1970–[1983]. 4 v. **CJ443**

Vol. 4 has title: *Bibliography : Pakistan government and administration, 1970–1981*, and is ed. by Mohamed Jameelur Rehman Khan (Islamabad : Public Admin. Res. Ctr.). Vol. 3 is continued by v. 3A, publ. 1987.

Broad topical arrangement (including sections for fiction and autobiography). Vol. 1 lists books, articles, government publications, theses and dissertations on Pakistan from independence to 1968; v. 2 covers 1968–70 publications, excluding government documents; v. 3 lists 1970 materials (adding agriculture); v. 4 covers 1970–81. Principally English-language materials. Includes Pakistani newspaper articles, theses and dissertations. Author index.

§ *Pakistan : a comprehensive bibliography of books and government publications with annotations, 1947–1980* (Islamabad : Inst. of Islamic History, Culture and Civilization, Islamic Univ., 1981. 515 p.) lists more than 8,300 books, pamphlets, government publications, and theses. Z7165.P3J65

Sri Lanka

Peiris, H. A. Political parties in Sri Lanka since independence : a bibliography. New Delhi : Navrang, 1988. 161 p. **CJ444**

Lists English-language books, periodical articles, theses, dissertations, party manifestos, and seminar and conference papers on political parties in Sri Lanka from its independence in 1948 through 1984. Excludes election literature, parliamentary debates, and newspaper articles. In three sections: (1) historical essays on majority, minority, and leftist parties; (2) aims and limitations of the work as well as sources for further research; and (3) an annotated bibliography. The 487 entries in the bibliography are grouped into reference, general, and political party categories, then arranged alphabetically by main entry. Personal author index. Z7164.P8P45

Vietnam

Phan Thiên Châu. Vietnamese communism : a research bibliography. Westport, Conn. : Greenwood, 1975. 359 p. **CJ445**

"An attempt to present a systematic assessment of research materials available in North America as of June 1974 on Vietnamese nationalism, communism and revolution."—*Introd.* A classed, computer-produced list of books and articles in Vietnamese, English, and French. The introductory bibliographic guide (p. 3–19) critically annotates major primary and secondary sources. Author and title indexes.

Z7165.V5P48

Australia and Oceania

Political parties of Asia and the Pacific : a reference guide / editors, D. S. Lewis and D. J. Sagar. Detroit : Gale, c1992. 369 p. **CJ446**

Also published in the U.K. by Longman.

Country chapters, arranged alphabetically, begin with a summary of the country's political history, constitutional structure, electoral system, recent elections, and evolution of suffrage, followed by entries for political parties. These entries are in sections for major, minor, defunct, and guerrilla or illegal groups. Indexes; personal name, political party.

§ For more detailed and historical information, *see* Haruhiro Fukui, *Political parties of Asia and the Pacific* (CJ414). JQ39.A45P645

Australia

Commonwealth government directory. 1977– . Canberra : Australian Government Publ. Service, 1977– . Annual.
                                                 CJ447

Supersedes: *A guide to Commonwealth government departments and authorities* (1976); *Australian government directory* (1973–75); and *Commonwealth of Australia directory* (1961–72).

For executive, parliamentary, judicial, and ministerial agencies, provides name, address, brief notes on creation, role, and function, and names of personnel. For ministries, also includes enactments administered. Acts, personal names, and organization/subject indexes.
                         JQ4021.C65

Macintyre, Clement. Political Australia : a handbook of facts. Oxford : Oxford Univ. Pr., 1991. 394 p.   **CJ448**

For annotation, *see* DF36.

Parliamentary handbook of the Commonwealth of Australia. 20th ed. (1978)– . Canberra : Australian Government Publ. Service, 1978– . Irregular.   **CJ449**

Continues *Biographical handbook and record of elections* (v. 1–7; v. 1 covers 1901–15); *Parliamentary handbook and record of elections* (v. 8–11, 1936–53); *Parliamentary handbook of the Commonwealth of Australia* (v. 12–17, 1956–71); *Australian parliamentary handbook. Suppl. 1* (Ed. 18–19, 1973–76).

Presents biographical sketches and lists of current members of parliament, records of parliaments and ministries, records of elections, etc. General index.

Rydon, Joan. A biographical register of the Commonwealth Parliament, 1901–1972. Canberra : Australian Nat. Univ. Pr., 1975. 229 p. (Australian parliaments: Biographical notes, 5).
                                         CJ450

An alphabetical arrangement of entries that include personal biography, career outside parliament, political career, and sources of further information. Details of ministries and dates of parliaments have been excluded, as they are available in the *Parliamentary handbook* (CJ449).   JQ4054.R93

New Zealand

The New Zealand politics source book / ed. by Paul Harris and Stephen Levine ... [et al.]. Palmerston North, N.Z. : Dunmore Pr. Ltd., 1992. 448 p.   **CJ451**

Reprints extracts from primary documents of New Zealand politics (e.g., Treaty of Waitangi), including charters, laws, regulations, judicial opinions, party manifestos, and treaties. In eight parts (each beginning with an introductory discussion): (1) The constitution; (2) Parliamentary elections; (3) Political parties; (4) Parliament; (5) Cabinet; (6) State sector; (7) Local government; and (8) International relations. No index.   JQ5800.A2

PARLIAMENTARY PROCEDURE

Cann, Marjorie Mitchell. Point of order : the ready reference for simple rules of order and parliamentary procedure. Rev. ed. N.Y. : Putnam, 1991. 71 p. : ill.   **CJ452**

1st ed., 1990, had title: *Cann's keys to better meetings.*

Provides a simplified approach, in layman's language, to fundamentals of parliamentary procedure, steps in forming a new organization, and techniques for organization participation. Seven topical chapters: voluntary organizations, forming new organizations, officers, meetings, committees and committee reports, motions, and paraticipation. Glossary. No index.

§ Another work with simple, basic procedure is *Goers' guide to parliamentary procedure*, by Sue Goers (Godfrey, Ill. : Pinkerton Publishing, 1990. 95 p.).   JF515.C32

Davidson, Henry A. Handbook of parliamentary procedure. 2nd ed. N.Y. : Ronald Pr. Co., [1968, c1955]. 300 p.   **CJ453**

1st ed., 1955.

Presents simple rules and practices of parliamentary procedure; especially suitable for small organizations. Glossary. Subject index.
                                       JF515.D32

Deschler, Lewis. Deschler's rules of order. Englewood Cliffs, N.J. : Prentice-Hall, 1976. 221 p.   **CJ454**

A system of parliamentary procedure based on the author's experience as parliamentarian of the U.S. House of Representatives. "In preparing this book, I have taken the approach that the House parliamentary system is readily adaptable to any membership organization that needs some form of parliamentary procedure. I have simplified and generalized that system in such a way that it will be applicable to any membership organization, large or small, legislative or nonlegislative."—*Pref.*   JF515.D45

Keesey, Ray E. Modern parliamentary procedure. Boston : Houghton Mifflin, 1974. 176 p.   **CJ455**

"A manual of simplified parliamentary procedure, entirely compatible with accepted parliamentary principles but free of the traditional mysterious jargon of the professional parliamentarian."—*Pref.* Intends to simplify the conduct of meetings and to make for easier participation by members of a group. Includes a critically annotated bibliography of parliamentary procedure manuals. Name and subject index.
                                       JF515.K395

Mason, Paul. Mason's manual of legislative procedure / the American Society of Legislative Clerks & Secretaries in cooperation with the National Conference of State Legislatures. Rev. ed. St. Paul, Minn. : West Publ. Co. ; Denver, Colo. : NCSL, 1989. 677 p.   **CJ456**

Rev. ed. of: *Manual of legislative procedure for legislative and other governmental bodies* (Sacramento, Calif. : Senate, Calif. Legislature, 1979).

Reflects current legislative practices and procedures. Covers law and rules; debate; motions; quorum, voting, elections; legislative and administrative bodies; conduct of business; relations with the executive and with the other house; sessions and meetings; and investigations and public order. Includes table of cases cited, brief and detailed subject indexes, and a list of motions.   JF515.M33

Robert, Henry Martyn. The Scott, Foresman Robert's rules of order newly revised. A new & enl. ed. by Sarah Corbin Robert ... [et al.]. Glenview, Ill : Scott, Foresman and Co., 1990. xliv, 706 p.   **CJ457**

First published in 1876 with the title *Pocket manual of rules of order for deliberative assemblies.* Frequently revised and reprinted. 1970 ed. publ. under title: *Robert's rules of order newly revised.* Scott, Foresman ed. first publ. 1981.

The standard guide to parliamentary rules, with charts, tables, and lists. This edition has been expanded, revised, updated, and reset in larger type. Indexed.

Other modern versions include:

The new Robert's rules of order, Mary A. De Vries (N.Y. : New American Library, 1989. 258 p.). Intended to be a modern version of the 1893 ed. of the *Pocket manual.* Also offers a section on meeting arrangements (program development, publicity, facilities, etc.).

Robert's rules of order revised (N.Y. : Morrow, 1971 [c1915]. 323 p.) is a revision of the 1876 *Pocket manual.* Somewhat simpler than the Scott, Foresman version.

Robert's rules of order. Modern ed., completely revised, by Darwin Patnode (Nashville : T. Nelson, 1989. 155 p.). Based on the 1876 edition. Attempts to retain Robert's style and content while modernizing the work for current use. Less detailed than the Scott, Foresman edition.   JF515.R692

Sturgis, Alice. Standard code of parliamentary procedure. 3rd ed., new and rev. N.Y. : McGraw-Hill, c1988. 275 p.   **CJ458**

1st ed., 1950, and 2nd ed., 1966, had title *Sturgis standard code of parliamentary procedure.*

Details standard parliamentary procedure. A committee of the American Institute of Parliamentarians has revised Sturgis' classic work to clarify wording, minimize gender bias, eliminate rarely used motions, and validate "tabling" a motion. New chapters contain often-asked questions and answers, and a guide to dealing with disapproved or obsolete motions. Appendixes give rules relating to governmental boards, councils, commissions, and committees; by-law provisions for a local organization; and model minutes. Includes definitions of parliamentary terms. Lists principal rules governing motions, incidental motions, and chief purposes of motions. Bibliographic notes. Subject index.   JF515.S88

PUBLIC ADMINISTRATION

Guides

Cherry, Virginia R. Public administration research guide / Virginia R. Cherry, Marc Holzer. N. Y. : Garland, 1992. 253 p. (Public affairs and administration, v. 26 ; Garland reference library of social science, v. 537).   **CJ459**

Treats the process of doing library research in public administration in 15 topical chapters (e.g., search strategy, indexing/abstracting services, CD-ROMs and online computers), each containing an explanatory narrative followed by brief annotated citations to relevant sources. Title index.

§ Earlier, still occasionally useful, works are Mary G. Rock, *A handbook of information sources and research strategies in public administration* (San Diego, Calif. : Institute of Public and Urban Affairs, San Diego State Univ., 1979) and Anthony E. Simpson, *Guide to library research in public administration* (N.Y. : Center for Productive Public Management, John Jay College of Criminal Justice, 1976). See also *Public administration desk book* (CJ460).   Z7164.A2C48

Coleman, James R. Public administration desk book / James R. Coleman and Robert E. Dugan. Newton, Mass. : Govt. Research Publ., c1990. 270 p.   **CJ460**

Intended as a guide for practitioners, researchers, and students of American public administration. Divided into chapters covering reference tools or providing information on: (1) People and organizations; (2) Statistics; (3) Terminology, research, and publishing; (4) Abstracts, indexes and periodicals; (5) Electronic information; (6) Law and reporter services; and (7) Associations and institutes. Entries are annotated and are alphabetically arranged within topical chapter subdivisions. Appendixes include a list of books for a basic public administration library and a list of other guides to public administration information. Title and subject indexes.

§ See also *Public administration research guide*, by Virginia R. Cherry and Marc Holzer (CJ459).   Z7164.A2C59

Cutchin, D. A. Guide to public administration. Itasca, Ill. : F.E. Peacock, c1981. 159 p. : ill.   **CJ461**

A still useful publication comprised primarily of alphabetically arranged explanations of terms, phrases, laws, organizations, and individuals relevant to public administration. Also includes an annotated bibliography of reference books and periodicals and organization charts for the executive branch of the U.S. government. Subject index.   JA61.C87

Ethics, government, and public policy : a reference guide / ed. by James S. Bowman and Frederick A. Elliston. N.Y. : Greenwood, 1988. 341 p. : ill.   **CJ462**

Considers "the ethical questions that affect government policy and administration."—*Introd.* Consists of 12 topical chapters containing essays (most including literature reviews and case studies) by scholars in governmental administration, in four sections covering: Analytical approaches; Ethical dilemmas and standards for public servants; Techniques and methods in ethical policy-making; and Studies of systemic issues in government. A final essay provides a comparative analysis of ethics, public policy, and public service. Bibliography; general index.   JA79.E824

Bibliography

American public administration : a bibliographical guide to the literature / Gerald E. Caiden ... [et al.]. N.Y. : Garland, 1983. 201 p. (The public affairs and administration series, 3 ; Garland reference library of social science, v. 169).   **CJ463**

Lists basic reference sources, leading journals, and significant books, but excludes government publications and journal articles. An introductory essay describing the scope of the field is followed by chapters including: (1) annotated citations for relevant abstracts, indexes, and continuing bibliographies; (2) annotated citations for professional journals; and (3) unannotated citations for selected books. Within chapters, entries are alphabetically arranged by main entry within subdivisions for subject or type of publication. Author index, journal title index, and index of abstracts, indexes, and continuing bibliographies.   Z7164.A2A53

Dynes, Patrick S. Program evaluation : an annotated bibliography / Patrick S. Dynes, Mary K. Marvel. N.Y. : Garland, 1987. 241 p. (The public affairs and administration series, 17 ; Garland reference library of social science, v. 172).   **CJ464**

Focuses on program evaluation as it relates to public administration. Lists selected books and articles published 1970–1985, arranged in four categories: Overviews of program evaluation, Methodology, Organization and management, and Utilization. Entries treat a wide range of issues (e.g., program design, standards and ethics, experimental methods, communicating results) and applications in politics, personnel administration, organization theory, decision making, administrative leadership, budgeting, regulation, management, and legislation. A brief but helpful introduction defines program evaluation, gives criteria for selection, describes the organization of the book, and suggests sources for further information. Excludes newspaper articles, government publications, occasional papers, and some dissertations. Author index.   Z7164.A2D95

Grasham, W. E. Canadian public administration : bibliography = Administration publique canadienne : bibliographie / comp. by W. E. Grasham [and] Germain Julien. Toronto : Institute of Public Administration of Canada, c1972. 261 p.   **CJ465**

Updated by supplements issued at three- to five-year intervals.

In English and French. Contains unannotated citations to books, articles, dissertations, and government publications, 1930–71. The classified arrangement presents subject chapters (e.g., Municipal administration, Public finance, Administrative sectors) subdivided for more specific topics. Within each section, English language entries are followed by French entries, both arranged alphabetically. No index.   Z7165.C2G7

Holzer, Marc. Public sector productivity : a resource guide / Marc Holzer, Arie Halachmi. N.Y. : Garland, 1988. 166 p. (Public affairs and administration series, 21 ; Garland reference library of social science, v. 386).   **CJ466**

Cites literature (mostly 1980–87) and organizations focusing on productivity improvement, primarily in the public sector. A lengthy introduction giving an overview of the topic is followed by five chapters of alphabetically arranged entries for books, reports, articles, periodicals and newsletters, and organizations. All entries are annotated except those for articles, which list keywords instead. Title index. Lack of a subject index or classified arrangement limits usefulness.   JF1525.P67H65

Huddleston, Mark W. Comparative public administration : an annotated bibliography. N.Y. : Garland, 1984. 245 p. (Public affairs and administration series, 5 ; Garland reference library of social science, v. 146). **CJ467**

Offers more than 600 annotated citations to books and journal articles published 1962–81; most works cited are in English. Begins with a helpful user's guide. Nine topical chapters (administrative history, public budgeting, etc.), in which entries are arranged alphabetically. Cross-references; author and country/geographical area indexes.

§ For an earlier bibliography in this field, *see* Ferrel Heady and Sybil Stoke, *Comparative public administration* (2nd ed. Ann Arbor : Institute of Public Administration, University of Michigan, 1960).

Z7164.A2H8

Jreisat, Jamil E. Administration and development in the Arab world : an annotated bibliography / Jamil E. Jreisat, Zaki R. Ghosheh. N.Y. : Garland, 1986. 259 p. **CJ468**

Intends to examine "the literature on administration, human resources, and development in the Arab world" (*Introd.*), with emphasis on contemporary societies and internal affairs of the 21 member countries of the Arab League, but excluding their foreign policies and international relations. English-language books, articles, and dissertations, 1970–85, are listed in four topical chapters plus a dissertation chapter subdivided by topic. The introduction includes a list of English-language journals cited in the text and another of Arabic-language journals focusing on administration and development. Author and country indexes.

Z7165.A67J73

Martin, Daniel. The guide to the foundations of public administration. N.Y. : Dekker, c1989. 454 p. (Public administration and public policy, 37). **CJ469**

Serves as "an annotated bibliographic guide to the development of the literature in public administration" (*Pref.*), emphasizing English-language articles, books, government publications, court cases, and legislation. In two parts, The emergence and impacts of public administration and The internal operation of public administration, each arranged in topical chapters that begin with a background paragraph, contain chronologically arranged and annotated citations, and end with a continuing concerns essay and notes. Emphasizes "formative" literature rather than the frequently cited works found in Howard E. McCurdy's *Public administration* (CJ470). Offers an introduction and a final essay of concluding observations. Name and subject indexes.

Z7164.A2M27

McCurdy, Howard E. Public administration : a bibliographic guide to the literature. N.Y. : M. Dekker, c1986. 311 p. (Public administration and public policy, 29). **CJ470**

Limited to monographs, this self-styled guide begins with two long essays, one on recent trends in public administration, the other on the history of the development of the field. There follows a list of the 181 most frequently cited books in public administration, in alphabetic order by author or title, with a lengthy review of each that summarizes the work's reputation and its contribution to the field; an unannotated list of monographs in classed order that includes the titles in the preceding part; and at the end, an index. Not for casual users, and not successful as a guide, since its principal section is highly selective, includes only monographs, and is in alphabetic rather than classed order. Author index.

Z7164.A2M29

Murin, William F. Delivering government services : an annotated bibliography / William F. Murin, Judith Pryor. N.Y. : Garland, 1988. 315 p. (Public affairs and administration series, 22 ; Garland reference library of social science, v. 426). **CJ471**

Contains 926 annotated citations, mostly to English-language books, articles, and reports on delivery systems for services provided by local and county levels of government. Specifically excluded are trade journal and newspaper articles; most references are from the past 20 years. Entries are arranged in seven broad topical chapters (some with further subdivisions), then alphabetically by main entry. Subject and author indexes.

Z7164.L8M96

Payad, Aurora T. Organization behavior in American public administration : an annotated bibliography. N.Y. : Garland, 1986. 264 p. (The public affairs and administration series, 15 ; Garland reference library of social science, v. 320). **CJ472**

Particularly useful, since it focuses on organization behavior in public administration; earlier bibliographies emphasized the private sector. Sections deal with: Organizational behavior in government; The ecology of public organizations (e.g., budgetary strategies and constraints, technology and office modernization); Individual behavior; Intergroup and intragroup behavior; and Managerial behavior. Includes journal articles, books, book chapters, reviews, and dissertations, 1940–84, although most were published 1974–84. List of professional associations; author and subject indexes.

Z7164.A2P39

Public administration. [1st ed. (1963)]– . [London : Overseas Development Administration Library, 1963]– . Irregular. **CJ473**

Kept up-to-date by supplements, 1964–1978.
Name of issuing body varies.
Unannotated citations in 27 subject categories, such as civil service, project management, urbanization. Coverage generally includes books and selected documents published since, or not included in, the previous edition. Author and country indexes.

§ *See also* the British Council's *Public administration : a select list of books and periodicals* (London : Longman, Green, 1964).

Z7164.A2P79

Public administration series. P-1–P-3120. Monticello, Ill. : Vance Bibliographies, 1978–1991. Irregular. **CJ474**

Ceased with P-3120 in July 1991.
Offers short, usually unannotated bibliographies on topics relevant to public administration (e.g., employment, health care, state government). Most bibliographies were generated by searching machine-readable sources. Author, title, subject, and number indexes published at varying intervals.

Rouse, John Edward. Public administration in American society : a guide to information sources. Detroit : Gale, [1980]. 553 p. (American government and history information guide series, v. 11). **CJ475**

An annotated bibliography of about 1,700 books and periodical articles covering the past 50 years, but focusing on the growing impact of the public bureaucracy in the 1970s. Chapters on federalism, governmental divisions and the administrative process, evaluation, policy making, accountability, human organization, personnel administration, productivity, budgeting, etc. Addendum of about 200 titles from 1979–80. Appendixes provide directory information on the American Society for Public Administration and the National Association of Schools of Public Affairs and Administration. Author, title, and subject indexes.

JK421.R63

Indexes; Abstract journals

Sage public administration abstracts. v. 1 (Apr. 1974)– . Beverly Hills, Calif. : Sage Publ., 1974– . Quarterly. **CJ476**

Each issue contains some 250 abstracts. Coverage is international in scope and includes books, articles selected from 120 journals, government documents, pamphlets, and research reports. Abstracts are grouped in broad subject areas (e.g., administration and economy, subnational government), which are further subdivided by topic. Following the abstracts is a list of unannotated citations. Quarterly author and subject indexes cumulate annually.

JA1.S27

Encyclopedias; Dictionaries

Chandler, Ralph C. The public administration dictionary / Ralph C. Chandler, Jack C. Plano. 2nd ed. Santa Barbara, Calif. : ABC-Clio, c1988. 430 p.   **CJ477**
1st ed., 1982.
Groups key concepts alphabetically within seven topical chapters (e.g., public policy, personnel administration, public law and regulation). Entries include descriptive definitions, cross-references, and a paragraph discussing the concept's historical and contemporary significance. Bibliography. General index.   JA61.C47

Shafritz, Jay M. The Facts on File dictionary of public administration. N.Y. : Facts on File, c1985. 610 p.   **CJ478**
Brief entries in alphabetic order treat all aspects of public administration: terms, concepts, processes and practices, significant individuals and organizations, statutes and judicial decisions, journals. Although a roster of 24 contributors is given, entries are unsigned. Some entries end with brief bibliographies, some include legal citations. Two appendixes give the U.S. Constitution and list members of the National Association of Schools of Public Affairs and Administration. Entries contain cross-references, but there is no index.
§ Ralph C. Chandler and Jack C. Plano's *The public administration dictionary* (CJ477) contains fewer entries but provides more depth.   JA61.S54

Terminology

Thésaurus multilingue international en administration publique = Multilingual international thesaurus of public administration = Tesauro multilingue internacional de administración pública / [sous la direction de Jean-Marc Alain et Jorge Avilés]. Montreal : Encyclopédie d'administration publique = Encyclopedia of Public Administration, 1987–1988. 2 v.
                                                            CJ479
In French, English, and Spanish.
Seven sections, including a Thematic Thesaurus, which divides the field into 15 themes, (e.g., Public policy, Organization, and Personnel administration), which are subdivided in turn into 116 subthemes, augmented by other descriptors, and arranged hierarchically. Other sections include a conventional alphabetic thesaurus and a permuted alphabetic index of descriptors. The sections attempt to show relationships among the themes, subthemes, and descriptors by the use of diagrams and a system of numerical codes to which the various indexes refer.   Z695.1.P79T43

Handbooks

Handbook of comparative and development public administration / ed. by Ali Farazmand. N.Y. : M. Dekker, c1991. 782 p. (Public administration and public policy, 41).   **CJ480**
Presents "essays that analyze basic issues and major aspects of the fields of comparative and development public administration, and comparative bureaucratic politics and public policy."—*Pref.* Written by experts, the signed essays are in two sections: (1) eight chapters covering public administration and public policy in both developed and developing countries; and (2) seven chapters focusing on bureaucratic politics and administrative theory (e.g., power, reform, women, effects of political revolution). General index.   JF1351.H267

Handbook of public administration / James L. Perry, ed. San Francisco : Jossey-Bass, 1989. 660 p.   **CJ481**
Written primarily for professional administrators, covers "a broad range of problems and situations that confront [them] at all levels of government and in all types of services."—*Pref.* Also valuable for faculty and students as it attempts to convey "the accumulated body of

knowledge" of the profession. Each of the 43 signed chapters treats a specific role, function, or aspect of the field, is written by an expert, and concludes with a bibliography. Name and subject indexes.
                                                            JF1351.H276

Handbook of public administration / ed. by Jack Rabin, W. Bartley Hildreth, Gerald J. Miller. N.Y. : M. Dekker, c1989. 1095 p. : ill. (Public administration and public policy, 35).
                                                            CJ482
A detailed review of the literature of public administration, intended more for students or scholars than James L. Perry's practically-oriented *Handbook of public administration* (CJ481). Contains 13 topical sections (e.g., Public budgeting and financial management, Policy sciences, Public law and regulation), each containing a chronological essay describing major concepts, theories, and applications and a "great ideas" essay consisting of the five most significant ideas or concepts. The lengthy essays are signed and have individual bibliographies. General index.   JF1351.H275

Public administration in the Third World : an international handbook / ed. by V. Subramaniam. N.Y. : Greenwood, 1990. 447 p. : ill.   **CJ483**
Describes the evolution, structure, and processes of public administration for selected Third World countries. Chapters on individual countries by specialists; the editor adds an introduction, a conclusion describing features common to all the countries, and an appendix discussing the sociohistorical characteristics of the countries' middle classes. Extensive bibliography; name and subject indexes.   JF60.P86

PUBLIC OPINION

An American profile : opinions and behavior, 1972–1989 : opinion results on 300 high-interest issues derived from the General Social Survey conducted by the National Opinion Research Center / Floris W. Wood, ed. ; Chronology of world events, 1972–1989 by Edward Weilant. Detroit : Gale, c1990. 1065 p   **CJ484**
Extracts data from the General Social Surveys (GSS) carried out annually 1972–89 (except 1979 and 1981) by the National Opinion Research Center of the Univ. of Chicago. 305 questions are grouped in three major sections: (1) Demography (e.g., How many children have you ever had?), (2) Opinions (e.g., Would you be for or against sex education in the public schools?), (3) Behavior (e.g., How often do you spend a social evening with friends?). For each question, separate tables provide results by total population, gender, age, and race, and include year of the survey, percentage of responses for each answer, and number of respondents. The tables are preceded by "A chronology of world events, 1972–1989" and followed by seven appendixes (e.g., a listing of questions and their corresponding GSS variable name; U.S. crime index, 1972–88; U.S. unemployment rate, 1972–88). Keyword index.
● Data is also available on tape through the Roper Center for Public Opinion Research or the Inter-university Consortium for Political and Social Research.
§ Similar data may be found in Richard G. Niemi's *Trends in public opinion* (CJ492).   HN90.P8A52

American public opinion index. 1981– . Louisville, Ky. : Opinion Research Service, [1981]– . Annual.   **CJ485**
A subject index to questions asked in nonproprietary public opinion polls with scientifically drawn random samples. From 1981 through 1984, it indexed only questions about the opinions of respondents, but since 1985 has also included behavioral questions. Questions, listed under alphabetically arranged topics, include response categories offered, polling group, and date of the poll. Ends with a section giving the full names, addresses, and phone numbers for the organizations conducting the polls, when the poll was released, the sample size, the poll method, the poll universe, and the special topic of the poll, if applicable.

§ Designed to be used with its companion microfiche publication, *American public opinion data* (1981– . [Louisville, Ky. : Opinion Research Service, 1981– .] Annual), which contains tabulated responses to most of the questions listed in the *Index*, the exact question wording, and detailed information about polling methodology for most of the polls. Arrangement is alphabetical by polling organization as given in the *Index*.

•A machine-readable version, *Polling the nation* (Bethesda, Md. : ORS Publ., 1986–), is available in CD-ROM. Updated annually.

HM261.A463

The Gallup international public opinion polls, France, 1939, 1944–1975 / George H. Gallup, gen. ed. N.Y. : Random House, 1976. 2 v. (1257 p.).   **CJ486**

Contents: v. 1, 1939, 1944–1967; v. 2, 1968–1975.

Chronologically arranged entries contain survey questions and results, usually expressed in percentages, but omit editorial and interpretive material. Subject index.

§ *The Gallup international public opinion polls, Great Britain, 1937–1975* (N.Y., 1976. 2 v. [1578 p.]) has the same arrangement and indexing.   HN440.P8G35

The Gallup poll : public opinion. 1978– . Wilmington, Del. : Scholarly Resources, [1979]– . Annual.   **CJ487**

George H. Gallup, ed.

An annual compilation of public opinion polls on political and social issues conducted by the Gallup organization. Polls are arranged chronologically. Entries provide date, question, and results; often results are analyzed by age, sex, race, income level, geographic region, education, political affiliation, etc. Subject index.

§ Two retrospective editions: *The Gallup poll : public opinion, 1935–1971* (N.Y. : Random House, 1972. 3 v.); *The Gallup poll : public opinion, 1972–1977* (Wilmington, Del. : Scholarly Resources, 1978. 2 v.).

§ For current U.S. polls, see: *The Gallup poll monthly* (Princeton, N.J. : The Gallup Poll, 1989–), formerly published as *The Gallup report* (1981–89), *The Gallup opinion index* (1967–81), and *The Gallup political index* (1965–66). A similar source is *The Harris poll* (Los Angeles : Creators Syndicate, Inc., 1988–), formerly published as *The Harris survey* (1981–87), *ABC News-Harris survey* (1979–80), and *The Harris survey* (1972–78).   HN90.P8G35

Gilbert, Dennis A. Compendium of American public opinion. N.Y. : Facts on File, c1988. 438 p. : ill.   **CJ488**

A selection of results of polls conducted primarily from 1984–86. Findings were originally disseminated via newspapers, journals, reports, press releases, and broadcasts. In 20 chapters, each treating a broad area (e.g., Foreign Policy, Health, Women). Contains numerous graphic representations of poll results. Sources are cited, but there is no index.   HN90.P8G56

Index to international public opinion. 1978/79– . Westport, Conn. : Greenwood, [1980]– . Annual.   **CJ489**

Prep. by Survey Research Consultants International.

Now in two main sections: (1) single nation surveys (arranged by topic and then by country); and (2) multinational surveys (divided by geographic area; includes world surveys). Each entry lists date and organization responsible for conducting the survey, sample size, questions, and responses, usually in percentages. Bibliography. Indexed by topic, by countries and regions in which surveys were conducted, and by countries and regions referenced in the surveys.   HM261.I552

The international Gallup polls : public opinion. Wilmington, Del. : Scholarly Resources, [1980–81]. 2 v.   **CJ490**

Vol. 1 covers 1978; v. 2, 1979. Planned as an annual.

Still of historical interest. Covers approximately 70 countries and includes mostly national surveys; reports findings of member companies of Gallup International. Entries give date, question, and results, but omit name of sponsoring organization and sample size. Subject and country index.

§ For more recent polls, see: *Index to international public opinion* (CJ489).   HM261.G276

Lake, Celinda C. Public opinion polling : a handbook for public interest and citizen advocacy groups / Celinda C. Lake with Pat Callbeck Harper. Wash. : Island Pr., c1987. 166 p.   **CJ491**

Prepared for the Montana Alliance for Progressive Policy.

Presents information on (1) how to plan, administer, and analyze a poll and (2) how to analyze the sampling, interpretation, and question-wording of polls conducted by others. Topical chapters (e.g., Questionnaire wording and construction; Interviewing; Sampling) proceed step-by-step through the polling process and feature tips for success, checklists, and possible problems. Includes an annotated bibliography and several appendixes (e.g., sample questionnaires, grids, and tabulations, a case study, and a glossary of terms). Subject index.

•A software package, *POLLSTART*, is also available.

HM261.L18

Niemi, Richard G. Trends in public opinion : a compendium of survey data / Richard G. Niemi, John Mueller, Tom W. Smith. N.Y. : Greenwood, 1989. 325 p.   **CJ492**

A collection of survey data that facilitates comparisons of public opinions over time, covering 1972–88 with some results from earlier years. Features the annual General Social Surveys (GSS) conducted by the National Opinion Research Center of the Univ. of Chicago but also reports on surveys from a number of other organizations. Topical chapters (e.g., Role of women, Race relations, International affairs) begin with a summary of the survey trends on that topic and a list of references. The data tables which follow include the survey question with the GSS mnemonic code if applicable, month and year of the survey, the percentage of responses for each answer, the number of respondents, and an abbreviation for the survey source (full source names are given in the introduction). Index of GSS mnemonics and a subject index.   HN90.P8N53

Noelle-Neumann, Elisabeth. The Germans : public opinion polls 1947–1966 / ed. by Elisabeth Noelle and Erich Peter Neumann. Allensbach ; Bonn : Verlag für Demoskopie, 1967. 630 p. : ill.   **CJ493**

Offers the results of surveys conducted in the Federal Republic of Germany and in West Berlin. Entries are organized by topic (e.g., family, law and justice) within broad headings (e.g., The people, The nation), and generally include date of survey and results, which are usually expressed in percentages and occasionally presented by sex, age, occupation, educational level, or region. Subject index.

§ Continued by: *The Germans—public opinion polls, 1967-1980*, ed. by Elisabeth Noelle-Neumann for the Institut für Demoskopie Allensbach (Westport, Conn. : Greenwood, 1981. 516 p.).

DD259.2.N62

•**Public opinion location library** : POLL [database]. Storrs, Conn. : The Roper Center for Public Opinion Research.   **CJ494**

Coverage: 1940– . Updated daily.

More than 200,000 questions and answers from public opinion surveys conducted throughout the U.S. on topics relating to politics and government, public affairs, business, social issues and attitudes, and consumer behavior. Records provide text of and responses to the questions; subjects; survey dates, population, and sponsor; name of survey organization; interview methods; number of respondents; and source of the data. Draws records from numerous groups (e.g., Gallup, National Opinion Research Center, Roper, CBS/New York Times).

Walden, Graham R. Public opinion polls and survey research : a selective annotated bibliography of U.S. guides and studies from the 1980s. N.Y. : Garland, 1990. 306 p. (The public affairs and administration series, 24 ; Garland reference library of social science, v. 575).   **CJ495**

Entries are arranged alphabetically in topical chapters (e.g., Sampling, Interviewing, Questions) and cite instructional guides, handbooks, reference works, textbooks, research studies, and evaluative and critical studies by American authors published in the U.S. Generally limited to 1980s publications although all relevant U.S. dissertations, 1941 to date, are incorporated. Specifically excludes newspaper articles, reviews of journals, book reviews, university occasional papers, most proceedings, master's theses, and mass market periodicals. Concludes with an unannotated addendum, eight appendixes (e.g., acronyms, bibliographic sources, organizations), an author index, and a selective keyword index. Z7164.P956W34

Young, Michael L. Dictionary of polling : the language of contemporary opinion research. N.Y. : Greenwood, 1992. 266 p. **CJ496**

Defines approximately 400 of the most important terms and phrases used in public opinion research. Intended as a ready reference source for pollsters and as a guide to practice and usage for poll users. American emphasis. Includes only those terms for which there were at least five citations in books or journals, and excludes highly technical or specialized terms. Alphabetically arranged entries contain cross-references to other entries and references to information sources, but acronyms are not cross-referenced under their spelled-out forms. Introductory essay on the literature of modern polling. Bibliography. Subject index. HM261.Y684

COMMUNISM AND SOCIALISM

Bibliography

Andréas, Bert. Le manifeste communiste de Marx et Engels : histoire et bibliographie, 1848–1918. Milano : Feltrinelli, [1963]. 429 p., plus 23 p. facsim. (Institut Giangiacomo Feltrinelli. Bibliografie, 6). **CJ497**

Facsimile reproduction of the 1st ed. of the *Communist manifesto* (23 p.) at end.

Proposes to trace the dissemination of the *Communist manifesto* through a chronologically-arranged bibliography of editions, paraphrases, extracts, and summaries. Detailed annotations describe bibliographic differences and degrees of accuracy in the editions. An introductory essay details the respective roles of Marx and Engels in the document's composition. Alphabetical list of publications in which the *Manifesto* was reproduced or cited. Index of countries and cities in which the *Manifesto* was published; indexes of names and libraries noted in the text.

Collotti, Enzo. Die Kommunistische Partei Deutschlands, 1918–1933 : ein bibliographischer Beitrag. Milan : Feltrinelli, [1961]. 217 p. (Istituto Giangiacomo Feltrinelli. Bibliografie, 4). **CJ498**

Important for historical research, as it aims to describe works relevant to the study of the Kommunistische Partei Deutschlands (KPD) from its founding to its suppression by the Nazis. A historical essay on the KPD in the context of German political events is followed by citations in two parts: (1) general literature; (2) sources on the KPD, arranged in chronological sections. The section for each time period begins with an introductory essay describing the activities of the KPD, with numbered references to the sources that follow. Three appendixes: (1) results of the Reichstag elections, 1919–33; (2) membership numbers of the KPD, 1919–32; (3) members of the Central Committee of the KPD, 1919–24. Name index. Z1009.M58 no.4

Communism in the world since 1945 : an annotated bibliography / Susan K. Kinnell, ed. Santa Barbara, Calif. : ABC-Clio, c1987. 415 p. **CJ499**

A bibliography of 4,151 entries on communism in all parts of the world since World War II, drawn from the publisher's databases for *America : history and life* (DB24) and *Historical abstracts* (DA176). Arranged by geographic region, with entries in each region alphabetical by author. Entries cover "the political history of the larger Communist and socialist nations, ... [or] topics [such] as the McCarthy era in the United States and the impact of communism in Southeast Asia."—*p. xi.* Lengthy author and subject indexes; lists of periodicals, abstractors, acronyms, abbreviations. Z7164.S67C594

Eubanks, Cecil L. Karl Marx and Friedrich Engels : an analytical bibliography. 2nd ed. N.Y. : Garland, 1984. 299 p. (Garland reference library of social science, v.100). **CJ500**

1st ed., 1977.

Intended to be "a comprehensive bibliography of those writings by and about Marx and Engels either written or translated into English, including books ... , articles, chapters from books and doctoral dissertations ... . Marx and Engels—not Lenin, not Mao and not the history of various communist revolutions—were the primary focus of attention."—*Introd.* Introductory bibliographic essay. Primary materials include individual and collected works of Marx, Engels, and Marx and Engels. Secondary literature is arranged by type—books, articles, and doctoral dissertations. Subject indexes to books, articles, and dissertations. Z8551.67.E94

Hammond, Thomas Taylor. Soviet foreign relations and world communism : a selected, annotated bibliography of 7,000 books in 30 languages. Princeton, N.J. : Princeton Univ. Pr., 1965. 1240 p. **CJ501**

Includes references to books, parts of books, periodical articles, and graduate theses on Soviet diplomatic and economic relations and on communist movements and tactics throughout the world since 1917. In three main parts: (1) Soviet relations by chronological periods, listing works treating of Soviet dealings with more than one country; (2) Soviet foreign relations and communism by regions and countries; and (3) Special topics. Most items are annotated. Index of authors, editors, compilers, and anonymous titles. Z2517.R4H3

Haynes, John Earl. Communism and anti-communism in the United States : an annotated guide to historical writings. N.Y. : Garland, 1987. 321 p. (Garland reference library of social science, v. 379). **CJ502**

Focuses on the Communist Party of the U.S., with some material on its splinter groups; omits studies of theoretical Marxism unless they deal directly with the American Communist movement. Anticommunism is treated only so far as it opposed the American movement. Primarily concerned with the period from the party's founding shortly after the Bolshevik Revolution through its near-disintegration in the mid-50s, although some items deal with the pro-Bolshevik movements out of which American communism developed, and some with the 1960s and 1970s. Contains 2,086 citations for books, published and unpublished essays, articles, dissertations, and theses, most of which are scholarly or historical in nature. Arranged in 37 chapters covering such subjects as Communism and the churches and Espionage. Author index. Z7164.S67H4

Kahan, Vilém. Bibliography of the Communist International (1919–1979). Leiden ; N.Y. : E.J. Brill, 1990. v. 1. (In progress). **CJ503**

Designed to be a three-volume bibliography of publications by and about the Communist International (Comintern) that have been published in more than 20 European languages. Based on several published bibliographies and the catalogs and holdings of 15 research institutions. Vol. 1 offers 3,186 unannotated entries grouped in sections by form (Bibliographies; Reference books, yearbooks; Documents and other primary sources; Memoirs; Literature on the Comintern—books and pamphlets published 1919–79 and periodical articles 1943–79). Entries are arranged alphabetically by main entry except for documents and materials relating to Comintern meetings, plenums, and congresses, which are arranged chronologically. Titles published in languages other than German, French, Italian, Spanish, and Portuguese have been translated into English or French. Includes summaries of Comintern congresses and Executive Committee plenums, chronologies of congresses and meetings, and lists of Comintern members and candidates. Author index.

Vol. 2 will list publications of and studies on organizations affiliated with the Comintern (e.g., Communist Youth International) and v. 3 will cover the national Communist parties that were members of the Comintern. When complete, will be more comprehensive than Witold S. Sworakowski's *The Communist International and its front organizations* (CJ511). Z7164.S67K34

Lachs, John. Marxist philosophy : a bibliographical guide. Chapel Hill : Univ. of North Carolina Pr., [1967]. 166 p.
CJ504

Covers "the group of theories that is usually thought to constitute the world view of dialetical and historical materialism."—*Introd.* Entries in chapters by topic or by form (e.g., documents, journals), with an essay beginning each chapter. Includes both critical and expository books written in English, French, and German. Author index.
Z7128.D5L3

Lubitz, Wolfgang. Trotsky bibliography : a classified list of published items about Leon Trotsky and Trotskyism. 2nd, totally rev. and expanded ed. München ; N.Y. : K.G. Saur, 1988. 581 p.
CJ505
1st ed., 1982.
Presents 5,009 citations to books, articles, dissertations, government publications, etc., written in European languages 1917–87. Unannotated entries in eight chapters (e.g., biographical items, Trotsky's literary and cultural thought, the international Trotskyist movement) further subdivided by topic. Author, anonymous title, source, and dissertation indexes.
Z8886.5.L8

Nursey-Bray, Paul F. Anarchist thinkers and thought : an annotated bibliography / comp. and ed. by Paul Nursey-Bray with the assistance of Jim Jose and Robyn Williams. N.Y. : Greenwood, 1992. 284 p. (Bibliographies and indexes in law and political science, no. 17).
CJ506
"Focuses on the nature and development of anarchism as a tradition of political thought."—*Introd.* Offers sections on anarchist philosophers and thinkers (e.g., Mikhail Bakunin, Pierre-Joseph Proudhon); related theorists and theories; general anarchist theory and history; anarchist movements in 18 countries; theses and dissertations; journals; and bibliographies. Entries, generally annotated, cover mainly English-language materials. Personal name and subject indexes.
§ Older but still useful bibliographies: Robert Goehlert and Claire Herczeg, *Anarchism : a bibliography* (Monticello, Ill. : Vance Bibliographies, 1982) and *L'Anarchisme : catalogue de livres et brochures des XIXe et XXe siècles*, by Janine Gaillemin, Marie-Aude Sowerwine-Mareschal and Diana Richet, under the direction of Denise Fauvel-Rouif (Paris ; N.Y. : K.G. Saur, 1982).
Z7164.A52N87

Seidman, Joel Isaac. Communism in the United States : a bibliography / comp. and ed. by Joel Seidman, assisted by Olive Golden and Yaffa Draznin. Ithaca, N.Y. : Cornell Univ. Pr., [1969]. 526 p.
CJ507
A "substantial revision, along with an expansion and updating" (*Pref.*) of the Fund for the Republic's *Bibliography on the communist problem in the United States* (N.Y., 1955).
Presents nearly 7,000 annotated citations of English-language books, pamphlets, and journal articles published through 1959, arranged alphabetically by author. The majority of the works deal with the official Communist Party of the U.S.; a preliminary section lists works on leftist movements preceding communism. Subject index.
Z7164.S67S38

Sharma, Jagdish Saran. Indian socialism : a descriptive bibliography. Delhi : Vikas, [1975]. 349 p.
CJ508
Intends to document the growth and development of Indian socialism through a classed bibliography of books, periodical and newspaper articles, pamphlets, government documents, etc. Some entries are briefly annotated. Author index.
Z7164.S67S44

Spiers, John. The left in Britain : a checklist and guide / John Spiers, Ann Sexsmith, Alastair Everitt. Hassocks, Sussex, Eng. : Harvester Pr., 1976. 168 p.
CJ509
Subtitle: With historical notes to 37 left-wing political movements and groupings active in Britain between 1904–1972 whose publications comprise the Harvester/Primary Sources Microfilm Collection.
A checklist of the publications of various groups; also serves as a guide to the 71,000 pages reproduced by the publishers in microform. Although the collection goes back to 1904 (largely based on materials from the Socialist Party of Great Britain), most of the material is from the 1950s and later. The background of each group is briefly sketched

before the main text of the checklist, which is divided into four parts. Each part has, when appropriate, an author, title, and chronological index, and consolidated author and title indexes are also provided. While a number of Marxist, Leninist, Trotskyist and Maoist groups are represented, the Communist Party of Great Britain is not included.
Updated by supplementary indexes, ed. by William Pidduck et al., *The left in Britain during [...]* (1978–). Published approximately every two years.
Z7165.G8S65

Stammhammer, Josef. Bibliographie des Socialismus und Communismus. Jena : Fischer, 1893–1909. 3 v.
CJ510
Repr.: Aalen : Zeller, 1963–64.
A classic bibliography on socialism and communism as well as related topics, such as anarchism. Includes references to books, articles, and pamphlets in German, French, English, and Italian, arranged alphabetically within each volume. The volumes cover successive dates of publication; v. 2–3 add works omitted from the earlier volume(s). Vols. 1–2 each have subject indexes; v. 3 has a cumulative subject index.
Z7164.S67S7

Sworakowski, Witold S. The Communist International and its front organizations : a research guide and checklist of holdings in American and European libraries. Stanford, Calif. : Hoover Institution on War, Revolution, and Peace, 1965. 493 p. (Hoover Institution on War, Revolution, and Peace. Biographical series, v. 21).
CJ511
A checklist of "holdings of 44 American and four European libraries of books and pamphlets published by and on ... the principal organizations which, during the time of the operation of the Communist International, from March 1919 to June 1943, promoted, sustained, and directed the communist movement in all corners of the world."—*Pref.* More than 2,200 entries. Classed arrangement. Subject/author index.
See also Vilém Kahan, *Bibliography of the Communist International (1919–1979)* (CJ503).
Z7164.S67S86

Uyehara, Cecil H. Leftwing social movements in Japan : an annotated bibliography. Tokyo ; Rutland, Vt. : Tuttle, [1959]. 444 p.
CJ512
Repr.: Westport, Conn. : Greenwood, 1972.
Publ. for the Fletcher School of Law and Diplomacy, Tufts University.
An extensive listing of books, periodicals, and documents published in Japanese, primarily since World War I. Entries arranged in topical chapters, each with a textual introduction. Titles are transliterated, followed by Japanese characters. Provides U.S. and Japanese library locations for each entry. Author-title index.
Z7164.S67U9

Vanden, Harry E. Latin American Marxism : a bibliography. N.Y. : Garland, 1991. 869 p. (Garland reference library of social science, v. 137.).
CJ513
Lists books, pamphlets, articles, and government documents either written by Latin American Marxists or dealing with Marxism or Marxist revolutionary thought or practice in Latin America. Approximately 6,300 entries (some briefly annotated) in four chronological chapters (1920 and before, 1921–45, 1946–60, 1961–80s), which are subdivided into general and country sections. Most citations are to English- or Spanish-language literature; selected items in Portuguese, French, German, Italian, and Russian. Author index.
§ Earlier, still often useful works are: Ludwig Lauerhass, *Communism in Latin America, a bibliography : the post-war years (1945–1960)* (Los Angeles : Center of Latin American Studies, Univ. of California, 1962. 78 p.) and Martin Sable and M. Wayne Dennis, *Communism in Latin America, an international bibliography : 1900–1945, 1960–1967* (Los Angeles : Latin American Center, Univ. of California, 1968. 220 p.).
Z7164.S67V36

Vigor, Peter Hast. Books on communism and the communist countries : a selected bibliography. [3rd ed.]. London : Ampersand, [1971]. 444 p.
CJ514
1st ed. by R. N. Carew Hunt, 1959; 2nd ed. by Walter Kolarz, 1964, had title: *Books on communism : a bibliography.*

A selected, annotated bibliography of some 2,600 English-language items in classed arrangement within three main sections: (1) Studies of communism in general and in the U.S.S.R; (2) Communism in other countries; and (3) Official documents and publications. Revision for this edition resulted in about 350 titles being dropped and 500 added. Although in-print status was a consideration in the selection, many older, out-of-print works (including important books from the 1920s and 1930s) are included. Coverage extends into 1970. No index.

Z7164.S67V5

Weinrich, Peter. Social protest from the left in Canada, 1870–1970. Toronto ; Buffalo : Univ. of Toronto Pr., 1982. 627 p. **CJ515**

A chronological listing, mostly of primary documents, from political parties, trade unions, cooperatives, leftist movements, and groups involved in riots, rebellions, and strikes. Excludes material relating to Quebec, and selectively includes secondary works and government documents. Canadian library locations are indicated. Separate lists of annual reports and serials. Indexed by author, organization, and title.

Z7165.C2W44

Periodicals

The left index. no.1 (Spring 1982)– . Santa Cruz, Calif. : Left Index, [1982]– Quarterly **CJ516**

Indexes journals with a "Marxist, radical or left perspective."—*Pref.* International in scope; primarily covers topics in the humanities and social sciences. Four main sections: (1) author list with full bibliographic entries; (2) subject index (cumulates annually); (3) book review index; (4) journal index. List of periodicals indexed.

§ See also *Alternative press index* (AD259). Z7164.S67L34

Lubitz, Wolfgang. Trotskyist serials bibliography 1927–1991 : with locations and indices / ed. by Wolfgang and Petra Lubitz. Munich ; N.Y. : Saur, 1993. 475 p. **CJ517**

Treats serials published by groups "which claim adherence to the theories and politics of Leon Trotsky" (*Introd.*); works cited are in 28 European languages and originate in 34 countries. Entries, arranged alphabetically by title, provide a full bibliographic description (including price), cross-references for title variations, language, country of publication, issuing group's affiliation, and holding libraries. Lists literature, sources, persons, and groups consulted. Indexes by organization, affiliation, and ISSN. HX73.Z99L83

Encyclopedias

Carver, Terrell. A Marx dictionary. Totowa, N.J. : Barnes & Noble Books, 1987. 164 p. **CJ518**

Intended for students and general readers. The body of the book consists of 16 short chapters, each treating one of the major Marxian concepts "that need careful explanation before his works can be grasped and criticized adequately" (*Pref.*) and an introductory chapter tying them together. Other terms are explained in the context of these 16, and readers are directed toward specific terms by an "Entry finder" section that refers to the appropriate chapter, and by a general index. The 16 key terms are printed in upper case when they occur in the text. Includes a bibliographic essay. HX17.C37

A dictionary of Marxist thought / ed. by Tom Bottomore. 2nd ed. Cambridge, Mass. : Harvard Univ. Pr., 1991. 647 p. **CJ519**

1st ed., 1983.
Describes terms, concepts, individuals, and schools of thought. The lengthy signed entries are alphabetically arranged, have cross-references, and end with brief bibliographies. Includes list of entries new to this edition; list of contributors. Two-part bibliography of cited works: (1) writings of Marx and Engels, and (2) other works. General index. HX17.D5

Draper, Hal. The Marx-Engels cyclopedia / by Hal Draper ; with the assistance of the Center for Socialist History. N.Y. : Schocken Books, 1985–1986. 3 v. **CJ520**

Contents: v. 1, The Marx-Engels chronicle: a day-by-day chronology of Marx and Engels' life and activity; v. 2, The Marx-Engels register: a complete bibliography of Marx and Engels' individual writings; v. 3, The Marx-Engels glossary: a glossary to the chronicle and register, and index to the glossary.

Serves as a guide to the lives and works of Marx and Engels. Vol. 1, the chronology, covers 1818–1895. Vol. 2, the bibliography, includes a title index. Vol. 3 is both a dictionary describing the importance of all proper names (e.g., people, organizations, parties, places, periodicals) referred to in v. 1–2 and an index to names. It also includes a personal name index (excluding Marx and Engels) to v. 3.

HX39.5.D69

Marxism, communism and Western society : a comparative encyclopedia / ed. by C. D. Kernig. [N.Y.] : Herder and Herder, [1972–73]. 8 v. : ill. **CJ521**

Long, signed articles by an international team of scholars attempt to survey "all the areas in which there is disagreement between East and West."—*Pref.* Emphasizes "the differences as mirrored in the thought and language of the corresponding disciplines."—*Pref.* Opposing views are presented and a comparison or a critical appraisal offered. Extensive bibliographies. AE5.M27

Wilczynski, Jozef. An encyclopedic dictionary of Marxism, socialism and communism : economic, philosophical, political and sociological theories, concepts, institutions and practices—classical and modern, East-West relations included. Berlin ; N.Y. : W. de Gruyter, 1981. 660 p. **CJ522**

Brief entries, alphabetically arranged and containing cross-references, cover relevant terms, phrases, doctrines, theories, writings, political parties, organizations, and individuals.

§ An older but still occasionally useful work is Lester de Koster's *Vocabulary of communism* (Grand Rapids, Mich. : Eerdmans, 1964. 224 p.). HX17.W54

Dictionaries

Russell, James. Marx-Engels dictionary. Westport, Conn. : Greenwood, 1980. 140 p. **CJ523**

Provides brief definitions of only those terms appearing in the writings of Marx and Engels which may present difficulty to the general reader because they are no longer commonly used, have a particular Marxian meaning, or are technical historical, economic, and philosophical terms. Where available, definitions given by Marx or Engels are provided. An appendix groups terms by broad subject area. Cross-references; bibliography. HX17.R87

Quotations

Brassey's Soviet and communist quotations / comp. and ed. by Albert L. Weeks. Wash. : Pergamon-Brassey's, c1987. 387 p. **CJ524**

A "comprehensive ... compilation of major statements by those whose ideas drive the Soviet Union today ... the words that reflect and have shaped the world view of the Soviet Union."—*Pref.* Includes pronouncements by Marx, Stalin, Gorbachev, etc., as well as by lesser-known figures (among whom are obscure officers whose statements may have been used by leaders to send signals the leaders did not wish attributed to themselves). Much material is drawn from official publications (e.g., *Pravda*, *Military thought*) and from transcripts of official radio broadcasts. The 2,117 quotations are arranged in 17 chapters (e.g., Class and class warfare, Foreign policy), each of which is further subdivided. Quotations vary in length. The index is arranged by chapter. HX73.B7

Handbooks

Atlas of communism / ed. by Geoffrey Stern ; [contributors, Terrell Carver ... et al.]. N.Y. : Macmillan, c1991. 256 p. : ill. (some col.), maps in color ; 31 cm.   **CJ525**

Summarizes, through essays and maps, the ideology, history, and current prospects of communism. In five chronological chapters: (1) The roots of Communism, 1848–1917; (2) The Soviet experience, 1917–45; (3) Cold War Communism, 1945–62; (4) New perspectives, 1962–85; and (5) Reform and revolution, 1985–present. Includes, besides maps, many sidebars, illustrations, and photographs. Subject/name/illustration index.   HX36.A87

Communist and Marxist parties of the world. 2nd ed. Chicago : St. James, 1990. 596 p.   **CJ526**

1st ed., 1986, by Charles Hobday.

Rev. by David S. Bell [et al.], under the general editorship of Roger East.

In three parts: (1) a historical essay on the development of communism; (2) descriptions of individual and Marxist parties arranged alphabetically within countries (grouped into broad geographic areas), followed by descriptions of international communist organizations and fronts; (3) selected documents illustrating Marxist view of the party, the state, and the role of the state in world affairs. Bibliography. Name index.   JF2051.C576

Egbert, Donald Drew. Socialism and American life / editors: Donald Drew Egbert and Stow Persons. Princeton, N.J. : Princeton Univ. Pr., 1952. 2 v. : ill. (Princeton studies in American civilization, no.4).   **CJ527**

Bibliographer (v. 2) : T. D. Seymour Bassett.

Provides a detailed treatment; still useful for historical research. Vol. 1 features signed essays, written by specialists, on the subject of socialism. Vol. 2 is a bibliography in essay form, arranged by topic roughly corresponding to the essays in v. 1. Includes books and articles, primarily in English, although some other languages are represented. Each volume has an author/subject index.   HX83.E45

Marxist governments : a world survey / ed. by Bogdan Szajkowski. N.Y. : St. Martin's Pr., 1981. 3 v. (822 p.) : maps.   **CJ528**

Primarily of historical value. Offers profiles by scholars of 24 countries that are or were ruled by Marxist-Leninist parties. Arranged alphabetically by country, each profile consists of the party's history, structure, constitution, electoral system, mass organizations and membership, and data on the country's economy, domestic policies, and foreign relations; footnotes and bibliographies are included. Afghanistan, Madagascar, and San Marino are excluded. Indexed.   JC474.M3512

Sworakowski, Witold S. World communism : a handbook, 1918–1965. Stanford, Calif. : Hoover Inst. Pr., 1973. 576 p. (Hoover Institution publication, 108).   **CJ529**

Contains signed essays written by scholars on "each of the 106 countries in which a communist party was or is active" (*Pref.*), on international communist organizations, and on developments in Latin America and sub-Saharan Africa. Essays arranged alphabetically by country, organization name, or geographic area. An appendix lists communist parties by country (with party name changes), 1918–65. List of contributors. Name and subject indexes.

§ Intended as a companion to *Yearbook on international communist affairs* (CJ530), providing historical background to the *Yearbook*'s more current information.   HX40.S89

Yearbook on international communist affairs. 1966–1991. Stanford, Calif. : Hoover Inst. on War, Revolution, and Peace, Stanford Univ., 1967–[1991?].   **CJ530**

Assembles "data concerning the individual communist parties and their activities, together with material pertaining to the international communist movement and its problems."—*Pref., 1966*. The major section of each volume offers profiles arranged by region and country that contain names of communist parties, founding dates, membership, leadership, dates of last congress, dates and results of last elections, auxiliary organizations, publications, and descriptive essays on each party's history, ideology, and activities. Other contents vary: usually included are international communist conferences/congresses, international communist organizations, biographies, a bibliography, and an index or biography, name, and subject indexes. Some volumes also have a section of relevant documents.   HX1.Y4

Biography

Biographical dictionary of Marxism / ed. by Robert A. Gorman. Westport, Conn. : Greenwood, 1986. 388 p.   **CJ531**

Describes the careers and theories of more than 200 Marxist philosophers from 45 countries, including extensive treatment of Third World Marxists who "have retooled materialist Marxism for the postcolonial liberation struggles ... without, however, altering its philosophical base."—*Pref*. Five entries describe groups of theorists. Biographies are arranged alphabetically; most are followed by two-part bibliographies of primary and secondary sources. An appendix lists subjects by nationality, which facilitates the relating of theorists and movements to national and regional cultures. List of contributors. General index.

§ Does not include nonmaterialist (i.e., nonorthodox) Marxists, who are treated by the editor's *Biographical dictionary of neo-Marxism* (CJ532), to which the present volume provides references.   HX23.B568

Biographical dictionary of neo-Marxism / ed. by Robert A. Gorman. Westport, Conn. : Greenwood, 1985. 463 p.   **CJ532**

Surveys some 200 nonmaterialist Marxists, complementing *Biographical dictionary of Marxism* (CJ531), which treats materialists. Ten additional entries treat groups, movements, or journals. The articles were written by "scholars with an intimate interest in and knowledge of a particular entrant."—*Pref*. Not complete, since some subjects (mostly East Europeans) were omitted at their own request, and others asked that some information be excluded. Entries, alphabetically arranged, are followed by two-part bibliographies of primary and secondary works. The index associates key terms with their originators, permitting readers to trace the "source and meaning of technical words and phrases that have turned many radical journals into lexical nightmares." Appendixes: list of contributors; list of subjects by nationality.   HX23.B57

Lazić, Branko M. Biographical dictionary of the Comintern / by Branko Lazitch in collaboration with Milorad M. Drachkovitch. New, rev., and expanded ed. Stanford, Calif. : Hoover Institution Pr., 1986. 532 p.   **CJ533**

1st ed., 1973.

Offers 753 alphabetically arranged biographies of: (1) members of tthe Comintern's directorate; (2) individuals who spoke at or were delegates to congresses or meetings and who also played important roles in the communist movements of their own countries or in the Comintern; (3) emissaries and functionaries of the Comintern; (4) leaders of related international organizations; and (5) graduates of the four principal Comintern schools who later played significant roles in the communist movement. Includes a guide to abbreviations and lists of biographees and pseudonyms.   HX23.L35

INTELLIGENCE AND ESPIONAGE

Becket, Henry S. A. The dictionary of espionage : spookspeak into English. N.Y. : Stein and Day, 1986. 203 p. **CJ534**

A helpful guide, alphabetically arranged, to the language of the espionage community, defining terms such as "access permit," "disinformation," and "paper merchant." Cross-references; bibliography of printed sources consulted.   UB270.B35

Blackstock, Paul W. Intelligence, espionage, counterespionage, and covert operations : a guide to information sources / Paul W. Blackstock, Frank L. Schaf, Jr. Detroit : Gale, 1978. 255 p. (International relations information guide series, 2). **CJ535**

"Designed primarily for the general American public" (*Introd.*), this selective, annotated bibliography includes mainly books and articles in the English language and concentrates on the post-1945 period. Classified arrangement in four sections: general bibliographic resources; strategic intelligence; espionage and counterespionage; covert operations. Bibliography of the 50 most essential books. Author and title indexes. Z6724.I7B55

Buranelli, Vincent. Spy/counterspy : an encyclopedia of espionage / Vincent and Nan Buranelli. N.Y. : McGraw-Hill, 1982. 361 p. **CJ536**

Comprises about 400 articles on individual spies, organizations, incidents, and techniques from the 16th century to the 1980s. International in scope; alphabetically arranged entries include cross-references and brief bibliographies. Name and subject index.

§ For biographies of spies, *see also* Wendell L. Minnick's *Spies and provocateurs* (CJ540). UB250.B87

Constantinides, George C. Intelligence and espionage : an analytical bibliography. Boulder, Colo. : Westview Pr., 1983. 559 p. **CJ537**

The main portion of the book offers descriptive and evaluative annotations for some 500 English-language books on the intelligence process and the history of intelligence, arranged alphabetically by author, with cross-references. Covers 17th–20th centuries, with emphasis on the latter. Preceding the annotated list is an "intelligence category index" that cites works from the annotated list by topic (e.g., American intelligence—World War II, Censorship and economic warfare, Photographic intelligence). Combined glossary and abbreviations list; title and subject/author indexes. Z6724.I7C66

Georgetown University. Library. Scholar's guide to intelligence literature : bibliography of the Russell J. Bowen Collection in the Joseph Mark Lauinger Memorial Library, Georgetown University / ed. by Marjorie W. Cline, Carla E. Christiansen and Judith M. Fontaine. Frederick, Md. : Univ. Publications of America, 1983. 236 p. **CJ538**

Publ. for the National Intelligence Study Center.

A classed but unannotated international bibliography of some 6,000 books, documents, and articles on espionage, counterintelligence, covert action, subversion, etc., including histories of wars and warfare from the American Revolution to the Vietnamese conflict. Author index; index of selected titles.

Mahoney, M. H. Women in espionage : a biographical dictionary. Santa Barbara, Calif. : ABC-Clio, c1993. 253 p. : ill. **CJ539**

Presents 150 women with various expertise and field experience in espionage, both the well-known and the less famous. Alphabetically arranged entries vary in length from a few paragraphs to several pages, sometimes include a photograph, and feature biographical information and a discussion of the significance of each woman's intelligence activities. Bibliography. List of acronyms and abbreviations. Name/subject index. JF1525.I6M25

Minnick, Wendell L. Spies and provocateurs : a worldwide encyclopedia of persons conducting espionage and covert action, 1946–1991. Jefferson, N.C. : McFarland, c1992. 310 p. **CJ540**

Discusses the activities of more than 700 individuals involved in espionage or covert action during the post-World War II (Cold War) era. Coverage is worldwide but emphasizes Western operatives because less information is available on communist agents. Numbered and cross-referenced entries, alphabetically arranged, include sources. Chronology of major Cold War espionage events; glossary; bibliography; general index.

§ See also Vincent and Nan Buranelli, *Spy/counterspy* (CJ536).

Other occasionally useful titles providing biographies of spies and spymasters are: Ronald Seth, *Encyclopedia of espionage* (Garden City, N.Y. : Doubleday, 1972); Christopher Dobson and Ronald Payne, *Who's who in espionage* (N.Y. : St. Martin's, 1984. Publ. in London as *The dictionary of espionage*); and Richard Deacon, *Spyclopaedia* (London : Macdonald, 1988). JF1525.I6M56

O'Toole, G. J. A. The encyclopedia of American intelligence and espionage : from the Revolutionary War to the present. N.Y. : Facts on File, c1988. 539 p. : ill. **CJ541**

The five major types of articles treat: American intelligence organizations; the role of intelligence in the principal wars of American history; subjects of importance in American intelligence history (e.g., cryptology); events, and individuals. Some of the other entries further explicate the major articles. Entries are arranged alphabetically and vary in length from a paragraph to 16 pages (Vietnam War). Articles include cross-references and source notes. List of abbreviations and acronyms. Extensive bibliography; general index. UB271.U5O85

Parrish, Michael. Soviet security and intelligence organizations, 1917–1990 : a biographical dictionary and review of literature in English. N. Y. : Greenwood, 1992. 669 p. **CJ542**

Pt. 1 contains biographies of nearly 4,000 senior and mid-level officials who served in Soviet security and intelligence organizations. Alphabetically arranged entries give (when available) nationality, highest rank, birth and death dates, education, career, other positions, and honors. Pt. 2 is an annotated, alphabetically arranged, bibliography of English language books dealing with Soviet security and intelligence. Several appendixes, including: lists of abbreviations, sources consulted, and Soviet journals and newspapers; a chart showing the development and leaders of Soviet security organizations; and an addendum to the biography section. No index. JN6529.I6P37

Peake, Hayden B. The reader's guide to intelligence periodicals. Wash. : NIBC Pr., c1992. 250 p. : ill. **CJ543**

Serves "to identify and briefly describe periodical sources of intelligence-related information."—*Pref.* Eight sections: (1) Intelligence periodicals; (2) Intelligence-related periodicals; (3) Limited distribution intelligence periodicals; (4) Intelligence periodicals no longer in print; (5) Periodicals occasionally containing intelligence articles; (6) Periodic bibliographies of intelligence literature; (7) Intelligence databases; and (8) Databases with intelligence-related material. Entries are for English-language publications and include perspective, content, publication, and subscription data. Title index. JF1525.I6P43

Petersen, Neal H. American intelligence, 1775–1990 : a bibliographical guide. Claremont, Calif. : Regina Books, 1992. 406 p. (New war/peace bibliographical series, 2). **CJ544**

Note on title page: Published sources on espionage, covert action, counterintelligence, domestic intelligence, technical collection, cryptology, research and analysis, policy and process, organization and oversight, and other aspects of U.S. intelligence operations since the American Revolution.

"Designed as a practical guide for the scholarly study of intelligence," covering "topics that are commonly treated in present-day professional intelligence journals, which are widely regarded by practitioners as part of their heritage, and which are considered part of intelligence by the informed public."—*Introd.* Cites more than 6,000 English-language monographs, articles from scholarly and professional journals, and selected articles from newspapers and popular magazines. No annotations. Entries are in chronological chapters; many sections have an introductory paragraph that describes the topic and leading sources. Also includes chapters on reference and general works, intelligence production, technical intelligence collection, and intelligence-related topics (e.g., terrorism, narcotics control, psychological warfare). Author and subject indexes. Z6724.I7P48

Rocca, Raymond G. Bibliography on Soviet intelligence and security services / Raymond G. Rocca and John J. Dziak with the staff of the Consortium for the Study of Intelligence. Boulder, Colo. : Westview Pr., 1985. 203 p. **CJ545**

The compilers (experts with government and teaching experience) attempt to provide scholars and policy analysts with "an analytic aid for research and teaching about Soviet intelligence and its role in both Soviet domestic politics and contemporary world affairs."—*Foreword.* Citations (many annotated) to more than 500 books, articles, and government documents are arranged in five sections: (1) Selected bibliographies and other reference works, (2) Russian/Soviet accounts, (3) Defector/first-hand accounts, (4) Secondary accounts, and (5) Congressional and other government documents. Appendixes provide a brief glossary, leadership lists, and a chart showing the development of Soviet intelligence/security operations. Author/source and title indexes.   Z6724.I7R6

Smith, Myron J. The secret wars : a guide to sources in English. Santa Barbara, Calif. : ABC-Clio, 1980–1981. 3 v. (War/Peace bibliography series, no. 12–14).   **CJ546**
Contents: v. 1, Intelligence, propaganda, and psychological warfare, resistance movements, and secret operations, 1939–1945; v. 2, Intelligence, propaganda and psychological warfare, covert operations 1945–1980; v. 3, International terrorism, 1968–1980.
An impressive compilation of more than 9,000 books, papers, periodical articles, government documents, doctoral dissertations and master's theses. Detailed table of contents and chronologies. Author and subject indexes in v. 1; author index only in v. 2 and v. 3.
                    Z6724.I7S63

United States intelligence : an encyclopedia / ed. by Bruce W. Watson, Susan M. Watson, Gerald W. Hopple. N.Y. : Garland, 1990. 792 p. (Garland reference library of social science, v. 589).   **CJ547**
"Intended for the serious researcher of the U.S. Intelligence Community" (*Introd.*); entries treat major terms, persons, and organizations since World War II. Lists of acronyms and major weapon systems, a chronology, and a bibliography are followed by the alphabetical list of entries, which contain cross-references and end with bibliographies. Ends with appendixes containing 25 relevant executive and congressional statements issued since 1941.   JK468.I6U57

TERRORISM

Atkins, Stephen E. Terrorism : a reference handbook. Santa Barbara. Calif. : ABC-Clio, c1992. 199 p.   **CJ548**
Includes an introductory essay on terrorism in its political context; a selected chronology, 1894–1992; short biographies of leading terrorists, 1945–90; selected documents; a directory of terrorist organizations, 1940–92 (giving founder, membership, acts of violence); and an annotated bibliography. Suitable for novices or undergraduates. General index.   HV6431.A87

Global terrorism : a historical bibliography / Suzanne Robitaille Ontiveros, ed. Santa Barbara, Calif. : ABC-Clio, c1986. 168 p. (ABC-Clio research guides, 16).   **CJ549**
Draws from *Historical abstracts* (DA176) and *America : history and life* (DB24) databases. Annotated citations to journal articles, most published in the 1970s and 1980s, grouped in seven chapters: General; Europe; Middle East; Asia and the Pacific Region; Latin America and the West Indies; North America; Africa. Chronology, 1975–85. Subject and author indexes.   Z7164.T3G57

Lakos, Amos. International terrorism : a bibliography. Boulder, Colo. : Westview Pr. ; London : Mansell, 1986. 481 p.   **CJ550**
Unannotated citations to English-language books, journal articles, reports, government publications, and dissertations publ. mid-1960s through 1990. Entries are grouped by broad category, then by form. Author and subject indexes.
Updated by Lakos's *Terrorism 1980–1990 : a bibliography* (1991. 443 p.), which has the same arrangement and scope.
§ *See also*: Augustus R. Norton and Martin H. Greenberg, *International terrorism : an annotated bibliography and research guide*

(c1980. 218 p.) and *Terrorism : an annotated bibliography*, by Susheela Bhan ... [et al.] (Boulder, Co. : Westview Pr., 1989. 338 p.). The latter cites many Indian sources.   Z7164.T3L34

Lentz, Harris M. Assassinations and executions : an encyclopedia of political violence, 1865–1986. Jefferson, N.C. : McFarland, c1988. 275 p.   **CJ551**
Chronologically arranged entries cover political assassinations, executions (such as those resulting from political purges), and unsuccessful assassination attempts, 1865–1986, with earlier activities summarized in the prologue. Includes information on heads of state, ambassadors, leading national figures, and military officers. Provides a description of the incident, manner of and motive for the assassination, name(s) of assailant(s), brief biography of the victim, immediate effect on politics, and fate of the assassin(s). Bibliography; personal and geographic name index.   HV6278.L45

Mickolus, Edward F. The literature of terrorism : a selectively annotated bibliography. Westport, Conn. : Greenwood, 1980. 553 p.   **CJ552**
————. *Terrorism, 1980–1987 : a selectively annotated bibliography*, comp. by Edward F. Mickolus with Peter A. Flemming (N.Y. : Greenwood, 1988. 314 p.).
Both works contain citations to books, articles, government documents, and dissertations, most in English. Many citations are annotated. Entries are grouped alphabetically within topic chapters (e.g., tactics, philosophies, responses to terrorism). Author and title indexes.
————. *Terrorism, 1988–1991 : a chronology of events and a selectively annotated bibliography* (Westport, Conn. : Greenwood, 1993. 913 p.). In three parts: update on terrorist incidents, 1960–87; 1988–1991 incidents; selectively annotated bibliography of books and journal articles organized by topic. No indexes.
•A machine-readable version with the title *ITERATE 3* (covering 1978–91 for numeric data and 1978 to the present for textual material) is available from Vinyard Software Inc., Falls Church, Va.
§ Related works: John L. Scherer, *Terrorism : an annual survey* (Minneapolis, Minn. : Scherer, 1982–1983); *InTer* (Jerusalem : Publ. for the Jaffee Center for Strategic Studies by the Jerusalem Post ; Boulder, Colo. : Distr. by Westview Pr., 1984–); *The Rand chronology of international terrorism for [date]* (Santa Monica, Calif. : Rand Corporation, 1990–); and *The [date] annual on terrorism* (Dordrecht ; Boston : M. Nijhoff, 1986–1989).   Z7164.T3M53

————   Transnational terrorism : a chronology of events, 1968–1979. Westport, Conn. : Greenwood, 1980. 967 p.   **CJ553**
With its companion publication, *International terrorism in the 1980s : a chronology of events* by Mickolus, Todd Sandler, and Jean M. Murdock (Ames : Iowa State Univ. Pr., 1989. 2 v.), provides a detailed chronology of international terrorism from 1968–1987, with a few earlier incidents. Includes skyjackings, but excludes declared wars, government military actions, and attacks between ethnic groups within a disputed area (e.g., Northern Ireland). Entries give date, place, and a description of the incident. Both titles have tables (e.g., number and type of attacks) and indexes for locations, types, and groups. *International terrorism* provides an eight-digit code for each incident, and includes appendixes giving codes used in the *International terrorism : attributes of terrorist events* (ITERATE) data project.
•A machine-readable version of the *ITERATE 2* data (covering 1968–77) is available through the Inter-university Consortium for Political and Social Research (Ann Arbor, Mich.). Accompanying codebook has title: *International terrorism : attributes of terrorist events 1968–1977 (ITERATE 2)* (1982). For information on *ITERATE 3*, see CJ552.   HV6431.M5

Schmid, Alex Peter. Political terrorism : a new guide to actors, authors, concepts, data bases, theories, and literature / Alex P. Schmid and Albert J. Jongman, with the collaboration of Michael Stohl ... [et al.]. Rev., expanded and updated ed. Amsterdam ; N.Y. : North-Holland Pub. Co. ; New Brunswick : Distr. by Transaction Books, c1988. 700 p.   **CJ554**
1st ed. (1983) had subtitle: a research guide to concepts, theories, data bases and literature.

At head of title: SWIDOC: Royal Netherlands Academy of Arts and Sciences, Social Science Information- and Documentation Centre; Centre for the Study of Social Conflicts (C.O.M.T.), State University of Leiden; Program on Nonviolent Sanctions in Conflict and Defense (PNS), Harvard Univ.

Has chapters on definitions and topologies, theories, data and databases, and literature; a bibliography; and a world directory of relevant organizations. Author index to bibliography.   HV6431.S349

Shafritz, Jay M. Almanac of modern terrorism / Jay M. Shafritz, E.F. Gibbons, Jr., Gregory E.J. Scott. N.Y. : Facts on File, c1991. 290 p.   **CJ555**

The major section is comprised of alphabetically arranged and cross-referenced entries (some with bibliographies) for individuals, organizations, events, terms, and phrases. Also offers a chronology, 1946–90; selected quotations; definitions of terrorism (chronologically arranged); bibliography; general index.   HV6431.S465

Sifakis, Carl. Encyclopedia of assassinations. N.Y. : Facts on File, c1991. 228 p. : ill.   **CJ556**

Relates details of successful and attempted political assassinations. Entries arranged alphabetically by name of victim, some with a photograph or illustration. List of victims by country. Cross-references; bibliography; general index.   HV6278.S54

Terrorism : an international resource file. Index. Ann Arbor, Mich. : U.M.I, 1987– . Annual.   **CJ557**

Publication began in 1987 with issue dated 1986; issue for 1980/85 publ. 1989; 1970–79 publ. 1990.

Although designed as the index to the microfiche collection of the same title, this publication includes additional materials accessible elsewhere. Indexes articles, documents, pamphlets, papers, press releases, etc.; author, title, subject, geographic area, document type, and microfiche number access.

§ A companion title is Yonah Alexander, *Terrorism : an international resource file : 1970–89 bibliography* (1991. 241 p.).

Z7164.T3T47

Thackrah, John Richard. Encyclopedia of terrorism and political violence. London ; N.Y. : Routledge & Kegan Paul, 1987. 308 p.   **CJ558**

Entries treat terms, phrases, events, countries, organizations, and individuals; cross-references. Western emphasis; concentrates on 20th century activities. Bibliography; general index.   HV6431.T56

ARMED FORCES

For wars, battles, and specific aspects of military history, *see also* the History and Area Studies sections.

General works

Guides

Arkin, William M. Research guide to current military and strategic affairs. Wash. : Institute for Policy Studies, 1981. 232 p.   **CJ559**

Dated but still useful. In five sections: (1) introduction; (2) general information sources; (3) U.S. government documents; (4) U.S. military; (5) worldwide military and strategic affairs. Within each section are listed bibliographies, recurrent statistical data sources, periodicals, other reference sources, and important monographs. Emphasizes current resources and periodicals. Appendixes list some 600 periodicals and serials, as well as relevant organizations. No index.   UA10.5.A7

Bibliography

Anderson, Martin. Conscription : a select and annotated bibliography / ed. by Martin Anderson ; comp. by Martin Anderson and Valerie Bloom. Stanford : Hoover Inst. Pr., 1976. 452 p. (Hoover bibliographical series, 57).   **CJ560**

More than 1,385 entries organized into 17 chapters representing major subjects; within most chapters writings are classified as books, unpublished manuscripts, articles, pamphlets, reprints, speeches, and government documents. Emphasis is on U.S. experience, "particularly from the viewpoint of public policy recommendations" (*Introd.*), but material relevant to England and other foreign countries is included. Separate chapter on bibliographies. Author and title indexes.

Z6724.C63A53

Craig, Hardin, Jr. A bibliography of encyclopedias and dictionaries dealing with military, naval and maritime affairs, 1577–1971. 4th ed. rev. & corr. Houston, Tex. : Dept. of History, Rice Univ., 1971. 134 p.   **CJ561**

1st ed., 1960; 3rd ed., 1965.

Still valuable for its historical information. A chronological listing of encyclopedias, dictionaries, and wordbooks, plus a few miscellaneous items of interest to the user. International in scope; numerous brief annotations. Author index.   Z6724.D5C7

Pohler, Johann. Bibliotheca historico-militaris : Systematische Uebersicht der Erscheinungen aller Sprachen auf dem Gebiete der Geschichte der Kriege und Kriegswissenschaft seit Erfindung der Buchdruckerkunst bis zum Schluss des Jahres 1880. Leipzig : Lang, 1887–1899. 4 v.   **CJ562**

Repr.: N.Y. : B. Franklin, 1962.

An extensive military bibliography of some 50,000 titles, including materials in many languages and covering 26 countries and all periods from ancient times to 1880. Broad in scope; includes military history and science, tactics, weapons, etc., economics, politics, biography. Author index at end of v. 4.   Z6721.P74

Tillema, Herbert K. International armed conflict since 1945 : a bibliographic handbook of wars and military interventions. Boulder, Colo. : Westview Pr., 1991. 360 p.   **CJ563**

Covers 269 selected international armed conflicts, Sept. 2, 1945–Dec. 31, 1988, including limited engagements short of war (e.g., Entebbe airport raid) as well as minor and major wars. Omits civil conflicts (such as that in Ireland) or crises where no overt military intervention took place (e.g., Cuban missile crisis). Arranged by region, then country. Brief entries (usually one page or less) are cross-referenced, describe who intervened where, when, how, why, and to what effect; each closes with bibliographical references. Chronology by geographic area; list of reference works; bibliography; geographic/conflict name index.   Z6204.T53

Current

Air University Library index to military periodicals. v. 14, no. 1 (Jan.–Mar. 1963)– . Maxwell Air Force Base, Ala. : Air Univ. Libr., 1963– . Quarterly.   **CJ564**

Superintendent of Documents classification: D301.26/2: .

Supersedes *Air University periodical index*, 1949–1962.

Issue no. 4 is annual cumulation for each year.

Triennial cumulations issued 1952–67.

Provides "a subject index to significant articles, news items, and editorials appearing in … English language military and aeronautical periodicals … ."—*Pref.* Currently indexes about 81 periodicals. Subject coverage is broad, including the technical aspects of military art and science, supplies, equipment, military history, military-civil relations, arms control, etc. Beginning with 1990, issues include author entries for articles and books; prior issues included only selected author entries.

Current military & political literature. Oxford : Military Pr., c1989– . **CJ565**

Continues *Current military literature*, which ceased with the volume covering 1984 (publ. 1988).

Provides citations, some with abstracts, to articles and occasional papers drawn from an international list of periodicals in the fields of international relations, strategic studies, military-political science and history, theory and conduct of military action, peace studies, and conflict resolution. Entries are arranged in classed order with cross-references. Author, source, and geographical indexes in each issue; the first issue of each volume has a list of titles scanned with publishers' addresses.

Current world affairs : a quarterly bibliography. v. 14, no. 1 (Spring 1990)– . Alexandria, Va. : John C. Damon, c1990– . Quarterly. **CJ566**

Continues *Quarterly strategic bibliography* which ceased with v. 13 (1989). That title continued *Current bibliographic survey of national defense*, which was publ. 1975–76.

Cites periodical articles, government documents, research reports, and monographs that relate to the U.S. and world affairs (e.g., foreign policy, arms control, environmental protection). Arranged by form (periodicals, books, documents) and indexed by subject; contains a list of periodicals consulted and a glossary. Z1361.D4Q37

Periodicals

Unsworth, Michael. Military periodicals : United States and selected international journals and newspapers. N.Y. : Greenwood, 1990. 404 p. **CJ567**

Presents historical sketches of selected periodicals (primarily American) that have influenced the armed forces and military thought of the U.S. In three sections, each alphabetically arranged by periodical title: Long profiles (of the more prominent journals), Short profiles (of the less prominent), and Multiple-edition profiles (of journals having special editions, supplements, etc.). Also contains an appendix listing journals by subject, a chronology, and a general index. Z6723.U57

Encyclopedias

Clodfelter, Micheal. Warfare and armed conflicts : a statistical reference to casualty and other figures, 1618–1991. Jefferson, N.C. : McFarland, 1991. 2 v. (1414 p.). **CJ568**

Describes more than 680 conflicts since 1600, giving casualty statistics and other details of the conflict, including reasons for and effects of the engagement. Arranged by century and then by region; covers every war for which statistics exist, including civil wars, riots, pogroms, etc. Bibliography. Name index. D214.C55

The complete encyclopedia of arms & weapons / ed. by Leonid Tarassuk and Claude Blair. N.Y. : Simon and Schuster, [1982]. 544 p. : ill. **CJ569**

Subtitle: The most comprehensive reference work ever published on arms and armor from prehistoric times to the present—with over 1,250 illustrations.

Translation of *Enciclopedia ragionata delle armi* (Milan : Mondadori, 1979).

A dictionary arrangement of cross-referenced articles on individual weapons and types of armor, with emphasis on their component parts, and tracing developments through history. Sections of color plates group illustrations of arms and armor by periods; numerous black-and-white illustrations appear in proximity to the descriptive articles. Select bibliography.

§ See also: *Weapons : an international encyclopedia from 5000 B.C. to 2000 A.D.*, prepared by the Diagram Group. (CJ581). U815.E5313

Gunston, Bill. The illustrated encyclopedia of rockets and missiles : a comprehensive technical directory and history of the military guided missile systems of the 20th century. N.Y. : Crescent Books, 1979. 264 p. : ill. **CJ570**

Divided into 11 sections, according to the missile's function and deployment; e.g., surface-to-surface land tactical, air-to-surface strategic, anti-submarine, etc. Descriptions of the missiles are arranged chronologically by nation within each section and include historical development, use, specifications, and illustration. Indexed by name, code-name, missile type, country of origin, designer, and manufacturer. Brief glossary. Good for historical information.

§ For current information, consult annual publications such as *Jane's air-launched weapons* (Alexandria, Va. : Jane's Information Group, 1989–). UG1310.G86

International military and defense encyclopedia / ed. in chief, Trevor N. Dupuy ... [et al.]. Wash. : Brassey's, c1993. 6 v. (lxxvi, 3132 p.) : ill. **CJ571**

Aims to be a definitive, comprehensive, multi-disciplinary, and multi-cultural encyclopedia of military and defense information. Covers, in 786 alphabetically arranged articles written by an international group of scholars and experts, topics in 17 major subject areas (e.g., aerospace forces and warfare, history and biography, logistics, materiel and weapons, military and international security law). Focusing primarily on post-World War II events and developments, the signed articles range in length from 100 to 10,000 words, contain cross-references, end with bibliographies, and often feature illustrations, charts, graphs, or photographs. Includes lists of articles, articles by subject, contributors, and abbreviations and acronyms. General index. U24.I58

The international military encyclopedia / ed. by Norman Tobias ... [et al.]. Gulf Breeze, Fla. : Academic International Pr., 1992. v. 1. (In progress). **CJ572**

Contents: v. 1, A-I Skyraider–Acre, Siege of, 1799.

Covers history, strategy, tactics, weapons, equipment, battles, and significant individuals from ancient times to the present, with emphasis on the 20th century. Entries vary in length from a few paragraphs to several pages, and are generally signed and contain cross-references and bibliographies of primary and secondary sources. Planned as a 50-volume set, to be published during the next 10–15 years, the work is to include supplementary volumes and indexes at 10-volume intervals. U24.I59

Luttwak, Edward. The dictionary of modern war / Edward Luttwak and Stuart Koehl. N.Y. : HarperCollins, c1991. 680 p. **CJ573**

An earlier ed. by Edward Luttwak had title: *A dictionary of modern war* (N.Y. : Harper & Row, 1971).

Presents detailed yet concise entries defining concepts, organizations, weapons, military technologies, methods of warfare, negotiations, and treaties. Intended as a reference source and a readable guide for both experts and general readers. "Too short to be an encyclopedia [but] more than a dictionary because it explains and does not merely describe its contents ... ." (*Introd.*) and includes its authors' opinions (e.g., statements as to whether a weapon really works). Alphabetically arranged, with extensive cross-references. A glossary lists popular names of weapon systems and vehicles and their nationalities. No illustrations; no index. U24.L93

Macksey, Kenneth. The Penguin encyclopedia of modern warfare : 1850 to the present day / Kenneth Macksey and William Woodhouse. London ; N.Y. : Viking, 1991. 373 p. : maps. **CJ574**

Produced by two retired British officers. Gives quick access to personalities, battles, campaigns, strategy, tactics, intelligence handling, logistics, and technology. Alphabetically arranged entries include cross-references; many have maps or diagrams. Chronology; bibliography; general index. U39.M3

Nicolle, David. Arms and armour of the crusading era, 1050–1350. White Plains, N.Y. : Kraus International Publ., c1988. 2 v. : ill. **CJ575**

Contents: v. 1, Commentary; v. 2, Illustrations.

Shows the arms and armor of the Christian, Islamic, and Turco-Mongol civilizations. Vol. 1 contains detailed commentary on the illustrations in v. 2. The illustrations (line drawings) are grouped by geographic and cultural areas, then arranged chronologically. Also included in v. 2 are a dictionary of terms and abbreviations, bibliographies, and a general index.   U810.N5

Parkinson, Roger. The encyclopedia of modern war. N.Y. : Stein and Day, 1977. 226 p. : maps.   **CJ576**

Attempts to cover battles, weapons, and individuals, plus "conceptual topics such as strategy, tactics and various theories and principles."—*Pref.* Alphabetically arranged entries cover 1793–1975. Maps depict campaigns in various wars. Cross-references; general index.

U24.P37

The Rand McNally encyclopedia of military aircraft, 1914–1980 / [conceived and ed. by] Enzo Angelucci ; [written by Paolo Matricardi]. Chicago : Rand McNally, 1981. 546 p. : ill.   **CJ577**

Translation of *Atlante enciclopedico degli aerei militari del mondo dal 1914 a oggi*, publ. by Mondadori, 1980.

Provides color illustrations, photographs, silhouettes, and specifications for about 800 models, arranged by historical period (i.e., World Wars I and II, 1919–39, and the post-1945 period). Numerous charts and graphs complement the text. Bibliography; index. A *Library journal* review (Mar. 1, 1982, p. 553) called this "the most useful one-volume reference on military aircraft available." Revised and updated, N.Y. : Gallery Books, 1990.

§ Designed as a companion to the editor's *World encyclopedia of civil aircraft : from Leonardo da Vinci to the present.* (English-language ed. supervised by John Stroud. N.Y. : Crown, [1982]. 414 p.).   UG1240.A8413

Robertson, David. Guide to modern defense and strategy : a complete description of the terms, tactics, organizations and accords of today's defense. Detroit : Gale, c1987. 324 p.

CJ578

British ed. has title: *A dictionary of modern defence and strategy* (London : Europa, 1987).

Intended to go further "than a standard dictionary in that the entries are not confined to mere definitions. The main aim ... is to set out the policy implications and theoretical arguments that lie behind the concepts and the physical specifications."—*Pref.* Alphabetically arranged entries, typically from one-half to two pages in length, define not only standard technical terms, but also such popular or colloquial usages as "Dr. Strangelove," and "Blue Water Navy," as well as describe significant individuals (e.g., McNamara, Clausewitz). Extensive cross-referencing, including the use of boldface for terms within entries that are themselves the subjects of entries. Table of abbreviations.   U24.R63

Taylor, Michael John Haddrick. Encyclopedia of the world's air forces. N.Y. : Facts on File, 1988. 211 p. : col. ill.

CJ579

Though now somewhat dated, still useful, as it describes the air forces of 150 nations, indicating air bases, number of specific models of planes, number of personnel, etc. Discusses the purposes of the force (e.g., for Benin, transport and liaison) and the world events and national conditions that have affected them. Short, fact-filled entries, arranged alphabetically by country, are followed by an appendix describing the speed, range, armaments, etc., for each type of aircraft, thus facilitating assessment of a nation's air strength. Includes a glossary and an index to specific models of aircraft.   UG628.T39

Warry, John. Warfare in the classical world : an illustrated encyclopedia of weapons, warriors and warfare in the ancient civilizations of Greece and Rome. N.Y. : St. Martin's, c1980. 224 p. : ill., maps.   **CJ580**

A handsomely illustrated, chronologically arranged survey of warfare as practiced by the Greeks, Romans, and those who came into conflict with them from Homeric times until the 5th century CE. Illus-

trations include color photographs, original art work (especially of soldiers and their equipment), battle diagrams, etc. Glossary; index.

U33.W37

Weapons : an international encyclopedia from 5000 BC to 2000 AD / the Diagram Group. [Updated ed.]. N.Y. : St. Martin's Pr., 1990. 336 p. : ill.   **CJ581**

1st ed., 1980.

Weapons are grouped by function, simple (handheld weapons) to complex (biological weapons), with explanations of function and many illustrative examples. Also contains a chapter on weapons developed in the 1980s and those projected for the 1990s. Includes short biographical sketches. Chronological tables for major topics. "Visual indexes" arrange Western weapons by historical periods, and others by region. Bibliography; index.

§ See also *The complete encyclopedia of arms & weapons* (CJ569).   U800.D55

Dictionaries

Ammer, Christine. Fighting words : from war, rebellion, and other combative capers. N.Y. : Paragon House, 1989. 266 p. : ill.   **CJ582**

Provides, for general readers, etymology of some 750 terms and phrases (e.g., cardigan, goldbrick, task force) that have entered the English language through use in warfare or the military. Arranged alphabetically. Term index.   U24.A55

Brassey's multilingual military dictionary = Brassey's dictionnaire multilingue militaire = Brassey's, diccionario polígloto militar = Brassey's, Militär-Wörterbuch in sechs Sprachen = [Brassi, mnogoĭazychnyĭ voennyĭ slovar'] = [Qāmūs Brāysīs al-' askarī al-muta'addid al-lughāt]. London ; Wash. : Brassey's Defence Publishers, 1987. 815 p.   **CJ583**

Designed to "meet the general needs of the service user and to provide the basic military vocabulary for a wide variety of situations in which direct word-for-word translation is required in an Army, Navy, or Air Force context."—*Introd.* Gives French, Spanish, German, Russian, and Arabic equivalents in a base list of 6,960 American English terms, with separate indexes for each language that refer to the base list. The Russian and Arabic indexes use Cyrillic and Arabic alphabets; there is also a brief index of British English. Appendixes give terms for ranks, units/formations, numerals/notation, tools, etc.

U25.B66

Department of Defense dictionary of military and associated terms / Joint Chiefs of Staff. 3 Jan. 1972– . Wash. : Joint Chiefs of Staff : U.S. Govt. Print. Off., 1972– . Irregular.

CJ584

Superintendent of Documents classification: D 5.12: .

Continues *Dictionary of United States military terms for joint usage* (Wash. : Joint Chiefs of Staff, 1955–68).

Serves as a glossary of standard military and associated terms, including terms for important modern weapons. Each definition indicates whether it has been standardized and approved for use by the Department of Defense (DOD) or NATO.   U24.D46

Dupuy, Trevor Nevitt. Dictionary of military terms : a guide to the language of warfare and military institutions / comp. by Trevor N. Dupuy, Curt Johnson, Grace P. Hayes. N.Y. : H.W. Wilson, 1986. 237 p.   **CJ585**

Intends to provide military professionals with the first comprehensive dictionary in the field, offering 2,500 concise definitions pertaining to all aspects of modern and historical military and naval affairs. Includes basic military terms (e.g., attack) that were omitted from the *Department of Defense dictionary of military and associated terms* (CJ584). Neglects such lexicographic concerns as etymology in favor of a strict concern for "military meanings and derivations ... including those that enjoy popular usage."—*Introd.*   U24.D87

International code name directory. 3rd ed. (1984)– . New-town, Conn. : Forecast International/DMS, Inc., 1983– . Annual.   **CJ586**

Title varies: some issues called *DMS international code name handbook*, *DMS international code name directory*, or *Code name directory. International.*

Place and publisher vary; some issues published in Greenwich, Conn., by DMS, Inc.

Designed to provide industry and government officials with a comprehensive listing of all past and current aerospace and defense code names and acronyms assigned by foreign governments and industries, including Warsaw Pact nations. An alphabetical listing, letter-by-letter, with succinct definitions, several words to two lines in length. Cross-references to other publications.

§ Also has a U.S. version: *Code name directory, US* (Greenwich, Conn. : Defense Marketing Services, 1984–).   U26.C568

Jane's defence glossary / comp. by Ian Kay, Mary Walker. Coulsdon : Jane's Information Group, 1993. 295 p.   **CJ587**

Lists more than 11,000 acronyms and abbreviations, giving their full form and often a designation for country or organization in which the term is used. 16 appendixes offer a variety of information, such as officer ranks for NATO countries.

•A machine-readable version is included on all Jane's CD-ROM products.   UF530.J36

Pretz, Bernhard. Dictionary of military and technological abbreviations and acronyms. London ; Boston : Routledge & Kegan Paul, 1983. 496 p.   **CJ588**

Alphabetically arranged and international in scope. Entries refer to country of use or origin where applicable. Includes equipment model numbers. Bibliography.   U26.P73

Shafritz, Jay M. The Facts on File dictionary of military science / Jay M. Shafritz, Todd J.A. Shafritz, David B. Robertson. N.Y. : Facts on File, c1989. 498 p.   **CJ589**

Focuses on the strategy, tactics, and technology of warfare, but does "not ignore peripheral yet critical concerns such as logistics, law, administration, and history." Aimed at both professionals and concerned citizens, but "essential for any commissioned or noncommissioned officer ... [as it contains] the vocabulary of his or her profession and brief discussions of all its major strategic doctrines and concerns."—*Pref.* Entries vary in length from two words to half a page. Some entries end with bibliographies, and cross-references are used liberally; those that refer to other entries are printed in upper case.
                                                              U24.S47

Quotations

Leadership : quotations from the military tradition / Robert A. Fitton, ed. Boulder, Co. : Westview Pr., 1990. 382 p.   **CJ590**

Topically arranged quotations on leadership (emphasizing military leadership) by statesmen, philosophers, corporate leaders, scholars, and authors as well as military leaders. International in scope; covers all time periods. Includes a short section of readings on leadership. Author index.   UB210.L396

Shafritz, Jay M. Words on war : military quotations from ancient times to the present. N.Y. : Prentice Hall, c1990. 559 p.
                                                              CJ591

Presents quotations and short anecdotes by commanders, theorists, writers, historians, soldiers, sailors, diplomats, and wartime leaders, from ancient to contemporary times. Also includes memorable war movie lines. Quotes are arranged chronologically within approximately 500 subjects arranged alphabetically. Appendix gives birth and death (if appropriate) dates and brief identification for the quoted public figures. Author/subject index.

§ For additional anecdotes, *see* Max Hastings, *The Oxford book of military anecdotes* (Oxford; N.Y. : Oxford Univ. Pr., 1985). *See also* the standard older work, Robert Heinl, *Dictionary of military and*

naval quotations (Annapolis, Md. : U.S. Naval Institute, c1966). Other similar and useful titles are Trevor Royle, *A dictionary of military quotations* (N.Y. : Simon & Schuster, 1989), Peter Tsouras, *Warrior's words* (N.Y. : Sterling, 1992), and Justin Wintle, *The dictionary of war quotations* (N.Y. : Free Press, 1989).   PN6084.W35S5

Handbooks

Conway's all the world's fighting ships, 1947–1982 / [ed., Robert Gardiner ; contributors, Norman Friedman ... et al.]. Annapolis, Md. : Naval Institute Pr., c1983. 2 v. : ill. **CJ592**

This work and its companion titles (below) provide a wealth of historical information on the fleets of the world, 1860–1982. Although each title groups countries in a different manner, entries for each country follow a standard format, beginning with a general introduction, followed by a description of fleet strength in the first year of the time period covered, and detailed information on ship classes (dimensions, personnel, armament, launch date, fate, etc.) with illustrations and photographs. Index by ship name for each title.

Companion works:

Conway's all the world's fighting ships, 1860–1905, ed. by Roger Chesneau and Eugene M. Kolesnik ; contrib., N.J.M. Campbell [et al.] (N.Y. : Mayflower Books, c1979. 440 p.).

Conway's all the world's fighting ships, 1906–1921, editorial director, Robert Gardiner ; ed., Randal Gray ... [et al.] (Annapolis, Md. : Naval Institute Pr., [1986], 1985. 439 p.).

Conway's all the world's fighting ships, 1922–1946, ed. by Roger Chesneau. (London : Conway Maritime Pr., 1980. 456 p.).

§ For more current information, see *Jane's fighting ships* (CJ594).   V765.C663

Flintham, Victor. Air wars and aircraft : a detailed record of air combat, 1945 to the present. N.Y. : Facts on File, c1990. 415 p. : ill.   **CJ593**

Describes wars and conflicts involving the use of military or, occasionally, civil aircraft. Chapters covering individual wars or conflicts are grouped geographically. Includes tables showing combat and support units involved; descriptions of aircraft markings; photographs of aircraft; and maps. Several appendixes (e.g., U.S., British, and Soviet military aircraft designations); bibliography; glossary; index.
                                                              UG630.F55 1990

Jane's fighting ships. 1916– . N.Y. : McGraw-Hill, [1916]– . Annual.   **CJ594**

Title varies: 1898–1904, *All the world's fighting ships*; 1905–15, *Fighting ships.*

Imprint varies.

Founded and for many years ed. by F.T. Jane.

Arranged alphabetically by country, subdivided by class of ship. Gives numbers and names of ships in each class; builders; dates of laying down, launching, and completion; a photograph of a ship in the class; and specifications for the class. For each country, gives statistics, names of naval personnel, and strength of fleet. Includes a variety of other features (e.g., flags and ensigns, identification silhouettes). Indexes of named ships, classes, and aircraft.

§ Jane's also publishes numerous other handbooks of military systems, among them *Jane's armour and artillery* (1979/80–) and *Jane's military communications* (1989–90–). The Naval Institute has published similar handbooks, e.g., *The Naval Institute guide to combat fleets of the world* (1990/91– . Annapolis, Md. : Naval Inst. Pr., c1990–) and *The Naval Institute guide to world naval weapons systems* (1989/90– . Annapolis, Md. : Naval Inst. Pr., 1990–).

•Jane's Information Group produces many of the *Jane's* titles on CD-ROM, with current coverage.   VA40.J34

Knötel, Richard. Uniforms of the world : a compendium of army, navy, and air force uniforms, 1700–1937 / with 1,600 ill. of uniforms by Richard Knötel and Herbert Knötel, Jr. ; trans. from the 1956 ed. by Ronald G. Ball. Rev., brought up to date, and enl. by Herbert Knötel, Jr. and Herbert Sieg. N.Y. : Scribner, 1980. 483 p. : ill.   **CJ595**

Revised translation of the work publ. in 1956 under title: *Handbuch der Uniformkunde.*

Organized by armed forces division—army, navy, air force—then by country. Narrative descriptions with line drawings; colors are carefully noted in the text. Glossary. No index.

§ Another useful work in the area is I.T. Schick, *Battledress* (Boston : Little, Brown, 1978), which covers the period from 1700 to the 1970s. There are three useful series on the topic: Arco's "Key uniform guides," the "Blandford colour series" from Blandford Press, and Osprey's "Men-at-arms" series. Sample titles: Howard P. Davies, *United States infantry, Europe 1942–45* (N.Y. : Arco, 1974); Andrew Mollo, *Army uniforms of World War I* (Poole, Eng. : Blandford Pr., c1977); Terence Wise, *Armies of the Crusades* (London : Osprey, 1978).   UC480.K513

The military balance. 1959/60– . London : Brassey's for the International Inst. for Strategic Studies, 1959– . Annual.   **CJ596**

Title varies: 1959/60, *Soviet Union and the NATO powers : the military balance; 1960/61, Communist bloc and the free world : the military balance; 1961/62–1962/63, Communist bloc and the western alliances : the military balance.*

Publisher varies; previously issued by the Institute under its earlier name: Institute for Strategic Studies.

A standard statistical assessment of military forces and defense expenditures, presented in tabular form for countries and regional organizations such as NATO and the Warsaw Pact.

§ Supplemented by the Institute's *Strategic survey* (CJ601). Another useful title in this area is *World military expenditures and arms transfers* (Wash. : U.S. Arms Control and Disarmament Agency, 1976– . Superintendent of Documents classification: AC 1.16:), an annual publication with comparative data for a 10-year period in each volume.   UA15.L65

The nuclear weapons world : who, how & where / ed. by Patrick Burke. Westport, Conn. : Greenwood, 1988. 383 p. : ill.   **CJ597**

A handbook of information on the official nuclear weapons states and organizations of the world, in seven chapters covering the U.S., Soviet Union, U.K., France, People's Republic of China, NATO, and Warsaw Pact. Each chapter has two cross-referenced parts, the first describing the decision-making organizations (e.g., committees, agencies, contractors) and their decision-making processes, the second containing alphabetically arranged biographies of decision-makers. Each chapter ends with a list of references. Name and subject indexes.   U264.N84

Small, Melvin. Resort to arms : international and civil wars, 1816–1980 / Melvin Small, J. David Singer ... [et al.]. Beverly Hills, Calif. : Sage, 1982. 373 p.   **CJ598**

A rev. ed. of the authors' *The wages of war, 1816–1965* (N.Y. : Wiley, 1972).

A detailed statistical analysis of 224 wars. Two parts: international war and civil war; sections of each give rationale and procedures, data on the wars, and patterns at various levels. Appendixes provide notes and references on wars included in the work and a list of those not included. Bibliography. No index.   U21.2.S6

World armies / [ed. by] John Keegan. 2nd ed. Detroit : Gale, 1983. 688 p. : ill.   **CJ599**

1st ed., 1979.

Intends "to provide a portrait of each army in its domestic context, historical, social and political as well as military."—*Pref.* Alphabetically arranged and signed entries for each country include: history; strength and budget; command and constitutional status; role, commitment, deployment and recent operations; organization; recruitment, training, and reserves; equipment and arms industry; rank, dress and

distinctions; and current developments. Although much of the data is no longer current, this title remains useful for its historical discussions. No index.

§ For more up-to-date statistics, see *The military balance* (CJ596).   UA15.W68

Chronologies

Pemsel, Helmut. A history of war at sea : an atlas and chronology of conflict at sea from earliest times to the present / tr. by G. D. G. Smith. [Annapolis, Md.] : Naval Inst. Pr., [1978]. 176 p. : ill., maps.   **CJ600**

Tr. from the 1975 German ed., *Von Salamis bis Okinawa.* (Munich : J. F. Lehmanns, 1975).

1st English-language ed. publ. as *Atlas of naval warfare* (London : Arms and Armour Press, 1977).

Chronicles armed conflicts at sea from the Persian Wars to the Yom Kippur War of 1973 and stresses fleet engagements rather than single ship encounters. Features many battle maps and line drawings of ships. Includes several appendixes (ship catalog of the Iliad, Allied shipping losses in World War II, etc.). Bibliography. Index.   D27.P2713

Yearbooks

Strategic survey. 1966– . London : International Inst. for Strategic Studies, 1966– . Annual.   **CJ601**

1966–71 issued by the Institute under its earlier name: Institute for Strategic Studies.

Supplements *The military balance* (CJ596), giving narrative summaries of the strategic situation in countries and regions of the world. Includes chronology.   U162.S77

World armaments and disarmament : SIPRI yearbook. 1972– . Stockholm : Almqvist & Wiksell ; N.Y. : Humanities Pr., 1972– . Annual.   **CJ602**

Continues: *SIPRI yearbook of world armaments and disarmament*, 1968/69–71.

Issued by the Stockholm International Peace Research Institute.

Attempts to provide factual and statistical information on the world's armaments and efforts to control arms proliferation. Includes signed essays on a variety of topics (e.g., weapons, military expenditures, arms trade, armed conflicts, arms control). Appendixes offer summaries of and data on major multilateral arms control agreements and a chronology of relevant events in the previous year. Subject index.

§ A cumulative index for 1968–1979 is useful for access to early volumes (London : Taylor & Francis; distr. by Crane, Russak & Co., 1980. 90 p.).   UA10.S69

Atlases

Kidron, Michael. The war atlas : armed conflict—armed peace / Michael Kidron and Dan Smith. N.Y. : Simon & Schuster, 1983. 128 p. : maps in color ; 26 cm.   **CJ603**

Graphic representation on 40 two-page colored maps of the wars and military situation since 1945. Source notes and comments on sources; bibliography.   G1046.R1K5

Individual countries

United States

Bibliography

Champion, Brian. Advanced weapons systems : an annotated bibliography of the cruise missile, MX missile, laser and space weapons, and stealth technology. N.Y. : Garland, 1985. 206 p.
CJ604

Intended for a wide audience, from general readers to those with a substantial background in science and technology. The citations, mostly to scholarly and professional journals and newspapers, are arranged in individual chapters on specific weapons. Within chapters, organization is chronological to show how particular weapons systems have developed. Author and subject indexes.   Z6724.W4C47

Fredriksen, John C. Shield of republic, sword of empire : a bibliography of United States military affairs, 1783–1846. N.Y. : Greenwood, [1990]. 433 p. (Bibliographies and indexes in American history, no. 15).   **CJ605**

A topical arrangement of 6,783 books, articles, and some state and federal publications covering the period from the Revolution through the Mexican War. In five sections: (1) a general overview of the period; (2) U.S. Army; (3) U.S. Navy; (4) Militia, Canada, Indians; (5) biographies. Subsections for wars and battles, and for contemporary accounts. Cross-references; indexes of authors/titles and subjects.

§ Serves as a companion to the author's *Free trade and sailor's rights* (Westport, Conn. : Greenwood, c1985. 399 p.).   Z1249.M5F73

Lawrence, Robert M. Strategic Defense Initiative : bibliography and research guide. Boulder, Colo. : Westview Pr. ; London : Mansell, 1987. 352 p.   **CJ606**

Less a research guide than a literature survey, this work's chief value lies in its bibliographies that cite some 1,000 items. 84 key citations (with substantial abstracts) occur in chapters summarizing writings favoring SDI, those opposing it, and works providing technical background. Includes documents and treaties related to SDI and arms control, and a glossary of acronyms and terminology. No index.

UG743.L38

Moran, John B. Creating a legend : the complete record of writing about the United States Marine Corps. Chicago : Moran Andrews, [1973]. 681 p. : ill.   **CJ607**

Written for Marines by an ex-Marine officer. Aims to include everything written about the Marine Corps: books, government documents, articles, plays, poems, short stories, songs, children's books, and movies. Entries, some with brief annotations, in ten subject chapters (e.g., World War II, career Marines), further subdivided by topic. Author index.   Z6725.U5M67

Research guides in military studies. N.Y. : Greenwood, 1988–1993. v. 1–6. (In progress).   **CJ608**

Contents: no. 1, The peacetime army, 1900–1941, by Marvin Fletcher (1988. 177 p.); no. 2, Special operations and elite units 1939–1988, by Roger A. Beaumont (1988. 243 p.); no. 3, The late 19th century U.S. Army, 1865–1898 : a research guide, by Joseph G. Dawson III (1990. 252 p.); no. 4, U.S. military logistics, 1607–1991, by Charles R. Shrader (1992. 356 p.); no. 5, Celluloid wars, by Frank Joseph Wetta, and Stephen J. Curley (1992. 296 p.); no. 6, Military intelligence, 1870–1991, by Jonathan M. House (1993. 165 p.); no. 7, The militia and the national guard in America since colonial times, by Jerry Cooper (1993. 185 p.).

A series of annotated bibliographies on a variety of military topics. Number of entries, arrangement, and coverage vary. Most volumes have subject and author indexes.

Smith, Myron J. American naval bibliography. Metuchen, N.J. : Scarecrow, 1972–74. 5 v.   **CJ609**

Contents: v. 1, Navies in the American Revolution : bibliography (1973. 219 p.); v. 2, The American Navy, 1789–1860 : a bibliography (1974. 489 p.); v. 3, American Civil War navies : a bibliography (1972. 347 p.); v. 4, The American Navy, 1865–1918 : a bibliography (1974. 372 p.); v. 5, The American Navy, 1918–1941 : a bibliography (1974. 429 p.).

Bibliographies of books, journal articles, scholarly papers, government publications, theses, and dissertations. Entries cite English-language sources (except for some materials in other languages in v. 1) and occasionally have very brief annotations. Subject index in each volume.

§ Continued by Smith's *The United States Navy and Coast Guard, 1946–1983* (CJ610).   Z1242.S63

———————— The United States Navy and Coast Guard, 1946–1983 : a bibliography of English-language works and 16mm films / comp. by Myron J. Smith, Jr. ; foreword by E.R. Zumwalt, Jr. ; historical note by John D.H. Kane, Jr. Jefferson, N.C. : McFarland, 1984. 539 p.   **CJ610**

Includes English-language books, articles, research projects, reports, government documents, theses, and dissertations. Citations (some briefly annotated) arranged in six topical chapters (e.g., reference works, balance of power and arms control). Separate chapter on films. Author and subject indexes.

§ Continues the author's *American naval bibliography* (CJ609).
Z1249.N3S63

United States Military Academy. The centennial of the United States Military Academy at West Point, New York, 1802–1902. Wash. : U.S. Govt. Print. Off., 1904. 2 v. : ill.   **CJ611**

Repr.: N.Y. : Greenwood, 1969.

Comp. by E. S. Holden and W. L. Ostrander.

Contents: v. 1, Addresses and histories; v. 2, Statistics and bibliographies.

Originally issued as House Document no. 789, 58th Congress, 2nd session.

In spite of its title, v. 2 does not provide statistics but contains extensive bibliographies of West Point, arranged chronologically for 1694–1902; of the U.S. Military Academy, arranged chronologically for 1776–1902; and of the writings of Academy graduates, 1802–1902, arranged alphabetically. No index.   U410.L1A2

Manuscripts; archives

American women and the U.S. armed forces : a guide to the records of military agencies in the National Archives relating to American women / comp. by Charlotte Palmer Seeley ; rev. by Virginia C. Purdy and Robert Gruber. Wash. : National Archives and Records Administration, 1992. 355 p. : ill. **CJ612**

Serves as a guide to holdings of the National Archives that "discuss women as wives and mothers of soldiers, suppliers of military goods and services, and participants in and victims of war."—*Pref.* Pt. 1 contains references to federal records, arranged by National Archives record group number; pt. 2 lists related materials in presidential libraries. Entries describe the records and give examples of relevant documents. Includes references to some photographs. Appendixes list acronyms, microfilm publications cited, National Archives regional archives, and give the War Department Decimal Classification Scheme (used from 1944 to the 1960s). Index refers to paragraph numbers.
U21.75.S44

Paszek, Lawrence J. United States Air Force history : a guide to documentary sources. Wash. : Off. of Air Force History, 1973. 245 p. : ill.   **CJ613**

Dated but still useful. Locates and describes more than 700 collections of primary and secondary documents on the Air Force. In five sections: (1) official Air Force depositories; (2) National Archives, Federal Records Centers, and presidential libraries; (3) university collections; (4) Library of Congress, federal and local government depositories and historical societies; (5) other sources on astronautics and aviation in general. Glossary. Index to depositories and general index.

CD3034.5.P37

Encyclopedias

Historical dictionary of the U.S. Air Force / ed. by Charles D. Bright ; Robin Higham, advisory ed. N.Y. : Greenwood, 1992. 713 p., [14] p. of plates : ill. **CJ614**

Covers all subjects relevant to the Air Force and its antecedent organizations. Signed entries are alphabetically arranged and end with bibliographical references. Includes a brief history of the Air Force and a list of contributors. Cross-references; general index. UG633.B75

Dictionaries

Air University. Aerospace Studies Institute. The United States Air Force dictionary / ed. by Woodford Agee Heflin. Princeton, N.J. : Van Nostrand, [1956]. 578 p. **CJ615**

Despite its age, still useful for words and abbreviations used historically and currently in the U.S. Air Force. Includes specialized terms in the many fields of aeronautics, aerodynamics, meteorology, electronics, nuclear energy, and supersonics. UG630.U637

Elting, John Robert. A dictionary of soldier talk / John R. Elting, Dan J. Cragg, Ernest L. Deal. N.Y. : Scribner's, 1984. 383 p. **CJ616**

Offers brief definitions of U.S. Army language, with an appendix of Navy and Marine Corps terms. Indicates historical as well as current usage. Cross-references. Emphasizes slang, and includes the "bawdy ... profane, [and] foul."—*Introd.* Bibliography. U24.E38

Gutzman, Philip C. Dictionary of military, defense contractor & troop slang acronyms. Santa Barbara, Calif. : ABC-Clio, c1990. 392 p. **CJ617**

Offers approximately 32,000 initialisms, acronyms, and abbreviations used by the U.S. military and the defense industries. U26.G88

Noel, John Vavasour. Naval terms dictionary / by John V. Noel, Jr. and Edward L. Beach. 5th ed. Annapolis, Md. : Naval Institute Pr., c1988. 316 p. **CJ618**

1st ed., 1952; 4th ed., 1978.

Provides brief definitions for terms and phrases in current usage. Entries contain cross-references. Excludes most acronyms, as they can be found in the *Dictionary of naval abbreviations* comp. by Bill Wedertz (CJ621). V23.N6

The United States Army : a dictionary / ed. by Peter Tsouras, Bruce W. Watson, Susan M. Watson. N.Y. : Garland, 1990. 898 p. (Garland reference library of social science, v. 696). **CJ619**

Intended for serious researchers. Defines major terms in use during the period since World War II, with emphasis on recent vocabulary. In three major sections: (1) a list of acronyms; (2) definitions, with extensive cross-references, ending with source notes; and (3) a bibliography.

§ Two companion volumes by Bruce W. Watson and Susan M. Watson:

The United States Air Force : a dictionary (N.Y. : Garland, 1992. 861 p.).

The United States Navy : a dictionary (N.Y. : Garland, 1991. 948 p.), which includes a separate list of acronyms for major types of ships. UA25.U49

Waldman, Harry. The dictionary of SDI. Wilmington, Del. : Scholarly Resources, 1988. 182 p. : ill. **CJ620**

"Nearly 800 items are defined in the areas of ballistic missile defense, arms control, research and development, countermoves to defense, Soviet capabilities, the roles of U.S. allies, personalities in the

field, and SDI software and hardware."—*Introd.* Most definitions are brief, although some are a page or more in length. Numerous drawings, diagrams, charts, and tables. Also includes relevant treaties and documents, and a list of the members of the Defense Technologies Study Team. UG743.W35

Wedertz, Bill. Dictionary of naval abbreviations. 3rd ed. Annapolis, Md. : Naval Institute Pr., 1984. 330 p. **CJ621**

1st ed., 1970; 2nd ed., 1977.

Contains abbreviations and acronyms currently in use in the U.S. Navy. V23.W43

Zurick, Timothy. Army dictionary and desk reference. Harrisburg, Pa. : Stackpole Books, c1992. 263 p. : ill. **CJ622**

"Attempts to catalog the working language of the Army."—*Pref.* Each brief definition of an acronym or term is followed by an acronym denoting field of usage (e.g., MI for military intelligence). Contains numerous reference tables; the Code of Conduct; sample memorandum and letters. UA25.Z86

Directories

Cragg, Dan. Guide to military installations. 3rd ed. Harrisburg, Pa. : Stackpole Books, c1991. 470 p. : ill., maps. **CJ623**

1st ed., 1983; 2nd ed., 1988.

Provides coverage of overseas bases. Omits Coast Guard, National Guard, and Reserve facilities. In three sections: (1) U.S. installations (alphabetical by state, then by service branch); (2) overseas installations (alphabetical by country, then by service branch); and (3) maps (divided by service branch and geographic area) showing locations of bases mentioned. Narrative entries typically give base's history and mission, housing and schools, personal services (e.g., medical care, commissary), recreational facilities, and locale. Each also includes an address and, for U.S. bases, telephone number of office to contact for more information. Base index.

§ Complements William R. Evinger's *Directory of military bases in the U.S.* (CJ624). UC403.C7

Directory of military bases in the U.S. Phoenix : Oryx, 1991. 197 p. **CJ624**

Ed. by William R. Evinger.

"The only single source to comprehensively list the Army, Navy, Air Force, Marines, Coast Guard, National Guard, Reserve, and Joint Service Installations, as well as Department of Defense agencies, military camps and stations, recruiting offices, and command headquarters offices."—*Introd.* The main section lists bases/installations alphabetically by state and city. Brief entries indicate the facility's address and size, telephone numbers of key officers, number of personnel, expenditures, major units, history, and services for personnel and their families (e.g., housing, commissaries, recreational opportunities). List of abbreviations. Appendix of facilities that are candidates for possible closing or realignment. Indexed. UA26.A26

Johnson, Richard S. How to locate anyone who is or has been in the military : armed forces locator directory. 5th ed., completely rev. San Antonio, Tex. : Military Information Enterprises, c1993. 247 p. : ill. **CJ625**

1st ed., 1988; 4th ed., 1991.

Information on locating present, former, or retired members of the Air Force, Army, Coast Guard, Marine Corps, National Guard, and Reserves. In topical chapters (e.g., locating active duty military, locating people for a military reunion). Includes charts of service and social security numbers for individuals, and addresses and telephone numbers for military bases, posts, associations, federal and state offices, etc. Subject index. UA23.J58

United States Navy and Marine Corps bases, domestic / Paolo E. Coletta, ed., K. Jack Bauer, assoc. ed. Westport, Conn. : Greenwood, 1985. 740 p. **CJ626**

Lists by location in alphabetical order all "important and historically significant bases and facilities, extant and extinct. Each entry discusses the form and function of the base or facility and gives something of its history and development."—*Pref.* Entries include bibliographies of primary and secondary sources. Appendixes: listings of bases by subject, geographic area, and time. General index.

§ Companion work: *United States Navy and Marine Corps bases, overseas* (1985. 459 p.) *Bases, domestic* treats bases and facilities within U.S. boundaries; *Bases, overseas,* those in other countries.

VA67.U55

Handbooks

The Air Force officer's guide. 23rd ed (1976)– . Harrisburg, Pa. : Stackpole Books, c1976– . Irregular.   **CJ627**

Editor varies.

Continues: *The air officer's guide* (1948–7?).

Gives information on all aspects of life in the Air Force in four sections covering: (1) the Air Force officer (e.g., appointment and assignments, customs, uniforms and insignia); (2) career and advancement (e.g., officer evaluation system, educational system); (3) family (e.g., social life, life overseas); (4) the Air Force (e.g., organization). Appendixes list U.S. and overseas bases, professional reading, selected Air Force publications, selected acronyms and abbreviations, and provide photographs of U.S. Air Force aircraft. General index.

UG633.A1A49

Army lineage series. Wash. : Office of the Chief of Military History, U.S. Army : for sale by U.S. Govt. Print. Off., 1968–92. v. [1–8]. (In progress).   **CJ628**

Contents: [1] Armor-cavalry, by Mary Lee Stubbs and Stanley Russell Connor, pt. 1, Regular Army and Army Reserve (1968. 477 p.), and pt. 2, Army National Guard (1972. 297 p.); [2] Infantry, pt. 1, Regular Army, by John K. Mahon and Romana Danysh (2nd ed., 1972. 938 p.); [3] The Continental army, by Robert K. Wright, Jr. (1983. 451 p.); [4] Field artillery : Regular Army and Army Reserve, by Janice E. McKenney (1985. 761 p.); [5] Air defense artillery, by Janice E. McKenney (1985. 429 p.); [6] Aviation, by Wayne M. Dzwonchyk (1986. 155 p.); [7] Armies, corps, divisions, and separate brigades, by John B. Wilson (1987. 736 p.); [8] Military police, by Robert K. Wright, Jr. (1992. 226 p.).

Companion volumes provide history/campaigns, lineage, heraldic data, honors/decorations, and bibliographic information on individual Army units.

§ For unit bibliographies, *see also*: Charles E. Dornbusch, *Histories, personal narratives : United States Army* (Cornwallville, N.Y. : Hope Farm Pr., 1967. 399 p.); James T. Controvich, *United States Army unit histories* (Manhattan, Kan. : Military Affairs/Aerospace Historian, [1983]. 591 p.); George S. Pappas, *United States Army unit histories* (Rev. ed.; Carlisle Barracks, Pa. : U.S. Army Military History Institute, 1978–).

For unit bibliographies of other branches, *see*: United States. Office of Military History, *Unit histories of World War II : United States Army, Air Force, Marines, Navy* (Wash. : Office of the Chief of Military History, [1950]. 141 p.) and its *Supplement, 1951* (Wash. : Library Section, Special Services Div., Dept. of the Army, 1951. 50 p.); and Charles E. Dornbusch, *Unit histories of the United States Air Forces* (Hampton Bays, N.Y. : Hampton Books, 1958. 56 p.).

The Army officer's guide. 39th ed.– . [Harrisburg, Pa.] : Stackpole, [1977]– .   **CJ629**

Continues *Officer's guide* (1930–75).

Place of publication varies.

Serves as "a trustworthy and convenient first place of reference on matters of interest to the officer corps."—*Foreword, 46th ed., 1993.* While not an official U.S. Army publication, the work is supported by and contains contributions from Army personnel. Currently in five parts: (1) Selection of an Army career; (2) Your life and family (e.g., military courtesy, customs); (3) Building your career (e.g., Army schools, assignments); (4) Regulations at a glance (e.g., pay and allowances, uniforms); (5) The Army (e.g., organization and missions). Includes an appendix with additional duty descriptions, a list of acronyms, and color plates of medals and badges. General index.

U133.A6O48

Borklund, Carl W. U.S. defense and military fact book. Santa Barbara, Calif. : ABC-Clio, c1991. 293 p.   **CJ630**

Offers basic information on the U.S. Department of Defense in four chapters: (1) The defense budget; (2) Basic facts; (3) History, including a chronology of key events and biographies of key people; (4) References and resources. An appendix summarizes important documents detailing the organizational structure, authority, and responsibilities of the department. Index.   UA23.6.B67

Estes, Kenneth W. The Marine officer's guide. 5th ed. Annapolis : Naval Institute Pr., c1985. 523 p. : ill.   **CJ631**

1st ed., 1956. 4th ed., 1977, ed. by Robert Debs Heinl.

Describes the position and function of the Marine Corps within the national defense network; the history, traditions, social customs and usages of the Corps; career and professional matters for the new officer. Glossary. Index.   VE153.E85

Holt, Dean W. American military cemeteries : a comprehensive illustrated guide to the hallowed grounds of the United States, including cemeteries overseas. Jefferson, N.C. : McFarland, 1992. 512 p. : ill., maps.   **CJ632**

For each of the national military cemeteries gives location, founding, history, notables buried there, etc.; often includes a photograph or map. The introduction describes the history and operations of the National Cemetery System (NCS) of the Department of Veteran Affairs. Also contains entries for Confederate cemeteries; soldiers' lots; monuments; cemeteries no longer maintained by the NCS; national cemeteries maintained by the Department of the Army or the National Park Service (the latter are mostly Civil War battlefields); and American Battle Monuments Commission cemeteries and monuments. Lists of state veterans cemeteries; installations by state; NCS cemeteries by date of establishment; soldiers' lots, plots, and monuments by date of establishment. Appendixes also include descriptions of headstones and markers used, the Medal of Honor award, and Memorial Day orders. Name index; Medal of Honor recipient name index.

§ See also *American battle monuments : a guide to military cemeteries and monuments maintained by the American Battle Monuments Commission*, ed. by Elizabeth Nishiura (BF390).   UB393.H65

Mack, William P. Naval ceremonies, customs, and traditions / by William P. Mack and Royal W. Connell. 5th ed. Annapolis, Md. : Naval Inst. Pr., 1980. 386 p. : ill.   **CJ633**

1st ed., 1934; 4th ed., 1959. Previous eds. by Leland P. Lovette had title: *Naval customs, traditions & usage.*

Traces the historical development and describes the modern status of various traditions, ceremonies, customs, and usages for the United States Navy and Marine Corps. Devotes a chapter to the derivation of nautical words and naval expressions. Useful appendixes offer biographical sketches and further rules of etiquette. Bibliography; index.

V310.L6

Military uniforms in America : from the series produced by the Company of Military Historians / John R. Elting, ed. San Rafael, Calif. : Presidio Pr., 1974–1988. v. 1–4 : color ill. (In progress?).   **CJ634**

Vols. 3–4 ed. by Elting and Michael J. McAfee.

Place of publication varies.

Contents: v. [1], The era of the American Revolution, 1755–1795; v. 2, Years of growth, 1796–1851; v. 3, Long endure, the Civil War period, 1852–1867; v. 4, The modern era—from 1868.

Chronologically arranged color plates depict period uniforms by military unit. Accompanying text describes parts of the uniform and their functions, weapons and military equipment, and the history of unit depicted. Vols. 1–3 contain glossaries; general index in each volume.

§ Another, briefer, volume covering American military uniforms is Michael Bowers, *North American fighting uniforms* (Poole, Eng. : Blandford Pr. ; N.Y. : distr. by Sterling Publ., 1984). *See also* Richard Knötel and Herbert Knötel, Jr., *Uniforms of the world* (CJ595).

UC480.C6

The naval officer's guide / William P. Mack with Thomas D. Paulsen. 10th ed. Annapolis, Md. : Naval Inst. Pr., 1991. 511 p. : ill.   **CJ635**

    1st ed., 1943; 9th ed., 1983. 1st–8th, ed. by Arthur A. Ageton.

    Provides information and advice for U.S. Navy officers on military and ship organization, conduct, assignments, education, sea duty, traditions and customs, etc. Includes appendixes giving competencies for officer accession programs, lists of recommended reading, the Code of Conduct, and essentials of military law. Bibliography. Subject index.   V133.A6

Yearbooks

American defense annual. 1985–1986– . Lexington, Mass. : Lexington Books, c1985– . Annual.   **CJ636**

    Sponsored by the Mershon Center at Ohio State University.

    Offers "an authoritative annual assessment of major issues in American defense policy."—*Foreword (1985)*. Each volume features articles (written by authors from a broad political spectrum) covering standard topics (e.g., the budget, forces, personnel, arms control) as well as topics of current interest. Usually contains a defense chronology and a bibliography for the previous year. Extensively illustrated with photographs, tables, and charts. Index.   UA23.A1A47

Biography

Brown, Russell K. Fallen in battle : American general officer combat fatalities from 1775. N.Y. : Greenwood, 1988. 243 p.   **CJ637**

    Gives brief biographical data, career highlights, and circumstances of death of each military or naval general officer killed in battle or its aftermath, from colonial times through Vietnam. Includes Confederate fatalities. Appendixes contain several statistical tables and descriptive listings (e.g., deaths by war or campaign, noncombat fatalities). Bibliography. Name index.   E181.B886

Callahan, Edward William. List of officers of the Navy of the United States and of the Marine Corps from 1775 to 1900 / comp. from the official records of the Navy Dept. ; ed. by Edward W. Callahan. N.Y. : L.R. Hamersly & Co., 1901. 749 p.   **CJ638**

    Repr.: N.Y. : Haskell House, 1969.

    Subtitle: Comprising a complete register of all present and former commissioned, warranted, and appointed officers of the United States Navy, and of the Marine Corps, regular and volunteer.

    Entries, in two separate alphabetical lists, for officers of the Navy and, since 1798, of the Marine Corps. Each entry shows date of entrance into service, ranks, and manner of leaving service. Also has a section listing superintendents; midshipmen, acting midshipmen, and naval cadets; and cadet engineers at the U.S. Naval Academy. Includes a variety of other information (e.g., officers, 1775–98; Secretaries of the Navy; Chiefs of Bureaus; lists of vessels, 1797–1900). No index.   V11.U7C2

Cogar, William B. Dictionary of admirals of the U.S. Navy. Annapolis, Md. : Naval Institute Pr., c1989–91. 2 v. : ill. (In progress).   **CJ639**

    Contents: v. 1, 1862–1900; v. 2, 1901–1918.

    "Intends to provide as reliable and as complete information as possible on every admiral of the United States Navy" (*Introd.*) since 1862, when the rank of admiral was adopted. Entries arranged alphabetically within chronological volumes, give personal data, a list of ranks and dates of promotions, a chronological career summary, career highlights, descriptions and locations of personal papers, and a bibliography of works by or about the officer. Includes an essay explaining ranks in the U.S. Navy, information on administration and management with names of bureau chiefs, a list of abbreviations, and a bibliographical note.

    § Other sources of detailed biographical information on admirals and other naval officers include three works by James C. Bradford: *Command under sail* (Annapolis, Md. : Naval Inst. Pr., 1985), *Captains of the old steam navy* (1986), and *Admirals of the new steel navy* (1990). *See also* Charles E. Claghorn, *Naval officers of the American Revolution* (Metuchen, N.J. : Scarecrow, 1988).   V62.U64

Cullum, George Washington. Biographical register of the officers and graduates of the U.S. Military Academy at West Point, N.Y : from its establishment in 1802 to 1890, with the early history of the United States Military Academy. 3rd ed., rev. and extended. Boston : Houghton-Mifflin, 1891. 3 v.   **CJ640**

    1st ed. covered the period to 1867; 2nd ed., to Jan. 1, 1879.

    A chronological list, with brief biographical and service history information. Name indexes.

    Supplements continue the volume numbering of the basic set: v. 4, 1890–1900, ed. by E. S. Holden; v. 5, 1900–10, ed. by Lieut. Charles Braden; v. 6, A and B, 1910–20, ed. by Col. Wirt Robinson; v. 7, 1920–30, ed. by Capt. W. H. Donaldson; v. 8, 1930–40, ed. by Lt.Col. E. E. Farman; v. 9, 1940–50, ed. by Col. Charles N. Branham. Subtitle varies slightly.   U410.H52

Dictionary of American military biography / Roger J. Spiller, ed.; Joseph G. Dawson III, assoc. ed.; T. Harry Williams, consulting ed. Westport, Conn. : Greenwood, 1984. 3 v. (1368 p.)   **CJ641**

    Presents lengthy biographical essays (about 1,500 words each) on some 400 individuals important in U.S. military history, including Native Americans and selected civilians. Entries are signed, cross-referenced, and end with brief bibliographies. Appendixes include a chronology of American military developments, as well as lists of American military ranks, of military units, and of individuals by birthplace, conflict, and service. General index.

    § *Webster's American military biographies*, ed. by Robert McHenry (CJ648), has more entries, but fewer details in each.   U52.D53

DuPre, Flint O. U.S. Air Force biographical dictionary. N.Y. : Watts, [1965]. 273 p.   **CJ642**

    Brief biographical sketches of outstanding members of the Air Force.

    § Companion volumes, both by Karl Schuon: *U.S. Marine Corps biographical dictionary : the corps' fighting men, what they did, where they served* (N.Y. : Watts, 1963. 278 p.); *U.S. Navy biographical dictionary* (N.Y. : F. Watts, 1964. 277 p.).   UG633.D8

Hawkins, Walter L. African American generals and flag officers : biographies of over 120 blacks in the United States military. Jefferson, N.C. : McFarland, c1993. 264 p. : ill.   **CJ643**

    Offers biographics of "all African American officers [both men and women] who have attained the rank of general or its naval equivalent."—*Introd.* Entries are arranged alphabetically and include biographical information, service record, awards and decorations, and, typically, a photograph. Chronology of African Americans in the military. Appendixes include names by rank, birth state, and colleges or universities. General index does not include personal names.   E181.H38

Heitman, Francis Bernard. Historical register and dictionary of the United States Army from its organization, Sept. 29, 1789, to March 2, 1903 : publ. under act of Congress approved March 2, 1903. Wash. : U.S. Govt. Print. Off., 1903. 2 v.   **CJ644**

    57th Cong., 2nd Session. House doc. 446.

    Repr.: Urbana : Univ. of Illinois Pr., 1965.

    An earlier ed. had title: *Historical register of the United States Army* (Wash. : The National Tribune, 1890) and covered 1789–1889.

    Vol. 1 is primarily an alphabetical dictionary of officers of the U.S. Army, giving their service records with some preliminary lists. Vol. 2 includes an alphabetical list of officers of the regular army who were killed, wounded in action, or taken prisoner; strength of the army and losses in the several wars; dates of certain wars, campaigns; alphabetical list of battles, actions, etc., 1775–1902; chronological list of battles, actions; list of forts, batteries, named camps, redoubts, reservations, general hospitals, national cemeteries, etc.; and various statistical tables. No index.

§ *See also* William Henry Powell, *List of officers of the army of the United States from 1779 to 1900* (CJ646).   U11.U5H6

——————— Historical register of officers of the Continental Army during the war of the Revolution, April 1775 to Dec. 1783. New, rev., and enl. ed. Wash. : Rare Book Shop Pub. Co., 1914. 685 p.   **CJ645**

Repr.: Baltimore : Genealogical Pub. Co., 1973.

1st ed., 1893.

An alphabetical register of officers, including service records. Various supplemental lists (aides-de-camp to General Washington, French officers who served with the American army, etc.). No index.   E255.H48

Powell, William Henry. List of officers of the army of the United States from 1779–1900 : embracing a register of all appointments ... in the volunteer service during the Civil War and of volunteer officers in the service of the United States June 1, 1900, comp. from the official records. N.Y. : Hamersly, 1900. 863 p.   **CJ646**

Repr. : Detroit : Gale, 1967.

A list of officers, 1779–1815, is arranged by years, followed by the army list, 1815–1900, which is arranged alphabetically by name with brief biographical information. Numerous other lists include officers of volunteers, general officers of the Revolution, etc. Name index for the chronological listing. Known also as the *United States army list.*

§ For additional information, *see also* Francis Bernard Heitman, *Historical register and dictionary of the United States Army ...* (CJ644).   U11.U5P7

——————— Officers of the army and navy (regular) who served in the Civil War / ed. by William H. Powell and Edward Shippen. Philadelphia : Hamersley, 1892. 487 p. : ports.   **CJ647**

Biographies of officers who served on the side of the Union during the Civil War. Entries (each with a photograph or portrait) include dates of birth and death (if available), education, family background, prewar or preservice life, military record, and postwar or postservice activities. Name index.

§ Companion work: *Officers of the army and navy (volunteer) who served in the Civil War* (1893. 419 p.).   E467.P88

Webster's American military biographies / ed. by Robert McHenry. Springfield, Mass. : G. & C. Merriam, 1978. 548 p.   **CJ648**

Repr.: N.Y. : Dover, 1984.

Presents more than 1,000 biographies of persons important to the military history of the nation, including "not only the battlefield heroes and the great commanders, but also the frontier scouts, nurses, Indian leaders, historians, explorers, shipbuilders, and inventors ... ."—*Introd.* Biographies average 450 words and cover the entire career. Bibliographies are not provided. Addenda section offers lists of relevant officials (e.g., Secretaries of War, commanders of NATO) and chief service officers; chronological lists of wars, battles, expeditions, etc., for the Army, Navy, and Marine Corps; and a listing of career categories (e.g., engineers, physicians).

§ The *Dictionary of American military biography* (CJ641) has fewer but more detailed entries.   U52.W4

Decorations and insignia

See Orders and decorations in Section AL.

Ships

Dictionary of American naval fighting ships. Wash. : Navy Dept., Office of the Chief of Naval Operations, Naval History Division, 1959–1981. 8 v. : ill.   **CJ649**

Superintendent of Documents classification: D 207.10.

Editors and issuing body vary.

"An alphabetical arrangement of the ships of the Continental and United States navies, with a historical sketch of each one."—*Pref.* Appendixes appear in v. 1–7: in v. 1, chronological listings of battleships, cruisers, submarines, torpedo boats and destroyers, escort vessels; in v. 2, aircraft carriers; Confederate forces afloat (historical sketches); in v. 3, historic ship exhibits; monitors; Civil War naval ordnance; in v. 4, amphibious warfare ships; aviation auxiliaries; destroyer tenders; ships of the line; classification of naval ships and service craft; in v. 5, stone fleet; mine craft; new ships; aircraft; in v. 6, submarine chasers; eagle-class patrol craft; in v. 7, tank landing ships. Lists of abbreviations; bibliographies.

Beginning 1991, supplemented by enhanced narratives for ships previously included in v. 1 (Wash. : Naval Historical Center. Ed. by James L. Mooney). Arranged alphabetically by name of ship.

§ For detailed, illustrated guides to current U.S. ships and naval aircraft, see *The Naval Institute guide to the ships and aircraft of the U.S. fleet* (15th ed. Annapolis, Md. : Naval Institute Pr., 1993) and *The almanac of seapower* (Arlington, Va. : Navy League of the United States, 1983–).   VA61.A53

Canada

Cooke, O. A. The Canadian military experience, 1867–1983 : a bibliography. 2nd ed. Ottawa : Directorate of History, Dept. of Nat. Defense, 1984. 329 p. (Canada. Department of National Defense. Directorate of History. Monograph series, 2).   **CJ650**

1st ed., 1979, had title *The Canadian military experience, 1867–1967.*

Prefatory matter and indexes in English and French; title also in French.

Contains unannotated citations to English- or French-language books, pamphlets, government publications, and journal titles (but not individual articles). Entries in sections covering bibliographies; defense policy and general works; naval forces, land forces, and air forces (each subdivided by time period through 1967); and the unified forces since 1968. Subject, person, and service, branch, formation, and unit indexes.   Z1387.M54C66

Europe

Great Britain

Chant, Christopher. The handbook of British regiments. London ; N. Y. : Routledge, 1988. 313 p.   **CJ651**

Aims "to trace the order of battle and antecedents of the regular corps and regiments of the current British army."—*Introd.* Presents corps and regiments in order of military precedence and lists for each: badge, name and numbers of the 1881 regiments that went into the present regiment, current colonel-in-chief and colonel, battle honors, administrative headquarters and museum, marches, mottoes, nicknames, full dress uniform, allied and affiliated regiments, and regiment history. List of Territorial Army units. Index to regiments and corps.   UA649.C47

Gander, Terry. Encyclopaedia of the modern British Army. 3rd ed. Wellingborough, Eng. : P. Stephens, 1986. 312 p. : ill. **CJ652**

1st ed., 1980; 2nd ed., 1982.

Other branches of the British armed services are treated by: Terry Gander, *Encyclopaedia of the modern Royal Air Force* (2nd ed. Wellingborough : P. Stephens ; N.Y. : Sterling Publ. Co., 1987. 256 p.) and Paul Beaver, *Encyclopaedia of the modern Royal Navy : including the Fleet Air Arm and Royal Marines* (3rd ed., 1987. 329 p.).

These companion titles provide a wealth of information about the military services of Great Britain (e.g., history since 1945, organization, weapons and equipment, uniforms and insignia). Each includes illustrations and an index. UA649.G26x

Uden, Grant. A dictionary of British ships and seamen / Grant Uden and Richard Cooper. N.Y. : St. Martin's, 1980. 591p. : ill., maps. **CJ653**

Treats the British naval heritage from early times to 1980. Alphabetically arranged entries, with illustrations and cross-references, cover terms, phrases, people, ships, equipment, wars, and battles.

VK57.U33

Union of Soviet Socialist Republics

Bibliography

Green, William C. Soviet nuclear weapons policy : a research and bibliographic guide. Boulder, Colo. : Westview Pr., 1987. 399 p. **CJ654**

Designed for Sovietologists and strategic analysts, but also useful for those interested in Soviet nuclear weapons policy. Contains an introductory essay and seven topical chapters of extensively annotated entries for books, articles, and reports. Six of the chapters cite post-war materials with a Western—primarily U.S.—perspective; most works cited were published after 1970. The seventh chapter is a guide to Soviet sources. Author index. UA770.G735

Smith, Myron J. The Soviet navy, 1941–1978 : a guide to sources in English. Santa Barbara, Calif. : ABC-Clio, 1980. 211 p. (War/peace bibliography series, no. 9). **CJ655**

Companion volumes:
The Soviet army, 1939–1980 (1982. 441 p.).
The Soviet air and strategic rocket forces, 1939–1980 (1981. 321 p.).

Classed subject bibliographies of English-language books, periodical articles, government documents, dissertations, theses, and reports. Each main section begins with an introduction, is usually subdivided by type of publication, and often ends with a concluding note on related sources in other sections of the work. Includes reference works and appendixes giving some or all of the following: late entries, journals consulted, charts, brief biographies of relevant individuals. Author index in each volume. Z6835.R9S64

Encyclopedias

Menaul, Stewart. The illustrated encyclopedia of the strategy, tactics and weapons of Russian military power / comp. by Stewart Menaul ; [ed. by Ray Bonds]. [New ed.]. N.Y. : St. Martin's Pr., 1980. 249 p. : ill. (some col.), coat of arms, col. maps, ports. **CJ656**

Earlier ed. published in 1976 under title: *The Soviet war machine: an encyclopedia of Russian military equipment and strategy* (London : Salamander Books, 1976). Title of 1980 British ed. (London : Salamander Books) varied slightly.

Though now dated, provides historically useful organizational charts, color photographs and illustrations, line drawings, and model

specifications of Soviet military aircraft, ships, armored vehicles, missiles, and other weapons. Also includes uniforms. Index of weapons systems. UA770.M46

The military-naval encyclopedia of Russia and the Soviet Union / ed. by David R. Jones. Gulf Breeze, Fla. : Academic International Pr., 1978–84. 4 v. : ill. **CJ657**

Contents: v.1–4, "A" (gliders)–Adzhariia.

Intended as a comprehensive encyclopedia of military leaders; ships, regiments, and formations; weapons; battles, campaigns and wars; military institutions; armed forces; treaties, etc. Lengthy, signed articles are alphabetically arranged; almost all have bibliographies. Originally planned to be in about 50 volumes, with indexes and supplements.

Publisher states that publication is expected to continue under (tentative) title *Central Eurasia military-naval encyclopedia*, ed. by John C. K. Daly. UA770.M56

Polmar, Norman. The Naval Institute guide to the Soviet navy. 5th ed. Annapolis, Md. : Naval Institute Pr., c1991. 492 p. : ill. (some col.). **CJ658**

1st ed., 1970, was an updated and expanded translation of *Die Seerustung der Sowjetunion* (Munich : J.F. Lehmann, 1964); 2nd, 3rd, and 4th ed. (1986) had title: *Guide to the Soviet navy*.

Covers all aspects of the Soviet Navy in topical chapters (e.g., missions and tactics, personnel and training, submarines, naval electronics). Provides data and illustrations or photographs for ships, naval aircraft, and naval weapons. Includes a glossary and appendixes giving names of senior naval officers; order of battle, 1945–90; ships transferred to other countries; and flags and insignia. General index; ship name and ship class index. VA573.P598

Sovetskaia voennaia entsiklopediia / [In-t voen. istorii] ; Gl. red. komis., Marshal Sov. Soiuza A. A. Grechko ... [et al.]. Moskva : Voenizdat, 1976–1980. 8 v. : ill. **CJ659**

Emphasizes post-revolutionary military history, biography, theory, and technology. Many articles are signed, cross-referenced, and contain brief bibliographies. A 2nd ed., ed. by M. A. Moiseev, began publication in 1990, but only two volumes of a projected thirteen were issued when publication was suspended following the August 1991 coup attempt.

§ A useful single volume work is *Voennyi entsiklopedicheskii slovar'*, ed. by S. F. Akhromeev (2nd ed. Moscow : Voen. izd-vo, 1986. 863 p.). U24.S72

Soviet military encyclopedia. Abridged English language ed. / ed. and trans. by William C. Green and W. Robert Reeves. Boulder, Colo. : Westview, 1993. 4 v. : ill. **CJ660**

Contents: v. 1–3, A–Z; v. 4, Index.

An abridged English ed. of *Sovetskaia voennaia entsiklopediia* (CJ659).

"Includes the most crucial theoretical and descriptive articles, with enough of the others present to convey the flavor of the Soviet original."—*Introd.* Arranges entries in English alphabetical order, giving entry term in English and in transliterated Russian, a translation of the complete article, author, location in the Soviet edition, references, and illustrations. Omits maps and photographs but provides their captions. Index volume can be used both with this abridged translation and with the original Russian edition: articles in the English version are listed in English alphabetic order with Russian titles in brackets, then articles in the Russian original are listed in Russian order with English titles in brackets. U24.S69

Yearbooks

Soviet armed forces review annual. v. 1 (1977)– . Gulf Breeze, Fla. : Academic Internat. Pr., 1977– . Annual. **CJ661**

Designed to assemble and organize in a standard format the available public information on Soviet military affairs, with analytical topical discussion, documentation, and bibliography. Consists of surveys of the current military situation, signed reviews by specialists, documents, and bibliography. No index.

Vol. 12 (publ. 1993; covering 1988) states in the preface: "future volumes ... will address the military aspects of the unfolding situation in the USSR and its eventual breakup. ... this will require some reorganization of the volumes, a broader range of materials presented, and a title change beginning with the volume covering 1992."

UA770.S657

ARMS CONTROL AND PEACE RESEARCH

Bibliography

Arms control and disarmament : a quarterly bibliography with abstracts and annotations. v. 1 (Winter 1964/65)–9, no. 2 (Spring 1973). Wash. : U.S. Govt. Prt. Off., 1964–1973. Quarterly.   **CJ662**

Comp. by the Arms Control and Disarmament Bibliography Section of the Library of Congress. Ceased publication with issue for Spring 1973.

Helpful for historical research. Originally included abstracts or brief annotations of books, periodical articles, government documents, and publications of international organizations "selected from a survey of the literature received by the Library of Congress that is likely to be available in the larger research and public libraries in the United States."—*Pref.* Beginning with v. 2, no. 1, Winter 1965/66, coverage was extended to include abstracts and annotations of current literature in French, German, and Russian, as well as of materials in English. Classed arrangement within issues; cumulated subject and author indexes for each volume.   JX1974.A1A7

Atkins, Stephen E. Arms control and disarmament, defense and military, international security, and peace : an annotated guide to sources, 1980–1987. Santa Barbara, Calif. : ABC-Clio, c1989. 411 p.   **CJ663**

Presents annotated citations for 1,596 monographs, hearings, papers, and reports (mostly English-language) published 1980–87. Within topical chapters (Arms control and disarmament, Defense and military, International security, and Peace) entries are alphabetically arranged by type of material (e.g., bibliographies, guidebooks, hearings, newsletters). List of publishers. Author/title and subject indexes.

Z6464.D6A85

Boulding, Elise. Bibliography on world conflict and peace / comp. by Elise Boulding, J. Robert Passmore, and Robert Scott Gassler. 2nd ed. Boulder, Colo. : Westview Pr., 1979. 168 p.   **CJ664**

1st ed., 1974.

Publ. in cooperation with the Consortium on Peace Research and the Section on the Sociology of World Conflicts of the American Sociological Association.

Focuses on English-language literature, published 1945–78, on world conflict, armament and disarmament, nonviolence, and peace research. Unannotated citations arranged alphabetically within four sections: (1) books, articles, and essays; (2) collections, annuals, and serials; (3) periodicals; and (4) bibliographies. Although the first section includes subject headings with the citations, the subject guide preceding the citations provides no direct subject access, as it lacks reference numbers.   Z6464.Z9B68

Burns, Grant. The atomic papers : a citizen's guide to selected books and articles on the bomb, the arms race, nuclear power, the peace movement, and related issues. Metuchen, N.J. : Scarecrow, 1984. 309 p.   **CJ665**

A topically arranged, annotated bibliography of English-language books (published 1945–79) and periodical articles (published 1980–83); includes a section on literature with nuclear themes. Subject and author indexes.   Z6464.D6B85

————— The nuclear present : a guide to recent books on nuclear war, weapons, the peace movement, and related issues, with a chronology of nuclear events, 1789–1991. Metuchen, N.J. : Scarecrow, 1992. 633 p.   **CJ666**

Updates the author's *The atomic papers* (CJ665) with annotated citations to English-language books and U.S. government publications arranged in topical chapters (e.g., reference works, nuclear weapons and nuclear war, arms control and disarmament). Includes a guide to periodicals and a nuclear chronology, 1789–1991. List of publishers and distributors. Author/editor, title, subject, and chronological indexes.   Z6464.D6B855

Burns, Richard Dean. Arms control and disarmament : a bibliography. Santa Barbara, Calif., ABC-Clio, 1977. 430 p. (War/peace bibliography series, no.6).   **CJ667**

An important source for English-language materials on the theory and practice of arms control and disarmament. More than 8,000 unannotated citations to books, articles, and government publications are grouped in topical chapters (e.g., research resources, limitation of weapons), which are further subdivided by subject. Subject and author indexes.   Z6464.D6B87

Doenecke, Justus D. Anti-intervention : a bibliographical introduction to isolationism and pacifism from World War I to the early cold war. N.Y. : Garland, 1987. 421 p. (Garland reference library of social science, v. 396).   **CJ668**

Contains citations to 1,581 books, articles, dissertations, and primary sources on the opposition of both isolationists and pacifists to U.S. overseas involvement from World War I to the mid-1950s. Entries (most briefly annotated) are organized in five topical chapters featuring general works, World War I and its aftermath, the 1920s to the mid-1950s, opinion-making, and groups and leaders. Within chapters, entries are chronologically or topically subdivided, then listed alphabetically by main entry. Includes a detailed table of contents and indexes by author, topic, and personal name.   Z6465.U5D62

Fenton, Thomas P. Third World struggle for peace with justice : a directory of resources / comp. and ed. by Thomas P. Fenton and Mary J. Heffron. Maryknoll, N.Y. : Orbis Books, c1990. 1 v.   **CJ669**

Provides access to readily available English-language material related to peace efforts in the Third World. Begins with a helpful introduction explaining definitions, selection criteria, geographic scope, political orientation, and format. Five chapters (Organizations, Books, Periodicals, Pamphlets and articles, and Audiovisuals) subdivided into annotated entries, supplementary lists, and further information sources (each alphabetically arranged). Organization, personal author, title, geographic area, and subject indexes.   Z7164.U5F45

Gay, William. The nuclear arms race / William Gay and Michael Pearson. Chicago : Amer. Libr. Assoc., 1987. 289 p. (The last quarter century, no. 1).   **CJ670**

Covers the major issues and literature of the nuclear arms race. Eight topical chapters provide historical background, describe consequences, and discuss deterrence and alternatives to the arms race and nuclear warfare. Each chapter summarizes the relevant issues in an essay and contains an extensive bibliography, often with annotations. The appendix serves as a guide to conducting further research on the topic. Includes a glossary, author-title index, and subject index.

Z6724.A9G39

Green, Marguerite. Peace archives : a guide to library collections of the papers of American peace organizations and of leaders in the public effort for peace. Berkeley, Calif. : World Without War Council, 1986. 66 p. **CJ671**

Brings together information on library collections containing papers of American peace organizations and of individuals active in peace efforts. Developed by the Historians Project of the World Without War Council. 30 major collections are listed alphabetically by institution name, giving address, telephone, director, description of the collection and its holdings, services available for researchers, and services provided for donors. An additional section lists, with locations, 72 individual peace collections (alphabetic by name). Appendixes give the archival methods of 27 peace organizations, a summary of the standards for record keeping and archiving used by the Swarthmore College Peace Collection, and a bibliography. No index.

Z6464.Z9G74

Howlett, Charles F. The American peace movement : references and resources. Boston : G.K. Hall, 1991. 416 p. **CJ672**

Offers nearly 1,700 annotated citations to primary sources, books, articles, dissertations, and selected government documents concerned with American peace activism from the 1600s to the present. After an extensive historical introduction, the bibliography is in 12 topical chapters (e.g., general works, leaders and thinkers, peace education). Appendix provides a list of peace research organizations with addresses and descriptions and an essay on American peace historiography. Author and subject indexes. Z6464.Z9H7

Lloyd, Lorna. British writing on disarmament from 1914–1978 : a bibliography / Lorna Lloyd and Nicholas A. Sims. London : F. Pinter ; N.Y. : Nichols, 1979. 171 p. **CJ673**

Complements Richard D. Burns, *Arms control and disarmament* (CJ667) by stressing titles written in Great Britain during this period. In two sections: pre 1914 to 1941, and 1941 to 1978; subject subdivisions within sections. Author index. Z6465.G7L56

McClean, Andrew. Security, arms control, and conflict reduction in East Asia and the Pacific : a bibliography, 1980–1991. Westport, Conn. : Greenwood, 1993. 551 p. (Bibliographies and indexes in law and political science, no. 19). **CJ674**

Selectively annotated citations to some 8,100 English-language books, articles, dissertations, working papers, reports, and government publications, arranged in four geographical sections: (1) East Asia and the Pacific, (2) Northeast Asia and the North Pacific Ocean, (3) Southeast Asia, and (4) Oceania. Each section contains a regional overview and country chapters, further subdivided by topic. Appendix lists relevant publishers, periodicals, and research institutions. Author and subject indexes. Z6724.N37M37

Meulen, Jacob ter. From Erasmus to Tolstoy : the peace literature of four centuries : Jacob ter Meulen's bibliographies of the peace movement before 1899 / Jacob ter Meulen ; ed., with an introduction by Peter van den Dungen. N.Y. : Greenwood, c1990. 145 p. (Bibliographies and indexes in law and political science, no. 14). **CJ675**

Lists in chronological order nearly 4,000 titles published from the beginning of printing until the end of the 19th century. In two sections, 1480–1776 and 1776–1898, each with its own author index. A reprinting of two titles published in limited editions: *Bibliography of the peace movement before 1899 (provisional lists)* = *Bibliographie du mouvement de la paix avant 1899 (liste provisoires)* (Hague : Library of the Palace of Peace, 1934) and *Bibliography of the peace movement before 1899 (provisional lists, 1480–1776)* = *Bibliographie du mouvement de la paix avant 1899 (listes provisoires periode 1480–1776)* (Hague : Library of the Palace of Peace, 1936). This version adds a 50-page introduction which has its own general index.

Z6464.Z9M38

Müller-Brettel, Marianne. Bibliography on peace research and peaceful international relations : the contributions of psychology 1900–1991 = Bibliographie Friedensforschung und Friedenspolitik : der Beitrag der Psychologie 1900–1991 / Marianne Müller-Brettel ; comp. by Gerhild Richter. München : Saur, 1993. 383 p. **CJ676**

Prefatory matter and headings in English and German.

Documents the contributions of psychology to war and peace research through more than 2,600 numbered citations to books, book chapters, and journal articles in English or German. Unannotated entries, arranged chronologically with topical subdivisions, contain descriptors used in the subject index. Also includes author index.

JX1952.Z99M85

Musto, Ronald G. The peace tradition in the Catholic Church : an annotated bibliography. N.Y. : Garland, 1987. 590 p. (Garland reference library of social science, v. 339). **CJ677**

Serves as a detailed (1,485 entries), critically annotated bibliography for the author's earlier study, *The Catholic peace tradition* (Maryknoll, N.Y. : Orbis Books, 1986). Entries cover Catholic church history from apostolic times to the present, and include books, articles, tracts, papal bulls, and dissertations in English, French, German, Italian, Spanish, Portuguese, and Latin up to November 1986. Arranged by broad chronological classification (e.g., Peace in the New Testament, The era of the Crusades) and subdivided by topic. Indexes of titles; authors, editors, and translators; and proper names.

Z7838.P54M87

Ridinger, Robert B. Marks. The Peace Corps : an annotated bibliography. Boston : G.K. Hall, c1989. 366 p. **CJ678**

Contains annotated citations to selected literature by and about the Peace Corps, 1961–86, including government and Peace Corps publications, books, articles, memoirs, dissertations, and videotapes. In three sections: (1) Creation and development of the agency and its programs, (2) Individual country programs, and (3) Roles and influence of returned volunteers. Sec. 1 and 3 are alphabetic by main entry, sec. 2 alphabetic by country. Appendixes list Peace Corps directors, 1961–86, and periodicals published by the Peace Corps (alphabetic by country). Subject and name index; no author index. Z7164.P3R53

Scrivener, David. Bibliography of arms control verification / David Scrivener and Michael Sheehan. Aldershot, England : Dartmouth Pub. Co. ; Brookfield, Vt. : Gower Pub., c1990. 161 p. **CJ679**

Cites books, book chapters, journal articles, reports, dissertations, proceedings, yearbooks, newspaper articles, and government publications on verification of compliance with arms control agreements. Consists of a general introductory overview followed by four chapters: General issues in arms control verification, Compliance issues and compliance diplomacy, Verification aspects of arms control negotiations and agreements, and Arms control verification in Soviet writings. Chapters 2–4 are topically subdivided. Detailed table of contents, but no index. Z6724.A73S38

Bibliography of bibliography

Carroll, Berenice A. Peace and war : a guide to bibliographies / Berenice A. Carroll, Clinton F. Fink, and Jane E. Mohraz. Santa Barbara, Calif. : ABC-Clio, 1983. 580 p. (War/peace bibliography series, 16). **CJ680**

An annotated bibliography of 1,398 bibliographies published in a variety of formats, 1785 through 1980. International in scope; focuses on works of general application rather than particular conflicts (except for the two World Wars). Subject arrangement; author and subject indexes. Z6464.Z9C55

Indexes; Abstract journals

Peace research abstracts journal. v. 1 (June 1964)– . Oakville, Ont. [etc.] : Canadian Peace Research Institute, 1964– .   **CJ681**

Provides abstracts of books, journal articles, conference papers, government publications, and other materials, grouping them in ten major areas (e.g., International organizations, Pairs of nations and crisis areas) with subsections (e.g., U.N. General Assembly, France and Germany). Each monthly issue treats only part of the field, sometimes considering portions of several major areas; a year's issues may not cover the entire field. Monthly issues have author indexes, but subject indexes are found only in an annual cumulative index, which consists of: (1) authors; (2) a "Complete subject index" that cites entry numbers for all items treating a topic, and (3) a "Primary code index" that lists only the works for which the topic is the principal focus. The latter is especially useful to pinpoint the most relevant entries when topics in the subject index are heavily posted.

————. *Revised coding manual* (Dundas, Ont. : Peace Research Inst., c1990. 36 p.) explains the organization, coding system, and use of the abstract journal.   JX1901.P38

Encyclopedias

Ali, Sheikh Rustum. The peace and nuclear war dictionary. Santa Barbara, Calif. : ABC-Clio , c1989. 294 p.   **CJ682**

Like *The arms control, disarmament, and military security dictionary* (CJ683), by Jeffrey M. Elliot and Robert Reginald, this book is designed to be used as a supplementary resource for college courses. Thus, its "over 300 entries, arranged alphabetically, have been systematically selected and organized to complement most standard works on the subject."—*Pref.* Headwords overlap with those of Elliot and Reginald; each concise definition is followed by a paragraph on the historical and contemporary significance of the concept. Extensive cross-references; subject index.   U263.A434

Elliot, Jeffrey M. The arms control, disarmament, and military security dictionary / Jeffrey M. Elliot, Robert Reginald. Santa Barbara, Calif. : ABC-Clio, c1989. 349 p.   **CJ683**

Designed as a supplementary resource for college classes, hence organized by subject areas that "parallel chapter topics in most leading books in the field" (*Pref.*) rather than alphabetically. The 268 entries, typically a page in length, overlap with those in Sheikh Rustum Ali's *The peace and nuclear war dictionary* (CJ682). The subject arrangement makes the general index essential. Extensive cross-references and copious notes.   JX1974.E55

Encyclopedia of arms control and disarmament / Richard Dean Burns, ed. in chief. N. Y. : Scribner's ; N. Y. : Maxwell Macmillan International, c1993. 3 v. (1692 p.).   **CJ684**

International in scope and written for a wide audience. Attempts "to bring together an informed survey of those processes that seek to prevent or, if that is not possible, to contain war and ameliorate its violence."—*Pref.* Vols. 1–2 contain 76 signed articles, with cross references and annotated bibliographies, in four sections: (1) national and regional dimensions (alphabetical by country or region); (2) themes and institutions (alphabetical by subject); (3) historical dimensions to 1945; and (4) arms control activities since 1945. Vol. 3 has excerpts from 141 significant treaties, a chronological list of the excerpted treaties, and lists of contributors and acronyms. Index.   JX1974.E57

Seeley, Robert A. The handbook of non-violence : including Aldous Huxley's An encyclopedia of pacifism. Westport, Conn. : L. Hill ; Great Neck, N.Y. : Lakeville Pr., c1986. 344 p.   **CJ685**

Reprints and updates Aldous Huxley's *An encyclopedia of pacifism* (N.Y.; London : Harper, 1937) and adds Seeley's *Handbook of non-violence*. Huxley's alphabetically arranged *Encyclopedia* has entries for terms, concepts, and organizations related to nonviolence and pacifism—e.g., armaments race, sanctions, Peace Pledge Union (PPU), War Resisters International (WRI)—and has cross-references, a general index, and two new appendixes that provide updated information on the PPU and the WRI. Seeley's *Handbook* is also alphabetical with cross-references and concentrates on more recent terminology, organizations, and individuals (e.g., nuclear free zones, Bishops' Pastoral Letter, Helen Caldicott). Bibliography; list of groups that work for peace (with addresses) but no index.   JX1952.S43

World encyclopedia of peace / honorary ed. in chief, Linus Pauling, exec. editors, Ervin Laszlo, Jong Youl Yoo. Oxford ; N.Y. : Pergamon Pr., 1986. 4 v.   **CJ686**

Contents: v. 1–2, A–Z; v. 3, Treaties, chronology of the peace movement, Nobel peace prize laureates; v. 4, Peace institutes and organizations, bibliography, journals, indexes.

Vols. 1–2 consist of alphabetically arranged, signed articles on topics and individuals. Articles vary in length from two to six pages and conclude with cross-references and bibliographies. Vol. 3 provides the text of 39 major treaties, a chronology of the peace movement (reprinted from Harold Josephson's *Biographical dictionary of modern peace leaders*, CJ700), and biographies of Nobel Peace prize winners through 1985. Vol. 4 includes an international directory of peace institutes and organizations, an unannotated bibliography on peace studies and peace research, lists of relevant journals and contributors, and name and subject indexes covering material in all four volumes.   JX1944.W67

Dictionaries

Disarmament terminology / comp. by the Language Services Division of the Foreign Office of the Federal Republic of Germany. Berlin ; N.Y. : W. de Gruyter, 1982. 645 p. (Terminological series, v.1).   **CJ687**

Title also in German, French, Spanish, and Russian.

A polyglot dictionary of terms, phrases, organizations, conferences, and agreements. Base language is English, with indexes in all five languages.   JX1974.D548

Thesauruses

Guides to Library of Congress subject headings and classification on peace and international conflict resolution. Wash. : United States Inst. of Peace, 1990. 488 p.   **CJ688**

Based on the 12th ed. of *Library of Congress subject headings* (AK220 *note*) and changes to them through Oct. 11, 1989, and on LC classification schedules through 1988. Facilitates access to cataloged materials on peace, war, international conflict resolution, and related topics. In two sections: subject headings and classification. The first offers an introduction to the construction of LC subject headings, then the headings themselves divided into three parts: topics and events, place-names, and wars and conflicts. The classification section has excerpts from the LC classification schedules, an appendix giving Cutter numbers for regions and countries, and a subject index to the classification.   Z695.1.P38G84

Quotations

Larson, Jeanne. Seeds of peace : a catalogue of quotations / comp. by Jeanne Larson & Madge Micheels-Cyrus. Philadelphia : New Society Publishers, c1986. 276 p.   **CJ689**

Presents some 1,600 quotations on peace, war, and nonviolence. In five sections: (1) Waging war; (2) The lighter side of a serious subject; (3) Patriotism; (4) Bumper stickers, buttons, T-shirts, and graffiti;

and (5) Waging peace. Longer sections are subdivided. Quotes the compilers feel contain sexist language are starred. Authors are cited (where known) but sources are not always given. Author index.

PN6084.P45L3

Directories

International affairs directory of organizations : the ACCESS resource guide / ed. by Bruce Seymore II. Santa Barbara, Calif. : ABC-Clio, c1992. 326 p. : ill. **CJ690**

1st ed., 1988, had title: *The ACCESS resource guide: an international directory of information on war, peace, and security* (Cambridge, Mass. : Ballinger Publ. Co., c1988).

Lists more than 800 international organizations (nearly half in the U.S.) providing information on international affairs, with emphasis on war, peace, and security. Entries for U.S. organizations are given first, followed by those for other countries, arranged alphabetically. Entries contain name, address, telephone, contact person, purpose, subject areas or specialization, publications, etc. Includes an annotated list of research publications and several indexes: (1) organizations by topics, (2) organizations by product or service, (3) organizations by title, (4) U.S. organizations by state, (5) personal name, and (6) title.

U104.I54

The international peace directory / ed. by T. Woodhouse (University of Bradford, School of Peace Studies). Plymouth, U.K. : Northcote House, 1988. 189 p. **CJ691**

Lists "organisations which concern themselves with the promotion of peaceful relationships and the constructive resolution of conflicts, whether within or between states, and at either the practical or academic and theoretical levels."—*p.19*. The 584 entries, arranged alphabetically within country name, contain information compiled from questionnaire responses. The standardized format for each entry lists the name, address, telephone, membership and affiliations, meeting times and publication, etc. Indexes include: lists of other directories and guides, bibliographies, a guide to current periodicals, organizations identified by issues covered and membership type, and an alphabetical index of organizations. JX1905.5.I58

Meyer, Robert S. Peace organizations, past and present : a survey and directory. Jefferson, N.C. : McFarland, c1988. 266 p. : ill. **CJ692**

Offers profiles of 92 peace organizations (primarily U.S.). Following a chapter describing historical peace efforts, information on the organizations is presented in three sections: (1) Personal, focusing on friendship, pacifism, service, understanding, unity; (2) Instructional, emphasizing knowledge and action in research, publishing, education; (3) Structural, aiming for world unity, organization, federation, citizenship, justice, law, and order. The entries, from one to five pages in length, usually cover the group's history, aims, efforts, and accomplishments. Included in the eight appendixes are a copy of the survey form, the U.N. Universal Declaration of Human Rights, and the Delhi Declaration of the Five Continent Peace Initiative. Bibliography; general index. JX1905.5.M48

Peace movements of the world / ed. by Alan J. Day. Burnt Mill, Essex, England : Longman ; Phoenix : distr. by Oryx, [1986]. 398 p. **CJ693**

Lists peace movements, chiefly post-1945, in various categories: international; Western Europe, Eastern Europe and the Soviet Union; North America; the Pacific region; Asia and the Indian Ocean; other regions (e.g., Middle East, Africa, Latin America and the Caribbean). Entries, in structured format, give address, aims and objectives, formation, activities, membership, publications, and where appropriate, affiliations. Based on information from the movements themselves, published sources, and the resources of *Keesing's contemporary archives* (now *Keesing's record of world events*, DA187). Indexes of movements and publications. JX1905.5.P426

Peace resource book : a comprehensive guide to issues, groups, and literature / from the Institute for Defense & Disarmament Studies. Cambridge, Mass. : Ballinger Pub. Co., c1986–c1988. 2 v. **CJ694**

Vol. 1 (1986) ed. by Elizabeth Bernstein [et al.]; volume for 1988–89 ed. by Carl Conetta.

A greatly expanded successor to *American peace directory* (Cambridge, Mass. : Ballinger, 1984), intended for those active in arms control, disarmament, and world peace. In three parts: (1) Peace issues and strategies, offering introductory essays describing the world military system, arms control negotiations, and peace movements; (2) (the major section) Directory of U.S. peace groups, consisting of a user's guide and lists of national peace groups and peace-oriented programs (arranged alphabetically with descriptive information), national and local peace organizations (arranged alphabetically and by zip code), and members of Congress by state and congressional district; (3) Guide to peace-related literature, a topical, annotated bibliography of books, articles, government publications, and pamphlets with an author index and a publisher/distributor address list. JX1905.5.A64

UNIDIR repertory of disarmament research / United Nations Institute for Disarmament Research. 1990– . N.Y. : United Nations, 1990– . **CJ695**

An updated and revised version of *Repertory of disarmament research* (Geneva : UNIDIR, 1982. 449 p.). The earlier version is still useful for its coverage of international publications, 1970–80.

Drawn from the U.N. Institute for Disarmament Research's (UNIDIR) computerized Research Institute Data Base. This edition focuses on research institutes and their activities. In two parts: Pt. 1, Research institutes, a directory of 730 research institutes and organizations (alphabetically arranged by country) gives name, acronym, address, description, date established, type of organization and activities, sources of funding, languages used, staff, periodical publications, research activities, and references to recent publications. Includes alphabetical lists of institutes by country and city and by name, an alphabetical index of periodical publications of the institutes, a subject index to research projects, and a personal name index. Pt. 2, Publications, features unannotated citations for 1988–90 publications of the institutes included in Pt. 1. Arranged alphabetically within topical divisions (e.g., Arms race, Nuclear weapons and disarmament). Includes author index. An appendix provides a questionnaire used to update UNIDIR's database. Z6464.D6U43

World directory of peace research and training institutions = Répertoire mondial des institutions de recherche et de formation sur la paix = Repertorio mundial de instituciones de investigación sobre la paz / prepared at UNESCO by the Social and Human Sciences Documentation Centre. 7th ed. Paris : UNESCO, 1991. 354 p. **CJ696**

1st ed., 1967; 6th ed., 1988. Title varies: *International repertory of institutions specializing in research on peace and disarmament*; *Peace research : trend report and world directory*, etc.

Describes 418 institutions, organized by country, with an initial international category. Entries include date of creation, director, number of staff, activities, research, publications, etc. Six indexes: institution names and acronyms; research subjects; countries/geographical areas; names of senior staff; courses and subjects taught; and institutions providing scholarships. JX1904.5.W67

Handbooks

Menos, Dennis. Arms control fact book. Jefferson, N.C. : McFarland, c1985. 140 p. **CJ697**

A nontechnical guide to arms control intended "to help the layman understand the basic issues underlying arms control, its accomplishments to date, and the challenges for the future."—*Pref.* Individual sections feature: encyclopedic entries of significant terms; descriptions of arms control organizations; reference data (e.g., acronyms, chronology, legislation); and a bibliography. General index.

JX1974.7.M45

Yearbooks

Unesco yearbook on peace and conflict studies. 1980–1988. Westport, Conn. : Greenwood ; Paris : UNESCO, 1980–90.
CJ698

Ceased with volume for 1988, publ. 1990.

Gives "an up-to-date overview of research on disarmament [and] a review of the basic concepts, issues, and literature that are essential to further research and teaching."—*Pref. to 1988 ed.* Useful for information on the activities of peace research institutions.

§ Continued by an unnumbered monographic series, *Unesco studies on peace and conflict*.   JX1904.5.U52

United Nations disarmament yearbook. v. 1 (1976)– . N.Y. : United Nations, 1977– . Annual.   **CJ699**

Prepared by the United Nations Centre for Disarmament.

Reviews "the main developments and negotiations in the field of disarmament taking place each year, together with a brief history of the major issues."—*Editorial note, 1992 ed.* Now in two parts: (1) Major trends and developments; (2) U.N. disarmament activities. Both parts are subdivided by topic (e.g., chemical weapons, economic aspects). Appendixes include status of agreements, text of selected treaties, tables of resolutions and decisions including sponsorship, and a list of abbreviations and acronyms. Subject index.   JX1974.U546

Biography

Biographical dictionary of modern peace leaders / ed. in chief, Harold Josephson. Westport, Conn. : Greenwood, 1985. 1133 p.   **CJ700**

Offers signed entries on "individuals [from 41 countries] who either contributed to the organized peace effort or who influenced others to question wars and organized violence."—*Introd.* Most biographees are from the U.S. or Europe and lived in the 19th and 20th centuries; all are now deceased. Entries, one to three pages long, are alphabetically arranged, cross-referenced, and contain: (1) an introductory paragraph with biographical data; (2) a discussion of the person's work, thought, and activities related to peace; and (3) a bibliography of works by and about the individual and the location of manuscript collections. Includes an introductory essay, a chronology of the peace movement, and an appendix grouping the biographees by their national affiliation. General index.

§ A companion to Warren F. Kuehl's *Biographical dictionary of internationalists* (CJ66); the two works cross-reference each other.   JX1962.A2B56

Roberts, Nancy L. American peace writers, editors, and periodicals : a dictionary. N. Y. : Greenwood, 1991. 362 p.   **CJ701**

Treats writers, editors, and periodicals associated with peace movements. An introductory essay describes periodicals devoted to peace advocacy. Entries, arranged alphabetically, offer information on 400 writers and editors, and contain personal information (e.g., birth and death dates, religion) importance/activities, affiliations, selected works, a bibliography, and location of personal papers. A section on periodicals provides 200 entries with place and dates of publication, description, and names of publishers and editors. Includes a chronology of U.S. peace movements and a list giving organizational affiliations for the biographees. Selected bibliography. Name and subject index.   JX1962.A2R63

Who's who in the Peace Corps. 1993 ed.– . Greenwich, Conn. : Reference Pr. International, c1993– . Annual.   **CJ702**

Contains current biographical information on approximately 50,000 former and present Peace Corps volunteers and staff. Entries, arranged alphabetically, give country and dates of service, foreign language(s) spoken, personal data (where available), and current address. A separate section provides entries for deceased volunteers and staff.

Includes a list of organizations serving returned volunteers. Geographic indexes by U.S. residence and by foreign residence, country of service index.   HC60.5.W46

CK

Law

This section emphasizes reference works that make legal literature accessible to a wider audience. Nonetheless, many works listed will be held only in specialized law libraries. Some law libraries are independent institutions, but most larger law libraries are connected with universities or state libraries.

A general library can refer complicated legal questions to a nearby law library, but will still need a basic collection to answer historical, political and general legal questions. A minimum collection would include: (1) the *United States code* (CK177) or *United States code annotated* (CK178); (2) the current compilation of the laws of the home state; (3) the charter and ordinances of the home city, if available; (4) the current edition of the United States *Treaties in force* (CK93); (5) reference works on the Constitution and the Supreme Court; (6) general guides and handbooks on legal matters; (7) a law dictionary; (8) a directory of federal and state courts; and (9) a guide to United States legal research.

Much legal research and reference work in libraries is conducted through two major database systems, LEXIS (Dayton, Ohio : Mead Data Central) and WESTLAW (St. Paul, Minn. : West Publishing). Both contain thousands of machine-readable files searchable by full text, including decisions of federal and state courts, federal and state statutes and legislative documents, legal periodical articles, specialized legal materials, and legal documents from other countries and international organizations. Access to these systems in law libraries is often restricted by contract to law school faculty and students, but a growing number of general libraries also have contracts with one system or the other.

GENERAL WORKS

Guides

Germain, Claire M. Germain's transnational law research : a guide for attorneys. Ardsley-on-Hudson, N.Y. : Transnational Juris Publications, c1991– . 1 v. (loose-leaf).   **CK1**

A comprehensive guide to materials in comparative and international legal research. The first two chapters introduce major procedural and substantive issues and provide extensive research references. Chapter 3 is an annotated bibliography of general research sources, including translations and digests of foreign laws, textbooks, and current awareness materials. The final two chapters survey the literature for about three dozen subjects and for 17 European countries. Most sections begin with useful discussions of background, current issues, and "where to start." K85.G47

Manual of law librarianship : the use and organization of legal literature / ed. by Elizabeth M. Moys. 2nd ed. Boston : G.K. Hall, 1986. [915] p. **CK2**
1st ed., 1976.
A standard work, published for the British and Irish Association of Law Librarians. Pt. 1 contains introductions to law libraries, legal systems, and legal literature. Pt. 2 provides a bibliographic treatment of the law of the British Isles and other common law systems, focusing primarily on English legislation, law reports, and government publications, but including discussion of historical sources, Commonwealth and U.S. materials, and general reference sources. Pt. 3 introduces the literature of other legal sytems, including the European Communities, international law, civil law, Roman law, and religious legal systems. Pt. 4 discusses procedures and practices of law librarianship. A highly recommended overview of the field and its literature. Z675.L2M27

Reynolds, Thomas H. Foreign law : current sources of codes and basic legislation in jurisdictions of the world / Thomas H. Reynolds, Arturo A. Flores. 1989– . Littleton, Colo. : Rothman, 1989– . 3 v. (looseleaf). **CK3**
Contents: v. 1, The Western hemisphere; v. 2, Western and Eastern Europe and the European Communities. Vol. 3, Africa, Asia, and Australasia.
Designed to identify the major laws of all countries of the world other than the U.S. and to help researchers find the texts, either in the original language or in English translation. The chapter for each country begins with a narrative description of the country's legal system, including a brief history and the nature of the legal literature. This is followed by references to major publications, including codifications, official gazettes, and court reports. Finally, laws and sources for each country are listed under about 60 subjects. Updated annually.
K38.R49

Bibliography

Adams, J. N. A bibliography of eighteenth century legal literature : a subject and author catalogue of law treatises and all law related literature held in the main legal collections in England / by J.N. Adams and G. Averley, with historical and technical assistance from F.J.G. Robinson for the BELL Project at the University of Kent in Canterbury. Newcastle upon Tyne, England : Avero (Eighteenth-Century) Publications, 1982. 900 p. + 6 microfiches in pocket. **CK4**
A classified subject listing of books and pamphlets dealing with legal issues, based on the catalog of 14 British and Irish libraries. Entries are alphabetical by author within each subject class. A microfiche author index is included, but the lack of subject and title indexes sometimes hinders access. KD56.A33

——————— A bibliography of nineteenth century legal literature : an author and subject catalogue of law treatises and all law related literature held in the legal collections of the Inns of Court in England, the British copyright libraries, Harvard University Library, and the Library of Congress / by J. N. Adams and M. J. Davies. [Newcastle upon Tyne, Eng.] : Avero Publications, Ltd. & Chadwyck-Healey, Ltd., 1992–93. v. 1–2. (In progress). **CK5**
Contents: v. 1, A–G; v. 2, H–Q. Subject index in microfiche in looseleaf binder.
A union catalog of English-language law books and law-related materials published between 1801 and 1870 and held in 12 major libraries in the U.K., Ireland, and the U.S. Entries indicate editions, publication data, and holding libraries. Books are listed by author, with a subject index issued on microfiche. When the bibliography is finished, a comprehensive CD-ROM version is expected to replace the microfiche subject index. K40.A33

Bibliographie juristischer Festschriften und Festschriftenbeiträge : Deutschland, Schweiz, Österreich = Bibliography of legal festschriften : titles and contents : Germany, Switzerland, Austria. 1864–1944– . Berlin : Berlin Verlag A. Spitz, 1984– . **CK6**
Eight volumes to date (1864–1944, 1945–61, 1962–66, 1967–74, 1975–79, 1980–84, 1985–87, 1988–90) providing subject and author access to the contents of more than 1,000 commemorative volumes of legal essays. The 1864–1944 volume includes an index to all volumes through 1979. In German, with some prefatory matter also in English.
KJC158.5.B53

Bibliography of law and economics / ed. by Boudewijn Bouckaert and Gerrit de Geest. Dordrecht ; Boston : Kluwer Academic, c1992. 667 p. **CK7**
A classified, unannotated list of more than 7,000 publications dealing with the economic approach to law. Includes as pt. 2 national surveys of publications from 11 European countries. Name index.
K38.B52

A bibliography on foreign and comparative law / comp. and annotated by Charles Szladits. [1790–Apr. 1, 1953]– . N.Y. : Parker School of Foreign and Comparative Law, Columbia Univ. in the city of New York : distr. by Oceana, 1955– . Irregular. **CK8**
Volumes for 1984–1986 ed. by Vratislav Pechota have title: *Szladits' bibliography on foreign and comparative law.*
A classified listing of materials on legal systems outside the U.S. or on the comparative study of law, with indexes by geographic area and author. Coverage before 1984 was limited to non-common-law systems, but entries on the U.K., Canada, Australia, New Zealand and other common-law countries are now included. Entries for books, but not articles, include brief descriptive annotations. Publication lags about five years behind dates of coverage. K38.B53

Cooper, Jeremy. Keyguide to information sources in public interest law. London ; N.Y. : Mansell, 1991. 208 p. **CK9**
A guide to both documentation and organizations. Pt. 1 gives an overview of public interest law and its literature, pt. 2 provides a well-annotated subject bibliography, and pt. 3 is a subject directory of organizations. Largely, but not exclusively, British and American sources. Indexed.
§ Lee Epstein, Tracey E. George, and Joseph F. Kobylika, *Public interest law: an annotated bibliography and research guide* (N.Y. : Garland, 1992) is a more slender work with a similar focus.
K118.P82A13

DeCoste, F. C. Feminist legal literature : a selective annotated bibliography / comp. by F. C. DeCoste, K. M. Munro, Lillian MacPherson. N.Y. : Garland, 1991. 499 p. (Garland reference library of social science, v. 671). **CK10**
A subject list of periodical articles written from feminist perspectives and published 1980–90. Limited to English-language and French Canadian works. Treatises and monographs are not covered, but Chapter 16, "Book Reviews," provides some access to this literature. Indexes by author (including those discussed in others' articles), journal name, and keyword. K644.A12D43

Harvard Law School. Library. The Harvard legal bibliography, 1961–1981 / [comp. by] Harvard Law Library [and] Law Library Microform Consortium [microform]. [Honolulu, Hawaii] : LLMC, 1985. 335 microfiches. **CK11**
A comprehensive listing of materials received in the Harvard Law School Library, cumulating on microfiche more than 575,000 entries from the 21 volumes of the library's *Annual legal bibliography*. Coverage includes treatises, government documents, conference proceedings, and articles in over 500 legal journals not indexed in either *Index to legal periodicals* (CK26) or *Index to foreign legal periodicals* (CK24). "Quick Survey Tables" indicate subjects under which materials on specific jurisdictions can be found.

Introduction bibliographique à l'histoire du droit et à l'ethnologie juridique = Bibliographical introduction to legal history and ethnology / publiée sous la direction de ... John Gilissen. Bruxelles : Editions de l'Institut de Sociologie, Université Libre de Bruxelles, [1963]–88. 9 v. (looseleaf) : maps.   **CK12**

Two volumes on ancient, medieval, and early modern legal systems, followed by 7 v. on individual national systems arranged geographically. Each chapter includes lists, with brief annotations, of bibliographies and reference works, general histories, legal histories, collections of legislation and law reports, and works on specific legal subjects. Most chapters are in French, with some in English or other languages. Most of the material was issued in the 1960s and early 1970s and is now quite dated. An index was prepared only for v. A, covering the ancient world.   K201.I58

Law books, 1876–1981 : books and serials on law and its related subjects. N.Y. : Bowker, [1981]. 4 v.   **CK13**

Contents: v. 1–3, Books—Subject index; v. 4, Books—Author and title indexes, Serials—Subject and title indexes, Publishers, Online database producers and vendors.

Lists about 130,000 books and 4,000 serial titles published or distributed in the U.S. since 1876. Arranged by subject, with author and title indexes. Excludes looseleafs, pamphlets, juvenile literature, and materials published by the U.S. Government Printing Office and the U.N.   KF1.L36

A legal bibliography of the British Commonwealth of Nations. 2nd ed. London : Sweet & Maxwell, 1955–64. 7 v.   **CK14**

1st ed. 1925–49 (7v.) had title *Sweet & Maxwell's complete law book catalogue.*

Contents: v. 1, English law to 1800, including Wales, the Channel Islands and the Isle of Man (1955); v. 2, English law from 1801 to 1954, including Wales, the Channel Islands and the Isle of Man (1957); v. 3, Canadian and British-American colonial law from earliest times to Dec. 1956 (1957); v. 4, Irish law to 1956 (1957); v. 5, Scottish law to 1956, together with a list of Roman law books in the English language (1957); v. 6, Australia, New Zealand and their dependencies, from earliest times to June 1958, with lists of reports of cases, digests, and collections of statutes and rules (1958); v. 7, The British Commonwealth, excluding the United Kingdom, Australia, New Zealand, Canada, India and Pakistan (1964).

Vol. 1 lists early English law books and later items dealing with the pre-1800 period. It is arranged by subject, includes annotations for some items, and is indexed by subject, place, author and title. The remaining volumes generally list primary sources chronologically and secondary sources alphabetically by author within each jurisdiction; each volume has a subject index.

Bibliography of bibliography

Lansky, Ralph. Bibliographisches Handbuch der Rechts– und Verwaltungswissenschaften : erläuternde Bibliographie nationaler und internationaler Bibliographien und anderer Nachschlagewerke und Informationsmittel = Bibliographical handbook on law and public administration : annotated bibliography of national and international bibliographies and other reference guides and information sources. Frankfurt am Main : Klostermann, c1987. v. 1. (In progress).   **CK15**

Contents: Bd. 1, Allgemeines und Europa.

Projected for three volumes. Vol. 1 covers general works and Europe. If published, v. 2 will treat the rest of the world (much of which was treated in Lansky's earlier *Handbuch der Bibliographien zum Recht der Entwicklungsländer*, CK16); and v. 3 will provide a supplement and index to the set. While the work focuses on bibliographies and indexes, it also lists other basic reference works such as encyclopedias, dictionaries, directories, and introductory surveys. "Works that are especially useful, e.g. because they are current, complete, particularly reliable or easy to use, are indicated by asterisks."—*Pref.* Intro-

ductory matter and section headings are in German and English; lists of contents are in the original languages; annotations are in German. No separate index to v. 1.   K37.L357

——————— Handbuch der Bibliographien zum Recht der Entwicklungsländer = Handbook of bibliographies on law in the developing countries. Frankfurt am Main : Klostermann, [1981]. 621 p. : map, in color.   **CK16**

Preliminary ed., 1977.

In German, English, French, and Spanish.

An annotated bibliography of about 1,450 bibliographies and other legal reference sources on countries in Africa, Asia, Oceania, and Latin America. General bibliographies are discussed first; then for each continent or region, multijurisdictional works precede bibliographies for individual countries. Works of special importance are marked with one or two asterisks. Annotations are in German, but an English-language summary (p. 515–532) provides a useful overview. Indexed.   K37.L36

Legal bibliography index. 1978–90. San Jose, Calif. [etc.] : Publ. by L.E. Dickson [etc.], 1978–90. Annual.   **CK17**

Editors: W. S. Chiang and L. E. Dickson.

A subject index to English-language bibliographies, published either separately or as parts of other publications. Prefatory sections list regularly published bibliographies and serials that feature bibliography sections. Cumulative two-volume compilations cover 1978–82 and 1983–87.   KF1.L43

Current

Bowker's law books and serials in print. 1984/85– . N.Y. : Bowker, c1984– . Annual.   **CK18**

Continues: *Law information* (1982–83. 6 v.) and *Law information update* (v. 1–2 [1983–84]).

Issued annually in three volumes: v. 1, Books—Subject index; v. 2, Books—Author index; v. 3, Books—Title index, Subject index to cataloged titles, Serials—Subject index, Title index, Publishers and distributors abbreviations.

Lists English-language legal materials, primarily U.S., including microforms, software packages, online databases, and audio and video material. Books are indexed by subject, author and title. Many entries contain brief descriptive annotations. Includes listings for more than 3,000 publishers. Kept up-to-date by quarterly supplements.

Catalog of new foreign and international law titles. v. 1, no. 1 (Jan./Feb. 1989)– . Ann Arbor, Mich. : Ward and Associates, [1989]– . Bimonthly.   **CK19**

Continues in part *National legal bibliography* (Buffalo, N.Y. : W.S. Hein, 1984–88).

Lists books and other materials recently acquired by several dozen major law libraries. Each issue includes "hot sheets" of titles acquired by at least 25% of contributing libraries, followed by listings of new periodicals, works on international law in general, works on specific regions and countries, and works on religious and early legal systems. Author and title indexes.

§ For similar coverage of U.S. law, see: *Catalog of current law titles* (CK120).   K40.C38

International legal books in print : an annotated bibliography. London ; N.Y. : Bowker-Saur, 1992. 2 v.   **CK20**

Rev. ed. of *International legal books in print, 1990–1991*, publ. 1990.

A comprehensive bibliography of more than 20,000 English-language texts and treatises published or distributed in the U.K., Western Europe, and the Commonwealth. Vol. 1 is an author/title listing, and v. 2 contains a subject guide and list of publishers. Some entries are annotated.   K38.I58

Triffin, Nicholas. Law books in print : law books in English published throughout the world and in print through 1990 / comp. and ed. by Nicholas Triffin with the assistance of Alice Pidgeon. 6th ed. [Dobbs Ferry, N.Y.] : Glanville Publ., c1991. 6 v.   **CK21**

  1st ed., 1957; 5th ed., 1987.

  Contents: v. 1–2, Authors/titles; v. 3–4, Subjects; v. 5, Publishers A–N; v. 6, Publishers O–Z. Series list.

  A bibliography of English-language law books from around the world, including microforms, video and audio cassettes, software packages, and CD-ROMs. Full bibliographical information included with all entries. Includes list of publishers and indexes by author/title, subject, and publisher. Updated by *Law books published* (semiannual).
                                                                   KF1.T75

Indexes

Current law index. v. 1 (Jan. 1980)– . Foster City, Calif. : Information Access Co., 1980– . Monthly, with two-volume annual cumulations.   **CK22**

  Publ. in cooperation with the American Association of Law Libraries.

  Indexes more than 700 law periodicals from the U.S., Canada, the U.K., Ireland, Australia and New Zealand. Separate subject and author/title indexes. Subject index uses detailed entries based on Library of Congress subject headings. Author/title index includes authors of articles, but lists only titles of books reviewed (not article titles). Tables of cases and statutes list articles discussing judicial opinions, legislative acts, court rules, and treaties.

  •Machine-readable versions: *Legal resource index* (Foster City, Calif. : Information Access Co., 1980–), available online, updated monthly, and *LegalTrac on InfoTrac* (1980–), available on CD-ROM, updated monthly. The electronic versions add coverage of *National law journal* and several other legal newspapers.   K33.C87

Index to Canadian legal literature. v. 1 (1981)– . Toronto : Carswell Co., 1981– . Eight issues per year, with annual bound cumulation.   **CK23**

  At head of title: The Canadian abridgement, second edition.

  An index to books and periodicals of interest to the Canadian legal community. Subject index; author index; table of cases; table of statutes; book review index. The subject index contains cross-referenced English and French headings, with entries listed under the heading for the language in which they are written. Two volumes publ. 1981 provide subject access to material published through 1980, and v. 3 (1981–84) includes a cumulative author index to the first three volumes.

  § *Index to Canadian legal periodical literature* (Montreal : Index to Canadian Legal Periodical Literature, 1961–) is a less comprehensive work, published quarterly with annual bound volumes and cumulations covering 1961–70, 1971–75, 1976–80, and 1981–85. KE1.I53

Index to foreign legal periodicals. v. 1 (1960)– . Berkeley, Calif. : Univ. of California Pr. for the American Association of Law Libraries, 1960– . Quarterly.   **CK24**

  Cumulations: triennial, 1960–83; annual, 1984– .

  Publisher varies: 1960–83, London : Inst. of Advanced Legal Studies, Univ. of London.

  Indexes selected legal periodicals and collections of essays dealing with international law, comparative law, and the domestic law of countries other than the U.S. and common-law members of the Commonwealth. Overlaps some in coverage of English-language journals with other legal periodical indexes, but also provides access to hundreds of journals in other languages. Articles are indexed by subject, with supplementary indexes by country and by author providing cross-references to subject listings.   Z695.1.L315

Index to legal periodical literature. Boston : C. C. Soule, 1888–1939. 6 v.   **CK25**

Imprint varies.

  Vol. 1–2, ed. by Leonard A. Jones; v. 3–6, ed. by Frank E. Chipman.

  Contents: v. 1, To 1886; v. 2, 1887–98; v. 3, 1898–1908; v. 4, 1908–22; v. 5, 1923–32; v. 6, 1932–37.

  The leading index to early legal periodicals. Consists of subject/title and author indexes. Vol. 1 covers both law journals and articles on legal subjects in more than 100 general periodicals dating back to the 18th century. Useful for historical research in both general libraries and law libraries.   Z6453.I38

Index to legal periodicals. Jan. 1908– . N.Y. : H.W. Wilson, 1909– . Monthly.   **CK26**

  Cumulations: triennial, 1926–79; annual, 1979– .

  An index to more than 600 journals and yearbooks published in the U.S., Canada, Great Britain, Ireland, Australia and New Zealand. Contains a main subject/author index; tables of cases and statutes (listing articles that focus on these primary sources); and a book review index. Subject headings tend to be broader than in the competing *Current law index* (CK22). The only comprehensive index to articles published before 1980 in English-language legal journals.

  •A machine-readable version with the same title (N.Y. : H.W. Wilson, 1981–) is available online (updated twice weekly), on CD-ROM (updated quarterly), and on magnetic tape.   K9.N32

Index to periodical articles related to law. v. 1 (Oct. 1958)– . Dobbs Ferry, N.Y. : Glanville, 1958– . Quarterly, with annual cumulations.   **CK27**

  A selective index to articles in general interest periodicals and other journals not covered by *Current law index*, (CK22), *Index to foreign legal periodicals* (CK24), or *Index to legal periodicals* (CK26).

  Cumulation: *Index to periodical articles related to law : thirty year cumulation, volumes 1–30 (1958–1988)*, ed. by Roy M. Mersky and J. Myron Jacobstein (1989. 4 v.).

Legal journals index. v. 1 (1986)– . Hebden Bridge, West Yorkshire : Legal Information Resources Ltd., 1986– . Monthly, with quarterly and annual cumulations.   **CK28**

  An index to some 150 law and law-related journals published in the U.K., with separate sections for subjects, authors, cases, legislation, and book reviews.

  § Journals focusing specifically on European law, formerly covered here, are now indexed separately in *European legal journals index* (1993–).   K33.L45

Encyclopedias

International encyclopaedia for labour law and industrial relations / ed. in chief, R. Blanpain. Deventer, Netherlands : Kluwer, 1977–[94]. 23 v. (loose-leaf) : ports.   **CK29**

  A collection of national monographs surveying the laws governing individual workers and collective organizations in more than 55 countries, as well as chapters on international and European labor law. Also includes volumes providing the texts of international instruments, case law from international tribunals, and legislation from some 20 countries. Each section has a separate index.

  § In recent years, the same publisher and editor-in-chief have launched several similar works in other subject areas, under the series title "International encyclopaedia of laws." These have the potential to become important transnational reference sources, although to date none has provided coverage of more than a handful of countries. Titles include *Commercial and economic law*, Jules Stuyck, ed. (1993–); *Constitutional law*, André Alen, ed. (1992–); *Contracts*, Jacques Herbots, ed. (1993–); *Corporations and partnerships*, Koen Geens, ed. (1991–); *Criminal law*. Lieven Dupont and Cyrille Fijnaut, eds. (1993–); *Environmental law*, Marc Boes, ed. (1991–); *Insurance law*, Simon Fredericq and Herman Cousy, eds. (1992–); and *Medical law*, Herman Nys, ed. (1993–).   K1705.I5

International encyclopedia of comparative law. Tübingen : Mohr (Siebeck) ; The Hague : Mouton, [1971–85?]. v. 1–17. **CK30**

Prep. under the auspices of the International Assoc. of Legal Science.

Chapters in each volume are being issued in fascicles.

Contents: v. 1, National reports, V. Knapp, ed.; v. 2, The Legal systems of the world, D. René, ed.; v. 3, Private international law, K. Lipstein, ed.; v. 4, Persons and family, M. Rheinstein, ed.; v. 5, Succession, K. H. Neumayer, ed.; v. 6, Property and trust, F. H. Lawson, ed.; v. 7, Contracts in general, A. T. von Mehren, ed.; v. 8, Specific contracts, K. Zweigert, ed.; v. 9, Letters of credit, B. Kozolchyk, ed.; v. 10, Quasi-contracts, E. von Caemmerer, ed.; v. 11, Torts, A. Tunc, ed.; v. 12, Law of transport, R. Rodière, ed.; v. 13, Business and private organizations, A. Conard, ed.; v. 14, Copyright and industrial property, E. Ulmer, ed.; v. 15, Labour law, O. Kahn-Freund, ed.; v. 16, Civil procedure, M. Cappelletti, ed.; v. 17, State and economy, B. T. Blagojevic, ed.

A major enterprise, intended to be complete in about 17,000 pages. Chapters in each volume are being issued in fascicles. Vol. 1 will incorporate a detailed description of the legal system of about 140 nations; the remaining 16 volumes will offer comparative analyses of the main issues in civil and commercial law throughout the world. Each section is by an individual scholar and includes extensive footnotes and bibliography. Publication has slowed considerably since the initial burst of activity in the 1970s. After two decades, only the Torts section has been published in its final bound format. **K530.I57**

Modern legal systems cyclopedia / gen. ed., Kenneth Robert Redden ; contributors, William Brock ... [et al.]. Buffalo, N.Y. : W.S. Hein, 1984– . 21 v. in 10 (loose-leaf). **CK31**

Kept up-to-date by supplements and revised volumes.

Contents: v. 1, North America; v. 2, Pacific basin; v. 3–4, Western Europe; v. 5, Middle East; v. 6, Africa; v. 7, Central America and Caribbean; v. 8, Eastern Europe; v. 9, Asia; v. 10, South America.

Attempts to describe all the world's legal systems, covering forms of government, law-making processes, and basic legal doctrines. Arranged geographically, with each volume containing both country studies and general studies. Many of the country studies on each jurisdiction's legal system are excellent encyclopedic treatments; the scope and coverage of other chapters are somewhat idiosyncratic. An index volume contains a complete table of contents for the set, brief subject and country indexes, and a copy of *World law school directory* (CK63). **K530.M62**

Walker, David M. The Oxford companion to law. Oxford : Clarendon Pr. ; N.Y. : Oxford Univ. Pr., 1980. 1366 p. **CK32**

A popular and respected source for concise information on legal doctrines and institutions. Defines terms and concepts; explains historical background and structure of courts and legal systems; provides brief biographies of major jurists and lawyers. Emphasizes British law, but includes broad coverage of all Western legal systems. An appendix lists the holders of various offices since 1660. **K48.W34**

Dictionaries

Black, Henry Campbell. Black's law dictionary : definitions of the terms and phrases of American and English jurisprudence, ancient and modern. 6th ed. / by the publisher's editorial staff ; contributing authors, Joseph R. Nolan ... [et al.]. St. Paul, Minn. : West Publ. Co., 1990. 1657 p. **CK33**

1st ed., 1891; 5th ed., 1979.

This comprehensive work is the standard U.S. law dictionary. The 6th ed. includes more than 5,000 new or revised entries, as well as thousands of archaic or little-used legal terms. Many entries include references to cases or statutes. Appendixes include a table of abbreviations and the text of the U.S. Constitution.

•A machine-readable version is available on disk and online through *WESTLAW*, the publisher's database system. **KF156.B53**

A concise dictionary of law / ed., Elizabeth A. Martin. 2nd ed. Oxford ; N.Y. : Oxford Univ. Pr., 1990. 448 p. **CK34**

1st ed., 1983.

A dictionary of English law designed for nonlawyers. Provides excellent coverage of basic legal concepts, with brief definitions that provide background information and avoid technical legal jargon. Includes some references to English statutes, but does not include citations to cases in which terms are used.

§ Three respected shorter English legal dictionaries, with references to both cases and statutes: Leslie B. Curzon, *A dictionary of law* (4th ed. London : Pitman Publ., 1993); E.R. Hardy Ivamy, *Mozley and Whiteley's law dictionary* (11th ed. London : Butterworths, 1993); and Leslie Rutherford and Sheila Bone, eds., *Osborn's concise law dictionary* (8th ed. London : Sweet & Maxwell, 1993). **KD313.C66**

Dukelow, Daphne A. The dictionary of Canadian law / by Daphne A. Dukelow, Betsy Nuse. Scarborough, Ont., Canada : Thomson Professional Pub. Canada, c1991. 1176 p. **CK35**

A dictionary of words, phrases, and abbreviations used in the common law Canadian jurisdictions, with most definitions based on federal and provincial statutes, regulations, and legal textbooks (but not case law). Includes Latin phrases but very few French terms. Cross-references from words to phrases in which they appear. **KE183.D85**

Garner, Bryan A. A dictionary of modern legal usage. N.Y. : Oxford Univ. Pr., 1987. 587 p. **CK36**

Designed to improve the writing of lawyers and law students, but also useful for general readers trying to decipher legal prose. Most entries provide advice on specific terms; some are more extensive essays on usage, word formation, pronunciation, and punctuation. These longer entries are listed in a classified guide at the beginning of the book. One of the most browsable of legal reference works, filled with humorous examples and a lively condemnation of archaic and obfuscatory legal writing. **KF156.G367**

Gifis, Steven H. Law dictionary. 3rd ed. N.Y. : Barron's, c1991. 537 p. **CK37**

1st ed., 1975; 2nd ed., 1984.

Intended as a ready reference source in paperback for students. More than 3,000 terms are defined, many with references to cases, statutes, and legal treatises. Pronunciation indicated for Latin and French terms.

§ An abridged edition, covering 2,000 terms and omitting the references to other legal sources, is published as *Dictionary of legal terms : a simplified guide to the language of law* (2nd ed. Hauppage, N.Y. : Barron's, 1993). This version includes as an appendix a consumer's guide to law and lawyers. **KF156.G53**

Jowitt, William Allen Jowitt. Jowitt's dictionary of English law / by Earl Jowitt and Clifford Walsh. 2nd ed. / by John M. Burke. London : Sweet & Maxwell, 1977. 2 v. (1935 p.). **CK38**

1st ed., 1959.

The standard English legal dictionary. Somewhat similar in purpose and scope to the American *Black's law dictionary* (CK33), although many entries are longer and more encyclopedic. Updated by second cumulative supplement (1985. 176 p.). **KD313.J6**

Mellinkoff, David. Mellinkoff's dictionary of American legal usage. St Paul, Minn. : West Publ. Co., 1992. 703 p. **CK39**

A dictionary of words and phrases commonly used in legal practice, attempting to provide definitions in ordinary English. Explains distinctions among varying uses and similar terminology, with cross-references and examples of usage. Very few references to cases and statutes. Arranged alphabetically, but all entries and cross-references are also listed on green pages at the beginning of the book. **KF156.M45**

Oran, Daniel. Oran's dictionary of the law / Daniel Oran ; contributing author, Mark Tosti. 2nd ed. St. Paul, Minn. : West Publ. Co., c1991. 500 p. : ill., maps. **CK40**

1st ed., 1983.

A basic dictionary designed for students and nonlawyers, with clear and straightforward definitions. Pronunciation given only for problem words. No references to cases. A 40-page appendix provides a concise introduction to legal research.

§ A condensed version, with 2,500 frequently used words, is published as *Law dictionary for nonlawyers* (3rd ed., 1991).   KF156.O69

Abbreviations

Kavass, Igor I. World dictionary of legal abbreviations / general editors, Igor I. Kavass, Mary Miles Prince. [Buffalo, N.Y.] : W.S. Hein, 1991– . 1 v. (loose-leaf).   **CK41**

A multilingual dictionary, with separate sections for each language. Chapters to date cover abbreviations in English (from non-U.S. sources only), French, Hebrew, Italian, Portuguese, and Spanish. There is no single alphabetical listing, so readers must know what language is being abbreviated in order to decipher the abbreviation.   K89.K38

Prince, Mary Miles. Bieber's dictionary of legal abbreviations : reference guide for attorneys, legal secretaries, paralegals, and law students. Prince's 4th ed. Buffalo, N.Y. : W.S. Hein, 1993. 791 p.   **CK42**

1st ed., 1979; 3rd ed., 1988.

Contains more than 20,000 abbreviations and acronyms found in legal literature. The latest edition omits foreign-language abbreviations included in earlier editions.   KF246.B46

Raistrick, Donald. Index to legal citations and abbreviations. 2nd ed. London ; N.Y. : Bowker-Saur, c1993. 496 p.   **CK43**

1st ed., 1981.

The most comprehensive dictionary of legal abbreviations, mostly but not exclusively English-language. More than 25,000 entries, with dates of publication or coverage indicated for most court reports and journals. Strongest in coverage of U.K., Commonwealth, and European sources.   KD400.R35

Foreign terms

Multilingual

Herbst, Robert. Dictionary of commercial, financial and legal terms / by Robert Herbst and Alan G. Readett. 4th ed., rev. and enl. Thun, Switzerland : Translegal, c1985–[1989?]. 3 v.   **CK44**

Contents: v. 1, English-German-French, 4th ed., 1985; v. 2, Deutsch-Englisch-Französisch, 4th ed., 1989; v. 3, Français-Anglais-Allemand, 2nd ed., 1982.

1st ed., 1955–66; 3rd ed., 1968–79.

A standard work providing comprehensive coverage of legal and commercial terminology, with separate volumes for each base language.   HB61.H46

Lindbergh, Ernest. International law dictionary. London : Blackstone Pr., 1992. 439 p.   **CK45**

Published in the U. S. as: *Modern dictionary of international legal terms* (Boston : Little, Brown and Co., 1993).

A shorter polyglot dictionary, with three sections listing legal and law-related terms in one of three languages (English, French and German), and provides translations to the other two languages. Does not include definitions or explanations.   JX1226.L56 1992

West's law and commercial dictionary in five languages : definitions of the legal and commercial terms and phrases of American, English, and civil law jurisdictions. St. Paul, Minn. : West Publ. Co., c1985. 2 v.   **CK46**

A major multilingual dictionary, providing detailed definitions in English, followed by equivalent terms and explanations in German, Spanish, French, and Italian. Focuses more on legal phrases and terms of art than on easily translated words. Appendixes include tables of legal abbreviations in the five languages and an international telephone code directory.

§ Lawrence Deems Egbert and Fernando Morales-Macedo, *Multilingual law dictionary : English-Français-Español-Deutsch* (Alphen aan den Rijn : Sijthoff ; Dobbs Ferry, N.Y. : Oceana ; Baden-Baden : Nomos, 1978) is a simpler work, listing 6,300 English terms and providing equivalents in the other languages.   K54.W47

Chinese

Bilancia, Philip R. Dictionary of Chinese law and government : Chinese-English. Stanford, Calif. : Stanford Univ. Pr., 1981. 822 p.   **CK47**

About 25,000 Chinese terms are entered under Wade-Giles romanized equivalents. Each main entry consists of the romanized term, the Chinese characters, pronunciation guide, definitions, cross-references, and examples of usage. Includes transliteration conversion tables and a radical index.   KQK.B59

French

Dictionnaire économique et juridique = Economic and legal dictionary / Jean Baleyte ... [et al.]. 3. éd., rev. et augm. Paris : L.G.D.J., c1992. 667 p.   **CK48**

1st ed., 1977, had title *Dictionnaire juridique* and served as a successor to Th. A. Quemner's 1953 work of the same title. 2nd ed., 1989.

"Français/anglais, English/French"—*Cover.*

Emphasizes phrases and legal terms in both languages. Some differences in American and British usage noted.

§ Michel Doucet, *Dictionnaire juridique et economique : français-anglais, anglais-français = Legal and economic dictionary : French-English, English-French* (Paris : Maison du Dictionnaire, 1979) is a comparable, somewhat more concise work.   K52.F7D53

German

Dietl, Clara-Erika. Wörterbuch für Recht, Wirtschaft und Politik : mit Kommentaren in deutscher und englischer Sprache / von Clara-Erika Dietl, Egon Lorenz ; unter Mitarbeit von Wiebke Buxbaum. 5., völlig neu bearb. und erw. Aufl. München : Beck, 1990. v. 1. (In progress).   **CK49**

Added title page: Dictionary of legal, commercial and political terms.

1st ed., 1964; 3rd ed., 1985–88. The current German-English volume is the 4th ed. (1992).

The most highly respected of several German legal dictionaries. Provides extensive explanatory notes, including differences between American and British usage.

§ Another reputable dictionary is: Alfred Romain, *Wörterbuch der Rechts- und Wirtschaftssprache = Dictionary of legal and commercial terms* (München : Beck, 1985–89. 2 v.).   K52.G4D54

Italian

De Franchis, Francesco. Dizionario giuridico = Law dictionary. Milano : Giuffrè, 1984. v. 1. (In progress).   **CK50**

An encyclopedic work, with lengthy explanatory entries and an extensive introduction (in Italian) on American and English usage. Only an English-Italian volume has so far been published.   K52.I73D4

Japanese

Ei-Beihō jiten = Dictionary of Anglo-American law / henshū daihyō Tanaka Hideo. Shohan. Tōkyō : Tōkyō Daigaku Shuppankai, 1991. 1025 p. : ill.   **CK51**
 An English-Japanese dictionary of American and British legal concepts, including major institutions and sources. All prefatory and explanatory matter in Japanese. A separate biographical section at the end covers major historical figures. Appendixes provide information on the U.S. and U.K. legal systems, including lists of officeholders and charts of court jurisdiction and government organization. Concludes with a brief Japanese-English glossary.
 § The major Japanese-English work is Jujiro Ito, *A Japanese-English dictionary of legal terms, with supplement* (Tokyo : Daigaku Shobo, 1952), which is quite extensive but too old to include many neologisms or technological terms.   KF156.E323

Latin

Berger, Adolf. Encyclopedic dictionary of Roman law. (*In* Transactions of the American Philosophical Society, n.s. 43, pt. 2 [1953] : 303–809).   **CK52**
 Definitions of Roman legal terms, as well as major institutions, jurists, and writings. Entries include references to Roman sources and to secondary literature. The dictionary is followed by a brief English-Latin glossary and a classified general bibliography.

Latin words & phrases for lawyers / R. S. Vasan, ed. Don Mills, Ontario ; N.Y. : Datinder S. Sodhi for Law and Business Publications (Canada), 1980. 335 p.   **CK53**
 A dictionary of Latin terms appearing in legal writing. One alphabetical list contains words, short terms of art, and longer maxims. Some entries include references to sources such as Coke and Blackstone. A cross-reference index lists maxims under about 40 legal topics.   KF156.L37

Portuguese

Mello, Maria Chaves de. Dicionário jurídico português-inglês, inglês-português = Portuguese-English, English-Portuguese law dictionary. 5. ed., aum. Rio de Janeiro : Barrister's Editora, 1992. 512 p.   **CK54**
 1st ed., 1984; 4th ed., 1991.
 A well-researched and thorough dictionary. Most explanatory material is in Portuguese only.   K52.P67M45

Spanish

Solís, Gerardo. West's Spanish-English/English-Spanish law dictionary : translations of terms, phrases, and definitions of concepts of modern Spanish and English legal terminology / by Gerardo Solís ; contributing authors, Eduardo Stagg ... [et al.] ; and Raúl A. Gasteazoro, Jr., ed. St. Paul, Minn. : West Publ. Co., 1992. 747 p.   **CK55**
 Added t.p. and title in Spanish: *Diccionario legal Español-Inglés/Inglés-Español.*
 One of the most useful of several recent dictionaries in this field. Most entries include brief explanations of the legal terms, in everyday English or Spanish.
 § Henry S. Dahl, *Dahl's law dictionary / Diccionario juridico* (Buffalo, N.Y. : Hein, 1992) provides some encyclopedic entries, taken from authoritative sources such as codes and case law. Guillermo Cabanellas de las Cuevas and Eleanor C. Hoague, *Butterworths Spanish/English legal dictionary / Diccionario jurídico español/inglés Butterworths* (Austin, Tex. : Butterworth, 1991) is an extensive, two-

volume work with more than 150,000 entries. It provides explanations of terms without direct translations, but most definitions are very brief. Enrique Alcarez Varó and Brian Hughes, *Diccionario de términos jurídicos : inglés-español, Spanish-English* (Barcelona : Editorial Ariel, 1993) includes extensive treatment of legal phrases and idioms.
K52.S6S65

Thesauruses

Burton, William C. Legal thesaurus. 2nd ed. N.Y. : Macmillan ; Toronto : Maxwell Macmillan Canada ; N.Y. : Maxwell Macmillan Internat., c1992. 1011 p.   **CK56**
 1st ed., 1980.
 An authoritative work, evenly divided into Main entries and Index sections. The alphabetically arranged main entries provide synonyms, associated legal concepts, and related foreign phrases (usually Latin maxims). The comprehensive index lists all terms and indicates the main entries under which they appear.
 § William P. Statsky, *West's legal thesaurus/dictionary* (St. Paul, Minn. : West, 1985) is a less extensive work, providing straightforward definitions and a smaller number of synonyms.   KF156.B856

Quotations

The Oxford dictionary of American legal quotations / Fred R. Shapiro. N.Y. : Oxford Univ. Pr., 1993. 582 p.   **CK57**
 The latest of several books of legal quotations, containing more than 3,500 entries from verified sources. Like its predecessors, arranged by subject and indexed by keyword and author.
 § Of earlier works, *A dictionary of legal quotations*, ed. by Simon James and Chantal Stebbins (London : Croon Helm ; N.Y. : Macmillan, 1987) is a short but useful British collection of briefer extracts. Eugene C. Gerhart, *Quote it! : memorable legal quotations* (N.Y. : Boardman, 1969) and *Quote it II : a dictionary of memorable legal quotations* (Buffalo, N.Y. : Hein, 1988) include a wide variety of material under several hundred idiosyncratic headings. David S. Shrager and Elizabeth Frost, *The quotable lawyer* (N.Y. : Facts on File, 1986) is a rather unimpressive collection lacking page references for quotations from books.   KF159.S53

Directories

Guide to foreign law firms / prepared by the American Bar Association, Section of International Law and Practice ; ed. by James R. Silkenat and Howard B. Hill. 2nd ed. Wash. : The Section, c1993. 274 p.   **CK58**
 Cover title: ABA guide to foreign law firms.
 1st ed., 1988.
 A concise and relatively inexpensive listing of lawyers in more than 130 countries. Arranged geographically by region, then by country. Brief entries list firm name, address, telephone, and names of partners. Based on suggestions and personal experiences of ABA members. Excludes foreign offices of U.S. firms.   K68.G85

International directory of legal aid / ed. by Judy Lane and Simon Hillyard. London : International Bar Assoc. Educational Trust : Sweet & Maxwell, 1985. 244 p.   **CK59**
 A survey of legal aid practices in more than 90 countries, with information on procedures followed in civil and criminal cases. The entry for each country includes the name and address of the agency from which further information is available.

The international financial law review 1000. 1991 ed.– . London : Euromoney Publications, c1990– . Annual.   **CK60**

A highly selective directory of international business law firms in some 100 countries, arranged geographically. Introductory summaries for each country discuss the business environment, legislative developments, the legal market, firms' areas of expertise, and billing practices. A general introduction provides a worldwide survey of law firms and legal business.   K68.I573

Kime's international law directory. 1892– . London : Bowden, Hudson & Co., 1892– . Annual.   **CK61**

Broader coverage than other international directories (almost 200 countries), although many countries have very few lawyers listed and some have none. Each country's entry begins with brief notes on the legal system, including designation of legal practitioners, professional education, and official language of legal proceedings. Includes a subject index of listed lawyers' areas of practice.

§ Another British-based international directory, *The international law list* (London : Corper-Mordaunt, 1867– . Annual), covers about 115 countries. It has no background information but includes useful lists of law societies, bar associations, and patent offices.

Martindale-Hubbell international law directory. 123rd year (1991)– . New Providence, N.J. : Martindale-Hubbell, c1991– . Annual.   **CK62**

Contents: v. 1, Europe, Asia, Australasia, Middle East, Africa; v. 2, North America, the Caribbean, Central America, South America.

The most extensive international legal directory, with information concerning more than 100,000 lawyers and 4,000 law firms in about 130 countries. Provides biographical data on firm partners and associates in a format similar to the domestic *Martindale-Hubbell law directory* (CK151). For Canada there is also a comprehensive alphabetical listing of lawyers, not limited to those who have purchased biographical entries. Includes U.S. practitioners in international law. Each volume contains an alphabetical index and an index of areas of practice.   K68.M37

World law school directory. 1993 ed. [Buffalo, N.Y.] : W.S. Hein, 1993. 333 p.   **CK63**

Covers law schools in 141 countries. Indicates addresses, telephone and fax numbers, key personnel, degrees offered, primary language spoken, and whether foreign students are admitted. Based on responses to a 1991 questionnaire. Also published as part of the *Modern legal systems cyclopedia* (CK31).   K100.A4W67

Handbooks

Codes of professional responsibility / ed. by Rena A. Gorlin. 2nd ed. Wash. : Bureau of National Affairs, c1990. 555 p.   **CK64**

For annotation, *see* CK160.   BJ1725.C57

World Peace Through Law Center. Law and judicial systems of nations / ed. by Charles S. Rhyne. 3rd rev. ed., covering 144 nations. Wash. : World Peace Through Law Center, 1978. 919 p.   **CK65**

1st ed., 1968.

Brief narrative sketches of the legal systems of 144 countries, covering the legal profession and organization of the bar, legal education, courts of justice (explaining the various components of each judicial system), and the legal system generally (common law or civil law basis; major influences). A handy source for general information, although unfortunately not updated.   K583.W64

Style manuals

The bluebook : a uniform system of citation. 15th ed.– . Cambridge, Mass. : Harvard Law Review Association, c1991– . Irregular.   **CK66**

"Compiled by the editors of the Columbia Law Review, the Harvard Law Review, the University of Pennsylvania Law Review, and the Yale Law Journal"—*t.p.*

Previous editions had title: *A uniform system of citation.*

The standard source for style and citation formats in U.S. legal journals. The first half of the book prescribes somewhat arcane rules, but blue pages in the second half provide (1) very useful tables of sources for court opinions, statutes, and administrative materials in each U.S. jurisdiction and in 21 other countries; and (2) lists of abbreviations used in law reviews.

§ The Canadian counterpart, with similar appendix tables of sources and abbreviations, is *Canadian guide to uniform legal citation = Manuel canadien de la référence juridique* (3rd ed. Toronto : Carswell, 1992).   KF245.B58

Digests and collections

Copyright laws and treaties of the world. Paris : United Nations Educational, Scientific and Cultural Organization and the Bureau of National Affairs, Washington, c1956– . 3 v. (loose-leaf).   **CK67**

An English-language compilation of the copyright laws of more than 140 countries, as well as information on international treaties by which each country is bound. Includes the text of several multilateral conventions.   K1419.2 1956

Digest of commercial laws of the world / Lester Nelson, ed. Rev. ed. Dobbs Ferry, N.Y. : Oceana, [1975]– . 11 v. (loose-leaf).   **CK68**

Published for the National Association of Credit Management.

A country-by-country summary of laws governing such matters as contracts, business organizations, investments, and commercial litigation. Covers more than 80 countries; each national section is published as a separate pamphlet and revised periodically. Vol. 7 includes major international conventions and a bibliography on international commercial law.

§ A companion 3-v. set, *Digest of intellectual property laws of the world* (Dobbs Ferry, N.Y. : Oceana, 1975– . looseleaf. Title varies.) provides similar coverage of patent, trademark and copyright laws. It also includes international conventions and a bibliography.   K1005.4.D54

International digest of health legislation. v. 1, no. 1 (1948)– . Geneva : World Health Organization, [1948]– . Quarterly.   **CK69**

Publ. also in French: *Recueil international de législation sanitaire.*

A subject selection of new national and international legislation dealing with such matters as disease control, food safety, and environmental protection. Most items are abstracted, but some documents are reprinted in full. An index in the front of each issue lists items by country and then chronologically. Also contains articles on recent developments, book reviews, and abstracts of current literature.

§ *Food and agriculture legislation* (Rome : Food and Agriculture Organization, 1952–), and *Labour law documents* (formerly *Legislative series*) (Geneva : International Labour Office, 1919–) are similar collections of current national legislation and international documents.

Investment laws of the world. Dobbs Ferry, N.Y. : Oceana, c1972– . 15 v. (loose-leaf).   **CK70**

Prep. by the International Centre for Settlement of Investment Disputes.

Provides the texts of investment laws in almost 100 countries. Separate pamphlets for each country are in English, French, Portuguese or Spanish; some foreign-language pamphlets include English translations. The set also includes five volumes of investment treaties, indexed alphabetically and chronologically.   K1112.A48

Martindale-Hubbell international law digest. 125th year (1993)– . New Providence, N.J. : Martindale-Hubbell, c1993– . Annual.   **CK71**

Continues *International law digest* volume of the *Martindale-Hubbell law digest*, which was formerly issued as v. 8 of *Martindale-Hubbell law directory* (CK151). Each set retains the numbering of the work it continues.

Useful overviews of laws in more than 60 countries, most prepared by law firms in each country. Each country's chapter contains about 10–20 pages summarizing laws under about 100 topics, with references to codes and other authoritative sources. Also includes the text of nine major international conventions.

Constitutions

Blaustein, Albert P. Constitutions of the countries of the world : a series of updated texts, constitutional chronologies and annotated bibliographies / Albert P. Blaustein, G. H. Flanz. Permanent ed. Dobbs Ferry, N.Y. : Oceana, [1971]– . 21 v.   **CK72**

Separate pamphlets for more than 160 countries, filed alphabetically in looseleaf binders. Replacement and supplementary pamphlets are issued several times a year. For each country, gives a chronology of national constitutional development, text of the constitution in English, and a brief annotated bibliography. Many pamphlets also include the text in the original language.

§ A companion series, Albert P. Blaustein and Eric P. Blaustein, *Constitutions of dependencies and special sovereignties* (Dobbs Ferry, N.Y. : Oceana, [1975]– , 8 v. looseleaf) covers U.S. territories, British dependencies, Spanish autonomous regions, the Vatican City State, and a variety of other jurisdictions.   K3157.A2B58

Peaslee, Amos Jenkins. Constitutions of nations. Rev. 4th ed. / by Dorothy Peaslee Xydis. The Hague : Nijhoff, 1974–85. v. 1–2 : ill. (In progress).   **CK73**

1st ed., 1950; 3rd ed. 1965–70, 4 v. in 7.

Contents: v. 1, Africa (1974); v. 2, pts. 1–2, Asia/Australia/Oceania (1985).

Provides texts of constitutions in English, in volumes grouped by continent. Brief introductory notes for each country summarize its international status, describe its form and branches of national government, and list constitutional rights guaranteed to its people.

K3157.E5P4

INTERNATIONAL LAW

Guides

Guide to international legal research / the George Washington journal of international law and economics. Stoneham, Mass. : Butterworth Legal Publishers, 1990. 400 p.   **CK74**

1981 ed. had title: *Research tips in international law.*

Originally publ. in *The George Washington journal of international law and economics* 20, no. 1–2 (1986).

An introductory overview of research procedures, followed by a bibliography of basic resources in international law. Coverage includes primary sources (codified law and case law), secondary sources (serials and analytical tools), and research tools (practice aids and reference sources). Most sections include brief introductions and descriptive annotations. No index.   JX1297.G84

Bibliography

Andrews, John A. Keyguide to information sources on the international protection of human rights / J.A. Andrews and W.D. Hines. London ; N.Y. : Mansell, 1987. 169 p.   **CK75**

A guide to the literature and organizations of human rights. Pt. 1 provides an overview of the field and its literature; pt. 2 is an annotated topical bibliography of treaties, law reports, official documentation, and secondary sources; and pt. 3 lists selected intergovernmental and nongovernmental organizations. Indexed.   K3236.A53

Beyerly, Elizabeth. Public international law : a guide to information sources. London ; N.Y. : Mansell, 1991. 331 p. **CK76**

An extensive, annotated bibliography of resources in international law. Pt. 1 lists major primary sources (treatises, international customary law, judicial decisions, and official publications); secondary sources (including treaties, periodicals, encyclopedias and dictionaries); and reference aids (research guides, bibliographies, directories, and libraries). Pt. 2 is a selected subject bibliography of books and articles on various substantive aspects of international law.   Z6461.B49

Human rights bibliography : United Nations documents and publications, 1980–1990 / comp. by the United Nations Library, Geneva, in cooperation with the Centre for Human Rights. N.Y. : United Nations, 1993. 5 v. (2048 p.).   **CK77**

Contents: v. 1, main list by category; v. 2, author index; v. 3–5, subject index.

An extensive listing of U.N. materials relating to human rights issues including civil and political rights, self-determination, discrimination, and the role of international organizations and other institutions. Author and subject indexes provide U.N. document numbers and references to descriptive entries in the main list.

§ Earlier, more general bibliographies in the field include J. Paul Martin, ed., *Human rights : a topical bibliography* (Boulder, Colo. : Westview Pr., 1983), which is limited to English-language books and articles but has a detailed subject arrangement; and Julian R. Friedman and Marc I. Sherman, editors, *Human rights : an international and comparative law bibliography* (Westport, Conn. : Greenwood, 1985), covering a wider range of sources under broader subject headings.

K3236.H863

Kleckner, Simone-Marie. Public international law and international organization : international law bibliography. Revised and updated. N.Y. : Oceana, 1988. 126 p. (A Collection of bibliographic and research resources, [1]).   **CK78**

1st ed., 1983.

A bibliography of official publications, collections, and other basic resources in international law. The first four parts list primary sources (treaty collections; documentary collections and digests of state practice; general principles of law; and judicial decisions), followed by a subject listing of treatises and commentaries, materials on international organizations, periodicals, yearbooks, and reference aids.

The law of the sea : a bibliography on the law of the sea, 1968–1988 : two decades of law-making, state practice, and doctrine (bilingual, English/French) = Le droit de la mer : bibliographie du droit de la mer, 1968–1988 : deux décennies de législation, de pratique des états et de doctrine (bilingue, anglais/français). N.Y. : Office for Ocean Affairs and the Law of the Sea, United Nations, 1991. 472 p.   **CK79**

Lists books and articles on legal issues concerning the world's oceans, including territorial seas and polar regions. Materials are listed alphabetically within each broad subject area; chapter 27, National policies and practice, is further divided by country. Limited to works in English or French. Author index.

———. *Multilingual supplement* (1993. 406 p.) consists of six parts listing publications in Chinese, German, Italian, Russian, Spanish, and Arabic.

§ An earlier extensive listing of books, articles and documents is Nikos Papadakis, *International law of the sea : a bibliography* (Alphen aan den Rijn ; Germantown, Md. : Sijthoff & Noordhoff, 1980), supplemented by *International law of the sea and marine affairs : a bibliography* (The Hague : Nijhoff, 1984).   Z6464.M2L34

Tutorow, Norman E. War crimes, war criminals, and war crimes trials : an annotated bibliography and source book / comp. and ed. by Norman E. Tutorow with the special assistance of Karen Winnovich. N.Y. : Greenwood, [1986]. 548 p. (Bibliographies and indexes in world history, 4).   **CK80**

A classified bibliography of 4,500 items mainly relating to World War II war crimes and the subsequent trials, but including material on earlier and more recent war crimes. Most items noted are in English. Also contains introductory sections of reference sources and general works. Appendixes reproduce major documents and provide tabular information on major trials. List of abbreviations; glossary; author and subject index.

§ John Rodney Lewis, *Uncertain judgment : a bibliography of war crimes trials* (Santa Barbara, Calif. : ABC-Clio, 1979) is a somewhat less comprehensive work focusing more specifically on the judicial proceedings, with sections on background and subsidiary issues. Its 3,300 entries are unannotated. Author index.   Z6464.W33T87

Current

Marine affairs bibliography. v. 1, [no. 1]– . Charlottesville, Va. : Univ. of Virginia Law School, [1980]– . Quarterly, with annual cumulations.   **CK81**

Subtitle: A comprehensive index to marine law and policy literature.

Originally comp. and ed. by Christian L. Wiktor and Leslie A. Foster ; prep. under the auspices of Dalhousie Ocean Studies Programme.

Publisher varies; 1980–87, Halifax, N.S. : Dalhousie Law School.

A detailed classed index to international literature on the law of the sea and maritime issues. Covers government and international documents as well as books and journal articles. Some entries include brief annotations. Indexed by author, corporate names and conferences, geographical area, and case name. A cumulation covering 1980–85 has been published (Dordrecht, Neth.; Boston : Nijhoff, 1987).   Z6464.M2W54

Public international law : a current bibliography of books and articles. v. 1, no. 1 (1975)– . Berlin [etc.] : Springer-Verlag, 1976– . Semiannual.   **CK82**

A classed listing of current writing on international law. Articles are selected from more than 1,000 journals and collections. Books are included beginning with v. 16 (1990). International and multilingual in scope. Author and subject indexes.   Z6461.P83

Refugee abstracts. v. 1, no. 1 [Mar. 1982]– . Geneva : Internat. Refugee Integration Resource Centre, 1982– . Quarterly.   **CK83**

Abstracts of a wide variety of books and articles, arranged by subject. Also includes abstracts of resource materials, book reviews, texts of major new documents, and announcements of upcoming conferences. Author and subject indexes.   HV640.R37

Treaties

Collections and Indexes

Bowman, M. J. Multilateral treaties : index and current status / comp. and annotated within the Univ. of Nottingham Treaty Centre by M. J. Bowman and D. J. Harris. London : Butterworths, 1984. 516 p.   **CK84**

One of the most useful indexes to multilateral conventions, with information on the published sources, dates, parties, and territorial scope of more than 900 treaties. Brief notes for each treaty summarize its purpose and provide references to related documents. Treaties are listed in chronological order, with subject and word indexes. Updated by annual supplements.   JX171.B68

The consolidated treaty series / ed. and annotated by Clive Parry. Dobbs Ferry, N.Y. : Oceana, [1969–81]. 231 v.   **CK85**

A retrospective collection of more than 10,000 treaties, covering the period from 1648 until the beginning of the League of Nations *Treaty series* (CK86) in 1919. Includes the text of each treaty in the language of one of the signatories, accompanied by a French or English translation if available. Index volumes include chronological list (5 v.), special chronologies (colonial treaties; postal and telegraph agreements) (2 v.), and index to parties listing dates, signatories and citations (5 v.). There is no subject index.   JX120.P35

League of Nations. Treaty series : publication of treaties and international engagements registered with the Secretariat of the League. London : Harrison, 1920–46. 205 v.   **CK86**

Includes Treaty no. 1–no. 4834.

Continued by United Nations *Treaty series* (CK90).

Contains treaties ratified from the formation of the League to the creation of the U.N. Includes English and French translations accompanying reprints of the official texts. Nine index volumes, issued after every 500 treaties, provide access chronologically and by country and subject.

Multilateral treaties deposited with the Secretary-General. 1981– . N.Y. : United Nations, 1982– . Annual.   **CK87**

Earlier title: *Multilateral treaties in respect of which the Secretary-General performs depositary functions* (U.N., 1967–79).

An annual listing of conventions and agreements concluded under U.N. auspices. Arranged by subject in 28 chapters, and chronologically within each chapter. Entries provide effective dates, U.N. *Treaty series* citations, list of parties with dates of signature and ratification or accession, and the texts of parties' declaration, reservations, and objections. Updated by the monthly *Statement of treaties and international agreements* (New York . U.N., 1947–), which also includes references to bilateral treaties and other agreements registered or filed with the Secretariat.   JX171.U372a

Organization of American States. General Secretariat. Inter-American treaties and conventions : signatures, ratifications, and deposits with explanatory notes. Rev. ed. Wash. : General Secretariat of the Organization of American States, 1993. 1 v. (looseleaf). (Treaty series, no.9).   **CK88**

1st ed., 1954.

Also publ. in Spanish. *Tratados y convenciones interamericanos : firmas, ratificaciones y depositos con notas explicativas.*

Lists multilateral treaties and conventions among the American states, with information on national signatures and ratifications. Provides references to sources for documents.

Rohn, Peter H. World treaty index. 2nd ed. Santa Barbara, Calif. : ABC-Clio, [1983–84]. 5 v.   **CK89**

Contents: v. 1, Reference volume; v. 2–3, Main entry section, pts. 1–2, 1900–59, 1960–80; v. 4, Party index; v. 5, Keyword index.

1st ed., 1974.

An index to more than 44,000 bilateral and multilateral treaties appearing in the League of Nations and U.N. *Treaty series* (CK86, CK90) and in the national treaty collections of 120 countries. Vol.1 includes a table of abbreviations, other explanatory matter, and an extensive series of tables ranking parties by subject and by treaty partner. References in the main entry section contain names of instruments; parties; dates of signature and entry into force; and references to sources. Indexes provide access by country, subject, date, and international organization.

A companion to his *Treaty profiles* (1976. 256 p.).   JX171.R63

United Nations. Treaty series : treaties and international agreements registered or filed and recorded with the Secretariat of the United Nations. N.Y. : United Nations, 1947– . v. 1 (1946/47)– .   **CK90**

Continues the *Treaty series* issued by the League of Nations (CK86).

The most comprehensive source for treaties since the Second World War. Treaties are published in their original languages, as well as in English and French translations. Noncumulative indexes cover every 100 (v. 1–400) or 50 volumes (v. 401–). There is a substantial time lag of several years before treaties are published, and several more before indexes are issued.   JX170.U35

Weiss, Edith Brown. International environmental law : basic instruments and references / by Edith Brown Weiss, Daniel Barstow Magraw, Paul C. Szasz. [Dobbs Ferry, N.Y.] : Transnational, c1992. 749 p.   **CK91**

A subject collection of 85 treaties, declarations, resolutions and other documents, current through mid-1991. Editors' notes provide valuable background information. A list by subject provides references to more than 800 additional documents. Includes a useful index of popular names.

§ Harald Hohmann, ed., *Basic documents of international environmental law* (London : Graham & Trotman, 1992. 3 v.) is another respected collection, more extensive and considerably more expensive.   K3583.W45

United States

Consolidated treaties & international agreements : current document service, United States. 1990– . [Dobbs Ferry, N.Y.] : Oceana, 1990– . Quarterly.   **CK92**

A commercial publication providing the English texts of new treaties within three months, usually years before they are available in the official sources *Treaties and other international acts* (inf92-17906) and *United States treaties* (CK95). Each issue includes appendixes indexing treaties by country and by subject.

•Also available in a machine–readable form as part of *TIARA CD-ROM : treaties and international agreements researchers' archive*, which includes the full text of over 4,500 treaties, an index, and a citation table.

§ Another commercial publication, *Hein's United States treaties and other international agreements—current microfiche service* (Buffalo, N.Y. : Hein, 1990–) provides the texts of new treaties in microfiche, accompanied by looseleaf paper index.   JX236 1990.U54a

United States. Department of State. Treaties in force : a list of treaties and other international agreements of the United States in force. Wash. : U. S. Govt. Print. Off., [1929?]– . Annual.   **CK93**

Superintendent of Documents classification: S9.14: .

Published irregularly until 1958, when annual publication began.

The basic guide to current treaties and agreements to which the U.S. is a party. In two parts: pt. 1 lists bilateral treaties by country and within each country by subject; pt. 2 lists multilateral treaties and conventions by subject. Indicates dates of signature and entry into force and provides citations, if available, to major treaty publications such as *Statutes at large, TIAS, UST,* Bevans, League of Nations *Treaty series,* and United Nations *Treaty series.* An appendix covers copyright treaties and conventions. Supplemented by the "Treaty Actions" section of the *U.S. Department of State dispatch* (Wash. : U. S. Govt. Print. Off., 1990–).

§ A commercial *Guide to the United States treaties in force* (Buffalo, N.Y. : Hein, 1982–) is also issued annually and provides several additional means of access to current treaties, including a numerical list of all treaties in force and a subject index to both bilateral and multilateral treaties.   JX236.1929c

United States. Treaties. Treaties and other international agreements of the United States of America, 1776–1949 / comp. under the direction of Charles I. Bevans. Wash. : U. S. Govt. Print. Off., 1968–76. 13 v.   **CK94**

Contents: v. 1, Multilateral, 1776–1917; v. 2, Multilateral, 1918–1930; v. 3, Multilateral, 1931–1945; v. 4, Multilateral, 1946–1949; v. 5, Afghanistan-Burma; v. 6, Canada-Czechoslovakia; v. 7, Denmark-France; v. 8, Germany-Iran; v. 9, Iraq-Muscat; v. 10, Nepal-Peru; v. 11, Philippines-United Arab Republic; v. 12, United Kingdom-Zanzibar; v. 13, General index.

The definitive historical compilation of pre-1950 U.S. treaties originally published in *Statutes at large* (CK176). Multilateral treaties are arranged chronologically, and bilateral treaties alphabetically by country. Only English-language texts are provided. Indexed by country and subject.   JX236 1968.A5

——————— United States treaties and other international agreements. v. 1 (1950)– . Wash. : U. S. Govt. Print. Off., 1952– . Annual.   **CK95**

Superintendent of Documents classification: S 59.12: .

The official source since 1950 for all treaties and international agreements to which the U.S. is a party. (Earlier treaties were published in *Statutes at large* [CK176] and have been compiled by Charles I. Bevans [CK94]). Treaties are first published individually as pamphlets in the *Treaties and other international acts* (TIAS) series (inf92-17906), then compiled into *UST* volumes after several years. Subject and country index.   JX231.A34

United States treaty index : 1776–1990 consolidation / comp. and ed. by Igor I. Kavass. Buffalo, N.Y. : W.S. Hein, 1991–93. 12 v.   **CK96**

Contents: v. 1–5, numerical master guide; v. 6–7, chronological index; v. 8–9, country index; v. 10–11, subject index; v. 12, geographical subject index.

Indexes the major collections and series of U.S. treaties and international agreements. The numerical guide lists all treaties and agreements, with names, citations, parties, subjects, dates, and references to earlier treaties amended or extended. Indexes by date, country, and subject provide references to the numerical list. Updated by *Supplement I* (1993) and the semiannual *Current treaty index,* which provides information on new agreements not yet published in the official sources.

•Cumulative electronic coverage is provided by *Hein's United States treaty index CD-ROM* [database] (Buffalo, N.Y. : Hein, 1991–).   JX231.U58 1991

Canada

Canada. Department of External Affairs. Treaty Section. Treaties in force for Canada : a list of treaties of Canada in force as of January 1, 1988 / comp. by Treaty Section, Bureau of Legal Affairs. [Ottawa] : External Affairs Canada, [1988]. 1 v. (various pagings).   **CK97**

Pt. 1 lists bilateral treaties by country; pt. 2 lists multilateral treaties by subject. Provides references to Canada's *Treaty series* (Ottawa : Queen's Printer for Canada, 1938–) and other sources. Combined subject index to multilateral and bilateral treaties.

§ Retrospective coverage of Canadian treaties is provided in Christian L. Wiktor, *Canadian treaty calendar = Répertoire des traités du Canada, 1928–1978* (London : Oceana, 1982).

Great Britain

Parry, Clive. An index of British treaties, 1101–1968 / Clive Parry and Charity Hopkins. London : H. M. S. O., 1970. 4 pts. in 3 v. (1816 p.).   **CK98**

Comp. under the auspices of the International Law Fund and the British Institute of International and Comparative Law.

Contents: v. 1, pt. 1, Index of multilateral treaties by subject; pt. 2. Index of bilateral treaties by country; pt. 3, Index of bilateral treaties by subject; v. 2, Chronological list of treaties, 1101–1925; v. 3, Chronological list of treaties, 1926–1968. (v. 2–3 comprise pt. 4.).

A comprehensive index of British treaties, providing citations to the U.K.'s *Treaty series* (London : H.M.S.O., 1892–), as well as to international collections and other British sources. A supplementary v. 4 (1991. 795 p.), compiled by D. J. Harris and J. A. Shepard, updates entries in volumes 2 and 3, lists new treaties entered into from 1969 to 1988, and includes indexes by subject and country.   JX636 1970.P37

Encyclopedias

Encyclopedia of human rights / [comp. by] Edward Lawson. N.Y. : Taylor & Francis, c1991. 1907 p.   **CK99**

A major work providing an overview of human rights concepts, activities of international organizations, and practices in 150 countries. Articles are in alphabetical order, with full texts or excerpts of many conventions, declarations, and other documents. Appendixes include an extensive bibliography in two parts, by country and by subject; a glossary of human rights terms; and lists of instruments and other documents. Subject index.   JC571.E67

Encyclopedia of public international law / publ. under the auspices of the Max Planck Institute for Comparative Public Law and International Law, under the direction of Rudolf Bernhardt. Amsterdam ; N.Y. : North-Holland, 1992. v. 1. (In progress).   **CK100**

Contents: v. 1, A–D.

An extensive, highly respected encyclopedia with informative articles by leading international law scholars from several countries. Articles are accompanied by brief bibliographies with references to English, French, and German sources. Originally published in 12 v. arranged by subject (1981–90), the work is being reissued with the articles in alphabetical order. Some articles have brief updating addenda, and a few new articles have been added.   JX1226.E5

Dictionaries

Bledsoe, Robert L. The international law dictionary / Robert L. Bledsoe, Boleslaw A. Boczek. Santa Barbara, Calif. : ABC-Clio, c1987. 422 p.   **CK101**

Lengthy definitions of more than 300 major concepts and doctrines in international law, arranged by subject in 12 chapters. Each entry is in two parts, first defining the term and then explaining its significance. Indexed.   JX1226.B57 1987

Fox, James R. Dictionary of international & comparative law. [Dobbs Ferry, N.Y.] : Oceana, c1992. 495 p.   **CK102**

Brief definitions of some 4,000 terms used in international law, including acronyms and foreign-language terms. Some entries provide references to source documents and journal articles.   JX1226.F69 1992

Paenson, Isaac. English-French-Spanish-Russian manual of the terminology of public international law (law of peace) and international organizations. Brussels : Bruylant ; Deventer, Netherlands : Kluwer, [1983]. xlviii, 846p.   **CK103**

"Publ. for the Graduate Institute of International Studies, Geneva, and 'INTERCENTRE'."—*t.p.*

A textual discussion of basic doctrines and concepts in international law, consisting of parallel columns in English, French, Spanish, and Russian with important terms highlighted in boldface type. There is a general index in each language, as well as separate indexes of conventions, declarations, conferences, and cases.   JX1226.P26

———— English-French-Spanish-Russian manual of the terminology of the law of armed conflicts and of international humanitarian organizations. Brussels : Bruylant ; Boston : M. Nijhoff ; Norwell, Mass. : distr. by Kluwer Academic Publ., 1989. 844 p.   **CK104**

A continuation of Paenson's earlier manual (CK103), focusing on the laws of war and neutrality. General index and index of international legal transactions, declarations and conferences in each language.   JX4281.P33

Parry, Clive. Parry and Grant encyclopaedic dictionary of international law / general editors, Clive Parry, John P. Grant ... [et al.] with assistance from some members of the Scottish Group of International Lawyers. N.Y. : Oceana, 1986. 564 p.   **CK105**

An extensive, alphabetically arranged dictionary providing definitions of terms and concepts, as well as information on international conventions, organizations, and leading cases. Lengthier entries include references to treaties, cases, and scholarly writings. A documentary appendix includes the text of the U.N. Charter and other basic documents of international law.   JX1226.P33

Directories

World directory of teaching and research institutions in international law = Répertoire mondial des institutions de formation et de recherche en droit international. 2nd ed. Paris : UNESCO, 1990. 387 p.   **CK106**

Introductory material in English, French, and Spanish.

1st ed., 1986.

A list of institutes and schools with international law programs in 70 countries, providing addresses, application procedures, and information on courses. Indexed by names of faculty members mentioned in entries and by subject. Also includes lists of associations and periodicals specializing in international law.

§ *World directory of human rights research and training institutions*, 2nd ed. (Paris : UNESCO, 1992) is a similar work covering a more specialized field.   JX1291.W69

Handbooks

Treaties and alliances of the world. 5th ed. / ed. by Nicholas Rengger. Burnt Mill, England : Longman ; Detroit : distr. by Gale, 1990. 579 p. : ill., maps.   **CK107**

1st ed., 1968; 4th ed., 1986. Earlier editions comp. by Henry W. Degenhardt.

Summaries of principal treaties, alliances, and international organizations, and regional agreements. Pt. 1 surveys the role of treaties in international politics and discusses recent developments. Pt. 2 includes extensive coverage of the U. N. and discussion of other international agreements and organizations arranged by subject. Pt. 3 covers NATO and other Cold War pacts. Pt. 4 covers regional agreements and includes lists of bilateral treaties. Pt. 5 discusses cultural, religious and other affiliations. Excerpts from some treaties are provided, but not references to treaty series or other full-text sources. Includes about a dozen maps. Bibliography; brief index.   JX4165

Annuals and current surveys

Anuario interamericano de derechos humanos. 1968– . Dordrecht ; Boston : Martinus Nijhoff.   **CK108**

Title also in English : Inter-American yearbook on human rights.

Imprint varies: Washington : General Secretariat of the Organization of American States, 1968–70.

Provides information on the work of the Inter-American Commission on Human Rights and the Inter-American Court of Human Rights. Pt. 1 reprints basic documents and provides a general overview, pts. 2 and 3 contains selected decisions of the Commission and the Court, and pt. 4 covers resolutions and other activities of the Organization of American States. Facing pages in English and Spanish. Volumes published cover 1968–70 and 1985– .

§ *Yearbook of the European convention on human rights = Annuaire de la Convention européenne des droits de l'homme* (Dordrecht, Netherlands; Boston : Nijhoff, 1958–) provides similar coverage for the European Commission of Human Rights, the European Court of Human Rights, and the Council of Europe, with facing pages in English and French.   KDZ574.A85I68

Humana, Charles. World human rights guide. 3rd ed. N.Y. : Oxford Univ. Pr., 1992. 393 p. : maps.   **CK109**

1st ed., 1983; 2nd ed., 1986.

Provides evaluative comparisons of the human rights situation in 104 countries, based on guidelines set in the Universal Declaration of Human Rights and various U.N. treaties. Covers rights ranging from free speech to freedom from summary executions and torture. The section on each country begins with a general human rights rating and an introductory section providing basic background information.

§ Annual country-by-country surveys of human rights practices include the Dept. of State's *Country reports on human rights practices* (Wash. : U.S. Govt. Print. Off., 1979–); *Critique : review of the U.S. Department of State's country reports on human rights practices* (N.Y. : Lawyers Committee for Human Rights, 1980–); *The Amnesty International report* (London : Amnesty International Publications, 1961–); *Freedom in the world* (N.Y. : Freedom House, 1978–); *Human rights watch world report* (N.Y. : Human Rights Watch, 1990–); and *Human rights in developing countries* (Oslo : Norwegian Univ. Pr., 1985–). The U.N. publishes a *Yearbook on human rights* (1946–) after a delay of several years.   JC571.H788

International Court of Justice. Yearbook. 1946/ 47– . [The Hague] : [International Court of Justice], 1947– . Annual.   **CK110**

Published also in French: *Annuaire.*

Basic information on the World Court, describing its jurisdiction and procedures and summarizing its work for the year. Includes biographies of current judges and comprehensive lists of cases and publications from the Court and its predecessor, the Permanent Court of International Justice (1920–46).

§ The Court also publishes an annual *Bibliography of the International Court of Justice* (1964/65–) listing books and articles discussing its work. The bibliography was included as part of the *Yearbook* from 1946/47 to 1963/64. *Documents on the International Court of Justice,* ed. by Shabtai Rosenne (3rd ed. Dordrecht, Netherlands; Boston : Nijhoff, 1991) is a useful compilation of basic source materials.   JX1971.6.A25

United Nations. United Nations juridical yearbook. 1962– . N.Y. : United Nations, 1963– . Annual.   **CK111**

Treaties, judicial decisions, and other documentary materials concerning the legal status and legal activities of the U.N. and related intergovernmental organizations. Each volume includes a bibliography of the year's books and articles on legal issues concerning the U.N. and related organizations. Published after a delay of several years.   JX1977.A1U54

Digests and collections

Basic documents of international economic law / gen. eds., Stephen Zamora and Ronald A. Brand. Chicago : Commerce Clearing House, c1990. 2 v.   **CK112**

Includes about 55 conventions, agreements, and other documents governing international trade, international finance, foreign investment, intellectual property rights, regional economic organizations, international litigation, arbitration, and other commercial matters. Each document is prefaced with a signed introduction providing historical background, summary of important provisions, and a bibliography.

•Machine-readable version: *International economic law documents* [database] (Wash. : American Soc. of International Law). Available online.

§ Philip Kunig, Niels Lau and Werner Meng, eds., *International economic law : basic documents* (2nd ed. Berlin ; N.Y. : Walter de Gruyter, 1993) is a shorter but somewhat more current collection of major treaties and other documents.   K3820.A35B37

Human rights : a compilation of international instruments / Centre for Human Rights, Geneva. N.Y. : United Nations, 1993. v. 1. (In progress).   **CK113**

1st ed., 1968; 5th ed., 1988.

Includes the texts of conventions, declarations, and recommendations on human rights adopted by the U.N. Vol. 1, in two parts, contains 94 universal instruments arranged by subject, with a chronological listing in the back of each part. Vol. 2 is to contain regional instruments of the Organization of American States, Council of Europe, Organization of African Unity, and Conference on Security and Cooperation in Europe.

§ Information on reservations and declarations of individual countries is found in the companion publication *Human rights : status of international instruments,* also issued every five years by the Centre for Human Rights. Current information on status is in a supplementary *Chart of ratifications* published every six months. Other recent compilations of human rights instruments include Ian Brownlie, *Basic documents on human rights* (3rd ed. Oxford : Clarendon Pr.; N.Y. : Oxford Univ. Pr., 1992); and Winston E. Langley, ed., *Human rights : sixty major global instruments* (Jefferson, N.C. : McFarland, 1992).   K3238.H8

International legal materials. v. 1, no. 1 (Aug. 1962)– . Wash. : American Society of International Law, [1962]– . Bimonthly.   **CK114**

Reproduces selected current documents in international law, including international agreements, U.N. resolutions, International Court of Justice decisions, and other judicial proceedings. Often the first widely distributed print source for new treaties and other important documents.   JX68.I5

NATIONAL LEGAL SYSTEMS

North America

United States

General works

Guides

Cohen, Morris L. How to find the law / by Morris L. Cohen, Robert C. Berring, and Kent C. Olson. 9th ed. St. Paul, Minn. : West Publ. Co., 1989. 716 p. : ill.   **CK115**

1st ed., 1931; 8th ed., 1983.

A standard text on U.S. legal research, discussing both printed sources and computer-based research methods. Extensive treatment of case law, statutes, regulations, and secondary sources, with sample pages from materials discussed. Includes chapters covering international law, English and Commonwealth materials, and foreign and comparative law. Appendixes include state-by-state lists of legal research guides and primary legal resources.

§ Available in an abridged version, limited to U.S. materials: *Finding the law* (2nd ed., St. Paul, Minn. : West Publ. Co., 1989).

Morris L. Cohen and Kent C. Olson, *Legal research in a nutshell* (5th ed., St. Paul, Minn. : West Publ. Co., 1992) is a useful shorter treatment by two of the same authors.   KF240.C538

Corbin, John. Find the law in the library : a guide to legal research. Chicago : Amer. Libr. Assoc., 1989. 327 p. : ill.   **CK116**

Designed primarily for librarians and library school students. An introduction to legal research techniques is followed by 20 chapters on specific fields, such as divorce, real property, criminal law, and pensions. These chapters treat specific research problems, so their reference value is minimal. Each, however, has a helpful introductory section and a bibliography of basic works on its subject. Table of legal abbreviations and glossary; no index.   KF240.C63

Elias, Stephen. Legal research : how to find and understand the law / by Stephen Elias and Susan Levinkind. 3rd national ed. Berkeley, Calif. : Nolo Pr., 1992. 1 v. (various pagings) : ill., forms.   **CK117**

1st ed., 1982; 2nd ed., 1986.

Intended for general readers. Explains the basic procedures of legal research, concentrating on materials for statutory and case law. Succinct explanations, with examples and many illustrations. A good basic guide.   KF240.E35

Jacobstein, J. Myron. Fundamentals of legal research / by J. Myron Jacobstein and Roy M. Mersky. 5th ed. Westbury, N.Y. : Foundation Pr., 1990. 734 p.   **CK118**

1st ed., 1977; 4th ed., 1987.

An extensive and well-illustrated guide, intended as an aid to beginning law students. Includes chapters on federal tax materials and legal citation form, a glossary of terms used in legal research, and an extensive table of legal abbreviations.

§ Available in an abridged version as: *Legal research illustrated* (5th ed., 1990).   KF240.J3

Specialized legal research / Leah F. Chanin, gen. ed. ; with contributions from Joseph James Beard ... [et al.]. Boston : Little, Brown, c1987– . 1 v. (looseleaf).   **CK119**

Each chapter describes the primary and secondary literature in a legal specialty. Covers admiralty, banking law, copyright, customs, environmental law, federal employment law, government contracts, immigration, income tax, military and veterans law, patents and trademarks, securities regulation, and Uniform Commercial Code. General bibliography of specialized legal research sources; subject index.

§ Guides specifically published for the extensive and highly specialized field of tax research: Robert L. Gardner and Dave N. Stewart, *Tax research techniques* (4th ed. N.Y. : American Inst. of Certified Public Accountants, 1993); and Gail Levin Richmond, *Federal tax research : guide to materials and techniques* (4th ed. Westport, N.Y. : Foundation Pr., 1990).   KF240.S69

Bibliography

Catalog of current law titles. 1990– . Ann Arbor, Mich. : Ward and Associates, 1990– . Bimonthly.   **CK120**

Previously published (1989–90) by W. S. Hein, Buffalo, N.Y. Continues in part *National legal bibliography*, publ. by Hein 1984–1988.

Lists books and other materials recently acquired by several dozen major law libraries on general or U.S. legal subjects. Arranged by jurisdiction (national, then individual states), then by subject. Author and title indexes in bimonthly issues; annual volumes add subject index. "Hot sheets" in each issue list items acquired by at least 25% of contributing libraries.

§ A companion publication, *Lawyer's monthly catalog* (1989–), provides coverage of federal and state documents of interest to the legal profession. For similar coverage of other countries and international law, see: *Catalog of new foreign and international law titles* (CK19).   KF4.C395

Doyle, Francis R. Searching the law, the states : a selective bibliography of state practice materials in the 50 states. Dobbs Ferry, N.Y. : Transnational, c1989. 525 p.   **CK121**

A bibliography of books focusing on the laws of specific states. Arranged by state and then by subject; unannotated. Updated by *Supplement 1* (1990. 236 p.) and *Supplement 2* (1991. 246 p.).   KF1.D69

Eis, Arlene L. Legal looseleafs in print. 1981– . Teaneck, N. J. : Infosources Publ., c1981– . Annual.   **CK122**

Earlier eds. publ. under compiler's former name, Arlene L. Stern.

Looseleaf services, many updated weekly or biweekly, are important sources of current legal information and major research tools in specialized fields such as taxation or securities. New material is interfiled with older pages, providing access to current statutes and regulations, recent court decisions, news of other developments, editorial analysis, and extensive subject indexing. This title listing of publications in looseleaf format available in the U.S. includes both regularly updated services and less frequently supplemented works. Entries include publisher, number of volumes, price, and frequency. Detailed subject index.

§ Shorter subject listings of looseleaf services are included as appendixes in Morris L. Cohen's *How to find the law* (CK115) and J. Myron Jacobstein's *Fundamentals of legal research* (CK118).   KF1.S73

———— Legal newsletters in print. 1985– . Teaneck, N.J. : Infosources Publ., c1985] . Annual.   **CK123**

A directory of more than 2,000 newsletters published in the U.S. Although newsletters are often ephemeral or expensive, they may be the leading current awareness sources in developing areas of the law. Excludes newsletters from government sources. Title listing, with indexes by publisher and subject.   KF1.L45

Encyclopedia of legal information sources : a bibliographic guide to approximately 29,000 citations for publications, organizations, and other sources of information on 480 law-related subjects / ed. by Brian L. Baker and Patrick J. Petit. 2nd ed. Detroit : Gale, c1993. 1083 p.   **CK124**

1st ed., 1988.

A topical list of selected books, serials, databases, and organizations. Subheadings under most of the 480 subjects include: looseleaf services and reporters; handbooks, manuals, formbooks; textbooks and general works; law reviews and periodicals; newsletters and newspapers; directories; associations and professional societies; and online databases. Entries are unannotated but include publishers' or organizations' addresses. A particularly useful section, States, lists primary and secondary legal materials for each jurisdiction.   KF1.E53

Hall, Kermit. A comprehensive bibliography of American constitutional and legal history, 1896–1979. Millwood, N.Y. : Kraus Internat., c1984. 5 v. (3443 p.).   **CK125**

A topically arranged bibliography of books and articles dealing with legal history. Organized in seven main sections: general surveys; institutions (e.g., executive, judiciary and courts); constitutional doctrine (judicial review, separation of powers); legal doctrine (corporations, procedure); biographical; chronological; geographical. Instead of using cross-references, the set lists most entries in several sections. Author and subject indexes in v. 5 are extensive, but include multiple locations for each item.

———. ———. *Supplement, 1980–1987* (1991. 2 v. [956 p.]). Adds some 4,000 entries.   KF4541.H34

Houdek, Frank G. Law for the layman : an annotated bibliography of self-help law books. Littleton, Colo. : Rothman, 1991. 1 v. (loose-leaf).   **CK126**

A descriptive list of law books designed for nonlawyers (such as Nolo Press publications), arranged under about 50 subject headings. Both general publications and works for specific states are noted. Includes indexes by author, title, and jurisdiction as well as a list of publishers' addresses and phone numbers.   KF1.H68

National Indian Law Library. Catalogue. v. 1 (1973/74)– . [Boulder, Colo.] : The National Indian Law Library, Native American Rights Fund, 1974– . Irregular.   **CK127**
Cumulative eds. issued at irregular intervals. Each cumulative ed. has four cumulative supplements.

An index of more than 5,000 books, documents, and articles received by the library and relating generally to Native American legal concerns. A subject listing, table of cases, and author/title table provide references to a numerical listing, which contains complete bibliographic information. The 1982 cumulative edition is updated by supplements issued in 1984, 1985, and 1989.   KF8201.A1N38

Recommended law books / ed. by James A. McDermott. 2nd ed. Chicago : Committee on Business Law Libraries, Section of Corporation, Banking and Business Law, American Bar Assoc., 1986. 152 p.   **CK128**
A selective listing of the most respected works in 59 legal subjects and 12 reference categories. Includes excerpts from reviews and comments by lawyers and law librarians. Designed specifically for the needs of practicing lawyers, but useful for learning what are considered the major works in a subject area.   KF1.R426

Encyclopedias

Chandler, Ralph C. The constitutional law dictionary / Ralph C. Chandler, Richard A. Enslen, Peter G. Renstrom. Santa Barbara, Calif. : ABC-Clio, c1985–91. 2 v. (Clio dictionaries in political science, 8).   **CK129**
Contents: v. 1, Individual rights (1985. 507 p.); Suppl. 1 (1987. 138 p.); suppl. 2 (1991. 251 p.); v. 2, Governmental powers (1987. 715 p.).

A guide to leading Supreme Court decisions, describing the cases and explaining their significance in constitutional law. Both volumes include chapters on constitutionalism and legal words and phrases, as well as appendixes providing the text of the Constitution and lists of Supreme Court justices.   KF4548.5.C47

Encyclopedia of the American Constitution / Leonard W. Levy, ed. in chief. N.Y. : Macmillan, c1986. 4 v.   **CK130**
An excellent resource for information on almost any aspect of constitutional law and Supreme Court history. More than 2,000 signed articles, arranged alphabetically and liberally cross-referenced, covering doctrinal concepts, individuals, judicial decisions, legislation, and historical periods. Articles vary in length; many include bibliographies. Appendixes of documents, chronologies, and a brief glossary. Case, name and subject indexes. Updated by a one-volume *Supplement 1* (1992).

Issued in a 2 v. "complete and unabridged" edition in 1990.
KF4548.E53

Encyclopedia of the American judicial system : studies of the principal institutions and processes of law / Robert J. Janosik, ed. N.Y. : Scribner, c1987. 3 v. (1420 p.).   **CK131**
A collection of 88 signed articles on various aspects of the U.S. legal system, written as introductory essays for readers without legal training. Arranged by subject in six broad categories: Legal history, Substantive law, Institutions and personnel, Process and behavior, Constitutional law and issues, Methodology. Articles end with lists of cases discussed and annotated bibliographies. Index in v. 3.
KF154.E53

The guide to American law : everyone's legal encyclopedia. St. Paul [Minn.] : West Publ. Co., c1983–c1985. 12 v. : ill. (some col.), ports.   **CK132**
A legal encyclopedia written for general readers and students, containing more than 5,000 entries and 420 major signed articles. Thoroughly illustrated, with some 3,600 photographs and other reproductions. Entries range from legal principles to historical events to federal regulatory agencies. An appendix volume (v. 11) reproduces sample legal forms and important historical documents; an index volume

(v. 12) contains tables of cited cases and acts and indexes by name and subject. Kept up to date by a 1987 yearbook and annual supplement volumes beginning in 1990.

§ The two standard U.S. legal encyclopedias, *American jurisprudence 2d* (Rochester, N.Y. : Lawyers Cooperative, 1962– . 133 v.) and *Corpus juris secundum* (St. Paul, Minn. : West, 1936– . 155 v.) are thorough, exhaustive treatments of legal doctrine. They have extensive footnotes providing references to federal and state case law, are accompanied by multivolume subject indexes, and are updated with annual pocket supplements in each volume. Because they are designed almost solely for a legal audience, however, they include little background or historical information useful for other researchers.
KF154.G85

Johnson, John W. Historic U.S. court cases, 1690–1990 : an encyclopedia. N.Y. : Garland, 1992. 754 p. (Garland reference library of social science, v. 497 ; Garland reference library of social science. American law and society, v. 2.).   **CK133**
171 signed articles on landmark court decisions, explaining their place in U.S. history in straightforward, nontechnical language. Most cases are from the U.S. Supreme Court, but other federal, state and colonial courts are also represented. Arranged in six parts (Crime and criminal law; Governmental organization, power, and procedure; Economics and the law; Race and gender in American law; Civil liberties; Law in critical periods of American history). Each part includes an introduction and most are subdivided by subject. Each article includes a brief bibliography. Index of cases; index of names and subjects.
KF385.A4J64

McCarthy, J. Thomas. McCarthy's desk encyclopedia of intellectual property. Wash. : Bureau of National Affairs, c1991. 385 p.   **CK134**
A brief encyclopedia of copyright, patent, and trademark terms and concepts, providing definitions and discussion of various applications. Includes references to treatises, cases, statutes, and legislative history documents. Appendixes provide historical lists of federal government officials and statistics on numbers of patents issued since 1790 and trademarks registered since 1870.   KF2976.4.M38

Reader's digest family legal guide : a complete encyclopedia of law for the layman. Pleasantville, N.Y. : Reader's Digest Assoc., c1981. 1268 p.   **CK135**
2,600 alphabetically arranged articles of varying length, from brief definitions to lengthier treatments of legal topics with illustrative case histories and highlight summaries. 17 signed articles on practical aspects of common legal situations are interspersed through the text. At the end, 34 charts and tables outline state laws on a variety of topics but do not include citations to statutes. Numerous cross-references; index.   KF387.R4

Renstrom, Peter G. The American law dictionary. Santa Barbara, Calif. : ABC-Clio, c1991. 308 p.   **CK136**
323 brief articles on major concepts and frequently used terminology in the U.S. judicial system, arranged in seven broad subject chapters (e.g. criminal, civil and appellate processes). Each article defines a term and then explains its significance. The index includes boldface entries providing an alphabetical list of terms defined.   KF156.R46

Directories

AALL directory and handbook. 27th ed. (1987–88)– . Chicago : publ. for the American Assoc. of Law Libraries with the compliments of Commerce Clearing House, Inc., 1987– . Annual.   **CK137**
Title varies: 1940–62/63, *Law libraries in the United States and Canada*; 1964–87, *Directory of law libraries*.
Frequency varies; biennial, 1940–80.
Includes a two-part directory of law libraries. Pt. 1 is an alphabetical listing of association members; pt. 2 a geographical listing of law libraries in the U.S., as well as AALL member libraries in Canada and

other countries. Entries include contact information, personnel, and library size. An alphabetical index of libraries indicates their locations.
Z675.L2L384

The AALS directory of law teachers / prepared by the Association of American Law Schools. 1988-89– . St. Paul, Minn. : West Publ. Co. ; Westbury, N.Y. : Foundation Pr., 1988– . Annual. **CK138**
Previously issued as 1922–56, *Directory of teachers in member schools*; 1957–69, *Directory of law teachers in American Bar Association approved law schools*; 1970–1987, *Directory of law teachers*. Suspended 1943–45; resumed with issue for 1946/47.
A biographical directory of U.S. law professors, listed alphabetically. A list of law schools at the front provides addresses and telephone numbers. There are also lists of organizations related to legal education, of professors by subject, and of administrators by function.
KF266.D552

Almanac of the federal judiciary / ed., Barnabas D. Johnson … [et al.]. Chicago : LawLetters, [1984]– . 2 v. (looseleaf). **CK139**
Contents: v. 1, Profiles and evaluations of all judges of the United States District Courts; v. 2, Profiles and evaluations of all judges of the United States Circuit Courts.
Biographical information on federal judges, listed by district or circuit. In addition to standard directory data, includes narrative sections on noteworthy rulings, media coverage, and lawyers' evaluations. The comments on judges' abilities and temperament are anonymous and can be rather interesting. KF8700.A1A45

The American bench : judges of the nation. 1st ed. (1977)– . Minneapolis : R. B. Forster & Associates, 1977– . Biennial. **CK140**
Frequency varies; annual, 1977–79.
The only directory with biographical information on judges from all levels of federal and state courts. The section for each jurisdiction includes descriptive information on each court in the state, maps of the judicial divisions and subdivisions, and an alphabetically arranged series of biographies of the judges. A name index at the beginning indicates title, court, and state of all judges. KF8700.A19A47

The best lawyers in America / Steven Naifeh and Gregory White Smith. 1983 . N.Y. : Woodward/White, 1983– . Biennial. **CK141**
Frequency varies: irregular, 1983–87; biennial. 1991–.
A directory of lawyers chosen by their peers as the leading practitioners in each state in 13 specialized areas. State-by-state listings of names, addresses, and telephone numbers of individual lawyers, arranged within each state by specialty. Based on surveys of more than 7,500 lawyers. KF190.B47

Directory of corporate counsel. 1980/81– . Englewood Cliffs, N.J. : Prentice Hall Law & Business, 1981– . Annual. **CK142**
For some 7,000 companies and organizations, provides information on law departments including biographical data on attorneys. A separate section in v. 2 covers nonprofit organizations. Each volume includes indexes of individual names, geographic locations, and names of parent and subsidiary organizations. Vol. 2 also has a subject index to nonprofit organizations and a law school alumni index.
§ The same publisher also issues the following annual directories, each providing biographical information on attorneys in a specialized area: *Directory of bankruptcy attorneys* (1988–), *Directory of environmental attorneys* (1992–), *Directory of intellectual property attorneys* (1993–), and *Directory of litigation attorneys* (1990–).
KF195.C6D57

Directory of lawyer referral services. Jan. 1976– . Chicago : American Bar Association, 1976– . Annual. **CK143**
A geographic listing of 348 lawyer referral programs in the U.S. and 17 programs in Canada, providing addresses, phone numbers, and brief information on additional legal services provided and methods of funding.

Directory of legal aid and defender offices in the United States. 1933– . Wash. : National Legal Aid & Defender Association, 1933– . Annual. **CK144**
Name of issuing body varies. Title varies slightly.
Geographic listings of civil legal aid offices and of public defenders, providing addresses, telephone numbers, and directors' names. A third section lists programs for special needs in 21 categories.
§ Similar information is available in Anthony J. Bosoni's *Legal resource directory : a guide to free or inexpensive assistance for low income families, with special sections for prisoners* (Jefferson, N.C. : McFarland, 1992). KF336.A332

Dispute Resolution Program directory / comp. by the Special Committee on Resolution of Minor Disputes of the Public Services Activities Division, American Bar Association. 1981– . Wash. : The Committee, [c1980]– . Irregular. **CK145**
Describes more than 400 dispute resolution services in the U.S. and Canada, arranged by state and province. Entries include information on caseloads, types of cases handled, and program procedures. Appendixes list a variety of other mediation and conciliation services, including better business bureaus and ombudsman contacts.
KF9084.A15D58

Hermann, R. L. The federal legal directory : a guide to the legal offices and key legal personnel of the U.S. Government / comp. and ed. by Richard L. Hermann, Linda P. Sutherland. Phoenix : Oryx, 1990. 547 p. **CK146**
A comprehensive directory of U.S. government legal offices. Entries for executive departments and independent commissions describe the legal offices' functions, list hours and access restrictions for law libraries, and note databases and publications of interest. Shorter sections cover the legislative and judicial branches. An extensive annotated bibliography of federal legal databases and publications is included. Topical index. KF299.G6H47

Human rights organizations and periodicals directory / Ann Fagan Ginger, Beverly Wilson, Linton Hale, editors. 7th ed. Berkeley, Calif. : Meiklejohn Civil Liberties Institute, 1993. 232 p. **CK147**
1st ed., 1973; 6th ed., 1990.
More than 1,000 entries cover a wide variety of organizations working in areas of civil and human rights. Entries provide addresses and phone numbers, describe organizational purposes, and list publications. Organizations are listed alphabetically, with subject, periodical and geographical indexes. Includes excerpts from major human rights documents. KF4741.H84

Judicial Conference of the United States. Bicentennial Committee. Judges of the United States. 2nd ed. Wash. : The Committee : For sale by U.S. Govt. Print. Off., 1983. 681 p. **CK148**
Superintendent of Documents classification: Ju 10.2 : J89/4/983.
1st ed., 1978.
A historical directory with biographical information for every federal judge since the 18th century. Indexed by appointing president and by year of appointment. KF353.J83

Judicial staff directory. 1986– . Mt. Vernon, Va. : Staff Directories, 1986– . Annual. **CK149**
A directory of the federal court system, listing addresses and telephone numbers for more than 15,000 individuals in the judiciary and the Department of Justice. Also provides biographical information for almost 2,000 judges, court staff, U.S. attorneys, and other Department of Justice personnel. Includes maps of circuit and district court jurisdictions, indexes of judges by year of appointment and by appointing president, and a comprehensive index of names.
§ Names, addresses, and telephone numbers of federal court personnel are also listed in *United States court directory* (Wash. : Administrative Office of the United States Courts : distr. by U.S. Govt. Print. Off., 1978– . Annual), available in most depository libraries.

•Machine-readable version: *Staff directories on CD-ROM* [database] (Mt. Vernon, Va. : Staff Directories). Updated biennially. Combines *Judicial staff directory, Congressional staff directory* (CJ215), and *Federal staff directory* (CJ137).   KF8700.A19J83

Law and legal information directory. 1st ed. (1980)– . Detroit : Gale, 1980– . Biennial.   **CK150**

Provides information on more than 30,000 institutions, services and facilities, including national and international law-related organizations, bar associations, legal and paralegal education, libraries, legal periodicals, publishers, lawyer referral services, and legal aid offices. By far the most extensive chapter (more than 900 pages) lists local law enforcement agencies.   KF190.L35

Martindale-Hubbell law directory. 63rd ed. (1931)– . New Providence, N.J. : Martindale-Hubbell, 1931– . Annual.   **CK151**

Consolidation of *Martindale's American law directory*, 1868–1930 (continues its volume numbering) and *Hubbell's legal directory*, 1870–1930. Now published annually in 19 v.

Place of publication varies.

Vols. 1–15 are arranged geographically by state, then by city. The first section of each volume provides basic data on almost all members of the bar; the second section provides biographical information on law firms and attorneys. Vol. 16 provides similar information for corporate law departments and law schools. A two-volume alphabetical index and a one-volume areas of practice index list attorneys and provide references to city and state under which they are listed.

•Machine-readable version: *The Martindale-Hubbell law directory* [database] (New Providence, N.J. : Martindale-Hubbell). Available in CD-ROM; updated annually. Each annual issue corresponds to the most recent printed version.

§ A one-volume directory from the same publisher, *Martindale-Hubbell bar register of preeminent lawyers* (1921– . Annual), provides information on leading practitioners in general-practice firms and in about two dozen specialized areas.   KF190.H813

The national directory of prosecuting attorneys. Alexandria, Va. : National District Attorneys Association, [1976?]– .   **CK152**

Place of publication varies.

Names, addresses, and telephone numbers for district attorneys and other prosecutors in each state. Does not include federal prosecutors. An appendix provides a brief overview of each state's prosecution system. Indexes by jurisdiction and name.

O'Connor, Karen. Public interest law groups : institutional profiles / Karen O'Connor and Lee Epstein. N.Y. : Greenwood, 1989. 261 p.   **CK153**

A descriptive directory of more than 3,000 organizations, noting history, major cases, and ongoing projects. Addresses are provided but not phone numbers. For some organizations, sources for further information are noted. Table of cases; index.   KF336.A4

The official guide to U.S. law schools. 1986–87– . [Newtown, Penn.] : publ. by Law School Admission Council/Law School Admission Services in cooperation with the American Bar Assoc. and the Assoc. of American Law Schools, c1986– . Annual.   **CK154**

Issued 1967–86 under title: *Prelaw handbook*.

Two-page entries supplied by all ABA-accredited law schools, including descriptions of facilities, curriculum, activities, and admissions. For some schools, graphs indicate prospects for admission based on GPA and LSAT scores. Prefatory chapters provide general information on preparing for and applying to law school and financing a legal education.

§ Other directories of law schools include *Barron's guide to law schools* (9th ed. N.Y. : Barron's Educational Series, 1990), S. F. Goldfarb's *Inside the law schools* (6th ed. N.Y. : Plume, 1993) and *The Princeton Review student guide to the best law schools* (N.Y. : Villard Books, 1993).   KF273.A87

United States lawyers reference directory. 1967– . Los Angeles : Legal Directories Publ. Co., 1967– . Annual.   **CK155**

Each annual issue in 5 v.

Imprint varies: Dallas, Tex., 1991– .

An extensive directory of federal and state government offices and personnel. The federal section in v. 1 has executive, legislative, and judicial branch names and addresses; a separate section for each state lists legislators, state and country officials, courts, law schools, and other information. Some states also have blue pages with paid listings for law firms.   KF190.U5

Want's federal-state court directory. 1984 ed.– . Wash. : WANT Publ. Co., c1984– . Annual.   **CK156**

A concise source for a wide variety of information on federal and state court systems. Provides addresses and telephone numbers for federal judges and court clerks and for U.S. attorneys, U.S. magistrates, probation officers, and federal administrative law judges. Each state system is featured on a separate page, with a diagram showing the hierarchy of the court system and the jurisdiction of each court. Contact information is provided for state supreme courts, governors, attorneys general, and secretaries of state. Other features include directories of major Canadian courts and of state bar associations, a guide to the federal court system, and a glossary.

§ *BNA's directory of state and federal courts, judges, and clerks : a state-by-state and federal listing* (Wash. : BNA Books, 1986– . Biennial) provides similar charts and addresses, with a more extensive listing of state appellate and trial court judges. Information on lower state courts is also available in *Directory of state court clerks & county courthouses* (Wash. : WANT Publ. Co., 1989– . Annual). Mark J. A. Yannone's *National directory of courts of law* (Arlington, Va. : Information Resources Pr., 1991) is an extensive listing of addresses and phone numbers for federal, state, territorial and tribal courts, but includes no information on judges or other personnel.   KF8700.A19F42

Where to write for vital records. May 1982– . Hyattsville, Md. : U.S. National Center for Health Statistics ; Wash. : U.S. Govt. Print. Off., 1982– . Triennial.   **CK157**

Superintendent of Documents classificaton: HE 20.6210/2: .

Frequency varies: biennial, 1982–84.

A brief state-by-state listing of sources for birth, death, marriage and divorce records. Provides addresses for state vital records offices, indicates required fees, and includes a variety of additional information for each state. An appendix discusses procedures for obtaining records of foreign or high-seas births or deaths.   HA38.A493

Who's who in American law. Ed. 1– . Chicago : Marquis, 1978– . Irregular.   **CK158**

In a format similar to *Who's who in America* (AH82) provides biographical information concerning more than 27,000 judges, lawyers, legal educators, and others in the legal community. Includes an index by fields of practice or interest.   KF372.W48

Handbooks

Belli, Melvin M. Everybody's guide to the law / Melvin M. Belli, Sr., & Allen P. Wilkinson. San Diego : Harcourt Brace Jovanovich, c1986. 649 p.   **CK159**

Twenty chapters on a wide range of legal topics, including marriage and divorce, automobiles, wills, real estate, and consumer credit. Among the most useful chapters are those on small claims court and finding the right lawyer. Indexed.   KF387.B38

Codes of professional responsibility / ed. by Rena A. Gorlin. 2nd ed. Wash. : Bureau of National Affairs, c1990. 555 p.   **CK160**

Presents the official codes for 37 major professional associations, grouped in 3 categories: business, health, and law. For each organization, information generally includes: address and telephone, date founded, number of members, name of the ethics committee, and the title of its code of ethics; the organization's activities and goals, implementation and enforcement of the code, and development and sources of code; and the full text of the code itself. Also includes a resources section (organizational, periodical, bibliographic, and other resources on ethics) and indexes of issues, professions, and organizations.

BJ1725.C57

The legal researcher's desk reference. 1990– . Teaneck, N.J. : Infosources Publ., 1990– . Biennial. **CK161**

Title varies: 1982–84, called *The law librarian's professional desk reference and diary*; 1986–89, called *Lawyer's diary and desk reference*.

A variety of legal information, including the text of the U.S. Constitution, diagrams of state court systems, bar admission requirements, and directories of federal and state agencies, federal judges, bar associations, and law schools. One of the handiest and most modestly priced collections of its genre. Indexed.

§ Several other, larger compendiums are also published, including *American jurisprudence desk book* (2nd ed. Rochester, N.Y. : Lawyers Cooperative, 1992); *The lawyer's almanac* (Englewood Cliffs, N.J. : Prentice Hall Law & Business, 1981– . Annual); and William P. Statsky et al., *West's legal desk reference* (St. Paul, Minn. : West, 1991). All provide a wide range of information, including reprinted documents, directories, charts, and other material reprinted from various sources. Z675.L2L3832

The state-by-state guide to women's legal rights / NOW Legal Defense and Education Fund and Renée Cherow-O'Leary. N.Y. : McGraw-Hill, c1987. 523 p. **CK162**

Earlier ed. published as *Shana Alexander's state-by-state guide to women's legal rights* (Los Angeles : Wollstonecraft, 1975).

Pt. 1 provides a general overview of women's legal rights in several areas (the legal process; home and family; education; employment; women in the community). Pt. 2 explains each state's laws in these areas, focusing primarily on laws concerning marriage, divorce, domestic violence, inheritance rights, reproductive rights, and unmarried couples. References to state statutes are provided.

KF478.Z95S73

You and the law / American Bar Association. Lincolnwood, Ill. : Publications International, c1990. 608 p. : ill., maps. **CK163**

A general introduction to the U.S. legal system, covering such topics as home ownership, consumer credit, automobiles, and personal injury. The text is in a question-and-answer format, with important points summarized in the margins. Includes sample forms and several tables outlining specific laws state by state. Glossary; index.

KF387.Y66

Formbooks

West's legal forms. 2nd ed. St. Paul, Minn. : West Pub. Co., 1981. 29 v. in 33 : forms. **CK164**

Some volumes updated to Rev. 2nd ed. Includes unnumbered index volume.

Contents: v. 1–6A, Business organizations, with tax analysis; v. 7, Domestic relations, with tax analysis; v. 8, Retirement plans, with tax analysis; v. 9–11, Debtor and creditor relations; v. 12–15, Commercial transactions; v. 16–18, Estate planning, with tax analysis; v. 19–23, Real estate transactions; v. 24, Employment—Agency—Service agreements; v. 25, Patents—Trademarks—Copyrights; v. 26–29, Specialized forms.

An extensive collection of forms for use in litigation and in handling personal and commercial affairs. Sample forms are accompanied by explanatory text and checklists. Updated by annual pocket supplements in each volume. A general index pamphlet covers the entire set.

§ Forms for use in federal courts are published in a separate 18-volume set, *West's federal forms* (St. Paul, Minn. : West, 1952–). Other legal publishers issue similar multivolume collections, including *American jurisprudence legal forms* (Rochester, N.Y. : Lawyers Cooperative, 1971–); *American jurisprudence pleading and practice forms, annotated*, rev. ed. (Rochester, N.Y. : Lawyers Cooperative, 1967–); and Jacob Rabkin and Mark H. Johnson, *Current legal forms,*

with tax analysis (N.Y. : Bender, 1948–). All these sets are designed primarily for use by lawyers. There are also much simpler volumes of forms designed specifically for use by general readers, such as Carl W. Battle's *Legal-wise : self-help legal forms for everyone* (2nd ed. N.Y. : Allworth Pr., 1991). KF1384.A65W47

Digests and collections

Credit manual of commercial laws for .... N.Y. : National Association of Credit Management, [1908?]– . Annual. **CK165**

Title varies slightly.

A compendium of federal and state laws on a variety of topics relevant to business, including contracts, corporations, liens, collections, sales taxes, and bankruptcy. Arranged in 34 chapters by subject, with general introductions and state-by-state tables or summaries. Useful information, although most sections do not provide the citations to statutory sources that would facilitate further research. Brief glossary of legal terms; indexed by subject and state.

Martindale-Hubbell law digest. 123rd year (1991)– . New Providence, N.J. : Martindale-Hubbell, c1990– . Annual. **CK166**

Formerly issued as v. 8 of *Martindale-Hubbell law directory* (CK151).

Contents: v. 1, Alabama–New Hampshire; v. 2, New Jersey–Wyoming; Uniform acts; A.B.A. codes.

Concise summaries of the laws of each state, the District of Columbia, Puerto Rico, and the Virgin Islands, compiled and revised annually by a law firm in each jurisdiction. Provides information on nearly 100 topics, with sample forms and citations to statutory codes and major cases. Vol. 2 also contains digests of U.S. copyright, patent, and trademark law; a brief section on the federal court system; texts of uniform and model acts; and the American Bar Association "Model rules of professional conduct" and "Model code of judicial conduct".

KF190.M3

Statistics

Curran, Barbara A. The lawyer statistical report : a statistical profile of the U.S. legal profession in the 1980s / by Barbara A. Curran with Katherine J. Rosich, Clara N. Carson, and Mark C. Puccetti. Chicago, Ill. : American Bar Foundation, c1985. 618 p. : ill. **CK167**

Provides statistics on size, composition and employment of the U.S. lawyer population in 1980. Includes data and rankings for states, metropolitan areas, and principal cities. Updated by supplements covering 1985 (published 1986) and 1988 (published 1991). KF301.C86

State court caseload statistics : annual report. 1980– . Williamsburg, Va. : National Center for State Courts, 1975– . Annual. **CK168**

Issued by the U.S. Department of Justice, 1975–79 (Superintendent of Documents classification: J 26.10: SD-C-).

Also available in microform.

Statistics on trial and appellate court caseloads in state judicial systems. Includes introductory comparative summaries, extensive tables and charts of each state's court structure. KF180.S83

United States. Administrative Office of the United States Courts. Annual report of the Director for the twelve month period ending [...]. Wash. : Administrative Office of the United States Courts : distr. by U.S. Govt. Print. Off. Annual. **CK169**

Superintendent of Documents classification: JU 10.1: .

Pt. 2, Judicial business of the United States courts, provides a narrative and statistical summary of all aspects of the federal court system, including workload, case dispositions, trials, and expenditures. Detailed tables provide data by specific court and by subject on civil and criminal commenced, terminated, and pending.   KF8732.A825

Constitutions

Constitutions of the United States, national and state. 2nd ed. Dobbs Ferry, N.Y. : Oceana, 1974– . 6 v. (looseleaf).
        CK170
1st ed., 1962.
Publ. for the Legislative Drafting Research Fund, Columbia University.
Current texts, with amendments, of the U.S. Constitution and the constitutions of the 50 states, Puerto Rico, the U.S. Virgin Islands, Samoa, Guam, and other U.S. territories. Only two topical indexes, covering fundamental liberties (1980) and legislative procedures (1982), have been published.   KF4530.C6

Federal

The founders' constitution / ed. by Philip B. Kurland and Ralph Lerner. Chicago : Univ. of Chicago Pr., 1987. 5 v.
        CK171
Excerpts from documents leading up to the Constitution and its first 12 amendments, as well as early interpretations up to 1835. Vol. 1 covers major themes, with a brief introduction to each chapter. The remaining volumes reprint material pertinent to particular clauses or amendments. Each volume has an index of constitutional provisions, a table of cases, and an index of authors and documents.   KF4502.F68

Sources and documents of United States constitutions, second series / ed. and annotated by William F. Swindler. Dobbs Ferry, N.Y. : Oceana, 1982–87. 5 v.   **CK172**
Vols. 2–4 comp. and ed. by Donald J. Musch.
Reprints documents on national constitutional development, 1492–1977, including texts leading up to the Constitution and major Supreme Court decisions. Vol. 5 is also separately published as Bernard A. Reams Jr. and Stuart D. Yoak, *The Constitution of the United States : a guide and bibliography to current scholarly research.*
        KF4530.S68

United States. Constitution. The Constitution of the United States of America : analysis and interpretation : annotations of cases decided by the Supreme Court of the United States to July 2, 1982 / prep. by the Congressional Research Service, Library of Congress ; Johnny H. Killian, ed. ; Leland E. Beck, assoc. ed. Rev. and annotated, 1982. Wash. : U.S. Govt. Print. Off., 1987. 2308 p. (Senate document, 99–16).   **CK173**
First issued 1923.
The text of the Constitution, with each provision followed by an extensive commentary on historical background and judicial developments. A useful place to begin research on a particular constitutional section or amendment. Updated, but not frequently, by a pocket supplement. Appendixes provide lists of Acts of Congress, state statutes, and ordinances held unconstitutional; and Supreme Court cases overruled by subsequent decisions. Table of cases; index.
§ The Constitution is also reprinted in numerous other sources, including compilations of federal and state statutes, legal compendiums, and legal and general dictionaries; and is published in several pamphlet and paperback editions, including *Congressional Quarterly's guide to the U.S. Constitution: history, text, index, and glossary* by Ralph Mitchell (Wash. : Congressional Quarterly, 1986). *The Constitution of the United States of America, as amended*, H. R. Doc. 102–188 (Wash. : U. S. Govt. Print. Off., 1992) is available in most depository libraries and includes unratified amendments and an extensive analytical index.   KF4527.K55

State

Browne, Cynthia E. State constitutional conventions from independence to the completion of the present Union, 1776–1959 : a bibliography. Westport, Conn. : Greenwood, [1973]. 250 p.   **CK174**
Lists the publications of state constitutional conventions and constitutional revision commissions or committees, chronologically by state. Published with a microfiche set of all documents listed.
§ Continued by: *State constitutional conventions, commissions & amendments, 1959–1978* (Project manager, Mark Vonderhaar ; Bibliography ed., Nicholas Olcott. Wash. : Congressional Information Service, 1981. 2 v.), and *State constitutional conventions, commissions & amendments, 1979–1988* (Bethesda, Md. : Congressional Information Service, c1989. 284 p.); these are also published to accompany microfiche collections of documents.   KF4501.B76

Swindler, William F. Sources and documents of United States constitutions. Dobbs Ferry, N.Y. : Oceana, 1973–88. 12 v. in 11.   **CK175**
A collection of the basic instruments recording the development of each state's constitution. States are in an alphabetical sequence; documents for each state appear chronologically. Bibliography and index for each state. Vol. 11 also separately published as Bernard D. Reams, Jr. and Stuart D. Yoak, *The constitutions of the states : a state by state guide and bibliography to current scholarly research* (1988).   KF4530.S94

Statutes

Federal

United States. [Laws, etc.]. The statutes at large of the United States of America ... : containing the laws and concurrent resolutions enacted ... and reorganization plans and proclamations, 1789–1873; 1873– . Boston : Little, 1845–73 ; Wash. : U.S. Govt. Print. Off., 1875– . v.1–17; v. 18 .   **CK176**
Title varies slightly.
The present series of *Statutes at large* starts with v. 18 (1873–75). It was preceded by the *Laws of the United States:* Folwell edition, for the first 13 Congresses, 1789–1813; Bioren and Duane edition, for the first 28 Congresses, 1789–1845; Little, Brown edition, called *Statutes at large,* covering the first 42 Congresses, 1789–1873, and ending with v. 17. This series was taken over by the federal government, v. 18– .
Contents vary, but beginning with v. 65, 1951, each volume contains public laws, reorganization plans, private laws, and concurrent resolutions and proclamations. Arrangement is chronological by date of passage of the act under the divisions: Public laws, Private laws, etc. A subject index and a personal-name index in each volume.
Slip laws are published separately, as soon as enacted, in two series: (1) Public Acts (cited as Public Law), and (2) Private Acts (cited as Private Law), and are superseded upon publication of the *Statutes at large.* Slip laws and resolutions are listed in the *Monthly catalog* (AG51) under "Congress" and then by number.
Treaties to which the United States was a party (1776–1949) were published in the *Statutes at large,* 1848–1949. Since Jan. 1, 1950, they have been contained in *United States treaties and other international agreements* (CK370).

———————— United States code : containing the general and permanent laws of the United States, in force on January 3, 1989 / prep. and publ. under authority of Title 2, U.S. code, section 285b, by the Office of the Law Revision Counsel of the House of Representatives. 1988 ed. Wash. : U.S. Govt. Print. Off., 1989– .   **CK177**
1st ed., 1926.
The standard official source for current federal laws of a general and permanent nature. A new edition is issued every six years, with bound cumulative supplements in intervening years. Statutes are ar-

ranged in broad subject topics, known as titles, and within each title divided into numbered sections. Citations to the *U.S. code* are to title and section rather than to volume and page (e.g., 50 U.S.C. § 1541). Includes tables providing references from Public Law numbers and *Statutes at large* (CK176) citations to *U.S. code* sections; a table of acts by popular name, which lists laws alphabetically; and a detailed multivolume index.

•Machine-readable versions are available online through LEXIS and WESTLAW and on CD-ROM as: *United States code* [database] (Wash. : Office of the Law Revision Counsel of the House of Representatives, 1991–). KF62 1988.A2

United States code annotated. St. Paul, Minn. : West Pub. Co., 1927– . v. 1–236. **CK178**

Contains federal statutes under the same arrangement as the *United States code*, with additional research aids. The most important of these are notes of court decisions that have interpreted or applied each statutory section. Kept up-to-date by cumulative annual pocket supplements containing amendments and notes of new cases, and by replacement volumes issued as needed. Also includes an extensive multivolume index, parallel conversion tables, and a table of acts by popular name.

§ *United States code service* (Rochester, N.Y. : Lawyers Cooperative, 191 vols., 1972–) is very similar, also providing the text of the statutes with notes of relevant court decisions, updated by annual pocket parts and replacement volumes.

•Machine-readable versions of both *United States code annotated* and *United States code service* are available online through LEXIS and WESTLAW. The latter is also available in CD-ROM as *US code service* [database] (Rochester, N.Y. : Lawyers Cooperative Publ. Co.; distr. Dayton, Ohio : Mead Data Central).

State

Alabama. [Laws, etc.]. Code of Alabama, 1975 : with provision for subsequent pocket parts / prepared under the supervision of the Code Revision Subcommittee of the Legislative Council .... Charlottesville, Va. : Michie Co., 1977– . **CK179**

This entry lists collections of state statutes in force, or *codes*, which are arranged by subject and generally divided into numerical titles and sections. All include the texts of the U.S. Constitution and the constitution of the state; most also provide court rules. *Annotated* codes provide references to judicial decisions that apply to constitutional and statutory sections, usually in the form of paragraphs summarizing rulings and providing case citations. Many annotated codes also include references to legal encyclopedias, law reviews, and treatises.

Most codes consist of a fluctuating number of bound volumes, replaced as necessary; a few are made up of pamphlets published in binders. Each volume is updated by a cumulative annual supplement containing recent statutes and annotations, usually in the form of a *pocket part* stored in a pocket inside the back cover. Many sets are further updated during the year by interim pamphlets containing new annotations, and by *session law services* or *legislative services* that provide the texts of new laws. Every code is accompanied by an extensive index of one or more volumes. Some states also have official unannotated codes; several of the larger states have two competing annotated code publications.

Although general reference collections will find it impractical to collect codes for all the states, it will be useful to have a set of the local state code, and if the weight of inquiry justifies, those of one or two neighboring states. Inquiries that require the codes of other states may be referred to the nearest law school library or governmental law library.

§Annotated codes for states of the U.S. are cited briefly below in alphabetical order by state. Library catalogs usually enter state codes under the name of the state followed by "Laws, etc.," as in the Alabama example above.

Alaska statutes, 1962 ... (Charlottesville, Va. : Michie Co., 1962–); *Arizona revised statutes, annotated* (St. Paul, Minn. : West Publ. Co., 1956–); *Arkansas code of 1987 annotated* (Michie, 1987–); *West's annotated California codes* (West, 1954–); *West's*

Colorado revised statutes annotated (West, c1989–); *Connecticut general statutes annotated* (West, [1960–]); *Delaware code annotated* (Michie, 1975–); *District of Columbia code, annotated* (Michie, 1981–); *West's Florida statutes annotated* (West, 1943–); *Official code of Georgia annotated* (Michie, 1982–).

Hawaii revised statutes annotated (Michie, 1988–); *Idaho code : containing the general laws of Idaho annotated* (Michie, [1948–]); *West's Smith-Hurd Illinois compiled statutes annotated* (West, c1992–); *Burns Indiana statutes annotated* (Michie, [1972–]); *Iowa code annotated* (West, [1949–]); *Kansas statutes annotated* ... (Topeka : printed by H. "Bud" Timberlake, State Printer, 1964–); *Kentucky revised statutes, annotated* (Michie, [1971–]); *West's Louisiana statutes annotated* (West, 1951–); *Maine revised statutes annotated, 1964* (West, c1964–); *The annotated code of the public general laws of Maryland* (Michie, 1957–).

Massachusetts general laws annotated ... (West, [1958–]); *Michigan compiled laws annotated* (West, 1967–); *Minnesota statutes annotated* (West, [1946–]); *Mississippi code 1972, annotated* (Atlanta, Ga. : Harrison Co. ; Rochester, N.Y. : Lawyers Cooperative Publ. Co., c1972–); *Vernon's annotated Missouri statutes* (West, [c1951–]); *Montana code annotated* (Helena, Mont. : Montana Legislative Council, 1978–); *Revised statutes of Nebraska* ... [[Lincoln] : Revisor of Statutes, [c1944–]); *Nevada revised statutes, annotated* (Michie, 1986–); *New Hampshire revised statutes annotated, 1955* (Orford, N.H. : Equity Publ. Co., 1955–); *New Jersey statutes annotated* ... (West, [1939–]).

New Mexico statutes, 1978 annotated (Michie, c1978–); *McKinney's consolidated laws of New York annotated* ... (West, [1939–]); *The general statutes of North Carolina* ... (Michie, 1950–); *North Dakota century code* ... (Michie, 1959–); *Page's Ohio revised code annotated* ... (Cincinnati : Anderson Publ. Co., [1953–]); *Oklahoma statutes annotated* (West, c1936–); *Oregon revised statutes annotated* (Seattle, Wash. : Butterworth Legal Publishers, c1983–); *Purdon's Pennsylvania statutes, annotated* (Philadelphia : G.T.Bisel Co. ; St. Paul, Minn. : West, c1930–); *Laws of Puerto Rico annotated* (Orford, N.H. : Equity Publ. Co., [c1954–]); *General laws of Rhode Island, 1956 : completely annotated* (Michie, [1957–]).

Code of laws of South Carolina, 1976, annotated ... (Rochester, N.Y. : Lawyers Cooperative Publ. Co., c1977–); *South Dakota codified laws* ... (Michie, 1968–); *Tennessee code annotated* (Michie, [1955–]); *Vernon's annotated Texas statutes and codes* (West, 1925–); *Utah code annotated 1953* (Michie, 1953–); *Vermont statutes annotated* (Orford, N.H. : Equity Publ. Co., [1958–]), *Virgin Islands code, annotated* (Orford, N.H. : Equity Publ. Co., [1957–]); *Code of Virginia, 1950* ... (Michie, [1949–]); *West's revised code of Washington annotated* (West, 1961–); *West Virginia code, annotated* (Michie, 1966–); *West's Wisconsin statutes annotated* ... (West, [1957–]); *Wyoming statutes, annotated* (Michie, 1977–).

•Machine-readable versions of state statutes, often with annotations, are available online through LEXIS and WESTLAW and in a variety of CD-ROM products. KFA30 1975.A24

National survey of state laws / Richard A. Leiter, ed. Detroit : Gale, c1993. 427 p. **CK180**

Summarizes state laws in 36 subjects. Divided into general legal categories: consumer, criminal, employment, family, real estate, tax, and other fields. Each subject is described in general terms, with tables providing specifics on the law in each state. Includes citations to sources in state statutory compilations. KF386.N38

Subject compilations of state laws. 1960-79– . Westport, Conn. : Greenwood, 1981– . Irregular. **CK181**

Imprint varies.

Editors: 1960–79, Lynn Foster and Carol Boast; 1979–83, Cheryl Rae Nyberg and Carol Boast; 1983–85– , Cheryl Rae Nyberg.

An annotated subject bibliography of treatises, reference books, journal articles, documents, looseleaf services and cases that list, summarize or reprint state laws on specific topics. Most sources simply list relevant state laws, but they can be good starting places for further research. Extensive cross-references within and between volumes. Author and publisher indexes. The first two volumes include brief research guides on doing comparative state statutory or administrative law research.

§ Jon S. Schultz, *Statutes compared : a U.S., Canadian, multinational research guide to statutes by subject* (Buffalo, N.Y. : Hein, 1991– . Looseleaf) is another subject listing of sources of multistate or multiprovince surveys summarizing or reprinting laws, limited to regularly revised or supplemented publications.   KF240.S795

Regulations

Code of federal regulations. 1949– . [Wash.] : U.S. Office of the Federal Register : for sale by U.S. Govt. Print. Off., [1949]– . Annual.   **CK182**

Cited as *CFR*.

Supersedes *Code of federal regulations of the United States of America ...* (1st ed., 1938).

A subject arrangement of administrative agency rules and regulations, consisting of more than 200 paperback volumes revised and reissued each year. Arranged in a subject scheme of 50 titles divided into chapters, each of which contains the regulations of a specific agency. A list in the back of each volume lists the title and chapter of each agency's regulations. Title 3 contains presidential documents, including proclamations and executive orders. An "Index and finding aids" volume provides access by agency name and subject.

§ New rules as they are promulgated appear in the daily *Federal register* (Wash. : U.S. Govt. Print. Off., 1936–). Each issue has a cumulative table for the month, noting which parts of the *CFR* are affected by new regulations. An index by agency is published monthly and cumulates references since the beginning of the year. A detailed explanation of the *Federal register* is provided in *The federal register : what it is and how to use it* (Rev. ed. Wash. : Office of the Federal Register, 1992).

•Both *CFR* and *Federal register* have machine-readable counterparts:

U.S. code of federal regulations (CFR) [database] (Wash. : Office of the Federal Register, 1981–). Available online; includes full text of all titles of printed *CFR*.

Federal register [database] (Wash. : Office of the Federal Register, 1980–). Available online; updated daily.   KF70.A3

Supreme Court

Blandford, Linda A. Supreme Court of the United States, 1789–1980 : an index to opinions arranged by Justice / Linda A. Blandford, Patricia Russell Evans. Millwood, N.Y. : Kraus Internat., 1983. 2 v. (1133 p.).   **CK183**

Sponsored by the Supreme Court Historical Society.

Provides the names and citations of all Supreme Court opinions written by each justice, organized by category (opinion of the Court, separate opinion, dissent, etc.). Justices are listed chronologically, but opinions in each category are listed alphabetically by name of case. Brief appendixes in v. 2 provide tabular information on the justices.   KF101.6.B57

Guenther, Nancy Anderman. United States Supreme Court decisions : an index to excerpts, reprints, and discussions. 2nd ed. Metuchen, N.J. : Scarecrow, 1983. 856 p.   **CK184**

1st ed., 1976.

Designed "to provide students a means of locating reprints, excerpts, and discussions of Supreme Court decisions available in publications printed from 1960 to 1980 that are generally accessible to undergraduate students."—*Pref.* Covers books and journals, excluding newspapers and legal periodicals. Arranged chronologically; indexed by case name and subject. A useful resource, but increasingly out of date.   KF101.6.G83

Lieberman, Jethro Koller. The evolving Constitution : how the Supreme Court has ruled on issues from abortion to zoning. N.Y. : Random House, 1992. 751 p.   **CK185**

A reference book on constitutional law, consisting mostly of brief alphabetically arranged essays on basic doctrines and issues. Less

comprehensive than similar works on either the Constitution or the Supreme Court, but well reviewed for its clear, jargon-free style designed for general readers. Appendixes include a concordance to the Constitution, brief biographical information on each Justice, and a table of more than 2,000 major Supreme Court decisions.   KF4548.L54

Martin, Fenton S. The U.S. Supreme Court : a bibliography / Fenton S. Martin, Robert U. Goehlert. Wash. : Congressional Quarterly, c1990. 594 p.   **CK186**

An unannotated bibliography of books, articles, dissertations, essays, and research reports in two major sections: (1) activities of the Supreme Court, arranged in 14 topical areas; (2) materials on individual justices, arranged alphabetically by name. Excludes government publications. An excellent introduction surveys selected research sources. Author and subject indexes.

§ The authors' more recent *How to research the Supreme Court* (Wash. : Congressional Quarterly, 1992) is little more than a simplified and updated version of the same work.   KF8741.A1M37

The Oxford companion to the Supreme Court of the United States / ed. in chief, Kermit L. Hall ; editors, James W. Ely, Jr., Joel B. Grossman, William M. Wiecek. N.Y. : Oxford Univ. Pr., 1992. 1032 p. : ill.   **CK187**

An encyclopedia of constitutional law, the Supreme Court, and the American judicial system, with more than 1,000 signed alphabetically arranged entries. Ranging in length from one paragraph to a 30-page History of the Court, articles cover major cases, terms and legal concepts, constitutional law issues, and justices and other historical figures. Illustrated with portraits of justices. Appendixes: The Constitution of the United States; Nominations and successions of the justices; Trivia and traditions of the Court. Case index; topical index.

KF8742.A35O9

The Supreme Court A to Z : a ready reference encyclopedia / Elder Witt, advisory ed. Wash. : Congressional Quarterly, 1993. 528 p. : ill. (CQ's encyclopedia of American government, v. 3).   **CK188**

Less comprehensive than other encyclopedias, perhaps better suited for general readers. Contains some 300 brief articles on the Court, including doctrinal issues, procedures, and a few major cases. Biographies of justices are accompanied by portraits. Other illustrations include photographs of litigants whose names have become synonymous with constitutional doctrines. Appendixes provide a Court chronology and the text of the Constitution. Bibliography; index.   KF8742.A35S8

The Supreme Court justices : illustrated biographies, 1789–1993 / ed. by Clare Cushman (the Supreme Court Historical Society) ; foreword by William H. Rehnquist. Wash. : Congressional Quarterly, c1993. 576 p. : ill.   **CK189**

Brief biographies of the first 106 justices of the Supreme Court. Each five-page article provides information on the justice's background and education, nomination, and major opinions. Thoroughly illustrated with portraits, photographs, and political cartoons. Bibliography; index.

§ A more extensive scholarly treatment is offered by Leon Friedman and Fred L. Israel, eds., *The justices of the United States Supreme Court, 1789–1969 : their lives and major opinions* (N.Y. : Chelsea House, 1969–78. 5 v.), which has unfortunately been updated only to 1978.   KF8744.S86

United States. Supreme Court. United States reports : cases adjudged in the Supreme Court. v. 108 (Oct. term 1882...Oct. term 1883)– . Wash. : U.S. Govt. Print. Off., 1884– . Irregular.   **CK190**

Imprint varies.

Reporters of early volumes: v. 1–4 (1790–1800), A.J. Dallas; v. 5–13 (1801–15), William Cranch; v. 14–25 (1816–27), Henry Wheaton; v. 26–41 (1828–42), Richard Peters; v. 42–65 (1843–60), Benjamin Howard; v. 66–67 (1861–62), J.S. Black; v. 68–90 (1863–74), J.W. Wallace.

The official source for opinions of the Supreme Court of the U.S. Each decision is preceded by a *Syllabus*, preliminary paragraphs summarizing the case and the Court's holding. Decisions are published first as individual slip opinions, then in a paperbound preliminary print after two years, and eventually in a bound volume. Each volume includes a table of cases reported and an index.

§ Because *U.S. reports* are published so slowly, it is necessary to use commercial publications for recent decisions. Two permanent bound editions are published: *Supreme Court reporter* (St. Paul, Minn. : West, 1882–), and *United States Supreme Court reports, lawyers' edition* (Rochester, N.Y. : Lawyers Cooperative, 1882–). These versions are available within a few weeks of the date of decision and include additional research aids useful in research. For the quickest printed sources for Supreme Court cases, see *United States law week* (CK191).

•Project Hermes, the Supreme Court's electronic access program, makes new decisions available online the same morning they are announced. Complete retrospective coverage is available online.

KF101.A212

The United States law week. v. 1, no. 1 (Sept. 5, 1933)– . Wash. : Bureau of National Affairs, [1933]– . Fifty no. a year. **CK191**

One of the most promptly published sources for Supreme Court opinions, usually available within a few days of decision. Also provides information about new *certiorari* filings, pending cases, and oral arguments. A second volume, General law, summarizes important weekly developments in the legal world.

§ *United States Supreme Court bulletin* (Chicago : Commerce Clearing House, 1936– . Weekly) also provides the text of new decisions and information about the Court's docket, but does not have the general law component of *U.S. law week*.

•Machine-readable versions of *United States law week* and an electronic-only daily update are available online.

Witt, Elder. Congressional Quarterly's guide to the U.S. Supreme Court. 2nd ed. Wash. : Congressional Quarterly, c1990. 1060 p. : ill. **CK192**

1st ed., 1979.

An extensive overview of the Court's history and workings. Surveys the origins and development of the Court, and discusses its cases dealing with the federal system and with individual rights. Also includes brief biographies of each justice and capsule summaries of major decisions. An appendix provides the texts of major documents. Subject and case indexes.

§ Stephen P. Elliot, ed., *A reference guide to the United States Supreme Court* (N.Y. : Facts on File, 1986) is a less exhaustive but similar work providing commentary on major issues, summaries of landmark cases, and biographies of the justices. KF8742.W567

Canada

Works listed elsewhere which cover Canadian law include *A legal bibliography of the British Commonwealth of Nations*, v. 3 (CK14); *Index to Canadian legal literature* (CK23); *Dictionary of Canadian law* (CK35); and *Treaties in force for Canada* (CK97).

Canada. [Laws, etc.]. Revised statutes of Canada, 1985 = Lois révisées du Canada (1985) / prep. under the authority of the Statute Revision Act. Ottawa : Queens's Printer for Canada, 1985. 8 v. **CK193**

The current official compilation of Canadian federal statutes, arranged alphabetically by name of act. An appendix contains constitutional documents and the Canadian Bill of Rights; supplements contain legislation enacted from 1985 to 1988 and the Income Tax Act. English-language subject access is provided through a paperback index volume (2nd ed., 1991).

§ New federal statutes are published in Part III of the *Canada gazette* (Ottawa : Queen's Printer, 1974–) upon assent, and then appear in the annual volumes of *Acts of the Parliament of Canada / Lois de Parlement du Canada* (Ottawa : Queen's Printer, 1867–), also known

as *Statutes of Canada*. The provincial governments have similar publication schemes, with infrequent revisions updated by sessional volumes. KE891985

The Canadian law list. 1883– . Agincourt, Ont. : Canada Law Book [etc.], 1883– . Annual. **CK194**

A comprehensive legal directory, listing legal practitioners by city and providing alphabetical indexes of judges and of barristers and solicitors. Also lists federal and provincial courts, government offices, law societies, and law schools. Paid entries at the beginning provide biographical information on some practitioners. A general index provides convenient access to the institutional entries.

§ *Canada legal directory* (Scarborough, Ont. : De Boo, 1911–) is a competing work of similar scope and design.

MacEllvan, Douglass T. Legal research handbook / Douglass T. MacEllven ; with special assistance by Michael J. McGuire. 3rd ed. Toronto : Butterworths, c1993. 407 p. **CK195**

1st ed., 1983; 2nd ed., 1986.

The most extensive guide to Canadian legal research, covering both common law jurisdictions and Quebec. Includes research checklists, a table of abbreviations, and a brief glossary of legal research terms. Index.

§ Margaret A. Banks, *Banks on using a law library : a Canadian guide to legal research* (5th ed. Toronto : Carswell, 1991), is a more descriptive approach designed for law students; Jacqueline R. Castel and Omeela K. Latchman, *The practical guide to Canadian legal research* (Toronto : Carswell, 1993) is a shorter work with a useful bibliography of reports, services and texts listed by subject. KE250.M32

Mexico

Avalos, Francisco. The Mexican legal system. N.Y. : Greenwood, 1992. 254 p. (Reference guides to national legal systems, no. 1). **CK196**

A subject bibliography of primary sources, articles and monographs on Mexican law. Lists the major laws and regulations in more than 40 subject areas, and sources for texts in Spanish and English. Items are unannotated except for translations of Spanish titles. An introduction provides an overview of the legal system. KGF150.A95

Clagett, Helen Lord. A revised guide to the law and legal literature of Mexico / Helen L. Clagett, David M. Valderama. Wash. : Library of Congress, 1973. 463 p. (Latin American series, no. 38). **CK197**

1945 ed. by John T. Vance and Helen L. Clagett had title: *A guide to the law and legal literature of Mexico*.

Dated, but useful for historical or background information on the Mexican legal system and its publications. Describes the history, major texts, and literature of more than a dozen substantive and procedural areas; also has chapters on general works, court reports and digests, legal periodicals, legal dictionaries and encyclopedias, and bibliographies. Bibliographic footnotes throughout; name index.

Z663.5.G8M4

Latin America

Medina, Rubens. Nomenclature and hierarchy—basic Latin American legal sources / by Reubens Medina and Cecilia Medina-Quiroga. Wash. : Library of Congress, 1979. 123 p. **CK198**

Discusses the function and relative importance of legal instruments (constitutions, treaties, laws, decrees) in 20 Central American, South American and Caribbean countries (including Haiti). Bibliographic references. Z663.5.N65

Villalón Galdames, Alberto. Bibliografía jurídica de América Latina, 1810–1965. [Santiago de Chile] : Editorial Jurídica de Chile, 1969–84. v.1–2. (In progress). **CK199**

"Precedida de una introducción al estudio: la bibliografía; las bibliografías universales y nacionales; las bibliografías por temas y, en especial, las bibliografías jurídicas; los indices periódicos de artículos; las bibliografías de bibliografías; los métodos de investigación; la técnica bibliográfica; la mecanización; la cooperación internacional, y la situación actual de la bibliografía en América Latina."—*title page.*

Contents: v. 1, Introducción; Argentina, Bolivia; v. 2, Brazil, Colombia, Costa Rica, Cuba.

Bibliographies for individual Latin American countries in alphabetical order, with annotated entries for codes, compilations of treaties, treatises, periodical articles, and other sources. Listings are generally in main-entry order with subject, geographical, and author indexes. The set is projected for eventual completion in five volumes.

               KG1.V54

Caribbean and Islands of the Western Atlantic

Newton, Velma. Commonwealth Caribbean legal literature : a bibliography of all primary sources to date and secondary sources for 1971–85. 2nd [ed.]. Barbados : Faculty of Law Library, Univ. of the West Indies, Cave Hill Campus, 1987. 492 p. **CK200**

1st ed., 1979, had title *Legal literature and conditions affecting legal publishing in the Commonwealth Caribbean.*

Pt. 1, Primary sources, lists historical and current legislation, constitutions, and law reports for 20 Caribbean jurisdictions. Pt. 2, Secondary sources, has alphabetical lists of bibliographies and periodicals; a combined subject listing of books and articles; and a subject listing of theses. Author index.   KGJ1.N49

Europe (by region)

Council of Europe. Judicial organisation in Europe. London : Morgan-Grampian, 1975. 159 p. (25 fold.) : ill. **CK201**

Descriptions of the judicial systems in 17 European countries (Austria, Belgium, Cyprus, Denmark, France, Germany, Iceland, Ireland, Italy, Luxembourg, Malta, Netherlands, Norway, Sweden, Switzerland, Turkey, and the U.K.), focusing on the jurisdiction of the various courts and agencies. For each country, a foldout chart provides a detailed analysis of court hierarchies and routes of appeal.

Europe, Western

Guide to foreign legal materials : Belgium, Luxembourg, Netherlands / by Paul Graulich ... [et al.]. Dobbs Ferry, N.Y. : Oceana, 1968. 258 p. (Parker School studies in foreign and comparative law. Parker School guides to foreign law, v. 3).   **CK202**

A dated but useful overview of basic Benelux legal resources. Separate sections for each country outline the sources of law, describe the major publications, and provide bibliographies and lists of abbreviations. Author and title index; subject index.

European Communities

Directory of community legislation in force and other acts of the community institutions. 5th ed. (1984)– . Luxembourg : Office for Official Publications of the European Communities, c1984– . Semiannual. **CK203**

At head of title: Official Journal of the European Communities. Frequency varies: annual, 1984–86; semiannual, 1987– . 1985– issued in 2 v.

Lists agreements, decisions, directives and regulations governing the European Community. Vol. 1, Analytical register, lists legislation by subject under 17 chapters, with references to sources in *Official journal of the European Communities*; v. 2 provides a chronological listing of legislation and an alphabetical index of subjects.

Issued also in Danish, Dutch, French, Greek, German, and Italian.

●*CELEX*, The legal database of the European Communities, includes the full text of legislation listed in the directory, as well as cases, preparatory documents, treaties, and other materials.

            KJE920.5.D57

Sheridan, Maurice. EC legal systems : an introductory guide / Maurice Sheridan, James Cameron ; consultant ed., John Toulmin. London : Butterworths, 1992. 1 v. (various pagings).   **CK204**

Overviews of the legal system of the 12 member states of the European Community. Each national section is divided into 11 chapters, covering sources of law, fundamental rights, jurisdiction of the courts, administration of justice, structure of the legal profession, civil procedure, criminal procedure, remedies, matrimonial disputes, property transactions, recognition and enforcement of foreign judgements. Also provides for each country a simplified chart of the court structure and a brief bibliography. Table of legislation; multilingual glossary of terms.

§ The same editors provide similar coverage of Austria, Finland, Iceland, Liechtenstein, Norway, Sweden, and Switzerland in *EFTA legal systems : an introductory guide* (London : Butterworths, 1993).

Toth, A. G. The Oxford encyclopaedia of European Community law. Oxford : Clarendon Pr. ; N.Y. : Oxford Univ. Pr., 1990. v. 1. (In progress). **CK205**

Contents: v. 1, Institutional law. To be complete in 3 v.

An authoritative guide to the law of the European Community, with references to relevant cases, acts, and treaties. Vol. 1 deals with general principles of Community law and institutions such as the European Parliament, the Commission, the Council, and the Court of Justice. Alphabetically arranged entries provide brief definitions followed by more detailed discussion, cross-references, and brief bibliographies. The volume has no index, but the list of entries at the beginning includes cross-references and there are tables of cases, Community treaties, Community acts, international agreements, and U.K. statutes. Vols. 2 and 3 are projected to cover substantive law and community policies.   KJE926.T67

Europe (by country)

Austria

Dosoudil, Ilse. Grundliteratur zum österreichischen Recht = Basic literature on Austrian law. Hamburg : Arbeitsgemeinschaft für Juristisches Bibliotheks- und Dokumentationswesen, 1988. 119 p. (Arbeitshefte der Arbeitsgemeinschaft für Juristisches Bibliotheks- und Dokumentationswesen, Nr. 12).   **CK206**

A bibliography of basic works on Austrian law, based on the organization of Ralph Lansky's *Grundliteratur Recht* (CK211). A subject listing of major periodicals, legislation, commentaries and treaties, with essential titles marked by asterisks. Subject headings and index entries in English as well as in German.   KJJ3.D67

Denmark

Dansk juridisk bibliografi = Bibliography of Danish law. 1950–1971– . København : Juristforbundets Forlag, 1973– . Irregular.   **CK207**

Vol. 1, 1950–71 (publ. 1973); v. 2, 1972–80 (1983); v. 3, 1981–84 (1986); v. 4, 1985–87 (1990).

Comp. by Jens Søndergaard, 1950/71–1985/87; by Lotte Jacobsen, 1988/89– .

Supplements Torben Lund's *Juridiske literaturhenvisninger* (1950).

A comprehensive national legal bibliography. Periodicals, books and articles are listed alphabetically in separate sections, and together in a classified subject section. Includes a section of Danish legal publications in English, French, and German. Table of contents and preface also in English. Annual volumes beginning with 1988–89 are published by the National Library of Denmark.

France

Szladits, Charles. Guide to foreign legal materials : French / by Charles Szladits and Claire M. Germain. 2nd rev. ed. Dobbs Ferry, N.Y. : Oceana, c1985. 205 p. : facsims.   **CK208**

Pubished for the Parker School of Foreign and Comparative Law, Columbia Univ.

Rev. ed. of pt. 1 of Szladits's *Guide to foreign legal materials : French, German, Swiss* (1959).

A guide for the common law lawyer to the use of French laws, court reports, legal reference works, and scholarly writing. Pt. 1 provides a general introduction to the materials, followed by more detailed bibliographic discussion in pt. 2. A conclusion gives some general advice in doing research in a foreign legal system. Appendixes of publishers' addresses and French legal abbreviations; subject and author-title indexes.   KJV140.S96

Tanguy, Yann. La recherche documentaire en droit. Paris : Presses universitaires de France, 1991. 283 p.   **CK209**

A guide to French legal research. Pt. 1 discusses the organization of legal literature, including official journals, codes, legal periodicals and databases; pt. 2 explains research methods. Includes sample pages and computer screens. Appendixes provide lists of periodicals, databases, and libraries and information centers. Subject index.   KJV140

Germany

Kearley, Timothy. Charles Szladits' guide to foreign legal materials : German / by Timothy Kearley, Wolfram Fischer. 2nd rev. ed. Dobbs Ferry, N.Y. : Oceana, 1990. 318 p.   **CK210**

Rev. ed. of pt. 2 of Szladits' *Guide to foreign legal materials : French, German, Swiss* (1959).

Publ. for the Parker School of Foreign and Comparative Law, Columbia University in the City of New York.

A comprehensive guide for English-speaking researchers to the legal literature of the Federal Republic of Germany (pre-reunification). Includes a general introduction to the German legal system and discussion of primary sources of law, bibliographies and other reference works, and doctrinal writings in major subject areas. Covers works published through 1987. Appendixes of legal abbreviations, publishers' addresses, and a useful list of English-language titles; author-title and subject indexes.   KK76.K42

Lansky, Ralph. Grundliteratur Recht : Bundesrepublik Deutschland: eine Auswahl-Bibliographie = Basic literature on law : Federal Republic of Germany : selective bibliography. 3. Aufl. München : J. Schweitzer, 1984. 172 p.   **CK211**

1st ed., 1974, publ. as *Arbeitshefte der Arbeitsgemeinschaft für juristisches Bibliotheks- und Dokumentationswesen*, no. 1; 2nd ed., 1978.

Recommends basic works on German law, in German and English. Lists bibliographies, periodicals, dictionaries, commentaries, treatises and other sources by subject, with essential titles marked by asterisks. Index includes subject entries in both German and English. Appendix provides information on German publishing houses.

§ *Deutsche rechtsbibliographie* (Baden-Baden : Nomos Verlagsgesellschaft, 1984–) is an annual subject bibliography of legal titles published in Germany. Selected works up to 1978 are listed in the German Association of Comparative Law's *Bibliographie des deutschen Rechts in englischer und deutscher Sprache = Bibliography of German law in English and German* (Karlsruhe : Müller, 4 vols. 1964–81). Both sets include subject indexing in English as well as in German.   KK3.L37

Great Britain

Works listed elsewhere which cover English law include *Manual of law librarianship* (CK2); *A legal bibliography of the British Commonwealth of Nations*, v. 1–2 (CK14); *A concise dictionary of law* (CK34); *Jowitt's dictionary of English law* (CK38) and *An index of British treaties* (CK98).

Beale, Joseph Henry. Bibliography of early English law books. Cambridge, Mass. : Harvard Univ. Pr., 1926. 304 p.   **CK212**

A listing of law books printed before 1600, with chapters for statutes, decisions, and treatises. Chapter 4 discusses the printers and their law books. Appendixes reproduce woodcuts and list holding libraries. A supplement (1943) by Robert B. Anderson adds some new material and provides revisions and corrections.   KD51.B3

Directory of British and Irish law libraries / ed. by Judith Barden. 4th ed. Hebden Bridge : publ. for the British and Irish Association of Law Librarians by Legal Information Resources Limited, c1992. 177 p.   **CK213**

1st ed., 1976; 3rd ed., 1988.

A listing of law libraries, indicating addresses, telephone numbers, contact persons, hours, and services. Covers England, Wales, Scotland, Northern Ireland, Republic of Ireland, Channel Islands, Isle of Man, and Isle of Wight, with entries arranged alphabetically by town in each region. Indexes by name of institution, type of organization, contact person, and special collections.   Z675.L2D57

Great Britain. [Laws, etc.]. Halsbury's statutes of England and Wales. 4th ed. London : Butterworths, 1985–93? v. 1–50.   **CK214**

1st ed., 1929–47, 40 v.; 3rd ed., 1968–85, 58 v.

A subject collection of legislation in force for England and Wales, with annotations providing brief descriptions of citing cases and other explanatory data. Kept up-to-date by revised volumes, annual supplements and looseleaf volumes containing new statutes. A *Table of statutes and general index* volume is published annually.

§ The official sources for English statutes are *Public general acts* (London : Incorporated Council of Law Reporting, 1866–), the chronological session law publication; and *Statutes in force : official revised edition* (London : H.M.S.O., 1972–date), a subject compilation in which each act is published in a separate pamphlet without annotations. H.M.S.O. also publishes an annual *Index to the statutes* providing subject access, and a *Chronological table of statutes* listing enactments since 1235 and providing information on current status.
KD135.H3G74

Halsbury's laws of England. 4th ed. London : Butterworths, 1973– . 56 v.   **CK215**

1st ed. (1901–17) had title *The laws of England*.

A comprehensive encyclopedia of English law, covering both cases and legislation. Updated by revised volumes, cumulative annual supplements and a *Monthly review* containing notices of legal developments. Tables of statutes and cases cited; consolidated index.

§ A comparable encyclopedia for Scots law, *The laws of Scotland : Stair memorial encyclopaedia* (Edinburgh : Law Society of Scotland/Butterworths, 1987–), is in progress.   KD310.H34

Hazell's guide to the judiciary and the courts, with the Holborn Law Society's bar list / ed. by the editorial staff of R. Hazell & Co. Henley-on-Thames, Oxfordshire, England : R. Hazell & Co., 1985– . Annual.   **CK216**

A directory of courts and other judicial offices in England and Wales, combined with listings of barristers by chambers and alphabetically. Courts and lawyers in Northern Ireland, Scotland, the Isle of Man, and the Channel Islands are listed separately at the end of the volume.

§ *Shaw's directory of courts in the United Kingdom* (London : Shaw & Sons, 1972–) is another annual listing of courts in England, Wales, Northern Ireland, and Scotland. Appendixes list prosecution offices and penal establishments.

Hines, W. D. English legal history : a bibliography and guide to the literature / W.D. Hines ; with contributions by R.W. Ireland, P.J. Rawlings, C.P. Rodgers. N.Y. : Garland, 1990. 201 p. (Garland reference library of the humanities, vol. 1011).   **CK217**

Three bibliographical essays—for the medieval period, for 1485–1815, and for criminal justice and punishment (including a short section on crime literature)—discuss collections of the law, commentaries and secondary works, procedures and traditions, court records, the legal profession; "significant gaps in the published work" are noted. The concluding two essays—Periodicals and periodical indexes, Introduction to bibliography—survey the most important periodicals, library catalogs, and other reference works. Bibliography with complete citations for all titles discussed.   KD532.A1H56

Holborn, Guy. Butterworths legal research guide. London ; Boston : Butterworths, 1993. 352 p. : ill.   **CK218**

A substantial new treatment of English legal research, with a narrative explanation of basic sources and techniques followed by a quick reference guide for specific inquiries and problems. European Communities materials are fully integrated into the discussion, as are CD-ROM and online databases. Sample pages from major sources are included. Intended for both students and experienced researchers.

§ Two useful research guides written primarily for law students are Peter Clinch, *Using a law library* (London : Blackstone Pr., 1992), and Jean Dane and Philip A. Thomas, *How to use a law library* (2nd ed. London : Sweet & Maxwell, 1987).   KD392.H65

Information sources in law / ed. R.G. Logan. London ; Boston : Butterworths, 1986. 370 p.   **CK219**

A narrative bibliography of contemporary English legal literature. Introductory chapters by the editor on law libraries and legal research are followed by more specialized treatments of particular types of publications and specialized subject areas. Includes chapters on the law of Scotland, Ireland, and the Commonwealth.   KD392.I54

Raistrick, Donald. Lawyers' law books : a practical index to legal literature. 2nd ed. [Abingdon, Eng.] : Professional Books, 1985. 604 p.   **CK220**

1st ed., 1977.

An unannotated bibliography of British law books, listing encyclopedia entries, journals, and texts under more than 500 subjects. Appendixes indicate regnal years and law reports of the U.K. and Ireland. Author index.   KD51.R33

Waterlow's solicitors' and barristers' directory. 1991– . London : Waterlow Directories, c1991– .   **CK221**

Earlier title: *Solicitors' and barristers' directory and diary.*

Provides a geographical listing of law firms, with alphabetical indexes of firms and individual solicitors; listings of barristers by chambers and by name; and information on selected organizations and legal services.

§ Courts, government offices, and local authorities are listed in an annual companion volume, *Waterlow's solicitors' and barristers' diary* (1991–). *Butterworth's law directory* (London : Martindale-Hubbell, 1985–) also provides listings of British solicitors and barristers, with biographical information, in a format familiar to users of *Martindale-Hubbell law directory* (CK151). *The legal 500* (London : Legalease, 1988–) has descriptive listings for many law firms and an extensive introduction on the British legal environment.   KD336.W38

Italy

Grisoli, Angelo. Guide to foreign legal materials : Italian. Dobbs Ferry, N.Y. : publ. for the Parker School of Foreign and Comparative Law, Columbia Univ., by Oceana, 1965. 272 p. (Parker School studies in foreign and comparative law. Parker School guides to foreign law, v. 2).   **CK222**

A bibliographical survey of Italian legal materials, dated but useful for standard and historical sources. Pt. 1 discusses the major sources of law; pt. 2 lists resources, including legislative materials, case law, and an extensive descriptive listing of doctrinal writings. Includes a list of legal abbreviations and indexes by subject and author/title.

Russia and the U.S.S.R.

Kavass, Igor I. Demise of the Soviet Union : a bibliographic survey of English writings on the Soviet legal system, 1990–1991. Buffalo, N.Y. : W.S. Hein, 1992. 288 p.   **CK223**

Author and subject bibliographies of books and articles on recent legal developments in the former Soviet Union. The author section includes annotations for many entries. Also contains a useful introductory section on legal research in the post–Soviet era.

§ The bibliography is a sequel to the author's earlier works, *Soviet law in English: research guide and bibliography, 1970–1987* (Buffalo, N.Y. : Hein, 1988), and *Gorbachev's law: a bibliographic survey of English writings on Soviet legal developments, 1987–1990* (Buffalo, N.Y. : Hein, 1991). The latest installment, "Sources for post–Soviet law in Russia and the other republics: an annotated bibliography of books and articles in English, 1992," appeared as v. 21, no. 3 (1993) of *International journal of legal information.*   KLA3.K38

Switzerland

Bibliographie des schweizerischen Rechts = Bibliographie du droit suisse. 1970– . Basel : Helbing & Lichtenhahn, 1970– . Annual.   **CK224**

French title, 1970–86: *Bibliographie juridique suisse.*

A classed bibliography of books and articles, indexed by author. All headings and editorial matter are in both French and German. Originally issued as unnumbered supplements to *Zeitschrift für schweizerisches Recht.*

Africa

Vanderlinden, Jacques. African law bibliography = Bibliographie de droit Africain. [v. 1] (1947–66)– . Bruxelles : Presses universitaires de Bruxelles, [1972–].   **CK225**

Contents: 1947–66 (publ. 1972), 1967–76 (3 v., 1985), 1977–86 (3 v., 1988), 1987–89 (1991).

A bibliography of books, periodicals, and government reports. The first volume has a subject arrangement, with country subdivisions and an author index; later volumes are alphabetical by author, with indexes by subject and country.

§ Vanderlinden is now editor of *Bibliographies internationales de la doctrine juridique africaine* (Moncton, N.B. : Editions du Centre International de la Common Law en Français, 1992–), being published in separate volumes for each country.   Z6458.A35V3

Nigeria

Jegede, Oluremi. Nigerian legal bibliography : a classified list of legal materials related to Nigeria. 2d ed. Dobbs Ferry, N.Y. : publ. for the Nigerian Inst. of Advanced Legal Studies, Lagos, by Oceana, [1983]. 332 p.   **CK226**
1st ed. 1975.
A bibliography of books, articles, dissertations and other materials relating to Nigerian law and legal history. A section of primary sources is followed by general works, a subject arrangement of 24 doctrinal and procedural areas, and listings of bibliographic sources and periodicals. Indexes by personal name and subject.
§ Journal articles are also covered in the narrower but more current *Nigerian legal periodicals: a subject index, 1946–1988* (Lagos : Nigerian Institute of Advanced Legal Studies, 1989).

Asia (by region)

Asia, West

Amin, S. H. Middle East legal systems. Glasgow, UK. : Royston, 1985. 434 p.   **CK227**
An overview of the legal systems of Afghanistan, Bahrain, Iran, Iraq, Jordan, Kuwait, North Yemen, Oman, Qatar, Saudi Arabia, South Yemen, Sudan, Syria, Turkey, and United Arab Emirates. The chapter for each country provides a general background and discusses legal history, the development of the legal system, sources of law, the judiciary, the legal profession, and legal education. Bibliographies at the end of chapters list materials in Arabic, Persian, and European languages. Indexed.

Asia (by country)

China

Pinard, Jeanette L. The People's Republic of China : a bibliography of selected English-language legal materials. 1985 ed. Wash. : Law Library, Library of Congress, 1985. 108 p.   **CK228**
1st ed., 1983.
Lists secondary materials and translations of Chinese laws in 26 subject categories. An introduction explains the sources and categories of Chinese law and basic legal terminology.
§ Continued by: Constance A. Johnson, *Chinese law: a bibliography of selected English-language materials* (Wash. : Far Eastern Law Div., Law Library of Congress, 1990. 138 p.), covering 1985–89.
Z663.5.P397

India

Jain, Hem Chandra. Indian legal materials : a bibliographical guide. Bombay : N. M. Tripathi ; Dobbs Ferry, N.Y. : Oceana, 1970. 123 p.   **CK229**

A list of basic Indian primary source material and secondary texts. The list of texts in pt. 1, Current Material, is outdated, but the discussion of legislative and judicial publications is still useful. Pt. 2 deals with historical materials. An introduction provides a brief overview of the Indian legal system.

Indonesia

Indonesian law 1949–1989 : a bibliography of foreign-language materials with brief commentaries on the law / ed. by S. Pompe. Dordrecht ; Boston : Nijhoff, 1992. 439 p.   **CK230**
A topical listing of materials on the Indonesian legal system in English and other non-Indonesian languages, with titles of works in Chinese, Dutch, Japanese and Russian translated into English. Entries are not annotated, but most sections include introductory overviews. Author index.   KNW3.I53

Israel

Sanilevici, Renée. Bibliography of Israeli law in European languages. Jerusalem : Hebrew Univ. of Jerusalem, Faculty of Law, Harry Sacher Institute for Legislative Research and Comparative Law, 1985. 221 p.   **CK231**
A classified list of articles and books, including collections of laws and judgements as well as secondary sources. Incorporates references in earlier bibliographies by Ernest Livneh, *Israel legal bibliography in European languages* (Jerusalem : Hebrew Univ. Students Pr., 1965. 118 p.) and Judith Romney Wegner, *A bibliography of Israel law in English and other European languages* (Jerusalem : Inst. for Legislative Research and Comparative Law, 1972. 124 p.).
————————. *[Supplement] 1985–1990* (1991. 88 p.).
§ Ruth Levush, *Introductions to research in foreign law : Israel* (Washington : Law Library of Congress, 1992) is a brief (11 p.) guide to basic sources.   KMK47.S25

Japan

Coleman, Rex. An index to Japanese law : a bibliography of Western language materials, 1867–1973 / by Rex Coleman and John Haley. [Tokyo : Univ. of Tokyo Pr.], 1975. 167 p.   **CK232**
On cover: *Law in Japan; an annual*, special issue, 1975.
A classed bibliography of translations of Japanese legal materials, as well as books and articles about Japanese law in European languages. No index. Updated irregularly by supplements in *Law in Japan: an annual*; most recent, supplement no. 6 by T. Susanne Lee, was published in v. 23 (1990), pp. 130–231, and covers material through 1983.
§ Also continued by Matthias K. Scheer, *Japanisches Recht in westlichen Sprachen, 1974–1989 : eine Bibliographie = Japanese law in Western languages, 1974–1989 : a bibliography* (Hamburg : Deutsch-Japanische Juristenvereinigung, 1992. 880 p.). Sung Yoon Cho, *Introductions to research in foreign law: Japan* (Washington: Law Library of Congress, 1991) is a recent but brief (15 p.) bibliography of major resources.

Australia and Oceania

Australian legal directory. 1979– . [Melbourne] : Law Council of Australia, 1979– . Annual.   **CK233**
A geographical directory of law firms, accompanied by alphabetical listings of legal practitioners and firms. Does not provide biographical information other than year of admission. A short section of legal institutions provides addresses and telephone numbers for courts, government offices, law schools, and law societies.

§ *New Zealand law register* (Sydney : Law Book Co., 1950– . Annual) is arranged in a similar manner and provides comparable information for New Zealand legal practitioners and institutions.

Elliott, Jacqueline D. Pacific law bibliography. 2nd ed. Hobart, Tas., Australia : Pacific Law Pr., 1990. 627, 32 p.   **CK234**

1st ed., 1988.
An annotated bibliography of more than 2,500 books and articles about jurisdictions of the Pacific. Pt. 1 lists bibliographies, statutes, law reports, periodicals, and other items under 32 subject headings, subdivided by jurisdiction; pt. 2 lists items under 20 jurisdictions, subdivided by subject. Author index.   KVC2.E45

Legal research : materials and methods / by Enid Campbell ... [et al.]. 3rd ed. North Ryde, N.S.W. : Law Book Co., 1988. 326 p.   **CK235**

1st ed., 1967; 2nd ed., 1979.
A general guide to the use of legal publications in Australia. Includes chapters on law reports of England, Australia, and other jurisdictions; Commonwealth and state statutes; treaties; legal periodicals; laws of Australian territories; international law; government publications; and Australian legal citation form. Indexed.
Legal materials in New Zealand as well as Australia are discussed in a less comprehensive work by Gwen Morris et al., *Laying down the law: the foundations of legal reasoning, research and writing in Australia and New Zealand* (3rd ed. Sydney : Butterworths, 1992).   KTA.L44

South Pacific islands legal systems / Michael A. Ntumy, general ed. Honolulu : Univ. of Hawaii Pr., c1993. 660 p. : map.   **CK236**

Discussion of the legal systems of 23 states and territories, from the Republic of Palau to Pitcairn Island. Summarizes sources of law, constitutional system, government, basic legal doctrines, and legal profession. Each chapter concludes with a brief bibliography or research guide.   KVC117.S68

RELIGIOUS LEGAL SYSTEMS

Canon law

Canon law abstracts : a half-yearly review of periodical literature in canon law. v. 1– . Melrose, Scotland : Canon Law Society of Great Britain, 1958– . Semiannual.   **CK237**

Abstracts of texts and articles on historical and contemporary canon law, arranged by subject. International in scope.

The code of canon law : a text and commentary / commissioned by the Canon Law Society of America ; ed. by James A. Coriden, Thomas J. Green, Donald E. Heintschel. N.Y. : Paulist Pr., c1985. 1152 p.   **CK238**

An English translation of the official Latin text of the revised code governing the Catholic Church, as promulgated on January 25, 1983; and an extensive commentary prepared by 23 scholars under the auspices of the Canon Law Society of America. Each section includes a bibliography. Tables provide correlations between the 1983 Code and its 1917 predecessor. Analytical index.
§ Shorter versions of the 1983 code include the authoritative *Code of canon law : Latin-English edition* (Wash. : Canon Law Society of America, 1983), with Latin and English on facing pages; and the convenient paperback *Code of canon law in English translation* (London : Collins ; Grand Rapids, Mich. : Eerdmans, 1983).

Jewish law

Encyclopedia Talmudica : a digest of halachic literature and Jewish law from the Tannaitic period to the present time, alphabetically arr[anged] ... / ed.: Shlomo Josef Zevin ... ; English tr. and ed. by Isidore Epstein and Harry Freedman. Jerusalem : Talmudic Encyclopedia Inst., [1969–1992]. v. 1–4. (In progress).   **CK239**

For annotation, *see* BC549.   BM500.5.E613

Raḳover, Naḥum. The multi-language bibliography of Jewish law. Jerusalem : Jewish Legal Heritage Society, [1990]. 871, 39 p.   **CK240**

Title on added t.p.: *Bibliyografyah rav-leshonit la-mishpaṭ ha-'Ivri.*
A bibliography of almost 15,000 books, articles, festschriften, and dissertations in languages other than Hebrew. 17 chapters, further subdivided by subject, with items listed by author under each subheading. Indexes in English and Hebrew to subjects, place names, rabbinical scholars, and authors.
§ Phyllis Holman Weisbard and David Schonbert, *Jewish law : bibliography of sources and scholarship in English* (Littleton, Colo. : Rothman, 1989) is a less comprehensive listing and uses broader subject divisions, but includes a useful introduction and sections on general works, literary sources, and Jewish history.   Z6374.L4R35

Welch, John W. A biblical law bibliography : arranged by subject and by author. Lewiston, N.Y. : E. Mellen Pr., c1990. 339 p. (Toronto studies in theology, v. 51).   **CK241**

An unannotated bibliography of books and articles, designed to supplement surveys of current literature published in *The Jewish law annual* (v. 1, 1978–). Covers works on the ancient Near East and the New Testament as well as the Old Testament.   Z7770.W44

CRIMINOLOGY

Guides

Lutzker, Marilyn. Criminal justice research in libraries : strategies and resources / Marilyn Lutzker and Eleanor Ferrall. N.Y. : Greenwood, 1986. 167 p.   **CK242**

Useful for both experienced and novice researchers. Includes a discussion of the organization of information in criminal justice, research design and control, and bibliographic searching, including computer database searching. Presents suggested research sources, special areas of research, and lists of subject headings and directories.   Z5703.4.C73L87

Bibliography

Beirne, Piers. Comparative criminology : an annotated bibliography / compiled by Piers Beirne and Joan Hill. N.Y. : Greenwood, 1991. 144 p. (Research and bibliographical guides in criminal justice, no. 3).   **CK243**

Lists articles, books and book chapters dealing with cross-national study of crime. 500 entries, listed alphabetically within 11 chapters. Author and subject indexes.   Z5703.B44

Berens, John F. Criminal justice documents : a selective, annotated bibliography of U.S. government publications since 1975. N.Y. : Greenwood, 1987. 236 p. (Bibliographies and indexes in law and political science, no. 7).   **CK244**

Lists more than 1,000 hearings, reports and other government documents in a detailed topical arrangement. Author, subject, geographic, and association/organization indexes.   Z5703.4.C73B47

Farson, Anthony Stuart. Criminal intelligence and security intelligence : a selective bibliography / comp. by A. Stuart Farson and Catherine J. Matthews. Toronto : Centre of Criminology, Univ. of Toronto, 1990. 77 p.   **CK245**

Compiled to help "scholars who want to draw distinctions between security and criminal intelligence work and to understand the context in which security intelligence work developed."—*Introd.* Focuses primarily on English-language materials about Canadian intelligence in the 1970s and 1980s. In two sections of unannotated entries, arranged alphabetically by author. The first section contains citations to books, articles, conference papers, theses, and dissertations; the second is comprised of citations to Australian, Canadian, British, and U.S. government documents. Appendix lists sources searched. Lack of index or subject arrangement hampers access.   Z5703.4.C728F37

Jerath, Bal K. Homicide : a bibliography / Bal K. Jerath, Rajinder Jerath. 2nd ed. Boca Raton, Fla. : CRC Pr., c1993. 788 p.   **CK246**

1st. ed., 1982.

An extensive interdisciplinary bibliography in 12 chapters (e.g., statistics, causes of murder, prevention and control), further subdivided by subject. Each unannotated item is assigned a brief keyword heading, which also serves as its only entry in the unsatisfactory subject index. Author index.

§ Ernest Abel, *Homicide : a bibliography* (Westport, Conn. : Greenwood, 1987) is a shorter, unannotated listing of articles and books by author, with a brief subject index. Michael Newton, *Mass murder : an annotated bibliography* (N.Y. : Garland, 1988) provides both a descriptive list of general works and case histories of over 600 murderers, with references to books, articles, and encyclopedia entries.   Z5703.4.M87J47

Ross, John M. Trials in collections : an index to famous trials throughout the world. Metuchen, N.J. : Scarecrow, 1983. 204 p.   **CK247**

An index to more than 300 compilations of trials, limited to English-language publications. Useful for finding trials that are not the subjects of separate volumes. Sources are listed by main entry and indexed by defendant or popular name and by criminal offense or other subject. The title index indicates the place and date for each trial.   K546.R67

Indexes; Abstract journals

Criminal justice abstracts. v. 9 (Mar. 1977)– . Monsey, N.Y. [etc.] : Willow Tree Pr. [etc.], 1977– . Quarterly.   **CK248**

Earlier titles: *Information review on crime and delinquency* and *Selected highlights of crime and delinquency literature*, 1968–69; *Crime and delinquency literature*, 1970–76. Publ. 1968–83 by the National Council on Crime and Delinquency.

Abstracts of books, journal articles, dissertations and reports, arranged alphabetically by author in six broad sections (Crime, the offender, and the victim; Juvenile justice and delinquency; Police; Courts and the legal process; Adult corrections; Crime prevention and control strategies). Some issues include specialized bibliographies or literature reviews. Subject and geographical index; author index. A cumulative index covering 1968–85 was published in 1989.   HV6001.C67

Criminal justice periodical index. 1975– . [Ann Arbor, Mich.] : Indexing Services, Univ. Microfilms, 1975– . 3 issues per year, including annual bound cumulation.   **CK249**

Indexes by author and subject more than 100 U.S., British and Canadian journals in the fields of corrections, criminal law, criminology, drug abuse, family law, juvenile justice, police studies, prison administration, rehabilitation, and security systems. Includes extensive coverage of trade bulletins and newsletters as well as academic journals.

•In machine-readable form as: *Criminal justice periodical index (CJPI)* [database] (Ann Arbor, Mich. : Univ. Microfilms Internat., 1975–). Available online, updated monthly.   Z5118.C9C74

Criminology, penology, and police science abstracts. Vol. 32, no. 1 (Jan./Feb. 1992)– . Amsterdam ; N.Y. : Kugler Publications, 1992– . Bimonthly.   **CK250**

Subtitle: An international abstracting service covering the etiology of crime and juvenile delinquency, the control and treatment of offenders, criminal procedure, the administration of justice, and police science.

Formed by the union of *Criminology & penology abstracts* (1980–91; former titles: *Excerpta criminologica*, 1961–68; *Abstracts on criminology and penology*, 1969–79) and *Police science abstracts* (1980–91); continues the volume numbering of the former.

English-language abstracts of books and articles in more than 200 journals, arranged by nine broad subject sections. Classified arrangement of 13 broad subjects with extensive subdivisions. Subject and author indexes.   HV6001.C74

Encyclopedias

Encyclopedia of crime and justice / Sanford H. Kadish, ed. in chief. N.Y. : Free Pr., c1983. 4 v. (1790 p.).   **CK251**

An impressive interdisciplinary survey of the nature and causes of criminal behavior, crime prevention, and the many components of the criminal justice system. American in emphasis, with international comparisons. 286 alphabetically arranged articles vary in length from 1 to 20 pages; each includes a short bibliography. A helpful "Guide to legal citations" in v. 1 not only defines abbreviations but explains both the formats of case and statutory citations and the legal significance of cited works. Glossary; legal index (tables of cases and other legal documents); general index.   HV6017.E52

The encyclopedia of police science / ed., William G. Bailey. N.Y. : Garland, 1989. [734 p.]. (Garland reference library of social science, v. 413.).   **CK252**

Contains 143 signed articles on methods and issues in criminology, major historical figures, and selected institutions. Articles, ranging in length from two to 12 pages, are arranged alphabetically and include bibliographies. Appendixes provide a bibliography of police history and a bibliography of bibliographies. General index and index of legal cases.   HV7901.E53

Encyclopedia of security management : techniques & technology / ed. by John J. Fay. Boston : Butterworth-Heinemann, c1993. 792 p. : ill.   **CK253**

Covers all aspects of the security business, including issues such as access control, executive protection, fire safety, lighting, and surveillance. Signed articles by more than 70 contributors, generally two to three pages in length, are arranged alphabetically and include bibliographic references. Index.   HV8290.S365

Encyclopedia of world crime : criminal justice, criminology, and law enforcement dictionary / [ed. in chief] Jay Robert Nash. Wilmette, Ill. : CrimeBooks, 1989–90. 6 v.   **CK254**

Contents: v. 1–4, A–Z and suppl.; v. 5, Dictionary; v. 6, Index.

Contains more than 50,000 articles on all aspects of crime and law enforcement, many with illustrations and bibliographic references. Vol. 4 contains more than two dozen supplements, including chronologies of major crimes such as assassinations and bombings; descriptions of methods of capital punishment; photographs of organized crime figures; and lists of western lawmen and outlaws. The dictionary volume covers 20,000 terms, indicating sources for definitions, and contains supplements listing acronyms, landmark court cases, and major crime legislation. Vol. 6 includes a 328-page bibliography and indexes by subject and name.

§ In 1992, Paragon House (N.Y.) published portions of the encyclopedia separately as: *Dictionary of crime : criminal justice, criminology & law enforcement*; *World encyclopedia of organized crime*; and *World encyclopedia of 20th century murder*.

Two one-volume encyclopedias by Carl Sifakis, *The encyclopedia of American crime* (N.Y. : Facts on File, 1982) and *The mafia encyclopedia* (N.Y. : Facts on File, 1987), are similar but narrower in scope. Works limited to discussion of famous and infamous homicides include J. H. H. Gaute and Robin Odell, *The new murderers' who's who* (London : Harrap, 1989 ; N.Y. : International Polygonics, 1991); Colin Wilson and Patricia Pitman, *Encyclopedia of murder* (London : Barker, 1961 ; N.Y. : Putnam, 1962); and Colin Wilson and Donald Seaman, *Encyclopedia of modern murder* (Rev. ed. London : Pan Books, 1989).   HV6017.E54

Kurian, George Thomas. World encyclopedia of police forces and penal systems. N.Y. : Facts on File, c1989. 582 p. : ill.   **CK255**

Describes the national law enforcement systems of 183 countries. Each country's entry provides information on the history and structure of its police forces, recruitment and training procedures, and penal systems. Tables of crime statistics are included for many countries. Concludes with information on Interpol, a world police directory, a bibliography, and an index.   HV7901.K87

Dictionaries

Benmaman, Virginia. Bilingual dictionary of criminal justice terms (English/Spanish) / by Virginia Benmaman, Norma C. Connolly, Scott Robert Loos. Binghamton, N.Y. : Gould Publications, c1991. 216 p. : ill.   **CK256**

A dictionary of terminology used in criminal procedure in the U.S. Equivalent Spanish terms are provided for about 900 English terms, including about 200 penal offenses. Definitions are provided in both languages, with notes on distinctions in usage and variations among state laws. A Spanish index provides references to English terms. Includes a bibliography and flow charts showing the major steps in criminal justice procedures.   KF9617.B46

De Sola, Ralph. Crime dictionary. Rev. and exp. ed. N.Y. : Facts on File, c1988. 222 p.   **CK257**

1st ed., 1982.

Concise definitions of more than 10,000 terms, including legal, medical and psychiatric terms relating to crime and drug addiction; abbreviations; weapons; nicknames; slang; gangs; and crime-fighting agencies. Appendixes provide definitions of foreign terms, place-name nicknames, and a selected bibliography.

§ Shorter dictionaries, also with brief definitions, include Erik Beckman, *The criminal justice dictionary* (2nd ed. Ann Arbor, Mich. : Pierian Pr., 1983); Julian A. Martin and Nicholas A. Astone, *Criminal justice vocabulary* (Springfield, Ill. : Thomas, 1980); and George E. Rush, *Dictionary of criminal justice* (3rd ed. Guilford, Conn. : Dushkin Publ. Group, 1991), which includes summaries of major Supreme Court cases in criminal law.   HV6025.D43

Elsevier's dictionary of criminal science in eight languages : English/American, French, Italian, Spanish, Portuguese, Dutch, Swedish, and German / comp. and arranged on an English alphabetical base by Johann Anton Adler. Amsterdam ; N.Y. : Elsevier, 1960. 1460 p.   **CK258**

A multilingual dictionary, exceedingly dated but still of some use. Includes some slang and technical terms which may not appear in general dictionaries. More than 10,000 terms are listed alphabetically in English with equivalents in seven other languages. Indexes for the other languages provide references to the main listing.   HV6017.E4

Fay, John. The police dictionary and encyclopedia. Springfield, Ill. : C.C. Thomas, c1988. 370 p.   **CK259**

Concise definitions for a wide range of terms used in law enforcement. Appendixes list minimum and maximum felony sentences, capital offenses and methods of execution by state. Bibliography.   HV7901.F39

Ferdico, John N. Ferdico's criminal law and justice dictionary. St. Paul : West Publ. Co., c1992. 476 p.   **CK260**

Some 5,000 definitions of terms used in criminal justice, from pretrial investigation and detection of crime through corrections, appeals, and postconviction remedies. Includes references to cases and examples of usage.   KF9217.F47 1992

Directories

Directory, juvenile & adult correctional departments, institutions, agencies & paroling authorities / American Correctional Association. 1993– . Laurel, Md. : The Association, c1993– . Annual.   **CK261**

Issued 1979–92 as: *Juvenile and adult correctional departments, institutions, agencies and paroling authorities, United States and Canada* and under several earlier titles.

A directory of institutions and personnel involved in correctional service in the U.S. and Canada. An introductory section provides statistics on expenditures, facilities, offender populations, and personnel. Name index.   HV9463.D57

Directory of criminal justice information sources. Wash. : U.S. Dept. of Justice, Office of Justice Programs, National Institute of Justice, 1976– . Biennial.   **CK262**

Superintendent of Documents classification: J 28.20: .

5th–7th eds. had title: *A network of knowledge : directory of criminal justice information sources.*

An alphabetical list of some 176 organizations offering criminal justice-related information services, such as database searches, document dissemination, reference services, or technical assistance. Entries include contact information, user restrictions, services offered, and publications. Subject and geographical indexes.   HV9950.D59

International directory of correctional administrations / American Correctional Association. College Park, Md. : The Association, c1987. 232 p. : ill.   **CK263**

Arranged by geographic region. Entries for 57 countries include brief summaries of national demographics and the legal system, a description of the corrections system, and names and addresses of administrators. Shorter entries for 85 other countries simply provide names or titles and addresses. Includes maps and a brief selected bibliography.   HV9443.I58 1987

National directory of law enforcement administrators, correctional institutions, and related governmental agencies. Milwaukee, Wis. : National Police Chiefs and Sheriffs Information Bureau, [1983?]– . Annual.   **CK264**

Title varies.

Lists county sheriffs, prosecuting attorneys, and municipal chiefs of police. Provides addresses and telephone numbers for state highway patrols, criminal investigation units, and correctional agencies; federal law enforcement and criminal justice agencies; selected Canadian and foreign police agencies; and law enforcement and related associations.   HV8130.N37

National jail and adult detention directory. 1978– . [College Park, Md. : American Correctional Assoc.], 1978– .   **CK265**

A state-by-state listing of city and county jails, providing addresses, phone numbers, names of sheriffs, and information on capacity, population, personnel, and expenditures. A dozen introductory tables provide nationwide statistics, and each state has a separate statistical summary.   HV9463.N37

National prison directory : a prison reform organizational and resource directory, with a special section on public library service to prisoners. 3rd ed., ed. by Mary Lee Bundy and Alice Bell. College Park, Md. : Urban Information Interpreters, [1984]. 205 p. **CK266**

> 1st ed., 1975; 2nd ed., 1979.

> Profiles of institutions and associations working towards reform of the penal system. Organized by state, with listings by name and subject. Also lists prison periodicals, national organizations working on prison issues, and public library services to prisoners. Becoming quite dated. HV8987.N37

Probation and parole directory : adult and juvenile probation and parole services, United States and Canada. 1st ed. (1981)– . College Park, Md. : American Correctional Assoc., c1981– . Triennial. **CK267**

> Frequency varies: Quadrennial, 1981–84; triennial, 1985–.

> Names, addresses, and telephone numbers for state, regional, and local probation and parole boards and offices, for both adults and juveniles. Appendixes summarize beginning salaries, educational requirements, and mandated training for parole officers in each state. Includes a brief bibliography of probation and parole terms.

> HV9304.P76

A world directory of criminological institutes / comp. and ed. by Carla Masotti Santoro. 5th ed. Rome, Italy : UNICRI, 1990. 661 p. **CK268**

> Lists more than 400 international and national organizations and research centers in 72 countries. Entries, based on questionnaire responses, vary widely in detail; each provides contact information and some information on organizational structure and activity.

> HV6024.5.W67

Statistics

Sourcebook of criminal justice statistics. 1973– . Wash. : U.S. Bureau of Justice Statistics : For sale by U.S. Govt. Print. Off., 1974– . Annual. **CK269**

> Superintendent of Documents classification: J1.42/3:SD-SD- .

> A wide variety of statistics relating to crime. Major sections are: Characteristics of the criminal justice system (expenditures, personnel, facilities); Public attitudes toward crime and criminal justice-related topics (including matters such as gun ownership and legality of homosexual relations); Nature and distribution of known offenses (including victimization, high school delinquency, and drug-related emergency room episodes); Characteristics and distribution of persons arrested; Judicial processing of defendants; Persons under correctional supervision. Includes an annotated list of sources, addresses of publishers, appendixes explaining statistical methodologies, and an extensive index.

> HV7245.N37b

Uniform crime reports for the United States. v. 1, no. 1 (Aug. 1930)– . Wash. : Bureau of Investigation, U.S. Dept. of Justice ; U.S. Govt. Print. Off., 1930– . Annual. **CK270**

> Superintendent of Documents classification: J 1.14/7: .

> Frequency varies: monthly, 1930–31; quarterly, 1932–41; semiannual with annual cumulation, 1942–57; annual, 1958– .

> Cover title: *Crime in the United States.*

> A compilation of criminal statistics gathered from federal, state and local authorities. Introductory summaries and charts indicate national rates for major offenses (homicide, rape, robbery, aggravated assault, burglary, larceny, motor vehicle theft, and arson), and more than 80 tables provide detailed statistical data by state and locality on crimes, persons arrested, and law enforcement personnel.

> § Similar annual publications from other countries include *Canadian crime statistics = Statistique de la criminalité de Canada* (Ottawa : Canadian Centre for Justice Statistics, 1983–) and *Criminal statistics England and Wales* (London : H.M.S.O., 1928–). The International Criminal Police Organization (Interpol) publishes a biennial *Sta-*

tistiques criminelles internationales = International crime statistics (Saint-Cloud, France : Secrétariat général de l'O.I.P.C.-Interpol, 1952–). HV6787.A3

CL

Geography

GENERAL WORKS

Guides

Brewer, James Gordon. The literature of geography : a guide to its organisation and use. 2nd ed. London : Bingley ; Hamden, Conn. : Linnet Books, [1978]. 264 p. : ill. **CL1**

> 1st ed., 1973.

> Subject chapter arrangement, with information on scope and use of geographical literature followed by bibliographic essays on types of material. Includes a chapter on cartobibliography. Z6001.B74

A guide to information sources in the geographical sciences / ed. by Stephen Goddard. London : Croom Helm ; Totowa, N.J. : Barnes & Noble, 1983. 273 p. : ill. **CL2**

> Thirteen chapters by academics and librarians provide bibliographical reviews of the literature and reference works of thematic fields of geography (e.g., agricultural), regional areas (Africa, South Asia, the United States, the Soviet Union), and tools (maps, aerial photographs and satellite data, statistical analysis and computers, and archival materials). Some British emphasis; no index. Z6001.G84

The student's companion to geography / ed. by Alisdair Rogers, Heather Viles, and Andrew Goudie. Oxford ; Cambridge, Mass. : Blackwell, 1992. 386 p. : ill., map. **CL3**

> Thorough introduction to the discipline provided by more than 50 widely recognized experts from Australia, Canada, New Zealand, the U.K., and the U.S. Organized in six parts: introductions to the field, reviews of the subfields and current issues, methodologies and techniques, biographies and bibliographies, directories of resources, and career options. Subfields range from physical geography (geomorphology, biogeography, climatology) to human geography (economic, social, cultural). Methodologies include statistical applications, remote sensing, laboratory work, archives research, and geographical information systems. Directories list libraries and museums, data sources (both in print and electronic), funding sources, and major institutions. Each chapter includes a list of references. General index. G116.S78

Wright, John Kirtland. Aids to geographical research : bibliographies, periodicals, atlases, gazetteers, and other reference books / by John Kirtland Wright and Elizabeth T. Platt. 2nd ed., compl. rev. N.Y. : publ. for the American Geographical Soc. by Columbia Univ. Pr., 1947. 331 p. (American Geographical Society. Research series, no. 22). **CL4**

> 1st ed., 1923.

> A valuable manual, though now out-of-date. In three main sections: (1) General aids; (2) Topical aids; (3) Regional aids and general

geographical periodicals from each country. The coverage is comprehensive and includes materials in many languages. Annotations are descriptive and evaluative. Author, subject, and title index. Includes, as an appendix, a classified index of American professional geographers, libraries of geographical utility, and institutions engaged in geographical research, p. 276–94.   Z6001.A1W9

Bibliography

A bibliography of geographic thought / comp. by Catherine L. Brown and James O. Wheeler. N.Y. : Greenwood, 1989. 520 p. (Bibliographies and indexes in geography, no. 1). **CL5**
     Rev. and expanded ed. of Wheeler's *Bibliography on geographic thought, 1950–1982* (Athens : Univ. of Georgia, Dept. of Geography, 1983).
     A comprehensive bibliography of approximately 6,000 English-language journal articles and 600 books on the history, philosophy, and methodology of geography. Books are listed in the first chapter alphabetically by author; articles are divided into nine chapters by topic, then listed alphabetically by author. Separate author, subject, and biographical indexes, but the subject index covers only citations in the chapter Subdisciplines in geography.   Z6001.B5814

Bibliotheca geographica / Gesellschaft für Erdkunde zu Berlin. Bd. 1 (1891/92)–19 (1911/12). Berlin : W. H. Kuhl, 1895–1917.   **CL6**
     Subtitle varies.
     Volumes 1, 18, and 19 each cover two years, 1891/92, 1909/10, and 1911/-12 respectively.
     An important annual bibliography, international in scope, of books and periodical articles, listing more titles than the *Bibliographie géographique internationale* (CL23 *note*), but without annotations. Classified, with author index. No more published.   Z6001.B582

Cox, Edward Godfrey. A reference guide to the literature of travel / including voyages, geographical descriptions, adventures, shipwrecks and expeditions. Seattle : Univ. of Washington, 1935–49. 3 v. (University of Washington Publications in language and literature, v. 9–10, 12).   **CL7**
     Repr.: N.Y. : Greenwood, 1969.
     Contents: v. 1, The Old World (401 p.); v. 2, The New World (591 p.); v. 3, Great Britain (732 p.).
     Classified with author index. Lists "in chronological order, from the earliest date ascertainable down to and including the year 1800, all the books on foreign travels, voyages and descriptions printed in Great Britain, together with translations from foreign tongues and continental renderings of English works."—*Pref.*   Z6011.C87

Documentatio geographica. Jan./Feb. 1966–1973. Bonn-Bad Godesberg : Bundesanstalt für Landeskunde und Raumforschung, 1966–73.   **CL8**
     Issued by the Institut für Landeskunde, Bad Godesberg, 1966–1970.
     Frequency varies: originally bimonthly with annual cumulation; 1971/72 combined; 1973, quarterly with annual cumulation.
     Subtitle (Geographische Zeitschriften- und Serien-Literatur) also in English (Papers of geographical periodicals and serials), French, Spanish, and Russian.
     An international bibliography of geographical literature appearing in periodicals and monographic series. Arranged by Universal Decimal Classification; the annual cumulation includes a separate *Register* volume which provides indexes by author, subject, and region, plus a UDC index offering references to related subject areas for each article.
     § Continued by: *Dokumentation zur Raumentwicklung* (Jahrg. 1974/75–1978. Bonn-Bad Godesberg : Bundesforschungsanstalt für Landeskunde und Raumordnung, 1975–79.).
     Subtitle: Vierteljahreshefte zur Literaturdokumentation aus Raumforschung, Raumordnung, Regionalforschung, Landeskunde und Sozialgeographie = A current and annotated bibliography of regional science, regional planning and social geography.

Published in two volumes per year: v. 1, Titelband (comprising 4 quarterly issues); v. 2, Registerband (issued annually in publisher's binding). A classed bibliography, with author, subject, and regional index.   Z6001.D63

Dunbar, Gary S. The history of modern geography : an annotated bibliography of selected works. N.Y. : Garland, 1985. 386 p. (Bibliographies of the history of science and technology, v. 9 ; Garland reference library of the humanities, v. 445).   **CL9**
     An international bibliography of works in western and central European languages on the history of geography from the mid-18th century to the early 1980s. 1,717 citations are classed within 22 chapters in three main parts: general and topical; geography in various countries; biographical works. Author and keyword subject indexes.
     ———. *The history of modern geography : corrigenda and addenda* (privately publ. by the author, 1987). Includes an additional 200 entries, primarily published since 1983. Corrects typographical errors and provides additional author index entries.   Z6001.D86

A geographical bibliography for American libraries / ed. by Chauncy D. Harris [et al.]. [Wash.] : Assoc. of American Geographers, 1985. 437 p.   **CL10**
     "A joint project of the Association of American Geographers and the National Geographic Society."—*t.p.*
     "Since the predecessor volume, *A geographical bibliography for American college libraries* (CL17), still provides an excellent guide to works published before 1970, the current bibliography focuses on publications for the period 1970–1984."—*Introd.* Entries and brief annotations for many new sections, including publications suitable for school libraries, were prepared by more than 70 contributors. 2,903 citations to monographs, bibliographies, serials, and atlases in detailed classed/regional arrangement. Brief, critical annotations; indexed. A major and indispensable work.   Z6001.G44

Goodman, Edward J. The exploration of South America : an annotated bibliography. N.Y. : Garland, 1983. 174 p. (Garland reference library of social science, v.148 ; Themes in European expansion, v. 4).   **CL11**
     General sections on bibliographies, documents collections, and contemporary accounts are followed by chapters arranged by historical period, then by geographic area. 915 entries, well annotated. Author and subject indexes. A 20-item addendum is indexed with wrong item numbers.
     § Can be supplemented by "Recent literature in discovery history," comp. by Barbara B. McCorkle, in the journal *Terrae incognitae.*   Z1212.G66

Harris, Chauncy Dennison. Bibliography of geography. Chicago : Univ. of Chicago, Dept. of Geography, 1976–84. Pt. 1–2. (University of Chicago. Department of Geography. Research paper, no. 179, 206).   **CL12**
     Contents: pt. 1, Introduction to general aids (276 p.); pt. 2. Regional: v. 1, United States of America (178 p.). No more published?
     Does not intend to supersede John Kirtland Wright and Elizabeth T. Platt, *Aids to geographical research* (CL4); although "many items in Wright and Platt are out of date or superseded by later or better works, yet the essential core of older works of enduring value published up to 1946, carefully selected and expertly annotated, remains recorded there and does not need to be repeated."—*Pref.* Chapters on bibliographies of bibliographies (guides, comprehensive retrospective and current bibliographies of geography, specialized bibliographies) are followed by sections for bibliographies of books, serials, government documents, dissertations, photographs, maps and atlases, gazetteers, place-name dictionaries, dictionaries, encyclopedias, statistics, and methodology.
     In each chapter, introductory remarks are followed by carefully annotated lists of bibliographies. The sections on comprehensive current and retrospective bibliographies are particularly precise and detailed. Appendix 1 lists gazetteers of the U.S. Board on Geographic Names; Appendix 2 is an annotated list comprising "A small geographical reference collection." Indexed.

Pt. 2, Regional geography, was planned to consist of five segments: the U.S.; the Soviet Union; the Americas; Europe; and Africa, Asia, Australia, and the Pacific. The U.S. volume emphasizes bibliographies, reference works, and data sources in four main areas: general aids; physical geography, earth science and environment; human geography; and individual regions, states, and cities. 1,257 entries, mostly annotated, for English-language sources published since 1969. Indexed.　　H31.C514

———————— Guide to geographical bibliographies and reference works in Russian or on the Soviet Union : annotated list of 2660 bibliographies or reference aids. Chicago : Univ. of Chicago, Dept. of Geography, 1975. 478 p. : maps. (University of Chicago. Dept. of Geography. Research paper, no.164). **CL13**

Intended as an aid to individuals outside the Soviet Union who wish to become informed on "the corpus of serious scientific work in geography and related disciplines published in Russian or in other languages of the Soviet Union or dealing with the geography of the Soviet Union."—*Pref.* Classed arrangement with author-title-subject index. Primarily non-Western language materials; entries are given in transliteration, with an English translation of the title.　　H31.C514 no.164

Kinauer, Rudolf. Lexikon geographischer Bildbände. Wien : Brüder Hollinek, [1966]. 463 p.　　**CL14**

A bibliography designed to enable the user to find easily pictures and photographs illustrating various aspects of geography.　　Z6001.K5

Kish, George. Bibliography of International Geographic Congresses, 1871–1976. Boston : G.K. Hall, c1979. 540 p. (Series of studies of the history of geography, v. 1). **CL15**

Publ. under the auspices of the Commission on the History of Geographical Thought, International Geographical Union.

Lists almost 7,000 papers presented at the 23 International Geographical Congresses held between 1871 and 1976. Arranged chronologically by congress, and within congress by group presentation, with complete bibliographical references to the published proceedings. Classed subject and author indexes.　　Z6001.K55

Lee, David R. Women and geography : a comprehensive bibliography. Boca Raton, Fla. : David Lee, Department of Geography, Florida Atlantic Univ., [1986?]. 1 v. (various pagings). **CL16**

Includes "works appearing in a known geography publication which make reference to women or gender issues" and "works dealing with women which are written by individuals identified as geographers ... irrespective of where they appear."—*Introd.* Emphasizes English-language titles. Arranged alphabetically by author with personal name and subject indexes.

————. *Supplement*, 1988, 1989, 1990.　　Z6001.L43

Lewthwaite, Gordon Rowland. A geographical bibliography for American college libraries / comp. and ed. by Gordon R. Lewthwaite, Edward T. Price, and Harold A. Winters. Rev. ed. Wash. : Assoc. of Amer. Geographers, Commission on College Geography, [1970]. 214 p. (Assoc. of Amer. Geographers. Comm. on College Geography, Pubn. 9). **CL17**

"A revision of *A basic geographical library; a selected and annotated book list for American colleges.* Original ed. compiled and edited by Martha Church, Robert E. Huke [and] Harold A. Winters [1966]."—*title page.*

A list of 1,760 items "selected as a core for the geography collection of an American undergraduate college library."—*Introd.* Emphasizes recent books in English, but "many books in foreign languages and older books, even though not currently available, have been included where their subject or quality seemed needed." Classed arrangement; brief annotations; author index.　　Z6001.L48

Owens, Peter L. Radical geography : an annotated bibliography / comp. and ed. by Peter L. Owens and Richard House. Norwich, [Eng.] : Geo Books, 1984. 260 p. (Geo abstracts bibliography, no. 13).　　**CL18**

1,314 citations, drawn from the database of *Geo abstracts* (CL32 *note*), which illustrate the left-oriented approach to social and economic geography. Topical arrangement with author and keyword subject indexes.　　Z6001.O9

Royal Geographical Society (London). New geographical literature and maps. v. 1–9. London : Royal Geographical Soc., 1951–80. Semiannual (irregular). **CL19**

Issued 1918–41 as *Recent geographical literature, maps, and photographs* ... as a supplement to *Geographical journal.* No more publ.

Lists books and articles in leading British and foreign geographical journals, and new maps and atlases. Also contains annual lists of completed theses in geography from British universities.　　Z6009.R882

Sanguin, André Louis. Géographie politique : bibliographie internationale. Montréal : Presses de l'Université du Québec, 1976. 232 p.　　**CL20**

An attempt to distinguish political geography from geopolitics. Subject-classed list of works on cultural geography; the nation and the state; the frontier; territorial conflicts; oceans and international rivers; space; military, administrative, and electoral geography; international affairs and regionalism; and colonialism. Within each topic, citations are usually arranged by general or regional content, with subdivisions by book or article format. Author index.　　Z6004.P7S3

Sukhwal, B. L. South Asia : a systematic geographic bibliography. Metuchen, N.J. : Scarecrow, 1974. 827 p.　　**CL21**

More than 10,300 entries. Within geographic divisions (South Asia, India, Pakistan, Bangladesh, Sri Lanka, Tibet, Kingdom of Nepal, Kingdoms of Bhutan and Sikkim, Indian Ocean and islands), materials are listed in classed arrangement. Author index.　　Z3185.S94

Current

Current geographical publications : additions to the Research catalogue of the American Geographical Society. v.1 (1938)– . N.Y. : The Society, 1938– . Monthly, except July and Aug.　　**CL22**

. Repr.: N.Y. : Kraus Reprint, 1966– .

Publisher varies; now issued by the Library, Univ. of Wisconsin, Milwaukee.

A classified index to current books, pamphlets, government publications, and periodical articles in the field of geography. Vol.1 has no index; v.2– have indexes by subject, author, and regions. From Oct. 1940 through Dec. 1952, each issue contained a supplement listing photographs in publications received in the library of the American Geographical Society. Since Nov. 1964 selected maps are listed in a separate section.　　Z6009.A47

FRANCIS. Bibliographie géographique internationale : 531. v. 96, no. 1 (1991)– . Nancy : Institut de l'Information Scientifique et Technique [and] Laboratoire de Communication et de Documentation en Géographie, 1991– . Quarterly. **CL23**

Issued as "Bibliographie géographique annuelle" in *Annales de géographie,* v. 1 (1891/92)–v. 23/24 (1914/15). Published separately thereafter, continuing the volume numbering, as: *Bibliographie géographique,* v. 25/29 (1915/19)–v. 40 (1930); *Bibliographie géographique internationale,* v. 41 (1931)–v. 95 (1990).

An important international bibliography of the holdings of the major French geographical institutions. Analyzes journals, conference proceedings, monographs, reports, theses and dissertations, and atlases and maps. Classed arrangement with detailed table of contents. Annotations are primarily in French, with some in English. List of publications indexed in each issue. Indexes by subject, place, author; annual cumulated index.

For full description of *FRANCIS,* see: AD254.　　Z6001.B57

Periodicals

Harris, Chauncy Dennison. Annotated world list of selected current geographical serials. 4th ed. Chicago : Univ. of Chicago, Dept. of Geography, 1980. 165 p. (University of Chicago. Department of Geography. Research paper, 194).   **CL24**
    1st ed., 1960.
    "443 current geographical serials from 72 countries, with a study of serials most cited in geographical bibliographies."—*t.p.*
                                                                HC31.C514

————— International list of geographical serials / comp. by Chauncy D. Harris and Jerome D. Fellmann. 3rd ed., rev., exp., & updated. Chicago : Univ. of Chicago, Dept. of Geography, 1980. 457 p. (University of Chicago. Department of Geography. Research paper, 193).   **CL25**
    1st ed., 1960. An earlier version had title: *Union list of geographical serials* (2nd. ed., 1950).
    "A comprehensive retrospective inventory of 3,445 geographical serials from 107 countries in 55 languages with locations in union lists."—*t.p.*   HC31.C514

Dissertations

Browning, Clyde Eugene. Bibliography of dissertations in geography, 1901 to 1969 : American and Canadian universities. Chapel Hill : Univ. of North Carolina, Dept. of Geography, 1970. 96 p. (University of North Carolina. Department of Geography. Studies in geography, no. 1).   **CL26**
    The compilation is based mainly on the dissertation lists published in the periodical *The professional geographer.*
    —————. *A bibliography of dissertations in geography, 1969 to 1982 : American and Canadian universities* (Chapel Hill : Univ. of North Carolina, Dept. of Geography, c1983. 145 p. [Studies in geography, no. 18]). Forms a supplement to the above, listing 2,270 dissertations from the 1969–82 period. Based on the listings appearing in *The professional geographer* and *Guide to programs in geography in the United States and Canada* (CL55). Classed arrangement with author index.   Z6001.B89

Stuart, Merrill M. A bibliography of master's theses in geography : American and Canadian universities. Tualatin, Ore. : Geographic and Area Study Publ., 1973. 275 p.   **CL27**
    More than 5,000 entries in classified arrangement, with author and regional indexes. Includes items from the lists appearing in *The professional geographer*, plus other titles reported by various degree-granting institutions.   Z6001.S78

Library catalogs

American Geographical Society of New York. Research catalogue of the American Geographical Society. Boston : G.K. Hall, 1962. 15 v. (10,432 p.).   **CL28**
    A photographic reproduction of the cards in the Research Catalogue of the Society's library, arranged by a systematic classification and a regional classification. Includes books, periodical articles, pamphlets, and government documents.
    —————. *Map supplement* (1962. 24 p. : maps ; 36 cm.).
    —————. *Supplement* 1–2. (Boston : G.K. Hall, 1972–78. 6 v.).
    Contents: Suppl. 1, 1962–71: [pt. 1] Regional (2 v.); [pt. 2] Topical (2 v.); Suppl. 2, 1972–76: v. 1, Topical; v. 2, Regional.
    Cumulates the citations first published in *Current geographical publications* (CL22), v. 25–39.   Z6009.A48

Harvard University. Library. Geography and anthropology : classification schedules; classified listing by call number; chronological listing; author and title listing. Cambridge : Publ. by the Harvard Univ. Library; distr. by Harvard Univ. Pr., 1979. 270 p. (Widener Library shelflist, 60).   **CL29**
    For annotation, *see* CE29.   Z6009.H37

Indexes; Abstract journals

•**GEOBASE** [database]. Norwich, England : Elsevier/Geo Abstracts, 1980– .   **CL30**
    Machine-readable version of *Geographical abstracts. Human geography* (CL31) and *Geographical abstracts. Physical geography* (CL32) and their predecessors.
    Also contains relevant records from *International development abstracts* (CH44), *Geological abstracts* (Norwich, Eng. : GeoAbstracts, Ltd., 1977–), *Ecological abstracts* (EG63), and *Mineralogical abstracts* (EF177). Available online.

Geographical abstracts. Human geography. 1989– . Norwich [England] : Elsevier/Geo Abstracts, 1989– . Monthly.   **CL31**
                                                                GF1.G47

Geographical abstracts. Physical geography. 1989– . Norwich, [England] : Elsevier/Geo Abstracts, c1989– . Monthly.   **CL32**
    Title history: Called *Geographical abstracts* (1966–71). Superseded by *Geo abstracts* (1972–85), which had the following parts: A, Landforms and the quaternary; B, Climatology and hydrology; C, Economic geography; D, Social and historical geography; E, Sedimentology; F, Regional and community planning; G, Remote sensing, photogrammetry and cartography. In 1986, *Geo abstracts*, pts. A, B, E, and G changed title to *Geographical abstracts*, pts. A, B, E, and G, and pts. C, D, and F to *Geographical abstracts*, pts. C, D, and F. In 1989, pts, A, B, E, and G merged to form *Geographical abstracts. Physical geography* and pts. C, D, and F merged to form *Geographical abstracts. Human geography.*
    The topical arrangement of the earlier titles has been retained. Each issue has a regional index, and regional and author indexes cumulate annually.   GB54.5.G46

National geographic index, 1888–1988. [Wash.] : National Geographic Society, 1989. 1215 p. : ill. (some col.).   **CL33**
    Compiled to commemorate the 100th anniversary of the National Geographic Society and publication of *National geographic* magazine. Contains a brief chronology of milestones in the history of the Society and a list of winners of Society medals and awards. The index proper, more than 1,000 pages, has author, title, and subject entries, with photographs in color and symbols to identify books, maps, and television programs.   G1.N27

Book reviews

Van Balen, John. Geography and earth sciences publications : an author, title and subject guide to books reviewed, and an index to the reviews. [Ann Arbor, Mich.] : Pierian Pr., 1978. 2 v.   **CL34**
    Contents: v. 1, 1968–1972; v. 2, 1973–1975.
    Vol. 1 contains about 3,400 entries and 4,900 book review citations from 21 geographical journals; v. 2, about 2,500 entries and 3,700 book review citations from 38 geographical journals. Author listing, with broad subject, geographical area, and title indexes.
                                                                Z6001.V33

Encyclopedias

Day, Alan Edwin. Discovery and exploration : a reference handbook. N.Y. : K. G. Saur ; London : Clive Bingley, 1980. 1 v. **CL35**

Contents: [v. 1] The old world (295 p.). A second volume, intended to cover the new world, appears to have never been published.

Presents 455 alphabetically arranged entries for persons, institutions, and published sources relevant to the exploration of Europe, Asia, and the Arctic. Indexed by region and authors/titles of published sources. G80.D36

The discoverers : an encyclopedia of explorers and exploration / ed. by Helen Delpar. N.Y. : McGraw-Hill, c1980. 471 p. : ill. **CL36**

Emphasizes the age of discovery that began in 15th-century Europe and continued up to the 20th century, with main stress on explorers of Western European origin. Articles are of three types: (1) biographical; (2) geographical, on continents or regions, reviewing the history of their exploration; (3) topical, on themes such as ancient or medieval exploration. Articles are signed; most have bibliographies. Cross-references; index. G200.D53

Huber, Thomas Patrick. Dictionary of concepts in physical geography / Thomas P. Huber, Robert P. Larkin, and Gary L. Peters. N.Y. : Greenwood, 1988. 291 p. (Reference sources for the social sciences and humanities, no. 5). **CL37**

For each of more than 150 terms, provides definitions (from earliest to most recent), historical development of the use of the term with brief literature review, a bibliography of important references, and a list of other sources of information. Cross-references. Appendix provides outline of concepts included. General index. GB10.H82

Larkin, Robert P. Dictionary of concepts in human geography / Robert P. Larkin, Gary L. Peters. Westport, Conn. : Greenwood, 1983. 286 p. (Reference sources for the social sciences and humanities, no. 2). **CL38**

For some 100 English-language terms, brief essays provide definitions, historical development, bibliographic references, and sources of additional information. Indexed. GF4.L37

Modern geography : an encyclopedic survey / ed. by Gary S. Dunbar. N.Y. : Garland, 1991. 219 p. (Garland reference library of the humanities, vol. 1197). **CL39**

Contains approximately 400 signed entries for "personalities, institutions, major concepts, subfields and the evolution of the discipline" (*Introd.*) of geography, 1890 to the present. Biographical entries cite major publications and biographies; other entries include brief bibliographies. Major terms and concepts only are defined; reference is made to appropriate subject dictionaries for other definitions. Cross-references; index of personal names. G63.M57

Westermann Lexikon der Geographie / hrsg. im Auftrag des Georg Westermann Verlages von Wolf Tietze. [Braunschweig] : G. Westermann, [1968–1972]. 5 v. : ill. **CL40**

Some 20,000 entries, mainly for place-names and geographical areas, but including numerous personal names and terms relating to geography. Extensive bibliographies for many of the longer articles; numerous maps, charts, tables, and line drawings. Vol. 5 is an index. G103.W47

The World book encyclopedia of people and places. Chicago : World Book, c1993. 6 v. : col. ill. **CL41**

Alphabetical arrangement of entries for individual countries and other political and geographic units. Comprised of a series of two-page articles; some countries have more than one article. Summary information on history, geography, economy, people, culture, and current political situation; physical/political map and "fact box." Numerous color photographs and maps; statistical charts and time lines. Detailed cumulative index. AE5.5W563

Dictionaries

British Association for the Advancement of Science. Research Committee. A glossary of geographical terms : based on a list prepared by a committee of the British Association for the Advancement of Science / ed. by Dudley Stamp and Audrey N. Clark. 3rd ed. London ; N.Y. : Longman, 1979. 571 p. **CL42**

1st ed., 1961.

Provides comparative definitions of geographical terms from various reference sources and texts. Many foreign-language terms are included. This edition has added new entries in the areas of human geography, cartography, biogeography, and climatology. G107.9.B74

Clark, Audrey N. Longman dictionary of geography : human and physical. London ; N.Y. : Longman, 1985. 724 p. : map. **CL43**

Definitions for the geographical terms are based on the fuller information in *Glossary of geographical terms* (CL42) and are complemented by *Chisholm's handbook of commercial geography* (CL67).

§ Abridged version published in 1990 with title: *The new Penguin dictionary of geography* (London : Penguin. 359 p.). G63.C56

Dictionary of human geography / ed. by R. J. Johnston, Derek Gregory, and David M. Smith. 3rd ed., rev. and updated. Oxford ; Cambridge, Mass. : Blackwell Reference, 1994. 724 p. : ill. **CL44**

1st ed., 1981; 2nd ed., 1986.

Provides about 500 signed definitions of basic concepts, major topics, subfields of human geography (urban, cultural, economic, Marxist, etc.), and organizations; definitions are followed by references and bibliography. Indexed. GF4.D52

Dictionnaire de la géographie / sous la direction de Pierre George. 5e éd. refondue / réalisée avec le concours de Fernand Verger. Paris : Presses Universitaires de France, 1993. 498 p. : ill. **CL45**

1st ed., 1970, 4th ed., 1990.

Provides variant terms in different languages, definitions organized by subfields (meteorology, human geography, geomorphology, etc.), and bibliographic references for some entries.

The encyclopedic dictionary of physical geography / ed. by Andrew Goudie ... [et al.]. 2nd ed. Oxford ; Cambridge : Blackwell, [1994]. 1 v. : ill. **CL46**

1st ed., 1985.

Contains more than 2,000 entries consisting of both short definitions and longer signed articles from the discipline and its subdivisions, including biogeography, climatology, geomorphology, hydrology, and quaternary studies. Longer definitions include brief bibliographies. Extensive cross-references and index. GB10.E53

The international geographic encyclopedia and atlas. Boston : Houghton Mifflin, c1979. 890, 115 p. : maps ; 28 cm. **CL47**

"Houghton Mifflin Company adapted, revised, and supplemented the encyclopedic text entries that originally appeared as geographic entries in *The New Columbia Encyclopedia* [4th ed., 1975], published by Columbia University Press."—[*p. iv*].

Provides entries for about 25,000 geographic names and terms, and a 64-page atlas of four-color maps produced by Rand McNally, plus an index to these maps. More than 200 black-and-white maps are distributed throughout the text. G105.I57

Mayhew, Susan. The concise Oxford dictionary of geography / Susan Mayhew and Anne Penny. Oxford ; N.Y. : Oxford Univ. Pr, 1992. 247 p. **CL48**

Includes more than 5,000 definitions, covering both human geography and physical geography terms. Fields covered range from cartography, surveying, and remote sensing to climatology, ecology, and migration. Entries range from several words to several paragraphs in length and are cross-referenced. Useful as a general reference.   G63.M39

Monkhouse, Francis John. A dictionary of geography. 2nd ed. Chicago : Aldine Publ., 1970. 378 p. : ill., maps.   **CL49**
2nd ed. repr. with corrections: London : Edward Arnold, 1972.
1st ed., 1965.
Besides words used to describe the various features of the earth's surface, includes those terms that have been used "in a specific geographical context, or in a specialist sense which differs from general practice or popular usage."—*Pref.* Nearly 4,000 entries.   G108.E5M6

———————— A dictionary of the natural environment / F. J. Monkhouse, John Small. N.Y. : Wiley, 1978. 320 p. : ill.
     CL50
Based in part on the revisions prepared for a new edition of Monkhouse's *A dictionary of geography* (CL49), with 465 new definitions, line diagrams, and photographs. Emphasizes terms used by physical geographers and environmental scientists.   GB10.M64

Small, Ronald John. A modern dictionary of geography / John Small and Michael Witherick. 2nd ed. London ; N.Y. : E. Arnold : Distr. by Routledge, Chapman and Hall, 1989. 247 p. : ill.   **CL51**
1st ed., 1986.
This edition reflects recent changes in the discipline. 2,000 entries, including 100 new and many revised from the 1st ed., cover both human and physical geography. 1,135 illustrations and maps. Terms limited to those likely to be encountered by advanced high school and undergraduate students; excludes highly specialized, unusual, and local terms, as well as those covered in standard college dictionaries.
     G63.S53

United States. Defense Mapping Agency. Topographic Center. Glossary of mapping, charting, and geodetic terms. 4th ed. Wash. : [for sale by U.S. Govt. Print. Off.], 1981. 281 p.   **CL52**
1st ed., 1967; 3rd ed., 1973.
Prep. for Department of Defense.
Definitions, for the most part, taken from existing dictionaries and glossaries. Includes "only those terms considered germane to some specific aspect of mapping, charting, and geodesy …"—*Introd.* Provides cross-references and a list of sources.   GA102.D43

Bibliography

Meynen, Emil. Bibliography of mono- and multilingual dictionaries and glossaries of technical terms used in geography, as well as in related natural and social sciences. Wiesbaden : Steiner, 1974. 246 p.   **CL53**
Title page and all explanatory material in English and French.
Comp. and ed. by the International Geographical Union Commission, "International Geographical Terminology."
A selective, classed list of dictionaries and glossaries published 1920 and later in monographic and periodical article format. Excludes gazetteers of geographical names and dictionaries of regional data, with the more comprehensive treatment given to multilingual, rather than monolingual works. Includes bibliographical references and a supplement. Author index includes titles if they are the main entry. Each citation indicates languages used in the work.   Z6004.D5M48

Quotations

Wheeler, James O. Dictionary of quotations in geography / comp. by James O. Wheeler and Francis M. Sibley. N.Y. : Greenwood, 1986. 257 p.   **CL54**

Uses quotations, "many by the most prominent American geographers of this century," to describe a wide range of views on geography, to review the development of geographic thought, and "to characterize a variety of themes as the discipline has evolved."—*Pref.* Five sections, including four that cover the main traditions of American geography (earth science, man-land, area studies, and spatial) and one on other aspects. Sections are subdivided topically, and quotations arranged chronologically within topics. Quotations are drawn primarily from the major American geographical journals, listed in "Sources cited."   G63.W47

Directories

Guide to programs of geography in the United States and Canada. 1991–92– . Wash. : Association of American Geographers, c1991– . Annual.   **CL55**
Title varies: 1968/69–1983/84 had title: *Guide to graduate departments of geography in the United States and Canada*; 1984/85–1990/91 had title: *Guide to departments of geography in the United States and Canada.* Also known as *AAG directory of geographers.*
Expanded to include government agencies, research institutions, and private companies that employ geographers, 1988–89; two-year institutions with geography courses, 1989–90; directory of Association of American Geographers members, 1990–91. Lists theses and dissertations completed during the previous year. Departmental specialties, name, and geographic indexes.   G76.5.U5G8

Orbis geographicus = Adressar géographique du monde = World directory of geography = Geographisches Weltadressbuch. 1952– . Wiesbaden : F. Steiner, 1952– . Irregular.
     CL56
Comp. and ed. in cooperation with the International Geographical Union by Eckart Ehlers.
1992/1993 ed. (issued 1992) in English and French.
With the 6th ed. (1988), format and organization changed. Entries arranged alphabetically by country; within country, the following structure is used: national committees and IGU, geographical societies, central institutions and academies, departments of geography and their members, agencies engaged in geography, and agencies engaged in cartography. Personal name index.   G67.W92

Handbooks

Cities of the world : a compilation of current information on cultural, geographical, and political conditions in the countries and cities of six continents, based on the Department of State's "Post reports" / Monica M. Hubbard and Beverly Baer, editors. 4th ed. Detroit : Gale, c1993.   **CL57**
1st ed., 1982; 3rd ed., 1987.
Contents: v. 1, Africa; v. 2, The Western Hemisphere (exclusive of the United States); v. 3, Europe and the Mediterranean Middle East; v. 4, Asia, the Pacific, and the Asiatic Middle East; Cumulative index.
Provides information on 451 major cities and 2,865 other cities in 140 countries; contains illustrations and maps.   G153.4.C56

Deserts of the world : an appraisal of research into their physical and biological environments / ed. by William G. McGinnies, Bram J. Goldman, Patricia Paylore. [Tucson] : Univ. of Arizona Pr., [1968]. 788 p. : ill.   **CL58**
For annotation, *see* EF17.   GB612.D4

Fitzpatrick, Gary L. Direct-line distances—international edition / by Gary L. Fitzpatrick and Marilyn J. Modlin. Metuchen, N.J. : Scarecrow, 1986. 275 p. : maps.   **CL59**
     G109.F53

——————— Direct-line distances—United States edition / by Gary L. Fitzpatrick and Marilyn J. Modlin. Metuchen, N.J. : Scarecrow, 1986. 275 p. : maps. **CL60**

Taken together, these volumes consist of tables of distances between 1,001 cities, towns, and other selected geographic places. The international edition includes only 120 U.S. cities and gives distances in kilometers; the U.S. edition includes 312 U.S. cities and gives distances in miles. Distances are computed mathematically and recorded as "geodesic" distances (roughly equivalent to "air miles"); the introduction explains the computational methodology. Alphabetical list of cities with coordinates and reference maps that locate cities.

G109.F54

Gresswell, R. Kay. Standard encyclopedia of the world's rivers and lakes / R. Kay Gresswell, Anthony Julian Huxley. N.Y. : Putnam, [1965]. 384 p. : ill. **CL61**

For annotation, *see* EF8. GB1203.G73

Huxley, Anthony Julian. Standard encyclopedia of the world's mountains. N.Y. : Putnam, [1962]. 383 p. : ill., maps. **CL62**

For annotation, *see* EF9. GB501.H8

——————— Standard encyclopedia of the world's oceans and islands. N.Y. : Putnam, [1962]. 383 p. : ill., maps. **CL63**

For annotation, *see* EF10. GB471.H9

Kurian, George Thomas. World encyclopedia of cities. Santa Barbara, Calif. : ABC-Clio, c1994. v. 1–2. : ill., maps. (In progress). **CL64**

Contents: v. 1, North America (United States, A–M). v. 2, North America (United States, N–Z, and Canada).

For each state and province, provides information concerning one to five cities. Each entry includes a one-page black-and-white city map, basic data, and environment, weather, demographic, government, economic, education, health, transportation, housing, crime, and cultural and recreational data. The preface provides the sources for the information (primarily federal publications) included in each section. To be complete in six volumes; v. 6 will be a gazetteer. HT108.5.K87

Shanks, Thomas G. The international atlas : world latitudes, longitudes, and time changes. 3rd rev. ed. San Diego, Calif. : ACS Publications, c1991. 426, [1] p. **CL65**

1st ed., 1985; 2nd ed., 1988.

American atlas covers only the U.S.; *International atlas* excludes U.S. place-names. Each title functions as a gazetteer of 100,000 cities and towns; both are arranged alphabetically by country or state, then by place-name. For each place-name, gives county code, then latitude and longitude coordinates to the minute. Designed to aid astrologers in calculating birthplace distance from Greenwich and birth hour in sidereal time, so only populated places are listed (no physical features). Index to geographic place-names also provides variant forms of county names. Most changes in various editions deal with improved techniques in calculating historical time for astrological purposes.

QB205.U373

——————— The American atlas : U.S. longitudes & latitudes, time changes and time zones. 5th ed., expanded. San Diego, Calif. : ACS Publications, 1990. 617 p. **CL66**

1st ed., 1978; 4th ed., 1987. QB205.U37

Stamp, L. Dudley. Chisholm's handbook of commercial geography / entirely rewritten by Dudley Stamp. 20th ed. / rev. by G. Noel Blake and Audrey N. Clark. London ; N.Y. : Longman, 1980. 983 p. : ill. **CL67**

1st ed., 1889; 19th ed., 1975.

"A factual and objective reference work which contains comprehensive information on the commodities of international commerce; the factors affecting their production, distribution and exchange; and a compact regional geography for each of the trading nations of the world."—*Pref.* Four sections: factors affecting production and distribution (climate, labor, power); factors affecting exchange (transport, communications, language); the commodities themselves (agricultural, aquacultural, mineral); and the regional geographies (at the country level). Appendixes include a section of maps showing world distribution of resources, and several statistical tables with demographic and trade data. Detailed index with both geographic and subject terms.

HF1025.S689

The world factbook. 1981– . Wash. : Central Intelligence Agency, 1981– . Annual. **CL68**

Continues *National basic intelligence factbook* (197?–1980).

For each country of the world (in alphabetical order), provides brief data on geography, people, government, economy, membership in international intergovernmental organizations, communications, and defense forces. Small maps of each country; regional maps in color. Includes introductory notes, definitions, and abbreviations.

Handbook of the nations (12th ed. Detroit : Gale, 1993) is a reprint of *World factbook* in a smaller format, without the regional maps.

•Machine-readable versions: *World factbook plus navigator* [database] (St. Paul, Minn. : Quanta Pr., 1989–). Available on CD-ROM, updated annually. Also available on CD-ROM as part of *National trade data bank* [database] (CH497). Available on CD-ROM and computer laser optical disc as *The CIA world factbook*.

G122.U56a

United States

America's top-rated cities : a statistical handbook / Rhoda Garoogian, editor ... [et al.]. 2nd ed. Boca Raton, Fla. : Universal Reference Publications, c1993. 5 v. : ill., charts. **CL69**

Contents: v. 1, Southern region. v. 2, Western region. v. 3, Central region. v. 4, Eastern region. v. 5, Northeastern region.

Data on 62 cities, arranged alphabetically within geographical regions. Selection criteria are based on magazine surveys of "choice places for companies and individuals on the move."—*Introd.* Entries range in length from 10 to 20 pages. Each entry has two sections, the business environment and the living environment; numerous statistical charts and tables. Sources are listed in the introduction. HT123.A669

Cities of the United States : a compilation of current information on economic, cultural, geographic, and social conditions / Linda Schmittroth, Mary Kay Rosteck, editors. 2nd ed. Detroit : Gale, 1994. 4 v. : ill. **CL70**

1st ed., 1988–90.

Contents: v. 1, The South (611 p.); v. 2, The West (485 p.); v. 3, The Midwest (537 p.); v. 4, The Northeast (515 p.).

Offers comprehensive current descriptions of selected major cities, one to five per state. Arrangement is alphabetical by state, then by city. Concise "State in brief" and "City in brief" overviews are followed by detailed descriptions of cities, each including introduction, geography and climate, history, population profile, municipal government, economy, education and research, health care, recreation, convention facilities, transportation, and communications. Illustrated with black-and-white photographs and general maps of each state and urban area. Index cumulates with each volume. HT123.C49677

Gannett, Henry. Dictionary of altitudes in the United States. 4th ed. Wash. : U.S. Govt. Print. Off., 1906. 1072 p. (United States. Geological Survey Bulletin, no. 106). **CL71**

Repr. : Detroit : Gale, 1967.

1st ed., 1884; 3rd ed., 1899.

Arranged alphabetically by state, and under state by city; gives altitude and refers to authority. GB494.G3

Marlin, John Tepper. Cities of opportunity : finding the best place to work, live, and prosper in the 1990's and beyond / John Tepper Marlin with David Lampe ... [et al.]. N.Y. : MasterMedia, c1988. 410 p. **CL72**

Delineates the economic environment and quality of life characteristic of 42 selected communities. Although there is a certain vagueness about the compiler's criteria, the cities were chosen primarily on the basis of economic strength, job opportunities, and large size, although variables such as weather, health facilities, and cultural attractions were also considered. Individual brief chapters treating each city are supplemented by others on smaller cities and on the best communities for specific populations (e.g., women, retirees). Designed to help with decisions about where to live, but useful to general readers desiring succinct information about these locations.   HT123.M2985

Moving and relocation sourcebook : a reference guide to the 100 largest metropolitan areas in the United States / comp. by Diane Barlow and Steven Wasserman ; Frank R. Abate, executive ed. Detroit : Omnigraphics, c1992. 1 v. (various pagings) : ill., maps.   **CL73**

For 100 of the largest metropolitan areas in the U.S. gives information concerning: background; population; location and climate; taxes; higher education; transportation; economic indicators; quality of life indicators, phone numbers of community agencies. Data are compiled from the latest federal, state, and local sources. Appendixes include: state maps of metropolitan statistical areas; 1990 census of population and ranking for MSAs; cost of housing survey, 1990–91. Indexed.   HT334.U5M5

Savageau, David. Places rated almanac : your guide to finding the best places to live in America / David Savageau & Richard Boyer. All new ed. N.Y. : Prentice Hall Travel, c1993. 485 p. : ill., maps.   **CL74**

1st ed., 1981; previous ed., 1989.

Ranks 343 metropolitan areas according to ten factors: climate, jobs, housing, health care and environment, crime, transportation, education, recreation, the arts, and cost of living. Each chapter on a particular factor lists cities in rank order, then alphabetically, and presents capsule descriptions of metropolitan area features. Many tables and lists of related statistical data, with sources indicated. A new appendix (Metropolitan place finder) lists smaller cities and towns considered to lie within metropolitan areas. List of tables, maps, and diagrams, but no index.   HN60.S284

Thomas, G. Scott. The rating guide to life in America's small cities. Buffalo, N.Y. : Prometheus Books, c1990. 538 p. : map.   **CL75**

Presents ratings based on a 20-point distribution, high to low, for 219 micropolitan areas (populations of 15,000–50,000). Ten chapters cover lifestyle factors (e.g., Climate, Economics, Education, Sophistication, Health care, Housing). For each factor, presents national ratings, then lists micropolitan areas alphabetically within states, with assigned scores. Sources of data are given. Concludes with "report card" summaries of scores for each micropolitan area, alphabetically listed by state. Glossary of terms; subject index to tables of national rankings.

§ A companion to David Savageau and Rick Boyer, *Places rated almanac* (CL74), which ranks metropolitan areas.   HA214.T46

Van Zandt, Franklin K. Boundaries of the United States and the several states : with miscellaneous geographic information concerning areas, altitudes, and geographic centers. Wash. : U.S. Govt. Print. Off., 1976. 191 p. : ill. (Geological Survey professional paper, 909.).   **CL76**

Original ed. prep. by Henry Gannett and issued 1885 as Geological Survey *Bulletin* 13. A 1930 revision by Edward M. Douglas appeared as *Bulletin* 817; the 1966 revision by Van Zandt as *Bulletin* 1212.

A useful compilation, giving the histories and changes of the boundaries of the U.S. and of the individual states and territories, with references to sources. "The revisions include clarification and modification of descriptions of certain boundaries, some of which are based on court decisions or international agreements; they also include more accurate figures for certain statistical data and numerous minor additions and deletions as appropriate."—*Pref.*   E179.5.V34

Willis, Alan. American suburbs rating guide and fact book / text by Alan Willis ; statistical data compiled by Bennett Jacobstein. Milpitas, CA : Toucan Valley Publications, c1993. 846 p. : maps.   **CL77**

Places included have populations of 10,000 or more within the 50 largest metropolitan areas. Scores and ranks for such criteria as income, housing, crime, open space, education, commuting, and community stability.   HA214.W55

Yearbooks

Geographic information : the yearbook of the Association for Geographic Information. 1991– . London ; N.Y. : Taylor & Francis ; Oxford : Miles Arnold, c1991– . Annual.   **CL78**

Continues *The Association for Geographic Information yearbook*, 1989–90.

Essays on research and technology developments; commonly includes sections on GIS/LIS marketplace, trade directories, standards, GIS worldwide, research, education and training, and the year ahead.   G70.2.A84

International GIS sourcebook. 1991–92– . Fort Collins, Colo. : GIS World, c1991– . Annual.   **CL79**

"This book is intended as a reference work in geographic information systems (GIS) technology."—*verso of t.p.*

Describes advances in a rapidly expanding discipline. Chapters include industry summaries, directories, technical applications, international GIS, education, data sources, and professional associations. Appendixes include events list, lexicon, acronyms, and literature. General and advertiser indexes.

Biography

Dunbar, Gary S. A biographical dictionary of American geography in the twentieth century. Baton Rouge, La. : Geoscience Publications, Dept. of Geography and Anthropology, Louisiana State Univ., c1992. 93 p.   **CL80**

Approximately 540 entries for geographers, American by birth or by length of residence, and all deceased. Provides brief biographical data of the type reported in various *Who's who* publications including educational background (with dissertation information) and professional experience.   G67.D86

Explorers and discoverers of the world / ed. by Daniel B. Baker. Detroit : Gale, c1993. 637 p. : ill.   **CL81**

"Presents biographical information on more than 320 world explorers. Beginning with early Greek scholars and travelers and extending to 20th-century underwater and space exploration....expands coverage beyond the standard well-known explorers to include contributions of women and non-Europeans."—*Pref.* Entries range from one to three pages in length, and include cross-references and sources for additional information. Illustrated with photographs and maps. Appendixes provide a glossary, bibliography, list of explorers by area explored, and list of explorers by place of birth. General index.   G200.E88

Geographers : biobibliographical studies. v. 1–12. [London] : Mansell, 1977–1988.   **CL82**

Ed. by T. W. Freeman, Marguerite Oughton and Philippe Pinchemel on behalf of the International Geographical Union Commission on the History of Geographical Thought.

Presents studies on deceased figures important in the history of geography. The biographical section of each study deals with personal background, career development, and contribution to the field; the bibliographies are selective, usually including primary, secondary, and archival sources. International in scope. Indexed.   Z6001.G425

Larkin, Robert P. Biographical dictionary of geography / Robert P. Larkin and Gary L. Peters. Westport, Conn. : Greenwood, 1993. 361 p. **CL83**

Each entry for 77 geographers includes a two- to three-page summary followed by a selected bibliography, a chronology, and references to additional biographical information. International in scope (covering 14 countries) although most entries are from the U.S., U.K., and Germany. Covers from ancients (Herodotus and Aristotle) through contemporary academics. Three appendixes list entries alphabetically, chronologically, and by country of birth. General index. G67.L37

GAZETTEERS

General works

Chambers world gazetteer : an A–Z of geographical information / ed. by David Munro. 5th ed. Edinburgh : Chambers ; Cambridge ; N.Y. : Cambridge Univ. Pr., 1988. 733 p., 112 p. of plates : ill. (some col.). **CL84**

Previous ed., 1965, called *Chambers's world gazetteer and geographical dictionary.*

Contains more than 20,000 place names. Includes, for many entries, a current geographical description and brief history, as well as location (including coordinates), area, and population. Uses pinyin romanization for Chinese place names. Provides a small uncluttered map with each country entry in addition to the maps by John Bartholomew and Son, appended as a 120-page "World atlas." Introductory pages explain inclusion criteria and give a sample entry and other notes. G103.5.C44

Columbia Lippincott gazetteer of the world / ed. by Leon E. Seltzer with the geographical research staff of Columbia University Press and with the cooperation of the American Geographical Society. With 1961 supplement. N.Y. : Columbia Univ. Pr., [1962]. 2148 p. **CL85**

1st ed., 1952.

A successor to *Lippincott's new gazetteer* (published in various editions, 1855–1931) but essentially a completely new work. Lists, in one alphabet, the places of the world, both political subdivisions and geographic features, giving variant spellings, pronunciation, population (with date), geographical and political location, altitude, trade, industry, agriculture, natural resources, communications, history, cultural institutions, and other pertinent facts. Comprises some 130,000 names with more than 30,000 cross-references. The supplement includes the major politico-geographical changes since 1952, with identification of new nations. Contains 1960 U.S. census figures. Although dated, continues to be a useful and important work. G103.L7

Fisher, Morris. Provinces and provincial capitals of the world. 2nd ed. Metuchen, N.J. : Scarecrow, 1985. 248 p. **CL86**

1st ed., 1967.

For each of 224 countries, gives number, type, and name of major administrative units or provinces and their capitals. Country arrangement; name index. G103.5.F57

Foreign gazetteers [of the] U.S. Board on Geographic Names [microform]. [California, Md.] : Congressional Information Service, [1987]–1990. c.1500 microfiches : negative, maps. **CL87**

A republication in microform of the gazetteers published by the U.S. Defense Mapping Agency, containing geographic names approved by the U.S. Board on Geographic Names. (For earlier versions of gazetteers published in printed format, see the Board's *Gazetteer,* CL95). The basic microform set contains 181 volumes, consisting of the most recent editions of the gazetteers as of May 1987; the supplement (Group 2 in the microform set) contains 22 country updates plus the current edition of *Gazetteer of conventional names* (3rd ed.

Wash. : Defense Mapping Agency, 1988). The printed guide that accompanies the microform set lists gazetteers in the original set and is keyed to the microfiche numbers.

Geograficheskiĭ entsiklopedicheskiĭ slovar' : geograficheskie nazvaniia / glav. red. A. F. Trëshnikov ; red. kollegiia E. B. Alaev ... [et al.]. Izd. 2., dop. Moskva : "Sov. Entsiklopediia", 1989. 591 p. : ill. **CL88**

1st ed., 1983.

A geographic dictionary of places, international in scope. Numerous maps, and some illustrations. G103.5.G45

Kratkaia geograficheskaia entsiklopediia / Glav. red., A.A. Grigor'ev. Moskva : Sovetskaia entsiklopediia, 1960-66. 5 v. : ill., maps. **CL89**

Primarily a gazetteer with descriptions and locations for place-names and geographical areas, with numerous maps, illustrations and charts. Also includes some definitions of geographical terminology. G103.K76

Kurian, George Thomas. Geo-data : the World Almanac gazetteer. Detroit : Gale, 1989. 544 p. **CL90**

Earlier version publ. 1983.

In four main sections: (1) detailed data about towns and cities in the U.S. with population of more than 10,000, and information on counties, states, and territories; (2) a variety of geographic, demographic, and political information about foreign countries; (3) geographic information on natural features such as continents, oceans, rivers, mountains, etc.; (4) rankings. U.S. population data based on 1980 census. Bibliography and index. G103.5.K87

Lana, Gabriella. Glossary of geographical names in six languages : English, French, Italian, Spanish, German & Dutch / comp. and arranged by Gabriella Lana, Liliana Iasbez and Lidia Meak. Amsterdam ; N.Y. : Elsevier, 1967. 184 p. (Glossaria interpretum, 12). **CL91**

Lists geographical proper names which vary from language to language. The basic table employs the English form followed by variants in other languages. Consolidated index. G104.5.L3

Paxton, John. The statesman's year-book world gazetteer. 4th ed. N.Y. : St. Martin's, 1991. 693 p. **CL92**

1st ed., 1975; 3rd ed., 1986.

Intended as a companion to *The statesman's year-book* (CJ62). Gives brief information on places of size and importance. Some statistical tables and a glossary of about 800 statistical terms are supplied. G102.5.P38

Room, Adrian. Place-name changes 1900–1991. Metuchen, N.J. : Scarecrow, 1993. 296 p. **CL93**

1st ed., 1979, had title: *Place-name changes since 1900: a world gazetteer.*

Lists more than 4,500 places; each entry provides present name, identification, location, former name or names, and year or years of renaming. Cross-references are provided from earlier names. Appendix of official country names; extensive bibliography of place-name sources. Majority of names are Russian or Chinese. G103.5.R657

Times, London. Index-gazetteer of the world. London : Times Publ. Co., 1965 ; Boston : Houghton, 1966. 964 p. **CL94**

Lists about 345,000 geographical features with latitude and longitude. The approximately 198,000 locations shown in the Mid-Century edition of *Times atlas of the world* (CL292) formed the basis of this work, and map references are given for locations in that series of atlases. Longitude and latitude coordinates, however, make the volume useful with any map marked with lines of parallels and meridians. G103.T5

United States. Defense Mapping Agency. Gazetteer. no. 1–130 [etc.]. Wash. : U.S. Govt. Print. Off., 1955–90. **CL95**

Prior to 1976, issued by the U.S. Board on Geographic Names.

Each number treats special country, listing places and geographical features, with approved names and cross-references from variant names, latitude and longitude, and location on specified official maps. Numbered through 130 (Surinam, 1974), then without numbers since 1974. The contents note below provides geographical area, number, edition, and date of publication.

Contents: Afghanistan (3rd ed., 1992); Africa and Southwest Asia, Gazetteer suppl. (126, 1972); Africa, British East (1, 1955); Albania (2nd ed., 1992); Algeria (127, 1972); Americas, Gazetteer suppl. (120, 1971); Andorra (51, 1961); Angola (2nd ed., 1986); Antarctica (4th ed., 1989); Arabian Peninsula (54, 1961); Argentina (103, 1968); Asia, Gazetteer suppl. (124, 1972); Asia, Southwest, Gazetteer suppl. (126, 1972); Australia (40, 1957); Australia, New Zealand, and Oceania, Gazetteer suppl. (125, 1972); Austria (66, 1962); Bahrain (1st ed., 1983; formerly issued as Bahrain, Kuwait, Qatar, and United Arab Emirates, 1976); Bangladesh (1976); Belgium (73, 1963); Belize (2nd ed., 1993); Berlin, East (43, 1959); Berlin, West (47, 1960); Bermuda (7, 1955); Bolivia (2nd ed., 1992); Borneo, British (10, 2nd ed., 1970); Brazil (71, 1963); Brunei (10, 2nd ed., 1970); Bulgaria (2nd ed., 1987); Burma (9, 1955; 96, 1966); Burundi (84, 1964); Cambodia (74, 2nd ed., 1971); Cameroon (60, 1962); Canal Zone (110, 1969); Cape Verde Islands (50, 1961); Central African Republic (64, 1962); Chad (2nd ed., 1989); Chile (6, 2nd ed., 1967); China, People's Republic (2nd ed., 1990); China, Suppl. (pinyin to Wade-Giles, Wade-Giles to pinyin, 1988); China, Republic of (5, 1955; 1974); Colombia (86, 1964); Comoro Islands (2, 1955); Congo (Brazzaville) (61, 1962); Congo (Léopoldville) (80, 1964); Costa Rica (18, 2nd ed. 1983); Cuba (3rd ed., 1991); Czechoslovakia (1955);

Dahomey (91, 1965); Denmark (53, 1961); Djibouti (1983); Dominican Republic (33, 2nd ed., 1972); Ecuador (2nd ed., 1987); Egypt (2nd ed., 1987); El Salvador (26, 1956); Ethiopia (1982); Europe, Gazetteer suppl. (118, 1971); Faeroe Islands (53, 1961); Fiji (1974); Finland (62, 1962); France (83, 2v., 1964); French Guiana (2nd ed., 1993); French West Indies (34, 1957); Gabon (59, 1962); Gambia (107, 1968); Germany, East (2nd ed., 1983); Germany, West (47, 1960); Ghana (102, 1967); Gibraltar (2nd ed., 1984); Greece (11, 1955); Greenland (2nd ed., 1983); Guatemala (94, 2nd ed., 1984); Guinea (90, 1965); Guinea, Portuguese (105, 1968); Guyana (2nd ed., 1993); Haiti (3rd ed., 1993); Hawaiian Islands (24, 1956); Honduras (27, 2nd ed., 1983); Honduras, British (16, 1956); Hong Kong (5, 1955; 128, 1972); Hungary (2nd ed., 1993); Iceland (57, 1961); Indian Ocean (32, 1957); Indonesia (13, 3rd ed., 1982, 2 v.); Iran (19, 2nd ed., 1982, 2 v.); Iraq (3rd ed., 1990); Israel (114, 2nd ed., 1983); Italy (1988); Ivory Coast (89, 1965); Japan (12, 1955); Jordan (2nd ed., 1990); Kenya (78, 1964); Korea, North (75, 2nd ed., 1982); Korea, South (95, 1965); Kuwait (1st ed., 1986); Laos (69, 2nd ed., 1973); Lebanon (115, 1970); Liberia (106, 2nd ed., 1976); Libya (3rd ed., 1988);

Macao (5, 1955; 128, 1972); Madagascar (2nd ed., 1989); Malawi (113, 1970); Malaya (10, 2nd ed., 1970); Mali (93, 1965); Malta (121, 1971); Mauritania (100, 1966); Mexico (3rd ed., 1992); Mongolia (2nd ed., 1988); Morocco (112, 1970); Mozambique (109, 1969); Namibia (1st ed., 1988); Nauru (1974); Netherlands (2nd ed., 1982 [i.e., 1986]); New Caledonia (1974); New Guinea (13, 2nd ed., 1968); New Hebrides (1974); Nicaragua (3rd ed., 1985); Niger (99, 1966); Nigeria (117, 1971); Norway (1990); Nyasaland (17, 1956); Oman (1983); Pakistan (67, 3rd ed. 1983); Panama and the Canal Zone (3rd ed., 1990); Papua New Guinea (1986); Paracel and Spratly Islands (1987); Paraguay (2nd ed., 1992); Peru (2nd ed., 1989); Philippines (2nd ed., 1988); Poland (2nd ed., 1988); Portugal (50, 1961); Puerto Rico (38, 1958); Qatar (1st ed., 1986); Réunion (2, 1955); Rhodesia (17, 1956); Rumania (48, 1960); Rwanda (85, 1964);

São Tomé e Principe (63, 1962); Senegal (2nd ed., 1990); Sierra Leone (101, 1966); Singapore (10, 2nd ed., 1970); Solomon Islands (1974); Somalia (1982); South Africa (2nd ed., 1992); South Atlantic (31, 1957); South Pacific (39, 1957); Southern Rhodesia (129, 1973); Southwest Pacific (29, 1956); Spain (51, 1961); Spanish Sahara (108, 1969); Sri Lanka (3rd ed., 1993); Sudan (2nd ed., 1989); Suriname (2nd ed., 1993); Sweden (3rd ed., 1989); Syria (104, 2nd ed. 1983); Taiwan (5, 1956; 1974); Tanzania (92, 1965); Thailand (1987); Tibet (5, 1955); Togo (98, 1966); Tonga (1974); Tunisia (81, 1964); Turkey (46, 2nd ed., 1984, 2 v.); Uganda (82, 1964); Underseas features (4th ed., 1990); United Arab Emirates (1st ed., 1987); Upper Volta (87, 1965); Uruguay (1993); U.S.S.R. (42, 2nd ed., 1970, 7 v.; 118, 1971); Venezuela (56, 2nd ed., 1993); Vietnam, Northern (79, 1964); Viet-

nam, Southern (58, 2nd ed., 1971); Virgin Islands (38, 1958); West Bank and Gaza Strip (1992); West Indies, British (7, 1955); Yemen, People's Democratic Republic of (1976); Yemen Arab Republic (1976); Yugoslavia (55, 2nd ed. 1983); Zambia (2nd ed., 1983); Zanzibar (76, 1964).

Vivien de Saint Martin, Louis. Nouveau dictionnaire de géographie universelle. Paris : Hachette, 1879–1895. 7 v.
                                                                CL96

Vols. 5–7 ed. by Louis Rousselet.

The most complete of the general gazetteers, covering physical, political, economic, and historical geography, ethnography, etc. The longer articles are by specialists and are of a high grade; information is much fuller than that given in *Columbia Lippincott gazetteer of the world* (CL85); and many names are included, especially minor European or Asian names which are not given in works in English. Out-of-date and less useful for ordinary questions than *Columbia Lippincott,* but more useful than that work when very detailed or out-of-the-way information is needed. Includes names of tribes and races, as well as place-names.

————. *Supplement* (1895–1900. 2 v.).

Webster's new geographical dictionary. Springfield, Mass. : Merriam-Webster, c1988. 1376 p., [2] p. of plates : maps.
                                                                CL97

Represents a thorough revision of *Webster's geographical dictionary* which was first published 1949 and reprinted from time to time with limited revisions.

A pronouncing dictionary of more than 47,000 geographical names, including not only current but also historical names from biblical times, ancient Greece and Rome, medieval Europe, World Wars I and II, etc. Some 15,000 cross-references are provided for equivalent and alternate spellings of foreign language names and former names. Gives the usual gazetteer information, e.g., location, area, population, altitudes of mountains, etc.; for the largest cities, important countries, and each of the United States, also gives geographical features, points of interest, and a concise history. Includes full-page and smaller inset maps by C. S. Hammond Co. Introductory material includes a list of geographical terms with language of origin and English equivalents.

The authority for place-names used in cataloging by the Library of Congress. This edition continues to use Wade-Giles romanization for Chinese place-names without cross-references from pinyin versions.

Also available in a Braille edition.   G103.5.W42

Wilcocks, Julie. Countries and islands of the world : a guide to nomenclature. 2nd ed. London : C. Bingley, 1985. 124 p.
                                                                CL98

An alphabetical dictionary of the changes in name and government that have occurred since the 15th century in independent countries, islands, states and provinces of federations, and former kingdoms and principalities that have been important in modern history.

                                                                G103.5.W54

Bibliography

Library of Congress. Geography and Map Division. Geographic names & the federal government : a bibliography / United States Board of Geographic Names ; comp. by Donald J. Orth with the assistance of Elizabeth Unger Mangan. Wash. : The Division, [1990]. 59 p.   **CL99**

Annotated listing of 594 sources published by various U.S. government agencies, primarily the Board on Geographic Names. Section 2, BGN foreign gazetteers (1943–1990) is especially useful. Author, title, and place-name indexes.   G105.O78

Meynen, Emil. Gazetteers and glossaries of geographical names of the member-countries of the United Nations and the agencies in relationship with the United Nations : bibliography 1946–1976. Wiesbaden : Steiner, 1984. 518 p.   **CL100**

Title and prefatory matter also in French.

A bibliography, including atlases which have place-name indexes. In five parts: lists of country and territory names; world gazetteers and indexes; gazetteers by continent, regions and oceans; gazetteers and indexes by countries; glossaries of generic, oceanographic, and foreign terms; gazetteers being published 1977–82.   Z6004.D5M49

Ancient and medieval

Deschamps, Pierre. Dictionnaire de géographie ancienne et moderne. Paris : Firmin-Didot, 1870. 1592 p.   **CL101**

Repr.: Geneva : Slatkine, 1990.

Also issued as v. 9 of Jacques Charles Brunet's *Manuel du libraire et de l'amateur de livres* (AA88).

Arranged alphabetically by the medieval name (Latin or Greek); gives under each name an indication of the modern name and brief information about the place with special emphasis on the history of printing in that place, establishment of presses, etc. Index of modern names.   Z1011.B9M5

Grant, Michael. A guide to the ancient world : a dictionary of classical place names. [Bronx, N.Y.] : H.W. Wilson, 1986. 728 p. : maps.   **CL102**

About 700 places, primarily cities and towns of the ancient Greek, Etruscan, and Roman worlds, are described in entries that range from one-half to one page in length. "Each entry includes data of a historical, geographical, archaeological and (where appropriate) artistic and mythological character."—*Introd.* Numerous cross-references. Introductory section of locator maps; extensive bibliography.   DE25.G72

Grässe, Johann Georg Theodor. Orbis Latinus : Lexikon lateinischer geographischer Namen des Mittelalters und der Neuzeit / [Johann Georg Theodor] Grässe, [Friedrich] Benedict, [Helmut] Plechl. Grossausgabe / bearb. und hrsg. von Helmut Plechl unter Mitarbeit von Sophie-Charlotte Plechl. Braunschweig : Klinkhardt & Biermann, [c1972]. 3 v.   **CL103**

1st ed., 1866.

A listing of medieval Latin place-names with their modern equivalents.   G107.G8

The new Century handbook of classical geography / ed. by Catherine B. Avery. N.Y. : Appleton-Century-Crofts, [1972]. 362 p. : maps.   **CL104**

"Presents concise discussions of the major geographical locations, incorporating the facts *and* legends drawn from such diverse sources as modern archaeology and ancient poetry."—*Pref.* Includes pronunciation guides and other classical forms of the names. Cross-references. Some signed articles. "Most of the entries…are derived from *The new Century classical handbook.*" [Englewood Cliffs, N.J. : Prentice-Hall, 1962]".—*Pref.*   DE25.N48

Smith, William. A dictionary of Greek and Roman geography. London : Murray ; Boston : Little, 1873–78. 2 v. : ill., maps.   **CL105**

Repr. : N.Y. : AMS Pr., 1966.

A standard work of the 19th century, still useful for its detailed articles on places of the ancient world. Includes many references to classical authors.   DE25.S664

North America

United States

Grim, Ronald E. Historical geography of the United States : a guide to information sources. Detroit : Gale, [1982]. 291 p. (Geography and travel guide information series, v. 5).   **CL106**

An annotated bibliography in three parts: cartographic sources, archival and historical materials, and secondary topical literature produced or reprinted since 1965. Each section is subdivided by topic or type of source material. Author, title, and subject indexes.

§ Intended to complement Douglas R. McManis, *Historical geography of the United States* (CL107).   Z1247.G74

McManis, Douglas R. Historical geography of the United States : a bibliography, excluding Alaska and Hawaii. [Ypsilanti? Mich. : Div. of Field Services, Eastern Michigan Univ., 1965]. 249 p.   **CL107**

Includes citations to monographs and scholarly periodical articles, especially state and local historical society publications. Arranged by region, state, and topic (such as exploration and settlement, population, agriculture, urban developments). Covers through the 19th century. No index.

§ Complements Ronald E. Grim, *Historical geography of the United States : a guide to information sources* (CL106).   Z1236.M3

The national gazetteer of the United States of America. [Wash.] : U.S. Govt. Print. Off. ; Alexandria, Va. : for sale by the Distribution Branch, U.S. Geological Survey, 1983–1992. [v. 1–8] : maps. (Geological Survey professional paper, 1200). (In progress).   **CL108**

Prepared in cooperation with the U.S. Board on Geographic Names.

Contents: New Jersey (1983); Delaware (1983); Kansas (1984); Arizona (1986); Indiana (1988); South Dakota (1989); North Dakota (1990); Florida (1992).

Derived from the Geographic Names Data Base of the Geological Survey, which presently contains information for about two million names. Separate volumes for states or territories will provide for each geographic name: type of feature, official status, variant names, county location, geographic coordinates, elevation, and location on the Geological Survey's topographic maps. Also available in microfiche from the National Cartographic Information Center, Reston, Virginia.

Also publ. in a concise edition: *The national gazetteer of the United States of America : United States concise 1990*, prep. by the U.S. Geological Survey in cooperation with the U.S. Board on Geographic Names (Wash. : U.S. Govt. Print. Off. ; Denver, Colo. : for sale by the Books and Open-File Reports Section, U.S. Geological Survey, 1990). Superintendent of Documents classification: I 19.16:1200-US.

Includes about 45,000 entries for populated places, administrative areas, and major physical features. Provides official name, feature type, elevation, county and state location, and geographic coordinates. Brief glossary.

•Machine-readable version: *Geographic names information system (GNIS)* [database] (Reston, Va. : U.S. Geological Survey, [1991]). Available on CD-ROM.   E154.N3

Omni gazetteer of the United States of America / Frank R. Abate, ed. Detroit : Omnigraphics, Inc., c1991. 11 v.   **CL109**

Based primarily on the Geographic Names Information System, the database used by the U.S. Geological Survey to compile the *National gazetteer of the United States of America* (CL108), but supplemented by several other governmental sources. Provides the first complete and comprehensive coverage for the U.S., more than 1.5 million entries.

The states are presented in alphabetical order in the first nine regional volumes: New England, Northeastern, Southeastern, South central, Southwestern, Great Lakes, Plains, Mountain, and Pacific. Each entry includes name, type of feature, county, and source code. Additional information may include zip code, population (1988 estimates), map name, coordinates, and elevation.

Vol. 10 is a national index, listing all entries in a single alphabet; v. 11 contains seven appendixes: USGS topographic maps names index; Index of feature types and generic names; National Register of Historic Places; State and county FIPS codes; Indian reservations; U.S. airports; and Elevated landmarks and structures.

Extensive background information on the compilation of the gazetteer is presented in each of the regional volumes, as well as essays on the place names, genealogical research, and map use, a glossary, and detailed instructions.

•Also available in machine-readable form, in CD-ROM.

E154.O45

Place guide / ed. by Donna Andriot ... [et al.]. 1990 ed. McLean, Va. : Documents Index, c1990. 561 p.   **CL110**

An alphabetical list of place names in the U.S., giving county and state for each. Compiled from U.S. Census Bureau publications. A preface describes various political subdivisions within states and lists abbreviations.   E155.P63

Canada

Canada. Board on Geographical Names. 18th–19th reports containing all decisions to July 31, 1927. Ottawa, 1924–27. 2 v.   **CL111**

18th report, Decisions to March 1924; 19th report, Decisions, April 1924–July 1927.

Alphabetical lists of place-names, with index by provinces, counties, etc. The main alphabet in each report gives form of name decided on, location of place, and origin of name when known, with cross-references from superseded names. Supersedes the earlier reports of the Board except for certain appendixes which are still useful for the fuller or special information they contain. These appendixes (also issued as separates) are:

9th report, 1910: pt. 2, Place-names in Quebec, by James White, p. 153–219; pt. 3, Place-names, Thousand Islands, St. Lawrence River, by James White, p. 221–29; pt. 4, Place-names in Northern Canada, by James White, p. 229–455.

17th report, 1922: Meaning of Canadian city names, by R. Douglas, p. 34–52; Place-names on Anticosti Island, by W. P. Anderson, p. 53–65; Place-names on Magdalen Islands, by R. Douglas, p. 66–74.

Additional lists issued by the Geographic Board include: Place-names of Prince Edward Island, with meanings, by R. Douglas (1925. 55 p.); Place-names of Alberta (1928. 138 p.); Place-names of Manitoba (1933. 95 p.).   G104.C2

Gazetteer of Canada = Répertoire géographique du Canada. Ottawa : Canadian Board on Geographical Names, 1952– . [v. 1–]. (In progress).   **CL112**

Issuing agency varies.

The following volumes have been published: Alberta (2nd ed., 1974); British Columbia (3rd ed., 1985); Manitoba (3rd ed., 1981); New Brunswick (2nd ed., 1972); Newfoundland and Labrador (1968); Northwest Territories (1980); Yukon (4th ed., 1981); Ontario (2nd ed., 1974); Prince Edward Island (1973); Saskatchewan (2nd ed., 1969); Southwestern Ontario (1952); Nova Scotia (2nd ed., 1977). Volumes published since 1967 have been cataloged separately by most libraries.

Special supplement (Ottawa, 1964–). Contents: no. 1, A list of named glaciological features in Canada, by C. F. Stevenson (1964); no. 2, Geographical features in Canada named for surveyors, by T. Jolicoeur (1966).   F1004.A2

Répertoire toponymique du Québec : 1987 / Commission de toponymie. Québec : Gouvernement du Québec, c1987. 1900 p., [2] leaves of plates : maps.   **CL113**

1st ed., 1969; 2nd ed., 1979.

More than 93,000 place names. Indicates type of feature, administrative division, latitude and longitude coordinates, and sheet number (1:50,000 map series) for location.

————. *Supplement cumulatif 1991* (Quebec : Les Publications du Quebec, 1991. 306 p.).   F1051.4.R47

Mexico

Nomenclátor de Aguascalientes. México, D.F. : Secretaría de Programación y Presupuesto, Coordinación General de los Servicios Nacionales de Estadística, Geografía e Informática, 1981–88. [v. 1–18]. (In progress).   **CL114**

A series of gazetteers has been published by this agency that cover each state of the Mexican republic. Each gazetteer has five sections: human settlements, other man-made features, mountains, continental water features, and coastal water features. In each section, entries are listed alphabetically. Each entry provides place-name, feature type, coordinates, and locator map sheet number.

Other gazetteers in the series: *Nomenclátor de Baja California* (1981); ... *estado de Coahuila* (1983); ... *Colima* (1981); ... *Guanajuato* (1980); ... *Jalisco* (1980); ... *estado de Mexico* (1981); ... *estado de Michoacan* (1985); ... *Morelos* (1981); ... *Nayarit* (1981); ... *Nuevo Leon* (2nd ed., 1986); ... *estado de Puebla* (1987); ... *estado de Queretaro* (1986); ... *San Luis Potosi* (1981); ... *estado de Tabasco* (1986); ... *Tamaulipas* (1981); ... *Tiaxcala* (1981); ... *estado de Veracruz* (1988); ... *Zacatecas* (1981).

Central America

El Salvador

Instituto Geográfico Nacional (El Salvador). Diccionario geográfico de El Salvador / Ministerio de OO.PP., Instituto Geográfico Nacional. San Salvador : El Instituto, 1970 [i.e., 1971–1976]. 4 v. : ill.   **CL115**

Name of issuing agency varies.

A gazetteer, with detailed historical, geographical, and statistical information on 24,519 names. Each volume contains data on a number of "departamentos": v. 1, Ahuachapán, Santa Ana and Sonsonata; v. 2, La Liberad, Chalatenango, San Salvador, and Cuscatlán; v. 3, La Paz, Cabañas and San Vicente; v. 4, Usulután, San Miguel, Morazán, and La Unión.

————. ————. *Index* (1978. 2 v.).   F1482.S35

Guatemala

Diccionario geográfico de Guatemala / compilación crítica, Francis Gall. 2a ed. Guatemala : Instituto Geográfico Nacional, 1976–1983. 4 v. : maps.   **CL116**

1st ed., 1961–62.

A geographical dictionary listing the place-names, cities, towns, villages, rivers, mountains, etc. For the larger places, gives considerable detail on history, demography, ethnography, geology, archaeology, etc.   F1462.D53

Honduras

Instituto Geográfico National (Honduras). Diccionario geográfico de Honduras. [Tegucigalpa] : Ministerio de Comunicaciones, Obras Públicas y Transporte, Instituto Geográfico Nacional, 1976–1993. v. 1–3, 5–6 : ill., some maps in color. (In progress).   **CL117**

Imprint varies.

Contents: t. 1, Departamento de Atlántida; t. 2, Departamento de Cortés; t. 3, Departamento de Copán; t. 5, Departamento de Comayagua; t. 6, Departamento de Colon.

Each volume serves as a gazetteer for one of the 18 departments in Honduras. Volumes will be published in alphabetical order according to department name and, upon completion, will be consolidated alphabetically in a single-volume, official geographical dictionary.

F1502.I57

South America

Argentina

Latzina, Francisco. Diccionario geográfico argentino : con ampliaciones enciclopédicas rioplatenses. 3. ed. Buenos Aires : Peuser, 1899. 814 p. **CL118**
1st ed., 1891.
Long historical and statistical articles on places in the Argentine.
———. *Suplemento, que contiene las adiciones, correcciones y ampliaciones aplicables á la 3.ª ed. de dicha obra* ... (Buenos Aires : Compañía Sud-americana de Billetes de Banco, 1908. 762 p.).

Toponimia de la República Argentina / Ejército Argentino, Instituto Geográfico Militar. Buenos Aires : El Instituto, 1982. v. 1, pt. 1 : maps. **CL119**
Contents: v. 1, Territorio Nacional de la Tierra del Fuego, Antártida e Islas del Atlántico Sur: pt. 1, Tierra del Fuego.
No more published?
An official gazetteer of place names, with notes on historical derivation, references to map series, and bibliographical references.

F2804.T66

Bolivia

Gonzales M., René. Diccionario geográfico boliviano / René Gonzales Moscoso. La Paz : Editorial Los Amigos del Libro, 1984. 257 p. : ill., maps. **CL120**
A basic dictionary of brief entries. A more detailed version, *Diccionario geográfico general de Bolivia*, was planned; publication cannot be verified.

Brazil

Dicionário de geografia do Brasil : com terminologia geográfica / Organização geral, Departamento Editorial das Edições Melhoramentos; redação de temas e verbetes, Erasmo d'Almeida Magalhaes [et al.]. 2. ed. São Paulo : Edições Melhoramentos, 1976. 544 p. **CL121**
1st ed., 1973.
Combines gazetteer information on major cities and states, and definitions of geographical terms and concepts, with emphasis on Brazilian aspects. Supplementary list of cities with more than 20,000 people is based on 1970 census figures. Bibliography. F2504.D48

Dicionário geográfico brasileiro : com numerosas ilustrações, inclusive mapas dos estados e territórios. 2. ed. Pôrto Alegre : Editôra Globo, 1972. 621 p. : ill., maps. **CL122**
1st ed., 1966.
Offers far more detailed gazetteer information on a greater number of geographical features, cities, towns, states, and territories in Brazil than does *Dicionário de geografia do Brasil* (CL121). Provides population figures based on 1970 census estimates. Bibliography.

F2504.D5

Colombia

Diccionario geográfico de Colombia / Instituto Geográfico Agustín Codazzi. 2a ed. rev. y augm. Bogotá : La Subdirección, 1980. 2 v. (1813 p.) : ill., maps. **CL123**
1st ed., 1971.
A gazetteer of about 60,000 names, with many longer articles.
F2254.A55

Ecuador

Instituto Geográfico Militar (Ecuador). Indice toponímico de la República del Ecuador. [Quito] : El Instituto, [1978?–82?]. v. 1–8. (In progress?). **CL124**
Contents: v. 1–8, A–Q.
A gazetteer of place-names, indicating type of feature, location, administrative division, and coordinates of latitude and longitude. Intended to be complete in 10 volumes. F3704.E28

Peru

Catálogo de nombres geográficos del Perú. [Lima] : Instituto Geográfico Militar, 1979. v. 1. (In progress?). **CL125**
Contents: v. 1, IGM-001–1979.
A gazetteer of place-names, providing latitude, longitude, altitude, and administrative location. Arranged by department and province; indexed by geographic name. F3404.C37

Caribbean and Islands of the Western Atlantic

Puerto Rico

Arana Soto, Salvador. Diccionario geográfico de Puerto Rico. San Juan de Puerto Rico, 1978. 228 p. : ill. **CL126**
Presents brief gazetteer information on about 8,000 place-names. Some longer entries, and numerous lists of rivers, sugar plantations, forests, etc. Bibliography.

Europe

Cohen, Chester G. Shtetl finder : Jewish communities in the 19th and early 20th centuries in the pale of settlement of Russia and Poland, and in Lithuania, Latvia, Galicia, and Bukovina, and with names of residents. Los Angeles : Periday Co., 1980. 145 p. : maps. **CL127**
For some 2,500 cities, towns, and villages, provides locations by directions from major reference cities. Also provides brief historical notes and reference to key shtetl geography sources. Listed by Jewish pronunciation, with cross-references to current place names. Covers more limited area than Gary Mokotoff and Sallyann Amdur Sack, *Where once we walked* (CL128), but includes some additional information. DS135.R9C58

Mokotoff, Gary. Where once we walked : a guide to the Jewish communities destroyed in the holocaust / Gary Mokotoff and Sallyann Amdur Sack. Teaneck, N.J. : Avotaynu, c1991. 514 p. : ill. **CL128**
Identifies more than 21,000 towns in Central and Eastern Europe.

For each entry, provides coordinates, direction and distance from closest major city, and Jewish population. Cross-references from alternate place names (Yiddish, former political regimes, variant spellings). Detailed information on methodology of compilation and a select bibliography of sources. Three clear black-and-white maps provide historical orientation. Index by Daich-Mokotoff soundex (phonetic) system.

DS135.E83M65

Albania

Permanent Committee on Geographical Names for British Official Use. A gazetteer of Albania. London : pr. by Williams, Lea & Co., 1946. 210 p. **CL129**
Prepared in conjunction with the Royal Geographical Society.
Includes locator maps and sources of information.

DR701.S495P4

Belgium

Seyn, Eugène de. Dictionnaire historique et géographique des communes belges. 3. éd., augm. et mise à jour. Turnhout : Brepols, [1940?]. 2 v. (1562 p.) : ill., maps. **CL130**
1st ed., 1924–26, in 2 v.
Gives detailed information on each place with historical notes, coats of arms, population to 1938, etc. DH414.S42

Czechoslovakia

Chromec, Břetislav. Místopisný slovník Československé republiky. 2. doplněné a rozmnožené vyd. V Praze : Nákl. Československého Kompasu, 1935. 778 p. **CL131**
1st ed., 1929.
A detailed gazetteer with accompanying postal information.

DB194.C5

Denmark

Trap, Jens Peter. Danmark. 5. Udg. red. af Niels Nielsen, Peter Skautrup [og] Povl Engelstoft. København : Gad, 1953–72. Bd. 1–15 in 32 v. : ill., maps. **CL132**
1st ed., 1860; 4th ed., 1919–32 (11 v.).
Originally publ. as *Statistik-topografisk beskrivelse af Kongeriget Danmark* (1858–59. 3 v. in 5).
Gives historical and descriptive notes about places in Denmark. A detailed and exhaustive work. DL109.T74

France

Joanne, Paul Bénigne. Dictionnaire géographique et administratif de la France. Paris : Hachette, 1890–1905. 7 v. : ill., maps. **CL133**
1st and 2nd ed. (1865, 1869) included Alsace-Lorraine.
The standard geographical dictionary of France, containing much historical information, with detailed articles on early place-names, as well as later ones, and various geographical features. Long articles, many illustrations, but no bibliographies. Adequate for most questions, but for special work needs to be supplemented by the many regional dictionaries of the provinces, *départements*, etc. DC14.J63

Germany

Müller, Friedrich. Müllers Grosses deutsches Ortsbuch, Bundesrepublik Deutschland : vollständiges Gemeindelexikon. 25., überarbeitete und erweiterte Aufl. / bearb. von Joachim Müller. Wuppertal : Post- und Ortsbuchverlag, 1994/95 [1993]. 1223 p. **CL134**
A frequently updated gazetteer of West German place names, originally produced by a postmaster. More than 110,000 names in this edition. DD14.M8

Great Britain

Bartholomew gazetteer of places in Britain / comp. by Oliver Mason. Rev. and repr. Edinburgh : J. Bartholomew, 1986. 270, 120 p. : maps in color. **CL135**
1st ed., 1977, had title: *Bartholomew gazetteer of Britain.* An earlier work by John G. Bartholomew was first publ. 1904 as *Survey gazetteer of the British Isles* and in 1966 as *Gazetteer of the British Isles.*
This edition updates the statistical section to include data for all places with more than 5,000 inhabitants (England) or 2,000 (Scotland and Wales), according to 1981 census; population estimates as of 1984 are also listed. Includes postal code area maps. DA640.B26

Census 1981 / Office of Population Censuses and Surveys. London : H.M.S.O., 1983–85. Issued in parts. **CL136**
Volumes are designated by initials corresponding to the subject (e.g, CB, Country of birth; KSUA, Key statistics for urban areas).
Vol. IPN (in 2 v.) is an alphabetical listing of English and Welsh place-names, including counties, boroughs, urban and rural districts, civil parishes, and many "localities" having a name but no legally defined boundaries. Location (i.e., within county, parish, etc.) is given, as is population at the time of the 1981 census. A similar index was published in 1977 for the 1971 census, 1965 in connection with the 1961 census, and 1955 for the 1951 census; prior to that, the latest index of this kind was the 1924 publication in the 1921 census series.

DA640.A25

Lewis, Samuel. Topographical dictionary of England. 5th ed. London : Lewis, 1845. 4 v. : ill. **CL137**
Subtitle: Comprising the several counties, cities, boroughs, corporate and market towns, parishes, and townships, and the islands of Guernsey, Jersey, and Man, with historical and statistical descriptions: and embellished with engravings of the arms of the cities, bishoprics, universities, colleges, corporate towns, and boroughs; and of the seals of the various municipal corporations.
Still useful for the historical information to be found in the long, detailed articles about places of all sizes.
———. *Atlas to the Topographical dictionaries of England and Wales : comprising a general map of England and Wales, a map of London, and maps of the counties* ... (London : S. Lewis, 1848. 58 l : 57 maps (most in color, some folded) ; 30 cm. DA625.L676

Mason, Oliver. The gazetteer of England : England's cities, towns, villages and hamlets: a comprehensive list with basic details on each. [Totowa, N.J.] : Rowman and Littlefield, [1972]. 2 v. **CL138**
Aims to provide "a comprehensive list of English places, from the largest cities down to all but the smallest hamlets, with certain essential information about each."—*Expl. notes.* Each place-name is followed by the name of the county in which it is situated, map reference to the Ordnance Survey National Grid System, and distance and direction from another place. Indication of administrative status and population is also given; additional notes and descriptive matter appear with many entries. DA640.M35

The Ordnance Survey gazetteer of Great Britain : all names from the 1:50,000 landranger map series. 3rd ed. London : Macmillan, 1992. 797 p. : ill., maps. **CL139**

1st ed., 1987; 2nd ed., 1989.

"This Gazetteer comprises some 250,000 names taken from the Landranger Map Series. The names are listed strictly in alphabetical order across the whole country."—*How to use the Gazetteer.* Each entry contains a place name, country, National Grid reference, coordinates, feature code, and sheet number to the Series. DA13.O73

Scotland

Johnston & Bacon. Johnston's gazetteer of Scotland : including a glossary of the most common Gaelic names. 3rd ed. / rev. by R. W. Munro. Edinburgh : Johnston & Bacon, 1973. 353 p. **CL140**

1st ed., 1937; 2nd ed., 1958.

Includes population figures from official 1969 estimates.

DA869.J74

Lewis, Samuel. Topographical dictionary of Scotland. London : Lewis, 1846. 2 v. and atlas. : ill. **CL141**

Repr. : Baltimore : Genealogical Publ. Co., 1989.

Subtitle: Comprising the several counties, islands, cities, burgh and market towns, parishes, and principal villages with historical and statistical descriptions, embellished with a large map of Scotland and engravings of the seals and arms of the different burghs and universities.

Still useful for the historical information to be found in the long, detailed articles about places of all sizes. The atlas consists of a sectional map of Scotland.

Also available in microfiche (Salt Lake City, Utah : Tradition Publishers) and microfilm (Ann Arbor, Mich. : University Microfilms). DA865.L67

Greece

Permanent Committee on Geographical Names for British Official Use. A gazetteer of Greece / prep. for the Admiralty and War Office at the House of the Royal Geographical Society. London : [pr. by W. Clowes], 1942. 161 p. : maps. **CL142**

Bibliography of books and articles consulted. DF714.P4

Ireland

Lewis, Samuel. Topographical dictionary of Ireland. 2nd ed. London : Lewis, 1846. 2 v. and atlas : maps. ; ill. **CL143**

Repr.: Baltimore : Genealogical Pub. Co., 1984.

Subtitle: Comprising the several counties, cities, boroughs, corporate, market, and post towns, parishes and villages with historical and statistical descriptions, embellished with engravings of the arms of the cities, bishoprics, corporate towns, and boroughs; and the seals of the several municipal corporations.

1st ed., 1837.

Still useful for the historical information to be found in the long, detailed articles about places of all sizes. DA979.L48

Italy

Amati, Amato. Dizionario corografico dell' Italia : opera illustrata da circa 1000 armi comunali colorate e da parecchie centinaia di incisioni intercalate nel testo rappresentanti i principali monumenti d'Italia. Milano : Vallardi, [1875?-1986?]. 8 v. in 9 : ill. (coats of arms). **CL144**

Long articles, some with extensive bibliographies. Colored coats of arms. Includes many more names than *La nuova Italia* (CL145).

DG415.A48

La nuova Italia : dizionario amministrativo, statistico, industriale, commerciale dei comuni del regno e dei principali paesi d'Italia oltre confine e colonie / compliato col concorso delle rappresentanze comunali e provinciali e [di] P. Battaini ... [et al.]. Milano : Vallardi, [1908?-10?]. 3 v. : ill., atlas of 26 color plates (coats of arms). **CL145**

A successor to, but not a substitute for, *Dizionario corografico dell' Italia* (CL144).

Compiled to show the development of industrial, commercial, and agricultural Italy during the first 40 years of its life as a nation, with detailed articles by place-name. DG415.N8

Netherlands

Laan, Kornelis ter. Van Goor's aardrijkskundig woordenboek van Nederland. 3e druk geheel opnieuw / bewerkt door A. G. C. Baert. Den Haag ; Brussel : [G.B.] van Goor, [1968]. 528 p. : ill. **CL146**

1st ed., 1942; 2nd ed., 1948.

Includes names of cities, villages, minor places, church groups, and geographical terms. Lists fewer names than *Lijst der aardrijkskundige namen* (CL147), but gives more information about each item and more up-to-date figures. DJ14.L2

Lijst der aardrijkskundige namen van Nederland / uitgegeven door het Koninklijk Nederlandsch Aardrijkskundig Genootschap ; met steun van het Ministrie van Onderwijs, Kunsten en Wetenschappen. Leiden : Brill, 1936. 492 p. **CL147**

"Commissie ... A.A. Beekman, Ph. G. Rapp en J. W. Muller"— *3rd preliminary page.*

An extensive list which includes many names but gives very brief information about each, usually merely the location. DJ15.N35

Poland

Słownik geograficzny Królestwa polskiego i innych krajów słowiańskich / wydany pod red. Filipa Sulimierskiego, Bronisława Chelbowskiego, Władysława Walewskiego. Warszawa : Druk "Wieku", 1880–1902. 15 v. in 16. **CL148**

Repr.: Warszawa : Wydawnictwa Artsytyczne i Filmowe, 1975–77.

Vol. 15 is a supplement in two volumes.

Each entry identifies geographical feature and location, and provides brief historical information. Cross-references. Small black-and-white maps of towns and cities; illustrations of city crests. Includes a section of small regional maps; one country map in pocket.

DJK7.S46

Spain

Diccionario geográfico de España. Madrid : Ed. del Movimento, 1956–1961. 17 v. **CL149**

Publisher varies.

A detailed gazetteer of Spanish places. Some long, signed articles with quite extensive information on physical characteristics, climate, vegetation, agriculture, industries, cultural opportunities, history, etc. Some articles are much shorter, with gazetteer information only.

DP12.D5

Switzerland

Knapp, Charles. Dictionnaire géographique de la Suisse / publié sous les auspices de la Société Neuchâteloise de Géographie, et sous la direction de Charles Knapp ... Maurice Borel, cartographe, et de V. Attinger, éditeur .... Neuchâtel : Attinger, 1902–1910. 6 v. : ill., maps. **CL150**
   One of the finest regional dictionaries, with authoritative articles and excellent illustrations. Articles contain more scientific geographical and geological information than is usual in local gazetteers. Vol. 6 includes a supplement, p. 685–1136.   DQ14.D5

Union of Soviet Socialist Republics

Library of Congress. Reference Department. Soviet geography : a bibliography / Nicholas R. Rodionoff, ed. Wash., 1951. 668 p.   **CL151**
   Repr. : N.Y. : Greenwood, 1969.
   Contents: pt. 1, U.S.S.R. geography by subject; pt. 2, Administrative, natural and economic regions.
   Geography "is construed herein as the science describing the land, sea, air and the distribution of plant and animal life, excluding man but not his industries."—*Pref.* Material is largely in Russian. Locates copies.   Z2506.U58

Russisches geographisches Namenbuch / begründet von Max Vasmer ; bearb. von Ingrid Coper [et al.] ; hrsg. von Max Vasmer und Herbert Brüauer. Wiesbaden : O. Harrassowitz, 1964–1989. 12 v.   **CL152**
   At head of title: Akademie der Wissenschaften und der Literatur, Mainz.
   Consists of nine volumes of gazetteer entries and a twelfth volume of locator maps. Vol. 1 includes 41 pages of introductory material and a bibliography of sources. Entries are in Cyrillic, with text and location in German. Each entry identifies location to lowest level administrative area and refers to sources listed in v. 1. Includes areas in Eastern Europe that were formerly under Russian administration (e.g., parts of Poland, Slovakia, and Transcarpathia).   DK14.R9

Slovar' geograficheskikh nazvaniĭ SSSR / [sost. N. P. Aniskevich ... et al.]. Izd. 2–e, perer. i dop. Moskva : Nedra, 1983. 296 p.   **CL153**
   1st ed., 1968.
   At head of title: Glavnoe upravlenie geodezii i kartografii pri Sovete Ministrov SSSR. TSentral'nyĭ ordena "Znak Pocheta" nauchno-issledovatel'skiĭ institut geodezii, aėros̆ëmki i kartografii im F. N. Krasovskogo.
   A dictionary of geographical names, identifying them as to type of feature, and providing general location.   DK14.S53

Volostnova, M. B. Slovar' russkoĭ transkriptsii geograficheskikh nazvaniĭ. Moskva : Uchpedgiz, 1955–59. 2 v.   **CL154**
   Contents: pt. 1, Geograficheskie nazvaniĭa na territorii SSSR; pt. 2, Geograficheskie nazvaniĭa na territorii zarubezhnykh stran'.
   A dictionary of transcription into Russian of geographic names, designed to stabilize usage for school maps and geography texts. Pt. 1 lists the names of cities, towns, lakes, mountains, etc., in non-Russian territories of the U.S.S.R. in one alphabet (Russian), with latitude and longitude; cross-references are given from variants. Pt. 2 lists the same type of information for countries outside the U.S.S.R.
   ———. *Dictionary of Russian geographical names* (N.Y. : Telberg Book. Co., [1958]. 82 p.) is an English edition of pt. 1, transliterated and translated by T. Deruguine.   G103.V93

Africa

Kirchherr, Eugene C. Place names of Africa, 1935–1986 : a political gazetteer. Metuchen, N.J. : Scarecrow, 1987. 136 p. : maps.   **CL155**
   A political gazetteer of African territories in four parts: general introduction, place names of the principal African states and adjacent islands, supplementary notes and maps, selected bibliography. Place names are listed alphabetically based on common spellings of territorial names with variant spellings included. Entries give both the common name and the official title of each state, cross-references, and map locations. Supplemental notes; list of maps; bibliography arranged by types of sources.
   § Updates Kirchherr's *Abyssinia to Zimbabwe : a guide to the political units of Africa in the period 1947–1978* (3rd ed. Athens : Ohio Univ. Center for International Studies, 1979).   DT31.K53

South Africa

Amptelike plekname in die Republiek van Suid-Afrika en in Suidwes-Afrika, goedgekeur tot 1 April 1977 = Official place names in the Republic of South Africa and in South-west Africa approved to 1 April 1977 / comp. by the Place Names Committee. Pretoria : Die Staatsdrukker, 1978. 329 p. **CL156**
   Prefatory matter in Afrikaans and English.
   A revised and supplemented edition of a 1952 list of official place names of townships, agricultural holdings, post offices, railway stations, etc.; does not cover names of geographical features. Includes some names from Transkei, Swaziland, Lesotho, Botswana, and Zimbabwe.   DT752.A63

Zimbabwe

Smith, Robert C. Avondale to Zimbabwe : a collection of cameos of Rhodesian towns and villages. Borrowdale [Rhodesia] : Smith , [1978]. 314 p. : ill., map.   **CL157**
   Contains a concise history of 130 cities and villages, along with their latitude, longitude, altitude, and rainfall.   DT962.5.S44

Asia

Afghanistan

India. Army. General Staff Branch. Historical and political gazetteer of Afghanistan / ed. by Ludwig W. Adamec. Graz : Akadem. Druck- u. Verlagsanst., 1972–85. v. 1–6. : maps. (In progress)   **CL158**
   Contents: v. 1, Badakhshan Province and northeastern Afghanistan; v. 2, Farah and southwestern Afghanistan; v. 3, Herat and northwestern Afghanistan; v. 4, Mazar-i-Sharif and north-central Afghanistan; v. 5, Kandahar and south-central Afghanistan; v. 6, Kabul and southeastern Iran.
   The present edition includes the formerly secret *Gazetteer of Afghanistan* (1st ed., 1871, with revisions at intervals through 1914), "with corrections and additions of maps and considerable new material to take into account developments up to 1970."—*Pref., v. 1.*   DS351.I5

Burma

Spearman, Horace Ralph. The British Burma gazetteer. Rangoon : Pr. at the Government Pr., 1879–1880. 2 v. : fronts., photos. **CL159**

Repr. as: *Gazetteer of Burma* (Delhi : Cultural Publ. House, 1983).

Vol. 1 (first publ. 1880) presents a natural history of the country: physical geography, geology, ethnology, history, arts, and fauna. Vol. 2 contains gazetteer information. Entries range from several lines to several pages. Numerous explanatory footnotes. DS485.B8S7

China

Playfair, George M. H. The cities and towns of China : a geographical dictionary. 2nd ed. Shanghai : Kelly and Walsh, 1910. 582 p., lxxvi p. **CL160**

Repr.: Taipei : Ch'eng Wen, 1978.

1st ed., 1879.

"In the main a revisal of [E. C.] Biot's *Dictionnaire des villes chinoises.*"—*Pref.*

Brief information on towns. Names are given in transliteration and in Chinese characters. DS705.P7

Tien, H. C. Gazetteer of China / H. C. Tien, Ronald Hsia, Peter Penn. Hong Kong : Oriental Book Co., 1961. 237 p. **CL161**

Gives name of locality, pronunciation, name in Chinese characters, province, longitude and latitude. Index. DS705.T54

United States. Defense Mapping Agency. Gazetteer of the People's Republic of China. Wash. : The Agency, 1979. 919 p. **CL162**

Superintendent of Documents classification: D5.319:C44.

Contains the names of approximately 22,000 populated places and physical features. In three parts: (1) pinyin names cross-referenced to Wade-Giles names; (2) Wade-Giles names with the corresponding pinyin names; (3) conventional names with the corresponding pinyin names.

———. *Supplement to the Gazetteer of the People's Republic of China: pinyin to Wade-Giles, Wade-Giles to pinyin.* (Wash. : Defense Mapping Agency, [1988]. 315 p.). DS705.D43

India

Gazetteer of India : Indian Union / [Comp. by] Central Gazetteers Unit, Govt. of India. [Delhi] : Publications Division, Ministry of Information and Broadcasting, [1965–78]. 4 v. **CL163**

Contents: v. 1, Country and people; v. 2, History and culture; v. 3, Economic structure and activities; v. [4] Administration and public welfare.

Plans for updating the *Imperial gazetteer* (CL164) call for revision or compilation of district gazetteers by the state governments, and for simultaneous work by the central government on revision, rewriting, and amplification of the Indian volumes. Chapters are contributed by one or more experts; a bibliography is provided at the end of each chapter.

District gazetteers published by the individual states have been appearing in parts since 1957 for Arunachal Praesh, Assam, Bihar, Goa, Daman and Diu, Gujarat, Haryana, Himachal Pradesh, Karnataka, Kerala, Madhya Pradesh, Madras, Maharashtra, Mysore, Nagaland, Orissa, Pondicherry, Punjab, Rajasthan, Tripura, Uttar Pradesh, West Bengal. DS407.G37

Imperial gazetteer of India / publ. under the authority of His Majesty's Secretary of State for India in Council. New ed. Oxford : Clarendon Pr., 1907–1909. 26 v. : maps. **CL164**

1st ed. (9 v.), 1881, and 2nd ed. (14 v.), 1885–87, ed. by Sir William Wilson Hunter. Considered to be a new work, rather than a new edition.

Editor for India: 1902–1904, William Stevenson Meyer; 1905–1909, Richard Burn. Editor in England: James Sutherland Cotton.

Contents: v. 1–4, Indian Empire (v. 1, Descriptive; v. 2, Historical; v. 3, Economic; v. 4, Administrative); v. 5–24, Gazetteer; v. 25, General index; v. 26, Atlas (new rev. ed., 1931).

Includes historical, topographical, ethnic, agricultural, industrial, administrative, and medical aspects of the various districts of British India.

For updating of v. 1–4, see: *Gazetteer of India* (CL163). DS405.H95

Iran

Adamec, Ludwig W. Historical gazetteer of Iran. Graz, Austria : Akademische Druck- u. Verlagsanstalt, 1976–88. v. 1–4. : maps. (In progress). **CL165**

Contents: v. 1, Tehran and northwestern Iran; v. 2, Meshed and northeastern Iran; v. 3, Abadan and southwestern Iran; v. 4, Zahidan and southeastern Iran.

This work adds to and updates material originally presented in the General Staff of British India's *Gazetteer of Persia* (1914; republ. 1918); the text has been reprinted, with new entries and passages added. Includes geographical features, villages and towns, ethnographic groups, etc., arranged alphabetically, plus a glossary, index of subtribes, and a map section. Statistics are based on the 1966 census. To be complete in 5 v. DS253.A54

Japan

Gerr, Stanley. A gazetteer of Japanese place names in characters and in Rōmaji script giving latitudes and longitudes. Cambridge : Harvard Univ. Pr., 1942. 269, 225 p. **CL166**

Two lists dealing with the same places, one in Rōmaji script (Latin alphabet), the other in Sino-Japanese character. Besides the names of cities, towns, etc., includes the names of mountains, rivers, islands, etc. "Based on the map of the Japanese Empire published in 1937 by the Japanese Kokusai Bunka Shinkōkai (Society for International Cultural Relations). It contains about 4500 place names covering Japan proper, Korea, Formosa, Kwangtung leased territory, Saghalien, and the Japanese mandated islands, but does not include Manchuria or other territory recently occupied by Japan. ..."—*Pref. note.* DS805.G4

United States. Hydrographic Office. Gazetteer of the Japanese Empire : containing place names from the Japanese hydrographic charts and sailing directions on issue in 1936. Wash., 1943. 378 p. (United States. Hydrographic Office. Publication, no. 880). **CL167**

A listing of some 15,000 place-names, arranged alphabetically by Rōmaji transcription, giving the Japanese form and the latitude and longitude. DS805.U45

Philippines

United States. Bureau of Insular Affairs. Pronouncing gazetteer and geographical dictionary of the Philippine Islands. Wash. : U.S. Govt. Print. Off., 1902. 933 p. : ill., maps. (Philippine culture series, 53). **CL168**

Detailed information on all aspects of life in the Philippines at turn of the century.

Also available on microcard: Wash. : Micro-card Editions, 1963. 15 cards.   DS654.U56

Australia and Oceania

New Zealand

Wises New Zealand guide. Auckland : Wises Publications, 1952– . Irregular.   **CL169**

Title, subtitle, and name of publisher vary.

Arranged alphabetically by place-name and geographical location. Frequently gives history, legends, origin of name, etc., as well as the usual gazetteer information.   DU405.N55

GEOGRAPHICAL NAMES AND TERMS

General works

Egli, Johann Jacob. Nomina geographica : Sprach- und Sacherklärung von 42000 geographischen Namen aller Erdräume. 2. verm. und verb. Aufl. Leipzig : Brandstetter, 1893. 1035 p.   **CL170**

Repr.: N.Y. : B. Franklin, 1971.

Gives the origin of place-names in various countries of the world, with references to sources.   G105.E3

Gazetteer of undersea feature names, 1987 = Répertoire des noms d'entités sous-marines, 1987 / Advisory Committee on Names for Undersea and Maritime Features, Canadian Permanent Committee on Geographical Names. [2nd ed.]. Ottawa : Information and Publication Branch, Dept. of Fisheries and Oceans, c1987. 155 p.   **CL171**

1st ed., 1983.

"The purpose of this guide is to familiarize specialists in the marine sciences, editors of scientific journals, geographers, and cartographers, with approved names, terms, definitions, principles, and procedures when naming undersea features."—*Pref.* Each entry includes a place name, feature designation, locator map or chart number, and coordinates. Also has sections on terminology, terms and definitions, and explanatory notes.

Names & nicknames of places & things / ed. by Laurence Urdang. Boston : G.K. Hall, c1987. 327 p.   **CL172**

A selective compilation of "names and nicknames as might qualify for consideration as being universal or, at least, important."— *Foreword.* Geographic names are interspersed with names of buildings, foods, institutions, modes of transportation, in a single alphabet. Well indexed.   G105.N36

Sharp, Harold S. Handbook of geographical nicknames. Metuchen, N.J. : Scarecrow, 1980. 153 p.   **CL173**

Both generally accepted names and nicknames appear in one alphabetical list. Nicknames are cross-referenced to the accepted names or main entries; the latter are followed by a brief notation giving locations and description, and a list of applicable nicknames. American nicknames are excluded since they are covered by Joseph N. Kane and Gerard L. Alexander's *Nicknames and sobriquets of U.S. cities, states and counties* (CL179).   G105.S5

United States Board on Geographic Names. Decisions on geographic names in the United States. Wash. : Dept. of the Interior, 1963– .   **CL174**

Superintendent of Documents classification: I 33.5/2: .

Frequency varies; annual, 1990– . Title varies: *Decisions, Decision lists.*

Contains general lists of decisions; some lists were issued for special locations (e.g., National parks) or on specific foreign countries (e.g., Tibet, Mongolia, Italy).   E154.U54a

United States Geographic Board. Sixth report, 1890–1932. Wash. : U.S. Govt. Print. Off., 1933. 834 p.   **CL175**

Repr.: Detroit : Gale, 1967.

Includes: (1) Geographic names, discussion of characteristics, problems, etc.; (2) The U.S. Geographic Board, its method of work, history, etc.; (3) Decisions, arranged alphabetically by approved form of name, with cross-references from other forms, p. 76–834.

The *Decisions* form a dictionary of many thousand place-names throughout the world, incorporating in one alphabetical list: the material of the *Fifth report* (1921); subsequent decisions; the 2,500 foreign place-names included in the *First report on foreign geographic names* (1932); and the Philippine and Hawaiian names given in separate lists in the *Fifth report*. For each name gives approved form, locates the place, indicates rejected forms, and, in some cases, marks pronunciation.

"This report contains, with the exception of a comparatively small number, all the decisions rendered by the Board from its organization in 1890 through June, 1932, and supersedes all previous reports. Not included ... are such decisions as have either been vacated, or being revised, have been replaced by new decisions listed under the revised name or spelling."—*Foreword.*

§ For current information, see *Decisions on geographic names in the United States* (CL174).   G105.U5

North America

Harder, Kelsie B. Illustrated dictionary of place names, United States and Canada. N.Y. : Van Nostrand Reinhold, 1976. 631 p. : ill.   **CL176**

Repr. : N.Y. : Facts on File, 1985.

"The names of all provinces, states, provincial and state capitals, counties and county seats are listed. An attempt is also made to include a comprehensive selection of the most viable and interesting United States cities and towns, based on current census reports and ZIP code directories."—*Introd.* Major geographical features are also covered. Illustrations depict persons for whom places were named, the site itself, or a historical event related to the site. Bibliography.   E155.H37

Sealock, Richard B. Bibliography of place-name literature : United States and Canada / Richard B. Sealock, Margaret M. Sealock, and Margaret S. Powell. 3rd ed. Chicago : Amer. Libr. Assoc., 1982. 435 p.   **CL177**

1st ed., 1948, by R. B. Sealock and P. A. Seely; 2nd ed., 1967.

More than 4,800 items, both books and periodical articles. Separate sections for the U.S. and Canada; each begins with listings of general studies and gazetteers, followed by sections for individual states and provinces. Many brief annotations; index.   Z6824.S4

United States

Kane, Joseph Nathan. The American counties. 4th ed. Metuchen, N.J. : Scarecrow, 1983. 546 p.   **CL178**

1st ed., 1960; 3rd ed., 1972.

Subtitle: Origins of county names, dates of creation and organization, area, population including 1980 census figures, historical data, and published sources.   E180.K3

——————— Nicknames and sobriquets of U.S. cities, states, and counties / Joseph Nathan Kane & Gerard L. Alexander. 3rd ed. Metuchen, N.J. : Scarecrow, 1979. 429 p.

     CL179

The 1st ed., 1965, had title: *Nicknames of cities and states of the U.S.*, which combined and expanded the lists in Kane's *1,000 facts worth knowing* (1938) and Alexander's *Nicknames of American cities, towns, and villages* (1951). The 2nd ed. (1970) was published as: *Nicknames and sobriquets of U.S. cities and states.* The new edition is a further expansion. Explanatory notes are frequently given, but source of the information is not indicated. Includes indexes.   E155.K24

Stewart, George Rippey. American place-names : a concise and selective dictionary for the continental United States of America. N.Y. : Oxford Univ. Pr., 1970. 550 p.   **CL180**
Repr., 1985.
About 12,000 entries. The principal categories of names treated are: (1) names of well-known places; (2) repeated names, i.e., those which appear on several or many places; and (3) unusual names, i.e., those which attract attention and arouse curiosity or controversy. Good introduction on the general background and classification of place names; bibliography.   E155.S79

Canada

Hamilton, William B. The Macmillan book of Canadian place names. Toronto : Macmillan of Canada, 1978. 340 p.   **CL181**
Begun as a revision of George Henry Armstrong, *Origin and meaning of place names in Canada* (Toronto : Macmillan, 1930. 312 p.), but in effect a new work.
Selection criteria included: (1) size (i.e., "major centres of population and the most important physical features."—*Pref.*); (2) historical significance; and (3) human interest. Bibliography, p. 333–40.   F1004.H35

Harder, Kelsie B. Illustrated dictionary of place names, United States and Canada. N.Y. : Van Nostrand Reinhold, 1976. 631 p. : ill.   **CL182**
For annotation, *see* CL176.   E155.H37

South America

Brazil

Souza, Bernardino José de. Dicionário da terra e da gente do Brasil. São Paulo : Compania Ed. Nacional, 1961. 346 p. (Brasiliana. Série grande formato, v. 19).   **CL183**
5th ed. of *Onomástica geral da geografia brasileira* (1927).
Explanations of Brazilian place-names. No bibliography or references, but includes brief list of sources in introduction.   F2504.S73

Europe

Austria

Zwanziger, Ronald. Bibliographie der Namenforschung in Österreich. Wien : Österreichische Gesellschaft für Namenforschung, 1980. v. 1. (Österreichische Namenforschung. Sonderreihe, 3.).   **CL184**
No more published?
1,172 citations to books, articles, and dissertations are grouped according to geographic region in v. 1. International in scope. Author index.   Z6824.Z93

France

Dauzat, Albert. Dictionnaire étymologique des noms de lieux en France / Albert Dauzat, et Ch. Rostaing. 2. éd. rev. et complétée par Ch. Rostaing. Paris : Guénégaud, 1978. 738 p.   **CL185**
1st ed., 1963.
A reprinting of the earlier edition with a list of corrections and a supplement (p. i–[xxiv]) of some 800 names, either new to this edition or with additional or corrected information.   DC14.D28

——————— Dictionnaire étymologique des noms de rivières et de montagnes en France / par A. Dauzat, avec la collaboration de G. Deslandes ; rev. et corrigé par Charles Rostaing. Paris : Klincksieck, 1978. 233 p. (Études linguistiques, 21).   **CL186**
In two parts, Noms de rivières and Noms de montagnes. Each entry provides etymological derivation, as well as any name variants, with accompanying dates; numerous cross-references.   GB1293.D37

Dictionnaire topographique de la France comprenant les noms de lieu anciens et modernes / publié par ordre du Ministère de l'Instruction Publique et sous la direction du Comité des Travaux Historiques et Scientifiques. Paris : Impr. Nationale, 1861–1992. v. [1–]. (In progress?).   **CL187**
Imprints vary; some volumes available in microform.
A monumental work, still in process of publication, one volume for each *département*. Each volume lists all place-names of its *département*, even names of farms, giving for each: location; derivation; variations in form from the earliest period to the present, with date when each form was used and exact references to manuscripts or printed authorities; and, in the case of important names, a brief history and description of the place. Entry in the dictionary proper is under the modern form of name; cross-references from old forms are given in a table at the end of the volume.
Volumes thus far published are: Ain, by E. Philipon, 1911; Aisne, by A. Matton, 1871; Aube, by Th. Boutiot and E. Socard, 1874; Aude, by the Abbé Sabarthès, 1912; Calvados, by C. Hippeau, 1883; Cantal, by E. Amé, 1897; Cher, by H. Boyer and R. Latouche, 1926; Côte d'Or, by A. Roserot, 1924; Deux-Sèvres, by B. Ledain, 1902; Dordogne, by A. J. D. de Gourgues, 1873; Drôme, by J. Brun-Durand, 1891; Eure, by B. E. P. de Blosseville, 1878; Eure-et-Loir, by L. Merlet, 1861; Gard, by E. Germer-Durand, 1868; Hautes Alpes, by J. Roman, 1884; Hérault, by E. Thomas, 1865; Loire (Haute), by A. Chassaing and A. Jacotin, 1907; Marne, by A. Longnon, 1891; Marne (Haute), by A. Roserot, 1903; Mayenne, by L. Maitre, 1878; Meurthe, by H. Lepage, 1862; Meuse, by F. Lienard, 1872; Morbihan, by L. Rosenzweig, 1870; Moselle, by E. de Bouteiller, 1874; Nièvre, by J. H. G. R. de Soultrait, 1865; Pas-de-Calais, by A. C. H. Menche de Loisne, 1908; Pyrénées (Basses), by P. R. L. Raymond, 1863; Pyrénées (Haute), by Louis-Antoine Lejosne (1865), rev. 1992 by R. Aymard; Rhin (Haut), by G. Stoffel, 1868; Sarthe, by E. Vallée, rev. et pub. by R. Latouche, 1950–52; Seine et Marne, by H. Stein and J. Hubert, 1954; Vienne, by L. Rédet, 1881; Vosges, by P. Marichal, 1941; Yonne, by M. Quantin, 1862; Seine-Maritime, by C. de Beaurepaire, revu, complété, entièrement refondu et publié par J. Laporte, 1982–84 (2 v.).

Mulon, Marianne. L'onomastique française : bibliographie des travaux publiés jusqu'en 1960. Paris : Documentation Française, 1977. 454 p.   **CL188**
At head of title: Archives Nationales.
Aims to present an exhaustive, noncritical bibliography of works on French personal and place names. In three main sections: (1) Études générales: (2) Études régionales; (3) Études locales par départements. About 6,900 items. Indexed.   Z2181.G37M84

Germany

Bach, Adolf. Deutsche Namenkunde. Heidelberg : C. Winter, 1952–1956. 3 v. in 5 : ill.   **CL189**
  Repr.: 1974–81.
  Contents: Bd.1, Die deutschen Personennamen. 2. stark erw.; Bd. 2, Die deutschen Ortsnamen: Hlbbd.1, Einleitung. Zur Laut- und Formenlehre, zur Satzfügung, Wortbildung und bedeutung der deutschen Ortsnamen; Hlbbd. 2, Die deutschen Ortsnamen in geschichtlicher, geographischer, soziologischer und psychologischer Betrachtung. Ortsnamenforschung im Dienste anderer Wissenschaften; Bd. 3, Registerband, bearb. von Dieter Berger. A 2nd ed. of Bd. 2, Hlbbd. 2 was publ. 1981.
  1st ed. of Bd. 1 appeared in 1943 as v. 18 of Herman Paul, *Grundriss der germanischen Philologie unter Mitwirkung zahlreicher Fachgelehrter.*
  A detailed treatment of German names; the first volume deals with personal names, the second with place-names. The third provides indexes to the other two.   PF3576.B33

Bahlow, Hans. Deutschlands geographische Namenwelt : etymologisches Lexikon der Fluss- und Ortsnamen alteuropäischer Herkunft. Frankfurt am Main : V. Klostermann, [1965]. 554 p.   **CL190**
  Repr. : Frankfurt am Main : Suhrkamp, 1985.
  Provides abundant cross-references from variant forms. List of sources for further reading.   PF3576.B34

Oesterley, Hermann. Historisch-geographisches Wörterbuch des deutschen Mittelalters. Gotha : Perthes, 1883. 806 p.   **CL191**
  A history of medieval German place-names.   DD14.O29

Great Britain

Cameron, Kenneth. English place-names. [4th ed.]. London : Batsford, 1988. 264 p., [8] p. of plates : ill.   **CL192**
  1st ed., 1961; 3rd ed., 1977.
  A discussion of the elements of English place-names. Indexes of place-names, street-names, and field-names. Bibliography.
                DA645.C3

Ekwall, Eilert. Concise Oxford dictionary of English place-names. 4th ed. Oxford : Clarendon Pr., 1960. 546 p.   **CL193**
  1st ed., 1936; 3rd ed., 1951.
  "Embraces names of the country, of the counties, and other important divisions, towns (except those of late origin), parishes, villages, some names of estates and hamlets, or even farms whose names are old and etymologically interesting, rivers, lakes—also names of capes, hills, bays for which early material is available. Names of hundreds, as being no longer in use, have been omitted."—*Introd.* The 4th ed. has been reset, incorporating corrections and addenda from the earlier editions; many articles were rewritten. Lists about 15,000 names.
  While the concise information given is considerably less full than that in the place-name records issued by the English Place-Name Society, (CL195) it includes in general: modern form, location (in county), derivation of meaning, older forms with dates, and some references to sources. Pronunciation is given in some cases.   DA645.E38

———————— English river names. Oxford : Clarendon Pr., 1928. 488 p.   **CL194**
  Gives detailed etymology for river names, with references to sources of information.   DA645.E5

English Place-Name Society. [Survey of English place-names]. Cambridge : Univ. Pr., 1924–1992. v. 1–63 : maps. (In progress).   **CL195**
  Contents: v. 1, pt. 1, Introduction to the survey of English place-names, by A. Mawer and F. M. Stenton (1924. 201 p.); v. 1, pt. 2, Chief elements used in English place-names, by A. Mawer (1924. 67

p; for rev. ed. *see* CL201); v. 2, Place-names of *Buckinghamshire*, by A. Mawer and F. M. Stenton (1925. 274 p.); v. 3, Place-names of *Bedfordshire* and *Huntingdonshire*, by A. Mawer and F. M. Stenton (1926. 316 p.); v. 4, Place-names of *Worcestershire*, by A. Mawer and F. M. Stenton (1927. 420 p.); v. 5, Place-names of the *North Riding of Yorkshire*, by A. H. Smith (1928. 352 p.); v. 6–7, Place-names of *Sussex*, by A. Mawer and F. M. Stenton (1929–30. 2 v.); v. 8–9, Place-names of *Devon*, by J. E. B. Gover, A. Mawer and F. M. Stenton (1931–32. 2 v. and case of maps); v. 10, Place-names of *Northamptonshire*, by J. E. B. Gover, A. Mawer and F. M. Stenton (1933. 311 p.); v. 11, Place-names of *Surrey*, by J. E. B. Gover, A. Mawer and F. M. Stenton (1934. 445 p.); v. 12, Place-names of *Essex*, by P. H. Reaney (1935. 698 p.); v. 13, Place-names of *Warwickshire*, by J. E. B. Gover, A. Mawer and F. M. Stenton (1936. 409 p.); v. 14, Place-names of the *East Riding of Yorkshire and York*, by A. H. Smith (1937. 351 p.);
  v. 15, Place-names of *Hertfordshire*, by J. E. B. Gover, A. Mawer and F. M. Stenton (1938. 342 p.); v. 16, Place-names of *Wiltshire*, by J. E. B. Gover, A. Mawer and F. M. Stenton (1939. 547 p.); v. 17, Place-names of *Nottinghamshire*, by J. E. B. Gover, A. Mawer and F. M. Stenton (1940. 348 p.); v. 18, Place-names of *Middlesex*, apart from the city of London, by J. E. B. Gover, A. Mawer and F. M. Stenton (1942. 235 p.); v. 19, Place-names of *Cambridgeshire* and the *Isle of Ely*, by P. H. Reaney (1943. 396 p.); v. 20–22, Place-names of *Cumberland*, by A. M. Armstrong, A. Mawer, F. M. Stenton and Bruce Dickins (1950–52. 3 pts. 565 p.); v. 23–24, Place-names of *Oxfordshire*, by Margaret Gelling, based on material collected by Doris Mary Stenton (1953–54. 2 v.); v. 25–26, English place-name elements, *see* CL201; v. 27–29, Place-names of *Derbyshire*, by Kenneth Cameron (1959. 3 v.); v. 30–37, Place-names of the *West Riding of Yorkshire*, by A. H. Smith (1961–63. 8 v.); v. 38–41, The place-names of *Gloucestershire*, by A. H. Smith (1964–65. 4 v.); v. 42–43, The place-names of *Westmorland*, by A. H. Smith (1967. 2 v.); v. 44–48, 54, The place-names of *Cheshire*, by J. McN. Dodgson (1970–81. 6 v.; pt. 5 still in prep.); v. 49–51, The place-names of *Berkshire*, by Margaret Gelling (1973–76. 3 v.); v. 52–53, Place-names of *Dorset*, pts. 1–2, by A. D. Mills (1977–80); v. 55, Place-names of *Staffordshire*, pt. 1, by J. P. Oakden (1984). v, 56/57, *Cornish* place-name elements, by O. J. Padel (1985); v. 58, 64/65–66– , The place-names of *Lincolnshire*, pt. 1, 2, 3– , by Kenneth Cameron (1985–1992); v. 61– , The place-names of *Norfolk*, pt. 1– , by Karl Inge Sandred and Bengt Lindstrom (1989–); v. 62/63– , The place-names of *Shropshire*, pt. 1– , by Margaret Gelling and H. D. G. Foxall (1990–).   DA645.A4

Field, John. Place-names of Great Britain and Ireland. London : David & Charles ; Totowa, N.J. : Barnes and Noble, 1980. 208 p. : maps.   **CL196**
  A selective alphabetical dictionary of place-names in England, Scotland, Wales, the Isle of Man, and the Irish island, intended for the general reader. Early forms of less common names are provided, with dates of usage. Includes glossary of common elements of place names and brief bibliography. No guide to pronunciation.   DA645.F53

Gelling, Margaret. The names of towns and cities in Britain / comp. by Margaret Gelling, W. F. H. Nicolaisen, and Melville Richards. London : Batsford, [1970]. 215 p.   **CL197**
  Repr.: London : Batsford, 1986.
  Treats town and city names of England, Scotland, and Wales in a single alphabet. The names included "have been chosen for one reason only: they are the names of those places—towns and cities—in which most people in Great Britain live to-day" (*Introd*)—i.e., names were not chosen merely for intrinsic interest or because they illustrate some linguistic peculiarity. Separate section for Greater London names. Brief bibliography.   DA645.G44

Mills, A. D. A dictionary of English place names. Oxford ; N.Y. : Oxford Univ. Pr., 1991. 388 p. : maps ; 21 cm.   **CL198**
  Provides "the most likely meaning and origins of over 12,000 English place-names in a clear, concise, and easily accessible form"—*Introd.* Inclusion in this work is related to the appearance of the name in generally available touring atlases. Covers physical (rivers, coastal features) and administrative (counties, districts) features,

as well as cities, towns and villages. Appendix: Glossary of some common elements in English place-names. Selected bibliography, organized by format. DA645.M55

Rivet, Albert Lionel Frederick. The place-names of Roman Britain / by A. L. F. Rivet and Colin Smith. Princeton, N.J. : Princeton Univ. Pr., 1979. 526 p. **CL199**
Also publ. London : B.T. Batsford.
Chapters (The literary authorities, Ptolemy's geography, Itineraries, The Ravenna cosmography, and Inscriptions) precede the alphabetic list of names (about half of the book) which gives derivations and identifications. Index of modern names in Britain. DA645.R58

Room, Adrian. A concise dictionary of modern place-names in Great Britain and Ireland. Oxford ; N.Y. : Oxford Univ. Pr., 1983. xliii, 148 p. **CL200**
Explains derivations of more than 1,000 names that have arisen since 1500. Bibliography. DA645.R66

Smith, Albert Hugh. English place-name elements. Cambridge [Eng.] : Univ. Pr., 1956. 2 v. (Survey of English place-names, v. 25–26). **CL201**
Repr., 1970.
Contents: pt. 1, Introduction, bibliography, the elements A–Iw, maps; pt. 2, The elements Jafn–Ytri, index and maps.
A detailed study of the derivation of the elements found in English place-names, with bibliographical references to sources.
§ Expands and revises A. Mawer, *Chief elements used in English place-names* (Cambridge : Univ. Pr., 1924. v. 1, pt. 2). DA645.A4

Scotland

Hogan, Edmund. Onomasticon goedelicum locorum et tribuum Hiberniae et Scotiae. Dublin : Hodges, 1910. 695p. map. **CL202**
For annotation, *see* CL208. DA979.H6

Johnston, James B. The place-names of Scotland. [3rd ed. enl.]. London : Murray, 1934. 335 p. **CL203**
Repr.: Wakefield : S. R. Publishers, 1970.
1st ed., 1892; 2nd ed., 1903.
Gives the origin and meaning of place-names in Scotland. Brief bibliography. DA869.J72

Mackenzie, William Cook. Scottish place-names. London : K. Paul, Trench, Trubner, 1931. 319 p. **CL204**
Discusses the elements in a selected list of Scottish place-names in such chapters as: The rivers and their burns, The nesses and the lochs, The bogs and the marshes, etc. DA869.M14

Nicolaisen, Wilhelm Fritz Hermann. Scottish place-names : their study and significance. London : Batsford, 1976. 210 p. : maps. **CL205**
Aims to provide "a cohesive and systematic, although not a comprehensive, account of the study of Scottish place names."—*Pref.* Bibliography and list of sources; index. DA869.N53

Wales

Lewis, Samuel. Topographical dictionary of Wales. 5th ed. London : Lewis, 1849. 2 v. and atlas. : ill. **CL206**
Subtitle: Comprising the several counties, cities, boroughs, corporate and market towns, parishes, chapelries, and townships, with historical and statistical descriptions: embellished with engravings of the arms of the bishoprics, and of the arms and seals of the various cities and municipal corporations, and illustrated by maps of the different counties.
1st ed., 1833; 2nd ed., 1840.

Still useful for the historical information to be found in the long, detailed articles about places of all sizes.
See also *Atlas to the Topographical dictionaries of England and Wales* by Lewis (CL137 *note*) and *Census 1981* (CL136).

Hungary

Kiss, Lajos. Földrajzi nevek etimológiai szótára. 4., bőv. és jav. kiad. Budapest : Akadémiai Kiadó, 1988. 2 v. **CL207**
1st ed., 1978; 3rd ed., 1983.
An etymological dictionary of place-names, with extensive references to some 4,000 geographical sources of reference for further data. Not limited to Hungarian place-names, but fullest treatment is offered to them. PH2576.K5

Ireland

Hogan, Edmund. Onomasticon goedelicum locorum et tribuum Hiberniae et Scotiae. Dublin : Hodges, 1910. 695p. map. **CL208**
Repr.: Dublin : Four Courts Pr., 1993.
Subtitle: An index, with identifications, to the Gaelic names of places and tribes.
"List of manuscripts and printed sources,"—*p. xi–xiv.* In Gaelic and English. DA979.H6

Joyce, Patrick W. Origin and history of Irish names of places. 7th ed. London ; N.Y. : Longmans, 1901–02. 2 v. **CL209**
Repr. (of 4th ed.): Wakefield : E. P. Publishing, 1972.
The best dictionary of Irish place-names, giving for each name its location, derivation, meaning, and an explanation of the meaning where necessary. Vols. 1–2, originally published 1869–71, are treatises, arranged in chapters with alphabetical indexes, but v.3 is a regular dictionary list. As v.3 does not duplicate many of the names in v.1–2, use must still be made of those earlier volumes.
§ *See also* John Field, *Place-names of Great Britain and Ireland* (CL196) and Adrian Room, *A concise dictionary of modern place-names in Great Britain and Ireland* (CL200). DA920.J893

Netherlands

Flou, Karel de. Woordenboek der toponymie van Westelijk Vlaanderen, Vlaamsch Artesië, het Land van den Hoek : de graafschappen Guines en Boulogne, en een gedeelte van het graafschap Ponthieu. Brugge : Poelvoorde, 1914–38. 18 v. **CL210**
Repr. : Torhout : Flandria Nostra, 1983–88.
Vols. 13–18 ed. by Joseph de Smet.
Vols. 1–2 publ. Gent : W. Siffer, Drukker der Koninklijke Vlaamsche Academie.
Sponsored by the Vlaamsche Academie voor Taal en Letterkunde.
An extensive listing, in dictionary arrangement, of Flemish place-names with explanations and references to original usages, etc. DH14.F6

Poland

Taszycki, Witold. Bibliografia onomastyki polskiej / Opracował Witold Taszycki ... [et al.]. Kraków : [Nakł Uniwersytetu Jagielleńskiego], 1960–92. v. 1–4. (Varia, t. 5, 76 [etc.]). (In progress?). **CL211**
Editor varies; publisher varies.

At head of title, v. 3–4: Polska Akademia Nauk. Instytut Jezyka Polskiego.

Contents: [t. 1] Do roku 1958 wlacznie; t. 2, Od roku 1959 do roku 1970 wlacznie; t. 3, Od roku 1971 do roku 1980 wlacznie; t. 4, Od roku 1981 do roku 1990 wlacznie.

A classed bibliography of Polish place-name literature, international in scope. Indexed by methodology, geographic names, and authors.   Z6824.T3

Switzerland

Hubschmid, Johannes. Bibliographia onomastica helvetica. Bern : Wyss, 1954. 50 p. : ill.   **CL212**

Some 750 citations are arranged by topical geographical region. Indexed by author and detailed subject.   Z6824.H8

Jaccard, Henri. Essai de toponymie : origine des noms de lieux habités et des lieux dits de la Suisse romande. Lausanne : Bridel, 1906. 558 p. (Société d'Histoire de la Suisse Romande. Mémoires et documents, 2. sér., t. 7).   **CL213**

Repr. : Geneva : Slatkine, 1985.

An extensive listing showing the development of Swiss place-names with references to sources.   DQ.S72

Studer, Julius. Schweizer Ortsnamen : ein historisch-etymologischer Versuch. Zürich : Schulthess, 1896. 288 p.   **CL214**

A listing of German-Swiss names, giving early usages and etymologies.

Africa

Mozambique

Cabral, António Carlos Pereira. Dicionário de nomes geográficos de Moçambique : sua origem. Lourenço Marques : [s.n.], 1975. 180 p. : ill.   **CL215**

Discusses the background of some 850 names. Cross-references. Bibliography.   DT452.C3

South Africa

Nienaber, Grabriel Stefanus. Hottentot (Khoekhoen) place names / G. S. Nienaber & P. E. Raper ; tr. by P. S. Rabie. Durban : publ. for the Onomastic Research Centre, Human Sciences Research Council, by Butterworth, 1983. 243 p. : ill. (Southern African place names, 1).   **CL216**

Translated from Afrikaans.

Based on the authors' Toponymica hottentotica (Pretoria, 1977–80. 3 v.). Bibliography p. 227–42.   DT752.5.N48

Raper, P. E. Bronnegids vir toponimie en topologie = Source guide for toponymy and topology. Pretoria : S. A. Naamkundesentrum, Raad vir Geesteswetenskaplike Navorsing, 1976. 478 p. (Naamkundereeks, 5).   **CL217**

Also publ. in 1975 in limited edition of 250.

In Afrikaans and English.

A bibliography for "the study of places and place names."—Pref. Includes books, pamphlets, periodical and newspaper articles, and theses. In two sections, the first arranged by subject or place name; the second by author. Full information is given in both sections.   Z3608.A5R36

Australia and Oceania

Australia

Reed, A. W. Aboriginal place names and their meanings. Sydney ; Wellington : Reed, [1967]. 144 p.   **CL218**

List of Australian place-names with meanings, followed by a word list with a subject approach to the aboriginal names. Relates present-day names to earlier aboriginal ones.   DU91.R4

New Zealand

Reed, A. W. A dictionary of Maori place names. 2nd ed. Wellington : Reed ; Beaverton, Ore. : distr. by ISBS, 1982. 144 p. : ill.   **CL219**

First publ. as Maori place names and their meanings, 1950.

1st ed., 1961.

In most cases, the explanation for an entry divides the place-name into its component parts. Brief historical references are included as available. Introductory material provides "Hints on pronunciation." Appendix of European place-names with Maori equivalents.   DU405.R42

ATLASES AND MAPS

General works

Guides

Information sources in cartography / editors, C.R. Perkins, R.B. Parry. London ; N.Y. : Bowker-Saur, c1990. 540 p. : ill., maps.   **CL220**

International in scope; arranges current and retrospective sources in a "sensible logical sequence to reflect a contemporary overview of a range of cartographic concerns"—Introd. 30 chapters with references, in five parts: General; History of cartography; Map production; Map librarianship; Types of mapping, map use and promotion. Appendixes include lists of cartographic periodicals, geographical arrangement of cartographic societies, and map publishers. Detailed subject and name indexes; list of contributors.   Z6021.I53

Kister, Kenneth F. Kister's atlas buying guide : general English-language world atlases available in North America. Phoenix : Oryx, 1984. 236 p. ; 24 cm.   **CL221**

For 105 atlases, provides complete bibliographic data and critical evaluations, including review citations. Also features general guide to atlas evaluation (p. 5–29), comparative charts, annotated bibliography, and directory of dealers for out-of-print materials. Indexed.   Z6021.K5

Lister, Raymond. How to identify old maps and globes : with a list of cartographers, engravers, publishers, and printers concerned with printed maps and globes from c.1500 to c.1850. Hamden, Conn. : Archon Books, [1965]. 256 p.   **CL222**

Gives attention to methods of map production, decorations and conventional signs, etc.   GA201.L56

Walsh, S. Padraig. General world atlases in print, 1972–1973 : a comparative analysis. [4th ed., enl.]. N.Y. : Bowker, 1973. 211 p.   **CL223**

1st ed., 1966.

Intended as a practical guide for nonspecialists in the choice of a general reference world atlas. Treats 40 major atlases and about 100 smaller ones, all of which were published in the U.S. or the U.K., or are translations or adaptations for the English-speaking user of foreign atlases. Gives information on publisher; publishing history and revision program; editors, cartographers, and contributors; home sale and retail prices; purpose and age suitability; size and number of pages; total map pages and types of maps; scale; balance; indexing; scope, contents, and arrangement; a summary of features, strengths and weaknesses; and references to critical reviews and sources of information on the atlas. Indicates overall quality and gives graded recommendations.   Z6028.W27

Bibliography and indexes

Alexander, Gerard L. Guide to atlases : world, regional, national, thematic; an international listing of atlases published since 1950. Metuchen, N.J. : Scarecrow, 1971. 671 p. **CL224**

Atlases are listed by date, then alphabetically within four main groups: (1) world, (2) regional, (3) national, and (4) thematic. Publisher, pagination, and size in centimeters are indicated. Indexed.

————. *Guide to atlases supplement : world, regional, national, thematic* (1977. 362 p.). "An international listing of atlases published 1971 through 1975 with comprehensive indexes."—*t.p.* Includes some entries from the 1950–70 period overlooked in the basic volume. Indexed by publisher and by author/cartographer/editor.   Z6021.A43

American Geographical Society of New York. Map Dept. Index to maps in books and periodicals. Boston : G.K. Hall, 1968. 10 v. **CL225**

Photoreproduction of a card catalog maintained by the Society's Map Department. Entries are alphabetical by subject and geographical-political division.

————. *First supplement* (1971. 603 p.).

————. *Second supplement* (1976. 568 p.). Covers the period 1972–75; format remains the same.

————. *Third supplement* (1987. 668 p.). Covers 1976–86 and includes 12,200 entries, format remains the same.   Z6028.A5

Bibliographie cartographique internationale. 1938–1979. Paris : Colin, 1938–1975. **CL226**

Title varies: 1936–45, *Bibliographie cartographique française.* 1936 and 1937 published as *Suppléments au Bulletin du Comité National Français de Géographie,* 1938–39. 1938/45, 1946/47 each published in one volume. 1948– , published annually under the auspices of the Comité National Français de Géographie and the Union Géographique Internationale by M. Foncin and P. Sommer, with the aid of Unesco and the Centre national de la recherche scientifique.

Lists general, political, and topographical maps and atlases; road maps; maps of cities, etc., from all parts of the world.   Z6021.B5

Bibliotheca cartographica. Hft. 1 (1957)–30 (1972). Bonn : Bundesanstalt für Landeskunde [etc.]. Semiannual (some issues combined). **CL227**

Place of publication and name of publisher vary.

Continues *Die Kartographie 1943–1954 : eine bibliographische Übersicht* by Hans-Peter Kosack and Karl-Heinz Meine (CL232). Continued by *Bibliographia cartographica* (CL247). Issued by the Institut für Landeskunde in the Bundesanstalt für Landeskunde und Raumforschung, in cooperation with the Deutsche Gesellschaft für Kartographie.

Lists books and periodical articles on cartography in classified arrangement, including materials from several countries of Europe, South Africa, South America, and the U. S. Tables of contents and subject headings in German, English, and French.   Z6021.B55

Chubb, Thomas. Printed maps in the atlases of Great Britain and Ireland : a bibliography, 1579–1850 / by Thomas Chubb, with an introduction by F. P. Sprent and biographical notes on the map makers, engravers and publishers by T. Chubb, assisted by J. W. Skells and H. Beharrell. With numerous reproductions of title pages, etc. London : Homeland Assoc., [1927]. 479 p. : ill., maps. **CL228**

Repr.: Folkestone, Kent, Eng. : Dawson, 1977.

Contents: (1) Atlases of England and Wales; (2) of Scotland; (3) of Ireland; (4) biographical notes on the map makers, engravers, and publishers. Index.   Z6027.G7C5

Claussen, Martin Paul. Descriptive catalog of maps published by Congress : 1817–1843 / comp. by Martin P. Claussen and Herman R. Friis. Wash., 1941. 104 p. **CL229**

"This is a catalog of the 503 maps that are scattered throughout v. 1–429 of the 'Congressional series' ... 15th through the 27th Congress, between 1817 and 1843."—*Introd.*

Arranged chronologically by Congress with index to area, place-names that appear in title, names of persons, government agencies, and institutions involved in compiling the maps.   Z6027.U5C6

Great Britain. Public Record Office. Maps and plans in the Public Record Office. London : H.M.S.O., 1967–1982. 3 v. (In progress). **CL230**

Contents: [v. 1] British Isles, c.1410–1860; [v. 2] America and the West Indies; [v. 3] Africa.

A catalog of maps listed or indexed in records of the Colonial and Foreign Offices and in other classes of records retained by the Public Record Office. Geographical arrangement; descriptive notes for each map. Personal name index.   Z6028.G767

Kartograficheskaia letopis' : organ gosudarstvennoĭ bibliografii SSSR. 1931–1940, 1946– . Moskva : Vsesoiuznaia Knizhnaia Palata, 1932?– . Frequency varies. **CL231**

1931–40 and 1946, quarterly. Publication suspended 1941–45. Title for 1939 and 1940: *Bibliografiia kartograficheskoĭ literatury i kart.* Index, *Svodny ukazatel',* 1941–50, publ. 1953. Publisher varies. Some details of publishing history uncertain.

A section of the Soviet national bibliography which lists the year's output of maps and atlases (scientific, school, tourist, etc.) with full bibliographic description and annotation.   Z6021.K3

Kosack, Hans-Peter. Die Kartographie, 1943–1954 : eine bibliographische Übersicht / [von] Hans-Peter Kosack [und] Karl-Heinz Meine. Lahr-Schwarzwald : Astra Verlag, 1955. 216 p. (Kartographische Schriftenreihe, Bd. 4). **CL232**

Includes material in many languages, although German titles predominate. Lists books, periodical articles, and serial publications of societies and governments, on all phases of cartography. Classed arrangement with author index.

Continued by: *Bibliotheca cartographica* (CL227).

Library of Congress. Maps and charts of North America and the West Indies, 1750–1789 : a guide to the collections in the Library of Congress / comp. by John R. Sellers and Patricia Molen Van Ee. Wash. : Library of Congress ; for sale by U.S. Govt. Print. Off., 1981. 495 p. : ill. **CL233**

An annotated bibliography of 2,146 items, arranged by geographic area. Bibliography; index.   Z6027.N68U54

Library of Congress. Geography and Map Division. Panoramic maps of cities in the United States and Canada : a checklist of maps in the collections of the Library of Congress, Geography and Map Division / comp. by John R. Hébert. 2nd ed. / rev. by Patrick E. Dempsey. Wash. : Library of Congress ; for sale by U.S. Govt. Print. Off., 1984. 181 p. : ill. **CL234**

1st ed., 1974, had title *Panoramic maps of Anglo-American cities.*

Lists 1,726 panoramic maps of cities in 47 states, the District of Columbia, and Canada. Arranged by state, then by city. Indicates artist, publisher, lithographer or printer, and map size. Indexed.

Z6027.U5L5

Library of Congress. Geography and Map Division. Reference and Bibliography Section. Fire insurance maps in the Library of Congress : plans of North American cities and towns produced by the Sanborn Map Company : a checklist. Wash. : Library of Congress : for sale by U.S. Govt. Print. Off., 1981. 773 p. : ill.   **CL235**
A checklist of some 700,000 items in a "uniform series of large-scale maps, dating from 1867 to the present and depicting the commercial, industrial, and residential sections of some twelve thousand cities and towns in the United States, Canada, and Mexico ... an unrivaled source of information about the structure and use of buildings in American cities."—*Pref.* Arranged by country, state and town; indexed by county, city and town.   Z6026.I7U54

Library of Congress. Map Division. List of maps of America in the Library ... preceded by a list of works relating to cartography / by P. Lee Phillips. Wash. : U.S. Govt. Print. Off., 1901. 1137 p.   **CL236**
Repr. : N.Y. : B. Franklin, 1967.
Lists maps to be found in books and atlases as well as those separately issued. Describes many old state and county maps and city plans.   Z663.35.L55

———————— United States atlases : a list of national, state, county, city, and regional atlases in the Library of Congress / comp. by Clara Egli LeGear. Wash. : U.S. Govt. Print. Off., 1950–53. 2 v.   **CL237**
Repr. : N.Y. : Arno, 1971 with cover title: United States atlases in the Library of Congress.
Vol. 2 adds "and cooperating libraries" to title.
The two volumes list more than 7,000 atlases. Vol. 2 lists not only atlases received by the Library of Congress between 1949 and 1953, but also those held by some 180 other libraries. Location of copies is shown.   Z881.U5

Mickwitz, Ann-Mari. The A. E. Nordenskiöld collection in the Helsinki University Library : annotated catalogue of maps made up to 1800 / comp. by Ann–Mari Mickwitz and Leena Miekkavaara. [Helsinki] : Helsinki Univ. Library ; Atlantic Highlands, N.J. : Humanities Pr. [distributor], 1979. 1 v. : ill., maps.   **CL238**
Contents: v. 1, Atlases A–J. No more published?
The Nordenskiöld Collection is one of the world's outstanding collections of geographical and cartographic literature. "The catalogue lists all the pre-nineteenth-century maps in the ... Collection, contained in atlases, books, or as loose sheets. The facsimiles are also catalogued. ... In addition to the area depicted on each map, all the important information concerning their preparation and identification has been taken into account for cataloguing purposes."—*p.xxix.* Arranged by author or publisher, with anonymous works entered by title (or, if lacking a title, under "Collection").   Z6028.M52

National and regional atlases : a bibliographic survey (up to and including 1978) / W. Stams. [The Netherlands?] : International Cartographic Association, [1980?]. 249 p.   **CL239**
Translated from German.
Comprehensive listing, by continent or other geographic region, of approximately 2,000 atlases that meet the Association's detailed qualifications. Each listing includes language, format, contents (coded), and type (coded), in addition to bibliographic information. Bibliographies and index.   Z6021.S72

Ristow, Walter William. Guide to the history of cartography : an annotated list of references on the history of maps and map-making. Wash. : Library of Congress, 1973. 96 p.   **CL240**
Revised version of a work originally entitled *A guide to historical cartography* (1st ed., 1954; 2nd ed., 1960, repr. 1962), comp. by W. W. Ristow and Clara E. LeGear, issued by the Map Division, Library of Congress.
This is a greatly expanded edition, listing nearly 400 items on the history of maps and mapmaking (not specifically historical maps). Includes 19th- and early 20th-century references (almost entirely mono-

graphs) as well as earlier periods. Alphabetical main entry listing with index of subjects, geographical areas, and secondary authors.
Z6021.R57

Shirley, Rodney W. The mapping of the world : early printed maps, 1472–1700. London : Holland Pr., 1983. xlvi, 669 p. : ill., maps; 35 cm. (Holland Press cartographica, 9).   **CL241**
Lists, annotates, and illustrates 639 pre-18th century printed world maps, excluding Oriental works and globes, with references to about 90 lost or apochryphal titles. Chronological arrangement, with locations in major map collections and bibliographic references. Chronological charts; appendixes; index.   Z6028.S48

United States. National Archives and Records Service. Guide to cartographic records in the National Archives / [by Charlotte M. Ashby (et al.)]. Wash. : U.S. Govt. Print. Off., 1971. 444 p.   **CL242**
Offers descriptive notes on the maps and aerial photographs in the Cartographic Branch of the National Archives as of July 1, 1966. Arrangement is according to the order in which the agencies generating the records are listed in the *United States government manual* (CJ151). Detailed index.   Z6028.U575

Walsh, Jim. Maps contained in the publications of the American bibliography, 1639–1819 : an index and checklist. Metuchen, N.J. : Scarecrow, 1988. 367 p.   **CL243**
In three parts: an "index and checklist of all map separates and maps contained in books" (*Introd.*) (1) in Charles Evans's *American bibliography*, 1639–1800 (AA405), arranged by Evans numbers; (2) in Ralph R. Shaw and Richard H. Shoemaker's *American bibliography*, 1801–1819 (AA417), arranged by Shaw-Shoemaker numbers; and (3) six indexes. Indexes by date of publication, place of publication, personal or corporate name, book title, map title, and geographic name.
Z6027.U5W35

Wheat, Carl Irving. Mapping the Transmississippi West, 1540–1861. San Francisco : Inst. of Historical Cartography, 1957–63. 5 v. in 6 : maps ; 37 cm.   **CL244**
Contents: v. 1, The Spanish *Entrada* to the Louisiana Purchase, 1540–1804; v. 2, From Lewis and Clark to Frémont, 1804–1845; v. 3, From the Mexican War to the Boundary Surveys, 1846–1854; v. 4, From the Pacific Railroad surveys to the onset of the Civil War, 1855–1860; v. 5, From the Civil War to the Geological Survey, 1861–1870s (2 v.).
A beautifully produced work with detailed textual descriptions, facsimile maps, "biblio-cartographies," and references to sources. Discusses many hundreds of maps.   GA405.W5

Wheat, James Clements. Maps and charts published in America before 1800 : a bibliography / by James Clements Wheat and Christian F. Brun. Rev. ed. London : Holland Pr., c1978. 215 p. (Holland Press cartographica, 3).   **CL245**
Repr.: London : Holland Pr., 1985.
1st ed., 1969.
The "rev. ed." is merely a reprint of the 1969 ed. with the addition of a new preface followed by four additional entries. The 1985 reprint is called the 2nd rev. ed.
A bibliography "which attempts to describe the entire known cartographical contribution of the American press prior to 1800."—*Pref.* Includes maps and charts appearing in books, pamphlets, almanacs, and magazines, as well as those published separately. Z6027.U5W47

Yonge, Ena L. A catalogue of early globes made prior to 1850 and conserved in the United States : a preliminary listing. N.Y. : Amer. Geographical Soc., 1968. 118 p. (American Geographical Society. Library series, 6).   **CL246**
The first published work in a series proposed by the Committee on Ancient Cartography of the International Geographical Congress to provide a worldwide inventory of the present locations of early globes.
GA193.U5Y6

Current

Bibliographia cartographica. no. 1 (1974)– . München ; N.Y. : K.G. Saur, [1974]– .   **CL247**

Issued by Staatsbibliothek Preussischer Kulturbesitz in cooperation with the Deutsche Gesellschaft für Kartographie.

Except for structural publishing changes and a new section on school cartography, this is a continuation of *Bibliotheca cartographica* (CL227). Author index.   Z6021.B48

Bibliographic guide to maps and atlases. 1979– . Boston : G. K. Hall, [1980]–. Annual.   **CL248**

Lists selected publications cataloged during the year of coverage by the Research Libraries of the New York Public Library and the Library of Congress. Includes individual and set maps, atlases, globes, books about maps, history and study of mapmaking, techniques, computer cartography, and cartobibliographies. Journal articles and analytics covered by the New York Public Library, as well as selected articles in non-map sources, are also included. Serves as a supplement to the New York Public Library's *Dictionary catalog of the Map Division* (CL255).

Guide to USGS geologic and hydrologic maps. McLean, Va. : Documents Index, 1983. 644 p.   **CL249**

Covers maps published by the U.S. Geological Survey since 1879; entries and annotations were taken from the Survey's *Publications* lists. Arranged by series, with area, subject, and coordinate indexes. Brief descriptive annotations for some entries. A list following each section shows maps currently available and their prices.

Supersedes *Guide to United States government maps : geologic and hydrologic maps* (1975–82).   Z6034.U49G95

Library catalogs

Bancroft Library. Index to printed maps. Boston : G. K. Hall, 1964. 521 p.   **CL250**

Photographic reproductions of the catalog cards of the map collection. Library's special strengths include Mormon materials, the Catholic church in Mexico, early New Spain and California, and the pioneer West.

A supplement with about 12,000 additional entries was published 1975.

§ For the catalog of the Bancroft Library, *see* DB163.
                              Z6028.C17

British Museum. Map Room. Catalogue of printed maps, charts and plans. Photolithographic ed. complete to 1964. London : British Museum, 1967. 15 v.   **CL251**

An earlier catalog was published in 1885 in two volumes and was kept up-to-date by a series of accessions lists. This new set lists pertinent materials acquired by the British Museum through 1964, whether part of the Map Room collection or of other parts of the library.

Supplemented by:

——. ——. *Corrections and additions* (London : The Museum, 1968. 55 p., alternate pages blank) chiefly adds cross-references. Post-1964 imprints are not included.

——. ——. *Ten year supplement, 1965–1974* (London : British Museum Publications, 1978). 1380 columns) contains entries for "(a) maps, atlases, globes and related materials, including literature on them, acquired by the Map Library during 1965–1974, and (b) the more important cartographic materials in other collections of the Department of Printed Books and of the Department of Oriental Manuscripts and Printed Books of the British Library Reference Division catalogued during the same period."—*Pref.* The first in a projected series of ten-year supplements.

Catalogue of cartographic materials in the British Library, 1975–1988 (London ; New York : Saur, 1989). "The British Library Catalogue of Cartographic Materials contains bibliographic records for atlases, single-sheet maps, map series, maritime charts, plans, globes and related reference materials acquired by the British Library Map Library since 1974."—*Explanatory note.* Includes records for current map accessions to the Manuscripts Collection and for remote-sensing and digital cartographic databases throughout the U.K. Vols. 1–2 contain the author/title index, v. 3 the geographic names and subject indexes.   Z6028.B863

Library of Congress. Library of Congress catalog : a cumulative list of works represented by Library of Congress printed cards. Maps and atlases. Wash., 1953–55. 3 v.   **CL252**

Contains entries for maps, relief models, globes, and geographical atlases, received by the Library of Congress and other American libraries participating in the cooperative cataloging program, insofar as these works are represented by Library of Congress printed cards. Arrangement is alphabetical by geographical area, with name and subject indexes.

Before 1953 and after 1955, entries are included in the *National union catalog* and its predecessors.

NUC. Cartographic materials [microform]. (Wash. : The Library, 1983– .) Issued in sections: Register, name index, LC subject index, LC series index, Title index, and Geographic classification code index. Each issue of indexes cumulates previous issues which may be discarded; issues of the Register are continuous and should be retained.
                              Z881.A1C327

Library of Congress. Geography and Map Division. The bibliography of cartography. Boston : G.K. Hall, 1973. 5 v.   **CL253**

Reproduces the cards from a file maintained in the Geography and Map Division, containing some 90,000 entries relating to maps, mapmakers, and the history of cartography.

——. ——. *First supplement* (Boston : G.K. Hall, 1980. 2 v. [1028 p.]). Adds about 21,500 entries, including new articles from 275 periodicals in cartography, geography, and library science, as well as a collection of approximately 4,000 pamphlets, offprints and reprints.
                              Z6028.U49

Library of Congress. Map Division. A list of geographical atlases in the Library of Congress, with bibliographical notes. Wash. : U.S. Govt. Print. Off., 1909–1992. 9 v.   **CL254**

Contents: v. 1, Titles 1–3265 (1909); v. 2, Author list and index (1909); v. 3, Titles 3266–4087 (acquired 1909–14) (1914); v. 4, Titles 4088–5324 (acquired 1914–20) (1920); v. 5, Titles 5325–7623 (acquired 1920–55) (1958); v. 6, Titles 7624–10254 (acquired 1920–60) (1963); v. 7, Titles 10255–18435 (acquired 1920–69) (1973); v. 8, Index to v.7 (1974); v. 9, comprehensive author list (1992).

An important catalog of an outstanding collection which includes many rare and early atlases. Vols. 1–4 form the record of 5,324 atlases in the Library of Congress in 1920, giving for each full description and contents. Vol. 2 is an index volume containing an author list and a detailed analytical index referring to all maps listed in the contents notes. Vols. 3–4 are supplements to the main work, listing new acquisitions, each containing an author list and an analytical index. The author list in v. 4 cumulates, combining the author lists to vols. 1–4, and is also published separately (1920. clxiii p.).

Vols. 5–6 bring forward the record with the same minute detail: v. 5 lists world atlases acquired 1920–55; v. 6 describes atlases of Europe, Asia, Africa and Oceania, the polar regions and the oceans, and includes some 800 Oriental atlases, mainly Chinese, Japanese, and Korean. Each includes full tables of contents for atlases published before 1820 and for some miscellaneous volumes published later; an author list; and a detailed analytical index to areas, subjects, maps, engravers, publishers, etc. Vol. 7 describes atlases of the Western hemisphere received in the Library of Congress between 1920 and 1969 (excluding atlases published after 1967). Vol. 8 is an index to v. 7. Vol. 9 is a comprehensive author index to the 18,435 atlases described in v. 1–8.
                              Z6028.U56

New York Public Library. Map Division. Dictionary catalog of the Map Division. Boston : G.K. Hall, 1971. 10 v.   **CL255**

Lists about 280,000 sheet maps, 11,000 volumes on cartography, periodical articles, and bibliographies, and some 6,000 atlases (with many analytics for atlases published before 1800). Also includes manuscript maps in the Manuscript Division, early printed maps in the Rare Book Division, and the Phelps Stokes American Historical Views in the Prints Division.

Updated by: *Bibliographic guide to maps and atlases* (CL248).

Lists selected publications cataloged during the year of coverage by the Research Libraries of the New York Public Library and the Library of Congress. Includes individual and set maps, atlases, globes, books about maps, history and study of mapmaking, techniques, computer cartography, and cartobibliographies. Journal articles and analytics covered by the New York Public Library, as well as selected articles in nonmap sources, are also included.   Z6028.N58

Directories

Cobb, David A. Guide to U.S. map resources / comp. by David A. Cobb ; regional editors, Brent Allison ... [et al.]. 2nd ed. Chicago : Amer. Libr. Assoc., 1990. 495 p.   **CL256**
1st ed., 1986.

Provides directory and access information, size, holdings and collection strengths for 974 U.S. map collections at a wide variety of institutions: academic, geoscience, private, public and governmental. Entries are arranged alphabetically by state, then by city and institution. 13 tables for collection size, classification systems, preservation techniques, public access policies, equipment and staff, and collection strengths. Three appendixes list addresses for federal and state mapping and cartographic information agencies. Indexes by library/institution, collection strengths, and personal names.   GA193.U5C62

Ehrenberg, Ralph E. Scholars' guide to Washington, D.C. for cartography and remote sensing imagery : (maps, charts, aerial photographs, satellite images, cartographic literature, and geographic information systems) / Ralph E. Ehrenberg ; ed., Zdeněk V. David. Wash. : Smithsonian Institution Pr., 1987. 385 p. (Scholars' guide to Washington, D.C., no. 12).   **CL257**

Provides comprehensive information on location, collections, organization and accessibility for institutions in Washington, D.C. metropolitan area. Arranges 180 sources of cartographic information in 11 sections, four for research collections and seven for organizations. The entry for each source includes address and telephone, number of volumes, scope of collections, and hours of service; additional information may include collection history, facilities description, special events, and access information. Contains six appendixes, five indexes, and short bibliography. Three appendixes provide information on Map stores; Housing, transportation, and other services; and Federal government holidays. Indexes include personal names, subjects, geographic headings (one each for maps and remote sensing imagery), and names of organizations and institutions.   GA193.U5E37

International directory of tactile map collections / Frank Kurt Cylke, Judith M. Dixon, managing editors. [The Hague, Netherlands?] : Section of Libraries for the Blind, International Federation of Library Associations and Institutions ; [Wash.] : National Library Service for the Blind and Physically Handicapped. Library of Congress, 1985. 19 p.   **CL258**

The first international directory describing collections of maps intended for the visually handicapped. Arranged alphabetically by country, then city; organizations are listed alphabetically under city. Entry includes address of institution, description of collections, and availability of maps, whether for sale or for loan. Alphabetical list of organizations.   GA135.I57

Map collections in the United States and Canada : a directory / David K. Carrington and Richard W. Stephenson, editors. 4th ed. N.Y. : Special Libraries Assoc., 1985. 178 p.   **CL259**

A project of the Geography and Map Division, Special Libraries Association.

1st ed., 1954.

Describes 804 map collections in the U.S. and Canada. Arranged alphabetically by city within states or provinces. For each collection gives: name, staffing level, size of collection and annual accessions, area and subject specialization, dates, special collections, depository status, clientele, service facilities, and publications. Indexed.   GA193.U5M36

Sheppard's international directory of print and map sellers / [comp. by Yvonne Eshelby]. 2nd ed. Farnham, Surrey : R. Joseph, 1992. 444 p.   **CL260**
1st ed., 1987.

Data supplied from questionnaires distributed through trade associations. More than 1,600 entries, 863 with full replies. Introductory information also in French, German, Italian, and Spanish. Full entries are listed alphabetically by country, then by city or town. Entry includes access information (postal and telecommunications), hours, stock, and speciality. Indexed by business, proprietors, and subject specialty.   GA102.25.S477

World directory of map collections / comp. by the Section of Geography and Map Libraries ; ed. by Lorraine Dubreuil. 3rd ed. Münich ; N.Y. : K.G. Saur, 1993. 405 p. (IFLA publications, 63).   **CL261**
1st ed., 1976; 2nd ed., 1986.

A directory of major map collections as of 1991–92 containing 522 entries from 67 countries. Lists "national libraries and archives, principal geographical, cartographical and historical society and institute collections, the collections of military geographical institutes or departments, and all other map collections, archives, or libraries of special significance."—*Pref., 2nd ed.* More selective for countries with published national directories of map collections (Australia, Canada, Federal Republic of Germany, France, Netherlands, U.K., U.S.). Detailed information on each collection lists location, person responsible, size, reference services, access policies, reproduction facilities, classification, specializations, and publications.   GA192.W67

Handbooks

Cartographical innovations : an international handbook of mapping terms to 1900 / ed. by Helen M. Wallis and Arthur H. Robinson. [Tring, Herts.] : publ. by Map Collector Publications in association with the International Cartographic Association, 1987. 353 p. : ill.   **CL262**

"Documents a wealth of innovative ideas and concepts which led to the advance of the art, craft and science of mapmaking in the past. The book covers all aspects of the field ranging from types of maps to concepts and from techniques of production to those of symbolization."—*Foreword.* International in scope. Contains 191 entries in eight sections: Types of maps; Maps of human occupation and activities; Maps of natural phenomena; Reference systems and geodetic concepts; Symbolism; Techniques and media; Methods of duplication; and Atlases. Entries are alphabetical within section; each entry includes a definition (citing *Multilingual dictionary of technical terms in cartography* [Wiesbaden : F. Steiner, c1973] where appropriate), a description of its innovative aspects, and bibliographical references. 25 black-and-white photographs illustrate significant entries. General index.   GA102.2.C37

Clark, Suzanne M. Cartographic citations : a style guide / by Suzanne M. Clark, Mary Lynette Larsgaard and Cynthia M. Teague. Chicago : Map and Geography Round Table, Amer. Libr. Assoc., 1992. 23 p. (MAGERT circular, no. 1).   **CL263**

"This guide provides assistance on how to cite—other than a detailed cartobibliography—cartographic materials of all formats; this includes printed and computer-generated maps, three-dimensional models, remote-sensing imagery, diagrams, globes, profiles, sections, views, and atlases, whether commercially or governmentally published."—*Introd.* Includes an "Explanation of map citation elements" and a glossary. Index.

Larsgaard, Mary Lynette. Map librarianship : an introduction. 2nd ed. Littleton, Colo. : Libraries Unlimited, 1987. 382 p. : ill. **CL264**
1st ed., 1978.
Treats all forms of cartographic materials (maps, atlases, diagrams, globes, models, profiles, sections, views, and remote sensing imagery). Much changed and enlarged from previous edition.
Z692.M3L37

Manual of federal geographic data products / Federal Geographic Data Committee ; information provided by U.S. Dept. of Agriculture ... [et al.] ; comp. under contract for Office of Information Resources Management, U.S. Environmental Protection Agency. Reston, Va. : The Committee, 1992. 1 v. (looseleaf) : ill., maps. **CL265**
"Describes Federal geographic data products that are national in scope and commonly distributed to the public. Geographic data products include maps, digital data, aerial photography and multispectral imagery, earth science, and other geographically-referenced data sets."—*Pref.* Organized by federal agency; for each data set, includes data product keywords, summary explanation, extent of program, available product coverage, information content, product delivery format, and ordering information. All information current to January 1993. GA406.M36

The map catalog : every kind of map and chart on earth and even some above it / Joel Makower, ed., Cathryn Poff, Laura Bergheim, assoc. editors. 3rd ed., newly rev. N.Y. : Random House, c1992. 364 p. : ill.; some maps in color ; 26 cm. **CL266**
1st ed., 1986; 2nd ed., 1990.
A compilation of "information about the many types of maps available, the major sources of each map type, and descriptions or examples of the map products available from each source."—*About this book.* Chapters include Travel maps; Maps of specific areas; Boundary maps; Scientific maps; History through maps; Utility and service maps; Water maps; Sky maps; Images as maps; and Atlases and globes. Includes information on map accessories, software and organizations. Numerous illustrations, some in color, provide examples of each type of map. Contains cross-references and a comprehensive index. Four appendixes list addresses for state and federal map agencies, map stores, and libraries. Z6028.M23

Permanent Committee on Geographical Names for British Official Use. Glossaries. London : House of the Royal Geographical Society, 1942–1954. 8 v. **CL267**
Contents: v. 1, Modern Greek (1942); v. 2, Russian (1942); v. 3, Albanian (1943); v. 4, Serbo-Croat and Slovene (1943); v. 5, Romanian (1944); v. 6, Thai (Siamese) (1944); v. 7, Turkish (1945); v. 8, Japanese (1954). Titles in series also cataloged separately.
Glossaries not of place-names but of words, abbreviations, and contractions found on official maps, charts, and geographical texts of the country concerned, with transliteration (if from a nonroman alphabet), meaning, and application.
§ More countries were covered, but much more briefly, in a series of *Short glossaries* published by the General Staff, Geographical Section, War Office (G.S.G.S.), 1943–45 in 23 numbers. G108.A1P4

Thompson, Morris Mordecai. Maps for America : cartographic products of the U.S. Geological Survey and others. 3rd ed. Reston, Va. : U.S. Geological Survey, 1987. 265 p. : ill. (some col.). **CL268**
1st ed., 1979; 2nd ed., 1981.
Offers detailed descriptions of kinds of maps and map data, as well as various sources of maps and related information, which are available from U. S. government agencies. "The third edition ... is intended primarily to replenish the supply of copies of the book, but it also contains a number of changes to correct or update the text."—*Foreword.* The most significant changes occur in sections on digital cartographic data. Glossary and bibliographic references; index.
GA405.T46

World mapping today / [ed. by] R.B. Parry, C.R. Perkins ; graphic indexes prepared by Cartographic Unit, Department of Geography, Portsmouth Polytechnic, U.K. London ; Boston : Butterworths, 1987. 583 p. : maps. **CL269**
Systematically lists maps (primarily series), atlases and gazetteers of the world and its continents and countries. Introductory matter treats the state of world mapping, map acquisition, map evaluation, maps and remote sensing, digital mapping, and future trends in digital mapping. Entries are arranged by continent then listed alphabetically by country. Each country entry includes a brief description of that country's mapping activities, addresses of mapping agencies, and bibliographies of maps, atlases, and other cartographic sources available as of approximately 1984–86. Does not include commercial road and tourist maps. 122 graphic indexes to major series. Brief glossary, geographical index, and publishers index. GA105.3.W67

Yearbooks

International yearbook of cartography = Annuaire international de cartographie = Internationales Jahrbuch für Kartographie. 1 (1961)– . Ulm [etc.] : Universitätsverlag Ulm GmbH [etc.]. Annual. **CL270**
Issued under the auspices of the International Cartographic Association, 1965–87.
Publishes review articles on historical, methodological and technical aspects of cartography and mapping. Articles are primarily in German or English; summaries are in German, English and French. Many extensive bibliographies. Cumulative index, 1961–81.
GA101.I55

World cartography. v. 1 (1951)– . N.Y. : United Nations, Dept. of Social Affairs, [1951]– . Irregular. **CL271**
Frequency and issuing agency vary; annual, 1951–55.
Annual summary of world mapping activity. Updates the status of topographic and cadastral mapping projects and satellite mapping technology. Also includes statistics on budgets and staffing of national mapping programs. GA101.W6

Biography

Bonacker, Wilhelm. Kartenmacher aller Länder und Zeiten. Stuttgart : A. Hiersemann, 1966. 243 p. **CL272**
Lists mapmakers from all countries and periods, giving dates, place, and special field of activity. Reference is provided to standard biographical sources where possible. Z6021.B69

Karrow, Robert W. Mapmakers of the sixteenth century and their maps : biobibliographies of the cartographers of Abraham Ortelius, 1570 : based on Leo Bagrow's A. Ortelii Catalogus cartographorum. Chicago : Publ. for the Newberry Library by Speculum Orbis Pr., 1993. 846 p. : maps. **CL273**
Originally planned as an English-language edition of Leo Bagrow's *A. Ortelii Catalogus cartographorum* (Gotha : J. Perthes, 1928–1930. 2 v.), this work significantly expands and extends the original research to include lengthy biographical essays of 88 cartographers with detailed cartobibliographical information on more than some 2,000 maps. Illustrated by 23 maps, many reproduced for the first time. Comprehensive bibliography of more than some 2,000 references; general index to personal names, plates, subjects and map titles. GA198.K37

Tooley, Ronald Vere. Tooley's dictionary of mapmakers. N.Y. : A.R. Liss ; Amsterdam : Meridian Publ. Co., 1979. 684 p. : ill. **CL274**
"Originally, the first half of the work appeared in parts in *Map Collectors' Circle*, which has now been discontinued."—*Foreword.*
Gives brief information on persons concerned with production of maps from earliest times to 1900. Aims to give for each: "name, dates of birth and death (whenever known), titles of honour (if any), working

addresses and changes of addresses, … main output of maps or atlases, with dates wherever known."—*Foreword.* Many entries provide only title and date of a published work.

———. *Supplement* (N.Y. : A.R. Liss, c1985. 116 p.), adds approximately 4,000 names.   GA198.T66

Regional and National

World

Akademii͡a nauk SSSR. Fiziko-geograficheskii atlas mira / Red. koll. I. P. Gerasimov i dr. Moskva, 1964. 289 p. : maps in color; 51 cm.   **CL275**
249 colored plates are supplemented by explanatory text. Includes relief and physical maps: geology, meteorology, hydrology, soil, vegetation, zoology, etc. Plates 2–76 contain maps of the world, the Arctic, and the Antarctic; 78–190, the continents; 192–249, U.S.S.R.
§ Legends and explanatory text have been published as *Soviet geography : review and translation. Physical-geographic atlas of the world.* (Moscow, 1964; N.Y. : American Geographical Society, 1965. 403 p. [A.G.S. Special issue of May–June 1965]).
"A translation of the legend matter and explanatory text of the *Fiziko–Geograficheskiy Atlas Mira …*"—p.1.

Centre d'Études de Géographie Tropicale. Atlas des départements français d'outre-mer / Réalisé par le Centre de Géographie Tropicale du C.N.R.S., Bordeaux-Talence …. Paris : Institut géographique national, 1975–1979. 4 v. : ill., maps ; 49 x 59 cm.   **CL276**
Contents: v. 1, La Réunion; v. 2, La Martinique; v. 3, La Guadeloupe; v. 4, La Guyane.
Comprehensive atlases of French overseas departments.
                                                            G1835.C4

Esselte kartor (Firm). Earth book world atlas. Boulder, Colo. : Graphic Learning International Pub., c1987. 327 p. : ill. (some col.), maps in color ; 34 cm.   **CL277**
In three sections: Encyclopedia of the earth, The world in maps, Index. The heavily illustrated encyclopedia section presents current topics from the physical and biological sciences clustered around environmental themes of air, water, earth and fire. World in maps section covers regions, not individual states and countries; a new mapping technique depicts landscape, especially vegetation, as the map base rather than the more traditional political or relief base. The index includes approximately 57,000 place names; brief glossary.
                                                            G1021.E784

Goode, J. Paul. Goode's world atlas / ed., Edward B. Espenshade, Jr. ; sr. consultant, Joel L. Morrison. 18th ed., rev. Chicago : Rand McNally, c1993. 367 p. : maps in color ; 29 cm.   **CL278**
Formerly *Goode's school atlas*, first publ. 1923. Frequently revised. 17th ed., 1986.
Emphasizes physical and political maps, and maps showing resources and products. Thematic maps include information on the world economic situation, U.S. health and economic conditions, ethnic situation in the Middle East and Caribbean, etc. List of source materials; glossary of foreign geographical terms. The U.S. is given by sections but not by individual states. Maps of environs. Index by subject to thematic maps; an index of more than 30,000 names indicates pronunciation and coordinates.   G1021.G6

Hammond Inc. Hammond world atlases. Maplewood, N.J. : Hammond, [1982, etc.]. [various paginations].   **CL279**
Over the years the Hammond Company has published a number of series of reputable atlases of varying size and content, and using some of the same titles to distinguish the different versions (e.g., an *Ambassador world atlas* first appeared in 1954). In 1982 the Hammond series included *Gold medallion, Ambassador, International*, and *Citation* volumes.

In addition to general updating of information, several innovations of the 1970s distinguish the atlases from their predecessors: a smaller page size (recommending the volumes for more convenient home and office use), the inclusion of postal zip code numbers for U.S. communities, and (in the larger volumes) three new sections of historical maps representing biblical, world, and U.S. history. There is also a section entitled Environment and life. As in the earlier editions, an index with population figures (incorporating 1980 census data for the U.S., as well as for Mexico, the Soviet Union, and the Democratic Republic of the Congo) accompanies each political map. There is also an index of more than 100,000 names for the world map section; U.S. zip codes appear in both indexes. Small topographical maps, reproductions of flags, and tables of salient facts about each country are provided with the political maps. Despite the smaller page size, maps of all but the largest and most populous political units are fairly uncluttered, legible, and generally attractive.

Kidron, Michael. The new state of the world atlas / Michael Kidron and Ronald Segal. 4th ed. N.Y. : Simon & Schuster, c1991. 159 p. : ill. ; maps in color ; 25 cm.   **CL280**
1st ed., 1981, had title: *The state of the world atlas*; 2nd ed., rev. and updated, 1987.
A graphic presentation of major topics of popular concern—the proliferation of nations and their claims on resources, the military situation, natural resources, government, business, labor, societal problems, the environment, protest movements and crises. Information sources and notes are provided for each of the 65 colored double-page maps. Subject index.   G1021.K46

Maps on file. N.Y. : Facts on File, c1981– . 2 v. (loose-leaf) : maps ; 30 cm.   **CL281**
A collection of approximately 450 maps designed for easy photocopying. In 14 sections arranged by continent, theme (demography, resources, economic, social, etc.), historical period, or type (e.g., outline maps). Index; annual supplements.   G1046.A1M16

Martin Greenwald Associates. Historical maps on file. N.Y. : Facts on File, c1984. 1 v. [looseleaf]) : 30 cm.   **CL282**
The 323 black-and-white maps were designed to be photocopied, hence are very simple, without much detail, and concentrate on depicting one aspect of historical development. Maps vary in size from about 6 ¼ x 4 ½ in. to 6 x 8 ½ in., and cover from the Ice Age to after the Korean War. Arranged in nine main sections: Ancient civilizations; Europe to 1500; Europe, 1500–1815; Europe, 1815 to the present; U.S.; Western hemisphere; Africa and the Middle East; Asia; Australia. 29-page index for geographical names.
§ *Time lines on file* (N.Y. : Facts on File, 1988. 300 p.), another looseleaf service, has about 200 charts giving time lines in world, European and American history, with separate displays for religion and ideas, culture and the arts, and science and technology.   G1030.M37

Meyers grosser Weltatlas / hrsg. vom Geographisch-Kartographischen Institut Meyer unter Leitung von Adolf Hanle. 4th rev. & enl. ed. Mannheim : Bibliographisches Institut, 1985. 624 p.   **CL283**
3rd ed., 1979.
A new work designed to accompany the *Meyers enzyklopädisches Lexikon* (AB52) and designated as Bd. 27 of that work. Includes both political and physical maps in color (many of them folded) and an extensive index. The maps offer a wealth of detail, but unfortunately the numerous double-page spreads do not lie flat, and a great deal is lost at the inner margin.   G1021.M26

National Geographic Society. National Geographic atlas of the world. Rev. 6th ed. Wash. : National Geographic Society, 1992. (133, 136 p.) : col. ill., maps in color ; 47 cm.   **CL284**
1st ed., 1963; 6th ed. first issued 1990.
Well-drawn maps based on those produced for the *National geographic magazine.* Well balanced in coverage between the U.S. and the rest of the world, with maps by area rather than by state or country. While some maps have a crowded appearance, they are legible and generally up-to-date. Includes a fold-out map of the world using the re-

cently adopted Robinson projection, and a number of spacecraft images of the earth and the planets. Indexes more than 150,000 place names.   G1021.N38

The New York times atlas of the world. 3rd rev. concise ed. (3rd U.S. ed.). N.Y. : Times Books, 1992. 43, 244 p. : maps in color ; 39 cm.   **CL285**

1st ed., 1972; 2nd ed., 1988.

A version of *The Times atlas*, "Comprehensive edition," reduced both in size and content. Maps by J. Bartholomew; physical earth maps by Duncan Mackay. "Originally published in Great Britain as *The Times atlas of the world: concise edition*, sixth edition in 1992"—*t.p. verso.*   G1019.N57

Oxford University Press. The new Oxford atlas / prep. by the Cartographic Dept. of the Oxford Univ. Pr. Rev. ed. Oxford : Oxford Univ. Pr., 1978. 202 p. : ill., maps ; 39 cm.   **CL286**

1st ed. (1951, frequently reprinted with revisions), entitled *The Oxford atlas*.

Termed "a development rather than a straightforward second edition" (*Pref.*), the work "retains the scales, projections, sheet lines, and general colouring of its topographic maps, whilst incorporating complete revision of all information liable to change and a re-styling of certain elements of map design in the interests of greater clarity. Its thematic or special subject maps, which are particularly concerned with the basic aspects of physical geography and demography, incorporate the results of modern research and latest available information and are presented by newly-evolved cartographic techniques." Index of towns and topographical features shown on the maps (plus, in italics, some historical place-names not shown but located by reference to places shown on the maps).   G1021.O9

Peters, Arno. Peters atlas of the world / cartography, Kümmerly + Frey [and] Oxford Cartographers. N.Y. : Harper & Row, 1990. 188, [39] p. : ill. (some col.), maps in color ; 35 cm.   **CL287**

Includes 43 shaded-relief and 246 thematic maps. Relief is shown with a combination of shading, spot heights, and photography of relief models; color indicates vegetation, not relief. Thematic maps cover the usual subjects (Precipitation, Languages, Economic growth) and some not so usual (The direction of writing, Monogamy/polygamy, a series on Sport). Lists sources of data used in thematic section. Maps use an equal area representation (Peters projection); illustrates areal significance of equatorial regions. Index includes both local and relevant English forms of place names.   G1021.P4

Rand McNally and Company. The new cosmopolitan world atlas. Census/environmental ed., rev. ed. Chicago : Rand McNally, c1992. 36 p., 304 p. : ill., maps in color; 39 cm.   **CL288**

1st ed., 1949; 1965, 1966, and 1967 editions had title *Rand McNally new cosmopolitan world atlas*; 1981 ed. had title *Rand McNally cosmopolitan world atlas.*

Cartography by Michael W. Dobson … [et al.].

In this atlas the world has been mapped on a regional basis, centered around a major country or group of countries, with a special preliminary section on the world's environment. Maps are clear and up-to-date. Includes maps for individual states of the U.S. and the Canadian provinces, with small insets for areas of large cities. There is also a special section of world metropolitan area maps. Special tables include world political information by country, tables of distances, list of principal lakes, rivers, islands, etc. Economic and historical maps appearing in some earlier editions of the *Cosmopolitan* atlas are omitted here.   G1021.R35

—————— The new international atlas = Der neue internationale Atlas = El nuevo atlas internacional = Le nouvel atlas international = O nôvo atlas internacional. 25th anniversary ed. Chicago : Rand McNally, c1994. [320, 200 p.] : col. ill., maps in color ; 39 cm.   **CL289**

Issued regularly; previous ed., 1993.

In the interest of wide international usage, the metric system is employed, and there is strong emphasis on the local language for geographic names throughout, with English used only for names of major features extending across international borders. Maps were designed as components of five series: (1) continents portrayed in natural colors at 1:24,000,000; (2) political maps of major regions of the world, at 1:12,000,000; (3) inhabited areas of the earth at 1:6,000,000 or 1:3,000,000, depending on population density; (4) key regions of the world at 1:1,000,000; and (5) major urban areas at 1:300,000. Map sequences follow from world to metropolitan maps; individual map layouts depict geographic and economic regions rather than individual countries. Concluding portion of the atlas offers a series of thematic maps, glossary, tables of geographic changes, population of cities and towns, and an index of 160,000 names. Maps are exceptionally clear and easy to interpret.   G1021.R23

Rand McNally atlas of the oceans. N.Y. : Rand McNally, c1977. 208 p. : ill., maps ; 38 cm.   **CL290**

For annotation, *see* EF224.   GC11.2.R35

Stieler, Adolf. Stieler's atlas of modern geography : 263 maps on 114 sheets, engraved on copper. 10th ed. International ed. / publ. by Dr. Hermann Haack, with the cooperation of Dr. Berthold Carlberg and Rudolf Schleifer. Gotha : Perthes, 1934–1938. 34 pts. : maps in color ; 41 cm.   **CL291**

One of the best of the prewar German atlases. This edition appeared in parts and was to have been completed in some 114 sheets. It was a thorough revision—with addition of various, entirely new sheets—of the 10. Aufl. of *Stieler's Handatlas* (1931/32), which included 108 sheets of maps, most of them double spreads, and an index of 337 pages. In the International edition, the maps are in the language of the country mapped; explanatory notes, etc., are in English, French, German, Italian, Portuguese, and Spanish. Also published with French title.

The Times atlas of the world. Mid-century ed. / ed. by John Bartholomew. London : Times Pub. Co., 1955–1959. 5 v. : maps in color; 50cm.   **CL292**

Earlier ed., 1920.

A thoroughly revised edition of a famous atlas designed for general, official, and library use. Gives as many place-names as possible, preferably in the form of spelling officially used by the inhabitants of a given country. "In the case of important places where English practice has familiarized an alternative form of the name" (*Pref., v. 3*), this is also shown, in brackets, both forms appearing in the index. Elevation is shown by color tints. Main roads, airports, etc., are indicated.

Each volume covers a different section of the world, and each has its own index-gazetteer: v. 1, World, Australasia and East Asia (1958); v. 2, Southwest Asia and Russia (1959); v. 3, Northern Europe (1955); v. 4, Southern Europe and Africa (1956); v. 5, The Americas (1957). Although dated, continues to be a useful source.   G1019.T52

—————— 9th comprehensive ed. N.Y. : Times Books, 1992. xlvii, 221 p. : col. ill., maps in color ; 46 cm.   **CL293**

Repr. with revisions, 1994.

1st ed., 1967; 8th ed., 1990.

Published simultaneously in Canada by Random House, Toronto.

Offers 47 pages of prefatory information; graphic size comparisons of continents, oceans, river drainage basins, islands, and inland water bodies; eight pages of world thematic mapping; and an index that includes more than 210,000 place names and continues to provide latitude and longitude coordinates.   G1021.T55

Touring Club Italiano. Atlante internazionale del Touring Club Italiano. 8. ed. Milan : Touring club italiano, 1968. 300 p. : maps in color ; 50 cm.   **CL294**

Repr., 1977, 1978.

"Opera redatta … sotto la direzione di Luigi V. Bertarelli, Olinto Marinelli, Petro Corbellini. Nuova edizione interamente rielaborata a cura di Manilio Castiglioni e Sandro Toniolo."—*verso of t.p.*

1st ed., 1927; 5th ed., 1938.

One of the finest of the European atlases, devoted to physical and political geography. Most of the maps are double-page spreads, hinged so that they lie flat and nothing is lost at the inner margin; some have an additional fold-out section. Maps are beautifully produced, include great detail, and have insets for major metropolitan areas. Place-names are in the spelling of the country concerned.

————. ————. *Indice dei nomi* (Milan, 1968. 1032 p.) indexes some 250,000 names from the atlas.   G1019.T6

The World book atlas. Chicago : World Book, 1994. 288, 144 p. : ill., maps in color ; 38 cm.   **CL295**

First published 1964; frequently reprinted with minor updating. Maps by Rand McNally & Company.

Designed as a complement to the *World book encyclopedia of people and places* (AB22), and planned for student use. Arranged by large groupings; under each has physical, political, and historical maps. Individual maps for states of the United States. Population tables are followed by a general index, which includes place-names, islands, rivers, mountains, etc. Maps and index are essentially the same as *Goode's world atlas* (CL278).   G1019.R5285

World ocean atlas / ed. by Sergei Georgievich Gorshkov. Oxford ; N.Y. : Pergamon, 1976–83. 3 v. : maps ; 46 cm. **CL296**

For annotation, *see* EF226.

North America

United States

Andriot, John L. Township atlas of the United States. McLean, Va. : Documents Index, c1991. 1508 p. : 29 cm.   **CL297**

1st ed., 1977; [3rd ed.], 1987.

"The purpose of this volume is to provide a handy atlas showing the named townships which exist today, their relative size and location within the county, and a detailed index to the 46,900 townships…"— *Foreword*. Includes information from the 1980 census. Each section on a particular state contains a state map showing all counties with a county location index, and a state name index of all incorporated places and unincorporated places of 1,000 or more population, giving the name of the county where each is located. County maps, which show subdivisions, are alphabetically arranged within each state section. Includes a seven-page explanation of the Public Land Surveys. Does not include Alaska or Hawaii. The township index, which includes incorporated and unincorporated place names, concludes the volume.

    G1201.F7A5

Geological Survey (U.S.). The national atlas of the United States of America / [Arch C. Gerlach, ed.]. Wash., 1970. 417 p. : maps in color ; 49 cm.   **CL298**

An impressive work "designed to be of practical use to decision makers in government and business, planners, research scholars, and others needing to visualize countrywide distributional patterns and relationships between environmental phenomena and human activities."—*Introd*. In plan and progress for more than 20 years, the work was produced with the cooperation and assistance of 84 federal agencies and bureaus.

Includes 765 maps, many of them double-page spreads, presenting in cartographic format "the principal characteristics of the country, including its physical features, historical evolution, economic activities, socio-cultural conditions, administrative subdivisions, and place in world affairs." Sources of information represented on the special subject maps are indicated either on the map itself or in an introductory note. Index of 41,000 entries for names of political entities, populated places, and physical and cultural features appearing on the maps. Although dated, continues to be a useful resource.   G1200.U57

A guide to Civil War maps in the National Archives. Wash. : National Archives, National Archives and Records Administration, 1986. 139 p. : ill.   **CL299**

1st ed., 1964, had title: *Civil War maps in the National Archives*.

Lists about 8,000 Civil War maps, charts, and plans housed in the Cartographic and Architectural Branch of the National Archives. Pt. 1 describes all maps by Record Group number. Pt. 2 deals with maps of "exceptional interest" (*p. 73*); these are arranged by state and are described in more detail. Added to this edition are maps of Record Group 109, War Department Collection of Confederate Records. Index for place names and for cartographers.   Z1242.G85

Historical atlas and chronology of county boundaries, 1788–1980 / John H. Long, ed. Boston : G. K. Hall, 1984. 5 v. : maps ; 29cm.   **CL300**

Produced in cooperation with the Hermon Dunlap Smith Center for the History of Cartography, the Newberry Library.

Contents: v. 1, Delaware, Maryland, New Jersey, Pennsylvania; v. 2, Illinois, Indiana, Ohio; v. 3, Michigan, Wisconsin; v. 4, Iowa, Missouri; v. 5, Minnesota, North Dakota, South Dakota.

For each state provides a chronology of county boundary developments, followed by maps of individual counties and chronology of that county's boundary changes; bibliographies. Regional history maps show development of county boundaries every ten years.

    G1201.F7H47

Library of Congress. Geography and Map Division. Civil War maps : an annotated list of maps and atlases in the Library of Congress / comp. by Richard W. Stephenson. 2nd ed. Wash. : Library of Congress, 1989. 410 p. : maps (some col.).   **CL301**

For annotation, *see* DB122.   Z6027.U5L5

Martin Greenwald Associates. State maps on file. N.Y. : Facts on File, [1984]. 7 v. : maps. 30cm.   **CL302**

Contents: [v. 1] New England; [v. 2] Mid-Atlantic; [v. 3] Southeast; [v. 4] Midwest; [v. 5] Mountain and prairie; [v. 6] Southwest; [v. 7] West.

Scales vary widely. For each state, maps generally illustrate county and legislative district boundaries, topographic areas, rivers and waterways, precipitation, agricultural and mineral products, population density, historical Indian tribes, early exploration and settlement. There is great variation in the historical maps. Volumes are sold separately or as a set.   G1200.F3

Mattson, Mark T. Atlas of the 1990 census. N.Y. : Macmillan, c1992. 168 p. : col. ill., maps in color ; 32 x 26 cm.

    CL303

"The Atlas of the 1990 census is divided into six parts—population, households, housing, race and ethnicity, economy, and education. These sections are followed by regional county locator maps, a Metro Fact Finder, and a glossary of census terms."—*Introd*. Clear, concise color maps at the state, regional and national level. Supplemented by tables and charts. Source of the map data is the 1990 Census of Population and Housing STF-1A.   G1201.E2M3

Rand McNally and Company. Rand McNally commercial atlas and marketing guide. 114th ed. (1983)– . N.Y. : Rand McNally, 1983– . Annual; maps in color ; 54 cm.   **CL304**

Date appears in title.

Maps are indexed individually by state. Index entries include information on population, administration, and zip code, as well as location. Includes many statistical tables of population, business and manufacturers, agriculture, and other commercial features.

A road atlas of the United States, Canada, and Mexico is issued as a supplement.   G1019C734

————   Standard highway mileage guide. 1934– . Chicago : Rand McNally & Co., 1934– . Irregular.   **CL305**

Issued in two volumes beginning in 1993. Vol. 1 contains key point city index; v. 2 contains vicinity and state road maps.

In the 1993 edition, mileage charts list distances between 1474 ("key point") major and medium-sized U.S. and Canadian cities. Alphabetical index to key point cities. The atlas section includes 155 pages of indexed highway maps by state and region and 50 urban vicinity maps; it designates key point cities in bright green circles.

    G1201.P1R3

Thorndale, William. Map guide to the U.S. federal censuses, 1790–1920 / William Thorndale and William Dollarhide. Baltimore : Genealogical Pub. Co., 1987. 420 p. : maps ; 23 x 30 cm. **CL306**

Shows U.S. county boundary maps for the census decades superimposed on modern county boundaries. Gives background information on each census, including census availability for each county.

G1201.F7T5

Canada

Canada. Energy, Mines and Resources Canada. The national atlas of Canada. 5th ed. Ottawa : Energy, Mines and Resources Canada, 1985– . folded maps in color ; 46 X 40 cm.; in box, 49 X 47 cm. **CL307**

1st ed., 1906; 4th ed., 1974.

"The fifth edition of the National Atlas of Canada is a serial publication of separate maps to be published over a period of time. The subject matter is organized into 44 separately titled and numbered realms of information ... which encompass all aspects of geographical information relating to Canada."—*Pref.* Most maps at a scale of 1:7,500,00. Also issued in French under title: *L'atlas national du Canada.* G1115

Canada gazetteer atlas. [Montreal] : Macmillan of Canada, in co-operation with Energy, Mines and Resources Canada and the Canadian Government Publishing Centre, Supply and Services Canada, 1980. [9], 164 p. : 48 maps in color ; 46 cm. **CL308**

Also published in French under title *Canada atlas toponymique.*

"A completely new reference work, consisting of 48 [double-page] maps and an index giving the name, status, population, and position of the populated places recorded in the 1976 Census of Canada. Selections of physical features, roads, railways, and important national and provincial parks are also included. ..."—*Introd.* Names are given "in the language actually approved by the respective name authorities for the provinces and territories." Serves as a complement to *The national atlas of Canada* (CL307). G1115.C6313

Nicholson, Norman Leon. The maps of Canada : a guide to official Canadian maps, charts, atlases, and gazetteers / N. L. Nicholson, L. M. Sebert. Folkestone, Kent, England : Wm. Dawson ; Hamden, Conn. : Archon Books, 1981. 251 p. : ill., maps ; 26 cm. **CL309**

A survey of official publications and their uses. Appendixes; bibliographic notes and references; index. GA471.N52

Mexico

Atlas of Mexico / Stanley A. Arbingast ... [et al.]. [2nd ed.]. [Austin] : Bureau of Business Research, Univ. of Texas at Austin, [1975]. 164 p. : some maps in color ; 28x37cm. **CL310**

1st ed., 1970.

A section of physical maps is followed by groups of topical maps showing population distribution, agricultural production, transportation, commerce, and industry. G1545.A9

El territorio mexicano / Víctor M. Ruiz Naufal ... [et al.]. México : Instituto Mexicano del Seguro Social, 1982. 2 v. : ill., maps ; 39 cm. **CL311**

Contents: v. 1, La nación; v. 2, Los estados. Accompanied by a portfolio of maps and plans, issued in a case.

A monumental work of historical geography focusing on the mid-16th century until about 1930. Both volumes are heavily illustrated with facsimile plans and maps which include descriptive contents notes. The portfolio contains facsimile plates of about 36 maps dating from the mid-16th century to 1980. General and cartographic bibliographies. F1226.T47

Central America

Atlas of Central America / Stanley A. Arbingast ... [et al.] ; cartography by William L. Hezlep. Austin : Bureau of Business Research, Univ. of Texas at Austin, c1979. 62 p. : maps in color ; 28 x 37 cm. **CL312**

Presents relief, thematic, and geological maps for the area and for Guatemala, Belize, Honduras, El Salvador, Nicaragua, Costa Rica, and Panama. Statistical sources are noted. G1550.A8

Costa Rica

Sánchez Chinchilla, Luis Angel. Atlas estadístico de Costa Rica, no. 2 / prep. en la Sección de Cartografía Censal por Luis Angel Sánchez Chinchilla y Eusebio Flores Silva. 2a ed. San José, Costa Rica : Dirección General de Estadística y Censos : Oficina de Planificación Nacional y Política Económica, 1981. 184 p. : ill. (some col.), maps in color; 30x45 cm. **CL313**

A revised edition of *Atlas estadístico de Costa Rica* (1953).

Presents maps, city plans, diagrams and graphs based on the censuses of 1950, 1963 and 1973. G1580.S2

South America

Argentina

Randle, Patricio H. Atlas del desarrollo territorial de la Argentina. Buenos Aires : OIKOS Asociación para la Promoción de los Estudios Territoriales y Ambientales, c1981. 3 v. : maps in color ; 37–55 cm. **CL314**

Contents: v. 1, Memoria; v. 2, Serie de estadísticas históricas; v. 3, Atlas.

Atlases in four sections: El territorio se configura; La producción y la población; El equipamiento territorial; El proceso de urbanización.

A major national atlas illustrating both historical and contemporary geography. Scale approximately 1:10,000,000. The Memoria provides explicative text for the atlas maps; the statistics section includes figures presented graphically in the socioeconomic maps. G1755.R3

Bolivia

Instituto Nacional de Estadística (Bolivia). Atlas censal de Bolivia. La Paz, Bolivia : El Instituto, 1982. 294 p. : some maps in color ; 33 cm. **CL315**

Data is based on the 1976 census; includes statistics on population, housing, language, etc. G1746.E1I5

Brazil

Ira, Rudolf. Atlas do Brasil Globo : com os mapas político e físic o do Brasil e os mapas dos seus estados e territórios / cartografia d e Rudolf Ira e Edgar Klettner ; índice remissivo e descritivo dos topônimos pelo Des. Lourenço Mario Prunes ; parte relativa aos Estados e territórios pelo Gen. Amyr Borges Fortes. Rio de Janeiro : Ed. Globo, [1960]. 98 p. : maps. 45cm. **CL316**

Also produced in microcard : Louisville, Ky. : Falls City Microcards, 1959.

Plates of colored maps, physical and political, national and regional. Index-gazetteer. G1775.I7

Colombia

Instituto Geográfico "Agustín Codazzi". Atlas de Colombia. 4. ed., rev. y aumentada. Santafé de Bogotá : Instituto Geografico Agustín Codazzi, 1992. 321 p. : ill., maps in color; 49 cm.   **CL317**

1st ed., 1967; 3rd ed., 1977.

A national atlas with historical, physical, and thematic maps; also includes maps of smaller administrative divisions such as *departamentos* and cities.

§ The Instituto has published regional atlases of Colombia: *Atlas regional andino* (1982. 168 p. 49x40 cm.) and *Atlas regional pacifico* (1983. 96 p. 49 cm.).   G1730.C65

Venezuela

Atlas de Venezuela. 2. ed., rev., actualizada, y ampliada. Caracas, Venezuela : Distribuidora Escolar (Discolar), 1987. 320 p. : col. ill., maps in color ; 28 cm.   **CL318**

1st ed., 1969; 2nd ed., 1979.

A national atlas with many thematic maps for demography, economic conditions, communications, etc., as well as physical and political maps.   G1725.V4

Caribbean and Islands of the Western Atlantic

Atlas regional del Caribe / realizado por el Departamento de Geografía económica, Instituto de Geografía, Akademia de Ciencias de Cuba. [Havana] : Editorial Científico-Técnica, Ministerio de Cultura, c1979. 69 p. : ill., maps ; 33 x 53 cm.   **CL319**

Table of contents in Spanish and English.

Maps, with text, are topically arranged within categories such as general political and economic structures, agriculture, population, industry, transport, foreign trade, national income.

Cuba

Atlas de Cuba / Instituto Cubano de Geodesia y Cartografía. Havana : El Instituto, 1978. 143 p. : ill., maps ; 26 x 36cm.   **CL320**

"XX aniversario del triunfo de la revolución cubana"—*t.p.*

Presents thematic and relief maps, most on a 1:300,000 scale, with a place-name index.

§ More thematic maps are available in the *Atlas demográfico de Cuba*, prepared by the Comité Estatal de Estadísticas (Havana : Instituto Cubano de Geodésia y Cartografía, 1979. 99 p.).   G1605.I5

Europe

The Economist atlas of the new Europe. N.Y. : H. Holt, 1992. 288 p. : col. ill., col. maps ; 38 cm.   **CL321**

"Originally published in Great Britain in 1992 by Century Business" (*t.p. verso*) with title: *Europe : a thematic atlas.*

Divided into nine topical sections: History, Communications, Business, Finance, Politics, International relations, War and defence, Environment, and People and culture. Numerous photographs and statistical charts supplement thematic maps. Brief introductory essays to each section. Cross-references. Country analysis section, in geographical arrangement, provides current summary statistical information. Time line, index, and list of sources.   G1797.2.E2

Czechoslovakia

Česká Akademie Věd a Umeadní, Prague. Atlas Republiky Československé / vydala Česká Akademia věd a umění za podpory Ministerstva zahraničních věcí Republiky Československé ; vrchní redakci vedl prof. dr. ing. Jar. Pantoflíček …. Praha : Vyšlo nákladem akc. spol. Orbis, 1935. 2 v. : maps ; 44 cm.   **CL322**

In two parts: (1) atlas of 55 double plates of maps (442 maps); and (2) accompanying text (43 p.), ed. by Václav Láska.

A good, detailed atlas, covering economic and physical geography, demography, political and culural aspects, etc.

Geodetický a kartografický podnik v Praze. Atlas ČSSR : [spracovala Geodetický a kartografický podnik v Praze ; zodpovědny redaktor Josef Ščipák]. 2., nezmenené vyd. Bratislava : Slovenská kartografia, 1986. 54, 12 p. : maps in color ; 33 cm.   **CL323**

1st ed., 1972; previous ed., 1984.

A small, up-to-date atlas with some city maps.   G1945.K3

Denmark

Atlas over Danmark : serie II / red. N. Kingo Jacobsen. København : Kongelige Danske Geografiske Selskab, 1976–86. 4 v. : some maps in color ; 34 cm.   **CL324**

Original series, publ. 1949–61, ed. by Niels Nielsen.

Contents: v. 1, Opgivne og tilplantede landbrugsarealer i Jylland; v. 2, Topografisk, atlas Danmark; v. 3, Danske Byers vakst; v. 4, Landbrugsatlas Danmark.

In Danish and German, with English summaries.   G2055.N5

Finland

Finland. Maanmittaushallitus. Fennia : suuri Suomi-kartasto : kartverk över Finland = Finland in maps = Finnischer Atlas. [Espoo] : Weilin & Göös, 1979. 224 p. : maps in color ; 30 cm.   **CL325**

Title and prefatory matter also in Swedish, English and German.

Colored topographic maps with road and highway information, on a 1:250,000 scale. Based on information and maps derived from the National Board of Survey's *Road map of Finland* (1:200,000) and its *Basic map of Finland* (1:20,000) of about 1977. Includes maps of major city centers. Index of about 9,000 place names.   G2075.F44

Geografiska Sällskapet i Finland, Helsingfors. Suomen kartasto = Atlas of Finland = Atlas över Finland. 5th ed. Helsinki : Maanmittauschallitus : Suomen maantieteellinen seura, 1976–1984. 1 v. in folios : map in color ; 49 cm.   **CL326**

1st ed., 1899; 4th ed., 1961.

Texts in English issued as appendix in pocket of each folio. Covers physical, economic, and social geography.

France

Atlas de France / Comité national de géographie. 2. éd. Paris : Éd. Géographiques de France, 1951–59. 80 pts. : maps in color (in portfolio) ; 50 cm.   **CL327**

1st ed., 1933–45.

A regional atlas of the highest grade, covering geomorphology, climatology, hydrography, biogeography, agriculture, industry, commerce, and human and political geography.   G1840.C6

Atlas départemental / cartes conçues et réalisées par la société française d'études et de réalisations cartographiques ; documentation rassemblée par Jean Barbier et Nicole Boubounelle, avec la collaboration de René Oizon. Paris : Larousse, 1983. 313 p. : maps in color ; 18 cm. **CL328**

Small maps in color of each département are accompanied by statistical notes based on censuses from 1975–82. Place-names index.

G1844.20.A78

Sélection du Reader's Digest. S.A.R.L. Grand atlas de la France. [Paris] : Sélection du Reader's Digest, [1969]. 244 p. : ill., maps ; 41 cm. **CL329**

A national atlas, with 48 physical maps on the scale of 1:500,000. Includes a section of small thematic maps, a pictorial section, and an index. G1840.S4

Luxembourg

Luxembourg. Ministère de l'éducation nationale. Atlas du Luxembourg. [St. Paul, 1971–76]. 1 v. (looseleaf) : ill. ; 50 cm. **CL330**

In six main sections: historical, physical, administrative, demographic, economic, and social. G1870.L8

Portugal

Atlas de España y Portugal / realización, Victoria Zalacain, con la colaboración de B. Blanc … [et al.]. Paris : Zalacain, 1982. 144 p. : ill., maps in color ; 22 x 29cm. **CL331**
For annotation, *see* CL333. G1960.A8

Girão, Aristides de Amorim. Atlas de Portugal = Atlas of Portugal. 2. ed. Coimbra : Inst. de Estudos Geográficos, Faculdade de Letras, 1957–58. [177] p. : some maps in color ; 43 cm. **CL332**
1st ed., 1941.

Issued in parts, in portfolio. In Portuguese and English. Maps cover geology, topography, climate, vegetation, population, agriculture, industries, etc. G1976.G1G5

Spain

Atlas de España y Portugal / realización, Victoria Zalacain, con la colaboración de B. Blanc … [et al.]. Paris : Zalacain, 1982. 144 p. : ill., maps in color ; 22 x 29cm. **CL333**

Presents maps illustrating physical geography, climate, soils, migration, economic situation, social conditions, and population (based on the 1970 censuses). Particularly strong on economic themes. Place name index. G1960.A8

Atlas nacional de España. Madrid : Instituto Geográfico Nacional., 1982. 2 v. : 100 folded maps in portfolio ; 56 cm.

CL334

1st ed., 1965.

An impressive national atlas with detailed physical and thematic maps. Includes geology, climate, hydrology, population, energy, industry, agriculture, commerce, communications, culture, etc. The two bound volumes comprise *Reseña geográfica de España* and *Indice toponímico*.

Updated by: Instituto Geográfico Nacional (Spain), *Atlas nacional de España* (Madrid : Dirección General del Instituto Geográfico Nacional, [1992]–). G1965.S65

Sweden

Svenska Sällskapet för Antropologi och Geografi. Atlas över Sverige. Stockholm : Generalstabens Litografiska Anstalts Förlag, [1953–71]. 26 parts : ill., maps ; 44 cm. **CL335**
Issued in fascicles.

A regional atlas of Sweden on some 150 folio-size sheets (including 520 maps in all) with descriptive text. Arranged in sections, with material on geophysics and geology, meteorology and hydrography, pasturage and animal husbandry, population, agriculture, forestry, industry, communications, trade, economic conditions, social conditions, cultural development, political geography, and history. Extensive English summaries of the Swedish textual material in each folio section, and parallel English headings for all maps and tables.

Updated by: *National atlas of Sweden* (Stockholm : SNA Publ., 1990– .). G2070.S8

Union of Soviet Socialist Republics

Dewdney, John C. The U.S.S.R. in maps. N.Y. : Holmes & Meier, [1982]. 117 p. : maps ; 27x24 cm. **CL336**

"This volume contains 49 [full-page] maps and diagrams, each with a page (or more) of supporting text, designed to illustrate the present-day geography physical, human and economic—of the Union of Soviet Socialist Republics. … "—*Introd.* Black-and-white maps. Classed bibliography; index. G2110.D5

Africa (by region)

Institut géographique national (France). The atlas of Africa / Régine van Chi-Bonnardel, ed. N.Y. : Free Pr., [1974]. 335 p. : ill., maps in color ; 42 cm. **CL337**

Also publ. in French as *Grand atlas du continent africain* by Éditions Jeune Afrique.

General physical and thematic maps are followed by maps for individual countries. Each country section has accompanying text.

G2445.F72

Africa, West

West African international atlas = Atlas international de l'Ouest Africain. [Dakar : Univ. de Dakar, Inst. Fondamental d'Afrique Noire], 1968–78. 2 v. (looseleaf). : maps in color ; 53 cm. **CL338**

Running title: *International atlas of West Africa.*

Folded plates with explanatory matter issued in installments.

On cover: Under the auspices of the Organisation of African Unity, Scientific, Technical and Research Commission, and with the assistance of the Ford Foundation.

Explanatory text in French and English. Detailed physical and relief maps, plus maps of geology, climate, zoogeography, sources of energy, administrative and political boundaries, etc. G2640.W4

Africa (by country)

Les atlas Jeune Afrique. Paris : Jeune Afrique. [v. 1–]. **CL339**

This publisher's series includes several good atlases of francophone sub-Saharan Africa; they offer color thematic maps and accompanying text, with glossary and index, in a 29–30 cm. format. The list includes:

Atlas de la République Unie du Cameroun. Georges Laclavère (1979. 72 p.).

Atlas de la République Centrafricaine. Pierre Vennetier. (1984. 64 p.).

Atlas de la République Populaire du Congo. Pierre Vennetier. (1977. 64 p.).

Atlas de la Côte d'Ivoire. Pierre Vennetier [et al.] (2e. éd., rev. et mise à jour. 1983. 72 p.).

Atlas de la Haute-Volta. Yves Péron. (1975. 47p.).

Atlas du Mali. Mamadou Traoré [et al.] (1980. 64 p.).

Atlas de la République Islamique du Mauritanie. Charles Toupet and Georges Laclavère. (1977. 64p.).

Atlas du Niger. Edmond Bernus and Sidikou A. Hamidou. (1980. 64p.).

Atlas du Sénégal. Paul Pélissier. (2nd ed. 1983. 72p.).

Atlas du Togo. Yema E. Gu-Konu. (1981. 64p.).

Atlas de Tunisie. Mohamed Fakhfakh. (1979).

Atlas de la Republique du Zaire. Georges Laclavere. (1978).

Ethiopia

Ya'Ityo p̄yā kārtā s̄erā derejet. National atlas of Ethiopia / [prepared and comp. by Geography Division]. 1st U.S. ed. Addis Ababa : Ethiopian Mapping Authority, 1988. 76 [i.e. 156] p. : ill., maps in color ; 40 cm.   **CL340**

Preliminary ed. issued 1981.

Natural conditions, socioeconomic activities, and historical development are depicted in 76 color maps, most at a scale of 1:5,000,000. Government, international, and educational institutions provided sources of data; information is current to 1984. Maps are accompanied by charts, tables and explanatory text. Index to place names.

G2505.E8

Kenya

Survey of Kenya. National atlas of Kenya. 3rd ed. [Nairobi] : The Survey, 1970. 103 p. : ill., some maps in color ; 41 cm.   **CL341**

1st ed., 1959. Previously published under the title *Atlas of Kenya.*

About 40 full-page maps with descriptive text and illustrations on facing pages; some historical maps and city plans. Gazetteer-index.

G2530.K42

Liberia

Gnielinski, Stefan. Liberia in maps. N.Y. : Africana Publishing Company, 1972. 111 p.   **CL342**

Offers a series of black-and-white line maps on physical geography, history, social conditions, agriculture, rural and urban life, economic conditions, communications, transport, etc. Explanatory text; bibliography; glossary.

§ The same publisher has issued *Malawi in maps*, by Swanzie Agnew and Michael Stubbs (1972. 143 p.); *Nigeria in maps*, by K. Michael Barbour [and others] (1982. 148 p.); *Sierra Leone in maps*, by John I. Clarke (2nd ed., 1972. 120 p.); *Tanzania in maps*, by L. Berry (1972. 172 p.); and *Zambia in maps*, by D. Hywel Davies (1972. 128 p.).

Namibia

National atlas of South West Africa (Namibia) = Nasionale atlas van Suidwes-Afrika (Namibié) / ed., J. H. van der Merwe. Goodwood, Cape [Town] : Nat. Book Printers, 1983. [184] p. : ill., maps. 31cm.   **CL343**

In English and Afrikaans.

Presents 92 maps, mostly thematic, in seven sections: orientation; natural environment; settlement structure; population structure; economic structure; infrastructure; urban structure. No index.   G2580.N3

Rwanda

Atlas du Rwanda / réalisateurs Christian Prioul [et] Pierre Sirven ; [réalisé avec le concours du Ministère de la Coopération de la République Française pour le compte de Univ. de Kigali, i.e., Univ. Nationale du Rwanda]. [Nantes] : Assoc. pour l'Atlas des Pays de Loire, 1981. 75 p. : ill., some maps in color ; 32 x 45cm.   **CL344**

Contains 33 full-page maps with descriptive text on facing pages. Bibliography.   G2539.5.A8

South Africa

Reader's Digest Association South Africa. Reader's digest atlas of Southern Africa / produced in conjunction with the Directorate of Surveys and Mapping, Dept. of Community Development. [Cape Town : Reader's Digest Assoc. of S.A., 1984]. 256 p. : ill., maps in color ; 44 cm.   **CL345**

Thematic maps of South Africa begin the volume (p.1–75) and are followed by six-color relief maps based on the official topographic maps prepared by the South African Directorate of Surveys and Mapping (p. 76–213). Scales range from 1:50,000 to 1:1,000,000. An index map is included in pocket. Gazetteer index of about 30,000 place names (some both in English and Afrikaans); subject index to thematic maps.   G2565.R4

Talbot, A. M. Atlas of the Union of South Africa / by A. M. Talbot and W. J. Talbot ; prep. in collaboration with the Trigonometrical Survey Office, and under the aegis of the National Council for Social Research. Pretoria : Govt. Printer, 1960. lxiv, 178 p. : some maps in color ; 45x58cm.   **CL346**

English and Afrikaans; added title page in Afrikaans.

Maps, in black-and-white, cover: relief; geology; vegetation; fisheries; climate and water resources; population; agriculture; industries and occupations; transportation; external trade.   G2566.J1T3

Asia (by region)

Asia, South

Dutt, Ashok K. Atlas of South Asia : fully annotated / Ashok K. Dutt, M. Margaret Geib. Boulder, Colo. : Westview Pr., 1987. 231 p. : ill. ; 28 cm.   **CL347**

Updates the authors' *India in maps* (Dubuque, Iowa : Kendall/ Hunt, 1976. 124 p.).

"Includes maps, figures, and narratives that provide comprehensive coverage of political, physical, economic, historical, and cultural aspects of South Asia."—*About the book and authors.* Covers Bangladesh, Bhutan, India, Nepal, Pakistan, and Sri Lanka with national-level maps. More than 300 black-and-white maps clearly illustrate the substantial text. Statistical data is now dated, but useful for comparison. Bibliography.   G2260.D8

Asia, Southeast

Atlas of South-east Asia / with an introduction by D. G. E. Hall. London : Macmillan ; N.Y. : St. Martin's, 1964. 84 p. : ill., maps in color ; 35 cm.   **CL348**

Maps produced by Djambatan Publishers and cartographers, Amsterdam.

Comprises 60 colored maps of the countries and islands of southeast Asia, usually showing climate, agriculture, population, minerals and industries, communications, etc. Includes plans of the larger cities.
G2360.D5

Arab states

Dempsey, Michael W. Atlas of the Arab world. N.Y. : Facts on File, 1983. c.118 p. : ill., maps ; 25 cm. **CL349**

About 40 double-page four-color maps, graphically present geographic and socioeconomic aspects of the Arab world. Brief gazetteer entries are made for each country. Statistical sources are indicated for each map in a descriptive notes section. DS63.7.D45

Asia (by country)

Afghanistan

National atlas of the Democratic Republic of Afghanistan / [editing, Organization for Surveying and Cartography GEOKART ; co-operation, Afghan Geodesy and Cartography Head Office ; authors and contributors, Abdul Satar ... et al.]. [Warsaw] : Organization for Surveying & Cartography GEOKART, [1985?]. [27] *l* of plates (some folded) : maps in color ; 37 cm. **CL350**

"Issued in two language versions, in English and in Dari"—*Foreword.*

"Not only Afghanistan's first National Atlas but also its first original collection of thematic maps, made in co-operation with that country's specialists."—*Foreword.* Contains 63 maps depicting physical, political, social and economic information; data is current to 1975–81, and administrative division is current to 1984. Bibliography of sources and index. G2265.N3

Bangladesh

Bangladesh in maps / gen. editors, M. Aminul Islam, M. Maniruzzaman Miah ... [et al.]. Dacca, Bangladesh : Univ. of Dacca, [1981?]. 77 p. : maps in color ; 40 cm. **CL351**

" ... a book of maps equivalent to the national Atlas in many a country..."—*Pref.* Clear national level maps in color give physical, agricultural, economic and demographic characteristics. No index, bibliography or list of sources. G2275.B3

China

Chang, Ch'i-yün. National atlas of China. 2nd ed. Yang Ming Shan, Taiwan : National War College, 1964–67. 5 v. : some maps in color. **CL352**

Vol. 2–3 (1st ed.) have title *Atlas of the Republic of China.*

Contents: v. 1, Taiwan (3rd ed., 1967); v. 2, Hsitsang (Tibet), Sinkiang and Mongolia; v. 3, North China; v. 4, South China; v. 5, General maps of China.

Place-names appear both in Chinese characters and in romanization; indexes from both forms. The general maps illustrate communications, climate, soils, vegetation and forestry, agriculture, fishing, livestock, minerals, population, and major languages.

Hsieh, Chiao-min. Atlas of China / by Chiao-min Hsieh ; ed. by Christopher L. Salter. N.Y. : McGraw-Hill, 1973. 282 p. : ill. **CL353**

Maps are grouped in four main sections: (1) Physical; (2) Cultural; (3) Regional; and (4) Historical. Background text and explanatory text accompany the maps. Indexed (separate index for the historical section). G2305.H83

The Times atlas of China. London : Times Books ; N.Y. : Quadrangle/New York Times Book, 1974. 145, 27 p. : chiefly maps in color ; 39 cm. **CL354**

Editors and chief contributors: P. J. M. Geelan, D. C. Twitchett; Cartographic consultant, John G. Bartholomew and Son, Ltd.

Offers maps and explanatory text representing a variety of historical, economic, and physical topics, maps of the provinces of China, and a section of city plans. Wade-Giles system of transcription of Chinese names is used on the maps. In the index, names are arranged alphabetically by Wade-Giles transcription with the pinyin transcription following; cross-references are provided from the old Post Office spellings. It is clearly stated in the Introduction that some of the information is fairly tentative since "detailed geographical and particularly statistical information at the time of writing is, by Western standards, hard to come by." G2305.T47

United States. Central Intelligence Agency. People's Republic of China—atlas. Wash. : U.S. Govt. Print. Off., 1971. 82 p. : ill., maps in color; 44cm. **CL355**

"This volume goes beyond the scope of a conventional atlas. It presents a wider variety of information, including geographic, economic, historical, and cultural data. ... To make so much information ... as meaningful as possible, a great deal of it is placed in a familiar context—that is, by drawing comparisons between China and the United States."—*Pref.*

Issued commercially as *Rand McNally illustrated atlas of China* (Chicago : Rand McNally, 1972. 80 p. 39 cm.). G2305.U55

India

An atlas of India / [designed, comp., cartographed, and pr. by TT. Maps & Publications Ltd ; ed. in chief, S. Muthiah ; chief cartographer, P. Poovendran]. Delhi ; N.Y. : Oxford Univ. Pr., 1990. 185 p. : maps in color ; 35 cm. **CL356**

A collection of 18 general national level maps, followed by a series of state level maps. "Each state and union territory of India has been allotted nine maps" that "deal with the following subjects: (1) physical features, (2) administration, (3) urban and rural population, (4) transport and tourist centres, (5) agriculture and irrigation, (6) industries and market potential, (7) mineral resources, (8) economic development, and (9) audio-visual communication."—*Introd.* All data is current to 1989 to allow comparison. Five tables of additional primarily economic data and an index of 12,000 place names. List of agency sources of data in introduction. G2280.T7

Israel

Israel. Agaf ha-medidot. Atlas of Israel : cartography, physical and human geography. 3rd ed. (English-Hebrew). Tel-Aviv : Survey of Israel ; N.Y. : Macmillan, 1985. [7], 40 [i.e. 160], 80 p. : maps in color; 50 cm. **CL357**

1st ed., 1956–64; 2nd ed., 1970.

Includes 40 double-page plates of bilingual maps (Hebrew and English) in color, portraying climatic, population, and economic aspects. Gives special attention to urban geography; new maps cover Jerusalem, Haifa, Tel-Aviv and 13 medium-sized and small towns. 80 pages of text in English, with numerous tables, provide supplementary information. Although listed as a 3rd ed., does not replace two older editions (CL358), each of which has special strengths. G2235.I77

Israel. Mahleket ha-Medidot. Atlas of Israel : cartography, physical geography, history, demography, economics, education. Jerusalem, 1956–64. 1 v. (looseleaf) : maps ; 50 cm. **CL358**

Title page and text in Hebrew; above title from added title page.

Includes about 100 double sheets of maps grouped in sections for Cartography, Geomorphology, Geology, Climate, Hydrology, Zoology, Botany, History, Population, Agriculture, Industry, etc. Maps are handsomely printed in as many as 15 colors, with explanatory texts overleaf. While some maps are restricted to Israel, Palestine is represented wherever reliable information is available.

§ *Atlas of Israel : cartography, physical geography, human and economic geography, history* ([2nd ed.] Amsterdam : publ. by Survey of Israel, Ministry of Labour, Jerusalem, and Elsevier, 1970. 1 v., various pagings : maps in color ; 49 cm.).

Represents a 2nd, English-language, edition of the looseleaf edition published in Hebrew (above). The work has been revised, slightly condensed, and brought up-to-date for this edition.

These works contain information not replaced by the publication of the 3rd ed. (CL357).   G2235.I8

Nepal

Sill, Michael. The atlas of Nepal in the modern world / Michael Sill and John Kirkby. London : Earthscan Publ., 1991. 159 p. : ill., maps. ; 27 x 23 cm.   **CL359**

Significantly more text than maps. Maps are black-and-white; also includes black-and-white photographs, charts and tables. Introductory text includes bibliographies; select bibliography provided for atlas sections.   G2295.S55

Pakistan

Survey of Pakistan. Atlas of Pakistan. Rawalpindi : Survey of Pakistan, 1990. 129 p. : maps in color ; 45 cm.   **CL360**

1st ed., 1985; repr. with minor amendments, 1986.

"In four sections of World relation maps, Regional maps of Pakistan, Thematic maps of Pakistan and Continental maps, constitutes 137 maps over 106 pages. A section of Gazetteer, Tables of Distances, Heights and Areas of major administrative units of the country have been included ... ."—*Pref.* No bibliography, but Acknowledgements mentions agencies that supplied information.   G2270.S8

Philippines

Fund for Assistance to Private Education. Philippine atlas. Manila : The Fund, 1975. 2 v. (304 p., 125 p.) : ill., maps in color.   **CL361**

Contents: v. 1, A historical, economic and educational profile of the Philippines; v. 2, Directory of schools, assistance groupings, and index.

Vol. 1 surveys the situation of the Philippines in the world in terms of land area, population and education; describes, through text, maps, and illustrations, the physical geography, history, culture, population, and economy; and describes the educational structure. Vol. 2 gives descriptive data on 695 higher education institutions, identifies public and private sources of educational funding, and includes name/place and general index.   G2391.G1F8

Hendry, Robert S. Atlas of the Philippines / Robert S. Hendry; assoc. editors, Lawrence R. Doran [and] Armando Malay. [Manila? : Phil-Asian Pub., 1959]. 228 p. : ill., maps in color ; 49 cm.   **CL362**

Political and economic maps of the islands, with separate maps for each province, and historical sketch. Gives area and population, roads, etc.   G2390.H4

Sri Lanka

Sri Lanka. Minindōru Depārtamēntuva. The national atlas of Sri Lanka. [Colombo] : Survey Dept., c1988. 142 p. : col. ill., maps in color ; 52 cm.   **CL363**

Contains 71 map pages and numerous other illustrations with the text. Most national maps at 1:1,000,000 scale. Nine sections cover: location; physical; archaeology and history; people; agriculture; industry, power and transport; commerce; and government, administration and justice. References to sources are provided in contents and in explanatory texts. Index.   G2290.S65

Australia and Oceania

Australia

Australia. Division of National Mapping. Atlas of Australian resources. 3rd series. Canberra : Division of National Mapping, 1980–1990. 6 v. : maps ; 44 cm.   **CL364**

Issued in sheets, each accompanied by a commentary.

1st series, 1952–60 and 2nd series, 1962–75, publ. by Dept. of National Development.

Contents: Landforms; Geology; Mineral deposits; Climate; Temperature; Rainfall; Surface water resources; Groundwater; Water use; Soils; Natural vegetation; Land use; Croplands; Crop production; Fish and fisheries; Mineral industry; Electricity; Manufacturing industries; Population distribution; Immigration; Railways; Roads and aerodromes; Ports and shipping; Government; Major urban areas; Livestock; Sheep and wool; Grasslands; Forest resources; Locational index.

Maps range in scale from 1:36,000,000 to 1:250,000. Each map is accompanied by an illustrated booklet written by specialists especially for this series. The series designation indicates a process of continuous revision.   G2751.G3A3

New Zealand

New Zealand atlas / ed. by Ian Wards. Wellington : A. R. Shearer, Govt. Printer, 1976. 291 p. : ill., maps in color ; 32 cm.   **CL365**

Although undertaken as a revised edition of *A descriptive atlas of New Zealand* ed. by A. H. McLintock (Wellington : R.E. Owen, Govt. Printer, 1960), only two maps are carried over from that work; the rest of the compilation, cartographic and textual, is new. "The aim has been an even balance between cartographic exposition, textual explanation and photographic illustration, each complementary to the other."—*Introd.* In addition to topographic maps (including numerous maps of urban areas), there are maps showing discovery and settlement, population distribution, climate, geology, forests, fauna, fishing, mineral resources, etc. Index gazetteer. Beautifully illustrated.

G2795.N4

New Zealand in maps / ed. by A. Grant Anderson ; cartography by Don Branch, Denis Kelsall, Jacqueline Malcolm. N.Y. : Holmes & Meier, 1978. 141 p. : maps ; 34 cm.   **CL366**

Black-and-white line maps with accompanying text, prepared by the faculty of the Dept. of Geography, Univ. of Auckland. In five main parts: physical environment; biological environment; population and settlement; economic organization; economic and social infrastructure. Bibliography.   G2796.G1N4

Oceania

Atlas of the South Pacific. 2nd ed. Wellington : Government Printing Office, 1986. 48 p. : maps in color ; 47 cm.   **CL367**

1st ed., 1979.

About 20 maps of South Pacific countries with text on facing pages giving facts on land area, geology, soil types, vegetation, climate, population, ethnic groups, language, land use, and the economy. Scales vary. Relief maps, with index map and gazetteer index. G2862.S6A8

Kennedy, Thomas Fillans. A descriptive atlas of the Pacific islands : New Zealand, Australia, Polynesia, Melanesia, Micronesia, Philippines / by T. F. Kennedy ; maps by Julius Petro and Lionel Forsdyke. 3rd ed., rev. and extended. Wellington, N. Z. : Reed Education, [1974]. 79 p. : ill., maps. **CL368**

Black-and-white maps with descriptive text. Intended for school use in the Pacific Islands and surrounding countries but of value for bringing together maps of the main island groups and the more important individual islands. G2860.K4

Polar regions

Antarctica

American Geographical Society of New York. Antarctic map folio series / Vivian C. Bushnell, ed. N.Y. : Amer. Geographical Soc., 1964–1975. 19 v. : some maps in color ; 44 cm. **CL369**

"The objective of the ... Series is to summarize in a succinct manner the present knowledge of the Antarctic ... [with each folio] devoted to one subject or scientific discipline."—*Ed. note.* Each folio consists of introductory text and bibliographic references, and numerous plate maps. Topics covered include hydrographic data, birds, fishes, morphology, marine sediments, mammals, and the history of Antarctic exploration and scientific investigation. G3100.A4

Sovetskaía antarkticheskaía ekspeditsiía. Atlas Antarktiki / glav. red. E. I. Tolstikov. Moskva : Glavnoe Upravlenie Geodezii i Kartografii MG SSSR, 1966–69. 2 v. : ill., maps in color ; 60 cm. **CL370**

A major atlas with sections on history, physical geography, geology, climate, morphology, oceanography, biology, etc. G3100.S6

TRAVEL AND TOURISM

General works

Cure, Karen. The travel catalogue. N.Y. : Holt, Rinehart & Winston, [1978]. 191 p. : ill. **CL371**

A guide to recreation and travel in the U.S., Canada, and the Caribbean, arranged in four main divisions: (1) resorts, inns, and lodgings; (2) historic sites and attractions; (3) crafts, music, dance activities; (4) miscellaneous vacation ideas and activities. A preliminary chapter deals with the mechanics of travel; a directory of travel bureaus, tourist boards, etc., is appended. Guidebook references are noted throughout the text. Indexed. G151.C67

Bibliography

Corley, Nora Teresa. Travel in Canada : a guide to information sources. Detroit : Gale, [1983]. 294 p. (Geography and travel information guide series, v.4). **CL372**

About 800 entries, most of them annotated, for books, periodicals, series, and agencies which are sources of information about travel in Canada. In three main sections (1) Canada; (2) Canada by region; (3) Canada by province and territory. Each section is appropriately subdi-

vided by focus of publication (e.g., guidebooks, periodicals, atlases and maps, transportation, accommodations, cities, recreation). Fully indexed. Z1382.C67

Edgar, Neal L. Travel in Asia : a guide to information sources / Neal L. Edgar, Wendy Yu Ma. Detroit : Gale, [1983]. 413 p. (Geography and travel information guide series, v.6). **CL373**

An annotated listing of materials in English, with emphasis on publications since 1969. Arranged by country, with author, title, and subject indexes. Nearly 1,200 entries. Z3001.E22

Goeldner, Charles R. Bibliography of tourism and travel research studies, reports, and articles / by C. R. Goeldner and Karen Dicke. Boulder, Colo. : Business Research Div., Graduate School of Business Admin., Univ. of Colo. ; [Salt Lake City, Utah] : Travel Research Assoc., 1980. 9 v. (762 *l.*). **CL374**

Contents: v. 1, Information sources; v. 2, Economics; v. 3, International tourism; v. 4, Lodging; v. 5, Recreation; v. 6, Transportation; v. 7, Advertising-Planning; v. 8, Statistics-Visitors; v. 9, Index.

Earlier ed.: *Travel research bibliography,* 1976.

Aims "to provide a ready source of research references on travel, recreation, and tourism for use in business, government, and academic fields."—*Pref.* Entries are mainly for post-1970 publications. Z6004.T6G63

Hachette. (firm, publishers, Paris). Avec les "Guides bleues" à travers la France et le monde : (Bibliothèque des voyages). Paris : Hachette, 1959. 304 p. : ill. **CL375**

A listing of some 4,000 titles (published in French, and in print at the time of compilation of the list) of guidebooks and volumes of geographical and artistic description of interest to tourists.

———. *Supplément* 1960–62 (Paris : Hachette, 1962. 116 p.).

Kaul, H. K. Travels in South Asia : a selected and annotated bibliography of guide-books and travel-books on South Asia. Delhi : Arnold-Heinemann ; [Atlantic Highlands, N.J.] : Humanities Pr., [1979]. 215 p. **CL376**

In two parts: (1) Guide-books; (2) Travel-books (i.e., accounts written by travelers). Author, title, and geographical indexes. Extensive annotations. Z3185.K38

Post, Joyce A. Travel in the United States : a guide to information sources / Joyce A. Post, Jeremiah B. Post. Detroit : Gale, [1981]. 578 p. (Geography and travel information guide series, 3). **CL377**

Provides references to printed sources (books, atlases, magazines, maps) and to organizations, information centers, which offer information on various aspects of travel in the U.S. General and regional sections are followed by sections for the individual states. Annotations; indexes. Z1245.P67

The travel and tourism index. 1984– . Laie, Hawaii : Business Division, Brigham Young University—Hawaii Campus, 1984– . Quarterly. **CL378**

An index to journals issued by local or national travel bureaus, petroleum companies, and airlines, as well as several titles published for travel agents. Infirm indexing. Of interest primarily to the travel industry. Z6004.T6T7

The traveler's reading guide : ready-made reading lists for the armchair traveler / Maggy Simony, ed. Completely revised and updated. N.Y. : Facts On File, c1993. 510 p. **CL379**

Rev., expanded ed., 1987.

"Originally self-published as a three-volume paperback series" (*Pref.*), this edition "is intended to make it easier for armchair travelers, writers, teachers, travel professionals and...librarians...to locate interesting background books, place-set novels and mysteries, travel memoirs, special guides, travel articles for the destination of choice." Arranged geographically by continent or region, then alphabetically by country or province. Headings under each place-name include guidebooks, background reading, history, novels, and travel articles. Citations are brief, excluding place and pagination; travel articles are arranged by journal title, then chronologically. Author index.

Z6004.T6T73

Encyclopedias

Encyclopedia of world travel / ed. by Nelson Doubleday and C. Earl Cooley. 3rd rev. ed. / by John J. Corris and Seth Goldstein. Garden City, N.Y. : Doubleday, [1979]. 2 v. (1292 p.) : ill.   **CL380**
1st ed., 1961.
Contents: v. 1, United States, Canada, Mexico, Central America, Bermuda, the Bahamas, the Caribbean, South America; v. 2, Europe, Africa, the Middle East, Asia, the Pacific.
Each article sketches the geography, climate, history, agriculture, industry, cities, special events, sports and recreation facilities, and dining and shopping opportunities. Most articles are country guides; the U.S. and Canada are covered on the state and provincial level. Indexed.   G153.4.E52

Dictionaries

Dervaes, Claudine. The travel dictionary. Tampa, Fla. : Solitaire Pub., c1994. 336 p.   **CL381**
First publ. 1985 as *The travel agent's dictionary*; previous ed., 1992.
Provides brief definitions for more than 2,800 terms, codes, acronyms, and abbreviations commonly used in the travel industry. Includes 19 sections (some 100 pages) of additional information, including metric conversion chart, comparative clothing size chart, world and U.S. time-zone tables, country currency codes, airport and airline codes, and communication and transportation codes.   G155.A1D47

Metelka, Charles J. Dictionary of hospitality, travel, and tourism. 3rd ed. Albany, N.Y. : Delmar Publishers, c1990. 194 p.   **CL382**
1st ed., 1981; 2nd ed., 1986. Both had title: *The dictionary of tourism.*
Substantially augmented, now including definitions of some 2,700 terms and phrases related specifically to the travel industry. Two appendixes list organizations and governmental agencies involved in tourism, and journals and newsletters of the trade.   G155.A1M443

Quotations

The travellers' dictionary of quotations : who said what, about where? / ed. by Peter Yapp. London ; Boston : Routledge & Kegan Paul, 1983. 1022 p.   **CL383**
A compilation of quotations "from the literature of travel, from letters and diaries, verse and song, history, fiction, journalism and drama."—*Introd.* Quotations, primarily in English, 15th century to the present, are arranged alphabetically by country. Source and date given for all quotations; asterisks identify entries from fiction. Special sections cover the earth, sun, moon, and universe. Indexes of places and peoples and of persons quoted.   PN6084.P55T72

Directories

Hecker, Helen. Travel for the disabled : a handbook of travel resources and 500 worldwide access guides. Portland, Ore. : Twin Peaks Pr., c1985. 185 p.   **CL384**
In 18 chapters, lists sources of information on all aspects of travel: travel agencies and clubs; modes of transportation; medical and respite services; accessible recreation spots; and travel books and mag-

azines. A final bibliography contains citations to, and sources for, access guides in two sections, U.S. and foreign; includes information for obtaining these guides, many of them free. Geographical index.

HV1568.6.H43

Worldwide travel information contact book. 1st ed. (1991–92)– . Detroit : Gale, c1991– . Biennial.   **CL385**
A comprehensive directory of addresses, telephone, telex, and fax numbers for more than 25,000 contacts in 309 countries or subdivisions of countries. Arranged by continent; countries listed alphabetically. Ten categories of information including tourism agencies at various governmental levels, recreational activities, transportation, and publications. Coverage is better for other countries, especially in Europe, than for the U.S.

Handbooks

Tourism's top twenty : fast facts on travel and tourism. [1988 ed.]. Boulder, Colo. : Business Research Division, Univ. of Colorado ; Wash. : U.S. Travel Data Center, c1987. 118 *l.*   **CL386**
1st ed., 1980; 2nd ed., 1984.
"A compilation of frequently requested facts and figures on travel, tourism, recreation and leisure."—*Introd.* 93 tables cover such topics as advertising, air travel, automobile travel, cities/ports, countries, hotels/motels, outdoor recreation, sports, and travel destinations. Primarily U.S. facts; information source listed with each table. Two appendixes: address of sources and state and territory abbreviations, and subject index.   G155.A1T5928

Guidebooks

American guide series / comp. by the Federal Writers' Project (later called Writers' Program). [Publ. variously by different publishers], 1937–49. ill.   **CL387**
Includes guides to each state (of the 48 that then made up the U.S.), many cities and regions, and some special subjects. The state guidebooks are particularly useful, giving accurate information about points of interest with some historical and background material and sidelights on unusual features.
Began as a New Deal project to provide employment for writers. Now out of date, but of considerable interest for the history of regions of the U.S. Many individual guides are out of print, although some have been reprinted and some revised and issued in new editions, notably by Hasting House, N.Y.
Jeff Dykes has compiled a bibliography of the series, *American guide series : a catalog and checklist* (College Park, Md. : author, [1966?]. 36 p.), and Marc S. Selvaggio an index, *American guide series: works by the Federal Writers' Project* (Pittsburgh, Pa. : Arthur Scharf : Schoyer's Books, [1990?]. 176 p.).

General

Braganti, Nancy L. European customs and manners : how to make friends and do business in Europe / Nancy L. Braganti and Elizabeth Devine. N.Y. : Meadowbrook Pr. : distr. by Simon & Schuster, 1992. 276 p. : ill.   **CL388**
Rev. ed. of: *The travelers' guide to European customs and manners*, by Braganti and Devine (Deephaven, Minn. : Meadowbrook Books, c1984).
Entries, each 10–12 pages, arranged alphabetically by country, are designed to acquaint prospective travelers with cultural aspects of that country. Topics covered include: greetings, conversation, public manners, meals and foods, hotels and private homes, currency and tipping, business practices, holidays, transportation, legal matters and safety, and key phrases.

Companion titles for Asia, Kevin Chambers, *The travelers' guide to Asian customs & manners* (Deephaven, Minn. : Meadowbrook Books; N.Y. : distr. by Simon & Schuster, c1988. 375 p.); for Africa, Elizabeth Devine, *The travelers' guide to African customs & manners* (N.Y. : St. Martin's Pr., 1995); for West Asia and North Africa, Devine's *The travelers' guide to Middle Eastern and North African customs and manners* (N.Y. : St. Martin's Pr., c1991); for Latin America, Devine's *The travelers' guide to Latin American customs and manners* (N.Y. : St. Martin's Pr., c1988).   D909.B722

Bibliography

Greenwood Press. Baedeker's handbook(s) for travellers : a bibliography of English editions published prior to World War II. Westport, Conn. : Greenwood, 1975. 38 p.   **CL389**

A bibliography of Baedeker guides, arranged by Baedeker series designations, that serves as a guide to the publisher's microfiche set, *Baedeker handbooks*. No index.

§ Another brief bibliography, Alex Hinrichsen, *Baedeker's Reisehandbucher 1828–1945 : vollstandiges Verzeichnis der deutschen, englischen und Französischen Ausgaben mit chronologischen Ubersichtstafeln und 6 Abbildungen* (Holzminden : Ursula Hinrichsen Verlag, 1979. 67 p.) lists editions individually and provides tables of derivation for the various guide series. Geographic index.
                                                           Z6016.T7G73

Hayes, Gregory. Going places : the guide to travel guides / Greg Hayes and Joan Wright. Harvard, Mass. : Harvard Common Pr., c1988. 772 p.   **CL390**

A selective bibliography, with annotations, of travel guides, including specialty guides (e.g., for photography, hiking, canoeing, cycling). An opening section describes travel guide series; individual guides are then listed geographically by continent or region, then by country. Four appendixes list phrase books, travel stores and mail order agents, travel book publishers, and travel newsletters and magazines. Subject and geographic indexes.   Z6011.H37

Neal, Jack A. Reference guide for travellers. N.Y. : Bowker, 1969. 674 p.   **CL391**

An annotated list of English language guidebooks and background readings for the traveler, most items drawn from in-print lists of 1968. Geographical arrangement, with author/title and place-name indexes.   Z6011.N4

Travel guidebooks in review / ed. by Jon O. Heise. 3rd ed., rev. Syracuse, N.Y. : Gaylord Professional Pubns., 1978. 187 p.   **CL392**

Eds. 1–2 (1974–75), publ. by the International Center of the University of Michigan, had title: *Suit your spirit*.

78 travel guides and series of guidebooks are grouped by continent, then by type: the European section includes annually revised guides; specialty guides; series guides about specific countries, cities or regions; accomodation and restaurant guides; train guides; motoring and camping guides; and bicycling and walking guides. Individual guides to countries or cities, and North American guides are excluded. Each entry indicates the purpose, audience, what information is included, and gives an evaluation. Various appendixes serve as indexes to the books, publishers' directories, guidebooks published in series, etc.
                                                           Z6016.T7S9

Hotels

Financial times world hotel directory. 1975/76– . [London : Financial Times, 1975]– . Annual.   **CL393**

Publisher varies.

Arranged by country, then by city. Geographical index; numerous city maps.   TX907.F47a

OAG business travel planner : North American ed. v. 32, no. 3 (Sept.–Nov. 1990)– . Oak Brook, Ill. : Official Airline Guides, 1990– . Quarterly.   **CL394**

Continues: *United States official hotel directory and railroad indicator* (N.Y. : Hotel Publ. and Advertising Co., 1886–92); *United States official hotel directory* (N.Y. : Hotel Red Book and Directory Co., 1893–1902); *The official hotel red book and directory* (N.Y. : Official Hotel Red Book and Directory Co., 1904–54); *Hotel red book* (N.Y. : American Hotel Assoc. Directory Corp., 1955–62); *Hotel & motel red book* (N.Y. : American Hotel Assoc. Directory Corp., (N.Y. : American Hotel Assoc. Directory Corp., 1963–86); *OAG travel planner, hotel & motel red book* (Oak Brook, Ill. : Official Airline Guides, 1987–90).

Editions also available for Asia-Pacific and Europe.

Arranged by city. For larger cities, gives airline and airport information, local transportation, climate, brief list of events, downtown street map. For hotels, gives addresses, general location, telephone, number of rooms, special services (e.g., swimming pool, airport pick-up), rates.   TX907.O45

Timetables

Russell's official national motor coach guide. Cedar Rapids, Iowa : Russell's Guides, 1927– . Monthly.   **CL395**

Now offers timetables "of the majority of intercity motor bus operators in the United States, Canada, Mexico, and Central America."—*Dec. 1985 issue.*   HE5623.A1R8

D

History and Area Studies

DA

General History

GENERAL WORKS

Guides

American Historical Association. Guide to historical literature / George Frederick Howe, Chairman, Board of Editors. N.Y. : Macmillan, 1961. 962 p.   **DA1**

A successor to the *Guide to historical literature,* ed. by George M. Dutcher [et al.] (N.Y. : Macmillan, 1931). The new *Guide,* generally similar in plan, is a selective, annotated bibliography of treatises and source materials, arranged in broad subject and country groups, each group selected and described by specialists. Within each section, materials are arranged as practicable by form, e.g., bibliographies, encyclopedias and dictionaries, general and specialized histories, biographies, government documents, printed collections of sources, etc.

Even though coverage ends with 1960 publications, it remains an important first aid for students and librarians who seek lists of printed collections of documents, journals, society publications and contemporary diaries, letters, and autobiographies.

A new edition has been announced by for 1995 (ed., Mary Beth Norton. N.Y. : Oxford Univ. Pr.).   Z6201.A55

Fritze, Ronald H. Reference sources in history : an introductory guide / Ronald H. Fritze, Brian E. Coutts, Louis A. Vyhnanek. Santa Barbara, Calif. : ABC-Clio, 1990. 319 p.
DA2
"Designed to provide an introduction to the major reference works for all periods of history and for all geographical areas."—*Pref.* Cites mainly English-language materials, arranged by format (bibliographies, newspaper lists, archives and manuscript guides) subdivided geographically or by period, with lengthy, well-written annotations. Strongest for Europe and North America, but includes major reference works on Asian, African and Latin American history. Indexed by broad field (e.g., Ethnic studies, Medieval studies), and by author and title.

§ Intended to extend Helen J. Poulton's *The historian's handbook: a descriptive guide to reference works* (Norman : Univ. of Oklahoma Pr., [1972]. 304 p.). which can still be used for discussions of major reference sources; e.g., newspaper indexes, quotation dictionaries, library catalogs, statistical guides, and summaries.   Z6201.F72

Historical method

Barzun, Jacques. The modern researcher / Jacques Barzun, Henry F. Graff. 5th ed. Boston : Houghton Mifflin Co., c1992. 409 p. : ill.   **DA3**
1st ed., 1957.
The 5th ed. is a thorough revision of the text, with much new illustrative material. The authors have skillfully combined a manual of research methods, an essay on the evaluation and interpretations of facts, and a textbook on the writing of acceptable expository English. Designed for researchers, it is probably most useful to graduate students in the humanities and the social sciences since examples and bibliographical citations emphasize research in the field of history. New

material on the use of computers, word processors, and data banks and "the place and function in the contemporary mind of psycho-history, quantified history, and the vast literature of retrospective sociology."—*Note.* DB13.B334

Bibliography

C.R.I.S : the combined retrospective index set to journals in history, 1838–1974 / Annadel N. Wile, exec. ed. ... introduction and user's guide by Evan I. Farber. Wash. : Carrollton Pr., 1977–78. 11 v. **DA4**

Contents: v. 1–4, World history; v. 5–9, United States history; v. 10–11, Author index.

Offers selective indexing of more than 900 journals in history, political science, and sociology under four or five keyword or subject headings. Topical arrangement within geographical areas. Author index. Similar to the same publisher's combined indexes for political science (CJ18) and sociology (CC12).

Inasmuch as indexing was done by computer, and because entries are not duplicated and cross-referencing is skimpy, care should be taken to check all relevant sections. Z6205.C18

Gilmore, William J. Psychohistorical inquiry : a comprehensive research bibliography. N.Y. : Garland, 1984. 317 p. (Garland reference library of social science, v. 156). **DA5**

A bibliography of the literature of psychohistory. Coverage aims to be comprehensive for English-language materials, with a selection of citations in other languages. Sections on bibliography and methodology are followed by geographical sections listing psychohistorical studies; the sections for European and U.S. civilizations are further subdivided topically and by time period. Author index; lack of a subject index lessens the work's usefulness.

§ For a selective bibliography of the most outstanding examples of psychohistory, see Henry Lawton, *The psychohistorian's handbook* (DA43). Z6208.P78G54

International Committee of Historical Sciences. Bibliographie internationale des travaux historiques publiés dans les volumes de "Mélanges" = International bibliography of historical articles in festschriften and miscellanies / Établie avec le concours des comités nationaux sous la direction de Hans Nabholz par Margarethe Rothbarth et U. Helfenstein. Éd. par le Comité International des Sciences Historiques. Paris : Armand Colin, 1955–65. 2 v. **DA6**

Contents: v. 1, 1880–1939; v. 2, 1940–1950, avec compléments au Tome 1.

Mélanges are grouped by country, with a classified index and a name index. Vol. 2 has two additional indexes which combine references to both v. 1 and v. 2 for the complete 1880–1950 period: one of persons treated in the studies, the other of geographical subjects dealt with. Z6201.I5

Kaplan, Jonathan. International bibliography of Jewish history and thought. Munich : K.G. Saur ; Jerusalem : Magnes Pr., 1984. 483 p. **DA7**

At head of title: Rothberg School for Overseas Students, The Hebrew University; Dor Hemschech Institutes, The World Zionist Organisation.

Text in English and Hebrew.

A selective bibliography designed "to furnish the educator, the student and the librarian with a basic list of books that are of major importance for the study of Jewish history and the history of Jewish thought, and to assist them in the selection of books best suited to their respective needs and interests."—*Introd.* More than 2,000 items (briefly annotated) in Hebrew, English, German, Spanish, Portuguese and French; selection criteria are spelled out in the introduction. A section on general works is followed by four chronological sections (topically subdivided) and one on Jewish communities throughout the world. Index of names.

§ The final chapter is supplemented by Morris Fine's *Israel-Diaspora relations : a selected annotated bibliography, 1973–1983* (N.Y. : Inst. on American Jewish–Israeli Relations, American Jewish Committee, c1983. 45 p.). Z6366.K34

King, H. G. R. Atlantic Ocean. Oxford ; Santa Barbara, Calif. : Clio Pr., c1985. 250 p. (World bibliographical series, v. 61). **DA8**

Aims to treat man's activity in the Atlantic region, Atlantic Ocean nature and wildlife, and aspects of islands or island groups not already covered by a volume in this series. 913 entries, mostly for English-language books published up to early 1985, with some government documents and periodical articles, and including works of the imagination. Author/title/subject index. Z6004.P6K5

Koner, Wilhelm. Repertorium über die vom Jahre 1800 bis zum Jahre 1850 in Akademischen Abhandlungen, Gesellschaftsschriften und wissenschaftlichen Journalen auf dem Gebiete der Geschichte und ihrer Hülfswissenschaften erschienenen Aufsätze. Berlin : Nicolai, 1852–56. 2 v. **DA9**

Repr. : Graz : Akademische Druck- und Verlagsanstalt, 1968.

A closely classified bibliography with subject index of articles on historical subjects appearing in some 500 periodicals and society publications in various languages. Includes some American publications. Vol. 2, p. 76–169, lists biographical articles arranged alphabetically by subject. The names of these biographees do not appear in the index.

§ For an index to publications of learned societies of various countries up to 1800, *see* T. 8, Historia, *Repertorium commentationum a societatibus litterariis editarum*, by Jeremias David Reuss (EA21). Z6205.K82

Munro, D. J. Microforms for historians : a finding-list of research collections in London libraries. London : Univ. of London, Institute of Historical Research, 1991. 110 p. **DA10**

Based on responses to a survey designed to identify microforms of collections or groups of materials held by libraries in the Greater London area. The 1,200 items are arranged by broad subject areas. Title index; provenance index (owners of original material); name and subject index. Z1033.M5.M86

Third World resource directory, 1994–1995 : an annotated guide to print and audiovisual resources from and about Africa, Asia and Pacific, Latin America and Caribbean, and the Middle East / ed. by Thomas P. Fenton and Mary J. Heffron. Maryknoll, N.Y. : Orbis Books, c1994. 785 p. : ill. **DA11**

First published 1984.

Lists resources on "United States involvement in the affairs of Third World nations and peoples" (*Pref.*) in two principal sections, Areas (Third World, Africa, Asia and the Pacific, Latin America and Caribbean, Middle East) and Issues (food, human rights, militarism, transnational corporations, women). Each subsection lists organizations, printed resources (books, periodicals, pamphlets and articles), audiovisual resources, other resources. Entries for resources are annotated. Index of organizations; seven indexes (titles only) of resources by type (books, audiovisuals, etc.).

Several sections of the 1984 ed. were revised and expanded into separate titles. See, for example, *Middle East : a directory of resources* (DE21). Z7164.U5T46

Current

International bibliography of historical sciences. v. 1 (1926)– . Oxford : Univ. Pr. ; N.Y. : Wilson, 1930– . Annual. **DA12**

Repr.: N.Y. : Kraus, 1963. v. 1–14, 16–41.

Subtitle: Internationale Bibliographie der Geschichtswissenschaften; Bibliografía internacional de ciencias históricas; Bibliographie internationale des sciences historiques; Bibliografia internazionale delle scienze storiche.

Ed. for the International Committee of Historical Sciences.

Imprint varies: Paris : Colin; Rome : P. Maglione; Berlin : W. de Gruyter; Madrid : Ed. Hernando; beginning 1980, publ. by K.G. Saur, München.

A very useful selected, classified list of historical publications, interpreted in a wide sense to include political, constitutional, religious, cultural, economic, and social aspects; international relations; etc. Includes references to critical reviews. Interrupted during World War II; v. 15, to cover 1940–46, has not been published; latest received is v. 57 (covering 1988), publ. 1992.

§ To partially fill the World War II gap, *see* Pier Fausto Palumbo, *Bibliografia storica internazionale, 1940–1947* (Roma : Ed. del Lavoro, 1950. 241 p.) and Walther Holtzmann, *Die deutsche Geschichtswissenschaft in zweiten Weltkrieg: Bibliographie des historischen Schrifttums deutscher Autoren 1939–1945* (Marburg/Lahn : Simons Verlag, 1951. 149, 512 p.).

Bibliography of historical works issued in the United Kingdom 1940/45–1971/75 (London : Univ. of London, Institute of Historical Research, 1947–77. 6 v.) was a listing of books and often periodical articles published in Great Britain and, for some years, the Commonwealth on all aspects of history. Z6205.I61

Periodicals

Fyfe, Janet. History journals and serials : an analytical guide. N.Y. : Greenwood, 1986. 351 p. (Annotated bibliographies of serials : a subject approach, no. 8). **DA13**

Limited to English-language journals with international reputations or "general or specialized interest" from which completed questionnaires were received, plus local history serials "of interest to more than a few enthusiasts ... aimed primarily at helping the librarian select journals for a library and the historian to select journals for personal reading or submission of manuscripts."—*Pref.* Topical listings, with complete publishing information and annotations. Arranged in 35 geographical and topical sections, indexed by title and geographical area. Directory of publishers.

§ Related work: David P. Henige, *Serial bibliographies and abstracts in history : an annotated guide* (Westport, Conn. : Greenwood, 1986. 220 p.), which lists 874 relatively current bibliographies published at least every two years. Subject index. Z6956.G6F94

Historical periodicals directory / Eric H. Boehm, Barbara H. Pope and Marie S. Ensign, eds. Santa Barbara, Calif. : ABC-Clio, [1981–86]. 5 v. **DA14**

Contents: v. 1, USA and Canada; v. 2, Europe: West, North, Central and South; v. 3, Europe: East and Southeast; USSR; v. 4, Latin America and the West Indies; v. 5, Australia and New Zealand.

Intended as a "comprehensive, authoritative source of accurate, up-to-date information on journals and selected serial publications in the field of history ... for all current publications, both scholarly and popular, and those that have ceased publication since 1960."—*Introd.* Information is presented in a standard format and includes a statement of scope or purpose for each journal. "Interdisciplinary journals and those devoted to disciplines other than history are included if at least thirty percent of the articles are historical in content." Vol. 5 includes a title, subject, and geographic index to the full set.

Replaces *Historical periodicals*, Eric Boehm and Lalit Adolphus (Santa Barbara, Calif. : ABC-Clio, 1961), which may still be useful for information on discontinued publications.

§ For a listing of general historical periodicals published in Europe, *see* Heinrich Kramm, *Bibliographie historischer Zeitschriften, 1939–1951* (Marburg : Otto Rasch, 1952–54. 366 p.). Z6205.H654

Steiner, Dale R. Historical journals : a handbook for writers and reviewers / Dale R. Steiner and Casey R. Phillips. Jefferson, N.C. : McFarland, 1993. 274 p. **DA15**

1st ed., 1981.

A guide for the writer interested in placing works for publication in historical journals. Brief sections offering advice on articles and book reviewing are followed by an alphabetical listing of about 700

historical journals. For each, gives directory information and its policies regarding acceptance of manuscripts and book reviews. Based on responses to a questionnaire. Subject index. Z6205.S73

Dissertations

Doctoral dissertations in history. v. 1 (Jan./June 1976)– . [Wash.] : American Historical Association, Institutional Services Program, 1976– . **DA16**

Vol. 1 no. 1 was preceded by an unnumbered issue dated July/ Dec. 1975. With the July–Dec. 1976 issue the issue number is included in the numbering (i.e., v. 1, no. 2). Frequency varies.

Each issue follows a chronological (Ancient, Medieval, Modern)/geographical arrangement. The U.S. section is subarranged by subject. Within each section "in progress" listings precede the completed dissertations. Author index. Entries include author abstracts. Vol. 15/16 (1992) covering Jan. 1990–Dec. 1991 is a double volume, arranged alphabetically by institution and listing dissertations in progress. For this issue, information was solicited from history departments in the U.S. and Canada. Indexes for authors, broad subjects, geographic names, and time periods. Vol. 17 (Mar. 1993) covered Jan. 1992–Mar. 1993 while v. 18 (fall 1994) will list dissertations Apr.–Dec. 1993.

Continues: *List of doctoral dissertations in history in progress or recently completed in the United States, 1909–1970/73* (Wash. : American Historical Association, 1909–74. 50 v.) and for 1971–75, *Titles of dissertations in progress registered ... and completed dissertations reported during that period* (Wash. : American Historical Association, 1971–75).

§ For a similar publication for Canadian dissertations in progress, see *Register of post-graduate dissertations in progress in history and related subjects* (DB191). Z6205.D6

Jacobs, Phyllis M. History theses, 1901–70 : historical research for higher degrees in the universities of the United Kingdom. [London] : Univ. of London, Inst. of Historical Research, 1976. 456 p. **DA17**

Attempts to provide a comprehensive list of theses "completed and approved for the degree of B. Litt. and for doctor's and master's degrees in universities of the United Kingdom."—*Introd.* More than 7,600 entries; classed arrangement with author and subject indexes. Unfortunately, it is "not a list of theses which are necessarily available for consultation, since in nearly all British universities it is only in relatively recent years that students have been required to place a copy of their work on deposit." The compiler, however, has gone beyond a mere cumulation of the printed lists, attempting to verify citations, correct errors, and winnow out theses which may have been listed as completed but which were, in fact, never approved.

Continued by: *History theses, 1971–80 : historical research for higher degrees in the universities of United Kingdom*, comp. by Joyce M. Horn (London : Univ. of London, Inst. of Historical Research, 1984. 294 p.).

Adds an additional 4,416 titles drawn from the Institute's thesis lists and verified against *Index to theses accepted for higher degrees by the universities of Great Britain and Ireland* (London : Aslib, 1953–).

§ The Institute of Historical Research has also issued lists of research for university degrees in history from 1920 to 1953 (*Historical research for university degrees in the United Kingdom*), and since 1954, the annual *Historical research for university degrees in the United Kingdom* in two parts (Theses completed and Theses in progress). For more information, *see* DC284. Z6201.J23

Kuehl, Warren F. Dissertations in history : an index to dissertations completed in history departments of United States and Canadian universities. [Lexington] : Univ. of Kentucky Pr., 1965–85. 3 v. **DA18**

Contents: [v. 1], 1873–1960; v. 2, 1961–June 1970; v. 3, 1970–June 1980.

Intends to include "only those doctoral dissertations which have been written under formally organized departments of history and for which the degree of doctor of philosophy has been conferred."—*Introd.*, *v. 1*. It does not, therefore, include dissertations of a historical nature completed in related disciplines. The first volume lists more than 7,600 dissertations; the second, about 5,900, including some from the 1873–1960 period omitted from the earlier volume. Arrangement is alphabetical by author, with detailed subject index. (Indexing of v. 2 was done largely from abstracts rather than title alone, and is therefore more complete.) No attempt has been made to indicate publication information. Vol. 3, published by ABC-Clio, is topically arranged and gives University Microfilms order numbers for obtaining copies. Author and subject indexes. Z6201.K8

Encyclopedias; Dictionaries

See also CJ, Political Science—Armed Forces.

Cornell, James. The great international disaster book. 3rd ed. N.Y. : Scribner's, [1982]. 472 p. : ill. **DA19**
1st ed., 1976.
An encyclopedia of natural and man-made disasters, classified by category. "Each category begins with a list of the worst disasters of that particular type, as measured by loss of life. This is followed by a short introductory definition of the disaster phenomenon itself ... followed by an extensive summary of all major disasters in that category, in chronological order."—*Introd.* Excludes war, mass murders, massacres, and pogroms. Indexed. D24.C65

Dupuy, Richard Ernest. The Harper encyclopedia of military history : from 3500 BC to the present / R. Ernest Dupuy and Trevor N. Dupuy. 4th ed. N.Y. : HarperCollins, c1993. 1654 p. : ill., maps. **DA20**
1st ed., 1970; 2nd ed., 1977; 2nd rev. ed., 1986.
Wars, warfare, and military affairs are treated in a series of chronologically and geographically arranged chapters. Covers through the late 1980s with a few entries for 1990–91. Exhaustive general index for names and events with separate index sections for battles and sieges and for wars. Bibliography, p. 1573–83, keyed to text.
D25.D86

Eggenberger, David. An encyclopedia of battles : accounts of over 1,560 battles from 1479 BC to the present. N.Y. : Dover, 1985. 533 p. : maps. **DA21**
Rev. ed. of: *A dictionary of battles*, 1967.
The most detailed of the dictionaries of battles. "Attempts to provide the essential details of all the major battles in recorded history."—*Pref.* Covers more than 1,500 separate engagements "from the first battle of Megiddo in 1479 BC to the fighting in Vietnam in the 1960s." Includes approximately 100 battle maps. Index of names and places. This Dover edition adds an appendix containing essays on the Vietnam War, Russia's invasion of Afghanistan, the Falkland War, the Yom Kippur War, the Israeli invasion of Lebanon, the U.S. invasion of Grenada, and a supplementary index for the appendix. Also added is a 25-title Suggestions for further reading.
§ *See also*: Michael W. B. Sanderson, *Sea battles : a reference guide* (Middletown, Conn. : Wesleyan Univ. Pr., [1975]. 199 p.). Offers concise accounts of more than 250 naval battles, 494 BCE to 1944 CE. D25.A2E37

Harbottle, Thomas Benfield. Dictionary of battles. 3rd rev. ed. / by George Bruce. N.Y. : Van Nostrand ; London : Granada, 1981. 303 p. **DA22**
Repr.: London : Paladin, 1986, under title *Paladin dictionary of battles*.
1st ed., 1904.
Battles, sieges, raids, etc., are listed alphabetically by place-names, with indication of the war or campaign, dates, and a brief description of the fighting and outcome. In the 2nd ed. (1971) errors were corrected, sequences standardized, and 20th-century battles

added (often in some detail); for the 3rd ed., Vietnam and the Sino-Vietnamese War have been updated to early 1979, otherwise there are few changes. D25.A2H2

Kohn, George C. Dictionary of historic documents. N.Y. : Facts on File, c1991. 408 p. **DA23**
Identifies more than 2,200 documents and indicates their significance. Includes Western-language treaties, government acts, court cases, speeches, constitutions, and a few books (e.g., *Mein Kampf*) that have had "sufficient force to influence people and events."—*Pref.* Bibliography of collections of documents that contain the texts (though they are not keyed to the entries in the alphabetical arrangement). Extensive index. D9.K63

————— Dictionary of wars. N.Y. : Facts on File, c1986. 586 p. **DA24**
Intended to be a concise but comprehensive source for the major wars, revolutions, and rebellions, 2000 BCE to the present. Of primary concern in this work "is the military information, though political, social, and cultural influences are often specified."—*Pref.* Entries, arranged alphabetically, give the name(s) of the conflict, dates, how it began, opponents, leaders, concise descriptions or summaries of events, and outcome or significance. A geographic index is arranged by country, region, or polity, then chronologically. Name index.
§ Another popular survey is David G. Chandler's *Dictionary of battles : the world's key battles from 405 BC to the present* (N.Y. : Holt, [1987]. 255 p.). Heavily illustrated with photographs of statues, paintings, etc. (not named in the index or located in the text), and battle plans and maps. Topical index. D25.A2K63

Laffin, John. Brassey's battles : 3,500 years of conflict, campaigns, and wars from A–Z. London ; Wash. : Brassey's Defence Publ., 1986. 484 p. : ill., maps. **DA25**
Treats about 7,000 battles in dictionary arrangement. In general, follows the principle of "the more recent the event the longer the entry .... Recent conflicts deserve greater space if only because it is difficult for the average reader to find adequate consolidated information about events which are still in the news."—*Introd.* Includes various engagements not in David Eggenberger's *An encyclopedia of battles* (DA21), but entries tend to be much less detailed. Ends with 1982 and the Falkland Islands conflict. D25.A2L23

Wetterau, Bruce. Macmillan concise dictionary of world history. N.Y. : Macmillan, [1983]. 867 p. **DA26**
An alphabetical arrangement of about 17,000 entries for persons, places, terms, and events relating to world history of all periods up to 1982. Entries for individual countries, major wars, etc., usually consist mainly of a chronology. Uneven in coverage (e.g., a surprising number of entries for mythological figures; emphasis on American persons and events). D9.W47

Directories

Directory of history departments and organizations in the United States and Canada. 16th ed. (1990–91)– . Wash. : American Historical Association, Institutional Services Program, c1990– . Annual. **DA27**
1st–15th eds. (1975/76–1989/90) called: *Guide to departments of history.*
The "most up-to-date and comprehensive directory of historians in the United States and Canada and the departments and organization in which they work"—*p. iii*. For history departments gives: address, tuition, application deadlines, enrollment, departmental specializations, faculty profiles, titles of dissertations by recent graduates, fax number, and mailing address. For organizations (e.g., societies, state archives, associations) gives: address, description of collections, library, publications, editions in progress, awards and fellowships offered, and historians on the staff. Indexes of historians, doctoral degree recipients, schools by state or province, organizations by state or province.
D16.3.G83

Financial aids; Grants

Grants, fellowships & prizes of interest to historians. [Wash.] : American Historical Association, Institutional Services Program, 1987– . Annual.   **DA28**
Continues *Grants and fellowships of interest to historians* (1977–86).

    Listing is by name of the fund or the grant-giving agency. Indicates requirements for eligibility, amount and term of the grant, application deadline, etc.
    The 1991/92 edition is updated to contain more than 400 listings for organizations. The title change reflects a new section: Books, essays, and article awards and prizes.   D16.25.G69

Chronologies, outlines, tables

Carruth, Gorton. The encyclopedia of world facts and dates. N.Y. : HarperCollins, c1993. 1310 p.   **DA29**
    Provides chronology from 18,000,000,000 BCE and the Big Bang up to December 31, 1992. Paragraph-length entries arranged in categories (e.g., Vital statistics and demographics, Politics and war), within a time span that varies according to currency (e.g., 1900– has one-year, while 1500–1799 has ten-year increments). Extensive index.
    § Companion work: Carruth's *Encyclopedia of American facts and dates* (DB58).   CB69.C37

Everyman's dictionary of dates. 7th ed. / rev. by Audrey Butler. London : J.M. Dent, [1986], c1985. 631 p.   **DA30**
1st ed., 1911; 6th ed., 1971.
    Pt. 1 is a dictionary arrangement of definitions, surveys, lists (e.g. heads of state, treaties, popes), etc., of most interest to a British reader, although the coverage is international. Pt. 2 is a 73-page Chronology of events: from 30,000 BCE to 1985. Tables to reconcile Jewish and Gregorian calendars. Cross-references but no index.   D9.D5

Gribetz, Judah. The timetables of Jewish history : a chronology of the most important people and events in Jewish history / Judah Gribetz and Edward L. Greenstein and Regina Stein. N.Y. : Simon & Schuster, c1993. 808 p. : ill., maps.   **DA31**
    A chronology of key figures and important events from 9000 BCE–Dec. 1991 CE. Displays events in parallel columns (9000 BCE–500 CE): General history, Jewish history, Jewish culture. With 502 CE, adds columns for Jews in Europe and Jews in Middle East and North Africa. With 1492 CE, adds a column for Jews in North and South America. Brief information; occasional, well-chosen, photographs. Glossary, maps, tables (e.g., Yiddish daily newspapers published in New York in 1916, Soviet Jewish immigration 1968–1991). Topical index.
    § Máttis Kantor, *The Jewish time line encyclopedia* (New updated ed. Northvale, N.J. : Jason Aronson, c1992. 364 p.), is stronger for the biblical and talmudic periods.   DS114.G68

Grun, Bernard. The timetables of history : a horizontal linkage of people and events. New 3rd rev. ed. N.Y. : Simon & Schuster, c1991. 724 p. : ill.   **DA32**
1st ed., 1975.
    Contemporary names and events in various fields are presented in parallel columns: (A) History, politics; (B) Literature, theater; (C) Religion, philosophy, learning; (D) Visual arts; (E) Music; (F) Science, technology, growth; (G) Daily life. Much of the material is directly translated from Werner Stein's *Kulturfahrplan,* first published 1946. This edition covers events through 1990.
    § G. S. P. Freeman-Grenville's *Chronology of world history : a calendar of principal events from 3000 BC to AD 1976* (2nd ed. London : Collings ; Totowa, N.J. : Rowman & Littlefield, 1978. 746 p.) presents events and developments in tabular form, in six columns on facing pages. The 2nd ed. is updated to 1976, with added entries mainly in the "Religion & culture" column.   D11.G78

Haydn, Joseph Timothy. Dictionary of dates and universal information relating to all ages and nations / by the late Benjamin Vincent. Rev. and brought up to date by eminent authorities. 25th ed. London, Ward, Locke, 1910; N.Y., Putnam, 1911. 1614 p.   **DA33**
Repr.: N.Y. : Dover, 1969.
1st ed., 1841.
    A dictionary of history and general information alphabetically arranged with information under each heading given mainly in chronological lists. Convenient for specific facts of history and for its various lists, e.g., Lord Mayors of London, famous fires, inundations, etc. Addenda list includes events to Oct. 1910.   D9.H45

Johnson, David E. From day to day : a calendar of notable birthdays and events. Metuchen, N.J. : Scarecrow, 1990. 850 p.   **DA34**
    Compiled to "present chronologically the highlights in history of each day of the year, and consider which noteworthy events occurred and which famous persons were born on the day."—*Pref.* At the beginning of each month discusses the name of the month and its length, followed by the list of events and the list of birthdays, each in chronological order. More than 15,000 entries with name index. A review in *Booklist* 87 (15 Feb. 1991): 1248 finds that "*From Day to Day* covers western history, American pop culture, and sports so extensively that it is a welcome addition to this body of literature."
    § *See also* AL143 for Robert Lewis Collison, *Hamlyn dictionary of dates and anniversaries,* and Cyril Leslie Beeching, *Dictionary of dates.*   CT105.J64

Langer, William Leonard. The new illustrated encyclopedia of world history. N.Y. : H.N. Abrams, [1975]. 2 v. (1368 p.) : ill.   **DA35**
1st ed., 1940; 5th ed., 1972.
    The first edition constituted a new version of Karl Julius Ploetz's useful *Manual of universal history* (Boston : Houghton, 1925), giving concise, accurate outlines, not tables. Devoted primarily to political, military, and diplomatic history. Includes outline maps and genealogical tables. A 3rd ed. (1952) added new sections on the Second World War and the postwar world. The 4th ed. was fully revised and reset, with much new material added and numerous corrections made. The 1975 ed. includes world developments through 1970, adds a chapter on the recent period with sections devoted to the exploration of space and scientific and technological advances, and is heavily illustrated with photographs, maps, charts, drawings (often without attribution); however, the text is the same as the 1972 edition.   D21.L276

Paxton, John. Calendar of creative man / John Paxton and Sheila Fairfield. N.Y. : Facts on File, 1980. 497 p. : ill. **DA36**
    Repr. as: *Chronology of culture ... from 3000 BC to the present* (N.Y. : Van Nostrand, 1984).
    Entries covering artistic and literary development, 5th century CE–1975, are presented in eight columns: historical events, literature, dance and drama, music, architecture, three-dimensional art, visual arts, inventions and discoveries. Survey articles of up to 500 words for most categories are very sketchy. No index.   NX447.5.P38

The Random House timetables of history. N.Y. : Random House, 1991. 360 p. : ill.   **DA37**
    "Portions of this work were originally published in different form in the *Random House encyclopedia* new revised Third Edition"–*verso of t.p.*
    Chronology covering the first civilization, 4000–2000 BCE through 1989. Gives brief paragraph within each time span for Art and archeology, Music, Science and technology, Literature, Religion, Principal events. Index of names.   D11.R325

Steinberg, Sigfrid H. Historical tables, 58 BC–AD 1990. 12th ed. / updated by John Paxton. N.Y. : Garland, c1991. 324 p.   **DA38**
1st ed., 1939.
    A chronology of world history, arranged in six parallel columns by period, beginning with 58 BCE when Caesar subdued Gaul, and

covering through the 1990s. Up to World War I, political history is subdivided by geographic areas, with additional headings for constitutional and economic history, ecclesiastical history, and cultural life (these vary slightly according to period). After 1914, the columns are divided only by geographic area. Index of countries; personal names; events. D11.S83

Trager, James. The people's chronology : a year-by-year record of human events from prehistory to the present. Rev. and updated ed. N.Y. : H. Holt, c1992. 1237 p. : ill. **DA39**
1st ed., 1979.
More than 30,000 entries for major events in a broad range of topics—political affairs, technology, art and photography, environment, consumer protection, food and drink—designated by symbols. Much is found here that is not readily located in similar chronologies. Indexed. Coverage to 1991.
•Available in machine-readable form as part of *Microsoft bookshelf '94* [database] (AB27). D11.T83

Wetterau, Bruce. The New York Public Library book of chronologies. N.Y. : Prentice Hall, c1990. 634 p. **DA40**
Provides 250 chronologies arranged by broad topic (e.g., under "Technology" are chronologies for prehistoric tools, clocks, photography, development of ships, the quest for speed). Boxes within some of the chronologies give added information, usually lists such as winners of Nobel prizes, British prime ministers, U.S. Supreme Court justices. Name index. D11.W47

Historiography

Cook, Chris. Dictionary of historical terms. 2nd ed. N.Y. : Peter Bedrick Books, 1990. 350 p. **DA41**
1st ed., 1983. 2nd ed. also published as *Macmillan dictionary of historical terms* (London : Macmillan Reference, 1989).
Aims to cover "historical terms that are frequently encountered by both undergraduates and research students."—*Pref.* Included are foreign words, very new terms, technical terms, etc. Users should follow up on *see also* references since many terms given a one-sentence definition receive fuller treatment in another, related entry.
The 2nd ed. is mainly an updating with a few new terms, such as "perestroika," or with a sentence or two added to cover the 1980s in such articles as those for PLO and ZAPU, or the addition of a death date (e.g., Harold Macmillan's death date added in the article "Wind of change"). No index. D9.C67

Dictionnaire des sciences historiques / publié sous la direction de André Burguière. Paris : Presses universitaires de France, c1986. 693 p. **DA42**
A dictionary of broad topics (e.g., Africa, Bourgeoisie, Women, Revolution) with discussion of how they have been treated by French historians. Each article has a short bibliography of fairly recent materials (a few publications from the 1980s are included). Numerous page-length articles on noted French and German historians (e.g, Bloch, Froissart, Monod). Not indexed. D9.D57

Lawton, Henry. The psychohistorian's handbook. N.Y. : Psychohistory Pr., c1988. 241 p. **DA43**
Both a guide to psychohistory research and a bibliography of books and articles leading the researcher deeper into the field. The overview of the field cites major journals and associations, and considers such aspects as training, methodology, types of psychohistory, getting published, and teaching psychohistory. An appendix lists notable psychohistorical work. No index.
§ For a more extensive bibliography see William J. Gilmore, *Psychohistorical inquiry* (DA5). D16.16.L38

Pók, Attila. A selected bibliography of modern historiography. N.Y. : Greenwood, 1992. 284 p. (Bibliographies and indexes in world history, no. 24). **DA44**

Prep. under the auspices of the Institute of History of the Hungarian Academy of Sciences.
Updates and expands Lester D. Stephens, *Historiography : a bibliography* (Metuchen, N.J. : Scarecrow, 1975. 271 p.).
Entries for some 2,500 books and articles of the 19th and 20th centuries, in all languages and for all countries, on the development of the historical sciences, in general or in a given age or field. A section of general works is followed by lists for continent and country. Strongest on Eastern Europe, the Soviet Union, and Germany. Index: author, persons discussed, subjects.
§ Strongest for English-language materials is R.C. Richardson, *The study of history : a bibliographical guide* (Manchester ; N.Y. : Manchester Univ. Pr. ; N.Y. : Distr. by St. Martin's, c1988. 98 p.). Z6208.H5P64

Ritter, Harry. Dictionary of concepts in history. Westport, Conn. : Greenwood, 1986. 490 p. (Reference sources for the social sciences and humanities, no. 3.). **DA45**
About 100 "key concepts of contemporary historical analysis" (*Pref.*) are discussed in short essays (e.g., Feudalism, Alienation, New history). For each, gives a short definition; historical development, usage, and evolution of the term; and sources of additional information. Cross-references; subject index. D13.R49

Biography

The Blackwell dictionary of historians / ed. by John Cannon ... [et al]. N.Y. ; Oxford : Blackwell Reference, 1988. 480 p. **DA46**
Contains articles on terms, movements, historiography of particular countries, and "450 biographical entries which indicate the scholarly reputation of historians, the circumstances in which they worked, and the extent to which their work has subsequently been confirmed or refuted."—*Pref.* Includes about 50 entries for living historians. Most articles are two to three paragraphs in length and often end with a list of principal publications and secondary works. Entries are signed with the initials of contributing scholars, most of them British. Indexed. D14.B58

Epstein, Catherine. A past renewed : a catalog of German-speaking refugee historians in the United States after 1933. N.Y. : Cambridge Univ. Pr., 1993. 386 p. **DA47**
A biobibliography of scholars who received their formal training and who began their careers in Germany or Austria-Hungary, and who emigrated and taught history in the U.S. after 1933. Gives birth, death, and emigration dates; education; positions held; archival sources; primary and secondary bibliography (i.e., works about followed by works by); festschriften. Index of names and institutions. E175.45.E67

Great historians from antiquity to 1800 : an international dictionary / Lucian Boia, ed. in chief. N.Y. : Greenwood, [1989]. 417 p. **DA48**
Sponsored by the Commission on the History of Historiography of the International Commission on the Historical Sciences.
Two criteria for inclusion were: " 'absolute' merit of those individuals in the development of universal historiography and their significance within each national culture."—*Pref.* Signed articles are arranged by country or geographical area, e.g. Austrian, African, Southeast Asian, Islamic. Each entry covers the subject's life and contributions and includes a short bibliography of secondary works. Indexes of historians, subjects. D14.G74

Atlases

Atlas of world history / [general ed., R. I. Moore]. Chicago : Rand McNally, 1992. 192 p. : ill., 31 cm. **DA49**

1st ed., 1957.

Earlier eds. had title: *Rand McNally atlas of world history*.

Publ. in U.K. as: *Philip's atlas of world history* (London : Philip's, 1992).

Well-made maps, about 87 from 23 contributors, plus an additional section of 11 maps and three statistical tables for U.S. history. Textual comment for each map ends with a section of further readings that has been updated for this edition. Maps are intended to be up-to-date as of 1990. A "Survey of maps by date and region" acts as an index, and there is an "Index of alternative place names."   G1030.R36

Banks, Arthur. A world atlas of military history. N.Y. : Hippocrene Books, [1973–84]. v. 1, [3–4]. : ill., maps.   **DA50**

First publ. in London by Seeley Service and Co.; v. 4 publ. in London by Leo Cooper in assoc. with Secker & Warburg.

Contents: v. 1, To 1500 [reissued 1982 as *Atlas of ancient and medieval warfare*]; [v. 3] 1861–1945 (publ. 1978); [v. 4] 1945–1984 by T. Hartman.

Black-and-white maps with notes printed on the maps. Some general maps in addition to those for wars, particular battles, defense systems, etc. Indexes of battles, individuals, groups of peoples, and places.   G1030.B27

Georg Westermann Verlag. Grosser Atlas zur Weltgeschichte / hrsg. von Hans-Erich Stier [et al.]. Bearb. von Hans-Erich Stier [et al.]. Unter Mitarbeit von Ekkehard Aner … . [Aufl. 10]. Braunschweig : Westermann, [1983?]. 170 p. of maps in color, 78 p.   **DA51**

1st ed., 1956.

A good modern atlas primarily of Europe, Africa, and western Asia. Covers from ancient times to about 1980. Includes many detailed maps of cities and other special areas. Indexes of place-names, of subjects, and by continent and country.   G1030.W448

Gilbert, Martin. The Dent atlas of Jewish history. 5th ed. London : J.M. Dent, 1993. 132 p. [i.e. 136] : maps. in color ; 26cm.   **DA52**

1st–4th eds. (1969–92) had title: *Jewish history atlas*.

Mainly single-page maps in black-and-white tracing "the worldwide Jewish migrations from ancient Mesopotamia to modern Israel."—*Pref.* Some maps have been revised and expanded, (e.g., number of Jews worldwide; Hebrew language newspapers and libraries in the Soviet Union, 1992). The number of maps in this edition has increased to 132 (from 123). The index of the earlier edition was dropped; the bibliography has been retained with little change.

§ A recent compilation with more text and illustrations is N. R. M. DeLange's *Atlas of the Jewish world* (Oxford : Phaidon; N.Y. : Facts on File, 1984. 240 p.).   G1030.G46

Grosser historischer Weltatlas. Munich : Bayerischer Schulbuch-Verlag, 1978–81. 3 v. : maps in color; 33cm.   **DA53**

Individual volumes revised at intervals.

Contents: T. 1, Vorgeschichte und Altertum (6. Aufl., 1978); T. 2, Mittelalter (2. Aufl., 1980?); T. 3, Neuzeit (4. Aufl., 1981).

An excellent example of German map-making. Clear, comprehensive maps with detailed table of contents and place-name index for each part. T. 1 covers prehistory to approximately 1200; T. 3, from late 15th century to the present.

Accompanied by *Erläuterungen*, by Hermann Bengtson … [et al.] (Munich : Bayerischer Schulbuch-Verlag, 1976–84. 3 v.).

Contents: T. 1, Vorgeschichte und Altertum; T. 2, Mittelalter; T. 3, Neuzeit.

Explains the context of each map and provides bibliography.   G1030.B38

The Harper atlas of world history. Rev. ed. N.Y. : Harper-Collins, c1992. 355 p. : ill., maps in color; 30 cm.   **DA54**

Translation of *Histoire de l'humanité* (Paris : Hachette, 1992). Ed. by Pierre Vidal-Naquet; Jacques Bertin, cartographer.

Presents colorful graphs, maps, reproductions, chronologies, texts, and photographs from the period of the Rift Valley to early 1992, with in some cases projections to the year 2000. Scales vary.

The addition of a table of contents would be of great help; topical index. This new edition adds new maps and revises existing maps for the period from the Cold War to the present.   G1030.G68513

Martin Greenwald Associates. Historical maps on file. N.Y. : Facts on File, c1984. 1 v. [looseleaf]) : 30 cm.   **DA55**

For annotation, *see* CL282.   G1030.M37

Natkiel, Richard. Atlas of maritime history / Richard Natkiel, Antony Preston. N.Y. : Facts on File, c1986. 256 p. : ill., maps in color; 28 cm.   **DA56**

Published in U.K. as *The Weidenfeld atlas of maritime history* (London : Weidenfeld and Nicolson, 1986).

Offers textual commentary with well-integrated maps, drawings, and photographs covering from the Phoenicians to maritime trade in the 1980s. Emphasizes naval battles, explorations, and the evolving patterns of trade and commerce. Two-page glossary. Index of topics and names of people, places, and ships.

§ See also: *Atlas of maritime history*, comp. by Christopher Lloyd (N.Y. : Arco, 1975. 144 p. 34 cm.).   G1059.N3

Shepherd, William Robert. Historical atlas. 9th ed. N.Y. : Barnes & Noble, 1964. 226, 115p. : col. maps (part folded).   **DA57**

Repr. with revisions: Totowa, N. J. : Barnes & Noble, 1980.

1st ed., 1911; 7th ed., 1929, the last published under Shepherd's direction.

For many years the standard and most used historical atlas. Covers from 1450 BCE to 1964. The 9th ed. contains all the maps of the 7th ed. and a special supplement (plates 218–26) of maps for the period since 1929, prepared by C. S. Hammond & Company.

The index is in three parts: (1) Original index; (2) Index-Supplement, which includes names contained in the maps for the period 1911–29, as well as some earlier ones, but does not include the new section, 1930–64; (3) Additional changes.

Sections have also been published separately, e.g., *Atlas of ancient history*; *Atlas of medieval and modern history*.

§ Another older atlas, still useful for maps depicting political history, is *Muir's historical atlas : ancient and modern*, ed. R.F. Treharne and Harold Fullard (10th ed., N.Y. : Barnes & Noble, 1964. 116 p. of colored maps). Both atlases are Eurocentric (and emphasize Western Europe).   G1030.S4

The Times atlas of world history / ed. by Geoffrey Barraclough. 4th ed. / ed. by Geoffrey Parker. London : Times Books ; Maplewood, N.J. : Hammond, 1993. 360 p. : ill., maps. 37cm.   **DA58**

3rd ed., 1989.

Aims "to present a view of history which is world-wide in conception and presentation and which does justice, without prejudice or favour, to the achievements of all peoples in all ages and in all quarters of the globe."—*Introd.* Plates, with accompanying text by contributing scholars, are grouped in seven main sections: (1) The world of early man; (2) The first civilisations; (3) The classical civilisations of Eurasia; (4) The world of divided regions; (5) The world of the emerging West; (6) The age of European dominance; (7) The age of global civilisation. Glossary, p.297–334; index, p.335–60.

Plates show considerable revision especially in the prehistoric and post-1945 sections (e.g., the chapter "Origins of man" is totally revised and rewritten). The chronology is updated to 1991–92.   G1030.T54

ARCHAEOLOGY AND ANCIENT HISTORY

For archaeology of a particular country, *see* under the name of that country.

General works

Guides

Bengtson, Hermann. Introduction to ancient history. Berkeley : Univ. of California Pr., 1970. 213 p.   **DA59**

Translated by R. I. Frank and Frank D. Gilliard from the 6th ed. of *Einführung in die alte Geschichte.*

Pt. 1 is a series of essays followed by bibliography on broad areas of historiography (e.g., "The scope of ancient history," "The sources," "The monuments," "The history of the study of antiquity from Renaissance to the present"). Pt. 2 is a bibliography of studies, organized to follow the *Cambridge ancient history* (1924–39); many of the titles cited are in English. Name and topical indexes. Although dated and lacking any mention of electronic resources, it is still useful for identifying basic printed materials.   Z6202.B413

Heizer, Robert Fleming. Archaeology : a bibliographical guide to the basic literature / Robert Fleming Heizer, Thomas R. Hester, Carol Graves. N.Y. : Garland, 1980. 434 p. (Garland reference library of social science, v. 54).   **DA60**

A compilation of more than 4,800 English-language references published up to 1979 and grouped as: Nature and purpose of archaeology; History of archaeology; The work of the archaeologist; Archaeology as a profession; Sources of primary data. Sections are subdivided as appropriate. Intends to identify "those publications which are important reference and research aids" (*Pref.*); emphasis is on New World archaeology, although an effort was made "to include reasonable coverage of the Old World, Africa, and Asia." Author index only. Though dated, still useful especially for beginning resources and New World archaeology.   Z5131.I144

Woodhead, Peter. Keyguide to information sources in archaeology. London ; N.Y. : Mansell, 1985. 219 p.   **DA61**

A discussion of archaeological research, its relationship to other disciplines, and to forms of archaeological literature is followed by an annotated bibliography of reference sources, topically arranged. The third part lists an archaeological organization for each country. Index of names, titles, and subjects.   CC120.W66

Bibliography

Allen, Peter S. Archaeology on film : a comprehensive guide to audio-visual materials / Peter S. Allen, Carole Lazio. [Boston] : Archaeological Inst. of America, [1983]. 240 p.   **DA62**

A title listing of films and videotapes currently available in the U.S. which "deal explicitly with archaeology or artifacts recovered from scientific excavation."—*Introd.* Gives production information, distributor, audience level, references to reviews, and brief description. Broad subject and geographic area index.

A 1995 edition, comp. by Mary Downs [et al.], was announced by the Archaeological Institute of America.

Deutsches Archäologisches Institut. Römische Abteilung. Bibliothek. Kataloge der Bibliothek des Deutschen Archaeologischen Instituts, Rom. Boston : G.K. Hall, 1969. 13 v.   **DA63**

In three sections: Autoren- und Periodica Kataloge; Systematischer Katalog; Zeitschriften-Autorenkatalog. The sections are available separately: the author and periodical catalogs in 7 v.; the classified catalog in 3 v.; and the author catalog of periodical references in 3 v.

Reproduces the catalog cards of one of the world's strongest archaeological libraries, representing some 91,000 volumes in all areas of European and Near Eastern archaeology and philology, from the prehistoric to the Byzantine period. Coverage of the *Zeitschriften-Autorenkatalog* begins with articles published in 1956 in periodicals, festschriften, and other special publications; articles indexed are limited to classical archaeology and epigraphy.

An earlier edition of the catalog is still useful for its references to journal articles of the pre-1956 period and the more complete book citations: *Katalog der Bibliothek des Kaiserlich Deutschen Archäologischer Instituts in Rom* ... (Berlin : W. de Gruyter, 1913–32. 2 v. in 4) and supplement (1930. 516 p.).

Continued by the institute's microfiche subject catalog (1985) and *DYABOLA* database (DA70).

§ The Institut has also issued a useful list of journals received in the library: *Zeitschriftenverzeichnis* (Wiesbaden : Steiner, 1964. 327 p.). It gives publication history and indicates title changes.

Z5134.R764

Ellis, Linda. Laboratory techniques in archaeology : a guide to the literature, 1920–1980. N.Y. : Garland, 1982. 419 p. (Garland reference library of social science, v. 110).   **DA64**

A thorough bibliography of some 3,755 items (in English, German, French, Italian, Spanish, or Russian) dealing with the application of any of the sciences to archaeology. Arranged by problem areas (remote sensing, chronometry, environmental reconstruction, materials analysis, data management) plus a general section, each appropriately subdivided. Indexed by author, geographic area, method of analysis, type of material analyzed.

§ A related bibliography somewhat older is *Bibliographie der archäologischen Konservierungstechnik*, comp. by Paul Gaudel (2. verb. Aufl. Berlin : Hessling, 1969. 374 p.) which provides extensive annotations for 1,800 books and periodical articles in a classed arrangement.   Z5131.E43

Harvard University. Library. Ancient history : classification schedule, classified listing by call number, chronological listing, author and title listing. Cambridge : Publ. by Harvard Univ. Libr.; distr. by Harvard Univ. Pr., 1975. 363 p. (Widener Library shelflist, 55).   **DA65**

For a note on the Widner shelflist series, *see* AA115.

"This volume ... lists more than 11,000 titles concerning the history, civilization, government, economic and social conditions, and geography of the Mediterranean region and Western Asia down to the Barbarian invasions in Europe and the Arab conquest in Asia and Africa. Also included are works on Egyptian and Assyro-Babylonian literatures and on the archaeology of Assyria and Babylonia. In general, archaeological works and works on prehistoric times are excluded."—*Pref.*

§ Related title from the shelflist series: *Archaeology : classification schedules; classified listing by call number; chronological listing; author and title listing* (1979. 442 p. [Widener Library shelflist, 56]). About 14,300 shelf list entries for the Widener *Arc* class, including the related disciplines of paleography and diplomatics, sigillography, and numismatics.   Z6202.H37

Kerber, Jordan E. Coastal and maritime archaeology : a bibliography. Metuchen, N.J. : Scarecrow, 1991. 400 p.   **DA66**

Offers 2,800 citations to books, essays, articles, theses, conference papers (often unpublished) dealing with "hunting, gathering, fishing and, to a limited extent, horticulture practiced as coastal and maritime adaptations by indigenous groups predominantly during the prehistoric period."—*Introd.* Divided into four chapters: Prehistoric worldwide; Prehistoric, North American Atlantic; Shellfish and shell middens, worldwide; History and ethnography, worldwide. Author index. Needs a subject or site index.   Z5133.U53K47

Rounds, Dorothy. Articles on antiquity in festschriften : the ancient Near East, the Old Testament, Greece, Rome, Roman law, Byzantium; an index. Cambridge : Harvard Univ. Pr., 1962. 560 p.   **DA67**

An index of festschriften, including in one alphabet: names of scholars and institutions honored, names of authors of articles, and all significant words in the titles of the articles.   Z6202.R6

Vogt, Joseph. Bibliographie zur antiken Sklaverei / im Auftrag der Kommission für Geschichte des Altertums der Akademie der Wissenschaften und der Literatur hrsg. von Joseph Vogt und Heinz Bellen ; neu bearb. von Elisabeth Herrmann in Verbindung mit Norbert Brockmeyer. Bochum : Brockmeyer, 1983. 2 v. (391 p.).   **DA68**

1st ed., 1971.

A classed bibliography of slavery in antiquity (5,162 entries). A high percentage of citations relates to Greece and Rome, but there are references to slavery in other parts of Europe, Egypt, the Middle East, East Asia, etc. Indexed.   Z7164.S6V64

Current

Archäologische Bibliographie. 1913– . Berlin : W. deGruyter, 1914– . Annual.   **DA69**

Title varies; publisher varies. Issued by the Deutsches Archäologisches Institut.

Continues the bibliographies previously included in the "Archäologischer Anzeiger" section of the Institut's *Jahrbuch,* 1889–1912; vols. for 1913–72 issued as "Beilage" to the *Jahrbuch.* Frequency varies: annual except 1916/17, 1918/19, 1923/24, and 1944/48.

A useful, topically arranged bibliography of books, periodical articles, and book reviews; broad in scope, international in coverage. Originally indexed by name (personal and place); beginning 1976, has name index, reviewer index, and a topical index (which includes names of periodicals devoted to a given topic). From 1986, superseded for the most part by *DYABOLA* [database] (DA70).

§ For its brief period of coverage, 1952–1959/60, the *Annuario bibliografico di archaeologia* (Modena : Soc. Tipografica, 1954–66) is a useful complement. See also: *Art and archaeology technical abstracts* (BF198).   Z5132.A67

•DYABOLA : alphabetic conversion of alphabetic and subject catalogues [database]. Enneptetal : Biering und Brinkmann, 1956– .   **DA70**

Produced for the Deutsches Archäologisches Institut.

Available on CD-ROM, updated annually. Issued in installments covering 1956–69, 1970–85, 1986–90.

Offers retrieval of citations to books, journal articles, reports, etc., by author, subject, keyword, title, and year of publication. Includes, from 1956, all entries in *Archäologische Bibliographie* (DA69), including those in its subject catalogue on microfiche, except those covering the early Christian period and the ancient Near East.

Sovetskai͡a arkheologicheskai͡a literatura : bibliografii͡a, 1918/40–1979/81 / sostaviteli T. N. Zadneprovskai͡a, R. Sh. Levina, L. M. Vseviov. Leningrad : "Nauka," Leningradskoe otd-nie, 1959–89. v. 1–8. (In progress).   **DA71**

1976/78 and subsequent volumes have subtitle: *Bibliograficheskiĭ ukazatel'.*

At head of title: Akademii͡a Nauk SSSR. Biblioteka Akademii nauk SSSR, and Institut Arkheologii.

Issued as follows: 1918–40, ed. by N. A. Vinberg (1965. 376 p.); 1941–57, ed. by N. A. Vinberg (Moscow, 1959. 773 p.); 1958–62, ed. by T. N. Zadneprovskai͡a (1969. 414 p.); 1963–67, ed. by T. N. Zadneprovskai͡a (1975. 471 p.); 1968–72, ed. by T. N. Zadneprovskai͡a (1980. 557 p.); 1973–75, ed. by T. N. Zadneprovskai͡a (1983. 376 p.); 1976–78, ed. by T. N. Zadneprovskai͡a, R. Sh. Levina, L. M. Vseviov (1986. 383 p.); 1979–1981, ed. by R. Sh. Levina, T. N. Zadneprovskai͡a, L. M. Vseviov (1989. 471 p.).

A classified bibliography of Soviet publications in archaeology, covering paleolithic times to the 17th century. In addition to books and periodical articles, there are citations to dissertations and parts of books, as well as reviews of major publications. Indexes for authors, archaeological monuments, and related subjects such as numismatics, sphragistics, and history of technology.

§ Updated by: *Novai͡a sovetskai͡a literatura po obshchestvennym nauckam : istorii͡a, arkheologii͡a, etnografii͡a* (Moskva : Akademii͡a Nauk SSSR, In-t nauch. informatsii po obshchestvennym naukam), a monthly begun in 1976 and continuing an older series. Lists books and articles by Soviet (now Russian) scholars. No cumulative indexes.   Z5131.Z33

Swedish archaeological bibliography. 1939/48–1971/75. Uppsala ; Stockholm : Almqvist & Wiksell, 1951–78.   **DA72**

Since the initial volume, each covered a five- or six-year period as follows: 1939–48, ed. by Sverker Janson and Olof Vessberg (1951. 360 p.); 1949–53, ed. by Christian Callmer and Wilhelm Holmqvist (1956. 294 p.); 1954–59, ed. by Wilhelm Odelberg and Hilding Thylander (1965. 259 p.); 1960–65, ed. by Marten Stenberger and Anders Hedvall (1968. 289 p.); 1966–70, ed. by Marten Stenberger and Anders Hedvall (1972. 331 p.); 1971–75, ed. by Sverker Janson and Hilding Thylander (1978. 338 p.).

A survey, in English, sponsored by the Svenska Arkeologiska Samfundet, listing Swedish archaeological literature.

§ Continued by: *Swedish archaeology,* 1976/80–1981/85. ([Stockholm] : Svenska Arkeologiska Samfundet, [c1983–87]) and by *Current Swedish archaeology* (1993–), an annual with 5-year cumulations (the first to cover 1986–90, publ. 1995).

Offers bibliographical essays by Swedish scholars discussing trends in the fields of archaeology with citations to the works discussed ending each essay. Citations to works on Norwegian archaeology are now incorporated into *Nordic archaeological abstracts* (v. 1 [1971]– . Viborg, 1974– . Annual), but references to classical archaeology remain in *Swedish archaeology.*   Z5111.S86

Dissertations

Drexhage, Hans-Joachim. Deutschsprachige Dissertationen zur alten Geschichte, 1844–1978. Wiesbaden : Franz Steiner Verlag, 1980. 142 p.   **DA73**

An author listing of about 2,700 German-language dissertations (including those from Austrian and Swiss universities) on ancient history. Three indexes: Personen– und Völkernamen, Orts– und Ländernamen, Sachregister.   Z6207.G7D73

Encyclopedias; Dictionaries

The Cambridge encyclopedia of archaeology / ed., Andrew Sherratt. N.Y. : Crown/Cambridge Univ. Pr., [1980]. 495 p. : ill., maps.   **DA74**

A topically arranged encyclopedia, each of its 64 chapters contributed by a specialist. A work for the educated general reader rather than for the scholar. In three main sections, the first treating the development of modern archaeology; the second (and most extensive) treating the various archaeological periods, regions, empires, etc., of archaeological study; and the third devoted to "Frameworks: dating and distribution." Chapter-by-chapter bibliography, p. 453–67. Indexed.   CC165.C3

Champion, Sara. A dictionary of terms and techniques in archaeology. Oxford : Phaidon ; N.Y. : Facts on File, 1980. 144 p. : ill.   **DA75**

A well-written dictionary "for the non-professional archaeologist" (*Introd.*), covering terms used in the scientific and technical aspects of archaeology; thus, considerable attention is given to matters such as dating techniques, but there are no definitions for cultures or artifacts. For major articles on techniques (e.g., aerial photography) a single, carefully chosen bibliographical reference is provided, and there is a general bibliography.

The review in *Booklist* 77 (1 June 1981) : 1310 points out that despite the "decided British emphasis in the examples and illustrations used," the dictionary "covers American work and usage quite adequately." CC70.C48

Collins dictionary of archaeology / ed. by Paul Bahn. Denver, Colo. : ABC-Clio, 1993. 654 p. **DA76**

A useful dictionary for theoretical and technical terms, sites, and archeologists, with "comparatively few entries from postclassical/historical/colonial periods, and none at all from industrial archaeology."—*Introd.* Illustrations (often line drawings) are occasionally found on pages following the entry. Cross-references in small caps; appendix with maps showing sites. Topically arranged reading list. CC70.C58

Cottrell, Leonard. Concise encyclopedia of archaeology. 3rd ed. London : Hutchinson, [1974]. 430 p. : maps; charts; photographs. **DA77**

1st ed., 1960.

A dictionary for the "intelligent amateur." Entries for archaeological discoveries and techniques, as well as for archaeologists. Emphasis is on archaeology outside Greece and Rome and medieval Europe. Useful, although depth of treatment is uneven. Maps, charts, photographs.

§ A similar work, *The illustrated encyclopedia of archaeology*, ed. by Glyn Daniel (N.Y. : Crowell, 1977. 244 p.), offers short articles and surveys; it is especially strong in Egyptian archaeology. CC70.C6

Dictionnaire de la préhistoire / directeur de la publication, André Leroi-Gourhan. Paris : Pr. universitaires de France, c1988. 1222 p. (16 p. of plates) : ill. **DA78**

Contains definitions of terms and descriptions of the most important sites, together with entries for names of early cultures, prehistoric periods, etc. Signed articles, most of which end with one to three bibliographical references.

§ See also *Encyclopedia of human evolution and prehistory* (CE40). GN710.D53

The Facts on File dictionary of archaeology / ed., Ruth D. Whitehouse. N.Y. : Facts on File, 1984. 597 p. : ill. **DA79**

Publ. in the U.K. as: *The Macmillan dictionary of archaeology* (London : Macmillan, [1983]).

International in coverage. So far as possible, uses non-technical language. Entries for terms, sites, persons, surveys of geographical areas, etc. Cross-references; subject index (including a geographical approach); select bibliography. One of the most complete sources. CC70.F32

Reallexikon der Assyriologie, unter Mitwirkung zahlreicher Fachgelehrter / hrsg. von Erich Ebeling ... und Bruno Meissner ... [et al.]. Berlin und Leipzig : W. de Gruyter & Co., 1928–94. v. 1–8³⁻⁴ : ill. (In progress). **DA80**

Contents: v. 1–8³⁻⁴, A–Moab.

A scholarly encyclopedia on Assyriology, with signed articles and extensive bibliographies. DS69.1.R4

Handbooks

Handbuch der Archaeologie : im Rahmen des Handbuchs der Altertumswissenschaft / hrsg. von Walter Otto. Munich : Beck, 1939–54. v. 1–2, 3¹, 4¹ : ill. (I. P. E. Müller, Handbuch der Altertumswissenschaft, 6. Abt.). **DA81**

A heavily documented history, each volume accompanied by a section of plates.

A new edition has begun to appear as: *Handbuch der Archäologie*, neu hrsg. von Ulrich Hausmann (München : Beck, 1969–88. v. 1–4. [In progress]).

Contents: [v. 1], Allgemeine Grundlagen der Archäologie, mit Beiträgen, von Hellmut Brunner [et al.]; [v. 2], Vorderasien I: Meso-

patamien, Babylonien, Iran, und Anatolien, von Barthel Hrouda; [pt. 2], Vorderasien II: Palestina in verhellenistischer Zeit, von Helga Weippert; [v. 3], Die antiken Gemmen, von Peter Zazoff; [v. 4], Römische Sarkophage, von Guntran Koch und Hellmut Sichtermann; [unnumbered], Die griechische Plastik, von Werner Fuchs. CC65.H3

Müller-Karpe, Hermann. Handbuch der Vorgeschichte. München : Beck, 1966–80. 4 v. in 10 : ill., maps, plates. **DA82**

Contents: v. 1, Altsteinzeit (1. Aufl., 1966; 2. Aufl., 1977. 2 v.); v. 2, Jungsteinzeit (1968. 2 v.); v. 3, Kupferzeit (1974. 3 v.); v. 4, Bronzerzeit (1980. 3 v.); v. 5, Frühe Eisenzeit (never publ.).

Discussions of the state of knowledge of each period (covering chronology, art, religion, social life, etc.) are followed by surveys of relevant sites arranged by country and giving for each a brief description and bibliography. Heavily illustrated with plates showing tools and art works; well indexed.

§ Max Ebert's *Reallexikon der Vorgeschichte* ... (Berlin : W. de Gruyter, 1924–32. 15 v.) may still prove useful, particularly in view of its dictionary arrangement. GN739.M8

Chronologies

Chronologies in Old World archaeology / ed. by Robert W. Ehrich. 3rd ed. Chicago : Univ. of Chicago Pr., 1992. 2 v. : ill., maps. **DA83**

1st ed., 1954; 2nd ed., 1965.

A survey of geographic areas (e.g., Egypt, northwest Europe, southwest Asia arid zone) from the "earliest settlements down to a breaking point of between 2000 and 1500 BC" with concentration on "1) sequences, 2) distribution and relationships, 3) calibrated radiocarbon and relative dates, 4) pertinent bibliography and sources."—*Foreword.* Vol. 1 is limited to the texts; v. 2 covers tables of radiocarbon dates, synchronic charts, drawings of pottery, maps, and bibliographics. Each chapter is indexed separately. D54.5.C48

Smithsonian timelines of the ancient world / [ed. in chief], Chris Scarre. [Wash.] : Smithsonian Institution ; N.Y. : D. Kindersley, c1993. 256 p. : ill., maps in color. **DA84**

A very handsome, heavily illustrated chronology covering from earliest times to 1500 CE. Consists of "18 chapters with each chapter built around a sequence of timecharts" (*p. 14*) divided by theme (e.g. Food and environment, Shelter and architecture, Technology and innovation, Art and ritual). The timecharts designate five regions (the Americas; East Asia and Australasia; Middle East and South Asia; Europe; Africa). Selected topics are presented in more detail in special features pages. Index of topics and locations. D54.5.S65

General histories

Cambridge ancient history. 1st–3rd eds. Cambridge ; London : Cambridge Univ. Pr., 1923– . [v. 1–12]. (In progress). **DA85**

Contents: v. 1 pt. 1, Prolegomena and prehistory, ed. by I. E. S. Edwards, C. J. Gadd, and N. G. L. Hammond (3rd ed., 1970); v. 1 pt. 2, Early history of the Middle East, ed. by I. E. S. Edwards, C. J. Gadd, and N. G. L. Hammond (3rd ed., 1971); v. 2 pt. 1, History of the Middle East and the Aegean region, c. 1800–1380 B.C., ed. by I. E. S. Edwards ... [et al.] (3rd ed., 1973); v. 2 pt. 2, History of the Middle East and the Aegean region, c. 1380–1000 B.C., ed. by I. E. S. Edwards ... [et al.] (3rd ed., 1975); v. 3 pt. 1, The prehistory of the Balkans and the Middle East and the Aegean World, tenth to eighth centuries, B.C., ed. by John Boardman ... [et al.] (2nd ed., [1982]); v. 3 pt. 2, The Assyrian and Babylonian empires and other states of the Near East, from the eighth to the sixth centuries B.C., ed. John Boardman ... [et al] (2nd ed., 1991); v. 3 pt. 3, The expansion of the Greek world, eighth to sixth centuries, B.C., ed. by John Boardman, N. G. L. Hammond (2nd ed., [1982]); v. 4, The Persian Empire and the West, ed. by J. B. Burry, S. A. Cook, F. E. Adcock (2nd ed., 1988); v. 5, Athens,

478–401 B.C., ed. by J. B. Burry, S. A. Cook, F. E. Adcock (1st ed., [1927]; repr. with corrections, [1935]); v. 6, The fourth century B.C., ed. D. M. Lewis (2nd ed., 1994); v. 7 pt. 1, The Hellenistic world, ed. by F. W. Walbank ... [et al.] (2nd ed., 1984); v. 7 pt. 2, The Hellenistic monarchies and the rise of Rome, ed. by S. A. Cook, F. E. Adcock, M. P. Charlesworth (2nd ed., 1989); v. 8, Rome and after the Mediterranean, to 133 B.C., ed. by A. E. Astin ... [et al.] (2nd ed., 1989); v. 9, The last age of the Roman Republic, 46–43 B.C., ed. J. A. Crook, A. Lintott, E. Rawson (2nd ed., 1994); v. 10, The Augustan Empire, 44 B.C.–A.D. 60, ed. by S. A. Cook, F. E. Adcock, M. P. Charlesworth (1st ed., 1934; repr. with corrections, 1952); v. 11, The Imperial peace, A.D. 70–192, ed. by S. A. Cook, F. E. Adcock, M. P. Charlesworth (1st ed., 1936; repr. with corrections, 1954); v. 12, The Imperial crisis and recovery, A.D. 193–324, ed. by S. A. Cook ... [et al.] (1st ed., 1939).

Volumes of plates: v. 1, to illustrate v. 1–4, ed. by C. T. Seltman (1927. Later editions issued as Plates to v. 1–2, ed. by I. E. S. Edwards [new ed., 1977]; Plates to v. 3, ed. by John Boardman [new ed., 1984]; Plates to v. 4, ed. by John Boardman [new ed., 1988]); v. 2, Plates to v. 5–6, ed. by C. T. Seltman (1928. Repr. 1977); v. 3, Plates to v. 7–8, ed. by C. T. Seltman (1930); new ed. Plates to v. 7 pt. 1, ed. R. Ling [1984]; v. 4, Plates to v. 9–10, ed. by C. T. Seltman (1934. Repr. 1960); v. 5, Plates to v. 11–12, ed. by C. T. Seltman (1939. Repr. 1960).

The original edition was publ. in 12 v. with 5 v. of plates and maps, 1923–39. Revisions of individual chapters began to appear in 1961 as fascicles of a revised edition. These fascicles have not been published in chronological sequence, and pages are renumbered for the completed bound volumes. Fascicles for yet another edition, called the 3rd, began appearing in 1970. Some parts of the original edition have never been revised; some unrevised parts have been reprinted with corrections.

An excellent reference history. Each chapter has been written by a specialist, with full bibliographies at the end of each volume. Footnotes, extensive bibliographies, index. The volumes of plates contain illustrations without comment.   D57.C25

Atlases

Beek, Martinus Adrianus. Atlas of Mesopotamia : a survey of the history and civilisation of Mesopotamia from the Stone Age to the fall of Babylon / Tr. by D. R. Welsh; ed. by H. H. Rowley. London : Nelson, 1962. 164 p. : ill., 22 maps in color ; 36cm.   **DA86**
Published also in German and in Dutch.
A historical survey with many plates showing the art and archaeology of the country, and historical maps.   G2251.E6B42

Manley, John. The atlas of past worlds : a comparative chronology of human history 2000 BC–AD 1500. London : Cassell Publishers ; N.Y. : Distr. by Sterling Pub., 1993. 224 p. : ill. (some col.), maps.   **DA87**
Offers discussion of a representative site for each of five regions (Europe, western Asia and Oceania, Africa, and the Americas) in 2000 BCE, 1000 BCE, 1 CE, 1000 CE, and 1500 CE, aiming to provide contrast. The sites are selected to "illustrate a central theme" (*Prologue*), e.g., The first gods, Ways of life, Cities of the world. Short bibliography for each site; topical index.   CC165.M32

Past worlds : the Times atlas of archaeology. Maplewood, N.J. : Hammond, [1988]. 319 p. : ill., maps in color; 27 x 37 cm.   **DA88**
Intended to be a companion volume to *The Times atlas of world history* (DA58).
Also called *Hammond past worlds*.
A handsome presentation through maps, photographs, charts and drawings of "world history, from the beginnings of human life down to the emergence of the modern world" (*Introd.*), i.e., from about 16 million BCE to 1800 CE. Representative sites or cultures are pictured

within six broad chronological divisions. Includes a 10-page comparative chronology, a glossary of terms, an extensive name and subject index, and a short bibliography for each map.

§ Similar to *The world atlas of archaeology* (DA90), in that both are handsome volumes with much thought given to visual presentation, but each addresses areas or sites not covered by the other. While *Past worlds* employs a chronological framework with more attention to the European world, the geographical framework of the *World atlas* covers all areas more comprehensively.   G1046.E15P3

Whitehouse, David. Archaeological atlas of the world / David and Ruth Whitehouse ; with 103 maps drawn by John Woodcock and Shalom Schotten. London : Thames and Hudson ; San Francisco : W.H. Freeman, 1975. 272 p. : maps ; 25 cm.   **DA89**
Small maps, with explanatory notes, "pinpointing some 5,000 pre- and proto-historic sites."—*Introd.* Suggestions for further reading accompany the notes. Index with map grid references.
     G1046.E15W5

The world atlas of archaeology. Boston : G.K. Hall, c1985. 423 p. : col. ill., maps in color ; 37 cm.   **DA90**
English edition of *Le grand atlas de l'archéologie* (Paris : Encyclopaedia Universalis, 1985).
Brief chronological surveys within a geographical arrangement, with photographs, maps, and line drawings. Covers from "The origin of man and his first habitats" (under Africa) through "Industrial archaeology" (under Modern period—a catch-all section and the only one that is not geographical). Bibliography (p. 394–403); glossary; index by topic.   G1046.E15W6

Classical studies

See also the section for Classical languages in BE, Literature.

Guides

Poucet, Jacques. Introduction aux études classiques : guide bibliographique / par J. Poucet et J.-M. Hannick. 2. éd., rev. et aug. [Louvain-la-Neuve, Belgium] : CIACO, 1989. 242 p.
     DA91
A guide for the student, with special emphasis on sources and reference works (e.g., encyclopedias, bibliographies, manuals). Many of the works cited are in French, but some English-language materials are also given. Name and subject index.

Bibliography

See also BE998.

Calder, William M. An introductory bibliography to the history of classical scholarship chiefly in the XIXth and XXth centuries / William M. Calder III, Daniel J. Kramer. Hildesheim [Germany] : G. Olms, 1992. 410 p.   **DA92**
A critical, partially annotated bibliography of books and festschriften, plus a few articles, dissertations, and monographic series. Arranged in general chapters, followed by a section for institutions, then by entries for individual scholars interspersed with separate lists of offprints. Somewhat idiosyncratic, based on a private collection. Index of scholars. Four-page addendum for omissions.   Z7016.C35

Halton, Thomas P. Classical scholarship : an annotated bibliography / Thomas P. Halton and Stella O'Leary. White Plains, N.Y. : Kraus Internat., c1986. 396 p.   **DA93**
For annotation, *see* BE997.   Z6207.C65H34

Rollins, Alden M. Rome in the fourth century A.D. : an annotated bibliography with historical overview. Jefferson, N.C. : McFarland, c1991. 324 p. **DA94**

A topical listing of 1,408 English-language books, articles, theses and dissertations, conference papers, and a few novels, published during the 20th century up to 1988. Reviews are cited whenever possible. Arrangement is by broad topic, e.g., Society and art, Monetary matters, Christianity. Includes an introductory survey of the period and an Appendix for 1989–90 entries, listed alphabetically. Subject index, but unfortunately no author index.

§ For a general bibliography of Rome through the fifth century CE, see Karl Christ, *Römische Geschichte, eine Bibliographie* (Darmstadt : Wissenschaftliche Buchgesellschaft, 1976. 544 p.).

Z2340.R653

Sociedad Española de Estudios Clásicos. Bibliografia de los estudios clásicos en España. Madrid : Sociedad, 1956–91. 3 v. (Publicaciones, 1). **DA95**

Contents: v. [1], 1939–55 (1956); v. [2], 1956–65 (1968); v. 3, 1965–84 (1991).

Lists books and articles in all areas of classical studies published in Spain. Arranged by broad topic, with author index.

Continued by: A. Alvar Ezquerra, *Bibliografia de los estudios clasicos en España, 1985* (Madrid : Sociedad, 1987), following the same arrangement.

§ James K. Demetrius's *Greek scholarship in Spain and Latin America* (Chicago : Agronaut, 1965. 144 p.) is useful for its listing of studies on specific Greek authors and also for its non-Spanish language entries.

Z7016.B55

Current

Fasti archeologici : annual bulletin of classical archaeology. v.1 (1946)– . Firenzi : Sansoni, 1948– . Annual. **DA96**

At head of title: International Association for Classical Archaeology.

An extensive bibliography of books, catalogs, reports, and periodical articles, topically arranged in six sections: General; Prehistoric and classical Greece; Italy before the Roman Empire; The Hellenistic world and the Eastern provinces of the Roman Empire; The Roman West; Christianity and late antiquity. Most sections are subdivided for regions and sites; many brief annotations; fully indexed.

Publication runs late; e.g., v. 36/37, covering 1981/82, was publ. 1992. GN700.I552

Dissertations

Thompson, Lawrence Sidney. A bibliography of American doctoral dissertations in classical studies and related fields. [Hamden, Conn.] : Shoe String Pr., 1968. 250 p. **DA97**

"All aspects of the culture of Greece and Rome, from the prehistory of Greece and Italy through the arbitrary terminal date of 500 A.D., are included ..."—*Pref.* Author listing with detailed subject and title index. Cutoff date is generally 1964, with some 1965 dissertations included.

§ Continued by: *A bibliography of dissertations in classical studies : American, 1964–1972; British, 1950–1972; with a cumulative index, 1861–1972* (Hamden, Conn. : Shoe String Pr., 1976. 296 p.). This is "somewhat more than a supplement to *A Bibliography of American Doctoral Dissertations in Classical Studies ...*" (*Pref.*) since, in addition to listing American doctoral studies of the 1964–72 period (as well as some earlier ones omitted from the previous compilation), it lists British master's theses and doctoral dissertations for 1950–72. The cumulative index serves both volumes. Z7016.T48

Encyclopedias; Dictionaries

Civilization of the ancient Mediterranean : Greece and Rome / ed. by Michael Grant and Rachel Kitzinger. N.Y. : Scribner's, c1988. 3 v. (1980 p.) : ill. **DA98**

Some 100 signed articles arranged topically within broad subject areas—e.g., Political and social life—with articles thereunder on topics such as folklore, athletes, and medicine. Each article is thorough and well written and concludes with a substantive bibliography. Coverage is from 1000 BCE to the fifth century CE. Index; chronology.

§ For works on Rome, see also Lesley Adkins, *Handbook to life in ancient Rome* (N.Y. : Facts on File, 1994. 404 p. : ill. ; maps).

DE59.C55

Daremberg, Charles Victor. Dictionnaire des antiquités grecques et romaines d'après les textes et les monuments / Charles Victor Daremberg, Edmond Saglio. Paris : Hachette, 1873–1919. 5 v. and index. : ill. **DA99**

Repr. : Graz : Akad. Druck– und Verlagsanstalt, 1962–63. 5 v. in 10.

A work of the highest authority, with long, signed articles by specialists and very detailed bibliographical references. Covers public and private life, manners and customs, institutions, arts, sciences, industries, religion, costume, furniture, military affairs, money, weights and measures, etc. Does not include biography and literature. Indexes of authors, Greek words, Latin words, and subjects. DE5.D21

Illustrated encyclopaedia of the classical world / [by] Michael Avi-Yonah and Israel Shatzman. N.Y. : Harper & Row, c1975 ; Maidenhead : Sampson Low, 1976. 509 p. : ill. (some col.), maps. **DA100**

Intended "to satisfy the requirements of those who have no direct training in the classical disciplines."—*Foreword*. Consists of about 2,300 articles "comprehending the main themes, persons and places of Greek and Roman history, classical mythology and religion, philosophy and thought, together with the most important writers, artists and statesmen, the chief sites, the topography and the social background of the ancient world." Some brief bibliographical citations. Index of names, terms and subjects which are not entries in the main body of the encyclopedia.

§ For a heavily illustrated presentation on warfare, with notes on ancient literary sources and the political background, see John Warry's *Warfare in the classical world* (CJ580). DE5.I44

Der kleine Pauly : Lexikon der Antike / Auf der Grundlage von Pauly's Real-Encyclopädie der classischen Altertumswissenschaft unter Mitwirkung zahlreicher Fachgelehrter, bearb. und hrsg. von Konrad Ziegler und Walther Sontheimer. Stuttgart : Alfred Druckenmüller Verlag, 1964–75. 5 v. : ill. **DA101**

Frequently reissued; latest: 8 Aufl., 1989, in 5 v.

An abridgment of *Pauly-Wissowa* (DA104), including a high percentage of its articles in concise form. Articles are signed with initials. New advances in scholarship, where relevant, are reflected, and bibliographic references have been updated as necessary. Reference to the longer article in the parent work is often given (cited as *RE*). Note should also be taken of the *Nachträge* in v. 1 and v. 3 of the abridgment. Corrigenda and addenda in v. 5. DE5.K5

Nash, Ernest. Pictorial dictionary of ancient Rome / prep. with the collaboration of the Deutsches Archaeologisches Institut. Rev. ed. London : Thames & Hudson ; N.Y. : Praeger, 1968. 2 v. (544 p.) : ill., maps, plans. **DA102**

Repr.: N.Y : Hacker, 1981.

1st ed., 1961.

An authoritative dictionary presenting each surviving monument of ancient Rome through photographs and drawings, with exhaustive bibliography for each. Index of names of places (including categories such as streets, squares, churches).

Companion to: Ioannes N. Traulos, *Pictorial dictionary of ancient Athens* (DA106). NA310.N28

Oxford classical dictionary. 2nd ed., ed. by N. G. L. Hammond and H. H. Scullard. Oxford : Clarendon Pr., 1970. 1176 p.   **DA103**

1st ed., 1949.

A scholarly dictionary, with signed articles, covering biography, literature, mythology, philosophy, religion, science, geography, etc. Most of the articles are brief, but there are some longer survey articles, e.g., Rome, music, scholarship, etc. Bibliographies are appended to most articles, and are usually limited to a few of the best works on the subject, in English and foreign languages. Bibliographies for the articles on the great classical writers usually include texts, commentaries, translations, lexicons, style, life, criticism, etc.

For the second edition all articles were reviewed for revision or replacement; bibliographies were updated to about 1967–68; and new material on the archaeological background was added. The number of entries for persons and places was increased, and an "Index of names etc. which are not titles of entries" makes a useful addition.   DE5.O9

Pauly, August Friedrich von. Paulys Real-Encyclopädie der classischen Altertumswissenschaft / neue Bearb. begonnen von Georg Wissowa, unter Mitwirkung zahlreicher Fachgenossen hrsg. von Wilhelm Kroll und Karl Mittelhaus. Stuttgart : Metzler, 1894–1978. v. 1–24¹; 2. Reihe, v. 1–10A; Suppl. v. 1–15. : maps.   **DA104**

Repr. : Munich : Artemis, 1981.

Called *Pauly-Wissowa.*

Contents: Bd. 1–24¹, A–Quosenus; 2. Reihe (R–Z), Bd. 1–10A, R–Zythos; Suppl., Bd. 1–15. (Volumes were not published in sequence, but in two series with a supplement).

The standard scholarly German work covering the whole field of classical literature, history, antiquities, biography, etc. Long, signed articles by specialists, with extensive bibliographies. Generally cited as *Pauly-Wissowa;* in German references sometimes cited as *RE.* Indispensable for scholarly work in classical antiquities.

The arrangement and the alphabetization are sometimes complicated. Many volumes include *"Nachträge und Berichtigungen,"* which in the later volumes are quite extensive. The volumes of the *Supplement* are geared to the volumes of the main set, each supplementary volume starting with A and continuing to a later part of the alphabet.

Significant additions to articles in the main set may appear in several supplementary volumes. Because some subjects treated in the supplement may not appear in the basic set, and because some articles in the supplements replace those in earlier volumes, two separately published indexes are especially welcome:

(1) *Paulys Realencyclopadie der classischen Altertumswissenschaft: Register der Nachträge und Supplemente,* by Hans Gartner and Albert Wunsch (München : Druckenmuller, 1980. 250 p.) indexes only the articles, corrections, and the addenda in the supplementary volumes and the Nachträge, but not the main alphabet. Each volume contains a short summary as well as the index reference.

(2) *Index to the supplements and suppl. volumes of Pauly-Wissowa's R.E.,* by John P. Murphy (Chicago : Ares, 1980. 144 p.). Gives the reference plus a symbol for the type of article: replacement, new entry, major addition, minor addition.

See also *Der kleine Pauly* (DA101), which can often be used as an index.   DE5.P33

The Princeton encyclopedia of classical sites / Richard Stillwell, ed. Princeton : Princeton Univ. Pr., 1976. 1019 p. : plates, maps.   **DA105**

Aims "to provide a one-volume source of information on sites that show remains from the Classical period."—*Pref.* (The "Classical period" is understood to cover from about 750 BCE to the sixth century CE). In general, entry is under the form of the name of the site as it was known in classical times, with the modern name, when it differs, following. Location and historical notes are given, together with dates of excavations, and a general summary of the extent of the work done. Bibliographical references are provided and indication is made of those works which include site maps, plans, or illustrations. Some corrections and additions are included in the review in *L'antiquité classique,* XLVI (1977), p. 345–47.   DE59.P7

Traulos, Ioannes N. Pictorial dictionary of ancient Athens / John Travlos. London : Thames & Hudson ; N.Y. : Praeger, 1971. 590 p. : ill., maps, plans.   **DA106**

Repr.: N.Y. : Hacker, 1980.

Prep. in collaboration with the Deutsches Archäologisches Institut. Translated from the Greek.

Similar in intent to Ernest Nash's *Pictorial dictionary of ancient Rome* (DA102). A dictionary of monuments, temples, and other extant structures from prehistoric through classical times in Athens. Includes photographs, plans, and extensive bibliographies. Topical index.

NA280.T68

Handbooks

In addition to the works listed below, research workers in classical antiquities will often need to refer to Iwan Müller's *Handbuch der Altertumsweissenschaft* (München : Beck, 1923–), a series of scholarly treatises on subjects in classical literature, antiquities, etc., the various volumes of which have appeared in many different editions. Some of the volumes are the most comprehensive and definitive works in their fields; others are much briefer. For a partial list of contents, see *Les sources du travail bibliographique* by Louise-Noëlle Malclès, v. 2, pt. 1, p. 105–6 (AA352).

Pfeiffer, Rudolf. History of classical scholarship from the beginnings to the end of the Hellenistic age. Oxford : Clarendon Pr., 1968. 311 p.   **DA107**

Following a brief survey of the nature of historical writing in the pre-Hellenic periods and the oriental backgrounds, the work concentrates on "the foundation laid by Greek poets and scholars in the last three centuries B.C. for the whole future of classical scholarship."— *Pref.* Extensive footnotes and references to original sources; brief selection of modern secondary literature.

Continued in time by the author's *History of classical scholarship from 1300 to 1850* (1976. 214 p.).

A survey of classical studies, editions, commentaries, transmission, and effect of major scholarship from pre-humanism to German neohellenism. Extensive notes and bibliographies.

§ The standard briefer history is U. von Wilamowitz-Moellendorff, *History of classical scholarship,* ed. by Hugh Lloyd-Jones (Baltimore : Johns Hopkins Univ. Pr., 1982. Tr. from *Geschichte der philologie,* first publ. 1921).   AZ301.P4

Sandys, John Edwin. Companion to Latin studies. 3rd ed. Cambridge : Univ. Pr. ; N.Y. : Macmillan, 1921. 891 p. : ill.   **DA108**

1st ed., 1910; 2nd ed., 1913. Repr., 1925, 1929.

A handbook covering such subjects as the geography and ethnology of Italy, fauna and flora, history, religion and mythology, private and public antiquities, art, literature, epigraphy, paleography, etc. Includes bibliographies.

§ Related work: Leonard Whibley, *Companion to Greek studies* (DA109).   DG77.S3

Whibley, Leonard. Companion to Greek studies. 4th ed., rev. Cambridge : Univ. Pr., 1931. 790 p. : ill.   **DA109**

Repr.: N.Y. : Hafner, 1968.

1st ed., 1905; 3rd ed., 1916.

Prepared on the same plan and general arrangement as John Edwin Sandys, *Companion to Latin studies* (DA108). Each consists of a series of articles, by specialists, on topics of importance such as geography, ethnology, flora, science, chronology, coins, ships, buildings, population, slavery, etc. Articles are well written, with useful bibliographies, and each volume has four indexes: (1) persons, deities, and races; (2) places, rivers, and mountains; (3) scholars and modern writers; (4) Greek (or Latin) words and phrases. Very useful for supplementing the various classical dictionaries.   DF77.W5

Chronologies

Bickerman, Elias Joseph. Chronology of the ancient world. Rev. ed. [London] : Thames & Hudson ; Ithaca, N.Y. : Cornell Univ. Pr., [1980]. 223 p. : ill. **DA110**
1st ed., 1968.
This English edition is based on the author's *Chronologie* (2. Aufl. Leipzig, 1963), with much supplementary material added. "The plan of the book is therefore to explain the structure of the ancient calendar, the principles followed in antiquity in computing the years, and the rules which we can derive from those principles in relating ancient dates to our own time reckoning."—*Introd.* Tables include the astronomical canon, rising and setting of stars, Olympic years, lists of rulers, etc., and chronological tables of Greek and Roman history.
D54.5.B5

Lauffer, Siegfried. Daten der griechischen und römischen Geschichte. München : Deutscher Taschenbuch Verlag, [1987]. 444 p. **DA111**
Arranged by year within two broad sections: Greece 5000–30 BCE; Rome 5000 BCE–500 CE. For each year, gives a sentence identifying each major event. Indexes for personal names and for places and topics.
DE86.L37x

Samuel, Alan Edouard. Greek and Roman chronology : calendars and years in classical antiquity. München : Beck, [1972]. 307 p. (Handbuch der Altertumswissenschaft, Abt. I, t. 7). **DA112**
A scholarly and carefully documented work. A discussion of the astronomical background is followed by chapters on Greek astronomical calendars, Greek civil calendars, calendars of the Hellenistic kingdoms, the Roman calendar, calendars of the Eastern Roman provinces, Greek chronography, and Roman chronography.
PA25.H24

Biography

Classical scholarship : a biographical encyclopedia / ed. by Ward W. Briggs and William M. Calder III. N.Y. : Garland, 1990. 396 p. : ports. (Garland reference library of the humanities, vol. 928). **DA113**
Presents biographies of some 50 outstanding scholars active in the "modern period" of 1977–86, "whose lives amounted to more than just bibliographies."—*Pref.* For each classicist there is a signed essay describing career and importance to the field, with a photograph or portrait. Appended to each is a bibliography of the subject's books and articles, and sources subdivided into Autobiography, Bibliography, Biography, Letters, Papers. Chronological list of biographies; list of contributors.
§ *See also* Rudolf Pfeiffer, *History of classical scholarship ....* (DA107) and John Edwin Sandys, *History of classical scholarship* (BE1022).
Some 600 classicists are given biographical coverage of about one page, plus extensive bibliographies, in *Biographical dictionary of North American classicists*, ed. by Ward W. Briggs, Jr. (Westport, Conn. : Greenwood, 1994. 800 p.), prepared under the auspices of the American Philological Association. Two introductory essays describe the history of classical scholarship in the U.S. and Canada.
PA83.C58

Who was who in the Greek world, 776 BC–30 BC / ed. by Diana Bowder. Oxford : Phaidon ; Ithaca, N.Y. : Cornell Univ. Pr., 1982. 227 p. : ill. **DA114**
Similar in design and purpose to the same editor's *Who was who in the Roman world* (DA115). Bibliographic references; illustrations drawn from works of art, coins, portrait busts, etc. Index of persons mentioned but not accorded an entry in the text. DF208.W48

Who was who in the Roman world, 753 BC–AD 476 / ed. by Diana Bowder. Oxford : Phaidon ; Ithaca, N.Y. : Cornell Univ. Pr., 1980. 256 p. : ill. **DA115**
Aims "to provide a biographical reference work of scholarly accuracy and reliability that is easily accessible to the student and general reader of Roman history, and ... to unite with it an important collection of pictorial documentation. ... "—*Introd.* One or more bibliographic citations follows each entry.
A companion to the same compiler's *Who was who in the Greek world* (DA114).
§ *See also* Michael Grant, *The Roman emperors : a biographical guide to the rulers of imperial Rome, 31 BC–AD 476* (N.Y. : Scribner's, 1985. 367 p.) Chronological presentation of very readable sketches. Includes genealogical tables, portraits from coins, list of Latin technical terms.
DG203.W46

Atlases

See C. Foss, "Classical atlases" in *Classical world* 80 (1987): 337–65, for an evaluation and comparison of 12 historical atlases for their coverage of the classical world. The atlases range from the general, e.g. William Robert Shepherd, *Historical atlas* (DA57) to the most specific, e.g. *Atlas of the Roman world*, by Tim Cornell and John Matthews (DA119).

Atlas of classical archaeology / ed. by M. I. Finley ; maps and plans by John Flower. London : Chatto and Windus ; N.Y. : McGraw-Hill, 1977. 256 p. : ill. **DA116**
Intended for students "and other 'stay-at-home' readers" but primarily for travelers. "We have omitted cities and districts regardless of their importance in antiquity, if, for one reason or another, the visible *classical* remains are scanty or uninteresting to the specialist."—*Introd.* Arranged by country, moving from west to east; each chapter presents an overview of a particular site, with a map of the region, plan of the site, photographs of representative art of the site, and a short bibliography. Appendixes: chronological table; Roman emperors; Greek vase types; Greek architectural orders; glossary. Indexed.
§ For Greece, see *Wings over Hellas : ancient Greece from the air*, comp. by Raymond V. Schoder (N.Y. : Oxford Univ. Pr., 1974. 256 p.) which for each ancient excavated site gives an aerial photograph, a site plan, an outline of the major visible monuments, and a brief overview of the site's historical and cultural interest.
G1046.E15A8

Atlas of classical history / ed. by Richard J. A. Talbert. London : Croom Helm ; N.Y. : Macmillan, c1985. 217 p. : 26 cm. **DA117**
Reissued: London : Routledge, [1988].
"A volume in which lucid maps [offer] the high school student and the undergraduate a reasonably comprehensive, up-to-date, and scholarly coverage of classical history down to the time of Constantine, accompanied by modest elucidation of the material and by some suggestions for further reading."—*Pref.* Covers Greek and Roman history from Troy and Knossos to the Roman Empire in 314 CE. The black-and-white maps, though small, are very clear. Many city maps. The text is brief, in many cases good mainly for identification, a skeletal history, or verification of a few key dates. Suggestions for further reading, p. 179–89. Place-name index with name, page, and coordinates.
§ Another atlas for students is: *Ancient history atlas*, comp. by Michael Grant with cartography by Arthur Banks (4th ed. London : Weidenfeld and Nicolson, 1986. 87 p. 26 cm.) which has very clear maps in black and white, each illustrating a single point. Covers 1700 BCE–sixth century CE for political, economic, religious, and agricultural history; includes city maps. Index of place-names (though not as many as Talbert).
G1033.A833

Atlas of the Greek and Roman world in antiquity / Nicholas G. L. Hammond, ed. in chief. Park Ridge, N.J. : Noyes Pr., 1981. 56 p. : 46 col. maps ; 41 cm. **DA118**

47 maps cover the Neolithic period (1 map) to sixth century CE, including site maps. Cartography is very clear, in shades of brown on white with black lettering. Lengthy gazetteer.   G1033.A84

Cornell, Tim. Atlas of the Roman world / Tim Cornell, John Matthews. Oxford : Phaidon ; N.Y. : Facts on File, [1982]. 240 p. : ill., maps.   **DA119**

A survey of "the Roman world in its physical and cultural setting" (*Introd.*) presented through a combination of text, maps, photographs and drawings. Covers from the founding of Rome to the Byzantine reconquest of Italy in 540 CE. Selected bibliography; gazetteer; index.

§ A similar atlas for Greece is by Peter Levi, *Atlas of the Greek world* (Oxford : Phaidon ; N.Y. : Facts on File, 1984. 239 p. Repr. : Alexandria, Va. : Stonehenge, 1991 with title: *The Greek world*).   DG77.C597

Heyden, A. A. M. van der. Atlas of the classical world / A. A. M. van der Heyden, Howard Hayes Scullard. London : Nelson, 1959. 221 p.   **DA120**

Originally published as *Atlas van de antieke wereld* (Amsterdam : Elsevier, 1958).

An excellent atlas depicting the life and cultures of the classical world in maps and pictures, with textual comment. The photographs of art and archaeological subjects are outstanding.

§ *Shorter atlas of the classical world* (London : Nelson, 1963. 239 p.) is the work of the same compilers and includes good illustrations.   DE29.H463

Ancient Egypt

Bibliography

Annual Egyptological bibliography = Bibliographie égyptologique annuelle. 1947– . Leiden : Brill, 1948– . Annual.   **DA121**

At head of title (1948–70): International Association of Egyptologists.

Publisher varies.

An alphabetical, annotated list, begun to fill the need of an annual bibliography caused by the cessation of the "Bibliografia metodica degli studi de egittologia e di papirologia," published in *Aegyptus*, 1920–43. Annotations are in either French or English.

—— *Indexes, 1947–1956*, by Jozef M. A. Janssen (Leiden : Brill, 1960. 475 p.) include an alphabetical index by authors, giving titles and full information; followed by many specialized indexes, e.g., topography, pharaohs, hieroglyphs, divinities, biblical references and Hebrew words, classical authors, and subjects.

—— *Late reviews AEB, 1947–1984*, comp. by L. M. J. Zonhoven with the collaboration of A. Egberts and W. Hovestreydt (Leiden : Internat. Assoc. of Egyptologists, in cooperation with Nederlands Instituut voor het Nabije Oosten, 1989. 74 p.). Contains book reviews that appeared after the annual publication, listed by *AEB* citation number. An earlier list appended to *AEB* 1973 (publ. 1977) is incorporated into this volume. Beginning with *AEB* 1985 (publ. 1989), a section of late reviews appears at the end of each annual volume.   Z3656.A2A6

Weeks, Kent R. An historical bibliography of Egyptian prehistory / comp. by Kent R. Weeks ... [et al.]. Winona Lake, Ind. : Publ. for the American Research Center in Egypt by Eisenbrauns, c1985. 138 p. (American Research Center in Egypt. Catalogs, no. 6).   **DA122**

An unannotated author list of 2,515 books, articles, and essays on the archaeology of Egypt to the end of the Old Kingdom. Chiefly English language materials, with other European languages represented. No index, but includes a selective subject guide in the introduction. Some cross-references; list of periodical titles cited.   Z5113.W43

Encyclopedias; Dictionaries

Bunson, Margaret. The encyclopedia of ancient Egypt. N.Y. : Facts on File, c1991. 291 p. : ill.   **DA123**

A quick reference resource. Covers Egypt "from the predynastic period to the close of the New Kingdom (1070 BC)" (*How to use this book*) in an alphabetical arrangement of overview articles (e.g., Religion, Dress) and shorter, more specific entries (e.g., solar cults, specific rulers or gods or goddesses). Little coverage of Egypt's contact with peoples outside the country. Cross-references at end of longer articles; suggested reading list. Index: list of broad terms, each followed by a list of specific terms related to that heading.

§ *Dictionary of Egyptian civilization*, by Georges Posener, with the assistance of Serge Sauneron and Jean Yoyotte (N.Y. : Tudor, [1962?]. 323 p.) is a small, popular dictionary with copious illustrations in color and in black-and-white.   DT58.B96

David, A. Rosalie. A biographical dictionary of ancient Egypt / by Rosalie and Antony E. David. London : Seaby, 1992. 179 p. : maps.   **DA124**

Offers brief biographies of important historical and cultural figures of Egypt, but also includes individuals or groups that had an impact on the country (e.g., Sea Peoples, Solomon). For each gives a brief identification, reigns and dates of relevant king or pharaoh, and one bibliographical reference. Maps depict major sites in Egypt as well as the classical world and the Middle East. General bibliography; glossary; chronology; index of persons mentioned in the text.   DT76.D38

Lexikon der Ägyptologie / hrsg. Wolfgang Helck und Eberhard Otto. Wiesbaden : O. Harrassowitz, 1972–1992. 7 v. : ill., maps, plans.   **DA125**

Beginning with v. 4, ed. by Wolfgang Helck und Wolfhart Westerdorf.

Contents: v. 1–6, A–Zypresse; v. 7, Nachträge, Korrekturen und Indices.

An authoritative encyclopedia of Egyptian civilization, intended for both the specialist and the student. Signed articles with lengthy bibliographies; a few articles are in English or French. Focus is on Egypt of the Pharoahs to the Hellenistic period, with sketchy treatment given to later periods, prehistory, and countries of conquest (the user being referred to more comprehensive encyclopedias such as *Reallexikon für Assyriologie*, DA80). Excellent indexes for each volume. The *Nachträge* includes a list of abbreviations, additions and corrections, general index, and place name, gods, pharoah, Egyptian, Coptic, Papyri word, and ancient author indexes.

§ Wolfhart Westendorf issued privately *Bemerkungen und Korrekturen zum Lexikon der Ägyptologie* (Göttingen : Göttinger Miszellen, Seminar für Ägyptologie und Koptologie, Universität Göttingen, 1989. 134 p.).   DT58.L49

Atlases

Baines, John. Atlas of ancient Egypt / by John Baines and Jaromír Málek. N.Y. : Facts on File ; Oxford : Phaidon, [1980]. 240 p. : ill., maps.   **DA126**

Repr.: N.Y. : Facts on File, 1989.

A historical atlas with maps, plans and illustrations (mainly in color) presented in conjunction with the text. In three sections: (1) The cultural setting; (2) A journey down the Nile; (3) Aspects of Egyptian society. Includes a list of museums with Egyptian collections, a glossary, bibliography, gazetteer, and index.   DT56.9.B34

MEDIEVAL AND RENAISSANCE

See also section for Diplomatics, handwriting and scripts, Section AA.

General works

Guides

Caenegem, R. C. van. Guide to the sources of medieval history / R. C. van Caenegem, with the collaboration of F. L. Ganshof. Amsterdam, etc. : North-Holland Publ. Co., 1978. 428 p. (Europe in the Middle Ages. Selected studies, v. 2). **DA127**

Earlier versions appeared in Dutch (*Encyclopedie van de Geschiedenis der Middeleeuwen*. Ghent, 1962) and German (*Kurze Quellenkunde des west-europäischen Mittelalters*. Göttingen, 1964); this is a revised and expanded edition, not merely a translation.

In five main sections: (1) Typology of the sources of medieval history; (2) Libraries and archives (i.e., repositories of medieval manuscripts); (3) Great collections and repertories of sources; (4) Reference works for the study of medieval texts; (5) Bibliographical introduction to the auxiliary sciences of history. Each section consists of a number of explanatory or bibliographic chapters citing and describing a wide range of sources for the many aspects of medieval studies. Detailed table of contents; index of names and anonymous titles.   Z6203.C25

Dolcini, Carlo. Guida allo studio della storia medievale. Torino : UTET libreria, 1992. 135 p.   **DA128**

Offers extensive descriptions of major bibliographies (including serial bibliographies), encyclopedias, catalogs for the student in medieval history. The first chapter discusses historiography.

§ Dated but still useful for its organization of reference materials: *Medieval and Renaissance studies : a location guide to selected works and source collections in the libraries of the University of North Carolina at Chapel Hill and Duke University*, prep. by the Reference Staff of the Humanities Division, University of North Carolina Library, under the supervision of Louise McG. Hall (Chapel Hill : Univ. of North Carolina, 1974. 325, [15] p.).   Z6203.D65

Medieval studies : an introduction / ed. by James M. Powell. 2nd ed. Syracuse, N.Y. : Syracuse Univ. Pr., 1992. 438 p.   **DA129**

1st ed., 1976.

Designed to offer the student "a convenient orientation in the field."—*Introd.* Essays by various authors on all aspects of medieval studies. Bibliographical footnotes and/or substantial bibliographies at the end of each chapter cover to the mid- to late 1980s. Includes paleography, diplomatics, chronology, literature, music, archaeology, law, and science.   D116.M4

Bibliography

Chevalier, Cyr Ulysse Joseph. Répertoire des sources historiques du moyen âge. Paris : Picard, 1894–1907. 2 v. in 4.   **DA130**

Repr.: N.Y. : Kraus, 1959–60. 4 v.

Publisher varies.

In two parts: (1) *Bio-bibliographie*, issued in 4 fasc., 1877–83, with Supplément (fasc. 5), 1888; nouv. éd., refondue, "corr. et considérablement augm.," 1905–07; and (2) *Topo-bibliographie*, issued in 6 fasc., 1894/99–1900/03.

Of first importance for the literature of medieval history. The first part is arranged alphabetically by personal name (in the French form), the second by place and topic. Under each name, references are given

to sources. An immense mass of material is indexed, but with no critical indication of value. For further information on the biobibliographical section, see AH11.   Z6203.C52

Crosby, Everett U. Medieval studies : a bibliographical guide / Everett U. Crosby, C. Julian Bishko, Robert L. Kellogg. N.Y. : Garland, 1983. 1131 p.   **DA131**

About 9,000 items (books and monographs) in classed arrangement; nearly all entries are briefly annotated. Lists "the major collections of sources and the secondary literature considered to be of basic importance for the history and the culture of the western European Middle Ages, Byzantium, and medieval Islamic civilization."—*Introd.* Detailed table of contents; indexes of authors and topics.

Z5579.5.C76

Davidson, Linda Kay. Pilgrimage in the Middle Ages : a research guide / Linda Kay Davidson, Maryjane Dunn-Wood. N.Y. : Garland, 1993. 480 p. : ill. (Garland medieval bibliographies, vol. 16 ; Garland reference library of the humanities, vol. 1379).   **DA132**

Covers materials on the journeys to religious shrines in Western Europe and the Middle East. Works listed are primarily in English; a few foreign language original sources, although not translated, are included. Pt. 1 is a narrative introduction to pilgrimage—the sites, outcomes, symbolism, etc. (p. 213–473). Pt. 2 is an annotated bibliography of 1,100 primary and secondary works—books, essays, chapter, articles—arranged by author. Not indexed.   BV5067.D38

Istoriia srednikh vekov / [Sostaviteli I. I. Korndorf ... et al.] ; Pod red. IU. M. Saprykina, M. S. Meĭera. Moskva : Izd-vo Moskovskogo universiteta, 1968–84. v. 1–2, pts. 1–3.   **DA133**

Contents: v. 1, 1918–1957 comp. and ed. by K. R. Simon; v. 2, pt. 1–3, 1958–68.

A bibliography of historical works on the Middle Ages published in the USSR. Classed arrangement with personal and geographical name indexes. Each volume has an index for authors, translators, editors, etc. The index for v. 2 includes a special index for medieval authors in either volume.   Z6203.S44

Paetow, Louis John. A guide to the study of medieval history. Rev. and corr. ed. with errata comp. by Gray C. Boyce and an addendum by Lynn Thorndike. Millwood, N.Y. : Kraus Reprint, [1980]. cxii, 643 p.   **DA134**

"Prep. under the auspices of the Medieval Academy of America."—*t.p.*

A reprinting of the 1931 ed. (repr. 1959) with the addition of an errata section, p. xxi–1i, and an addendum section, p. liii–cxii, of titles of books and articles not cited in previous editions. Items in this latter section are keyed to appropriate sections of the main work; only works published through 1930 are included.

§ Supplemented by: Gray Cowan Boyce, *Literature of medieval history, 1930–1975* (Millwood, N.Y. : Kraus Internat., 1981. 5 v.). Extends and follows much the same arrangement. Like the earlier work, concentrates on medieval studies of Western Europe with "restricted attention to Eastern and Northern Europe" (*Pref.*) and excludes material specifically on English history. Coverage of medieval culture has been expanded to the year 1500. The index (v. 5) is only of personal names as either author or subject. Sponsored by the Medieval Academy of America.   Z6203.P25

Quirin, Heinz. Einführung in das Studium der mittelalterlichen Geschichte. 4. Aufl. mit einer neuen Einleitung. Stuttgart : F. Steiner, 1985. 363 p. : maps, charts.   **DA135**

1st ed., 1950; 3rd ed., 1964.

A useful handbook supplementing Louis John Paetow's *A guide to the study of medieval history* (DA134). Gives much information on location and use of source materials. Bibliography, p. 292–363.

The "Quellentabeln" (overview of sources), p. 243–58, is revised, enlarged, and translated in: *Medieval narrative sources : a chronological guide (with a list of major letter collections)*, comp. by János M. Bak with the assistance of Heinz Quirin and Paul Hollingsworth (N.Y. : Garland, 1987. 117 p. Garland reference library of the humanities, 734). In roughly chronological order, Bak lists printed editions with translations. Indexes by author and anonymous title and by regions and place-names.   D116.Q82

Repertorium fontium historiae medii aevi : primum ab Augusto Potthast digestum, nunc cura collegii historicorum e pluribus nationibus emendatum et auctum. Romae : Istit. Storico Italiano per il Medio Evo, 1962–89. v. 1–6.   **DA136**

At head of title: Istituto Storico Italiano per il Medio Evo. Unione Internazionale degli Istituti di Archeologia, Storia e Storia dell' Arte in Roma.

Contents: v. 1, Series collectionum; v. 2–6, Fontes, A–K.

Constitutes a new edition of August Potthast's *Bibliotheca historica medii aevi : Wegweiser durch die Geschichtswerke des europäischen Mittelalters bis 1500* (2. verb. und verm. Aufl. Berlin : Weber, 1896. 2 v. Repr. : Graz : Akademische Druck– u. Verlagsanstalt, 1954.).

The first volume of the "new Potthast" corresponds generally to the first major section of the old work, i.e., an alphabetical listing of sets of chronicles, miscellanies, and other collections, together with their contents of sources of medieval history up to 1500. It contains some sets omitted by Potthast and many published since that work appeared, including Byzantine, Arabic, Jewish, and Turkish sets, not covered in Potthast. Bibliographic treatment is good. Introductory and explanatory material is in Latin.

The "Fontes" section offers a repertory of medieval writings arranged by individual author's name or anonymous title of the chronicle or document treated. Whereas the listings in Potthast were limited to works relating to historical studies in the strict sense, the new work extends coverage to works of theology, philosophy, law, economics, art, and literature. As in the earlier work entries include, as far as possible, an identifying note together with references to manuscripts, translations, facsimiles, editions, and commentaries.

§ *Additamenta* (Rome : Istituto Storico Italiano per il Medio Evo, 1977– . 1 v. [In progress]).

Contents: v. 1, Series collectionum continuata et aucta (1962–1972; 181 p.).

Cites new collections and additions to those listed in v. 1; corrections to listings in v. 1, p. 175–81.   Z6203.R427

Rouse, Richard H. Serial bibliographies for medieval studies / Richard H. Rouse, assisted by J. H. Claxton and M. D. Metzger. Berkeley : Univ. of California Pr., 1969. 150 p. (Center for Medieval and Renaissance Studies. Publications, 3).   **DA137**

An annotated listing of 283 serial publications (national and regional bibliographies and archival publications as well as periodicals and bibliographical annuals), useful to the research worker in medieval studies. Items are grouped by field of interest, with numerous cross-references. Title index.   Z6203.R66

Toronto medieval bibliographies. Toronto : Univ. of Toronto Pr., 1967–88. no. 1–11. (In progress?).   **DA138**

Contents: no. 1, Old Norse-Icelandic studies, H. Bekker-Nielsen (1967. 94 p.); no. 2, Old English language, F.C. Robinson (1970. 68 p.); no. 3, Medieval rhetoric, J.J. Murphy (2nd ed., 1989. 100 p.); no. 4, Medieval music, A. Hughes (rev. ed., 1980. 360 p.); no. 5, Medieval Celtic literature, R. Bromwich (1974. 109 p.); no. 6, Medieval monasticism, G. Constable (1976. 171 p.); no. 7, La littérature occitane du Moyen Âge, R.A. Taylor (1977. 166 p.); no. 8, Medieval Latin palaeography, L. Boyle (1984. 399 p.); no. 9, Medieval Latin liturgy, R.W. Pfaff (1982. 129 p.); no. 10, Chaucer : a bibliographical introduction, by John Leyerle and Anne Quick (1986. 321 p.); no. 11, Medieval Christian literary imagery : a guide to interpretation, R.E. Kaske (1988. 247 p.).

A series of authoritative, annotated bibliographies.

Williams, Harry Franklin. An index of mediaeval studies published in festschriften, 1865–1946 : with special reference to Romanic material. Berkeley : Univ. of California Pr., 1951. 165 p.   **DA139**

An index of the contributions concerning medieval art, customs, history, philosophy, literature, language, and science of Western Europe found in anniversary or homage volumes published in honor of scholars, occasions, or institutions, covering more than 5,000 items from about 500 volumes of such studies. Not all volumes are fully indexed, since material not pertinent to medieval studies is omitted. The emphasis is on Romanic material. Includes a list of the festschriften, a list of reviews of some 170 festschriften, an index of authors, and one of subject matter.   Z6203.W5

Current

Bibliographie internationale de l'humanisme et de la renaissance. v. 1 (1965)– . Genève : Droz, 1966– . Annual.   **DA140**

Prepared for the Fédération internationale des sociétés et instituts pour l'étude de la renaissance, of the Conseil international de la philosophie et des sciences humaines.

Lists books and articles in all areas—literature, philosophy, history, religion, the arts, economics, political science, law, science—of study on the 15th and 16th centuries in Europe. Arrangement: pt. 1: Personnages et oeuvres anonymes; pt. 2: Matières. Author index. Much delayed; v. 24 covering 1988 publ. 1992.   Z6207.R4B5

Cahiers de civilisation médiévale : bibliographie. 1958– . Poitiers : Centre d'Études Supérieures de Civilisation Médiévale, Université de Poitiers, 1958– . Annual.   **DA141**

The bibliography was issued as part of the journal 1958–68; beginning 1969 the bibliography is issued separately.

An extensive subject listing of articles and books, primarily on European history and civilization of the 10th–12th centuries; to a lesser extent includes materials relating to Byzantine, Islamic, Slavic, and Middle Eastern civilizations. Annual author index; index for v. 1–5 of names, places, texts, etc. Liberal use of cross-references.   CB3.C3

Deutsches Archiv für Erforschung des Mittelalters. 1. Jahrg. (1937)– . Köln : Graz, 1937– . Twice yearly.   **DA142**

Title varies; v. 1–7 (1937–44) called *Deutsches Archiv für Geschichte des Mittelalters*.

Title page note, v. 2–7: namens des Reichsinstituts für Ältere Deutsche Geschichtskunde (Monumenta Germaniae Historica); v. 8– , namens der Monumenta Germaniae Historica.

Publisher varies.

Publication suspended 1945–49.

A bibliography (the bibliographical portion is called: Besprechungen und Anzeigen) of articles and books concerning medieval studies. Topical arrangement under broad headings; descriptive annotations. Name and subject indexes end each volume.

DD126.A1D4

International medieval bibliography. 1967– . [Leeds, Eng.] : Univ. of Leeds ; Minneapolis : Univ. of Minnesota, Dept. of History, [1968]– .   **DA143**

Frequency varies.

Originally issued in card form. The first volume reproduces (in reduced size) the cards issued during 1967; beginning with 1968, the bound volumes appear semiannually. Covers the whole range of medieval studies. Articles indexed are drawn from journals and festschriften; critical reviews are noted. Arrangement is by subject, with indexes of authors and of personal and place-names mentioned in the titles. Considered a standard bibliography for the period.   Z6203.I63

Medioevo latino : bollettino bibliografico della cultura europea dal secolo VI al XIII. v. 1– . Spoleto : Centro Italiano di Studi Sull'Alto Medioevo, 1980– . Annual.   **DA144**

Claudio Leonardi, ed.

Vol. 2 and following called 1979 (etc.). Bibliographical appendix to *Studi medievali*, v. 20– .

Although a high percentage of items in v. 1 were published in 1978, numerous publications from 1977 and earlier are included.

An extensive bibliography of primary and secondary sources often annotated. Classed arrangement, with indexes of authors and manuscripts. Includes citations to critical reviews. Considered one of the standard bibliographies for this period.

Dissertations

Monumenta Germaniae Historica. Hochschulschriften zur Geschichte und Kultur des Mittelalters 1939 bis 1972/74 : (Deutschland, Österreich, Schweiz). München : Monumenta Germaniae Historica, 1975. 3 v. (1051 p.). (Monumenta Germaniae Historica : Hilfsmittel, 1).   **DA145**

A classed listing of some 8,400 dissertations, both published and unpublished. Author and subject indexes in v. 3.   Z5579.M66

Encyclopedias; Dictionaries

Bergin, Thomas Goddard. Encyclopedia of the Renaissance / Thomas G. Bergin, Jennifer Speake. N.Y. : Facts on File, c1987. 454 p., [32] p. of plates : ill. (some col.).   **DA146**

Brief articles on all aspects of the Renaissance (the period of 1300–1620 in Europe) in alphabetical arrangement, with cross-references. A bibliography for further reading is divided into primary and secondary materials. Includes a chronological table with columns for politics and secular events, religion, emperors, kings and princes.   CB361.B43

Broughton, Bradford B. Dictionary of medieval knighthood and chivalry. N.Y. : Greenwood, 1986–1988. 2 v.   **DA147**

Contents: v. 1, Concepts and terms; v. 2, People, places, and events.

Intended "to help students understand the background of some of the literary works they were reading in medieval literature courses."—*Acknowledgments*. Provides definitions, explanations, or identification of ideas and concepts, major figures, social customs and mores, events, and information a knight was expected to know (e.g. conduct, weapons, feast days, currency). Concentrates on England and France, 1050–1400. Most entries include reference to a specific title in a numbered bibliography of 394 books and articles. Topical index for each volume.   CR4505.B76

Dictionary of the Middle Ages / Joseph R. Strayer, ed. in chief. N.Y. : Scribner's, c1982–1989. 13 v. : ill., maps.   **DA148**

Comprises some 5,000 signed articles ranging in length from about 100 to 10,000 words dealing with various aspects of the many disciplines and interests of medieval scholarship, and intended to be useful at all levels, from high school student to specialist scholar. Chronological limits are roughly CE 500 to 1500, with geographic scope "limited to the Latin West, the Slavic world, Asia Minor, the lands of the caliphate in the East, and the Muslim-Christian areas of North Africa."—*Pref.* Among the contributors, U.S. and Canadian scholars predominate; as far as possible, bibliographies emphasize English-language works. *See* and *see also* references; numerous black-and-white maps; illustrations relate mainly to art history.

The index (v. 13) offers entries for people, places, and concepts; and includes cross-references which do not "entirely replace the existing system of parenthetical and blind-entry headings and *see also* references at the end of the articles." —*Accessus.* There is a list of contributors with titles of articles written by each; an errata list for v. 1–12; and a discussion of the treatment and alphabetizing of particular languages (e.g., Arabic), titles (e.g., anonymous works), or topics (e.g., law).   D114.D5

Echols, Anne. An annotated index of medieval women / by Anne Echols and Marty Williams. N.Y. : M. Wiener Publ., c1992. 635 p.   **DA149**

For annotation, *see* CC575.   CT3220.A56

Lexikon des Mittelalters / [hrsg. von Robert Auty ... et al.]. München ; Zürich : Artemis-Verlag, [1977–1995]. Bd. 1–Bd. 7, Lfg. 5. (In progress).   **DA150**

Liselotte Lutz given as editor in early volumes.

Contents: Bd. 1–7⁵, Aachen–Russiche Literatur.

A new work with signed contributions by an international roster of scholars. Entries for persons, places, terms, etc. Bibliographies. Covers the period 300–1500 CE, concentrating on Europe.   D101.5.L49

Meyer, Otto. Clavis mediaevalis : kleines Wörterbuch der Mittelalterforschung / Otto Meyer, Renate Klauser. Wiesbaden : Harrassowitz, 1962. 311 p. : ill.   **DA151**

Reissued 1966.

A small handbook giving encyclopedic articles on terms used in medieval studies, with bibliographical references.   D114.M4

The Middle Ages : a concise encyclopaedia / general ed., H.R. Loyn. N.Y. : Thames and Hudson, 1989. 352 p. : ill., maps.   **DA152**

"The overriding aim throughout has been to provide both beginner and specialist with a single volume that presents a summary of current thought on the key protagonists, events and themes relating to the history of Europe from c.400 to c.1500."—*p. [5]*. Entries for individuals, battles, events, and sites are brief, usually only a paragraph; the "theme" articles (e.g., Jews, Climate, Handwriting) are several columns in length and are signed. Most articles have at least one bibliographic citation. Not indexed. Very useful for ready reference; good illustrations.

§ Two useful one-volume dictionaries of the Middle Ages are the *Dictionary of medieval civilization*, by Joseph Dahmus (N.Y. : Macmillan, 1984. 700 p.) and *The illustrated encyclopedia of medieval civilization*, by Arveh Grabois (London : Octopus ; N.Y. : Mayflower ; Jerusalem : Jerusalem Publ. House, 1980. 751 p.). Both are meant for general readers and both treat all countries. Because Dahmus offers short definitions, identifications, etc., his work appears to cover more topics (but includes no bibliographies and has no index); Grabois has longer articles (often surveys) with illustrations, provides short bibliographies, and includes a chronology and an index.   CB351.M565

Directories

Eisenbichler, Konrad. International directory of Renaissance and Reformation associations and institutes / comp. by Konrad Eisenbichler, Lesley B. Cormack, Jacqueline Murray. Toronto : Centre for Reformation and Renaissance Studies, 1990. 79 p.   **DA153**

Includes some text in French.

Alphabetical list of 214 centers and institutes of research concerning early modern Europe. Based on results of a questionnaire, each entry gives address, phone number (and occasionally the e-mail address of the director), size, date founded, parent body, accessibility, publications, main focus of interest, seminars of courses offered, conferences sponsored, and fellowships. Indexes for persons mentioned in an entry, cities (under country name), titles of journals and series; and general subjects.   CB359.E37

Répertoire international des médiévistes = International directory of medievalists / Fédération Internationale des Instituts d'Études Médiévales. 7 éd. [Turnhout, Belgium] : Brepols, c1990. 646 p.   **DA154**

1st ed., 1971; 6th ed., 1987.

Provides names, addresses, and fields of specialization for 16,000 medievalists worldwide. Indexes for fields and country of origin.   D112.R512

Handbooks

Mas-Latrie, Louis, *Comte de.* Trésor de chronologie d'histoire et de géographie pour l'étude et l'emploi des documents du moyen âge. Paris : Palme, 1889. 2300 col.   **DA155**
Repr.: Torino : Bottego d'Erasmo, 1962, 1969.
An extremely useful compilation (though at times unreliable), including perpetual calendars; historical chronologies; lists of saints and Fathers of the church, popes, cardinals, bishops, and archbishops; rulers of many countries in Europe, Asia, and Africa, etc.   D114.M139

Chronologies

Storey, R. L. Chronology of the medieval world, 800 to 1491 / gen. ed., Neville Williams. N.Y. : David McKay ; London : Barrie & Jenkins, 1973. 705 p.   **DA156**
Political events are shown chronologically on the left-hand pages, with contributions to religious, intellectual and artistic developments appearing on the corresponding right-hand pages. Index of persons, places, subjects, titles of works of literature and art, occupations by nationality.   D118.S855

General histories

Cambridge mediaeval history / planned by J. B. Bury. …. Cambridge : Cambridge Univ. Pr. ; N.Y. : Macmillan, 1911–36. 8 v. : maps.   **DA157**
Contents: v. 1, The Christian Roman Empire and the foundation of the Teutonic kingdoms (2nd ed., 1924); v. 2, Rise of the Saracens and the foundation of the Western Empire; v. 3, Germany and the Western Empire; v. 4, Eastern Roman Empire; v. 5, Contest of empire and papacy; v. 6, Victory of the papacy; v. 7, Decline of empire and papacy; v. 8, Close of the Middle Ages.
An excellent reference history, written by specialists, with full bibliographies at the end of each volume.
New edition: *Cambridge mediaeval history* (2nd ed., Cambridge : Cambridge Univ. Pr., 1966–67. v. 4 in 2 v.).
Contents: v. 4, ed. by J. M. Hussey: pt. 1, Byzantium and its neighbors; pt. 2, The Byzantine empire: government, church and civilisation.
These first published parts represent a complete reworking of the earlier volume for the Byzantine Empire. The limiting dates of the 1st ed., 717–1453, have been retained, but two new introductory chapters have been added to sketch the background from the time of Constantine to 717. Fully indexed; extensive bibliography.
Abridgment: *The shorter Cambridge mediaeval history*, by Charles William Previté-Orton (Cambridge : Cambridge Univ. Pr., 1952. 2 v.). Also available in paperback.   D117.C3

Atlases

Atlas of the Renaissance / C. Black … [et al.]. London : Cassell, 1993. 240 p. : ill. ; 31 cm.   **DA158**
A heavily illustrated narrative presented basically by chronological period, then by country. Inserts of "special features" offer short discussions of narrower topics (e.g., Ladies of learning, Symbolism and allegory, Sistine Chapel ceiling). Maps, photographs, reproductions are used throughout. Gazetteer; topical index; one-page bibliography; list of illustrations.   CB361.A88

Beinart, Haim. Atlas of medieval Jewish history / Haim Beinart ; [cartography, design, and production, Carta, Jerusalem ; English translation, Moshe Shalvi]. N.Y. : Simon & Schuster, c1992. 144 p. : ill., col. maps ; 31 cm.   **DA159**

Translation of: Aṭlas Karṭa le-toldot 'am Yiśra'el bi-Yeme ha-benayim.
Presents text, maps and other visual material "illustrating the changes that occurred in the Holy Land and in the Diaspora … : emigration, expulsion from cities and countries, and forced conversion" (*Introd.*) from the 4th and 5th centuries to the 17th. Indexes for geographical names, for subjects and for persons.   G1034.B413

Riley-Smith, Jonathan Simon Christopher. The atlas of the Crusades. N.Y. : Facts on File, 1990. 192 p. : col. ill., maps.
DA160
A chronological presentation with narrative supplemented by colored maps, photographs, and drawings. Chronology; glossary; place-name index with some subject entries and cross-references.
G1034.R5

Byzantine studies

Bibliography

Dölger, Franz Joseph. Byzanz / Franz Joseph Dölger, Alfons Maria Schneider. Bern : A. Francke, 1952. 328 p. (Wissenschaftliche Forschungsberichte. Geisteswissenschaftliche Reihe, Bd. 5).   **DA161**
A survey of Byzantine studies published 1938–50, with bibliographical footnotes. The first section covers history, literature, and language; the second, early Christian and Byzantine art. Author index for each section.
§ Charles Diehl's bibliography in *Byzantium : greatness and decline* (New Brunswick, N.J. : Rutgers Univ. Pr., 1957, p. 301–57) emphasizes English language works.   Z6207.B9D6

Dumbarton Oaks. Dictionary catalogue of the Byzantine collection of the Dumbarton Oaks Research Library, Washington, D.C. Boston : G.K. Hall, 1975. 12 v.   **DA162**
At head of title: Harvard University.
Provides photographic reproductions of catalog cards of one of the richest libraries on Byzantine civilization, including strong collections relating to "antecedent cultures which exerted an important influence on the development of Byzantium as well as contemporary cultures which influenced or were influenced by Byzantium [i.e., late Graeco-Roman world, early and medieval Islam, and the world of the Orthodox Slavs] … "—*Introd.* Dictionary arrangement of main and added entries and subject entries for books, journals, documents, etc.
§ The Dumbarton Oaks Research Library and Collection has issued the *Byzantine Library serials list* (Wash., 1990. 277 p.) which cites about 1,670 titles covering "all aspects of Byzantium, as well as the antecedent cultures of Greece and Rome and the contemporary Slavic, Islamic and Western Latin societies in contact with Byzantium."—*p. ii.* No index; copious cross-references.   Z6207.B9D85

Current

Byzantinische Zeitschrift : III. Abteilung : Bibliographische Notizien und Mitteilungen. Bd. 1 (1892)– . München : Beck, 1892– . Semiannual/annual.   **DA163**
Bd. 1–41 (1892–1941), repr. : N.Y. : Johnson Reprint, 1964.
An important current listing of books, articles, and essays published in Europe and North America in all European languages on the Byzantine period (325–1453). Classified arrangement with some annotations and references to reviews. Annual author index.
§ A cumulation of the entries on Byzantine art has been published as *Literature on Byzantine art, 1892–1967*, ed. by Jelisaveta S. Allen (BF9) and on epigraphy as *Literature in various Byzantine disciplines, 1892–1977 : v. 1 : Epigraphy*, by Jelisaveta S. Allen and Ihor Ševčenko (London : Mansell, 1981. 386 p.), both in the "Dumbarton Oaks bibliographies" series.

§ The Center for Byzantine Studies at Dumbarton Oaks has compiled *Author index of Byzantine studies* [microform] ([Zug, Switzerland] : IDC, [1986?]. 170 microfiches) which lists: (1) all citations in the bibliographies in *Byzantine Zeitschrift*, v. 1–47 (1892–1981); (2) author entries to articles in 77 pre-1917 Slavic (especially Russian) journals; and (3) references in Karl Krumbacher, *Geschichte der byzantinischen Literature von Justinian bis zum Ende des Oströmischen Reiches (527–1453)* (München : Beck, 1897. 1193 p.). The fiche are arranged as follows: Primary and secondary sources, including book reviews if written by a scholar associated with Dumbarton Oaks; Anonymous titles; Festschriften by honoree; Scholars' names citing necrologies, personalia; Dissertations; Congresses under best-known name; Symposia, usually under place but occasionally under best-known name. The last fiche is a name index to Jacques Paul Migne, *Patrologiae cursus completus … Series graeca* (Paris : Migne, 1857–66. 161 v. in 166. Repr.: N.Y. : Adlers, 1965–71).

A lengthy bibliography of recent books and articles, with emphasis on the Balkans, is published in each issue of *Byzantinoslavica : revue internationale des études byzantines* (v. 1 [1929]– . Prague : Československá Akademie Věd, 1929– . Two no. a year).

Translations

Hanawalt, Emily Albu. An annotated bibliography of Byzantine sources in English translation. Brookline, Mass. : Hellenic College Pr., c1988. 37 p.   **DA164**
An alphabetically arranged bibliography of books and articles which are translations into English of Byzantine materials. Only about half the entries have annotations, usually about one sentence long. Based on Clarissa Palmer Farrar and Austin Patterson Evans, *Bibliography of English translations from medieval sources* (BE45) and Mary Anne Heyward Ferguson, *Bibliography of English translations from medieval sources, 1943–1967* (N.Y. : Columbia Univ. Pr., 1974. 274 p.). Compiled for a panel on Byzantine Studies in the Undergraduate Curriculum.   Z6207.B9H36

Encyclopedias; Dictionaries

Nicol, Donald MacGillivray. A biographical dictionary of the Byzantine Empire. London : Seaby ; Braintree, Essex : distr. by B.T. Batsford, 1991. 156 p. : ill.   **DA165**
Covers "most of the persons of note and influence in the Byzantine Empire from its founding in AD330 to its conquest … in 1453. Only those who were native to the Byzantine world based on Constantinople" (*Pref.*) are included. For each, gives a brief description (usually a long paragraph) with bibliographical references for additional material. Chronology; 13 genealogical tables; index of other persons; index of foreign names.   DF506.N53

The Oxford dictionary of Byzantium / Alexander P. Kazhdan, ed. in chief. N.Y. : Oxford Univ. Pr., 1991. 3 v. (li, 2232 p.) : ill., maps.   **DA166**
Prepared at Dumbarton Oaks, Washington, D.C.
A major reference source for information on Byzantine "saints, patriarchs, all emperors, writers, places, fiscal and administrative concepts" (*Pref.*) of the 4th–15th centuries, including a few classical authors with focus "on the transmission and knowledge of their writings in Byzantium." Over 100 contributors; emphasizes interdisciplinary coverage. Major survey articles (with cross-references designated by small capitals) and many shorter articles on lesser topics. Special attention to everyday life: e.g., articles on diet, the family, gesture, emotions. Bibliographical notes at the end of articles include references to the most recent scholarship, to the best editions of texts, and to major studies. Illustrations include photographs of art works, buildings, etc., and there are maps and genealogies. No index.   DF521.O93

Crusades

Atiya, Aziz Suryal. The crusade : historiography and bibliography. Bloomington : Indiana Univ. Pr., 1962. 170 p. **DA167**
A companion volume to the author's *Crusade, commerce and culture* (Bloomington : Indiana Univ. Pr., 1962).
Includes chapters on historiography with descriptions of the great historical collections and a bibliography of books and periodical articles in various languages on the Crusades.   Z6207.C97A8

Mayer, Hans Eberhard. Bibliographie zur Geschichte der Kreuzzüge. Hannover : Hahnsche Buchhandlung, 1960. 272 p.   **DA168**
Repr., 1965, as 2. unveränd. Aufl.
Lists almost 5,400 numbered entries on the age of the Crusades up to about 1453 in a classified arrangement. Includes both books and periodical articles published before 1957/58 in Western languages and also in Arabic, Hebrew, and Chinese. The field is interpreted broadly to include the church, legal, economic, social, and intellectual history of the time.
§ Mayer is also the author of a standard text, *The Crusades*, tr. from his *Geschichte der Kreuzzüge* by John Gillingham (2nd ed. Oxford : Oxford Univ. Pr., 1990. 354 p.), which offers little bibliography.

MODERN

General works

Bibliography

Bibliographie zur Zeitgeschichte, 1953–1989 / im Auftrag des Instituts für Zeitgeschichte München, hrsg. von Thilo Vogelsang und Hellmuth Auerbach unter Mitarbeit van Ursula van Laak. Münich : K.G. Saur, 1982–91. 4 v.   **DA169**
Contents: Bd. 1, Allgemeiner Teil; Bd. 2, Geschichte des 20. Jahrhunderts bis 1945; Bd. 3, Geschichte des 20. Jahrhunderts seit 1945; Bd. 4, Bibliographie zur Zeitgeschichte, 1953–1989.
A cumulation of the citations in the quarterly "Bibliographie zur Zeitgeschrifte," published as a *Beilage* to the *Vierteljahrsbefte für Zeitgeschichte*, Jahrg. 1–38, (1985–90) and continued as a section of that publication. Classed arrangement; includes monographs, periodical articles, and dissertations.
§ The catalog of the Institut's library has been published in several parts: *Alphabetischer Katalog* (Boston : G.K. Hall, 1967. 5 v.); *Biographischer Katalog* (1967. 764 p.); and an *Erster Nachtragsband* (1973. 588 p.). An earlier compilation of the Institut's catalog is Franz Herre's *Bibliographie zur Zeitgeschichte und zum Zweiten Weltkreig für die Jahre 1945–50* (Munich : Selbstverlag des Instituts, c 1955. 254 p. [Repr. : N.Y. : Johnson Reprint, 1966]). G.K. Hall has also published the catalog of the Bibliothek für Zeitgeschichte, Stuttgart under the title *Bibliothek für Zeitgeschichte—Weltskreisbücherei, Stuttgart : systematischer Katalog* (Boston, 1968. 20 v.).   Z6204.B59

Bibliographies of battles and leaders. N.Y. : Greenwood, 1990–94. v. 1–13. (In progress).   **DA170**
Formerly called: *Meckler's bibliographies of battles and leaders.*
Contents: v. 1, The battle of Antietam and the Maryland Campaign of 1862 : a bibliography, by D. Scott Hartwig (1990. 129 p.); v. 2, The central Pacific campaign, 1943–1944 : a bibliography, by James T. Controvich (1990. 152 p.); v. 3, American warplanes 1908–1988 : a bibliography, by Myron J. Smith, Jr. (1991. 900 p.); v. 4, The battle of Pearl Harbor : a bibliography, by Myron J. Smith, Jr. (1991. 210 p.); v. 5, The battles of Coral Sea and Midway, May–June 1942 : a bibliography, by Myron J. Smith, Jr. (1991. 169 p.); v. 6, The Falklands/Malvinas campaign : a bibliography, by Eugene L. Rasor (1991. 196 p.); v. 7, The battle of Jutland : a bibliography, by Eugene L. Ra-

sor (1991. 176 p.); v. 8, General Matthew B. Ridgeway : an annotated bibliography, by Paul M. Edwards (1993. 144 p.); v. 9, The Normandy campaign, 1944 : a selected bibliography, by Colin F. Baxter (1992. 167 p.); v. 10, The Spanish Armada of 1588 : historiography and annotated bibliography, by Eugene L. Rasor (1993. 277 p.); v. 11, The Pusan perimeter, Korea, 1950 : an annotated bibliography, by Paul M. Edwards (1993. 160 p.); v. 12, General Douglas MacArthur, 1880–1964 : a historiography and annotated bibliography, by Eugene L. Rasor (1994. 217 p.).; v. 13, The Inchon Landing, Korea, 1950 : an annotated bibliography, by Paul M. Edwards (1994. 111 p.). Forthcoming: v. 14, Dangerous sky : a resource guide to the Battle of Britain, by Eunice Wilson (1995?).

An ambitious series of bibliographies covering armed conflicts and military leaders. Arrangement and type and quality of indexing vary from volume to volume. Included are "books, memoirs, monographs, periodical/journal articles, documents, theses and dissertations, and several newspapers."—*Series editor's foreword.*

§ *Bibliographie internationale d'histoire militaire* (t. 2 [1975/77]– . [Berne : Comité de Bibliographie de la CIHMC], 1979– .) provides an international survey of monographic publications on military history. Main entry listing with chronological, geographic, name, and subject indexes. Strongest for Europe. A first volume covering selected publications of 1974/76 was published 1978 as *Bulletin de bibliographie* of the Comité International des Sciences Historiques, Commission Internationale d'Histoire Militaire Comparée, Comité de Bibliographie.

Dale E. Floyd's *The world bibliography of armed land conflict from Waterloo to World War I : wars, campaigns, battles, revolutions, revolts, coups d'état, insurrections, riots, armed confrontations* (Wilmington, Del. : Michael Glazier, Inc., [1979]. 2 v.) cites some 4,000 books, periodical articles, pamphlets, and doctoral dissertations in a topical arrangement. Lacks an index.

For more recent times, see *The Second World War and the atomic age, 1940–1973,* comp. by E. David Cronon and Theodore Rosenof (Northbrook, Ill. : AHM Publ. Corp., c1975. 146 p.). A topical listing of some 2,700 books, articles, doctoral dissertations, memoirs, and printed documentary collections. Very useful for beginning researchers. Author index.

Foreign Relations Library. Catalog of the Foreign Relations Library, Inc., New York. Boston : G. K. Hall, 1969. 9 v.   **DA171**

An author, subject, and selective title catalog of a collection which aims to "cover all phases of international relations since 1918, but reference and source material necessary to an understanding of pre-World War I diplomatic and economic relations are also included."—*Pref.* Includes books, pamphlets, government publications (especially those of the United States) and publications of international organizations (except League of Nations).

————. ————. *First supplement* (Boston : G. K. Hall, 1979. 3 v.).

Reflects cataloging of the 1968–78 period.

§ The catalog is complemented by the Royal Institute of International Affairs Library's *Index to periodical articles, 1950/64, 1965/72,* and *1973/78* (Boston : G. K. Hall, 1964–79. 4 v.); it follows a classified arrangement and is based on that Library's collection.

For the *Catalogue of the Foreign Office Library, 1926–1968,* see DC274.

Hoover Institution on War, Revolution and Peace. The library catalogs of the Hoover Institution on War, Revolution, and Peace, Stanford University : catalog of the Western language collections. Boston : G. K. Hall, 1969. 63 v.   **DA172**

Reproduces the catalog cards for the Western-language books, pamphlets, and special collections of one of the major libraries of late 19th- and 20th-century economic, social and political history of Europe and Asia. The same publisher has issued a separate catalog of Western-language periodicals and newspapers (3 v.), and catalogs of materials in the Chinese- (13 v.), Japanese- (7 v.), Arabic- (1 v.), and Turkish and Persian- (1 v.) language collections.

Two *Supplements* were issued by the same publisher. The first supplement (1972) contains a catalog of the Western language collection (5 v.), the Chinese collection (2 v.), and the Japanese collection (1

v.). The second (1977) continued the catalogs of the Western language collections (6 v.), the Chinese collection (2 v.), and the Japanese collection (1 v.). The supplements cover materials catalogued July 1969–June 1973. Unlike the main set, the supplements do not include government documents, society publications, Western-language serials and newspapers, and archives and manuscripts.

§ An extensive guide to the library's archival and manuscript holdings acquired to 1978 is: *Guide to the Hoover Institution archives,* comp. by Charles G. Palm and Dale Reed (Stanford : Hoover Inst. Pr., 1980. 418 p. [Hoover bibliographical series, 59]).   Z881.S785

Huck, Burkhardt J. Informationshandbuch internationale Beziehungen und Länderkunde = Information handbook international relations and area studies / Dietrich Seydel (Hrsg.) ; bearb. von Burkhardt J. Huck. Baden-Baden : Nomos, [1989]. 752 p. (Internationale Politik und Sicherheit, Bd. 26).   **DA173**

A classed arrangement of handbooks, encyclopedias and dictionaries, bibliographies, databases (and directories of databases), journals, and guides to government publications. Indexes of authors, sponsoring bodies, titles, and geographical areas.

Novaia istoriia : ukazatel' literatury, izdannoĭ v SSSR na russkom iazyke, 1917–1940 / [sostaviteli I.I. Korndorf ... et al.]. Moskva : Izd-vo Moskovskogo universiteta, 1980–1988. v. 1–2, pt. 1–2.   **DA174**

At head of title: Moskovskii Gosudarstvennyi Universitet imeni M. V. Lomonsova. Nauchnaia Biblioteka imeni A. M. Gor'kogo.

Contents: chast 1, Obshchii otdel pervyi period novoi istorii 1640–1870gg., pod red. A.V. Ado i M. S. Meiera; chast II, vyp. 1, Vtoroĭ period noveĭsheĭ istorii, 1871–1918 gg.; chast II, vyp. 2, Vtoroĭ period novoĭ istorii, 1871–1918 gg.

A classed bibliography of Russian writings on modern history published during the 1917–40 period. Includes books, parts of books, and periodical articles.   Z6204.N683

Manuscripts; Archives

Vázquez de Parga, Margarita. International bibliography of directories and guides to archival repositories = Bibliographie internationale des guides et annuaires relatifs aux dépôts d'archives. München ; N.Y. : K.G. Saur, 1990. 195 p. **DA175**

"A study prepared by Margarita Vázquez de Parga with the collaboration of Soledad Garcia Fernandez and of Mercedes Gómez Montejano, and updated by the Editorial Committee of Archivum with assistance from the correspondents of the review."—*t.p.*

Cites directories and guides for an entire country, region, locality, or repository; also those treating a subject, a historical period, or geographical area. A section for international organizations precedes the arrangement by continents followed by country in the French form of the name. Under country name the entries are subdivided by type of repository, e.g., Central archives, Church, Local administrative archives, Archives of political papers, Private archives. Index of authors and places (in language of the country).

§ Companion work: *International directory of archives* (AK185).   CD1.A18 v.36

Indexes; Abstract journals

Historical abstracts. v. 17, no. 1 (Spr. 1971)– . Santa Barbara, Calif. : ABC-Clio, 1971– . Quarterly.   **DA176**

Issued in two parts: pt. A, Modern history abstracts, 1450–1914; pt. B, Twentieth century abstracts. No. 4 of each volume is a cumulative index.

Selectively indexes some 2,200 journals, articles in festschriften and homage volumes, and, with v. 31 (1980), includes citations for books and dissertations. Dissertation citations are drawn from *Dissertation abstracts international* (and therefore the list is not exhaustive); book citations are selected from reviews in *Choice, Library journal,* and 11 English-language history journals. Indexed by SPIndex, a rotated index of names and topics that refers to citation numbers in the bibliographic index.

Vol. 26 (1980)–30 (1984) provide retrospective indexing of journal articles omitted from *Historical abstracts* prior to 1971 (when scope was expanded to include the period 1450 to the present), as well as indexing of earlier volumes of numerous journals added to *Historical abstracts* at various periods over the years.

"List of periodicals surveyed for *America : history and life* and *Historical abstracts* (rev. 1992)" appeared in v. 43 following the index, giving years of coverage for each journal indexed.

Continues *Historical abstracts, 1775–1945 : bibliography of the world's periodical literature*, Erich H. Boehm, ed. (v. 1 [1955]–16 [1970]. Santa Barbara, Calif. : Clio Pr. with the Internat. Social Science Inst., 1955–70. Quarterly). Classified arrangement with annual author, biographical, geographical, and subject indexes (these vary). After 1964 coverage of the U.S. and Canada are excluded (*see America : history and life*, DB24).

•*Historical abstracts on disc.* Available on CD-ROM from ABC-Clio. Issued three times a year, with each a cumulation. Coverage (1982–) corresponds to the two printed parts.   D299.H5

Encyclopedias; Dictionaries

The Blackwell companion to Jewish culture : from the eighteenth century to the present / ed. by Glenda Abramson ; advisory editors, Dovid Katz … [et al.]. Oxford ; Cambridge, Mass. : Blackwell Reference, 1989. 853 p. : ill.   **DA177**

A dictionary arrangement of signed articles, mostly in the areas of literature, politics, popular culture, history and religion, with little in the sciences except psychoanalysis. Strongly bibliographical (including the living) with occasional survey and topical articles. Some articles have one or two references for further reading. Topical index.

DS102.8.B46

The Blackwell encyclopedia of industrial archaeology / ed. by Barrie Trinder … [et al.]. Oxford ; Cambridge, Mass. : Blackwell, 1992. 964 p. : ill., maps.   **DA178**

"Provides a guide to the monuments, settlements, landscapes and museums holding artifacts of the industrial societies which evolved in the West from the mid-eighteenth century."—*Introd.* Organized by country, with references to relevant political subdivisions and other general locations. Additional entries define technical terms used in industrial archeology or give biographies of persons prominent in the field. Appendixes include subject guide to the contents, an extensive bibliography, and a standard index.   T37.B55

Brownstone, David M. Dictionary of 20th-century history / David M. Brownstone, Irene M. Franck. N.Y. : Prentice Hall, c1990. 444 p.   **DA179**

"Our main aim has been to identify and briefly discuss the central events, people, movements, ideas and discoveries of the twentieth century. Our main focus has been on political, military, economic, religious, scientific and medical matters."—*Pref.* A few cultural topics are included but the publishers plan to issue a dictionary for 20th-century culture. Most entries are one paragraph long, giving identification or definition and a brief history, although a few entries are quite lengthy (e.g., nearly two columns on AIDS). Events covered are as recent as Ivan Boesky and the insider trading scandal (1986), but the country entries are more current; for example, coverage for the Philippines extends to December 1989. No bibliography; cross-references.

§ *See also* S. R. Gibbons, *A handbook of modern history* (London : Longmans, 1986. 271 p.) which is an alphabetical arrangement of about 450 articles on world history since 1870. Indexed.   D419.B76

Facts on File encyclopedia of the 20th century / gen. ed., John Drexel. N.Y. : Facts on File, [c1991]. 1046 p. : ill., maps.   **DA180**

Dictionary of about 8,000 entries for events, cities, popular books, plays, films but especially for people. Short entries, usually 100–200 words. 750 black-and-white illustrations. Some entries cover to 1991. Topical index.

§ An older work found in many libraries is *Harper encyclopedia of the modern world : a concise reference history from 1760 to the present*, ed. by Richard B. Morris and Graham W. Irwin (N.Y. : Harper, [1970]. 1271 p.). In two parts: "a 'Basic Chronology,' which deals with political, military, and diplomatic history by state, region, and area; and a 'Topical Chronology,' in which are handled, on a worldwide basis, economic, social, and constitutional history, and the history of science, thought, and culture."—*Pref.* The detailed index is essential for use.   D419.F33

Teed, Peter. A dictionary of twentieth century history : 1914–1990. Oxford ; N.Y. : Oxford Univ. Pr., 1992. 520 p.   **DA181**

Provides short-entry definitions of terms, people, movements, events, etc., of the period. Though emphasis is on political and military history, attention is paid to cultural, social, and economic affairs. No index; asterisks are used to indicate cross-references for works or names with separate entries.

§ *Dictionary of 20th-century history*, by David M. Brownstone and Irene M. Franck (DA179) overlaps very much with this work, but is stronger for the U.S. and does not provide as thorough coverage of Europe.

Chronologies

Chase's annual events. 1984 (27th year)– . Chicago : Contemporary Books, c1983– . Annual.   **DA182**

Subtitle: An almanac and survey of the year: a calendar of holidays, holy days, national and ethnic days, seasons, astronomical phenomena, festivals and fairs, anniversaries, birthdays, special events and traditional observances of all kinds, the World over.

Compiled by William D. and Helen M. Chase.

Formerly: *Chase's calendar of annual events*, 1958–83.

The 1994 edition covers some 10,000 events in a chronological arrangement. Besides the categories listed in the subtitle, includes significant historical events from the past 50 years, presidential proclamations, names and addresses of sponsoring organizations, and birthdays of famous people. Special tables of hurricanes, time zones, major awards, and an anniversary gift list. Well indexed.   GT4803.C48

Events : a chronicle of the twentieth century / ed. by Philip L. Cottrell. N.Y. : Oxford Univ. Pr., 1992. 250 p. : ill.   **DA183**

Covers 1900 to mid-1991. For each year offers a double-page spread with four columns (Politics, Society, Culture, Science) and one illustration chosen to typify the most important event of the year. Cross-references connect events. Index of people and of topics.

CB425.E85

Williams, Neville. Chronology of the expanding world, 1492–1762. N.Y. : McKay ; London : Barrie & Rockliff, 1969. 700 p.   **DA184**

———. *Chronology of the modern world, 1793–1965* (Rev. ed. Harmondsworth, Eng. : Penguin, 1975. 1020 p.).

The two chronologies include events in the fields of arts and sciences as well as political and international events of historical interest. Extensive indexes.

§ A related work is R. L. Storey's *Chronology of the medieval world, 800 to 1491* (DA156).   D11.5.W48

Annuals; Current surveys

Annual register : a record of world events. 1758– . London : Longmans ; N.Y. : St. Martin's Pr., 1761– . Annual.   **DA185**

Title varies: Annual register, 1758–1953; Annual register of world events, a review of the year, 1954–63; Annual register: world events, in 1964–74. Publisher varies.

Vols. 1–205 (1758–1963) available on microfilm from Research Publications, Woodbridge, Conn., in its "Early English newspapers" series.

Contents vary. 19th– and early-20th-century volumes are strong in biographical information in the obituary sections. Recent volumes have very few obituary notices. Includes survey articles on the year's developments in the United Kingdom, the Commonwealth, and other countries of the world; international organizations; and chapters on religion, science, law, the arts, economics, etc.

Includes some public documents, and many abstracts of political speeches. Gives English affairs with more fullness than those of other countries.

Facts on file : world news digest with index. v. 1 (Oct./Nov. 1940)– . N.Y. : Facts on File, 1940– . Looseleaf, updated weekly, with annual bound volumes available. **DA186**
Subtitle varies.

A weekly classified digest of news arranged under mainly geographical headings: United States, Europe, Other world news, Sports, Obituaries, Miscellaneous, etc. Indexes are published twice monthly and are cumulative throughout the year. The annual bound volume is called *Facts on file yearbook*. Spinoffs include *News dictionary* (annual, 1964–80) and *Latin America* (annual, 1972–78).

――――. *Five year index* (1957–).
Volumes published to date: 1946–50 (publ. 1958) to 1986–90 (publ. 1992).
•*Facts on File news digest CD-ROM* [database] (N.Y. : Facts on File, 1980–).
Machine-readable version, including full text of printed version. Updated quarterly.

Keesing's record of world events. v. 33, no. 1 (Jan. 1987)– . London : Longman, 1987– . Eleven no. a year. **DA187**
Continues *Keesing's contemporary archives* (v. 1–32, no. 12, July 1, 1931–Dec. 1986). Subtitle varies.

Published monthly until April 1991.

A diary of important events in all countries, including texts of speeches and documents, obituaries, statistics, etc., with source of report cited. Detailed indexes cumulate fortnightly, quarterly, annually, and biennially, two years completing a volume. (Until 1954, three years made up a volume.) Beginning in 1959/60, an index of names was added, published quarterly, cumulating annually and biennially. Contents organized into chronological, geographical, and topical sections. A cumulative outline index in each issue supplements the quarterly and annual indexes.
•Also available from the publisher on CD-ROM.

Atlases

Chaliand, Gérard. Atlas des diasporas / Gérard Chaliand, Jean-Pierre Rageau. Paris : O. Jacob, [c1991]. 182 p. : ill., maps ; 25 x 19 cm. **DA188**
Maps, chronologies, statistical tables, photographs, text used to portray migrations of Jews, Armenians, blacks, Chinese, Indians, Irish, Greeks, Lebanese, Palestinians, Vietnamese, and Koreans. Not indexed. An English-language edition, *The Penguin atlas of the diasporas* is announced for publication in 1995 (N.Y. : Viking).

Dockrill, Michael L. Atlas of twentieth century world history. N.Y. : HarperCollins, 1991. 160 p. : ill., maps in color, ports. ; 26 cm. **DA189**
Also publ. in Glasgow as: *Collins atlas of twentieth century world history*.

Presents 94 maps, arranged by broad periods, to demonstrate the "global shifts in territorial control and political power and ... to scrutinize a particular region revealing, for example, how wars were won or lost or how the patchwork of ethnic distribution has been—or may

prove to be—a major cause of historical change."—*Pref*. Brief discussion with maps, charts and photographs. Glossary. Index by place-name.

§ Another 20th-century atlas is *Atlas of modern world history*, editorial advisers, Haydn Middleton, Derek Heater (Oxford : Oxford Univ. Pr., c1989. [64] p. : ill. (some col.), maps in color ; 29 cm.), with small maps concentrating on a single feature. D394

Friesel, Evyatar. Atlas of modern Jewish history. Rev. from the Hebrew ed. N.Y. : Oxford Univ. Pr., 1990. 159 p. : col. ill., maps in color ; 31 cm. **DA190**
Revised and updated from Hebrew edition, Aṭlas Karṭa le-toldot 'Am Yiśra'el ba-zeman he-ḥadash, 1983.

Offers maps, charts, and drawings portraying Jewish history in the world from the late 19th century to the 1980s. Concentrates on demography and history, but economic, ideological and religious developments are also featured. Four-page bibliography; index of geographical names; general index of other names. G1030.F6513

The World Wars

General works

Mayer, Sydney L. The two World Wars : a guide to manuscript collections in the United Kingdom / Sydney L. Mayer, William J. Koenig. London ; N.Y. : Bowker, [1976]. 317 p. **DA191**
"The primary material covered ... concentrates on military and naval records in the public domain as well as the diplomatic and political records which impinge directly on the course of the wars themselves. With one or two exceptions, material still in private ownership has not been included."—*Introd*. Intended as an introductory tool to identify repositories and the nature of their contents rather than as a comprehensive guide. Arranged by place, then by repository. Subject index. Z6611.H5M38

Wedborn, Helena. Women in the First and Second World Wars : a checklist of the holdings of the Hoover Institution on War, Revolution, and Peace. [Stanford, Calif.] : Hoover Institution, Stanford Univ., c1988. 73 p. (Hoover Press bibliography, 72). **DA192**
Both the print and manuscript holdings of the Hoover Institution up to 1987 arranged by L.C. subject heading in either of two sections, 1914–18, or 1939–45. Correspondence is not listed, although diaries and memoirs are. Cross-references, but no author approach.
Z6207.E8W38

World War I

Bibliography

Enser, A. G. S. A subject bibliography of the First World War : books in English, 1914–1987. [Aldershot, England] ; Brookfield, Vt. : Gower, [1990]. 412 p. **DA193**
Companion to *A subject bibliography of the Second World War* (DA200). A topical arrangement of books, including memoirs, published 1914–87. Cross-references are used sparingly. Author and anonymous title indexes; list of subject headings used.

§ Two specialized bibliographies:
James Philip Noffsinger, *World War I aviation books in English : an annotated bibliography*. (Metuchen, N.J. : Scarecrow, 1987. 305 p.), which cites more than 1,650 books and government publications, most with short annotations.
Myron J. Smith, *World War I in the air : a bibliography and chronology* (Metuchen, N.J. : Scarecrow, 1977. 271 p.). Adds coverage of periodical articles. Z6207.E8E58

Markmann, Sigrid. Women and the First World War in England : a selective bibliographical guide = Frauen und Erster Weltkrieg in England : Auswahlbibliographie / Sigrid Markmann mit Dagmar Lange. Osnabrück : H. Th. Wenner, 1988. 66 p. **DA194**

In four parts: (1) Situation of women in the First World War, including bibliographies, official publications, surveys of the period; (2) Nonfictional texts by women commenting on the period through autobiographies, published diaries, and letters; (3) Biographical accounts; (4) Fictional accounts. Title/author index. Z6207.E8M37

Neue Forschungen zum Ersten Weltkrieg : Literaturberichte und Bibliographien von 30 Mitgliedstaaten der "Commission internationale d'histoire militaire comparée" / hrsg., Jürgen Rohwer. Koblenz : Bernard & Graefe, c1985. 406 p. (Schriften der Bibliothek für Zeitgeschichte, Bd. 25). **DA195**

A state-of-the-art account of research as of 1989/90 on World War I, for "as many countries as possible with a select bibliography."—*Pref.* For some countries the author includes a brief survey of that country's participation in the war. Author/editor index.

§ A companion volume is *Neue Forschungen zum Zweiten Weltkrieg : Literaturberichte und Bibliographien aus 67 Ländern*, in Zusammenarbeit mit dem Comité internationale d'histoire de la Deuxième Guerre Mondiale und der Commission Internationale d'Histoire Militaire Comparée, hrsg. von Jürgen Rohwer und Hildegard Müller (Koblenz : Bernard & Graefe, c1990. 564 p. Schriften der Bibliothek für Zeitgeschichte, Bd. 28).

Follows the same pattern, with surveys of research and bibliographies of publications from each of 67 countries. Each state-of-the-art summary is current as of 1989. Lists 3,560 titles. Author/editor index. D522.42.N48

New York Public Library. Reference Department. Subject catalog of the World War I collection. Boston : G. K. Hall, 1961. 4 v. **DA196**

During World War I and its reconstruction period the New York Public Library attempted to obtain everything relevant to the war and its aftermath published in the United States and Europe—about 35,000 items. Relevant subject cards from the catalog in the Reference Department are reproduced here; material from the Slavonic, Oriental and Jewish Divisions are not included. Entries for books, pamphlets, and important periodical articles.

§ *Subject catalog of the World War II collection* of the New York Public Library, Research Libraries (Boston : G. K. Hall, 1977. 3 v.) is especially strong for its listings of military and diplomatic history, prisoners, propaganda (with many examples of clandestine publications), post-war planning, the effect of the war on art, literature and philosophy, and more than 3,000 personal accounts. Z6207.E8N48

Woodward, David R. America and World War I : a selected annotated bibliography of English-language sources / David R. Woodward, Robert Franklin Maddox. N.Y. : Garland, 1985. 368 p. (Wars of the United States, vol. 6 ; Garland reference library of social science, v. 259). **DA197**

A classified, briefly annotated bibliography of some 2,500 items, with author and subject indexes. Encompasses works published prior to 1984 which examine the war's impact on society as well as those relating to military operations.

§ Ronald Schaeffer's *The United States in World War I : a selected bibliography* (Santa Barbara, Calif. : ABC-Clio, 1978. 224 p.) can be used to supplement this work, especially for contemporary narrative accounts. Also useful for first-person accounts is Charles V. Genthe, *American war narratives 1917–1918 : a study and bibliography* (N.Y. : D. Lewis, 1969. 194 p.). Z6207.E8W67

Encyclopedias; Dictionaries

Gray, Randal. Chronicle of the First World War / Randal Gray and Christopher Argyle. N.Y. : Facts on File, 1990. 2 v. **DA198**

Contents: v. 1, 1914–16 (352 p.); v. 2, 1917–21 (383 p.).

A chronology arranged in nine parallel columns, each column (with subheading) representing a military site or theater of war: The Western front, Home fronts, Eastern front, African operations, Southern fronts, Turkish front, Sea war, International events, Air war. Each volume gives tables of statistics for important military operations and for the overall war; a glossary defining wartime terminology and abbreviations; maps of fronts and battles; a bibliography arranged by topic; and an index to main events. Vol. 2 adds a who's-who section, with categories and names (e.g., War poets, Russian admirals). D523.G634

The Marshall Cavendish illustrated encyclopedia of World War I. N.Y. : M. Cavendish, 1984. 12 v. **DA199**

A comprehensive encyclopedia, heavily illustrated (5,000 photographs, maps, drawings, etc.). Vol. 1 gives an outline of origins and major events; vols. 2–11 cover the war in 540 articles (e.g., artists and poets, songs and slang, battles, etc.) with references to further reading at the end of each article. Vol. 12 offers an essay on consequences and outcome, with profit and loss charts, a 21-page bibliography, and a topical index followed by special indexes for military commanders, statesmen, ships, contributors, illustrations, and drawings.

§ A. P. C. Bruce, *An illustrated companion to the First World War* (London ; New York : Joseph, 1989. 424 p.) provides an alphabetical arrangement of some 800 entries, mainly political, military, and biographical with 200 contemporary photographs, most of them drawn from the collections of the Imperial War Museum, London.

Biographical dictionary of World War I, by Holger H. Herwig and Neil Heyman (Westport, Conn. : Greenwood, [1982]. 424 p.) offers biographical sketches of about 325 key World War I figures with emphasis on their roles in the war.

World War II

Bibliography

Enser, A. G. S. A subject bibliography of the Second World War : books in English 1939–1974. Boulder, Colo. : Westview Pr. ; London : Deutsch, [1977]. 592 p. **DA200**

Intended as a guide for "both the general reader and the research er."—*Pref.* Lists, by subject, items appearing in the British Museum subject catalog, the *Cumulative book index,* the *British national bibliography* and *Whitaker.* Author index.

———. *A subject bibliography of the Second World War, and aftermath : books in English, 1975–1987* ([Aldershot, England] ; Brookfield, Vt., : Gower, c1990. 287 p.) continues the earlier bibliography and supersedes its continuation covering 1975–83 (1985). Adds an additional 1,600 titles, including a section under each country on the aftermath of the war. Arrangement is by subject as in earlier volumes and there is a list of headings at the end of the volume. Author index.

§ Many bibliographies have appeared on the conduct of the war by a specific country. A few examples:

Derek G. Law, *The Royal Navy in World War Two : an annotated bibliography* ([London] : Greenhill Books, [1988]. 305 p.).

Michael Parrish, *The U.S.S.R. in World War II : an annotated bibliography of books published in the Soviet Union, 1945–1975; with an addenda for the years 1975–1980* (N.Y. : Garland, 1981. 2 v.).

Myron J. Smith, *World War II at sea : a bibliography of sources in English* (Metuchen, N.J. : Scarecrow, 1976. 3 v.) and its supplement for 1974–89 (1990. 304 p.);.

Myron J. Smith, *World War II : the European and Mediterranean theaters; an annotated bibliography* (N.Y. : Garland, 1984. 450 p.). Z6207.W8E57

Funk, Arthur Layton. The Second World War : a select bibliography of books in English published since 1975. Claremont, Calif. : Regina Books, [1985]. 210 p. **DA201**

Publ. for the American Committee on the History of the Second World War, for the 1965 meeting of the International Congress of Historical Sciences.

A topical arrangement of 4,519 books and government publications from 1975–84, with some titles published in 1985. Index.

§ For earlier works, *see*: Janet Ziegler, *World War II books in English 1945–1965* (Stanford, Calif. : Hoover Inst. Pr., 1971. 194 p.) and its supplement, *A selected bibliography of books on the Second World War in English published in the United States, 1966–1975*, comp. by Arthur L. Funk ... [et al.] (Gainesville, Fla. : American Committee on the History of the Second World War, [1976?]. 33 p.).

Z6207.W8F79

Sbrega, John J. The war against Japan, 1941–1945 : an annotated bibliography. N.Y. : Garland, 1989. 1050 p. (Wars of the United States, v. 10 ; Garland reference library of social science, v. 258). **DA202**

Lists English-language books, articles, novels, and documents (including declassified military reports) issued through 1987. Arrangement is by broad subject, subdivided topically. All aspects are included—diplomatic, political, economic, military, social and cultural, religious. Author and subject indexes; chronology.

Z6207.W8S299

Tutorow, Norman E. War crimes, war criminals, and war crimes trials : an annotated bibliography and source book / comp. and ed. by Norman E. Tutorow with the special assistance of Karen Winnovich. N.Y. : Greenwood, [1986]. 548 p. (Bibliographies and indexes in world history, 4). **DA203**

For annotation, *see* CK80. Z6464.W33T87

Manuscripts; Archives

Cantwell, John D. The Second World War : a guide to documents in the Public Record Office. 2nd ed. London : H.M.S.O., 1993. 218 p. (Public Record Office handbooks, 15). **DA204**

1st ed., 1972.

Describes the files of the archives, which deal with "the prosecution of the war but [which also] embrace to some extent records of activities arising from or affected by it [i.e., World War II]"—*Introd.* The 1st ed. was issued to accompany the opening of the records in 1972; this ed. adds coverage of additional files subsequently opened. Includes useful historical notes on the ministries, departments, offices, etc. Appendixes add coverage of the war crimes files and lists of official histories. Topical index.

§ *See also*: Frances Thorpe and Nicholas Pronay, *British official films in the Second World War : a descriptive catalog* (Oxford ; Santa Barbara, Calif. : Clio Pr., [1980]. 321 p.), providing descriptions of 1,887 films "produced or distributed by an accredited agency of the British government" (*Pref.*) and indicating location of copies. Indexes of titles and credits. CD1046

Encyclopedias; Dictionaries

Ellis, John. The World War II databook : the essential facts and figures for all the combatants. [London] : Aurum, [1993]. 315 p. : maps. **DA205**

Aims to cover the "administrative, industrial and logistical basis of military operations between 1939 and 1945" (*Pref.*) through 28 black-and-white maps, statistical tables and charts, lists of the command structure, etc. Not indexed, but there is a detailed table of contents. Sources are not given, but a bibliography, pp. 309–15 cites books most useful in compiling the databook. D744.E46

Hogg, Ian V. Encyclopaedia of the Second World War / by Ian V. Hogg & Bryan Perrett. [Novato, Calif.] : Presidio Pr., c1989. 447 p. : ill., maps. **DA206**

A general dictionary of "personalities, campaigns, battles, events, warships, aircraft, land warfare weapons, electronic warfare, intelligence, abbreviations, and operational codenames."—*Pref.* Short articles give a person's career during the war, summary of a battle, definition of term or abbreviation, location of a place name. Three-page bibliography; cross-references. Lacks an index.

§ Also useful for military aspects is *Rand McNally encyclopedia of World War II* (Chicago : Rand McNally, 1977. 256 p.), with its articles on every major weapon and weapons system, ship classes, aircraft, tanks and armored vehicles, though it has no bibliography or index. D740.H64

Polmar, Norman. World War II : America at war, 1941–1945 / Norman Polmar, Thomas B. Allen. N.Y. : Random House, c1991. 940 p. : ill., maps. **DA207**

Aims to address "how the war touched and even shaped the American way of life if not the American character ... "—*Introd.* Alphabetical arrangement of entries for weapons, battles, places, events, people (including "young future American leaders," e.g., George Bush, John F. Kennedy), plus an Epilogue to the War. Appendix for comparisons of military ranks; Personal name index; Code and project names index. D743.5.P56

The Simon and Schuster encyclopedia of World War II / ed. by Thomas Parrish. N.Y. : Simon & Schuster, [1978]. 767 p. : ill. ; maps. **DA208**

An attempt to present an accurate and balanced account of World War II through a series of alphabetically arranged, mainly short articles dealing with the events, persons, places, equipment, terms and abbreviations, etc., that figured prominently in the war. A list of contributing writers, with credentials, is given, but most articles are unsigned. *See* references are provided, and *see also* references are signaled by use of small capitals within the text; there is also a detailed subject index. Chronology, p. 708-15; selected bibliography, p. 716-21. Table of equivalent ranks.

§ *The historical encyclopedia of World War II*, ed. by Marcel Baudot [et al.] (N.Y. : Facts on File, [1980]. 548 p. : maps, charts) is a translation from the French *Encyclopédie de la guerre 1939–1945* but lacking the index of the French original.

Louis L. Snyder's historical guide to World War II (Westport, Conn. : Greenwood, 1982. 838 p.) emphasizes the non-military aspects of the war. D740.S57

Chronologies

10 eventful years : a record of events of the years preceding, including and following World War II, 1937 through 1946 / prep. under the editorial direction of Walter Yust, ed. of Encyclopaedia Britannica. Chicago : Encyclopaedia Britannica, [1947]. 4 v. : ill. **DA209**

An alphabetically arranged encyclopedia covering events, personalities, and developments in science, technology, literature, etc., of a crucial period. Does not supersede the annual *Britannica book of the year* (Chicago : Encyclopaedia Britannica, 1938– .) for the period, as many articles in the annuals are not included, but it cumulates, summarizes, and surveys the events of the era. Includes useful chronologies, tables, and summaries. Many articles are signed, bibliographies are included, and illustrations are clear, as is the typography. Comprehensive index.

§ A similar publication, i.e., a chronology published contemporaneously, is *Chronology and index of the Second World War 1938–1945*, comp. by the Royal Institute of International Affairs and issued quarterly. It was cumulated and published by the Institute in 1948. Newspaper Archives Developments of Reading, England, reprinted the *Chronology* (1975) and added an index by John G. Ames. This later edition was reprinted by Meckler (Westport, Conn., 1990. 446 p.). AG5.T35

Goralski, Robert. World War II almanac, 1931–1945 : a political and military record. N.Y. : Putnam, [1981]. 486 p. : ill. **DA210**

A heavily-illustrated chronology of events leading up to the war, and virtually day-by-day summaries of developments during the war years themselves. Statistical tables for the cost of the war, strength of the combatants, casualties, lists of weapons and equipment, comparison of ranks; bibliography. Index includes references to illustrations (given in italics).

§ *United States naval chronology: World War II* (Wash. : U.S. Govt. Print. Off., 1955. 214 p.), prepared by the Naval History Division of the Office of the Chief of Naval Operations, includes "a record of the loss or damage of every U.S. naval vessel of any size, as well as every ship sinking by U.S. forces."—*Foreword.*   D743.5.G64

Atlases

Pitt, Barrie. The chronological atlas of World War II / Barrie and Frances Pitt. London : Macmillan, c1989. 178 p. : some maps in color ; 36 x 27 cm.   **DA211**

Published in U.S. as *The month-by-month atlas of World War II.*

Offers a month-by-month account of the war, emphasizing "the panorama of the war ... so that not only could the progress of each individual compaign and battle be followed, but also their relationship to the whole global conflict."—*Author's note.* For each month, a double-page spread gives: a world map showing advances and contractions in the territory controlled by the Germans and Japanese; more detailed maps for specific battles; and a summary of military events. Also includes essays on compaigns (e.g., Barbarossa, D-Day) or political history (e.g., The world in Autumn 1945). Index of place names divided by Eastern, European and Middle Eastern, and Pacific fronts; index of political and military names and events.

§ A similar atlas by Charles Messenger: *World War Two: chronological atlas : when, where, how and why* ([London] : Bloomsbury, [1989]. 255 p. : maps in color ; 30 cm.).   G1038.P6

The Times atlas of the Second World War / ed. by John Keegan. London : Times Books ; N.Y. : Harper & Row, c1989. 254 p. : ill. (some col.), some maps in color ; 37 cm.   **DA212**

Covers the war in maps, charts, photographs, and brief essays, beginning with Europe after the First World War and continuing through 1945. The arrangement is roughly chronological, then area by area. Besides military aspects, sections for The world war economies, The casualties, Resistance in Eastern Europe. One-page bibliography, glossary of personal names, lists of abbreviations and of battles (locating them); index of place names (referring to specific maps); chronology for each area.   G1038.T6

Holocaust

Bibliography

Braham, Randolph L. The Hungarian Jewish catastrophe : a selected and annotated bibliography. 2nd ed., rev. and enl. [N.Y.] : Social Science Monographs and Institute for Holocaust Studies, City Univ. of N.Y. : distr. by Columbia Univ. Pr., 1984. 501 p. (East European monographs, no. 162).   **DA213**

1st ed., 1962.

"Aims ... to bring under one cover all the important references" to both separately published and periodical literature on the subject for "scholars, researchers and officials, as well as interested laymen."—*Introd.* About 2,500 entries in many languages; classified arrangement. Includes general reference works, background studies on Jews in Hungary, the Holocaust in that country, and events of the postwar era. Author, name, geographic, and subject indexes.   Z6373.H8B7

Cargas, Harry J. The Holocaust : an annotated bibliography. 2nd ed. Chicago : Amer. Libr. Assoc., 1985. 196 p.   **DA214**

1st ed., Haverford, Pa. : Catholic Library Assoc., 1977.

Contains critical annotations in classified arrangement of approximately 500 books published in English in the U.S. Includes a chapter on "Researching the Holocaust, guidance for students." Regional in-

dexes by nation and by concentration camp; index by author and title. Compiler calls himself "a post-Auschwitz Catholic." Author/title index. Useful for work with undergraduates and high school students.

§ Another useful bibliography for undergraduates is by Marty Bloomberg, *The Jewish holocaust : an annotated guide to books in English* (San Bernardino, Calif. : Borgo Pr., 1991. 248 p.).   Z6374.H6C37

Edelheit, Abraham J. Bibliography on Holocaust literature / Abraham J. Edelheit and Hershel Edelheit. Boulder, Colo. : Westview Pr., 1986. 842 p.   **DA215**

Contains 9,014 entries for English-language books, periodicals, and pamphlets; selected book entries are annotated. Entries are arranged chronologically by four periods and in classified order within periods. Detailed table of contents; index of authors.

——. —— *Supplement* (Boulder, Colo. : Westview Pr., 1990–93. v. 1–2 [In progress]).

Contains additional English-language entries, also arranged by period; v. 1 adds sections on: Reflections on the Holocaust, The Holocaust in literature and art, Distorting the Holocaust, Historiography, Dissertations, Bibliographies, Guides. Vol. 2 has an appendix of periodicals and newsletters that contain considerable information on anti-Semitism, fascism, Naziism, and the Holocaust but were not indexed.

§ Companion work by the same authors: *The Jewish world in modern times : a selected, annotated bibliography* (Boulder, Colo. : Westview Pr. ; London : Mansell, 1988. 569 p.).

See also:

(1) Leo Eitinger and Robert Krell, *The psychological and medical effects of concentration camps and related persecutions on survivors of the Holocaust : a research bibliography* (Vancouver : Univ. of British Columbia Pr., 1985. 168 p.), an unannotated listing of 1,650 items (mostly books and articles) published to 1984, indexed by broad subject.

(2) For Yiddish-language materials, *Bibliography of Yiddish books on the catastrophe and heroism* (N.Y. : Yivo Inst. for Jewish Research, 1962. *Supplement*, 1970. [Bibliographical series 3, 11]).   Z6374.H6E33

The Holocaust : an annotated bibliography and resource guide / ed. by David M. Szonyi. [Hoboken, N.J.] : Ktav Publ. House for the National Jewish Resource Center, New York, c1985. 396 p.   **DA216**

Identifies and annotates a wealth of material: primary and secondary print sources, audiovisual materials, music, exhibits, education centers, U.S. and Canadian memorials and landmarks, survivor groups, resources for religious services, and funding sources for research and programming. Arranged in classified order, but there is no index.

Supplemented by: *The Holocaust : catalog of publications and audio-visual materials 1988–1990* (N.Y. : International Center for Holocaust Studies, 1988[?]. 111 p.). The Center also publishes a journal, *Dimensions : a journal of Holocaust studies* (1985–) that lists current publications.

§ *See also:*

(1) Martin Sable, *Holocaust studies : a directory and bibliography of bibliographies* (Greenwood, Fla. : Penkeville, [1987]. 115 p.) for a listing with addresses of relevant organizations, associations, information and research centers, government agencies, libraries and archives, schools and universities, and monuments and sculptures.

(2) Judith Herschlag Muffs and Dennis B. Klein, eds., *The Holocaust in books and films : a selected, annotated list* (3rd ed. N.Y. : Hippocrene Books, 1986. 158 p.), sponsored by the Anti-Defamation League of B'nai B'rith, intended for teachers in junior and senior high schools.   Z6374.H6H65

Holocaust literature : a handbook of critical, historical, and literary writings / ed. by Saul S. Friedman. Westport, Conn. : Greenwood, 1993. 677 p.   **DA217**

Essays written by specialists, designed to guide researchers, teachers, and librarians to recommended texts. In three sections: Conceptual approaches ("Selected biographies and interpretations of Hitler," "Church and the holocaust"); Holocaust by area (Holland, Arab countries, American response); Holocaust in education and the arts (diaries and memoirs, movies). Author/title index; subject index.

D804.3.H6475

Jewish immigrants of the Nazi period in the USA / Herbert A. Strauss, ed. N.Y. : K.G. Saur ; Detroit : distr. by Gale, 1978–c1992. 6 v. in 8 : ill.   **DA218**
For annotation, *see* DB126.   E184.J5J558

Yad Vashem Martyrs' and Heroes Memorial Authority, Jerusalem. Joint documentary projects : bibliographical series / Yad Vashem Martyrs' and Heroes Memorial Authority, Jerusalem [and] Yivo Institute for Jewish Research, N.Y. N.Y. : [Yivo Inst.], 1960–74. v. 1–14. (In progress?).   **DA219**
Contents: v. 1, Guide to Jewish history under Nazi impact, by Jacob Robinson and Philip Friedman (1960. 425 p.); v. 2, Bibliography of books in Hebrew on the Jewish catastrophe and heroism in Europe, ed. by Philip Friedman (1960. 433 p. In Hebrew); v. 3, Bibliography of Yiddish books on the catastrophe and heroism, by Philip Friedman and Joseph Gar (1962. 330 p. In Yiddish); v. 4, The Hungarian Jewish catastrophe: a selected and annotated bibliography, by Randolph L. Braham (1962. 86 p.; for rev. ed. *see* DA213); v. 5–8, The Jewish holocaust and heroism through the eyes of the Hebrew press; a bibliography, ed. by Mendel Piekarz (1966. 4 v. In Hebrew), continued by his *ha-Shoah u Sefiheha be-Asparklaryat Kitue 'Et' Iviijim* for the period 1951–75 (1978. 493 p.); v. 9–10, Bibliography of articles on the catastrophe and heroism in Yiddish periodicals, by Joseph Gar (1966–69. 2 v. In Yiddish); v. 11, Bibliography of Yiddish books on the catastrophe and heroism, ed. by David Bass [additions for 1960–70, to v. 3, above] (1970. 54 p. In Yiddish).; v. 12, The holocaust and after : sources and literature in English, by Jacob Robinson, assisted by Mrs. Philip Friedman (1973. 353 p.); v. 13–14, The holocaust and its aftermath : Hebrew books published in the years 1933–1972, by Mendel Piekarz (1974. 2 v. In Hebrew).
A series of bibliographies essential for the study of the Holocaust. Most volumes are in Hebrew, but all include English title page and front matter.

Filmography

Ringelheim, Joan Miriam. A catalogue of audio and video collections of Holocaust testamony. 2nd ed. N.Y. : Greenwood, 1992. 209 p. (Bibliographies and indexes in world history, no. 23).   **DA220**
1st ed., 1986.
A directory of repositories of oral history holocaust testimony, arranged by state. Based on responses to questionnaires; for each, gives address, access, summary of content, finding aids, additional holocaust material available. Appendixes identify collections of Jewish survivors by nation of birth, ghettos, concentration camps, and liberators. This ed. adds information on six new collections, for a total of 20.
§ The Fortunoff Video Archive for Holocaust testimonies at Yale University has published its own *Guide to Yale University Holocaust video testimonies* (N.Y. : Garland, 1990; 2nd ed., 1994. 245 p.).

D804.3.R55

Skirball, Sheba F. Films of the Holocaust : an annotated filmography of collections in Israel. N.Y. : Garland, [1990]. 273 p., [8] p. of plates : ill. (Garland filmographies, 2 ; Garland reference library of social science, v. 463).   **DA221**
Sponsored by the Steven Spielberg Jewish Film Archive, Jerusalem.
An inventory of films and videotapes in libraries and archives in Jerusalem and Tel Aviv, including newsreels, television clips, commercially produced films, etc. Arranged by title, with a separate listing by date for untitled films. Subject index; language index.
§ *See also*: Frances Lawrence Gellert, *The Holocaust, Israel and the Jews : motion pictures in the National Archives* (Wash. : publ. for NARA by National Archives Trust Fund Board, 1989. 117 p.) which lists, describes, and indexes about 600 films.   D804.3.S59

Chronologies

Edelheit, Hershel. A world in turmoil : an integrated chronology of the Holocaust and World War II / Hershel Edelheit and Abraham J. Edelheit. N.Y. : Greenwood, 1991. 450 p. (Bibliographies and indexes in world history, no. 22).   **DA222**
Covers January 30, 1933–May 14, 1948, concentrating on events in Europe and the Middle East, with less attention to Africa, the Americas, and Asia. Brief entries; glossary of terms; nine-page bibliography arranged by author. Personal name, place-name, and subject indexes.

D804.3.E34

Atlases

Gilbert, Martin. Atlas of the Holocaust. 1st U.S. ed. N. Y. : William Morrow, [c1993]. 256 p. : ill., maps ; 25 cm.   **DA223**
U.K. 2nd ed. entitled *Dent atlas of the Holocaust*.
1st ed., 1982, entitled *Macmillan atlas of the Holocaust*; repr. 1988, entitled *Atlas of the Holocaust*.
Presents 316 black-and-white maps with photographs that "show in chronological sequence, the destruction of each of the main Jewish communities of Europe, as well as acts of resistance and revolt, avenues of escape and rescue, and the fate of individuals."—*Introd.* An 8½ page list of sources includes the map number for each (but the alphabetical arrangement of the sources means that the accompanying map numbers are not in sequence). Indexes of places and of individuals.   G1797.21.E29G58

DB

The Americas

GENERAL WORKS

Bibliography

Brown, John Carter. Bibliotheca americana : a catalogue of books relating to North and South America in the library of John Carter Brown of Providence, R.I / with notes by John Russell Bartlett. Providence : [printed by H. O. Houghton and company, Cambridge], 1865–71. 3 pts. in 4 v.   **DB1**
Available in microform from Readex Microprint. Pt. 3 repr.: N.Y. : Kraus, 1963. 2 v.
Contents: pt.1, 1482–1600; pt.2, 1601–1700; pt.3, 1701–1800. 2v. 2nd ed., 1875–82, of pts. 1–2 only.
The catalog of a very rich collection now in the Brown University Library. The set lists 4,173 numbered, annotated items, arranged chronologically with alphabetical index of authors. Detailed bibliographic information. The Kraus reprint includes additions and corrections made by Wilberforce Eames in the New York Public Library copy.

Pts. 1–2 are largely superseded by the following:

§ *Bibliotheca Americana : catalogue of the John Carter Brown Library in Brown University, Providence, Rhode Island* (Providence : The Library, 1919–1931. 3 v. in 5) is still said to be the most complete chronological list available for this period. Lists 3,737 items, including books and pamphlets in all languages as well as translations. Contents: v.1, pt.1, to 1569; v.1, pt.2, 1570–99; v.2, pt.1, 1600–34; v.2, pt.2, 1634–58; v.3, 1659–74. (Repr.: N.Y. : Kraus, 1961–1975).

An additional catalog covering books printed 1675–1700 (Providence, 1973. 484 p.) was followed by a short-title list of additions, 1471–1700 (Providence, 1973. 167 p.), thus completing the record of books printed before 1701 that were in the Library on July 1, 1971.

Z1203.B87

Church, Elihu Dwight. Catalogue of books relating to the discovery and early history of North and South America : forming a part of the library of E. D. Church / comp. and annotated by George Watson Cole. N.Y. : Dodd ; Cambridge : Univ. Pr., 1907. 5 v. : ill. **DB2**

Repr. : N.Y. : P. Smith, 1951. Also available in microform from Readex Microprint.

A monumental work which includes 1,385 entries of books about America, arranged chronologically by date of publication from the earliest period to 1884, with author and title index. Gives for each book: full title, collation, and important historical and bibliographical annotations, with notes of differences in copies and location of copies in some 50 public and private libraries. Gives many facsimile reproductions of title pages, colophons, etc. The Church collection is now part of the Huntington Library, San Marino, Calif. Z1203.C55

Harrisse, Henry. Bibliotheca americana vetustissima : a description of works relating to America published between the years 1492 and 1551. N.Y. : Philes, 1866. 519 p. **DB3**

Frequently reprinted.

A standard early work listing, with great bibliographical detail, 304 works relating to America publ. 1492–1551. Copious footnotes; references to sources.

————. ———— *Additions* (Paris : Librairie Tross, 1872. 199 p. Repr. both parts: Chicago : Argonaut, 1967).

"Not a continuation of the *Bibliotheca americana vetustissima*, but a series of notes and additions intended to aid towards forming a complete list of works relating to American, printed previous to the year 1551."—*Introd.*

Revised and expanded by: Carlos Sanz, *Bibliotheca americana vetustissima : últimas adiciones* (Madrid : Librería General V. Suárez, 1960. 2 v.) and his *Comentario crítico e índice general cronológico* (1960. 79 p.).

The first two volumes are "final" supplements to Harrisse, the other an index to the Harrisse volumes, the two new volumes, and two other works by Sanz, *Henry Harrisse...* (1958) and *El gran secreto de la carta de Colón* (1959). In 1958 Suárez reprinted the original Harrisse volumes and issued all seven volumes under the series title, *Bibliotheca americana vetustissima*.

James Ford Bell Library. The James Ford Bell Library : an annotated catalog of original source materials relating to the history of European expansion, 1400–1800, University of Minnesota. Boston : G. K. Hall, 1981. 493 p. **DB4**

A main entry listing of the Bell Library's holdings as of Dec. 31, 1980. The collection is strong in accounts of the discovery and exploration of America; includes books, maps, and manuscripts. This volume incorporates the listings in the Library's earlier published catalogs: *Jesuit relations and other Americana in the library of James Ford Bell* (1950) and the lists of additions to the collection published 1955, 1961, 1967, 1970 and 1975. (Those catalogs remain useful for their chronological approach and for the fuller descriptions, collations, and facsimiles of titles found in the basic volume.).

Occasional supplements appear in *The merchant explorer*, (no. 1 [Apr. 1961]– . Minneapolis : Univ. of Minnesota Library, 1961–), a publication of the library. Z1212.J35

New York Public Library. Reference Department. Dictionary catalog of the history of the Americas. Boston : G.K. Hall, 1961. 28 v. **DB5**

Reproduction of nearly 600,000 author, subject, and other catalog cards of an outstanding collection in North and South American history and related topics. Many subject cards are included for periodical articles indexed by the Library.

————. ————. *First supplement* (Boston : G.K. Hall, 1973. 9 v.) reproduces cards for all materials added to the collection through Dec. 31, 1971. After that date, additions appear in the Library's *Dictionary catalog of the Research Libraries* (AA116) and the *Bibliographic guide to North American history* (DB25). Z1201.N4

Newberry Library. Dictionary catalog of the Edward E. Ayer collection of Americana and American Indians in the Newberry Library. Boston : G. K. Hall, 1961. 16 v. (8062 p.). **DB6**

This collection of some 90,000 pieces is particularly strong in early discoveries and explorations of America, the American Indian, missionary activities, western exploration and travel, cartography, the history of Latin America, the Philippines, and the Hawaiian Islands. The volumes are a reproduction of the entire Ayer dictionary catalog, but do not include the Greenlee (Portuguese history and literature) or Graff (Western Americana) collections.

Supplements (1st, 1970. 3 v.; 2nd, 1980. 4 v.).

The 1st suppl. adds 9,500 books, pamphlets and serials cataloged for the Ayer Collection and 285 titles added to the Everett D. Graff Collection of Western Americana. The 2nd suppl. adds another 9,500 titles for the Ayer Collection (including selected materials from its holdings on Indian linguistics and dissertations on the American Indian). In addition, the Graff Collection is now fully represented, including additions not included in the 1st suppl. The Graff collection was formerly accessible only through its *Catalogue of the Everett D. Graff Collection of Western Americana*, comp. by Colton Storm (Chicago : Univ. of Chicago Pr., 1968. 854 p.).

§ The Newberry Library has also published *Checklist of manuscripts in the Edward E. Ayer collection*, comp. by Ruth Lapham Butler (Chicago : Newberry Library, 1937. 295 p.). While old, it is still useful in identifying materials.

Statistics

Mitchell, Brian R. International historical statistics : the Americas 1750–1988. 2nd ed. N.Y. : Stockton Pr., 1993. 817 p. **DB7**

For annotation, *see* CG70. HA175.M55

NORTH AMERICA

United States

General works

Guides

Prucha, Francis Paul. Handbook for research in American history : a guide to bibliographies and other reference works. 2nd ed. rev. Lincoln : Univ. of Nebraska Pr., c1994. 214 p. **DB8**

1st ed., 1987.

A "bibliography of bibliographies and other reference books which will in turn direct the researcher to useful books, articles, and other sources."—*Introd.* Arranged into essays on types and formats of reference books (e.g., periodical indexes and abstracts, manuscript catalogs, picture sources, statistics, databases). Incorporates information on new technologies (Internet, CD-ROMs, etc.). Pt. 2 of the 1st ed. covered individual disciplines; this has been dropped; some of the citations have been incorporated into other sections. Author, title, subject indexes. A major guide for historians.　　　　Z1236.P78

Bibliography

See also the Diaries and letters section in BE, American literature, as well as CC for specific ethnic groups and women, and CJ for political and military affairs of the U.S.

Beers, Henry Putney. Bibliographies in American history : guide to materials for research. N.Y. : Wilson, 1942. 487 p.
　　　　　　　　　　　　　　　　　　　　　　　　DB9

1st ed., 1938.

A classified list of more than 11,000 bibliographies including separate works, analytics, compilations in progess, and manuscript bibliographies, with author and subject index. Covers many aspects of American history, including political, diplomatic, economic, military, religious, cultural, local, etc.

————. *Bibliographies in American history, 1942–1978 : guide to materials for research* (Woodbridge, Conn. : Research Publications, 1982. 2 v. [946 p.]).

Lists nearly 11,800 works that are primarily bibliographic in nature or include relevant lists of publications, descriptions and inventories of archival and manuscript collections, and similar research aids. Index of main entries and subjects.　　　　Z1236.A1B4

Church and state in America : a bibliographical guide / ed. by John F. Wilson. N.Y. : Greenwood, 1986–87. 2 v.　**DB10**

Contents: v. 1, The colonial and early national periods (433 p.); v. 2, The Civil War to the present day (452 p.).

Sponsored by the Princeton Project of Church and State.

In signed bibliographical essays devoted mostly to historical periods, with additional chapters on education, law, and gender relations, the compilers cite books, articles, bibliographies, and primary sources of the last 25 years (with a few older materials). Index for authors and subjects cited in the essays but not for the bibliographies that follow the essays, which include additional citations.

§ See also: *Cities and churches : an international bibliography*, by Loyde H. Hartley (Metuchen, N.J. : American Theological Library Assoc. and Scarecrow, 1992. 3 v.) which lists books, articles, dissertations, essays, pamphlets, films, and serials on the church in the U.S., 1800–1991; and *Religion and society in North America : an annotated bibliography*, ed. by Robert deV. Brunkow (BC30) which cites some 4,300 articles published 1973–1980, drawn from the database for *America : history and life* (DB24), relating to religion and religious experience in the U.S. and Canada since the 17th century. Another format-specific bibliography is Arthur P. Young and E. Jens Holley's *Religion and the American experience, 1620–1900: a bibliography of doctoral dissertations* (Westport, Conn.: Greenwood, 1992. 479 p.).
　　　　　　　　　　　　　　　　　　　　　　　Z7776.72.C48

Cole, Garold. Travels in America from the voyages of discovery to the present : an annotated bibliography of travel articles in periodicals, 1955–1980. Norman : Univ. of Oklahoma Pr., 1984. 291 p.　　　　　　　　　　　　　　　　　**DB11**

Brings together citations to travel narratives (mostly from the 18th and 19th centuries) which have appeared as articles in some 220 periodicals. 1,028 entries are grouped by region, state, and date of content. Indexed by traveler, place, subject, author, editor, and translator.
　　　　　　　　　　　　　　　　　　　　　　　　Z1236.C64

The craft of public history : an annotated select bibliography / David F. Trask and Robert W. Pomeroy III, gen. editors. Westport, Conn. : Greenwood, 1983. 481 p.　　　**DB12**

"Prep. under the auspices of the National Council on Public History."—*t.p.*

Intended as a basic guide to the literature of "public history"—a term denoting "the practice of history and history-related disciplines in settings elsewhere than in educational institutions."—*Pref.* Some 1,700 items (books and periodical articles) are topically arranged and annotated within 11 chapters edited and introduced by contributing scholars. Chapters include research and writing, training, and business management in the field of public history; archives and records management; genealogy and family history; historical editing; historical resource management; library science; media; oral history; and policy history. Emphasis is on "how-to-do-it" aspects. Author index.
　　　　　　　　　　　　　　　　　　　　　　　Z6208.H5C73

Freidel, Frank B. Harvard guide to American history. Rev. ed. / Frank Freidel, ed., with the assistance of Richard K. Showman. Cambridge : Belknap Pr. of Harvard Univ. Pr., 1974. 2 v. (1290 p.).　　　　　　　　　　　　**DB13**

The 1st ed. (1954), was the successor to and a revision of Edward Channing, Albert B. Hart, and Frederick J. Turner's *Guide to the study and reading of American history* (Rev. and augm. ed. Boston ; London : Ginn, 1912. 650 p.). The editions for 1954 and 1967 were ed. by Oscar Handlin [et al.]. Repr., 1980.

This is a greatly revised and expanded edition citing publications through June 1970 (with occasional later listings). About a third of the entries are new to this edition.

The basic reference bibliography for American history. A selective listing covering the whole range of American history, and including citations to both book and periodical materials. Entries in v. 1 are arranged by topic; the arrangement of v. 2 is chronological, then by topic within historical period. The first chapters are again devoted to "Research methods and materials," and successive parts are: (2) Biographies and personal records; (3) Comprehensive and area histories; (4) Histories of special subjects. The major chronological divisions in v. 2 are: America to 1789; United States, 1789–1860; Civil War and reconstruction; Rise of industry and empire; Twentieth century. There are numerous subdivisions within each major section of both volumes; a detailed table of contents; a list of serial abbreviations; and separate name and subject indexes (the former including entries for authors of specific books and articles cited). Though dated, still an indispensable first source for this field.

§ Another dated work which is still useful is the *Guide to the study of the United States of America : representative books reflecting the development of American life and thought*, sponsored by the General Reference and Bibliography Div. of the Library of Congress, and prep. by Donald H. Mugridge and Blanche P. McCrum (Wash. : U.S. Govt. Print. Off., 1960. 1193 p.). Provides a topical arrangement of 6,500 annotated entries for books, and documents published up to about 1955. *Supplement 1956–65* (Wash., 1976. 526 p.), prep. under the direction of Roy P. Basler, Oliver H. Orr, Jr., and the staff of the Bibliography and Reference Correspondence Section. A few pre-1956 titles are included, but most works cited were published 1956–65.
　　　　　　　　　　　　　　　　　　　　　　　　Z1236.F77

Gerhan, David R. A retrospective bibliography of American demographic history from colonial times to 1983 / comp. by David R. Gerhan and Robert V. Wells. N.Y. : Greenwood, [1989]. 474 p. (Bibliographies and indexes in American history, no. 10).　　　　　　　　　　　　　　　**DB14**

For annotation, *see* CG92.　　　　Z7165.U5G43

Guide to American foreign relations since 1700 / ed. by Richard Dean Burns. Santa Barbara, Calif. : ABC-Clio, c1983. 1311 p. : maps.　　　　　　　　　　　　　　　**DB15**

Sponsored by the Society for Historians of American Foreign Relations.

A successor to the *Guide to the diplomatic history of the United States, 1775–1921* by Samuel Flagg Bemis and Grace Gardner Griffin (Wash. : U.S. Govt. Print. Off., 1935. Repr. : Gloucester, Mass. : Peter Smith, 1959. 979 p.), but emphasizing foreign relations rather than the more narrowly defined "diplomatic history" of that work. Bemis and Griffin remains useful for references to earlier materials, and particularly for references to manuscript collections. The new work follows a chronological/topical plan and provides "a ready introduction to basic printed (and occasionally microfilmed) books, monographs, essays, documents, and reference works related to the topics that make up America's diplomatic record."—*Introd.* Descriptive annotations, with some critical comment; the great bulk of materials is in English. A cooperative effort; contributing editors and scholars are listed for each chronological/topical chapter. The introduction to each chapter briefly surveys the scholarship of the field and points out areas for further research; sections for Resources and overviews and for Personalities precede the further topical subdivisions. Separate author and subject indexes (the latter subdivided for topics and for individuals).

§ For bibliography of the Federalist period, *see* Ian Mugridge, *United States foreign relations under Washington and Adams : a guide to literature and sources* (N.Y. : Garland, 1982. 88 p.). 411 books, dissertations, collections of documents, periodical articles cover both primary and secondary material. Author and topical indexes.

Z6465.U5G84

Guide to the sources of United States military history / ed. by Robin Higham. Hamden, Conn. : Archon Books, 1975. 559 p. **DB16**

Offers bibliographical essays by historians; surveys the field of U.S. military history, with sections on specific wars, periods, or topics (e.g., military and naval medicine). Each chapter indicates important general references or histories, documents, journals, primary sources, specialized articles and books, and suggests areas for further research; full bibliographic citations appear at the end of each chapter. Materials are judiciously selected with no intention of being comprehensive. No index.

——. *Supplement 1–3*, ed. by Robin Higham and Donald J. Mrozek ([Hamden, Conn.] : Archon Books, 1981–93. 3 v.).

Extends coverage through about 1990, with the bibliographical essays again written by scholars. The first supplement adds new chapters for the U.S. Marine Corps; nuclear war and arms control; and military law, martial law and military government. The second surveys publications of 1978–83. The third supplement includes "assessments and recommendations of works...which seem to have had special continuing value and influence."—*Pref.* Entries are numbered consecutively in the corresponding chapters throughout the three volumes. Not indexed. Z1249.M5G83

Guide to the study of United States history outside the U.S., 1945–1980 / ed. by Lewis Hanke ... [et al.]. White Plains, N.Y. : Kraus Internat., [1985]. 5 v. **DB17**

Edited "with the assistance of many historians in many lands. Sponsored by the American Historical Association & the University of Massachusetts, Amherst."—*t.p.*

Contents: v. 1, Introductory material, perspectives, essays and reports; Africa through China; v. 2–3, Essays and reports : Colombia through Venezuela; author index; v. 4–5, Bibliography.

Intended to "inform historians of the U.S. of the studies made by foreign scholars ... [show them] new sources and fresh perspectives on their own history, and ... help broaden their views. It should also foster communication between historians in the U.S. and abroad."—*p. 2.* Pt. 1 (v. 1–3) contains essays contributed by foreign specialists on U.S. history describing the teaching and research carried out in their countries between the end of World War II and 1980. Also includes essays describing archival materials in the various countries relating to any aspect of U.S. history. Pt. 2 (v. 4–5) is a classified annotated bibliography of 3,100 books, articles and dissertations, published abroad, arranged topically within period divisions. Author index; detailed table of contents. No subject index. E175.8.G85

Historical documentary editions. 1986– . Wash. : National Historical Publications and Records Commission, National Archives, 1986– . Irregular. **DB18**

Superintendent of Documents classification: AE 1.110:H 62/ .

Continues: National Historical Publications and Records Commission, *Publications catalog.*

An irregularly published listing of editions, usually of letters, diaries, etc., either in paper or microfilm, which have been "supported financially or endorsed by the NHPRC."—*Foreword.* For each, gives name of editor or project director, title, format, publisher, price (though some entries indicate out-of-date print status), description (often with detailed list of contents), ISBN. Title arrangement with no index. List of publishers with addresses.

Hoy, Suellen M. Public works history in the United States : a guide to the literature / by the Public Works Historical Society ; comp. and ed. by Suellen M. Hoy and Michael C. Robinson. Nashville, Tenn. : American Association for State and Local History, c1982. 477 p. **DB19**

An annotated bibliography in 14 sections (Waterways, Flood control and drainage, Sewers and wastewater treatment, Urban mass transportation, Energy, etc.). The main criterion for inclusion was that a work be written as history; primary sources and technical literature are generally excluded. Name and title index. Z7164.P97H68

Pamphlets in American history : a bibliographic guide to the microform collection / Henry Barnard, ed. Sanford, N.C. : Microfilming Corp. of Amer., 1979–1984. 5 v. **DB20**

Contents: Group 1, Biography (general), Indians, Revolutionary War, Revolutionary War biography, women; Group 2, Civil liberties, labor, tariffs and free trade; Group 3, Cooperative societies, finance, Mexican War 1846–1848, socialism, War of 1812; Group 4, Catholicism and anti-Catholicism; Group 5, Church of Jesus Christ of Latter-Day Saints, World War 1914–1918, Civil War.

Serves as a bibliography of selected pamphlet literature as well as a guide to the collection *Pamphlets in American history* [microform] (Sanford, N.C. : Microfilming Corp. of America, 1979–84), which is based on the collection at the State Historical Society of Wisconsin, augmented by other special collections. A numerical index for each category of pamphlets lists the items in the order in which they appear on the microfiche. Author, title, and subject indexes.

Z1236.P27E178

Philippine-American relations : a guide to manuscript sources in the United States / comp. and ed. by Shiro Saito. Westport, Conn. : Greenwood, 1982. 256 p. **DB21**

For annotation, *see* DE249. Z1361.R4P47

Sorenson, John L. Pre-Columbian contact with the Americas across the oceans : an annotated bibliography / John L. Sorenson and Martin H. Raish. Provo, Utah : Research Pr., c1990. 2 v. **DB22**

5,613 numbered entries, alphabetically arranged, cite books, essays and articles "that more or less follow a scholarly format... including citing sources." *Introd.* Abstracts often refer to reviews and reprints. Topical index for terms (e.g., acculturation), cultural group (Algonquin), country (Zanzibar), or artifact (axe). E59.F53S67

Writings on American history. 1902–1961. Wash. : American Historical Assoc. ; Millwood, N.Y. : Kraus-Thomson, 1904–1978. Annual. **DB23**

No bibliographies issued for 1904–05, 1941–47.

Subtitle varies: 1906–35, A bibliography of books and articles on United States and Canadian history ... with some memoranda on other portions of America.

Imprint varies.

Index: 1902–40 (publ. 1956).

An excellent annual bibliography and index employing a classified arrangement, with author, title, and subject index. Includes many contents and descriptive notes and, through 1940, cites critical reviews.

Through 1935 included all books and articles, wherever published, which contained anything of value on the history of the U.S. and British Canada, and all books published in the U.S. or Europe on Latin America and the Pacific Islands. Beginning with 1936, the scope was changed to include only writings on the history of the U.S. and its outlying possessions. The index volume covering 1902–40 expands the indexing of the annual volumes and "contains references and subject classifications which will not be found in the separate indexes."—*Foreword.*

When the series resumed with coverage for 1948, scope, arrangement, and indexing were again somewhat changed: e.g., (1) only books and articles having any research value for the history of the U.S. are included; (2) reviews are not cited; (3) titles are cited chronologically according to the beginning date of the subject matter rather than alphabetically by author; (4) indexing is much expanded. Other changes are noted in the preface to the volumes. The list of "Periodicals cited" is a valuable serials record.

Continued by: *Writings on American history : a subject bibliography of articles* (1962/73–1989/90. Millwood, N.Y. : KTO Pr., 1973–90), issued by the American Historical Assoc. and comp. by J. J. Dougherty [et al.].

The period between the two series is covered by *Writings on American history, 1962–1973 : a subject bibliography of articles*, by James J. Dougherty (Wash. : American Historical Assoc. ; Millwood, N.Y. : KTO Pr., 1976. 4 v.), which lists 33,000 citations from 510 journals. Books of the period are cited in *Writings on American history, 1962–1973 : a subject bibliography of books and monographs based on a compilation by James R. Masterson* (White Plains, N.Y. : Kraus, 1985. 10 v.), which was created from Library of Congress catalog cards. Both titles are arranged under broad topics in three sections: Chronological, Geographical, Subjects. Author index but no detailed subject index.   Z1236.L331

Current

America : history and life : a guide to periodical literature. v. 1, no. 1 (July 1964)– . Santa Barbara, Calif. : ABC-Clio, c1964– . Quarterly.   **DB24**

Abstracts "articles on the history of the United States and Canada published throughout the world, and ... articles dealing with current American life and times."—*Note.* Some 2,200 serial publications are now surveyed, including annuals and festschriften. Arranged by broad geographical areas and chronological periods, subdivided by topic, then by format.

Initially, nos. 1–3 of each volume contained abstracts, and no. 4 was the annual index. Beginning 1974, issued in four parts: A, Article abstracts and citations (Spring, Summer, Fall); B, Book reviews (Spring, Fall); C, American history bibliography (i.e., articles cited in pt. A, books cited in pt. B, and dissertations; annual); D, Annual index (title index added with v. 16 [1979]). Now issued in five parts: issues 1–4 contain abstracts and citations for articles, book reviews, and dissertations, while issue 5 is the annual index. Also cites reviews of films, videos, and nonprint media.

Reviews are drawn from 140 U.S. and Canadian journals, dissertations from *Dissertation abstracts international* (AG13).

The index, called "SPIndex," is a rotated index of names and topics that refers to citation numbers in the bibliographic listing.

————. *Supplement to volumes 1–10 (1964–1973)* (Santa Barbara, [1980]. 2 v. [759 p.]).

Contents: pt. 1, Article abstracts and citations; pt. 2, Index.

Provides abstracts and indexing of some 8,744 articles "originally omitted from *America : History and Life* because either the journals were not received or there were not enough abstracters and editors to complete them."—*Introd.* Also includes some coverage for 1954–62.

Five five-year indexes covering 1964–69 through 1984/88 have been published (Santa Barbara, 1970–90). The index covering v. 11–15 (1974–78) also includes indexing for the supplement to v. 1–10.

•Machine-readable version: *America, history and life on disc* [database] (Santa Barbara, Calif. : ABC-Clio, 1991–). Available on CD-ROM, updated three times per year, with each disc being cumulative.

A manual for searching the database is now available: *Searching America : history and life (AHL) and Historical abstracts (HA) on DIALOG*, by Joyce Duncan Falk and Susan K. Kinnell (Santa Barbara, Calif. : ABC-Clio, c1987. 31 p.).   Z1236.A482

Bibliographic guide to North American history. v. 1 (1978)– . Boston : G.K. Hall, 1979– . Annual.   **DB25**

A dictionary catalog of the monographs and serials cataloged by the Research Libraries of the New York Public Library and by the Library of Congress during the year of coverage. North America is defined as including the United States and Canada, although a few general works on the Americas are included, as is material on the American Indian. Full bibliographic information appears only under the main entry, with briefer information under other entries.

According to the introduction, this is to be the annual supplement to the "United States local history catalog," the two-volume supplement to the New York Public Library Local History and Genealogy

Division's *Dictionary catalog of the Local History and Genealogy Division* (Boston : G.K. Hall, 1974. 18 v.), but it would seem to supplement the Library's *Dictionary catalog of the history of the Americas* (DB5) as well.   Z1236.B47

Manuscripts; Archives

Beers, Henry Putney. The French and British in the Old Northwest : a bibliographical guide to archive and manuscript sources. Detroit : Wayne State Univ. Pr., 1964. 297 p.   **DB26**

"Presents an historical account of the acquisition, preservation and publication ... of the original records ... in the Old Northwest (the region south of the Great Lakes) chiefly during the 18th century, and of officials and governing bodies of Canada relating to that region."—*Pref.* Bibliographical sources, p. 195–255.

§ Beers has compiled similar guides to archives: *French and Spanish records of Louisiana : a bibliographical guide to archive and manuscript sources* (Baton Rouge : Louisiana State Univ. Pr., 1989. 371 p.); *The French in North America : a bibliographical guide to French archives, reproductions, and research missions* (Baton Rouge : L.S.U. Pr., 1957. 413 p.); *Spanish & Mexican records of the American Southwest : a bibliographical guide to archive and manuscript sources* (DB171).   F478.2.B4

Brooks, Phillip Coolidge. Research in archives : the use of unpublished primary sources. Chicago : Univ. of Chicago Pr., [1969]. 127 p.   **DB27**

A manual for the beginning research worker rather than for the archivist. Includes a good section on "Limitations on access and use." Concerned almost wholly with American sources, with special attention to the Library of Congress and the National Archives. Selected bibliography; index.   D16.B87

Carnegie Institution of Washington. Guides to manuscript materials for the history of the United States. Wash. : The Institution, 1906–43. 23 v.   **DB28**

Repr.: Millwood, N.Y. : Kraus Reprint, 1965. Title of series from reprint.

Contents: *American*: Guide to the archives of the government of the United States in Washington, by C. H. Van Tyne and W. G. Leland (Rev. ed. 1907. 327 p.); Diplomatic archives of the Department of State, 1789–1840, by A. C. McLaughlin (Rev. ed. 1906. 73 p.); Inventory of unpublished material for American religious history in Protestant church archives and other repositories, by W. H. Allison (1910. 254 p.); Calendar of papers in Washington archives relating to the territories of the United States (to 1873), by D. W. Parker (1911. 476 p.).

British and British American: Guide to the manuscript materials for the history of the United States to 1783 in the British Museum, in minor London archives and in the libraries of Oxford and Cambridge, by C. M. Andrews and F. G. Davenport (1908. 499 p.); Guide to the materials for American history, to 1783, in the Public Record Office of Great Britain, by C. M. Andrews: v. 1, State papers. v. 2, Departmental and miscellaneous papers, 1912–14. 2 v.; Guide to materials in London archives for the history of the United States since 1783, by C. O. Paullin and F. L. Paxon (1914. 642 p.); Guide to British West Indian archive materials in London and in the Islands, for the history of the United States, by H. C. Bell and D. W. Parker (1926. 435 p.); Guide to materials in Canadian archives, by D. W. Parker (1913. 339 p.).

European (except Spanish): List of manuscripts concerning American history preserved in European libraries and noted in their published catalogues and similar printed lists, by D. M. Matteson (1925. 203 p.); Guide to the manuscript materials relating to American history in German state archives, by M. D. Learned (1912. 352 p.); Guide to materials for American history in the libraries and archives of Paris, by W. G. Leland (1932–43. v. 1–2); Guide to the materials for American history in Roman and other Italian archives, by C. R. Fish (1911. 289 p.); Guide to materials for American history in Russian archives, by F. A. Golder (1917–37. 2 v.); Guide to the materials for American history in Swiss and Austrian archives, by A. B. Faust (1916. 299 p.).

Spanish and Spanish American: Guide to the materials for American history in Cuban archives, by L. M. Pérez (1907. 142 p.); Descriptive catalogue of the documents relating to the history of the United States in the Papeles Procedentes de Cuba, deposited in the Archivo General de Indias at Seville, by R. R. Hill (1916. 594 p.); Guide to materials for the history of the United States in the principal archives of Mexico, by H. E. Bolton (1913. 553 p.); List of documents in Spanish archives ... which have been printed or of which transcripts are preserved in American libraries, by J. A. Robertson (1910. 368 p.); Guide to materials ... in Spanish archives, by W. R. Shepherd (1907. 107 p.).

A series of publications compiled to help the research worker find the materials for the history of the U.S. located in foreign archives and libraries. Still useful, although in many cases more recent inventories have been made.

A very useful article placing the Carnegie guides in context of more recently published guides for American historians (and also pointing out lacunae) is John J. McCusker's "New guides to primary sources on the history of early British America" in *William and Mary quarterly*, 3rd ser., 41 (Apr. 1984): 277–95.

DeWitt, Donald L. Guides to archives and manuscript collections in the United States : an annotated bibliography. Westport, Conn. : Greenwood, c1994. 478 p. (Bibliographies and indexes in library and information science, no. 8). **DB29**

Aims to present "finding aids to unpublished materials ... including the numerous calendars, directories, inventories, checklists and registers ... for collections of photographs, oral histories, maps and motion pictures in addition to the more traditional manuscript and archival collection."—*Introd.* Arrangement is by subject; 2,062 entries, most annotated. Cites guides to foreign archives when they describe records or papers relating specifically to U.S. history. Indexes for authors, subjects, and repository name. CD3022.A2D48

Directory of archives and manuscript repositories in the United States / National Historical Publications and Records Commission. 2nd ed. Phoenix : Oryx, 1988. 853 p. **DB30**
1st ed., 1978.

Serves as a companion to United States National Historical Publications Commission, *A guide to archives and manuscripts in the United States*, ed. by Philip M. Hamer (New Haven, Conn. : Yale Univ. Pr., 1961. 775 p.) and gives citations to the earlier work and to *National union catalog of manuscript collections* (DB34).

"The second edition of the *Directory* ... is a revision of the 1978 edition and includes descriptions of approximately 1,400 repositories not described in the earlier volume, as well as updated entries for previously listed institutions."—*Pref.* Based on the results of questionnaires, telephone calls and site visits, now includes some 4,225 repositories in the U.S., Puerto Rico, and the Virgin Islands. Arranged by state, then city, then institution. For each repository, gives address, telephone, hours, access, copy facilities, total holdings, brief description and any finding aids. Repository and subject indexes. CD3020.D49

Guide des sources de l'histoire des États-Unis dans les archives françaises / Madeline Astorquia [et al.], comp. Paris : France Expansion, 1976. 390 p. **DB31**

A survey of documents relating to American history in the Archives Nationales, Services d'Archives de la Guerre et de la Marine through 1940, and through 1929 for the Ministère des Affaires Étrangères. Includes: 16th–17th centuries, America in general; 18th century–1815, North America and the Caribbean; after 1815, only the United States. For the most part, the papers in the municipal libraries are pre-20th century. No indexes.

§ *French consuls in the United States: a calendar of their correspondence in the Archives Nationales* by A. P. Nasatir and G. E. Monell (Wash. : Library of Congress, 1967. 605 p.) is a guide to the microfilm copy on deposit at the Library of Congress of early consular records relating to the U.S. to about 1834; appendixes include lists of French ministers and diplomatic agents, and biographical sketches of French consular agents. CD1192.A2G84

A guide to manuscripts relating to America in Great Britain and Ireland : a revision of the guide ed. in 1961 by B. R. Crick and Miriam Alman / ed. by John W. Raimo under the general supervision of Dennis Welland. Rev. ed. Westport, Conn. : Publ. for the British Association for American Studies by Meckler Books, 1979. 467 p. **DB32**

A revised and expanded edition of this important guide which "seeks to draw attention to the location and to give a brief description of all manuscripts in Great Britain and Ireland relating to the history and literature of the American colonies and the United States which did not fall within the scope of the ... volumes published by the Carnegie Institution [DB28]."—*Introd.* Descriptions are of collections of papers, not of individual manuscripts. Arranged by county, then by repository. Detailed index of personal and geographical names, subjects, and repositories.

Many of the collections are available in microform (particularly in the series "British records relating to America" published by Microform Ltd., East Ardsley, Eng.) but such availability is not indicated in this guide.

§ Grace Gardner Griffin's *Guide to manuscripts relating to American history in British depositories reproduced for the Division of Manuscripts of the Library of Congress* (Wash., 1946. 313 p.) remains useful. Z1236.C74

Meckler, Alan M. Oral history collections / comp. and ed. by Alan M. Meckler and Ruth McMullin. N.Y. : Bowker, 1975. 344 p. **DB33**

In two main sections: (1) name and subject index, which includes both the names of persons interviewed and those prominently mentioned in the interviews, and (2) directory of oral history centers (subdivided as United States and foreign centers). The compilers plan future editions with the hope of achieving a "comprehensive annotated listing of oral history collections located in libraries, oral history centers, and archives. The names of those whose memoirs are included comprise a list of the people most active in recent and contemporary history."—*Foreword.*

§ For more recent information, see *Oral history index : an international directory of oral history interviews*, ed. by Ellen A. Wasserman (Westport, Conn. : Meckler, 1990. 434 p.). More than 30,000 oral history transcripts in the U.S., Canada, Great Britain, and Israel are listed by name of the person interviewed, giving the location and a brief description. AI3.M4

National union catalog of manuscript collections. 1959/61– . Wash. : Library of Congress, 1962– . Annual. **DB34**
"Based on reports from American repositories of manuscripts."—*t.p., 1959–61.*

Comp. by the Manuscripts Section, Descriptive Cataloging Division of the Library of Congress, 1975– . Publisher and compiling division vary. Biennial, 1986/1987–1988–89.

Each volume includes reproductions of catalog cards for collections reported by repositories throughout the United States during the period covered. Each entry gives number of items, physical description, scope and content, location, restrictions on access, finding tools, availability of microfilm copies, etc.

The collections consist largely of personal papers: "manuscripts or typescripts, originals or copies, of letters, memoranda, diaries, accounts, log books, drafts, and the like. ..."—*Introd.* Volumes for 1965– indicate holders of duplicates and holders of original materials as reported by repositories holding reproductions. Beginning 1970, lists oral history interview transcripts and collections containing sound recordings.

Indexes: [v. 3], 1959–62 (732 p.); 1963–66 in volume for 1966; 1967–69 in volume for 1969; 1970–74 in volume for 1974; 1975–79; 1980–84; 1986–90. 1985 issued separately. Beginning 1975, indexes are issued in separate volumes which cumulate annually, then quinquennially. In alphabetical arrangement, listing names, places, subjects, and named historical periods.

§ *Index to personal names in the National union catalog of manuscript collections, 1959–1984*, ed. under the supervision of Harriet Ostroff (Alexandria, Va. : Chadwyck-Healey, [1988]. 2 v.), cumulates all personal name entries (including family names) used in the indexes of *NUCMC* through 1984. Item numbers in italics refer to descriptions of major collections.

See also *Index to subjects and corporate names in the National union catalog of manuscript collections, 1959–1984* (Alexandria, Va. : Chadwyck-Healey, 1994. 3 v.).

•The Archives and Manuscripts component of the RLIN database is a useful tool for making the search more comprehensive.

For a very good comparison of *NUCMC, National inventory of documentary sources in the United States* (*NIDS*), and RLIN, *see* "Finding manuscript collections: NUCMC, NIDS, and RLIN" in *National Genealogical Society quarterly* 77 (Sept. 1989): 208–18.

Z6620.U5N3

Researcher's guide to archives and regional history sources / ed. by John C. Larsen. Hamden, Conn. : Library Professional Publications, [1988]. 167 p.   **DB35**

A general introduction designed to "help the researcher whose work requires the use of archival records, for resources which go beyond printed library materials [by] identifying basic procedures and tools."—*Pref.* 14 essays, each written by an experienced archivist, deal with such topics as archival sources, ethics and archives, oral histories, preservation, reference tools.   CD3021.R47

Smith, Allen. Directory of oral history collections. Phoenix : Oryx, 1988. 141 p.   **DB36**

Based on responses to questionnaires sent to Oral History Association members and to institutions listed in library and oral history directories. Arranged geographically, covering some 500 oral history collections in the U.S. Subject and interviewee indexes. Describes some collections not treated in Alan Meckler and Ruth McMullin's *Oral history collections* (DB33) but the latter includes a section on foreign repositories and has fuller descriptions and better indexing.

Z6208.O7S54

Szucs, Loretto Dennis. The archives : a guide to the National Archives field branches / by Loretto Dennis Szucs & Sandra Hargreaves Luebking. Salt Lake City, Utah : Ancestry, 1988. 340 p. : ill.   **DB37**

The 11 National Archives Field Branches were established to preserve and make available "original records created by field offices of federal agencies" as well as to house and make available, on microfilm or microfiche, records from the National Archives of the decennial censuses 1790–1910, U.S. diplomatic missions, "large bodies of material relating to Indian affairs, the Revolutionary and Civil Wars, German records captured at the end of World War II, and territorial papers."—*Introd.* Section 1 describes each field office, giving brief summaries of its distinctive holdings, services, and activities. Section 2 lists holdings in common, and Section 3 provides an administrative history and listing of each record group held by a branch office, arranged alphabetically (e.g., Census, Bureau of; Centers for Disease Control; Courts, District), with indications of printed guides. Includes descriptions of record groups, microfilm call numbers, bibliographies, illustrations. Excludes the National Archives itself, the National Records Center in Suitland, Md., and the newest branch in Anchorage, Alaska. Indexed by agency, title of finding aid, and some topics. A very useful guide that also discusses how to use the archives.

§ For notes on the contents and a discussion of presidential libraries, *see*: Dennis A. Burton, *A guide to manuscripts in the presidential libraries* (CJ176); Frank Schick, *Records of the presidency* (CJ174); and Fritz Veit, *Presidential libraries and collections* (CJ175). For guides to the records of the House of Representatives and Senate, see: *Guide to research collections of former members of the U.S. House of Representatives 1789–1987* (CJ201); *Guide to research collections of former U.S. Senators 1789–1982* (CJ202); and *Members of Congress : a checklist of their papers in the Manuscript Division, Library of Congress* (Wash. : Library of Congress, 1980. 217 p.).   CD3026

United States. National Archives and Records Administration. Guide to the National Archives of the United States / new pref. by Frank B. Evans. Wash. : The Archives, 1987. 896 p.   **DB38**

1948 ed. had title: *Guide to the records in the National Archives.*

"Except for this Preface, the new Foreword and an appendix describing the record groups newly assigned to the National Archives between 1970 and 1977 the text of the 1974 guide has been reproduced without modification."—*Pref.* Appendix D lists 20 record groups added 1970–77; these are not included in the index.

§The National Archives has also published guides for special topics (e.g., *Guide to materials on Latin America in the National Archives* [DB280]; *Guide to cartographic records in the National Archives* [CL242]); and *Prologue : journal of the National Archives* (v. 1 [Spring 1969]– ; Wash., 1969. 3 times a year), which contains articles describing activities of the National Archives and various of its special collections.   CD3023.U53

Women's history sources : a guide to archives and manuscript collections in the United States / ed. by Andrea Hinding. N.Y. : Bowker, 1979. 2 v.   **DB39**

"In association with the University of Minnesota."—*t.p.*

Contents: v.1, Collections; v.2, Index.

Records the results of the "Women's History Sources Survey" conducted under auspices of the Social Welfare History Archives at the University of Minnesota with additional funding from the National Endowment for the Humanities. Entries describe "18,026 collections in 1,586 repositories, arranged geographically by state and city."—*Pref.* The bulk of the information was obtained by questionnaire, but field workers conducted on-site surveys at various institutions which were unable to report their own holdings. Included are collections devoted to: (1) Papers of a woman; (2) Records of a women's organization; (3) Records of an organization, institution, or movement in which women played a significant but not exclusive part; (4) Records of an organization, institution, or movement that significantly affected women; (5) Groups of materials assembled around a theme or type of record that relates to women; (6) Papers of a family (in which there are papers of female members); (7) Collections with "hidden" women. Descriptions are good; indexing is detailed; but unfortunately there are some surprising omissions.   Z7964.U49W64

Encyclopedias; Dictionaries

Dictionary of American history. Rev. ed. N.Y. : Scribner, 1976–1978. 8 v.   **DB40**

Louise Bilebof Ketz, managing ed.

1st ed., 1940.

In general, consists of 7,200 clear, compact articles each dealing with a separate and definite aspect of American history and each signed with full name of contributor. Also contains a number of articles on broader subjects, which include cross-references to related articles on specific aspects. Covers political, economic, social, industrial, and cultural history, but omits biography as this is considered the province of the *Dictionary of American biography* (AH62). However, the activities of prominent persons may frequently be traced through the references under their names in the analytical index (v. 8). Includes many catchwords and popular names of bills and laws, etc., e.g., Hawley-Smoot Act, Wade-Davis bill. The bibliographies are usually very brief, in most cases consisting of two or three items chosen "so far as possible, with a view to accessibility in the average library."

E174.D52

Dictionary of American immigration history / ed. by Francesco Cordasco. Metuchen, N.J. : Scarecrow, 1990. 784 p.   **DB41**

Entries, varying in length from a paragraph to a long essay, are arranged alphabetically and cover a broad range of topics relating to immigration: ethnic groups, individuals, societies, legislation, and conceptual themes (e.g., assimilation, pluralism, ethnicity). Includes Canada. Entries end with brief bibliographies of one to three items. The introduction provides a brief history of immigration law. Cross-references; select bibliography.

§ For bibliographies and guides to specific immigrant groups, *see* the subsection "Ethnic groups" in Section CC, Sociology.

JV6450.D53

Encyclopedia of American economic history : studies of the principal movements and ideas / Glenn Porter, ed. N.Y. : Scribner, [1980]. 3 v. (1286 p.) : ill. **DB42**

72 signed articles by prominent scholars are grouped in five sections extending over the three volumes: historiography; chronology; economic growth; the institutional framework; the social framework. Most articles have extensive annotated bibliographies. List of contributors and general index in the final volume. Similar to the publisher's *Encyclopedia of American political history* (DB45). HC103.E52

Encyclopedia of American foreign policy : studies of the principal movements and ideas / ed., Alexander De Conde. N.Y. : Scribner, 1978. 3 v. (1201 p.). **DB43**

Offers some 95 well-written and researched "essays of original scholarship ... [which] explore concepts, themes, large ideas, theories, and distinctive policies in the history of American foreign relations."—*Pref.* Conventional accounts of major episodes are excluded. Brief but judiciously selected bibliographies are appended; cross-references to related essays are provided. A biographical dictionary, p. 995–1138, is based on information from *Concise dictionary of American biography* (1st ed.; *see* AH60) and the 5th suppl. to *Dictionary of American biography* (AH62). Extensive name and subject index.

JX1407.E53

Encyclopedia of American history. 6th ed. / ed. by Richard B. Morris. N.Y. : Harper & Row, [1982]. 1285 p. : maps. **DB44**

1st ed., 1953.

A standard work, frequently revised. This ed. in four main parts: (1) basic chronology, which lists the major political and military events of American history from aboriginal times to Dec. 1981; (2) topical chronology, which lists events under such headings as the expansion of the nation, population and immigration, leading Supreme Court decisions, the American economy, science and technology, thought and culture, and mass media; (3) 500 notable Americans, with biographical sketches; (4) structure of the federal government, giving lists of Presidents and their cabinets, tables of party strength in Congress, list of Supreme Court justices, and texts of the Declaration of Independence and the Constitution.

A chronological manual with index rather than an encyclopedia as usually understood. No bibliography and no references to sources.

E174.5.E52

Encyclopedia of American political history : studies of the principal movements and ideas / Jack P. Greene, ed. N.Y. : Scribner, [1984]. 3 v. (1420 p.). **DB45**

An authoritative, scholarly encyclopedia of some 90 articles on "major issues, themes, institutions, processes and developments as they have been manifest throughout the whole of United States history from before the decision for independence to the present."—*Pref.* Each article is by a contributing scholar and gives a detailed account of the topic (e.g., Agricultural policy, Historiography of American political history, Women's rights); each has a good bibliography. Well indexed.

E183.E5

Encyclopedia of American social history / Mary Kupiec Cayton, Elliott J. Gorn, Peter W. Williams, editors. N.Y. : Scribner : Maxwell Macmillan International, c1993. 3 v. (2653 p.) : ill. **DB46**

Seeks to provide "a history of everyday life."—*Pref.* 180 contributor-signed subject-specific essays (Oral history, Appalachia) are grouped into 14 thematic sections (e.g., methods and contexts, social identity, regional subcultures, etc.). Each essay ends with copious *see also* references and bibliography. Topical index. HN57.E58

Encyclopedia USA : the encyclopedia of the United States of America past & present / ed. by R. Alton Lee. Gulf Breeze, Fla. : Academic International Pr., c1983–1994. v. 1–20. (In progress). **DB47**

Vols. 4–11 ed. by Archie P. McDonald; v. 12–20 ed. by Donald W. Whisenhunt.

Contents: v. 1–20, AAA (Agriculture Adjustment Administration)–Detective story.

Attempts to "produce an encyclopedia that will encompass all major facts, events, personalities, and institutions important in American life ... those of most interest and use to a wide readership ... . Designed primarily for the general public from the beginning researcher to the specialist in any field who needs an authoritative statement on a topic not in his specialty ... ."—*From the editor.* The articles are clear, very readable, seem to cover the topic adequately, are signed, and end with brief bibliographies. The overall product is scholarly and workmanlike. Topical index.

An index, ed. by Donald W. Whisenhunt, covers v. 1–10, AAA–Chicano movement (Gulf Breeze, Fla., 1992– . [In progress]).

E156.E52

Handbook of American women's history / Angela Howard Zophy, ed., Frances M. Kavenik, associate ed. N.Y. : Garland, 1990. 736 p. (Garland reference library of the humanities, vol. 696). **DB48**

Signed articles, alphabetically arranged, with appended bibliographies on concepts, events, organizations, and people. Cross-references; subject index. HQ1410.H36

Historical dictionary of North American archaeology / Edward B. Jelks, ed., Juliet C. Jelks, assistant ed. N.Y. : Greenwood, 1988. 760 p. **DB49**

An alphabetical arrangement of more than 1,800 entries for prehistoric cultures, archaeological sites, and major artifact types. Bibliography, p. [555]–705. E77.9.H57

Newton, Michael. The Ku Klux Klan : an encyclopedia / by Michael and Judy Ann Newton. N.Y. : Garland, c1991. 639 p., [32] p. of plates : ill. (Garland reference library of the social sciences, vol. 499). **DB50**

A short-entry encyclopedia whose entries cover topics, people, and organizations associated with the Ku Klux Klan from its inception in 1866 until the mid-1980s. The information was gathered from newspaper and wire service reports, general interest magazines, and books, all listed in a bibliography. Entries are arranged alphabetically and are linked to the bibliography. Four alphabetical lists of entries are designed to substitute for an index: a general list, a geographic list, an organization list, and a list of people. A preface provides a short history of the Klan. HS2330.K63N49

Reference guide to United States military history / Charles Reginald Shrader, gen. ed. N.Y. : Facts on File, 1991–1994. 5 v. : ill., maps. **DB51**

Contents: v. 1, 1607–1815; v. 2, 1815–65; v. 3, 1865–1919; v. 4, 1919–1945; v. 5, 1945–1993.

Narrative chapters on the organization of military forces and on the various wars are followed by entries for American leaders and opponents and for principal events and battles. Some articles have short bibliographies attached; most signed by contributor. Bibliographies and topical index at the end of each volume. E181.R34

Handbooks

The American history sourcebook / Joel Makower, ed. N.Y. : Prentice Hall, c1988. 548 p. : ill. **DB52**

A directory of about 3,000 museums, historical societies, and libraries, giving for each: address, phone number (usually), hours, access, and a brief description of the content of the collection. Arrangement is alphabetical within state. Appendixes: Key dates in American history, and an "American history bibliography" giving an alphabetical list of bibliographies, manuals, and guides. Organization name and subject indexes.

§ A related guide to museums is Jay Anderson's *Living history sourcebook* (Nashville : American Association for State and Local History, 1985. 469 p.), which offers addresses and descriptions of 360 museums, events, magazines, books, articles, organizations, supplies, games, and films—all of which feature the simulation or reenactment of life in another time. Glossary. Z1236.A5144

Austin, Erik W. Political facts of the United States since 1789 / Erik W. Austin ; with the assistance of Jerome M. Clubb. N.Y. : Columbia Univ. Pr., 1986. 518 p.   **DB53**

A collection of selected data, chiefly in tabular form, with emphasis on politics and government at the national level. Includes sections on: National leadership; State politics; Parties and elections; Foreign affairs; Armed forces; Wealth, revenue, taxation, and public expenditure; and Demographics. Tables can be located from the table of contents, but lack of an index limits the item's usefulness for quick reference. Sources of the data are cited at the end of the work. E183.A97

Noël Hume, Ivor. Historical archaeology. N.Y. : Knopf, 1969. 355 p.   **DB54**

For the amateur, the student of archaeology, or the professional. Describes methods of excavation based on the extensive experience of the author, who was director of the Department of Archaeology at Colonial Williamsburg. Emphasis is on work in the U.S. Includes a substantial bibliography.

§ Another work by Noël Hume treats identification of artifacts, a topic the author chose to omit from the earlier work. *A guide to artifacts of colonial America* (N. Y. : Knopf, 1970. 323 p.) presents information to help identify objects which have been or could be dug up on British American sites inhabited during the 17th and 18th centuries. Arranged alphabetically by name of artifact (e.g., bayonet, buckles), with a bibliography for each entry.   CC73.N6

The United States / ed. by Godfrey Hodgson. N.Y. : Facts on File, c1992. 3 v. (1762 p.) : ill., maps.   **DB55**

Essays by scholars and researchers, about one-third from countries other than the U.S. In four main sections: history since 1945; politics; economics; social affairs. Special section of basic information for each state. Most essays include bibliographies. Topical index.   E156.U54

Chronologies

The almanac of American history / Arthur M. Schlesinger, Jr., gen. ed. N.Y. : Putnam, 1983. 623 p. : ill.   **DB56**

Basically a chronology with summaries of important events. In five chronological sections, each with an introductory essay by a contributing scholar. Biographical sketches and extended notes on specific events and developments are interspersed with the chronologies. Index is not sufficiently detailed.   E174.5A45

Brune, Lester H. Chronological history of United States foreign relations / Lester H. Brune ; consulting ed., Donald R. Whitnah. N.Y. : Garland, 1985–91. 3 v. : maps. (Garland reference library of social science, v. 196, 586).   **DB57**

Contents: v. 1–2: 1776 to January 20, 1981 (1289 p.) ; v. 3: The Reagan years, January 21, 1981–January 20, 1989 (362 p.).

A listing, with some description, of events in the U.S. and foreign countries which had an impact on American political life and foreign policy. Topical index in v. 2 for v. 1–2 and in v. 3 for v. 3 only. Bibliography, v. 2, p. 1198–1209 by period; v. 3, by broad topics such as geographical area.   E183.7.B745

Carruth, Gorton. The encyclopedia of American facts and dates. 9th ed. N.Y. : HarperCollins, 1993. 1039 p.   **DB58**

1st ed., 1986; 8th ed., 1987.

Chronologically arranged in columnar form, covering: (1) Exploration and settlement, wars, civil rights, government, statistics; (2) Publishing, arts and music, popular entertainment, architecture, theater; (3) Business and industry, education, philosophy, religion, science; (4) Sports, social issues and crime, folkways, fashions, holidays. Information to Nov. 1, 1992. Detailed index.   E174.5.C3

Gross, Ernie. This day in American history. N.Y. : Neal-Schuman, c1990. 477 p.   **DB59**

A chronology containing some 11,000 entries arranged by date. "Each day's listings begin with the earliest date available."—*Pref.* Includes both people chosen for their "impact on American life through

their positions or actions—U.S. presidents and vice presidents and their wives, Supreme Court justices, key legislators, inventors and pioneers, military and business leaders, scientists and doctors, artists, sports figures, and entertainment personalities … [and] scientific inventions and geographical discoveries, landmark government actions, manmade and natural disasters." The index of names and events could be more extensive: some place-names mentioned in the text and all professions are omitted. Intended for "the harried newswriter and other print and media professionals, speechwriters, planners of special events, teachers and students, the general reader."   E174.5.G76

Sweetman, Jack. American naval history : an illustrated chronology of the U.S. Navy and Marine Corps, 1775–present. 2nd ed. Annapolis, Md. : Naval Institute Pr., c1991. 376 p. : ill., maps.   **DB60**

1st ed., 1984.

Covers Apr. 19, 1775–Mar. 8–10, 1991, listing significant events (battles, technological firsts, etc.) along with some typical, though relatively minor, ones. Entries include indication of effect as well as description of the event. Calendar index by month and day; indexes of American naval vessels, of other vessels, and general index. Updated bibliography.   VA58.4.S94

Sourcebooks

Documentos relativos a la independencia de Norteamérica existentes en archivos españoles. Madrid : Ministerio de Asuntos Exteriores, Dirección General de Relaciones Culturales, 1976–1985. 11 v. in 14.   **DB61**

Contents: v. 1, Medina Encina, P. Archivo General de Indias, Sección de Gobierno (años 1752–1822) (2 v.); v. 2, Siles Saturnino, R. Archivo General de Indias, Sección Papeles de Cuba, Correspondencia y documentación oficial de los Gobernadores de Luisiana (1777–1803); v. 3, León Tello, P. Archivo histórico nacional, correspondencia diplomatica (años 1801–1820) (3 v.); v. 4, León Tello, P. Archivo histórico nacional, expedientes (años 1801–1820); v. 5, Represa Fernández, M.F. [et al.] Archivo General de Simancas, Secretaría de Estado: Inglaterra (años 1750–1820) (2 v.); v. 6, Archivo general de Simancas secretaría de estado: Francia (años 1774–1786); v. 7, Archivo General de Indias, Sección Papeles de Cuba: correspondencia y documentación oficial de varias autoridades de Luisiana y de las dos Floridas (años 1778–1817); v. 8, Archivo Histórico Nacional : correspondencia diplomática (años 1821–1833); v. 9, Siles Saturnino, R., Medina Encina, P. Archivo General de Indias : Sección Papeles de Cuba : correspondencia y documentatión oficial de autoridades de Luisiana y de Florida occidental (años 1764–1819); v. 10, León Tello, P. Archivo Histórico Nacional: expedientes (años 1821–1850); v. 11, Alarios Trigueros, M., Camino Represa Fernámdez, M. Archivo General de Simancas : Secretaria de Guerra : Florida y Liusiana (años 1779–1802).

Provides a calendar for the papers of each archive.   Z1238.D62

Documents of American history / ed. by Henry Steele Commager and Milton Cantor. 10th ed. Englewood Cliffs, N.J. : Prentice-Hall, 1988. 2 v.   **DB62**

1st ed., 1934; 9th ed., 1973.

Contents: v. 1, To 1898 (640 p.); v. 2, Since 1898 (896 p.).

Includes significant documents from 1492 through the report of the Congressional Committees investigating the Iran-Contra affair, Nov. 13, 1987. As in previous revisions, a few earlier documents were dropped and new ones added from the period since 1966. For each document gives title, date, source, references to studies, a brief statement of historical significance, and a complete reprinting of the document. Index by topic and personal name in each volume.   E173.D66

New American world : a documentary history of North America to 1612 / ed., with a commentary by David B. Quinn. N.Y. : Arno Pr. and Hector Bye, 1979. 5 v. (2602 p.) : ill.   **DB63**

Contents: v. 1, America from concept to discovery; Early exploration of North America; v. 2, Major Spanish searches in Eastern North America; The Franco-Spanish clashes in Florida; The beginnings of

Spanish Florida; v. 3, English plans for North America; The Roanoke voyages; New England ventures; v. 4, Newfoundland from fishery to colony; Northwest passage searches; v. 5, The extension of settlement in Florida, Virginia, and the Spanish Southwest; Index.

Brings together a vast collection of documents (translated, if not originally in English), drawn from printed sources and from archive and manuscript collections throughout Europe and North America. Designed to portray the discovery and settlement of North America up to 1612, the documents chosen include narrative accounts, administrative records, diplomatic correspondence, business records, broadsides, 147 contemporary maps, etc. Almost all are printed in full. Headnotes provide reference to original sources, other available translations, problems with the texts, etc. Each of the principal sections has an introduction which "attempts to point to the major characteristics of the selection in that volume and to bring out major comparative points of relationship."—*Introd.* Vol. 5 includes a general index to the set and a bibliography of all manuscript and printed sources used.   E101.N47

The United States and Russia : the beginnings of relations, 1765–1815 / ed. by Nina N. Bashkina … [et al.]. Wash. : U.S. Govt. Print. Off., 1980. 1184 p. : ill.   **DB64**

Prep. under the direction of a Joint Soviet-American Editorial Board.

A collection of some 560 documents selected by Russian and American archivists and historians; documents were drawn from repositories in both countries.   E183.8.R9U59

Biography

American historians 1607–1865 / ed. by Clyde N. Wilson. Detroit : Gale, [1984]. 382 p. : ill., ports. (Dictionary of literary biography, v.30).   **DB65**

Long signed essays on 46 writers on American history whose careers fall within the period. Bibliographies.

Continued by the same editor's *American historians, 1866–1912* (Detroit : Gale, c1986. 429 p. : ill., ports. [Dictionary of literary biography, v. 47]), which profiles 50 American historians, most of whom wrote about the U.S. Emphasizes their careers in history, and provides bibliography, locations of papers, and supplementary reading list. An appendix features two articles on the historiography of the Civil War.

§ See also: *Twentieth-century American historians*, ed. by Wilson (Detroit : Gale, 1983. 519 p. [Dictionary of literary biography, v. 17]) which covers 59 American historians whose careers belong to the 20th century. Includes bibliographies and career assessments.

     E175.45.A48

Arksey, Laura. American diaries : an annotated bibliography of published American diaries and journals / Laura Arksey, Nancy Pries, and Marcia Reed. Detroit : Gale, c1983–87. 2 v.   **DB66**

For annotation, *see* BE507.   Z5305.U5A74

A bibliography of American autobiographies / comp. by Louis Kaplan … [et al.]. Madison : Univ. of Wisconsin Pr., 1961. 372 p.   **DB67**

For annotation of this and of Mary Louise Briscoe's *American autobiography, 1945–1980*, see AH89.   Z1224.K3

Historians of the American frontier : a bio-bibliographical sourcebook / ed. by John R. Wunder. N.Y. : Greenwood, 1988. 814 p.   **DB68**

Signed essays treat 57 historians, giving for each a biography, themes treated, analysis of work, and bibliography of writings by and (often) about the historian. Index of titles cited in the bibliographies and of topics.   E175.45.H57

Atlases

The American heritage pictorial atlas of United States history / by the editors of American heritage. N.Y. : American Heritage, [1966]. 424 p. : ill., maps ; 29 cm.   **DB69**

Attractive maps (in color) with accompanying text. Chapter texts are unsigned, but the title page credits them to a list of distinguished contributors. Although the atlas includes material not found in either Charles Oscar Paullin's *Atlas of the historical geography of the United States* (DB75) or Clifford L. and Elizabeth H. Lord's *Historical atlas of the United States* (Rev. ed. N.Y. : Holt, c1953. 238 p. Repr.: N.Y. : Johnson, 1972), it does not truly supersede either of those standard works. There is a particularly good section on U.S. operations in World War II. Elaborate color spreads, or "pictorial maps," of major battles of the Revolutionary and Civil wars, and of the National parks are unusual features.   G1201.S1A4

Atlas of American history. 2nd rev. ed. N.Y. : Scribner, 1984. 306 p. : maps ; 29 cm.   **DB70**

1st ed. (James Truslow Adams, ed. in chief), 1943; rev. ed. (Kenneth T. Jackson, ed.), 1978.

Designed to accompany *Dictionary of American history* (DB40).

Black-and-white maps describe U.S. history to about 1984. No text, but the 200 maps are clear and detailed. Includes a supplement, Current issues 1978–84. Extensive index.   G1201.S1J3

Ferrell, Robert H. Atlas of American history / Robert H. Ferrell, Richard Natkiel. Updated ed. N.Y. : Facts on File, 1993. 192 p. : ill., col. maps ; 29 cm.   **DB71**

1st ed., 1987. An earlier "updated edition" (1990) added 1988 election results.

Arranged by broad periods (e.g., The Colonial era, Founding a nation, Expansion and Civil War, Imperial democracy, The two World Wars, America in a divided world). For each period, a short essay of three to five pages is followed by maps, photographs, and drawings. Index by topic to text and illustrations. The 1993 ed. adds 1992 election results and three pages of maps on the Gulf War and a brief chronology on Iraq, Jan. 1991–Jan. 18, 1993.   G1201.S1F4

Gilbert, Martin. The Dent atlas of American history. 3rd ed. London : Dent, 1993. 138 p. : ill., maps ; 26 cm.   **DB72**

Originally published as: *American history atlas* (N.Y. : Macmillan, 1968; rev. ed. 1985).

Offers 138 very clear black-and-white maps with little text. Most maps treat a single subject. Developed for use with a course. Not indexed. The 3rd ed. adds 26 new maps, bringing coverage to 1991.

Martis, Kenneth C. The historical atlas of political parties in the United States Congress, 1789–1989 / Kenneth C. Martis, author and ed. ; Ruth Anderson Rowles, cartographer ; Gyula Pauer, production cartographer. N.Y. : Macmillan ; London : Collier Macmillan, c1989. 518 p. : maps in color ; 34 x 46 cm.   **DB73**

For annotation, *see* CJ258.   G1201.F9M26

National Geographic Society. Historical atlas of the United States. Wash. : National Geographic Society, c1988. 289 p. : ill. ; 47 cm.   **DB74**

Heavily illustrated with reproductions of paintings, charts, graphs, photographs, maps with relevant text, chronologies, and time lines. An accompanying portfolio contains 18 maps for regions and for the entire U.S. The presentation in six major areas (The land, People, Boundaries, Economy, Networks, Communities) is interspersed with five chronological sections: 1400–1606, 1607–1788, 1789–1860, 1861–1916, 1917–88. The illustrative material is very well chosen and clearly presented, but since much of it runs across or up to the inner margin, the book can never be satisfactorily rebound. The bibliography cites sources for the illustrations and text of each page and the consultants used. Topical index for illustrations and text.

§ Two extremely useful specialized atlases expand coverage for women and ethnic groups: James P. Allen and Eugene J. Turner, *We* the people : an atlas of America's ethnic diversity (CC358) and Barbara G. Shortridge, *Atlas of American women* (N.Y. : Macmillan ; London : Collier Macmillan, c1987).   G1201.S1N3

Paullin, Charles Oscar. Atlas of the historical geography of the United States / by Charles O. Paullin, ed. by John K. Wright. [Wash. ; N.Y.] : Publ. jointly by Carnegie Inst. of Wash. and the American Geographical Soc. of N.Y., 1932. 162 p. : 688 maps ; 37 cm. (Carnegie Institution of Washington. Publication, no. 401).   **DB75**
 Repr. : Westport, Conn. : Greenwood, 1975.
 The first adequate atlas of American history, with good maps, including reproductions of early maps, and descriptive text for each with lists of sources; indispensable in any library doing much work in U.S. history. Indexed.   G1201.S1P3

This remarkable continent : an atlas of United States and Canadian society and culture / gen. editors, John F. Rooney, Jr., Wilbur Zelinsky, and Dean R. Louder ; cartographic ed., John D. Vitek. College Station, [Tex.] : Publ. for The Society for the North American Cultural Survey by Texas A & M Univ. Pr., c1982. 316 p. : ill., maps ; 24x32cm.   **DB76**
 Offers 390 black-and-white maps chosen to show "how the inhabitants of this continent, past and present, differ from place to place in terms of origins, traditions, beliefs, patterns of thought and behavior, and ways of organizing themselves upon the land."—*Introd.* Maps are grouped in 13 chapters introduced by scholars; sources of the maps are given at the end of the volume. Indexed.   G1201.E1T5

United States Military Academy. Dept. of Military Art and Engineering. The West Point atlas of American wars / chief ed., Vincent J. Esposito. N.Y. : Praeger, [1959]. 2 v. : maps in color ; 27x37cm.   **DB77**
 Contents: v. 1, 1689–1900; v. 2, 1900–1953.
 Includes maps of campaigns, battles, etc. Text and maps on facing pages.
 The Civil War material is also available separately in the Academy's *West Point atlas of the Civil War* (N.Y. : Praeger, 1962. 154 maps in color ; 27 x 37 cm.).   G1201.S1U5

17th and 18th centuries

Bibliography

Ammerman, David L. Books about early America : 2001 titles / comp. by David L. Ammerman and Philip D. Morgan. Williamsburg, Va. : Institute of Early American History and Culture, c1989. 126 p.   **DB78**
 1st ed., 1954, entitled *Readable books about early America*; 4th ed., 1970, had title *Books about early America.*
 A selective bibliography of major studies. In three sections: narrative (by period, subdivided by topic); thematic (e.g., migration and population); collections and biography (e.g., travel accounts, documentary collections). A brief introduction to each section cites review essays and surveys. Index for authors and editors.   Z1237.A54

Greene, Evarts Boutell. A guide to the principal sources for early American history (1600–1800) in the city of New York. 2nd ed. rev. by Richard B. Morris. N.Y. : Columbia Univ. Pr., 1953. 400 p.   **DB79**
 1st ed., 1929.
 A guide to manuscript and printed sources for the study of early American history to be found in the libraries and other depositories in the city of New York. Classed arrangement with general index.
 § Harry J. Carman and Arthur W. Thompson published a similar guide for the period 1800–1900 (DB98).   Z1236.G82

Lydon, James G. Struggle for empire : a bibliography of the French and Indian War. N.Y. : Garland, [1986]. 272 p. (Wars of the United States, v. 7 ; Garland reference library of social science, v. 188).   **DB80**
 An annotated bibliography of books, documents and journal articles, with "emphasis placed on contemporary accounts ... and upon twentieth century writers covering through 1983."—*Pref.* Topically arranged, with author and subject indexes.   Z1237.L93

Wehmann, Howard H. A guide to pre-federal records in the National Archives / comp. by Howard H. Wehmann ; rev. by Benjamin L. DeWhitt. Wash. : National Archives and Records Administration, 1989. 375 p.   **DB81**
 Superintendent of Documents classification: AE 1.108:P91.
 Describes the "holdings of the National Archives that relate directly to, or were created during, the period before the Constitution went into effect on March 4, 1779."—*Pref.* Each record group and series is discussed with indications of organization, brief history, availability on microform (and reel numbers) and any finding aid. Subject index for names, offices, places and a few topics.   CD3045.W44

Encyclopedias; Dictionaries

The encyclopedia of colonial and revolutionary America / gen. ed., John Mack Faragher. N.Y. : Facts on File, c1990. 484 p. : ill.   **DB82**
 Some 1,500 short entries, alphabetically arranged, cover from the Norse exploration to the end of the American Revolution. Emphasis is on the English colonies, with some treatment of the Spanish, French and Russian colonies. Very useful cross-references. Topic guides, which accompany major articles, give a list of related, shorter articles to which the reader is referred for greater detail in a specialized area; list of further reading. Not indexed.   E188.E63

Encyclopedia of the North American colonies / ed. in chief, Jacob Ernest Cooke ... [et al.]. N.Y. : Scribner, c1993. 3 v. : maps.   **DB83**
 Attempts to cover all North American colonies. Signed essays are grouped within broad topics or themes; each essay concludes with bibliography and cross-references. List of contributors with titles of their essays. Subject index uses boldface to indicate full articles on the subject, and italics for tables. Chronology begins with Erik the Red and ends in 1867 when Russia sold its North American possessions.
                                    E45.E53

American Revolution

Bibliography

Several earlier bibliographies are still useful: *The era of the American Revolution*, ed. by Dwight L. Smith (Santa Barbara, Calif. : ABC-Clio, 1975. 381 p.), is a classified listing of 1,400 entries from *America : history and life*; Robert W. Coakley and Stetson Conn's *The War of the American Revolution* (Wash. : U.S. Army Center of Military History, 1975. 257 p.) includes a brief narrative, a chronology, and a select bibliography; and John Shy's *The American Revolution* (Northbrook, Ill. : AHM Publ. Corp., 1973. 134 p.) lists books, articles, and dissertations for the period 1763–1783.

Adams, Thomas Randolph. The American controversy : a bibliographical study of the British pamphlets about the American disputes, 1764–1783. Providence, R.I. : Brown Univ. Pr. ; N.Y. : Bibliographical Society of America, 1980. 2 v. (1102 p.).   **DB84**
 A census of some 1,400 titles in about 2,350 editions or issues. For each, gives transcription of title page, collation, and notes which

"include bibliographical information, information concerning the circumstances surrounding the printing and publication, the extent of its publication in America, and the appearance of the text or some part of it in London newspapers and magazines" *(p. xx)*, original price, and number of copies printed. Title index and general index of names, places, and subjects.   Z1238.A39

———————— American independence : the growth of an idea; a bibliographical study of the American political pamphlets printed between 1764 and 1776 dealing with the dispute between Great Britain and her colonies. Austin, Tex. : Jenkins and Reese, 1980. 264 p. (Contributions to bibliography, 5).
                                                          DB85

"First appeared in the Publications of the Colonial Society of Massachusetts, Transactions, v. 43."—*verso of t.p.* Subsequently publ. by Brown Univ. Pr., 1965.

Pamphlets are listed chronologically by first imprint date with indication of later editions. Gives brief transcription of title page, census of copies and, in many cases, information about circumstances leading to publication. Also includes a short-title list of some 19 pamphlet exchanges. This edition includes additions and corrections (p. 183–86) and a study, "The British pamphlet press and the American controversy, 1764–1783," reprinted from *Proceedings* of the American Antiquarian Society, 89 (Apr. 1979).   Z1238.A4

Blanco, Richard L. The War of the American Revolution : a selected annotated bibliography of published sources. N.Y. : Garland, 1984. 654 p. (Wars of the United States, v. 1 ; Garland reference library of social science, v. 154).   **DB86**

Lists more than 3,700 books, journals, articles and essays, government publications, and dissertations published to 1980 in topical arrangement with author and subject indexes. The compiler has "blended items about traditional military, naval and diplomatic subjects with topics representative of the newer 'social' history, such as crowd behavior, prisoners of war, and women in the Revolution."—*Pref.* Little emphasis on primary source material since the work is meant for students and the interested public.   Z1238.B55

Clark, David Sanders. Index to maps of the American Revolution in books and periodicals illustrating the Revolutionary War and other events of the period 1763–1789. [2nd ed.]. Westport, Conn. : Greenwood, [1974]. 301 p.   **DB87**
1st ed., 1969.

An index to maps in monographs, journals, general histories, textbooks and standard reference books which portray any part of the United States, Canada, the Caribbean and West Indies of the period 1763–89. Although the maps are largely military and naval, many show population, roads and boundaries, towns, etc. Geographical arrangement; extensive subject and name index.   Z6027.U5C57

Gephart, Ronald M. Revolutionary America, 1763–1789 : a bibliography. Wash. : Library of Congress, 1984. 2 v. (1671 p.) : ill.   **DB88**
Superintendent of Documents classification: LC 1.12/2: R 32/ 4/ 763–769.

Designed as "a guide to the more important printed primary and secondary works" in the Library of Congress, "the bibliography represents a comprehensive review of monographs, doctoral dissertations, collected works, festschriften, pamphlets, and serial publications in both general and special collections."—*Pref.* Arranged in 12 topical/ chronological chapters, with numerous subsections, it intends to encompass a broad range of interests, needs, and approaches to the study of the Revolution and its historical, social and cultural setting. Extensive section of biographies and personal primary sources, and a chapter on the preservation and publication of documentary sources on the American Revolution. Selectively annotated. Cutoff date is Dec. 31, 1972. "The index is limited, for the most part, to proper names (authors, editors, compilers, historical figures, corporate bodies, geographic locations, etc.) with descriptive subdivisions." Detailed table of contents.   Z1238.G43

White, J. Todd. Fighters for independence : a guide to sources of biographical information on soldiers and sailors of the American Revolution / ed. by J. Todd White and Charles H. Lesser. Chicago : Univ. of Chicago Pr., 1977. 112 p.
                                                          DB89

A discussion of the types of records deemed useful for research in this area, followed by an annotated bibliography of published and unpublished lists of soldiers and sailors. Includes a bibliography of diaries, journals, memoirs, and autobiographies, and a bibliography of more general works. Subject index.   Z1238.W45

Manuscripts; Archives

Koenig, William J. European manuscript sources of the American Revolution / W. J. Koenig & S. L. Mayer. London ; N.Y. : Bowker, c1974. 328 p.   **DB90**

Aims "to provide … the scholar, particularly the graduate student, an introduction to the source material in Europe so that research can be more effectively planned. This volume is really … a tool which the scholar can use to identify repositories, with summaries of their contents and notices of relevant bibliography."—*Gen. Introd.* Arranged by country, then by city and repository. Provides references to published descriptions of the collections, of individual manuscripts, etc. General index.   CD1002.K63

Library of Congress. Manuscript sources in the Library of Congress for research on the American Revolution / comp. by John R. Sellers … [et al.]. Wash. : Library of Congress : [For sale by the U.S. Govt. Print. Off.], 1975. 372 p.   **DB91**
Superintendent of Documents classification: LC 1.2:M31/3.

"In the preparation of this guide virtually every collection in the Library's Manuscript Division, Rare Book Division, and Law Library was surveyed for documents from the Revolutionary era [1763 to 1789]."—*Introd.* Includes photostats, transcripts, and microfilms as well as original manuscripts. In two main sections: (1) Domestic collections, and (2) Foreign reproductions. Descriptive notes vary according to the specific item or collection in question: "Collections that are extremely large and uniform in content may receive more cursory treatment than smaller collections containing a variety of documents." Index to repositories and a detailed subject index.   Z1238.U57

Encyclopedias

The American Revolution, 1775–1783 : an encyclopedia / Richard L. Blanco, ed.; Paul J. Sanborn, contributing ed. N.Y. : Garland, 1993. 2 v. (1857 p.) : ill. ; maps ; portraits. (Garland reference library of the humanities, v. 933 ; Military history of the U.S., 1).   **DB92**

More than 800 signed entries, varying from 250–2,500 words, cover all facets of the Revolution: battles, raids, skirmishes; impact of war on society; biographies of statesmen and diplomats (used to explain political and diplomatic themes); role of women, blacks, Indians, etc. Alphabetical arrangement; bibliographical references ending each entry. Topical index; no cross-references in text. Includes a chronology, April 19, 1775–November 25, 1783; 58 maps; glossary, and list of contributors.

§ An older quick-reference dictionary in which biographical sketches predominate is Mark Mayo Boatner's *Encyclopedia of the American Revolution* (N.Y. : D. McKay, [1974]. 1290 p.).
                                                          E208.A433

The Blackwell encyclopedia of the American Revolution / ed. by Jack P. Greene and J. R. Pole. Cambridge, Mass. : Blackwell Reference, 1991. 845 p. : ill., maps.   **DB93**

Information is presented in "75 substantive articles [which] cover all the major topics relating to the Revolution, including its central events, the context in which it occurred, its causes, its effects, and the principal concepts associated with it."—*Pref.* The essays appear in sections: Context; Themes and events; External effects of the Revolution; Internal development after the Revolution; Concepts. The essays are followed by a biographical section and a chronology, December 11, 1688–December 1, 1791 (divided into columns by subject, e.g, political and legal; military campaigns). Topical index; no cross-references.

§ Not as useful for quick reference as Richard L. Blanco, *The American Revolution, 1775–1783* (DB92), but the essay format allows more discussion and development of ideas.   E208.B635

Handbooks

Dupuy, Trevor Nevitt. People & events of the American Revolution / ed. by Trevor N. Dupuy, Gay M. Hammerman. N.Y. : Bowker, 1974. 473 p. : maps.   **DB94**
In two main sections: a chronology of events 1733–83, and an alphabetical section of names with short biographies. Index covers events listed in the chronology.   E209.D86

Stember, Sol. The bicentennial guide to the American Revolution. N.Y. : Saturday Review Pr. ; [distr. by Dutton], 1974. 3 v. : maps.   **DB95**
Contents: v. 1, The war in the North; v. 2, The Middle Colonies; v. 3, The war in the South.
On cover: *Touring guide to Revolutionary War sites.*
Sites are considered area by area, and as much in chronological sequence of the war as is feasible without constant back-tracking over the same region. Includes bibliographies.   E230.S74

Atlases

Atlas of early American history : the Revolutionary era, 1760–1790 / Lester J. Cappon, ed. in chief ; Barbara Bartz Petchenik, cartographic ed. ... [et al.]. [Princeton, N.J.] : publ. for the Newberry Library and the Inst. of Early American History and Culture by Princeton Univ. Pr., 1976. 157 p. : maps in color ; 47 cm.   **DB96**
An impressive historical atlas containing 74 pages of colored maps of varying size, followed by extensive explanatory text and a detailed index. "The basic framework ... is chronological, conceived as a work of history rather than one of historical geography. Three periods are easily recognized in the table of contents: (1) the colonial years before 1776; (2) the War of the American Revolution; and (3) the postwar years of Confederation period."—*Introd.*   G1201.S3A8

Nebenzahl, Kenneth. Atlas of the American Revolution / map selection and commentary by Kenneth Nebenzahl ; narrative text by Don Higginbotham. Chicago : Rand McNally, 1974. 218 p. : ill., maps ; 39 cm.   **DB97**
Reproductions of 18th-century maps with commentary and narrative text. Indexed.   G1201.S3N4

19th century

Bibliography

See also DB147.

Carman, Harry James. A guide to the principal sources for American civilization, 1800–1900, in the city of New York / by Harry J. Carman and Arthur W. Thompson. N.Y. : Columbia Univ. Pr., 1960–1962. 2 v.   **DB98**
Chronological successor to E. B. Greene's *A guide to the principal sources for early American history, (1600–1800)* (DB79).
Contents: v. 1, Manuscripts; v. 2, Printed materials.

Basic arrangement of each volume is topical; within chapters materials for the country are presented first, then for each state. Name index in each volume.   Z1236.C25

Glenn, Robert W. The Haymarket affair : an annotated bibliography. Westport, Conn. : Greenwood, 1993. 363 p. (Bibliographies and indexes in American history, no. 25).   **DB99**
1,513 books, pamphlets, articles and documents (both primary and secondary material), arranged in four areas: (1) Context, for background information on the period and personalities; (2) History, including trial records, appellate court decisions, and secondary material; (3) Argument, for polemical writing and speeches, with special attention to anarchist and labor journals; (4) Imagination, covering literary and visual interpretations. Good annotations. Author/title/subject index.   Z7164.A52G58

Smith, Dwight La Vern. The War of 1812 : an annotated bibliography. N.Y. : Garland, 1985. 340 p. (Wars of the United States, v. 3 ; Garland reference library of social science, v. 250).   **DB100**
1,400 topically arranged entries for books, essays, articles, diaries, memoirs, speeches, satires, pamphlets, poems, songs, novels, juvenile literature, dissertations, and sermons. Excludes broadsides and government documents. The war is presented from Canadian, American, and British perspectives; political, social, and economic aspects are included along with the military. Cutoff date is 1981. Author and subject indexes.   Z1240.S65

Venzon, Anne Cipriano. The Spanish-American War : an annotated bibliography. N.Y. : Garland, 1990. 255 p. (Garland reference library of the humanities, vol. 1120 ; Wars of the United States, vol. 11).   **DB101**
Cites books, articles, government publications, and a few dissertations in English published 1898–1986 on the Spanish-American War, including the Philippine-American War. Arranged by broad topics, subdivided for books and articles. Includes fiction and music; most articles have brief annotations. Author and subject indexes.
                    Z1243.V45

Encyclopedias; Dictionaries

Foner, Eric. Freedom's lawmakers : a directory of Black officeholders during Reconstruction. N.Y. : Oxford Univ. Pr., 1993. xlv, 290 p. : ill.   **DB102**
Published in cooperation with the Schomburg Center for Research in Black Culture, New York.
A lengthy introduction provides a survey with numerous charts on black public officials who held office immediately after the Civil War followed by an alphabetical dictionary of biographical sketches giving citations to primary and secondary sources. Indexes by state, occupation, office, topic and birth status (free, slave, or free before the Civil War).   E185.96.F64

Gale, Robert L. A cultural encyclopedia of the 1850s in America. Westport, Conn. : Greenwood, c1993. 472 p.
                    DB103
Covers the period 1849–60 with entries for names, significant titles, events, and a few subjects. Topical index includes *see* references; asterisks in the text indicate cross-references. Bibliography subdivided by broad topics; Appendix is a classified list of biographical entries for occupations and professions.   E426.G147

———— The gay nineties in America : a cultural dictionary of the 1890s. Westport, Conn. : Greenwood, 1992. 457 p.   **DB104**
Covers the key "writers, inventors, painters and illustrators, politicians, sculptors, social workers and critics, explorers, soldiers and sailors, boxers, educators, editors, and photographers ... [along with] especially significant literary works and magazines" (*Pref.*), 1888–

1901. *See also* references; asterisks signal cross-references. Topical index with italics used to indicate main entries. Ten-page bibliography; a table lists biographical entries by occupation.   E169.1.G26

Trefousse, Hans Louis. Historical dictionary of Reconstruction. N.Y. : Greenwood, 1991. 284 p.   **DB105**

Provides short entries for "the major personalities of Reconstruction, the principal issues, ... the ideas current.... Those statistics involved in the process ... as well as the most important decisions of the Supreme Court."—*Pref.* Cross-references; bibliography at end of each article; chronology, 1862 to about 1877; select bibliography. Topical index with italicized numbers for main entries.   E668.T66

Civil War

Bibliography

Aimone, Alan Conrad. A user's guide to the official records of the American Civil War / by Alan C. and Barbara A. Aimone. [Shippensburg, Penn.] : White Mane Pub. Co., c1993. 125 p. : ill., maps.   **DB106**

An expanded version of *The official records of the American Civil War, a researcher's guide* (West Point, 1978).

Offers information on the "historical background, editorial policy, purpose and organization of the *Official Records* along with an understanding of the finding aids."—*Introd.* Appendixes include: Annotated list of selected reference sources; Congressional documents relating to the Civil War; Confederate documents and sources outside the *Rebellion records*; Civil War map sources in the *Rebellion records*; *Rebellion records* in the House miscellaneous documents; Index to principal events in the *Official records* and the *Naval official records*. Topical index.   E464.A35

Cole, Garold. Civil War eyewitnesses : an annotated bibliography of books and articles, 1955–1986. Columbia, S.C. : Univ. of South Carolina Pr., c1988. 351 p.   **DB107**

Lists 1,400 books, collected essays, memoirs, autobiographies, popular and scholarly periodical articles. In three parts: (1) The North, (2) The South, (3) Anthologies and studies, with subdivisions for military, civilian and foreign accounts. Index of authors, editors, titles, troops by state, battles, places mentioned, and a few subjects (e.g., recreation, vices, character, effect of war on soldiers).

§ *See also* Albert J. Menendez, *Civil War novels : an annotated bibliography* (BE477).   Z1242.C78

Coulter, Ellis Merton. Travels in the Confederate states : a bibliography. Norman : Univ. of Oklahoma Pr., 1948. 289p. (American exploration and travel series, [no.11]).   **DB108**

Lists more than 500 accounts of travels in the South during the Civil War, written either at the time or at a later date. Fills in, for 1861–65, the *Travels* series edited by T. D. Clark (DB155).

Text of titles listed are available on microcard from Lost Cause Press, Louisville, Ky.   Z1251.S7C68

Dornbusch, Charles Emil. Military bibliography of the Civil War. N.Y. : New York Public Library, 1962–1987. 4 v.   **DB109**

Contents: v. 1, Northern states (originally issued in 7 pts.): pt. 1, Illinois; pt. 2, New York; pt. 3, New England states; pt. 4, New Jersey and Pennsylvania; pt. 5, Indiana and Ohio; pt. 6, Iowa, Kansas, Michigan, Minnesota, and Wisconsin; pt. 7, Index of names; v. 2, Regimental publications and personal narratives: Southern, Border, and Western states and territories; Federal troops; Union and Confederate biographies; v. 3, General references; armed forces; and campaigns and battles; v. 4, Union and Confederate biography (continuation); General references (supplement); armed forces (supplement); campaigns and battles (supplement).

The first volume appeared under the title: *Regimental publications and personal narratives of the Civil War.* The new title was introduced to signal the broadened scope of the later volumes which include more general references to the military aspects of the war.

Much of the material cited has been reprinted on microfiche in two series: *Regimental histories of the Civil War* (Univ. Microfilms), and *Civil War unit histories* (Univ. Publ. of America).   Z71242.D612

Freemon, Frank R. Microbes and minie balls : an annotated bibliography of Civil War medicine. Rutherford, N.J. : Fairleigh Dickinson Univ. Pr., c1993. 253 p.   **DB110**

Bibliography of every published "letter and diary by a doctor or nurse who participated in ... the War even if they made no medical observations ... [and] includes the most important contemporary medical publications ... [as well as] reports by individual soldiers and officers who were wounded or were hospitalized."—*Introd.* Well-annotated; primary and secondary materials, books, articles, and journals. Index by author and subject. A few illustrations, mostly portraits.   Z1242.F74

Nevins, Allan. Civil War books : a critical bibliography / ed. by Allan Nevins, James I. Robertson, Jr., Bell I. Wiley. Baton Rouge : Publ. for the U.S. Civil War Centennial Commission by Louisiana State Univ. Pr., [1967–69]. 2 v.   **DB111**

Contents: v. 1, Military aspects; Prisons and prisoners of war; The Negro; The navies; Diplomacy; v. 2, General works; Biographies, memoirs, and collected works; The Union; The Confederacy; Cumulative index.

A selective bibliography, intended for both scholars and general readers. Restricted to books and pamphlets bearing solely on the war years, not on causes and results of the war. Citations are reproduced from Library of Congress catalog cards, with the addition of a critical note for each. Each section compiled by a specialist scholar. General index in v. 2.   Z1242.N35

Parrish, T. Michael. Confederate imprints : a bibliography of Southern publications from secession to surrender / by T. Michael Parrish & Robert M. Willingham, Jr. Austin, Tex. : Jenkins Publ. Co. ; Katonah, N.Y. : G.A. Foster, [ca.1984]. 991 p., [132] p. of plates : ill.   **DB112**

Expands and revises Marjorie Lyle Crandall, *Confederate imprints : a check list based principally on the collection of the Boston Athenaeum* ([Boston] : Athenaeum, 1955. 2 v.) and Richard Barksdale Harwell, *More Confederate imprints* (Richmond : Virginia State Library, 1957. 2 v.).

Aims to list "any book, pamphlet, broadside, map, piece of sheet music, pictorial print, newspaper, magazine or other serial publication, published in Confederate-held territory ... [including] official imprints: national, state, and local government publications, as well as army, militia, or other military publications."—*Introd.* The entries are divided into official publications (arranged by state) and nonofficial publications (arranged by topic). Location symbols; table of cross-references from the 5,121 Crandall and Harwell numbers to the entries in this volume. Index of authors, titles, and broad subjects. Works listed are reproduced on microfilm by Research Publications, Inc.   Z1242.5.P37

United States. Army. Military History Institute. The era of the Civil War—1820–1876 / by Louise Arnold ; with accompanying essays by Richard Sommers and Michael Winey. Carlisle Barracks, Penn. : U.S. Army Military History Inst., 1982. 704 p. (Special bibliography, 11).   **DB113**

An extensive bibliography based on the holdings of the Army Military History Institute. Topical arrangement of published books, pamphlets, and government documents, together with brief essays on the Institute's manuscript holdings and museum collections. Not indexed.

§ An earlier bibliography of the same title, by B. Franklin Cooling, was publ. 1974.   Z1242.U588

Manuscripts; Archives

Beers, Henry Putney. Guide to the archives of the government of the Confederate States of America. Wash. : Nat. Archives, Nat. Archives and Records Service, 1968. 536 p. (National Archives publication, no.68–15).   **DB114**
  Superintendent of Documents classification: GS 4.6/2:C 76.
  Repr., 1986, as *The Confederacy : a guide to the archives.*
  Describes, as far as possible, "all the records of the Confederacy in the National Archives, the Library of Congress, and in other custody."—*Pref.* Arrangement is by agency, with a subject index.
                                                          CD3047.B4

Library of Congress. Manuscript Division. Civil War manuscripts : a guide to collections in the Manuscript Division of the Library of Congress / comp. by John R. Sellers. Wash. : Library of Congress : For sale by the U.S. Govt. Print. Off., 1986. 391 p. : ill.   **DB115**
  Superintendent of Documents classification: LC4.2: C49.
  The collections consist mainly of personal papers (as opposed to government records held by the National Archives). The guide lists and briefly describes materials dealing directly in whole or in part with the Civil War. Listing is by name of the individual or agency whose papers are described. Subject index. Does not include materials in other parts of the library.   Z1242.L48

Munden, Kenneth White. Guide to federal archives relating to the Civil War / by Kenneth W. Munden and Henry Putney Beers. Wash. : National Archives, National Archives and Records Service, 1962. 721 p. (National Archives and Records Service publication, no. 63–1).   **DB116**
  Repr. (1986) as *The Union: guide to federal archives relating to the Civil War.*
  Describes the records, relating to the Civil War, of the various agencies of the federal government. Arranged by agency with a subject index.   CD3047.M8

Encyclopedias

Encyclopedia of the Confederacy / Richard N. Current, ed. in chief … [et al.]. N.Y. : Simon & Schuster, c1993. 4 v. (1916 p.) : ill., maps.   **DB117**
  Provides extensive coverage through more than 1,400 articles signed by scholars and emphasizing the role and perspective of the Confederacy. Offers accounts of campaigns and battles; biographical sketches; discussion of the government and its conduct of economic and foreign affairs; roles of ethnic minorities, women, and the free and slave African American; the cultural life of the South. Extensive cross-references and index. Illustrations include specially commissioned maps, contemporary etchings and photographs—all with the sources identified in captions. Appendix reprints key documents (e.g., Constitution of the Confederate States, terms of surrender, Lee's farewell). Synoptic outline lists articles by categories (e.g., Union and dissension, Society and culture, Confederate legacy).   E487.E55

Historical times illustrated encyclopedia of the Civil War / Patricia L. Faust, ed. N.Y. : Harper & Row, c1986. 849 p. : ill.   **DB118**
  The 2,100 signed articles are strongly biographical, but include entries for newspapers, battles, towns, organizations, and weapons. Illustrated with photographs and maps. According to *Booklist* 83 (1987): 1108, "Readers familiar with other single-volume works on the Civil War such as [Mark M.] Boatner's *The Civil War dictionary* [Rev. ed. N.Y. : McKay, c1988. 974 p.] and *Civil War almanac* [exec. ed., John S. Bowman. N.Y. : Facts on File, 1983. 400 p.] will find that this book combines the best features of each … . At this price, [it] is a good value."
  § Frances H. Kennedy has compiled *The Civil War battlefield guide* (Boston : Houghton Mifflin, 1990. 317 p.), a guidebook to bat-

tlefields that can be visited. The chapter on each area is written by a specialist and includes a narrative, maps, and brief directions. The appendix includes complete lists of Civil War battles, lost Civil War battlefields, combat strengths and casualities, war statistics, and a glossary. Topical index.   E468.H57

Handbooks

Dyer, Frederick Henry. Compendium of the war of the rebellion : comp. and arranged from official records of the Federal and Confederate armies, reports of the adjutant generals of the several states, the army registers, and other reliable documents and sources. Des Moines, Iowa : Dyer, 1908. 1796 p.   **DB119**
  Repr. in three volumes, with a new introd. by Bell Irwin Wiley: N.Y., Yoseloff, 1959. Repr. of 1909 ed., in two volumes: Dayton, Ohio : National Historical Society, in cooperation with the Press of Morningside Bookshop, 1979.
  Contents: pt. 1, Number and organization of the armies of the United States; pt. 2, Chronological record of the campaigns, battles, engagements, actions, combats, sieges, skirmishes, etc., in the United States, 1861 to 1865; pt. 3, Regimental histories.
  § Frank Johnson Welcher, *The Union army, 1861–1865 : organization and operation* (Bloomington : Indiana Univ. Pr., 1989. 2 v.) provides expanded coverage for the Union army, with descriptions of the formation, composition, and organization of the armies.
                                                          E491.D99

Chronologies

Long, Everette Beach. The Civil War day by day : an almanac, 1861–1865 / [by] E. B. Long with Barbara Long. Foreword by Bruce Catton. Garden City, N.Y. : Doubleday, 1971. 1135 p. : maps.   **DB120**
  A concise account of the war in chronological order, November 1860–December 18, 1865 (with two paragraphs for April 2 and August 20, 1866). Introduction for each year and month. Special studies offer discussion of population, casualties, prisoners, economics, cost of the war, with charts and tables. Extensive bibliography, pp. 730–840, which is actually an author listing of the articles, books, and manuscript collections used for research toward Bruce Catton's *Centennial history of the Civil War* (1961–65). Topical index referring to specific dates (not to pages).
  § Robert E. Denny's *Civil War years: a day-by-day chronicle of the life of nation* (N.Y. : Sterling, [1992]. 606 p. ill., maps) offers much the same coverage: January 1, 1861–May 30, 1865, with an epilogue June, July, September, November 1865 and April 1866. Denny often reprints excerpts from newspaper stories, diaries, and contemporary accounts; The special studies section of Long is summarized by Denny in a prologue. Topical index to page instead of date; no bibliography.
  The *Civil War naval chronology, 1861–1865*, is compiled by the Naval History Division of the Dept. of the Navy (Washington : U.S. Govt. Print. Off., 1961–66. 6 v.; reissued 1971 in 1 volume).
                                                          E468.3.L6

Biography

Sifakis, Stewart. Who was who in the Civil War. N.Y. : Facts on File, c1988. 766 p. : ill.   **DB121**
  Some 2,500 entries deal with principal Union and Confederate military figures, together with politicians, activists, journalists, artists, medical personnel, diplomats and foreign observers, and engineers. Each entry includes sources for further information, if available. Concludes with a monthly chronology, list of officers who received thanks of the U.S. Congress, select annotated bibliography. Indexed.
  § See also: *Generals in blue : lives of the Union commanders* ([Baton Rouge] : LSU Pr., 1964. 670 p. Repr. 1981) and *Generals in gray : lives of the Confederate commanders* ([Baton Rouge] : LSU Pr.,

1959. 520 p. Repr. 1981), both compiled by Ezra J. Warner. These two dictionaries present biographical sketches, often with photographs and statistics for 583 Union commanders and 425 Confederate.

Warner and Buck Yates have also compiled *Biographical register of the Confederate Congress* (Baton Rouge : LSU Pr., 1975. 319 p.) which provides biographical sketches of 267 members of the Confederate Congress. Appendixes for sessions of the Congress, standing committees, and membership by state. E467.S56

Atlases

Library of Congress. Geography and Map Division. Civil War maps : an annotated list of maps and atlases in the Library of Congress / comp. by Richard W. Stephenson. 2nd ed. Wash. : Library of Congress, 1989. 410 p. : maps (some col.). **DB122**

1st ed., 1961.

Superintendent of Documents classification: LC 1.12/2:C49.

"Expanded to include descriptions of 2,240 maps and charts and 76 atlases and sketch books in the Geography and Map Division [and] ... 162 maps from the collections of the Manuscript Division."—*Pref.* Arranged by geographical area (i.e., the nation as a whole, then state). Title and general indexes. Z6027.U5L5

United States. War Dept. The official atlas of the Civil War / introd. by Henry Steele Commager. N.Y. : T. Yoseloff, 1958. 29 p., 175 plates ; 45 cm. **DB123**

Reproduction of the *Atlas to accompany the official records of the Union and Confederate armies* ... (Wash. : U.S. Govt. Print. Off., 1891–95).

The plates, often with several maps each, cover military operations: battles, engagements, campaigns, defenses, etc.; topographical maps; military divisions and departments. Four of the plates show uniforms, ordnance, transportation of sick or wounded, and corps flags, badges, etc.

§ Craig L. Symonds, *A battlefield atlas of the Civil War* (Annapolis, Md. : Nautical and Aviation Publ. Co., 1983. 106 p.) is well adapted to student use. G1201.S5U6

20th century

Bibliography

Bloxom, Marguerite D. Pickaxe and pencil : references for the study of the WPA. Wash. : Library of Congress, 1982. 87 p. : ill. **DB124**

Superintendent of Documents classification: LC 1.12/2:P 58.

A selective bibliography of books and periodical articles on various aspects of the WPA—what it was, what it did, and what became of many of the projects. Nearly 400 entries, both contemporary with the WPA and retrospective; numerous annotations. Separate list of doctoral dissertations. Author index. Z7164.P97B58

Buenker, John D. Progressive reform : a guide to information sources / John D. Buenker, Nicholas C. Burckel. Detroit : Gale, 1980. 366 p. (American government and history information guide series, v.8). **DB125**

An annotated bibliography of more than 1,600 books, periodical articles, and doctoral dissertations on the progressive reform period in the United States from the depression of the 1890s to the end of World War I. Broad topical arrangement, with author and subject indexes.

§ Though even older, Louis Filler's *Progressivism and muckraking* (N.Y. : Bowker, 1976. 200 p.) is useful for its bibliographic essays and its heavier emphasis on biography. Z1242.8.B84

Jewish immigrants of the Nazi period in the USA / Herbert A. Strauss, ed. N.Y. : K.G. Saur ; Detroit : distr. by Gale, 1978–c1992. 6 v. in 8 : ill. **DB126**

Sponsored by the Research Foundation for Jewish Immigration.

Contents: v. 1, Archival resources, comp. by Steven W. Siegel; v. 2, Classified and annotated bibliography of books and articles on the immigration and acculturation of Jews from Central Europe to the USA since 1933, comp. by Henry Friedlander ... [et al.]; v. 3, pt. 1, Guide to the oral history collection of the Research Foundation for Jewish Immigration, New York, comp. by Joan C. Lessing; v. 3, pt. 2, Classified list of articles concerning emigration in Germany : Jewish periodicals, Jan. 30, 1933 to Nov. 9, 1938, comp. by Daniel R. Schwartz, with Daniel S. Niederland; v. 4, Jewish emigration from Germany, 1933–1942 : a documentary history: pt. 1, Programs and policies until 1937, ed. by Norbert Kampe; pt. 2, Restrictions on emigration and deportation to Eastern Europe, ed. by Norbert Kampe; v. 5, The individual and collective experience of German-Jewish immigrants, 1933–1984 : an oral history record, comp. by Dennis Rohrbaugh; v. 6, Essays on the history, persecution, and emigration of German Jews, by Herbert A. Strauss.

A major research project which documents "the immigration, resettlement, and acculturation in the USA of Jews from Germany and Austria who were uprooted by Nazi persecution."—*Pref., v. 1.* Deals with archival sources, published materials, and oral history interviews. Indexed. E184.J5J558

Killen, Linda. Versailles and after : an annotated bibliography of American foreign relations, 1919–1933 / Linda Killen, Richard L. Lael. N.Y. : Garland, 1983. 469 p. (Garland reference library of social science, v. 135 ; American diplomatic history, v. 2). **DB127**

Cites "English-language books, articles, dissertations, indexes, guides, bibliographies, and manuscript collections which provide insight into the diverse diplomatic issues facing the nation" (*Introd.*) during the period indicated. Classed arrangement; subject and author indexes. Omits citations to articles in *Foreign affairs*, *Current history*, *Annals* of the American Academy of Political and Social Sciences, and the *Proceedings* of the Academy of Political Science. Z6465.U5K4

Kyvig, David E. New day/New Deal : a bibliography of the Great American Depression, 1929–1941 / comp. by David E. Kyvig and Mary-Ann Blasio with contributions by Dawn Corley. N.Y. : Greenwood, 1988. 306 p. (Bibliographies and indexes in American history, no. 9). **DB128**

Cites 4,600 books, articles, dissertations in classed arrangement subdivided by format. Separate section for biographies. Cutoff date is early 1987. Indexed by author with reference to topical number.

§Two earlier bibliographies are still useful for their depth of coverage of retrospective material and for their arrangement (respectively): Robert E. Burke and Richard Lowitt's *The new era and the New Deal, 1920–1940* (Arlington, Ill. : Harlan Davidson, 1981. 215 p.) which includes 4,200 books and articles, and *The great depression : a historical bibliography* (Santa Barbara, Calif. : ABC-Clio, 1984. 260 p.) which is a classified listing of 959 journal articles and abstracts with author and subject indexes. Z1244.K95

Encyclopedias; Dictionaries

Encyclopedia of the American left / ed. by Mari Jo Buhle, Paul Buhle, Dan Georgakas. N.Y. : Garland, 1990. 928 p. : ill. (Garland reference library of social science, v. 502). **DB129**

A dictionary arrangement of articles treating "that segment of society which has sought fundamental changes in the economic, political and cultural systems" (*Introd.*), but also including political parties, conventions, organizations, issues, literature, etc., from about 1870 to the early to mid-1980s. The signed articles are based on primary sources and include one to five bibliographic citations. Indexes of names and subjects. HX86.E58

The Harlem Renaissance : an historical dictionary for the era / ed. by Bruce Kellner. Westport, Conn. : Greenwood, 1984. 476 p. : ill. **DB130**

Repr. : N.Y. : Methuen, 1987.

Covers significant figures, events, and locales relating to the "rich surge of black arts and letters" (*Introd.*) during the period 1917–35, with entries for politicians, educators, poets, clergymen, musicians, churches, journals, theaters, and including plots and notes on the critical reception of representative literary and theatrical works. Bibliographies at the end of each article cite both primary and secondary sources. Appendixes offer chronologies (including literary and dramatic events), a list of newspapers and other serial publications, and a glossary of Harlem slang. Indexed. NX511.N4H37

Historical dictionary of the New Deal : from inauguration to preparation for war / ed. by James S. Olson. Westport, Conn. : Greenwood, [1985]. 611 p. **DB131**
Offers articles on persons, agencies, terms, slogans, etc., relative to U.S. domestic policy during the 1933–40 period. Contributed articles are signed, others are by the editor. One or more bibliographic references for each article. Also has a chronology, a select bibliography of New Deal programs, and a list of New Deal acronyms. Indexed by subject. E806.H58

Historical dictionary of the Progressive Era, 1890–1920 / ed. by John D. Buenker and Edward R. Kantowicz. N.Y. : Greenwood, c1988. 599 p. **DB132**
Focuses on "the emergence of the United States as a modern, urban industrial, multi-cultural world power between 1890-1920"—*Pref.* Alphabetically arranged, signed articles cover people, events, organizations, concepts, significant states and cities. Each entry includes a short bibliography of works for further study. Cross-references indicated by asterisks. Indexes: people; books, periodicals and newspapers; subjects. Chronology gives a list of major events for the year. E661.H6

Olson, James Stuart. Historical dictionary of the 1920s : from World War I to the New Deal, 1919–1933. N.Y. : Greenwood, 1988. 420 p. **DB133**
Offers brief articles, alphabetically arranged, on "the most prominent individuals, social movements, organizations, legislation, treaties, political events, and ideas of the era" (*Pref.*) in the U.S., with emphasis on individuals and events. Each article ends with at least one bibliographical reference. Detailed index, chronology, and topically arranged bibliography of books and articles on the period. E784.O44

Chronologies

Dickson, Paul. Timelines. Reading, Mass. : Addison-Wesley, c1990. 357 p. **DB134**
Gives the "dates and events, ... fads, trends, names, statistics and slogans that defined a given year ... from the end of World War II [January 20, 1945] to the present [November 10, 1989]"—*Introd.* Chronologically arranged by date, with special lists for many of the years, e.g., list of button and bumper stickers prominent during that particular year, or list of words and phrases invented or in heavy use. Topical index. E741.D53

Gordon, Lois G. American chronicle : seven decades in American life, 1920–1989 / Lois Gordon, Alan Gordon. Rev. ed. N.Y. : Crown, 1990. 709 p. : ill., ports. **DB135**
Supersedes their 1987 publication, *American chronicle : six decades in American life, 1920–1980.*
A chronology presenting in columnar form for each year: Facts and figures, In the news, Deaths, Quotes, Ads, Radio and television, The arts, Science and technology, Sports, Fashion, and a "Kaleidoscope" which aims to give the flavor of the year by listing, e.g., food prices, new words. At the beginning of each decade a brief narrative describes trends and presents vital, economic, social, and consumer statistics. Not indexed. E169.1.G665

Sourcebooks

The dynamics of world power : a documentary history of United States foreign policy, 1945–1973 / gen. ed., Arthur Meier Schlesinger. N.Y. : Chelsea House, 1973. 5 v. **DB136**
Repr. 1983, 5 v. in 10.
Contents: v. 1, Western Europe, ed. by R. Dallek; v. 2, Eastern Europe and the Soviet Union, ed. by W. La Feber; v. 3, Latin America, ed. by R. Burr; v. 4, The Far East, ed. by R. Buhite; v. 5, The United Nations, ed. by R. C. Hottelet; Subsaharan Africa, ed. by J. Herskovits.
Brings together in convenient form, on a region-by-region basis, the essential documents in the history of American foreign policy for the period 1945–73. E744.S395

Historic documents. 1972– . [Wash.] : Congressional Quarterly, Inc., 1973– . Annual. **DB137**
The year appears in the title.
A chronological arrangement of "statements, court decisions, reports, special studies, speeches" (*Foreword*), with a brief introduction for each giving background, source (not always published), frequently a short summary, and indication of subsequent events. Well indexed, each index cumulating over a five-year period (e.g., the 1985 index covers 1981–85). E839.5.H57

Regional and local

Bibliography

Dare, Philip N. American communes to 1860 : bibliography. N.Y. : Garland, 1990. 203 p. (Sects and cults in America. Bibliographical guides, v. 12 ; Garland reference library of social science, v. 347). **DB138**
More than 1,900 books, articles, and archival materials are grouped by name of commune or utopian society, with a brief historical note for each community. The volume begins with a listing of bibliographies and general works on communal movements. Topical index.
§ Continued by: Timothy Miller's *American communes, 1860–1960 : a bibliography* (N.Y. : Garland, 1990. 583 p. [Sects and cults in America. Bibliographical guides, v. 13 ; Garland reference library of social science, v. 402]).
An alphabetical listing of communes, giving for each a brief description (usually a paragraph) followed by a list of secondary works and any published primary material available—e.g., periodicals issued by the commune or works by a leader. The bibliographies list mostly English-language books and articles, plus a few theses. A separate chapter contains an annotated list of other bibliographical works and research aids. Name index of authors of works cited, communes, and those associated with the history and development of any commune. Z7164.C69D37

Filby, P. William. A bibliography of American county histories. Baltimore, Md. : Genealogical Publ., 1985. 449 p. **DB139**
Aims to replace Clarence S. Peterson's *Consolidated bibliography of county histories in fifty states in 1961* (Baltimore, 1961. 186 p.). Listing is by state, then by county, giving full bibliographic information. Not indexed. Z1250.F54

Jones, Houston Gwynne. Local government records : an introduction to their management, preservation and use. Nashville : Amer. Assoc. for State and Local History, 1980. 208 p. **DB140**
Aims to be an introduction to the topic rather than a guide or how-to-do-it manual. Pt. 1, Management and preservation, discusses general principles and is directed to local officials, encouraging them to develop and/or evaluate a records management program. Pt. 2, Use

of local records, is intended for the researcher and explains the various government divisions that produce records, the types of records (e.g., records of orphans, apprentices, and the disadvantaged; tax records), and briefly discusses how to approach those records. Appendixes describe records management services for each state and give names and addresses of sources of information. CD3024.J66

Library of Congress. A guide to the microfilm collection of early state records / collected and comp. under the direction of William Sumner Jenkins ; ed. by Lillian A. Hamrick. Wash. : Library of Congress, 1950. various pagings. **DB141**

Begun in 1941 as a joint project of the Library of Congress and the University of North Carolina to locate and reproduce early state legislative proceedings. When the project was resumed after World War II, the coverage was expanded to include also statutory laws; constitutional, administrative, executive, and court records; some local records; records of American Indian nations; and a miscellaneous group.

The *Guide* is an index to more than 2,500,000 pages of records represented on 160,000 feet of microfilm. General arrangement is by the classifications noted above for each state. Items within these classifications are arranged chronologically. Library locations and reel numbers are given for each item.

In 1951, Jenkins published a *Supplement*, providing information on some 170 reels of microfilm remaining after the regular project had been completed, under five special classes: (1) local records, (2) records of American Indian nations, (3) newspapers, (4) records of rudimentary states, and (5) miscellany.

─────── United States local histories in the Library of Congress : a bibliography / ed. by Marion J. Kaminkow. Baltimore : Magna Carta Book Co., 1975–1976. 5 v. **DB142**

Contents: v. 1–2, Atlantic States; v. 3, Middle West, Alaska, Hawaii; v. 4, The West; v. 5, Supplement and index.

"Includes all the books cataloged and classified under the local history portion of the Library of Congress classification schedule (F1–F975) for which cards had been filed in the Library's shelflist by mid-1972."—*Pref.* Arrangement is by classification number (which provides a state-by-state listing). For each state a classification schedule is given, as is a supplementary index of places. The supplement adds citations from cards filed mid-1972 to beginning of 1976. General index of personal names in all volumes; corrections to v. 1–4 in v. 5, p. 567–69. Z1250.U59

Neagles, James C. The Library of Congress : a guide to genealogical and historical research / by James C. Neagles ; assisted by Mark C. Neagles. Salt Lake City, Utah : Ancestry, c1990. 381 p. : ill. **DB143**

Discusses major subject areas in the Library of Congress collections, but emphasizes genealogical and historical resources. Includes helpful background material, cites many bibliographies, and provides LC call numbers. Useful for genealogists and reference librarians. Z1250.N4

Reference guides to state history and research. N.Y. : Greenwood, [1982–1993]. 7 v. (In progress). **DB144**

Contents: A guide to the history of Louisiana, ed. by Light Townsend Cummins and Glen Jeansonne (1982. 298 p.); … Massachusetts, ed. by Martin Kaufman, John W. Ifkovic, and Joseph Carvalho III (1988. 313 p.); … Texas, ed. by Light Townsend Cummins and Alvin R. Bailey, Jr. (1988. 307 p.); … Florida, ed. by Paul S. George (1989. 300 p.); … California, ed. by Doyce R. Nunis, Jr. and Gloria Ricci Lothrop (1989. 309 p.); … Illinois, ed. by John Hoffman (1991. 349 p.); … Pennsylvania, ed. by Dennis B. Downey and Francis J. Bremer (1993. 486 p.).

Intended for researchers of state and local history. Volumes follow a standard pattern: Pt. 1, Historical essays, presents chapters arranged by periods or topics (urban, women's, oral history), written by specialists and designed to cover "major sources and interpretations … while surveying the major historical literature, including books, articles, and dissertations"—*Introd., Massachusetts*. Pt. 2, Archives and sources, describes major archival repositories of the state's history. Subject index. Some volumes include a chronology of the state's history; all give brief biographies of the contributors.

Shearer, Barbara Smith. Periodical literature on United States cities : a bibliography and subject guide / Barbara Smith Shearer, Benjamin F. Shearer. Westport, Conn. : Greenwood, 1983. 574 p. **DB145**

Lists selected periodical articles published 1970–81 on 170 United States cities with a population of 100,000 or more. Arrangement is alphabetical by name of city, with subsections for general articles, arts and architecture, education and media, environment, government and politics, housing and urban development, social and economic conditions, and transportation. Author and subject indexes. Z5942.S464

Steiner, Michael. Region and regionalism in the United States : a source book for the humanities and social sciences / Michael Steiner, Clarence Mondale. N.Y. : Garland, 1988. 495 p. (Garland reference library of social science, v. 204). **DB146**

A topical listing of 1,652 books, articles and essays on cultural regions as a concept and as an object of study. Headnotes to each section or subsection; annotations. Author index only. Z1247.S73

Stephens, W. B. Sources for U.S. history : nineteenth-century communities. Cambridge [Eng.] ; N.Y. : Cambridge Univ. Pr., 1991. 558 p. **DB147**

Presents a discussion of archival, statistical, and historical sources for "research into the history of individual nineteenth-century U.S. communities, large and small. The book is arranged topically (covering demography, ethnicity and race, land use and settlement, religion, education, politics and local government, industry, trade and transportation, and poverty, health and crime)."—*Adv.* Includes a very useful section on the use of primary sources. Topical index.

§ Similar in scope to Stephens' *Sources for English local history* (DC351). E180.S74

Dissertations

Young, Arthur P. Cities and towns in American history : a bibliography of doctoral dissertations. N.Y. : Greenwood, [1989]. 438 p. (Bibliographies and indexes in American history, no. 13). **DB148**

Lists 4,314 doctoral dissertations through 1987, identified in *Comprehensive dissertation index* (AG12), that treat the urban experience. "All subject areas—culture, economics, education, ethnicity, health, politics, religion, and social structure—are reflected in the compilation … " (*Pref.*) if they have a historical orientation. Pt. 1 lists dissertations by state, then city; cities with more than 25 entries are subdivided by topic, and New York City by neighborhood, borough, and street. Pt. 2 lists works by topic (e.g., cultural and intellectual life, labor). Gives University Microfilms order numbers when available, but omits references to *Dissertation abstracts international*. Author and subject indexes. Z7164.U7Y7

Handbooks

Fogarty, Robert S. Dictionary of American communal and utopian history. Westport, Conn. : Greenwood, 1980. 271 p. **DB149**

Presents biographical sketches of more than 140 prominent leaders and descriptions of 59 of the most important or interesting colonies. An additional 270 settlements are briefly noted in an annotated chronology of communal and utopian societies established between 1787 and 1919. Each biographical and communal entry has a list of sources noted. An appendix provides a review of the literature. Selected bibliography; index. HX653.F65

Regional differences in America : a statistical sourcebook / Alfred N. Garwood, ed. Seattle, Wash. : Numbers & Concepts, c1988. 590 p. **DB150**

Information drawn from census publications, surveys, and polls (especially Gallup polls) is organized by broad topic (e.g., Health and vital statistics; Transportation; Income, poverty, subsidy, and wealth; Education, the arts, culture, recreation). Data is presented in tables mostly covering 1982–85, with a few beginning as early as 1970. Glossary of terms; subject index.   HA215.R43

Shearer, Benjamin F. State names, seals, flags, and symbols : a historical guide / Benjamin F. Shearer and Barbara S. Shearer. Rev. and expanded. Westport, Conn. : Greenwood, 1994. 438 p. : ill.   **DB151**
For annotation, *see* AL192.   E155.S44

New England

Bibliographies of New England history. Boston : G. K. Hall, 1976–89. v. 1–8. (In progress).   **DB152**
Under the auspices of the Committee for a New England Bibliography. Publisher varies.
Contents: v.1, Massachusetts, ed. by John Haskell. 583 p.; v. 2, Maine, ed. by John D. Haskell. 279 p.; v. 3, New Hampshire, ed. by John D. Haskell and T. D. Seymour Bassett. 330 p.; v. 4, Vermont, ed. by T. D. Seymour Bassett. 391 p.; v. 5, Rhode Island, ed. by R. Parks. 229 p; v. 6, Connecticut, ed. by Roger Parks (571 p.); v. 7, New England, ed. by Roger Parks (259 p.); v. 8, New England : additions to the six state bibliographies, ed. by Roger Parks (776 p.).
Citations for books, collected series, journal articles are arranged alphabetically within a geographical framework. Cutoff date for Massachusetts is generally Dec. 1972; for the Maine volume, 1975; for New Hampshire, 1977; for Vermont, 1979; for Rhode Ilsand, 1981; for Connecticut, 1984; for New England, 1987, with a few later publications cited. If no location is indicated in the *National union catalog* or the printed catalogs of the Library of Congress, a location symbol is given. Indexes cite authors, editors, subjects, and geographical places (including variant names and extinct places).
Vol. 7 "contains entries that pertain to the history of the region and to more than one New England state. It also includes writings about the Northeastern United States in which New England is prominently mentioned and works on certain subjects in the American past that are nearly synonymous with New England: [e.g.,] Puritan history."—*Introd.* Also of interest is a historiographic essay, "Reassessing the local history of New England," by David D. Hall and Alan Taylor.
Vol. 8 "lists additions and corrections to the state bibliographies and updates them through 1987 with additional entries for 1988 and early 1989."—*Introd.* Plans call for additional volumes in 1994 or 1995 with updating and corrections.
For a description of the project and guidelines for compilation, see *New England quarterly* 43 (Sept. 1970): 523–26.

The encyclopedia of New England / ed. by Robert O'Brien with Richard D. Brown. N.Y. : Facts on File, c1985. 613 p. : ill., maps.   **DB153**
Concerned with the states of Connecticut, Maine, Massachusetts, New Hampshire, Rhode Island, and Vermont. Includes entries for historical works, cultural institutions and developments, geographical topics, statistical and political information, and more general themes as they relate to New England. Dictionary arrangement with cross-references and select bibliography.   F2.E43

The South

Bibliography

See also the annual bibliography, "Southern history in periodicals," in *Journal of Southern history*.

Brown, Catherine L. The urban South : a bibliography. N.Y. : Greenwood, 1989. 455 p. (Bibliographies and indexes in American history, no. 12).   **DB154**

Lists 7,370 books and pamphlets, periodical articles, theses, and doctoral dissertations concerned with cities, towns, Indian settlements, ghost towns, etc. in the South (West Virginia to Oklahoma, Texas to Maryland). Arranged by format subdivided by broad topic (e.g., Archaeology, Artisans and crafts, History and geography). Does not give *Dissertation abstracts* references for dissertations. Geographic index, subject index.   Z7164.U7B69

Clark, Thomas Dionysius. Travels in the old South : a bibliography. Norman : Univ. of Oklahoma Pr., 1956–59. 3 v. (American exploration and travel series, no. 19).   **DB155**
Contents: v. 1, The formative years, 1527–1783. From the Spanish explorations through the American Revolution; v. 2, The expanding South, 1750–1825. The Ohio Valley and the cotton frontier; v. 3, The ante-bellum South, 1825–1860. Cotton, slavery and conflict.
Each volume is divided into sections, each compiled by a specialist. Annotations are descriptive and often include critical comments; location of copies is indicated. Each volume has an index of authors, subjects, and names of persons and places.
§ Companion volumes: E. M. Coulter, *Travels in the Confederate states* (DB108) and Clark's *Travels in the new South* (Norman, 1962), completing the series. Contents of *Travels in the new South*: v. 1, The postwar South, 1865–1900. An era of reconstruction and readjustment; v. 2, The twentieth-century South, 1900–1955. An era of change, depression and emergence.
Titles listed in these three works are available on microcard from Lost Cause Press.   Z1251.S7C4

Green, Fletcher M. The old South / Fletcher M. Green, J. Isaac Copeland. Arlington Heights, Ill. : AHM Publ. Corp., [1980]. 173 p.   **DB156**
A selective bibliography of major books and periodical articles, topically arranged. Designed for advanced undergraduates and entering graduating students. Emphasis on the economic, cultural, and social history of the South since the Civil War. Author index.
Z1251.S7G69

Ross, Charlotte T. Bibliography of Southern Appalachia : a publication of the Appalachian Consortium, Inc / comp. by Appalachian State University ... [et al.]. Boone, N.C. : Appalachian Consortium Pr., 1976. 260, 235, 16 p.   **DB157**
A union list of the books, monographs and films relating to Southern Appalachia held by the thirteen libraries of the Appalachian Consortium. Author/main entry listing with subject index; separate section for films.   Z1251.A7B53

Encyclopedias

Encyclopedia of Southern culture / Charles Reagan Wilson & William Ferris, coeditors ; Ann J. Abadie & Mary L. Hart, assoc. editors. Chapel Hill : Univ. of North Carolina Pr., c1989. 1634 p. : ill.   **DB158**
Sponsored by The Center for the Study of Southern Culture, Univ. of Mississippi.
Signed, short articles, with bibliographies, are arranged under broader topics (e.g., "We shall overcome" under Black life; Stoicism under Philanthropy; Northern under History and manners; Jonathan Daniels under Media). Cross-references; index of contributors; general index. An excellent, authoritative survey.   F209.E53

The encyclopedia of Southern history / ed. by David C. Roller and Robert W. Twyman. Baton Rouge : Louisiana State Univ. Pr., 1979. 1421 p.   **DB159**
Designed "to answer those questions about the South most frequently asked by scholars, teachers, students, and laymen."—*Pref.* Features authoritative signed articles (most of them with select bibliographies) on events, terms, persons, places, etc., relevant to southern history from earliest times to the present. "The South" is defined "as encompassing the District of Columbia and those states that accepted the practice of slavery in 1860." Articles on the region's 16 states are an important feature of the work. Indexed.   F207.7.E52

The Midwest

Carpenter, Allan. The encyclopedia of the Midwest / by Allan Carpenter ; contributor, Randy Lyon. N.Y. : Facts on File, c1989. 544 p. : ill.   **DB160**

Treats the states of Illinois, Indiana, Iowa, Michigan, Minnesota, Missouri, Ohio, and Wisconsin by presenting "information of the widest variety" (*Pref.*), including local events, institutions, statistics, etc., in alphabetical arrangement. Cross-references; general index. Brief bibliography, p. 505–506.   F351.C33

Hubach, Robert Rogers. Early midwestern travel narratives : an annotated bibliography, 1634–1850. Detroit : Wayne State Univ. Pr., 1961. 149 p.   **DB161**

Lists books and periodical articles in chronological order by period, with full descriptive annotations. Includes journals and diaries, published and unpublished. Author and place-name index.

"Midwest" is here understood to include the western border of Pennsylvania and all territory north of the present states of Arkansas and Oklahoma to the Canadian border.   Z1251.W5H8

The West

Bibliography

Adams, Ramon Frederick. Six-guns and saddle leather : a bibliography of books and pamphlets on western outlaws and gunmen. New ed., rev. and greatly enl. [Norman : Univ. of Oklahoma Pr., 1969]. 808 p.   **DB162**

Repr.: Cleveland : Zubal, 1982.

1st ed., 1954.

2,491 numbered items, arranged alphabetically, dealing with western outlaws. Detailed index; annotations.

§ Similar bibliographies by the same compiler: *Burs under the saddle : a second look at books and histories of the West* (Norman, 1964. Repr., 1989), *More burs under the saddle : books and histories of the West* (Norman, 1978. Repr., 1989), and *The rampaging herd : a bibliography of books and pamphlets on men and events in the cattle industry* (Norman, 1959. Repr., Cleveland : Zubal, 1982.).   Z1251.W5A3

Bancroft Library. Catalog of printed books. Boston : G. K. Hall, 1964. 22 v.   **DB163**

Photographic reproduction of the cards of the dictionary catalog, representing some 150,000 printed books, pamphlets, scrapbooks, government documents, broadsides, magazines, special issues of modern newspapers, as well as extensive files of early western papers. The scope of the library is broad, but generally covers historical materials for the study of the western half of North America, including all of Mexico and Central America. Particularly strong in the history, religion, politics, economics, and social conditions of the region, with special collections on the Mormons, the Catholic church in Mexico, early California printing, voyages and travels, maps from the 16th–20th centuries, etc.

————. ————. *Supplements 1–3* (1969–1979. 17 v.) cover materials added 1964–68, 1969–73 and 1974–78, dealing with western North America from Alaska through Panama. Of special interest is the acquisition of a collection of Mexican political pamphlets from the 1880s to the 1960s.

§ Manuscripts are described in *A guide to the manuscript collections of the Bancroft Library,* ed. by Dale L. Morgan and George P. Hammond (Berkeley : Univ. of Calif. Pr., 1963–72. 2 v.). See also *Index to printed maps* (CL250).   Z881.C1523

Borderlands sourcebook : a guide to the literature on northern Mexico and the American Southwest / ed., Ellwyn R. Stoddard, Richard L. Nostrand and Jonathan P. West. Norman : Univ. of Okla. Pr., publ. under sponsorship of the Assoc. of Borderlands Scholars, [1983]. 445 p. : maps.   **DB164**

Sixty bibliographic essays survey all areas of research on this region. In three main sections: (1) Delineating the U.S.-Mexican borderlands; (2) Specific border phenomena (e.g., Society and culture, History and archaeology, Economics); (3) Borderlands information resources. A bibliography gives full citations to all works mentioned in the essays and includes sections for documents and theses (topically arranged). Enhanced by maps, time scales, tables and charts.

Z1251.S8B67

The frontier experience : a reader's guide to the life and literature of the American West / ed. by Jon Tuska and Vicki Piekarski. Jefferson, N.C. : McFarland, [1984]. 434 p.   **DB165**

A critically annotated bibliography of books on "the entire American frontier experience but with special emphasis on the American West."—*Introd.* In two sections (The life, The literature), each consisting of numerous chapters (e.g., Frontier professionals, Transportation and communication, Western films). An introductory survey of each topic is followed by the annotated bibliography, then a list of suggested fiction and suggested films. Name and title indexes only.

§ A useful annotated bibliography of periodical articles is Dwight L. Smith's *The American and Canadian West* (Santa Barbara : ABC-Clio, 1979. 558 p.) which is a collection of 4,157 abstracts drawn from *America : history and life* (DB24), 1964–73.   Z1251.W5F76

Townley, John M. The trail west : a bibliography-index to western American trails, 1841–1869. Reno, Nev. : Jamison Station Pr., [1988]. 309 p. : maps.   **DB166**

Begins with the first California-bound settlers in 1841 and ends with the completion of the transcontinental railroad in 1869. Includes staging and freight lines and the telegraph. The main portion of the work is an alphabetical listing of diaries, recollections, books, articles, theses, and maps, with complete bibliographical information. Indexes refer to the author's name in the main section: Chronological index by year, Subject index, Trail segment index. For this last index, the trails have been divided into 42 geographical segments; each segment is listed with the author's names, subdivided by year.   Z1251.W5T68

Valk, Barbara G. BorderLine : a bibliography of the United States-Mexico borderlands. Los Angeles : UCLA Latin American Center Publications ; Riverside : UC MEXUS, Univ. of California Consortium on Mexico and the United States, c1988. 711 p. (UCLA Latin American Center Publications. Reference series, v. 12).   **DB167**

Arrangement of the 8,692 entries is topical, divided geographically within chapters. Covers Arizona, California, New Mexico, Texas, Baja California, Chihuahua, Coahuila, Nuevo Léon, Sonora, Tamaulipas. Topics include history, demography, urbanization, agriculture, emigration and immigration, business and industry, commerce and trade, science and medicine, mass media, language, literature, arts, anthropology, religion, and mythology. Primarily in English, although some Spanish-language materials are included. Most materials were published 1960–85, and include books, government documents, conference proceedings, theses and dissertations, unpublished papers, maps, films and other audiovisual materials. Each citation is listed only once with no cross-references, but scope notes appear in the table of contents. Author index.   Z1251.M44V35

Wagner, Henry R. The plains & the Rockies : a critical bibliography of exploration, adventure and travel in the American West, 1800–1865 / Henry R. Wagner, Charles L. Camp. 4th ed. rev., enl. and ed. by Robert H. Becker. San Francisco : John Howell Books, 1982. 745 p. : ill.   **DB168**

1st ed., 1920 (corrected reissue 1921); 3rd ed., 1961.

A descriptive bibliography of some 1,800 issues and editions of about 690 individual works, arranged by year, then by author. This is a complete reworking of the 3rd ed., aiming to provide a "standard bibliographical form," and with notes edited and usually shortened; it retains the numbering scheme of the earlier editions. Locates copies. Indexed.

§ A series based on the 3rd ed. and on R. F Adams' *Burs under the saddle* (DB162 *note*), is issued by the Lost Cause Press, Louisville, Ky., and makes most of the items available on microcard.

Z1251.W5W2

Winther, Oscar Osburn. A classified bibliography of the periodical literature of the trans-Mississippi West (1811-1957). Bloomington : Indiana Univ. Pr., 1961. 626 p. (Indiana University. Social science series, no. 19).   **DB169**

Lists 9,244 items in classified arrangement with author index. Supersedes the author's *The trans-Mississippi West (1811–1938)*.

Winther and Richard Van Orman published a supplement in 1970, updating the bibliography through 1967 and adding more than 4,500 entries. The two works were reprinted as one in 1972 (Westport, Conn. : Greenwood. 340 p.).   Z1251.W5W53

Yale University. Library. Catalog of the Yale collection of Western Americana. Boston : G. K. Hall, [1961]. 4 v. **DB170**
Contents: v.1–3, A–Z; v.4, Shelflist.

A photographic reproduction of the card catalog of the Western Americana collection, which consists of a number of special collections in the field, mostly of a rare book nature, including early imprints of books, pamphlets, and periodicals. Authors, titles, and subjects are in one alphabet. The shelflist serves as a classed guide. The catalog includes only those books cataloged for the collection at time of publication; this means that some notable collections are omitted, and materials in the general library are not included.

§ See also: *A catalogue of the Frederick W. and Carrie S. Beinecke collection of Western Americana : manuscripts*, comp. by Jeanne M. Goddard and Charles Kritzler; ed. by Archibald Hanna (New Haven : Yale Univ. Pr., 1965. 114 p.). This work lists and describes 285 items in the collection, which emphasizes materials "on the Spanish Southwest and California, from the period of discovery and exploration by the Spanish down through the Mexican War and the gold rush."—*Introd.*   Z1251.W5Y35

Manuscripts; Archives

Beers, Henry Putney. Spanish & Mexican records of the American Southwest : a bibliographical guide to archive and manuscript sources. Tucson : Univ. of Arizona Pr., 1979. 493 p. : maps.   **DB171**

Offers "a historical account of the acquisition, preservation, and publication, by American institutions and individuals, of the original records created by Spanish and Mexican officials in what became the American Southwest, from the beginning of settlement in the early 1600s to the mid-nineteenth century. The historical treatment primarily concerns public records that have been preserved in official custody. ... Descriptive information regarding the records, derived from a wide variety of finding aids and other publications, is included, and records of the Franciscan and Jesuit missions are also described."—*Pref.* Records of New Mexico, Texas, California, and Arizona are treated in separate chapters. Bibliography, p. 385–454. Detailed index.

Z1251.S8B4

Women in the West : a guide to manuscript sources / editors, Susan Armitage ... [et al.]. N.Y. : Garland, 1991. 422 p. (Women's history and culture, 5 ; Garland reference library of the humanities, vol. 1086).   **DB172**

Includes repositories in 20 western states, Minnesota to Hawaii. For each gives address, hours, services, description of major collections, guides. Arranged geographically. Not indexed.

Supplements Andrea Hinding, *Women's history sources* (DB39).

Z7964.U49W6

Encyclopedias; Dictionaries

Carpenter, Allan. The encyclopedia of the Central West. N.Y. : Facts on File, c1990. 544 p. : ill.   **DB173**

Covering Colorado, Kansas, Montana, Nebraska, New Mexico, North Dakota, Oklahoma, South Dakota, Texas, and Wyoming, the work presents in a dictionary arrangement information on people, places, colleges and universities, native American groups, and topics (Adobe architecture, Agriculture—pueblo) relating specifically to this region. State entries describe population, archeology, etc. of that state. Short bibliography; topical index.

§ From the same editor and publisher, *The encyclopedia of the Far West* (1991) covers Alaska, Arizona, California, Hawaii, Idaho, Nevada, Oregon, Utah, Washington, and the U.S. territories in the Pacific (e.g., Guam).   F351.C325

The reader's encyclopedia of the American West / ed. by Howard R. Lamar. N.Y. : T. Y. Crowell, [1977]. 1306 p. : ill.
DB174

"Historically the term *American West* has meant either any part of the continental United States in its formative or frontier period or the entire trans-Mississippi West from the time of first exploration to the present. The editor has employed both these approaches. Thematically the *Encyclopedia* embraces the story of Indian-white relations; the diplomacy of American expansion; the overland trails experience; the era of the fur trader, the miner, the cowboy, and the settler; and those western subcultures we call Texas and Mormon."—*Pref.* Includes entries for persons, places, organizations, events, terms, etc. About 2,400 entries by some 200 contributors. Articles are signed with initials; many include bibliographic references.   F591.R38

Thrapp, Dan L. Encyclopedia of frontier biography. Glendale, Calif. : A.H. Clark Co., 1988. 3 v.   **DB175**

Short biographic sketches of all "who came to attention through the significance of their deeds or simply were of interest in some connection with the evolving drama" (*Introd.*)—trappers, traders, cowboys, scouts, explorers, miners, heroes, desperadoes, etc. Omits people in the mining industry and those noted only through "formal and declared wars." Each entry gives dates, brief biography, significance or influence, and sources for further research. Indexed by topic, names, locations, Indian tribes, occupations.   F596.T515

Atlases

Beck, Warren A. Historical atlas of the American West / by Warren A. Beck and Ynez D. Haase. Norman : Univ. of Oklahoma Pr., c1989. [156 p.] ; 32 cm.   **DB176**

Presents 78 black-and-white maps with discussion on facing pages. Covers 17 Western states from Texas to Canada "along the hundredth meridian and westward."—*Pref.* Bibliography of works used for each map. Index mainly of names. Appendix: Spanish-American land grants—Lower Rio Grande Valley, west of the Nueces River, Texas.   G1381.S1B4

Canada

General works

Guides

Guide du chercheur en histoire canadienne / [rédaction, Gilbert Caron ... et al.]. Québec : Presses de l'Université Laval, 1986. 808 p.   **DB177**

Intended as a starting point for those researching Canadian history. Treats reference books, documents collections, journals, statistical compilations, and secondary studies on specific topics. Describes relevant collections and lists finding aids, inventories, guides, etc., for archives. Topical and name indexes.   Z1382.G85

Bibliography

See also BE825.

Aubin, Paul. Bibliographie de l'histoire du Québec et du Canada = Bibliography of the history of Quebec and Canada. [Québec : Inst. Québecois de Recherche sur la Culture, 1981– [1990?]. pts. 1–4. (In progress).   **DB178**

Contents: [Pt. 1], 1946–65 (1987. 2 v.); [pt. 2], 1966–75 (1981. 2 v.); [Pt. 3], 1976–80 (1985. 2 v.); [Pt. 4], 1981–85 (1990?. 2 v.).

More than 20,000 citations to books, articles, and dissertations drawn from standard bibliographies and some 400 journals. In three sections: (1) classed order; (2) analytic (i.e., names of persons, places, organizations, and subject terms in alphabetical order); (3) authors.
Z1382.A88

Bibliographic guide to North American history. v. 1 (1978)– . Boston : G.K. Hall, 1979– . Annual.   **DB179**
For annotation, *see* DB25.   Z1236.B47

Black, J. L. Soviet perception of Canada, 1917–1987 : an annotated bibliographic guide. Kingston, Ont. : R.P. Frye, c1989. 2 v. in 1 [139, 242 p.]. (The Centre for Canadian Soviet Studies bibliographic series, no. 1).   **DB180**

In two parts: Pt. 1 is "a list of all books, articles from periodical literature, chapters in books, and dissertations written in the USSR about Canada since 1917" (*Introd.*), arranged by format; Pt. 2 is a listing by date of Soviet newspapers reporting on Canada, 1945–87. Author index for each part.

§ Black also wrote *Soviet perception of Canada, 1945–1987 : an overview of the literature* (Toronto : Centre for Russian and East European Studies, 1990. 78 p.) which focused on literature of the postwar decade and the 1970s, written or published in the Soviet Union, concerning history, continentalism and free trade, the Canadian North, and Canadian authors translated for Soviet readers.   Z6465.C2B58

Day, Alan Edwin. Search for the Northwest Passage : an annotated bibliography. N.Y. : Garland, 1986. 632 p. (Garland reference library of social science, v. 186).   **DB181**

"The search for a passage by the northwest is traced in print from the late fifteenth-century voyages of the Cabots ... to the voyage of a Royal Canadian Mounted Police schooner through the passage in both directions in the early 1940s."—*Pref.* A section of general works is followed by a chronological arrangement of entries for the various voyages and expeditions. 5,160 entries, indexed by author.
Z6016.N67D39

Gagnon, Philéas. Essai de bibliographie canadienne : inventaire d'une bibliothèque comprenant imprimés, manuscrits, estampes, etc., relatifs à l'histoire du Canada et des pays adjacents, avec des notes bibliographiques. Québec : L'auteur, 1895–1913. 2 v. : ill.   **DB182**

Contents: v. 1, Books, pamphlets, periodicals, no. 1–3747; Autographs and manuscripts, no. 3748–4406; Prints, etc., no. 4407–4745; Ex-libris, no. 4746–5018; v. 2, Additions to the collection, 1895–1909, ed. by Frédéric Villeneuve. Vol. 1 also available in microform (Ottawa : Canadian Institute for Historical Microreproductions, 1983. 8 microfiche).

Contains both English and French material. Information given for each book includes: author, full title, place, publisher, date, paging, size, with occasional bibliographical notes, facsimiles of title pages, etc. The Gagnon collection was acquired in 1909 by the city of Montreal as a nucleus for the Public Library.

§ Patricia Fleming has provided full bibliographic descriptions of works published in 1801–20 in *Atlantic Canadian imprints, 1801–1820: a bibliography* (Toronto : Univ. of Toronto Pr., 1991. 188 p.).
Z1365.G2

Ingles, Ernest Boyce. Canada. Oxford ; Santa Barbara, Calif. : Clio Pr., c1990. 393 p. : map. (World bibliographical series, v. 62).   **DB183**

An annotated bibliography of 1,316 books (including some government documents), topicaly arranged. Indexes: author, title, subject.
Z1365.I56

Jones, Linda M. Canadian studies : foreign publications and theses. 4th ed. Ottawa : International Council for Canadian Studies, 1992. 525 p.   **DB184**

Title and text in French and English.

2nd ed., 1987 had title *Monographs and periodicals published abroad in the context of Canadian studies*; 3rd ed., 1989.

Books, journals, and dissertations drawn from such compilations as the LC-MARC database, dissertation lists, and published bibliographies, arranged in broad categories (e.g., Bibliography—History, civilisation). Most titles published since 1979. Name index.   Z1385.M65

Matthews, William. Canadian diaries and autobiographies. Berkeley : Univ. of California Pr., 1950. 130 p.   **DB185**

Lists 1,276 published and unpublished diaries and autobiographies of Canadians of both British and French origin. Arrangement is alphabetical with topical index.   Z5305.C3M3

Page, Donald M. Bibliography of works on Canadian foreign relations, 1945–1970. [Toronto] : Canadian Inst. of Internat. Affairs, [1973]. 441 p.   **DB186**

More than 6,000 books, pamphlets, documents, periodical articles, and dissertations appearing since 1945 are listed by broad topics and geographical areas, with detailed subject and author indexes. Sec. 6 is a "Chronological list of statements and speeches issued by the Department of External Affairs," followed by an "Index to the Monthly report on Canadian external relations and International Canada, 1962–1970."

Three supplements have been issued: 1971–75, comp. by Donald M. Page (1976. 300 p.); 1976–80, comp. by Jane R. Barrett and Jane Beaumont (1982. 306 p.); and 1981–85, comp. by Jane R. Barrett with Jane Beaumont and Lee-Anne Broadhead (1987. 157 p.). All follow an arrangement similar to the basic work, covering books, parts of books, collections, and government publications, with personal name and subject indexes.   Z6465.C2P33

A reader's guide to Canadian history. Toronto : Univ. of Toronto Pr., 1982. 2 v.   **DB187**

On cover: An authoritative critical bibliographical guide to Canadian historical writing ... what is good and why.

Contents: v. 1, Beginnings to confederation, ed. by D. A. Muise; v. 2, Confederation to the present, ed. by J. L. Granatstein and P. Stevens.

Vol. 2 was previously publ. as *Canada since 1867: a bibliographical guide* (2nd ed., 1977).

Bibliographic essays by contributing scholars assessing the best and most useful publications for the study of Canadian history. Emphasis is on recent materials; book citations predominate, but some periodical articles are discussed. Follows a thematic arrangement within a regional context. Index of subjects, but not of authors.

§ *The history of Canada : an annotated bibliography*, ed. by Dwight L. Smith (Santa Barbara, Calif. : ABC-Clio, 1983. 327 p.), lists some 3,362 articles, with abstracts, drawn from the *America : history and life* database, 1973–78 (DB24).   Z1382.R4

Toronto Public Libraries. A bibliography of Canadiana : being items in the Public Library of Toronto, Canada, relating to the early history and development of Canada / ed. by Frances M. Staton and Marie Tremaine. Toronto : Public Library, 1934. 828 p. : ill.   **DB188**

An author catalog of 4,646 numbered items from the Reference Department of the Library, described with full titles, collations, many contents notes, and references to bibliographic sources. Covers the period 1534–1867.

———. ———. *First supplement* ... ed. by Gertrude M. Boyle, assisted by Marjorie Colbeck (Toronto : Public Library, 1959. 333 p. [Repr. 1969]).

Continues the item numbering of the main volume, adding 1,640 entries.

————. ————. *Second supplement*, ed. by Sandra Alston, assisted by Karen Evans (Toronto : Metropolitan Toronto Library Board, 1985–89. 4 v.).

Contents: v. 1–3, 1512–1857; v. 4, Indexes.

Adds 3,254 titles received by the Library since 1959. Arranged by imprint date; index in each volume. Vol. 4 is a cumulative index to v. 1–3 and covers names of individuals and corporate bodies, titles, places of publication, printers and publishers, subjects, maps and plans, and illustrations, each in a separate section. Vol. 3, p. 13–19, has key to bibliographic sources.

§ A related title: Freda Farrell Waldon, *Bibliography of Canadiana published in Great Britain, 1519–1763 = Bibliographie des ouvrages sur le Canada publiés en Grand-Bretagne entre 1519 et 1763*, rev., enl. and ed. by W.F.E. Morley ([Ottawa] : National Library of Canada; Toronto : ECW Pr., 1990. 535 p.), which provides full bibliographic information for 865 books and pamphlets including price, collation, notes on variants, notes on the title's relevance to Canada, verification sources, and locations in Canadian libraries. NUC references to American locations are noted. Cross-references; author/title index.   Z1365.T64

Waterston, Elizabeth. The travellers, Canada to 1900 : an annotated bibliography of works published in English from 1577 / Elizabeth Waterston ; with Ian Easterbrook, Bernard Katz, and Kathleen Scott. Guelph, Ontario : Univ. of Guelph, 1989. 321 p., [13] leaves of plates : ill. ; 28 cm.   **DB189**

A listing of about 700 travelers' accounts that cover more than one region of Canada. Each entry gives full title, birth and death dates of the author, collation, publishing information for first edition, microfiche number if available from the Canadian Institute for Historical Microreproduction, and an annotation summarizing the content. The extensive secondary bibliography includes sections for: Bibliographies, collections and histories; Reference books; Articles, books and dissertations on Canadian travel and exploration literature to 1900; Books and dissertations on other travel and exploration literature to 1900. Author/title index; topical index. The topical index includes sections for places, climatic conditions, institutions, people, social customs, language patterns, health care, modes of transportation, native tribes.   Z1382.W37

Dissertations

Dossick, Jesse John. Doctoral research on Canada and Canadians, 1884–1983 = Thèses de doctorat concernant le Canada et les Canadiens, 1884–1983. Ottawa : National Library of Canada, 1986. 559 p.   **DB190**

More than 12,000 items on Canadian topics from Canadian, U.S., and British institutions. Subject arrangement, with author index. An introductory note to each subject gives statistical information on dissertations in that field. The name index includes the microfilm number of dissertations filmed by the National Library.

§*Sub-doctoral theses on Canada accepted by universities in the United Kingdom & Ireland 1899–1986*, by Elspeth Reid ([Edinburgh] : British Assoc. for Canadian Studies, 1987. 10 p.) lists dissertations not included by Dossick as well as nondoctoral theses and theses submitted for the Fellowship of the Library Association. Covers all fields related to Canada, topically arranged, with author index.   Z1365.D67

Register of post-graduate dissertations in progress in history and related subjects = Répertoire des thèses en cours portant sur des sujets d'histoire et autres sujets connexes. no. 1 (1966)–. [Ottawa] : Canadian Historical Assoc., [1966]– . Annual.   **DB191**

Under the auspices of the Public Archives of Canada.

Continues the list published in the *Canadian historical review*, 1927–65. Concerned with dissertations and MA theses in progress at Canadian universities at both the master's and the doctoral level. Arranged in three parts: Completed theses, Abandoned theses, In progess. Author index.

Manuscripts; Archives

National Archives of Canada. Government Archives Division / comp. by Cynthia Lovering. [Rev. and updated ed.]. Ottawa, Ont. : National Archives of Canada, c1991. 154 p.   **DB192**

Text in English and French.

Title on added t.p. : Division des archives gouvernementales.

Revision of *Historical records of the government of Canada*, by Terry Cook and Glen T. Wright (1st ed., 1978; 2nd ed., 1981).

The Government Archives Division (as did its predecessor, Federal Records Division) houses and provides access to all permanently retained records of the departments and agencies of the government of Canada since 1867. Listing is by record group, giving brief administrative history, years covered, and amount of material in each of the subfiles. Indexed by broad subject and by agency.

The Archives' bimonthly journal *Archivist* occasionally provides updated information.   CD3626

Public Archives Canada. Guide to the reports of the Public Archives of Canada, 1872–1972 / Françoise Caron-Houle. Ottawa : [Public Archives Canada] : available from Information Canada, 1975. 97 p. : ports.   **DB193**

Provides an index to the calendars and inventories of private and public papers, documents, maps, plans, and photographs to be found in the *Annual reports* of the Public Archives. Indexed.

§ Reproduction of these calendars and inventories of the National Archives of Canada are available on microfiche as unit 1 of the *National inventory of documentary sources in Canada* (Alexandria, Md. : Chadwyck-Healey, 1991–). Also included in that series are the finding aids for the National Library of Canada.   Z5140.P82

Public Archives of Canada. General inventory : manuscripts = Inventaire général: manuscrits. Ottawa, 1971–77. v. 1–5, 7–8.   **DB194**

Contents: v. 1, MG1–MG10: Archives des colonies, Archives de la marine, Archives nationales, Archives de la guerre; Ministère des affaires étrangères, Archives départementales, municipales, maritimes, et de bibliothèques, Paris; Bibliothèques de Paris; Documents relatifs à la Nouvelle-France et au Québec (XVIIᵉ–XXᵉ siècles); Provincial, local, territorial records; Records of foreign governments; v. 2, MG11–16: Public Record Office, London: Colonial Office, Admiralty, War Office, Audit Office, Treasury, Foreign Office; v. 3, MG17–21: Archives religieuses, Documents antérieurs à la cession, Fur trade and Indians, Hudson's Bay Company archives, Transcripts from papers in the British Museum; v. 4, MG22–MG25: Autographs; Late 18th century papers; 19th century pre-Confederation papers; Genealogy; v. 5, MG26–MG27: Papers of the prime ministers; Political figures, 1867–1950; v. 7, MG29: Nineteenth century post-Confederation manuscripts; v. 8, MG80: Manuscripts of the first half of the twentieth century ("accessions completed before 1 April 1976").

"Intended to provide researchers with a complete guide to all documents kept in the Manuscript Division of the Public Archives of Canada ... [the series] will cover about 100 groups of public records (RGs) and 30 groups of manuscripts (MGs)."—*Introd.*

Preliminary inventories for both groups were published between 1951 and 1967. Entries have been revised for the *General inventory*, descriptions completed, and a more systematic arrangement devised. Covers accessions prior to Jan. 1, 1972. Includes descriptions of microfilm copies of documents from archives outside Canada as well as the Canadian documents in the Public Archives. Detailed index in each volume.

The Archives' "General inventory series" describes specific record groups as to content and availability (no. 1–9 publ. 1975–77, plus unnumbered issues publ. 1979–81).   DC3626

Union list of manuscripts in Canadian repositories = Catalogue collectif des manuscrits des archives canadiennes / Robert S. Gordon, director ; E. Grace Maurice, ed. Rev. ed. Ottawa : Public Archives, 1975. 2 v. (1578 p.).   **DB195**

Cooperative project of the Public Archives of Canada and the Humanities Research Council of Canada.

Title also in French; text in English or French.

1st ed., 1968.

Represents about 27,000 collections in 171 repositories. Arranged by name of the collection with an index of names, subjects, and cross references. An added feature is a Catalogue-by-repositories, which brings together the names of all collections in a given repository.

————. ————. *Supplement*, 1976–1981/82 (issued annually; no more published?). Adds new acquisitions from a varying number of institutions; in addition, the 1976 publication includes some 1,000 entries omitted from the basic work. CD3622.A2U54

Wilson, Bruce. Manuscripts and government records in the United Kingdom and Ireland relating to Canada = Manuscrits et documents gouvernementaux au Royaume-Uni et Irlande concernant le Canada / Bruce G. Wilson, ed. ; Anita Burdett, Bruce G. Wilson, compilers. Ottawa : National Archives Canada, 1992. 705 p. **DB196**

Text in English and French.

Surveys 872 repositories and private collections in Great Britain and Ireland for original materials (including microfilms) significant to the study of Canadian political, economic, social, intellectual, cultural, and scientific life. Geographically arranged by repository. For each gives address, any published guides, and a brief description of the relevant portions. Many of the materials described have been copied and are available in the National Archives of Canada. Detailed subject index. F1029.9.W559

Encyclopedias; Dictionaries

Bercuson, David Jay. The Collins dictionary of Canadian history : 1867 to the present / David J. Bercuson and J. L. Granatstein. Toronto : Collins, 1988. 270 p. : ill. **DB197**

An alphabetical arrangement of 1,600 articles covering "people, institutions, and events [together with] key terms to answer the most commonly asked queries about our collective past."—*Pref.* Short entries with cross-references indicated by small capitals, with many black-and-white illustrations. Chronology in five parallel columns: Major political events; Major social, economic and industrial events; Science and technology; Artistic and cultural events; Sporting events. Appendix of statistical tables, maps, and chronological list by province of governors-general, prime ministers, all provincial premiers. Not indexed. F1033.B488

The Canadian encyclopedia. 2nd ed. Edmonton : Hurtig, c1988. 4 v. (2736 p.) : ill., maps in color, ports. **DB198**

Editor in chief, James H. Marsh.

1st ed., 1985.

Includes entries for all aspects of Canadian life—e.g., places, people, political themes, flora and fauna, historical background, ethnic groups, titles of literary works. Signed articles by specialists, many with short bibliographies. General index; excellent illustrations. This edition adds much new material, updates statistics to incorporate 1986 census figures, and expands the index (p. 2365–2736). A supplementary volume is planned.

§ An older set, widely held and still useful, is *Encyclopedia Canadiana*, ed., Kenneth H. Pearson (Toronto : Grolier, 1977. 10 v.) with well written articles, plentiful and well-chosen illustrations, and an extensive atlas.

For French Canada *see*: Jean Marie Le Jeune, *Dictionnaire général de biographie, histoire, littérature, agriculture, commerce, industrie et des arts, sciences, moers, coutumes, institutions politiques et religieuses du Canada* ([Ottawa] : Univ. d'Ottawa, [1931]. 2 v.). A general encyclopedia heavily illustrated, with bibliographies ending most articles, and strongest on matters dealing with French Canada. F1006.C35

Directories

National Library of Canada. Research collections in Canadian libraries. Ottawa : Information Canada, 1972–1984. 2 v. in 15 pts. : maps. (In progress). **DB199**

Portions having particular relevance for history and area studies include: Section I, Universities; v. 1, Prairie provinces; v. 2, Atlantic provinces; v. 3, British Columbia; v. 4, Ontario; v. 5, Quebec; v. 6, Canada. Section II, Special studies: v. 2, Federal government libraries; v. 3, Law library resources in Canada; v. 5, Collections of official publications in Canada; v. 9, Resources for native peoples studies. For complete information, *see* AK128. Z735.A1N37

———————— Canadian directories, 1790–1987 : a bibliography and place-name index = Annuaires canadiens, 1790–1987 : une bibliographie et un index des noms de lieux / Mary E. Bond. Ottawa : National Library of Canada, 1989. 3 v. : ill. **DB200**

A directory of 1,200 directories arranged chronologically then by province, city, town, township, county, district, or region. Based on the collections at the National Library of Canada and the library of the National Archives. Vol. 1 is the bibliography; v. 2–3, place-name indexes. Z5771.4C3N37

Répertoire international des études canadiennes = International directory of Canadian studies. [1992]– . Ottawa : Conseil international d'études canadiennes = International Council for Canadian Studies, c[1992]– . Biennial (irregular). **DB201**

Continues: *International directory to Canadian studies = Répertoire international des études canadiennes*, publ. 1980/1981–1988/89. Also absorbed *Directory of Canadianists*.

Directory of programs, courses, publications, and specialists in Canadian studies in America, Europe, Asia and Australia. Based on questionnaires. Text in English and French. Subject and name indexes. F1025.I57

Handbooks

Canada / ed. by Mel Watkins. N.Y. : Facts on File, c1993. 701 p. : maps. **DB202**

Survey articles by scholars and researchers (many Canadian) are grouped in five areas: Provinces and territories, History, Politics, Economy, Social Affairs. Maps; tables in Comparative statistics section. Suggestions for further reading at end of each article. Topical index. F1008.C2

General histories

The Canadian centenary series : a history of Canada / ed. by W. L. Morton, D. G. Creighton, Ramsey Cook. Toronto : McClelland & Stewart ; N.Y. : Oxford Univ. Pr., 1963–1989. 19 v. **DB203**

Contents: v. 1, Early voyages and northern approaches, 1000–1632, by T. J. Oleson; v. 2, The beginnings of New France, 1524–1663, by Margaret Trudel; v. 3, Canada under Louis XIV, 1663–1701, by W. J. Eccles; v. 4, New France 1701–1744, by D. Miquelon; v. 5, New France: the last phase, 1744–1760, by G. F. G. Stanley; v. 6, Quebec: the revolutionary age, 1760–1791, by H. M. Neatby; v. 7, Upper Canada: the formative years, 1784–1841, by G. M. Craig; v. 8, Lower Canada, 1791–1840, by F. Ouellet; v. 9, The Atlantic provinces: the emergence of colonial society, 1712–1857, by W. S. MacNutt; v. 10, The union of the Canadas: the growth of Canadian institutions, 1841–1857, by J. M. S. Careless; v. 11, The fur trade and the Northwest to 1857, by E. E. Rich; v. 12, The critical years: the union of British North America, 1857–1873, by W. L. Morton; v. 13, Canada 1874–1896: arduous destiny, by P. B. Waite; v. 14, Canada, 1896–1921; a nation transformed, by Robert Craig Brown and Ramsey Cook; v. 15, Canada 1922–1939, by J. H. Thompson; v. 16, The opening of the Canadian North, 1870–1914, by M. Zaslow; v. 17, The northward expansion of Canada 1914–1967, by M. Zaslow; v. 18, The forked road: Canada 1939–1957, by D. Creighton; v. 19, Canada, 1957–1967, by J. L. Granatstein.

Each period is treated by a specialist, and the series forms the definitive history of Canada. Copious notes, lengthy bibliographies. Index.

Vol. 2 is mainly a condensation of v. 1–3 of Marcel Trudel, *Histoire de la Nouvelle-France* (Montreal, 1963–75). Vol. 8 is a translation and abridgment of Ouellet's *Le Bas-Canada* (Ottawa, 1976, 1980).

Current surveys

Canadian news facts. v.1, no.1 (Jan. 16, 1967)– . Toronto : Marpep, 1967– .   **DB204**
   Subtitle: The indexed digest of Canadian current events.
   Biweekly with monthly indexes cumulating quarterly and annually.

   A looseleaf synopsis of Canadian news events (similar to *Facts on file*) under such headings as: Canada in the world, Canada-U.S. relations, Economy, Energy, Federal-provincial relations, Sports, Names in the news, Obituaries.

Sourcebooks

Canadian historical documents series. Scarborough, Ont. : Prentice-Hall of Canada, [1965–66]. 3 v.   **DB205**
   Contents: v. 1, The French régime, ed. and tr. by C. Nish; v. 2, Pre-Confederation, ed. by P. B. Waite; v. 3, Confederation to 1949, ed. by R. C. Brown and M. E. Prang.
   Offers collections of important Canadian historical documents, indicating original sources, and with introductory notes. Bibliography of primary and secondary sources in each volume.
   § A very useful one-volume selection of texts is John William Michael Bliss, *Canadian history in documents, 1763–1966* (Toronto : Ryerson Pr., c1966. 397 p.) which presents documents topically. Each has a headnote which gives brief context and bibliographical citation of the original. Topical index.

Documenting Canada : a history of modern Canada in documents / Dave De Brou and Bill Waiser, editors. Saskatoon, Sask. : Fifth House Publishers, c1992. 702 p.   **DB206**
   Reprints "the [212] most significant federal documents in Canadian history"—*Introd*. Some documents are not completely rendered. An explanatory paragraph accompanies each document. Emphasizes the post-World War II period and concentrates on documents at the federal level: acts, charters, treaties, orders in council and judicial rulings. Topics range from the study of gender relations to aboriginal peoples and the environment. Index by subject and title; no bibliography.
                                                            F1033.D63

Atlases

Historical atlas of Canada / R. Cole Harris, ed. ; Geoffrey J. Matthews, cartographer/designer. Toronto ; Buffalo, N.Y. : Univ. of Toronto Pr., [1987–93]. 3 v. : ill., maps in color ; 38 cm.   **DB207**
   Also publ. in French as: *Atlas historique du Canada*.
   Contents: v. 1, From the beginning to 1800 (1987. 198 p.); v. 2, The land transformed 1800–1891 (1993. 184 p.); v. 3, Addressing the twentieth century, 1891–1961 (1990. 197 p.).
   "Our aim was to use the latest research in historical geography, history, and related disciplines to present the social and economic evolution of Canada."—*Foreword*. Vol. 1 presents maps, drawings, and charts for the prehistorical period, with subsequent periods treated under geographical divisions; e.g., The Atlantic realm, Inland expansion, The St. Lawrence settlements, The Northwest, and ending with

Canada in 1800. Notes for each plate list primary and secondary sources. Vol. 2 emphasizes themes reflecting the "transformation of a thinly populated, marginally viable group of colonies in 1800 to consolidated Canada of the 1890s, poised for industrial expansion."—*Pref.* Vol. 3 has two sections: The great transformation 1891–1929, and Crisis and response, 1930s–1961. The 66 plates "examine Canada's past through specific groups and individuals in specific times and places."—*Pref.* Within each section the maps are presented chronologically, but each features multivariables. Source is given for each map and there are often suggestions for further reading.
   § Donald Gordon Grady Kerr's *Historical atlas of Canada* (3rd rev. ed. Don Mills, Ont. : Nelson, 1975. 100 p.) is still a very useful one-volume atlas for the history of Canada up to the early 1970s.
                                                            G1116.S1H5

Trudel, Marcel. Atlas de la Nouvelle-France = An atlas of New France. Québec : Presses de l'Université Laval, 1968. 219 p. : ill, maps ; 30 cm.   **DB208**
   Repr., 1973.
   A further revision and expansion of the author's 1948 work *Collection de cartes anciennes et modernes pour servir à l'étude de l'histoire de l'Amérique et du Canada* which was published in a revised edition in 1961 under the title *Atlas historique du Canada français des origines à 1867*.
   General maps, grouped by century, are presented first, followed by special maps of settlements, population, and cities.   G1116.S1T7

Statistics

Historical statistics of Canada. 2nd ed. / F. H. Leacy, ed. [Ottawa] : Publ. by Statistics Canada in joint sponsorship with the Social Science Federation of Canada, c1983. ca.900 p.
                                                            DB209
   For annotation, *see* CG113.   HA745.H57

Regional and local

Artibise, Alan F. J. Canada's urban past : a bibliography to 1980 and guide to Canadian urban studies / Alan F. J. Artibise and Gilbert A. Stelter. Vancouver : Univ. of British Columbia Pr., [1981]. 396 p.   **DB210**
   A major reference compilation of some 7,000 entries (books, articles, and theses) topically arranged within a general section and sections for each province. Author, geographical, and subject indexes. Supplements appear in *Urban history review* (1981–84, Oct. issue).
   § A similar publication, *Bibliography of Canadian urban history*, comp. by F. H. Armstrong, A. F. J. Artibise, and Melvin Baker (Monticello, Ill. : Vance Bibliographies, 1980. 6 v.) follows much the same arrangement.   Z7165.C2A77

———————— Western Canada since 1870 : a select bibliography and guide. Vancouver : Univ. of British Columbia Pr., c1978. 294 p. : ill.   **DB211**
   A selective bibliography of books, pamphlets, periodical articles, theses and dissertations on any area of Western Canadian studies (i.e., Manitoba, Saskatchewan, Alberta, British Columbia). Topical arrangement; author index. Select subject index for ethnic groups and political parties and politicians.   Z1392.N7A77

Bishop, Olga B. Bibliography of Ontario history, 1867–1976 : cultural, economic, political, social / by Olga B. Bishop, assisted by Barbara I. Irwin, Clara G. Miller. Toronto : Univ. of Toronto Pr., 1980. 2 v. (1760 p.).   **DB212**
   1st ed., 1978, had title: *Ontario since 1867*.
   An extensive bibliography covering all periods. Topically organized; includes books, periodicals, and government reports.

§ Updated by: *Annual bibliography of Ontario history* (1980–85. Sudbury, Ont. : Laurentian Univ. Pr., 1980–86), sponsored by the Ontario Historical Society. Z1392.O6O67

Canadian local histories to 1950 : a bibliography / W. F. E. Morley, ed. [Toronto] : Univ. of Toronto Pr., [1967–78]. 3 v. **DB213**

Contents: v. 1, The Atlantic provinces, by W. F. E. Morley (137 p.); v. 2, Quebec, by André Beaulieu (328 p.); v. 3, Ontario and the Canadian North, by W. F. E. Morley (322 p.).

Extensive bibliographies with locations of copies.

§ *Atlantic provinces checklist: a guide to current information in books, pamphlets, government publications, magazine articles and documentary films relating to the four Atlantic provinces* (Halifax, N.S. : Maritime Library Assoc., 1958–74. 10 v.) lists relevant publications of 1957–72.

The Prairie provinces are dealt with in Bruce Braden Peel's *A bibliography of the Prairie Provinces to 1953* (DB216).

Dekin, Albert A. Arctic archaeology : a bibliography and history. N.Y. : Garland, 1978. 279 p. (Garland reference library of science and technology, v. 1). **DB214**

For the most part, the Arctic is here defined as Alaska, the present Tundra regions of Canada and Greenland, and parts of the coasts of Quebec, Labrador, and Newfoundland. The bulk of the volume is a history of the research and publications on Arctic archaeology; the bibliography is an author listing of books, articles and book reviews, essays, dissertations and conference papers, and technical reports. Includes a short directory of museums with extensive Arctic archaeological materials, and a list of serial publications with significant content on the subject. No index. E99.E7D36

Messier, Jean-Jacques. Bibliographie relative à la Nouvelle-France. Montréal : L'Aurore, c1979. 198 p. **DB215**

A classed bibliography of books, theses and periodical articles. Includes agriculture, archaeology, art, cartography, commerce, costume, exploration, economy, folklore, religious history, military affairs, money, population, etc. About 2,300 entries. Mainly French-language material. Author index. Z1383.M47

Peel, Bruce Braden. A bibliography of the Prairie Provinces to 1953 : with biographical index. 2nd [enl.] ed. [Toronto] : Univ. of Toronto Pr., [c1973]. 780 p. **DB216**

1st ed., 1956; suppl., 1963.

Lists books and pamphlets on the region defined by the compiler as "that agricultural arc resting on the international boundary." Chronological arrangement with author and subject indexes. The new edition was expanded to include a selection of post-1953 publications, as well as earlier books and documents not previously noted. Z1392.P7P43

Mexico

Bibliography

Beltrán Bernal, Trinidad. Bibliografía histórica del Estado de México / Trinidad Beltrán Bernal, Eliva Montes de Oca N. [Zinacantepec, Edo. de México] : El Colegio Mexiquense, 1989–1992. 3 v. (In progess). **DB217**

An annotated listing of books, articles, government publications, and pamphlets. Arranged by period up to the 1940s, with subdivisions for topics such as archaeology, literature, history, economics. Vol. 3 is a supplement to both, listing 2,100 books, articles, pamphlets, and government documents following the same arrangement. Each volume has its own author index. Z1427.M61B45

Bibliografía comentada sobre la mujer mexicana / María Soledad Arbeláez A. ... [et al.]. Col. Roma, México, D.F. : Dirección de Estudios Históricos, Instituto Nacional de Antropología e Historia, 1988. 438, [19] p. : ill. **DB218**

1,046 entries for books, pamphlets, documents, theses, articles, and mimeographed studies, mostly published 1960–85, though some are earlier. Alphabetical by author; annotated. Subject index.

§ See also *Bibliografía sobre la mujer* (México : Comisión Nacional de la Mujer, 1986. 248 p. 1st ed., 1984 [55 p.]) for books, articles, and U.N. documents. Not indexed. Z7964.M4B5

Bibliografía general del desarrollo económico de México 1500–1976 / Jorge Ceballos ... [et al.]. México : SEP, Inst. Nacional de Antropología e Historia, Departamento de Investigaciones Historicas, 1980. 3 v. (1177 p.). (Colección científica, 76). **DB219**

An extensive, annotated bibliography, topically arranged, but with no period divisions. Especially strong for 19th century material. Particularly useful for 20th century study is a description of the content of each census taken since 1895. Author index; locates copies in 34 Mexican and U.S. libraries. Z7165.M45B525

Bustamante, Jorge A. México—Estados Unidos : bibliografía general sobre estudios fronterizos / Jorge A. Bustamante asistido por Francisco Malagamba A. México : El Colegio de México, 1980. 251 p. **DB220**

Following a lengthy introduction (which includes statistical tables), 2,290 books, articles, theses, and films are listed under 14 broad topics such as Mexican–U.S. relations, Sociopolitical movements, Chicanos. Author index.

§ Two annuals cover relations with the United States: *Mexico–Estados Unidos*, 1982– (Mexico : El Colegio de México, 1982–) and *Relaciones México–Estados Unidos : bibliografío anual*, 1980– (México : El Colegio de México, 1982–). Z1361.R4B87

Cole, Garold. American travelers to Mexico, 1821–1972 : a descriptive bibliography. Troy, N.Y. : Whitston, 1978. 139 p. **DB221**

An annotated author bibliography of some 477 accounts (excluding guidebooks, promotional literature, etc.) in books or parts of books. Lacks an index. Z1425.C64

Cosío Villegas, Daniel. Cuestiones internacionales de México : una bibliografía. México : Secretaría de Relaciones Exteriores, 1966. 588 p. (Archivo Histórico Diplomático Mexicano. Guías para la historia diplomática de México, 4). **DB222**

Presents 10,776 items in classed arrangement on all aspects of Mexican international relations and diplomatic affairs. Indexed.

Extranjeros en México, 1821–1990 : bibliografía / Dolores Pla ... [et al.]. México, D.F. : Instituto Nacional de Antropología e Historia, 1993. 153 p. **DB223**

Locates copies in Mexican libraries. Topical arrangement for Western language titles on foreigners in Mexico, 1821–1990. Broad section on immigration followed by sections on specific groups, e.g., Chinese, Mennonites, Spanish refugees. Lengthy reviews of academic publications in Spanish. Appendix for 1991 92 publications. Not indexed. Z7164.I3E28

Flores Villela, Carlos Arturo. México, la cultura, el arte y la vida cotidiana. México, D.F. : Coordinación de Humanidades, Universidad Nacional Autónoma de México, 1990. 2 v. (561 p.). (Cuadernos del CIIH. Serie fuentes, 7). **DB224**

Almost 7,000 references are arranged in 51 broad headings (e.g., Architecture, Literature, Kitsch, Urbanism, Chicanos) with subsections for categories such as general works, theory, biographies. Cites books and articles. Author index. Z1429.C58F57

Gerhard, Peter. A guide to the historical geography of New Spain. Rev. ed. Norman : Univ. of Oklahoma Pr., 1993. 484 p. **DB225**

Offers a "regional listing of contemporary source material descriptive of central and southern Mexico throughout the three centuries of Spanish rule, and a synthesis of certain data gleaned from these documents."—*Pref.* Includes bibliographical references to governors, agriculture, church, population, and settlements.

§ Two companion volumes by Gerhard: *The North frontier of New Spain* (Princeton, N.J. : Princeton Univ. Pr., 1982. 454 p.) and *The Southeast frontier of New Spain* (Princeton, 1979. 213 p.).
F1231.G37

González y González, Luis. Fuentes de la historia contemporánea de México : libros y folletos / estudio preliminar, ordenamiento y compilación de Luis González, con la colaboración de Guadelupe Monroy y Susana Uribe. México : El Colegio de México, 1961–1962. 3 v.   **DB226**
Contents: v. 1, Generalidades. Territorio. Sociedad; v. 2, Economía. Política. Religión; v. 3, Educación. Filosofía y ciencias. Letras y artes.
An extensive bibliography on the whole range of Mexican culture, 1910–40. Vol. 3 contains general and title indexes.   Z1426.5.G6

Köppen, Elke. Movimientos sociales en México (1968–1987). México : Coordinación de Humanidades, Universidad Nacional Autónoma de México, 1989. 136 p. (Cuadernos del CIIH. Serie Fuentes, 4).   **DB227**
At head of title: Centro de Investigaciones Interdisciplinarias en Humanidades.
Lists 1,268 entries for books, essays, pamphlets, articles on social movements in Mexico. Topical arrangement (e.g., student, women, religious), with indexes for author and state.   Z7164.S66K66

López Cervantes, Gonzalo. Ensayo bibliográfico del periodo colonial de México / Gonzalo López Cervantes y Rosa García García. México, D.F. : Instituto Nacional de Antropología e Historia, 1989. 235 p.   **DB228**
An extensive bibliography of 2,424 books, articles and documents, published 16th–20th centuries. Arranged by broad topics, e.g., Conquest and colonization, Architecture, Religion, Literature, Bibliographies and guides to archives. Author index.   F1426.L67

López Rosado, Diego H. Bibliografía de historia económica y social de México. México : Univ. Nacional Autónoma de México, 1979–1982. 13 v. (Instituto de Investigaciones Bibliográfias. Serie: Bibliografías, 8).   **DB229**
Contents: v. 1, Fuentes para el estudio de la agricultura, la ganadería y la silvicultura de México; v. 2, ... propiedad de la tierra y colonización; v. 3, ... mineria y el petróleo; v. 4, ... industria y la promoción industrial; v. 5, ... comunicaciones y transportes; v. 6, ... relaciones de trabajo; v. 7, ... comercio interior y exterior; v. 8, ... sistemas monetario y del crédito; v. 9, ... finanzas públicas; v. 10, ... obras publicas; v. 11, ... clases sociales; v. 12, ... organización politica y los partidos políticos; v. 13, índice general; bibliografía general; índice de materias.
A bibliography of Spanish-language books, articles, government documents, etc., covering economic and social history of Mexico from pre-Hispanic times through 1925. Classified arrangement within period divisions; works are closely analyzed.   Z7165.M45L66

México. Comisión de Estudios Militares. Biblioteca del Ejército. Apuntes para una bibliografía militar de México, 1536–1936 : recopilación de fichas bibliográficas hecha por los delegados de la Secretaría de guerra y marina, con ocasión del primer Congreso bibliográfico, convocado por el Ateneo nacional de ciencias y artes de México / Sección de estudios militares del Ateneo, mayor M. C. Néstor Herrera Gómez, mayor Silvino M. González. México : Talleres gráficos de la nación, 1937. 469 p. : ill.; facsims.   **DB230**
A bibliography of more than 1,800 titles on Mexican military history, 1536–1936.   Z6725.M6M6

Philip, George D.E. Mexico. Rev. and expanded ed. Oxford, Eng. ; Santa Barbara, Calif. : Clio Pr., c1993. 195 p. (World bibliographical series, 48).   **DB231**
Previous ed., 1984, comp. by Naomi C. Robbins.
Presents 640 annotated entries arranged in 48 subject categories. Highly selective, with all but a few items in English. Author, title, subject indexes.   Z1411.P45

Raat, W. Dirk. The Mexican Revolution : an annotated guide to recent scholarship. Boston : G. K. Hall, [1982]. 275 p.   **DB232**
Nearly 1,250 items (both books and periodical articles) are listed in classed arrangement, with subject and name indexes. Does not replace Roberto Ramos, *Bibliografía de la revolución mexicana* (DB233) for older materials.   Z1426.5.R15

Ramos, Roberto. Bibliografía de la revolución mexicana. 2. ed. México : Instituto Nacional de Estudios Históricos de la Revolución Mexicana, 1959–60. 3 v. (Biblioteca del Instituto Nacional de Estudios Históricos de la Revolución Mexicana., 15).   **DB233**
More than 5,000 items on the Mexican revolution, 1910–22. Vols. 1–2 are reprints of the edition published 1931–35. v. 3, originally published in 1940, has been considerably expanded, listing nearly 2,000 items published since 1935.   Z1426.5.R2

Ross, Stanley Robert. Fuentes de la historia contemporánea de México : periódicos y revistas. [México] : Colegio de México, [1965]–1978. 5 v. (Serie Bibliografías, 4).   **DB234**
Publisher varies.
A classed bibliography of articles from Spanish-language magazines, newspapers, and journals published in Mexico and the southwestern United States between 1908 and 1968. Brief annotations; indexes of authors, names, and places in vols. 2 and 5.   Z1426.5.R6

Sutro Library. Catalogue of Mexican pamphlets in the Sutro collection (1623–[1888]) / prep. by the personnel of the Works Progress Administration Project no. 665-08-3-236. A. Yedidia, supervisor. P. Radin, ed. Sponsored by the California State Library. San Francisco, 1939–1940. 10 pts. (963 p.).   **DB235**
A chronological listing of a large collection of pamphlets, in the Spanish language, on Mexico or printed in Mexico.
———. ———. *Supplement (1605–1887)* (1941. 3 pts. [290 p.].
———. ———. *Author index* (1941. 65 p.) covers both the main work and the supplement. Both the supplement and the author index were reprinted with the main work by Kraus in 1971; separate pagination retained.

Tutorow, Norman E. The Mexican-American war : an annotated bibliography. Westport, Conn. : Greenwood, 1981. 427 p. : maps.   **DB236**
About 4,500 items in eight main sections: (1) Reference works; (2) Manuscript collections; (3) Government documents; (4) National archives of the U.S.; (5) Periodical literature; (6) Books; (7) Theses and dissertations; (8) Miscellaneous works: graphics, cartography, and addenda. Sections are topically or geographically subdivided as appropriate. Indexed.   Z1241.T87

Dissertations

Catálogo de tesis sobre historia de México / supervisión, Enrique Florescano ... [et al.]. México : Comité Mexicano de Ciencias Históricas, 1976. 173 p. : ill.   **DB237**
Dissertations and masters theses from Mexican and some U.S. universities, arranged by broad topic, e.g., archeology; political history; regional history by state. Name index.
§ Continued by: *Segundo catalog de tesis sobre historia de México / Cecilia Greaves ... [et al.] (1984. 365 p.).*   Z1425.C37

Guides to records

Archivo General de la Nación. México : guía general / coordinacíon general, Juan Manuel Herrera Huerta, Victoria San Vicente Tello. México, D.F. : Secretaría de Gobernación, 1990. 525 p. : ill., ports, facsims, maps; 32 cm.   **DB238**
Following a brief history and discussion of how to use the archive, gives brief description of each file including period covered, size, any finding aids, and related sources. Appendixes for colonial and

national administrators, 1521–1990, maps. Indexes by categories of material, e.g., archives of individuals, archives of colonial institutions, illustrations, and maps. Alphabetical list of documentary groups.

§ See also *Serie archivos estatales y municipales de México* (México : El Caballito, 1984–87. 5 v.), which is a guide to holdings of archives in Mexico City.   CD3656

Bieber, León Enrique. Katalog der Quellen zur Geschichte Mexikos in der Bundesrepublik Deutschland, 1521–1945 = Catálogo de las fuentes para la historia de México en la República Federal de Alemania, 1521–1945. Berlin : Colloquium Verlag, 1990. 405 p. (Bibliotheca Ibero-Americana, Bd. 35).   **DB239**

A list of files of archives in West Germany, first those in the Central Archives and then files in official archives of the various states. Most of the materials cited are 20th century, but earlier years are represented. For each file gives title, number of pages, and a classmark. A directory lists names of archives with address, phone number and hours. Topical index.   Z1425.B55

Greenleaf, Richard E. Research in Mexican history : topics, methodology, sources and a practical guide to field research / Richard E. Greenleaf, Michael C. Meyer. Lincoln : Univ. of Nebraska Pr., [1973]. 226 p.   **DB240**

"Comp. for the Committee on Mexican Studies, Conference on Latin American History."—*t.p.*

An extremely useful guide to doing research in Mexican archives. Offers chapters by contributing scholars on specific archives, periods, or topics. Includes practical information and suggestions for topics needing research.   F1225.5.G73

Universidad Nacional Autónoma de México. Instituto de Investigaciones Bibliográficas. Serie guías. México : Univ. Nacional Autónoma de México, Inst. de Invest. Bibliograficas, 1969–78. 6 v.   **DB241**

Contents: v. 1, Grajales Ramos, G. Guía de documentos para la historia de México en archivos ingleses (siglo XIX) (1969. 455 p.); v. 2, Moreno Valle, L. Catálogo de la Colección Lafragua de la Biblioteca Nacional de México, 1821–1853 (1975. 1203 p.); v. 3, Río, I. Guía del Archivo Franciscano de la Biblioteca Nacional de México (1975. 499 p.); v. 4, Yhmhoff Cabrera, J. Catálogo de obras manuscritas en Latin de la Biblioteca Nacional de México (1975. 459 p.); v. 5, Fernández de Zamora, R. M. Las publicaciones oficiales de México, guía de publicaciones periódicas y seriadas, 1937–1970 (1977. 238 p.); v. 6, Quínones Melgoza, J. Catálogo de obras de autores latinos en servicio en la Biblioteca Nacional de México (1978. 133 p.). No more published?

Encyclopedias

Diccionario histórico y biográfico de la Revolución Mexicana. México, D.F. : Instituto Nacional de Estudios Históricos de la Revolución Mexicana, Secretaría de Gobernación, 1990–92. 7 v.   **DB242**

A short-entry dictionary of people, political parties, battles, and other acts of war, publications, congresses, popular songs, etc. relating to the Mexican Revolution, 1890–1920. Arranged by state; each section begins with a survey of the Revolution in that state and ends with a chronology, a list of governors and a short bibliography. Lacks an index.

§ The material for the state of Mexico has been expanded and published separately: *Diccionario biográfico y histórico de la Revolución Mexicana en el Estado de México*, ed, Roberto Blancare (Zinacantepec : El Colegio Mexiquense, 1992. 298 p.).   F1234.D595

Diccionario Porrúa de historia, biografía y geografía de México. 5. ed. corr. y aum., con un suplemento / ed. Miguel León Portilla. México, D. F. : Editorial Porrúa, 1986. 3 v. (3282 p.) : ill., maps.   **DB243**

1st ed., 1964; 4th ed., 1976.

An encyclopedia of Mexican affairs, running heavily to entries for personal and place names. The fifth edition reprints the third edition, with some articles added from the fourth edition supplement. Not indexed.   F1204.D56

Enciclopedia de México / director, José Rogelio Alvarez. Ed. especial. Ciudad de México : Enciclopedia de México : Secretaría de Educación Pública, 1987–1988. 14 v. (8460 p.) : ill.   **DB244**

1st ed., 1966–71; v. 5–12 are 3rd. ed.

Some articles are signed; some carry bibliographies. Heavily illustrated. Statistics are current to 1986. Vol. 14 is a kind of index with the articles classed by broad topics and biographical articles classed by profession.   F1204.E46

Enciclopedia yucatanense. 2. ed. / patrocinada por el Gobierno del Estado de Yucatán a cargo del Dr. Francisco Luna Kan; publicada bajo la dirección de la Comisión Reeditora de la Enciclopedia Yucatanense, integrada por Luis H. Hoyos Villanueva [et al.]. México : Gobierno de Yucatán, 1977–1981. 12 v. : ill.   **DB245**

1st ed., 1944–47, ed. C. A. Echánove Trujillo. This set is a reprint of the 1st ed., with an additional three volumes of new material. Vol. 8 of the earlier edition, a general Yucatan bibliography, is now divided between v. 8 and v. 9, with indexes of subjects, names, and illustrations added; also contains a supplement updating the bibliography to 1947. Vols. 10 and 11 are supplements.

A classed encyclopedia aiming to cover all aspects of Yucatan history and life. Each section is written by an authority, and most have bibliographies. Vol. 7, *Biografías*, deals with only 14 individuals, but more biographical material is included in an extensive alphabetical list of works published in and on the Yucatan.   F1376.E55

Musacchio, Humberto. Diccionario enciclopédico de México. México, D.F. : A. León, ed., 1989. 4 v. : ill.   **DB246**

Short articles about people, places, organizations, journals, and newspapers, together with longer articles on topics such as political parties or education. Special emphasis on art and the cinema. Alphabetical arrangement. Lacks an index or cross references.   F1204.M95

Nieto López, J. de Jesús. Diccionario histórico del México contemporáneo, 1900–1982. México, D.F. : Alhambra Mexicana, 1986. 214 p.   **DB247**

Short entries for events, terms, political movements, personalities, and trends are arranged alphabetically. Chronology, 1900–1982, with events listed under each year. Useful for identification, definition, etc. Not indexed.   F1234.N53

Handbooks

Atlas cultural de México. [México, D.F.] : Secretaría de Educación Pública, Instituto Nacional de Antropología e Historia : Grupo Editorial Planeta, 1987–1988. 12 v. : ill. (some col.).   **DB248**

Contents: v. [1], Arqueología; v. [2], Turismo; v. [3], Artesanías; v. [4], Flora; v. [5], Museos; v. [6], Monumentos históricos; v. [7], Fauna; v. [8], Gastronomía; v. [9], Lingüística; v. [10]–[11], Cartográfico; v. [12], Música. Volume designation is arbitrary.

A collection of essays, heavily illustrated. Some volumes have bibliographies; some have subject indexes.

§ Also useful is *Atlas histórico de México*, comp. by Enrique Florescano and Alejandra Moreno Toscano (Mexico : Siglo Veintiuno Ed., 1983. 222 p. ; 30 x 34 cm.), with 105 black-and-white maps to illustrate the history of Mexico, 35,000 BCE to the 1970s. Cites sources.   F1216.5.A88

Barnes, Thomas Charles. Northern New Spain : a research guide / Thomas C. Barnes, Thomas H. Naylor, Charles W. Polzer. Tucson : Univ. of Arizona Pr., c1981. 147 p. : maps.
                                                            DB249
A very helpful aid for research in colonial history of Northern Mexico and the U.S. Southwest. Through discussion, tables and descriptions covers archives in Mexico, U.S. and Europe; structure of the colonial government; money and currency; weights and measures; nomenclature of native groups; and lists of colonial officials. Maps; glossary; bibliography with each chapter.   Z1251.S8B37

The border guide : institutions and organizations of the United States-Mexico borderlands / by Milton H. Jamail and Margo Gutiérrez. 2nd updated and rev. ed. Austin, Tex. : Center for Mexican American Studies, Univ. of Texas at Austin, 1992. 193 p.   **DB250**
Rev. ed. of: *The United States-Mexico border : a guide to institutions, organizations, and scholars* (1980).

A handbook for the region giving descriptions and local listings for border communities; directories of U.S., Mexican and state government offices, and lists of television stations, educational resources, chambers of commerce; select bibliography of borderland topics, and a guide to conducting library research. Based on questionnaires, on-site visits, and published guides. Appendix provides population and border crossing statistics and a directory of public health organizations in the region.   F787.J35

LATIN AMERICA

General works

Guides

Latin America and the Caribbean : a critical guide to research sources / ed. by Paula H. Covington ... [et al.]. N.Y. : Greenwood, 1992. 924 p. (Bibliographies and indexes in Latin American and Caribbean studies, no. 2).   **DB251**
A major reference work, the starting point for the advanced student, researcher and scholar. It intends to identify "relevant bibliographic research sources ... [as well as] principal sources beyond their own specialization."—*Introd.* Arranged by discipline, subdivided by country. Each section begins with an essay written by a specialist offering a "general discussion of research and access to information within the discipline and its subfields, along with a description of the nature and evolution of the source material, and recent research trends." The essay is followed by a bibliography of the major resources with lengthy, well-written annotations. The sections often end with a brief listing of relevant special collections. Very basic resources are cited in several sections. Coverage is strongest for materials published up to 1988, with some later titles. Author, title, and subject indexes.
                                                            Z1601.L3225

Latin American studies : a basic guide to sources / Robert A. McNeil, ed. ; Barbara G. Valk, associate ed. 2nd ed., rev. and enl. Metuchen, N.J. : Scarecrow, 1990. 458 p.   **DB252**
1st. ed., by Julia Garlant [et al.], ed. by Laurence Halliwell, had title: *Latin American bibliography*.

A basic handbook for researchers, compiled by a group of librarians. Discusses major Latin American library collections in Great Britain, Western Europe, and the U.S., and describes how to use them; indicates major bibliographies available (subject, national, and personal) and notes other kinds of reference sources (e.g., dictionaries, newspapers, etc., including nonprint resources such as databases, visual materials). Ends with a discussion of career development in the field and lists institutions with Latin American programs, opportunities for study abroad, societies, conferences, travel guides. Subject and author/title indexes.   Z1601.L324

Bibliography

Alcina Franch, José. Bibliografía básica de arqueología americana. [Madrid] : Ediciones Cultura Hispánica, Instituto de Cooperación Iberoamericana, [1985]. 475 p.   **DB253**
1st ed., 1960.
A major source for bibliography, listing 7,610 entries for printed books, articles, essays or important chapters, mostly in Spanish and English but with a few in other Western European languages. Arranged by period then by country or region. Author, geographical and topical indexes.
§ The bibliography "Current research" in the October and January issues of *American antiquity* updates this work.   Z1208.A2A45

Chilcote, Ronald H. Revolution and structural change in Latin America : a bibliography on ideology, development, and the radical left (1930–1965). Stanford, Calif. : Hoover Institution on War, Revolution and Peace, 1970. 2 v. (Hoover Institution on War, Revolution and Peace. Bibliographical series, 40).   **DB254**
A country-by-country listing of books, pamphlets, and periodical articles. Emphasis is on the period 1930–65, with some earlier materials noted. Most references are in English, French, Portuguese, or Spanish, but some Russian and German materials are listed. Vol. 2 includes an author index and a subject approach by broad topical categories.
                                                            Z1601.C496

Dahlin, Therrin C. The Catholic left in Latin America : a comprehensive bibliography / Therrin C. Dahlin, Gary P. Gillum, Mark L. Grover. Boston : G. K. Hall, 1981. 410 p.
                                                            DB255
A bibliography of materials published 1960–78, in any language, which the compilers felt could be located in the U.S. Concerned with the Catholic Left movement in any area of Latin America, including the Caribbean and any dependencies. Topical arrangement within geographical areas; author and title indexes. Since there is no subject index, items dealing with several topics or geographic areas are listed more than once.   Z7165.L3D33

Delorme, Robert. Latin America : social science information sources, 1967–1979. Santa Barbara, Calif. : ABC-Clio, 1981. 262 p.   **DB256**
A listing of some 5,600 books and journal articles published 1967–79 on all areas of Latin America. Geographical arrangement, subdivided by form of publication. Entries are repeated for items which deal with as many as three countries. Most citations are to English-language materials, but many Spanish, French or Portuguese items are included. Author and subject indexes, the latter somewhat lacking in detail.
Continued by:
———. *Latin America, 1979–1983 : a social science bibliography* (1984. 225 p.). Adds 3,728 citations in English, Spanish, and Portugueses for books, parts of books, and periodical articles published mid-1978 through Sept. 1983.
———. *Latin America, 1983–1987 : a social science bibliography* (N.Y. : Greenwood, 1988. 391 p. [Bibliographies and indexes in sociology, no. 14]). Lists more than 3,900 books, essays, and periodical articles in English and Spanish. Both these more recent works follow the organizational pattern of the 1981 publication.   Z7165.L3D44

Griffin, Charles Carroll. Latin America : a guide to the historical literature. Austin : publ. for the Conference on Latin American History by the Univ. of Texas Pr., [1971]. 700 p. (Conference on Latin American History. Publication, 4).
                                                            DB257
A cooperative effort sponsored jointly by the Conference on Latin American History and the Hispanic Foundation, Library of Congress. It attempts "to provide a selective scholarly bibliography, accompanied by critical annotations, covering the whole field of Latin American history."—*Introd.* Sections have been compiled by scholar specialists who have also contributed introductory notes and annotations. More than 7,000 items; cutoff date for publications included is 1966. Sec-

tions on reference works and general materials are followed by period sections, each with numerous subdivisions. There is an author index, but the detailed table of contents provides the only subject approach. Despite its age, still considered essential, especially for its listing of archival and document guides.

§ Other older bibliographies which may still prove useful because of their extensive coverage, include: S. A. Bayitch, *Latin America and the Caribbean : a bibliographical guide to works in English* (Coral Gables : Univ. of Miami Pr., 1967. 943 p.); and R. A. Humphreys, *Latin American history : a guide to the literature in English* (London : Oxford Univ. Pr., 1958. 197 p.).   Z1601.G75

Latin American military history : an annotated bibliography / ed. by David G. LaFrance and Errol D. Jones. N.Y. : Garland, 1992. 734 p. : map. (Military history bibliographies, vol. 12 ; Garland reference library of the humanities, vol. 1024).   **DB258**

Bibliographic essays on military history for particular periods and countries. Written by a specialist, each essay "includes sections on general works, bibliographies, archival guides and sources, published documents, memoirs, journals and eyewitness accounts, specialized works as well as periodicals and concludes with suggestions for further research."—*Pref.* The works discussed are listed alphabetically at the end of each chapter. Not indexed; no cross-references.   Z1621.L38

Monteiro, John M. América Latina colonial : bibli[o]grafía básica / John M. Monteiro, Francisco Moscoso. São Paulo : CELA, Universidade Estadual Paulista, 1990. 238 p. (Série Bibliografiás básicas, no. 1).   **DB259**

Some 3,000 books and articles on the Spanish, Portuguese, English, French, and Scandinavian colonies in Latin America and the Caribbean. Materials cited are in Spanish and English. Geographically arranged. Author index.   Z1601.M575

Okinshevich, Leo. Latin America in Soviet writings : a bibliography / comp. by Leo Okinshevich ; ed. by Robert G. Carlton. Baltimore : Publ. for the Library of Congress by the Johns Hopkins Pr., [1966]. 2 v.   **DB260**

Presents 8,688 entries, topically arranged, and covers 1917–1964. Supersedes and extends the coverage of the bibliography of the same title by Okinshevich and C. J. Gorokhoff (Wash. : Library of Congress, 1959. 257 p.), that covered 1945–1958.

§ For discussions of Soviet bibliography and historiography in the writing of Latin American history, on research trends, and on 18th- and 19th-century travelers' accounts, see *Soviet historians on Latin America : recent scholarly contributions*, ed. by Russell H. Bartley (Madison : Univ. of Wisconsin Pr., 1978. 345 p.). For additional Soviet titles and Eastern European titles, see Martin H. Sable, *Latin American studies in the non-Western world and Eastern Europe : a bibliography on Latin America in the languages of Africa, Asia, the Middle East and Eastern Europe, with transliterations and translations in English* (Metuchen, N.J. : Scarecrow, 1970. 701 p.).   Z1601.O55

Phillips, Gillian. Canada's relations with Latin America and the Caribbean, 1970–1990 : a bibliography = Les relations du Canada avec l'Amérique latine et la Caribes: une bibliographie / Gillian Phillips and Claude Morin for the Canada-Latin America Resource Centre. [Ottawa] : Canadian Association of Latin American and Caribbean Studies, 1993. 1172 p.   **DB261**

Text in English and French.

Although 30 libraries and information centers in Ontario and Québec were searched, this bibliography is based on collections at University of Montreal and the Canada-Latin American Resource Centre. Topical listing subdivided by country and subject for 13,000 books, theses, government publications, journals, and newspapers (but not articles). Location code for each item cited. Author, title, subject indexes.   Z6465.C25P55

Stoner, K. Lynn. Latinas of the Americas : a source book. N.Y. : Garland, 1989. 692 p. (Garland reference library of social science, v. 363).   **DB262**

For annotation, see CC617.   Z7964.L3S76

Welch, Thomas L. Travel accounts and descriptions of Latin America and the Caribbean, 1800–1920 : a selected bibliography / Thomas L. Welch, Myriam Figueras. Wash. : Columbus Memorial Libr., 1982. 293p.   **DB263**

A geographically arranged bibliography of "impressions and observations" recorded between 1800 and 1920 by a "writer who was not a native of the area," and including "such items as prospectuses for would-be investors and railroad and commercial guides ... since they provide information that may not be available elsewhere."—*Introd.* Excludes archaeological reports, manuscript materials, technical treatises on development programs. No index.

§ Alva Curtis Wilgus, *Latin America in the nineteenth century : a selected bibliography of books of travel and description published in English* (Metuchen, N.J. : Scarecrow, 1973. 174 p.) includes guidebooks, geographies, diaries, letters, memoirs and reminiscences, autobiographies, selected collections of private and public documents and papers, and occasional fiction. For French travelers, *see* Jean-Georges Kirchheimer, *Voyageurs francophones en Amérique hispanique au cours du XIXe siècles : repertoire bio-bibliographie* (Paris : Bibliothèque Nationale, 1987. 140 p.).

Wolf, Ulrike. Bibliography of Western European-Latin American relations. Madrid : Institute for European-Latin American Relations, c1986. 207 p. (Working paper, 1).   **DB264**

Approximately 1,800 entries for books, articles, and documents published over the past 25 years. Alphabetical arrangement by author, with subject and geographical indexes.   Z1609.R4W64

Current

Bibliographic guide to Latin American studies. v. 1 (1978)– . Boston : G. K. Hall, 1979– . Annual.   **DB265**

Added title page in Spanish; prefatory matter in English and Spanish.

A continuation of the *Catalog of the Latin American Collection* of the Library of the University of Texas at Austin and its supplements (DB270).

Reflects cataloging done for the University of Texas Latin American Collection from OCLC tapes during the year indicated, supplemented by relevant material from Library of Congress MARC tapes for that year. Full bibliographical information is given under main entry, with briefer information under added entries.

The University of Texas Library continues its policy of acquiring all materials written by Latin American authors or concerning Latin America in any language, including Indian dialects of Latin America.   Z1610.B52

Handbook of Latin American studies. v. 1 (1935)– . Gainesville : Univ. of Florida Pr. ; Austin : Univ. of Texas Pr., 1936– . Annual.   **DB266**

Publisher varies. Prepared by the Hispanic Division, Library of Congress.

Of first importance. An extensive, annotated bibliography of material relating to Latin America, prepared by a group of scholars. Coverage varies; e.g., v. 25 (publ. 1963) covers anthropology, art, economics, education, geography, government, history, international relations, language and literature, law, music and philosophy, sociology, and travel. Each volume also contains special articles on particular phases of life and culture or inter-American relations.

With the 1964 issue, divided into two sections—social sciences and humanities—now published in alternate years; i.e., v. 26, *Humanities*, covers art, history, language, literature, music, and philosophy; v. 27, *Social sciences*, includes anthropology, economics, education, geography, government and international relations, law, and sociology.

———. *Author index to ... nos. 1–28, 1936–1966*, comp. by Francisco José and Maria Elena Cardona (Gainesville : Univ. of Florida Pr., 1968. 421 p.). Prepared at the University of Florida for the Library of Congress Hispanic Foundation.

• Machine-readable version: *Latin American studies* [database] (Baltimore, Md. : National Information Services Corp., 1970–). Available on CD-ROM, updated semiannually. The CD-ROM includes *HAPI: Hispanic American periodicals index* (AD296).　Z1605.H23

Dissertations

Hanson, Carl A. Dissertations on Iberian and Latin American history. Troy, N.Y. : Whitston, 1975. 400 p.　**DB267**

In addition to U.S. and Canadian dissertations on Latin America completed in history departments, the bibliography includes studies on: "Iberia and its non-Latin American holdings; other European possessions, past and present, on the perimeter of Latin America; dissertations completed in British and Irish universities and colleges; and titles from disciplines other than history."—*Introd.* Geographical/chronological arrangement. More than 3,500 entries. Author index.
　Z1601.H32

Library catalogs

Biblioteca Nacional (Spain). Catálogo de obras iberoamericanas y filipinas de la Biblioteca Nacional de Madrid / Luisa Cuesta [y] Modesta Cuesta. Madrid : Dirección General de Archivos y Bibliotecas, Servicio de Publicaciones del Ministério de Educación Nacional, 1953. 322 p.　**DB268**

On cover: Obra núm. 15 de Publicaciones de Educación Nacional.

Some 3,364 items on Latin America and the Philippines are listed in this volume, which is devoted to general works. Other volumes were planned for individual countries but only this volume was published.

§ *See also* its *Catálogo de manuscritos de América existentes en la Biblioteca Nacional*, by Julín Paz (Madrid : Tip. de Archivos, 1933. 724 p.) for a calendar with brief descriptions. Geographic and name indexes.　Z945.M22

University of Florida. Libraries. Catalog of the Latin-American collection. Boston : G. K. Hall, 1973. 13 v.　**DB269**

Reproduction of the cards from this author/subject catalog representing 120,000 books, pamphlets, periodicals and government documents in original form and 9,000 units of microform, dealing with Latin America including the Caribbean. The collection is especially strong in materials relating to Brazil and the Caribbean, and in official documents and periodicals.

———. ——— *Supplement* (Boston : G.K. Hall, 1979. 7 v.). Reproduces an additional 99,000 cards representing cataloging May 1973–78.

§ One of the strongest European libraries for Latin American and Caribbean materials is that of the Ibero-Amerikanisches Institut (Berlin, Germany). Their catalog, *Schlagwortkalog des Ibero-Amerikanisches Institute, Preussischer Kulturbesitz in Berlin = Subject catalog of the Ibero-American Institute, Prussian Cultural Heritage Foundation in Berlin* (Boston: G. K. Hall, 1977. 30 v.), has separate volumes indexing persons and places.

Catalog of the Latin American Library of Tulane University Library, New Orleans (Boston : G. K. Hall, 1970. 9 v. Suppls. 1–3, 1973–78. 6 v.) is particularly strong in Central American materials.
　Z1610.F6

University of Texas at Austin. Library. Latin American Collection. Catalog of the Latin American collection. Boston : G. K. Hall, 1969. 31 v.　**DB270**

Reproduction in book form of the dictionary catalog of this outstanding collection. Includes cards for about 175,000 books, pamphlets, serials, and microforms.

———. ——— *Supplement* 1–4 (Boston : G. K. Hall, 1971–1977. 19 v.) cover materials processed for the collection 1969–74. *Suppl. 1* includes cards for "Hilea–Hispanidad A" which were omitted from the 1969 catalog. *Suppl. 3–4* include a number of pre-1970 imprints from the cataloging backlog.

Continued by: *Bibliographic guide to Latin American studies* (DB265).

§ The University of Texas Library also issued *Latin American serials list* from the Benson Collection ([1984]. 9 microfiche); includes title index, country of publication index, Mexican-American serials index.

The Widener shelflist, no. 5–6, covers Harvard's holdings in *Latin America and Latin American periodicals* (Cambridge : The Library, 1966. 2 v. *See* AA115 for a note on the series).　Z1610.T48

Yale University. Library. Guide to Latin American pamphlets from the Yale University Library : selections from 1600–1900 / ed. by Lofton Wilson ; comp. by Lisa Browar, Anna Fernicola, Miryam A. Ospina. N. Y. : Clearwater Pub. Co., c1985. 7 v.　**DB271**

Lists more than 6,300 pamphlets for Mexico, 2,000 for Peru, and 1,325 for the rest of Central and South America. Principally concerned with social, political, and economic history, 17th–20th centuries. Each geographical part is divided by subject, author, and imprint date. Accompanies *Latin American pamphlets from the Yale University Library*, a microfiche reproduction of pamphlets.　Z1431.Y34

Guides to records

Archives nationales (France). Guide des sources de l'histoire de l'Amérique latine et des Antilles dans les archives françaises. Paris : Archives nationales : Diffusé par la Documentation française, 1984. 711 p., [8] p. of plates : ill.　**DB272**

Forms part of the series *Guides to the sources for the history of the nations* (DB275).

A list of inventories covering materials, 18th century to about 1952, for: Archives nationales, Archives départementales et communales, Archives of ministries (e.g., Relations exterièures, Defense, Economie et des finances), Archives parlementaires, Archives des Chambres de Commerce, Bibliothèque nationale, Archives missionaires, and some private collections. For each, gives address, brief history and terms of access, finding aids, and detailed inventories. Appendix lists ministers, secretaries of state, colonial administrators for the French colonies in the Antilles, and government representatives in territorial Latin America. Not indexed.　Z1610.F72

Grow, Michael. Scholars' guide to Washington, D.C. for Latin American and Caribbean studies / Michael Grow ... [et al.]. 2nd ed. / rev. by Craig VanGrasstek. Wash. : Woodrow Wilson Center Pr. ; Baltimore : Johns Hopkins Univ. Pr., 1992. 427 p. (Scholars' guide to Washington, D.C., 2).
　DB273

1st ed., 1979.

Publ. for the Latin American Program of the Woodrow Wilson International Center for Scholars.

Intended as "a descriptive and evaluative survey of research resources" (*Introd.*) primarily for the serious scholar. In two main sections: (1) Collections (which lists, briefly describes and evaluates pertinent libraries, archives, museums and art collections, music and sound recording collections, map collections, film collections, and data banks); (2) Organizations (both public and private, "which deal with Latin America and are potential sources of information or assistance to researchers"). Covers some 500 collections, organizations, and agencies, with information current as of June 30, 1991. Indexed.
　Z1601.G867

Guide to manuscript sources for the history of Latin America and the Caribbean in the British Isles / ed. by Peter Walne. Oxford : Univ. Pr. in collaboration with the Inst. of Latin American Studies, Univ. of London, 1973. 580 p.
　DB274

Sponsored by the International Council on Archives.

This is the first comprehensive survey of archival and manuscript materials for this area. Also includes the Philippine Islands. Entries are arranged alphabetically by English counties, followed by listings for

Scotland, Wales, and Ireland; within geographical area, arrangement is alphabetical by name of repository or owner of the papers described. References to any published descriptions or guides to particular collections are noted. Includes archives of business firms preserved in public and private hands. Subject index includes names of collections, owners and holders of records. CD1048.L35G84

Guide to the sources of the history of the nations : A. Latin America. The Hague : Govt. Publ. Office, [1966–69]. v. 3–4. (In progress?). **DB275**

At head of title: Conseil International des Archives. International Council on Archives. Consejo Internacional des Archivos.

Contents: v. 3, fasc. 2, Guides to the sources in the Netherlands for the history of Latin America, by M. P. H. Roessingh (1968. 232 p.); v. 4, Guía de fuentes para la historia de Ibero-Americo conservadas en España, ed. for Direccion General de Archivos y Bibliotecas, Spain (1966–69. 2 v.).

§ Inter Documentation (Zug, Switz.) has assembled a microfiche series consisting of inventories from various publishers of materials in archives and libraries that are important for research in Latin American studies:

Guide des sources de l'histoire d'Amérique Latine conservées en Belgique, by L. Liagre (Brussels, 1967. 132 p.); *Übersicht über die Quellen zur Geschichte Lateinamerikas in Archiven der D.D.R.*, comp at the Staatliche Archivverwaltung of the German Democratic Republic (Potsdam, 1971. 122 p.); *Führer durch die Quellen zur Geschichte Lateinamerikas in der Bundesrepublik Deutschland*, v. 2, pt. 1, by R. Hauschild-Thiessen (Bremen, 1972. 437 p.); *A guide to the manuscript sources for the history of Latin America and the Caribbean in the British Isles*, by P. A. Walne (DB274); *Guida delle fonti per la storia dell'America latina esistenti in Italia*, by E. Lodolini (Rome, 1976. 403 p.); *Fuentes para la historia de Ibero-América : Escandinavia*, by M. Mörner (Stockholm, 1968. 105 p.); *Guide to materials on Latin America in the National Archives*, comp. at the U.S. National Archives (DB280); *Guida delle fonti per la storia dell'America Latina negli archivi della Santa Sede e negli archivi ecclesiastici d'Italia*, by L. Pásztor (Vatican, 1970. 665 p.).

See also: *Sources of the history of Africa, Asia, Australia and Oceania in Hungary, with a Supplement, Latin America* (3rd series, v. 8, DD75). CD941.G83

Hanke, Lewis. Guía de las fuentes en hispanoamérica para el estudio de la administracion virreinal española en Mexico y en el Perú, 1535–1700. Wash. : Secretaría General, OAS, 1980. 523 p. **DB276**

A survey of materials dealing with the colonial period (1535–1700) in Mexico and Peru as found in the archives of individual South American nations. For some countries (e.g., Bolivia) the information is quite full.

§ Hanke has also compiled *Guía de las fuentes en el Archivo General de Indias para el estudio de la administración virreinal española en México y en el Perú, 1535–1700* (Köln : Böhlau, 1977. 3v.), of which v.1 is particularly useful since, besides providing an overview of viceregal sources, it gives short biographies and bibliographies of the viceroys of Mexico and Peru. Z1426.H36

Misiones americanas en los archivos europeos. México : Inst. Panamericano de Geografía e Historia, 1949–57. 10 v. (Instituto Pan-Americano de Geografía e Historia. Comisión de Historia. Publication, 8 [etc.]). **DB277**

Contents: no.1, Mexican, by Manuel Carrera Stampa (1949); no.2, American, by Roscoe R. Hill (1951); no.3, Cuban, by Manuel Moreno Fraginals (1951); no.4, Brazilian, by Virgilio Correa Filho (1952); no.5, Colombian, by Enrique Ortega Ricaurte (1951); no.6, Chilean, by Alejandro Soto Cárdenas (1953); no.7, Argentinian, by Raúl A. Molina (1955); no.8, Venezuelan, by Joaquín Gabaldón Márquez (1954); no.9, Ecuadorian, by José María Vargas (1956); no.10–11, not published; no.12, Nicaraguan, by Carlos Molina Argüello (1957).

The series offers calendars of copies of documents in European archives relating to the individual Latin American countries; the copies were acquired by various "missions" sent out by the Latin American countries.

Nauman, Ann Keith. A handbook of Latin American & Caribbean national archives = Guía de los archivos nacionales de America Latina y el Caribe. Detroit : Blaine Ethridge–Books, [1983]. 127 p. **DB278**

For annotation, *see* AK130. CD3680.N38

Research guide to Andean history : Bolivia, Chile, Ecuador, and Peru / John J. TePaske, coordinating ed. Durham, N.C. : Duke Univ. Pr., 1981. 346 p. **DB279**

A collection of contributed articles (a few of them in Spanish), each describing a particular archive or a group of repositories having materials relating to a specific historical period or topic. Articles are grouped by country, with an introductory note for each country section. Includes directory information for many of the individual archives, as well as references to published guides and descriptions. The index is limited to a listing of the archives and libraries by country, including references to repositories outside the four countries under consideration. Z1656.R47

United States. National Archives and Records Service. Guide to materials on Latin America in the National Archives of the United States / by George S. Ulibarri and John P. Harrison. Wash. : National Archives & Records Service, 1974. 489 p. **DB280**

"This guide supersedes the *Guide to Materials on Latin America in the National Archives* (vol. I, 1961), compiled by Dr. John P. Harrison, and includes the records descriptions contained in that guide. In addition, it includes descriptions of pertinent records of the executive, legislative, and judicial branches of the Government that were not included in the earlier guide."—*Introd.* The 1961 guide was intended to be in two volumes; the present work results from a decision to present the earlier material in revised form together with much new information. CD3023.U54

Encyclopedias; Dictionaries

The Cambridge encyclopedia of Latin America and the Caribbean / gen. editors, Simon Collier, Thomas E. Skidmore, Harold Blakemore. 2nd ed. Cambridge ; N.Y. : Cambridge Univ. Pr., 1992. 480 p. : ill., some maps in color. **DB281**

Provides discussion of all of Latin America and the Caribbean within six topical sections: Physical environment, The economy, The peoples, History, Politics and society, Culture, each subdivided and with short bibliographies appended to each signed subsection. Heavily illustrated with maps, photographs, charts. Subject index. A review of the 1st ed. in *TLS* 16 May 1986 : 522, concludes that the encyclopedia provides "a very valuable means to help understand the issues facing Latin America and the Caribbean, to see all dimensions of this continent's past and present, and to appreciate the nature of both its enormous problems and its enormous potential." F1406.C36

Latin American historical dictionaries / A. Curtis Wilgus, gen. ed. Metuchen, N.J. : Scarecrow, 1970–1991. v. 1–24. (In progress). **DB282**

Contents: v. 1, Guatemala, ed. by Richard E. Moore (rev. ed., 1973); v. 2, Panama, ed. by Basil C. and Anne K. Hedrick (1970); v. 3, Venezuela, ed. by Donna Keyse and G. A. Rudolph (1971); v. 4, Bolivia, ed. by Dwight B. Heath (1972); v. 5, El Salvador, ed. by Philip F. Flemion (1972); v. 6, Nicaragua, ed. by Harvey K. Meyer (1972); v. 7, Chile, ed. by Salvatore Bizzarro (1972; 2nd ed. rev., 1987); v. 8, Paraguay, ed. by Charles J. Kolinski (1973. Replaced by v. 24); v. 9, Puerto Rico and the U.S. Virgin Islands, by Kenneth R. Farr (1973); v. 10, Ecuador, by Albert Bork and Georg Maier (1973); v. 11, Uruguay, by Jean Willis (1974); v. 12, British Caribbean, by William R. Lux (1975); v. 13, Honduras, by Harvey K. Meyer (1976); v. 14, Colombia, by Robert H. Davis (1977. Replaced by v. 23); v. 15, Haiti, by Roland I. Perusse (1977); v. 16, Costa Rica, by Theodore S. Creedman (1977. 2nd ed., 1991); no. 17, Argentina, by Ione S. Wright and Lisa M. Nikhom (1977. Tr. into Spanish, Buenos Aires : Emecí, 1990); v. 18, French and Netherlands Antilles, by Albert Gastmann (1978); v. 19,

Brazil, by Robert M. Levine (1979); v. 20, Peru, by Marvin Alisky (1979); v. 21, Mexico, by Donald C. Briggs and Marvin Alisky (1981); v. 22, Cuba, by Jaime Suchlicki (1988); v. 23, Colombia, by Robert H. Davis (1977; 2nd ed., 1993); v. 24, Paraguay, by R. Andrew Nickson (2nd ed., rev. 1993).

A series of historical dictionaries with brief entries for personal names, places, and events of individual Latin American nations. Quality of the individual volumes in somewhat uneven.

Political and economic encyclopaedia of South America and the Caribbean / ed. by Peter Calvert ... [et al.]. Harlow, Essex : Longman ; Detroit : Distr. by Gale, c1991. 363 p. : col. ill. **DB283**

Treats personalities, political parties, geographical areas, and problems or topics common to a number of countries. Each article is signed with initials, though not all the initials are identified. Cross-references in bold. Sketchy chronology, 2300 BCE–1991 CE. Indexed under broad headings. F1410.P69

Shavit, David. The United States in Latin America : a historical dictionary. N.Y. : Greenwood, 1992. 471 p. **DB284**

Short entries give "information about persons, institutions, and events that affected the relationships between the United States and Latin America" (*Pref*), from Mexico to Argentina and including the Caribbean. Appendix for lists of chiefs of American diplomatic missions in Latin America 1823–1900 and of individuals by profession and occupation. Bibliographical essay; index by subject.

§ Similar to Shavit's volumes on Africa (DD96), Middle East (DE56), and Asia (DE15). F1418.S494

Directories

Directorio latinoamericano : socio-económico, político, académico = Latin American directory. Quito, Ecuador : EDIEC Latina, c1985. 4 v. **DB285**

Contents: v. 1, México y Centro América; v. 2, Caribe y Brasil; v. 3, Group Andino; v. 4, Cono sur y extrarregionales.

Contains "15,000 names of institutions and personalities, mass media, governments, companies, chambers of commerce, labour unions, inter-regional organizations, academic centers, political parties, and a variety of different Latin American associations, and also the names of its leaders."—*Foreword*. Arranged by country, then by type of organization; for each entry gives name of organization, address, title or name of person in charge, and occasionally phone numbers. Vol. 4 covers organizations in other countries of interest to Latin America (e.g., branches of Latin American banks, university departments, government offices). Lists of countries and topics used.
F1406.5.D57

Manual para las relaciones Europeo-Latinoamericanas = Handbook for European-Latin American relations / comp. by Brigitte Farenholtz and Wolfgang Grenz. Madrid : Instituto de Relaciones Europeo-Latinoamericanas, c1987. 772 p. **DB286**

Offers directory information based on questionnaire responses from about 500 organizations—academic, government, business, religious, technical—with interests in one or more Latin American countries. Includes short biographies of individuals. Arranged by country, then by city (using Spanish form of name). Indexed by personal name, region, subject, institution, and acronym. An appendix lists diplomatic missions, periodical publications, banks, cultural institutes, and organizations in Austria, Switzerland, and Sweden. AS97.M3

National directory of Latin Americanists : biographies of 1422 specialists / comp. in collaboration with the Hispanic Division of the Library of Congress. 4th ed. / ed. by Jacqueline M. Nickel. Dallas : Taylor Pub. Co., 1992. 188 p. **DB287**

1st ed., 1966; 3rd ed., 1985, issued by the Library of Congress (1011 p.).

Provides information on active Latin Americanists, based on responses to questionnaires. According to the preface, the criteria for inclusion are: (1) command of at least one of the major languages of the

area; (2) broad knowledge of the area, often demonstrated in graduate study in three or more disciplines; (3) at least one year in field of research. Index by subject specialty and by geographical area.

§ The European equivalent is *Latinoamericanistas en Europa 1990 : registro biobibliografico*, (Amsterdam : Centrum voor Studie in Dokumentatie van Latijns Amerika, [1990]. 240 p.). F1409.8.A2N37

Tinker guide to Latin American and Caribbean policy and scholarly resources in metropolitan New York / ed. by Ronald G. Hellman & Beth Kempler Pfannl. [N.Y.] : Bildner Center for Western Hemisphere Studies, Graduate School and Univ. Center, City Univ. of New York, c1988. 217 p. **DB288**

Lists 212 organizations and collections interested in public policy, international relations, and social sciences. For each gives name, address, phone number, and activities and collections related to Latin American and the Caribbean. Appendix lists bookstores, publishers, and scholars at the City University of New York interested in this subject. Name and subject indexes. F1409.95.U6T56

Handbooks

Handbook of Latin American popular culture / ed. by Harold E. Hinds, Jr. and Charles M. Tatum. Westport, Conn. : Greenwood, c1985. 259 p. **DB289**

Surveys scholarship concerning Spanish and Portuguese Latin America in ten chapters: Popular music, Popular religion, Comics, Television, Sport, Photonovels, Film, Festivals and carnivals, Single-panel comics, Newspapers. Each chapter ends with sections on research centers and collections, and suggestions for future research. Topical index. F1408.3.H316

Mitchell, Brian R. International historical statistics : the Americas 1750–1988. 2nd ed. N.Y. : Stockton Pr., 1993. 817 p. **DB290**

For annotation, *see* CG70. HA175.M55

Histories

The Cambridge history of Latin America / ed. by Leslie Bethell. Cambridge ; N.Y. : Cambridge Univ. Pr., 1984–1990. v. 1–8 : ill. (In progress). **DB291**

Contents: v. 1, Colonial Latin America (1985. In 2 v., now designated v. 1–2); v. 3, From independence to c.1870 (1985. 945 p.); v. 4–5, 1870–1930 (1986. 2 v.); v. 6, Latin America since 1930 : economy, society, and politics (1994); v. 7, Latin America since 1930 : Mexico, Central America and the Caribbean (1990. 775 p.); v. 8, Latin America since 1930 : Spanish South America (1991. 919 p.).

To be in 9 v. Similar in plan to other Cambridge histories, this aims to be the "first large-scale authoritative survey of Latin America's unique historical experience during almost five centuries from the first contacts between the Native American Indians and Europeans (and the beginnings of the African slave trade) in the late fifteenth and early sixteenth centuries to the present day."—*Pref.* Each chapter is by a specialist, and each is accompanied by an extremely useful bibliographic essay.

Cambridge Univ. Pr. has republished parts or chapters of various of these volumes under new titles: e.g., *Colonial Spanish America* (1987) is taken from v. 1–2; *The independence of Latin America* (1987) is from part of v. 3; *Spanish America after independence, c.1820–c.1870* (1987), part of v. 3; *Central America since independence* (1991) reissues chapters from v. 3, 5, 7; *Latin America : economy and society, 1870–1930* (1989) is part of v. 4; *Colonial Brazil* (1987) and *Brazil : empire and republic, 1822–1930* (1989) are reprints of chapters from v. 1–2, 3 and 5 respectively; *Mexico since independence* (1991), *Chile since independence* (1993), *Cuba : a short history* (1993), *Argentina since independence* (1993), all from v. 3, 5, and 8. F1410.C1834

New Iberian world : a documentary history of the discovery and settlement of Latin America to the early 17th century / ed. with commentaries by John H. Parry and Robert G. Keith. N.Y. : Times Books : Hector & Rose, c1984. 5 v. : ill. **DB292**

Contents: v. 1, The conquerors and the conquered; v. 2, The Caribbean; v. 3, Central America and Mexico; v. 4, Andes; v. 5, Coastlines, rivers, and forests.

Offers translations of travel narratives, government accounts, chronicles and descriptions of Latin America. Many of the documents are newly translated for this work, though most are "ruthlessly excerpted"—*Introd.* General introduction for each section; headnotes for individual documents indicate source. Glossary of terms (especially nautical and legal ones) common in the 16th-century documents. Contemporary or near-contemporary maps in each volume; bibliography (v. 5, p. 497–506) lists works mentioned or quoted in the text. Index.

F1411.N49

Current surveys

ISLA / Information Services on Latin America. [v. 1, no. 1] (July 1970)– . Oakland, Calif. : ISLA, [1970]– . Monthly. Looseleaf. **DB293**

Reproduces articles from ten English-language newspapers (seven American, three European) which deal primarily with political, social, and economic news of all areas of Latin America, including Central America and the Caribbean. Arrangement is geographical, then chronological within country sections; each issue ranges from 300–450 pages.

§ Other similar services include *Latin America weekly report* (London : Latin American Newsletters, 1979–). The same publisher issues *Latin American regional reports* (1979– . Monthly) for the Andean Group, Brazil, the Caribbean, Central America, Mexico and NAFTA, and the southern cone. Business International also issues regional reports: *Latin American monitor*, 1984– (London. Monthly) for the Andean Group, Caribbean, Central America, Mexico and Brazil, southern cone. Most of these services are also available through NEXIS.

For Central America and the Caribbean, besides the titles listed above, see: *Central America newspak*, (Austin : Central American Resource Center, 1986– . Biweekly) and *Caribbean basin databook* (Wash. : Caribbean/Latin America Action, 1991– . Annual).

Latin America and Caribbean contemporary record. v. 1 (1981/82)– . N.Y. : Holmes & Meier, [1983]– . Annual. **DB294**

Offers current, authoritative, analytical surveys (e.g., the role of the Catholic Church; debt crisis) in five major sections: Current issues; Country-by-country review; Documents; Economic, social, and political data; Book abstracts. Names and subjects index.

§ Similar to *Africa contemporary record* (DD59) and *Middle East contemporary survey* (DE61).

South America, Central America, and the Caribbean. 1st ed. (1986)– . London : Europa Publications Ltd., 1985– . Biennial. **DB295**

Covers 43 countries and territories. In three parts: (1) Background to the region, which includes essays by scholars on such topics as Church and politics in Latin America, The politics of cocaine in Latin America, Ecology in Latin America; (2) Country surveys, featuring "historical and economic essays written by experts on the country, statistical surveys, directory and bibliography" (*Foreword*); (3) The region, which lists regional organizations, major commodities, research institutes, bibliography of periodical titles. Index to regional organizations. Contributors are mainly British, with a few Americans represented.

F1401.S68

Biography

Thomas, Jack Ray. Biographical dictionary of Latin American historians and historiography. Westport, Conn. : Greenwood, 1984. 420 p. **DB296**

Provides biographical sketches, with notes on their work, of Latin American historians from the colonial period to the present (i.e., includes 20th century writers who died prior to 1983). "The major considerations for inclusion were that the writer either produced a significant amount of historical writing or that a portion of his scholarly production was so important to the discipline of history that he could not be excluded."—*Pref.* Bibliography at the end of each article, and a general bibliography, p. 403–411. Extensive introductory essay; index.

§ See also *Guide to the writings of pioneer Latinoamericanists of the United States* by Martin Sable (N. Y. : Haworth, 1989. 159 p.) which concentrates on those Latin Americanists born 1700–1900. Also of interest is the article discussing the writing of Latin American history in the U.S. 1885–1984 by John J. Johnson, "One hundred years of historical writing on modern Latin America by United States historians" in *Hispanic American historical review* 65 (1985): 745–65.

F1409.8.A2T48

Atlases

Lombardi, Cathryn L. Latin American history : a teaching atlas / Cathryn L. Lombardi, John V. Lombardi. Madison : Publ. for the Conference on Latin American History by the Univ. of Wisconsin Pr., 1983. 104 p., 40 p. : maps. 29cm. **DB297**

Offers 104 clear, simple black-and-white maps covering all areas of Latin America and the Caribbean from discovery and conquest until about 1976; there is a 1982 map of the Falklands. Basic presentation is chronological, with many maps depicting economics, culture, the environment, etc. Index of names and topics. G1541.S1L6

CENTRAL AMERICA

In addition to those works listed here, many general works in the section on Latin America include coverage of Central America.

Garst, Rachel. Bibliografía anotada de obras de referencia sobre Centroamérica y Panamá en el campo de las ciencias sociales. San José, Costa Rica : Instituto de Investigaciones Sociales, Universidad de Costa Rica ; [S.l.] : Friends World College, Latin American Center, 1983. 2 v. (662 p.). **DB298**

Lists some 1,445 books and journals in Spanish and English, addressing socioeconomic and political study of the area, 1968–82. Arranged by region or country, subdivided by topic. Annotated; subject, author, and title indexes. Appendix lists relevant libraries in Central America. Z7165.C4G37

Grieb, Kenneth J. Central America in the nineteenth and twentieth centuries : an annotated bibliography. Boston : G.K. Hall, c1988. 573 p. **DB299**

Lists books (including codification of laws and compilations of documents and treaties) for the period 1810–1980 on Guatemala, Honduras, El Salvador, Nicaragua, Costa Rica, and Belize, in Spanish and English. Indicates library locations. Annotations are well written and balanced. Author and subject indexes. Z1437.G74

Nordquist, Joan. Current Central American–U.S. relations. Santa Cruz, Calif. : Reference and Research Services, 1987. 68 p. (Contemporary social issues, no. 5). **DB300**

An annotated bibliography developed for use by undergraduates. Lists books, articles, government publications, and pamphlets. Appendix of religious organizations and periodicals, with addresses.
F1436.C4N670

Research guide to Central America and the Caribbean / Kenneth J. Grieb, ed. in chief. Madison : Univ. of Wisconsin Pr., 1985. 431 p.   **DB301**
Signed contributions describe major archives or discuss areas for future research on various topics. Topical index. A major resource for scholars.   Z1595.R47

Tropical Science Center (San José, Costa Rica). Occasional paper = Estudio ocasional. San José : Tropical Science Center, 1965–67. no. 2–7.   **DB302**
Research conducted in association with the Associated Colleges of the Midwest.
Contents: no. 2, Anthropological bibliography of aboriginal Panama, by E.W. Shook (1965); no. 3, Anthropological bibliography of aboriginal Nicaragua, by J.A. Lines (1965); no. 4, Anthropological bibliography of aboriginal El Salvador, by J.A. Lines (1965); no. 5, Anthropological bibliography of aboriginal Honduras, by J.A. Lines (1966); no. 6, Anthropological bibliography of aboriginal Guatemala, British Honduras, by J.A. Lines (1967); no. 7, Anthropological bibliography of aboriginal Costa Rica, by J.A. Lines (1967).
Bibliographies of the principal studies from colonial times up to the recent present (i.e., citations and references up to the end of 1965) for each Central American country. Author listing; no index.

Belize

Woodward, Ralph Lee. Belize / Ralph Lee Woodward, Jr., compiler ; ed. by Sheila R. Herstein. Oxford, Eng. ; Santa Barbara, Calif. : Clio Pr., c1980. 229 p. : map. (World bibliographical series, v. 21).   **DB303**
Offers an "annotated compilation of the most significant and useful publications on Belize" (*Introd*)—books, periodical articles, documents, and theses. Topical arrangement with author/title/subject index.
Z1441.W59

Costa Rica

Elizondo, Carlos L. Research guide to Costa Rica / prep. by Instituto Geográfico Nacional, Oficina de Investigaciones Geográficas ; Carlos L. Elizondo, Juan B. González, Luis F. Martínez. [Mexico] : Pan American Inst. of Geography and History, 1977. 138 p. : maps.   **DB304**
Tr. of *Guía para investigadores de Costa Rica* (1977).
An inventory of published and unpublished maps on Costa Rica (listed by type) is followed by a topically arranged bibliography of books, pamphlets, and articles, mainly in Spanish (with occasional English entries) and mainly published 1960–74. Intended as a "guide to contemporary resources of information for studies on the development of Costa Rica, and the planning of resources, both physical and human, by means of index maps, descriptive texts, and bibliography."—*Introd.*
§ A supplementary bibliography by Manuel J. Carvajal, *Bibliography of poverty and related topics in Costa Rica* ([Wash.] : Rural Development Division, Agency for Internat. Development, 1979. 329 p.), cites books, articles and government documents published since about 1960; it is well indexed.   Z6027.C83E4313

Stansifer, Charles L. Costa Rica. Santa Barbara, Calif. : Clio Pr., c1991. 292 p. (World bibliographical series, v. 126).
DB305
760 books, articles and essays, primarily in English. Topical arrangement; author, title, and subject indexes. Separate listing of U.S. and Canadian dissertations on Costa Rica.

§ *See also*: Richard J. Jenkins, "Historical sources in Costa Rica" in *Latin American research review* 23, no. 3 (1988): 117–27, which discusses seven archives and libraries in Costa Rica that support research on the history of Costa Rica, giving for each a background sketch and discussion of its resources; and *Materiales para la historia de las relaciones internacionales de Costa Rica : bibliografía fuentes impresas*, comp. by Manuel E. Araya Incera (San Pedro : Univ. Costa Rica, Centro Investigaciones Historicas, 1980. 91 p.), which lists 533 books, articles, theses, and government publications (including U.N. publications).   Z1451.S7

El Salvador

García, Miguel Angel. Diccionario histórico-enciclopédico de la República de El Salvador. San Salvador : Tipografía "La Luz", 1927–1951. 13 v.   **DB306**
Contents: v. 1–13, A–Col. Imprint varies. No more published.
Historical and biographical articles in one alphabet, often including reproduction of documentary sources.   F1483.G21

Woodward, Ralph Lee. El Salvador. Oxford ; Santa Barbara, Calif. : Clio Pr., c1988. 213 p. (World bibliographical series, v. 98).   **DB307**
"Guide to the most significant publications in the field with annotations that should help the reader to identify both the scope and utility of individual items."—*Introd.* Cites 659 books and articles (mainly in English with some Spanish) plus a few theses and dissertations. Topically arranged in 40 sections. Author/title/subject index. Z1491.W66

Guatemala

Laporte Molina, Juan Pedro. Bibliografía de la arqueología guatemalteca. Guatemala : Ed. de la Dirección General de Antropología e Historia, 1981. 1 v.   **DB308**
Contents: v. 1, A–I. No more published.
An extensive bibliography arranged by topic. Sections include general works on Mayan archeology; physical characteristics of the area (including geological analysis, soil condition, flora and fauna); specific archeological areas; epigraphy, the calendar, and religion; ethnohistory and historical sources; individual authors.   Z1209.2.G9L36

Woodward, Ralph Lee. Guatemala. Rev. and expanded ed. Oxford, Eng. ; Santa Barbara, Calif. : Clio Pr., c1992. 269 p. (World bibliographical series, v. 9).   **DB309**
1st ed., 1981, comp. by Woodman B. Franklin.
843 books and articles in English and Spanish. Topical arrangement with author, title, and subject indexes.   Z1461.W66

Honduras

Arqueta, Mario. Investigación y tendencias recientes de la historiografía hondureña : un ensayo bibliográfico. Tegucigalpa : Ed. Universitaria, 1981. 28 p. (Colección cuadernos universitarios, 3).   **DB310**
A good bibliographical essay covering scholarship in the 1970s.
§ Arquita has also written a bibliographical essay describing material relevant for research on colonial Honduras: *Guía para el investigador de la historia colonial hondureña* (Tegucigalpa : Ed. Universitaria, 1985. 43 p.).

Enciclopedia histórica de Honduras : obra fundamental de información y consulta e imprescindible auxiliar pedagógico para maestros, padres de familia y estudiantes de todos los niveles / editada bajo la dirección de Ramiro Colindres Ortega ... [et al.]. Tegucigalpa : Graficentro Editores, 1988–1989. 12 v. in 11 : ill. **DB311**

Contents: t. 1–2, Honduras precolombina. Período colonial; t. 3, La independencia y anexión a México; t. 4, La Federación Centroamericana; t. 5, Génesis del estado republicano; t. 6, Regímenes prereformistas; t. 7, La reforma liberal; t. 8, Consolidación del estado liberal; t. 9, Dependencia e injerencia externa; t. 10, Guerra civil y paz autoritaria; t. 11, Gobiernos contemporáneos; t. 12, El paisaje, la gente y las instituciones.

A heavily illustrated encyclopedia intended for use in schools and the home. Arranged chronologically, from pre-Columbian to contemporary times. F1506.E53

Howard-Reguindin, Pamela F. Honduras. Oxford, Eng. ; Santa Barbara, Calif. : Clio Pr., c1992. 258 p. (World bibliographical series, v. 139). **DB312**

788 books, government publications, dissertations, journal articles in English and Spanish topically arranged. Indexes for author, title and subject. Z1471.H68

Nicaragua

Barquero, Sara Luisa. Gobernantes de Nicaragua : 1825–1947. 2. ed. [Managua] : Ministerio de Instrucción Pública y E.F., [1945]. 248 p. **DB313**

Biographical sketches, three to four pages in length, of the heads of Nicaraguan government. F1522.7.B36

Realidad y perspectiva : bibliografía nacional anotada sobre la mujer en Nicaragua. Managua : Ministerio de la Presidencia, Oficina de la Mujer : Centro de Documentacíon de la Mujer, [1987]. 50l. **DB314**

A broad topical arrangement of books, documents, essays, and unpublished studies, mostly published in the 1980s in Nicaragua. Annotated; index of authors and editors and of titles.

§ Supplemented by a bibliographic essay on the state of research and describing the most important research, 1976–86, on the status of women in Nicaragua: *10 años de investigaciones sobre la mujer en Nicaragua 1976–1987 : informes* by Paola Pérez and Pamela Diaz (Managua : Oficina de la Mujer, 1986. 61 p.). Z7964.N5R321

Sandinista Nicaragua : an annotated bibliography with analytical introductions / by Neil Snarr and associates. Ann Arbor, Mich. : Pierian Pr., 1989–1990. 2 v. **DB315**

Contents: Pt. 1, Revolution, religion, and social policy: an annotated bibliography with analytical introductions (1989. 188 p.); Pt. 2, Economy, politics, and foreign policy: an annotated bibliography with analytical introductions (1990. 191 p.).

Chapters signed by scholars address various topics of the ten years of Sandinista Nicaragua. Critical introductions and lengthy annotated bibliography form each chapter. Lists English and some Spanish books, with a few government publications and periodical articles. Author and title indexes in each volume. Appended in v. 2 is a chronology of 20th-century Nicaragua. Z1487.P65S26

Woodward, Ralph Lee. Nicaragua / Ralph Lee Woodward, Jr., comp.; Sheila R. Herstein, ed. Oxford, ; Santa Barbara, Calif. : Clio Pr., 1983. 254 p. (World bibliographical series, v. 44). **DB316**

A "guide to the most significant publications in each field" (*Introd.*) of Nicaraguan studies, emphasizing English-language materials when available. Books, articles, and theses are arranged by subject, with brief annotations. Indexed.

§ Omits the *Bibliografía socioeconómica de Nicaragua* by G. Gutiérrez (Managua : Univ. Nac. Autónoma de Nicaragua, 1977. 45 p.) which is based on the collection of the Biblioteca del Banco Central de Nicaragua. Z1481.W66

Panama

Alba C, Manuel María. Cronología de los gobernantes de Panamá, 1510–1967. Panamá : [s.n.], 1967. 399 p. **DB317**

Offers biographical sketches of heads of state, including juntas, in chronological order. Brief bibliography, p. 389–92. F1566.A317

Canal Zone. Library-Museum, Balboa Heights. Subject catalog of the special Panama Collection of the Canal Zone Library-Museum : the history of the Isthmus of Panama as it applies to interoceanic transportation. Boston : G. K. Hall, 1964. 341 p. : ill., maps. **DB318**

7,000 cards representing nearly 500 subject headings have been reproduced. Although the strength of the collection lies in materials on the planning and construction of the Canal, there is much on exploration, travelers' accounts, and political and social life. Works cited are in English and Spanish. Z1500.C35

Gasteazoro, Carlos Manuel. Introducción al estudio de la historia de Panamá : fuentes de la época hispánica / prólogo de Celestino Andrés Araúz. 2a. ed. Panamá Rep. de Panamá : Editores Manfer, 1990. 157 p. : ill., maps. **DB319**

Bibliographic essay with discussion of sources. Very good historical maps. Not indexed.

§ Christopher Ward's "Panamanian historical sources," *Latin American research review* 21, no. 3 (1986) : 129-36 surveys six archives in Panama considered most important for historical research, giving for each a description of its contents. Z1500.G3

Langstaff, Eleanor De Selms. Panama / Eleanor De Selms Langstaff, comp. ; Sheila R. Herstein, ed. Oxford, ; Santa Barbara, Calif. : Clio Pr., 1982. 184 p. (World bibliographical series, v. 14). **DB320**

Books, articles, documents of international organizations, and a few dissertations are arranged by topic, with brief annotations. Spanish-language materials are included on topics for which English sources were not available. Z1500.L36

SOUTH AMERICA

Amazon River Region

Amazônia : bibliografia. Rio de Janeiro : Instituto Brasileiro de Bibliografia e Documentação, 1963–1977. 4 v. **DB321**

Contents: v. 1, 1614–1962; v. 2, 1601–1970; v. 3, 1971–72; v. 4, 1973–74.

Includes references to books, periodical articles, and other documents; arranged by Universal Decimal Classification. Author index.

§ *Documentação Amazônica: catalogo colectivo* (Belém : SUDAM, 1974–75. 3 v.) reproduces catalog cards for books, journals, monographic serials, and documents dealing with the Amazon added by cooperating libraries 1960–74. Author, subject and geographic indexes. Z1694.A55R5

Amazonía ecuatoriana : reseña bibliográfica comentada 1950–1992 / Marco Restrepo G. ; colaboración, Marco Andrade, Patricia Ortiz. Quito, Ecuador : CEDIME ; [Mexico] : CONACYT, 1992. 373 p. **DB322**

Author arrangement of books, essays, pamphlets, government and research reports, and periodical articles on all facets of the Amazon region. Materials included were published mostly in the 1970s and 1980s; annotations; one library location for each entry. Subject index; library location index. Z1784.A46R47

Argentina

Bibliography

Academia Nacional de la Historia (Argentina). Catálogo analítico de las publicaciones de la Academia Nacional de la Historia, 1903–1986 / presentación del presidente, Enrique M. Barba ; introducción y compilación, Néstor E. Poitevin y Graciela G. Barcala de Moyano. Buenos Aires : La Academia, 1987. 359 p. : facsim. **DB323**
"Edición de homenaje al quinto centenario del descubrimiento de América"—*p.iii.*
Index to all publications of the Academia Nacional. Some 4,300 entries arranged by topic, with author and subject indexes.
Z1626.A28

Biggins, Alan. Argentina. Oxford, Eng. ; Santa Barbara, Calif. : Clio Pr., c1991. 460 p. (World bibliographical series, v. 130). **DB324**
Cites 1,350 books and some periodical articles in English unless there is no equivalent to the Spanish-language work. Emphasizes publications of the 1960s–1980s. Topical arrangement; author, title, and subject indexes.
§ *See also*: Universidad de Buenos Aires, *Bibliografía argentina : catálogo de materiales argentinos en las bibliotecas de la Universidad de Buenos Aires* (AA497). Z1611.B62

Etchepareborda, Roberto. Historiografía militar argentina. Buenos Aires : Círculo Militar, 1984. 205 p. (Biblioteca del oficial, v. 717). **DB325**
A comprehensive bibliography of publications–newspapers, government documents, books, articles–on military actions up to 1943, including wars of revolution, coup d'états, civil wars, border wars, and the "conquest of the Indians." Mostly Argentinian publications.
F2832.E83

Fúrlong Cárdiff, Guillermo. Bibliografía de la Revolución de Mayo, 1810–1828 / por Guillermo Fúrlong y Abel Rodolfo Geoghegan. Edición especial con motivo del Sesquicentenario de la Revolución de Mayo de 1810. Buenos Aires : Biblioteca del Congreso de la Nación, 1960. 704 p. **DB326**
A detailed, classified listing of materials on the period of the Argentine revolt from Spain. Nearly 10,000 items—monographs, periodical articles, and documents—are included, with annotations and often tables of contents for the more significant works. Author index.
Z1629.F8

Horvath, Laszlo. Peronism and the three Perons : a checklist of material on Peronism and on Juan Domingo, Eva, and Isabel Peron, and their writings, in the Hoover Institution library and archives and in the Stanford University Libraries. Stanford, Calif. : Hoover Institution, Stanford Univ., c1988. 170 p. (Hoover Press bibliography, 71). **DB327**
A checklist of books, pamphlets, offprints, and archival material at Stanford. Arranged in four sections: (1) Works on Peronism and on Don Domingo Peron; (2) Works on Eva Peron; (3) Works on Isabel Peron; (4) All published writings of the three Perons at Stanford. Not indexed.
§ *See also* Horvath's *A half century of Peronism, 1943–1993 : an international bibliography* (Stanford: Hoover Institution, 1993. 375 p. [Hoover Press bibliography, 76]). Z1630.3.H67

Matijevic, Nicolás. Bibliografía patagónica y de las tierras australes / Nicolás Matijevic, Olga H. de Matijevic. Bahía Blanca : Centro de Documentación Patagónica, Univ. Nacional del Sur, 1973–78. 2 v. **DB328**
Contents: v. 1, Historia; v. 2, Geografía. Other volumes were intended but were never completed.
Each volume is a topically arranged bibliography of more than 2,000 entries, with indexes of names and of geographic areas. Further volumes were to cover: (3) Indígenas; (4) Botánica y zoología; (5) Geología y paleontología; (6) Recursos naturales y desarrollo.
Z1634.P58M38

Santos Gómez, Susana. Bibliografía de viajeros a la Argentina. Buenos Aires : Fundación para la Educación, la Ciencia y la Cultura, c1983. 2 v. (650 p., [8] leaves of plates) : facsims. **DB329**
Lists about 3,000 published accounts by travelers to Argentina, written 16th–20th centuries. Includes books, articles, pamphlets, government documents, and anthologies, in French, English, Spanish and German. Gives location in an Argentine library. Author index.
Z1626.S32

Encyclopedias; Dictionaries

Gran enciclopedia argentina / [por] Diego A. de Santillán. Buenos Aires : Ediar, 1956–64. 9 v. : ill., maps. **DB330**
Subtitle: Todo lo argentino ordenado alfabeticamente; geografía e historia, toponimias, biografías, ciencias, artes, letras, derecho, economía, industria y comercio, instituciones, flora y fauna, folklore, léxico regional.
Vol. 9: Apendice (460 p.).
A national rather than a general encyclopedia, providing a large body of reference material not easily available otherwise. Biographical entries are numerous, including living persons.

Vázquez-Presedo, Vicente. Estadísticas históricas argentinas (comparadas). Buenos Aires : Ediciones Macchi, [1971]-1988. 3 v. **DB331**
For annotation, *see* CG137. HA957.V39

Historiography

Bohdziewicz, Jorge C. Bibliografía de bibliografías individuales : historia y antropología. Buenos Aires, Instituto Bibliográfico "Antonio Zinny", 1979. 56 p. **DB332**
An annotated bibliography arranged by name of Argentine scholar; includes lengthy bibliographies published in books and periodical articles.

Historiografía argentina, 1958–1988 : una evaluación crítica de la producción histórica nacional / Comité Internacional de Ciencias Históricas, Comité Argentino, 1988. Buenos Aires : Comité Internacional de Ciencias Históricas, Comité Argentino, 1990. 625 p. **DB333**
Scholarly, signed articles reporting on historiography in Argentina. Surveys cover all history, but are especially strong on Argentina. Arranged topically, e.g., regions , colonial history, demography. Not indexed.
§ For the earlier period *see* Elisabeth Feigen de Roca and Alicia Gaer de Sabulsky, *Historiografía Argentina 1930–1970* (Buenos Aires : Servicio de Documentación Libreria Piolot, 1972. 2 v.) which cites almost 5,100 books and articles. A supplementary work is the survey by Héctor José Tanzi, *Historiografía argentina contemporánea* (Caracas, 1976. 167 p. [Instituto Panamericano de Geografía e Historia, 339. Historiografías, 9]). F2829.H57

Bolivia

Barnadas, Josep M. Introducción a los estudios bolivianos contemporáneos, 1960–1984 : manual de bibliografía / Josep Barnadas ; [revisado y corregido por Carlota Rosasco de Chacón]. Cusco : Centro de Estudios Rurales Andinos "Bartolomé de las Casas", c1987. 514 p. (Archivos de historia andina, 6). **DB334**
 An extensive bibliography of 6,227 books, articles, theses, essays in collections, and government publications on all aspects of Bolivia, 1960–84, though especially strong for history (with more than 3,050 entries). Topically arranged under broad headings, each with a brief bibliographical essay. Subject index. F3308.B37

Bibliografía de la mujer boliviana, 1920–1985 : La Paz, Sucre, Cochabamba y Santa Cruz / Miriam Agramont Virreira … [et al.]. La Paz : [Ediciones CIDEM, 1986]. 158 p. : ill. (Serie Mujer bibliografía, 1). **DB335**
 687 books, pamphlets, and theses, listed alphabetically by author or title. Gives at least one location in a library in Bolivia. Emphasizes feminist literature. Subject index. Z7964.B5B53

Cajías, Lupe. Las relaciones de Bolivia, Chile y Perú : el problema marítimo boliviano : guía mínima bibliográfica. La Paz, Bolivia : Ediciones CERID, 1992. 124 p. **DB336**
 Based on material available in the libraries of La Paz. An author listing of 345 books, including histories, commentaries, poetry and novels, government documents, and unpublished studies. Brief annotations. Broad topical index (e.g., economics, literature, foreign relations). Gives locations in La Paz. Z6465.B5C35

Lora, Guillermo. Diccionario político, histórico, cultural. La Paz, Bolivia : Ediciones Masas, 1985. 603 p. **DB337**
 Cover subtitle: Lora y Bolivia.
 Marxist approach. Mainly short biographical entries, but also includes political parties, movements, laws, events. Not indexed; no cross-references; no bibliography. F3304.L66

Yeager, Gertrude Matyoka. Bolivia. Oxford, Eng. ; Santa Barbara, Calif. : Clio Pr., c1988. 228 p. (World bibliographical series, v. 89). **DB338**
 Offers 816 annotated entries for books, government reports, periodical articles, and dissertations. Topically arranged in 36 sections. Author/title/subject indexes.
 § See also José Vázquez Machicado's archival guide, Catálogo descriptivo del material del Archivo de Indias referente a la historia de Bolivia (La Paz : Ministerio de Educación y Cultura, Instituto Boliviano de Cultura, 1989. 525 p.; ill).
 Although dated, Maruja Uribe and Margarita Hernandez, Bibliografía selectiva sobra desarrollo rural en Bolivia (Bogotá : Biblioteca IICA, 1980. 134 p.) is still useful for historical research. Arranged in broad topical divisions, it cites 1,000 books, documents, and articles published 1960–80. Z1641.Y43

Brazil

Guides

Lacombe, Américo Jacobina. Introdução ao estudo da história do Brasil. São Paulo : Companhia Editora Nacional, [1974]. 208 p. (Brasiliana, v. 349). **DB339**
 A useful manual. Chapters on sources include archives, periods of history, regional history, academies and associations. F2520.7.L32

Rodrigues, José Honório. A pesquisa histórica do Brasil. 4. ed., rev. e atualizada. São Paulo : Companhia Editora Nacional, 1982. 314 p. (Brasiliana. Serie grande formato, v. 20). **DB340**
 1st ed., 1952.
 A guide for the student of Brazilian history. Includes discussions of archives, sources, historiography, etc. This edition includes notes, additions, revisions to the 2nd ed. (1968), p. 294–302, and an appendix of new editions with emphasis on those relating to archives, p. 273–93. F2520.4.R6

Bibliography

Bryant, Solena V. Brazil / Solena V. Bryant, comp. ; ed. by Sheila R. Herstein. Oxford, Eng. ; Santa Barbara, Calif. : Clio Pr., c1985. 244 p. (World bibliographical series, v. 57). **DB341**
 Presents 802 annotated entries for books, essays, and articles arranged in 36 topical sections. Emphasizes English-language materials published in the 1970s and early 1980s. Author/title/subject index.
 § For a bibliography of politics in Brazil see Bibliografia do pensamento político republicano (1870/1980) comp. by Evelyse Maria Freire Mendes, rev. by Edson Nery da Fonseca (2nd ed. Brasilia : Camâra des Deputados, 1983. 205 p.). Z1671.B78

Chilcote, Ronald H. Brazil and its radical left : an annotated bibliography on the communist movement and the rise of Marxism, 1922–1972. Millwood, N.Y. : Kraus Internat. Pubns., 1980. 455 p. **DB342**
 In three sections: the first two are author listings of more than 3,000 books, pamphlets and periodical articles on the communist, socialist, anarchist, and leftist-oriented labor movements in Brazil since the founding of the Brazilian Communist Party in 1922; the third is a list of periodicals, with library locations. Brief annotations. Index to periodicals cited and a general index. Z7164.S67C54

Fundação Carlos Chagas. Mulher brasileira : bibliografia anotada. São Paulo : Editora Brasiliense, 1979–81. 2 v. **DB343**
 Contents: v. 1, História, família, grupos éthnicos, feminismo; v. 2, Trabalho, direito, educacão, artes e meios de comunicacáo.
 Extensive bibliography of books, articles, theses topically arranged. Annotated; author index.
 § Updated by June Edith Hahner, "Recent research on women in Brazil," in Latin American research review 20, no. 3 (1985) : 163–79, for books and articles published 1977–85. HQ1542.F86

Hartness, Ann. Brazil in reference books, 1965–1989 : an annotated bibliography. Metuchen, N.J. : Scarecrow, 1991. 351 p. **DB344**
 Aims to satisfy the "need for reference materials to provide bibliographic data, define terms, locate places, identify individuals and supply statistics."—Introd. Books, pamphlets, reprints, annuals, and whole issues of journals are arranged by broad topic, subdivided by format, geographic area, or subtopic as needed. Cites reference material at the regional, country, state, and city levels. Annotations indicate scope of the work. Author and subject indexes. Z1671.H38

Levine, Robert M. Brazil, 1822–1930 : an annotated bibliography for social historians. N.Y. : Garland, 1983. 487 p. (Garland reference library of social science, v. 132). **DB345**
 An annotated bibliography of books, collections of essays, articles, and dissertations on Brazilian society and culture, as well as its historical and political evolution from independence to 1830. About half the entries are in English, the others in Portuguese, Spanish, French, and German; cutoff date for publications is 1981. Author and subject indexes.
 Coverage continued in Levine's earlier work, Brazil since 1930 : an annotated bibliography for social historians (1980. 336 p.). Z1671.L478

Moraes, Rubens Borba de. Bibliographia brasiliana : rare books about Brazil published from 1504 to 1900 and works by Brazilian authors of the colonial period. Rev. and enl. ed. Los Angeles : UCLA Latin American Ctr. Pubns., Univ. of Calif. ; Rio de Janeiro : Livraria Kosmos Editôra, [1983]. 2 v. (1074 p.) : ill. (University of California, Los Angeles. Latin American Center. Publications. Reference series, v. 10). **DB346**

1st ed., 1958.

The purpose is "to describe and comment upon rare books about various aspects of Brazil and upon books by Brazilian authors which were printed outside the borders of Brazil before or shortly after Independence in 1822. I have incorporated the entries from my *Bibliografia brasileira do periodo colonial* ... [1969] and shortened the commentaries. In this revised edition, there is more emphasis on entries for books of the sixteenth, seventeenth, and eighteenth centuries than on books published in the nineteenth century when production increased. ... "—*Pref.*

Commentaries emphasize the importance of the book in relation to Brazil; short biographies of the author or printer are supplied in some cases. Subject index; works cited in the commentaries are indexed by subject as well as by author and title.

§ *See also* Anatole Louis Garraux, *Bibliographie brésilienne : catalogue des ouvrages français et latins relatifs au Brésil (1500–1898)* (2nd ed. Rio de Janeiro : J. Olympio, 1962. 519 p.).

Z1671.M6

Porter, Dorothy Burnett. Afro-Braziliana : a working bibliography. Boston : G. K. Hall, [1978]. 294 p. **DB347**
For annotation, *see* CC475. Z1697.N4P67

Pôrto, Angela. Processo de modernização do Brasil, 1850–1930 : economia e sociedade, una bibliografia / elaboração, Angela Pôrto, Lilian de A. Fritsch, Sylvia F. Padilha. Rio de Janeiro : Fundação Casa de Rui Barbosa : Biblioteca CREFISUL, 1985. 364 p. **DB348**

2,053 annotated entries for books are topically arranged (e.g., works of reference; biographies; economics, subdivided by industry; finance, subdivided by topic). Materials cited were published from late 19th century to 1981. Author, title, and very broad subject indexes.

Z7165.B7P67

Library resources

France. Ministère des affaires étrangères. Archives. Guide des sources de l'histoire du Brésil aux archives du Ministère français des affaires étrangères / Pascal Even. Paris : Publications de l'I.H.E.A.L., 1987. 63 p. : ill. (Travaux & mémoires de l'Institut des hautes études de l'Amérique latine. Collection "Textes & documents", 38). **DB349**

Lists files of materials relevant to Brazil in the Archives. Appendix lists French representatives to Brazil. Not indexed. Z1699.F73

Guia preliminar de fontes para a história do Brasil : instituições governamentais do Município do Rio de Janeiro / supervisão geral, Maria Amelia Porto Migueis ... [et al.]. Rio de Janeiro : Fundação Casa de Rui Barbosa : Fundação Getúlio Vargas, CPDOC, 1979. 128 p. **DB350**

A guide to repositories of federal, state, and municipal archives in Rio de Janeiro. Gives name and address, collecting interest, and brief descriptions of contents, including films. Institution index.

§ For similar coverage of Portuguese archives, *see* Caio C. Boschi, *Roteiro sumario dos arquivos portugueses de interesse para o pesquisador da história do Brasil* (Saõ Paulo : Ed. Arquivo do Estado, 1986. 113 p.). The archives in Brasília are covered by *Guia preliminar de fontes para a história de Brasília* (Brasília : Arquivo Público do Distrito Federal, 1988. 145 p.).

The Arquivo Nacional in Rio has published a list of some 600 publications that catalog, describe, or print materials which are part of the Arquivo : *Publicacões de Arquivo Nacional 1886–1990* (Rio de Janeiro : [Arquivo Nacional], 1991. 192 p.). The volume ends with indexes for titles, authors, and subjects. Z1694.B7G85

Jackson, William Vernon. Library guide for Brazilian studies. Pittsburgh : Distr. by the Univ. of Pittsburgh Book Centers, 1964. 197 p. **DB351**

A survey describing the holdings in 1963–64 of resources for Brazilian studies in the major research collections of the United States. Includes chapters on general materials, humanities, social sciences, science, and technology, with indications of strengths and weaknesses in specific subject areas. Contains a bibliography of published guides, catalogs, and descriptions of specific collections; useful appendixes include a union list of selected Brazilian periodicals in the humanities and social sciences, and indexes to the Library of Congress classification schemes for Brazilian history and literature. The index of libraries, plus a number of maps and tables, add to the value of the guide.

§ Jackson also compiled *Resources for Brazilian studies at the Bibliothèque Nationale* (Austin : Jackson, 1980. 57 p.). Z1671.J3

Encyclopedias

Brasil A/Z : enciclopédia alfabética em um único volume. São Paulo : Editora Universo, c1988. 867 p. : ill., maps in color. **DB352**

Cover title: Larousse cultural, Brasil A/Z.

A short entry encyclopedia covering any aspect of Brazil. Statistics as recent as 1988. Appendix lists flora and fauna entries.

F2508.B78

Dicionário de história do Brasil : moral e civismo / organização geral, Departamento Editorial das Edições Melhoramentos ; redação de temas e biografias, Brasil Bandecchi ... [et al.]. 4. ed. São Paulo : Melhoramentos, 1976 [c1973]. 618 p. **DB353**

1st ed. (1970) entitled: *Novo dicionário de história do Brasil.*

Offers brief unsigned articles on persons and events. Supplementary sections of national dates, description of the organization of the federal government, and sections on moral and civic education (including a summary of the laws and a description of the commission of that name).

§ See also *Dicionário biobibliográfico de historiadores, geógrafos e antropólogos brasileiros* (Rio de Janeiro : Instituto Histórico e Geográfico Brasileiro, 1991–93. v. 1–3 [In progress]).

F2504.D49

Dicionário histórico-biográfico brasileiro, 1930–1983 / coordenação de Israel Beloch e Alzira Alves de Abreu. Rio de Janeiro-RJ : Forense-Universitária : FINEP, 1984. 4 v. (3634 p.) : ports. **DB354**

Although primarily biographical, there are entries for parties, governmental bodies, and other organizations. For annotation, *see* AH124. F2504.D53

Handbooks

Donato, Hernâni. Dicionário das batalhas brasileiras. São Paulo : Instituição Brasileira de Difusão Cultural, [1987], c1986. 542 p. (Biblioteca "Estudos brasileiros", 15). **DB355**

Cover title: Dos conflitos com indígenas ás guerrilhas políticas urbanas e rurais.

Includes a list of popular names of battles, a chronology, surveys of wars, and a short-entry dictionary of people, battles, places, etc.

F2522.D66

Ludwig, Armin K. Brazil : a handbook of historical statistics. Boston : G.K. Hall, c1985. 487 p. : maps. **DB356**

Social, economic, and political statistics, arranged in broad subject sections. Tables cover varying time periods; sources of data are cited. Serves as a guide to the statistics of Brazil.   HA984.L83

Historiography

Rodrigues, José Honório. História da história do Brasil. São Paulo : Companhia Editora Nacional, 1979–1988. 3 v. (Brasiliana, v. 21, 23–24.).   **DB357**
An extensive, authoritative discussion of writings on colonial Brazil constitutes v. 1, replacing the compiler's *Historiografía del Brasil* (México, 1957–63. 2 v.). Vol. 2, in two parts, covers historiography of the 19th and 20th centuries.   F2520.4.R615

Chile

Bibliography

Blakemore, Harold. Chile. Oxford, Eng. ; Santa Barbara, Calif. : Clio Pr., c1988. 197 p., [2] p. of plates : maps. (World bibliographical series, v. 97).   **DB358**
Presents 642 annotated entries for books and longer periodical articles topically arranged in 29 sections. Most are English-language works although Spanish-language materials are included where there is little or no coverage of the topic in English. Emphasizes recent publications. Author, title, and subject indexes.
§ See also two works by Guillermo Feliú Cruz: *Viajes relativos a Chile* (Santiago : Fondo Historico y Bibliografico José Toribio Medina, 1962. 2 v.) which covers travelers accounts. 16th–19th centuries; *Historia de las fuentes de la bibliografía chilena* (Santiago : Biblioteca Nacional, 1966–69. 4 v.), a collection of critical essays on historians, bibliographers, and chroniclers of Chile.
More recent information can be found in "A survey of recent Chilean historiography, 1965–1976," in *Latin American research review* 14, no. 2 (1979): 55–88.   Z1701.B56

Portales, Carlos. Bibliografía sobre relaciones internacionales y política exterior de Chile, 1964–1980. Santiago de Chile : Facultad Latinoamericana de Ciencias Sociales, [1981]. 19 p. (Documento de trabajo. Programa FLACSO, 108).   **DB359**
An author listing of books, articles, essays and documents in Spanish and English. Subject index.

Williams, Lee H. The Allende years : a union list of Chilean imprints, 1970–1973, in selected North American libraries, with a supplemental holdings list of books published elsewhere for the same period by Chileans or about Chile or Chileans. Boston : G. K. Hall, 1977. 339 p.   **DB360**
The Chilean holdings of 14 U.S. libraries are cited in three main sections: (1) Chilean monographs published 1970–73; (2) books published outside Chile, 1970–73, about Chile or by Chileans; (3) serial publications issued in Chile, 1970–73. The first two sections are subdivided by topic. Personal and corporate name index.
§ *See also* Manuel A. Garretón and Eugenia Hola A., *Bibliografía del proceso chileno 1970–1973* (Santiago : Facultad Latinoamericana de Ciencias Sociales, 1978. 393, 93 p.), which is an extensive listing of 3,400 books, pamphlets, documents, Chilean magazines and newspapers, and political party publications in a topical arrangement.
   Z1701.W55

Library resources

Sehlinger, Peter J. A select guide to Chilean libraries and archives. Bloomington : Latin American Studies Program, Indiana Univ., 1979. 35 p. (Latin American studies working papers, 9).   **DB361**
For each library or archive is given: name, address, person in charge, and description of relevant collections, together with references to any published guides or finding aids.   Z771.A1S43

Handbooks

Céspedes, Mario. Gran diccionario de Chile : (biográfico-cultural) / Mario Céspedes, Lelia Garreaud. 2a ed. Santiago, Chile : Importadora Alfa, 1988. 2 v. (888 p.) : ill., ports.   **DB362**
Primarily consists of biographical articles for political, literary, and cultural figures in Chile but also includes events, places, and political groups and movements. Occasional cross-references. Appendix lists Governantes de Chile 1540–1974; Principales batallas, 1536–1891; political and administrative units. Six pages of bibliography. No index.
§ Almost all the topics found in Jordi Fuentes' *Diccionario histórico de Chile* (10th ed. Santiago : Zig-Zag, 1988. 663 p.) are found in the Céspedes work, though not always at as much length.
   F3060.C4

Colombia

Bibliography

Bernal Villa, Segundo. Guía bibliográfica de Colombia de interés para el antropólogo. Bogotá : Ediciones Universidad de los Andes, 1969. 782 p. : maps.   **DB363**
An extensive bibliography with emphasis on cultural anthropology but with some attention to archaeology, geography, history, and linguistics. A general section is followed by regional sections. Author index.   Z1731.B44

Cardona Grisález, Guillermo. Para un estudio sobre la violencia en Columbia : bibliografía. Bogotá, Colombia : Centro de Investigación y Educación Popular, 1989. 271 p. (Documentos ocasionales, 55).   **DB364**
An unannotated bibliography of 1,807 books, documents, theses, and articles published in Colombia, with library locations. Entries are mostly from the 1970s and 1980s up to about 1987, although earlier materials are present. Topical arrangement with author index.
   HN310.V5C37

Davis, Robert H. Colombia. Oxford, Eng. ; Santa Barbara, Calif. : Clio Pr., c1990. 204 p. (World bibliographical series, v. 112).   **DB365**
Intends to present "a good representative sample for an English-language reader" (*Pref.*) with a preference for materials of the last 25 years. About 660 annotated entries, arranged topically. Indexed by author, title, and subject.   Z1731.D38

Giraldo Jaramillo, Gabriel. Bibliografía colombiana de viajes. Bogotá : Editorial ABC, 1957. 224 p. (Biblioteca de bibliografía colombiana, 2).   **DB366**
An alphabetical listing of travelers accounts by Colombians or by non-Colombians journeying to Colombia. Brief annotations; no index.
   Z1746.G5

Ocampo López, Javier. Historiografía y bibliografía de la emancipación del Nuevo Reino de Granada. Tunja : Universidad Pedagogica y Tecnológica de Colombia, 1969. 555 p. **DB367**

A brief historiographical section is followed by a lengthy bibliography of the emancipation of Colombia, covering mainly the years 1810–1819. In addition to the listing of archives, documents, and contemporary sources, there is a broad subject arrangement of secondary materials. Author, biographical, and subject indexes.   Z1749.O23

Handbooks

Gómez Aristizábal, Horacio. Diccionario de la historia de Colombia. 2a ed., condensada y corr., 1a ed. en SCC. Bogotá : Plaza & Janes, 1985. 287 p. : ill. (Selección cultura colombiana, 10). **DB368**

Offers brief entries (about 1 or 1½ columns) for topics, biographies, and some historical events. Appendix includes a short bibliography, chronological lists of governors and vice-regents (1550–1810) and presidents and other rulers (1810–1986).   F2254.G58

Ecuador

Bibliography

Corkill, David. Ecuador. Oxford, Eng. ; Santa Barbara, Calif. : Clio Pr., c1989. 155 p. : map. (World bibliographical series, v. 101). **DB369**

A topical arrangement of 557 annotated entries for books and articles in Spanish and English. Indexed by author, title, and subject.   Z1761.C67

Ecuador. Junta Nacional de Planificatión y Coordinación Económica. Sección de Investigaciones Sociales. Bibliografía social, económica y política del Ecuador. [Quito] : La Sección, [1973?]. 2 v. (708 p.). **DB370**

Preliminary ed. (1972?) had title: *Listado parcial de la bibliografía social, socio-éconómica y política del Ecuador.*

Cites some 4,000 books, articles, and dissertations in Spanish or English published approximately 1890–1969 in all areas of the social sciences; includes a long section for history, subdivided by period and region. Most citations are annotated; topical arrangement; no index.

§ A more recent bibliography covering some of the same subjects is *Ecuador, aspectos socio-económicos: bibliografía* by Lucia Alzamora C. (2.ed. Quito : Junapla, 1977. 212 p.). It lists approximately half the number of books, documents and articles in Spanish, English, French, and German in topical arrangement, but without annotations. No index.   Z7165.E28E26

Rosero, Rocío. Bibliografía sobre la mujer en el Ecuador / Rocío Rosero, Jackeline Contreras. Quito, Ecuador : ILDIS, c1988. 164 p. **DB371**

About 500 books, journal articles, theses, conference proceedings and unpublished research on the condition of women in Ecuador are cited in a broad topical arrangement. Annotated; author and subject indexes. Gives one location for each item.   Z7964.E2R67

Uribe, Maruja. Bibliografía selectiva sobre desarrollo rural en el Ecuador / Maruja Uribe, Blanca Cecilia Salazar, Margarita Hernández. Bogotá : Instituto Interamericano de Ciencias Agrícolas-OEA, 1979. 203 p. (Documentación e Información Agrícola, no.75). **DB372**

An extensive bibliography of 1,549 references, published mainly 1960–79, on broad topics such as planning, cooperatives, legislation, and historical aspects. Includes a directory of 121 organizations and 139 periodicals. Author index.

Manuscripts; Archives

Archivo Nacional de Historia (Ecuador). Guía del Archivo Nacional de Historia. Quito : Edit. Casa de la Cultura Ecuatoriana, 1981. 219 p. **DB373**

Describes collections available in the Archivo Nacional. Most files of government departments end in the 19th century; files of personal papers close prior to World War II.

§ *See also* Grecia Vasco de Escudero, *Los archivos quiteños* (Quito : Instituto Panamericanos de Geografía y Historia, Sección Nacional del Ecuador, 1977. 178 p.). For calendars of Foreign office materials (FO25, FO368, FO371) held by the Public Record Office (London), see *Guía de la documentación diplomática británica sobre Ecuador*, comp. Enrique Ayala Mora (Quito : Facultad Latinoamericana de Ciencias Sociales, Sede Quito, 1986. 85 p.). Citations are also given to relevant years in the printed reports from the Department of Overseas Trade, which include information on economic and financial conditions in Ecuador.   CD4126 1981

Falkland Islands

Islas Malvinas. Buenos Aires : OIKOS, Asociación para la Promoción de los Estudios Territoriales y Ambientales, [1982]. 242 p. : ill. **DB374**

Contents: Reseña geográfica, by Federico A. Daus; Bibliografía (1955–1982), by Raúl C. Rey Balmaceda.

The bibliography (p. 89–242) lists books, newspaper and periodical articles, documents, and conference proceedings, January 1955–June 1982 (the end of the hostilities with Argentina). Broad coverage (e.g., water circulation). No index.

§ For the period 1965–1982, *see* the historiographical article by Roberto Etchepareborda, "La bibliografia reciente sobre la cuestion Malvinar," in *Revista interamericana de bibliografia* 34, no. 1 (1984): 1–52; 34, no. 2 (1984): 227–88.   F3031.I82

Orgill, Andrew. The Falklands War : background, conflict, aftermath : an annotated bibliography. ; N.Y. : Mansell, 1993. 132 p. **DB375**

Bibliographical essay followed by an annotated listing of 822 books, government and international organization documents, and periodical (not newspaper) articles, mostly in English and Spanish. Arranged in five subject areas, further subdivided: bibliographies, sovereignty dispute, 1982 crisis, war, and aftermath. Cutoff date for coverage is December 1991. Author/subject index; index of journal and serial titles.

§ Eugene L. Rasor's *The Falklands/Malvinas campaign : a bibliography* (N.Y. : Greenwood, 1992. 196 p.) seeks to cite all published books, oral histories, government publications, periodical articles, dissertations, and conference papers, in English, Spanish, French and German. Includes creative works, e.g., fiction, drama, film, art. 554 titles. Indexed by author and subject.   Z1945.O74

Torre Revello, José. Bibliografía de las Islas Malvinas : obras, mapas y documentos; contribución. Buenos Aires : Impr. de la Universidad, 1953. 260 p. : maps, facsims. (Universidad de Buenos Aires. Facultad de Filosofía y Letras. Publication del Inst. de Investigaciones Históricas, no. 99). **DB376**

A bibliography of more than 800 items on the history and geography of the Falkland Islands, with a section listing unpublished documents, 1534–1953. Many of the works listed are in Spanish, but some titles in other languages are included.

§ *See also* Sara de Mundo Lo's *The Falkland/Malvinas Islands: a bibliography of books, 1619–1982* (Urbana, Ill. : Albatross, 1983. 65 p.) for an author listing of books, government publications, and pamphlets covering "discovery and exploration to wildlife" (*Introd.*) of the Falkland Islands. Subject index.   Z1945.T6

French Guiana

Abonnenc, Émile. Bibliographie de la Guyane Française / E. Abonnenc, J. Hurault, R. Savan ... [et al.]. Paris : Éd. Larose, 1957. v. 1.   **DB377**

Contents: t.1, Ouvrages et articles de langue française concernant la Guyane et les territoires avoisinants (78 p.). No more published.

A comprehensive bibliography of books and periodical articles which appeared from the end of the 16th century to 1955. Listing is alphabetical by author with subject index. A second volume was planned to cover non-French materials.   Z1811.A2

Guyana

Chambers, Frances. Guyana. Oxford, Eng. ; Santa Barbara, Calif. : Clio Pr., c1989. 206 p. (World bibliographical series, v. 96).   **DB378**

Provides 606 annotated entries for books, periodical articles, and government publications, topically arranged. Author, title, and subject indexes.   Z1791.C48

Malvinas

See Falkland Islands.

Paraguay

Jones, David Lewis. Paraguay : a bibliography. N.Y. : Garland, 1979. 499 p. (Garland reference library of social science, v. 51).   **DB379**

Aims "to present a fairly comprehensive list of works relating to Paraguay for the use of students in other countries."—*Introd.* Includes books in European languages and Guarani, and articles from Paraguayan periodicals deemed "reasonably accessible in British, United States and Canadian libraries." Classed arrangement with author/subject index. More than 4,400 entries.   Z1821.J66

Nickson, R. Andrew. Paraguay. Oxford, Eng. ; Santa Barbara, Calif. : Clio Pr., c1987. 212 p. (World bibliographical series, v. 84).   **DB380**

Offers 600 annotated entries organized into 33 topical chapters. Cross-references; indexed by author, title, and subject.   Z1821.N53

Peru

Bibliography

Basadre, Jorge. Introducción a las bases documentales para la historia de la República del Perú : con algunas reflexiones. [Lima] : Ediciones P.L.V., [1971]. 3 v.   **DB381**

An extensive bibliography of Peruvian history from independence in 1822 to 1933, including diplomatic and military history, legal and legislative affairs, statistics, material on the theater, literature, memoirs, etc. Arranged by topic within period divisions; good introductory chapters on archival and library guides, bibliographies, collections of documents. Indexes of personal names, geographical names, serial publications, and topics by chapter.   Z1851.B35

Fisher, John Robert. Peru. Oxford, Eng. ; Santa Barbara, Calif. : Clio Pr., c1989. 193 p. (World bibliographical series, v. 109).   **DB382**

A selective annotated bibliography of 705 recent publications in English (with some in Spanish): books, U.N. publications, and a few articles. Topically arranged in 31 sections. Cross-references; author, title, and subject indexes.   Z1851.F57

Martínez, Héctor. Bibliografía indígena andina peruana (1900–1968) / Héctor Martínez, Miguel Cameo C., Jesús Ramírez S. [Lima : Centro de Estudios de Población y Desarrollo, 1969]. 157 p.   **DB383**

A multigraphed edition in 2 v. was publ. 1968.

A classed bibliography of 1,700 items. A general section is followed by sections for northern, central, and southern areas of Peru, each with geographical and topical subdivisions. Indexes of authors, subjects, and places.   Z1209.2.P3M37

Muñoz de Linares, Elba. Bibliografía de tesis peruanos sobre indigenismo y ciencias sociales / Elba Muñoz de Linares, Alicia Céspedes de Reynaga. Lima : Instituto Indigenista Peruano, 1983. 2 v. (733 p.). (Serie bibliográfica, 4).   **DB384**

Topical arrangement; chapter headings are given for each work cited. Indexed by author, subject, ethnic group, place-name, and institution.

§ Among the other useful bibliographies in the Institute's series: *Bibliografía sobre identidad cultural en el Perú* (1982. 126 p.); *Legislación peruanos sobre comunidades y comunidades nativas* (1985. 206 p.); *Indices y resúmenes de "Perú indígena" y "Perú integral"* (1982. 259 p.).

Ravines, Rogger. Introducción a una bibliografía general de la arqueología del Perú, 1860–1988. Lima : Editorial Los Pinos, 1989. 296 p. : ill.   **DB385**

3,600 entries for books, essays, conference papers, and articles; listed by author, with indexes by subject and personal name. All languages. Includes sketch of archaeology in Peru with a synopsis of the relevant laws.

§ See also *The Incas : a bibliography of books and periodical articles*, comp. by Thomas L. Welch and René L. Gutiérrez (CC478).   Z1208.1.4R38

Manuscripts; Archives

Peru. Archivo General de la Nación. Guía del archivo histórico. Lima : Archivo General de la Nación : Fondo del Libro del B.I.P., 1987. 44 p., [2] leaves of plates : ill.   **DB386**

Descriptions of files in the Archivo, focusing on those from 1708 till about 1940. A few contain material as late as 1985.   CD4223.P47

Encyclopedias; Dictionaries

Diccionario histórico y biográfico del Perú, siglos XV–XX / dirección, producción, revisión, ilustración, epígrafes, diagramación y edición, Carlos Milla Batres. Lima : Editorial Milla Batres, 1986. 9 v. : ill.   **DB387**

An encyclopedia of Peruvian history with a preponderance of biographical entries. Some living persons are included; bibliography appended to many articles.

§ Supplemented by *Diccionario histórico biográfico de los conquistadores del Perú*, comp. José Antonio del Busto Duthurburu (Lima : Librería Studium Ediciones, 1986–87. v. 1–2. [In progress?]), which gives information on the Spanish conquerors with reference to chronicles and secondary sources.   F3404.D53

Tauro, Alberto. Enciclopedia ilustrada del Perú : síntesis del conocimiento integral del Perú, desde sus orígenes hasta la actualidad. 2a ed. Lima, Perú : PEISA, c1988. 6 v. (2352 p.) : ill. **DB388**

"Biografías, historia, geografía, toponimias, folklore, peruanismos, flora y fauna, el territorio, los recursos naturales, los hombres en sus gestas y sus creaciones."   F3404.T38

Statistics

Portocarrero S., Felipe. Compendio estadístico del Perú, 1900–1990 / Felipe Portocarrero S., Arlette Beltrán B., María Elena Romero P. Lima, Perú : Universidad del Pacífico, Centro de Investigacíon (CIUP) : Consorcio de Investigacíon Económica, 1992. 184 p. : ill.   **DB389**

Compilation of mostly post-1945 statistics.

§ Another compilation of statistics is *Perú : series estadísticas 1970–92* (Direccíon Técnica de Indicadores Económicos, Dirección Ejecutiva de Previsíon y Estudios. Lima, Perú : Instituto Nacional de Estadística e Informática, 1993. 391 p.) Includes tables of statistics, economic, social, demographic, mainly from Peruvian sources. See also *Anuario estadístico del Perú* (CG157).   HC227.P67

Suriname

Brown, Enid. Suriname and the Netherlands Antilles : an annotated English-language bibliography. Metuchen, N.J. : Scarecrow, 1992. 275 p.   **DB390**

Based on collections in libraries in Guyana, Suriname, and the Caribbean for books, articles, documents, essays, and dissertations in English. Author or main entry arrangement of 1,223 entries; indexes for joint authors and topics. Gives addresses of libraries used.   Z1806.B76

Encyclopedie van Suriname / Hoofdredactie, C. F. A. Bruijning, J. Voorhoeve; samensteller, W. Gordijn. Amsterdam : Elsevier, 1977. 716 p. : ill.   **DB391**

A national encyclopedia with articles relating to the immediate area (natural and political history, physical features, flora, fauna, places, personalities, etc.).   F2404.E5

Hoefte, Rosemarijn. Suriname. Oxford, Eng. ; Santa Barbara, Calif. : Clio Pr., 1990. 227 p. : map. (World bibliographical series, v. 117).   **DB392**

A topical listing of 731 books and a few journal articles in English, Spanish, German, French, and Dutch. Indexed by author, title and subject.   Z1806.H64

Nagelkerke, Gerard A. Suriname : a bibliography, 1940–80. Leiden : Dept. of Caribbean Studies, R. Institute of Linguistics & Anthropology ; The Hague : Smits Drukkers-Uitgevers, 1980. 316 p.   **DB393**

A revision of the compiler's 1972 work, *Literatuur-overzicht van Suriname 1940 tot 1970.*

Citations to more than 2,600 monographs and articles are arranged by author, with subject and author index. The topic of Surinamers in the Netherlands is selectively treated. Based on the collection in the Library of the Royal Institute of Linguistics and Anthropology.

§ Continued by *Suriname: a bibliography 1980–1989*, compiled by Jo Derkx and Irene Rolfes (Leiden, 1990. 297 p.) with about 2,000 entries. Subject and name indexes.   Z1806.N33

Uruguay

Araújo, Orestes. Diccionario popular de historia de la República o. del Uruguay : desde la época del descubrimiento de su territorio, hasta la de su independencia. Montevideo : Dornaleche y Reyes, 1901–1903. 3 v.   **DB394**

A dictionary of persons, places, and events; includes documentary sources.   F2704.A67

Diccionario biográfico de la mujer en el Uruguay / Osvaldo A. Fraire [ed.]. [Montevideo, Uruguay : Impr. Rosgal], 1983. 163 p.   **DB395**

For annotation, *see* AH143.   CT3290.D53

Finch, M. H. J. Uruguay / Henry Finch ; with the assistance of Alicia Casas de Barrán. Oxford, Eng. ; Santa Barbara, Calif. : Clio Pr., c1989. 232 p. : map. (World bibliographical series, v. 102).   **DB396**

Offers 667 annotated entries arranged in 34 topical sections. Covers River Plate area. Indexed by author, title, and subject. Theses and dissertations on Uruguay, p. xxvii–xxix; this section not indexed.   Z1881.F56

Latin American Center for Research in the Social Sciences. Estratificación y movilidad social en el Uruguay : fuentes bibliograficas, 1880–1958. Rio de Janeiro, 1959. 60 p. (Centro Latino-Americano de Pesquisas em Ciências Sociais. Publicación, 5).   **DB397**

An annotated bibliography of some 327 books, plus a few articles and essays. Works are grouped as (1) Theory, (2) Before 1930, (3) Contemporary, and (4) Documentation (which includes statistical studies, biography, autobiography, and legislation). Entries are graded for importance on a scale of 1 to 4.

Venezuela

Guides

Lovera De-Sola, Roberto J. Guía para el estudio de la historia de Venezuela. Caracas : Academia Nacional de la Historia, 1982. 217 p. (Biblioteca de la Academia Nacional de la Historia. Estudios, monografías y ensayos, 23).   **DB398**

The 700 annotated entries for reference materials include bibliographies and guides for the study of Latin American as well as Venezuelan history, together with historical encyclopedias, chronologies, collections of documents, and archival guides. An author listing of books, pamphlets, periodicals and articles. Not indexed.

§ An older archival guide, *Estudio bibliográfico de los archivos venezolanos y extranjeros de interés para la historia de Venezuela*, comp. Agustín Millares Carlo (Caracas : Archivo General de la Nación, 1971. 367 p.), surveys state, local, and ecclesiastical archives, mostly in Venezuela.   Z1926.L68

Bibliography

Lombardi, John V. Venezuelan history : a comprehensive working bibliography / John V. Lombardi, Germán Carrera Damas, Roberta E. Adams ... [et al.]. Boston : G. K. Hall, 1977. 530 p.   **DB399**

Intended as "a starting place for the study of Venezuelan history."—*Pref.* More than 4,600 entries arranged under the following main headings: (1) General reference; (2) History; (3) Bolivar; (4) Church; (5) Civilization; (6) Education; (7) Geography; (8) Petroleum; (9) Population; (10) Urbanization. There is an author index, but none of detailed subjects.   Z1911.L64

Sullivan, William M. Dissertations and theses on Venezuelan topics, 1900–1985. Metuchen, N.J. : Scarecrow, 1988. 274 p. **DB400**

An annotated listing of master's theses and doctoral dissertations accepted in the U.S., Canada, the U.K., France, Austria, Venezuela, Germany, and Belgium, arranged by broad topics. Author and subject indexes. Z1911.S84

Waddell, D. A. G. Venezuela. Oxford, Eng. ; Santa Barbara, Calif. : Clio Pr., c1990. 206 p. (World bibliographical series, v. 110). **DB401**

Presents 800 annotated entries in a topical arrangement. Indexed by author, title, and subject. Z1911.W33

Encyclopedias

Diccionario de historia de Venezuela. Caracas, Venezuela : Fundacíon Polar, 1988 [i.e. 1989]. 3 v. **DB402**

A scholarly encyclopedia covering Venezuela from pre-Conquest up to about 1985–86 and offering an alphabetical arrangement of 10,000 entries for people, places, events, institutions, historiography, and similar topics. Articles are signed with initials; most have bibliographies of books and articles, and cross-references to related articles. Appendixes list chronicles and travelers' accounts, rulers and administrators, bishops, administrative divisions, oil towns, treaties, etc. Authoritative but not indexed. F2321.D55

Chronologies

Arellano Moreno, Antonio. Guía de historia de Venezuela. 3a. ed. Caracas : Ediciones Centauro, 1977. 262 p. **DB403**
1st ed., 1955.

A chronology of Venezuelan history, 1498–1977, with tables and lists of presidents, coups, buccaneers and pirates, constitutions, etc. F2319.5.A8

ISLANDS OF THE CARIBBEAN AND WESTERN ATLANTIC

General works

Bibliography

See also AA33.

Cohen Stuart, Bertie A. Women in the Caribbean : a bibliography. [The Hague] : Smits ; Leiden : Dept. of Caribbean Studies, Royal Inst. of Linguistics and Anthropology, 1979–1992. v. 1–3. (In progress?). **DB404**
Vol. 3 ed. by Irene Rolfes.

An annotated, classified bibliography dealing with Suriname, French Guiana and Guyana, the Bahamas and Bermuda, and the islands of the Antillean archipelago. Entries are coded according to the geographical codes used in Lambros Comitas, *The complete Caribbeana, 1900–1975* (DB405). Author index. Z7964.C38C64

Comitas, Lambros. The complete Caribbeana, 1900–1975 : a bibliographic guide to the scholarly literature. Millwood, N.Y. : KTO Pr., c1977. 4 v. **DB405**

Prep. under the auspices of the Research Institute for the Study of Man.

Contents: v. 1, People; v. 2, Institutions; v. 3, Resources; v. 4, Indexes.

Based on the same author's *Caribbeana 1900–1965* (1968), but representing a thorough revision thereof, expanding the geographical coverage to include Bermuda and the Bahamas along with the other non-Hispanic areas, and extending the period of coverage through 1975. Now lists "over seventeen thousand complete references to authored publications such as monographs, readers, conference proceedings, doctoral dissertations, master's theses, journal articles, reports, pamphlets, and other miscellaneous works."—*Pref.* Vols. 1–3 are each divided into three main sections with numerous subdivisions: v. 1, Introduction to the Caribbean; The past; The people; v. 2, Elements of culture; Health, education and welfare; Political issues; v. 3, Socioeconomic activities and institutions; The environment and human geography; Soils, crops and livestock. Separate author and geographical indexes. Library location indicated for most items.

§ Updated by: *Bibliography of the English-speaking Caribbean : books, articles and reviews in English from the arts, humanities and the social sciences*, 1978–84 (Parkersburg, Ia. : R. J. Neymeyer, 1979–); by *CARICOM bibliography*, 1977– (Georgetown, Guyana : Caribbean Community Secretariat Lib., 1977–86); and by *CARINDEX : social sciences and humanitites*, 1977– (St. Augustine, Trinidad : ACURIL, Indexing Committee, 1977– . Semiannual). Z1595.C63

Hughes, Roger. The Caribbean : a basic annotated bibliography for students, librarians and general readers. London : Commonwealth Institute Library Services, 1987. 71 p. (Commonwealth bibliographies, no. 6). **DB406**

"A selective list of the main publications available … including a short annotation to indicate the level and coverage of the publication."—*Introd.* Subdivided under the headings Caribbean experience, Lifestyle, Communication, Education, Arts. Index by name of island. Covers only books and documents. Z1501

Ragatz, Lowell Joseph. A guide for the study of British Caribbean history, 1763–1834 : including the abolition and emancipation movements. Wash. : U.S. Govt. Print. Off., 1932. 725 p. (American Historical Association. Annual report, 1930, v.3). **DB407**
Repr.: N.Y. : DaCapo, 1970.

An extensive, classified, annotated list of books, manuscripts, documents, and periodical articles, with author, title, subject, and name index. Z1502.B5R22

University of Miami. Cuban and Caribbean Library. Catalog of the Cuban and Caribbean Library, University of Miami, Coral Gables, Florida. Boston : G. K. Hall, 1977. 6 v. **DB408**

"Books chosen for inclusion are those whose subject headings or titles indicate content specifically within the scope of the Catalog; books by known authors important to the Caribbean, Cuban, Dominican, Puerto Rican literature, history, art, music, etc., as could be determined by classification in our shelf list."—*Introd.* Government publications and periodicals are not included. Geographic areas covered are Cuba, the Antilles, Guyana, Venezuela, Mexico, Colombia, and all of Central America except San Salvador. Z1595.M5

Welch, Thomas L. Travel accounts and descriptions of Latin America and the Caribbean, 1800–1920 : a selected bibliography / Thomas L. Welch, Myriam Figueras. Wash. : Columbus Memorial Libr., 1982. 293p. **DB409**

For annotation, *see* DB263.

Wilkinson, Audine. Economic literature on the Commonwealth Caribbean : a select bibliography : based on material available in Barbados / Audine C. Wilkinson and Andrew S. Downes. Cave Hill, Barbados : Institute of Social and Economic Research (Eastern Caribbean), Univ. of the West Indies, c1987. 503 p. (Occasional bibliography series, no. 8). **DB410**

Aims to show the state of the art and then indicate research needs; also provides background information through citations of historical surveys. Lists books, journal articles, and some unpublished research reports for all of the Caribbean countries in the Commonwealth except for the Bahamas, which is "excluded explicitly due to the unavailability of material."—*Introd.* Arrangement is by topic (e.g., External debt, Agriculture, Economic integration, Human resources) subdivided first as general then by specific country. One location symbol is given for each item. Author index.   Z7165.W5W55

Dissertations

Baa, Enid M. Theses on Caribbean topics, 1778–1968. San Juan : Inst. of Caribbean Studies, Univ. of Puerto Rico, 1970. 146 p. (Caribbean bibliographic series, 1).   **DB411**

A preliminary edition, computer-produced, appeared in 1969.

Doctoral dissertations and master's theses appear in separate listings, alphabetical by author. Indexes by university at which the work was done, by country studied, by subject, and by date of completion.   Z1501.C33

Manuscripts; Archives

In addition to the works listed here, many manuscript and archival guides for Latin America cover the Caribbean.

Ingram, Kenneth E. Manuscripts relating to Commonwealth Caribbean countries in United States and Canadian repositories. St. Lawrence, Barbados : Caribbean Universities Pr., 1975. 422 p.   **DB412**

Describes repositories in the United States, Canada, and the Canal Zone relevant for the study of Bermuda, Bahamas, British Honduras, Jamaica, British Virgin Islands, Anguilla, St. Kitts, St. Lucia, St. Vincent, Barbados, Grenada and the Grenadines, Trinidad and Tobago, Guyana. Arranged by state and city; especially strong for coverage of family, estate and mercantile papers. Chronology; indexed by name (person, place, ship), title, genre (e.g., diary), and a few topics (e.g., plantation management, slave trade).   CD3002.I53

———————— Sources for West Indian studies : a supplementary listing, with particular reference to manuscript sources. Zug, Switzerland : Inter Documentation Co., [1983]. 412p.   **DB413**

Describes collections in archives of Great Britain, Ireland, Holland, Denmark, Australia, Barbados, Jamaica, St. Kitts, Trinidad & Tobago dealing with the Commonwealth Caribbean, especially Jamaica. Very comprehensive. Name and broad subject index.   Z1502.B5I47

Research guide to Central America and the Caribbean / Kenneth J. Grieb, ed. in chief. Madison : Univ. of Wisconsin Pr., 1985. 431 p.   **DB414**

For annotation, see DB301.   Z1595.R47

Tyson, George F. A guide to manuscript sources in United States and West Indian depositories relating to the British West Indies during the era of the American Revolution. Wilmington, Del. : Scholarly Resources, 1978. 96 p.   **DB415**

United States repositories are listed by state, then by library or institution; for the West Indies, listing is by island, then by library. Individual collections are briefly described. Indexed.   Z1238.T954

Bahamas

Boultbee, Paul G. The Bahamas. Oxford ; Santa Barbara, Calif. : Clio Pr., c1989. 195 p. : map. (World bibliographical series, v. 108).   **DB416**

Offers 703 annotated entries for books, articles, and a few government documents, topically arranged in 35 sections. Author/title/subject index.

The *Bahamas index*, 1986–89, now *The Bahamas index and yearbook* (1990– . Decatur, Ill. : White Sound Pr., 1987–), is a selective, annual index of the *Nassau guardian* and *The tribune.*   Z1503.B68

———————— Turks and Caicos Islands. Santa Barbara, Calif. : Clio Pr., c1991. 97 p. (World bibliographical series, v. 137).   **DB417**

305 entries for books, articles, dissertations, and some government documents; topical arrangement. Because so little has been published, includes many references to more general works on the Bahamas. Author/title/subject indexes.   Z1507.T87B68

Saunders, D. Gail. Guide to the records of the Bahamas / D. Gail Saunders, E. A. Carson. Nassau : Govt. Print. Dept., Commonwealth of the Bahamas, 1973. 109, 28 p.   **DB418**

An inventory of the Public Record Office in Nassau and of other relevant repositories, e.g., British Library, Archivo General de Indias in Seville, the Anglican Church of the Bahamas. Includes a list from the Bahamian Public Record Office of microfilms of records in foreign repositories. Separately paged topical and name indexes.

————. *Supplement* (Nassau : Public Records Office, Archives Section, Ministry of Education and Culture, 1980. 55 p.) concentrates on records in Bahama not recorded by the earlier *Guide.* Not indexed.   CD3882.S27

Barbados

Chandler, Michael John. A guide to records in Barbados. Oxford : B. Blackwell for the Univ. of the West Indies, 1965. 204 p.   **DB419**

Records are grouped according to class—central government, local government, semipublic, ecclesiastical, private—and listed by repository as they existed in 1961. Historical notes on government departments are given. Subject index.

§ First of a series surveying the records of the English-speaking territories of the West Indies. Two companion works by E. C. Baker cover the Windward Islands (DB460) and Leeward Islands (DB444).   CD3985.B3C5

Handler, Jerome S. A guide to source materials for the study of Barbados history, 1627–1834. Carbondale : Southern Illinois Univ. Pr., 1971. 205 p.   **DB420**

Lists books, pamphlets, parliamentary papers, newspapers, and manuscript collections relevant to the early history of Barbados. Detailed index.

Continued by: *Supplement to a guide to source materials for the study of Barbados history, 1627–1834* (Providence : publ. by the John Carter Brown Library and The Barbados Museum and Historical Society, 1991. 89 p.). Well annotated; topical index; gives locations.   Z1561.B3H34

Potter, Robert B. Barbados / Robert B. Potter, Graham M. S. Dann. Oxford, Eng. ; Santa Barbara, Calif. : Clio Pr., c1987. 356 p. (World bibliographical series, v. 76).   **DB421**

Lists books, theses, and articles deemed significant and readily available in large libraries or through interlibrary loan. 958 annotated entries are arranged in broad categories. Author, title, and subject indexes.   Z1561.B3P67

Bermuda

Rowe, Helen. A guide to the records of Bermuda. Hamilton : Bermuda Archives, 1980. 1 v. (looseleaf) : ill.   **DB422**

A guide to the records kept in the Bermuda Archives, the Maritime Museum, and the historical societies, schools, and churches of Bermuda, together with material in archives in Great Britain, the United States, Canada, Ireland, Spain, and the West Indies. Also includes a list of records on microfilm in the Bermuda Archives. Indexed.

CD3985.B47R68

Cuba

Chilcote, Ronald H. Cuba, 1953–1978 : a bibliographic guide to the literature / ed. and comp. by Ronald H. Chilcote with Sheryl Lutjens. White Plains, N.Y. : Kraus Internat., c1986. 2 v. (lxii, 1376 p.). **DB423**

Similar in plan to Lambros Comitas' *The complete Caribbeana* (DB405). Offers a comprehensive, classed listing of books, periodical articles, pamphlets, and dissertations. Principal sections include: Structure of society; Culture; Politics; Economics; International affairs; Periodization of the revolution; Revolutionary leadership. The latter has separate extensive sections for Ché Guevara and Fidel Castro, listing their speeches and writings as well as works about them. English translations of Spanish titles are given in brackets. Appendix: Annotated list of Cuban newspapers. Author index, but no detailed subject approach. Z1511.C48

Cuba en la mano : enciclopedia popular ilustrada. La Habana : Imprenta Ucar, García y cía., 1940. 1302 p. : ill. **DB424**

Esteban Roldán Oliarte, ed.

Includes sections on geographical names, natural history, history, printing, biography, education and culture, communications, politics, statistics, etc. F1754.C8

Pérez Cabrera, José Manuel. Historiografía de Cuba. México, 1962. 394 p. (Instituto Pan-Americano de Geografía e Historia. Comisión de Historia. Publication, 106). **DB425**

A résumé of historical writings, 15th century to about 1900, with annotated bibliographies throughout.

Pérez, Louis A. Cuba : an annotated bibliography. N.Y. : Greenwood, 1988. 301 p. (Bibliographies and indexes in world history, no. 10). **DB426**

Consists of 1,120 annotated entries in topical arrangement, including English and Spanish books, articles, and journals. Author/title/subject indexes. Z1511.P43

———— A guide to Cuban collections in the United States. N.Y. : Greenwood, 1991. 179 p. (Reference guides to archival and manuscript sources in world history, no. 1). **DB427**

Emphasizes "collections of substantial and varied holdings ... [but] exceptions have been made ... where records deal with a particularly critical period in Cuban history or if the records are related to persons involved in these events in some important fashion."—*Introd.* Arranged by state, then by repository. For each, gives for each address and brief description of each file. A collection index provides access from names of individual record files. Subject index. Z1525.P44

Schroeder, Susan. Cuba : a handbook of historical statistics. Boston : G. K. Hall, 1982. 589 p. : ill., maps. **DB428**

For annotation, *see* CG171. F1778.S37

Cuban Revolution

Pérez, Louis A. Historiography in the Revolution : a bibliography of Cuban scholarship, 1959–1979. N.Y. : Garland, 1982. 318 p. (Garland reference library of social science, v.90). **DB429**

In three parts: (1) a general section followed by sections on specific historical periods; (2) topical sections (e.g., women, communism in Cuba, labor, peasantry); (3) biography. Nearly 3,800 entries; author and subject indexes. Z1511.P44

———— The Cuban revolutionary war, 1953–1958 : a bibliography. Metuchen, N.J. : Scarecrow, 1976. 225 p. **DB430**

A classed bibliography of nearly 2,500 items. Author index. Z1525.P43

Suchlicki, Jaime. The Cuban revolution : a documentary bibliography, 1952–1968. Coral Gables, Fla. : Univ. of Miami, Research Inst. for Cuba and the Caribbean, 1968. 83 p. **DB431**

A chronological listing of speeches, editorials, manifestos, communiqués, etc., relating to the Cuban revolution. Index of names. Z1525.S93

Dominica

Myers, Robert A. Dominica. Oxford, Eng. ; Santa Barbara, Calif. : Clio Pr., c1987. 190 p. (World bibliographical series, v. 82). **DB432**

Offers 93 items, mostly in English but a few in French or Caribe, including books, articles and chapters. Author/title/subject index.

§ The same author has compiled a comprehensive bibliography, *Resource guide to Dominica 1493–1986* (New Haven, Conn. : HRAF, 1987. 3 v. [649 l.]), which includes archival materials, films, recordings, paintings, and photographs as well as books, articles, theses, etc., with a name and subject index. Z1561.D65M93

Dominican Republic

Bibliography

Schoenhals, Kai P. Dominican Republic. Oxford, Eng. ; Santa Barbara, Calif. : Clio Pr., c1990. 210 p. (World bibliographical series, v. 111). **DB433**

Arranges 913 annotated entries for books, articles, dissertations, and government publications (e.g., *Congressional record*)—mostly English and Spanish-language materials—in 40 sections. Author/title/subject indexes. Z1536.S36

Wiarda, Howard J. Materials for the study of politics and government in the Dominican Republic, 1930–1966. [Santiago de los Caballeros] : UCMM, [1968]. 142 p. (Univesidad Católica Madre y Maestra. Colección estudios, 5). **DB434**

A listing of books, articles, and manuscripts arranged in sections for the Trujillo and post-Trujillo periods; each entry has a one-line annotation. Includes lists of relevant libraries and of journals and newspapers. No index.

§ Wolf Grabendorff's *Bibliographie zu Politik und Gesellschaft der Dominikanischen Republik, neuere Studien, 1961–1971* (München : Weltforum Verlag, 1973. 103 p.) is useful for extending the coverage of this work and of Deborah S. Hitt and Larman C. Wilson, *A selected bibliography of the Dominican Republic* (Wash., D.C. : American Univ., Center for Research in Social Systems, 1968. 142 p.). Z7165.D6W5

Encyclopedias

Enciclopedia dominicana. 3a ed. ampliada, corr. y actualizada. Santo Domingo, R.D. : Enciclopédica Dominicana, S.A., 1986–1988. 8 v. : ill. (some col.). **DB435**

1st ed., 1976; 2nd ed., 1978.

Contents: v. 1–7, A–Z; v. 8, Antología poética.

An encyclopedia of Dominican affairs, with many biographical and historical articles, statistical tables, maps, etc. F1932.E52

Rutinel Domínguez, Ulises. Diccionario histórico dominicano / Ulises Rutinel Domínguez, Manuel Darío De León. Santo Domingo : Editora Universitaria, 1986. 365 p. : ill., maps, ports. (Coleción historia y sociedad, 69 ; Publicaciones de la Universidad Autónoma de Santo Domingo, 499).   **DB436**
Offers short entries for places, subjects, and people. Includes a list of prelates 1510–1986, governors 1492–1821, presidents and governors 1844–1990, and reproduction of significant documents. Not indexed. Although there are interesting maps and illustrations, they are not well produced.   F1932.R875

Grenada

Schoenhals, Kai P. Grenada. Oxford, Eng. : Clio Pr., 1991. 179 p. (World bibliographical series, 119.).   **DB437**
Citations to 793 books, dissertations and periodical articles are arranged by topic. Author/title/subject index.   Z1561.G76536

Haiti

Chambers, Frances. Haiti. Oxford, Eng. ; Santa Barbara, Calif. : Clio Pr., 1983. 177 p. (World bibliographical series, v. 39).   **DB438**
Provides 550 citations (primarily English language) to books and periodical articles, arranged in 37 categories. Brief annotations. Aims to meet the "needs of the general reader, undergraduate college student, and the librarian interested in building a library collection."— *Introd.* Index.   Z1531.C47

Haiti : guide to the periodical literature in English, 1800–1990 / comp. and ed. by Frantz Pratt. N.Y. : Greenwood, c1991. 314 p. (Bibliographies and indexes in Latin American and Caribbean studies, no. 1).   **DB439**
5,045 citations (nos. 4998–5045 in an Addendum) arranged in nine categories (e.g., Physical setting, Cultural environment, Historical background), subdivided by subject. Author and journal title indexes, with separate author and journal title indexes for the Addendum.   Z1531.H35

Laguerre, Michel S. The complete Haitiana : a bibliographic guide to the scholarly literature, 1900–1980. Millwood, N.Y. : Kraus Internat. Pubns., 1982. 2 v.   **DB440**
Prep. under the auspices of the Research Institute for the Study of Man.
A classed bibliography of books, parts of books, periodical articles, and government publications. Detailed table of contents; author index. Includes writings on the ecological setting as well as Haitian history, population, social and cultural affairs, politics, education, etc. Complements *The complete Caribbeana* by L. Comitas (DB405) which omits Haiti.   Z1531.L33

Lawless, Robert. Haiti : a research handbook / by Robert Lawless ; with contributions from Ilona Maria Lawless ... [et al.]. N.Y. : Garland, 1990. 354 p. (Garland reference library of social science, v. 546).   **DB441**
Intended for both specialists and general readers. Cites 2,040 books, journal articles, dissertations, and masters essays in a numbered topical arrangement (e.g., History—general or by period, Fiction, Health, AIDS, Butterflies, Mammalogy). Each section begins with a bibliographic essay of two to four pages that emphasizes published materials widely available in major libraries. Includes a list of Creole language item numbers and an author index.
§ Expanded from Lawless' *Bibliography on Haiti: English and Creole items* (Gainsville, Fla. : Center for Latin American Studies, Univ. of Florida, 1985. 146 p. Caribbean Migration Program, Occasional paper no. 6).   Z1531.L39

Jamaica

Ingram, Kenneth E. Jamaica. Santa Barbara, Calif. : Clio Pr., 1984. 369 p. (World bibliographical series, 45).   **DB442**
Lists more than 1,180 books, periodical articles, dissertations, government publications, and technical reports on all aspects of Jamaican life and culture. Topically arranged; good annotations. Index of authors, titles, and subjects.
§ The *Jamaican national bibliography* (AA568) can be used for continuous updating since it lists books about Jamaica or by Jamaicans regardless of place of publication.   Z1541.I52

——————— Sources of Jamaican history, 1655–1838 : a bibliographical survey with particular reference to manuscript sources. Zug, Switz. : Inter Documentation Co., 1976. 2 v. (1310 p.).   **DB443**
Revision of the author's thesis, University of London, 1970.
A survey of manuscript collections in British and Jamaican repositories, with some attention to European and North American archives. The only printed sources included are newspapers, almanacs, legislative documents, etc., and these are listed chronologically with library locations. A supplement, p. 1124–93, adds materials discovered since 1970 when the survey was originally made. Extensive index of names and subjects.   Z1541.I53

Leeward Islands

Baker, Edward Cecil. A guide to records in the Leeward Islands. Oxford : B. Blackwell for the Univ. of the West Indies, 1965. 102 p.   **DB444**
A section on federal records, followed by sections on the records of Antigua, Montserrat, Nevis, St. Christopher, and the British Virgin Islands, each arranged by repository and including historical and descriptive notes.
§ Companion works: M. J. Chandler, *A guide to records in Barbados* (DB419) and Baker's *A guide to records in the Windward Islands* (DB460).   CD3985.W5B3

Martinique

Jardel, Jean Pierre. Bibliographie de la Martinique / Jean-Pierre Jardel, Maurice Nicolas, Claude Relouzat. Fort-de-France : Centre d'Études Régionales Antilles-Guyane, 1969. v. 1. (Les cahiers de CERAG, no. 3).   **DB445**
No more published.
A classified bibliography of books and periodical articles on Martinique and the Antilles in general. Vol. 2 was to be a subject and author index.   Z1561.M3J37

Martinique. Archives. Guide des Archives de la Martinique / Liliane Chauleau, comp. Fort-de-France : Archives Départementales, 1978. 68 p. : ill., facsims.   **DB446**
Offers a description of the arrangement and contents of each file in the Archives, plus a chapter on copies of items from the Archives Nationales in Paris which are also available for use.   CD3985.M47A7

Montserrat

Berleant-Schiller, Riva. Montserrat. Santa Barbara, Calif. : Clio Pr., c1991. 102 p. (World bibliographical series, v. 134).   **DB447**

Books, journal and newspaper articles, and government documents in topical arrangement. 341 entries; because of the small amount of material available, the compiler has tried to be inclusive. Author, title, subject indexes. Z1561.M67B47

Netherlands Antilles

Encyclopedie van de Nederlandse Antillen. 2. herziene druk / onder redactie van J. Ph. de Palm. Zutphen : De Walburg Pers, c1985. 552 p. : ill. **DB448**

1st ed., 1969.

Covers social, economic, political, and cultural life up to about 1983. Clear illustrations. Many articles include bibliographies. Cross-references listed at end of volume. Not indexed. F2141.E5

Nagelkerke, Gerard A. Netherlands Antilles : a bibliography, 17th century–1980. Leiden : Dept. Caribbean Studies, Royal Institute of Linguistics & Anthropology ; The Hague : Smits Drukkers-Uitgevers, 1982. 422 p. **DB449**

Text in Dutch; introduction in Dutch, English and Papiamento.

Offers "a survey of the collection of books, articles, manuscripts, etc., relating to the Netherland Antilles kept in the library of the Royal Institute of Linguistics and Anthropology (KITLV) in Leiden."—*Introd.* The library has tried to collect everything available in the humanities and social sciences dealing with this area. Listing is by author/title, with indexes for names and title "catchwords/subjects." Z1502.D7N33

Puerto Rico

Bibliography

Castro Arroyo, María de los Angeles. Los primeros pasos : una bibliografía para empezar a investigar la historia de Puerto Rico / María de los Angeles Castro, María Dolores Luque de Sánchez, Gervasio Luis García. 2a ed. rev. y aum. Río Piedras, P.R. : Ediciones Huracán, 1987. 130 p. **DB450**

A guide to research on Puerto Rico with chapters on formats (e.g. dictionaries and encyclopedias, document collections) and discussion of archives. Not indexed. F1971.Z99C37

Cevallos, Elena E. Puerto Rico. Oxford, Eng. ; Santa Barbara, Calif. : Clio Pr., c1985. 193 p. (World bibliographical series, v. 52). **DB451**

Consists of 605 annotated entries for books, government publications, and articles, topically arranged. For the "non-specialist, English speaking reader."—*Introd.* Most entries are in English, except for Spanish-language materials which are classics or the only available source. Other than classic works, publications date from 1970 to about 1984. Emphasis on economics and politics. Author/title/subject index.

§ *See also*: Luis A. Cardona, *An annotated bibliography on Puerto Rican materials and other sundry matters* (Bethesda, Md. : Carreta, 1983. 156 p.), which groups citations by type of material—books, government reports, conference reports, journals, oral history, National Archives. F1958.Z99C48

Fowlie-Flores, Fay. Annotated bibliography of Puerto Rican bibliographies. N.Y. : Greenwood, 1990. 167 p. (Bibliographies and indexes in ethnic studies, no. 1). **DB452**

Lists, in topical arrangement, book or pamphlet-length bibliographies published (some in mimeographed form) in Spanish or English through 1987. Attempts to include "all significant bibliographies on … Puerto Rico in general, special topics or specific individuals, and Puerto Ricans in the United States"—*Pref.* Annotations are two to three sentences in length, usually descriptive. Author/title/subject indexes. Z1551.F69

Pedreira, Antonio Salvador. Bibliografía puertorriqueña (1492–1930). Madrid : Impr. de la Librería y Casa Ed. Hernando, 1932. 707 p. (Monografías de la Universidad de Puerto Rico. Series A. Estudios hispánicos, núm. 1). **DB453**

Repr.: N.Y. : B. Franklin, 1974.

Includes works by natives and foreigners about Puerto Rico, the artistic literary works of Puerto Ricans, and a selected list of works by Puerto Ricans on various subjects—cf. *Introd., p. xvii.* Classified, with author and subject indexes.

§ Continued by: Augusto Bird, *Bibliografía puertorriqueña de fuentes para investigaciones sociales, 1930–1945* (Ed. provisional. Río Piedras : Centro de Investigaciones Sociales, Universidad de Puerto Rico, 1946–1947. 2 v. [547 p.]). Z1551.P37

Encyclopedias; Dictionaries

La gran enciclopedia de Puerto Rico. Madrid : [Ed. R], 1976–1980. 15 v. : ill. **DB454**

Vincente Baez, ed.

Contents: v. 1, Historia; v. 2, Política; v. 3, Poesía; v. 4, Cuento; v. 5, Novela; v. 6, Teatro; v. 7, Música; v. 8, Artes plásticas; v. 9, Arquitectura. Leyes; v. 10, Educación, flora, fauna, economía; v. 11, Deportes; v. 12, Folklore; v. 13, Municipios; v. 14, Diccionario histórico-biografico; v. 15, Geografía.

A heavily illustrated general encyclopdia. Each volume is made up of essays by specialists on the topics covered; Vol. 14 is a biographical dictionary. Name index and brief bibliography in each volume. F1954.G72

Hostos, Adolfo de. Diccionario histórico bibliográfico comentado de Puerto Rico. [San Juan] : Academia Puertorriqueña de la Historia, 1976. 952 p. **DB455**

Includes entries for names, events, terms, etc., in Puerto Rican history. Articles are usually quite brief, bibliographic references are cited in many entries.

§ For a more specialized dictionary *see* Luis de la Rosa Martinez, *Lexicón histórico-documental de Puerto Rico (1812–1899)* (San Juan : Centro de Estudios Avanzados de Puerto Rico y el Caribe, 1986. 139 p. ill.). F1954.H67

Tesauro de datos históricos : índice compendioso de la literatura histórica de Puerto Rico, incluyendo algunos datos inéditos, periodísticos y cartográficos / preparado en la Oficina del Indice Histórico de Puerto Rico, bajo la dirección de Aldofo de Hostos. Río Piedras, P.R. : Editorial de la Universidad de Puerto Rico, 1990–1994. v. 1–4. (In progress). **DB456**

Contents: v. 1–4, A–R.

1st ed., 1948, covered A–Epid and has been reprinted as v. 1.

A brief-entry dictionary covering organizations, peoples, topics (e.g., medicine, minerals), and states, with references to sources (articles, collections of documents, histories), marked by a roman numeral referring to a list in the front of each volume. F1971.T47

St. Vincent and the Grenadines

Potter, Robert B. St. Vincent and the Grenadines. Santa Barbara, Calif. : Clio Pr., c1992. 212 p. (World bibliographical series, v. 143). **DB457**

631 books, articles, and some government documents, mostly in English and reasonably accessible. Topical arrangement; author, title, subject indexes. Z1561.S35P67

Trinidad and Tobago

Chambers, Frances. Trinidad and Tobago. Oxford, Eng. ; Santa Barbara, Calif. : Clio Pr., c1986. 213 p. (World bibliographical series, v. 74).   **DB458**

A selective list of some 640 entries from books, journal articles, and a few government documents. Topical arrangement. Annotations, author/title/subject index.   Z1561.T7C43

Virgin Islands

Moll, Verna P. Virgin Islands. Oxford, Eng. ; Santa Barbara, Calif. : Clio Pr., c1991. 210 p. (World bibliographical series, v. 138).   **DB459**

614 publications, books, and some articles and documents, considered most significant and useful. Separate sections for British and U.S. Virgin Islands, each topically arranged. Indexes also so divided: author/title and subject indexes for each.   Z1561.V8M65

Windward Islands

Baker, Edward Cecil. A guide to records in the Windward Islands. Oxford : B. Blackwell for the Univ. of the West Indies, 1968. 95 p.   **DB460**

Surveys the records of Grenada, Saint Vincent, Saint Lucia, and Dominica. Indexed.

§ A companion to Baker's records guide for the Leeward Islands (DB444) and M. J. Chandler's volume for Barbados (DB419).   CD3985.W5B3

DC

Europe

GENERAL WORKS

Bibliography

See also *Widener Library shelflist* (AA115).

Aldcroft, Derek Howard. Bibliography of European economic and social history / comp. by Derek H. Aldcroft and Richard Rodger. 2nd ed. Manchester, Eng. ; N.Y. : Manchester Univ. Pr. ; N.Y. : St. Martin's Pr., 1993. 292 p.   **DC1**

1st ed., 1984.

Covers writings on the period 1700–1939 relating to continental Europe (including Turkey in Europe, but not Great Britain) in about 9,000 books, journal articles, and a few government reports published mainly in the 20th century. Arranged by region or country within about a dozen topical headings. Author index.

§ Great Britain is treated by a companion work, William Henry Chaloner and R. C. Richardson, *Bibliography of British economic and social history* (DC272). *See also* Barry Taylor, *European economic and social history, 1450–1789* (Manchester ; N.Y. : Manchester Univ. Pr. ; distr. by St. Martin's Press, c1989. 303 p.) for books, articles, and essays, 1945–87.   Z7165.E8A4

Europe / préparé par la Commission internationale pour l'histoire des villes] ; sous la direction de Philippe Wolff. Paris : Éditions Klincksieck, 1977. 544 p. (Guide international d'histoire urbaine, v.1).   **DC2**

Brief sections on "La ville antique" and "La ville byzantine" are followed by entries for the individual countries of Europe in alphabetical sequence. Each country section begins with a brief historical introduction, followed by a review of the principal sources, published and unpublished, for urban history research (with attention to archives and their organization), a list of institutes and periodicals concerned with urban history, and a selected bibliography.   HT131.I44

Ferguson, Chris D. Europe in transition : a select, annotated bibliography of the twelfth-century renaissance. N.Y. : Garland, 1989. 156 p. (Garland reference library of the humanities, vol. 875).   **DC3**

A topical arrangement of books, articles, and dissertations, most published since World War II and preponderantly in English, French, and German (but with a few in Spanish and Italian) "that examine the major social, political, cultural and economic currents."—*Pref.* Annotations are usually a paragraph in length, and there is a good discussion of bibliographies. Indexes of authors and of persons as subjects.   Z2000.F45

Ferreiro, Alberto. The Visigoths in Gaul and Spain, A.D. 418–711 : a bibliography. Leiden ; N.Y. : E.J. Brill, 1988. 822 p.   **DC4**

"Covers the Visigoths from their sojourn in Toulouse beginning AD418 through the dissolution of the Kingdom of Toulouse in AD711. For other barbarians, it covers Iberian history from AD400–711." —*Introd.* Topical listing for primary sources, editions in Migne's *Patrologia latina* and the *Monumenta Germania historiae*, subsequent editions, and secondary literature (books, articles, essays in collections). Three indexes: (1) periodicals, (2) modern authors, (3) subjects. List of collected essays, *Studia honoraria*, festschriften, which are indexed.   Z2177.F47

Frey, Linda. Women in Western European history : a select chronological, geographical, and topical bibliography / comp. and ed. by Linda Frey, Marsha Frey, and Joanne Schneider. Westport, Conn. : Greenwood, 1982–1984. 2 v.   **DC5**

Contents: [v.1] From antiquity to the French Revolution; [v.2] The nineteenth and twentieth centuries.

A selective bibliography of nearly 12,000 references to Western language books and periodical articles; primary and literary sources have been excluded. Arrangement is by period, further subdivided by country, then by subject. Detailed tables of contents with subject, name, and author indexes.

———. ———. *First supplement*, publ. 1987 (699 p.), adds some 6,500 entries.   Z7961.F74

Hachmann, Rolf. Ausgewählte Bibliographie zur Vorgeschichte von Mitteleuropa. Wiesbaden ; Stuttgart : Steiner, 1984. lxiii, 390 p.   **DC6**

Sponsored by Römisch-Germanische Kommission des Deutschen Archäologischen Instituts.

Offers some 10,821 entries for books and articles in classed arrangement, with author index. Covers all of Europe (except Greece and Albania) through the Iron Age. Good section on cultural life. List of serial abbreviations, p.xxxiii–lxiii.

§ See also *Verzeichnis vor- und frühgeschichtlicher Bibliographien*, by Gudrun Gerlach and Rolf Hachmann (Berlin : de Gruyter, 1971. 269 p. maps), with 3,013 entries.

Hacken, Richard D. Central European economic history from Waterloo to OPEC, 1815–1975 : a bibliography. N.Y. : Greenwood, 1987. 270 p. (Bibliographies and indexes in economics and economic history, no. 6). **DC7**

Lists 5,300 monographs, bibliographies, dissertations, and articles from journals and festschriften, grouped in five broad categories (Economic conditions, Agriculture, Industry, Business and commerce, and Finance) subdivided geographically and chronologically. German-speaking and mixed-language areas of central Europe are covered; non-German-speaking areas are not. Concerned with secondary rather than primary source materials published in Western languages, particularly English and German. Cross-references; author index.
Z7165.C42H33

Halstead, John P. Modern European imperialism : a bibliography of books and articles, 1815–1972 / John P. Halstead and Serafino Porcari. Boston : G. K. Hall, 1974. 2 v. **DC8**

Contents: v.1, General and British Empire; v.2, French and other empires, regions.

A classed bibliography of more than 33,000 entries. Historical treatments of imperialism are given emphasis, but "the searcher will find a wide selection of materials ranging from primary sources to fiction."—*Pref.* Although "designed as a guide to secondary works for the serious scholar or student," most sections include a selection of documents and papers as an indication of the kinds of primary sources available. Detailed table of contents for each volume, but no index.
Z6204.H35

Krewson, Margrit B. The German-speaking countries of Europe : a selective bibliography. 2nd ed., rev. and enl. Wash. : Library of Congress, 1989. 318 p. **DC9**

1st ed., 1985.

Superintendent of Documents classification: LC 43.9:G31.

"Intends to provide researchers and students with a current guide to sources on the German-speaking countries of Europe: Austria, the Federal Republic of Germany, the German Democratic Republic, Liechtenstein, and Switzerland."—*Introd.* Preference is given to English-language books and documents published in the 1980s, although publications of the 1970s and publications in German are also among the 1,485 items cited. Arranged by broad topic under country. LC call numbers are given. Indexed by main entry.

§ Krewson has also compiled *Immigrants from the German-speaking countries of Europe: a bibliography* (Wash. : Library of Congress, 1991. 76 p.), and, with Stephan H. Lindner, *The economies of the German-speaking countries of Europe* (Wash. : Library of Congress, 1986. 98 p.).
Z2000.K73

Messick, Frederic M. Primary sources in European diplomacy, 1914–1945 : a bibliography of published memoirs and diaries. N.Y. : Greenwood, [1987]. 221 p. : maps. (Bibliographies and indexes in world history, no. 6). **DC10**

For annotation, *see* CJ316.
Z2000.M395

Sheehan, Michael M. Domestic society in medieval Europe : a select bibliography / comp. by Michael M. Sheehan and Jacqueline Murray. Toronto : Pontifical Institute of Mediaeval Studies, c1990. 57 p. **DC11**

"Intended to provide preliminary orientation for the study of medieval European demography and kinship, family and marriage, various special groups ... and the attitudes of the population to each of these institutions and groups."—*Pref.* 453 well-chosen entries are topically arranged, each with a very brief annotation (usually a phrase) and a note indicating the time period covered. Index of authors and editors.
Z7164.M2S46

Zophy, Jonathan W. An annotated bibliography of the Holy Roman Empire. N.Y. : Greenwood, [1986]. 398 p. (Bibliographies and indexes in world history, no. 3). **DC12**

A classed listing of more than 3,000 items that includes sections for rulers, relations with the church, the nobility, the peasantry, economic and social history, etc. Annotations are brief. Author and subject indexes.

§ Companion work: *The Holy Roman Empire : a dictionary handbook*, also by Zophy (Westport, Conn. : Greenwood, 1980. 551 p.).
Z2236.Z66

Library resources

See also *Guide to libraries in Western Europe*, ed. by Peter Dale (AK132).

Brogan, Martha L. Research guide to libraries and archives in the Low Countries. N.Y. : Greenwood, 1991. 546 p. (Bibliographies and indexes in library and information science, no. 5). **DC13**

For annotation, *see* AK133.
813.A1B76

Dillon, Kenneth J. Scholars' guide to Washington, D.C. for Central and East European studies : Albania, Austria, Bulgaria, Czechoslovakia, Germany (FRG & GDR), Greece (Ancient & Modern), Hungary, Poland, Romania, Switzerland, Yugoslavia. Wash. : Smithsonian Inst. Pr., 1980. 329 p. (Scholars' guide to Washington, D.C., no. 5) **DC14**

Publ. for the Woodrow Wilson International Center for Scholars.

Like other volumes in the series this is intended as a "descriptive and evaluative survey of research resources" (*Introd.*) and is presented in two parts: (1) collections (offering information on libraries, archives, databanks, etc.) and (2) organizations which deal with Central and Eastern Europe and are potential sources of information or assistance to researchers. Indexed.
Z2483.D54

Higbee, Joan Florence. Scholars' guide to Washington, D.C. for southwest European studies : France, Italy (including Ancient Rome), Malta, Portugal, Spain, the Vatican / Joan Florence Higbee ; ed., Zdenek V. David. Wash. : Wilson Center Pr. ; Lanham, Md. : distr. by Univ. Pr. of America, 1989. 475 p. (Scholars' guide to Washington, D.C., 13). **DC15**

Similar to other guides in the series—e.g., for Central and East European studies (DC14) and for Northwest Europe (DC16). Describes about 500 organizations, government agencies (including embassies), library collections, museums, academic programs and departments, noting their resources and any finding aids, along with pertinent directory information (address, phone number, hours, etc.). Appendixes: directory of bookstores in the Washington area; housing and travel information; government holidays. Indexes: Oral histories and personal papers; Artists; Library subject strengths; Subject; Organizations and institutions.
Z2000.H5

Pitschmann, Louis A. Scholar's guide to Washington, D.C. for northwest European studies. Wash. : Smithsonian Inst. Pr., 1984. 436 p. (Scholar's guide to Washington, D.C., no.10). **DC16**

Concerned with Belgium, Denmark, Finland, Great Britain, Greenland, Iceland, Ireland, Luxembourg, The Netherlands, Norway, Sweden. Like the other guides in the series sponsored by the Woodrow Wilson International Center for Scholars, it lists and describes collections (libraries, archives, museums, etc.) and organizations (research centers, academic programs, government agencies, associations, etc.) which have resources or provide services to scholars.
Z2551.P57

Guides to records

Cook, Chris. Sources in European political history / Chris Cook and Geoff Pugh. N.Y. : Facts on File, 1987–91. 3 v. **DC17**

Contents: v. 1, The European left (237 p.); v. 2, Diplomacy and international affairs (190 p.); v. 3, War and resistance (260 p.).

U.K. ed. published by Macmillan; v. 2 of that edition has title, *Diplomacy and imperialism*.

Locates and describes unpublished personal papers of major Western European political figures of the 19th and 20th centuries. Similar in arrangement to Cook's *Sources in British political history, 1900–1951* (DC335)—i.e., alphabetical under personal name, each entry giving dates, very brief biographical information, location of manuscripts and papers. Occasionally, a citation will mention an inventory or cite published papers. Excludes figures from Britain and Ireland. Not indexed.   Z2000.C57

Thomas, Daniel H. The new guide to the diplomatic archives of Western Europe / ed. by Daniel H. Thomas and Lynn M. Case. [Rev. ed.]. [Philadelphia] : Univ. of Pennsylvania Pr., 1975. 441 p.   **DC18**

1st ed., 1959, publ. as *Guide to the diplomatic archives of Western Europe*.

21 chapters, each by a specialist, describe the diplomatic archives of 18 countries and 3 international collections. For each, gives an account of the history, content, administration, and conditions of use of the collections, and usually a bibliography. Subject index. Chapters on Finland, Greece, and Luxembourg have been added in this revised and updated edition, and there are new subsections for the International Labour Organisation and the International Telecommunication Union.   CD1001.T4

Encyclopedias; Dictionaries

The Blackwell companion to the Enlightenment / John W. Yolton … [et al.]. Oxford ; Cambridge, Mass. : Blackwell, 1992. 581 p. : ill.   **DC19**

For annotation, *see* BE749.   CB411.B57

Columbia dictionary of European political history since 1914 / gen. ed., John Stevenson. N.Y. : Columbia Univ. Pr., 1992. 437 p.   **DC20**

Also publ. London : Macmillan, 1991, as *Macmillan dictionary of British and European history since 1914*.

Covers European history since 1914 from a British perspective. Alphabetically arranged entries on "personalitites, topics and events … [with] an attempt to provide some pointers to current assessments of some of the issues of the period … and extra-European events in terms of their significance in European affairs. Also included are major American figures who impinge directly upon European history."—*Pref*. Most articles conclude with short bibliographies of two to five citations. Cross-references, but no index.   D419.M33

Cook, Chris. The Longman handbook of modern European history, 1763–1985 / Chris Cook and John Stevenson. 2nd ed. London ; N.Y. : Longman, 1992. 201 p. : ill.   **DC21**

Offers "chronological, statistical and tabular information … biographies of important individuals, a glossary of commonly used historical terms and a topic bibliography … . The coverage of the volume is European-wide in its broadest sense, including events in the former Soviet Union, the Balkans and Scandinavia," (*Pref.*) updated to 1990–91. Complements Cook and Stevenson's *Longman handbook of modern British history, 1714–1987* (DC294).   D299.C627

Palmer, Alan. An encyclopaedia of Napoleon's Europe. London : Weidenfeld and Nicolson ; N.Y. : St. Martin's, 1984. 300 p. : ill., maps.   **DC22**

Offers entries for leading political, military, and literary institutions, events, and people in all countries of Europe, 1797–1815. General headings for social, economic and religious themes. Brief bibliography (p. 299–300).   DC147.P34

Williams, E. Neville. The Facts on File dictionary of European history, 1485–1789. N.Y. : Facts on File, 1980. 509 p.   **DC23**

Also published as *The Penguin dictionary of English and European history*.

Offers entries on important personalities and topics (but not themes). Aims to "follow the mainstream of political history without diverging too far into economic history, cultural history, and so on."—*Pref.* Cross-references; general subject index; no bibliographies.   D231.W54

Handbooks; Current surveys

Although *Keesing's record of world events* (DA187) is strongest for European coverage, other services also concentrate on Europe—e.g., *Europe* (Brussels : Agence internationale d'information pour la presse, 1952–), a daily newsletter with much local information and statistics. Separately numbered supplements are published: *Economic interpenetration in Europe and the rest of the world* (daily); *Europe weekly selected statistics, Europe brief notes* (irregular), and *Europe documents* (irregular). For Western Europe, see *Western Europe : a political and economic survey* (1993), and for the European Community, *European access* (Cambridge, Eng. : Chadwyck-Healey, 1988–) and *European Communities encyclopedia and directory* (London : Europa, 1991–).

Mitchell, Brian R. International historical statistics, Europe, 1750–1988. 3rd ed. N.Y. : Stockton Pr., 1992. 942 p.   **DC24**

For annotation, *see* CG189.   HA1107.M5

REFORMATION

See also DC128, DC226, DC227.

Archiv für Reformationsgeschichte : Beiheft, Literaturbericht. v. 1– . Gütersloh : G. Mohn, 1972– . Annual.   **DC25**

Added title page (varies): Archive for Reformation history, an international journal concerned with the history of the Reformation and its significance in world affairs. Supplement: Literature review.

Published under the auspices of the Verein für Reformationsgeschichte and the American Society for Reformation Research.

A selective bibliography of books, collections of essays, and periodical articles arranged topically or by geographic area. Brief abstracts; no index.   Z7830.A7

Bainton, Roland Herbert. Bibliography of the continental Reformation : materials available in English / by Roland H. Bainton and Eric W. Gritsch. 2nd ed., rev. and enl. [Hamden, Conn.] : Archon Books, 1972. 220 p.   **DC26**

1st ed., 1935, by R. H. Bainton.

A topically arranged bibliography without author index.   Z7830.B16

Commission Internationale d'Histoire Ecclésiastique Comparée. Bibliographie de la réforme, 1450–1648. Leiden : Brill, 1958–82. 8 v.   **DC27**

Contents: fasc.1, Allemagne, Pays-Bas; fasc.2, Belgique, Suède, Norvège, Danemark, Irlande, États-Unis d'Amérique; fasc.3, Italie, Espagne, Portugal; fasc.4, France, Angleterre, Suisse; fasc.5, Pologne, Hongrie, Tchécoslovaquie, Finlande; fasc.6, Autriche; fasc.7, Écosse; fasc.8, Benelux. No more published.

Subtitle varies to reflect period of coverage.

Lists books, dissertations, and periodical articles on the Reformation published in the countries indicated.

§ A companion work from the Commission's British Sub-Commission: *The bibliography of the Reform, 1450–1648 : relating to the United Kingdom and Ireland for the years 1955–70*, ed. by Derek Baker ... [et al.] (Oxford : Blackwell, 1975. 242 p.). In three main sections: (1) England and Wales; (2) Scotland; and (3) Ireland. Books, periodical articles, reviews, and theses. Author listing within subsections, no subject index.   Z7830.I5

Reformation Europe : a guide to research / ed. by Steven Ozment. St. Louis : Center for Reformation Research, 1982. 390 p.   **DC28**

Offers 16 surveys by American and English scholars on as many subjects in Reformation history (e.g., Martin Luther, pamphlet literature of the German Reformation, social history). Designed to assess the present state of research on a topic, to indicate key issues requiring scholarly investigation, and to identify research collections for a given subject. Bibliography for each essay. Index of names.

§ Continued by: *Reformation Europe : a guide to research II*, ed. by William S. Maltby (1992. 348 p.). Some of the articles of the first volume have been updated (e.g. Calvin, Luther) while others are new (e.g. Jews and new Christians in Reformation Europe, Studies of women, the family and gender), Index of names. The essay in *Reformation Europe I* on Catholic reform was expanded into an entire volume, *Catholicism in early modern history : a guide to research*, ed. by John W. O'Malley (BC413).   BR305.2.R39

BY REGION

Europe, Eastern

Guides

Slavic studies : a guide to bibliographies, encyclopedias, and handbooks / comp. and ed. by Murlin Croucher. Wilmington : Scholarly Resources, 1993. 2 v.   **DC29**

A topical listing of major reference materials—bibliographies, directories, catalogs, encyclopedias, dictionaries, gazetteers, handbooks, travel guides—in English, French, German, and the Slavic languages. Good annotations. Listing is by Library of Congress subject heading under broad topics, e.g., Area studies (works on the whole region including the former Soviet Union), Eastern Europe and the Balkans (works on the whole area but excluding the Soviet Union), Czechoslovakia, Poland, Soviet Union, Yugoslavia. Author and subject indexes. A major resource for beginning researchers.   Z2483.S554

Bibliography

Abstracts of Soviet and East European émigré periodical literature. [v. 1, no.] 1–v. 8, no. 4. [Pacific Grove, Calif.] : Abstracts of Soviet and East European Émigré Periodical Literature., [1981]–1992. Quarterly.   **DC30**

Also called *ASEEPL*.

Provides abstracts of articles originating in 50 to 75 Russian- and East European-language newspapers and periodicals published in the United States, Western Europe, and Israel, including such titles as *Novaia zhizn', Novoe russkoe slovo,* and *Russkaia mysl'*. Broad subject arrangement, with subject and author indexes.

§The same publisher issued *Review of Russian emigré books* (1 [1984]–no. 4/5 [1985/1987]. Publ. 1984–1989. No. 1 reissued with no. 2 in 1986).

Church and state in postwar eastern Europe : a bibliographical survey / comp. by Paul Mojzes. N.Y. : Greenwood, [1987]. 109 p. (Bibliographies and indexes in religious studies, no. 11).   **DC31**

"The subject of this bibliography is the literature on the relationship between Soviet and Eastern European churches and the societies in which they have existed since the end of World War II. Covered are Albania, Bulgaria, Czechoslovakia, East Germany, Hungary, Poland, Romania, and Yugoslavia."—*Pref.* Two survey chapters on the mutual relations between the churches and society are followed by country sections listing books and articles. Author, title, and subject indexes.   Z7776.72.C5

Horak, Stephan M. Russia, the USSR, and Eastern Europe : a bibliographic guide to English language publications, 1964–1974 / comp. by Stephan M. Horak ; ed. by Rosemary Nieswender. Littleton, Colo. : Libraries Unlimited, 1978. 488 p.   **DC32**

"Although initially intended as a revision of the compiler's *Junior Slavica* [N.Y., 1968], a bibliography of basic English-language publications in the social sciences ... coverage has been broadened to include titles in literature, linguistics, and the fine arts."—*Introd.* Classed arrangement with author/title and subject indexes. Entries are annotated, with most of the annotations excerpted from reviews appearing in leading American, Canadian, and British journals of Slavic studies.

Supplemented in 1982 by Horak's work of the same title, covering 1975–1980, and by a 2nd supplement in 1987, covering 1981–1985. Each volume adds about 1,000 items.

§ Horak is also the compiler of *The Soviet Union and Eastern Europe: a bibliographic guide to recommended books for small and medium-sized libraries and school media centers* (Littleton, Colo. : Libraries Unlimited, 1985. 373 p.).   Z2483.H54

Horecky, Paul Louis. East Central Europe : a guide to basic publications. Chicago : Univ. of Chicago Pr., [1969]. 956 p.   **DC33**

Intended as "a highly selective and judiciously evaluated inventory of the most important publications" (*Pref.*) relating to the area. The bibliography is presented in six main sections: (1) a bibliographical overview of the area; (2) Czechoslovakia; (3) East Germany; (4) Hungary; (5) Poland; and (6) Sorbians (Lusatians) and Polabians. For each of the four countries represented there are sections for general reference aids and bibliographies, the land, the people, history, the state, the economy, the society, and intellectual and cultural life. Entries are annotated; each subsection is the work of one or more area specialists. Despite its age, still useful for its older materials which provide background. Also valuable for collection development and assessment.

§ Companion work, also edited by Horecky: *Southeastern Europe : a guide to basic publications* (DC59).   Z2483.H56

Hundert, Gershon David. The Jews in Poland and Russia : bibliographical essays / Gershon David Hundert and Gershon C. Bacon. Bloomington : Indiana Univ. Pr., [1984]. 276 p.   **DC34**

Offers two bibliographical essays, The Jews in Poland-Lithuania from the twelfth century to the first partition, and East European Jewry from the first partition of Poland to the present; each essay ends with a bibliography of books, articles, and published documents cited in the text.

Updated by Hundert's essay, "Polish Jewish history," *Modern Judaism* 10 (1990) : 259–70, which includes suggestions for areas of research.   Z6373.P7H86

Magocsi, Paul R. Galicia : a historical survey and bibliographic guide. Toronto : Publ. in assoc. with the Canadian Inst. of Ukrainian Studies and the Harvard Ukrainian Research Inst. by Univ. of Toronto Pr., 1983. 299 p. : maps.   **DC35**

"Intended to serve as an introduction to the basic historical problems of Galicia and to direct the reader to the major published primary and secondary sources dealing with those problems."—*Introd.* Bibliographic essays (arranged by period) treat some 3,000 items on political, socioeconomic, and literary matters. DK511.G14M34

Remington, Robin Alison. The international relations of Eastern Europe : a guide to information sources. Detroit : Gale, 1978. 273 p. **DC36**

An annotated bibliography for students, listing books, essays and articles published through about 1975. A general chapter on the region is followed by sections on Albania, Bulgaria, Czechoslovakia, East Germany, Hungary, Poland, Romania, and Yugoslavia. Title and subject indexes.

§ For publications (books and articles) for 1967–71, see *Soviet and East European foreign policy : a bibliography of English- and Russian-language publications 1967–71* (Santa Barbara, Calif. : ABC-Clio, 1974. 208 p.), an author listing of 3,200 items with subject index. Z6465.E853R45

Schmidt, Christian D. Bibliographie zur osteuropäischen Geschichte : Verzeichnis der zwischen 1965 und 1974 veröffentlichten Literatur in westeuropäischen Sprachen zur osteuropäischen Geschichte bis 1945 / Christian D. Schmidt ... [et al.]. Wiesbaden : Harrassowitz, 1983. lxix, 1059 p. (Bibliographische Mitteilungen des Osteuropa-Instituts an der Freien Universität Berlin, 22). **DC37**

Added title page in English: Bibliography of Russian and East European history: list of books published between 1965 and 1974 in Western European languages on Russian and East European history to 1945.

An extensive bibliography of almost 18,000 books, essays, articles relating to Russia and the Soviet Union, Poland, Finland, and the Baltic States. Geographical arrangement with many subdivisions. Author index.

§ Continues: *Bibliographie zur osteuropäischen Geschichte : Verzeichnis der zwischen 1939 und 1964 veröffenilichen literatur in westeuropäischen Sprachen zur osteuropäischen Geschichte bis 1945* by Klaus Meyer (Berlin ; Wiesbaden : Harrassowitz, 1972. 434 p.) which includes about 12,000 books and periodical articles.

Z2483.S34

Current

Abstracts, Russian and East European series : ABREES. v. 101– . London : ABREES Ltd., 1993– . **DC38**

Issues for 1993 and following also numbered v. 23, no. 1– .

Replaces the former "Information supplement" to the journal *Soviet studies* and *ABSEES: Soviet and East European abstract series* (v. 1 [1970]–22 [1992]; also called no. 27–100).

Now sponsored by the British Association of Slavonic and East European Studies.

Covers the former U.S.S.R., Albania, Bulgaria, Czechoslovakia, Germany, Hungary, Poland, Romania, Russia, and Yugoslavia, providing abstracts of periodical and newspaper articles and books on these areas. Classed arrangement within country divisions. Each issue includes a select bibliography on a specific topic. Each number is issued as a printed pamphlet which includes microfiche in pockets interleaved with printed pages. Arrangement is by classed listing within country divisions for citations to periodical and newspaper articles. Each citation is followed by a very brief abstract; for most citations a longer abstract appears on the accompanying microfiche. The latter abstracts are very full, even reproducing statistical tables from the articles; occasionally the entire text is reproduced. Topical index for each issue.

DK1.A2

American bibliography of Slavic and East European studies. 1967– . Stanford, Calif. : American Association for the Advancement of Slavic Studies, 1972– . Annual. **DC39**

Publisher and place of publication vary.

Continues *American bibliography of Russian and East European studies* (Bloomington : Indiana Univ., 1957–67), which in turn continued Robert Francis Byrnes, *Bibliography of American publications on East Central Europe, 1945–1957* (1958. 213 p.).

Topical lists of books and articles, including book reviews, on Eastern Europe and Soviet Union. The arrangement is by country, subdivided by broad topics.

•An online version called *ABSEES* is available via the University of Illinois. Updated daily. Z2483.A65

Bibliographic guide to Soviet and East European studies. 1978– . Boston : G. K. Hall, 1979– . Annual. **DC40**

Represents materials cataloged by the New York Public Library and the Library of Congress from Sept. of the previous year through Aug. of the year of coverage and supplements NYPL's *Dictionary catalog of the Slavonic Collection* (DC45). Includes all book and nonbook materials published in or dealing with any East European country or the Soviet Union, together with any materials written in an East European, Baltic, or Slavonic language. A dictionary catalog with full information only under main entry. Z2483.B48

European bibliography of Soviet, East European and Slavonic studies. v.1 (1975)– . Birmingham, Eng. : Univ. of Birmingham, 1977– . Annual. **DC41**

Title and prefatory matter also in French and German.

Incorporates "Travaux et publications parus en français ... sur la Russie et l'URSS" (publ. in *Cahiers du monde russe et soviétique*) and "Soviet, East European and Slavonic studies in Britain" (publ. in *ABSEES : Soviet and East European abstracts series*; see DC38).

Sponsored by the International Committee for Soviet and East European Studies, with various other institutions.

A comprehensive annual bibliography of books, essays, and periodical articles, together with references to major articles in British newspapers on Russia and the eight countries of Eastern Europe. Strong coverage in the social sciences and humanities; "materials relating to science and technology included only where relevant to political, economic and social life."—*Introd.* A topically arranged general section is followed by geographical sections also subdivided by topic. Name index.

•To supplement, see the bibliographic database on Hytelnet, *German language publications on Russia/USSR/CIS.* E2483.E94

Kaloeva, I. A. Sovetskoe slavi̐anovedenie : literatura o zarubezhnykh slavi̐anskikhy stranakh na russkom i̐azyke, 1961/62. Moskva : Akad. Nauk SSSR. Institut Nauchnoĭ Informatsii po obshchestvennym naukam [INION], 1973. 7 pts. **DC42**

Continues *Sovetskoe slavi̐anovedenie,* ed. by Kaloeva and issued by the Akademii̐a nauk SSSR, Fundamental nai̐a biblioteka obshchestvennykh nauk.

A bibliography of Soviet publications, in the Russian language, for Soviet and East European countries. In addition to history and philology, it includes economics, law and state, and social structure. Name index.

Continued by publications covering 1963–68 (publ. began 1973); 1969–73 (1976); 1974–77 (1978); 1978–82 (1983); 1983–87 (1988). Each is issued in seven volumes. Z6207.S6A45

Novai̐a otechestvennai̐a i inostrannai̐a literatura po obshchestvennym naukam. Slavi̐anovedenie i balkanistika : Rossiĭskai̐a akademii̐a nauk, Institut nauchnoĭ informatsii po obshchestvennym naukam. [v.] 1 (1992)– . Moskva : RAN INION, 1992– . Six issues yearly. **DC43**

Continues: *Novai̐a sovetskai̐a i inostrannai̐a literatura po obshchestvennym naukam. Problemy slavi̐anovedenii̐a i balkanistiki,* 1976–91.

Indexes Eastern European and Russian books and articles on the area. Citations arranged by broad topics; e.g., agriculture subdivided by country. A current awareness resource, as each issue has author and subject indexes but does not cumulate. List of publications used.

Z5118.S6N68

Library catalogs

Johann Gottfried Herder-Institut, Marburg. Bibliothek.
Bibliothek des Johann Gottfried Herder-Instituts, Marburg/
Lahn, Germany : alphabetischer Katalog. Boston : G.K. Hall,
1964. 5 v.   **DC44**

The library's holdings "cover East Central Europe, the territory itself; the inhabitants and all their activities through the course of history, from prehistoric times to the present; and all aspects of cultural
life— law, government, economics, religion and church, art and literature."— *Foreword.* Photoreproduction from catalog cards. Chiefly
main entries, with some subject cards.

———. ———. *Nachtrag* (1971. 2 v.).
———. ———. *Nachtrag* 2. (1981. 3 v.).

The first supplement covers new material cataloged through 1970,
including a specialized library on Polish and Baltic history that was
given to the Institut. The second supplement adds acquisitions 1971–
77.   Z2483.J6

New York Public Library. Slavonic Division. Dictionary
catalog of the Slavonic collection / the New York Public Library, the Research Libraries. 2nd ed., rev. and enl. Boston :
G.K. Hall, 1974. 44 v.   **DC45**

1st ed., 1959.

A photographic reproduction of the catalog cards for Slavic and
Baltic materials, and for materials in other languages on these areas
published through 1971. The basic collection in literature and social
science was augmented later by science and technology titles. The
724,000-entry catalog is notable for analytics and references to periodical articles. Transliteration differs from the Library of Congress system.

§ Beginning January 1972, all additions to the collection of the
Slavonic Division (regardless of publication date) are included in the
Dictionary catalog of the Research Libraries (AA116), and since
1978, included in *Bibliographic guide to Soviet and East European
studies* (DC40).   Z881.N59

Library resources

Budurowycz, Bohdan. Slavic and East European resources in
Canadian academic and research libraries. Ottawa : Collections Development Branch, Resources Survey Division, Nat.
Lib. of Canada, 1976. 595 p. (Research collections in Canadian libraries, II: Special studies, no.4).   **DC46**

A survey of 67 Canadian libraries, reporting for each the extent
and nature of the collections of printed materials, microforms, and
manuscripts in whatever language originating in or dealing with the
following countries: Albania, Bulgaria, Czechoslovakia, Hungary, Poland, Romania, the U.S.S.R. (including Estonia, Latvia and Lithuania),
and Yugoslavia. Extensive index.

§ For a complete list of the *Research collections in Canadian libraries* set, *see* AK128.

East Central and Southeast Europe : a handbook of library
and archival resources in North America / Paul L. Horecky,
chief ed. ; David H. Kraus, assoc. ed. Santa Barbara, Calif. :
Clio Pr., 1976. 466 p. (Joint Committee on Eastern Europe.
Publications series, no.3).   **DC47**

Intends "to provide scholars, librarians, students, and researchers
with a basic reference tool for the study of the essential collections
available in major libraries, archives, and research institutions in the
United States and Canada, by outlining the profiles of these collections
and offering broad guidance to their subject and area contents. The
focus is on the humanities and the socioeconomic and political sciences."—*Foreword.* Covers material on Albania, Bulgaria, Czechoslovakia, East Germany, Greece, Hungary, Poland, Romania, and Yugoslavia. Collections of some 40 libraries, archives, and research institutions are described, with major surveys of up to 5,000 words in length.

Descriptions are signed by contributors and include bibliographic citations. Institutions are arranged alphabetically. An "Area and subject
guide" serves as an index.

A careful review appears in *Slavic review* 37 (Mar. 1978): 146–
48.   Z2483.E2

Guide to libraries in Central and Eastern Europe / comp.
by Maria Hughes. London : British Library, [1992]. 82 p.
    DC48

Based on results of a questionnaire, though in a few cases when
no response was received, data were compiled from secondary sources.
For each gives: name, telephone, fax if available, director, brief statement of holdings, availability, hours, publications, and in most cases,
address. Covers libraries in the former Communist bloc and adds eight
"key" collections of related materials in British libraries. Arranged alphabetically by country. Not indexed.   Z674.5.E8H95

Hoover Institution on War, Revolution, and Peace. Russia,
the Soviet Union, and Eastern Europe : a survey of holdings at
the Hoover Institution ... / ed. by Joseph D. Dwyer. Stanford :
Hoover Inst. Pr., 1980. 233 p. (Hoover Press survey, 6).
    DC49

A survey of Hoover holdings, published and unpublished, on each
of the Central (including the Balkan states and Greece) and East European countries. Not indexed.   Z2491.H57

Lewanski, Richard Casimir. Eastern Europe and Russia/
Soviet Union : a handbook of West European archival and library resources. N.Y. [etc.] : K.G. Saur, 1980. 317 p. (American Council of Learned Societies/Social Science Research
Council. Joint Committee on Eastern Europe. Publications series, 3).   **DC50**

Intended as "an inventory in directory format of the principal research resources, facilities, and services available in some 1,000 repositories—institutions of higher learning and research, libraries, archives,
and museums—in various European countries."—*Pref.* Arranged by
country, then by city and repository; broad subject index. For each repository usually indicates scope of collection or subject profile, notes
on special collections, number of volumes, type of catalog or catalogs,
restrictions, availability of interlibrary loan, etc.   Z2483.L48

Walker, Gregory. Library resources in Britain for the study
of Eastern Europe and the former U.S.S.R / comp. by Gregory
Walker and Jackie Johnson. Wheatley : G. Walker, 1992. 92 p.
    DC51

Revision of Walker's *Resources for Soviet, East European and
Slavonic studies in British libraries* (Birmingham, 1981. 240 p.),
which is a successor to Crosby Lockwood, *Directory of libraries and
special collections on Eastern Europe and the USSR* (1971).

"Intended primarily for those undertaking study or research at
first-degree level or on Eastern Europe and the area covered by the
former USSR"—p. 2. Entries for some 95 libraries, arranged by city
then by repository, are revised in consultation with the library. For
each, gives addresses (including phone, fax and telex numbers), name
of chief librarian, description of collection, hours, admission conditions, various services, guides, catalogs, etc. "The former German
Democratic Republic is now excluded save that relating to the Serbs as
a Slavonic minority"—*Pref.* Subject index.   Z2483.W36

Encyclopedias

**Political and economic encyclopaedia of the Soviet Union
and Eastern Europe** / ed. by Stephen White. Harlow, Essex :
Longman ; Chicago : St. James, 1990. 328 p. : maps.   **DC52**

Articles on the political and economic background of each country, political parties, leaders, and topics (e.g., women, sports) are alphabetically arranged. Emphasizes the most recent period up to March
31, 1990. Articles are signed with the initials of the contributors.
Chronology, 1945–90. Cross-references; index for topics.
    JN96.A2P64

Polska Akademia Nauk. Komitet Słowianoznawstwa. Słownik starożytności słowiańskich : encyklopedyczny zarys kultury słowian od czasów najdawniejszych / pod red. Władyslawa Kowalenki, Gerarda Labudy i Tadeusza Lehra-Splawińskiego. Wrocław : Zklad Narodowy im. Osolińskich, 1961–91. v. 1–8 : ill., maps : 31 cm. (In progress?).   **DC53**

  Contents: v. 1–6 (1961–80); v. 7–8, Suplementy A–J (1982–91).

  A scholarly, authoritative encyclopedia covering all Slavic people with some treatment of neighboring peoples; e.g., Balts, Avars. Signed articles with bibliographies cover Slavic antiquities—their history, societies, relations with other groups.   D147.P6

Biography

Istoriki-slavisty SSSR : biobibliograficheskii slovar— spravochnik. Moskva : Izd-vo "Nauka", 1981. 205 p.   **DC54**

  At head of title: Akademiia Nauk SSSR. Nauchnyi Sovet po Kompleksym Problemam Slavianovedeniia i Balkanistiki. Institut Slavianovedeniia i Balkanistiki.

  Comp. by S. I. Sidelnikov and others.

  A dictionary of 20th century Russian scholars (living or deceased) whose specialty was a Slavic country. Gives academic or other affiliation, dissertation subject, and most important publications. Indexes of names and of organizations/institutions. Includes a survey of the development of Slavic studies in Russia.

  § Updated by: *Slavianovedenie v SSSR : Izuchenie iuznykh i zapadnykh slavian : biobibliograficheskii slovar'*, red. IU. V. Bromlei, V. A. D'iakov (N. Y. : publ. for the Institut Slavianovedenie i Balkanistike by Norman Ross, 1993. 525 p.), which gives biographical details and a list of their more important works for 1,500 Soviet humanists and social scientists who study the western or southern Slavs, 1917–85. Based on information from questionnaires, reference sources, and archival materials. Articles are signed. A lengthy essay surveys historical work completed during this period.   Z2483.I84

Slavianovedenie v dorevoliutsionnoi Rossii : biobibliograficheskii slovar' / [Otv. red. V.A. Diakov]. Moskva : Nauka, 1979. 426 p.   **DC55**

  At head of title: Akademiia Nauk SSSR. Institut Slavianovedeniia i Balkanistiki.

  A biobibliography of pre-Revolutionary Russian scholars in the fields of history, archaeology, ethnography, literature, linguistics, paleography, and art of Slavic countries. Indexed.   Z2483.S55

Atlases

Magocsi, Paul R. Historical atlas of East Central Europe / Paul Robert Magocsi ; cartographic design by Geoffrey J. Matthews. Seattle ; London : Univ. of Washington Pr., 1993. 218 p. : maps in color ; 31 cm. (A history of East Central Europe, v. 1.).   **DC56**

  Some 89 maps covering, for 400 CE–1992, the Poles, Czechs, Slovaks, Hungarians, Romanians, Yugoslav peoples, Bulgarians, and Greeks, with lesser coverage of Finns, Estonians, Latvians, Lithuanians, Belorussians, and Ukrainians (i.e., those on the borders). Chronologically arranged with explanatory text. Bibliography of sources; sources for individual maps are keyed to the printed works in the bibliography. Name index.

  § *An atlas of Russian and East European history*, by Arthur E. Adams, Ian M. Matley, and William O. McCagg. (N.Y. : Praeger, [1967]. 204 p. 21 cm.) is dated but still useful.

Sellier, André. Atlas des peuples d'Europe centrale / André Sellier et Jean Sellier ; cartographie Anne Le Fur. Paris : La Découverte, c1991. 192 p. : ill. (some color) ; 18 x 24 cm.   **DC57**

Presents maps depicting Central Europe (Finland to Greece), 12th century to 1991, with references to languages, religions, alphabets, politics. Index of place names and a few personal names (e.g., Charlemagne).   DJK26.S45

Balkan states

Bibliography

Historische Bücherkunde Südosteuropa / hrsg. von Mathias Bernath ; Leitung u. Red. Gertrud Krallert. München ; Wien : Oldenbourg, 1978–1988. v. 1^{1-2}, 2^1. (Südosteuropäische Arbeiten, 76). (In progress).   **DC58**

  Vol. 2, pt. 1 ed. by Mathias Bernath and Karl Nehring.

  Contents: Bd. 1, Mittelalter: pt. 1, Historische Zeitschriften aus und über Südosteuropa. Byzanz. Südosteuropa. Die Slawen. Bulgarien. Serbien. Albaner (1978); pt. 2, Die pannonische Raum von 6. bis Ende des 9. Jahrhunderts. Die Slawenen. Ungarn. Ragusa-Dubrovnik. Bosnia. Rümanien (1980); Bd. 2, Neuzeit: pt. 1, Osmanisches Reich. Makedonien. Albanien (1988). Bd. 2, pt. 2, is to cover the Habsburg Empire.

  Provides a guide to scholarly books and articles on the history of southeastern Europe irrespective of the date of publication and including all known editions, reprints, translations, and revisions. Topical arrangement; author index in v. 1, pt. 2 and in v. 2, pt. 1.   Z2831.H57

Horecky, Paul Louis. Southeastern Europe : a guide to basic publications. Chicago : Univ. of Chicago Pr., [1969]. 755 p.   **DC59**

  Together with its companion volume, *East Central Europe* (DC33), the bibliography was prepared by a Subcommittee on East Central and Southeast European Studies appointed by the Joint Committee on Slavic Studies of the American Council of Learned Societies and the Social Science Research Council.

  Both works are still valuable despite their age, particularly for collection development and assessment. A bibliographical overview of the area is followed by separate sections for Albania, Bulgaria, Greece, Romania, and Yugoslavia. Each section is further subdivided as: general reference aids and bibliographies; general and descriptive works; the land; the people; history; the state; the economy; the society; intellectual and cultural life. Subsections comprise annotated bibliographies contributed by area specialists. More than 3,000 items. Detailed index.

  § For 19th-century publications *see* George Begescu, *Essai d'une notice biobibliographique sur la question d'Orient : Orient européen, 1821–1897* (Paris : Le Soudier, 1897. 327 p.), which lists chronologically 2,100 works published in France and Belgium 1821–97, with author and anonymous works indexes.

  Léon Savadjian's *Bibliographie balkanique 1920–1938* (Paris : Soc. Générale d'Impr. et d'Edit., 1933–39. 8 v. Repr.: Nedeln, Liechtenstein : Kraus, 1969. 2 v.) covers Albania, Bulgaria, Greece, Romania, Turkey, and Yugoslavia, in French, Germany, Italian, and English publications.   Z2831.H67

Jessup, John E. Balkan military history : a bibliography. N.Y. : Garland, 1986. 478 p. (Military history bibliographies, vol. 8 ; Garland reference library of social science, v. 234).   **DC60**

  Bibliographical essays on Balkan military history during chronological periods from the late 14th century through 1984. Each essay is followed by a bibliography of the works cited. Author and subject indexes.   Z2851.M5J47

Kornrumpf, Hans-Jürgen. Osmanische Bibliographie mit Besonderer Berücksichtigung der Türkei in Europa / Hans-Jürgen Kornrumpf ; Unter Mitarbeit von Jutta Kornrumpf. Leiden : Brill, 1973. 1378 p. (Handbuch der Orientalistik. 1 Abt. Der Nahe und der Mittlere Osten. Ergänzungsband, 8).   **DC61**

  For annotation, *see* DC536.   Z2831.K67

Lazarov, Mikhail. Bŭlgariĭa na balkanite, 1944–1974 : bibliografiĭa. Sofiĭa : BAN, 1975. 371 p.   **DC62**
    For annotation, *see* DC114.   Z2831.L39

List of British diplomatic records for Balkan history, 1879–1905 : from general correspondence, classes FO 32 (Greece), FO 103 (Montenegro), FO 104 (Roumania), FO 105 (Serbia), FO 78 (Turkey). Sofia : Centre international d'information sur les sources de l'histoire balkanique et méditerranéenne, 1984. 278 p. (Balcanica. II, Inventaires et catalogues, v. 4).   **DC63**
    Detailed listing (arranged under Public Record Office class, then chronologically) giving volume number, statement of content, and repository in the Balkans of microfilm copies. Name and geographical area indexes.   Z6465.G7L53

Nationalism in the Balkans : an annotated bibliography / Gale Stokes. N.Y. : Garland, 1984. 243 p. (Canadian review of studies in nationalism, v.3 ; Garland reference library of social science, v.160).   **DC64**
    A reissue, with some updating, of bibliographies originally published as research aids for scholars in the *Canadian review of studies in nationalism*. Covers post-World War II literature relating to the nationalism of a country or a national group (with countries defined according to present-day political boundaries). There are annotated bibliographies for Greece, Romania, Bulgaria, and Yugoslavia (plus seven additional chapters for ethnic groups within Yugoslavia). Books, articles, and theses in all languages are listed; author index.   Z2846.N37

Südost-Institut München. Bibliothek. Bestandskatalog der Bibliothek des Südost-Instituts München / Gerhard Seewann, unter Mitarbeit von Gerda Bartl und Wilma Kömives. München : R. Oldenbourg, 1990. v. 1. (Südosteuropa-Bibliographie. Ergänzungsband, 1). (In progress).   **DC65**
    Contents: v. 1, Druckschriften 1529–1945 (840 p.); v. 2, Periodica (in preparation).
    A topical arrangement under geographical area follows a general section. Strongest for materials on the countries that make up the Balkans. Authors, editors, titles index.   Z2483.S85

Current

Bibliographie d'études balkaniques / Académie bulgare des sciences. Institut d'études balkaniques "Ludmila Jivkova." Centre d'information et de documentation balkaniques. v.1 (1966)– . Sofia : Le Centre, 1968– . Annual.   **DC66**
    Issuing body varies.
    An extensive bibliography, international in scope, covering the history, culture, language, folklore, and ethnography of the people and countries of the Balkans (including Cyprus, Greece and Western Turkey). Originally in classified arrangement with personal name, geographic name, and subject indexes; beginning with v. 8 (1973), arranged alphabetically by topic with personal name and geographic name indexes. Historical period covered was originally from the mid-14th century; with v. 13 (1978) the beginning point is the seventh century. Latest published: v. 23 (1988), publ. 1990.
    § A complementary bibliography is *Valkanikē vivliographia*, ed. K.A. Dēmadēs (v. 1 [1973]–9 [1985]. Thessalonikē : Hidryma Meletōn Chersonēsou tou Haimon, 1973–85), an annual bibliography of books, reviews, and articles, topically arranged. Covers the period from the fall of the Byzantine empire until the end of World War II. All major languages included.   Z2831.B5

Dissertations

Scherer, Anton. Südosteuropa-Dissertationen, 1918–1960 : eine Bibliographie deutscher, österreichischer und schweizerischer Hochschulschriften. Graz : Hermann Böhlau, 1968. 221 p.   **DC67**
    Dissertations on the political, social, and cultural history of southeastern European countries are listed in topical groups within country sections. Author index.   Z2831.S3

Handbooks

Südosteuropa-Handbuch = Handbook on South Eastern Europe / hrsg. Klaus-Detlev Grothusen in Verbindung mit dem Südosteuropa-Arbeitskreis der Deutschen Forschungsgemeinschaft. Göttingen : Vandenhoeck u. Ruprecht, 1975–93. v. 1–7. (In progress).   **DC68**
    Contents: Bd. 1, Jugoslawien; Bd. 2, Rumänien; Bd. 3, Griechenland; Bd. 4, Türkei; Bd. 5, Ungarn; Bd. 6, Bulgarien; Bd. 7, Albanien.
    Individual volumes in this series contain articles contributed by authorities from Germany, the U.S., Yugoslavia, etc., that survey the political and legal structure, the economic system, social and cultural life. Each includes an extensive bibliography and a brief biographical dictionary of contemporary politicians of the country.

Baltic States

See also DC137.

The Baltic states : a reference book. Tallin : Estonian Encyclopaedia Publishers ; Riga : Latvian Encyclopaedia Publishers ; Vilnius : Lithuanian Publishers, 1991. 272 p. : ill. (some col.), maps.   **DC69**
    Begins with a short statistical survey of the region followed by country coverage. For each country, describes language, natural environment, population, political system, history, national economy, culture, religion and church, social welfare; offers useful information for visitors, a dictionary and a who's who. Phrase book from English to each of the other languages. No index.   DK502.4.B35

Smith, Inese A. The Baltic states : Estonia, Latvia, Lithuania / Inese A. Smith and Marita V. Grunts, comps. Oxford, Eng. ; Santa Barbara, Calif. : Clio, c1993. lxxvii, 199 p. : maps. (World bibliographical series, v. 161).   **DC70**
    A topical listing of 554 books, essays, and a few articles mostly published 1970s–1990 on the region or any of the three countries. English-language material predominates. Separate listing by author of dissertations, p. lxxiii–lxxvii. Chronology of the 20th century in the Baltic world. Author, title, subject indexes.   DK502.35.S65

Scandinavia

Bibliography

Guide to Nordic bibliography / general ed., Erland Munch-Petersen. [Copenhagen] : Nord, c1984. 235 p. : ill.   **DC71**
    An excellent guide, produced in collaboration by lecturers at five library schools in Denmark, Norway, Iceland, Sweden, and Finland. In two parts: (1) essays on each country's history, language, computerized library and information systems, and national bibliographic systems; (2) annotated entries for retrospective and current national bibliographies and for more than 800 author and subject bibliographies in print, microform, or online, arranged by UDC. The second part is indexed by author and title.

————. ———— *Supplement I*, 1983–86, and *Supplement II*, 1987–1990 (ed. by Munch-Petersen, Mona Madsen, et al. Publ. 1988 and 1992), extend coverage, include sections on changes to the national bibliographies, add some bibliographies published before 1983 that were omitted from the earlier work, and include recommended bibliographies of Nordic authors and composers.   Z2551.G84

International bibliography of urban history : Denmark, Finland, Norway, Sweden. Stockholm : Swedish Inst. for Urban History, Univ. of Stockholm, 1960. 73 p.   **DC72**

The first of a projected series of bibliographies dealing with the history of cities. The plan is to present each country separately. In this volume the Scandinavian countries are treated individually; in each case, general bibliographies and other materials are followed by histories of individual cities.   Z7164.U7I56

Meyen, Fritz. The North European nations as presented in German university publications, 1885–1957 : a bibliography. Bonn : H. Bouvier ; Charlottesville : Bibliographical Soc. of the Univ. of Virginia, 1959. 124 p. (Bonner Beiträge zur Bibliotheks- und Bücherkunde, 4).   **DC73**

Added title page in German: Die nordeuropäischen Länder im Spiegel der deutschen Universitätsschriften, 1885–1957. Contents, preface, and headings in English and German.

Lists 1,099 dissertations and habilitation theses "that exclusively or preponderatingly, treat a theme relative to Denmark, Sweden, Norway, Iceland, or Finland."—*Pref.* Includes both published and unpublished works. Topical arrangement; author and subject indexes.   Z2000.M4

Oakley, Stewart P. Scandinavian history, 1520–1970 : list of books and articles in English. London : Historical Assoc., [1984]. 232p. (Helps for students of history, 91).   **DC74**

Lists some 2,478 items by century, subdivided by country and by topic. Introductory notes for each chapter point up significant publications and provide cross references. Aims to "include all secondary material published in English between 1880 and 1980 on all aspects of the history of Scandinavia as well as some items of special interest which appeared earlier and accounts by travellers in the region before the middle of the nineteenth century."—*Pref.* Author index.   Z2551.O26

Encyclopedias

Kulturhistorisk Leksikon for nordisk Middelalder fra Vikingetid til Reformationstid / administrator, Lis Jacobsen ; Dansk redaktør, John Danstrup. København : Rosenkilde og Bagger, 1956–78. 22 v. : ill.   **DC75**

Editors vary.

Written by the leading medievalists in Denmark, Norway, Sweden, and Finland. Each article signed, and most include bibliography; Vol. 21 includes a supplement; v. 22 is an index.   DL30.K8

Medieval Scandinavia : an encyclopedia / Phillip Pulsiano, ed. ; Kirsten Wolf and Donald K. Fry, co-editors … [et al.]. N.Y. : Garland, 1993. 768 p. : ill., maps. (Garland reference library of the humanities, vol. 934 ; Garland encyclopedias of the Middle Ages, v. 1).   **DC76**

Signed, scholarly articles of 150–5,000 words cover Denmark, Finland, Iceland, Norway and Sweden from about 900 CE to the Reformation. Entries range from "detailed descriptions of, for example, individual works, artifacts, and historical figures, to broad surveys…such as genres, historical movements, art, and broader still, particular countries" (*Pref*) and thus planned to supplement *Kulturhistorisk Leksikon* … (*see* DC75). Each article includes bibliographies with full citations and cross-references. Topical index; well illustrated with line drawings, maps, and reproductions of art works.   DL30.M43

Directories

Directory of Scandinavian studies in North America / Robert B. Kvavik, ed. Madison, Wis. : Publ. for the Society for the Advancement of Scandinavian Study by Grote Deutsch, 1989. 280 p.   **DC77**

A discussion of the state-of-the-art of Scandinavian studies in America in the humanities, language, history, and the social sciences, and of relevant resources in American libraries. Directory of departments, programs, instructors and professors. Plans call for new editions every ten years.   PT7037.N67D5

BY COUNTRY

Albania

Bland, William B. Albania. Oxford, Eng. ; Santa Barbara, Calif. : Clio Pr., c1988. 290 p. : map. (World bibliographical series, v. 94).   **DC78**

A topical arrangement of 893 books and a few articles in English, French, Albanian, and German. "In the annotations information has often been provided concerning the institutional affiliation of the authors."—*Introd.* Indexes for authors, titles, and subjects.   Z2886.B54

Daniel, Odile. Albanie, une bibliographie historique. Paris : Editions du Centre national de la recherche scientifique, [1985]. 616 p.   **DC79**

A topically arranged bibliography covering all periods of Albanian history up to 1945. Cites Western-language materials (books, articles, and some essays) and within 24 libraries locates at least one copy of each item. Author index and index to journals cited.   Z2886.D36

Hetzer, Armin. Albanien : ein bibliographischer Forschungsbericht mit Titelübersetzungen und Standortnachweisen = Albania, a bibliographic research survey with location codes / Armin Hetzer, Viorel S. Roman. München : K. G. Saur, 1983. 653 p. (Bibliographien zur regionalen Geographie und Landeskunde, 3).   **DC80**

A classed bibliography with sections for general works, history (including politics), law, and business and economics. International coverage; includes books, periodical articles, pamphlets, official documents. Cutoff date is mainly 1980. Author index; detailed table of contents, but no subject index.

§ Parts of a supplementary bibliography by Hetzer were published as *Arbeitsmaterialien zu einer Landesbibliographie, Albanien : Geschichte, Politik, Recht, Wirtschaft, in sechs Heften* (Bremen : Univ. Bremen, Bibliothek, 1980. Abteilung Jura. 4 Heft, Recht; 5 Heft, Wirtschaft).   Z2854.A5H47

Jubani, Bep. Bibliografi e arkeologjisë dhe historisë së lashtë të shqipërisë : 1945–1971. Tiranë : Nëntori, 1972. 222 p.   **DC81**

At head of title: Universiteti i Tiranës. Instituti i Historisë. Sektori i Arkeologjisë e Historisë Lashtë të Shqipërisë.

Added title page in French: Bibliographie de l'archéologie et de l'histoire antique de l'Albanie.

An annotated author listing of about 700 items. Entries are first given in the original language, with annotations in Albanian, then repeated in a second section with titles translated into French and with annotations in French.

§ Continued by: Faik Drini, *Bibliografie arkeologjisë dhe e historisë së lashtë të Shqipërisë, 1972–83* (Tiranë : Academia e Shkencave e RPS të Shqipërisë, Qendrda e Kërkimeve Arkeologjike, 1985. 316 p.). Cites 656 books and articles alphabetical by author. Annotations are in Albanian and French; index by sites and by districts.   Z2854.A5J82

Andorra

Taylor, Barry. Andorra. Oxford ; Santa Barbara, Calif. : Clio Pr., 1993. 97 p. : map.   **DC82**

Offers 268 entries for books, articles, and essays, mostly in English and Spanish with a few French titles. Based on the collection in the British Library. Cross-references. Separate listing of 26 theses and dissertations accepted by American, French, German, and Spanish universities. Chronology, 806–February 2, 1993. List of rulers including French co-rulers. Author, title, and subject indexes.

§ Taylor commends *Materials per una bibliografia d'Andorra*, by Lidia Armengol, Monica Batlle, and Ramon Gual ([Andorra] : Institut d'Estudis Andorrans, Centre de perpinya, 1978. 106 p.), as the "only substantial printed Andorran bibliography."   DC924.T39

Armenia

Armen, Garbis. Historical atlas of Armenia = Hayastani patmakan atlas / text, Garbis Armen ; editing, Vrej-Armen Artinean ; maps and design, Hamo Abdalian. N.Y. : Armenian National Education Committee, c1987. 50 p. text, 51 p. maps : ill., maps in color ; 23 x 35 cm.   **DC83**

In Armenian and English.

Maps depict geographical, historical, and cultural aspects of Armenia's past, with brief text and photographs. Covers 3000 BCE to ca.1975, including the Armenian diaspora.   G2157.61.S1A7

Avakian, Anne M. Armenia and the Armenians in academic dissertations. Berkeley, Calif. : Professional Pr., 1974. 38 p.   **DC84**

An author listing of some 260 dissertations and master's essays completed through 1972 at foreign as well as American universities. Topical index.

———. ———. *Supplement one* (1987. 53 p.) provides an author listing of 386 master's essays and doctoral dissertations, including a few from the previous list. Only Western language titles included. Topical index.   Z3461.A85

Nersessian, Vrej. Armenia. Oxford ; Santa Barbara, Calif. : Clio, c1993. 304 p. : maps. (World bibliographical series, v. 163).   **DC85**

Topical bibliography of 879 annotated entries for books and articles in English with important materials in French, German, and Armenian also included. Author, title, and subject indexes.

§ See also: *The Armenians : a colossal bibliographic guide to books published in the English language* (Glendale, Calif. : Armenian Reference Books, 1993. 206 p.), an author/title listing of about 1,900 books on Armenian history and culture. No cross-references; not indexed.   DS165.N47

——————— An index of articles on Armenian studies in Western journals. London : Luzac, [1976]. 95 p.   **DC86**

A classed bibliography without index. Includes religion and theology, history, numismatics, mythology and folklore, paleography, philology and linguistics, and the arts.   Z3461.N5

Austria

Bibliography

Behrmann, Lilly-Ralou. Bibliographie zur Aussenpolitik der Republik Österreich seit 1945 : (Stand: 31. Dez. 1971) / Lilly-Ralou Behrmann, Peter Proché, Wolfgang Strasser. Wien : W. Braunmüller, 1974. 505 p. (Schriftenreihe der österreichischen Gesellschaft für Aussenpolitik und internationale Beziehungen, Bd. 7).   **DC87**

Lists books, pamphlets, periodical articles, and essays in a chronological/topical arrangement with author index; country breakdown within chronological sections.

Low, Alfred D. The Anschluss movement, 1918–1938 : background and aftermath; an annotated bibliography of German and Austrian nationalism. N.Y. : Garland, 1984. 186 p. (Canadian review of studies in nationalism, v.4 ; Garland reference library of social science, vol. 151).   **DC88**

An annotated bibliography of books, pamphlets, Austrian and American academic theses, essays, and articles, together with a representative listing of Nazi propaganda materials. In three chronological sections: (1) Roots of the Anschluss movement 1848–1918; (2) The Anschluss movement, 1918–1938; (3) Allied occupation and the rebirth of the Austrian state and nation, 1945 to the present. In many copies the number eight must be added to the index number in order to find the correct page.   Z2120.L68

Malina, Peter. Bibliographie zur österreichischen Zeitgeschichte, 1918–1985 : eine Auswahl / Peter Malina, Gustav Spann. Wien : Verlag für Geschichte und Politik, 1985. 107 p. (Politische Bildung [Vienna, Austria], Hft. 47–50).   **DC89**

Updates Malina and Spann's earlier bibliography, covering 1918–78, publ. 1978.

A very selective, annotated bibliography of German-language books and a few periodical articles, most of them published after 1970. Sections for general bibliographies and handbooks on Austria, general histories of Austria for the period, histories of Austria for more specific periods, and specialized topics (e.g., foreign relations, neofascism, minorities). Author index.   Z2120.3.M35

Rausch, Wilhelm. Bibliographie zur Geschichte der Städte Österreichs. Linz/Donau : Österreichischer Arbeitskreis für Stadtgeschichtsforschung, 1984. 329 p., [2] leaves of plates : 1 map.   **DC90**

More than 4,250 citations to books, dissertations, essays, and articles on the cities, towns, and states of Austria (including Südtirol) are arranged alphabetically by geographic area with author index.   Z2123.R38

Salt, Denys. Austria / comp. Denys Salt, with the assistance of Arthur Farrand Radley. Oxford ; Santa Barbara, Calif. : Clio Pr., c1986. 318 p. : ill. (World bibliographical series, v. 66).   **DC91**

Intends to provide a "broad and representative spectrum" (*Introd.*) of English- and German-language books and articles. 847 entries with good annotations in topical arrangement. Author/title/subject index. Chart of Austrian rulers. A good starting point for beginning researchers.   Z2101.S27

Strassmayr, Eduard. Bibliographie zur oberösterreichischen Geschichte, 1891–1926. Linz a. Donau : Winkler, 1929. 280 p. (Bibliographie zur Geschichte, Landes- und Volkskunde Oesterreichs. 1.Abt.: Oberösterreich, Bd.1–4).   **DC92**

A topical listing of books, articles, and essays; includes a good biographical section. Name and subject indexes.

Continued by the following, each in the same style:

———. ———. *1927–1934* (Linz : J. Feichtinger, 1937. 166 p.).

———. ———. *1935–1948*, hrsg. von Oberösterreichischen Landesarchiv (Linz, 1950. 255 p.). These three works also were issued as one volume by F. Winkler in 1950.

————. ————. *1949–1953* (Graz : Oberösterreichischen Landesarchiv In Kommission bei H. Böhlaus Nachf., 1957. 186 p.).

Bibliographie zur oberösterreichischen Geschichte, 1954/65 (Wien ; Köln ; Graz : Bohlaus, 1972–). v. 1 comp. by Alfred Marks, v. 2–5 by Johannes Wunschheim.

Contents: [v. 1], 1954/65 (1972. 429 p.); [v. 2], 1966/75 (1980. 518 p.); [v. 3], 1976/80 (1982. 308 p.); [v. 4], 1981/85 (1987. 311 p.); [v. 5], 1986/90 (1992. 407 p.). Each volume is a topical listing of books, articles, and essays, with name and subject indexes. Good biographical section.   Z2124.A9S83

Uhlirz, Karl. Handbuch der Geschichte Österreichs und seiner Nachbarländer Böhmen und Ungarn / begonnen von Karl Uhlirz ; bearb. von Mathilde Uhlirz. Graz : Leuschner und Lubensky, 1927–1944. 4 v. in 5.   **DC93**
A guide to research on the history of Austria, Bohemia, and Hungary, with extensive bibliographies.

Vol. 1 (to 1526) of a new edition was issued in 1963: *Handbuch der Geschichte Österreich-Ungarns*, by Mathilde Uhlirz (Graz : Böhlaus, 1963).   DB38.U4

Current

Österreichische historische Bibliographie = Austrian historical bibliography. 1945/1964– . Santa Barbara, Calif. : Clio Pr., 1967– . Annual.   **DC94**
Volume for 1945/1964 publ. in 1985. Annual coverage began with 1965.
A classed bibliography of historical literature published in Austrian periodicals or by Austrian publishing houses, the bulk of the material relating to Austria. Author index.
————. *Liste der Zeitschriften 1945–1979 (List of periodicals 1945–1979)*, comp. by Herbert and Hermine Paulhart, gives title, place, issuing body, and volumes/years covered in the bibliography (Salzburg : Neugebauer ; Santa Barbara : Clio Pr., 1980. 32 p.).
———— *Fünf-Jahres-Register (Austrian historical bibliography, five-year-index)* 1965/69/-1985/89, bearb. von Günther Hödl [et. al] (Salzburg : W. Neugebauer ; Santa Barbara : Clio Pr., [1974–93] 5 v.). Author index; subject, personal name, and place index.   Z2116.O48

Encyclopedias

Die Habsburger : ein biographisches Lexikon / hrsg. von Brigitte Hamann. München : Piper, c1988. 447 p. : ill. (some col.), geneal. tables, ports.   **DC95**
A somewhat popular account, giving brief facts (family relationship, birth, dates, burial place) followed by a biographical sketch written by a scholar and signed with initials. Genealogies; cross-references. Not indexed.
§ F. R. Bridge's *The Hapsburg monarchy, 1804–1918 : books and pamphlets published in the United Kingdom between 1918-1967 : a critical bibliography* (London : School of Slavonic and East European Studies, 1967. 82 p.) is an annotated bibliography of 649 titles concluding with a section listing biographies and memoirs.
DB36.3.H3H32

Österreich-Lexikon / hrsg. Richard Bamberger und Franz Maier-Bruck. Wien : Österreichischer Bundesverlag, [1966–67]. 2 v. (1320 p.) : ill., maps.   **DC96**
Offers extensive coverage of topics relating to Austria during all periods. Short articles predominate, with about 100 long entries (e.g., Beethoven, Biedermeier, Kaffeehaus). Most entries include bibliographies.   DB14.O48

Chronologies

Kleindel, Walter. Die Chronik Österreichs. 3., durchgesehene Aufl. Dortmund : Chronik Verlag, 1989. 672 p. : ill., maps, ports.   **DC97**
A history of Austria, 5000 BCE–1988 CE, presented as short newspaper articles. Heavily illustrated. Chronological arrangement; name and subject indexes. Appendix of population and economic statistics, and lists of prime ministers and presidents, and of mayors of Vienna. Name and topic indexes.   DB38.K5

Belarus

Korobushkina, Tat'iâna Nikolaevna. Arkheologiiâ Belorussi : bibliograficheskiĭ ukazatel', 1932–1975. Minsk : Gos. biblioteka BSSR im. V. I. Lenina : Akademiiâ nauk Belorusskoĭ SSR, In-t istorii, 1988. 162 p.   **DC98**
A topical arrangement of 2,419 entries; author and place-name index.   DK507.3K67

Belgium

See also Netherlands.

Bibliography

Bibliographie de l'histoire de Belgique. Louvain : Éd. Nauwelaerts, 1960–1986. 4 v. (Centre Interuniversitaire d'Histoire Contemporaine. Cahiers, 15, etc.).   **DC99**
Vols. 2–4 have title also in Flemish : Bibliografie van de geschiedenis van België.
Contents: [v. 1], 1789–21 juillet 1831, by Paul Gérin (1960. 429 p.); [v. 2], 1831–1865, by Solange Vervaeck (1965. 303 p.); [v. 3], 1865–1914, by J. de Belder and J. Hannes (1965. 301 p.); [v. 4], 1914–1940, by Micheline Heyse and Romain van Eenoo (1986. 410 p.).
Classed arrangement. Covers all areas of history: political, military, social, economic, religious, cultural, etc., with indexes by author and subject.

Pirenne, Henri. Bibliographie de l'histoire de Belgique : catalogue méthodique et chronologique des sources et des ouvrages principaux relatifs à l'histoire de tous les Pays-Bas jusqu'en 1598 et à l'histoire de Belgique jusqu'en 1914. 3. éd., rev. et compl. avec la collaboration de Henri Nowé et Henri Obreen. Bruxelles : Lamertin, 1931. 440 p.   **DC100**
Repr.: Hildesheim : G. Olms, 1979.
The standard bibliography of Belgian history, listing 4,151 titles. Classed arrangement within two parts: Recueils et ouvrages généraux; Histoire par époques. Author index.   Z2416.P67

Riley, Raymond Charles. Belgium. Oxford ; Santa Barbara, Calif. : Clio Pr., c1989. 271 p. (World bibliographical series, v. 104).   **DC101**
Cites 819 books and articles, published from earliest times to the present day, "encompassing those territories that eventually came to be Belgium."—*Pref.* Topically arranged; author, title, and subject indexes. "Theses and dissertations on Belgium," p. xxix–xxxviii.
Z2401.R55

Vingt ans de recherche historique en Belgique, 1969–1988 / publié sous la direction de Léopold Genicot. [Bruxelles] : Crédit communal, 1990. 569 p. (Collection Histoire. Série in-8°, no. 82).   **DC102**

Continues J. A. Van Houtte, "Un quart de siècle de recherche historique en Belgique 1944–1968" in *Bulletin critique d'histoire de Belgique* (1969–71).

Sponsored by the Comité National Belges des Sciences Historiques.

A survey of historical writing in Belgium. Bibliographical essays, signed by scholars, in two sections, subdivided by period: Histoire générale, Histoire belge. Indexes by topic, author, place-name, personal name as subject.

Wachter, Leo de. Repertorium van de Vlaamse gouwen en gemeenten : heemkundige dokumentatie. Antwerpen : De Sikkel, 1942–57. 6v.   **DC103**

Contents: v.1, Algemeen gedeelte en gewesten; v.2–4, Gemeenten, A–Z. Register; v.5–6, 1940–1950, Algemeen gedeelte en gewesten. Gemeenten A–Z. Register.

A bibliography of book and periodical material on Flemish local history. Indexes some 500 periodicals in various languages.

Z2423.W3

Current

Bibliographie de l'histoire de Belgique = Bibliografie van de geschiedenis van Belgie. 1952– . (*In* Revue belge de philologie et d'histoire : v. 31 [1953]–). Annual.   **DC104**

Continues the series published in *Revue du nord* 1947–49 in v. 32; 1950 in v. 33; 1951 in v. 34 (publ. 1950–52). Item numbers run consecutively through both series. Classified arrangement. No indexes to date.

Dissertations

Hendrickx, Jean-Pierre. Répertoire des mémoires de licence et des thèses de doctorat présentés dans les départements d'histoire contemporaine des universités belges. Louvain : Editions Nauwelaerts, 1986. v. 1. (In progress?).   **DC105**

Contents: v. 1, 1945–1975 (214 p.).

Topical arrangement with author and subject indexes. Almost all theses listed deal with Belgium in some way.   DH403.C42

Manuscripts; Archives

See also *Research guide to libraries and archives in the Low Countries* (AK133).

Nicodème, Jacques. Répertoire des inventaires des archives conservées en Belgique, parus avant le 1ᵉʳ Janvier 1969. Bruxelles : [Commission Belge de Bibliographie], 1970. 121 p. (Bibliographia belgica, 107 ; Archives et bibliothèques de Belgique. Numéro spécial, 2).   **DC106**

A bibliography of inventories and descriptions of documents presented as (1) general inventories; (2) published inventories of the Archives Générales du Royaume and the Archives de l'État in the provinces and in other central governmental archives; and (3) inventories of archives of towns, parishes, and public and private institutions arranged by place. Indexes of topics, authors, and places.

Het Rijksarchief in de provinciën : overzicht van de fondsen en verzamelingen. Brussel : Het Rijksarchief, 1974–1975. 2 v. : maps.   **DC107**

Contents: v.1, De Vlaamse provinciën; v.2, Les provinces wallonnes.

An extensive listing of government archives, giving brief histories, descriptions of collections, including church records, legal records, and special collections (e.g., genealogical lists, parish registers). Arranged by province, then by city. Index of people and places cited in the text.   Z5140.B44

Encyclopedias

Grande encyclopédie de la Belgique et du Congo. Bruxelles : Wauthoz-Legrand, 1938–52. 2 v. : ill.   **DC108**

Non-alphabetical. Signed articles with some bibliography. Maps. Vol. 1 deals with the Royal family, the geology, geography, demography, and history of Belgium to the end of the war in 1918; v. 2, with the fine arts and the sciences.   DH418.G7

Winkler Prins encyclopedie van Vlaanderen / Hoofdredactie: R. F. Lissens … [et al.]. [Brussels] : Elsevier Sequoia, [1972–74]. 5 v. : ill.   **DC109**

A regional encyclopedia concentrating on political, cultural, economic, and historical aspects of the Flemish area of Belgium and closely related matters. An introductory section on the physical and economic milieu of the area precedes the alphabetical sequence of articles. Vol. 4 begins with introductory essays on Flemish art; v.5 with essays on Flemish literature, language, music, and science. Vol. 5 also includes supplementary articles updating introductory essays throughout the set.

§ Also of interest is *Flandria nostra : ons land en ons volk…* van J. L. Broeckx [et al.] (Antwerp : Standaard-Boekhandel, 1957–60. 5 v.) which includes long, signed articles and extensive bibliographies.   DH801.F4W562

Bulgaria

Bibliography

Angelova, Stefka. Gŭrtsiia i bŭlgaro-grŭtskite otnosheniia v bŭlgarskata nauchna knizhnina, 1878–1980 : anotirana bibliografiia / [sŭstaviteli Stefka Angelova, Aleksandra Grigorova, redaktori Nadia Danova, Liliana Shandanova]. Sofiia : In-t za balkanistika "Liudmila Zhivkova", 1983. 339 p.   **DC110**

At head of title: Bŭlgarska akademiia na naukite. Institut za balkanistika "Liudmila Zhivkova." TSentŭr za informatsiia i Dokumentatsiia po balkanistika.

Added title page: La Grèce et les rapports bulgaro-greco dans la littérature scientifique bulgare, 1878–1980.

Annotated bibliography of 967 books and periodical articles published in Bulgaria 1878–1980 and concerned with socio-economic, political and cultural influences between Bulgaria and Greece. Works are mainly from the 18th century. Each annotation is in Bulgarian and French. Indexes for personal and place name. List of sources used.   Z2296.A54

Bŭlgarskata istoricheska nauka : Bibliografiia. 1960/64–1980/84. Sofia : BAN, 1965–85. t. 1–5. (In progress?).   **DC111**

At head of title: Bŭlgarskata Akademiia na Naukite. Institut za Istoriia.

Title on added title page: La science historique bulgare. Preface and table of contents also in French.

Each volume was published on the occasion of a meeting of the International Congress of Historical Sciences, and each is a topical listing of books and articles written in Bulgaria on Bulgarian history. With the 1965/69 volume a section of theses is added. Includes indexes for personal names, geographic names, and topics.

Crampton, R. J. Bulgaria. Oxford ; Santa Barbara, Calif. : Clio Pr., c1989. 232 p. (World bibliographical series, v. 107).   **DC112**

Lists 794 books and a few articles (mostly in English) topically arranged. Author, title, and subject indexes.

§ Still useful is Marin V. Pundeff's *Bulgaria : a bibliographic guide* (Wash. : Library of Congress, 1965, 98 p. Repr.: N.Y. : Arno Pr., 1968) for its bibliographic essays on sources for the study of Bulgaria.   Z2896.C7

Diabina, N. I. Sovetskaia bolgaristika : ukazatel literatury, 1945–1980 / sost. N. I. Diabina, I. A. Kaloeva, L. A. Rozhova. Moskva : Akademiia Nauk SSSR, Inst. Nauch. Informatsiĭ po Obshchestvennym Nauka, 1981. 3 v.   **DC113**

Topical arrangement of citations to almost 5,000 books, articles, and parts of books published in Russia on Bulgaria. Indexed.   Z2896.D44

Lazarov, Mikhail. Bŭlgariia na balkanite, 1944–1974 : bibliografiia. Sofiia : BAN, 1975. 371 p.   **DC114**

At head of title: Bŭlgarska akademiia na naukite. Institut za balkanistika.

Title also in English: *Bulgaria in the Balkans.*

A classified listing of books, essays, articles, and reviews published in Bulgaria "which directly refer to the Balkans, individual Balkan countries and the relations of the People's Republic of Bulgaria with them and such as treat problems of the Danube, the Black Sea, etc."—*Notes.* In addition to historical, economic, and political studies, materials on art, the cinema, the press, religion and atheism, linguistics, etc., are also cited.

§ Lazarov's *Development and achievements of bibliography on the history of Bulgaria* (Sofia : CIBAL, Centre International d'Information sur les Sources de l'Histoire Balkanique, 1977. 98 p.) is a bibliographical essay concerning about 250 bibliographies published over the last century relating to Bulgaria and the Balkans.   Z2831.L39

Petrova, Ivanka Apostolova. Istoriiata na Bŭlgariia v memoarnata literatura : bibliografski ukazatel / [sŭstaviteli Ivanka Petrova, Ivanka Vangelova ; redaktori Nikolaĭ Zhechev, Elena Statelova]. Sofiia : Nar. biblioteka "Kiril i Metodiĭ", 1985–1990. 3 v.   **DC115**

Vol. 3 has title: Edin vek kultura na Bŭlgariia, otrazena v memoarnata literatura.

An annotated bibliography of Bulgarian memoir literature located in books, pamphlets and anthologies. Arranged topically by very broad periods, then by profession or other topic. Vol. 3 features musicians, writers, dancers in ballet, etc. Each volume has its own index by memoirist, artist, etc.   Z2896.P47

Voenna istoriia na Bŭlgariia, 681–1945 : bibliografiia / [sŭstav. L. Venkova-Ilieva ... et al.]. Sofiia : Voen. izd., 1977–1987. 2 v.   **DC116**

A bibliography of works on Bulgarian military history for 681–1945, mostly in Bulgarian. Cites materials published from 1850s to 1972. Vol. 1 covers books, collections of documents, albums of pictures and drawings; v.2 lists articles from 119 journals. Topically arranged (mostly in chronological sections); annotations; indexed for authors and anonymous titles.   Z2898.M5

Archives

Bŭlgarski istoricheski arkhiv. Obzor na arkhivnite fondove, kolektsii i edinichni postŭpleniia, sŭkhraiavani v Bŭlgarski istoricheski arkhiv / Narodna biblioteka "Kiril i Metodiĭ," Bŭlgarski istoricheski arkhiv ; sŭstavili Elisaveta Miladinova ... [et al.] ; pod. red. na Kirila Vŭzvŭzova-Karateodorova. Sofiia : Narodna biblioteka "Kiril i Metodii", Bŭlgarski istoricheski arkhiv, 1966–86. v. 1–7. (In progress?).   **DC117**

Title also in English: Guide to the archive groups, collections, and single documents preserved in the Archives of Bulgarian History.

An inventory with notes on finding aids and detailed descriptions of the scope and character of each collection. Index of compilers, geographical areas, and subjects in each volume.   CD19541981

Encyclopedias; Dictionaries

Cholov, Petur. Bŭlgarski istoritsi : biografichno-bibliografski spravochnik. Sofiia : Nauka i izkustvo, 1981. 527 p.   **DC118**

Offers about 750 biobibliographies of 20th century Bulgarian historians, giving education, career, and publications. Includes all Bulgarian historians, but the great majority are concerned with Bulgarian history. Subject and geographic indexes.   Z2896.C49

Entsiklopediia Bŭlgariia / [glav. redaktor Vladimir Georgiev]. Sofiia : BAN, 1978–1988. v. 1–6. : ill., maps. (In progress?).   **DC119**

At head of title: Bŭlgarska Akademiia na naukite. Bulgarska entsiklopediia.

Contents: v. 1–6, A–Tu.

An encyclopedia of Bulgarian history, cultural affairs, etc. Numerous biographical sketches; bibliographies appended to some articles.

§ For a very recent historical dictionary, see: *Krat'uk spravochnik po istoriia na Bŭlgariia,* comp. by Kristo Matanov, Todor Dakov, and Bobi Bobev (Sofiia : Bulvest 2000, 1993. 302 p.). Offers short topical and biographical entries in two sections: 1700–1878 and 1878–1944 with chronologies. Not indexed.   DR53.E57

Commonwealth of Independent States

See Union of Soviet Socialist Republics.

Croatia

See Yugoslavia.

Cyprus

See also DC374.

Kitromilides, Paschalis. Cyprus / Paschalis M. Kitromilides, Marios L. Evriviades. Oxford ; Santa Barbara, Calif. : Clio Pr., 1982. 193 p. (World bibliographical series, 28).   **DC120**

An annotated bibliography, mainly of recent or easily accessible works in English. Topical arrangement with author, title, and subject index.

§ *See also* Evangelos Coufoudakis, "A bibliography on Cyprus," in *Modern Greek society,* v.12, no.1 (Dec. 1984) : 4–92. A broad topical listing of books, articles, government documents and dissertations (primarily in English, but with some Greek, Turkish, and French citations) focusing on the relationship between Cyprus and Greece/Turkey.   Z3496.K57

Megalē Kypriakē enkyklopaideia / [genikē euthynē ekdosēs Antros Paulidēs]. Leukōsia, Kypros : Philokypros, 1984-91. 14 v. : ill. (some col.).   **DC121**

Covers Cyprus and its relations to other countries, as well as flora and fauna, personalities, events, history, etc., within the island (e.g., the article on Egypt discusses Cyprus under the Ptolemies, that on Adonis addresses cult sites on Cyprus). Includes maps of cities and archaeological sites. Some longer articles are signed and include bibliographies. A supplement concludes v. 14.   DS54.A3M44

Czechoslovakia

In keeping with the focus of much of the literature produced prior to the separation, the heading Czechoslovakia is used here.

Bibliography

Bibliografie české historie za rok 1904–41. Praha : Nákl. Klubu Historického, 1905–51. Annual. **DC122**
Very comprehensive, annual record of material in Czech and other languages on the history of Czechoslovakia.
Volumes for 1904–14, 1930–36 published in—and later as a supplement to—*Český časopis historický* (Prague). Other volumes published separately.
Continued by the following:
(1) *Bibliografie československé historie za rok 1955–65* (Praha : Nákl. Československa Akademie Věd, 1957–68. 9 v.).
Annual volumes covering 1955–58 were published 1957–62; 1959–60 published in 1 v., 1964; 1961 published in 1 v., 1965; 1962–63 published in 1 v., 1967; 1964 published in 1 v., 1968. The subject classification was revised with the 1961 volume.
(2) *Bibliografie dějin Československa* (1971– . Annual).
"A specialized bibliography of Czech and Slovak historical works on the problems of Czech, Slovak, and world history" (*Foreword*) for books, essays, articles, and reviews. Classified arrangement in three sections: (1) "general works ... targeting the present state of historical sciences and related scientific disciplines;" (2) "history of Bohemian lands and Slovakia;" and (3) "Czech and Slovak works on world history including translations." Cross-references; personal name, geographic name, and title indexes. The 1980/81 volume was published 1993.
Z2136.B58

Hejzlar, Zdeněk. Czechoslovakia, 1968–1969 : chronology, bibliography, annotation / Zdeněk Hejzlar, Vladimir V. Kusin. N.Y. : Garland, 1975. 316 p. **DC123**
Includes a bibliography of publications of 1968–74 on the "Prague spring," a bibliography of Czech and Slovak articles relating to 1968–70, major documents in English translation, etc.
DB215.6.H44

Historiografie v Československu, 1970–1980 : v výběrová bibliografie / [sestavili Bohumila Houbová, et al.]. Praha : Ústav Československých a Světových Dějin ČSAV, 1980. 385 p. **DC124**
Lists more than 6,300 monographs, essays, documents, biographics, articles, etc., published in Czechoslovakia or elsewhere on Czech or Slovak history, together with Czech publications on world history. Author and title indexes.
§ Later publications cover 1980–85 (1985. 257 p.) and 1985–89 (1990. 376 p.). Both ed. by Miloslav Kudelásek. Z6201.H578

Jilek, Heinrich. Bibliographie zur Geschichte und Landeskunde der Böhmischen Länder von den Anfängen bis 1948 : Publikationen der Jahre 1850 bis 1975. Köln : Böhlau, 1986–1988. v. 1–2. (Ostmitteleuropa in Vergangenheit und Gegenwart, 19/I, 19/II). (In progress). **DC125**
Offers 23,884 numbered entries for books and articles in a topical arrangement for all fields of history, including the history of literature, publishing, art, and music. Vol. 3 (which will complete the set) is to be an index of authors and editors, anonymous works, and personal and place names. Z2131.J54

Short, David. Czechoslovakia. Oxford ; Santa Barbara, Calif. : Clio Pr., c1986. 409 p. (World bibliographical series, v. 68). **DC126**
Consists of 1,000 annotated entries, mostly English-language books, topically arranged. Author/title/subject index.

§ For earlier materials *see* Rudolf Sturm's *Czechoslovakia : a bibliographic guide* (Wash. : Library of Congress, 1967. 157 p.).
Z2131.S5

Wildová Tosi, Alena. Bibliografia degli studi italiani sulla Cecoslovacchia (1918–1978). Rome : Bulzoni, [1980]. 318 p. (Il bibliotecario, 4). **DC127**
A topically arranged bibliography of Italian works on the social sciences, literature, and arts of Czechoslovakia. Name index.
Z2136.W54

Zeman, Jarold K. The Hussite movement and the reformation in Bohemia, Moravia and Slovakia (1350–1650) : a bibliographical study guide (with particular reference to resources in North America). Ann Arbor : publ. under auspices of the Center for Reformation Research by Michigan Slavic Publications, 1977. 390 p. (Reformation in Central Europe, no.1). **DC128**
An inventory of some 50 research libraries in the U.S. and Canada, designed to identify "manuscripts, microfilms of manuscripts, rare books, unpublished theses and a few important modern critical works, both sources and literature."—*Purpose*. Includes a bibliography of books, essays, articles, and festschriften. Topically arranged, with indexes by name and format.
Z7845.H85Z45

Encyclopedias

Encyklopédia slovenska / [hlanva redakcia Vladimír Hajko ... et al.]. Bratislava : Slovenskej Akadémie Vied, 1977–1982. 6 v. : ill. **DC129**
A regional encyclopedia emphasizing Czech and Slovak topics, personalities, and events after 1968. DB2707.E5

Denmark

See also section for Scandinavia.

Bjerg, Hans Christian. Dansk marinehistorisk bibliografi, 1500–1975. København : Marinehistorisk Selskab, Akademisk Forlag, 1975. 166 p. (Marinehistorisk selskabs skrift, 12). **DC130**
A topical listing of more than 2,000 books and articles. Includes a section for biographies of individual officers. Author index.
§ See also *Den tyske marines arkiv 1848–1945* which is v. 1 of *Tyske arkivalier om Danmark 1848–1945* (København : Rigsarkivet, 1978. *Forelobige arkivregistraturer*, ny ser. 15). Z2581.N3B64

Erichsen, Balder. Dansk historisk bibliografi : systematisk Fortegnelse over Bidrag til Danmarks Historie til Udgangen af 1912, i tilslutning til Bibliotheca danica / ved B. Erichsen og Alfr. Krarup ... . Udg. paa Carlsbergfondets Bekostning. København : I kommission hos G.E.C. Gad, 1917–1927. 3 v. **DC131**
A very full list, including books, pamphlets, and many analytical references to articles in periodicals and other composite works. Vols. 1–2, published in parts, are a classified list of more than 20,000 references on history, topography, etc., with detailed indexes of authors and titles. Vol. 3 is a list of published biographies of persons living between 1830 and 1912, in continuation of a similar section in v. 3 of Henry Bruun, *Bibliotheca danica* and including some names of the earlier period omitted from Bruun; for more information, *see* AH185.
§ Continued by: *Dansk historisk bibliografi*: v. 1, pt. 1–6, 1913–42, comp. Henry Bruun (1966–77. 6 v.); v. 2, 1943–47, comp. by Henry Bruun (1956. 594 p.). Z2576.E68

Jansen, Henrik M. A select bibliography of Danish works on the history of towns published 1960–1976. Odense : [Odense Universitet, Institut for Historie og Samfundsvidenskab], 1977. 85 p. (Byhistoriske hjlpemidler, 2 ; Odense Universitet. Institut for Historie og Samfundsvidenskab. Historie, 21).   **DC132**
    Extends the coverage of the *International bibliography of urban history : Denmark, Finland, Norway, Sweden* (DC72) for Danish towns and for towns outside Denmark if the work was written by a Dane. Includes books, articles, essays, and archival lists.
                  Z7165.D4J35

Miller, Kenneth E. Denmark. Oxford ; Santa Barbara, Calif. : Clio Pr., c1987. 216 p. (World bibliographical series, v. 83).   **DC133**
    A selective (730 items) bibliography of books and a few articles, mostly in English, arranged topically. A chapter is devoted to basic materials on Greenland and the Faroe Islands. Cross-references; author/title/subject index.   Z2561.M55

Estonia

See also section for Baltic States.

Blumfeldt, Evald. Bibliotheca Estoniae historica, 1877–1917 / von Evald Blumfeldt und Nigolas Loone ; Nachdruck mit einer Einführung neu hrsg. von Paul Kaegbein. Wien : Böhlau Verlag Köln, 1987. 632 p. (Quellen und Studien zur baltischen Geschichte, Bd. 10).   **DC134**
    Reprint. Originally issued as: *Eesti ajaloo bibliograafia, 1877–1917* (Tartu : Loodus, 1933–39).
    Topical arrangement of 14,256 books and some articles within broad headings (e.g., Art and literature, Ethnography, Local history). Cross-references.   DK511.E6.B55

British Library. Reference Division. Catalogue of books and periodicals on Estonia in the British Library Reference Division / comp. by Salme Pruuden [et al.]. London : British Lib. ; N.Y. : Garland, 1981. 309 p.   **DC135**
    A comprehensive, topical listing of books and journals with materials relating to Estonia. Includes all areas except fiction and poetry; encompasses materials in any language. Index of authors, editors, and compilers.
    § Also of interest is *History (archaeology, history, history of art, music, religion, and church), 1945–1983 : a bibliography of works published by Estonian scholars in exile*, comp. by Meemo Mäelo (Stockholm : Institutum Litterarum Estonicum, 1985. 108 p. [Folia bibliographica, 7]). 1st ed., 1969, by Aino Ränk.   Z2533.B75

Finland

See also section for Scandinavia.

Bako, Elemer. Finland and the Finns : a selective bibliography. Wash. : Library of Congress, 1993. 276 p. : ill.   **DC136**
    A broad topical arrangement of 1,716 monographs and 392 serial titles available at the Library of Congress, about half of them published 1980–91. Preference is given to English-language material, but Finnish and Scandinavian language titles are included. Index of personal names, index of titles.   Z2520.B33

Harvard University. Library. Finnish and Baltic history and literatures : classification schedule; classified listing by call number; chronological listing; author and title listing. Cambridge : publ. by Harvard Univ. Libr., distr. by Harvard Univ. Pr., 1972. 250 p. (Widener Library shelflist, 40).   **DC137**
    For a note on the series *see* AA115.

    About 8,600 titles representing "the classes *Balt* and *Balt Doc* which provide for works on the history and literatures of Finland, Estonia, Latvia, and Lithuania, and for writings in other Finno-Ugrian languages except Hungarian."—*Pref.*   Z2520.H37

Paloposki, Toivo J. Quellenkunde zur Geschichte Finnlands / Toivo J. Paloposki ... [et al.]. Wiesbaden : Harrassowitz, 1988. 145 p. (Veröffentlichungen des Osteuropa-Institutes München. Reihe Geschichte, Bd. 55).   **DC138**
    A discussion of resources and guides to Finnish archives. Arranged by subject, e.g., Reichsrat, Archive der Kirche und der Pfarrgemeinden, Die Presse. Not indexed.   Z2520.P35

Ruokonen, Kyllikki. Finland—sources of information : a selective list of publications / Kyllikki Ruokonen, Erkki Vaisto. Helsinki : Helsinki School of Economics Library, 1979–89. 2 v. (Helsingin kauppakorkeakoulun Selvityskiä E, 54, 56.).   **DC139**
    Vol. 1 reissued, 1988.
    A classed bibliography of English-language titles with author and subject listings. In each section, Finnish publications are followed by those from outside Finland. Vol. 1 concentrates on economics and business; v. 2 is broader in scope: "...periodical articles, books, pamphlets, research reports dealing with the Finnish way of life."—*Pref.*

Screen, J. E. O. Finland. Oxford : Santa Barbara, Calif. : Clio, 1981. 212 p. (World bibliographical series, 31).   **DC140**
    A brief introductory survey of Finnish history and life is followed by an annotated bibliography of 768 books, periodical titles (not articles), and documents, mainly in English. Arranged by broad topic; author, title, subject index.   Z2520.S24

Suomen historiallinen bibliografia = Finsk historisk bibliografi = Bibliografie historique finlandaise = Finnish historical bibliography. Helsinki, 1940–1992. v. [1–7]. (Suomen historiallinen Seura. Käsikirjoja, 2, 4–6, 9, 11, 14). (In progress).   **DC141**
    Contents: v. [1], 1544–1900, by J. Vallinkoski and H. Schauman (1961); v. [2], 1901–1925, by A. H. Maliniemi and E. Kivikoski (1940); v. [3], 1926–1950, by J. Vallinkoski and H. Schauman (1955–56); v. [4], 1951–1960, by P. Laminén (1968); v. [5], 1961–1970, by T. Rantanen and L. Pärssinen (1983); v. [6], 1971–1980, by Tuula Rantanen and Raija Mankki (1988); v. [7], 1986–1990, by Kirsti Antin (1992). 1980–1985 not yet published.
    Beginning with 1986–90, also available on microfiche.
    A series of comprehensive bibliographies of Finnish historical works, including both books and periodical articles. Classed arrangement with author indexes. Headings are given in Finnish, Swedish, and French. Most of the material is in Finnish, though some titles are in Swedish, German, and other languages. History is interpreted in its broadest sense to include not only political and economic history of all periods, but also allied interests, e.g., history of the church, education, literature, folklore, etc., and local history.   Z2520.S94

France

General works

Guides

Barbier, Frédéric. Bibliographie de l'histoire de France. Paris ; N.Y. : Masson, 1987. 283 p.   **DC142**
    Covers basic reference sources in French history published through June 1985. Includes descriptive notes. French-language materials predominate but other languages are included.   Z2187.C55B37

Bibliography

Bibliothèque Nationale (France). Département des Imprimés. Catalogue de l'histoire de France. Paris : Didot, 1855–1879. 11 v.   **DC143**

Repr. w. supplements: Paris : Bibliothèque Nationale, 1968–69. 16 v. Parts of v. 9–16 available on microfilm from the Bibliothèque. Also available on microfiche (Chadwick Healey Paris).

Ed. by J. A. Schmit.

A very comprehensive catalog of books, pamphlets, etc., printed before 1875 on the history of France prior to 1875. Classed (15 main and 904 subclasses), with author index.

Contents: v. 1, Préliminaires et généralités. Histoire par époques. Histoire par règnes [à Louis XIII]; v. 2, Louis XIV–Louis XVI; v. 3, 1792–1848; v. 4, 1848–1856. Journaux et publications périodiques; v. 5, Histoire religieuse; v. 6, Histoire constitutionnelle; v. 7, Histoire constitutionnelle [suite]. Histoire administrative, diplomatique, militaire. Moeurs et coutumes. Archéologie; v. 8, Histoire locale; v. 9, Histoire locale [suite]. Biographie; v. 10, Biographie [suite]; v. 11, Supplément [suite].

Six *Suppléments*, ed. by Schmit and Paul Marchal, began publication in 1880, and correspond to chapters: no. 10, Moeurs et coutumes; no. 11, Archéologie française; no. 12, Histoire locale; no. 14, Histoire des familles française; no. 15, biographie française. *Ouvrages généraux sur l'histoire de France, 1807–1959*, Séries L32–L42, ed. by Jeannine Boghen and Marie-Renée Morin, form a 2nd supplement (1972. 327 p.).

———. ———. *Biographies individuelles 1879–1943*. Carnets d'inventaire (1973. 1 v., unpaged).

———. ———. *Table des auteurs* (1895. 798 p.).

———. ———. *Table des divisions* (1966. 75 p.) Outline of v. 1–10 only.

———. ———. *Table générale alphabétique des ouvrages anonymes* (1905–32. 15 v.) covers titles in the main catalogue and its supplements. Contents: v. 1–4, Table des noms de personnes (1905–9); v. 5–15, Tables des noms de lieux (1911–32).

Chambers, Frances. France. Rev. and expanded ed. Oxford ; Santa Barbara, Calif. : Clio Pr., 1990. 290 p. (World bibliographical series, 13).   **DC144**

1st ed., 1980.

Lists 942 books and articles selected as "a 'core' collection of books about France for an English-speaking reader who has a serious interest in the country and its culture, but who is not a specialist."— *Introd.* For this edition several new sections have been added, e.g., Paris; Dreyfus affair; Family, marriage and sexuality; Landscape architecture; Sport. Author, title, subject indexes.   Z2161.C5

Heggoy, Alf Andrew. The military in imperial history : the French connection / Alf Andrew Heggoy, John M. Haar. N.Y. : Garland, 1984. 302 p. (Military history bibliographies, v.4 ; Garland reference library of social science, v.192).   **DC145**

Introductory chapters on topics such as Organization of the French military, French Foreign Legion, and Colonialism are followed by chapters for each country or area in the French empire. A brief survey of the role of the French army in a given area precedes the bibliographic listings for that area. Covers books and articles; name index.   Z2181.C7H43

Ross, Steven T. French military history, 1661–1799 : a guide to the literature. N.Y. : Garland, 1984. 305 p. (Military history bibliographies, v. 6 ; Garland reference bibliography of social science, v. 190).   **DC146**

Running title: *French Army bibliography*.

A comprehensive bibliography of books, articles, and manuals relating to the army in the foreign and domestic affairs of France; includes works on the evolution of the French army, campaigns, and leaders. In three main sections: General works; The old régime; The French Revolution. Author index.   Z2181.M5R67

Les sources de l'histoire de France depuis les origines jusqu'en 1815 / par A. Molinier … [et al.]. Paris : Picard, 1901–35. pt. 1–3 in 18 v.   **DC147**

Repr. : 1. pt., N.Y. : B. Franklin, 1964; 2. pt., Nendeln : Kraus, 1966.

A valuable bibliography listing printed sources. The volumes to cover the period 1715–1815 were never published.

§ An expanded version of 1. pt., t. 1 was published as *La Gaule jusqu'au milieu de Ve siècle*, by Paul-Marie Duval (Paris : Picard, 1971. 2 v.).   Z2176.S75

Current

Bibliographie annuelle de l'histoire de France du cinquième siècle à 1939. Année 1955– . Paris : Éd. du Centre National de la Recherche Scientifique, 1956– . Annual.   **DC148**

Date in title varies according to period of coverage.

Issued by the Comité Français de Sciences Historiques and the Centre National de la Recherche Scientifique.

A detailed, classified bibliography with author and subject indexes.   Z2176.B5

Bibliographie en langue française d'histoire du droit. v. 1 (1926/56)– . Paris : Montchrestien, [1961?]–   **DC149**

Continuation of Gabriel Lepointe, *Éléments de bibliographie sur l'histoire des institutions et des faits sociaux, 987–1875* (1958. 232 p.) which was prepared to accompany his *Histoire des institutions et des faits sociaux de la France* (1956).

1957–59 issued in one volume; annual, 1960–69; 1957/59–62 issued without volume numbering; 1963– called v. 6– .

Lists books and articles in French on the social history of France from 987 to 1875. A few articles on other countries are included. Arranged alphabetically with an index by subject.   Z2161.L572

Manuscripts; Archives

Archives nationales (France). État des inventaires / publié sous la direction de Jean Favier. Paris : Archives nationales : Diffusé par La Documentation française, 1985–91. v. 1–2, 4. (In progress).   **DC150**

Contents: v. 1, L'ancien régime (1985); v. 2, 1789–1940 (1991); v. 4, Fonds divers (1986). To be complete in 4 v.

A comprehensive listing of registers, indexes and other finding aids, and similar research tools for French public archives as of January 1, 1983. Arranged by major chronological periods, subdivided by *série*.

§ Gerard Ermisse, *Guide du lecteur* (6th ed. Paris : Archives Nationales, 1993. 77 p.) is a guide for first-time users.

Chadwyck-Healey France has begun issuing *Les inventaires des Archives Nationales* on microfiche (1988–) along with *Guide de l'utilisateur des Inventaires des Archives nationales*, by Isabelle Carbonnel and Ghislain Brunel (1990. 112 p.). The aim is to reproduce the inventories themselves.   CD1196

——— État général des fonds / publié sous la direction de Jean Favier. Paris : Archives Nationales : Diffusé par La Documentation française, 1978–88. v. 1–5. (In progress).   **DC151**

Contents: v. 1, L'ancien régime; v. 2, 1789–1940; v. 3, Marine et outre-mer; v. 4, Fonds divers et additions et corrections aux tomes I, II, et III; v. 5, 1940–58, Fonds conservé à Paris.

Offers a detailed inventory of the contents of each file in the Archives Nationales, including materials added up to July 1, 1976. Each section begins with a headnote giving a brief description and an indication of any registers or published guides to the collections. Vol. 4 covers descriptions of private archives, notarial records and maps, and corrections to previous volumes, and also includes a list of microfilms of collections in other archives, p. 328–93. Vol. 5 extends coverage of vols. 2 and 4 for archives in Paris, thereby excluding the Centre des Archives Contemporaines at Fontainebleau. Includes an extensive list of members of French cabinets, 1940–58.

§ The papers of the Minutier Central des Notaires de Paris described in v. 4 have been treated in more detail and by special subject in publications issued by the Archives Nationales: *Documents du Minutier central des notaires de Paris. Inventaires après décès*, comp. by Madeleine Jurgens (v. 1, 1483–1547. Paris, 1982. [In progress]); *Ronsard et ses amis*, comp. by Madeleine Jurgens (1985. 442 p.); *Histoire de l'art au XVIe siècle, 1540–1600* (1985–86. 2 v.); *Documents inedits sur les artistes français du XVIIIe siècle, conservés au Minutier central des notaires de la Seine …*, comp. by Daniel Wildenstein (1966. 171 p.).

Another portion of the Archives Nationales receiving its own published guide is: *L'administration parisienne à la veille de la Révolution : délibérations du Bureau de la Ville de Paris, 1784–1790 : inventaire des minutes H(2) …* (1989. 137 p.).   CD1196

─────────── Guide des papiers des ministres et secrétaires d'État de 1871 à 1974 / par Chantal de Tourtier-Bonazzi et François Pourcelet. 2e éd. rev. et augm. Paris : Archives nationales : Diffusé par la Documentation française, 1984. 282 p.   **DC152**

1st ed., 1978.

Cabinet ministers are listed alphabetically; for each, gives a biographical sketch followed by descriptions of any papers in national, departmental, and private archives, mentioning any finding aids and noting terms of access.   CD1196

Bruguière, Michel. Guide du chercheur pour la période 1789–1815 : les sources de l'histoire financière et économique / Michel Brugière, Pierre-François Pinaud. Genève : Droz, 1992. 195 p.   **DC153**

An inventory of national and département archives in France of interest to economic historians. Arranged by département. For each series, information includes brief description of contents and organization of file, any other inventories or document collections using this series, list of contents. Index of personal names; topical index which includes names of organizations and government departments.

Z2179.B78

État des inventaires des archives départementales, communales et hospitalières au 1er janvier 1983 / par les Services d'archives départementaux et communaux et le Service technique de La Direction des archives de France. Paris : Archives nationales : Diffusé par la Documentation française, 1984. 2 v. (1275 p.).   **DC154**

Supersedes Henri Courteault, *État des inventaires des archives nationales, départementales, communales et hospitalières au 1 janvier 1937* (Paris : Didier, 1938. 703 p.) and its *Supplément*, ed. by Robert H. Boutier (Paris : Impr Nationale, 1955. 344 p.).

Covers departmental, regional, and private papers on deposit in those archives, listing for each the inventories and other finding aids available as of January 1, 1983. In two parts: (1) general aids arranged by historical period and subject; (2) aids listed by département. See appendix for list of laws, statutes, etc. applying to archives, and a list of chief archivists.   CD1192.A2E72

France. Ministère des affaires étrangères. État général des inventaires des archives diplomatiques. Paris : Impr. nationale, 1987. 249 p.   **DC155**

A catalog of inventories of archives of diplomatic and consular posts that also includes descriptions of the records of the French occupation of Germany and Austria after World War II.

§ For students working in the archives, valuable assistance is provided by Paul Pitman's *Short guide to the archives of the Quai d'Orsay* (Paris : Assoc. des Amis des Archives Diplomatiques, 1993. 97 p.).   CD1201

France. Ministère des relations extérieures. Archives et documentation. Les archives du Ministère des relations extérieures depuis les origines : histoire et guide : suivis d'une étude des sources de l'histoire des affaires étrangères dans les dépôts parisiens et départementaux. Paris : Impr. nationale, 1984–1985. 2 v. : ill.   **DC156**

Pt. 1 is a history of the Archives of the Ministère, discussing the applicable laws, the development, relevant finding aids and bibliographies, general organization, and staffing. Pt. 2 is the guide to individual files, indicating their organization, dates covered, size, and a summary list of finding aids. Pt. 3 describes related files in other archives and libraries in Paris, such as Bibliothèque Nationale, Archives de la Marine, Bibliothèque de la Sorbonne. An appendix in v. 2 gives names and terms of ministers, secretaries and undersecretaries. Names and subject indexes for each volume.   CD1201

Guide des centres de documentation en histoire ouvrière et sociale / sous la responsabilitié de Michel Dreyfus. Paris : Editions ouvrières, 1983. v. 1.   **DC157**

No more published?

A directory of libraries, parties, centers of research, museums, and government agencies giving address, hours, telephone, brief history, catalogs of holdings, conditions of access, and list of publications. Indexes of personal names, periodical publications, organizations.

Z7164.T7G83

Welsch, Erwin K. Archives and libraries in France : with 1991 supplement. N.Y. : Council for European Studies, 1991. 147 p.   **DC158**

For annotation, *see* AK136.   Z797.A1W44

Encyclopedias; Dictionaries

Charlton, D. G. France : a companion to French studies. 2nd ed. London : Methuen, 1979. 690 p.   **DC159**

1st ed., 1972.

Offered "as a detailed introduction and guide to the history and culture of France from the time of the Renaissance to the present day."—*Pref.* Each chapter, written by a contributing scholar, deals with a facet of French life and provides a bibliographical essay. Indexed.   DC33.C478

Dictionnaire d'histoire de France Perrin / sous la direction de Alain Decaux et André Castelot. Paris : Perrin, c1981. 1076 p. : ill.   **DC160**

Reissued as "Nouv. ed." in 1986, with little change.

Includes entries for persons, places, terms, and events important to the understanding of French history from earliest times to the recent past. Certain events of unusual significance (Diên Biên Phu, the Resistance) are given extended treatment and appear on pages with colored borders. Heavily illustrated; occasional *see* references; no bibliography.   DC35.D53

Chronologies

Jouette, André. Toute l'histoire par les dates et les documents : chronologie de l'histoire de France et regards sur le monde. Paris : Perrin, 1989. 973 p.   **DC161**

A chronology presented in three main columns: (1) In France, (2) Outside France, (3) Civilization, science and technology. A fourth column gives quotations, facts, lists, etc., relevant to the year(s) covered in the other columns. Prehistoric times through 18th century treated in 80 pages. Appendix for genealogies, lists, calendars, reprinting of texts, etc. Index from name of event, place, or person to the date in the chronology section.

Historiography

Bibliographical foundations of French historical studies / Lawrence J. McCrank, ed. N.Y. : Haworth Pr., c1992. 255 p. : ill. **DC162**

Selected papers from the annual conference of the Association for the Bibliography of History held in conjunction with the American Historical Association in San Francisco, Calif., Dec. 27–28, 1989.

Articles on specific archives (outside Paris), libraries, bibliographic resources, the new National library, booksellers, collectors, etc. are presented in four sections: (1) Bibliographic methods and French historical studies; (2) French archives and libraries: historical perspectives and research possibilities; (3) Post-Revolution French bibliographic connections with the New World; (4) French Revolution archives and libraries: from royal to national and from private to public institutions. Subject index. Z2178.B47

Biography

Les historiens français de la période moderne et contemporaine. Paris : Éditions du Centre National de la Recherche Scientifique, 1991. 313 p. **DC163**

At head of title: Centre National de la Recherche Scientifique. Institut d'Historie Moderne et Contemporaine.

1st ed., 1983, comp. by Arlette Faugères and Régine Ferré, had title: *Répertoire des historiens français pour la période moderne et contemporaine.*

A directory of French historians with information derived from questionnaires distributed in 1991 to affiliates of CNRS, universities, archives, libraries, and museums in France. In addition to address and institutional affiliation, aims to include titles of theses, specialties, works in progress or published. Topical, period, geographic area, and specialty indexes. Directory of organizations. DC36.95.H57

Atlases

Ardagh, John. Cultural atlas of France / by John Ardagh, with Colin Jones. N. Y. ; Oxford : Facts on File, 1991. 260 p. : col. ill., col. maps ; 31 cm. **DC164**

Through maps, text, photographs of sites, paintings, illuminations, etc., describes France in general sections: Geology, History, French society including the role of the state, Life-styles, Intellectual life, Regions. Each region receives 4–6 pages. Topical index; gazetteer.

§ Similar in presentation and still useful is *Atlas historique et culturel de France* (Paris : Elsevier, 1957. 214 p. ; ill.). G1844.21.E64.A7

Atlas historique : Provence, Comtat Venaissin, principauté d'Orange, comté de Nice, principauté de Monaco / [sous la direction de] Édouard Baratier, Georges Duby, Ernest Hildesheimer … [et al.]. [Paris] : Librairie Armand Colin, [1969]. 208 p. : ill. ; 326 maps in portfolio. 35 cm. **DC165**

Added t.p. : Atlas Belfram.

Historical, geographical, and linguistic maps of southern France. The volume of commentary gives sources for the information depicted on the maps, plus lists of cardinals, bishops, genealogical charts, county officials, and a gazetteer. G1843.P7A3

Atlas historique de la France / préface de Pierre Miquel ; [conçu, écrit et réalisé par Edimages]. [Paris] : Plon, c1985. 150 p. : maps in color ; 30 cm. **DC166**

Colored maps with textual commentary are arranged by period from prehistoric time to that of the European Community. List of maps. "Chronologie de l'histoire de France," p. 7–39, gives, in columns, political, military, and international events.

§ A less elegantly produced (in black-and-white) but often clearer work is: *Atlas de géographie historique de la France et de la Gaule, de la conquête césarienne à nos jours,* by Stéphane Sinclair (Paris: SEDES, [1985]. 260 p.), which includes an index of names of places and people and a bibliography of sources. G1844.21.S1A8

Reverdy, Georges. Atlas historique des routes de France. Paris : Presses de l'École nationale des ponts et chaussées, c1986. 182 p. : some maps in color ; 38 cm. **DC167**

Reproduces maps of the roads in France with explanatory text and notes on the cartographers. Arranged chronologically in five parts: (1) Jusqu'en 1550; (2) 1550–1750; (3) 1750–1800; (4) 1800–1900; (5) De 1900 à nos jours [i.e., to 1986]. One-page index of geographical names. G1844.21.P2R4

Early to 1789 (including archaeology)

Bibliography

Bibliographie de l'histoire médiévale en France (1965–1990) / Société des historiens médiévistes de l'enseignement supérieur ; textes réunis par Michel Balard. Paris : Publications de la Sorbonne, 1992. 486 p. **DC168**

A bibliographical survey of works published on the study of medieval France, arranged by broad topics such as art history, urban history, and computer sciences. Mostly in French but with a few Italian, Spanish, German, British, and American titles. Author index.

§ Companion work: *Histoire médiévale en France : bilan et perspectives,* by Françoise Autrand … [et al.] (Paris : Seuil, c1991. 566 p.). Z2177.B52

Lindsay, Robert O. French political pamphlets, 1547–1648 : a catalog of major collections in American libraries / comp. by Robert O. Lindsay and John Neu. Madison : Univ. of Wisconsin Pr., 1969. 510 p. **DC169**

More than 6,700 items; chronological arrangement, with author-title index. Locates copies.

§ Most of the items listed are available on microfilm from Research Publications, New Haven, Conn. (86 reels; publ. 1978). That company has also issued *French political pamphlets 1547–1648 : a supplement listing the microform additions to the original edition,* comp. by R. O. Lindsay and J. Neu (Woodbridge, Conn., 1981. 40 p.). For a similar collection, *see* Newberry Library, *A checklist of French political pamphlets 1560–1653 in the Newberry Library,* comp. by Doris Varner Welsh (Chicago : The Library, 1950–1955 2 v. [204, 190 p.]). More than 2,500 items, most unavailable elsewhere in the U.S. Z2177.5.L54

Margolis, Nadia. Joan of Arc in history, literature, and film : a select, annotated bibliography. N.Y. : Garland, 1990. 406 p. (Garland reference library of the humanities, 1224). **DC170**

An annotated bibliography of books, essays in collections, periodical articles, films, and early French television productions. Arranged in three categories: histories, literature, film; each is subdivided by genre or period. For example, History is subdivided under headings, such as Chronicles, Biographies, Military aspects, Regional interest; Literature is divided as primary literature and critical literature under century. No index. Z8451.M37

Montandon, Raoul. Bibliographie générale des travaux palethnologiques et archéologiques (époques préhistorique, protohistorique et gallo-romaine). France … . Genève : Georg, 1917–38. 5 v. : maps. **DC171**

A comprehensive bibliography of books and periodical articles, arranged by geographical division.

———. ——— *Supplément du t. 1–3* (1921–29. 3 v.

————. ———— *Supplément* (Le Mans : Monnoyer, 1952. [Société préhistorique française. Bullétin, v. 49, no. 9, Sept. 1952]). Includes "2^ieme suppl. du t. 3; 2^ieme suppl. du t. 1; 1^ier suppl. du t. 4."
Z5117.M75

Répertoire archéologique de la France / pub. par ordre du Ministre de l'Instruction Publique et sous la direction du Comité des Travaux Historiques et des Sociétés Savantes. Paris : Impr. Nationale, 1861–1888. 8 v. (Collection de documents inédits sur l'histoire de France. Series vii, 7).   **DC172**
> Contents: *Alpes* (*Hautes*), by Joseph Roman (1888); *Aube*, by Henri d'Arbois de Jubainville (1861); *Morbihan*, by Louis Rosensweig (1863); *Nièvre*, by J. H. G. R. de Soultrait (1875); *Oise*, by Emmanuel Woilez (1862); *Seine-Inférieure*, by J. B. D. Cochet (1872); *Tarn*, by Hippolyte Crozes (1865); *Yonne*, by Maximilien Quantin (1868).

Saulnier, Eugène. Bibliographie des travaux publiés de 1866 à 1897 sur l'histoire de la France de 1500 à 1789 / Eugène Saulnier, André Martin. Paris : Presses Universitaires, 1932-38. v. 1–2, fasc. 2. (Publication de la Société d'Histoire Moderne).   **DC173**
> Contents: v.1, Histoire intérieure, Histoire des institutions, Histoire diplomatique, Histoire militaire, Histoire de la marine militaire, Histoire religieuse; v.2, fasc.1–2, Histoire économique et sociale, Histoire coloniale, Histoire des familles, Biographies. No more published.

> A comprehensive listing of books and periodical articles, with references to reviews. Classified arrangement. Not completed, and lacks indexes.

Dictionaries; Handbooks

Cabourdin, Guy. Lexique historique de la France d'ancien régime / Guy Cabourdin, Georges Viard. 2. éd., rev. et corr. Paris : Armand Colin, 1981. 324 p.   **DC174**
> 1st ed., 1978.

> Not intended as an encyclopedia, but as an introductory dictionary for the period. Covers all areas from institutions to art and science; bibliographical citations conclude most articles. Liberal use of cross-references.   DC35.C3

Dictionnaire archéologique de la France. Paris : Editions Atlas, c1989. 2 v. : ill. (chiefly color), maps.   **DC175**
> An alphabetical presentation of about 900 articles on sites, monuments, techniques, principal museums, artifacts, and archaeologists in France and adjacent parts of Belgium and Switzerland. Some entries are essay length, e.g., Corsica, dating, prehistoric climates, Gallo-Roman divinities. Covers from prehistoric to ca.500 CE. Cross-references but no index nor bibliography. Well illustrated with portraits of archaeologists, maps, and photographs of sites and artifacts.

> § See also *Dictionnaire archéologique de la Gaule, époque celtique*, by the Commission de la Topographie der Gaules (Paris : Imprimerie nationale, 1875–1923. 2 v. [Collection de documents inédits sur l'histoire de France, séries 6, t. 20]), which offers older treatment of the archeological remains of France. In alphabetical order by name of site.   GN811.D53

French Revolution

Bibliography

Bibliographie de la Révolution française, 1940–1988 / sous la direction de Alfred Fierro. Paris : Références, c1989. 2 v. (1334 p.).   **DC176**
> An extensive bibliography (31,960 books and articles) on the French Revolution, mainly French- and English-language materials in topical arrangement; long sections on biography and local history. Indexes for authors and for names and places.

Continues:
> André Monglond, *La France révolutionnaire et impériale : annales de bibliographie méthodique et description des livres illustrés* (Paris : Impr. Nationale, 1930–78. 10 v.).
> Gérard Walter, *Répertoire de l'histoire de la Révolution française : Travaux publiés de 1800 à 1940* (Paris : Bibliothèque Nationale, Dép. des Imprimés, 1941–51. 2 v.).   DC148.Z9F465

Bibliothèque Nationale (France). Département des Imprimés. Catalogue de l'histoire de la révolution française / par André Martin et Gérard Walter. Paris : Éd. des Bibliothèques Nationales, 1936–1969. 6 v. in 7.   **DC177**
> Contents: v.1–4^1, Écrits de la période révolutionnaire—Auteurs; v.4^2, Anonymes; v.5, Journaux et almanachs; v.6, Table analytique, par G. Walter.

> A very comprehensive bibliography of works published during the French Revolution.   Z2179.P27

Caldwell, Ronald J. The era of the French Revolution : a bibliography of the history of western civilization, 1789–1799. N.Y. : Garland, c1985. 2 v. (Garland reference library of social science, v. 284).   **DC178**
> Companion to the author's *The era of Napoleon* (DC191).

> "A partly annotated topical listing of 42,420 books, articles, theses, and dissertations on the general and national history of Europe and the Western hemisphere" (*Pref.*) in the period of the French Revolution. "Since it is principally a bibliography of writings on history, it includes only the most important works published during the Revolution." Relatively few annotations. Cross-references; detailed table of contents; index of names and subjects.   Z2178.C34

Dallet, Sylvie. Filmographie mondiale de la Révolution française / Sylvie Dallet, Francis Gendron. Montreuil : Centre d'action culturelle de Montreuil, c1989. 229 p. : ill.   **DC179**
> An international list of films with production information and plot summary for each. Very inclusive, even embracing films with only a few scenes on the Revolution, e.g., *Singin' in the rain*. Arrangement is by year of release, then by country name (in French), and finally alphabetical by title. Indexed by title and by country.   DC149.5.D35

Fierro, Alfred. Bibliographie critique des mémoires sur la Révolution écrits ou traduits en français. [Paris] : Service des travaux historiques de la ville de Paris, 1988. 482 p.   **DC180**
> Cover title: Mémoires de la Révolution.

> An annotated bibliography of diaries, correspondence, memoirs, etc., concerning the French Revolution, written or translated into French and appearing as books, parts of books or articles. Cross-references; index by geographical area or by topic, e.g., emigration, women.   Z2178.F54

Miraval, Paule. Répertoire des travaux universitaires inédits sur la période révolutionnaire / préparé par Paule Miraval et Raymonde Monnier. Paris : Société des études robespierristes, 1990. 325 p.   **DC181**
> At head of title: Institut d'histoire de la Révolution française.

> An author listing, mainly of theses but also including reports from university research institutes in France. For each gives author, title, name of institution, degree, date, usually number of pages, and a location. Indexes for place-names and for topics. Lists of authors by period and by place of deposit. Appendix gives addresses of universities, institutes and centers of research.   Z2178.M57

Manuscripts; Archives

Archives nationales (France). Guide des papiers privés d'époque révolutionnaire / par Françoise Hildesheimer. Paris : Archives nationales : Documentation française [distributor], 1987. 301 p.   **DC182**
> In two parts: (1) a listing by name of collections of papers of persons (e.g., Danton, Marie Antoinette) prominent during the French Revolution, with archival location and brief description of contents; (2)

Archives départmentales, communales et hospitalières, listing by département and then by repository with indications of holdings of papers. Name index for the second part. CD1192.A2F74

Encyclopedias; Dictionaries

A critical dictionary of the French Revolution / ed. by François Furet and Mona Ozouf ; transl. by Arthur Goldhammer. Cambridge, Mass. : Belknap Pr. of Harvard Univ. Pr., 1989. 1063 p., [32] p. of plates : ill. (some col.). **DC183**

Translation of *Dictionnaire critique de la Révolution française* ([Paris] : Flammarion, [1988]).

A summary of contemporary scholarship presented as a collection of essays arranged in five groups: Events, Actors, Institutions and creations, Ideas, Historians and commentators. Short bibliographies; cross-references. Indexes by theme and proper name to name of article; alphabetical listing of articles within the sections. Good illustrations in color. DC148.D5313

Dictionnaire historique de la Révolution française / publié sous la direction scientifique de Jean-René Suratteau et François Gendron. Paris : Pr. universitaires de France, c1989. 1132 p.; maps. **DC184**

At head of title: Albert Soboul.

Offers signed articles, with bibliographies, on the French Revolution, including biographies, events, cities, and topics, such as Administration locales, Musique. Index of names as subjects. Includes an essay on the historiography of the Revolution and a chronology with events divided by topics in parallel columns (e.g., Politiques et religions, Literature et philosophie). DC147.D52

Historical dictionary of the French Revolution, 1789–1799 / ed. by Samuel F. Scott and Barry Rothaus. Westport, Conn. : Greenwood, 1985. 2 v. (1143 p.). **DC185**

About 525 articles by 96 contributing scholars cover various aspects of the French Revolution—personalities, events, constitutional developments, etc. Short bibliography with each entry; numerous cross-references; chronology of principal events. Indexed. Continued by *Historical dictionary of Napoleonic France, 1799–1815* (DC197).

§ An older work is *Dictionnaire historique et biographique de la Révolution et de l'Empire, 1789–1815*, by J. F. E. Robinet [et al.] (Paris : Librairie Historique de la Révolution et de l'Empire, 1899. 2 v.). DC147.H57

Manceron, Claude. La Révolution française / Claude Manceron, avec la collaboration d'Anne Manceron. Paris : Renaudot : Diffusion Stendhal, c1989. 2 v. **DC186**

Contents: v. [1], Dictionnaire biographique (571 p.); v. [2], Dictionnaire général : evenements, institutions (385 p.).

Each volume presents an alphabetical arrangement of brief articles. Cross-references; no bibliography. DC147.M36

Handbooks

Jones, Colin. The French Revolution : a companion. London ; N.Y. : Longman, 1988. 473 p. **DC187**

Published in U.K. as: *The Longman companion to the French Revolution*.

A quick reference guide that includes chronologies, biographical dictionary, glossary, explanation of calendar, government machinery, political groups and parties, statistical tables portraying social and economic data, select bibliography, and subject index.

§ A similar quick reference guide is John Paxton's *Companion to the French Revolution* (N.Y. : Facts on File, [1988]. 231 p.).

DC148.J57

Tulard, Jean. Histoire et dictionnaire de la Révolution française : 1789–1799 / par Jean Tulard, Jean-François Fayard, Alfred Fierro. Paris : R. Laffont, c1987. 1213 p.; maps. **DC188**

Gives brief discussions of events, a chronology, tables of conversion for Gregorian and revolutionary calendars, a dictionary of short entries for people and topics, a historiography, and a filmography. Topical index. DC147.T85

Sourcebooks

Roberts, John Morris. French Revolution documents / John Morris Roberts, Richard Charles Cobb. Oxford : Blackwell, 1966–73. 2 v. **DC189**

Contents: v.1, 1787–1792; v.2, 1792–1795.

Official documents, memoirs, letters, etc., are presented in chronological arrangement. Headnotes and detailed indexes add to the usefulness of the work. DC141.R6

Atlases

Atlas de la Révolution française / sous la direction de Serge Bonin et Claude Langlois. Paris : Editions de l'École des hautes études en sciences sociales, 1987–1993. v. 1–7 : ill. ; some maps in color ; 30 cm. (In progress). **DC190**

Contents: v. 1, Routes et communications; v. 2, L'enseignement, 1760–1815; v. 3, L'armée et la guerre; v. 4, Le territoire (1) : Réalités et représentations; v. 5, Le territoire (2): les limites administratives; v. 6, Les sociétés politiques; v. 7, Médecine et santé.

Maps, tables, charts, and text portray the Revolution and often the Napoleonic era to 1815 or 1820. Detailed list of sources and good bibliography in each volume. DC148.A84

Napoleonic era

Bibliography

Caldwell, Ronald J. The era of Napoleon : a bibliography of the history of western civilization, 1799–1815. N.Y. : Garland, 1991. 2 v. (1447 p.). (Garland reference library of the humanities, vol. 1097). **DC191**

"A topical, partially annotated, listing of 48,136 books, articles, and doctoral dissertations and theses on the general and national history of Europe and the Western Hemisphere in this period."—*Pref.* Cites works published up to 1986, arranged topically under six broad headings: v. 1, General history; France; Biography of Napoleonic France; Local history of Napoleonic France; v. 2, National history of Europe; National history of the Americas. Author/subject index.

§ Companion to the author's *The era of the French Revolution : a bibliography of the history of Western civilization, 1789–1799* (DC178). Z5579.6.C35

Horward, Donald D. Napoleonic military history : a bibliography. N.Y. : Garland, 1986. 689 p. (Military history bibliographies, vol. 9 ; Garland reference library of social science, v. 194). **DC192**

In 24 chapters, Horward and contributing scholars deal with specific wars, campaigns, and military activities in particular countries or regions during the Napoleonic era. A bibliographic essay introduces each section. Lacks an index. Z2181.M5H67

Meyer, Jack Allen. An annotated bibliography of the Napoleonic era : recent publications, 1945–1985. N.Y. : Greenwood, 1987. 288 p. (Bibliographies and indexes in world history, no. 8). **DC193**

Scholarship since World War II is cited under broad topics (e.g., Napoleon) with subdivisions (e.g., Napoleon's family). Excludes journal articles. Annotations are intended to be a "rough guide to the contents of the volume."—*Introd.* Author/editor index only.　Z2179.M49

Tulard, Jean. Nouvelle bibliographie critique des mémoires sur l'époque napoléonienne, écrits ou traduits en français / Jean Tulard ; avec le concours de Jacques Garnier, Alfred Fierro et Charles d'Huart. Nouv. éd. rev. et enrichie. Genève : Droz, 1991. 312 p. (Hautes études médiévales et modernes, 67).　　　　**DC194**

1st ed., 1971.

An author arrangement of 1,527 memoirs (including correspondence and diaries) on the Napoleonic era; works cited have been published as books, parts of books, or journal articles. Annotated; topical index; few cross-references. All works cited are in French.

Z2179.T85

Encyclopedias; Handbooks

See also DC22.

Dictionnaire Napoléon / sous la direction de Jean Tulard. [2nd ed.]. [Paris] : Fayard, [1989]. 1866 p., [16] p. of plates : ill. (some col.).　　　**DC195**

1st ed., 1987.

Signed articles offer coverage of major topics (e.g. continental blockade, conscription) and biographies of major and some minor figures; each usually ends with a brief bibliography. An "Index thématique" groups articles under broad topics (e.g. Mémoires [auteurs de], Nourriture). More comprehensive than *Historical dictionary of Napoleonic France, 1799–1815* (DC197). This edition adds a supplementary section, p. 1761–1855, for new articles on people and subjects (e.g., list of Sous-préfectures, Mikhail Sokolniki). The Index thématique prints the new entries in italics.　DC147.D53

Haythornthwaite, Philip J. The Napoleonic source book. N.Y. : Facts on File ; London : Arms and Armour, 1990. 414 p. : ill., maps.　　**DC196**

Pt. 1 is a chronological narrative of the Napoleonic wars and their treaties. Pt. 2 surveys weaponry and tactics "which would be familiar to every capable company officer of the period."—*Introd.* Pt. 3 offers a country-by-country review of military participation. Pt. 4 gives brief biographical descriptions of the leading military participants. Pt. 5 discusses Napoleonic literature and art. Pt. 6, Miscellanea, provides lists and charts—e.g., the calendar, expenses, measurements, colors. Pt. 7 is a glossary of military terms in use at the time. Each section includes bibliographies of representative works, usually books. Heavily illustrated with reproductions of prints, drawings, pictures of medals, portraits, maps. Subject index to broader topics.　DC151.H32

Historical dictionary of Napoleonic France, 1799–1815 / ed. by Owen Connelly. Westport, Conn. : Greenwood, 1985. 586 p.　　　**DC197**

Reissued: London : Greenhill ; N. Y. : Simon & Schuster, 1993.

Emphasis is on Napoleon's Empire, its "events, politics, economy and economic developments, society and its evolution, and the institutions and culture of the era."—*Pref.* Brief articles are included on campaigns and battles but the reader is referred to David G. Chandler's *Dictionary of the Napoleonic wars* (N.Y. : Macmillan, 1979. 570 p.) for fuller information. Topical articles (e.g., Naples, women) and biographical articles (for writers, artists, actors, scientists prominent in the period) provide good coverage, give a list of secondary references and end with a list of related entries. Some entries, (e.g., Campaigns; Spain: ministers) provide a list of the names of articles relating to that topic. Chronology, 1768–1840; general bibliography subdivided by topic; topical index. Series continues with *Historical dictionary of France from the 1815 restoration to the Second Empire* (DC204) and is preceded by the *Historical dictionary of the French Revolution* (DC185).

§ Note that *An encyclopedia of Napoleon's Europe* by Alan Palmer (DC22) addresses the period 1797–1815 in Europe as a whole, so that, in addition to political and military matters, it includes entries for major writers (such as Jane Austen and William Blake) who lived during the period but may not have commented on the war or on Napoleon, and for issues such as the slave trade or the Enclosure Act. Illustrated with black-and-white reproductions of portraits, paintings, maps, etc.　　DC201.H673

Since 1815

Bibliography

Caron, Pierre. Bibliographie des travaux publiés de 1866 à 1897 sur l'histoire de la France depuis 1789. Paris : Cornély, 1912. 831 p.　　**DC198**

Repr.: Geneva : Slatkine, 1974.

A valuable bibliography including 13,496 titles of books, pamphlets, and articles in periodicals, society publications, and other composite works. Indicates book reviews and abstracts of important items. Indexes the historical articles in some 394 French and 260 foreign periodicals. Classified arrangement with two indexes: (1) authors and persons, (2) places. Forms the main volume in Caron's series of indexes of the history of France since 1789.

§ Continued by: *Répertoire méthodique de l'histoire moderne et contemporaine de la France pour les années 1898–1913* (Paris : G. Bellzis [etc.], 1899–[1932]).　Z2179.C25

Echard, William E. Foreign policy of the French Second Empire : a bibliography. N.Y. : Greenwood, 1988. 416 p. (Bibliographies and indexes in world history, no. 12).　　**DC199**

A topical bibliography of books, articles, and dissertations published between the mid-1880s and the mid-1980s in English, French, German, Italian, or Spanish on the French world role and foreign policy together with general studies of major diplomatic history topics "where French interest was paramount, or, in some instances, peculiar."—*Pref.* Author and subject indexes. To be used with *Select bibliography of the French Second Empire* (not yet published) and *Historical dictionary of the French Second Empire, 1852–1870* (DC206).

Z6465.F7E26

Evleth, Donna. France under the German occupation, 1940–1944 : an annotated bibliography. N.Y. : Greenwood, 1991. 220 p. (Bibliographies and indexes in world history, no. 20).　　**DC200**

Arranged under seven headings with appropriate subdivisions: Vichy France; Daily life in France under the Occupation; Collaboration and the collaborationists outside the government; The resistance; The position of the Communists; The liberation; The purge. Annotations consist of a brief identification of the author plus a sentence (with citation) from one or more reviews. The final two chapters offer brief discussions of newspapers published during the period in France and a guide to major French archives. Author, reviewer, and subject indexes.　Z6207.W8E84

Menyesch, Dieter. France-Allemagne, relations internationes et interdépendances bilatérales : une bibliographie 1963–1982 / Dieter Menyesch, Bérénice Manac'h …. München : Saur, 1984. 793 p.　　**DC201**

Title also in German; text in French and German.

An extensive bibliography of books, articles, essays, theses, and some archival materials arranged under five broad headings (general, political relations, government relations, economic relations, and cultural relations) with some subdivision. Topical and name indexes.

A supplement covering French-German relations, 1983–90, was published in 1994 by Saur.　Z6465.F7M46

University of Sussex. Library. The Paris commune, 1871 : inventory of the collection in the University of Sussex Library / introduction by Eugene W. Schulkind. Brighton : The Library, 1975. 231 p. : ill.   **DC202**

Listing is alphabetical by author under type of material, e.g., bibliographies and reference books, newspapers, imaginative literature (including criticism), posters, audiovisuals, etc. Place-name index.
                                                                    Z2179.B74

Young, Robert J. French foreign policy, 1918–1945 : a guide to research and research materials. Rev. ed. Wilmington, Del. : Scholarly Resources, 1991. 339 p.   **DC203**

1st ed., 1981.

Introductory chapters describe the conduct of foreign policy in France and the relevant contents of archives, libraries, research institutions, etc. The remainder of the volume is a bibliography of some 2,090 entries for reference sources, documentary series, memoirs, and secondary sources. Includes a section for dissertations in progress. Appendixes provide registers and brief biographical data on ministers and administrators. Partial subject and name indexes.   JN2681.D53

Encyclopedias

Historical dictionary of France from the 1815 restoration to the Second Empire / ed. by Edgar Leon Newman ; Robert Lawrence Simpson, assistant ed. N.Y. : Greenwood, c1987. 2 v. (1241 p.).   **DC204**

Consists of 950 articles by 75 scholars that cover the period from the end of the reign of Napoleon Bonaparte to the beginning of that of Louis Napoleon and deal with movements, cultural life, influences, and political figures. List of references and related articles at the end of each article. Chronology; general index.

§ For similar coverage of an earlier period, see: *Historical dictionary of the French Revolution, 1789–1799* (DC185) and *Historical dictionary of Napoleonic France, 1799–1815* (DC197). The following publications continue this work.   DC256.II57

Historical dictionary of the French Fourth and Fifth Republics, 1946–1991 / Wayne Northcutt, ed. in chief. N.Y. : Greenwood, 1992. 527 p.   **DC205**

Consists of 269 signed articles "ranging from politics to economics, to foreign and defense policy to society and culture" (*Pref.*), arranged alphabetically. Each article includes definition, explanation of significance, select bibliography, and a list of relevant and related entries. Appendixes: chronology; list of entries according to categories; presidents and prime ministers of France. Topical index. DC401.H57

Historical dictionary of the French Second Empire, 1852–1870 / ed. by William E. Echard. Westport, Conn. : Greenwood, c1985. 829 p.   **DC206**

Some 350 articles by contributing scholars, plus unsigned articles written by the editor with bibliographies and references to related articles. Chronology. A detailed index complements the dictionary arrangement.   DC276.H57

Historical dictionary of the Third French Republic, 1870–1940 / Patrick H. Hutton, ed. in chief ; Amanda S. Bourque and Amy J. Staples, asst. eds. N.Y. : Greenwood, [1986]. 2 v.
                                                                    DC207

With "over 750 entries written largely by American scholars, the volume scans all aspects of French civilization between 1870 and 1940" (*Pref.*) for political, social, economic, and cultural issues. Many articles are quite extensive, especially 24 interpretive essays. Each article is signed and includes a short bibliography and a list of related articles. Appendix: Entries classified by topic; Presidents and premiers of the Third Republic. Topical index.   DC337.H57

Dictionaries

Aplin, Richard. A dictionary of contemporary France / by Richard Aplin with the collaboration of Joseph Montchamp. London : Hodder & Stoughton, 1993. 488 p.   **DC208**

Attempts to identify and define those terms and acronyms used in newspapers with wide distribution, such as *L'Express*, *Le Monde*, and *Le Point*, when reporting on France since 1970. Tends to concentrate on institutions, public figures, and events. Alphabetical arrangement; *see also* references. No index.   DC415.A65

Handbooks

Handbook of French popular culture / ed. by Pierre L. Horn. N.Y. : Greenwood, 1991. 307 p.   **DC209**

Bibliographic essays on advertising, comics, detective stories, science fiction, cartoons, film, broadcasting, culinary matters, leisure, love, music, serial publications and sports. Each provides historical background, analyzes trends and relevant studies, and offers suggestions for further research. List of museums; index by topic and cited author.   DC33.7.H29

Chronologies

Guillaume, Sylvie. La France contemporaine, 1946–1990 : chronologie commentée. Paris : Perrin, c1990–91. 2 v. : ill.
                                                                    DC210

Contents: v. 1, La IVe République, 1944–58 (327 p.); v. 2, La Ve République, 1959–89 (583 p.).

A detailed chronology with paragraph-length entries. Appendixes for members of the governments, election results and some statistical economic tables. Index of names cited in the text.   DC401.G85

Biography

Dictionnaire des ministres de 1789 à 1989 / sous la direction de Benoît Yvert ; [auteurs, Antoine de Baecque … et al.] …. Paris : Perrin, c1990. 1028 p.   **DC211**

Biographical accounts of cabinet ministers are presented alphabetically within chronological periods. For each gives dates, place of birth, cabinet posts with dates, family and educational background and political career. Indexed by name.

§ For similar dictionaries of members of parliament, see *Dictionnaire des parlementaires français*, by Adolphe Robert, Edgar Bourloton, and Gaston Cougny (CJ329).

Regional and local

Dollinger, Philippe. Bibliographie d'histoire des villes de France / Philippe Dollinger, Philippe Wolff, Simonne Guenée. Paris : Klincksieck, 1967. 756 p.   **DC212**

At head of title: Commission Internationale pour l'Histoire des Villes.

Nearly 10,000 references (book and periodical materials) on more than 300 cities, arranged geographically. Not indexed. Z2176.D6

Lasteyrie du Saillant, Robert Charles. Bibliographie générale des travaux historiques et archéologiques publiés par les sociétés savantes de la France : dressée sous les auspices du Ministère de l'Instruction Publique. Paris : Impr. Nationale, 1888–1918. 6 v.   **DC213**

Repr.: N.Y. : B. Franklin, 1972.

Publication of the Comité des Travaux Historiques et Scientifiques. Issued in parts, 1885–1918.

Vols. 1–4 cover the literature published to the year 1885; vols. 5–6 deal with publications of 1886–1900.

A monumental undertaking, the most important work on French societies. Arranged alphabetically first by département, then by town, and under each by society. For each society gives: brief history, changes of name, suspensions, mergers, etc.; full titles, dates, etc., of all of its publications; full contents of each volume. An index of societies (arranged by département) at the end of v. 6 links together references to the same society in the main part and the supplement. Includes also societies in the French colonies and French societies abroad. Most useful at present for the historical matter about the societies and for the titles, collation, and contents of the sets of their publications, but cannot be used rapidly for the analytical material. An alphabetical author and subject index was projected but never published.

§ Continued on the same plan and scale by *Bibliographie annuelle des travaux historiques et archéologiques publiés par les sociétés savantes de la France* (1901/02–1909/10. Paris : Impr. Nationale, 1906–1914. 3 v. in 9 pts.).

Contents: v.1, 1901/02–1903/04; v.2, 1904/05–1906/07; v.3, 1907/08–1909/10.

An annual continuation of the *Bibliographie générale*, listing in the nine annuals 42,612 analytics. Indexes to be noted: v.3, no.3, 1909/10, has general index of societies (but not of analytics) in vols. 1–3; v.1, no.1, 1901/02, has both an author and a subject index to the analytical material in that issue.

Further continued by René Gandilhon's *Bibliographie générale des travaux historiques et archéologiques publiés par les sociétés savantes de la France ... Période 1910–1940* (Paris : Impr. Nationale, 1944–61. 5 v.) Follows the plan of the original work, with slightly increased coverage, adding to history and archaeology such related materials as geography, folklore, prehistoric studies, obituaries, etc.

    Z2183.L34

Germany

General works

Bibliography

Bird, Keith W. German naval history : a guide to the literature. N.Y. : Garland, 1985. 1121 p. (Military history bibliographies, v.7 ; Garland reference library of social science, 215).
    DC214

In two sections: (1) overview and discussion of research, with chapters on the writing of German naval history, sources of German naval history, and on the German navy in various historical periods up to 1945–83; and (2) a bibliography of the works discussed—some 4,871 items (books, essays, articles)—listed by author, with reference to page or section where cited.   Z2241.N3B57

Dahlmann, Friedrich Christoph. Dahlmann-Waitz Quellenkunde der deutschen Geschichte : Bibliographie der Quellen und der Literatur zur deutschen Geschichte. 10. Aufl. unter Mitwirkung zahlreicher Gelehrter hrsg. im Max-Planck-Institut für Geschichte von Hermann Heimpel und Herbert Geuss. Stuttgart : A. Hiersemann, 1965–1993. Lfg. 1–75. (In progress).   **DC215**

Originally by F.C. Dahlmann and Georg Waitz.

Contents: A, Allgemeiner Teil, v. 1–4; B, Die einzelnen Zeitalter, v. 5–7. Publication has proceeded as follows: v. 1, Abschnitt 1–38, Lfg. 1, 4–11 (complete); v. 2, Abschnitt 39–57, Lfg. 12–20 (complete); v. 3, Abschnitt 58–120, Lfg. 21–23/24, 48 (complete); v.4, Abschnitt 108–136, Lfg. 43–47, 49–50, 52–53, 55–57 (complete); v.5, Abschnitt 158–236, Lfg. 25–34/35 (complete); v. 6, Abschnitt 237–279, Lfg. 36–41/42, 51, 54, 58 (complete); v.7, Abschnitt 280–351, Lfg. 59–65, 67, 70–71 (complete); v. 8, Abschnitt 352–356, 361–379, 393–402, Lfg. 2–3, 66, 68/69, 72–85 (in progress).

The 9th ed. (Leipzig : Koehler, 1931–32. 2 v. [1292 p.]) was ed. by Hermann Haering. Contents: v. 1, Bibliography; v.2, Index. Contains 16,337 entries in classified arrangement.

The standard bibliography of German history in all its phases, covering to the end of world War II with German and non-German works. Represents a substantial reworking of the various sections, though the general plan remains the same. The publisher estimates three times as many entries as for the 9th ed., but since numerous citations are being dropped, most libraries will want to retain the 9th ed. in the reference collection. The detailed table of contents for each completed volume is essential in working with this enormous bibliography.

———. ———. *Register* (Stuttgart : Hiersemann, 1985–1991 [In progress]). Contents: Band 1 und 2 (496 p.); Band 3 und 4 (684 p.). Provides indexes of authors and of personal and geographic names as subjects.   Z2236.D34

Krewson, Margrit B. Hidden research resources in the German collections of the Library of Congress : a selective bibliography of reference works. Wash. : Library of Congress, 1992. 170 p.   **DC216**

A bibliography of dictionaries, bibliographies, and works of secondary literature which have received minimal level cataloging (with no subject approach) and which the compiler feels has unique research value. 918 volumes arranged by broad topics with author/title index.   Z2000.K74

Current

Jahrbuch der historischen Forschung in der Bundesrepublik Deutschland. 1974– . München : Saur, 1975– . Annual.
    DC217

Hrsg. von der Arbeitsgemeinschaft Ausseruniversitäter Historischer Forschungseinrichtungen in der Bundesrepublik Deutschland.

Imprint varies.

A topically arranged listing of in-progress, in-press, or recently published historical research (including dissertations) in Germany; includes all geographical areas and all periods. Indexed by author, persons, place names, and institutions.

§ Two ten-year cumulative records of research in East Germany are provided by Gerhard Becker's *Historische Forschungen in der DDR 1960–1970* and *Historische Forschungen in der DDR 1970–1980 : Analysen und Berichte* (Berlin : Deutscher Verlag der Wissenschaften, 1980. 2 v.).   DD86.J255

Jahresberichte für deutsche Geschichte. 1. Jahrg. (1925)–15/16. Jahrg. (1942); n.f. 1. Jahrg. (1949)– . Berlin : Akademie-Verlag, 1927– . Annual.   **DC218**

Sponsoring body varies; Akademie der Wissenschaften der DDR, 1971– . Issued in two parts: 1.T., Bibliographie; 2. T., Forschungsberichte.

Topical listing of writings on German history from the earliest times through World War II. Author and subject indexes. Volumes for 1941–48 not yet published.

§ Preceded by *Jahresberichte der Geschichtswissenschaft*, 1878–1918 (Berlin : Mittler, 1880–1916. Annual). *See also* Walter Holtzmann, *Die deutsche Geschichtswissenschaft im zweiten Weltkrieg* (Marburg/Lahn : Simons Verlag, 1951. 149, 512 p.).

Dissertations

Gabel, Gernot U. Theses on Germany accepted for higher degrees by the universities of Great Britain and Ireland, 1900–1975 : a bibliography / comp. by Gernot U. Gabel and Gisela R. Gabel. Hamburg : Gemini, 1979. 89 p.   **DC219**

A bibliography of theses at both the master's and doctoral level, arranged by broad subject classes (e.g., philosophy, religion, history/politics, science), with author and subject indexes. Language and literature are excluded as having been covered in the University of London's *Theses in Germanic studies* (BE1237).   Z2221.G25

Handbooks

Gebhardt, Bruno. Handbuch der deutschen Geschichte. 9. neu bearb. / Aufl. hrsg. von Herbert Grundmann. Stuttgart : Union, 1970–76. 4 v. in 5. **DC220**

Contents: v.1, Frühzeit und Mittelalter; v.2, Von der Reformation bis zum Ende des Absolutismus; v.3, Von der Französischen Revolution bis zum Ersten Weltkrieg; v.4, Der Zeit der Weltkriege (2 v.).

A very useful compendium, arranged chronologically, covering up to 1946–50. Chapters offer a survey of the history of a period followed an extensive bibliography. The work of several scholars, it originally appeared 1891–92 and has been issued in revised editions under various editors. Each volume has name and subject indexes. Vol. 4, pt.2 includes an appendix of lists and tables for 20th century statistics, political memberships of cabinets, parties, and government departmennt. A new edition has been announced. DD90.G32

Lexikon der deutschen Geschichte : Personen, Ereignisse, Institutionen, von der Zeitwende bis zum Ausgang des 2. Weltkrieges / unter Mitarbeit von Historiken und Archivaren hrsg. von Gerhard Taddey. 2. überarbeitete Aufl. Stuttgart : Kröner, 1983. 1391 p. **DC221**

1st ed., 1977.

Brief, signed articles on persons, events, and institutions important in German history. Bibliographic references accompany many entries. DD84.L48

Rössler, Hellmuth. Sachwörterbuch zur deutschen Geschichte / Hellmuth Rössler, Günther Franz. München : Oldenbourg, 1956–58. 2 v. (1472 p.). **DC222**

Repr.: Nendeln : Kraus, 1978.

Dictionary arrangement, dealing with "events, institutions, countries, peoples and ideas," including the cultural, political, and economic aspects, of all periods. Includes bibliographies.

§ A companion volume is Rössler and Franz, *Biographisches Wörterbuch zur deutschen Geschichte* (AH215). DD84.R6

Chronologies

Grotefend, Hermann. Zeitrechnung des deutschen Mittelalters und der Neuzeit. 2. Neudruck. Hannover : Hahn, 1891–1898. 3 pts. in 2 v. **DC223**

Repr.: Aalin : Scientia-Verlag, 1984.

Contents: Bd. 1, Glossar und Tafeln (1891); Bd. 2, Abt. 1, Kalendar der diöcesen Deutschlands, der Schweiz und Skandinaviens (1892); Abt. 2, Ordenskalendar. Heiligenverzeichniss. Nachträge zum Glossar (1898).

Glossaries, calendars, and tables showing the chronology of German history in the Middle Ages.

§ Published in various abridged editions, the latest of which is: *Taschenbuch der Zeitrechnung des deutschen Mittelalters und der Neuzeit* (12. erw. Aufl. Hrsg. von Jürgen Asch. Hannover : Hahn, 1982. 222 p.).

§ See also: Gerhard Hellwig's *Daten zu deutschen Geschichte* (Berlin : Golmann, 1977. 384 p.). CE61.G3G83

Jung, Kurt Michael. Weltgeschichte in einem Griff. Neubearb. und erg. Ausg. / von Peter Wiench. Berlin : Ullstein, 1985. 1367 p. : ill. **DC224**

Represents a new edition of *Weltgeschichte in Stichworten* (Berlin, 1965), extending coverage to early 1980. Previous ed. publ. 1968.

A chronology of events from earliest times, set forth in parallel columns for German, European, world, social, economic, and cultural history. Name and subject index. Emphasis is on European history, especially German history. Illustrated with photographs and maps.

D11.J8

Biography

Weber, Wolfgang. Biographisches Lexikon zur Geschichtswissenschaft in Deutschland, Österreich und der Schweiz : die Lehrstuhlinhaber für Geschichte von den Anfängen des Faches bis 1970. 2., durchgesehene und durch ein Vorwort erg. Aufl. Frankfurt am Main ; N.Y. : P. Lang, c1987. 697 p. **DC225**

Limited to historians in Germany, Austria, and Switzerland who achieved an academic position during the years 1800–1970. Offers much information about career and educational background but nothing about publications, although each entry includes a short bibliography of other sources. DD86.5.W43

To 1600

Bibliography

Dotzauer, Winfried. Das Zeitalter der Glaubensspaltung (1500–1618). Darmstadt : Wissenschaftliche Buchgesellschaft, 1987. 182 p. (Quellenkunde zur deutschen Geschichte der Neuzeit von 1500 bis zur Gegenwart, Bd. 1). **DC226**

A topical listing of the principal sources for the history of the Reformation. Each section concludes with a brief discussion of the documents, ending with references to other bibliographies, e.g., *Dahlmann-Waitz* … (DC215). An appendix lists documentary sources for this period for non-German countries. Indexed by title, compiler or editor, and subject.

§ For other guides and bibliographies on the Reformation *see* Karl Schottenloher's *Bibliographie* … (DC227) and the Reformation section in General History (DA). Z2237.5.D66x

Schottenloher, Karl. Bibliographie zur deutschen Geschichte im Zeitalter der Glaubensspaltung 1517–1585. 2. Aufl. Stuttgart : Hiersemann, 1956–66. 7 v. **DC227**

Vols. 1–6, initiated and supported by the Kommission zur Erforschung der Geschichte der Reformation und Gegenreformation, first publ. beginning 1933. Vol. 7, 1966, ed. by Ulrich Thürauf.

Contents: Bd.1–2, Personnen, A–Z. Orte u. Landschaften; Bd.3, Reich u. Kaiser. Territorien u. Landesherren; Bd.4, Gesamtdarstellungen der Reformationszeit. Stoffe; Bd.5, Nachträge und Ergänzungen. Zeittafel; Bd.6, Verfasser und Titelverzeichnis; Bd.7, Das Schrifttum von 1938–1960.

A very comprehensive bibliography of books and periodical articles, including those published during the period as well as later works about the period. Z2237.S37

Wattenbach, Wilhelm. Deutschlands Geschichtsquellen im Mittelalter bis zur mitte des dreizehnten Jahrhunderts. 6. Aufl. Berlin : W. Hertz, 1893–94. 2 v. **DC228**

Repr.: Darmstadt : Wissenschaftliche Buchgesellschaft, 1976.

An important guide to the printed sources of German history. Vol. 1, *Vorzeit und Karolinger*, covers from early times through the Carolingians to the treaty of Verdun in 843; v. 2, *Deutsche Kaizerzeit*, covers through the Ottos, 900–1050.

Revised parts have begun to appear as:

(1) ———. ———. *Vorzeit und Karolinger*, bearb. von Wilhelm Levison und Heinz Löwe (Weimar : Böhlaus, 1952–78. v. 1–6, Beiheft. [In progress]).

Contents: Heft 1, Die Vorzeit von Anfängen bis zur Herrschaft der Karolinger; Heft 2, Die Karolinger von Anfang des 8. Jahrhunderts biz zum Tode Karls des Grossen; Heft 3, Die Karolinger vom Tode Karl des Grossen bis zum Vertrag von Verdun; Heft 4, Die Karolinger vom Vertrag von Verdun bis zum Herrschaftsantritt der Herrscher ais dem sächsischen Hause: Des westfränkische Reich; Heft 6, Die Karolinger vom Vertrag von Verdun bis zum Herrschaftsantritt der Herrscher aus dem sächsischen Hause: Das ostfränkische Reich; Beiheft, Rechtsquellen von Rudolf Buchner.

(2) Robert Holtzmann, *Deutschlands Geschichtsquellen im Mittelalter : die Zeit der Sachsen und Salier.* Neuaisgabe, besorgt von Franz-Josef Schmale (Köln : Böhlau Verlag, 1967–71. Teil 1–3. [In progress]).

Contents: Teil 1 (Heft 1–2), Das Zeitalter des Ottonischen Staates (900–1050); Teil 2 (Heft 3–4), Das Zeitalter des Investiturstreits (1050–1125); Teil 3, Italien (1050–1125), England (900–1135), Nachträge zum ersten und zweiten Teil.

Revision of the first part of v. 2 of Wattenbach's basic work.

(3) Franz-Josef Schmale, unter Mitarbeit von Irene Schmale-Ott and Dieter Berg, *Deutschlands Geschichtsquellen im Mittelalter vom Tode Kaiser Heinrichs V. bis zim Ende des Interregnum* (Darmstadt : Wissenschaftliche buchgesellschaft, 1976– . v. 1, [In progress]).

Contents: v. 1, Vom Tode Kaiser Heinrichs V. bis zum Ende des Interregnums.

Supersedes the second half of v. 2 of Wattenbach's basic work.

§ Continued by: Ottokar Lorenz, *Deutschlands Geschichtsquellen im Mittelalter seit der Mitte des 13. Jahrhunderts* (3. in Verbindung mit Arthur Goldmann umgearb. Aufl. Berlin : Hertz, 1886–87. 2 v. Repr.: Graz : Akademische Druck– und Verlagsanstalt, 1966). Continues from the middle of the 13th century, where the 6th ed. of Wattenbach ceases.

Willemsen, Carl Arnold. Bibliographie zur Geschichte Kaiser Friedrichs II. und der letzten Staufer. München : Monumenta Germaniae Historica, 1986. 205 p. (Monumenta Germaniae historica : Hilfsmittel, 8).   **DC229**

A scholarly bibliography of books, articles, essays, and dissertations concerning Friedrich II (1194–1250) and later Staufen family members. Arranged by format; name indexes.   Z2237.W54

Handbooks

Reallexikon der germanischen Altertumskundes / Begründet von Johannes Hoops. 2. völlig neu bearb. und stark erw. Aufl. Hrsg. Herbert Jankuhn … [et al.]. Berlin : W. de Gruyter, 1968–1993. Lfg.1–8³/⁴. (In progress).   **DC230**

Contents: Bd. 1–8, Lfg. 3/4, Aachen–Fibeltracht.

1st ed., 1911–1919 in 4 v.

Signed articles; bibliographies. A valuable reference source for archaeology, Germanic philology, and related fields.   DD51.R42

18th–20th Centuries

See also sections in DA on World Wars and Holocaust.

Bibliography

Buse, Dieter K. German nationalism : a bibliographic approach / Dieter K. Buse, Juergen C. Doerr. N.Y. : Garland, 1985. 230 p. (Canadian review of studies in nationalism, 5 ; Garland reference library of social science, 161).   **DC231**

An annotated bibliography of English and German language books, articles, and essays dealing with nationalism, national consciousness, and national identity in Germany. Arranged by period (each spanning about 30–50 years), with lengthy introduction to each period. Author and subject indexes.

§ A companion bibliography compiled by Doerr, *The big powers and the German question 1941–1990 : a selected bibliographic guide* (N.Y. : Garland, 1992. 403 p.) indexes 530 German- and English-language books, government publications, and a few periodical articles for 1941–49 and 1949–90. Author and subject indexes.

Z2241.N28B88

Detwiler, Donald S. West Germany : the Federal Republic of Germany / Donald S. Detwiler, Ilse E. Detwiler. Oxford ; Santa Barbara, Calif. : Clio Pr. : c1987. 353 p. (World bibliographical series, v. 72).   **DC232**

Covers post-1945 West Germany including West Berlin. About 500 entries with lengthy annotations which cite about another 500 titles. Includes English and German publications. Author/title/subject index.

§ For earlier publications, *see* Arnold Hereward Price, *The Federal Republic of Germany : a selected bibliography of English-language publications* (2nd rev. ed. Wash. : Library of Congress, 1978. 116 p.).

Z2240.3.D37

Goguel, Rudi. Antifaschistischer Widerstand und Klassenkampf : die faschistische Diktatur 1933 bis 1945 und ihre Gegner : Bibliographie deutschsprachiger Literatur aus den Jahren 1945 bis 1973 / Rudi Goguel ; unter bibliographischer Mitarbeit von Jutta Grimann, Manfred Püschner, Ingrid Volz. Berlin : Militärverlag der Deutschen Demokratischen Republik, 1976. 567 p.   **DC233**

A classed listing of some 4,700 items, with author and subject indexes on opposition to Nazisim and class conflict, 1933–1945.

Z2241.A53G63

Henning, Herzeleide. Bibliographie Friedrich der Grosse, 1786–1986 : das Schrifttum des deutschen Sprachraums und der Übersetzungen aus Fremdsprachen / bearb. von Herzeleide und Eckart Henning. Berlin ; N.Y. : W. de Gruyter, 1988. 511 p.   **DC234**

In two sections: primary sources arranged by format, and secondary literature arranged by topic. Includes German-language material only; indexed by author and by cited personal and place names.

Z8397.13.H46

Hess, Jürgen C. Bibliographie zum deutschen Liberalismus / Jürgen C. Hess, E. van Steensel van der Aa. Göttingen : Vandenhoeck & Ruprecht, 1981. 148 p. (Arbeitsbücher zur modernen Geschichte, Bd. 10).   **DC235**

About 1,200 German books, dissertations, essays and periodical articles on liberalism in Germany, 1815–1980, are listed in topical arrangement under broad periods. Not indexed.   Z7165.G3H47

Kehr, Helen. The Nazi era, 1919–1945 : a select bibliography of published works from the early roots to 1980 / comp. by Helen Kehr and Janet Langmaid. London : Mansell ; Bronx, N.Y. : Distr. by H.W. Wilson, 1982. 621 p.   **DC236**

A selective, classified bibliography of about 6,500 items, almost exclusively works published in book form. Selectivity for the World War II period was particularly stringent, the primary aim being "to represent the German outlook of the time, while including a number of bibliographies and basic works which can point the way for further research."—*Introd.* Intended for the interested layman as well as the serious student. Indexed.   Z2240.K44

Kimmich, Christoph M. German foreign policy, 1918-1945 : a guide to research and research materials. Rev. ed. Wilmington, Del. : Scholarly Research, c1991. 264 p.   **DC237**

1st ed., 1981.

The first two chapters describe the conduct of German foreign policy and the materials held in libraries, archives, and research institutes in Germany, Europe and the U.S. The bibliography (largely annotated) of reference sources, documentary series, memoirs, and secondary literature is arranged in broadly chronological order. Indexed by author, documentary series title, and subject.

§ For a bibliography of research since 1949 on German relations with Russia and Poland, 1917–91, see *Sowjetische Forschungen zur Geschichte der deutsch-russischen Beziehungen von den Anfängen bis 1949 : Bibliographie*, by Karin Borck (Berlin : Academie Verlag, 1993. 366 p.), which includes books, collections of essays, articles, and party publications arranged in chronological periods subdivided by subject. Author index.   Z6465.G4K54

Merritt, Anna J. Politics, economics, and society in the two Germanies, 1945–75 : a bibliography of English-language works / comp. by Anna J. Merritt and Richard L. Merritt, with the assistance of Kathleen Kelly Rummel. Urbana : Univ. of Illinois Pr., 1978. 268 p.   **DC238**

A computer printout listing more than 8,500 titles of books and periodical articles published before mid-1976 and relating to the post-war Germanies. Arrangement is by subject within six major divisions: (1) general (including the historical and demographic background); (2) the Occupation; (3) political systems; (4) economic systems; (5) social systems; and (6) foreign policy issues. Each item is cited only once in the bibliography. Author index.

§ See also an earlier bibliography by Gisela Hersch, *A bibliography of German studies, 1945–1971* (Bloomington : Indiana Univ. Pr., [1972]. 603 p.).   Z7165.G3M47

Paul, Barbara Dotts. The Germans after World War II : an English-language bibliography. Boston : G.K. Hall, 1990. 190 p.   **DC239**

Annotated bibliography of books and articles, government publications, doctoral dissertations, motion pictures, and filmstrips on Germany, 1945–48. In 9 sections: German experiences, Foreign observers, Civilian relief efforts, Journal articles, Fiction by Germans, Non-German fiction, Films about Germany, Historical studies, Bibliographies. Author/title index.   Z2240.3.P38

Showalter, Dennis E. German military history, 1648–1982 : a critical bibliography. N.Y. : Garland, 1984. 331 p. (Military history bibliographies, v.3 ; Garland reference library of social science, v. 113).   **DC240**

A section of general works is followed by chapters on nine historical periods, each with an introductory essay discussing the bibliographic listings which follow. Author index.   Z2241.M5S5

Snyder, Louis Leo. The Third Reich, 1933–1945 : a bibliographical guide to German national socialism. N.Y. : Garland, 1987. 284 p. (Canadian review of studies in nationalism, v. 7 ; Garland reference library of social science, v. 384).   **DC241**

A selection of citations to 850 books and articles mostly in English, but some in German. Topical arrangement. Annotations provide a brief summary of contents; asterisks appear before those entries considered most important. Introduction to each chapter is an overview of the research on that topic. Author index.

§ To expand periodical coverage, see *The Third Reich 1933–1939 : a historical bibliography* (Santa Barbara, Calif. : ABC-Clio, 1984. 239 p.) and *The Third Reich at war : a historical bibliography* (Santa Barbara : ABC-Clio, 1984. 270 p.). Both of these compilations provide citations derived from the *Historical abstracts* database (DA176) with author and detailed subject indexes.   Z2241.N27S65

Stachura, Peter D. The Weimar era and Hitler, 1917–1933. Oxford : Clio Pr., 1977. 276 p.   **DC242**

A topically arranged bibliography of Western-language books, pamphlets, festschriften, theses, and other secondary materials published mainly between May 1945 and early 1975. Aims to be comprehensive, but critical annotations distinguish the more useful from the slighter studies. Author and subject indexes.

§ *Weimar Republic : a historical bibliography* (Santa Barbara, Calif. : ABC-Clio, 1984. 285 p.) offers some updating.   Z2240.S74

Wallace, Ian. East Germany : the German Democratic Republic. Oxford ; Santa Barbara, Calif. : Clio Pr., c1987. 293 p. (World bibliographical series, v. 77).   **DC243**

Presents topically arranged entries for books, articles, essays, and a few documents on all aspects of East Germany since 1945. Nothing on pre-World War II Germany or West Germany is included unless it has great significance for East Germany. Well annotated; author/title/subject index.

§ For earlier publications, *see* Arnold Hereward Price's *East Germany: a selected bibliography* (Wash.: Library of Congress, 1967. 133 p.).   Z2250.W34

Wiener Library, London. Persecution and resistance under the Nazis. London : Institute of Contemporary History, 1978. 500 p. (Wiener Library. Catalogue series, no. 7).   **DC244**

Pt. 1 originally publ. 1949 under title *Books on persecution, terror and resistance in Nazi Germany*; rev. 2nd ed., 1959. Pt 2 entitled New material and amendment.

Pt. 1 ed. by I. R. Wolff; pt. 2 ed. by H. Kehr.

Topical arrangement of citations to more than 4,700 books, pamphlets, documents, and a few periodical articles. Pt. 1 is a reprinting of the 2nd ed. which expanded coverage to Jews in any Nazi-occupied territory and added new sections for individual cities or regions and on the after-effects on the health of the persecuted. Pt. 2, also topically arranged, lists publications added to the Wiener Library from about 1959–74. Appendixes list unpublished eyewitness reports, unpublished Nuremberg documents, periodicals of Germans in exile, illegal pamphlets and periodicals. Full index to both parts.

Continued by: Wiener Library. *After Hitler Germany, 1945-1963*, comp. by Helen Kehr (London : publ. for the Wiener Library by Vallentine, Mitchell, 1963. 265 p.). See also the Library's *From Weimar to Hiltler : Germany, 1918-1933* (2nd, rev. and enl. ed. London : Vallentine, Mitchell, 1964. 268 p.).   Z2240.W5

Guides to records

Deutsche Wirtschaftsarchive : Nachweis historischer Quellen in Unternehmen, Kammern und Verbänden der Bundesrepublik Deutschland / hrsg. im Auftrag der Gesellschaft für Unternehmensgeschichte e.V. von Klara van Eyll … [et al.]. 2., völlig neu bearb. Aufl. Stuttgart : F. Steiner Verlag Wiesbaden, 1987–88. 2 v.   **DC245**

1st ed., 1978–83.

Contents: Bd. 1 [without special title] (471 p.); Bd. 2, Kreditwirtschaft (557 p.).

Describes archives in companies, banks, and foundations. For each, indicates address, archivist, contents, hours, and any finding aids. Name and place indexes, plus an index to branch names by broad topic in each volume.   HC282.2.D48

Frohn, Axel. Guide to inventories and finding aids of German archives at the German Historical Institute, Washington, D.C / Axel Frohn, with the assistance of Anne Hope. Wash. : German Historical Institute, 1989. 84 p. (Reference guides of the German Historical Institute, no. 2).   **DC246**

A listing of published inventories and finding aids arranged alphabetically by city, then by the name of the archive. Index for names of archives and for titles. Appendixes cover a few archives in Austria and Switzerland and a list of *Guides to German records microfilmed at Alexandria, Va.* (DC254).   CD1222.A2G47

Haase, Carl. The records of German history in German and certain other record offices : with short notes on libraries and other collections. Boppard (am Rhein) : Boldt, 1975. 194 p.   **DC247**

Title also in German; text in German.

A guide for historians, treating archives and libraries in both East and West Germany, and giving for each the address, hours of opening, and a statement of collection size. Name index.

§ Updated by: *Archives and libraries in a new Germany*, by Erwin K. Welsch and Jürgen Danyel (AK139), a directory and handbook for those scholars or students in German history, social science, or literature who are planning research trips.   CD1220.H37

Verzeichnis der schriftlichen Nachlässe im deutschen Archiven und Bibliotheken. Boppard am Rhein : H. Boldt, [1971–83]. 2 v. in 3.   **DC248**

Contents: v.1, Die Nachlässe in den deutschen Archiven, bearb. W. A. Mommsen (2 v.); v.2, Die Nachlässe in den Bibliotheken der Bundesrepublik Deutschland, bearb. Ludwig Denecke (2. Aufl. völlig neu bearb. Tilo Brandis. 538 p.

A survey of collections of papers; listing is by personal name, with dates, profession, and brief description of the papers and their location. Fully indexed.

1867–1945

The German archives were captured at the end of World War II and microfilmed in England and the United States. Guides to these documents are listed below, arranged by dates of coverage. All microfilms are available through the National Archives, Washington; the original files were returned to Germany.

Weinberg, Gerhard L. Guide to captured German documents / prep. by Gerhard L. Weinberg and the WDP staff under the direction of Fritz T. Epstein. [Maxwell Air Force Base, Ala. : Human Resources Research Inst., 1952]. 90 p. (United States. Human Resources Research Institute. Research memorandum, no.2, v.1).   **DC249**

At head of title: War Documentation Project. Study no.1.

Pts.1–2 list books and periodical articles which include German documentary material; pt.3 lists, by location, files of captured documents in various depositories, including the Library of Congress, the National Archives, the Hoover Institution, etc. Annotated; indexed.

————. ————. *Supplement* (Wash. : National Archives and Records Service, 1959. 69 p.).   Z2240.W4

American Historical Association. Committee for the Study of War Documents. A catalogue of files and microfilms of the German Foreign Ministry archives, 1867–1920. Oxford : Univ. Pr., 1959. 1290 col.   **DC250**

Repr.: N.Y. : Kraus, 1970.

Designed to present a complete record of the files of the Political Dept. of the German Foreign Ministry for the period 1867–1920, and at the same time to give details of the filming programs which have been carried out on these files. Indicates holders of negative copy. Serves as an index to U.S. National Archives Record Group 242.   CD1261.A52

———————— A list of archival references and data of documents from the archives of the German Foreign Ministry, 1867–1920 / microfilmed at Whaddon Hall for the American Committee for the Study of War Documents. Buckinghamshire : Whaddon Hall, 1957. 179 *l*.   **DC251**

The microfilms have been deposited in the National Archives in Washington (National Archives Record Group 242), and in the Public Record Office in London.

§ See also *List of archival references to matérial in the German Foreign Ministry Archives filmed under grant from the Old Dominion Foundation, Whaddon Hall, Buckinghamshire, Eng.* (1958. 49 *l*.).   CD1261.A53

Schwändt, Ernst. Index of microfilmed records of the German Foreign Ministry and the Reich's Chancellery covering the Weimar period, deposited at the National Archives. Wash. : Nat. Archives, 1958. 95 p.   **DC252**

One of a series of indexes of microfilms of German documents which make up National Archives Record Group 242. Covers the period of the Weimar Republic, 1919–33.   Z2240.S3

United States. Department of State. Historical Office. A catalog of files and microfilms of the German Foreign Ministry archives, 1920–1945 / comp. and ed. by George O. Kent. Stanford, Calif. : Hoover Inst., Stanford Univ., 1962–72. 4 v.   **DC253**

Vol. 4 issued as Hoover Institution Publication no. 120.

"Continues and completes the work of the *Catalogue of German Foreign Ministry files and microfilms, 1867–1920* [DC250]."—*Pref.*

Published as a joint project of the U.S. Dept. of State and the Hoover Institution on War, Revolution, and Peace.

Lists all files from the *Politisches Archiv* of the German Foreign Ministry, 1920–1945, which were seized by the American and British armies at the end of World War II, and indicates which have been microfilmed. The films make up National Archives Record Group 242.

"The availability of new materials, specifically the files from various German missions and consulates in Europe as well as from some of the overseas offices, necessitated publication" (*Pref.*) of this final volume of the series.   CD1261.A65

United States. National Archives and Records Service. Guides to German records microfilmed at Alexandria, Va. Wash. : Nat. Archives and Records Service, General Services Admin., 1958–1993. Pts. 1–94. 20 x 36 cm. (In progress).   **DC254**

Initiated by the Committee for the Study of War Documents of the American Historical Association and continued in July 1963 by the National Archives and Records Service.

Each part describes the filmed records of one of the Reich ministries or other record groups. The microfilms have been deposited in the National Archives, Record Group 242.

Issued in microfiche, no. 85 (1990)– .   Z2240.A7

Encyclopedias; Dictionaries

The encyclopedia of the Third Reich / ed. by Christian Zentner and Friedemann Bedürftig ; English translation ed. by Amy Hackett. N.Y. : Macmillan ; London : Collier Macmillan, c1991. 2 v. (1150 p.) : ill.   **DC255**

Translation of *Grosse Lexikon des Dritten Reiches* (München : Sudwest Verlag, 1985. 686 p.).

A richly illustrated dictionary of the people, organizations, jargon (e.g., blood sacrifice, final solution), events, movements, politics, culture, etc., of German history 1933–45. 22 overview essays (e.g., Women in the Third Reich, Concentration camps, Opposition, Attempts to assassinate Hitler) are designed to provide context and link the shorter articles together. The more than 3,000 entries, signed by German historians, are alphabetically arranged. Cross-references; subject index. The topical bibliography, p. 1083–1103, has been updated for the N.Y. edition, especially with English-language titles (which are starred).   DD256.5.G76313

Fest, Wilfried. Dictionary of German history, 1806–1945. N.Y. : St. Martin's Pr. ; London : Prior, 1978. 189 p.   **DC256**

Attempts to provide "salient facts and dates of Germany's political, social and economic history ... from the dissolution of the Holy Roman Empire of the German nation in 1806 to the collapse of the German Reich in 1945."—*Pref.* Most of the approximately 700 articles include at least one bibliographic reference. Chronological table; cross-references. No index.   DD203.F47

Sachwörterbuch der Geschichte Deutschlands und der deutschen Arbeiterbewegung / Horst Bartel, ed. Berlin : Dietz, 1969–70. 2 v. : ill. ; maps.   **DC257**

A dictionary of modern German history presented in terms of the working-class movement from the time of the French Revolution to the present, and emphasizing socialist and communist theories and developments, organizations, congresses, party publications, etc.   DD84.S2

Snyder, Louis Leo. Encyclopedia of the Third Reich. N.Y. : McGraw-Hill, 1976. 410 p. : ill.   **DC258**

Repr.: N.Y. : Paragon, 1989.

Entries for persons, places, terms, events, etc. "The major area covered is the period from the rise of National Socialism to the fall of the Third Reich in 1945. There are selected entries from the time of the Weimar Republic, which preceded Hitler, and from the Bonn Republic, which succeeded him. ... The names of the biographees selected are those that would be recognized by most historians of the Third Reich as of some significance."—*Pref.* Brief bibliographies appended to many articles (English translations are cited in preference to the German originals); general bibliography, p. 389–410. Terms are entered under the German form with cross-references from the English equivalent.   DD256.5.S57

Taylor, James. The Third Reich almanac / James Taylor and Warren Shaw. N.Y. : World Almanac, c1987. 392 p., [21] p. of plates : ill. **DC259**

Published in England as *A dictionary of the Third Reich* (London : Grafton, 1987).

An alphabetical dictionary of people, parties, events, government organizations, concentration camps, battles, military units, etc., intended for the general reader. Includes chronologies, maps, charts, photographs. Not indexed; cross-references. Some odd choices of headings: "Diary of Anne Frank" but no entry or cross-reference under "Frank"; "Cinema in the Third Reich" with no cross-reference from "film" or "motion pictures," though the term "film" is used in the preface. A section of quotations give source but not page. Brief bibliography.

§ Overlaps with Louis Leo Snyder, *Encyclopedia of the Third Reich* (DC258), in that both give chronologies and cover the same people, battles, events, etc., though with varying amounts of information. Snyder also lacks an index but has a much longer bibliography.

DD256.5.T283

Chronologies

Overesch, Manfred. Chronik deutscher Zeitgeschichte : Politik, Wirtschaft, Kultur / [Manfred] Overesch, [Friedrich Wm.] Saal. Düsseldorf : Droste, c1982–1986. v. 1–3, pt. 1–2. (In progress). **DC260**

At head of title: Droste Geschichts-Kalendarium.

Contents: Bd. 1, Die Weimarer Republik; Bd. 2¹, Das Dritte Reich, 1933–1939; Bd. 2², Das Dritte Reich, 1939–1945; Bd. 3¹, Das besetze Deutschland 1945–1947; Bd. 3², Das besetze Deutschland 1948–1949.

To be complete in four volumes. Each volume offers a day-by-day summary of events and includes an index of names. DD232.O9

Biography

Biographisches Lexikon zur Weimarer Republik / hrsg. von Wolfgang Benz und Hermann Graml. München : C.H. Beck, c1988. 392 p. **DC261**

Signed articles of one or two columns for about 500 individuals active in Germany and Austria during the Weimar Republic. Bibliographical references to each subject's primary and secondary works and location of archives. List of German ministers, 1919–33, and a chronology of German political events, 1918–33. CT1062.B56

Stachura, Peter D. Political leaders in Weimar Germany : a biographical study. N.Y. : Simon and Schuster, 1993. 230 p. **DC262**

Short essays on 135 political leaders in Germany, 1918–1933. Alphabetically arranged entries range from 400–1,000 words, and give backgrounds, career, a "critical assessment of the subject's significance and contribution to Weimar politics at the top" (*Introd.*), and a bibliography citing works by and about the subject. Glossary of abbreviations and terms; chronology covers September 1918–January 1933; select bibliography of works for understanding events and developments; topical index. DD244.S64

Atlases

Freeman, Michael J. Atlas of Nazi Germany / Michael Freeman ; consulting ed., Tim Mason. N.Y. : Macmillan, c1987. 205 p. : ill. (some col.), some maps in color. **DC263**

Also published: London : Croom Helm, 1987.

Diagrams, charts, tables, maps, photographs, and historical summaries are used "to provide a graphic presentation of the outward face and inward structures of the Third Reich and, where applicable, the manner of their evolution."—*Introd.* Topical index.

DD256.5.F73354

Hilgemann, Werner. Atlas zur deutschen Zeitgeschichte, 1918–1968 / Werner Hilgemann ; Kartografie, Jürgen Taufmann. München : Piper, c1984. 207 p. : ill., maps (chiefly in col.) ; 20 x 26 cm. **DC264**

A chronological framework for maps and text on facing tables illustrates the history of Germany 1918–68. Arranged in five sections: Das Ende des Kaiserreiches (1918); Die Weimarer Republik (1919–33); Das Dritte Reich (1933–45); Deutschland unter Besatzungsmächten (1945–49); Bundesrepublik Deutschland und Sowjetische Besatzungszone DDR (1949–58). Ends with a chronology of the period. Not indexed. G1911.S1H5

Local history

Keyser, Erich. Bibliographie zur Städtegeschichte Deutschlands : unter Mitwirkung zahlreicher Sachkenner. Köln : Böhlau, 1969. 404 p. **DC265**

At head of title: Acta collegii historiae urbanae societatis historicorum internationalis.

Similar to (and published in the same series with) *Bibliographie d'histoire des villes de France*, by Philippe Dollinger, Philippe Wolff, and Simonne Guenée (DC212), for the history of French cities. More than 4,700 items in geographical arrangement, with indexes of place-names and of authors. Z2243.K48

Schröder, Brigitte. Bibliographie zur deutschen historischen Städteforschung / bearb. von Brigitte Schröder und Heinz Stoob. Köln : Böhlau, 1986. v. 1–2 : ill. (Städteforschung. Reihe B, Handbücher, Bd. 1, etc.). (In progress). **DC266**

For annotation, *see* BF274. DD91.S36

Sperling, Walter. Landeskunde DDR : eine kommentierte Auswahlbibliographie : Ergänzungsband, 1978–1983. München ; N.Y. : K.G. Saur, 1984. 623 p. (Bibliographien zur regionalen Geographie und Landeskunde, Bd. 5). **DC267**

Cites 4,323 books, essays, and articles on East Germany, mainly German-language publications with a few English titles. Arranged by topic: e.g., Wirtschaft, Die brandenburgische Bezirke, Bildung und Wissenschaft. Each section has an introductory overview. Indexes for author, title and subject.

§ The period up to 1978 is covered by *Landeskunde DDR : eine annotierte Auswahlbibliographie*, also by Walter Sperling (München : Verlag Documentation, 1978. 456 p. [Bibliographien zur regionalen Geographie und Landeskunde, 1]). Z2250.S65

Gibraltar

Green, Muriel M. A Gibraltar bibliography. London : Univ. of London, Inst. of Commonwealth Studies, 1980. 108 p. **DC268**

Subtitle: based on holdings of the British Library Reference Division and of the libraries of the Royal Institute of International Affairs, Commonwealth Institute, Ministry of Defence, Foreign and Commonwealth Office, Gibraltar Garrison Library, Imperial War Museum, Rhodes House (Oxford), and Royal Commonwealth Society.

Lists 984 books, periodical articles, government publications, and unpublished materials under ten broad subject headings. Author index. Locates copies in English and Gibraltar libraries.

———. *Supplement* (1981. p. 109–136). Adds material inadvertently omitted from the earlier work as well as new titles.

Z2704.G44G74

Shields, Graham J. Gibraltar. Oxford ; Santa Barbara, Calif. : Clio Pr., c1987. 100 p. (World bibliographical series, v. 87). **DC269**

A selective bibliography (260 entries) of books, government publications, maps, and British dissertations. Clear and frequently critical annotations. Author, title, and subject indexes. Z2704.G44S56

Great Britain

General Works

Bibliography

See also Widener Library shelflist (AA115).

Bibliography of British history / issued under the direction of the American Historical Association and the Royal Historical Society of Great Britain. Oxford : Clarendon Pr., 1951–77. 6 v.   **DC270**

Contents: A bibliography of English history to 1485 (DC304); Tudor period, 1485–1603 (DC318); Stuart period, 1603–1714 (DC315); The eighteenth century, 1714–1789 (DC317); 1789–1851 (DC328); 1851–1914 (DC330). Some volumes in revised editions.

Covers all aspects of history: political, constitutional, legal, ecclesiastical, economic, military, cultural, and social, including discovery and exploration, colonization, etc. Each volume is a selected, classified-subject list—with author index—of book, pamphlet, and document material, with a liberal inclusion of articles in periodicals and society transactions. Indispensable for the student of history, and useful also for literature and social studies.

Bruce, A. P. C. A bibliography of British military history, from the Roman invasions to the Restoration, 1660. München : K. G. Saur, 1981. 349 p.   **DC271**

A classed bibliography of books and periodical articles. Author index; many brief annotations. Nearly 3,300 items.

§ Continued chronologically by Bruce's *A bibliography of the British Army, 1660–1914* (N.Y. : Garland, 1975. 255 p.).

Books, periodical articles, government documents, and unpublished official and personal papers are grouped in four broad subject chapters: (1) Bibliographies, guides, indexes and general works; (2) Organization, management and personnel; (3) Military theory, tactics, drill and equipment; (4) Military operations and overseas garrisons. Each chapter is subdivided by type of material, subjects, or chronological period. Index.   Z2021.M5B78

Chaloner, William Henry. Bibliography of British economic and social history / W. H. Chaloner, R. C. Richardson. [2nd ed.]. Manchester, Eng. : Manchester Univ. Pr., 1984. 208 p.   **DC272**

1st ed., 1976, had title: *British economic and social history.*

A companion to D.H. Aldcroft and R. Rodger, *Bibliography of European economic and social history* (DC1).

A select bibliographic guide to books and periodical articles in English. A brief general section is followed by four main chronological sections (1066–1300; 1300–1500; 1500–1700; 1700–1970), plus separate sections for Wales, Scotland, and Ireland, each with appropriate subdivisions. About 5,800 items; some brief annotations. Detailed table of contents and author index, but no alphabetical subject index.   Z7165.G8C46

Day, Alan Edwin. England. Oxford : Clio, c1993. 591 p. : map. (World bibliographical series, v. 160).   **DC273**

Extensive bibliography, mostly of recent books with a few periodical articles and government publications, arranged by broad topics. In addition to the 2,364 numbered entries, related works are cited in annotations. Indexed by author, title, and subject.   DA27.5.D29

Great Britain. Foreign Office. Library. Catalogue of the Foreign Office Library, 1926–1968. Boston : G. K. Hall, 1972. 8 v.   **DC274**

Lists works relating to politics, government, economic development, and international relations between Britain and countries outside the Commonwealth. Author, title, subject, and classified indexes. Builds on an earlier compilation, *Catalogue of the printed books in the Library of the Foreign Office, London* (London : H.M.S.O., 1926).

§ The Foreign Office merged with the Colonial Office in 1968 to form the Foreign and Commonwealth Office; for supplements to this catalog see *Catalogue of the Colonial Office Library* (DC342), which represents holdings of the combined library of the two offices, beginning with the 2nd supplement, 1972.

For the earliest holdings, see *A short title catalogue of books printed before 1701 in the Foreign Office Library*, comp. by Colin L. Robertson (London : H.M.S.O., 1966. 177 p.).   Z921.G682

Guide to the historical publications of the societies of England and Wales. London : Longmans, 1930–48. 13 v.   **DC275**

Issued as Supplement no. 1–13, Nov. 1930–1948, of the *Bulletin* of the Institute of Historical Research.

Prepared by a committee of the Institute and of the Congress of Archaeological Societies to supplement a work which was never published. Planned to do for the societies of England and Wales what Charles Sanford Terry (*Catalogue of the publications of Scottish historical and kindred clubs and societies ... , 1780–1908*, DC362) and C. Matheson (*Catalogue of the publications of Scottish historical and kindred clubs and societies ... , 1908–27*, DC362 *note*) do for those of Scotland, and also to take the place of the discontinued *Index of archaeological papers* by George Gomme for indexing of English archaeological periodicals and transactions of local antiquarian societies for 1665–1890 and 1891–1910 (London: Constable, 1907–14. 21 v.). The supplements merely record issues for the years covered; the historical information about the societies and the records of publication, index, etc., were to have been published in the basic work.

E. L. C. Mullins, *Guide to the historical and archaeological publications ... 1903–1933* (DC279), provides a list of contents of the series.

Hartigan, Maureen. The history of the Irish in Britain : a bibliography. [London : The Irish in British History Group, 1986]. 85 p.   **DC276**

Lists books, articles, and some theses and conference papers on all aspects of the contact. Works range from general histories to local studies and autobiographies, but exclude novels and government publications. Alphabetically arranged by author with subject and chronological period indexes. Two bibliographical articles, The Irish in other parts of the world and Some general studies on migration, are appended but not indexed.   Z2027.I75H37

Higham, Robin D. S. A guide to the sources of British military history. Berkeley : Univ. of California Pr., 1971. 630 p.   **DC277**

"Sponsored by the Conference on British Studies."—*title page.*

Scholar specialists have contributed bibliographic essays on the whole range of British military history from earliest times to the present. Attention is given to the general histories, bibliographies, selected special studies, and sources. Each chapter includes a section on research opportunities, pointing out areas where initial research is needed or where reappraisals are in order. Mention is also made of archives and special collections of papers and documents, with suggestions on how to obtain access to them. No general index.

§ Continued by: *British military history*, Gerald Jordan, ed. (N.Y. : Garland, 1988. 586 p. [Military history bibliographies, v. 10 ; Garland reference library of the humanities, v. 715]). Updates Higham to about 1984. An excellent introduction to reference materials begins each chapter. No index.   Z2021.M5H54

Jackson, Paul. British sources of information : a subject guide and bibliography. London ; N.Y. : Routledge & Kegan Paul, 1987. 526 p.   **DC278**

In three sections: (1) a bibliography of books "recognized as useful introductions or as authoritative studies on a given topic" (*Pref.*), subdivided for specific subject areas (e.g., Government and administration—cabinet); (2) periodicals, journals, and magazines "which provide general or specific coverage of major topics"; (3) sources of information (e.g., organizations and institutions "which stock information on particular fields," films, videocassettes, audiovisual aids). Appendix of addresses and suppliers: publishers, distributors of films, video workshops. No index. Z2001.J33

Mullins, Edward Lindsay Carson. A guide to the historical and archaeological publications of societies in England and Wales, 1903–1933 / comp. for the Institute of Historical Research. London : Athlone Pr., 1968. 850 p. **DC279**

Lists and indexes the books and articles issued by more than 400 local and national societies of England, Wales, Isle of Man, and the Channel Islands during the period in question. Listing is under name of the society, with an author index and a detailed subject index.

§ Serves as a complement to *Writings on British history* (DC281). Z5055.G6M8

——————— Texts and calendars : an analytical guide to serial publications. London : Royal Historical Soc., 1958–83. 2 v. (Royal Historical Society. Guides and handbooks, no. 7, 12). **DC280**

Contents: v. [1], 1802–57 (674 p.); v. 2, 1957–82 (323 p.).

"An analytical guide to printed texts and calendars relating to English and Welsh history" (*Pref.*) issued in general collections such as the Rolls series, the Historical Manuscripts Commission reports, etc., and in the publications of societies such as the Hakluyt Society, the English Historical Society, the Camden Society, and numerous others. Some organizations founded after 1957 are included in v. 2, which also includes corrections to the first volume. Z2016.M8

Writings on British history / comp. by Alexander Taylor Milne. 1934–73/74. London : J. Cape, 1937–86. **DC281**

Contents: 1940–45 publ. 1960 in 2 v.; 1946/48, ed. by D.J. Munro; 1949/51, ed. by D.J. Munro; 1952/54, ed. by J.M. Sims; 1955/57, ed. by J.M. Sims and P.M. Jacobs; 1958/59, ed. by H.J. Creaton; 1960/61, ed. by C.H.E. Philpin and H.J. Creaton; 1962/64–1973/74, ed. by H.J. Creaton.

Sponsored by the Institute of Historical Research and the Royal Historical Society.

A bibliography of books and articles on the history of Great Britain from about 400 CE to 1914, published during the years 1934–74, with an appendix containing a select list of publications in these years on British history since 1914.

A comprehensive, classified bibliography, arranged topically under broad time periods, with detailed indexes. Prior to the issue covering 1946–48, book reviews were noted; review articles were included throughout the publication's life. Publications of societies are generally excluded, these being listed in E. L. C. Mullins' *Guide to the historical and archaeological publications of societies in England and Wales, 1903–1933* (DC279), C. S. Terry's *Catalogue of the publications of Scottish historical and kindred clubs and societies … 1780–1908* (DC362), and C. Matheson's *Catalogue of the publications of Scottish historical and kindred clubs and societies … 1908–27* (note, DC362).

Because of the time lag in publication, the series ceased with coverage for 1973/74. For subsequent years, see: *Annual bibliography of British and Irish history* (DC282), which began its coverage with 1975.

§ A retrospective bibliography is provided by *Writings on British history 1901–1933* (London : J. Cape, 1968–70. 5 v.), which follows an arrangement similar to the 1934–73/74 series. Z2016.W74

Current

Annual bibliography of British and Irish history : Publications of 1975– . Brighton, Sussex : Harvester Pr. for the Royal Historical Soc. ; Atlantic Highlands, N.J. : Humanities Pr., 1976– . Annual. **DC282**

Designed to provide interim coverage in view of the long delays in publishing *Writings on British history* (DC281) which ceased with 1973/74.

"Auxiliary" and "General" sections are followed by chronological sections for England/Britain, Medieval Wales, Scotland before the

Union, and Ireland, each with appropriate subdivisions (e.g., Politics, External affairs, Religion, Social structure and population). Separate author and subject indexes. Items covering more than one category are entered only once, with cross-references from the other sections. Z2016.A55

Dissertations

Gilbert, Victor Francis. Labour and social history theses : American, British and Irish university theses and dissertations in the field of British and Irish labour history, presented between 1900 and 1978. London : Mansell ; N.Y. : H. W. Wilson, 1982. 194 p. **DC283**

For annotation, *see* CH295. Z7164.L1G5

Historical research for university degrees in the United Kingdom. 1931/32–1952. London : Longmans, 1933–53. **DC284**

Issued as *Bulletin of the Institute of Historical Research. Theses supplement*, no. 1–14.

Each number is in two parts: (1) Theses completed during the year; (2) Theses in progress. "The former follows on the lists published annually in *History* from 1920 to 1929 [covering 1911/19–1927/28], and in the *Bulletin* from 1930 to 1932; the latter is an innovation suggested by the Anglo-American Historical Committee."—*Pref. note to no. 1.*

§ Superseded by:

(1) *Historical research for higher degrees in the United Kingdom. Pt. I, Theses completed* (1953– . London : Univ. of London, Inst. of Historical Research, 1954– . Annual).

(2) ———. *Pt. II, Theses in progress* (1954– . London : Univ. of London, Inst. of Historical Research, 1954– . Annual).

Issues for 1954–66 published as *Theses supplement* no. 15–27 to the *Bulletin*. Beginning 1967 (list no. 28) the lists appear as separate publications of the Institute.

Each section, 1953–59, was arranged by university with author index (for completed theses there were also subject indexes). Beginning with 1960, each section is arranged under "broad chronological and topographical headings" with indexes of authors. Again, for completed theses, there are also subject indexes. Titles changed from "university degrees" to "higher degrees" with no. 47, 1985.

§ For a complete list of theses in history accepted in the United Kingdom see: *History theses, 1901–70* compiled by Phyllis M. Jacobs and its supplement *History theses, 1971–80* compiled by Joyce M. Horn (DA17). Z5055.G695

Guides to records

Great Britain. Historical Manuscripts Commission. A guide to the reports on collections of manuscripts of private families, corporations and institutions in Great Britain and Ireland / issued by the Royal Commissioners for Historical Manuscripts. London : H.M.S.O., 1914–38. 2 v. in 3. **DC285**

Ed. by Francis Bickley.

Contents: Pt. 1, Topographical index (1914. 233 p.); pt. 2, v. 1–2, Index of persons (1938. 859 p.).

Pt. 2 has title: *Guide to the reports of the Royal Commission on Historical Manuscripts, 1870–1911*, and is an alphabetical index of names, with reference under each to the report or reports in which some letter or document connected with the person is listed or calendared.

Continued by: *Guide to the reports of the Royal Commission on Historical Manuscripts, 1911–1957*, ed. by A. C. S. Hall (London : H.M.S.O., 1966–73. 2 v. in 4). Contents: pt. 1, Index of places; pt. 2, Index of persons, 3 v. DA25.M25

Great Britain. Public Record Office. Guide to the contents of the Public Record Office. London : H.M.S.O., 1963–1968. 3 v. **DC286**

A revision of *A guide to the manuscripts preserved in the Public Record Office*, by M. S. Giuseppi, published 1923–24.

Contents: v. 1, Legal records, etc.; v. 2, State papers and departmental records; v. 3, Documents transferred 1960–1966.

Vols. 1–2 are based on, and in large measure a revision and updating of Giuseppi's *Guide*, adding the records transferred to the Public Record Office, 1923–60, many of which fall into new classes. Vol. 3 "takes account of transfers of new classes of records and of changes in existing classes" (*Introd.*) effected 1960–66.

A cumulation and updating of the *Guide* is being issued on microfiche as *Current guide to the contents of the Public Record Office* (Kew : P.R.O., 1983–). Only v. 2–3 have been issued thus far, covering material in the paper edition of v. 2 and the relevant portion of v. 3; the microform v. 3 is an index. The earlier set will continue to be useful for its introductory materials, brief histories of the departments, notes on finding aids, etc.

Those classes (or parts of classes) available for purchase on microfiche or microfilm are listed in *PRO microfilm catalogue* [microform] (1983).

§ The "Public Record Office handbooks" series includes various items of interest, e.g.: no. 3, *The records of the Colonial and Dominions Offices* (1964); no. 8, *List of Colonial Office confidential prints* (1965); no. 13, *Records of the Foreign Office, 1782–1939* (1969); no. 15, *The Second World War*, by John D. Cantwell (DA204); no. 17, *The Cabinet Office to 1945 (1975)*.

See also Stella Colwell, *Dictionary of genealogical sources in the Public Record Office* (London : Weidenfeld & Nicolson, 1992. 206 p.), which is very useful as a guide to working in the P.R.O.
　　　　　　　　　　　　　　　　　　　　　CD1043.A553

Guides to sources for British history based on the National Register of Archives. London : H.M.S.O., [1982–90]. v. 1–8. (In progress).　　　　　　　　　　　　　**DC287**

At head of title: Royal Commission on Historical Manuscripts.

Contents: v. 1, Papers of British cabinet ministers, 1782-1900; v. 2, The manuscript papers of British scientists, 1600-1940; v. 3, Guide to the locations of collections described in the Reports and calendars series, 1870-1980; v. 4, Private papers of British diplomats, 1782-1900; v. 5, Private papers of British colonial governors 1782-1900; v. 6, Papers of British churchmen 1780-1940; v. 7, Papers of British politicians 1782-1900; v. 8, Records of British business and industry, 1760-1914: textiles and leather.

The series aims to publish systematically revised digests of selected segments of the unpublished information accumulated by the Commission in the National Register of Archives, concentrating "on the areas of historical study for which the information itself is most comprehensive and most obviously in scholarly demand."—*Pref., v. 1*. The listing is by individual.　　　　　　CD1042.A2.G8

Record repositories in Great Britain : a geographical directory / the Royal Commission on Historical Manuscripts. 9th ed. London : H.M.S.O., 1991. 46 p.　　　　　　**DC288**

1st ed., 1964; 8th ed., 1987.

More than 200 repositories are included, along with details of about twenty other institutions. Each entry gives address, hours, telephone, and facilities for providing photographs or microfilm. Arranged alphabetically under city; indexed by name of repository.
　　　　　　　　　　　　　　　　　　　　　CD1040.R43

Encyclopedias; Dictionaries

The Cambridge historical encyclopedia of Great Britain and Ireland / ed., Christopher Haigh. Cambridge ; N.Y. : Cambridge Univ. Pr., 1985. 392 p. : ill. (some col.).　**DC289**

Signed articles are organized within a chronological framework, with an overview introducing each period. Emphasis is on political, diplomatic, economic, social, and economic history. In the margins are definitions, identifications (of events, of documents), etc., that relate to the broader articles. Heavily illustrated with photographs,

drawings, and maps, well-chosen and well-placed in the text. Concludes with brief biographies and a bibliography. Cross-references; subject index.　　　　　　　　　　　　　　DA34.C28

The Cambridge illustrated dictionary of British heritage / ed. by Alan Isaacs and Jennifer Monk. Cambridge ; N.Y. : Cambridge Univ. Pr., 1986. 484 p. : ill.　　　**DC290**

Intended for foreigners or those not well acquainted with England. Provides short descriptions or definitions of terms and topics not always easily found in similar works (e.g., Arts and Crafts movement, Arts Council of Great Britain, Arundel Castle, Ascot races). Heavily illustrated with small black-and-white photographs and drawings. Select bibliography, p. 480–83. Not indexed.　　　　DA110.C254

Day, Alan Edwin. History : a reference handbook. London : C. Bingley ; Hamden, Conn. : Linnet Books, 1977. 354 p.
　　　　　　　　　　　　　　　　　　　　　DC291

Concerned with the "political and constitutional history of the English people from the earliest times of which we have a true historical record ... , Great Britain and its expansion overseas ... [encompassing] the history of Australia, Canada and the United States and to a lesser degree ... the history of New Zealand, India and British Africa."—*Foreword*. Aims to "provide a guide to ... reference aids and, at the same time ... indicate the main purposes and features" thereof. 787 numbered entries deal with noted scholars, major texts, bibliographies, publications of historical societies, lecture series, collections of documents and other primary sources. Author/title index.　Z2016.D38

Gascoigne, Bamber. Encyclopedia of Britain. N.Y. ; Basingstoke, Eng. : Macmillan, 1993. 320 p. : col. ill.　**DC292**

A dictionary of about 6,000 articles that includes "mainstream facts about Britain and the British"—i.e., information about Britain "people are most likely to look up."—*Pref*. Includes British cities, authors, sports personalities, musicians known as British, current affairs, scandals and disasters, the 50 largest British corporations, television, pop groups, all Commonwealth countries. Northern Ireland and the Anglo-Irish are included. Asterisks indicate cross-references; there is no index. Well-illustrated with line drawings, tables, photographs of places, art works. The most frequently used sources are cited in a bibliography at the end.　　　　　　　　　　　　　DA27.5.G37

Steinberg, Sigfrid H. Steinberg's dictionary of British history / ed. by S. H. Steinberg and I. H. Evans ; contributors, P. M. Barnes ... [et al.]. 2nd ed. N.Y. : St. Martin's, [1971]. 421 p.
　　　　　　　　　　　　　　　　　　　　　DC293

Previous ed., 1963, had title: *A new dictionary of British history*; a successor to *A dictionary of British history* by J. A. Brendon (London : E. Arnold, 1937).

A dictionary of brief articles written by a group of scholars, covering England and her overseas possessions so long as they maintained their British connection. Biographies are omitted; no bibliographical references.

§ See also: *The Cambridge historical encyclopedia of Great Britain and Ireland*, ed. Christopher Haigh (DC289), for lavishly illustrated essays grouped by period.　　　　　　　　DA34.S7

Handbooks

Cook, Chris. The Longman handbook of modern British history, 1714–1987 / Chris Cook and John Stevenson. 2nd ed. London ; N.Y. : Longman, [1988]. 418 p.　　　**DC294**

1st ed., 1983.

Offers a variety of chronologies, statistical tables (updated to 1985–87), lists of principal ministers, biographical sketches, etc., relating to British political, social, religious, and economic history. Subject index.　　　　　　　　　　　　　　　DA470.C65

Chronologies

Handbook of British chronology / ed. by E. B. Fryde ... [et al.]. 3rd ed. London : Royal Historical Society, 1986. 605 p. (Royal Historical Society. Guides and handbooks, no. 2). **DC295**

1st ed., 1939, and 2nd ed., 1961, comp. by F. M. Powicke and Fryde.

Partial contents: Bibliographical guide to the lists of English office-holders; Chronological lists of rulers of England, Wales, Scotland and the Isle of Man; Officers of State of England, Ireland and Scotland; Bishops of England, Wales, Scotland, Ireland; Dukes, Marquesses, and Earls 1066–1714, English parliaments to 1832; Provincial and national councils of the Church in England to 1536.

Includes tables current through 1985. No index.

§ A section from the first edition, "Reckonings of time," has been reprinted in revised form in R. C. Cheney, *Handbook of dates for students of English history* (London : Offices of the Royal Historical Soc., 1945. 164 p.).   DA34.P6

General histories

Oxford history of England / ed. by Sir George Clark. 2nd ed. Oxford : Clarendon Pr., 1937–62. 15 v. in 16. **DC296**

1st ed., 1934–65, 15 v. The 2nd ed. began publication before the 1st ed. was completed. Some volumes have appeared in a 3rd ed.; others appear in reprint.

Contents: v. 1A, Roman Britain, by P. Salway; v. 1B, Roman Britain and the English settlements, R. G. Collingwood and J. N. L. Myers; v. 2, Anglo-Saxon England, by F. M. Stenton; v. 3, From Domesday Book to Magna Carta, 1087–1216, by Austin L. Poole; v. 4, The thirteenth century, 1216–1307, by F. M. Powicke; v. 5, The fourteenth century, 1307–1399, by M. McKisack; v. 6, The fifteenth century, 1399–1485, by E. F. Jacob; v. 7, The earlier Tudors, 1485–1558, by J. D. Mackie; v. 8, The reign of Elizabeth, 1558–1603, by J. B. Black; v. 9, Early Stuarts, 1603–1660, by G. Davies; v. 10, The later Stuarts, 1660–1714, by G.N. Clark; v. 11, Whig supremacy, 1714–1760, by B. Williams, rev. by C. H. Stuart; v. 12, The reign of George III, 1760–1815, by J. S. Watson; v. 13, Age of reform, 1815–1870, by E. L. Woodward; v. 14, England, 1870–1914, by R. C. K. Ensor; v. 15, English history, 1914–1945, by A. J. P. Taylor.

Richard Raper has merged the indexes of all 16 v. into one, which required some reindexing: *Consolidated indexes* (Oxford : Clarendon Pr. ; N.Y. : Oxford Univ. Pr., 1991. 622 p.).

Sourcebooks

English historical documents / gen. ed., David C. Douglas. London : Eyre and Spottiswoode, 1953–1977. 12 v. : ill. **DC297**

Contents: v. 1, English historical documents, ca.500–1042, ed. by Dorothy Whitelock (1955); v. 2, 1042–1189, ed. by David C. Douglas and George W. Greenaway (1953); v. 3, 1189–1327, ed. by Henry Rothwell (1975); v. 4, 1327–1485, ed. by A. R. Myers (1969); v. 5, 1485–1558, ed. by C. H. Williams (1967); v. 6, 1558–1603, ed. by D.F. Price; v. 7, 1603–1660, ed. by Ivan Roots; v. 8, 1660–1714, ed. by Andrew Browning (1953); v. 9, American colonial documents to 1776, ed. by Merrill Jensen (1955); v. 10, English historical documents, 1714–1783, ed. by D. B. Horn and Mary Ransome (1957); v. 11, 1783–1832, ed. by A. Aspinall and E. Anthony Smith (1959); v. 12, pt. 1, 1833–1874, ed. by G. M. Young and W. D. Handcock (1956); v. 12, pt. 2, 1874–1914, ed. by W. D. Handcock (1977).

Covers the complete span of English history from 500 CE to 1914. The early documents are given in English translation from the original Latin, French, or Anglo-Saxon. A valuable collection, with extensive introductions and bibliographies.

§ A second edition began publication in 1979 (London : Eyre Methuen ; N.Y. : Oxford Univ. Pr., 1979–1981. v. 1–2. [In progress?]). Contents: v. 1, ca.500–1042, ed. by Dorothy Whitelock; v. 2, 1042–1189, ed. by D. C. Douglas and G. W. Greenaway.   DA26.E56

Biography

Who's who in British history / ed. Geoffrey Treasure. London : Shepheard-Walwyn ; Chicago : St. James Pr., 1988–1992. v. 1, 3–6 : maps. (In progress). **DC298**

Contents: v. 1, Who's who in Roman Britain and Anglo-Saxon England, by Richard A. Fletcher (1989. 245 p.); v. 3, ... late medieval England 1272–1485, by Michael A. Hicks (2nd ed., 1991. 382 p.); v. 4, ... Tudor England, by C.N.R. Routh, rev. and enl. by Peter Holmes (1990. 476 p.); v. 5, ... Stuart England, by C.P. Hill, rev. and enl. by Hill (1988. 466 p.); v. 6, ... early Hanoverian Britain 1714–1789, by Geoffrey Treasure (1992. 450 p.) Announced for publication is a volume for Victorian Britain.

The first editions of the revised volumes in this series were originally published in the *Who's who in history* series.

Biographical essays, very readable and well-researched, are arranged chronologically in order to give a picture of an age. Each essay concludes with a reference to an original source in English or a good secondary work. Glossary, maps, and, in some volumes, genealogical charts. A brief subject index in each volume also refers from variant names to the page number of the form chosen by the author.

Atlases

Atlas of British social and economic history since c. 1700 / ed. by Rex Pope. N.Y. : Macmillan, [1989]. [250] p. : ill. ; maps ; 26 cm. **DC299**

Publ. in U.K. : London : Routledge.

Chapters, written by scholars, on particular topics, (e.g., The textile and chemical industries, Demographic changes) discuss British social and economic history and development through a narrative summary followed by a graphic presentation using maps with extensive explanatory text. "The different sections of the Atlas contain roughly equal proportions of maps and supporting text." *Introd.* Notes at the end of each section provide bibliographies of source materials; suggestions for further reading, p. 236–245; topical index. Does not include Ireland.   HC253.A86

Atlas of industrializing Britain 1780–1914 / ed. by John Langton and R.J. Morris. London ; N.Y. : Methuen, [1986]. 246 p. ; 26 cm. **DC300**

The social and economic history of the Industrial Revolution in England, Scotland, and Wales, presented through maps, graphs, and detailed explanations. Arranged under 31 headings, such as The physical environment, Population, Wages, Wind and water power, Religion, and Electoral system. Sources of maps, p. 228–235; bibliography, p. 236–246. Not indexed.   G1812.21.G1A8

Freeman-Grenville, Greville Stewart Parker. Atlas of British history / G. S. P. Freeman-Grenville ; cartography, Lorraine Kessel. London : Rex Collings, 1979. [96 p.] (unpaged) ; 25 cm. **DC301**

Comprises 140 maps of various sizes which aim to portray "the principal themes and events in the history of the British Isles from prehistoric times until 1978."—*Pref.* Chronological arrangement. Indexed.

§ More recent is *Atlas of British history* by Martin Gilbert (2nd ed. N.Y. : Oxford Univ. Pr., 1993. 144 p. ; 26 cm.) with clear black-and-white maps and charts but little text. Extends from the Celts (about 50 BCE) to the amount of public spending budgeted for 1993/94.   G1812.21.S1F7

Historical atlas of Britain / [gen. editors] Malcolm Falkus, John Gillingham. [Rev. ed.]. N.Y. : Crescent Books : Distr. by Crown, 1987. 223 p. : ill. (some col.), maps in color ; 30 cm.
DC302

1st ed., 1981.

Also publ. London : Kingfisher Books.

Aims to present in text, maps, and pictures a comprehensive view of British history—political, economic, and social—from earliest times to the present. Gives attention to overseas possessions. Except for occasional updating, there is very little change from the previous edition. Indexed.   G1812.21.S1H5

Early to 1485

Bibliography

Altschul, Michael. Anglo-Norman England, 1066–1154. [London] : Univ. Pr., 1969. 83 p.   **DC303**

Slightly more than 1,800 items in subject sections, with author index.

§ Part of the series of bibliographic handbooks published by the Conference on British Studies that cover periods of British history. *See also* Bertie Wilkinson, *The high Middle Ages in England, 1154–1377* (DC308); DeLloyd J. Guth, *Late-medieval England, 1377–1485* (DC307); Mortimer Levine, *Tudor England, 1485–1603* (Cambridge : Univ. Pr., 1968. 115 p.); William L. Sachse, *Restoration England, 1660–1689* (DC319); Robert A. Smith, *Late Georgian and Regency England, 1760–1837* (DC320); Josef Lewis Altholz, *Victorian England, 1837–1901* (DC325); and Alfred F. Havighurst, *Modern England, 1901–1984* (DC331).   Z2017.A43

A bibliography of English history to 1485 : based on The sources and literature of English history from the earliest times to about 1485 by Charles Gross / ed. by Edgar B. Graves. Oxford ; N.Y. : Clarendon Pr., 1975. 1103 p.   **DC304**

Part of the series, Bibliography of British history. For a note on the series, *see* DC270.

"Issued under the sponsorship of the Royal Historical Society, the American Historical Association and the Mediaeval Academy of America."—*t.p.*

Like Charles Gross's *Sources* ... (2nd ed., rev. and enl. London : Longmans, 1915. 820 p.), which is largely superseded, this edition is planned as "a systematic survey of the printed materials relating to the political, constitutional, legal, social, and economic history of England, Wales and Ireland down to 1485."—*Pref.* Older standard or seminal works have been retained and recent writings added, "especially those which set forth new or controversial interpretations or include modern specialized bibliographies." Includes works published through Dec. 1969 for the pre-1066 period; through Dec. 1970 for the period 1066–1485. The sections for economic and cultural and social history are considerably expanded. Extensive index.   Z2017.B5

Bonser, Wilfrid. A prehistoric bibliography / Wilfrid Bonser, extended and ed. by June Troy. Oxford : Blackwell, 1976. 425 p.   **DC305**

About 9,000 items in classed arrangement with an author/subject index. In five main sections: (1) Men and methods in archaeology; (2) Field archaeology; (3) Specific sites; (4) Material finds; (5) Culture.

Continued by two of Bonser's works: *A Romano-British bibliography, 55 B.C.–A.D. 449* (Oxford : B. Blackwell, 1964 [i.e. 1965]. 2 v.) and *Anglo-Saxon and Celtic bibliography 450–1087* (Berkeley : Univ. of California Pr., 1957. 2 v.).   Z2007.A67B65

British archaeological bibliography. v. 1, no. 1 (Apr. 1992)– . London : British Archaeological Bibliography, 1992– . Semiannual.   **DC306**

Produced for the Council for British Archaeology. Issues for Apr. 1992– cover material published July-Dec. 1991– .

Continues *British archaeological abstracts*, v. 1–24 (1968–1991), and *Archaeological bibliography for Great Britain and Ireland* (1950–1981).

Indexes journals for materials about archeology in Great Britain and Ireland to 1600 CE. Less international in scope than *British archaeological abstracts*. Topical arrangement within a generally chronological framework. Plans call for compilation of the bibliography on computer to make it available on disk, via JANET, or through an on-line service.

§ The Council also issued *Archaeological site index to radiocarbon dates for Great Britain and Ireland* (London, 1971).   DA90.B822

Guth, DeLloyd J. Late-medieval England, 1377–1485. Cambridge ; N.Y. : Univ. Pr., for the Conference on British Studies, 1976. 143 p.   **DC307**

Classified arrangement listing some 2,500 printed materials published through Dec. 1974 and dealing with England and Wales (plus a few references to Scotland and Ireland), 1377–1485. Some annotations. Index of editors, authors, and translators.

§ Part of the bibliographical handbooks series from the Conference on British Studies, covering periods of British history. For a list of these works, *see* Michael Altschul, *Anglo-Norman England, 1066–1154*, DC303.   Z2017.G87

Wilkinson, Bertie. The high Middle Ages in England, 1154–1377. Cambridge : Univ. Pr. for the Conference on British Studies, [1978]. 130 p.   **DC308**

A select bibliography for the student and scholar. Classed arrangement, with author index. Includes books and periodical articles. 2,259 items.

§ Part of the bibliographical handbooks series from the Conference on British Studies, covering periods of British history. For a list of these works, *see* Michael Altschul, *Anglo-Norman England, 1066–1154* (DC303).   Z2017.W54

Encyclopedias; Dictionaries

Adkins, Lesley. A thesaurus of British archaeology / Lesley Adkins and Roy A. Adkins. Newton Abbott, Eng. : David & Charles ; Totowa, N.J. : Barnes & Noble, 1982. 319 p. : ill.
DC309

Also publ. as *The handbook of British archaeology* (London, Macmillan, 1983).

Concerned with the archaeology of England, Scotland and Wales, from the palaeolithic to the medieval periods. Arranged by period, then topically within chapters. Select bibliography and detailed index.
    DA90.A6

The Plantagenet encyclopedia : an alphabetical guide to 400 years of English history / ed. by Elizabeth Hallam. N.Y. : Grove Weidenfeld, c1990. 224 p. : ill. (some col.), maps.
DC310

Publ. in U.K. : London : Weidenfeld and Nicolson.

Designed as a companion to three chronicles translated and edited by Hallam: *The Plantagenet chronicles* (London : Weidenfeld & Nicolson ; Markham, Ont. : Viking, 1987. 352 p.), *Chronicles of the age of chivalry* (London : Weidenfeld & Nicolson, 1987 ; publ. in the U.S. as *Four Gothic kings*, N.Y. : Weidenfeld & Nicolson, 1987. 320 p.), and *The chronicles of the Wars of the Roses*, N.Y. : Weidenfeld & Nicolson, 1988. 320 p.). The set covers English history from before the coronation of Henry II in 1154 to the death of Richard III in 1485.

A lavishly illustrated dictionary of short entries identifying places, giving short biographies of notables, and treating a few subjects (e.g., Travel) or government bodies (e.g., Parliament). Each article ends with specific citations to one or more of the chronicles. Includes a 2½-page bibliography, a list of manuscripts, and an index of names.
    DA225.P54

Saul, Nigel. The Batsford companion to medieval England. London : Batsford ; Totowa, N.J. : Barnes & Noble, 1983. 283 p. : ill.   **DC311**

A dictionary arrangement of relatively short articles on people, institutions, events, and various aspects of life and culture in medieval

England. Aims to provide "a reference work to which a non-specialist, though not just a non-specialist, may turn with profit and with pleasure."—*Pref.* Bibliographies are generally limited to one or two citations.   DA175.S38

Atlases

Hill, David. An atlas of Anglo-Saxon England. Toronto : Univ. of Toronto Pr. ; Oxford : B. Blackwell, 1981. 180 p. : maps. 29cm.   **DC312**

Attempts "to display all the evidence on Anglo-Saxon England that can be placed in a topographic or chronological framework."—*Pref.* Black-and-white maps with accompanying text and a number of tables and charts are grouped in five main sections: (1) the background; (2) the events; (3) administration; (4) the economy; (5) the church. Bibliography; index.   G1812.21.S2H5

Jones, Barri. An atlas of Roman Britain / Barri Jones and David Mattingly. Cambridge, Mass. : Blackwell, 1990. 341 p. : ill., maps ; 29 cm.   **DC313**

Black-and-white maps, photographs, charts, and tables, accompanied by extensive commentary, cover recent scholarship and excavations. Begins with Britain before the Roman conquest and ends with "The Saxon inheritors." Subject index; bibliography arranged to coordinate with the chapters.   G1812.21.S2J6

Manley, John. Atlas of prehistoric Britain. N.Y. : Oxford Univ. Pr., 1989. 160 p. : some maps in color ; 31 cm.   **DC314**

Publ. in U.K. : Oxford : Phaidon.

A popular work in which photographs, maps, drawings, and text "depict the principal concentration of major prehistoric monuments in Britain and Ireland."—*Pref.* Topical index.   GN805.M36

16th–18th centuries

See also DC328.

Bibliography

Davies, Godfrey. Bibliography of British history, Stuart period, 1603–1714 / issued under the direction of the American Historical Association and the Royal Historical Society of Great Britain. 2nd ed. / [ed. by] Mary Frear Keeler. Oxford : Clarendon Pr., 1970. 734 p.   **DC315**

Part of the series, Bibliography of British history. For a note on the series, *see* DC270.

Extensive scholarly bibliography with emphasis on materials from the century itself and "on those later works whose interpretations have been significant"—*Foreword.* Covers government publications, essays, books, articles; cut-off date 1961–63. Index for author, some titles and subjects.   Z2018.D25

Morgan, William Thomas. Bibliography of British history (1700–1715) with special reference to the reign of Queen Anne. Bloomington, Ind., 1934–42. 5 v. (Indiana University. Studies, no.18–19, 23–26, 94–95, 114–24).   **DC316**

Repr.: N.Y. : B. Franklin, 1973.

Vols. 2–3 and v. 5 by W. T. Morgan and Chloe S. Morgan.

Contents: v. 1–2, Pamphlets and memoirs, 1700–1715; v. 3, Source materials published in 1717 and later. Correspondence, autobiographies, diaries, and journals. Periodicals, including newspapers and annuals (1700–1715). Plays and other dramatic works. Secondary materials (to about June 1938); v. 4, Unpublished manuscripts with index; v. 5, Addenda and corrigenda. Supplements to v. 1–3. Appendixes. Comprehensive index to v. 1, 2, 3, and 5.   Z2018.M6

Pargellis, Stanley. The eighteenth century, 1714–1789 / Issued under the direction of the American Historical Association and the Royal Historical Society of Great Britain ; ed. by Stanley Pargellis and D. J. Medley. Oxford : Clarendon Pr., 1951. 642 p.   **DC317**

Repr.: Totowa, N.J. : Rowman and Littlefield, 1977.

Part of the series, Bibliography of British history. For a note on the series, *see* DC270.

A major scholarly bibliography for this period. Concentrates heavily on source material, attempting "to provide some sort of guide through the mass of contemporary literature, much of which is yet undiscovered by students."—*Pref.* Within each topical section entries are arranged by date of publication or date of coverage, earliest first. Includes sections for the American colonies and India, as well as local history, Scotland, Ireland, and Wales. Brief commentary; indexed by main entry and subject.   Z2018.P37

Read, Conyers. Bibliography of British history, Tudor period, 1485–1603. 2nd ed. Oxford : Clarendon Pr., 1959. 624 p.
                                                          DC318

Repr.: Hassocks : Harvester ; Totowa, N.J. : Rowman and Littlefield, 1978.

1st ed., 1933.

A major scholarly bibliography of books, articles, documents and pamphlets. Topical listing; each subsection has an introductory note emphasizing the more important works. Exhaustive to Jan. 1, 1957, with some later works included.

Part of the series, Bibliography of British history. For a note on the series, *see* DC270.   Z2018.R28

Sachse, William Lewis. Restoration England, 1660–1689. Cambridge : Univ. Pr. for the Conference on British Studies, [1971]. 114 p.   **DC319**

A selected, classified bibliography similar to the other works in the series. Index of authors and editors.

Part of the bibliographical handbooks series from the Conference on British Studies, covering periods of British history. For a list of these works, *see* Michael Altschul, *Anglo-Norman England, 1066–1154,* DC303.   Z2018.S3

Smith, Robert A. Late Georgian and Regency England, 1760–1837. Cambridge, Eng. ; Univ. Pr. for the Conference on British Studies, [1984]. 114 p.   **DC320**

A topically arranged bibliography of "the best of the voluminous literature on later eighteenth and early nineteenth century England."—*Pref.* 2,514 entries; author index. With a few exceptions, publications are pre-1981.

§ Part of the bibliographical handbooks series from the Conference on British Studies, covering periods of British history. For a list of these works, *see* Michael Altschul, *Anglo-Norman England, 1066–1154,* DC303.   Z2041.S64

Union Theological Seminary (New York, N.Y.). Library. Catalogue of the McAlpin collection of British history and theology / comp. and ed. by Charles Ripley Gillett. N.Y. : [Union Theological Seminary], 1927–30. 5 v.   **DC321**

Valuable for historical material published 1500–1700. For complete information, *see* BC227.   Z7757.E5N5

Encyclopedias; Dictionaries

Historical dictionary of Tudor England, 1485–1603 / Ronald H. Fritze, ed. in chief.; Walter Sutton, asst. ed. N.Y. : Greenwood, 1991. 594 p.   **DC322**

295 articles written by scholars. Primary focus on political, military, and religious topics, but with some coverage of social, economic and intellectual history. Cross-references are indicated by small capitals. References usually end the articles. Indexed mostly by personal names with a few topics. Appendixes: Chronology, Select bibliography.   DA315.H5

Handbooks

Powell, Ken. English historical facts, 1485–1603 / Ken Powell and Chris Cook. Totowa, N.J. : Rowman & Littlefield, 1977. 228 p.   **DC323**

Offers a variety of lists, chronologies, and background information on historical events and developments of the Tudor period, presented in chapters on: The crown and central government; Parliament; The judicature and the courts; Local government; The church; Education; War, rebellion and diplomacy; Scotland and Ireland; Tudor economic legislation; Population and growth of towns. Selected Tudor biographies, p. 206–20; brief bibliography, p. 221–28. Lacks an index which would have greatly enhanced the ready reference value.

§ Continued by the following:

Chris Cook and John Wroughton, *English historical facts, 1603–1688* (1980. 231 p.). Similar in choice of topics and arrangement, this volume covers the Stuart and Cromwell periods, with tables, lists, chronologies, etc., in chapters on the monarchy, selected holders of public office, central government, Parliament, local government, the church, armed forces, overseas trade and the colonies, education, population, and towns. Selected biographies; select bibliography. No index.

Chris Cook and John Stevenson, *British historical facts, 1688–1760* (N.Y. : St. Martin's Pr., 1988. 252 p.).

Chris Cook and John Stevenson, *British historical facts, 1760–1830* (Hamden, Conn. : Archon Books, 1980. 197 p.). Presents various lists, tables, chronologies, etc., within sections such as: The monarchy; Ministries and administrations; Selected holders of public office; Parliament and elections; Foreign affairs; Armed forces; Law and order; The press; Religion; The economy.

Chris Cook and Brendan Keith, *British historical facts, 1830–1900* (London : Macmillan, 1975. 279 p. Repr.: N.Y. : St. Martin's, 1984). A compilation of lists, tables, etc., bringing together a great deal of political information from many sources. Emphasis is on people, listing "almost all those who held high political, judicial, military or administrative office in Britain between 1830 and 1900."—*Pref.*

DA315.P68

Atlases

Atlas of the English civil war / Peter Newman. N.Y. : Macmillan, 1985. 126 p. ; 26 cm.   **DC324**

Simultaneously published: London : Croom Helm, c1985.

In 56 maps, with text on facing pages, depicts campaigns and battles of the English Civil War, 1642–51, plus a few maps that show the state of the country overall. Scotland and Ireland are included. Chronological arrangement; index for geographical and personal names.

G1812.21.S4N42

19th–20th centuries

For a discussion of materials and approaches, *see* Charles Mowat, *Great Britain since 1914* (Ithaca, N.Y. : Cornell Univ. Pr., 1971).

Bibliography

Altholz, Josef Lewis. Victorian England, 1837–1901. Cambridge, [Eng.] : publ. for the Conference on British Studies at the Univ. Pr., 1970. 100 p.   **DC325**

A selective bibliography, "the chief criterion being that of potential scholarly utility."—*Pref.*

§ Part of the bibliographical handbooks series from the Conference on British Studies, covering periods of British history. For a list of these works, *see* DC303.   Z2019.A56

Aster, Sidney. British foreign policy 1918–1945 : a guide to research and research materials. Rev. ed. Wilmington, Del. : Scholarly Resources, 1991. 391 p.   **DC326**

1st ed., 1984.

A survey of archives and libraries is followed by a bibliography of 1,950 printed primary and secondary literature grouped as Parliament and the government, memoirs, and period divisions. Includes a discussion of the Foreign Office and how policy is made; appendix of names of secretaries and undersecretaries of state, ambassadors and consuls. Name index to the archives and bibliography section.

Z6465.G7A85

Batts, John Stuart. British manuscript diaries of the nineteenth century : an annotated listing. Totowa, N.J. : Rowman and Littlefield ; Fontwell : Centaur Pr., 1976. 345 p.   **DC327**

For annotation, *see* BE724.   Z6611.B6B38

Brown, Lucy M. Bibliography of British history, 1789–1851 / Lucy M. Brown, Ian R. Christie. Oxford : Clarendon Pr., 1977. 759 p.   **DC328**

Part of the series, Bibliography of British history. For a note on the series, *see* DC270.

"Issued under the direction of the American Historical Association and the Royal Historical Society of Great Britain."—*t.p.*

Very selective in its inclusiveness. "The various sections and subsections have been prepared with the object of providing, first, a representative sample of the more prolific forms of contemporary imprints, such as pamphlets and essays; secondly, an outline of each field as treated in the literature concerned with it, drawing attention to leading features and/or personalities; thirdly, reference, where this is possible, to up-to-date authoritative treatment; and fourthly, an indication of further immediate guidance to be found, for instance, in specialist bibliographies, in reading lists of books, or by reference to specialist journals or series."—*Pref.* Cutoff date appears to have been approximately 1973, with some items as late as 1975 noted.   Z2019.B76

Catterall, Peter. British history, 1945–1987 : an annotated bibliography. Oxford ; Cambridge, Mass. : B. Blackwell, 1991. 843 p.   **DC329**

A classified bibliography of books, articles, and some British and American theses published through 1989 (with a few from 1990). Includes special sections for Scotland, Wales, and Northern Ireland, with some treatment of former colonies. "The objective in researching this bibliography, as well as demonstrating the areas where further research is required, has been to establish the range and quality of the material available."—*Pref.* Headnotes discuss scholarship; cross-references link sections together. Good annotations, often including citations to related works. Author and subject indexes.

§ Complements *Bibliography of British history* (DC270) and, like those volumes, should be a starting point for research in the period.

Z2020.3.C37

Hanham, Harold John. Bibliography of British history, 1851–1914. Oxford : Clarendon Pr., 1976. 1606 p.   **DC330**

Part of the series, Bibliography of British history. For a note on the series, *see* DC270.

"Issued under the direction of the American Historical Association and the Royal Historical Society of Great Britain."—*t.p.*

Aims "to list the major works which a student is likely to wish to consult, a selection of other works which makes clear the scope of contemporary printed materials, and a selection of biographies and autobiographies."—*Pref.* Cutoff date is generally 1970, but some publications as late as 1973 have been included. Extensive author and subject index.

Z2019.H35

Havighurst, Alfred F. Modern England, 1901–1984. 2nd ed. Cambridge ; N.Y. : Cambridge Univ. Pr. for the North American Conference on British Studies, [1987]. 109 p.   **DC331**

1st ed., 1976, covers 1901–1970.

"The selection of books and articles here presented rests upon a comprehensive search of historical literature published before 1984, though a few important items published in 1984 are included. Of the major aspects of English life only literature per se is excluded."—*Pref.*

A new category "Labour history" has been added. Arranged by broad topics subdivided by format (e.g., printed sources, surveys, monographs). Occasional annotations; author/editor/translator index.

§ Part of the bibliographical handbooks series from the Conference on British Studies, covering periods of British history. For a list of these works, *see* DC303.   Z2020.H38

Perks, Robert. Oral history : an annotated bibliography. London : British Library National Sound Archive, 1990. 183 p.   **DC332**

Lists 2,132 "books, pamphlets, periodicals, articles, catalogs and published recordings about, based on or using oral history, together with relevant coverage of related topics like sound archives and reminiscent therapy."—*Introd.* Intended to be comprehensive for the U.K. and selective for the rest of the world. Materials cited were published 1945–89. Arranged alphabetically by interviewee; cross-references; index of names, places, topics and concepts.   Z6208.O7P47

Rasor, Eugene L. British naval history since 1815 : a guide to the literature. N.Y. : Garland, 1990. 841 p. (Military history bibliographies, vol. 13 ; Garland reference library of the humanities, vol. 1069).   **DC333**

In two parts: (1) Historiographical narrative, which discusses "trends and developments and points to areas for further contribution" (*Pref.*); and (2) Bibliographical listing, which lists 3,125 "standard, popular, and official histories, surveys, monographs, articles, anthologies, dissertations, published documents, review articles, essays, guides, bibliographies," most published since 1960. Arranged in chronological and topical chapters. Cross-references but no index.   Z2021.N3R38

Dissertations

Bell, S. Peter. Dissertations on British history, 1815–1914 : an index to British and American theses. Metuchen, N.J. : Scarecrow, 1974. 232 p.   **DC334**

In five main sections. (1) political history; (2) economic history; (3) social history; (4) ecclesiastical history; (5) history of education. Sections are subdivided as necessary. Indexes of authors, persons, places and subjects. About 2,300 entries. British master's essays are included, but not American; also not included are theses submitted prior to 1914.   Z2016.B43

Guides to records

Cook, Chris. Sources in British political history, 1900–1951 / comp. for the British Library of Political and Economic Science by Chris Cook ... [et al.]. London : Macmillan ; N.Y. : St. Martin's, 1975–85. 6 v.   **DC335**

Contents: v. 1, A guide to the archives of selected organisations and societies; v. 2, A guide to the private papers of selected public servants; v. 3–4, A guide to the private papers of Members of Parliament; v. 5, A guide to the private papers of selected writers, intellectuals and publicists; v. 6, First consolidated supplement.

A report on "the results of a survey of twentieth-century British political archives."—*Foreword.* The project was "intended to locate the papers of all persons and organisations influential in British politics between 1900 and 1951, encourage their preservation, and publish a guide," but certain priorities have necessarily been established: "Whilst a comprehensive search is being made for the papers of all members of the House of Commons, the papers of individual members of other categories are being sought more selectively, on the basis either of their rank or of their known political activity."

Vol. 5 includes journalists, Fabians, businessmen, religious leaders, trade unionists, etc. Vol. 6 records changes in location of materials, new deposits, and reorganization or new information gathered between 1977 and July 1, 1984.   Z2020.C66

Encyclopedias; Dictionaries

Lines, Clifford John. Companion to the Industrial Revolution. N.Y. : Facts on File, c1990. 262 p. : ill.   **DC336**

"In addition to essential information about industrial and technological developments and the people who made these possible, [the dictionary] also includes organizations and events which affected the lives of working people."—*Introd.* Short articles of one to three paragraphs identify, define, or briefly describe; most end with one bibliographic citation for a relevant study or a site open to the public. Cross-references; not indexed. A chronology, 1702–1867, is arranged in columns for Industry, Transport, Society. Maps and charts for age distribution in 1841, canals and railways, coalfields and industrial regions in 1820, etc.   HC254.5.L72

Victorian Britain : an encyclopedia / Sally Mitchell, ed. ... [et al.]. N.Y. : Garland, 1988. 986 p. : ill. (Garland reference library of social science, v. 438).   **DC337**

Intends to provide an "overview and point of departure" for the study of "persons, events, institutions, topics, groups, and artifacts in Great Britain between 1837 and 1901."—*Pref.* Arranged alphabetically, the signed articles end with bibliographies of sources. A seven-page annotated bibliography of key reference sources concludes the dictionary. Cross-references; general index. Chronology, p. xi–xxi.   DA550.V53

Weigall, David. Britain & the world, 1815–1986 : a dictionary of international relations. N.Y. : Oxford Univ. Pr., 1987. 240 p., [12] p. of plates : maps.   **DC338**

"Intended ... as a standard work of reference on British foreign policy and international relations."—*Pref.* Features historical and biographical entries (e.g., Boer War, Winston Churchill, every British foreign secretary since 1815); definitions of terms and concepts used in diplomacy and foreign relations (e.g., Balkanization, Reparations); and extended articles on bilateral relations between Britain and major powers (e.g., France, Germany). Entries are arranged alphabetically, contain cross-references, and many end with short bibliographies; they are followed by a chronological table giving events and treaties of British significance and a map section.   DA45.W45

Handbooks

Butler, David. British political facts, 1900–1985 / by David Butler and Gareth Butler. 6th ed. N.Y. : St. Martin's Pr., 1986. 536 p.   **DC339**

1st ed., 1963; 5th ed., 1980.

Provides lists of political personnel, tables of political statistics, and statistical data on many aspects of British politics, economics, and society, 1900–85. Organizes information in 22 topical chapters (e.g., Parties, Parliament, Elections). Bibliographical note. Index of ministers; subject index.   JN231.B8

Biography

The Blackwell biographical dictionary of British political life in the twentieth century / ed. by Keith Robbins. Oxford ; Cambridge, Mass. : Blackwell Reference, 1990. 449 p. : ill.   **DC340**

Offers "succinct summaries of the careers of leading figures in twentieth-century British political life, together with concise estimates of their stature and significance."—*Editor's introd.* Political life is interpreted broadly: besides party leaders, "front-rank" politicians, and prominent civil servants, includes newspaper publishers and editors, archbishops, trade union leaders, and scientists; biographies range from Gilbert Murray to Rupert Murdock. Signed articles with bibliographies, many including a photograph. Subject index.   DA566.9.A1B57

British Empire and Commonwealth

Bibliography

See also John P. Halstead and Serafino Pocari, *Modern European imperialism*, DC8.

Gipson, Lawrence Henry. A bibliographical guide to the history of the British Empire, 1748–1776. N.Y. : Knopf, 1968. 478 p. (The British Empire before the American Revolution, v.14).   **DC341**

A classified listing of books, pamphlets, and periodical articles. Detailed index.

§ Gipson's companion volume dealing with manuscripts is *A guide to manuscripts relating to the history of the British Empire, 1748–1776* (N.Y. : Knopf, 1970. 490 p.). Arrangement is by depository, with notes on the manuscript holdings in general, and descriptions of special collections of papers. Indexed.

Great Britain. Colonial Office. Library. Catalogue of the Colonial Office Library, London. Boston : G. K. Hall, 1964. 15 v.   **DC342**

Lists works relating to all aspects of the organization and development of any country that has been a member of the British Commonwealth at any time during the last 300 years. For former members, the collection is complete through the date on which the country left the Commonwealth; thereafter, the collection is selective, devoted to administration, external relations, and economic and social development of the nation. Material acquired before 1950 is in a subject catalog and an author index; post-1950 acquisitions are arranged by authors and titles, by subjects, and in classified order by the LC system. In 1968 the Library was merged with the Foreign Office Library, now Foreign and Commonwealth Office Library; supplements 2–3 reflect the merger.

————. ————. *1st–3rd supplements* (Boston : G. K. Hall, 1967–79. 7 v.).

Contents: 1st suppl., 1963–67 (1967. 894 p.); 2nd suppl., 1968–71 (1972. 2 v.); 3rd suppl. entitled: *Foreign and Commonwealth Office, Accessions to the Library, May 1971–June 1977* (1979. 4 v.). The 3rd suppl. includes accessions to the Ministry of Overseas Development Library.   Z921.L388

Palmegiano, Eugenia M. The British Empire in the Victorian press, 1832–1867 : a bibliography. N.Y. : Garland, 1987. 234 p. (Themes in European expansion, vol. 8 ; Garland reference library of social science, vol. 389).   **DC343**

Contains 3,000 entries drawn from 50 popular London-based magazines. Author index; broad subject index. Includes checklist of 37 magazines treating imperial matters exclusively or extensively.   Z2021.C7P32

Royal Commonwealth Society. Library. Subject catalogue of the Library of the Royal Empire Society, formerly Royal Colonial Institute / Evans Lewin. [London : The Society], 1930–1937. 4 v.   **DC344**

Repr.: London : Dawsons, 1967.

Contents: v. 1, British Empire generally, and Africa; v. 2, Commonwealth of Australia, Dominion of New Zealand, South Pacific, general voyages and travels, and Arctic and Antarctic regions; v. 3, Dominion of Canada and its provinces, Dominion of Newfoundland, the West Indies, and Colonial America; v. 4, Mediterranean colonies, Middle East, Indian Empire, Burma, Ceylon, British Malaya, East Indian Islands, and the Far East.

A fine catalog, particularly for the history, description, etc., of certain regions for which no separate bibliographies exist. Arranged geographically and by subject under each country. Entries are chronological under subject. Includes books, pamphlets, periodical articles, etc. Author index in each volume.

Continued by:

(1) *Subject catalogue of the Royal Colonial Society* (Boston : G. K. Hall, 1971. 7 v. (4477 p.).

Contents: v. 1, British Commonwealth and Europe, Asia in general, Mideast, India; v. 2, Other Asian areas, Africa in general, North Africa; v. 3, West Africa, East Africa; v. 4, Noncommonwealth Africa including former foreign colonies, Republic of South Africa, other southern African countries; v. 5, The Americas; v. 6, Australia, New Zealand, Pacific; v. 7, Biography, voyages and travels, World War I and II.

Supplements the 1930–37 edition of the *Subject catalogue* (above) and the *Biography catalogue* (AH238) "by reproducing all the cards between their publication and March 1971."—*Pref.*

(2) *First supplement* (Boston : G. K. Hall, 1977. 2 v.).

Covers additions to the Library for Mar. 1971–Dec. 1976 and adds a list of periodical holdings, as well as indexing of certain albums and collections of photographs and volumes of engravings.

§ *The manuscript catalogue of the Library of the Royal Commonwealth Society*, ed. by Donald H. Simpson, (London : Mansell, 1975. 199 p.) lists some 600 items. Supplements were published in the Society's *Library notes* Jan./Mar. 1976 and Jan./Mar. 1978.   Z7164.C7R82

Guides to records

Burdett, Anita L. P. Summary guide to the archive and manuscript collections relevant to the former British colonial territories in the United Kingdom for the Joint Copyists Standing Committee of the Commonwealth Archivists' Association. London : Commonwealth Archivists Association, 1988. 97 p.   **DC345**

Intends to provide a "list of all known accessible repositories with relevant collections" (*Introd.*) relating to colonies of the British Empire in libraries or archives in the U.K. Does not inventory the Public Record Office, regimental museums, or repositories in the Republic of Ireland. Excludes materials on Canada, Australia, New Zealand, and Kenya because separate studies for those countries are planned. For each repository gives address, major publications describing the collection, examples of documents held, and other useful details including travel tips and backgound notes on the institution. Intended to update *Guide to manuscript sources for the history of Latin America and the Caribbean* (Oxford : Oxford Univ. Pr., 1973) and Noel Matthews and M. Doreen Wainwright's *Guide to manuscripts and documents in the British Isles relating to Africa* (DD39 *note*). Indexes to repositories and geographical locations.

§ The same organization has issued *Commonwealth sources in British official records : Colonial and Dominion Offices* (1985. 93 p.), describing the relevant classes in Public Record Office, London; Australian National Library; Public Archives Canada; Public Archives Bahamas. Also indicates availability of microfilm.   Z2021.C7B87

Atlases

Atlas of the British Empire / [ed., C.A. Bayly ; contributors, Alan Atkinson ... et al.]. N.Y. : Facts on File, c1989. 256 p. : ill. (some col.); 31 cm.   **DC346**

Also publ.: London : Hamlyn, 1989.

"Organized not only to show the rise and subsequent decline of British dominance but also to analyse and map the evolution of the states and peoples of the modern world as they interacted, traded and fought with the British over 400 years."—*Introd.* Narrative discussion copiously illustrated with maps, photographs of art objects and places, etc. Begins with World politics and trade in the 15th century and ends with The Commonwealth today. Index by topic, place and personal name.

§ See also *Atlas of British overseas expansion*, ed. A.N. Porter (N.Y. : Simon & Schuster ; London : Routledge, 1991. 279 p.), compiled to assist undergraduate teaching. Offers about 140 maps, covers late 15th century to the 1970s–80s, and provides black-and-white maps with explanatory text. Bibliography for reference and further reading; place-name index that includes some topics.   DA16.A8

Regional and local

Anderson, John Parker. The book of British topography : a classified catalogue of the topographical works in the library of the British Museum relating to Great Britain and Ireland. London : Satchell, 1881. 472 p.   **DC347**

Various reprints.

Lists historical works about the places of England, Wales, Scotland, and Ireland, arranged by county and then by place.   Z2023.A54

Gross, Charles. A bibliography of British municipal history. 2nd ed. Leicester : Leicester Univ. Pr., 1966. 461 p.   **DC348**

1st ed., 1897. The "2d ed." is a photographic reprint of the 1897 ed., with only a preface by G. H. Martin added.

A comprehensive bibliography, giving general authorities, including public records, followed by histories of particular towns, p. 150–430.

§ Continued by G. H. Martin and Sylvia McIntyre, *A bibliography of British and Irish municipal history*. ([Leicester] : Leicester Univ. Pr. ; N.Y. : Humanities Pr., 1972. v. 1. [In progress?]).

Z7164.L8G8

Humphreys, Arthur Lee. Handbook to county bibliography : being a bibliography of bibliographies relating to the counties and towns of Great Britain and Ireland. London : Strangeways, 1917. 501 p.   **DC349**

Repr.: London : Dawsons, 1974.

An indispensable record of bibliographies relating to the topography of Great Britain and Ireland, including those published in periodicals and society publications.   Z2001.A1H84

Riden, Philip. Record sources for local history. London : B.T. Batsford, 1987. 253 p.   **DC350**

A "guide to classes of the public records which can be searched reasonably expeditiously and profitably for local studies" (*Pref.*), "setting out what is available, where it is likely to be found and what finding aids exist."—*p. 9*. The chapters follow a chronological arrangement, beginning with the Middle Ages and ending with a discussion of "Local material amongst the modern records of central government." Very helpful for students or beginning researchers. Topical index.

§ Complements W. B. Stephens, *Sources for English local history* (DC351).   Z2023.R53

Stephens, W. B. Sources for English local history. [Rev. & exp. ed.]. Cambridge ; N.Y. : Cambridge Univ. Pr., 1981. 342 p.   **DC351**

1st ed., 1973; reprinted with minor amendments, 1975.

A detailed guide (to both published and unpublished source materials) intended to be of use "to undergraduates reading history, to college of education students, to postgraduate students training for teaching or archive work, to those beginning research for higher degrees, to members of adult education classes, and to teachers at various levels, as well as to the many interested amateurs who wish to pursue seriously the study of their neighbourhood."—*Pref.* An introductory section is followed by chapters on population and social structure; local government and politics; poor relief, charities, prices and wages; industry, trade and communications; agriculture; education; religion. Besides correcting and augmenting various sections, the revised edition adds new information on the use of sources and new material on family history, oral history, and housing. Indexed.

§ A more popularly written guide is *A companion to local history research*, by John Campbell-Kease (London : A & C Black, 1989. 384 p.), which aims to "identify ... the principal material available for the study of local history ... indicate where it may be found ... provide information on a range of related subjects such as archaeology, architecture, place and field names, and palaeography."—*Introd.* Index by names, events, and topics but not to works cited.   Z2023.S8

Victoria history of the counties of England. London : Oxford Univ. Pr., 1901–93. 42 parts : ill. (In progress).   **DC352**

First published by Constable, then by the St. Catherine Press, and later by the Oxford University Press for the University of London, Institute of Historical Research. Many volumes reprinted by Dawsons of Pall Mall.

Of first importance for its large amount of detailed information on the natural history, archaeology, industries, religious houses, political and social history, manorial history, topography, biography, and genealogy of each county. Contains numerous excellent illustrations and maps and many references to sources of information. Indispensable in any library doing much research in English local history.

Contents: *The Victoria history of the counties of England : general introduction*, by Ralph B. Pugh. 1970. *General introduction : supplement 1970–90*, C. R. Elrington. 1990. 67 p. Lists by county the contents of the volumes published since 1970 and indexes by author and title the articles in each volume.

Bedford, ed. by H. A. Doubleday and William Page. 1904–14. 3 v. and index. (Complete).

Berkshire, ed. by P. H. Ditchfield and William Page. 1906–27. 4 v. and index. (Complete).

Buckingham, ed. by William Page. 1905–28. 4 v. and index. (Complete).

Cambridge and the Isle of Ely: v. 1–2, ed. by L. F. Salzman. 1938–48; v. 3, ed. by J. P. C. Roach. 1959; v. 4, ed. by R. B. Pugh. 1953; v. 5, ed. by C. R. Elrington. 1973; v. 6, ed. by A. P. M. Wright. 1978; v. 7, Roman Cambridgeshire, ed. by J. J. Wilkes and C. R. Elrington. 1978; v. 8, ed. by A. P. M. Wright. 1982; v. 9, A. P. M. Wright and C. P. Lewis. 1989; Index to v.1–4.

Chester: v. 1, Physique, prehistory, Roman, Anglo-Saxon and Domesday, B.E. Harris. 1987; v. 2–3, ed. by E. B. Harris. 1979–80.

Cornwall, ed. by William Page. 1906. v. 1; v. 2, pts. 5 and 8 bound with v. 1.

Cumberland, ed. by James Wilson. 1901–1905. v. 1–2.

Derby, ed. by William Page. 1905–1907. v. 1–2.

Devon, ed. by William Page. 1906. v. 1.

Dorset: v. 2, ed. by William Page. 1908; v. 3, ed. by R. B. Pugh. 1968 (includes index to v. 2).

Durham, ed. by William Page. 1905–28. v. 1–3.

Essex: v. 1, ed. by H. A. Doubleday and William Page. 1903; v. 2, ed. by William Page and J. H. Round. 1907; v. 3, with index to v. 1–3, ed. by W. R. Powell. 1963; v. 4–8, ed. by W. R. Powell. 1956–83; Bibliography, ed. by W. R. Powell. 1959. Bibliography supplement, ed. by Frank Sansbury. 1987.

Gloucester: v. 2, ed. by William Page. 1907; v. 4, The City of Gloucester, ed. N. M. Herbert. 1988; v. 6, ed. by G. R. Elrington. 1965; v. 7, ed. by N. M. Herbert. 1981; v. 8, ed. by G. R. Elrington. 1968; v. 10, ed. by G. R. Elrington and N. M. Herbert. 1972; v. 11, ed. by N. M. Herbert. 1976.

Hampshire and the Isle of Wight: v. 1–2, ed. by H. A. Doubleday. 1900–1903; v. 3–5, ed. by William Page. 1908–12; Index. 1914. 5 v. and index. (Complete).

Hereford, ed. by William Page. 1908. v. 1.

Hertford, ed. by William Page. 1902–23. 4 v. and index. (Complete).

Hertfordshire families, ed. by Duncan Warrand. 1907. 325 p. (Complete).

Huntingdon, ed. by William Page. 1926–38. 3 v. and index. (Complete).

Kent, ed. by William Page. 1908–32. v. 1–3.

Lancaster: v. 1–2, ed. by William Page. 1906–1908; v. 3–8, ed. by William Farrar and J. Brownbill. 1907–14. (Complete).

Leicester: v. 1, ed. by William Page. 1907; v. 2–3, ed. by W. G. Hoskins. 1954–55; v. 4, ed. by R. A. McKinley. 1958; v. 5, ed. by J. M. Lee and R. A. McKinley. 1964.

Lincoln, ed. by William Page. 1906. v. 2.

London, ed. by William Page. 1909. v. 1.

Middlesex: v. 1, ed. by J. S. Cockburn, H. P. F. King and K. G. T. McDonnell. 1969; v. 2, ed. by William Page. 1911; v. 3, with index, v. 2–3, ed. by Susan Reynolds. 1962; v. 4, ed. by J. S. Cockburn and T.F.T. Baker. 1971; v. 5–8, ed. by T.F.T. Baker. 1976–85; v. 9, Hampstead and Paddington parishes, ed. by T.F.T. Baker. 1989.

Norfolk: v. 1, ed. by H. A. Doubleday. 1901; v. 2, ed. by William Page. 1906.

Northampton: v. 1–2, ed. by W. Ryland, D. Adkins and R. M. Serjeantson. 1902–1906; v. 3, ed. by William Page. 1930; v. 4, ed. by L. F. Salzman. 1937.

Northamptonshire families, ed. by Oswald Barron. 1906.

Nottingham, ed. by William Page. 1906–10. v. 1–2.

Oxford: v. 1, ed. by L. F. Salzman. 1939; v. 2, ed. by William Page. 1907; v. 3, The University of Oxford, ed. by H. E. Salter and M. D. Lobel. 1957–64; v. 4, The City of Oxford, ed. by Alan Crossley. 1979; v. 5–8, ed. by M. D. Lobel. 1957–64; v. 9, Bloxham Hundred, ed. by M. D. Lobel. 1969; v. 10–11, ed. by Alan Crossley. 1972–83; v. 12, Wooten Hundred (South) including Woodstock, ed. by Alan Crossley. 1990.

Rutland, ed. by William Page. 1908–36. 2 v. and index. (Complete).

Shropshire: v. 1, ed. by William Page. 1908; v. 2 and index to v. 1–2, ed. by A. T. Gaydon. 1973; v. 3, ed. by G. C. Baugh. 1979; v. 4, Agriculture, ed. by G.C. Baugh. 1989; v. 8, ed. by A. T. Gaydon. 1968; v. 11, ed. by G. C. Baugh. 1985.

Somerset: v. 1–2, ed. by William Page. 1906–11; v. 3–6, ed. by R. N. Dunning. 1974–92; Extracts from v. 3 (Huish Episcopi, Langport and Somerton), ed. by R. J. E. Bush and R. W. Dunning. 1983.

Stafford: v. 1, ed. by William Page. 1908; v. 2 and index to v. 1–2, ed. by M. W. Greenslade and J. G. Jenkins. 1967; v. 3, ed. by M. W. Greenslade. 1970; v. 4, Staffordshire Domesday and West Cuttlestone Hundred, ed. by L. M. Midgley. 1958; v. 5, East Cuttlestone Hundred, ed. by L. M. Midgley. 1959; v. 6, ed. by M. W. Greenslade and D. A. Johnson. 1979; v. 8, ed. by J. G. Jenkins. 1963; v. 14, Lichfield, ed. by M.W. Greenslade, 1990; v. 17, ed. by M. W. Greenslade. 1976; v. 20, Seisdon Hundred (part), ed. by M. W. Greenslade. 1984.

Suffolk, ed. by William Page. v. 1, 1911; v. 2, 1907.

Surrey, ed. by H. E. Malden. 1902–14. 4 v. and index. (Complete).

Sussex: v. 1–2, ed. by William Page. 1905–1907; v. 3, ed. by L. F. Salzman, 1935; v. 4, The Rape of Chichester, ed. by L. F. Salzman. 1953; v. 6, pt. 1, Bramber Rape (Southern part), ed. by T. P. Hudson. 1980; v. 6, pt. 2, Bramber Rape (Northwestern part) including Horsham, ed. by T. P. Hudson. 1986; v. 6, pt. 3, Bramber Rape (Northeastern part) including Crawley New Town, ed. by T. P. Hudson. 1987; v. 7, The Rape of Lewes, ed. by L. F. Salzman. 1940; v. 9, The Rape of Hastings, ed. by L. F. Salzman. 1937; Index v. 1–4, 7, 9, ed. by S. M. Keeling and C. P. Lewis. 1984.

Warwick: v. 1, Warwickshire, ed. by H. Arthur Doubleday and William Page. 1904; v. 2, Warwickshire, ed. by William Page. 1908; v. 3, Barlichway Hundred, ed. by L. F. Salzman. 1945; v. 4, Hemlingford Hundred, ed. by L. F. Salzman. 1947; v. 5, Kington Hundred, ed. by L. F. Salzman. 1951; v. 6, Knightlow Hundred, ed. by L. F. Salzman. 1951; Index to v. 1–6. 1955; v. 7, The City of Birmingham, ed. by W. B. Stephens. 1964; v. 8, The City of Coventry and Borough of Warwick, ed. by W. B. Stephens. 1969.

Wiltshire: v. 1, pt. 1, ed. by R. B. Pugh and Elizabeth Crittall. 1955; v. 1, pt. 2, ed. by Elizabeth Crittall. 1973; v. 2–5, ed. by R. B. Pugh and Elizabeth Crittall. 1955–57; v. 6, ed. by Elizabeth Crittall. 1962; v. 7, ed. by R. B. Pugh and Elizabeth Crittall. 1953; v. 8–10, ed. by Elizabeth Crittall. 1965–75; v. 11–12, ed. by D. A. Crowley. 1980–83; v. 13, South-West Wiltshire, D. A. Crowley. 1987; v. 14, ed. by D. A. Crowley. 1991.

Worcester: v. 1, ed. by J. W. Willis-Bund and H. A. Doubleday. 1901; v. 2–4, ed. by J. W. Willis-Bund and William Page. 1906–24; Index. 1926. 4 v. and index. (Complete).

York, ed. by William Page. 1907–25. 3 v. and index. (Complete).

York, East Riding: v. 1, The City of Kingston upon Hull, ed. by K. J. Allison. 1969; v. 2–4, A history of Yorkshire East Riding, ed. by K. J. Allison; v. 5, Holderness : southern part, ed. by K. J. Allison. 1974–84; v. 6, The Borough and Liberties of Beverley, ed. by K. J. Allison. 1989.

York, North Riding, ed. by William Page. 1914–25. 2 v. and index. (Complete).

Yorkshire: the City of York, ed. by P. M. Tillott. 1961. (Complete).

West, John. Town records. [Chichester, Sussex] : Phillimore, [1983]. 366 p., [16] p. of plates : ill.   **DC353**

Serves as a handbook identifying documentary materials available for the study of English towns. All the 375 towns discussed had borough status in 1971. Place-name index.

§ A companion to the author's *Village records* ([2nd ed.] Chichester, Eng. : Phillimore, 1982. 248 p.).

Several pamphlets in the Historical Association's *Helps for students of history* series supplement this work: no.69, *English local history handlist* (4th ed., 1969); no.85, *Local record sources in print and in progress, 1971–72* (1972).   DA690.A1W47

Atlases

Historic towns : maps and plans of towns and cities in the British Isles, with historical commentaries from earliest times to 1800 / gen. ed., M. D. Lobel. [N.Y.] : Oxford Univ. Pr. in conjunction with Historic Towns Trust, 1969–1985. v. 1–3. (In progress).   **DC354**

Contents: v. 1, Banbury, Caernarvon, Glasgow, Gloucester, Hereford, Nottingham, Reading, Salisbury (151 p.); v. 2, Bristol, Cambridge, Coventry, Norwich (various pagings); v. 3, The City of London from prehistoric times to c. 1520 (99 p., [20] p. of plates).

The British atlas of historic towns series is a project of the International Commission for the History of Towns and the British Committee of Historic Towns. Publisher varies; each town also published separately.

"Not facsimiles of early maps, but modern scientific plans which should incorporate data derived from early maps, documents, and material remains."—*Introd.* The base map is "a large-scale plan (1:5000 scale) of each selected town as it was in the first quarter of the 19th century before it had been much affected by the Industrial Revolution and the accompanying rise in population." On this map are imposed features of the medieval town, including medieval street names; it is preceded by maps showing the site within the region, with principal roads. The historical introduction for each town presents "the relevant factors in the story of the town's origin, physical growth or contraction." No index.   G1814.A1H5

Ireland, Northern

Shannon, Michael Owen. Northern Ireland. Oxford, Eng. ; Santa Barbara, Calif. : Clio Pr., c1991. 603 p. (World bibliographical series, 129).   **DC355**

Aims to "list all major published works on Northern Ireland which are readily obtainable."—*Introd.* Covers books, pamphets, government publications and titles of newspapers and periodicals, mostly issued 1920–1990. Those works on the whole of Ireland which have "particular relevance to the North" are included so there is overlap with Shannon's bibliography, *Modern Ireland* (Westport, Conn. : Greenwood ; London : Library Assoc., 1981. 733 p.). Author, title, and subject entries.   Z2043.N6S5

A social science bibliography of Northern Ireland, 1945–1983 : material published since 1945 relating to Northern Ireland since 1921 / comp. by Bill Rolston ... [et al.]. Belfast : Queen's Univ., 1983. 270 p.   **DC356**

A bibliography of books, periodical articles, essays, pamphlets, government publications, and academic theses. The social sciences are broadly interpreted to include history, psychology, and medicosocial material. Classed arrangement; author, subject, and geographic indexes.   Z7165.G82N676

Scotland

Bibliography

Grant, Eric G. Scotland. Oxford ; Santa Barbara, Calif. : Clio, 1982. 408 p. (World bibliographical series, 34).　**DC357**

An annotated bibliography of more than 1,400 books and pamphlets, most published since 1960, on Scottish history and culture. Topically arranged; author/title/subject index.　Z2051.G7

Great Britain. General Register Office (Scotland). Guide to the public records of Scotland deposited in H. M. General Register House, Edinburgh : by M. Livingstone. Edinburgh : General Register House, 1905. 233 p.　**DC358**

Contents: (1) Crown, parliament, revenue, and administration; (2) Judicial records; (3) Titles to land, dignities, and offices; (4) Ecclesiastical and miscellaneous.　CD1072.A3

Haythornthwaite, J. A. Scotland in the nineteenth century : an analytical bibliography of material relating to Scotland in parliamentary papers, 1800–1900 / by J.A. Haythornthwaite ; with the assistance of N.C. Wilson and V.A. Batho. Aldershot, Hants, England : Scolar Pr. ; Brookfield, Vt. : Ashgate Pub. Co., c1993. 360 p.　**DC359**

"A detailed, annotated bibliography (1) of parliamentary papers relating solely to Scotland and (2) of materials concerning Scottish affairs buried in reports pertaining to the whole of the United Kingdom."—*Pref.* Arranged by broad topic (e.g., culture, health and living conditions) with topical subdivisions. For each report, gives title, date, location in parliamentary papers, chairman, brief history and description of the report, and its major recommendation. Appendix for annual reports of government departments which include Scotland. Topical index; index of statutes.　Z2061.H38

Mitchell, Arthur. A contribution to the bibliography of Scottish topography / by the late Sir Arthur Mitchell, K.C.B., and C. G. Cash. Edinburgh : Printed by T. and A. Constable for the Scottish History Society, 1917. 2 v. (Scottish Historical Society. Publications. 2nd series, v.14–15).　**DC360**

Reproduced in microform: La Crosse, Wis. : Northern Micrographics for Brookhaven Press, 1982.

A detailed record of books and periodical articles on Scottish history, life, and culture. Vol. 1 indexes material by place; v. 2, by subject.

§ Continued by: P. D. Hancock, *A bibliography of works relating to Scotland, 1916–1950* (Edinburgh : Univ. Pr., [1959–60]. 2 v.). Follows the arrangement of the original work, with a somewhat more detailed subject classification in the second part.

Stevenson, David. Scottish texts and calendars : an analytical guide to serial publications / David and Wendy B. Stevenson. London : Royal Historical Society ; Edinburgh : Scottish History Society, 1987. 233 p. (Guides and handbooks, no. 14 ; Scottish History Society. 4th ser., 23).　**DC361**

A companion to Edward Mullin's *Texts and calendars* for England and Wales (DC280).

Lists primary sources published in series from 43 private societies in Scotland. Occasional brief annotations. Topical index, but no author or editor index.

§ Updates and partially replaces Charles Sanford Terry, *Catalogue of the publications of Scottish historical and kindred clubs and societies ... 1780–1908* and Cyril Matheson's *Catalogue ... 1908–1927*; see DC362.　DA750.S25

Terry, Charles Sanford. Catalogue of the publications of Scottish historical and kindred clubs and societies and of the volumes relative to Scottish history issued by His Majesty's Stationery Office, 1780–1908, with a subject-index. Glasgow : MacLehose, 1909. 253 p.　**DC362**

Contents: (1) Catalog of the publications of societies, arranged alphabetically, continuing Terry's *Catalogue* from 1908 and referring to pages in Terry for earlier titles; (2) Author and subject index; (3) Index to Terry's *Catalogue*; (4) Index to papers relating to Scotland in Historical Mss. Commission's reports.

§ Continued by: Cyril Matheson, *Catalogue of the publications of Scottish historical and kindred clubs and societies and of the papers relative to Scottish history issued by H. M. Stationery Office, including the reports of the Royal Commission on Historical Mss., 1908–27, with a subject index* (Aberdeen : Milne and Hutchison, 1928. 232 p.).　Z2061.T32

Encyclopedias; Dictionaries

A companion to Scottish culture / ed. by David Daiches. London : Arnold ; N.Y. : Holmes & Meier, 1982. 441 p. : ill., maps.　**DC363**

Offers a "compendium of information about all significant aspects of Scottish culture ... throughout history with articles on both movements, institutions and individuals."—*Pref.* Articles, some quite lengthy, are alphabetically arranged. "Further reading," p.408–18, lists books and periodical articles in topical arrangement. Indexed.

§ See also *Companion to Gaelic Scotland*, ed. Derick S. Thomson (Oxford : Blackwell Reference, 1983. 363 p.).　DA772.C63

Donaldson, Gordon. A dictionary of Scottish history / Gordon Donaldson and Robert S. Morpeth. Edinburgh : John Donald Publ., 1977. 234 p.　**DC364**

A short-entry dictionary stressing events, institutions, titles, and offices, with some biographical and geographical entries. Brief chronology.　DA757.9.D66

Handbooks

Donnachie, Ian L. Companion to Scottish history : from the Reformation to the present / Ian Donnachie and George Hewitt. N.Y. : Facts on File, 1990. 245, 17 p.; maps, charts.　**DC365**

Publ. in U.K. : London : B.J. Batsford, [1989].

Covers people, events, themes, and topics beginning with the 16th century, placing less emphasis on 20th-century Scotland. Copious cross-references; bibliographies follow most articles. Chronology; statistical tables; genealogies; 18 pages of maps.　DA757.9.D68

Sourcebooks

Dickinson, William Crofts. A source book of Scottish history / ed. by William Croft Dickinson, Gordon Donaldson, Isabel A. Milne. 2nd ed., rev. and enl. London : Nelson, 1958–61. 3 v.　**DC366**

Contents: v. 1, From earliest time to 1424; v. 2, 1424 to 1567; v. 3, 1567–1707.

A collection of documents and extracts with commentaries.　DA755.D52

Atlases

An historical atlas of Scotland, c.400–c.1600 / ed. Peter McNeill and Ranald Nicolson; cartographer W. J. Davie. St. Andrews : Atlas Committee of Scottish Medievalists, 1975. 213 p. : maps ; 29 cm.　**DC367**

Offers very clear, black-and-white maps with accompanying text (signed by contributors) and selected bibliography. No index.　G1826.S1H5

Wales

Holt, Constance Wall. Welsh women : an annotated bibliography of women in Wales and women of Welsh descent in America. Metuchen, N.J. : Scarecrow, 1993. 834 p. **DC368**

Attempts to "document the lives and contributions of the women in the histories and cultures of Wales and the United States from prehistory to the present."—*Introd.* Broad topical listing of "books, journal articles, biographies, bibliographies, published speeches, letters, diaries, videorecordings, doctoral dissertations, manuscripts, typescripts and pamphlets … and a few works of fiction and juvenile literature." The 2,179 annotated entries are in English, with Welsh materials cited separately. Book reviews are cited in the annotations; one location is given for each title. Indexes: subject, author and title, periodical title. Cutoff date is end of 1991.   Z7964.G72W345

Huws, Gwilym. Wales / Gwilym Huws, D. Hywel E. Roberts. Oxford, Eng. ; Santa Barbara, Calif. : Clio Pr., c1991. 247 p. (World bibliographical series, v. 122).   **DC369**

An annotated bibliography, mostly in English, of books and journal articles published from mid-1960s to the present. Welsh language materials are mainly in the language and literature section. Author, title, subject indexes.   Z2071.H89

Jones, Philip Henry. A bibliography of the history of Wales / comp. for the History and Law Committee of the University of Wales Board of Celtic Studies, by Philip Henry Jones [microform]. 3rd ed. Cardiff : Univ. of Wales Pr., 1989. 21 microfiches.   **DC370**

1st ed., 1931; 2nd ed., 1962.

This microfiche edition cites 22,000 works in classed arrangement. Does not cover prehistoric or Roman Wales. The accompanying guide includes a list of abbreviations, classification chart, and instructions.

§ See also *Llyfryddiaeth Cymru = A bibliography of Wales* (AA698 *note*) which is a continuation of *Bibliotheca celtica*, 1909–1981/84, 1985/86- . This series includes a listing of works on the Celtic people.   Z2081.W229

Greece

Clogg, Mary Jo. Greece / Mary Jo Clogg, Richard Clogg, compilers. Santa Barbara, Calif. : Clio Pr., 1980. 224 p. (World bibliographical series, 17).   **DC371**

An annotated bibliography of books, essays, and articles on medieval and modern Greece; primarily English-language materials. Not intended for the specialist, but for those "who wish to acquire an informed understanding of the present state of Greece and of the forces that have helped to shape her present society."—*Introd.* Annotations; index of names and subjects.   Z2281.C58

Fleischer, Hagen. Greece in the 1940s : a bibliographic companion / bibliographies by Hagen Fleischer, Steven Bowman. Hanover, N. H. ; London : Univ. Pr. of New England, 1981. 94 p. (Modern Greek Studies Association series, 5).   **DC372**

In two parts: Greece under the Axis occupation : a bibliographical survey, by Fleischer; Jews in wartime Greece: a select annotated bibliography, by Bowman. Both bibliographies cover published and unpublished material in all languages, although most entries are in Greek. There are separate listings for unpublished primary sources, published primary sources, and secondary literature; the latter entries are coded to indicate specific subject matter or source. Most entries are annotated; no index.

§ Companion to *Greece in the 1940s : a nation in crisis.* Both works have been translated into Greek; *Hē Hellada stē dekaetia 1940–50* (Athens : Themelio, 1984).   Z2296.F56

Gennadius Library. Catalogue. Boston : G. K. Hall, 1968. 7 v.   **DC373**

Photoreproduction of the catalog cards for this collection of more than 50,000 volumes concerning "the history and achievement of Greece in its entirety, from earliest antiquity to the present."—*Introd.* The library is affiliated with the American School of Classical Studies in Athens.

————. ———— Supplements 1–2 (Boston : G.K. Hall, 1973–81). The first supplement adds acquisitions of Dec.1968–Feb. 1973, plus revised cataloging of many items in the main catalog. The second supplement reflects cataloging of Mar. 1973–Mar. 1979, together with titles recataloged under the heading "Newspapers and periodicals—Gennadeion Collection" (which constitutes an alphabetical title listing of all the Library's serials).   Z2309.A46

Richter, Heinz A. Greece and Cyprus since 1920 : bibliography of contemporary history = Griechenland und Zypern seit 1920 : Bibliographie zur Zeitgeschichte. Heidelberg : Wissenschaftlicher Verlag Nea Hellas, c1984. 437 p.   **DC374**

History is here defined broadly to include economics, art, education, etc. In three sections: Greece's contemporary history; Greek communism, socialism and trade unionism; Contemporary history of Cyprus. Sections are subdivided by period, then by format; e.g., bibliographies, documents, memoirs and diaries, articles in periodicals. All Western languages are included. Index of personal and corporate names.   Z2300.3.R5

University of Cincinnati. Library. Catalog of the Modern Greek collection. Boston : G. K. Hall, 1978. 5 v.   **DC375**

Reproduction of the catalog cards (in dictionary arrangement) for this outstanding collection. Lists both monographic and serial holdings. The collection was originally devoted to "works of Greek scholars on Ancient Greek authors, history and archaeology" (*Introd.*), but collecting policy was soon extended to encompass works "on Byzantium, Modern Greek literature, linguistics, history, folklore, religion, philosophy, economics and sociology."

An earlier catalog was published 1960.   Z2281.C55

Greenland

See also section DH, Polar regions.

Greenland since 1979 : an annotated, cross-referenced bibliography / ed. by France Benoit. [Ottawa : Circumpolar & Scientific Affairs Directorate, Dept. of Indian Affairs and Northern Development], 1989. 92 p.   **DC376**

A topically arranged bibliography of 1,575 books, government publications, and articles published between 1979 and Jan. 1989, mostly in Danish, French, English, and Greenlandic. All aspects of life in Greenland are covered: culture and language, economic development, housing and settlement policies, transport, etc. Annotations are brief, usually one sentence; about two-thirds of the entries are annotated. At least one location is cited for each title. Good topical index but no author index.

Miller, Kenneth E. Greenland. Oxford, Eng. ; Santa Barbara, Calif. : Clio Pr., c1991. 111 p. (World bibliographical series, v. 125).   **DC377**

A selective, annotated bibliography of 375 books, essays, articles, and government publications with "preference to recently published works but including older ones when they remain among the best sources of information…or when they are of historical interest."—*Introd.* Author/title/subject index.   Z6005.P7M48

Hungary

Bibliography

See also *Widener Library shelflist* (AA115).

Apponyi, Sándor. Hungarica : Ungarn betreffende im Auslande gedruckte Bücher und Flugschriften. München : Rosenthal, 1903–27. 4 v.   **DC378**

Repr.: Nendeln, Liechtenstein : Kraus, 1969.

Contents: Bd.1, 15. und 16. Jahrhundert; Bd.2, 17. und 18. Jahrhundert (bis 1720); Bd.3, Neue Sammlung. I, 15. und 16. Jahrhundert besorgt von L. Dézsi; Bd.4, 17. und 18. Jahrhundert besorgt von L. Dézsi.

Includes works on Hungary in languages other than Hungarian, published both in and outside of Hungary, 1470–1798. Each volume has its own index.

§ For non-Hungarian books on Hungary, *see also* Károly Szabó, *Régi magyar Könyvtár* (AA714), and Károly Mária Kertbeny, *Bibliografie der ungarischin nationalen und internationalen Literatur* (1880. clxxxiv, 760, 14 p.).   Z2141.A65

Banner, János. Bibliographia archaeologica hungarica, 1793–1943. Szeged : Ed. Inst. Archaeologicum Universitatis de Nicolao Horthy, 1944. 558 p. (Fontes rerum archaeologicarum hungaricarum, t.1).   **DC379**

This and *Bibliographia Hungariae : Verzeichnis der 1861–1921 erschienen …* (Berlin : de Gruyter, 1923–29. 4 v.) offer retrospective coverage for Hungarian archaeology. A classified list of current Hungarian literature on archaeology appears annually in the periodical *Archaeológiai ertesitö*, 1949– .

Halász de Beky, I. L. A bibliography of the Hungarian Revolution, 1956. Toronto : Univ. of Toronto Pr., 1963. 179 p.   **DC380**

"Published under the auspices of the Canadian Institute of International Affairs."—*title page.*

A listing of 2,136 items: books and pamphlets, periodical articles, monitored broadcasts, and motion pictures, covering the period Oct. 1956–Dec. 1960. Arranged by language (15 languages).

Continued by: ———. *Supplement, 1956–1965* (Wash., 1967. *In* Francis S. Wagner, *The Hungarian Revolution in perspective*, p. 256–350). A second supplement appeared in the *Canadian review of Hungarian studies*, v. 3, pt. 2 (1976): 195–202.

§ Halász de Beky has also compiled *The medieval Hungarian historians* which is v. 1 of *Hungarian historiography : a bibliography of works in the University of Toronto John P. Robarts Research Library* (1976).   Z2148.A5H3

Kabdebó, Thomas. Hungary. Oxford ; Santa Barbara, Calif. : Clio Pr., 1980. lvi, 280 p. : map. (World bibliographical series, 15).   **DC381**

Lists 1,094 items, almost all in English, providing an introductory survey of Hungarian life. Topical arrangement with author, title, and subject index.   Z2146.K32

Kosáry, Domokos G. Bevezetés a magyar történelem forrásaiba és irodalmába. Budapest : Közoktatásügyi Kiadóvállalat, 1951–58. 3 v.   **DC382**

At head of title: A Magyar Tudományos Akadémia Történettudományi Intézet.

Publisher varies.

Contents: v. 1, [to 1711] (1951); v. 2, 1711–1824 (1954); v. 3, Supplement and index (1958).

A bibliographical guide to Hungarian history. Includes chapters on general materials and guides to archives, with specific chapters by locality and period. International in scope; textual annotations.

The first volume (*Áalános rísz I–II*) has appeared in a revised edition (Budapest : Tankönyvkiadó, 1970).   DB921.5.K6

Magyar Tudományos Akadémia. Történettudományi Intézet. Magyar történeti bibliográfia, 1825–1867 : szerkesztette a Töténettudományi Intézet Munkaközössége / I. Tóth Zoltán vezetésével. Budapest : Akadémiai Kiadö, 1950–59. 4 v.   **DC383**

Contents: v. 1, General works (1950. 118 p.); v. 2, Economics (1952. 260 p.); v. 3, Politics and ideology (1950. 407 p.); v. 4, History of non-Hungarian people (1959. 675 p.).

Classified arrangement. Imprints as late as 1948 are included; monographs and periodical and newspaper articles, in various languages, are covered. As yet, no author index.

§ Continued by: *A magyar történettudomány válogatott bibliográfiája, 1945–1968* (Budapest : Akadémiai Kiadö, 1971. 855 p.) Similar arrangement, with index by personal and place names. Lists books and articles published in Hungary for the period indicated, plus some articles about countries outside Hungary. Annotated.

An additional series, for the years 1867–1945, was planned.   Z2146.M3

Miska, John P. Canadian studies on Hungarians, 1886–1986 : an annotated bibliography of primary and secondary sources. Regina, Sask. : Canadian Plains Research Center, Univ. of Regina, 1987. 245 p. (Canadian plains bibliography, 1).   **DC384**

Monographs, periodicals and newspapers, theses, book reviews, and research papers, topically arranged in two sections: (1) Writings about Hungary and the Magyars; (2) Writings by and about Hungarian Canadians (the larger portion). Includes brief descriptions of archival collections of Hungarian material. Author/title/subject index.

§ A supplement appeared in *Canlit bibliographic series*, no. 6 (Ottawa : Microforms Biblos, 1992. 80 p.).   Z1395.H94M57

Telek, J. History of Hungary and the Hungarians, 1848–1971 : a select bibliography. Toronto : [Pannonia Books, 1972–78]. 2 v. (Hungarian historical studies, 1, 3).   **DC385**

Repr. with additions and corrections, 1980–81.

Vol. 2 has title: History of Hungary and the Hungarians, 1848–1977.

Based on the collections of the University of Toronto Library, the Library of Congress, and the British Library. Topical arrangement; index of names and serials.   Z2148.A5T44

Manuscripts; Archives

Guide to the archives of Hungary / [ed. by Péter Balázs]. Budapest : Archival Board, Ministry of Culture, 1976. 229 p., [7] leaves of plates : 7 ill.   **DC386**

Extensive descriptions of about 65 archives, giving general statements about major collections, rules of access, and address, and citing printed guides. The Magyar Országos Levéltár and the Új Magyar Központi Levéltár are treated first, followed by the regional archives and special archives (including church archives) in alphabetical order. Not indexed.   CD1170.G84

Kurucz, György. Guide to documents and manuscripts in Great Britain relating to the Kingdom of Hungary from the earliest times to 1800. N.Y. : Mansell, 1992. 708 p.   **DC387**

Intended to identify, "itemize and describe the contents of the most important documents and in particular those in the Public Record Office."—*Pref.* Libraries are arranged alphabetically by city; for each library or collection gives brief description of each manuscript or class, noting published and unpublished finding aids. Index of personal and place names.   CD1048.H9K87

Handbooks

Erdei, Ferenc. Information Hungary. Budapest : Akadémiai Kiadó, 1968. 1144p. : il. (Countries of the world information series, v.2).   **DC388**

"The organization and compilation of this work was undertaken
... by an editorial committee appointed by the Hungarian Academy of
Sciences. ... This is the Hungarian view of Hungary."—*Pref.*

Could still be useful because of the attitude of the contributors in
the 1960s. DB906.E7

Historiography

Guide to research and scholarship in Hungary / ed. by
Márton Tolnai, Péter Vas-Zoltán ; [trans. by Barbara
Harasztos ; English text ed. by Gloria Deák]. Budapest :
Akadémiai Kiadó ; Bloomington : Distr. by Indiana Univ. Pr.,
c1988. 2 v. (1127 p.). **DC389**

At head of title: International Research and Exchanges Board/
American Council of Learned Societies—Hungarian Academy of Sciences, Commission on the Humanities and Social Sciences.

The history and present state (as of 1985/86) of Hungarian scholarly research is reviewed in two sections: (1) a series of ten signed essays on the development of individual areas of Hungarian scholarship,
including philosophy, language, history, medicine, science, and technology; and (2) a directory of research institutions in Hungary, including the Hungarian Academy of Sciences, university and college departments and institutes, industrial research units, museums, archives, and
libraries. Entries list name, address, telephone, principal scientists and
staff, recent publications, and research programs. Alphabetic index by
research unit.

§ For a state-of-the-art survey of historical research in Hungary,
see *Études historiques hongroises 1990*, ed. Ferenc Glatz (Budapest :
Inst. of History, 1990. 7 v.). Vol. 7 is a Selected bibliography of Hungarian historical science 1985–89. Q180.H8G85

Iceland

See also section for Scandinavia.

Hill, Dennis Auburn. Icelandic libraries and archives : a selective guide for researchers. Madison, Wis. : Dept. of Scandinavian Studies, Univ. of Wisconsin-Madison, 1988. 34 p. : ill.
DC390

Following the format of Erwin Welsch's compilations on libraries
in France and Germany (AK139, AK136), describes 11 major libraries
and archives, giving for each: address, hours, holdings, specialization,
terms of access, catalogs, publications, photocopying facilities. Not indexed. Z823.R49H55

Horton, John J. Iceland. Santa Barbara, Calif. : Clio Pr.,
1983. 346 p. (World bibliographical series, 37). **DC391**

A classified, annotated bibliography of English-language materials relating to Iceland. 960 items, plus references to many additional titles in the annotations. Index of authors, titles and subjects.
Z2590.A3H67

Ireland

Bibliography

Asplin, P. W. A. Medieval Ireland c.1170–1495 : a bibliography of secondary works. Dublin : Royal Irish Academy, 1971.
139 p. (A new history of Ireland. Ancillary publications, 1).
DC392

Classed bibliography of more than 700 items. Many annotations;
general index.

§ For information on the Ancillary publications series, *see*
DC411. Z2041.A85

Brady, Anna. Women in Ireland : an annotated bibliography.
N.Y. : Greenwood, 1988. 478 p. (Bibliographies and indexes
in women's studies, no. 6). **DC393**

For annotation, *see* CC591. Z7964.I73B7

Hayes, Richard J. Sources for the history of Irish civilisation : articles in Irish periodicals. Boston : G. K. Hall, 1970.
9 v. **DC394**

Contents: v. 1–5, Persons; v. 6–8, Subjects; v. 9, Places-Dates.

"Catalog of all articles, poems and reviews ... in the periodicals
published in Ireland, which contained material likely to be of value for
research into every aspect of the intellectual life and cultural activities
of the country" (*Introd*), 1800–1969. Popular and news periodicals and
trade journals are not included. Indexed in four ways: (1) persons, institutions, societies, titles, (2) subjects (with list of headings at beginning of v. 5, (3) places in Ireland (places outside Ireland are in the subject volumes), (4) dates in chronological order. For each entry gives
author, title, journal, volume, date and pages. Z2034.H35

Kenney, James Francis. Sources for the early history of Ireland : ecclesiastical : an introduction and guide. N.Y. : Columbia Univ. Pr., 1929. 807 p. (Records of civilization: sources
and studies, v.11). **DC395**

Repr.: N.Y. : Octagon Books, 1966; Dublin : P. O'Tailluir, 1979.

Cover title: The early history of Ireland : ecclesiastical. Designated as v. 1; no more published.

An introduction and guide to the manuscript and printed sources
for the ecclesiastical history of Ireland up to the 12th century. Gives
detailed analysis of 659 manuscript sources with bibliographic references for each. Z2041.K362

Maguire, Maria. A bibliography of published works on Irish
foreign relations, 1921–1978. Dublin : Royal Irish Academy,
1981. 136 p. **DC396**

About 1,300 items—books, articles, pamphlets, government publications, and doctoral dissertations—in classed arrangement, with author index. Z6465.I73M33

National Library of Ireland. Bibliography of Irish history /
by James Carty. Dublin : Publ. for the Dept. of Education by
the Stationery Office, 1936–1940. 2 v. **DC397**

Contents: [v. 1], 1912–1921 (1936); [v. 2], 1870–1911 (1940).

Lists books and periodical articles on the history of Ireland during
these periods. Classified arrangement; author index. Z2041.D8

Shannon, Michael Owen. Irish Republic. Oxford ; Santa Barbara, Calif. : Clio Pr., c1986. 404 p. (World bibliographical series, v. 69). **DC398**

A "sampling of some of the better or more popular general works
on Ireland" (*Introd.*) after 1922. 1,459 books and a few articles published through 1985 are topically arranged. Author/title/subject index.

§ *See also* another work by Shannon, *Modern Ireland : a bibliog-
raphy on politics, planning, research, and development* (Westport,
Conn. : Greenwood ; London : Library Assoc., 1981. 733 p.).
Z2031.S53

Writings on Irish history. 1984– . Dublin : Irish Committee
of Historical Sciences, 1986– . Annual. **DC399**

Comp. by Clara Cullen and Monica Henchy, 1986– .

Classified by chronological period following the order of the *New
history of Ireland* (DC413). Includes books, essays, and periodical articles; if a work relates to two periods, it is cited twice. Excludes works
of reference, newspaper articles and parliamentary publications. Author index. The latest received covers 1987, publ. 1991.

Continues: *Writings on Irish history* for 1936–1978, which was
part of the journal *Irish historical studies*; arranged by author. This
was continued by *Writings on Irish history* 1979–1983, which follows
the same arrangement. Issued in microfiche by the Irish Committee of
Historical Sciences. The 1984 edition of the current publication incorporated addenda from 1973–1984.

§ A "Select bibliography of writings on Irish economic and social history" appears annually in *Irish economic and social history* (v. 1 [1974]–) with coverage of books, essays, articles, and conference proceedings beginning with 1973. Author arrangement. Z2041W75

Library resources (including archives)

Directory of Irish archives / ed. by Seamus Helferty & Raymond Refaussé. 2nd ed. [Dublin] : Irish Academic Pr., 1993. 154 p. **DC400**

1st ed., 1988.

Covers both the Republic and Northern Ireland libraries and archives. Arranged alphabetically by name; for each gives address, phone, hours, person to whom to direct inquiries, facilities, brief descriptions of major collections. Index by name and broad subject. This edition has added 74 new archives (particularly in the area of religious institutions) to the 155 in the original publication. CD1101.D57

Ireland. Public Record Office. The public record : sources for local studies in the Public Record Office of Ireland / [comp. by S.J. Connolly]. [Dublin] : Co-ordinating Committee for Educational Services Based on the Institutions of Science and Art, 1982. 48 p. : ill. **DC401**

A brief guide to using both the Public Record Office and the State Paper Office in Dublin. Arranged by type of record; e.g., parish records, census returns. No index.

§ For earler periods the guide by Herbert Wood, *A guide to the records deposited in the Public Record Office of Ireland* (Dublin : Stat. Office, 1919. 334 p.) is still useful. Z2043.A1I73

Lester, DeeGee. Irish research : a guide to collections in North America, Ireland, and Great Britain. N.Y. : Greenwood, 1987. 348 p. (Bibliographies and indexes in world history, no. 9). **DC402**

A companion to Jack W. Weaver and DeeGee Lester's *Immigrants from Great Britain and Ireland* (CC332). Covers all aspects of Irish life in the U.K., U.S., Canada, Northern Ireland, and Eire by describing book collections of university and college libraries and publishing efforts of organizations. Based on responses to a questionnaire. Entries, arranged alphabetically under geographic headings, describe the institution and its library, giving for the latter contents, access, special services, address, and telephone. Organization and subject index. Appendixes: Bookstores and bookdealers; Irish local newspapers.

§ Overlaps somewhat with Susan Eleuterio-Comer's *Irish American material culture: a directory of collections, sites, and festivals in the United States and Canada* (N.Y. : Greenwood, 1988. 107 p.), since both include publications, but Eleuterio-Comer concentrates on the U.S. and focuses more fully on festivals, historic sites, objects, and audio and video tapes. Z2031.L47

National Library of Ireland. Manuscript sources for the history of Irish civilisation / Richard J. Hayes, ed. Boston : G. K. Hall, 1965. 11 v. **DC403**

Contents: v. 1–4, Persons; v. 5–6, Subjects; v. 7–8, Places; v. 9–10, Dates; v. 11, Lists of manuscripts.

An inventory of manuscript materials relating to Irish civilization and history from the 5th to the 20th centuries as found in 678 libraries and archives in 30 countries and in more than 600 private collections. Gives brief description, location (if not in the National Library of Ireland), and source if printed. Separate list of Gaelic manuscripts in v. 11.

———. ———. *First supplement, 1965–1975* (Boston : G. K. Hall, 1979. 3 v.). Covers materials "newly added to the collections of the National Library ... and other repositories, or newly noted, in the period 1965–1975; the volumes also include itemised treatment of some materials dealt with in summary form in 1965 and make good some earlier omissions."—*Introd.*

§ The Irish Manuscript Commission's *Catalogue of publications issued and in preparation 1928–1966* (Dublin, 1966. 79 p.) offers an annotated list of the Commission's publications, some of which describe manuscript publications or, in some cases, publishes them. Z2041.D85

Prochaska, Alice. Irish history from 1700 : a guide to sources in the Public Record Office. [London] : British Records Association, 1986. 96 p. (Archives and the user, no. 6). **DC404**

Offers brief descriptions of record classes, arranged by Public Record Office number, in two main sections: Summary of classes of public records 1750–1950 which contain material of relevance to Irish history; Classes of records related entirely to Irish affairs. Indexed by subject and agency. Z2041.P76

Encyclopedias; Dictionaries

Flanagan, Laurence. A dictionary of Irish archaeology. Savage, Md. : Barnes & Noble Books, 1992. 221 p. : ill. **DC405**

Covers from the Mesolithic period to the end of medieval times, providing definitions and descriptions of artifacts and sites. References to fuller studies at end of the articles; line drawings. No cross-references; not indexed. DA920.F57

Hickey, D. J. A dictionary of Irish history since 1800 / D. J. Hickey, J. E. Doherty. [Dublin] : Gill and Macmillan ; Totowa, N.J. : Barnes & Noble, 1980. 615 p. **DC406**

A dictionary of brief articles covering both Irelands since 1800 (the year of the Act of Union), with history broadly interpreted to include articles on the arts, literature, folk customs, religion, and economics as well as political and military affairs. Cross-references, but no index; no bibliographies. DA949.7.H53

Ireland : a cultural encyclopaedia / gen. ed., Brian de Breffny. London : Thames and Hudson ; N.Y. : Facts on File, 1983. 256 p. ; ill. **DC407**

"Culture" is here broadly interpreted "to mean the aesthetic endeavor of a people and the manifestation of their intellectual, artistic and even social development."—*Introd.* Offers brief, signed articles on persons, places, terms and objects relating to language, literature, fine arts, architecture, decorative arts, music, theater, applied arts, etc. Some bibliographic references. NX546.A1I73

Newman, P. R. Companion to Irish history, 1603–1921 : from the submission of Tyrone to partition. Oxford [England] ; N.Y. : Facts On File, c1991. 244 p. : maps. **DC408**

Dictionary arrangement of articles relating to institutions, events, movements, organizations and individuals. Includes a chronology and lists of viceroys, deputies, and chief secretaries in Ireland. DA912.N485

Quotations

O'Clery, Conor. The dictionary of political quotations on Ireland, 1886–1987 : phrases make history here. Boston : G.K. Hall, [1987]. 232 p. **DC409**

Publ. in Ireland as: *Phrases make history here : a century of Irish political quotations, 1886–1986* (Dublin : O'Brien Pr., 1986. 229 p.).

A chronological arrangement of "telling phrases ... touching on the great issues and arguments of the day, the political and social preoccupations and passing distractions."—*Introd.* Notes with each quotation identify the speaker, date, and situation in which the statement was made. Introductory chapters discuss key issues and outline important political developments. Indexes of speakers and subjects. DA959.O25

Handbooks

Edwards, R. Dudley. Sources for early modern Irish history, 1534–1641 / R.W. Dudley Edwards and Mary O'Dowd. Cambridge ; N.Y. : Cambridge Univ. Pr., 1985. 222 p.   **DC410**

Guide to using written sources (e.g., administrative records, civil and ecclesiastical, central and local, English and foreign) in research on Ireland 1534–1641. Includes chapters on historiography, contemporary maps and drawings, and archival collections. Topical index.

DA905.E38

A new history of Ireland. Ancillary publications. Dublin : Royal Irish Academy, 1971–1992. no. 1–5. (In progress).   **DC411**

Contents: no. 1, Medieval Ireland c.1170–1495, P. W. A. Asplin (DC392); no. 2, Irish historical statistics : population, 1821–1971, W. E. Vaughan and A. J. Fitzpatrick (CG253); no. 3, Giraldus Cambrensis. Expugnatis hibernica/The conquest of Ireland, ed. A. B. Scott and F. X. Martin. 1978; no. 4, Parliamentary election results in Ireland, 1801–1922, Brian M. Walker. 1978 (CJ379): no. 5, Parliamentary election results in Ireland, 1918–92 : Irish elections to parliaments and parliamentary assemblies at Westminister, Belfast, Dublin, Strasbourg, ed. by Brian M. Walker. 1992 (CJ379 *note*).

Chronology

Doherty, J. E. A chronology of Irish history since 1500 / J. E. Doherty, D. J. Hickey. Savage, Md. : Barnes & Noble, 1990. 395 p.   **DC412**

Publ. in Ireland : [Dublin] : Gill and Macmillan, [1989].

A companion to the same authors' *A dictionary of Irish history since 1800* (DC406).

Although coverage begins with 1500, the emphasis is on the 19th and 20th centuries to Nov. 30, 1988. History is interpreted broadly to include religious, social, cultural and sporting events as well as military and political affairs. Extensive subject index.   DA910.D66

General histories

A new history of Ireland / ed. by T. W. Moody, F. X. Martin, F. J. Byrne. Oxford : Clarendon Pr. ; N.Y. : Oxford Univ. Pr., 1976–1993. v. 2–5[1], 8–9 : ill. (In progress).   **DC413**

Comp. under the auspices of the Royal Irish Academy.

Contents: v. 2, Medieval Ireland, 1169–1534; v. 3, Early modern Ireland, 1534–1691; v. 4, Eighteenth century Ireland, 1691–1800; v. 5, pt. 1, Ireland under the Union, 1801–70; v. 8, A chronology of Irish history to 1976 (A companion to Irish history, v. 1); v. 9, Maps, genealogies, lists (A companion to Irish history, v. 2).

Planned for 10 volumes. Other volumes are to cover: v. 1, Prehistoric and early medieval Ireland; v. 6, Ireland under the union, II (1870–1921); v. 7, Ireland since 1921; v. 10, Illustrations, statistics, bibliography, documents.

§ For information on the Ancillary publications series, *see* DC411.   DA912.N48

Historiography

Moody, T. W. Irish historiography, 1936–70. Dublin : Irish Committee of Historical Sciences, 1971. 155 p.   **DC414**

A revision and updating of a series entitled "Thirty years' work in Irish history" which appeared in *Irish historical studies,* 1967–69. Offers surveys by various scholars of work done in any English-speaking country on Irish history during the period indicated.

Continued by *Irish historiography, 1970–79,* ed. by Joseph Lee (Cork : Cork Univ. Pr., 1981. 238 p.). Covers chronological periods, economic history, and ecclesiastical history. Not indexed.

Z2041.M65

Sourcebooks

Irish historical documents since 1800 / ed. by Alan O'Day and John Stevenson. N.Y. : Barnes and Noble, c1992. 252 p. : maps.   **DC415**

142 documents focus on political life but also include economic, social, intellectual, and religious matters. Documents include polls, tables, newspaper articles, and radio broadcasts as well as official reports. Most are excerpted, with source cited in an appendix. In eight chronological periods, with brief introduction for each section. Not indexed.   DA950.I69

Atlases

Edwards, Ruth Dudley. An atlas of Irish history. 2nd ed. London ; N.Y. : Methuen, 1981. 286 p. : maps ; 24 cm.   **DC416**

Repr.: London ; New York : Routledge, 1989.

1st ed., 1973.

Primarily concerned with social and political developments and characteristics of the Irish people. Includes a section on the Irish abroad.   G1831.S1E3

Italy

Bibliography

See also *Widener Library shelflist* (AA115).

Antonini, Rosalba. Bibliografia dell'Italia antica : epigrafia, linguistica e scienze ausiliarie, 1950–1984 / R. Antonini, L. Del Tutto Palma, S. Renzetti Marra. Urbino : Università degli studi di Urbino, 1985. 2 v. (Quaderni dell'Istituto di linguistica dell'Università degli studi di Urbino, 3).   **DC417**

T. 1 is a bibliography of general works: periodicals, catalogs, festschriften, guides to museums. T. 2, Epigrafia—linguistica, archeologia, storia, bibliografia, offers subject listings subdivided by geographical area. The arrangement within each section is chronological by date of publication, then by author. 9,400 articles, reviews, monographs and essays are cited. Indexes of authors and reviewers at end of t. 1 cover both volumes.   Z2357.A58

Bibliografia italiana di storia e studi militari, 1960–1984. Milano : F. Angeli, c1987. 580 p.   **DC418**

2,905 books, articles, essays, chapters, with one-sentence annotations. Covers the history of the military in Italy, 19th–20th centuries. Personal and place name index; subject index with broad topics divided by periods. The subject headings used are included with each entry.   Z2361.M5B53

Cassels, Alan. Italian foreign policy, 1918–1945 : a guide to research and research materials. Rev. ed. Wilmington, Del. : Scholarly Resources, 1991. 261 p.   **DC419**

1st ed., 1981.

Introductory chapters that discuss how foreign policy was made in Italy are followed by listings with descriptions of international archives, libraries, research institutes, and newspaper collections. The remainder of the volume is an annotated bibliography, topically arranged.

The revised edition features expanded coverage of the Archivio Storico del Ministerio degli Affari Esteri and the addition of several more repositories. Older works have been dropped from the bibliography, especially those published more than 25 years ago, or articles expanded into book-length studies if the book is included. Name index to the bibliography (which has grown to 993 entries). Z6465.I8C37

Coppa, Frank J. Modern Italian history : an annotated bibliography / comp. by Frank J. Coppa and William Roberts. N.Y. : Greenwood, c1990. 226 p. : ill. (Bibliographies and indexes in world history, no. 18). **DC420**

Books, journals, and dissertations in English and Italian are arranged under seven headings: (1) General and reference works; (2) Monographic studies encompassing more than one period; (3) Eighteenth century, 1700–1796; (4) Risorgimento, 1796–1861; (5) Liberal Italy, 1861–1922; (6) Fascist Italy, 1922–1945; (7) Italian republic, 1945 to the present. Annotations are succinct but capture the scope of contents. Author and subject indexes.

§ Intended as a companion to *Dictionary of modern Italian history* (DC431), ed. by Coppa. Z2358.C67

D'Andrea, Anna. Il secondo dopoguerra in Italia, 1945–1960 : proposte per una bibliografia ragionata. [Cosenza : Edizioni Pellegrini, 1977]. 229 p. (Collana interventi, 2). **DC421**

A classed bibliography of the socioeconomic and political history of the post–World War II period in Italy. In two main sections: (1) Gli anni 1945–1950: ricostruzione democratica o restaurazione capitalistica? (2) Gli anni cinquanta: espansione economica e sue contraddizioni. Items are listed chronologically within subsections; index of names. Z7165.I8D35

Evola, Niccoló Domenico. Origini e dottrina del fascismo. Firenze : Sansoni, 1935. 166 p. (Guide bibliografiche dell' Istituto Nazionale Fascista di Cultura., I). **DC422**

Repr.: N.Y. : AMS, 1975.

A bibliography of books and periodical articles on the origin and development of fascism in its political, legal, economic, and social aspects. Still useful for materials contemporary to the period. Z2361.F2E8

Fay, George Emory. A bibliography of Etruscan culture and archaeology, 1498–1981. Greeley, Colo. : Univ. of Northern Colo., 1981. 2 v. (Occasional publications in classical studies, monograph no.1). **DC423**

An author listing of books, articles, and parts of books on archeological and linguistic studies of Etruscan culture.

Pine-Coffin, R. S. Bibliography of British and American travel in Italy to 1860. Florence : Olschki, 1974. 371 p. (Biblioteca di bibliografia italiana, 76). **DC424**

British and American works are listed in separate chronological sections. Brief annotations. Indexes of (1) persons; (2) anonymous titles; (3) places; (4) publishers, printers and booksellers. Z2356.P55

Current

Bibliografia storica nazionale / Giunta centrale per gli studi storici. 1939 (1)– . Bari : Laterza, 1942– . Annual. **DC425**

Publisher varies; some years combined.

A classified record of books and periodical articles, published in Italy about Italy. Name index. In many cases indicates location of reviews. Follows the general form of the *International bibliography of historical sciences* (DA12). Z6201.B54

Periodicals

Istituto Nazionale per la Storia del Movimento di Liberazione in Italia. Catalogo della stampa periodica della Biblioteche dell' Istituto Nazionale per la Storia del Movimento di Liberazione in Italia e degli Istituti associati, 1900/1975 / a cura di Francesca Ferratini Tosi … [et al.]. Milano : [The Institute], 1977. 374 p. **DC426**

A catalog of periodicals relating to antifascism and the Italian resistance. Locates files in some 23 Italian libraries.

§ The Istituto also published *Guida agli archivi della resistenze*, comp. by Gaetano Grassi (Rome : Ministero per i beni culturali e ambientali, 1983. 974 p.).

For periodicals published in Italian during World War I, see *Periodici italiani 1914–1919*, ed. by Maria Lucia Cavallo and Ettore Tanzarella based on the collection at the Biblioteca di Storia Moderna e Contemporanea (Roma : La Biblioteca, 1989. 209 p.). Includes titles published outside Italy but in Italian—e.g., in Kansas City, Peru, Paris. Index by sponsoring body and by place. Z6945.I75

Manuscripts; Archives

Bibliografia dell'Archivio centrale dello Stato, 1953–1978 / a cura di Sandro Carocci … [et al.] ; coordinamento di Maura Piccialuti Caprioli. Roma : Ministero per i beni culturali e ambientali : Distribuzione e vendita, Istituto poligrafico e zecca dello Stato Libreria dello Stato, 1986. 457 p. (Pubblicazioni degli archivi di Stato. Sussidi, 1). **DC427**

A bibliography of monographs, articles, biographies, editions, etc., whose authors made use of documents in the state archives. Arrangement is alphabetical; each entry gives complete bibliographic information for the published work and a list of documents used in the Archivio. Pt. 1 covers 1953–68 and is an expanded version of Costanzo Casucci's "Saggio di bibliografia dell'Archivio Centrale dello Stato (1953–1968)," *Rassegna degli Archivi di Stato* 31 (1971): 335–96. Pt. 2 adds publications for the 1969–78 period. About 80% of the journals covered are Italian, the rest English, German, and French. Indexes of documents, subjects, and year of publication.

§ A supplement appeared in 1992. *Bibliografia. le fonti documentarie nelle pubblicazioni dal 1979 al 1985* (542 p.). Z2360.B33

Dolci, Fabrizio. L'associazionismo operaio in Italia (1870–1900) nelle raccolte della Biblioteca nazionale centrale di Firenze : catalogo / a cura di Fabrizio Dolci … [et al.]. Firenze : Giunta Regionale Toscana : La Nuova Italia, 1980. 506 p. : facsims., plates. (Inventari e cataloghi toscani, 5). **DC428**

An extensive catalog of the papers of labor organizations (unions, clubs, societies, etc.) held by the Biblioteca Nazionale in Florence, with very brief annotations. Arranged by geographic area; indexed by subject (e.g., decorative arts, metals) and by province; list of printers by city. Z7164.T7D64

Guida generale degli archivi di Stato italiani / direttori, Piero D'Angiolini, Claudio Pavone. Roma : Ministero per i beni culturali e ambientali, Ufficio centrale per i beni archivistici, 1981–86. v. 1–3. (In progress?). **DC429**

For annotation, *see* AK150. CD1424.G84

Encyclopedias; Dictionaries

A concise encyclopaedia of the Italian Renaissance / ed. by J. R. Hale. N.Y. : Oxford Univ. Pr. ; London : Thames and Hudson, 1981. 360 p. : ill. **DC430**

Offers brief signed articles on the people, institutions, events, etc., of Renaissance Italy. "It is designed to answer questions about what went on but also to suggest what it might have been like to have lived then."—*[p.5]* A subject index lists the entries topically. Bibliographies.   DG445.C66

Dictionary of modern Italian history / Frank J. Coppa, ed. in chief. Westport, Conn. : Greenwood, 1985. 496 p.   **DC431**

A dictionary arrangement of brief articles covering Italian political, economic, cultural, social, and religious life from the 18th century to the present. Many entries include at least one bibliographic reference; an appendix gives chronologies and lists of political and religious leaders. Indexed.

§ Companion to *Modern Italian history : an annotated bibliography*, ed. by Coppa and William Roberts (DC420).   DG545.D53

Enciclopedia dell'antifascismo e della Resistenza .... Milan : La pietra, 1968–c1989. 6 v. : ill.   **DC432**

Concerned primarily with people and events important to Italian history of the period 1919–45, but including many articles on a wide range of related figures and topics. A one-vol. appendix was issued in 1971; v. 6 includes an appendix of 400 articles (p. 473–573) but does not duplicate the articles published in the 1971 volume. A list of authors with titles of the articles each wrote appears at the end of v. 6.

DG571.A2E5

Historical dictionary of fascist Italy / Philip V. Cannistraro, ed. in chief. Westport, Conn. : Greenwood, [1982]. 657 p. : maps.   **DC433**

Concentrates on "the Italian variety of fascism" (*Pref.*), offering signed articles—some of considerable length—on individuals, organizations, events and movements, terms, etc. Sources of further information are cited; useful appendixes; index.   DG571.A1H57

Latvia

See also section for Baltic States.

Caune, Andris. Latvijas PSR arheologija, 1940–1974 : literatūras rādītājs / A. Caune, C. Caune. Rīgā : Vila Lācā Latvijas PSR Valsts Bibliotēka, 1976. 290 p.   **DC434**

Added title page, table of contents, introduction and chapter/section headings in Russian and German.

Topical arrangement of books and articles published mainly in Latvia and Russia (with a few German titles) during the 1940–Jan. 1975 period and concerned with archaeology in Latvia. Person, place, and subject indexes.   Z2535.C36

Enciklopēdiskā vārdnīca : 2 sējumos / [galvenais redaktors A. Vilks]. Rīga : Latvijas enciklopēdiju redakcija, 1991. 2 v. : ill. (some col.).   **DC435**

General encyclopedia, with strongest emphasis on Latvia. Short entries, good for identification, verification, etc. Appendix for economic statistics up to 1989, deputies in 1991, etc. No index.

AG35.5.E53

Latvijas PSR mazā enciklopēdija / [Galvenais redaktors V. Samsons]. Riga : Izdevnieciba "Zinātne", 1967–72. 3 v.

   DC436

Concerned with Latvian culture and affairs. Many biographical sketches. Most articles are signed; some carry bibliographies.

A 1972 supplement, *Personu un prieksmetu alfabetiskais rādiltājs*, indexes the main work.   AE57.L34

Ozols, Selma Aleksandra. Latvia : a selected bibliography. Wash. : K. Karusa, 1963. 144 p.   **DC437**

Issued also as a thesis, Catholic University of America, 1958.

Classed arrangement with author-title index. Includes publications to 1957 only. Locates copies.   Z2535.O9

Liechtenstein

Meier, Regula A. Liechtenstein. Oxford ; Santa Barbara, Calif. : Clio Pr., c1993. 123 p. (World bibliographical series, v. 159.).   **DC438**

Some 267 entries in English and German in a topical arrangement. Books and some articles; author, title, subject index.

DB886.M45

The Principality of Liechtenstein : a documentary handbook / ed. by Walter Kranz ; [tr. from the German by J. A. Nicholls]. 5th rev. & enl. ed. [Vaduz, Liechtenstein] : Press and Information Office of the Govt. of the Principality of Liechtenstein, 1981. 302 p. : ill.   **DC439**

Translation of *Fürstentum Liechtenstein*.

Brief essays by various authors survey "the history of the Principality and the Princely House, the State with its legal, social and fiscal institutions, culture and folklore, ... economy and the educational system."—*Foreword*.   DB886.F8713

Roeckle, Heidi. Liechtensteinische Bibliographie 1960–1973. Vaduz : Liechtensteinische Landesbibliothek, 1979. 278 p.

   DC440

Classed arrangement of some 1,840 citations to books, maps and plans, articles, and journals dealing with any subject area relating to Liechtenstein; materials are primarily those published in Liechtenstein. Name and keyword indexes.

§ Continued by: *Liechtensteinische Bibliographie* (AA740).

Z2820.R63

Lithuania

See also section for Baltic States.

Encyclopedia Lituanica / [ed. by Simas Sužiedėlis]. Boston : [Juozas Kapočius], 1970–78. 6 v. : ill.   **DC441**

Attempts to provide information in English "about Lithuania and the Lithuanian nation from the earliest times until the most recent events."—*Pref.* Many articles are signed with the initials of the contributor; many include bibliographies; most were written in Lithuanian and translated into English. Vol. 6 includes a supplement (p. 365–486), a list of contributors, and a general index to the set.   DK511.L2E5

Kantautas, Adam. A Lithuanian bibliography : a check-list of books and articles held by the major libraries of Canada and the United States / Adam & Filomena Kantautas. Edmonton : Univ. of Alberta Pr., 1975. 725 p.   **DC442**

A classed bibliography with author and title indexes. More than 10,000 items. Locates copies. Includes sections for Lithuanians abroad.

————. *Supplement to A Lithuanian bibliography : a further check-list of books and articles held by the major libraries of Canada and the United States*, Adam and Filomena Kantautas (Edmonton : Univ. of Alberta Pr., 1979. 316 p.). Lists materials cataloged 1972–77.   Z2537.K33

Lietuviškoji tarybinė enciklopedija / [vyriausiasis redaktorius J. Zinkus]. Vilnius : Mokslas, 1976–85. 12 v. : ill.

   DC443

A general encyclopedia with strong national and regional emphasis. Occasional brief bibliographies.

§ Supplement: ———— *Papildymai A-Ž* / [vyriausiasis redaktorius J. Zinkus] (Vilnius : Vyriausioji enciklopedijų redakcija, 1985. 640 p.).

Contains: (1) new articles on topics not covered "for one reason or another" (*Pref*) in the earlier volumes (some reflecting more recent developments, but many others covering topics that date well before 1975), and (2) supplementary material to articles in the main set (marked with an asterisk).   AE35.55.L54

Lithuania : an encyclopedic survey / [ed. in chief, Jonas Zinkus ; contributors, Tadas Adomonis … et al.]. Vilnius : Encyclopedia Publishers, 1986. 431 p. : ill.   **DC444**

     Some 50 scholars have contributed to chapters that survey Lithuanian science, folk art, literature and art, public health, history, etc. Statistics are current to about 1983. Heavily illustrated; not indexed. A description of Lithuania by Lithuanians.   DK511.L2L478

Šešplaukis, Alfonsas. Lituanica collections in European research libraries : a bibliography. Chicago : Lithuanian Research and Studies, 1986. 215 p.   **DC445**

     The bibliography is based on the collections of Dr. Vilius Gaigalaitis, Professor Eduard Hermann, Professor Ernst Fraenkel, and Petras Klimas.

     Based on four collections (one still in a private library) this topically arranged listing of books in any language (mostly 20th-century with some 19th-century publications) treats all aspects of Lithuania. Author and subject indexes.   DK511.L2S475

Luxembourg

Bibliographie d'histoire luxembourgeoise. 1964– . Luxembourg : Bibliothèque nationale, 1965– .   **DC446**

     Added t.p. in German: Bibliographie zur Geschichte Luxemburgs für das Jahr 1964– .

     Topical listing of books and periodical articles significant for the study of Luxembourg history. Author index.   Z2461.B48

Hury, Carlo. Luxembourg / Carlo Hury, Jules Christophory. Oxford, Eng. ; Santa Barbara, Calif. : Clio Pr., [1981]. 184 p. (World bibliographical series, 23).   **DC447**

     Lists about 480 books and articles in topical arrangement; many items are in English, but French and German titles are included. Name and subject index.   Z2461.H87

Malta

Thackrah, John Richard. Malta. Oxford ; Santa Barbara, Calif. : Clio Pr., c[1985]. 163 p. (World bibliographical series, v. 64).   **DC448**

     Offers 588 annotated entries for primarily English-language materials, topically arranged in 35 sections. Indexed by author, title, subject.   Z2375.T47

Monaco

Hudson, Grace L. Monaco. Oxford, Eng. ; Santa Barbara, Calif. : Clio Pr., c1991. 193 p. (World bibliographical series, v. 120).   **DC449**

     Updates Geoffrey Handley-Taylor, *Bibliography of Monaco* (2nd ed. Chicago : St. James Pr., 1968. 62 p.).

     "Selected, annotated…guide to serious works on all aspects of the country which will be of interest to the general reader, student, librarian, researcher and business traveller."—*Pref.* Even though emphasis is on the English-language material, about two-thirds of the almost 550 titles are in French. Author/title/subject index. Appendix gives list of the reigns of the Lords and Princes of Monaco, House of Grimaldi.   Z2191.H83

Netherlands

Bibliography

Bibliographia neerlandica. [New enl. ed.]. The Hague : Nijhoff, 1962. 598 p.   **DC450**

     1st ed., 1951.

     Contents: Pt.1, Books on the Netherlands in foreign languages, 1940–57, comp. by A. M. P. Mollema; pt. 2, Translations of Dutch literature, 1900–1957, comp. by P. M. Morel. Indexes.

     Title, introductory material, and captions in English, French, German, and Spanish.

     § E. van Raan's *Het Nederlandse boek in vertaling, 1958–1967 : bibliografie van vertalingen van Noord- en Zuidnederlandse werken* ('sGravenhage : Staatuitgervij, 1974. 233 p.) serves as a continuation of the Morel section above, and is continued by: *Het Nederlandse boek in vertaling : bibliografie van vertalingen van Noord- en Zuidnerlandse werken* (1968/72–1983/87. 'sGravenhage : Staatsuitgeverij, 1969–87. Annual with 5-year cumulations). Issued by Koninklijke Bibliotheek, Hague, and Koninklijke Bibliotheek, Brussels.   Z2446.M64

Buck, Hendrik de. Bibliografie der geschiedenis van Nederland / Door H. de Buck. Samen gesteld in opdracht van het Nederlands Comité voor Geschiedkundige Wetenschappen. met Medewerking van E. M. Smit. Leiden : Brill, 1968. 712 p.   **DC451**

     Repr.: Utrecht : HES, 1979.

     Comp. under the auspices of the Nederlands Comité voor Geschiedkundige Wetenschappen.

     Modeled on Henri Pirenne, *Bibliographie de l'histoire de Belgique* (DC100). A classed bibliography of more than 8,600 items covering the whole range of Netherlands history through 1945. Indexes of authors, personal names, and place-names.   Z2446.B8

Coolhaas, Willem Philippus. A critical survey of studies on Dutch colonial history. 2nd ed. / rev. by G. J. Schutte. The Hague : Nijhoff, 1980. 264 p. (Bibliographical series / Koninklijk Instituut voor Taal- Land- en Volkenkunde, 4).   **DC452**

     1st ed., 1960.

     Offers bibliographical essays describing and evaluating published works on the colonial empire of the Netherlands. Presentation is mainly chronological, but there are separate chapters on archives; journals, institutes and university chairs; bibliographies; travel accounts. This edition adds post-1960 material and earlier important items inadvertently omitted previously. Includes a list of titles discussed; indexes of personal and geographic names.   Z2457.5.C66

Herwijnen, G. van. Bibliografie van de stedengeschiedenis van Nederland / samengesteld door G. van Herwijnen … [et al.]. Leiden : Brill, 1978. 355 p.   **DC453**

     At head of title: Acta collegii historiae urbanae societatis historicorum internationalis.

     A general section on the history of towns in the Netherlands is followed by sections for individual provinces, each further subdivided by specific cities and towns, and thereunder by topic. 3,331 items. Indexes of place names and of authors.   Z2423.H47

King, Peter. The Netherlands / Peter King and Michael Wintle. Oxford ; Santa Barbara, Calif. : Clio Pr., c1988. 308 p. (World bibliographical series, v. 88).   **DC454**

     A selective bibliography (1,025 entries) of Dutch- and English-language books, topically arranged. Author, title, and subject indexes; cross-references.   Z2431.K56

Klashorst, G. O. van de. Bibliography of Dutch seventeenth century political thought : an annotated inventory, 1581–1710 / G.O. van de Klashorst, H.W. Blom & E.O.G. Haitsma Mulier. Amsterdam : APA-Holland Univ. Pr., c1986. 162 p., [7] p. of plates : ill. (Bibliotheca historico-politica, 1).   **DC455**

More than 360 books, dissertations and disputations, pamphlets published in Holland by Dutch or by foreigners who studied there. Arrangement is alphabetical under year of publication. Annotated indexes for: anonymous titles; authors, students, editors, translators; countries and places of origin of students; printers, publishers and booksellers; subjects. Locates copies in one library in Western Europe, or, if no location, a reference to a printed bibliography. Z7165.N4K58

Krewson, Margrit B. The Netherlands and Northern Belgium : a selective bibliography of reference works. Rev. ed. Wash. : Library of Congress, 1989. 152 p. **DC456**

Superintendent of Documents classification: LC 1.12/2:N38.

A revision and expansion of *The Netherlands : a selective bibliography of reference works*, 1986.

Based on collections at the Library of Congress. Lists books and government publications (most published in the 1980s, with a few from the 1970s) in a broad topical arrangement. Includes studies, reference works, histories, and travel accounts, in Dutch, English, French, and German. Appendix of institutions concerned with the Netherlands and northern Belgium; indexed by main entry. Z2431.K73

Repertorium der verhandelingen en bijdragen betreffende de geschiedenis des vaderlands, in tijdschriften en mengelwerken. Leiden : Brill, 1907–1953. 5 v. **DC457**

Vol. 1 is a revision of the 1st ed. (1863) and its supplements. Lists publications through 1900.

Contents: v. 1, through 1900; v. 2, 1901–10 (884 col.); v. 3, 1911–20 (904 col.); v. 4, 1921–29 (1132 col.); v. 5, 1930–39 (764 col.).

A comprehensive, classified bibliography of analytical material on all aspects of Dutch history, indexing articles on the subject in more than 1,000 periodicals, society transactions, composite books, etc., principally Dutch publications but including some in other languages. List of titles indexed varies in the different volumes.

§ Continued by: *Repertorium van boeken en tijdschriftartikelen betreffende de geschiedenis van Nederland* (Leiden : Brill, 1943– . Irregular.). Very delayed; volume for 1987 published in 1993.

For pre-1901 publications, see *Repertorium der verhandelingen en bijdragen betreffende en mengelwerken tot op 1900 verschenen (Leiden : Brill, 1907. 1638 col.).* Z2416.R46

Archives

See also Martha Brogan's *Research guide to libraries and archives in the Low Countries* (AK133).

De Rijksarchieven in Nederland / eindred. L. P. L. Pirenne, ... met medew. van P. van Iterson en P. G. J. M. Wagenaar. 'sGravenhage : Staatsdrukkerij– en Uitgeverijbedrijf, 1973. 2 v. : maps. **DC458**

A listing of government archives, giving for each: name, address, hours, and lengthy descriptions of contents, together with lists of published catalogs. Indexed.

§ *Overzichten van de archieven en verzamelingen in de openbare archiefbewaarplaatsen in Nederland* (Alphen aan den Rijn : Samson, 1979–85. v.1–11. [In progress]) provides an extensive listing of archives; each volume is devoted to one province. CD1692.A2R54

Dictionaries

Volmuller, H. W. J. Nijhoffs geschiedenislexicon Nederland en België / samengesteld door W. W. J. Volmutter, in samenwerking met de redactie van De Grote Oosthoek. 'sGravenhage : Nijhoff, 1981. 655 p. : ill. **DC459**

Offers brief entries for personal and place names, events, etc., relating to the history of the Low Countries. Bibliographical references are appended to many articles. DH101.V64

Chronologies

Strubbe, Egied I. De chronologie van de middeleeuwen en de moderne tijden in de Nederlanden / door Eg. I. Strubbe en L. Voet. Antwerp : Standaard-Boekhandel, 1960. 551 p. **DC460**

Chiefly tables, including a calendar for the years 396–2000, and chronological lists of popes, bishops of Dutch sees, selected European dynasties, and early Dutch rulers and landholders. DH101.S7

Biography

Haitsma Mulier, E. O. G. Repertorium van geschiedschrijvers in Nederland, 1500–1800 / samengesteld door E. O. G. Haitsma Mulier, G. A. C. van der Lem ; med medewerking van P. Knevel. Den Haag : Nederlands Historisch Genootschap, 1990. 470 p. (Bibliografische reeks van het Nederlands Historisch Genootschap, v. 7). **DC461**

A biographical dictionary treating 533 Dutch historians who were active 1500–1800, giving brief biographical details, lists of works by the historians, and references to secondary literature. Index to works of the historians. DJ97.H35

Atlases

Geschiedkundige atlas van Nederland. 'sGravenhage : Nijhoff, 1913–1938. 3 v. : maps in color ; 37 x 53 cm. **DC462**

Vols. 1–2 issued by the Commissie voor den geschiedkundigen atlas.

Historical maps of the various sections of the Netherlands, with detailed textual comment.

Norway

See also section for Scandinavia.

Bibliografi til Norges historie. 1916–1974/75. Oslo : Universitetsforlaget, 1916–1975. **DC463**

Issued as supplements to *Historisk tidsskrift* (Oslo).

Full bibliography, including books, pamphlets, and analytical material in periodicals, etc. General title pages and general author indexes are issued for 10-year periods, 1916–25, 1926–35, 1936–45, 1946–55, 1956–65, 1966–75. Items are numbered consecutively throughout the 10-year period.

Continued by: *Bibliografi til Norges historie* [microform] / utarbeidet ved Universitetsbiblioteket i Oslo (1976–1977– . [Oslo] : Den Norske historiske forening, 1977– . Biennial). Title on eye-readable header: Historisk bibliografi.

Coverage and arrangement are similar to the earlier work. Fully indexed. Now produced from a database at the Universitetsbibliothek in Oslo and based on the collection at that institution. Z2606.N83

Johnsen, Arne Odd. Norsk militarhistorisk bibliografi / red.: Arne Odd Johnsen [og] Gunnar Christie Wasberg ; av Forsvarets krigshistoriske avdeling. Oslo : Gyldendal, 1969. 373 p. **DC464**

A topical listing of materials, mainly in Norwegian, on Norwegian military history of all periods. Author, place, and subject indexes.

§ Supplemented by Harald Sandvik's *Norsk militærhistorisk bibliografi : tillegg* (Oslo : Gyldendal, 1977. 59p.). Z2611.M5J64

Nysæter, Egil. Norske arkivkatalogar : oversikt over katalogar, register, mikrofilm, kjeldeutgaver m.m. i norske arkiv. 2. utg. Oslo : Riksarkivet, 1992. 612 p. **DC465**

1st ed., 1982.

Comprehensive listing of catalogs of holdings of municipal archives. CD1812.A2N95

Ørvik, Nils. Norwegian foreign policy : a bibliography, 1905–1965. [Oslo] : Universitetsforlaget, 1968. 91 p. (Norsk bibliografisk bibliotek, 34). **DC466**

Topical listing within sections for books, articles, and government publications. Author index.

§ Updated by Ørvik, *Norsk utenrikspolitisk litteratur, 1965–1970 = Norwegian foreign policy, a bibliography, 1965–70* (Oslo : Universitetsforlaget, [c1973]. 74 p.). Z2617.R4O382

Sather, Leland B. Norway / Leland B. Sather, comp. ; ed. by Hans H. Wellisch. Oxford, England ; Santa Barbara, Calif. : Clio Pr., c1986. 293 p. : map. (World bibliographical series, v. 67). **DC467**

Offers 942 annotated entries arranged in 41 sections covering from the Vikings to the present. Indexed by author, title, and subject. Z2591.S28

Schiötz, Eiler H. Utlendingers reiser i Norge : en bibliografi. Oslo : Universitetsforlaget, 1970–1986. 2 v. : ill. (Norsk bibliografisk bibliotik, 44, 54). **DC468**

Contents: v. 1, Itineraria Norvegica, a bibliography on foreigners' travels in Norway until 1900; v. 2, Itineraria Norvegica ... [until 1900] and Supplementer (595 p.).

The first volume lists more than 1,278 accounts, in any language, of travels to any area of Norway, with indication of every place mentioned in each. Personal name index; topographic and chronological register; index of books relating to the Lapps. Vol. 2 offers supplementary material in three parts: (1) books not listed in the 1970 volume; (2) list of foreign painters in Norway before 1900; (3) additional information concerning books in the earlier volume. Index of names, geographic areas, historical periods, and nationalities, and of books on the Lapps. Two additional indexes of privately printed books, and books on hunting and angling cover both volumes. Z2606.S32

Universitetsbiblioteket i Oslo. Norsk lokalhistorisk litteratur, 1946–1970. Oslo : Universitetsbiblioteket i Oslo, 1976–1981. 19 v. : maps. **DC469**

Devotes a volume to each province or major city; in each there is a general section followed by subdivisions for local areas. Lists books, pamphlets, etc., many of them published locally. Indexed by author and by Universal Decimal Classification.

§ Continued by: *Norsk lokalhistorisk litteratur, 1971–90* (Oslo : Universitetsbiblioteket i Oslo, 1993– . [In progress]).

Contents: (v. 1) Ostfold; (v. 2) Akershus; (v. 3) Oslo; (v. 4) Hedmark; (v. 5) Oppland; (v. 6) Buskerud; (v. 7) Vestfold; (v. 8) Telemark; (v. 9–10) Agder; (v. 11) Rogaland; (v. 12) Hordaland; (v. 13) Sogn og Fjordane; (v. 14) More og Romsdal; (v. 15–16) Trondelag; (v. 17) Nordland; (v. 18–19) Troms. Finnmark; (v. 20) Norge med landsdeler. Svalbard. Jan Mayen.

See also *Norwegian local history: a bibliography of material in the collections of the Memorial Library, University of Wisconsin-Madison,* comp. by Dennis Auburn Hill (Jefferson, N.C. : McFarland, 1989. 125 p.). Z2606.O7

Poland

Bibliography

Kanka, August Gerald. Poland : an annotated bibliography of books in English. N.Y. : Garland, 1988. 395 p. (Garland reference library of the humanities, v. 743). **DC470**

"Attempts to be the most exhaustive and the most comprehensive list of works in the English language."—*Pref.* A topical listing of books, government publications written by individuals, and pamphlets. Excluded are articles, translations of literary works by Poles, and government statistical materials. Author and title indexes. Z2526.K28

Lerski, Jerzy J. Jewish-Polish coexistence, 1772–1939 : a topical bibliography / comp. by George J. Lerski and Halina T. Lerski. N.Y. : Greenwood, 1986. 230 p. (Bibliographies and indexes in world history, no. 5). **DC471**

Lists 3,000 books, pamphlets, and articles in scholarly journals on the relations between the Jews and the rest of the people living in Poland, 1772–1939. The citations are arranged alphabetically within 34 topical sections, e.g., Economics, Jews in Polish literature, Town communities and shtetls. Author index only. Z6373.P7L47

La Pologne au XIIIᵉ Congrès International des Sciences Historiques à Moscou. Warsaw : Éditions Scientifiques de Pologne, 1970. 2 v. **DC472**

Added title page in Polish.

Contents: v. 1, La recherche historique en Pologne, 1945–1968, rédigé par Andrzej Wyczański; v. 2, Bibliographie sélective des travaux des historiens polonais parus dans les années 1945–1968, rédigé par Janusz Tazbir.

Vol. 1 offers essays on historical research and training in Poland, followed by directories of Polish archives, libraries, etc. Vol. 2 is a topically arranged bibliography of Polish works on history published during the period indicated. Not indexed.

§ See also: *La science historique polonaise dans l'historiographie mondiale,* sponsored by the 17th International Congress of Historical Sciences (Warsaw : Ossolineum, 1990. 448 p.).

Polska Akademia Nauk. Instytut Historii. Bibliografia historii Polski / Pod red. Heleny Madurowicz-Urbańkiej opracowali Wiesław Bieńkowski [et al.]. Warszawa : Państwowe Wydawnictwo Naukowe, 1965–78. 3 v. in 7. **DC473**

Contents: v.1, pt.1, Do roku 1454; pt.2, 1454–1795; pt.3, Do roku 1795, indeksy; v.2, pt.1, 1795–1918; pt.2, Indeksy; v.3, pt.1, 1918–45; pt.2, Indeksy.

Explanatory notes in English, French, and Russian.

A bibliography of Polish history from earliest times to 1945. The first section of pt. 1 is a general guide to bibliographic and reference aids, methodology, historiography, archives and libraries, and auxiliary studies; it is followed by a bibliography of Polish history arranged by periods to 1454, with appropriate subdivisions. The second part continues the period sections to 1795, and the third part provides indexes to the nearly 20,000 items listed. Vol. 2 deals with Polish history to 1918, and v. 3 covers the years following. Although coverage extends to such subjects as statistics, economics, and sociology, the bibliography is meant to be selective rather than exhaustive. Both books and periodical articles are included; there are some brief annotations.

§ While this work extends the period of coverage, as well as updates, the listings in Ludwik Finkcl's *Bibliografia historyi polskiej* (Krakow : Nakł. Komisyi Historycznej Akademii, 1891–1906), the older bibliography will still be found useful.

Publications of 1935–39 are listed in Wiesław Bieńkowski's *Bibliografia polskiej* (Wrocław : Zakł. Narrod. im. Ossolińskich, 1976–81. 2 v.). Z2526.P64

Rister, Herbert. Bibliographie der ehemaligen preussischen Ostprovinzen : übergreifende Themen, 1971–1985. Marburg/Lahn : Johann-Gottfried-Herder-Institut, 1988. 2 v. (Bibliographien zur Geschichte und Landeskunde Ostmitteleuropas, Nr.8). **DC474**

Extensive bibliography of 5,513 books, articles, essays and chapters in books, mainly in German and Polish, on western Poland. Much material also on Central Europe. Vol. 2 is the Register, an index to authors, place names, topics. Z2527.P78.R57

Sanford, George. Poland / George Sanford and Adriana Gozdecka-Sanford, compilers. Rev. ed. Oxford ; Santa Barbara, Calif. : Clio Pr., c1993. 250 p. (World bibliographical series, v. 32). **DC475**

1st ed., 1984, comp. by Richard C. Lewański.

Lists 914 books and articles, mostly in English with a few French and Polish titles; broad topical arrangement. Annotated. The new edition concentrates on materials published since 1980, so only about one-quarter of the earlier references are present, essentially those considered to be classics or still of major importance. Indexed by author, title, and subject. Z2526.S26

Schrifttum über Polen (ohne Posener Land) : (Auswahl) : im Auftrage der Historisch-Landeskundlichen Kommission für Posen und das Deutschtum in Polen. Marburg/Lahn : J. G. Herder-Instituts, 1953–1983. 7 v. (Wissenschaftliche Beiträge zur Geschichte und Landeskunde Ost-Mitteleuropas, 90, etc.). **DC476**

Title varies: *Schrifttum über Polen mit besonderer Berücksichtigung des posener Landes*. Dates of coverage appear in title.

Comp. by Herbert Rister until 1966; comp. by Johanna Stiller, 1971–83.

Contents: 1943–51 (1953); 1952–53 (1955); 1954–55 (1958); 1956–58 (1960); 1959–60 (1966); 1961–62 (1971); 1966–1970 (1980); 1971–73 (1983).

§ Because the literature for the Poznań region became so extensive, a separate bibliography was published for that area: *Schrifttum über das Posener Land 1961–1970*, ed. by Herbert Rister (Marburg/Lahn, 1976. 168 p.).

Current

Bibliografia historii polskiej ... / Polska Akademia Nauk, Instytut Historii, Pracownia Informacji Naukowej. 1938/39– . Wrocław : Zakład Narodowy im. Ossolińskich, 1948– . Annual. **DC477**

Title varies.

Began publication with volume for 1948. 1944/47 published 1962; 1938–39 publ. 1981.

An extensive classified list of books and articles in various languages on Polish history and related fields. Author indexes. Z2526.B53

Dissertations

Wielewinski, Bernard. Doctoral dissertations and masters theses regarding Polish subjects, 1900–1985 : an annotated bibliography. Boulder, Colo. : East European Monographs ; N.Y. : Distr. by Columbia Univ. Pr., 1988. 200 p. (East European monographs, no. 235). **DC478**

Published jointly with the Commission on History and Archives of the Polish National Catholic Church.

An author listing of theses accepted in U.S., Canada, and Great Britain. Subject, title, discipline, and school indexes. Z2526.W54

Manuscripts; Archives

Płaza, Stanisław. Żródła rékopišmienne do dziejów wsi w Polsce feudalnej : studium archiewoznawcze. Warszawa : Państ. Wydaw. Naukowe, 1976. 440 p. **DC479**

A guide to church and national archives containing material on medieval history. Indexed by topics, localities, and persons. CD1742.P55

Encyclopedias; Dictionaries

Polish encyclopaedia / Publ. by the Committee for the Polish Encyclopaedic Publications at Fribourg and Geneva. Geneva : Atar, 1922–26. 3 v. : maps. **DC480**

An English edition of portions of the *Encyclopédie polonaise* (Lausanne : Comité des Publications Encyclopédiques sur la Pologne, 1916–20. v. 1–4, pt. 1).

Repr.: N.Y. : Arno, 1972.

Contents: v. 1, The Polish language. History of literature. History of Poland; v. 2, Territory and population of Poland; v. 3, Economic life of Poland.

Sponsored by the Polish National Committee of America.

Sienkiewicz, Witold. Mały słownik historii Polski. Warszawa : Wideza Powszechna, 1991. 251 p. **DC481**

A quick reference dictionary for Polish history that concentrates on the period 1939–89 not well covered by other historical dictionaries. Includes names of individuals, political parties, movements, etc. Name index. DK4123.S54

Atlases

The historical atlas of Poland / [editors, Władysław Czapliński and Tadeusz Ładogórski ; authors, Irena Gieysztorowa ... et al. ; translator, Maria Paczyńska]. Warszawa : Państwowe Przedsiębiorstwo Wyd. Kartograficzynch, 1986. 54, 56 p. : maps in color ; 31 cm. **DC482**

Translation of *Atlas historyczny Polski*.

Contains 54 pages of maps in color followed by 39 pages of explanatory material. Covers from the early stone age to about 1975, with roughly half the maps devoted to 800–1600. Index of places.

§ A less authoritative English-language publication, Iwo Pogonowski's *Poland : a historical atlas* (N.Y. : Hippocrene Books, 1987. 321 p.) depicts Poland from prehistoric times to the 1980s in black-and-white maps. Tables of dynasties, chronology, bibliography, index by subject and place-name. Gives a few statistics (e.g., number of Holocaust victims). G1951.S1P33

Portugal

Bibliography

Biblioteca Nacional de Lisboa. Subsidios para a bibliografia da história local portuguêsa. Lisbon : [Tipografia Henrique Torres], 1933. 425 p. **DC483**

Ed. by Antonio Mesquita de Figueiredo.

A bibliography of local history. Z2733.L77

Coutinho, Bernardo Xavier da Costa. Bibliographie franco-portugaise : essai d'une bibliographie chronologique de livres français sur le Portugal. Porto : Lopes da Silva, 1939. 409 p. **DC484**

On cover: Publiée sous les auspices de l'Institut Français au Portugal et de l'Instituto para a Alta Cultura, avec le concours du Secrétariado da Propaganda Nacional.

Arranged chronologically from the 16th to 20th centuries; lists almost 3,000 items. Z2737.R4C6

Guia da bibliografia histórica portuguesa. Lisboa : Academia Portuguesa da História, 1959. v. 1, fasc. 1. **DC485**

Organized by the commission headed by Marcelo Caetano.

No more published.

Planned to constitute, when complete, a comprehensive bibliography of Portuguese history from the 9th century to 1910. Despite the fact that only one fascicle was published, still very useful, for it lists collections of sources (documents, diplomatic records, etc.). No index. Z2726.G84

Marques, Alfredo Pinheiro. Guia de história dos Descobrimentos e expansão portuguesa : estudos. Lisboa : Biblioteca Nacional, 1987. 188 p. **DC486**

1988 "2nd ed." appears to be a reissue.

A topical arrangement of books and articles concerning Portuguese discoveries and expansion through the 18th century. Most citations are to Portuguese-language materials, although some are in French, English, and Spanish. Not indexed; cross-references to related sections. DP583.M36

Marques, António Henrique R. de Oliveira. Guia de história de la República Portuguesa. Lisboa : Estampa, 1981. 662 p. **DC487**

A bibliography in essay form covering Portugal during the period 1910–32; indicates bibliographies, sources, studies, and periodicals. Broad topical arrangement with subdivisions. Includes all forms of history—cultural, demographic, etc.—and "auxiliary sciences of history" extending to cinematography and chronology. Indexed.

——————— Guia do estudante de história medieval portuguesa. 3a. ed. Lisbon : Editorial Estampa, 1988. 294 p. **DC488**

1st ed., 1964; 2nd ed., 1979.

Intended as a researcher's manual or guide to principal sources and published studies in the field. Includes special sections for archives and manuscript repositories. This edition includes publications as late as 1987. Indexed.

Newberry Library. A catalog of the Greenlee collection. Boston : G. K. Hall, 1970. 2 v. (1465 p.). **DC489**

An outstanding, comprehensive collection of Portuguese history and literature. Dictionary arrangement.

§ The earlier catalog, ed. by Doris Varner Welsh (*A catalog of the William B. Greenlee collection of Portuguese history and literature and the Portuguese materials in the Newberry Library*. Chicago, 1953. 342 p.), should still be used since it includes additional materials at the Newberry Library which are not in the Greenlee collection. Z2739.N483

Unwin, P. T. H. Portugal. Oxford ; Santa Barbara, Calif. : Clio Pr., c1987. 269 p. (World bibliographical series, v. 71). **DC490**

An annotated, topically arranged bibliography of 787 English-language books and some articles. Author, title, subject index. Z2711.U59

Dissertations

Kettenring, N. Ernest. A bibliography of theses and dissertations on Portuguese topics completed in the United States and Canada, 1861–1983. Durham, N.H. : International Conference on Modern Portugal, Dept. of History, Univ. of New Hampshire, 1984. 87 p. **DC491**

An author listing, with index by country and broad topic. Includes a small number of South African theses and research papers; thorough coverage for the U.S. and Canada. Z2711.K4

Dictionaries

Wheeler, Douglas L. Historical dictionary of Portugal. Metuchen, N.J. : Scarecrow, 1993. 288 p. (European historical dictionaries, no. 1). **DC492**

Covers all facets of Portuguese history, up to about 1990, with entries mostly under names of people, places, organizations, buildings, and treaties, plus occasional topics such as the colonial empire or relations with other countries. Extensive and excellent English and Portuguese bibliography (p. 184–283). Chronology; brief history. Appendixes: Monarchs 1140–1910; Presidents since 1910; Prime ministers since 1922. Not indexed. DP535.W44

Romania

Ancel, Jean. Bibliography of the Jews in Romania / comp. by Jean Ancel and Victor Eskenasy. [Tel Aviv] : Goldstein-Goren Centre for the History of the Jews in Romania, Diaspora Research Institute, Tel Aviv Univ., 1991. 125, 50 p. **DC493**

Title on added t.p.: Bibliyografyah le-toldot ha-Yehudim be-Romanyah.

Lists 2,000 books, articles, government documents, encyclopedia articles (primarily from *Encyclopaedia Judaica*, BC546) in Romanian, English, French, German, Spanish, Polish, Hungarian, Yiddish (in Roman transliteration) and Hebrew. Includes much coverage of Eastern Europe. Arranged alphabetically by author; an occasional descriptive phrase is provided. Indexes for names, places and subjects. Z6373.R6A54

Bibliografia istorica a României. Bucureşti : Editura Academiei Republicii Socialiste România, 1970–1990. v. 1–7. (In progress). **DC494**

Contents: v.1, 1944–1969: Bibliografie selectiva; v.2,t.1, Secolul XIX: Cadrul general. Tara si locuitorii; v. 3, t. 5, Secolul XIX: Biografi; v.4, 1969–1974: Bibliografie selectiva; v. 5, 1974–1979: Bibliografie selectiva; v. 6, 1979–1984: Bibliografie selectiva; v. 7, 1984–1989: Bibliografie selectiva.

An extensive bibliography of books and articles on history published in Romania. Emphasis is on Romanian history, with brief sections on world history in some volumes. Each volume has its own author index. Z2926.B5

Buonincontro, Pasquale. La presenza delle Romania in Italia nel secolo XX : contributo bibliografico, 1900–1980. Napoli : De Simone, [1988]. 211 p. **DC495**

Lists by date, then by author, 2,553 books, pamphlets, articles, collections of documents, proccedings of conferences, plus 80 translations on Romania and important Romanians published in Italy 1900–80. Author index. DR205.A12.B86

Deletant, Andrea. Romania / Andrea Deletant, Dennis Deletant, compilers. Oxford ; Santa Barbara, Calif. : Clio Pr., c1985. 236 p. (World bibliographical series, v. 59). **DC496**

A topically arranged bibliography of primarily English-language books, but including French, German and Romanian publications when there is no equivalent English-language work. 797 annotated entries index by author, title and subject.

§ Still useful for older materials is Stephen A. Fischer-Galati, *Rumania : a bibliographic guide* (Wash. : Slavic and Central European Division, Library of Congress, 1963. 75 p. Repr.: N.Y. : Arno Pr., 1968) which lists some 748 books and periodicals.

For bibliography for 1914–19, *see* Glenn E. Torrey, "Romania in the First World War," *Emporia State research studies* 29, no. 4 (1981), which covers books, dissertations, newspapers, periodicals, and a few journal articles published mostly in Romania. DR205.Z99D44

Enciclopedia istoriografiei româneşti / coordonator ştiintific, Stefan Stefănescu. Bucureşti : Editura Ştiinţificăşi Enciclopedică, 1978. 470 p. **DC497**

Biobibliography of Romanian historians, including archaeologists, of the 17th–20th centuries, giving information about their careers and a bibliography of their publications and of secondary works. Also gives lists of institutes, periodicals, and documentary collections with brief descriptions and full bibliographic information. Not indexed. DR216.8.E52

Enciclopedia României. [Bucharesti : Asociatia Ştiinţifică Pentru Enciclopedia României], 1938–43. 4 v. : ill. **DC498**

Contents: A. Organizarea politica-administrativa: v.1, Statul; v.2, Tara româneasca. B. Economia; v.3, Economia nationala. Cadre si productie; v.4, Economia nationala. Circúlatie, distributie si consum. (Two projected volumes have not been published: C. Cultura: v.5, Cultura nationala; v.6, Institutii si personalitati culturale).

Scholarly, monographic articles arranged by large classes, with detailed tables of contents and indexes in each volume. Articles are signed by authorities and include bibliographies except in v.2, which presents gazetteer information and includes an index to all places in Rumania.

§ A historical dictionary covering Romania through the 10th century: *Dictionar de istorie veche a Romănie : paleolithic—sec. X*, by D.M. Pippidi (Bucureşti : Ed. Ştiinţifică si enciclopediă, 1976. 625 p.). Poor illustrations.

Slovakia

See Czechoslovakia.

Spain

General works

Bibliography

See also *Widener Library shelflist* (AA115).

Aguilar Piñal, Francisco. Bibliografía de estudios sobre Carlos III y su época. Madrid : Consejo Superior de Investigaciones Científicas, 1988. 428 p.   **DC499**

Companion to Aguilar Piñal's *Bibliografía de autores españoles del siglo XVIII* (BE1431).

A topically arranged bibliography of 18th-century Spain, including coverage of architecture, painting, and literature as well as economic affairs and social life. Lists 8,176 books, articles, and pamphlets in Spanish, English, German, and French. Author index.

DP199.A253

Burgo, Jaime del. Bibliografía del siglo XIX : guerras carlistas, luchas políticas. 2. ed. rev. y puesta al día. Pamplona : [Diputación Foral de Navarra], 1978. 1072 p.   **DC500**

1st ed. 1953–66 had title *Bibliografía de las guerras carlistas* .

An extensive bibliography of books and pamphlets (with a few periodical articles) dealing with political strife in Spain in the 19th century. Includes works published to 1975.   Z2699.B87

Cadenas y Vicent, Vicente de. Bibliografía del Emperador Carlos V. Madrid : Instituto Salazar y Castro (C.S.I.C.), 1986. 245 p.   **DC501**

A long bibliographical essay (p. 5–36) is followed by a bibliography of books, documents, and articles arranged by author. Mostly Spanish and Italian works with some in German and French. Covers 16th century Spain and Europe. No index.

Cortada, James W. A bibliographic guide to Spanish diplomatic history, 1460–1977. Westport, Conn. : Greenwood, 1977. 390 p.   **DC502**

Organized by reign, then by country (with occasional topical subdivisions). Author index, but none of subjects. Only published books, pamphlets, government documents, and periodical articles are included.   Z2696.C67

González Ollé, Fernando. Manual bibliográfico de estudios españoles. Pamplona : Ediciones Universidad de Navarra, 1976. 1375 p.   **DC503**

A classed bibliography covering the whole range of Spanish studies, and a useful starting point for almost any subject in the discipline. Arranged in 22 main categories, each closely subdivided, with chronological and geographical subsections where appropriate. Author and subject indexes in addition to a very detailed table of contents.

Z2681.G58

Kinder, A. Gordon. Spanish Protestants and reformers in the sixteenth century : a bibliography. London : Grant & Cutler, 1983. 108 p. (Research bibliographies and checklists, 39).   **DC504**

Covers "the reform-minded heterodox antecedents of Spanish Protestantism, its brief flourishing in its homeland, and its dying echoes abroad" (*Introd.*)—i.e., mainly 1500–1600. Listing is divided: (1) Manuscripts and (2) Editions and studies. Cutoff date is 1979. Indexed.   Z7830.K66

Rasor, Eugene L. The Spanish Armada of 1588 : historiography and annotated bibliography. Westport, Conn. : Greenwood, 1993. 277 p. (Bibliographies of battles and leaders, no. 10).   **DC505**

In two parts: pt. 1, a historiographical essay with evaluation of the writings on the Armada; pt. 2, a bibliography of 1,114 annotated entries for books (including fiction, drama, and poetry), official publications, articles, dissertations, and primary source mterial on Anglo-Spanish relations during the 16th century. Bracketed numbers refer from the essay to the bibliography. Chronology; index of authors and a few subjects.   DA360.R37

Sánchez Alonso, Benito. Fuentes de la historia española e hispanoaméricana. 3. ed. corr. y puesta al día. Madrid : Consejo Superior de Investigaciones Científicas, 1952. 3 v. (Revista de filología española. Publicaciones, 8).   **DC506**

Subtitle: Ensayo de bibliografía sistemática de impresos y manuscritos que ilustran la historia política de España y sus antiguas provincias de ultramar.

A comprehensive bibliography of books and periodical articles covering Spanish history from early times through the 19th century. An author index and three subject indexes: (1) biographical, (2) geographical, and (3) miscellaneous.

§ Sánchez Alonso has also written a standard historiography: *Historia de la historiografía española* (Madrid, 1943–50. 3 v.) covering historical writing up to 1684.   Z2696.S21

Shields, Graham J. Spain. Oxford ; Santa Barbara, Calif. : Clio Pr., c1985. 340 p. (World bibliographical series, v. 60).   **DC507**

A selected, annotated bibliography of 982 books and periodical articles. Emphasizes recently published English-language material. The annotations often include references to related titles. Topical arrangement; author/title/subject index.   DP17.Z99S54

Simón Díaz, José. Bibliografía regional y local de España. Madrid : CSIC, 1976. 1 v. (Cuadernos bibliográficos, 33).   **DC508**

Contents: v.1, Impresos localizados (siglos XV–XVII). No more published.

Lists, for each local area (city, bishopric, etc.), all publications from the 15th–17th centuries relating to that area—books, documents, histories, etc. Arranged by area, then by date of publication. Locates copies in libraries of Western Europe and the U.S. Index of personal names and topics.   Z2703

Current

Índice histórico español. v. 1 (enero/marzo 1953)– . Barcelona : Ed. Teide, 1953– . 3 no. a year.   **DC509**

Issued also in biennial cumulations.

An extensive bibliography which aims to list books and articles on Spanish history published in Western Europe and the Americas, with a section on the history of Latin America. Titles are annotated and evaluated by experts, and references to critical reviews are often given. Annual author and subject indexes. Very slow in appearing; v. 29, publ. 1992, covers publications of 1983–91.

§ Vol. 1, fasc.1–8, also issued in bound form (859 p.) with title *Bibliografía histórica de España e Hispanoamérica*.   Z2696.I6

Dissertations

Hanson, Carl A. Dissertations on Iberian and Latin American history. Troy, N.Y. : Whitston, 1975. 400 p. **DC510**
For annotation, *see* DB267. Z1601.H32

Manuscripts; Archives

Spain. Subdirección General de Archivos. Guía de los archivos estatales españoles : guía del investigador / Ministerio de Cultura, Dirección General de Bellas Artes y Archivos, Subdirección General de Archivos, Inspección Tecnica de Archivos. 2a. ed. Madrid : The Inspección, 1984. 244 p. : ill. **DC511**
Text of earlier ed., 1977, by the Inspección Tecnica de Archivos.
Describes government and other historical archives; for each gives name, address, size, outline of contents, any printed descriptions. Appendix lists archives by geographical area, functionaries in the archive, and archives by type. Not indexed. CD1850.S67

Encyclopedias; Dictionaries

Diccionario de historia de España / dirigido por Germán Bleiberg. 2. ed., corr. y aum. Madrid : Ediciones de la Revista de Occidente, [1968–69]. 3 v. **DC512**
1st ed., 1952.
Repr.: Madrid : Alianza, 1979.
An alphabetical dictionary of persons, events, and subjects in the history of Spain, compiled by a group of scholars. Articles are generally brief, though some of the more important entries cover several pages; all are signed. Treatment of the 1931–68 period is confined largely to the chronology and the bibliographical section appended to v. 3 (p. 1083–1113).
§ Still useful for local history is a much older work by Tomás Muñoz y Romero, *Diccionario bibliográfica-histórico de los antiguos reinos, provincais, ciudades, villas, iglesias y santuarios de España* (1858. 329 p.). DP56.D5

Enciclopedia de historia de España / dirigida por Miguel Artola. Madrid : Alianza, 1988–93. 7 v. **DC513**
Contents: v. 1, Economía. Sociedad; v. 2, Instituciones políticas. Imperio; v. 3, Iglesia. Pensamiento. Cultura; v. 4, Diccionario biográfico; v. 5, Diccionario temático; v. 6, Cronología. Mapas. Estadísticas; v. 7, Fuentes. Indice.
A scholarly encyclopedia with signed articles. Cross-references in the text from variant forms of entry. Vol. 5 gives an outline of concepts, listing relevant articles under each concept. Vol. 6 covers from 500,000 BCE to 1988 in columns for Spain, culture, international relations, Europe-America; the statistics end in the mid-1980s; maps; tables of genealogy; lists of secretaries of state, governors. Vol. 7 begins with a discussion of archives and libraries; the index to the set is mostly by name although some topical entries appear. DP56.E63

Historical dictionary of modern Spain, 1700–1988 / Robert W. Kern, ed. in chief, Meredith D. Dodge, associate ed. N.Y. : Greenwood, [1990]. 697 p. : ill.; maps. **DC514**
Offers signed articles by scholars from the U.S., Britain, Spain, Canada, and Latin America in areas of politics, government, diplomacy, institutions, culture, society, and the military. Gives little attention to the Spanish Civil War because of the coverage by *Historical dictionary of the Spanish Civil War 1936–1939* ed. by James W. Cortada (DC517). "The objective of this dictionary is not to provide definitive, detailed history for Spain, but to offer a quick reference on a broad range of material for those interested in basic information."—*Pref.* Bibliographic references with each article; cross-references; subject index; chronology of Spanish history; selected bibliography. Very useful. DP192.H57

Historical dictionary of the Spanish Empire, 1402–1975 / James S. Olson, ed. in chief ; Sam L. Slick, senior ed. ; Samuel Freeman … [et al.], associate editors. N.Y. : Greenwood, 1992. 702 p. **DC515**
Offers brief essays written by scholars on "colonies, individuals, political institutions, legislation, treaties, conferences, wars, revolutions, technologies, social and religious groups and military battles."—*Pref.* Cross-references within the text are indicated by asterisks. Most articles have a few bibliographic references at the end, not all of which are cited in the Select bibliography. Index by topic. Appendixes: Chronology and Colonial viceroys, 1535–1824. DP56.H57

Spanish Civil War

García Durán, Juan. La guerra civil española, fuentes : archivos, bibliografía y filmografía. Barcelona : Crítica, c1985. 443 p. **DC516**
In three parts: (1) archivos, colecciones, bibliografías, museos; (2) bibliografías, antologías, indices de publicaciones periodicas; (3) filmes, filmstecas, filmografías. Geographical arrangement. Listings are extensive, in the case of archives describing the files of records. List of pseudonyms with real names. Not indexed. Z2700.G33

Historical dictionary of the Spanish Civil War, 1936–1939 / ed. by James W. Cortada. Westport, Conn. : Greenwood, 1982. 571 p. : maps. **DC517**
Offers signed articles on persons, places, organizations, events, etc., relating to the Spanish Civil War. A high percentage of the short articles was contributed by the editor. Bibliographies accompany many articles. Numerous appendixes, including a detailed chronology and a concise military history of the war. Indexed. DP269.H54

Ruhl, Klaus-Jörg. Der spanische Bürgerkrieg : Literaturbericht und Bibliographie. München : Bernard & Graefe, [1982–1988]. v. 1–2. (Schriften der Bibliothek für Zeitgeschichte, N.F., Bd. 22, 26). (In progress). **DC518**
Contents: Bd. 1, Der politische Konflikt; Bd. 2, Der militärische Konflikt.
A topically arranged bibliography of documents, books, and articles in any language relating to the Spanish Civil War; includes much contemporary writing. Vol. 2 extends the earlier volume's coverage of publications on the political conflict through 1986–87, adding citations for economic and military topics. Name index in each volume. Z2700.R83

Sweden

See also section for Scandinavia.

Bring, Samuel Ebbe. Itineraria svecana : bibliografisk förteckning över resor i Sverige fram till 1950. Stockholm : Almqvist & Wiksell, [1954]. 586 p. : ill. (Svenska bibliotekariesamfundets skriftserie, 3). **DC519**
A bibliography of almost 3,250 works of travel in Sweden, in various languages. Arranged chronologically, 944–1950, with author index. Z2636.B83

Sather, Leland B. Sweden / Leland B. Sather, Alan Swanson, compilers ; ed. by Hans H. Wellisch. Oxford : Clio, 1987. 370 p. (World bibliographical series, 80.). **DC520**
1,015 entries, arranged in 44 topical sections; lists books and some articles, mostly in English but including significant works by Swedish scholars. Cross-references; author/title/subject index. Z2621.S28

Svensk historisk bibliografi. [1] (1880)– . Stockholm : Svenska historiska föreningen [etc.], 1881– . Annual. **DC521**

v. 1–3 repr.: Nendeln : Kraus, 1975.

An annual bibliography of books and periodical articles. Vols. 1–70 (1880–1949) issued as a supplement to the quarterly *Historisk tidsskrift.*

§ A cumulation is issued irregularly: 1771–1874 (publ. 1937); 1875–1900 (1907); 1901–20 (1923); 1921–35 (1956); 1936–50 (1964); 1951–60 (1968); 1961–70 (1984); 1971–75 (1987). Publisher varies. Issued as the series "Skrifter utg. av Svenska historiska föreningen".

For earlier publications, *see* Kristian Setterwall, *Svensk historisk bibliografi 1771–1874,* rev. by S. Ågren (Uppsala, 1937. 911 p.).

                             Z2636.S9

Switzerland

Bibliography

Barth, Hans. Bibliographie der schweizer Geschichte enthaltend die selbständig erschienenen Druckwerke zur Geschichte der Schweiz bis Ende 1912. Basel : Basler Buch– und Antiquariatshandlung, 1914–15. 3 v. (Quellen zur schweizer Geschichte hrsg. von der Allgemeinen Geschichtforschenden Gesellschaft der Schweiz. n. F., 4. Abt. Handbücher).   **DC522**

Contents: v. 1, General history, by periods; v. 2–3, Special subjects, e.g., biography, religious history, etc. Author and title index.

A very comprehensive bibliography, including more than 32,000 entries.

§ May be supplemented by the following:

(1) For material after 1912, by the annual *Bibliographie der Schweizergeschichte* (DC528).

(2) For analytical material before 1900, by the two volumes of the *Repertorium über die in Zeit- und Sammelschriften* (DC523).

                             Z2786.B28

Brandstetter, Josef Leopold. Repertorium über die in Zeit- und Sammelschriften der Jahre 1812–1890 enthaltenen Aufsätze und Mitteilungen schweizergeschichtlichen Inhaltes / hrsg. von der Allgemeinen Geschichtforschenden Gesellschaft der Schweiz von Josef Leopold Brandstetter .... Basel : A. Geering, 1892. 467 p.   **DC523**

Classed list—arranged by topic with alphabetical index of authors—for articles on Swiss history, biography, etc., in more than 300 periodicals and society transactions. The sections on biography give, in addition to the references to the articles, the dates of birth and death and a brief characterizing phrase, and thus supply some direct biographical information.

§ Continued by: Hans Barth, *Repertorium über die in zeit- und sammelschriften der jahre 1891–1900 enthaltenen aufsätze und mitteilungen schweizergeschichtlichen inhaltes* (Basel : Basler Buch– und Antiquariatshandlung, 1906. 359 p.).

Both works were reprinted by H. Lang, Bern, in 1967.

                             Z2786.B81

Guyer, Paul. Bibliographie der Städtegeschichte der Schweiz. Zürich : Verlag Leemann, 1960. 70 p. (Schweizerische Zeitschrift für Geschichte. Beiheft, 11).   **DC524**

Contains 763 entries for books and periodical articles. Geographical arrangement; name index. Gives population of each town in 1850 and in 1950.   Z2793.G8

Kaufmann, Uri R. Bibliographie zur Geschichte der Juden in der Schweiz : auf der Basis des Werkes von Annie Fraenkel. München ; N.Y. : Saur, 1993. 151 p. (Bibliographien zur deutsch-jüdischen Geschichte, Bd. 4).   **DC525**

A topical geographical arrangement for books, articles, and essays of the 18th–20th centuries, though a few go back to 1500. 1,576 entries. Indexes: name as subject, place as subject, topic, authors.

                             Z6373.S9K38

Meier, Heinz K. Switzerland / Heinz K. Meier, Regula A. Meier. Oxford ; Santa Barbara, Calif. : Clio Pr., c1990. 409 p. (World bibliographical series, v. 114).   **DC526**

A bibliography of 974 annotated entries, arranged by topic, with chapters on major periodicals, reference books, and bibliographies. Intends to provide "a representative sample of works available in each of the subject areas."—*Introd.* Most titles cited are in English, but a good number are in French, German, or Italian. Author, title, and subject indexes.   Z2771.M45

Santschy, Jean-Louis. Manuel analytique et critique de bibliographie générale de l'histoire suisse. Berne : Herbert Lang, 1961. 250 p.   **DC527**

A guide to sources—general, archival, periodical, and monographic—rather than a bibliography as such. Chapter arrangement, according to type and date of material. Annotations are full; author and subject indexes. Still useful as an introduction to sources.   Z2786.S3

Current

Bibliographie der Schweizergeschichte = Bibliographie de l'histoire suisse. Jahrg. 1913– . [Bern : Eidegenössische Drucksachen- und Materialzentrale], 1914– . Annual (some years combined).   **DC528**

Publisher varies.

Continues Hans Barth's *Bibliographie der schweizer Geschichte* (DC522).

Vols. for 1913–19 publ. as supplements to the *Anzeiger für schweizerische Geschichte*; those for 1920–34, as supplements to the *Zeitschrift für schweizerische Geschichte.*

Classed arrangement. Includes material on history, bibliography, biography, church, art, literature, music, customs, etc. Later volumes have author and subject indexes.   Z2786.B58

Encyclopedias

Dictionnaire historique et biographique de la Suisse. Neuchâtel : Admin. du Dictionnaire, 1921–34. 9 v. : ill., maps.   **DC529**

Also issued in German as: *Historisch-biographisches Lexikon der Schweiz.*

Publié avec la recommandation de la Société Générale Suisse d'Histoire.

Contents: v. 1–7, A–Z; suppl., A–Z, p. 1–184; 2nd suppl., A–Z, p. 185–208. Table systématique.

May be considered a companion work to the *Dictionnaire géographique de la Suisse* (CL150), published by Attinger. Covers the fields of general, political, local, economic, and social history; topography; genealogy; and biography of the country. Signed articles, bibliographies, and many good illustrations. Many biographical articles, including some on persons still living at time of compilation.   DQ51.D5

Schweizer Lexikon 91 : in sechs Bänden. Lucerne : Verlag Schweizer Lexikon, 1992–93. 6 v.   **DC530**

For annotation, *see* AB100.   AE27.S39

Turkey

Bibliography

Battersby, Harold R. Anatolian archaeology : a bibliography. New Haven, Conn. : Human Relations Area Files, 1976. 2 v. (Anatolian studies, 1).   **DC531**

Entries for 5,169 articles, essays, books, and periodical titles are listed in two alphabetical author sequences, with index by topic or excavation site.

§ For an additional bibliography, see *Türk arkeologi dergisis makaleler bibliografyasi*, comp. M. Asif Išik (Ankara : Eski Eserler ve Müzeler Genel Müdürlügü, 1982. v. 1, 1930–80). For an encyclopedia, *see* Pars Tuğlaci, *Çağdaş Türkiye* (Istanbul : Cem Yayınevi, 1987–1990. 3 v. [1978 p.]). Devoted to Atatürk and Turkey at the time of Atatürk; heavily illustrated. **Z2857.A67B38**

Bibliografiíà Türtsii, 1713–1917 / A. K. Sverchevskaíà, T. P. Cherman. Moskva : Izd-vo Vostochnoi Lit-ry, 1961. 266 p. **DC532**

At head of title: Akademiíà Nauk SSSR. Institut Narodov Azii.

Bibliography of scientific and popular Soviet writings on Turkey and Turkology, and of Turkish authors translated into Russian.

Continued by: *Bibliografiíà Türtsii, 1917–1975* by Sverchevskaíà and Cherman (Moskva : Nauka, 1982. 742 p.). **Z2846.S89**

Bodurgil, Abraham. Kemal Atatürk : a centennial bibliography (1881–1981). Wash. : Near East Section, African and Middle Eastern Div., Library of Congress, 1984. 214 p. **DC533**

1st ed., 1974, had title: *Atatürk and Turkey.*

A topically arranged bibliography of some 2,000 books, articles, dissertations, conference papers, and motion pictures. Author index and a very full subject index.

Continued by the author's *Turkey—politics and government : a bibliography, 1938–1975* (Wash. : Library of Congress, 1978. 156 p.), citing 2,020 books, journal articles, Turkish and U.S. publications.

§ For other reference materials on Atatürk, see *Atatürk kaynakçasi*, a bibliography comp. by Leman Senalp (Ankara : Türk Tarih Kurumu Basimevi, 1984. 2 v.) and *Atatürk ve devrimleri tarihi bibliyografyas*, by Muzaffer Gökman (Ankara : Kültür Bakanliği, 1982–84. v. 1–3), subtitled *Bibliography of the history of Atatürk and his reforms.* **Z2850.A85B6**

Güçlü, Meral. Turkey. London ; Santa Barbara, Calif. : Clio Pr., [1981]. 331 p. (World bibliographical series, 27). **DC534**

Citations to 993 books and a few periodical articles are arranged topically; good annotations. All arc English-language materials except for a few recent Turkish titles chosen arbitrarily as examples. Author, title, subject index. **Z2831.G83**

Koray, Enver. Türkiye tarih yayinlari bibliyografyasi. Istanbul : Maarif Basimevi, 1959–87. [v. 1–4]. (In progress). **DC535**

Contents: [v. 1, 2. basim] 1729–1955 (1959); [v. 2, 1. basim] 1955–1968 (1970); v. 3, 1968–1977 (1979); v. 4, 1978–84 (1987).

Vol. 1 supersedes an earlier edition covering 1729–1950 (publ. 1952).

A bibliography of Turkish historical writings. Lists general works, collections, encyclopedias, etc., followed by books on the history of individual countries, and then works in related fields such as archaeology, biography, and ethnology. Author and title indexes. **Z2846.K62**

Kornrumpf, Hans-Jürgen. Osmanische Bibliographie mit Besonderer Berücksichtigung der Türkei in Europa / Hans-Jürgen Kornrumpf ; Unter Mitarbeit von Jutta Kornrumpf. Leiden : Brill, 1973. 1378 p. (Handbuch der Orientalistik. 1 Abt. Der Nahe und der Mittlere Osten. Ergänzungsband, 8). **DC536**

Pages 1–726 comprise an alphabetical author listing of books (including book reviews), essays, and articles in all languages. A second section, p. 729–1378, provides a listing in classed arrangement of the items in the first section. A useful feature is the indication at the end of each entry in the author part of the classification used for that item in the subject section. **Z2831.K67**

Mikhov, Nikola V. Bibliografskii iztochnitsi za istoriíàta na Turtsíà i Bulgaríà = Sources bibliographiques sur l'histoire de la Turquie et de la Bulgarie. Sofiia : Durzhavna pechatnitsa, 1914–34. 4 v. **DC537**

Text in French, German, and other Western languages; preface in Bulgarian and French.

A bibliography of works of the 19th and 20th centuries, in various languages, on the history of Turkey and Bulgaria. Cumulated author and subject indexes to all four volumes in v. 4. **Z6464.E1M6**

————— Bibliographie des articles de périodiques allemands, anglais, français et italiens sur la Turquie et la Bulgarie. Sofià : Imprimerie de la Cour, 1938. 686 p. **DC538**

At head of title: Académie Bulgare des Sciences.

A comprehensive compilation of more than 10,000 titles of articles appearing in the periodicals of Western Europe from 1715 to 1880 (with some additional entries to 1891), arranged chronologically by year, with indexes by author and personal name and by subject and place-name. List of abbreviations of periodical titles, p. 1–58.

§ See also Mikhov's *Naselenieto na Turtsíà na Bulgaríà priez XVIII i XIX vekovete : bibliografisko-statistichni izslíedvaníà = La population de la Turquie et la Bulgarie au XVIIIe et au XIXe siécles : recherches bibliographiques avec données statistiques etnographiques* (Sofià : Durzhavna pechatnitsa, 1915–67. 5 v.) for books and articles on population and other demographic statistics. **Z2846.M63**

Tamkoç, Metin. A bibliography on the foreign relations of the Republic of Turkey, 1919–1967, and brief biographies of Turkish statesmen. Ankara : Orta Dogu Teknik Universitesi, Idari Ilimler Facultesi, 1968. 248 p. (Ankara. Orta Dogu Teknik Universitesi. Yayinlar, 11). **DC539**

A classed bibliography of about 1,800 entries. Turkish and foreign sources are listed in separate sections, English translations of the Turkish titles are added. Index of names.

§ For relations between Turkey and Western Europe since 1973, *see* Erol Esen, *Bestandsaufnahme der Literatur und Forschungen in der Bundesrepublik Deutschland sowie der EG-Veröffentlichungen zum Thema der politischen und wirtschaftlichen Beziehungen zwischen der Türkei und Westeuropa seit 1973* (Istanbul : Friedrich Ebert Stiftungt, 1989. 101 p.), which includes listings of European Community publications. **Z2857.R4T3**

Witherell, Julian W. The Republic of Turkey : an American perspective : a guide to U.S. official documents and government-sponsored publications. Wash. : Library of Congress : For sale by the U.S. Govt. Print. Off., 1988. 211 p. **DC540**

Superintendent of Documents classification: LC 1.6/4: T84.

"Records a selection [i.e. 1,702] of publications on Turkey issued by or for agencies of the U.S. government in the period 1919–1986."—*Pref.* Arranged topically; includes Library of Congress call number or library location if not in LC. Does not include classified documents, Congressional bills and resolutions, preliminary or program reports on government contracts. Author/title/subject index. May serve as a guide to the microfilm collection, *Republic of Turkey*, produced by Univ. Publications of America. **Z6465.U5W56**

Dissertations

Suzuki, Peter T. French, German, and Swiss university dissertations on twentieth century Turkey : a bibliography of 593 titles, with English translations. Wiesbaden : WDS-Schnelldruck, 1970. 138p. (Newsletter for European researchers on modern Turkey. Supplement, no.1, rev.). **DC541**

An author listing with broad subject index. Covers French dissertations accepted 1900–67; German dissertations, 1900–65; Swiss dissertations, 1900–68. Includes some works completed at the universities of Graz and Vienna.

Encyclopedias

Yurt ansiklopedisi : Türkiye, il dünü bügünü, yarini. Istanbul : Anadolu Yayincilik, 1981–84. 11 v. : ill. ; maps. **DC542**

Contents: v. 1–10, A–Z; v. 11, Türkiye/genel.

Arranged by place-name, giving extensive information in all subject areas—historical, political, cultural, literary, etc.

Ukraine

For an archival guide, *see* DC561 *note*.

Encyclopedia of Ukraine / ed. by Volodymyr Kubijovyč. Toronto ; Buffalo : Univ. of Toronto Pr., c1984–c1993. 5 v. : ill.
DC543

Published for the Canadian Institute of Ukrainian Studies, the Shevchenko Scientific Society and the Canadian Foundation for Ukrainian Studies.

Translation and revision of *Entsyklopediia ukraïnoznavstva* (1949–73).

Covers all areas of Ukrainian studies, including information on Ukrainians living outside the U.S.S.R. Some long survey articles (e.g., Anthropology, Botany); much biographical information. Longer articles are signed and usually give bibliographical references. Handsome illustrations. Includes an atlas and gazetteer. DK508.E613

Magocsi, Paul R. Ukraine, a historical atlas / Paul Robert Magocsi ; Geoffrey J. Matthews, cartographer. Toronto ; Buffalo : Univ. of Toronto Pr., c1985. 25 [i.e. 59] p. : maps in color. **DC544**

Reprinted with a few revisions, 1987.

Text and maps on facing pages cover "the present-day Ukrainian Soviet Socialist Republic and the Ukrainian ethnolinguistic territory" (*Pref.*) from the time of the Greek colonies through World War II. Very clear presentation. G2151.S1M34

Ukrainskai͡a Sovetskai͡a Sotsialisticheskai͡a Respublika : ėntsiklopedicheskiĭ spravochnik / glavnai͡a redaktsionnai͡a kollegii͡a B.M. Babiĭ, F.S. Babichev. … [et al.]. Kiev : Glav. red. Ukrainskoĭ Sov. ėntsiklopedii, 1987. 513 p., [75] p. of plates : ill. (some col.). **DC545**

Russian ed. of *Ukraïns'ka Radi͡ans'ka Sotsialistychna Respublika*, 1986.

A single-volume encyclopedia, covering 500 BCE–1986, published and translated in the Ukraine. Articles treat broad topics, such as history or culture. Heavily illustrated. DK508.A4U4717

University of Toronto. Library. Ucrainica at the University of Toronto Library : a catalogue of holdings / comp. by Paul Robert Magocsi with the assistance of Nadia Odette Diakun. Toronto ; Buffalo : Univ. of Toronto Pr., c1985. 2 v. (1845 p.).
DC546

About 11,000 titles published up to 1980 held by the University of Toronto Library are topically arranged in 31 chapters with 80 subdivisions. Covers "all materials in whatever language or form that deal in some way in the Ukraine or which are produced by individuals working within a Ukrainian historical and cultural environment."—*Introd*. Not indexed. Z2514.U5U55

Wynar, Bohdan S. Ukraine : a bibliographic guide to English-language publications. Englewood, Colo. : Ukrainian Academic Pr., 1990. 406 p. **DC547**

A bibliography of 1,084 English-language books, theses, pamphlets, essays, and articles, with critical annotations that often cite reviews. Subsumed in the annotations are citations to other works in English or Ukrainian. Arrangement is topical, well divided, even to individual authors in the Literature section. Author/title/subject index (with subject headings in boldface). Z2514.U5W9

Union of Soviet Socialist Republics

Materials on pre-Revolutionary Russia and on the republic of Russia since the Soviet breakup are presented here together with works on the Soviet Union.

General works

Bibliography

See also *Slavic studies* DC29.

Fundamental'nai͡a biblioteka obshchestvennykh nauk. (Akademii͡a nauk SSSR). Istorii͡a SSSR : ukazatel' sovetskoi literatury za 1917–1952 gg / [Sostaviteli: I. P. Doronin, i dr. Otvetstvennyĭ redaktor K. R. Simon]. Moskva : Izd-vo Akademii nauk SSSR, 1956–81. v. 1–2, 3^2,4. **DC548**

Compilers vary on later volumes.

Contents: v. 1, Istorii͡a SSSR s drevneishikh vremen do vstupleniia Rossii v period kapitalizma; v. 2, Istorii͡a SSSR v period kapitalizma 1861–1917; v. 3, Istorii͡a sovetskogo obshchestva: vyp. 2, Velikaia oktiabrskaia sotsialisticheskaia revoliutsita i Grazhdanskaia voina (mart 1917–1920gg.); vyp. 4, SSSR v gody Velikoi Otechestvennoi voiny (iiun 1941–Sent. 1945g.).

A major bibliography of Soviet historical writing, published between 1917 and 1952, on Russian history. Originally planned in three main chronological divisions.

———. ———. *Prilozhenie. Skhema klassifikatsii. Vspomogatel'nye ukazateli*.

These separate appendixes (with one published for each volume of the primary work) contain an outline of the classification, and name, subject, and other indexes.

Glavatskikh, G. A. Istorii͡a SSSR : annotirovannyi ukazatel' bibliograficheskikh posobii, opublikovannykh na russkom iazyke s nachala XIX v. po 1982 g.; v dvukh chastiakh / [G. A. Glavatskikh, N. V. Kadushkinda, L. M. Maslova]. 3–e izd., dop. i perer. Moskva : Gos. Biblioteka SSSR imeni V. I. Lenina, 1983–84. 2 v. **DC549**

1st ed., 1957, had title: *Bibliografiia russkoi bibliografii po istorii SSSR*. Compilers vary.

At head of title: Gosudarstvennaia Publichnaia Istoricheskaia Biblioteka RSFSR.

An annotated bibliography of bibliographies of historical works, topically arranged with extensive annotations. This edition includes materials published up to 1982. Not indexed. Z2506.G53

Horecky, Paul Louis. Basic Russian publications : an annotated bibliography on Russia and the Soviet Union. Chicago : Univ. of Chicago Pr., 1962. 313 p. **DC550**

A selective bibliography, representing the judgments of numerous area-study specialists and providing a "rigorously pruned inventory of Russian and Western publications."—*Introd*. Major sections: General reference aids and bibliographies; The land; The people: ethnic and demographic features; The nations; Civilizations and politics; History; The state; The economic and social structure; The intellectual and cultural life. Works relevant to the organizational, research, and socio-economic aspects of science and technology are represented. Despite its age, still very useful for older materials.

§ Companion volume follows the same arrangement: *Russia and the Soviet Union : a bibliographic guide to Western-language publications* (Chicago : Univ. Of Chicago Pr., 1965. 473 p.). Z2491.H6

Nerhood, Harry W. To Russia and return : an annotated bibliography of travelers' English-language accounts of Russia from the ninth century to the present. [Columbus] : Ohio State Univ. Pr., [1968]. 367 p. **DC551**

More than 1,400 items. Arrangement is chronological by date of the visit to Russia; author and title indexes.   Z2491.N435

Thompson, Anthony. Russia/U.S.S.R : a selective, annotated bibliography of books in English. Oxford ; Santa Barbara, Calif. : Clio Pr., 1979. 287 p. (World bibliographical series, 6).   **DC552**

Lists 1,247 books selected for the undergraduate or general reader "which will serve to stimulate interest in, and to illuminate the geography, history, social and economic system, and other aspects of the Soviet Union and its peoples."—*Introd.* Author, title, subject index.   Z2491.T45

Dissertations

Bruhn, Peter. Russika und Sowjetika unter den deutschsprachigen Hochschulschriften, 1961–1973 : bibliographisches Verzeichnis. Wiesbaden : Harrassowitz ; Berlin : Osteuropa-Inst. an d. Freien Univ., 1975. 166 p. (Bibliographische Mitteilungen des Osteuropas-Instituts an der Freien Universität Berlin, 11).   **DC553**

Serves as a continuation of Gerhard Hanusch's list of "Osteuropa-Dissertationen" covering the period 1945–60, which appeared as supplements in the *Jahrbücher für Geschichte Osteuropas,* 1953–60.

§ Continued by: *Russika und Sowjetika unter den deutschsprachigen Hochschulschriften (1973–1975) : mit Nachträgen für 1963 bis 1972* (Berlin : Osteuropa-Inst. an der Freien Univ. ; Wiesbaden : Harrassowitz, 1981. 437 p. Bibliographische Mitteilungen des Osteuropas-Instituts an der Freien Universität Berlin, 21).   Z2491.B88

Dossick, Jesse John. Doctoral research on Russia and the Soviet Union. N.Y. : New York Univ. Pr., 1960. 248 p.   **DC554**

Arranged by subject, with American and Canadian works in one scheme and British works in a second, similar scheme. Bibliography of bibliographies of doctoral dissertations. No index.

§ Continued by: *Doctoral research on Russia and the Soviet Union, 1960–1975 : a classified list of 3,150 American, Canadian, and British dissertations with some critical and statistical analysis* (N.Y. : Garland, 1976. 345 p. [Garland reference library of social science, 7]).

Supersedes the annual supplements appearing in the *Slavic review* 1964–1974, and adds some items missed in the earlier volume. Indexes of Russian/Soviet names, American and Canadian authors, and British authors.   Z2491.D6

Seydoux, Marianne. Répertoire des thèses concernant les études slaves : l'U.R.S.S. et les pays de l'Est européen et soutenues en France de 1824 à 1969 / Marianne Seydoux, Mieczyslaw Biesiekierski. Paris : Institut d'études slaves, 1970. 157 p. (Travaux publiés par l'Institut d'études slaves, 30).   **DC555**

Listing is by country, then classified. More than 1,300 items. Author index.

Reprinted in the Institut's *Guide du slaviste* as issued in looseleaf form in 1971. Looseleaf supplements adding some new theses as late as 1972 (together with some from the pre-1969 period) were issued in 1972.   Z2483.S49

Library resources

Grant, Steven A. Scholars' guide to Washington, D.C. for Russian, Central Eurasian, and Baltic studies : Armenia, Azerbaijan, Belarus, Estonia, Georgia, Kazakhstan, Kyrgyzstan, Latvia .... 3rd ed. / rev. by William E. Pomeranz ... [et al.]. Wash. : Woodrow Wilson Center Pr. ; Baltimore : Johns Hopkins Univ. Pr., 1994. 293 p. (Scholars' guide to Washington, D.C., no. 15).   **DC556**

1st ed., 1977; 2nd ed., 1983.

Published for the Kennan Institute for Advanced Russian Studies, Woodrow Wilson International Center for Scholars.

One of a series of scholars' guides to the Washington, D.C. area. Covers collections (i.e., libraries, archives, museums, data banks, etc.) and organizations (i.e., associations, government agencies, research centers, etc.). Indexed.   Z2491.G67

Manuscripts; Archives

Archives in Russia : a brief directory / comp. by Patricia Kennedy Grimsted ... [et al.] ; ed. by Mikhail Dmitrivich Afanas'ev .... Preliminary English version. Wash. : International Research & Exchanges Board, c1993– . v. (loose-leaf).   **DC557**

Contents: pt. 1, Moscow and St. Petersburg; pt. 2, Russian Federation outside Moscow and St. Petersburg (In progress).

Updates archival data in the appendixes of *Handbook for archival research in the U.S.S.R.* (DC562).

Offers extensive discussion of the new archival laws, new organizations, and use of the archives, followed by a directory based on responses to questionnaires. For each archive, gives: Russian name in transliteration, address, phone, hours, director, nearest Metro stop, short history with previous names, brief characteristics, size, and inclusive dates of holdings, published and unpublished finding aids, IDC reference for microfiche publication of finding aids. Indexes for previous names and acronyms.

§ Through interviews with archival officials, Theodore Karasik has gathered information in *The post-Soviet archives : organization, access and declassification* (Santa Monica, Calif. : Rand Corp., 1993. 68 p.) on the "structure, access, and declassification procedures for Soviet-era civil and military archives located in Moscow" (*Pref.*) as of Oct. 1992. His book is divided into six areas: Russian state archive system, Russian Foreign Ministry archives, Russian presidential archives, Committee for State Security (KGB) archives, Chief Intelligence Directorate (GRU) archives, Commonwealth of Independent States (CIS) military archives.

Bakhmeteff Archive of Russian and East European History and Culture. Russia in the twentieth century : the catalog of the Bakhmeteff Archive of Russian and East European History and Culture / the Rare Book and Manuscript Library, Columbia University. Boston : G.K. Hall, 1987. 187 p.   **DC558**

Lists more then 900 collections pertaining to people and institutions of late 19th- and 20th-century Eastern Europe and Russia. Arranged alphabetically by author with descriptions of contents and indication of extent of collection and access (but not of provenance). Index of names and subjects.   CD1739.N483B35

Bolkhovitinov, N. N. Russia and the United States : an analytical survey of archival documents and historical studies / trans. and ed. by J. Dane Hartgrove. Armonk, N.Y. : M.E. Sharpe, c1986. 79 p.   **DC559**

Also issued as *Soviet studies in history*, 25, no. 2 (1986).

Translation of *Rossiĩa i SShA* (Moscow : INION AN SSSR, 1984).

A discussion of the archival guides and a survey of the holdings of the state archives and of major libraries in Moscow and Leningrad, plus a summary of research in the U.S.S.R. on U.S.-Russian relations. Selected bibliography of finding aids, and of English- and Russian-language material. Not indexed.   Z6465.U5B64

Grant, Steven A. The Russian Empire and the Soviet Union : a guide to manuscripts and archival materials in the United States / Steven A. Grant and John H. Brown ; Kennan Institute for Advanced Russian Studies, the Wilson Center. Boston : G.K. Hall, 1981. 632 p.   **DC560**

Lists and briefly describes "materials in U.S. archives and manuscript repositories that relate to the Russian Empire, Soviet Union, and the many distinct nationalities therein."—*Introd.* Covers the "broadest possible range of subjects" and includes collections found in public and private institutions, libraries, museums, ethnic organizations, church and business archives, historical societies, and some private collections. Arranged by state, then by city and repository, with detailed subject index. References are given to published descriptions and finding aids for individual collections.   Z2491.G66

Grimsted, Patricia Kennedy. Archives and manuscript repositories in the USSR : Moscow and Leningrad. Princeton : Princeton Univ. Pr., [1972]. 436 p.   **DC561**

Intended "first to serve as a starting point for the foreigner planning research in the Soviet Union" (*Pref.*), but also as a guide for scholars, librarians, and others who need information about holdings and published finding aids of the various collections.

For each repository there is information on contents (usually with an historical note), working conditions, and published descriptions and inventories. An historical survey of Russian archives, a chapter on procedural information, and a bibliography of general Russian archival and research aids are followed by sections treating the individual repositories grouped as: (1) Central state archives; (2) Archives and manuscript collections of the Academy of Sciences; (3) Special archives; (4) Manuscript divisions of libraries and museums in Moscow; (5) Manuscript divisions of libraries and museums in Leningrad; (6) Republic and local state archives in Moscow and Leningrad.

A microfiche series, *Archives and manuscript repositories in the USSR* (Zug, Switzerland : InterDocumentation Co., 1975–81) reproduces all the catalogs and other findings cited in the published work, its supplement, and the companion works (below).

————. ————. *Supplement 1 : Bibliographical addenda* (Zug, Switzerland : InterDocumentation Co., 1976. 203 p.). Lists publications appearing through the end of 1973 (and including numerous pre-1970 publications which were omitted from the original volume) plus a few 1974 imprints. Items in the supplement which are available in the publisher's (i.e., IDC) microfiche series are so noted, and a "microfiche correlation table" for items in the main volume is provided.

Companion works:

————. *Archives and manuscript repositories in the USSR : Estonia, Latvia, Lithuania, and Belorussia* (Princeton, N.J. : Princeton Univ. Pr., [1981]. 929 p.).

Aims "to serve as a starting point for the foreign scholar planning research in the Baltic republics and Belorussia" (*Pref.*) by providing descriptions of archival and manuscript collections and providing references to additional published descriptions, finding aids, and guides to those collections. Each of the four republics is treated separately, and there is an introductory historical survey and general bibliography for each section. Author/title and subject indexes.

————. *Archives and manuscript repositories in the USSR : Ukraine and Moldavia* (Princeton, N.J. : Princeton Univ. Pr., c1988. v. 1 ; maps. [In progress]).

To be in two parts: "Book 1 [the volume at hand] provides a bibliography of general reference literature relating to archives and manuscript collections in both union republics, followed by a comprehensive directory of archives and other manuscript repositories with bibliographies of their respective finding aids. Book 2, to be published later, will present a historical survey of the development of archives and recordkeeping practices in Ukraine and Moldavia."—*Pref.* Format follows that of previous volumes.   CD1711.G7

———— A handbook for archival research in the USSR. [N.Y.?] : International Research and Exchanges Board ; [Wash.] : Kennan Institute for Advanced Russian Studies, c1989. 430 p.   **DC562**

"The aim ... is to provide an updated general orientation for the beginning researcher, with selected bibliographic leads for further reference."—*Pref.* Discusses the state administration of the archives in U.S.S.R, their general arrangement, access, how to prepare for on-site use, and duplication services. Also includes a bibliographical essay on reference aids and a directory of major archives, libraries, and manuscript repositories in Moscow and Leningrad, as well as state archives of the other republics. The latter gives for each: address, staff, brief description of holdings, and published guides and finding aids. General index. A necessity for anyone planning research in the U.S.S.R.

Updated by: *Archives in Russia : a brief directory* (DC557).

§ An earlier work by Grimsted discusses bibliographies of archival literature, with emphasis on repositories in Moscow and Lenin-

grad: *Recent Soviet archival literature: a review and preliminary bibliography of selected reference aids* (Wash. : Kennan Institute for Advanced Russian Studies, 1987. 122 p. Occasional paper 8).   CD1711.G68

Hartley, Janet M. Guide to documents and manuscripts in the United Kingdom relating to Russia and the Soviet Union. London ; N.Y. : Mansell, 1987. 526 p.   **DC563**

The result of "a three-year research project undertaken at the School of Slavonic and East European Studies, University of London, from 1982 to 1985."—*Introd.* Information is based mainly on responses to questionnaires sent to libraries, museums, record offices, and professional, religious and cultural organizations; many repositories were also visited. Geographical arrangement with address, finding aids and brief descriptions. Indexed.

§ The School sponsored a conference (Apr. 1984) in order to demonstrate "the richness and variety of sources in Britain for the study of Anglo-Russian and Anglo-Soviet relations and Russian and Soviet history and to show how these sources could be used as a basis for scholarly research."—*Introd.* The papers were published as: *The study of Russian history from British archival sources*, ed. Janet M. Hartley (London ; N.Y. : Mansell, 1986. 184 p.). Some papers discuss specific archival collections (e.g., Leeds Russian archives), other particular topics (e.g., Britons in 17th-century Russia).   Z2491.H37

Hoover Institution on War, Revolution, and Peace. Guide to the collections in the Hoover Institution archives relating to Imperial Russia, the Russian revolutions and civil war, and the first emigration / comp. by Carol A. Leadenham. Stanford, Calif. : Hoover Institution Pr., Stanford Univ., c1986. 208 p. (Hoover Press bibliographical series, 68).   **DC564**

A guide to one of the great Western repositories concentrating on 20th-century Russian political, diplomatic, and military affairs, gathered from émigrés, relief workers, Russian consulates in Germany, Tsarist military officers, government officials, and embassies in France. The archives also include motion pictures, films, posters, and art works. Collections are listed alphabetically, with notes on size and content, within period or broad category (e.g., Mongolia, Relief agencies). Indexed by subject.   Z2510.H66

Soviet Union. Glavnoe arkhivnoe upravlenie. Lichnye arkhivnye fondy v gosudarstvennykh kranilishchakh SSSR : ukazatel' / [Red. IU. I. Gerasimova ... et al. ; Sost. E. V. Kolosova ... et al.]. Moskva, [1962–80]. 3 v.   **DC565**

At head of title: Gosudarstvennaia Biblioteka SSSR imeni V. I. Lenina. Arkhiv Akademiia Nauk SSSR.

Editor varies; publisher varies.

A directory of personal and family papers in the Soviet Union. Vol. 1–2 concerned mainly with the pre-Revolutionary period; v. 3 concentrates on figures active during the Soviet period and adds collections not previously covered.   CD1734.R87

Encyclopedias; Dictionaries

The modern encyclopedia of Russian and Soviet history / ed. by Joseph L. Wieczynski. [Gulf Breeze, Fla.] : Academic International Pr., 1976–94. 58 v.   **DC566**

Contents: v. 1–55, Aachen–Zvenigorod; v. 56, Index of entries and authors; v. 57, Index of entries by topics; v. 58, Index of entries by time period.

Aims "to become the most comprehensive aid to the study of the Russian past ever created in the English language" (*v. 1, p. vi*), with information encompassing "all major facts, events, personalities and institutions important to the history of the Russian Empire and the Soviet Union." While the editor's note states that the work "will reproduce in English information contained in the many standard Russian reference series," the sources of specific articles are not given (nor is there an indication whether the information is a direct translation from a single source). Additional information is derived from monographs and research studies, and new articles have been contributed by an international roster of contemporary scholars. Longer articles are signed, and include bibliographies of both Russian- and English-language materials. Intended to be useful "to undergraduate students, government and private researchers and even high school students as well as to professional historians and scholars," but highly specialized information of narrow interest is omitted on the assumption that the specialist can obtain it from Russian-language sources.

With v. 46 begins a supplement designed to cover topics previously omitted, especially material on the history and development of cites and towns, articles from the *Great Soviet encyclopedia* (AB87), and biographies of people who died since publication of earlier volumes. Note especially v. 46–47, which include discussion of archives in the Soviet Union, in the Union Republics, and in Tsarist Russia.

§ Also being published by Academic International Pr. and in progress are: *The modern encyclopedia of religions in Russia and the Soviet Union*, ed. Paul D. Steeves (Gulf Breeze, Fla. : Academic International Pr., 1988–93. v. 1–5 [In progress]) and *Military-naval encyclopedia of Russia and the Soviet Union*, ed. David R. Jones (CJ657).

DK36.M55

Paxton, John. Encyclopedia of Russian history : from the Christianization of Kiev to the break-up of the U.S.S.R. Santa Barbara, Calif. : ABC-Clio, c1993. 483 p. : maps.   **DC567**

Rev. ed. of *Companion to Russian history* (London : Batsford ; N.Y. : Facts on File, 1983. 503 p.).

A dictionary of some 2,500 brief entries covering Russian history from the 10th century to about 1990. Entries include places, movements, arts, foreign influences, people, often with brief bibliographies. Statistics used are meant to be current as of late 1980s. Chronology; select bibliography; historical maps. Offers 11 black-and-white maps, but without reference to or from the text.   DK36.P39

Shavit, David. United States relations with Russia and the Soviet Union : a historical dictionary. Westport, Conn. : Greenwood, 1993. 233 p.   **DC568**

Beginning with the 18th century, "includes entries on policies, summit meetings, treaties, industries, institutions, organizations and business firms ..." (*Pref*), individuals who played a significant role in political and economic, cultural and scientific relations. Cross-references indicated by an asterisk. Bibliographical essay discusses relevant books. Topical index.

§ Similar to Shavit's volumes on Africa (DD96), Middle East (DE56), and Asia (DE15).   E183.8.R9S487

Sovetskaia istoricheskaia entsiklopediia / glavny red. E. M. Zhukov. Moskva : Sovetskaia Entsiklopediia, 1961–80. 16 v. : ill., maps, facsims.   **DC569**

Offers some 25,000 articles (often with chronologies, maps, tables, bibliographies) on biographical, historical, political and similar subjects. Universal in coverage; strongest on Russian topics, but much attention is given to history, etc., of developing countries.   D9.S64

Historiography

Gosudarstvennaia publichnaia istoricheskaia biblioteka RSFSR. Istoriia istoricheskoi nauki v SSSR : Dooktiabr'skii period; bibliografiia / [Otv. red. M. V. Nechkina]. Moskva : Nauka, 1965. 702 p.   **DC570**

On page preceeding t.p.: Akademiiaa nauk SSSR. Institut istorii. Gosudarstvennia publichnaia biblioteka RSFSR.

A bibliography of historiographical literature published in the U.S.S.R. and dealing with pre-revolutionary history. Includes writings on the activities of historical societies and institutions. Classed arrangement with index.

Continued by: *Istoriia istoricheskoi nauki v SSSR—sovetskii period oktiabr' 1917–1967 g. : bibliografiia* / [sostaviteli R. G. Eimontova ... et al. ; red. kollegiia M. V. Nechkina (otvetstvennyi red.) ... et al.]. Moskva : Izd-vo "Nauka," 1980. 732 p.).   Z2511.H5I84

Atlases

Gilbert, Martin. Atlas of Russian history. 2nd ed. N.Y. : Oxford Univ. Pr., 1993. [9], 161, [35] p. : 161 maps ; scales differ ; 26 cm.   **DC571**

Rev. ed. of the author's *Russian history atlas*, 1972.

Black-and-white maps with effective use of shading, covering up to the breakup of the Soviet Union. Text accompanying maps gives background information, brief chronology, or significant dates. Index includes cross-references and dates. Bibliography of works consulted.

§ Allen F. Chew's *An atlas of Russian history : eleven centuries of changing borders* (Rev. ed. New Haven, Conn. : Yale Univ. Pr., 1970. 127 p. ; maps ; 28 cm.) can still be found in many reference departments because of its interest in boundaries and possessions, 9th century to 1945.   G2111.S1G52

Milner-Gulland, R. R. Cultural atlas of Russia and the Soviet Union / by Robin Milner-Gulland with Nikolai Dejevsky. N.Y. : Facts on File, 1989. 240 p. : ill. (some col.), some maps in color ; 31 cm.   **DC572**

U.K. edition entitled: *Atlas of Russia and the Soviet Union* (Oxford : Phaidon, 1989).

Essentially a narrative history of Russia and the Soviet Union up to 1985, heavily illustrated with maps, diagrams, and photographs. A final section gives "a concise geographical and cultural 'portrait' in maps, words and pictures of each of the republics ... so as to give the reader a sense of its location within the USSR, its people, its resources, its past and its individuality."—*p. 185*. A chronological table, 800–1979, is presented in parallel columns for: Politics and rulers; Religion; International relations; Territorial expansion; Art and architecture; Learning, science and literature. Bibliography arranged by themes; glossary; list of illustrations; gazetteer; index by topic.

§ Older but with useful maps: *Atlas historique et culturel de las Russie et de monde slav*, by Pierre Kovalevsky (Paris : Elsevier, 1961).   DK32.M62

Pre-1917

Bibliography

Bibliografiia trudov po otechestvennomu istochnikovedeniiu i spetsial'nym istoricheskim distsiplinam izdannykh v XVIII v / [sost. A. I. Aksenov ... i dr.] ; pod. red. V.I. Buganova. Moskva : Akademiia Nauk SSSR, 1981. 209 p.   **DC573**

An annotated bibliography of 18th-century publications useful to students of history. Includes materials on sources, genealogy, heraldry, numismatics, and reports of archaeological commissions. Name index.

Clendenning, Philip. Eighteenth century Russia : a select bibliography of works published since 1955 / Philip Clendenning, Roger Bartlett. Newtonville, Mass. : Oriental Research Partners, 1981. 262 p. (Russian bibliography series, 2).   **DC574**

Intended for the undergraduate and beginning graduate student. Aims "to provide up-to-date and representative coverage of recent writing on Russia in the eighteenth century."—*Pref.* Includes books and periodical articles in English, French and German, as well as Russian materials. Classed arrangement with index of names. Detailed table of contents, but no alphabetical subject approach.   Z2508.C58

Crowther, Peter A. A bibliography of works in English on early Russian history to 1800. Oxford : Blackwell ; N.Y. : Barnes & Noble, 1969. 236 p.   **DC575**

More than 2,000 items in classed arrangement, with name and subject index.

§ Continued by David Shapiro, *Select bibliography of works in English on Russian history, 1801–1917* (Oxford : Blackwell, 1962. 106 p.) for books and articles published up to Dec. 1961.   Z2506.C75

Dmitrieva, Rufina Petrovna. Bibliografiia russkogo leto-pisaniia / sostavila R. P. Dmitrieva ; [otvettstvennyĭ redaktor IA. S. Lure]. Leningrad : Izd-vo Akademii Nauk SSSR, 1962. 352 p. **DC576**

At head of title: Akademiia nauk SSSR. Institut russkoi literatury. Comprehensive bibliography of editions of the early Russian chronicles and of the historical and literary commentary and research concerning them. Russian, Ukrainian, and Belorussian publications of the years 1674–1917; Soviet work for the period 1918–1959; and selected foreign publications are included. Chronologically arranged, with various indexes. Z2506.D5

Dvizhenie dekabristov : ukazatel' literatury 1960–1976 / otvetstvennyi redaktor M. V. Nechkina ; [redaktor-sostavitel' R.G. Eimontova ; sostaviteli V. S. Barashkova ... [et al.]. Moskva : Izd-vo "Nauka", 1983. 301 p. **DC577**

At head of title: Akademiia Nauk SSSR. Institut Istorii SSSR. Gosudarstvennaia Publichnaia Istoricheskaia Biblioteka RSFSR. Continues the coverage of R. G. Eimontova's *Dvizhenie dekabris-tov: ukazatel' literatury 1928–1959* (Moskva, 1960. 434 p.), listing some 3,800 Soviet books, articles (including articles in provincial newspapers), and chapters in textbooks on the Decembrists. Topical arrangement with name and title index. Z2509.D88

Egan, David R. Russian autocrats from Ivan the Great to the fall of the Romanov dynasty : an annotated bibliography of English language sources to 1985 / David R. Egan and Melinda A. Egan. Metuchen, N.J. : Scarecrow, 1987. 512 p. **DC578**

Aims to provide a comprehensive listing of English-language monographs, chapters from general works, essays, articles, memoirs, letters, and doctoral dissertations, plus a selection of reviews. Includes translations from French, German and Russian. Annotations, some quite lengthy, are descriptive. Asterisks are "provided for sources that focus upon one or more monarchs and are comprehensive, scholarly, or unique in some way."—*Introd.* Arranged chronologically by tsar, with an author index and a subject index arranged alphabetically by ruler. Items in the General section are not indexed. Z2506.E35

Istoriia dorevoliutsionnoĭ Rossii v dnevnikakh i vospom-inaniiakh : [annotirovannyĭ ukazatel' knig i publikatsii v zhur-nalakh / sostaviteli G.A. Glavatskikh ... et al. ; nauchnoe ruko-vodstvo, red. i vvedenie P.A. Zaĭonchkovskogo]. Moskva : Kniga, 1976–89. 5 v. in 13. **DC579**

At head of title: Nauchnaia Biblioteka imeni A. M. Gor'kogo, Moskovskogo Gosudarstvennogo Universiteta imeni M. V. Lomonoso-va, Gosudarstvennaia Biblioteka SSR imeni V. I. Lenina. Contents: t. 1, XV–XVIII veka; t. 2, 1801–1856 (2 pts.); t. 3, 1857–1894 (4 pts.), t. 4, 1895–1917 (4 pts.); t. 5, ch. 1, Literatura; t. 5, ch. 2, Dopolmeniia t. 1–5 (completes the volume).

An annotated bibliography of pre-revolutionary Russian diaries, memoirs, travel accounts, etc., published in books, journals and collections. Foreign-language accounts are cited if published in Russia. Topically arranged within historical period. Indexes in v. 1; Names and titles cited; Geographic and ethnic names; Collections used for v. 1; Periodicals and other serials used for v. 1–4.

Vol. 5, Chap. 1 deals specifically with seven authors: Pushkin, Saltykov-Shchedrin, Tolstoi, Chekov, Blok, Gorkii, and Maiakovskii. These writers were omitted in the earlier volumes because they were already subjects of comprehensive bibliographies; the compilers have reconsidered and feel the set would be incomplete without citations to memoirs relating to them. Vol. 5, Chap. 2 is a supplement to v. 1–4[1], following the same arrangement as the earlier volumes; it also includes a consolidated table of contents for the full set, telling where the same section heads appear in each volume. Each volume includes its own author and place or ethnic group indexes. Z2506.I87

Mezhov, Vladimir Izmailovich. Russkaia istoricheskaia bibli-ografiia, 1800–54. St. Petersburg : Sibiriakov, 1892–93. 2 v. **DC580**

Added title page in French: Bibliographie des livres et articles russes d'histoire et sciences auxiliaires de 1800–1854.

Contents: v.1, Documents historiques et histoire politique de la Russie; v.2, Biographies. Sciences auxiliaires: généalogie, la science héraldique, chronologie, archéologie, paléographie, numismatique, sphragistique, mythologie; v.3, Géographie, hydrographie, orographie, cartographie, voyages, statistique, éthnographie, histoire des cultes et de l'église, agiologie, histoire de l'instruction publique. 34,994 entries. No index.

§ Continued by: *Russkaia istoricheskaia bibliografiia 1855–64*, compiled by Petr Petrovich Lambin (1861–84. 10 v.) and *Russkaia is-toricheskaia bibliografiia, 1865–76* (1882–90. 8 v.). compiled by Mezhov.

Schmidt, Christoph. Ausgewählte Bibliographien und Biblio-thekskatalog zur russischen Sozialgesichte (1861–1917). Wiesbaden : In Kommission bei O. Harrassowitz, 1989. 108 p. **DC581**

A guide to 77 major bibliographies and catalogs relevant to the study of Russian social history, most published before 1916 (though a few were published up to 1936). Subjects include social classes, minority groups, prostitution, local history, alcoholism, etc. Alphabetical arrangement with substantive annotations; subject index.

Z7165.S65S35

Spravochnik po istorii dorevoliutsionnoi Rossii : bibliograf-icheskii ukazatel' / [sost. G. A. Glavatskikh ... et al.] ; nauch. rukovodstvo, red. i vstup. statia P. A. Zaĭonchkovskogo. 2-e izd., peresmotr. i dop. Moskva : Kniga, 1978. 639 p. **DC582** 1st ed., 1971.

A bibliography of materials on pre-revolutionary Russia, topically arranged. Cites many statistical works and directories. Z2506.S65

Encyclopedias

Lexikon der Geschichte Russlands : von den Anfängen bis zur Oktober Revolution / hrsg. von Hans-Joachim Torke. München : Beck, c1985. 446 p. : ill. **DC583**

Signed articles cover from about 850 to 1917, each ending with a brief bibliography. Cross-references; no index. Brief chronology, 860–1917. A table gives translation of Russian terms to German titles of articles. DK36.L48

Historiography

Pushkarev, Sergei Germanovich. Dictionary of Russian historical terms from the eleventh century to 1917 / comp. by Sergei G. Pushkarev ; ed. by George Vernadsky and Ralph T. Fisher, Jr. New Haven, [Conn.] : Yale Univ. Pr., 1970. 199 p. **DC584**

"Designed to assist English-speaking readers to understand the specialized terms they encounter in Russian historical sources and in English-language works on Russia, terms explained very briefly if at all in an ordinary Russian-English dictionary."—*Pref.*

§ Vol. 1, Le monde rural, of Denise Eeckaute's *Thesaurus des in-stitutions de l'ancienne Russie (XIe–XVIIIe siècle)* (Paris : Éditions de la Maison des sciences de l'homme, [1986]–) has begun covering such areas as property and the practices of agriculture. Definitions incorporate the most recent scholarship. DK36.P78

Post-1917

Bibliography

Harvard University. Library. Russian history since 1917 : classification schedule, classified listing by call number, alphabetical listing by author or title, chronological listing. Cambridge : publ. by the Harvard Univ. Library ; distr. by the Harvard Univ. Pr., 1966. 698p. (Widener Library shelflist, no.4).   **DC585**

For a note on the series, *see* AA115.

13,772 titles encompassing general histories and descriptive works on the Soviet Union since 1917, including works on all aspects of the poliical, economic, and social life of the period. Local histories and geographies of the individual autonomous republics, cities, etc., are not found in this segment of the shelflist.   Z2510.H35

Johnston, Robert H. Soviet foreign policy, 1918–1945 : a guide to research and research materials. Wilmington, Del. : Scholarly Resources, [1991]. 236 p.   **DC586**

In four sections: (1) discussion of the People's Commissariat of Foreign Affairs—its organization and activities; (2) brief biographical notes on those people most involved, both Russian and foreign; (3) description of the archives, libraries and research institutes, both Russian and foreign repositories, indicating "their known or potential usefulness as primary sources for Soviet foreign policy materials" (*Introd.*); (4) listing of published resources arranged by format—bibliographies, documentary and official publications, memoirs and diaries, secondary literature, arranged by broad period. The last section contains 907 annotated items which are indexed by author or editor and by title if that is the main entry.

§ Companion to similar guides for Great Britain (DC326), France (DC203), Germany (DC237), Italy (DC419), and International organizations (AF1).

For extensive coverage of works published 1945–1978, *see* V. N. Egorov, *Mezhdunarodnye otnoseniĭa : bibliograficheskii spravochnik 1945–1960* (Moscow, 1961. 405 p.) and Johnny Christensen, *International relations and foreign policy—by countries and subjects : a bibliography of Soviet publications 1960–1978 : 1500 titles* (Aarhus : Arkona, 1979. 198 p.).   Z6465.S65J64

Luckert, Yelena. Soviet Jewish history, 1917 1991 : an annotated bibliography. N.Y. : Garland, 1992. 271 p. (Garland reference library of social science, v. 611).   **DC587**

A comprehensive, selected bibliography of 1,146 books, documents, newspaper and periodical articles, covering Soviet Jewish history, politics, culture, emigration, and religion. Helpful annotations. Chronological and subject chapters subdivided by topics. Although the topical arrangement is useful, a subject index would have enhanced access. Author index.

§ For recent Russian materials, *see* Boris Korsch, *Soviet publications on Judaism, Zionism, and the State of Israel, 1984–1988 : an annotated bibliography* (N.Y. : Garland, 1990. 126 p.).   Z6373.R9L83

Metzger, Wolfgang. Bibliographie deutschsprachiger Sowjetunion-Reiseberichte, -Reportagen und -Bildbände, 1917–1990. Wiesbaden : O. Harassowitz, c1991. 445 p.   **DC588**

Citations to about 5,000 German books, pamphlets, articles giving travel accounts, journalistic reports, and pictorial works, with some Soviet publications. Arranged by year. Not annotated; index to authors and main entry titles only.   Z2510.M495

The rise and fall of the Soviet Union : a selected bibliography of sources in English / ed. by Abraham J. Edelheit and Hershel Edelheit. Westport, Conn. : Greenwood, 1992. 430 p. (Bibliographies and indexes in world history, no. 27).   **DC589**

A selective bibliography of 2,016 English-language books and articles (from 28 journals), most published since 1970. Topically ar-

ranged by period, 1917–1991, with a background chapter on Tsarist Russia. Occasional annotations for books. Glossary; cross-references; author/title and subject indexes.   Z2510.3.R57

Sovetskaĭa strana v period vosstanovleniĭa narodnogo khoziaĭstva, 1921–1925 gg : bibliograficheskiĭ ukazatel' dokumental'nykh publikatsiĭ / pod red. E. B. Genkinoi ; sost. L. A. Kotel'nikova ... [et al.]. Moskva : Kniga, 1975. 692 p.   **DC590**

At head of title: Gosudarstvennaĭa Publichnaĭa Istoricheskaĭa Biblioteka RSFSR.

Offers citations to 9,611 documents published 1921–25, arranged topically and with a geographical index. Published in series with *Velikaĭa oktiabr'skaĭa sotsialisticheskaĭa revoliutsiĭa* (DC601) and *Sovetskaĭa strana v period grazhdanskoi voiny (1918–1922 gg.)* (Moscow, 1961).   Z2510.S67

Soviet studies guide / ed. by Tania Konn. London : Bowker-Saur, 1992. 237 p. : map.   **DC591**

Ten essays of approximately 5,000 words, each dealing with the literature of a particular subject (history, geography, etc.) over the past decade. Each essay is followed by an annotated bibliography of about 100 books and articles, mostly in English but also including major Russian works. Main entry index.   DK266.S68

Library resources (including archives)

A researcher's guide to sources on Soviet social history in the 1930s / ed. by Sheila Fitzpatrick and Lynne Viola. Armonk, N.Y. : M.E. Sharpe, c1990. 296 p.   **DC592**

A collection of essays by archivists, bibliographers, librarians, and historians that aim "to cover the basic types of existing source material on the social history of the 1930s: archives, statistics, newspapers and journals, laws and regulations, directories, memoirs and biographical data."—*Introd.* Subject index. Appendixes: National, republican and regional newspapers; Stenographic reports of party, Soviet, and other meetings (which are lists with no discussion).   Z7165.S65R47

A scholars' guide to humanities and social sciences in the Soviet successor states / Institute of Scientific Information in the Social Sciences (INION), Russian Academy of Sciences [and] Kennan Inst. for Advanced Russian Studies, Woodrow Wilson International Center for Scholars. 2nd ed. Armonk, N.Y. : M.E. Sharpe, c1993. 228 p.   **DC593**

For annotation, *see* AL59.   AS258.S36

Encyclopedias

The Blackwell encyclopedia of the Russian Revolution / ed. by Harold Shukman. Oxford ; N.Y. : Blackwell, 1988. 418 p. : ill., ports.   **DC594**

Treats organizations, events, and individuals important in Russian history, 1860s–1921. Contributors are mostly British. Pt. 1 is arranged basically in chronological chapters (unsigned) with cross-references in the text, each article ending with suggestions for further reading. Pt. 2, a biographical dictionary, deals with fewer people than *Dictionary of the Russian Revolution* (DC595), since here coverage begins with the roots of the revolution; no bibliographies in this part. Topical index. Heavily illustrated.   DK265.B54

Dictionary of the Russian Revolution / George Jackson, ed. in chief ; Robert Devlin, assistant ed. N.Y. : Greenwood, 1989. 704 p. : ill.   **DC595**

Approximately 300 signed articles on "revolutionary leaders and governing institutions ... social classes and social problems, workers, peasants, the agrarian question, the national question, the army, the navy, and the trade unions ... [and] national minorities.—*Pref.* Articles include bibliographic citations and cross-references. Contributors are mostly American. Much broader in coverage of the Revolution than *The Blackwell encyclopedia of the Russian Revolution* (DC594), but not as extensive for the earlier period. Chronology, 1898–1922. Name and subject indexes.   DK265.D49

Grazhdanskaía voina i voennaía interventsiía v SSSR : entsiklopediía / glavnyĭ red. S. S. Khromov ... [et al.]. Moskva : "Sov. entsiklopediia", 1983. 702 p. : ill., maps.   **DC596**

An encyclopedia relating to Allied intervention in Russia, 1918–1920. Articles cover biography, cities, battles, weaponry, etc. Bibliography, p. 683–97.   DK265.4.G7

Wilson, Andrew. Russia and the commonwealth A to Z / Andrew Wilson & Nina Bachkatov. N.Y. : HarperPerennial, c1992. 258 p.   **DC597**

Expanded from the French work, *Nouveaux Soviétiques de A á Z* (Paris: Calmann-Lévy, 1991). British ed. has title: *Russia revised.* Bachkatov's name appears first in the French edition.

Identifies persons and organizations and explains concepts. Occasional bibliographic references. Thematic index lists relevant articles under broad headings, e.g., Agriculture, Enterprises.   DK286.W5513

Handbooks

Batalden, Stephen K. The newly independent states of Eurasia : handbook of former Soviet republics / by Stephen K. Batalden and Sandra K. Batalden. Phoenix : Oryx, 1993. 205 p.   **DC598**

Twelve chapters, each covering a former Soviet republic (excluding Estonia, Latvia, and Lithuania) grouped in four sections: The Russian Federation (an overview), European republics (Belarus, Moldova, Ukraine), Transcaucasia, Central Asia. For each, gives a statistical profile based on the 1989 Soviet census followed by a narrative that touches on the history of that republic and an "examination of the contemporary issues facing each newly independent state."—*Pref.* Glossary; topical index.   DK17.B34

McLane, Charles B. Soviet-African relations. London : Central Asian Research Centre; distr. by Columbia Univ. Pr., 1974. 190 p. (Soviet-Third world relations, v.3).   **DC599**

Surveys "Soviet relations with 36 sovereign African nations south of the Sahara" (*Pref.*), excluding those countries which were still colonies or dependencies in 1972 as well as South Africa and Rhodesia. Soviet relationship with each country is presented in tabular form— political, economic, cultural—chronologically arranged. List of references for each country section. A Regional perspective section offers a "discussion of the broad tendencies of Soviet interest in Africa from the late 1950s to the end of 1972, as measured by the substance of Soviet press commentaries, the volume of aid and trade and the diplomatic response to competition from other non-African powers, notably China. ..."—*Pref.*

§ See also: *India and the Soviet Union : a chronology of political and diplomatic cooperation*, compiled by A. Roy (Calcutta : Firma, 1982. 194 p.). Two companion volumes in this series by McLane: *Soviet-Asian relations* (1973. 150 p.), and *Soviet-Middle East relations* (1973. 126 p.).   DT38.9.R8M27

Twining, David Thomas. Guide to the republics of the former Soviet Union. Westport, Conn. : Greenwood, 1993. 213 p. : maps.   **DC600**

Also published in paperback under title *The new Eurasia.*

Treats the 15 former republics and new states giving "basic data on their history, populations, economic development, governments, and key issues" (*Introd.*) such as The road to independence, Separatist/territorial disputes. Arranged by country under a broad geographical grouping, e.g., Western area subdivided into Belarus, Moldavia and the Ukraine. Topical index.   DK293.T85

Velikaía Oktiabr'skaía sotsialisticheskaía revoliutsiía : entsiklopediía / pod red. G. N. Golikova, M. I. Kuznetsova ; otv. sekretar izd. IU. IU. Figatner. Moskva : Izd. "Sovetskaía Entsiklopediía", 1977. 711 p. : ill.   **DC601**

Brief articles, in dictionary arrangement, concerning persons, places, events, etc., of the 1917 Russian revolution. Selected bibliography, p. 700–709. Based on a 1968 work of the same title.

Regional and local

Bibliographia studiorum uralicorum, 1917–1987 = Uralistiikan tutkimuksen bibliografia = Bibliography on Uralic studies / [bibliografian toimitusneuvosto, Esko Häkli, puheenjohtaja, Helsinki ... et al. ; V.A. Vinogradov, puheenjohtaja, Moskova ... et al.]. Helsinki : Suomalaisen Kirjallisuuden Seura, 1988–93. v. 1–2, 4. (Suomalaisen Kirjallisuuden Seuran toimituksia, 494, etc.). (In progress).   **DC602**

Contents: v. 1, Archaeology (1988. 397 p.); v. 2, Ethnography and folklore (1990); v. 4, Literary studies. Future volume(s?) to include Linguistics.

Joint project of Akademiia Nauk SSSR and Suomen Akatemian ja Neuvostoliiton.

Lists monographs, essays, journals, abstracts of conferences, and dissertations written by Soviet or Finnish scholars 1917–87 on this part of western Russia. Topical arrangement within geographical areas or period divisions. Index in Russian for names of authors, compilers, and editors; indexes in Russian and English for subjects.   Z7045.A16

Collins, David Norman. Siberia and the Soviet Far East. Oxford, England ; Santa Barbara, Calif. : Clio Pr., c1991. 217 p. : maps. (World bibliographical series, v. 127).   **DC603**

A selective bibliography of 735 English-language books and periodical articles. Excludes materials on the Arctic. Indexed by author, title and subject.   Z3401.C65

Sibirskaía sovetskaía entsiklopediía / pod obshcheĭ redaktsie M.K. Azadovskogo ... [et al.]. [Novosibirsk] : Sibirskoe kraevoe izd-vo, 1929–32, 1992. v. 1–4. (In progress).   **DC604**

Vols. 2–3 ed. by B.Z. Shaumiatskiĭ, A.A. Anson, M.M. Basov.

Contents: v. 1–4, A–Sézdy.

Vols. 1–3 cover A–N; v. 4, to have been published in 1936, existed in proof copy until published in 1992 (N.Y. : Norman Ross). Vol. 4 also has a list of entries planned for v. 5.

Extensive articles, compiled by leading specialists of the period, treat the "geography, history, culture, peoples, productive capacity and natural history" (*Introd.*) of Siberia.

United Kingdom

See Great Britain.

Vatican

Walsh, Michael J. Vatican City State. Oxford ; Santa Barbara, Calif. : Clio Pr., 1983. 105 p. (World bibliographical series, 41).   **DC605**

Cites 368 items (mainly English-language publications) in a topical arrangement. Author, title, subject index.   Z2373.W34

Yugoslavia

Bibliography

Friedman, Francine. Yugoslavia : a comprehensive English-language bibliography. Wilmington, Del. : Scholarly Resources, 1993. 547 p. **DC606**

An extensive bibliography of published books, articles, chapters and essays, theses and dissertations, documents and pamphlets together with working papers, unpublished manuscripts, and conference papers from 17th century the 1980s, with less thorough coverage for the early 1990s. Alphabetically arranged by topics in seven categories: Reference works and aids, Geography, History, Economics, Politics and government, Anthropology, Culture (which includes education and the sciences). Author and subject indexes. Z2956.F75

Horton, John J. Yugoslavia. Rev. and expanded ed. Oxford ; Santa Barbara, Calif. : Clio Pr., c1990. 279 p. (World bibliographical series, v. 1). **DC607**

1st ed., 1977.

Offers 921 annotated entries, mostly English-language publications, topically arranged in 42 sections. Many more references are subsumed in the annotations. Indexed by author, title, and subject. Z2951.H67

Prpič, George J. Croatia and the Croatians : a selected and annotated bibliography in English. Scottsdale, Ariz. : Associated Book Publishers, 1982. lvii, 315 p. : maps. **DC608**

An annotated listing by broad topics within sections for books and pamphlets, articles, theses and dissertations. Includes a section on Croatian emigrants. Appendixes; author and title indexes. Z2957.C7P75

Terry, Garth M. Yugoslav history : a bibliographic index to English-language articles. 2nd rev. ed. Nottingham, Eng. : Astra Pr., 1990. 165 p. (Astra Soviet and East European bibliographies, v. 10). **DC609**

1st ed., 1985.

Attempts to list "all articles on the history—in its broadest sense—of Yugoslavia contained in *Festschriften*, conference proceedings, collected papers and journals in the English language from 1945 to 1990."—*Introd.* Includes areas such as diplomacy, economics, intellectual life, religious development as well as history. Topically ar-

ranged in four main sections: (1) General; (2) To 1945; (3) 1945– ; (4) History of the Yugoslav republics. List of subject headings; name index for authors, compilers, editors, translators, and any other person mentioned in an entry.

§ For coverage of much older material, *see* Michael B. Petrovich, *Yugoslavia : a bibliographic guide* (Wash. : Library of Congress, Slavic and Central European Div., 1974. 207 p.) and Rusko Matulič, *Bibliography of sources on Yugoslavia* (Palo Alto, Calif. : Ragusan Pr., 1981. 252 p.). Z2956.T47

Titova reč u publikacijama JNA 1941–1980 : anotirana bibliografija / [glavni urednik Rula Dragon ... et al.]. Beograd : Centar za Vojnonaučnu Dokumentaciju i Informacije, 1982. 682 p. **DC610**

A chronologically arranged bibliography of books, journals, articles and chapters, government and communist party publications concerning the career of Tito. About 2,700 items. Topical and name indexes. Z2958.A5T57

Guides to records

Jovanovič, Slobodan. A guide to Yugoslav libraries and archives / Slobodan Jovanovič, Matko Rojnič, compilers ; Paul L. Horecky, chief ed.; Elizabeth Beyerly, tr. and assoc. ed. [Columbus, Ohio : American Assoc. for the Advancement of Slavic Studies, 1976]. 108 p. (Joint Committee on Eastern Europe publication series, 2). **DC611**

Offers historical notes on the libraries, descriptions of book and manuscript collections, and references to published writings on the libraries. Z841.A1J68

Encyclopedias

Enciklopedija jugoslavije / [glavni redaktor: Mirloslav Krleža]. Zagreb : Leksikografskog zavoda FNRJ, 1955–71. 8 v. : ill. **DC612**

A well-produced encyclopedia dealing with the life and culture of the Yugoslav peoples. Articles, many of considerable length, are signed and include bibliographies. Illustrations and maps are excellent.

§ A new edition is in progress, also ed. by Miroslav Krleža. (Zagreb : Jugoslavenski leksikografski Zavod, 1980–90. v. 1–6. ill., maps.) Contents: v. 1–6, A-Kat.

Although there are some general articles, they often show a strong national orientation (e.g., country articles emphasize relations with Jugoslavia); biographical sketches are almost exclusively on Yugoslav figures. Signed articles; bibliographies. DR304.E5

DD

Africa

African studies, like any program in area studies, is cross-disciplinary by definition, drawing materials from many fields of study that are useful in understanding the region. Past editions of the *Guide* have listed only the most general cross-disciplinary titles in the African area studies section, but many more were to be found in other sections by topic, a practice this edition continues. Researchers looking for reference sources on African music should consult the Music section (BJ), on African literature the Literature section (BE), and so on. At the same time, materials on African music, literature, etc., can also be found in the more general sources listed here.

This section contains no machine-readable sources. Although many general online or CD-ROM sources are useful for African studies, few focus specifically on Africa, and none is broad enough in scope to be included.

Students or researchers looking for a suitable starting point for research concerning particular African countries may like to begin with the sources found in three broad series: *African historical dictionaries* (DD48), *World bibliographical series* (DD18), or *Foreign country studies/Area handbooks* (DD62). In some cases, these may be the best (or the only) reference sources available in English. Individual volumes in these series are entered by subject in the index.

GENERAL WORKS

Bibliography

Asamani, J. O. Index Africanus. Stanford, Calif. : Hoover Institution Pr., [1975]. 659 p. (Hoover Institution bibliographies series, 53). **DD1**
"A catalogue of articles in Western languages dealing with Africa and published from 1885 to 1965 in periodicals, Festschriften or memorial volumes, symposia, and proceedings of congresses and conferences."—*Pref.* A general section is followed by regional sections, each subdivided by country, then by subject. More than 24,600 entries; author index. A more detailed table of contents or a subject index would have greatly facilitated use of the volume. Z3501.A73

Brüne, Stefan. Die französische Afrikapolitik : Auswahlbibliographie = La politique africaine de la France : bibliographie sélectionnée = French policy in Africa : a selected bibliography / Stefan Brüne, Christine Weiss. Hamburg : Deutsches Übersee-Institut, 1988. 149 p. : maps. (Dokumentationsdienst Afrika. Reihe A, 25). **DD2**
In German, English, French, and Russian.
One in a series of outstanding bibliographies on African topics; consists of 916 entries in Western languages, with concise abstracts in German. Period covered is "1970–1987 except for some overview studies ... articles, contributions to collective works, monographs, and

grey literature currently indexed by the Africa Documentation Centre."—*Prelim. note.* Arranged by type of policy—colonial, foreign, military, economic, cultural, and development aid—followed by a country section. Author index. DT33.7.B78

DeLancey, Mark W. African international relations : an annotated bibliography. Boulder, Colo. : Westview Pr., [1981]. 365 p. **DD3**
Lists 2,840 items, 1960–78, with some entries through 1980. "Books, journal articles, pamphlets, and a few documents have been included."—*Introd.* Broad subject arrangement with some annotations.
§ A more recent title that focuses on a single set of foreign interactions is Beverly Ann Gray and Angel Batiste's *Japanese-African relations : a selected list of references.* (Wash. : African Section, African and Middle Eastern Div., Library of Congress, 1988), which presents 178 annotated references to selected government documents, books, pamphlets, and periodical articles. Z6465.A36D44

Fontán Lobé, Juan. Bibliografía colonial : contribución a un índice de publicaciones africanas. Madrid : "Selecciones Gráficas", 1946. 669 p. **DD4**
An alphabetical catalog of nearly 17,000 titles of books and periodical articles in various languages. Particularly rich in Spanish and Portuguese materials. Geographical and subject indexes.
§ For the period since 1945, *see* the two excellent bibliographic essays in *The transfer of power in Africa,* ed. by Prosser Gifford and W.R. Louis (New Haven, Conn. : Yale Univ. Pr., 1982). Z3501.F6

Hogg, Peter C. The African slave trade and its suppression : a classified and annotated bibliography of books, pamphlets and periodical articles. London : Cass, [1973]. 409 p. **DD5**
An excellent bibliographic essay precedes the bibliography of 4,675 entries, most with brief annotations. Indexes of authors, personal names, geographic names, and anonymous titles. Includes some government publications and academic theses.
§ For more recent scholarship, *see* Joseph C. Miller, *Slavery and slaving in world history : a worldwide bibliography, 1900–1991* (CC328). Z7164.S6H63

Kersebaum, Andrea. Integrationsbestrebungen in Afrika : zwischenstaatliche Organisationen und regionale Zusammenarbeit : eine Auswahlbibliographie = Integration efforts in Africa : international organizations and regional co-operation : a selected bibliography. Hamburg : Deutsches Übersee-Institut, Übersee-Dokumentation, Referat Afrika, 1986–1987. 2 v. : map. (Dokumentationsdienst Afrika. Reihe A, 23). **DD6**
Vol. 1 covers organizations continent-wide, and v. 2 regional organizations, 1970 through 1985. Selectively cites 2,377 reports, books, and journal articles chiefly in French, German, and English, with brief annotations in German. Author and organization index in each volume.
§ *See also* Mark W. DeLancey and Terry M. Mays, *Historical dictionary of international organizations in sub-Saharan Africa* (Metuchen, N.J. : Scarecrow, 1994), which includes an extensive 198-p. topical bibliography. Z7165.A4K47

Maurer, Margarete. Leben und Arbeit von Frauen, Frauenforschung und Frauenbewegung in Afrika : (Kapitel 400. bis 499.) / von Margarete Maurer und Barbara Smetschka ; unter Mitarbeit von Martina Gajdos... [et al.]. Wien : Verein für Interdisziplinäre Forschung und Praxis, Rosa-Luxemburg-Institut : Harald Fischer Verlag, 1993. 523 p. : ill., maps. **DD7**
More than 4,000 annotated entries, chiefly 1970–92, for monographs, collected works, government publications, and periodical and newspaper articles, with special attention to gray literature, primarily in European languages, but others, including Arabic, are also represented. This very thorough work is arranged by broad subjects, then geographically. Index of ethnic and linguistic groups and author index which refers to page, not entry numbers.

Melville J. Herskovits Library of African Studies. The Africana conference paper index. Boston : G. K. Hall, 1982. 2v. **DD8**

The Herskovitz Library (Northwestern Univ.) holds papers from 562 conferences that were held chiefly in the 1960s and 1970s (although some were earlier), both published and unpublished, about half in English, the remainder mostly in other Western languages. The index consists of a register of conferences arranged by main entry, with the papers listed by author under each conference. Author and keyword indexes. "All papers ... are available for either loan or photocopy."—*Introd.* DT1.5.M45

Miliavskaia, S. L. Bibliografiia stran Afriki i Arabskogo Vostoka : ukazatel' literatury na russkom iazike, opublikovannoi v SSSR v 1917–1967 gg. Moskva : Glavnaia Redaktsiia Vostochnoi Literatury Izdatel'stvo Nauka, 1979–80. 2 v. **DD9**

Contents: v. 1, Obshchie raboty; Afrika (tropicheskaia i iuzhnaia); v. 2, Arabskie strany.

A classed bibliography of Russian-language publications on Africa and the Arab States. Vol. 1 offers a section of general works followed by sections for Africa as a whole, specific regions, and individual countries of Africa. Detailed table of contents; index. Vol. 2 follows the same plan, covering Northern Africa and the Arab States.

Z3551.M54

——————— Izuchenie kul'tury i iazykov narodov Afriki v Sovetskom Soiuze : 1917–1985 / [otvetstvennyi red. R. N. Ismagilova …. Moskva : Izd-vo "Nauka," Glav. red. vostochnoi lit-ry, 1986. 223 p. **DD10**

At head of title: Akademiia nauk SSSR. Institut Afriki.

Contents: pt. 1, Study of cultures; pt. 2, Study of languages.

Translation of title: *The study of the culture and languages of people of Africa in the Soviet Union 1917–1985.*

An annotated, descriptive bibliography of Soviet books and articles, with an overview article on Soviet research 1917–1985. Classified by subject. Z3508.C58M55

Passé de l'Afrique par l'oralité = African history from oral sources / under the direction of Claude Hélène Perrot … [et al.]. Paris : Ministère de la coopération et du développement : La Documentation française, c1993. 304 p. : ill. **DD11**

Summaries in English and French of 90 French-language works on precolonial Africa that draw on oral as well as other sources. Written over the past 30 years, these works were previously unpublished even in summary form. Attempts to "situate the works examined in their contexts, and to underscore the originality of the research carried out in the region's history."—*Introd.* Author and subject indexes, the latter in English and French. DT13.A12P3

Pélissier, René. Africana : bibliographies sur l'Afrique luso-hispanophone : 1800–1980. Montameta : Éditions Pélissier, [c1980]. 205 p. **DD12**

Reprints a review essay and bibliographies published 1965–79 in *Revue française d'études politiques africaines* and in *Genève-Afrique.* Concentrates on areas that were formerly Spanish and Portuguese colonies; includes publications of all countries. Index by geographical area.

Updated by Pélissier's *Du Sahara à Timor : 700 livres analysés (1980–1990) sur l'Afrique et l'Insulinde ex-ibériques* (Orgeval, France : Pélissier, c1991. 349 p.). Z3871.P44

Ridinger, Robert B. Marks. African archaeology : a selected bibliography. N.Y. : G.K. Hall : Maxwell Macmillan International, c1993. 311 p. **DD13**

717 extensively annotated entries published 1826–1989 in many languages, arranged by country, then chronologically. Includes dates of the Pan African Congress on Prehistory and Quarternary Studies and identifies legislation that regulates archaeological activity in 38 countries. For "both the expert and novice with a representative sampling of both monographic and periodical literatures on African archaeology, including exhibition catalogs."—*Pref.* Index. Z5118.A6R5

Schmidt, Nancy J. Children's books on Africa and their authors : an annotated bibliography. N.Y. : Africana Publ. Co., 1975. 290 p. **DD14**

More than 800 annotated entries, 1880–1973, with biographical information on authors. "Primarily the annotations seek to convey whether the book contributes to an understanding of African people and whether an African viewpoint is conveyed in the book."—*Introd.* Geographic, name, series, title, subject, and tribal indexes.

——————. *Supplement* (N.Y. : Africana, 1979) which lists 700 additional titles published through 1977. In the introduction, six tables analyze themes, topics, geographic and ethnic distribution, dates, and series. Exceptionally well-indexed. Z3508.C5S35

Vellut, Jean Luc. Guide de l'étudiant en histoire du Zaïre. Kinshasa : Éditions du Mont Noir, [1974]. 207 p. ([Collection "Objectif 80"] : Série "Essais", no. 8 ; Collection Cours universitaires, no. 1). **DD15**

For annotation, *see* DD245. Z3631.V4

Williams, Michael W. Pan-Africanism : an annotated bibliography. Pasadena, Calif. : Salem Pr., 1993. 142 p. **DD16**

Approximately 480 descriptive and usefully evaluative annotations "locate the best and most accessible secondary (and some primary) literature."—*Introd.* Selections arranged in categories: overview; history; organizations and movements; political and cultural expressions; biographies; and theoretical issues. Defining Pan-Africanism broadly, includes widely available books, chapters of books, and journals. Index. Z3508.P35W55

Witherell, Julian W. The United States and Africa : guide to U.S. official documents and government-sponsored publications on Africa, 1785–1975. Wash. : Library of Congress, 1978. 949 p. **DD17**

A selective, partially annotated bibliography of more than 8,800 publications issued by or for the U.S. government relating to any part of Africa, except Egypt. Sections covering 1820–1951 are "limited primarily to congressional and presidential documents, commercial reports, diplomatic papers and treaties," whereas those for 1952–75 also include "translations issued by JPRS and printed and mimeographed studies concerning American assistance programs prepared by or for federal government agencies."—*Pref.* Chiefly lists materials held at the Library of Congress, with additions from 45 other libraries arranged geographically. The 1952–75 section is subdivided by topic. Index by topics, issuing bodies, main entries.

Continued in part by Witherell's *The United States and sub-Saharan Africa : a guide to U.S. official documents and government-sponsored publications, 1976–1980* (Wash. : Library of Congress, 1984), a geographical/topical listing of 5,047 publications that includes ERIC, JPRS, and NTIS reports but omits classified documents, congressional bills and resolutions, and Congressional Research Service reports. Useful annotations vary in length; author/title/subject index. Z3501.W57

World bibliographical series : [Africa]. Santa Barbara, Calif. ; Oxford : ABC-Clio, 1979– . v. 3– . (In progress). **DD18**

An important monographic series that, for many African countries, is one of the best places for nonspecialists to begin research. A few early volumes were more comprehensive and intended for scholars, but since 1981, the series has been oriented toward English-speaking general readers. Volumes follow a standardized format, beginning with a historically-based overview essay, followed by topical sections containing useful annotated citations. Recent monographic publications are favored over older, briefer works. Volumes end with a dictionary index, an outline map, and sometimes a chronology.

The following volumes have appeared to date. Each is rated on a four-point scale (*E=excellent, G=good, F=fair, P=poor*), based on expertise of the authors, errors of fact, sensitivity to the material, important omissions, currency on date of publication. Reviews in the scholarly press have also been considered. Vols. 4 and 162 were not available for examination.

v. 3, *Lesotho*, by Shelagh M. Willet and David P. Ambrose (1980. 496 p. *E*).

v. 4, *Zimbabwe*, by Deborah Potts (1993. 368 p.).

v. 7, *South Africa*, by Reuben Musiker (1979. 194 p. *P*).

v. 8, *Malawi*, by Robert P. Boeder (1979. 165 p. *G*).

v. 11, *Uganda*, by Robert L. Collison (1981. 159 p. *F*).

v. 19, *Algeria*, by Richard I. Lawless (1980. 215 p. *E*).

v. 24, *Swaziland*, by Balam Nyeko (1982. 135 p. *E*).

v. 25, *Kenya*, by Robert L. Collison (1982. 157 p. *F*).

v. 33, *Tunisia*, by Allan M. Findlay and Richard I. Lawless (1982. 251 p. *G*).

v. 40, *Sudan*, by M. W. Daly (rev. ed., 1992. 195 p. *E*).

v. 47, *Morocco*, by Anne M. Findlay, Allan M. Findlay, Richard I. Lawless (1984. 311 p. *G*).

v. 51, *Zambia*, by Anne M. Bliss and J. A. Rigg (1984. 233 p. *E*).

v. 53, *Namibia*, by Stanley Schoeman and Elna Schoeman (1984. 186 p. *F*).

v. 54, *Tanzania*, by Colin Darch (1985. 316 p. *E*).

v. 63, *Cameroon*, by Mark W. DeLancey and Peter J. Schraeder (1986. 201 p. *E*).

v. 78, *Mozambique*, by Colin Darch (1987. 360 p. *E*).

v. 79, *Libya*, by Ronald Bruce St. John (1991. 192 p. *G*).

v. 85, *Indian Ocean*, by Julia J. Gotthold (1988. 329 p. *E*).

v. 86, *Egypt*, by Ragai N. Makar (1988. 306 p. *G*).

v. 91, *The Gambia*, by David W. Gamble (1988. 135 p. *E*).

v. 92, *Somalia*, by Mark W. DeLancey [et al.] (1988. 191 p. *E*).

v. 100, *Nigeria*, by Robert A. Myers (1989. 462 p. *G*).

v. 118, *Djibouti*, by Peter J. Schraeder (1991. 239 p. *E*).

v. 121, *Guinea-Bissau*, by Rosemary E. Galil (1990. 180 p. *F*).

v. 123, *Cape Verde*, by Caroline S. Shaw (1991. 190 p. *G*).

v. 124, *Ghana*, by Robert A. Myers (1991. 436 p. *E*).

v. 136, *Equatorial Guinea*, by Randall Fegley (1991. 118 p. *G*).

v. 140, *Mauritius*, by Pramila Ramgulam Bennett (1992. 151 p. *E*).

v. 141, *Mauritania*, by Simonetta Calderini [et al.] (1992. 165 p. *E*).

v. 145, *Burundi*, by Morna Daniels (1992. 135 p. *G*).

v. 148, *Sierra Leone*, by Margaret Binns and Tony Binns (1992. 235 p. *G*).

v. 149, *Gabon*, by David E. Gardinier (1992. 178 p. *E*).

v. 150, *Botswana*, by John A. Wiseman (1992. 187 p. *E*).

v. 151, *Angola*, by Richard Black (1992. 176 p. *E*).

v. 152, *Central African Republic*, by Pierre Kalck (1993. 153 p. *E*).

v. 153, *Seychelles*, by George Bennett (1993. 117 p. *E*).

v. 154, *Rwanda*, by Randall Fegley (1993. 161 p. *E*).

v. 162, *Congo*, by Randall Fegley (1993. 168 p.).

Current

Africa bibliography. 1984– . Manchester, Eng. ; Dover, N.H. : Manchester Univ. Pr., c1985– . Annual.   **DD19**

Annual coverage of books, essays, and articles "principally in the social sciences, environmental sciences, humanities and arts, though a selection of items from the medical, biological and physical sciences is also included ... African government publications, and works of creative literature are not covered, but there are no other a priori exclusions."—*Introd.* Based on materials received by the Edinburgh University Library and the International African Institute. Arranged by region and country, with further subdivisions into broad subjects. Author and subject (keyword) indexes.   Z3503.A34

The African book publishing record. v. 1, no. 1 (Jan. 1975)– . [Oxford, Eng. : Hans Zell Ltd.], 1975– . Quarterly.   **DD20**

"Africana reference works," an annotated list, appears annually. For complete information, *see* AA847.   Z465.7.A35

A current bibliography on African affairs. v. l, no. 1 (Apr. 1962)– . [Farmingdale, N.Y.] : Baywood Publ. Co., 1962– . Quarterly.   **DD21**

Frequency varied in early volumes. Also called "new series," 1968–73.

Publ. for the African Bibliographic Center.

In three parts: (1) original studies, bibliographies or bibliographic essays; (2) book reviews; (3) bibliography of newly published books, articles, government documents, and visual aids, arranged by general subject or geographical area. Although extensive, the bibliography would be more useful if periodical coverage and subject classification were more consistent. Author index in each issue; regional index in the 4th issue of each volume.

§ The Center also issued a *Special bibliographic series* (v. 1–8, 1963–73; n.s. v.1–6, 1975–78) devoted to longer bibliographies.

     Z3501.C87

Current contents Africa. v. 4, no. 1– . Oxford : publ. on behalf of the Stadt- und Universitätsbibliotek, Frankfurt am Main by Hans Zell, c1978– . Quarterly.   **DD22**

Called "New series," but continues the numbering of *CCA : Current contents Afrika*.

Germany's largest Africana collection publishes this valuable source providing "fascimile reproductions of the title or contents pages, of current contents of almost 200 major Africanist periodicals."–*Introd.* These serials are augmented by other periodicals when they contain important Africana material. Gives place of publication, volume and issue/part number, and date, as well as frequency for each title. Excludes titles in medicine, natural science, modern law, and economics. Indexed since 1992; includes some African titles not indexed elsewhere.

International African bibliography = Bibliographie internationale africaine. v. 1 (1971)– . London : Mansell, 1971– . Quarterly.   **DD23**

Subtitle: Current books, articles and papers in African studies.

Publisher varies: 1971, International African Institute; 1973– in association with the Univ. of London School of Oriental and African Studies (SOAS).

Continues the bibliography of current publications which appeared in the journal *Africa*, 1929–70; *see* below.

Based on regular scanning of about 1,000 periodicals and selected monographs, chiefly holdings of the SOAS Library. The most comprehensive index of Africana, listing annually more than 4,000 articles, chapters in edited volumes, and monographs; excluded are Egypt and Madeira. Since 1992, in two sections: Articles and Monographs. Classification is geographic within each section, then subdivided by broad subjects. "The last issue of each year contains indexes ... of Authors/ Personalities, Ethnic Groups, Languages, and Special Terms and Other Names. It also has a cumulated Subject-index."—*Editorial note, v. 23:4.*

J.D. Pearson's *International African bibliography, 1973–1978 : books, articles and papers in African affairs* (London : Mansell, 1982. 343 p.) cumulates v. 3–8 (about 20,000 citations), plus an additional 3,000 entries not appearing in the quarterly issues. Arranged geographically, then topically; index of authors, editors, and translators. The International African Institute's *Cumulative bibliography of African studies ... Classified catalogue* (Boston : G.K. Hall, 1973. 3 v.) and its *Author catalogue* (Boston : G.K. Hall, 1973. 2 v.) provide access to the quarterly bibliography published in *Africa*, 1929–70. These catalogs reproduce cards from files maintained at the Institute and contain some items not appearing in the published bibliographies.

Joint acquisitions list of Africana. v. 1 (1962)– . Evanston, Ill. : Melville J. Herskovits Library of African Studies, Northwestern Univ., 1962– . Bimonthly.   **DD24**

Often referred to as *JALA*.

Comp. 1962–72 by African Dept., Northwestern University Library.

A bimonthly cooperative listing of Africana in all languages published over the previous five-year period and reported to the Herskovits Library by major Africana libraries in the U.S. Provides full cataloging records and holdings at Northwestern. Issues for 1972–77, with re-editing and further authority work, were cumulated in an author/title arrangement and published in v. 5–6 of the 1st suppl. of the Herskovits catalog (DD34).

Annual cumulations covering 1978–80 have been publ. by G.K. Hall. A *Cumulated edition (1978–1988)* is available on microfiche from Northwestern Univ. Library. This version contains about 35,000 records, most with full cataloging, and includes a geographic index.

United Nations. Economic Commission for Africa. Library. Africa index : selected articles on socio-economic development = Catalogue Afrique : articles choisis sur le développement économique et social. no. 1 (Apr. 1971)– . [Addis Ababa, Ethiopia?] : Economic Commission for Africa, United Nations, 1971– . Quarterly. **DD25**

Issued three times per year by the Library of the U.N. Economic commission for Africa. Indexes "periodical articles, titles of series and occasional papers, as well as titles of chapters of books when felt essential."—*Foreword*. Arranged by 38 broad subject categories, with author and title indexes. HC800.A1U54c

Periodicals

Library of Congress. Serial and Government Publications Division. African newspapers in the Library of Congress / comp., John Pluge, Jr. 2nd ed. Wash. : Library of Congress, 1984. 144 p. **DD26**

1st ed., 1977.

A comprehensive list of 931 newspapers from 52 African countries held by the Library. "These holdings include both hard copy and positive microfilm."—*Pref*. Supplies date of establishment and includes frequency of publication when known. Geographical arrangement; title index.

§ A related title is *African newspapers available on positive microfilm*, (Wash. : Photoduplication Service, Library of Congress, 1984), which lists newspapers and the dates for which microfilm may be ordered from LC. For sub-Saharan newspapers, *see also* Mette Shayne, *African newspapers currently received by American libraries* (Evanston, Ill. : Northwestern Univ. Library, 1994. 20 p.), which lists newspapers and libraries subscribing to them. Does not provide holdings, but does give frequency when known. Z6959.Z9L53

Mullan, Anthony Páez. Africana serials in microform in the Library of Congress. Wash. : Library of Congress, 1978. 36 p. **DD27**

"Prepared as an operational document in an edition of 250 copies for internal use in the Library of Congress and limited outside distribution."—*[p.ii]*.

Lists "a selection of serials in microform relating to Africa. ... Most of the serials are in European and African languages that use the Roman alphabet. However, since the scope of the list covers all of Africa, a number of Arabic publications are also listed."—*Pref*.

Travis, Carole. Periodicals from Africa : a bibliography and union list of periodicals published in Africa / comp. and ed. by Carole Travis and Miriam Alman. Boston : G. K. Hall, 1977. 619 p. **DD28**

For annotation, *see* AD238. Z3503.T73

Dissertations

Dinstel, Marion. List of French doctoral dissertations on Africa, 1884–1961. Boston : G.K. Hall, 1966. 336 p. **DD29**

At head of title: Boston University Libraries.

Lists 2,981 titles arranged by country or area. Author and very broad subject index.

§ Mireille Lafond's *Recueil de theses africanistes, droit et science politique 1967–1984* (Paris : Section des droits Africains, Centre d'etudes jurisiques comparatives, [1985] 183 p.) provides roughly 1,200 additional citations for the fields of law and political science. Z3501.D5

Köhler, Jochen. Deutsche Dissertationen über Afrika : ein Verzeichnis für die Jahre 1918–1959 / zusammengestellt von Jochen Köhler [hrsg. vom Wissenschaftlichen Ausschluss, Deutsche Afrika-Gesellschaft e. V. Bonn, durch H. Abel, E. Ackermann, und W. Fröhlich]. Bonn : Kurt Schroeder, 1962. 1 v., unpaged. **DD30**

Prepared under auspices of the Deutsche Afrika Gesellschaft, Bonn.

A list of 795 titles classified geographically, with keyword and author indexes.

§ Continued by: Barbara Maurer and Klaus Schwarz, *Hochschulschriften zu Schwarz-Afrika, 1960–1978 : Deutschland-Österreich-Schweiz* (Freiburg : Klaus Schwarz Verlag, 1979. 226 p. [Materialen zur Afrikakunde, 1]). Lists 1,238 dissertations, with coverage extended to Austrian and Swiss dissertations (including Swiss dissertations written in French). Classed arrangement; author and subject indexes. Z3501.K6

Répertoire des thèses africanistes françaises / Centre d'études africaines–CARDAN, École des hautes études en sciences sociales. 1977–[1988/89?]. Paris : CARDAN, 1980–[1991?]. **DD31**

Represents a merger of the *Inventaire de thèses africainistes de langue française en cours* (1970–76) and *Inventaire de thèses et mémoires africainistes de langue française soutenus* (1970–76).

Appears to have ceased with 1988/89, publ. 1991.

Lists theses in the humanities and social sciences concerning any part of Africa. In two sections: Thèses soutenues, and Thèses inscrites. Geographical arrangement with topical subdivisions; author and subject indexes. Z3501.R44

Sims, Michael. American & Canadian doctoral dissertations & master's theses on Africa, 1886–1974 : comp. by Michael Sims and Alfred Kagan. Waltham, Mass. : African Studies Assoc., Brandeis Univ., [1976]. 365 p. **DD32**

Expands *American doctoral dissertations on Africa 1886–1972* by Anne Schneller and Michael Bratton (1973); adds master's theses and Canadian titles, extending coverage through 1974. Cites 6,070 titles arranged by country or geographic area, then by broad subject field. Subject and author indexes.

Continued by: *American and Canadian doctoral dissertations and master's theses on Africa, 1974–1987*, comp. by Joseph J. Lauer, Alfred Kagan, and Gregory V. Larkin (Atlanta: Crossroads Pr., Emory Univ., c1989. 1 v. [377p.]). Cumulates the annual lists in *ASA news* (1981–89; sponsored by the African Studies Association). Presents 8,537 entries by country and region, then by broad discipline. Subject, author, and institution indexes.

§ *See also* Oliver B. Pollak, *Theses and dissertations on Southern Africa : an international bibliography* (Boston, G.K. Hall, [1976].). Covers 1884–1974 for 30 countries. Z3501.S5

Standing Conference on Library Materials on Africa. Theses on Africa accepted by universities in the United Kingdom and Ireland. Cambridge : Heffer, 1964. 74 p. **DD33**

Lists 1,142 titles, 1920–62, by region and country, subdivided by topic. Author index.

Continued by: *Theses on Africa, 1963–1975* ... comp. by J. H. St. J. McIlwaine (London : Mansell, 1978. 123 p.), a classed list with author index that "contains 2,231 items ... in addition, 124 theses submitted *before* 1962 but omitted from the original volume have been included in an Appendix." (*Introd*); and *Theses on Africa, 1976–1988* ... comp. by Helen C. Price and Colin Hewson (London ; N.Y. : publ. for SCOLMA [by] Hans Zell Publ., 1993), which adds more than 3,600 entries, arranged by region, subdivided by country and topic, with author and subject indexes. Z3501.S83

Library catalogs

Melville J. Herskovits Library of African Studies. Catalog of the Melville J. Herskovits Library of African Studies, Northwestern University Library and Africana in selected libraries, Evanston, Ill. Boston : G.K. Hall, 1972. 8 v.   **DD34**
1962 ed. publ. as: *Catalog of the African collection* by Northwestern University Library.
Author, title, and added entries for some 60,000 volumes of books, periodicals, newspapers, manuscripts, maps, photographs, phonograph records, microforms, etc. Emphasizes Africa, south of the Sahara, especially West Africa. Includes cards from libraries contributing to *JALA* (Joint acquisition list of Africana, DD24).
————. ————. *First supplement* (1978. 6 v.). Vols. 1–4 reproduce catalog cards for materials added to the Herskovitz Library during the period 1972–77, together with revised records for some materials cited in the basic set. Vols. 5–6 cumulate reports of African materials cataloged at selected libraries in the U.S. which were included in *JALA*, 1962–77.   Z3509.M45

University of London. School of Oriental and African Studies. Library. Library catalogue. Boston : G. K. Hall, 1963. 28 v.   **DD35**
Reproduces the catalog cards for this outstanding collection, covering intensively all aspects of Africa, Asia, and Oceania, except science, medicine and technology which are treated less thoroughly. All types of materials are cited, including manuscripts, maps, and sound recordings.
Continued by:
————. ————. *Supplement 1–3* (Boston : G.K. Hall, 1968-1979). Suppl. 1, 16 v.; Suppl. 2, 16 v.; Suppl. 3, 19 v. The supplements reflect cataloging, 1963 through summer 1978, following the earlier arrangement.
————. ————. *Fourth supplement, 1978–1984* [microform] (Zug, Switzerland : IDC, [1985]. 363 microfiches). Entries for 430,000 titles acquired 1978–84. Also reproduces the complete Manuscripts Catalogue of the School. Main entry by title, with author and subject entries.

Library resources

African studies information resources directory / comp. and ed. by Jean E. Meeh Gosebrink. Oxford ; N.Y. : H. Zell, 1986. 572 p.   **DD36**
Publ. for the African Studies Association.
Lists institutional sources of information about Africa in the U.S. in 437 entries (many with extensive subdivisions). "Conceived ... as a partial revision of Peter Duignan's *Handbook of American Resources for African Studies* [DD37]."—*Introd.* The main section describes collections and information services in libraries and special collections, archival repositories, documentation centres and information services, government agencies, museums, learned societies, and professional organizations, providing full detail on holdings, conditions of access, and publications. Other sections cover 86 church and mission organizations, 43 distributors of Africa-related books and films, and 48 publishers. "Because of the two reference guides by Aloha South, the *Guide to Federal Archives relating to Africa* [DD42], and the *Guide to Non-Federal Archives and Manuscripts in the United States relating to Africa* [DD42], which comprise the United States contribution to the series "Guides to the Sources of African History"—no attempt has been made to provide a comprehensive and detailed survey of archival and manuscript materials on Africa in American collections." Notes some collections on African art, without surveying them systematically. An index of subjects, persons, places, and institutions or organizations is supplemented by a listing of entries by state.   Z3501

Duignan, Peter. Handbook of American resources for African studies. [Stanford, Calif.] : Hoover Institution on War, Revolution, and Peace, Stanford Univ., 1967. 218 p. (Hoover Inst. bibliographical ser., 29).   **DD37**
Describes "95 library and manuscript collections, 108 church and missionary libraries and archives, 95 art and ethnographic collections, and 4 business archives. No systematic effort was made to cover North Africa, but if librarians supplied data on their North African holdings this information was left in."—*Pref.* Although partially updated by Jean Gosebrink's *African studies information resources directory* (DD36), covers art and ethnographic collections more fully, and treats 22 church and missionary collections not covered by Gosebrink.
Z3501.D8

Guide to the sources of the history of the nations : B. Africa. Zug, Switzerland : Inter Documentation, 1970–83. 9 v.
                    DD38
Publisher varies.
At head of title: Conseil International des Archives. International Council on Archives. Consejo Internacional des Archivos.
Contents: v. 1, Quellen zur Geschichte Afrikas südlich der Sahara in dem Archiven der Bundesrepublik Deutschland (1970); v. 2, España. Guía de fuentas para la historia de Africa Subsahariana (1971); v. 3–4, Africa: sources de l'histoire de l'Afrique au Sud du Sahara dans les archives et bibliothèques françaises (1971–76. 4 v.); v. 5–6, Guida delle fonti per la storia dell'Africa a Sud del Sahara esistenti in Italia (1972–74. 2 v.); v. 7, Guida delle fonti per la storia dell'Africa a Sud del Sahara negli Archivi Santa Sede e negli Archivi Ecclesiastici d'Italia (1983; Collectana archivi vaticana, 3); v. 8, Scandinavia. Sources in Denmark, Norway and Sweden (1971); v. 9, Guide to the sources of the history of Africa south of the Sahara in the Netherlands (1978).
"The volumes for Belgium, the United Kingdom and the United States will appear separately."—[v.] 1, p. xi. For the U.S., *see*: Aloha South, *Guide to federal archives relating to Africa* (DD42), and for the U.K., J. D. Pearson's new edition of Noel Matthews and M. Doreen Wainwright, *A guide to manuscripts and documents in the British Isles relating to Africa* (DD39). *See also* for North Africa: *Guides to the sources for the history of the nations : 3rd series, North Africa, Asia, and Oceania* (DD75) and Matthews and Wainwright, *A guide to manuscripts and documents in the British Isles relating to the Middle East and North Africa* (DE50), also ed. by Pearson.
Surveys of library and archival materials important for research in African studies. Some volumes lack indexes.   CD941.G84

Pearson, J. D. A guide to manuscripts and documents in the British Isles relating to Africa. London ; N.Y. : Mansell, 1993. 2 v. (In progress).   **DD39**
Contents: v. 1, London (375 p.); v. 2, British Isles (excluding London).
A new edition of Noel Matthews and M. Doreen Wainwright's *A guide to manuscripts and documents in the British Isles relating to Africa* (1980).   CD1048.A3P43

Porgès, Laurence. Sources d'information sur l'Afrique noire francophone et Madagascar : institutions, répertoires, bibliographies. Paris : Ministère de la coopération : La Documentation française, c1988. 389 p.   **DD40**
At head of title: ORSTOM, Institut française de recherche scientifique pour le développement en coopération.
A comprehensive 1,498-item guide to sources of information concerning francophone black Africa and Madagascar. Pt. 1 is an annotated list of research institutions, associations and societies, libraries and documentation centers, official publications, journals, theses, and general and specialized bibliographies. Pt. 2 continues with a country-by-country inventory of bibliographies, directories, archives and manuscripts, and other sources, most with annotations. For each country also provides information about research centers, universities, museums, and other institutions. Indexes: journals cited, databases, authors, and institutions.

§ Updates: *Sources bibliographiques de l'Afrique de l'Ouest et de l'Afrique equatoriale d'expression française*, by Paule Brasseur and Jean-François Maurel (Dakar : Bibliothèque de l'Université de Dakar, 1970). Z3681.P77

The SCOLMA directory of libraries and special collections on Africa in the United Kingdom and Western Europe. 5th rev. and exp. ed. / comp. and ed. by Tom French. London ; N.Y. : Hans Zell Publishers, 1993. 355 p. **DD41**

4th ed., 1983, ed by. Harry Hannam.

Lists 237 libraries in 24 European countries and 155 in the U.K. Directory information includes full name and address; telephone and fax numbers; electronic mail address; opening hours; terms of access; size, scope, and depth of each collection; loan and reference facilities; CD-ROM and online databases; audiovisual resources; and publications issued. Index of institutions, organizations, subjects, and countries. Z3501.S8

South, Aloha. Guide to federal archives relating to Africa. Waltham, Mass. : Crossroads Pr., c1977. 556 p. **DD42**

Indexed and prepared for publ. by the African Studies Association.

Detailed descriptions of the "known Africa-related records in the National Archives of the United States. The records, which include textual material, maps, sound recordings, motion and still pictures, are located in the National Archives Building, the General Archives Division in the Washington National Records Center, Presidential libraries, and the regional archives branches that are part of the Federal Archives and Records Centers."—*Introd.* Arranged alphabetically by name of agency, then by subordinate agencies. Indexes of subjects, of places, of proper names, of ships, and of ethnic groups. Although published separately, is part of *Guides to the sources for the history of the nations : Africa* (DD38).

§ A companion volume is the same author's *Guide to non-federal archives and manuscripts in the United States relating to Africa* (London ; N. Y. : Zell, 1989. 2 v. [1250 p.]. Publ. for the National Archives and Records Administration, Washington, D.C.). Arranged by state, then by city, it describes, often in considerable detail, textual and non-textual records from more than 440 public and private depositories. Complements but does not supersede Jean M. Gosebrink's *African studies information resources directory* (DD36). Will "remain an indispensable work of reference for all Africanist scholars"—*Journal of African history*, 33 (1992): 524. Alphabetical list of repositories; extensive name and topical index that lacks page headers and has severely abbreviated entry numbers. Z3509.S67

Filmography

Wiley, David S. Africa on film and videotape, 1960–1981 : a compendium of reviews / David S. Wiley [et al.]. East Lansing : African Studies Center, Michigan State Univ., 1982. 551 p. **DD43**

Evaluates 7,500 films for their utility in education about Africa according to "accuracy, balance, organization, and objectivity."—*Introd.* For each film, provides "overview critique," quality rating, citations to other reviews, as well as suggestions for use, and appropriate educational level, (K–12 through higher education). Indexed by topic, country, and language.

§ Two somewhat more recent sources are: the Univ. of Illinois Film Center's *Film and video resources about Africa available from the University of Illinois Film Center* Champaign, Ill : The Center, [c1985]) and Media Network's *Guide to films on apartheid and the southern African region* (N.Y. : Media Network, 1985). *See also* Nancy J. Schmidt, *Sub-Saharan African films and filmmakers, 1987–1992 : an annotated bibliography* (London : Hans Zell, 1994). DT19.8.Z9W54

Indexes; Abstract journals

Africa index to continental periodical literature. v. 3 (1978)–9 (1982). Oxford : Hans Zell (Publ. for the African Bibliographical Centre), 1981–1989. Annual (slightly irregular). **DD44**

Continues *Africa index*, v. 1–2 (1976–78); apparently ceased with No. 7, (1989) which covered 1982.

An index to "selected scholarly and semi-scholarly journals published but not necessarily printed within the African continent excluding South Africa ... Report literature, conference papers, and papers presented to seminars in African countries are also included."—*Introd.* It also selectively indexes popular magazines and review articles, but excludes book reviews. Arranged by broad topic, with code letters next to entries to indicate geographical area treated; author and subject indexes.

§ A new index, *The index of African social science periodical articles* (v. 1– . Dakar : CODESRIA, 1989–) extends coverage retrospectively to 1985 titles, and thus offers a partial coverage of the 1980s for sub-Saharan periodicals. As of Spring 1994, two volumes have been published. Vol. 1 listed 216 items from 24 journals, in chronological order, with abstracts in the language of publication. Emphasis on social research and economic development.

A second new index, for which only one issue has been produced, is *Nigerian periodicals index* (no. 1 [June 1986]– . Jos : Committee of Univ. Librarians of Nigerian Universities). Offers retrospective coverage, in this case for 1972–85. It aims to cover Nigerian scholarly and academic journals, and includes book reviews. Easy to use, "this is a major achievement; the index is well produced and will be an invaluable research tool for scholars ..."—*The African book publishing record*, 13 no. 2 (1987): 113. Z3501.A43

African studies abstracts : the abstracts journal of the African Studies Centre, Leiden. v. 25, no. 1– . London : Hans Zell, c1994– . Quarterly. **DD45**

Continues: *Documentatieblad* of the Leiden Afrika-Studiecentrum (v. 1–24 [1968–93]. Leiden : De Centrum, 1968–93).

An essential, timely index, offering some 460 abstracts in each issue. Draws abstracts from more than 100 leading periodicals on African studies, many journals that treat developing nations, and edited works on Africa in the humanities and social sciences. Arranged by broad geographic regions, then by country. Each issue has a geographical/subject/author index and a list of journals and edited works abstracted in that issue. Z3501.L37

Book reviews

Easterbrook, David L. Africana book reviews, 1885–1945 : an index to books reviewed in selected English-language publications. Boston : G. K. Hall, [1979]. 247 p. **DD46**

Lists 1,725 reviews of appearing in 44 English-language journals, by main entry of the work under review. Title index. Z3501.E35

Henige, David P. Works in African history : an index to reviews, 1960–1974. Waltham, Mass. : African Studies Assoc., Brandeis Univ., [1976]. 54 p. **DD47**

Lists book reviews and review essays (the latter marked with asterisks) of 442 books dealing with Africa south of the Sahara, drawn from 75 journals. Arranged by author of book; no index.

Supplements, covering 1974–78 (Waltham, Mass. : Crossroads Pr., 1978. 58 p.) and 1978–82 (Los Angeles : Crossroads Pr., 1984. 127 p.) add about 5,000 reviews, drawn from about 500 journals, of 1,003 additional books. Includes reviews of important reference works. Attempts to include works on "the history of Africa from the beginnings (Egyptology aside) to the era of independence in the 1960s."—*[p. ii].* Z3508.H5H46

Encyclopedias; Dictionaries

African historical dictionaries. Metuchen, N.J. : Scarecrow, 1974– . no. 1– . (In progress).   **DD48**

Each dictionary in this series offers a brief chronology and a survey of the country's history and economics, followed by entries for basic contemporary and historical information and brief biographies of important persons. Most volumes end with a selective and sometimes extensive bibliography. Breadth, depth, and quality of coverage vary widely from one volume to another. Historians have criticized the series (*see* especially David Henige, "African historical dictionaries : through the looking glass," *Africana journal* 10 [1979]: 120–128). On the whole, the 2nd series (since 1987) has been of higher quality than the 1st, which nevertheless contained some excellent works.

The following volumes have appeared to date. Each is rated on a four-point scale (*E=excellent, G=good, F=fair, P=poor*), based on expertise of the authors, balance of current political with historical entries, errors of fact, sensitivity to the material, exclusion of important material while including trivia, correct orthography, accurate and sufficient bibliographies, format, currency on date of publication, and inclusion of indexes. Reviews in the scholarly press have also been considered. Nos. 56 and 58 were not available for examination. Superseded volumes are omitted.

no. 2, *People's Republic of the Congo*, by V. McLean Thompson and R. Adloff (2nd ed., 1984. 139 p. *E*).

no. 3, *Swaziland*, by John J. Grotpeter (1975. 251 p. *G*).

no. 4, *Gambia*, by H. A. Gailey (2nd ed., 1987. 176 p. *F*).

no. 6, *Somalia*, by Margaret Castagno (1975. 213 p. *E*).

no. 7, *Benin*, by S. Decalo (2nd ed., 1987. 349 p. *G*).

no. 8, *Burundi*, by Warren Weinstein (1976. 368 p. *G*).

no. 9, *Togo*, by S. Decalo (2nd ed., 1987. 331 p. *G*).

no. 10, *Lesotho*, by Gordon Haliburton (1977. 223 p. *G*).

no. 11, *Mali*, by Pascal J. Imperato (2nd ed., 1986. 359 p. *F*).

no. 12, *Sierra Leone*, by C. P. Foray (1977. 279 p. *F*).

no. 13, *Chad*, by S. Decalo (2nd ed., 1987. 532 p. *G*).

no. 14, *Upper Volta*, by D. M. McFarland (1978. 239 p. *F*).

no. 15, *Tanzania*, by L. S. Kurtz (1978. 363 p. *P*).

no. 16, *Guinea (Republic of Guinea/Conakry)*, by Thomas E. O'Toole (2nd ed., 1987. 204 p. *G*).

no. 19, *Zambia*, by John J. Grotpeter (1979. 410 p. *F*).

no. 20, *Niger*, by S. Decalo (2nd ed., 1989. 234 p. *G*).

no. 21, *Equatorial Guinea*, by Max Liniger-Goumaz (2nd ed., 1988. 238 p. *G*).

no. 22, *Republic of Guinea-Bissau*, by Richard A. Lobban and J. Forrest (2nd ed., 1988. 210 p. *G*).

no. 23, *Senegal*, by L. G. Colvin (1980. 355p. *G*).

no. 24, *Morocco*, by W. Spencer (1980. 152 p. *G*).

no. 28, *Algeria*, by A. Heggoy (1981. 247 p. *F*).

no. 29, *Kenya*, by B. A. Ogot (1981. 279 p. *E*).

no. 31, *Mauritania*, by A. G. Gerteiny (1981. 98 p. *F*).

no. 33, *Libya*, by Ronald Bruce St. John (2nd ed., 1991. 192 p. *P*).

no. 35, *Western Sahara*, by T. Hodges (1982. 431 p. *E*).

no. 36, *Egypt*, by J. Wucher King (1984. 719 p. *E*).

no. 37, *South Africa*, by C. C. Saunders (1983. 241 p. *E*).

no. 38, *Liberia*, by D. Elwood Dunn and Svend E. Holsoe (1985. 274 p. *E*).

no. 39, *Ghana*, by D. M. McFarland (1985. 296 p. *G*).

no. 40, *Nigeria*, by Anthony Oyewole (1987. 391 p. *G*).

no. 41, *Ivory Coast*, by Robert J. Mundt (1987. 246 p. *F*).

no. 42, *Cape Verde*, by Richard A. Lobban and Marilyn Halter (2nd ed., 1988. 171 p. *G*).

no. 43, *Zaire*, by F. Scott Bobb (1988. 349 p. *F*).

no. 44, *Botswana*, by Fred Morton, Andrew Murray, and Jeff Ramsay (1989. 216 p. *E*).

no. 45, *Tunisia*, by Kenneth J. Perkins (1989. 234 p. *G*).

no. 46, *Zimbabwe*, by R. Kent Rasmussen and Steven C. Rubert (2nd ed., 1990. 502 p. *E*).

no. 47, *Mozambique*, by Mario Azevedo (1991. 250 p. *P*).

no. 48, *Cameroon*, by Mark W. Delancey and H. Mbella Mokeba (1990. 297 p. *G*).

no. 49, *Mauritius*, by Sydney Selvon (2nd ed., 1991. 253 p. *G*).

no. 51, *Central African Republic*, by Pierre Kalck (2nd ed., 1992. 188 p. *G*).

no. 52, *Angola*, by Susan H. Broadhead (2nd ed., 1992. 296 p. *E*).

no. 53, *Sudan*, by Carolyn Fluehr-Lobban, Richard A. Lobban Jr., and John Obert Voll (2nd ed., 1992. 409 p. *E*).

no. 54, *Malawi*, by Cynthia A. Crosby (2nd ed., 1993. 202 p. *G*).

no. 56, *Ethiopia and Eritrea*, by Chris Prouty and Eugene Rosenfeld (2nd ed., 1994. 614 p.).

no. 58, *Gabon*, by David E. Gardinier (1994. 467 p.).

Afrika : ėntsiklopedicheskiĭ spravochnik / glavnyĭ redaktor An.A. Gromyko ; chleny redaktsionnoĭ kollegii V.M. Vasev … [et al.]. Moskva : "Sov. ėntsiklopediia", 1986–1987. 2 v. : ill. (some col.).   **DD49**

The 2nd ed. of an encyclopedic handbook on Africa. Pt. 1 consists of signed articles on varied topics, e.g., film, communist movements, law, literature, Soviet-American relations; pt. 2 is illustrated and includes biographical sketches. Some entries are signed. Very good for the Soviet perspective.   DT2.A34 1986

The Cambridge encyclopedia of Africa / general editors, Roland Oliver, Michael Crowder. Cambridge ; N.Y. : Cambridge Univ. Pr., 1981. 492 p. : ill. (some col.).   **DD50**

This handsomely illustrated volume, in four parts by 99 contributors, offers wide-ranging coverage of both recent and historical topics. Sections are: The African continent; The African past before European colonisation; Contemporary Africa; Africa and the world. Bibliography, p. 485–491. "There is really no other work on the market at present that is so comprehensive and useful as this handsome publication."—*Choice* 19 (June 1982): 1374.   DT3.C35

Thesauruses

Otchere, Freda E. African studies thesaurus : subject headings for library headings. N.Y. : Greenwood, 1992. 435 p. (Bibliographies and indexes in Afro-American and African studies, no. 29).   **DD51**

Lists some 4,000 subject heading terms pertaining specifically to Africa south of the Sahara for which it provides LC classification numbers. Includes "names of over 600 African peoples and nearly 600 African languages, as well as cross-references from unused synonyms and references to broader, related, and narrower terms."—*Introd.*

Z695.1.A37085

Directories

Danaher, Kevin. Beyond safaris : a guide to building people-to-people ties with Africa. Trenton, N.J. : Africa World Pr., c1991. 193 p.   **DD52**

Intended to facilitate U.S.-African interactions. Lists organizations and resources dealing with aid, studying and volunteering, people-to-people contacts, travel with a purpose, fair trade, and the environment, as well as corporate and government accountability. Appendix of highly selective general resources; reference books, periodicals, organizations, and African Studies programs in the U.S. Index.

Directory of African and African-American studies in the United States. 8th ed.– . Atlanta : African Studies Association Pr., c1993– .   **DD53**

Title varies: 1971/72–74/75 entitled: *Directory of African studies in the United States*; 1976–87 entitled: *Directory of African & Afro-American studies in the United States*.

The 1993 ed. lists 326 programs by state, and provides information on courses, faculty members, library holdings, regional emphases, special features, student enrollment, degrees offered, etc. "Institutions that did not answer our requests for information are not included."— *Pref.* Index of institutions. DT19.9.U5D56

International guide to African studies research = Études africaines : guide international de recherches / ed. by the International African Institute ; comp. by Philip Baker. 2nd fully rev. and expanded ed. London ; N.Y. : Zell, 1987. 264 p. **DD54**

1st ed., 1971, had title: *International register of organizations undertaking Africanist research*; rev. ed., 1975, had title: *International guide to African research studies.*

Publ. for the International African Institute, London.

Entries, many extensively subdivided, for 1,139 research bodies, academic institutions, and international organizations throughout the world. Provides telephone numbers, details regarding staff, library collections, research, courses offered, degrees awarded, and publications. Indexes by institution, scholar, subjects of research, specialization by region, country, or ethnic group. A 3rd rev. and exp. ed., also comp. by Baker, is projected for Oct. 1994.

§ For an excellent, annotated list of 881 research projects in 42 African countries, see: *Register of development research projects in Africa = Répertoire des projets de recherche en matière de développement in Afrique* (Paris : OECD, 1992. 346 p.). A more massive, though now dated, work covering Europe is: *Etudes africaines en Europe* (Paris : A.C.C.T. : Karthala, c1981. 2 v.). DT19.8.I58

Zell, Hans M. The African studies companion : a resource guide & directory. London ; N.Y. : Zell, 1989. 165 p. (Hans Zell resource guides, no. 1). **DD55**

Includes some 667 "annotated listings of the major reference tools; bibliographies and continuing sources; journals and magazines; major libraries and documentation centres; publishers with African studies lists; dealers and distributors of African studies associations; foundations and donor agencies supporting African studies research or which are active in Africa; and awards and prizes in African studies."—*Pref.* Appendix of abbreviations and acronyms in African studies and name index. DT19.8.Z45

Chronologies

Freeman-Grenville, Greville Stewart Parker. Chronology of African history. [London ; N.Y.] : Oxford Univ. Pr., 1973. 312 p. **DD56**

"These historical tables display, in a calendrical fashion, the whole course, so far as it is known, of the principal events and dates in the whole continent of Africa from c.1000 BC until the end of 1971."—*Introd.* Indexed. DT17.F73

General histories

The Cambridge history of Africa / gen. editors, J. D. Fage and Roland Oliver. Cambridge ; N.Y. : Cambridge Univ. Pr., 1975–86. 8 v. : ill. **DD57**

Contents: v. 1, From the earliest times to c.500 B.C., ed. J. Desmond Clark (1981. 1157 p.); v. 2, From c.500 B.C. to A.D. 1050, ed. J. D. Fage (1978. 840 p.); v. 3, From c.1050 to c.1600, ed. Roland Oliver (1977. 803 p.); v. 4, The sixteenth and seventeenth centuries, ed. Richard Gray (1975. 738 p.); v. 5, From c.1790 to c.1870, ed. John E. Flint (1977. 617 p.); v. 6, From 1870 to 1905, ed. Roland Oliver and G. N. Sanderson (1985. 956 p.); v. 7, From 1905–40, ed. A. D. Roberts (1986. 1063 p.); v. 8, From c.1940–1975, ed. Michael Crowder (1984. 1011 p.).

Chapters written by specialists include full bibliographies, and each volume ends with a bibliographical essay. Detailed index; maps. Of the same excellence as other Cambridge histories. DT20.C28

General history of Africa / UNESCO International Scientific Committee for the Drafting of a General History of Africa. London : Heinemann Educational Books ; Berkeley : Univ. of California Pr., 1981–92. v. 1–7 : ill., maps, ports. (In progress). **DD58**

Contents: v. 1, Methodology and African prehistory, ed. Joseph Ki-Zerbo (1981); v. 2, Ancient civilizations of Africa, ed. G. Mokhtar (1981); v. 3, Africa from the seventh to the eleventh century, ed. M. Elfasi; assoc. ed. Iran Hrbek (1988); v. 4, Africa from the twelfth to the sixteenth century, ed. D. T. Niane (1984); v. 5, Africa from the sixteenth to the eighteenth century (1992); v. 6, Africa in the nineteenth century until the 1880s, ed. J. F. Ade Ajayi (1989); v. 7, Africa under colonial domination 1880–1935, ed. Adu Boahen (1985). To be in 8 v.

An interdisciplinary history sponsored by Unesco, and informed by extensive reliance upon the oral tradition, whose aim is to present African history as viewed by African scholars themselves. An International Scientific Committee for the Drafting of General History of Africa (two-thirds African members, one-third non-African) supervised an initial gathering of sources published as *Guide to the sources for the history of the nations : Africa* (DD38) and the subsequent publication of the series. "Description of the project" notes that each volume presents some 30 chapters, each the work of a principal author, with preference given to qualified African scholars (*v. 7, p. xxvi*).

§ Also presenting the African point of view is *The arts and civilization of black and African peoples*, ed. by Joseph Okpaku, Alfred Opubor, and Benjamin Oloruntimehin (Lagos : Centre for Black and African Arts and Civilization, 1986. 10 v.). Essays in this work originated in a Colloquium on Black Civilization held during the 2nd World Black and African Festival of Arts and Culture in Lagos, Nigeria, in 1977. Presents information on black people worldwide in the arts, philosophy, literature, languages, history, education, religion, science and technology, government, and mass media. DT20.G45

Current surveys

Africa contemporary record : annual survey and documents. 1968/69– . London : Africa Research Ltd., 1969– . Annual. **DD59**

Survey and analysis of political, economic, social and international affairs for the entire continent. Three sections: essays by specialists on current issues and developments; a detailed country-by-country review of the year's events (with relevant statistics and other key data); reprints of essential political and economic documents from such organizations as the Organization of African Unity and the U.N.; as well as other bi-lateral and multi-lateral agreements, treaties, statistics, etc. Index. DT1.L43

Africa research bulletin. v.1 (Jan. 1964)– . Exeter, Eng. : Africa Research Ltd., 1964– . Monthly. Looseleaf. **DD60**

In two parts: A, Political, social and cultural series; B, Economic, financial and technical series.

Among the most useful current publications in African Studies, these news digests take directly from African newspapers, radio braodcasts (e.g., the B.B.C. reporting from Luanda), news agencies, U.N. publications, European newspapers, and journals, giving full credit to original sources. A similar format is followed in both series, with news arranged in seven subject categories, then by country. Monthly indexes cumulate annually.

Africa review. 1985– . Saffron Walden, Essex, Eng. : World of Information, c1984– . Annual. **DD61**

17th ed. covers 1993–94.

Chiefly a country-by-country business and economics review, with signed articles, a profile, summary analysis of the year's events, key indicators, key facts, and a business directory and business guide for each country. 17th ed. has currency tables for 1990–July 1993.

§ For Northern Africa, *see* the companion volume, *Middle East review* (CH191). HC501.A532

Area handbook series. 196?– . [Wash.] : U.S. Gov. Print. Office, Superintendent of Documents, 1992– .   **DD62**

Formerly called "Foreign area studies."

A series developed at American Univ. by academics but published for the U.S. Department of Defense. The most recent volumes have been produced by the Library of Congress. All are book-length monographs that serve as excellent introductions to the history, politics, economics, and culture of each country, and include very good bibliographies, maps, graphics, and photographs.

Published to date:

Algeria, by Harold D. Nelson (1986. 414 p.); *Angola*, by Thomas Collelo (1991. 318 p.); *Area handbook for the United Republic of Cameroon*, by Harold D. Nelson (1974. 335 p.); *Chad*, by Thomas Collelo (1990. 254 p.); *Area handbook for the Democratic Republic of the Congo (Congo Kinshasa)*, by Gordon C. McDonald (1971. 587 p.); *Area handbook for People's Republic of the Congo (Congo Brazzaville)*, by Gordon C. McDonald (1971. 255 p.); *Côte d'Ivoire*, by Robert E. Handloff (1991. 262 p.); *Egypt*, by Helen Chapin Metz (1991. 428 p.); *Ethiopia*, by Harold D. Nelson (1981. 366 p.); *Area handbook for Ghana*, by Irving Kaplan (1971. 449 p.);

Indian Ocean: five island countries, by Frederica M. Bunge (1983. 346 p.); *Kenya*, by Irving Kaplan (1984. 334 p.); *Liberia*, by Harold D. Nelson (1985. 340 p.) *Libya*, by Harold D. Nelson (1989. 351 p.); *Malawi*, by Harold D. Nelson (1987. 353 p.); *Mauritania*, by Robert E. Handloff (1990. 218 p.); *Morocco*, by Harold D. Nelson (1986. 448 p.); *Mozambique*, by Harold D. Nelson (1985. 342 p.); *Nigeria*, by Helen Chapin Metz (1992. 394 p.); *Rwanda*, by Richard F. Nyrop (1982. 214 p.);

Area handbook for Senegal, by Harold D. Nelson (1974. 410 p.); *Area handbook for Sierra Leone*, by Irving Kaplan (1976. 400 p.); *Somalia*, by Helen Chapin Metz (1993. 282 p.); *South Africa*, by Harold D. Nelson (1981. 464 p.); *Sudan*, by Helen Chapin Metz (1992. 365 p.); *Tanzania*, by A. B. Herrick (1987. 344 p.); *Tunisia*, by Harold D. Nelson (1987. 380 p.); *Uganda*, by Rita M. Byrnes (1992. 298 p.); *Zaire*, by Helen Chapin Metz (1992. 394 p.); *Zambia*, by Irving Kaplan (1979. 308 p.); *Zimbabwe*, by Harold D. Nelson (1983. 360 p.).

New African yearbook. 7th ed. (1987–88)– . London : IC Magazines Ltd. ; N.Y. : Franklin Watts, Inc., c1987–88– . Annual.   **DD63**

9th ed. covers 1993/94.

Covers basic factual material annually for 52 African countries and for the major regional organizations of the continent. For each country gives selected statistics, a fair-sized map, current political and economic summaries, and much additional information.   DT1.N473

Atlases

Clark, John Desmond. Atlas of African prehistory. Chicago : Univ. of Chicago Pr., [1967]. 62 p., : 50 maps ; 52cm.   **DD64**

Comp. under auspices of the Pan-African Congress on Prehistory and Quaternary Studies.

Designed to meet the "need for maps to show the distribution of prehistoric industries in Africa and their relations to ecological data," concentrating on the Stone Age. Base maps show ecological data (e.g., topography, soils, hypothetical rainfall, vegetative zones); transparent overlays indicate "industrial and other significant distributions" such as fossil pollen sites, fossil man sites. A supplement provides a gazetteer of important prehistoric sites.   G2446.E1C5

Historical atlas of Africa / gen. eds., J. F. Ade Ajayi and Michael Crowder. Cambridge ; N.Y. : Cambridge Univ. Pr. ; Essex : Longman, 1985. 167 p. : maps. 40cm.   **DD65**

An excellent work reflecting the editors' desire to "bring together experts on different periods of African history to produce an atlas in full colour that made use of the latest cartographic techniques."—*Pref.* Maps and text (by contributing scholars) on facing pages; photographs are also employed. Maps are of three kinds: (1) event oriented; (2) historical process oriented (e.g., "before and after"); (3) quantitative (especially for economic topics). Sources are sometimes indicated. A review in *The Journal of African History* 28 (1987):152, states "it is dif-

ficult to find anything negative to say ... unlikely to be surpassed as the standard reference work for years to come." Indexes more than 4,000 personal, corporate, and place names, with many cross-references, and lists 57 prominent historian contributors.

§ Worthwhile atlases intended for student or school use include John D. Fage's *An atlas of African history* (2nd ed. London : E. Arnold, 1978. 84 p.); G. S. P. Freeman-Grenville's *New atlas of African history* (N.Y. : Simon & Schuster, c1991. 144 p.); *African history in maps*, comp. by Michael Kwamena-Poh (London : Longman, 1982. 76 p.), and *Africa today : an atlas of reproducible pages* (Rev. ed. Wellesley, Mass. : World Eagle, 1990. 172 p.).   G2446.S1H5

AFRICA (by region)

Africa, North

See also the section for "Asia, West" in Section DE and the entries for the following works: *Index Islamicus* and its supplements (BC502); *Encyclopedia of Islam* (BC505); and issues of the *Middle East review* (CH191).

Bibliography

Bibliographie analytique de l'Afrique antique. v. 1 (1961/62)– . [Roma] : Ecole française de Rome, 1969– . Annual.   **DD66**

Frequency varied in early volumes.

Some issues are reprints of *Bulletin d'archéologie algérienne*. Continues a bibliography published annually in *Libyca*, 1953–61.

Topical arrangement of North African archaeology, covering the ancient Egyptian, Greco-Roman, and early Christian eras. Lists European language books, articles, and essays, with brief annotations. In paragraph, not list, form, which makes it a little difficult to examine quickly. Author index.   Z3511.B5

Blaudin de Thé, Bernard. Essai de bibliographie du Sahara français et des régions avoisinantes / éd. avec le concours de l'Organisation Communes des Régions Sahariennes. 2. éd. Paris : Arts et Métiers Graphiques, Librairie C. Klincksieck, 1960. 258 p.   **DD67**

1st ed., 1959.

Lists some 9,300 items in two parts. Pt. 1 is a partial reprint of *Les territoires du sud de l'Algérie*, (Alger, 1930), with titles arranged by topic, then chronologically, concentrating on materials from the 19th century, but including materials from as far back as 1550. Pt. 2, also arranged by topic then alphabetically by author, lists materials published through 1958. Both parts cover a broad range of subjects and contain materials in French and other European languages. No annotations. Author index.   Z3709.B55

Chaker, Salem. Une décennie d'études berbères (1980-1990) : bibliographie critique : langue, littérature, identité. Alger : Bouchene, 1992? 256 p.   **DD68**

A recompilation of the "Langues et littérature berbères" sections appearing in *L'annuaire de l'Afrique du Nord*, 1980–89 (Paris : Centre Nationale de la Recherche Scientifique). Includes materials on Maghrebian as well as Sahara-Sahel region Berbers. In addition to an annotation, each of the 1,408 entries includes an appropriate geopolitical and dialect designation. Arranged by author. Covers books, articles, and serial publications in many different languages, though chiefly in French. The introduction includes a history of research in Berber studies. Indexed by dialect, country or area, and general subjects.

§ Continues Lionel Galand's *Langue et littérature berbères : vingt cinq ans d'études* (Paris : Centre National de la Recherche Scientifique, 1979). More than 1,500 items covering the years 1954–77, and including materials from the 1965–77 editions of *L'annuaire*.

France. État-major de l'armée. L'Afrique française du nord : Bibliographie militaire des ouvrages français ou traduits en français et des articles des principales revues françaises relatifs à l'Algérie, à la Tunisie et au Maroc de 1830 à 1926. Paris : Imprimerie Nationale, 1930–35. 4 v. **DD69**

Repr. : N.Y. : AMS Pr., 1975 (2 v.).

At head of title: Ministère de la guerre. État-major de l'armée. Service historique.

A comprehensive bibliography, annotated and classified. In v. 1–2, *L'Algérie*, the arrangement in each class is alphabetical by author; in v. 3–4, *La Tunisie*, it is chronological by date of publication.

Vols. 1–2 contain works published from 1830 to 1926; v. 3–4, publications issued up to 1927, and those published prior to 1830 as well.

§ Also published by the Service Historique are unannotated catalogs of materials in the Army Archives: *Inventaire des archives de la Tunisie : sous-série 2 H, 1881–1960*, by Jean Nicot and Jeannine Duru (Vincennes, 1985), and *Répertoire des archives du Maroc : série 3H (1877–1960)*, by Arnaud de Menditte and Jean Nicot (Vincennes, 1982). Z3515.F81

García-Arenal, Mercedes. Repertorio bibliográfico de las relaciones entre la península Ibérica y el Norte de África, siglos XV–XVI : fuentes y bibliográfia / Mercedes García-Arenal, Miguel Ángel de Bunes, Victoria Aguilar. Madrid : Consejo Superior de Investigaciones Centíficas, Instituto de Filología, 1989. 303 p. **DD70**

Pt. 1 provides unannotated citations to 97 Castilian and Portuguese-language sources written between 1415 and 1610, published or in manuscript. Pt. 2 is a bibliography, arranged by author, of 725 secondary sources (books, chapters, articles), most of which are annotated. Extensive introduction; no index. DT197.5.S7G37

McClintock, Marsha Hamilton. The Middle East and North Africa on film : an annotated filmography. N.Y. : Garland, 1982. 542 p. (Garland reference library of the humanities, v.159). **DD71**

For annotation, *see* DE34. DS44.M43

Moatassime, Ahmed. Langues, cultures et éducation au Maghreb . bibliographie thématique / sous la direction d'Ahmed Moatassime ; avec la collaboration de Hafida Mouaziz, Hédi Chenchabi, Aziz Cherkaoui. Paris : Université de Paris I-Panthéon-Sorbonne, Institute d'étude du développement économique et social, [1986]. 154 p. **DD72**

At head of title: Centre d'études comparatives sur le développement.

Approx. 950 unannotated entries covering works 1960–86 on Morocco, Algeria, Tunisia, Mauritania, Libya, and the Maghreb in general. Arranged by country, then subject (language, culture, and education), then by type of publication (dissertations and studies, books and articles). The section on the Maghreb lists general sociological works on the area, plus topics such as immigration. Author index, plus bibliographic appendixes.

Shinar, Pessah. Essai de bibliographie sélective et annotée sur l'Islam maghrébin contemporain : Maroc, Algérie, Tunisie, Libye (1830–1978). Paris : Éditions du Centre National de la Recherche Scientifique, 1983. 506 p. **DD73**

For annotation, *see* BC501. Z7835.M6S5

Dissertations

Sluglett, Peter. Theses on Islam, the Middle East and North-West Africa, 1880–1978, accepted by universities in the United Kingdom and Ireland. London : Mansell, 1983. 147 p. **DD74**

For annotation, *see* DE44. Z3013.S57

Library resources

Guides to the sources for the history of the nations : 3rd series, North Africa, Asia and Oceania = Guides des sources de l'histoire des nations : 3ème série, Afrique du Nord, Asie et Océanie. München : Saur ; Detroit : Gale, 1972–91. v. 1–10. (In progress). **DD75**

Publisher varies; [v. 1] publ. Brussels : Archives Générales.

Contents: [v. 1] Guide des sources de l'histoire … conservées en Belgique, comp. E. Vandewoude et A. Vanrie; v. 2, Sources … dans les archives et bibliothéques françaises (2 v.); v. 3, Sources … in Finland, Norway and Sweden (2 v.); [v. 4–5] Guide to the sources in the Netherlands concerning the history of Asia and Oceania 1796–1949 (2 v.; also available on microfiche); v. 6, Quellen zur Geschichte Nordafrikas, Asiens und Ozeaniens in der Bundesrepublik Deutschland bis 1945, ed. Ernst Ritter; v. 7, Guía de fuentes para la historia de Asia en España, by Luis Sanchez Belda (1987. 242 p.); v. 8, Quellen zur Geschichte Afrikas, Asiens und Ozeaniens im Österreichischen Staatsarchiv bis 1919 (1986. 273 p.); v. 9, Sources of the history of Africa, Asia, Australia and Oceania in Hungary (with a supplement: Latin America) (1991. 451 p.); v. 10, Sources of the history of Africa, Asia and Oceania in Yugoslavia, ed. by Union of Societies at Archivists in Yugoslavia.

Offers inventories of archive and manuscript collections dealing with North Africa, Asia (including West Asia), and Oceania. CD941.G85

Encyclopedias

Ronart, Stephan. Concise encyclopaedia of Arabic civilization : the Arab West / Stephan Ronart, Nandy Ronart. N.Y. : Praeger, [1966]. 410 p. : maps. **DD76**

Covers history, politics, people, culture, and philosophies of the Maghreb and parts of the Iberian peninsula which historically had been under Muslim control. Includes cross-references, maps, lists of political parties/groups and place names, plus suggested readings.

§ Companion work by the same authors: *Concise encyclopaedia of Arabic civilization : the Arab East* (Amsterdam : Djambatan, 1959 ; N.Y. : Praeger, 1960. 589 p.). DT173.R6

Current surveys

Annuaire de l'Afrique du Nord. v. 1 (1962)– . Paris : Centre National de la Recherche Scientifique, 1964– . Annual. **DD77**

Covers Algeria, Libya, Morocco, Tunisia. Includes reports on various phases of constitutional and economic development; chronologies of diplomatic, political, and economic life; documents; bibliography. DT181.A74

Africa, South of the Sahara

Bibliography

Afrika-Schrifttum : Bibliographie deutschsprachiger wissenschaftlicher Veröffentlichungen über Afrika südlich der Sahara = Literature on Africa = Études sur l'Afrique / [Mitarbeiter: H. Becker (u.a.) ; Generalredaktion: Geo. T. Mary]. Wiesbaden : Steiner in Kommission, [1966–71]. 2 v. **DD78**

A massive bibliography of German-language scholarly publications 1871–1963 on sub-Saharan Africa. Vol. 1 is arranged by broad fields: geography, ethnology, linguistics, theology and education, tropical medicine, zoology, and botany. To facilitate use, in v. 1 "essential keywords … are appended as marginal notes in English and French in special type."—*Pref.* Vol. 2 is a subject index in German, French, and English.

§ For German-language publications since 1960, see: *Afrika Bibliographie* (Bonn : Kurt-Schroeder-Verlag, 1963–), which provides "a valuable supplementation to this present bibliographie."—*Pref.*

Z3501.A53

Bibliographie de l'Afrique sud-saharienne, sciences humaines et sociales. 1978– . Tervuren, Belgium : Musée Royal de l'Afrique Centrale, 1982– . Annual.   **DD79**
Continues: *Bibliographie ethnographique du Congo Belge et des régions avoisinantes*, 1925/30–58; *Bibliographie ethnographique du Congo et des régions avoisinantes*, 1959; *Bibliographie ethnographique de l'Afrique sud-saharienne*, 1960–77.
Lists periodical articles in seven Western languages by author, with subject index. Earlier issues included annotated citations to books and essays as well as periodical articles, but since 1980 has included only the latter. The volume for 1988/89 (publ. 1992) cites 3,578 articles. Earlier volumes provided annotations, but recent volumes give only subject descriptors.   Z5113.T33

Bridgman, Jon. German Africa : a select annotated bibliography / by Jon Bridgman and David E. Clarke. Stanford, Calif. : Hoover Inst. on War, Revolution and Peace, Stanford Univ., 1965. 120 p. (Hoover Institution bibliographical series, 19).
                    DD80
Lists 907 partially annotated items, some of them substantial runs of newspapers and other serials held by the Hoover Institution, on German activity in Africa from 1870 to the mid-1960s, "concentrating on German government, politics, foreign relations, military activity and territorial expansion."—*Pref.* Coverage of the period from World War I, when the "recovery of the colonies became a domestic political issue" through the Nazi era and World War II is particularly extensive.
                    Z3751.B7

Cooperative Africana Microform Project. CAMP catalog. 1985 cumulative ed. Chicago : Cooperative Africana Microform Project and the Center for Research Libraries [etc.], [1986]. 642 p.   **DD81**
Previous cumulative editions issued in 1977 and 1981. This supersedes all earlier editions and is cumulative to May 1985.
Photoreproduction of cards for 7,590 entries, arranged by main entry, with limited cross-references and a 41-p. subject index. This edition supersedes all earlier editions.
§ CAMP (founded 1963) is a joint effort by research libraries and the Center for Research Libraries (CRL) to preserve sub-Saharan Africana by acquiring expensive microform sets; authorizing filming of newspapers, journals, government publications, personal and corporate archives, and African-language materials; and making these materials available through interlibrary loan to CAMP subscribers and to CRL members and others according to CRL policy. Records of CAMP materials are found in CRL's online bibliographic database and in both RLIN and OCLC.   Z3509.C66

Duignan, Peter. A bibliographical guide to colonialism in sub-Saharan Africa / Peter Duignan and L. H. Gann. Cambridge : Cambridge Univ. Pr., 1973. 552 p.   **DD82**
Vol. 5 of Gann's *Colonialism in Africa, 1870–1960*.
Covers publications on the historical, political, societal, and related problems, 1870–1960. Stress is on historical material, but works in anthropology, law, economics, and geography are also cited. Includes publications to early 1972. Provides a guide to reference sources, libraries, archives, etc., as well as a subject guide to the literature.

———— Guide to research and reference works on sub-Saharan Africa / by Peter Duignan and Helen F. Conover. Stanford, Calif. : Hoover Institution Pr., [1972?]. 1102 p. (Hoover Institution bibliographical series, 46).   **DD83**
This authoritative source describes, as of 1968–70, "African library and archival materials important in reference, research, and

teaching. It aims to serve especially the librarian and the student."—*Pref.* Presents 3,127 fully annotated entries arranged topically and geographically, with a general index.   Z3501.D78

Hess, Robert L. Semper ex Africa : a bibliography of primary source[s] for nineteenth-century tropical Africa as recorded by explorers, missionaries, traders, travelers, administrators, military men, adventurers, and others / by Robert L. Hess and Dalvan M. Coger. [Stanford, Calif. : Hoover Inst., 1972]. 800 p. (Hoover Institution bibliographical series, 47).   **DD84**
Lists more than 7,700 items concerned with "that area of the continent exclusive of the Muslim Arab North and of the Afrikaner-controlled Republic of South Africa."—*Introd.* Geographical arrangement with author index. Includes both books and periodical articles.
                    Z3501.H47

Library of Congress. Library of Congress Office, Nairobi, Kenya. Accessions list, Eastern and Southern Africa. v. 1, no. 1. (Jan. 1968)–v. 25 no. 6 (Nov./Dec. 1992). Nairobi : Library of Congress, 1968–[1993].   **DD85**
Covers books, serials, and government publications of 22 eastern and southern African countries, with occasional acquisitions from others. Lists monographs by country, then language. "Each bimonthly Accessions List includes a main and added entry index of monograph entries, and a list of publisher's addresses."—*Introd.* Annual cumulations of both appear in no. 6. An *Annual serial supplement* lists all serial titles currently received by the Office. Includes occasional lists of nonbook materials and significant U.N. publications. Microfiche version available from Photoduplication Service, Library of Congress.
                    Z3516.U52

McIlwaine, John. Africa : a guide to reference material. London ; N.Y. : Hans Zell Publishers, 1993. 507 p. (Regional reference guides, no. 1).   **DD86**
Annotations for 1,766 nonbibliographic reference works cover chiefly the past 100 years. Arrangement is continent-wide first, followed by five regions, each subdivided by individual countries. Categories are: handbooks, yearbooks, statistics, directories, biographies, atlases, and gazeteers. Chronological by date of publication within each section, with combined author, title, and subject index. A preface of outstanding clarity sets the present work in context, and for excluded works directs readers to other sources. Provides references to all substantial reviews in several major journals. An essential source, "highly recommended for all scholarly collections, not just for African studies."—*Library journal* 118, no. 18 (15 Nov. 1993): 68.
                    Z3501.M3

Obdeijn, Herman. The political role of Catholic and Protestant missions in the colonial partition of Black Africa : a bibliographical essay. Leiden : [Leiden Center for the History of European Expansion], 1983. 95 p. : ill. (Intercontinenta, no. 3).
                    DD87
Offers "a survey of recent [post-1950] studies on the political role of missionary work in Africa south of the Sahara at the time this continent was divided among European powers."—*Introd.* Each essay covers a different geographical area; publications discussed are in English, French, German, or Dutch. Not indexed.   BV3520.O23

Scheven, Yvette. Bibliographies for African studies, 1970–1986. London ; N.Y. : Zell, 1988. 615 p.   **DD88**
Provides an overview of 17 years of African studies scholarship through annotations of 3,245 bibliographies from some 40 specific disciplines and 57 sub-Saharan nations and geographic areas. Cumulates the compiler's earlier volumes for 1970–75, 1976–79, and 1980–83, adding new materials published through 1986. Notable for its international coverage, including bibliographies published in periodicals and series, and its comprehensiveness. Topical and geographic arrangement, with an extensive index of subjects, authors, and some titles.
                    Z3501.S34

U.S. imprints on Sub-Saharan Africa / African Section, African and Middle Eastern Division, Research Services. v. 1 (1985)– . Wash. : Library of Congress : for sale by the U.S. Govt. Print. Off., 1986– . Biennial.   **DD89**

Superintendent of Documents classification: LC 41.12/2.

Subtitle: a guide to publications cataloged at the Library of Congress.

Each biennial issue has a combined numeric designation (i.e., 1990/91 is called v. 6/7). Frequency varies.

Each volume focuses on monographs, cataloged at the Library of Congress and published in the U.S., about sub-Saharan Africa within the previous three years. For example, v. 6–7 "focuses on monographs published or distributed in the United States about sub-Saharan Africa and catalogued by the Library of Congress from 1988 to 1991 ... Belles-lettres works are not included unless geographic area codes appear on their machine-readable records."—*Pref., v. 6–7*. The majority of the titles are in English; arrangement is by author. Vol. 1 provides 652 citations, v. 6–7, cites 1,648. Each volume includes a list of titles and a combined list of subjects, geographic terms, and personal authors. Appendix: list of publishers' and distributors' addresses.

Z3509.U18

Young, Josiah U. African theology : a critical analysis and annotated bibliography. Westport, Conn. : Greenwood, 1993. 257 p. (Bibliographies and indexes in religious studies, no. 26).   **DD90**

For annotation, *see* BC35.   BT30.A438Y68

Indexes

Library of Congress. African Section. Africa south of the Sahara : index to periodical literature, 1900–1970. Boston : G.K. Hall, 1971. 4 v.   **DD91**

A massive index to more than 1,500 periodicals, based on records of three European research institutes, the International African Institute (London), and the Library of Congress. Covers all sub-Saharan countries of Africa, arranged by area, then region or country, then subject. "Most of the references are to articles published in the last ten years in the major scholarly journals of Africa, Asia, Europe, and North America."—*Pref.* Despite the dates in the subtitle, some articles from the 129th century are included, especially in anthropology, description and travel, and linguistics. Emphasizes the social sciences, but also indexes material on virtually all aspects of African life and culture, including agriculture, the arts, medicine, sports, etc. An appendix cites some 3,000 African literary works.

————. ————. *1st–3rd supplements* (Boston : G.K. Hall, 1973–85. 3 v.).

Entries for materials added Jan. 1971–Dec. 1977. Each supplement has author index. Suppl. 3 departs from the pattern of earlier supplements, arranging entries by six broad subject categories. Publication suspended with Suppl. 3.   Z3503.U47

Quarterly index to periodical literature, Eastern and Southern Africa. v. 1, no. 1 (1991)– . Nairobi, Kenya : Library of Congress, Library of Congress Office, 1991– . Quarterly.   **DD92**

Superintendent of Documents classification: LC 1.30/8-4: .

Fills a longstanding need for a timely, regularly published index of periodicals published across the African continent. Indexes more than 200 journals, most scholarly, from 23 countries; most are not indexed elsewhere. Citations, arranged by 30 broad subject categories, are followed by five indexes: author, geographic area, subject, article title, journal title. A "Register of citations" includes subject terms; the journal title index gives addresses. Annual cumulative index in no. 4.

Z3503.Q37

Directories

Fenton, Thomas P. Africa : a directory of resources / comp. and ed. by Thomas P. Fenton and Mary J. Heffron. Maryknoll, N.Y. : Orbis Books, c1987. 144 p. : ill.   **DD93**

An updated and greatly expanded version of the corresponding chapter in Fenton and Heffron's 1984 *Third World resource directory* (DA11).

Cites with extensive annotations, organizations, publishers, audiovisual materials, books and pamphlets that focus on Africa south of the Sahara. Indexes for organizations, author, title, subject, and geographic area. Emphasizes "social-change resources" that present alternative views regarding African development.   Z3501.F45

Handbooks; Current surveys

Africa south of the Sahara. Ed. 1 (1971)– . London : Europa Publ., 1971– . Annual.   **DD94**

An essential handbook and directory of information in three parts: (1) Background to the continent, with essays by specialists on varied aspects of African studies, and a well-chosen bibliography of select periodicals for the field; (2) Regional organizations, with details of their activities; (3) Country surveys for 51 countries, covering key political, social and economic developments of the preceding year, with select bibliographies. Also provides overview essays; statistics on economic, demographic, and other data; directory of names and addresses of major institutions, e.g., banks, governmental officials, media, newspapers, political parties, trade unions, etc.

"A new examination of 'Africa in Retrospect and Prospect,' together with an in-depth evaluation of Economic Trends in the region, and comprehensive coverage of the production, marketing and world-price trends in the principal African commodities. Extensive directory coverage of international organizations and research institutions active in Africa is once again included."—*Foreword, 22nd ed., 1993.*

DT351.A37

Morrison, Donald George. Black Africa : a comparative handbook / Donald George Morrison, Robert Cameron Mitchell, John Naber Paden. 2nd ed. N.Y. : Paragon House : Irvington Publishers, c1989. 716 p. : ill.   **DD95**

1st ed., 1972.

Although this volume contains information no more up-to-date than 1982, it retains importance for its essays on theoretical and methodological issues, for its rankings of interdisciplinary and comparative data by 200 key trends, and for its aggregate data for 1955, 1961, 1966, 1972, and 1977. Covers demographic, developmental, ecological, economic, educational, political, international, linguistic, and societal statistics and other information for 41 Sub-Saharan countries.

DT352.8.M67

Shavit, David. The United States in Africa : a historical dictionary. N.Y. : Greenwood, [1989]. 298 p.   **DD96**

Brief entries for individual Americans, missionary societies, other institutions, and events concerned with Africa south of the Sahara and adjacent islands over the past 200 years. Includes a chronology, lists of chiefs of American diplomatic missions in Africa, 1863–1986, individuals by profession and occupation, and bibliographical essay. Combined personal and geographic name and limited subject index. Entries frequently cite additional sources.   DT38.1.S53

Africa, West

Bibliography

Brasseur, Paule Marion. Bibliographie générale du Mali (anciens Soudan Français et Haut-Sénégal-Niger). Dakar : IFAN, 1964. 461 p. : map. (Institit Français d'Afrique Noire. Catalogues et documents, XVI).   **DD97**

A classified listing of 4,873 numbered items—books and periodical articles—almost entirely in French, on all phases of life, culture, and history of francophone West Africa. Many titles are annotated.

§ Continued by: *Bibliographie générale du Mali (1961–1970)* (Dakar : Nouvelles Éditions Africaines, 1976. 184 p. [Inst. Fondamental d'Afrique Noire. Catalogues et documents, no. 16–2]).

Adds almost 3,000 documents, books, periodical articles, mimeographed reports. Entries are mainly in French; brief annotations. Topical arrangement; author and subject index.   Z3711.B7

Cardinall, Allan Wolsey. Bibliography of the Gold Coast. Accra : Govt. Pr., [1932]. 384 p.   **DD98**

Repr.: Westport, Conn. : Negro Univ. Pr., 1970.

Issued as a companion volume to the census report of 1931.

Cites 5,168 titles in many languages concerning the Gold Coast and neighboring regions, now Ghana, Togo, Benin, Burkina Faso, and Côte d'Ivoire. Cardinall describes his aim as "the systematic list, description and history of books and articles dealing with the Gold Coast."—*Introd.* A classic bibliography.   Z3785.C3

Fage, J. D. A guide to original sources for precolonial western Africa published in European languages. Madison, Wis. : African Studies Program, Univ. of Wisconsin-Madison, c1987. 192 p. : map. (Studies in African sources, 2).   **DD99**

Annotations, chiefly descriptive but sometimes critical, for 700 published sources. Arranged chronologically according to years covered, ca.800–1871. Includes books, parts of collections, and articles on the region from Senegal to Angola. Indexes of authors, editors, translators, and geographical areas.   Z3516.5.F34

Irele, Modupeola. The Economic Community of West African States (ECOWAS) : a bibliography and sourcebook. Lagos, Nigeria : Nigerian Inst. of International Affairs, 1990. 221 p. (NIIA bibliography series, no. 17).   **DD100**

Cites 524 entries for ECOWAS publications and secondary works that focus on the history of the organization, general information on the subregion, and on ECOWAS projects. Annotated list of administrative decisions pertaining to ECOWAS and basic information on the 16 ECOWAS states. Provides substantial documentation for the period 1962–85. Appendixes present texts of ECOWAS treaties and protocols. Subject index.   HC1000.I74

Joucla, Edmond A. Bibliographie de l'Afrique occidentale française. Paris, Soc. d'Éditions Géographiques, Maritimes et Coloniales, 1937. 704 p.   **DD101**

A massive bibliography of 9,543 maps, books and articles, (primarily in French), arranged by main entry. Detailed subject and geographical indexes.   Z3711.J68

M'baye, Saliou. Sources de l'histoire démographique des pays du Sahel conservées dans les archives : 1816–1960. [Ouagadougou, Burkina Faso] : CILSS : Institut du Sahel, 1986. 328 p.   **DD102**

For annotation, *see* CG307.   Z7164.D3M38

RESINDEX / CILSS, Institut du Sahel, Programme RESADOC. No. 1– . Bamako, Mali : Le Programme, 1985– . Semiannual.   **DD103**

Cites books and articles on 20 broad topics with emphasis on agriculture and desert ecology. Entries originated from institutions in nine West African countries: Burkina Faso, Cape Verde, Chad, Gambia, Guinea-Bissau, Mali, Mauritania, Niger, and Senegal. Much of this material may not be indexed elsewhere. Indexes by subject, geographical areas, institutions and authors.

§ For earlier coverage, see: *Bibliographie de documents et rapports sur les pays du Sahel, 1977–1985*, jointly compiled by the Sahel Antenna of the Development Centre and the Club de Sahel. (Paris : OCDE, 1989). More than 900 books, articles, papers and documents dealing with agricultural and economic development in the Sahel collected by Michigan State University's Sahel Documentation Center, plus about 100 related American doctoral dissertations, are available on microfiche from University Microfilms International. The fiches are accompanied by a printed pamphlet, *Sahel: a guide to the microfiche collection* (Ann Arbor, Mich., 1981).   Z3515.R48

Periodicals

Bibliothèque Nationale (France). Les publications en série éditées au Sénégal, 1856–1982 : liste provisoire / par Marie-Elisabeth Bouscarle. Paris : Bibliothèque Nationale, 1987. 107 p. (Collection Etudes, guides et inventaires, no 7).   **DD104**

For annotation, *see* AD176.   Z3715.B54

Archives

Guides to materials for West African history in European archives. London : Univ. of London, Athlone Pr., 1962–73. 5 v.   **DD105**

Contents: no.1, Materials for West African history in the archives of Belgium and Holland, by Patricia Carson (1962); no.2, ... Portuguese archives, by A. F. C. Ryder (1965); no.3, ... Italian archives, by Richard Gray and D. S. Chambers (1965); no.4, ... French archives, by Patricia Carson (1968); no.5, ... archives of the United Kingdom, by Noel Matthews (1973).

§ Largely superseded by the series *Guide to the sources of the history of the nations : B. Africa* (DD38), but material for Belgium and Portugal is not covered by the newer series. For British archives, see: J. D. Pearson, *A guide to manuscripts and documents in the British Isles relating to Africa* (DD39).   CD1000.G8

M'baye, Saliou. Guide des archives de l'Afrique occidentale française. Dakar : Archives du Sénégal, 1990. 204 p.   **DD106**

The introduction describes the organization and history of the archives, arguably the best-organized in West Africa. After each collection of materials from the former French West Africa, a bibliography lists works resulting from research in the collection. Reprints laws and other regulations governing the archives. Index of subjects and names.   CD2491.S38S25

Africa, East

See also Davis Bullwinkle's *Women of eastern and southern Africa : a bibliography, 1976–1985* (CC593).

Bibliography

Darch, Colin. A Soviet view of Africa : an annotated bibliography on Ethiopia, Somalia and Djibouti. Boston : G. K. Hall, c1980. 200 p. : map (on lining paper).   **DD107**

A classified bibliography of writings from the USSR and pre-revolutionary Russia on the Horn of Africa. About 1,200 items, including printed monographs, collections, and periodical articles in Russian that deal wholly or in part with the history, linguistics, social sciences, natural science and medicine of the Horn of Africa. Newspaper articles and book reviews have been relegated to appendixes; maps are omitted. Publication dates range from the 19th century to about 1975. Titles are given in transliteration, with English translation. Indexes of names and subjects.

§ Darch is also the compiler of *Russian writings on Tanganyika, Zanzibar, and Tanzania* ([Dar es Salaam] : Bureau of Resource Assessment and Land Use Planning, Univ. of Dar es Salaam, 1976. 68 p. [Research report, n.s., 19]). *See also*: Charles B. McLane, *Soviet-African relations* (DC599).   Z3521.D37

Ofcansky, Thomas P. British East Africa, 1856–1963 : an annotated bibliography. N.Y. : Garland, 1985. 474 p. (Themes in European expansion, v. 7 ; Garland reference library of social science, v. 158).   **DD108**

3,086 mostly nonofficial books and pamphlets, mostly in English, on British East Africa generally including sections for Kenya, Uganda, Tanganyika, and Zanzibar. Includes special headings for exploration, religion, agriculture, education, Mau Mau revolt, medicine, slavery, and wildlife. Author index.

§ *See also*: Library of Congress. African Section, *Official publications of British East Africa*, comp. by Helen F. Conover and Audrey A. Walker (AF223); and John B. Webster, *A bibliography on Kenya* (DD167).   Z3516.O33

Stella, Gian Carlo. Africa orientale (Eritrea, Abissinia, Somalia) e colonialismo italiano : bibliografia : catalogo descrittivo delle opere possedute. 2a ed. notevolmente aum. Ravenna [Italy] : G. C. Stella, 1986. 571 p.   **DD109**

At head of title: Biblioteca privata di Gian Carlo Stella.

An interesting catalog of a private library dealing with Italian colonialism in East Africa. 2,051 citations arranged alphabetically by author, with indexes by periodical title and personal name. No general subject index.   Z3521.A32

Wilding, Richard. Swahili bibliography of the East African coast. [Nairobi] : Lamu Society, 1990. 1 v. (unpaged).   **DD110**

Concerns the Swahili people and their influence in the region. Language materials are excluded. Covers published and unpublished works, but only in Western languages. Each citation was coded by broad subject and geographic location, but the arrangement is difficult to use and the work needs a subject index. Citations are often cryptic because important information (e.g., publisher) is omitted.   Z3516.W55

Africa, Central

Hategekimana, Grégoire. Sources bibliographiques des états de l'ancien domaine colonial belge d'Afrique centrale : Rwanda, Burundi, Zaire. Éd. abrégée. Kigali : Author, [1983], c1979. 204 p.   **DD111**

At head of title: Contribution à la recherche bibliographique sur les états de la Communauté économique des pays des Grands Lacs, I.

A topically arranged bibliography of bibliographies, the first part dealing with the countries mentioned in the title, the second with Africa in general. Cites some 1,017 books, pamphlets, and articles in various Western languages. Some annotations; no index.

Africa, Southern

See also Davis Bullwinkle's *Women of eastern and southern Africa : a bibliography, 1976–1985* (CC593).

Bibliography

Andor, L. E. The USSR and the Soviet bloc : policies and influences in Southern Africa, 1975–1986 : a select and annotated bibliography. Braamfontein, Johannesburg : South African Institute of International Affairs, 1987. 275 p. (South African Institute of International Affairs. Bibliographical series, no. 15).   **DD112**

An establishment publication listing 1,046 entries including books, chapters, articles, and pamphlets in a single listing sequence for all countries. Author and subject indexes.

§ For previous works, *see* Mary Holdsworth, *Soviet African studies, 1918–59 : an annotated bibliography* (Oxford : Oxford Univ. Pr., 1961), pt. 2: Regional studies, p. 51–66. *See also* Charles B. McLane, *Soviet-African relations* (DC599).   Z3518.A63

Böhmer, Elizabeth W. Left-radical movements in South Africa and Namibia 1900–1981 : a bibliographical and historical study. Cape Town : South African Library, 1986. 2 v. (liv, 1249 p.). (Grey-bibliografieë, 14.).   **DD113**

Written from the apartheid mind-set, this bibliography was compiled for the South African Sources on Communism project of the University of Stellenbosch. "Left-radical movements" are defined as any organization opposing apartheid (including church groups, humanitarian organizations or multiracial organizations, labor unions, and branches of international organizations portrayed as infiltrated by Communists). The compiler makes an an unsuccessful effort to distance herself from the labels. There are 5,039 entries for materials available in South Africa, including banned materials. The main listing includes sections on Southern Africa generally, South Africa, Namibia and Lesotho. Addenda: List of banned persons, organizations and periodicals; Consolidated alphabet of all persons listed in terms of the Suppression of Communism Act to 30 June 1983. Indexes of subjects, names as subject, periodicals, and court cases.   HN801.Z9R33

Gowan, Susan Jean. Portuguese-speaking Africa 1900–1979 : a select bibliography. Braamfontein, South Africa : South African Inst. of Internat. Affairs, [1982–83]. 4 v. in 3 : ill. (South African Institute of International Affairs. Bibliographical series, no.9–11).   **DD114**

Contents: v. 1, Angola; v. 2, Mozambique; v. 3, Portuguese Guinea/Guinea Bissau, Cape Verde, São Tomé e Principe, Portuguese-speaking Africa as a whole; v. 4, United Nations documentation on Portuguese-speaking Africa, by Elna Schoeman.

Lists selected books, essays, periodical articles, and government publications, mainly in Portuguese or English, covering the period 1900–1979. Vols. 1–2 arranged by broad topics within two larger sections, Pre-Independence and Post-Independence, with author and subject indexes. Vol. 3 lists works on the whole of Portuguese-speaking Africa, on Angola and Mozambique together, and on any of the former Portuguese colonies in topical or geographical arrangement, with author and subject indexes. Vol. 4 is exclusively a listing of 197 U. N. documents "on the decolonization process of the Portuguese colonies and their subsequent attainment of independence."—*Pref.* It includes annotations and author and subject indexes.

§ *See also* Mary Jane Gibson, *Portuguese Africa : a guide to official publications* (AF220).   Z3871.P67

Hofmeyr, J. W. History of the church in southern Africa / comp. and ed. by J. W. Hofmeyr and K. E. Cross. Pretoria : Univ. of South Africa, 1986–93. v. 1–3. (Studia composita, 4.). (In progress).   **DD115**

Contents: v. 1, A select bibliography of published material to 1980; v. 2, A select bibliography of published material 1981 to 1985; v. 3, A select bibliography of published material 1985–1989.

An impressive work in four parts: general, denominations, missions and missionary societies, and topics. The base volume (v. 1) contains 5,735 entries. Includes books, pamphlets, chapters in books, sermons, liturgies, and church laws and regulations. The sections on denominations and missions are arranged chronologically by date of the organizations appearance in South Africa; other sections are alphabetically arranged. The last section includes 12 topics, including: Church and race relations, and Church and society. Name and subject indexes.
Z7778.S57H64

Löfgren, Ake. SADCC literature and literature on SADCC. Uppsala : Southern Africa Programme, Scandinavian Inst. of African Studies, 1990. 64 p.   **DD116**

An important work about the organization that was established to foster regional cooperation and break away from economic dependence on South Africa under apartheid. SADCC documents are difficult to find, since many are not published by SADCC, but by many other publishers. Nonofficial topical books, articles, reports, and conference papers are included. 32 key monographs are listed with critical evaluative annotations.

§ *See also*: Elna Schoeman, *Southern African Development Coordination Conference (SADCC) : a select and annotated bibliography* (Braamfontein, South Africa : South African Inst. of International Affairs, 1986. 131 p.), with 438 citations; and her *Economic interdependence in southern Africa, 1961–1989 : a select and annotated bibliography* (Johannesburg : South African Inst. of International Affairs, 1990. 377 p.), with 1,316 citations.

Parsons, Quentin Neil. The High Commission territories, 1909–1964 : a bibliography. Kwaluseni : Univ. of Botswana, Lesotho, and Swaziland, 1976. 18 *l.* (Swaziland libraries publications, no. 3).   **DD117**

A bibliography of 146 unannotated entries that include government publications and are divided into seven historical sections, 1909–73, that correspond to South Africa's attempts to incorporate the High Commission Territories (Basutoland, later Lesotho; Bechuanaland Protectorate, later Botswana; and Swaziland). Includes works that treat one, two, or all three territories. Author/main entry index.
Z3559.P37

Pélissier, René. Africana : bibliographies sur l'Afrique luso-hispanophone : 1800–1980. Montameta : Éditions Pélissier, [c1980]. 205 p.   **DD118**
For annotation, *see* DD12.   Z3871.P44

Rhodes-Livingstone Institute. A selected bibliography of the Federation of Rhodesia and Nyasaland / comp. by R. M. S. Ng'ombe. [Lusaka, Zambia], 1957. 68 p.   **DD119**

Arranged by "tribe" and territory. Useful to supplement country bibliographies for the pre-independence period for both Zambia and Malawi. No index.

Thompson, Leonard Monteath. Southern African history before 1900 : a select bibliography of articles / by Leonard Thompson, Richard Elphick and Inez Jarrick. Stanford, Calif. : Hoover Institution Pr., [1971]. 102 p. (Hoover Institution bibliographical series, 49).   **DD120**

1,136 articles arranged in 26 subject or country sections with subsections. Covers 34 "major" journals and seven "minor" journals as well as selected articles from elsewhere. Author index.   Z3518.T5

Université de la Réunion. Service commun de la documentation. Iles du sud-ouest de l'océan Indien : catalogue des monographies / rédigé par Roucaya Safla. 4e éd., rev. et augm. Saint Denis : Université de la Réunion, Service commun de la documentation ; Paris : Diffusion, Harmattan, 1991. 349 p.   **DD121**

The most current general bibliography on the Indian Ocean islands of Réunion (with 44% of the entries), Mauritius (14%), Madagascar (14%), and the Seychelles, Comoros, and Mayotte (3%).The first quarter of the citations consist of general works treating more than one island. Entries are arranged by island, then subdivided by nine

broad subject categories. This edition includes 2,828 citations, of which the majority are French-language monographs. Although there are no annotations, citations for volumes of collected conference papers show the individual paper titles.   Z3499.U54

Women in development in Southern Africa : Botswana, Lesotho, Malawi, and Zambia : an annotated bibliography / comp. by L. Ramore ... [et al.]. Wageningen, Netherlands : Technical Centre for Agricultural and Rural Cooperation, 1991. 4 v. : ill.   **DD122**

Contents: v. 1, Botswana, comp. by L. Ramore; v. 2, Lesotho, comp. by M. M. Chadzingwa; v. 3, Malawi, comp. by G. W. P. Kishindo; v. 4, Zambia, comp. by M. Misengo and K. L. Chanda.

Lists published and unpublished materials, with author and subject indexes. The volumes differ considerably in size and arrangement. Vol. 1 lists 324 citations in 11 broad subject sections, v. 2 lists 157 citations in one alphabet, v. 3 lists 415 citations in six sections, and v. 4 lists 392 citations in ten subject sections.

§ For Botswana, *see*: Francine I. Henderson, *Women in Botswana : an annotated bibliography* (Gaborone : National Inst. of Development and Cultural Research, Univ. College of Botwana, Univ. of Botswana and Swaziland, 1981. 20 p.).

For Lesotho, *see*: Thokozile Nkabinde, E. R. M. Mapetia, and M. M. Moshoeshoe, *Women in Lesotho : an annotated bibliography* ([2nd ed.]. Roma, Lesotho : Women's Research Collective, National Univ. of Lesotho, 1989. 76*l.*); Shelby Lewis, Mathetha Molapo, and Bunie Sexwale, *Women in Lesotho : an annotated bibliography* (Roma, Lesotho : Women's Research Collective, National Univ. of Lesotho, 1984. 27*l.*); and for an overview monograph, M. Shale ... [et al.], *The situation of women in Lesotho* (Maseru? : Dept. of Social Anthropology/Sociology, National Univ. of Lesotho, 1985).   Z7963.E18W66

Women in Southern Africa : a bibliography / comp. by Heather Hughes ... [et al.]. Rev. ed. Durban, South Africa : Durban Women's Bibliography Group, Univ. of Natal, c1991. 181 p.   **DD123**
1st ed., 1985.

This edition is in 17 sections. The authors did not view the titles.
§ See also *Resistance, war and liberation : women of Southern Africa* (N.Y. : Women's International Resource Exchange, [1980?]).   Z7964.A336W65

Current

Southern African update. v. 1, no. 1 (Apr. 1986)– . [Braamfontein, South Africa] : Univ. of the Witwatersrand Library, c1986– . Semiannual.   **DD124**
Subtitle: "A bibliographical survey."

Annotated bibliographies of publications on Southern Africa (widely defined), arranged in topical chapters. Some numbers update previous issues. Topics covered are mostly political; e.g., v. 7, no. 2 includes a chapter on the Convention for a Democratic South Africa (CODESA) and an update on Nyerere's Tanzania. Author, title and subject indexes.

AFRICA (by country)

For specific countries, *see also* collective entries *World bibliographical series* (DD18), *African historical dictionaries* (DD48), and *Area handbook series* (DD62).

Algeria

Maynadies, Michel. Bibliographie algérienne : répertoire des sources documentaires relatives à l'Algérie. Alger : Office des publications universitaires, c1989. 337 p.   **DD125**

Cites 1,133 items, mostly bibliographies and other reference works. Pt. 1 lists general reference works, plus research centers, libraries, and archives; pt. 2 lists works by topics, ranging from the natural to the social sciences. Most entries are annotated and indicate if items can be found at Bibliothèque nationale d'Algérie, Bibliothèque universitaire d'Alger, Bibliothèque de l'Institut des Sciences Économiques de l'Université d'Alger, or Bibliothèque Nationale (Paris). Primarily materials in French, but also includes works in other European languages. Author/anonymous title and serial title indexes.

§ An important catalog not included in the above is *Papiers du Consulat de France à Alger : inventaire analytique des volumes de correspondance du consulat de France à Alger, 1585–1798,* by Pascal Even (Paris : Impr. nationale, 1988).   Z3681.M38

Ruhe, Ernstpeter. Algerien-Bibliographie : Publikationen aus der Bundesrepublik Deutschland, Österreich und der Schweiz 1962–1989. Wiesbaden : Harrassowitz, 1990. 181 p.   **DD126**

Chiefly German-language items, with a few French and English entries, arranged by topics covering the natural sciences, social sciences, and the arts. Lists 1,262 books, articles, and other materials. No annotations. Author index and list of periodical titles cited.   Z3681.R84

Stora, Benjamin. Dictionnaire biographique de militants nationalistes algériens : E.N.A., P.P.A., M.T.L.D., 1926–1954. Paris : Harmattan, c1985. 404 p., [8] p. of plates : ill.   **DD127**

Offers biographical information ranging from a paragraph to several pages concerning Algerian nationalists active 1926–54 in the Étoile Nord Africaine, Parti du Peuple Algérien, or Mouvement pour le Triomphe des Libertés Démocratiques—the major political organizations of the Algerian independence movement. In three main parts: (1) nationalists active in France, 1926–54; (2) those active in Algeria, 1933–54; and (3) members of schisms that developed within the P.P.A. and M.T.L.D., 1946–54. Entries are arranged alphabetically by the most commonly used name or pseudonym. Entries provide summary biographies and cite sources of information. Bibliography of archival and secondary sources, p. 365–382; indexes by biographee and by other names mentioned in the entries.   DT294.7.A1S76

Angola

Borchardt, Paul. Bibliographie de l'Angola : (Bibliotheca Angolensis) 1500–1910. [Bruxelles : Misch et Thron, 1912]. 61 p. (Institut de sociologie. Monographies bibliographiques, no. 2).   **DD128**

Covers a broad range of topics including the natural sciences, early explorations, and cartography. There are no annotations or index, but its arrangement and format make it easy to use.

§ *See also* Margaret Joan Greenwood, *Angola : a bibliography* (Cape Town : Univ. of Cape Town School of Librarianship, 1967. 52 p.), with 183 citations. For an overview of Angola with bibliography: Keith Somerville, *Angola : politics, economics, society* (Boulder, Colo. : Lynn Rienner, 1986. 207 p.); and for U.S. involvement, John Stockwell, *In search of enemies : a CIA story* (N.Y. : Norton, 1978. 285 p.). M. L. Rodrigues de Areia's *Angola : bibliografía antropologica* (Coimbra : Centro de Estudos Africanos, Inst. de Antropologia, Univ.,

de Coimbra, 1984. 165 p.) is an alphabetical list without annotations or indexes. About half the citations are in Portuguese, the rest in other European languages. Anthropology is broadly construed.

Benin

Allen, Christopher. The Peoples Republic of Benin : a bibliography, covering the period since 1972 with some background materials. Edinburgh : Centre of African Studies, Edinburgh Univ., [1985]. 31 p. (University of Edinburgh. Centre of African Studies. Occasional papers, no. 11).   **DD129**

Focuses "on political and economic change since the declaration of the former Dahomey Republic as a socialist state, and its renaming as the People's Republic of Benin, in 1975 ... relatively weak on material published in Benin, on fugitive literature generally, and on dissertation[s]."—*Introd.* Includes a brief list of dissertations in progress. 277 entries, with subject index.   Z3686.A46

Botswana

Henderson, Francine I. A guide to periodical articles about Botswana, 1965–80 / ed. and comp. by Francine Henderson and Tiny Modisakeng. Gaborone : Nat. Inst. of Development and Cultural Research, Documentation Unit, Univ. College of Botswana, 1982. 147 p. (Working bibliography, 9).   **DD130**

A broad subject listing of some 1,232 English-language entries compiled from bibliographies and indexes. Includes any area of study on Botswana. Author index.

§ *Botswana's environment* by Henderson and Johannes Opschoor (Gaborone, 1981. 83 p.) covers socioeconomic development and environmental impact since 1966.   Z3559.H46

Kerven, Carol. Bibliography on the society, culture, and political economy of post-independence Botswana / comp. by Carol Kerven & Pamela Simmons. Gaborone : Nat. Migration Study, Central Statistics Off., 1981. 131 p.   **DD131**

At head of title: National Migration Study.

1,936 citations arranged in ten broad subject categories. Includes some older materials and some materials on Lesotho and Swaziland. Limited to works found in Gaborone. Author-keyword and subject indexes.

§ See also *Women in development in Southern Africa* (DD122).   Z7165.B65K47

Mohome, Paulus. A bibliography on Bechuanaland / comp. by Paulus Mohome [and] John B. Webster. Syracuse, N.Y. : Bibliographic Section, Program of Eastern African Studies, Syracuse Univ., 1966. 58 p. (Program of Eastern African Studies. Occasional bibliography, no. 5).   **DD132**

Compiled as a Peace Corps project. Arranged by 17 subject categories, without annotations. Author and subject/keyword indexes.

———. ———. *Supplement,* comp. by John B. Webster, Paulus Mohome, [and] M. Catherine Todd (1968. 38 p.) [Program of East African Studies. Occasional bibliography, 12]).

§ For a history, *see:* F. Morton and J. Ramsay, *The birth of Botswana : a history of the Bechuanaland Protectorate from 1910 to 1966* (Gaborone : Longman Botswana, 1987. 206 p.).   Z7165.A42S9

Burkina Faso

Izard, Françoise. Bibliographie générale de la Haute-Volta, 1956–1965. Paris : CNRS-CVRS, 1967. 300 p. (Recherches voltaïques, 7).   **DD133**

A topical listing of more than 1,500 articles, books, seminar papers, and government documents. Some annotations. Well indexed.

Burundi

Pabanel, Jean-Pierre. Femmes et enfants au Burundi : guide bibliographique / Jean-Pierre Pabanel ; avec la collaboration de Étienne Bisengimana, Joséphine Kamanzi. [S.l.] : UNICEF ; Curdes, 1985. 67 *l*.   **DD134**

A partially annotated bibliography on women and children in Burundi. In 13 sections, citing books, articles, and reports published 1970–85, mostly at 13 institutions in Burundi itself.

Rodegem, F. M. Documentation bibliographique sur le Burundi. Bologna : EMI, 1978. 346 p.   **DD135**

Cites about 5,800 books, articles, government reports, films, sound recordings, and maps within broad topics, with author and subject indexes. Covers pre-1976 publications and provides a list of periodicals published in Burundi.

Updated by the author's unannotated, unindexed *Bibliographie du Burundi* (Bruxelles : Editions Rundi, 1986. 73 p.).

§ *See also* Julian W. Witherell, *French-speaking central Africa : guide to official publications in American libraries* (AF229); or for a scholarly overview, Emile Mworoha, *Histoire du Burundi: des origines à fin du XIXe siècle* (Paris : Hatier, c 1987. 272 p.); or Joseph R.A.M. Clément, *Essai de bibliographie du Ruanda-Urundi* (Usumbara : Service des A.I.M.O., 1959. 201 p.); or Théodore Heyse, *Bibliographie du Congo Belge et du Ruanda-Urundi* (DD244).

Cameroon

DeLancey, Mark W. A bibliography of Cameroon / by Mark W. DeLancey and Virginia H. DeLancey. N.Y. : Africana Publ. Co., [1975]. 673 p. (African bibliography ser., 4).   **DD136**

"From the onset of German colonization (1884) through the beginning of 1972"—*Introd.* Lists 6,061 titles by broad subjects. Includes books, articles, pamphlets, and some documents and recordings, and provides references to book reviews and appropriate entries in *African abstracts, Forestry abstracts,* and *Tropical abstracts.* Indexed by ethnic, linguistic, and geographic terms; author and personal names, and subject.

§ An equally comprehensive work that lists only German-language research is Max F. Dippold, *Une bibliographie du Cameroun: les écrits en langue allemande* (Burgau, Germany: Impr. Otto Boeck, 1971).   Z3761.D44

L'Encyclopédie de la République unie du Cameroun / préface de Ahmadou Ahidjo ; présentation de Guillaume Bwele. Abidjan : Nouvelles éditions africaines, c1981. 4 v. : ill. (some col.), maps, ports.   **DD137**

Contents: t. 1, Le milieu et les hommes; t. 2, L'histoire et l'état t. 3, L'economie; t. 4, La vie de la nation.

In French and English, these vividly illustrated volumes present information on all aspects of Camerounian geography, life, and culture. Articles vary in length, with some signed, and longer ones accompanied by bibliographies.   DT563.E5

Schilder, Kees. State formation, religion, and land tenure in Cameroon : [a bibliographical survey]. Leiden, Netherlands : African Studies Centre, Dept. of Political and Historical Studies, c1988. 257 p.   **DD138**

An annotated bibliography of approximately 800 social science titles, very broadly defined, chiefly of the 1970s and 1980s. Includes particularly important earlier studies "still often cited, and those studies which deal with themes about which no recently published material is available."—*Introd.* Short bibliographical essays throughout "present the relevant literature as a coherent body, i.e., the main themes, debates, and gaps are reviewed." Cites Mark W. DeLancey and Peter J. Schraeder's *Cameroon,* (see *World bibliographical series: Africa* v. 63, DD18] as 'the most useful introduction to the major books and articles on Cameroon."

§ Another fairly exhaustive social scientific bibliography is Patrick Gubry, *Bibliographie generale des études de population au Cameroun* (Yaounde : Ministère de l'enseignement supérieur et de la recherche scientífique, Institut des sciences humaines, Centre de recherches économiques et demographiques, 1984). Includes 2,472 entries, some annotated, and covers the literature "des origines jusqu'au 31 mars 1984."—*Introd.*   DT561.S35

Central African Republic

Banville, Christian de. Bibliographie centrafricaine. Bangui [Central African Republic] : C. de Banville, 1990. 71 *l*.   **DD139**

Cites approximately 1,500 books and articles by author. Provides subject terms in right margin, but no indexes.   Z3694.B36

Chad

Bibliographie du Tchad : (sciences humaines). 2. éd. rev., corr. et suivi d'un supplément / par Jacqueline Moreau et Danielle Stordeur. Fort-Lamy : Inst. Nat. Tchadien pour les Sciences Humaines, 1970. 353 p. (Études et documents tchadiens, sér. A, 5).   **DD140**

1st ed., 1968.

Lists almost 2,450 books, articles, films, and theses published to Dec. 31, 1969. Indexed.

Continued by Marie-Magdeleine Bériel's *Complément à la Bibliographie du Tchad* ... (N'Djaména : Inst. Nat. des Science Humaines, 1974. 103 p. [Études et documents tchadiens, sér A, 6]). Adds about 500 items publ. 1970–73.   Z3695.B5

A concise bibliography of Northern Chad and Fezzan in Southern Libya / Mohamed A. Alawar, gen. ed. Outwell, Cambridgeshire : Arab Crescent Pr. ; Boulder, Colo. : distr. by Westview Pr., [1983]. 229 p.   **DD141**

Aims to include "all major items that concern the border issue in the Chad-Libya dispute; documents concerned with Libyan-Chad relations in general; and materials relating to the geography, history, economics and political backgrounds..."—*Introd.* 2,991 entries, chiefly in English or French, arranged topically with author index.   Z3695.C66

Comoros

Newitt, M. D. D. The Comoro Islands : struggle against dependency in the Indian Ocean. Boulder, Colo. : Westview Pr. ; London : Gower, 1984. 144 p. : ill., maps.   **DD142**

An overview with a bibliographic essay. Indexed.

§ See also: *Iles du sud-ouest de l'océan Indien : catalogue de monographies,* ed. by Roucaya Safla (DD121).   DT469.C7N49

Congo (Brazzaville)

Carozzi, Carlo. Congo Brazzaville : bibliografia generale = Congo Brazzaville : bibliographie générale / Carlo Carozzi, Maurizio Tiepolo. Torino : Cortina, 1991. 289 p. : maps. (Collana di studi e ricerche / Dipartimento interateneo territorio del Politecnico e dell'Università di Torino, n. 4).   **DD143**

A bibliography of more than 3,400 citations in all formats, 1870 to the present, although most citations are from the period beginning 1960. Citations are in alphabetical order in a single sequence and there are no annotations. Includes a coded subject index, journal list, and a few maps. The authors did not see all the materials and take no responsibility for citation errors. Introduction in Italian and French.

Z3696.C37

Perrot, Claude Hélène. République du Congo-Brazzaville : répertoire bibliographique / établi par Cl. Perrot avec la collaboration de Hélène Sauvalle. [Paris : Bureau pour le développement de la production agricole, 1966?]. 112 *l.* **DD144**

867 citations in 5 sections: Ouvrages generaux, Milieu naturel, Science de l'homme, Economie. Author index. Z3696.P47

Côte d'Ivoire

Borremans, Raymond. Le grand dictionnaire encyclopédique de la Côte d'Ivoire. Abidjan : Nouvelles Editions africaines, [1986–c1988]. v. 1–4 : ill. (some col.), maps, ports. **DD145**

Contents: v. 1–4, A–M. Two more volumes planned.

Heavily illustrated. Gives terms in several national languages. Biographies and geographical articles, as well as good coverage of such topics as flora and fauna. Most entries are relatively brief; longer articles include bibliographies. DT545.15.B67

Janvier, Geneviève. Bibliographie de la Côte d'Ivoire. [Abidjan] : Université d'Abidjan, 1972–85. v. 1–5:1. (In progress?). **DD146**

Issued as supplements to *Annales de l'Université d'Abidjan.*

Contents: v. 1, Sciences de la vie; v. 2, Sciences de l'homme; v. 3, Sciences physiques et de la terre, by G. Janvier and G. Peron; v. 4, Sciences de la terre, Sciences de la vie, 1970–76, by G. Janvier and G. Peron; v. 5:1, Sciences de l'homme [exceptée l'economie] (1970–82), by T. Aye-Pimanova.

Classed arrangement of books, articles, theses and dissertations with author and subject indexes. Vol. 5:1 also includes a geographic index and index for names cited. Z3689.N34

Djibouti

Aubry, Marie-Christine. Djibouti : bibliographie fondamentale (domaine francophone). Paris : L'Harmattan, 1990. 169 p. : maps. **DD147**

Much expanded from *Bibliographie de la RDD* (Djibouti: Centre Culturel Arthur Rimbaud, 1980. 77 p.). An alphabetical listing of about 1,600 books, chapters, articles in periodicals and newspapers, proceedings, and a few government publications. Topically arranged in four sections: Vues d'ensemble; La nature; Les hommes; Visions litteraires. Some entries have annotations. Location in a library in Djibouti or France is given for each item. Index by names, and by sponsoring body for anonymous works. List of periodicals indexed is quite extensive and includes locations.

§ *See also*: Colin Darch, *A Soviet view of Africa : an annotated bibliography on Ethiopia, Somalia and Djibouti* (DD107). DT411.22A9

Egypt

See also Egyptian Antiquities in Section DA.

Ibrahim-Hilmy, *Prince.* The literature of Egypt and the Soudan, from the earliest times to the year 1885 [i.e., 1887] inclusive : a bibliography, comprising printed books, periodical writings and papers of learned societies; maps and charts; ancient papyri, manuscripts, drawings, etc. London : Trübner, 1886–1887. 2 v. **DD148**

Repr. : Nendeln, Liechtenstein : Kraus, 1966.

An author list of roughly 20,000 titles, with some subject and form headings. Materials listed are in European languages as well as Arabic. Appendix of additional works to May 1887 in v. 2, p. 371–459. Z3651.I14

Maunier, René. Bibliographie économique, juridique et sociale de l'Égypte moderne, (1798–1916). Cairo : Impr. de l'Inst. Français d'Archéologie Orientale, 1918. 372 p. (Société sultanich d'économie politique, de statistique et de législation. Travaux spéciaux, no.1). **DD149**

Repr.: N.Y. : Lenox Hill, 1971.

A classified bibliography of almost 6,700 titles of books and periodical articles primarily in French, but with some in other European languages, on the economic, legal, and social activities of early modern Egypt. Author and subject indexes. Includes a "Liste chronologique des revues publiées (en langues européennes) en Égypte de 1798 à 1916," p.xxiii–xxxi. Z3651.M45

Equatorial Guinea

Liniger-Goumaz, Max. Guinea ecuatorial : bibliografía general. Berne : Commission Nationale Suisse pour l'Unesco, 1974–91. v. 1–5, 7. (In progress). **DD150**

Vols. 5 and 7 publ. Geneva : Les Editions du Temps. Vol. 5 said to be "vol. recapitulativo … referencís 1–8125."—*Introd.* Vol. 7 contains referencís 11,302–13,120. Vol. 6 appears not yet to have been published.

A bibliography of books, articles, and government publications, 1705 onward, in an author listing with geographic and topical indexes. Each volume contains 1,000–2,000 entries. Cumulative index in v. 5 indexes entries in v. 1–5 by chronology, geography, subjects, ethnic groups, movements, organizations, parties, and personal names in titles. Z3937.L56

———— La Guinée équatoriale : un pays méconnu. Paris : L'Harmattan, c1979. 511 p. : maps. **DD151**

Encompasses biographical, geographical, historical, economic, and political information. Similar in overall structure and choice of entry to his *Historical dictionary* (*see* DD48) but somewhat fuller in content. Includes a chronology and a highly selective bibliography, p. 485–504. DT620.15.L56

Who's who de la dictature de Guinée équatoriale : les Nguemistes, 1979–1993 / Max Liniger-Goumaz. Geneva : Editions du temps, 1993. 351 p. **DD152**

Includes a section, in dictionary format, of current social and political information, and a biography of political personalities, 1979 on.

Eritrea

Bibliography on Eritrea / Research and Information Centre on Eritrea. Rome ; N.Y. : The Centre, 1982. 235 p. **DD153**

Cites some 3,376 publications on Eritrean society, past and present, under 20 main headings. Gives five Italian library locations. Index by main heading and subheadings. For more material on Eritrea, *see* general works on Ethiopia. Z3523.E74B52

Ethiopia

Abbink, J. Ethiopian society and history : a bibliography of Ethiopian studies, 1957–1990. Leiden, The Netherlands : African Studies Centre, 1990. 407 p. (Rijksuniversiteit te Leiden. Afrika-Studiecentrum. Research reports, 45.). **DD154**

An impressive bibliography of 5,433 items, nearly comprehensive except for its exclusion of works in Amharic and in southern and eastern European languages. "Society and history" is defined broadly; linguistics is excluded. Ethiopian names are generally indexed as name statements, hence entry is by first element; well-known names, however, are inverted.

§ For a general history, *see*: Bahru Zewde, *A history of modern Ethiopia, 1855–1974* (Athens, Ohio : Ohio Univ. Pr., 1991. 244 p.).   Z3521.A64

Brown, Clifton F. Ethiopian perspectives : a bibliographical guide to the history of Ethiopa. Westport, Conn. : Greenwood, 1978. 264 p. (African Bibliographic Center. Special bibliographic series, n.s., no.5).   **DD155**

The best bibliography up to the date of its publication on Ethiopia. "Ethiopian history" is interpreted in the broadest sense, so that ethnology, health, religion, etc., are included. Books and periodical articles in all languages are listed in 41 topical sections, alphabetically arranged. Some problems with spellings of Ethiopian names. Index of authors and anonymous titles.

Fumagalli, Giuseppe. Bibliografia etiopica ... . Milan : Hoepli, 1893. 288 p.   **DD156**

Repr.: Farnsborough : Gregg, 1971.

Subtitle: Catalogo descrittivo e ragionato degli scritti pubblicati dalla invenzione della stampa fino a tutto il 1891, intorno alla Etiopia e regioni limitrofe.

A classified, partially annotated bibliography, with author index, of writings on Ethiopia, published from the 15th century to 1891.

Continued by Silvio Zanutto, *Bibliografia etiopica in continuazione alla "Bibliografia etiopica" di G. Fumagalli* (Rome : Sindicato Italiano Arti Grafiche, 1932–36. 2 v.). *See also*: Alula Hidaru and Dessalegn Rahmato, *A short guide to the study of Ethiopia : a general bibliography* (Westport, Conn. : Greenwood, 1976. 176 p.).   Z3521.F97

Lockot, Hans Wilhelm. Bibliographia Aethiopica : die äthiopienkundliche Literatur des deutschsprachigen Raums. Wiesbaden : Steiner, 1982. 441 p. (Äthiopistische Forschungen, Bd. 9).   **DD157**

A bibliography of about 7,779 citations to German-language books, articles, book reviews, and serials; covers to about 1976, with a few listings as late as 1979. Covers all areas of study; topical listing with author/editor index and source list.   Z3521.L62

Paulos Milkias. Ethiopia : a comprehensive bibliography. Boston : G.K. Hall, c1989. 694 p. : ill.   **DD158**

With more than 19,000 published and unpublished citations gathered from 680 sources and from libraries around the world, this is the most comprehensive bibliography on Ethiopia, with sources in numerous languages including Russian and Greek (beginning with the 1st century CE). Thousands of titles in Amharic are transliterated, and works in other Ethiopian languages are listed. There are 21 topical sections, but a subject index is badly needed. The author index is of limited value. There are no sections for ethnology, anthropology, or sociology, and typographical and other errors are numerous. Best for entries before 1957.

§ *See also*: Colin Darch, *A Soviet view of Africa* (DD107); *Ethiopia & Amharica: a list of works in the New York Public Library*, comp. by George F. Black (N.Y. : New York Public Library, 1928. 87 p.); *Dictionary of African biography* (AH314), v. 1 of which has about 150 entries for Ethiopians; Harold G. Marcus, *The modern history of Ethiopia and the horn of Africa: a select and annotated bibliography* (Stanford, Calif. : Hoover Inst. Pr., [1972]).   Z3521.M55

Gabon

Darkowska-Nidzgorska, Olenka. Connaissance du Gabon : guide bibliographique. Libreville : Univ. Nationale el Hadj Omar Bongo, 1978. 151 p. (Projet documentaire, pubn. no.1).   **DD159**

A classed bibliography of 1,025 items relating to all aspects of Gabon—geography, demography, politics, education, history, etc. Index of names.   Z3697.D37

The Gambia

Gamble, David P. A general bibliography of the Gambia, up to 31 December 1977 / David P. Gamble, with Louise Sperling. Boston : G. K. Hall, [1979]. 266 p.   **DD160**

Classed arrangement with detailed table of contents and indexes of personal names, organizations, place names, etc. Nearly 4,500 items.

———. ———. *Supplement* 1 (1987), 2 (1987), and 3 (1990), publ. in San Francisco by the author (Gambian studies no. 18, 19, and 24), add respectively 935, 2,450, and 1,851 items and cover the years 1978–87. All topically arranged and have indexes of personal names, organizations, Gambian place-names, items in languages other than English, periodicals, conferences, seminars, theses and dissertations, etc.   Z3735.G33

Ghana

Bibliography

Afre, S. A. Ashanti region of Ghana : an annotated bibliography, from earliest times to 1973. Boston : G. K. Hall, [1975]. 494 p.   **DD161**

Attempts "to list all books, pamphlets and periodical articles; academic theses, dissertations, and project reports; maps and atlases; and unpublished seminar and conference papers relating or containing important references to Ashanti published or produced up to and including the year 1973"—*Introd.* Broad subject listing of 2,781 mostly annotated items with author and subject indexes.   Z3785.A64

Aguolu, Christian Chukwunedu. Ghana in the humanities and social sciences, 1900–1971 : a bibliography. Metuchen, N.J. : Scarecrow, 1973. 469 p.   **DD162**

An outstanding classed bibliography of 4,309 partially annotated items, including books, articles, conference papers, research reports, pamphlets, theses, and dissertations. A knowledgeable introductions surveys the bibliographic situation in Ghana, the best developed in sub-Saharan Africa apart from the Republic of South Africa. Author index.

§ Aguolu's work supplements A. W. Cardinall, *A bibliography of the Gold Coast* (DD98). *See also*: Albert Frederick Johnson, *A bibliography of Ghana, 1930–1961* (Accra : publ. for the Ghana Library Board by Longmans, 1964), which lists 2,608 publications and includes selected periodical articles.   Z3785.A65

Ardayfio-Schandorf, Elizabeth. Women in Ghana : an annotated bibliography / Elizabeth Ardayfio-Schandorf and Kate Kwafo-Akoto. Accra : Woeli Publ. Services, 1990. 427 p.   **DD163**

Published for United Nations Population Fund.

Cites 754 monographs, periodicals, conference papers, government publications, and theses, published early 20th century through 1988, in nine topical sections. Lengthy abstracts; author and subject indexes.   Z7964.G43A73

Kenya

Kenya : an official handbook. [Nairobi, Kenya : Ministry of Information and Broadcasting, 1989?]. pagination varies ; [48] p. of plates : ill. (some col.).   **DD164**

Issued to commemorate the 25th anniversary of the independence of Kenya. Offers 23 articles written by Kenyan academics with numerous statistical charts, maps, and photographs.   DT433.522.K4634

Norgaard, Ole. Kenya in the social sciences : an annotated bibliography 1967–1979. [Nairobi] : Kenya Literature Bureau, [1980]. 372 p.   **DD165**

Cites 5,981 books, articles, dissertations, and working papers on Kenyan population, language, religion, history, government and politics, economic development and planning, and education. Includes a literature review and articles on education and development, economy, and historiography. Topically arranged, partially annotated; author and keyword indexes.

Updates John B. Webster, *Bibliography on Kenya* (DD167).

See also Simon Bell, *Women in rural development in Kenya, Tanzania and Zimbabwe : a partially annotated bibliography* (Norwich, U.K. : School of Development Studies, Univ. of East Anglia, 1985. 40 p.).

Socio-economic profiles : Kwale District, Kitui District, Embu District, Baringo District, Kisumu District, South Nyanza District, Nairobi City, Mombasa Municipality, Kisumu Municipality / ed. by John E. Odada, James O. Otieno. Nairobi, Kenya : Government of Kenya, Ministry of Planning and National Development of Kenya and UNICEF, [1990]. 303 p. : ill.   **DD166**

Includes much information and many statistics concerning infrastructure, community organizations, household income, health and nutrition, water and sanitation, and education and literacy.

§ See also:

Robert A. Obudho, *Demography, urbanization, and spatial planning in Kenya : a bibliographical survey* (Westport, Conn. : Greenwood, 1985. 285 p.).

Carol Sicherman, *Ngugi wa Thiong'o, the making of a rebel : a sourcebook in Kenyan literature and resistance* (London ; N.Y. : H. Zell, 1990. 486 p.).

Who is who in Kenya (AH320).

For Kenyan history, William R. Ochieng', *A modern history of Kenya, 1895–1980 : in honor of B. A. Ogot* (Nairobi : Evans Brothers [Kenya] ltd., 1989. 260 p.) and *Themes in Kenyan history*, ed. by William R. Ochieng' (Nairobi : Heinemann Kenya ; Athens, Ohio : Ohio Univ. Pr., 1991. 261 p.).   HC865.S65

Webster, John B. A bibliography on Kenya / comp. by John B. Webster, with Shirin G. F. Kassam, Robert S. Peckham [and] Barbara A. Skapa. [Syracuse, N.Y.] : Program of Eastern African Studies, Syracuse Univ., [1967]. 461 p. (Syracuse University Eastern African bibliographical series, no. 2, Kenya).   **DD167**

7,210 citations in 28 topical chapters with author and subject/key words indexes. Most chapters have sections on East Africa as well as Kenya. The chapter on language and linguistics is further subdivided by topics such as flora and fauna, health, pedagogy, etc.

§ *See also*: John Bruce Howell, *Kenya : subject guide to official publications* (AF232).   Z3583.K4W4

Women & development : a Kenya guide. Nairobi : Mazingira Institute, 1992. 136 p. : ill.   **DD168**

Information concerning 188 organizations working on women in development and on gender issues. Coverage ranges from local women's cooperatives to international agencies with brief descriptions of their work, how to contact them, programs for women. Special sections on libraries and resource centers and on women's groups movements in Kenya, its history and growth. Index organized by categories.

§ See also *Women in rural development in Kenya, Tanzania and Zimbabwe : a partially annotated bibliography* (Norwich, U.K. : School of Development Studies, Univ. of East Anglia, 1985).   HQ1240.5.K4W64

Lesotho

Gordon, Loraine. Lesotho : a bibliography. Johannesburg : Univ. of the Witwatersrand, Dept. of Bibliography, Librarianship and Typography, 1970. 47 p.   **DD169**

587 citations in 14 broad topical sections, excluding language and literature. Includes books, chapters, articles, and government publications, 1947–66. Author and subject indexes.

§ For earlier works, *see*: Julie te Groen, *Basutoland : a bibliography* (Cape Town : School of Librarianship, Univ. of Cape Town, 1946. 30 *l.*); D. L. Shaskolsky, *Basutoland bibliography* (Cape Town : School of Librarianship, Univ. of Cape Town, 1960. 20 *l.*); Paulus Mohome and John B. Webster, *A bibliography on Lesotho* (Syracuse, N.Y. : Program of Eastern African Studies, Syracuse Univ., 1968. 59 p.). The latter offers 531 citations.   Z3558.G65

Lesothana : an annotated bibliography of new and newly located Lesotho materials. no. 1 (Aug. 1982)–9 (May 1987). Roma, Lesotho : Documentation Centre, Inst. of Southern African Studies, Nat. Univ. of Lesotho, 1982–87. Irregular.   **DD170**

Intended as an ongoing supplement to Shelagh M. Willet and David P. Ambrose, *Lesotho* (Roma, Lesotho : Documentation Centre, Inst. of Southern African Studies, National Univ. of Lesotho, 1982–). Includes book and periodical references, most to works published outside Lesotho. Early issues were devoted mainly to control of a backlog of older materials; format and indexing have changed over time.

§ *See also*: Quentin Neil Parsons, *The High Commission territories, 1909–1964 : a bibliography* (DD117).

Women in development in Southern Africa : Botswana, Lesotho, Malawi, and Zambia : an annotated bibliography / comp. by L. Ramore ... [et al.]. Wageningen, Netherlands : Technical Centre for Agricultural and Rural Cooperation, 1991. 4 v. : ill.   **DD171**

Vol. 2, Lesotho. For full annotation, *see* DD122.

Z7963.E18W66

Liberia

Gray, Beverly Ann. Liberia during the Tolbert era : a guide / Beverly Ann Gray, Angel Batiste. Wash. : Library of Congress, 1983. 79 p.   **DD172**

A selection of 451 annotated entries for Liberian government documents, and for books, pamphlets, periodical articles, and dissertations about the country during the presidency of W. R. Tolbert, 1971–80. Classed arrangement with author/subject index.   Z3821.G7

Holsoe, Svend E. A bibliography on Liberia / by Svend E. Holsoe. Newark : Published at the Dept. of Anthropology, Univ. of Delaware, by Liberian Studies Association in America, 1971–76. 3 v.   **DD173**

In three parts: Pt. 1, Books (1971. 117 p. 1,078 items); index of subjects, co-authors, and authors of introductions. Pt. 2, Publications concerning colonization (1971. 63 p. 444 books and articles); includes works from the American Colonization Society. Author index. Pt. 3, Articles (1976. 169 p. 2,250 items); index of co-authors and persons mentioned in titles.

§ A more recent bibliography, Robert Kappel and Werner Korte's *A bibliography of books and articles on Liberia as edited in German speaking countries since 1960* (Bremen : Liberia Working Group, 1989) lists about 400 books, statistical sources, manuscripts, pamphlets, dissertations, and articles. Arranged by subject, with author and subject index. The compilers plan an expanded edition, and credit Holsoe's bibliography as "the main and outstanding bibliographical source on Liberia."—*Foreword.*   Z3821.H6

Libya

Witherell, Julian W. Libya, 1969–1989, an American perspective : a guide to U.S. official documents and government-sponsored publications. Wash. : Library of Congress : For sale by the U.S. Govt. Print. Off., 1990. 180 p. : map. (Near East series, no. 4).   **DD174**

Superintendent of Documents classification: LC 41.9: L61.

Topical arrangement of a "selection of publications on Libya issued by or for agencies of the U.S. government [since 1969, including] reports on its agriculture, commerce, economic situation, labor force, petroleum industry, and politics and government."—*Pref.* Most of the 669 documents are housed in the Library of Congress, with some in the Dept. of State, Pentagon, Air University, and Air Force libraries. Omits classified materials, Congressional bills and resolutions, and materials prepared exclusively for Congress. Author/title/subject index.   DT215.W57

Madagascar

Grandidier, Guillaume. Bibliographie de Madagascar. Paris : Comité de Madagascar, 1905/06–1957. 3 v.   **DD175**

Contents: [v.1], 1500–1904 (publ. 1905–1906. 905 p.); [v. 2], 1904–1933 (Paris : Soc. d'Édit. Géographiques, Maritimes et Coloniales, 1935. p.759–1350); v. 3, 1934–1955 (Tananarive : Inst. de Recherche Scientifique de Madagascar, 1957. p. 1351–1910). Volumes are paged continuously, disregarding the supplement in v. 1.

A comprehensive bibliography of 23,003 citations including manuscripts, books, pamphlets, and periodical articles on Madagascar published 1500–1955. Includes author indexes by subject classification.

§ *See also*:

Madagascar and adjacent islands: a guide to official publications, by Julian W. Witherell for the Library of Congress, African Section (AF222).

Iles du sud-ouest de l'ocean Indien : catalogue des monographes, ed. by Roucaya Safla (DD121).

(3) *Madagascar : society and history*, ed. by Conrad Phillip Kottak ... [et al.] (Durham, N. C. : Carolina Academic Pr., 1986. 443 p.), an overview with extensive bibliography.

(4) For materials publ. 1964–69: *Bibliographie annuelle de Madagascar* (AA863).   Z3701.G85

Malawi

Brown, Edward E. A bibliography of Malawi / comp. by Edward E. Brown, Carol A. Fisher, John B. Webster. [Syracuse, N.Y.] : Program of Eastern African Studies, Syracuse Univ., [c1965]. 161 p. (Syracuse University Eastern Africa, bibliographical series, no. 1, Malawi).   **DD176**

Covers all subjects in 22 sections, but excludes government publications. Author and unsigned title indexes.

———. ———. *Supplement.* (1969. 62 p.).

§ *See also*: R. M. S. Ng'ombe, *A selected bibliography of the Federation of Rhodesia and Nyasaland* (DD119); Francis Michael Glenn Willson and Gloria C. Passmore, *Catalogue of the parlimentary papers of Southern Rhodesia, 1899–1953* (AF242); Norman W. Wilding, *Catalogue of the parliamentary papers of Southern Rhodesia and Rhodesia, 1954–1970, and the Federation of Rhodesia and Nyasaland, 1954–1963* (AF241); Audrey A. Walker, *The Rhodesias and Nyasaland : guide to official publications* (AF226); Augustine W.C. Msiska, *Malawi : an annotated bibliography of bibliographies* (Zomba : Chancellor College, 1989).   Z3573.M3B7

Malawi National Library Service. Books about Malawi : a select reading list. Blantyre : the Service, 1969. 23 p.   **DD177**

250 citations in 14 broad subject categories.

Mauritania

Robert, Dieter. Recueils bibliographiques concernant la Mauritanie. 2nd ed. Nouakchott : D. Robert, [1985]. 252 p. (various pagings).   **DD178**

1st ed., 1984–85.

Contents: Liste sommaire d'ouvrages concernant la Mauritanie (5 p.); Recueil bibliographique d'intérêt général concernant la Mauritanie (60 p.); Recueil d'études sectorielles...(126 p.); Recueil d'études traitant des régions administratives et géographiques...(58 p.).

An extensive listing of books, chapters, articles, and research reports. Topical arrangement within each section; not indexed.

Z7165.M37R63

Mauritius

Mauritius. Archives Dept. Bibliography of Mauritius, (1502–1954) : covering the printed record, manuscripts, archivalia and cartographic material / by A. Toussaint and H. Adolphe. Port Louis : Esclapon, 1956. 884 p.   **DD179**

A comprehensive bibliography of 8,865 entries, covering printed materials (including periodical and newspaper articles and government publications), manuscripts, and caartographic materials. Mauritius' dependencies, Rodrigues Island, and the Oil Islands are covered, and there are many references to Madagascar, Réunion, and the Seychelles. In six sections by format, each with a descriptive introduction. Some parts contain brief annotations. General index.

§ *See also*: Larry W. Bowman, *Mauritius : democracy and development in the Indian Ocean* (Boulder, Colo. : Westview Pr., 1991. 208 p.), an overview; S. Deerpalsingh, *A bibliography of Mauritian government publications, 1955–1978* (AF234); and Université de la Réunion. Service commun de la documentation, *Iles du sud-ouest de l'océan Indien : catalogue des monographies* (DD121).

Z3703.M3A5

Morocco

Cenival, Pierre de. Bibliographie marocaine, 1923–1933. Paris : Librairie Larose, 1937. 606 p.   **DD180**

Repr. from the quarterly journal *Hespéris*. Continued at intervals in *Hespéris* and its successor *Hespéris tamuda*.

At head of title: Pierre de Cenival, Christian Funck-Brentano et Marcel Bousser.

A comprehensive, unannotated bibliography of books and periodical articles on all aspects of life in Morocco. Arranged by year of publication, then by subject. Most materials are in French. Brief subject index.   Z3836.C38

La grande encyclopédie du Maroc. Rabat : GEM ; Bergamo, Italy : Gruppo Walk Over, c1986–89. 12 v. : ill.   **DD181**

Ed. by Mustapha Sehimi, with the participation of Me. Ahmed Rída Guedira, councillor to S. M. Hassan II.

Contents: v. 1, Institutions; v. 2, Economie et finances; v. 3, Géographie physique et géologie; v. 4, Flore et végétation; v. 5, Culture, arts et traditions (v. 1); v. 6, Culture, arts et traditions (v. 2); v. 7, Agriculture et pêche; v. 8, Histoire; v. 9, Géographie humaine; v. 10, Faune; v. 11, Sports et loisirs. Education; v. 12, Index.

Short articles, heavily illustrated, covering all aspects of Moroccan life. The last volume is an index to the set. An appendix to v. 1 gives the 1972 amended Constitution.   DT304.G66

Mozambique

Bibliografia anotada multidisciplinar sobre população desenvolvimento em Moçambique / República de Moçambique, Comissão Nacional do Plan, o Direcção Nacional de Estatística, Unidade de População e Planificação. Maputo : A Unidade, [1991]. 135 p. (Série População e desenvolvimento, doc. no. 4). **DD182**

A bibliography of 792 entries in various formats, arranged in reverse chronological order in subject sections. Not all entries are annotated. No indexes. Z7165.M85B53

Chonchol, Maria Edy. Guide bibliographique du Mozambique : environnement naturel, développement et organisation villageoise. Paris : L'Harmattan, 1979. 135 p. : maps. **DD183**

Four sections with introductory essays. Emphasis is on development and natural resources, but includes material on colonization and village life. Extensive annotations.

§ *See also: Catálogo dos livros sobre Moçambique existentes no CDI do Banco em Lourenço Marques* from the Banco Nacional Ultramarino, Lourenço Marques, Centro de Documentação e Informação (1972), which provides 1,353 citations in one sequence, almost all in Portuguese, with no index. Z3881.C45

Costa, Mario Augusto da. Bibliografia geral de Moçambique : (contribuição para um estudo completo). Lisbon : Divisão de publicações e biblioteca, Agência geral das colónias, 1946. 2 v. **DD184**

At head of title: Republica portuguesa. Ministério das colónias.

Also available in microfiche from IDC.

Vol. 1 has 35 topical sections with author and subject indexes. The second volume noted in the preface is not readily located.

§ *See also:*

Allen F. Isaacman and Barbara Isaacman, *Mozambique : from colonialism to revolution, 1900–1982* (Boulder, Colo. : Westview Pr., 1983. 235 p.), the best general history.

Mary Jane Gibson, *Portuguese Africa : a guide to official publications* (AF220).

Susan Jean Gowan, *Portuguese-speaking Africa 1900–1979 : a select bibliography* (DD114).

A. Rita-Ferreira, *Bibliografia etnologica de Moçambique (das origens a 1954)* (Lisboa : Junta de Investigações do Ultramar, 1961. 254 p.). 968 annotated citations. Z3881.C6

Namibia

Eriksen, Tore Linné. The political economy of Namibia : an annotated critical bibliography / by Tore Linné Eriksen, with Richard Moorsom. 2nd ed. Uppsala, Sweden : The Scandinavian Inst. of African Studies, c1989. 370 p. : map. **DD185**

1st ed., 1985.

Publ. in cooperation with the U.N. Inst. for Namibia and the Norwegian Inst. of International Affairs.

The best bibliography on Namibia, including 2,169 entries with special attention to the South West African Peoples Organization (SWAPO). In 20 sections by topic or format; most sections include valuable critical annotations. Theses, conference papers, and new titles 1985–89 are not annotated. Author index but no subject index.

§ *See also:* Elna Schoeman, *The Namibian issue 1920–1980 : a selected and annotated bibliography* (Boston : G.K. Hall, 1982), which does not cover the liberation movement; and *Transnational corporations in South Africa and Namibia : a selective bibliography* (N.Y. : United Nations, 1989). For a history of SWAPO, see: *To be born a nation : the liberation struggle for Namibia*, Dept. of Information and Publicity, SWAPO of Namibia (London : Zed Pr., 1981. 357 p.).

Evborokhai, A. O. A descriptive list of United Nations reference documents on Namibia (1946–1978). Lusaka, Zambia : United Nations Institute for Namibia, [1979]. 161 *l.* **DD186**

The U.N. revoked South Africa's mandate over Namibia in 1966, and the International Court of Justice declared South Africa's presence illegal in 1971. Listed here are 721 publications (some annotated) relating to these events from the General Assembly, Security Council, Economic and Social Council, and International Court of Justice. Arranged by organ and document number, hence almost chronological, but without an index.

———. *Supplement one*, comp. by D. H. Shivangulula (Lusaka : U.N. Inst. for Namibia, [1981]. 46 p.), includes documents for the same time period that were not available to Evborokhai. Z3771.E9

Moorsom, Richard. Namibia in transition : a select list of titles on economic, political and development themes. Bergen, Norway : Chr. Michelsen Institute DERAP, (Development Research and Action Programme), [1989]. 59 p. **DD187**

A product of the Namibia Socio-economic Database Project, a cooperative initiative of the Michelsen Inst. and the U.N. Inst. for Namibia. An alphabetical list, with locations, of 770 titles mostly from the 1980s. A sequel to the author's earlier *Namibia : a provisional list of titles in the libraries of the Chr. Michelsen Institute and the Scandinavian Institute of African Studies* (Bergen : CMI, 1985). The newer work does not contain titles from the Scandinavian Institute. Z7165.N27M66

Namibia : the facts / [prep. by IDAF Research, Information, and Publications Department]. [New ed.]. London : IDAF Publications ; Cambridge, Ma : IDAFSA-US, 1989. pagination varies : ill. **DD188**

1st ed., 1980.

A good basic overview of the history of Namibia as a South African colony by a respected human rights organization. Bibliography and index. DT1645.N36

Pütz, Joe. Namibia handbook and political who's who : post-election edition 1990 / Pütz, Von Egidy & Caplan. 2nd ed. Windhoek, Namibia : Magus, 1990. 448 p. : ill., maps. (Namibia series, v. 2). **DD189**

1st ed., 1989.

"Incorporates the *Political who's who of Namibia*, first published in 1987."—t.p. verso.

An excellent sourcebook for Namibia on the eve of independence. Includes important U.N. documents and chronologies, as well as entries for numerous political parties, government agencies, pressure groups, nongovermental organizations, churches, etc. Short biographies of leaders appear in chapters on their political parties. Written by journalists. JQ3549.A795P87

Scheven, Yvette. Namibia bibliographies. Urbana-Champaign, Ill. : [Y. Scheven], [1985]. 16, [9] p. **DD190**

Prepared for the Seminar on Namibian Bibliography and Documentation, United Nations Institute for Namibia, Lusaka, Zambia.

Cumulates the Namibia entries in Scheven's *Bibliographies for African studies* (DD88) together with any other recent bibliographies the compiler could trace, into an annotated bibliography of books, articles, and bibliographic essays. Arranged chronologically within each topic. Includes information on databases. 86 annotated entries, with author and chronological indexes. Z3771.S33

Nigeria

Coles, Catherine M. Nigerian women in development : a research bibliography / by Catherine M. Coles and Barbara Entwisle, with the assistance of Margaret Hardner. Los Angeles : Crossroads Pr., c1986. 170 p. **DD191**

For annotation, *see* CC598. Z7964.N6C65

DeLancey, Mark W. Nigeria : a bibliography of politics, government, administration, and international relations / Mark DeLancey, Elizabeth L. Normandy. [Los Angeles] : Crossroads Pr., [1983]. 188 p.   **DD192**

Covers the period from Nigerian independence in 1960 to the end of 1980. Lists 2,207 books, articles, dissertations, and some government publications. Provides annotations for about half the entries, with frequent references to book reviews. "References to traditional Nigerian political systems are excluded."—*Introd.* Personal name and subject indexes.   Z3597.D45

Eitner, Kurt. Nigeria : Auswahlbibliographie : a selected bibliography. Hamburg : Institut für Afrika-Kunde im Verbund der Stiftung Deutsches Übersee-Institut, Dokumentations-Leitstelle Afrika, 1983. 2 v. : ill. (Dokumentationsdienst Afrika. Reihe A, 20).   **DD193**

Contents: v. 1, Country studies, politics, law; v. 2, Economics, society.

Lists 1,883 books, pamphlets, serials, and articles in topical arrangement. Prefatory matter, explanatory notes, topical headings, and index of subject headings in German and English; concise annotations in German. Publications are in German, English, and French, and date from 1975–82. Chiefly a social scientific, policy orientation; other subjects include culture, public health, education, language and law. Maps of federal states, agriculture, mineral resources, industries, and traffic. Indexes of subject headings and corporate authors in each volume cover both volumes.   Z3597.E34

Le Nigeria contemporain / sous la direction de Daniel C. Bach. Paris : Editions du Centre national de la recherche scientifique, 1986. 336 p., [20] p. of plates : ill. maps.   **DD194**

Offers surveys written by specialists on all aspects of Nigeria (e.g., history, culture, urbanization). Pt. 2 is a union list of Nigerian periodicals in collections in Belgium, France, and Switzerland. Pt. 3 is a topical bibliography of 1,538 books, articles, and theses in French. Author index to the bibliography.   DT515.22.N533

University of Ibadan. Library. Africana catalogue of the Ibadan University Library, Ibadan, Nigeria. Boston : G.K. Hall, 1973. 2 v. (1605 p.).   **DD195**

Reproduction of more than 5,000 cards representing "Africana acquisitions from 1948 to April, 1972," (*Pref*) chiefly focusing on West Africa, and particularly Nigeria.

§ For another important category of Nigeriana, see: *A catalogue of the Arabic manuscripts preserved in the University Library, Ibadan, Nigeria,* by W. E. N. Kensdale (Ibadan : Ibadan Univ. Library, c1955–58).   Z3509.I228

Who's who in Nigeria / ed., Nyaknno Osso. Lagos, Nigeria : Newswatch, 1990. 803 p.   **DD196**

For annotation, *see* AH323.   CT2522.W45

Rwanda

Hategekimana, Grégoire. Bibliographie annotée sur la population du Rwanda / prép. par Grégoire Hategekimana, Alphonse Ngoga. Addis Abéba, Ethiopie : Unité de coordination, Réseau d'information en matiere de population pour l'Afrique (POPIN-AFRICA), Division de la population, CEA, 1991. 272 p. (Population in Africa, no. 5).   **DD197**

For annotation, *see* CG352.   Z7164.D3H38

Hertefelt, Marcel d'. Société, culture et histoire du Rwanda : encyclopédie bibliographique 1863–1980/87 / Marcel d'Hertefelt, Danielle de Lame. Tervuren, Belgique : Musée royal de l'Afrique centrale, 1987. 2 v. (1849 p.).   **DD198**

Cites 5,550 books, essays, and articles published 1863–1987 concerning Rwandan social and cultural anthropology, archaeology, history, sociology, demography, politics, economics, education, linguistics,

oral tradition, literature, musicology, and religion. Annotations are excellent. Reviews and library holdings are noted. Subject index. A magnificent work.

Supplemented by: *Documentation sur le Rwanda : catalogue du centre de documentation du Ministère du Plan* (Kigali : The Centre, 1988. 140 *l.*) and Albert Lévesque, *Contribution to the national bibliography of Rwanda, 1965–1970* (AA871).

§ *See also* Joseph R.A.M. Clement, *Essai de bibliographie du Ruanda-Urundi* (Usumbura : Service des A.I.M.O., 1959) and Théodore Heyse, *Bibliographie du Congo Belge et du Ruanda-Urundi* (DD244).   Z3721.H47

Mugwaneza, Annie. Recueil des études et ouvrages ayant trait à la femme rwandaise / Grégoire Hategekimana, Annie Mugwaneza. Kigali : Fonds des Nations Unies pour l'enfance : Réseau des femmes oeuvrant pour le développement rural, 1992. 291 p.   **DD199**

An impressive annotated bibliography on Rwandan women's issues including 809 references in five subject sections. Entries include headings used in the subject index. The table of contents is at the end, following the subject and author indexes.

Senegal

Les elites sénégalaises. Paris : Ediafric, La Documentation africaine, 1984. 169 p.   **DD200**

Brief biographies for approximately 1,000 persons, chiefly governmental officials. Includes a directory of prominent officials as of April 3, 1983.   JQ3396.A69E94

Hue, Pascal. Senegal : bibliographie / réalisée à partir de la Banque de données IBISCUS triée par grands domaines par Pascal Hue. Paris : Ministère de la coopération et du développement, 1991. 295 p.   **DD201**

This excellent bibliography reflects contents of the IBISCUS data base, and provides access to 1,257 references of the 1970s and 1980s. Classed by broad themes, the chief subjects are health, education, the environment, business, economics, demography, agriculture, and energy. Annotations in French, with author, subject, and geographical indexes. Also includes a section on audiovisual materials and a section of summary information on the country, plus a fine map.

Porgès, Laurence. Bibliographie des régions du Sénégal. Dakar, 1977. 705 p.   **DD202**

At head of title: République du Sénégal. Ministère du Plan et du Développement.

A general bibliography of works on the region from early times through 1965, with emphasis on publications since 1945. Arranged by geographical area, with author and subject indexes.

————. ————. *Compliment pour la période des origines á 1965 et mise á jour 1966–1973* (Paris, Mouton, 1977. 637 p.). Updates the bibliography through 1973, bringing the number of entries covered by both volumes to 7,274.

Seychelles

Franda, Marcus F. The Seychelles : unquiet islands. Boulder, Colo. : Westview Pr., 1982. 140 p. : ill.   **DD203**

An overview with bibliographic references.

§ *See also* Université de la Réunion. Service commun de la documentation, *Catalogue du fonds "Iles de l'océan Indien,"* rédigé par Roucaya Safla (3e éd. [Saint-Denis] : le Service, 1989).   DT469.S422F7

Sierra Leone

Freetown, Sierra Leone. Fourah Bay College. Library. Catalog of the Sierra Leone collection, Fourah Bay College Library, University of Sierra Leone. Boston : G. K. Hall, c1979. 411 p.   **DD204**
This collection, recorded on approximately 6,000 cards, "is comprised of published and unpublished works written about Sierra Leone and by Sierra Leoneans. It also includes materials from other West African countries whenever a work or journal devotes a chapter or article to Sierra Leone."—*Introd.* "For almost nine decades, Fourah Bay College alone served the needs of the country and indeed of all West Africa for university education."—*Pref.*   Z3598.F73

Williams, Geoffrey J. A bibliography of Sierra Leone, 1925–1967. N.Y. : Africana Publ. Corp., [1971]. 209 p.   **DD205**
A classified listing of 3,047 books, articles, and government publications, accompanied by author and geographical indexes. Intended to supplement a much earlier bibliography of 1,103 items by Harry Luke, *Bibliography of Sierra Leone*, (2nd enl. ed. London : Oxford Univ. Pr., 1925).
§ *See also* Hans M. Zell, *Bibliography of non-periodical literature on Sierra Leone, 1925–1966* (Freetown : Fourah Bay College Bookshop, Univ. of Sierra Leone, 1966. 44 p).   Z3553.S5W55

Somalia

Carboni, Fabio. Bibliografia somala : primo contributo. [Rome] : Ministero degli affari esteri, Dipartimento per la cooperazione allo sviluppo : Comitato tecnico linguistico per l'Università somala, [1983]. 309 p. (Studi somali, 4).   **DD206**
A bibliography of 7,552 citations (mostly Italian) publ. up to 1973 with an addendum of 14 new titles. Arranged by Dewey Decimal numbers; author and geographic indexes.   Z3526.C37

Salud, Mohamed Khalief. Somalia : a bibliographical survey. Westport, Conn. : Greenwood, 1977. 468 p. (African Bibliographic Center. Special bibliographic series, n.s., no. 4).   **DD207**
A bibliography of nearly 4,000 books, journal and newspaper articles, grey literature, and maps. Covers all disciplines; treats Somalia and Somalis without regard to current borders. No index.
§ *See also*: Helen F. Conover, *Official publications of Somaliland, 1941–1959 : a guide* (AF237); and Colin Darch, *A Soviet view of Africa : an annotated bibliography on Ethiopia, Somalia and Djibouti* (DD107). For history, *see*: David D. Laitin and Said S. Samatar, *Somalia : nation in search of a state* (Boulder, Colo. : Westview Pr., 1987. 198 p.); and I. M. Lewis, *A modern history of Somalia : nation and state in the horn of Africa* (rev., updated, exp. ed. Boulder, Colo. : Westview Pr., 1988. 297 p.).

South Africa

Davies, Robert H. The struggle for South Africa : a reference guide to movements, organizations, and institutions / Robert Davies, Dan O'Meara, Sipho Dlamini. New ed., rev. and updated. London ; Atlantic Highlands, N.J. : Zed Books, 1988. 2 v. : ill.   **DD208**
1st ed., 1984.
The best directory of the government, corporations, liberation movements, and other organizations that have been contesting for power in South Africa. The ten chapters begin with introductory essays, continue with individual entries, and conclude with bibliographies. Classified arrangement. Good index, with cross-references.   JQ1931.D38

Race relations survey / South African Institute of Race Relations. Vol. 38 (1984)– . Johannesburg : The Institute, 1985– . Annual.   **DD209**
Continues: *Survey of race relations in South Africa* (1951/52–1983).
The most respected annual analysis of South African events, covering a wide variety of events, including business, education, employment, health, labor, politics, etc., with an appendix of legislation. Excellent subject and name index.   DT763.S79

Riley, Eileen. Major political events in South Africa, 1948–1990. Oxford ; N. Y. : Facts on File, c1991. 250 p. : maps.   **DD210**
A chronology of South African history from 1948 through the freeing of Nelson Mandela in February 1990. Introductory historical essay, biographical sketches, bibliography, and maps. Index.   DT1945.R54

South African review / ed. and comp. by SARS (South African Research Service). 1 (1983)– . Johannesburg : Ravan Pr., 1983– . Annual.   **DD211**
Analyzes current conditions in South Africa in scholarly essays by anti-apartheid writers.
§ For history, *see*:
Leonard Monteath Thompson, *A history of South Africa* (New Haven, Conn. : Yale Univ. Pr., c1990. 288 p.), a scholarly but accessible treatment by a distinguished scholar.
Monica Wilson and Leonard Thompson, *The Oxford history of South Africa* (N.Y. : Oxford Univ. Pr., 1969–71. 2 v.), a more complete history.
Edward Roux, *Time longer than rope : a history of the black man's struggle for freedom in South Africa* (2nd ed. Madison : Univ. of Wisconsin Pr., 1964. 469 p.), the first history of South Africa from the viewpoint of the oppressed majority. Covers the full history of the country, but emphasizes the 1920s–1930s when Roux was an active participant, and gives special attention to the labor movement and the Communist Party.
Bernard Magubane, *The political economy of race and class in South Africa* (N.Y. : Monthly Review Pr., c1979. 364 p.), an important contribution by a member of the ANC. A sociohistorical account of the evolution of racial oppression in South Africa.   HC905.A1S67

Who's who in South African politics / ed. by Shelagh Gastrow. 4th rev. ed. London ; N.Y. : Zell, 1993. 333 p. : ports.   **DD212**
Also publ. as *Bowker-Saur who's who in South African politics.* 1st ed., 1985; 3rd ed., 1990.
Offers alphabetically-arranged biographies of 122 key figures in contemporary South African politics. Each profile contains a photograph, basic biographical information, the biographee's political history and views, and a list of sources. Includes lists of office holders and members of various political parties, the Parliament, and relevant organizations. Earlier editions are useful for historic purposes, since many names are dropped with each revision. No index.   DT1774.G37

Bibliography

Bibliographies on South African political history / ed. by O. Geyser, P. W. Coetzer, J. H. Le Roux. Boston : G. K. Hall, 1979–82. 3 v.   **DD213**
Comp. for the Institute for Contemporary History, University of the Orange Free State.
Contents: v. 1, Register of private document collections on the political history of South Africa since 1902, ed. by O. Geyser, P. W. Coetzer, J. H. Le Roux; v. 2, General sources on South African political history since 1902, comp. by P. W. Coetzer, J. H. Le Roux; v. 3, Index to periodical articles on South African political and social history since 1902.
Not a bibliography of bibliographies as the title suggests, but a register of collections of primary sources and a classed bibliography of

secondary materials. Vol. 1, the register, lists and describes the larger and more important collections (although some important collections not fully inventoried and arranged are excluded), and lists smaller collections in the "annexure." Vol. 2 is a bibliography of monographic secondary sources classed in 20 subject areas; political history is broadly interpreted to include social welfare, justice, culture, and sport. Vol. 3 follows the classification scheme of the previous volume.

Z3608.A5B5

Kagan, Alfred. The African National Congress of South Africa : a bibliography. [N.Y.] : U.N. Centre Against Apartheid, Dept. of Political and Security Council Affairs, 1982. 40 p. **DD214**

A special issue of: *Notes and documents of the United Nations Centre Against Apartheid* (May 1982).

Includes 484 partially annotated entries, organized in seven sections by provenance or format, concentrating on ANC publications and authors, with various other materials published mostly 1960–80. Includes audiovisual materials. Reprinted with an introduction in *A current bibliography of African affairs* 15, no. 1 (1982/83): 2–35.

§ *See also* short bibliographies in *Southern African update* 4, no. 1 (1989): 1–19; 4, no. 2 (1989): 63; 8, no. 1 (1993): 100–104.

Z3608.N35K33

Kalley, Jacqueline Audrey. Pressure on Pretoria : sanctions, boycotts, and the divestment/disinvestment issue, 1964–1988 : a select and annotated bibliography. Braamfontein, South Africa : South African Institute of International Affairs, c1988. 299 p. (Bibliographical series ; no. 17). **DD215**

1,161 citations treating the worldwide economic boycott of South Africa. Excellent annotations and author and subject indexes.

§ *See also*: Elna Schoeman, *South African sanctions directory, 1946–1988 : actions by governments, banks, churches, trade unions, universities, international and regional organizations* (Johannesburg : South African Inst. of International Affairs, 1988. 235 p.), a chronological listing of 621 entries; and United Nations Centre on Transnational Corporations, *Transnational corporations in South Africa and Namibia : a selective bibliography* (N.Y. : United Nations, 1989).

Z6464.S2K35

———— South Africa under apartheid : a select and annotated bibliography. Westport, Conn. : Meckler, c1989. 544 p. **DD216**

Publ. in South Africa: Pietermaritzburg : Shuter & Shooter in association with Institute of Social and Economic Research, Rhodes University, 1987 (Occasional paper 31).

Praised by reviewers, this bibliography lists 1,123 articles, books, government publications, and book reviews. Annotations are deliberately nonevaluative. Author and subject indexes are thorough and have numerous cross-references.

Kalley followed with *South Africa's road to change 1987–1990 : a select and annotated bibliography* (N.Y. : Greenwood, 1991. 432 p.), which offers 1,517 entries.

§ *See also* Newell M. Stultz, *South Africa : an annotated bibliography with analytical introductions* (Ann Arbor, Mich. : Pierian Pr., 1989. 191 p.), which has good annotations.   Z3608.R3K34

Kessel, Ineke van. Aspects of the apartheid state : a bibliographical survey. Leiden, The Netherlands : African Studies Centre, Dept. of Political Historical Studies, 1989. 251 p. **DD217**

An excellent selective work of 850 entries including books, articles, and conference papers, mostly published after 1975 and covering the period after 1945. Its theme is the nature of the conflict in South Africa, especially the "race-class debate." Several essays introduce the topics. No indexes.   Z3608.R3K47

Keto, C. Tsehloane. American–South African relations, 1784–1980 : review and select bibliography. Athens, Ohio : Ohio Univ. Center for International Studies, Africa Studies Program, 1985. 159 p. (Monographs in international studies. Africa series, no. 45). **DD218**

Covers books, articles, reports and theses. Divided into two parts and an author index. Pt. 1 is an introductory review essay that includes key works. Pt. 2 is a select bibliography that includes four chapters: Study aids, American-African relations, Chronological categories (5 periods), and Subject categories (13 categories). Includes a section on "African-Americans and South Africa."

§ Updated by Y. G.-M. Lulat, *U.S. relations with South Africa : an analytical survey and annotated bibliography* (Boulder, Colo. : Westview Pr., 1989–91. 2 v.). 4,500 items in poor format.

Z6465.U5K47

Knox-Davies, Laetitia. Russian and Soviet perspectives on South Africa : a selected annotated bibliography of English-language translations from the Russian. Stellenbosch : Unit for Soviet Studies, Univ. of Stellenbosch, c1991. 132 p. **DD219**

Cites 197 English translations (or summaries) of books, articles, and pamphlets originally written in Russian. Annotations are long and descriptive. Chapters are arranged chronologically. Name and subject indexes.

§ *See also*: L. E. Andor, *The USSR and the Soviet bloc : policies and influences in southern Africa, 1975–1986* (DD112).

DK69.4.S6K59

Potgieter, Pieter Jacobus Johannes Stephanus. Index to literature on race relations in South Africa, 1910–1975 / comp. for the Potchefstroom University for Christian Higher Education by P. J. J. S. Potgieter. Boston : G. K. Hall, 1979. 555 p. **DD220**

Includes books and periodicals that concern the policy of apartheid, its implementation, and the divided society; problems of multiracialism and multinationalsim; and alternative policies and actions in opposition to apartheid. Excludes U.N. publications but includes some South African government publications. The author index lists different forms of the same name; the subject index, which includes many racist terms, is a keyword index with some added headings.

§ See also *Race relations survey* (DD209).   Z3608.R3P67

Rogaly, Gail Lynda. South Africa's foreign relations, 1961–1979 : a select and partially annotated bibliography. Braamfontein : South African Inst. of Internat. Affairs, [1980]. 462 p. (South African Institute of International Affairs. Bibliographical series, 7.). **DD221**

Includes books, government publications, journal articles, and conference papers concerning "bilateral relations with other states, Southern African questions, relations with international organizations and such specific questions as the involvement of multinational corporations in the Republic."—*Pref.* Arranged by main entry with author and subject indexes.

The latter has some interesting features, such as headings Economic relations, Foreign investment, and Foreign trade, under specific countries. Since this work was compiled in South Africa, it reflects lack of access to opposition sources; there is hence very little on liberation movement activities in the international arena.

Continued by: Jacqueline A. Kalley, *South Africa's foreign relations, 1980–1984* (Braamfontein : South African Inst. of Internat. Affairs, 1984. 283 p.), which provides a better mix of materials over the political spectrum than Rogaly, but excludes South African documents.

Z6465.S6R63

Seekings, Jeremy. South Africa's townships 1980–1991 : an annotated bibliography. Stellenbosch : Univ. of Stellenbosch, [1992]. 236 l. (Univ. of Stellenbosch. Dept. of Sociology. Occasional paper, no. 16). **DD222**

Includes books, articles, reports, and dissertations that bear directly or indirectly on township political organizations and protest activities. More than 500 entries arranged alphabetically by author. There is an index by township and subject and an index for secondary authors and other names. Publications of political organizations are excluded. Annotations are descriptive. A long introduction constitutes a critical review of the literature and includes a section listing works by themes.

HN801.A8

South African history and historians : a bibliography / ed. by C.F.J. Muller [et al.]. Pretoria : Univ. of South Africa, 1979. 411 p. (Documenta-Unisa, 21). **DD223**

An update of Reuben Musiker's *A select bibliography of South African history* (Pretoria, 1966; *Suppl.*, 1974).

4,518 unannotated entries in three parts: General, Periods, and Subjects. Aims to "include most of the more important items appearing before August 1978, together with certain new editions and published theses which came to our attention while the book was in its final stages."—*Introd.* "History" is intrepreted broadly to include language, arts and crafts, armed forces, etc.

§ Updated by *A bibliography of South African history, 1978–1989*, ed. by B.J. Liebenberg, K.W. Smith, S.B. Spies (Pretoria : Univ. of South Africa, 1992. 401 p.). *See also* Naomi Musiker, *South African history : bibliographical guide with special reference to territorial expansion and colonization* (N.Y. : Garland, 1984. 297 p.); and Leonard Monteath Thompson, Richard Elphick, and Inez Jarrick, *Southern African history before 1900 : a select bibliography of articles* (DD120).

Z3606.S67

United Nations Centre Against Apartheid. Publications list and comprehensive indexes (1967–1982). N.Y. : U.N. Centre Against Apartheid, [1983]. 75 p. **DD224**

A special issue (Oct. 1983) of U.N. Centre Against Apartheid, *Notes and documents*.

Includes 575 publications of the U.N. Centre Against Apartheid and its predecessor, the U.N. Unit Against Apartheid. Subject, personal author, and organization indexes.

§ Updated by: *UNDOC : current index* (AF48). *See also*: Elna Schoeman, *South Africa and the United Nations : a select and annotated bibliography* (Braamfontein : South African Inst. of International Affairs, 1981. 244 p.), which offers 1,007 entries, 1946–80, concentrating on U.N. publications but also including books, articles, conference papers, theses, and South African government publications.

DT763.U55

Sudan

El-Singaby, Talaat. La République Démocratique du Soudan : bilan des recherches en France et en R.F.A. : bibliographie sélective, 1900–1986. Aix-en-Provence : I.R.E.M.A.M., 1987. 139 p. : maps, ports. **DD225**

The first part surveys research activities in France and Germany on Sudan and lists researchers. The second part is an unannotated bibliography of 1,475 entries by subject, and includes a list of archives. No index.

Hill, Richard Leslie. A bibliography of the Anglo-Egyptian Sudan : from the earliest times to 1937. London : Oxford Univ. Pr., 1939. 213 p. **DD226**

Called "the first comprehensive bibliography of the Sudan" by M.W. Daly (*see* DD18). Topical arrangement of unannotated entries, including books and periodical articles. Primarily English language works, with some materials in European languages. Indexes of persons and subjects.

Continued by Abdel Rahman el Nasri's *A bibliography of the Sudan, 1938–1958* (London, 1962. 171 p.). 2,763 items. Retains the arrangement used by Hill, but includes materials in Arabic (titles are transliterated). Z3711.H64

Khartoum (Sudan). Jāmi'at al-Kharṭūm. al-Maktabah. al-Fihris al-musannaf li-majmū'at al-Sūdān = The classified catalogue of the Sudan collection in the University of Khartoum Library. Khartoum : Univ. of Khartoum Library, 1971. 1 v. (unpaged). **DD227**

In Arabic and English.

More than 5,000 entries for books, periodicals, pamphlets, government publications, and newspapers, arranged by classification number. Reputed to be the most comprehensive collection anywhere of printed material about the Sudan. Author index.

Supplements were published in 1973 and 1974. Z3665.K48

Wawa, Yosa H. Southern Sudan : a select bibliography / by Yosa H. Wawa, Amal Eisa El-Fadil, Fatima Shalaby Sid Ahmed. Khartoum : Univ. of Khartoum, Inst. of African Studies, Library & Documentation, 1988. 138 leaves. **DD228**

Title on added t.p. : Janūb al-Sūdān.

"This unannotated bibliography includes materials in the fields of politics, socio-economics, anthropology, education, language, history, and administration on Southern Sudan"—*p. i.* Lists English, French, and Arabic books, pamphlets, theses, conference proceedings, government publications, journal articles, letters, and press releases. All materials are housed in the I.A.S. Documentation Center. Author and subject indexes.

§ Also of interest by Wawa and El-Fadil is the *Bibliography on Sudan international relations* (Khartoum : Univ. of Khartoum, Inst. of African and Asian Studies, Library & Documentation, 1990).

Z3665.W39

Swaziland

Ngcobo, Zipho G. An annotated bibliography on women : Swaziland / prep. and comp. by Zipho G. Ngcobo for the Women and Law in Southern Africa Research Project. [Kwalusensi, Swaziland? : Social Science Research Unit, Univ. of Swaziland, 1991]. 82 p. **DD229**

Originally publ. by the Women and Law in Southern Africa Project, 1989.

Offers 158 entries organized in 12 subject categories. Materials are in various formats and annotations are descriptive. The materials include works on women broadly construed; many are locally published. Includes an author/title index.

Swaziland. Economic Planning Office. Socio-economic development bibliography. Mbabane : Economic Planning Office, Dept. of Economic Planning and Statistics, Prime Minister's Office, [1989]. 375 p. **DD230**

This classified bibliography of about 850 documents, compiled locally by consulting government agencies, nongovernmental organizations, offices of donor countries, and academic institutions, includes studies, reports and plans for the period 1983–89. There are no annotations, but library locations are given. Z7165.S795S95

University College of Swaziland. Library. Swaziana : an annotated bibliography of materials relating to Swaziland in the libraries of the University College of Swaziland / comp. by Thokozile Nkabinde. Kwaluseni : Univ. Coll. of Swaziland, 1978. 45 *l.* (Swaziland libraries publications, no. 4). **DD231**

A bibliography arranged by broad topical headings, with separate sections for microfiche and tape cassettes. Excludes periodical articles and government publications. Author/title index.

§ See also: *Swaziland official publications, 1880–1972 : a bibliography of the original and microfiche edition* (AF238). For history, see: J. S. M. Matsebula, *A history of Swaziland* (Cape Town : Longman Southern Africa, 1972. 131 p.), which provides a history of the Swazi nation, and includes a genealogical table of the royal dynasty, executive officers, chronology, and a short bibliography; and Alan R. Booth, *Swaziland : tradition and change in a southern African kingdom* (Boulder, Colo. : Westview Pr., 1983. 156 p.). Z3560.U54

Wallace, Charles Stewart. Swaziland : a bibliography. Johannesburg : Univ. of the Witwatersrand, Dept. of Bibliography, Librarianship and Typography, 1967. 87 p. **DD232**

An unannotated student bibliography of 1,191 entries arranged in 26 topical sections with author, geographical, mineral, and biographical indexes.

§ Updates Johanna Arnheim, *Swaziland : a bibliography* (Cape Town : School of Librarianship, Univ. of Cape Town, 1950. 20*l.* Repr. 1963, 1969); 150 citations. *See also*: John B. Webster and Paulus Mohome, *A bibliography on Swaziland* (Syracuse, N.Y. : Program of

Eastern African Studies, Syracuse Univ., 1968. 32*l.*), 178 citations; and Quentin Neil Parsons, *The High Commission territories, 1909–1964 : a bibliography* (DD117).   Z3607.S9W34

Tanzania

See also Zanzibar.

Howell, John Bruce. Tanganyika African National Union : a guide to publications by and about TANU. Wash. : General Reference and Bibliography Division, Reader Services Dept., Library of Congress, 1976. 52 p.   **DD233**

An annotated guide to the beginning period of Tanzania's long-standing ruling party, 1954–74. Includes official documents, books, articles, dissertations and papers.   Z7165.T3H68

Makaidi, Emmanuel J. E. A dictionary of historic records of Tanzania (1497–1982). Dar-es-Salaam : Sunrise Publ., c1984. 73 p.   **DD234**

Brief entries. No index.   DT444.M34

Mascarenhas, Ophelia. Women in Tanzania : an analytical bibliography / by Ophelia Mascarenhas and Marjorie Mbilinyi. Uppsala : Scandinavian Inst. of African Studies ; Stockholm : Swedish International Development Authority, 1983. 256 p.   **DD235**

An excellent bibliography of 400 extensively annotated citations arranged by 18 topics. Each section includes an introductory essay with references to citations that follow.

§ *See also*: Volkhard Hundsdörfer and Wolfgang Küper, *Bibliography for social science research on Tanzania* (München : Weltforum Verlag, 1974) and Simon Bell, *Women in rural development in Kenya, Tanzania and Zimbabwe : a partially annotated bibliography* (Norwic U.K. : School of Development Studies, Univ. of East Anglia, 1985. 40 p.). For an overview history with foldout maps and reading list, *see*: I. N. Kimambo and A. J. Temu, *A history of Tanzania* (Nairobi : publ. for Historical Assoc. of Tanzania by East African Publ. House, 1969. 276 p.).   Z7964.T34M37

Serkkola, Ari. Rural development in Tanzania : a bibliography. Helsinki : Institute of Development Studies, Univ. of Helsinki, 1987. 252 p.   **DD236**

An excellent source for works published 1970–85 and a few earlier titles of special significance. Intended to be a comprehensive work of materials gathered from six DIALOG databases and five Commonwealth Agricultural Bureau databases. Gives complete citations, some with annotations. Arranged by nine broad subject headings; author index.

Togo

Bibliographie sur la population et le développement au Togo : tirée de la base de données POPTOGO / Tilate Agboli ... [et al.]. Lomé : Unité de recherche démographique, 1992. 190 p. : forms.   **DD237**

Cites 1,566 entries, most of which are annotated, organized by subject. Index by author, subject, and geographic area.

Tunisia

Tunisia. Maktabah al-Qawmīyah. Bibliographie historique sur la Tunisie, 1881–1955 : livres se trouvant à la Bibliothèque Nationale, Tunis. Tunis : La Bibliothèque, [197?]. 98 *l.*   **DD238**

More than 900 books, journal and newspaper articles, arranged by historical period then by author. Chiefly French language materials. No annotations or index.   Z3685.M35

Uganda

Gertzel, Cherry J. Uganda, an annotated bibliography of source materials : with particular reference to the period since 1971 and up to 1988. London : Hans Zell, 1991. 228 p.   **DD239**

A first-rate user-friendly bibliography that emphasizes government publications and begins with an excellent bibliographic essay that will save researchers much time and energy. The beginning sections are in chronological order by government administration; most others are organized by provenance—materials from political parties, human rights organizations, international organizations, Makerere University. The remaining sections are organized alphabetically by format: books, articles and conference papers, theses, pamphlets, and local newspapers and journals. Many citations include annotations. Despite the subtitle, includes sections on the British colonial period and the first Obote administration (1962–71), but the author claims nearly comprehensive coverage of official sources only for the dates named. Rudimentary subject index.

§ For history, *see* Jan Jelmert Jorgensen, *Uganda : a modern history* (N.Y. : St. Martin's Pr., 1981. 381 p.), which Gertzel calls the "most useful single monograph" for a general introduction to Uganda. *See also* Mahmood Mamdani, *Politics and class formation in Uganda* (N.Y. : Monthly Review Pr., 1976) and Amii Omara-Otunnu, *Politics and the military in Uganda, 1890–1985* (N.Y. : St. Martin's Pr., 1987. 218 p.).   Z3586.G47

Kleinschmidt, Harald. Amin collection : bibliographical catalogue of materials relevant to the history of Uganda under the military government of Idi Amin Dada. Heidelberg : P. Kivouvou, Editions Bantoues, c1983. 107 p.   **DD240**

Aims to "function as a step into the historical research in the social and political aspects of Uganda under the Amin government and to provide materials apt to connect the 'Amin' period with earlier periods of Ugandan history."—*Pref.* About 1,500 entries arranged by date of publication, 1900–80, with author and inadequate subject indexes.

§ Also useful is M. O. Afolabi's "President Idi Amin Dada of Uganda, a bibliography" in *Current bibliography on African affairs*, 10, no. 4 (1977/78): 309–27, a partially annotated list of 256 items. *See also*: Beverly Ann Gray's *Uganda : subject guide to official publications* (AF240).   Z3586.K57

Mutibwa, Olivia M. N. Women in Uganda : a bibliography. Kampala, Uganda : Uganda Association of Univ. of Women, 1986. 23 p.   **DD241**

A useful bibliography of 149 annotated, mostly local, sources, arranged in 15 broad subject sections.   Z7964.U49M87

Western Sahara

Western Sahara is the former Rio de Oro, or Spanish Sahara.

Sipe, Lynn F. Western Sahara : a comprehensive bibliography. N.Y. : Garland, 1984. 418 p. (Garland reference library of social science, v. 178).   **DD242**

Cites with many annotations 3,345 books and articles published 1884 to early 1983. "Language of publication is limited to Western European languages written in the Latin alphabet."—*Introd.* Topical arrangement. Indexed.   Z3933.S57

Zaïre

Bibliographies analytiques sur l'Afrique centrale. no. 1 (1978)–no. 7 (1985). Bruxelles : Centre d'Étude et de Documentation Africaines, 1978–85.   **DD243**

Contents: no. 1, Les périodiques Zaïrois 1970–77; no. 2, Les périodiques Congolais 1960–69; no. 3, Les périodiques Zaïrois 1970–77, supplément; no. 4, L'education en République du Zaïre 1960–1979; no. 5, L'économie de la République du Zaïre 1960–1er semestre 1980; no. 6, La politique en République du Zaïre 1955–1er semestre 1981; no. 7, L'économie de la République du Zaïre.

Nos. 1–3 list periodicals published in Zaïre, with tables of contents for each, and with author and subject indexes.   Z3517.B5

Heyse, Théodore. Bibliographie du Congo Belge et du Ruanda-Urundi. Bruxelles : Campenhout, 1946–53. 15 v. in 1. and suppl. (Cahiers belges et congolais, no. 4–7, 9–12, 16–22).   **DD244**

Contents: no. 4, Géologie et mines (1939–45); no. 5, Régime foncier; no. 6, Littérature, arts oraux indigènes (1939–47); no. 7, Agriculture, élevage, produits et industries agricoles, forêts, chasse, pêche, parcs, flore, et faune (1939–47); no. 9, Transports, travaux publics, P.T.T. et radio-diffusion, forces hydro-electriques (1939–48); no. 10, Économie générale, industrie et commerce, effort de guerre, banques et finances, matières économiques spéciales, main d'oeuvre (partie non-legislative) (1939–48), no. 11, Beaux-arts, urbanisme, arts-indigènes, cinéma (1939–49); no. 12, Documentation générale, histoire et expansion belge, biographies, Stanley, articles et ouvrages généraux (1939–49); no. 16, Politique générale, politique indigène, enseignement, cultes et missions (1939–50); no. 17, Hygiène et assistance sociale, service médical, éthnographie, langues et linguistique, suivi d'un complément à la "Politique indigène" (période antérieure à 1940) (1939–50); no. 18, Sciences coloniales: répertoire suivi d'un complément à la "Politique indigène," période antérieure à 1940 (1939–51); no. 19, Documentation générale: bibliographies et centres d'études, expositions, presse et propagande; répertoire suivi d'un complément à la "Politique indigène" ... (1939–51); no. 20, Documentation générale: folklore, philatélie, sports, tourisme; répertoire suivi d'un complément à la "Politique indigène" ... (1939–51); no. 21–22, L'Afrique centrale dans le conflit mondiale (1939–51. 2 v.).

Z3631.H51b

Vellut, Jean Luc. Guide de l'étudiant en histoire du Zaïre. Kinshasa : Éditions du Mont Noir, [1974]. 207 p. ([Collection "Objectif 80"] : Série "Essais", no. 8 ; Collection Cours universitaires, no. 1).   **DD245**

At head of title: Presses universitaires du Zaïre.

Much broader than its title would indicate, half this book is a guide to the study of history in Africa, including classical Greek, Roman, and Islamic and precolonial European sources. The second half, a guide to the study of the history of Zaïre, includes an indexed classified bibliography of 545 citations.

§ *See also:* Alphonse Jules Wauters, *Bibliographie du Congo, 1880–1895 : catalogue méthodique de 3,800 ouvrages, brochures, notices et cartes rélatifs à l'historie, à la géographie et à la colonisation du Congo* (Bruxelles : Administration du Mouvement Géographique, 1895. 356 p.); Mandjumba Mwanyimi-Mbonba, *Chronologie générale de l'histoire du Zaïre (des origines à 1988)* (2nd ed. Kinshasa : Centre de Recherches Pédagogiques, 1989); *Dictionary of African biography* (AH314) with about 150 entries for Zaïreans; Marcel Walraet, *Bibliographie du Katanga* (Bruxelles : Inst. Royal Colonial Belge, 1954–60. 3 v.), covering the entire country.   Z3631.V4

Zambia

Chitambo, A. M. Women in Zambia : a bibliographical guide and directory. [Lusaka, Zambia] : Women and Law in Southern Africa Research Project, [1991]. 89 p.   **DD246**

Contains a bibliography of 307 annotated entries and a brief directory of organizations. Most of the materials are not monographs but articles, research reports, government publications, theses, and conference papers.

§ Useful companion works are: Susan Antkiewicz, *Women and development in Zambia : an annotated bibliography* (Addis Ababa, Ethiopia : U.N. Economic Commission for Africa, 1983. 98 p.), and following it chronologically, *An annotated bibliography of research on Zambian women* (Lusaka, Zambia : Zambia Assoc. for Research and Development [ZARD], 1985. 159 p.). See also *Women in development in Southern Africa* (DD122) and Raj Bardouille, *Research on Zambian women in retrospect and prospect : an annotated bibliography* (Lusaka : SIDA, 1992), which offers 154 citations and a directory of organizations.   Z7963.E18C495

Mwanza, Ilse. Bibliography of Zambiana theses and dissertations, 1930s–1989. [Lusaka, Zambia] : Univ. of Zambia, Inst. for African Studies, Office of the Research Secretary, 1990. 95 p.   **DD247**

For annotation, *see* AG50.

Rau, William E. A bibliography of pre-independence Zambia : the social sciences. Boston : G.K. Hall, 1978. 357 p.   **DD248**

The content is broader than the title implies. 3,925 unannotated citations are arranged by broad discipline and subtopics, e.g., anthropology, linguistics, history, and wildlife. Includes indexes by ethnic groups, personal and place names, and authors, but there is no subject index.

§ *See also:* R.M.S. Ng'ombe, *A selected bibliography of the Federation of Rhodesia and Nyasaland* (DD119).   Z3579.R38

Williams, Geoffrey J. Independent Zambia : a bibliography of the social sciences, 1964–1979 / Geoffrey J. Williams. Boston : G.K. Hall, c1984. 538 p., [4] p. of plates : maps.   **DD249**

Like William E. Rau's *A bibliography of pre-independence Zambia* (DD248), the content of this volume is broader than its title suggests. Williams provides 5,023 citations (some annotated), including government publications, arranged by broad discipline and by subtopics like Rau. There is some overlap with Rau, as Williams notes in his extensive introduction. Some reviews are cited. Not all materials were seen by the author. Includes indexes by ethnic groups, personal names, geography, and authors, but there is no general subject index.

Z3579.W54

Zanzibar

Zanzibar merged with Tanganyika in 1964, forming Tanzania.

Bennett, Norman Robert. The Arab state of Zanzibar : a bibliography. Boston : G. K. Hall, [1984]. 231 p.   **DD250**

An important work whose "primary emphasis is on the period from the late eighteenth century through the revolution of January 1964"—*Pref*; the 2,492 entries cite works published from the 18th century to mid-1984 in Britain, France, Germany, Belgium, Portugal, and the U.S. Topical arrangement with indexes of persons, places, and subjects.

§ For history, *see:* Sir John Milner Gray, *History of Zanzibar, from the Middle Ages to 1856* (London : Oxford Univ. Pr., 1962. 314 p. Repr.: Westport, Conn. : Greenwood, 1975) and *Zanzibar under colonial rule*, ed. by Abdul Sheriff and Ed Ferguson (Athens : Ohio Univ. Pr., 1991. 278 p.).   Z3589.B46

Zimbabwe

Doro, Marion E. Rhodesia/Zimbabwe : a bibliographic guide to the nationalist period. Boston : G.K. Hall, c1984. 247 p. **DD251**

A selective bibliography of the period 1960–80, from just before the Universal Declaration of Indepedence by the white minority (1965) to majority rule and political independence. There are many annotations and explanatory sections, including appendixes concentrating on the first independence election. Lists books, articles, and government publications issued through 1981. Unfortunately, there are many errors in citations and some errors of fact in the text. Includes a minimal subject index, and an author index for books only.

§ *See also*: Goswin Baumhögger, *Simbabwe—Geschichte, Politik, Wirtschaft, Gesellschaft : Auswahlbibliographie = Zimbabwe— history, politics, economics, society : a selected bibliography* (Hamburg : Institut für Afrika-Kunde im Verbund der Stiftung Deutsches Übersee-Institut, Dokumentations-Leitstelle Afrika, 1984. 266 p.). 1,701 citations for works published 1970–84, annotations in German. Z3578.D67

Johnstone, I. J. Zimbabwean political material published in exile, 1959–1980 : a bibliography. Harare : National Archives, 1987. 31 p. (Bibliographical series [Zimbabwe. National Archives], no. 3.). **DD252**

Lists political materials published in exile by the Zimbabwe liberation movement, 1959–80, including pamphlets, posters, leaflets, and serials. Includes "bogus publications" used against the liberation movement. General index. Z3578.J64

Macnamara, Eve. Women in Zimbabwe : an annotated bibliography. Harare, Zimbabwe : Dept. of Sociology, Univ. of Zimbabwe, c1989. 170 p. **DD253**

670 annotated entries, including materials specifically about women and topics important to women (e.g., AIDS, literacy, family planning). Covers colonial materials and grey literature. Author and subject indexes.

§ For the debate on the role of women in society just after independence, *see*: "Women in the press" section of Olivia N. Muchena, *Women and development in Zimbabwe : an annotated bibliography* (Addis Ababa : U.N. Economic Commission for Africa, 1984). *See also*: Simon Bell, *Women in rural development in Kenya, Tanzania and Zimbabwe : a partially annotated bibliography* (Norwich, U.K. : School of Development Studies, Univ. of East Anglia, 1985. 40 p.), and for an overview, Elinor Zatezat and Margaret Mwalo, *Women in Zimbabwe* (Harare : SAPES Trust, 1989. 73 p.). Z7965.Z55M33

DE

Asia

GENERAL WORKS

Guides

Nunn, Godfrey Raymond. Asia : reference works; a select annotated guide. London : Mansell, 1980. 365 p. **DE1**

Although based on Nunn's *Asia, a selected and annotated guide to reference works* (Cambridge, Mass. : M.I.T. Pr., 1971), this is virtually a new work, fewer than a third of the 1,567 titles in the present edition having been retained without change from the earlier publication. Employs a regional/country arrangement, providing annotated listings of encyclopedias, handbooks, yearbooks, dictionaries, directories, atlases, gazetteers, chronologies, statistical sources, and bibliographies within each geographical section. Asian and Western-language (mainly English) materials are cited. Author/title index. Does not include the Middle East or Central Asia.

§ Companion works by Nunn: *East Asia : a bibliography of bibliographies* ([Honolulu] : East-West Center Libr., 1967. 92 p.) and *South and Southeast Asia : a bibliography of bibliographies* ([Honolulu] : East–West Center Libr., 1966. 59 p.). Z3001.N79

Bibliography

Asien-Bibliographie. Jahrg. 1 (Sep. 1949)–134 (May 1986). Frankenau/Hessen : Asien-Bücherei. Quarterly. **DE2**

Lists new publications in the German language on all parts of Asia, plus some materials on North Africa, and Oceania. Some entries are annotated. Includes periodical articles. *Bibliographia asiatica*, publ. by Asien-Bücherei in Frankenau, Hesse, 1953–77, merged into *Asien-Bibliographie*. Z3001.A84

Bryson, Thomas A. United States/Middle East diplomatic relations, 1784–1978 : an annotated bibliography. Metuchen, N.J. : Scarecrow, 1979. 205 p. **DE3**

About 1,350 English-language items—books, periodical articles, documents, and dissertations. Arrangement is mainly chronological, with separate sections for general materials and for dissertations. Author index.

§ *See also* Sanford R. Silverburg and Bernard Reich, *United States foreign policy and the Middle East/North Africa* (DE40) for its more current coverage. Bryson's work, however, addresses a wider period, and its arrangement is easier to use. Z3014.R44B79

Cumulative bibliography of Asian studies, 1941–1965 : author bibliography. Boston : G. K. Hall, 1969 [i.e, 1970]. 4 v. **DE4**

This work and its companion, *Cumulative bibliography of Asian studies, 1941–1965 : subject bibliography*, cumulate the entries from the *Bibliography of Asian studies* (DE8) and its predecessors. The subject part follows the same general arrangement as the original bibliographies.

§ The Association of Asian Studies issued updates for both bibliographies, covering 1966–1970 (Boston : G.K. Hall. Author, 1972; subject, 1973). Each appears in three volumes.

De Silva, Daya. The Portuguese in Asia : an annotated bibliography of studies on Portuguese colonial history in Asia, 1498–c.1800. Zug, Switzerland : IDC, 1987. 313 p. (Bibliotheca Asiatica, 22). **DE5**

An annotated listing of 2,773 books, pamphlets, and articles in European languages, with emphasis on published primary source material. Literature is excluded unless it is significant "in terms of the development of historiography of Portuguese Asia."—*Introd.* Arranged under five broad subjects subdivided by geographic area: Travel and description; Conquest : expansion and decline; Religion : encounter, confrontation and conversion; Economic foundations; Impact on Asian society. Index of authors, editors, translators, compilers, etc. 1,000 of the titles cited in the bibliography and considered scarce are available on microfiche from IDC. Z3001.D32

Gotthold, Julia J. Indian Ocean / Julia J. Gotthold, comp., with the assistance of Donald W. Gotthold. Oxford ; Santa Barbara, Calif. : Clio Pr., c1988. 329 p., [1] leaf of plates : map. (World bibliographical series, v. 85). **DE6**

Offers 804 annotated entries for books, articles, atlases, maps, and bibliographies on the Indian Ocean, including the Red Sea and the Persian Gulf. Broad subject arrangement with appropriate subdivisions; mostly English-language titles with a few in French. Author/title/subject index. Z3499.G67

Orientalische Bibliographie. Vol. 1–26. Berlin : Reuther, 1887–[1926]. **DE7**

Repr.: Munich : Kraus, 1980.

Publication suspended 1912–1925. Vols. 23/24 (1909/10) were issued in one volume publ. 1912–15; v. 25 (1911) publ. 1917–22.

An important annual bibliography, including books, pamphlets, periodical articles, and reviews in the whole field of Oriental studies: language, literature, geography, ethnology, folklore, history, etc.

§ For material before 1887, the following should be consulted: Julius Theodor Zenker's *Bibliotheca orientalis*, 1846–61; *Wissenschaftlicher Jahresbericht über die morgenländischen Studien*, 1859–81; Karl Friederici's *Bibliotheca orientalis*, 1876–83; and *Litteraturblatt für orientalische Philologie*, 1883–86.

Current

Bibliography of Asian studies. 1956– . [Ann Arbor, Mich.] : Association for Asian Studies. Annual. **DE8**

Formerly entitled "Far Eastern bibliography," appearing in the *Far Eastern quarterly*, 1936–55 (title varies slightly). Volumes for 1956–68 issued as the September number of the *Journal of Asian studies*.

An extensive, classified listing of books, pamphlets, and periodical articles on all phases of life and culture in Asia, in the English language. Coverage varies. Earlier volumes treated East and Southeast Asia, but, beginning with 1956, coverage was extended to include also South and Central Asia, the Philippines, etc. Z3001.B49

Dissertations

Bloomfield, Barry Cambray. Theses on Asia accepted by universities in the United Kingdom and Ireland, 1877–1964. London : Cass, 1967. 127 p. **DE9**

Contains information on 2,571 theses. The main listing is geographical, with appropriate subdivisions. Author index. Z3001.B56

Grunendahl, Reinhold. Hochschulschriften zu Süd– und Südostasien : Deutschland, Österreich, Schweiz (1959–1979). Wiesbaden : Harrassowitz, 1981. 254 p. **DE10**

A bibliography of some 1,352 dissertations and *Habilitationsschriften* (post-doctoral theses required for qualification as a university lecturer). Topical arrangement within country divisions, subarranged chronologically. Name and subject indexes. Z3185.G78

Library resources

Asia and Oceania : a guide to archival & manuscript sources in the United States / G. Raymond Nunn, ed. London : Mansell, 1985. 5 v. **DE11**

A major finding aid for manuscripts and archival collections in the U.S. Covers from Afghanistan to the Pacific (including Turkey and Persia, but not the rest of the Middle East), the Pacific Islands (excluding Hawaii and Australia, and material relating to overseas Asians and Pacific Islanders). Excludes major manuscript collections in East Asian, Turkish, and Persian languages. Arrangement is by state and city, then by name of repository (with address, hours, restrictions, etc.). Descriptions of collections (some given in much detail) include type, size, dates, guides or Binding Bids, NUCMC listing if any, and content. Extensive index in v. 5.

§ Serves for U.S. resources the same purpose as *Guides to the sources for the history of the nations* (DD75). Z3001.A78

Pearson, J. D. A guide to manuscripts and documents in the British Isles relating to South and South-East Asia. London ; N.Y. : Mansell, 1989–90. 2 v. **DE12**

A supplement to M.D. Wainwright and Noel Matthew's *A guide to Western manuscripts and documents in the British Isles relating to South and South East Asia* (DE13).

Contents: v. 1, London (319 p.); v. 2, British Isles (excluding London).

Based on visits to repositories and on published and unpublished lists and articles. Vol. 1 describes changes in locations and additions to collections, and includes information concerning India Office holdings in the British Library (but is not so detailed as either Amar Kaur Jasbir Singh, *A guide to source materials in the India Office Library and Records for the history of Tibet, Sikkim and Bhutan 1765–1950* (DE86) or India Office Library and Records, *A general guide to the India Office Records*, ed. by Martin Moir (DE83). Also lists finding aids and publications where blocks of manuscripts are printed. Topical index. CD1048.A8P43

Wainwright, M. D. A guide to Western manuscripts and documents in the British Isles relating to South and South East Asia / M. D. Wainwright and Noel Matthews. London : Oxford Univ. Pr., 1965. 532 p. **DE13**

Lists, by depository, collections of manuscripts in all subject groups: history, literature, sciences, social sciences, and humanities. Includes some private collections, but collections of the India Office Library are excluded. Index of names and subjects. CD1048.A8W3

Encyclopedias

Encyclopedia of Asian history / Ainslie T. Embree, ed. in chief. N.Y. : Scribner's ; London : Collier Macmillan, c1988. 4 v. : ill. **DE14**

Prepared under the auspices of the Asia Society.

Signed articles by scholars, well-written and informative, are aimed toward a non-specialist audience. Asia is defined as covering Iran to the Philippines and excludes the U.S.S.R except for the Central Asian republics. Most of the articles include short bibliographies of English-language works. Features a synoptic outline; numerous *see* and *see also* references; topical index; directory of contributors. Black-and-white photographs and maps are well chosen and clearly reproduced. DS31.E53

Shavit, David. The United States in Asia : a historical dictionary. N.Y. : Greenwood, 1990. 620 p.   **DE15**
"Attempts to be comprehensive, including all persons, institutions, and events that brought the U.S. in contact with Asia."—*Pref.* All of Asia is included except the Middle East. Short articles with bibliographies appended. Brief chronology; bibliographic essays; cross-references; topical index.
§ Companion to Shavit's *The United States in Africa* (DD96) and *The United States in the Middle East* (DE56).   DS33.4.U6S46

Handbooks

Asia and the Pacific / ed. by Robert H. Taylor. N.Y. : Facts on File, c1991. 2 v. (1879 p.) : ill., maps.   **DE16**
Vol. 1 contains two separate country-by-country sequences, first for basic information, and, second, general essays. Vol. 2 has general regional essays on history, political affairs, economic affairs, and social affairs. Subject index.   DS5.A79

Fenton, Thomas P. Asia and Pacific : a directory of resources / comp. and ed. by Thomas P. Fenton and Mary J. Heffron. Maryknoll, N.Y. : Orbis Books, c1986. 137 p.   **DE17**
Updates and expands the Asia and Pacific chapter of Fenton and Heffron's 1984 *Third World resource directory* (DA11).
Lists, with annotations, books, organizations, periodicals, pamphlets and articles, audiovisuals, news services, etc., which aim to promote fundamental reform in the designated areas. Arranged by format. Indexes by name, title, and geographical area.   Z3001.F46

Historiography

University of London. School of Oriental and African Studies. Historical writing on the peoples of Asia. London ; N.Y. : Oxford Univ. Pr., 1961–1962. 4 v.   **DE18**
Contents: [1], Historians of India, Pakistan, and Ceylon, ed. by C. H. Philips; [2], Historians of South East Asia, ed. by D.G.E. Hall; [3], Historians of China and Japan, ed. by W. G. Beasley and E.G. Pulleyblank; [4], Historians of the Middle East, ed. by B. Lewis and P.M. Holt.   DS32.5.L6

Current surveys

Asian recorder : a weekly digest of outstanding Asian events. v.1 (Jan. 1/7, 1955)– . New Delhi : K.K. Thomas at Recorder Pr., 1955– . Weekly.   **DE19**
Publisher varies.
A specimen copy entitled *Asian archives* was issued Sept. 26/Oct. 3, 1954.
Arranged by country, each issue giving a summary of events occurring during the previous week. Source of information (newspaper, periodical, radio broadcast, etc.) is given. Quarterly indexes cumulate annually; indexing is under 33 broad subject headings.   DS1.A4747

Biography

Who's who in Asian and Australasian politics. London ; N.Y. : Bowker-Saur, c1991. 475 p.   **DE20**
Contains biographies of 3,000 governmental, political, or trade union leaders from 37 countries, emphasizing contributions to government and politics. A second part contains a country-by-country political directory and index providing membership lists, leaders in government, government agencies, and political parties.   DS35.2.W48

ASIA (by region)

Asia, West

General works

Guides

Middle East : a directory of resources / comp. and ed. by Thomas P. Fenton and Mary J. Heffron. Maryknoll, N.Y. : Orbis Books, c1988. 144 p. : ill.   **DE21**
Updates and expands a chapter in Fenton and Heffron's 1984 *Third World resource directory* (DA11).
Covers the Middle East and North Africa as a region, as well as the individual countries. Cites organizations, periodicals, books, articles and pamphlets, and audiovisual materials. Entries contain extensive annotations and lists of information sources. Index for organizations, individuals, titles, and geographical areas.   Z3014.P64M53

Middle East and Islam : a bibliographical introduction / ed. by Diana Grimwood-Jones. Rev. and enl. ed. Zug, Switz. : Inter Documentation, [1979]. 429 p. (Bibliotheca asiatica, 15).   **DE22**
At head of title: Middle East Libraries Committee.
1st ed., 1972.
A cooperative effort, with sections on individual topics (e.g., Islamic history, Islamic law, Anthropology, Political science) contributed by scholars and librarians.
"The pattern of the volume is substantially the same as the first edition, though the range of subjects has been broadened considerably, and thus some papers, e.g. Islamic Philosophy, Islamic Theology, Oil, Berber Studies are completely new."—*Introd.*   Z3013.M48

Tuttle guide to the Middle East / ed. by Peter Sluglett and Marion Farouk-Sluglett. Boston : C.E. Tuttle Co., 1992. 320 p. : maps.   **DE23**
A country-by-country survey; includes regions (Maghrib) and ethnic groups (Kurds, Palestinians). Each chapter provides a basic overview and concentrates upon recent history. Appendixes concentrate on wars in the region. Index is primarily to individuals.
DS44.T881992

Bibliography

Articles on the Middle East, 1947–1971 : a cumulation of the bibliographies from the Middle East journal / ed. by Peter N. Rossi, Wayne E. White. Ann Arbor, Mich. : Pierian Pr., 1980. 4 v. (1646 p.).   **DE24**
"Reproduced from original bibliographies and items appear as they did in the pages of the journal."—*Foreword.*
Covers the Muslim world from Morocco to Pakistan (with Palestine and Israel added since 1964). Emphasis is on modern history, politics, social conditions, language and literature from the late 18th century to the present. Broad topical arrangement; separate section for book reviews. Includes materials in all European and Middle Eastern languages. Annotations. Indexes in v. 4.   Z3013.A76

Atiyeh, George Nicholas. The contemporary Middle East, 1948–1973 : a selective and annotated bibliography. Boston : G. K. Hall, [1975]. 664p.   **DE25**
A classed bibliography with author and subject indexes. Emphasis is on the social sciences. Materials are mainly in English, French, German, Italian and Spanish, with some works in Arabic, Turkish and Persian included "either because they represent new trends in their fields

or because they complete the coverage of topics that otherwise would not be well represented."—*Introd.* Nearly 6,500 items. Intended for the student and beginning researcher. Z3013.A85

Banuazizi, Ali. Social stratification in the Middle East and North Africa : a bibliographic survey. London : Mansell, [1984]. 248p. **DE26**

Goes beyond social stratification and inequality to include related areas of social history, geography, and anthropology. Covers Afghanistan to Morocco. Includes 19th-century to contemporary times in order to demonstrate social continuities. Some 2,000 books, essays, dissertations, research reports and periodical articles in English and French, publ. 1946–82. Geographical arrangement; author and subject indexes. Z7165.N35B36

Bevis, Richard W. Bibliotheca cisorientalia : an annotated checklist of early English travel books on the Near and Middle East. Boston : G. K. Hall, 1973. 317 p. **DE27**

Provides " a reasonably complete checklist of books reporting at first hand on the Mideast after the Moslem conquest, published in English before 1915."—*Introd.* Author listing within five sections: English language travel books; Translations into English; Collections; Biography, criticism and scholarship; Bibliography. Most entries are briefly annotated; library locations are indicated. Z3013.B47

Bibliographie de la culture arabe contemporaine / sous la direction de Jacques Berque. [Paris] : Sindbad/Presses de l'Unesco, [1981]. 483 p. **DE28**

A classified, partially annotated bibliography on various aspects of contemporary Arabic culture, including the social, political, historical and religious background. Arabic titles are given in transliteration in the body of the work, but there are author and title indexes in Arabic as well as a general index of names. Annotations in French or English. Z3013.B49

Bibliographie der Deutschsprachigen Arabistik und Islamkunde : von den Anfängen bis 1986 nebst Literatur über die arabischen Länder der Gegenwart. Frankfurt am Main : Institut für Geschichte der Arabisch-Islamischen Wissenschaften an der Johann Wolfgang Goethe-Universität, 1990. v. 1–6. (Veröffentlichungen des Institutes für Geschichte der Arabisch-Islamischen Wissenschaften. Reihe A, Texte und Studien, Bd. 3). (In progress). **DE29**

Contents: v. 1, Allgemeines und Hilfsmittel der Forschung, hrsg. von Fuat Sezgin (308 p.); v. 2, Islam. Religion und Theologie. Recht und Sitte; v. 3, Arabische Sprache. Philologie; v. 4, Poesie und Prosa; v. 5, Wissenschaftsgeschichte. Philosophie, Medezin und Naturwissenschaften; v. 6, Kulturgeschichte. Gewerbe, Handwerke und Künste.

To be in 8 v. covering all areas and topics relative to the Islamic world (language, literature, history, medicine, art, geography, religion, etc.), concluding with an author/title/subject index. Vol. 1 is the general volume and includes entries for general bibliographies, major journals, festschriften, bibliographies relating to scholars, guides to papyrology, publishers, the press, manuscripts and archives, etc. Citations are mainly to German publications, most of them issued in the 20th century, but with some 18th- and 19th-century publications included. Major reviews are cited. DS61.9.B53

Groot, Alexander H. de. A bibliography of Dutch publications on the Middle East and Islam 1945–1981. Nijmegen : Nederlandse Vereniging voor de Studie van het Midden-Osten en de Islam, 1981. 80 p. **DE30**

1st ed., 1976.

Aims to provide "a representative listing of all the various currents of research undertaken in the Netherlands at the present time" (*Pref.*) on the Arab world, including studies on the European parts of Turkey, the Ottoman Empire, and Afghanistan. Broad topical arrangement; author index.

Hazai, György. Bibliographisches Handbuch der Turkologie : eine Bibliographie der Bibliographien vom 18. Jahrhundert bis 1979 / zusammengestellt von György Hazai und Barbara Kellner-Heinkele. Budapest : Akadémiai Kiadó, 1986. v. 1. (Bibliotheca orientalis Hungarica, v. 30). (In progress). **DE31**

Consists of numbered bibliographic citations woven into a systematic survey of Turkic studies, in 14 major subject sections (General international bibliographies; General bibliographies of major Turkic-speaking countries; Bibliographies of Near-Eastern, Middle-Eastern, and Islamic studies; Oriental-studies bibliographies for various countries; Regional bibliographies for Turkic studies; various subject-specialized bibliographies for Turkic studies; Linguistics; Ethnography and Folklore; Literary studies; History; Archeology, anthropology, numismatics, and art history; Religious studies; Geography; and Travel accounts); subarranged by the various Turkic nations with other subdivisions as appropriate. Vol. 1 contains 2,967 entries.

Planned for 2 v.; v. 2 is to contain catalogs of library and manuscript collections, personal bibliography, coverage of areas geographically and conceptually bordering on Turkic studies, and indexes to the entire set. Z7049.T87H39

Hussain, Asaf. Islamic movements in Egypt, Pakistan and Iran : an annotated bibliography. [London] : Mansell, [1983]. 168 p. **DE32**

Designed to examine the political role of Islamic movements in the countries mentioned by providing an annotated listing of books and journal articles (mainly in English). Country arrangement; annotations intend to "bring out the essential points of the article or book and in many cases the viewpoint of the authors."—*Introd.* Author index. Z7835.M6H9

Internationale Jahresbibliographie Südwestasien = International annual bibliography South West Asia : SWA. Jahrg. 1 (1985)– . Osnabrück : F. Dietrich, 1988– . Annual. **DE33**

Editors, 1988– , Otto and Wolfram Zeller.

Based on the collection of the Univ. of Tübingen. A subject listing of books, articles, book reviews, festschriften, and conference proceedings. Southwest Asia is here understood to cover from India to the Sudan. Similar in organization and appearance to *IBZ* (AD255); the topical headings are listed in a subject index under 16 broad fields. An index of authors and reviewers refers to the appropriate subject heading. DS44.Z99I58

McClintock, Marsha Hamilton. The Middle East and North Africa on film : an annotated filmography. N.Y. : Garland, 1982. 542 p. (Garland reference library of the humanities, v.159). **DE34**

A listing of films and videotapes produced between 1903 and Jan. 1980; limited to "English, English sub-titled and silent films in 8, super 8, 16 and 35mm and tapes in ½, ¾ and 2 inch formats."—*Introd.* Includes films about Algeria, Egypt, Ethiopia, Libya, Morocco, Sudan, Tunisia, and North African generally. Geographical arrangement, with country divisions subdivided topically. Title/series index and distributor/location index. Gives full information for each film, together with brief annotation and location. DS44.M43

McLachlan, Keith Stanley. A bibliography of the Iran-Iraq borderland / Keith McLachlan & Richard N. Schofield. Wisbech : Middle East & North African Studies, 1987. 383 p. **DE35**

Based on the collection developed at the School of Oriental and African Studies at the Univ. of London, this is an extensive listing of books, essays, dissertations, government publications, and maps in Western languages. Topical arrangement (e.g., Geography, Geology, Geomorphology, International relations, Modern history). Appendix lists relevant materials in the India Office and the Public Record Office. Addendum for recent publications or for works inadvertently omitted. Author index only. Z3366.I55M2

The Middle East in conflict : a historical bibliography. Santa Barbara, Calif. : ABC-Clio, [1985]. 302 p. (Clio bibliography series, 19). **DE36**

A topical/geographical arrangement of entries drawn from *Historical abstracts* (DA176), 1973–82. Covers Pakistan to Morocco and the Western Sahara in the 20th century. Subject and author indexes.

DS62.4.M53

Olson, William J. Britain's elusive empire in the Middle East, 1900–1921 : an annotated bibliography. N.Y. : Garland, 1982. 404 p. (Themes in European expansion, exploration and the impact of empire, v.2 ; Garland reference library of social science, v. 109). **DE37**

Covers "British policy in the Middle East from 1900 to 1921, beginning roughly with the Baghdad Railway Concession to the Germans, and ending with the Cairo Conference which set out the main features of Britain's post-war policy in the area."—*Pref.* Cites monographs, articles, and book reviews (mainly post-1950 publications) in topical arrangement. Annotations; cross references; index.

Z3014.R44O47

Ponko, Vincent. Britain in the Middle East, 1921–1956 : an annotated bibliography. N.Y. : Garland, 1990. 513 p. (Themes in European expansion, v. 9 ; Garland reference library of social science, v. 357). **DE38**

Lists publications "dealing in some way with the British presence in the Middle East from about 1921 to the period of the 1956 Suez Canal crisis."—*Pref.* The Middle East is defined as encompassing Iran, Iraq, Jordan, Israel, Egypt, and the Arabian peninsula. Topical arrangement of books and documents, with extensive annotations and cross-references. There is a separate list of doctoral dissertations accepted in the U.S., 1980–87 (in no order), and an appendix of periodical articles, 1980–88, arranged by year of publication; entries in these sections are not included in the author index.   Z3014.R44P66

Silverburg, Sanford R. Middle East bibliography. Metuchen, N.J. : Scarecrow, 1992. 564 p. (The Scarecrow area bibliographies, 1). **DE39**

"Geographic coverage is a triangle from Egypt to Iran to Turkey."—*Pref.* Treats books only, primarily in English, with a minimum number of works in other languages. Concentrates upon works published after 1980. Cites 4,435 titles. Subject arrangement; author index.

Z3013.S54

————————— United States foreign policy and the Middle East/North Africa : a bibliography of twentieth-century research / Sanford R. Silverburg, Bernard Reich. N.Y. : Garland, 1990. 407 p. (Garland reference library of social science, v. 570). **DE40**

Concentrates on English-language books, essays, articles, dissertations, master's essays, NTIS reports, and government documents that treat the relationship between the U.S. and the Middle East and North Africa (defined as from Turkey and Iran to South Yemen and Morocco). 3,676 numbered items, arranged alphabetically by author, with a subject index.   Z3515.S55

Current

Bibliographic guide to Middle Eastern studies. 1990– . Boston, Mass. : G.K. Hall & Co., c1991– . Annual.   **DE41**

"An interdisciplinary subject bibliography that covers all fields of Middle Eastern Studies."—*Introd.* Based on holdings of the New York Public Library and the Library of Congress. Cites items in Arabic, Hebrew, Persian, and Turkish published in the Middle East, as well as works published elsewhere dealing with the Middle East.   Z3013.B48

Dissertations

Dix ans de recherche universitaire française sur le monde arabe et islamique de 1968–69 à 1979. Paris : publié avec le concours du ministère [sic] de l'Education Nationale et du ministère [sic] des Relations Extérieures [par] Editions Recherche sur les Civilisations, 1982. 438 p.   **DE42**

Almost 6,000 dissertations accepted by French universities concerning the Islamic world are topically arranged within broad geographic divisions: e.g., Monde arabe contemporain, Maghreb contemporain, Monde turc. Index of thesis advisors only. Brief bibliography and directory of major sources in France.   Z3013.D59

Saliba, M. Arab Gulf states : doctoral dissertations & graduate theses in English, French & German (1881–1981). [Antélias, Lebanon] : M. Saliba, 1983. 171 p. (Middle East bibliographical serials, 1).   **DE43**

Aims "to identify all dissertations and theses written in English, French, and German in fields of history, geography, politics, economics, law, social studies, arts, sciences, etc. and [which] are directly concerned with the following states: Iraq, Saudi Arabia, Kuwait, United Arab Emirates, Bahrain, Oman, Qatar, North and South Yemen."—*Introd.* Arranged alphabetically by country, with author and subject indexes.   Z3026.S235

Sluglett, Peter. Theses on Islam, the Middle East and Northwest Africa, 1880–1978, accepted by universities in the United Kingdom and Ireland. London : Mansell, 1983. 147 p.   **DE44**

A classed listing of more than 3,000 theses at both the master's and doctoral level. Sections on Islamic studies, Islam outside the Middle East and Northwest Africa, Arabic studies, and Christianity in the Middle East and North Africa precede the geographical sections (including Cyprus and Malta) with their topical subdivisions. Author index.   Z3013.S57

Translations

Anderson, Margaret. Arabic materials in English translation : a bibliography of works from the pre-Islamic period to 1977. Boston : G. K. Hall, [1980]. 249 p.   **DE45**

A classed listing with sections for Islamic studies, philosophy, music, history of science, history, geography, social sciences, and Arabic literature. Brief descriptive annotations for many items. Indexed.

Z3014.L56A52

Library catalogs

Library of Congress. Library of Congress Office, Cairo. Accessions list, Middle East. v. 12, no. 7 (1974)– . [Cairo] : Library of Congress Office, Cairo. Bimonthly, 1982– . **DE46**

Frequency varies.

Vol. 1–12, no. 5/6 (Jan. 1963–May/June 1974) available on microfiche from the Library of Congress Office, New Delhi.

Also issued in microfiche, v. 20– (Wash. : Supt. of Docs.).

Lists publications, both commercial and government, acquired by the Office from any of the Arab world countries (except Djibouti, Somalia and Sudan which are covered in the Eastern Africa list, DD85), for distribution to participants in the PL480 program. Alphabetical arrangement until 1983; now a country listing with separate lists of monographs and serials. Cumulative serials list issued annually in the July/Aug. number. Beginning Sep. 1982, availability of selected items on microfiche through Library of Congress is noted.

————. ————. *Annual index.* v. 17 (1979)– . ([Cairo] : Library of Congress Office, Cairo). Annual.

Prior to 1979, the annual index was publ. in the Dec. issue of *Accessions list, Middle East.*   Z3013.U54

Weber, Shirley Howard. Voyages and travels in Greece, the Near East and adjacent regions made previous to the year 1801 : being a part of a larger catalogue of works on geography, cartography, voyages and travels, in the Gennadius Library in Athens. Princeton, N.J. : Amer. School of Classical Studies at Athens, 1953. 208 p. (Catalogues of the Gennadius Library, II).   **DE47**

The Gennadius Library is a rich and unique collection of more than 55,000 books, pictures, and maps relating to Greece, the Balkans, and the Near East from medieval to modern times. This is a companion to the Weber's *Voyages and travels in the Near East made during the XIX century* (DE48), covering from the first century to 1801. Lists travel accounts, voyages, descriptive and topographic works, and guide books of Greek Orthodox pilgrims; appendix of works which are mainly pictorial. Indexed.   Z6016.L6W4

———————— Voyages and travels in the Near East made during the XIX century : being a part of a larger catalogue of works on geography, cartography, voyages, and travels, in the Gennadius Library in Athens. Princeton, N.J. : Amer. School of Classical Studies at Athens, 1952. 252 p. (Catalogues of the Gennadius Library, I).   **DE48**

Contains 1,206 annotated titles, representing only a portion of the material on geography and travel in the Library. The titles are entered by date of publication; a general index and a name index of travelers and authors are given at the end of the volume.

The author's companion volume: *Voyages and travels in Greece, the Near East and adjacent regions made previous to the year 1801* (DE47).   Z3013.W4

Library resources

Dorr, Steven R. Scholars' guide to Washington, D.C. for Middle Eastern studies : Egypt, Sudan, Jordan, Lebanon, Syria, Iraq, the Arabian peninsula, Israel, Turkey, Iran. Wash. : Smithsonian Inst. Pr., 1981. 540 p. (Scholars' guide to Washington, D.C., no. 7).   **DE49**

Another in the series of guides sponsored by the Woodrow Wilson International Center for Scholars. Lists and describes collections, research facilities, services, etc., available in libraries, archives, museums, research centers, and organizations concerned with the Middle East in the Washington, D.C. area.   Z3013.6.D67

Matthews, Noel. A guide to manuscripts and documents in the British Isles relating to the Middle East and North Africa / Noel Matthews, M. Doreen Wainwright; ed. by J. D. Pearson. Oxford : Oxford Univ. Pr., 1980. 482 p.   **DE50**

A guide to collections of Western-language manuscripts and documents in United Kingdom repositories. "The area covered here encompasses the Arab countries of the Middle East and North Africa, Israel, Cyprus, Turkey, Iran and certain regions of the Caucasus, Central Asia and the Crimea."—*Pref.* Briefly describes the collections and lists important documents in each. Detailed index.

A companion to the volumes surveying British manuscript collections relating to South and South East Asia (DE13), Africa (new ed., DD39), and the Far East (DE105).   CD1048.N4M37

Netton, Ian Richard. Middle East materials in United Kingdom and Irish libraries : a directory. London : Libr. Assoc., publ. in assoc. with the Centre for Arab Gulf Studies, Univ. of Exeter, [1983]. 136 p.   **DE51**

"A MELCOM [Middle East Libraries Committee] guide to libraries and other institutions in Britain and Ireland with Islamic and Middle Eastern books and materials."—*t.p.*

Indicates hours of opening, terms of access, etc., as well as providing brief descriptions of holdings. Bibliography of catalogs and directories cited in the text; index.   Z3013.6.N47

Indexes; Abstract journals

The Middle East : abstracts and index. v. 1, no. 1 (Mar. 1978)– . Pittsburgh : Northumberland Pr., 1978– . Quarterly.   **DE52**

Amy C. Lowenstein, ed.

Volumes for Mar./Sep. 1978 publ. by the Library Information and Research Service.

Offers citations, with abstracts, of English-language materials in the humanities and social sciences relating to countries of the Middle East. A section of general materials applicable to the entire area is followed by one on the Arab-Israeli conflict and another on the Arab World; then follow sections on individual countries. Within sections the materials are grouped by type: journal articles (drawn from a wide range of periodicals), editorials, government documents, interviews, NTIS documents, speeches and statements, doctoral dissertations, reprints, statistics, books and reviews. Each issue has author and subject indexes which cumulate annually in the December issue.

Mideast file. v. 1, no. 1 (Mar. 1982)– . Oxford, Eng. ; [Medford], N.J. : Learned Information, 1982– . Quarterly.   **DE53**

Issued by the Shiloah Center, Dept. of Middle Eastern and African History, Tel-Aviv Univ.

An index to books, book reviews, scholarly periodical articles, important newspaper articles, government publications, and research reports from institutions and corporations. Covers the Mideast between Iran and Libya, Turkey and Sudan; regional or country arrangement; emphasis on social sciences and religion. Author and subject indexes.   DS42.4.M53

Encyclopedias

The Cambridge encyclopedia of the Middle East and North Africa / executive ed., Trevor Mostyn ; advisory ed., Albert Hourani. Cambridge ; N. Y. : Cambridge Univ. Pr., 1988. 504 p. : ill. (some col.).   **DE54**

Companion to *Cambridge atlas of the Middle East and North Africa* (DE68).

Offers an overview of various subject areas for the region: e.g., history, quick survey by major periods; culture, including religion, literature, arts, music, Islamic science, Islamic law; economics, with statistics as current as 1986. Pt. 5 is a survey of individual countries, Mauritania to Afghanistan to Somalia. The volume ends with "peoples without a country," e.g., Kurds, Armenians, Palestinians. Suggestions for further reading. Subject index.   DS44.C37

Gresh, Alain. An A to Z of the Middle East / Alain Gresh and Dominique Vidal; transl. by Bob Cumming. London : Biddles Ltd. ; Atlantic Highlands, N.J. : Zed Books, 1990. 261 p., [3] p. of plates : ill., maps.   **DE55**

Translation and updating of *Les cent portes du Proche-orient* (Paris : Autrement, 1986).

Covers countries, people, events, movements, and problems relating to the Middle East. 112 alphabetically arranged entries, generally concentrating on the last half of the 20th century, average two pages in length, and combine description with analysis. Includes a chronology of events (through Iraq's invasion of Kuwait, August 2, 1990), maps, tables, and 13 appendixes of important documents (e.g., The Balfour Declaration, Camp David Framework). Bibliography; personal name index.

§ Less comprehensive than Lawrence Ziring's *The Middle East : a political dictionary* (CJ420), Yaacov Shimoni's *Political dictionary of the Arab World* (CJ424), or *Political dictionary of the State of Israel*, ed. by Susan H. Rolef (CJ439).   DS43.G7413

Shavit, David. The United States in the Middle East : a historical dictionary. N.Y. : Greenwood, 1988. 441 p.   **DE56**

Provides "information about persons, institutions, and events that affected the relationships between the United States and the Middle East" (*Pref.*), Morocco to Afghanistan. Most entries are single paragraphs, followed by bibliographic references. Appendix: Chiefs of American diplomatic missions in the Middle East, 1831–1986.

§ A companion to Shavit's *The United States in Africa* (DD96) and *The United States in Asia* (DE15).　　DS63.2.U5S384

Ziring, Lawrence. The Middle East : a political dictionary. Santa Barbara, Calif. : ABC-Clio, c1992. 401 p.　　**DE57**
　　For annotation, *see* CJ420.　　DS61.Z58

Handbooks

Bacharach, Jere L. A Middle East studies handbook. Seattle : Univ. of Washington Pr., [1984]. 160 p. : ill., maps.　　**DE58**
　　1st ed., 1974 (rev. 1976), entitled *A Near East studies handbook.*
　　A useful handbook which aims to bring together pertinent information for the beginner. Includes discussion of problems of converting dates and of transliteration, lists of standard abbreviations for periodicals and reference works, tables of dynasties, rulers, etc. Lengthy chronology; historical atlas. Indexed.　　DS61.B3

Izady, Mehrdad R. The Kurds : a concise handbook. Wash. : Crane Russak, c1992. 268 p. : ill., maps.　　**DE59**
　　In ten broad topical section, further divided in subsections. Each subsection concludes with a bibliography. No index.
　　　　　　　　　　DS59.K86I93 1992

The Middle East / ed. by Michael Adams. N.Y. : Facts on File, 1987. 865 p. : maps.　　**DE60**
　　At head of title: *Handbooks to the modern world.*
　　An overview by 41 English- and American-trained scholars giving basic information on each country, 34 pages of comparative statistics, and essays on the region (e.g., Zionism and the Arab question, Foreign aid and investment, Archaeology). North Africa is not included except for Libya. Subject index.　　DS44.H35

Middle East contemporary survey. 1976/77– . N.Y. : Holmes & Meier, 1978– . Annual.　　**DE61**
　　Colin Legum, ed.
　　Each annual volume comprises a series of essays by scholars from the United States, Great Britain, and Israel "which study developments relating to internal and external issues, both regionally and internationally," (e.g., The Red Sea in the Arab/African context, The Soviet bloc and the Middle East) followed by "a country-by-country survey of each of the Middle East entities excluding the three North African states of Tunisia, Algeria and Morocco."—*Pref.* Maps, tables, charts. Indexed.　　DS62.8.M53

Chronologies

Mostyn, Trevor. Major political events in Iran, Iraq, and the Arabian Peninsula, 1945–1990. N.Y. : Facts on File, c1991. 308 p. : maps.　　**DE62**
　　Serves as an introduction to politics in the Arab world (Iran, Iraq, Saudi Arabia, Kuwait, Qatar, Bahrain, the United Arab Emirates, Oman, and Yemen). The major portion of the work is a descriptive chronology of events from 1945 to the beginning of the 1991 Gulf War. Also contains biographical sketches, glossary, brief bibliography, and maps. Subject index.　　DS326.M64

Rahman, H. U. A chronology of Islamic history, 570–1000 CE. Boston : G.K. Hall, [1989]. 181 p., [6] p. of plates : ill.
　　　　　　　　　　DE63
　　From the birth of the Prophet to the expeditions of Mahmud of Ghazna into India. Short articles describe the events, the people involved, and the exact locations. Index by name of person or place.
　　　　　　　　　　DS38.3.R35

Sourcebooks

Hurewitz, Jacob Coleman. The Middle East and North Africa in world politics : a documentary record. 2nd ed., rev. & enl. New Haven, Conn. : Yale Univ. Pr., 1975–79. 2 v.　**DE64**
　　1st ed., 1956, had title: *Diplomacy in the Near and Middle East.*
　　Contents: v.1, European expansion, 1535–1914; v.2, British-French supremacy, 1914–1945.
　　A collection of English translations of important documents relating to Western European and American contacts with countries of the Middle East—Afghanistan to non-Soviet southwest Asia—and North Africa. Each document is preceded by a short essay indicating its importance. Lengthy bibliography at the end of v. 1.　　DS42.H87

The Middle East, 1914–1979 / T. G. Fraser, comp. London : E. Arnold ; N.Y. : St. Martin's, 1980. 205 p. : maps.　　**DE65**
　　A selection of documents (most of them previously unpublished) on three major areas: the conflict between Arab nationalism and Zionism; the role of the "Great Powers" and the United States; the growth of the oil industry. Section notes place documents in context. Indexed.
　　　　　　　　　　DS119.7.M4717

Biography

Shimoni, Yaacov. The biographical dictionary of the Middle East. N.Y. : Facts on File, c1991. 255 p. : ill., maps.　　**DE66**
　　"Provides 500 biographies of personalities who have played a role in the present and recent past of the Middle East."—*Foreword.* Does not provide sources of biographical data.　　DS62.4.S53

Atlases

Beek, Martinus Adrianus. Atlas of Mesopotamia : a survey of the history and civilisation of Mesopotamia from the Stone Age to the fall of Babylon / Tr. by D. R. Welsh; ed. by H. H. Rowley. London : Nelson, 1962. 164 p. : ill., 22 maps in color ; 36cm.　　**DE67**
　　For annotation, *see* DA86.　　G2251.E6B42

The Cambridge atlas of the Middle East and North Africa / [ed. by] Gerald Blake, John Dewdney, Jonathan Mitchell. Cambridge ; N.Y. : Cambridge Univ. Pr., 1987. 124 p. : maps in color ; 26 x 36 cm.　　**DE68**
　　Companion to *Cambridge encyclopedia of the Middle East and North Africa* (DE54).
　　A topical presentation of 58 maps with text, tables, and some statistics (e.g., Soils, Irrigation, Ottoman Empire to 1556, World oil movements). Each chapter ends with a list of key references. Most maps treat the whole region. No indexes.　　G2205.C3

An historical atlas of Islam / ed. by William C. Brice under the patronage of The encyclopaedia of Islam. Leiden : Brill, 1981. 71 p. : maps.　　**DE69**
　　Maps are arranged chronologically within broad regional divisions (e.g., Near and Middle East; Anatolia and the Balkans). Covers down to the time of World War I. Index of place-names and ethnics (including alternate forms of the names); astronomical index; economic index.
　　A review in *TLS* 10 (Sep. 1982): 970, asserts that "its patchy coverage reflects work in progress rather than a balanced survey of Islamic history" and points out numerous inconsistencies and shortcomings.
　　　　　　　　　　G1786.S1H6

Karta (Firm). Atlas of the Middle East / ed. by Moshe Brawer ; prepared by Carta, Jerusalem. N.Y. : Macmillan ; London : Collier Macmillan, c1988. 140 p. : maps in color ; 29 cm.
　　　　　　　　　　DE70

Companion to *Political dictionary of the Arab world* (CJ424) and *Political dictionary of the state of Israel* (CJ439).

Covers from Turkey to Iran to Sudan to Libya. Arranged in 2 parts: (1) The region (with maps, narrative, and tables on geology, climate, flora and fauna, population, oil, etc.), (2) The countries, which treats political, cultural, and historic life of each nation. Current in its coverage to 1988. Bibliography and list of further readings. Index to geographical names. G2205.K33

Robinson, Francis. Atlas of the Islamic world since 1500. N.Y. : Facts on File ; Oxford : Phaidon, [c1982]. 238 p. : ill., maps ; 31cm. **DE71**

Using a combination of text, maps, and illustrations, aims "to demonstrate how Islamic society has been maintained, how it has been transmitted from generation to generation, and how it has been spread throughout the world."—*Pref.* Illustrations tend to outnumber the maps. Bibliography; gazetteer; index. DS35.6.R6

Arab-Israeli conflict

Bibliography

The Arab-Israeli conflict 1945–1971 : a bibliography / John Sherman, gen. ed. N.Y. : Garland, 1978. 419 p. (Garland reference library of social science, v.52). **DE72**

Lists books, pamphlets, government documents, and articles in English chronologically by date of publication. Some annotations; translations into other languages are noted. Author and subject indexes. Z3479.R4A7

DeVore, Ronald M. The Arab-Israeli conflict : a historical, political, social, and military bibliography. Santa Barbara, Calif. : Clio Books, [1976]. 273 p. **DE73**

Directed toward the undergraduate student, the bibliography concentrates almost exclusively on important English-language books and articles published before 1974. "An attempt was made to include works which present a diversity of views on a given subject in order to give the user a broad perspective on the evolution of the conflict."—*Note.* Detailed subject arrangement with name index. Z3479.R4D48

Atlases

Gilbert, Martin. The Arab-Israeli conflict : its history in maps. 5th ed. London : Weidenfeld & Nicolson, 1992. 136 p. : maps ; 26 cm. **DE74**

1st ed., 1974.

Traces "the history of Arab-Jewish conflict from the turn of the century to the present day. The majority of the maps depict wars, conflict and violence."—*Pref.* 136 black-and-white maps. No index. G2206.S1G5

Asia, Central

Lee, Don Y. An annotated bibliography on inner Asia : premodern. Bloomington, Ind. : Eastern Pr., 1983. 183p. **DE75**

In two parts: (1) Northern Asia; (2) Inner Asia and Tibet; each section is subdivided for prehistorical and historical eras. Lists books and articles in any language. Useful despite the lack of a subject approach. Z3126.L44

Asia, South

Bibliography

Case, Margaret H. South Asian history, 1750–1950 : a guide to periodicals, dissertations and newspapers. Princeton, N.J. : Princeton Univ. Pr., 1968. 561 p. **DE76**

A selective, annotated bibliography of periodical articles, together with a list of about 650 doctoral dissertations accepted through 1965 and a list of newspapers (with locations) published in South Asia since 1800. Well indexed. Z3185.C3

Center for Research Libraries. SAMP catalog. 1980 cumulative ed. Chicago, [1980]. 246 p. **DE77**

1st ed., 1974; suppl., 1976–78.

"The South Asia Microform Project (SAMP) exists to make available in microform [to member libraries] research materials related to the study of South Asia. This catalog represents all titles acquired by SAMP through the early part of 1979."—*Introd.* Items are listed alphabetically by main entry; index is mainly geographic. Includes relevant holdings from the ARL Foreign Newspaper Microform Project. Z3499.C45

Kozicki, Richard J. International relations of South Asia, 1947–1980. Detroit : Gale, [1981]. 166 p. (International relations information guide series, v.10). **DE78**

A selective, annotated bibliography of English-language books, pamphlets, essays, articles, and government publications on India, Pakistan, Bangladesh, Sri Lanka, Nepal, Sikkim, Bhutan, Afghanistan, but excluding Burma. Topical arrangement; author index. Z3185.K69

Library of Congress. Library of Congress Office, New Delhi. Accessions list, South Asia. v. 1, no.1 (Jan. 1981)– . New Delhi : The Office, 1981– . Monthly. **DE79**

Also issued in microfiche to depository libraries (Superintendent of Documents classification: LC1.30/10-3).

Represents a merger of the accessions lists for India (1962–79), Pakistan (1962–79), Bangladesh (1972–79), Sri Lanka (1973–79), Nepal (1966–79), and Afghanistan (1978–79); those lists, in turn, might be considered a continuation of the *Southern Asia accessions list* (1952–60) issued by the Orientalia Division of the Library of Congress.

Lists government and commercial publications of the countries noted above and adds coverage for Bhutan and Maldives. Country listing subdivided for monographs, serials, and special materials. Annual cumulation; cumulative author, title, and subject indexes. A serials supplement is published irregularly, cumulating new titles and changes. Beginning Jan. 1982, availability of selected items on microfiche through Library of Congress is noted. Z3185.L52

Patterson, Maureen L. P. South Asian civilisations : a bibliographic synthesis. Chicago : Univ. of Chicago Pr., [1981]. 853 p. **DE80**

Lists books, theses, and long review articles on South Asia "between the Himalayas and the Indian Ocean, and adjacent islands" (*Introd.*) in a finely classified arrangement. About 28,000 entries; based on the collection at the University of Chicago. Outline of headings used; author and keyword indexes. Z3185.P37

South Asian bibliography / comp. and ed. by the South Asia Library Group ; gen. ed., J. D. Pearson. Sussex, Eng. : Harvester Pr. ; Atlantic Highlands, N.J. : Humanities Pr., 1979. 381 p. **DE81**

An important guide which is the "product of a series of seminars organized by the South Asia Library Group and held over a period of several years with the aim of compiling a guide to works of reference …."—*Pref.* Offers essays describing archives and manuscript collections of South Asian materials in various countries, together with bibliographies of theses. A second section deals with reference works for published sources, including maps, periodicals and newspapers. Indexed.   Z3185.S65

Library resources

Directory of South Asian library resources in the UK and the Republic of Ireland / ed. by S. Gunasingam. [London] : South Asia Library Group, 1988. 182 p.   **DE82**

Based on replies to a questionnaire. Gives operating details of each library (hours, address, staff members, admission, etc.), relevant catalogs, and an overview of the South Asian material. Geographic arrangement. Index of libraries; index to language collections.

DS336.D58

India Office Library and Records. A general guide to the India Office Records / Martin Moir. [London] : British Library, 1988. 331 p. : ill.   **DE83**

Now a part of the British Library, the collections of the India Office (formerly the East India Company) were until recently part of the Foreign and Commonwealth Office. This work presents information on the administrative background of the Office followed by a descriptive inventory of the archives. Does not totally supersede William Foster's *Guide to the India Office Records 1600–1858* (London : Eyre and Spottiswoode, 1919) for the earlier period. Indexed.

CD1052.I4I53

Low, Donald Anthony. Government archives in South Asia : a guide to national and state archives in Ceylon, India and Pakistan / Donald Anthony Low, J. C. Iltis, M. D. Wainwright. [London] : Cambridge Univ. Pr., 1969. 355 p.   **DE84**

Information on each archive generally includes name, address, and officer in charge, followed by "a note about the latest available information on rules of access; a short historical account of the territory whose archives are described; a short account of the history of its archival administration; a note about the nature and extent of the holdings the archives possess; and a brief guide to any published aids to reference."—*Pref.*   CD2081.L6

Rahim, Enayetur. Scholars' guide to Washington, D.C. for South Asian studies : Afghanistan, Bangladesh, Bhutan, India, Maldives, Nepal, Pakistan, Sri Lanka. Wash. : Smithsonian Inst. Pr., 1981. 438 p. (Scholars' guide to Washington, D.C., no. 8).   **DE85**

Prepared for the Woodrow Wilson International Center for Scholars.

Describes relevant scholarly resources available in libraries, archives and manuscript repositories, museums, galleries, map collections, film collections and data banks, together with information on organizations, associations, and agencies which may be helpful to the scholar. Indexed.   Z3185.R34

Singh, Amar Kaur Jasbir. A guide to source materials in the India Office Library and Records for the history of Tibet, Sikkim and Bhutan 1765–1950. [London] : British Library, 1988. 187 p.   **DE86**

Primarily a guide to archives (both official and private) held in the India Office, but also offers information on the Office's maps, drawings, and printed books. Brief notes on other archival sources; index by topic.   Z6005.H6A

South Asian library resources in North America : a survey prep. for the Boston Conference, 1974 / ed. by Maureen L. P. Patterson. Zug, Switz. : Inter Documentation, 1975. 23, 223 p. (Bibliotheca Asiatica, 12).   **DE87**

Sponsored by the Committee on South Asian Libraries and Documentation of the Association for Asian Studies.

An inventory based on responses to questionnaires. For each institution indicates teaching and research interests, description of relevant library holdings, access, and cooperative arrangements.   Z3185.B67

South Asian studies : papers presented at a colloquium, 24–26 April 1985 / ed. by Albertine Gaur. London ; Wolfeboro, N.H. : British Library, 1986. 327 p. (British Library occasional papers, 7).   **DE88**

Sessions dealt with resources for the study of South Asia within the U.K., and projects, facilities, and bibliographical research around the world. Brief descriptions of resources in Czechoslovakia, Denmark, France, Germany, Italy, the Netherlands, and Poland.

Z3185.S69

University of Cambridge. Centre for South Asian Studies. Cambridge South Asian archive : records of the British period in South Asia relating to India, Pakistan, Ceylon, Burma, Nepal and Afghanistan held in the Centre / Mary Thatcher, comp. and ed. [London] : Mansell, 1973. 346 p.   **DE89**

Describes "primary source material [such] as papers, letters, and photographs, written or collected by those who had served and lived in South Asia, which were capable of throwing light on economic, social and political conditions during the period of British rule in the former Indian Empire and Ceylon."—*Introd.* Also includes tapes, records, etc. Arranged by name of collection, with chronological, subject, and donor indexes.   Z6616.A2C35

Encyclopedias

The Cambridge encyclopedia of India, Pakistan, Bangladesh, Sri Lanka, Nepal, Bhutan, and the Maldives / ed., Francis Robinson. Cambridge ; N.Y. : Cambridge Univ. Pr., [1989]. 520 p. : ill.   **DE90**

A heavily illustrated encyclopedia intended for the general reader, and topically arranged under broad headings: Land; Peoples; History to independence; Politics; Foreign relations; Economics; Religion; Societies; Culture. Statistics are current to about 1983, although references in the bibliographies are as recent as 1986–87. Topical index.

DS334.9..C36

Atlases

A historical atlas of South Asia / ed. by Joseph E. Schwartzberg ; with the collaboration of Shiva G. Bajpai ... [et al.] ; final map drafts by the American Geographical Society of New York ; principal sponsors, Charles Lesley Ames ... [et al.]. 2nd impression, with additional material. N.Y. ; Oxford : Oxford Univ. Pr., 1992. 376 p. : ill., maps in color ; 41 cm. (Association for Asian Studies. Reference series, no. 2).   **DE91**

1st ed., 1978.

Provides "a comprehensive cartographic record of the history of South Asia from the Old Stone Age to the present day. Five principal parts: the maps in the body of the work, the text, the bibliography, the index, and the inserts."—*Introd.* This impression updates certain portions of the text summarizing research since the original edition and expands the bibliography. Photographs in the text illustrate area utilization and landscape. The inserts consist of two overlay maps and three chronological charts in a pocket.   G2261.S1H5

Asia, Southeast

The Cambridge history of Southeast Asia / ed. by Nicholas Tarling. Cambridge, U.K. : N.Y. : Cambridge Univ. Pr., 1992. 2 v. : ill., maps.   **DE92**

Contents: v. 1, From early times to c.1800; v. 2, The nineteenth and twentieth centuries.   DS525.T37

Guides

Johnson, Donald Clay. A guide to reference materials on Southeast Asia : based on the collections in the Yale and Cornell University Libraries. New Haven, Conn. : Yale Univ. Pr., 1970. 160 p. (Yale Southeast Asia studies, 6). **DE93**

A classed bibliography of reference sources for all aspects of Southeast Asia studies. No annotations. Author index. Z3221.J63

Bibliography

ASEAN : a bibliography / project co-ordinator, Patricia Lim ; contributors, IDE, Tokyo … [et al.]. Singapore : Institute of Southeast Asian Studies, 1984. 487 p. **DE94**

Based on the collection at the Institute of Southeast Asian Studies, this basic bibliography lists 6,300 books, articles, theses, official publications, conference papers, press releases, and radio monitoring reports with some archival materials and unpublished seminar and conference reports. All languages are represented, with the focus more on the region of Southeast Asia than on individual countries. Employs a topical arrangement with author index.

§ *ASEAN : a bibliography, 1981–85* (project co-ordinator, Patricia Lim Pui Huen ; ed. by Ajita Thuraisingham, with contributions from Violeta V. Encarnacion … [et al.]) adds an additional 6,397 items, follows the same arrangement, and gathers the same type of material from the Library of the Institute. Z3221.A72

Burns, Richard Dean. The wars in Vietnam, Cambodia and Laos, 1945–1982 : a bibliographic guide / Richard Dean Burns and Milton Leitenberg. Santa Barbara, Calif. : ABC-Clio, 1984. 290 p. (War/peace bibliography series, 18). **DE95**

Updates the same compilers' *Vietnam conflict* (Santa Barbara : ABC-Clio, 1973), but does not include every item listed in that work. Aims to provide a selected guide to the "important contemporary and retrospective books, dissertations, research papers and essays" *(p.3)*, including periodical articles and some government documents. Topical arrangement, with introductory notes for each chapter. Author index; detailed table of contents, but no subject index. Z3228.V5B87

Cordier, Henri. Bibliotheca indosinica : dictionnaire bibliographique des ouvrages relatifs à la péninsule Indochinoise. Paris : Impr. Nationale, Leroux, 1912–15. 4 v. (École Française d'Extrême-Orient. Publications., v. 15–17). **DE96**

Repr.: N.Y. : B. Franklin, 1967 (includes index; 5 v. in 3).

An extensive, classified bibliography of materials in Western languages on the peninsula formerly called Indochina.

Index, by M.A. Roland-Cabaton (Paris : G. van Oest, 1932. 309 p. [Publications de l'École Française d'Extrême-Orient, v. 18). Contains both author and subject indexes. Z3221.C78

Iwasaki, Ikuo. Japan and Southeast Asia : a bibliography of historical, economic and political relations. [Tokyo] : Library Institute of Developing Economies, 1983. 176p. **DE97**

For annotation, *see* DE200. DS525.9.J3I93

Library of Congress. Library of Congress Office, Jakarta. Accessions list, Southeast Asia. v. 1, no. 1–3 (Jan./Mar. 1975)– . Jakarta, Indonesia : Library of Congress Office, Jakarta. Bimonthly. **DE98**

Frequency varies; bimonthly since Jan./Apr. 1982.

Supersedes *Accessions list, Indonesia, Malaysia, Singapore and Brunei*, 1964–74.

Also issued in microfiche, v. 13– (Wash. : Supt. of Docs.).

Lists commercial and government publications in country arrangement subdivided for monographs and serials. Annual author/title index. Beginning Sep. 1979, coverage includes Burma, Laos, and Thailand as well as Indonesia, Malaysia, Singapore and Brunei. From Apr. 1978 availability of selected items on microfiche through the Library of Congress is noted.

Separate cumulative lists of serials issued irregularly as supplements: Burma, Thailand, and Laos (New Delhi Office); Malaysia, Singapore, and Brunei (Jakarta Office); Indonesia (Jakarta Office). Z3221.U54

Lim, Patricia Pui Huen. The Malay world of Southeast Asia : a select cultural bibliography. Singapore : Programme on the Cultural Heritage of Southeast Asia, Institute of Southeast Asian Studies, c1986. 456 p. **DE99**

The Malay world comprises Brunei, Indonesia, Singapore, Thailand, Malaysia, and the Philippines. Topical arrangement, emphasizing culture (e.g., history, anthropology, literature, sociology, political science), subdivided by geographical area or time period. Lists 5,327 books, articles and dissertations, most published mid-1960s to 1983, with a few as late as 1986. Author index. Z3221.L547

Those who were there : eyewitness accounts of the war in Southeast Asia, 1956–1975 & aftermath; annotated bibliography of books, articles & topic-related magazines, covering writings both factual & imaginative. [Paradise, Calif. : DustBooks, 1984]. 297 p. **DE100**

Merritt Clifton, coordinating ed.

Includes "veterans of all military and guerilla forces active or stationed in Vietnam, Laos, Cambodia, and Thailand; civilians of these nations; journalists who actually witnessed combat or traveled with military units; & any others … whose writings describe or reflect their first-hand experience."—*Introd.* Arranged by genre; not indexed. Z3228.V5T46

Library resources

Mayerchak, Patrick M. Scholars' guide to Washington, D.C. for Southeast Asian studies : Brunei, Burma, Cambodia, Indonesia, Laos, Malaysia, Philippines, Singapore, Thailand, Vietnam. Wash. : Smithsonian Inst. Pr., 1983. 411 p. (Scholar's guide to Washington, D.C., no. 9). **DE101**

Sponsored by the Woodrow Wilson International Center for Scholars.

More than 400 collections, organizations, and agencies and their services are described, giving name, address, hours of opening, collection strengths, unique features. Appendixes list Vietnam War archives, bookstores, libraries by size of collection. Indexes by subject strength, subject, and name. Z3221.M37

Indexes

Johnson, Donald Clay. Index to Southeast Asian journals, 1960–1974 : a guide to articles, book reviews, and composite works. Boston : G. K. Hall, [1977]. 811 p. **DE102**

Indexes articles and book reviews in 44 journals published 1960–74 which are "internationally oriented" and deal with several countries for a single discipline. The reviews were used to identify collections of essays, and some 120 of these "composite works" are indexed by subject. Author index.

A supplement covering 1975–79 was publ. 1982 (265 p.). Z3221.J64

Asia, East

Library resources

Kim, Hong N. Scholars' guide to Washington, D.C. for East Asian studies : China, Japan, Korea, and Mongolia. Wash. : Smithsonian Inst. Pr., 1979. 413 p. (Scholar's guide to Washington, D.C., no. 3). **DE103**

Third in the series of guides to scholarly resources in Washington, D.C., prepared under the auspices of the Woodrow Wilson International Center for Scholars. Describes collections of East Asian materials in libraries, archives, museums, etc., and gives information regarding governmental and non-governmental organizations of interest to researchers in this field. Indexed.   Z3001.K49

Lee, Thomas H. A guide to East Asian collections in North America. N.Y. : Greenwood, c1992. 158 p. (Bibliographies and indexes in world history, no. 25).   **DE104**
For annotation, *see* AK108.   Z3001.L4

Matthews, Noel. A guide to manuscripts and documents in the British Isles relating to the Far East / Noel Matthews and M. Doreen Wainwright. [London] : Oxford Univ. Pr. for the School of Oriental and African Studies, 1977. 182 p.   **DE105**
A survey of English, Welsh, Scots, and Irish (both Northern Ireland and the Republic) depositories, including some papers in private custody.   CD1048.A77M37

Yang, Teresa S. East Asian resources in American libraries / Teresa S. Yang, Thomas C. Kuo, Frank Joseph Shulman. N.Y. : Paragon Book Gallery, 1977. 143 p.   **DE106**
An outgrowth of Teresa Yang and Winston L. Y. Yang's *Asian resources in American libraries* (N.Y. : Foreign Area Materials Center, Univ. of the State of New York, 1968), but concentrating on East Asia rather than sources relating to the whole of Asia.

Contains two essays, "American library resources on East Asia," by T. S. Yang, and "East Asian collections in American libraries," by T. C. Kuo; a bibliographical guide to East Asian resources by F. J. Shulman; and a directory of East Asian collections in American libraries by T. S. Yang. The bibliographic guide concentrates on publications of the 1968–76 period—i.e., works appearing since publication of the earlier guide mentioned above. Index of authors and other main entries.   Z3001.Y35

ASIA (by country)

Afghanistan

Adamec, Ludwig W. A biographical dictionary of contemporary Afghanistan. Graz, Austria : Akademische Druck– u. Verlagsanstalt, 1987. 252 p. : ill.   **DE107**
Entries for some 1,600 persons, including government officials, politicians, clergy, military officers, writers, artists, and other professionals. Includes an index of government officers, with names and dates of tenure for government ministers and their deputies, as well as diplomats from Afghanistan and foreign representatives to Afghanistan, 1919–35.   DS371.A2A33

——————— Historical dictionary of Afghanistan. Metuchen, N.J. : Scarecrow, 1991. 376 p. : map. (Asian historical dictionaries, no. 5).   **DE108**
Provides a "concise reference work on Afghanistan, including major political events, important places, leading personalities, and significant aspects of culture, religion, and economy. Focus is on the political history of contemporary Afghanistan."—*User's notes.* Chronology; bibliography; series of family trees for the most notable families.   DS356.A27

Ball, Warwick. Catalogue des sites archéologiques d'Afghanistan = Archaeological gazetteer of Afghanistan. Paris : Éd. Recherches sur les Civilisations, 1982. 2 v. : ill., maps. (Synthèse, 8).   **DE109**
An extensive catalog and bibliography of all known sites and monuments within the modern day borders of Afghanistan, from the lower palaeolithic period to the Timurids. Includes published and unpublished materials. Main listing is by site name, giving location, date,

description, field work, collections of artifacts, and sources. The bibliography is arranged by broad topic and is fairly comprehensive. Atlas of site plans and of regional and period maps. Appendixes include listing of sites by date and by date of field work; listing of study collections; glossary. Subject index.   DS353.B35

Hanifi, M. Jamil. Annotated bibliography of Afghanistan. 4th ed. rev. New Haven, Conn. : Human Relations Area Files, 1982. 545 p.   **DE110**
1st ed., 1956.
A classified list of book and periodical items on physical, social, and humanistic aspects of the country. Author-title index. Includes material in Western languages and in Russian, Arabic, Persian, and Pushtu, published both within and outside Afghanistan. Cutoff date for this edition is Jan. 1982.   Z3016.H36

Jones, Schuyler. Afghanistan. Oxford ; Santa Barbara, Calif. : Clio Pr., c1992. 279 p. : map. (World bibliographical series, v. 135).   **DE111**
Presents 1,014 annotated entries, most in English, arranged by broad subject. Uneven coverage of disciplines. Author, title, and subject indexes.   Z3016.J66

McLachlan, Keith Stanley. A bibliography of Afghanistan : a working bibliography of materials on Afghanistan with special reference to economic and social change in the twentieth century / Keith Stanley McLachlan, William Whittaker. Wisbech, Cambridgeshire : Middle East & North African Studies Pr., 1983. 671 p.   **DE112**
Aims to present an "up-to-date classified list of western language materials ... for use by social scientists and other researchers with interests in the development of Afghanistan."—*Introd.* Includes books, government publications, dissertations, periodical articles, and maps. Indexes for personal names, organization names, and authors of dissertations. Cutoff date is 1979; brief addendum of 1979–81 (and a few 1982) publications.   Z3016.M4

Nursai, Ata M. Bibliographie zur Afghanistan-Literatur 1960–1987. Köln : Bundesinstitut für Ostwissenschaftliche und Internationale Studien, c1988. 360 p.   **DE113**
A topical arrangement of books, documents, essays, and occasional articles held by libraries in West Germany. Much of the material is in English but German, French, and Russian publications are also included. A 40-page author index was issued separately (1989).   Z3016.N87

Witherell, Julian W. Afghanistan : an American perspective : a guide to U.S. official documents and government-sponsored publications. Wash. : Library of Congress : For sale by U.S. Govt. Print. Off., 1986. 158 p. (Near East series, no. 3).   **DE114**
"Records a selection of publications on Afghanistan issued by or for the United States government from the time of initial official contacts between the two nations in the 1920s to 1984."—*Pref.* 631 items in classed arrangement; author/subject index.   Z3016.W58

Bahrain

Unwin, P. T. H. Bahrain. Santa Barbara, Calif. : Clio Pr., c1984. 265 p. (World bibliographical series, v. 49).   **DE115**
Books and some government documents in Western European languages (but primarily English) are arranged by broad topics. About 900 annotated entries; author, title, subject index.   Z3028.B34U58

Bangladesh

Satyaprakash. Bangla Desh : a select bibliography. Gurgaon : Indian Documentation Service, 1976. 218p. (International bibliography series, 3).　**DE116**

Lists some 2,500 titles (3,699 entries) of books, book reviews, journal articles and articles from the *Times of India* dealing with Bangladesh and published 1962–76. Arranged by author and topic.

Z3186.S27

Zafarullah, Habib Mohammad. Government and politics in Bangladesh : a bibliographical guide. Dacca, Bangladesh : Center for Administrative Studies, [1981]. 140 p.　**DE117**

Some 1,000 books, articles, official publications, and newspapers are listed by topic in three chronological sections: 1947–71, 1971, 1971–80. Author index.　Z3186.Z34

Bhutan

Dogra, R. C. Bhutan. Oxford ; Santa Barbara, Calif. : Clio Pr., c1990. 124 p. : maps. (World bibliographical series, v. 116).　**DE118**

403 annotated entries for works published in English since the British period. Chronology; glossary; author, title, and subject index.

Z3210.5.D64 DS491

Burma

Bernot, Denise. Bibliographie birmane, années 1950–1960. Paris : Éditions du Centre National de la Recherche Scientifique, 1968. Atlas ethno-linguistique. 3.série: Bibliographies.

DE119

Intended to supplement the Burma sections of Henri Cordier's *Bibliotheca indosinica* (DE96) and John Fee Embree and Lillian Ota Dotson's *Bibliography of the peoples and cultures of mainland Southeast Asia* (New Haven, Conn. : Yale Univ., 1950). Items are listed both in classed arrangement and alphabetically by author.

A continuation, following the arrangement of the main work and covering 1960–70, was publ. in facicles 1982–85. Contents: v. 1, Partie méthodique (2 fasc.); v. 2, Partie Alphabétique (fasc. 1–2, A-L). No more published.　Z3216.B4

Burma, a study guide. Wash. : Wilson Center Pr. ; Lanham, Md. : Distr. in North America by UPA Inc., c1988. 1 v.

DE120

Contents: Burma studies worldwide, ed. by Ronald A. Morse and Helen L. Loerke; Burma, a selective guide to scholarly resources, ed. by Anita Hibler and William P. Tuchrello; Burma, a selective guide to periodical literature (1970–1986), ed. by Anita Hibler and William P. Tuchrello.

Intended to be used with F. J. Shulman's *Burma: an annotated bibliographical guide to international dissertation research* (Lanham, Md. : Univ. Pr. of America ; Wash. : Wilson Center, c1986) and Patrick M. Mayerchak's *Scholar's guide to Washington D.C. for Southeast Asian studies* (DE101). The first section contains reports arranged by country summarizing research on Burma. The selective guide is an updating of an earlier publication, with 340 new entries, including 19th-century material and works in Burmese. The guide to periodical literature includes 1,618 citations arranged in alphabetical order by author. The latter two sections have their own topical indexes.　Z3216.B86

Herbert, Patricia M. Burma. Oxford ; Santa Barbara, Calif. : Clio Pr., c1991. 327 p. : map. (World bibliographical series, v. 132).　**DE121**

"Contains references to recent political events in Burma as well as older source material. The first multi-disciplinary guide to English-language publications to appear in twenty years."—*Pref.* 850 citations, extensive annotations to most entries. Separate author, title, and subject indexes.　Z3216.H47

Cambodia

Zaleha Tamby. Cambodia : a bibliography. Singapore : Inst. of Southeast Asian Studies, 1982. 61 p. (Institute of Southeast Asian Studies. Library bulletin, 12).　**DE122**

A topical listing of about 700 books, serials, official publications, and articles from books and newspapers, mainly in English. Based on the collection of the Institute. Emphasis is on political life and international relations. Author, personal and corporate name indexes.

Z3228.C3Z34

China

Guides

Teng, Ssu-yü. An annotated bibliography of selected Chinese reference works / Ssu-yü Teng, Knight Biggerstaff. 3rd ed. Cambridge : Harvard Univ. Pr., 1971. 250 p. (Harvard-Yenching Institute studies, 2).　**DE123**

1st ed., 1936; 2nd ed., 1950.

Arranged by form (bibliographies, encyclopedias, dictionaries, geographical works, tables, yearbooks, Sinological indexes); lengthy annotations. This edition includes some 200 new titles (mostly indexes) of which 25 are in Japanese. About 100 works from the 2nd ed. were dropped. Index of titles, authors and compilers.

§ Lists very few works devoted entirely to events since 1949 since this period is well covered by Peter Alexander Menquez Berton and Eugene Wu, *Contemporary China : a research guide* (Stanford, Calif. : Hoover Institution on War, Revolution, and Peace, 1967).

Z1035.T32

Wilkinson, Endymion. The history of imperial China : a research guide. Cambridge, East Asian Research Center, Harvard Univ.; distr. by Harvard Univ. Pr., 1973. 213p. (Harvard East Asian monographs, 49).　**DE124**

A survey of "primary sources and the reference aids to them in Chinese, Japanese, and Western languages."—*Pref.* Concentrates on the period from the third century BCE to the 18th century. An introductory section, Research hints, discusses the main problems (i.e., converting dates, locating places, finding biographical information, etc.) encountered in using primary materials. Subject and author/title indexes.　DS734.7.W5

Wolff, Ernest. Chinese studies : a bibliographic manual. San Francisco : Chinese Materials Ctr., 1981. 152 p. (Bibliographical series, 1).　**DE125**

A manual of basic reference tools for "the topics and problems of Chinese bibliography or Chinese research methodology."—*Pref.* Works are described and their usefulness discussed in chapters presented in a mainly topical arrangement. No index.

§ A similar guide for students preparing for thesis research is *Chinese studies research methodology,* by P. A. Herbert and T. Chiang (Hong Kong : Chinese Materials Ctr., 1982. 269 p.).　Z3106.W64

Bibliography

Cheng, Peter. China. Oxford, Eng. ; Santa Barbara, Calif. : Clio Pr., [1983]. 390 p. : map. (World bibliographical series, 35).   **DE126**

"The goal is to present a selection of over 1,450 works in English which will provide basic information on China, including its culture, its place in the world and the qualities which make it unique."—*Introd.* Most citations are to works published 1970–82. Topical arrangement; only books are included. Indexed.   Z3106.C465

Cordier, Henri. Bibliotheca sinica : dictionnaire bibliographique des ouvrages relatifs à l'Empire Chinois. 2nd éd., rev., corr. et considérablement augm. Paris : Guilmoto, 1904–08. 4 v.   **DE127**

Repr. with suppl.: Taipei: Ch'eng-wen Publ. Co., 1966. 5 v.

An exhaustive listing of books and periodical articles in many languages, primarily of the 19th century, on all aspects of life in China.

———. ——— *Supplément* (Paris : Geuthner, 1922–24. 4 v. in 1).

The lack of an author index, which seriously hampered use of this work, has been at least temporarily filled by the issue in multigraphed form of: *Author index to the Bibliotheca sinica*, comp., issued, and distr. by the East Asiatic Library, Columbia Univ. Libraries (N.Y., 1953. 84 p.).

See also T'ung-li Yüan, *China in Western literature : a continuation of Cordier's Bibliotheca sinica* (DE138).

Hsieh, Winston. Chinese historiography on the Revolution of 1911 : a critical survey and a select bibliography. Stanford, Calif. : Hoover Inst. Pr., 1975. 165 p. (Hoover Institution studies, 34).   **DE128**

A bibliographical essay (p.3–103) is followed by "A selected bibliography on the 1911 Revolution, with addenda," p.104–42, giving citations to Chinese works with English translation of titles, and notes on any English translation or summary of the complete work. Subject index.   DS773.H7

Lust, John. Index sinicus : a catalogue of articles relating to China in periodicals and other collective publications, 1920–1955. Cambridge, Eng. : W. Heffer, [1964]. 663 p.   **DE129**

A classified listing of some 20,000 articles in Western languages, dealing with China, in periodicals, memorial volumes, proceedings of conferences and congresses, etc. Supplements Henri Cordier's *Bibliotheca sinica* (DE127), which lists works to 1924, and T. L. Yüan's *China in Western literature* (DE138), covering 1921–57. Author and subject indexes.   Z3101.L8

Modern Chinese society : an analytical bibliography. Stanford, Calif. : Stanford Univ. Pr., 1973. 3 v. : maps.   **DE130**

Title also in Chinese. Sponsored by the Subcommittee on Research on Chinese Society, Joint Committee on Contemporary China.

Contents: v. 1, Publications in Western languages 1644–1972, G. W. Skinner, ed. (802 p.); v. 2, Publications in Chinese 1644–1969, G. W. Skinner and W. Hsieh, eds. (801 p.); v. 3, Publications in Japanese 1644–1971, G. W. Skinner and S. Tomita, eds. (531 p.).

Cites published secondary works and unpublished dissertations. Includes periodical articles, but not newspaper articles. Classified arrangement, with each entry coded as to library location, type of place (urban, rural, etc.), geographic location, historical period, and subject.

Indexes: (1) Historical index (a subject index to entries arranged by historical period and showing nature of the source); (2) Geographical index (a subject index to entries, arranged by geographic location and indicating historical era and type of place); (3) Author index; (4) Institutional author index; (5) General index (an alphabetical index of selected topics, terms, events, and proper names, with references to coding categories and to the analytical indexes as well as to particular entries).   Z7165.C6M62

Morton, Andrew. Union list of Chinese local histories in British libraries. Oxford : China Library Group, 1979. 140 p.   **DE131**

Based on a survey of seven British libraries. Identifies and locates 1,100 original and 1,700 reprinted titles of official gazetteers, including 64 analyzed collections. Arranged by province with indexes of place-names in pinyin transliteration and in Chinese characters.

§ *Chinese local histories* (Chicago : distr. by the Univ. of Chicago Bookstore, 1969. 139 p.) is a finding aid for relevant materials in the University of Chicago's Far Eastern Library. Fang-hua Chang's *Checklist of Chinese local histories* (Berkeley : Stanford-Berkeley Joint East Asia Ctr., 1980. 470 p.) offers similar coverage for the libraries at Stanford and the University of California, Berkeley.

Z3109.M66

Müller, Meike. China nach Mao : Auswahlbibliographie = China after Mao : a selected bibliography. Hamburg : Deutsches Übersee-Institut, Referat Asien und Südpazifik, 1987. 239 p. (Dokumentationsdienst Asien. Reihe A, 19).

DE132

Table of contents, introductory material and subject headings in German and English.

Cites some 1,300 books, essays, and periodical articles selected for their focus "on reforms in the areas of domestic and foreign policy, economic planning and development strategy. Publications on geography, history, law and the constitution, population and society, health and culture were included, too."—*Pref.* Classed arrangement. Most entries are annotated, with library locations, usually in Germany, but including a few European libraries outside Germany. Author index.

Z3108.A5M85

Posner, Arlene. China : a resource and curriculum guide / Arlene Posner, Ann J. de Keijzer. 2nd ed., rev. Chicago : Univ. of Chicago Pr., [1976]. 317 p.   **DE133**

1st ed., 1972.

Aims to list "a wide range of materials currently available to the public and offering representative views of the social, economic, political and cultural aspects of China's society and international relations, both past and present."—*Pref.* Offers essays on teaching about China; lists of audiovisual materials, books, and periodicals with evaluative annotations; resource materials from the People's Republic of China; and lists of resource centers, publishers and distributors.

§ Mary Robinson Sive's *China : a multimedia guide* (N.Y. : Neal Schuman, 1982. 245 p.) offers partial updating.   Z3106.P67

Revue bibliographique de Sinologie. Année 1 (1955)–14 (1968/70); n.s. 1 (1983)– . Paris : Mouton, 1957– . Annual.

DE134

Sponsored by the École Pratique des Hautes Études (later the École Pratique des Hautes Études en Sciences Sociales).

Lists books and articles (not necessarily in Chinese) on China in topical arrangement with a brief review in English or French. Long delays in publication.   Z7059.R4

A Sung bibliography = Bibliographie des Sung / initiated by Etienne Balazs ; ed. by Yves Hervouet. [Hong Kong] : Chinese Univ. Pr., [1978]. 598 p.   **DE135**

Introduction and instructions to the reader in English and French; notices in English or French.

A bibliography with extensive descriptive notes for texts issued during the Sung dynasty, with references to the most important later editions. Topical arrangement, e.g., official records, encyclopedias, works on bureaucracy, *The classic of filial purity*. Indexes of names, titles, and subjects.   Z3102.S77

Teng, Ssu-Yü. Protest & crime in China : a bibliography of secret associations, popular uprisings, peasant rebellions. N.Y. : Garland, 1981. 455 p. (Garland reference library of social science, v.86).   **DE136**

Lists about 4,000 articles, books, reviews, dissertations, etc., in any language covering all periods to 1981. Separate sections for occidental and oriental language materials, plus an addenda section in all languages. Subject index.   Z7164.S36T46

University of London. School of Oriental and African Studies. Library. Western books on China published up to 1850 in the Library of the School of Oriental and African Studies, University of London : a descriptive catalogue / John Lust. London : Bamboo, 1987. [336] p. : ill.   **DE137**

A classified listing of 1,283 books and pamphlets on China, eastern central Asia including Tibet, Manchuria and Mongolia, Taiwan, and Hong Kong. For each entry, gives a transcription of the title page, annotation, indication of a major catalog where cited—e.g., *NUC*, British Museum *Catalogue*, Henri Cordier's *Bibliotheca sinica* (DE127), Tōyō Bunko in Tokyo. Author and title indexes; Supplementary subject index.   Z3101

Yüan, T'ung-li. China in Western literature : a continuation of Cordier's Bibliotheca sinica. New Haven, Conn. : Far Eastern Publ., Yale Univ., 1958. 802 p.   **DE138**

For Henri Cordier's *Bibliotheca sinica*, see DE127.

"The bibliography represents a comprehensive survey of all types of writings on China, with no attempt to select or reject, but rather to record and describe."—*Pref.* This supplementary list covers books and monographs published from 1921 to 1957 in English, French, German, and Portuguese but does not include periodical articles. The classed arrangement differs somewhat from that used by Cordier, and there is an author index.

§ Supplemented by John Lust, *Index sinicus* (DE129).

     Z3101.Y8

Indexes

Yu, Ping-Kuen. Chung-kuo shih hsüeh lun wên yin tê = Chinese history : index to learned articles. Hong Kong : East Asia Inst., Univ. of Hong Kong ; Cambridge, Mass. : Harvard-Yenching Libr., 1963–1970. 2 v.   **DE139**

Text in Chinese; prefatory matter in English and Chinese.

Contents: v. 1, 1902–1962, comp. in the Fung Ping Shan Library, Univ. of Hong Kong; v. 2, 1905–1964, based on the collections in American and European libraries. Vol. 2 has series statement: Harvard-Yenching Library. Bibliographical series, 1.

An author listing of articles published in Chinese periodicals. Vol. 1 indexes articles on Chinese history to the end of the Ch'ing dynasty in 335 periodicals, and includes a subject index. Vol. 2 lists articles on Chinese history, philosophy, language and literature in 599 periodicals.   Z3106.Y79

Encyclopedias

The Cambridge encyclopedia of China / ed., Brian Hook ; consultant ed., Denis Twitchett. 2nd ed. Cambridge [Eng.] ; N.Y. : Cambridge Univ. Pr., 1991. 502 p. : col. ill., maps.   **DE140**

1st ed., 1982.

"A source of information about all aspects of Chinese civilization, traditional and contemporary."—*Pref.* A considerably revised and expanded edition, reflecting recent events in China. Almost a third of the volume is a dynasty-by-dynasty review of Chinese history. Subject index and bibliography; glossary of Chinese terms with pinyin and Wade-Giles transliteration, and Chinese characters.   DS70.C35

Encyclopedia of China today / ed. by Frederic M. Kaplan, Julian M. Sobin, Stephen Andors. 3rd ed. rev. & exp. N.Y. : Eurasia Pr. (distr. by Harper & Row), [1981]. 446 p. : ill.   **DE141**

1st ed., 1979.

A handsome and readable one-volume encyclopedia on the People's Republic of China, concentrating on the last 30 years. The information is given in nine broad subject divisions, and presentation is enhanced by photographs, maps, charts, glossaries, and a large number of statistical tables. Other interesting features: travel information for both private and commercial travelers; an overview of information sources (including translation services); and a bibliography (p. 301–20). This edition adds a new section for pre-1949 matter and expands coverage of art, culture, and health.   DS705.E54

Historical dictionary of revolutionary China, 1839–1976 / ed. by Edwin Pak-wah Leung. N.Y. : Greenwood, 1992. 566 p. : map.   **DE142**

Signed articles by more than 70 contributors. Bibliography, p. 521–43. Index has both Wade-Giles and pinyin romanization.   DS740.2.H57

O'Neill, Hugh B. Companion to Chinese history. N.Y. : Facts on File, c1987. 397 p. : maps.   **DE143**

Aims "to provide basic information on several hundred topics and a number of individuals."—*Introd.* Many articles are quite lengthy and include bibliographic references. Five-page chronology, 1506–1985. Cross-references; not indexed.   DS705.O63

Dictionaries

Dillon, Michael. Dictionary of Chinese history. London : Frank Cass, 1979. 239 p.   **DE144**

A short-entry dictionary covering Chinese history from the prehistoric period to 1977; useful for quick identification or definition. Terms included are those which "occur most frequently in English-language works on China and which can usefully be explained in a few hundred words."—*Pref.* The transliterated form of a word is that most frequently encountered in English-language books. No bibliography.   DS733.D54

Handbooks

Information China : the comprehensive and authoritative reference source of new China / ed. ... by C. V. James. Oxford ; N.Y. : Pergamon Pr., 1989. 3 v. (1621 p., [60] p. of plates) : ill. (some col.).   **DE145**

Organized by the Chinese Academy of Social Sciences ; comp. and tr. by the China Social Sciences Publishing House.

"Covers all major aspects of the physical, political, social, economic and cultural life of the [People's Republic of China]. Volume 1 [provides] an overall view of China; Volume 2 [gives] economic and socio-economic [data]; Volume 2 [provides] specialist information on contemporary Chinese society. Includes a special section on China in figures containing 178 tables of statistics provided by the Chinese State Statistical Bureau."—*Pref.* Vol. 3 contains name, place, and subject indexes.   DS706.I5

General histories

Cambridge history of China / gen. editors, Denis Twitchett and John K. Fairbank. Cambridge : Cambridge Univ. Pr., 1978–91. v. 1, 3, 7, 10–15. (In progress).   **DE146**

Contents: v. 1, The Ch'in and Han Empires, 221 B.C.–A.D. 220; v. 3, Sui and T'ang China, 589–906. Pt. 1; v. 7, The Ming Dynasty, 1368–1644. Pt. 1.; v. 10, Late Ch'ing, 1800–1870. Pt. 1; v. 11, Late Ch'ing, 1800–1911. Pt. 2.; v. 12, Republican China. Pt. 1; v. 13, Republican China, 1912–1949. Pt. 2; v. 14, The People's Republic. Pt. 1. The emergence of Revolutionary China, 1949–1965; v. 15, The People's Republic. Pt. 2. Revolutions within the Chinese Revolution, 1966–1982.

Similar to the other "Cambridge histories," and with sections written by specialists, the series will offer a survey of the "current state of knowledge" of the history of China, excluding the pre-dynastic period.   DS735.C3I45

Lieberthal, Kenneth. A research guide to central party and government meetings in China, 1949–1986 / Kenneth G. Lieberthal, Bruce J. Dickson. Rev. and expanded ed. Armonk, N.Y. : M.E. Sharpe, c1989. lvi, 339 p.   **DE147**

1st ed., 1976.

A chronological listing of 513 meetings, giving topic, dates, place, major agenda items, attendance, summaries of speeches and reports, indication of documents passed, reference to published accounts of the meeting and to any important secondary works. Sources of information include U.S. government translation services (e.g., JPRS) as well as Chinese print media. Index to meeting summaries.

JQ1519.A5L474

Mackerras, Colin. The Cambridge handbook of contemporary China / by Colin Mackerras and Amanda Yorke. Cambridge, U.K. ; N.Y. : Cambridge Univ. Pr., 1991. 266 p. : ill.   **DE148**

Focuses on the People's Republic of China, with occasional mention of Taiwan and Hong Kong. Includes: surveys of the history, economics, population, minority nationals, culture and society, etc.; biographies of one-half to one column in length; a 58-page chronology, 1900–April 1990, divided into categories such as foreign affairs, economics, natural disasters, births and deaths; an annotated bibliography of English-language books arranged by broad categories; gazetteer; topical index. Cutoff date is April 30, 1990. Very useful.

DS706.M24

Sourcebooks

The People's Republic of China, 1949–1979 : a documentary survey / Harold C. Hinton, ed. Wash. : Scholarly Books, 1980. 5 v.   **DE149**

A careful selection of Chinese government publications, newspaper articles, speeches, press releases, radio broadcasts, etc., which aims to provide an overview of the period. Full text is given in English in a basically chronological arrangement; source of the translation of each document is given; headnotes indicate importance of the document. (Title of the document is the only indication of its original source.) Brief index in each volume.

Continued by: *The people's republic of China, 1979–1984: a documentary survey* (Wilmington, Del. : Scholarly Resources, 1986. 2 v.).

DS777.55.P4243

Hong Kong

Research material for Hong Kong studies / ed. by Alan Birch, Y.C. Jao, and Elizabeth Sinn. [Hong Kong] : Centre of Asian Studies, Univ. of Hong Kong, 1984. [340 p.] : ill. (Centre of Asian Studies bibliographies and research guides, no. 23).   **DE150**

Consists of papers presented at a conference called to assess the current state of research materials, institutions, and studies of Hong Kong. Thus the article on reference materials points out the major sources but also notes lacunae—e.g., a bibliography of literary works set in Hong Kong, updating H. Anthony Rydings's *A Hong Kong union catalogue* (Hong Kong : Centre of Asian Studies, Univ. of Hong Kong, 1976). The article on institutions covers contents of and access to the Public Record Office in Hong Kong, the Hongkong and Shanghai Bank Corporation, the Hung On-To Memorial Library, and the Information Services Department of the government. Not indexed.

DS796.H74R47

Roberts, Elfed Vaughan. Historical dictionary of Hong Kong & Macau / Elfed Vaughan Roberts, Sum Ngai Ling, Peter Bradshaw. Metuchen, N.J. : Scarecrow, 1992. xlvii, 357 p. : ill. (Asian historical dictionaries, no. 10).   **DE151**

Three-fourths of the volume treats Hong Kong, one-fourth Macau. The Hong Kong sections also offers a 32-page bibliography and the Macau section an 8-page bibliography.   DS796.H757R64

Scott, Ian. Hong Kong. Oxford ; Santa Barbara, Calif. : Clio Pr., c1990. 248 p. : map. (World bibliographical series, v. 115).   **DE152**

Since the audience is expected to be general readers, focus is on books, articles, and a few government publications in English. 838 citations arranged by topic. Cross-references; author, title, subject indexes.   Z3107.H7S36

India

Bibliography

Annotated bibliography on the economic history of India : 1500 A.D. to 1947 A.D. / [chief ed., V. D. Divekar]. Pune : Gokhale Institute of Politics & Economics ; New Delhi : Indian Council of Social Science Research, 1977–80. 4 v. in 5.   **DE153**

For annotation, *see* CH194.   Z7165.I6A8

Annual bibliography of Indian archaeology / Kern Institute, Leyden. [v. 1] (1926)–v. 23 (1970–1972). Leyden : E. J. Brill, 1928–c1984.   **DE154**

Title varies slightly.

An extensive, annotated bibliography, including books and periodical articles in various languages, and sometimes reviews of books.

Z5133.I4I6

Chambard, Jean-Luc. Bibliographie de civilisation de l'Inde contemporaine. [Paris] : Publications Orientalistes de France, [1977]. 340 p.   **DE155**

A classed bibliography covering Indian geography, history, sociology/ethnography, demography, economics, agricultural economy, politics, and foreign relations. Predominantly English-language materials. Detailed table of contents, but no author or subject index.

Z3206.C44

A guide to reference materials on India / comp. and ed. by N. N. Gidwani and K. Navalani. Jaipur : Saraswati Publ., 1974. 2 v. (1536 p.).   **DE156**

Some 20,000 annotated entries for reference books and "contributions lying buried in a vast number of journals, conference proceedings, festschrifts and other composite works."—*Introd.* Provides contents of many scholarly series and sets. Author/subject index.

Z3206.G84

Gupta, Brijen K. India / Brijen K. Gupta, Datta S. Kharbas. Oxford, Eng. ; Santa Barbara, Calif. : Clio Pr., [1984]. 264 p. : map. (World bibliographical series, 26).   **DE157**

A selective and annotated bibliography intended to express India's "unique culture and its importance in the family of nations."—*Introd.* Topical arrangement; only English-language materials were chosen. Indexed.   Z2306.G86

India Office Library. Catalogue of European printed books / India Office Library, Commonwealth Relations Office (London). Boston : G. K. Hall, 1964. 10 v.   **DE158**

The collection covers all aspects of the study of India. Accessions until 1936 are listed only by author; after 1936, there are both author and subject entries.   Z3209.I53

Riddick, John F. Glimpses of India : an annotated bibliography of published personal writings by Englishmen, 1583–1947. N.Y. : Greenwood, 1989. 195 p. (Bibliographies and indexes in world history, no. 15). **DE159**

Offers 580 entries, arranged by period (e.g., 1583–1740, 1740–1818, 1920–47), for published memoirs, autobiographies, collections of personal letters, diaries and journals, travel narratives. Coverage is wider than India since many accounts include other parts of South Asia (e.g., Nepal, Tibet, Afghanistan, Burma). Annotations give a brief note identifying the author and a description of the contents. Name index.
Z3206.R5

Saha, Santosh C. Indo-U.S. relations, 1947–1988 : a guide to information sources. N.Y. : P. Lang, [1990]. 213 p. (American university studies., vol. 95). **DE160**

Following an overview of relations between the U.S. and India 1947–89, describes relevant portions of presidential archives and related holdings in the Detroit Public Library and the United Nations Library. These are complemented by a bibliography of books, journal articles, newspaper articles, and economic documents from U.S. government agencies. Author and subject indexes. Z6465.U5S24

Scholberg, Henry. Bibliography of Goa and the Portuguese in India / Henry Scholberg, with the collaboration of Archana Ashok Kakodker and Carmo Azevedo. New Delhi : Promilla ; Atlantic Highlands, N.J. : Humanities Pr., 1982. 413 p. **DE161**

An extensive bibliography of books and pamphlets focusing on the period between 1497 and 1961. Topical arrangement with author and subject index. Locates copies. A supplement discusses archival materials in India, Portugal, and Great Britain and offers bibliographical essays on Goan independence. Z3207.G6S36

Manuscripts; Archives

Guide to the sources of Asian history : 3, India / International Council on Archives. New Delhi : National Archives of India, 1987. v. 1. (In progress). **DE162**

Part of the UNESCO project, Guide to the sources of the history of nations, begun in 1959. The segment for India is projected for 6 v., to survey holdings of archival repositories and other custodial institutions in India.

Vol. 1 deals with the National Archives of India, surveying ministries of the government of India and calendars of holdings.
DS480.45.G79

India Office Library. Index of post-1937 European manuscript accessions / India Office Library, Commonwealth Relations Office (London). Boston : G. K. Hall, 1964. 156 p. **DE163**

Indexes private papers of many secretaries of state for India, viceroys and governors of India and Indian provinces, and prominent Indian citizens from 1801. To a lesser extent, the collection also deals with Burma and Ceylon. Z6621.G78E92

Encyclopedias

Balfour, Edward Green. Cyclopædia of India and of eastern and southern Asia, commercial, industrial, and scientific : products of the mineral, vegetable and animal kingdoms, useful arts and manufactures. 3rd ed. London : Quaritch, 1885. 3 v. **DE164**

Repr.: Graz : Akad. Druck– u. Verlagsanstalt, 1967–78.

A comprehensive, alphabetically arranged encyclopedia still valuable for its geographical, historical, and ethnographical material.
DS405.B18

Chopra, Pran Nath. Encyclopaedia of India / P. N. Chopra, Prabha Chopra. Delhi : Agam Prakashan, 1988. 2 v. (628 p., [44] p. of plates) : ill., maps, ports. **DE165**

Intends to be the standard encyclopedia of India, with articles on people, places, companies and industries, religions, arts, fairs and festivals, mathematics, etc. For each topic, information is meant to be current through 1981. Short bibliographies end most articles. Includes a gazetteer of India, giving population figures from the Census of 1981 and a chronology, 4000 BCE–1986. Index of article titles under broad topics, e.g., Books, Castes. DS405.C47

An encyclopaedia of Indian archaeology / ed. by A. Ghosh. Leiden ; N.Y. : E.J. Brill, 1990. 2 v. : ill. **DE166**

Contents: v. 1, Subjects; v. 2, A gazetteer of explored and excavated sites in India.

Encompasses "the major findings of Indian archaeology during the last hundred and fifty years, on prehistory, protohistory, and the ancient historical period."—Introd. DS418.E53

Kurian, George Thomas. Historical and cultural dictionary of India. Metuchen, N.J. : Scarecrow, 1976. 307 p. : map. (Historical & cultural dictionaries of Asia, no. 8). **DE167**

Approximately 2,000 entries with brief annotations and numerous cross-references. Bibliography, p. 263–306. DS405.K87

Mehra, Parshotam. A dictionary of modern Indian history, 1707–1947. Delhi ; N.Y. : Oxford Univ. Pr., 1987. 823 p. : maps. **DE168**

About 400 alphabetically arranged entries cover places, events, leaders, parties, etc. Some articles are lengthy and all end with a brief bibliography of one to nine entries. Cross-references; topical index. Appendix includes chronology, glossary of Indian terms, list of governors general and viceroys, 1774–1947. DS433.M33

The new Cambridge history of India / [gen. ed., Gordon Johnson ; assoc. editors, C.A. Bayly and John F. Richards]. Cambridge ; N.Y. : Cambridge Univ. Pr., 1987–1993. v. 1^{1-2}, $^{4-5}$; pt. 2^{1-2}; pt. 3^{1-2}; pt. 4^1 : maps; ill. (In progress). **DE169**

1st ed., 1922–37, had title Cambridge history of India.

The plan of the new edition is to divide Indian history beginning with the 16th century into "four overlapping chronological volumes, each containing about eight short books on individual themes or subjects."—General editor's pref. Each volume is a monograph written by a specialist on an aspect of Indian history; some include bibliographies, others bibliographic essays. DS436.N47

Saletore, Rajaram Narayan. Encyclopaedia of Indian culture. Atlantic Highlands, N.J. : Humanities Pr. ; New Delhi : Sterling, 1981–1985. 5 v. **DE170**

Indian culture is defined to be Brahmanical, Buddhist, and Jaina; the Muslim contribution is omitted. Articles are arranged alphabetically and conclude with brief bibliographies. Index, v. 5.

A 2nd rev. ed. (New Delhi : Sterling Publ.) began in 1985.
DS423.S218

Chronologies

Sharma, Jagdish Saran. India since the advent of the British : a descriptive chronology from 1600 to Oct. 2, 1969. Delhi : S. Chand, 1970. 817 p. (National bibliography, 7). **DE171**

A chronology with comprehensive index of names of places, events, subjects, newspapers, important books, etc. DS433.S47

Atlases

Habib, Irfan. An atlas of the Mughal Empire : political and economic maps with detailed notes, bibliography and index. [Aligarh] : Centre of Advanced Study in History, Aligarh Muslim Univ. ; Delhi ; N.Y. : Oxford Univ. Pr., 1982. 105 p. : 34 maps ; 44cm.   **DE172**
Repr. "with corrections", 1986.
An outstanding atlas of political and economic maps of the Indian subcontinent, 1550–1750. Black-and-white maps; extensive notes; bibliography of 250 items; detailed index.   G2282.M6H3

Indonesia

Cribb, Robert B. Historical dictionary of Indonesia. Metuchen, N.J. : Scarecrow, 1992. lxxiv, 663 p. : maps. (Asian historical dictionaries, no. 9).   **DE173**
"Emphasis is on political and economic history and on the period since 1800; no attempt has been made to deal comprehensively with the many traditional social institutions and cultural forms."—*Pref.* Includes 23-page chronology and a bibliography of more than 1,000 items. Appendixes cite rulers, governors-general, Republic of Indonesia cabinets and office holders.   DS633.C75

Bibliography

Chijs, Jacobus Anne van der. Proeve eener Ned : Indische bibliographie (1659–1870). [Batavia : Bruining & Wijt, 1875. 325 p. (Verhandelingen van het Bataviaasch Genootschap van Kunsten en Wetenschappen, deel 37).   **DE174**
A chronological listing of works on the Netherlands East Indies, primarily in Dutch but with some works in other languages.
————. ————. *Supplement* [I] (Batavia : W. Bruining, 1879. 93 p.).
————. ————. *Supplement* [II] (Batavia : Albrecht ; 'sGravenhage : M. Nijhoff, 1903. 64 p.).
The supplements give additions and corrections for the years 1720–1870.   AS522.L418

Hooykaas, J. C. Repertorium op de koloniale litteratuur : of, Systematische inhoudsopgaaf van hetgeen voorkomt over de koloniën (beoosten de Kaap) in mengelwerken en tijdschriften van 1595–1865 uitg. in Nederland en zijne overzeesche bezittingen. .... Amsterdam : van Kampen, 1874–80. 2 v.   **DE175**
Contents: 1. deel; I, Het land. II, Het volk; 2. deel; III, Het bestuur. IV. de Wetenschap.
An extensive bibliography—listing more than 21,000 items—of Dutch materials on Dutch colonies throughout the world.
Continued by *Repertorium op de literatuur betreffende de Nederlandsche koloniën : voor zoover zij verspreid is in tijdschriften en mengelwerken ... samengesteld door A. Hartmann ('sGravenhage : Nijhoff, 1895–1935. 454 p. and suppl. 1–8).
Basic volume: East Indies, 1866–93; West Indies, 1840–93. Supplements 1–8: v. 1, 1894–1900 (1901. 224 p.); v. 2, 1901–1905 (1906. 233 p.); v. 3, 1906–10 (1912. 271 p.); v. 4, 1911–15 (1917. 378 p.); v. 5, 1916–20 (1923. 508 p.); v. 6, 1921–25 (1928. 522 p.); v. 7, 1926–30 (1935. 712 p.); v. 8, 1931–32 (1934. 189 p.).
Treats Dutch colonies in the East Indies and the West Indies.
Z2451.C7H75

Kemp, Herman C. Annotated bibliography of bibliographies on Indonesia. Leiden, Netherlands : KITLV Pr., 1990. 433 p.
DE176
For annotation, *see* AA78.   Z3271.A1K46

Rowland, Ian. Timor : including the islands of Roti and Ndao. Oxford, England ; Santa Barbara, Calif. : Clio Pr., c1992. 117 p. : ill. (World bibliographical series, v. 142).   **DE177**
Bibliography contains 359 entries, with some citations to works in Portuguese. Over 20% of the citations relate to relations with Indonesia and the eventual incorporation of Portuguese Timor into Indonesia. Cites many general works on Indonesia that have a chapter on Timor. Follows the standard format of the *World bibliographical series.* Author, title, and subject index.   Z3277.T5R69 1992

Stuart-Fox, David J. Bibliography of Bali : publications from 1920 to 1990. Leiden : KITLV Pr., 1992. 708 p.   **DE178**
Intended as a continuation of Frederick Albert Liefrinck's *Bali en lombok* (Amsterdam : J. H. de Bussy, 1927. 542 p.).
A selective bibliography, with 8,000 unannotated entries. Arranged in broad sections (e.g., Social sciences; Economy and agriculture; Religion; Art) with numerous subdivisions. Lists 227 serials dealing with Bali. Author, corporate author, and subject indexes.
DS647.B2.S78

Current

Excerpta Indonesica. No. 1 (Jan. 1970)– . Leyden, The Netherlands : Centre for Documentation on Modern Indonesia of the Royal Institute of Linguistics and Anthropology, 1970– . Twice yearly.   **DE179**
Offers "abstracts of selected periodical articles ... and annotations of selected books on Indonesia in the field of the social sciences and humanities" (*t.p.*) in many languages. About 200 citations per issue; indexed by author and subject. Cumulative indexes for every ten issues (i.e., no. 1–10 publ. 1975; no. 11–20 publ. 1981).
§ The Institute also publishes periodic surveys of research: *Current Indonesian studies in the Netherlands, 1978/79* was published 1979; earlier surveys for 1970, 1973 and 1976 were published in *Excerpta Indonesia,* no. 2, 7 and 11, respectively.   Z3273.E83

Iran

Bibliography

Berghe, Louis van den. Bibliographie analytique de l'archéologie de l'Iran ancien. Leiden : Brill, 1979. 329 p.
DE180
"Avec la collaboration de B. Wulf et E. Haerinck."—*t.p.*
Cites publications issued from the end of the 19th century through 1977, arranged by topic under three broad categories: general, region or site, period. Index of authors and places.
Supplements by Berghe and Haerinck cover 1978–80 (1981. 109 p.) and 1981–85 (1987. 102 p.).

Bibliographic guide to Iran : the Middle East Library Committee guide / L. P. Elwell-Sutton, ed. Brighton, Sussex : Harvester Pr. ; Totowa, N.J. : Barnes & Noble, [1983]. 462 p.
DE181
A companion to the Committee's *Arab Islamic bibliography* (BC492).
A topically arranged bibliography of "the most useful and significant books and articles in each of the fields ... and as far as possible [indicates] the scope and usefulness of each."—*Foreword.* A joint effort of some 30 scholars, covering from pre-Islamic times to the departure of the Shah. International coverage, but English-language materials predominate. Topical arrangement; brief annotations; author index.
Z3366.B5

Ehlers, Eckart. Iran : ein bibliographischer Forschungsbericht, mit Kommentaren und Annotationen = a bibliographic research survey, with comments and annotations. N.Y. : K.G. Saur ; Detroit : Gale, 1980. 441 p. : map. (Bibliographies on regional geography and area studies, v. 2).   **DE182**

A comprehensive bibliography of all aspects of Iranian studies; topically arranged, with author index. Includes materials in all Western languages, but a high percentage of publications is in English. Chapter introductions in English and German.

Ghanī, Sīrūs. Iran and the West : a critical bibliography. London ; N.Y. : Kegan Paul, 1987. 967 p.   **DE183**

Based on a personal collection of works on Persia published in the 19th and 20th centuries, mainly in English. Alphabetically arranged in four sections: (A) History, politics, and travel; (B) Literature, religion, science, language including fiction with an Eastern setting; (C) Arts, archaeology, books of illustrations, photography albums, art sale catalogs; (D) Pamphlets, articles, journals, occasional papers, museum catalogs, newspaper and news magazine articles. Author index.   Z3366.G46

Gitisetan, Dariush. Iran, politics and government under the Pahlavis : an annotated bibliography. Metuchen, N.J. : Scarecrow, 1985. 201 p.   **DE184**

Lists books, articles, government publications, and dissertations (mainly in English, but including French, German, Italian and Spanish publications) in topical arrangement with name index. Includes social and economic conditions as well as politics and government. Descriptive annotations. Thorough for the period of coverage.   Z3366.G58

Navabpour, Reza. Iran. Oxford ; Santa Barbara, Calif. : Clio Pr., c1988. 308 p. : map. (World bibliographical series, v. 81).   **DE185**

Offers 1,787 annotated entries for books, articles, essays in English. Priority was given to titles in print and those "which can reasonably be expected to be found in the Middle East sections of universities or large public libraries."—*Introd.* Author/title/subject index; cross-references.   Z3366.N37

Nawabi, Y. M. A bibliography of Iran : a catalogue of books and articles on Iranian subjects, mainly in European languages. [Tehran] : Cultural Studies & Research Institute, 1969–[1987?]. v. 1–8. (Iranian Culture Foundation, v. 53 [etc.]). (In progress?).   **DE186**

Added t.p. in Persian.

Contents: v. 1, Studies on Avesta, Mani & Manichaeism, Old Persian, Pahlavi (Parsik & Parthian), Parsis of India and Zoroaster & Zoroastrianism; v. 2, Persian language and literature; v. 3, Archaeology, architecture and art; v. 4, Travel and description; v. 5, History, mythology & foreign relations; v. 6, Religion, philosophy & science; v. 7, Linguistics; v. 8, Geography and related sciences.

A bibliography of book and periodical materials; author listing within broad subject classes; no index.   Z3366.N38

Pearson, J. D. A bibliography of pre-Islamic Persia. [London] : Mansell, 1975. 288 p. (Persian studies series, 2).   **DE187**

About 7,300 items in classed arrangement. The principal sections are: (A) Languages and literatures; (B) History; (C) Religion; and (D) Art and archaeology; each is appropriately subdivided. Full table of contents but no detailed subject index. International in coverage (but omitting Russian materials); generally speaking, the cutoff date is 1970. Author index.   Z3366.P36

Encyclopedias

Encyclopædia Iranica / ed. by Ehsan Yarshater. London ; Boston : Routledge & Kegan Paul, 1983–1993. v. 1–6. (In progress).   **DE188**

Contents: v. 1–v. 6, Āb-Dārā. Each volume complete in eight fascicles.

Aims "to provide accurate and up-to-date presentations on topics of archaeological, geographic, ethnographic, historical, artistic, literary, religious, linguistic, philosophical, scientific, and folkloric interest" (*Introd.*) for scholars, specialists and students in Iranian studies and related fields. Covers from prehistoric times to the present, but biographies of living persons are not included. Gives careful attention to reciprocal cultural influences between Iran and its neighbors. Signed articles (in English) by specialists; bibliographic references. Entry is usually under the transliterated Persian or Arabic form of a term or name, with adequate cross-referencing promised. Includes entries for individual book titles. Figures and plates are generally limited to maps, plans of architectural monuments, sketches of archeological artifacts, or representative works by an artist or calligrapher.   DS253.E53

General histories

Cambridge history of Iran. Cambridge : Univ. Pr., 1968–1991. 7 v. in 8 : ill., maps, plates.   **DE189**

A. J. Arberry [and others], eds.

Contents: v. 1, The land of Iran, ed. by W. B. Fisher; v. 2, The Median and Achaemenian periods, by I. Gershevitch; v. 3, The Seleucid, Parthian, and Sasanian period, ed. by E. Yarshater (2 v.); v. 4, The period from the Arab invasion to the Saljugs, ed. by R. N. Frye; v. 5, The Saljuq and Mongol periods, ed. by J. A. Boyle; v. 6, The Timurid and Safavid periods, ed. by Peter Jackson and Laurence Lockhart; v. 7, From Nadir Shah to the Islamic Republic, ed. by Peter Avery, Gavin Hambly, and Charles Melville.

Chapters are contributed by scholar specialists. Each volume has its own bibliography and index. Vol. 8 contains a bibliography, a survey of research, and indexes for the set.   DS272.C34

Iraq

'Abd al-Rahmān, 'Abd al-Jabbār. Iraq. Oxford, Eng. ; Santa Barbara, Calif. : Clio Pr., 1984. 162 p. (World bibliographical series, 42).   **DE190**

"The aim has been to list material which will provide the general reader, researcher, and librarian with a reasonably comprehensive picture of Iraq … focussing his attention on books while referring to a wide range of periodicals rather than citing articles."—*Introd.* Primarily English-language materials. Topically arranged; annotated; well indexed. Separate list of theses and dissertations.   Z3036.A653

Israel

Bibliography

Alexander, Yonah. A bibliography of Israel / comp. and ed. by Yonah and Miriam Alexander and Mordecai Chertoff. N.Y. : Herzl Pr. : Dept. of Education and Culture, World Zionist Organization, American Section, 1981. 263 p.   **DE191**

A topically arranged, annotated listing of English-language books, including biographies, autobiographies, fiction and poetry. Emphasis is on social and political life in contemporary Israel, but there is some treatment of Palestine and biblical Israel. Author and title indexes.   Z3476.A66

Encyclopedias

Reich, Bernard. Historical dictionary of Israel. Metuchen, N.J. : Scarecrow, 1992. lxv, 353 p. : map. (Asian historical dictionaries, no. 8).   **DE192**
    Serves both as a reference source for events in Israel and for the Zionist movement in Europe during the 19th and 20th centuries. Includes a chronology of the Jewish people and bibliography.
                                             DS126.5.R38

Atlases

Gilbert, Martin. The Dent atlas of Jewish history. 5th ed. London : J.M. Dent, 1993. 132 p. [i.e. 136] : maps. in color ; 26cm.   **DE193**
    For annotation, *see* DA52.   G1030.G46

Japan

The Cambridge history of Japan / [general editors, John W. Hall … et al.]. Cambridge [Eng.] ; N.Y. : Cambridge Univ. Pr., 1988–93. v. 1, 3–6. (In progress).   **DE194**
    Contents: v. 1, Ancient Japan; v. 3, Medieval Japan; v. 4, Early modern Japan; v. 5, Nineteenth century; v. 6, Twentieth century.
                                              DS835.C36

Bibliography

Berlin. Japan-Institut. Bibliographischer Alt-Japan-Katalog, 1542–1853 / bearb. und hrsg. vom Japan-Institut in Berlin und vom Deutschen Forschungsinstitut in Kyoto. Kyoto : Deutsches Forschungsinstitut, 1940. 415 p.   **DE195**
    Repr.: Munich : Verlag Dokumentation, 1977.
    An excellent bibliography of older Western materials on Japan, giving complete bibliographical information and also location (in 1940) of copies in German and Japanese libraries.
    § Complements Henri Cordier's *Bibliotheca japonica* (DE198).
                                                Z3306.B4

Catalogue of books in English on Japan, 1945–1981 / [comp. by The Japan Foundation]. [Tokyo] : The Foundation, 1986. 726 p.   **DE196**
    Lists some 9,000 books published 1945–81 in humanities, social sciences, art, and the history of science. Entries were drawn from collections of the National Diet Library, the Japan Foundation Library and from lists in the *Bibliography of Asian studies* (DE8). Classified arrangement with indexes for authors and titles.
    § A much shorter listing of English-language books is *Japan reading guide : a select list of books on Japan with annotations* (Tokyo : International House of Japan Library, 1986. [109] p.), a topical arrangement of 300 basic books on Japan. Also provides a list of government publications and periodicals in English. For general readers.
                                                Z3306.C34

Catalogue of books on Japan translated from the Japanese into English, 1945–1981 = Eiyaku Nihon kankei hōbun tosho mokuroku / [comp. by The Japan Foundation] ; Henshū Kokusai Kōryū Kikin]. Tokyo : The Foundation, 1988. 109 p.   **DE197**
    A classified arrangement of books identified while compiling *Catalogue of books in English on Japan 1945–1981* (DE196). Entry indicates title of the Japanese original. Author and title indexes.
                                                Z3301.C38

Cordier, Henri. Bibliotheca japonica : dictionnaire bibliographique des ouvrages relatifs à l'Empire Japonais rangés par ordre chronologique jusqu'à 1870, suivi d'un appendice renfermant la liste alphabétique des principaux ouvrages parus de 1870 à 1912. Paris : Leroux, 1912. 762 col. (École des Langues Orientales Vivantes. Publications. 5. séries, v.8).   **DE198**
    A chronological, annotated listing of materials in Western languages from pre-Marco Polo times to 1870. The appendix lists, alphabetically, the principal works published from 1870 to 1912.
                                                Z3301.C7

Hoover Institution on War, Revolution and Peace. East Asian Collection. A checklist of monographs and periodicals on the Japanese colonial empire : in the East Asian collection… / Michiko Kiyohara, comp. Stanford : Hoover Inst. Pr., [1981]. 334 p.   **DE199**
    All relevant monographs, newspapers, and periodicals listed in the Japanese card catalog at Hoover are here arranged by colony and then by topic: colonial empire, Korea, Taiwan, Kwantung, leased territories, Micronesia, Sakhalin, Kurile Islands. Lists materials on each area from the time it became a colony. Author and title indexes.
                                                Z3308.C7H65

Iwasaki, Ikuo. Japan and Southeast Asia : a bibliography of historical, economic and political relations. [Tokyo] : Library Institute of Developing Economies, 1983. 176p.   **DE200**
    Covers relations between Japan and southeast Asian countries, Burma to Thailand, from the 16th century to 1983. Arranged by country, then topically, with separate sections for Western language and Chinese/Japanese materials. Author index.
                                              DS525.9.J3I93

Japan and the world, 1853–1952 : a bibliographic guide to Japanese scholarship in foreign relations / ed. by Sadao Asada. N.Y. : Columbia Univ. Pr., c1989. 462 p.   **DE201**
    "A project of the Japan Association of International Relations."—*t.p.*
    Translates, revises, and much expands the chapter on Japanese diplomatic relations in *Sengo Nihon no kokusai seijigaku* (Tokyo : hatsubai Yūhikaku, 1979). Scholars discuss the "range and content of what Japanese historians have been writing during the past forty years … in the field of international studies both historical and theoretical" (*Pref.*) on the period 1853 through the Allied Occupation (1945–52). At the end of each chapter is a bibliography of the books, articles, archives, and personal papers discussed. Cutoff date is 1986–87. Author and subject indexes.
                                                Z3308.R4J36

Japanese studies from pre-history to 1990 : a bibliographical guide / comp. by Richard Perren. Manchester : Manchester Univ. Pr. ; N.Y. : St. Martin's, c1992. 172 p.   **DE202**
    The aim is "to provide an introduction to Japanese studies by detailing the most important Western-language publications on Japan."—*Pref.* Arranged by five broad historical periods with thematic sections within each. 4,069 entries, briefly annotated. Author index.
                                                Z3301.J36

King, Norman D. Ryukyu Islands : a bibliography. Wash. : Headquarters, Dept. of the Army, 1967. 105 p.   **DE203**
    Department of the Army pamphlet 550-4.
    Lists about 2,100 English-language publications arranged by broad subject areas. Includes books, articles, government publications. Some annotations; name index.   Z3307.R9K55

Nachod, Oskar. Bibliographie von Japan, 1906–[1943] : Enthaltend ein ausführliches Verzeichnis der Bücher und Aufsätze über Japan, die seit der Ausgabe des zweiten Bändes von Wenckstern "Bibliography of the Japanese Empire" bis 1926 in europäischen Sprachen erschienen sind. Leipzig : Hiersemann, 1928–70. 7 v. in 9.   **DE204**
    Vols. 1–2 also published with English title: *Bibliography of the Japanese Empire, 1906–26* (London : Goldston, 1928).

Contents: v. 1–2, Books and articles, 1906–26 (1928); v. 3, 1927–29 (1931); v. 4, 1930–32, von Hans Praesent (1935); v. 5, 1933–35, von Hans Praesent und Wolf Haenisch (1937); v. 6, 1936–37, von Wolf Haenisch und Hans Praesent (1940); v.7, 1938–43, von Hans Praesent (1970).

A comprehensive, classified list, including books, pamphlets, and periodical articles. Each volume includes some titles of earlier dates omitted from previous volumes. Continues Friedrich von Wenckstein's *Bibliography of the Japanese Empire* (Leiden : Brill, 1895. 2v. [Repr.: Stuttgart : Hiersemann ; Nendeln : Kraus, 1970) covering 1859–1906. Z3301.W472

Shulman, Frank Joseph. Japan. Oxford ; Santa Barbara, Calif. : Clio Pr., c1989. 873 p. : maps. (World bibliographical series, v. 103). **DE205**

Provides 1,615 annotated entries for books, with special emphasis on those published in the 1970s and 1980s. Topical arrangement. Cross-references; author, title, and subject indexes. Z3301.S475

Library resources

Fukuda, Naomi. Survey of Japanese collections in the United States. Ann Arbor : Ctr. for Japanese Studies, Univ. of Michigan, 1980. 180 p. (Michigan papers in Japanese studies, 4). **DE206**

Presents profiles of the Japanese collections at each of 28 universities and the Library of Congress. Gives background, organization, strenghs, size, etc. Appendix of statistics from all the libraries presented in tabular form. Z3306.F84

Encyclopedias

The Cambridge encyclopedia of Japan / editors, Richard Bowring, Peter Kornicki. N.Y. : Cambridge Univ. Pr., 1993. 400 p. : ill. **DE207**

Essays on "everything from early Japan to the use of robots"—*Pref*. Bibliography notes key works for each essay. More useful for the general reader than for specialists. Lavish use of color illustration. Index. DS805.C36

Dictionnaire historique du Japon / sous la direction de Iwao Seiichi. Tokyo : Librairie Kinokuniya, 1963–1992. Fasc. 1–10, 13–18. (In progress). **DE208**

An extensive dictionary of Japanese history and culture; articles cover most aspects of Japanese civilization. Brief bibliographies of one to five entries attached to each article. DS833.D5

Kodansha encyclopedia of Japan. [Tokyo] : Kodansha, [1983]. 9 v. : ill., maps. **DE209**

For annotation, *see* AB71. DS805.K633

Handbooks

Focus Japan II : a resource guide to Japan-oriented organizations : a joint project of National Planning Association [and] University of Maryland at College Park / presented by Gateway Japan ; ed. by Erland Heginbotham, Gretchen Shinoda. Wash. : Gateway Japan, c1993. 691 p. **DE210**

For annotation, *see* AL43. DS801.F625

Hunter, Janet. Concise dictionary of Japanese history. Berkeley : Univ. of Calif. Pr., [1984]. 347 p. **DE211**

Aims to be a "handy source of information on the individuals, events, and organizations that have played a significant role in Japan's modern history" (*Pref.*) during the 1853–1980 period. Material covering earlier periods is included when important to the understanding of

modern developments. Brief entries in alphabetical arrangement; most include at least one bibliographic reference. Glossary; appendixes of tables, charts, and lists of names. DS881.9.H86

Jordan

Seccombe, Ian J. Jordan. Oxford, Eng. ; Santa Barbara, Calif. : Clio Pr., [1984]. 278 p. (World bibliographical series, 55). **DE212**

Aims to "provide a range of basic references on all key aspects of the country."—*Pref.* Except for a very few important works in French and German, coverage is limited to English-language books, articles, and government publications. Topical arrangement; annotations; author/title/subject index. Z3471.S43

Korea

Bibliography

McFarland, Keith D. The Korean War : an annotated bibliography. N.Y. : Garland, 1986. 463 p. (Wars of the United States, v. 8 ; Garland reference library of social science, v. 189). **DE213**

A classified bibliography of more than 2,300 English-language items, including books, articles, theses, and government publications. Author and subject indexes; chronology. Z3319.K6M38

Studies on Korea : a scholar's guide / ed. by Han-Kyo Kim with the assistance of Hong-Kyu Park. Honolulu : Univ. Pr. of Hawaii, [1980] 438 p **DE214**

A guide to materials in 14 academic disciplines intended for "the college-level readers and others in the United States and elsewhere who may not have much background knowledge in Korean studies but who wish to read materials available in English or other Western languages on Korea."—*Pref.* Each chapter has an introductory essay giving an overview of research, followed by an annotated bibliography subdivided by period, form, or topic. Chapter 15 deals with North Korea; chapter 16 with Russian-language materials on Korea. Author index. Z3316.S78

Encyclopedias

Historical dictionary of the Korean War / ed. by James I. Matray. N.Y. : Greenwood, 1991. 626 p. : maps. **DE215**

Focuses on "diplomatic and political developments with a secondary emphasis on military affairs. Concentrates on the period [from] June 25, 1950 to the armistice agreement [of] July 27, 1953."—*Pref.* Most of the signed entries are several paragraphs long and conclude with bibliographies. A 15-page chronology in the appendixes provides an overview of the war. Indexed. DS918.H536

Nahm, Andrew C. Historical dictionary of the Republic of Korea. Metuchen, N.J. : Scarecrow, 1993. lxi, 272 p. : maps. (Asian historical dictionaries, no. 11). **DE216**

Includes data on Korea previous to partition in 1948 as well as the resulting state of South Korea. Treats political, social, cultural, and economic history. Biographical data limited to major political and historical figures. Chronology; bibliography. DS909.N34

Handbooks

Handbook of Korea. 8th ed. Seoul : Korean Overseas Information Service, 1990. 574 p. : ill. (some col.), maps.   **DE217**
1st ed., 1978.
    A heavily illustrated handbook on South Korea and its people. Topical arrangement; name and subject indexes. Bibliography, p. 549–61.   DS902.H2864

Summers, Harry G. Korean War almanac. N.Y. : Facts on File, c1990. 330 p. : ill.   **DE218**
    Covers the Korean War by means of the following sections: (1) Essays on the setting: Geographical realities, Historical realities, The two Koreas; (2) Chronology 1950–1953; and (3) a dictionary in a single alphabet of short entries on people, places, battles, military groups, and topics. The dictionary is the largest section, each entry concluding with suggestions for further reading. Selected bibliography arranged by author; cross-references; topical index.   DS918.S86

Korea, People's Republic of

An, Tai Sung. North Korea : a political handbook. Wilmington, Del. : Scholarly Resources, 1983. 294 p. : map.   **DE219**
    For annotation, *see* CJ441.   DS932.A76

Kuwait

Clements, Frank A. Kuwait. Oxford, Eng. ; Santa Barbara, Calif. : Clio Pr., [1985]. 195 p. map. (World bibliographical series, 56).   **DE220**
    Aims to present a "comprehensive picture of Kuwait for the general reader, the librarian, or researcher."—*Introd.* 799 annotated entries for English-language materials. Publications on the Gulf are "deliberately excluded" except in the fields of language and literature where there is little material in English. Indexed.   D247.K82Z992

Laos

Cordell, Helen. Laos. Oxford ; Santa Barbara, Calif. : Clio Pr., c1991. 215 p. : map. (World bibliographical series, v. 133).   **DE221**
    "Aims to offer broad subject coverage but reflects the dominance of works on recent history. A feature which hampers the bibliographer is the semi-published nature of much material, such work has been included where it has been relatively easily found in research libraries."—*Introd.* 548 entries. Separate author, title, and subject indexes.   Z3233.C67

Lafont, Pierre-Bernard. Bibliographie du Laos. Paris : École Française d'Éxtrême-Orient, 1964–80. 2 v. (École Française d'Extrême-Orient. Publication, v. 50).   **DE222**
    Contents: v. 1, 1666–1962; v. 2, 1962–75.
    A classified listing of books and periodical articles on all phases of history, life, and culture of Laos. Titles are largely in French, but some material in English and other languages is included; v. 2 extends coverage of English and German materials. Separate indexes for publications in Lao, Thai, Vietnamese, and Russian; author indexes include corporate bodies such as national governments and political parties.
    Supplemented by: William W. Sage and Judith A. N. Henchy, *Laos : a bibliography* (DE223).   Z3228.L3L3

Sage, William W. Laos : a bibliography / comp. by William W. Sage and Judith A.N. Henchy. Singapore : Institute of Southeast Asian Studies, 1986. 253 p. (Library bulletin, Institute of Southeast Asian Studies, no. 16).   **DE223**
    Based on Sage's own collection and that of the Institute, meant to supplement Pierre-Bernard Lafont's *Bibliographie du Laos* (DE222).
    An extensive listing of mostly English-language (with some French, Vietnamese, and Lao) materials published 1975–84, arranged by topic (including refugees and resettlement). Covers books, pamphlets, articles, government and international agency reports, mimeographed papers, and radio monitoring services. Subject and author indexes.   Z3228.L3S24

Stuart-Fox, Martin. Historical dictionary of Laos / by Martin Stuart-Fox and Mary Kooyman. Metuchen, N.J. : Scarecrow, 1992. xlix, 258 p. : ill. (Asian historical dictionaries, no. 6).   **DE224**
    Emphasizes "recent events and those who have played a central role in them. Both the classical kingdom of Lan Xang and its successor kingdoms, and the French colonial interlude have been relatively neglected."—*Pref.* Ten pages of maps and a 20-page chronology provide background data. A 69-page bibliography and appendixes citing rules, members of government ministries, and population data end the work.   DS555.5.S78

Lebanon

Bleaney, C. H. Lebanon. Rev. and expanded ed. Oxford ; Santa Barbara, Calif. : Clio Pr., 1991. 230 p. : map. (World bibliographical series, 2).   **DE225**
    1st ed. (1979) comp. by Shereen Khairallah.
    "This revised edition focuses on material published since the appearance of the first edition in 1979. The majority of new publications have concentrated on the civil war which broke out in 1975. Changes in academic fashion are reflected in a substantial number of publications in the field of women's studies and in the availability of many new translations of modern literature."—*Pref.* 724 entries, in a classed arrangement. Index.   Z3483.L4K48

Macao

Edmonds, Richard L. Macau. Oxford ; Santa Barbara, Calif. : Clio Pr., c1989. lv, 110 p. : map. (World bibliographical series, v. 105).   **DE226**
    Includes "almost all available English or French references as well as a considerable number of Portuguese items" (*Introd.*) and a few selected Chinese publications. Lists 381 books, articles and documents, topically arranged with cross-references and an author/title/subject index.   Z3107.M24E35

Malaysia

Ding, Choo Ming. A bibliography of bibliographies on Malaysia / Ding Choo Ming. Petaling Jaya : Hexagon Elite Publications, c1981. 184 p.   **DE227**
    An annotated listing of more than 650 bibliographies, indexes, catalogs, checklists, etc., "containing bibliographic data wholly or partially pertinent to Malaysia."—*Introd.* Author and title indexes.   Z3246.A1D56

Heussler, Robert. British Malaya : a bibliographical and biographical compendium. N.Y. : Garland, 1981. 193 p. (Themes in European expansion, v.1 ; Garland reference library of social science, v.79).   **DE228**

In two parts: (1) a topically-arranged bibliography covering the years 1867–1942; (2) biographical sketches of personnel of the Malayan civil service (both British and Malayan). Author index.

Z3246.H48

Karni, Rahadi S. Bibliography of Malaysia & Singapore. Kuala Lumpur : Penerbit Universiti Malaya, 1980. 649 p. **DE229**

Books, government publications, periodical articles in all Western languages are listed in topical arrangement. Coverage ends with 1966; not indexed. Useful because of depth of coverage.   Z3236.K37

Kaur, Amarjit. Historical dictionary of Malaysia. Metuchen, N.J. : Scarecrow, 1993. 300 p. : maps. (Asian historical dictionaries, no. 13).   **DE230**

Includes, in addition to the historical dictionary, a 104-page bibliography, appendixes of political leaders, and 27 pages of tables, primarily on economics.   DS596.K36

Malaysian studies : archaeology, historiography, geography, and bibliography / John A. Lent and Kent Mulliner, editors. [De Kalb, Ill.] : Northern Illinois Univ., Center for Southeast Asian Studies : Distr. by the Cellar Bookshop, Detroit, 1985. 240 p. (Northern Illinois University. Center for Southeast Asian Studies. Occasional paper, no. 11).   **DE231**

Presents state-of-the-art papers and surveys, with bibliographies.

DS592.M348

Mongolia

Information Mongolia : the comprehensive reference source of the People's Republic of Mongolia (MPR) / comp. and ed. by the Academy of Sciences, MPR. Oxford ; N.Y. : Pergamon, 1990. 505 p., [45] p. of plates : ill., some maps in color.   **DE232**

B. Lhamsüren, ed. in chief.

"Offers encyclopaedic coverage of all aspects of contemporary Mongolian life within a detailed historical framework ... beginning with a background survey of the land and people and their history from ancient times right up to the present day."—*Pref.* Arranged by topics within broad categories (e.g., Industry under National economy or Written literature under Mongolian culture). Each broad topical section ends with a bibliography; most references are in Russian or Mongolian. Heavily illustrated with photographs, charts, and maps. Directory; chronology; subject index. Last chapter: MPR in figures.

DS798.I54

Nordby, Judith. Mongolia. Oxford, Eng. ; Santa Barbara, Calif. : Clio Pr., 1993. 192 p. : map. (World bibliographical series, v. 156).   **DE233**

"Prepared for the use of students, (and) academics wishing to read on a subject outside their field of expertise. Preference given to monographs written in English. However Mongolia does not command a large body of literature in English and not all that has been published can be recommended as reliable and informative."—*Introd.* Of the 489 entries, more deal with the humanities than the social sciences. Author, title, and subject index.

Myanmar

See Burma.

Nepal

Bibliographie du Népal. Paris : Éditions C.N.R.S., 1969–1984. v. 1 and suppl., v. 3¹⁻³. (In progress).   **DE234**

Contents: v.1, Sciences humaines : Références en langues européennes / L. Boulnois et H. Millot; v. 1, suppl., References en langues europeenes, 1967–1973; v. 3, Sciences naturelles : pt. 1, Cartes du Népal dans les bibliothèques de Paris et de Londres / L. Boulnois; pt. 2, Botanique / J.-F. Dobremez, F. Vigny, L. H. J. Williams; pt. 3, Géologie de l'Himalaya Central / I. Cloître-Trincano.

Publisher varies.

An attempt to provide an extensive bibliography of works relating to Nepal, in classed arrangement. Contains occasional descriptive notes and references to reviews. Author index for each volume. Vol. 2 is to provide reference in Oriental languages to the humanistic sciences.   Z3210.B5

Bibliography of Nepal / comp. and ed. by Khadga Man Malla. Kathmandu : Royal Nepal Academy, 1975. 529 p. **DE235**

Title and introductory matter in English and Nepali.

A classified bibliography of some 8,300 books and periodical articles on various aspects of Nepalese history, life and culture published up to 1972. Annotations in Nepali. Indexed.   Z3207.N4B52

Whelpton, John. Nepal / John Whelpton, comp., with the assistance of Lucette Boulnois ... [et al.]. Oxford ; Santa Barbara, Calif. : Clio Pr., c1990. 294 p. : map. (World bibliographical series, v. 38).   **DE236**

Lists 917 works, mainly books with a few articles and essays. Mostly English-language materials, but some in French, German, or Nepalese. Topical arrangement; annotations. Cross-references; author/title/subject index.   Z3210.W45

Oman

Clements, Frank A. Oman. Oxford ; Santa Barbara, Calif. : Clio Pr., c1981. 216 p. : map. (World bibliographical series, v. 29).   **DE237**

"Material listed should provide a comprehensive picture of Oman for the general reader, the library or researcher. Arrangement is by broad subject head and within that breakdown is alphabetical. Annotations reflect my (i.e., compiler's) views as well as illustrating the content of the material. Only English-language or translated items have been listed."—*Introd.* 890 entries. Author, title, subject index.

Z3028.O5C57

Shannon, Michael Owen. Oman and southeastern Arabia : a bibliographic survey. Boston : G. K. Hall, [1978]. 165 p.   **DE238**

Aims "to record to the fullest extent possible all the major works which have appeared in the West on this Sultanate and surrounding Arab territories."—*Introd.* Main entry listing with subject/author/title index. Includes books and periodical articles; 988 items. Intends to be reasonably complete through 1976, with some 1977 items listed.

Z3028.O5S52

Pakistan

Guide to the sources of Asian history. 8. Pakistan / International Council on Archives. Islamabad : National Archives of Pakistan, 1990. v. 1. (In progress).   **DE239**

Part of the UNESCO project, Guide to the sources of the history of nations, begun in 1959. Intends to note resources for historical research in Pakistan in public archives, archives of semipublic bodies, libraries, museums, universities, and archives in private hands (e.g., political organizations, religious institutions, businesses).

Vol. 1 deals with the National Archives, provincial archives, and district archives, giving general guides to holdings.

CD2104.5.P18G84

Bibliography

Bhatty, Khan Mohammad. Annotated bibliography of social research in Pakistan. Peshawar : Pakistan Academy for Rural Development, [1986]. 141 p., [1] leaf of plates : col. ill.   **DE240**

A topical arrangement under 18 subjects of 540 annotated entries for organization and government publications, articles, mimeographs and typewritten research reports, and a few books. Author index.

Z7165.P3B43

Jones, Garth N. A comprehensive bibliography : Pakistan government and administration / by Garth N. Jones, Shaukat Ali. [Lahore : All Pakistan Public Admin. Research Centre], 1970–[1983]. 4 v.   **DE241**

For annotation, see CJ443.   Z7165.P3J65

Taylor, David D. Pakistan. Oxford ; Santa Barbara, Calif. : Clio Pr., c1990. 255 p., [1] leaf of plates : map. (World bibliographical series, v. 10).   **DE242**

Lists 797 English-language books and a few articles, topically arranged and annotated. Chronology; list of heads of state. Author, title, and subject indexes; cross-references.   Z3196.T39

Palestine

Jones, Philip. Britain and Palestine, 1914–1948 : archival sources for the history of the British mandate. [Oxford] : publ. for the British Academy by Oxford Univ. Pr., [1979]. 246 p.   **DE243**

Presents the findings of a survey conducted by the Anglo-Palestinian Archives Committee "to locate and list briefly the unpublished papers and records of those individuals and organisations, whose base was in Britain, that had involvement or interest in events in Palestine during the first half of this century."—*Introd.* Most of the collections described are in England. Divisions include: Personal papers, Records of selected organisations, Official archives in Britain, Archives outside Britain. Not indexed.   Z6374.Z5J65

Perry, Glenn E. The Palestine question : an annotated bibliography. Belmont, Mass. : Assoc. of Arab-American Univ. Graduates, 1990. 138 p. (AAUG bibliography series, no. 6).   **DE244**

A selected, annotated bibliography limited to English titles. Covers primarily materials on the Palestinians with minimal entries on the Israeli perspective. Books only. Entries are listed alphabetically with subject index.   Z3479.R4P47

Philippines

Biblioteca Nacional (Spain). Catálogo de obras iberoamericanas y filipinas de la Biblioteca Nacional de Madrid / Luisa Cuesta [y] Modesta Cuesta. Madrid : Dirección General de Archivos y Bibliotecas, Servicio de Publicaciones del Ministério de Educación Nacional, 1953. 322 p.   **DE245**

For annotation, see DB268.   Z945.M22

Blair, Emma Helen. The Philippine Islands, 1493–1898 / ed. and annotated by Emma Helen Blair and James Alexander Roberts, with historical introduction and additional notes by Edward Gaylord Bourne. Cleveland, Ohio : Arthur H. Clark Co., 1903–1909. 55 v.   **DE246**

Various reproductions.

The set is a collection of English translations of original source materials from the time of discovery to the end of Spanish rule. Vol. 53 is an extensive annotated bibliography: (1) a bibliography of bibliographies published in various countries concerning the Philippines, p.55–99; (2) other printed books, pamphlets, etc., mostly published in whole or in part in *The Philippine Islands, 1493–1898*; (3) Philippine manuscripts, arranged chronologically by authors, p. 143–419.   DS653.B63

Documentary sources of Philippine history / comp., ed., and annotated by Gregorio F. Zaide ; additional notes by Sonia M. Zaide. Metro Manila, Philippines : National Book Store, 1990. 12 v. : ill., maps.   **DE247**

Makes available the contents of many works damaged or destroyed in the Second World War. Vol. 12 contains an index to the set.   DS668.D6

Hilton, Sylvia L. Bibliografía hispanoamericana y filipina : manual de repertorios bibliográficos para la investigación de la historia y la literatura hispanoamericanas y filipinas / Sylvia-Lyn Hilton, Amancio Labandeira. Madrid : Fundación Universitaria Española, 1983. 411 p. (Publicaciones de la Fundación Universitaria Española. Biblioteca histórica hispanoamericana, 6).   **DE248**

A student's guide to reference materials useful for the study of South American and the Philippines. Chapters for bibliography of bibliographies, national bibliography, biographical dictionaries (subdivided by categories, e.g., governors, artists, women), periodical indexes (general and also cumulated indexes for individual journals), library catalogs, and bibliographies of Hispanic literature and Hispanic and Philippine history. Some categories are subdivided for general works, works on a specific country, and, in some cases, for works on a state or city. Author indexes.   Z1601.H55

Philippine-American relations : a guide to manuscript sources in the United States / comp. and ed. by Shiro Saito. Westport, Conn. : Greenwood, 1982. 256 p.   **DE249**

A guide to the location and general content of collections of "unpublished materials, manuscripts, and official records providing contemporary descriptions or records of the various phases of the Philippine-American encounter."—*Pref.* Includes relevant official, diplomatic, business, shipping, missionary records, etc. Information was collected through literature search, questionnaires, and visits to repositories. Listing is alphabetical by personal or institutional name of collection; general index, repository index, and chronological index.

Z1361.R4P47

Richardson, Jim. Philippines. Oxford ; Santa Barbara, Calif. : Clio Pr., c1989. 372 p. : map. (World bibliographical series, v. 106).   **DE250**

The compiler offers "a fully annotated listing of selected books, articles and other materials on every major aspect of the Philippines and its people ... [seeking to] reflect cultural diversity [yet provide a] fair balance between major geographical regions."—*Introd.* 955 entries in topical arrangement; titles listed are in English or Pilipino. Author, title, and subject indexes.   Z3296.R53

Qatar

Unwin, P. T. H. Qatar. Oxford, Eng. ; Santa Barbara, Calif. : Clio Pr., [1982]. 162 p. (World bibliographical series, 36).   **DE251**

Intends to present a "wide spectrum of basic texts on all major aspects of the country ... in English."—*Pref.* Topical listing, with annotations, of 574 books, government publications, articles, and essays. Well indexed.   Z3828.Q3U58

Saudi Arabia

Clements, Frank A. Saudi Arabia. Rev. and expanded ed. Oxford ; Santa Barbara, Calif. : Clio Pr., c1988. 354 p. : map. (World bibliographical series, v. 5). **DE252**
  1st ed., 1979.
  Lists English-language books and periodical articles in topical arrangement. Annotations; author/title/subject index. Updated through 1986. Z3026.C57

Peterson, John. Historical dictionary of Saudi Arabia. Metuchen, N.J. : Scarecrow, 1993. 245 p. (Asian historical dictionaries, no. 14). **DE253**
  Concentrates on the events and people of the 20th century which have influenced Saudi Arabia. Includes numerous geographic terms. An 18-page chronology similarly concentrates upon 20th century events. Five appendixes deal with the genealogy of the royal family. Concludes with a 30-page bibliography. DS221.P48 1993

Philipp, Hans-Jürgen. Saudi Arabia : bibliography on society, politics, economics = Saudi-Arabien : Bibliographie zu Gesellschaft, Politik, Wirtschaft : Literatur seit dem 18. Jahrhundert in westeuropäischen Sprachen mit Standortnachweisen. München ; N.Y. : Saur, 1984–1989. 2 v. (Bibliographies on regional geography and area studies = Bibliographien zur regionalen Geographie und Landeskunde, 7). **DE254**
  Title page, table of contents, introduction, and index in English and German.
  A topically arranged bibliography of more than 9,200 books, periodical articles, government publications, corporation reports, and reports from international organizations and research institutions, etc., covering from 1745 to the present. Limited to Western language materials with a high percentage in English. Indexes of subjects, authors, corporate authors, and editors in each volume cover that volume only. Locates copies in German libraries. Z3026.P48

Singapore

Karni, Rahadi S. Bibliography of Malaysia & Singapore. Kuala Lumpur : Penerbit Universiti Malaya, 1980. 649 p. **DE255**
  For annotation, *see* DE229. Z3236.K37

Mulliner, K. Historical dictionary of Singapore / by K. Mulliner and Lian The-Mulliner. Metuchen, N.J. : Scarecrow, 1991. 251 p. : map. (Asian historical dictionaries, no. 7). **DE256**
  Consists of several sections: Chronology of important events; Introductory overview of general information on Singapore; Dictionary; Appendixes citing heads of government, elections, ethnicity, and percentage of Chinese dialects in the population. 59-page bibliography; maps; index. DS610.4.M85

Quah, Stella R. Singapore / Stella R. Quah, Jon S.T. Quah, compilers. Oxford ; Santa Barbara, Calif. : Clio Pr., c1988. 258 p. : maps. (World bibliographical series, v. 95). **DE257**
  Includes English-language "works dealing with Singapore as the only, or the major topic" (*Introd.*), published 1980–88, except for a few significant older materials. Lists 764 books and articles in a topical arrangement. Author, title, and subject indexes. Z3285.Q33

Sri Lanka

De Silva, Daya. Sri Lanka since independence : a reference guide to the literature / Daya de Silva and Chandra R. de Silva. New Delhi : Navrang Booksellers and Publishers, 1992. 312 p. **DE258**
  Update of *Sri Lanka (Ceylon) since independence (1948–1974)* (1978).
  Intended as a "guide to the literature on society, economy, religion and politics in contemporary Sri Lanka."—*Introd.* Lists Western-language publications—books, government publications, dissertations, annual reports, journal articles—under broad subject headings. 2,456 works cited, most with brief annotations. Author index. Z3211.D48

Goonetileke, H. A. I. A bibliography of Ceylon. Zug : Inter Documentation, [1970–83]. 5 v. (Bibliotheca asiatica, 5). **DE259**
  Subtitle: A systematic guide to the literature on the land, people, history and culture published in Western languages from the sixteenth century to the present day.
  A classed bibliography of more than 11,600 items. Books, parts of books, pamphlets, periodical articles, and government publications are included. Some brief annotations. Vol. 3–5 are supplements adding materials to Dec. 1978. Author index in v. 5. Z3211.G65

Rupesinghe, Kumar. Ethnic conflict and human rights in Sri Lanka : an annotated bibliography / Kumar Rupesinghe & Berth Verstappen. London ; N.Y. : Zell ; Oslo : Publ. for the International Peace Research Institute, 1989. 565 p. **DE260**
  "The purpose of this bibliography is to record the literature concerning the escalating phase of the internal conflict in Sri Lanka, with an emphasis on the period 1983–88."—*Introd.* A topical listing with good annotations of 2,311 books, pamphlets, government publications, articles, and documents of organizations. Author, subject, and geographical indexes. Z3211.R855

Samaraweera, Vijaya. Sri Lanka. Oxford ; Santa Barbara, Calif. : Clio Pr., c1987. 194 p. : map. (World bibliographical series, v. 20). **DE261**
  An annotated list of books, government publications, and periodical articles. Topical arrangement with author/title/subject index.
  Z3211.S26

Syria

Seccombe, Ian J. Syria. Oxford ; Santa Barbara, Calif. : Clio Pr., c1987. 341 p. : map. (World bibliographical series, v. 73). **DE262**
  An annotated bibliography of 903 books, government publications, and articles, primarily in English but some in French, German, or Italian. Emphasis is on history, politics, and archaeology. Author, title, subject indexes. Z3481.S43

Taiwan

Copper, John Franklin. Historical dictionary of Taiwan. Metuchen, N.J. : Scarecrow, 1993. 178 p. : map. (Asian historical dictionaries, no. 12). **DE263**
  In addition to the entries in the body of the work, includes a chronology of important events, a general overview, and a 58-page bibliography. Appendix provides information on the presidents and premiers. No index. DS798.96.C67

Lee, Wei-chin. Taiwan. Oxford ; Santa Barbara, Calif. : Clio Pr., c1990. 247 p. : map. (World bibliographical series, v. 113). **DE264**

A topical listing of 825 books, articles, doctoral dissertations, and government publications, most of them in English and published after 1980. Cross-references; author, title, subject indexes.   Z3116.L44

Republic of China yearbook. 1989– . Taipei, Taiwan, R.O.C. : Kwang Hwa Pub. Co., 1989– . Annual.   **DE265**
Surveys events and developments of the year, with chapters on language, history, central government, political parties, science and industry, etc., each chapter ending with a short bibliography and a listing of relevant institutions, organizations, government agencies, etc. Appendix: Who's who in the R.O.C.; Chronology, Jan. 1911–June 1987; Constitution; The Republic of China in figures; National holidays; Directory of legislators; Diplomatic representatives. Topical index.
DS798.92.R46

Thailand

Smith, Harold Eugene. Historical and cultural dictionary of Thailand. Metuchen, N.J. : Scarecrow, 1976. 213 p. (Historical and cultural dictionaries of Asia, no. 6).   **DE266**
Entries cover "history, Thai Buddhism and other religions, ethnolinguistic groupings, the economy, geography, governmental patterns, Thai customs and values, communication, and artistic production."—*Introd.* Discusses each of the 72 Thai provinces as well as its capital.
DS563.S56

Watts, Michael. Thailand. Oxford, England ; Santa Barbara, Calif. : Clio Pr, 1986. 275 p. : map. (World bibliography series, v. 65).   **DE267**
818 annotated entries primarily representing works in English but with some French and German works. Designed as a general introduction. 63-page author, title, and subject index.   Z3236.W38

Tibet

Bibliography of Tibetan studies / comp. by Hallvard Kåre Kuløy, Yoshiro Imaeda. Narita-shi Chiba-ken, Japan : Naritasan Shinshōji, 1986. 735 p. (Naritasan Institute for Buddhist studies. Monograph series, 2).   **DE268**
Amasses 11,822 entries to produce a comprehensive bibliography of books and articles, in all languages, "published up to (and including) 1975, and which deal with 'Tibetan' civilisation: all aspects of 'Tibetan'-speaking people and followers of Mahāyāna Buddhism … and in the strictly cultural, linguistic and ethnical context."—*p. v.* Author arrangement, with cross-references to variant form of name, etc., but no index.   Z3107.T5B53

Pinfold, John R. Tibet. Oxford ; Santa Barbara, Calif. : Clio Pr., c1991. 158 p. (World bibliographical series, v. 128.).   **DE269**
"Aimed at students or researchers or intellectually curious individuals who may be approaching the subject for the first time and want to know where to start."—*Introd.* 559 entries, overwhelmingly in English, of books and articles, with brief annotations. Author, title, and subject indexes.   DS786.P56

United Arab Emirates

Clements, Frank A. United Arab Emirates. Oxford, Eng. ; Santa Barbara, Calif. : Clio Pr., [1983]. 162 p. (World bibliographical series, 43).   **DE270**
Covers the Federation of Abu Dhabi, Dubai, Sharjah, Ajman, Umm al-Qaiwain, Ras al-Khaimah and Fujairah, listing books, articles, and a few government documents in English or translated into English. Topical arrangement; annotations; good index.   Z3028.U54C57

Vietnam

Cotter, Michael. Vietnam : a guide to reference sources. Boston : G. K. Hall, [1977]. 272p.   **DE271**
Presented as the "first known compilation of reference works about Vietnam. It lists about 1400 books, periodical articles, serials, government publications, and other materials in the human and natural sciences, primarily in romanized Vietnamese (quôc-ngũ), French and English from 1651 (the date of the first dictionary using romanized Vietnamese …) until 1976."—*Introd.* Classified arrangement; annotations; name/title index.   Z3228.V5C68

Descours-Gatin, Chantal. Guide de recherches sur le Vietnam : bibliographies, archives et bibliothèques de France / Chantal Descours-Gatin, Hugues Villiers. Paris : L'Harmattan, [1983]. 259 p.   **DE272**
In two parts, the first listing bibliographies and other works of reference (library catalogs, periodical indexes, maps and atlases, yearbooks, chronologies, biographical dictionaries, language dictionaries, official documents, etc.). The second part provides a guide to French libraries and archives, with descriptions of holdings related to Vietnam. Covers materials from early times to the recent past. Detailed table of contents, but no index.   Z3228.V5D47

Duiker, William J. Historical dictionary of Vietnam. Metuchen, N.J. : Scarecrow, 1989. 269 p. : maps. (Asian historical dictionaries, no. 1).   **DE273**
"Recent events and individuals receive priority treatment over those from the remote past. Primary emphasis is on history and politics" (*Pref.*) with secondary treatment of economic, social, and cultural issues. A 43-page bibliography and appendixes citing statistics complete the volume.   DS556.25.D85

Marr, David G. Vietnam. Oxford ; Santa Barbara, Calif. : Clio Pr., c1992. lxxviii, 393 p. : map. (World bibliographical series, v. 147).   **DE274**
"The vast majority of English books about 'Vietnam' appearing in the past quarter century have in fact concentrated on Americans in Vietnam. Very little attention has been given to the Vietnamese people, much less to Vietnam's rich culture and extensive history prior to 1945, or developments in the country since 1975."—*Introd.* 1,038 annotated entries. Author, title, and subject indexes.   Z3226.M39

Peake, Louis A. The United States in the Vietnam War, 1954–1975 : a selected annotated bibliography. N.Y. : Garland, 1986. 406 p. (Wars of the United States, vol. 4 ; Garland reference library of social science, vol. 256).   **DE275**
More than 1,500 English-language items in classed arrangement, including books, articles, government publications, films, and recordings. Author and subject indexes; chronology; glossary; four-page list of addenda.   Z3226.P43

Sugnet, Christopher L. Vietnam War bibliography : selected from Cornell University's Echols Collection / Christopher L. Sugnet, John T. Hickey. Lexington, Mass. : Lexington Books, 1983. 572 p.   **DE276**
Lists more than 3,000 books, pamphlets, government publications, manuscripts, and maps, plus notes on the content of journals, newspapers and press releases relating to "U.S. involvement (1945–1975) including the War's international context and its interaction with U.S. domestic politics."—*Introd.* Title listing with topical index; some annotations.   Z3226.S9

Vietnam : the definitive documentation of human decision / Gareth Porter, comp. Stanfordville, N.Y. : Coleman Enterprises, 1979. 2 v.   **DE277**
A chronological presentation of documents from 1941 to May 1975 which the compiler feels "will illuminate the ideology, assumptions, strategy, and tactics of the two sides, as well as the interaction between decisions made by both sides" (*Introd.*) during the Vietnam conflict. Documents are derived from both U.S. and Vietnamese

sources; Vietnamese documents are given in English translation. Each document has a headnote giving source and a summary. Public figure index; broad subject index. DS556.8.V53

Wittman, Sandra M. Writing about Vietnam : a bibliography of the literature of the Vietnam Conflict. Boston : G.K. Hall, c1989. 385 p. : ill. **DE278**
For annotation, *see* BE417. Z3226.W58

Encyclopedias

Dictionary of the Vietnam War / ed. by James S. Olson. N.Y. : Greenwood, 1988. 585 p. : maps. **DE279**
An encyclopedia with "brief descriptive essays on most people, legislation, military operations, and controversies important to American participation in the Vietnam War."—*Pref.* Articles not written by Olson are signed with the contributor's name. Most articles have short bibliographies. Cross-references; subject index. Appendix of tables showing population in South Vietnam and of minority groups in South Vietnam; glossary of acronyms and slang; select bibliography; chronology.
§ See also *Words of the Vietnam War* by Gregory R. Clark (AC121). DS557.7.D53

Yemen

Smith, Gerald Rex. The Yemens : the Yemen Arab Republic and the People's Democratic Republic of Yemen. Oxford, Eng. ; Santa Barbara, Calif. : Clio Pr., [1984]. 161 p. map. (World bibliographical series, 50). **DE280**
A topical arrangement of 130 entries for materials "reasonably accessible" in the United Kingdom—mainly English and French materials, with a few Italian and German items. Annotations; separate list of theses; author/title/subject index. Z3028.Y39S65

DF

Australia and Oceania

GENERAL WORKS

Bibliography

An annotated bibliography of the Southwest Pacific and adjacent areas / with an introduction by Douglas MacArthur. [s.l.], 1944–45. 4 v. : fold map. **DF1**
Repr. : Queensland : Pacific Books, 1990 (230 p.).
At head of title: Allied Geographical Section. Southwest Pacific Area.

Contents: v. 1, The Netherlands and British East Indies and the Philippine Islands; v. 2, The Mandated Territory of New Guinea, Papua, the British Solomon Islands, the New Hebrides and Micronesia; v. 3, Malaya, Thailand, Indo China, the China coast and the Japanese Empire; v. 4, Supplement.
Features more than 5,000 citations to books and articles arranged by geographic region, then by author. Most include annotations indicating the presence of maps, photographs, and other illustrations as well as holdings in Australian libraries.
§ European imprints related to exploration are identified in Willem Carel Hendrik Robert's *Contributions to a bibliography of Australia and the South Sea Islands* (Amsterdam : Philo Pr., 1964– . Some volumes in 2nd ed. *Supplement*, 1972–). Z4501.A4

Bibliography of periodical articles relating to the South Pacific. v. 1 (1974)–4/5 (1977/78). Suva, Fiji : Univ. of the South Pacific Libr., 1976–82. Annual. **DF2**
Esther Dam, comp. and ed.
A classed listing within geographical sections for Oceania, Melanesia, Micronesia, Polynesia. Author index. References are drawn from about 200 periodicals received in the University of the South Pacific Library. Continued by the University's Pacific Information Centre, *South Pacific periodicals index*, v. 6–8 (1979/81)– , publ. 1984– . Z4501.B53

Fry, Gerald. Pacific Basin and Oceania / Gerald W. Fry, Rufino Mauricio, compilers. Oxford ; Santa Barbara, Calif. : Clio Pr., c1987. 468 p. : map. (World bibliographical series, v. 70). **DF3**
Lists 1,178 English-language books and periodical articles, most of them published 1975–85, with a few earlier works "of enduring value or special interest."—*Introd.* Arrangement is by broad topic; the annotations are meant to be evaluative and descriptive. Covers Melanesia, Micronesia, and Polynesia; specific countries (e.g., Australia, Indonesia) are not included because they are accorded separate volumes in this series. The compilers made an effort to include "a sizable portion of indigenous publications." Author/title/subject index. Z4501.F79

Hamnett, Judith D. A guide to films about the Pacific Islands [Honolulu, Hawaii] : Pacific Islands Studies Program, Center for Asian and Pacific Studies, Univ. of Hawaii at Manoa, 1986. 148 p. **DF4**
Lists films and videocassettes in three sections: 1) Pacific Islands excluding Hawaii; 2) Hawaii; 3) Pacific Islands films available outside the U.S. Excluded are films and videos whose sole purpose is entertainment. Each entry includes name of film, country or culture, length, format, color or black-and-white, year of release, producer, distributor, and a brief annotation. List of producers' names and addresses. Not indexed.
§ A more narrowly focused compilation is the New Zealand Film Archive's *Maori and Pacific films from New Zealand 1901–1984* (Wellington : New Zealand Film Archive, 1984). DU28.2.H36

Marshall, Mac. Micronesia, 1944–1974 : a bibliography of anthropological and related source materials / by Mac Marshall and James D. Nason. New Haven, Conn. : HRAF Pr., 1975. 337 p. : ill. **DF5**
For annotation, *see* CE114. Z5116.M37

Pacific Island studies : a survey of the literature / Miles M. Jackson, ed. in chief. N.Y. : Greenwood, [1986]. 244 p. (Bibliographies and indexes in sociology, no. 7). **DF6**
Based on the collection of the library of the University of Hawaii, Manoa, the guide provides "a concise synthesis of the significant literature" (*Pref.*) on history, political change, popular accounts, language, and sources of information (e.g., newspapers and journals). Presented as a series of bibliographic essays on Polynesia subdivided for Pacific Islands and Hawaii, Micronesia, Melanesia, and Australian aboriginal studies with a list of full citations at the end of each. Subject/author index. Z4501.P33

Snow, Philip A. A bibliography of Fiji, Tonga, and Rotuma. Prelim. working ed. Coral Gables, Fla. : Univ. of Miami Pr., 1969. 418 p.   **DF7**

More than 10,000 items. Classified arrangement within geographical sections; author index. Includes books, periodical articles, government publications, vernacular language items, and references to pertinent material in selected British newspapers.   Z4651.S65

Taylor, Clyde Romer Hughes. A Pacific bibliography : printed matter relating to the native peoples of Polynesia, Melanesia and Micronesia. 2nd ed. Oxford : Clarendon Pr., 1965. 692 p.   **DF8**

1st ed., 1951.

A bibliography of books and periodical articles in various languages dealing with Pacific Island groups. Arrangement is by island group, subdivided by such headings as: bibliography, ethnology, physical and mental characteristics, origins and migrations, culture contacts, tribal and family organizations, religion, medicine, language, folklore, music, arts, archaeology, dress, houses, handicrafts. Listings are as complete as possible up to 1960.

§ The New Zealand and Maori section was revised, updated, and issued separately as *A bibliography of publications on the New Zealand Maori and the Moriori of the Chatham Islands* (Oxford : Clarendon Pr., 1972. 161 p.).   Z4501.T3

Where the whalers went : an index to the Pacific ports and islands visited by American whalers (and some other ships) in the 19th century / ed. by Robert Langdon. Canberra : Pacific Manuscripts Bureau, Research School of Pacific Studies, Australian National Univ., 1984. 298 p. : ill., maps.   **DF9**

Supersedes *Thar she went* ... (Canberra : Pacific Manuscripts Bureau, Research School of Pacific Studies, The Australian National University, 1979).

A bibliography of logbooks kept by 19th century American whaling, trading, and naval ships with ports of call in Australia, New Zealand, and the Pacific Islands. Arranged by place and date; each entry gives precise dates, captain/logkeeper, and citation to microfilm number if reproduced in the New England Microfilming Project sponsored by the Pacific Manuscripts Bureau. Index of captains/logkeepers.

§ Francis X. Hezel's *Foreign ships in Micronesia : compendium of ship contacts in the Caroline and Marshall Islands 1521–1885* (Saipan, Mariana Is. : publ. in cooperation with the Trust Territory Historic Preservation Office and the U.S. Heritage Conservation and Recreation Service, 1979) gives chronological listings for Palau, Yap, Truk, Ponape, Kosrai, Marshalls and Carolines.   SH382.6.W44

Library resources

Bernice Pauahi Bishop Museum. Library. Dictionary catalog of the Library. Boston : G.K. Hall, 1964. 9 v.   **DF10**

Photoreproduction of the author, subject, and title cards from the Library's catalog. The Museum "confines its efforts entirely to study of the peoples and natural areas of the Pacific," and concentration of interest is in "cultural anthropology, archaeology, marine zoology, malacology, entomology, music, further recording of linguistic material, astronomy, bibliography."—*Pref.*

Supplements were issued in 1967 and 1969. *Supplement 1* represents holdings added through Aug. 1967. *Supplement 2* provides access to the Fuller Library, a collection of about 2,500 volumes on Pacific history and exploration.

§ Another important collection: University of California, Santa Cruz. University Library. *Catalog of the South Pacific collection* (Santa Cruz : The Library, 1978. 722 p.). *Supplement, 1978–1985* (1985?. 2 v. in 6).

Bloomfield, Valerie. Resources for Australian and New Zealand studies : a guide to library holdings in the United Kingdom. London : Australian Studies Centre : British Library, 1986. 284 p.   **DF11**

Aims "to provide a guide to the holdings of printed and audiovisual materials in the United Kingdom relating to Australia and New Zealand."—*Introd.* Manuscripts and archives are excluded because they are treated by Phyllis Mander-Jones's *Manuscripts in the British Isles relating to Australia, New Zealand and the Pacific* (DF15). Based on responses to a questionnaire and on personal visits. Covers 172 libraries and institutions, giving for each: name and address, hours, access, lending policies, details of holdings, and any publications about the library. Arranged alphabetically under name of city. Index of names, subjects and categories (e.g. maps, information retrieval services, audiovisual materials).   Z4009.B54

Thompson, Anne-Gabrielle. The Southwest Pacific : an annotated guide to bibliographies, indexes and collections in Australian libraries. Canberra : Research School of Pacific Studies, the Australian National Univ. in association with the Academy of Social Sciences in Australia, 1986. 127 p. (Aids to research series, no. A/6).   **DF12**

Lists reference materials on the Southwest Pacific: Fiji, New Caledonia, Papua New Guinea, the Solomon Islands, and Vanuatu (formerly New Hebrides). Includes sections for general and subject bibliographies, thesis catalogs, and guides to archives and manuscripts, to newspaper and journal articles, to official publications, to holdings of special libraries, and to serial publications. Author and subject indexes.   DU3.T56

Manuscripts; Archives

Asia and Oceania : a guide to archival & manuscript sources in the United States / G. Raymond Nunn, ed. London : Mansell, 1985. 5 v.   **DF13**

For annotation, *see* DE11.   Z3001.A78

Australian National University. Pacific Manuscripts Bureau. Complete annotated catalogue PMB manuscript series microfilms PMB 1–1030 / ed. by Gillian Scott. Canberra : Pacific Manuscripts Bureau, Research School of Pacific Studies, Australian National Univ., 1991. 822, 48 p.   **DF14**

Lists a variety of primary materials, including correspondence and journals related to exploration and settlement.   DU17.C66

Mander-Jones, Phyllis. Manuscripts in the British Isles relating to Australia, New Zealand, and the Pacific. Honolulu : Univ. of Hawaii Pr., 1972. 697 p.   **DF15**

Sponsored by the National Library of Australia and the Australian National University.

Lists "manuscript material in Great Britain and Ireland relating to Australia and New Zealand, New Guinea, Melanesia, Micronesia, Polynesia, Antarctica, the sub-Antarctic islands in southern Pacific and Indian Oceans."—*Pref.* Arranged by county, with London holdings described first. Detailed index.   CD1048.A85M35

Dictionaries

Craig, Robert D. Historical dictionary of Polynesia. Metuchen, N.J. : Scarecrow, 1993. 298 p. : map. (Oceanian historical dictionaries, no. 2).   **DF16**

Descriptive entries for people, places, political and economic developments, and related issues, arranged alphabetically by topic. Includes a chronology and general bibliography as well as selected bibliographies on the Cook Islands, Easter Island, French Polynesia, Hawaii, New Zealand, Niue, Pitcairn, Samoa, Tokelau, Tonga, Tuvalu, and Wallis and Futuna. Appendixes: names of Polynesian islands, rulers and adminstrators.

Planned in the series are companion volumes on Micronesia and Melanesia.   DU510.C73

Historical dictionary of Oceania / ed. by Robert D. Craig and Frank P. King. Westport, Conn. : Greenwood, 1981. 392 p. : maps.   **DF17**

Signed entries, in alphabetical order, each with a list of sources. Various appendixes give chronologies, prehistoric settlements, individuals by occupation. Select bibliography; name and subject indexes.

DU10.H57

Handbooks

Hoadley, Steve. The South Pacific foreign affairs handbook. North Sydney, N.S.W. : Allen & Unwin, 1992. 258 p. : ill., maps.   **DF18**

Publ. in association with the New Zealand Institute of International Affairs.

Provides four chapters of introductory material giving a historical, economic, and political overview of the region, followed by individual chapters covering Cook Islands and Niue; Fiji; Kiribati and Tuvalu; Northern Marianas, Guam, American Samoa; Marshall Islands, Federated States of Micronesia, Palau; Nauru; New Caledonia, French Polynesia, Wallis and Futuna; Papua New Guinea; Solomon Islands; Tonga; Vanuatu; and Western Samoa. More than 50 tables feature historical and economic data. List of references; subject index.

Oceania, a regional study / Foreign Area Studies, the American University ; ed. by Frederica M. Bunge and Melinda W. Cooke. 2nd ed. Wash. : for sale by U.S. Govt. Print. Off., 1985. 572 p. : ill. (DA pam, 550-94).   **DF19**

The first chapter provides a historical overview followed by separate chapters by experts on Melanesia, Micronesia, and Polynesia, with a final chapter on "strategic perspective." Bibliography, glossary, index.   DU17..026

Biography

Who's who in Asian and Australasian politics. London ; N.Y. : Bowker-Saur, c1991. 475 p.   **DF20**

For annotation, *see* DE20.   DS35.2.W48

AUSTRALIA

See also CF99.

Bibliography

Adelaide, Debra. Australian women writers : a bibliographic guide. London : Pandora, 1988. 208 p.   **DF21**

For annotation, *see* BE845.   PR9608.A3

APAIS, Australian public affairs information service : a subject index to current literature. no.1 (July 1945)– . Canberra : National Library of Australia, 1945– . Monthly (except Dec.).   **DF22**

For annotation, *see* CA23.   Z7165.A8A8

Australian national bibliography. Jan. 1961– . Canberra : National Library of Australia, 1961– . Monthly issues superseded by annual cumulation.   **DF23**

For annotation, *see* AA944.   Z4015.A96

A bibliography of Australian multicultural writers / comp. by Sneja Gunev … [et al.]. Geelong, Vic. : Centre for Studies in Literary Education, Humanities, Deakin Univ., 1992. 291 p.   **DF24**

PR9608.2.M55

Bodi, Leslie. Image of a continent : a bibliography of German Australiana from the beginnings to 1975 = Bild eines Kontinents : eine Bibliographie deutscher Australiana von den Anfängen bis 1975 / Leslie Bodi, Stephen Jeffries, Susan Radvansky. Wiesbaden : O. Harrassowitz, c1990. 587 p.   **DF25**

"A comprehensive checklist of printed materials on Australian subjects in German … (and) a listing of works of German-language settlers in Australia … in German or in English."—*Introd.* Cites more than 6,700 books and articles. Arranged by main entry, with an extremely broad subject index and a chronological index.   Z4001.B63

Ferguson, John Alexander. Bibliography of Australia. Sydney ; London : Angus & Robertson, 1941–69. 7 v.   **DF26**

Contents: v. 1, 1784–1830; v. 2, 1831–1838; v. 3, 1839–1845; v. 4, 1846–1850; v. 5–7, 1851–1900.

Arranged chronologically. Indexes are not cumulative. Vols. 2–4 include lists of Addenda. A promised index and further addenda were not published.

The standard bibliography of Australia, which aims to include all books, pamphlets, broadsides, newspapers, magazines, and government papers printed from 1784 to 1900. Does not include manuscripts. Extensive annotations. Locates copies in ten Australian libraries and the British Museum.

———. ——— Addenda, *1784–1850* (Canberra : National Library of Australia, 1986. 706 p.). Includes titles omitted from v. 1–4 and addenda in v. 2–4. Arranged chronologically with general author/title/subject index.   Z4011.F47

Kepars, I. Australia. 2nd ed. Oxford : Santa Barbara, Calif. : Clio Pr., 1994. 260 p. (World bibliographical series, 46).   **DF27**

An annotated bibliography of recent books in English, arranged by topic (e.g., environment, Australian aborigines, food and drink). Author, title, subject index.   Z4011.K46

Thawley, John. Bibliographies on the Australian aborigine : an annotated listing / by John Thawley and Sarah Gauci. 2nd ed. Bundoora, Vic. : Borchardt Library, La Trobe Univ., 1987. 44 p. (Library publications [La Trobe University. Library], no. 32).   **DF28**

1st ed., 1979.   Z5116.T46

Wantrup, Jonathan. Australian rare books, 1788–1900. Sydney : Horden House ; London ; N.Y. : Kegan Paul International, 1987. 468 p. : ill. (some col.).   **DF29**

Offers two introductory chapters on book collecting followed by six covering the founding period 1788–1806, the Bligh-Macquarie era 1806–23, post-Cook exploration along the coast, interior discovery from 1788 to 1850 and from 1850 to 1900, and books featuring color plates. Includes an analytical bibliography of the books discussed in each chapter. Glossary; general index; index of artists and engravers.   Z1029.W367

Library resources

Albinski, Nan Bowman. Directory of resources for Australian studies in North America. Clayton, Vic. : National Centre for Australian Studies, Monash Univ. ; University Park, Penn. : Australia-New Zealand Studies Center, Pennsylvania State Univ., 1992. 211 p.   **DF30**

A "first attempt to systematically locate and record Australian materials in the libraries, galleries and museums of North America."—*Introd.* An initial section lists and describes relevant holdings in general libraries. Remaining subject-based sections cover such topics as ethnographic papers, maritime and mercantile records, travel diaries and letters. Select bibliography; index of repositories and of personal names.   Z4029.A5

Directory of special collections in Australiana / comp. by Jennifer Alison, Margaret Medcalf, and Catherine Santamaria. Sydney : NSW Group, LAA Acquisitions Section, 1988. 150 p.   **DF31**
    Z4011.A45

Guide to collections of manuscripts relating to Australia [microform]. Microfiche ed. 1986– . Canberra : National Library of Australia, 1986– . Irregular.   **DF32**

Encyclopedias; dictionaries

The Australian people : an encyclopedia of the nation, its people, and their origins / gen. ed., James Jupp. North Ryde, Australia : Angus & Robertson Publishers, 1988. 1040 p. : ill., plates.   **DF33**
    "Seeks to serve two major purposes: to provide detailed information on the Aboriginal people and the later settlers of Australia; and to look at historical and contemporary interactions between the Australian people in a chronological and thematic way."—*Introd.* Signed entries. Appendixes provide 1986 census data and a chronology of Australian history. Select bibliography; index.
    § Also useful: *The Cambridge encyclopedia of Australia*, ed. by Susan Hambrick (N.Y. : Cambridge Univ. Pr., 1994).   DU120.A718

Docherty, James C. Historical dictionary of Australia. Metuchen, N.J. : Scarecrow, 1992. 284 p. (Oceanian historical dictionaries, no. 1).   **DF34**
    Brief entries in alphabetical order. Appendixes include a chronology, list of the governors-general and prime ministers, and historical statistics. Concludes with brief bibliographies on 35 topics.
    DU90.D63 1992

Grant, Ian. A dictionary of Australian military history. Milsons Point, N.S.W. : Random House, 1992. 414 p.   **DF35**
    Provides in an alphabetical arrangement about 500 brief entries describing people, places, things, and events related to military history, with lengthier discussions of Gallipoli, the two World Wars, and the Royal Australian Navy and Air Force. Extensive cross-references, but no index or list of sources.

Handbooks

Macintyre, Clement. Political Australia : a handbook of facts. Oxford : Oxford Univ. Pr., 1991. 394 p.   **DF36**
    Individual chapters provide historical data (including names, dates, and statistics) for elections, ministries, parties, Parliament, Vice-Regal appointments, the judiciary, royal commissions, public service, and social and economic indicators. Brief bibliography. Name/subject index; index to ministers and portfolios.

General histories

Australians : a historical library. Broadway, N.S.W., Australia : Fairfax, Syme & Weldon, 1987. 11 v. : ill. (some col.), maps, ports.   **DF37**
    General editors: Alan D. Gilbert and K. S. Inglis for v. 1–5, Frank Crowley and Peter Spearritt for v. 6–10. Chairman of the Management Committee: Oliver MacDonagh.
    Contents: v. 1, Australians to 1788, ed. by D. J. Mulvaney and J. Peter White; v. 2, Australians 1838, ed. by Alan Atkinson and Marian Aveling; v. 3, Australians 1888, ed. by Graeme Davison, J. W. McCar-

ty and Ailsa McLeary; v. 4, Australians 1938, ed. by Bill Gammage and Peter Spearritt; oral history coord., Louise Douglas; v. 5, Australians from 1939, ed. by Ann Curthoys, A. W. Martin, and Tim Rowse; v. 6, Australians : a historical atlas, ed. by J. C. R. Camm and John McQuilton; cartographic ed., Trevor W. Plumb; 40 cm.); v. 7, Australians : events and places, ed. by Graeme Aplin, S. G. Foster and Michael McKernan; v. 8, Australians : a historical dictionary, ed. by Graeme Aplin, S. G. Foster, Michael McKernan; v. 9, Australians : a guide to sources, ed. by D. H. Borchardt and Victor Crittenden; v. 10, Australians : historical statistics, ed. by Wray Vamplew; v. 11, Australians : the guide and index.
    Written to commemorate the bicentenary of European settlement in Australia, each volume is intended to stand alone and has its own index, but all are meant to complement each other. The set is composed of five historical volumes, of which three are "slice" volumes (i.e., describing a single year); the others are reference volumes. General index (v. 11 unites the individual indexes).   DU96.A87

Clark, Charles Manning Hope. A history of Australia. [Carlton, Victoria] : Melbourne Univ. Pr. ; London ; N.Y. : Cambridge Univ. Pr., [1962] i.e., 1963–1987. 6 v. : illus.   **DF38**
    Contents: v. 1, From the earliest times to the age of Macquarie; v. 2, New South Wales and Van Diemen's Land, 1822–1838; v. 3, The beginning of an Australian civilization, 1824–1851; v. 4, The earth abideth for ever, 1851–1888; v. 5, The people make laws, 1888–1915; v. 6, The old dead tree and the young tree green, 1916–1935.
    The classic narrative of Australian history.   DU110.C48

The Oxford history of Australia / [gen. ed., Geoffrey Bolton]. Melbourne ; N.Y. : Oxford Univ. Pr., 1986–1992. v. 2–5 : ill. (In progress).   **DF39**
    Contents: v. 2, 1770–1860, Possessions, by Jan Kociumbas; v. 3, 1860–1900, Glad, confident morning, by Beverley Kingston; v. 4, 1901–1942, The succeeding age, by Stuart Macintyre; v. 5, 1942–1988, The middle way, by Geoffrey Bolton.
    The standard survey of Australia's past. A projected first volume will cover Aboriginal Australia.   DU110.O94

Biography

Australian dictionary of biography. [Melbourne] : Melbourne Univ. Pr. ; London ; N.Y. : Cambridge Univ. Pr., [1966]–1991. 13 vol.   **DF40**
    For annotation, *see* AH371.   CT2802.A95

NEW CALEDONIA

O'Reilly, Patrick. Bibliographie méthodique, analytique et critique de la Nouvelle-Calédonie. Paris : Musée de l'Homme, 1955. 361 p. (Société des océanistes. Publications, no.4).   **DF41**
    A comprehensive, annotated bibliography of some 4,100 entries, covering the voyages, geology, botany, zoology, geography, ethnology, history, economy, medicine, and literature of the area. Texts in the native language are grouped with the ethnology section.
    § Continued by: George Pisier, *Bibliographie méthodique, analytique et critique de la Nouvelle-Calédonie, 1955–1982* (Noumía : Société d'Études Historiques de la Nouvelle-Calédonie, 1983. 350 p.). A topical listing of 3,338 books, articles, theses, and book reviews. Nonevaluative. Name index.   Z4805.O7

NEW ZEALAND

Bibliography

Bagnall, Austin Graham. New Zealand national bibliography to the year 1960. Wellington : A.R. Shearer, Govt. Printer, 1970–85. 5 v. : ill. **DF42**
> For annotation, *see* AA946. Z4101.B28

Encyclopedias

Encyclopaedia of New Zealand / A. H. McLintock, ed. Wellington : R. E. Owen, Govt. Printer, 1966. 3 v. : ill. **DF43**
> Prepared under government auspices, and more than six years in preparation, this is the first really comprehensive encyclopedia for New Zealand. An alphabetical arrangement is employed, but, where practicable, closely related topics are grouped under broad subject headings (e.g., universities are treated under Education; Army under Defense), with appropriate subdivisions and cross-references. There are, of course, lengthy articles on New Zealand history, literature, etc., and an extensive series on aspects of Maori life and culture. Biographies given separate entries are largely confined to deceased persons; a section on expatriates offers biographical sketches of a considerable number of New Zealanders who are more or less permanently living or working abroad. Most articles (particularly the longer ones) are signed with the initials of the contributors, and many carry bibliographies. Numerous line drawings, maps, and statistical tables (1961 census figures are used) are scattered throughout the text, and there are plates of black-and-white photographs. Good general index in v. 3.
> § More up-to-date is *Bateman New Zealand encyclopedia* ([3rd ed.]. Auckland : David Bateman, 1992). DU405.E5

Handbooks

Hoadley, Steve. The New Zealand foreign affairs handbook. Auckland ; N.Y. : Oxford Univ. Pr. in association with New Zealand Institute of International Affairs, 1989. 176 p. : ill., maps. **DF44**
> "Presents facts and statistics that reflect the main elements of New Zealand's relations with the rest of the world."—*Pref.* Chapters devoted to history, diplomacy, aid, trade, immigration, and related topics provide text, figures, glossaries, tables and notes. Subject index. DU421.H63

General histories

The Oxford history of New Zealand / ed. by Geoffrey M. Rice. 2nd ed. Auckland, N.Z. ; N.Y. : Oxford Univ. Pr., 1992. 755 p. : ill., maps. **DF45**
> 1st ed. ed. by W. H. Oliver with B. R. Williams.
> Twenty-two chapters by various contributors are divided into four parts, emphasizing social history: Beginnings, Growth and conflict, A time of transition, and Precarious maturity. Tables, maps, graphs, notes, bibliography, subject index. DU420.O9

Biography

The book of New Zealand women = Ko kui ma te kaupapa / ed. by Charlotte Macdonald, Merimeri Penfold, and Bridget Williams. Wellington, N.Z. : B. Williams Books, 1991. 772 p. **DF46**
> For annotation, *see* AH377. CT3805.B66

The dictionary of New Zealand biography. Wellington : Dept. of Internal Affairs : Allen & Unwin, 1990–93. v. 1–2. (In progress). **DF47**
> For annotation, *see* AH378. CT2886.S35

PAPUA NEW GUINEA

Butler, Alan. A New Guinea bibliography. Waigani : Univ. of Papua New Guinea Pr., 1984–1990. 5 v. **DF48**
> Vols. 3–4 comp. by Alan Butler and Gary Cummings; v. 5 comp. by Alan Butler and Inge Butler.
> Based on the New Guinea collection at Michael Somare Library, University of Papua New Guinea. A topical listing of all books, pamphlets, theses, reports, government documents, seminar papers, journals, etc., either published in New Guinea or which deal with Papua New Guinea or Irian Jayan topics. Z4811.B88

McConnell, Fraiser. Papua New Guinea. Oxford ; Santa Barbara, Calif. : Clio Pr., [1988]. 378 p. : map. (World bibliographical series, v. 90). **DF49**
> A bibliography of published works (primarily books, with some series and government publications) issued before April 1987. Topical arrangement with good annotations; indexed by author and subject.
> § Topical bibliographies are also listed in Ann Turner's *Historical dictionary of Papua New Guinea* (Metuchen, N.J. : Scarecrow, 1994). DU740.A12P261

SOLOMON ISLANDS

Edridge, Sally. Solomon Islands bibliography to 1980. Suva, Fiji : Institute of Pacific Studies, the Univ. of the South Pacific, 1985. 476 p. : map. **DF50**
> Also issued by Alexander Turnbull Library, Wellington, N.Z. and the Solomon Islands National Library, Honiara.
> A retrospective bibliography of "books, pamphlets and periodical articles published within the Solomon Islands, or relating to those Islands. Works published by Solomon Islanders are included regardless of subject."—*Introd.* Classed arrangement with author and title/subject indexes. Z4898.E37

TAHITI

O'Reilly, Patrick. Bibliographie de Tahiti et de la Polynésie française / Patrick O'Reilly, Édouard Reitman. Paris : Musée de l'Homme, 1967. 1046 p. (Société des Océanistes. Publications, 14). **DF51**
> A classified, annotated bibliography of 10,501 items. Z4501.O72

VANUATU

O'Reilly, Patrick. Bibliographie méthodique, analytique et critique des Nouvelles-Hébrides. Paris : Musée de l'Homme, 1958. 304p. (Société des océanistes. Publications, no. 8).   **DF52**

A comprehensive, annotated bibliography of books and periodical articles which refer to many aspects of life in the islands of the New Hebrides (now Vanuatu).

§ For biographical material on this region, *see* the author's *Hébridais : répertoire bio-bibliographique des Nouvelles-Hébrides* (AH383).   Z4820.O7

WESTERN SAMOA

Holmes, Lowell Don. Samoan Islands bibliography. Wichita, Kan. : Poly Concepts, 1984. 329 p.   **DF53**

Books, chapters and page references in books, essays, periodical articles, newspaper articles (from the *New York times* and the *Samoan reporter*), theses, films, archives and manuscript collections, and documents are cited within broad subject sections. All periods of history and many languages are represented. No index.   Z4891.H65

Pereira, Janet Aileen. A check list of selected material on Samoa. Western Samoa : Samoan History Writing Project, Univ. of the South Pacific, Extension Centre, 1983. v. 1–2.   **DF54**

Contents: v. 1, General bibliography (437 p.); v. 2, Agriculture (112 p.).

A topical bibliography of books, articles, government publications, manuscripts and archives; coverage is predominantly of Western Samoa. Name index.   Z4891.P47

DG

Polar Regions

BIBLIOGRAPHY

Antarctic bibliography. v. 1 (1965)– . Wash. : Library of Congress : For sale by U.S. Govt. Print. Off., 1965– . Annual.   **DG1**

Prep. by the Library of Congress ; sponsored by the Division of Polar Programs, National Science Foundation. George A. Doumani, ed.

An ongoing series which, with the Naval Photographic Interpretation Center's *Antarctic bibliography* (Wash. : U.S. Govt. Print. Off., 1951) and the Library of Congress' *Antarctic bibliography, 1951–1961* (Wash. : The Library, 1970) now offers continuous coverage for Antarctic materials. (The first volume provided references, with abstracts, of items published between 1962 and 1964.) Arranged by broad sub-

ject category (biological sciences; expeditions; geological sciences; ice and snow; political geography, etc.) with subject, author, geographic, and grantee indexes. International coverage. Locates copies.

New volumes appear at irregular intervals (i.e., whenever 2,000 abstracts have been compiled, they are assembled for publication in form of a bound volume).

———. *Indexes* (Wash., 1977–84. 2 v.).

Contents: [v. 1], v. 1–7; [v. 2], v. 8–12.

Cumulates the volume indexes. Anonymous journal articles are indexed under journal title.

•In machine-readable form as part of *Arctic & antarctic regions* [database] (DG2).   Z6005.P7A55

•Arctic & antarctic regions [database]. College Park, Md. : National Information Services Corp., c1989– .   **DG2**

Accompanied by user manual.

Available on CD-ROM; updated semiannually.

Worldwide collection of cold regions research compiled by the Library of Congress, Science and Technology Division.

With more than 600,000 entries for journal articles, reports, and documents, this CD-ROM provides comprehensive coverage for the Antarctic regions. It includes all data available for 40 years of *COLD : cold regions data base* [database] (Wash. : Library of Congress, Cold Regions Bibliography Project, 1950–) and over 25 years of *Antarctic bibliography* (DG1). For the Arctic regions, the coverage is selective with emphasis on science and technology. New iterations of the disk increase coverage and the next version will contain nearly a million records. The software makes searching exceptionally easy.

Arctic information and data : a guide to selected resources / Arctic Research Consortium of the United States, Data and Information Resources Working Group. [Fairbanks, Alaska] : The Consortium, 1992. 50 p.   **DG3**

This brief guide is an important gateway to the data and information resources available to researchers and students interested in the Arctic regions. It describes selected Arctic information resources, Arctic data resources, Alaskan information resources, Arctic research entities, and major Arctic conferences. Emphasizes information generated or published in the U.S.   G606.A73

Arctic Institute of North America. Arctic bibliography. Wash. : U.S. Govt. Print. Off., 1953–75. 16 v. : maps.   **DG4**

Imprint varies.

Also available on microfilm: Ann Arbor, Mich. : University Microfilms.

Prepared under the general direction of Marie Tremaine. Vols. 1–3 form the basic bibliography, and list some 20,000 publications in many languages representing all phases of the subject: geographical, scientific, and sociological. Emphasizes the 19th and 20th centuries. In two parts: (1) Alphabetical author list with full title in the original language, imprint, and collation. Russian titles are given in LC transliteration. Translations into English are added for foreign titles. Entries include books, government documents, and periodical articles. There are brief annotations or abstracts, and location is given for the copy used. (2) A comprehensive subject-geographic index of some 100,000 entries, arranged under 18,000 subject and geographic headings.

Vol. 4 emphasizes material published 1950–52; v. 5 covers material published 1950–53, but in both volumes earlier material is included.

Vols. 6–16 were published annually, each listing as many current or recent items as possible, as well as older materials not previously included. Emphasizes scientific, technical, and medical materials; the number of items in foreign languages, particularly in Russian, is increased.   Z6005.P7A72

•Polar pac [database]. Lacey, Wash. : Western Library Network, 1990– .   **DG5**

Available on CD-ROM. Updated irregularly; entire file is replaced.

Provides access to the Arctic resources of more than 50 libraries in 15 nations. In its third iteration (1993), it contains some 100,000 bibliographic records and nearly 100,000 citations to articles. It also contains specialized indexes for Alaskan literature. There is a strong emphasis on humanities and social sciences as well as excellent coverage of science and technology.

ATLASES

National Foreign Assessment Center (U.S.). Polar regions atlas / [produced by the National Foreign Assessment Center, CIA]. [Wash.] : Central Intelligence Agency, 1978. 66 p., [2] fold. leaves of plates : ill. (some col.), col. maps. (ACSM Map Design Competition Collection, 1978–5).　　**DG10**

The most comprehensive atlas of the polar regions available. The volume has been reprinted by several commercial publishers. It provides clear and complete coverage of both regions and is very well indexed. The maps are based on satellite photographs and other mapping devices. Updated by single-sheet maps produced by the same agency.
G1054.N36

ENCYCLOPEDIAS

Fogg, G. E. A history of Antarctic science. Cambridge ; N.Y. : Cambridge Univ. Pr., 1992. 483 p. : ill.　　**DG6**

Providing both a general history and discipline-specific information, this volume is an important reference tool. Coverage is from the earliest sighting of the continent to the present. Of particular importance is the emphasis on equipment and logistics, information often difficult to locate. The complete index and massive bibliography are of great use.　　G860.F64

Holland, Clive. Arctic exploration and development, c.500 B.C. to 1915 : an encyclopedia. N.Y. : Garland, 1994. 704 p. : maps. (Garland reference library of the humanities, v. 930).　　**DG7**

Lists and describes in chronological order more than 2,000 Arctic expeditions from earliest times to 1915. Excluded are commercial ventures (such as whaling and sealing) and all of Iceland. The entire Arctic region is treated, although emphasis is placed on the American and European Arctic. Included are short biographies of explorers, concentrating on those not covered in standard biographical reference tools. An alphabetical list of all expedition members and their Arctic service ties many of the expeditions together. The indexes and maps are excellent.　　G606.H66

Stewart, John. Antarctica : an encyclopedia. Jefferson, N.C. : McFarland, c1990. 2 v. (1193 p.).　　**DG8**

"Incorporating geographical features, expeditions, people, scientific subjects, and entries of general interest" (*Pref.*), offers thorough coverage of the continent (south of 60°) for the "average reader." Short articles define, identify, locate, or describe a wide variety of topics relating to Antarctica, even discussing churches, fossils, penguins, stamps, etc. Alphabetical arrangement. Copious cross-references; chronology; list of expeditions. A bibliography, p. 1173–93, cites 420 books with some annotations.　　G855.S74

CHRONOLOGIES

Headland, Robert. Chronological list of Antarctic expeditions and related historical events. Cambridge, [Eng.] ; N.Y. : Cambridge Univ. Pr., 1989. 730 p. : ill.　　**DG9**

Based on Brian Roberts's "Chronological list" published in the *Polar record* of the Scott Polar Research Institute, v. 9 (1958): 97–134, 191–239.

Aims to record "as concisely as possible the history of discovery, exploration, exploitation, mapping, scientific investigation, administration ... in Antarctic regions."—*p. 2.* A chronological list of about 2,800 expeditions and events, giving for each: nationality, purpose, leader, and brief annotations containing other details; this section constitutes most of the work. Bibliography of Antarctic chronology, p. 604–21, gives sources of further information. Index of personal and place names, ship names, and institutions.　　G860.H36

E

Science, Technology, and Medicine

EA

General Science

The increasing use of electronic publishing has had two pronounced effects on scientific, technical, and medical reference
materials. For traditional print sources, there has been a
marked decrease in the time between editions of major works,
such as subject-specific encyclopedias and multivolume handbooks. Libraries today often decide that the latest edition of a
very expensive work is not needed, since the added value will
not justify the considerable cost. The information in this section is intended to assist in making such determinations. At the
same time, reference works are increasingly available in electronic formats as well as in printed form; indeed, some reference works are now available only in electronic form. Readers
will need to check the latest edition of a source such as *Gale
directory of databases* to determine whether a given work is
available in electronic form.

Cost considerations play an increasing role in libraries'
decisions to purchase reference works. Today libraries may
purchase a single work in subject areas where once they would
have bought several, and libraries are less likely to purchase
reference works in fields of peripheral interest. Comparative
evaluation of reference works is therefore emphasized here.

GENERAL WORKS

Guides

Aluri, Rao. A guide to U.S. government scientific and technical resources / Rao Aluri, Judith Schiek Robinson. Littleton,
Colo. : Libraries Unlimited, 1983. 259 p.   **EA1**
"This guide is organized to reflect the normal patterns of scientific communications where the information goes through a number of
successive stages. ... [It] is a guide to the literature and *not* a current
bibliography."—*Introd.* Emphasizes the type of information available
and the means of gaining access to it. Indexed.   Q224.3.U6A43

Chen, Ching-chih. Scientific and technical information
sources. 2nd ed. Cambridge, Mass. : MIT Pr., c1987. 824 p.
                                                          EA2
  1st ed., 1977.
  An essential guide to current sources of information in science
and technology, " ... intended primarily as a basic one-volume reference guide for science and engineering information professionals and
their assistants and as a textbook for library and information science
school students."—*Pref.* The new edition has been revised and expanded to 5,300 sources, many published 1980–86. Arranged by type
of material (e.g. handbook, directory, manual), then by subject. Many
entries are annotated and include critical notes and citations to both
scientific and library reviewing sources. Complete name and title indexes.   Z7401.C48

Grogan, Denis Joseph. Science and technology : an introduction to the literature. 4th ed. London : C. Bingley ; distr. by
Shoe String Pr., 1982. 400 p.   **EA3**
  1st ed., 1970.
  Introduces students to the forms of the literature of science and
technology both in print and online. Examples illustrate the uses of ref-

erence sources; however, there is neither a subject emphasis nor an attempt to provide a defined level of listing for any form. Subject index, but none of titles. Q223.G76

Hurt, Charlie Deuel. Information sources in science and technology. 2nd ed. Englewood, Colo. : Libraries Unlimited, 1994. 412 p. **EA4**

1st ed., 1988.

This selective bibliography provides a basic introduction to the literature of science, medicine, and technology. Some 2,000 English-language reference works are arranged in 20 subject chapters. Within each chapter, entries are grouped by form or type of material (e.g., abstracts, dictionaries, atlases). Annotated entries include descriptive and critical comments about each publication. Lists of electronic sources have been asdded for this edition. Author/title and subject indexes.

§ Similar in scope and content to H. Robert Malinowsky and Jeanne M. Richardson's *Science and engineering literature* (EA5).
Z7401.H85

Malinowsky, H. Robert. Science and engineering literature : a guide to reference sources / H. Robert Malinowsky, Jeanne M. Richardson. 3rd ed. Littleton, Colo. : Libraries Unlimited, 1980. 342 p. **EA5**

1st ed., 1967, had title: *Science and engineering reference sources.*

A guide for students and librarians. The text has been rewritten, restructured, and reduced, and the number of reference sources expanded from 1,096 to 1,273. Annotated entries are arranged by form and by subject, and emphasize recent American and British sources. Author/title/subject index.

§ *Reference sources in science, engineering, medicine, and agriculture,* by Malinowsky (Phoenix : Oryx, 1994) contains some 2,400 annotated entries. Recommended as an introduction to the literature of a discipline, and for those needing cross-disciplinary works.
Z7401.M28

Parker, C. C. Information sources in science and technology : a practical guide to traditional and online use / C.C. Parker, R.V. Turley. 2nd ed. London ; N.Y. : Butterworths, 1986. 328 p. : ill. **EA6**

1st ed., 1975.

A selective guide to current information sources which also discusses strategies for finding and using information. Addressed to librarians, scientists, engineers, and students, this combination bibliography and reader's adviser is particularly useful for its description of British sources and research methods. Name and subject index.
Q224.P37

Primack, Alice Lefler. Finding answers in science and technology. N.Y. : Van Nostrand Reinhold, 1984. 364 p. : ill. **EA7**

"This book is intended for use by 'hobby' scientists, advanced high school, junior college, and undergraduate college students, and the teachers and librarians helping these users."—*Pref.* A subject arranged narrative guide to using printed and online science resources. Indexed. Z7401.P86

Smith, Robert V. Graduate research : a guide for students in the sciences. 2nd ed. N.Y. : Plenum Pr., c1990. 292 p. : ill. **EA8**

1st ed., 1984.

Offers an expanded and updated overview of the issues confronting graduate students in the sciences. Topics range from the principles of research and professional ethics to time management and grantsmanship. The section about libraries is brief, but does mention online catalogs and computerized literature searching. Q180.55.M4S58

Talbot, Dawn E. Japan's high technology : an annotated guide to English-language information sources. Phoenix, Ariz. : Oryx, 1991. 171 p. **EA9**

A "guide to over 500 English-language sources of information in science, technology, and business."—*Introd.* Annotated entries are grouped by topic in 13 chapters (e.g., bibliographies, newsletters and magazines, online databases, patents). Appendixes list booksellers, libraries, and noncommercial organizations specializing in Japanese materials. An excellent reference source for both general and special library collections. Z7916.T35

Walford's guide to reference material. 6th ed. London : Library Association Publ., 1993. v. 1. **EA10**

1st ed., 1959; 5th ed., 1989–91 (AA363).

Contents: v. 1, Science and technology / ed. by Marilyn Mullay and Priscilla Schlicke.

The new edition of this standard source includes more than 7,000 entries in the physical and life sciences and in anthropology, engineering and technology, medicine, and agriculture. Remains an essential source for science reference collections, containing sufficient revision to justify purchase of this new edition. For 5th ed., *see* AA363.
Z1035.W174

Bibliography

Blackwell, Richard J. A bibliography of the philosophy of science, 1945–1981. Westport, Conn. : Greenwood, 1983. 585 p. **EA11**

"Our purpose is to provide assistance to both the neophyte and the expert in finding one's way around within the vast contemporary literature on the philosophy of science."—*Introd.* Citations to books and articles are arranged in seven major categories with subdivisions. Entries within subdivisions are by author. Appendixes include lists of major series and periodicals cited. Index of personal names.
Z7405.P74B57

British Museum (Natural History). Library. Catalogue of the books, manuscripts, maps and drawings in the British Museum (Natural History). London : Trustees, 1903–1940. 8 v. **EA12**

Repr.: N.Y. : Stechert-Hafner, 1964 ; N.Y. : Maurizio Martino, [1990?] (4 v)

Comp. and ed. by B. B. Woodward.

Contents: v. 1–5, A–Z; v. 6–8, Supplement, A–Z.

An author catalog of one of the world's finest collections on natural history. Includes many analytics and occasional descriptive notes. A subject approach is provided for atlases, dictionaries, encyclopedias, and gazetteers. Titles of words in nonroman alphabets are transliterated, then translated. Z7409.B85

British scientific and technical books. v. 1 (1935/52)–v. 2 (1953/57). London : publ. for Aslib by J. Clarke ; [N.Y.] : Hafner, 1956–60. **EA13**

Supplements the British Science Guild's *Catalogue of British scientific and technical books* (3rd ed., comp. by Daphne Shaw. London : sold by A. and F. Denny, for the Guild, 1930).

A listing of the "most important and useful books on science and technology published in the United Kingdom and the Dominions ..." —*Introd.* Reappraises the books listed in the *Aslib book list* (currently the *Aslib book guide*, EA32), omitting some and adding others, in order to present a comprehensive bibliography of books published by commercial publishers during the period. "Books in all the divisions of pure and applied science are represented together with those publications in such fields as psychology, documentation, architecture and photography which are of interest to technical readers." Notes presence of illustrations or bibliographies, date of previous edition, and level of difficulty. Arranged by Universal Decimal Classification with author and subject indexes. Z7407.G7B85

Encyclopedia of physical sciences and engineering information sources / Steven Wasserman, Martin A. Smith, and Susan Mottu, editors. Detroit : Gale, c1989. 736 p. **EA14**

Subtitle: a bibliographic guide to approximately 16,000 citations for publications, organizations, and other sources of information on 425 subjects relating to the physical sciences and engineering.

Citations are organized under topical subject headings, often narrowly defined, which are subdivided by type of source (e.g., abstract services, directories, statistics sources, databases). Individual citations include the bibliographic description or address, telephone, and publication or subscription price. Information sources are frequently repeated under related subject headings. An outline of contents serves as a guide to subjects and related terms. No index.   Z7401.E56

A guide to the culture of science, technology, and medicine / gen. ed., Paul T. Durbin. N.Y. : Free Pr., 1984. 735 p.   **EA15**

Originally publ. 1980.

Specialists have contributed nine survey articles, with extensive bibliographies, on the state of the art of the history, philosophy, and sociology of science, technology, and medicine. Focus of the work is on value issues in the sciences and the place of science, technology, and medicine in contemporary culture. Bibliographic introductions to the individual essays vary in content, some discussing major reference sources, others citing classic or standard works. An 11-page bibliographic update includes works identified since the original edition was published. Indexed.   Q175.5.G84

International catalogue of scientific literature / publ. for the Internat. Council by the Royal Soc. of London. v. 1 (1901)–v. 14 (1914). London : Harrison, 1902–21.   **EA16**

Repr.: N.Y. : Johnson Repr., 1968.

An outgrowth of the *Catalogue of scientific papers* (EA22), this annual bibliography covers scientific books, articles, memoirs, and pamphlets.

Each annual issue consists of 17 sections: A, Mathematics; B, Mechanics; C, Physics; D, Chemistry; E, Astronomy; F, Meteorology; G, Mineralogy; H, Geology; J, Geography, mathematical and physical; K, Paleontology; L, General biology; M, Botany; N, Zoology; O, Human anatomy; P, Anthropology; Q, Physiology; R, Bacteriology.

Each part includes: (1) schedules and indexes in four languages; (2) an author catalog; and (3) subject index. The purpose is to record the titles of all original contributions since Jan. 1, 1901, in certain branches of science.

At the time of its issue, this was the most important current bibliography covering all the sciences. Publication was suspended after the volumes for 1914 were issued.

§ Related works: *List of journals with abbreviations used in the Catalogue as references* (1903. 312 p.) and *Supplementary list of journals* (1904. 68 p.), in which titles are arranged alphabetically by country of publication.

John Crerar Library. Author-title catalog. Boston : G.K. Hall, 1967. 35 v.   **EA17**

Photoreproduction of the catalog of about 563,000 cards, which describe the historical and modern collections held by this major scientific, medical, and technical library of 1.1 million volumes.

———. *Classified subject catalog* (Boston : G.K. Hall, 1967. 42 v.). Includes about 700,000 entries in a modified Dewey classification arrangement. Vol. 42, Subject index, links subject terms to classification numbers.   Z881.C5212

Mitcham, Carl. Bibliography of the philosophy of technology / comp. by Carl Mitcham and Robert Mackey. Chicago : Univ. of Chicago Pr., 1973. 205 p.   **EA18**

Originally published as v. 14, no. 2, pt. 2 (April 1973) of *Technology and culture.*

In four main sections: (1) Comprehensive philosophical works; (2) Ethical and political critiques; (3) Religious critiques; (4) Metaphysical and epistemological studies.

Lists works showing an "awareness of the philosophical significance of modern technology."—*Introd.* Concentrates on works of the period 1925–72. Where it seemed advisable, foreign-language titles have been translated and placed in brackets. Important and/or hard-to-secure sources are annotated more extensively than others. Only articles worthy of special notice are cited independently of general collections. There are appendixes of "Classical documents" and "Background materials." No index.

Powell, Russell H. Core list of books and journals in science and technology / ed. by Russell H. Powell and James R. Powell, Jr. Phoenix : Oryx, 1987. 134 p.   **EA19**

A selective bibliography of some 1,500 English-language publications, emphasizing recent imprints, standard editions of textbooks, and current serials used in college and advanced educational programs. Titles are organized in ten subject sections: agriculture, astronomy, biology, chemistry, computer science, engineering, geology, mathematics, physics, reference. A complete bibliographic citation is given for each entry, plus a critical annotation for books. Indexed by author or editor, title, and subject.   Z7401.P778

Pure & applied science books, 1876–1982. N.Y. : Bowker, 1982. 6 v. (7784 p.).   **EA20**

Subtitle: Subject index, author index, title index.

This listing "of over 220,000 titles in science and technology published and distributed in the United States and spanning publication dates from before 1800 through 1982 covers all aspects of the physical and biological sciences and their applications ... as well as every type of technology, engineering, agriculture, domestic arts and science and manufactures."—*Pref.* Despite the beginning date in the title, about 5,000 works published before 1876 are included. Entries are arranged by LC subject heading and include full LC cataloging data. Indexed by author (personal and corporate) and by title.   Z7401.P89

Reuss, Jeremias David. Repertorium commentationum a societatibus litterariis editarum / secundum disciplinarum ordinem digessit I. D. Reuss .... Gottingae : apud Henricum Dieterich, 1801–21. 16 v.   **EA21**

Repr. : N.Y. : B. Franklin, 1961.

Contents: (1) Historia naturalis, generalis et zoologia; (2) Botanica et mineralogia; (3) Chemia et res metallica; (4) Physica; (5) Astronomia; (6) Oeconomia; (7) Mathesis, mechanica, hydrostatica, hydraulica, hydrotechnia, aerostatica, pnevmatica, technologia, architectura civilis, scientia navalis, scientia militaris; (8) Historia; (9) Philologia, linguae, scriptores graeci, scriptores latini, litterae elegantiores, poesis, rhetorica, ars antiqua, pictura, musica; (10–16) Scientia et ars medica et chirurgica.

A very valuable index to the publications of the learned societies of various countries from the time of the founding of each society to 1800, thus preceding the Royal Society of London's *Catalogue of scientific papers* (EA22). Sections are arranged topically and include an author index.   Z5051.R44

Royal Society (Great Britain). Catalogue of scientific papers, 1800–1900. London : Clay, 1867–1902 ; Cambridge : Univ. Pr., 1914–25. 19 v.   **EA22**

Imprint varies. Repr.: N.Y. : Johnson Reprint, 1965; Metuchen, N.J. : Scarecrow, 1968. Republished in microform: London : Eyre & Spottiswoode, 1970.

Continued by: *International catalogue of scientific literature* (EA16).

Contents: v. 1–6, 1st ser., 1800–63; v. 7–8, 2nd ser., 1864–73; v. 9–11, 3rd ser., 1874–83; v. 12, Supplementary volume, 1800–83; v. 13–19, 4th ser., 1884–1900.

A monumental index of the first importance in scientific or large reference libraries. Papers of a purely literary, technical, or professional nature are excluded; medicine is excluded unless the material relates to anatomy or physiology. An author index, for the whole of the 19th century, to 1,555 periodicals in various languages including the transactions of the European academies and other learned societies. Gives, for each article entered: author's name in full when it can be found, full title, title of periodical, volume, date, and inclusive paging. For Russian articles the original title is given followed by French, German, or English translation in brackets. A listing of abbreviations and sources consulted precedes each series, giving considerable bibliographic information and noting instances when particular volumes were not available for review.

———. ———. *Subject index* (Cambridge : Univ. Pr., 1908–14. 3 v. in 4).

Contents: v. 1, Pure mathematics; v. 2, Mechanics; v. 3, Physics: pt. 1, Generalities, heat, light, sound; pt. 2, Electricity and magnetism.

Covers the same material as the author catalog. Arranged by the classification schedules used in *International catalogue of scientific literature*. The original plan was to publish separate index volumes for each of the 17 sections of the *International catalogue*, but only the first three were issued. These index 116,687 articles from 1,555 periodicals. The *Subject index* gives sufficiently full information to be used independently of the author volumes—i.e., author's name, brief title, periodical, volume date, and pagination—but for full title, reference must be made to the author catalog. Z7403.R88

Royal Society (Great Britain). Library. Book catalogue of the Library of the Royal Society / comp. by Alan J. Clark. [Frederick, Md.] : Univ. Publications of America, 1982. 5 v. **EA23**

Photographic copies of catalog cards for 62,500 books and pamphlets cataloged through November 30, 1981. Entries are in alphabetical order by personal or corporate name; personal name is preferred. A valuable source for historians of science since the Library of the Royal Society was established in 1667. Z921.R76R69

Selin, Helaine. Science across cultures : an annotated bibliography of books on non-western science, technology, and medicine. N.Y. : Garland, 1992. 431 p. (Garland reference library of the humanities, v. 1597). **EA24**

Contains some 836 annotated references to recent English-language literature describing the history and development of science in Native American, Asian, Islamic, and Pacific societies. Citations are grouped in national or regional chapters, then arranged alphabetically by author. Short essays on the nature of the particular scientific tradition introduce each section. Author, title, and subject indexes. Z7405.S6S4

General and juvenile

AAAS science film catalog / Ann Seltz-Petrash, project ed. and comp. ; Kathryn Wolff, managing ed., AAAS Publications Program ; prep. with the assistance of the National Science Foundation. Wash. : American Assoc. for the Advancement of Science, 1975. 398 p. **EA25**

Provides information for about 5,600 science films (pure sciences, technology, and social sciences) for elementary grades through adult level available from U.S. producers or distributors. Arranged by subject; indexed by title. Kept up-to-date in part by annual lists in *Science books & films* (EA34). Q192.A17

Appraisal : science books for young people. v. 1, no. 1 (1967)– . Boston, Mass. : Children's Science Book Review Committee, 1967– . 3 times a yr. **EA26**

Sponsored by the Science Education Dept., Boston Univ. School of Education and the New England Round Table of Children's Librarians.

Succinct criticisms by a specialist and a librarian for each title covered, with ratings by each reviewer. Intended for children's librarians, teachers, and other buyers and users of children's books. Z7401.A63

Deason, Hilary J. The AAAS science book list : a selected and annotated list of science and mathematics books for secondary school students, college undergraduates and nonspecialists. 3rd ed. Wash. : Amer. Assoc. for the Advancement of Science, 1970. 439 p. **EA27**

1st ed., 1959; 2nd ed., 1964.

An annotated list of 1,530 titles, arranged according to Dewey classification, in the biological, physical, behavioral, medical, engineering, agricultural, and mathematical sciences. Contains evaluative annotations and designation of level of difficulty. Indexed by author, subject and title.

Supplements:

AAAS science book list supplement, by Kathryn Wolff and Jill Storey (Wash. : AAAS, 1978. 457 p.). "A selected and annotated list of science and mathematics books ... for secondary school students, undergraduates, teachers and nonspecialist readers."—*t.p.*

AAAS science book list, 1978–1986, comp. and ed. by Kathryn Wolff, Susan M. O'Connell, and Valerie J. Montenegro (Wash. : AAAS, 1986. 668 p. [AAAS publ., 85-24]). Based on reviews published in *Science books & films* (EA34).

Kennedy, DayAnn M. Science & technology in fact and fiction : a guide to children's books / DayAnn M. Kennedy, Stella S. Spangler, Mary Ann Vanderwerf. N.Y. : Bowker, c1990. 319 p. **EA28**

An annotated guide to children's literature for ages up to 11 years that arranges entries for some 500 recommended works of fiction and nonfiction under the two broad categories of science and technology. Each entry includes a complete bibliographic description, a summary of the work, and evaluative comments on the literary and scientific qualities of the book. Indexed by author, title, illustrator, subject, and reading level.

§ Similar in purpose and arrangement, the same authors' *Science and technology in fact and fiction : a guide to young adult books* (N.Y. : Bowker, c1990. 363 p.) is an evaluative bibliography that reviews fiction and nonfiction for reading levels grade three to 12+. Excludes works about the life sciences. Author, title, subject, and reading level indexes. Z7401.K46

Malinowsky, H. Robert. Best science and technology reference books for young people. Phoenix : Oryx, 1991. 216 p. **EA29**

Guide to sci-tech reference books for children and teens (grades 3–12). 669 titles are grouped, first by broad subject categories, then by type of publication. Entries include full bibliographic citation, short abstract, sources for reviews, and grade level. Title, name, subject, and grade level indexes. Z7401.M277

Richter, Bernice. The Museum of Science and Industry basic list of children's science books, 1973–1984 / comp. by Bernice Richter and Duane Wenzel. Chicago : Amer. Libr. Assoc., 1985. 154 p. **EA30**

"This bibliography of science trade literature is an extension of the Museum of Science and Industry's Kresge Library and its annual Children's Science Book Fair."—*Pref.* Some 1,100 entries include bibliographic description; contents summary; reading level; evaluative rating; citations to reviews. Appendixes list publishers, adult sourcebooks, children's science magazines, and review journals. Author and title indexes.

Continued by the annual *The Museum of Science and Industry basic list of children's science books* (Chicago : Amer. Libr. Assoc., c1985–88). Z7401.R49

Science fair project index, 1960–1972 / ed. by Janet Y. Stoffer. Metuchen, N.J. : Scarecrow, 1975. 728 p. **EA31**

Comp. by the staff of the Science and Technology Division of the Akron-Summit County Public Library.

An index, based on Library of Congress subject headings, to books and general science periodicals that describe projects, experiments, and display techniques useful for teachers and secondary school students. References are alphabetical by article titles, or by authors when an entire book is cited. A bibliography provides complete citation for monographs.

Supplements: ———. *1973–1980* (1983. 723 p.), in which, since "an increasing number of elementary school students are preparing science projects, the indexing has been extended to include materials appropriate for grades 5 through high school."—*Pref.*

———. *1981–1984*, ed. by Cynthia Bishop and Deborah Crowe (1986. 686 p.), which provides better access to subjects by adding more *see* references and increasing the number of subject headings per entry.

———. *1985–1989 for grades K–8*, ed. by Cynthia Bishop, Katherine Ertle, and Karen Zeleznik (1992. 555 p.). Includes ten monographs published before 1985 but excludes periodicals, and changes audience to students in kindergarten through eighth grade and their teachers and librarians. Q182.3.S34

Current

Aslib book guide / Aslib. v. 57, no. 1 (Jan. 1992)– . London : Aslib, c1992– . Monthly. **EA32**
Continues: *Aslib book list* (v. 1–57, 1935–92).
A classed list of selected books in science, technology, medicine, and the social sciences. Intended as a selection guide for librarians; annotations are evaluative and indicate reading level. Author index for each issue.
§ See also: *British scientific and technical books* (EA13).
Z7403.A84

New York Public Library. New technical books. v. 1 (June/ Aug. 1915)– . N.Y. : New York Public Library, 1915– . Bimonthly. **EA33**
Subtitle varies. Frequency varies.
A "selective list of current English language books. Subject emphasis is on the pure and applied physical sciences, mathematics, engineering, industrial technology, and related disciplines."—*Pref.* Annotations usually consist of full tables of contents followed by descriptive notes. Level of content ranges from introductory college to advanced specialist. Arranged by broad Dewey classification with annual classified, author, and subject indexes. Z5854.N542

Science books & films. v. 11 (May 1975)– . [Wash.] : American Assoc. for the Advancement of Science, 1975– . 9 nos. a year. **EA34**
Title varies: some issues called *AAAS science books & films*.
Continues *Science books : a quarterly review* (v. 1–10, 1965–75).
An annotated, classified listing of new printed, audiovisual, and electronic resources in the pure and applied sciences. Provides a useful selection guide for libraries serving students from the elementary grades through the first two years of college. Symbols indicate reading level, recommendation, etc. Annual index.
§ Selective compilations of evaluations appearing in *Science books & films* have been published: *The best books for children : a selected and annotated list of science books for children ages five through twelve*, comp. and ed. by Kathryn Wolff and others (Wash. : Amer. Assoc. for the Advancement of Science, 1983. 271 p. [AAAS publ. 83-5]); *Films in the sciences : reviews and recommendations; selected science and mathematics films for students, teachers, professional, and general audiences*, comp. and ed. by Michele M. Newman and Madelyn A. McRae (Wash. : Amer. Assoc. for the Advancement of Science, 1980. 172 p. [AAAS publ. 80-9]); Kathryn Wolff, *The best science films, filmstrips, and videocassettes for children* (Wash. : Amer. Assoc. for the Advancement of Science, 1982. 140 p. [AAAS publ. 82-6]); *The best science books & A-V materials for children*, ed. by Susan M. O'Connell, Valerie J. Montenegro, and Kathryn Wolff (Wash. : Amer. Assoc. for the Advancement of Science, 1988. 335 p. [AAAS publ. 87-11]). Z7403.S33

Science tracer bullets : a reference guide to scientific, technological, health, and environmental information sources / ed. by Helene Henderson. Detroit : Omnigraphics, 1990. 4 v. **EA35**
Contents: v. 1, Earth and natural sciences; v. 2, High technology; v. 3, Medical and biological sciences; v. 4, Socio-political aspects of science and technology.
Annually, about 10 new or revised subject bibliographies, based on the holdings of the Library of Congress, are issued as *LC science tracer bullet* (TB72– . Wash. : Library of Congress, Science and Technology Div., 1972–). Each contains a scope note, lists of relevant LC subject headings, sources for additional information, and references categorized by type (e.g., basic and advanced texts, handbooks, bibliographies, abstracting and indexing services, journals). Some entries are annotated.

Tracer bullets publ. 1972–89 have here been reissued in bound form. Each volume contains revised versions of the original bibliographies, in order by series number, with indexes by subject, corporate name, and compiler. Z7409.S343

Scientific and technical books and serials in print. 1972– . N.Y. : Bowker, 1972– . Annual. **EA36**
Title varies.
An author, title, and subject index to scientific and technical books and serials available from U.S. publishers. Derived from *Books in print* (AA425), *Ulrich's international periodicals directory* (AD18), and related Bowker databases.
•Machine-readable version: *Scientific and technical books and serials in print* [database] (N.Y. : Bowker, 1990–). Available online (updated monthly) and in CD-ROM as part of *SciTech reference plus* [database] (EA37).

•**SciTech reference plus** [database]. N.Y. : Bowker, c1989– . **EA37**
Available in CD-ROM, updated annually.
Represents the merger of six scientific and technical information sources and databases: (1) *American men & women of science* (EA170); (2) science and technology titles from *Books in print* (AA425); (3) *Directory of American research and technology* (EA213); (4) scientific and technical periodicals from *Ulrich's international periodicals directory* (AD18); (5) scientific books and serials from *Medical and health care books and serials in print* (EH23); (6) *Corporate technology directory (Corptech)* [database], a CD-ROM source. Sources may be searched individually or in combination. A variety of formatted displays and printouts is available.

Periodicals

See also *Journals in translation* (AD25).

BioSciences Information Service of Biological Abstracts. Bibliographic guide for editors & authors / Biosciences Information Service of Biological Abstracts, Chemical Abstracts Service, Division of the American Chemical Society [and] Engineering Index, Inc. Wash. : American Chemical Society, 1974. 362 p. **EA38**
Prepared through the combined efforts of BIOSIS, CAS, and EI, Inc. to aid in improving the reliability and usefulness of bibliographic information found in scientific and technical publications. Contents divided into three sections: (1) Guideline for use of the coded bibliographic strip; (2) Bibliographic standards, an annotated list of international standards especially relevant for editors and authors; (3) Serial titles, abbreviations and codes, giving the complete titles with the standardized abbreviations and ASTM CODEN for some 27,700 serial publications.
§ Superseded in part by *International serials catalogue* (EA43). Z6945.A2B55

Bolton, Henry Carrington. Catalogue of scientific and technical periodicals, 1665–1895 : together with chronological tables and a library check-list. 2nd ed. Wash. : Smithsonian Inst., 1897. 1247 p. (Smithsonian miscellaneous collections, v. 40). **EA39**
Repr. : N.Y. : Johnson, 1965.
8,603 titles. Pt. 1 (4,954 titles) is a reprint of the 1st ed., 1885, with changes to date; pt. 2 includes additions to titles in pt. 1, and titles 5001–8477; addenda, titles 8478–8603.
"Intended to contain the principal independent periodicals of every branch of pure and applied science, published in all countries from the rise of this literature to the present time."—*Pref.* Excludes medicine but includes anatomy, physiology, and veterinary science. Usually omits publications of learned societies. Gives full titles, names of editors, changes of titles, dates, etc. The chronological tables permit the finding of volume numbers for specific years. Z7403.B69

British Museum (Natural History). Library. Serial publications in the British Museum (Natural History) Library. 3rd ed. London : Trustees of the British Museum (Natural History), 1980. 3 v. (British Museum [Natural History]. Library. Publication, no. 778). **EA40**

1st ed., 1968, had title: *List of serial publications in the British Museum (Natural History) Library.*

An alphabetical listing of about 20,000 serials held by the library. Emphasis is on the life sciences, geology, mineralogy, general science, and natural history.

§ Continued by: *Serial publications in the British Museum (Natural History) Library* [microform] (1984– . London : [The Museum], 1985– . Microfiche. Semiannual). The first microfiche edition (Jan. 1985) contains approximately 24,000 entries. Issues are cumulative.

Z7403.B844

Chemical Abstracts Service source index : 1907–1989 cumulative. [Columbus, Ohio] : American Chemical Society, [1990]. **EA41**

For annotation, *see* EE18. The principal source for titles and abbreviations in the physical sciences, the life sciences, and engineering.

Z5523.A52

Gascoigne, Robert Mortimer. A historical catalogue of scientific periodicals, 1665–1900 : with a survey of their development. N.Y. : Garland, 1985. 205 p. (Garland reference library of the humanities, v. 583). **EA42**

A companion to Gascoigne's *A historical catalogue of scientists and scientific books,* 1984 (EA193). Pt. 1 contains citations to some 900 scientific periodicals, arranged chronologically by subject. Pts. 2–3 analyze and review the development of periodical literature for the sciences. Bibliography of sources; general index by author, title, and place. More selective than Henry C. Bolton's *Catalogue of scientific and technical periodicals 1665–1895* (EA39). Z7403.G3

International Council of Scientific Unions. Abstracting Board. International serials catalogue. Paris : International Council of Scientific Unions, Abstracting Board ; Philadelphia : distr. by Biosciences Information Service, c1978. 2 v. **EA43**

Contents: Pt. 1, Catalogue; Pt. 2, Index/concordance.

The *Catalogue* lists in alphabetical order the serial publications abstracted and indexed by the member services of the ICSUAB, and includes journal abbreviation, CODEN, ISSN, and the initials of the services indexing the journal. The *Index/concordance* includes an ISSN to CODEN list in numerical order and a CODEN to ISSN list in alphabetical order; each is associated with corresponding page numbers in the *Catalogue.*

Linda Hall Library. Serials holdings in the Linda Hall Library [as of April 30] 1989. Kansas City, Mo. : The Library, 1989. 800 p. **EA44**

First issued 1967; previous ed., 1986.

An alphabetical arrangement of some 24,000 serial titles at the library through April 1989. Holdings information and frequent cross-references make this a useful directory for the identification and location of scientific and technical serial publications. Z7403.L65a

Union list of scientific serials in Canadian libraries / comp. and ed. in the Library of the National Research Council. [1st ed.]– . Ottawa : The Library, 1957– . Biennial, 1967– . **EA45**

At head of title: National Research Council Canada. Conseil national de recherches Canada. Title on added t.p.: Catalogue collectif des publications scientifiques dans les bibliothèques canadiennes.

Lists more than 65,000 scientific, technical, and medical serial titles representing the holdings of 294 Canadian libraries. Entries are arranged by title and include complete bibliographic description and holdings information. The file "is available for online searching on CISTI's [Canada Institute for Scientific and Technical Information] CAN/OLE system (Union File) and on DOBIS."—*Pref.*

Z7403.U3425

World list of scientific periodicals published in the years 1900–1960. 4th ed. / ed. by Peter Brown and George Burder Stratton. Wash. : Butterworths, 1963–65. 3 v. **EA46**

1st ed., 1925–27.

More than 60,000 titles of periodicals concerned with the natural sciences, of which issues were published during the period 1900–60. Periodicals first published at any time before 1900 are listed so long as they continued publication into the 20th century. Some 10,000 titles which appeared in the 3rd ed. have been omitted as being of social or commercial rather than of scientific interest. Arrangement is alphabetical by title with standard abbreviation, location, dates of publication, and coverage given where known. Holdings of British participating libraries are given. "Titles in the Cyrillic and Greek alphabets are arranged according to their transliterated form, but the transliteration and original alphabet are both given in the entries; titles in other nonroman alphabets are given only in transliteration."—*Editors' note.*

§ Continued in *British union-catalogue of periodicals, incorporating World list of scientific periodicals* (AD237). Z7403.W923

Abbreviations

International CODEN directory [microform]. 1980– . Columbus, Ohio : Chemical Abstracts Service, 1980– . Quinquennial, with cumulative annual supplement. **EA47**

1st ed., 1963. Previously entitled: *Coden for periodical titles (including) non-periodical titles and deleted coden*; publisher varies.

A directory of all CODEN (unique six-character codes which identify serial publications) assigned since 1950—approximately 175,000. In three parts: an index in CODEN order, an alphabetical index by full title, and a KWOC title index. Includes "Introduction and user's guide" (some years in printed booklet, some in microfiche).

Japanese

Directory of Japanese scientific periodicals = Nihon kagaku gijutsu kankei chikuji kankōbutsu mokuroku. 1962– . Tokyo : National Diet Library, 1962– . Irregular. **EA48**

Japanese title varies.

A comprehensive, classified listing of current serials published in Japan in science, medicine, agriculture, and technology. Entries include title in Japanese, romanized Japanese, and Western language; publisher name and address; price; language of text; and ISSN. Indexes by romanized and Western-language title and by editor and publisher. Z7403.K79

Gibson, Robert W. Japanese scientific and technical literature : a subject guide / Robert W. Gibson, Jr., and Barbara K. Kunkel. Westport, Conn. : Greenwood., 1981. 560 p. **EA49**

A preliminary section entitled "Analysis of information activities and bibliographic control in Japan: scientific and technical literature," is followed by a "Subject guide to Japanese scientific and technical journals." The latter lists some 9,116 science and technology journals published in Japan. Arrangement is by modified Universal Decimal Classification, with a title index. Titles are given in romanized Japanese with English translation. Sources in which a journal is indexed or abstracted are indicated by symbols. Z699.5.S3G5

Science Reference Library (British Library). Japanese journals in English / Betty Smith and Shirley V. King. London : British Library Lending Division : British Library Science Reference Library, 1985. 138 p. : ill. **EA50**

Subtitle: A list of Japanese scientific, technical, and commercial journals held by the British Library Science Reference Library and/or the British Library Lending Division.

Lists English-language serials, including cover-to-cover translation journals and journals containing selected articles, published in Japan, 1960–84. Three sections: (1) English language journals published in Japan arranged by subject keyword; (2) translated journals and journals with translations arranged by subject keyword; (3) alphabetic list by romanized Japanese title of journals from section 2.

Z7403.S34

Russian

Library of Congress. Science and Technology Division. Scientific and technical serial publications of the Soviet Union, 1945–1960 / prep. by Nikolay T. Zikeev. Wash. : [for sale by U.S. Govt. Print. Off.], 1963. 347 p.   **EA51**

Alphabetical arrangement of Soviet journals, annuals, monographic series, etc. Titles are given in transliteration, with bracketed English translation, followed by beginning date, frequency, and LC classification number. Index by Soviet institute and subject.

Z7403.U5368

Mezhenko, ÎU. A. Russkaîa tekhnicheskaîa periodika 1800–1916 : bibliograficheskiĭ ukazatel'. Moskva : Izd-vo Akademii Nauk SSSR, 1955. 298 p. : facsims.   **EA52**

An annotated, descriptive bibliography, with subject and other indexes, of 415 Russian periodicals in technological fields, published between 1800 and 1916.   Z7403.M57

Book reviews

Science and technology annual reference review. 1989–1991. Phoenix : Oryx, c1989–1991.   **EA53**

Ed. by H. Robert Malinowsky.

Also referred to as *STARR*.

Reviews a broad range of scientific and technical reference publications, including textbooks, manuals, directories, and bibliographies. Title, author, subject, and type of library indexes.

§ Complements the science section of *American reference books annual* (AA346).   Z7401.S357

Technical book review index. v. 1 (1917)–v. 12 (1928). Pittsburgh : [Technology Dept. of the Carnegie Library of Pittsburgh, 1917–29].   **EA54**

An index listing much material not found in *Book review digest* (AA365). Gives title of book, bibliographic data, references to periodicals, and brief quotations.

§ Suspended 1928–35, then continued by: *Technical book review index*, v. 1 (1935)–v. 54 (1988) (Pittsburgh : JAAD Publ. Co., 1935–88).

Publisher varies; issued 1935–76 by Special Libraries Assoc.

A very useful guide to reviews in scientific, technical, and trade journals, with brief quotations from the reviews cited. Classed arrangement; annual author index only. Beginning with v. 39, no. 1 (Jan. 1973) coverage was expanded to include "all scientific, technical and medical (except clinical) subjects, including life sciences and mathematics. Management and behavioral sciences will be included in the cases where they interface with science or technology."—*v. 39, no. 1. p. 4.*

Dissertations

Inventaire des thèses de doctorat soutenues devant les universités françaises : Sciences / Ministère de l'éducation nationale, Direction générale des enseignements supérieurs et de la recherche. 1981– . Paris : Université de Paris I, Bibliothèque de la Sorbonne, Direction des bibliothèques, des musées et de l'information scientifique et technique, 1982– . Annual.   **EA55**

Continues in part *Catalogue des thèses de doctorat soutenues devant les universités françaises* (AG26).

A classified subject listing of theses awarded in the physical and life sciences, agriculture, and engineering by universities in France. Brief listings include author, thesis title, and locator code. Indexed by author and university granting degree.   Z7403.I68

Lavaud, Suzanne. Catalogue des thèses de doctorat ès sciences naturelles, soutenues à Paris de 1891 à 1954. Paris : Person, 1955. 257 p.   **EA56**

A partial continuation of Albert Maire's *Catalogue des thèses de sciences soutenues en France de 1810 à 1890 inclusivement* (EA57). Arranged chronologically with author and subject indexes.

Maire, Albert. Catalogue des thèses de sciences soutenues en France de 1810 à 1890 inclusivement. Paris : Welter, 1892. 224 p.   **EA57**

Lists more than 2,100 theses, giving publication information, format, and pagination, date, and brief biographical information for each author. Arranged by university, then chronologically. Author and subject indexes.   Z7403.M22

Masters theses in the pure and applied sciences accepted by colleges and universities of the United States and Canada. v. 1 (1955/56)– . N.Y. : Plenum, 1957– . Annual.   **EA58**

Title varies: v. 1–2, *Master's theses accepted by U.S. colleges and universities in the fields of chemical engineering, chemistry, mechanical engineering ...* ; v.3, *Master's theses and doctoral dissertations in the pure and applied sciences ...* .

Publisher varies: the first 12 v. were produced, published, and distributed by the Thermophysical Properties Research Center, School of Mechanical Engineering, Purdue University, Lafayette, Ind.; v. 13–17 (1969–73) were produced by the Center and printed and distributed by Xerox University Microfilms; v. 18 (1974)– published and distributed by Plenum Press.

An annual list of master's theses completed at accredited colleges and universities. Arrangement is alphabetical by discipline, subdivided by university, then alphabetically by author. "Mathematical and most life sciences have been excluded from this publication, on a purely arbitrary basis. ... Biochemistry, biophysics, and bioengineering are included in the coverage when titles in these areas are reported together with chemistry, physics and engineering and not as a separate discipline."—*Contents page.* Covers theses completed since 1955. Subject indexing discontinued after 1960. Canadian theses are listed beginning with v. 18 (1974).   Z7401.M35

Translations

Great Britain. Department of Scientific and Industrial Research. Translated contents lists of Russian periodicals. no. 1 (1940)–117 (Dec. 1958). London : The Dept., 1949–58. Monthly.   **EA59**

Subtitle: With list of recent accessions of Russian scientific and technical books and parts of serial publications available in the British Museum.

Each issue contains a list of periodicals whose contents are included, the translated contents pages, translations of periodical articles available from the Science Museum Library, and a list of accessions of Russian scientific and technical books and individual periodical issues received by the British Museum in the weeks preceding publication.

§ Continued by: *NLL translations bulletin* (EA61).   Z7403.G65

National Translations Center (U.S.). Consolidated index of translations into English. N.Y. : Special Libraries Assoc., 1969. 948 p.   **EA60**

Brings together "information on the availability of translations which have appeared in a number of different lists issued by different agencies at different times. ... Cover-to-cover translations of journals are not listed article by article. ... Items included ... are restricted to translations (in English) of serially published originals such as journals, patents, standards, etc."—*Introd.* In two sections: Serial citation index and Patent citation index. In the serial section, listing is alphabetical by title of the journal, followed by indication of year of publication, volume, issue, pages, and source from which the translation is available. Patents are listed under the name of the country issuing the patent.

Continued by: *Consolidated index of translations into English II : 1967–1984 cumulation of Translations register-index* (Chicago : National Translations Center, 1986. 3 v.). Cover title (all vols.): *CITE II*. Cumulates information previously listed in *Translations register-index* (EA62) for 250,000 translations of scientific and technical articles originally published in reports and serials. Listing is alphabetical by title of journal, then year of publication, volume, issue, and pages. CODEN, ISSN, and a source for obtaining copy are indicated in each entry. A directory of sources appears in each volume.   Z7403.N273

NLL translations bulletin. v. 1 (1959)–12 (1970). London : National Lending Library for Science and Technology, 1959–70. Monthly.   **EA61**

Title varies: v. 1–2, *LLU translations bulletin*, issued by Great Britain. Dept. of Scientific and Industrial Research, Lending Library Unit.

Issues contain listings of new books received from the U.S.S.R. with introduction or author's preface given in translation, new cover-to-cover translations available from the National Lending Library or from other sources, and translations of articles available from the Library, but giving only citation and shelf number.   Q4.N12

Translations register-index. v. 1–20. [Chicago] : National Translations Center, John Crerar Library, 1967–86.   **EA62**

Frequency varies.

The National Translations Center was a depository and information source for unpublished translations into English in the whole range of natural, physical, medical, and social sciences. *Translations register-index* lists (in classed arrangement) accessions to the Center, together with references to translations available from the National Technical Information Service (formerly the Clearinghouse for Federal Scientific and Technical Information) and from commercial sources. Semiannual and annual cumulated indexes.

Continued by: *World translations index* (EA63).

§ The *Register-index* is the direct successor to *Technical translations* (Wash. : U.S. Dept. of Commerce, Office of Technical Services, 1959–67), which in turn superseded *Translation monthly* (Chicago : Special Libraries Assoc., 1955–58). Holdings of the National Translations Center are listed in those earlier publications, as well as in *S.L.A. list of translations* (N.Y., 1953) and its 1954 supplement (both publ. by the Special Libraries Association's Translations Activities Committee), and in *Bibliography of translations from Russian scientific and technical literature*, prep. by the Scientific Translations Center of the Library of Congress (List 1–39, Oct. 1953–Dec. 1956).   Z7401.T72

World translations index : a joint publication of International Translations Centre [and] Centre national de la recherche scientifique in cooperation with the National Translations Center. v. 1, no. 1 (1987)– . Delft, Netherlands : International Translations Centre, 1987– . Ten no. per year.   **EA63**

Publishing history: began as *World index of scientific translations* (v. 1–5. Delft : European Translations Centre, 1967–1971); superseded by *World index of scientific translations and list of translations notified to the ETC* (v. 6–10. Delft : ETC., 1972–1976); superseded by *World index of scientific translations and list of translations notified to the International Translations Centre* (v. 11. Delft : International Translations Centre, 1977); superseded by *World transindex* (v. 1–9. Delft : ITC, 1978–86). *World translations index* formed by merger of *World transindex* and *Translations register-index* (EA62).

Indexes translations of periodical articles, patents, and standards from all languages into English and other Western European languages for all fields of science and technology. Lists additions to the Centre's collections as well as translations available from other national and international translation sources. Author and source indexes.

•In machine-readable form as: *World translations index (WTI)* [database] (Delft : International Translations Centre, 1977–). Available online, updated monthly.   Z7403.W95

Technical reports

Government reports announcements & index. v. 75, no. 7 (4 Apr. 1975)– . [Springfield, Va.] : National Technical Information Service, 1975– . Semimonthly.   **EA64**

Formed by merger of *Government reports announcements* and *Government reports index* (both below).

The National Technical Information Service (NTIS) is "the central source for the public sale of U.S. government-sponsored research, development, and engineering reports and for sales of foreign technical reports and other analyses prepared by national and local government agencies and their contractors or grantees. NTIS is the central source for federally-generated computerized datafiles, databases, and software [and] licensing U.S. government-owned patents."—*About NTIS*.

Includes abstracts arranged in 38 broad subject categories, further divided into 350 subcategories. Each issue includes five indexes: keyword, personal author, corporate author, contract/grant number, NTIS order/report number.

Indexed by: *Government reports annual index* (v. 75 [1975]– . [Springfield, Va.] : NTIS, 1976–). Cumulates the indexes from individual issues of *Government reports announcements & index*.

§ Continues: *Government reports announcements* (v. 1 [1946]–v. 75, no. 6 [21 Mar. 1975]. [Springfield, Va.] : NTIS, 1946–75).

Title varies: Jan. 1946–June 1949, *Bibliography of scientific and industrial reports*; July 1949–Sept. 1954, *Bibliography of technical reports* (varies slightly); Oct. 1954–1964, *U.S. government research reports*; 1965–Mar. 1971, *U.S. government research and development reports*.

Frequency and issuing agency vary.

English abstracts of reports arranged by 22 subject fields with appropriate subdivisions.

Indexed by: *Government reports index* (v. 1 [15 Feb. 1965]–v. 74 [1974]. [Springfield, Va.] : NTIS, 1965–75). Frequency, issuing agency, and coverage vary. Title varies: 1965–67, *Government-wide index*; 1968–71, *U.S. government research and development reports*. Indexed all reports announced in *Government reports announcements* by corporate author, subject, personal author, contract number, and accession/report number.

•Machine-readable version: *NTIS bibliographic database* [database] (Springfield, Va. : NTIS, 1964–). Available online (updated biweekly), on CD-ROM (updated quarterly), and on magnetic tape.

Corresponds in large part to *Government reports announcements & index* and its index and predecessors (above). Cites federally produced or sponsored technical reports, machine-readable data files, software, translations, and licensable government inventions as well as references to some foreign government research publications.

Report series codes dictionary / Eleanor J. Aronson, ed. 3rd ed. Detroit : Gale, c1986. 647 p.   **EA65**

1st ed., 1962, and 2nd ed., 1973, had title: *Dictionary of report series codes* and were issued by Special Libraries Assoc., Rio Grande Chapter.

Subtitle: A guide to more than 20,000 alphanumeric codes used to identify technical reports, arranged both by code and by corporate author.

Section 1 is arranged alphabetically by report code series and Section 2 by the name of the issuing organization. The "information is derived from the unclassified and unlimited cataloging records of the National Technical Information Service (NTIS), the Office of Scientific and Technical Information (OSTI) under the Department of Energy (DOE), the Defense Technical Information Center (DTIC), and the National Aeronautics and Space Administration (NASA), as received in NTIS during the period 1979–May 1985."—*Introd.* Previous edition contains information about report codes prior to 1979, hence will continue to be useful.   Z6945.A2R45

Special Libraries Council of Philadelphia and Vicinity. Correlation index : document series and PB reports / comp. by the Science-Technology Group, Special Libraries Council of Philadelphia and Vicinity, with the cooperation of Office of Technical Services, U.S. Dept. of Commerce, Wash., D.C. ; ed. by Gretchen E. Runge. N.Y. : Special Libraries Assoc., 1953. 271 p. **EA66**

"Many of the unclassified and declassified documents listed as PB Reports in the *Bibliography of Technical Reports* [EA64 note] have also appeared under other series designations. ... This correlation has been compiled to show the relationship of these miscellaneous document series to the PB Report numbers. ..."—*Pref.* Z7916.S65

Indexes; Abstract journals

Applied science and technology index. v. 46 (1958)– . Bronx, N.Y. : H.W. Wilson, 1958– . Monthly, with quarterly and annual cumulations. **EA67**

Continues: *Industrial arts index* (v. 1 [1913]–45 [1957]), which divided in 1958 into *Applied science and technology index*, which carried on the old volume numbering, and *Business periodicals index* (CH37).

A cumulative subject index to about 335 English-language periodicals in the fields of aeronautics and space science, automation, chemistry, computer technology, construction, earth and atmospheric sciences, electricity and electronics, engineering, industrial and mechanical arts, materials, mathematics, metallurgy, physics, telecommunication, transportation, and related subjects. No author entries except for a separate listing, by author, of book reviews. Beginning 1991, also has index to product reviews.

•Machine-readable version: *Applied science & technology index* [database] (Bronx, N.Y. : H.W. Wilson, 1983–). Available online (updated twice weekly), in CD-ROM (updated quarterly), and on magnetic tape. The electronic versions provide multiple approaches, including some unavailable in the printed version (e.g., authors and titles of articles). Z7913.I7

Current contents. 1961– . Philadelphia : Inst. for Scientific Information, 1961– . Weekly. **EA68**

A series of "current awareness" publications that has appeared in various sections since 1961, continuing in part *Current contents of pharmacomedical publications*. Each weekly number reproduces the tables of contents from the most recent issues of journals in the relevant fields. Each issue provides a list of first authors with addresses and an index of words appearing in titles.

Presently published in seven sections, each available separately:

(1) *Current contents. Agriculture, biology & environmental sciences* (1973–).

(2) *Current contents. Clinical medicine* (1987–).

(3) *Current contents. Engineering, technology & applied sciences* (1975–).

(4) *Current contents. Life sciences* (1967–).

(5) *Current contents. Physical, chemical & earth sciences* (1979–).

(6) *Current contents. Social & behavioral sciences* (1974–).

(7) *Current contents. Arts & humanities* (1979–).

•Machine-readable versions: *Current contents search* [database] (Philadelphia : Inst. for Scientific Information). Includes the most recent two years of all seven sections of the printed version. Available online, updated weekly. Also available on diskettes as *Current contents on diskette* [database] (Philadelphia : Inst. for Scientific Information, 1989–), updated weekly. Available for all the printed sections except *Arts & humanities*. Article abstracts are available for *Agriculture, biology & environmental sciences, Clinical medicine, Life sciences*, and *Physical, chemical & earth sciences* sections. Information on weekly diskettes does not cumulate. User's guide.

Also available on CD-ROM as: *Current contents on CD-ROM : Life sciences*; ... *Clinical medicine*; ... *Agriculture, biology & environmental sciences*; ... *Physical, chemical & earth sciences*. Each is published in 51 weekly discs, each of which contains a 52-week rolling file, and an annual archival disc containing the calendar year. Includes abstracts if they are published with the articles.

General science index. v. 1 (July 1978)– . N.Y. : Wilson, 1978– . Monthly except June and Dec., with annual cumulations. **EA69**

A cumulative subject index to more than 100 English-language general science periodicals not completely covered by other indexes or abstracting journals. An author listing of citations to book reviews follows the main body of the index. No other author entries are included.

•Machine-readable version: *General science index* [database] (Bronx, N.Y. : H.W. Wilson, 1984–). Available online (updated twice weekly), on CD-ROM (updated quarterly), and on magnetic tape. The electronic versions provide multiple approaches, including some unavailable in the printed version (e.g., authors and titles of articles).

Index to scientific book contents : ISBC. (1986)– . Philadelphia : Institute for Scientific Information, c1986– . Quarterly with annual cumulations. **EA70**

Indexes chapters from multiauthored scientific books and books that are part of multiauthored series. Disciplines covered include the life sciences and clinical medicine, the physical sciences, and agriculture. Complete descriptive entries for works are arranged by code number; access is provided through indexes to author/editor, book and chapter title keywords, author affiliation, and geographic location of author. A unique index to information generally unavailable from most other abstracting and indexing sources.

•Available online as part of *ISTP&B search* [database] (Philadelphia : Inst. for Scientific Information, 1982–). Updated monthly. Z7401.I37

Index to scientific reviews : an international interdisciplinary index to the review literature of science, medicine, agriculture, technology, and the behavioral sciences. 1974– . Philadelphia, Pa. : Inst. for Scientific Information, Inc., [1974?]– . Semiannual. **EA71**

Covers reviews and review articles in science, medicine, and technology. Indexes all articles in the monographic review series and review journals covered and selected reviews in journals scanned for *Science citation index* database (EA75). The source index arranges articles by author and carries the bibliographic description and codes for research specialty. Indexes by research specialty, author's affiliation, and permuterm subject index. Good description of purpose and scope, lists of source publications, and other information are given in the introduction. Z7403.I42

PASCAL. 1984– . Paris : Centre Nationale de la Recherche Scientifique, 1984– . Frequency varies; most sections 10 issues per year. **EA72**

Publisher varies; recent issues publ. Vandoeuvre-les-Nancy Cedex: Institut de l'Information Scientifique et Technique.

Title varies: v. 1–8 had title: *Bulletin analytique*; v. 9–16, in a new pattern of organization, also called *Bulletin analytique*; 1960–84 called *Bulletin signalétique* (a title still carried by some issues); 1984– , assumed present title.

An international abstract journal, exhaustive in coverage, surveying more than 5,000 periodicals from many countries. Titles are translated into French; abstracts are in French. Sources include books, journals and other serials, dissertations, technical reports, and conference proceedings.

Presently published in two principal sections: *FRANCIS. Bulletin signalétique* (AD254) for humanities and social sciences, and *PASCAL* for the sciences, technology, agriculture, and medicine.

Vols. 9–21 in two parts: pt. 1, Mathématiques, astronomie, physique, chimie, sciences de l'ingénieur, sciences de la terre; pt. 2, Sciences biologiques, sciences pharmacologiques, industries alimentaires, agriculture.

As *Bulletin signalétique*, published in the following sections which continued the volume numbering of the earlier series: Sec. 1, Mathématiques pures et appliquées; Sec. 2, Astronomie et astrophysique; Physique du globe; Sec. 3, Physique I, Généralités—physique mathématique, mécanique, acoustique, optique, chaleur, thermodynamique; Sec. 4, Physique II, Électricité; Sec. 5, Physique nucléaire; Sec. 6, Structure de la matière; Sec. 7, Chimie I, Chimie générale, chimie physique, chimie minérale, chimie analytique, chimie organique; Sec. 8, Chimie II, Chimie appliquée, métallurgie; Sec. 9, Sciences de l'ingénieur; Sec. 10, Sciences de la terre I, Minéralogie, géochimie, pétrographie; Sec. 11, Sciences de la terre II, Physique du globe, géologie, paléontologie; Sec. 12, Biophysique. Biochimie. Chimie analytique biologique; Sec. 13, Sciences pharmacologiques, toxicologie; Sec. 14, Microbiologie. Virus. Bactériophages. Immunologie; Sec. 15, Pathologie générale et experimentale; Sec. 16, Biologie et physiologie animales; Sec. 17, Biologie et physiologie végétales; Sec. 18, Sciences agricoles, zootechnie, phytiatrie et phytopharmacie, aliments et industries alimentaires; Sec. 19, Sciences humaines, philosophie; Sec. 20, Psychologie. Pédagogie; Sec. 21, Sociologie. Sciences du langage; Sec. 22, Histoire des sciences et des techniques.

After v. 29 (1968), the organization of the series was again changed, the sections renumbered, and many previous subsections issued as separate abstract journals. Several new sections devoted to areas not previously covered in depth were also added. Library of Congress entered each section under title, *Bulletin signalétique*, with numerical designation of the section. These include:

101. Information scientifique et technique; 110, Mathématiques pures et appliquées; 120, Astronomie, physique spatiale, géophysique; 130. Physique I, Généralités, physique mathématique, mécanique, acoustique, optique, chaleur, thermodynamique; 140, Physique II, Électricité; 145, Électronique; 150, Physique, chimie et technologie nucléaires; 160, Structure de la matière I, Physique de l'état condensé, physique atomique et moléculaire; spectroscopie; 161, Structure de la matière II, Crystallographie; 170, Chimie—chimie générale et chimie physique, chimie minérale, chimie analytique, chimie organique; 210, Sciences de la terre I, Minéralogie, géochimie, géologie extraterrestre pétrographie; 214, Sciences de la terre II, Géologie appliquée; 216, Sciences de la terre III, Géologie, paléontologie; 320, Biochimie. Biophysique. Génie biologique et médical; 330, Sciences pharmacologiques, toxicologie; 340, Microbiologie, virologie, immunologie; 346, Ophtalmologie; 347, Otorhinolaryngologie; 348, Dermatologie; 350, Pathologie générale et experimentale; 360, Biologie et physiologie animales; 361, Endocrinologie et reproduction. Génétique; 370, Biologie et physiologie végétales; 380, Sciences agricoles, zootechnie, phytiatrie et phytopharmacie, aliments et industries alimentaires; 390, Psychologie, psychopathologie; 522, Histoire des sciences et des techniques; 730, Combustibles, énergie thermique; 740, Métaux, métallurgie; 761, Microscopie électronique, diffraction électronique; 780, Polymères, chimie et technologie; 880, Chimie appliquée, génie chimique, céramique, eaux, corps gras, papier, pollution atmosphérique; 890, Sciences de l'ingénieur.

Beginning 1984, title changed to *PASCAL* (Program appliqué à la selection et à la compilation automatiques de la littérature), the number of sections expanded form 49 to more than 70, and the sections issued in three series, "Explore," "Folio," and "Théma." Some sections have ceased, while others began publication after 1984. Current lists may be found in *Ulrich's international periodicals directory* (AD18). Sections published as follows:

PASCAL. Explore: E11, Physique atomique et moléculaire, plasmas; E12, État condensé; E13, Structure des liquides et des solides, cristallographie; E18, Chromatographie; E20, Électronique et télécommunications; E26, Sciences économiques, problèmes de gestion; E27, Méthodes de formation et traitment des images; E29, Semiconducteurs, matèriaux et composants (ceased 1989); E30, Microscopie électronique et diffraction électronique; E31, Tribiologie; E32, Métrologie et appareillage en physique et physiochemie; E33, Informatique; E34, Robotique, automatique automisation des processes industriels (ceased 1989); E35, Télédétection; E36, Pollution de l'eau, de l'air et du sol; E48, Environnement cosmique terrestre astronomie et géologie extraterrestre; E49, Météorologie; E58, Génétique (numbered E60 1984–85); E61, Microbiologie, bactériologie, virologie, mycologie, protozaires pathogènes; E62, Immunologie; E63, Toxicologie; E64, Endocrinologie humaine et expérimentales, endocrinopathies; E65, Psychologie, psychopathologie, psychiatrie (ceased 1989); E68, Génétique humaine (ceased 1989); E71, Ophthalmologie; E72, Otorhinolaryngologie, atomatologie, pathologie cervicofaciale; E73, Dermatologie, maladies sexuellement transmissibles; E74, Pneumologie; E75, Cardiologie et appareil circulatoire; E76, Gastroénterologie, foie,

pancréas, abdomen; E77, Néphrologie, voies urinaires; E78, Neurologie; E79, Pathologie et physiologie ostéoarticulaires; E80, Hématologie; E81, Maladies métaboloques; E82, Gynécologie, obstétrique, andrologie; E83, Anésthesie et réanimation; E84, Génie biomedical, informatique biomédicale; E85, Radiodiagnostic, exploration radioisotopique, exploration par ultrasons, imagerie RMN; E86, Gérontologie, gériatrie; E89, Cancer; E99, Congrés, rapports, thèses.

PASCAL. Folio: F10, Mécanique, acoustique et transfert de chaleur; F16, Chimie analytique minérale et organique; F17, Chimie générale, minérale et organique; F21, Electrotechnique; F23, Génie chimique. Industries chimiques et parachimiques; F24, Polymères, peintures, bois; F25, Transports terestres et maritimes; F40, Minéralogie, géochemie, géologie extraterrestre; F41, Gisements métalliques et non métalliques; F42, Roches cristallines; F43, Roches sédimentaires, géologie marine; F44, Stratigraphie, géologie régionale, géologie générale; F45, Tectonique, géophysique interne; F46, Hydrologie, géologie de l'ingénieur, formations superficielles; F47, Paléontologie; F52, Biochimie, biophysique moléculaire, biologie moléculaire et cellulaire; F53, Anatomie et physiologie des vertébrés; F54, Reproduction des vertébrés, embryologie des vertébrés et des invertébrés; F55, Biologie végétale; F56, Ecologie animale et végétales; F70, Pharmacologie, traitements médicamenteux.

PASCAL. Thèma: T022, Sciences de la terre (ceased 1989); T195, Bâtiment, travaux publiques; T205, Sciences de l'information, documentation; T210, Industries agrimentaires; T215, Biotechnologies; T230, Energie; T235, Médecine tropicale; T240, Métaux, métallugie; T245, Soudage, brasage et techniques connexe; T251, Cancérologie; T260, Zoologie fondamentale et appliquées des invertébrés (milieu terrestre, eaux douces); T280, Science agronomiques, productions végétales.

•Machine-readable version: *PASCAL* [database] (Vandoeuvreles-Nancy Cedex : Institut de l'Information Scientifique et Technique, 1973–). Available online; updated monthly.

With completion of issues for 1994, the publisher intends to issue *PASCAL* only in machine-readable form, terminating the printed version.

Referativnyĭ zhurnal. Moskva : VINITI [Vsesiouznyi Institut Nauchnoi Tekhnicheskoi Informatsii], 1953–   **EA73**
Publisher varies.

A major abstracting journal, published in sections that cover most branches of science and technology. Bibliographic information is given in Russian followed by the original language.

Titles and coverage of the various series have varied greatly since establishment of the journal. As of 1993, published in 74 subject series covering the entire range of science and technology; mathematics and agriculture are included but not clinical medicine. A listing of current sections is found in the "Abstracts and indexing services" section of *Ulrich's international periodicals directory* (AD18).

For a good description of the series, a list of its subject sections, and a key to distribution of specific subjects, *see*: Eric James Copley, *A guide to Referativnyi zhurnal* (London : National Reference Library of Science and Invention, 1975. 20 p.).

Repertorium der technischen Journal-Literatur, 1823–1908. Berlin : Heymann, 1856–1909. 40 v.   **EA74**
Title and publisher vary.

Contents: 1823–53, publ. 1856 (1049 p.); 1854–68, publ. 1871–73 (2 v.); 1869–73, publ. 1876–78 (2 v.); 1874–1908, publ. 1875–1909 (35 v.).

1823–76, hrsg. im Auftrage des Königlich Preussischen Ministeriums für Handel, Gewerbe und öffentliche Arbeiten; 1877–1908, hrsg. im Auftrage des Kaiserlichen Patentamts.

A subject index to more than 400 periodicals in various languages, arranged alphabetically by the German subject word followed, in volumes from 1892 on, by the French and English equivalents. Each volume has a detailed subject index to this subject list which, in volumes before 1892, is an index of German words only, but from 1892 includes French and English words in the same alphabet; volumes from 1897 on have an author index also. Still useful for older and foreign material.

§ Continued by *Fortschritte der Technik* (1.–2. Jahrg., [1909–11]. Berlin : Bibliographisch Zentralverlag, 1910–11. 9 v.).   Z7913.R42

Science citation index. 1961– . Philadelphia : Inst. for Scientific Information, 1961– . Bimonthly with annual cumulations.   **EA75**

Subtitle (varies): An international interdisciplinary index to the literature of science, medicine, agriculture, technology, and the behavioral sciences.

In four sections: Citation index, Source index, Permuterm index, Corporate index. Based on the concept of citation indexing which links current and past publications, *SCI* indexes current publications (more than 3,800 journals and monographic series) and lists current works in the Source index by first author. Works cited in the current publications are listed by the original (first) author in the Citation index. The Permuterm index provides subject access, based on the words in the titles of articles, to the current publications listed in the Source index. The Corporate index lists affiliations of first authors of articles listed in the Source index. Instructions for use are given on the front endpapers.

Ten-year cumulations for 1945–54 and 1955–64 provide coverage for periods predating the annual format. Five-year cumulations have been issued for 1965–69 through 1985–89.

•Machine-readable versions: *SCISEARCH* [database] (Philadelphia : Inst. for Scientific Information, 1974–). Available online and on magnetic tape, updated weekly. Covers materials indexed in *SCI* plus some additional periodicals listed in *Current contents* (EA68). User guide available from publisher. Available on CD-ROM as *Science citation index : compact disc edition* [database] (Philadelphia : Inst. for Scientific Information, 1980–). One disc per year; current disc updated quarterly. User guide.

Also available as: *Science citation index compact disc edition with abstracts* [database] (1991–), available on CD-ROM, updated quarterly, two discs for each year.   Z7401.S365

Bibliography

Owen, Dolores B. Abstracts and indexes in science and technology : a descriptive guide. 2nd ed. Metuchen, N.J. : Scarecrow Pr., 1985. 235 p.   **EA76**
1st ed., 1974.

Gives descriptions of 223 abstracting and indexing services arranged in 11 subject categories, with information on arrangement, coverage, scope, a description of the abstracts, characteristics of the indexes, and existence of online databases. Title index.   Z7403.O95

Correlation indexes

United States. Department of Commerce. Office of Technical Services. Correlation index of technical reports (AD-PB reports). Wash., 1958. 184 p.   **EA77**

A cross index from ASTIA document numbers (AD) to the ones assigned by the Office of Technical Services (PB) in making the reports available for sale to the public.

Encyclopedias

Durbin, Paul T. Dictionary of concepts in the philosophy of science. N.Y. : Greenwood, 1988. 362 p. (Reference sources for the social sciences and humanities, no. 6).   **EA78**

Summarizes 100 basic controversies in philosophy of science. Topics are arranged alphabetically, with historical and contemporary issues discussed in encyclopedia-length articles. Excellent bibliographies. Accessible to advanced undergraduate and graduate students and educated general readers.   Q174.7.D87

Encyclopedia of physical science and technology / Robert A. Meyers [editor]. 2nd ed. San Diego : Academic Pr., c1992. 18 v. : ill.   **EA79**
1st ed., 1987 (15 v.).

Revised, updated and expanded by 155 new articles, the basic arrangement of the work is retained. Signed articles by specialists, each begins with a table of contents, glossary, and introductory definitions of the subject. Technical levels of the articles vary, but most are more sophisticated than those in the *McGraw-Hill encyclopedia of science & technology* (EA81). The index (v. 18) includes the contributor list, a relational index to groups of similar articles, and a subject index. The excellent index overcomes the difficulty of locating topics under the sometimes idiosyncratic titles in the alphabetic volumes. Kept up to date by *Encyclopedia of physical science and technology yearbook* (EA165).   Q123.E497

Gardner, Martin. Fads and fallacies in the name of science. Rev. ed. N.Y. : Dover Publications, [1957]. 363 p.   **EA80**

"A revised and expanded edition of the work first published in 1952 under the title *In the name of science*."—t.p.

A collection of essays giving information about modern pseudoscientists and their theories, e.g., Voliva's flat earth, Velikovsky's worlds in collision, Bates's perfect sight without glasses, etc. New bibliographic information is included in the appendix, Index of names.   Q173.G35

McGraw-Hill encyclopedia of science & technology : an international reference work in twenty volumes including index. 7th ed. N.Y. : McGraw-Hill, c1992. 20 v. : ill.   **EA81**
1st ed., 1960; 6th ed., 1987.

Provides authoritative coverage for all disciplines in science and engineering with new or revised entries based on advances in knowledge and new technological achievements. This edition contains 7,500 signed entries alphabetically arranged, each including a definition, general overview of the subject, relationships to other broader or more specialized topics, and cross-references to other articles. Biographical and historical articles are excluded. Measurements are expressed both in the U.S. customary system and the International system (SI). Articles are well-illustrated and include maps, charts, photographs, and tables. Bibliographies follow most longer articles. Vol. 20 includes a list of contributors, tables on scientific notation, study guides, a topical index that groups entries under 79 major subject areas, and the alphabetic analytical index. Kept up-to-date between editions by: *McGraw-Hill yearbook of science and technology* (EA167).

§ The publisher has derived other works from this edition: *McGraw-Hill encyclopedia of astronomy* (2nd ed., 1993. 531 p.); *McGraw-Hill dictionary of chemistry* (EE43); *McGraw-Hill encyclopedia of engineering* (2nd ed., 1993. 1,414 p.); *McGraw-Hill encyclopedia of environmental science & engineering* (3rd ed., 1993. 749 p.); *McGraw-Hill encyclopedia of physics* (2nd ed., 1993. 1,624 p.).   Q121.M3

Van Amerongen, C. The way things work : an illustrated encyclopedia of modern technology. N.Y. : Simon & Schuster, [1967–71]. 2 v. : ill.   **EA82**

Translated and adapted from *Wie funktioniert das?* and *Und wie funktioniert dies?* by "an English-American team," using English terminology with footnotes giving American equivalents. " ... not a reference book in the ordinary sense. It has been designed to give the layman an understanding of *how things work*, from the simplest mechanical functions of modern life to the most basic scientific principles and complex industrial processes that affect our well-being."—*Foreword*. Subject index.   T47.W3913

Van Nostrand's scientific encyclopedia / Douglas M. Considine, ed. ; Glenn D. Considine, managing ed. 7th ed. N.Y. : Van Nostrand Reinhold, c1989. 2 v. (3180 p.) : ill.   **EA83**
1st ed., 1968; 6th ed., 1983.

The new edition of this standard encyclopedia is conveniently published in two volumes. Although emphasis is on short, concise entries, longer, frequently signed articles are included, many with revised and updated bibliographies. More than 3,000 black-and-white illustrations; some 500 tabular summaries. Now includes an extensive alphabetic index of terms. A new edition is planned for 1994. Q121.V3

Dictionaries

Academic Press dictionary of science and technology / ed. by Christopher Morris. San Diego, Calif. : Academic Pr., c1992. 2432 p. : ill. (some col.). **EA84**

A major new source of brief definitions for terms in science, medicine, and engineering with 133,007 entries, of which 112,227 are main entries. Definitions include field of specialty, related and cross-references, and sometimes a pronunciation key. Biographical entries for historical and living scientists are included. Black-and-white line drawings and photographs accompany some entries, and 12 color plates illustrate special themes. The International system of units (SI) is used. Appendix includes tables of symbols and units, fundamental physical constants, conversion tables, and some basic tables and charts in astronomy, biology, chemistry, and geology. No index. Intended for students and knowledgeable general readers.

§ Should be compared to *McGraw-Hill dictionary of scientific and technical terms* (EA93). Large reference and science collections will need both. Q123.A33

Ballentyne, Denis William George. A dictionary of named effects and laws in chemistry, physics, and mathematics / D. W. G. Ballentyne and D. R. Lovett. 4th ed. London ; N.Y. : Chapman and Hall, 1980. 346 p. : ill. **EA85**

1st ed., 1958.

A dictionary of terms known by the names of the scientists who discovered them or worked in the fields with which their names have become connected, e.g., Curie's law, Einstein's principle of relativity, Fourier's series, etc. Gives brief definitions of the law or theory, but no indication as to who the scientist was or when he or she lived. Q123.B32

Barnhart, Robert K. The American heritage dictionary of science / Robert K. Barnhart ; with Sol Steinmetz, managing ed. Boston : Houghton Mifflin, c1986. 740 p. : ill. **EA86**

Originally publ. 1986 as: *Hammond Barnhart dictionary of science.*

"Designed to support the student in his or her introduction to a first systematic study of the physical and biological sciences."—*Pref.* Defines more than 15,000 words and phrases; definitions indicate subject, and may give derivative or variant forms, a pronunciation key for difficult words, notes about related terms, examples of usage, and word etymologies. Black-and-white line illustrations. A useful, non-technical source for a variety of scientific disciplines. Q123.B35

Cailleux, André. Dictionnaire des racines scientifiques / André Cailleux, Jean Komorn. 3ᵉ éd., rev. et augm. de plus 1200 entrées nouvelles. Paris : Editions SEDES-CDU réunis, c1981. 263 p. **EA87**

1st ed., 1961.

A dictionary of word roots in the pure and applied sciences. About 1,200 entries added in this edition. Q123.C3

Cambridge dictionary of science and technology / gen. ed. Peter M. B. Walker. Cambridge ; N.Y. : Cambridge Univ. Pr., [1990]. 1008 p. **EA88**

Rev. ed., 1975, had title: *Dictionary of science and technology.*

British ed., 1988, had title: *Chambers science and technology dictionary.* A direct successor to *Chambers's technical dictionary* (1st–3rd eds., 1940–58).

Defines 45,000 terms in 100 scientific and technical areas. Short definitions identify a field of specialty for each term and often refer to related headwords. British spelling and usage. Appendixes contain tables of chemical formulas, chemical elements, SI conversion factors, physical constants, animal and plant classifications, SI units, geological eras, paper sizes, and a periodic table. The work is "useful both to

the layman and to the professional but will not replace the expert's own specialist dictionaries."—*Pref.* Compact size and sturdy binding make this a good choice for smaller library collections. Q123.C482

Concise science dictionary. 2nd ed. Oxford ; N.Y. : Oxford Univ. Pr., c1991. 758 p. : ill. **EA89**

1st ed., 1984.

"Aims to provide school and first-year university students with explanations of unfamiliar words they might come across in the course of their studies, in their own or adjacent disciplines."—*Pref.* The new edition totals 7,500 terms with additions in physics, chemistry, environmental science, genetics, and immunology. Standard collection of physical tables and charts in appendix. Q123.C68

Emiliani, Cesare. Dictionary of the physical sciences : terms, formulas, data. N.Y. : Oxford Univ. Pr., c1987. 365 p. : ill. **EA90**

A convenient compilation of terms, formulas, and data for the disciplines of physics, chemistry, the geological sciences (including related areas in biology), and cosmology (astronomy and astrophysics). Definitions are arranged alphabetically, and often include useful formulas, diagrams, or references to one of the 70 supplementary data tables. A separate bibliography of sources is provided for the tables and illustrations. Q123.E46

The encyclopedic dictionary of science / [ed., Candida Hunt ; contributing consultants, Bernard Dixon ... et al.]. N.Y. : Facts on File, c1988. 256 p. : col. ill. **EA91**

A general science dictionary that defines some 7,000 terms and includes biographical listings for historical and modern scientists. Definitions are usually three to four sentences in length and are written for beginning college students and general readers. Cross-references within the text point to useful related terms. 34 color illustrations. Incorporates some material from *Concise encyclopedia of the sciences* (N.Y. : Facts on File, 1980. 590 p.). Q123.E498

Greenstein, Carol Horn. Dictionary of logical terms and symbols. N.Y. : Van Nostrand Reinhold, c1978. 188 p. : ill. **EA92**

"The primary objective of the *Dictionary* ... is to present compactly, concisely, and side by side a variety of alternative notational systems currently used by logicians, computer scientists, and engineers."—*Pref.* Notations are arranged by function, e.g., logical gate notation, truth tables, etc. Includes list of abbreviations, glossary, and bibliography. QA9.G698

McGraw-Hill dictionary of scientific and technical terms / Sybil P. Parker, ed. in chief. 5th ed. N. Y. : McGraw-Hill, 1993. 2088, 49 p. : ill. **EA93**

1st ed., 1974; 4th ed., 1989.

Provides 122,600 brief definitions for 105,100 terms, an increase of 5,000 terms over the previous edition. Each entry notes field of interest, acronyms, synonyms, abbreviations, and pronunciation. Small black-and-white line drawings, photographs, tables, and charts illustrate 3,000 terms. U.S. customary values are given with equivalent SI metric units. The appendix includes a selection of standard tables and charts—the periodic table, fundamental constants, etc.—as well as a biographical listing of 1,500 noted historical and modern scientists.

A 3½-in. disk for DOS-based computers containing a customized spell-checking dictionary is included, but information on installation and use of the disk is limited and found only on the disk itself. A review in *Wilson library bulletin*, 68, no. 10 (June 1994): 99–100 compares this work with *Academic Press dictionary of science and technology* (EA84). Larger science reference collections will need both. Q123.M34

Nybakken, Oscar Edward. Greek and Latin in scientific terminology. Ames : Iowa State College Pr., [1959]. 321 p. **EA94**

Repr., 1985.

Deals with the "construction of the technical terms, names, and specific epithets used in the medical and biological sciences."—*Pref.*

Includes discussion on language in general and the Latin and Greek languages in particular, especially in regard to scientific terminology. Includes alphabetical lists of Latin and Greek root words with the English scientific terms which are derived from them. Bibliography and index.   Q179.N9

Bibliography

International bibliography of specialized dictionaries = Fachwörterbücher und Lexika, ein internationales Verzeichnis / [ed. by Helga Lengenfelder]. 6th ed. München ; N.Y. : K.G. Saur ; Detroit : Distr. by Gale, 1979. 470 p. (Handbook of international documentation and information, v.4).   **EA95**
For annotation, *see* AC192.   Z7004.D5I55

Abbreviations

Murith, Jean. Dictionnaire des abréviations et acronymes scientifiques, techniques, médicaux, économiques, juridiques = Dictionary of scientific, technical, medical, economic, legal abbreviations and acronyms / Jean Murith, Jean-Marc Boca-beille. 2e éd. rev. et augmentée. Paris ; Londres ; N.Y. : Tec et Doc-Lavoisier, c1992. 949 p.   **EA96**
1st ed., 1984, had title: *Dictionnaire des abréviations & acro-nymes scientifiques, techniques, économiques = Dictionary of scientif-ic, technical & economic abbreviations & acronyms.*
This greatly expanded edition lists French and English uses for some 60,000 alphabetically arranged acronyms and abbreviations.
                                               Q179.M8

Ocran, Emanuel Benjamin. Ocran's acronyms : a dictionary of abbreviations and acronyms used in scientific and technical writing. London ; Boston : Routledge & K. Paul, 1978. 262 p.
                                               EA97
A collection of abbreviations and acronyms found in journal arti-cles and technical reports. Excludes foreign abbreviations and acro-nyms and those for associations, institutions, and governmental bodies. Entries in the main alphabetical section are subdivided and listed by 47 subject fields.   Q179.O24

Wennrich, Peter. Anglo-amerikanische und deutsche Abkur-zungen in Wissenschaft und Technik = Anglo-American and German abbreviations in science and technology. München : Verlag Dokumentation, 1976–78. 3 v.   **EA98**
A compilation of more than 150,000 German and Anglo-American abbreviations taken from some 800 international journals. "More than 60% [of the abbreviations] are found in the Anglo-American sphere. ..."—*Foreword.* German and English words are in-terfiled in a single alphabetical sequence.
———. ———. *Teil 4, Nachtrage = Part 4, supplement* (München : K.G. Saur, 1980. 618 p.).   Q179.W45

Zimmerman, Oswald Theodore. Scientific and technical ab-breviations, signs and symbols / by O. T. Zimmerman and Ir-vin Lavine. 2nd ed. Dover, N.H. : Industrial Research Service, 1949. 541 p.   **EA99**
1st ed., 1948.
Arranged by categories including: General list of abbreviations and symbols, Chemistry, Mechanics, Shop terms, Electricity, Map-ping, etc. Brief subject index, but no general index to abbreviations. The chief purpose is to answer the question "What is the standard ab-breviation for ... ?" rather than "What does this abbreviation stand for?"   Q179.Z5

Foreign terms

Multilingual

Dictionary of scientific and technical terminology / A. S. Markov ... [et. al.]. The Hague ; Boston : Martinus Nijhoff ; Hingham, Mass. : Distr. by Kluwer Boston, 1984. 496 p.
                                               EA100
A five-language polyglot dictionary of 9,000 terms, arranged al-phabetically by English term with equivalents in the other languages. German, French, Dutch, and Russian indexes.   T10.D564

Te Ying Han tsung ho kỏ chi ta tzủ tien = Deutsch-Englisch-Chinesisch polytechnisches Wörterbuch = German-English-Chinese polytechnical dictionary / Lü Wen-chảo chu pien. [Peking] : Kỏ hsüeh chi shu wen hsien chủ pan she : Hsin hua tien kỏ chi fa hsing so fa hsing, 1988. 2 v. (2660 p.).
                                               EA101
120,000 entries in German with English and Chinese equivalents cover the physical sciences, engineering, medicine, and agriculture. Vol. 2 has English and Chinese indexes with entries keyed to page number in German section.   Q123.T34

Technologisches Wörterbuch. 6. vollkommen neubearb. Aufl. / hrsg. von Alfred Schlomann. Berlin : Springer, 1944. 3 v.   **EA102**
English subtitle: Crafts and industries, engineering and engineer-ing science, mining and metallurgy; raw and finished materials ...; electrical and communication engineering; metrology; ... optical, med-ical, and sanitary engineering; safety engineering; civil engineering and chemical technology; agriculture and forestry; foodstuffs, textile and clothing industries; trade, banking, and fair practice; traffic, ... motor engineering; shipbuilding and navigation; patents, law, and cus-toms [etc.].
Contents: v.1, German-English-French; v.2, English-German-French; v.3, French-German-English.
A general technical dictionary that attempts to cover the entire field of technology and its allied subjects. There is a preface to each volume in the first-named language of the volume. Includes 100,000 terms in each of the languages covered. "Expressions which are pre-ferred, or are used almost exclusively, in the United States, are marked (A)."—*Pref., v.2.*   T10.T27

Arabic

Khaṭib, Ahmad Shafiq. A new dictionary of scientific and technical terms : English-Arabic. 6th ed. Beirut : Librarie du Liban, 1987. 751 p. : ill.   **EA103**
Added title page in Arabic.
1st ed., 1971.
Some 65,000 English terms with Arabic equivalents. Appendix includes scientific tables and charts, some with Arabic descriptions.
                                               Q123.K53

Mu'jam al-muṣṭalaḥāt al-fannīyah = Dictionary of technical terms : English-Arabic. [2nd ed.]. Cairo : Govt. Print. Off., 1967. 40, 847, 78 p.   **EA104**
Comp. by Idārat al-Tadrīb al-Mihnī lil-Qūwāt al-Musallaḥah.
Repr: al-Qāhirah : al-Waṭan al-'Arabī, 1984.
Some 40,000 English headwords with Arabic equivalents. Ap-pendix includes tables of common scientific and technical formulas and data.   T9.M83

Bulgarian

Kratük bŭlgarsko-angliĭski politekhnicheski rechnik / [avtori Simeon Todorov Todoriev ... et al.]. Sofiĭa : Izd-vo "Tekhnika", 1990. 464 p.   **EA105**

Title on added t.p.: Concise Bulgarian-English technical dictionary.

Contains 35,000 terms in the basic sciences and engineering.
    T10.K773

Czech

Anglicko-český technický slovník / [Zdeněk Bažnt ... et al.]. 5. vyd. Praha : SNTL ; Brno : Littera, 1992. 1026 p.   **EA106**

Added title page: English-Czech technical dictionary.

1st ed., 1969; 4th ed., 1985.

Lists 78,000 English terms from all branches of engineering and technology with their Czech equivalents.

§ Companion volume: *Česko-anglický technický slovník,* [by Zdeněk Bažnt ... et al.] (5. vyd. Praha : SNTL, 1992. 944 p.). 1st ed., 1963; 4th ed., 1986. Added title page: Czech-English technical dictionary.   T10.A57

French

DeVries, Louis. French-English science and technology dictionary. 4th ed. / rev. and enl. by Stanley Hochman. N.Y. : McGraw-Hill, c1976. 683 p.   **EA107**

1st–3rd eds. (1940–62) publ. under title: *French-English science dictionary for students in agricultural, biological, and physical sciences.*

"This new edition has been revised to include some 4,500 terms. ... The new entries have been incorporated into the Supplement which follows the main body of the dictionary."—*Introd.*   Q123.D37

Dorian, Angelo Francis. Dictionary of science and technology : English-French. N.Y. ; Amsterdam : Elsevier, 1979. 1586 p.   **EA108**

Added title page: Dictionnaire de science et technologie.

A massive dictionary with more than 150,000 terms from more than 100 fields. Entries indicate the field to which the term belongs and the French equivalent. Definitions are given only when necessary to obviate ambiguity.

Companion volume: *Dictionary of science and technology : French-English* (1980. 1085 p.). Added title page: Dictionnaire de science et technologie.   Q123.D672

Ernst, Richard. Comprehensive dictionary of engineering and technology : with extensive treatment of the most modern techniques and processes. Cambridge, [Eng.] ; N.Y. : Cambridge Univ. Pr. ; Wiesbaden : Brandstetter, 1985. 2 v.   **EA109**

For annotation, *see* EK9.   T10.E747

Harrap's French and English science dictionary / consultant ed., D. E. Hathway. London : Harrap, 1985. 320, 302 p.   **EA110**

Arranges about 20,000 terms in the physical and life sciences in two sections, English-French and French-English. Entries note the discipline associated with the term and give brief definitions when necessary for clarification. Medical and pharmaceutical terms and taxonomic names are excluded.   Q123.H265

German

De Vries, Louis. German-English science dictionary / Louis De Vries ; updated and expanded by Leon Jacolev, with the assistance of Phyllis L. Bolton. 4th ed. N.Y. : McGraw-Hill, c1978. 628 p.   **EA111**

1st ed., 1954; 3rd ed., 1959, had title: *German-English science dictionary for students in chemistry, physics, biology, agriculture, and related sciences.*

"The Fourth Edition introduces the newly specialized terminologies of nuclear science and engineering, computer science and data processing, solid state physics, molecular biology, genetics, automation, soil and environmental sciences, electronics, etc. ... For the sake of expediency ... the new terms have again been ... incorporated into the Addendum."—*Pref.* About 65,000 entries.   Q123.D42

DeVries, Louis. German-English technical and engineering dictionary / by Louis DeVries and Theo M. Herrmann. 2nd ed., rev. and enl. N.Y. : McGraw-Hill, [1965, c1966]. 1178 p.   **EA112**

1st ed. 1950; supplement, 1959.

Gives English equivalents of German words and expressions. This edition "has been completely revised, antiquated terms removed and the valid material of the supplement incorporated."—*Pref.*

§ Companion work: *English-German technical and engineering dictionary,* by Louis DeVries and Theo M. Herrmann (2nd ed., rev. and enl. N.Y. : McGraw-Hill, [c1967]. 1154 p.). 1st ed., 1954; suppl., 1959.   T9.D48

Dorian, Angelo Francis. Dictionary of science and technology : English-German. 2nd rev. ed. Amsterdam ; N.Y. : Elsevier, 1978. 1401 p.   **EA113**

Added title page: Handwörterbuch der Naturwissenschaft und Technik : Englisch-Deutsch.

1st ed., 1967.

"A large number of terms which could rightly be regarded as ballast has been eliminated and about 16,000 new lemmata inserted, mainly relating to those branches of science and technology which are being constantly developed in our times."—*Pref.*

Companion work: *Dictionary of science and technology : German-English,* by A. F. Dorian (2nd rev. ed. Amsterdam ; N.Y. : Elsevier, 1981. 1119 p.). Added title page: Handwörterbuch der Naturwissenschaft und Technik : Deutsch-Englisch. 1st ed., 1970.   Q123.D67

Ernst, Richard. Dictionary of engineering and technology : with extensive treatment of the most modern techniques and processes. 5th ed. N.Y. : Oxford Univ. Pr., [1985–89]. 2 v.   **EA114**

For annotation, *see* EK10.   T10.E76

Hungarian

Magyar-angol műszaki szótár / [szerk., Nagy Ernő, Klár János, és Katona Lóránt]. 6., változatlan kiad. Budapest : Akadémiai Kiadó, 1990. 752 p.   **EA115**

1st ed., 1957.

Added title page: Hungarian-English technical dictionary.

The first Hungarian-English dictionary of scientific and technical words and terms. Lists about 120,000 Hungarian technical terms with English equivalents.

Companion work: *Angol-magyar műszaki szótár,* szerk., Nagy Ernő, Klár János, [munkatársak, Herz Elza ... et al.] (7., változatlan kiad. Budapest : Akadémiai Kiadó, 1990. 791 p.). Added title page: English-Hungarian technical dictionary. 1st ed., 1951.   T10.M22

Italian

Denti, Renzo. Dizionario tecnico italiano-inglese, inglese-italiano : abbreviazioni tecniche anglo-americane aggiornate ed aumentate : tabelle di conversione e riduzione, ecc. 11a ed. riv., ampliata ed aggiornata. Milano : Edit. U. Hoepli, c1985. 2023 p.   **EA116**
    Added title page: Technical dictionary English-Italian, Italian-English.
    1st ed., 1946.
    Updated to incorporate current scientific terminology. A useful abbreviations section includes equivalent terms in English and Italian.
                                           T10.D45

Gatto, Simon. Dizionario tecnico scientifico illustrato : italiano-inglese, inglese-italiano = A dictionary of technical and scientific terms : English-Italian, Italian-English. Milan : Ceschina, [1960]. 1381 p. : ill.   **EA117**
    A 1965 printing, claiming to be a 2nd ed., revised and corrected, shows no difference in pagination.
    A collection of some 60,000 terms covering both engineering and other scientific fields, including many new terms culled from scientific literature.   T9.G35

Marolli, Giorgio. Dizionario tecnico, inglese-italiano, italiano-inglese = Technical dictionary, English-Italian, Italian-English. 12a ed. interamente riveduta e ampliata. Milano : Edit. U. Hoepli, c1991. 1960 p.   **EA118**
    A comprehensive bilingual dictionary. Most headwords and derivatives indicate specialty or field of interest. Abbreviations incorporated into text in alphabetical order. Portfolio of plates gives detailed diagrams of machinery, engines, vehicles, etc. with bilingual terminology.   T9.M18

Japanese

Intā Puresu-ban kagaku gijutsu 35–mango daijiten = Inter Press dictionary of science and engineering / [kikaku hensan Fujioka Keisuke]. 3rd ed. Tōkyō : IPC, 1990. 2 v.   **EA119**
    Contents: v. 1, Japanese-English; v. 2, English-Japanese.
    This massive dictionary includes more than 150,000 headwords in each volume and is particularly strong in engineering and technology. Includes idioms, abbreviations, acronyms, and technical phrases, but lacks any introduction or explanation in English.   T10.I57

Tung, Louise Watanabe. Japanese/English English/Japanese glossary of scientific and technical terms / Louise Watanabe Tung = [Wa-Ei Ei-Wa kagaku kōgaku yōgo jiten / Watanabe Hisako]. N.Y. : Wiley, c1993. 1146 p.   **EA120**
    A bilingual glossary of 22,000 terms compiled for use by "translators and interpreters, scientists and engineers, patent process experts, media researchers, teachers and students of language, and others who look up English as well as Japanese terms."—*Pref.* The Japanese/English section is arranged by the romanized form, followed by the *kanji/kana* forms and the English equivalent. Pronunciation keys and specialty fields for terms are provided. The helpful explanatory matter and reasonable price make this a good alternative to the larger and considerably more expensive *Inter Press dictionary of science and technology* (EA119).   Q123.T844

Norwegian

Ansteinsson, John. Norsk-engelsk teknisk ordbok. 3. revid. og omarb. utg. / av Olav Reiersen. Trondheim : F. Brun, 1990. 358 p.   **EA121**
    1st ed., 1948.

    Added title page: Norwegian-English technical dictionary.
    A glossary of Norwegian technical terms and their English equivalents. Entries are grouped by root words with related expressions.
    Companion volume: *Engelsk-norsk teknisk ordbok*, by John Ansteinsson and Olav Reiersen (5. revid. og omarb. utg. Trondheim : Brun, 1991. 583 p.). Added title page: English-Norwegian technical dictionary.

Polish

Słownik naukowo-techniczny polsko-angielski / redagowali Sergiusz Czerni i Maria Skrzyńska. Wyd. 6., niezmienione. Warszawa : Wydawnictwa Naukowo-Techniczne, 1986. 846 p.   **EA122**
    Added title page: *Polish-English dictionary of science and technology.*
    1st ed., 1962, had title: *Słownik techniczny polsko-angielski = Polish-English technological dictionary.*
    Contains 80,000 Polish terms with their English equivalents. Revisions have emphasized such rapidly changing topics as electronics, computer science, and nuclear engineering.
    § Companion volume: *Słownik naukowo-techniczny angielsko-polski*, redagowali Maria Skrzyńska ... [et al.] (Wyd. 10. Warszawa : Wydawnictwa Naukowo-Techniczne, c1992. 1032 p.). Added title page: *English-Polish dictionary of science and technology.* T10.S623

Portuguese

Fürstenau, Eugênio. Novo dicionário de termos técnicos inglês-português. 15a. ed. São Paulo, Brasil : Editora Globo, [1989]. 2 v. (1413 p.) : ill.   **EA123**
    1st ed., 1947.
    About 30,000 terms, including words from such rapidly growing fields as astronautics, nuclear physics, and computer sciences.
                                            T10.F87

Russian

Alford, Mark Hugh Tankerville. Russian-English scientific and technical dictionary / M. H. T. and V. L. Alford. Oxford ; N.Y. : Pergamon, [1970]. 2 v. (1423 p.).   **EA124**
    About 100,000 entries, drawing on terminology from 94 specialized fields. Stresses are shown for all terms; irregular verb forms are included. Does not cover belles lettres or popular science. Also includes instructions for learning large vocabularies; instructions for use of dictionary; reference sources; and in v. 2, supplementary dictionary of Russian word endings.   Q123.A4

Chakalov, G. Elsevier's dictionary of science and technology : Russian-English / compiled by G. Chakalov. Amsterdam ; N.Y. : Elsevier, 1993. 1243 p.   **EA125**
    About 120,000 entries from all branches of technology and from mathematics, information science, economics, and finance. The dictionary is "a translation into Russian from an unpublished Bulgarian-English version."—*Pref.*   Q123.C4817

Chernukhin, Adol'f Efimovich. Anglo-russkiĭ politekhnicheskiĭ slovar' : okolo 87,000 terminov. Izd. 4., stereotipnoe s dopolneniami. Moskva : Russkiĭ Iazyk, 1979. 687 p.   **EA126**
    Added title page: English-Russian polytechnical dictionary.
    Updated to about 87,000 terms.   T10.C52

Macura, Paul. Elsevier's Russian-English dictionary. Amsterdam ; N.Y. : Elsevier ; N.Y. : distr. [by] Elsevier Science Publ. Co., 1990. 4 v. (3208 p.).   **EA127**
    For annotation, *see* AC677.   Q123.M182

Transliterated dictionary of the Russian language : an abridged dictionary consisting of Russian-to-English and English-to-Russian sections / Eugene Garfield, ed. Philadelphia : ISI Pr., 1979. 382 p. **EA128**

For annotation, *see* AC682. PG2640.T7

Zalucky, Henry K. Dictionary of Russian technical and scientific abbreviations : with their full meaning in Russian, English, and German ; comp. and arr. on a Russian alphabetical basis. Amsterdam ; N.Y. [etc.] : Elsevier, 1968. 400 p. **EA129**

About 7,300 entries including obsolete but historically important terms. Except in the largest collections where there may be call for the German equivalents, most libraries will not need this, but will find the more comprehensive *Glossary of Russian abbreviations and acronyms* (AC688) fully adequate. PG2693.Z3

Zimmerman, Mikhail G. Russian-English translators dictionary : a guide to scientific and technical usage / Mikhail G. Zimmerman, Claudia Vedeneeva. 3rd ed. N.Y. : Wiley, c1991. 735 p. **EA130**

Title on added t.p.: Russko-angliiskii nauchno-tekhnicheskii slovar perevodchika.

1st ed., 1967.

"Not a dictionary of terms or idioms, but a collection of typical examples from scientific and technical sources."—*Introd.* Rather than merely giving equivalent English terms for the Russian words and idioms, this work gives a number of examples of English usage of the equivalent terms drawn from scientific and technical literature. Q123.T83

Spanish

Castilla's Spanish and English technical dictionary. London : Routledge and Paul, 1958. 2 v. **EA131**

Contents: v. 1, English-Spanish (1611 p.); v. 2, Spanish-English (1137 p.).

A comprehensive modern dictionary. "Only the fields of engineering technology are included, and the physical, chemical and biological sciences are excluded, except for those words which are of importance to engineers."—*Introd.* Abbreviations are given at the beginning of each letter of the alphabet. Important commercial and legal terms are included, as well as some words of significance in everyday language. The words selected are in current usage, not obsolete terms, and "the language used is that of Spain and Latin America in the Spanish language and of England and the United States in the English language." The field to which a term belongs is indicated only in cases of ambiguity. T9.C34

Collazo, Javier L. Encyclopedic dictionary of technical terms : English-Spanish, Spanish-English. N.Y. : McGraw-Hill, c1980. 3 v. **EA132**

Added title page in Spanish.

Pt. 1, in two volumes, is an English-Spanish lexicon with nearly 100,000 entries, many of which have extended definitions including subentries and synonyms. Pt. 2, is a Spanish-English lexicon of 43,000 entries providing English equivalents of Spanish words but not definitions. T10.C593

Diccionario de términos científicos y técnicos / Daniel N. Lapedes, redactor jefe. Barcelona : Marcombo, c1981. 5 v. (2839, 53 p.) : ill. **EA133**

Translation of: *McGraw-Hill dictionary of scientific and technical terms*, 2nd ed., 1978 (5th ed., EA93).

Entries in v. 1–4 give the Spanish term, the English term, the field of science or technology, and a brief definition. Vol. 5 is an alphabetical list of English terms with the Spanish equivalent.

Thomann, Arthur E. Elsevier's dictionary of technology : English-Spanish = Elsevier diccionario de tecnología : inglés-español. Amsterdam ; N.Y. : Elsevier, 1990. 2 v. **EA134**

Includes some 250,000 terms drawn from such fields as metallurgy, mining, drilling, engineering, electronics, and management. Prefers internationally accepted forms of Spanish terms, but gives geographical indications when local forms are used.

Companion work, also comp. by Thomann: *Elsevier's dictionary of technology : Spanish-English = Elsevier diccionario de tecnología : Español-inglés* (Amsterdam : Elsevier, 1993. 2 v. [1741 p.]). T10.T46

Swedish

Engström, Einar. Svensk-engelsk teknisk ordbok = Swedish-English technical dictionary. 10. uppl. Stockholm : Svensk Trävarutidning, 1977. 973 p. **EA135**

Repr. 1989.

3rd ed., 1947.

This edition revised and updated to include some 90,000 terms.

Companion work: *Engelsk-svensk teknisk ordbok = English-Swedish technical dictionary*, by Einar Engström (13. uppl., 1978. 1026 p.). Repr. 1985. 3rd ed., 1946. T9.E5

Periodicals

SCI JCR [microform]. 1989– . [Philadelphia : Inst. for Scientific Information], c1989– . Annual. **EA136**

Publ. 1975–88 as part of the annual cumulation of *Science citation index* (EA75).

"A bibliometric analysis of science journals in the ISI database."—*t.p.* Organized in six parts: journal rankings, source data listing, journal half-life listing, subject category listing, citing journal listing, and cited journal listing. A printed guide, *Science citation index journal citation reports*, supplements the microfiche. A unique classification and measurement of the patterns of use for some 5,000 scientific periodicals.

Directories

Current contents address directory : science & technology. 1984–87. Philadelphia : Inst. for Scientific Information, c1985–1988. **EA137**

Subtitle: An international directory of scientists and scholars.

Supersedes in part *Current bibliographic directory of the arts & sciences*, 1978–83 (Philadelphia : ISI, 1979–), which itself superseded *Who is publishing in science*, 1971–78.

Information is derived from other current awareness and indexing sources published by ISI. In three sections: author, organization, and geographic, of which the author section is most important and also lists each author's recent publications. The organization section (corporate and governmental) refers to country and city. The geographic section is arranged by states of the U.S., then by foreign countries. Each state and country is subdivided according to the place-names in the author's address, then further subdivided by organization name. Under the organization name, authors giving that affiliation are listed. Vol. 1 contains statistical summaries based on the geographic data.

Companion publication: *Current contents address directory : social sciences/arts & humanities* (1985–88). Q145.C86

Current research in Britain : physical sciences : CRB. [1st. ed.]– . Boston Spa, Wetherby, West Yorkshire : British Library Lending Division, c1985– . Annual. **EA138**

Supersedes *Research in British universities, polytechnics and colleges*.

Each edition is in four parts: *Physical sciences* (2 v.); *Biological sciences* (EG47); *Social sciences* (CA46); *The humanities* (BA8).

Provides information on more than 75,000 research projects at some 300 British institutions. The main arrangement is by institutional and departmental code numbers; within code numbers, listings are in alphabetical order by the name of the principle investigator and include the names of all researchers, a brief description of the project, project dates, sponsors, and publications. Departmental addresses and the names of department heads are also included. Indexed by researcher name, area of study, and project title keywords.

•Machine-readable version: *Current research in Britain* [database] (Boston Spa : British Library Document Supply Centre). File is current; available online and on CD-ROM, both updated annually.

H62.5.G7C87

Directory of Japanese technical resources in the United States. 1988– . Springfield, Va. : National Technical Information Service, c1988– . Annual.   **EA139**

Superintendent of Documents classification: C 51.19:J 27/ .

Prep. by the U.S. Department of Commerce, National Technical Information Service, Office of International Affairs.

In three sections: (1) Directory of information services, giving for each entry: organization name, address, contact person, and a good description of organization mission and service, with indexes for organization name, type of service, area of expertise, and location; (2) Recent federally-funded translations, arranged by subject; and (3) University programs and internships in technical Japanese, arranged alphabetically by program name.   T10.63.A1N37

Directory of technical and scientific directories : a world bibliographic guide to medical, agricultural, industrial, and natural science directories. 6th ed. Harlow : Longman ; Phoenix : Oryx, 1989. 302 p.   **EA140**

1st–4th eds. had title: *Directory of scientific directories*. Previous ed., 1988.

Listings are relatively current for some 1,500 titles. New to this edition are technical encyclopedias, dictionaries, and handbooks. Indexes: author/editor/compiler; directory title; publisher (with address).

Z7405.D55D57

European research centres. 5th ed. (1982)– . Harlow, Essex, U.K. ; Longman : Detroit : Gale, 1982– . Irregular.   **EA141**

Subtitle (varies): a directory of scientific, industrial, agricultural and biomedical laboratories.

Continues: *European research index* (1st–4th ed. Guernsey : F. Hodgson, 1965–77) and *East European research index* ([Guernsey] : F. Hodgson, 1977. 1 v,).

The 9th ed. (1993) lists more than 12,000 research centers in 31 countries (excluding former Soviet republics). Entries are grouped by country, then alphabetically by name. Listings typically include official name, address, telephone and telex numbers, contact person, activities, annual expenditures, and publications. Subject and organization name indexes.   Q180.E9E88

European sources of scientific and technical information. 10th ed. Harlow, Essex, Eng. : Longman ; Detroit : Gale, 1993. 412 p.   **EA142**

1st–4th eds. (1957–76) had title: *Guide to European sources of technical information*.

Publisher varies.

A directory of some 2,000 East and West European organizations and information centers organized into 26 general and subject fields, each subarranged by country. Entries include official name, address, telephone/telex/fax numbers, parent organization or affiliation, year founded, contact name, subject coverage, library facilities and holdings, information services, consultancy services, courses, and publications. Organization name and subject indexes.   T10.65.E8E84

Industrial research in the United Kingdom : a guide to organisation and programmes. 14th ed. [London] : Longman, 1991. 592 p.   **EA143**

Describes more than 3,000 organizations, grouped by type: industrial firms, research organizations, government departments and laboratories, universities and polytechnics, trade associations, learned and professional societies. Research areas include aerospace, agriculture, materials, earth, electronics, engineering and biomedical sciences. Entries provide directory information, affiliation, products, organizational

type, names of staff, annual expenditure, activities, publications, and clients. Four indexes: personnel, subject, title of establishment, and establishment by broad subject category.

Libraries, information centers and databases in science and technology : a world guide = Bibliotheken, Informationszentren und Datenbasen für Wissenschaft und Technik : ein internationales Verzeichnis. 1st ed.– . München ; N.Y. : K.G. Saur, 1984– . Biennial.   **EA144**

A directory of 14,000 scientific and technical libraries, information and documentation centers, and database producers in 141 countries. Entries are arranged by country and include name in original language, address, telephone, year founded, director, collecting interests, holdings. online and loan services. Some 300 databases are briefly described. Name and subject indexes.

§ Similar information is found in *World guide to libraries* (AK121).   Z675.T3L56

Longman guide to world science and technology. v. 1 (1982)– . London ; N.Y. : Longman ; Detroit : Gale, 1982– . Irregular.   **EA145**

Contents: v. 1, Middle East (1982); v. 2, Latin America (1983); v. 3, China (1984); v. 4, Japan (2nd ed., 1991); v. 5, USA (1986); v. 6, USSR (1988); v. 7, France and Belgium (1988); v. 8, Eastern Europe (1988); v. 9, Scandinavia (1989); v. 10, Africa (1989); v. 11, Australia, Antarctica and the Pacific Islands (1990); [v. 12], India, Pakistan, Bangladesh and Sri Lanka (1990); [v. 13], Federal Republic of Germany (1990); v. 14, United Kingdom (1991); [v. 15], Canada (1993).

A series of individually authored volumes reporting on the current state of the scientific and technical enterprise in various countries. Volumes vary in organization and style, but generally provide detailed reviews of the development, current activities, and research programs of official governmental bureaus, semiofficial agencies, private-sector industrial organizations, and professional associations. Addresses and some statistical data are given. Subject and organization indexes.

Pacific research centres. 1st ed. (1986)– . Harlow, Essex, U.K. : Longman Group Ltd., Professional and Information Publ. Div. ; Detroit : Gale, c1986– .   **EA146**

A directory of more than 3,500 laboratories and industrial companies active in research and technology in 21 countries in the Pacific area (excluding the former Soviet Union). Entries are arranged alphabetically by country in the original language, and include translated name (if needed), telephone/fax numbers, address, size of organization, major personnel, a description of activities, corporate affiliations, and publications. An appendix lists trade associations and societies in the region. Subject index; alphabetic and classified index to organization names.   Q180.P16P33

Research centers directory. 2nd ed. (1965)– . Detroit : Gale, 1965– . Irregular.   **EA147**

For annotation, *see* AL82.   AS25.D5

Swannack-Nunn, Susan. Directory of scientific research institutes in the People's Republic of China / by Susan Swannack-Nunn ; executive ed., Nicholas H. Ludlow. Wash. : National Council for U.S.-China Trade, 1977–78. 3 v. in 4.

EA148

Contents: v. 1, Agriculture, fisheries, forestry; v. 2, Chemicals, construction; v. 3 (in 2 pts.), Electrical and electronics; energy; light industry; machinery, including metals and mining; transportation.

Contains introductory material on the organization and state of scientific research in the People's Republic of China, followed by listings of research organizations by subject area. Includes institutional names both in English and in Chinese characters, address, organizational structure, journals in which the institution has recently published, areas of research activity, staff when known; sometimes includes abstracts of recent publications.   Q180.C5S92

Handbooks

Composite index for CRC handbooks. 3rd ed. Boca Raton, Fla. : CRC Pr., 1990. 3 v.   **EA149**

1st ed., 1971; 2nd ed., 1977.

Provides access to "information and data contained in over 14,000 pages from 317 handbook volumes [298 discrete titles] published by CRC Press [from 1969 through 1990]. Indexes from these volumes have been merged to form a single, unified composite index."—Pref. The 1st ed. indexed ten volumes, the 2nd ed. 58; this edition indexes most of the volumes published since 1977, and a few before that, and includes the 71st ed. (1990) of *CRC handbook of chemistry and physics* (EE70). In spite of its high price, this work and its companion CD-ROM (below) are essential to the efficient use of CRC publications and give readers full access to the content of all volumes, including those not held locally.

————. *1991 supplement* (Boca Raton, Fla. : CRC Pr., c1992. 413 p.).

•Included with the printed edition is a CD-ROM version that permits searching combined terms using Boolean operators.   QD65.C74

Diagram Group. Comparisons of distance, size, area, volume, mass, weight, density, energy, temperature, time, speed and number throughout the universe. N.Y. : St. Martin's, c1980. 240 p. : ill.   **EA150**

Provides graphic representations of measurable phenomena. "By making comparisons between like and like and between like and unlike we can evaluate the different properties of the known world."—*Foreword*. Indexed.   QC39.D5

Lewis, Adele Beatrice. Best resumes for scientists and engineers / Adele Lewis, David J. Moore. 2nd ed. N.Y. : Wiley, c1993. 215 p. : ill.   **EA151**

1st ed., 1988.

Uses worksheets and samples to assist technical professionals in the preparation and use of résumés. Chapters cover the elements of a résumé, i.e., career objectives, experience, education, and references as well as the cover letter, sources of employment information, and interview techniques. Index to résumé samples by job title.   Q148.L47

Powell, Russell H. Handbooks and tables in science and technology. 2nd ed. London : Libr. Assoc., c1983. 297 p.   **EA152**

1st ed., 1979.

A guide to approximately 3,400 publications. Entries provide full bibliographic information, LC number, ISBN, document or report access number, price, and series. Most entries are annotated. Subject index; author/editor index. Publisher's directory. New edition planned for 1994.   Z7405.T3P68

Science and technology desk reference : 1,500 answers to frequently-asked or difficult-to-answer questions / the Carnegie Library of Pittsburgh Science and Technology Department. Wash. : Gale, c1993. 741 p. : ill.   **EA153**

Based on the Carnegie Library of Pittsburgh's reference file of questions, this handbook aims to answer typical or time-consuming questions, especially for those librarians in smaller libraries with limited access to scientific sources. Questions are arranged under 20 broad subject categories, then subarranged by topics. Answers are written in nontechnical language and include a source for additional information. Subject index and excellent bibliography of sources.   Q173.S397

Tables

Geigy scientific tables / ed. by C. Lentner. 8th rev. & enl. ed. [Basel ; West Caldwell, N.J.] : Ciba-Geigy [Corp.], 1981–92. v. 1–6. (In progress).   **EA154**

Contents: v. 1, Units of measurement, body fluids, composition of the body, nutrition; v. 2, Introduction to statistics, statistical tables, mathematical formulae; v. 3, Physical chemistry, composition of blood, hematology, somatometric data; v. 4, Biochemistry, metabolism of xenobiotics, inborn errors of metabolism, pharmacogenetics and ecogenetics; v. 5, Heart and circulation; v. 6, Bacteria, fungi, protozoa, helminths.

The tables aim to "provide scientists and, in particular, doctors with a concise compendium of scientific data backed by literature references."—*By way of explanation*. Indexed.   QP33.5.G45

Landolt, Hans Heinrich. Zahlenwerte und Funktionen aus Physik, Chemie, Astronomie, Geophysik und Technik. 6. Aufl. Berlin : Springer, 1950–80. v. 1–4 (No more published?).   **EA155**

This edition aims to present "the compilation of all the certain results of physical, chemical, and technological research, characterized by both the greatest possible completeness and a critical attitude."—*Pref., New series*. Uniformity of presentation is achieved by dividing the work into major units on atomic and molecular physics, macrophysics and chemistry, astronomy and geophysics, and technology, each consisting of several subdivisions. Data are presented largely in tabular and graphic form. Extensive references to primary sources.

New series: *Landolt-Börnstein Zahlenwerte und Funktionen aus Naturwissenschaften und Technik : neue Serie*, Gesamtherausgabe : K. H. Hellwege (Berlin : Springer, 1961–89. [In progress]).

Contents: Gruppe 1, Kern- und Teilchenphysik=Nuclear and particle physics; Gruppe 2, Atom- und Molekularphysik=Atomic and molecular physics; Gruppe 3, Kristall- und Festkörperphysik=Crystal and solid state physics; Gruppe 4, Makroskopische und technische Eigenschaften der Materie=Macroscopic and technical properties of matter; Gruppe 5, Geophysik und Weltraumforschung=Geophysics and space research; Gruppe 6, Astronomie, Astrophysik und Weltraumforschung=Astromony, astrophysics, and space research; Gruppe 7, Biophysik=Biophysics.

Not a 7th ed., but a new series having "as principal feature, that the inflexible division into a few subdivided volumes, i.e., the principle of planned subdivision, is given up. In the future, volumes will be published in simple succession: closed fields will be supplemented by new volumes, whereas new treatments will appear with greater frequency for fields which are being newly opened up or are evolving rapidly "—*Pref., New series*. Much material appears in English; later volumes have text in both German and English, with some in English only.

Indexes:

————. ————. *Gesamtregister für 6te Auflage 1950–1980 und Neue Serie 1961–1985*, hrsg., H. K. Hellwege (Berlin ; N. Y. : Springer, 1987).

————. ————. *Gesamtregister* (Berlin ; N. Y. : Springer, 1988– . Irregular).   QC61.L33

National Research Council. International critical tables of numerical data, physics, chemistry and technology / prep. under the auspices of the International Research Council and the National Academy of Sciences by the National Research Council of the United States of America ; ed. in chief, Edward W. Washburn ... associate editors: Clarence J. West .... N.Y. : publ. for the National Research Council by McGraw-Hill, 1926–33. 7 v. and index : diagrams.   **EA156**

Data based on the material in *Tables annuelles de constantes ...* (Paris : Gauthier-Villars ; Chicago : Univ. of Chicago Pr., 1912–).

Represents the efforts of a large number of specialists, each charged with the critical compilation of the quantitative information available on the topic. "Critical" means the "best" value the expert could derive with an estimate of its probable reliability. Derived from the literature published up to 1924, data are presented in the form of text, equations, tables, graphs, and charts. Cites publications from which information was obtained. In 300 sections, such as Laboratory technique, Physical properties of chemical substances, and Astronomic and geodetic data. Detailed index.   Q199.N32

Style manuals; Report writing

Booth, Vernon. Communicating in science : writing a scientific paper and speaking at scientific meetings. 2nd ed. Cambridge, Eng. ; N.Y. : Cambridge Univ. Pr., 1993. 78 p. : ill.
EA157

1st ed., 1985, based on an essay written in 1970.

A succinct guide, focusing on the oral and written presentation of scientific papers. Bibliography and subject index.   Q223.B665

Day, Robert A. How to write & publish a scientific paper. 3rd ed. Phoenix : Oryx, 1988. 211 p. : ill.   **EA158**

1st ed., 1979; 2nd ed., 1983.

"The purpose of this book is to help scientists and students of the sciences in all disciplines to prepare manuscripts that will have a high probability of being accepted for publication and of being completely understood when they are published."—*Pref.* Chapters are updated to present new developments in scientific publishing for beginning students and researchers. Indexed. 4th ed. planned for 1994.   T11.D33

Freedman, George. The technical editor's and secretary's desk guide / George Freedman & Deborah A. Freedman. N.Y. : McGraw-Hill, c1985. 538 p. in various pagings : ill.
EA159

In two parts: (1) Technical narration and notation; (2) Reference section. "This book is addressed to those who transcribe or type scientific or technical material."—*Pref.* Provides descriptive, contextual assistance rather than being a prescriptive style manual. Includes a 147-page dictionary of technical terms. Indexed.   T11.4.F74

Locke, Lawrence F. Proposals that work : a guide for planning dissertations and grant proposals / Lawrence F. Locke, Waneen Wyrick Spirduso, Stephen J. Silverman. 3rd ed. Newbury Park : Sage Publications, c1993. 323 p. : ill. **EA160**

1st ed., 1976.

Aims to address the problem of writing a research proposal, rather than how to do research. The basic issues of proposal writing, thesis preparation, grant applications, and oral presentations are addressed in the first nine chapters. In pt. 2, specimen proposals are critically evaluated. Appendix with annotated supplementary references and sample consent forms. Subject index.   Q180.55.P7L63

The Oxford dictionary for scientific writers and editors. Oxford : Clarendon Pr. ; N.Y. : Oxford Univ. Pr., 1991. 389 p.
EA161

Companion to: *Oxford dictionary for writers and editors* (AA277).

Aims "to provide scientists, science writers, and editors of scientific texts with a guide to the style for presenting scientific information most widely used within the scientific community" (*Pref*), hence does not emphasize definitions of terms so much as usage or accepted form. Difference between British and American spelling or usage is shown. Complies with the house style of the Oxford Univ. Pr. and the recommendations of the International Union of Pure and Applied Physics and the International Union of Pure and Applied Chemistry. Appendix of common scientific tables and symbols.   T11.O94

Patrias, Karen. National Library of Medicine recommended formats for bibliographic citation. Bethesda, Md. : U.S. National Library of Medicine, Reference Section, [1991]. 190, [15] p. : ill.   **EA162**

Provides recommended citation formats for 14 categories of published and unpublished materials. Each chapter provides a list of required and optional elements for a citation, with a clearly labeled sample and a list of examples. Citation style is drawn from three sources: *MEDLARS indexing manual*, comp. by Thelma Charen (Bethesda, Md. : NLM, 1964–); *American national standard for bibliographic references* (N.Y. : American National Standards Institute, 1977. [ANSI Z39.29-19771]); and *Documentation—bibliographic references—content, form and structure* (2nd ed. Geneva : International Organ-

ization for Standardization, 1987. [ISO 690]). Style preference is given to the NLM format. Two appendixes provide lists of references consulted and commonly abbreviated words.

Weisman, Herman M. Basic technical writing. 6th ed. N.Y. : Merrill ; Toronto : Maxwell Macmillan Canada, 1992. 602 p. : ill.   **EA163**

1st ed., 1960.

A textbook emphasizing expository techniques, technical report writing, and short forms of technical writing such as correspondence and proposals. Revised to include details on computer word processing and graphics programs. Useful descriptions of the context and stages of technical writing. Contains examples, chapter reading lists, and bibliography. Subject index.   T11.W43

Bibliography

Society of Technical Writers and Publishers. An annotated bibliography on technical writing, editing, graphics, and publishing, 1950–1965 / ed. by Theresa Ammannito Philler, Ruth K. Hersch, and Helen V. Carlson. Wash., [1966]. 1 v. unpaged.   **EA164**

Published jointly by Society of Technical Writers and Publishers and Carnegie Library of Pittsburgh.

A computer-produced bibliography of 2,000 entries. Permuted title index and author index.

Continued by: *An annotated bibliography on technical writing, editing, graphics, and publishing, 1966–80*, ed. by Helen V. Carlson ... [et al.] (Wash. : Soc. for Technical Communication, c1983. 1 v. unpaged).   Z7405.T4S6

Yearbooks

Encyclopedia of physical science and technology yearbook. (1989)– . San Diego, Calif. : Academic Pr., c1989– . Annual.
EA165

Intended to supplement *Encyclopedia of physical science and technology* (EA79) by covering rapidly changing fields; follows the *Encyclopedia*'s format. The 1991 edition includes 39 signed articles written by scientists and engineers and grouped in 2 sections: Feature articles and A-Z articles. The subject index cumulates entries from the previous *Yearbook* editions.   Q123.E4973

The Facts on File scientific yearbook. N.Y. : Facts on File, c1985–92.   **EA166**

Well-illustrated articles report on current, popular topics in science. Glossary of terms; index to names and topics. Useful for secondary school students and general readers, but lacks bibliographies or sources for additional reading.   Q9.F32

McGraw-Hill yearbook of science and technology. 1962– . N.Y. : McGraw-Hill, 1962– .   **EA167**

Serves as an annual review of recent achievements in science and engineering as well as an update to the last edition of *McGraw-Hill encyclopedia of science & technology* (EA81). Signed artricles are written by subject specialists and are directed to students, teachers, and educated scientific readers. Articles are often several pages in length, with illustrations and a selective bibliography. Subject index.
Q121.M312

Science year : the World book science annual. 1965– . Chicago : World-Book Childcraft International, 1965– . Annual.
EA168

Publisher varies.

Offers clear and detailed articles by specialists on specific topics, plus a "Science file" that provides (in alphabetical arrangement) reports on the recent developments in various areas of science. Good color illustrations. Indexed. Useful beyond the juvenile level.   Q9.S33

Yearbook of science and the future. 1975– . Chicago : Encyclopaedia Britannica, [1976]– . Annual. **EA169**

Continues: *Britannica yearbook of science and the future*, 1969–74.

Designed to provide those who have little or no background in science with authoritative, up-to-date information about current scientific and technological efforts and advances. A useful reference source for the general reader. Name and subject index. Q9.B78

Biography

American men & women of science. 17th ed. (1989/90)– . N.Y. : Bowker, 1989– . Irregular. **EA170**

Title varies: 1st–11th eds., 1906–68, called *American men of science*. New editions publ. at irregular intervals; content has varied. 18th ed. publ. 1992.

This edition contains full biographical data for 122,817 living U.S. and Canadian scientists in the physical and biological sciences, including public health scientists, engineers, mathematicians, statisticians, and computer scientists. 7,021 are new to this edition. Criteria for inclusion are: distinguished achievement, research activity of high quality, or attainment of position of substantial responsibility. "The biographies of engineers and scientists constitute seven of the eight volumes and provide birthdates, birthplaces, field of specialty, education, honorary degrees, professional and concurrent experiences, awards, memberships, research information and addresses... The eighth volume, the discipline index, organizes biographees by field of activity"—*Pref.*

Cumulative index: *American men & women of science : editions 1–14 cumulative index*, comp. by Jacques Cattell Pr. (N.Y. : Bowker, 1983. 847 p.).

•Included in the CD-ROM source *SciTech reference plus* (EA37). H50.A47

Asimov, Isaac. Asimov's biographical encyclopedia of science and technology. 2nd rev. ed. Garden City, N.Y. : Doubleday, 1982. 941 p., [24] p. of plates : ill. **EA171**

Subtitle: The lives and achievements of 1510 great scientists from ancient times to the present chronologically arranged.

1st ed., 1972.

Biographies ranging in time from Imhotep (fl.2980–2950 BCE) to Stephen W. Hawking (b.1942), of varying length, and written in an informal, nontechnical style. Index of subjects and names not included as biographees. Q141.A74

A biographical dictionary of scientists / ed. by Trevor I. Williams ; assistant ed., Sonia Withers. 3rd ed. N.Y. : Wiley, 1982. 674 p. **EA172**

1st ed., 1969.

Brief sketches of deceased scientists are signed with the initials of the contributor; a limited number of bibliographical references are usually appended. International in scope with broad coverage from science, technology, and medicine. Biographies added since the 2nd ed. are listed separately as "Additional biographies." There is a chronological list of anniversaries, an appendix listing names occurring in the book but for whom there is not a full biography, and a subject index. Q141.B528

The biographical dictionary of scientists / gen. ed., David Abbott. N.Y. : Peter Bedrick Books, 1983–1985. 6 v. : ill. **EA173**

Contents: [v. 1], Biologists (EG60); [v. 2], Chemists (EE100); [v. 3], Astronomers (EC63); [v. 4], Physicists (ED54); [v. 5], Mathematicians (EB101); [v. 6], Engineers and inventors.

In each volume, a historical introduction is followed by brief narrative biographies, alphabetically arranged, of living and deceased scientists. No bibliographies; brief glossary; index to areas of research pursued by biographees. Q141.B56

A biographical encyclopedia of scientists / John Daintith ... [et al.]. 2nd ed. Bristol ; Philadelphia : Inst. of Physics Publ., c1994. 2 v. (1075 p.) : ill. **EA174**

1st ed., 1981.

Includes living and deceased scientists with some biographies drawn from medicine and technology. Entries provide limited biographical data and a discussion of the importance of the biographee. Few portraits. There is a chronology, list of scientific institutions, book list, index of names, and index of subjects. Q141.B53

Concise dictionary of scientific biography. N.Y. : Scribner, c1981. 773 p. **EA175**

Published under the auspices of the American Council of Learned Societies.

Based on the *Dictionary of scientific biography* (EA176). All entries from the parent work including the supplement have been retained, but the text is substantially reduced. Q141.C55

Dictionary of scientific biography / Charles Coulston Gillispie, ed. in chief. N.Y. : Scribner, [1970–80]. 16 v. **EA176**

Repr., 1981 in 8 v.

Contents: v. 1–14, Abailard–Zwelfer; v. 15, Suppl. 1, Biographies and topical essays; v. 16, Index.

"Published under the sponsorship of the American Council of Learned Societies with the endorsement of the History of Science Society."—*Pref.*

A completely new work, international in coverage, including scientists from all periods of history (excluding living persons), and encompassing the fields of astronomy, biology, chemistry, the earth sciences, mathematics, and physics. "Technology, medicine, the behavioral sciences, and philosophy are included only in the instances of persons whose work was intrinsically related to the sciences of nature or to mathematics."—*Pref.* An important selection criterion was whether or not a person's contributions to science "were sufficiently distinctive to make an identifiable difference to the profession or community of knowledge." The Editorial Board notes a certain imbalance in coverage of 20th-century figures and of ancient Indian, Chinese, Japanese, and Near Eastern scientists owing mainly to the shortage of technically qualified contributors for these areas.

Articles are signed by the contributing scholars (in some cases different scholars have treated specific aspects of an individual scientist's work); include bibliographies of original and secondary works; and emphasize the scientific accomplishments and careers of the biographees. In some cases the article is the first or the most comprehensive study of a figure's total contribution to science.

Vol. 15 is in two parts: the first part consists of biographical articles on scientists not included in the main work, either because they only recently died, or because the article was planned for the *Dictionary* but not included in the main work (in which case there is a reference to the Supplement under the scientist's name in the main work) or simply because the scientist was previously overlooked. The second part offers topical essays "on the scientific outlook and accomplishments of certain ancient civilizations."—*Pref.*

Vol. 16 includes the following sections: Index, Contributors, Societies indexed, Periodicals indexed, Lists of scientists by field, Errata.

———. *Supplement II*, Frederic L. Holmes, ed. in chief (N.Y. : Scribner, c1990. 2 v.).

Also issued as v. 17–18 of the *Dictionary*.

Maintains the principles of selection and subject scope developed for the original work, but extends coverage to scientists active during the 20th century. The majority of the 445 biographees died between 1970 and 1981. Name and topics index and list of scientists by field in v. 2. Q141.D5

Elliott, Clark A. Biographical dictionary of American science : the seventeenth through the nineteenth centuries. Westport, Conn. : Greenwood, 1979. 360 p. **EA177**

"This *Dictionary* is deliberately designed as a retrospective companion to *American men of science*. ... The *Dictionary* includes major entries, averaging between 300 to 400 words, for nearly 600 scientists never included in AMS."—*Pref.* Also includes about 300 important 19th-century scientists from *American men & women of science*

(EA170). Appendixes list biographees by year of birth, place of birth, education, occupation, and fields of science. Name and topic index.
Q141.E37

Liŭdi russkoĭ nauki : ocherki o vydaĭushchikhsiĭa deĭateljakh estestvoznaniĭa i tekhniki / pod red. I. V. Kuznetsova. Moskva : Gos. Izd-vo Fiziko-Matematicheskoĭ Lit-ry, 1961–65. 4 v. : ill.   **EA178**
Contents: [v. 1], Matematika, mekhanika, astronomiĭa, fizika, khimiĭa (1961); [v. 2], Geologiĭa, geografiĭa (1962); [v. 3], Biologiĭa, meditsina, sel'skokhoziĭaistvennye nauki (1963); [v. 4], Tekhnika (1965).
A biographical dictionary of major Russian scientists of the 19th and 20th centuries. No living persons are included. Articles are signed, and include bibliographies of principal works and additional biographical and scientific references.

McGraw-Hill modern scientists and engineers. N.Y. : McGraw-Hill, c1980. 3 v. : ill.   **EA179**
1st ed., 1966–68, had title: *McGraw-Hill modern men of science*.
Intended to be a biographical supplement to the 4th ed. (1977) of *McGraw-Hill encyclopedia of science & technology* (EA81, 7th ed.). A revised and expanded edition of the earlier work; 300 of the 1,140 biographies are new. "The individuals were selected by the editors from recipients of major awards and prizes given by the leading societies, organizations, and institutions of the world. The scope is international and extends in time from the leaders of the 1920s to the 1978 Nobel Prize winners."—*Pref*. Discusses research achievements and provides sketchy biographical data for each biographee, frequently includes a portrait; gives references to background articles in the encyclopedia. Field index and analytical (name and subject) index. Most of the entries were written by the biographee. Q141.M15

Ogilvie, Marilyn Bailey. Women in science : antiquity through the nineteenth century : a biographical dictionary with annotated bibliography. Cambridge, Mass. : MIT Pr., c1986. 254 p.   **EA180**
Includes some 200 women who made significant contributions to science prior to 1910. Biographical entries vary in length from a few lines to several pages. All listings include references to the extensive bibliography of sources. Name index. Q141.O34

Poggendorff, Johann Christian. Biographisch-literarisches Handwörterbuch zur Geschichte der exakten Wissenschaften. Berlin : Akademie Verlag, 1863– . v. 1–7b.   **EA181**
Issued in parts.
Frequently reprinted.
Title varies.
Publisher varies: 1863–1904, Leipzig : J.A. Barth; 1926–40, Leipzig : Verlag Chemie; 1955– , Berlin : Akademie Verlag.
Contents: Bd. 1–2, to 1857; Bd. 3, 1858–83; Bd. 4, 1883–1904; Bd. 5, 1904–22 (2 v.); Bd. 6, 1923–31 (4 v.); Bd. 7a, T. 1–4, A–Z, Anhang und Schlusswort; Bd. 7a Suppl., A–Z; Bd. 7b, 1932–62, T. 1–9², A–Wi.
The standard and indispensable work for information about the life and works of mathematicians, astronomers, physicists, chemists, mineralogists, geologists, and other scientists of all countries. For each scientist gives a brief biographical sketch, followed by a detailed bibliography of writings, including periodical articles.
From 1955 published as: *Biographisch-literarisches Handwörterbuch der exakten Naturwissenschaften*, unter Mitwirkung der Akademien der Wissenschaften zu Berlin, Göttingen, Heidelberg, München und Wien, hrsg. von der Sächischen Akademie der Wissenschaften zu Leipzig, red. von Rudolph Zaunick und Hans Salié (Berlin : Akademie Verlag, 1955–85. v. 7a–7b¹⁻⁹. [In progress]).
This series includes supplementary material for names mentioned in earlier volumes as well as new biographical sketches. Bd. 7a contains biobibliographies of scientists, technologists, and physicians from Germany, Austria, and Switzerland, 1932–53; Bd. 7b treats scientists of other countries, 1932–62. Z7404.P74

Royal Society (Great Britain). Obituary notices of Fellows of the Royal Society. [v. 1], no. 1 (Dec. 1932)–v. 9, [no. 23] (1954). London : [Printed and publ. for the Royal Society by] Harrison & Sons, 1932–1954.   **EA182**
Imprint varies.
Long biographical articles with excellent autographed portraits of deceased fellows of the Royal Society, including foreign members. Usually includes bibliographies, some quite extensive.
Previous obituary notices were publ. in *Proceedings* of the Royal Society. Vol. 75 (1905) of *Proceedings* contained obituaries of deceased fellows chiefly for 1898–1904 with a general index to previous obituary notices that covered 1860–99.
Continued by: *Biographical memoirs of fellows of the Royal Society* (EA189). Q171.R8

Sammons, Vivian O. Blacks in science and medicine. N.Y. : Hemisphere Pub. Corp., c1990. 293 p.   **EA183**
Presents biographical information, based on published sources, for more than 1,500 living and deceased individuals who have contributed to the development of science, medicine, and technology, focusing on contributions by African Americans in the U.S. Entries are brief, in who's who style, but include citations to the source material. Extensive bibliography. A very useful index to biographees is arranged by such categories as occupation, discipline, or invention, and notes "first black" and "first (black or white)" achievements. Q141.B58

Who was who in American history—science and technology. Chicago : Marquis Who's Who, c1976. 688 p.   **EA184**
"A component of *Who's who in American history*."—*t.p.*
A compilation of biographical information for "some 90,000 deceased American notables within the covers of the [*Who was who in America*] volumes ... from the early days of the colonies to mid-1973."—*Pref*. Q141.W43

Who's who in frontiers of science and technology. 2nd ed. Chicago : Marquis Who's Who, c1985. 606 p.   **EA185**
Continues: *Who's who in frontier science and technology*, 1984.
Uses the same format and selection as the earlier title, providing brief, standardized biographical information. Includes approximately 14,000 scientists and technologists currently working in North America. Fields and subspecialties index.

Who's who of British scientists, 1980/81. 3rd ed. Dorking, Surrey : Simon Books : [distr. by St. Martin's], 1980. 589 p.   **EA186**
1st ed., 1969.
An alphabetical listing of scientists in British universities and polytechnics, research establishments, and industry. Biographical section is followed by an addendum of names and two organizational directories: Scientific research establishments and Scientific societies and professional institutions. Q145.W46

Women in chemistry and physics : a biobibliographic sourcebook / ed. by Louise S. Grinstein, Rose K. Rose, and Miriam H. Rafailovich. Westport, Conn. : Greenwood, 1993. 721 p.   **EA187**
Aims to be "a comprehensive collection of biobibliographies of women in the physical sciences over nearly three centuries."—*Foreword*. Includes biographies of 75 women, deceased or born before 1933, alphabetically arranged. Essays average five pages in length and provide personal history, scientific contributions, and a bibliography of scientific publications. Appendixes include sources of additional information and lists of biographees by date and place of birth, place of work, and field of scientific interest. Index. QD21.W62

Current

National Academy of Sciences. Biographical memoirs. v. 1– . Wash. : National Academy of Sciences, 1877– . Irregular.   **EA188**

Deceased members of the National Academy of Sciences are the subjects of biographical essays written by colleagues. Articles include a portrait and bibliography of the subject's published scientific work. Recent volumes have a cumulative index to the series. Q141.N2

Royal Society (Great Britain). Biographical memoirs of fellows of the Royal Society. v. 1 (1955)– . London : The Society, 1955– . Annual. **EA189**

Follows the scope and arrangement of its predecessor, *Obituary notices of fellows of the Royal Society* (EA182). Vol. 26 (1980) includes a subject index (i.e., by biographee) for *Obituary notices* (v. 1 [1932]–v. 9 [1954]) and *Biographical memoirs* (v. 1 [1955]–v. 26 [1980]); v. 35 (1990) has a similar index for *Biographical memoirs* (v. 27 [1981]–v. 35 [1990]). Q41.R9

Who's who in science and engineering. 1992–93– . Wilmette, Ill. : Marquis Who's Who, c1992– . **EA190**

Contains biographies for some 22,000 scientists, engineers, and physicians, generally from the U.S. Includes all specialties in the physical and life sciences, applied sciences, and medicine, plus some individuals from the humanities and social sciences. Basic biographical data is supplemented with more detailed professional and career information, including publications, awards and principal achievements, and current business address. Geographic and professional area indexes. The appendix covers major scientific awards for the past three years. More detail on the criteria for selection of biographees is needed for this work to find a place among other major biographical sources in science and medicine. Q141.W576

Who's who in science in Europe. 1st ed. (1967)– . Guernsey, Channel Islands : F. Hodgson, 1967– . Biennial. **EA191**

1st ed., 1967; 8th ed., 1993.

Frequency and publisher vary.

Provides current biographical and professional information for approximately 30,000 scientists and engineers from Europe (excluding the former Soviet republics). Each volume has two sections: biographical entries for each country in alphabetic order by surname, and a subject specialty index arranged by country. Lacks comprehensive name index. Q141.W59

Indexes

Elliott, Clark A. Biographical index to American science : the seventeenth century to 1920. N.Y. : Greenwood, 1990. 300 p. (Bibliographies and indexes in American history, no. 16). **EA192**

Supplements in part the author's *Biographical dictionary of American science : the seventeenth through the nineteenth centuries* (EA177).

Biographical entries have been compiled from standard biographical directories, dictionaries, and indexes for 2,850 American scientists deceased prior to 1920; for lesser-known individuals information is drawn from sources such as obituaries and local histories. Principal focus is on the natural and physical sciences, but some engineers, inventors, and physicians are included if relevant to the development of American science. Entries are arranged alphabetically by name and include year of birth and death, scientific field, occupation, any references in the *National union catalog of manuscript collections*, 1959–84 (DB34), and citations to sources of additional information. Index of names by scientific field. Q141.E373

Gascoigne, Robert Mortimer. A historical catalogue of scientists and scientific books : from the earliest times to the close of the nineteenth century. N.Y. : Garland, 1984. 1177 p. (Garland reference library of the humanities, v. 495). **EA193**

Contents: pt. 1, Ancient and medieval periods; pt. 2, Early modern period (ca.1450–1700); pt. 3, Eighteenth and nineteenth centuries.

"This catalogue is designed to serve both as a general reference work and as a research tool for historians of science. It is ... a chronological list of 13,300 persons who were of some degree of significance in the development of science ... for whom biographical information is available in reference books."—*Introd*. Consists of 15,918 entries grouped by historic period; most include reference to major sources of biographical data. There are four indexes—a main index which includes persons, institutions, and ships, an index of selected titles, an index of dictionaries and encyclopedias, and an index of bibliographies and book catalogs. Q141.G38

Herzenberg, Caroline L. Women scientists from antiquity to the present : an index : an international reference listing and biographical directory of some notable women scientists from ancient to modern times. West Cornwall, Conn. : Locust Hill Pr., 1986. 200 p. **EA194**

Identifies 2,500 women who worked in or contributed to the development of science, medicine, engineering, and technology. Brief alphabetical listings provide name, birth and death dates or date of activity, nationality, field of work, and reference to the bibliography of sources. Index of names by specialty and field of work. Q141.H475

Ireland, Norma Olin. Index to scientists of the world from ancient to modern times : biographies and portraits. Boston : Faxon, 1962. 662 p. (Useful reference series, no. 90). **EA195**

Indexes 338 collections in the English language, covering all phases of science, with listings for 7,475 world scientists from ancient to modern times. Emphasizes the indexing of portraits. Gives full name, years of birth and death, and distinguishing identification. Intended as an aid for group assignments. General nonreference books as well as many basic juvenile books have formed the core of works indexed; encyclopedias generally excluded. Z7404.I7

Pelletier, Paul A. Prominent scientists : an index to collective biographies. 2nd ed. N.Y. : Neal-Schuman, c1985. 356 p. **EA196**

1st ed., 1980.

Coverage extended to 12,211 scientists, living and dead, with citations from 262 sources published primarily 1960–83. Principal list is by surname; additional lists by field. 3rd ed. due in 1994. Q141.P398

Prizes and awards

Special Libraries Association. Science-Technology Division. Handbook of scientific and technical awards in the United States and Canada, 1900–1952 / ed. by Margaret A. Firth. N.Y. : Special Libraries Assoc., [1956]. 491 p. **EA197**

"A selected listing of the most important awards presented by certain of the scientific and technical societies in the United States and Canada to individuals in recognition of their meritoriuos achievements in scientific fields." —*Introd*.

Arranged alphabetically by name of society with the awards listed chronologically under society, giving names of the recipients and, from 1929 to 1952, citations of published references concerning the awards. Also describes the award, the criteria for selecting the recipient, and whether there is a monetary reward, a citation or a medal. Provides biographical facts about recipients and specific accomplishments for which award was granted. Canadian awards appear as a separate listing following American awards. An index of recipients and award titles, and a separate subject index.

Supplemented by: *Handbook of scientific and technical awards : supplement no. 1 : Chemistry (ACS)-Physics (AIP)-Geophysics (AGU)*, [comp. under the direction of Johanna E. Tallman] (1981. 26, 11, 6 p.). A partial update for selected scientific societies. Q141.S63

SOCIETIES AND CONGRESSES

Directories

Bates, Ralph Samuel. Scientific societies in the United States. 3rd ed. Cambridge, Mass. : M.I.T. Pr., [1965]. 326 p.   **EA198**
1st ed., 1945.
A history of the growth of American scientific societies from 1727. Covers the main national societies and the specialized and technical societies of the various states. Bibliography, p. 245–93. Indexed.
Q11.A1B3

Fundamental'naiā biblioteka obshchestvennykh nauk (Akademiiā nauk SSSR). Nauchnye s'ezdy, konferentsii i soveshchaniiā v SSSR : bibliograficheskiĭ ukazatel'. [Moskva] : Nauka, 1958–1966. [v. 1–3]. (In progress?).
  EA199
Contents: [v. 1], 1946–53 (1958. 222 p.); [v. 2–3], 1954–60 (1966. 2 v.).
Lists Russian-language publications of and about scholarly congresses, conferences, and meetings in the Soviet Union. Includes both natural and social sciences.   AS258.A55

Scientific and technical organizations and agencies directory. 3rd ed. / Peter D. Dresser, ed. ; Amy Lynn Emrich, associate ed. Detroit : Gale, c1994. 2 v. (2618 p.).   **EA200**
Subtitle: A guide to over 25,000 organizations and agencies concerned with the physical sciences, engineering, and technology.
1st ed., 1985; 2nd ed., 1987.
Expanded to include 15,000 U.S., Canadian, and international organizations in the physical and applied sciences and engineering. Entries are grouped in 19 chapters based on type of organization (e.g., federal government agencies, state agencies, standards organizations). Name and keyword indexes.   Q145.S36

World guide to scientific associations and learned societies / ed. by Michael Sachs. 5th ed. Munich ; N.Y. : K.G. Saur, 1990. 672 p. (Handbook of international documentation and information, 13).   **EA201**
For annotation, *see* AL24.   Q145.W9267

Meetings

MInd, the meetings index : Series SEMT, science, engineering, medicine, technology. v. 1 (Feb. 1984)– . Harrison, N.Y. : InterDok, 1984– . Bimonthly.   **EA202**
"Classifies and indexes forthcoming meetings (congresses, conferences, courses, symposia, seminars, summer schools and similar meetings) to be held worldwide."—*Pref.* The main section is arranged by keyword with supplemental indexes by sponsoring organization, date, and location of meeting. A cumulative keyword index covers previous issues of the volume. A contact list for further information is included.

Scientific meetings. v. 1 (1957)– . [Poway, Calif.] : Scientific Meetings Publications, 1977– . Quarterly.   **EA203**
Subtitle (varies): Describing future meetings of technical, scientific, medical, and management organizations and universities.
Imprint varies: v. 1 (1957)-v. 20 (1976), N.Y. : Special Libraries Assoc.
Frequency varies.
An alphabetical listing of organizations "sponsoring future national, international, and regional meetings, symposia, colloquia, and institutes."—*t.p. verso.* Includes a chronological listing and a subject index.

World meetings: United States and Canada. v. 1, no. 1 (Sept. 1963)– . N.Y. : Macmillan Information, 1963– . Quarterly.   **EA204**
Subtitle: A two-year registry of future scientific, technical, and medical meetings; completely revised and updated quarterly.
Issues for Sept. 1963–Jan. 1967 had title: *Technical meetings index.*
Publisher varies.
Full information on the meetings is given in the "Main entry section" which is divided into eight parts, one for each calendar quarter of the 2-year period following the publication date of a particular issue. Gives location, date, sponsors, source of general information, technical sections or brief meeting description, number of papers to be presented, languages and translation facilities, projected attendance, availability of abstracts or papers, and information regarding exhibits. Indexes by date of meeting, keyword of meeting name, location, deadline for abstracts or papers, and by sponsor.

World meetings outside U.S.A. and Canada. v. 1, no. 1 (Jan. 1968)– . N.Y. : Macmillan Information, 1968– . Quarterly.   **EA205**
Subtitle: A two-year registry of future scientific, technical, and medical meetings; completely revised and updated quarterly.
Publisher varies.
A companion to *World meetings : United States and Canada* (EA204), following the arrangement of that publication.

Publications

British Library. Document Supply Centre. Index of conference proceedings. ICP 256 (Jan. 1989)– . Boston Spa, U.K. : The Centre, 1989– . Monthly, with annual cumulation.
  EA206
For annotation, *see* AL26.   Z5051.B862

Conference papers index. v. 6 (Jan. 1978)– . Louisville, Ky. : Data Courier, 1978– . Monthly, with cumulated annual index available separately.   **EA207**
Continues *Current programs*, v. 1 (1973)–5 (1977), and assumes its numbering. Frequency of indexing varies.
Monthly issues have programs of scientific and technological conferences grouped by subject. Information includes the full title of the meeting, inclusive dates, location, names of sponsoring organizations, ordering information for publications, and a list of papers presented. This list includes the name and mailing address for the first author, complete title of paper, and any order number assigned to the paper in the printed program. Beginning with v. 7 (1979) each monthly issue includes both author and keyword indexes which cumulate into the separate annual index volume.
•Machine-readable version: *Conference papers index* [database] (Bethesda, Md. : Cambridge Scientific Abstracts, 1973–). Available online, updated monthly.

Deniker, Joseph. Bibliographie des travaux scientifiques : (sciences mathématiques, physiques et naturelles) pub. par les sociétés savantes de la France depuis l'origine jusqu'en 1888 / dressée sous les auspices du Ministère de l'instruction publique. Paris : Impr. Nationale, 1916–22. 2 v.   **EA208**
Publ. in parts, 1895–1922; v. 1, ed. by Joseph Deniker; v. 2, by René Descharmes. No more published.
Contents: v. 1–2, pt. 1, Ain–Sarthe.
A companion work to Robert Charles Lasteyrie du Saillant's *Bibliographie générale des travaux historiques …* (DC213); on the same scale and intended to do for scientific societies what Lasteyrie has done for historical societies. Unfortunately not finished.
Arranged by *département,* then by city. Complete contents are given for each volume of the publications of the societies included. No index.   Z7403.D39

Directory of published proceedings. Series SEMT : Science, engineering, medicine, technology. v. 1 (Sept. 1965)– . Harrison, N.Y. : InterDok Corp., 1965– . Monthly, except July–Aug., with annual cumulation.   **EA209**

At head of title: InterDok.

Vol. 1–2 lacked the series designation, and included proceedings for the social sciences and humanities. Beginning 1968, the latter disciplines are covered in a separate (*SSH*) series (*see* AL27).

"A bibliography citing preprints and published proceedings of congresses, conferences, summer schools, symposia, meetings, and seminars that have taken place worldwide from 1964 to date."—*Pref.* Arranged chronologically by date of conference, and indexed by editor, location, and keywords of conference name and sponsor.

Five-year cumulated indexes were published for v. 1–5, Sept. 1965–June 1970; v. 6–10, Sept. 1970–June 1975; v. 11–15, Sept. 1975–June 1980.   Z7409.D56

Index to scientific and technical proceedings. v. 1 (Jan. 1978)– . Philadelphia : Institute for Scientific Information, 1978– . Monthly with annual cumulations.   **EA210**

Indexes published conference proceedings at the individual paper level with Permuterm indexing of keywords from titles of papers, an author/editor index, and an index of authors' corporate affiliation. Also indexes conferences by category (i.e., subject), sponsor, and meeting location, but does not index by date of conference. Publishes full information about published proceedings including title, date, and place held, sponsor, editors, how published, price, and order information. Includes tables of contents of papers presented, giving title of paper, authors' names and corporate affiliation, and page number. Does not attempt to give comprehensive coverage of published proceedings but selects the more important proceedings.

•Machine-readable version: *ISTP search* [database] (Philadelphia : Inst. for Scientific Information, 1978–). Available online; updated annually.

Proceedings in print. v. 1, no. 1/2 (Oct. 1964)– . [Arlington, Mass. : Proceedings in Print, Inc.], 1964– . Bimonthly.   **EA211**

v. 1, no. 1/2–v. 3, no. 2, publ. by the Aerospace Division, Special Libraries Association.

Originally meant as an index to "all conference proceedings pertinent to aerospace technology" (*v. 1, no. 1*), coverage was soon expanded to "the various fields of science, technology and medicine" (*v. 2, no. 1*) and, beginning with v. 3, no. 3, to all published conference proceedings regardless of subject. Currently covers proceedings of a broad range of meetings, e.g., hearings, seminars, institutes, colloquia, in all languages. Since 1981, entries are arranged alphabetically in one sequence by conference name. Entries include place and date of conference, sponsoring agencies, publisher, and order information. A single index includes corporate authors, sponsoring agencies, editors, and keyword or subject headings. Cumulative index for each volume.   Z5063.A2P7

Union catalogue of scientific libraries in the University of Cambridge : scientific conference proceedings, 1644–1974. London : Mansell, 1975. 2 v. (2441 col.).   **EA212**

"Compiled at the Scientific Periodicals Library, University of Cambridge."—*t.p.*

A computer-produced catalog of "about 25,000 entries for approximately 6,000 conferences and symposia" (*Pref.*) for the period 1644–1974. A name and keyword catalog with entries for each conference under several headings—official name of conference, title of published proceedings, corporate bodies involved, and venues.   Z7409.C35

LABORATORIES

Directory of American research and technology / ed. by Jaques Cattell Press. 20th ed. (1986)– . N.Y. : Bowker, c1986– . Annual.   **EA213**

Subtitle: Organizations active in product development for business.

Continues:*Industrial research laboratories of the United States* (1st–19th ed., 1920–85).

Listings cover nongovernmental facilities currently active in basic and applied research, including the development of products and processes. Of the 13,007 organizations in the 1994 edition, 7,783 are parent companies listed alphabetically by name and 5,224 are subsidiaries listed under a parent company entry. Each entry includes name, address, telephone, executive officers, professional staff, and research and development interests. Geographic, personnel, and research and development classification indexes.

•The *Directory* is available online and in CD-ROM as part of *Sci-Tech reference plus* (EA37).   T176.I65

Directory of federal laboratory & technology resources : a guide to services, facilities, and expertise / prepared by the Center for the Utilization of Federal Technology, U.S. Dept. of Commerce, National Technical Information Service. Springfield, Va. : NTIS, 1986–87– . Biennial.   **EA214**

Superintendent of Documents classification: C 51.19/2-2: .

Continues *Directory of federal technology resources* (1984).

Lists some 1,000 federal government research centers, testing facilities, laboratories, and special technology centers that will share expertise, equipment, or facilities with commercial businesses and universities. Information includes name, address, telephone, contact person, and description of facility. Indexed by subject, state, facility name, and government agency.   T21.D57

International directory of testing laboratories / comp. by ASTM. 1993 ed.– . Philadelphia : American Society for Testing and Materials, c1992– . Annual.   **EA215**

Continues: *Directory of testing laboratories*, 1987–92, which in turn continued *Directory of testing laboratories, commercial-institutional*, 1952–82.

A geographical listing by country of about 1,400 commercial testing laboratories, with some 200 outside the U.S. In addition to name, address, and telephone/fax numbers, provides information on the laboratory's specialty, equipment, testing capabilities, and staff. Alphabetic organization and subject/geographic indexes.   TA416.5.U6D55

MUSEUMS AND HISTORIC SITES

Danilov, Victor J. America's science museums. N.Y. : Greenwood, c1990. 496 p.   **EA216**

The nature, history, facilities, collections, and programs of 480 scientific and technologic museums and related institutions such as botanic gardens, zoos, and observatories are described. Institutions are selected for their stature in the field, speciality, age, or novelty. Entries are organized in 12 subject categories. The introduction to each category reviews the development and present state of the particular type of science museum. Selected bibliography and name index. Lacks a geographical index.   Q105.U5D36

The official museum directory. 1971– . Wash. : American Association of Museums, 1971– . Annual since 1980.   **EA217**

For annotation, *see* AL90.   AM10.A2O4

Tanford, Charles. The scientific traveler : a guide to the people, places, and institutions of Europe / Charles Tanford, Jacqueline Reynolds. N.Y. : Wiley, c1992. 335 p. : ill., maps.   **EA218**

A guidebook about places significant to the history of European science. A general review of important scientific events for 16 countries is followed by descriptive details of principle sites. Includes some illustrations, in addition to small-scale maps for each country. Indexed by personal name, subject, and place. While subjective and personal in the selection of sites, this is a unique effort to place the history of scientific development in a geographic context.   Q127.E8T36

SCIENTIFIC EXPEDITIONS

Terek, Eugenie. Scientific expeditions. Jamaica, N.Y. : Queens Borough Public Libr., 1952. 176 p.   **EA219**
A list of scientific expeditions compiled primarily to assist catalogers in establishing correct forms of entry. Expeditions are listed alphabetically with many cross-references. Under each expedition is given, insofar as possible, the source, purpose, members, equipment, and sponsors. Contains supplementary lists showing geographical distribution, subject classification, bibliography of sources, and indexes of members and sponsors.   Q115.T35

SCIENTIFIC ILLUSTRATION

Bridson, Gavin D. R. Plant, animal & anatomical illustration in art & science : a bibliographical guide from the 16th century to the present day / comp. by Gavin D. R. Bridson and James J. White. Winchester : St Paul's Bibliographies in assoc. with Hunt Inst. for Botanical Documentation ; Detroit : Omnigraphics, 1990. 450 p.   **EA220**
Some 7,670 references, organized in seven general sections: (1) bibliographies; (2) nature in general; (3) plants; (4) animals; (5) the human body; (6) artist biographies; and (7) periodicals. The "major sections each include four categories of literature: primary literature on hand-created illustration methods from the 16th century to the present day; secondary literature on the history and criticism of natural history illustration; selected literature on the history of plant, animal, and anatomical representation in art; and primary and secondary literature on illustrative photography from 1840's to the present day … Artist biographies include secondary literature on the biography and work of individual artists, illustrators, and photographers. Title, subject and name indexes provide access to these classified lists."—*Introd.* Within sections, entries are arranged chronologically except for collections and exhibitions subsections where entries are by country and institution, and section 6, which is alphabetical by artist. Entries contain full bibliographic details with some notes to reference sources and catalogs consulted.
§ A recommended work for locating illustrations of specific plants or animals is Beth Clewis, *Index to illustrations of animals and plants* (N.Y. : Neal-Schuman, 1991. 217 p.). Earlier works include *Index to illustrations of the natural world*, comp. by John W. Thompson, ed. by Nedra G. Slauson (EG73) and *Index to illustrations of living things outside North America*, by Lucile Thompson Munz and Nedra G. Slauson (EG72).   QH46.5.P43

Council of Biology Editors. Scientific Illustration Committee. Illustrating science : standards for publication. Bethesda, Md. : The Council, c1988. 296 p. : ill. (some col.).   **EA221**
A style manual that aims to "develop specific standards and guidelines for publication of illustrated scientific materials."—*Pref.* Chapters review illustration techniques emphasizing standards of reproduction and publication. Glossary of graphic arts terms, annotated bibliography, and topics index.   Q222.C68

The Guild handbook of scientific illustration / ed. by Elaine R.S. Hodges … [et al.]. N.Y. : Van Nostrand Reinhold, c1989. 575 p., [12] p. of plates : ill. (some col.).   **EA222**

Sponsored by the Guild of Natural Science Illustrators.
A comprehensive review, with more than 600 black-and-white and color illustrations, of the principles and techniques of scientific illustration. An appendix lists sources for artist's materials and equipment, degree programs, professional organizations, business information, and a bibliography. Subject index and index to illustrators.   Q222.G85

Zweifel, Frances W. A handbook of biological illustration. 2nd ed. Chicago : Univ. of Chicago Pr., 1988. 137 p. : ill.
EA223
For annotation, *see* EG58.   QH318.Z97

HISTORY OF SCIENCE

Guides

Information sources in the history of science and medicine / editors, Pietro Corsi, Paul Weindling. London ; Boston : Butterworth Scientific, 1983. 531 p. : ill.   **EA224**
Consists of 23 topical chapters (e.g., The history of technology, Scientific instruments, Medicine since 1500) written by authorities. Each chapter includes background and history, a discussion of the literature, and an extensive list of references. Remains the best guide and overview to the field. Indexed.   R118.2.I53

Bibliography

American Philosophical Society. Library. Catalog of books in the American Philosophical Society Library, Philadelphia, Pennsylvania. Westport, Conn. : Greenwood, [1970]. 28 v.
EA225
Reproduction of the catalog cards for this important collection "concentrating on particular aspects of the history of science and related fields."—*Introd.* Includes extensive holdings of publications of scientific academies. In addition, there are strong collections on Franklin, evolution, and 19th-century natural history. Mainly an author and subject catalog, but with some title entries as well as many entries for journal articles in the areas of the Society's special interests.
Z881.P5318

——————— Catalog of manuscripts in the American Philosophical Society Library, including the archival shelflist. Westport, Conn. : Greenwood, [1970]. 10 v.   **EA226**
Reproduction of the catalog cards for this collection which contains "much of great value for scholars interested in the general history of America before 1800 and the history of science since about 1700."—*Introd.* (The Franklin papers, for which a separate catalog was published in 1908, are not included.).   Z881.P5319

Batschelet, Margaret. Early American scientific and technical literature : an annotated bibliography of books, pamphlets, and broadsides. Metuchen, N.J. : Scarecrow, 1990. 136 p.
EA227
Offers 833 annotated citations to works published in the U.S., 1665–1799. Entries are arranged by date within three sequences: medical; technical science; nature and physical science. Author and subject indexes.   Z7402.B38

Ferguson, Eugene S. Bibliography of the history of technology. Cambridge, Mass. : Society for the History of Technology, [1968]. 347 p. (Society for the History of Technology. Monograph series, v.5).   **EA228**
"The purpose of this book is to provide a reasonably comprehensive introduction to primary and secondary sources in the history of technology."—*Pref.* "Technology" is defined as those "activities of

man that result in artifacts." Intended for the serious student. Includes many general guides and reference sources as well as an extensive chapter listing monographs, articles, and bibliographies in specific subject fields. Entries are annotated, often at some length. Indexed. An important work for this field. Earlier versions of parts of the book appeared in *Technology and culture*, v. 3–6 (1962–65).

§ Supplemented by: *Current bibliography in the history of technology* (EA242). Z7914.H5F4

Forbes, Robert James. Bibliographia antiqua : philosophia naturalis. Leiden : Nederlandsch Inst. voor het Nabije Osten, 1940–50. 10 pts. in 1 v. **EA229**

A listing of nearly 11,000 books and periodical articles in various languages published through 1939. Each of the ten parts treats an area of ancient science and technology, such as mining and geology, building materials, and pottery, faience, glass, glazes, beads. No index.

———. ———. *Supplement 1, 1940–50* (1952); *Supplement 2, 1950–60* (1963). The supplements give greater attention to ancient mathematics, physics, and astronomy.

Harkanyi, Katalin. The natural sciences and American scientists in the revolutionary era : a bibliography. N.Y. : Greenwood, 1990. 520 p. (Bibliographies and indexes in American history, no. 17). **EA230**

An extensive bibliography of primary and secondary works including monographs, serials, pamphlets, and documentary sources concerning science and scientists of the American revolutionary period, 1760–89. Entries are arranged alphabetically under nine topics and often include descriptive annotations. Appendixes give biographical details of scientists. Subject index. Arrangement and typography are drawbacks to effective use. Z7405.H6H37

The history of women and science, health, and technology : a bibliographic guide to the professions and the disciplines. 2nd ed. / gen. ed., Phyllis Holman Weisbard ; assoc. ed., Rima D. Apple. Madison : Univ. of Wisconsin System, Women's Studies Librarian, 1993. 100 p. **EA231**

1st ed., 1988, ed. by Susan E. Searing.

Designed to assist in preparation of gender-centered courses, this edition expands and updates citations to 1992. Covers feminist scholarship on the history of women in the workplace, professional education for women, and the relationship between science and social conventions. Entries are arranged under six major topics: (1) Overviews; (2) Women in the scientific professions; (3) Health and biology; (4) Home economics/domestic science; (5) Technology; (6) Books for older children and young adults. Sources for individual and collective biographies are highlighted. Author index. HQ1397.H57

Horblit, Harrison D. One hundred books famous in science : based on an exhibition held at the Grolier Club. N.Y. : Grolier Club, 1964. 449 p. : ill., facsims. **EA232**

Examples of early scientific works in theoretical, experimental, and applied science, including technology. Full bibliographical descriptions with facsimiles of title pages, and with brief notes on the importance of these books in the history of science. Entries are sometimes accompanied by references to other books or papers which introduce, amplify, or complete their meaning. Alphabetical author arrangement. Z7401.H6

Isis cumulative bibliography : a bibliography of the history of science formed from *Isis* critical bibliographies 1–90, 1913–65 / ed. by Magda Whitrow. [London] : Mansell, in conjunction with the History of Science Society, 1971–84. 6 v. **EA233**

Contents: v. 1, Personalities, A–J; v. 2, Personalities, K–Z and Institutions A–Z; v. 3, Subjects; v. 4, Civilizations and periods, prehistory to Middle Ages; v. 5, Civilizations and periods, 15th to 19th centuries, Addenda to v. 1–3; v. 6, Author index.

A classed arrangement of the listings appearing in the *Isis* critical bibliographies. Serves as a "guide to the literature of the history of science during fifty most significant years [and] an analytical guide to *ISIS* itself [since] throughout most of its history *ISIS* has been fully an-

alyzed in the Critical Bibliographies."—*Foreword, v. 1.* The bibliography, while massive, is selective in keeping with George Sarton's intentions for the critical bibliographies.

Entries without reference to period or civilization, those that refer to two centuries in the modern period, those that deal with two or more civilizations but are not restricted to a particular period, and those dealing with the 20th century or the 19th and 20th centuries together are included in v. 3. Vol. 5 includes a subject index to v. 4 and v. 5. Vol. 6 is an author index for v. 1–5.

Continued by:

———. *1966–1975 : a bibliography of the history of science formed from* Isis *critical bibliographies 91–100 indexing literature published from 1965 through 1974,* ed. by John Neu (1980–85. 2 v.). Vol. 1, Personalities and institutions; v. 2, Subjects, periods and civilizations.

———. *1976–1985 : a bibliography of the history of science formed from* Isis *critical bibliographies 101–110 indexing literature published from 1975 through 1984,* ed. by John Neu (c1989. 2 v.). Vol. 1, Persons and institutions; v. 2, Subjects, periods and civilizations. Z7405.H6I2

Jayawardene, S. A. Reference books for the historian of science : a handlist. London : Science Museum, 1982. 229 p. (Occasional publications / Science Museum Library, 2). **EA234**

A classified list of 1,034 titles. Major works are annotated. Author/title and subject indexes. Z7405.H6J3

John Crerar Library. A list of books on the history of science, January 1911 / prep. by A. G. S. Josephson. Chicago : print. by order of the Board of Directors, 1911. 297 p. **EA235**

Repr. : N.Y. : Kraus, 1966.

"Includes the social, physical, natural and medical sciences, but omits the applied sciences. ... Publications on the history of learned institutions have not been included ... and only such biographies as have a direct bearing on the position of their subjects in the history of science."—*Pref.* Includes monographs printed in serials, contents of proceedings and congresses, and festschriften. Entries occasionally give scope notes and tables of contents. Arranged by large class, then by period, then by author. Author index.

———. ———. *Supplement, December 1916* (Chicago, 1917. 139 p.); *Second supplement,* prep. by R. B. Gordon (Chicago, 1942–46. Pts. 1–6).

Richardson, R. Alan. Science and technology in Canadian history : a bibliography of primary sources to 1914 / comp. by R. Alan Richardson and Bertrum H. Macdonald [microform]. Thornhill, Ont. : HSTC Publications, 1987. 105 microfiches. (Research tools for the history of Canadian science and technology, no. 3). **EA236**

Accompanied by a 17-p. guide.

Contains "over 58,000 entries to works (articles and monographs) in science, engineering, architecture, and technology published by Canadians or about Canada from the 16th century to 1914."—*Scope of the bibliography.* Excludes secondary works and medicine. Complete bibliographic entries are arranged by author, title, and by classified subject. All entries include a location code for copies and some include content annotations. Keyword-out-of-context index to titles; alphabetic monograph title index. Z7402.R53

Rink, Evald. Technical Americana : a checklist of technical publications printed before 1831. Millwood, N.Y. : Kraus Internat., [1981]. 776 p. **EA237**

For annotation, *see* EK3. Z7912.R56

Rothenberg, Marc. The history of science and technology in the United States : a critical and selective bibliography. N.Y. : Garland, 1982. 242 p. (Bibliographies of the history of science and technology, 2 ; Garland reference library of the humanities, 308). **EA238**

A guide to secondary literature in English on the history of American science and technology (excluding medicine) published 1940–80. The 832 annotated entries are arranged by subject within six chapters—Bibliographies and general studies, Special themes, The physical sciences, The biological sciences, The social sciences, and Technology and agriculture. Author and subject indexes.

Updated by: ———. ———. *Volume II* (1993. 197 p. [Bibliographies of the history of science and technology, 17 ; Garland reference library of the humanities, 815]), whose 653 entries describe books, articles, dissertations, and review articles published in English 1980–87. One new category—Science, technology, and government—has been introduced to the topical scheme carried over from the basic volume. Author and subject indexes.   Z7405.H6R67

Sarton, George. A guide to the history of science : a first guide for the study of the history of science with introductory essays on science and tradition. Waltham, Mass. : Chronica Botanica Co., 1952. 316 p. : ill.   **EA239**

At head of title: Horus.

In two parts: the first and shorter explains the purpose and meaning of the history of science through a series of three lectures; the second is a bibliographic survey prepared for students and scholars. The bibliography is in four parts, each consisting of six to eight chapters: (1) history; (2) science (dealing with method, philosophy, periodicals, and national academies and societies); (3) history of science; (4) organization of the study and teaching of the history of science. The entries are not annotated, but many contain detailed notes. Evaluative remarks often appear at the beginning or end of chapters.   Q125.S24

Thornton, John Leonard. Scientific books, libraries and collectors : a study of bibliography and the book trade in relation to science / by John L. Thornton and R. I. J. Tully. 3rd ed. London : Libr. Assoc., 1971. 508 p., 17 plates : facsims.   **EA240**

1st ed., 1954.

In 12 chapters, presents "an introductory history of the production, distribution and storage of scientific literature from the earliest times."—*Pref., 1st ed.* Includes material on the rise of scientific societies, the growth of the scientific periodical literature, scientific bibliographies and bibliographers, scientific publishing, and scientific libraries. Records the writings of prominent scientific authors and lists the more important printed editions of their work. Bibliography; index.

———. ———. *Supplement, 1969–75* (London : Libr. Assoc., 1978. 172 p.).   Z7401.T45

Current

Critical bibliography of the history of science and its cultural influences. (*In* Isis, v. 46 [June 1955]– . Chicago : Univ. of Chicago Pr., 1955–). Annual.   **EA241**

Publisher varies.

A continuation, with a reorganized classification of the 79 lists, with slightly different title, compiled by George Sarton and covering 1912–52, which appeared in *Isis*, v. 13 (1913)–44 (1953). None published 1954.

Issues usually include: A, History of science. General references and tools; B, Science and its history from special points of view; C, Histories of the special sciences; D, Chronological classification. Each section is subdivided into more specific categories. Entries list books and articles, and many entries are annotated and give references to reviews. Index of all personal names appearing in the bibliography.

Cumulated in three series: 1–90 (1913–65), 91–100 (1966–75), and 101–110 (1976–85) (*see* EA233).

•Available online through Research Libraries Information Network (RLIN) for 1976 and after.

Current bibliography in the history of technology. 1990– . Chicago : Univ. of Chicago Pr. : 1992– . Annual.   **EA242**

Issued by: Society for the History of Technology.

Previously appeared annually in issues of *Technology and culture*. Carries numbering from previous title.

A classified bibliography of current materials intended to survey the literature of a given year. There is a gap of about two years between the date of publication and the year of focus. Items omitted from one year's compilation may appear in following years. Many brief annotations. Author and subject indexes.

•Available online through Research Libraries Information Network (RLIN), 1987– .

Periodicals

Kronick, David A. Scientific and technical periodicals of the seventeenth and eighteenth centuries : a guide. Metuchen, N.J. : Scarecrow, 1991. 332 p.   **EA243**

Lists periodicals and serials relevant to the history of science with national union lists and other sources indicated. Titles are arranged alphabetically word by word with entry under latest title with reference to preceding titles. Citations include bibliographic details, source list consulted, union list identifiers, subject heading, and reprint information when known. Indexed by subject, personal name, institutional name, and title. Bibliography of references.   Z7403.K76

Manuscripts

The manuscript papers of British scientists, 1600–1940. London : H.M.S.O., 1982. 109 p. (Guides to sources for British history, 2).   **EA244**

Initiated by the Royal Commission on Historical Manuscripts and the Royal Society. Lists 635 scientists with the location of manuscript materials both in Great Britain and other countries. Excludes living scientists; however, scientists who died up to 1980 are included if their substantive work was completed by 1940. Index of locations.   Z7407.G7M35

Encyclopedias

Archiv der Geschichte der Naturwissenschaften : Biographien, Sachwörter und Bibliographien. Wien : Hollinek, 1980–83. Heft 1–8/9. (In progress).   **EA245**

Supersedes *Lexikon der Geschichte der Naturwissenschaften* (EA247) and continues its contents. The article on "Edelsteinkunde" left incomplete in Bd. 2, Lfg. 8 is reprinted in full. Now published in looseleaf format; articles are not in progressive alphabetical sequence. Issues include notices and occasional original articles.   Q141.A2

Bynum, W. F. Dictionary of the history of science / ed. by W. F. Bynum, E. J. Browne, Roy Porter. Princeton, N.J. : Princeton Univ. Pr., c1981. 494 p. : ill.   **EA246**

"We have planned this *Dictionary* in the hope of explaining—to lay people as well as the scientifically trained—core features of recent Western science within the context of its development."—*Introd.* In alphabetical order, signed entries consist of one or more paragraphs that discuss terms and concepts. There are extensive cross-references from specific terms to the more general articles. Some entries include bibliographical references. The biographical index gives dates, field of interest, and subject reference in the dictionary.   Q125.B98

Lexikon der Geschichte der Naturwissenschaften : Biographien, Sachwörter und Bibliographien, mit einer Einführung "Die Zeitalter der Naturforschung" und einer Übersichtstabelle / von Josef Mayerhöfer ... [et al.]. Wien : Hollinek, [1959–76]. 2 v.   **EA247**

Contents: Bd. 1 (Lfg. 1–6)–2 (Lfg. 7–8), Aachen–Edelsteinkunde. No more published.

Deals with the history of science from ancient times to the end of the 19th century, with much biography as well as articles on scientific subjects and geographical areas. Includes quite extensive bibliographies at the end of articles; in the case of biographical articles, bibliographies include works both by and about the person.

§ Continued by: *Archiv der Geschichte der Naturwissenschaften : Biographien, Sachwörter und Bibliographien* (EA245). Q141.L49

Directories

Guide to the history of science. 1980– . Philadelphia : Dept. of History and Sociology of Science, Univ. of Pennsylvania, 1980– . Triennial. **EA248**

At head of title: Isis.

Supersedes: *Directory of members.*

Serves as the official membership directory for the History of Science Society as well as guide to the field. Lists graduate programs, associations and research centers, and journals and newsletters in the history of science. Indexes for institutions, societies, and organizations; members' subject interests, national culture interests, and locations.

Q125.I8

Chronologies

Asimov, Isaac. Asimov's chronology of science and discovery. N.Y. : Harper & Row, c1989. 707 p. : col. ill. **EA249**

Chronicles scientific, medical, and technical discoveries and achievements from the advent of human bipedality in 4,000,000 BCE to the greenhouse effect in 1988. Written for a general readership, this year-by-year historical record emphasizes developments of interest to a modern American audience. Index of names and subjects. No bibliography or list of works consulted. Q125.A765

Bunch, Bryan H. The timetables of technology : a chronology of the most important people and events in the history of technology / Bryan Bunch and Alexander Hellemans. N.Y. : Simon & Schuster, c1993. 490 p. **EA250**

Chronological tables present historical data, inventions, discoveries, etc. from the Stone Age to 1993. Text is placed in columns under such headings as communication, transportation, tools and devices, and food and agriculture. Short, inset paragraphs provide greater detail on important events and developments. Name and subject indexes. T15.B73

Darmstaedter, Ludwig. Handbuch zur Geschichte der Naturwissenschaften und der Technik ... . 2. umgearb. und verm. Aufl. / unter Mitwirkung von R. Du Bois-Reymond und D. C. Schaefer, hrsg. von L. Darmstaedter. Berlin : Springer, 1908. 1262 p. **EA251**

Repr.: N.Y. : Kraus, 1978.

Chronological list of about 12,000 important scientific discoveries and inventions, dating from 3500 BCE to 1908 CE giving for each its date, name of discoverer or inventor, and other brief data. Alphabetical indexes of names and of subjects. Q125.D26

Hellemans, Alexander. The timetables of science : a chronology of the most important people and events in the history of science / Alexander Hellemans and Bryan Bunch. N.Y. : Simon and Schuster, c1988. 656 p. **EA252**

Chronologically organized tables record events, discoveries, and inventions from the time of the appearance of hominids to 1988. Each table's entries are grouped under headings such as astronomy, physics, earth sciences, and medicine. Short overviews of major scientific periods and brief information inserts in the tables themselves provide historical context. The timetable format promotes examination of simultaneous events, but limits the amount of information conveyed. Name and topical indexes. Q125.H557

Mount, Ellis. Milestones in science and technology : the ready reference guide to discoveries, inventions, and facts / by Ellis Mount and Barbara A. List. 2nd ed. Phoenix : Oryx, 1994. 206 p. : ill. **EA253**

1st ed., 1987.

An alphabetically arranged selection of 1,250 significant topics in science and technology from the prehistoric period to 1992. Entries from the 1st ed. were reviewed and revised. "Topics cover basic discoveries as well as practical inventions, and range from relativity and genetics to the electric motor and DDT."—*Foreword, 1st ed.* Each entry gives a brief description of the topic, and includes dates, relevant persons, and a source for additional reading. Indexes by personal name, date, place, and field of study. Annotated bibliography of references. Q199.M68

Parkinson, Claire L. Breakthroughs : a chronology of great achievements in science and mathematics, 1200–1930. Boston : G.K. Hall, c1985. 576 p. : ill. **EA254**

Events and accomplishments important for the development of western science are listed chronologically in nine categories: astronomy, biology, chemistry, earth sciences, health sciences, mathematics, meteorology, physics, and supplemental topics. Each event is described briefly, referring to important figures, published works, and the subsequent influence or use of the development. Subject and name indexes, the latter enhanced with birth/death dates, nationality, and alternate names. Bibliography of original and secondary sources. Useful for college libraries and history of science collections; more specialized than *Asimov's chronology of science and discovery* (EA249) or Alexander Hellemans and Bryan Bunch's *The timetables of science* (EA252). Q125.P327

History

Companion to the history of modern science / ed. by R.C. Olby ... [et al.]. London ; N.Y. : Routledge, 1990. 1081 p. **EA255**

An introduction to the history of Western science from the 16th century to the present, excluding medicine and technology. Succinct, authoritative essays written by scholars are grouped in two sections: the study of the history of science and selected writings in the history of science. Essays include bibliographies and further readings. Name and subject indexes. Q125.C565

Sarton, George. Introduction to the history of science. Baltimore : publ. for the Carnegie Institution by Williams & Wilkins, 1927–48. 3 v. in 5. (Carnegie Institution of Washington. Publication, no. 376). **EA256**

Contents: v. 1, Homer to Omar Khayyam; v. 2, Rabbi Ben Ezra to Roger Bacon; v. 3, Science and learning in the 14th century.

An important reference history, rich in biography and bibliography, covering European and Asian countries. With the exception of the first four chapters, which cover longer periods, treatment is by periods of a half century. Each period is introduced with a simplified survey, followed by detailed analyses. A general index in v. 3 is relatively complete for v. 3, but for v. 1–2 lists only the main personalities treated, giving the page of the main article and the page of the index in v. 1 or 2 where other references may be found. Addenda and errata are included in "Critical bibliography of the history and philosophy of science ..." appearing in *Isis* (EA241). Q125.S32

PATENTS; TRADEMARKS

Burge, David A. Patent and trademark tactics and practice. 2nd ed. N.Y. : Wiley, c1984. 213 p. : forms. **EA257**

1st ed., 1980.

Intends "to outline fundamental principles that should be understood by inventors and businesspersons engaged in the development, protection, and management of intellectual property."—*Pref.* In narrative form, concentrating on patents and trademarks but also dealing with other forms of intellectual property and other issues such as design patents, plant protection, copyrights, computerware, and biotechnology. Glossary; index.   KF3120.B87

Fenner, Terrence W. Inventor's handbook / Terrence W. Fenner and James L. Everett. N.Y. : Chemical Publ. Co., 1969. 309 p. : ill.   **EA258**
   Remains useful for its practical information for the inventor on how to proceed from idea through model building, patenting, marketing, etc.   T212.F44

Index of patents issued from the United States Patent and Trademark Office. 1974– . Wash. : The Office : for sale by U.S. Govt. Print. Off., 1974– . Annual.   **EA259**
   Superintendent of Documents classification: C 21.5/2 .
   Continues: *Index of patents issued from the United States Patent Office* (1920–73. 54 v.), which continues *Annual report of the Commissioner of Patents,* 1876–1925. The latter forms an annual index to the *Official gazette* (EA264) and to *Specifications and drawings of patents* (1871–1912) and replaced U.S. Patent Office *General index of the Official gazette and monthly volumes of patents,* 1872–1875 (Wash. : U.S. Govt. Print. Off., 1872–76. 4 v.).
   Contents vary, but include a name index to inventors and assignees and a subject or classified subject index to inventions.   T223.D3

Index of trademarks issued from the United States Patent and Trademark Office. 1974– . Wash. : The Office : for sale by U.S. Govt. Print. Off., 1975– . Annual.   **EA260**
   Superintendent of Documents classification: C 21.5/3.
   Continues: *Index of trademarks issued from the United States Patent Office* (1927–73. 47 v.), which continues *Annual report of the Commissioner of Patents* (1876–1925). The latter forms an annual index to the *Official gazette* (EA265) and to *Specifications and drawings of patents* (1871–1912).   T223.V4A2

Information sources in patents / ed. by C. P. Auger. London ; N.Y. : Bowker-Saur, c1992. 187 p. : ill.   **EA261**
   Thirteen topical chapters review: the history of the patent process: patents in Europe, Great Britain, Japan, and the U.S.; print and online information sources; and the use of patents in engineering, chemistry, and the life sciences. Valuable for its emphasis on patents as sources of information and for the international perspective of the contributors. Brief glossary and sources list. Subject index.   T210.I53

Levy, Richard C. Inventing and patenting sourcebook : how to sell and protect your ideas / Richard C. Levy ; Annette Piccirelli, editor. 2nd ed. Detroit : Gale, c1992. [84], 1024 p. : ill.
                                                          EA262
   1st ed., 1990.
   Serves as a "practical "how-to" guide to developing, patenting, licensing, and marketing." (*Introd.*) and a classified directory to agencies, professionals, and other resources of interest to the inventor or patentee. Appendixes include the U.S. patent classification schedule, telephone directory to the U.S. Patent and Trademark Office, and an alphabetical index to the directory section.   T339.L38

Maynard, John T. Understanding chemical patents : a guide for the inventor / John T. Maynard, Howard M. Peters. 2nd ed. Wash. : American Chemical Soc., 1991. 183 p. : ill.
                                                          EA263
   1st ed., 1978.
   Aimed at chemists or engineers who need to understand patents and the invention process, and deal with the legal aspects of patent protection and infringements. Readable discussion of a broad range of patent issues, including some coverage of copyrights and trademarks. Glossary, bibliography of sources, and subject index.   QD39.2.M38

Official gazette of the United States Patent and Trademark Office. Patents. v. 931 (Feb. 4, 1975)– . [Wash.] : U.S. Dept. of Commerce, Patent and Trademark Office : [U.S. Govt. Print. Off., distr.], 1975– . Weekly.   **EA264**
   Superintendent of Documents classification: C 21.5: .
   Continues: U.S. Patent Office *Official gazette of the United States Patent Office* (v. 1 no. 1 [Jan. 3, 1872]–v. 882 no. 4 [Jan. 26, 1971]) and *Official gazette of the United States Patent Office. Patents* (v. 883 no. 1 [Feb. 2, 1971]–v. 930 no. 4 [Jan. 28, 1975]).
   Contains brief advance descriptions and simple drawings of the patents issued each week. Reports decisions of the Commissioner of Patents and the U.S. courts in patent cases, as well as general information on patent procedures, rule changes, and Patent and Trademark Office notices.
   § For an index of patents, *see* EA259.   T223.A23

Official gazette of the United States Patent and Trademark Office. Trademarks. v. 931, no. 2 (Feb. 11, 1975)– . [Wash.] : U.S. Dept. of Commerce, Patent and Trademark Office : [distr. by U.S. Govt. Print. Off.]. Weekly.   **EA265**
   Superintendent of Documents classification: C 21.5/4: .
   Continues: U.S. Patent Office *Official gazette of the United States Patent Office* (v. 1 no. 1 [Jan. 3, 1872]–v. 882 no. 4 [Jan. 26, 1971]) and *Official gazette of the United States Patent Office. Trademarks* (v. 883 no. 1 [Feb. 2, 1971]–v. 930 no. 1 [Feb. 4, 1975]).
   Carries illustrations and brief descriptions of the trademarks registered each week. Contains important notices, decisions of the Patent and Trademark Office, and information on trademark registrations and claims.   T223.V13A34

Phillips, John B. Directory of patent depository libraries / originally comp. by John B. Phillips ; recompiled, rev., and ed. by James A. Arshem. 1st ed., revision "f", including changes through September 1989. [Wash.?] : Patent and Trademark Office, U.S. Dept. of Commerce, Patent Depository Library Program, [1988]. 179 [i.e. 251] *l.* : charts.   **EA266**
   1st ed., 1986.
   A geographic listing of all U.S. patent depository libraries; describes the staff, collections, and services available for public use.
                                                          Z675.D4P55

Rimmer, Brenda M. International guide to official industrial property publications / Brenda M. Rimmer ; rev. and updated by Stephen Van Dulken. 3rd ed. London : British Library, Science Reference and Information Service, 1992. 1 v. (looseleaf) : ill.   **EA267**
   1st ed., 1985, had title: *Guide to official industrial property publications.*
   This handbook describes the official literature that records patents, designs, and trademarks for some 50 nations and international patenting authorities. The principles of industrial property registration are described in an introductory chapter. Invaluable information is included about the historical development of patent systems and contemporary legislation and publications. Subject/title index.   T210.R545

STANDARDS

American national standards ... catalog / ANSI. 1993– . N.Y. : American National Standards Institute, 1993– . Annual.   **EA268**
   Continues: *Catalog of American national standards* (N.Y. : ANSI, 1977–92. 15 v.).
   Earlier catalogs of standards issued under the Institute's earlier names: American Standards Association, and United States of America Standards Institute.
   Lists ANSI and ANSI-approved standards by numeric code. Subject index. Updated by bimonthly supplements.

American Society for Testing and Materials. Annual book of A.S.T.M. standards including tentative standards. 1939– . Philadelphia : A.S.T.M., 1939– . Annual. **EA269**

Frequency and title vary.

Number of parts varies; 1993 ed. consists of 16 sections in 68 v.

The American Society for Testing and Materials is a scientific and technical organization formed for "the development of standards on characteristics and performance of materials, products, systems, and services; and the promotion of related knowledge." Included are "all current formally approved ASTM standard and tentative test methods, definitions, recommended practices, classifications, and specifications, and other related material, such as proposed methods."—*Introd., 1973 rev.* Sections appear at various times throughout the year, each section devoted to a particular topic. Length may range from a few hundred to more than a thousand pages, and numbers of standards from less than 50 to 300. About 30 % of each part is new or revised annually. Each part contains its own index; there is also a general index. TA401.A653

BSI standards catalogue / British Standards Institution. 1987– . London : BSI, 1987– . Annual, with monthly cumulative supplements. **EA270**

Continues BSI's *Yearbook*, 1937–83 (title varies) and *BSI catalogue*, 1984–86.

Lists British standards in numerical order, with date of standard, description, amendments, and number of pages. Also lists work in progress, revised standards, withdrawn standards, European standards, corresponding international and British standards, and locations of depository sets of standards. Subject index. T59.2.G7B74

Directory of international and regional organizations conducting standards-related activities / Maureen Breitenberg, ed. Gaithersburg, Md. : U.S. Dept. of Commerce, National Institute of Standards and Technology ; Wash. : for sale by U.S. Govt. Print. Off., [1989]. 436 p. (NIST special publication, 767). **EA271**

Distr. to depository libraries in microfiche. Superintendent of Documents classification: C 13.10:767.

Repr.: Irvine, Calif. : Global Professioanl Publ., [1989?].

1st ed., 1983 (NBS special publication, 649).

Contains detailed information on "338 international and regional organizations which conduct standardization, certification, laboratory accreditation, or other standards-related activities."—*Abstract.* Entries include organization name in official language with English name provided, address, scope, activities, library and information services, names and addresses of any official U.S. members or related U.S. organizations, and lists of member countries. Organizational index by English name, acronyms and initials list, and organizational index by subject/product. Essential directory for work with international standards. QC100.U57 no. 767

Index and directory of industry standards. 1989/90– . Englewood, Colo. : Information Handling Services ; Irvine, Calif. : distr. by Global Engineering Documents, c1989– . Annual. **EA272**

Lists more than 138,000 standards from some 400 national and international standards developing organizations. Indexes by subject and organization/numeric listing. Includes directory of standards organizations.

•Machine-readable versions: *IHS international standards & specifications* (Englewood, Colo. : IHS, 1930–). Available online; updated weekly. *Worldwide standards service* (Englewood, Co. : IHS, 1896–). Available on CD-ROM; updated monthly. T59.2.U6I5

International Organization for Standardization. ISO catalogue. [Geneva] : The Organization. Quarterly, the final issue being the annual cumulation. **EA273**

A classified list of more than 7,000 international standards, giving title, edition, pagination, price, and ISO standard number. Includes list of withdrawn and superseded standards. Numeric, subject, and technical committee indexes.

§ Also useful is *KWIC index of international standards* (5th ed.

Geneva : ISO/IEC, 1991. 694 p.), which provides keyword access to existing international standards from the ISO, International Electrotechnical Commission (IEC), and 27 other international standards agencies. Z7914.A22I61

National Institute of Standards and Technology. Publications of the National Institute of Standards and Technology ... catalog. 1988– . Gaithersburg, Md. : The Institute ; Wash. : for sale by the U.S. Govt. Print. Off., 1989– . Annual. **EA274**

Summarizes research and lists publications of the chief U.S. governmental standards testing and formulating agency.

Supersedes:

National Bureau of Standards (U.S.). *Publications of the Bureau of Standards complete from the establishment of the Bureau (1901) to June 30, 1947* (Wash. : U.S. Govt. Print. Off., 1948. 375 p. [NBS circular, 460]).

Includes brief abstracts.

Publications of the National Bureau of Standards (1966/67–1970. Wash. : U.S. Govt. Print. Off., 1961–71. [NBS special publication, 305 ; miscellaneous publication, 240]).

Supplements NBS circular 460 (above).

Publications of the National Bureau of Standards (1971–87. Wash. : NBS : for sale by U.S. Govt. Print. Off., 1972–88. [NBS special publication, 305, suppl. 14–19]).

Ricci, Patricia. Standards : a resource and guide for identification, selection, and acquisition. 2nd ed. Woodbury, Minn. : P. Ricci Enterprises, 1992. 336 p. **EA275**

1st ed., 1990.

A convenient inventory of national and international governmental and industrial organizations that develop voluntary standards and specificiations. Additional features of the directory include listings of libraries, standards vendors, consultants, standards newsletters, and a bibliography of standards publications. Indexes: standards prefix, subject, name. Addendum has index by acronym. T59.R48

Standards activities of organizations in the United States / Robert B. Toth, ed. Gaithersburg, Md. : National Institute of Standards and Technology : for sale by U.S. Govt. Print. Off., [1991]. 729 p. (NIST special publication, 806). **EA276**

1st ed., 1984.

Supersedes *Directory of United States standardization activities*, ed. by Sophie Chumas (Wash. : Nat. Bureau of Standards, 1975. [NBS special publication, 417]).

A directory to more than 750 federal and nongovernmental agencies and organizations that produce mandatory and voluntary standards. Contains information concerning standards vendors, libraries, union lists of standards repositories, and defunct standards agencies. Individual entries include name, address, telephone, and a summary of the scope and activities of the organization. Indexes by subject and acronym/initials. QC100.U57

FORMULAS AND RECIPES

Chemical formulary : a collection of formulas for making thousands of products in many fields. v. 1 (1933)– . Brooklyn, N.Y. : Chemical Publ. Co., 1933– . Irregular. **EA277**

Subtitle varies.

Useful both to general readers and to chemists requiring information on chemical compounding and treatment. Formulas have been provided and reviewed by chemists and engineers engaged in many industries. Each volume presents a collection of new, up-to-date formulas not appearing in previous volumes. Grouping is under broad headings such as: Adhesives, Cosmetics and drugs, Foods and beverages, Paints and lacquers, Soaps and cleaners. Includes lists of chemicals and suppliers. Indexed.

———. *Cumulative index* for v. 1–25 (N.Y. : Chemical Publ. Co., 1987. 473 p.).

Hiscox, Gardner Dexter. Henley's twentieth century book of formulas, processes and trade secrets. New rev. and enl. ed., by T. O'Conor Sloane. N.Y. : Books, 1957. 867 p. : ill.
EA278

Subtitle: A valuable reference book for the home, factory, office, laboratory and the workshop, containing ten thousand selected household, workshop and scientific formulas, trade secrets, chemical recipes, processes and money-saving ideas for both the amateur and professional worker.

First issued 1907 as *Henley's twentieth century book of recipes, formulas and processes.* A standard work which has gone through many editions and was frequently reissued with slight changes. Includes a glossary of technical terms and their corresponding common names, information on materials needed for compounding formulas, and a section on workshop and laboratory methods. Indexed.   T49.H6

Swezey, Kenneth M. Formulas, methods, tips, and data for home and workshop / by Kenneth M. Swezey ; updated and expanded by Robert Scharff. 2nd ed., rev. and expanded. N.Y. : Popular Science : [distr. by] Harper & Row, 1979. 670 p.
EA279
1st ed., 1969.

Offers a wide range of practical information for the do-it-yourself enthusiast. Among the topics treated are: wood selection, finishing, and preservation; paints and paint removers; finishing, plating, and working metals; working with concrete, brick, and plaster; adhesives and sealing compounds; laundering, stain removing, and dyeing; photography; calculations and conversions.   TT153.S88

EB

Mathematics

GENERAL WORKS

Guides

A guide to library service in mathematics : the non-trivial mathematics librarian / ed. by Nancy D. Anderson, Lois M. Pausch. Greenwich, Conn. : JAI Pr., c1993. 402 p. (Foundations in library and information science, v. 30).
EB1

Section 1 presents chapters on providing mathematics library service in academic, special, and public libraries. Section 2 includes two comprehensive annotated bibliographies: Reference materials for a mathematics library, and Books for a contemporary mathematics collection. Lists currently published journals of interest to mathematicians. Author and subject indexes.   Z675.M37G85

Loria, Gino. Guida allo studio della storia delle matematiche : generalità, didattica, bibliografia. Appendice: Questioni storiche concernenti le scienze esatte. 2. ed. rif. e aum. Milan : Hoepli, 1946. 385 p.
EB2

A comprehensive guide to the literature of the history of mathematics, covering all periods and all countries. Includes material on the history, manuscripts, biographical sources, reviews, periodicals, etc. Unfortunately, many typographical errors.

Parke, Nathan Grier. Guide to the literature of mathematics and physics including related works on engineering science. 2nd rev. ed. N.Y. : Dover, [1958]. 436 p. : facsims.   **EB3**
1st ed., 1947.

A useful handbook for mathematicians, scientists, and librarians. Pt. 1 comprises chapters on principles of reading and study, literature searching, types of materials, and library use. Pt. 2 is a bibliography of some 5,000 titles published up to 1956, arranged by subject, with notes for each section. Author and subject index.   Z6651.P3

Pemberton, John E. How to find out in mathematics : a guide to sources of information. 2nd rev. ed. Oxford ; N.Y. : Pergamon, [1969]. 193 p.   **EB4**
1st ed., 1963.

Presents an overview of the mathematics literature. Chapters are arranged by Dewey Decimal Classification for mathematics. Appendixes: Sources of Russian mathematical information, Mathematics and the government, and Actuarial science. Subject and author indexes.   Z6651.P4

Schaefer, Barbara Kirsch. Using the mathematical literature : a practical guide. N.Y. : Dekker, c1979. 141 p.   **EB5**
"The purpose of this book is to provide an insight into the vast and varied amount of mathematical literature and to act as a guide to its exploitation."—*Pref.* For students, teachers, and practitioners of mathematics, scientists in other fields, and students and practitioners in library science. Chapters discuss the history, nature, and organization of the mathematical literature, and the specific categories of materials. Chapter bibliographies and subject index.   QA41.7.S3

Use of mathematical literature / ed., Alison Rosemary Dorling. London ; Boston : Butterworths, 1977. 260 p.   **EB6**
Chapters on mathematical literature, organizations, reference materials, mathematics education, and the history of mathematics are followed by nine chapters on topical areas in mathematics, with bibliographies. Author and subject indexes.   QA41.7.U83

Bibliography

Anderson, Nancy D. French mathematical seminars : a union list. 2nd ed. Providence, R.I. : Amer. Mathematical Soc., 1989. 178 p.   **EB7**
1st ed., 1978.

A bibliography of proceedings of French mathematical seminars that includes library locations. Designed to "provide a means for librarians to verify the existence of published French mathematical seminars."—*Pref.* This edition includes 95 new seminar titles plus additional cross-references; first edition entries have been "corrected, revised, and augumented." Arranged alphabetically by the form most frequently cited in the literature. Entries include, as appropriate, sponsoring body, inclusive publication dates, variant titles, cross-references to former and later titles, series titles and numeration, titles of individual volumes, library cataloging entry, references from *Mathematical reviews* (EB27), publisher name and address, and holdings of almost 100 academic libraries in the U.S. and Canada.   Z6655.A53

Dauben, Joseph Warren. The history of mathematics from antiquity to the present : a selective bibliography. N. Y. : Garland, 1985. 467 p. : ill., ports. (Bibliographies of the history of science and technology, v. 6 ; Garland reference library of the humanities, v. 313).   **EB8**
The 2,384 entries in this bibliography are divided into six main sections: (1) General reference works; (2) Source materials; (3) General histories of mathematics; (4) The history of mathematics: chronological periods; (5) The history of mathematics: sub-disciplines; (6) The history of mathematics: selected topics. All entries have been read critically and annotated by 49 expert contributors. A 19-page introduction by the author on the historiography of mathematics includes

references. This book and Kenneth Ownsworth May's *Bibliography and research manual of the history of mathematics* (EB14) are indispensable tools for the historian of mathematics. Indexed. Z6651.D38

Harter, H. Leon. The chronological annotated bibliography of order statistics. Columbus, Ohio : Amer. Sciences Pr., c1983–c1993. 8 v. (American series in mathematical and management sciences, v. 7, etc.). **EB9**

Vol. 1 originally publ. 1978 by U.S. Govt. Print. Off.

Vol. 8: H. Leon Harter, with N. Balakrishnan.

Contents: v. 1, Pre-1950; v. 2, 1950–59; v. 3, 1960–61; v. 4, 1962–63; v. 5, 1964–65; v. 6, 1966–67; v. 7, 1968–69; v. 8, Indices, with a Supplement on 1970–1992.

Lists books, journal articles, dissertations, theses, technical reports, and other papers relating to the methods and applications of order statistics. Entries, arranged chronologically and then alphabetically by author, include bibliographic information, citations for abstracts and reviews, summary, and list of references. A list of citations is included for each entry in v. 1–2; v. 8 includes citation lists for publications in v. 3–7. Vols. 1 and 2 contain subject indexes; v. 8 includes author and subject indexes for entire set. Z6654.O73H37 1983

International catalogue of scientific literature / publ. for the Internat. Council by the Royal Soc. of London. v. 1 (1901)–v. 14 (1914). London : Harrison, 1902–21. **EB10**

Section A, Mathematics. For description of the full set, *see* EA16.

Karpinski, Louis Charles. Bibliography of mathematical works printed in America through 1850 / by Louis C. Karpinski, with the cooperation for Washington Libraries of Walter F. Shenton. Ann Arbor : Univ. of Michigan Pr. ; London : Oxford Univ. Pr., 1940. 697 p. : ill. (incl. facsims.). **EB11**

Repr. : N.Y. : Arno, 1980. Includes main volume and first two supplements.

A chronological record of mathematical works in various languages printed in America. Later editions and issues of each title are listed under the 1st edition. Includes more than 1,000 titles and some 3,000 editions. Locates copies in more than 100 libraries. Indexes: General index of authors' names and anonymous titles; Topical indexes; Index of non-English and Canadian works; Index of printers and publishers.

———. ———. *Supplements 1–3* (In *Scripta mathematica* 8 [Dec. 1941]: 233–36; 11 [June 1945]: 173–77; 20 [Sept.–Dec. 1954]: 197–202).

Kendall, Maurice George. Bibliography of statistical literature / Maurice G. Kendall and Alison G. Doig. Edinburgh : Oliver & Boyd ; N.Y. : Hafner, 1962–68. 3 v. **EB12**

Repr.: N.Y. : Arno, 1981.

Contents: v. [1], 1950–58; v. 2, 1940–49; v. [3], Pre-1940, with supplements to the volumes for 1940–49 and 1950–58.

A comprehensive author list of significant "papers (mostly in Western languages) on statistical method, statistical theory, and probability from the sixteenth century up to the end of 1958."—*Pref. to v. 1*. Excludes papers on applications and all books. Designed to provide access to the early statistical periodical literature and to precede *International journal of abstracts, statistical theory and method* (v. 1 [1959]–v. 4 [1963]) and its successor, *Statistical theory and method abstracts* (EB29). Z7551.K42

Lancaster, Henry Oliver. Bibliography of statistical bibliographies. Edinburgh ; London : publ. for the Internat. Statistical Inst. by Oliver & Boyd, [1968]. 103 p. **EB13**

Lists biographies and bibliographies of statisticians and mathematicians who have advanced statistical theory. Includes sections for national and subject bibliographies. Covers both book and periodical literature. Author and subject index.

Updated annually by articles in *Revue* of the International Statistical Institute (1969–71), *International statistical review* (1972–87), and *The mathematical scientist* (1988–89). Z7551.L3

May, Kenneth Ownsworth. Bibliography and research manual of the history of mathematics. [Toronto] : Univ. of Toronto Pr., [1973]. 818 p. **EB14**

Designed as a "complete bibliography of published writings on the history, biography, and bibliography of mathematics" (*Introd. to Part II*) for historians and mathematicians. Pt. 1, Research manual, consists of brief comments on information retrieval and storage, and historical analysis and writing. Pt. 2, Bibliography, has five main sections: Biography; Mathematical topics; Epimathematical topics; Historical classification; Information retrieval. Lists about 31,000 entries, alphabetically arranged by author within the five sections. Also lists mathematical serials, which includes but is not limited to those cited in the bibliography section. No subject index. Z6651.M38

[Omega]—bibliography of mathematical logic / ed. by Gert H. Müller in collaboration with Wolfgang Lenski. Berlin ; N.Y. : Springer-Verlag, c1987. 6 v. **EB15**

Contents: v. 1, Classical logic; v. 2, Non-classical logics; v. 3, Model theory; v. 4, Recursion theory; v. 5, Set theory; v. 6, Proof theory and constructive mathematics.

A comprehensive compilation of significant works in mathematical logic, 1879–1985. Each volume is in four sections: subject index, author index, source index, and miscellaneous indexes. Bibliographic citations to books, journal articles, and proceedings papers are contained in the alphabetical author index; cross-references are included. The subject index is arranged according to a subject classification scheme similar to those used in *Mathematical reviews* (EB27) and *Zentralblatt für Mathematik und ihre Grenzgebiete* (EB31); within subject classes, author/title entries are arranged chronologically, then by author; complete citations are given in the author index. The source index contains full title and publishing information for journals, series, proceedings, and collections that are cited in abbreviated form in the author index. Z6654.M26O47

Royal Society (Great Britain). Catalogue of scientific papers, 1800–1900. London : Clay, 1867–1902 ; Cambridge : Univ. Pr., 1914–25. 19 v. **EB16**

Vol. 1 of the *Subject index* has title: Pure mathematics. For full description, *see* EA22. Z7403.R88

Sachs, Lothar. A guide to statistical methods and to the pertinent literature = Literatur zur Angewandten Statistik. Berlin ; N.Y. : Springer-Verlag, 1986. 212 p. **EB17**

A guide to intermediate statistical methods designed for students, professional statisticians, and nonprofessional users of statistics. An alphabetical subject index, composed of title keywords and subject headings for journal articles and book contents, refers the user to entries in the bibliography section, which contains 1,449 citations. Coverage is through 1985. Z6654.M33S23

Smith, David Eugene. Rara arithmetica : a catalogue of the arithmetics written before the year MDCI, with a description of those in the library of George Arthur Plimpton, of New York. Boston ; London : Ginn, 1908. 507 p. : ill., facsims. **EB18**

Some versions issued in 2 pts., paged continuously.

Chronological arrangement. Gives brief identification of authors, full bibliographic entries, other editions printed before 1601, and other descriptive and historical notes. Includes many facsimiles of title pages. Index of dates. Index of names, places, and subjects. This extensive collection was presented to the Columbia University Libraries in 1936.

———. ———. *Addenda* ... (Boston ; London : Ginn, 1939. 52 p.). A 1970 reprint (N.Y. : Chelsea Pub. Co.) includes both works.

Wallis, R. V. Biobibliography of British mathematics and its applications / R.V. and P. J. Wallis. Letchworth, Eng. : Epsilon Pr., 1986. v. 2 : ill. **EB19**

On title page: Project for Historical Biobibliography (PHIBB), Newcastle upon Tyne.

Contents: v. 2, 1701–1760 (502 p.). No more published?

Provides bibliographic information for books and periodical articles "written in English although published elsewhere, notably in America, or in translation on the continent; works by foreign authors in whatever language, published in Britain; and works by authors of British origin living and publishing abroad."—*Pref.* Entries, organized by year and then by author, contain brief biographical information and lists of publications with Dewey class numbers and library locations. All works by an author appear in a single listing in the "year of appearance of his [sic] first known printed mathematical work." Indexes for names, dedicatees, places, occupations, printers and publishers, and societies.

Indexes; Abstract journals

American Mathematical Society. Index to translations selected by the American Mathematical Society. 1949/65–1966/73. Providence, R.I. : The Society, 1966–73. 2 v.   **EB20**

Indexes all translations published in the *American Mathematical Society translations*, Series 1 (1949–54) and Series 2 (1955–72) and in *Selected translations in mathematical statistics and probability* (1961–73). Author and subject indexes.   Z6651.A55

CompuMath citation index : CMCI. Philadelphia : Inst. for Scientific Information, 1981– . Semiannual.   **EB21**

For annotation, *see* EK160.   Z6653.C84

Current index to statistics, applications, methods and theory. v. 1 (1975)– . Wash. : Amer. Statistical Assoc., [1976]– . Annual.   **EB22**

Sponsored by American Statistical Association and Institute of Mathematical Statistics.

A comprehensive index to journal and monographic literature, covering statistics in a very broad sense. The author index, giving bibliographic citations, is followed by a permuted-term/keyword subject index. All titles and keywords are in English. Includes book reviews and software reviews. Some entries are taken from published abstracts; abstract source and number are given.

•Machine-readable versions: (1) *MathSci* (EB28); (2) *CIS cumulative database* [database] ([Hayward, Calif.] : IMS, 1990?–). 1980– . Available on disk (annual) or on CD-ROM as *CIS extended database*, updated annually.   QA276.A1

Current mathematical publications. v. 7 (Jan. 10, 1975)– . [Providence, R.I.] : Amer. Mathematical Soc., 1975– . Every three weeks.   **EB23**

Continues *Contents of contemporary mathematical journals and new publications*, (v. 4–6, 1972–74) and assumes its numbering. Frequency varies.

Indexes the current mathematical literature, both periodical and monographic. Items are arranged by the AMS classification, so may appear in several sections. Each issue contains an author index plus cumulative author and key subject indexes. Most items will eventually be included in *Mathematical reviews* (EB27).

•Available in machine-readable form as part of *MathSci* [database] (EB28).   Z6653.C85

Dolby, J. L. The statistics cumindex / [by] James L. Dolby and John W. Tukey ... [et al.]. Los Altos, Calif. : R & D Pr., [1973]. 498 p. (Information access series, v. 1).   **EB24**

A subject index to book contents that is in fact a cumulation of indexes from a highly selective group of 113 books, published 1927–71.   Z7551.D64

Index of mathematical papers. v. 1 (1970)–9 (1977). Providence, R.I. : Amer. Mathematical Soc., 1972–[79]. Annual.   **EB25**

Frequency varied: v. 1–4 semiannual.

An author and subject index of all papers and books reviewed in *Mathematical reviews*. The subject index is arranged according to the AMS (MOS) Subject Classification Scheme (1970). Superseded by *Mathematical reviews* annual indexes (EB27).   Z6653.I5

Jahrbuch über die Fortschritte der Mathematik. Bd. 1 (1868)–68[1] (1942). Berlin : Georg Reimer, 1871–1944. Annual.   **EB26**

Issued by Preussische Akademie der Wissenschaften, 1925-42. Editor and publisher vary.

Absorbed with its t. 37 *Revue semestrielle des publications mathématiques*, t. 1 (1893)–39 (1934), a bibliography of mathematical materials in various languages with very few abstracts.

International coverage. Brief, signed abstracts. Classed arrangement with author index.   Z6653R45

Mathematical reviews. v. 1, no. 1 (Jan. 1940)–v.58, no. 6 (Dec. 1979); Issue 80a (Jan. 1980)– . Providence, R.I. : Amer. Mathematical Soc., 1940– . Monthly.   **EB27**

Cosponsored by American Mathematical Society and Mathematical Association of America.

Provides comprehensive coverage of the pure and applied mathematics literature, both monographs and journals. Entries include abstracts or author summaries or, in many cases, critical reviews, many signed and most in English. Currently arranged by Mathematics Subject Classification; prior to 1980, the AMS (MOS) Subject Classification Scheme was used. Monthly author and keyword indexes; annual cumulated author and subject indexes.

Separately published indexes: (1) ——— *Author index* (v. 1–20 [1940–59]; v. 21–28 [1960–64]; v. 29–44 [1965–72]; v. 45–58 [1973–79]; v. 80–84 [1980–84]. Providence, R.I. : AMS, 1961–86. 21 v.). Gives author, full title, full citation, and abstract number.

(2) ——— *Cumulative subject index* (v. 1–19 [1940–58]. (Providence, R.I. : AMS, 1983. 413 p.). Combines annual subject indexes in one volume. Contains original cross-references augmented by cross-references from each major word in any main heading or subheading.

(3) ——— *Subject index* (v. 20–44 [1959–72]; v. 45–58 [1973–79]; v. 80–84 [1980–84]. (Providence, R.I. : AMS, 1973–86. 14 v.). Arranged by AMS (MOS) Subject Classification Schemes (1968–80) and after 1980 by the Mathematics Subject Classification. Entries give author, full title, and abstract number.

(4) ——— *Annual indexes* (1978– . Providence, R.I. : AMS, 1979–). Author index entries include author, full title, and abstract number. Subject index originally arranged by 1970 AMS (MOS) Subject Classification; entries give author, title, and abstract number. Supersedes *Index of mathematical papers* (EB25).

•Available in machine-readable form as part of *MathSci* [database] (EB28).

•**MathSci** [database]. Providence, R.I. : American Mathematical Society, 1959– .   **EB28**

Formerly known as *MATHFILE*.

Provides comprehensive coverage of literature in mathematics and statistics and their applications to other fields, including physics, computer science, and engineering. Available online and in CD-ROM. Online file draws records from *Mathematical reviews*, 1940– (EB27); *Current mathematical publications*, 1985– (EB23); *Current index to statistics*, 1975– (EB22); *Index to statistics and probability* (The Tukey index), 1910–68; *Computing reviews*, 1960– (EK166); *ACM guide to computing literature*, 1986– (EK159); and *Technical reports in computer science*, 1954– . Abstracts and reviews are included for *Mathematical reviews*, 1980– . Available online, updated monthly. The CD-ROM version (*MathSci disc*) contains records from the *Mathematical reviews* and *Current mathematical publications* sections of the online file; updated semiannually.

Statistical theory and method abstracts. v. 1 (1959)– . Edinburgh : Longman Group, for the Internat. Statistical Inst., 1959– . 4 issues a year, plus index supplement.   **EB29**

Publisher varies.

Title varies: v. 1–4 (1959–63), *International journal of abstracts. Statistical theory and method.*

An international abstract journal covering journals, conference proceedings, and selected monographs. Classified arrangement with author index. Titles are translated into English, and abstracts are in English. Annual author index.

Tukey, John Wilder. Index to statistics and probability / John W. Tukey, with the assistance of Verna Bertrand … [et al.]. Los Altos, Calif. : R & D Pr., 1973–75. 5 v. (Information access series, v. 2–6).   **EB30**

Contents by series volume number: v. 2, Citation index; v. 3–4, Permuted titles; v. 5, Locations and authors; v. 6, Permuted index to minimum abbreviations.

Provides access to "the great bulk of the literature of statistics and probability through 1966."—*Introd.* While these volumes contain a wealth of information, their organization and the extensive use of coded information make them difficult to use. The "Citation index" provides cryptic references to cited items, which include journal articles, books, and reports; entries are arranged by source title codes. The "Permuted titles" volumes contain a Keyword index of titles with coded citation information. The "Locations and authors" provides full titles of items, arranged by source and by author. "Permuted index to minimum abbreviations" gives full title and place of publication for journals and other publications included in this set of volumes.

• Available in machine-readable form as part of: *MathSci* [database] (EB28).   Z6654.M33T84

Zentralblatt für Mathematik und ihre Grenzgebiete. Berlin : Springer, 1931– .   **EB31**

Subtitle varies. Later issues also have title *Mathematics abstracts.* Suspended Nov. 1944–June 1948.

A classified arrangement of signed abstracts of books, journal articles, and conference proceedings in pure and applied mathematics, statistics, and applications of mathematics to science and engineering. International in scope, historically stronger in coverage of non-English publications than *Mathematical reviews* (EB27). Currently arranged by the Mathematics Subject Classification. Author and subject indexes in each volume; cumulative indexes every 10th and 50th volume.

• Machine-readable version: *Mathematics abstracts (MATH)* [database] (Karlsruhe [Germany] : Fachinformationszentrum Karlsruhe GmbH [FIZ Karlsruhe], 1972–). Includes abstracts, 1984– . Available online, updated monthly, and on CD-ROM as *CompactMATH*, updated annually.   QA1.Z4

Book reviews

Grinstein, Louise S. Mathematical book review index, 1800–1940. N.Y. : Garland, 1992. 448 p. (Garland reference library of social science, v. 527).   **EB32**

Provides "a central source for reviews of works appearing in the periodical literature of mathematics, science, philosophy, and education."—*Pref.* Lists more than 3,200 English-language works that were published or distributed in the U.S. or Canada. Entries are alphabetical by author and include title, publisher, publication date, topic and type descriptors, and review citations. List of periodicals surveyed, list of references, and basic subject index.   Z6651.G75

Encyclopedias

Encyclopaedia of mathematics : an updated and annotated translation of the Soviet "Mathematical encyclopaedia" / [managing ed., M. Hazewinkel]. Dordrecht ; Boston : Reidel ; Norwell, Mass. : Distr. by Kluwer Academic Publ., c1988–1994. 10 v.   **EB33**

A translation of *Matematicheskaîa éntsiklopediîa* (Moskva : 1977–85. 5 v.) with updating and editorial comment. Contains three levels of entries: general survey articles on main topics; more specialized articles on concrete problems, techniques, and results; and brief definitions. Most articles include bibliographies, cross-references, and classification numbers in the scheme developed by the American Mathematical Society. Vol. 10: subject and author indexes.   QA5.M3713

Encyclopedia of statistical sciences / editors in chief, Samuel Kotz, Norman L. Johnson. N.Y. : Wiley, c1982–89. 9 v. : ill.   **EB34**

Provides information on an extensive selection of topics in statistical theory and applications of statistical methods, "intended primarily to be of value to readers who do not have detailed information about the topics but have encountered references … that they wish to understand."—*Pref.* Signed articles, many with bibliographies; some biographical articles. Cross-references. Cumulative subject index in v. 9.

———— *Supplement volume*, editors in chief, Samuel Kotz, Norman L. Johnson ; associate ed., Campbell B. Read. (N.Y. : Wiley, 1989. 289 p.).

Contains full, detailed articles for topics not covered in the basic set, plus additional cross-references. Cumulative index for basic set and supplement.   QA276.14.E5

Encyclopedic dictionary of mathematics / by the Mathematical Society of Japan ; ed. by Kiyosi Itô. 2nd ed. Cambridge, Mass. : MIT Pr., c1987. 4 v. (2148 p.) : ill.   **EB35**

1st ed., 1977.

Translation of *Iwanami sūgaku jiten.*

An English version of the 3rd Japanese edition (1985). "Intended to be a compact, up-to-date source of information comprising, as completely as possible, all significant results in all fields of our Science, pure and applied, from the elementary to the advanced level."—*Foreword.* Contains 450 articles on broad mathematical subjects, with extensive subdivisions and literature references; includes some biographical entries. Vol. 4 contains appendixes (tables of formulas, numerical tables, lists of journals and publishers, tables of special notations, systematic and alphabetical lists of articles, and lists of contributors and translators), as well as name and detailed subject indexes.   QA5.I8313

Encyklopädie der mathematischen Wissenschaften mit Einschluss ihrer Anwendungen / hrsg. im Auftrage der Akademien der Wissenschaften zu Göttingen, Leipzig, München und Wien, sowie unter Mitwirkung zahlreicher Fachgenossen. Leipzig : Teubner, 1898/1904–1904/35. 6 v. in 23 : ill., plates, diagrs.   **EB36**

Contents: [1], Arithmetik und Algebra; [2], Analysis; [3], Geometrie; [4], Mechanik; [5], Physik; [6^1], Geodäsie und Geophysik; [6^2], Astronomie.

An important encyclopedia, containing long articles by specialists, with full bibliographic notes, although in some cases articles are now out of date. For advanced students and specialists. A French edition (Paris : Gauthier-Villars, 1904–16. 7 v.) was never completed, but included some revision.

Parts of a 2nd ed. appeared as *Enzyklopädie der mathematischen Wissenschaften mit einschluss ihrer anwendungen* (2. völlig neubearb. Aufl. hrsg. von M. Deuring, H. Hasse, E. Sperner. Leipzig : Teubner, 1939–58).

Contents: Bd. 1, Algebra und Zahlentheorie: 1. T.: A, Grundlagen. B, Algebra; 2. T.: C, Reine Zahlentheorie. D, Analytische Zahlentheorie.   QA36.E56

International encyclopedia of statistics / ed. by William H. Kruskal and Judith M. Tanur. N.Y. : Free Pr., c1978. 2 v. (1350 p.) : ill.   **EB37**

For annotation, *see* CG20.   HA17.I63

Dictionaries

Clapham, Christopher. A concise dictionary of mathematics. Oxford ; N.Y. : Oxford Univ. Pr., 1990. 203 p. : ill.   **EB38**

Cover title: *A concise Oxford dictionary of mathematics.*

Similar in scope and intended audience to J.A. Glenn and G. H. Littler's *Dictionary of mathematics* (EB39), but assumes a more thorough background in mathematics and contains fewer entries. Some biographical entries. Cross-references and appendixes of formulas and symbols.   QA5.C53

Glenn, J. A. Dictionary of mathematics / J.A. Glenn, G.H. Littler. Totowa, N.J. : Barnes & Noble Books, 1984. 230 p. : ill. **EB39**

Contains approximately 2,500 entries, covering basic concepts in mathematics, with understandable definitions and helpful illustrations. Some brief biographical entries. Designed primarily for undergraduate students but appropriate for any user with some basic mathematical knowledge. Appendix of mathematical symbols. QA5.G623

International dictionary of applied mathematics / W. F. Freiberger, ed. in chief. Princeton, N.J. : Van Nostrand, [1960]. 1173 p. : diagrs. **EB40**

"Defines the terms and describes the methods in the application of mathematics to 31 fields of physical science and engineering" in order to provide the means "to obtain the necessary mathematical results by the best available methods."—*Pref.* Indexes in French, German, Spanish, and Russian. QA5.I5

James, Robert C. Mathematics dictionary / [Robert C.] James [and Glenn] James ... [et al.]. 5th ed. N.Y. : Van Nostrand Reinhold, c1992. 548 p. : ill. **EB41**

1st ed., 1942; 4th ed., 1976.

Provides definitions of terms and phrases in pure and applied mathematics; brief biographical entries. Designed for "students, scientists, engineers, and others interested in the meaning of mathematical terms and concepts."—*Pref.* Contains sections on Denominate numbers, Mathematical symbols, Differentiation formulas, and Integral tables. Indexes in French, German, Russian, and Spanish. QA5.J33

Karush, William. Webster's new World dictionary of mathematics. N.Y. : Webster's New World : distr. by Prentice Hall Trade, c1989. 317 p. : ill. **EB42**

Rev. ed. of William Karush, *The crescent dictionary of mathematics* (N.Y. : Macmillan, 1962).

Provides basic definitions for more than 1,400 mathematical terms; some entries have cross-references. Designed for general readers, students, and teachers at high school and college levels. Appendixes contain a list of famous mathematicians with brief biographical information, a table of mathematical symbols, and basic mathematical tables. QA5.K27

Marriott, F. H. C. A dictionary of statistical terms. 5th ed. / prep. for the Internat. Statistical Inst. by F.H.C. Marriott. Burnt Mill, England : Publ. for the Institute by Longman Scientific & Technical ; N.Y. : Wiley, 1990. 223 p. **EB43**

For annotation, *see* CG25. HA17.K4

Naas, Josef. Mathematisches Wörterbuch mit Einbeziehung der theoretischen Physik / Josef Naas, Hermann Ludwig Schmid. 2. unveränderte Aufl. Berlin : Akademie Verlag ; Stuttgart : Teubner, 1962. 2 v. : ill. **EB44**

"Im Auftrage des Instituts für Reine Mathematik an der Deutschen Akademie der Wissenschaften zu Berlin."—*title page.*

An encyclopedia and dictionary containing definitions and current terminology in mathematics and physics, including principles, formulas, some biographical sketches of outstanding mathematicians, and (in many cases) bibliographies at the ends of articles. Alphabetical arrangement. No indexes. QA5.N25

Tietjen, Gary L. A topical dictionary of statistics. N.Y. : Chapman and Hall, 1986. 171 p. **EB45**

For annotation, *see* CG32. QA276.14.T54

Universal encyclopedia of mathematics. N.Y. : Simon & Schuster, 1964. 715 p. : ill. **EB46**

"Designed to serve the needs of high school and college students."—*Foreword.* Provides clear, concise definitions with many line drawings and formulas. Includes sections of mathematical formulae and mathematical tables. QA5.U5413

Foreign terms

Multilingual

Eisenreich, Günther. Dictionary of mathematics : in four languages: English, German, French, Russian. Amsterdam ; N.Y. : Elsevier Scientific ; Berlin : VEB Verlag Technik, 1982. 2 v. **EB47**

Vol. 1, alphabetized by English-language terms, gives the corresponding terms in the other three languages; v. 2 has sections alphabetized by each of the other languages, with references to the entry number of v. 1. Because of the complexity of synonyms and homonyms, each term is assigned one or more subject categories; many terms are followed by brief explanatory notes. The emphasis is on pure mathematics. QA5.E35

Chinese

DeFrancis, John. Chinese-English glossary of the mathematical sciences. Providence, R.I. : Amer. Mathematical Soc., 1964. 275 p. **EB48**

Gives English equivalents for 16,540 Chinese terms. Characters are "arranged on the basis of first, the radical of a character, and second, the number of strokes in the character apart from the radical."—*Pref.* QA5.D4

French

Lyle, William David. Dictionnaire française et anglais de terminologie mathématique = French and English dictionary of mathematical vocabulary. [Montréal] : Didier, [1971]. 137 p. **EB49**

In two parts: French-English and English-French.

Provides equivalent words in English and French; entries include pronunciation, gender, part of speech, and some synonyms.

QA5.L94

German

Herland, Leo Joseph. Dictionary of mathematical sciences. 2nd ed., rev. and enl. N.Y. : Ungar, [1965]. 2 v. **EB50**

1st ed., 1951–55.

Added t. p. in German.

Contents: v. 1, German-English; v. 2, English-German with a supplement of new words.

Covers mathematics and its applications to other fields, including mathematical logic, statistics, physics, and astronomy. Statistical entries by Gregor Sebba; commercial entries by Robert Grossbard.

QA5.H42

MacIntyre, Sheila. German-English mathematical vocabulary / Sheila MacIntyre and Edith Witte, with a grammatical sketch by Lilias W. Brebner. 2nd ed. Edinburgh : Oliver & Boyd ; N.Y. : Interscience, 1966. 95 p. **EB51**

1st ed., 1956.

Lists German terms and their English equivalents in the field of pure mathematics, excluding applied mathematics, statistics, and mathematical logic. QA5.M36

Russian

Efimov, Oleg P. Russian-English dictionary of mathematics. Boca Raton, Fla. : CRC Pr., c1993. 419 p. **EB52**
Provides English equivalents for more than 27,000 Russian mathematical terms, reflecting both contemporary and historical usage; terms are grouped "within articles under the principal term ... rather than alphabetically."—*Pref.* Designed to be a "comprehensive vocabulary aid for present-day readers or writers of Russian mathematical literature." QA5.E33

Lohwater, A. J. A.J. Lohwater's Russian-English dictionary of the mathematical sciences / ed. by R.P. Boas. 2nd ed., rev. and expanded / with the assistance of Alana I. Thorpe. Providence, R.I. : Amer. Mathematical Soc., c1990. 343 p. **EB53**
1st ed., 1961.
A comprehensive dictionary that provides English equivalents for some 15,000 Russian terms, reflecting current usage in mathematics. "The vocabulary has been extensively enlarged and brought up to date, although it retains some obsolete terms that may be needed by users who have to consult older literature."—*Pref.* This edition adds stress markings on Russian words and contains a revised brief Russian grammar section with appendixes that contain noun declensions, verb conjugations, list of numerals, and root list. QA5.L64

Spanish

García Rodríguez, Mariano. Diccionario matemático : español-inglés, inglés-español = Mathematics dictionary : Spanish-English, English-Spanish. N.Y. : Hobbs, Dorman, [1965]. 78 p. **EB54**
Limited to presentation of equivalent words and phrases in Spanish and English. QA5.G36

Quotations

Moritz, Robert Edouard. On mathematics and mathematicians. N.Y. : Dover, [1958, c1942]. 410 p. **EB55**
Unabridged and unaltered republication of *Memorabilia mathematica; or, The philomath's quotation-book* (N.Y. : Macmillan, 1914).
Contains more than 2,100 quotations about mathematics, its nature, value, philosophy, application, etc., grouped by class with an extensive index. Quotations from foreign authors are given only in English, but references to original sources are cited. QA3.M7

Directories

American Mathematical Society. Combined membership list of the American Mathematical Society, the Mathematical Association of America, and the Society for Industrial and Applied Mathematics. 1962/63– . Providence, R.I. : American Mathematical Society, 1963?– . Annual. **EB56**
Lists all individual members of the American Mathematical Society (AMS), the Mathematical Society of America (MAA), and the Society for Industrial and Applied Mathematics (SIAM). Access by name and geographical location. Geographical list of academic and institutional members. QA1.A523

American Statistical Association. Directory of members / the American Statistical Association, the Biometric Society, Eastern and Western North American regions. 1981– . Alexandria, Va. : The Association, [1981]– . Every four years. **EB57**
For information, *see* CG35. HA1.D52

Assistantships and graduate fellowships in the mathematical sciences / comp. under the direction of the AMS-MAA Joint Committee on Employment and Educational Policy. 1989-90– . [Providence, R.I.] : Amer. Mathematical Soc., c1988– . Annual. **EB58**
Formerly published as special issues of the *Notices of the AMS*, entitled "Assistantships and fellowships in mathematics" (1960/61–1979/80) and "Assistantships and fellowships in mathematical sciences" (1980/81–1988/89).
1993–94 volume provides information about graduate programs in about 380 departments of mathematics, statistics, computer science, and related disciplines in the U.S. and Canada. Entries are organized by state and include number of faculty and students, type and number of degrees awarded, and type and amount of financial aid available. QA13.A88

Mathematical sciences professional directory. 1983– . Providence, R.I. : Amer. Mathematical Soc., c1983– . Annual. **EB59**
Continues *Mathematical sciences administrative directory* (1977).
Provides basic information about North American mathematical organizations. Includes officers and committee members for professional organizations, mathematical personnel in selected government agencies, editors of mathematical journals, and chairmen of academic mathematics departments. QA1.M765

World directory of mathematicians / publ. under the auspices of the Internat. Mathematical Union. 1958– . Bombay : School of Mathematics, Tata Inst. of Fundamental Research, 1958– . **EB60**
Publisher varies; 9th ed., Helsinki : International Mathematical Union; Providence, R.I. : distr. by American Mathematical Society.
Published quadrennially; 9th ed., 1990.
A comprehensive alphabetical listing of mathematicians, with geographic index. Geographical list of mathematical organizations. QA30.W6

Handbooks

Bartsch, Hans-Jochen. Handbook of mathematical formulas. N.Y. : Academic Pr., 1974. 528 p. : ill. **EB61**
"Translation of the 9th ed. of *Mathematische Formeln* by Herbert Liebscher, Leipzig."—*verso of t.p.*
"The scope of this collection of formulas covers the whole field from the fundamental rules of arithmetic, via analytic geometry and infinitesimal calculus through to Fourier's series and fundamentals of probability calculus." *Pref.* Arranged by topics; includes illustrations. Subject index. QA41.B313

Bronshteĭn, I. N. Handbook of mathematics / I. N. Bronshteĭn, K. A. Semendyayev ; English translation ed. by K. A. Hirsch. 3rd rev. ed. Frankfurt : Verlag Harri Deutsch ; N.Y. : Van Nostrand Reinhold [distributor], 1985. 973 p. : ill. **EB62**
This English translation is based on the 19th and 20th German editions of the standard handbook, *Taschenbuch der Mathematik.* The 19th ed. (Leipzig : Teubner, 1979) represented a major revision undertaken by a team of mathematicians primarily from the Karl Marx Univ. of Leipzig; the 20th German edition (Leipzig : Teubner, 1981) was basically a reprint of the 19th. The original version, *Spravochnik po matematike : dlia inzhenerov i uchashchikhsia vtuzov*, was published in Russian (6th ed., Moskva : Gos. izd-vo tekhniko-teoret. lit-ry, 1956).
Provides in-depth coverage of all aspects of mathematics, including analysis, probability theory, and mathematical information processing. Useful for students, teachers, and mathematicians. Organized in broad subject sections that contain definitions, equations, and tables. Bibliography and subject index. QA40.B869

Burington, Richard Stevens. Handbook of probability and statistics, with tables / Richard Stevens Burington and Donald Curtis May, Jr. 2nd ed. N.Y. : McGraw-Hill, [1970]. 462 p. **EB63**

1st ed., 1953.

"The book is intended to provide a convenient summary of theory, working rules, and tabular material useful in the study and solution of practical problems involving probability and statistics."—*Pref.* Designed to complement Burington's *Handbook of mathematical tables and formulas* (EB83). Topical arrangement, with indexes to names, Greek symbols, numerical tables, and subjects. QA273.B925

Grazda, Edward E. Handbook of applied mathematics / ed. by Edward E. Grazda, Morris Brenner, assoc. ed., [and] William R. Minrath. 4th ed. Princeton, N.J. : Van Nostrand, [1966]. 1119 p. : ill. **EB64**

Repr. : Huntington, N.Y. : R.E. Krieger, 1977.

1st ed., 1933.

Presents basic mathematical concepts and operations, which are then applied to practical problem-solving in engineering, construction trades, and business. Many illustrations and tables; subject index. TA330.G7

Handbook of statistics. Amsterdam ; N.Y. : North-Holland, 1980– . v. 1–12 : ill. (In progress). **EB65**

General editor: Paruchuri R. Krishnaiah.

Contents: v. 1, Analysis of variance; v. 2, Classification, pattern recognition and reduction of dimensionality; v. 3, Time series in the frequency domain; v. 4, Nonparametric methods; v. 5, Time series in the time domain; v. 6, Sampling; v. 7, Quality control and reliability; v. 8, Statistical methods in biological and medical sciences; v. 9, Computational statistics; v. 10, Signal processing and its applications; v. 11, Econometrics; v. 12, Environmental statistics.

An authoritative set providing comprehensive coverage of statistics. Each volume is devoted to a specific subject, is organized by topical chapters, and has a subject index.

Korn, Granino Arthur. Mathematical handbook for scientists and engineers : definitions, theorems, and formulas for reference and review / Granino Arthur Korn and Theresa M. Korn. 2nd enl. and rev. ed. N.Y. : McGraw-Hill, [1968]. 1130 p. **EB66**

1st ed., 1961.

"A comprehensive reference collection of mathematical definitions, theorems, and formulas for scientists, engineers, and undergraduate and graduate students."—*Pref.* Topically arranged chapters attempt to survey entire mathematical subjects but exclude proofs. Numerical tables and a glossary of symbols and notations. Cross-references; index. QA40.K598

Pearson, Carl E., *ed.* Handbook of applied mathematics : selected results and methods. 2nd ed. N.Y. : Van Nostrand Reinhold, [1983]. 307 p. : ill. **EB67**

1st ed., 1974.

"Most of the topics in applied mathematics dealt with in this handbook can be grouped rather loosely under the term *analysis*. They involve results and techniques which experience has shown to be of utility in a very broad variety of applications."—*Pref.* Emphasis on technique. Consists of 21 chapters, contributed by 20 mathematicians. Bibliographic references; extensive index. QA40.H34

Spanier, Jerome. An atlas of functions / Jerome Spanier, Keith B. Oldham. Wash. : Hemisphere Publ. Corp., c1987. 700 p. : ill. (some col.). **EB68**

A useful compendium concerning groups of functions, in 64 chapters. Data are presented in a standardized format that includes notation, behavior, definitions, special cases, interrelationships, expansions, particular values, numerical values, approximations, operations of the calculus, complex argument, generalizations, cognate functions, and related topics. Valuable to researchers, teachers, and students. Contains extensive tables and more than 180 multicolored computer-

generated graphs. Appendixes of general algorithms and of useful data (e.g., conversion factors, units, constants, and Greek alphabet). Bibliography; subject and symbol indexes. QA331.S685

The VNR concise encyclopedia of mathematics / W. Gellert ... [et al.], editors ; K. A. Hirsch, H. Reichardt, scientific advisors. 2nd ed. N.Y. : Van Nostrand Reinhold, 1989. 776 p., 56 p. of plates : ill. (some col.). **EB69**

1st American ed., 1977.

Originally published in German: *Kleine enzyklopädie der mathematik* (Leipzig : VEB Bibliographisches Institut, 1973).

Intended to "describe mathematical interrelations as briefly and precisely as possible" and to "smooth out access to the specialist literature for as many readers as possible."—*Pref.* Organized in three parts (46 sections): Elementary mathematics, Steps toward higher mathematics, Brief reports on selected topics. Topics are clearly explained. Includes extensive illustrations, diagrams, and tables; color is used to clarify diagrams and to separate and highlight elements of the presentations. Subject index; separate section of plates. QA40.V18

Zwillinger, Daniel. Handbook of differential equations. 2nd ed. Boston : Academic Pr., c1992. 787 p. : ill. **EB70**

1st ed., 1989.

"A compilation of the most important and widely applicable methods for solving and approximating differential equations."—*Introd.* Useful for students and practitioners; assumes a basic understanding of differential equations. Entries include not only procedures and examples but also the idea behind the method and types of equations to which a particular method can be applied. Includes references for each technique and an index of named differential equations. QA371.Z88

———————— Handbook of integration. Boston : Jones and Bartlett, c1992. 367 p. : ill. **EB71**

"A compilation of the most important and widely applicable methods for evaluating and approximating integrals."—*Introd.* Organized like the author's *Handbook of differential equations* (EB70). Subject index. QA299.3.Z85

Tables

Bibliography

Fletcher, Alan. An index of mathematical tables. 2nd ed. / by A. Fletcher [et al.]. Reading, Mass. : Publ. for Scientific Computing Service by Addison-Wesley, 1962. 2 v. (994 p.). **EB72**

1st ed., 1946.

Contents: v. 1, Introduction. pt. 1, Index according to functions; v. 2: pt. 2, Bibliography; pt. 3, Errors; pt. 4, Index to introduction and pt. 1.

An important index to well-known tables of functions published in books and periodicals. Entries in the main index, arranged topically in 24 chapters, provide brief citations; complete citations are found in the bibliography. This edition adds a useful section on errors in tables; both new error listings and references to corrections published elsewhere are given. Author and subject index. QA47.F55

Greenwood, Joseph Arthur. Guide to tables in mathematical statistics / J. Arthur Greenwood, H. O. Hartley. Princeton, N.J. : Princeton Univ. Pr., 1962. lxii, 1014 p. : diagrs. **EB73**

Sponsored by the Committee on Statistics of the Division of Mathematics of the National Academy of Sciences–National Research Council.

"A sequel to the guides to mathematical tables produced by and for the Committee on Mathematical Tables and Aids to Computation of the National Academy of Sciences–National Research Council" (*Pref.*); that is, to Derrick H. Lehmer, *Guide to tables in the theory of numbers* (EB75); Harry Bateman and R. C. Archibald, "Guide to tables of Bessel functions," *Mathematical tables and other aids to computation* 1 (July 1944): 205–63; and Alan Fletcher, "Guide to tables of elliptic functions," *ibid.* 3 (Jan. 1948): 229–81.

Classified arrangement of explanatory text and references to specific tables which have been published separately or in the periodical literature. Includes a section listing contents of books of tables. Author index gives full citations. Subject index. Z6654.T3G7

Lebedev, Aleksandr Vasil'evich. A guide to mathematical tables / by A. V. Lebedev and R. M. Fedorova. English ed., prep. from the Russian by D. G. Fry. N.Y. ; Oxford : Pergamon, 1960. 586 p. **EB74**
"This book has been prepared from the original Russian edition by a photographic process. The Russian text has been replaced by English, but the tabular matter has been reproduced direct from the original."—*Translator's pref.* Organizes references to tables in topical chapters; full bibliographic citations are provided in a separate section. Includes tables published in separate editions through 1952, some published in 1953 and 1954, and those published in periodicals through 1953. Author index.
———. ——— *Supplement no. 1*, by N. M. Burunova (N.Y. ; London : Pergamon, 1960. [Mathematical tables series, 6]). No more published. Prepared and organized like the main volume. Includes tables published through 1959. Author index.

Lehmer, Derrick Henry. Guide to tables in the theory of numbers. Wash. : Nat. Research Council, Nat. Academy of Sciences, 1941. 177 p. incl. tables. (Bulletin of the National Research Council, no.105). **EB75**
Contents: pt.1, Descriptive account of existing tables; pt.2, Bibliography, arranged alphabetically by author, giving exact references to the sources of the tables referred to in pt.1; pt.3, Lists of errata in the tables.
Bibliography, with location of copies in libraries of the U.S. and Canada, p. 85–125. QA241.L53

Compendiums

Abramowitz, Milton. Handbook of mathematical functions with formulas, graphs, and mathematical tables / ed. by Milton Abramowitz and Irene A. Stegun. Wash. : U. S. Bureau of Standards : U.S. Govt. Print. Off., 1964. 1046 p. (United States. National Bureau of Standards. Applied mathematics series, v. 55). **EB76**
Frequently reprinted with corrections, e.g., "10th printing with corrections," 1972 and a "7th corr. Dover printing" (N.Y. : Dover, 1970).
Intended to update and expand the classic *Tafeln höherer Funktionen* by E. Jahnke and Fritz Emde (6th ed., rev. by Friedrich Lösch, publ. in German and English as *Tables of higher functions*, N.Y. : McGraw-Hill, 1960) and "designed to provide scientific investigators with a comprehensive and self-contained summary of the mathematical functions that arise in physical and engineering problems."—*Introd.* Tables are divided into topical chapters, edited by specialists, and include bibliographic references. Subject index and index of notations. QA47.A34

Apelblat, Alexander. Table of definite and indefinite integrals. Amsterdam ; N.Y. : Elsevier Scientific, 1983. 457 p. (Physical sciences data, v. 13). **EB77**
Presents a classified arrangement of more than 3,000 integrals with emphasis on those "not included in previous publications. ... For convenience, equivalent reducible forms ... and particular cases of existing integrals of special interest, are also presented."—*Pref.* Includes references. QA310.A63

Applied mathematics series / National Bureau of Standards. no. 1 (1948)– . Wash. : The Bureau : For sale by the U.S. Govt. Print. Off., 1948– . Irregular. **EB78**

"The Applied Mathematics Series contains mathematical tables, manuals and studies of special interest to physicists, engineers, chemists, biologists, mathematicians, computers, and others engaged in scientific and technical work. Some of the volumes are reissues of the mathematical tables prepared by the Project for the Computation of Mathematical Tables conducted by the Federal Works Agency, Works Project Administration for the City of New York. ..."—*U.S.N.B.S. Publications of the National Bureau of Standards, 1966–67, p. 35.* QA3.U5

Bateman Manuscript Project. Higher transcendental functions : based, in part, on notes left by Harry Bateman, and compiled by the staff of the Bateman Manuscript Project / director: Arthur Erdélyi ... [et al.]. N.Y. : McGraw-Hill, 1953–55. 3 v. : diagrs. **EB79**
Prepared at the California Institute of Technology under contract with the Office of Naval Research.
An extensive compilation of functions notable for its breadth of scope and depth of treatment. Functions are arranged in 19 topical chapters with chapter bibliographies. Each volume has a subject index and an index of notations. QA351.B2

——————— Tables of integral transforms : based, in part, on notes left by Harry Bateman, and comp. by the staff of the Bateman Manuscript Project / Arthur Erdélyi, ed. ... [et al.]. N.Y. : McGraw-Hill, 1954. 2 v. **EB80**
Prepared at the California Institute of Technology under contract with the Office of Naval Research.
Intended as a companion to the Bateman Project's *Higher transcendental functions* (EB79), this very extensive compilation of integral transforms was designed to "be used in conjunction with other existing tables" and "concentrate[s] mostly on integrals involving higher transcendental functions"—*Introd.* Functions are organized in topical chapters with chapter bibliographies. Each volume has an index of notations. QA351.B22

Beyer, William H. CRC handbook of tables for probability and statistics. 2nd ed. Cleveland : Chemical Rubber Co., [1968]. 642 p. **EB81**
1st ed., 1966.
The 2nd ed. incorporates corrections of errors detected in the 1st ed., and includes expanded and additional tables and graphs. Offers a brief textual survey on important theorems and functions, extensive sections of statistical tables and graphs, and a section of commonly used mathematical tables. Indexed. QA276.B44

British Association for the Advancement of Science. Mathematical tables. Cambridge : Publ. for the Assoc. at the Univ. Pr., 1931–52. 12 v. **EB82**
Contents: v. 1, 3rd ed. (1951), Circular and hyperbolic functions, exponential and sine and cosine integrals, factorial function and allied functions, hermitian probability functions; v. 2, Emden functions, being solutions of Emden's equation together with certain associated functions; v. 3, Minimum decompositions into fifth powers, prep. by L. E. Dickson; v. 4, Cycles of reduced ideals in quadratic fields, prep. by E. L. Ince; v. 5, Factor table, giving the complete decomposition of all numbers less than 100,000, prep. by J. Peters, A. Lodge, E. J. Ternouth, E. Gifford; v. 6, Bessel functions: pt. 1, Functions of orders zero and unity; v. 7, The probability integral, by W. F. Sheppard; v. 8, Number-divisor tables, designed and in part prep. by J. W. L. Glaisher; v. 9, Table of powers, giving integral powers of integers, initiated by J. W. L. Glaisher; v. 10, Bessel functions: pt. 2, Functions of positive integer order, by W. G. Bickley [and others]; [v. 11] pt. v. A, Legendre polynomials; [v. 12] pt. v. B, The Airy integral, giving tables of solutions of the differential equation y = xy, prep. by J. C. P. Miller.
Continued as: *Royal Society mathematical tables* (EB94). QA47.B7

Burington, Richard Stevens. Handbook of mathematical tables and formulas. 5th ed. N.Y. : McGraw-Hill, [1973]. 500 p. **EB83**
1st ed., 1933; 4th ed., 1965.

Intended "to meet the needs of students and workers in mathematics, engineering, physics, chemistry, science, and other fields in which mathematical reasoning, processes, and computations are required."— *Pref.* Pt. 1 offers summaries of the more important formulas and theorems of algebra, trigonometry, analytical geometry, calculus, and vector analysis; pt. 2 contains tables of logarithms, trigonometric functions, etc. Index of tables and subject index.

§ Serves as a companion to the *Handbook of probability and statistics, with tables* by R. S. Burington and D. C. May (EB63).

QA47.B8

CRC handbook of mathematical sciences. 5th ed. (1978)– . West Palm Beach, Fla. : CRC Pr., 1978– .   **EB84**

Title varies: 1st–2nd eds. (1962–64), *Handbook of mathematical tables*; 3rd–4th eds. (1967–75), *Handbook of tables for mathematics*.

Extensive compilation of formulas, tables, and other reference material in pure and applied mathematics of value to scientists, mathematicians, teachers, and students. In 13 topical sections with a subject index.

§ See also: *CRC standard mathematical tables and formulae* (29th ed. [1991]– . Boca Raton, Fla. : CRC Pr., c1991– . Irregular).

Title varies: 1st–9th eds. (1931–48), *Mathematical tables from the Handbook of chemistry and physics*; 10th–28th eds. (1954–87), *CRC standard mathematical tables*.

Currently a condensed version of the *CRC handbook*, but more frequently updated.

Gradshtein, Izrail Solomonovich. Table of integrals, series, and products / I. S. Gradshtein and I. M. Ryzhik ; Alan Jeffrey, ed. 5th ed. Boston : Academic Pr., c1994. xlvii, 1204 p. : ill.   **EB85**

4th ed., 1965; corr. and enl. ed., 1980.

Translated from the Russian by Scripta Technica, Inc.

A "corrected and expanded version of the previous English edition based on a translation of the fourth Russian edition" (*Pref.*): *Tablitsy integralov, summ, riadov i proizvedenii* (Moscow : Gosundarstvennoe Izdatel'stvo Fiziko-Matematicheskoy Literatury, 1963).

Provides comprehensive coverage of elementary functions and special functions and their definite and indefinite integrals. Integrals are organized within a unique classification system. Entries are keyed to bibliographic sources listed at the end of the volume, and the original numbering system for entries has been retained. List of supplementary references.   QA55.G6613

Haan, David Bierens de. Nouvelles tables d'intégrales définies. Ed. of 1867, corr.; with an English translation of the introd. by J. F. Ritt. N.Y. : Stechert, 1939. 716 p.   **EB86**

Reissued : N.Y. : Hafner, 1957.

Classified arrangement of 8,339 functions of definite integrals. Includes references to discussions of the functions in earlier works of the author.

Hansen, Eldon R. A table of series and products. Englewood Cliffs, N.J. : Prentice-Hall, [1975]. 523 p.   **EB87**

A systematic table of series and products. Provides systematic access not only to series involving elementary and special functions, but also to numerical power series, which are written "in a canonical form so that a given numerical power series can be found … about as easily as one finds a given numbered page in a book. … The 'average' reader finding a series in the literature will almost certainly also find his [sic] series in this table." —*Pref.*   QA295.H25

Mathematical Tables Project. [Mathematical tables] / prep. by the Mathematical Tables Project, Work Projects Administration of the Federal Works Agency. Conducted under the sponsorship of the Nat. Bureau of Standards. …. N.Y. : Columbia Univ. Pr., 1939–44. 40 v.   **EB88**

Originally published by the Work Projects Administration for the City of New York under sponsorship of the National Bureau of Standards. After 1942, when the WPA was discontinued, the work was taken over by the National Bureau of Standards; later volumes were published by Columbia University Press. Many of the tables have been reissued by the NBS in its *Applied mathematics series* (EB78).

Mathematics of computation. v. 14, no. 69 (Jan. 1960)– . Wash. : Nat. Academy of Sciences-Nat. Research Council, [1960]– . Quarterly.   **EB89**

Continues: *Mathematical tables and other aids to computation* (v. 1 [1943] – 13 [1959]).

Serves as a "clearing-house for information concerning mathematical tables and other aids to computation."—*Introd to v. 1.* Each issue includes a section entitled Reviews and descriptions of tables and books (former title: Recent mathematical tables), which provides extensive reviews of new tables and a listing of reported errors in published tables.   QA47.M29

Pearson, Egon Sharpe. Biometrika tables for statisticians / ed. by E. S. Pearson and H. O. Hartley. 3rd ed., repr. with corrections. London : Biometrika Trust, 1976. 2 v.   **EB90**

Vol. 1 is a corrected reprint of the 3rd ed., 1976 (originally publ. 1954; 2nd ed. 1958); v. 2 is a corrected reprint of the 1st ed. of that volume published 1972. The work represents a revision and expansion of *Tables for statisticians and biometricians*, ed. by Karl Pearson (1st ed., Cambridge : Cambridge Univ. Pr., 1914; 3rd ed., 1948).

Taken together, these two volumes of tables cover the vast majority of situations encountered by statisticians. Vol. 1 contains all the more commonly used tables; more specialized tables are in v. 2. Each volume has an extensive introduction defining the functions covered and describing their use; illustrative examples are given.

QA276.P431

Prudnikov, Anatoliĭ Platonovich. Integrals and series / A. P. Prudnikov, IU. A. Brychkov, O. I. Marichev ; tr. from the Russian by N. M. Queen. N.Y. : Gordon & Breach, c1986–92. v. 1–5. (In progress).   **EB91**

Translation of: *Integraly i riady* (Moskva : Nauka, 1981–).

Contents: v. 1, Elementary functions; v. 2, Special functions; v. 3, More special functions; v. 4, Direct Laplace transforms; v. 5, Inverse Laplace transforms.

An extensive collection of up-to-date mathematical tables. Each volume includes a detailed table of contents, bibliography, and index of notations.   QA308.P7813

Råde, Lennart. Beta mathematics handbook : concepts, theorems, methods, algorithms, formulas, graphs, tables / Lennart Råde, Bertil Westergren. 2nd ed. Lund [Sweden] : Studentlitteratur ; Boca Raton, Fla. : CRC Pr., 1990. 494 p. : ill.   **EB92**

1st ed., 1988.

A well-formatted handbook that organizes information in pure and applied mathematics, probability and statistics, and numerical analysis in 19 topical chapters. "Intended for students and teachers of mathematics, science and engineering professionals working in these areas."—*Pref.* Subject index.   QA41.R33

Rand Corporation. A million random digits : with 100,000 normal deviates. Glencoe, Ill. : Free Pr., [1955]. 400, 200 p.   **EB93**

Contains exclusive tables of random digits and Gaussian deviates, useful for statistical sampling. Introduction includes information on how to use these tables effectively.   QA276.5.R3

Royal Society (Great Britain). Royal Society mathematical tables. Cambridge : Univ. Pr., 1950–68. 11 v.   **EB94**

Continues: *Mathematical tables* issued by the British Association for the Advancement of Science (EB82).

Contents: v. 1, E. H. Neville. Farey series of order 1025 (1950); v. 2, E. H. Neville. Rectangular-polar conversion tables (1956); v. 3, J. C. P. Miller. Table of binomial coefficients (1954); v. 4, H. Gupta [and others]. Tables of partitions (1958); v. 5, H. Gupta [and others]. Representations of primes by quadratic forms (1960); v. 6, C. B. Haselgrove and J. C. P. Miller. Tables of the Riemann Zeta function (1960); v. 7, F. W. J. Olver. Bessel functions, pt. 3: Zeros and associated values (1960); v. 8, W. E. Mansell. Tables of natural and common logarithms to 110 decimals (1964); v. 9, A. E. Western and J. C. P. Miller. Tables of indices and primitive roots (1968); v. 10, A. Young and A. Kirk. Bessel functions, pt. 4: Kelvin functions (1964); v. 11, A. R. Curtis. Coulomb wave functions (1964).

Selected tables in mathematical statistics. Providence, R.I. : Amer. Mathematical Soc., 1970–1988. v. 1–11. (In progress). **EB95**

Vol. 1 originally publ. : Chicago : Markham.

Volumes issued jointly by the Institute of Mathematical Statistics and the American Mathematical Society.

Each volume contains one or more sections of tables on specific topics, with introductory notes and references for each. Further volumes are planned. QA276.25.S43

Thompson, Alexander John. Logarithmetica Britannica : being a standard table of logarithms to 20 decimal places. Cambridge : Univ. Pr., 1924–52. 9 v. (Tracts for computers, no. 11, etc.). **EB96**

Repr. : 1952, 1967, each in two volumes, by Cambridge Univ. Pr. Contents: pt. 1, no.10,000–20,000 (1934); pt. 2, no. 20,000–30,000 (1952); pt. 3, no. 30,000–40,000 (1937); pt. 4, no. 40,000–50,000 (1928); pt. 5, no. 50,000–60,000 (1931); pt. 6, no. 60,000–70,000 (1933); pt. 7, no. 70,000–80,000 (1935); pt. 8, no. 80,000–90,000 (1927); pt. 9, no. 90,000–100,000 (1924). QA55.T4

Style manuals

Chaundy, Theodore W. The printing of mathematics : aids for authors and editors and rules for compositors and readers at the University Press, Oxford / by T. W. Chaundy, P. R. Barrett and Charles Batey. 2nd impression, rev. London : Oxford Univ. Pr., 1957. 109 p. : ill. **EB97**

First publ. 1954.

A reference work for authors and printers that discusses "technical problems which are peculiar to the composition of mathematics."—*Pref.* Includes sections on: (1) The mechanics of mathematical printing; (2) Recommendations to mathematical authors; (3) Rules for the composition of mathematics at the University Press, Oxford. Subject index. Z250.6.M3C5

Higham, N. J. Handbook of writing for the mathematical sciences. Philadelphia : Soc. for Industrial and Applied Mathematics, 1993. 241 p. : ill. **EB98**

A guide to mathematical writing designed primarily for graduate students. Includes chapters on standard English usage, writing papers and talks, the publishing process, and using computers for writing and research. Appendixes of Greek symbols, TeX and LaTeX symbols, GNU EMACS commands, mathematical organizations, and expository writing prize winners. Brief glossary, extensive bibliography, and subject index. QA42.H54

Swanson, Ellen. Mathematics into type : copy editing and proofreading of mathematics for editorial assistants and authors. Rev. ed. Providence, R.I. : Amer. Mathematical Soc., 1979. 90 p. **EB99**

1st ed., 1971.

"Covers the publication of mathematics from manuscript to the printed book or journal, with emphasis on the preparation of copy for the compositor and the proofreading and makeup of the publication."—*Pref.* Glossary, bibliography, and index.

Biography

Biographical dictionary of mathematicians : reference biographies from the Dictionary of scientific biography. N.Y. : Scribner : Maxwell Macmillan International, 1991. 4 v. (2696 p.) : ill. **EB100**

Publ. under the auspices of the American Council of Learned Societies.

A collection of 1,023 essays from *Dictionary of scientific biography* (EA176). Most entries are for mathematicians, but also included

are "many intellectual giants outside the formal profession of mathematics" who enriched the "science of numbers"—*Pref.* Name and subject index; list of mathematicians by field; chronology index. QA28.B534

The biographical dictionary of scientists : mathematicians / gen. ed., David Abbott. 1st American ed. N.Y. : P. Bedrick Books, 1986. 175 p. : ill. **EB101**

First publ. London : Blond Educational, 1985.

Presents concise biographical articles for a select group of 179 prominent mathematicians, predominantly historical figures. Includes brief historical introduction, glossary of mathematical terms, and name index. QA28.B54

Taylor, Eva Germaine Rimington. The mathematical practitioners of Hanoverian England, 1714–1840. London : Cambridge Univ. Pr. for the Inst. of Navigation, 1966. 503 p. : front., 12 plates (incl. ports.). **EB102**

"A sequel to *The mathematical practitioners of Tudor and Stuart England* [EB103] by the same author."—*t.p.* With that work, an important reference source for the history of science.

A narrative of the scientific and technical advances of the period is followed by 2,282 biographical sketches of mathematicians, including teachers, philosophers, and makers of mathematical, optical, and nautical instruments. Indexed.

An index to The mathematical practitioners of Hanoverian England, 1714–1840 by E. G. R. Taylor, comp. by Kate Bostock, Susan Hurt, Michael Hurt from the 1966 edition, publ. by Cambridge Univ. Pr. (London : H. Wynter, 1980. 23 p.).

A listing in one alphabetical sequence of all of the practitioners in the biographical section of Taylor's book; in that work the biographies are divided into 14 groups by dated period, and only those accorded six lines or more are indexed. QA27.G7T28

———————— The mathematical practitioners of Tudor and Stuart England. Cambridge : publ. for the Inst. of Navigation at the Univ. Pr., 1954. 442 p., [10] leaves of plates : ill., facsim., fold. map, ports. **EB103**

Repr. : Costa Mesa, Calif. : Knowledge Resources, Inc., 1985.

In three parts: (1) a narrative account of mathematical practice and the work of outstanding mathematicians of the period 1485–1715; (2) biographies of 582 practitioners; and (3) a list of "Works on mathematical arts and practices, with descriptive notes," plus a "Bibliography of secondary works consulted." Indexed. QA27.G7T3

Women of mathematics : a biobibliographic sourcebook / ed. by Louise S. Grinstein and Paul J. Campbell. N.Y. : Greenwood, 1987. 292 p. **EB104**

Contains 43 essays about important women mathematicians from ancient times to the present. Written primarily by women mathematicians, each essay includes biographical information, a detailed discussion of the individual's mathematical work, and a bibliography of works by and about the individual. Broader in scope than either L. M. Osen's *Women in mathematics* (Cambridge, Mass. : MIT Pr., 1974) or T. Perl's *Math equals : biographies of women mathematicians + related activities* (Menlo Park, Calif. : Addison-Wesley, 1978), both of which emphasize biographical rather than mathematical information. QA28.W66

EC

Astronomy

GENERAL WORKS

Guides

Databases & on-line data in astronomy / ed. by Miguel A. Albrecht and Daniel Egret. Dordrecht ; Boston : Kluwer Academic Publishers, c1991. 273 p. : ill., maps. (Astrophysics and space science library, v. 171).   **EC1**

Describes current and developing astronomical archives, data repositories, and information systems derived from space missions and from large, ground-based observatories as well as online bibliographic and reference sources. Chapters are written by practicing astronomers and astrophysicists and describe the history, purpose, content, method of access, and products of a variety of astronomical systems and networks. List of acronyms; general index. Updates and extends guides of printed information sources.   QB51.3.E43D38

Kemp, D. Alasdair. Astronomy and astrophysics : a bibliographical guide. London : Macdonald Technical and Scientific ; Hamden, Conn. : Archon Books, 1970. 584 p.   **EC2**

A standard reference source for astronomy. Most of the 3,642 annotated entries are for materials published post-World War II to 1969. Arrangement is chronological within a unique classification system of 75 sections that begins with reference media, star catalogs, and ephemerides and ends with sections on stellar evolution, cosmology, abundance and origin of the elements, and cosmo-, gamma-, and x-ray astronomy. Author and subject indexes.

§ Robert A. Seal and Sarah S. Martin's *A bibliography of astronomy, 1970–1979* (EC18) provides an update.   Z5151.K45

Lusis, Andy. Astronomy and astronautics : an enthusiast's guide to books and periodicals. N.Y. : Facts on File, c1986. 292 p.   **EC3**

Intends to "provide a comprehensive, annotated list of books and periodicals on astronomy and astronautics in English ... below the professional or undergraduate level."—*Introd.* There are seven topical sections: General astronomy; Practical astronomy; History of astronomy; Astronomy plus (multi- and interdisciplinary works); Astrophysics; The solar system; and Astronautics. Within each section, entries are arranged alphabetically by author under form or topical subheadings. Informative annotations indicate readership level, special features, and note comparable publications. Emphasizes works published since 1977, excluding maps, nonprint media, and computer software. Author, title and subject indexes.   Z5151.L87

Seal, Robert A. A guide to the literature of astronomy. Littleton, Colo. : Libraries Unlimited, 1977. 306 p.   **EC4**

Serves as an introduction to the literature of astronomy. "Full bibliographic data, annotations, and a brief evaluation are provided for each work. The guide is intended mainly for those individuals who are totally unfamiliar with astronomical information, or who wish to gain better knowledge of the literature than they currently possess."—*Introd.* Indexed.   Z5151.S4

Bibliography

Baranowski, Henryk. Bibliografia kopernikowska. Warszawa : Państwowe Wydawnictwo Naukowe, 1958– . v. 1–2. (In progress?).   **EC5**

At head of title: Polska Akademia Nauk. Komitet Historii Nauki. Contents: v. 1, 1509–1955; v. 2, 1956–71.

Lists some 5,000 works by and about Copernicus; supersedes earlier bibliographies. Aims to be universal in scope, although a high percentage of titles is in Polish. Includes books, periodical articles, and parts of books. Author index.   Z8192.5.B3

Collard, Auguste. L'astronomie et les astronomes. Bruxelles : Van Oest, 1921. 119 p.   **EC6**

A classed catalog with author index, of works published after 1880; supplements Jean Charles Houzeau and Albert Lancaster's *Bibliographie générale de l'astronomie jusqu'en 1880* (EC13).   Z5151.C69

Collea, Beth A. A selected bibliography on Native American astronomy / Beth A. Collea and Anthony F. Aveni. Hamilton, N.Y. : Colgate Univ., Dept. of Physics and Astronomy, 1978. 148 p.   **EC7**

A bibliography compiled from the literature of "archaeology, ethnology, geography and architecture as well as astronomy to examine the evidence of the practice of astronomy ... [among] the aboriginal inhabitants of the two New World continents. Information included deals with astronomy before European contact as well as post-contact survivals of these practices."—*Pref.* The 1,480 citations from books and journals are arranged by author. Subject index.

Supplement to a selected bibliography on Native American astronomy, by Beth A. Collea, Anthony F. Aveni, Marilyn C. Wyzga ([s.l. : s.n., 1982]. 29 l.). 303 citations to books and articles published between 1970–81 with some earlier references. No introduction or index.   Z5151.C65

Collins, Mike J. Astronomical catalogues, 1951–75. [London] : INSPEC, c1977. 325 p. (INSPEC bibliography series, no. 2).   **EC8**

"Presents a collection of nearly 2500 catalogues ... covering ... 1951 to 1975 inclusive. Some catalogues published in 1976 and 1977 are also included. The bibliography contains lists of celestial objects, phenomena and equipment as well as books and slides. Each entry contains full bibliographic details and most have an abstract and a summary."—*Abstract.* Author, corporate author, and designation indexes.   Z5154.S8C64

DeVorkin, David H. The history of modern astronomy and astrophysics : a selected, annotated bibliography. N.Y. : Garland, 1982. 434 p. (Bibliographies of the history of science and technology, v. 1; Garland reference library of the humanities, 304).   **EC9**

The period covered "begins with the invention and application of the telescope to astronomy ... emphasis is placed upon the literature of recent astronomy, dating from the middle of the 19th to the middle of the 20th century."—*Introd.* Contains popular and scholarly works which are reasonably accessible in major public and university libraries. The 1,417 annotated citations are grouped as: Bibliographies; General histories; National and institutional histories; Instrumentation; Descriptive astronomy; Theoretical astronomy; Positional astronomy; Astrophysics; Biographical, autobiographical and collected works; and Textbooks and popular works. The index merges author, institution, and subject entries.   Z5154.H57D48

Drake, Milton. Almanacs of the United States. N.Y. : Scarecrow, 1962. 2 v.   **EC10**

For annotation, *see* AB103.   Z1231.A6D7

Freitag, Ruth S. Halley's comet : a bibliography. Wash. : Library of Congress : For sale by U.S. Govt. Print. Off., 1984. 555 p. : ill.   **EC11**

Superintendent of Documents classification: LC 33.9/2:H15.

An extensive bibliography that lists works about the history, popular reaction to, and scientific study of Halley's comet. Most entries cite "books, parts of books, pamphlets and reports, and articles in journals, selected newspapers, conference proceedings, encyclopedias, and other collections" (*Pref.*), but personal recollections, letters, fiction, drama, music, and early broadsides and news sheets are also included. The 3,235 entries are alphabetically arranged by main entry; many are annotated and cite additional sources. Locations and call numbers at the Library of Congress or other North American and European libraries are provided. Bibliography of sources; a list of perihelion dates for the appearance of the comet (1404 BCE–1986); name and topical indexes. Z5154.H2F74

Grassi, Giovanna. Union catalogue of printed books of 15th, 16th and 17th centuries in European astronomical observatories. Manziana, Roma : Vecchiarelli, 1989. 1040 p. **EC12**

Contains some 6,000 alphabetically arranged entries for works in all areas of the physical sciences, including astronomy, astrology, chemistry, mathematics, and physics as reported by 51 European astronomical institutes. Listings are concise and arranged by author, then title. Anonymous works are listed by subject. Includes chronological index and index of printers and publishers for the 15th and 16th centuries. Based on an earlier work, *Union catalogue of printed books of the XV and XVI centuries in astronomical European observatories* (Rome : Rome Astronomical Observatory Library, 1977. 105 p.).
Z5152.G73

Houzeau, Jean Charles. Bibliographie générale de l'astronomie jusqu'en 1880 / par J. C. Houzeau et A. Lancaster. Nouv. éd. / avec. introd. et table des auteurs par D. W. Dewhirst. London : Holland Pr., 1964. 2 v. in 3. **EC13**

Added title page in English: General bibliography of astronomy to the year 1880.

Contents: v. 1, pt. 1–2, Ouvrages séparés, tant imprimés que manuscrits; v. 2, Mémoires et notices insérés dans les collections académiques et les revues.

A major bibliographic source for historical references, first published 1880–89, 2 v. in 3. This edition is largely a reprint of the original work (which was issued in 5 pts.), retaining the original page numbering of the bibliography proper, with some additional material—chiefly a new "Editorial introduction" and a name index to v. 1, pts. 1–2, by D. W. Dewhirst. A third volume intended to cover astronomical observations was never published. Z5151.H84

International Astronomical Union. Bibliography of astronomy, 1881–1898, on microfilm. Buckinghamshire, Eng. : Univ. Microfilms Ltd., 1970. 18 reels. **EC14**

Prepared by P. Stroobant, 1932–1936, and by the Belgian National Committee for Astronomy, 1938–1965.

Accompanying guide (16 p.) by J. B. Sykes.

The literature of this period, more than 52,000 items, was recorded by the Observatoire Royal de Belgique. The purpose "is to fill the gap which previously existed between two great works of astronomical bibliography: the *Bibliographie générale de l'astronomie jusqu'en 1880* by J. C. Houzeau and A. Lancaster [EC13], which dealt with publications up to 1880 and the *Astronomischer Jahresbericht* [EC22]."—*Guide, p. 15.* Arrangement is by subject within nine two-year periods, and is based on that used in *Astronomischer Jahresbericht.*

International catalogue of scientific literature / publ. for the Internat. Council by the Royal Soc. of London. v. 1 (1901)–v. 14 (1914). London : Harrison, 1902–21. **EC15**

Section E, Astronomy. For full description, *see* EA16.

Lalande, Joseph Jérôme le Français de. Bibliographie astronomique : avec l'histoire de l'astronomie depuis 1781 jusqu'à 1802. Paris : Impr. de la République, 1803. 966 p. **EC16**

Repr. : Amsterdam : Gieben, 1970.

Covers the period 480 BCE through 1803 CE. Approximately 5,000 titles are arranged chronologically. Coverage predates that of *Bibliography of astronomy 1881–1898* (EC14). Author and subject indexes. Z5151.L19

Reuss, Jeremias David. Repertorium commentationum a societatibus litterariis editarum / secundum disciplinarum ordinem digessit I. D. Reuss …. Gottingae : apud Henricum Dieterich, 1801–21. 16 v. **EC17**

T. 5, Astronomia. For full description, *see* EA21. Z5051.R44

Seal, Robert A. A bibliography of astronomy, 1970–1979 / Robert A. Seal, Sarah S. Martin. Littleton, Colo. : Libraries Unlimited, 1982. 407 p. **EC18**

An updating of D. Alasdair Kemp's *Astronomy and astrophysics : a bibliographic guide* (EC2). The arrangement of the text is by the classification system of *Astronomy and astrophysics abstracts* (EC23). The list of 2,119 items "is fairly comprehensive in its coverage of review and bibliographic sources … Exclusions [include] primarily those items only indirectly related to astronomy, such as general optics, plasma physics, time astronautics, etc."—*Introd.* History is covered only by bibliographic materials. The appendix includes listings of the International Astronomical Union Symposia 1969–1979, and the abbreviations used. Indexes for monographic title/conference proceedings, author and subject. Z5151.S38

Sunal, Dennis W. Astronomy education materials resource guide / Dennis W. Sunal and V. Carol Demchik, editors. 3rd ed. Morgantown, W. Va. : West Virginia Univ., c1985. 187 p. **EC19**

1st ed., 1982.

"A project completed under the Astronomy Education Materials Network, Division of Education, College of Human Resources and Education, West Virginia University and supported by the V.M. Slipher Fund of the National Academy of Sciences."—*t.p.*

Attempts to facilitate the dissemination of "non-published or difficult to find educational materials used with pre-school through college and adult students."—*Introd.* The 230 entries are arranged by type of instructional material, e.g., laboratory and field activities, assessment instruments, films, slides, video tapes, games, simulations, planetarium lessons, and computer programs. Each entry includes source and address, cost, educational level, and a general description. Supplemented by abstracts for astronomy publications indexed in the ERIC database, 1966–85. No index. QB62.N4

Zinner, Ernst. Geschichte und Bibliographie der astronomischen Literatur in Deutschland zur Zeit der Renaissance. Stuttgart : Anton Hiersemann, 1964. 480 p. **EC20**

1st ed., 1941.

An unaltered reprint of the 1941 ed., together with a new supplement. Covers 1448–1630 in chronological arrangement, with author index. Includes astronomical works and works in related fields if they affected the development of astronomy as a science. Z5152.Z5

Periodicals

Lola, Judith A. Union list of astronomy serials. [S.l.] : Special Libraries Association, Physics-Astronomy-Mathematics Div., 1983. 170 p. **EC21**

Brief listings for some 2,300 current and retrospective serial titles in astronomy, astrophysics, and related subjects. Augmented by holdings information for 14 major American academic and observatory libraries. Z5153.L65

Abstract journals

Astronomischer Jahresbericht. Bd. 1 (1899)–68 (1968). Berlin : W. de Gruyter, 1900–1969. Annual. **EC22**

A comprehensive, classed bibliography covering the literature from all countries appearing in the year preceding publication. Titles are given in the language of publication, with transliteration provided for Russian-language entries. Abstracts, appearing more frequently in the earlier volumes, are in German. Classed arrangement, e.g., Instrumente; Sonne; Erde; Interplanetare Objekte; Sterne; Doppelsterne; Mehrfachsterne. Author and subject indexes.

§ Continued by *Astronomy and astrophysics abstracts* (EC23).

QB1.A797

Astronomy and astrophysics abstracts. v. 1 (1969)– . Berlin ; N.Y. : Springer-Verlag, 1969– . Semiannual.   **EC23**
Continues *Astronomischer Jahresbericht* (EC22).
"A publication of the Astronomisches Rechen-Institut Heidelberg produced in cooperation with the Fachinformationszentrum Karlsruhe, *Astronomy and astrophysics abstracts* is prepared under the auspices of the International Astronomical Union."—*t. p., v. 56, 1992.*
"Aims to present a comprehensive documentation of the literature concerning all aspects of astronomy, astrophysics, and their neighbouring fields."—*Pref., v. 56.* The text of the abstracts is primarily in English with some in French or German. Popular articles are not abstracted. Abstracts are arranged in a unique classification system. There is a "concordance relation" between it and *International classification system for physics* (2nd ed. Paris : International Council of Scientific Unions Abstracting Board, 1978). Each volume includes: list of abbreviations; periodicals, proceedings, books, and activities; author, subject, and (since v. 39), object indexes.
Author, subject, and object (v. 39–) indexes are issued periodically as numbered volumes of the set: v. 1–10, 1969–73 in v. 15/16; v. 11–14 and v. 17–22, 1974–78 in v. 23/24; v. 25–34, 1979–83 in v. 35/36; and v. 37–46, 1984–1988 in v. 47/48.
•Most of the information in recent volumes of *Astronomy and astrophysics abstracts* has been incorporated into *Physics briefs online* [database] (N.Y. : American Institute of Physics, 1979–). For complete information, *see* ED10.   Z5153.A862

Encyclopedias

The astronomy and astrophysics encyclopedia / ed. by Stephen P. Maran ; foreword by Carl Sagan. N.Y. : Van Nostrand Reinhold, c1992. 1002 p. : ill.   **EC24**
The 403 topical articles "attempt to provide an authoritative summary of current knowledge of astronomy and astrophysics, including the exploration of the solar system."—*Pref.* Directed to the scientifically literate reader, teacher, or writer, the articles are written by astronomers and other professionals in the discipline. Numerous black-and-white illustrations, tables and diagrams, article bibliographies, and detailed subject index make this the new, standard reference encyclopedia for college and university library collections.   QB14.A873

The Cambridge encyclopaedia of astronomy / ed. in chief, Simon Mitton. N.Y. : Crown, 1977. 481 p. : ill.   **EC25**
Prepared by astronomers, the encyclopedia retains its usefulness as a broad-based survey of astronomy. The 23 major topics, which have "been gathered into cohesive themes in order to present a more accurate and understandable guide to the new Universe" (*Introd.*), are intended for amateur and professional. The index is specific and extensive with references to the main text, photographs, and diagrams. A 14–page "Star atlas" of stars visible to the naked eye in the Northern and Southern hemispheres, and "An outline of physics" are provided in the appendixes.   QB43.2.C35

Encyclopedia of astronomy and astrophysics / Robert A. Meyers, ed. ; Steven N. Shore, scientific consultant. San Diego, Calif. : Academic Pr., c1989. 807 p. : ill.   **EC26**
Contains 41 signed essays, many derived from *Encyclopedia of physical science and technology* (EA79), arranged alphabetically by topic. Each includes a glossary and short bibliography. There are more than 300 black-and-white photographs and illustrations, numerous tables, and a general subject index. Intended for a broad audience, but

most useful to those with some knowledge of the subject, since there are variations in coverage and style. Reviewed in *Sky and telescope* 79 (Feb. 1990): 169–70.   QB14.E53

Encyclopedia of cosmology : historical, philosophical, and scientific foundations of modern cosmology / ed. by Norriss S. Hetherington. N.Y. : Garland, 1993. 686 p. : ill. (Garland reference library of the humanities, v. 1250).   **EC27**
Arranged alphabetically, combining lengthy, signed essays with shorter, factual definitions and biographical notes. The 53 contributors include scientific researchers and historians and philosophers of science. Historical and contemporary Western cosmological theories are described as are those of some Asian, Islamic, and Native American cultures. Article bibliographies, cross-references, and name/subject index.   QB980.5.E53

Handbuch der Astrophysik / hrsg. von G. Eberhard, A. Kohlschütter, H. Ludendorff .... Berlin : Springer, 1928–36. 7 v. in 10. : ill.   **EC28**
Contents: v. 1–3, W. E. Bernheimer [et al.], Grundlagen der Astrophysik; v. 4, Georgio Abetti, Das Sonnensystem; v. 5–6, Friedrich Becker [et al.], Das Sternsystem; v. 7, Ergänzungsband, Berücksichtigend die Literatur bis ende 1934. Generalregister.
A classic source that remains useful for retrospective literature reviews and articles on basic astronomical principles. Chapters by specialists are in German or English.   QB461.H3

Handbuch der Physik / hrsg. von S. Flugge. Berlin : Springer, 1955–88. v. 1–55 in 78 parts.   **EC29**
Vols. 50–54, Astrophysik/Astrophysics, contain authoritative articles with extensive bibliographies. For full annotation, *see* ED17.   QC21.H327

The international encyclopedia of astronomy / ed. by Patrick Moore. N.Y. : Orion Books, c1987. 464 p. : ill. (some col.).   **EC30**
Seven longer essays on the universe, the "big bang," space exploration, interstellar matter, moons, pulsars, and superclusters are interspersed in an alphabetic arrangement of about 2,500 short articles. Most articles are signed and many are illustrated with diagrams, charts, and photographs; many biographical entries include portraits. A four-page supplement has standard data about stellar objects. No index. Useful as a general reference to both historic and contemporary developments in astronomy and astrophysics.   QB14.I58

Lewis, Richard S. The illustrated encyclopedia of the universe : exploring and understanding the cosmos. N.Y. : Harmony Books, c1983. 320 p. : ill. (some col.).   **EC31**
Twelve space scientists and science journalists offer 20 essays on the origin of the universe, the solar system, and space exploration. Emphasis is placed on the details of space exploration, with extensive descriptions of the lunar and planetary missions undertaken by the U.S. and the Soviet Union. The color photographs, charts, maps, and drawings make this work atlas-like in presentation. Short bibliographies supplement each essay section. Subject index.   QB501.2.L48

Dictionaries

The Facts on File dictionary of astronomy / ed. by Valerie Illingworth. 2nd ed. N.Y. : Facts on File, 1985. 437 p. : ill.   **EC32**
1st ed., 1979.
Publ. in U.K. as *Macmillan dictionary of astronomy*.
Containing more than 2,300 entries, this revised and expanded edition covers all areas of astronomy and astrophysics. Definitions are written for the educated reader and astronomy student, and include arithmetical and astrophysical notations and helpful cross-references. 12 tables with general astronomical data supplement the text. No index.   QB14.F3

Heck, André. Acronyms & abbreviations in astronomy, space sciences, & related fields. Strasbourg, France : Observatoire Astronomique, 1990. 218 p. (Publication spéciale du C.D.S., no. 15). **EC33**

An alphabetical list of some 15,000 acronyms and abbreviations with their parent terms for organizations, procedures, equipment, etc., in astronomy, space sciences, and several related disciplines in the physical sciences and engineering. Prepared as a complement to the directory, *Astronomy, space sciences, and related organizations of the world* (EC44). No index. QB14.H42

Hopkins, Jeanne. Glossary of astronomy and astrophysics. 2nd ed. Chicago : Univ. of Chicago Pr., [1980]. 224 p. **EC34**

1st ed., 1976.

"This volume is published under the auspices of *Astrophysical journal*."—*verso of t. p.*

Offers brief definitions of the most commonly used terms in astronomy and astrophysics. An expanded and updated revision. QB14.H69

Mitton, Jacqueline. A concise dictionary of astronomy. Oxford ; N.Y. : Oxford Univ. Pr., 1991. 423 p. : ill. **EC35**

Publ. in paperback as: *The Penguin dictionary of astronomy* (London ; N.Y. : Penguin, 1993).

More than 2,400 brief entries on all aspects of astronomy and related fields. Appendix includes useful bibliography of sources and general astronomical tables. No index. Does not replace the older, more detailed *Facts on File dictionary of astronomy* (EC32). Reviewed and compared favorably with Dianne F. Moore's *HarperCollins dictionary of astronomy and space science* (N.Y. : HarperPerennial, 1992) in *Sky and Telescope* 84 (Sept. 1992): 289. QB14.M56

Moore, Patrick. Patrick Moore's A–Z of astronomy. N.Y. : Norton, 1987. 240 p. : ill. (some col.). **EC36**

First publ. as *The amateur astronomer's glossary*, 1967; rev. 1976 as *A–Z of astronomy*.

This all-purpose dictionary, intended for a general readership, combines short descriptive definitions with many photographs and diagrams of astronomical objects and instruments. Also has useful historical and biographical data. Indexed. QB14.M6

Room, Adrian. Dictionary of astronomical names. London ; N.Y. : Routledge, 1988. 282 p. : ill. **EC37**

Describes origins of the names for about 600 astronomical objects. Two lengthy appendixes list the names of lunar craters and minor planets (asteroids). Includes a short astronomical glossary and select bibliography of sources. No index. QB14.R66

Foreign terms

Anglo-russkiĭ astronomicheskiĭ slovar' : Okolo 20 000 terminov / Sost. ... O. A. Mel'nikov ... [et al.]. Moskva : "Sov. Éntsiklopediíã," 1971. 504 p. **EC38**

Added t.p.: English-Russian astronomical dictionary.

About 20,000 terms. English words and phrases are given with Russian equivalents. Separate listing for abbreviations and acronyms; specific names of galaxies, asteroids, etc., are grouped in another list. Observatory names, societies, and astronomical publications make up a fourth alphabetical arrangement. An index under Russian terms refers only to the word and phrase section. QB14.A54

Chinese-English glossary of astro-science terms / ed. by the Chinese-English Translation Assistance Group. Kensington, Md. : Dunwoody Pr., 1986. 129 p. **EC39**

Some 7,000 terms are represented in traditional Chinese characters followed by the pinyin romanization, the Standard telegraphic code number, and an English translation. QB14.C48

Chiu, Hong-yee. Chinese-English, English-Chinese astronomical dictionary. N.Y. : Consultants Bureau, 1966. 173 p. **EC40**

More than 3,000 terms with many Chinese characters represented by simplified stroke forms. The Chinese-English part is taken, in slightly modified form, from a Chinese-Russian-English astronomical nomenclature published by the Scientific Publishing House, Peking, in 1959; the English-Chinese section is new. QB14.C5

Kleczek, Josip. Space sciences dictionary / Josip Kleczek, Helena Kleczková. Amsterdam ; N.Y. : Elsevier, 1990–93. v. 1–4. (In progress). **EC41**

Contents: v. 1, Radiation/matter; v. 2, Motion/space flight/data; v. 3, Space technology/space research; v. 4, Earth sciences/solar system/deep space.

Contains terms used in space sciences, space technology, space research, and allied disciplines for six languages: English, French, German, Spanish, Portuguese, and Russian. Each volume consists of two parts: (1) terms in all languages arranged topically and (2) alphabetic indexes for each language. Invaluable source for college and university reference collections. QB497.K58

Vocabulaire d'astronomie : index allemand, anglais, italien, néerlandais / Conseil international de la langue française. Paris : Hachette, 1980. 329 p. : ill. **EC42**

About 1,000 terms are defined in French and give German and English equivalent terms. Indexes for German, English, Italian, and Dutch terms give French equivalent. Supplemental sections include an index to individuals cited in the text and a list of constellations. QB14.V6

Periodicals

Sky and telescope. v. 1 (1941)– . Cambridge, Mass. : Sky Publ. Corp., Harvard College Observatory, 1941– . Monthly. **EC43**

An excellent source for general current information and articles on popular topics. Illustrated, with fine color photography. Contains review articles, articles on current events, monthly star maps and calendars, reviews of important professional and amateur meetings, book reviews, etc. Good for all levels of interest. Indexed by author, title, departments and features, and selected topics and celestial objects.

—— *Cumulative index : volumes 1–70, 1941 November–1985 December*, comp. by Judith Lola Bausch (Cambridge, Mass. : Sky Publ. Corp., c1988. 297 p.).

Five separate cumulative indexes (title, author, department and features, topic and celestial object, and special supplement) were prepared from the annual indexes of the journal. QB1.S536

Directories

Astronomy, space sciences and related organizations of the world : A.Sp.Sc.R.O.W. .... 1991– . Strasbourg, France : Observatoire astronomique, c1991– . **EC44**

Merges and supersedes: *International directory of astronomical associations and societies* (Strasbourg, France : Centre de données de stellaires, Observatoire astronomique, 1985–90) and *International directory of professional astronomical institutions* (Strasbourg, France : Centre de données de Strasbourg, 1986–90).

An international directory of 6,000 associations, societies, scientific committees, agencies, companies, institutions, data centers, and related organizations serving astronomy, space sciences, and related disciplines in the physical and engineering sciences. Entries are alphabetical by country and include postal and electronic address, telephone and fax numbers, and brief descriptions of activities or purpose. Name and acronym index. Supplementary section on the size and foundation of astronomical societies and institutions. QB61.I59

Directory of physics & astronomy staff members. 1975/
76– . N.Y. : American Inst. of Physics, 1975/76– . Biennial
(1982/83–). **EC45**
  For annotation, *see* ED31. QC47.N75D57

Earth and astronomical sciences research centres. 3rd ed.
[Harlow, Essex, Eng.] : Longman ; Detroit : distr. by Gale,
1993. 605 p. **EC46**
  For annotation, *see* EF16. QE40.E25

Kirby-Smith, H. T. U.S. observatories : a directory and travel
guide. N.Y. : Van Nostrand Reinhold, [1976]. 173 p. : ill.
EC47
  A compilation of information about U.S. observatories and some
important museums and planetariums. Gives descriptions of facilities,
equipment, and the kind of work done, as well as histories and information on the availability of public tours. Indexed. QB81.K57

Handbooks

Allen, Clabon Walter. Astrophysical quantities. 3rd ed., repr.
with corrections. London : Athlone Pr. ; Atlantic Highlands,
N.J. : Humanities Pr., c1976. 310 p. : graphs. **EC48**
  1st ed., 1955; 2nd ed., 1963. 3rd ed. originally publ. 1973.
  "The intention of this book is to present the essential information
of astrophysics in a form that can be readily used. ... The information
is as up to date as possible."—*Pref*. "The book should contain all experimental and theoretical values, constants, and conversion factors
that are fundamental to astrophysical arguments."—*Introd*. Indexed.

CRC handbook of laser science and technology / ed., Marvin J. Weber. Boca Raton, Fla. : CRC Pr., [1982–90]. 5 v. and
suppl. **EC49**
  For annotation, *see* ED34. TA1675.L38

Gibson, Bob. The astronomer's sourcebook : the complete
guide to astronomical equipment, publications, planetariums,
organizations, events, and more. Rockville, Md. : Woodbine
House, 1992. 302 p. : ill. **EC50**
  Written for amateur observers, this astronomy vade mecum includes sources for astronomical supplies and computer software; book,
serial, and computer bulletin board lists; directories to observatories,
planetariums, museums, educational programs, and astronomical societies; historical and biographical notes; general astronomical data tables, and a glossary. Useful corporate, publication and subject indexes.
QB64.G43

Howard, Neale E. The telescope handbook and star atlas. Updated ed. N.Y. : Crowell, [1975]. 226 p. : ill. **EC51**
  First published 1967.
  An introduction and guide to telescopes and to observing the
heavens, for students and other beginning astronomers. The "Star
atlas" section includes the atlas, a gazetteer to 234 named stars, numerous tables of data for the observer, and the Messier Catalog with 104
familiar astronomical objects listed on a day-to-day basis. Appendixes
are mainly conversion tables. Glossary; index. QB63.H68

Kronk, Gary W. Comets : a descriptive catalog. Hillside,
N.J. : Enslow Publ., [1984]. 331 p. **EC52**
  Provides details about the discovery, magnitude, and physical
characteristics of some 650 comets observed from 371 BCE to 1982
CE. In two sections: long-period and non-period comets arranged by
date; and short-period comets arranged alphabetically by proper name.
Precise orbital information is not supplied. Brief reference list and
index by comet name. QB722.K76

Lang, Kenneth R. Astrophysical data. N.Y. : Springer-
Verlag, c1992–[1993?]. 2 v. : ill. **EC53**
  Contents: v. 1., Planets and stars; v. 2, Galaxies and the universe.

Provides "basic data for use by all scientists, from the amateur astronomer to the professional astrophysicist."—*Pref*. The text is
grouped topically into sections and consists of well-referenced tables
with occasional introductory notes. Compiled from both printed and
electronic sources, this handbook will serve the scientific and technical
community as a standard reference source. Well-indexed with a bibliography of sources. QB461.L35

———————— Astrophysical formulae : a compendium for
the physicist and astrophysicist. 2nd corrected and enl. ed.
Berlin ; N.Y. : Springer-Verlag, 1980. 783 p. : ill. **EC54**
  1st ed., 1974.
  A handbook of fundamental concepts in astrophysics and physics.
Five major sections: Continuum radiation; Monochromatic (line) radiation; Gas processes; Nuclear astrophysics and high energy particles;
Astrometry and cosmology. Equations, formulae, and short explanations are grouped topically within each section. Extensive bibliography. The 2nd ed. lists misprints and errors, and adds supplemental references for 1974–80 as an appendix, where they are grouped by chapter headings. Author and subject indexes. QB461.L35

Meeus, Jean. Astronomical algorithms. Richmond, Va. :
Willmann-Bell, c1991. 429 p. : ill. **EC55**
  An extensive revision of Meeus's *Astronomical formulae for calculators* (Richmond, Va. : Willmann-Bell, c1988. 208 p.), this edition
"intends to be a guide for the professional or amateur astronomer who
wants to do calculations."—*Introd*. Chapters are organized by specific
application or object and present the formulae and mathematical processes necessary to write microcomputer programs for astronomical observations. Subject index. QB51.3.E43M42

Robinson, J. Hedley. Astronomy data book / J. Hedley Robinson and James Muirden. 2nd ed. N.Y. : Wiley, c1979.
272 p., [1] fold. leaf of plates : ill. **EC56**
  1st ed., 1972.
  "This book is intended as a reference tool for the student and amateur astronomer and for those interested in the earth sciences. ... It is
intended that the observer shall use this book in conjunction with a
Star Atlas."—*Introd*. Brings together basic data and information on
such topics as the sun, the moon, planets, comets, etc. Includes a glossary and important historical dates. Index. QB64.R58

Royal Astronomical Society of Canada. The observer's
handbook. 1907– . Toronto : The Society, 1907– . Annual.
EC57
  Continues *Canadian astronomical handbook*.
  Narrative information and tabular data to assist amateur astronomers in their observations. Emphasizes the sky over Canada and the
northern U.S. QB9.R7

Zombeck, Martin V. Handbook of space astronomy and astrophysics. 2nd ed. Cambridge ; N.Y. : Cambridge Univ. Pr.,
1990. 440 p. **EC58**
  1st ed., 1982.
  A diversified reference work using tables, graphs, charts, and formulas drawn from sources in classical astronomy, astrophysics, physics, geophysics, and mathematics. Although intended for the practicing
astronomer and astrophysicist, it is a useful general compilation of the
most recent data for astrophysical quantities and events. Short bibliographies for each chapter and a general topical index. QB136.Z65

History

The general history of astronomy / gen. ed., Michael A.
Hoskin. Cambridge ; N.Y. : Cambridge Univ. Pr., 1984–1989.
v. 2, pt. A; v. 4, pt. A. : ill. (In progress). **EC59**
  Contents: v. 2, René Taton and Curtis Wilson, editors, Planetary
astronomy from the Renaissance to the rise of astrophysics : Pt. A,
Tycho Brahe to Newton; v. 4, Owen Gingerich, ed., Astrophysics and
twentieth-century astronomy to 1950 (Pt. A, 1984).

Published under the auspices of the International Astronomical Union and the International Union for the History and Philosophy of Science.

Written for nonspecialist readers, this set when complete will survey the development of astronomy from earliest times to the mid-1950s. Each volume consists of essays of 15–20 pages written by historians of astronomy, and includes short bibliographies and a volume index.   QB15.G38

Native American astronomy / ed. by Anthony F. Aveni. Austin, Tex. : Univ. of Texas Pr., 1977. 286 p.   **EC60**

"Edited version of papers presented at a symposium held … 1975."—*verso of t.p.*

Consists of contributed papers by specialists in both astronomy and astrophysics and on Native Americans. The subject coverage includes the records of astronomical events, use of solar observatories and calendars, and religious astronomical rites as evidenced by archaeological findings. Notes on contributors, references, and subject index.   E59.A8N37

Pannekoek, Antonie. A history of astronomy. N.Y. : Interscience, 1961. 521 p. : ill.   **EC61**

Translation of *De groei van ons wereldbeeld* (Amsterdam, 1951).

A comprehensive and scholarly history from antiquity to the late 1930s. Appendix A: Aristarchus' derivation of the sun's distance; Appendix B: Apollonius' derivation othe planets' stations; Appendix C: Newton's demonstration of the law of areas; Appendix D: Newton's derivation of the force of attraction. Indexed.   QB15.P283

Shapley, Harlow. A source book in astronomy / by Harlow Shapley and Helen E. Howarth. N.Y. : McGraw-Hill, 1929. 412 p. : ill.   **EC62**

Intends to be "a fairly comprehensive synopsis of the great contributions to astronomy of the past four hundred years (1500–1900)"—*Author's pref.* Consists of extracts from the classic works in the astronomical sciences, avoiding very technical and mathematical explanations. Indexed.

Continued by:

Source book in astronomy, 1900–1950, by Harlow Shapley (Cambridge, Mass. : Harvard Univ. Pr., 1960. 423 p.). 69 new contributions, arranged by topic, with name index.

A source book in astronomy and astrophysics, 1900–1975, ed. by Kenneth R. Lang and Owen Gingerich (Cambridge, Mass. : Harvard Univ. Pr., 1979. 922 p.). 132 selections with brief critical introductions. To some extent supersedes Shapley's 1900–50 work (above) but differs from it in selection of articles. Author and subject indexes.   QB3.S5

Biography

The biographical dictionary of scientists : astronomers / gen. ed., David Abbott. N.Y. : P. Bedrick Books, 1984. 204 p. : ill.   **EC63**

Presents 200 alphabetically arranged articles about historical figures as well as modern scientists. Few illustrations and no portraits. Includes a name and topics index and a glossary of astronomical terms. No principles for selection are given, articles are unsigned, and there is no bibliography.   QB35.B56

Atlases

Briggs, Geoffrey. The Cambridge photographic atlas of the planets / Geoffrey Briggs, Fredric Taylor. Cambridge : Cambridge Univ. Pr., 1982. 255 p. : ill., maps.   **EC64**

A compilation of 200 illustrations and maps with detailed description and information about Mercury, Venus, Earth and moon, Mars, the Jovian system, and the Saturnian system. No index.   QB605.B74

The Cambridge atlas of astronomy / ed. by Jean Audouze and Guy Israël. 2nd ed. Cambridge ; N.Y. : Cambridge Univ. Pr., c1988. 431 p. : ill. (some col.).   **EC65**

1st ed., 1985.

Translation of *Grand atlas de l'astronomie*.

Signed essays by 26 French astronomers and scientists are organized in five main sections: The sun; The solar system; Stars and the galaxy; Extragalactic domain; Scientific perspective. Heavily illustrated with photographs, satellite imagery, maps, and diagrams. Glossary, reading list, and alphabetic index of topics and objects supplement the text. A general astronomy encyclopedia for the educated reader, containing more scientific detail and greater coverage of extra-solar system bodies and phenomena than Patrick Moore's *The new atlas of the universe* (EC67).   QB65.G6813

Kopal, Zdeněk. A new photographic atlas of the moon. London : Hale ; N.Y. : Taplinger, [1971]. 311 p. : ill.   **EC66**

An earlier work (1965) had title: *Photographic atlas of the moon*.

Consists of about 200 photographs with explanatory text. Includes pictures taken from earth-based apparatus and from cameras on space vehicles near the moon. Tables of data on lunar spacecraft; glossary of terms; indexed.   QB595.K59

Moore, Patrick. The new atlas of the universe. N.Y. : Crown, c1984. 271 p. : ill. (some col.).   **EC67**

Title varies: 1st ed., 1970, called *The atlas of the universe*; rev. ed., 1974, called *The concise atlas of the universe*.

Completely revised from earlier editions, this atlas, intended for general readers, has four sections: The development of astronomy; The solar system; The outer universe; Into the future. A short introductory text precedes each pictorial feature. A catalog of stellar objects, glossary, "Beginner's guide to the heavens," and subject index complete the atlas. Many illustrations, photographs, maps, and charts are in color. The detailed maps of planetary surfaces, seasonal star maps, and list of constellations are useful.   QB44.2.M66

Rükl, Antonín. Atlas of the moon / Antonín Rükl ; ed. by T. W. Rackham. Waukesha, Wis. : Kalmbach Books, 1992. 224 p. : ill. (some col.).   **EC68**

A detailed map in 76 sections and based on an orthographic projection, portrays the near side of the moon at a scale of 1:2.5 million. Accompanying text for each section describes the principle features, locates lunar landing sites, and provides short, biographical notes about the names assigned to lunar formations. An introductory essay emphasizes observational details about the moon and recent developments in lunar cartography and nomenclature. A selection of lunar photographs, notes on observing, a list of future lunar eclipses, a glossary, and index of named formations supplement the atlas. The effective combination of photographic and cartographic imagery makes this atlas a good choice for general reference collections.   QB595.R8

The Times atlas of the moon / ed. by H. A. G. Lewis. London, [1969]. 110 p. : ill.   **EC69**

A brief introductory section covers: The moon; The far side; Mapping the moon; The lunar landscape; and Techniques of lunar flight. The atlas consists of 110 pages of maps at a scale of approximately 20 miles to 1 inch. Based on the work of the U.S. Air Force Aeronautical Chart and Information Center. Index and key to the maps.

STARS

Burnham, Robert. Burnham's celestial handbook. Rev. and enl. ed. N.Y. : Dover, [1978]. 3 v. : ill.   **EC70**

Subtitle: An observer's guide to the universe beyond the solar system.

1st ed., 1966, publ. by Celestial Handbook Publications.

Covers celestial objects outside our solar system that are within the range of 2– to 12–inch telescopes. Entries (arranged by constellations in which the objects appear) give names, celestial coordinates, classification, and descriptive notes. Includes an extensive introduction to fundamental observational astronomy. Vol. 1 includes lists of symbols and abbreviations and v. 3, indexes to names, topics, and data.

QB64.B85

Norton, Arthur P. Norton's 2000.0 : star atlas and reference handbook. 18th ed. / rev. under the editorship of Ian Ridpath. Harlow, England : Longman Scientific & Technical ; N.Y. : Wiley, 1989. 179 p. : ill.   **EC71**

1st ed., 1919, had title: *A star atlas and telescopic handbook (epoch 1920).* 17th ed., 1978.

The familiar features of this standard atlas of practical astronomy have been retained, but all maps have been redrawn to standard epoch 2000.0. Map projections have been standardized and computer-verified. The reference section has been rewritten and expanded; "the emphasis is on reference information and practical observing advice that is often difficult to obtain elsewhere."—*Pref.* Includes a glossary and a subject index to the reference handbook. No bibliography.

QB65.N7

Sky catalogue 2000.0 / by Alan Hirshfeld, Roger W. Sinnott, and François Ochsenbein. 2nd ed. Cambridge [Eng.] ; N.Y. : Cambridge Univ. Pr. ; Cambridge, Mass. : Sky Publ. Corp., 1991–[1993?]. v. 1–2 : ill. (In progress).   **EC72**

1st ed., 1982–85.

Contents: v. 1, Stars to magnitude 8.0; v. 2, Double stars, variable stars, and nonstellar objects.

Revised and corrected through extensive use of the SIMBAD database of astronomical data (Strasbourg, Centre de Données Stellaires, Observatoire de Strasbourg). Entries are arranged by right ascension and declination for the 2000.0 epoch. Introduction and correlation name indexes assist in locating objects. Serves as the reference gazetteer for Wil Tirion, *Sky atlas 2000.0* (EC76).   QB6.S54

Smithsonian Astrophysical Observatory. Smithsonian Astrophysical Observatory star atlas of reference stars and nonstellar objects / prep. by the staff. Cambridge, Mass. : M.I.T. Pr., [1969]. 1 case (13 p., 2 charts, 152 plates).   **EC73**

Title on case: Star atlas of reference stars and nonstellar objects.

A companion to the SAO *Star catalog* (EC74), which serves as gazetteer to this atlas. Shows about 260,000 stars and "is nearly complete to visual magnitude 9 but contains many fainter stars to 11 and occasionally beyond."—*Foreword.*   QB65.S65

——————————— Star catalog : positions and proper motions of 258,997 stars for the epoch and equinox of 1950.0. Wash. : Smithsonian Inst. : [For sale by U.S. Govt. Print. Off.], 1966. 4 v. : ill. (Smithsonian publication, 4652).   **EC74**

Repr., 1971.

"Sources for the catalog," v. 1, p. xx–xxiv. A companion to the SAO *Star atlas* ... (EC73).   QB6.S57

Tirion, Wil. Uranometria 2000.0 / Wil Tirion, Barry Rappaport, George Lovi. Richmond, Va. : Willmann-Bell, 1987–88. 2 v.   **EC75**

Repr. with corrections: Richmond, Va. : Willmann-Bell, 1988.

Contents: v. 1, The northern hemisphere to -6°; v. 2, The southern hemisphere to +6°.

A computer-plotted atlas that records some 332,000 stars and 10,300 deep sky objects. Data were compiled to 9.5 magnitude from several highly respected celestial atlases and catalogs: *Bonner Durchmusterung (BD)* of the Universitäts-Sternwarte zu Bonn (Bonn : A. Marcus, 1859–1903. 4 v.); *Bonner Durchmusterung : Südliche Teil (SBD)*, (2nd ed., rev. Bonn : Dümmler, 1951); *Cordoba Durchmusterung (CoD)* of the Observatorio Astronomico of the Universidad Nacional de Córdoba (Buenos Aires, 1892–1932. 5 v.); and Jack W. Sulentic and William G. Tifft's *The revised new general catalogue of nonstellar astronomical objects* (Tucson : Univ. of Arizona Pr., 1973). Includes an introductory essay and a selective bibliography on

the history of celestial cartography by George Lovi. The compact size, highly legible and well-labeled charts, and comprehensive coverage make this an important stellar atlas.   QB65.T55

——————————— Sky atlas 2000.0 : 26 star charts, covering both hemispheres. Deluxe ed. Cambridge, Mass. : Sky Publ. Corp. ; Cambridge, Eng. : Cambridge Univ. Pr., 1981. [2] folded p., 26 folded leaves : 26 maps.   **EC76**

"Contains some 43,000 stars to visual magnitude 8.0 and about 2,500 deep-sky objects, compiled from some of the best current sources."—*Introd.* Authoritative atlas for the new coordinate epoch makes good use of color (in Deluxe edition), type, styles, and projections to present astronomical details clearly. Reference list and index to constellations. Companion to *Sky catalogue 2000.0* (EC72).

QB65.T54

NAVIGATION

American practical navigator. 1st ed. (1802)– . Wash. : Defense Mapping Agency Hydrographic Center ; for sale by the U.S. Govt. Print. Off., 1802– . Irregular.   **EC77**

"An epitome of navigation, originally by Nathaniel Bowditch."—*t.p.*

First published under title: *The new American practical navigator.*

Imprint varies; issuing agency varies; now issued by Defense Mapping Agency, Hydrographic Topographic Center as *Pubn.* no. 9 (v. 1, 1984 ed., 1414 p.; v. 2, 1975 ed., 716 p.).

Intends to provide a compendium of navigational material understandable to the mariner. "Emphasis has been given to the fact that the aids provided by *science* can be used effectively to improve the *art* of navigation only if a well-informed person of mature judgment and experience is on hand to interpret information as it becomes available. Thus, the facts needed to perform the mechanics of navigation have been supplemented with additional material intended to help the navigator acquire the perspective in meeting the various needs that arise."—*Pref.*

Vol. 1 gives the necessary in-depth background or historical information needed to use the tables in v. 2; it contains sections on: Fundamentals, piloting and dead reckoning, Celestial navigation, Practice of navigation, Navigational safety, Oceanography, Weather, and Electronics and navigation, together with 25 appendixes with headings such as Greek alphabet, Navigational coordination, Constellations, Hand-held digital calculators, Sea state, and Geodesy for the navigator. Vol. 2 is "extensively revised ... provides the tables, formulas, data, and instructions needed by the navigator to perform many of the computations associated with dead reckoning, piloting, and celestial navigation."—*Pref.* Each volume is indexed.   VK555.A48

The astronomical almanac for the year 1981– . Wash. : Nautical Almanac Off., U.S. Naval Observatory : For sale by the U.S. Govt. Print. Off. ; London : Her Majesty's Nautical Almanac Off. : For sale by H.M.S.O., 1980– . Annual. **EC78**

Subtitle: Data for astronomy, space sciences, geodesy, surveying, navigation and other applications.

Formed by the merger of *The American ephemeris and nautical almanac* (1855–1980) and the *Astronomical ephemeris* (1767–1980), which, beginning with the editions for 1960, have been virtually identical, only some introductory pages differing.

"The principal ephemerides ... have been computed from fundamental ephemerides of the planets and the Moon prepared at the Jet Propulsion Laboratory, California in cooperation with the U.S. Naval Observatory."—*Pref.* A compendium of astronomical data useful for professionals and amateurs, including data on lunar and terrestrial phenomena, time scales and coordinate systems, and observational details for the solar system, stars, and stellar systems. Includes an index to observatories, data tables, a glossary, and a general index.

§ Related annual publications from the same publishers include:

(1) *Astronomical phenomena* (1950–), containing extracts and published in advance of the *Almanac*.

(2) *Air almanac* (1953–), with ephemerides at 10-minute intervals and additional data for marine navigation.

(3) *Nautical almanac* (1855–), with ephemeride intervals of one hour and additional data for marine navigation.

•Machine-readable version: *The floppy almanac* [database] (Wash. : Nautical Almanac Off., U.S. Naval Observatory ; distr. by National Audiovisual Center, National Archives and Records Administration). On diskettes; annual. Provides "to full precision most of the data in the *Astronomical almanac* including both positional and physical data interpolated to any date and time within the appropriate year."–*Related publications, p. viii.*   QB8.U6A77

Explanatory supplement to the Astronomical almanac / prep. by the Nautical Almanac Office, U.S. Naval Observatory ; with contributions from H.M. Nautical Almanac Office, Royal Greenwich Observatory ... [et al.] ; ed. by P. Kenneth Seidelmann. [Rev. ed.]. Mill Valley, Calif. : Univ. Science Books, c1992. 752 p. : ill.   **EC79**

Subtitle: A revision to the Explanatory supplement to the *Astronomical ephemeris* and the *American ephemeris and nautical almanac*.

"The primary purpose ... is to provide users of the *Astronomical almanac* with more complete explanations of the significance, sources, methods of computation, and use of the data given in the almanac than can be included annually in the almanac itself. The secondary purpose is to provide complementary information that doesn't change annually, such as conceptual explanations, lists of constants and other data, bibliographic references, and historical information."—*Pref*. Subject index.   QB8.U6A772

International code of signals. [Suitland, Md.] : Defense Mapping Agency Hydrographic/Topographic Center; for sale by authorized sales agents of the Defense Mapping Agency Support Center, 1990. 165 p. : ill. (Defense Mapping Agency Hydrographic/Topographic Center. Publication, no. 102).   **EC80**

Subtitle: As adopted by the fourth Assembly of the Inter-governmental Maritime Consultative Organization in 1965, for visual, sound, and radio communications.

Supersedes H.O. Publications 103 and 104, *International code of signals* (American ed. Wash. : U.S. Govt. Print. Off., 1952. 2 v.).

Also issued in microfiche.

The revised code pertains to the safety of navigation and persons and covers transmissions by all means of communication. Changes and corrections are published in the *Notice to mariners* (Wash. : Defense Mapping Agency Hydrographic/Topographic Center, 196?–). Index for signaling instructions and general signal code; index for medical signal code.

Dictionaries

Ansted, A. A dictionary of sea terms. 3rd ed. / rev. by Peter Clissold. Glasgow : Brown, Son & Ferguson, 1985. 355 p. : ill.   **EC81**

1st ed., 1920; 2nd ed., 1928.

Lengthy definitions and helpful illustrations for some 3,000 words emphasize sailing and yachting terminology. Entries retained from the 1st ed. make this work useful for historical references.

United States. Naval Oceanographic Office. Navigation dictionary. 2nd ed. Wash. : U.S. Govt. Print. Off., 1969. 292 p. (Hydrographic Office publication, no. 220).   **EC82**

1st ed., 1956, publ. by the U.S. Hydrographic Office.

Alphabetical listing of terms. Includes parts of speech, synonyms and antonyms, list of abbreviations, and bibliography of sources.   V23.U557

CHRONOLOGY

Bond, John James. Handy-book of rules and tables for verifying dates with the Christian Era. London : Bell, 1875. 465 p.   **EC83**

Repr. : N.Y. : Russell & Russell, 1966.

Republ. in microform: Wash. : Library of Congress, 19??

Subtitle: Giving an account of the chief eras, and systems used by various nations, with easy methods for determining the corresponding dates; with regnal years of English sovereigns from the Norman Conquest to the present time, 1066–1874.   CE11.B7

The book of calendars / Frank Parise, ed. N.Y. : Facts on File, c1982. 387 p.   **EC84**

Short introductory essays detail the history and special features of each calendar. Tables for some 60 calendars are translated to appropriate Julian or Gregorian dates. The lack of a bibliography or explanation of sources is unfortunate in a reference tool that simplifies and replaces many older calendrical works. Indexed.   CE11.B66

Cappelli, Adriano. Cronologia, cronografia e calendario perpetuo : dal principio dell'era cristiana ai giorni nostri : tavole cronologico-sincrone e quadri sinottici per verificare le date storiche 4. ed. aggiornata. Milano : Hoepli, 1978. 602 p.   **EC85**

1st ed., 1906; 3rd ed., 1969.

Christian, Islamic, and secular calendar systems are described. Most valuable are the historical chronologies for Roman times and those developed for the principal cities and locales in Western Europe. An appendix updates tables to 1977.

Fitzpatrick, Gary L. International time tables. Metuchen, N.J. : Scarecrow, 1990. 106 p., [2] p. of plates : col. maps.   **EC86**

Tables are arranged by country, and allow for 12- and 24-hour forms of notation, standard and advanced time periods, multiple time zones, and the effect of the International Dateline. Notes on use, examples, and several maps help to make this an excellent source for libraries.   QB211.F56

Ginzel, Friedrich Karl. Handbuch der mathematischen und technischen Chronologie : das Zeitrechnungswesen der Völker. Leipzig : J. C. Hinrichs, 1906–14. 3 v.   **EC87**

Contents: Bd. 1, Zeitrechnung der Babylonier, Ägypter, Mohammedaner, Perser, Inder, Südostasiaten, Chinesen, Japaner und Zentralamerikaner; Bd. 2, Zeitrechnung der Juden, der Naturvölker, der Römer und Griechen, sowie Nachträge zum 1. Bande; Bd. 3, Zeitrechnung der Makedonier, Kleinasier und Syrer, der Germanen und Kelten, des Mittelalters, der Byzantiner (und Russen), Armenier, Kopten, Abessinier, Zeitrechnung der neueren Zeit, sowie Nachträge zu den drei Bänden.

Remains useful for its scope and extensive bibliography. Each volume has its own index.   CE11.G5

Welch, Windon Chandler. Chinese-American calendar for the 102 Chinese years commencing Jan. 24, 1849, and ending Feb. 5, 1951. Wash. : U.S. Govt. Print. Off., 1928. 102 p., incl. tables.   **EC88**

At head of title: United States Department of Labor. Bureau of Immigration.

One page for each year: figures in black represent the Chinese day; red figures are used for the corresponding English day.

§ Supplemented by: *Chinese-American calendar for the 40th through the 89th year of the Chinese Republic, Feb. 6, 1951 to Jan. 23, 2001* (Rev. 1957. Wash. : Admin. Div., Immigration and Naturalization Service, 1957. 50 p.).

ED

Physics

Information sources in physics (ED1) is an up-to-date guide to materials in physics. For earlier literature, *see also* Parke's *Guide to the literature of mathematics and physics* (EB3) and Whitford's *Physics literature* (ED3). For more recent listings, *see* the current bibliographies noted under Section EA and *Technical book review index* (EA54). *See also* Nuclear Engineering, Section EK.

GENERAL WORKS

Guides

Information sources in physics / ed., Dennis F. Shaw. 3rd ed. London ; Bowker-Saur, c1994. 507 p.   **ED1**
 1st ed., 1975, ed. by Herbert Coblans, had title: *The use of physics literature*; 2nd ed., 1985.
 Most of the 20 chapters by physicists and specialist librarians deal with the literature in specific fields of physics; there are also chapters on: The scope and control of physics, its literature, and information sources, Science libraries, Reference material and general treatises, Grey literature, and Patent literature. Information on online services that had been in a separate chapter in the 2nd ed. is now incorporated into the topical chapters. Includes an appendix giving the most important physics journals, based on the number of physics articles abstracted by INSPEC. Indexed.

Parke, Nathan Grier. Guide to the literature of mathematics and physics including related works on engineering science. 2nd rev. ed. N.Y. : Dover, [1958]. 436 p. : facsims.   **ED2**
 For annotation, *see* EB3.   Z6651.P3

Whitford, Robert Henry. Physics literature : a reference manual. 2nd ed. Metuchen, N.J. : Scarecrow, 1968. 272 p.
                                                         ED3
 1st ed., 1954.
 A bibliographical manual for college students, describing available materials and outlining library methods. Arrangement is by "usual lines of inquiry," termed "approaches" (e.g., bibliographical, historical, experimental, topical), with subdivisions for form of literature or by nature of subject. Commentaries, annotations, and excerpts from the literature accompany the bibliographical entries. Author and subject indexes.   Z7141.W47

Bibliography

Datensammlungen in der Physik = Data compilations in physics / by H. Behrens ... [et al.]. Karlsruhe : Fachinformationszentrum Energie, Physik, Mathematik, 1976–85. 5 v.
                                                         ED4

Physik Daten = Physics data ; no. 3–1 through 3–5. No. 3–5 cumulates, revises, and extends the four earlier numbers.
 An index to about 3,600 data compilations, arranged under topical headings in German and English, with a subject index in English. Also includes author index, corporate index, report number index, journal index, and index of atomic numbers for nuclear structure and decay data compilations. Very useful in finding data in many fields of physics.   Z7405.T3B44

International catalogue of scientific literature / publ. for the Internat. Council by the Royal Soc. of London. v. 1 (1901)–v. 14 (1914). London : Harrison, 1902–21.   **ED5**
 Section C, Physics. For full description, *see* EA16.

Reuss, Jeremias David. Repertorium commentationum a societatibus litterariis editarum / secundum disciplinarum ordinem digessit I. D. Reuss .... Gottingae : apud Henricum Dieterich, 1801–21. 16 v.   **ED6**
 T. 4, Physica. For full description, *see* EA21.   Z5051.R44

Royal Society (Great Britain). Catalogue of scientific papers, 1800–1900. London : Clay, 1867–1902 ; Cambridge : Univ. Pr., 1914–25. 19 v.   **ED7**
 Vol. 3, Physics. For full description, *see* EA22.   Z7403.R88

Dissertations

Marckworth, M. Lois. Dissertations in physics : an indexed bibliography of all doctoral theses accepted by American universities, 1861–1959. Stanford, Calif. : Stanford Univ. Pr., 1961. 803 p.   **ED8**
 Comp. with the assistance of the staff of the Advanced Systems Development Division and Research Laboratories, International Business Machines Corporation, San Jose, California.
 In two sections: pt. 1, an alphabetical list of 8,216 dissertations; pt. 2, a permutation subject index coded by important words in the titles. Although the entries are primarily for physics subjects, some dissertations written under the auspices of a physics department are oriented toward astronomy, bio- and geophysics, electrical and mechanical engineering, and chemical, mathematical, or agricultural physics.
                                                         Z7141.M3

Indexes; Abstract journals

•**INSPEC** [database]. Stevenage, Herts., Eng. : Institution of Electrical Engineers, 1969– .   **ED9**
 Provides access to literature on physics, electrical engineering, electronics, control theory and technology, computing, and control engineering. Made up of four subfiles: Series A, Physics abstracts; Series B, Electrical & electronics abstracts; Series C, Computer & control abstracts; Series D, Information technology. Records correspond to those in the printed sources *Science abstracts: Series A, Physics abstracts* (ED11); *Series B, Electrical & electronics abstracts* (EK128); and *Series C, Computer & control abstracts* (EK162).
 •A CD-ROM version, *INSPEC ondisc* [database] (1989–), is updated quarterly. Subsets of this source, *INSPEC physics* and *INSPEC electronics & computing*, are also available.

Physics briefs = Physikalische Berichte. v. 1 (Jan. 15, 1979)– . Weinheim : Physik Verlag, 1979– . Semimonthly.
                                                         ED10
 Continues: *Physikalische Berichte* (Braunschweig : 1920–78; publ. suspended 1945–June 1947) which itself continued the abstracting service of *Fortschritte der Physik*, 1845–1918 (Braunschweig : 1847–1919. 74 v. in 141).
 A comprehensive abstract journal ed. by Deutsche Physikalische Gesellschaft and by Fachinformationszentrum: Energie, Physik, Mathematik, in cooperation with American Institute of Physics.

Abstracts, in English, are arranged by a classification scheme, with cross-references as appropriate. Each issue contains a subject guide with terms from the subject classification in keyword form, and an index to authors and editors. Semiannual cumulated author and subject indexes. Currently publishes about 130,000 abstract entries per year.

As of Jan. 1995, this publication and its online counterpart (below) will cease and Fachinformatioszentrum (FIZ) will join INSPEC in producing *Physics abstracts* (ED11).

•Available in machine-readable form as: *PHYS (Physics briefs online)* [database] (Karlsruhe, Germany : Fachinformationszentrum, 1979–). Available online, updated semiweekly. QC1.P6535

Science abstracts : Series A, Physics abstracts. v. 70 (Jan. 1967)– . London : Institution of Electrical Engineers, 1967– . Semimonthly. **ED11**

Publisher and frequency vary.

Title varies: 1898–1902, *Science abstracts, physics and electrical engineering*; 1903-65, issued in two sections: A, *Physics*; B, *Electrical engineering*; 1966, issued without section designations, *Physics abstracts*. Since 1967, issued as Section A, with *Electrical & electronics abstracts* issued as Section B.

Entries arranged according to a subject classification listed on the back cover of each issue. Coverage is international and includes periodicals, reports, books, dissertations, patents, and conference papers. A complete list of periodicals is issued as a part of the semiannual author indexes. Author and subject indexes, plus several "small indexes"—bibliographies, books, patents and reports, conferences. Now has more than 151,000 abstract entries per year.

Cumulated indexes:

———. *Cumulative author index*, 1955–1959 (1 v.), 1960–1964 (4 v.), 1965–1968 (2 v.), 1969–1972 (3 v.), 1973–1976 (4 v.), 1977–1980 (4 v.), 1981–84 (4 v.), 1985–88 (4 v.) (London : [1960–89]).

———. *Cumulative subject index*, 1955–1959 (1 v.), 1960–1964 (2 v.), 1965–1968 (3 v.), 1969–1972 (4 v.), 1973–1976 (8 v.), 1977–1980 (6 v.), 1981–84 (7 v.), 1985–88 (9 v.) (London : [1960–89]).

•Machine-readable form: *INSPEC : Physics ondisc* [database] (Stevenage, Herts., England : Institution of Electrical Engineers, 1989–). Available in CD-ROM, (updated quarterly) and online as *INSPEC* (ED9). QC1.P46

Encyclopedias

See also *Encyclopedia of physical science and technology* (EA79).

Besancon, Robert Martin. The encyclopedia of physics. 3rd ed. N.Y. : Van Nostrand Reinhold, [1985]. 1378 p. : ill. **ED12**

1st ed., 1966.

Concise, signed articles—most including bibliographic references—on physics in general, its major areas, divisions, and subdivisions as well as related topics such as astrophysics, geophysics, and biophysics. Intended for physicists who need information outside their special field of interest, librarians, teachers, engineers, and other scientists "who encounter physical concepts in pursuit of their professions."—*Pref.* As a rule, the technical level of the writing is higher for the more specialized areas than for the general topics. Useful cross-references. Indexed. QC5.B44

Encyclopaedic dictionary of physics : general, nuclear, solid state, molecular, chemical, metal and vacuum physics, astronomy, geophysics, biophysics and related subjects / ed. in chief, J. Thewlis. London ; N.Y. : Pergamon, 1961–64. 9 v. **ED13**

Contents: v. 1–7, A–Z; v. 8, Subject and author indexes; v. 9, Multilingual glossary: English, French, German, Spanish, Russian, Japanese.

Edited in England, with an international list of some 2,000 contributors. Not a modern version of Sir Richard Glazebrook's *Dictionary of applied physics* (London : Macmillan, 1922–23. 5 v.), but largely replaces that standard work. Articles are signed and range in length

from a few lines to approximately 3,000 words. Each is self-contained, but cross-references are provided to related articles, and bibliographies refer to more detailed works.

——— *Supplement* 1–5 (N.Y. : Pergamon, [1966–75]. 5 v.).

Volumes in the supplementary series "are designed to deal with new topics in physics and related subjects, new developments in topics previously covered and topics which have been left out of earlier volumes for various reasons. They will also contain survey articles covering particularly important fields."—*Foreword, Suppl. 1.* Bibliographies are included, as are sections of addenda and errata for the *Dictionary* and its supplements. Each volume has its own index.

Encyclopedia of applied physics / ed. by George L. Trigg ; associate editors, Eduardo S. Vera, Walter Greulich. N.Y. : VCH Publ., c1991–94. v. 1–11 : ill. (In progress). **ED14**

Contents: v. 1–11, Accelerators, linear–Nuclear structure. Expected to be complete in 20 v.

Temporary subject index issued for every third volume; final volume will include index to entire work.

Sponsored by the American Institute of Physics, Deutsche physikalische Gesellschaft, Japan Society of Applied Physics, and Physical Society of Japan.

Treating areas of physics which have or promise to have industrial applications, the alphabetically arranged articles are technical but not comprehensive; the level and depth of coverage are similar to those of *Encyclopedia of physical science and technology* (EA79). The signed articles each begin with a table of contents and have glossaries and lists both of works cited and recommended readings. Each volume has a list of recommended units and symbols. QC5.E543

Encyclopedia of modern physics / Robert A. Meyers, ed. ; Steven N. Shore, scientific consultant. San Diego, Calif. : Academic Pr., c1990. 773 p. : ill. **ED15**

Entries are derived from *Encyclopedia of physical science and technology* (EA79), with articles chosen to constitute a "survey of the most rapidly advancing fields of theoretical and applied physics."—*Pref.* May be of use in physics libraries lacking the parent work.
QC5.E544

Encyclopedia of physics / ed. by Rita G. Lerner, George L. Trigg. 2nd ed. N.Y. : VCH, 1990. 1408 p. : ill. **ED16**

1st ed., 1981.

Intended to be a comprehensive introductory reference. Brief articles (ranging in length from a page to more than 20 pages) are by authorities in their fields and include bibliographies and cross-references. Indexed. QC5.E545

Handbuch der Physik / hrsg. von S. Flugge. Berlin : Springer, 1955–88. v. 1–55 in 78 parts. **ED17**

Earlier edition 1926–29 (24 v. and index).

Added title page in English: *Encyclopedia of physics.*

Contents: v. 1, Mathematical methods, I (1956); v. 2, Mathematical methods, II (1955); v. 3, pt. 1, Principles of classical mechanics and field theory (1960); v. 3, pt. 2, Principles of thermodynamics and statistics (1959); v. 3, pt. 3, Non-linear field theories of mechanics (1965); v. 4, Principles of electrodynamics and relativity (1962); v. 5, pt. 1, Principles of quantum theory, I (1958); v. 6, Elasticity and plasticity (1958); v. 6a[1], Mechanics of solids (1972–74); v. 7, pt. 1, Crystal physics, I (1955); v. 7, pt. 2, Crystal physics, II (1958); v. 8, pt. 1, Fluid dynamics, I (1959); v. 8, pt. 2, Fluid dynamics, II (1963); v. 9, Fluid dynamics, III (1960); v. 10, Structure of liquids (1960); v. 11, pt. 1, Acoustics, I (1961); v. 11, pt. 2, Acoustics, II (1962); v. 12, Thermodynamics of gases (1958); v. 13, Thermodynamics of liquids and solids (1962); v. 14, Low temperature physics, I (1956); v. 15, Low temperature physics, II (1956): v. 16, Electric fields and waves (1958); v. 17, Dielectrics (1956); v. 18, pt. 1, Magnetism (1968); v. 18, pt. 2, Ferromagnetism (1966); v. 19, Electrical conductivity, I (1956); v. 20, Electrical conductivity, II (1957);

v. 21, Electron emission. Gas discharges, I (1956); v. 22, Gas discharges, II (1956); v. 23, Electrical instruments (1967); v. 24, Fundamentals of optics (1956); v. 25, pt. 1, Crystal optics. Diffraction (1961); v. 25, pt. 2a, Light and matter, Ia (1967); v. 25, pt. 2b, Light and matter, Ib (1974); v. 25, pt. 2c, Light and matter, Ic (1970); v. 25, pt. 2d, Light and matter, Id (1984); v. 26, Light and matter, II (1958); v. 27, Spectroscopy, I (1964); v. 28, Spectroscopy, II (1957); v. 29, Optical instruments (1967); v. 30, X-rays (1957); v. 31, Corpuscles and radiation in matter, I (1982); v. 32, Structural research (1957); v. 33, Corpuscular optics (1956); v. 34, Corpuscles and radiation in matter, II (1958); v. 35, Atoms, I (1957); v. 36, Atoms, II (1956); v. 37, pt.1, Atoms, III. Molecules, I (1959); v. 37, pt. 2, Molecules, II (1961); v. 38, pt.1, External properties of atomic nuclei (1958); v. 38, pt. 2, Neutrons and related Gamma ray problems (1959); v. 39, Structure of atomic nuclei (1957); v. 40, Nuclear reactions, I (1957);

v. 41, pt. 1, Nuclear reactions, II (1959); v. 41, pt. 2, Beta decay (1962); v. 42, Nuclear reactions, III (1957); v. 44, Nuclear instrumentation, I (1959); v. 45, Nuclear instrumentation, II (1958); v. 46, pt. 1, Cosmic rays, I (1961); v. 46, pt. 2, Cosmic rays, II (1967); v. 47, Geophysics, I: The earth's body (1956); v. 48, Geophysics, II (1957); v. 49, pts. 1–7, Geophysics III (1966–84); v. 50, Astrophysics, I (Stellar surface-binaries) (1958); v. 51, Astrophysics, II (Stellar structure) (1958); v. 52, Astrophysics, III (The solar system) (1959); v. 53, Astrophysics, IV (Stellar systems) (1959); v. 54, Astrophysics, V (Miscellaneous) (1962); v. 55, General index. No v. 43 was issued.

Volumes are arranged by topical group: (1) Mathematical physics; (2) Principles of theoretical physics; (3) Mechanical and thermal behavior of matter; (4) Electric and magnetic behaviour of matter; (5) Optics; (6) X-rays and corpuscular rays; (7) Atomic and molecular physics; (8) Nuclear physics; (9) Cosmic rays; (10) Geophysics; (11) Astrophysics. Vol. 55, General index, has a separate subject index for each topical group, an index of contributors, and a listing of all volumes issued with their contents. An encyclopedic treatment of all areas of physics. Many early volumes were largely in German, but most of the articles in the set are in English; a few are in French. The articles are authoritative and comprehensive treatments of the topics at the time they were written; the authors are distinguished and often eminent physicists. Each volume is fully indexed in English; early volumes were also fully indexed in German.   QC21.H327

Dictionaries

The Facts on File dictionary of physics / ed. by John Daintith ; consultant editors, Eric Deeson, J. W. Warren. Rev. and expanded ed. N.Y. : Facts on File, c1988. 235 p. : ill.   **ED18**
   First publ. in the U.K. in 1980.
   More than 2,000 entries defining the most important and commonly used terms related to physics; most entries are single paragraphs. British spellings used. Cross-references.   QC5.F34

Jerrard, Harold George. A dictionary of scientific units : including dimensionless numbers and scales / H. G. Jerrard and D. B. McNeill. 6th ed. London ; N.Y. : Chapman & Hall, 1992. 255 p.   **ED19**
   1st ed., 1963.
   More than 900 entries arranged alphabetically by name of unit. Gives definition, relevant historical facts, and, usually, some indication of the magnitude of the unit; cites sources by numbers with full citations given in an appendix. Other appendixes: table of fundamental physical constants, information on standardization committees and conferences, British and American weights and measures, conversion tables, and conversion factors for SI and centimeter/gram/second units. Indexed.   QC82.J4

Lexikon der Physik / hrsg. von Hermann Franke. 3. Aufl. Stuttgart : Franck, [1969]. 3 v. (1960, 98, 53 p.) : ill.   **ED20**
   1st ed., 1950–52.
   A dictionary-encyclopedia defining the words and concepts of modern physics, illustrated with line drawings, diagrams, tables and plates. Biographical articles are included, and references are given at the ends of many articles.   QC5.L42

Lord, M. P. Macmillan dictionary of physics. London : Macmillan, 1986. [331] p. : ill.   **ED21**

Brief definitions with cross-references. Includes some formulas, illustrations, and tables of SI units.   QC5.L67

McGraw-Hill dictionary of physics / Sybil P. Parker, ed. in chief. N.Y. : McGraw-Hill, [1985?]. 646 p.   **ED22**
   Entries, drawn from *McGraw-Hill dictionary of scientific and technical terms* (3rd ed., 1984; 5th ed., EA93) range from a single sentence to a brief paragraph. Definitions are preceded by abbreviations indicating the fields in which they are primarily used. Includes abbreviations, acronyms. Cross-references.   QC5.M23

Schubert, Joachim. Dictionary of effects and phenomena in physics : descriptions, applications, tables. Weinheim (Federal Republic of Germany) ; N.Y. : VCH, c1987. 140 p. : ill.   **ED23**
   Rev. translation of: *Physikalische Effekte*.
   Approximately 400 effects and phenomena are listed alphabetically, with a description of the effect, usually one or more references, the date of discovery, and a symbol indicating the field of physics to which the effect relates. Tables at the back list the fields and the effects that pertain to them, and a chronology lists the effects in order of discovery.   QC5.S3513 1987

Thewlis, James. Concise dictionary of physics and related subjects. 2nd ed., rev. and enl. Oxford ; N.Y. : Pergamon, 1979. 370 p.   **ED24**
   1st ed., 1973.
   "Covers not only Physics proper, but to a greater or lesser extent, such related subjects as Astronomy, Astrophysics, Aerodynamics; Biophysics, Crystallography, Geophysics, Hydraulics, Mathematics, Medical Physics, Meteorology, Metrology, Photography, Physical Chemistry, Physical Metallurgy and so on."—*Foreword.* Brief entries are restricted to single concepts. Many cross-references. Appendixes include the periodic table, conversion tables from CGS and Imperial units to SI units, and values of the general physical constants.
    QC5.T5

Foreign terms

German

De Vries, Louis. Dictionary of pure and applied physics / comp. by Louis de Vries and W. E. Clason. Amsterdam ; N.Y. : Elsevier, 1963–64. 2 v.   **ED25**
   Contents: v. 1, German-English; v. 2, English-German.
   More than 25,000 terms. Intended for students in science and technology in the U.S.   QC5.D4

Dictionary of physics and allied sciences. N.Y. : Ungar, c1978. 2 v.   **ED26**
   Added t.p. in German: Wörterbuch der Physik und verwandter Wissenschaften.
   Vol. 1, German-English, ed. by Charles J. Hyman with supplement by R. Idlin; v. 2, English-German with supplement, ed. by R. Idlin.
   Covers terms in theoretical physics and related sciences and their applications in technology and engineering.   QC5.D52

Russian

Emin, Irving. Russian-English physics dictionary / by Irving Emin and the Consultants Bureau staff of physicist-translators. N.Y. : Wiley, [1963]. 554 p.   **ED27**
   Compiled by specialists. Includes the terminology of all important branches of physics and the vocabulary of astronomy, astrophysics, chemistry, geophysics, and general technology. Russian abbreviations for scientific units, journal titles, institutions, and transliterations of the names of many scientsts are also included.   QC5.E48

Voskoboinik, David I. Anglo-russkiĭ iadernyĭ slovar' / David I. Voskoboinik and M. G. TSimmerman. Moscow : Glav. red. Inostr. Nauchno-Tekhn. Slovarei Fizmat., 1960. 400 p. **ED28**
> Added title page: English-Russian nuclear dictionary.
> 20,000 English terms and their Russian equivalents.
> Companion volume: ———. *Russko-angliiskiĭ iadernyĭ slovar'* (Moscow, 1960. 334 p.).
> Added title page: Russian-English nuclear dictionary.
> 20,000 Russian terms and their English equivalents. QC5.V6

Directories

American Institute of Physics. Graduate programs in physics, astronomy, and related fields. 1976/77– . N.Y. : American Institute of Physics, 1976– . Annual. **ED29**
> Supersedes *Graduate programs in physics and astronomy,* 1968.
> "Designed to provide easily accessible, comparative information on the graduate programs and research in physics and in fields based upon the principles of physics."—*Introd.* Organized geographically, with entries first for institutions in the U.S. arranged by state and within states alphabetically by institution; this section covers essentially all U.S. physics doctoral programs, almost all astronomy doctoral programs, most master's programs in both fields, and a number of related departments such nuclear engineering, electrical engineering, chemical physics, materials science, geophysics, and medical physics. The section on Canadian departments is less complete, but most major programs are included, arranged by province and within province by institution. The Mexican section includes two programs (1992–93 ed.).
> Information for each department includes address and telephone number; general information about the institution; tuition, admission, financial aid, and housing information; department enrollments and numbers of degrees granted; graduate degree requirements; departmental budgets; lists of faculty including fields of specialization and when and where they received their graduate degrees; and recent publications for some departments. QC30.A48

Directory of physicists from developing countries. 2nd version. Miramare, Trieste : International Centre for Theoretical Physics, [1987]. 399 p. **ED30**
> Entries are arranged by country, and within country alphabetically by name. Entries include year of birth, address, academic qualifications, field of research, nationality if other than country of residence. Indexed. QC16.2.D58

Directory of physics & astronomy staff members. 1975/76– . N.Y. : American Inst. of Physics, 1975/76– . Biennial (1982/83–). **ED31**
> Title varies slightly.
> Vols. for 1986/87– also issued as the December issue, pt. 2 of the *Bulletin* of the American Physical Society (publ. Dec. 1984–).
> Lists staff members of North American physics faculties, research centers, and government laboratories, giving address and telephone number, academic or other rank if supplied by institution. Currently lists about 30,000 staff members at 2,700 institutions. QC47.N75D57

Handbooks

American Institute of Physics. American Institute of Physics handbook / section editors: Bruce H. Billings [and others]. Coordinating ed.: Dwight E. Gray ... [et al.]. 3rd ed. N.Y. : McGraw-Hill, [c1972]. 1 v. (various pagings) : ill. **ED32**
> 1st ed., 1957.
> Each section edited by a specialist. Provides authoritative, up-to-date information on various aspects of physics. Treats mathematical aids to computation, mechanics, acoustics, heat, electricity and mag-

netism, optics, atomic and molecular physics, nuclear physics, and solid-state physics. Includes definitions, tables, formulas, bibliographic references, etc. Indexed. QC61.A5

Condon, Edward Uhler. Handbook of physics / ed. by E. U. Condon, Hugh Odishaw. 2nd ed. N.Y. : McGraw-Hill, [1967]. 1 v. (various pagings) : ill. **ED33**
> 1st ed., 1958.
> A standard handbook with chapters by specialists; encyclopedic in nature. In nine main sections: (1) Mathematics; (2) Mechanics of particles and rigid bodies; (3) Mechanics of deformable bodies; (4) Electricity and magnetism; (5) Heat and thermodynamics; (6) Optics; (7) Atomic physics; (8) Solid state; (9) Nuclear physics. Includes bibliographies; indexed. QC21.C7

CRC handbook of laser science and technology / ed., Marvin J. Weber. Boca Raton, Fla. : CRC Pr., [1982–90]. 5 v. and suppl. **ED34**
> Updates and considerably extends *CRC handbook of lasers,* ed. by Robert J. Pressley (1971).
> Contents: v. 1, Lasers and masers; v. 2, Gas lasers; v. 3, Optical materials, pt. 1: Nonlinear optical properties/radiation damage; v. 4, Optical materials, pt. 2: Properties; v. 5, Optical materials, pt. 3: Applications, coatings, and fabrication; suppl. 1, Lasers.
> "The object of this series is to provide a readily accessible and concise source of data in tabular and graphical form for workers in the areas of laser research and development."—*Pref.* Signed articles include tabular data and references. Indexed. TA1675.L38

Electrical resistivity handbook / ed. by G. T. Dyos and T. Farrell. London : Peter Peregrinus on behalf of the Inst. of Electrical Engineers, c1992. 735 p. : ill. (IEE materials & devices series, 10). **ED35**
> A compilation of graphs of resistivity data for elements and alloys, as a function of temperature. Sources of the data are given, most from the last 20 years; only sources giving purity of the materials used are included. Not included are pressure or magnetic effects, effects of crystalline resistivity, superconductivity, or irradiation damage. Compositions of alloys are given as atomic percentages. Introductory material discusses measurement techniques. Indexed by element.
> QC610.6.E38

Fischbeck, Helmut J. Formulas, facts, and constants for students and professionals in engineering, chemistry, and physics / H. J. Fischbeck, K. H. Fischbeck. 2nd rev. and enl. ed. Berlin ; N.Y. : Springer-Verlag, c1987. 260 p. : ill. **ED36**
> 1st ed., 1982.
> Divided into five sections: Basic mathematical facts and figures; Units, conversion factors, and constants; spectroscopy and atomic structure; Basic wave mechanics; Facts, figures and data useful in the laboratory. Indexed. A convenient compilation. QC61.F58

Handbook of optics / ed. by Walter G. Driscoll and William Vaughan. N.Y. : McGraw-Hill, [1978]. 1 v. (various pagings) : ill. **ED37**
> "Sponsored by the Optical Society of America."—*t.p.*
> Intended to fill "a need for a convenient compilation of optical information [as expressed by members of the Society, including] not only those engaged in optical physics, lens design, vision, color and other specializations traditionally associated with optics but also chemists, engineering scientists, and medical scientists. ..."—*Pref.*
> QC369.H35

Nordling, Carl. Physics handbook : elementary constants and units, tables, formulae and diagrams, and mathematical formulae / Carl Nordling, Jonny Österman. 4th ed. Lund, Sweden : Studentlitteratur ; Goch, Western Germany : Bratt Institut für Neues Lernen ; Bromley, Kent, England : Chartwell-Bratt, c1987. 430 p. : ill. **ED38**
> Accompanied by "Chart of the nuclides" (13th ed. 1 folded leaf), previously publ. separately in 1983.
> A translation of a popular Swedish handbook for physics students.

The handbook is in four parts: Pt. E, Elementary constants and units; Pt. T, Physical tables; Pt. F, Physical formulae and diagrams; Pt. M, Mathematical formulae. Each part is divided by subject area. Indexed.

QC61.N67 1987

Streeter, Victor Lyle. Handbook of fluid dynamics. N.Y. : McGraw-Hill, 1961. 1 v. (various pagings) : ill.   **ED39**
Repr., 1982.

Chapters written by specialists; the first half of the book "deals with fundamental concepts and principles, while the second half is devoted to applied fields."—*Pref.* Bibliography at the end of each chapter.   QA911.S85

Tuma, Jan J. Handbook of physical calculations. 2nd enl. and rev. ed. N.Y. : McGraw-Hill, c1983. 478 p. : ill.   **ED40**
1st ed., 1976.

"Definitions—formulas—technical applications—physical tables—conversion tables—graphs—dictionary of physical terms."—*t.p.*

Presents a concise summary of major definitions, formulas, tables, and examples of elementary and intermediate technical physics, arranged by field. Intended to "serve as a desk-top reference book for practicing engineers, architects, and technologists. ..."—*Pref.* Emphasizes practical applications; uses no mathematics beyond elementary calculus. Appendixes include tables of data and conversion factors. Includes references; brief bibliography. Indexed.   QC61.T85

Tables

See also Mathematics—Tables, Section EB.

Ardenne, Manfred. Tabellen zur angewandten Physik : Elektronenphysik, Ionenphysik, Vakuumphysik, Kernphysik, medizinische Elektronik, Hilfsgebiete. 2. umgearb. und stark erw. Aufl. der Tabellen. Berlin : Deutscher Verlag der Wissenschaften, 1962–64. 2 v. : ill.   **ED41**
1st ed., 1956, had title: *Elekronenphysik, Ionenphysik und Übermikroskopie.*

Contents: Bd. 1, Elektronenphysik, Übermikroskopie, Ionenphysik; Bd. 2, Physik und Technik des Vakuums, Plasmaphysik.

Presents, with short commentaries, the most important formulas, fundamentals, methods, groupings, conclusions, technical physical data, and characteristics of matter in tabular form, with references to the principal literature sources. Related fields of high-vacuum technology, optic, heat, magnetism, nuclear physics, and mathematics are included. Subject index and index to the literature cited.   QC61.A72

Browne, Edgardo. Table of radioactive isotopes / Edgardo Browne and Richard B. Firestone ; Virginia S. Shirley, ed. N.Y. : Wiley, c1986. 1 v. (various pagings) : ill.   **ED42**

A compendium of data for all known radioactive isotopes, derived in part from the related compendium *Table of isotopes* (ed. by Charles Michael Lederer and Virginia S. Shirley; ED46), the journal *Nuclear data sheets*, and other sources. The compilers have "tried to satisfy the ever increasing demand for *adopted* properties for *all* radiations emitted by nuclei. We have therefore included tables of adopted properties, which were derived from experimental data plus reliable calculations (e.g., continuous radiation spectra), along with those based on statistical analyses of existing experimental data alone ... . We further calculated other derived adopted properties (e.g. average photon energies per disintegration) for which we sensed strong user demand."—*Pref.* As with the *Table of isotopes*, the main table is ordered by mass number and subordered by atomic number.   QD601.2.B76

James, A. M. VNR index of chemical and physical data / Arthur James & Mary Lord. N.Y. : Van Nostrand Reinhold, c1992. 565 p. : 26 cm.   **ED43**

A concise and handy compilation of reference data in chemistry, physics, and related fields. Sources of data (and where to find both more extensive compilations and explanations of formulas) are given, but the data have not been critically evaluated by the editors. Tables of physical properties of organic compounds include references to Freidrich Beilstein, *Handbuch der organischen Chemie* (EE115) and to Aldrich spectral data (*The Aldrich library of NMR spectra*, EE142, and *The Aldrich library of FT-IR spectra*, EE140, both compiled by Charles J. Pouchert).   QC61.J36

Kaye, G. W. C. Tables of physical and chemical constants and some mathematical functions. 15th ed. London ; N.Y. : Longman, 1986. 477 p. : ill.   **ED44**
First published 1911; 14th ed., 1974.

"Originally compiled by G. W. C. Kaye and T. H. Laby ; now prepared under the direction of an editorial committee."—*t.p.*

A convenient compilation of physical and chemical data. Chapters are grouped into sections on general physics, chemistry, atomic and nuclear physics, and mathematical functions; this last section is very brief because of the availability of pocket calculators. References; index.   QC61.K3

Lang, Kenneth R. Astrophysical formulae : a compendium for the physicist and astrophysicist. 2nd corrected and enl. ed. Berlin ; N.Y. : Springer-Verlag, 1980. 783 p. : ill.   **ED45**
For annotation, *see* EC54.   QB461.L35

Lederer, Charles Michael. Table of isotopes / Charles Michael Lederer, Virginia S. Shirley, eds. 7th ed. N.Y. : Wiley, 1978. 1523 p. : ill.   **ED46**
Edgardo Browne, Janis M. Dairiki, and Raymond E. Doebler, principal authors.

Early editions appeared as articles by G. T. Seaborg and others in *Reviews of modern physics,* 1940–58; 6th ed., 1967.

"An Isotope Index, ordered by atomic number (Z) and subordered by mass number (A), precedes the main table. It contains all stable nuclei, radioisotopes, and isomers that appear in the *Table of isotopes* .... The main table is ordered by mass number and subordered by atomic number. For each mass number there is an abbreviated mass-chain decay scheme. ... Following the mass-chain decay scheme, tabulated data and detailed nuclear level schemes are given for individual isotopes. ... As in the 6th edition, each tabulated entry consists of a critical selection of reported data."—*Introd.*   QD466.L37

Menzel, Donald Howard. Fundamental formulas of physics. N.Y. : Prentice-Hall, c1955. 2 v. (741 p.) : ill.   **ED47**
Reprinted : N.Y. : Dover, 1960.

"Each chapter stands as a brief summary of the field represented" (*Pref.*) and is written by a specialist. Some chapters consist primarily of basic formulas, while others have considerable explanatory text. Includes bibliographies; indexed.   QA401.M492

A physicist's desk reference / Herbert L. Anderson, ed. in chief. N.Y. : American Institute of Physics, c1989. 356 p. : ill.   **ED48**
1st ed., 1981, had title: *AIP 50th anniversary physics vade mecum.*

The 22 chapters include tables, references, and formula compilations for subjects broadly representative of the fields of physics. A general section contains fundamental constants, units, conversion factors, magnitudes, basic mathematical and physical formulas, and a list of physics data centers; in the following sections the contributing editors provide about ten pages of the most useful formulas, numerical data, and references for each of the subfields. Indexed.   QC61.P49

Review of particle properties / Particle Data Group. 1957– . Berkeley, Calif. : Lawrence Berkeley Laboratory, 1957– . Biennial [irregular].   **ED49**

A critical review of data concerning elementary particles. A history of the Particle Data Group and its publications is found in A. H. Rosenfeld, *Annual review of nuclear science* 25 (1975) : 555-598. Current members of the group are listed in the current number of *Review of particle properties*, which also gives their institutional affiliations.

The *Review* appears every second year and has been variously published in the report and journal literature:

1st ed., 1957, issued as report UCRL-8030, had title: *Data for elementary-particle physics*, by Walter H. Barks and Arthur H. Rosenfeld.

In *Reviews of modern physics* 43, no. 2, pt. 2 suppl. (1971?), also issued as a separate (Lancaster, Pa. : American Inst. of Physics, 1971).

In *Physics letters* (Apr. 1972), also issued as a separate (Berkeley : Lawrence Berkeley Laboratory, 1972. Report LBL-100).

In *Physics letters*, ser. B, 50, no. 1 (Apr. 1974).

In *Reviews of modern physics*, 48, no. 2, pt. 2 (Apr. 1976).

In *Physics letters*, 75B, no. 1 (Apr. 1978).

In *Reviews of modern physics*, 52, no. 2, pt. 2 (Apr. 1980).

In *Physics letters*, 111B (Apr. 1988).

In *Reviews of modern physics*, 56, no. 2, pt. 2 (1984).

In *Physics letters*, 204B (14 Apr. 1988).

In *Physics letters*, 239B (12 Apr. 1990).

In *Physical review*, 45D, 3rd ser., v. 45, pt. 2 (1 June 1992).

In *Physical review*, 50D, 3rd ser., v. 50, no. 3, pt. 1 (1 Aug. 1994).

The data are also available on the Internet; the 1994 issue (p. 1188–1190) gives information for accessing the Internet version. The most convenient access point for those with a World Wide Web browser is at the Uniform Resource Locator (URL): http: //www-pdg.lbl.gov/ ; this site also has links to other nuclear data compilations and information on obtaining the *Review of particle properties* in booklet form.

Smithsonian Institution. Smithsonian physical tables. 9th rev. ed. / prep. by William E. Forsythe. Wash. : Smithsonian Inst., 1954. 827 p. : ill. (Smithsonian Institution. Smithsonian miscellaneous collections, v. 120). **ED50**

1st ed., 1896.

"Consists of 901 tables giving data of general interest to scientists and engineers, and of particular interest to those concerned with physics in the broader sense."—*Pref*. Indexed. QC61.S6

Style manuals

American Institute of Physics. AIP style manual / prepared under the direction of the AIP Publication Board. 4th ed. N.Y. : American Institute of Physics, 1990. 64 p. : ill. **ED51**

1st ed., 1951; 3rd ed., 1978. Title varies.

Previous editions were intended to provide guidance for submission of manuscripts to AIP publications; this edition "presents advice which, if followed, should result in the preparation of clear, concise, and well organized manuscripts eminently suitable for submission to any physics or astronomy journal editor's office."—*Pref*. Indexed. QC5.45.A45

History

Brush, Stephen G. The history of modern physics : an international bibliography / Stephen G. Brush, Lanfranco Belloni. N. Y. : Garland, 1983. 334 p. (Bibliographies of the history of science and technology, v. 4 ; Garland reference library of the humanities, v. 420). **ED52**

A classified bibliography that assumes the reader has access to J.L. Heilbron and Bruce J. Wheaton's *Literature on the history of physics in the 20th century* (ED53) and to *Isis cumulative bibliography* (EA233); thus in most cases it lists titles found in one of those sources only when it adds an annotation. Unlike Heilbron and Wheaton, this work includes short obituary notes, biographical articles on physicists active after the mid-1950s, and anthologies of reprints or translations of classic papers. Author and subject indexes. A useful supplement to Heilbron and Wheaton. Z7141.B78

Heilbron, J. L. Literature on the history of physics in the 20th century / J. L. Heilbron and Bruce R. Wheaton. Berkeley, Calif. : Office for History of Science and Technology, Univ. of California, Berkeley, 1981. 485 p. (Berkeley papers in history of science, 5). **ED53**

Accompanied by microfiche work by Wheaton entitled: *An inventory of published letters to and from physicists, 1900–1950* (1982).

A thorough bibliography of monographic and journal literature on the history of modern physics. Entries are arranged in an elaborate topical classification system, with cross-references. Short obituary notices are excluded, as are Nobel lectures (available from other sources). The biography section omits physicists active after the mid-1950s. Author index. Z7144.H55H44

Biography

The biographical dictionary of scientists : physicists / gen. ed., David Abbott. N.Y. : Peter Redrick, [1984]. 212 p. : ill. **ED54**

A six-page historical introduction is followed by brief narrative biographies, alphabetically arranged, of living and deceased physicists; no bibliographical references are included. Brief glossary; index to topics studied by the biographees. QC15.B56

The Nobel Prize winners : physics / ed. by Frank N. Magill. Pasadena, Calif. : Salem Pr., c1989. 3 v. (1364 p.) : ports. **ED55**

For annotation, *see* AL172. QC25.N63

Nobelstiftelsen. Physics. Amsterdam : Elsevier, 1964–[1992?]. v. 1–6 : ill. (In progress). **ED56**

For annotation, *see* AL175. QC71.N64

Women in chemistry and physics : a biobibliographic sourcebook / ed. by Louise S. Grinstein, Rose K. Rose, and Miriam H. Rafailovich. Westport, Conn. : Greenwood, 1993. 721 p. **ED57**

For annotation, *see* EA187. QD21.W62

COLOR

British Colour Council. The British Colour Council dictionary of colour standards : a list of colour names shown in the companion volume. 2nd ed. London : Council, 1951. 57 p. : atlas of mounted samples. **ED58**

"The purpose ... is to simplify work in connection with colour throughout all colour-using industries so that the standard name or standard number will always signify the colour so designated in this Dictionary."—*Note*.

Hope, Augustine. The color compendium / Augustine Hope, Margaret Walch. N.Y. : Van Nostrand Reinhold, c1990. 360 p. : ill. (some col.). **ED59**

An encyclopedic survey of all aspects of color, including not only physics, chemistry, biology, and engineering, but also psychology, symbolism, art, and communication. Entries are arranged alphabetically, and range from brief definitions to signed essays; biographical entries are included. The table of contents lists separately the essays and "color sections"—long, unsigned entries with many color illustrations—although these special entries are found at the expected locations in the alphabetic arrangement with the exception of the color section on sources of historic color, which appears at the end. Appendixes list names and addresses of color organizations, and color specifier systems. Bibliography; cross-references; index.

§ For earlier works, see *Color theory : a guide to information sources* by Mary L. Buckley and David W. Baum (Detroit ; Gale, 1974). QC494.2.H67

Kelly, Kenneth L. Color : universal language and dictionary of names / Kenneth L. Kelly and Deane B. Judd. [Wash.] : U.S. Dept. of Commerce, National Bureau of Standards; for sale by U.S. Govt. Print. Off., 1976. 19, 158 p. : ill. (National Bureau of Standards. Special Publication, 440).   **ED60**

Supersedes and combines *The ISCC-NBS method of designating colors and a dictionary of color names* by Kelly and Judd (1955. NBS Circular 553) and *A universal color language* by Kelly (1965).

"The purpose of this dictionary is to assist the scientist, businessman, and layman to understand the different color vocabularies used in the many fields of art, science, and industry.... The dictionary will serve not only as a record of the 7,500 individual color names listed but it will also enable anyone to translate from one color vocabulary to another." —*Pref.*

Supplemented by: Kelly's *Color-universal language and dictionary of names* [microform] (Wash.], 1985. 25 p. [NBS special publication 440/Add.]).   QC100.U57

Maerz, Aloys John. Dictionary of color / by A. Maerz, M. Rea Paul. 2nd ed. N.Y. : McGraw-Hill, 1950. 208 p. : 56 color plates.   **ED61**

1st ed., 1930.

Partial contents: Introduction; Table of terms found in literature; Table of principal color names; Polyglot table of principal color names; Bibliography; Color plates; Brief history of color standardization; Notes on color names; Index of color names.

"This work is primarily intended as a reference for the individual who seeks to relate colors with the names by which they are commonly identified."—*Pref.* Contains "the most extensive range of colors as yet published, together with a list of practically all recorded color names in use up to this time in the English language."   QC495.M25

Smithe, Frank B. Naturalist's color guide. N.Y. : Amer. Museum of Natural History, [1975–81]. Pt. I, 24 p. (looseleaf); pt. II, 229 p.; pt. III, 37 p.   **ED62**

Pt. I, Naturalist's color guide, consists of 86 swatches, named and numbered. Pt. II, Naturalist's color guide supplement, retains much of the terminology from Robert Ridgway's *Color standards and color nomenclature* (Wash., 1912), analyzes each color, correlates it with other colors, and mentions numerous others. Pt. III supplements the earlier parts.   QL767.S63

Society of Dyers and Colourists. Colour index. 3rd ed. Bradford, Eng. : Society of Dyers and Colourists ; Lowell, Mass. : American Association of Textile Chemists and Colorists, [1971–88]. 7 v.   **ED63**

1st ed., 1924–28.

A revised v. 5 was issued in 1982; v. 6 (1975) is a 1st suppl. to v. 1–4; v. 7 (1988) is a 2nd suppl. to both v. 1–4 and v. 6; v. 8 (1987) is a suppl. to v. 1–4, 6, and 7; v. 9 (1992) revises v. 5 and supplements v. 1–4, 6–8.

The standard work in the field. 7,898 Colour Index generic names. "Volumes 1–3 contain in tabular form the technical information for each C.I. Generic Name and Volume 4 gives structural formulae, where known, together with an outline of the method of preparation and literature references. The entries in Volumes 1–3 and Volume 4 are cross-referenced. Volume 5 contains lists of manufacturers and the code letters allocated to them, the C.I. Generic Names Index and the Commercial Names Index."—*Introd.*

Wyszecki, Günter. Color science : concepts and methods, quantitative data and formulas / Günter Wyszecki, W. S. Stiles. 2nd ed. N.Y. : Wiley, [1982]. 950 p. : ill.   **ED64**

1st ed., 1967.

A compilation of the quantitative tools for work on color, including working concepts, formulas, and tables, intended for those concerned with color problems in industry and for research workers in color—physicists, physiologists, or psychologists. In eight major sections: (1) Physical data; (2) The eye; (3) Colorimetry; (4) Photometry; (5) Visual equivalence and visual matching; (6) Uniform color scales; (7) Visual thresholds; (8) Theories and models of color vision. "For the most part, descriptive and qualitative material on color phenomena

which would properly find a place in a textbook or introductory treatise on color has not been included."—*Pref.* List of references; author and subject indexes.   QC495.W88

EE

Chemistry

A number of guides to the literature of chemistry are available. Both Wiggins, *Chemical information sources* (EE8) and Bottle and Rowland, *Information sources in chemistry* (EE3) are recent and very sound, and Wolman, *Chemical information* (EE9) is useful. Crane, Patterson, and Marr, *A guide to the literature of chemistry* (EE2), an older standard work, is still useful as a guide to the older literature. *Chemical abstracts* (EE22), one of the oldest and best-known abstract journals, is perhaps the largest single index to the scientific literature. It is indispensable for chemistry research, which is carried out increasingly through the online version. Its list of periodicals, *CASSI* (EE18), is one of the most useful bibliographies of scientific periodicals.

For the literature of inorganic chemistry, Gmelin (EE110) is still a key source, and for organic chemistry, Beilstein (EE115) remains important.

GENERAL WORKS

Guides

Antony, Arthur. Guide to basic information sources in chemistry. N.Y.: Wiley, [1979]. 219 p.   **EE1**

"This guide ... is primarily intended for the student of chemistry from college freshmen through graduate level."—*Pref.* Chapters treat types of sources—nomenclature, guides to techniques, access to primary publications other than journals, major reference tools. Author/title and subject indexes.   QD8.5.A57

Crane, Evan Jay. A guide to the literature of chemistry / Evan Jay Crane, Austin M. Patterson, Eleanor B. Marr. 2nd ed. N.Y. : Wiley, [1957]. 397 p.   **EE2**

1st ed., 1927.

Chiefly useful today for aid in searching the older literature; for example, an appendix gives a useful list of names and abbreviations for periodicals discontinued before 1910. General subject index.

   Z5521.C89

Information sources in chemistry / ed., R. T. Bottle, J. F. B. Rowland. 4th ed. London ; N.Y. : Bowker-Saur, c1992. 341 p. : ill.   **EE3**

1st ed., 1962. Earlier eds. had title *The use of chemical literature.*

17 chapters by various authors provide information on various aspects of the use of the chemical literature: primary literature, chemical structure handling by computer, patents, standard tables of physico-

chemical data, etc. A number of chapters emphasize British practice (e.g. "National and international governmental sources of information" allots half its space to U.K. sources); the only non-British author, from the Research Department of *Chemical abstracts* (EE22), contributed the chapter on "Online searching for chemical information." One of the most up-to-date guides for chemistry. Indexed, with a separate "Index-glossary of acronyms, databases, etc." QD8.5.B6

Maizell, Robert E. How to find chemical information : a guide for practicing chemists, educators, and students. 2nd ed. N.Y. : Wiley, c1987. 402 p. : ill. **EE4**
  1st ed., 1979.
  Subtitle: A guide for practicing chemists, educators, and students.
  Emphasizes the key tools and fundamental principles of chemical information, with in-depth coverage of *Chemical abstracts* (EE22), Beilstein (EE115) and Gmelin (EE110). QD8.5.M34

Mellon, Melvin Guy. Chemical publications : their nature and use. 5th ed. N.Y. : McGraw-Hill, [1982]. 419 p. : ill. **EE5**
  1st ed., 1928; 4th ed., 1965.
  The first part, Publications: kinds and nature, describes the principal sources for reference and research, including primary sources (periodicals, technical reports, patents, etc.), secondary sources (abstracts, reference compilations of various sorts, treatises, textbooks, etc.), and tertiary sources (guides and directories). The second part, Publications: storage and use, describes libraries and information centers and how to search manually and with on-line databases; it also includes, as Chapter 16, examples of library problems. Indexed. QD8.5.M44

Schulz, Hedda. From CA to CAS ONLINE : databases in chemistry / Hedda Schulz, Ursula Georgy. 2nd, completely rev. and enl. ed. Berlin ; N.Y. : Springer Verlag, c1994. 311 p. : ill. **EE6**
  1st ed., 1988, was a translation of *Von CA bis CAS ONLINE* (Weinheim ; Deerfield Beach, Fla. : VCH, c1985).
  This guide to *Chemical abstracts* and its online version is a very useful starting point for anyone needing to use the single most important source of information in chemistry and related fields. Users will need to consult Chemical Abstracts Service documents for the most recent changes in the online system (e.g., for information on the software package "STN Express," which facilitates searching *CAS ONLINE*). QD9.S3813

Skolnik, Herman. The literature matrix of chemistry. N.Y. : Wiley, [1982]. 297 p. **EE7**
  Intended to "delineate the scope and content of the literature matrix so that the reader can interact with and gain access to it effectively."—*Pref.* The author is a distinguished chemical information scientist. Indexed. QD5.S58

Wiggins, Gary. Chemical information sources. N.Y. : McGraw-Hill, 1991. 352 p. : ill. + 2 computer disks. **EE8**
  A textbook designed to give to the chemist, librarian, or student the command of the chemical literature which is needed to successfully solve most chemical information problems. Contains helpful and detailed information on the use of reference sources, and is particularly strong on the use of the Chemical Abstracts online file (*CA FILE*) as made available through STN International. A unique feature is a Pro-Cite database included with the book on a 3½-inch MS-DOS disk; the database includes records for more than 2,150 sources (bibliographic information and index terms) which can be searched for sources on particular topics, using the Pro-Cite search-only software which is also included with the book on a second 3½-inch disk. This database contains records for printed reference works, online databases, and software, including many reference sources not discussed in the parent work. An ASCII version of the database may be obtained from the author. The printed text is indexed, but does not have entries for all titles mentioned. Perhaps the best single text currently available for a course in chemical information; also useful for quick reference, particularly using the accompanying database. Z699.5.C5W54

Wolman, Yecheskel. Chemical information : a practical guide to utilization. 2nd rev. and enl. ed. Chichester [Eng.] ; N.Y. : Wiley, c1988. 291 p. : ill. **EE9**
  1st ed., 1983.
  Based on a course presented to undergraduate chemistry students. Emphasizes actual search problems and their solutions using current information sources. Accordingly, its organization is by sections on current awareness, obtaining numerical data, synthetic reaction search, etc., unlike the organization of most other guides to chemical literature, which it complements. Online searching is discussed throughout, in parallel to manual searching tools and sources, although the 2nd ed. includes a chapter on expert systems. Indexed; includes a glossary of acronyms. QD8.5.W64

Bibliography

Bolton, Henry Carrington. A select bibliography of chemistry, 1492–1892. Wash. : Smithsonian Institution, 1893. 1212 p. (Smithsonian Institution miscellaneous collections, 36 ; Smithsonian Institution publication, 850). **EE10**
  Repr. : Millwood, N.Y. : Kraus Reprint Corp., 1973 (basic vol.); 1967 (supplements).
  Eight sections: (1) Bibliography; (2) Dictionaries; (3) History; (4) Biography; (5) Chemistry, pure and applied; (6) Alchemy; (7) Periodicals; (8) Academic dissertations.
  Includes some 18,000 independent works but does not list analytics. Sec.8, Academic dissertations, is particularly strong for dissertations from the universities of France, Germany, Russia and the U.S.
  Supplements: ———. ——— *First supplement,* covering 1492–1897 (1899. 489 p. Miscellaneous collections, v. 39, art. 7; Publication 1170); *Second supplement,* covering 1492–1902 (1904. 462 p. Miscellaneous collections, v. 44 art. 5; Publication 1440); *Academic dissertations,* covering 1492–1897 (1901. 534 p. Miscellaneous collections, v. 41, art. 3; Publication 1253). Z5521.B69

Cole, William A. Chemical literature, 1700–1860 : a bibliography with annotations, detailed descriptions, comparisons, and locations. London ; N.Y. : Mansell, 1988. 582 p. **EE11**
  An elaborate descriptive bibliography that follows largely (but not entirely) the precepts of Philip Gaskell's *A new introduction to bibliography* (AA3). The wealth of detail makes this work an important addition to collections where much use is made of Henry Carrington Bolton's *A select bibliography of chemistry 1492–1892* and supplements (EE10), Denis I. Duveen's *Bibliotheca alchemica et chemica* (EE12), or *Bibliotheca chemica* by John Ferguson (EE16). Z5522.C73

Duveen, Denis I. Bibliotheca alchemica et chemica : an annotated catalogue of printed books on alchemy, chemistry and cognate subjects in the library of Denis I. Duveen. London : Weil, 1949. 669 p. : ill. **EE12**
  Repr.: Rijwijk, Utrecht : Krips/ Oosthoek, 1965; London : Dawsons, 1965.
  Includes works, with full bibliographical description, from the 16th to the 19th centuries. Collection now housed at the University of Wisconsin Libraries (*see* EE17). Z5526.D8

International catalogue of scientific literature / publ. for the Internat. Council by the Royal Soc. of London. v. 1 (1901)–v. 14 (1914). London : Harrison, 1902–21. **EE13**
  Section D, Chemistry. For full description, *see* EA16.

Pritchard, Alan. Alchemy : a bibliography of English-language writings. London : Routledge & Kegan Paul jointly with the Library Assoc., [1980]. 439 p. **EE14**
  A scholarly and "purposeful attempt to draw together into one document all writings in the English language on and about alchemy—texts and secondary works respectively. It adds to these, works which mention alchemy *en passant,* and works on some of the byways which seem … to be imbued with Hermetic thinking, or which throw

light on those works which are directly concerned with alchemy."—
Pref. In three main sections: (1) Alchemical texts; (2) Works about al-
chemy: countries; (3) Works about alchemy: subjects. Indexed.
Z5524.A35P75

Reuss, Jeremias David. Repertorium commentationum a societatibus litterariis editarum / secundum disciplinarum ordinem digessit I. D. Reuss …. Gottingae : apud Henricum
Dieterich, 1801–21. 16 v.   **EE15**
    T. 3, Chemia et res metallica. A valuable index to the publications
of learned societies up to 1800. Classed arrangement with author
index. For description of complete set *see* EA21.   Z5051.R44

**Royal College of Science and Technology (Glasgow, Scot-
land). Andersonian Library.** Bibliotheca chemica : A catalogue of the alchemical, chemical and pharmaceutical books in
the collection of the late James Young of Kelly and Durris / by
John Ferguson. Glasgow : Maclehose, 1906. 2 v.   **EE16**
    Repr.: Hildesheim ; N.Y. : Olms, 1974. Facsimile, called 2nd ed,
publ. London : Holland Pr., 1954.
    A rich collection of early works useful for the history of chemis-
try, particularly in alchemy. Detailed bibliographical descriptions.
Frequently mentioned are other editions, translations, and additional
works which are not included in the Young collection. Biographical information and an evaluation of an author's work are added features.
    Collection bequeathed to the chair of technical chemistry of An-
derson's College, now incorporated in the Royal Technical College,
Glasgow.   Z5524.A35G42

University of Wisconsin-Madison. Libraries. Chemical,
medical, and pharmaceutical books printed before 1800, in the
collections of the University of Wisconsin Libraries / ed. by
John Neu. Madison : Univ. of Wisconsin Pr., 1965. 280 p.
    EE17
    Full bibliographical listings of 4,442 items, including Denis I.
Duveen's *Bibliotheca alchemica et chemica* (EE12). No annotations.
Z5526.W5

Periodicals

Chemical Abstracts Service source index : 1907–1989 cumulative. [Columbus, Ohio] : American Chemical Society,
[1990].   **EE18**
    Cited as *CAS source index*; also cited as *CASSI*.
    The cumulative version of *CAS source index* was first publ. in
1975 and has appeared every five years since. It supersedes the publication of the same title that first appeared in 1971, superseding *Access*
(1969), which itself superseded the *List of periodicals* … issued irregularly in connection with *Chemical abstracts*.
    This cumulation contains information concerning 68,000 serial
and nonserial source publications; including cross-references, there are
about 125,000 entries.
    This most important publication is broad in scope since *Chemical
abstracts* (EE22) covers not only the chemical sciences but also related
biological, engineering, and physical sciences. Moreover, to the publications indexed there *CASSI* has added those indexed by *BIOSIS*
(EG13), *Engineering index* (EK7), and the Institute for Scientific Information, as well as those publications covered by *Chemisches Zentralblatt* (EE24) and its predecessors, 1830–1969, and those cited by
Friedrich Beilstein's *Handbuch der organischen Chemie* (EE115) prior
to 1907. *CASSI* includes both periodicals and nonserial publications
such as proceedings of nonrecurring meetings and other compilations
of articles.
    Each entry includes the full title with its abbreviated portions
printed in boldface; the entries are alphabetized letter-by-letter according to this abbreviated title. All titles are printed in the roman alphabet;
for titles not in Western European languages, a translation is included.
Entries also include: CODEN; ISBN; ISSN; previous and succeeding
titles; information on language(s) of publication, summaries and table
of contents; history and frequency of publication; current volume/year
correlation; address of publisher or source (or abbreviation if a stan-

dard source); indication of year of publication or date and place of
meeting for nonserial titles; cross-references, including references to
title-to-title translations journals if they exist (e.g., for Slavic titles);
abbreviated entry as cataloged under *Anglo-American cataloguing
rules* (2nd ed.); and information on location in libraries throughout the
world, with library holdings. There is also a list of the 1,000 journals
most frequently cited in *Chemical abstracts* v. 109–110 (July
1988–June 1989)—i.e., the journals which have had the most articles
abstracted during that period.
    Invaluable for determining full titles from abbreviations, for pub-
lication history including changes of titles and discontinuations, for
finding title-to-title translation journals for Slavic and Asian publications, for locating libraries holding obscure publications, for verification of bibliographic information, etc.
    Kept up-to-date by: *Chemical Abstracts Service source index :
quarterly supplement*, (1990– . [Columbus, Ohio] : American Chemical Soc., 1990– . Quarterly). Cited as *CAS source index, quarterly
supplement*; supersedes *Access quarterly* (1970). The 4th issue each
year is a cumulation for the year.
    Both *CASSI* and its *Quarterly supplement* are indexed by: *CASSI
keyword-out-of-context index, 1907–1989* [microform] ([Columbus,
Ohio] : American Chemical Soc., 1990– . Microfiche; annual). Accompanied by "User's guide," both in the fiche set and as a nine-page
pamphlet. Also cited as *CASSI KWOC*. Each annual edition cumulates
entries from the most recent ed. of *CASSI* and its supplements. An
index to all words from the title/reference data fields in each *CASSI*
record, omitting stopwords (a list of which is included) and nonindexed terms (words beginning with lower case letters—e.g., prepositions and articles—and words of more than 30 characters). About 50
titles consisting only of stopwords and nonindexed terms are listed
separately. Permits identification of titles for which only fragments are
known. Entries show keyword at the left, followed by title or reference
entry from *CASSI*, and the item's *CODEN*.
    ●Machine-readable form: *Chemical Abstracts Service source
index (CASSI)* [database] (Columbus, Ohio : Chemical Abstracts Service, 1830–). Available online, updated quarterly.   Z5523.A52

Periodica chemica : Verzeichnis der im Chemischen Zentralblatt referierten Zeitschriften mit den entsprechenden
genormten Titelabkürzungen / hrsg. von Maximilian Pflücke
und Alice Hawelek. 2. neubearb. Aufl. Berlin : Akademie-
Verlag, 1952. 411 p.   **EE19**
    1st ed., 1940.
    An international list of chemical periodicals indicating all changes
of title that have taken place since 1930, with abbreviations as used in
Chemisches Zentralblatt (EE24). Arrangement is alphabetical by title,
with separate listings of Russian periodicals in Cyrillic and in non-
Cyrillic alphabets.   Z5523.P45

Indexes; Abstract journals

See Wiggins, *Chemical information sources* (EE8), for a description of *Chemical abstracts* and other abstracting services;
and Schulz, *From CA to CAS online* (EE6) for more detail on
Chemical abstracts.

Analytical abstracts. v. 1 (Jan. 1954)– . [London] : Royal
Society of Chemistry, 1954– . Monthly.   **EE20**
    Continues: *British abstracts.* Pt. C, Analysis and apparatus
(EE21).
    Publisher varies: 1954–Oct. 1979, Society for Analytical Chemis-
try; Nov. 1979–June 1981, Chemical Society; July 1981– , Royal Society of Chemistry.
    Abstracts arranged under topical headings and subheadings;
monthly issues have brief subject indexes. Annual index of subjects
and authors.
    ●Available in machine-readable form as: *Analytical abstracts
(AA)* [database] (Cambridge, Eng. : Royal Society of Chemistry,
1980–). Available online, updated monthly.   QD71.A49

British abstracts. London : Bureau of Abstracts, 1926–53. A and B, monthly; C, quarterly. **EE21**

Title varies: 1926–37, *British chemical abstracts*; 1938–44, *British chemical and physiological abstracts*. Continues the abstract volumes previously published in *Journal* of the Chemical Society and *Journal* of the Society of Chemical Industry.

Publ. in three parts: A, Pure chemistry, divided 1937–53 into three sections: A1, General, physical, and inorganic chemistry, A2, Organic chemistry, A3, Physiology, biochemistry, anatomy; B, Applied chemistry, divided 1945–53 into three sections: B1, Chemical engineering & industrial inorganic chemistry, including metallurgy (renamed 1949–53, Chemical engineering, fuels, industrial electrochemistry and inorganic chemistry, and metallurgy), B2, Industrial organic chemistry, B3, Agriculture, foods, sanitation; C, Analysis and apparatus.

The list of periodicals abstracted duplicates to a considerable extent the list for *Chemical abstracts* (EE22), but includes some titles not covered there.

Ceased 1953. Superseded by several publications, of which only one continues as an abstracting journal in chemistry: *Analytical abstracts* (EE20), continuing Section C. QD1.B68

Chemical abstracts. 1907– . Columbus, Ohio : American Chemical Society, 1907– . Weekly. **EE22**

Imprint varies.

Now the most comprehensive of the abstract journals, with an international reputation for comprehensive coverage of the literature. More than 530,000 documents are selected annually for abstracting. Abstracts are prepared from publications in more than 50 languages. Initially issued biweekly; now weekly. Indexes in current issues: keyword, author, numerical patent, patent concordance. The keyword indexes should not be confused with the subject indexes.

Subject indexing is thorough. Beginning with v. 76 (1972), the subject index was divided into two parts: chemical substances and general subjects. Within the past few years a variety of indexes and aids have been introduced. The Index guide first appeared as pt. 1 of the subject index to v. 69; annual revisions are issued with the subject indexes for the odd-numbered volumes of *CA*. A Registry number index began in 1969 and an Index of ring systems with v. 66 (1967; see also: *Ring systems handbook*, EE86). The IIAIC (hetero atom in context) index was initiated prior to 1970 but discontinued.

Cumulated indexes:

(1) ———. *Decennial author and subject index*, 1907/16–1947/56.

(2) ———. *Collective index*, 1957/61; 1962/66; 1967/71; 1972/76; 1977/81; 1982/86; 1987/91. Each quinquennial Collective index has separate author, subject, and patent sections. The 1967/71 index introduced the Index guide. Beginning with 1972/76, separate chemical substances and general subject indexes replaced the former subject index.

(3) ———. *Formula index*, v. 14–40, 1920–46; v. 41–50, 1947–56; v. 51–55, 1957–61; v. 56–65, 1962–66; v. 66–75, 1967–71; v. 76–85, 1972–76; v. 86–95, 1977–81; v. 96–105, 1982–86; v. 106–115, 1987–91.

(4) *Patent index to Chemical abstracts, 1907–1936*, comp. by the Science-Technology Group of Special Libraries Association. ... (Ann Arbor, Mich. : Edwards, 1944. 479 p.). Numerical lists by country of all patents included in the first 30 v. of *CA*.

(5) ———. *Collective numerical patent index*, v. 31–40, 1937–46; v. 41–50, 1947–56; v. 51–55, 1957–61; v. 56–65, 1962–66; v. 66–75, 1967–71; v. 76–85, 1972–76; v. 86–95, 1977–81; v. 96–105, 1982–86; v. 106–115, 1987–91. The patent concordance appeared with the 1962–66 index. It "correlates patents issued by different countries for the same basic invention."—*Introd.*

•Available in machine-readable form as: *CA file* [database] (Columbus, Ohio : The Service, 1966–). Includes abstracts 1969– , to which CAS is adding abstracts for earlier records. Available online under various names; most vendors update biweekly. Versions available through various online services differ substantially in their indexing features and in the period for which full abstracts are available. This complex database may require sophisticated search techniques; it is important to study the documentation available from the service being used before starting a search. A CD-ROM version of the *Collective index* covering 1987–91 is available, but does not allow all the types of searching provided online. The collected abstracts for this period are also available in CD-ROM. CAS has begun to offer CD-ROMs covering the current literature for selected subsets covered under the title *CA surveyor* (e.g., Food and food chemistry, Organometallic chemistry). QD1.A51

Chemical titles. Apr. 1960– . Columbus, Ohio : American Chemical Society, 1960– . Biweekly. **EE23**

Subtitle: Current author and keyword indexes from selected chemical journals.

A computer-produced index to titles of chemical research papers. Each issue in three parts: (1) keywords arranged alphabetically down the center of the column; (2) a bibliographic listing of titles of current papers from selected journals, arranged as tables of contents of the journals; and (3) an index of authors. Titles are selected from more than 700 journals in pure and applied chemistry and chemical engineering. Serves as a current awareness listing and as a means of locating recent articles on a topic before they appear in *Chemical abstracts* (EE22).

Chemisches Zentralblatt. Jahrg. 1–140. Berlin : Verlag Chemie, 1830–1969. Weekly. **EE24**

Title and imprint vary: 1897–1945, publ. by the Deutsche Chemische Gesellschaft; v. 112–16, pt. 1, repr. by J. W. Edwards, Ann Arbor, Mich; 1946–69, hrsg. im Auftrage der Deutschen Akademie der Wissenschaften zu Berlin, der Chemischen Gesellscaft in der DDR, der Akademie der Wissenschaften zu Göttingen, und der Gesellschaft Deutscher Chemiker.

An abstracting journal for pure and applied chemistry, particularly valuable because of the length of the period covered. Many of the abstracts are more detailed than those in *Chemical abstracts* (EE22). Before 1919, did not include abstracts on applied chemistry, as these appeared in *Angewandte Chemie*. Author index in each issue; annual and cumulated author, subject, patent, and organic formula indexes (vary somewhat). QD1.C7

Encyclopedias

See also EK52, EK53.

Comprehensive dictionary of physical chemistry / editors, L. Ulický, T. J. Kemp. N.Y. : E. Horwood : PTR Prentice Hall, 1992. 472 p. : ill. **EE25**

Translated from the Slovak.

A concise encyclopedia of concepts and terms in physical and theoretical chemistry, and in physical techniques used in chemistry. Entries are brief, from a few paragraphs to a page in length, and are extensively cross-referenced. Some acronyms are included.

QD5.C4555

Concise encyclopedia chemistry / tr. and rev. by Mary Eagleson. Berlin ; N.Y. : W. de Gruyter, 1994. 1201 p. : ill. **EE26**

1st ed., 1965, had title: *ABC Chemie in zwei Bänden*; 2nd ed., 1967–70, publ. Frankfurt am Main with 1st ed. title and in Leipzig with title: *Brockhaus ABC Chemie in zwei Bänden*; 5th ed., 1987.

A very handy encyclopedia, with a remarkable amount of information in a single volume. Includes entries on individual elements and compounds, classes of compounds, chemical concepts, experimental techniques, etc. Hazards presented by substances are noted in distinctive boxes. Many cross-references. The clearly-written entries give numerical data but no literature references. Includes topics from technical chemistry and chemical engineering.

§ The related field of biochemistry has some entries, but is chiefly covered in the companion work: *Concise encyclopedia biochemistry* (EG315). QD4.A2313

Encyclopedia of industrial chemical analysis / ed. by Foster Dee Snell and Clifford L. Hilton. N.Y. : Interscience Publ., [1966–74]. 20 v. : ill.   **EE27**
Vols. 8–20 ed. by Snell and Leslie S. Ettre.
General techniques of analysis, especially instrumental methods, are discussed in v. 1–3. The remaining 17 v. contain articles on chemicals of industrial importance, emphasizing methods and techniques for identification and analysis. Subject index for v. 1–3 in v. 3; v. 20 has a subject index for v. 4–19, plus lists of contents and contributors for the whole encyclopedia.   QD131.E5

Encyclopédie des gaz = Gas encyclopaedia / [comp. by Société] L'Air Liquide, Division Scientifique. N.Y. & Amsterdam : Elsevier, [1976]. 1150 p. : ill.   **EE28**
Text in French and English.
Offers articles on 138 gases from air to xenon, with an "enormous scope of the subjects covered: chemical and physical properties, operating conditions, flammability limits, toxicity, biological properties, materials of construction, uses, etc. ... [with] short but effective bibliography."—*Pref.*   TP247.E52

Flood, Walter Edgar. The dictionary of chemical names. N.Y. : Philosophical Lib., [1963]. 238 p.   **EE29**
Published in U.K. as *The origins of chemical names.*
In two parts: (1) names of chemical elements; (2) compounds, minerals and other substances. Some entries include a number of related compounds. The date of the earliest use of the name is added when known.   QD5.F55

Hampel, Clifford A. Encyclopedia of the chemical elements. N.Y. : Reinhold, [1968]. 849 p. : ill.   **EE30**
Each of 103 elements is discussed in relation to its history, prevalence, sources, physical and chemical properties, applications, importance of the elements and its compounds, and biological and biochemical aspects (including toxicology). Data tables are used frequently. Articles are signed; subject index.   QD466.H295

Kingzett, Charles Thomas. Kingzett's chemical encyclopaedia : a digest of chemistry and its industrial applications / gen. ed., D. H. Hey. 9th ed. London : Baillière ; Princeton, N.J. : Van Nostrand, [1966]. 1092 p. : ill.   **EE31**
1st ed., 1919, had title: *Popular chemical dictionary*; 8th ed., 1952.
Entries for trade names, prefixes, methods, names of reactions, etc. Inorganic compounds usually are listed under a discussion of the parent element and its compounds. Very few tables; British spelling predominates. Index consists only of alternate names for entries appearing in the main portion of the book.   QD5.K4

Römpps Chemie-Lexikon. Völlig neubearb. und erw. 8. Aufl. / fortgeführt von Erhard Ühlein, neubearb. von Otto-Albrecht Neumüller. Stuttgart : Franckh, [1979–88]. 6 v.   **EE32**
1st–6th eds. had title: *Chemie Lexikon.*
An alphabetically arranged, comprehensive encyclopedia, revised, updated, and enlarged. Contains information on chemical compound types, trade name products, statistics, industrial chemicals, etc., as well as biographical sketches. Includes bibliographies.   QD5.R62

Van Nostrand Reinhold encyclopedia of chemistry / Douglas M. Considine, ed. in chief ; Glenn D. Considine, managing ed. 4th ed. N.Y. : Van Nostrand Reinhold, 1984. 1082 p. : ill.   **EE33**
1st ed., 1957; 3rd ed., 1973. Earlier eds. had title *Encyclopedia of chemistry.*
A very much revised edition containing more than 85% new text. The roughly 1,300 entries range from brief definitions to articles, some of them signed, which may include tabular data and references. Includes topics from fields related to chemistry, such as materials science, energy sources and conversion, biochemistry and biotechnology, wastes and pollution. Cross-references; index.   QD5.V37

Dictionaries

Bennett, H. Concise chemical and technical dictionary. 4th enl. ed. N.Y. : Chemical Publ. Co., c1986. 1271 p. : ill. **EE34**
1st ed., 1947; 3rd ed., 1974.
More than 85,000 very brief definitions of scientific terms, chemicals, trademark products, and drugs. Supplementary materials, including a key to pronunciation of chemical words, and miscellaneous tables and other matter, are hard to find since there is no table of contents; an essay on the nomenclature of organic chemistry is reprinted from a source more than 50 years old.   QD5.B4

Compendium of analytical nomenclature : definitive rules 1987 / prep. for publication by Henry Freiser and George H. Nancollas. 2nd ed. Oxford ; Boston : Blackwell Scientific Publ., 1987. 279 p. : ill.   **EE35**
At head of title: International Union of Pure and Applied Chemistry, Analytical Chemistry Division.
Gives recommendations, arranged in topical sections, for nomenclature in areas of analytical chemistry, including thermal and titrimetic analysis, electrochemical analysis, spectrochemical analysis, etc. Not yet a comprehensive manual; the table of contents lists chapter headings and subheadings for which the appropriate report is not yet available, with an indication of its absence.   QD75.3.C65

Compendium of chemical terminology : IUPAC recommendations / comp. by Victor Gold ... [et al.]. Oxford ; Boston : Blackwell Scientific, 1987. 456 p. : ill.   **EE36**
At head of title: International Union of Pure and Applied Chemistry.
A dictionary of terms compiled from material published up to the end of 1985 by the Physical, Inorganic, Organic, Macromolecular, and Analytical Chemistry divisions of IUPAC. Contains brief definitions, some with diagrams or formulas, and references to IUPAC source documents and other sources. Cross-references; related entries in definitions are italicized.   QD5.C455

Eklund, Jon. The incompleat chymist : being an essay on the eighteenth-century chemist in his laboratory, with a dictionary of obsolete chemical terms of the period. Wash. : Smithsonian Institution Pr., 1975. 49 p. : ill. (Smithsonian studies in history and technology, no. 33).   **EE37**
The essay on 18th-century chemical practices, with bibliographic references, is followed by a 30-page "Dictionary of British eighteenth-century chemical terms" which gives brief explanations or modern equivalents for the terms. Includes Latin and French phrases that were common in British journals and treatises. Cross-references.   QD14.E38

The Facts on File dictionary of chemistry / ed. by John Daintith. Rev. and expanded ed. N.Y. : Facts on File, 1988. 233 p. : ill.   **EE38**
"First edition published in the United Kingdom in 1981 by Intercontinental Book Productions Limited ... ."—*verso of t.p.* The U.S. version, publ. 1981 by Facts on File, called 2nd ed.
Some 2,200 entries define the most important and commonly used chemical terms; entries are carefully written and relatively long. British spellings are sometimes used (e.g., "aluminium" rather than "aluminum"). Many *see* references.   QD5.D26

Gardner's chemical synonyms and trade names / executive ed., Jill Pearce ; consultant, John Buckingham. 9th ed. Aldershots, Hants, Eng. ; Brookfield, Vt. : Gower Technical Pr., c1987. 1081 p.   **EE39**
1st ed., 1924.
Previous eds. had title: *Chemical synonyms and trade names*, ed. by William Gardner.
Brief definitions. In this edition material has been deleted for the first time; there are 12,000 new entries, and 45% of the material is new. British spellings are used, and *see* references lead from alternate

names. Entries give manufacturers, and a list at the end of the volume gives manufacturers' full names, addresses, and product trade names.

TP9.G28

Hackh, Ingo W. D. Grant & Hackh's chemical dictionary : American, international, European, and British usage. 5th ed. / completely rev. and ed. by Roger Grant, Claire Grant. N.Y. : McGraw-Hill, c1987. 641 p. : ill.   **EE40**

4th ed., 1969.

"Containing the words generally used in chemistry, and many of the terms used in the related sciences of physics, medicine, engineering, biology, pharmacy, astrophysics, agriculture, mineralogy, etc. Based on recent scientific literature."—*t.p.* Brief definitions in simple language for about 55,000 entries. Includes trade names (initial letters capitalized), symbols, prefixes, abbreviations, etc. Both American and British usage are noted; entries are listed under the American spelling. Internationally accepted terminology or symbols (from IUPAC) are starred. A few entries are substantially extended; for example, "Nomenclature" includes a two-page summary of the basics of IUPAC nomenclature, and "Enzymes" a page-long table of classification of enzymes.   QD5.H3

Hawley's condensed chemical dictionary. 12th ed, rev. by Richard J. Lewis, Sr. N.Y. : Van Nostrand Reinhold, c1993. 1275 p. : ill.   **EE41**

1st ed., 1919; 11th ed., 1987.

Concise definitions for terms relating to chemistry and the chemical industry. Includes short biographies of outstanding scientists and brief information about some American technical societies. Many *see* and *see also* references. Entries for compounds give other commonly accepted names, CAS Registry number, molecular formula, properties, source or occurence, commercial grades available, hazards, and uses in large-scale applications. Proprietary names in the alphabetical listings are set in quotation marks; a brief form of the manufacturer's name is given, while full names and addresses appear as an appendix. Other appendixes give the origins of some chemical names and highlights in the history of chemistry.   QD5.C5

Howard, Philip H. Dictionary of chemical names and synonyms / Philip H. Howard, Michael Neal. Boca Raton, Fla. : Lewis Publishers, c1992. 1 v. (various pagings) : ports. **EE42**

The main part lists chemical substances in order of their CAS Registry number, and includes chemical formulas, molecular weights, and synonyms. More than 130,000 chemical synonyms are included for the approximately 20,000 chemicals listed. The preferred name is indicated in boldface (usually the *Chemical abstracts* 9th Collective index name, indicated by "[9CI]") and tradenames are included. There follow an index by synonym, and an index by molecular formula.

TP9.H65

McGraw-Hill dictionary of chemistry / Sybil P. Packer, ed. in chief. 2nd ed. N.Y. : McGraw-Hill, c1993. 1236 p. : ill.   **EE43**

1st ed., 1983.

Most of the material in this work is taken from *McGraw-Hill encyclopedia of science & technology*, 7th ed. (EA81) or *McGraw-Hill yearbook of science and technology* (EA167). "Focuses on the vocabulary of theoretical and applied chemistry rather than on chemicals and materials … Synonyms, acronyms and abbreviations are given with the definitions and are also listed in the alphabetical sequence as cross-references."—*Pref.* Useful for chemistry libraries that do not own the parent work. Indexed.   QD5.M357

Miall's dictionary of chemistry / ed. by D. W. A. Sharp. 5th ed. [Harlow, Essex] : Longman, [1981]. 501 p.   **EE44**

1st ed., 1940, by Stephen Miall; 4th ed., 1968, by L. M. Miall and D. W. A. Sharp. Previous eds. had title *A new dictionary of chemistry*.

Intended for university teaching where chemical terms may be encountered, and for professionals outside their own specialty. Industrial processes, manufacture, and use are given particular attention in this edition; some data on annual production are included. Brief biographi-

cal information is given for prominent chemists, past and contemporary. Trade names are kept to a minimum; abbreviations are omitted. British spelling is used.   QD5.M52

Schramm, Laurier Lincoln. The language of colloid and interface science : a dictionary of terms. Wash. : American Chemical Society, 1993. 195 p.   **EE45**

A dictionary with brief entries, some with references, on topics in colloids, surface chemistry, and interface science. An appendix includes tables that classify types of colloidal dispersion, give various equations, and list techniques of surface science and their acronyms. Cross-references.   QD549.S37

Thorpe, Jocelyn Field. Thorpe's dictionary of applied chemistry / by Jocelyn Field Thorpe and M. A. Whitely. 4th ed. London ; N.Y. [etc.] : Longmans, Green, [1937–56]. 12 v. : ill.   **EE46**

Consists primarily of short entries, with some long articles. General index in v. 12.   TP8.T72

Foreign terms

Multilingual

Fouchier, Jean. Chemical dictionary = Dictionanaire de chemie = Fachwörterbuch für Chemie / by J. Fouchier and F. Billet, with the cooperation of H. Epstein. 3d ed. rev. and enl. [Amsterdam] : Netherlands Univ. Pr., 1970. 566 p., 421 p., 477 p.   **EE47**

1st ed., 1953.

Compound names and terms for pure and applied chemistry. In three parts: English-French-German; French-German-English; German-English-French. Preceding each part is an alphabetical listing of abbreviations and the full expression in the first language of the part. Tables of equivalent weights and measures are included for the three languages. Structural formulas appear only in pt.1, English section. About 20,000 entries for each language.   QD5.F6

French

Patterson, Austin McDowell. French-English dictionary for chemists. 2nd ed. N.Y. : Wiley, [1954]. 476 p.   **EE48**

1st ed., 1921.

Phrases and abbreviations are included among the 42,000 entries. Common forms of various irregular verbs are entered separately rather than being grouped under the parent verb. The introduction discusses some of the common French chemical suffixes and their English equivalents.   QD5.P25

German

De Vries, Louis. Dictionary of chemistry and chemical engineering. 2nd ed., rev. and enl. Weinheim ; N.Y. : Verlag Chemie, 1978–79. 2 v.   **EE49**

1st ed., 1970–72.

Added title page: Wörterbuch der Chemie … .

Contents: v. 1, German-English; v. 2, English-German.

Intended to be comprehensive for students, practicing scientists, and engineers. Brief entries. Includes trivial names of chemical substances.   QD5.D47

Fachwörterbuch, Chemie und chemische Technik : Deutsch-Englisch, mit etwa 62 000 Wortstellen / hrsg. von der Technischen Universit at Dresden Zentrum Fur Angewandte Sprachwissenschaft ; [erb. in der Entwicklungsstelle für fachwörterbücher des Zentrums für Angewandte Sprachwissenschaft von Wolfgang Borsdorf, Helmut Gross, Joachim Knepper]. Berlin : A. Hatier, c1992. 760 p.   **EE50**
    1st ed., 1976, had title: *Wörterbuch Chemie und chemische Technik: Deutsch-English*.
    This edition is based largely on the 4th ed. of its English-German predecessor, *Dictionary of chemistry and chemical technology. English-German* (Amsterdam; N.Y. : Elsevier, 1989).
    Contains about 62,000 entries for terms in analytical, inorganic, organic, and physical chemistry, laboratory techniques, industrial chemistry, and chemical process engineering. IUPAC nomenclature is consistently used for English and German names of chemical compounds; "C" spelling (instead of "K" and "Z" spelling of former editions) is used; e.g., "Carbonat" instead of "Karbonat." Brief entries of a few words each.

Patterson, Austin McDowell. Patterson's German-English dictionary for chemists / by Austin M. Patterson ; rev. by James C. Cox ; ed. by George E. Condoyannis. 4th ed. N.Y. : Wiley, 1992. liii, 890 p.   **EE51**
    Rev. ed. of *A German-English dictionary for chemists* (3rd ed., 1950).
    A substantial revision and expansion of an old classic, now including about 65,000 terms. As in past editions, a large number of general words are included, while obvious cognates are excluded except when they have additional or different meanings. Some obsolete or antiquated chemical terms, labeled "Old Chem.," have been dropped from this edition to make room for newer terms. Includes abbreviations, prefixes, and suffixes.   QD5.P3

Wohlauer, Gabriele E. M. German chemical abbreviations / comp. and ed. by Gabriele E.M. Wohlauer and H.D. Gholston. N.Y. : Special Libraries Assoc., 1965. 63 p.   **EE52**
    A project of the Chemistry Section of the Science-Technology Division of Special Libraries Association.
    In addition to technical abbreviations, gives some nontechnical and Latin entries. Information presented in parallel columns: the abbreviation in German (or Latin), the corresponding word or phrase written in full, and the English equivalent. About 2,500 entries.   QD7.W6

Russian

Callaham, Ludmilla Ignatiev. Russian-English chemical and polytechnical dictionary. 3rd ed. N.Y. : Wiley, [1975]. 852 p.   **EE53**
    1st ed., 1947, had title *Russian-English technical and chemical dictionary*; 2nd ed., 1962.
    Both technical and nontechnical terms are included, together with abbreviations, prefixes, frequently used suffixes, and terms occurring in the older literature. There is a listing of common Russian technical word endings and a review of declensions.   QD5.C33

Macura, Paul. Elsevier's dictionary of chemistry : Russian-English. Amsterdam ; N.Y. : Elsevier, 1993. 920 p.   **EE54**
    Provides entries for more than 95,000 words in a wide range of pure and applied areas related to chemistry, arranged alphabetically by the Russian alphabet, with English equivalents.   QD5.M262

Directories

Chemical industry Europe. 1991– . Tonbridge, Kent, U.K. : Benn Business Information Services, c1991– . Annual.   **EE55**

    Continues: *The chemical age yearbook* (1923–58); *Chemical age directory and who's who* (1959–63); *Chemical industry directory and who's who* (1964–88); *Chemical industry directory* (1989–90).
    A directory and guide to European (especially British) chemical manufacturers and suppliers and process plant manufacturing industries.   TP1.C34

Chemical research faculties : an international directory. [2nd ed.]. Wash. : American Chemical Society, c1988. 558, [129] p.   **EE56**
    1st ed., 1984.
    Provides, for departments of chemistry, chemical engineering, biochemistry, pharmaceutical/medicinal chemistry, polymer science, and toxicology outside the U.S. and Canada the same sort of information as the *Directory of graduate research* (EE59) provides for departments within the U.S. and Canada. In each subject field countries are listed alphabetically, and under each country institutions are listed alphabetically. For each department gives: address and telephone number; advanced degrees offered; fields of specialization; faculty members, with academic rank, year of birth, education, field of research, areas of current research interest, and a listing of one or two recent research publications. Statistical summaries for the subject areas list the institutions alphabetically under their countries to show numbers of full-time faculty, postdoctoral appointments, graduate enrollments, and graduate degrees granted for 1984–85 and for 1985–86. Also includes a directory of chemical and chemical engineering societies with current address and telephone, principal officer, date founded, major publications, size of membership, and purpose. Faculty are indexed by name and by research subjects. A merged alphabetical listing of all institutions gives the country under which the department is listed.   QD40.C4317

College chemistry faculties. 9th ed. Wash. : American Chemical Society, 1993. 197 p.   **EE57**
    1st ed., 1965; 8th ed., 1989.
    A directory of all chemistry teachers in universities, colleges, and junior colleges in the U.S. and Canada. Under each country, states or provinces are listed alphabetically, then institutions under state or province. Entries give address and telephone, degrees offered, and faculty with specialization. Indexed by individual and by institution.

Directory of chemistry software. Oxford : Cherwell Scientific Publ. ; [Wash.] : American Chemical Society, 1992.   **EE58**
    A convenient compilation of software programs applicable to chemistry. Programs are listed alphabetically, with entries including the functions of the program, publisher, distributors, pricing, and user support information. There is a separate listing of publishers and indexes by program function and by computer systems (platforms).   QD39.3.C6D57

Directory of graduate research. Wash. : American Chemical Society, [1953]– . Biennial.   **EE59**
    Subtitle (varies): Faculties, publications, and doctoral and master's theses in departments or divisions of chemistry, chemical engineering, biochemistry, pharmaceutical/medicinal chemistry, clinical chemistry, and polymer science at universities in the United States and Canada.
    Prepared by the Committee on Professional Training.
    Title varies in early volumes.
    In each subject field the institutions are listed alphabetically. For each department is given: degrees offered; fields of specialization; faculty members, with academic rank, year of birth, education, field of research, specific current research interests, and telephone number, followed by a list of research publications for the biennium covered and master's and doctoral candidates completing their degrees in the period covered, with the theses titles. Statistical summaries for the subject areas list the institutions alphabetically to show the numbers of full and part-time faculty, postdoctoral appointments, graduate enrollments, and graduate degrees granted for the two years. Index of instructional staff.   Z5525.U5A6

Noyes Data Corporation. Chemical guide to the United States. [Ed.1–] 1963/64– . Park Ridge : N.J., 1963– . Irregular. **EE60**

8th ed., 1989/1990.

Earlier volumes were issued by the Corporation under its previous name, Noyes Development Corporation.

Now describes some 400 of the largest chemical firms of the U.S. The same publisher issues similar guides for Canada, Europe, Latin America, etc., and guides for specific types of firms (cosmetics, pharmaceuticals, etc.) in the U.S. and elsewhere. TP12.N615

Handbooks

American Chemical Society. Reagent chemicals : American Chemical Society specifications, official from April 1, 1993. 8th ed. Wash. : The Society, 1993. 806 p. **EE61**

1st ed., 1950; 7th ed., 1986.

The standard reference work for specifications and analytical procedures relating to the most important reagents used in analytical work. Includes information on reagent solutions. QD77.A512

American Public Health Association. Standard methods for the examination of water and wastewater. [1st] (1905)– . Wash. : APHA, 1905– . Irregular. **EE62**

"Prepared and published jointly by American Public Health Association, American Water Works Association, Water Environment Federation."—t.p.

The major divisions of the text are: Introduction, Physical and aggregate properties, Metals, Inorganic nonmetallic constituents, Aggregate organic constituents, Individual organic compounds, Radioactivity, Toxicity, Microbiological examination, and Biological examination. Each section has a bibliography and/or references. Since the 17th ed. (1989), the organization of the work reflects a commitment to develop and retain a permanent numbering system, using section numbers based on multiples of 1,000 for main groupings (e.g., Pt. 2000, Physical and aggregate properties; Pt. 2310, Acidity). The standard reference in its field. Indexed. QD142.A5

Barin, Ihsan. Thermochemical data of pure substances. 2nd ed. Weinheim, Federal Republic of Germany ; N.Y. : VCH, c1993. 2 v. **EE63**

1st ed., 1989.

"In collaboration with Fried Sauert, Ernst Schultze-Rhonof, Wang Shu Sheng."—t.p.

The data presented in this edition are little changed from the 1st ed.; however, the introduction has been rewritten to call attention to the nonstandard numerical conventions, making this edition easier to use.

A compilation of thermodynamic data for some 2,400 pure substances that complements JANAF thermochemical tables (EE93), which were compiled for the U.S. Air Force and are concerned chiefly with substances related to propulsion, fuels, combustion, etc. The present work includes many additional elements and compounds of importance to metallurgy and other fields. Data are given for room temperature, for 300°K, and where possible are graduated in 100°K increments to 5,000°K. Data are given in SI units, and sources are cited; critically evaluated data are used when available. Thermodynamic functions are included; the layout of the tables corresponds to conventions used in standard works such as the JANAF tables. Apart from some 100 organic substances, these tables contain data on chemical elements and on inorganic compounds of two, three, or four elements; primary arrangement of the tables is in alphabetical order of the first element in the chemical formula. Six introductory sections discuss basic thermodynamic principles and explain how the tables were compiled and how they can be used, with examples. QD511.8.B369

Basic laboratory and industrial chemicals : a CRC quick reference handbook / David R. Lide. Boca Raton, Fla. : CRC Pr., c1993. 370 p. **EE64**

A handy reference giving basic information on a "core set" of about 1,000 substances that are frequently found in chemical laboratories or industrial facilities. Entries are alphabetical by substance name, and include identifying information (name, synonyms, molecular formula, molecular weight, CAS Registry Number, Merck number); physical properties (melting point, boiling point, critical temperature and pressure, electric dipole moment, ionization potential); transition properties (enthalpies of fusion and of vaporization, vapor pressures at 0°C, 25°C, 100°C); thermodynamic and transport properties at 25°C; and comments on unusual hazards. Not all properties are given for each substance. Indexed by synonyms, molecular formulas, and by CAS Registry Numbers. QD64.L53

Bretherick, L. Bretherick's handbook of reactive chemical hazards. 4th ed. London ; Boston : Butterworths, 1990. 2005 p. : ill. **EE65**

1st ed., 1975. Previous eds. had title: Handbook of reactive chemical hazards.

This handbook has two principal sections. Section 1, Specific chemicals, lists elements and compounds in formula order, giving name, CAS Registry Number, structural formula, and explosive or other reactive hazards of the compound, with references to the chemical literature. Subentries are given for compounds which interact violently with the entry compound. Section 2, Classes, groups and topics, lists topics and classes of reactive compounds in alphabetical order with literature references and references to individual chemicals giving the entry number from Section 1. Also includes general information on reactive chemical hazards, tabulated fire-related data (boiling point, flash point, auto-ignition temperature, explosive limit) for compounds considered to be unusually hazardous in a fire context. Extensively indexed by chemical name and synonym, class and general topic, and CAS Registry Number, and has a pictorial guide to compounds with cyclic structural formulas. A superb source of rapid, comprehensive access to this crucial information. T55.3.H3B73

Chem sources U.S.A. v. 1 (1958)– . Ormond Beach, Fla. : Directories Publ. Co., 1958– . Annual. **EE66**

Title varies: 1958–72, Chem sources.

An alphabetical listing by chemical name, giving CAS Registry Number with most listings and three- to five-letter codes for producers. Some 155,000 inorganic and organic compounds are listed either in the main (Chemicals) section or the Dyes/stains/indicators or Monomers/polymers subsections. Includes: trade name index; classified trade name index arranged by type of product; list of companies by letter code, including addresses and phone, telex, and fax numbers; index from company name to letter code.

§ Companion publication: Chem sources international (1986 ed.– . Clemson, S.C. : Directories Publ. Co., 1986– . Biennial).

Supersedes Chem sources Europe (1973–84); publisher varies.

Includes some 80,000 inorganic and organic compounds produced by chemical firms from 80 countries. Lists companies that produce the substances and has a section of agents or representatives, arranged alphabetically by country where they are located, giving address, telephone, telex, and fax.

•A machine-readable version, Chem sources [database] (Clemson, S.C. : Chemical Sources International) provides current information corresponding to the latest editions of both printed sources above. Available online and in CD-ROM. TP12.C44

Compendium of hazardous chemicals in schools and colleges / The Forum for Scientific Excellence, Inc. Philadelphia : Lippincott, c1990. 897 p. : ill. (some col.). **EE67**

A compilation of hazardous chemical data and assessments for the 900 hazardous chemicals most commonly found in educational facilities. Entries are listed alphabetically by compound name (to find the index name, consult Cross-reference index of hazardous chemicals, synonyms, and CAS Registry numbers [EE72]). Entries include synonyms; CAS Registry Number; DOT (Department of Transportation); PNSN (Prime Name Sequence Number), and RTECS (Registry of Toxic Effects of Chemical Substances) numbers; class of compound (e.g., mutagen, tumorigen); physical data including molecular formula, molecular weight, melting point, boiling point, flash point, properties, fire and explosion hazards; acute and chronic health effects with references; and environmental data including threshold value in air and water solubility.   T55.3.H3C646

Comprehensive coordination chemistry : the synthesis, reactions, properties & applications of coordination compounds / ed. in chief, Sir Geoffrey Wilkinson. Oxford ; N.Y. : Pergamon, 1987. 7 v. : ill.   **EE68**
  Contents: v. 1, Theory & background; v. 2, Ligands; v. 3, Main group & early transition elements; v. 4, Middle transition elements; v. 5, Late transition elements; v. 6, Applications; v. 7, Indexes.
  An encyclopedic collection of signed, authoritative articles including tabular data and literature references. The index volume contains subject and formula indexes, and an index of review articles and specialist texts.   QD474.C65

CRC handbook of bimolecular and termolecular gas reactions / ed., J. Alistair Kerr, assistant ed., Stephen J. Moss. Boca Raton, Fla. : CRC Pr., c1981–87. 3 v. in 4.   **EE69**
  Assistant ed., v. 3, Roger Michael Drew.
  A compilation of experimental data, with entries grouped by type of reaction and under type by reactants. Much of the data was taken from other compilations, and all sources are indicated. Vols. 1–2 cover the literature through 1977, and v. 3, (in 2 pts.) brings the coverage through 1982. Each part is indexed.   QD502.C18

CRC handbook of chemistry and physics : a ready-reference book of chemical and physical data / ed. in chief, Robert C. Weast. Ed. 1– . Boca Raton, Fla. : CRC Pr., 1913– . Annual.   **EE70**
  74th ed. publ. 1993.
  1st–57th eds. had title: *Handbook of chemistry and physics.*
  Publisher formerly called Chemical Rubber Co.
  "A ready-reference book of chemical and physical data"—*t.p.*
  An indispensable tool for scientists and engineers. Each new ed. is revised, incorporating new material, additional tables. Indexed.
  For supplementary volumes, see *CRC handbook of data on organic compounds*, EE149; *CRC handbook of tables for organic compound identification*, EE151.   QD65.H5

CRC handbook of laboratory safety. 3rd ed. / ed., A. Keith Furr. Boca Raton, Fla. : CRC Pr., c1990. 704 p. : ill.   **EE71**
  Completely rewritten, a different sort of resource than the 2nd ed. (EE88). "Not primarily intended for the safety and health specialist, but ... to guide research personnel in working with safety and health professionals to implement effective health and safety programs in their facilities."—*Foreword*. Gives much more emphasis to disposal of chemical and other hazardous wastes, and discusses newer topics such as recombinant DNA that were not mentioned in the previous edition. Detailed treatments of, for example, eye protection, chemical cyanosis, and flammability characteristics of combustible gases and vapors have not been carried over to this edition. Instead, it refers to other sources, often including the 2nd ed., for such information. This work significantly supplements, but does not supersede, the 2nd ed.   QD51.C73

Cross-reference index of hazardous chemicals, synonyms, and CAS registry numbers / The Forum for Scientific Excellence, Inc. Philadelphia : J.B. Lippincott, c1990. 576 p.   **EE72**
  An index to some 3,000 hazardous substances, including more than 35,000 synonyms. The "Chemicals by name" section lists the synonyms alphabetically, including trade names and special numbers (e.g., DOT [Department of Transportation] number). Order of listing is character-by-character, so chemical names beginning with numbers, such as 1,1'-Biphenyl, precede the main alphabetic sequence. Within this section each name is keyed to the CAS Registry Number; the following sections list entries in order of the CAS Registry Number and each entry includes all the synonyms in the previous list. Names that are used as entry points in *Compendium of hazardous chemicals in schools and colleges* (EE67) are indicated by asterisks. T55.3.H3C76

Emsley, J. The elements. 2nd ed. Oxford : Clarendon Pr. ; N.Y. : Oxford Univ. Pr., 1991. 251 p.   **EE73**

1st ed., 1989.
  Lists the elements in alphabetical order. Each two-page entry gives chemical and physical properties including radii, electronegativity, standard reduction potential, oxidation states, melting and boiling points, thermodynamic properties, density, conductivities, lattice structures, nuclear properties including NMR, electronic configuration, ionization energies, principal atomic lines, and other significant data. Entries also give brief descriptions of chemical properties, uses, history of discovery, biological roles and levels in humans, abundances in the earth, in seawater, and on the sun, and geologic data including world production. A key at the beginning explains the properties listed, giving units used, conversion factors to other units, and sources for the data. Tables at the back list 20 of the properties both in order of the elements and in numerical order of the property. A very convenient handbook.   QD466.E48

Gordon, Arnold J. The chemist's companion : a handbook of practical data, techniques, and references / Arnold J. Gordon, Richard A. Ford. N.Y. : Wiley, [1972]. 537 p. : ill.   **EE74**
  Information is presented in sections for: (1) Properties of molecular systems; (2) Properties of atoms and bonds; (3) Kinetics and energetics; (4) Spectroscopy; (5) Photochemistry; (6) Chromatography; (7) Experimental techniques; (8) Mathematical and numerical information; (9) Miscellaneous. Indexed.   QD65.G64

Hazards in the chemical laboratory / ed. by S. G. Luxon. 5th ed. Cambridge : Royal Society of Chemistry, 1992. 675 p. : ill.   **EE75**
  Editor varies.
  1st ed., 1971; 4th ed., 1986.
  Supersedes: *Laboratory handbook of toxic agents*, 1st ed., 1960.
  Publisher formerly called Chemical Society.
  Includes chapters on: Safety planning and laboratory design, Fire protection, Reactive chemical hazards, Chemical hazards and toxicology, Control of health hazards, First aid, Precautions against radiation, Electrical hazards. The principal chapter, Hazardous chemicals, is a listing in alphabetical order of 1,339 flammable, explosive, corrosive, or toxic substances commonly used in chemical laboratories. Entries include for each substance: description, solubility, melting and boiling points, risks, safety precautions, toxic effects, first aid recommendations, hazardous reactions, fire hazard, and spillage disposal methods. This edition includes a chapter on legislation (in the U.K.) and a new chapter on "Chemical laboratories—an American view" with an overview of OSHA and other U.S. regulations. An index of variant chemical names and an index of CAS Registry Numbers refer to the substance's entry number. Should be available for every chemical laboratory.   QD51.H35

Industrial chemical thesaurus / comp. by Michael and Irene Ash. 2nd ed. N.Y. : VCH Publishers, c1992. 2 v.   **EE76**
  Contents: v. 1, Chemical to tradename reference; v. 2, Tradename to chemical cross-reference and manufacturers directory.
  The first volume contains entries for some 6,000 chemicals listed alphabetically, including synonyms, CAS Registry number, formula, properties, precautions, toxicology, uses, trade name products, and trade names containing this chemical (with manufacturer). Vol. 2 lists some 40,000 trade names used for the chemicals listed in v. 1, or products containing those chemicals, with the manufacturer and the name of the compound used in v.1. A listing of the chemical manufacturers gives addresses, telephone numbers, and representatives in various countries.   Z695.1.C5I52

Lange, Norbert Adolph. Lange's handbook of chemistry / John A. Dean, ed. 14th ed. N.Y. : McGraw-Hill, 1992. 1 v., various pagings. : ill.   **EE77**
  1st ed., 1934; 1st–10th eds. had title *Handbook of chemistry.*
  A standard reference source for both students and professional chemists. Sections for: organic compounds; general information, conversion tables, and mathematics; inorganic chemistry; properties of atoms, radicals, and bonds; physical properties; thermodynamic properties; spectroscopy; electrolytes, electromotive force, and chemical

equilibrium; physicochemical relationships; polymers, rubbers, fats, oils, and waxes; and practical laboratory information. Index.

QD65.L36

Lefèvre, M. J. First aid manual for chemical accidents. 2nd English-language ed. / rev. by Shirley A. Conibear. N.Y. : Van Nostrand Reinhold, c1989. 261 p. **EE78**

1st English ed., 1980.

Chapters describe symptoms of poisoning and first aid measures in cases of inhalation, ingestion, skin contact, and eye contact; within each of these chapters are numbered sections on groups of chemical compounds having the same symptoms and treatment procedures. A chemical index gives the section number for each chapter and the CAS Registry Number of each particular compound. Appendixes include general instructions in case of poisoning by unknown chemicals, and a glossary of commercial and common pesticide names.

RC963.3.L4313

Lewis, Richard J. Hazardous chemical desk reference. 3rd ed. N.Y. : Van Nostrand Reinhold, 1993. 1742 p. **EE79**

1st ed., 1987; 2nd ed., 1991.

A compilation of basic hazard data concerning more than 5,630 chemicals, extracted from Lewis's *Sax's dangerous properties of industrial materials* (EE80). Typical entries, filed alphabetically by compound name, include CAS Registry Number, molecular formula, molecular weight, synonyms, a "hazard rating" on a scale of 1–3 (where 3 is high hazard) or "D" if the data are insufficient, Department of Transportation hazard code and classification, physical properties, indication of availability or consensus reports (such as from World Health Organization, International Agency for Research on Cancer, etc.), and a "safety profile" (a summary of reported hazards). Unlike the larger work from which these data are taken, no references are included. Indexes by synonym and by CAS Registry Number.

T55.3.H3L49

——————— Sax's dangerous properties of industrial materials. 8th ed. N.Y. : Van Nostrand Reinhold, c1992. 3 v. **EE80**

1st ed., 1957; previous editions had title *Dangerous properties of industrial materials.*

A standard compilation of hazardous properties, covering some 20,000 materials. Vol. 1 includes an introduction explaining the entries, formats, sources, and codes, and both a CAS Registry Number cross-index and a synonym cross-index; it also lists full references corresponding to the alphanumeric codes used in the entries. Vols. 2 and 3 contain the entries, alphabetical by substance name; typical entries include synonyms, molecular formula, molecular weight, CAS Registry Number, a "hazard rating" of 1–3 (or "D" if there is insufficient data), properties, toxicity data with references, references to consensus reports in the literature, a Department of Transportation hazard code, and standards and recommendations from various agencies (OSHA, NIOSH, DOT, etc.) as to toxic concentrations. Most entries are one or two paragraphs; a few, such as DDT, run one or two pages. In this edition, the information on carcinogenic and reproductive effects are reduced, since complete data are available in *Carcinogenically active chemicals* (c1991) and *Reproductively active chemicals* (c1991) from the same publisher, both edited by Lewis. T55.3.H3S3

Linke, William F. Solubilities, inorganic and metal organic compounds : a compilation of solubility data from the periodical literature. 4th ed. Wash. : American Chemical Society, 1958–65. 2 v. **EE81**

Publisher varies.

"A revision and continuation of the compilation originated by Atherton Seidell."—*title page.*

3rd ed., 1940–41; suppl. 1952.

Arranged in the form of short data tables; each table is preceded by a brief evaluation of the data taken from the original literature. All the numerical values were taken from publications covered by *Chemical abstracts.*

"Elements are listed alphabetically by their chemical symbol, and their compounds are listed alphabetically according to the chemical symbols of their anions or radicals."—*Pref.* Subject and author indexes for both volumes in v. 2.

Often cited as "Seidell's Solubilities." QD66.L5

Meites, Louis, *ed.* Handbook of analytical chemistry. N.Y. : McGraw-Hill, [1963]. 1 v. (various pagings) : ill. **EE82**

In 15 sections, each with a detailed table of contents. Descriptive material readily available elsewhere has been omitted. Three sections are "primarily intended to aid in selecting an analytical procedure to meet the requirements of a specific problem." The remainder of the book "presents the fundamental data that characterize the behaviors of different substances toward the techniques of separation and measurement most widely used in chemical analysis, and also outlines the most important and most reliable of the analytical methods and procedures based on them."—*Pref.* QD71.M37

The Merck index : an encyclopedia of chemicals, drugs, and biologicals / Susan Budavari, ed. 11th (centennial) ed. Rahway, N.J. : Merck, 1989. 1 v. (various pagings) : ill. **EE83**

1st ed., 1889; 10th ed., 1983. Subtitle varies.

Concise descriptions of more than 10,000 organic and inorganic chemicals, drugs, and biological substances, chosen for inclusion on the basis of their importance. Entries give formulas, alternate names, physical properties, uses, toxicity, and journal and patent references. A separate table gives CAS Registry Numbers. Miscellaneous tables include radioactive isotopes, standard solutions, conversion factors, prescription notation, and a list of entries from the 9th and 10th editions that have been deleted. The Organic name reactions section has been dropped. Includes a formula index, a detailed cross-index of alternate names, and an index by therapeutic category and biological activity.

•Machine-readable version: *The Merck index online* [database] / comp. by Merck & Co. (Rahway, N.J. : Merck). Available online. Updated semiannually. Includes full text of the latest edition of *The Merck index,* with additional entries added or revised since publication of that edition. Contains textual, numeric, and bibliographic data.

RS51.M4

Official methods of analysis of the Association of Official Analytical Chemists. 11th ed. (1970)– . Wash. : The Association, c1970– . Quinquennial. **EE84**

For annotation, *see* EJ59. S587.O38

Perrin, D. D. Purification of laboratory chemicals / D. D. Perrin and W. L. F. Armarego. 3rd ed. Oxford ; N.Y. : Pergamon Pr., 1988. 391 p. **EE85**

1st ed., 1966.

A very useful guide for chemists, biochemists, and other scientists who need to purify chemical reagents. After chapters on physical and chemical methods of purification, the core of the book is: Chap. 3, Purification of organic chemicals; Chap. 4, Purification of inorganic and metal-organic chemicals; Chap. 5, General methods for the purification of classes of compounds; and Chap. 6, Purification of biochemicals and related products. Within these chapters, substances are listed alphabetically; CAS Registry numbers are given for individual substances, along with melting points, brief descriptions of purification methods, and references. More than 4,000 organic and 750 inorganic and organometallic substances are included. Indexed by topic.

TP156.P83P47

Ring systems handbook. 1984– . Columbus, Ohio : American Chemical Society, 1984– . Irregular. **EE86**

Supersedes: *Parent compound handbook* (1976–83), which in turn superseded *The ring index* (1st ed., 1940; 2nd ed., 1960 with suppls. 1–3, 1963–65).

A publication of Chemical Abstracts Service.

"The *Ring systems handbook* is intended to be a major reference work for chemists and others who use *Chemical Abstracts (CA)*. ... The first part of the Handbook, the Ring Systems File (RSF), contains structural diagrams and related data for nearly 60,000 unique, representative *CA* index ring systems. The RSF also includes data on cage systems (polyboranes, metallocenes, etc.). Information accompanying each ring system includes a Ring File (RF) number, the CAS Registry Number, a structural diagram illustrating the numbering system, the current *CA* index name, the molecular formula, and the Wiswesser Line Notation. The ring systems are arranged by their ring analysis, which is given before each group of ring systems having a common ring analysis, except for cage systems. The Handbook also includes the Ring Formula Index (RFI) and the Ring Name Index (RNI) which are designed to provide access to the contents of the RSF by molecular formula and by ring name … Supplements to the RSF, RFI, and RNI are cumulative and are issued semiannually in one volume."—*Introd.*

1984 issued in four parts: Ring formula file I; Ring systems file II; Ring formula index [and] Ring name index; and Ring WLN index.

QD390.R56

Shugar, Gershon J. Chemist's ready reference handbook / Gershon J. Shugar, John A. Dean. N.Y. : McGraw-Hill, c1990. ca. 590 p. : ill.   **EE87**

A quick reference handbook for practicing chemists and college or graduate students. Gives details concerning a wide variety of analytical procedures, with illustrations and references, emphasizing practical matters with theory given only as needed for background.

§ Much of the material is derived from *Chemical technician's ready reference handbook*, by Gershon J. Shugar and Jack T. Ballinger (3rd ed., N.Y. : McGraw-Hill, c1990. 889 p.), which is somewhat more didactic (e.g., with worked-out examples of calculations) and better suited to beginners. Designed "to give 'every single step' to be followed in most of the conventional laboratory procedures" (*Pref.*), it is useful for technicians and students at all levels, since it gives sequential steps for procedures, detailed illustrations, safety precautions, and examples of calculations.   QD65.3.S537

Steere, Norman V. CRC handbook of laboratory safety. 2nd ed. Cleveland, Ohio : Chemical Rubber Co., [1971]. 854 p. : ill.   **EE88**

Intends "to provide convenient information for hazard recognition and control."—*Pref.* Detailed sections deal with particular classes of hazards. This remains a valuable resource both for planning safe laboratories and for responding to laboratory emergencies; it is not superseded by the 3rd ed. (EE71), and should be retained.   QD51.S88

Structure reports. v. 1 (1913/28)– . Utrecht : A. Oosthoek, 1928– .   **EE89**

Vols. 1–7 issued as suppl. to *Zeitschrift für Kristallographie, Mineralogie und Petrographie.* Since v. 8 (issued 1956), has been in English. From v. 30 (covering 1965, issued 1974–75) split into Section A: Metals and inorganic; Section B: Organic. Publication is faster for Section A; v. 57A, covering 1990, was publ. 1992, while the most recent coverage of organics is v. 52B, covering 1985 and publ. 1993. Some vols. publ. out of sequence in Section B.

Includes numerical data and diagrams of compounds that have been analyzed, as well as descriptions of the structures, with the bibliographic references. Each recent vol. has author, formula, permuted formula, subject (compound name), and permuted subject indexes. Occasional cumulated indexes, including v. 58A (subject and formula indexes for 1913–90 of metals and inorganics), v. 47B (subject, formula, and author index for 1971–80 of organics).   QD901.S8

Szymanski, Herman A. Infrared band handbook / [by] Herman A. Szymanski and Ronald E. Erickson. 2d ed. rev. and enl. N.Y. : IFI/Plenum, 1970. 2 v. : ill.   **EE90**

1st ed. and supplements, 1963–66.

Includes all the data in the 1st ed. and its supplements, plus much additional material. Entries are arranged in the order of ascending wave number and subarranged according to decreasing band strength. Each page contains data for 20 compounds, usually with structural formulas. No infrared spectra are given. Index for both parts in last volume; entries refer to wave numbers, not pages.   QC457.S983

Vsesoĭuznyĭ Institut Nauchnoĭ i Tekhnicheskoĭ informat͡sii (Russia). Solubilities of inorganic and organic compounds / ed. by Henry Stephen and T. Stephen. Oxford : Pergamon ; N.Y. : Macmillan, 1963–79. 3 v. in 7 : ill.   **EE91**

Added title page in Russian. Translation of *Spravochnik po rastrorimosti.*

Contents: v. 1, pts. 1–2, Binary systems; v. 2, pt. 1, Ternary systems; v. 2, pt. 2, Ternary and multicomponent systems; v. 3 in 3 v., Ternary and multicomponent systems of inorganic substances, ed. by Howard L. Silcock.

Contains tables of data without critical evaluation.

QD543.M7213

Welcher, Frank Johnson. Chemical solutions : reagents useful to the chemist, biologist, and bacteriologist. N.Y. : Van Nostrand, 1942. 404 p.   **EE92**

Repr. 1966.

"The purpose … is to collect in one place for convenient reference the methods for preparing those solutions most frequently required by the chemist."—*Pref.* Usually gives for each solution: the use, procedure for use, substances which interfere, sensitivity of the reagents, remarks, and literature reference. Alphabetical arrangement according to the most commonly known name. Cross-references. The index classifies the solutions according to their use.   QD77.W4

Tables

JANAF thermochemical tables. 3rd ed. N.Y. : American Institute of Physics, c1986. 2 v. (1856 p.).   **EE93**

Issued as: *Journal of physical and chemical reference data,* v. 14, suppl. no. 1 (1985).

Combines material revised and updated from the 2nd ed., 1971, with the four supplements published in *Journal of physical and chemical reference data* (1974, 1975, 1978, and 1982) and with previously unpublished tables. Provides, for elements, inorganic compounds, and simple organic compounds, "thermodynamic reference data of the highest quality and timeliness."—*Pref.* Tables are in SI units and "notation has been made consistent with current international recommendations."—*Foreword.* Gives thermodynamic properties of about 1,800 substances. Filing order of tables is according to the modified Hill indexing system; an index to the filing order is given before the tables.

•Available in machine-readable form as: *NIST JANAF thermochemical tables* [database] (Gaithersburg, Md. : U.S. National Institute of Standards and Technology). Available online. Much of the data is also contained in the diskette *NIST structures & properties database and estimation program* [database] (Gaithersburg, Md. : U.S. National Institute of Standards and Technology, [1991]).   QC100.U573

The NBS tables of chemical thermodynamic properties : selected values for inorganic and C_1 and C_2 organic substances in SI units / Donald D. Wagman … [et al.]. N.Y. ; Wash. : American Chemical Soc. and the American Inst. of Physics for the National Bureau of Standards, 1982. 392 p. (Journal of physical and chemical reference data, v. 11, suppl. 2).   **EE94**

A new ed. of NBS Technical Note 270, *Selected values of chemical thermodynamic properties,* issued in 8 pts., 1965–81; that publication in turn superseded NBS Circular 500, 1952, of the same title.

Provides recommended values of chemical thermodynamic properties. Includes careful discussion of the process used to evaluate the data.   QD511.8.N3

Style manuals

The ACS style guide : a manual for authors and editors / Janet S. Dodd, ed. ; Marianne C. Brogan, advisory ed. Wash. : American Chemical Society, 1986. 264 p. : ill.   **EE95**

Rev. and expanded version of *Handbook for authors of papers in American Chemical Society publications* (3rd ed., 1978).

A manual on manuscript preparation, "stressing those principles and practices that are desirable throughout the scientific literature."—*Foreword.* Includes chapters on the scientific paper; grammar, style and usage; illustrations and tables; copyright and permissions; manuscript submissions in machine-readable form; the literature; and making effective oral presentations. Appendix I gives editorial procedures for ACS publications. Other appendixes are on ethical guidelines to publication of chemical research; hints to the typist; proofreaders' marks; and symbols. Bibliography; index.   QD8.5.A25

History

Haynes, Williams. American chemical industry : a history. N.Y. : Van Nostrand, 1945–54. 6 v. : ill.   **EE96**
> Contents: v. 1, Background and beginning, 1608–1911; v. 2–3, The World War I period, 1912–1922; v. 4, The merger era, 1923–1929; v. 5, Decade of new products, 1930–1939; v. 6, The chemical companies.
> Subject and name indexes in each volume.   TP23.H37

Multhauf, Robert P. The history of chemical technology : an annotated bibliography. N. Y. : Garland, 1984. 299 p., [9] leaves of plates : ill. (Bibliographies of the history of science and technology, v. 5 ; Garland reference library of the humanities, v. 348).   **EE97**
> A critically annotated bibliography, with entries listed under topical headings, covering the period since 1700. Author and subject (called "title") indexes.   Z7914.C4M84

Partington, James Riddick. A history of chemistry. London : Macmillan ; N.Y. : St. Martin's, 1961–70. v. 1^1, 2–4. : ill.   **EE98**
> A heavily documented history. Vol. 1, pt. 1, covers the theoretical background; v. 2–3, the 16th–18th centuries; v. 4, the 19th and early 20th centuries. Vol. 1, pt. 2, unfinished at the author's death, was to cover the earliest period.   QD11.P28

Biography

American chemists and chemical engineers / ed. by Wyndham D. Miles. Wash. : American Chemical Society, 1976–1994. 2 v. (In progress?).   **EE99**
> Vol. 2 ed. by Miles and Robert F. Gould.
> Contains biographical sketches, ranging from a few paragraphs to several pages, of more than 500 deceased American chemists and chemical engineers. Biographies cover the period from colonial times to the present; bibliographies of biographical information are included. Index of names mentioned in the biographies.
> Vol. 2 offers biographies of deceased American alchemists, chemists, and chemical engineers (including mineralogists, metallurgists, pharmacists, and other related professionals). Names mentioned in the text are marked with a dagger (†) if that person's biography appears in v. 1. The index to v. 2 includes names, subjects, cities and towns, and titles of books and journals.   QD21.A43

The biographical dictionary of scientists : chemists / gen. ed., David Abbott. N.Y. : Peter Redrick, [1983]. 203 p. : ill.   **EE100**
> A historical introduction is followed by brief narrative biographies, alphabetically arranged, of living and deceased chemists; no references are included. Brief glossary and an index to topics studied by the biographees.   QD21.B48

Farber, Eduard. Great chemists. N.Y. : Interscience, 1961. 1642 p. : ill.   **EE101**
> A collection of more than 100 biographies of famous chemists from ancient times to the 20th century, not including living persons. The essays were written by scholars of the last two centuries, and some have been translated from other languages for this work. Includes bibliographies.   QD21.F35

——————— Nobel prize winners in chemistry, 1901–1961. Rev. ed. London ; N.Y. : Abelard-Schuman, 1963. 341 p. : ill.   **EE102**
> For annotation, *see* AL165.   QD21.F37

Nobel laureates in chemistry, 1901–1992 / Laylin K. James, ed. [Wash.] : American Chemical Society : Chemical Heritage Foundation, 1993. 798 p. : ill.   **EE103**
> For annotation, *see* AL166.   QD21.N63

The Nobel Prize winners : chemistry / ed. by Frank N. Magill. Pasadena, Calif. : Salem Pr., c1990. 3 v. (1246 p.) : ill.   **EE104**
> For annotation, *see* AL171.   QD35.N64

Nobelstiftelsen. Chemistry. Amsterdam : Elsevier, 1964–92. v. 1–6 : ill. (In progress).   **EE105**
> For annotation, *see* AL174.   QD39.N735

Women in chemistry and physics : a biobibliographic sourcebook / ed. by Louise S. Grinstein, Rose K. Rose, and Miriam H. Rafailovich. Westport, Conn. : Greenwood, 1993. 721 p.   **EE106**
> For annotation, *see* EA187.   QD21.W62

INORGANIC

Block, B. Peter. Inorganic chemical nomenclature : principles and practice / B. Peter Block, Warren H. Powell, W. Conard Fernelius. Wash. : American Chemical Society, 1990. 210 p. : ill.   **EE107**
> "… concerned with the nomenclature of all substances except those that have carbon as a central atom and contain carbon-to-carbon bonds. Its purpose is to provide the reader with a basic understanding of the principles currently in use for naming such substances and the background necessary for searching much of the older literature."—*Pref.* Includes references; indexed.   QD149.B59

Comprehensive inorganic chemistry / editorial board: J. C. Bailar, Jr. … [et al.]. [Oxford] : Pergamon Pr., [1973]. 5 v. : ill.   **EE108**
> Designed to fill the gap between single-volume works and the multivolume sets found only in larger libraries. "It was envisaged that the treatise would be of service to a wide range of readers many of whom would not be professional chemists. Convenience for all classes of reader was of paramount importance so that if a conflict arose between brevity and ease of use, the latter was preferred."—*Pref.* Each chapter by a specialist. Bibliographic footnotes. Vols. 1–4 are indexed individually, and there is a master index to the set in v. 5. All indexes cover subjects only.   QD151.2.C64

Dictionary of inorganic compounds / [executive ed., J. E. Macintyre]. London ; N.Y. : Chapman & Hall, 1992. 5 v. : ill.   **EE109**
> Contents: v. 1, Ac–C_{10}; v. 2, C_{11}–C_{45}; v. 3, C_{46}–Zr; v. 4, Structural type index, name index, CAS Registry Number index; v. 5, Element index.
> Complements: *Dictionary of organic compounds* (EE127) and related Chapman and Hall dictionaries.
> Entries, in order by empirical formula according to the Hill Convention (first C, the H, then other elements in alphabetic sequence), include structural formula, CAS Registry Number, formula weight, derivative salts, hazard data, sometimes physical data, a brief description of synthesis, uses, and other information. Entries also include references to articles on synthesis and properties. Indexed by structural type, by name, by CAS Registry Number, and by element. Kept up-to-date by annual supplements (beginning 1993).
> •Available in electronic form as *CHCD dictionary of inorganic compounds on CD-ROM* [database] (London : Chapman and Hall, 1993–), and included in the online database *HEILBRON* (EE133).   QD148.D53

Gmelins Handbuch der anorganischen Chemie. 8. Aufl. / hrsg. von der Deutschen Chemischen Gesellschaft, bearb. von R. J. Meyer, unter beratender Mitwirkung von Franz Peters. Berlin : Springer Verlag, 1924– . v. 1– . (In progress).   **EE110**

Publisher varies.

Earlier editions by Leopold Gmelin.

Vols. publ. since 1981 have title: *Gmelin handbook of inorganic chemistry*.

A monumental work, now occupying some 600 volumes, that attempts to include all inorganic compounds ever described, with references to the original articles. The material is critically evaluated according to current knowledge. Volumes are not published in numerical sequence. Tables of contents and paragraph headings in English have been used for a number of years. From 1981, most articles have appeared in English.

Supplementary works:

(1) ———. *Alphabetische Folge zur Systematik der Sachverhalte* (Weinheim : Verlag Chemie, 1959. 109 p.).

(2) ———. *Ergänzungswerk* (v. 1– . Berlin : Springer Verlag, 1970– . [In progress]). Publisher varies. This supplementary series is being compiled on a selective basis; since 1981, most articles appear in English.

(3) ———. *Index : formula index* (Berlin : Springer Verlag, 1975–1980. 12 v.). Covers all volumes of the main series that had appeared up to the end of 1974, and of the suppl. that had appeared up to the end of 1973. *1st supplement* (Berlin ; N.Y. : Springer Verlag, 1983–1986. 8 v.) continues indexing up to the end of 1979, and *2nd supplement* (Berlin ; N.Y. : Springer Verlag, 1988–1990. 10 v.) continues indexing from the period covered by the *1st supplement* to the end of 1987. No further supplements in printed form are contemplated.

•The indexing contained in *Formula index* and its supplements, and indexing for the most recent volumes of the parent set, are available in machine-readable form as: *Gmelin formula index (GFI)* [database] (Berlin : Fachinformationszentrum Chemie GmbH, 1975–). Available online. Allows searching by formula, element count, compound class identifier, and other controlled text.

Gmelin factual database (GFDB) [database] (Frankfurt am Main : Gmelin Inst. for Inorganic Chemistry), available online, provides critically evaluated structural and other factual data from *Gmelin*, as well as data not yet evaluated or included in *Gmelin* but taken from 111 important journals, 1988– .   QD151.G522

Mellor, Joseph William. A comprehensive treatise on inorganic and theoretical chemistry. London ; N.Y. : Longmans, 1922–37. 16 v. : ill.   **EE111**

Detailed treatment of the elements and their compounds. Extensive bibliographies. Sequence of elements discussed follows the periodic table. Indexes in each volume; complete index in v. 16.

Supplements: (1) ———. ——— *v. II, Supplement I–III* (London ; N.Y. : Longmans, [1956–63]. 3 v.).

(2) ———. ——— *v. V, Supplement I, pt. A* (London ; N.Y. : Longmans, [1980]. 1 v.).

(3) ———. ——— *v. VIII, Supplement I–III* ([London] : Longmans, [1964–71]. 3 v.). The supplements purposely omit theoretical aspects. Recent developments reported in the literature are presented, together with an evauation of the experimental work. No more supplements published.

Nomenclature of inorganic chemistry : recommendations 1990 / issued by the Commission on the Nomenclature of Inorganic Chemistry and ed. by G. J. Leigh. [3rd ed.]. Oxford, [Eng.] ; Boston : Blackwell Scientific, 1990. 289 p. : ill.   **EE112**

1st ed., 1959; 2nd ed., 1971.

Part I, a general expansion of the 2nd ed. "expounds the basic principles of inorganic chemical nomenclature …. Part II and subsequent volumes will deal with specialized areas of nomenclature, and some of the eventual contents have already appeared in *Pure and applied chemistry*."—*Introd.* "… the level of Part I should be such that its general principles will not be undermined, and … it should retain its currency for many years. Part II, more specialized, will appear in the

near future, and, by its nature, will require more frequent revision."—*Pref.* This edition appears in an instructional format rather than as a series of numbered rules as in past editions; it provides numerous examples and the text is more coherent and discursive. Also new are two introductory chapters: Chap. 1 gives a concise history of inorganic chemical nomenclature, and Chap. 2 summarizes "the usages of inorganic nomenclature" and is intended to be used in conjunction with other chapters. Indexed.   QD149.N66

ORGANIC

The Aldrich library of ^{13}C and ^{1}H FT NMR spectra / Charles J. Pouchert, Jacqlynn Behnke. Milwaukee : Aldrich Chemical Co., c1993. 3 v. : chiefly ill.   **EE113**

A very useful compilation of carbon-13 and proton nuclear magnetic resonance spectra; the 300 MHz Fourier-transform proton spectra given here supplement the 60 MHz proton spectra given in the author's *Aldrich library of NMR spectra* (EE142). As with the other Aldrich Library series, compounds are arranged by chemical class and by increasing complexity within a class. Entries give carbon-13 spectrum and tabulated peaks, proton spectrum and integrated proton spectrum, structural formula, formula weight, basic physical properties for the high-purity samples used, references to spectra in other Aldrich Library collections, and CAS Registry Number. Indexed by compound name, molecular formula, CAS Registry Number.   QC462.85.A44

Amino acids and peptides / ed. by J. S. Davies. London ; N.Y. : Chapman and Hall, 1985. 430 p.   **EE114**

With *Carbohydrates* (EE116), forms part of the "Chapman and Hall chemistry sourcebooks" series.

Despite the series title, these are dictionaries of organic substances. They contain material drawn for the most part from the publisher's dictionaries of organic compounds, but some entries do not occur in those dictionaries, and some are revised. Substances are listed alphabetically by chemical name, and there are indexes of names, molecular formulae, and CAS Registry Numbers.   QP561.A48

Beilstein, Friedrich. Handbuch der organischen Chemie. 4. Aufl. Die Literatur bis 1. Januar 1910 umfassend / hrsg. von der Deutschen Chemischen Gesellschaft; bearb. von Bernhard Prager … [et al.]. Berlin : Springer, 1918–40. 31 v. : tables.   **EE115**

Editors vary.

A monumental compilation, still in many ways the most important reference work in organic chemistry. The arrangement of entries by compound class, with running heads in the supplements (below) give the corresponding volume and pages in the parent work, allows readers who know the Beilstein system to find immediately information on the class of compounds of interest. Moreover, entries give physical properties and information concerning preparation as well as bibliographic citations to critically evaluated articles. The general plan of arrangement may be found in many works—e.g., Deutsche Chemische Gesellschaft, *System der organischen Verbindungen* (Berlin : Springer, 1929. 246 p.); Ernest Hamlin Huntress's *A brief introduction to the use of Beilstein's Handbuch der organischen Chemie* (2nd ed. rev. N.Y. : Wiley, 1938. 44 p.); and Oskar Weissbach's *The Beilstein guide : a manual for the use of Beilstein's Handbuch der organischen Chemie* (Berlin ; N.Y. : Springer Verlag, 1976. 95 p.); and brief summaries are given in guides such as Melvin Guy Mellon's *Chemical publications : their nature and use* (EE5). The Beilstein Institute has also produced a software package, *SANDRA*, which allows input of structures in graphic form and tells users where in the Beilstein volumes to find the compounds.

Beilstein does not, however, provide comprehensive coverage of current research; the 5th suppl. for 1960–79 (below) is still in progress. Use of Beilstein must therefore be supplemented by *Chemical abstracts* (EE22) and by the database *Beilstein current facts in chemistry* (below).

Supplements:

(1) ——. ——. *I. Ergäzungswerk, die Literatur von 1910–1919 umfassend*, hrsg. vom der Deutschen Chemischen Gesellschaft, bearb. von Friedriech Richter (Berlin : Springer, 1928–38. 27 v.).

(2) ——. ——. *II. Ergäzungswerk, die Literatur von 1920–1929 umfassend* ... (Berlin : Springer, 1941–57, v. 1–29$^{1-3}$).

(3) ——. ——. *III. Ergäzungswerk, die Literatur von 1930–1949 umfassend*, hrsg. vom Beilstein-Institut für Literatur der Organischen Chemie (Berlin : Springer, 1958–74. 16 v.).

(4) ——. ——. *III. und IV. Ergäzungswerk, die Literatur von 1930–1959 umfassend* ... (Berlin ; N.Y. : Springer, 1974–85. Bd. 17–27). Beginning with Bd. 17, the 3rd and 4th suppls. were combined in order to relieve some of the delay in coverage of the literature.

(5) ——. ——. *IV. Ergäzungswerk, die Literatur von 1950–1959 umfassend* ... (Berlin : Springer, 1972–86. 16 v.).

(6) ——. ——. *V. Supplementary series, covering the literature from 1960–79*, comp. by the Beilstein-Institut für Literatur der Organischen Chemie ... Executive ed., Reiner Luckenbach (v. 17– . Berlin ; N.Y. : Springer, 1984– . [In progress]). Title appears as: *Beilstein handbook of organic chemistry*. Vols. of the 5th suppl. are in English. Publication began with v. 17–27 (heterocyclic compounds) because "an extensive survey ... indicated a clear preference among users for information about these compounds. Publication of v. 1–16 ... will be undertaken as soon as possible."—*Foreword*.

Indexes:

(1) ——. ——. *Gesamtregister für das Hauptwerk und die Ergänzungswerk I, II, III, und IV. Die Literatur bis 1959 umfassend ... Sachregister* (Berlin ; N.Y. : Springer, 1975–88. Bd. 1–27 in 15 pts.). Subject indexes, volume by volume for the main work and first 4 suppls.

(2) ——. ——. *Gesamtregister für das Hauptwerk und die Ergänzungswerk I, II, III, und IV. Die Literatur bis 1959 umfassend ... Formelregister* (Berlin ; N.Y. : Springer, 1975–89. Bd. 1–27 in 15 pts.). Formula indexes, volume by volume for the main work and first 4 suppls.

(3) ——. ——. *Beilstein centennial index : general compound-name index. The literature until 1959* ... (Berlin ; N.Y. : Springer, 1991. In 10 pts.).

(4) ——. ——. *Beilstein centennial index : general formula index. The literature until 1959* ... (Berlin ; N.Y. : Springer, 1992. In 13 pts.). These two indexes, considered v. 28 and 29 of the 4th suppl., allow more convenient access than the volume indexing of the earlier indexes.

(5) ——. ——. *Collective indexes to supplementary series V. The literature from 1960–79 ... Subject index* (Berlin ; N.Y. : Springer, 1990– . v. 17– . [In progress]).

(6) ——. ——. *Collective indexes to supplementary series V. The literature from 1960–79 ... Formula index* (Berlin ; N.Y. : Springer, 1991– . v. 17– . [In progress]).

•Available in machine-readable form as: *Beilstein online* [database] (Frankfurt am Main [Germany] : Beilstein-Institut für Literatur der Organischen Chemie). Available online. Includes data and references, 1830– , corresponding to the 4th ed. of the main work, suppls. 1–4, and material already published in suppl. 5 as well as material not yet published there. Machine-readable data for the most recent literature, 1990– , not yet published in printed form, is given in: *Beilstein current facts in chemistry* [database] (Frankfurt am Main [Germany] : Beilstein-Institut für Literatur der Organischen Chemie). Available both online and in CD-ROM. QD251.B4

Carbohydrates / ed. by P. M. Collins ; principal contributor, V. R. N. Munasinghe. London ; N.Y. : Chapman and Hall, 1987. 719 p. : ill. **EE116**

With *Amino acids and peptides* (EE114), forms part of the "Chapman and Hall chemistry sourcebooks" series. QP701.C294

Comprehensive heterocyclic chemistry : the structure, reactions, synthesis, and uses of heterocyclic compounds / editorial board: Alan R. Katritzky, chairman; Charles W. Rees, co-chairman. Oxford ; N.Y. : Pergamon, 1984. 8 v. : ill. **EE117**

Contents: v. 1, Introduction, nomenclature, review literature, biological aspects, industrial uses, less-common heteroatoms; v. 2, Six-membered rings with one nitrogen atom; v. 3, Six-membered rings

with oxygen, sulfur or two or more nitrogen atoms; v. 4, Five-membered rings with one oxygen, sulfur or nitrogen atom; v. 5, Five-membered rings with two or more nitrogen atoms; v. 6, Five-membered rings with two or more oxygen, sulfur or nitrogen atoms; v. 7, Small and large rings; v. 8, Author, subject, ring and data indexes.

Signed, authoritative articles include literature references. QD400.C65

Comprehensive organic chemistry : the synthesis and reactions of organic compounds / editorial board: Sir Derek Barton, chairman; W. David Ollis, deputy chairman. Oxford ; N.Y. : Pergamon, 1979. 6 v. : ill. **EE118**

Contents: v. 1, Stereochemistry, hydrocarbons, halo compounds, oxygen compounds; v. 2, Nitrogen compounds, carboxylic acids, phosphorus compounds; v. 3, Sulphur selenium, silicon, boron, organometallic compounds; v. 4. Heterocyclic compounds; v. 5, Biological compounds; v. 6, Author, formula, subject, reagent, reaction indexes.

Signed, authoritative articles include literature references. ZD245.C65

Comprehensive organic synthesis : selectivity, strategy, and efficiency in modern organic chemistry / editor[s] Barry M. Trost, Ian Fleming. Oxford ; N.Y. : Pergamon Pr., 1991. 9 v. : ill. **EE119**

A supplement to *Comprehensive organic chemistry* (EE118). Provides up-to-date treatment of the synthetic aspects of organic chemistry, using the same approach: signed, authoritative articles with substantial bibliographies. Each volume includes indexes to authors cited in the bibliographies and subjects treated in that volumes; the index volume has cumulative author and subject indexes. QD262.C535

Comprehensive organometallic chemistry : the synthesis, reactions and structures of organometallic compounds / ed., Sir Geoffrey Wilkinson; deputy ed., F. Gordon A. Stone, executive ed., Edward W. Abel. Oxford ; N.Y. : Pergamon, 1982. 9 v. : ill. **EE120**

Each of the first seven volumes contains signed, authoritative articles, including tabular data and literature references, on the organic compounds of specific metals. Vol. 8 has articles on special topics such as the use of various organometallics in organic synthesis, polymer supported catalysts, etc. Vol. 9 contains subject, author, and formula indexes, an index of structures determined by diffraction methods, and an index of review articles and books. QD411.C65

Connolly, J. D. Dictionary of terpenoids / J. D. Connolly and R. A. Hill. London ; N.Y. : Chapman & Hall, 1991. 3 v. : ill. **EE121**

Part of a series being issued by this publisher; *see* EE123.

Contents: v. 1, Mono- and sesquiterpenoids; v. 2, Di- and higher terpenoids; v. 3, Indexes.

•In machine-readable form as part of *HEILBRON* (EE133). QD416.C75

Deutsche Chemische Gesellschaft. Literatur Register der organischen Chemie / geordnet nach M. M. Richter's Formelsystem; redigiert von Robert Stelzner. Bd. 1 (1910/11)–5 (1919/21). Braunschweig ; Berlin : Vieweg Chemie Verlag, 1913–26. **EE122**

Repr.: Ann Arbor, Mich. : Edwards, 1948.

Cited as "Stelzner." Publisher varies.

Arranged by formulas in continuation of Max Moritz Richter's *Lexikon der Kohlenstoff-Verbindungen* (EE143). Each volume covers the literature of from two to three years. Merged with Index to *Chemisches Zentralblatt* (EE24).

Dictionary of alkaloids / editorial board: G. A. Cordell ... [et al.]; comp. and ed. by I. W. Southon, J. Buckingham. London ; N.Y. : Chapman and Hall, 1989. 2 v. : ill. **EE123**

Part of a series, with *Dictionary of analytical reagents* (EE124), *Dictionary of antibiotics and related substances* (EE125), *Dictionary of drugs* (EE126), *Dictionary of organophosphorus compounds* (EE129), *Dictionary of steroids* (EE130), and *Dictionary of terpenoids* (EE121), that complements *Dictionary of organic compounds* (EE127) and *Dictionary of organometallic compounds* (EE128). The coverage of each dictionary is substantially discrete, for the most part not duplicating that of the more comprehensive works, or of one another.

●In machine-readable form as part of *HEILBRON* (EE133).

RS431.A53D53

Dictionary of analytical reagents / editorial board, A. Townshend ... [et al.] ; principal contributors, R. Lobin'ski, Z. Marczenko, P. Rhodes. London ; N.Y. : Chapman & Hall, 1993. 1370 p. : ill.   **EE124**

Part of a series being issued by this publisher; *see* EE123.

Entries are alphabetical by compound name and include synonyms, CAS Registry Number, analytical applications of the reagents, physical properties, structural formula, molecular weight, derivatives, toxicity, and literature references. Indexed by compound group, by use in analysis (e.g., as a stain, as an NMR shift reagent), by analyte (substance analyzed for), by synonym, by CAS Registry Number, and by molecular formula.

●In machine-readable form as part of *HEILBRON* (EE133).

QD77.D498

Dictionary of antibiotics and related substances / ed. by B. W. Bycroft ; contributors, A. A. Higton, A. D. Roberts. London ; N.Y. : Chapman and Hall, 1988. 944 p. : ill.   **EE125**

Part of a series being issued by this publisher; *see* EE123.

●In machine-readable form as part of *HEILBRON* (EE133).

RS431.A6D53

Dictionary of drugs : chemical data, structures, and bibliographies / editors, J. Elks, C. R. Ganellin. London ; N.Y. : Chapman and Hall, 1990. 2 v. : ill.   **EE126**

Part of a series being issued by this publisher; *see* EE123.

●In machine-readable form as part of *HEILBRON* (EE133).

RS51.D479

Dictionary of organic compounds. 5th ed. N.Y. ; London : Chapman and Hall, [1982]. 7 v. : ill.   **EE127**

1st ed., 1934.

This edition is the most radical and comprehensive revision of the publication ever undertaken. Entries are included for fundamental organic compounds of simple structures, compounds of widespread industrial or commercial value, important natural products, compounds frequently encountered as solvents, reagents or starting materials, and other compounds of particular interest because of their chemical, structural, or biological properties. Arrnged alphabetically by "DOC Name" (the name the editors believe is most likely to be known by most readers), entries also include synonyms considered useful or important. Names used by Chemical Abstracts Service during the 8th and 9th Collective Index periods are labeled with suffixes 8CI and 9CI; names recommended by various national or international organizations are also labeled. Information on derivatives is frequently included under the entry for the parent compound.

Entries include constitution, physical and chemical properties, use, and bibliographic references; this new edition also includes hazard and toxicity information and CAS Registry Numbers. A name index, listing in alphabetical order all "DOC names" and synonyms contained in the main work makes up v. 6.; v. 7 consists of a molecular formula index, a heteroatom index to the formulae of compounds containing atoms other than C, H, O, N, or halogens, and a CAS Registry Number index.

Kept up-to-date by: ———. *Supplement* (1st [1983]– . London ; N.Y. : Chapman and Hall, 1983– . Annual). Contains new and updated entries derived from the primary literature of the preceding year. The 2nd and subsequent supplements have cumulative indexes derived from the entries in all the preceding supplements. The 5th annual suppl. (1987) is in 2 v., of which the second is a cumulative index to suppl. 1–5. The 7th and subsequent supplements cumulate indexing from the 6th suppl. onwards.

●Machine-readable versions: *CHCD dictionary of organic compounds on CD-ROM* [database] (London : Chapman and Hall, 1993–). Available on CD-ROM; updated semiannually. Also included as part of the online database *HEILBRON* (EE133).

Dictionary of organometallic compounds. N.Y. ; London : Chapman and Hall, [1984]. 3 v. : ill.   **EE128**

Complements *Dictionary of organic compounds* (EE127) by providing for organometallics the same types of information that work supplies for organic compounds.

"Divided into element sections; within each section the arrangement of entries is in order of molecular formula according to the Hill convention (i.e., C, then H, then other elements in alphabetical sequence of element symbol ...). There is a section for every element except for the halogens, the noble gases, unstable radioactive elements for which no organometallic compounds have been well characterised, and the following: H, C, N, O, P, S, Se, and Te. (Entries for organic compounds containing only these elements are included in the companion ... *Dictionary of organic compounds*.) The entries for compounds which contain more than one type of metal atom are printed in full in all relevant sections, thus obviating the need for cross-references."—*Introd.*

Each element section begins with a brief description of physical properties, availability, analysis, handling, and toxicity of the element, with the name of the element in French, German, Spanish, Italian, Russian, and Japanese, plus references. Longer element sections also include a structure index with molecular structures displayed for rapid location. Each entry is numbered. Entries include names of compounds as reported in the literature, and *Chemical abstracts* names; the latter are identified by suffixes 8CI, 9CI, or 10CI depending on which collective index period they fall under. CAS Registry Numbers are also given. American spelling is used for all chemical names. Entries include structural formulae and stereochemical description as appropriate, physical and chemical information, use, hazard and toxicity, and bibliographic references.

Vol. 3 contains a name index listing every compound name or synonym; a molecular formula index in Hill convention order; and a CAS Registry Number index. All indexes refer to entry numbers.

Kept up-to-date by: ———. *Supplement* (1st [1984]– . London ; N.Y. : Chapman and Hall, 1985– . Annual). Substances are in order alphabetically by the metallic element, with indexes by molecular formula and CAS Registry Number. The 5th suppl. is in 3 v., of which v. 2–3 are cumulative indexes to suppl. 1–5; one of these is a cumulative index of structures, the first structure index since the parent work (1984). The 7th and subsequent supplements will cumulate indexing from the 6th suppl. onwards.

●In machine-readable form as part of *HEILBRON* (EE133).

QD411.D53

Dictionary of organophosphorus compounds / ed. and comp. by R. S. Edmundson. London ; N.Y. : Chapman and Hall, c1988. 1347 p. : ill.   **EE129**

Part of a series being issued by this publisher; *see* EE123.

●In machine-readable form as part of *HEILBRON* (EE133).

QD412.P1E36

Dictionary of steroids / editors, R. A. Hill ... [et al.]; principal contributors, A. Cooper, A. D. Roberts. London ; N.Y. : Chapman & Hall, 1991. 2 v.   **EE130**

Part of series being issued by this publisher; *see* EE123.

●In machine-readable form as part of *HEILBRON* (EE133).

QP752.S7D53

Fieser, Louis Frederick. Fieser and Fieser's reagents for organic synthesis / Louis F. Fieser, Mary Fieser. N.Y. : Wiley, [1967–94]. v. 1–17 : ill. (In progress).   **EE131**

Vol. 1–7 had title: *Reagents for organic synthesis*, some with order of authors reversed. Vol. 7 is the last with Louis Fieser as co-author.

Published approximately annually since v. 7.

Vol. 1 describes more than 1,000 reagents of use to organic chemists. Reagents are listed alphabetically, with structural formula, molecular weight, physical constants, and preferred methods of preparation given for each. Bibliographic references are included. Subsequent volumes describe additional reagents and add new information and references for reagents previously described. Each volume has author and subject indexes. An index volume (1990) covering v. 1–12 includes indexing by type of reaction, synthesis, type of compound, and reagent. QD262.F5

Giese, Friedo. Beilstein's index : trivial names in systematic nomenclature of organic chemistry. Berlin ; N.Y. : Springer-Verlag, c1986. 253 p. : ill. **EE132**

An index to organic compounds known by nonsystematic ("trivial") names. As the title indicates, intends to help find information in Friedrich Beilstein, *Handbuch der organischen Chemie* (EE115), but useful in finding information from other sources as well. Entries, alphabetical by trivial name, include formula, chemical structure, Beilstein and Chemical Abstracts systematic names, CAS Registry Number, Beilstein system number, and IUPAC rule number for IUPAC name. Indexed by ring system (see: *Ring systems handbook*, EE86), by chemical formula, and by CAS Registry Number. QD291.G53

•**HEILBRON** [database]. London : Chapman & Hall, Scientific Data Division. **EE133**

Available online; updated semiannually.

Drawn primarily from the producer's series of dictionaries of organic compounds: *Dictionary of organic compounds* and supplements (EE127), *Dictionary of organometallic compounds* and supplements (EE128), and the more specialized dictionaries described in EE123. The online file contains additional information not in the dictionaries. Full text is searchable, as is numeric data (e.g., melting point, density, optical rotation). Includes more than 200,000 substances.

Index of reviews in organic chemistry. London : Royal Society of Chemistry (distr. in U.S. by American Chem. Soc.), 1959–85. **EE134**

Publisher formerly named Chemical Society.

Originally prepared for internal use at Imperial Chemical Industries in 1959, this publication developed into a continuing series. Cumulation issued in 1971 supersedes all previous issues; a second cumulation issued in 1977 covers the literature 1971 May 1976. The 1979 suppl. (publ. 1980) covers May 1976–1978; 1981 suppl. covers 1979–November 1980. A volume covering 1981–82 was issued in 1983; volumes publ. in 1984 and 1985 cover the literature of the previous year.

Through the 1981 suppl., arranged in three sections: articles on individual compounds or classes of compounds; articles on "name reactions"; articles on specific chemical processes or phenomena. Subsequent issues omitted the section on "name reactions." Covers journals, books, monographs, technical reports, and conference proceedings. QD291.I523

Index to reviews, symposia volumes and monographs in organic chemistry. v. 1 (1940/60)–v. 3 (1963/64). N.Y. : Pergamon, 1962–65. **EE135**

Ed. by Norman Kharasch and Walter Wolf (with E. Harrison, 1940/60).

Contents: v. 1, 1940–60 (345 p.); v. 2, 1961–62 (260 p.); v. 3, 1963–64 (326 p.).

Each volume in three divisions: (1) Reviews in journals and periodic publications; (2) Reviews in symposia, collective volumes and non-periodical publications; (3) Monographs on organic chemistry. In the first two divisions the arrangement is by periodical or monograph, giving complete contents for each volume. The third section omits contents but includes full bibliographic information. Entries limited to French, German, English, and Russian (if an English translation is readily available). Author and subject indexes. Z5524.O8I5

International Union of Pure and Applied Chemistry. Commission on the Nomenclature of Organic Chemistry. Nomenclature of organic chemistry. 4th ed. Oxford ; N.Y. : Pergamon, 1979. 559 p. : ill. **EE136**

Prep. for publication by J. Rigaudy and S. P. Klesney.

1st ed., 1958; 3rd ed., 1971.

Contains 4th ed. of Sections A and B, 3rd ed. of Section C, 1st ed. of Sections D, E, F, H.

Contents: Section A, Hydrocarbons; Section B, Fundamental heterocyclic systems; Section C, Characteristic groups containing carbon, hydrogen, oxygen, nitrogen, halogen, sulfur, selenium and/or tellurium; Section D, Organic compounds containing elements that are not exclusively carbon, hydrogen, oxygen, nitrogen, halogen, sulfur, selenium and tellurium; Section E, Stereochemistry; Section F, General principles for the naming of natural products and related compounds; Section H, Isotopically modified compounds. QD291.I57

Krauch, Helmut. Organic name reactions : a contribution to the terminology of organic chemistry, biochemistry and theoretical organic chemistry / by Helmut Krauch and Werner Kunz. N.Y. : Wiley, 1964. 620 p. **EE137**

Translation of the authors' *Namenreaktionen der organischen Chemie*, 2nd rev. ed.; tr. by John M. Harkin.

Contains more than 500 reactions named for the discoverers and 15 reactions given title entry. Each reaction is explained in words, together with an equation, reaction conditions, and several literature citations. Entry length varies from one-half page to three pages. Author index includes persons identified with name reactions as well as authors mentioned in literature references. Subject index. QD291.K713

Methoden der organischen Chemie (Houben-Weyl). 4. völlig neu gestaltete Aufl. / hrsg. von Eugen Müller, unter besonderer Mitwirkung von O. Bayer, H. Meerwein [und] K. Ziegler. Stuttgart : G. Thieme, 1952–86. 15 v. in 67 : ill. **EE138**

1st ed., 1908–10.

The work of many specialists and a standard reference in the field. Discusses methods of preparation in terms of classes of compounds; the first 4 v. treat techniques and methods. Each volume has its own index.

A supplementary series, ———. *Erweiterungs- und Folgebände zur vierten Auflage*, hrsg. [von] K. H. Büchel … [et al.] (Stuttgart ; N.Y. : G. Thieme, 1982–93. v. 1–5, 7, 11–16, 18–20 in 41 pts. [In progress]), covers new developments and progress in preparative methods, including compound classes not previously described, and compound classes concerning which considerable progress has been made. Vols. 16[1] and 16[2], pts. a and b, consist of comprehensive indexes for the main works (all volumes) and for v. 1–5 and v. 11 of the suppl.; they include indexes to classes of substances, individual compounds, name reactions, and experimental procedures. Vol. 12b of the suppl. ("Organotellurium compounds") is in English. QD258.M44

Molecular structures and dimensions. Utrecht : Scheltema & Holkema ; distr. Pittsburgh, Pa. : Polycrystal Book Service, [1970]–84. 15 v. **EE139**

"Published for the Crystallographic Data Centre Cambridge and the International Union of Crystallography."—*t.p.*

A classified bibliography of organic and organometallic crystal structures, with author, formula, and transition metal indexes. Indexing both by standard formula and permuted formula; beginning with v. 8 includes a KWIC index of compound names. Vols. 1 and 2 cover the literature from 1935–69; v. 3, 1969–71; v. 4, 1971–72; subsequent volumes cover the literature of a 12-month period beginning in mid-year, after the pattern of v. 4. Vol. 15 covers 1982/83.

Partially indexed by: *Molecular structures and dimensions : guide to the literature 1935–1976 ; organic and organometallic crystal structures*, ed. by Olga Kennard, Frank H. Allen and David G. Watson (Utrecht : Scheltema & Holkema, [1977]. 1 v., various pagings).

Includes KWIC indexes of compound names for organic and organometallic compounds, molecular formula index, permuted formula index, and author index citing entries in *Molecular structures and dimensions*, v. 1–8; also an index arranged by those entry numbers and giving the journal citation from which the entry was taken.

•Machine-readable version: *Cambridge structural database (CSD)* [database] (Cambridge, England : Cambridge Crystallographic Centre, 1970–). Available online, updated every six weeks. Includes numeric and bibliographic data, 1935 to date. Z5524.C8M6

Pouchert, Charles J. The Aldrich library of FT-IR spectra. Milwaukee, Wis. : Aldrich Chemical Co., c1985. 2 v. : chiefly ill. **EE140**

Any college or university using Fourier-transform infrared spectrometers should have these volumes to supplement the *Aldrich library of infrared spectra* (EE141). Vols. 1 and 2 give spectra of compounds in the condensed phase, and v. 3 of compounds in the vapor phase; in both cases, compounds are arranged in order of chemical class and structural complexity. Entries include spectrum, structural formula, some physical properties (formula weight, and density, melting point, boiling point, index of refraction when available) for the high-purity samples used, listings of the main peak positions, references to spectra in other Aldrich Library collections, and CAS Registry Number. Indexed by compound name, molecular formula, CAS Registry Number.

QD96.I5P66

———————— The Aldrich library of infrared spectra. 3rd ed. [Milwaukee] : Aldrich Chemical Co., [1981]. 1867 p. : ill.   **EE141**

1st ed., 1970.

"The intention of this book [is] to present a large number of spectra on each of the important organic functional groups along with a short written description and graphic representation of their spectral features for the purpose of review by the average chemist who is not a specialist in infrared spectroscopy."—*Pref.* Compounds are grouped by category. Includes compound name and molecular formula indexes.

QD96.I5P67

———————— The Aldrich library of NMR spectra. 2nd ed. [Milwaukee] : Aldrich Chemical Co., [1983]. 2 v. : ill.   **EE142**

1st ed., 1974.

A compilation of spectra arranged by chemical class of compounds, "to assist the average chemist who is not a specialist in nmr spectroscopy."—*Pref.* Includes indexes of compound names and molecular formulas.

QD96.N8P68

Richter, Max Moritz. Lexikon der Kohlenstoff-Verbindungen. 3. Aufl. Hamburg ; Leipzig : Voss, 1910–12. 4 v. : diagrs.   **EE143**

A formula index to all compounds known to Dec. 31, 1909. Includes more than 144,000 compounds, with references to literature which describes preparation and properties, but not to purely theoretical papers. References to Beilstein refer to the 3rd ed. of the *Handbuch.*

§ Continued by: Deutsche Chemische Gesellschaft, *Literatur Register der organischen Chemie* (EE122).

Sittig, Marshall. Organic chemical process encyclopedia. 2nd ed. Park Ridge, N.J. : Noyes Development Corp., [1969]. 712 p. : ill.   **EE144**

1st ed., 1967.

Consists of 711 flow sheets showing the manufacture of the major organic chemicals, as of 1969. Petroleum chemicals are emphasized. Included in the standard format for each entry are reaction utilized, a labeled drawing showing feed materials and conditions (catalyst, solvent, temperature, pressure, etc.), major product and uses, coproducts where known, and references to one or more patents. No index.

TP690.S56

Sugasawa, Shigehiko. Reaction index of organic syntheses / Shigehiko Sugasawa, Seijirō Nakai. [Rev. ed.]. Tokyo : Hirokawa ; N.Y. : Wiley, [1967]. 251 p.   **EE145**

All reactions listed in the annual volumes of *Organic syntheses* have been classified into 31 types. No index.   QD262.S87

University of Cincinnati. Dept. of Chemistry. Organic Division. The vocabulary of organic chemistry / [by] Milton Orchin [et al.]. N.Y. : Wiley, 1980. 609 p. : ill.   **EE146**

"The purpose of this book is to ientify the fundamental vocabulary of organic chemistry and then to present concise, accurate definitions, with examples where appropriate, for the words and concepts. ... "—*Pref.* Arranged in topical chapters; numbered paragraphs within chapters present words and concepts placed in a sequence that makes pedagogical sense to the authors. Where possible, the authors

adhere to recognized definitions such as those prescribed in various publications of the International Union of Pure and Applied Chemistry. Includes bibliographic citations. Some cross-references. Indexed.

QD291.C55

Utermark, Walther. Melting point tables of organic compounds / [by] Walther Utermark [and] Walter Schicke. 2d rev. and supplemented ed. N.Y. : Interscience, 1963. 715 p.   **EE147**

Original German edition, 1951.

Added title page in German, French, and Russian.

Compounds are arranged in ascending order of melting point. Included with each entry are molecular and structural formulas, Beilstein citation, solubility, etc. Column headings are in German. The preface, list of abbreviations, and index of special terms appear in English, French, German, and Russian. The formula index refers only to the German name.   QD518.U7

Handbooks

Dean, John Aurie. Handbook of organic chemistry. N.Y. : McGraw-Hill, c1987. 1 v. (various pagings) : ill.   **EE148**

A compilation of numerical information in tabular form, designed to meet the needs of organic chemists. Includes a brief introduction to organic nomenclature. The main table includes basic properties and Beilstein references for 4,000 organic compounds; other tables give physical properties, thermodynamic properties, and spectroscopic data for some of the these compounds and for inorganic compounds considered useful to organic chemists. Also has chapters giving useful data for laboratory manipulations, data on polymers, rubbers, fats, oils and waxes, and miscellaneous data (e.g., conversion factors). Indexed.

QD251.2.D43

Handbook of data on organic compounds / editors, Robert C. Weast, Jeanette G. Grasselli. 2nd ed. Boca Raton, Fla. : CRC Pr., 1988–92. 11 v. : ill.   **EE149**

Rev. ed. of: *CRC handbook of data on organic compounds*, ed. by Weast and Melvin J. Astle (c1985. 2 v.).

A major expansion, the 2nd ed. consists of the basic work in 9 v. with supplementary volumes. The main body of the parent work consists of a compilation in alphabetical order of entries for the 26,000 most common organic compounds. Entries include a sequential number for indexing, the CAS Registry Number, Beilstein volume and page, compound name, synonyms, line formula, molecular formula, structure, molecular weight, boiling point, melting point, density, refractive index, specific rotation, color, and solubility. Spectral data, where available, are given as references to various of the Sadtler and other spectral compilations, as well as major peaks (or chemical shifts for magnetic resonance spectra). Vols. 7–9 of the main work provide indexes by synonyms, molecular formula, molecular weight, melting point, boiling point, spectral data arranged by type of spectra and within that by class of compound, and CAS Registry Number. Vols. 10–11 are supplements, each of which lists about 1,000 new compounds and updates about 1,000 compounds in the main work. A 3rd ed. has been announced for 1994.

• Machine-readable version: *Properties of organic compounds* [database] (Version 3.1. Boca Raton, Fla. : CRC Pr., 1993). Available on CD-ROM. Numerical indexes such as melting point can be searched by ranges of values.   QD257.7.C73

Mingotaud, Anne-Françoise. Handbook of monolayers / Anne-Françoise Mingotaud, Christophe Mingotaud, Larry K. Patterson. San Diego : Academic Pr., c1993. 2 v. (2726 p.) : ill.   **EE150**

Provides data on monolayers of more than 1,300 amphiphilic compounds and preparations, with entries including the structure of the compound and data taken from surface pressure–area isotherms. Literature references are given. Entries are arranged by category of compound (e.g., single-chain fatty acid) and within these by subcategory (such as hydrophilic groups present). Indexed by common names. Useful in a wide range of subject areas, e.g., chemical sensors, biophysics of cell membranes, nonlinear optics. QD506.M56

Rappoport, Zvi. CRC handbook of tables for organic compound identification. 3rd ed. Cleveland, Ohio : Chemical Rubber Co., [1967]. 564 p. **EE151**

Repr. : Boca Raton, Fla. : CRC Press, 1983.

1st ed. (1960) and 2nd ed. (1964) comp. by Max Frankel and others and published under title *Tables for identification of organic compounds.*

Compounds are arranged according to functional group, with subarrangement in order of increasing melting point, boiling point, etc. Includes more than 8,100 parent compounds. Indexed. QD291.R28

EF

Earth Sciences

GENERAL WORKS

Guides

Hopkins, Stephen T. Research guide to the arid lands of the world / by Stephen T. Hopkins and Douglas E. Jones. Phoenix, Ariz. : Oryx, 1983. 391 p. : maps. **EF1**

A comprehensive 3,199-entry bibliography for interdisciplinary research on countries and geographic areas which contain arid lands. Arrangement is geographical with subject and author indexes. The broad subject coverage includes geology, climatology, hydrology, biology, botany, agriculture, anthropology, urban geography, transportation and other fields. Z6004.A7H66

Information sources in the earth sciences / [ed. by] David N. Wood, Joan E. Hardy, and Anthony P. Harvey. 2nd ed. London ; N.Y. : Bowker-Saur, c1989. 518 p. **EF2**

Rev. ed. of Wood's *Use of earth sciences literature* ([Hamden, Conn.] : Archon Books, 1973).

For this completely revised edition, 19 librarians and earth scientists contributed detailed bibliographic essays. Introductory chapters describing the general nature of primary and secondary literature in the earth sciences are followed by reviews of reference sources, textbooks, and special format materials for specific earth sciences subdisciplines. Topical index with some title entries. Z6031.I55

Encyclopedias

The Cambridge encyclopedia of earth sciences / ed. in chief, David G. Smith. N.Y. : Crown Publ. : Cambridge Univ. Pr., 1981. 496 p. : ill., maps. **EF3**

A collection of long, signed articles written by specialists survey different earth sciences. "Designed to be used as a work of reference … but it is also a book that is designed to be picked up and read."— *Introd.* Includes glossary, index, and bibliography. QE26.2.C35

The encyclopedia of beaches and coastal environments / ed. by Maurice L. Schwartz. Stroudsburg, Pa. : Hutchinson Ross ; distr. by Van Nostrand Reinhold, 1982. 940 p. : ill., maps. (Encyclopedia of earth sciences, v.15). **EF4**

A survey of the field of coastal studies including the geomorphic, biologic, engineering, and human aspects of the world's coast. Signed articles, with cross-references and bibliographies, are arranged alphabetically. Cited author and subject indexes. GB450.4.E53

Encyclopedia of earth sciences / Rhodes Whitmore Fairbridge, series ed. N.Y. : Van Nostrand Reinhold, 1966–89? v. 1–8, 10–17 : ill. **EF5**

According to the publisher, plans for future volumes have been cancelled.

Contents: v. 1, *The encyclopedia of oceanography* (EF216); v. 2, *The encyclopedia of atmospheric sciences and astrogeology* (EF145); v. 3, *The encyclopedia of geomorphology* (EF7); v. 4A, *The encyclopedia of geochemistry and environmental sciences* (EF67); v. 4B, *The encyclopedia of mineralogy* (EF179); v. 6, *The encyclopedia of sedimentology* (EF64); v. 7, *The encyclopedia of paleontology* (EF235); v. 8, *The encyclopedia of world regional geology,* pt. 1, Western Hemisphere (including Antarctica and Australia) (EF68); v. 10, *Encyclopedia of structural geology and plate tectonics* (EF66); v. 11, *Encyclopedia of climatology* (EF144); v. 12, *The encyclopedia of soil science,* pt. 1, physics, chemistry, biology, fertility, and technology (EJ22); v. 13, *The encyclopedia of applied geology* (EF62); v. 14, *Encyclopedia of field and general geology* (EF63); v. 15, *The encyclopedia of beaches and coastal environments* (EF4); v. 16, *Encyclopedia of igneous and metamorphic petrology* (EF253); v. 17, *Encyclopedia of solid earth geophysics* (EF65).

A series of autonomous, single-volume encyclopedias with subject focus. Signed articles with bibliographic references appear in alphabetical arrangement. Numerous cross-references, including references to other volumes of the series. Detailed subject indexes.

Encyclopedia of earth system science / William A. Nierenberg, ed. in chief. San Diego, Calif. : Academic Pr., c1992. 4 v. ; ill., maps. **EF6**

The interactions of natural planetary processes, the earth, atmosphere, and oceans, are the special context of this work. About 230 lengthy, signed articles are alphabetically arranged. Following the format of the publisher's *Encyclopedia of physical science and technology* (EA79) each article includes a table of contents, bibliography, and glossary. Quick reference lookups are difficult due to the very specific titles used for articles, e.g., Analytical petrology, Water geochemistry. The detailed subject index is a more helpful entry point. Vol. 13 includes the list of contributors, a relational index that groups articles on similar topics, and a subject index. QE5.E514

Fairbridge, Rhodes Whitmore. The encyclopedia of geomorphology. N.Y. : Reinhold, [1968]. 1295 p. : ill. (Encyclopedia of earth sciences, v.3). **EF7**

Signed articles, with bibliographies, on the analytic physiography of the earth's surface and closely related topics. Topical index includes place-names used in text. GB10.F3

Gresswell, R. Kay. Standard encyclopedia of the world's rivers and lakes / R. Kay Gresswell, Anthony Julian Huxley. N.Y. : Putnam, [1965]. 384 p. : ill. **EF8**

A companion to Huxley's *Standard encyclopedia of the world's mountains* (EF9) and *Standard encyclopedia of the world's oceans and islands* (EF10), with a similar format. GB1203.G73

Huxley, Anthony Julian. Standard encyclopedia of the world's mountains. N.Y. : Putnam, [1962]. 383 p. : ill., maps. **EF9**

A companion to Huxley's *Standard encyclopedia of the world's rivers and lakes* (with Kay Gresswell; EF8) and *Standard encyclopedia of the world's oceans and islands* (EF10).

Written in popular style, arranged alphabetically by name of mountain; gives location, height, dates, and names of first climbers, etc., and a brief description and history. Illustrated with black-and-white and color photographs. Includes a gazetteer and an index.
GB501.H8

――――――――― Standard encyclopedia of the world's oceans and islands. N.Y. : Putnam, [1962]. 383 p. : ill., maps. **EF10**
A companion to Huxley's *Standard encyclopedia of the world's rivers and lakes* (with Kay Gresswell; EF8) and *Standard encyclopedia of the world's mountains* (EF9).
A work written in popular style, arranged alphabetically by name of ocean or island, giving location; dimensions, etc. (in case of oceans the maximum depth); and a brief description and history. Includes a gazetteer and an index.
GB471.H9

International dictionary of geophysics : seismology, geomagnetism, aeronomy, oceanography, geodesy, gravity, marine geophysics, meteorology, the earth as a planet and its evolution / ed. S. K. Runcorn ... [et al.]. Oxford ; N.Y. : Pergamon, [1967]. 2 v. : ill., maps + map portfolio (2 folded maps in color). **EF11**
Includes more than 700 articles contributed by an international roster of some 300 contributors. With the exception of certain brief definitions, entries consist of lengthy articles including bibliographies which refer to both standard and specialized works. An index supplements the dictionary arrangement.
QC801.9.I5

Magill's survey of science. Earth science series / ed. by Frank N. Magill ; consulting ed., James A. Woodhead. Pasadena, Calif. : Salem Pr., c1990. 5 v. : ill. **EF12**
Contains 377 signed articles by 130 contributors. All major aspects of the earth sciences are surveyed, including geology, paleontology, geochemistry, hydrology, oceanography, atmospheric sciences, and astronomy. The alphabetically arranged articles are written for general readers and organized for ease of use, with definitions of pertinent terms and short annotated bibliographies. Few tables, charts, or illustrations. Each volume contains a complete table of contents and topical index for the set. Glossary of terms and comprehensive index in v. 5. A more general source than R. W. Fairbridge's *Encyclopedia of earth sciences* (EF5).
QE28.M33

Dictionaries

Chambers earth sciences dictionary / gen. ed., P. M. B. Walker ; consultant ed., P. A. Sabine. Edinburgh : Chambers, 1991. 250 p. : ill., map. **EF13**
Short definitions, many with illustrations, for some 6,000 terms from geological, mineralogical, mining, and other solid earth subspecialities. Valuable as a current source in a rapidly developing discipline, although many entries are taken from *Chambers science and technology dictionary*, ed. by P. M. B. Walker (Edinburgh : Chambers ; Cambridge; N.Y. : Cambridge Univ. Pr., 1988. 1,008 p.).　　QE5.C452

The concise Oxford dictionary of earth sciences / ed. by Ailsa Allaby and Michael Allaby. Oxford ; N.Y. : Oxford Univ. Pr., 1990. 410 p. **EF14**
Some 6,000 alphabetically organized headwords from all disciplines in the earth sciences are defined and explained. Brief, two- to three-sentence definitions include biographical entries for important figures and cross-references to terms defined elsewhere in the dictionary. Prepared by 33 contributors and advisors, with about a third of the terms drawn from *The Oxford dictionary of natural history* (EG78). Useful bibliography of sources.　　QE5.C66

McGraw-Hill dictionary of earth sciences / Sybil P. Parker, ed. in chief. N.Y. : McGraw-Hill, c1984. 837 p. **EF15**
Defines briefly more than 15,000 terms from 18 different fields in the earth sciences. Most material was previously published in the

McGraw-Hill dictionary of scientific and technical terms (3rd ed., 1984. 5th ed., EA93). Useful for secondary school students and general readers. No index or bibliography.　　QE5.M365

Directories

Earth and astronomical sciences research centres. 3rd ed. [Harlow, Essex, Eng.] : Longman ; Detroit : distr. by Gale, 1993. 605 p. **EF16**
Subtitle (varies): a world directory of organizations and programmes.
1st ed., 1984; 2nd ed., 1991. Consultant ed., Jennifer M. Fitch.
Lists some 3,500 governmental, industrial, and academic laboratories, national geological and meteorological agencies, observatories, and professional societies. Entries are arranged alphabetically by country. In addition to name, address, and telephone, the entries frequently include the name of the director, size of staff, description of activities, and brief list of publications. Organization name and subject indexes.
§ The publisher has announced a new title, *Earth, astronomical and aerospace science research centres*, for 1994. Represents a merger of the above with *Aerospace technology centres*.　　QE40.E25

Handbooks

Deserts of the world : an appraisal of research into their physical and biological environments / ed. by William G. McGinnies, Bram J. Goldman, Patricia Paylore. [Tucson] : Univ. of Arizona Pr., [1968]. 788 p. : ill. **EF17**
Originally published in eight parts by the Office of Arid Lands Research, Univ. of Arizona (1967) as *An inventory of geographical research on desert environments*.
A summary and evaluation of the state of knowledge of the characteristics of all deserts of the world, "based upon critical reviews of the published literature augmented by consultations with specialists."—*Foreword*. Discusses climate, geomorphology, surface materials, vegetation, fauna, and groundwater hydrology. Includes extensive bibliographies.　　GB612.D4

Manual of remote sensing. 2nd ed. / ed. in chief, Robert N. Colwell. Falls Church, Va. : American Soc. of Photogrammetry, c1983. 2 v. (2440 p., [214] p. of plates) : ill. (some col.). **EF18**
1st ed., 1975.
Contents: v. 1., Theory, instruments, and techniques; v. 2. Interpretations and applications.
A substantial revision and expansion of the 1st ed. as well as of the American Society of Photogrammetry's *Manual of photographic interpretation* (1960), also using material from the Society's *Manual of photogrammetry* (3rd ed., 1966), *Manual of color aerial photography* (1968), and the periodical *Photogrammetric engineering*. Presents a comprehensive treatment of remote sensing theory and applications, with technical articles written by expert contributors. Articles include illustrations, diagrams, formulas, and lengthy reference lists. Complete index in v. 1 and v. 2; glossary in v. 2.　　G70.4.M36

Wedepohl, Karl Hans. Handbook of geochemistry / executive ed.: K. H. Wedepohl ; editorial board: C. W. Correns ... [et al.]. Berlin : Springer, 1969–78. 2 v. in 6. : ill. **EF19**
Vol. 1 (442 p.) is concerned with the "fundamental facts of geochemistry, geophysics and cosmochemistry, together with definitions, methods of evaluation, etc."—*Pref*. Vol. 2 was issued in looseleaf installments, each chapter dealing with a separate element, and giving tables, graphs, text, and references on abundance and on various aspects of the chemical and physical properties.　　QE515.W42

GEOLOGY

Guides

Ward, Dederick C. Geologic reference sources : a subject and regional bibliography of publications and maps in the geological sciences / Dederick C. Ward, Marjorie W. Wheeler, Robert A. Bier. 2nd ed. Metuchen, N.J. : Scarecrow, 1981. 560 p.
EF20

1st ed., 1972, by D.C. Ward and M.W. Wheeler. Earlier ed., 1967, by D.C. Ward.

This edition is "completely revised, being over 25 per cent larger … with only one-third of the citations carried over."—*Pref.* The general section (with subdivisions for general information sources, current awareness services, bibliography and abstracting services, indexes, encyclopedias, dictionaries, etc.) is followed by a subject section (subdivided as earth science, meteorology, oceanography, mineralogy, petrology, etc.), and a regional section (including maps). Items listed range from introductory works to highly technical ones, and from standard reference works to texts, treatises, and serials. Some brief annotations. Subject and geographic indexes.   Z6031.W35

Bibliography

Annotated bibliography of economic geology. v. 1 (July 1928)–v. 38 (1965). [Urbana, Ill.] : Economic Geology Pub. Co., 1929–66.
EF21

Comp. by the Bibliographic Staff of the Geological Society of America and prep. under the auspices of GSA and the Society of Economic Geologists.

A bibliography, with signed annotations of both book and periodical material in various languages. Covers about 150 periodicals.

Avnimelech, Moshe A. Bibliography of Levant geology : including Cyprus, Hatay, Israel, Jordania, Lebanon, Sinai and Syria. Jerusalem : Israel Program for Scientific Translations, 1965–1969. 2 v. : map.
EF22

Vol. 1 includes about 4,500 items in an author listing, covering the literature from about the years 1250 to 1963, with chronological and subject indexes. Vol. 2 adds another 200 items, largely from the years 1950 to 1968, with some earlier items.   Z6034.N35A9

Belikov, Evgeniĭ Fedorovich. Bibliograficheskiĭ ukazatel' geodezicheskoĭ literatury za 40 let 1917–1956 / sost. E. F. Belikov; pod. red., L. S. Khrenova. Moskva : Izd-vo Geodezicheskoĭ Lit ry, 1961. 535 p.
EF23

Books and articles, published in the U.S.S.R. from 1917 through 1956, on geodesy and related sciences. Some 8,800 items are arranged in 20 topical chapters and further subdivisions. Brief bibliographical identification. Author index.

§ The period to 1917 is covered by: *Bibliographicheskiĭ ukazatel' geodezicheskoĭ literatury s nachala knigopechataniia do 1917 g.*, sostaviteli E. F. Belikov i L. P. Solov'ev ; pod. red. L. S. Khrenova (Moskva : Nedra, 1971. 271 p.).   Z6000.B4

Clapp, Jane. Museum publications : a classified list and index of books, pamphlets and other monographs, and of serial reprints. N.Y. : Scarecrow, 1962. 2 v.
EF24

Pt. 2 covers publications in biological and earth sciences. For annotation, *see* AL86.   Z5051.C5

Corbin, John Boyd. An index of state geological survey publications issued in series. N.Y. : Scarecrow, 1965. 667 p.
EF25

Intended as a companion to Jane Clapp's *Museum publications* (AL86). Includes monographic publications issued in numbered series by the state geological surveys through 1962. Listing is by state, with author and subject indexes.

——. ——. *Supplement, 1963–1980.* (Metuchen, N.J. : Scarecrow, 1982. 449 p.).

Includes Alaska, Hawaii, and South Carolina, as well as older series which were omitted from the initial volume. Author and subject indexes.   Z6031.C6

Darton, Nelson Horatio. Catalogue and index of contributions to North American geology, 1732–1891. Wash. : Govt. Prt. Off., 1896. 1045 p. (United States. Geological Survey. Bulletin, no.127).
EF26

An author-subject index in one alphabet. "All composite works are segregated into the separate contributions of individual authors as far as practicable."—*Introd.* Geographic and stratigraphic subject entries are used. Includes both monographs and periodicals.

Faessler, Carl. Cross-index to the geological illustration of Canada. [Québec, 1947–58]. 4 v. in 3. (Université Laval. [Faculté des Sciences] Géologie et Minéralogie. Contribution no., 75, 117, 127).
EF27

Vols. 1–2 issued in 1 v. without general title.

Contents: v. 1–2, Cross-index to the maps and illustrations of the Geological Survey and the Mines Branch (Bureau of Mines) of Canada, 1843–1946 (incl.); v. 3, Geological illustrations published by Ontario Department of Mines 1891–1955; v. 4, Geological illustrations published by Quebec Department of Mines, 1898–1957.

Publications containing geological illustrations are listed by series, with author and subject indexes.

——. —— *Supplement, 1946–1956 : cross-index to the geological illustration of Canada* (Québec, 1956. 193 p. [Contribution no. 118]).

Ferrier, W. F. Annotated catalogue of and guide to the publications of the Geological Survey Canada, 1845–1917 / by W. F. Ferrier, assisted by Dorothy J. Ferrier. Ottawa : Taché, 1920. 544 p. : 10 folded maps.
EF28

Lists of publications are arranged by series, giving citations and some short explanatory notes. Index maps accompany "Finding lists" arranged by province and series. Author arrangement in separate section. Index of publication numbers.   Z6034.C19F3

Geological Survey of Canada. Index of publications of the Geological Survey of Canada, 1845–1958 / by A. G. Johnston. Ottawa : Dept. of Mines and Technical Surveys, [1961]. 378 p. : fold. col. map.
EF29

Pt. 1 lists all publications of the Geological Survey of Canada to the end of 1958, arranged according to series. Pt. 2 is classified by area. Includes National Topographic System index map.

——————— Index to publications = Index des publications. Ottawa : Geological Survey of Canada : available from Information Canada, 1975– . 4 v.
EF30

English and French.

Cumulations published as follows: 1959–74, comp. by P. J. Griffin (1975. 138 p.); 1975–79 (1980. 247 p.); 1980–84 (1985. 321 p.); and 1985–87 (c1989. 159 p.).

Publications are listed by series, author, and National Topographic System (NTS) area. Kept up-to-date by supplements in the Survey's *Papers* series.   Z6034.C19C214

——————— Index to reports of Geological Survey of Canada from 1927–50 / comp. by W. E. Cockfield, E. Hall and J. F. Wright. Ottawa : Dept. of Mines and Technical Surveys, [1962]. 723 p.
EF31

The 6th in a series: no. 1 covers 1863–84; no. 2, 1884–1904; no. 3, Separate reports, 1906–10. Summary reports, 1905–16; no. 4, Palaeontology reports, 1847–1916; no. 5, Memoirs, 1910–26. Bulletins, 1913–26. Summary reports, 1917–26.

Provides in one alphabet an author and subject index to Annual reports, Economic geology series, Geological bulletins, Maps without reports, and Museum bulletins, 1927–50; Geological papers, 1935–50; and Summary reports, 1927–33.

Hazen, Robert M. American geological literature, 1669 to 1850 / Robert M. Hazen and Margaret Hindle Hazen. Stroudsburg, Pa. : Dowden, Hutchinson & Ross, 1980. 431 p. **EF32**

"Conceived as a reference tool for historians of American geology, it includes geology-related books, reviews, maps, broadsides, pamphlets, journal articles, and other nonnewspaper sources ... in the United States."—*Pref.* The 11,129 entries are arranged alphabetically by author, then chronologically. Bibliography of sources. Index includes minerals, places, and broad concepts.   Z6034.U49H39

Leafloor, Lorne B. Publications of the Geological Survey of Canada, 1917–1952. Ottawa : Canada Dept. of Mines and Technical Surveys, Geological Survey of Canada : Cloutier, 1952. 82 p.   **EF33**

Z6034.C19L4

Margerie, Emmanuel de. Catalogue des bibliographies géologiques : rédigé avec le concours des membres de la Commission Bibliographique du Congrès. Paris : Gauthier-Villars, 1896. 733 p. (Congrès Géologique International. 5ᵉ session, Wash., 1891; 6ᵉ session, Zürich, 1894).   **EF34**

Repr.: Amsterdam : Meridian, 1966.

Covers monographs and serial publications containing bibliographies, published approximately 1726–1895. The first section covers general bibliographies; the rest of the work is arranged by country or region. Author index, but not complete subject or geographic indexes.

Z6031.M32

Mathews, Edward Bennett. Catalogue of published bibliographies in geology, 1896–1920 .... Wash. : Nat. Research Council, 1923. 228 p. (Bulletin of the National Research Council, no. 26 [v. 6, pt. 5] [Oct. 1923]).   **EF35**

Continues in a somewhat simplified form Emmanuel de Margerie's *Catalogue des bibliographies géologiques* (EF34). Arranged by subject with author index. Separate section for personal bibliographies.

Nickles, John Milton. Geologic literature on North America, 1785–1918. Wash. : U. S. Govt. Print. Off., 1923–24. 2 v. (U.S. Geological Survey. Bulletin, 746, 747).   **EF36**

An author list, with subject index, covering the geology, paleontology, petrology, and mineralogy of the continent of North America and the adjacent islands, Panama, and the Hawaiian Islands. Lists both books and periodical articles; indexes all articles on American geology in more than 500 periodicals, including some foreign journals. A cumulation of the annual bibliographies issued by the Geological Survey.

Pestana, Harold R. Bibliography of congressional geology. N.Y. : Hafner, 1972. 285 p.   **EF37**

Gives full citation to, and indexes all of the geologic documents published from 1818 to 1907 in the "Serial set" of U. S. government publications.   Z6034.U49P47

Richards, Horace Gardiner. Annotated bibliography of quaternary shorelines, 1945–1964 / [by] Horace G. Richards [and] Rhodes W. Fairbridge. Philadelphia : Academy of Natural Sciences, 1965. 280 p. (Academy of Natural Sciences. Special publication, 6).   **EF38**

Prepared for the VII International Congress of the International Association for Quaternary Research (INQUA) meeting, Boulder, Colo., August 30–September 5, 1965.

About 2,400 articles in geographical groupings with author index. International in coverage; annotations in English.

Kept up-to-date by supplements covering 1965–69 (1970. 240 p.); 1970–73 (1974. 214 p.); 1974–77 (Norwich : Geo Abstracts, 1979. 245 p.); 1978–83 (Charlottesville, Va. : Coastal Education and Research Foundation, 1986. 87 p.).   Z6033.S8R5

United States. Geological Survey. Publications of the Geological Survey, 1879–1961. Wash. : U.S. Govt. Print. Off., 1964. 457 p.   **EF39**

"A permanent catalog of books, maps, and charts issued by the Geological Survey through December 1961."—*title page.* Supersedes all earlier lists. Citations are arranged by series, with subject, geographic, and author indexes.

Supplemented by: ———. *Publications of the Geological Survey* (1962/70– . Wash. : U.S. Govt. Print. Off., 1972). A monthly publication that cumulates annually and at longer nine- to ten-year intervals.

Z6034.U49U53

Periodicals

GeoRef serials list. 1981?– . Alexandria, Va. : American Geological Inst., 1981– .   **EF40**

Occasionally published in microfiche with the title: *GeoRef serials list and KWOC index.*

Lists more than 14,000 titles covered in whole or in part in *GeoRef* database (EF53). Serves as a finding and verification source for serial titles in the earth sciences.   QE1.G467

Lomský, Josef. Soupis periodik geologických věd : periodica geologica, palaeontologica et mineralogica. Přiruční seznam s citačními zkratkami názvovými. Praha : Nakl. Československé Akademie Věd, 1959. 499 p.   **EF41**

An alphabetical listing by first word of title of the geological periodicals of the world, past and present. Classified index. Gives title, publishing body, place, dates, and abbreviation.   Z6032.L6

Dissertations

Bibliography of geoscience theses of the United States and Canada. Alexandria, Va. : American Geological Institute, 1993. 3 v. (3779 p.).   **EF42**

Contents: v. 1, Geoscience theses, degree recipients at each institution, thesis subject distribution by decade and by institution; v. 2–3, Subject and geographic index, A–Z.

Identifies "20,748 doctoral dissertations and 41,464 masters theses in the geosciences issued by academic institutions in the United States and Canada from 1867 through 1988."—*Introd.* Source documents include *Dissertation abstracts international*, the *GeoRef* database (EF53), and more than 20 geoscience theses bibliographies. The principal arrangement is alphabetic by recipient's name and includes thesis title, degree-granting institution, degree level, year, and number of pages. The extensive subject index is based on the *GeoRef thesaurus and guide to indexing* (EF73).   Z6034.U5B54

Chronic, John. Bibliography of theses written for advanced degrees in geology and related sciences at universities and colleges in the United States and Canada through 1957 / by John Chronic and Halka Chronic and Petroleum Research Corp. Boulder, Colo. : Pruett Pr., 1958. 1 v., unpaged.   **EF43**

An alphabetical author listing of 11,091 graduate theses written in 131 universities in the U.S. and Canada. Includes geology theses and those in such closely allied fields as geophysics, geochemistry, geological engineering, and petroleum engineering, as well as mining and meteorology when there is a geological connection. Index by geologic names, and general index arranged primarily by geographic area and secondarily by geologic time and subject matter.

Continued by the Chronics' *Bibliography of theses in geology, 1958–63* (Wash. : Amer. Geological Inst., c1964. 1 v., unpaged).

Lists an additional 5,886 theses. Extends subject coverage to space science, hydrology, and biological and meteorological subjects completed in earth science, geophysics, or geology departments.

Ward, Dederick C. Bibliography of theses in geology, 1964. [Wash. : American Geological Institute, 1965]. [37 p.]. **EF44**

Originally published as a special supplement in *Geoscience abstracts*, v. 7 no. 12, pt. 1 (Dec. 1965) : 101–37.

Continues John and Halka Chronic's *Bibliography of theses in geology, 1958–63* (see EF43), listing an additional 682 theses.

Continued by:

(1) Dederick C. Ward and T. C. O'Callaghan, *Bibliography of theses in geology, 1965–66* ([Wash.] : Amer. Geological Inst., [1969]. 255 p.).

"Published ... in cooperation with the Geoscience Information Society." *—title page.* Theses are arranged by field of interest with indexes by subject, author, and geologic name.

(2) Dederick C. Ward, *Bibliography of theses in geology, 1967–70* (Boulder, Colo. : Geological Soc. of America, 1973. 160, 274 p. [Geological Soc. of America. Special paper 143]).

A classed subject arrangement with subject, author, and geologic name indexes, and a directory of colleges and universities. The continuations for 1965–66 and 1967–70 were prepared using data processing equipment.

(3) From 1971– , citations to master's and doctoral theses in geology appear in monthly issues of *Bibliography and index of geology* (EF47).

Library catalogs

Geological Society of London. Library. List of geological literature added to the Geological Society's library, [July 1894]–1934. [no. 1]–37. London : Geological Soc., 1895–1935. **EF45**

Title varies.

Not published 1913–19; 1915–19 later issued in 1 v. Ceased with issue covering 1934.

Subject index in each annual number. Supplements the Society's *Catalogue of the Library* (London, 1881. 618 p.). Z6035.G34

United States. Geological Survey. Library. Catalog of the United States Geological Survey Library. Boston : G.K. Hall, 1964. 25 v. **EF46**

Reproduces the cards from the Library's catalog. Scope of the collection, the largest of its kind, makes this a valuable tool for bibliographic verification.

———. ———. *First supplement* (1972. 11 v.) records additions from late 1964 through Dec. 31, 1971. Z881.U597

Indexes; Abstract journals

Bibliography and index of geology. v.33, no.1 (Jan. 1969)– . [Boulder, Colo.] : publ. by the Geological Soc. of America in cooperation with the American Geological Inst., 1970– . Monthly with annual cumulation. **EF47**

Represents a change of title for *Bibliography and index of geology exclusive of North America* (EF48) and continues its numbering. Coverage expanded to include North American geology. Monthly issues are in four sections: (1) list of serials cited in the issue; (2) fields of interest, with entries grouped under 30 broad subjects or specialties; (3) subject index; (4) author index. The annual cumulation consists of a citation section alphabetically arranged by author; a subject index; a list of serials covered; and for 1967–73 and 1982– , a list of monographs cited.

"Photocomposed from citations in GeoRef, a database produced at the American Geological Institute." *—verso of 1994 t.p.*

•Included in online database *Geological reference file (GeoRef)* (EF53). Z6081.B57

Bibliography and index of geology exclusive of North America. v.1 (1933)–v. 32 (1968). Boulder, Colo. : Amer. Geological Inst., 1934–69. **EF48**

Imprint varies. Compilers vary.

Frequency varies: v.1–8, annual; v.9–11, biennial; v.12–30, annual; v.31–32, monthly with annual index.

A comprehensive bibliography of books, maps, and periodical articles dealing with the geology of all parts of the world except North America, thus complementing *Bibliography of North American geology* (EF49). Most entries include a brief annotation. Beginning with v. 31 (1967), issued as a monthly citation journal with an annual cumulative bibliography and index.

Superseded by: *Bibliography and index of geology* (EF47).

•Included in online database *Geological reference file (GeoRef)* (EF53). Z6031.G4

Bibliography of North American geology. 1919/28–1970. Wash. : Govt. Print. Off., 1931–73. Annual. **EF49**

Cumulations issued as follows: 1919–1928, comp. by John M. Nickles; 1929–39, comp. by Emma M. Thom; 1940–49, comp. by Ruth Reece King [and others]. Ceased with volume for 1970.

Issued in the *Bulletin* series of the U. S. Geological Survey. Volumes represent cumulations of bibliography numbers in the *Bulletin* series, with the addition for 1950–70 of annual (formerly biennial) supplements with the same title also published in the *Bulletin* series.

Each volume consists of a comprehensive bibliography with detailed index, covering the geology of the North American continent, including Greenland, the West Indies and other adjacent islands, Hawaii, Guam, and other island possessions of the U. S.

Superseded by: *Bibliography and index of geology* (EF47).

•Included in online database *Geological reference file : (GeoRef)* (EF53).

•**GeoArchive** [database]. Didcot, Oxon, Eng. : Geosystems, 1974– . **EF50**

Available online (updated monthly) and on CD-ROM (updated twice yearly).

Covers international literature of the earth sciences, including books, serials, and maps. Corresponds to the printed indexes, *Geotitles* (EF56), *Geoscience documentation* (London : Geosystems, 1969–); *Bibliography of vertebrate paleontology* (through 1984) (EF227); and *Bibliography of economic geology* (London : Geosystems, 1982–).

•**GEOBASE** [database]. Norwich, England : Elsevier/Geo Abstracts, 1980– . **EF51**

For annotation, *see* CL30.

Geological abstracts. 1989– . Norwich, U.K. : Elsevier/Geo Abstracts. Monthly. **EF52**

Merges: *Geological abstracts. Economic geology* (1986–88); *Geological abstracts. Geophysics & tectonics abstracts* (1982–88); *Geological abstracts. Palaeontology & stratigraphy* (1986–88); and *Geological abstracts. Sedimentary geology* (1986–88).

Indexes journals, books, conference proceedings, reports, and maps from the international earth sciences literature. Monthly issues include a subject and regional index; cumulative annual index by author, subject, and geographic location.

•Machine-readable version: *GEOBASE* (CL30). QE1.G1345

•**Geological reference file** : (GeoRef) [database]. Alexandria, Va. : American Geological Institute, GeoRef Information System, 1961– . **EF53**

Coverage: North American geology, 1785– ; other areas of the world, 1933– . Available online (updated monthly), in CD-ROM as *GeoRef* (updated quarterly), and on magnetic tape.

Corresponds to the printed versions of *Bibliography and index of geology* (EF47), *Bibliography of North American geology* (EF49), *Bibliography and index of geology exclusive of North America* (EF48), and *Geophysical abstracts* (EF54). Includes books, serials, maps, reports, and U.S. and Canadian dissertations. Search fields include author, source, subject, geographic descriptor, map coordinate. *GeoRef thesaurus and guide to indexing* (EF73) is needed for effective searching.

Geological Survey (U.S.). Geophysical abstracts. 1929–71. Wash. : [U.S.G.S.], 1929–73. Monthly. **EF54**

Frequency varies. Ceased publication with issue no. 299, Dec. 1971.

Abstracts 1–86 were issued in mimeographed form by the Bureau of Mines. On July 1, 1936, the geophysical section was transferred to the Geological Survey, which issued abstracts 87–111. By Departmental Order of Oct. 5, 1942, the geophysical section was again placed with the Bureau of Mines, and abstracts 112–27 were issued by that bureau. Beginning July 1, 1947, it was transferred again to the Geological Survey.

Offers worldwide coverage of literature pertaining to the physics of the solid earth and to geophysical exploration. Abstracts in English. Annual author and subject indexes. Index for 1971 published 1973. 1966–71 available in *Geological reference file : (GeoRef)* (EF53).

QE500.U5

Geologisches Zentralblatt : Anzeiger für Geologie, Petrographie, Palaeontologie und verwandte Wissenschaften .... Bd. 1 (1901)–Bd. 45 (1931). Leipzig : Borntraeger, 1901–31. **EF55**

Frequency varies.

Divided 1932–42 into: *Geologisches Zentralblatt. Abt. A, Geologie* and *Geologisches Zentralblatt. Abt. B, Palaeontologisches Zentralblatt*. Abt. B reprinted as *Palaeontologisches Zentralblatt* (Amsterdam : Swets & Zeitlinger, 1969. 17 v.).

Signed abstracts of book and periodical material in various languages in a subject arrangement, with author, geographical, and subject indexes in each volume. Cumulative indexes to Bd. 1–15, 16–30, 31–50.

Continued by: *Neues Jahrbuch für Mineralogie, Geologie und Paläontologie* (EF58).

QE1.G494

Geotitles. 62/732–734 (Mar. 1985)– . Didcot, Oxon, Eng. : Geosystems, c1987– . Monthly. **EF56**

Continues: *Geotitles weekly* (1969–84).

A classified listing of new publications, including monographs, serials, and maps. Author and serial source index in each issue.

•Included as part of *GeoArchive* [database] (EF50). Z6032.G36

International catalogue of scientific literature / publ. for the Internat. Council by the Royal Soc. of London. v. 1 (1901)–v. 14 (1914). London : Harrison, 1902–21. **EF57**

Section H, Geology. For full description, *see* EA16.

Neues Jahrbuch für Mineralogie, Geologie und Paläontologie. 1830–1949. Stuttgart : Schweizerbart'sche Verlagsbuchhandlung, 1830–1949. **EF58**

Title and frequency vary.

This bibliographical periodical has had a long and complicated history with varying coverage, but has usually included "Neues Literatur" and, from 1925 to 1942, "Referate." Abstracts generally presented in a subject arrangement, with yearly indexes. Some cumulated indexes were also published.

"Referate" became *Zentralblatt für Mineralogie, Geologie und Paläontologie*, 1943–49; superseded by *Zentralblatt für Geologie und Paläontologie* (EF60) and *Zentralblatt für Mineralogie* (EF178).

PASCAL. v. 4, Sciences de la terre = Earth sciences. 1992– . Vandoeuvre-les-Nancy, France : Centre National de la Recherche Scientifique, Institut de l'Information Scientifique et Technique, 1992– . Ten issues per year. **EF59**

Continues: *PASCAL. v. 4, Terre, ocean, espace* (1990–91) and *PASCAL thema. T022, Sciences de la terre* (1984–89).

A comprehensive index for the geosciences, including mineralogy, geochemistry, petrology, economic geology, paleontology, oceanography, and marine geology. Covers monographs, more than 3,000 serials, maps, documents, conference proceedings. Annual cumulative index.

For full information concerning *PASCAL*, see EA72.

Zentralblatt für Geologie und Paläontologie. v. 1 (1950)– . Stuttgart : Schweizerbart'sche Verlagsbuchhandlung, 1950– . T.1, Allgemeine, angewandte, regionale und historische Geologie (13 no. per yr.); T.2, Paläontologie (7 no. per yr.). **EF60**

Continues the same title publ. 1950–64 with section titles: T. 1, Allgemeine und angewandte Geologie einschl. Lagerstattengeologie, regionale Geologie; t. 2, Historische Geologie und Paläontologie. The earlier title superseded pts. 3–4 of *Zentralblatt für Mineralogie, Geologie und Paläontologie*.

International in scope. Signed abstracts (mainly in German) arranged by topic. Annual author, subject, and topographic indexes.

QE1.Z45

Encyclopedias

The encyclopaedia of the solid earth sciences / ed. in chief, Philip Kearey ... [et al.]. Oxford ; Boston : Blackwell Scientific Publications, 1993. 713 p. : ill., maps. **EF61**

Combines short-entry definitions with longer overview articles for some 2,700 headwords in all earth science subdisciplines, but excludes atmospheric and oceanic studies. Includes black-and-white illustrations, maps, and charts, plus many cross-references within articles and short reference lists following the longer entries. Intended for use by professional earth scientists and specialists in related fields; most articles are intelligible to college students and interested general readers. Detailed topical index.

QE5.E517

The encyclopedia of applied geology / ed. by Charles W. Finkl, Jr. N.Y. : Van Nostrand Reinhold, c1984. 644 p. : ill. (Encyclopedia of earth sciences, v. 13). **EF62**

"Topics in this volume largely center around the field of engineering geology and deal with landscapes, earth materials, or the management of geological processes."—*Pref.* Signed articles with bibliographic references appear in alphabetical arrangement. Numerous cross-references. Indexed.

QE5.E5

The encyclopedia of field and general geology / ed. by Charles W. Finkl. N.Y. : Van Nostrand Reinhold, c1988. 911 p. : ill. (Encyclopedia of earth sciences, v. 14). **EF63**

"The purpose of this volume is to provide an introduction to general fieldwork by way of selected topics that illustrate some specific technique or methodology."—*Pref.* Signed articles are alphabetically arranged, with many cross-references between subjects. Extensive bibliographies and many charts, tables, and photographs make this an excellent source for all libraries. May be used in combination with *The encyclopedia of applied geology* (EF62). Author citation and subject index.

QE5.E515

The encyclopedia of sedimentology / ed. by Rhodes W. Fairbridge, Joanne Bourgeois. Stroudsburg, Pa. : Dowden, Hutchinson & Ross ; [N.Y.] : distr. by Academic Pr., c1978. 901 p. : ill. (Encyclopedia of earth sciences, v. 6). **EF64**

A "comprehensive, alphabetical treatment of the discipline of sedimentology. It is intended to be a reference book for sedimentologists, geologists, and others who come in contact with sediments. ... Some attempt has been made to define terms and to adhere to definitions in this volume, but an encyclopedia is *not* a dictionary."—*Pref.* Signed articles have bibliographies and cross-references. Index. QE471.E49

The encyclopedia of solid earth geophysics / ed. by David E. James. N.Y. : Van Nostrand Reinhold, c1989. 1328 p. : ill. (Encyclopedia of earth sciences, [v. 17]). **EF65**

Surveys recent research in solid earth geophysics, drawing from specialities in physics, geology, and the space sciences with the intent of integrating that research with classical geophysics. Some 160 signed topical essays, alphabetically arranged, treat both introductory and technical issues and incorporate formulas, tables, diagrams, maps, cross-references, and short bibliographies. Written by specialists but accessible to a wide audience including students and knowledgeable general readers. Author and subject indexes. QE501.E58

The encyclopedia of structural geology and plate tectonics / ed. by Carl K. Seyfert. N.Y. : Van Nostrand Reinhold, c1987. 876 p. : ill., maps. (Encyclopedia of earth sciences, v. 10). **EF66**

Surveys the classic areas of geology as well as recent developments in continental drift and sea floor spreading. Alphabetically arranged articles are signed and generally include illustrations and a bibliography. Author citations and subject indexes. QE601.E53

Fairbridge, Rhodes Whitmore. The encyclopedia of geochemistry and environmental sciences. N.Y. : Van Nostrand Reinhold, [1972]. 1321 p. : ill. (Encyclopedia of earth sciences, v. 4A). **EF67**

"Geochemistry is coupled with Environmental Science in this volume because it is the chemical pollution of our planet's air and water that is claiming the attention of many geologists and chemists today."—*Pref.* Signed articles with bibliographic references appear in alphabetical arrangement. Numerous cross-references, including references to articles in other volumes of the "Encyclopedia of earth sciences" series. Detailed subject index. QE515.F24

——————— The encyclopedia of world regional geology. Stroudsburg, Pa. : Dowden, Hutchinson & Ross ; [N.Y.] : distr. by Halsted Pr., [1975]. 1 v. : ill. (Encyclopedia of earth sciences, v. 8). **EF68**

Contents: pt. 1, Western hemisphere (including Antarctica and Australia). An anticipated Pt. 2, Eastern hemisphere, was not published.

Provides geologic and geomorphic data by continent, region, country, and island group. Signed articles, with cross-references and bibliographies, are arranged alphabetically. Indexed. QE5.F33

McGraw-Hill encyclopedia of the geological sciences / Sybil P. Parker, ed. in chief. 2nd ed. N.Y. : McGraw-Hill, 1988. 722 p. : ill. **EF69**

1st ed., 1978.

Contains 520 signed articles that explore a broad range of topics in the earth sciences and include cross-references and brief bibliographies. Articles were drawn from *McGraw-Hill encyclopedia of science & technology* (6th ed., 1987; 7th ed., EA81). Numerous black-and-white illustrations, tables, and charts. Subject index. QE5.M29

Dictionaries

Bates, Robert Latimer. Glossary of geology / Robert L. Bates and Julia A. Jackson, editors. 3rd ed. Alexandria, Va. : American Geological Institute, c1987. 788 p. **EF70**

1st ed., 1972; 2nd ed., 1980.

Brief entry definitions. Coverage has been expanded to 37,000 headwords, with many new entries added for the fields of carbonate sedimentology, hydrogeology, marine geology, mineralogy, ore deposits, plate tectonics, and snow and ice. Terms and definitions recommended in the North American Stratigraphical Code (1983) are included. Syllabication and accents are given for headwords. List of references cited at end. QE5.B38

Challinor, John. Challinor's dictionary of geology / ed. by Antony Wyatt. 6th ed. N.Y. : Oxford Univ. Pr. ; Cardiff : Univ. of Wales Pr., 1986. 374 p. **EF71**

1st ed. (1961)–5th ed. (1978) had title: *A dictionary of geology.*

Definitions in this standard British work are longer than those in Robert L. Bates and Julia A. Jackson's *Glossary of geology* (EF72 note) and employ quotations from the geological literature to show usage. Classified index of terms. QE5.C45

Dictionary of geological terms / Robert L. Bates and Julia A. Jackson, editors. 3rd ed., Anchor Books ed. Garden City, N.Y. : Anchor Pr./Doubleday, 1984. 571 p. **EF72**

1st ed., 1957; 2nd ed., 1976.

Prep. under the direction of the American Geological Institute.

An abridgment of the same editors' 1980 *Glossary of geology.* Aims "to provide the non-specialist with accurate definitions of the working vocabulary of the earth sciences."—*Pref.* Syllabication and pronunciation are indicated and etymologies are given for some terms. QE5.D55 1984

GeoRef thesaurus and guide to indexing. 6th ed. / Barbara A. Goodman, ed. Alexandria, Va. : American Geological Institute, c1992. 803 p. : ill. **EF73**

1st ed., 1977; 5th ed., 1989.

A guide "to the index terms used in *GeoRef* [EF53]. It includes term relationships, usage notes, dates of addition, indexing rules, guidelines for searching, and lists of systematic and other terms."—

Introd. This edition contains 27,000 terms, of which 3,600 are new. Essential for using the printed *Bibliography and index of geology* (EF47) as well as the electronic versions of the database. Z695.1.G43G46

International Geological Congress. Commission de stratigraphie. Lexique stratigraphique international. Paris : Centre National de la Recherche Scientifique, 1956–77. 8 v. : ill. **EF74**

Contents: v. 1, Europe; v. 2, U.R.S.S.; v. 3, Asie; v. 4, Afrique; v. 5, Amérique Latine; v. 6, Océanie; v. 7, Amérique du Nord; v. 8, Termes stratigraphiques majeurs. No more published.

A lexicon of stratigraphic nomenclature in all continents and countries of the world, published in various parts, each covering a particular country. Gives a description of the formation, the type of locality, age, and reference wherein described.

A "Nouvelle série," v. 1 (1983)– apparently ceased after no. 1, *Afrique de l'ouest = West Africa,* by J. M. Bertraud.

Lapidus, Dorothy Farris. The Facts on File dictionary of geology and geophysics / Dorothy Farris Lapidus ; Donald R. Coates, scientific adviser ; Edmund H. Immergut, series ed. N.Y. : Facts on File, c1987. 347 p. : ill. **EF75**

Contains some 3,500 alphabetically arranged definitions for terms and concepts used in the geological sciences, including geophysical engineering. Lacks an introductory description of purpose or selection criteria. Useful for high school students and general readers. Black and-white illustrations. QE5.L29

Nelson, Archibald. Dictionary of applied geology : mining and civil engineering / by Archibald Nelson and Kenneth Davies Nelson. N.Y. : Philosophical Libr., [1967]. 421 p. : ill. **EF76**

Intended mainly "for school and college students, and engineers in the mining and civil engineering professions."—*Pref.* A work of British origin. QE5.N44

Wilmarth, Mary Grace. Lexicon of geologic names of the United States : (including Alaska). Wash. : U.S. Govt. Print. Off., 1938. 2 v. (U.S. Geological Survey. Bulletin, 896). **EF77**

Repr.: Grosse Pointe, Mich. : Scholarly Pr., 1968.

Superintendent of Documents classification: I 19.3.

Subtitle: Also includes the names and ages, but not the definitions, of the named geologic units of Canada, Mexico, the West Indies, Central America, and Hawaii.

Each name is followed by a definition, usually giving lithology, thickness, age, underlying and overlying formations, and type locality, with bibliographical references.

Updated by: Druid Wilson [et al.], *Geologic names of North America* (Wash. : U.S. Govt. Print. Off., 1959. 621 p. [U.S. Geological Survey. Bulletin 1056]).

Contents: A, Geologic names of North America introduced in 1936–1955 : a compilation of new geological names of North America, including Greenland, the West Indies, the Pacific Island possessions of the United States, and the Trust Territory of the Pacific Islands (1957); B, Index to the geologic names of North America : geologic names arranged by age and by area containing type locality.

Prepared to bring Wilmarth up-to-date and to serve as the first step in preparing a new edition.

Continued by:

Lexicon of geologic names of the United States for 1936–1960, by Grace C. Keroher [et al.] (Wash. : U.S. Govt. Print. Off., 1966. 3 v. [4341 p.]. [U.S. Geological Survey. Bulletin 1200]). "A compilation of the geologic names of the United States, its possessions, the Trust Territory of the Pacific Islands, and the Panama Canal Zone."—*t.p.* Brings Wilmarth further up-to-date but covers a smaller geographic area. Includes 14,634 names, of which 9,128 appeared in Wilmarth and 5,506 did not.

——————. *1961–1967,* by Grace C. Keroher [et al.] (Wash. : U.S. Govt. Print. Off., 1970. 848 p. [U.S. Geological Survey. Bulletin 1350]). Lists 2,860 names, including cross-references.

————. *1968–1975*, by Gwendolyn W. Luttrell [et al.] (Wash. : U.S. Govt. Print. Off., 1981. 342 p. [U.S. Geological Survey. Bulletin 1520]).

Lexicon of new formal geologic names of the United States, 1976–1980, by Gwendolyn W. Luttrell, Marilyn L. Hubert, and Virginia M. Jussen (Wash. : U.S. Govt. Print. Off., 1986. 191 p. [U.S. Geological Survey. Bulletin 1564]).

————. *1981–1985*, by Gwendolyn W. Luttrell, Marilyn L. Hubert, and Cynthia R. Murdock (Wash. : U.S. Govt. Print. Off., 1991. 376 p. [U.S. Geological Survey. Bulletin 1565]). U.S. and Puerto Rico only. Entries include geologic age, geographic location, geologic province, type locality, and other descriptive features. QE77.L88

Foreign language and multilingual

Multilingual

Geostatistical glossary and multilingual dictionary / members of the 1984–1989 IAMG Committee on Geostatistics ; Ricardo A. Olea, ed. N.Y. : Oxford Univ. Pr., 1991. 177 p. : ill. (Studies in mathematical geology, 3). **EF78**

Lists some 4,300 definitions in mathematical geophysics. Indexes to the English base are provided for seven languages: Chinese, French, German, Greek, Portuguese, Russian, and Spanish. QE33.2.M3G46

Multilingual thesaurus of geosciences / ed. by G. N. Rassam, J. Gravesteijn, R. Potenza. N.Y. : Pergamon, c1988. lii, 516 p. **EF79**

Sponsored by the International Council of Scientific and Technical Information (ICSTI) and International Union of Geological Sciences (IUGS).

Lists some 5,000 terms in six languages: English, French, German, Italian, Russian, and Spanish. The base list, in English, identifies terms by a reference number and by subject field; indexes in all six languages refer to the base list. There is also an index by subject field. Z695.1.G43M84

Nederlands Geologisch Mijnbouwkundig Genootschap. Geological nomenclature / ed. by W.A. Visser. Boston : M. Nijhoff, 1980. 540 p. **EF80**

At head of title: Royal Geological and Mining Society of the Netherlands.

1st ed., 1959, ed. by A.A.G. Schieferdecker.

This edition has ben expanded to more than 7,000 terms and subject coverage has been broadened. As with earlier editions, a principal list on an English base is followed by indexes to Dutch, French, German, and for the first time, Spanish. Also lists terms that lack English equivalents, some synonyms in languages other than the five of the text, and obsolete or antiquated terms. Fourteen supplementary geological data tables. QE5.N413

Zylka, Romauld. Geological dictionary : English-Polish-Russian-French-German. Warsaw : Wydawnictwa Geologiczne, 1970. 1439 p. **EF81**

Arranged alphabetically by English terms. Approximately 25,000 terms followed by Polish, Russian, French, and German renderings and important synonyms. Indexes from the other languages. QE5.Z95

Czech

Zeman, Otakar. Anglicko-český geologický slovník : s rejstříkem českých názvů / Otakar Zeman, Karel Beneš a kolektiv. 2. přepracované vyd. Praha : Academia, 1985. 497 p. **EF82**

1st ed., 1963.

An English word list with Czech equivalents for some 18,000 terms. The Czech term list is keyed to the English section. Appendix of crystallographic tables. QE5.Z39

French

Foucault, Alain. Dictionnaire de géologie / par Alain Foucault et Jean-François Raoult. 3e éd., rev. et augm. Paris : Masson, 1988. 352 p. : ill. **EF83**

Compact French dictionary provides short definitions for terms in geology, paleontology, stratigraphy, and mineralogy. Brief bibliography of sources. QE8.F68

Michel, Jean-Pierre. Dictionary of earth sciences : English-French, French-English = Dictionnaire des sciences de la terre : anglais-français, français-anglais / J.-P. Michel, R. W. Fairbridge. 2nd ed., rev. and expanded. Chichester ; N.Y. : Wiley ; Paris : Masson, 1992. 299 p. **EF84**

1st ed., 1980, had title: *Dictionary of earth science.*

Provides both current and obsolete terminology in geology and related areas for both languages. This edition has been expanded to include new terms in astronomy, geomorphology, paleontology, and soil science. The sizable vocabulary makes this dictionary suitable for students and professional users. QE5.M52

German

Dictionary of geosciences / ed. by Adolf Watznauer. Amsterdam ; N.Y. : Elsevier, 1982. 2 v. **EF85**

Translation of: *Wörterbuch Geowissenschaften.*

Contents: [v. 1], German-English; [v. 2], English-German.

Contains approximately 38,000 terms used in the earth sciences, but limits inclusion from allied fields. Charts of geologic time scale, scale of seismic intensity, and Beaufort scale. QE5.W6513

Russian

Bhatnagar, K. P. Elsevier's dictionary of geosciences : Russian-English / comp. by K. P. Bhatnagar ; ed. by S. K. Bhattacharya. Amsterdam ; N.Y. : Elsevier, 1991. 1023 p. **EF86**

Contains "approximately 56,000 Russian terms used in geochemistry and physical chemistry, geology and tectonics, meteorology and climatography, mineralogy, oceanology, paleontology, petroleum engineering ... petrology, petrography and rock mechanics, [and] sedimentology."—*Pref.* QE5.B46

Burgunker, Mark E. Russian-English dictionary of earth sciences. N.Y. : Telberg Book Co., 1961. 94 p. **EF87**

Gives English terms for Russian words, sometimes with explanations and definitions. Not comprehensive, but constitutes "the 'hard core' of the nomenclature of tectonics, geomorphology, hydrology, paleogeography and geophysics."—*Pref.* Includes personal names. QE5.B8

English-Russian dictionary of applied geophysics = [Anglo-russkiĭ slovar' po prikladnoĭ geofizike] / authors B. V. Gusev ... [et al.]. [Moskva : "Russkiĭ ĭazyk"] ; Oxford ; N.Y. : Pergamon, 1984. 487 p. **EF88**

A specialist's dictionary of 30,000 terms in geophysics and petroleum engineering. TN269.A5413

Timofeev, Petr Petrovich. Anglo-russkiĭ geologicheskiĭ slovar' : okolo 52,000 terminov / P.P. Timofeev, M.N. Alekseev, T.A. Sofiano ; pod redaktsieĭ P.P. Timofeeva i M.N. Alekseeva. Moskva : "Russkiĭ ĭazyk", 1988. 540 p. **EF89**

Title on added t.p.: *English-Russian dictionary of geology.*

Gives Russian equivalents for about 52,000 English terms, with explanations or definitions in Russian provided for some words. Alphabetic arrangement, with supplementary tables in English and Russian for geological time periods and paleomagnetic reversals.

QE5.T547

Directories

Directory of geoscience departments. 31st ed. (fall 1992)– . Alexandria, Va. : Amer. Geological Inst., 1992– . Annual. **EF90**

Continues: 1950/51–1956/57, *Departments of geological science in educational institutions of the United States and Canada*; 1958–69, *Directory of geoscience departments in the colleges and universities of the United States and Canada*; 1970–88, *Directory of geoscience departments, United States and Canada*; 1989–91, *Directory of geoscience departments, North America*. Editions 1–7 issued as *Reports* of the Institute.

Lists colleges and universities in the U.S., Canada, and Mexico that grant undergraduate and graduate degrees in the earth sciences. The 1993 ed. provides address, telephone/fax/internet numbers, and faculty in separate sections for the three countries. The U.S. section is subarranged by state, then alphabetically by university; Canadian and Mexican sections are alphabetical by university. Includes directories of U.S. state geological surveys, selected foreign geoscience departments, field courses and camps, financial aid and scholarships, and teaching and education programs. Indexed by faculty name and specialty.

Geophysical directory. v.1 (1948)– . Houston, Tex. : Geophysical Directory, Inc., 1948– . Annual. **EF91**

"Intended to be a comprehensive listing of all companies and individuals directly connected with, or engaged in the geophysical exploration for petroleum."—*Foreword*. A classified listing with company and personnel indexes. TN867.G46

Tinsley, Elizabeth J. Worldwide directory of national earth-science agencies and related international organizations / comp. by E.J. Tinsley and Joyce P. Hollander. Alexandria, Va. : Distribution Branch, Text Products Section, U.S. Geological Survey [distributor], 1984. 102 p. : maps. (U.S. Geological Survey circular, 934). **EF92**

Superintendent of Documents classification: I 19.4/2:934.

1st ed., 1975.

Subtitle: A listing of governmental earth-science agencies and selected major international organizations whose functions are similar to those of the U.S. Geological Survey.

Entries are arranged by country and have been updated through Nov. 1983. QE23.T56

Guidebooks

Union list of geologic field trip guidebooks of North America / comp. and ed. by the Geoscience Information Society Guidebooks Committee, Charlotte Derksen, chair. 5th ed. Alexandria, Va. : American Geological Inst., in cooperation with the Geoscience Information Soc., c1989. 223 p. **EF93**

1st ed., 1968, had title *Geologic field trip guidebooks of North America, a union list incorporating monographic titles*; 4th ed., 1986.

Alphabetically organized by the name of the sponsoring society, organization, conference, government agency, or commercial source responsible for the guidebook. Includes guidebooks for field trips scheduled through 1985. Within each corporate entry, guidebooks are listed chronologically, followed by library holdings. Includes a directory of participating libraries and their services and geographic and stratigraphic indexes to the guidebooks. Useful for college and university library collections. QE45.G48

Handbooks

American Geological Institute. Conference. (Duluth, 1959). Geology and earth sciences sourcebook for elementary and secondary schools / Robert L. Heller, ed. Prep. under the guidance of the American Geological Institute, National Academy of Sciences–National Research Council. N.Y. : Holt, [1962]. 496 p. : ill. **EF94**

Remains valuable as a textbook and practical handbook presenting various areas of the earth sciences, with introductions, suggestions for methods and activities, problems, teaching aids, and references. Geologic topics for biology, chemistry, and physics courses are discussed. Indexed; Sources/supplier index is out of date. QE41.A55

International Union of Geological Sciences. International Subcommission on Stratigraphic Classification. International stratigraphic guide : a guide to stratigraphic classification, terminology, and procedure. N.Y. : Wiley, [1976]. 200 p. : ill. **EF95**

Hollis D. Hedberg, ed.

An international standard to replace national and regional codes and unify stratigraphic usage; an essential reference. Has an extensive bibliography. Subject index. QE651.I57

Tables

Clark, Sydney P. Handbook of physical constants. Rev. ed. [N.Y.] : Geological Soc. of America, 1966. 587 p. : ill. (Geological Society of America. Memoir, 97). **EF96**

Contains an impressive amount of physical data needed for geological and geophysical calculations. The compilations of data are grouped by topic. Index to properties. This edition revised and greatly expanded from the 1942 edition. Q199.N25

History

Brush, Stephen G. The history of geophysics and meteorology : an annotated bibliography / Stephen G. Brush, Helmut E. Landsberg, wtih the assistance of Martin Collins. N.Y. : Garland, 1985. 450 p. (Bibliographies of the history of science and technology, 7). **EF97**

Includes general histories, biography, institutional history, and various subdivisions of geophysics and meteorology. Name and subject indexes. Z6041.B78

Challinor, John. The history of British geology : a bibliographical study. Newton Abbott : David & Charles ; N.Y. : Barnes & Noble, 1971. 224 p. **EF98**

In two main sections, the first listing works chronologically by date of publication; the second being a treatment of publications in a thematic context. QE13.G7C3

Geologists and ideas : a history of North American geology / ed. by Ellen T. Drake and William M. Jordan. Boulder, Colo. : Geological Society of America, 1985. 525 p. : ill. (Centennial special volume, 1). **EF99**

33 contributions from geologists and historians of science in four sections: (1) Evolution of significant ideas; (2) Contributions of individuals; (3) Contributions of organized groups; (4) Application of significant ideas. Well-illustrated with reference lists for each chapter. Name/subject index. QE13.U6G466

Gohau, Gabriel. A history of geology / by Gabriel Gohau ; rev. and tr. by Albert V. Carozzi and Marguerite Carozzi. New Brunswick : Rutgers Univ. Pr., c1990. 259 p. : ill. **EF100**

Translation of: *Histoire de la géologie* (Paris : La Decouverte, 1987) with additions and revisions.

A history of ideas that focuses on the observation of geological features and the theories developed to explain them. Good bibliography emphasizing the primary literature and a glossary of terms. Index of names.   QE11.G64

La Rocque, Aurèle. Contributions to the history of geology. Columbus : Ohio State Univ., Dept. of Geology, 1964. 3 v.   **EF101**

Contents: v.1, Biographies of geologists, 1961. Suppl. 1, [1962?]. Suppl. 2, 1964; v.2, Bibliography of the history of geology, 1964. Suppl. 1, 1960. Suppl. 2, 1962; v.3, Biographic index, 1964.

Preliminary paper presented at the Conference on the History of Geology supported by the National Science Foundation and held at the University of Nevada, Reno, Aug. 1964.

Biographies of geologists of all periods and countries from ancient times to the present. The length of articles varies from one to several columns. The index gives full name, years of birth and death, nationality, field of interest, and references to the literature.

Merrill, George Perkins. First 100 years of American geology. New Haven, Conn. : Yale Univ. Pr.; London : Milford, 1924. 773 p. : ill.   **EF102**

Repr.: N.Y. : Hafner, 1964.

A survey history including biographies of geologists but no bibliographical references. A revised version of the author's *Contributions to the history of American geology* (1904).   QE13.U6M6

Porter, Roy. The earth sciences : an annotated bibliography. N.Y. : Garland, 1983. 192 p., [15] p. of plates : ill. (Bibliographies of the history of science and technology, v. 3 ; Garland reference library of the humanities, v. 315).   **EF103**

Defines the "history of geology in a broad sense, to include a wide range of scientific inquiries in the nature and history of the earth."—*Introd.* Bibliographical citations with brief annotations are grouped in ten chapters, e.g., bibliography and reference works, specialist histories, cognate sciences, biographical studies. Provides a good introduction to American and British sources. Index of names includes some subject references.   Z6031.P67

Thompson, Susan J. A chronology of geological thinking from antiquity to 1899. Metuchen, N.J. : Scarecrow, 1988. 320 p.   **EF104**

Descriptions of discoveries, ideas, and significant findings in the history of geology, collected from some 200 primary and secondary sources, briefly paraphrased, and arranged in chronological order. Although not a comprehensive survey, the work provides an overview of the development of geological thought. Useful bibliography of sources. Name index.   QE11.T47

Zittel, Karl Alfred von. Geschichte der Geologie und Paläontologie bis Ende des 19. Jahrhunderts. München : Oldenbourg, 1899. 868 p. : ill.   **EF105**

English translation by Maria M. Ogilvie-Gordon, *History of geology and palaeontology to the end of the nineteenth century* (London : Walter Scott, 1901. Repr.: N.Y. : Hafner, 1962).

A standard history; treatment is by general subject area. Author and subject indexes.   QE11.Z7

Biography

Geikie, Archibald. The founders of geology. 2nd ed. London : Macmillan, 1905. 486 p.   **EF106**

Repr.: N.Y. : Dover, 1962.

1st ed., 1897.

A standard history of geology based on the lives and works of outstanding geologists. The major portion of the book emphasizes "the

history and development of geology during the period between the middle of the eighteenth and the close of the second decade of the nineteenth century."—*Pref.*   QE11.G3

Geological Society of America. Memorials. v. 1 (1973)– . Boulder, Colo. : Geological Society of America, 1973– .   **EF107**

Beginning with obituaries for Society members and honorary fellows deceased in 1969, the annual volumes review the professional career of the subjects in signed essays of two to three pages. A portrait and bibliography of works is included for each individual.   QE21.G46a

Sarjeant, William A. S. Geologists and the history of geology : an international bibliography from the origins to 1978. N.Y. : Arno, 1980. 5 v.   **EF108**

Contents: v. 1, Introduction, general histories of science, of geology and its subdivisions, and allied sciences. Historical accounts of institutions concerned with geology. Histories of the petroleum industry. Accounts of geological events; v. 2–3, Individual geologists; v. 4, Geologists index by country and speciality; v. 5, Index of authors, editors and translators. Appendix.

A short biography is included with the bibliography of each geologist.

————. ————. *Supplement, 1979-1984 and additions* (Malabar, Fla. : R. E. Krieger Publ. Co., 1987. 2 v.). Includes some 7,100 new references and 1,548 brief biographies. The index volume contains an appendix listing women geologists identified in both the main set and supplement.   Z6031.S28

Atlases

Atlas of landforms / ed. by H. Allen Curran ... [et al.]. 3rd ed. N.Y. : Wiley, 1984. 165 p. : ill., maps ; 32x38cm.   **EF109**

1st ed., 1966.

An instructional aid illustrating various geomorphic principles and features for introductory courses in earth sciences. Consists of maps and photographs of various land forms, with some explanatory text, in a topical arrangement; includes the lunar surface and submarine topography. Subject index.   G1046.C2A8

Derry, Duncan R. World atlas of geology and mineral deposits / Duncan R. Derry ; assisted by Laurence Curtis ... [et al.]. London : Mining Journal Books, 1980. 110 p. : some maps in color ; 25 x 33cm.   **EF110**

A whole world approach "intended for use of students, travelling amateurs and professional earth scientists."—*Introd.* The first part consists of a general survey intelligible to those with relatively little background in geology. The second part consists of ten land maps of the world with a geological history. Includes suggested readings, sources of additional information, and glossary.   G1046.C5D8

Guide to USGS geologic and hydrologic maps. McLean, Va. : Documents Index, 1983. 644 p.   **EF111**

For annotation, *see* CL249.   Z6034.U49G95

Owen, H.G. Atlas of continental displacement : 200 million years to the present. Cambridge ; N.Y. : Cambridge Univ. Pr., 1983. 159p. : maps ; 31cm.   **EF112**

The atlas is the "first of a two-part work designed to provide maps of the distribution of continental and oceanic crust during the last 700 million years of the Earth's history."—*Pref.* 76 maps in seven sections.   G1046.C55O9

Shell Oil Company. Exploration Department. Stratigraphic atlas of North America and Central America / prep. by the Exploration Department of Shell Oil Company, Houston, Texas ; ed. by T. D. Cook and A. W. Balley ; comp. by S. Milner ... [ct al.] ; cartography and drafting by W. C. Heuer ... [et al.]. Princeton, N.J. : Princeton Univ. Pr., c1975. 272 p. : ill., maps ; 43 cm.　　　**EF113**

Also publ. under title: *Stratigraphic atlas, North & Central America.*

A collection of black-and-white maps, on a scale of 1:25,000,000, and stratigraphic sections, together with extensive bibliographies.
G1106.C57S54

Snead, Rodman E. World atlas of geomorphic features. Huntington, N.Y. : Krieger, 1980. 301 p. : col. ill., maps in color ; 29cm.　　　**EF114**

103 maps grouped in six sections. Brief text defines the landforms and describes the major characteristics of the features. Bibliography and index.　　　G1046.C256

Ziegler, Peter A. Geological atlas of Western and Central Europe. 2nd ed. The Hague : Shell Internationale Petroleum, 1990. 1 v. : maps ; 31 cm.　　　**EF115**

1st ed., 1982.

Aims to provide an "updated overview of the tectonic and stratigraphic framework of Western and Central Europe and its evolution in a global context since the Mid-Paleozoic."—*Postscript.* Portfolio contains 52 maps (tectonic, geologic, palaeogeographic, isopach, and stratigraphic) plus separate charts of legends and abbreviations. Bibliography and geographic index.　　　QE260.Z53

CRYSTALLOGRAPHY

Backhaus, Karl-Otto. Wörterbuch Kristallografie : Englisch, Deutsch, Französisch, Russisch : mit etwa 3600 Fachbegriffen. Thun : H. Deutsch, 1983. 132 p.　　　**EF116**

Title on added t.p.: *Dictionary of crystallography : English, German, French, Russian.*

Some 3,600 words and phrases are arranged in four columns alphabetically by the English term. Indexes in the other three languages refer to the English section.　　　QD902.B33

International tables for crystallography. 3rd rev. ed. Dordrecht ; Boston : publ. for the International Union of Crystallography by Kluwer Academic Publishers, 1992–93. v. A, C. (In progress).　　　**EF117**

1st ed., 1983–93.

Contents: v. A, Space-group symmetry, ed. by Theo Hahn; v. C, Mathematical, physical, and chemical tables, ed. by A. J. C. Wilson. v. B to be Reciprocal space, ed. by U. Shmueli.

Continues work first publ. as *Internationale Tabellen zur Bestimmung von Kristallstrukturen* (Berlin : Gebrüder Brontraeger; N.Y. : Chemical Catalog Co., 1935) and *International tables for X-ray crystallography* (Birmingham : publ. for the International Union of Crystallography by Kynoch Pr., 1952–74).

"The aim of the present work is to provide data and text which are useful for all aspects of crystallography."—*Pref.* Topically arranged chapters by specialists include extensive charts, tables, and reference lists. Author and subject indexes for each volume. A standard reference work for university libraries.

PASCAL. 1984– . Paris : Centre Nationale de la Recherche Scientifique, 1984– . Frequency varies; most sections 10 issues per year.　　　**EF118**

Includes two sections of interest to crystallography, both in *PASCAL. Explore*: E12, *État condensé* and E13, *Structures des liquides et des solides, cristallographie.* For full information, *see* EA72.

World directory of crystallographers and of other scientists employing crystallographic methods. 1st ed. (1957)– . Utrecht : Publ. for the International Union of Crystallography by N.V.A. Oosthoek's Uitgeversmaatschappi, 1957– .　　　**EF119**

Publisher, place of publication, and compilers vary. 7th ed., 1986.

An international directory of scientists with active interests in crystallography. Lists some 9,000 scientists from 69 countries. Entries are arranged alphabetically by country and include: name and title; institutional address; birth date; highest academic degree awarded and granting university; present position; telephone; major fields of interest. Index by personal name.　　　QD903.5.W6

Wyckoff, Ralph W. G. Crystal structures. 2nd ed. N.Y. : Interscience, 1963–71. v.1–6$^{1-2}$. : ill.　　　**EF120**

Repr.: Malabar, Fla. : R. E. Krieger, 1982– .

A revision of the compilation previously published in loose-leaf form (1948–53), written for crystallographers, physicists, biochemists, geologists, and mineralogists. Gives detailed descriptions of structures with illustrations. Following the text of each chapter is a bibliography in tabular form. Individual volumes have name and formula indexes.
QD951.W82

GEODESY

Bibliographia geodaetica : internationale geodaetische Dokumentation. Jahrg. 1, no. 1 (Jan. 1963)–Jahrg. 29, no. 3 (1991). Berlin : Akademie Verlag, 1963–91.　　　**EF121**

Hrsg. vom Nationalkomitee für Geodäsie und Geophysik der Deutschen Demokratischen Republik bei der Deutschen Akademie der Wissenschaften zu Berlin.

Subtitle also in French, English (International geodetic documentation), and Russian.

A classed bibliography with annual author and subject indexes. Each issue includes sections in German, French, English, and Russian, the same citations appearing in each section but with brief abstracts in the different languages.

Geodetic glossary / National Geodetic Survey. Rockville, Md. : National Oceanic and Atmospheric Administration, National Ocean Service : for sale by the National Geodetic Information Center, NOAA, [1986]. 274 p.　　　**EF122**

Supersedes U.S. Coast and Geodetic Survey's *Definitions of terms used in geodetic and other surveys* (Wash. : U.S. Govt. Print. Off., 1948).

Contains some 5,000 alphabetically arranged terms covering the theory, standards, and instruments of geodesy and related disciplines. References and list of sources.　　　QB279.G46

Mueller, Ivan Istvan. Gravimetric and celestial geodesy : a glossary of terms / Ivan I. Mueller and John D. Rockie. N.Y. : Ungar, [1966]. 129 p. : ill., map.　　　**EF123**

Supplements and updates *Definitions of surveying, mapping, and related terms* (1954) prepared by the Committee on Definitions of Surveying Terms of the American Society of Civil Engineers, and H. C. Mitchell's *Definitions of terms used in geodetic and other surveys* (1949).

Intends to analyze and define "as accurately as possible, terminology in the fields of gravimetric (physical) geodesy, geodetic astronomy, and satellite geodesy."—*Pref.* Contains about 500 definitions with many cross-references. Tabular appendix includes list of major geodetic datums.　　　QB279.M8

Multilingual dictionary of geodesy / ed. Dénes Csatkai. Budapest, Hungary : Omikk Technoinform, 1989. 5 v. (In progress).　　　**EF124**

Contents: v. 1, Adjustment computation, higher geodesy, national survey, v. 2, Instrument, equipment, notions of instrumental technics; v. 3, Plane surveying, land organisation, city survey, land registry, evaluation of land; v. 4, Topography; v. 5, Photogrammetry, photography.

The base word list with definitions is Hungarian with equivalents for the five other languages. Indexes for each language: English, Esperanto, French, German, and Russian are keyed to the Hungarian section.   QB279.M95

GLACIOLOGY

Elsevier's dictionary of glaciology in four languages : English (with definitions), Russian (with definitions), French, and German / comp. by V.M. Kotlyakov and N.A. Smolyarova. Amsterdam ; N.Y. : Elsevier, 1990. 336 p.   **EF125**

All types of glaciological phenomena (atmospheric, glacial, sea, river, lake, and ground ice; snow cover; and paleoglaciology) are defined. Terms from closely related disciplines such as physics, meteorology, and geocryology are included. The base list contains about 1,200 English headwords with accompanying definitions. Russian, French, and German language indexes are keyed to the main section. Useful introductory essay on the development of glaciological science and terminology.   GB2401.E57

HYDROLOGY

Bibliography

American Geophysical Union. Annotated bibliography on hydrology (1951–54) and sedimentation (1950–54), United States and Canada. [Wash. : U.S. Govt. Print. Off., 1956]. 207 p. (U.S. Inter-Agency Committee on Water Resources. Joint hydrology-sedimentation bull., no.7).   **EF126**

Continues the Union's publications: *Bibliography of hydrology : United States of America for the year(s) 1935/6–1940* (Wash. : American Geophysical Union, Section of Hydrology, 1937–41. 5 v. in 1) and *Annotated bibliography on hydrology, 1941–1950* (Wash., 1952. 408 p.).

Arranged by author, with a list of organizations and their publications.

Continued by: U.S. Geological Survey, *Annotated bibliography on hydrology and sedimentation* (EF127).

Geological Survey (U.S.). Annotated bibliography on hydrology and sedimentation : United States and Canada. 1955/58– . Wash. : U.S. Govt. Print. Off., 1962– . Irregular.   **EF127**

Initial volume covering 1955–58 publ. as U. S. Geological Survey *Water supply paper* no.1546.

Includes papers, articles, books, data compilations, and data reports that are not part of a series. "Listings are arranged alphabetically by author, followed by a combined subject and geographic location or river basin index. Each article is indexed by primary subject, and by geographic area if applicable."—*Introd.*

Continues American Geophysical Union, *Annotated bibliography on hydrology (1951–54) and sedimentation (1950–54), United States and Canada* (EF126). Continued by a series of bibliographies with the same title prepared for the U.S. Interagency Committee on Water Resources and published as issues of the *Joint hydrology-sedimentation bulletin*: 1959/62, publ. 1964 (Bull. no. 8); 1963/65, publ. 1969 (Bull. no. 9); 1966/68, publ. 1970 (Bull. no. 10).   TC801.U2

Hydata. v.1 (Jan. 1965)–14 (Dec. 1978). Urbana, Ill. : American Water Resources Assoc., 1965–78. Monthly.   **EF128**

Contains tables of contents pages from current periodicals in the field of water resources and hydrology. In addition there are other lists: Selected article titles from other periodicals; Tables of contents of non-periodical literature (primarily conferences); Selected titles of non-periodical literature (reports).

Continued by *Hydro-index* (July 1980– . Minneapolis : Environmental Hydrology Corp.), a monthly index of titles of the world's literature on water.

Selected water resources abstracts. v.1 (Jan. 1968)–v. 24, no. 12 (1991). [Springfield, Va. : National Technical Information Service], 1968–1991. Monthly with annual index.   **EF129**

Superintendent of Documents classification: I 1.94/2: .

Vol. 1, no. 1–9, publ. by the Bureau of Reclamation, Denver, Colo. Frequency varies; semimonthly, 1968–1982.

Published for the Water Resources Scientific Information Center, U.S. Geological Survey, U.S. Dept. of the Interior.

Includes "abstracts of current and earlier pertinent monographs, journal articles, reports, and other publication formats" that "cover water resources as treated in the life, physical, and social sciences and the related engineering and legal aspects of the characteristics, supply condition, conservation, control, use, or management of water resources."—*Pref.* Topical arrangement with detailed subject, author, organizational, and accession number indexes in each issue.

•Available in machine-readable form as *Selected water resources abstracts* (continued as *Water resources abstracts*, 1990– , EF131).
                    TC1.S45

Van der Leeden, Frits. Geraghty & Miller's groundwater bibliography. 5th ed. Plainview, N.Y. : Water Information Center, Inc., c1991. 507 p.   **EF130**

1st ed., 1971, had title: *Ground water : a selected bibliography*; 4th ed., 1987.

Expanded to 5,600 entries that include standard works as well as significant new papers on ground water contamination, modeling, and regulations and legal issues. A general section contains citations to bibliographies, textbooks, and serial titles, while the subject section is arranged by topic and includes journal articles, reports, documents, and specialized monographs. Author index.   GB1003.2.V35

•**Water resources abstracts** [database]. Baltimore : National Information Services Corp., 1990– .   **EF131**

Continues: *Selected water resources abstracts* [database] (Wash. : WRSIC, 1967–91).

Available on CD-ROM, updated quarterly.

Indexes and abstracts the water resources literature published in the physical, life, and social sciences, in related branches of engineering, and in the legal literature. Compiled from publications by the Water Resources Scientific Information Center of the U.S. Geological Survey.

Dictionaries

Elsevier's dictionary of environmental hydrogeology : in English, French, and German / comp. by Hans-Olaf Pfannkuch. Amsterdam ; N.Y. : Elsevier, 1990. 332 p.   **EF132**

1st ed., 1969, had title *Elsevier's dictionary of hydrogeology in three languages*.

Expanded to 5,422 terms to include new areas of interest and interdisciplinary nature of the subject. English words are alphabetically arranged and are followed by French and German equivalents. Some definitions are provided for clarification. French and German term indexes refer to the English section. Bibliography of sources.
                    GB1003.E47

International glossary of hydrology = Glossaire international d'hydrologie / WMO/Unesco Panel on Terminology. 2nd ed. Paris : UNESCO ; Geneva, : World Meteorological Organization, 1992. 413 p. (WMO, no. 385).   **EF133**

Title also in Russian and Spanish.

1st ed., 1974.

1,800 terms, alphabetically arranged in English, with equivalents and definitions given in four languages. Indexes in English, French, Russian, and Spanish refer to the main section. Universal Decimal Classification for hydrology in appendix. GB655.I57

Lo, Shuh-shiaw. Glossary of hydrology. Littleton, Colo. : Water Resources Publications, c1992. 1794 p. **EF134**

Lists some 17,500 terms in surface and ground water hydrology as well as related areas of meteorology, geology, and engineering. Definitions are usually brief, but not overly technical, making the dictionary useful for general and college audiences. GB655.L6

Singer, Lothar. Russian-English-German-French hydrological dictionary. London : Scientific Information Consultants, [1967]. 151 p. **EF135**

About 1,500 terms arranged on a Russian base with indexes from the other languages. GB655.S5

Tuin, J. D. van der. Elsevier's dictionary of hydrology and water quality management : in five languages, English, French, Spanish, Dutch, and German. Amsterdam ; N.Y. : Elsevier, 1991. 527 p. **EF136**

Terms are drawn from the physical, chemical, and biological aspects of hydrology and surface and subsurface waters. Excludes study of the sea except as it impacts on inland waters. 5,928 numbered terms in English with equivalents for French, Spanish, Dutch, and German. Indexes for the other languages refer to the English section. GB653.2.T85

Handbooks

Chow, Ven Te. Handbook of applied hydrology : a compendium of water-resources technology. N.Y. : McGraw-Hill, [1964]. 1 v. (various pagings) : ill., maps. **EF137**

Contains 25 sections written by specialists. Designed for scientists, engineers, and consultants. Interdisciplinary aspects are stressed. Includes bibliographies. GB661.C56

Guide to hydrological practices / World Meteorological Organization. 4th ed. Geneva : Secretariat of the World Meteorological Organization, 1981. 2 v. (looseleaf) : ill. (WMO, no. 168). **EF138**

1st ed., 1965, called: *Guide to hydrometeorological practices*; 3rd ed., 1974.

Contains detailed descriptions of the practices, procedures, and instrumentation WMO countries should follow to be in compliance with regulations. Chapter references. Subject index in v. 2. QC925.W667

Handbook of hydrology / David R. Maidment, ed. in chief. N.Y. : McGraw-Hill, c1993. 1 v. (various pagings) : ill., maps. **EF139**

A "compendium of hydrologic practice" (*Pref.*) designed for hydrologists, professionals in related fields, and students with interests in research or engineering. Contributions emphasize the applied aspects of hydrology and are grouped in four major sections (hydrologic cycle; hydrologic transport; hydrologic statistics; hydrologic technology). Charts, tables, and black-and-white photographs illustrate the text. Updates and supersedes Ven Te Chow, *Handbook of applied hydrology* (EF137) for some topics. Subject index. GB662.5.M35

Van der Leeden, Frits. The water encyclopedia / Frits van der Leeden, Fred L. Troise, David Keith Todd. 2nd ed. Chelsea, Mich. : Lewis Publishers, c1990. 808 p. : ill., maps. **EF140**

For annotation, *see* EK96. TD351.V36

METEOROLOGY

Bibliography

International catalogue of scientific literature / publ. for the Internat. Council by the Royal Soc. of London. v. 1 (1901)–v. 14 (1914). London : Harrison, 1902–21. **EF141**

Section F, Meteorology, including terrestrial magnetism. For full description, *see* EA16.

United States. Army. Signal Corps. Bibliography of meteorology. Wash. : Signal Off., 1889–91. 4 v. **EF142**

Subtitle: A classed catalogue of the printed literature of meteorology from the origin of printing to the close of 1881; with a supplement to the close of 1887, and an author index. Prepared under the direction of Brigadier General A. W. Greely … ed. by Oliver L. Fassig.

Contents: v.1, Temperature; v.2, Moisture; v.3, Winds; v.4, Storms.

Includes some 60,000 titles by 13,000 authors. Vols. 3–4 include literature to 1889. Z6681.U58

Indexes; Abstract journals

Meteorological and geoastrophysical abstracts. v. 1 (Jan. 1950)– . Boston : Amer. Meteorological Soc., 1950– . Monthly. **EF143**

Title varies: v.1–10, *Meteorological abstracts and bibliography*.

A classified arrangement of abstracts in English on important meteorological, hydrological, physical, oceanographic, and geoastrophysical literature in all languages. Includes various lists of serial publications, and in 1960–70, occasional selective annotated bibliographies on subjects of special interest to meteorologists. Each issue has author, subject, and geographical indexes. Most yearly volumes have cumulated indexes.

A cumulated index has been published as: American Meteorological Society, *Cumulated bibliography and index to Meteorological and geoastrophysical abstracts, 1950–1969 : classified subject and author arrangements* (Boston : G.K. Hall, 1972. 9 v.). Cumulates the entries without the abstracts. Contents: Author sequence, 5 v.; Universal Decimal Classification cumulation, 4 v.

•Machine-readable version: *Meteorological and geoastrophysical abstracts* [database] (Boston : American Meteorological Soc., 1970–). Available online, 1970– (updated irregularly) and on CD-ROM, 1974– (updated quarterly).

Encyclopedias

The encyclopedia of climatology / ed. by John E. Oliver, Rhodes W. Fairbridge. N.Y. : Van Nostrand Reinhold, c1987. 986 p. : ill. (Encyclopedia of earth sciences, v. 11). **EF144**

Signed articles, many with extensive bibliographies, survey basic and applied research, with an emphasis on current studies of climate change. A comprehensive source useful to general readers as well as students and researchers. The text incorporates tables, charts, and some black-and-white photographs. Subject index and index to authors cited in the text. QC854.E525

Fairbridge, Rhodes Whitmore. The encyclopedia of atmospheric sciences and astrogeology. N.Y. : Reinhold, [1967]. 1200p. : ill. (Encyclopedia of earth sciences, 2). **EF145**

Intended "for all scientists, from those still in high school to the emeritus professor who would like to check on a few items."—*Pref.* A

dictionary arrangement is followed; articles are signed; an index complements the dictionary arrangement; bibliographies are included.
QC854.F34

Dictionaries

Glossary of meteorology / ed. by Ralph E. Huschke. Boston : Amer. Meteorological Soc., 1959. 638 p.   **EF146**
Frequently reprinted.
"Sponsored by U.S. Dept of Commerce, Weather Bureau [and others]."—*t.p.*
A dictionary compiled and written by specialists with definitions "understandable to an undergraduate in a technical college yet [with] sufficient detail to satisfy the working specialist."—*Pref.* Primarily U.S. usage, but with some terms used in other countries. QC854.G55

Great Britain. Meteorological Office. Meteorological glossary. 6th ed. London : H.M.S.O., 1991. 335 p. : ill.   **EF147**
1st ed., 1916; 5th ed., 1972.
Revises, corrects, and augments the 5th ed. Emphasizes terms that are used in the scientific and technical meteorological and climatological literature. Many definitions are lengthy and include formulas, graphs, charts, maps, and photographs. Bibliography.   QC854.G7

Foreign terms

Multilingual

World Meteorological Organization. International meteorological vocabulary. 2nd ed. Geneva : Secretariat of the World Meteorological Organization, 1992. 784 p.   **EF148**
1st ed., 1966.
Title also in French, Russian, and Spanish.
Brief definitions for some 3,500 terms arranged in English alphabetic order, accompanied by definitions in the other three languages. French, Russian, and Spanish indexes.

French

Proulx, Gerard-J. Standard dictionary of meteorological sciences : English-French/French-English. Montreal : McGill–Queen's Univ. Pr., 1971. 307 p.   **EF149**
Lists equivalents for terms and phrases in theoretical and applied meteorology, hydrometeorology, oceanography, and geomorphology.
QC854.P76

Spanish

Brazol, Demetrio. Dictionary of meteorological and related terms. Buenos Aires : Hachette, 1955. 557 p.   **EF150**
Contents: English-Spanish, Spanish-English.   QC854.B75

Directories

Curricula in the atmospheric, oceanic, hydrologic, and related sciences. 1992– . Boston : American Meteorological Society, 1992– . Biennial.   **EF151**
Issues for 1963/64–73 had title: *Curricula in the atmospheric sciences*; for 1974–83: *Curricula in the atmospheric and oceanographic sciences*; for 1984–91: *Curricula in the atmospheric, oceanic, and related sciences.*

A directory of American and Canadian college and university programs in atmospheric science and in closely related oceanic and other sciences. Alphabetically arranged listings include: course and degree offerings, financial aid sources, research grants and contracts in effect, faculty, and information on recently completed theses and dissertations. Alphabetic, geographic, and degree indexes to universities and colleges; faculty index.

Handbooks

American Meteorological Society. Committee on the Compendium of Meteorology. Compendium of meteorology / prep. under the direction of the Committee on the Compendium of Meteorology ; ed. by Thomas F. Malone. Boston : American Meteorological Society, 1951. 1334 p. : ill. **EF152**
Topical arrangement of 108 survey articles, each by a different author and including a list of references. Subject index.   QC852.A5

Guide to meteorological instruments and methods of observation. 5th ed. Geneva : Secretariat of the World Meteorological Organization, 1983. 1 v. (various pagings) : ill. (WMO, no. 8).   **EF153**
1st ed., 1954–4th ed., 1971, called *Guide to meteorological instrument and observing practices.*
Detailed outline of the approved methods of observation and reporting for meteorological agencies in WMO member countries. Bibliography. Subject index.   QC851.W6445

Handbook of applied meteorology / ed. by David D. Houghton. N.Y. : Wiley, 1985. 1461 p. : ill.   **EF154**
The handbook "presents, for the first time, an authoritative, concise, and comprehensive reference for meteorological knowledge and technology, designed for professionals and technicians outside the meteorological profession."—*Pref.* A chapter on resources includes bibliographic references, as well as directories to data, university departments, research centers, and societies. Glossary and index.
TA197.H36

United States. Air Force. Geophysics Laboratory. Handbook of geophysics and space environments / scientific ed., Adolph S. Jursa. 4th ed. Bedford, Mass. : Hanscom Air Force Base, 1985. 1 v. (various pagings) : ill., tables.   **EF155**
Superintendent of Documents classification: D 301.6/5:G29/985.
1st ed., 1957, called *Handbook of geophysics for Air Force designers.*
Completely revised to emphasize the Air Force's increased interest in space environment. Text, charts, and tables are used to survey the sun and solar phenomena, astronomy and astrophysics, geomagnetism, properties of the atmosphere and ionosphere, and the earth sciences. Meant for use in the design of aerospace systems. Appendix of units, constants, and conversion factors. Subject index.   QC806.U48

Climatology

Bair, Frank E. The weather almanac. 6th ed. Detroit : Gale, 1992. 855 p. : ill., maps, charts.   **EF156**
1st ed., 1974; 5th ed., 1987.
Subtitle: A reference guide to weather, climate, and air quality in the United States and its key cities, comprising statistics, principles, and terminology. Provides weather/health information and safety rules for environmental hazards associated with storms, weather extremes, earthquakes and volcanoes. Also includes world climatological highlights and special features on weather, climate, and society.
Collects information and data from a variety of U.S. government agencies. Subject index.   QC983.R83

Climate normals for the U.S. (base: 1951–80) : data elements / comp. by National Climatic Center, Environmental Data and Information Service, National Oceanic and Atmospheric Administration. Detroit : Gale, 1983. 712 p. **EF157**

Gives average temperature and precipitation data by state and station. QC983.C53

Climates of the states / new material by James A. Ruffner. 3rd ed. Detroit : Gale, c1985. 2 v. : maps. **EF158**

Subtitle: National Oceanic and Atmospheric Administration narrative summaries, tables, and maps for each state, with overview of state climatologist programs.

1st ed., 1974; 2nd ed., 1980.

Covers 2,138 weather stations and substations with climatological summary tables for 1951–80. State maps are collected at the end of v. 2. QC983.C56

Climatological data. v. 1 (Jan. 1914)– . Asheville. N.C. : U.S. Dept. of Commerce, National Climatic Center , 1914– . Monthly (with annual summaries). **EF159**

Title varies: *Climatological data … by sections.*

Previously issued by: U.S. Weather Bureau, U.S. Environmental Science Services Administration, and U.S. Environmental Data Service.

Contains weather statistics from 47 separate areas, most sections corresponding to a state. Printed in the various section centers and assembled and bound in Washington. QC983.A5

Climatological data : national summary. v.25? (1975)–30 (1980). Asheville, N.C. : National Climatic Center, 1975–80. Monthly and annual. **EF160**

Continues: Weather Bureau (U.S.), *Climatological data : national summary (Asheville, N.C., 1950–65) and Environmental Data Service (U.S.), Climatological data : national summary* (Asheville, N.C., 1966–75). Science Services Administration, and U.S. Environmental Data Service.

Provides tables and maps containing data from every state.

Grayson, Donald K. A bibliography of the literature on North American climates of the past 13,000 years. N.Y. : Garland, 1975. 206 p. (Garland reference library of natural science, v.2). **EF161**

Not an exhaustive bibliography of its subject area, nor a critical compilation of the literature, although it includes "much, perhaps even most, of the pertinent literature."—*Introd.* Publications are listed by author and numbered; an index gives access to the literature by seven broad geographic subdivisions of North America. Z6683.C5G66

Hatch, Warren L. Selective guide to climatic data sources. Rev. ed. Wash. : U.S. National Environmental Satellite, Data, and Information Service, 1988. 1 v. (various pagings). (Key to meteorological records documentation, no. 4.11). **EF162**

Previous editions, 1963, 1969, 1979. 1963 ed. had title: *Selective guide to published climatic data sources.*

Published and unpublished climatological data sources are grouped alphabetically by title within five categories: (1) Current serial publications; (2) Marine publications; (3) Decennial and intermittent publications; (4) Special publications including atlases; (5) Data catalogs and indexes. An essential reference for locating detailed U.S. climate information. Indexed by climatologic element. Z6685.U64

Pearce, E. A. The Times Books world weather guide / by E.A. Pearce and Gordon Smith. 2nd ed. N.Y. : Times Books/ Random House, 1990. 1 v. **EF163**

Published in U.K. as *World weather guide.*

1st ed., 1984.

A convenient compilation of climatic information, largely unchanged from the 1st ed. Climate summaries and data tables are arranged by continent, then country, and for some larger countries, by region. Tables for the several representative stations in each country include latitude, longitude, and altitude of the station; monthly maximum and minimum temperatures in Fahrenheit and Celsius scales; relative humidity; and precipitation. British Meteorological Office publications are the principal source for the climatic data. Helpful introduction, glossary, country maps, and geographic index. QC982.P43

Rudloff, Willy. World-climates : with tables of climatic data and practical suggestions. Stuttgart : Wissenschaftliche Verlagsgesellschaft, 1981. 632 p. **EF164**

For 1,474 weather stations throughout the world, gives tables presenting a general climatic description and monthly mean temperatures, precipitation, sunshine, recommended clothing, and scale of heat stress. For 116 select stations, hygrothermal diagrams show mean daily values of air temperature and humidity for every month, indicating conditions at about dawn and in the early afternoon. QC982.R83

Storm data for the United States, 1970–1974. Detroit, Gale, 1982. 884p. **EF165**

Subtitle: A quinquennial compilation of the U.S. Environmental Data Service's official monthly reports of storm activity logged by the National Weather Service with damage extent estimates, and counts of injuries and deaths.

Reprints of monthly, *Storm data,* issued by the U.S. Environmental Data Service. Listed alphabetically by state within month. Not indexed.

Continued by *Storm data for the United States, 1975–1979* (1982. 946 p.), which follows the format of the earlier volume. QC943.5.U6S83

The weather handbook : a summary of climatic conditions and weather phenomena for selected cities in the United States and around the world / ed. by McKinley Conway and Linda L. Liston. Rev. ed. 1990. Norcross, Ga. : Conway Data, 1990. 548 p. : ill., maps. **EF166**

1st ed., 1963.

A compilation of basic climatic data covering 250 U.S. cities and more than 600 foreign cities. Other features include small-scale state maps with weather risk profiles, U.S. summary climatic maps, charts of unusual weather phenomena, and a list by country of major weather-related disasters. Indexed by city. QC982.W38

World survey of climatology / H. E. Landsberg, ed. in chief. Amsterdam : Elsevier, 1969–84. 15 v. **EF167**

Contents: v. 1–3, General climatology; v. 4, Climate of the free atmosphere; v. 5, Climates of northern and western Europe; v. 6, Climates of central and southern Europe; v. 7, Climates of the Soviet Union; v. 8, Climates of northern and eastern Asia; v. 9, Climates of southern and western Asia; v. 10, Climates of Africa; v. 11, Climates of North America; v. 12, Climates of Central and South America; v. 13, Climates of Australia and New Zealand; v. 14, Climates of polar regions; v. 15, Climates of the oceans.

Each volume represents the contributions of a group of specialists, and the complete set is intended to provide a systematic appraisal of the state of knowledge in the field of climatology throughout the world. In each volume there is an index of bibliographical references, a geographic index, and a subject index. QC981.W67

World weather records, 1971–80. Wash. : National Climatic Data Center, 1987–91. v. 1–3. (In progress). **EF168**

Contents: v. 1, North America (1989); v. 2, Europe (1987); v. 3, West Indies, South and Central America (1991).

Continues:

Henry Helm Clayton, *World weather records, collected from official sources by Dr. Felix Exner [and others],* assembled and arranged for publication by H.Helm Clayton; publ. under a grant from John A. Roebling (Wash. : Smithsonian Inst., 1927. 1199 p., maps. [Smithsonian misc. collections, v. 79]).

———. ———. *Errata* (Wash., Smithsonian Inst., 1929. 28 p.).

———. *World weather records … 1921-1930* (Wash. : Smithsonian Inst., 1934. 616 p.).

———. ——— 1931-1940 (Wash. : Smithsonian Inst., 1937. 646 p.).

U.S. Weather Bureau, *World weather records, 1941–50* (Wash., 1959. 1361 p.).

————. ———— *1951–60* (Wash. : U.S. Govt. Print. Off., 1965-68. 6 v.). Contents: v. 1, North America; v. 2, Europe; v. 3, South America, Central America, West Indies, the Caribbean and Bermuda; v. 4, Asia; v. 5, Africa; v. 6, Antarctica, Australia, Oceanic Islands, and Ocean weather stations.

World weather records, 1961–1970 (Asheville, N.C. : National Climatic Center ; Wash. : Environmental Data and Information Service, 1979-82. v. 1–3, 6. [In progress]). Contents: v. 1, North America; v. 2, Europe; v. 3, West Indies, South and Central America; v. 6, Islands of the world.

Consists of statistical tables arranged geographically giving pressure at station level, temperature, and precipitation, by month. The 1921–30 volume includes atmospheric pressures over the northern oceans and sea-level pressures at selected land stations, late reports, and additional data; the 1931–40 volume includes lake and river levels. Indexes by country, station, etc.; indexes by latitude.   QC982.W6

Atlases

Climate Analysis Center. Daily weather maps : weekly series / National Oceanic and Atmospheric Administration, National Weather Service, National Meteorological Center, Climate Analysis Center. Wash. : The Center, 1968– . Weekly.
                                                    EF169
Superintendent of Documents classification: C 55.195.

Issuing agency varies: 1968–78, U.S. Environmental Data Service; 1978–83, U.S. Environmental Data and Information Service; 1983–84, U.S. National Environmental Satellite, Data, and Information Service.

A continuation of the principal charts of the former U.S. Weather Bureau publication, *Daily weather map,* which was discontinued April 14, 1968.

For each day of the week, provides maps of the 48 adjacent states and southern Canada, showing surface weather and station weather, 500-millibar height contours, precipitation amounts, and high and low temperatures.

Visher, Stephen Sargent. Climatic atlas of the United States. Cambridge : Harvard Univ. Pr., 1954. 403p. : 1031 maps. 30cm.   **EF170**
"The 1031 maps and diagrams are presented in 34 chapters grouped in seven parts. Five parts embrace the major elements of climate: temperature, wind, sunshine, humidity, and precipitation, and the other two, some consequences of climate and weather, and climatic regions and climatic changes. The consequences include those to agriculture, health, soil erosion, soil moisture, soil freezing, lakes, streams, and topography."—*Foreword.* Includes bibliographic references and sources of maps. Indexed.   G1201.C8V5

MINERALOGY

Guides

Kaplan, Stuart R. A guide to information sources in mining, minerals, and geosciences. N.Y. : Interscience, [1965]. 599 p. (Guides to information sources in science and technology, v. 2).   **EF171**
Covers "the fields of metallic and nonmetallic mining, metals, fuels, minerals, geology, geophysics, beneficiation and processing, geography and the broad area of pure and applied earth sciences."—*Introd.* Emphasizes current and continuing sources of information. In two parts: (1) organizations (arranged by geographical areas, with address, purpose, functions, publications, etc.); and (2) literature (arranged by subject field and listing bibliographies, handbooks, dictionaries, abstracts, journals, yearbooks). Separate indexes to the literature and to the organizations.   Z7401.G83

O'Donoghue, Michael. The literature of mineralogy. [London] : Science Reference and Information Service, The British Library, 1986. 85 p. : ill.   **EF172**
A brief guide to standard (and some specialized) reference sources in mineralogy. Descriptive annotations accompany many citations. Valuable for listings of regional mineralogy studies. Author/title index.   Z6033.M6

Bibliography

International catalogue of scientific literature / publ. for the Internat. Council by the Royal Soc. of London. v. 1 (1901)–v. 14 (1914). London : Harrison, 1902–21.   **EF173**
Includes Section G, Mineralogy. For full description, *see* EA16.

Repertorium der mineralogischen und krystallographischen Literatur, 1876–[1902] : und Generalregister der Zeitschrift für Krystallographie und Mineralogie ... Bd.1–40. Leipzig : Engelmann, 1886–1910. 4 v.   **EF174**
Contents of *Repertorium*: 1876–85, 1885–91, 1891–97, 1897–1902.

Each volume is in two parts: (1) a bibliography of material published during the period covered, and (2) an index to the *Zeitschrift*.   Z6033.M6R5

Ridge, John Drew. Annotated bibliographies of mineral deposits in the Western hemisphere. [Boulder, Colo.] : Geological Soc. of America, 1972. 681 p. : ill. (Geological Society of America. Memoir, 131).   **EF175**
Together with Ridge's *Annotated bibliographies of mineral deposits in Africa, Asia (exclusive of the USSR) and Australasia* (Oxford ; N.Y. : Pergamon, 1976) and *...Europe* (Oxford ; N.Y. : Pergamon, 1984–90. 2 v.), this will form a revised and expanded version of Ridge's *Selected bibliographies of hydrothermal and magmatic mineral deposits,* 1958.

"I have included in these bibliographies all deposits that have, in my opinion, been formed in whole or in part by magmatic or hydrothermal processes, including those produced by volcanic exhalations reaching the sea floor, for which I believe a worthwhile literature exists."—*Introd.* Thoroughly annotated. Arranged geographically; indexed by author, by deposit, by age of mineralization, by metals or minerals produced, and by Lindgren Classification Index.
                                                    Z6738.075.R5

Sinkankas, John. Gemology : an annotated bibliography. Metuchen, N.J. : Scarecrow, 1993. 2 v. (1179 p.) : ill. **EF176**
A descriptive bibliography based on the author's unique collection of works on gemology and related fields of jewelry making, lapidary work, and engraved gems. About 7,500 entries, alphabetically arranged by author, include detailed bibliographic notations and evaluative annotations. Lists of serial publications and bibliographies and references consulted. Subject index.   Z5998.S55

Indexes; Abstract journals

Mineralogical abstracts. v. 1 (1920)– . London : Mineralogical Society of Great Britain and Mineralogical Society of America, 1920– .   **EF177**
Publisher varies. Frequency varies: v. 1–13 (1920–58) issued only with *Mineralogical magazine*; v. 14– , published jointly by the Mineralogical Society of Great Britain and the Mineralogical Society of America.

A classified list of signed abstracts of current literature—books, pamphlets, reports, periodical articles, etc. International in coverage. Annual author and subject indexes. Supplements the record in the *International catalogue of scientific literature* (EA16. Section G, Mineralogy) by summarizing the mineralogical literature from 1915.

•Included in *GEOBASE* database (CL30) since 1980.
QE351.M35

Zentralblatt für Mineralogie. v. 1 (1950)– . Stuttgart : Schweizerbart, 1950– . **EF178**

Supersedes in part *Neues Jahrbuch für Mineralogie, Geologie und Paläontologie* (EF58).

In two sections: T.1, Kristallographie und Mineralogie (7 issues per yr.); T.2, Petrographie, technische Mineralogie, Geochemie und Lagerstättenkunde (title varies slightly; 13 issues per yr.).

Abstracts are arranged by subject; international coverage of serial and monographic literature. Author and subject indexes published two to three years after each volume is complete.
QE351.Z45

Encyclopedias

The encyclopedia of mineralogy / ed. by Keith Frye. Stroudsburg, Pa. : Hutchinson Ross, [1981]. 794 p. : ill. (Encyclopedia of earth sciences, v.4B). **EF179**

Consists of "articles by practicing mineralogists about the many aspects of their science."—*Pref.* Signed articles, with cross-references and bibliographies, arranged alphabetically. Contains a mineral glossary of nearly 3,000 entries, defined with chemical composition, structural group, and crystal system, plus cross-references to articles. Indexed.
QE355.E49

Webster, Robert. Gems, their sources, descriptions, and identification. 4th ed. / rev. by B.W. Anderson. London ; Boston : Butterworths, 1983. 1006 p. : ill. **EF180**

1st ed., 1962.

A useful, comprehensive work.
QE392.W37

Dictionaries

Bailey, Dorothy. An etymological dictionary of chemistry and mineralogy / by Dorothy Bailey and Kenneth C. Bailey. London : Edward Arnold, 1929. 307 p. **EF181**

Gives the "derivation of chemical and mineralogical names which have been current in the literaure ... at any period later than the middle of the 19th century."—*Pref.*

Bradley, J. E. S. Chinese-English glossary of mineral names / comp. by J.E.S. Bradley and A.C. Barnes. N.Y. : Consultants Bureau, 1963. 120 p. **EF182**

Basically a table of English equivalents of Chinese terms of minerals, based on the sounds of the Chinese characters, in an arrangement similar to Andrew Clark's *Hey's mineral index* (EF193). Includes an English index.
QE355.B75

Dorian, Angelo Francis. Elsevier's dictionary of mining and mineralogy : in English, French, German, and Italian. Amsterdam ; N.Y. : Elsevier, 1993. 300 p. **EF183**

Some 3,500 English-language entries are listed alphabetically, some with definitions, followed by equivalents in the other languages. French, German, and Italian indexes reference the English section.
TN10.D67

A manual of new mineral names, 1892–1978 / ed. by Peter G. Embrey and John P. Fuller. N.Y. : Oxford Univ. Pr., 1980. 467 p. **EF184**

"A collection of the thirty Lists of New Mineral Names that have been published in the *Mineralogical Magazine.*"—*Foreword.* Offers an alphabetical listing of mineral names with complete bibliographic citation for the first article that names and chemically identifies the mineral. Minerals that do not conform to the nomenclature of the new minerals and mineral names of the International Commission on Min-

eralogical Association have been included until new investigation can authenticate or relegate them to synonymy. Incorporates lists 1–21 by L. J. Spencer and 22–30 by M. H. Hey. Author index.
QE357.M36

Read, Peter G. Dictionary of gemmology. 2nd ed. London ; Boston : Butterworth Scientific, 1988. 266 p. : ill. **EF185**

1st ed., 1982.

A compact, alphabetical listing that provides "concise descriptions of the principal gem materials, as well as definitions of associated scientific terms and brief working explanations of the many types of gemmological instruments."—*Pref.* Some black-and-white illustrations, crystal system diagrams, and a data appendix.
TS722.R43

Roberts, Willard Lincoln. Encyclopedia of minerals / Willard Lincoln Roberts, Thomas J. Campbell, George Robert Rapp, Jr. 2nd ed. N.Y. : Van Nostrand Reinhold, c1990. 979 p., 48 p. of plates : ill. (some col.). **EF186**

1st ed., 1974.

A desk reference for mineralogical data, containing 3,200 alphabetically arranged entries. Entries include chemical composition, crystallographic data, physical properties, mode of occurence, best reference in English, and a color photograph.
QE355.R6

Shipley, Robert Morrill. Dictionary of gems and gemology : including ornamental, decorative and curio stones (excluding diamonds) / Robert Morrill Shipley ... [et al.]. 6th ed. Santa Monica, Calif. : Gemological Inst. of America, 1974. 230 p. **EF187**

1st ed., 1945.

"A glossary of over 4,000 English and foreign words, terms and abbreviations which may be encountered in English literature or in the gem, jewelry or art trades."—*title page.*

Includes names of some persons, societies, museums, journals, etc. Entries within quotation marks identify misnomers. Pronunciation included for difficult words.
TN980.S5

Thrush, Paul W. A dictionary of mining, mineral, and related terms / comp. and ed. by Paul W. Thrush and the staff of the Bureau of Mines. [Wash. : U.S. Bureau of Mines], 1968. 1269 p. **EF188**

Begun as a revision of the U.S. Bureau of Mines Bulletin 95, *A glossary of the mining and mineral industry*, by A. H. Fay (Wash., 1920; repr. 1947. 754 p.), the new work is greatly expanded and includes up-to-date terminology of new methods and technologies. It is a comprehensive and authoritative work of about 55,000 entries and 150,000 definitions. Foreign terms have been excluded, except where no satisfactory English equivalent was available and for those Spanish-American and Mexican terms still in use in the American Southwest. Authority for each entry is provided through a list of sources at the end of the volume.
TN9.T5

Directories

International Mineralogical Association. World directory of mineralogists / ed. by Fabien Cesbron ; comp. with the help of the representatives of the national mineralogical societies. Orléans, France : Bureau de Recherches Géologiques et Minières ; Marburg, West Germany : Internat. Mineralological Assoc., 1985. 361 p. : ill. **EF189**

1st ed., 1962.

Entries are arranged nationally and include name, address, education, and area of interest. Name index.
QE361.A115

Handbooks

Arem, Joel E. Color encyclopedia of gemstones. 2nd ed. N.Y. : Van Nostrand Reinhold Co., c1987. 248 p., [68] p. of plates : ill. (some col.).   **EF190**
1st ed., 1977.
Provides basic information to identify mineral species used or cut as gemstones. Physical, chemical, optical, occurrence, and dimensional characteristics are given for some 250 species. Introductory chapters help explain the data tables. Appendixes of trade names, gemological interest groups, periodic table, bibliography, and portfolio of color photographs. Topical index.   QE392.A69 1987

Bögel, Hellmuth. A collector's guide to minerals and gemstones / [tr. from the German by Eva Fejer and Patricia Walter]; ed. and rev. by John Sinkankas. London : Thames & Hudson, 1971. 304 p. : ill.   **EF191**
German edition, 1968, had title *Knaurs Mineralienbuch*. English translation also published with title *The studio handbook of minerals* (N.Y. : Viking, 1972).
An illustrated handbook for the amateur. Includes a section of "Determinative tables" for identification of minerals.   QE363.2.B6413

Börner, Rudolf. Minerals, rocks, and gemstones / tr. and ed. by W. Mykura. [English ed. repr. with additional plates and references]. Edinburgh ; London : Oliver & Boyd, [1966]. 250 p. : ill.   **EF192**
1st English ed., 1962.
A translation of Börner's *Welcher Stein ist das?* (Stuttgart : Franckh'sche Verlagshandlung W. Keller & Co., 1938).
Adapted for use in Great Britain with rock classifications conforming to current English usage.
Designed as an aid to identification of specimens in the field with only minimal equipment. In three parts: the first gives properties, uses, and localities of 200 important minerals; the second provides an introduction to rocks, their uses and properties, and includes a short glossary of important rocks; the third, an introduction to the study of gemstones. Much information in tabular form. Bibliography; index.   QE365.B613

Clark, Andrew. Hey's mineral index : mineral species, varieties, and synonyms. 3rd ed. London ; N.Y. : Chapman & Hall, c1993. 848 p.   **EF193**
1st. ed., 1955, and 2nd rev. ed., 1962, by Max H. Hey, had title: *An index of mineral species & varieties arranged chemically.*
An index of published mineral names with the mineralogical data and references arranged in an alphabetical section, followed by a much more concise chemical finding index.   QE357.C53

Dana, James Dwight. The system of mineralogy of James Dwight Dana and Edward Salisbury Dana, Yale University, 1837–1892. 7th ed., entirely rewritten and greatly enl. by Charles Palache, Harry Berman and Clifford Frondel. N.Y. : Wiley, 1944–62. 3 v.   **EF194**
1st ed., 1837.
Contents: v. 1, Elements, sulfides, sulfosalts, oxides; v. 2, Halides, nitrates, borates, carbonates, sulfates, phosphates, arsenates, tungstates, molybdates, etc.; v. 3, Silica minerals.
Essentially a new work because of the accumulation of new data, and the development of analytical techniques and new classification systems since the 6th ed. (1892). An exhaustive treatment for the professional geologist, in classed arrangement, with information on each mineral, usually including sections on classification, morphological crystallography, X-ray crystallography, habit, physical properties, optical properties, chemistry, occurrences, alteration, synthesis, name, nomenclature, synonymy, bibliography, and abbreviation. Each volume individually indexed. The format of v. 3 varies slightly in coverage of properties.   QE372.D23

Deer, William Alexander. Rock-forming minerals / [by] W.A. Deer, R.A. Howie and J. Zussman. London : Longmans, [1962–63]. 5 v. : ill.   **EF195**
Contents: v.1, Ortho– and ring silicates; v.2, Chain silicates; v.3, Sheet silicates; v.4, Framework silicates; v.5, Nonsilicates.
Covers the common minerals of igneous, metamorphic, and sedimentary rocks. Within each volume information on each mineral or mineral group is divided into five subsections: Structure, giving brief description of atomic structure and the use of X-rays to determine chemical composition; Chemistry, giving principal variations in chemical composition, structural formula, and synthesis and breakdown of the minerals; Optical and physical properties, relating them to structure and chemistry; Distinguishing features, giving means or tests by which minerals may be recognized; and Paragenesis, giving principal rock types and typical mineral assemblages. Condensed tables and references accompany each entry. Each volume individually indexed.
A 2nd ed. has begun publication (N.Y. : Halsted ; London : Longmans, [1978–86]. [In progress]). Contents: v. 1A, Orthosilicates; v. 1B, Disilicates and ring silicates; v. 2A, Single-chain silicates. A "completely new edition" that "maintains the general principles and organization adopted for the first edition."—*Pref.*

Dixon, Colin J. Atlas of economic mineral deposits. Ithaca, N.Y. : Cornell Univ. Pr., 1979. 143 p. : maps ; 26 x 39 cm.   **EF196**
"Forty-eight mineral deposits or groups of deposits are described with world distribution maps of five selected groups of commodities."—*Introd.* The five sections cover the geological environment of the earth's surface, sedimentary rock, felsic magmatic environments, basic and ultrabasic magmatic rocks, and mineral deposits. Each diagram or map has text giving location, history, mining, and geology of deposits. Excludes deposits in USSR, China, and Eastern Europe. Indexed.   TN263.D57

Fay, Gordon S. The rockhound's manual. N.Y. : Harper & Row, [1972]. 290 p. : ill.   **EF197**
A handbook for the hobbyist. "Determinative tables and how to use them," p.223–71.   QE365.F22

Handbook of mineralogy / John W. Anthony ... [et al.]. Tucson, Ariz. : Mineral Data Pub., c1990. v. 1. (In progress).   **EF198**
Contents: v. 1, Elements, sulfides, sulfosalts.
To be complete in 5 v. Projected contents: v. 2, Silica, silicates; v. 3, Halides, hydroxides, oxides; v. 4, Arsenates, phosphates, uranates, vanadates; v. 5, Borates, carbonates, sulfates.
This substantial set will "gather in convenient form the data crucial to identification of all mineral species and ... provide relatively up-to-date references containing information central to the definition of each species."—*Introd.* Alphabetically arranged entries record: physical, chemical, crystal, X-ray powder, and optical properties; occurrence and distribution; history of name; type specimen information; and bibliographic references for each mineral species. A specialist's source important for college and university library collections. No illustrations or index.   QE366.8.H36

Lefond, Stanley J. Handbook of world salt resources. N.Y. : Plenum, 1969. 384 p.   **EF199**
Concise accounts of salt resources and deposits in individual countries (and the individual states of the U.S.) are presented, together with tables of chemical analysis, statistics on production, and bibliographical references. Indexed.   TN900.L44

Minerals yearbook / prep. by the staff of the Bureau of Mines. 1932/33– . Wash. : The Bureau : for sale by U.S. Govt. Print. Off., 1933– . Annual.   **EF200**
Supersedes the Bureau's *Mineral resources of the United States*, 1882–1931, as well as various interim summaries.
The volumes dated 1932/33 through 1940 contain reviews of 1932 through 1939. In 1941, designation was changed to use the date of period covered. Therefore, two volumes bear the date 1940: (1) 1940 (review of 1939), and (2) the actual review of 1940.

Beginning 1952, issued in 3–4 volumes per year: v. 1, Metals and minerals; v. 2, Area reports: domestic; v. 3, Area reports: international.

Provides information on worldwide industrial performance for the year covered. The material is largely tabular in format, but background information is provided to permit interpretation of the year's developments. Contents of volumes in recent years have included chapters on metallic, nonmetallic, and mineral fuel commodities and their relationship to the domestic economy, a review of the mineral industries, technological trends, and area reports, which cover mineral production and economic indicators for states within the U.S. and for foreign countries. Arrangement of v. 1 is alphabetical by mineral, and by state or country in the area reports. No index.

———. *Statistical appendix … 1932/33–1935* (Wash. : U.S. Govt. Print. Off., 1934–36. 3 v.). No more published. Later statistical figures included in the *Yearbook*. TN23.U642

Nickel, Ernest H. Mineral reference manual / Ernest H. Nickel, Monte C. Nichols. N. Y. : Van Nostrand Reinhold, c1991. 250 p. : ill. **EF201**

An alphabetical listing of "all valid mineral species [that] includes the name, formula, current status, crystal system, appearance, hardness, measured and calculated density, type locality, mineral classification, a reference to the origin of the name, an indication of related species, and selected literature references."—*Introd.* Short, condensed entry format is useful for quick reference by students, and for field and laboratory use. No index. QE372.2.N53

Nicolay, H. H. Rocks and minerals : a guide for collectors of the eastern United States / by H.H. Nicolay and A.V. Stone. South Brunswick, N.J. : Barnes, [1967]. 255 p. : ill. **EF202**

A state-by-state, county-by-county guide indicating the types of rocks and minerals to be found in each area. For the amateur and hobbyist. QE364.N49

Picot, Paul. Atlas of ore minerals / P. Picot and Z. Johan … [et al.]. Orléans, France : Bureau de Recherches Géologiques et Minières ; Amsterdam : Elsevier, 1982. 458 p. : ill. **EF203**

Translation of: *Atlas des minéraux métalliques.*

Detailed criteria for determination and identification of more than 350 ore minerals. Criteria include color, reflectance, anisotopy, and structure; there is a color photograph for most entries. QE390.P52

Pough, Frederick H. A field guide to rocks and minerals. 4th ed. Boston : Houghton Mifflin, 1976. 317 p. : ill. **EF204**

1st ed., 1953.

A practical handbook for mineral identification. In two parts, the first describing matters pertaining to care and maintenance of a collection, geographical distribution of minerals, physical properties, crystal classifications, chemical classification, and testing techniques. In the second and major part, properties of individual minerals are described, each mineral appearing with related minerals in a classed arrangement by type. Gives details of environment, where found, description, composition, distinguishing characteristics, occurrence, etc. Numerous plates, some in color. Glossary, bibliography, and index. QE367.P6

Scalisi, Philip. Classic mineral localities of the world : Asia and Australia / [by] Philip Scalisi [and] David Cook. N.Y. : Van Nostrand Reinhold, 1983. 226 p. : ill., maps. **EF205**

Describes sites that are "generally acknowledged to have produced some of the finest examples of mineral species."—*Pref.* Includes descriptions of individual specimens, as well as photographs and crystal drawings. TN99.S28

Meteorites

Brown, Harrison Scott. A bibliography on meteorites / assoc. editors: Gunnar Kullerud, Walter Nichiporuk. Chicago : Univ. of Chicago Pr., 1953. 686 p. **EF206**

The first of a projected three-volume catalog of meteorites. This covers, in chronological order, literature published from 1491 to 1950, with an author index. Cites papers and books, giving references to abstracts where possible. Z6033.M5B7

Graham, A. L. Catalogue of meteorites : with special reference to those represented in the collection of the British Museum (Natural History) / by A. L. Graham, A. W. R. Bevan and R. Hutchison. 4th ed., rev. and enl. Tucson, Ariz. : Univ. of Arizona Pr., 1985. 460 p. **EF207**

1st ed., 1923.

"This edition incorporates and expands the information published in the third edition (1966) and its appendix (1977). It includes the names of all well-authenticated meteorites known up to January 1984, even if no material has been preserved."—*Introd.* Contains entries for 2,611 meteorites of which 1,435 are represented in the collection of the British Museum (Natural History). Classified lists of meteorites by country and by type serve as indexes to the alphabetically arranged entries. QB755.G73

Unesco. Directory of meteorite collections and meteorite research. Paris : UNESCO, c1968. 50 p. **EF208**

Title also in French.

Lists by country collections, catalogs, research institutions, researchers, and topics of research. QE395.U54

OCEANOGRAPHY

Bibliography

Library of the Marine Biological Laboratory and the Woods Hole Oceanographic Institution. Catalog. Boston : G. K. Hall, 1971. 12 v. **EF209**

Reproduction of the catalog cards for a collection of some 12,000 books and monographs, reports of 138 expeditions, and nearly 300,000 journal articles. Arranged alphabetically, except that periodicals (about 4,000 titles) are separately listed in v. 12, the Journal catalog. Z881.L72

Sears, Mary. Oceanographic index : author cumulation, 1946–1970. Boston : G. K. Hall, 1971. 3 v. **EF210**
Z6004.P6S43

——— Oceanographic index : regional cumulation, 1946–1970. Boston : G. K. Hall, 1971. 706 p. **EF211**
Z6004.P6S436

——— Oceanographic index : subject cumulation, 1946–1971. Boston : G. K. Hall, 1972. 4 v. **EF212**

Reproduction of a card file maintained by the compiler and based on the collection of books and journals held in the library of the Marine Biological Laboratory, Woods Hole, Mass. Emphasis is on biological oceanography, physical oceanography, marine chemistry, geology, and meteorology. Z6004.P6S44

United States. Environmental Science Services Administration. ESSA libraries holdings in oceanography and marine meteorology, 1710–1967. Rockville, Md. : The Administration, Scientific Information and Documentation Division, 1969. 4 v. **EF213**

Contents: v. 1, Bibliography; v. 2, Author and subject indexes; v. 3, Systematic indexes; v. 4, Keyword (KWIC) index.

A computer-produced catalog of about 3,000 references.

Current

Oceanic abstracts. v. 21, no. 1 (Feb. 1984)– . Bethesda, Md. : Cambridge Scientific Abstracts, [1984]– . Bimonthly. **EF214**

Continues and assumes the volume numbering of: *Oceanic index* (v. 1 [1964]–v. 3 [1966]; v. 5 [1968]–v. 8 [1971]. La Jolla, Calif. : Oceanic Research Inst., 1964–68); *Oceanic citation journals with abstracts* (v. 5 [1968]–v. 8 [1971]. La Jolla, 1968–72); *Oceanic abstracts with indexes* (v. 9 [Feb. 1972]–v. 20 [Dec. 1983]. Bethesda, Md. : Cambridge Scientific Abstracts, 1972–83).

A classified abstracts section is followed by "keytalpha" subject, author, geographic, and organism indexes. Covers aspects of biology, geology, oceanography, pollution, engineering, ships, and other marine-related subjects. Includes citations to foreign language materials, with abstracts in English. Annual cumulated indexes.

•Available in machine-readable form as: *Oceanic abstracts : OC* [database]. Available online as part of *CSA life sciences collection* and as part of *Pollution/toxicology CD-ROM*.   GC1.O24

Oceanographic literature review. v. 40 (1993)– . Oxford ; N.Y. : Pergamon Pr., 1993– .   **EF215**

Continues: *Deep-sea research. Part B : Oceanographic literature review* (v. 26 [1979] - v. 39 [1992]). Subtitle, frequency, and format vary: v. 1–13, entitled "Oceanographic abstracts" and "Oceanographic bibliography," were publ. in issues of *Deep sea research*; v. 14–23 publ. separately as "Oceanographic abstracts and oceanographic bibliography section"; v. 24–25 publ. separately as "Oceanographic abstracts and bibliography."

Classified abstracts, drawn from recent literature on oceanography and related disciplines, with subject and author indexes and annual cumulated index.

Encyclopedias

Fairbridge, Rhodes Whitmore. The encyclopedia of oceanography. N.Y. : Reinhold, [1966]. 1021 p. : ill. (Encyclopedia of earth sciences, v. 1).   **EF216**

Signed articles with bibliographies ranging from the general to the highly technical, and including closely allied topics such as navigation. Numerous charts, illustrations, and tables; cross-references and index.   GC9.F3

Firth, Frank E. The encyclopedia of marine resources. N.Y. : Van Nostrand Reinhold, [1969]. 740 p. : ill.   **EF217**

Signed articles by specialists on the most significant aspects of the ocean's resources and closely related topics. Oceanography and marine engineering are given only brief treatment. Many entries include bibliographical references. Cross-references; index.   SH201.F56

Groves, Donald G. Ocean world encyclopedia / [by] Donald G. Groves [and] Lee M. Hunt. N.Y. : McGraw-Hill, c1980. 443 p. : ill.   **EF218**

Intended for nonspecialists. Includes articles on physical, geological, chemical, and biological oceanography, oceanographic instrumentation, hurricanes, international marine science organizations, and biographies of famous oceanographers. Indexed.   GC9.G76

Dictionaries

Encyclopedia of marine sciences / J.G. Baretta-Bekker, E. K. Duursma, B. R. Kuipers, editors. Berlin ; N.Y. : Springer-Verlag, c1992. 311 p. : ill., maps.   **EF219**

Some 1,850 entries covering marine chemistry, physical oceanography, marine geology, and marine biology are described in short paragraphs. Compact size, concise definitions, and black-and-white illustrations make this useful for students as well as libraries. Reference list. No index.   GC9.E56

United States. Naval Oceanographic Office. Glossary of oceanographic terms / ed. by B. B. Baker, Jr., W. R. Deebel, and R. D. Geisenderfer. 2nd ed. Wash. : U.S. Naval Oceanographic Office, 1966. 204 p. : ill. (United States. Naval Oceanographic Office. Special publication, SP-35).   **EF220**

1st ed., 1960, issued by U.S. Hydrographic Office.

Provides definitions of technical terms which "represent current and, in some places, past usage in the marine aspects of physics, chemistry, biology, geology, geophysics, geography, mathematics, and meteorology, particularly in the manner that these terms are used in the U.S. Naval Oceanographic Office research, operations, and publications."—*Pref.* Appendixes list sources of definitions; abbreviations and acronyms; and oceanographic institutions, agencies, activities, and groups.   GC9.U5

Directories

International directory of marine scientists. 3rd ed. Paris : UNESCO, 1983. 488, 173 p.   **EF221**

1st ed., 1970.

"A product of the joint FAO/IOC/UN (OETB) Aquatic Sciences and Fisheries Information System (ASFIS) with support from Unesco."—*t.p.*

Identifies approximately 2,500 institutions and 18,000 specialists in marine sciences. Scientists are grouped by institution within country. Name and subject indexes.   GC10.I57

U.S. ocean scientists & engineers: 1987 directory. Wash. : American Geophysical Union, c1987.   **EF222**

Expanded version of *U.S. directory of marine scientists*, 1982.

A directory to some 6,600 American scientists and engineers teaching or working in marine science. Data were gathered by questionnaire in 1986. Individual entries are brief, listing name, current business address and telephone, and specializations. Entries are arranged in 3 sections: alphabetic; geographic by state and current employer; area of specialization.   GC10.D57

Handbooks

Handbook of marine science. Boca Raton, Fla., CRC Pr., 1974–76. 4 v.   **EF223**

Consists of tables assembled from many sources to provide a convenient source of information for oceanographers; each volume is separately indexed.

Atlases

Rand McNally atlas of the oceans. N.Y. : Rand McNally, c1977. 208 p. : ill., maps ; 38 cm.   **EF224**

A clearly written, profusely illustrated, and well-indexed encyclopedic guide for nonspecialists. Includes information on physical and biological oceanography and on human interactions with the ocean. The final chapter is a brief encyclopedia of marine life, arranged taxonomically.   GC11.2.R35

The Times atlas and encyclopedia of the sea / ed. by Alastair Couper. 2nd ed. N.Y. : Harper & Row ; London : Times Books, 1989. 272 p. : ill., col. charts, col. maps ; 37 cm.   **EF225**

1st ed., 1983, called *The Times atlas of the oceans*.

Organized into four main sections: The ocean environment; Resources of the ocean; Ocean trade; and The world ocean. Text, maps, and photographs are combined to illustrate details of the physical, economic, and political ocean environment. Appendixes for data, chronologies, and legal regulations. Glossary, bibliography, and subject index.

G2800.T5

World ocean atlas / ed. by Sergei Georgievich Gorshkov. Oxford ; N.Y. : Pergamon, 1976–83. 3 v. : maps ; 46 cm. **EF226**

Contents: v. 1, Pacific ocean; v. 2, Atlantic ocean; v. 3, Arctic Ocean.

Includes charts on ocean bed, climate, hydrology, hydrochemistry, biogeography, navigation, and many other topics, presented with great care on beautifully colored plates. Text, keys, and captions are in Russian. A translation (poorly done) is provided only for the brief introductory text and index.

PALEONTOLOGY

Bibliography

Bibliography of vertebrate paleontology and related subjects. 1945/46–72. [Chicago?] : Soc. of Vertebrate Paleontology, 1947–72. **EF227**

Nos. 1–20 prepared from periodicals received by the Library of the American Museum of Natural History in New York. Previously included in the *News bulletin* of the Society of Vertebrate Paleontology, no. 20 (1965/66)– , prepared from working files for forthcoming volumes of Charles Lewis Camp, *Bibliography of fossil vertebrates* (EF228).

Arranged alphabetically by author. Through 1964/65, each issue in two parts: (1) the preceding year and earlier, and (2) the year covered.

Continued by: *Bibliography of vertebrate paleontology* (v. 1 [1973]–v. 5 [1978]; London : Geosystems, 1973–78). Publ. in association with the Soc. of Vertebrate Paleontology.

• Through 1974, available in machine-readable form as part of *GeoArchive* [database] (EF50).

Z6033.P2B5

Camp, Charles Lewis. Bibliography of fossil vertebrates / by C. L. Camp and V. L. Vanderhoof. [N.Y.] : Geological Soc. of America, 1940–73. 9 v. (Geological Society of America. Special papers, 27, 42; Memoir, 37, 57, 84, 92, 117, 134, 141). **EF228**

Covers 1928–72.

Consists of author catalogs, international in scope, of serial and separate publications. Subject and systematic indexes.

Continued by: Morton Green, *Bibliography of fossil vertebrates, 1973–77* (Rapid City, S.D. : South Dakota School of Mines and Technology, 1979).

Z6033.P2C32

Fleury, Bruce E. Dinosaurs : a guide to research. N.Y. : Garland, 1992. 468 p. : ill. (Garland reference library of the humanities, v. 1196). **EF229**

A compilation of citations to recent (1960–91) English-language research publications, including articles, books, and conference papers, likely to be available in university libraries. The 1,153 annotated references are grouped in nine thematic chapters, e.g., dinosaur hunters, warm-blooded dinosaurs, dinosaur ecology, dinosaur evolution. Brief bibliographic essays introduce each chapter. Time charts, glossary, and abbreviated systematic classification in appendix. Index of curricular materials, authors, subjects.

Z6033.D55F54

Hay, Oliver Perry. Bibliography and catalogue of the fossil vertebrata of North America. Wash. : U.S. Govt. Print. Off., 1902. 868 p. (U.S. Geological Survey. Bulletin, 179). **EF230**

With Hay's *Second bibliography and catalogue of fossil vertebrata of North America* (Wash. : Carnegie Inst. of Wash., 1929–30. 2 v. [Carnegie Inst. of Wash. Publ. 390, v. 1–2]), provides comprehensive author bibliographies covering North America to 1927, with subject and systematic indexes. The second compilation extends the coverage to include Greenland, Mexico, and Central America.

Supplemented by: Charles Lewis Camp and V.L. Vanderhoof, *Bibliography of fossil vertebrates* (EF228).

Hiltermann, Heinrich. Bibliographie stratigraphisch wichtiger mikropaläontologischer Publikationen von etwa 1830 bis 1958 mit Kurzreferaten / zusammengestellt und bearb. von H. Hiltermann ... [et al.]. Stuttgart : E. Schweizerbart'sche Verlagsbuchhandlung, 1961. 403 p. **EF231**

A bibliography of microfossils in connection with stratigraphic problems. International scope. Classed arrangement, with author and subject/place indexes.

Z6033.P2H5

International catalogue of scientific literature / publ. for the Internat. Council by the Royal Soc. of London. v. 1 (1901)–v. 14 (1914). London : Harrison, 1902–21. **EF232**

Section K, Paleontology. For full description, *see* EA16.

Romer, Alfred Sherwood. Bibliography of fossil vertebrates exclusive of North America, 1509–1927 / Alfred Sherwood Romer ... [et al.]. N.Y. : Geological Soc. of America, 1962. 2 v. (1544 p.). (G.S.A., memoir 87). **EF233**

A comprehensive international bibliography of serial literature, separately published volumes, and pamphlets, through the year 1927, arranged alphabetically by author. No subject index.

§ Complements Oliver Perry Hay's *Bibliography and catalogue of the fossil vertebrata of North America* (EF230). Z6033.P2R6

Indexes; Abstract journals

Bibliography and index of micropaleontology. v. 1 (Jan. 1972)– . N.Y. : Micropaleontology Pr. of the American Museum of Natural History, 1972– . Monthly. **EF234**

"This specialized bibliography and index is produced in cooperation with the American Geological Institute's (AGI) bibliographic staff. ... These records are added to the Geological Reference File (GEO-REF [EF53]) of the AGI, which is a computerized indexed reference file supported by the National Science Foundation."—*Pref., v. 1, no. 1.* QE719.B5

Encyclopedias

The encyclopedia of paleontology. Stroudsburg, Pa. : Dowden, Hutchinson & Ross, 1979. 886 p. (Encyclopedia of earth sciences, v. 7.). **EF235**

Rhodes W. Fairbridge and David Jablonski, eds.

Attempts "to provide a survey of many of the objects and concepts encompassed by this multifaceted field within the limits of a single volume. The entries are written at several conceptual levels from the most basic [to] inclusive ... the extensive reference lists and cross-references at the end of each [entry] are designed to lead the reader deeper into the subject."—*Pref.* Subject index. QE703.E52

Fossil indexes

Andrews, Henry Nathaniel. Index of generic names of fossil plants, 1820–1965 : based on the Compendium index of paleobotany of the U.S. Geological Survey. Wash., 1970. 354 p. (U.S. Geological Survey, Bull. 1300). **EF236**

Arranged alphabetically according to genus, then by species. Gives names of authors and an abbreviated citation. Complete references are given in the bibliography.

Continued by: Anna M. Blazer, *Index of generic names of fossil plants, 1966–1973* (Wash. : U.S. Govt. Print. Off., 1975. 54 p.) and Arthur Dwight Watt, *Index of generic names of fossil plants, 1974–1978* (Wash. : U.S. Govt. Print. Off.; Alexandria, Va. : U.S. Geological Survey, 1982. 63 p.). QE906.A7

Bibliography of fossil vertebrates / American Geological Inst., Soc. of Vertebrate Paleontology. 1978– . Falls Church, Va. : Amer. Geological Inst., 1978– . Annual. **EF237**
Ed. and indexed by Judith A. Bacskal and George V. Shkurkin, under supervision of Joseph T. Gregory.
Publisher varies: 1983– , publ. by Soc. of Vertebrate Paleontology.
Largely a subset of citations from the *GeoRef* database, selected, edited, and indexed by editors at the Museum of Paleontology, University of California, Berkeley. Subject and systematic indexes.
Z6033.P2B48●

Catalogue of Foraminifera / by Brooks F. Ellis and Angelina R. Messina. N.Y. : Amer. Museum of Natural History, 1940. 30 v. and supplements (looseleaf). : ill. **EF238**
Vol. 30: Index to taxonomic changes and bibliography.
For each species, arranged alphabetically by genus, gives synonymy, type reference, type figure, type description, type level, type locality, and type specimen. In many cases, includes illustrations. Supplements (1945–) have similar arrangement.
§ The same authors' *Catalogue of index Foraminifera : special publication* (1965–67. 3 v.) records the geologic and geographic distribution of Foraminifera. Bibliographic references. QL368.F6E5

Ellis, Brooks Fleming. Catalogue of Ostracoda / by Brooks F. Ellis and Angelina R. Messina. N.Y. : Amer. Museum of Natural History, 1952–64. 20 v. and supplements. **EF239**
Provides the same type of information as the author's *Catalogue of index Foraminifera*, (EF238 *note*) but is arranged stratigraphically. Beginning 1964, about two supplements per year have been issued, containing units on new species, plus some units which update previous entries. Entire set is in looseleaf format. QL444.08.E38

Fossilium catalogus. Amsterdam : Kugler, Publ. by W. Junk, 1913–93. v. 1–2. (In progress). **EF240**
Publ. in two sections: I, Animalia, Pars 1–132 (1913–93); II, Plantae, pars 1–94 (1913–91).
The two sections make up an important, comprehensive series. Each published part, written by a specialist, consists of a catalog of known species and an index and bibliography pertaining to the class covered.

Purnell, Louis R. Catalog of the type specimens of invertebrate fossils. Wash. : Smithsonian Institution Pr., 1968. pt. 1 : ill. (United States. National Museum. Bulletin, 262). (In progress). **EF241**
Contents: pt. 1, Paleozoic cephalopoda.
First in a proposed series listing invertebrate fossil specimens in the collection of the Division of Invertebrate Paleontology of the Smithsonian Institution. Arranged by subclass, then alphabetically by species. Gives author and brief reference, type, catalog number, rock unit, and geographic source of the specimen. Complete citations in bibliography. Q11.U6

Shimer, Hervey Woodburn. Index fossils of North America / by Hervey Woodburn Shimer and Robert R. Shrock. N.Y. : Wiley ; London : Chapman & Hall, [1944]. 837 p. : ill. **EF242**
Subtitle: A new work based on the complete revision and reillustration of Grabau and Shimer's *North American index fossils.*
"An index fossil is one which identifies and dates the strata or succession of strata in which it lies."—*p. 1.* This work is a systematic arrangement of descriptions of index fossil animals, with brief inclusion of fossil plants. Index of genera; index of species. QE745.S48

Treatise on invertebrate paleontology / directed and ed. by Raymond C. Moore. [N.Y.] : Geological Soc. of America, 1953–83. Pt. [A–W]. : ill. (In progress.). **EF243**
Parts are assigned letters, A-W, with a view to indicating their systematic sequence, but are published at whatever time each is ready. Parts published to date: A, C-F (Suppl. 1), G-I, K-L, N$^{1-3}$, O-R(pt.3-4), S-W (Suppl. 1-2).
The parts are divided according to phylum, and the orders, classes, genra, species, etc., in each phylum are described: their growth and development, general features, charcteristics, etc., with references to the literature.
New editions of some parts have begun to appear as: *Treatise on invertebrate paleontology,* directed and ed. by Curt Teichert (2nd ed., rev. and enl. Boulder, Colo. : Geological Soc. of America, 1970– . [In progress]). To date, pts. E^1, G. and V have been published. QE770.T7

Directories

Cleevely, R. J. World palaeontological collections. London : British Museum (Natural History) : Mansell ; N.Y. : distr. by H.W. Wilson, 1983. 365p. **EF244**
Includes list of published catalogs, alphabetical index of collectors, geographic index of institutions, and collection holdings. QE716.G72

International Paleontological Association. Directory of paleontologists of the world / [comp.] by Rex A. Doescher. 5th ed. [Wash.] : International Paleontological Assoc., 1989. 447 p. **EF245**
2nd ed., 1968; 4th ed., 1984.
Alphabetic listings of some 7,600 paleontologists include name, address, telephone, and subject specialties. Geographic and taxonomic specialty indexes. QE707.A2I61

Handbooks

Kuhn-Schnyder, Emil. Handbook of paleozoology / Emil Kuhn-Schnyder, Hans Rieber. Baltimore : Johns Hopkins Univ. Pr., c1986. 394 p. : ill. **EF246**
Translation of *Paläozoologie.*
A selective guide that aims "to provide students with a well-illustrated, condensed introduction to the systematics of fossil animals."—*Foreword.* Entries are arranged by taxon and include morphological and ecological data and numerous illustrations. Appendixes include charts of temporal distribution of fossil groups and of geologic periods, and a tabular summary of the classificiation system. Indexes of subjects and of genera and species. QE761.K8413

Kummel, Bernhard. Handbook of paleontological techniques / ed. by Bernhard Kummel, David Raup. San Francisco : Freeman, [1965]. 852 p. : ill. **EF247**
Prep. under the auspices of the Paleontological Society.
A series of essays on various techniques, followed by a section of bibliographies on paleontological techniques and other bibliographies of use to workers in this area. Indexed. QE718.K8

Mayr, Helmut. A guide to fossils / Helmut Mayr ; tr. by D. Dineley & G. Windsor. Princeton, N.J. : Princeton Univ. Pr., c1992. 256 p. : ill. (some col.). **EF248**
A collection of excellent color photographs and short descriptions for some 500 plant and animal fossils. To aid amateur collectors and students, there is a brief introduction to the field and to collecting. List of works for further reading, glossary, and fossil name index. QE711.2.M3913

Piveteau, Jean, *ed.* Traité de paléontologie. Paris : Masson, [1952–69]. 7 v. in 10 : ill. **EF249**
An excellent series offering long articles on fossil families with bibliographies, glossaries, illustrations, and index. QE711.P62

Ransom, Jay Ellis. Fossils in America : their nature, origin, identification and classification, and a range guide to collecting sites. N.Y. : Harper, [1964]. 402p. : il. **EF250**
A popularly written work with detailed information on the origin, nature, and collecting of fossils. Fossil localities are arranged by state, with subdivisions. QE746.R3

Thompson, Ida. The Audubon Society field guide to North American fossils. N.Y. : Knopf, [1982]. 846 p. : ill. **EF251**
A detailed guide for the collector, with more than 500 color plates. Appendixes; index. QE718.T5

Biography

Lambrecht, Kalman. Palaeontologi : Catalogus bio-bibliographicus / Kalman Lambrecht and W. and A. Quenstedt. 'sGravenhage : W. Junk, 1938. 495 p. (Fossilium catalogus, I, Animalia, ed. by W. Quenstedt, pars 72). **EF252**
Repr.: N.Y. : Arno Pr., 1978.
An alphabetical list of paleontologists of many countries and periods, giving full name, places and dates of birth and death, identification data, and references to biographical data.

PETROLOGY

The encyclopedia of igneous and metamorphic petrology / ed. by D. R. Bowes. N.Y. : Van Nostrand Reinhold, c1989. 666 p. : ill. (Encyclopedia of earth sciences, [v. 16]). **EF253**
In 250 signed articles, provides detailed information on the mineralogical, chemical, and physical nature of igneous and metamorphic rock types as well as more general information on their formation, location, and investigation. Articles contain short bibliographies and cross-references as well as formulas, illustrations, charts, and tables. Author and subject indexes. QE461.E56

Handbook of physical properties of rocks / ed., Robert S. Carmichael. Boca Raton, Fla. : CRC Pr., c1982–84. v. 1–3 : ill. **EF254**
Compilation of data and information about the physical, electrical, spectroscopic, seismic, magnetic, mechanical, and engineering properties of rocks. Intended for use in geology, geochemistry, petrology, geophysics, and geotechnical engineering. Chapter references and a separate index for each volume. QE431.6.P5H36

International Union of Geological Sciences. Subcommission on the Systematics of Igneous Rocks. A classification of igneous rocks and glossary of terms / ed. by Roger W. Le Maitre ... [et al]. Oxford ; Boston : Blackwell, 1989. 193 p. **EF255**
A revised classification scheme approved after 20 years of deliberation and study. In two main sections: (1) classification scheme and nomenclature for igneous rocks with a summary of all published IUGS recommendations; (2) glossary of 1,586 rock names and related terms including description of properties, original source for the name, type locality, and references to additional sources of information about the rock type. Includes an extensive bibliography, appendixes on the history of the Subcommission's work, and a wall chart illustrating the classification scheme. QE461.I547

Johannsen, Albert. A descriptive petrography of the igneous rocks. Chicago : Univ. of Chicago Pr., 1931–38. 4 v. : ill. **EF256**

Contents: v.1, Introduction, textures, classifications, and glossary (2nd ed., 1939); v.2, The quartz-bearing rocks; v.3, The intermediate rocks; v.4: pt.1, The feldspathoid rocks; pt.2, The peridotites and perknites. Index of authors, of localities, of rock names.
A standard, basic work, with bibliographical footnotes. Vol. 1 includes appendixes: Miscellaneous definitions; Definitions of textural terms. QE461.J6

Mitchell, Richard Scott. Dictionary of rocks. N.Y. : Van Nostrand Reinhold, c1985. 228 p., [4] p. of plates : ill. (some col.). **EF257**
Physical properties of rocks and histories of the origin and use of rock names are given for some 4,000 alphabetically arranged rock types. Meteoritics, natural organic materials, and gemstones are included. Includes black-and-white and color plates of specimens, a glossary of terms, and a bibliography. QE423.M58

Telberg, Vladimir George. Russian-English petrographic dictionary. N.Y. : Telberg, [1967]. 250p. **EF258**
Russian terms with English equivalents. Names and abbreviations are omitted. QE425.T4

Tomkeieff, S.I. Dictionary of petrology / ed. by E.K. Walton ... [et al]. Chichester ; N.Y. : Wiley, 1983. 680 p. **EF259**
Repr. with corrections, 1985.
Approximately 10,000 terms, with bibliographic references to early usage. Synoptic classification tables provide a subject grouping of terms and serve as a thesaurus. QE425.T65

SEISMOLOGY

Ganse, Robert A. Catalog of significant earthquakes, 2000 B.C.–1979, including quantitative casualties and damage / Robert A. Ganse, John B. Nelson. Boulder, Colo. : World Data Center A for Solid Earth Geophysics, 1981. 154 p. (Report, SE-27). **EF260**
Includes 2,484 events meeting the following criteria: damage greater than $1 million, or more than 10 deaths, or magnitude greater than 7.5. Listed chronologically and by longitude and latitude. References.
Updated by: Paul K. Dunbar, Patricia A. Lockridge, and Lowell S. Whiteside, *Catalog of significant earthquakes, 2150 B.C.–1991 A.D. : including quantitative casualties and damage* (Boulder, Colo. : National Geophysical Data Center, [1992]. 320 p.).

Montessus de Ballore, Fernand, *Comte de.* Bibliografía general de temblores y terremotos / publicada por la Sociedad Chilena de Historia y Geografía. Chile : Impr. Universitaria, 1915–19. 7 pts. (1515 p.). **EF261**
Contents: 1. pt., Teorías sismológicas. Efectos geológicos de los terremotos. Catálogos sísmicos mundiales; 2. pt., Europa septentrional y central; 3. pt., Países circunmediterráneos; 4. pt., Asia, África, y Oceanía; 5. pt., América, Tierras antárticas y océanos; 6. pt., Fenómenos accesorios. El movimiento sísmico ... Literatura sísmica. Historia de la sismología. Misceláneas; 7. pt., Prólogo. Suplemento. Apéndice. Addenda. (Indexes not published?).
Also published in *Revista chilena de historia y geografía,* 1915–19.
Covers books and periodicals from all countries, with no chronological limitations. Z6033.E1M7

Stover, Carl W. Seismicity of the United States, 1568–1989 (revised) / by Carl W. Stover and Jerry L. Coffman. Wash. : U.S. Govt. Print. Off., 1993. 418 p. : ill., maps. (U.S. Geological Survey professional paper, 1527). **EF262**
Supersedes U.S. Coast and Geodetic Survey, *Earthquake history of the United States,* ed. by J.L. Coffman ... [et al.] (1963–82 editions. Wash : U.S. Govt. Print. Off.).

A history of principal earthquakes with information on the date, location, size, and effects of each event. Data has been added, reevaluated, and recalculated for this edition. Arranged by state, then chronologically, with many isoseismal maps, photographs, and tables. References are in two tables: hypocenter and intensity and magnitude.

QE535.2.U6S77

United States earthquakes. 1928– . Golden, Colo. : U.S. Geological Survey ; Wash. : for sale by U.S. Govt. Print. Off., 1930– . Annual. **EF263**

Issuing body varies: 1928–68, U.S. Coast and Geodetic Survey; 1969–72, National Oceanic and Atmospheric Administration; 1973–83, NOAA in cooperation with the U.S. Geological Survey; 1984– , U.S. Geological Survey.

An annual report of earthquakes felt in the U. S. Includes some general discussions and information, earthquake descriptions arranged by region, descriptions and charts on miscellaneous activities, and strong-motions seismograph data.

VOLCANOLOGY

International Volcanological Association. Catalogue of the active volcanoes of the world : including solfatara fields. Naples, 1951–75. 22 pts. : ill. (In progress). **EF264**

Each part treats a different area of the world.

Usually gives for each volcano: name and location, with information on type, geographical position, and height; form and structure, with a short description of the volcano; volcanic activity, with dates of eruptions and details of occurring events or phenomena; petrography, giving kind and analysis of rocks; and a bibliography, listing principal literature. Also included are maps of craters, and information on volcanoes which had eruptions in historic time but are now extinct.

QE522.I6

Volcanoes of the world / Tom Simkin ... [et al.]. Stroudsburg, Pa. : Hutchinson Ross ; [N.Y.] : Academic Pr., c1981. 232 p. : ill. **EF265**

Subtitle: A regional directory, gazetteer, and chronology of volcanism during the last 10,000 years.

Includes a gazetteer of 5,345 volcanic names, synonyms, and feature names; a chronology of 5,564 eruptions; a regional directory of 1,343 volcanoes; and a bibliography of 709 references. QE522.V92

EG

Biological Sciences

GENERAL WORKS

Guides

Davis, Elisabeth B. Using the biological literature. N.Y. : Marcel Dekker, c1981. 286 p. (Books in library and information science, v. 35). **EG1**

An expansion of handouts intended to familiarize undergraduate and graduate students with biological literature. Divides the literature into broad categories (e.g., botany, ecology, physiology), then into subcategories. Lists important primary journals for each category, with scope of coverage. Indexed. QH303.D39

Information sources in the life sciences / ed., H. V. Wyatt. 3rd ed. London ; Boston : Butterworths, 1987. 191 p. **EG2**

1st ed., 1966, and 2nd ed., 1971, had title: *The use of biological literature*, ed. by R. T. Bottle and H. V. Wyatt.

"A number of chapters have been omitted or completely changed in this new edition."—*Pref.* The major divisions in this edition are: Current awareness; Searching by computer; Abstracts, indexes and bibliographies; Major research databases; Guides to the literature; Biochemical sciences; Microbiology; Biotechnology; Genetics; Zoology; Ecology; Botany; and History of biology. Index to major formats, subjects, and book titles. QH303.6.I54

Magel, Charles R. Keyguide to information sources in animal rights. London : Mansell ; Jefferson, N.C. : McFarland, 1989. 267 p. **EG3**

In three main parts: a general overview of the literature, an annotated bibliography of 335 works arranged chronologically, and a list of selected organizations concerned with animal rights. A "literature cited" section lists approximately 1,000 additional articles and books. Appendixes include a declaration on animal rights and a brief list of magazines and journals. Indexed. Z7164.C45M36

Nicholas, Robin. Immunology : an information profile / Robin and David Nicholas. London ; N.Y. : Mansell, c1985. 216 p. : ill. **EG4**

In three parts: (1) topical coverage of history, organizations, conferences, and literature of the field; (2) a list of 529 bibliographic sources; (3) a directory of more than 800 organizations and database hosts. Index to titles and subjects. QR182.N53

Smith, Roger C. Smith's guide to the literature of the life sciences / Roger C. Smith, W. Malcolm Reid, Arlene E. Luchsinger. 9th ed. Minneapolis : Burgess, [1980]. 223 p. **EG5**

1st–7th eds. (1943–67) had title *Guide to the literature of the zoological sciences*; 8th ed. (1972) had title *Guide to the literature of the life sciences*.

"The aim ... is to present (1) an introduction to the most useful materials for the library phase of biological research, and (2) suggestions for the reporting of research to the scientific community."—*Pref.*

Arranged by topics such as "Abstracts and abstracting journals"; "Searching the literature"; and "Preparation for scientific writing." Includes library assignments. Indexed. QH303.S6

Bibliography

International catalogue of scientific literature / publ. for the Internat. Council by the Royal Soc. of London. v. 1 (1901)–v. 14 (1914). London : Harrison, 1902–21. **EG6**

Section L, General biology. 1st–14th annual issues, 1901–14. For description of the full set, *see* EA16.

Murray, Margaret Ransome. A bibliography of the research in tissue culture : 1884–1950; an index to the literature of the living cell cultivated in vitro / Margaret Ransome Murray, Gertrude Kopech. N.Y. : Academic Pr., 1953. 2 v. (1741 p.). **EG7**

"Tissue culture has been defined as the maintenance of isolated portions of multicellular organisms in artificial containers outside the individual for considerable periods of time."—*Introd.* Represents 15,000 original articles from serials and books, expanded to 86,000 entries by cross-indexing, using a comprehensive subject classification scheme. Authors and subjects arranged in one alphabet. Entries include references to abstracts in *Biological abstracts*.

———. ———. *Supplementary author list, 1950.* (Incomplete and unverified, Oct. 1953). N.Y. : Academic Pr., 1953. 11 p.

Smit, Pieter. History of the life sciences : an annotated bibliography. N.Y. : Hafner Pr., [1974]. 1074 p. **EG8**

Contents: Chap. 1, General references and tools; Chap. 2, Historiography of the life and medical sciences; Selected list of biographies, bibliographies, etc., of famous biologists, medical men, etc., including some modern reissues of their publications; Index of personal names.

"Originated as a plan to produce an extension of the parts of Sarton's 'Guide to the History of Science' [Waltham, Mass. : Chronica Botanica Co., 1952] that deal with the life sciences."—*Introd.* More than 4,000 entries with full bibliographical information and short summary review (about 90 words). Z5320.S55

Indexes; Abstract journals

•**BioBusiness** [database]. Philadelphia : BIOSIS, 1984– . **EG9**

Available online, updated monthly.

Covers the business aspects of biological and biomedical research, especially in the areas of agriculture, food technology, bioengineering, pharmaceuticals, and other fields with substantial economic impact. International coverage drawn from journals, books, trade and business publications (such as *Wall Street journal*), newsletters, and conference proceedings. Patents are included, especially in the pharmaceutical area.

Biological & agricultural index : a cumulative subject index to periodicals in the fields of biology, agriculture, and related sciences. v. 19 (1964)– . N.Y. : Wilson, 1964– . Monthly (except Aug.) with annual cumulation. **EG10**

Continues *Agricultural index* (EJ15).

An alphabetic subject index to approximately 200 English-language periodicals in the agricultural and biological sciences. Publications of U.S. and state government agencies and of university service and research facilities are not included. The list of periodicals indexed (decided by subscriber vote) gives subscription information. Book reviews are listed by author in a separate section; no other author entries.

•Machine-readable version: *Biological & agricultural index* [database]. N.Y. : H.W. Wilson, 1983– . Available online and in CD-ROM, both updated twice weekly. Draws some 200 journals of relatively high circulation. Especially good for undergraduates. Z5073.A46

Biological abstracts. v. 1 (Dec. 1926)– . Philadelphia : BioSciences Information Service, 1926– . Semimonthly. **EG11**

Frequency varies: 1926–75, monthly.

"Reporting worldwide research in life science."—*t. p.*

The principal abstracting journal for the subject matter of biology. Preceded by *Abstracts of bacteriology*, v. 1–9, 1917–25 (Baltimore : Williams & Wilkins), and *Botanical abstracts*, v. 1–15, 1918–26 (Baltimore : Williams & Wilkins), which merged to form *Biological abstracts*.

Each issue consists of five sections: Abstracts, Author index, Biosystematic index, Generic index, and Subject index. Entries are arranged within the abstracts section according to 84 major concept headings. All titles are given in English; the language of the original, when not English, is noted. Gives affiliation of the first author. Abstracts are detailed. The Author index includes both personal and corporate names; up to ten coauthors are indexed. The Biosystematic index gives access by taxonomic categories. The Generic index gives access according to genus or genus-species names. The Subject index gives access on the basis of all significant words in the author's title or text, or words added by BIOSIS; it is a keyword-in-context index.

•Machine-readable versions: *Biological abstracts* (BA) [database] (Philadelphia : BIOSIS, 1976–), available online, updated semimonthly; and *Biological abstracts on compact disc* [database] (Philadelphia : BIOSIS, 1985–), available on CD-ROM, updated quarterly. See also *BIOSIS previews* (EG13). QH301.B37

Biological abstracts/RRM. v. 18 (Jan. 1980)– . Philadelphia : BioSciences Information Service, 1980– . Monthly. **EG12**

"Reporting worldwide research in life science."—*t.p.*

Vol. 1–17 (1967–79) had title: *Bioresearch index.*

A supplement to *Biological abstracts* (EG11), concentrating on reports, reviews, meetings, and books. Entries do not include abstracts; however, concepts (key words) are listed after the bibliographic information. Author, biosystematic, generic, and subject indexes. Semiannual cumulative indexes.

•Available in machine-readable form as part of *BIOSIS previews* (EG13). Z5321.B672

•**BIOSIS previews** [database]. Philadelphia : BIOSIS, 1969– . **EG13**

Machine-readable version of the combined *Biological abstracts* (EG11) and *Biological abstracts/RRM* (EG12).

Available online, in CD-ROM, and on diskette or magnetic tape, updated weekly.

Draws from more than 9,000 publications, including books, journal articles, conference proceedings, patents, meeting announcements. Coverage is very broad, including substantial nonclinical medical publications. Records that mention chemical substances are combined with CAS Registry Numbers in *BIOSIS previews/RN* (available through STN International). A current awareness version, *BioExpress*, includes the latest eight weeks of *BIOSIS previews* without abstracts (available through Life Sciences Network).

•**CSA life sciences collection** [database]. Bethesda, Md. : Cambridge Scientific Abstracts, c1978– . **EG14**

Machine-readable version of abstracting journals issued by the publisher, each also available as a stand-alone database: *Animal behavior abstracts*; *Biochemistry abstracts : amino-acid, peptide, and protein*; *Biochemistry abstracts: biological membranes*; *Biochemistry abstracts: nucleic acids*; *Biotechnology research abstracts*; *Calcified tissues abstracts*; *Chemoreception abstracts*; *Ecology abstracts*; *Endocrinology abstracts*; *Entomology abstracts*; *Genetics abstracts*; *Immunology abstracts*; *Marine biotechnology abstracts*; *Microbiology abstracts : algology, mycology, and protozoology*; *Microbiology abstracts : industrial and applied microbiology*; *Neurosciences abstracts*; *Oncogenes and growth factors abstracts*; *Virology and AIDS abstracts*.

Dates of coverage vary. Available online, updated monthly, and in CD-ROM as *Compact Cambridge life sciences*. CD-ROM version covers 1982 to the present and is updated quarterly.

Provides good coverage of many applied and basic fields in the sciences, including biotechnology, genetic engineering, and clinical applications. Covers journal articles, reports, books, and conference proceedings.

•**Current awareness in biological sciences** : (CABS) [database]. Oxford : Pergamon, 1982– .   **EG15**

Available online, updated monthly.

Citations covering a mix of basic biological and clinical/medical subjects, collected from more than 2,500 journals.

Current awareness in biological sciences. v. 100 (1983)– . Oxford ; N.Y. : Pergamon, 1983– . Monthly.   **EG16**

Continues in part *International abstracts of biological sciences* (EG17).

A computer-generated, subject-arranged listing of periodical articles. Coverage: biochemistry, cell and developmental biology, ecological sciences, genetics, microbiology, plant science, physiology, pharmacology, toxicology, and immunology. Abstracts as found in the earlier title were discontinued. Author index.   QH301.I475

International abstracts of biological sciences. v. 1 (1954)–v. 99 (1982). London : Pergamon, for Biological and Medical Abstracts, 1954–82. Monthly.   **EG17**

Title varies: v. 1–3, *British abstracts of medical sciences*.

Attempted to cover "the important papers in experimental biology, approaching the subject from the fundamental point of view, with emphasis on anatomy, oral biology, biochemistry, immunology and experimental pathology, microbiology, pharmacology, physiology, animal behavior, cytology, genetics and experimental zoology."—*Aims and scope*. Titles of foreign-language articles are translated into English; language of article is indicated if other than English. Abstracts are signed; not all entries carry abstracts. Author and subject indexes. Continued (without abstracts) by *Current awareness in biological sciences* (EG16).   QH301.I475

Serial sources for the BIOSIS data base. Philadelphia : BioSciences Information Service, 1971– . Annual.   **EG18**

The 1984 list includes 16,520 serials contributing to *Biological abstracts* (EG11) and *Biological abstracts/RRM* (EG12). Full titles are entered but the list is arranged by the standard BIOSIS abbreviated title. Entries include CODEN, frequency, and a number keyed to the list of 6,404 publishers at the back.

Encyclopedias

Clark, George Lindenberg. The encyclopedia of microscopy. N.Y. : Reinhold, [1961]. 693 p. : ill.   **EG19**

Alphabetical arrangement of signed articles covering instruments, uses, techniques and theories of microscopy, techniques of preparation, and the structures and substances which can be studied using microscopy. Bibliographies follow most articles. No index.   QH211BC54

Encyclopedia of human biology / [ed. by] Renato Dulbecco. San Diego, Calif. : Academic Pr., 1991. 8 v.   **EG20**

Contains more than 600 articles, averaging about nine pages each, by more than 700 contributors. The topics covered encompass all biological fields relating to humans, including anthropology, behavior, biochemistry, biophysics, cytology, ecology, evolution, genetics, immunology, neurosciences, pharmacology, physiology, and toxicology. Vol. 8 contains the subject index and cross-index of related articles. A major survey work on human biology.   QP11.E53

Encyclopedia of immunology / ed. in chief, Ivan M. Roitt, executive ed., Peter J. Delves. London ; San Diego, Calif. : Academic Pr., c1992. 3 v. (li, 1578, xci p.).   **EG21**

Contents: v. 1, ABO blood group system to Epstein-Barr virus, infection and immunity; v. 2, Erythrocytes to maternal antibodies; v. 3, Maturation of immune responses to zinc and the immune system.

Provides "the largest comprehensive reference source of current immunological knowledge available." —*Pref.* The 650 entries are listed at the beginning of each volume, and each volume has a complete subject index to all three volumes.   QR180.4.E56

Encyclopedia of microbiology / ed., Joshua Lederberg. San Diego : Academic Pr., c1992. 4 v. : ill.   **EG22**

Contents: v. 1–3, A–R; v. 4, S–Z and index.

Intends "to survey the entire field coherently, complementing material that would be included in an advanced undergraduate and graduate major course of university study."—*Pref.* Each volume contains 50–60 chapters on topics concerning microorganisms, mainly bacteria and fungi, but with some coverage of protozoa.   QR9.E53

Gray, Peter. The encyclopedia of microscopy and microtechnique. N.Y. : Van Nostrand, [1973]. 638 p. : ill.   **EG23**

Comprises signed articles, in alphabetic sequence, on instruments in theory or practice, techniques of microscopy and preparation, disciplines, individual subjects and materials intended for examination, and reagents. A list of references follows each article. Indexed.   QH203.G8

——————— The encyclopedia of the biological sciences. 2nd ed. N.Y. : Van Nostrand Reinhold, [1970]. 1027 p. : ill.   **EG24**

1st ed., 1961.

An alphabetically arranged encyclopedia of signed articles with bibliographies, covering all aspects of the broad field of the biological sciences, including biographies, but excluding the applied biological sciences and the behavioral sciences except as they apply to animals. Prepared for the nonspecialist, the teacher, the librarian, and the student, although some highly technical articles on the more specialized subjects are included. Black-and-white drawings and photographs. Indexed.   QH13.G7

Magill's survey of science. Life science series / ed. by Frank N. Magill, consulting ed., Laura L. Mays Hoopes. Pasadena, Calif. : Salem Pr., c1991. 6 v. (liv, 2763, cxlii p.).   **EG25**

Contents: v. 1, A–Central and peripheral nervous system functions; v. 2, Central metabolism regulation–Eukaryotic transcriptional control; v. 3, Positive and negative eukaryotic transcriptional control–Mammalian hormones; v. 4, Hormones and behavior–Muscular contraction; v. 5, Muscular contraction and relaxation–Sexual reproduction in plants; v. 6, Reproductive behavior and mating–X inactivation and the Lyon hypothesis.

An alphabetic arrangement of about 350 signed short essays (usually about eight pages long) on selected major topics in the life sciences (e.g., Reproductive behavior, Neurotransmitters, Ribosomes, Systematics). Each essay has sections of principal terms, summary of the phenomenon, methods of study, context, bibliography, and cross-references. Each volume begins with a table of contents and ends with alphabetical and topical lists of essay headings. Vol. 6 contains a comprehensive index of subject terms. No illustrations or diagrams. This work is most suitable as an undergraduate or secondary school resource.   QH307.2.M34

Milner, Richard. The encyclopedia of evolution : humanity's search for its origins. N.Y. : Facts on File, c1990. 481 p.   **EG26**

Quirky and aimed at a popular audience, but of interest to all libraries for the variety of off-beat information its 500 entries contain. Emphasizes human evolution, includes biographies of many well-known researchers, and treats topics as diverse as "Planet of the apes" and "Minium's dead cow quarry" (a Miocene deposit in Kansas). Illustrations include photographs, circus posters, cartoons. Indexed.   GN281.M53

Singleton, Paul. Dictionary of microbiology and molecular biology / Paul Singleton, Diana Sainsbury. 2nd ed. Chichester [West Sussex] ; N.Y. : Wiley, c1987. 1019 p. : ill.   **EG27**

Rev. ed. of 1978 ed., which had title *Dictionary of microbiology*.

Very complete, with nearly 15,000 entries that vary in length from one line to more than three pages, often with citations to sources. Terms are defined "in a way which reflects their actual usage."—*Pref.*

Appendixes include metabolic pathway charts, a bibliography of major sources, and a key to journal title abbreviations used in the entries. QR9.S56

General taxonomy

Synopsis and classification of living organisms / Sybil P. Parker, ed. in chief. N.Y. : McGraw-Hill, [1982]. 2 v. : ill. **EG28**

"In these volumes, the systematic positions and affinities of all living organisms are presented in synoptic articles for all taxa down to the family level."—*Pref.* Organized into four kingdoms—virus, monera, plantae, and animalia. Consists of 8,200 signed synoptic articles with literature references. Indexed. QH83.S89

Dictionaries

Abercrombie, M. The Penguin dictionary of biology / M. Abercrombie, C. J. Hickman, M. L. Johnson. [New ed.]. [London] : Allen Lane ; [N.Y.] : Viking, [1977]. 311 p. **EG29**

1st ed., 1951.
"This hardback edition, based on sixth paperback edition, 1977."—*verso of t.p.*
For students and general readers. QH203.A2

Chambers biology dictionary / ed., Peter M.B. Walker. Cambridge ; N.Y. : Chambers : Cambridge Univ. Pr., c1989. 324 p. : ill. **EG30**

Offers definitions, nearly all less than 100 words in length, of some 10,000 words and phrases, plus more than 100 short special articles (many illustrated) on important or difficult topics. Uses British spelling. Some controversial terms, recently introduced, such as "protoctista" and "undulipodia," are excluded. Cross-references. QH302.5.C47

Cowan, Samuel Tertius. A dictionary of microbial taxonomy. Cambridge : Cambridge Univ. Pr., [1978]. 285 p. **EG31**

Ed. by L.R. Hill.
1968 ed. had title: *A dictionary of microbial taxonomic usage.*
Intended "for those whose work brings them to taxonomy, often reluctantly."—*Pref.* Modeled on Fowler's *Dictionary of modern English usage*, so that comparisons of terms and discussions of broader subjects generally accompany the definitions. QR9.C66

The dictionary of cell biology / ed. by J.M. Lackie and J.A.T. Dow. London : Academic Pr., c1989. 262 p. **EG32**

Offers more than 4,000 entries, which include most of the commonly used terms, although some controversial terms (e.g., "protoctista" and "undulipodia") are omitted. Definitions vary in length from about ten words to 250, averaging around 40. Uses British spelling. Some 27 tables of families of terms are interspersed; a list of these is given at the beginning. No illustrations. QH575.D53

Dictionary of immunology / ed. by W.J. Herbert, P.C. Wilkinson, D.I. Stott. 3rd ed. Oxford ; Boston : Blackwell Scientific ; St. Louis : Blackwell Mosby Book Distributors, 1985. 240 p. : ill. **EG33**

1st ed., 1971; 2nd ed., 1977.
"Our aim ... has been to include a range of terms wide enough to satisfy the needs of any biologist, clinician or biochemist who requires easy reference to current immunological usage."—*Pref.* 300 entries are new and about 100 have been deleted since the 2nd ed. Maximum entry length about 200 words; approximately 2,000 entries.
QR180.4.D53

Dictionary of life sciences / ed. by Elizabeth A. Martin. 2nd ed. rev. N.Y. : Pica ; distr. by Universe Books, [1983]. 396 p. : ill. **EG34**

1st ed., 1977.
A handy, easy-to-use, concise dictionary for the life sciences. QH302.5.D52

Dumbleton, C. W. Russian-English biological dictionary. Edinburgh : Oliver & Boyd, 1964. 512p. **EG35**

Gives equivalent English terms for Russian terms in the biological sciences, excluding pathology. Includes the scientific names of species. Assumes a knowledge of Russian grammar and syntax.
QH13.D78

The Facts on File dictionary of biology / ed. by Elizabeth Tootill. Rev. and expanded ed. N.Y. : Facts On File, c1988. 326 p. : ill. **EG36**

First publ. 1981; "2nd ed.", 1981, appears to be the 1st U.S. edition. An additional revision publ. 1984.
This edition exhibits many changes that attempt to account for rapidly developing fields such as biotechnology and AIDS research. Definitions are well written and longer than those in many comparable dictionaries. QH13.F35

Gray, Peter. The dictionary of the biological sciences. N.Y. : Reinhold, [1967]. 602 p. : ill. **EG37**

A work by the author of the *Encyclopedia of the biological sciences* (EG24), made up largely of brief definitions for terms which did not warrant entries in the *Encyclopedia.* Users should note that all words from a given root are listed under that root, usually without cross-reference. QH13.G68

International dictionary of medicine and biology / editorial board, E. Lovell Becker ... [et al.] ; consulting ed., Alexandre Manuila ; Sidney I. Landau, ed. in chief. N.Y. : Wiley, c1986. 3 v. (3200 p.). **EG38**

For annotation, *see* EH100. R121.I58

Jacobs, Morris B. Dictionary of microbiology / Morris B. Jacobs, Maurice J. Gerstein, William G. Walter. Princeton, N.J. : Van Nostrand, [1957]. 276 p. : ill. **EG39**

Provides definitions only for "terms commonly used in microbiology and the related fields of bacteriology, mycology, virology, cytology, immunology and immunochemistry, serology and microscopy."—*Pref.* Includes names of families, genera, etc., of organisms. Few illustrations. QR9.J18

Jaeger, Edmund Carroll. The biologist's handbook of pronunciations. Springfield, Ill. : Thomas, [1960]. 317 p. : ill. **EG40**

Gives pronunciation of some 9,000 scientific terms used in the biological sciences. "Many commonly used terms and generic names of obvious sound and accentuation have been omitted."—*Pref.* In some cases, lists less acceptable alternatives following the preferred pronunciation. QH13.J3

———— A source-book of biological names and terms. 3rd ed. Springfield, Ill. : Thomas, [1955]. 317 p. : ill. **EG41**

1st ed. 1944; 2nd ed., 1950. Rev. 2nd printing, 1959.
An alphabetical list of some 12,000 elements from which scientific biological names and terms are made, with their Greek, Latin, or other origins and their concise meanings, with examples of usage. This edition includes some corrections in the main text and adds a supplement of more than 1,000 entries, which include "a limited number of much used geographical place-name stems employed in forming adjectival trivial and varietal names of plants and animals and ... more than 280 short biographies of persons commemorated in botanical and zoological generic names."—*Pref.* QH83.J3

Jeffrey, Charles. Biological nomenclature. 2nd ed. N.Y. : Crane, Russak, [1977]. 72 p. **EG42**

1st ed., 1973.

"The purpose of this handbook is to provide a practical guide to the use of the nomenclatural parts of taxonomic literature, to promote understanding of the problems, principles and practice of biological nomenclature and to act as an introduction to the Codes of Nomenclature themselves."—*Pref.*   QH83.J43

Lawrence, Eleanor. Henderson's dictionary of biological terms. 10th ed. N.Y. : Wiley, 1989. 637 p. : ill.   **EG43**
1st ed., 1920; 9th ed., 1979. Title and editors vary.
This edition contains more than 22,000 entries, including expanded definitions and many new terms. Acronyms and biochemical terms are included; British spelling. Appendixes contain structural formulae of important biochemical compounds and outline classifications of the various kingdoms and phyla.   QH302.5.H65

Roe, Keith E. Dictionary of theoretical concepts in biology / Keith E. Roe, Richard G. Frederick. Metuchen, N.J. : Scarecrow, 1981. 267 p.   **EG44**
Lists 1,166 named concepts and cites "original sources and reviews in which these concepts are elucidated."—*Introd.*   QH302.5.R63

Steen, Edwin Benzel. Dictionary of biology. N.Y. : Barnes & Noble, [1971]. 630 p.   **EG45**
Provides brief definitions of about 12,000 terms. "Taxonomic names, except for some of the major groups, are not included as entries with definitions; however, under their common names, representatives of the principal groups are listed and the groups are characterized."—*Pref.*   QH13.S74

Woods, Robert S. An English-classical dictionary for the use of taxonomists. [Claremont, Calif.] : Pomona College, [1966]. 331 p.   **EG46**
"The purpose ... is to present in the most adaptable form all words found in unabridged classical Greek and Latin lexicons which could conceivably be used in scientific nomenclature ..."—*Pref.*   QH83.W58

Directories

Current research in Britain : Biological sciences : CRB. [1st ed]– . Boston Spa, England : British Library Lending Division, c1985– . Annual.   **EG47**
Supersedes *Research in British universities, polytechnics and colleges.*
Volume numbering for 1st ed. appears only in the introduction.
Each edition is in four parts: *Physical sciences* (EA138); *Biological sciences*; *Social sciences* (CA46); *The humanities* (BA8).
Contents: pt. 1, Research; pt. 2, Indexes.
"National register of current [biological] research being carried out in universities, polytechnics, colleges and other institutions within the United Kingdom."—*Introd.* Index to institutions and departments in pt. 1. Indexes in pt. 2 include names of researchers, study areas (subjects), and keywords.   QH320.G7C87

The directory of North American fisheries and aquatic scientists / Beth D. McAleer, ed. 2nd ed. Bethesda, Md. : American Fisheries Society, c1987. 363 p.   **EG48**
1st ed., 1984.
Consists of several lists arranged by scientist's name, geographic location (state, province, or country), area of expertise, and type of professional activity. About 20% larger than the 1st ed.   SH203.D57

Life sciences organizations and agencies directory / Brigitte T. Darnay, Margaret Labash Young, editors. Detroit : Gale, c1988. 864 p.   **EG49**
Some 7,600 entries, arranged into 18 chapters, cover agricultural sciences, veterinary sciences, biology, and biotechnology. Each entry gives name, address, telephone, officers, publications, meetings, etc. Six of the 18 chapters are based on material from other Gale directories. Indexed.   QH321.L54

Handbooks

Altman, Philip L. Environmental biology / ed. by Philip L. Altman, Dorothy S. Dittmer ; prep. under the auspices of the Committee on Biological Handbooks. Bethesda, Md. : Federation of American Societies for Experimental Biology, [1966]. 694 p. : ill.   **EG50**
A compilation, mainly tabular, of qualitative and quantitative data on the effects on living entities of various natural and synthetic external factors, including chemical constituents of the surrounding media, radiations, and temperature. The index includes all species covered in the tables, as well as the environmental conditions and constituents considered and the physiological characteristics measured.   QH310.A395

——— Biology data book / Philip L. Altman, Dorothy S. Dittmer. 2nd ed. Bethesda, Md. : Federation of American Societies for Experimental Biology, [1972–74]. 3 v.   **EG51**
1st ed., 1964.
"A three-volume compilation of evaluated reference data in the life sciences" (*Foreword, v.3.*) in tabular form. Consists largely of quantitative data but also includes some descriptive data, such as experimental results, interrelationships of organisms and of biochemical processes, and characteristics of organisms and conditions. Vol. 1 covers genetics, cytology, reproduction, development, and growth; v. 2, biological regulators and toxins; and v. 3, nutrition, digestion, and excretion; metabolism; respiration and circulation; and blood and other fluids. Each volume is indexed separately, but there is no index to the entire set.   QH3110.A392

——— Cell biology / Philip L. Altman, Dorothy Dittmer Katz. Bethesda, Md. : Federation of Amer. Societies for Experimental Biology, [1976]. 454 p. (Biological handbooks, n.s., v. 1).   **EG52**
A detailed tabulation of data on the cell, with emphasis on vertebrate cells. 102 tables are arranged in seven sections: (1) General cell characteristics; (2) Cell environment; (3) Cell periphery; (4) Mitochondria: (5) Endoplasmic reticulum, microsomes, ribosomes, and Golgi; (6) Lysosomes, peroxisomes, granules, and microbodies; (7) Nuclei. Includes appendixes of animal and plant names.   QH581.2.C34

——— Respiration and circulation / comp. and ed. by Philip L. Altman and Dorothy S. Dittmer. Bethesda, Md. : Federation of Amer. Societies for Experimental Biology, [1971]. 930 p.   **EG53**
Prep. under the auspices of the Committee on Biological Handbooks.
Constitutes a complete revision and combination of *Handbook of respiration* (1958) and *Handbook of circulation* (1959).
A collection of authoritative data, quantitative and descriptive, on respiration and circulation. For the most part concerned with man and other vertebrates but includes sections on invertebrates and on plants.   QP101.R47

CRC handbook of microbiology / editors, Allen I. Laskin, Hubert A. Lechevalier. 2nd ed. Boca Raton, Fla. : CRC Pr., c1977–c1988. 9 v. in 10 : ill.   **EG54**
Contents: v. 1, Bacteria; v. 2, Fungi, algae, protozoa, and viruses; v. 3, Microbial composition: amino acids, proteins, and nucleic acids; v. 4, Microbial composition: carbohydrates, lipids, and minerals; v. 5, Microbial products; v. 6, Growth and metabolism; v. 7, Microbial transformation; v. 8, Toxins and enzymes; v. 9A, Antibiotics; v. 9B, Antimicrobial inhibitors.

A comprehensive source of current information in microbiology. Each volume consists of signed articles; many have tabular data, illustrations, and lists of references. Some of the latter are extensive. References are listed at the end of each section. Each volume has taxonomic and subject indexes, but there is no general index.

An abbreviated edition has title: *Practical handbook of microbiology* (EG56). QR6.C2

LABFAX series. San Diego, Calif. : Academic Pr., 1991–93. v. 1–7. (In progress). **EG55**
Contents: Molecular biology (1991); Cell structure (1992); Cell biology (1992); Virology (1993); Plant molecular biology (1993); Immunochemistry (1993); Biochemistry (1993).
Convenient laboratory guides to selected standard methods and protocols used in each field.

Practical handbook of microbiology / ed. by William M. O'Leary. Boca Raton, Fla. : CRC Pr., c1989. 681 p. : ill. **EG56**
A condensed version of the most useful sections of *CRC handbook of microbiology* (EG54), covering bacteria, mycoplasmas, fungi, and viruses, and including both the table of contents and index from the parent work. QR72.5.P73

Style manuals

Council of Biology Editors. CBE Style Manual Committee. CBE style manual. 5th ed., rev. and expanded. Bethesda, Md. : Council of Biology Editors, Inc., [1983]. 324 p. **EG57**
Subtitle: A guide for authors, editors, and publishers in the biological sciences.
1st–4th eds. 1960–78; title varies.
Intended primarily as a guide for authors preparing articles for publication in biological journals. New chapters deal with ethical conduct, copyright, and illustrative material. There is an annotated list of other, similar works. Subject index. Z250.6.B5C65

Zweifel, Frances W. A handbook of biological illustration. 2nd ed. Chicago : Univ. of Chicago Pr., 1988. 137 p. : ill. **EG58**
1st ed., 1961.
"Intended primarily for the guidance of the student or professional biologist who is unfamiliar with materials and techniques of illustrating. ..."—*Pref.* A succinct how-to book, emphasizing black-and-white drawing, but including some discussion of color illustration. Does not include photography but does cover graphs, maps, and lettering. QH318.Z97

History

Dawes, Benjamin. A hundred years of biology. London : Duckworth, [1952]. 429 p. : ill. **EG59**
Bibliography, p.385–418. QH305.D3

Biography

The biographical dictionary of scientists : biologists / David Abbott, gen. ed. N.Y. : Peter Bedrick Bks., [1983]. 182 p. **EG60**
Includes a selection of significant biologists from ancient times through the present day. The dictionary emphasizes the nature and significance of the subjects' work. Biographees are clustered under one name in cases of collaboration, with *see* references in the text. Glossary. Subject and name index. QH26.B54

Statistics

Fisher, Ronald A. Statistical tables for biological, agricultural and medical research / Sir Ronald A. Fisher, Frank Yates. 6th ed. rev. and enl. N.Y. : Hafner ; Edinburgh ; London : Oliver and Boyd, [1963]. 146 p. **EG61**
1st ed., 1938.
34 tables, with introductions, providing solutions to statistical problems with direct application to biological, agricultural, and medical research. QH324.F52

ECOLOGY

Burke, John Gordon. Guide to ecology information and organizations / John Gordon Burke, Jill Swanson Reddig. N.Y. : Wilson, 1976. 292 p. **EG62**
Intended primarily for public libraries and their patrons. Includes "both print and nonprint materials, as well as names of persons who are willing to share their expertise."—*Introd.* In various sections: Citizen action guides, Indexes, Reference books, Histories, Monographs, Government publications, Nonprint media, Periodicals, Organizations, Government officials. Includes a directory of publishers and distributors, and a detailed index. Z5861.B87

Ecological abstracts. 1990– . [Norwich, Eng. : Geo Abstracts Ltd.]. Monthly. **EG63**
This service abstracts about 700 journals as well as books, conference proceedings, reports, and dissertations. Combines with the two sections of *Geographical abstracts* (Physical geography, CL32, and Human geography, CL31), *International development abstracts* (CH44) and other databases to form *GEOBASE* database (CL30). QH540.E27

Grzimek's encyclopedia of ecology / ed. in chief, Bernhard Grzimek. English ed. N.Y. : Van Nostrand Reinhold, [1976]. 705 p. : ill. **EG64**
Ed. by Bernhard Grzimek, Joachim Illies, Wolfgang Klausewitz. Translation of the 1973 German ed.
"A supplement to the thirteen-volume Grzimek's Animal Life Encyclopedia [EG226]."—*Foreword.*
Some 40 experts have made contributions to the 33 essays in this one-volume encyclopedia. In pt. 1, "The environment of animals," the 22 essays are arranged under four headings: (1) Adaptations to the abiotic environment; (2) Adaptations to the biotic environment; (3) Habitats and their fauna; (4) Man as a factor in the environment of animals. Pt. 2 entitled "The environment of man." Index. QL45.G7913

Lincoln, Roger J. A dictionary of ecology, evolution and systematics / Roger J. Lincoln, G. A. Boxshall, P. F. Clark. Cambridge : Cambridge Univ. Pr., [1982]. 298 p. **EG65**
Brief definitions of terms in the broad field of evolutionary biology. There are 21 brief appendixes with useful information. QH540.4.L56

Sheldon, Joseph Kenneth. Rediscovery of creation : a bibliographical study of the church's response to the environmental crisis. Metuchen, N.J. : Amer. Theological Libr. Assoc. : Scarecrow, 1992. 1 v. (ATLA bibliography series, no. 29). **EG66**
For annotation, *see* BC223. Z7799.8.S44

NATURAL HISTORY

Bibliography

American Museum of Natural History. Library. Research catalog of the Library of the American Museum of Natural History : authors. Boston : G. K. Hall, 1977. 13 v. **EG67**

"Provides access by personal, corporate, and joint authors, compilers, editors, and illustrators of note, as well as biographical and critical materials. ... Of particular value are author entries for journal articles and chapters in books."—*Pref.* Z7409.A43

A concordance to Darwin's Origin of species, first edition / ed. by Paul H. Barrett, Donald J. Weinshank, and Timothy T. Gottleber. Ithaca, N.Y. : Cornell Univ. Pr., [1981]. 834 p. **EG68**

A keyword-in-context concordance based on the 1964 Harvard Univ. Pr. reprint of the 1st ed. There is a list of stop words and their frequency. QH365.O8B37

Freeman, Richard Broke. British natural history books, 1495–1900 : a handlist. [Folkestone, Eng.] : Dawson ; [Hamden, Conn.] : Archon Books, [1980]. 437 p. **EG69**

Lists "all books about the fauna and flora of the British Islands, including all Ireland, the Channel Islands. ... all general natural history books written by inhabitants of these islands, and ... translations into English of relevant books by foreign authors and a few American books which have appeared in British editions."—*Introd.* Lists 4,206 publications by main entry, giving full bibliographic information. Includes a list by imprint date and a subject inex. Z7408.G7F73

———— The works of Charles Darwin : an annotated bibliographical handlist. 2nd ed. Rev. & enl. Folkestone, [Eng.] : Dawson ; [Hamden, Conn.] : Archon Books, [1977]. 235 p. **EG70**

1st ed., 1965.

Contents: pt. 1, Books and pamphlets; pt. 2, Publications in serials.

"The first part of the ... list contains all the editions and issues of books, pamphlets and circulars, both British and foreign, which I have seen, or seen reliably recorded, from the first in 1835 up to the end of 1975. ... The second part contains a list of papers, notes and letters which were originally published in serials."—*Pref.* A listing of 1,805 items. Includes a review of the publication history for each title listed in the books and pamphlets section. Indexed.

§ A complementary work is *A concordance to Darwin's Origin of the species, first edition* (EG68). Z8217.F7

Meisel, Max. Bibliography of American natural history : the pioneer century, 1769–1865. Brooklyn, N.Y. : Premier Pub. Co., 1924–29. 3 v. **EG71**

Subtitle continues: The role played by the scientific societies; scientific journals; natural history museums and botanic gardens; state geological and natural history surveys; federal exploring expeditions in the rise and progress of American botany, geology, mineralogy, paleontology and zoology.

Vol. 1, Annotated bibliography of the publications relating to the history, biography and bibliography of American natural history and its institutions during colonial times and the pioneer century, which have been published up to 1924; with a classified subject and geographical index and a bibliography of biographies; v.2 and 3, Chronological bibliography of the publications of institutions which have contributed to the rise and progress of American natural history which were founded or organized between 1769 and 1865, with short histories of the institutions. Bibliography of books, articles, and miscellaneous publications not published in the proceedings and transactions of scientific societies, etc. Chronological tables; index of authors and institutions; addenda. Z7408.U5M5

Indexes

Munz, Lucile Thompson. Index to illustrations of living things outside North America : where to find pictures of flora and fauna / Lucile Thompson Munz, Nedra G. Slauson. [Hamden, Conn.] : Archon Books, 1981. 441 p. **EG72**

"A companion volume to John W. Thompson's *Index to illustrations of the natural world ... [EG73].*"—*t.p.*

An index to illustrations of more than 9,000 species of animals and plants to be found in 209 books published since 1963. Subject entries are by common name; a scientific name index supplies the latter. Z7998.N67M85

Thompson, John W. Index to illustrations of the natural world : where to find pictures of the living things of North America / John W. Thompson, comp. ; Nedra Slauson, ed. Syracuse, N.Y. : Gaylord Professional Publ., 1977. 265 p. **EG73**

Approximately 6,200 entries for plants, birds, and animals. For each item is listed the common name, scientific name, and citations to three to ten illustrations. The pictures cited are found in a total of 178 books which "have been published since 1960, but some classic works published earlier have been included. ... The availability of the books in most medium-size and large libraries was an important criterion in selection."—*Introd.* Includes a 77-page index from the scientific name to the common name.

§ *See also*: Beth Clewis, *Index to illustrations of animals and plants* (N.Y. : Neal-Schuman, 1991. 217 p.), and "Scientific illustration" in Section EA. Z7998.N67T45

Encyclopedias

Grzimek's encyclopedia of evolution / ed. in chief, Bernhard Grzimek. English ed. N.Y. : Van Nostrand Reinhold, [1976]. 560 p. : ill. **EG74**

Ed. by Gerhard Heberer and Herbert Wendt.

Translation of the 1972 German ed.

More than 200 contributors from all the world have prepared the 23 essays in this encyclopedia. The many general aspects of evolutionary theory, phylogeny, genetics effect, paleontology, paleobotany, paleogeology, and the evolution of man are covered, as well as such subjects as the origin of life, early history of the earth, the path to warm-bloodedness, origin of mammals, the conquest of the air, etc. Includes supplementary readings and index. QE711.2.G79

Lincoln, Roger J. The Cambridge illustrated dictionary of natural history / R.J. Lincoln and G.A. Boxshall. Cambridge ; N.Y. : Cambridge Univ. Pr., 1987. 413 p. : ill. **EG75**

Based in part on the authors' *Dictionary of ecology, evolution and systematics* (EG65). "The major taxonomic groups ... are included, down to the level of order. For flowering plants, vertebrate animals and the economically more important insect groups, the coverage extends further, to include families."—*Pref.* Many common names are included, but only as cross-references to higher taxa. Defines virtually no organismal body parts. Includes about 700 small but clear stippled black-and-white drawings and some maps and charts.

§ Appropriate for both scientifically literate general readers and undergraduates, but both this work and *The Oxford dictionary of natural history* (EG78) are useful compendiums of terms even for specialists. The two works overlap less than 50%, the *Oxford* being somewhat more scholarly. QH13.L56

Dictionaries

Compton's dictionary of the natural sciences. Chicago : Compton, [1966]. 2 v. : ill. **EG76**

Ed. in chief, Charles A. Ford.

Written in simple, easily understandable language, this work is useful not only to young people, but to nonspecialists at all educational levels. Entries run heavily to plants, animals, birds, fishes, insects, and the like, but there are entries for terms in geology, astronomy, etc. Genus and scientific names are given for plants, etc., as applicable. An "Illustrated index and glossary of terms" offers definitions of numerous terms (with pronunciation) not included in the main text, together with references (mainly from variant forms) to articles in the text.

QH13.C65

Fitter, Richard Sidney Richmond. The Penguin dictionary of British natural history / Richard Sidney Fitter, Maisie Fitter. [Harmondsworth, Eng.], Penguin, [1967]. 348 p. **EG77**

"In this dictionary of the natural history of the British Isles the term 'natural history' is interpreted in the broadest sense to include all living things and natural phenomena of the earth and its atmosphere."—*Scope.* QH137.F539

The Oxford dictionary of natural history / ed. by Michael Allaby. Oxford ; N.Y. : Oxford Univ. Pr., 1985. 688 p. **EG78**

An alphabetical arrangement of about 14,000 entries, most less than 100 words in length. Intended primarily for students and amateur naturalists, this is nevertheless a good compilation of terms in common use by the several disciplines that make up the general field of natural history (e.g., earth and atmospheric sciences, genetics, taxonomy, elementary cell biology). No diagrams or illustrations. QH13.O9

Directories

Conservation directory. 1956– . Wash. : Nat. Wildlife Federation. Annual. **EG79**

Subtitle: A list of organizations, agencies and officials concerned with natural resource use and management.

Supersedes *Directory of organizations and officials concerned with the protection of wildlife and other natural resources* (title varies), first publ. 1900.

A classified directory which emphasizes U.S., international, and Canadian organizations and agencies. Includes national, state, and provincial governments. For most entries gives address, scope of work or concern, personnel information, subagencies or subprograms, and publications. Includes miscellaneous information such as U.S. national wildlife refuges, forests, parks, and seashores. Personal name index. S920.C64

The naturalists' directory and almanac (international). 43rd ed.– . Gainesville, Fla. : Sandhill Crane Pr., c1981– . **EG80**

Comp. and ed. by Ross H. Arnett and Mary E. Arnett. Publisher and place of publication vary.

Supersedes *The naturalist's directory* (began publ. 1877; some editions called *International scientist's directory*) and *The naturalist's directory, international* (1958–1975).

The directory section is an alphabetical listing of naturalists with addresses. The almanac section includes indexes to the naturalists by country, city, and reference number, a geographical list of museums and zoological and botanical gardens, and miscellaneous information. Has occasional supplements between editions. Q145.S4

Handbooks

Audubon Society field guide series. N.Y. : Knopf, 1977– . [v. 1–]. **EG81**

Each guide in the series is written by an authority. Virtually limited to the contiguous U.S.; illustrated with colored photographs. Generic and English name index in each volume.

Titles in the series are called *A field guide to North American*: birds, Eastern region edition; birds, Western region edition; butterflies; fishes; fossils; insects; mammals; reptiles and amphibians; rocks and minerals; seashells; seashore creatures; trees, Eastern edition; trees, Western edition; wildflowers, Eastern region; wildflowers, Western region; natural places of the mid-Atlantic states (v. 1, coastal; v. 2, inland).

Collins, Henry Hill. Harper & Row's complete field guide to North American wildlife : Eastern edition. N.Y. : Harper & Row, [1981]. 714 p. : ill. **EG82**

Subtitle: Covering 1500 species of birds, mammals, reptiles, amphibians, food and game fishes of both fresh and salt waters, mollusks, and the principal marine invertebrates occuring in North America east of the 100th meridian from the 55th parallel to Florida north of the Keys.

A substantial revision of *Complete field guide to American wildlife: east, central and north* (1959). Indexed. QL151.C62

Jaques, Harry Edwin. Pictured-key nature series. Dubuque, Ia. : Wm. C. Brown, 1946– . [v. 1–]. **EG83**

A series of popular, illustrated handbooks for identifying plants, animals, etc., suitable for the beginner but scientifically reliable. Titles begin *How to know …,* and include such topics as beetles, economic plants, insects, land birds, living things, plant families, protozoa, trees, water birds, weeds.

Metcalf, Robert Lee. Destructive and useful insects : their habits and control / Robert L. Metcalf, Robert A. Metcalf. 5th ed. N.Y. : McGraw-Hill, c1993. 1 v. (various pagings) : ill. **EG84**

4th ed., 1962, by C.L. Metcalf and W.P. Flint.

"Intended as a text … in entomology and also as a guide or reference book … [containing] up-to-date and reliable information about the many kinds of insect pests."—*Introd.* Contains chapters on topics in general entomology (e.g., morphology, development, classification) followed by chapters on 372 of the most important insect pests of crops and gardens, as well as those that atack and annoy humans and affect their health. Each description includes references. Index. Review: *Choice* 30 (June 1993): review 30-5572. SB931.M47

Peterson, Roger Tory. The Peterson field guide series. Boston : Houghton Mifflin, 1947– . [v. 1–]. **EG85**

Designed as basic guides for the nature student, beginner, or expert, each volume by a specialist in the subject.

Titles in the series are called *A field guide to*: birds; Western birds; shells of the Atlantic and Gulf coasts and the West Indies; butterflies; mammals; Pacific coast shells (including shells of Hawaii and the Gulf of California); rocks and minerals; birds of Britain and Europe; animal tracks; ferns and their related families of Northeastern and Central North America; trees and shrubs; reptiles and amphibians of Eastern and Central North America; birds of Texas and adjacent states; Rocky Mountain wildflowers; stars and planets; Western reptiles and amphibians; wildflowers of Northeastern and North-Central North America; mammals of Britain and Europe; insects of America north of Mexico; Mexican birds; birds' nests (found east of Mississippi River); Pacific states wildflowers; edible wild plants of Eastern and Central North America; Atlantic seashore; Western birds' nests; atmosphere; coral reefs of the Caribbean and Florida; Pacific coast fishes; beetles; moths; Southwestern and Texas wildflowers; Atlantic coast fishes.

Ransom, Jay Ellis. Harper & Row's complete field guide to North American wildlife. Western edition. N.Y. : Harper & Row, [1981]. 809 p. : ill. **EG86**

Subtitle: Covering 1800 species of birds, mammals, reptiles, amphibians, food and game fishes of both fresh and salt waters, mollusks, and the principal marine invertebrates occurring in North America west of the 100th meridian from the 55th parallel to the border of Mexico.

Indexed. QL151.R36

Annuals

Audubon wildlife report. 1985–1989/1990. N.Y. : National Audubon Society, c1985–c1990. Annual.   **EG87**
Published: Orlando, Fla. : Academic Pr., 1987; San Diego, Calif. : Academic Pr., 1988–90.
Each volume contains chapters by specialists on major problems, issues, and developments affecting fish and wildlife resources, a chapter on a featured agency, and chapters on species selected annually for each report (14 in 1988–89). A good source for information on the organization of, and important personnel in, governmental agencies concerned with the environment. Index to subjects.   QL84.2.A9

BOTANY

General works

Bibliography

Bay, Jens Christian. Bibliographies of botany : a contribution toward a bibliotheca bibliographica. Jena : Fischer, 1909. .   **EG88**
Originally publ. in *Progressus rei botanicae* 3, pt.2 (1909) : 331–456.
A valuable, annotated historical bibliography of bibliographies including detailed records of periodicals; general, local, and subject bibliographies; library catalogs; auction and sales catalogs, etc.   Z5351.A1B3

Beale, Helen Purdy. Bibliography of plant viruses and index to research. N.Y. : Columbia Univ. Pr., 1976. 1495 p.   **EG89**
This international bibliography of plant virus articles covers a span of 78 years, 1892–1970. More than 29,000 entries arranged alphabetically by author. The virus diseases included are chiefly those of higher plants. Extensive subject indexes.   Z5185.V5B42

Davis, Elisabeth B. Guide to information sources in the botanical sciences. Littleton, Colo. : Libraries Unlimited, 1987. 175 p.   **EG90**
Arranged by subject. "The purpose of this guide is to provide a useful survey of information sources for students, librarians, avocational and professional botanists."—*Pref.* Excludes agriculture, horticulture and gardening. Index to titles, authors, and major subjects.   Z5351.D38

Frodin, D. G. Guide to standard floras of the world. Cambridge : Cambridge Univ. Pr., [1984]. 619 p.   **EG91**
Subtitle: An annotated, geographically arranged systematic bibliography of the principal floras, enumerations, checklists and chorological atlases of different areas.
Geographical index; author index.   Z5351.F76

Nissen, Claus. Die botanische Buchillustration : ihre Geschichte und Bibliographie. 2. Aufl. Stuttgart : A. Hiersemann, 1966. 3 v. in 1.   **EG92**
1st ed. in 2 v., 1951–52.
Consists of a reproduction of the two volumes of the 1st ed. together with a 94-p. supplement as v. 3.
Vol. 1 offers a succinct presentation of the history of botanical book illustration, emphasizing German artists but including brief discussions on the art and artists of other countries. Vol. 2 contains an alphabetical listing of authors and their works, with references to the artists of the illustrations therein; an alphabetical list of anonymous works and serial publications, with references to artists; an index to ar-

tists, with codes designating the mediums in which they worked; subject and geographical indexes; an author index for both volumes; and addenda.   Z5351.N49

Stafleu, Frans Anthonie. Taxonomic literature : a selective guide to botanical publications and collections with dates, commentaries and types / Frans A. Stafleu and Richard S. Cowan. 2nd ed. Utrecht : Bohn, Scheltema & Holkema, 1976–88. 7 v.   **EG93**
Previous ed., 1967.
Attempts to give extensive information concerning the authors of botanical works "by going into more detail with respect to their collections, the biographical and bibliographical literature about them (one aspect of the book now is that it has become a 'bibliography of bibliographies'), and possibly further information of use for the systematist or for the historian of botany. We also provide information on outstanding botanical explorers and collectors."—*Introd.* Each volume includes indexes of titles and names.   QK96.R4

Swift, Lloyd H. Botanical bibliographies : a guide to bibliographic materials applicable to botany. Minneapolis : Burgess, [1970]. 804 p.   **EG94**
This is the first part of a projected "Guide to literature useful in botany" designed primarily for the beginning graduate student. Arranged in 65 numbered sections, the first seven of which are concerned with general bibliography and the remainder with bibliographies of particular subject areas. Introductory notes for each section indicate scope or special features of the more important bibliographies, and suggested subject headings for use in searching the general bibliographies are noted in each section. Index of authors, subjects, and titles.
Z5551.A1S8

Early

Hunt, Rachel McMasters Miller. Catalogue of botanical books in the collection of Rachel McMasters Miller Hunt. Pittsburgh : Hunt Botanical Lib., 1958–61. v. 1–2 in 3. : ill., facsims.   **EG95**
Contents: v. 1, Printed books, 1477–1700, with several manuscripts of the 12th, 15th, 16th & 17th centuries, comp. by Jane Quinby; v. 2, pt. 1, Introduction to printed books 1701–1800, comp. by Allan Stevenson; pt. 2, Printed books, 1701–1800, comp. by Allan Stevenson.
A catalog of the collection, which is now the property of Carnegie Institute of Technology, arranged chronologically by date of imprint. Each entry consists of a detailed bibliographic description, collation, physical description, and annotation, with a list of references. Each volume contains its own detailed index; in addition, v. 2, pt. 2, has an index to scientific names. v. 2, pt. 1, includes a comprehensive article on a bibliographical method for the description of botanical books, a list of bibliographic sources, and lists of symbols and abbreviations.
Z5360.H83

Jackson, Benjamin Daydon. Guide to the literature of botany : being a classified selection of botanical works, including nearly 6000 titles not given in Pritzel's "Thesaurus.". London : publ. for the Index Society by Longmans, 1881. 626 p. (Index Society, London. Publications, v. 8).   **EG96**
A selective listing of approximately 9,000 works in the form of a short-title catalog, classified by type of publication (for general works), or by subject. Individual articles from serials are not included, but serial publications are cited in a separate section. The addendum contains citations which were found too late for inclusion in the main text. The index covers all sections of the book.   Z5351.J12

Pritzel, Georg August. Thesaurus literaturae botanicae : omnium gentim, inde a rerum botanicarum initiis ad nostra usque tempora, quindecim millia operum recensens. Ed. novam reformatam. Lipsiae : Brockhaus, 1872–[77]. 576 p.   **EG97**
Repr.: Milan : Görlizh, 1950.

A bibliography attempting to include all separately published books which appeared through the third quarter of the 19th century. Arranged alphabetically by author, with some brief biographical information and references to *Catalogue of scientific papers.* "Anonyma et periodica" cited in a separate section. Systematic, topical and geographical, author, and anonymous titles indexes. Z5351.P96

Reuss, Jeremias David. Repertorium commentationum a societatibus litterariis editarum / secundum disciplinarum ordinem digessit I. D. Reuss .... Gottingae : apud Henricum Dieterich, 1801–21. 16 v. **EG98**
T. 2, Botanica et mineralogia; T. 6, Oeconomia. For full description, *see EA21.* Z5051.R44

Modern

Barton, Lela Viola. Bibliography of seeds. N.Y. : Columbia Univ. Pr., 1967. 858 p. **EG99**
More than 20,000 citations in author arrangement, with a plant index for both scientific and common names and a subject index. Based on a file of literature references maintained at the Boyce Thompson Institute for Plant Research. Coverage includes seed research, seed technology, and agricultural practices worldwide, to June 1, 1964. Z5354.S4B3

Blake, Sidney Fay. Geographical guide to floras of the world : an annotated list with special reference to useful plants and common plant names. Pts. 1–2. Wash. : U.S. Govt. Print. Off., 1942–61. v. 1–2. (U.S. Department of Agriculture. Miscellaneous publication, no. 401, 797.). (In progress?). **EG100**
Joint contribution from the U.S. Bureau of Plant Industry and the U.S. Dept. of Agriculture Library.
Contents: pt. 1, Africa, Australia, North America, South America, and Islands of the Atlantic, Pacific, and Indian Oceans; pt. 2, Finland, Sweden, Norway, Denmark, Iceland, Great Britain with Ireland, Netherlands, Belgium, Luxembourg, France, Spain, Portugal, Andorra, Monaco, Italy, San Marino, and Switzerland.
An annotated list of floras and floristic works, including those in periodical literature. Author index in each volume includes birth and death dates. Z5358.A12B5

Boureau, Édouard. Rapport sur la paléobotanique dans le monde = World report on palaeobotany / rassemblé par Ed. Boureau, avec la collaboration de C. A. Arnold [et al.]. Utrecht, 1956–71. v. 1–8. (Regnum vegetabile, 7, 11, 19, 24, 35, 42, 57, 78). **EG101**
Ed. by the International Organization of Palaeobotany and published by the International Bureau for Plant Taxonomy and Nomenclature.
An international bibliography of paleobotany. Covers 1950–65, each volume including additional entries for all previous volumes. Includes 16,186 consecutively numbered entries in the eight issues published to date.
Beginning with the second issue (1958) each bibliography (except no. 4) has been preceded by a directory of paleobotanists, "Paléobotanistes du monde."

British Museum. Department of Printed Books. A catalogue of the works of Linnaeus (and publications more immediately relating thereto) preserved in the libraries of the British Museum (Bloomsbury) and the British Museum (Natural History) (South Kensington). 2nd ed. London : Museum, 1933. 246 p., 68 p. : ill. **EG102**

———— An index to the authors (other than Linnaeus) mentioned in the Catalogue .... London : Museum, 1936. 59 p. **EG103**
Z8508.B86

Index londinensis to illustrations of flowering plants, ferns and fern allies : being an emended and enlarged edition continued up to the end of the year 1920 of Pritzel's Alphabetical register of representations of flowering plants and ferns comp. from botanical and horticultural publications of the XVIIIth and XIXth centuries / prep. under the auspices of the Royal Horticultural Society of London at the Royal Botanic Gardens, Kew, by O. Stapf. Oxford : Clarendon Pr., 1929–31. 6 v. **EG104**
Added title page: Iconum botanicarum index londinensis.
Includes almost all references found in Pritzel (2. ausg. Berlin, 1861–66) plus later material. Arrangement is alphabetic by genera. No list of references from abbreviations to full titles.
————. *Supplement for the years 1921–35,* prep. under the auspices of the Royal Horticultural Society of London at the Royal Botanic Gardens, Kew, by W. C. Worsdell under the direction of Arthur W. Hill (Oxford : Clarendon Pr., 1941. 2 v.).
"This supplement to the six volumes of the *Index londinensis …* now concludes that work. … Although no further supplements are to be issued, it has been arranged that references to new illustrations shall be given in the entries of new names included in future supplements of the *Index kewensis* [EG128]. from 1936 onwards. Such entries will be prefixed by an asterisk."—*Pref., v. 1.*
Includes references to illustrations from periodicals and independent works published during the years 1921–35, inclusive, and also some references from books prior to 1921 not included in the main work.

International catalogue of scientific literature / publ. for the Internat. Council by the Royal Soc. of London. v. 1 (1901)–v. 14 (1914). London : Harrison, 1902–21. **EG105**
Section M, Botany. 1st–14th annual issues, 1901–14. For description of the full set, *see EA16.*

Merrill, Elmer Drew. A bibliography of eastern Asiatic botany / by Elmer D. Merrill and Egbert H. Walker. Jamaica Plain, Mass. : Arnold Arboretum of Harvard Univ., 1938. 719 p. **EG106**
From title page: "Sponsored by the Smithsonian Institution, Arnold Arboretum of Harvard University, New York Botanical Garden, Harvard-Yenching Institute."
A comprehensive, briefly annotated bibliography of books and articles on the taxonomic botany of China, Japan, Formosa, Korea, Manchuria, Mongolia, Tibet, and eastern and southern Siberia, through 1936; where pertinent, papers pertaining to adjacent geographical areas and peripheral subject areas are included. Authors and titles are included in one alphabetic list. Appendixes: Older Oriental works; Reference lists of Oriental serials; Reference lists of Oriental authors. Subject, geographic, and systematic indexes.
————. ————. *Supplement 1–* , by Egbert H. Walker (Wash. : American Institute of Biological Sciences, 1960–). Covers through the year 1958 and includes pre-1936 references noted too late for inclusion in the original *Bibliography.*

National Agricultural Library (U.S.). Plant science catalog : botany subject index. Boston : Microphotography Co., 1958. 15 v. **EG107**
A photographic reproduction of the subject card catalog section of the Plant science catalog of the U.S. Dept. of Agriculture Library, compiled from 1903 to July 18, 1952, when work on it ceased because of lack of funds. Worldwide in scope; contains references to botanical literature from earliest times, as published in books and periodicals.

Sachet, Marie-Hélène. Island bibliographies : Micronesian botany; Land environment and ecology of coral atolls; Vegetation of tropical Pacific islands / Marie-Hélène Sachet, Frances Raymond Fosberg. [Wash.] : Nat. Academy of Sciences—Nat. Research Council, 1955. 577 p. (National Research Council (U.S.), no. 335). **EG108**
Compiled under the auspices of the Pacific Science Board.
In three separate sections, as indicated in the title, arranged alphabetically by author, and each with its own index to geographical locations and subjects.

Includes books, periodical articles, and some unpublished works, with no limitations on date or source, to Nov. 1954. List of serial abbreviations and addenda.

————. ————. *Supplement* (Wash. : National Academy of Sciences, 1971. 427 p.).

Follows the plan of the main volume. Lists new publications, some older items not included in the main work, and incorporates the addenda from that work.

Sandbergs Bokhandel, Stockholm. A catalogue of the works of Linnaeus issued in commemoration of the 250th anniversary of the birthday of Carolus Linnaeus, 1707–1778. Stockholm, [1957]. 179 p. : ill.   **EG109**

Based on the collection of Axel Liljedahl.

892 entries, giving short bibliographic, historic, and descriptive notes on most items. In sections according to form or topic. Includes biographies and bibliographies. Indexes to Linnaeus's works, to authors prior to 1850, and to selected subjects.

Simon, James E. Herbs : an indexed bibliography, 1971–1980 / James E. Simon, Alena F. Chadwick, Lyle E. Craker. Hamden, Conn. : Archon Books, 1984. 770 p.   **EG110**

Subtitle: The scientific literature on selected herbs, and aromatic and medicinal plants of the temperate zone.

Includes 64 commercially significant herbs. Arranged in two sections: (1) herbs, and (2) subject classifications. The first section gives cultural, commercial, or medicinal information and bibliographic references coded to the broad subject classifications of the second section. Author index; subject index.   Z5996.H37S56

Periodicals

Hunt Botanical Library. B-P-H : Botanico-Periodicum-Huntianum / George H. M. Lawrence [et al.], editors. Pittsburgh, 1968. 1063 p.   **EG111**

A list of abbreviations for more than 12,000 titles of serial publications "that regularly contain (or, in some period of their history, included) articles dealing with the plant sciences and botanical literature, and with persons who have contributed to botany and its literature."— *Pref.* An attempt to provide a set of standardized abbreviations for *Bibliographia huntiana* (*see* the yearbook *Huntia* 1 (1964) : 17–24). Arranged alphabetically, entries include full title, bibliographic information, title history, and a reference to the citation in *Union list of serials*. Includes 12,000 references from alternate abbreviations.   Z5353.H85

Indexes; Abstract journals

Botanisches Zentralblatt : referierendes Organ für das Gesamtgebiet der Botanik / im Auftrage der Deutschen Botanischen Gesellschaft .... 1.–40. Jahr. (Bd. 1–142), 1880–1919; Bd. 143–79 (Neue Folge, Bd. 1–37, no. 8), 1922–45. Cassell : T. Fischer, etc., 1880–1905 ; Jena : G. Fischer, 1906–45.

EG112

Frequency varies: weekly, 1880–1919; publication suspended, 1920–21; irregular, 1922–45. Ceased publication.

Title varies: *Botanisches Centralblatt*.

International coverage of the botanical literature. Provides lengthy signed abstracts for books and somewhat shorter abstracts for articles, in a classed arrangement. The "Neue Literatur" is a current awareness section (published separately, 1902–19, v. 91, 94, 97, etc. Each vol. of "Neue Folge" has two sections: "Referate" and "Literatur"). Most volumes include some kind of alphabetical author list.

"Generalregister," v. 1–60, 1880–94. "Generalregister" appears in "Neue Folge" at 5-year intervals.

————. *General register zu den Bänden 1 bis 30 [Neue Folge]* (*Bd. 143–72*), bearb. von Wilhelm Dörries. (Jena : Fischer, 1971–38. 3 v.).

Index to Australasian taxonomic literature. 1968– . Utrecht : Internat. Bureau for Plant Taxonomy and Nomenclature, 1970– . Annual.   **EG113**

An index to "current literature and names of new taxa relevant to the study of the systematics of vascular plants of Australasia and Polynesia." Modeled on *Index to European taxonomic literature* (EG114).

Index to European taxonomic literature. 1965– . Utrecht : Internat. Bureau for Plant Taxonomy and Nomenclature, 1966– . Annual.   **EG114**

An index to "current literature relevant to the study of the systematics of vascular plants of Europe and adjacent regions."—*Introd., 1965.* A general section is followed by listings of books and periodical articles arranged in taxonomic groups. New names are listed alphabetically under the relevant genus or family, following the references to papers.   QK96.R4

Torrey Botanical Club. Index to American botanical literature. (*In* Torrey Botanical Club. *Bulletin.* v. 15 [1888]– . Bimonthly).   **EG115**

Appears in each issue of the *Bulletin*. Alphabetical author arrangement of citations under general subject headings. Aims to include all literature on botany in the Western hemisphere.

Beginning with v. 21, 1894, the index has also been reprinted on cards for which annual subscriptions may be placed. From 1959, author cards are printed annually by G. K. Hall, Boston.

Cards covering the period 1886–1966 have been cumulated as:

————. *Index to American botanical literature, 1886–1966*. (Boston : G. K. Hall, 1969. 4 v.).

Photoreproduction of the card file cumulating the entries from the "index" feature which appeared serially in the *Bulletin* of the Torrey Botanical club (above). Includes works relating to "taxonomy, phylogeny, and floristics of the fungi, bryophytes, pteridophytes, and spermatophytes; morphology, anatomy, cytology, genetics, physiology, and pathology of the same groups; plant ecology; and general botany, including biography and bibliography."—*Pref.*

————. *Index to American botanical literature : first supplement. 1967–76.* (Boston : G. K. Hall, 1977. 740 p.).

A supplement to the above.

Encyclopedias

The American Horticultural Society encyclopedia of garden plants / ed. in chief, Christopher Brickell ; horticultural consultant, John Elsley. N.Y. : Macmillan, 1989. 608 p. : ill.

EG116

For annotation, *see* EJ231.   SB403.2.A46

Mabberley, D. J. The plant-book. Cambridge ; N.Y. : Cambridge Univ. Pr., 1987. 706 p.   **EG117**

Subtitle: A portable dictionary of the higher plants utilising Cronquist's *An integrated system of classification of flowering plants* (1981) and current botanical literature arranged largely on the principles of editions 1–6 (1896/97–1931) of Willis's *A dictionary of the flowering plants and ferns*.

An update of J. C. Willis's *Dictionary of the flowering plants and ferns*, 8th ed., 1973 (EG182). Attempts "to present all currently accepted generic and family names of flowering plants (including gymnosperms), ferns (and other Pteridophyta), as well as a wide range of English names encountered in the literature."—*Pref.* About 100 primary sources and 230 major botanical periodicals are also listed.

QK11.M29

Dictionaries

American Joint Committee on Horticultural Nomenclature. Standardized plant names : a revised and enlarged listing of approved scientific and common names of plants and plant products in American commerce or use / prep. by Harlan P. Kelsey and William A. Dayton. 2nd ed. Harrisburg, Penn. : J. Horace McFarland Co., 1942. 675 p.   **EG118**

1st ed., 1923.

Intends to establish a standardized "scientific" name and a standardized "common name" for every tree, shrub, and plant in American commerce. Alphabetic arrangement includes genera, subdivided by species, and general common name, subdivided by the specific common name of each plant. Also has entries for commercial names and plant patents issued from Aug. 18, 1931, to July 1, 1941. Many entries for hobby and commercial plants include names of originators or introducers, with date. Glossary.   QK11.A5

Authors of plant names : a list of authors of scientific names of plants, with recommended standard forms of their names, including abbreviations / ed. by R. K. Brummitt and C. E. Powell ; principal compilers: C. E. Powell... [et al.]. [London] : Royal Botanic Gardens, Kew ; Forestburgh, N.Y. : Lubrecht & Cramer, Ltd., 1992. 732 p.   **EG119**

"The intention is to include all authors who have published names of plants covered by the International Code of Botanical Nomenclature, which excludes bacteria. However, coverage of authors of names of fossil plants is very restricted."—*Pref.*   QK96.A87

Britten, James. Dictionary of English plant-names / James Britten, Robert Holland. London : publ. for the English Dialect Society by Trübner, 1886. 618 p.   **EG120**

Originally issued in three parts, 1878–84, as no. 22, 26, and 45 (forming v. 10) of *Publications* of the English Dialect Society.

Arranged by common name followed by scientific name with explanation of origin and references to uses in literature, frequently with quotations.

Carleton, R. Milton. Index to common names of herbaceous plants. Boston : G. K. Hall, 1959. 129 p.   **EG121**

Lists the common or vernacular names of plants as used in the U.S., or in English and American literature, with Latin equivalents.   QK13.C33

Carnoy, Albert Joseph. Dictionnaire étymologique des noms grecs de plantes. Louvain : Publ. Universitaires, Inst. Orientaliste, 1959. 277 p. (Bibliothèque du Muséon, v. 46).   **EG122**

The romanized form of the Greek name is followed by the word in the Greek alphabet together with an explanation of its meaning and derivation in French. Many references to the literature.   QK9.C3

Carpenter, John Richard. An ecological glossary. Norman : Univ. of Oklahoma Pr., 1938. 306 p. : ill.   **EG123**

Repr.: N.Y. : Hafner, 1956.

Defines nearly 3,000 terms, in many cases with references to the works in which the terms were originally used or discussed. Includes a discussion of the development of ecological nomenclature and several appendixes of charts and maps.   QH541.C3

The concise Oxford dictionary of botany / ed. by Michael Allaby. Oxford, [Eng.] ; N.Y. : Oxford Univ. Pr., 1992. 442 p.   **EG124**

Contains more than 5,000 terms drawn from "ecology, earth science, earth history, evolution, genetics, plant physiology, biochemistry, cytology and biogeography."—*Pref.* Many entries are short, "only two or three words. Other entries are longer, going beyond the simple definition to describe complex biological processes as succinctly as practicable." Almost a third of the entries "describe taxonomic groups of seed plants, ferns, algae, mosses, and liverworts, and also fungi, bacteria and slime molds." There are *see* and *compare* references. Many entries are updated extracts from *The Oxford dictionary of natural history* (EG78).

§ Companion work: *The concise Oxford dictionary of zoology* (EG227).   QK9.C67

Dictionary of gardening / ed. in chief Anthony Huxley ; ed., Mark Griffiths ; managing ed., Margot Levy. London : Macmillan ; N.Y. : Stockton Pr., 1992. 4 v. : ill.   **EG125**

At head of title: The new Royal Horticultural Society.

1st ed., 1951, had title: *The Royal Horticultural Society dictionary of gardening.*

Designed "to present a considerable volume of information in a clear and consistent form. Many of the entries in the main alphabetical sequence are [detailed] descriptions of plants arranged in alphabetical order by genus [3,983 genera; approx. 50,000 plants]; a brief description of each Family appears in the same sequence. Alongside these are the [178] general entries ... and ... [173] biographies; a list of the general entries and biographies is printed at the beginning of each volume."—*Using the dictionary.* Plant descriptions include genus description (genus author, popular name, derivation of name, family, and distribution of the genus), cultivation note (habit, garden, value and cultural requirements, instruction for cultivation, methods of propagation, and control of pests and diseases), key (based on features visible to the gardener), and species descriptions (name, author, popular name, distribution when different than the genus, climatic zones, cultivars, and synonymy). Includes in v. 1, Botanical glossary; Glossary of plant taxonomy; in v. 4, a glossary of pests, diseases, and disorders; Horticultural glossary; Glossary of common botanical epithets; Index of authors cited; Bibliography; and Index of popular names.   SB450.95.D53

Featherly, Henry Ira. Taxonomic terminology of the higher plants. Ames : Iowa State College Pr., 1954. 166 p.   **EG126**

Intended "for students in taxonomy, plant distribution, and speciation."—*Pref.* Omits obsolete and seldom-used words. In four sections, each of which deals with a particular area of terminology: (1) Glossary of botanical technical terms; (2) Subject classification; (3) Some specific epithets with their meanings; (4) Some Greek and Latin components of scientific words.   QK9.F4

Gerth van Wijk, H. L. Dictionary of plant names / Publ. by the Dutch Society of Sciences at Haarlem. The Hague : Nijhoff, 1911–16. 2 v.   **EG127**

Contents. v. 1, Latin names, A–Z, v. 2, Index of English, French, Dutch, and German names.

A dictionary of names and terms only; arranged alphabetically by the Latin name and giving under each Latin name the equivalent popular and literary names in the English, Dutch, French, and German languages. Aims to include names of all wild and cultivated plants, flowers and fruits, varieties and subvarieties, and parts of plants now or formerly used in medicine or industry. The only work of its kind; accurate.

Index kewensis : plantarum phanerogamarum nomina et synonyma omnium generum et specierum a Linnaeo usque ad annum MDCCCLXXXV complectens nomine recepto auctore patria unicuique plantae subjectis / sumptibus beati Caroli Roberti Darwin ductu et consilio Josephi D. Hooker confecit B. Daydon Jackson. .... Oxford : Clarendon Pr., 1893–95. 2 v.   **EG128**

Added title page in English: Index kewensis, an enumeration of the genera and species of flowering plants from the time of Linneaus to the year 1885 inclusive together with their authors' names, the works in which they were first published, their native countries and their synonyms.

Arrangement is alphabetical by names of genera, with species listed under their particular genera. No listing of references from serial abbreviation to full title is given.

———. *Supplementum ... nomina et synonyma omnium generum et specierum ab initio anni MDCCCLXXXVI usque ad finem anni MDCCCCLV nonulla etiam antea edita complectens ...* (Oxford : Clarendon Pr., 1901–74. v. 1–15. [In progress]).

Vol. 1, 1886–95, with quinquennial supplements to Suppl. 15, 1966/70 (publ. 1974).

Arrangement is the same as for original *Index*. From 1936 on, in order to further supplement *Index londinensis* (EG104), includes references to illustrations of new plants.

Index nominum genericorum (plantarum) / ed. Ellen R. Farr, Jan A. Leussink and Frans A. Stafleu. Utrecht : Bohn, Scheltema & Holkema ; The Hague : Junk, 1979. 3 v. (Regnum vegetabile, v. 100–102).   **EG129**
   Intended as an aid in stabilizing nomenclature, the index consists of an alphabetical list of validly published scientific names of all plant genera. Entries include citations to the authors to whom the names are attributed; citations to the first valid publication of names; a record of existing homonymy; an indication of taxonomic placement.
   ———. *Supplement 1*, Ellen R. Farr, Jan A. Leussink, and Gea Zijlstra, editors (The Hague; Boston : Bohn, Scheltema & Holkema, 1986. 126 p.).   QK96.R4 v.100–102

International Botanical Congress (*14th : 1987 : Berlin, Germany*). International code of botanical nomenclature : adopted by the 14th International Botanical Congress, Berlin, July–Aug. 1987 / prep. and ed. by W. Greuter ... [et al.]. Königstein : Koeltz Scientific Books, 1988. 328 p. (Regnum vegetabile, v. 118).   **EG130**
   Text and index in English, French, and German. The Code consists of 75 articles governing nomenclature and substantial appendixes—names of hybrids, names of families to be retained, and generic names retained and rejected.   QK96.R4

Jackson, Benjamin Daydon. Glossary of botanic terms with their derivation and accent. 4th ed. rev. and enl. Philadelphia : Lippincott, [1928]. 481 p.   **EG131**
   Repr.: London : Duckworth, 1949.
   1st ed., 1900.
   Does not include technical terms not relating to botany and gives only the botany-related definition of terms having meaning in other fields. The "Supplement of additional terms" from the 3rd ed. has not been incorporated into the main glossary but has again been appended.   QK9.J1

Kartesz, John T. A synonymized checklist of the vascular flora of the United States, Canada, and Greenland / John T. Kartesz and Rosemarie Kartesz. Chapel Hill : Univ. of North Carolina Pr., [1980]. 498 p. (The flora of North America, v. 2).   **EG132**
   "In confederation with Anne H. Lindsey and C. Ritchie Bell."—*t.p.*
   A computer-generated list of 56,941 names in three sections: pteridophyta, gymnospermae, and angiospermae. "Within each section all names of taxa are arranged sequentially and alphabetically by family, genus, species, subspecies, and variety."—*Introd.* This volume is intended to be the first of three. Indexed.
   2nd ed. to be released 1994.   QK110.K37

Keysers Lexikon der Pflanzen / von A. Schindlmayr. Heidelberg : Keyser, [1956]. 439 p. : ill.   **EG133**
   Alphabetically arranged by scientific name with cross-references from German common name; includes descriptions.   QK9.K3

Little, R. John. A dictionary of botany / John R. Little, Eugene C. Jones. N.Y. : Van Nostrand Reinhold, [1980]. 400 p. : ill.   **EG134**
   Provides brief definitions of about 5,500 terms, excluding taxonomic and common plant names. Bibliography.   QK9.L735

Marshall, William Taylor. Glossary of succulent plant terms / William Taylor Marshall and Robert S. Woods. [Pasadena, Calif. : Abbey Garden Pr.], 1945. 112 p. : ill.   **EG135**
   1st printing, 1938.
   Subtitle: A glossary of botanical terms and pronouncing vocabulary of generic and specific names used in connection with xerophytic plants.

Illustrated with photographs and line drawings. Includes etymology as part of entries for terms whose derivative elements are not defined elsewhere in the text.   QK10.M37

National list of scientific plant names. Rev. ed. Wash. : Soil Conservation Service, [1982]. 2 v.   **EG136**
   1st ed., 1971.
   "The revision ... contains symbols for scientific names; accepted names for genera, species, subspecies, and varieties; authors of plant names; symbols for source manuals; family names; symbols for plant habits; and symbols for regions of distribution."—*Pref.*   QK96.U57

A provisional checklist of species for flora North America (revised). [St. Louis] : Missouri Botanical Garden, 1978. 199 p. (Flora North America report, 84).   **EG137**
   Ed. by Stanwyn G. Shetler and Lawrence E. Skog.
   "This *Checklist* is being published in its highly provisional state to satisfy a growing need for a simple working list of the species of vascular plants in North America. It covers ... the United States (including Alaska), Canada, and Greenland—stopping at the Mexican boundary."—*Introd.* A computer-generated checklist in taxonomic order—family, genus, species. Gives name of author first identifying species, plant characteristics (in code), geographic regions, and primary source of species entry.   QK110.P76

Snell, Walter Henry. A glossary of mycology / Walter Henry Snell, Esther A. Dick. Rev. ed. Cambridge : Harvard Univ. Pr., 1971. 181 p. : ill.   **EG138**
   1st ed., 1957.
   Based on Walter H. Snell's *Three thousand mycological terms* (Providence, R.I., 1936).
   Defines about 7,000 terms in mycology. Includes color, obsolete, and nontechnical terms. Gives Latin and Greek derivations and references to the literature.   QK603.S53

Trehane, Piers. Index hortensis : a modern nomenclator for botanists, horticulturalists, plantsmen, and the serious gardener. Wimborne, [England] : Quarterjack Publishing, 1989. v. 1. (In progress).   **EG139**
   Contents: v. 1, Perennials.
   "An authoritative guide to the correct naming of our garden plants."—*Cover.* A modern nomenclator for botanists, horticulturalists, and serious gardeners. Indexed.   OK96.T7

Usher, George. A dictionary of botany : including terms used in biochemistry, soil science and statistics. London : Constable, 1966. 404 p.   **EG140**
   Brief definitions. Intended for high school and college students. "Definitions of all the phyla, classes, orders and families have been given, but descriptions of genera and species have been omitted."—*Pref.*   QK9.U8

Foreign terms

Bedevian, Armenag K. Illustrated polyglottic dictionary of plant names in Latin, Arabic, Armenian, English, French, German, Italian and Turkish languages : including economic, medicinal, poisonous and ornamental plants and common weeds .... Cairo : Argus and Papazian Pr., 1936. 2 pts. in 1 v. (644 p., 455 p.) : ill.   **EG141**

Davydov, Nikolai Nikolaevich. Botanicheskiĭ slovar' : russko-angliisko-nemetsko-frantsuzsko-latinskiĭ. Izd. 2. Moskva : Fizmatgiz, 1962. 335 p.   **EG142**
   1st ed., 1960.
   Compiled on a Russian base. Some 6,000 terms, including common names of plants. Gives equivalent terms in English, German, French, and Latin; for plant names, the Latin term given is the scientific name and family. For each of the four non-Russian languages, there is an index with references to the number of the equivalent Russian term. Preface in Russian, English, German, and French.   QK9.D3

Stearn, William T. Botanical Latin : history, grammar, syntax, terminology and vocabulary. 4th ed. Newton Abbot, [Eng.] : David & Charles, 1992. 546 p. : ill. **EG143**

1st ed., 1966; 3rd ed. rev., 1983.

"Aims to provide a working guide to the special kind of Latin internationally used by botanists for the description and naming of plants."—*Apologia.* Valuable both as a combination style manual and grammar and as a conventional dictionary (i.e., the vocabulary section). Indexed. QK10.S74

Steinmetz, E. F. Vocabularium botanicum : Plantenterminologie. Woordenlijst in zes talen (Latijn, Grieks, Nederlands, Duits, Engels en Frans) van de voornaamste wetenschappelijke woorden, die in de plantkunde gebruikt worden. 2. druk. Amsterdam : Steinmetz, [1953]. 149 p. **EG144**

1st ed., 1947.

Title page also in German, English, and French.

Arranged alphabetically by Latin and/or Greek term. Lists equivalent terms in Dutch, German, English, and French, in tabular form. QK9.S8

Directories

Ayensu, Edward S. Endangered and threatened plants of the United States / Edward S. Ayensu, Robert A. DeFilipps. Wash. : Smithsonian Inst. and World Wildlife Fund, 1978. 403 p. **EG145**

Contains diverse information about endangered plants, with sections arranged by species; by family, genus, and species; and by state. Includes extensive bibliographies. QK86.U6A93

Henderson, D. M. International directory of botanical gardens / D. M. henderson, H. T. Prentice. 3rd ed. Utrecht : Bohn, Scheltema & Holkema, 1977. 270 p. (Regnum vegetabile, v. 95). **EG146**

1st ed., 1963.

Arranged by country, then by city. Gives full directory information, including personnel. Index to personal names; index to towns and gardens. QK96.R4

Hortus third : a concise dictionary of plants cultivated in the United States and Canada. N.Y. : Macmillan, [1976]. 1290 p. : ill. **EG147**

"Initially compiled by Liberty Hyde Bailey and Ethel Zoe Bailey. Revised and expanded by the Staff of the Liberty Hyde Bailey Hortorium."—*t.p.*

1941 ed. had title: *Hortus second.*

"Provides a contemporary assessment of the kinds and the names of plants cultivated in the continental United States and Canada, Puerto Rico, and Hawaii. Initially planned as a simple revision of *Hortus second, Hortus third* evolved … into an essentially new work. … Innovations included are: author or authors for each botanical name, illustrations of representative members of most families, a separate glossary of botanical terms, an index to common names, and a list of authors cited."—*Pref.* SB45.H67

Hyams, Edward. Great botanical gardens of the world / Edward Hyams ; photography by William MacQuilty. [N.Y.] : Macmillan, [1969]. 288 p. : ill. **EG148**

A geographical arrangement of descriptions and histories of 42 of the largest botanical gardens in the world, plus a special section on gardens in Japan. More than half of the contents are black-and-white and color plates and other illustrations of garden scenes, buildings, grounds plans, and particular plants. Includes an index and a comprehensive list, with map, of the botanical gardens of the world. QK71.H9

The IUCN plant red data book : comprising red data sheets on 250 selected plants threatened on a world scale / International Union for Conservation of Nature and Natural Resources; comp. by Gren Lucas and Hugh Synge for the Threatened Plants Committee of the Survival Service Commission of IUCN, with the help and advice of experts throughout the world. Morges, Switzerland : IUCN, 1978. 540 p. **EG149**

For each entry gives status, distribution, habitat and ecology, conservation measures taken, conservation measures proposed, biology and potential value, description, and references. Species index. QK86A1.I58

Kingsbury, John Merriam. Poisonous plants of the United States and Canada. Englewood Cliffs, N.J. : Prentice-Hall, 1964. 626 p. : ill. **EG150**

Intended as a reference for physicians, veterinarians, and medical and veterinary students. Provides descriptions of the plants and their habitats and ranges, of poisonous principles, and of the symptoms and conditions of poisoning for each plant. Introductory material includes discussions of the chemistry of toxic compounds. Bibliographies; index. SB617.K5

Klein, Richard M. Research methods in plant science / Richard M. Klein and Deana T. Klein. Garden City, N.Y. : publ. for the American Museum of Natural History by the Natural History Pr., 1970. 756 p. : ill. **EG151**

A book of methods, covering such areas as acquisition and maintenance of plant collections; environmental control of plant growth; measurements; general procedures for the cultivation of plants; separation and analysis of plant components; reproduction; plant diseases; and preparation of manuscripts reporting research findings. Indexed. QK51.K53

Lampe, Kenneth F. AMA handbook of poisonous and injurious plants / Kenneth F. Lampe and Mary Ann McCann. Chicago : Amer. Medical Assoc., distr. by Chicago Review Pr., [1985]. 432 p. : ill. **EG152**

Contents: (I) Systemic plant poisoning; (II) Plant dermatitis; (III) Mushroom poisoning.

"The purpose … is to provide physicians and other health care professionals with an easily used reference for the management of plant intoxications. The format also makes it useful as a field guide."—*Pref.*

Entries for plants include information on symptoms and management, and references. Color illustrations. Indexed. RA1250.L27

Lanjouw, Joseph. Index herbariorum : a guide to the location and contents of the world's public herbaria / general ed., F. A. Stafleu. Utrecht : Bohn, Scheltema & Holkema ; The Hague ; Boston : W. Junk, 1981–88. Pt. 1; pt. 2, v. 5–7. (Regnum vegetabile, v. 106, 109, 114, 117.). (In progress). **EG153**

Contents: pt. 1, The herbaria of the world, comp. by Patricia K. Holmgren, Wil Keuken, and Eileen K. Schofield (7th ed.); pt. 2, Collectors, by I. Hettie Vegter.

Arranged alphabetically by city, pt. 1 lists address, dates, affiliation, amount, and type of material collected and research specializations, staff, publications, and loan and exchange information. Index to personal and scientific names. Pt. 2 is a coded alphabetical listing of collectors and their dates, types of plants and localities where specimens were collected, with dates, and final dispositions of their collections.

Martin, Alexander Campbell. Seed identification manual / Alexander Campbell Martin and William D. Barkley. Berkeley ; Los Angeles : Univ. of California Pr., 1961. 221 p. : ill. **EG154**

Black-and-white photographs and nontechnical descriptions of 600 seeds and seed-like dry fruits intended "to help agriculturists, foresters, wildlife biologists and others interested in land-use programs to identify the seeds in their particular ecological fields of interest."—*Introd.* Photographs are arranged by habitat and family; "Identification clues," including textual descriptions and graphic illustrations, are arranged by family. Index to common and scientific names.

QK661.M37

North American horticulture : a reference guide / comp. by the American Horticultural Society ; Thomas M. Barrett, ed. 2nd ed. N.Y. : Macmillan, c1992. 427 p. : ill.   **EG155**
1st ed., 1982.

A thorough but not all-inclusive listing of U.S. and Canadian amateur and professional horticultural institutions. Three types of entries: full (main entry for each organization); ancillary (cross-reference to or from full entries); abbreviations. Full and ancillary entries give two-part numbers that refer to chapter and entry numbers. Indexes of states and organizations.   SB317.56.U6N67

Handbooks

Belousova, L. S. Rare plants of the world / L. S. Belousova, L. V. Denisova ; [translator, B. R. Sharma]. Rotterdam : A. A. Balkema ; Brookfield, Vt. : Ashgate Publ. Co., 1992. 348 p., 64 p. of plates : ill. (some col.). (Russian translations series, v. 93).   **EG156**

"This book is compiled to illustrate the present status of the conversation of the diversity on plants in different parts of the world."—*Pref.* About 2,000 rare species (of the estimated 20,000) are described. The plants are divided taxonomically within major geographic sections. Index of Latin names.   QK86.A1B4513

Facciola, Stephen. Cornucopia : a source book of edible plants. Vista, Calif. : Kampong Publications, 1990. 677 p.

    EG157

A "compendium of the diversity of food plants available today to consumer, gardener and scientist. It includes thousands of cultivars of hundreds of crop species as well as many mushrooms and microorganisms."—*Pref.* More than 3,000 species recorded. Contains a bibliography and several indexes including names, usage and edible parts, and species native or naturalized in North America.   SB175.F33

Graf, Alfred Byrd. Exotica, series 4 international : pictorial cyclopedia of exotic plants from tropical and near-tropic regions. Library ed., 12th ed. East Rutherford, N.J. : Roehrs Co. Publishers, 1985. 2 v. (2576 p.) : ill. (some col.).   **EG158**
1st ed., 1978.

16,300 photographs, 405 in color, and 300 drawings. Index to genera illustrated at beginning of v. 1. Work composed mostly of photographs, four to nine per page, with a section in v. 2 giving a brief description of each plant and a code for care of each family (temperature, location, soil, light preference, and moisture level). Includes indexes.   SB407.G7

Gray, Asa. Gray's manual of botany : a handbook of the flowering plants and ferns of the central and northeastern United States and adjacent Canada. 8th (centennial) ed. / largely rewritten and expanded by Merritt Lyndon Fernald with assistance of specialists in some groups. N.Y. : Amer. Book Co., [1950]. 1632 p. : ill.   **EG159**
Repr.: Portland, Ore. : Dioscorides Pr., 1987.
1st ed., 1848, had title *A manual of the botany of the United States.*

A descriptive flora of 8,340 vascular plants arranged systematically. For each species, gives description, habitat, range, and sometimes an illustration, with further specifics on varieties and forms. Aids to locating information on a particular plant include a synopsis of orders and families, an artificial analytical key to the families, and indexes to Latin and colloquial names. Includes a glossary and a table showing the numbers of genera, species, varieties, and forms of the families of plants included.   QK117.G75

Human protein data / ed. by André Haeberli. Weinheim ; N.Y. : VCH, c1992– . 1 v. (looseleaf) : ill. (In progress).

    EG160

"The first and second installments contain data on 208 human proteins, chiefly consisting of plasma proteins belonging to the fields of blood coagulation and immunology. At least 60 new proteins will be added each year. ... Each contribution will be updated every 2 to 3 years."—*Introd.*   QP551.H845

Phytochemical dictionary : a handbook of bioactive compounds from plants / ed. by Jeffrey B. Harborne and Herbert Baxter ... [et al.]. London ; Wash. : Taylor & Francis, c1993. 791 p. : ill.   **EG161**

Contents: Pt. 1, Carbohydrates and Lipids; Pt. 2, Nitrogen containing compounds (excluding alkaloids); Pt. 3, Alkaloids; Pt. 4, Phenolics; Pt. 5, Terpenoids.

Each entry includes a dictionary registry number, trivial or systematic name, common synonyms, stereochemical diagram of chemical structure, molecular formula, molecular weight, natural occurrence (including plant genus and species), and biological activity (where known). "The index contains (1) names of main entries with entry numbers, (2) synonyms for these which are followed by 'See' and the entry number, and (3) the names of significant similar compounds referred to in the texts of some entries which are followed by 'See under' and the entry number."—*Index.*   QK898.B54P48

Plants in danger : what do we know? / Stephen D. Davis ... [et al.]. Gland, Switzerland : International Union for Conservation of Nature and Natural Resources, 1986. 461 p. : ill.

    EG162

A comprehensive guide to literature on endangered plant species from around the world, including the U.S., listed alphabetically by country. The data sheet for each country includes, when they exist, citations to checklists and floras, field guides, information sources on threatened plants, laws protecting plants, voluntary organizations, botanic gardens, useful addresses and a section called "Additional references." Annotations are very brief or nonexistent. Appendixes provide a list of additional general and regional references, a geographical index to these, and a list of the dates when each country implemented the various global conservation conventions. Index only to countries, islands, and island groups mentioned in the text.   QK86.A1P58

Takhtadzhi̇͡an, A. L. Floristic regions of the world. Berkeley : Univ. of California Pr., c1986. 522 p. : maps.   **EG163**

Translation of *Floristicheskie oblasti Zemli.*

A description of the five floristic kingdoms and 35 regions of the world. Appendix gives a distribution list of orders and families. Extensive bibliography arranged by floristic kingdom. Index is primarily of plant names and some important geographic locations.

QK101.T313

Uphof, Johannes Cornelis Theodorus. Dictionary of economic plants. 2nd ed., rev. and enl. Lehre : J. Cramer ; N.Y. : Stechert-Hafner ; Codicote, Herts. : Wheldon & Wesley, 1968. 591 p.   **EG164**
1st ed., 1959.

"Over 3,000 species have been added, bringing the total number of plant species to 9,500."—*Pref., 2nd ed.* Presents brief descriptions of economic plants, with their geographical distribution, products, and principal uses. Includes plants not only of commercial value but of any practical use to humanity. Entries under scientific names of plants, with references from common names and products. Classed bibliography.   QK9.U6

Biography

Desmond, Ray. Dictionary of British and Irish botanists and horticulturists including plant collectors and botanical artists. London : Taylor & Francis, 1977. 747 p.   **EG165**

1st ed., 1893; 2nd ed. (1931) had title: *A biographical index of deceased British and Irish botanists.*

"In this revision of the 1931 edition the number of entries has been almost quadrupled. This has been achieved not only by scanning books and periodicals published up to 1975, but also by substantially enlarging the scope of the work."—*Pref.* This edition adds horticulturalists but continues to be limited to deceased subjects. Entries include dates, education, qualifications, honors, biographical references in books and periodicals, location of plant collections, herbaria, etc., and any plant commemorating the individual. Subject index.

Z5358.G7B7

Ferns

Tryon, Rolla M. Ferns and allied plants : with special reference to tropical America / Rolla M. Tyron, Alice F. Tyron...[et al.]. N.Y. : Springer-Verlag, c1982. 857 p. : ill., maps. **EG166**

"This systematic treatment of the ferns and allied plants provides a modern classification of the Pteridophyta based on an assessment of the wealth of new data published during the last few decades."—*Pref.* Includes about 9,000 species arranged by family and genus. Gives citations to naming authors. Includes references. Scientific name index.

QK524.4.T78

Flora

Bailey, Liberty Hyde. Manual of cultivated plants most commonly grown in the continental United States and Canada. Rev. ed., compl. restudied. N.Y. : Macmillan, 1949. 1116 p. : ill. **EG167**

1st ed., 1924.

Completely revised and greatly enlarged edition of an important handbook for the identification of the most common species of plants for food, ornament, utility, etc. Arranged by scientific name, with indexes to scientific and common name.

QK110.B3

Clapham, A. R. Flora of the British Isles / A. R. Clapham, T. G. Tutin, D. M. Moore. 3rd ed. Cambridge ; N. Y., : Cambridge Univ. Pr., 1987. 688 p. : ill. **EG168**

2nd ed., 1962.

Arranged taxonomically, with a synopsis of the classification provided as a preface, along with a key to families. Provides authoritative coverage of each plant's natural history, including chromosome number, physical description, variability, habitat, and associated species. Illustrations are confined to fruits and seeds. Appendixes include a table of authorship of families, notes on the plant life forms, and a glossary. Index to vernacular names and to scientific names of families, genera, and species.

QK306.C57

The European garden flora : a manual for the identification of plants cultivated in Europe, both out-of-doors and under glass / ed. by S.M. Walters ... [et al.]. Cambridge ; N. Y. : Cambridge Univ. Pr., 1984–89. v. 1–3 : ill. (In progress). **EG169**

Contents: v. 1, Pteridophtya, Gymnospermae, Angiospermae—Monocotyledons (part 1) (1986); v. 2, Monocotyledons (part 2) (1984); v. 3, Dicotyledons (part 1) (1989).

"The present Flora...attempts to provide a scientifically accurate and up-to-date means for the identification of plants cultivated for amenity in Europe."—*Introd.* Does not include crops or garden weeds. The introduction includes details of the format and use of the Flora. Separate indexes for each volume.

SB406.93.E85E97

Flora Europaea / ed. by T. G. Tutin ... [et al.] ; with the assistance of P. W. Ball and A. O. Chater. 2nd ed. Cambridge ; N.Y. : Cambridge Univ. Pr., 1964–1980. 5 v. **EG170**

Contents: v. 1, Lycopodiaceae to Plantanaceae; v. 2, Rosaceae to Umbelliferae; v. 3, Diapensiaceae to Myoporaceae; v. 4, Plantaginaceae to Compositae (and Rubiaceae); v. 5, Alismataceae to Orchidaceae. Each volume indexed; index to families and genera in all volumes in v. 5 (green sheets).

A cooperative effort of many European scholars. Comprehensive to the level of subspecies. Gives synonyms, brief descriptions of structure, habitat, and European distribution, with references to the article where first identified, and diploid chromosome number where possible. Each volume includes a key to abbreviations, a glossary, Vocabularium Anglo-Latinum, an index to scientific names, and a section of maps. Each volume indexed. *Consolidated index to Flora Europaea*, G. Halliday and M. Beadle (Cambridge : Cambridge Univ. Pr., [1983]. 210 p.), was compiled from the separate indexes of v. 1–5.

————. Ed. by T. G. Tutin ... [et al.] ; assisted by J. R. Akeroyd and M. E. Newton ; appendices ed. by R. R. Mill (2nd ed. Cambridge ; N.Y. : Cambridge Univ. Pr., 1993. 1 v.). Contents: Psilotaceae to Plantanaceae.

Only v. 1, which was most out of date, will be revised. 350 new taxa have been added, 20 deleted, and numerous corrections made to 1st ed. Appendixes include a key to authors' names, keys to cited book and periodical title abbreviations, a brief glossary of technical terms, and an English-Latin vocabulary. Index to scientific names; alphabetic listing of families and genera with species listed under genus.

QK281.F59

Flora of North America : north of Mexico / ed. by Flora of North America Editorial Committee. N.Y. : Oxford Univ. Pr., 1993. v. 1–2 : ill., maps. (In progress). **EG171**

Contents: v. 1, Background essays; v. 2, Pteridophytes and gymnosperms. To be complete in 14 v.

The first comprehensive guide to the 20,000 plant species of North America north of Mexico. For all plant groups, gives distribution maps, morphological descriptions, diagrams of species relationships, identification keys, synonymies, chromosome numbers, summaries of habitat and geographic ranges, line drawings of all genera and more than a third of the species, and literature citations. Each volume has full index and bibliography.

Publication of these volumes represents culmination of the Flora of North America Project, begun in 1982. The Project also sponsors a botanical database, maintained at the Missouri Botanical Garden, which contains all published information in the volumes of the *Flora*, including references, as well as detailed additional information concerning morphology, type specimens, and documentation for chromosome counts.

QK110.F55

Flowering plants of the world / consultant ed., Vernon H. Heywood ... [et al.]. N.Y. : Oxford Univ. Pr., 1993. 336 p. : color ill. **EG172**

Entries for more than 300 families of plants. Includes distribution maps. Many illustrations, with 200 families illustrated by color plates. Each family is described by distribution, diagnostic features, classification, and economic uses of its members. Main entries are supplemented by an extensive glossary and a general introduction to the forms, structure, ecology, uses, and classification of flowering plants. Index to both Latin and common English names.

QK495.A1F58

Gleason, Henry Allan. The new Britton and Brown illustrated flora of the northeastern United States and adjacent Canada. [N.Y. : New York Botanical Garden, 1952]. 3 v. : ill. **EG173**

Original work by N. L. Britton and Addison Brown. 1st ed., 1896–98; 2nd ed., 1913 (frequently repr.); 3rd ed., 1952 (repr. 1963 with slight revisions).

The 3rd ed. has been entirely rewritten, and new material added. Attempts to describe all known species of native and successfully introduced seed plants, ferns, and fern allies. Intended "for the interested laity rather than the professional botanist."—*Pref.* A glossary defines the more technical terms used in the text.

For each species gives description, variant names, common name, habitat and range, and illustration. Vols. 1–2 have their own indexes. Vol. 3 contains the general index to all divisions, classes, subclasses, orders, families, genera and species, and English names. QK117.G5

Graf, Alfred Byrd. Hortica : a color cyclopedia of garden flora in all climates and indoor plants. East Rutherford, N.J. : Roehrs Co., 1992. 1216 p. : col. ill., maps (some col.).
EG174

A guide to a very broad range of the more basic species and cultivars worldwide. Primarily useful for the large number of plant photographs; there are more than 8,000, four to 12 per page. The text provides brief descriptions of each pictured plant, arranged by genus, with a guide to climate zones for plant hardiness. At the beginning is a common names index. In sections by very general plant types, e.g., Cacti and succulents, Bamboos and grasses, Fruits and nuts.   SB407.G72

Hay, Roy. The color dictionary of flowers and plants for home and garden / Roy Hay and Patrick M. Synge ; American consultant, George Kalmbacher. London : Joseph ; N.Y. : Crown, [1969]. 373 p. : ill.   **EG175**

Repr.: N.Y. : Crown, 1982. 584 p.

A section of color illustrations of more than 2,000 plants is followed by a dictionary section giving brief descriptions which are intended as useful notes to the pictures.   SB407.H292

Hickey, Michael. 100 families of flowering plants / Michael Hickey & Clive King. 2nd ed. Cambridge ; N.Y. : Cambridge Univ. Pr., 1988. 619 p. : ill.   **EG176**

A taxonomically arranged guide to differences between 100 important plant families (of the 300–400 now living). Each family is first treated generally, then detailed descriptions are given of one or two representative genera. Also contains additional natural history information on each family. Index of families and genera with a few vernacular group names (e.g., grass and rose families). References are confined to 25 listed at the end.   QK495.A1H53

Newcomb, Lawrence. Newcomb's wildflower guide. Boston ; Toronto : Little, Brown, [1977]. 490 p. : ill.   **EG177**

"An ingenious new key system for quick, positive field identification of the wildflowers, flowering shrubs and vines of Northeastern and North-central North America."—*t.p.*

"This guide provides a new and eminently workable key system, which is based on the most easily seen features that make each species unique."—*Introd.* Identification is based on examining a specimen for flower type, plant type, and leaf type and referring to the locator key with the information derived. The locator key refers the user to the page on which the wildflower is identified.   QK118.N38

Polunin, Oleg. Flowers of Europe : a field guide. London ; N.Y. : Oxford Univ. Pr., 1969. 662 p. : ill.   **EG178**

A work for students and serious amateurs. Attempts to describe and illustrate "the commoner and most attractive seed-bearing plants to be found throughout Europe."—*Pref.* Includes about 2,600 species. Arrangement is adapted from *Flora Europaea*, v. 1, 1964 (EG170). Indexes of popular names, of English names, and of Latin names. Bibliography.   QK281.P65

Popular encyclopedia of plants / Vernon H. Heywood, chief ed.; Stuart R. Chant, assoc. ed. Cambridge : Cambridge Univ. Pr., [1982]. 368 p. : ill.   **EG179**

"An illustrated guide to the main species of plants used by man [sic]."—*Introd.* This work consists of short entries arranged both by genus and by common name. Includes plant products and principal crop species. Provides information about distribution and uses of plants. Does not include cultural information. Generous number of color photographs. 31 special feature articles one or two pages in length. Indexed by scientific names and by common names.
SB107.P67

Rickett, Harold William. Wild flowers of the United States / gen. ed., William C. Steere... [et al.]. N.Y. : McGraw-Hill, [1966–73]. 6 v. in 14. : ill., maps in color.   **EG180**

Contents: v. 1, The Northeastern states. 2 v.; v. 2, The Southeastern states. 2 v.; v. 3, Texas. 2 v.; v. 4, The Southwestern states. 3 v.; v. 5, The Northwestern states. 2 v.; v. 6, The Central mountains and plains. 3 v.

A publication of the New York Botanical Garden.

A flora for general readers which attempts to include all wildflowers of the areas covered. Arranged in groups according to characteristics recognizable to amateurs. Gives concise descriptions of plants, habitats, seasons, etc., with color photographs of most species. Each volume has an illustrated general explanation and glossary, and its own index.

———. ———. *Complete index for the six volumes of Wild flowers of the United States* (N.Y., McGraw-Hill, [1975]. 152 p.).

Index comp. by Lee Pennington from the separate indexes in the six individual volumes.

Lists artists, photographers, common and botanical names. The latter gives families, genera, and species.   QK115.R5

United States. Agricultural Research Service. Selected weeds of the United States / [by Clyde F. Reed]. Wash. : U.S. Govt. Print. Off., 1970. 463 p. : ill.   **EG181**

Reprint ed. (N.Y. : Dover, 1971) has title *Common weeds of the United States*.

"The 224 species of weeds included in this handbook were selected by weed scientists largely from the composite list of 1,775 weeds published in *WEEDS* 14 (1966) : 347–386. Those selected are some of the prevalent weeds in croplands, grazing lands, noncroplands, and aquatic sites."—*Introd.* Illustrates and describes the weeds and indicates their geographical distribution in the U.S. Arranged by family, then alphabetically by genera and species according to scientific name. Glossary of terms. Index includes popular as well as scientific names.
SB612.A2A46

Willis, John Christopher. Dictionary of the flowering plants and ferns. 8th ed., rev. by H. K. Airy Shaw. Cambridge : Univ. Pr., 1973. 1245 p.   **EG182**

1st ed., 1897; 7th ed., 1966.

A corrected and enlarged edition of the 7th ed., which differs from earlier editions by being confined to generic and family names and excluding botanical terms, common and vernacular names, and economic products. Consists largely of short coded entries showing equivalents and taxonomic relationships; entries for families are more lengthy.   QK11.W53

Wit, H. C. D. de. Plants of the world / H.C.D. de Wit ; tr. by A. J. Pomerans. N.Y. : Dutton, 1966–69. 3 v. : ill.   **EG183**

Contents: v. 1, The higher plants I; v. 2, The higher plants, II (tr. of *Hogere planten I–II*. The Hague, 1963–65); v. 3, The lower plants (tr. of *Lagere planten*. The Hague, 1965).

Plants are grouped by family. In addition to physical descriptions (and illustrations) of the individual plants there are notes on uses, historical notes, etc. Indexed.   QK98.W7213

Fungi

Ainsworth, Geoffrey Clough. Dictionary of the fungi / Geoffrey Clough Ainsworth, Guy Richard Bisby. 6th ed. Farnham Royal : Commonwealth Mycological Inst., 1971. 663 p. : ill.
EG184

1st ed., 1943.

The main body of the work lists systematic position, distribution, and number of species for every genus of fungi, excluding bacteria and lichens; definitions and explanations of terms and concepts related to mycology; common and scientific names of important fungi, and explanations of the chief families, orders, and classes of fungi and of bacteria and lichens. Supplemented by a table showing the systematic arrangement of the genera of fungi; a key to the families of fungi, which lists major characteristics of the families within the various orders of fungi; and a section of figures which illustrate the forms and phases of some of the genera.   QK603.A5

——————— The fungi : an advanced treatise. N.Y. : Academic Pr., 1965–73. 4 v. : ill.   **EG185**

Contents: v. 1, The fungal cell; v. 2, The fungal organism; v. 3, The fungal population; v. 4 (in 2 pts.), A taxonomic review with keys.
"The object of this work is ... to summarize what is known about fungi as fungi. ... The work, as the subtitle implies, is also intended as a reference book."—*Pref.* QK603.A33

Fungi on plants and plant products in the United States / David F. Farr ... [et al.]. St. Paul, Minn. : American Phytopathological Society, 1989. 1252 p. (Contributions from the U.S. National Fungus Collections, no. 5). **EG186**
    Provides host-fungus, fungus, host, and host common name indexes, as well as a list of authors of the scientific names.
                            SB733.F9815

Lange, Morten. Collins guide to mushrooms and toadstools / Morten Lange, F. Bayard Hora. 2nd ed. London : Collins, 1975. 257 p. : ill. **EG187**
    1st ed., 1963, had title: *A guide to mushrooms & toadstools.*
    "With 96 colour plates from *Flora Agaricina Danica* by Jakob E. Lange with additions by Ebbe Sunesen and P. Dahlstrøm."—*title page.*

Lindau, Gustav. Thesaurus litteraturae mycologicae et lichenologicae ratione habita praecipue omnium quae adhuc scripta sunt de mycologia applicata quem congesserunt / Gustav Lindau, P. Sydow. Leipzig : Borntraeger, 1908–17. 5 v. **EG188**

    Repr.: N.Y. : Johnson, 1954.
    ———. ———. *Supplementum, 1911–1930,* by Raffaele Ciferri. (Papia, [Italy] : Cortina, 1957–60. 4 v.).

Rossman, Amy Y. A literature guide for the identification of plant pathogenic fungi / Amy Y. Rossman, Mary E. Palm, and Linda J. Spielman. St. Paul, Minn. : American Phytopathological Society, 1987. 252 p. (Contributions from the U.S. National Fungus Collections, no. 1). **EG189**
    In two sections, the first listing general references to major groups and the second providing an alphabetical listing of genera.
                            Z5356.F97R67

Smith, Alexander Hanchett. A field guide to western mushrooms. Ann Arbor : Univ. of Michigan Pr., [1975]. 280 p. : ill. **EG190**
    Seeks to provide information on 201 species of western mushrooms. "Seventy of the species included here were known only from the western area or were described from it originally but have since been found elsewhere. Over twenty-five poisonous or very undesirable species for the table from the areas are illustrated and described. Many species are in the 'edible' column meaning that as far as it is known they are not poisonous. About fifteen of these are considered to be of 'gourmet' calibre. Finally there is the residuum of species of which the edibility is still apparently unrecorded. These have for the most part been listed as 'not recommended'."—*Introd.* Glossary; bibliography; index. QK617.S55

——————— The mushroom hunter's field guide / Alexander Hanchett Smith and Nancy Smith Weber. Ann Arbor : Univ. of Michigan Pr., [1980]. 316 p. : ill. **EG191**
    1st ed., 1958.
    Intended for use in identifying fleshy fungi throughout the U.S. and Canada. Includes most edible species as well as most dangerous ones. Glossary; index. QK617.S56

Watling, Roy. A literature guide for identifying mushrooms / Roy Watling and Ann Elizabeth Watling. [Eureka, Calif. : Mad River Pr., 1980]. 121 p. **EG192**
    An annotated bibliographic guide to articles and books on fungi. In two principal sections: taxonomic and geographic. Includes a list of general works and mycological journals. Indexed. Z5356.F97W35

Mosses

Grout, Abel Joel. Mosses with a hand-lens : a popular guide to the common or conspicuous mosses and liverworts of the United States and Canada / by A. J. Grout. Liverworts by M. A. Howe ... [et al.]. Newfane, Vt. : The Author, [1947]. 344 p. : ill. **EG193**
    1st ed., 1900. QK541.G8

Trees

Elias, Thomas. The complete trees of North America : field guide and natural history. N.Y. : Outdoor Life/Nature Books : Van Nostrand Reinhold, c1980. 948 p. : ill., maps. **EG194**
    A guide by family to more than 652 native trees north of Mexico and 100 common introduced trees. Species are illustrated by drawings of branchlets, many showing spring and summer or fall characteristics. Ranges shown on maps. Indexed. QK481.E38

Hough, Romeyn Beck. Handbook of the trees of the northern states and Canada east of the Rocky Mountains : photodescriptive. N.Y. : Macmillan, 1947. 470 p. : ill. **EG195**
    First publ. 1907. This is a reprint of that edition.
    Descriptions of "the native and naturalized trees of the region of North America lying north of the northern boundaries of North Carolina, Tennessee, Arkansas and Oklahoma and east of the Rocky Mountains, and extending southward in the Appalachian region to northern Alabama and Georgia."—p. 1. Basic arrangement is by genus. Includes photographs of the leaves, fruit, and bark of each species but not of the overall appearance of the trees. Maps show the range of each species. QK481.H8

Krüssmann, Gerd. Manual of cultivated broad-leaved trees & shrubs. Beaverton, Ore. : Timber Pr., 1984–86. 3 v. **EG196**
    Translation of *Handbuch der Laugehölze.* Ed. by Gilbert S. Daniels; tr. by Michael E. Epp.
    Published in cooperation with the American Horticultural Society.
    An extensive guide to trees, shrubs, subshrubs, vines, and some herbaceous plants. In alphabetical order by genera with more than 5,000 species and over 6,000 cultivars. Emphasizes descriptive information and contains notes of interest to gardeners. SB435.K94

Little, Elbert Luther. Check list of native and naturalized trees of the United States (including Alaska). Wash. : U.S. Forest Service, 1953. 472 p. (Agriculture handbook, no. 41). **EG197**
    Listed by accepted scientific name with approved common names, giving current synonyms, arranged chronologically with citations to the literature. Used as the official standard for tree names in the U.S. Forest Service. QK481.L5

Oxford encyclopedia of trees of the world / consultant ed., Bayard Hora. Oxford ; N.Y. : Oxford Univ. Pr., 1981. 288 p. : ill., maps. **EG198**
    Repr.: N.Y. : Crescent Books, dist. by Crown Publ., 1986.
    A compilation of illustrations and descriptions of the principal trees of the world. Includes 149 genera and over 500 species. Illustrated with drawings and color photographs. Identification key, bibliography, glossary. Index of common names; index of Latin names. QK475.O8

Preston, Richard Joseph. North American trees : exclusive of Mexico and tropical Florida. 4th ed. Ames : Iowa State Univ. Pr., 1989. 407 p. : ill. **EG199**
    1st ed., 1948; 3rd ed., 1976.
    A taxonomic arrangement of both native and commonly planted exotic species. A general introduction is followed by a key to the genera, then by a general description of each major family, with a key to

each of its species and detailed descriptions of them, with illustrations of key features and small distribution maps. Index to common names and to genera as main headings with species as subheadings: e.g., Cupressus; arizonica, bakeri, goveniana, etc. Changes from the 3rd ed. lie mainly in nomenclature and accepted species designations, as well as in improvements in the distribution maps and key descriptions.

QK110.P74

Rehder, Alfred. Manual of cultivated trees and shrubs hardy in North America : exclusive of the subtropical and warmer temperate regions. 2nd ed. rev. and enl. N.Y. : Macmillan, 1940. 996 p.   **EG200**

1st ed., 1927.

A systematically arranged manual describing 2,685 varieties in full and briefly describing 1,400 other species and hybrids. Rarely cultivated genera, varieties, and garden forms are not included. Intended for the horticulturist, entries give concise descriptions of plants and indication of the origin and date of cultivation, plus the climatic zone in which each plant thrives. Glossary; key to authors' names; index to scientific and common names.

Supplemented by the author's *Bibliography of cultivated trees and shrubs hardy in the cooler temperate regions of the Northern Hemisphere* (EG204).   QK481.R4

Sargent, Charles Sprague. The silva of North America : a description of the trees which grow naturally in North America exclusive of Mexico .... Boston : Houghton, 1891–1902. 14 v. : 740 plates.   **EG201**

Repr.: 1947 (14 v. in 7).

Systematic arrangement of descriptions of "all woody plants which grow up from the ground with a single stem."—*Pref.* Includes complete descriptions of characteristics, habitats, and economic and medicinal uses of all genera included; not all species are completely described. Large, detailed engravings of leaves, flowers, and fruit. Extensive footnotes; no bibliography. General index in v. 14 includes scientific and common names, authors' names and subjects.

QK481.S24

Silvics of forest trees of the United States / prep. by the Division of Timber Management Research, Forest Service ; comp. and rev. by H. A. Fowells. Wash. : U.S. Dept of Agriculture, Forest Service, 1965. 762 p. : ill. (Agriculture handbook, no.271).   **EG202**

"An edited compendium of nearly 125 silvical leaflets prepared by specialists at the Forest Service experiment stations."—*Foreword.* Gives habitat conditions (climate, soils and topography, associated trees and shrubs), life history, and races and hybrids of the individual species. Includes bibliographic references. Indexes of common names and scientific names.   SD395.U5

Sinclair, Wayne A. Diseases of trees and shrubs / by Wayne A. Sinclair, Howard H. Lyon, and Warren T. Johnson. Ithaca, N.Y. : Comstock Pub. Associates, 1987. 574 p. : ill.   **EG203**

Provides a description of each disease and its causal agent, with a bibliography of some 2,000 references. Very fine photographs in color; index of common and scientific names of plants and fungi. Very useful.   SB762.S56

Bibliography

Rehder, Alfred. Bibliography of cultivated trees and shrubs hardy in the cooler temperate regions of the Northern Hemisphere. Jamaica Plain, Mass. : Arnold Arboretum of Harvard Univ., 1949. 825 p.   **EG204**

Designed to "give references to sources of the botanical names, valid names and synonyms, of the woody plants" (*Introd.*) arranged approximately the same as in the author's *Manual of cultivated trees and shrubs* (EG200), to which it is a companion volume. Index to scientific names.   Z5356.T8R42

ZOOLOGY

General works

Bibliography

Animal identification : a reference guide. London : British Museum (Natural History) ; Chichester, [Eng.] ; N.Y. : Wiley, [1980]. 3 v.   **EG205**

Ed. by R. W. Sims.

Contents: v. 1, Marine and brackish water animals; v. 2, Land and freshwater animals (*not* insects); v. 3, Insects (ed. by D. Hollis).

"It is the intention in these volumes to provide ... help by listing primary reference sources so that the non-specialist by himself will be able to set about identifying any animal from any part of the world."—*Introd.* Citations to articles and books are arranged by phylum. Within each phylum entries are subdivided into general, systematic, and geographical sections. Vol. 3 has a group name index; no other indexes.   Z7994.I34A54

Baker, Sylva. Endangered vertebrates : a selected, annotated bibliography, 1981–1988. N.Y. : Garland, 1990. 197 p. (Garland reference library of social science, v. 480).   **EG206**

A list of about 1,000 vertebrates which, following a general sources section, are arranged taxonomically from mammals to fishes. An appendix lists organizations concerned with endangered species and includes their publications. Indexes to common names, scientific names, authors, and geographic areas.   Z7996.V4B35

Blacker-Wood Library of Zoology and Ornithology. A dictionary catalogue of the Blacker-Wood library .... Boston : G.K. Hall, 1966. 9 v.   **EG207**

At head of title: McGill University, Montreal.

Reproduction of the catalog cards for this collection of about 60,000 volumes.   Z7991.B67

Blackwelder, Richard Eliot. Guide to the taxonomic literature of vertebrates. Ames : Iowa State Univ. Pr., [1972]. 259 p.   **EG208**

Intended for student use and based on material appearing in the *Zoological record*, this is a bibliography of items "published during the past 50 years or more which may be taxonomically useful themselves or may lead the student to the older literature."—*Pref.* Under each class of vertebrates, citations are grouped by type of work, i.e., bibliographies, faunas, glossaries, etc. Revisionary works are listed alphabetically by family name, with references to alphabetical author lists with complete citations. In general, works on fossils are not included. No indexes.

Engelmann, Wilhelm. Bibliotheca historico-naturalis : Verzeichniss der Bücher über Naturgeschichte, welche in Deutschland, Scandinavien, Holland, England, Frankreich, Italien und Spanien 1700–1846 erscheinen sind. ... Mit einem Namen– und Sach-Register. Leipzig : Engelmann, 1846. 786 p.   **EG209**

Citations are arranged in groups according to the types and topics of the works included. Each section is divided into subsections of German and "foreign" works. Covers anatomy and physiology, zoology, and paleontology.

§ Continued for zoology by:

Bibliotheca zoologica [I] : Verzeichnis der Schriften über Zoologie welche in den periodischen Werken enthalten und vom Jahre 1846–1860 selbständig erschienen sind. Mit Einschluss der allgemein-naturgeschichtlichen, periodischen und paleontologischen Schriften, bearb. von J. Victor Carus und Wilhelm Engelmann (Leipzig : Engelmann, 1861. 2 v. [Bibliotheca historico-naturalis, hrsg. von Wilhelm Engelmann. Supplement Bd.]).

Autoren- und Sach-Register.

Bibliotheca zoologica II : Verzeichnis der Schriften über Zoologie welche in den periodischen Werken enthalten und vom Jahre 1861–1880 selbständig erschienen sind, bearb. von O. Taschenberg (Leipzig : Engelmann, 1887–1923. 8 v.).

No indexes. These three works comprise an international classed bibliography covering the literature of zoology, 1770–1880.

Z7401.E56

Harvard University. Museum of Comparative Zoology. Library. Catalogue. Boston : G. K. Hall, 1968. 8v.   **EG210**

A main-entry catalog, but with many useful analytics under the author entries. The collection contains nearly 250,000 volumes.

———. ———. *First supplement.* (Boston : G.K. Hall, 1976. 770 p.).

"The First supplement ... includes new titles added to the Library since 1966 as well as cataloging information for many older titles revised according to the Anglo-American cataloging rules."—*Pref.*

Z7999.H32

International catalogue of scientific literature / publ. for the Internat. Council by the Royal Soc. of London. v. 1 (1901)–v. 14 (1914). London : Harrison, 1902–21.   **EG211**

Section N, Zoology, in the 1st–14th annual issues, 1901–14. Of this section, v. 6–14, 1906–14, were issued jointly with the *Zoological record,* v. 43–51. For description of the full set *see* EA16.

Nissen, Claus. Die zoologische Buchillustration : ihre Bibliographie und Geschichte. Stuttgart : A. Hiersemann, 1966–78. 2 v.   **EG212**

Contents: v. 1, Bibliographie; v. 2, Geschichte der zoologischen Buchillustration.

Issued serially in 16 pts. Vol. 1 is a bibliography of illustrated works listed alphabetically by first author and by illustrator, with indexes to subject, geographic area, animal, and author (including coauthors and editors). Vol. 2 is a history of zoological illustration and is indexed by author, illustrator, geographic area, subject and animal; it also includes a supplement to v. 1 which has a closing date of Sept. 1975.

Z7991.N5

Reuss, Jeremias David. Repertorium commentationum a societatibus litterariis editarum / secundum disciplinarum ordinem digessit I. D. Reuss .... Gottingae : apud Henricum Dieterich, 1801–21. 16 v.   **EG213**

T. 1, Historia naturalis, generalis et zoologia. For full description, *see* EA21.

Z5051.R44

Ruch, Theodore Cedric. Bibliographia primatologica : a classified bibliography of primates other than man ... v. 1. Springfield, Ill. ; Baltimore : Thomas, 1941. 241 p. (Yale Univ. School of Medicine. Yale Medical Library. Historical Library , Pubn. no.4).   **EG214**

Contents: pt. 1, Anatomy, embryology and quantitative morphology; Physiology, pharmacology and psychobiology; Primate phylogeny and miscellanea.

Covers material published through 1938. Classed arrangement; author index. 4,630 entries.

Z7996.P85R8

Wood, Casey Albert. An introduction to the literature of vertebrate zoology : based chiefly on the titles in the Blacker Library of Zoology, the Emma Shearer Wood Library of Ornithology, the Bibliotheca Osleriana and other libraries of McGill University, Montreal. London : Oxford Univ. Pr., 1931. 643 p.   **EG215**

Issued also as *McGill University publications, ser. XI (Zoology),* no. 24.

Contents: Introduction to the literature of vertebrate zoology, p. 1–146; Students' and librarians' ready index to short author-titles on vertebrate zoology arranged geographically and in chronological order, p. 147–72; A partially annotated catalog of the titles on vertebrate zoology in the libraries of McGill University, p. 173–643.

Z7996.V4W8

Indexes; Abstract journals

Bibliographia zoologica. v. 1 (1896)–43 (1934). Zurich : Sumptibus Concilii Bibliographici, 1896–1934.   **EG216**

Publisher varies.

Vols. 1–22 published as v. 19–35 of *Zoologischer Anzeiger,* continuing *Literatur* published in that periodical, v. 1–18.

An international classed bibliography of the periodical literature of zoology, similar in format to the earlier works of the related *Bibliotheca zoologica [I]* and *Bibliotheca zoologica II* (EG209 *note*), but with updated classification schemes. Includes paleozoology. Comprehensive coverage starts approximately with the literature for 1895. The individual volumes have no indexes, but the *Bibliographia zoologica* is indexed in the *Register* of the *Zoologischer Anzeiger,* Jahrg. 16–40, 1899–1922 (5 v.).

Z7991.B6

Wildlife abstracts. no. 1/66 (1935/51)– . Wash. : U.S. Dept. of the Interior, Fish & Wildlife Service, 1954– . Quinquennial.   **EG217**

Superintendent of Documents classification: I 49.17/2: .

Early volumes cover 1935/51, 1952/55, 1956/60 (issued by Bureau of Sport Fisheries and Wildlife), 1961/70.

Cumulations of the citations and indexing appearing in *Wildlife review* (EG218).

SK351.U52

Wildlife review. no.1 (Sept. 1935)– . [Ft. Collins, Colo. : Fish and Wildlife Service], 1935– . 6 no. a year.   **EG218**

Superintendent of Documents classification: I 49.17: .

Place of publication, issuing body, frequency, and format vary.

A subject-arranged index to serial and report literature on wildlife management. Entries are not annotated. Issues include author, geographical, and subject indexes. Indexes cumulated annually starting with no.180, 1981. Indexed by *Wildlife abstracts* (EG217).

•Available in machine-readable format as *Wildlife worldwide.*

SK351.W58

Zentralblatt für Zoologie : allgemeine und experimentelle Biologie. Leipzig : Teubner, 1912–18. 6 v.   **EG219**

Formed by the union of the *Zoologisches Zentralblatt,* 1894–1911, and the *Zentralblatt für allgemeine und experimentelle Biologie.* Includes surveys of the literature with abstracts for the most important papers.

The zoological record. v. 1 (1864)– . Philadelphia : BioSciences Information Service ; London : Zoological Soc. of London, 1865– . Annual.   **EG220**

Vols. 1–6 entitled *Record of zoological literature.*

Vols. 43–52, 1906–15, issued also as Sec. N of the *International catalogue of scientific literature* (EA16).

Jointly published by BIOSIS and the Zoological Society beginning with v. 115.

A comprehensive index to worldwide serials literature in systematic zoology. Now published in 20 sections. As applicable, each section consists of five indexes: author, subject, geographical, palaeontological, and systematic. Full bibliographical information is given in the author index; the remaining indexes refer to the numbers assigned to the author entries. The previous long delay between publication of the cited articles and their indexing is now substantially eliminated.

Z7991.Z87

•Zoological record online [database]. Philadelphia : BIOSIS, 1978– .   **EG221**

Machine-readable version of *The zoological record,* 1978 to the present (EG220).

Available online and on magnetic tape, updated monthly.

More up-to-date and generally easier to search than the printed version. Worldwide in scope; records are drawn from some 6,000 journals and consist mainly of systematic and taxonomic information about all living and extinct animals, divided into 27 groups. Records contain basic bibliographic data and include subject headings and systematic classification for each animal. No abstracts.

Zoologischer Bericht im Auftrage der Deutschen Zoologischen Gesellschaft. Jena : G. Fischer, 1922–1943/44. 55 Bd.
EG222

————. *General-Autoren Register*, Bd. 1–25, 1922–31; Bd. 26–50, 1931–40.

Contains abstracts of books and periodical material in various languages.

Zoologischer Jahresbericht / hrsg. von der Zoologischen Station zu Neapel. v. 1 (1879)–v. 35 (1913). Leipzig : Zoologischen Station zu Neapel, 1880–1924. Annual. v. 1–35.
EG223

————. *Autoren- und Sachregister*, 1886–90, 1891–1900, 1901–10.

A bibliographical and review journal covering the whole field of zoology through 1884. Subsequently, systematic zoology was omitted, as it was covered by *The zoological record* (EG220). Systematic arrangement, with various indexes in each volume.

Encyclopedias

George, J. David. Marine life : an illustrated encyclopedia of invertebrates in the sea / David J. George and Jennifer J. George. N.Y. : Wiley, [1979]. 288 p. : ill.   **EG224**

Includes only living species, arranged systematically by 27 invertebrate phyla with marine representatives. Entries are keyed to 128 pages of photographs, virtually all in color. Indexed.   QL121.G4

Gozmany, László. Seven-language thesaurus of European animals. London : Chapman and Hall, 1990. 2 v.   **EG225**

Vol. 1 contains 12,026 scientific names, listed alphabetically by genus or suprageneric category, of vertebrate and invertebrate animals, including insects and protozoa, which have vernacular names in at least two of six modern languages (English, German, French, Hungarian, Spanish, and Russian). The scientific name is considered the 7th language. Beneath each scientific name is a list of vernacular synonyms in each of the other languages in which they exist. Vol. 1 also contains a dictionary of the zoological taxa designations in each language (plus Latin) and an outline of the taxonomy used. Vol. 2 contains indexes to the first key word of the vernacular names in each language.   QL353.G69

Grzimek, Bernhard. Grzimek's animal life encyclopedia. N.Y. : Van Nostrand Reinhold, [1972–75]. 13 v. : ill. **EG226**

Translation of *Grzimeks Tierleben: Enzyklopädie des Tierreiches* (Zürich, 1968. 13 v.).

Contents: v. 1, Lower animals; v. 2, Insects; v. 3, Mollusks and echinoderms; v. 4, Fishes I; v. 5, Fishes II and amphibia; v. 6, Reptiles; v. 7–9, Birds I–III; v. 10–13, Mammals I–IV.

Each volume is made up of chapters by an international group of scholars treating the various classes, orders, families, etc., according to modern zoological classification and names. Profusely illustrated. Each volume includes an outline of systematic classification; an "Animal dictionary" giving corresponding names in English, German, French, and Russian; a list of supplementary readings; and an index to the volume in question.   QL3.G7813

Dictionaries

The concise Oxford dictionary of zoology / ed. by Michael Allaby. Oxford, [Eng.] ; N.Y. : Oxford Univ. Pr., 1991. 508 p.
EG227

Directed at "students, professional non-zoologists, and non-professional zoologists."—*Pref.* "Most of its entries are based on those pertaining to zoology which appeared earlier in *The Oxford dictionary of natural history* [EG78] but they have been extensively revised and more have been added, effectively making this a new and different work." Asterisks are placed next to all terms in definitions that have

their own entries. "Many new entries have been added to augment those on ecology and physiology in particular, and changes that have occured since 1985 in the classification." Definitions vary in length from one line to about one column in length. No illustrations.
QL9.C66

International code of zoological nomenclature / ed. by W.D.L. Ride … [et al.]. 3rd ed. [London] : International Trust for Zoological Nomenclature ; Berkeley : Univ. of California Pr., 1985. 338 p.   **EG228**

Adopted by the XX General Assembly of the International Union of Biological Sciences.

1st ed., 1961.

This edition "has one fundamental aim, which is to provide the maximum universality and continuity in the scientific names of animals compatible with the freedom of scientists to classify animals according to taxonomic judgments."—*Introd.* The text is in French and English on facing pages. There is a glossary and an index in each language and an index of scientific names.   QL353.I67

Leftwich, A. W. A dictionary of zoology. [3rd ed.]. London : Constable, [1973]. 478 p.   **EG229**

1st ed., 1963.

Offers concise definitions of about 6,700 technical terms relating to zoology and related branches of biology including taxonomy, comparative anatomy, physiology, histology, genetics, ecology, etc. There is a separate section with short entries and/or references for 800 English names of animals; a section on classification and nomenclature; and a bibliography.   QL9.L4

Pennak, Robert William. Collegiate dictionary of zoology. N.Y. : Ronald, [1964]. 583 p.   **EG230**

Intended for specialists as well as students. Gives succinct definitions of 19,000 terms in the zoological disciplines; includes paleontological terms, scientific and common names, and biographical entries. Appendix: Condensed taxonomic outline of the animal kingdom.
QL9.P4

Handbooks

Conn, David Bruce. Atlas of invertebrate reproduction and development. N.Y. : Wiley-Liss, c1991. 252 p. : ill.   **EG231**

"Outlines the major groups of invertebrate animals with respect to their major reproductive and developmental strategies."—*Pref.* Phylogenetically arranged. Glossary and index.   QL364.15.C67

Handbuch der Zoologie : eine Naturgeschichte der Stämme des Tierreiches / gegründet von Willy Kükenthal ; hrsg. von J. G. Helmcke [et al.]. 2. Aufl. Berlin : W. de Gruyter, 1968– . v. 4– : ill. (In progress).   **EG232**

The 1st ed. of this work, which began publication in 1923, is still in progress. The 2nd ed. begins with v. 4 (Arthropoda: Insecta). A comprehensive descriptive work covering all animals of the world. Includes discussions of paleontology and of all aspects of the biology of the various orders, classes, genera, etc. Basic arrangement is systematic. Mainly in German; some of the more recently published sections include occasional articles in English. Each of the major bibliographic sections has its own index. No general index.

International zoo yearbook. v.1 (1959)– . London : Zoological Soc., 1959– . Annual.   **EG233**

Contents vary from year to year with each edition including feature topics. A recurrent feature is "Zoos & aquaria of the world; new buildings and exhibits." Each volume includes a reference section listing species bred in captivity and multiple generation births, and a census of rare animals in captivity. Indexed.   QL76.A1I5

The IUCN invertebrate red data book. Gland, Switzerland : IUCN, 1983. 632 p.   **EG234**

"Compiled jointly by Susan M. Wells, Robert M. Pyle and N. Mark Collins of the IUCN [International Union for Conservation of Nature and Natural Resources] Conservation Monitoring Centre with the help and advice of the Species Survival Commission of IUCN and other experts throughout the world."—*t.p.*

For each entry gives summary, description, distribution, population, habitat and ecology, scientific interest and potential value, conservation measures taken, conservation measures proposed, captive breeding, and references. Indexed. QL362.I82

Melby, Edward C. CRC handbook of laboratory animal sciences. Cleveland : CRC Pr., 1974–76. 3 v. **EG235**

Vol. 1 deals with legislative regulations pertaining to laboratory animals for the U.S. and Canada, and includes general and specific information for the management and control of various types of animals, e.g., fish, dogs. Vol. 2 discusses neoplasias, zoonoses, and diseases of laboratory animals. Vol. 3 covers new and additional information about laboratory animals, such as: nutrition, physiological data, effect of drugs on nervous system, spontaneous viral infections, hematology, immunology, virology. Cumulated index in v. 3. QL55.M45

Microscopic anatomy of invertebrates / treatise ed., Frederick W. Harrison, Edward E. Ruppert. N.Y. : Wiley-Liss, c1991–93. 15 v. : ill. **EG236**

Contents: v. 1, Protozoa; v. 2, Placozoa, Porifera, Cnidaria, and Ctenophora; v. 3, Platyhelminthes and Nemertinea; v. 4, Aschelminthes; v. 5, Mollusca: Monoplacophora, Aplacophora, Polyplacophora, and Gastropoda; v. 6, Mollusca: Bivalvia, Scaphopoda, and Cephalopoda; v. 7, Annelida; v. 8, Chelicerate Arthropoda; v. 9, Crustacea; v. 10, Decapod Crustacea; v. 11, Insecta; v. 12, Onychophora, Muriapod Arthropoda, and Lesser Protostomat; v. 13, Lophophorates; v. 14, Echinodermata; v. 15, Hemichoradata, Chaetognatha, and the Invertebrate Chordates.

The 15 volumes are arranged phylogenetically. Each volume, where possible, adheres to the following outline: (1) external anatomy; (2) epithelia; (3) glands and secretion; (4) connective, skeletal and muscular tissue; (5) vascular elements and blood; (6) digestive system and associated organs; (7) respiratory structures and gas exchange; (8) excretory structures and fluid exhange; (9) reproductive components; (10) immune system; (11) nervous system and sensory elements. QL363.M53

The official World Wildlife Fund guide to endangered species of North America / [managing ed., David W. Lowe, editors, John R. Matthews, Charles J. Moseley]. Wash. : Beacham Pub., c1990. 2 v. : ill. (some col.). **EG237**

Contents: v. 1, Plants, mammals; v. 2, Birds, reptiles, amphibians, fishes, mussels, crustaceans, snails, insects, & arachnids.

An exceptional work that attempts to "consolidate information on native plants and animals that have been placed on the list of threatened and endangered species."—*Pref.* Each species is described in about two pages, which include: a brief physical description; behavior; habitat; historic and current distribution; an essay on conservation and recovery; a brief bibliography; a small black-and-white photograph, generally poor in quality; a diagrammatic distribution map; and contacts for further information. Appendixes include lists of U.S. Fish and Wildlife Service and National Marine Fisheries Service offices, State Heritage Programs, Bureau of Land Management and National Forest Service offices, National Wildlife Refuges, and state-by-state occurrence of each endangered species. Index to common and scientific names. QL84.2.O35

Whiteley, Derek. The Oxford book of vertebrates : cyclostomes, fish, amphibians, reptiles and mammals. London : Oxford Univ. Pr., 1972. 216 p. : ill. **EG238**

Illustrates and describes "the wide variety [about 340 species] of vertebrates found in and around the British Isles."—*Introd.* The book is one of the publisher's series of similar works such as *The Oxford book of birds*, by Bruce Campbell (London, 1964); *The Oxford book of insects*, by John Burton (London, 1968); and *The Oxford book of invertebrates*, by David Nichols and John Cooke (London, 1971). QL255.W48

Treatises

Halstead, Bruce W. Poisonous and venomous marine animals of the world. 2nd rev. ed. Princeton, N.J. : Darwin Pr., c1988. 1168 p., 288 p. of plates : ill. **EG239**

1st ed., 1965–70 (Wash. : U.S. Govt. Print Off. 3 v.).

Authoritative and exhaustive coverage of marine biotoxicology. Taxonomic arrangement of well over 500 species, with an exceptional set of plates. Citations are listed at the end of each chapter and in a brief list at end. Personal name and subject indexes. RA1255.H35

Hyman, Libbie Henrietta. The invertebrates. N.Y. : McGraw-Hill, 1940–67. v. 1–6^1. : ill. **EG240**

Contents: [v. 1], Protozoa through Ctenophora; v. 2, Platyhelminthes and Rhynchocoela, the acoelomate Bilateria; v. 3, Acanthocephala, Aschelminthes, and Entroprocta, the pseudocoelomate Bilateria; v. 4, Echinodermata; v. 5, Smaller coelomate groups; v. 6^1, Mollusca.

A comprehensive treatise, arranged by phylum, on all aspects of the biology of the invertebrates. Describes all phyla included, but does not discuss separate species in detail. Serves as a reference manual for students and researchers in zoology and for workers in allied fields. Includes a bibliography for each phylum and an index to each volume. QL362.H9

Pennak, Robert William. Fresh-water invertebrates of the United States : protozoa to mollusca. 3rd ed. N.Y. : Wiley, c1989. 628 p. : ill. **EG241**

1st ed., 1953; 2nd ed., 1978.

Chapters for each major group, in taxonomic order, Protozoa to Pelecypoda. Insects are included. Each chapter has a taxonomic key to members of the group and gives general descriptions of the group's biological characteristics, taxonomy, ecology, and techniques of culture and preservation. References are at the end of each chapter. The appendix lists and defines reagents, solutions, and laboratory items mentioned more than once in the text. Index to subjects and to scientific and common names. QL141.P45

Traité de zoologie : anatomie, systématique, biologie / pub. sous la direction de Pierre-P. Grassé. Paris : Masson, 1948– . 17 v. : ill., maps. (In progress.) **EG242**

An exhaustive, multivolume treatise, arranged systemically and including extinct and fossil forms. Volumes are published in parts and out of sequence. Many detailed black-and-white drawings; black-and-white and color photographs. Bibliography for each topical section. Each physical volume has its own index. QL45.T7

Generic indexes

Neave, Sheffield Airey. Nomenclator zoologicus : a list of the names of genera and subgenera in zoology from the tenth edition of Linnaeus 1758 to the end of [1945]. London : Zoological Soc. of London, 1939–50. 5 v. **EG243**

Contents; v. 1–4, A–Z and suppl.; v. 5, 1936–45.

Lists in alphabetical order, by name of genus or subgenus, the original reference for each name; in cases of doubt of validity or scarcity of the original work, additional references may be given. Does not include unapproved or hypothetical names.

Continued by *Nomenclator zoologicus* (EG244). QL354.N4

Nomenclator zoologicus. London : Zoological Soc. of London, 1966–75. v. 6–7. **EG244**

Continues the publication of v. 1–5 (EG243).

Contents: v. 6, 1946–55, ed. by Marcia A. Edwards and A. Tindell Hopwood; v. 7, 1956–65, ed. by Marcia A. Edwards and H. Gwynne Vevers.

Amphibians and reptiles

Cochran, Doris Mabel. The new field book of reptiles and amphibians : more than 200 photographs and diagrams. N.Y. : Putnam, [1970]. 359 p. : ill. **EG245**
For the beginner. Intended as "an introduction to the salamanders, frogs and toads, turtles, crocodilians, lizards, and snakes now known to occur in the United States, including Alaska and Hawaii."—*Pref.* QL644.C6

Ditmars, Raymond Lee. The reptiles of North America : a review of the crocodilians, lizards, snakes, turtles and tortoises inhabiting the United States and Northern Mexico. N.Y. : Doubleday, 1936. 476 p. : ill. **EG246**
A revision of the author's *Reptile book* (N.Y., 1907).
Comprehensive in scope and inclusion of species. Popular in approach, using common names of species and non-technical descriptions and narrative style in discussion of coloration, distribution, habits, etc., of better-known species. Large section of photographic plates; index to scientific and common names. QL651.D6

Ernst, Carl H. Turtles of the world / Carl H. Ernst and Roger W. Barbour. Wash. : Smithsonian Institution Pr., c1989. 313 p., 16 p. of plates : ill. **EG247**
Primarily a guide to identification of the 257 turtle species now living, presented in 12 chapters, one for each family. Good bibliography and glossary; adequate illustrations. Indexes of terminology and of scientific and common names. QL666.C5E77

Frost, Darrel R. Amphibian species of the world. Lawrence, Kan. : Allen Pr. and the Assoc. of Systematics Collections, [1985]. 732 p. **EG248**
Subtitle: A taxonomic and geographical reference.
"Compiled for the Parties to the Convention on International Trade in Endangered Species of Wild Fauna and Flora to serve as a standard reference to amphibian nomenclature under the auspices of the World Congress of Herpetology and its Checklist Committee, William E. Duellman, Chairman."—*verso of half t.p.*
An annotated checklist of 4,014 nominal species. Organization: higher taxonomy; scientific name, authority, year of publication, and citation; type species; type specimen(s); type locality; distribution; comments; attribution; and protected status. Taxonomic index. QL645.F76

Harding, Keith A. Venomous snakes of the world : a checklist / Keith A. Harding and Kenneth R.G. Welch. Oxford ; N.Y. : Pergamon Pr., [1980]. 188 p. **EG249**
Publ. as suppl. 1 to the journal *Toxicon.*
Main section arranged taxonomically. Gives original description for genera, original description reference, type locality, and distribution for species and subspecies. Geographical distribution section lists genera by country. Author and subject indexes. QL666.O6H34

The IUCN amphibia-reptilia red data book / comp. by Brian Groombridge; assisted by Lissie Wright, with the help and advice of the Species Survival Commission of IUCN and other experts throughout the world. Fully rev., expanded ed. Gland, Switzerland : IUCN, 1982. v. 1 (426 p.). (In progress?). **EG250**
Contents: pt. 1, Testudines, Crocodylia, Rhynchocephalia.
Earlier versions (1968–79), comp. by R. E. Honegger, appeared in looseleaf format as v. 3 of the *Red data book* published by the International Union for Conservation of Nature and Natural Resources.
For each entry gives summary, distribution, population, habitat and ecology, threats to survival, conservation measures taken, conservation measures proposed, captive breeding, remarks, and references. Indexed. QL641.G76

Leviton, Alan E. Reptiles and amphibians of North America. N.Y. : Doubleday, [1971]. 250 p. : ill. **EG251**
Offers popular descriptions of appearance, habits, habitat, etc., of families of amphibians and reptiles found north of Mexico. Includes short comments on specific species. Arranged by order, with an index to amphibians and an index to reptiles. Includes short general section on keeping reptiles, and a brief bibliography. QL651.L42

Obst, Fritz Jürgen. The completely illustrated atlas of reptiles and amphibians for the terrarium / Fritz Jürgen Obst, Klaus Richter, Udo Jacob ; English-language ed., Jerry G. Walls. Neptune City, N.J. : T.F.H. Publications, c1988. 830 p. : ill. **EG252**
Translation of *Lexikon der Terraristik und Herpetologie* (Hannover : Land-buch Verlag, 1984).
Athough not comprehensive, an impressive information source for domestic reptiles and amphibians. Includes more than 1,500 excellent full-color photographs and hundreds of drawings. Indexed. SF459.A45O27

Birds

The birds of North America. no. 1– . Wash. : American Ornithologists' Union, c1992– . Bimonthly. **EG253**
Issued jointly by American Ornithologists' Union and Academy of Natural Sciences of Philadelphia. QL681.B625

The Cambridge encyclopedia of ornithology / ed. by Michael Brooke and Tim Birkhead. Cambridge ; N.Y. : Cambridge Univ. Pr., 1991. 362 p. : ill. (some col.). **EG254**
Contents: (1) Introduction, (2) Anatomy & physiology, (3) Movement, (4) Birds, ancient and modern (survey of fossil and modern birds), (5) The daily activities of birds (e.g., feeding, sleep, disease), (6) Distribution, (7) Migration and navigation, (8) Bird populations, (9) Breeding, (10) Behavior, (11) People and birds (e.g., birds in art, domestic birds, conservation). Appendixes include a list of ornithological organizations, a glossary of terms, and a bibliography. Indexes to scientific names, common names, and subjects. QL672.2.C35

Check-list of North American birds : the species of birds of North America from the Arctic through Panama, including the West Indies and Hawaiian Islands / prep. by the Committee on Classification and Nomenclature of the American Ornithologists' Union. 6th ed. [Wash.] : The Union, 1983. 877 p. : port., maps. **EG255**
1st ed., 1889; 5th ed., 1957.
Taxonomic arrangement. Includes AOU numbers for each species, and lists species which have been introduced. Index of scientific and common names. QL681.C52

Clark, William S. A field guide to hawks : North America. Boston : Houghton Mifflin, 1987. 198 p. : ill., maps. (The Peterson field guide series, 35). **EG256**
"Sponsored by the National Audubon Society and the National Wildlife Federation."
A taxonomic arrangement of species of the U.S. and Canada only. A prefatory chapter treats the general topography of hawks. Provides a good description of each of 39 species, including sexual differences, both flight and stationary identification marks, geographic distribution, and behavior. An unusual feature of this guide is the set of photographs of virtually all the species, many both in flight and at rest. At the end is a list of more than 400 references indexed by both species and topics, and a general index to genera as main headings, to species as subheadings, and to common names. 24 plates in color. QL696.F3C59

A dictionary of birds / ed. by Bruce Campbell and Elizabeth Lack. Vermillion, S.D. : Publ. for the British Ornithologists' Union [by] Buteo Books, 1985. 670 p. : ill. **EG257**
A revised and rewritten edition of *A new dictionary of birds* (1964) which was a successor to Alfred Newton's *Dictionary of birds* (1896). "The Dictionary consists of articles on general subjects relat-

ing to birds, and on different kinds of birds mainly treated by family."—*Introd.* With contributions by more than 280 specialists, the work combines elements of a dictionary and an encyclopedia. Longer entries include references.   QL677.D53

Ehrlich, Paul R. The birder's handbook : a field guide to the natural history of North American birds : including all species that regularly breed north of Mexico / Paul R. Ehrlich, David S. Dobkin, Darryl Wheye. N.Y. : Simon & Schuster, c1988. 785 p. : ill.   **EG258**

In two parts: (1) taxonomically arranged essays treating nearly 650 species; (2) brief essays on aspects of their natural history. Separate subject, author, and scientific/common name indexes and a guide to essay topics. Extensive bibliography.   QL681.E37

———————— Birds in jeopardy : the imperiled and extinct birds of the United States and Canada including Hawaii and Puerto Rico / Paul R. Ehrlich, David S. Dobkin, and Darryl Wheye ; illustrations by Darryl Wheye. Stanford, Calif. : Stanford Univ. Pr., 1992. 259 p. : col. ill.   **EG259**

Descriptions and illustrations of 151 imperiled and 29 extinct species. Contents: Birds that are officially threatened or endangered; Birds that are not officially listed in the U.S.; Birds that have become extinct since 1776; Commentaries on imperilment; Regional quick check of birds in jeopardy; Reference materials. Index to English and scientific names.

Review: *Choice*, 30 (Sept. 1992): review 30-0297.

QL676.55.E38

The encyclopedia of birds / ed. by Christopher M. Perrins and Alex L. A. Middleton. N.Y. : Facts on File, [1985]. 447 p. : ill.   **EG260**

"We have tried to provide the reader with an encapsulated but up-to-date account of the world's birds."—*Pref.* Consists of articles dealing with single families or several families; recognizes 8,805 species. Gives information on distribution, habitat, dimension, plumage, voice, nests, eggs, and diet. Colored illustrations and maps. Indexed.   QL673.E53

Gruson, Edward S. Checklist of the world's birds : a complete list of the species, with names, authorities and areas of distribution. N.Y. : Times Books, [1976]. 212 p.   **EG261**

"It is the purpose of this book to provide as complete a listing of the species of birds of the world as possible, to give the scientific name and an English common name for each of the species, to provide a source to which the reader is referred if more information about the species is wanted and to give a gross idea of its range."—*Introd.*

QL677.G76

Handbook of the birds of Europe, the Middle East and North Africa : the birds of the Western Palearctic / Stanley Cramp, chief ed. ... [et al.]. Oxford ; N. Y. : Oxford Univ. Pr., 1977–1993. v. 1–7 : ill. (In progress).   **EG262**

Contents: v. 1, Ostrich to ducks (1977); v. 2, Hawks to bustards (1980); v. 3, Waders to gulls (1983); v. 4, Terns to woodpeckers (1985); v. 5, Tyrant flycatchers to thrushes (1989); v. 6, Warblers (1992); v. 7, Old World Flycatchers to Shrikes (1993). To be complete in 8 v.

Each species is described by field characters, habitat, distribution, movements, food, behavior, voice, breeding and detailed external morphology. Each volume has a separate index of scientific names as well as common English, French, and German names. Full-color illustrations are distributed through each volume with color plates of eggs at the end, along with an extensive list of cited references. Each later volume has a section of corrections to earlier volumes. Nonpasserine species are covered in v. 1–4, passerines in v. 5–8.   QL690.A1H25

Howard, Richard. A complete checklist of the birds of the world / Richard Howard, Alick Moore. 2nd ed. [Orlando, Fla.] : Academic Pr., 1991. 701 p.   **EG263**

Previous ed., 1980.

A taxonomically arranged checklist of more than 9,200 species;

arrangement of orders and families is given at the beginning. For each species gives geographic distribution and English name. Separate indexes to Latin and English names. Uses the Basel sequence of families. This may be the last major world list that does *not* depend on DNA hybridization studies.   QL677.H75

The illustrated encyclopedia of birds : the definitive reference to birds of the world / consultant-in-chief, Christopher M. Perrins. N.Y. : Prentice Hall Editions, c1990. 420 p. : ill. (some col.), maps (some col.).   **EG264**

Publ. in association with International Council for Bird Preservation.

Of 9,300 species listed, many are described and illustrated. Descriptions include range, habitat and size. Includes a word checklist of species (p. 366–412) and an index to scientific and common names. Introduction covers general aspects of structure and biology, evolution and classification, geography, ecology, migration, particularly unusual birds, threatened species, and conservation. Review: *Choice*, 29 (July–Aug. 1992): review 29-6032.   QL672.2.I45

Jobling, James A. A dictionary of scientific bird names. Oxford ; N.Y. : Oxford Univ. Pr., 1991. 272 p. : ill.   **EG265**

About 8,500 names arranged alphabetically with generic and specific names in one sequence. Each part of the name (genus and species) is entered separately. "My aims have been to provide a complete and accurate etymology for all currently valid genera and specific bird names described between January 1758 and June 1990, together with an eclectic selection of historical synonyms."—*Introd.*   QL677.J55

Johnsgard, Paul A. Hawks, eagles & falcons of North America : biology and natural history. Wash. : Smithsonian Institution Pr., c1990. 403 p., [31] p. of plates : ill., maps.   **EG266**

Begins with several chapters on general aspects of ecology and behavior, followed by a taxonomic arrangement of chapters on each species with distribution maps. Appendixes contain a taxonomic key to species, origins of both common and scientific names, a glossary, and field identification marks. A separate section at the end cites about 7,700 references. Indexed.   QL696.F3J6

Lever, Christopher. Naturalized birds of the world / Christopher Lever ...[et al.]. Burnt Mill, Harlow, Essex, England : Longman Scientific & Technical ; N.Y. : Wiley, 1987. 615 p. : ill.   **EG267**

Taxonomic arrangement of about 140 species. "Each species account is a monograph on an individual bird" whose collective intent is to describe "when, where, how and by whom various birds now living in the wild state were introduced, and what effects for good or ill, they have had on the native biota."—*Pref.* Indexed by common and scientific names and by geographic location. Provides small natural and naturalized distribution maps for each species. Bibliography of about 2,000 references.   QL677.4.L49

Miller, Melanie Ann. Birds : a guide to the literature. N.Y. : Garland, 1986. 887 p. (Garland reference library of the humanities, vol. 680).   **EG268**

An annotated bibliography of literature about birds, 1800–1984, readily accessible in libraries. Nearly 2,000 individual works are listed, as well as major periodicals and organization publications. Index of authors and anonymous titles.   Z5331.M54

Monroe, Burt L. A world checklist of birds / Burt L. Monroe, Jr., Charles G. Sibley. New Haven, Conn. : Yale Univ. Pr., c1993. 393 p.   **EG269**

Ql677.M75

Mountfort, Guy. Rare birds of the world : a Collins/ICBP handbook. Lexington, Mass. : S. Greene Pr., 1989. 1 v.   **EG270**

Lists about 1,000 species in a geographic arrangement with a taxonomic arrangement in each geographic group. Appendix 1 gives a systematic list of the species with vernacular and scientific names, endangered status, zoogeographic region, and range of distribution; Ap-

pendix 2 lists those birds presumed to have gone extinct since 1600 (about 100). Separate indexes of scientific and vernacular names.
QL676.7.M68

Palmer, Ralph S. Handbook of North American birds. New Haven, Conn. : Yale Univ. Pr., 1962–88. 5 v. **EG271**
Contents: v. 1, Loons through flamingoes; v. 2–3, Waterfowl; v. 4–5, Diurnal raptors.
An exceptional, very thorough standard ornithological work. Intended to be comprehensible by general readers, hence unfamiliar terminology and concepts are kept to a minimum. For each species, gives detailed textual description of both sexes, as well as of any known subspecies, including field identification marks, voice, habitat, distribution, banding status, reproduction, survival, general habits and food. Vol. 4 has its own index, v. 5 an index for both volumes and a list of literature cited in both volumes. Illustrations consist of a few simple ink drawings and distribution maps. QL681.P35

Peterson, Roger Tory. A field guide to the birds : a completely new guide to all the birds of eastern and central North America. 4th ed. Boston : Houghton Mifflin, 1980. 384p. : ill., maps. **EG272**
For list of other titles in the Peterson "Field guide" series, see EG85.
1st ed., 1934.
"This edition of *A Field Guide to the Birds*, the flagship book of the Peterson Field Guide Series, is more than a revision; it is completely new, with 136 plates, as against 60 in the previous edition. Every illustration is new or redrawn. All species are now shown in color; some are repeated in monochrome, but only when flight patterns are more clearly diagnosed in that way."—*Introd.* A classic in an updated version. Indexed. QL681.P45

Rickert, Jon E. A guide to North American bird clubs. Elizabethtown, Ky. : Avian Publ., 1978. 565 p. **EG273**
Lists over 835 bird clubs in North America. In six sections: National organizations (U.S. and Canada); State and local clubs in the U.S. (by state); Puerto Rico; Virgin Islands; Provincial and local clubs in Canada (by province); and other North American nations (by nation). Entries give person(s) to contact, birding report, publications, field trips, and meetings. No index. QL681.R52

Robbins, Chandler S. Birds of North America / Chandler S. Robbins, Bertel Bruun, and Herbert S. Zim. N.Y. : Golden Pr., [1966]. 340 p. : ill. **EG274**
At head of title: A guide to field identification.
A comprehensive, but inexpensive guide. Arranged by family, giving popular and scientific names, brief description, range, habitat, and verbal descriptions and "Sonograms" of songs or calls. Indexed. QL681.R59

Sibley, Charles Gald. Distribution and taxonomy of birds of the world / Charles G. Sibley and Burt L. Monroe, Jr. New Haven : Yale Univ. Pr., c1990. 1111 p. **EG275**
"This book has several goals: (1) to delineate the distribution of the species of birds of the world in moderate detail, and up-to-date to the beginning of 1990; (2) to arrange the species in a classification based primarily on evidence of phylogenetic relationships from comparisons of their DNAs; (3) to provide a numbering system for the species of living birds; (4) to include a gazetteer [of over 3,000 localities] with [25] maps indicating the positions of localities mentioned in the distributional accounts; and (5) to provide an index to the scientific and English names of species."—*Introd.* List of references, p. 907–939. Index to scientific names (by genus and species) and English common names, p. 940–1111.
———. ———. *Supplement* (1993. 112 p.). QL678.S54

Strong, Reuben Myron. A bibliography of birds : with special reference to anatomy, behavior, biochemistry, embryology, pathology, physiology, genetics, ecology, aviculture, economic ornithology, poultry culture, evolution, and related subjects. Chicago : Natural History Museum, 1939–59. 4 v. (Zoological series, Field museum of natural history., v. 25, pt. 1–4 ; Publication 442, 457, 581, 870). **EG276**
Compiled for the research worker in ornithology, pts. 1–2 are an author catalog of about 20,000 articles and books. Means to be comprehensive in coverage from earliest times through 1926, but includes additional titles through 1938. Authors' dates and references to biographies are included when known. Also gives library locations.
Pt. 3 is an extensive subject index. The "Finding index," pt. 4, helps the reader to find all entries for topics and names which occur in more than one place in the subject index. Z5331.S92

Terres, John K. The Audubon Society encyclopedia of North American birds. N.Y. : Knopf, 1980. 1109 p. : ill. **EG277**
"The encyclopedia is arranged alphabetically and includes the following categories: biographies of North American birds (and foreign visitors); major articles about bird life and bird biology and its study; definitions of ornithological terms; short biographies of some of the great ornithologists, naturalists and explorers whose names are associated with North American birds; and about 4,000 cross-references that link related articles and function as an index."—*Pref.* QL681.T43

Threatened birds of the Americas / N. J. Collar ... [et. al]. 3rd ed. Wash. ; London : Smithsonian Inst. Pr. in cooperation with International Council for Bird Preservation, c1992. 1150 p. : ill. (The ICBP/IUCN red data book, pt. 2.). **EG278**
Rev. ed. of Jack Vincent, *Aves* (c1966), later reissued as *Endangered birds of the world : the ICBP bird red data book*.
A comprehensive snapshot of about 300 threatened bird species in South America and the Caribbean. Those in North America and the neotropical Pacific are to be treated in a separate volume. Taxonomic and subject indexes.
Companion title: *Threatened birds of Africa and related islands*, comp. by N. J. Collar and S. N. Stuart (Cambridge, U.K. : Internat. Council for Bird Preservation ; Gland, Switzerland : Internat. Union for Conservation of Nature and Natural Resources, 1985. [The ICBP/IUCN red data book, pt. 1]). QL676.7.C69

World Association of Veterinary Anatomists. Nomina anatomica avium : an annotated anatomical dictionary of birds. London ; N.Y. : Academic Pr., 1979. 637 p. : ill. **EG279**
Prepared by the International Committee on Avian Anatomical Nomenclature, a committee of the World Association of Veterinary Anatomists.
Ed. by Julian J. Baumel, Anthony S. King, Alfred M. Lucas, James E. Breazile, and Howard E. Evans. Consultant for taxonomy: Richard L. Zusi; consultant for classical languages: Lubomir Malinovsky.
"An inescapable commitment of the NAA [Nomina anatomica avium] has been to produce Latin names for major structures which have been described but not named, or named only in the vernacular by the author. ... These broad objectives connected with usage can be summarized as follows: (1) To select one term where two or more are in general use for the same structure; (2) to replace terms which are grossly defective; (3) to produce new terms in Latin where none is available; and (4) within the limitations of the above, to codify prevailing usage."—*General introd.* Organized anatomically, e.g., osteology, digestive system, etc. Taxonomic list (scientific and common names); references; subject index. QL697.W79

Wynne, Owen E. Biographical key—names of birds of the world—to authors and those commemorated. Fordingbridge, Hants., Eng. : Author, [1969]. 246 p. **EG280**
An alphabetical list of names of persons commemorated in bird names, with birth and death dates if known, genus of bird in which the name is commemorated, a biographical note or identifying phrase, and a reference to a biographical source.

Fishes

American Fisheries Society. Committee on Names of Fishes. A list of common and scientific names of fishes from the United States and Canada. 4th ed. Bethesda, Md. : Amer. Fisheries Soc., 1980. 174 p. (Special pubn. no.12). **EG281**
By C. Richard Robins and others.
1st ed., 1948; 3rd ed., 1970.
"The present list purports to include all species of fishes known from the fresh waters of the continental United States and Canada, and those marine species inhabiting contiguous shore waters on or above the continental shelf, to a depth of 200 meters (656 feet)."—*Introd.* Lists 2,268 species in family order giving occurrence and accepted common name. Appendixes list changes from 1970 list and comments, established exotic fishes, exotic fishes formerly established or of local occurrence, and fishes known or suspected to be extinct. Indexed.
QL618.A48

The aquarium encyclopedia / by Gunther Sterba. Cambridge, Mass. : M.I.T. Pr., [1983]. 605 p. : ill. **EG282**
Translation of *Lexikon der Aquaristik und Ichthyologie* (Leipzig, 1978). Also publ. as *The aquarist's encyclopedia* (Poole, Dorset : Blandford Pr., 1983). Dick Mills, English ed.; Susan Simpson, tr.
Compiled as "a reference work for freshwater and sea-water aquarium-keeping [and to provide] basic information about general and specialist ichthyology, hydrology, fish economy, the biology of freshwater animals and marine biology."—*Foreword.* Emphasis on genera. SF456.5.L4913

Aquatic sciences & fisheries abstracts. v. 1– . London : Information Retrieval Ltd., 1971– . Monthly with annual index. **EG283**
Comp. by the Food and Agricultural Organization of the United Nations with the collaboration of Institut für Dokumentationswesen, Frankfurt, Bundesforschungsanstalt für Fischerei, Hamburg, [etc.].
An amalgamation and continuation of the *Current bibliography for aquatic sciences and fisheries*, produced by the FAO.
International coverage; abstracts in English.

Axelrod, Herbert R. Encyclopedia of tropical fishes : with special emphasis on techniques of breeding / Herbert R. Axelrod and William Vorderwinkler. 27th ed. Jersey City : T. F. H. Publs., [1983]. 631 p. : ill. **EG284**
1st ed., 1957. Frequently reissued. QL78.A86

——————— Handbook of tropical aquarium fishes / Herbert R. Axelrod and Leonard P. Schultz. Rev. ed. Neptune City, N.J. : T.F.H. Publs., 1983. 718 p. : ill. **EG285**
1st ed., 1955.
Designed for the hobbyist as well as the scientist.
The introductory chapters give a brief survey of ichthyology, the aquarium and its management, aquarium plants, and the diseases of fishes. The main part of the work illustrates and describes some 500 fishes, giving identification, range, size, temperament, sex differences, breeding, temperature requirements, food, color patterns, etc. Glossary; brief bibliography; index. QL78.A87

Dean, Bashford. A bibliography of fishes / Bashford Dean ; enl. and ed. by C. R. Eastman. N.Y. : Amer. Museum of Natural History, 1916–23. 3 v. **EG286**
The most comprehensive bibliography on fishes, "their habits, structure, development, physiology, pathology, distribution and kinds."—*Pref.* Vols. 1–2 are the author list; v. 3 offers a subject index, a list of general bibliographies, voyages, periodicals, etc. Z5971.D35

Herald, Earl Stannard. Living fishes of the world. Garden City, N.Y. : Doubleday, [1961]. 303 p. : ill. **EG287**
Arranged by systematic classification, with excellent underwater photographs, some in color. QL615.H45

Wheeler, Alwyne C. Fishes of the world : an illustrated dictionary. N.Y. : Macmillan, [1975]. 366 p. : ill. **EG288**
"The dictionary entries are arranged in alphabetical order, separate entries being made for families (cross-referenced to genera included), and under the scientific name of the species of fish. ... Widely used vernacular names mostly in the English language are also given and cross-indexed. The [500 color] plates are arranged in systematic order of families, thus bringing the closest related groups together."—*Introd.* More than 2,000 entries, which include some 700 line drawings. "Common names are fully cross-referred in the dictionary section."—*Contents.* QL614.7.W47

Mammals

Burton, John A. The Collins guide to the rare mammals of the world / John A. Burton with the assistance of Vivien G. Burton. Lexington, Mass. : S. Greene Pr. ; N.Y. : Distr. by Viking Penguin, 1988. 240 p. : ill., maps. **EG289**
A taxonomically arranged listing of the most threatened mammalian species. Verso pages have several one-paragraph descriptions of individual species, recto pages have color drawings of many of these species and distribution maps. A brief bibliography and a checklist of the species and their threatened status appear as appendixes. Index to genera and vernacular names. QL706.8.B87

Burton, Maurice. Systematic dictionary of mammals of the world / Maurice Burton ; illus. by David Pratt. 2nd ed. London : Museum Pr., [1965]. 307 p. : ill. **EG290**
1st ed., 1962.
General descriptions are given of the various subclasses, orders, suborders and families. For certain species, detailed descriptions are given, including general characters, habits, habitat, food, breeding, present status, range, and longevity. Species included are those "about which most information is available, adding where possible more shortened notes on related forms."—*Introd.* QL708.B85

Current primate references. Feb. 1965– . Seattle : Regional Primate Research Center, Univ. of Washington, 1966– . Weekly. **EG291**
A current awareness bibliography for publications dealing with all aspects of primate study. No cumulations to date.

The encyclopedia of mammals / ed. by David Macdonald. N.Y. : Facts on File, [1984]. 895 p. : ill. **EG292**
Contents: The carnivores; Sea mammals; The primates; Large herbivores—the ungulates; Small herbivores; Insect-eaters; Marsupials.
"The bulk of this encyclopedia is devoted to individual species, groups of closely related species or families of species. The text on these pages covers details of physical features, distribution, evolutionary history, diet and feeding behavior, social dynamics and spatial organization, classification, conservation and relationships with man."—*Pref.* Indexed. QL703.E53

Grzimek's encyclopedia of mammals. N.Y. : McGraw-Hill, 1989. 5 v. **EG293**
Translation of *Grzimeks Enzyklopädie Säugetiere*.
Offers more complete coverage of each mammalian group than *Grzimek's animal life encyclopedia* (EG226) but retains its general high quality, although the lack of adequate references in both works detract from their value. Arranged by subclasses and orders; each category includes an introduction, information on phylogeny and evolution of the group, detailed information about many species, and bibliographies. Good for summary accounts of the basic biology of each group and of selected individual species. Excellent photographs, although many are double page spreads in which detail is lost in the gutter. Index in each volume, but no general index.

•Laser optical version: *The multimedia encyclopedia of mammalian biology : incorporating Grzimek's encyclopedia of mammals* [laser optical disk] (Maidenhead, Berkshire, U.K. : McGraw-Hill, 1992).
QL701.G7913

Hall, Eugene Raymond. The mammals of North America. 2nd ed. N.Y. : Wiley, [1981]. 2 v. : ill., maps.   **EG294**
1st ed., 1959.
A summary of taxonomic studies of North American native mammals from 1492 to June 1977 arranged systematically by order and family. "Genera and species are arranged in order of inferred geologic age, oldest to youngest. Subspecies are arranged alphabetically."— *Pref.* For subspecies includes reference to the original description and, when necessary, reference to the first use of the current name. Includes descriptive information, marginal records, and keys to identification. Each volume contains a cumulative "Index to vernacular names" and a cumulative "Index to technical names."   QL715.H15

Institute of Laboratory Animal Resources. Committee on Care and Use of Laboratory Animals. Guide for the care and use of laboratory animals. Rev., 1985. Bethesda, Md. : National Institutes of Health, 1985. 83 p. (NIH publication, no. 85-23.).   **EG295**
Superintendent of Documents classification: HE20.3008:An 5/985.
1st ed., 1963, had title: *Guide for laboratory animal facilities and care.*
Divided into five topical chapters and meant to serve, in conjunction with other applicable federal laws, regulations, and policies, as a guide to the operation of institutional animal facilities and programs. Each chapter ends with a list of references. Appendixes include a substantial selected bibliography, certifying organizations, federal laws, and Public Health Service policy and government principles on care and use of animals. *See also* Trevor B. Poole, ed., *The UFAW handbook on the care and management of laboratory animals* (EJ129).
SF406.G8

The IUCN mammal red data book : Part 1: Threatened mammalian taxa of the Americas and the Australasian zoogeographic region (excluding Cetacea). Gland, Switzerland : IUCN, 1982. 516 p.   **EG296**
Comp. by Jane Thornback and Martin Jenkins of the IUCN Conservation Monitoring Centre with the help and advice of the Species Survival Commission of IUCN and other experts throughout the world.
Earlier eds. (1966–78) published in looseleaf format as v. 1 of the *Red data book* of the International Union for Conservation of Nature and Natural Resources.
For each entry gives summary, distribution, population, habitat and ecology, threats to survival, conservation measures taken, conservation measures proposed, captive breeding, remarks, and references. Indexed.   QL703.I86

Lever, Christopher. Naturalized mammals of the world. London ; N.Y. : Longman, 1985. 487 p. : ill.   **EG297**
Describes when, where, why, how, and by whom the various alien mammals now living in the wild throughout the world were introduced, how they subsequently became naturalized, and what effects they have had on native biota and vice versa. Indexes to common and scientific names. Extensive bibliography. Tables of species listed by country in appendix.   QL86.L48

Macmillan illustrated animal encyclopedia / ed. by Philip Whitfield. N.Y. : Macmillan, [1984]. 600 p. : ill.   **EG298**
Arranged in 5 sections: mammals, birds, reptiles, amphibians, and fishes. Seeks to be a comprehensive catalog of vertebrates at the family level, except for the fish section which is treated at the order level. A representative selection of species is included. Profusely illustrated with colored drawings. Indexed.   QL7.M33

Mammal species of the world : a taxonomic and geographic reference / ed. by Don E. Wilson and DeeAnn M. Reeder. 2nd ed. Wash. : Smithsonian Inst. Pr., c1993. 1206 p.   **EG299**
Published in association with the American Society of Mammalogists.
1st ed., 1982.
Describes 4,620 species, up from 4,170 in 1st ed. This edition abandons "the egalitarian approach of the first edition that allowed any mammalogist the opportunity to have dissenting opinions published along with the consensus taxonomic arrangement."—*Pref.* For each species, gives locality, distribution, status, synonyms, and list of references. Extensive cited literature listing. Index to genera and speices. Review: *Choice* 31(Sept. 1993): review 31–0037.   QL708.M35

Morris, Desmond. The mammals : a guide to the living species. London : Hodder and Stoughton ; N.Y. : Harper, [1965]. 448 p. : ill.   **EG300**
Provides notes on each of the mammalian orders, and lists the species within each order. Both scientific and popular names are included; geographical distribution of the order is indicated; and abbreviations are used to denote references to each species in standard technical writings. 300 representative animals (at least one from each order) have been selected for brief description and illustration. Though the text is popularly written, the lists of species have real reference value. Indexes of popular and scientific names.   QL703.M68

Napier, John Russell. A handbook of living primates : morphology, ecology and behaviour of nonhuman primates / John Russell Napier and Prue H. Napier. London ; N.Y. : Academic Pr., 1967. 456 p. : ill.   **EG301**
Major sections include a lengthy general presentation on the functional morphology of primates; alphabetically arranged, concise profiles of primate genera; and supplementary sections dealing with systematics, names, taxonomy, habitats, limbs and locomotion, data on macaques, and vital statistics. Lengthy bibliography. Index of animals.   QL737.P9

The new Larousse encyclopedia of animal life. N.Y. : Larousse, 1980. 640 p. : ill.   **EG302**
1st ed., 1967, was based largely on Léon Bertin's *La vie des animaux* (Paris, 1949–50), revised, updated, and with new material added.
A systematic arrangement of popular-level articles giving general discussions of each class followed by more detailed descriptions of orders and species. Includes a classification list for orders and families, a glossary, and an index.   QL50.N48

Nowak, Ronald M. Walker's mammals of the world. 5th ed. Baltimore : Johns Hopkins Univ. Pr., 1991. 2 v. (1629 p.) : ill.   **EG303**
4th ed., 1983.
Contents: v. 1, Monotremata, Marsupialia, Insectivora, Macroscelidea, Dermoptera, Chiroptera, Scandentia, Primates, Xenarthra, Pholidota, Lagomorpha, Rodentia (Sciuromorpha); v. 2, Rodentia (Myomorpha, hystricomorpha), Cetacea, Carnivora, Pinnipedia, Tubulidentata, Proboscidae, Hyracoidae, Sirena, Perissodactyla, Artiodactyla.
"I have tried to keep ... to Walker's original objectives. One of these ways was to emphasize the small and little known, as well as the large and popular animals."—*Foreword.* Text length is increased about 22% over the 4th ed. and substantive changes have been made in about 80% of the generic accounts, with 106 new ones added. "When possible the following topics have been covered for each genus: scientific and common name, number and distribution of species, measurements, physical description, habitat, locomotion, daily and seasonal activity, diet, population dynamics, home range, social life, reproduction, longevity, and relationships with people."—*Pref.* Nearly all genera are represented by photographs of living individuals. Complete index to all included genera and species in both volumes. Review: *Choice* 29 (Apr. 1992): review 29-4264.   QL703.N69

Orders and families of recent mammals of the world / ed. by Sydney Anderson, J. Knox Jones, Jr. ; sponsored by the American Society of Mammalogists. N.Y. : Wiley, 1984. 686 p. : ill. **EG304**

Arranged taxonomically by orders and families with a chapter for each major grouping. Each order or family is described by its general characteristics, habits, habitats, recent distribution, recent genera, geologic range and major fossil groups. Index to common and scientific names and a separate section of about 1,700 references to works cited in the text. QL703.O73

Simpson, George Gaylord. The principles of classification and a classification of mammals. N.Y. : American Museum of Natural History, 1945. 350 p. (American Museum of Natural History Bulletin, 85). **EG305**

In three parts: (1) Principles of taxonomy; (2) Formal classification of mammalia; (3) Review of mammalian classification.

Based both on the published literature and on new, original research. Pt. 1 is an introductory essay; pt.2 is intended as a working classification and includes literature references. Includes a bibliography arranged alphabetically by author. Indexes of technical and vernacular names.

Shells

Abbott, Robert Tucker. American seashells : the marine mollusca of the Atlantic and Pacific coasts of North America. 2nd ed. N.Y. : Van Nostrand Reinhold, [1974]. 663 p. : ill. **EG306**

1st ed., 1954.

For advanced amateurs and professionals. Describes in detail about 2,000 species and lists another 4,500. Basically a taxonomic survey of marine species found along the shores and continental shelf of North America. QL411.A19

Rogers, Julia Ellen. The shell book : a popular guide to a knowledge of the families of living mollusks, and an aid to the identification of shells, native and foreign. [Rev. ed.]. Boston : C. T. Branford, [1951, c.1936]. 503 p. : ill. **EG307**

1st ed., 1908. Preface to revised edition dated 1951. The text has not been changed, but a "List of modern names" has been appended to update the book.

Systematic arrangement of descriptions of the shells, animal behavior, and habitat of each species included. Index to scientific and common names. QL405.R72

BACTERIOLOGY

Approved lists of bacterial names. Wash. : Amer. Soc. for Microbiology, 1980. 420 p. **EG308**

A listing by genera and species of names valid as of Jan. 1, 1980. For each species or subspecies gives citation to the initial primary literature reference, type strain or species, and citation to descriptive literature reference. QR81.A66

Bergey's manual of systematic bacteriology / John G. Holt, ed. in chief. Baltimore : Williams & Wilkins, c1984–c1989. 4 v. (2648 p.) : ill. **EG309**

Vol. 1 ed. by Noel R. Krieg; v. 2 ed. by Peter Sneath; v. 3 ed. by James T. Staley; v. 4 ed. by Stanley T. Williams.

Based on *Bergey's manual of determinative bacteriology* (1st ed., 1923; 8th ed., 1974).

Intends to aid in bacterial identification and to indicate relationships between various bacteria. Divided into various taxonomic "sections" or chapters, each by specialists, which are based on general characteristics of each major taxonomic grouping. Light and electron

micrographs are interspersed. Each volume has a separate extensive bibliography and an index to scientific names of the bacteria within that volume. Vol. 4 has a cumulative index. QR81.B46

Grainger, Thomas H. A guide to the history of bacteriology. N.Y. : Ronald, [1958]. 210 p. (Chronica botanica, no. 18). **EG310**

An annotated, bibliographical guide to the literature and history of bacteriology. Originally compiled for use in a course in the history of microbiology at Lehigh University.

Institut Pasteur. Bulletin de l'Institut Pasteur : revues et analyses des travaux de bactériologie et de médecine, biologie générale, physiologie, chimie biologique dans leurs rapports avec la microbiologie. Paris : Masson, 1903–70. [v. 1–]. **EG311**

Through 1970, contains abstracts in French from world literature on bacteriology. Beginning 1971, the *Bulletin* continues as a journal publishing original articles, but no longer includes abstracts.

International catalogue of scientific literature / publ. for the Internat. Council by the Royal Soc. of London. v. 1 (1901)–v. 14 (1914). London : Harrison, 1902–21. **EG312**

Section R, Bacteriology. For full description of the set *see* EA16.

Zentralblatt für Bakteriologie, Parasitenkunde, Infektions-Krankheiten und Hygiene : Abt. 1, Medizinisch-hygienische Bakteriologie, Virusforschung und Parasitologie. Referate. Jena, 1902– . v. 31– . **EG313**

Title and coverage vary. This section currently published as *Zentralblatt für Bakteriologie* (irregular).

Provides lengthy abstracts of articles and books in a classified arrangement. International in scope, but includes mostly German publications. "Neue Literatur" section meant for current awareness purposes. Author and subject indexes in each volume.

BIOCHEMISTRY

Barman, Thomas E. Enzyme handbook. N.Y. : Springer, 1969. 2 v. **EG314**

Provides data on the physical and chemical characteristics and specificities of approximately 800 enzymes included in the Enzyme Commission's list. Arrangement follows the Enzyme Commission classification system in which the enzymes are grouped according to their activities and specificities. Indexed.

——. ——. *Supplement 1*. (N.Y., Springer, 1974. 517 p.).

"In the five years since the appearance of the *Enzyme Handbook* several hundred new enzymes have been described. The *Supplement* includes molecular and kinetic data on about half of these and also several enzymes omitted from the *Handbook*."—*Pref.* QP601.B26

Concise encyclopedia biochemistry. English language ed., 2nd ed. rev. and expanded by Thomas Scott and Mary Eagleson. Berlin ; N.Y. : W. de Gruyter, 1988. 649 p. : ill. **EG315**

A compact encyclopedia with entries ranging from a single sentence to several pages. Includes numerous tables, molecular structures, and metabolic pathways. Abundant *see* references. Not indexed. QD415.A25B713

Concise encyclopedia of biochemistry. Berlin ; N.Y. : W. DeGruyter, 1983. 509 p. : ill. **EG316**

Translation of *Brockhaus ABC Biochemie*, 2nd ed. 1981. Tr., rev., and enl. by Thomas Scott and Mary Brewer.

A compact encyclopedia with entries ranging from a single sentence to several pages. Includes numerous tables, molecular structures, and metabolic pathways. Abundant *see* references. Not indexed. QD415.B713

Croft, L. R. Handbook of protein sequence analysis : a compilation of amino acid sequences of proteins with an introduction to the methodology. 2nd ed. Chichester, [Eng.] ; N.Y. : Wiley, [1980]. 628 p.   **EG317**
1st ed., 1973 had title: *Handbook of protein sequences.*
Contains new sequences and complete reappraisal of sequence data published to the end of 1978. In two sections: an introduction containing 8 chapters covering enzymic and chemical cleavage, purification of peptides, sequenator, etc.; and a reference section arranged under 20 headings from "protein sequences," "enzymes," through "milk proteins," "miscellaneous proteins." Appendixes: human haemoglobins, amino acid replacements, etc. Author index and index of protein sources, protein names, and general methodology section.
QP551.C77

Data for biochemical research / Rex M.C. Dawson ... [et al.]. 3rd ed. Oxford : Clarendon Pr., 1986. 580 p. : ill. **EG318**
1st ed., 1959; 2nd ed., 1969.
Attempts to supply information of potential use to a majority of biochemists in a form sufficiently concise to be kept in the laboratory. Considerably expanded over the 2nd ed. Index mainly to chemical terms.   QP520.D37

Fruton, Joseph S. A bio-bibliography for the history of the biochemical sciences since 1800. Philadelphia : Amer. Philosophical Soc., 1982. 885 p.   **EG319**
A revision of a work first published in 1974 and revised in 1977.
Arranged in alphabetical order by author, each entry gives biographical references, if found, and bibliographical references to books and articles. Living persons born before 1911 are included in this edition.
———. ———. *Supplement* (1986. 262 p.).   Z5524.B54F78

Handbook of biochemistry and molecular biology / Gerald D. Fasman, ed. 3rd ed. Cleveland : CRC Pr., [1976–77]. 9 v.
EG320
1st–2nd eds., 1968–70, had title: *Handbook of biochemistry.*
Contents: Proteins—amino acids, peptides, polypeptides, proteins (3 v.); Nucleic acids—purines, pyrimidines, nucleotides, oligonucleotides, tRNA, DNA, RNA (2 v.); Lipids, carbohydrates, steroids (1 v.); Physical and chemical data, miscellaneous—ion exchange, chromatography, buffers, miscellaneous [e.g. vitamins] (2 v.); Cumulative series index.   QP514.H34

International Union of Biochemistry. Nomenclature Committee. Enzyme nomenclature 1984. Orlando, Fla. : Academic Pr., 1984. 646 p.   **EG321**
Subtitle: Recommendations of Nomenclature Committee of the International Union of Biochemistry on the nomenclature and classification of enzyme-catalysed reactions.
Copy prepared for publication by Edwin C. Webb.
1st ed., 1961; previous ed., 1974.
A classified list of 2,477 ezymes. Entries are arranged by Enzyme Classification number and give recommended name, reaction, other names, basis for classification (systematic name), comments, and references. Includes 4,478 published references. Name index.
QP601.I54

Long, Cyril. Biochemists' handbook / comp. by 171 contributors. London : Spon ; Princeton, N.J. : Van Nostrand, 1961. 1192 p.   **EG322**
Tabular data and short articles on specific biochemicals, reagents and analytic methods, and on topical areas: metabolic pathways; chemical composition of animal tissue and related data; chemical composition of plant tissues and related data; and physiological and nutritional data. Bibliographies; general index.   QD245.L6

National Research Council. Committee on Specifications and Criteria for Biochemical Compounds. Specifications and criteria for biochemical compounds. 3rd ed. Wash. : Nat. Academy of Sciences, 1972. 216 p.   **EG323**
1st ed., 1960.

"This publication is the result of a program to improve the quality of chemicals available for biochemical research by establishing criteria, standards, or specifications useful for describing such chemicals, particularly with regard to purity."—*Pref.* Lists 521 compounds by type of compound and specific name. Gives standard handbook data such as formula, structure, weight, sources, and methods of purification and assaying for purity. Many entries include references. Compound index.
———. ———. *Supplement: biogenic amines and related compounds.* (Wash. : Nat. Academy of Sciences, 1977. 20 p.).
QD415.7.N37

Stenesh, J. Dictionary of biochemistry and molecular biology. 2nd ed. N.Y. : Wiley, c1989. 525 p.   **EG324**
1st ed., 1975, had title: *Dictionary of biochemistry.*
Contains 4,000 more entries than the 12,000 in the 1st ed., mainly in the addition of names of compounds. Entries are direct rather than inverted, (e.g., "First law of cancer biochemistry" rather than "Cancer biochemistry, first law"). Cross-references.   QP512.S73

Williams, Roger John. The encyclopedia of biochemistry / Roger John Williams and Edwin M. Landsford. N.Y. : Reinhold, [1967]. 876 p. : ill.   **EG325**
For nonspecialists. Articles on broader topics presuppose only general scientific background; specialized topics are more technical. The alphabetically arranged articles cover general and specific topics in chemistry, physics, methodology, metabolism, nutrition, diseases, and disorders as related to biochemistry, as well as short biographies and more peripheral topics. Longer articles have appended references. Indexed.   QP512.W5

ENTOMOLOGY

Arnett, Ross H. American insects : a handbook of the insects of America north of Mexico. N.Y. : Van Nostrand Reinhold, [1985]. 850 p. : ill.   **EG326**
Intended to provide the nonspecialist with both identification and access to the source literature. "I have attempted to compile in a single reference book a tool that will be useful to those working without a major collection and library."—*Pref.* Arranged taxonomically; extensively illustrated with photographs and drawings. Indexed.
QL474.A76

Chamberlin, Willard Joseph. Entomological nomenclature and literature. 3rd ed. rev. and enl. Dubuque, Iowa : W. C. Brown, [1952]. 141 p.   **EG327**
Includes general discussions of the development and status of the nomenclature, instructions on bibliographic methods, bibliographies of principal entomological literature, and aids to preparing scientific articles.   Z5856.C5

Derksen, Walther. Index litteraturae entomologicae : Serie II: Die Welt-Literatur über die gesamte Entomologie von 1864 bis 1900 / von Walther Derksen [und] Ursula Scheiding. Berlin : Deutsche Akad. der Landwirtschaftswissenschaften zu Berlin, 1963–75. 5 v.   **EG328**
Contents: Bd. 1–4, A–Z; Bd. 5, Register.   Z5856.I53

Gilbert, Pamela. A compendium of biographical literature on deceased entomologists. London : British Museum (Natural History), 1977. 455 p.   **EG329**
Contains references to biographical information and bibliographical listings published before the end of 1975 for some 7,500 deceased entomologists.   Z5856.G55

——————— Entomology : a guide to information sources / [by] Pamela Gilbert [and] Chris J. Hamilton. 2nd ed. N.Y. : Cassell Publ. (Academic Div.), 1990. 272 p.   **EG330**

1st ed., 1983.

A guide to literature, libraries, and organizations. Arranged by subject. Annotated; indexed. QL468.2.G55

Horn, Walther. Index litteraturae entomologicae : Ser. I, Die welt-Literatur über die gesamte Entomologie bis inklusive 1863 / von Walther Horn und Sigm. Schenkling. Berlin-Dahlem, 1928–29. 4 v. **EG331**

A revision of H. A. Hagen's *Bibliotheca entomologica* (Leipzig, 1862–63. 2 v.), with the addition of some 8,000 titles, covering the field up to the beginning of *The zoological record* (EG220). Arranged alphabetically by author. No index, although Hagen included an author-subject index which may be used with either work for the material he covered. Z5856.H81

Howe, William H. The butterflies of North America. Garden City, N.Y. : Doubleday, 1975. 633 p. : ill. **EG332**

"*The Butterflies of North America* is a comprehensive volume on the butterflies and skippers of Canada and the United States, including Alaska and Hawaii."—*Pref.* QL548.H68

Johnson, Warren T. Insects that feed on trees and shrubs : an illustrated practical guide / Warren T. Johnson and Howard H. Lyon. Ithaca, N.Y. : Cornell Univ. Pr., [1976]. 464 p. : ill. **EG333**

"With the collaboration of C. S. Loehler, N. E. Johnson, and J. A. Weidhaas."—*t.p.*

Contents: Insects that feed on conifers; Insects that feed on broad-leaved evergreens, and deciduous plants; Sources of information on pest control; Selected references; Glossary; Index of insects, mites and animals; Index to insects by host plants.

"This book is a reference manual. It covers essential information about many of the important insects, mites, and other animals associated with woody ornamental plants. Its audience is intended to be agricultural advisor, teacher, student, nurseryman, arborist, forester, gardener, scientist, as well as any person having direct or peripheral responsibility for the maintenance of trees and shrubs. It deals in a pragmatic way with the science of entomology, and provides assistance in the identification of insects and related animals often considered pests."—*Introd.* More than 700 insects and mites are discussed, listed, or illustrated. More than 1,000 photographs of the pests and their damage to the host tree or shrub, including some 200 color plates. SB931.J64

Mallis, Arnold. American entomologists. New Brunswick, N.J. : Rutgers Univ. Pr., [1971]. 549 p. : ill. **EG334**

Biographical essays on some 200 American entomologists from the 18th century to the present. Arrangement is according to area of interest. Portraits; index of names. QL26.M24

Metcalf, Robert Lee. Destructive and useful insects : their habits and control / Robert L. Metcalf, Robert A. Metcalf. 5th ed. N.Y. : McGraw-Hill, c1993. 1 v. (various pagings) : ill. **EG335**

For annotation, *see* EG84. SB931.M47

Osborn, Herbert. A brief history of entomology : including time of Demosthenes and Aristotle to modern times, with over five hundred portraits. Columbus, Ohio : Spahr and Glenn, 1952. 303 p. : ill. **EG336**

Intended mainly for general readers. General outlines of the history of entomology, followed by an alphabetical list of "founders and leaders of entomological science," giving brief biographical data for each. The portraits, 12 on each plate, are taken from photographs or contemporary paintings. QL462.5.O7

Review of agricultural entomology. v. 78 (Jan. 1990)– . Wallingford, Oxon, U.K. : CAB International Information Services, 1990– . Monthly. **EG337**

An international abstract journal in classed arrangement. Each issue contains an author index; each volume a cumulative author and subject index.

Continues *Review of applied entomology. Series A: Agricultural* (1913–89) and assumes its numbering.

§ *Review of applied entomology. Series B: Medical and veterinary* similarly ceased in 1989 and was continued by *Review of medical and veterinary entomology.* SB599.R38

Torre-Bueno, José Rollin de la. The Torre-Bueno glossary of entomology / comp. by Stephen W. Nichols ; including Supplement A by George S. Tulloch ; managing ed., Randall T. Schuh. Rev. ed. N.Y. : New York Entomological Society in cooperation with the American Museum of Natural History, 1989. 840 p. **EG338**

1st ed., 1937, called *A glossary of entomology*; 2nd ed., 1960, by George S. Tulloch, called *Torre-Bueno's glossary of entomology.*

A greatly expanded edition; cross-references are extensive, more than one sense of a term is given where necessary, and the number and length of definitions have both been increased. Includes a bibliography and an ordinal classification. Anatomical plates and other figures used in earlier editions have been deleted. Computerization of the file will permit more frequent updates. The standard source for terminology in entomology. QL462.3.T67

GENETICS

King, Robert C. A dictionary of genetics / Robert C. King, William D. Stansfield. 4th ed. N.Y. : Oxford Univ. Pr., 1990. 496 p. **EG339**

1st ed., 1968; 3rd ed., 1985.

This edition contains some 6,000 entries for terms in both classical and molecular genetics. Appendixes give a chronology of events in the history of genetics, a list of major journals, a classification of organisms, and a list of domesticated species. QH427.K55

Knight, Robert L. Dictionary of genetics, including terms used in cytology, animal breeding and evolution. Waltham, Mass. : Chronica Botanica, 1948. 183 p. : ill. (Lotsya, a biological miscellany, v. 2). **EG340**

An attempt at standardizing terminology. Briefly defines about 2,500 older and modern terms. Nine appendixes consist mostly of standard genetics and statistical data. QH13.K5

Maclean, Norman. Dictionary of genetics & cell biology. N.Y. : New York Univ. Pr., 1987. 422 p. : ill. **EG341**

Contains both basic and specialized terms. Definitions are brief and clear, similar in length to those in J.M. Lackie and J.A.T. Dow's *The dictionary of cell biology* (EG32). Uses British spelling and the controversial classification of Lynn Margulis's *Five kingdoms* (San Francisco : W.H. Freeman, 1982; 2nd ed., 1988). A good companion to R.C. King and W.D. Stansfield's *A dictionary of genetics* (EG339). QH427.M33

McKusick, Victor A. Mendelian inheritance in man : catalogs of autosomal dominant, autosomal recessive, and X-linked phenotypes / Victor A. McKusick, with the assistance of Clair A. Francomano and Stylianos E. Antonarakis. 10th ed. Baltimore : Johns Hopkins Univ. Pr., 1992. 2 v. (ccxix, 2320 p.). **EG342**

Available both in printed and machine-readable versions; the printed version is derived from the machine-readable file.

This compilation of research on genetic disease is probably the best available. The printed version is well indexed, but the machine-readable version is more current and provides indexing for all keywords. The machine-readable version is available online through the Welch Medical Library of Johns Hopkins Univ., where, in combination with the *Genome data base (GDB)*, it gives mapping, linkage, and additional bibliographic data as well as a list of experts on various genetic diseases. Z6675.M4M33

Rieger, Rigomar. Glossary of genetics : classical and molecular / R. Rieger, A. Michaelis, M.M. Green. 5th ed. Berlin ; N.Y. : Springer-Verlag, 1991. 553 p.   **EG343**

1st ed., 1954, and 2nd ed., 1958, were published in German under the title *Genetisches und cytogenetisches Wörterbuch.* 4th ed., 1976, had title : *Glossary of genetics and cytogenetics.*

A new English-language edition, not a translation from German. Approximately 2,500 entries; lengthy definitions. Where possible, includes references to the specific paper in which the term or concept was introduced. Cross-references between related terms are designated by an arrow before each relevant term. Review: *Choice* 29 (Feb. 1992): review 29–3074. Bibliography.   QH427.R54

EH

Medical and Health Sciences

VIROLOGY

Fraenkel-Conrat, Heinz. The viruses : catalogue, characterization, and classification. N.Y. : Plenum Pr., c1985. 266 p., [2] p. of plates : ill.   **EG344**

Three sections: animal (including protozoan) viruses, plant viruses, and prokaryote (bacteria and blue-green algae) phage. Attempts "to list most if not all well established and studied viruses in alphabetical order ... ."—*Pref.* Animal and plant viruses are listed by common and scientific name and prokaryote phage by name or by identifying letters and/or numbers, or by host. Each virus is classified, as appropriate, to group, genus, family, and subfamily. Fairly complete descriptions of each family or major group are included with citations to the list of references at the end of each section. Provides good illustrations of most families or groups, mainly by electron micrographs of negatively stained specimens. No index.   QR394.F73

Hull, Roger. Virology : directory & dictionary of animal, bacterial, and plant viruses / Roger Hull, Fred Brown, Chris Payne. N.Y. : Stockton Pr. ; London : Macmillan, 1989. 1 v.   **EG345**

The authors "have attempted to list most, if not all, viruses of vertebrates, invertebrates, plants and bacteria."—*Introd.* A combined directory and dictionary section lists the "names of viruses and their higher order taxa as well as terms which are commonly used in the virological literature." Many entries include references to recent reviews and papers. The directory portion also includes appendixes, of which several (A–E) list viral isolates from various insect species and one (F) gives a list of nearly 2,000 known bacteriophage isolates. No separate index.   QR358.H85

Nicholas, Robin. Virology : an information profile. [London] : Mansell, distr. in U.S. by H.W. Wilson, [1983]. 236 p.   **EG346**

Contents: History and scope of virology; Organizations and their role in virology; Conferences; The literature of virology; Searching the literature; Culture collections; Legislation and laboratory safety; Bibliography; Directory; and Index.

"A one-place reference to all sources of information on virology."—*Pref.*   Z5185.V5N53

Stedman's ICTV virus words / [ed. by Charles H. Calisher, Claude M. Fauquet]. Baltimore : Williams & Wilkins, c1992. 271 p. : ill.   **EG347**

A publication of the International Committee on Taxonomy of Viruses.   QR394.S74

MEDICINE

Guides

Allan, Barbara. Guide to information sources in alternative therapy. Aldershot, Hants, Eng. ; Brookfield, Vt. : Gower, c1988. 216 p. : ill.   **EH1**

Pt. 1 provides an introduction to alternative therapy, i.e., "therapies ... primarily concerned with physical, emotional, psychic and spiritual development."—*Introd.* Pt. 2 contains a bibliography of general and specialized information sources, arranged in alphabetical order by subject. Pt. 3 provides information about people, organizations and activities, and training opportunities. Combined author, subject, and title index.   Z6675.A42A43

Blake, John Ballard. Medical reference works, 1679–1966 : a selected bibliography / John B. Blake, Charles Roos, editors. Chicago : Medical Libr. Assoc., 1967. 343 p. (Medical Library Association. Publication, no. 3).   **EH2**

Supersedes the bibliographies published as part of the 2nd ed. (1956) of the Medical Library Association's *Handbook of medical library practice* (EH4).

Lists more than 2,700 titles in classed arrangement within three main sections: Medicine, general; History of medicine; and Special subjects. Titles have been selected for their usefulness in answering questions in bioscience libraries; titles especially useful for smaller medical libraries are marked with an asterisk. "Handbooks and treatises in the basic sciences and clinical medicine have only rarely been included."—*Pref.* Brief annotations.

———. *Supplement* 1–3 (Chicago : Medical Libr. Assoc., 1970–75. 3 v.). Suppl. 1 comp. by Mary Virginia Clark; suppls. 2–3 by Joy S. Richmond.

The 1st supplement follows the pattern of the main work, but excludes references on the history of medicine "since material of this sort is listed in the annual *Bibliography of the history of medicine* [EH199]."—*Pref.* Includes more than 300 references with the emphasis on works published 1967–68. The 2nd and 3rd supplements are computer-produced from National Library of Medicine's *Current catalog* (EH49); therefore, these citations are arranged by author and subject. "General historical works, pharmacopoeias, reviews, and popular works have been excluded."—*Pref., suppl.* 2. A total of about 750 citations are added for the periods 1969–72 and 1973–74. Most references in the supplements are annotated.

Finding the source of medical information : a thesaurus-index to the reference collection / comp. by Barbara Smith Shearer and Geneva L. Bush. Westport, Conn. : Greenwood Pr., [1985]. 225 p.   **EH3**

Pt. 1 lists 447 reference books and textbooks, covering a wide range of subjects, selected by the authors with the assistance of librarians, physicians, pharmacists, and nurses. Pt. 2 is a detailed subject thesaurus/index for the core books using natural language terms. The subject terms range from general to specific and are cross-referenced to broader, narrower, and related terms when appropriate.   Z6658.S4

Handbook of medical library practice / Louise Darling, ed., David Bishop, Lois Ann Colaianni, associate editors. 4th ed. Chicago : Medical Library Assoc., 1982–88. 3 v. : ill.   **EH4**
1st ed., 1943; 3rd ed., 1970.
Contents: v. 1, Public services in health science libraries; v. 2, Technical services in health science libraries; v. 3, Health science librarianship and administration.
A guide to practices and policies in medical libraries, written by medical library specialists. All chapters include references. Indexed.
Z675.M4H33

Information sources in the medical sciences. 4th ed. / editors, L. T. Morton and Shane Godbolt. London ; N.Y. : Bowker-Saur, c1992. 608 p.   **EH5**
Imprint varies.
1st ed., 1974, and 2nd ed., 1977, had title: *Use of medical literature*; 3rd ed., 1984.
Individual chapters are written by experts. "Intended to serve as an evaluative guide to the most important sources of information that each contributor has recommended from experience of the subject."— *Pref.* Indexed. Companion to *Information sources in pharmaceuticals* (EH317).   R118.6.I54

Introduction to reference sources in the health sciences / by Fred W. Roper and Jo Anne Boorkman. 2nd ed. Chicago : Medical Libr. Assoc., c1984. 302 p. : ill.   **EH6**
1st ed., 1980.
"The purpose ... is to discuss various types of bibliographic and information sources and their use in reference work in the health sciences. Although written with library school students in mind, practicing librarians and health science library users should also find the book of value."—*Pref., 1980.* Arranged under broad headings such as Reference collection, Bibliographic sources, and Information sources. Each of the chapters covers specialized topics such as bibliographic sources for monographs, bibliographic sources for periodicals, terminology, medical and health statistics, and history sources. A new edition is expected in 1994.   Z6658.I54

Keyguide to information sources in paramedical sciences / ed. by John F. Hewlett. London ; N.Y. : Mansell, 1990. 270 p.   **EH7**
"Paramedical or allied health professionals are usually considered to be those groups of health care workers who are not doctors or nurses, but who have a part to play in the diagnosis or cure of disease, the rehabilitation of the patient or the maintenance of his or her health."—*Pref.* Serves as a guide to the literature for six groups of allied health workers: chiropodists, dietitians, occupational therapists, physiotherapists, radiographers, and speech therapists. Pt. 1 provides an overview of paramedical sciences and their literature, with chapters for each specific group, while pt. 2 provides a bibliography of sources for each subject area, subdivided by format. Pt. 3 lists selected organizations. Includes index.   R118.6.K49

Strickland-Hodge, Barry. Medical information : a profile / Barry Strickland-Hodge and Barbara Allan. White Plains, N.Y. : Knowledge Industry Publications, 1986. 145 p.   **EH8**
A survey of the major types of medical information sources. Provides a list of printed and other sources, shows how searches can be carried out, and discusses techniques for organizing information retrieved during online searches. Intended to be a practical guide, aimed at those beginning medical research. Emphasis on British sources.
Z6658.S92

Bibliography

Besterman, Theodore. Medicine : a bibliography of bibliographies. Totowa, N.J. : Rowman and Littlefield, 1971. 409 p.   **EH9**
Taken from Besterman's *World bibliography of bibliographies* (AA14).
Rather than listing citations alphabetically as they were in the parent publication, this source lists them topically as follows: medicine, anatomy, hygiene, pharmacology, pharmaceutics, psychiatry, and special subjects such as adrenal glands, balneology, and yaws. "Useful to those who seek primary signposts to information in varied fields of inquiry."—*Pref.* Wide subject and language coverage.   Z6658.A1B4

Brodman, Estelle. The development of medical bibliography. Baltimore : Medical Libr. Assoc., 1954. 226 p. : ill. (Medical Library Association, pubn. 1).   **EH10**
A comprehensive survey of medical bibliography since 1500, covering printed medical bibliographies in Western languages which pertain to medicine in general rather than to its subdivisions or specialties. Personal bibliographies and bibliographies which do not make up the main portion of a work have been excluded, as have catalogs (with the exception of the *Index-catalogue of the Library of the Surgeon General's Office ...* [EH47]). No distinction is made between indexes and abstracts as bibliographies.
"For each bibliography discussed there is a biographical sketch of the compiler, a description of the work emphasizing advances in technique, and a discussion of the importance of the work in the history of medical bibliography."—*Introd.* Appendix 1 lists references; Appendix 2 lists medical bibliographies since 1500 which were not discussed in the body of the text, arranged by century. General and author indexes.   Z6658.B7

Bruhn, John G. Medical sociology : an annotated bibliography, 1972–1982 / John G. Bruhn, Billy U. Philips, Paula L. Levine. N.Y. : Garland, 1985. 779 p. (Garland bibliographies in sociology, v. 6 ; Garland reference library of social science, v. 243).   **EH11**
For annotation, *see* CC6.   Z6675.S53B78

Cordasco, Francesco. American medical imprints, 1820–1910 : a checklist of publications illustrating the history and progress of medical science, medical education, and the healing arts in the United States : a preliminary contribution. Totowa, N.J. : Rowman & Littlefield ; Fairview, N.J. : Junius-Vaughn Pr., 1985. 2 v.   **EH12**
Continues *Early American medical imprints : a guide to works printed in the United States, 1668–1820*, by Robert B. Austin (EH25).
A "systematic and enumerative bibliography ... intended as a functional checklist" that includes "any item which could legitimately be related to the medical arts and their progress in the U.S."—*Introd.* Contains 36,612 entries arranged chronologically by decade of publication; within decades, entries are arranged alphabetically by author, then by date of publication. Each entry includes a transcription of the work's title page; for most items, only the principal pagination is given. Shows one to four library locations. Some items are annotated, and there is an index of names. Introductory material includes "A handlist of selected bibliographies, catalogues and related reference materials." An appendix, "Wood's library of standard medical authors" (a checklist of 100 medical textbooks published in N.Y. by William Wood & Co. from the 1870s to the 1890s), was originally published in *AB bookman's weekly* 73 (1984): 3333–56.   Z6661.U5C67

———————— Medical education in the United States : a guide to information sources / Francesco Cordasco, David N. Alloway. Detroit : Gale, [1980]. 393 p. (Education information guide series, v. 8).   **EH13**
A bibliography of 2,364 sources arranged as follows: (1) Bibliographies, dictionaries, directories, and general information; (2) History of medicine; (3) Medical school admissions; (4) Medical education;

(5) Health policy; (6) Women's medical education; (7) Hospitals; (8) Autobiographies, biographies, reminiscences and related materials; (9) Miscellaneous. Author, title, and subject indexes. Z5818.M43C67

Current bibliographies in medicine / National Library of Medicine. [Bethesda, Md.] : The Library ; [Wash. : Sold by U.S. Govt. Print. Off., 1988]– . **EH14**
Superintendent of Documents classification: HE20.3615/2.
Continues in part *Literature search* of the National Library of Medicine (EH22) which ceased in 1988; in 1989 absorbed the National Library of Medicine's "Specialized bibliography series." "Each bibliography ... covers a distinct subject area of biomedicine and is intended to fulfill a current awareness function."—*Pref.* Approximately 20 bibliographies are published per year. Contains citations to articles indexed for MEDLARS. A list of currently available bibliographies appears each month in *Index medicus* (EH65).

Encyclopedia of health information sources / Alan M. Rees, ed. 2nd ed. Detroit : Gale, c1993. 521 p. **EH15**
1st ed., 1987, ed. by Paul Wasserman and Suzanne Grefsheim.
Subtitle: a bibliographic guide to over 13,000 citations for publications, organizations, and databases on health-related subjects.
Intended as a starting point to locate information on health and medical subjects. Includes all types of information sources, listed alphabetically under each subject. International in scope. Detailed table of contents and cross-references. No index. Z6658.E54

Gilbert, Judson Bennett. Disease and destiny : a bibliography of medical references to the famous / with additions and an introd. by Gordon E. Mestler. London : Dawsons of Pall Mall, 1962. 535 p. **EH16**
A bibliography drawn largely from *Index-catalogue of the library of the Surgeon General's Office* (EH47), *Index medicus* (EH65), and the *Quarterly cumulative index medicus* (EH62) of writings that treat the medical history of famous people in history, the humanities, and the arts and sciences in all countries from ancient to modern times. Personalities are listed alphabetically and identified by dates of birth and death and a brief descriptive phrase. Books and papers about them are listed in chronological order. The introduction contains an excellent bibliography of monographic literature in the field of medico-biographical writing. Z6664.A1G5

Haselbauer, Kathleen J. A research guide to the health sciences : medical, nutritional, and environmental. N.Y. : Greenwood, 1987. 655 p. : ill. (Reference sources for the social sciences and humanities, no. 4). **EH17**
Cites more than 2,000 sources in four broad categories: General works, Basic sciences supporting clinical medicine, Social aspects of the health sciences, and Medical specialties. Intended for researchers at all levels, with emphasis on the needs of students and those working outside their specialty. Critical and evaluative annotations, many of them lengthy, compare similar sources. Cross-references are numerous. Indexed by author, title, and subject. Z6658.H35

Health affairs information guide series. Detroit : Gale, 1978–1983. 10 v. **EH18**
Contents: v. 1, Health care administration. Dwight A. Morris and Lynne D. Morris, eds. (1978. 264 p.); v. 2, Cross-national study of health systems; concepts, methods, and data sources. Ray H. Elling, ed. (1980. 293 p); v. 3, Cross-national study of health systems; countries, world regions, and special problems. Ray H. Elling, ed. (1980. 687 p.); v. 4, Health statistics. Frieda O. Weise, ed. (1980. 137 p.; for full information see EH235); v. 5, The professional and scientific literature on patient education. Lawrence W. Green, ed. (1980. 330 p.); v. 6, Health care costs and financing. Rita M. Keintz, ed. (1981. 258 p.); v. 7, Health maintenance through food and nutrition. Helen D. Ullrich, ed. (1981. 305 p.); v. 8, Bioethics. Doris Mueller Goldstein, ed. (1982. 366 p.; for full information see EH242); v. 9, Emergency medical service systems. Carlos Fernandez-Cabellero and Marianne Fernandez-Cabellero, eds. (1981. 183 p.); v. 10, Human ecology. Frederick Sargent, ed. (1983. 293 p.).
Each volume has subtitle "A guide to information sources."

Edited by authorities, each volume is designed to aid health care professionals, scientists, librarians, and students. Classified, annotated lists of books, articles, periodicals, audiovisual aids, organizations, and other types of information sources on specific topics make up each volume of the series. Z6663.N9U44

Health science books, 1876–1982. N.Y. : Bowker, 1982. 4 v. (4601 p.). **EH19**
"Prepared by the R.R. Bowker Company's Dept. of Bibliography."—*verso of t.p.*
Contents: v. 1–3, Subject index; v. 4, Author index.
Arranged by Library of Congress subject headings, the entries provide complete LC entry with tracings, call number, and ISBN. Includes a guide to MeSH/LC equivalents and a guide to LC/MeSH equivalents for the health sciences. Z6658.H4

Huber, Jeffrey T. How to find information about AIDS. 2nd ed. N.Y. : Haworth Pr., c1992. 290 p. **EH20**
1st ed., 1988, by Virginia A. Lingle and M. Sandra Wood.
Written for health care professionals and general readers. U.S. focus. Provides directory information and occasional brief descriptions for organizations; state health departments; research institutes; funding sources; hotlines; electronic, print, and audiovisual sources. This edition omits list of key journal articles, instead referring readers to periodical indexes. Indexes: titles, organizations, and personal names; geographic, general and state indexes. RC607.A26H9

Learning AIDS : an information resources directory / [editors, Trish Halleron, Janet Pisaneschi, Margi Trapani]. 2nd ed. N.Y. : American Foundation for AIDS Research : distr. by Bowker, c1989. 270 p. **EH21**
1st ed., 1988, had title: *AIDS information resources directory*.
Reviews and evaluates more than 1,700 AIDS/HIV educational resources of all types. Intended to be a first step in identifying suitable materials for a particular audience. Arranged by 21 target audiences. Entries include bibliographic description, reviewer comments, price, and ordering information. RA644.A25L438

Literature search / National Library of Medicine. no. 67-7 (1967)–no. 87-15 (1988). [Bethesda, Md.] : The Library, [1967–1988]. **EH22**
Continues: *New bibliographic series* (no. 1–65—no. 21–65; 1965. 21 v.); *National Library of Medicine literature search* (no. 22–65—no. 6–67. 3 v.).
Narrowly focused subject bibliographies, containing citations to articles indexed for NLM's computerized Medical Literature Analysis and Retrieval System (MEDLARS). Each citation lists descriptors drawn from *Medical subject headings (MeSH)* (EH143, EH144, EH145) used in indexing the article. Some typical topics: osteoporosis, hospices, Alzheimer's disease, recurrent mood disorders, AIDS, fetal surgery, adolescent alcoholism. A list of the currently available bibliographies appears each month in *Index medicus* (EH65).
§ Continued by: *Current bibliographies in medicine* (EH14) and *AIDS bibliography* (EH71).

Medical and health care books and serials in print. 1985– . N.Y. : R. R. Bowker Co., [1985]– . Annual. **EH23**
Continues: *Medical books and serials in print: an index to literature in the health sciences* (1972–84).
Derived from *Books in print* (AA425), *Ulrich's international periodicals directory* (AD18), and related Bowker databases.
A comprehensive and authoritative source for information on new titles. The available books in medicine, dentistry, nursing, and veterinary medicine are classified in more than 5,800 subject categories. Indexed by author and title. Z6658.B65

National Library of Medicine (U.S.). A catalogue of seventeenth century printed books in the National Library of Medicine / comp. by Peter Krivatsy. Bethesda, Md. : National Library of Medicine, 1989. 1315 p. (National Institute of Health publication, no. 89–2619). **EH24**
Superintendent of Documents classification: HE 20.3614:Se 8.

For some 13,300 books printed 1601–1700, "monographs, dissertations and corresponding program disputations, broadsides, pamphlets and serials" (*Introd.*), provides title page transcription, physical description, and reference to standard bibliographies. Entries are alphabetical by author, editor, compiler, occasionally by corporate body, and in a few instances by title. Most authors' names are in vernacular form with cross-references to latinized or other names. There is no index, but the National Library of Medicine's History of Medicine Division maintains indexes of printers, publishers, and vernacular imprints.

§ Complements earlier catalogs of pre-19th century holdings of NLM: *A catalogue of incunabula and manuscripts in the Army Medical Library*, by Dorothy M. Schullian and Francis E. Sommer, ([1948?]); *A catalogue of sixteenth century printed books in the National Library of Medicine*, comp. by Richard J. Durling (1967); *A catalogue of incunabula and sixteenth century books in the National Library of Medicine : first supplement*, comp. by Peter Krivatsy (1971); and *A short title catalogue of eighteenth century printed books in the National Library of Medicine*, comp. by John Ballard Blake (1979).

Z6659.N38

———————— Early American medical imprints : a guide to works printed in the United States, 1668–1820 / by Robert B. Austin. Wash. : U.S. Public Health Service, 1961. 240 p.   **EH25**

An alphabetical author listing of more than 2,100 separately published items, including books, pamphlets, theses, broadsides, and selected periodicals, with full bibliographical information and many annotations. Library holdings are indicated for 67 libraries. Appendixes include a chronological index and a list of 74 items in Charles Evans's *American bibliography* (AA405) that are not included because copies could not be located or because they could not be verified as having been printed.   Z6661.U5A44

Olson, James Stuart. The history of cancer : an annotated bibliography. N.Y. : Greenwood, 1989. 426 p. (Bibliographies and indexes in medical studies, no. 3).   **EH26**

A comprehensive bibliography that emphasizes documents in the history of the etiology, manifestations, diagnosis, and treatment of cancer, and on persons with distinguished careers in cancer research and treatment. Citations to approximately 3,000 articles are arranged in 30 categories. Helpful cross-references; author and subject index.   RC262.O47

Rees, Alan M. The consumer health information source book / by Alan M. Rees and Catherine Hoffman. 3rd ed. Phoenix : Oryx, 1990. 210 p.   **EH27**

1st ed., 1981; 2nd ed., 1984.

Provides brief evaluations of popular health publications in a variety of formats: books, popular magazines and newsletters, pamphlets, and professional publications. Also includes information clearinghouses and centers, toll-free hotlines, and health organizations that provide information to the general public. Separate subject, title, and author indexes. A 4th ed. is expected in 1994.   Z6673.R3

Thornton, John Leonard. Thornton's medical books, libraries, and collectors : a study of bibliography and the book trade in relation to the medical sciences / ed. by Alain Besson. 3rd rev. ed. Aldershot, England ; Brookfield, Vt. : Gower, c1990. 417 p. : ill.   **EH28**

1st ed., 1949, and 2nd ed., 1966, had title: *Medical books, libraries and collectors : a study of bibliography and the book trade in relation to the medical sciences.*

An introductory history of the literature of medicine from the earliest times through the 19th century. A separate chapter treats medical writings before the invention of printing. Medical literature of the 20th century is included in chapters on growth of the medical periodical literature and medical libraries of today. Intends "to record the chief writings of every prominent medical author and to chart the growth and development of medical bibliography."—*Introd.* Includes a bibliography and indexes of personal and institutional names, journal titles, and subjects.   Z286.M4T47

Watstein, Sarah. AIDS and women : a sourcebook / Sarah Barbara Watstein & Robert Anthony Laurich. Phoenix : Oryx, 1991. 159 p. : ill.   **EH29**

Covers "prevention, transmission, mental health, demographic and occupational issues and points the reader toward important resources to fill the support services gap for women with HIV infection and AIDS."—*Foreword.* Each of 14 chapters begins with a brief overview of a particular topic, followed by an annotated bibliography of selected sources. Includes statistical tables. Appendixes provide selected audiovisual resources; directory of national, state, and local resources; glossary of AIDS-related terms and discussion of materials and methods for continuing research on women and AIDS. Author, subject and title indexes.   RC607.A26W38

West, Ruth. Alternative medicine : a bibliography of books in English / comp. by Ruth West and Joanna E. Trevelyan. London ; N.Y. : Mansell, 1985. 210 p.   **EH30**

Lists more than 2,000 books relating to certain major systems for the treatment of illness. Entries are arranged alphabetically by author within broad subject categories (e.g., homeopathy, herbal medicine, naturopathy, clinical nutrition, osteopathy, chiropractic, Chinese medicine, acupuncture). Includes textbooks, manuals, reference books, pamphlets, mostly from Britain and the U.S. Some brief annotations; subject index.   Z6665.P49W47

Winter, Eugenia B. Psychological and medical aspects of induced abortion : a selective, annotated bibliography, 1970–1986. N.Y. : Greenwood, 1988. 162 p. (Bibliographies and indexes in women's studies, no. 7).   **EH31**

For annotation, *see* CC259.   Z6671.2.A2W56

Women in medicine : a bibliography of the literature on women physicians / comp. and ed. by Sandra L. Chaff ... [et al.]. Metuchen, N.J. : Scarecrow, 1977. 1124 p.   **EH32**

Provides "comprehensive coverage of the literature about women physicians in all parts of the world."—*Introd.* Includes 4,000 citations (books, medical and nonmedical journal articles, alumnae and alumni magazine articles), representing the literature from the 18th century through December 1975.   Z7963.M43W65

Incunabula

Klebs, Arnold Carl. Incunabula scientifica et medica : short title list. Bruges : Saint Catherine Pr., 1938 [i.e., 1937]. 359 p.   **EH33**

Repr. from *Osiris*, 4 (1938) : [1]–359.

"Intended ... to offer ... a survey in the briefest possible terms."—*Introd.* Arranged alphabetically by the names of authors (approximately 650 names) or by keyword in the case of anonymous works. The vernacular form of personal name is used whenever possible, otherwise the latinized name. Editions are arranged in ascending chronological order. There are approximately 3,000 editions, with dubious editions excluded. Cross-references at the end.   Z240.K62

Periodicals

EMBASE list of journals indexed. 1993– . Amsterdam ; N.Y. : Elsevier Science Publ., Electronic Publ. Div., c1993– . Annual.   **EH34**

Title varies: *Excerpta medica : list of journals abstracted*, 1979–82; *List of journals abstracted*, 1983–92.

Complete list of journals indexed in *EMBASE* (EH58) and *Excerpta medica* (EH59). Arranged in alphabetical order by abbreviated journal title; includes a classified list of journals.   R5.E946

List of journals indexed in Index medicus / National Library of Medicine. [Bethesda, Md.] : National Library of Medicine, 1960– . Annual.   **EH35**

Superintendent of Documents classification: HE 20.3612/4.
1962 not separately published.

Provides bibliographic information for journals indexed: entries are listed alphabetically by journal abbreviation, then by full title. Indicates titles that are selectively indexed. Includes separate listings of titles added and title changes during the preceding year, as well as subject and geographic listings. Published as part of both *Index medicus* (EH65) and *Cumulated index medicus* (EH66), as well as separately.

List of serials indexed for online users / (U.S.) National Library of Medicine. 1983– . [Springfield, Va.] : U.S. National Technical Information Service, 1983– . Annual.   **EH36**

Continues: *List of serials and monographs indexed for online users*, 1980–82.

Provides information on journals indexed in *MEDLINE* (EH67) *Health planning and administration* (EH75), and *POPLINE* (CC257). Titles are listed alphabetically by abbreviated journal title, and indicates those which are selectively indexed.   Z6660.L66

•**SERLINE** : (SERials onLINE) [database]. Bethesda, Md. : National Library of Medicine (U.S.).   **EH37**

Machine-readable version of *List of journals indexed in Index medicus* (EH35), *Index of NLM serial titles* (Bethesda, Md. : National Library of Medicine, 1972–), and *List of serials indexed for online users* (EH36).

Available online, updated monthly.

Provides bibliographic information for all serial titles catalogued by the National Library of Medicine.

Vaillancourt, Pauline M. Cancer journals and serials : an analytical guide. N.Y. : Greenwood, 1988. 259 p.   **EH38**

Provides full bibliographic descriptions for some 400 titles that devote a significant portion of their content to cancer, appear at least once per year, and are published for the most part in English. Where applicable, annotations give the International Cancer Research Data Bank (ICRDB) ranking (last made available in 1981). Publisher, geographic, subject, and sponsor indexes.   Z6664.C2V343

Vital notes on medical periodicals : a publication of the Medical Library Association. v. 1 (Oct. 1952)–v. 30 (Dec. 1982). [Philadelphia : The Association, 1952–1982]. Three no. a year.   **EH39**

Prepared by the Medical Library Center of New York.

Published by the Periodicals and Serial Publications Committee of the Medical Library Association.

The first issue (Oct. 1952) was arranged by births and deaths of periodicals under specific fields; subsequent issues are arranged alphabetically by title, giving address, birth or death date, frequency, and sometimes price.   Z6660.M458

World medical periodicals = Les périodiques médicaux dans le monde = Periódicos médicos del mundo = Medizinische Zeitschriften aller Länder. 3rd ed. N.Y. : World Medical Assoc., 1961. 407 p.   **EH40**

1st ed., 1953; 2nd ed., 1957.

Prep. by C. H. A. Fleurent for the World Medical Association, under the general editorship of H. A. Clegg.

The 3rd ed. includes the titles of more than 5,800 periodicals relating to medicine, pharmacy, dentistry, and veterinary medicine, as well as to hospital buildings, administration, and equipment. Gives address, frequency, language, and the *World list of scientific periodicals* (EA46) abbreviation of the title.

———. *Supplement*, prep. by C. H. A. Fleurent under the editorship of Martin Ware (1968). Includes approximately 700 journals that first appeared or changed title between 1961 and 1968. The numbering of entries is continuous with that of the 3rd ed.   Z6660.W6

Government publications

Chitty, Mary Glen. Federal information sources in health and medicine : a selected annotated bibliography / comp. by Mary Glen Chitty with the assistance of Natalie Schatz. N.Y. : Greenwood, 1988. 306 p. (Bibliographies and indexes in medical studies, no. 1).   **EH41**

Lists "about 1200 government publications and 100 databases from some 90 federal agencies, institutes and information centers."—*Pref.* Consists of subject bibliographies in the medical and health sciences fields, including many depository titles. Entries are numbered and include author, title, document availability, publication date, and Superintendent of Documents and NTIS numbers but not GPO stock number or format. Appendixes of discontinued publications and addresses of major federal agencies. Indexes of keywords in titles, database names, agencies, and subjects.   Z6658.C445

Audiovisual materials

•**AVLINE** [database]. Bethesda, Md. : U.S. National Library of Medicine, 1975– .   **EH42**

Machine-readable version of *National Library of Medicine audiovisuals catalog* (EH44).

Available online, updated weekly.

Contains bibliographic records for audiovisual materials, and since 1988, to microcomputer software catalogued by NLM. Includes primarily English-language material available in the U.S. and Canada.

Health media review index / Jill E. Provan, Joy W. Hunter, editors. Metuchen, N.J. : Scarecrow, 1985. 844 p.   **EH43**

Subtitle: A guide to reviews and descriptions of commercially-available nonprint material for the medical, mental, allied health, human service, and related counselling professions.

Provides excerpts and often includes several different critical reviews published 1980–83. Does not duplicate reviews cited in *AVLINE* (EH42) and the *National Library of Medicine audiovisuals catalog* (EH44), nor audiovisual reviews from journals and databases devoted to the review of software. Lists programs that have won awards.

Supplemented by: *Health media review index, 1984–86*, ed. by Deborah J. McCalpin, with Provan and Hunter as contributing editors (1988), which includes abstracts of reviews and descriptions of more than 3,000 audiovisual products and computer software programs.   RA440.55.H44

National Library of Medicine (U.S.). National Library of Medicine audiovisuals catalog. 1977– . Bethesda, Md. : National Library of Medicine ; Wash. : For sale by U.S. Govt. Print. Off., 1977– . Quarterly, with the fourth issue being the annual cumulation.   **EH44**

Superintendent of Documents classification: HE 20.3609/4.

Provides bibliographic citations to audiovisual materials, and since 1988 to microcomputer software, catalogued by the National Library of Medicine. Provides access to both monographs and serials by name and title and by subject, includes a section concerning procurement, and an appendix covering audiovisual serials.

•Citations to these materials are also available through *AVLINE* database (EH42).   R835.U49b

National Medical Audiovisual Center. National Medical Audiovisual Center catalog. 1974–81. Bethesda, Md. : The Center : for sale by U.S. Govt. Print. Off., 1974–81.   **EH45**

Subtitle (varies): Films for the health scientist.

Continues: *National Medical Audiovisual Center motion picture and videotape catalog* (1973) and *National Medical Audiovisual Center catalog* (1968–72), which in turn continued the U.S. Public Health Service *Film catalog* (1960–67).

Arranged by subject and title, giving purchase, rental, and loan policies. Sponsor and producer code indexes.   R835.N28

Library catalogs

•**CATLINE** : (CATalog onLINE) [database]. Bethesda, Md. : U.S. National Library of Medicine, 1966– .   **EH46**

Machine-readable version of *National Library of Medicine current catalog* (EH49).

Available online, updated weekly.

Contains bibliographic records for monographs and serials catalogued for the collection of the National Library of Medicine.

National Library of Medicine (U.S.). Index-catalogue of the library of the Surgeon General's Office, United States Army (Army Medical Library), authors and subjects. Wash. : U.S. Govt. Print. Off., 1880–1955. 58 v.   **EH47**

Contents: ser. 1, A–Z (1880–95. 16 v.); ser. 2, A–Z (1896–1916. 21 v.); ser. 3, A–Z (1918–32. 10 v.); ser. 4, v. 1–11, A–Mn (1936–55).

A dictionary catalog, including not only books and pamphlets but also a large number of references to periodical articles and other analytics. The National Library of Medicine (formerly the Surgeon General's Library, then the Army Medical Library) is one of the largest medical libraries in the world, and this monumental catalog is therefore a very important bibliography of all aspects of the subject. One of its special uses is for medical biography, since it indexes a large number of biographical and obituary articles.

———. ———. *5th series* (1959–61. 3 v.).

Contents: v. 1, Authors and titles (1959); v. 2–3, Subjects (1961). No more published.

These are the final volumes of the *Index-catalogue*, and are published as a supplementary series to include selected monographic material from the unpublished files of the *Index-catalogue* covering the 19th and first half of the 20th centuries. After a screening of these files, some 83,000 entries were selected, consisting of monographic imprints for 1950 or earlier and including "theses, project reports, monographic and series analytics, equipment and supply catalogs, legislative issuances and bibliographical reference works."—*Pref.*

Z6676.U6

——————— Catalog. 1948–1965. Wash. : Library of Congress, 1949–66. Annual, with quinquennial cumulations beginning 1950/54.   **EH48**

April/Dec. 1948 issue was published in the 1948 cumulative catalog of the Library of Congress as a continuously paged supplement but with separate title page. Also issued separately as v.1 of the present catalog.

Title varies: 1948, *Catalog cards;* 1949–50, *Author catalog.*

Library name varies: 1948–51, U.S. Army Medical Library; 1952–55, U.S. Armed Forces Medical Library.

Includes reproductions of catalog cards prepared for the NLM card catalog for newly received materials and for titles recataloged during the period.

Quinquennial cumulations cover 1950/54, 1955/59, 1960/65.

——————— National Library of Medicine current catalog. 1966– . Wash. : U.S. Govt. Print. Off., 1966– . Quarterly, with annual cumulations.   **EH49**

Supersedes *National Library of Medicine catalog* (N.Y. : Rowman & Littlefield, 1955–65. 12 v.).

Cumulations issued for 1965–70 and 1971–75 and for 1976–80 on microfiche.

Lists all printed monographs and printed and audiovisual serials acquired by NLM; after 1993, audiovisual serials no longer included. Citations also appear in the database *CATLINE* (EH46). Arranged in the following sections: monographs name and title section, serials name and title section, monographs subject section, serials subject section. From 1969 to December 1992, Medical Library Association in cooperation with NLM published citations to current English-language titles in the weekly *NLM current catalog proof sheets*, now ceased.

Z675.M4U578

New York Academy of Medicine. Library. Author catalog. Boston : G.K. Hall, 1969. 43 v.   **EH50**

———. ———. *1st supplement* (1974. 4 v.).

———. *Subject catalog* (Boston : G. K. Hall, 1969. 34 v.).

———.———. *1st supplement* (1974. 4 v.).

These two catalogs with their supplements reproduce the catalog cards for this important collection. The basic set includes entries for more than 373,200 volumes and more than 169,300 pamphlets.

——————— Illustration catalog. 3rd ed., rev. & enl. Boston : G.K. Hall, 1976. 264 p.   **EH51**

1st ed., 1960.

Photographic reproduction of an index to illustrative material in medical works, early as well as recent. Arranged by subject. More than 22,000 illustrations are cataloged.   Z6676.N54

——————— Portrait catalog. Boston : G.K. Hall, 1960. 5 v.   **EH52**

Reproduction of the catalog cards listing the 120,784 separate portraits—paintings, woodcuts, engravings, photographs—in the Academy and 151,792 entries for portraits appearing in books and journals. When a portrait is accompanied by biographical material or an obituary, this is indicated.

Supplements cover 1959–65 (publ. 1965. 842 p.); 1965–71 (1971. 593 p.); 1971–75 (1976. 589 p.).   R153.5.N4

University of Reading. Library. The Cole Library of early medicine and zoology : catalogue of books and pamphlets / Nellie B. Eales. Oxford : Alden Pr. [for] the Univ. of Reading Lib., 1969–75. 2 v. (Reading University Library publications, 1–2).   **EH53**

Contents: v. 1, 1472–1800; v. 2, 1800 to present day and supplement to v. 1.

A descriptive catalog of a distinguished collection. Chronological arrangement, with subject and author indexes.   Z6676.R35

Wellcome Institute for the History of Medicine. Subject catalogue of the history of medicine and related sciences. Munich : Kraus International Publ., 1980. 18 v.   **EH54**

Contents: v. 1–9, Subject section; v. 10–13, Topographical section; v. 14–18, Biographical section.

This subject card catalogue of the library "is not an index to the entire collection, but is probably one of the most comprehensive guides in existence to the modern secondary literature of the history of medicine and allied sciences."—*Pref.* Coverage is from 1954 to 1977. More than 200 journals are regularly indexed; articles from journals not directly related to the field are retrieved from MEDLARS. This catalogue includes more than is covered in the Library's *Current work in the history of medicine* (EH218) and, since it includes all the entries listed in *Current work*, it also serves as an index to the latter.

Z6660.8.W44

Classification

The International classification of diseases, 9th revision, clinical modification : ICD-9-CM. 4th ed. [Wash.] : U.S. Public Health Service, Health Care Financing Administration : for sale by U.S. Govt. Print. Off., [1991–]. 2 v. (DHHS publication, no. (PHS) 91–1260). (In progress).   **EH55**

Contents: v. 1, Diseases: tabular lists; v. 2, Diseases: alphabetic index.

Intended to "serve as a useful tool in the area of classification of morbidity data for indexing of medical records, medical care review,...and other medical care programs, as well as for basic health statistics.—*Foreword.* Based on *International classification of diseases,* 9th revision (Geneva: World Health Organization, 1978). ICD-9-CM is the U.S. modification of ICD-9. Updated by "official authorized" addenda.   RB115.I49

International statistical classification of diseases and related health problems. 10th revision. Geneva : World Health Organization, 1992. 3 v.   **EH56**

At head of title: ICD-10.

9th ed., 1977–78, had title: *Manual of the international statistical classification of diseases, injuries and causes of death.*

Contents : v. 1, Tabular list; v. 2, Instruction manual; v. 3, Alphabetical index.

A decimal classification system for diseases, in 21 broad areas, in which each disease is assigned an alphanumeric code. Vol. 2 contains a review of the historical background on the development of the ICD (p. 139-51).   RB115.I6

Indexes; Abstract journals

Consumer health & nutrition index. v. 1, no. 1 (July 1985)– . Phoenix : Oryx, c1985– . Quarterly.   **EH57**

Indexes articles related to symptoms and diagnoses of diseases and to nutrition found in general-interest magazines and health newsletters. From 1992, covers cost, quality, and access to health care. Uses modified MeSH headings. Includes references to book reviews. Annual cumulative subject index. Of interest to consumers and general readers.

•In machine-readable form as part of *Consumers reference disc* [database] (Baltimore, Md. : National Information Services Corp., 1985–). Available on CD-ROM, updated twice yearly. The disc also includes a machine-readable version of *Consumers index to product evaluations and information sources* (Ann Arbor, Mich. : Pierian Pr., 1973–).

•**EMBASE** [database]. Amsterdam : Excerpta Medica/ EMBASE Publ. Group, 1974– .   **EH58**

Machine-readable version of *Excerpta medica* (EH59).

Available online (updated weekly) and on CD-ROM, diskette, and magnetic tape.

Indexes more than 2,900 journals thoroughly, with selective coverage of an additional 600. Titles indexed are listed in *EMBASE list of journals indexed* (EH34). Provides access to biomedical literature on human medicine and related areas of the biological sciences, with extensive coverage of pharmacology, while excluding dentistry, nursing, and psychology. International in scope; 55% of the journals indexed are published in Europe. Approximately 25% of citations added annually do not appear in *Excerpta medica.*

Excerpta medica : the international medical abstracting service. 1947– . Amsterdam : Excerpta Medica, 1947– . Monthly.   **EH59**

An important abstracting service listing articles from medical journals in all countries. Article titles are given in English translation and sometimes in the original language. Monthly issues are published for each section, with annual author and subject indexes for each.

Section titles have varied over the years; new sections have been added; some sections have split into two or more sections for a period of years, and these subsections have later been assigned new section numbers (usually continuing the volume numbering of the original section). The current section designations are:

Sec. 1, Anatomy, anthropology, embryology and histology; Sec. 2, Physiology; Sec. 3, Endocrinology; Sec. 4, Microbiology, bacteriology, mycology, parasitology and virology; Sec. 5, General pathology and pathological anatomy; Sec. 6, Internal medicine; Sec. 7, Pediatrics and pediatric surgery; Sec. 8, Neurology and neurosurgery; Sec. 9, Surgery; Sec. 10, Obstetrics and gynecology; Sec. 11, Oto-, rhino-, laryngology; Sec. 12, Ophthalmology; Sec. 13, Dermatology and venereology; Sec. 14, Radiology; Sec. 15 Chest diseases, thoracic surgery and tuberculosis; Sec. 16, Cancer; Sec. 17, Public health, social medicine and epidemiology; Sec. 18, Cardiovascular disease and cardiovascular surgery; Sec. 19, Rehabilitation and physical medicine; Sec. 20, Gerontology and geriatrics; Sec. 21, Developmental biology and teratology; Sec. 22, Human genetics; Sec. 23, Nuclear medicine; Sec. 24, Anesthesiology; Sec. 25, Hematology; Sec. 26, Immunology, serology and transplantation; Sec. 27, Biophysics, bioengineering and medical instrumentation; Sec. 28, Urology and nephrology; Sec. 29, Clinical and experimental biochemistry; Sec. 30, Clinical and experimental pharmacology; Sec. 31, Arthritis and rheumatism; Sec. 32, Psychiatry;

Sec. 33, Orthopaedic surgery; Sec. 35, Occupational health and industrial medicine; Sec. 36, Health policy, economics, and management; Sec. 38, Adverse reaction titles; Sec. 40, Drug dependence, alcohol abuse and alcoholism; Sec. 46, Environmental health and pollution control; Sec. 48, Gastroenterology; Sec. 49, Forensic science; Sec. 50, Epilepsy; Sec. 51, Leprosy and related subjects; Sec. 52, Toxicology.

•Since 1974, citations are indexed in online database *EMBASE* (EH58).

Index medicus : a ... classified index of the current medical literature of the world. N.Y. ; Boston ; Wash., 1879–1927. v. 1 (Jan. 1879)–21 (April 1899); ser. 2, v. 1 (Jan. 1903)–18 (Dec. 1920); ser. 3, v. 1 (Jan. 1921)–6 (June 1927).   **EH60**

Publisher varies.

The 1st ser. ceased publication with April 1899; was revived by the Carnegie Institution of Washington in Jan. 1903. During the interval a similar index, *Bibliographia medica (Index medicus)*, was published by the Institut de Bibliographie of Paris.

From 1879 to 1927 the *Index* was a standard current bibliography of medicine, covering publications in all principal languages and including periodical articles and other analytical entries as well as books, pamphlets, and theses. Ser. 1–2, published monthly, consists of references in a classified listing with an author index, cumulated annually, and an annual subject index. Ser. 3 was published quarterly in an alphabetical subject arrangement with an author index cumulated annually, but has no annual subject index. Contains material not found in the *Index-catalogue* of the Surgeon General's Office. Discontinued June 1927, and merged into *Quarterly cumulative index medicus* (EH62).   Z6660.I4

Quarterly cumulative index to current medical literature. v. 1 (Jan./Mar. 1916)–v. 12 (July/Dec. 1926). Chicago : American Medical Assoc., 1917–27.   **EH61**

An important author-subject index to "original articles in the better and more accessible medical journals."—*Note*. Each annual volume includes, in addition to the index to periodicals, a bibliography of the important new books of the year, exclusive of new editions, and a list of government documents of interest to physicians. Titles of articles in foreign languages have been translated into English. In 1926, two semiannual volumes were issued instead of one annual. Should be used with the *Index medicus* for this period.

Continued by: *Quarterly cumulative index medicus* (EH62).
                                                            Z6660.A5

Quarterly cumulative index medicus. v. 1 (1927)–v. 60 (1956). Chicago : Amer. Medical Assoc., 1927–56. Quarterly with semiannual cumulations.   **EH62**

"This volume represents the culmination of efforts whereby the *Index Medicus*, published since 1879 under various auspices, and the *Quarterly Cumulative Index*, published since 1916 by the American Medical Association, are combined as the *Quarterly Cumulative Index Medicus*."—*Pref., 1927.*

An author-subject index to some 1,200 periodicals in many languages, forming a fairly comprehensive general index to the journal literature. Includes medical biography. Also includes a list of journals and publications indexed and a list of new books published during the period, arranged alphabetically by author and followed by a subject classification of the same material. All subject entries are in English and the title is frequently inverted, shortened, or expanded to indicate the contents of the article more clearly. Complete bibliographic information is found under the author entry (including the title of the article in the original language if English, French, German, Spanish, Italian, or Portuguese).

Continued by: *Current list of medical literature* (EH63).
                                                            Z6660.A51

Current list of medical literature. v. 1 (1941)–v. 36 (1959). Wash. : Army Medical Libr., 1950–59. Monthly.   **EH63**

1941–49, issued weekly, consists of the copied contents pages of English- and foreign-language journals in a classified arrangement. Foreign-language titles are not translated. Index to journals, but no subject approach to individual papers and no author index.

Beginning with v. 19 (July–Dec. 1950), published in a greatly expanded form, analyzing nearly 1,500 journals. The journals are listed alphabetically, and items are numbered. Author and subject index in each issue, with a cumulative index for each volume.

Superseded by: *Index medicus* (EH65). Z6660.C8

Bibliography of medical reviews. [v. 1] (1955)–v. 12 (1967). Bethesda, Md. : National Library of Medicine, 1955–67. **EH64**

Vol. 6 is a cumulation, 1955 through 1960, superseding the annual volumes previously published for that period.

Each volume includes references to review articles in thousands of journals in many languages. Review articles include "articles which are well-documented surveys of the recent biomedical journal literature."—*Introd.* Excluded are histories of a subject, case reports with reviews as adjuncts to the main presentation, statistical and epidemiological surveys, bibliographies comprising only a list of references, monthly summaries of subject areas published as regular features in journals, subject reviews which are more appropriately considered refresher courses, and theses. Although some journals not indexed in *Index medicus* (EH65) were covered prior to April 1965, all journals included since that date are also included in *Index medicus*. Subject arrangement with name index. Since January 1968, appears monthly in each issue of *Index medicus* and cumulated annually as part of *Cumulated index medicus* (EH66). Also issued as a separate publication, *Monthly bibliography of medical reviews*, 1968–77.

Index medicus. v. 1– . Wash. : Nat. Libr. of Medicine, 1960– . Monthly. **EH65**

Cumulates annually as *Cumulated index medicus* (EH66).

A comprehensive index to the international biomedical literature, indexing more than 3,000 journals either completely or selectively. In addition to journals in the medical and health sciences, representative journals in other biological sciences are included. All citations in *Index medicus* have been included since 1966 in the online database *MEDLINE* (EH67).

Monthly issues are in two parts: Pt. 1, Subject, A–P; and Pt. 2, Subject, Q–Z, Author, and Bibliography of medical reviews. In the alphabetical Subject section the following elements of the citation are provided: title of English-language article or translation of non-English title; author; journal title abbreviation, with volume, issue, inclusive paging; and date; and an abbreviation indicating original language of non-English articles. English-language articles appear first under each subject. The Author section gives authors' names (up to ten) and biographees; titles are given in the vernacular except for some of the lesser-known languages. *Medical subject headings* (EH143) and *List of journals indexed in Index medicus* (EH35) are published as part of this title as well as separately.

Issues for 1960–65 include a separate section, "Recent United States publications," that reproduces National Library of Medicine catalog cards for current titles.

From Jan. 1970, *Abridged index medicus* (Bethesda, Md. : National Library of Medicine) has been published monthly, intended for individual physicians and small libraries. This title currently indexes 118 English-language publications and is arranged like the parent title. Z6660.I42

Cumulated index medicus. v. 1 (1960)– . Chicago : Amer. Medical Assoc., 1961– . Annual. **EH66**

Imprint varies.

Continues *Quarterly cumulative index medicus* (EH62).

Cumulates *Index medicus* (EH65). Includes separate cumulated author and subject indexes for each year and an annual cumulation of *Bibliography of medical reviews* (EH64). Reprints *List of journals indexed in index medicus* (EH35) and *Medical subject headings : annotated alphabetic list* (EH143). Z666.I422

•**MEDLINE** [database]. Bethesda, Md. : National Library of Medicine, 1966– . **EH67**

Available online, updated weekly, and on CD-ROM, updated monthly.

Provides comprehensive bibliographic access to the international biomedical literature. Corresponds to *Index medicus* (EH65), *Index to*

dental literature (EH251) and *International nursing index* (EH276). Indexes more than 3,200 biomedical journals published in the U.S. and abroad, and chapters and articles from selected monographs, 1976–81. Abstracts are available for approximately 60% of the citations. A list of journals indexed is provided in *List of serials indexed for online users* (EH36).

Reuss, Jeremias David. Repertorium commentationum a societatibus litterariis editarum / secundum disciplinarum ordinem digessit I. D. Reuss …. Gottingae : apud Henricum Dieterich, 1801–21. 16 v. **EH68**

Contents: T. 10, Propaedeutica, anatomia et physiologia, hygieine, pathologia seu nosologia generalis, semeiotica; T. 11, Materia medica, pharmacia; T. 12–15, Therapia generalis et specialis, A–Z; Operationes chirurgicae, Medicina forensis, legalis et politica; T. 16, Ars obstetricia, Ars veterinaria. For full description, *see* EA21.

Z5051.R44

Specialized indexes

Abstracts of health care management studies. v. 15 (Sept. 1978)–v. 23 (July 1987). Ann Arbor, Mich. : Health Administration Pr., 1978–87. **EH69**

Vol. 1 (1964)–v. 14 (1977) had title: *Abstracts of hospital management studies.*

Indexes published and unpublished studies, periodical and other pertinent literature, in the field of health care management. Abstracts are arranged by classified system in broad subject categories. Author and subject indexes. Z6675.H75A27

Aerospace medicine and biology. Jan./Mar. 1964– . Wash. : Scientific and Technical Information Branch, National Aeronautics and Space Administration, 1964– . Monthly, with annual cumulative index. **EH70**

Superintendent of Documents classification: NAS 1.21:7011.

Supersedes an earlier publication of the same title, issued 1952–63 (1952–53 called *Aviation medicine*).

Subtitle and name of issuing agency vary.

References describe the "biological, physiological, psychological, and environmental effects to which man [and biological organisms of lower orders] is subjected during and following simulated or actual flight in the earth's atmosphere or in interplanetary space."—*Introd.* Although emphasis is placed on applied research, references to fundamental studies are also included. International coverage; signed annotations in English. Subject and personal author indexes in each volume are cumulated annually. Corporate source index. Z6664.3.A36

AIDS bibliography. v. 1, no. 1 (Jan. 1988 through Mar. 1988)– . Bethesda, Md. : National Library of Medicine, Reference Section ; Wash. : For sale by U.S. Govt. Print. Off., [1988]– . **EH71**

Superintendent of Documents classification: HE 20.3615/3: .

Frequency varies: quarterly, 1988; monthly, 1989– .

Continues in part *Literature search* of the National Library of Medicine (EH22), discontinued in 1987. In that series, 17 bibliographies on Acquired Immunodeficiency Syndrome (AIDS) were published between 1983 and 1987. Consists of citations from the National Library of Medicine's *AIDSLINE* (EH72), *CATLINE* (EH46), and *AVLINE* (EH42) databases. Citations are arranged by publication type in three sections: (1) journal articles, listed under alphabetically arranged subject headings and subheadings; (2) monographs, arranged alphabetically by author or editor, and (3) audiovisuals, alphabetically by title. The June and Dec. issues contain an additional section that lists all new serial titles on AIDS added during the previous six months.

Z6664.A27A39

•**AIDSLINE** [database]. Bethesda, Md. : U. S. National Library of Medicine, 1980– . **EH72**

Available online (updated three times per month) and on CD-ROM (updated annually).

Machine-readable version of the National Library of Medicine's *AIDS Bibliography* (EH71). Provides comprehensive coverage on all AIDS-related topics, 1980 to the present. Citations are drawn from several databases: *MEDLINE* (EH67), *Health planning and administration* (EH75), *CANCERLIT* (EH73), *CATLINE* (EH46), and *AVLINE* (EH42).

•CANCERLIT [database]. Bethesda, Md. : U.S. National Cancer Institute, International Cancer Information Center, 1963– . **EH73**
Available online (updated monthly) and on CD-ROM (updated quarterly).
Provides international coverage of literature pertaining to all aspects of cancer, including epidemiology, pathology, treatment, and research, from a variety of source documents. From 1963 to 1967, this database corresponded to *Carcinogenesis abstracts* and until 1967 to *Cancer therapy abstracts*. Since 1983, most citations to journals have been derived from *MEDLINE* (EH67).

Cumulative index of hospital literature, 1945–1977. Chicago : Amer. Hospital Assoc., 1950–79. 7 v.   **EH74**
Prepared by the Library of the American Hospital Association, Asa S. Bacon Memorial.
Cumulates *Hospital literature index* at five-year intervals, the 7th and last volume covering three years, 1975–77.
Continued by: *Hospital literature index* (EH77).
"The *Cumulative Index* is a subject-author index to journal literature on the delivery of health care published in the English language, containing three parts: Periodicals Indexed, Subject Section, and Author Section."—*Introd.*

•**Health planning and administration** : (HEALTH) [database]. Bethesda, Md. : U.S. National Library of Medicine, 1975– .   **EH75**
Available online and on CD-ROM, both updated monthly.
Provides bibliographic coverage of the international literature on health care delivery, including administration, management, finances, and planning. Approximately 30% of citations have abstracts. Citations are drawn from *MEDLINE* (EH67), from *Hospital literature index* (EH77), and from material submitted by the National Health Planning Information Center since 1983. Titles indexed are listed in *List of serials indexed for online users* (EH36).

Health service abstracts. v. 1, no. 1 (May 1985)– . London : Dept. of Health and Social Security Library, c1985– . Monthly.   **EH76**
Formed by the union of: *Current literature on health services*; *Current literature on general medical practice*; and *Hospital abstracts* (v. 1 [1961]–24 [1984]. London : H.M.S.O., 1961–84).
Produced from DHSS-DATA, the online database of the Department of Health and Social Security Library.

Hospital literature index. June 1955– . Chicago : Amer. Hospital Assoc., 1955– . Quarterly.   **EH77**
Title varies.
Frequency varies: 1945–61, semiannual; 1962– , quarterly with annual cumulation. 1945–77 cumulated as: *Cumulative index of hospital literature* (EH74).
A "primary guide to literature on hospital and other health care facility administration, including multi-institutional systems, health policy and planning, and the administrative aspects of health care delivery … Special emphasis is given to the theory of health care systems in general; health care in industrialized countries, primarily in the United States; and provision of health care both inside and outside of health care facilities."—*Introd.* Separate subject and author sections. Includes a list of recent acquisitions of the American Hospital Association Resource Center and list of journals indexed.
Since 1978, all citations are included in: National Library of Medicine, *Health planning and administration (HEALTH)* [database] (EH75).   Z6675.H75H67

•POPLINE [database]. Bethesda, Md. : National Library of Medicine, 1970– .   **EH78**
For annotation, *see* CC257.

Tropical diseases bulletin. v. 1 (Nov. 15, 1912)– . London : Bureau of Hygiene and Tropical Diseases, 1912– . Monthly.   **EH79**
Published in association with *Abstracts on hygiene and communicable diseases* (EH408). An international abstracting journal dealing with the various aspects of tropical diseases. Classified arrangement. Most articles are summarized; all summaries are in English. Includes a detailed table of contents and a listing of authors or sources in each monthly issue. Annual general index of subjects and index of authors or sources.   RC960.L78

Encyclopedias

The American Medical Association encyclopedia of medicine / medical ed., Charles B. Clayman. N.Y. : Random House, c1989. 1184 p. : ill.   **EH80**
Produced in response to growing public interest in health care, and to provide wider understanding of the language of medicine. The main section (more than 5,000 entries) includes symptoms, disorders, anatomy and physiology, medical tests, surgical procedures, and drugs, and is illustrated by flow charts, diagrams, etc. References in the text that refer to headwords of other articles are italicized. Also has a directory of self-help organizations and a drug glossary that cross-references brand and generic drug names and gives page numbers for related entries. General index.   RC81.A2A52

Ammer, Christine. The new A to Z of women's health : a concise encyclopedia. N.Y. : Facts on File, c1989. 472 p. : ill.   **EH81**
Revised edition of Ammer's *The A to Z of women's health* (1983).
Entries cover a broad range of topics related to women's health, emphasizing all aspects of reproduction and sexuality. Also discusses alternative health issues such as herbal remedies and astrological birth control. An appendix acts as a subject index, grouping related entries under 18 major topics (e.g., pregnancy and childbirth, cancer); an additional appendix provides addresses of related associations and organizations. Cross-references.   RA778.A494

Concise encyclopedia of biological & biomedical measurement systems / ed., Peter A. Payne. Oxford ; N.Y. : Pergamon Pr., 1991. 490 p. : ill.   **EH82**
85 major articles written in technical language, with *see also* references and bibliography appended to articles. Detailed subject index. Intended for physical scientists, and medical and health care personnel.   RC71.C65

Current medical diagnosis and treatment. 1974– . East Norwalk, Conn. : Appleton & Lange, 1974– . Annual.   **EH83**
Imprint varies: 1962–86 publ. by Lange Medical Publications; 1987– , Appleton & Lange.
Supersedes: *Current diagnosis & treatment* (1962–73).
Also issued in German, Italian, Portuguese, Romanian, Serbo-Croation, and Spanish editions.
Provides concise and up-to-date information on diseases and disorders and widely accepted methods currently available for diagnosis and treatment. Covers internal medicine, gynecology/obstetrics, dermatology, ophthalmology, otolaryngology, psychiatry, neurology, and imaging procedures. Includes information on nutrition, medical genetics, and an annual update on HIV infection and AIDS.   RC71.A14

Encyclopaedia of Indian medicine / ed., S.K. Ramachandra Rao. Bombay : Popular Prakashan on behalf of Dr. V. Parameshvara Charitable Trust, Bangalore, 1985– . v. 1–3 : ill. (In progress).   **EH84**

Contents: v. 1, Historical perspective; v. 2, Basic concepts; v. 3, Clinical examination and diagnostic methods.

Attempts to present "theoretical and practical issues as…formulated in Ayurveda several centuries ago" and to "introduce the reader to the basic principles guiding Indian medicine in the context of the country's geography, history and culture."—*Introd.* To be complete in 6 v.

R605.E53

Encyclopedia of immunology / ed. in chief, Ivan M. Roitt, executive ed., Peter J. Delves. London ; San Diego, Calif. : Academic Pr., c1992. 3 v. (li, 1578, xci p.).   **EH85**

For annotation, *see* EG21.   QR180.4.E56

Encyclopedia of medical devices and instrumentation / John G. Webster, ed. in chief. N.Y. : Wiley, c1988. 4 v. (3022 p.) : ill.   **EH86**

An alphabetically arranged collection of more than 250 articles by experts, providing a comprehensive treatment of the contributions of engineering, physics, and computers to the various areas of medicine. Broader than the title would indicate, the work covers not only devices and instrumentation, but also the scientific basis for medical biotechnology, including articles on topics such as blood rheology, statistical methods, and biomechanics of scoliosis. Articles include many illustrations and substantial bibliographies of the primary literature. Cross-references; index.   R856.A3E53

Encyclopedia of neuroscience / ed. by George Adelman. Boston : Birkhäuser, 1987. 2 v. : ill.   **EH87**

The first general encyclopedia in the field, with some 700 signed entries varying in length from several hundred words to several pages, and covering all clinical and basic aspects of neuroscience for both specialists and general readers. Both volumes begin with a list of all entries and end with an appendix of illustrations of the gross anatomy of the brain and name and subject indexes. Vol. 2 has two additional appendixes: a discussion of the use of animals in neuroscience research and concise biographies of contributors to neuroscience, 300 BCE to 1950.

Supplemented by: *Neuroscience year: supplement 1 to the Encyclopedia of neuroscience*, ed. by George Adelman (1989).

————. *Supplement 2*, ed. by Barry Smith and George Adelman (1992).

————. *Supplement 3*, ed. by Barry Smith and George Adelman (1993). Supplements provide brief descriptions of recent developments in neuroscience, and represent potential new entries to the encyclopedia. Name and subject indexes.   RC334.E53

The Oxford companion to medicine / ed. by John Walton, Paul B. Beeson, Ronald Bodley Scott. Oxford ; N.Y. : Oxford Univ. Pr., 1986. 2 v. : ill.   **EH88**

Contains essays that vary in length, some historical, some contemporary, on disciplines, specialties, and topics affecting the practice of medicine. Includes biographical entries and short definitions of selected medical terms. Essays are signed and include bibliographies. Appendixes give abbreviations and full names for major medical and related qualifications.   R121.O88

Physics in medicine & biology encyclopedia : medical physics, bioengineering, and biophysics / ed., T.F. McAinsh. Oxford ; N.Y. : Pergamon, 1986. 2 v. (980 p.) : ill.   **EH89**

Includes more than 200 signed comprehensive articles with bibliographies. Articles are predominantly clinical in nature; topics demanding a highly mathematical treatment have been omitted. A classified list, grouping material into broad fields, precedes the alphabetic list of articles. Glossary; author and subject index. Intended for "the reader who has a basic grounding in physics, but no particular knowledge of the specific topic under discussion."—*Foreword.*

R895.A3P47

Sardegna, Jill. The encyclopedia of blindness and vision impairment / Jill Sardegna and T. Otis Paul. N.Y. : Facts on File, c1991. 329 p.   **EH90**

A basic guide aimed at both professionals and general readers; treats all aspects of blindness, including health issues, education, adaptive aids, and organizations. More than 500 entries include both brief definitions and main articles (one to two pages in length), some of which include short lists of references. Provides an extensive bibliography. Appendixes list relevant companies (but do not list their services or products); organizations; schools; federal agencies; publications; databases; and services related to blindness and vision impairment. Five tables provide statistical information related to eye injuries and diseases in the U.S., containing data for 1978–79. Subject and name index.   RE91.S27

Wynbrandt, James. The encyclopedia of genetic disorders and birth defects / James Wynbrandt and Mark D. Ludman. N.Y. : Facts on File, c1991. 426 p. : ill.   **EH91**

Presents some 600 articles written for both health care professionals and general readers. Entries for disorders, selected on the basis of incidence and historical and clinical importance, discuss prognosis, prevalence, mode of inheritance, and the availability of both carrier screening and prenatal diagnosis; many include addresses of private organizations which can provide further information. Also included are brief discussions of subjects and terminology related to genetic disorders and congenital anomalies. Appendixes provide statistics and tables on congenital malformations and infant mortality, addresses for federal organizations and other associations in the U.S., support groups in the U.K., and Canadian organizations. Bibliography; subject and name index; numerous cross-references.   RB155.5.W96

Dictionaries

Black's medical dictionary. 37th ed. London : A. & C. Black, 1992.   **EH92**

1st ed., 1906; 36th ed., 1990.

A standard dictionary of British terminology. Each edition includes some new terms and revisions. Many cross-references.

R121.B598

Blakiston's Gould medical dictionary / Chairman of the editorial board, Arthur Osol. 4th ed. N.Y. : McGraw-Hill, [1979]. 1632 p.   **EH93**

1st ed., 1949, and 2nd ed., 1956, had title: *Blakiston's new Gould medical dictionary.* 3rd ed., 1972.

Subtitle: A modern comprehensive dictionary of the terms used in all branches of medicine and allied sciences; with illustrations and tables.

Based on George M. Gould's *Medical dictionary* (5 editions, 1926–41) and its predecessors, published with varying titles in 1890, 1894, and 1904. More than 75,000 words are defined. Includes tables of anatomic structure, chemical constituents of the blood, common radioactive pharmaceuticals, etc.   R121.B62

Butterworths medical dictionary / Macdonald Critchley, ed. in chief. 2nd ed. London ; Boston : Butterworths, 1978. 1942 p.   **EH94**

First published as: *The British medical dictionary*, ed. by Sir Arthur Salusbury MacNalty (London : Caxton, 1961).

Includes an appendix on anatomical nomenclature, relating Nomina Anatomica nomenclature to English equivalent.   R121.B75

Churchill's illustrated medical dictionary. N.Y. : Churchill Livingstone, 1989. 2120 p. : ill.   **EH95**

Some 100,000 entries, with "extensive coverage given to vocabulary … from medical research, advanced diagnostic technology and innovations in health care."—*Pref.* Pronunciations (for more than 32,000 terms) and some usage notes (for 750). Includes biographical data for eponymous terms.   R121.I58

Current medical information and terminology : CMIT. 5th ed. [Chicago : Americal Medical Assoc., 1981]. 801p.   **EH96**

1st ed., 1963, had title: *Current medical terminology*; 4th ed., 1971.

On cover: ... for the naming and description of diseases and conditions in practice and in areas related to medicine.

The main section consists of 3,262 "preferred terms and definitions," with a definition and description of the disease, cause, physical signs, complications, and laboratory data. There is a section of cross-references from French, German, and Spanish names of diseases, and a systematic classification of diseases. A KWIC index covering genus names, infections, geographic distributions of disease, genetic abnormalities, and organ involvements is included.

Dorland's illustrated medical dictionary. 27th ed. Philadelphia : Saunders, c1988. 1888 p. : ill.   **EH97**

Earlier editions published under title *The American illustrated medical dictionary*.

[1st] ed., 1900; 26th ed., 1981.

Japanese, Spanish, and Braille editions are also available.

Designed to satisfy the conventional use of a dictionary, that is, to discover spelling, meaning, and derivation of specific terms and to assist in the creation of words by defining prefixes, suffixes, and stems. Includes a chapter on "Fundamentals of medical etymology."

R121.D73

Dox, Ida. Melloni's illustrated medical dictionary / Ida G. Dox, B. John Melloni, Gilbert M. Eisner. 3rd ed. N.Y. : Parthenon Publ. Group, c1993. 533 p. : ill.   **EH98**

1st ed., 1979; 2nd ed., 1985.

A "compilation of over 26,000 terms comprising the common core of information for all the health sciences."—*Pref.* Many illustrations are keyed to specific terms; terms with accompanying illustrations are highlighted in brown. Phonetic pronunciations are included in a separate list at the front of the book. Includes a list of abbreviations, prefixes, suffixes, and combining forms.   R121.D76

Firkin, Barry G. Dictionary of medical eponyms / B.G. Firkin and J.A. Whitworth. Carnforth, U.K. ; Park Ridge, N.J. : Parthenon Publ. Group, 1987. 591 p. : ill.   **EH99**

Offers explanations of approximately 2,300 eponyms currently used in internal medicine; in general, eponymous terms from subspecialities have been excluded. Each entry includes a brief definition of the term, and provides biographical information about the person from whose name the term is derived; some entries include a photograph or portrait. Although the orientation is Australian, these terms are used in most English-speaking countries. Includes some cross-references, but there is no index. The introduction provides a brief list of reference sources, but individual entries do not provide bibliographic citations.

R121.F535

International dictionary of medicine and biology / editorial board, E. Lovell Becker ... [et al.] ; consulting ed., Alexandre Manuila ; Sidney I. Landau, ed. in chief. N.Y. : Wiley, c1986. 3 v. (3200 p.).   **EH100**

An unabridged dictionary of medicine and closely allied biological sciences, offering some 159,000 definitions and 30,000 etymologies. In addition to the standard current terminology from the various disciplines and specialties, it also includes many terms of historical interest.   R121.I58

Lorenzini, Jean A. Medical phrase index : a one-step reference to the terminology of medicine / Jean A. Lorenzini, Laura Lorenzini Ley. 3rd ed. Los Angeles : Practice Management Information Corp., c1994. 1261 p.   **EH101**

1st ed., 1978; 2nd ed., 1989.

"For medical transcribers, medical records librarians, medical assistants, legal secretaries, insurance claims examiners—for anyone who must capture medical terminology accurately and quickly."— *Publ. notes.* Includes both formal and informal phrases which are cross-indexed for each major word. Entries are arranged alphabetically. For words with more than one spelling, gives directions to common usage; sound-alikes are indicated.   R123.L84

Mosby's medical, nursing, and allied health dictionary / managing ed., Walter D. Glanze ; revision ed., Kenneth N. Anderson ; consulting ed. and writer, Lois E. Anderson. 3rd ed. St. Louis : Mosby, 1990. 1 v. (various pagings).   **EH102**

1st ed., 1983, and 2nd ed., 1986, had title: *Mosby's medical and nursing dictionary.*

Many definitions are discursive. Emphasizes allied health professions, with new categories of entries in physical therapy, occupational therapy, and respiratory care. 21 appendixes include, e.g., units of measure, symbols, prefixes and suffixes, and a 32-page color atlas of human anatomy.   R121M89

Segen, J. C. The dictionary of modern medicine. Carnforth, Lancs, U.K. ; Park Ridge, N.J. : Parthenon Publ. Group, 1992. 800 p. : ill.   **EH103**

"Modern" is meant to cover the last two to three decades. Intended to complement traditional medical dictionaries. Comprehensive and detailed definitions of more than 2,000 current medical terms not adequately addressed in standard medical dictionaries. Etymological information is not given. Many entries include citations from the journal literature.   R121.S429

Sloane, Sheila B. The medical word book : a spelling and vocabulary guide to medical transcription. 3rd ed. Philadelphia : Saunders, 1991. 1097 p., 16 p. of plates : ill. (some col.).

EH104

Designed for the purposes of medical transcription, providing lists of terms without definitions. In three major parts: pt. 1 provides illustrations of human anatomy and a list of general medical terms and general surgical terms; pt. 2, terms associated with 15 specialties; and pt. 3, a list of abbreviations and symbols, combining forms, and phonetic spelling.   R123.S57

Stedman, Thomas Lathrop. Stedman's medical dictionary. 25th ed. Baltimore : Williams & Wilkins, c1990. 95, 1784 p. : ill.   **EH105**

1st ed., 1911, entitled: *A practical medical dictionary*; titles of later editions varies slightly; 24th ed., 1982.

A standard work frequently revised. Offers approximately 100,000 entries and includes a section on medical etymology. Appendixes include: Comparative temperature scales, Temperature equivalents, Weights and measures, and Laboratory reference range values.

R121.S8

Taber's cyclopedic medical dictionary / ed. by Clayton L. Thomas. Ed. 17th ill. / ed. by Clayton L. Thomas. Philadelphia : F.A. Davis, c1993. 2590 p. : ill.   **EH106**

1st ed., 1940; 16th ed., 1989.

An updated edition of this standard work giving definitions of medical terms and words. Pronunciation is given for all but very common terms and the etymology of most words is included. Appendixes include such information as emergency treatment, dietetic charts, Latin and Greek nomenclature, and normal reference laboratory values.

R121.T144

Willeford, George. Webster's new World medical word finder. 4th ed. N.Y : Prentice-Hall, c1987. 433 p.   **EH107**

1st ed., 1967–3rd ed., 1983, had title: *Medical word finder.*

A compact, easy-to-use guide to spelling, syllabication, and accentuation of frequently used medical terms. Includes word and prescription abbreviations.   R123.W47

Specialized dictionaries

Altman, Roberta. The cancer dictionary / Roberta Altman, Michael Sarg. N.Y. : Facts on File, c1992. 334 p. : ill. **EH108**

Designed for general readers, this dictionary attempts to provide definitions for every term connected with cancer. Includes many cross-references, and capitalized terms within a definition have their own entry. Brief bibliography, appendixes (support organizations, comprehensive cancer centers, clinical trials cooperative groups, and drugs), and subject index. RC262.A39

Bennington, James L. Saunders dictionary & encyclopedia of laboratory medicine and technology / James L. Bennington ; assoc. ed., George Brecher ... [et al.]. Philadelphia : Saunders, c1984. 1674 p. : ill. **EH109**

This dictionary "was created to provide in a single source comprehensive and authoritative definitions of terms used in the field. ... [The compilers have] attempted to provide comprehensive coverage of currently used methods and techniques for laboratory analysis in the areas of clinical chemistry, biochemistry, toxicology, hematology ... and respiratory medicine. For each test, assay, or examination, the basic principles of the methods or instrumentation, or both, used for analysis are discussed, along with the conditions that affect the accuracy and precision of detection and measurement, fundamentals of quality control, reference values, pathophysiologic alterations that produce abnormal values, and the chemical use of some applications of the procedures."—*Pref.* Appendixes include: cancer chemotherapy drugs, bacteriologic specimen collections, and reference ranges and laboratory values of clinical importance. RB37.B453

Cassin, Barbara. Dictionary of eye terminology / Barbara Cassin, Sheila A. B. Solomon ; Melvin L. Rubin, ed. 2nd ed. Gainesville, Fla. : Triad Publ. Co., c1990. 286 p. : ill. **EH110**

A dictionary "geared to making ophthalmic terminology accessible and understandable to all who were not familiar with the field."—*Pref.* Brief definitions, with pronunciation guides only for difficult words. Each term is also assigned a general category—e.g., pathologic condition, optical device or surgical procedure—which provides a context for each definition. RE21.C37

A dictionary of dermatologic terms. 4th ed. / ed. by Robert L. Carter. Baltimore : Williams & Wilkins, c1992. 385 p. **EH111**

1st ed., 1965, through 3rd ed., 1976, by Morris Leider and Morris Rosenblum, had title: *A dictionary of dermatological words, terms, and phrases.*

Brief definitions of dermatologic terms, including pronunciations. Some entries have incomplete references to well-known dermatologic texts, which may confuse readers other than dermatologists; no bibliography. RL39.L44

Dictionary of obstetrics and gynecology / comp. by the editorial staff of Pschyrembel Klinisches Wörterbuch ; managing ed., Christoph Zink. Berlin ; N.Y. : W. de Gruyter, 1988. 277 p. : ill. (some col.). **EH112**

English translation of *Pschyrembel Wörterbuch Gynäkologie und Geburtshilfe* (1987), which supplemented and augmented *Pschyrembel's Klinisches Wörterbuch* (1986).

"This English version is primarily to be understood as the translation of a reference book which has its origins in the German scientific tradition. Nevertheless, also aspects specific to English-speaking countries have been included."—*Pref.* More than 2,600 entries are arranged alphabetically (except for plural forms). Derivation is given for words of Greek or Latin origin. Includes biographical entries. More than 400 illustrations, some in color; large number of tables and charts. Medical abbreviations have their own entries; general abbreviations are in an "Abbreviations list" (*p.xi*). Copious use of cross-references. RG45.P7813

Dictionary of visual science / [ed. by] David Cline, Henry W. Hofstetter, John R. Griffin. 4th ed. Radnor, Pa. : Chilton, c1989. 820 p. : ill. **EH113**

1st ed., 1960; 3rd ed., 1980.

A comprehensive dictionary providing succinct definitions for terms in all fields of visual science, including anatomy and physiology of the eye, optics, and ocular pharmacology. Includes entries for syndromes with ocular manifestations. Compound and eponymous terms are listed alphabetically under the noun ("artificial light" under "light," "Harada's disease" under "disease"), and pronunciation is given for

more difficult terms. An appendix lists terms, symbols and abbreviations, and there are reference tables related to visual science. RE21.D42

Gibson, John. A dictionary of medical and surgical syndromes / J. Gibson and O. Potparič. Carnforth, U.K. ; Park Ridge, N.J. : Parthenon Publ. Group, 1992. 202 p. **EH114**

Includes more than 1,000 definitions. Alphabetical arrangement; cross-references. RC69.G53

Goldstein, Arnold S. The Aspen dictionary of health care administration. Rockville, Md. : Aspen Publishers, 1989. 293 p. **EH115**

A dictionary of current health care terminology, focusing on health care administration. Cross-references to other terms are italicized. Appendix of abbreviations. RA971.G579

Haubrich, William S. Medical meanings : a glossary of word origins. San Diego : Harcourt Brace Jovanovich, c1984. 285 p. : ill. **EH116**

An etymological dictionary of medical terms, relating word origins to their current meaning. Cross-reference index. R123.H29

Hospital administration terminology / American Hospital Resource Center ; comp. by Anne Fox Kiger. 2nd ed. [Chicago] : American Hospital Pub., c1986. 61 p. **EH117**

1st ed., 1982.

Provides concise definitions of health care terms that "have application to the administration of hospitals and related health care institutions and to health care delivery in general."—*Pref.* Includes recent terminology in the areas of diversification, financial management, and multi-institutional arrangements. Includes some abbreviations. See also: *Acronyms and initialisms in health care administration* (EH129). RA962.2.H67

Jablonski, Stanley. Jablonski's dictionary of syndromes and eponymic diseases. Malabar, Fla. : Krieger Publ., 1991. 665 p. : ill. **EH118**

Rev. ed. of: *Illustrated dictionary of eponymic syndromes and diseases and their synonyms,* 1969.

"Included in the book are the names of syndromes and eponymous diseases which occur in the literature with reasonable frequency."—*Introd.* Entries under personal names may provide brief biographical information. Many cross-references, and some entries include references.

§ A complementary work is: *Eponymous syndromes : MEDLARS indexing instructions* (Wash. : National Library of Medicine, Index Section, 1970. 132 p.). Indicates the *MeSH* terms used for indexing the syndromes. Useful as a guide for machine searching as well as an aid for the user of *Index medicus* (EH65). R121.J24

Lockard, Isabel. Desk reference for neuroscience. 2nd ed. N.Y. : Springer-Verlag, c1992. 306 p. : ill. **EH119**

A dictionary of neuroscience terms based on Lockard's *Desk reference for neuroanatomy* (1977). "In this edition...many terms from the first edition have been amplified and the text has been expanded to include many more terms from various NEUROSCIENCES—neurophysiology, neuropathology, neuropharmacology, and the related clinical branches, in addition to neuroanatomy."—*Pref.* QM451.L625

Magalini, Sergio I. Dictionary of medical syndromes / Sergio I. Magalini, Sabina C. Magalini, Giovanni de Francisci. 3rd ed. Philadelphia : Lippincott, 1990. 1042 p. **EH120**

1st ed., 1971; 2nd ed., 1981.

Alphabetic arrangement by name of syndrome, giving for each: synonyms, symptoms and signs, etiology, pathology, diagnostic procedures, therapy, prognosis, and bibliography. Indexed. RC69.M33

Millodot, Michel. Dictionary of optometry. 3rd ed. Oxford ; Boston : Butterworth-Heinemann, 1993. 196 p. **EH121**

1st ed., 1986; 2nd ed., 1990.

Defines terms commonly used in optometry. Many cross-references.   RE939.7.M54

Nicolosi, Lucille. Terminology of communication disorders : speech-language-hearing / Lucille Nicolosi, Elizabeth Harryman, Janet Kresheck. 3rd ed. Baltimore : Williams & Wilkins, c1989. 354 p. : ill.   **EH122**

1st ed., 1978; 2nd ed., 1983.

A comprehensive dictionary, intended to be an "authoritative reference work for the Speech, Language and Hearing Professions."—*Foreword.* Brief definitions; illustrations; many cross-references. Includes list of tables, and appendixes.   RC423.N52

Rodin, Alvin E. Medicine, literature & eponyms : an encyclopedia of medical eponyms derived from literary characters / Alvin E. Rodin and Jack D. Key. Malabar, Fla. : R.E. Krieger Publ. Co., 1989. 345 p. : ill.   **EH123**

Defines more than 350 medical eponyms derived from literary characters; among the sources are mythology, fables, and cartoons. Each entry includes a synopsis of the medical condition, a description of the associated literary character and of how specific characteristics correspond to symptoms of the condition, further literary references to the medical state, and other related material. A list of references to both the literary character and the medical condition appear with each entry. Subject index.   R121.R62

Rosen, Fred S. Dictionary of immunology / Fred S. Rosen, Lisa A. Steiner, Emil R. Unanue. N.Y. : Stockton Pr. ; London : Macmillan, 1989. 223 p. : ill.   **EH124**

Repr. with corrections, 1990.

"Draws from the vocabulary of molecular biology, cell biology and genetics as well as from immunology itself ... . Many of the definitions are long and contain considerable detail."—*Introd.* May be useful to readers with little background in immunology.

QR180.4.R67

Slee, Vergil N. Health care terms / Vergil N. Slee, Debora A. Slee. 2nd ed. St. Paul, Minn. : Tringa Pr., c1991. 456 p.

EH125

1st ed., 1986.

Provides concise definitions for terms from a wide range of disciplines in the health care field, including health care administration and finance, statistics, and governmental regulation. Many cross-references; this glossary pays particular attention to sometimes incomprehensible acronyms. Terms used in definitions are italicized to indicate the term is defined elsewhere in the dictionary; related terms may be grouped together under one term, such as the many entries under the term "hospital." Intended for both health care professionals and general readers.   RA423.S55

Thornton, Spencer P. Ophthalmic eponyms : an encyclopedia of named signs, syndromes, and diseases in ophthalmology. Birmingham, Ala. : Aesculapius Pub. Co., [1967]. 324 p.

EH126

In two sections: (1) signs, syndromes, and diseases in medical, pediatric, and neuro-ophthalmology; and (2) eponyms in ophthalmic surgery. Arrangement is alphabetical within each section. Bibliographic references are included with most entries.   RE21.T54

Tver, David F. Encyclopedic dictionary of sports medicine / David F. Tver, Howard F. Hunt. N.Y. : Chapman and Hall, 1986. 232 p. : ill.   **EH127**

Provides brief definitions for terms related to injuries and illnesses associated with physical activities and sports. Also included are descriptions of parts of the body which may receive a greater proportion of injuries. Includes some illustrations and a glossary of terms.   RC1206.T88

——————— Industrial medicine desk reference / David F. Tver, Kenneth A. Anderson. N.Y. : Chapman and Hall, 1986. 307 p.   **EH128**

An encyclopedic dictionary that provides entries for a variety of terms related to industrial medicine, including types of chemicals and specific chemicals, diseases, and discussions of specific industries.

RC963.A3T94

Abbreviations

Acronyms and initialisms in health care administration / American Hospital Association Resource Center ; comp. by Anne Fox Kiger. Chicago : American Hospital Publ., c1986. 71 p.   **EH129**

Identifies terms primarily in health care administration, but also from areas such as statistics, data processing, economics, and organizational and regulatory processes. Excludes terms specific to countries other than the U.S., terms that are limited to regional, state, or local usage within the U.S., clinical terms, names of journals, and acronyms for commercial computer software. See also: *Hospital administration terminology* (EH117) where many terms included here are defined.

RA962.2.A28

Dupayrat, Jacques. Dictionary of biomedical acronyms and abbreviations. 2nd ed. Chichester, [Eng.] ; N.Y. : Wiley, c1990. 162 p.   **EH130**

Provides more than 7,000 definitions for 4,000 of the most common acronyms in medicine, biology, and biochemistry. Some chemical terms are included. Intended for researchers in chemistry, biochemistry, and biology, and for physicians and translators. Where necessary, a specific field or term (e.g., "Syndrome") is added in parentheses to define more clearly the abbreviation or acronym.   R123.D87

Heister, Rolf. Dictionary of abbreviations in medical sciences : with a list of the most important medical and scientific journals and their traditional abbreviations. Berlin ; N.Y. : Springer-Verlag, c1989. 287 p.   **EH131**

International in scope, providing definitions for approximately 15,000 abbreviations. Includes acronyms of many associations. Important or internationally used acronyms from languages other than English are included, the language indicated by a single-letter code. Indications of the specialty are occasionally provided (e.g., "mil" for military medicine). An appendix gives a short list of abbreviated titles of medical and scientific journals. Omitted are common, well-known abbreviations and physical and chemical symbols and formulae.   R123.H35

Jablonski, Stanley. Dictionary of medical acronyms and abbreviations. 2nd ed. Philadelphia, Pa. : Hanley & Belfus ; St. Louis : Mosby-Year Book, c1993. 330 p.   **EH132**

A selective dictionary of the most frequently used acronyms and abbreviations, arranged alphabetically. Includes a brief list of symbols and the Greek alphabet.   R123.J24

Mitchell-Hatton, Sarah Lu. The Davis book of medical abbreviations : a deciphering guide. Philadelphia : F.A. Davis Co., c1991. 1028 p.   **EH133**

Intended for medical transcriptionists and other medical personnel. Arranged alphabetically by abbreviation, with multiple definitions arranged alphabetically. Fields or specialties are indicated in parentheses. "Included are many odd, obsolete, profane, slang and utterly stupid abbreviations" (*Pref.*), as well as sports and some nonmedical abbreviations.   R123.M54

Stedman's abbrev. : abbreviations, acronyms & symbols. Baltimore : Williams & Wilkins, c1992. 664 p.   **EH134**

Spine title: Stedman's abbreviations, acronyms & symbols.

A "primary resource for anyone involved in transcribing, recording, copy editing or reading records, reports, and other material generated by health care professionals."—*Explanatory notes.* Abbreviations are in boldface; multiple meanings are listed alphabetically, with explanatory material in parentheses.   R123.S69

Steen, Edwin Benzel. Baillière's abbreviations in medicine. 5th ed. London ; Philadelphia : Baillière Tindall, [1984]. 255 p. **EH135**
1st ed., 1960.
A pocket book that lists more than 15,000 common medical and related abbreviations. Includes bibliography. R123.S84

Multilingual

Bunjes, Werner Ernst. Medical and pharmaceutical dictionary : English-German. 4th ed., with a supplement comprising more than 17,000 new entries. Stuttgart : G. Thieme, 1981. 556, 140 p. **EH136**
1st ed., 1953, and 2nd ed., 1968–69, also formed v. 2 of Fritz Lejeune's *German-English, English-German dictionary for physicians* (EH140). 2nd ed. also issued as v. 2 of Lejeune's *Deutsch-Englisches, Englisch-Deutsches Wörterbuch für Aerzte*.
A comprehensive dictionary that includes eponyms, abbreviations, and acronyms. Each entry consists of the English term, pronunciation, and German equivalents. R121.B86

Dictionary of medicine : English-German : containing about 55,000 terms / comp. by Jürgen Nöhring. Amsterdam ; N.Y. : Elsevier, 1984. 708 p. **EH137**
"Terms have been selected from all branches of medicine [with the] aim … to serve as a practical source … intended not only for physicians … and specialists, but also students of medicine and … ancillary staff."—*Pref.* R121.N63

Dictionary of medicine : German-English : containing about 75,000 terms / comp. by Jürgen Nöhring. Amsterdam ; N.Y. : Elsevier, 1987. 846 p. **EH138**
"In preparing this edition the terminology of the English-German volume has been revised and … some new terms have been added."—*Pref.* R121.N63

Dorian, Angelo Francis. Elsevier's encyclopaedic dictionary of medicine : in five languages, English, French, German, Italian, and Spanish. Amsterdam ; N.Y. : Elsevier, 1987–1989. v. 1–3. **EH139**
Contents: pt. A, General medicine (1987); pt. B, Anatomy (1988); pt. C, Biology, genetics and biochemistry (1989); pt. D, Therapeutic substances (1990).
Provides both a concise definition and a translation for each entry. The "Basic table" lists English entries in alphabetical order, each followed by an English definition and its French, German, Italian, and Spanish equivalents. The equivalents are listed alphabetically in four separate indexes. Part B, Anatomy, "is based on the English equivalents of the Nomina Anatomica as set forth by the sixth International Congress of Anatomists in Paris in 1955."—*Pref.* R121.D72

Lejeune, Fritz. German-English, English-German dictionary for physicians / by Fritz Lejeune and Werner E. Bunjes. 2nd ed. Stuttgart : Thieme Verlag ; N.Y. : Intercontinental Medical Book Corp., 1968–69. 2 v. **EH140**
Added title page in German.
Contents: v. 1, German-English (2nd ed., compl. rev.); v. 2, English-German (2nd ed., unrevised).
1st ed., 1951.
Includes some 85,000 entries covering all fields of medicine, but with restrictive coverage of peripheral fields and anatomical terms. Quasi-medical words, although formerly included, are omitted from this edition. R121.L373

Lépine, Pierre. Dictionnaire français-anglais, anglais-français des termes médicaux et biologiques. 2. éd. / prép. par Pierre Lépine et Philip R. Peacock. Paris : Flammarion, [1974]. 876 p. **EH141**
Added title on cover: *Dictionary, English-French, French-English, of medical & biological terms.*

Brief definitions are provided if necessary to comprehension. R121.L39

Ruiz Torres, Francisco. Diccionario de términos médicos, inglés-español, español-inglés. 6a ed., rev. y ampliada. Madrid : Editorial Alhambra, c1989. 880 p. **EH142**
1st ed., 1957; 5th ed., 1986.
Offers brief Spanish-language definitions of English medical terms and a separate section of Spanish medical terms with English equivalents (not definitions). R121.R93

Thesauruses

Medical subject headings : annotated alphabetic list. 1979– . Bethesda, Md. : Medical Subject Headings Section, National Library of Medicine ; [Springfield, Va. : National Technical Information Service], 1979– . Annual. **EH143**
Superintendent of Documents classification: HE 20.3602:H 34/ .
An alphabetic list of subject descriptors, often called "MeSH headings." Includes subject headings, cross-references, geographic headings, non-MeSH terms, check tags, tree numbers, and notes.
Z695.1.M48U52c

Medical subject headings. Supplementary chemical records / (U.S.) National Library of Medicine. 1983– . Bethesda, Md. : The Library ; [Springfield, Va.] : National Technical Information Service [distributor], 1982– . Annual. **EH144**
Superintendent of Documents classification: HE 20.3612/3-7: .
Contains records of approximately 22,000 chemicals which, since 1970, have been mentioned in a significant way in journals indexed in *MEDLINE* (EH67).

Medical subject headings. Tree structures 1972– . Bethesda, Md. : Medical Subject Headings Section, Library Operations, National Library of Medicine, 1972– . Annual. **EH145**
Superintendent of Documents classification: HE 20.3602:H 34/2/
MeSH headings are arranged hierarchially to show the relationship between terms. Beginning 1990, also contains *MeSH tree annotations.* Z695.1.M48U52b

Permuted medical subject headings / (U.S.) National Library of Medicine. Bethesda, Md. : The Library ; [Springfield, Va.] : U.S. National Technical Information Center, 1983– . Annual. **EH146**
Superintendent of Documents classification: HE 20.3602:H 34/3/ .
For each significant term used in MeSH headings, lists all headings that include that term. Z695.1.M48U52d

Physicians' current procedural terminology : CPT / American Medical Association. 3rd ed.– . Chicago : The Association, c1973– . Irregular. **EH147**
1st ed., 1966, and 2nd ed., 1970, had title: *Current procedural terminology.*
"Listing of descriptive terms and identifying codes for reporting medical services and procedures performed by physicians. The purpose of the terminology is to provide a uniform language … for reliable … communication among physicians, patients, and third parties."—*Foreword.* Terms are arranged by body systems and by a five-digit code. Appendixes; index. RB115.C17

Directories

International

Directory of technical and scientific directories : a world bibliographic guide to medical, agricultural, industrial, and natural science directories. 6th ed. Harlow : Longman ; Phoenix : Oryx, 1989. 302 p.   **EH148**
>   For annotation, *see* EA140.   Z7405.D55D57

Medical research centres : a world directory of organizations and programmes. 6th ed. (1983)– . Harlow, [Eng.] : Longman ; Detroit : Gale, c1983– . Irregular.   **EH149**
>   Title varies; 1st–5th eds. (1945–79) called: *Medical research index*.
>   Intends "to provide a comprehensive guide to ... organizations and people in the medical research world."—*Introd., 7th ed.* Lists 9,000 organizations and laboratories in 104 countries, arranged alphabetically by country. For each research establishment, gives address, scope of interest, key personnel. Indexes of establishments and subjects.
>   § Companion volume: *Medical sciences international who's who* (EH150).   R850.M43

Medical sciences international who's who. 3rd ed., (1987)– . Harlow, Essex : Longman ; Detroit : Gale, 1987– .   **EH150**
>   1st ed., 1980, and 2nd ed., 1985, had title: *International medical who's who : a biographical guide in the biomedical sciences.*
>   Provides information on approximately 8,000 biomedical scientists from more than 90 countries. Vol. 1 gives individual profiles in alphabetical order; v. 2 presents a listing of experts in 14 subject areas, by country. Subject areas include anatomy and physiology, biochemistry, biophysics, molecular biology, dental sciences, immunology and transplantation, clinical medicine and neoplasia. A companion to *Medical research centres* (EH149).   R134.I57

World directory of medical schools. [Ed. 1] (1953)– . Geneva : World Health Organization, 1953– . Irregular.   **EH151**
>   6th ed., 1983.
>   "Lists institutions of undergraduate medical education in 127 countries and areas and gives a few pertinent facts about each.

United States

Allied health education directory. Ed. 7 (1978)– . [Chicago : American Medical Assoc.], Committee on Allied Health Education and Accreditation, 1978– . Annual.   **EH152**
>   21st ed., 1993.
>   Continues: *Directory of accredited allied medical education programs*, 1969/70; *Directory of approved allied medical education programs*, 1971; and *Allied medical education directory*, 1972–76.
>   Contains information on educational programs in 28 allied health occupations, and on the accreditation process. Organized in five sections: CAHEA (Committee on Allied Health Education and Accreditation), occupational and educational programs, institutions sponsoring accredited programs, studies and reports, and appendixes (glossary, members of CAHEA key groups, and review committee information).   R847.D57

American Hospital Association guide to the health care field. 1972– . [Chicago] : The Assoc., 1972– . Annual.
>   **EH153**
>   Title varies: 1972–73, *AHA guide to the health care field.*
>   Continues, 1949–71, pt. 2 of Aug. issue (called "Guide issue," 1956–70) of *Hospitals*, which superseded *American hospital directory* (1945–48).

Provides "basic data reflecting the delivery of health care in the United States and associated territories." —*Introd.* Four major sections, each with a table of contents and explanatory information: Hospitals; Health care systems; Maps of hospital distribution; Health organizations, agencies, providers, alliances, networks. Index.
>   § Statistical information concerning hospitals is publ. as: *Hospital statistics* (Chicago : AHA, 1971–). Reprinted from annual section in *Hospitals.*

American Osteopathic Association. Yearbook and directory of osteopathic physicians. Ed. 44 (1952)– . Chicago : Amer. Osteopathic Assoc., [1952?]– .   **EH154**
>   1st ed., 1899; annual since 1904. 85th ed., 1994.
>   Continues: *Directory of osteopathic physicians.*
>   Includes alphabetic and geographic listing of members and certified physicians. Also includes AOA information—copies of basic documents, position papers, statistical tables, AOA history; licensing information; pre- and postdoctoral education and training requirements. Contains a glossary of osteopathic terminology. Index.

Directory of health care professionals. 1990 ed.– . Chicago : American Hospital Association, c1990– . Annual.
>   **EH155**
>   Some have title :*HCIA directory of health care professionals.*
>   Lists names, titles, addresses, and telephone numbers of health care professionals in U.S. hospitals. Arranged in separate alphabetical sections for state, city, and hospital. Other sections list health care systems headquarters professionals and names organized by job function in different job categories. A companion to *American Hospital Association guide to the health care field* (EH153).   R712.A1D49

Directory of nursing homes. [1st ed.]– . Phoenix : Oryx, 1982– . Annual.   **EH156**
>   Subtitle: A state-by-state listing of facilities and services.
>   Frequency varies: 1982–92(?), irregular; 1993– , annual.
>   Entries include name of home, administrators and medical personnel, licensure, ownership, admission requirements, facilities, activities, and description of specialties, e.g., language spoken, religious affiliation, patient transportation, recreation. Index for religious/fraternal/maternal affiliation. Alphabetic listing of facilities.
>   RA997.A2D49

Directory of physicians in the United States / American Medical Association. 33rd ed. (1992)– . Chicago : Div. of Survey and Data Resources, The Association, c1992– . Irregular.   **EH157**
>   Continues: *American medical directory*, 1st ed. (1906)–32nd ed. (1990).
>   Contents: pt. 1, Alphabetical index of physicians; pt. 2–4, Geographical register of physicians.
>   For 640,000 physicians, gives school of graduation, and licensing and American Board of Specialties (ABMS) certification information.

•DIRLINE : (Directory of information resources online) [database]. Bethesda, Md. : U.S. National Library of Medicine.
>   **EH158**
>   Available online, updated quarterly.
>   Lists primarily U.S. organizations that provide information services in areas related to health sciences: government agencies, information centers, professional societies, and voluntary and self-help agencies. Records provide organization name, address and telephone numbers, description of the organization, and types of services provided.

Encyclopedia of medical organizations and agencies : a subject guide to organizations, foundations, federal and state government agencies, research centers, and medical and allied health schools. 5th ed. (1994–95) / Karen Boyden, ed. Detroit : Gale, c1994. 1385 p.   **EH159**
>   1st ed., 1983; 4th ed., 1992.
>   Subtitle varies.
>   Arranged by subject from the most general to the specific. Major divisions include national and international associations, state and fed-

eral agencies, research centers, and computer-based information and database services. Entries provide organization's name, address, telephone number, key officials, founding year, number of members, number of employees, and publications. Name, keyword, and subject indexes. Derived from *Encyclopedia of associations* (AL41).

R712.A1U5

Graduate medical education directory. 1993–1994– . Chicago : American Medical Association, c1993– . Annual.

EH160

Title varies: 1948-51, *Approved internships and residencies in the United States*; 1952-1973/74, *Directory of approved internships and residencies*; 1974-75, *Directory of approved residencies*; 1975/76-1977/78, *Directory of accredited residencies*; 1978/79-1986/87, *Directory of residency training programs accredited by the Liaison Committee on Graduate Medical Education*; 1987/88-1992/93, *Directory of graduate medical education programs*. Also known as "The green book."

Has sections for: (1) Information about accreditation; (2) Requirements for accreditation of programs; (3) Graduate medical education programs for each specialty and subspecialty; (4) Newly accredited and withdrawn programs; (5) Directory of institutions and organizations participating in graduate medical education. Appendixes: Combined specialty training programs; Certification requirements of each specialty board; Medical licensure requirements; List of U.S. medical schools.

Lipp, Martin R. Medical landmarks USA : a travel guide to historic sites, architectural gems, remarkable museums and libraries, and other places of health related interest. N.Y. : McGraw-Hill, Health Professions Div., c1991. 550 p. : ill.

EH161

Lists teaching institutions, hospitals and clinics, museums, libraries and professional organizations, and special landmarks. Includes chapters on seven specific cities (Baltimore, Boston, Chicago, New York, Philadelphia, Rochester, Minn., and Washington, D.C.) as well as special attractions listed by state.

R151.L56

Medical and health information directory. 1st ed. (1977)– . Detroit : Gale, 1977– . Irregular. **EH162**

Subtitle: A guide to associations, agencies, companies, institutions, research centers, hospitals, clinics, treatment centers, educational programs, publications, audiovisuals, data banks, libraries and information services in clinical medicine, basic bio-medical sciences, and the technological and socioeconomic aspects of health care.

1st–5th ed., Anthony Kruzas, ed.

Contents, 6th ed., 1992: v. 1, Organizations, agencies, and institutions (1331 p.); v. 2, Publications, libraries, and other information services (730 p.); v. 3, Health services (870 p.).

Entries include name, address, membership, purpose, meeting, and publications. R118.4.V6M4

Medical school admission requirements, United States and Canada. Ed. 27 (1977/78)– . Wash. : Assoc. of American Medical Colleges, 1978– . Annual. **EH163**

Continues: *Admission requirements of American medical colleges* (1951–57); *Admission requirements of American medical colleges, including Canada* (1957/58–63/64); *Medical school admission requirements. U.S.A. and Canada* (1964/65–76/77).

Contents, 1993/94: Nature of medical education; Premedical planning; Deciding whether and where to apply to medical school; Medical College Admission Test (MCAT) and American Medical College Application Service (AMCAS); Medical school application and selection process; Financial information for medical students; Information for minority group students; Information for applicants not admitted to medical school; Information for high school students; Information about U.S. medical schools; Information about Canadian medical schools; and Information on medical schools offering combined college/M.D. programs for high school students.

§ The Association also publishes *AAMC curriculum directory* (1972/73–) which gives data on required courses, conferences, laboratory periods, electives, opportunities for early specialization, etc. The

annual *AAMC directory of American medical education* (title varies) lists member institutions, with information on their facilities and administration. R745.A8

The official ABMS directory of board certified medical specialists. 26th ed. (1994)– . New Providence, N.J. : Marquis Who's Who, c1993– . **EH164**

Formed by the merger of *Directory of medical specialists* (16th ed. [1974/75]–25th ed. [1991/92]. Chicago : Marquis Who's Who, 1975–92), assuming its edition numbering, and *ABMS compendium of certified medical specialists*, ed. 1–4 (1987–1992/93). Ed. 4 had title: *The official American Board of Medical Specialties (ABMS) directory of board certified medical specialists.*

Lists more than 428,000 certified physicians (practicing and retired), arranged by the 24 U.S. Medical Specialty Boards in alphabetical order, then by states, cities, and towns. For each physician, lists name, certification(s), type of practice, birth date and place, education, career history, teaching positions, military record, professional memberships, office address and phone number. Includes an outline of certification requirements for each specialty. Personal names index. The specialty in which the person's full sketch is found is printed in bold face. Foreign medical degrees appear in shortened form in the biographical sketches, but are shown in full in the index. R712.A1O335

Canada

Canadian hospital directory = Annuaire des hôpitaux du Canada. [Ed. 1] (1953)– . [Toronto : Canadian Hospital Assoc.], 1953– . Annual. **EH165**

Includes: Buyers' guide and statistical compendium.

Text in English and French.

Lists provincial hospital/health associations, Canadian Hospital Association (personnel), Association of Canadian Teaching Hospitals, Canadian Association of Paediatric Hospitals/Canadian Institute of Child Health, and outpatient health service centres. Includes comparison of provincial hospital plans and of their medical/health plans and education programs for personnel. RA983.A1C3

Canadian medical directory. 1st ed. (1955)– . Don Mills, Ont. : Southam Business Communications, 1955– . Annual.

EH166

Imprint varies.

39th ed., 1993.

Brief biographical information for Canadian physicians; alphabetical arrangement, with address, telephone number, medical school and year of degree, professional memberships, position, and hospital affiliation. A separate listing provides names of physicians by geographic location, in two sections: general practitioners and family physicians, and certified specialists. Also includes a section of related miscellaneous information, such as listings of hospitals, government agencies, and professional societies. R713.01.C3

Great Britain

Directory of medical and health care libraries in the United Kingdom and Republic of Ireland. 8th ed. / comp. by Derek J. Wright for the Medical, Health and Welfare Libraries Group of the Library Association. London : Library Assoc. Publ., 1992. 293 p. **EH167**

1st ed. 1957; 7th ed., 1990.

For each library listed gives location, stack policy, hours, holdings, classifications, computer facilities and availability, and user accessibility. Indexed by personal name, establishment, country, special collection, and library type. Z675.M4W88

The medical directory. 1845– . London : Churchill, 1845– . Annual. **EH168**

Subtitle varies.

Lists registered practitioners in London, the provinces, Wales, Scotland, Ireland, abroad, and in the armed forces, giving brief biographical information. Includes lists of universities, colleges, medical schools, hospitals, associations, etc., and geographical lists of physicians in London, England, Wales and Monmouthshire, Scotland, and Ireland.   R713.29.M4

Medical register : printed and publ. under the direction of the General Medical Council ... comprising the names and addresses of medical practitioners .... 1859– . London : publ. for the General Medical Council by Constable, 1859– . Annual.
                                                                EH169

Subtitle varies.

Brief directory information only, consisting of address, date and place of registration, qualifications. Includes names from the Commonwealth and foreign lists.

Handbooks

AIDS information sourcebook / ed. by H. Robert Malinowsky and Gerald J. Perry. 3rd ed., 1991–92. Phoenix : Oryx, 1991. 300 p.   **EH170**

1st ed., 1988; 2nd ed., 1989–90.

In four parts: (1) Chronology, listing events in the AIDS epidemic, June 1981–Jan. 1991; (2) Directory, listing approximately 1,000 facilities in the U.S. and Canada, arranged alphabetically by state or province, then by city and name of facility; (3) Bibliography, including citations to periodical articles, bibliographies, books, pamphlets, etc.; (4) an appendix containing selected statistical tables and a glossary of brief, nontechnical definitions.   RC607.A26A3475

The American Medical Association family medical guide / editors, Jeffrey R. M. Kunz, Asher J. Finkel. Rev. and updated ed. N.Y. : Random House, c1987. 832 p. : ill. (some col.).
                                                                EH171

1st ed., 1982; 3rd ed. expected 1994.

Aimed at general readers, this guide is in four main sections: general discussion of the healthy body, self-diagnosis symptom charts with visual aids to diagnosis, diseases and other disorders and problems, and caring for the sick, including a section on accidents and emergencies. Glossary and subject index.   RC81.A543

The American Medical Association handbook of first aid & emergency care / developed by the American Medical Association ; medical editors, Stanley M. Zydlo, James A. Hill. Rev. ed. N.Y. : Random House, c1990. 332 p. : ill.   **EH172**
1st ed., 1980.

Pt. 1 helps readers prepare for emergency situations, pt. 2 provides an alphabetical listing of injuries and illnesses, designed to be consulted at the time of an emergency, and pt. 3 deals with common sports injuries. Subject index.   RC87.A535

Cancer sourcebook / ed. by Frank E. Bair. Detroit : Omnigraphics, 1991. 932 p. : ill. (Health reference series, v. 1).
                                                                EH173

Compiles 37 individual pamphlets, fact sheets, papers, and bulletins issued by the National Institutes of Health (NIH) and its subagency, the National Cancer Institute (NCI), 1986–89. NIH publication numbers are listed (cf. *Preface* "Bibliographic note"). Written in nontechnical language. In four sections, provides information on the most common forms of cancer, cancer treatments and therapies, coping strategies, and a statistical overview on cancer rates and risks. References and bibliographies end each chapter. Useful for patients, their families, medical professionals, and librarians. Updates are planned.   RC261.C276

Clinical guide to laboratory tests / ed. by Norbert W. Tietz ... [et al.]. 2nd ed. Philadelphia : Saunders, 1990. 931 p.
                                                                EH174

1st ed., 1983.

Attempts "to establish and compile reference ranges for most of the laboratory tests conducted in modern clinical laboratories together with information related to specimen type, stability of specimens, drug interferences, diagnostic information and biological variables affecting the test results."—*Pref.* Three main sections: general clinical tests, therapeutic drugs, and microbiology, with test entries in the first two sections arranged alphabetically. The third section on microbiology is subdivided by broad class of disease (e.g., viral diseases), with test entries grouped by procedure. Indexed separately by test and disease.
                                                                RB38.2.C55

Codes of professional responsibility / ed. by Rena A. Gorlin. 2nd ed. Wash. : Bureau of National Affairs, c1990. 555 p.
                                                                EH175

For annotation, *see* CK160.   BJ1725.C57

Concise encyclopedia of medical & dental materials / ed., David Williams ; executive ed., Robert W. Cahn ; senior advisory ed., Michael B. Bever. Oxford, Eng. ; N.Y. : Pergamon Pr. ; Cambridge, Mass. : MIT Pr., 1990. 412 p. : ill.   **EH176**

A comprehensive encyclopedia "covering all aspects of medical and dental materials."—*Guide.* A spinoff of the *Encyclopedia of materials science and engineering* (EK262). Fairly long essays, arranged alphabetically, on a wide variety of subjects, (e.g., biocompatibility of dental materials, invasive sensors). Essays include bibliographies, with many cross-references. Generously illustrated with tables, photographs, and charts. Includes list of essays and subject index.
                                                                R857.M3C64

Conn's current therapy : latest approved methods of treatment for the practicing physician. 1949– . Philadelphia : Saunders, 1949– . Annual.   **EH177**

Title varies: 1949–83, *Current therapy.*

Ed. 1949–83 by Howard F. Conn; 1984– by Robert E. Rakel.

Presents authoritative, current methods of therapy. Arranged in 18 sections offering broad coverage of diseases and disorders of the various organ sytems, e.g., infectious diseases, respiratory system, cardiovascular system, and diseases of allergy. Each section contains articles by specialists on more specific topics. Index.   RM101.C87

Fry, John D. Disease data book / John Fry, Gerald Sandler, David Brooks. Lancaster, England ; Boston : MTP Pr., c1986. 405 p. : ill.   **EH178**

For each of 22 important medical conditions and problems, including high blood pressure, diabetes, epilepsy, etc., the same set of questions (what is it? who gets it when? what happens? what to do?) is posed, answers are given to each, and the nature, course, prognosis, and outcome of these conditions is described. Index.   RC55.F75

——————— The health care data source book : finding the right information and making the most of it / John D. Fry, Robert W. Young. Chicago : American Hospital Publishing, Inc., c1992. 137 p.   **EH179**

Provides information on health care-related issues, including inpatient, outpatient, and financial data in each state; sources of information, by state; and selected studies and reports.   RA407.3.F78

Griffith, H. Winter. Complete guide to medical tests. Tucson, Ariz. : Fisher Books, c1988. 932 p.   **EH180**

A comprehensive guide for general readers that contains descriptions of more than 400 physician-ordered medical tests, with an additional section on do-it-yourself tests. Although entries are arranged by most common test name, the table of contents provides access by test type (e.g., Blood gases and electrolytes). Has sections on "Before the test" (purpose, risks, precautions, etc.) and "Test" (what the patient will see and hear, equipment used, etc.), and includes advice on post-test care and interpretation of results. Provides a glossary of medical terms, a subject index, various appendixes, and a brief list of related titles.   RC71.3.G75

Handbook of bioengineering / co-editors, Richard Skalak, Shu Chien. N.Y. : McGraw-Hill, c1987. 1 v. (various pagings) : ill. **EH181**

"The purpose of this handbook is to collect, in one place, authoritative summary accounts of the various topics that comprise the field of bioengineering."—*Pref.* 41 signed chapters by experts include references to the primary literature. Indexed. R856.H36

Handbook of biomedical engineering / ed. by Jacob Kline. San Diego : Academic Pr., c1988. 733 p. : ill. **EH182**

" ... presents in one place authoritative summary accounts of the important areas in which significant advances have been made because of biomedical engineering ... it concentrates on ... an in-depth description of the most important currently used systems and materials."—*Pref.* 27 signed chapters include numerous references. Indexed. R856.H37

Handbook of clinical neurology / ed. by P. J. Vinken and G. W. Bruyn. Amsterdam : North-Holland ; N. Y. : Wiley-Interscience, [1968–91]. v. 1–52, 55–56, 58–60 : ill. (In progress). **EH183**

Vols. 45 and after are publ. in a "revised series," which continues the volume numbering of the original set but carries its own volume numbers as well.

Intends to present critical, balanced, and comprehensive views written by acknowledged experts to provide the clinical neurologist "with full information about any particular aspect of his subject with which he may find himself confronted."—*Pref.* RC332.H3

Handbook of neurochemistry / ed. by Abel Lajha. 2nd ed. N.Y. : Plenum, [1982–85]. 10 v. : ill. **EH184**

1st ed., 1969–72.

Contents: v. 1, Chemical and cellular architecture; v. 2, Experimental neurochemistry; v. 3, Metabolism in the nervous system; v. 4, Enzymes in the nervous system; v. 5, Metabolic turnover in the nervous system; v. 6, Receptors in the nervous system; v. 7, Structural elements of the nervous system; v. 8, Neurochemical systems; v. 9, Alterations of metabolites in the nervous system; v. 10, Pathological neurochemistry.

Each chapter is a concise and critical summary written by one or more specialists, with a supportive bibliography. Each volume is indexed. QP356.3.H36

Harrison, Ira E. Traditional medicine / Ira E. Harrison and Sheila Cosminsky. N.Y. : Garland, 1976–84. 2 v. (Garland reference library of social science, v. 19, 147). **EH185**

Vol. 1 has subtitle: Implications for ethnomedicine, ethnopharmacology, maternal and child health, mental health, and public health : an annotated bibliography of Africa, Latin America, and the Caribbean; v. 2, Current research with implications for ethnomedicine.

Contents: v. 1, 1950–75; v. 2, 1976–81.

Traditional medicine is defined as "native medical systems (healers, therapies and beliefs)."—*Introd.* Covers books, articles, dissertations, and papers, mostly in English, published 1950–81. Author and country-area index. Z5118.M4H3

Inglis, Brian. The alternative health guide / Brian Inglis and Ruth West. N.Y. : Knopf, 1983. 352 p. : ill. (some col.). **EH186**

Gives descriptions of many nontraditional therapies not covered in traditional medical books. The first part discusses history, theory, and practice, and gives short explanations of therapies (e.g., naturopathy, herbal medicine, homeopathy, chiropractic, and Alexander technique); psychotherapies (e.g., dream therapy and Gestalt); and paranormal therapies (e.g., exorcism, Christian Science, and psychic therapy). The second part deals with specific ailments such as allergies, cancer, and mental illness. Each condition is summarized, indicating the traditional medical therapy and where it fails; the guide then gives alternative therapies which have been shown to be effective. Bibliography and index. R733.I497

The injury fact book / Susan P. Baker ... [et al.]. 2nd ed. N.Y. : Oxford Univ. Pr., 1992. 344 p. : ill. **EH187**

1st ed., 1984.

Includes "detailed information on many of the factors surrounding injuries—the man-made systems and products involved, the groups of people at greatest risk, and effective ways to protect people from injuries."—*Introd.* Organization is related to International Classification of Diseases codes, each chapter covering a major category of injury (e.g., suicide, poisoning), with most providing information on age and sex, race and per capita income, geographic distribution, historical trends, and other topics appropriate to the type of injury addressed. No list of the many tables and illustrative graphs and charts; indexes of authors and subjects. RD93.8.B34

Iturralde, Mario P. Dictionary and handbook of nuclear medicine and clinical imaging. Boca Raton, Fla. : CRC Pr., c1990. 564 p. **EH188**

Designed to bridge the gap between highly specialized sources and general science dictionaries. The first part, a dictionary of brief definitions, also includes various lists (e.g., terms used to describe anatomical positions and planes, common abbreviations). The accompanying handbook consists of tables on subjects such as: properties of elements and radioisotopes, radionuclides and radiopharmaceuticals; radioactive decay; radiation dosimetry; Reference Man; SI units for the measurement of radioactivity and ionizing radiation; physical constants and conversion factors. The handbook includes a subject index. RC78.7.D53I88

McKusick, Victor A. Mendelian inheritance in man : catalogs of autosomal dominant, autosomal recessive, and X-linked phenotypes / Victor A. McKusick, with the assistance of Clair A. Francomano and Stylianos E. Antonarakis. 10th ed. Baltimore : Johns Hopkins Univ. Pr., 1992. 2 v. (ccxix, 2320 p.). **EH189**

For annotation, *see* EG342. Z6675.M4M33

Merck manual of diagnosis and therapy. Ed. 1 (1899)– . Rahway, N.J. : Merck, 1899– . Irregular. **EH190**

Title varies.

16th ed., 1992.

Periodically revised to provide up-to-date medical information that will facilitate accurate diagnosis and promote effective treatment. Most entries include a definition or description, etiology, symptoms and signs, diagnosis, prognosis, and treatment. Surgical procedures are rarely described. Includes tables and illustrations. Indexed. RC71.M4

The Merck manual of geriatrics / William B. Abrams, and Robert Berkow, editors ; Andrew J. Fletcher, assistant ed. Rahway, N.J. : Merck Sharp & Dohme Research Laboratories, 1990. 1267 p. : ill. **EH191**

Covers "all aspects of disease and the clinical management of elderly patients ... [following] the tradition set by the *Merck manual* [EH190] ... ."—*Pref.* Provides information on common problems among older patients, treatment approaches specific to the elderly, normal changes and diseases or disorders arranged by organ systems. Emphasizes age-related concerns, and treats epidemiological, social, ethical, financial, and legal issues specific to the elderly. Includes expected laboratory values and other data unique to the older population. Numerous cross-references in both text and index; in the index, page numbers in boldface signify major discussions of the topics. RC952.55.M555

Wallach, Jacques B. Interpretation of diagnostic tests : a synopsis of laboratory medicine. 5th ed. Boston : Little, Brown, c1992. 933 p. : ill. **EH192**

1st ed., 1970; 4th ed., 1986.

"The role of the laboratory in diagnosis and treatment continues to gain importance as newer tests and analytic methods allow diagnoses that were not possible before. Clinicians increasingly depend on laboratory test data."—*Pref.* Designed for clinicians, this handbook should also be of use in providing information to informed health consumers. Includes sections on normal values, specific laboratory examinations, diseases of organ systems, and drugs and laboratory test values. Appendixes include a list of abbreviations and acronyms and a table of conversion factors. Subject index.   RB38.2.W35

Style manuals

American Medical Association manual of style. 8th ed. / Cheryl Iverson, chair ... [et al.]. Baltimore : Williams & Wilkins, c1989. 377 p. : ill.   **EH193**
Title varies: 1st ed., 1962, called *AMA stylebook*; [6th ed., 1976] called *Stylebook: editorial manual*; 7th ed., 1981, called *Manual for authors and editors*. Compiler varies.
Presents guidelines for medical authors and editors in writing and preparing articles for publication. Offers advice on style, usage, nomenclature, statistics, and mathematical composition; also considers types of articles, fraud and plagiarism, grammar, the publishing process, online resources, sexist language, and duplicate publication. An appendix lists virus names. Indexed.   R119.A533

Huth, Edward J. How to write and publish papers in the medical sciences. 2nd ed. Baltimore : Williams & Wilkins, c1990. 252 p.   **EH194**
1st ed., 1982.
"19 chapters describe all the steps in writing and publishing a paper."—*Introd.* Punctuation, abbreviation, citation, formats for references, etc. are those specified in the author's *Medical style and format: an international guide for authors, editors and publishers* (Phildelphia: ISI Press, 1987). Includes a chapter on how to search the medical literature. Four appendixes, including a list of "Journals in the 'Uniform requirements' agreement as of September 1989." Index.   R119.H87

History

McGrew, Roderick E. Encyclopedia of medical history / Roderick E. McGrew, with the collaboration of Margaret P. McGrew. N.Y. : McGraw-Hill, c1985. 400 p.   **EH195**
Intends "to provide an easily accessible historical treatment of important medical topics."—*Pref.* Includes 103 essays, each with a bibliography of additional readings. Topical entries are arranged in alphabetical order. No biographical articles, but individuals' contributions to medical science are discussed in the essays. Index.   R133.M34

Rutkow, Ira M. The history of surgery in the United States, 1775–1900. San Francisco : Norman Publ., 1988. v. 1 : ill. (Norman surgery series, no. 2). (In progress).   **EH196**
Contents: v. 1, Textbooks, monographs, and treatises.
An annotated bibliography to be complete in 4 v. Vol. 1 lists 552 works "written by surgeons living in the U.S."—*Introd.* Most entries are either first editions of textbooks or the initial printing of a treatise or monograph. For each work includes a summary. Brief biographical sketches of authors. Includes 130 reproductions from various cited works and a short-title list of all items found in the volume. Name/subject index.   Z6666.R87

Wardwell, Walter I. Chiropractic : history and evolution of a new profession. St. Louis : Mosby-Year Book, c1992. 358 p. : ill.   **EH197**
A history of chiropractic since its beginning in 1895.
                    RZ225.U6W37

Women, health, and medicine in America : a historical handbook / ed. by Rima D. Apple. N.Y. : Garland, 1990. 580 p. : ill. (Garland reference library of social science, v. 483).   **EH198**

Includes chapters on a wide variety of subjects, including Childbirth in America, 1650–1990, Historical perspectives on women and mental illness, and Race as a factor in health. Extensive bibliography and index.   RA564.85.W664

Bibliography

Bibliography of the history of medicine / National Library of Medicine. no. 1 (1965)– . Bethesda, Md. : National Library of Medicine : For sale by U.S. Govt. Print. Off., 1966– . Annual, each 5th issue being a quinquennial cumulation.   **EH199**
Cumulations: 1964/69 (publ. 1972. 1475 p.); 1970/74 (1976. 1069 p.); 1975/79 (1980. 924 p.); 1980/84 (1985. 1300 p.); 1985/89 (1990. 1454 p.).
Superintendent of Documents classification: HE 20.3615: .
Now consists of citations drawn from NLM's *HISTLINE* [database] (Bethesda, Md. : National Library of medicine, 1970–). "Focuses on the history of medicine and its related sciences, professions, and institutions."—*Introd.* Includes journal articles, monographs, analytic entries for symposia, congresses, etc., and chapters in general monographs. Works on the general history and philosophy of science are largely excluded. Attempts to avoid extensive duplication of topics regularly covered in "Critical bibliographies" section of *Isis*, but there is considerable duplication with *Current work in the history of medicine* (EH218), although the latter is noncumulative. Subject and author listings.   Z6660.B582

Cordasco, Francesco. Homeopathy in the United States : a bibliography of homeopathic medical imprints, 1825–1925. Fairview, N.J. : Junius-Vaughn Pr., 1991. 231 p.   **EH200**
Intended in part to replace Thomas Lindsley Bradford's *Homeopathic bibliography of the United States, from the year 1825 to the year 1891, inclusive* (Philadelphia : Boericke & Tafel, 1892). Divided into three chronological periods, 1825–59, 1860–89, and 1890–1925, which correspond to periods in the history of the field. Historical and biographical works are included, while association and periodical literature are not. Includes a list of selected references and a subject and name index.   Z6675.H7C67

Erlen, Jonathon. The history of the health care sciences and health care, 1700–1980 : a selective annotated bibliography. N.Y. : Garland, 1984. 1028 p. (Garland reference library of the humanities, vol. 398).   **EH201**
Contains 5,004 entries with descriptive annotations; arranged alphabetically by topic. Includes English-language books, journal articles, government documents, unpublished masters' theses and Ph.D. dissertations. Index. Intended for researchers and students.
                    Z6660.8.E74

Guerra, Francisco. American medical bibliography, 1639–1783. N.Y. : L.C. Harper, 1962. 885 p. : facsims. (Yale University. Dept. of the History of Science and Medicine. Publication, 40).   **EH202**
Subtitle: A chronological catalogue, and critical and bibliographical study of books, pamphlets, broadsides, and articles in periodical publications relating to the medical sciences—medicine, surgery, pharmacy, dentistry, and veterinary medicine—printed in the present territory of the United States of America during British dominion and the Revolutionary War.
In three sections: (1) books, pamphlets, broadsides; (2) almanacs; and (3) periodical publications: magazines and newspapers. Gives detailed bibliographic information, with references to other historical sources.   Z6659.G8

Kelly, Emerson Crosby. Encyclopedia of medical sources. Baltimore : Williams & Wilkins, 1948. 476 p.   **EH203**
The author "kept a list of references to medical eponyms and original works. ... A search for the earliest *or* best article has been conducted and great care has been exercised in copying the correct title with exact reference."—*Pref.* This bibliography of first-to-publish arti-

cles is arranged alphabetically by investigator/author and gives the contribution with its citation in the literature. Includes an index to the specific condition, disease, medication, treatment, test, etc.

    Z6658.K4

Miller, Genevieve. Bibliography of the history of medicine of the United States and Canada, 1939–1960. Baltimore : Johns Hopkins Pr., [1964]. 428 p.   **EH204**

    Repr. : N.Y. : Arno Pr., 1979.

    A consolidation of the annual bibliographies reprinted from the *Bulletin of the history of medicine*, covering the years 1939 through 1960. Classified arrangement; author index. A section, "Biography," p. 1–126, lists books and periodical articles about persons under the names of the biographees.   Z666a.U5M52

Morton, Leslie Thomas. Morton's medical bibliography : an annotated check-list of texts illustrating the history of medicine / ed. by Jeremy M. Norman. 5th ed. Aldershot, Eng. : Scolar Pr. ; Brookfield, Vt. : Gower, c1991. 1243 p.   **EH205**

    1st ed., 1943; 4th ed., 1983. Title varies.

    A major revision of this classic work. A bibliography of 8,927 books and periodical articles in various languages and periods, early times to the present. Classed arrangement with brief annotations indicating the significance of the work in the history and development of the medical sciences; chronological arrangement within each subject category. Name and subject index.   Z6660.8.M67

Osler, William. Bibliotheca Osleriana : a catalogue of books illustrating the history of medicine and science / collected, arranged and annotated by William Osler and bequeathed to McGill University. Montreal : McGill-Queen's Univ. Pr., 1969. xli, 792 p.   **EH206**

    An earlier version (Oxford : Clarendon Pr., 1929) described the basic collection and had nearly as many entries as the 1969 ed.

    Some 8,000 entries in classed arrangement with index. Particularly valuable for its annotations.   Z676.O86

Rather, L. J. A commentary on the medical writings of Rudolf Virchow : based on Schwalbe's Virchow-Bibliographie, 1843–1901. San Francisco, Calif. : Norman Publ., 1991. 236 p. : ill. (Norman bibliography series, no. 3).   **EH207**

    An annotated bibliography that lists in chronological order Virchow's publications in pathology, parasitology, epidemiology, social medicine, public health and sanitation, medical history and philosophy, forensic medicine, military medicine, school hygiene, and medical therapy. "Commentary touches on most of the more important items in Schwalbe's first list."—*Pref.* Entries are numbered. Name and subject indexes.   Z8943.5.S393R37

Rogal, Samuel J. Medicine in Great Britain from the Restoration to the nineteenth century, 1660–1800 : an annotated bibliography. N.Y. : Greenwood, 1992. 258 p. (Bibliographies and indexes in medical studies, no. 8).   **EH208**

    Provides bibliographic citations, with brief descriptions, to more than 2,000 references published in "medical tracts, treatises, narratives, guides and references published in England, Ireland, Scotland and Wales during one of the most significant periods in the overall history of science in the Western world."—*Pref.* Entries may also provide brief biographical information about the author. References are arranged by topic: general subject, diseases, or anatomical region. Subject and name indexes.   Z6661.G7R63

Sir William Osler : an annotated bibliography with illustrations / ed. by Richard L. Golden, Charles G. Roland. San Francisco : Norman Publ., 1988. 214 p. : ill. (Norman bibliography series, no. 1).   **EH209**

    Rev. and updated ed. of Maude E. Abbott's *Classified and annotated bibliography of Sir William Osler's publications*, 2nd ed. (Montreal : The Medical Museum, McGill Univ., 1939).

    Contains 1,493 citations, some with annotations, arranged chronologically in 11 categories. This edition includes a checklist of Osler's

papers published under his pseudonym (Egerton Yorrick Davis) and a list of editions, printings, and translations of *The principles of medicine*.   Z8647.8.S55

Wellcome Historical Medical Library. A catalogue of printed books in the Wellcome Historical Medical Library. London : The Library, 1962–76. 3 v. (Wellcome Historical Medical Library. Publications. Catalogue series, PB1–PB3).   **EH210**

    Contents: v. 1, Books printed before 1641; v. 2–3, Books printed from 1641 to 1850: A–L. No more published?

    Vol. 1 includes almost 7,000 titles arranged by author, with indexes by place of publication and by printer and publisher, and a concordance for English books with STC numbers.   Z6676.W4

Historical surveys

Bordley, James. Two centuries of American medicine, 1776–1976. Philadelphia : Saunders, 1976. 844 p.   **EH211**

    Contents: pt. 1, The first century—1776–1876; pt. 2, Period of scientific advance—1987–1946; pt. 3, Period of explosive growth—1946–1976; Appendix A, Population figures; Appendix B, Chronological summary of major events in American medical history.

    The purpose is "to relate in language that can be understood by interested laymen, as well as the physician, an account of the extraordinary advances in medical education and in the prevention and treatment of disease that have taken place during the two centuries of this nation's political independence."—*Pref.* Includes bibliography and index.   R151.B58

The Cambridge world history of human disease / ed., Kenneth F. Kiple … [et al.]. Cambridge ; N.Y. : Cambridge Univ. Pr., 1993. 1176 p. : ill.   **EH212**

    A major work, the result of the Cambridge History and Geography of Human Disease Project which began in late 1985. Pt. 1 covers the "major historical roots and branches of medical thought from ancient times to the twentieth century," while pt. 2 "deals with concepts of disease in the East and West, as well as with concepts of complex physical and mental ailments."—*Introd.* Other sections treat medical specialties and disease prevention, the measurement of health, the history of human disease in Asia and elsewhere, and the geography of human disease. The final section covers major human diseases, past and present. A list of tables, figures, and maps is provided, and a bibliography is provided for each topic covered. Name and subject indexes.   R131.C233

Castiglioni, Arturo. A history of medicine / Arturo Castiglioni ; tr. from the Italian and ed. by E. B. Krumbhaar. 2nd ed., rev. and enl. N.Y. : Knopf, 1947. 1192, lxi p. : ill., ports.   **EH213**

    Translation of: *Storia della medicina* (rev. and enl. ed. Milan : A. Mondadori, 1936).

    A comprehensive and readable source, especially strong in coverage of Greek and Roman history of medicine. Includes a useful bibliography (p. 1147–92) arranged by subject. Index of subjects and index of names. Serves to supplement Fielding H. Garrison's *Introduction to the history of medicine* (EH214).   R131.C272

Garrison, Fielding Hudson. Introduction to the history of medicine : with medical chronology, suggestions for study and bibliographic data. 4th ed. rev. and enl. Philadelphia : Saunders, 1929. 996 p. : ill.   **EH214**

    Repr., 1967.

    1st ed., 1913; 3rd ed., 1921.

    The most valuable reference history in English, covering the whole history of medicine from the earliest times to the 1920s. Much biography and bibliography are included for every period. Appendixes include: a chronology of medicine and public hygiene; hints on the study of medical history; bibliographic notes for collateral reading including histories of medicine, medical biography, and histories of special subjects. Index of personal names and index of subjects.

R131.G3

Packard, Francis Randolph. History of medicine in the United States. N.Y. : Hoeber, 1931. 2 v. (1323 p.) : ill.   **EH215**
Repr. : N.Y. : Hafner, 1963.
    An enlargement of the author's earlier work (1901). Contains much useful reference material, in both text and illustrations, on American medical history, biography, and bibliography. Gives a bibliography of pre-Revolutionary medical publications and a general bibliography.

R151.P12

Biography

Nobel laureates in medicine or physiology : a biographical dictionary / ed. by Daniel M. Fox, Marcia Meldrum, and Ira Rezak. N.Y. : Garland, c1990. 595 p. (Garland reference library of the humanities, vol. 852).   **EH216**
For annotation, *see* AL169.   R134.N63

Sammons, Vivian O. Blacks in science and medicine. N.Y. : Hemisphere Pub. Corp., c1990. 293 p.   **EH217**
For annotation, *see* EA183.   Q141.B58

Bibliography

Current work in the history of medicine : an international bibliography. v. 1 (1954)– . London : Wellcome Institute for the History of Medicine, 1954– . Quarterly.   **EH218**
    A quarterly index of articles on the history of medicine, arranged by subject, with an author index in each issue. International coverage. A list of new books on the history of medicine and science is provided at the end of each issue. No cumulation of the references is published, but a retrospective cumulative index is maintained at the Wellcome Library.   R131.A1C8

Morton, Leslie Thomas. A bibliography of medical and biomedical biography / Leslie T. Morton and Robert J. Moore. Aldershot, England : Scolar Pr. ; Brookfield, Vt., : Gower Publ. Co., c1989. 208 p.   **EH219**
    Begun as a 3rd ed. of John L. Thornton's *A select bibliography of medical biography* (EH227) this work is broader in scope, including biographical references to more than 1,600 individuals in the biomedical sciences as well as in clinical medicine and surgery. Lists only English-language publications and provides references to biographies published in book form, to entries in *Dictionary of scientific biography*, (EA176), *Biographical memoirs of Fellows of the Royal Society* (EA189), *Obituary notices of Fellows of the Royal Society* (EA182), *Biographical memoirs* (of the National Academy of Sciences) (EA188), and selected periodical references. An initial section of individual biographies is alphabetic by biographee, giving nationality, field, and notable accomplishments; location of archival material is also indicated. A list of collective biographies follows, usually giving a brief description of the work, while a third section provides a short list of books on the history of medicine and related works, arranged by subject. Indexed by discipline; biographees are listed within each discipline by birth date. A 2nd ed. is expected in 1994.   Z6660.5.M67

International

Bailey, Hamilton. Bailey and Bishop's notable names in medicine and surgery. 4th ed. / rev. by Harold Ellis. London : H. K. Lewis, 1983. 272 p. : ill.   **EH220**
    1st ed., 1944–3rd ed., 1959, had title: *Notable names in medicine and surgery.*

Includes biographical sketches (with portraits) of persons whose names are associated with particular diseases or other medical discoveries, e.g., Potter's disease, Thomas's splint. Includes a list of biographies for additional reading. Indexed.   R134.B3

Bendiner, Jessica. Biographical dictionary of medicine / Jessica Bendiner and Elmer Bendiner. N.Y. : Facts on File, c1990. 284 p.   **EH221**
    Subjects are included on the basis of their importance to the history of medicine. Entries vary in length from one paragraph to several pages. Includes a chronology of important events in the history of medicine and a brief bibliography. Separate name and subject indexes.

R134.B455

Biographisches Lexikon der hervorragenden Ärzte aller Zeiten und Völker / unter Mitwirkung [von] E. Albert ... [et al.] ; ... hrsg. von August Hirsch. 2. Aufl. durchgesehen und ergänzt von W. Haberling, F. Hübotter und H. Vierordt. Berlin : Urban, 1929–35. 6 v. : ports.   **EH222**
    Repr. : München : Urban & Schwarzenberg, 1962 (called 3. unveränderte Aufl.).
    1st ed., 1884–88.
    The final volume, *Ergänzungsband : Nachträge zu den Bänden I–V* (1935) includes corrections and additions to the main set.
    A valuable medical biographical dictionary, international in scope, covering physicians who had achieved prominence before 1880. Includes biographical facts, bibliography of works, and sometimes bibliographical references.
    To a large extent replaces its own 1st ed. and *Biographisches Lexikon: hervorragender Ärzte des neunzehnten Jahrhunderts*, by Julius Leopold Pagel (Berlin ; Wien : Urban & Schwarzenberg, 1901), although both are occasionally useful for material omitted from the 2nd ed.
    § *Biographisches Lexikon der hervorragenden Ärzte der letzten 50 Jahre*, by Isidor Fischer (Berlin, 1932–33. 2 v.) serves as a continuation, covering 1880–1930. Similar in scope, although articles are somewhat briefer.   Z6658.B61

Komorowski, Manfred. Bio-bibliographisches Verzeichnis jüdischer Doktoren im 17. und 18. Jahrhundert. München ; N.Y. : Saur, 1991. 128 p. : ill. (Bibliographien zur deutsch-jüdischen Geschichte, Bd. 3).   **EH223**
    A chronological list, 1624–1799, of 412 Jewish physicians who completed their medical education at European universities. A typical entry includes name, home town, location of the university, brief Latin title of the dissertation, date pertaining to the completion of the dissertation ("Promotionsdatum"), and reference(s) to biographical works and sources where further information about the physician can be found. Indexed.   R512.A1K65

New York Academy of Medicine. Library. Catalog of biographies. Boston : G.K. Hall, 1960. 165 p.   **EH224**
    A photographic reproduction of the Library's shelflist, containing "single biographies of physicians and scientists, with a few autobiographies, family histories and occasional biographies written by physicians."—*Introd.*   R134.N4

The Nobel Prize winners : physiology and medicine / ed. by Frank N. Magill. Pasadena, Calif. : Salem Pr., c1991. 3 v. : ports.   **EH225**
    For sources concerning Nobel prizes, *see* AL173 and other titles in the same section.   R134.N633

Talbot, Charles H. The medical practitioners in medieval England : a biographical register / by C. H. Talbot and E. A. Hammond. London : Wellcome Historical Medical Libr., 1965. 503 p. (Publications of the Wellcome Historical Medical Library, v. 8).   **EH226**
    Inspired by Ernest Wickersheimer's *Dictionnaire biographique des médecins en France au Moyen Âge* (Paris : E. Droz, 1936), but entries are generally longer than in that work. The period covered is from Anglo-Saxon times to about 1518, and physicians of England, Scot-

land, and Wales are included. Bibliographical references follow the articles, and the general index offers geographical and a wide variety of topical subject approaches.   R489.A1T3

Thornton, John Leonard. A select bibliography of medical biography : with an introductory essay on medical biography. 2nd ed. London : Lib. Assoc., 1970. 170 p. : ill. (Lib. Assoc. Bibliographies, no.3).   **EH227**

1st ed., 1961, by Thornton, A. J. Monk and E. S. Brooke.

Contains citations to books in English published in the 19th and 20th centuries. Includes more than 400 biographees. Nearly 100 collective biographies are listed in a separate section. Indexed.   Z6660.5.T5

United States

Dictionary of American medical biography. Westport, Conn. : Greenwood, [1984]. 2 v. (1027 p.).   **EH228**

Martin Kaufman, Stuart Galishoff, and Todd L. Savitt, eds.

Includes more than 1,000 persons from the 17th century to those of the 20th century who had died prior to Dec. 31, 1976. "The major contribution of [this] work is the inclusion of biographical sketches representing developments which occurred after the publication of Kelly and Burrage [*Dictionary of American medical biography*. N.Y. : Appleton, 1928]."—*Pref.* Coverage extends outside the medical mainstream—blacks and women; nonphysicians such as biochemists, medical educators, administrators; and "health faddists, patent medicine manufacturers, unorthodox practitioners, and others whose major role was to provide alternatives to traditional medicine."

A typical entry gives full name, date and place of birth, date and place of death, occupation and area of specialization, parents' names and occupations, marital information, career information, contributions, and a maximum of five citations to important or representative works. The appendix gives a listing by date of birth, place of birth, state where prominent, occupation and specialty, medical college or graduate level college, and females. Indexed.

§A companion work is *Dictionary of American nursing biography* (EH288).   R153.D53

Kelly, Howard Atwood. Dictionary of American medical biography : lives of eminent physicians of the United States and Canada, from the earliest times / by Howard A. Kelly and Walter L. Burrage. N.Y. ; London : Appleton, 1928. 1364 p.   **EH229**

Repr. : Boston : Milford House, 1971.

Supersedes Kelly's *Cyclopedia of American medical biography* (Philadelphia : Saunders, 1910. 2 v.), which covered 1610-1910.

Biographies with bibliographies of 2,049 deceased American and Canadian physicians and surgeons from colonial days to 1927. Although each edition includes new biographical sketches, some material is dropped from each, and therefore the earlier editions may still be useful.   R153.K3

Great Britain

Plarr, Victor Gustave. Plarr's lives of the fellows of the Royal College of Surgeons of England / rev. by Sir D'Arcy Power. Bristol : Royal College ; London : Simkin, Marshall, 1930. 2 v.   **EH230**

Biographies of fellows from those elected in 1843 (founding date of the fellowship) through those who died before 1930. Much of the information was obtained from obituary notices or from friends and relatives of the fellows. For each fellow, includes references to publications sufficient to indicate the subjects in which each was interested.

Continued by:

Sir D'Arcy Power and William Richard Le Fanu, *Lives of the fellows of the Royal College of Surgeons of England, 1930–1951* (London : Royal College, 1953. 889 p.). Biographies of fellows who died from 1930 to the end of 1951, including some who died before 1930 but were omitted from Plarr's list. Includes lists of publications.

R.H.O.B. Robinson and W.R. Le Fanu, *Lives of the fellows of the Royal College of Surgeons of England, 1952–1964* (Edinburgh : E. & S. Livingstone, 1970. 470 p.).

James Paterson Ross and W.R. Le Fanu, *Lives of the fellows of the Royal College of Surgeons of England, 1965–1973* (London : Pitman Medical, 1981. 405 p.).   R489.A1P5

Royal College of Physicians of London. The roll of the Royal College of Physicians of London : comprising biographical sketches of all the eminent physicians whose names are recorded in the Annals... / by William Munk. 2nd ed., rev. and enl. London : publ. by the College, 1878–1984. v. 1–7. (In progress).   **EH231**

Vols. 4–7 have title: *Lives of the fellows.* Often cited as "Munk's roll."

Imprint varies.

Contents: v. 1, 1518 to 1700; v. 2, 1701 to 1800; v. 3, 1801 to 1825; v. 4, 1826–1925 (comp. by G. H. Brown); v. 5, Continued to 1965 (ed. by R. R. Trail); v. 6, Continued to 1975 (ed. by G. Wolstenholme); v. 7, Continued to 1983 (ed. by G. Wolstenholme).

Vols. 1–3 have subtitle: Comprising biographical sketches of all eminent physicians, whose names are recorded in the Annals from the foundation of the College in 1518 to its removal in 1825 from Warwick Lane to Pall Mall East.

Vol. 4 contains short biographies of 874 Fellows elected between 1826 and 1925, who died before Jan. 1, 1954.

Vol. 5 contains biographies of 422 Fellows who died since the end of 1953 or who died earlier, but were not included in the previous volume because they were elected to the Fellowship after 1925. Arranged alphabetically. Also designated as "Munk's roll, v. 5."

Statistics

Health, United States. 1975– . Rockville, Md. : National Center for Health Statistics ; Wash. : for sale by U.S. Govt. Print. Off., 1976– . Annual.   **EH232**

[17th ed.], 1992.

"Presents statistics concerning recent trends in the health care sector. The 143 detailed tables ... are organized around four major subject areas—health status and determinants, utilization of health resources, health care resources, and health care expenditures."—*Pref.* Provides, in a separate section, data on the disease prevention and health promotion initiative ("Healthy people 2000 review") which continues the section "Prevention profile," issued every third year in previous editions. Appendix 1 describes each data source used in this report and provides references for further information. Appendix 2 defines the terms used in the report.   RA407.3.U57a

Medical risks : trends in mortality by age and time elapsed : a reference volume / Edward A. Lew, project director and co-ed. ; Jerzy Gajewski, co-ed. N.Y. : Praeger, 1990. 2 v.   **EH233**

Sequel to: *Medical risks : patterns of mortality and survival* (Lexington, Mass. : D.C. Health ; Lexington Books, 1976), ed. by Richard B. Singer and Louis Levinson.

Sponsored by the Association of Life Insurance Medical Directors of America and the Society of Actuaries.

"Compendium of useful quantitative information on mortality and survival in a wide variety of medical risks, based on recent medical literature as well as investigation of mortality among insured lives and epidemiologic studies of special groups."—*Introd.* Information was obtained from major studies of epidemiological and medical research organizations. Twelve chapters examine different types of impairments and hazards, including lifestyle and occupational hazards; cancer; cardiovascular diseases; neurological and psychiatric diseases, etc. Author and subject indexes.   RA407.3.M43

Standard medical almanac. 2nd ed. Chicago : Marquis Academic Media, [1980]. 712 p.   **EH234**
1st ed., 1977.
Contents: pt.1, Expenditures; pt.2, Personnel; pt.3, Education and licensure; pt.4, Facilities and ancillary services; pt.5, Disease, disability and health status; pt.6, Government and health status; pt.7, Indexes—author, organization and geographic.
Data for the almanac were collected from a health insurer, professional organizations, and government sources.   RA407.3.S73

Weise, Frieda O. Health statistics : a guide to information sources. Detroit : Gale, [1980]. 137 p. (Health affairs information guide series, v. 4).   **EH235**
An annotated bibliography of "basic sources of vital and health statistics in the United States. Vital and health statistics are broadly defined here to include … natality and mortality, marriage and divorce, morbidity, health care facilities, health manpower, health services utilization, health care costs and expenditures, health profession education, [and] population characteristics."—*Pref.* Author, title, and subject indexes.   Z7553.M43W444

Medical illustration

The sourcebook of medical illustration : over 900 anatomical, medical, and scientific illustrations available for general re-use and adaptation free of normal copyright restrictions / ed. by Peter Cull ; drawings by Lois Hague … [et al.]. Carnforth, Lancs, U.K. ; Park Ridge, N.J. : Parthenon Publ. Group, 1989. 481 p. : chiefly ill.   **EH236**
A collection of line drawings, simple medical illustrations, and graphics designed to assist in the communication of medical and scientific information. Sections include body outlines and all anatomical features, as well as illustrations relating to obstetrics, anesthesia, cells and tissues, bacteria, yeasts, protozoans, helminths, viruses, arthropods, scientific symbols and maps.   QM25.S677

BIOETHICS

Bibliography of bioethics. v. 1– . Detroit : Gale, [1975]– . Annual.   **EH237**
Vol. 1–10 ed. by LeRoy Walters; v. 10– by LeRoy Walters and Tamar Joy Kahn.
Imprint varies: v. 1–6, 1975–80, publ. by Gale; v. 7–9, 1981–83 by Free Press/Macmillian; v. 10– by Kennedy Inst. of Ethics in cooperation with National Library of Medicine.
Sponsored by the Center for Bioethics, Kennedy Institute, Georgetown University.
Lists English-language books, essays in books, journal and newspaper articles, court decisions, bills and laws, and audiovisual materials concerned with ethical, legal, and public policy aspects of health-related topics. The product of "a unique information retrieval system designed to identify the central issues of bioethics, to develop an indexing language appropriate to the field, and to provide comprehensive, cross-disciplinary coverage of current English-language materials on bioethical topics."—*Introd.* Vol. 18 (publ. 1993) indexes material publ. primarily in 1990 and 1991, and treats bioethical issues of current concern—e.g., euthanasia, surrogate motherhood, abortion, AIDS, organ donation and transplantation. Includes as a section *Bioethics thesaurus*, developed for use in searching BIOETHICSLINE (EH238), also available as a separate publication from the Institute.
§ Less comprehensive but providing some annotations is: *Bibliography of society, ethics, and the life sciences*, comp. by Sharmon Sollitto and Robert M. Veach (Hastings-on-Hudson, N.Y. : Hastings Center, Inst. of Society, Ethics, and the Life Sciences, c1973–79/80. 6 v. Annual). Classified subject arrangement with author index. Vols. for 1976/77–79/80 had title: *A selected and partially annotated bibliography of society, ethics, and the life sciences.*   Z6675.E8W34

•BIOETHICSLINE [database]. Wash. : Center for Bioethics, Kennedy Institute of Ethics, Georgetown Univ., 1973– .   **EH238**
Machine-readable version of *Bibliography of bioethics* (EH237). Available online, updated bimonthly.
Provides coverage for all areas of biomedical ethics, including genetic intervention, abortion, professional ethics, and related public policy and legal issues. Sources indexed include other indexes (both online and print) and more than 70 journals and newspapers.
Bioethics thesaurus, developed for use in searching BIOETHICSLINE, is published as a section of *Bibliography of bioethics* and is also available separately (Wash : Kennedy Inst. of Ethics, 1984?–).

BioLaw. 1986– . Frederick, Md. : Univ. Publications of America, c1986– . Annual.   **EH239**
Editors: 1986– , James F. Childress [et al.].
Loose-leaf; updated between editions.
Continues: *Bioethics reporter* (1983–85).
Each annual consists of 2 v.: v. 1, Resource manual, contains essays on biological, medical, and health care issues with ethical and legal implications; v. 2 includes updates and special sections on laws, regulations, court cases, etc. Each update comes with a cumulative subject index covering both volumes and a cumulative index to court cases. A microfiche supplement containing the original source documents is available.

Dictionary of medical ethics / ed. by A. S. Duncan, G. R. Dunstan, and R. B. Welbourn. New rev. ed. N.Y. : Crossroad, 1981. 459 p.   **EH240**
1st ed., 1977.
In addition to supplying definitions, gives "access to a brief but authoritative statement on this or that subject which has moral or ethical implications."—*Introd. 1st ed.* Some entries include a bibliography; all entries are signed. Although a few of the contributors are from the U.S., most are British.   R724.D53

Encyclopedia of bioethics / Warren T. Reich, ed. in chief. N.Y. : Free Pr., c1978. 4 v. (1933 p.).   **EH241**
315 original, signed articles, with an average length of 3,400 words, focus on six core areas of bioethics: (1) concrete ethical and legal problems; (2) basic concepts and principles such as pain and suffering, life, death in Eastern and Western thought; (3) ethical theories; (4) religious traditions; (5) historical perspectives; (6) disciplines bearing on bioethics, such as the philosophy of biology, and the anthropology of medicine. No biographies. Most articles have extensive bibliographies. Articles are arranged alphabetically, with numerous cross-references; systematic classification of articles and index is also provided. Appendix gives the texts of codes and statements related to medical ethics. A revised edition is expected in 1995.   QH332.E52

Goldstein, Doris M. Bioethics : a guide to information sources / Doris Mueller Goldstein ; consulting ed., LeRoy Walters. Detroit : Gale, c1982. 366 p. (Health affairs information guide series, v. 8).   **EH242**
An annotated bibliography of approximately 1,000 selected documents published 1973–81. Also includes some significant pre-1973 citations. Organizations, programs, and library collections are described; there is a section on periodicals and reference sources. Index.   Z6675.E8G64

DENTISTRY

Guides

Clennett, Margaret A. Keyguide to information sources in dentistry. London ; N.Y. : Mansell, 1985. 287 p. : ill.   **EH243**

Offers "the information worker or non-dental researcher an overview of the major sources in the field as a whole, and in specialized subject areas."—*Introd.* Pt. 1, Survey of dentistry and its literature, includes a chapter on the history of dentistry. Pt. 2 contains a bibliography of 666 annotated entries, and pt. 3, a directory of organizations. Index.   RK28.7.C55

Kowitz, Aletha. Basic dental reference works. [9th ed.]. Chicago : Bureau of Library Services, American Dental Assoc., 1990. 23 p.   **EH244**

1st ed., 1975; 8th ed., 1989.

An "annotated listing of 131 titles ... [intended] to provide a guide to the most pertinent works that the dental reference librarian and others who use the dental literature cannot work without."—*Pref.* No index.   RK56.K69

Bibliography

New York Academy of Medicine. Library. Dental bibliography : ... literature of dental science and art as found in the libraries of the New York Academy of Medicine and Bernhard Wolf Weinberger / comp. by B. W. Weinberger. 2nd ed. [N.Y.] : First District Dental Society, [1929–32]. 2 v. in 1.   **EH245**

Subtitle : pt. 1, A reference index; pt. 2, A subject index.

1st ed., 1916.

"Though far from a complete dental bibliography, it contains every important dental publication that has been published, thereby enabling those who are interested in dental research and study to fulfill their needs."—*Pref.* Subject index covers only dental books, not dental periodicals. Includes sections on "Medical classics containing dental citations" (p. 178–183) and "Earliest dental books published, 1530–1810" (p. 220–222). Pt. 2 updates the previous volume.   Z6668.N53

Periodicals

Kowitz, Aletha. Dentistry journals and serials : an analytical guide. Westport, Conn. : Greenwood, 1985. 226 p. (Annotated bibliographies of serials, no. 3).   **EH246**

"Dental journals have proliferated since 1839 while the literature of related fields has also done so. The result is an extensive list of titles of widely varied styles and depths of content."—*Pref.* Includes 645 titles with descriptive annotations, arranged alphabetically by title. Geographical, publishers, and classified titles indexes.   Z6668.K68

Schmidt, Hans Joachim. Index der zahnärztlichen Zeitschriften der Welt = Liste des périodiques dentaires = List of dental periodicals. Stuttgart-Degerloch : Verlag der Deutschen Dokumentenstelle für Zahnärztliches Schrifttum, 1962. 125 p.   **EH247**

Title and introductory material also in French, English, Spanish, Italian, and Polish.

"Covers 1255 dental periodicals from 58 countries showing the full title, publisher's address and the abbreviated title. Both current and lapsed periodicals are listed."—[*Engl. pref.*].   Z6668.S3

Indexes; Abstract journals

Dental abstracts : a selection of world dental literature. v. 1 (1956)– . Chicago : American Dental Association, 1956– . Monthly.   **EH248**

Imprint varies: publ. 1990– , Chicago : Mosby-Yearbook.

Frequency varies: since 1990, bimonthly; previously monthly.

Fairly long, informative abstracts of state-of-the-art articles from English-language journals. Issues currently contain approximately 50 abstracts. Author and subject indexes appear since 1990 in the November/December issue.   RK1.A5416

Dental abstracts. no. 1 (Dec. 1941)–no. 5 (Nov. 1944); ser. 2, v. 1 (1945)–v. 6 no. 3/4 (Sept./Dec. 1950). N.Y. : Dental Abstracts Soc., School of Dental and Oral Surgery, Columbia Univ., 1941–50.   **EH249**

An index of "dental progress ... valuable to the research worker ... as a comprehensive guide to the literature."—*Pref.*   RK1.D46

Index of the periodical dental literature published in the English language. 1839/75–1936/38. Chicago : Amer. Dental Assoc., 1921–39. Irregular.   **EH250**

Arthur D. Black, comp.

Contents: 1839–75 (1923); 1876–85 (1925); 1886–90 (1926); 1891–95 (1927); 1896–1900 (1930); 1901–05 (1931); 1906–10 (1934); 1911–15 (1921); 1916–20 (1922); 1921–23 (1928); 1924–26 (1929); 1927–29 (1932); 1930–32 (1936); 1933–35 (1938); 1936–38 (1939).

Volumes are unnumbered and were not issued in regular chronological sequence. Imprint varies: issues for 1839/75–1927/29 publ. Buffalo, N.Y. : Dental Index Bureau.

Each volume is in two parts: (1) a classified subject index arranged by an extension of the Dewey Decimal Classification, and (2) an author index.

Continued by *Index to dental literature* (EH251).   Z6668.B62

Index to dental literature. 1962– . Chicago : American Dental Association, 1962– . Quarterly, with annual cumulation.   **EH251**

Continues: *Index of the periodical dental literature published in the English language* (EH250); *Index to dental periodical literature in the English language* (1939–61).

Publ. in cooperation with the National Library of Medicine.

An author and subject index to dental periodical literature. Since 1962, includes periodicals in foreign languages. Contains lists of dental books, and of theses and dissertations that have been accepted for degrees by schools of dentistry.

Beginning 1965, the index consists of citations retrieved from the *MEDLARS* database of the National Library of Medicine, and coverage has been expanded to include articles in nondental journals. Page and entry format follow that of *Index medicus* (EH60).   Z6668.I45

Dictionaries

Boucher's current clinical dental terminology : a glossary of accepted terms in all disciplines of dentistry / [ed by] Thomas J. Zwemer. 4th ed. St. Louis : Mosby, 1993. 433 p.   **EH252**

1st ed., 1963 and 2nd ed., 1974, ed. by Carl O. Boucher, had title: *Current clinical dental terminology*; 3rd ed., 1982.

The work of specialist contributors, defining several thousand terms. Appendixes (p. 338–433) include abbreviations, "Code on dental procedures and nomenclature," (7th revision), "Explanation of the American Dental Association tooth numbering systems ...," selected anatomical illustrations, and "Directory of American Dental Association, constituent societies, boards of dental examiners, and accredited dental schools."   RK28.B68

Fairpo, Jenifer E. H. Heinemann dental dictionary / Jenifer E. H. Fairpo and C. Gavin Fairpo. 3rd ed. London : Heinemann Medical Books, 1987. 311 p.   **EH253**

1st ed., 1962, and 2nd ed., 1973, had title: *Heinemann modern dictionary for dental students.*

Provides brief definitions of terms, including many obsolete terms from early dental literature. American terms are included, although the clinical terminology is based on the *British standard glossary of dental terms* (British Standard 4492; London : British Standards Inst., 1983). This edition omits pronunciations and illustrations included in earlier editions. Anatomical charts of the head and neck show arteries, muscles, nerves, and veins; an appendix lists dental periodicals, with country of origin and frequency of publication.   RK27

Freiberg, Marcos A. Bilingual dictionary of dental terms : Spanish-English = Diccionario bilingüe de términos odonto-lógicos : inglés-español. San Francisco : Ism Pr., c1990. 111 p.   **EH254**

Includes guide to both Spanish and English pronunciation.   RK27.F74

Harty, F. J. Concise illustrated dental dictionary / F. J. Harty, R. Ogston. Bristol : Wright, 1987. [304] p. : ill.   **EH255**

Offers brief definitions for a comprehensive range of dental terminology, including both common and more exotic terms. Designed to be an aid to practitioners, dental students, and dental surgery assistants. Includes cross-references and line drawings illustrating anatomical features and dental instruments. Appendixes include a chronological table of the development and eruption of the teeth, and addresses of selected dental schools and national dental organizations.   RK27

Illustrated dental terminology : with Spanish, French, and German correlations / ed. by John H. Manhold and Michael P. Balbo. Philadelphia : Lippincott, c1985. 370 p. : ill.   **EH256**

Brief definitions, with some illustrations. Separate section of foreign terminology, arranged by language. Concentrates on strictly dental terms: words easily found in standard or medical dictionaries are omitted, even when applicable to dentistry.   RK27.I45

International Dental Federation. A lexicon of English dental terms : with their equivalents in Español, Deutsch, Français / comp. by Fédération Dentaire Internationale ; principal investigator, Louis J. Baume. 2nd ed. London : The Federation, 1985. 400 p.   **EH257**

Rev. ed. of: *A lexicon of English dental terms*, 1966.

Intended for research workers, students, practitioners, and interpreters at dental meetings. The main section of the lexicon includes more than 7,000 terms arranged on an English base with equivalent terms in the other languages. Spanish, German, French, and Italian indexes refer to numbered entries in the main section. Includes some medical and technological terms.   RK27.I5

Jablonski, Stanley. Illustrated dictionary of dentistry. Philadelphia : Saunders, [1982]. 919 p. : ill.   **EH258**

Repr. : Malabar, Fla. : Krieger Publ. Co., 1992.

Entries consist of headword, phonetic pronunciation, etymological source, a descriptive definition, synonyms, trademarks if applicable, and cross-references. Appendixes include information about the American Dental Association, accreditation of schools and dental programs in the U.S. and Canada, and laboratory reference values of clinical importance.   RK27.J3

Directories

American Association of Dental Schools. Admission requirements of U.S. and Canadian dental schools. 1974/75– . Wash. : American Association of Dental Schools, 1975– . Annual.   **EH259**

Continues: *Admission requirements of American dental schools*, 1963–74. Publ. in cooperation with the Council on Dental Education, American Dental Association.

Provides an extensive range of information for each school: general information, description of programs, admission requirements, applications processes, costs, etc.   RK91.A582a

American dental directory. 1947– . [Chicago] : American Dental Association, 1947– . Annual.   **EH260**

American dentists are listed by state and city, with an alphabetical index. Gives address, and indicates specialization and dental school with year of graduation. There are separate sections for dentists of the armed forces and for specialists.   RK37.A25

The dentists register. 1879– . London : printed and publ. in pursuance of the Dentists Act 1957 under the direction of the General Dental Council, 1879– . Annual.   **EH261**

Publisher varies.

Gives the names and addresses of registered dental practitioners arranged in three alphabetical lists: (1) U. K. list, (2) Commonwealth list, and (3) foreign list. Recent editions include text of Dentists Act, 1957.   RK37.D5

Handbooks

Accepted dental therapeutics. 33rd ed. (1969/70)–40th ed. (1984). Chicago : Council on Dental Therapeutics of the Amer. Dental Assoc., 1970–84. Biennial.   **EH262**

Subtitle: Drugs used in dental practice, including a list of brands accepted by the Council on Dental Therapeutics of the American Dental Association.

Continues: *Accepted dental remedies* (1st–32nd ed. [1934–67]) and assumes its edition numbering. Merged 1990 with *Dentist's desk reference* (EH263) to form: *Monograph series on dental materials and therapeutics.*

Designed "to assist the dentist in selecting appropriate drugs and procedures for the prevention and treatment of oral diseases."—*Pref.* Includes sections on general principles of medication, therapeutic agents, and preventative agents. Includes index to selected Council reports, distributors, brand names, and a general index, as well as a directory of poison control centers.   RK701.A3

Dentist's desk reference : materials, instruments and equipment. 1st–2nd ed. Chicago : Amer. Dental Assoc., 1981–83.   **EH263**

Continues: *American Dental Association specifications for dental materials* (1955–61), *Guide to dental materials* (1963–66), and *Guide to dental materials and devices* (1969–78). Merged with *Accepted dental therapeutics* (EH262) to form *Monograph series on dental materials and therapeutics.*

Provides information on the use, properties and characteristics of dental materials, instruments and equipment, including a chapter on safety in the dental office. Includes index to manufacturers and distributors, and a general index. "Products appearing in boldface print throughout this book have been evaluated and classified under either the Certification Program or the Acceptance Program of the Council on Dental Materials, Instruments and Equipment of the American Dental Association."—*verso of t.p.*   RK652.5.D47

History

Asbell, Milton B. A bibliography of dentistry in America, 1790–1840. [Cherry Hill, N.J. : Sussex House, 1973]. 107 p. : ill.   **EH264**

Intends to list all books and articles on dentistry published during the period indicated. Separate chronological list of books and articles. Locates copies of the books. List of journals searched, p. 80–84.

Guerini, Vincenzo. A history of dentistry from the most ancient times until the end of the eighteenth century. Philadelphia : Lea & Febiger, 1909. 355 p. : ill., ports.   **EH265**

Frequently reprinted.

Publ. under the auspices of the National Dental Assoc. of the United States of America.

A classic work in this field, well documented by footnotes to sources. Includes name and subject index.   RK29.G8

Weinberger, Bernhard Wolf. An introduction to the history of dentistry : with medical & dental chronology & bibliographic data. St. Louis : Mosby, 1948. 2 v. : ill., ports., facsims.   **EH266**

Vol. 2 has title: *An introduction to the history of dentistry in America.*

Describes the steps in the origin, evolution, and growth of knowledge of dentistry through the 19th century; presents the history of dentistry "graphically and biographically."—*Pref.* Includes bibliography of important literature in the history of dentistry and a chronology of important related events in history, medicine, and dentistry. Index of personal names; subject index.

Based in part on the author's earlier work, *Orthodontics : an historical review of its origin and evolution* (St. Louis : Mosby, 1926. 2 v.).   RK29.W39

MEDICAL JURISPRUDENCE

Bander, Edward J. Medical legal dictionary / by Edward J. Bander and Jeffrey J. Wallach. Dobbs Ferry, N.Y.: Oceana, 1970. 114 p.   **EH267**

Intends "to provide the reader with a selective list of terms that should be familiar to those of the legal and medical professions. The stress has been on practical rather than definitive definitions. In many instances, readers are referred to more extensive texts and cases."—*Introd.* Includes more than 400 definitions and an appendix on the relationship of doctors and lawyers in medical legal matters.

KF2905.A68B3

Fiscina, Salvatore F. A sourcebook for research in law and medicine / Salvatore F. Fiscina ... [et al.]. Owings Mills, Md. : Nat. Health Publ., 1985. 348 p.   **EH268**

Contents: Problems analysis and research design, Medicolegal information sources, Medicolegal references, Law primer, Cases in law and medicine, and Medicolegal consultants. "The purpose is to provide an outline of medical and legal issues currently being addressed as well as a survey of resources available."—*Introd.* Includes bibliographies.   KF3821.A1S67

Sloane, Richard. The Sloane-Dorland annotated medical-legal dictionary. St. Paul, Minn.: West Publ. Co., c1987. 787 p. : ill.   **EH269**

Definitions of medical terms, taken from *Dorland's illustrated medical dictionary* (EH97), are combined with "judicial interpretations of the same terms ... drawn from court opinions, the testimony of medical experts, and extracts of lawyers' briefs found in those opinions."—*Pref.*

Updated by a supplement, 1992.   RA1017.S56

Stedman, Thomas Lathrop. Illustrated Stedman's medical dictionary / lawyers' section ed. by William H. L. Dornette. 5th unabr. lawyers' ed. Cincinnati : Anderson, c1982. xlvii, 1678 p. : ill.   **EH270**

For the standard edition *see* EH105.

In this edition, a 67-p. "Lawyers' section" has been added covering such topics as use of a medical library, institutional members of the Medical Library Association, standard abbreviations of medical terms used in medical records, and medicine from the lawyer's point of view. The latter section approaches jurisprudence and forensic medicine from the following viewpoints: nervous system, skeletal system, muscular system, mental illness, epilepsy and arthritis, introduction of hospital records as evidence, frequently recurring forensic problems, risk management, and codes and model statutes.   R121.S8

Ziegenfuss, James T. Law, medicine & health care : a bibliography. N.Y. : Facts on File, [1983]. 265 p.   **EH271**

On cover: With over 3500 citations on all aspects of law and medicine.

A classified bibliography of citations to articles dealing with various types of interactions in the fields of law, medicine, and health care. Four topics are emphasized: individual specialists and specialties, medical care organizations, medical services and process, and legal processes. No index, but the topical organization permits relatively direct use. Has a substantial section on law firms practicing in law, medicine, and health care.   KF3821.A1Z53

NURSING

Bibliography

Directory of educational software for nursing. 1987– . N.Y. : National League for Nursing, c1987– . Annual.   **EH272**

5th ed., 1993.

Intended for educators and others responsible for the selection and purchase of computer-assisted instruction (CAI) software for use in nursing. Divides CAI programs into two sections: those which use microcomputers, and those which use both microcomputers and videodisc players. Lengthy entries provide detailed description and evaluation, and information concerning hardware requirements, price, preview policy, warranty, published reviews, and support after purchase. Indexed by topic, mode of instructional style, and publisher (including address and telephone number). Glossary of terms; bibliography.

Thompson, Alice M. C. A bibliography of nursing literature. London : Library Association for the Royal College of Nursing and National Council of Nurses of the United Kingdom in assoc. with King Edward's Hospital Fund for London, 1968–76. 3 v.   **EH273**

Contents: v. 1, 1859–1960; v. 2, 1961–70; v. 3, 1971–76, ed. by Frances Walsh.

A guide to the first 125 years of nursing literature, covering periodical and monographic literature from English-speaking countries. In five main sections: (1) History of nursing; (2) Biography; (3) Nursing as a profession; (4) Specialties of knowledge and practice; and (5) Hospitals. No index.   Z6675.N7T5

Indexes; Abstract journals

Cumulative index to nursing & allied health literature. v. 22 (1977)– . Glendale, Calif. : Glendale Adventist Medical Center, 1977– . Five bimonthly issues and annual cumulation.   **EH274**

Supersedes: *Cumulative index to nursing literature* (EH277) and continues its numbering. Called *CINAHL.*

The change of title reflects the expanded coverage; now indexes all major nursing periodicals published in English, as well as selected periodicals for the following allied health professions: cardiopulmonary technology, health education, laboratory technology, medical assistant, medical records, occupational therapy, physical therapy and rehabilitation, radiologic technology, respiratory therapy, social service in health care.   Z6675.N7C8

•Nursing & allied health (CINAHL) [database]. Glendale, Calif. : CINAHL Corp., 1983– .   **EH275**

Available online (updated monthly) and on CD-ROM (updated bimonthly).

Accompanied by manual, database search guide, and subject heading list.

Issued for: Glendale Adventist Medical Center.

Online version of *Cumulative index to nursing & allied health literature* (EH274). Provides bibliographic access to the nursing literature, with some coverage of allied health and biomedicine. Indexes more than 330 English-language journals, as well as publications of the American Nurses' Association and the National League for Nursing, nursing dissertations, and new books. Subject access is provided by subject headings from *Nursing and allied health (CINAHL) subject headings* (EH280).

International nursing index. v. 1, no. 1 (1966)– . Philadelphia : American Journal of Nursing, 1966– . Quarterly, with annual cumulation.   **EH276**

Publ. in cooperation with the National Library of Medicine and sponsored by the American Nurses' Association and the National League for Nursing. Vols. for 1986–90 include the Institute for Scientific Information's (ISI) *Nursing citation index*.

"Over 270 nursing journals received from all over the world are indexed, as well as nursing articles in the 2,700 allied health and biomedical journals currently indexed for *Index medicus* [EH65], its recurring bibliographies, and *Health planning and administration* [EH75] data base."—*Pref.* (1992 cumulation).

A computer-produced index using MEDLARS (Medical Literature Analysis and Retrieval System) facilities. Because subject headings were originally chosen for a medical index, a "Nursing thesaurus," included in the annual cumulation, gives commonly used nursing terms as cross-references to the subject headings used in the index. Cross-references from *MeSH* are included in each annual cumulation since v. 7, 1972. Also includes brief sections listing nursing publications of organizations and agencies, and books published by or for nurses. A list of doctoral dissertations by nurses appears in the annual cumulative volume.   Z6675.N7I5

Cumulative index to nursing literature. v. 1/5 (1956–60)–v. 21 (1976). Glendale, Calif. : Seventh Day Adventist Hospital Assoc., 1961–76.   **EH277**

Frequency varies: v. 1/5, 1956/60, is a collection in one volume of five previously unpublished annual volumes, indexing, by author and subject, 17 journals; v. 6/8, 1961/63, v. 9/11, 1964/66, and v. 12/13, 1967/68 are also single volume cumulations; v. 14–21, 1969–76, are annual cumulations. In 1964 book reviews, films, filmstrips and recordings, and pamphlets were accorded a separate section. In 1967 the combined author-subject arrangement was changed to separate alphabetical listings by author and by subject. Indexed all major English-language nursing periodicals, plus selective indexing of various medical journals.

§ Continued by *Cumulative index to nursing & allied health literature* (EH274).

Nursing studies index / prep. by Yale University School of Nursing Index Staff under the direction of Virginia Henderson. Philadelphia : Lippincott, 1963–72. 4 v.   **EH278**

Contents: v. 1, 1900–29 (publ. 1972); v. 2, 1930–49 (publ. 1970); v. 3, 1950–56 (publ. 1966); v. 4, 1957–59 (publ. 1963).

Repr.: N.Y. : Garland, 1984.

Subtitle: An annotated guide to reported studies, research in progress, research methods and historical materials, in periodicals, books, and pamphlets published in English.

Provides retrospective coverage for a wide range of materials not treated elsewhere. The number of journals covered varies from 110 in v. 1 to 239 in v. 4, according to availability at the time of publication. Annotations note study methods used, nature and scope of the investigation, and frequently indicate the author's qualifications and the auspices under which the work was done. Includes unpublished doctoral dissertations but not master's theses. Subject arrangement with author index.

Dictionaries

Miller, Benjamin Frank. Encyclopedia and dictionary of medicine, nursing, and allied health / by Benjamin F. Miller and Claire Brackman Keane. 5th ed. Philadelphia : Saunders, 1992. 1427 p. : ill.   **EH279**

1st ed., 1972, had title: *Encyclopedia and dictionary of medicine and nursing*; 4th ed., 1987.

A concise work intended for students and workers in the nursing and paramedic fields. Pronunciation is indicated for all but the most common words. The greater emphasis on patient care and patient education is reflected in the title change.   R121.M65

Thesauruses

Nursing & allied health (CINAHL) ... subject heading list. 1986– . Glendale, Calif. : Glendale Adventist Medical Center, c1986– . Annual.   **EH280**

Continues: *CINAHL subject headings*, 1984.

The subject thesaurus used in compiling *Nursing & allied health database* [database] (EH275) and *Cumulative index to nursing & allied health literature* (EH274); useful in searching both. Published separately and as part of the latter.   Z695.1.N8N87

Directories

Allen, Sallie T. The directory of black nursing faculty : doctoral to diploma programs. 2nd ed. Lisle, Ill. : Tucker Publ., 1990. 330 p.   **EH281**

1st ed., 1988, had title: *Directory of black nursing faculty : baccalaureate and higher degree programs*.

Provides brief biographical data for African-American nursing faculty teaching at institutions accredited by the National League for Nursing. The directory is divided into six sections: sec. 1–3 cover faculty in baccalaureate, associate degree and diploma programs, arranged alphabetically by state and then by institution. Sec. 4–6 function as an index by name, noting institution and state where employed. Gives for each biographee: highest degree, RN, title, position or rank, telephone, educational background, areas of teaching and research, professional and community interests. Institutions with no African-American faculty are noted.   RT79.A38

Guide to programs in nursing in four-year colleges and universities : baccalaureate and graduate programs in the United States and Canada / ed. by Barbara K. Redman, Linda K. Amos ; managing ed., Ruth Lamothe. N.Y. : American Council on Education/Macmillan, c1987. 472 p.   **EH282**

Provides information on the more than 600 nursing education programs in the U.S. and Canada, including faculty research activities and admission and graduation requirements. Organized by state and province; each entry provides information about the institution and the programs offered, including library facilities and affiliations with health care facilities. Indexed by type of program and institution.

RT79.G85

Who's who in American nursing. 5th ed. (1993)– . New Providence, N.J. : Marquis Who's Who, 1993– . Biennial.
                                                          EH283

Continues: *Who's who in American nursing* (Wash. : Soc. of Nursing Professionals, 1984–89) and assumes its edition numbering. Original title split in 1990 into: *Who's who in American nursing. Administrators, educator and other nursing professionals*, and *Who's who in American Nursing. Primary care nurses in clinical settings*, which the present title merges.

Lists outstanding leaders in the field of nursing. Comp. by the Soc. of Nursing Professionals in association with the publisher.

RT25.U5W48

Handbooks

Suddarth, Doris Smith. The Lippincott manual of nursing practice. 5th ed. Philadelphia : Lippincott, c1991. 1607 p. : il. **EH284**

1st ed., 1974; 4th ed., 1986.
Gives a step-by-step explanation of a total physical examination and diagnostic procedures. The normal and abnormal conditions are identified and appropriate observations, with illustrations, for procedures, clinical manifestations, management, and health education are discussed. Covers a wide range of disorders and health problems. Indexed. RT51.B72

History

Bullough, Bonnie. Nursing : a historical bibliography / Bonnie Bullough, Vern L. Bullough, Barrett Elcano. N.Y. : Garland, 1981. 408 p. (Garland reference library of social sciences, v. 66). **EH285**

A bibliography of some 3,500 references collected from major sources. The cutoff date is 1978. Z6675.N7B84

Stewart, Isabel Maitland. A history of nursing, from ancient to modern times : a world view. 5th ed. / by Isabel M. Stewart and Anne L. Austin. N.Y. : Putnam, [1962]. 516 p. : ill. **EH286**

1st ed., 1920, by L. L. Dock and I. M. Stewart, had title: *A short history of nursing* and was based on Dock and M. Adelaide Nutting, *A history of nursing : the evolution of nursing systems from the earliest times to the foundation of the first English and American training schools for nurses* (N.Y. : Putnam, 1907–12, 4 v.).

Intended especially for student nurses. Pt. 1 consists of eight chapters sketching the history of nursing from ancient to modern times; pt. 2, 11 chapters on nursing today in various countries throughout the world. Includes a general classified bibliography and selected bibliographies for each chapter. Subject and name index. RT31.S7

Biography

American nursing : a biographical dictionary / ed. by Vern L. Bullough, Olga Church, Alice P. Stein. N.Y. : Garland, 1988–92. v. 1–2. (Garland reference library of social science, v. 368, 684). (In progress). **EH287**

Contains long entries for those who "made a significant contribution to nursing"—*Introd.* Vol. 1 contains entries for those who were born prior to 1890 or deceased, v. 2 entries for those born before 1915 or deceased. Entries include bibliographies. Each volume is indexed separately by decade of birth, first nursing school attended, area of interest or accomplishment, and state and country of birth. RT34.A44

Dictionary of American nursing biography / Martin Kaufman, ed. in chief. N.Y. : Greenwood, 1988. 462 p. **EH288**

Companion to *Dictionary of American medical biography* (EH228).

Contains "196 biographical sketches of persons who were important in the history of American nursing" (*Pref.*) and who died prior to January 31, 1987. For each individual, includes biographical data, summary of contributions to nursing, and a list of writings and references. Appendixes list persons by place of birth, state where prominent, and specialty or occupation. Indexed by personal name, organization, place, and special subject. RT34.D53

Statistics

Facts about nursing. 1935– . N.Y. : American Nurses' Association, 1935– . Annual. **EH289**

A statistical summary and basic data source book including information on nurse distribution, nursing education, the economic status of registered nurses, allied health personnel, functions and purposes of nursing organizations, and related information. Indexed by subject.

NUTRITION

Guides

Frank, Robyn C. The directory of food and nutrition information for professionals and consumers / ed. by Robyn C. Frank and Holly Berry Irving. 2nd ed. Phoenix : Oryx, 1992. 332 p. **EH290**

For annotation, *see* EJ214. TX353.D56

Szilard, Paula. Food and nutrition information guide. Littleton, Colo. : Libraries Unlimited, 1987. 358 p. : ill. **EH291**

A selection of predominantly English-language materials (most published during the last ten years) on human nutrition, dietetics, and food sciences and technology. Materials on animal nutrition are omitted unless considered useful for those interested in human nutrition. Contains publications from commercial publishers and international organizations (including FAO and WHO), and government publications. Most citations are annotated. Under topical headings, citations are arranged alphabetically. Detailed table of contents and extensive subject index. Intended for students, professionals, researchers, and librarians. Z5776.N8S94

Bibliography

Food and Agriculture Organization of the United Nations. Food composition tables : updated annotated bibliography. Rome : FAO, 1975. 181 p. **EH292**

For annotation, *see* EJ221.

Freedman, Robert L. Human food uses : a cross-cultural, comprehensive annotated bibliography. Westport, Conn. : Greenwood, 1981. 552 p. **EH293**

Offers more than 9,000 citations to a wide variety of materials, including theses, dissertations, and manuscripts. International in scope; author arrangement with keyword index.

———. ——— *Supplement*, comp. by Freedman (Westport, Conn. : Greenwood, 1983. 387 p.), provides an additional 4,025 citations.

Shih, Tian-Chu. Health-related cookbooks : a bibliography. Metuchen, N.J. : Scarecrow, 1991. 401 p. **EH294**

For annotation, *see* EJ223. Z6665.D53S54

Indexes; Abstract journals

Nutrition abstracts and reviews. v. 1 (Oct. 1931)–46 (1976). Farnham Royal, England : Commonwealth Agricultural Bureau, 1931–76. **EH295**

Name of issuing agency varies: publ. 1931–72 by Commonwealth Bureaux of Animal Nutrition (formerly Imperial Bureaux of Animal Nutrition).

Quarterly, with annual combined table of contents and author and subject indexes.

An international abstracting service in classed arrangement. Titles are given in the original language and in English translation. Signed abstracts in English.

Continued by: (1) *Nutrition abstracts and reviews. Series A: Human and experimental*, (v. 47 [Jan. 1977]– . Farnham Royal : Commonwealth Agricultural Bureaux, 1977– . Monthly). International in coverage. Abstracts appear in classed arrangement, with monthly subject index and annual cumulated subject and author indexes. Series B treats livestock feeds and feeding.

(2) ——— *Series B : Livestock feeds and feeding* (EJ104).

RM214.N8

Encyclopedias

The Columbia encyclopedia of nutrition / the Institute of Human Nutrition, Columbia University College of Physicians and Surgeons ; comp. and ed. by Myron Winick ... [et al.]. N.Y. : G.P. Putnam, c1988. 349 p. : ill. **EH296**

Provides authoritative summaries of current knowledge for selected major topics in nutrition, in language readily comprehensible to general readers. Entries vary in length from half a page to several pages, and cover a wide variety of topics (e.g., osteoporosis, obesity, cholesterol, nutrition in the workplace, seaweed). Indexed by subject.

QP141.C69

Encyclopaedia of food science, food technology, and nutrition / ed. by R. Macrae, R. K. Robinson, M. J. Sadler. London ; San Diego : Academic Pr., 1993. 8 v. **EH297**

Covers all aspects of food science, with a British emphasis. Entries vary in length, and include bibliographies. The final volume provides an index and list of contributors; the introduction and organization are included in each volume. TX349.E47

Foods & nutrition encyclopedia / Audrey H. Ensminger ... [et al.]. 2nd ed. Boca Raton, Fla. : CRC Pr., c1994. 2 v. (2415 p.) : ill. (some col.). **EH298**

For annotation, *see* EJ210. TX349.F575

Garrison, Robert H. The nutrition desk reference / Robert H. Garrison, Jr., and Elizabeth Somer. 2nd ed. New Canaan, Conn. : Keats, c1990. 306 p. : ill. **EH299**

Directed at health professionals and interested general readers. Combines basic nutritional information and recent nutritional research findings in six sections, each dealing with a major dietary topic: Dietary factors, Vitamin and mineral research, The relationships between nutrition and cancer, Cardiovascular disease, Other diseases, and Drugs. Separate section of dietary recommendations. List of figures and tables, glossary, and index. QP141.G33

Tver, David F. The nutrition and health encyclopedia / David F. Tver and Percy Russell. 2nd ed. N.Y. : Van Nostrand Reinhold, c1989. 639 p. : ill. **EH300**

1st ed., 1981.

This edition of this comprehensive dictionary contains 150 revised definitions and 86 new terms. Entries, which vary in length from short definitions to several pages, are arranged alphabetically and cover a wide range of nutritional topics. Food entries give a description of the food and its caloric value; includes food tables with nutritional values. 13 appendixes are included, such as a table of nutritive values, and height/weight ranges of men and women. QP141.T88

Dictionaries

Bender, Arnold E. Dictionary of nutrition and food technology. 6th ed. London ; Boston : Butterworths, 1990. 336 p. **EH301**

1st ed., 1960; 5th ed., 1982.

Designed to define the broad range of words used by individuals involved in nutrition and food technology. Many cross-references; bibliography; tables. TX349.B4 1990

Handbooks

Adams, Catherine F. Nutritive value of American foods in common units. Wash. : Agricultural Research Service : for sale by U.S. Govt. Print. Off., 1975. 291 p. (Agriculture handbook, no. 456). **EH302**

Superintendent of Documents classification: A 1.76:456.

Based on Agriculture handbook no. 8, *Composition of foods : raw, processed, prepared* (EJ220).

"This publication has been prepared to serve as a basic reference for data on nutrients in frequently used household measures and market units of food."—*Introd.* Two basic sections: Table 1, Nutritive values for household measures and market units of foods; Table 2, Fatty acid values for household measures and market units of foods. Uses generic names of foods. S21.A37 no. 456

Bowes, Anna De Planter. Bowes and Church's food values of portions commonly used. 16th ed. / rev. by Jean A. T. Pennington. Philadelphia : Lippincott, c1994. 483 p. : tables. **EH303**

For annotation, *see* EJ216. TX551.B64

CRC handbook of food additives / ed. Thomas E. Furia. 2nd ed. Cleveland ; Boca Raton, Fla. : CRC Pr., 1972–1980. 2 v. **EH304**

1st ed., 1968.

Sections by specialists, often with extensive bibliographies. Major sections on enzymes; vitamins and amino acids; antimicrobial food additives; antioxidants as food stabilizers; acidulants in food processing; sequestrants in foods; gums; starch in the food industry; surface active agents; polyhydric alcohols; natural and synthetic flavorings; flavor potentiators; nonnutritive sweeteners; color additives in food; phosphates in food processing. There is also an extensive section on "Regulatory status of direct food additives" and an index.

Vol. 2 gives updates on progress concerning oil-soluble polymeric antioxidants, some polymeric food dyes, and high intensity sweeteners. Reviews the traditional categories of food additives and updates the bibliography on saccharin and cyclamates. Indexed.

TX553.A3C2

Fenaroli, Giovanni. Fenaroli's handbook of flavor ingredients : adapted from [his] Italian language works. 2nd ed. Cleveland : CRC Pr., [1975]. 2 v. (928 p.) : ill. **EH305**

At head of title: CRC.

Ed., tr., and rev. by Thomas E. Furia and Nicolo Bellanca.

1st ed., 1971.

Contents: v. 1, pt. 1, General considerations; pt. 2, Natural flavor; v. 2, pt. 3, Synthetic flavor; pt. 4, Use of flavor ingredients.

The aim is the same as for the 1st ed., "to present a current, authoritative, first-source description of natural and synthetic flavor ingredients, their detailed characteristics, and their application in food. It is primarily intended for those using flavors rather than for the accomplished *flavorist.*"—*Editorial foreword, 1st ed.* "New material presented includes the following: (1) Data on new synthetic flavor ingredients; (2) Updating of natural occurrence of flavor ingredients; (3) Addition of references, augmenting many of the topics ... ; (4) Through the cooperation of CRC Press utilization of new, comprehensive reviews on significant flavor topics."—*Pref.* Indexed. TP418.F4613

Food chemicals code / Committee on Codex Specifications, Food and Nutrition Board, Division of Biological Sciences, Assembly of Life Sciences, National Research Council. 3rd ed. Wash. : Nat. Academy Pr., 1981. 735 p. : ill.   **EH306**
  For annotation, see EJ148.   TP455.F66

Igoe, Robert S. Dictionary of food ingredients. 2nd ed. N.Y. : Van Nostrand Reinhold, c1989. 225 p.   **EH307**
  For annotation, see EJ156.   TX551.I26

Leveille, Gilbert A. Nutrients in foods / Gilbert A. Leveille, Mary Ellen Zabik, Karen J. Morgan. Cambridge, Mass. : Nutrition Guild, 1983. 291 p.   **EH308**
  The introduction provides general information on human nutritional requirements and describes how to use and interpret the tables in this work. The information is compiled from the Michigan State University Nutrient Data Bank which includes data from the USDA *Agriculture handbook* no. 8 (EJ220). Additional information on processed foods was provided by 64 major food companies. The tables list the nutrient composition for more than 2,700 naturally occurring and processed foods. Tables include information on amino acids, vitamins, carbohydrates, ash, fibers (dietary and crude), minerals, and the US RDA (recommended daily allowance). Appendixes list caffeine and alcohol content of selected foods.   TX551.N56

Machlin, Lawrence J. Handbook of vitamins. 2nd ed., rev. and expanded. N.Y. : Dekker, c1991. 595 p. : ill. (Food science and technology, 40).   **EH309**
  1st ed., 1984, had title: *Handbook of vitamins: nutritional, biochemical, and clinical aspects.*
  Intends "to provide a relatively brief but authoritative and comprehensive source of information on the vitamins for the human and animal nutritionist, the dietician, clinician, biochemist, and interested lay person. [Each entry includes information on the vitamin's] chemistry, availability and content in food, metabolism, function, and deficiency symptoms; methods for evaluating overt or marginal deficiencies; nutritional requirements; the interaction of vitamins with environmental and disease factors, and the efficacy and safety when used at high levels."—*Pref.* There are bibliographic references with each essay. Indexed.   QP771.H36

Modern nutrition in health and disease / ed. by Maurice E. Shils, James A. Olson, Moshe Shike. 8th ed. Philadelphia : Lea & Febiger, 1994. 2 v. : ill.   **EH310**
  1st ed., 1955; 7th ed., 1988.
  Contents: Pt. 1, Specific dietary components; pt. 2, Nutrition in integrated biologic systems; pt. 3, Dietary and nutritional assessment of the individual; pt. 4, Diet and nutrition in disease; pt. 5, Diet in the health of populations.
  Serves as a "major authoritative textbook and reference source in basic and clinical nutrition."—*Pref.* Each volume contains a full table of contents, index, and appendixes (text and tables). Provides information on basal metabolic rate data, WHO recommended dietary allowances of vitamins and minerals, WHO energy and protein requirements, height-weight tables, information on various kinds of diets (sodium-restricted, fat-restricted, lactose intolerance, etc.), and recommended national nutrient intakes for U.S. (1989), Canada (1990), U.K. (1991), Japan (1991) and Korea (1989).   QP141.M64

National Research Council. Committee on Diet and Health. Diet and health : implications for reducing chronic disease risk. Wash. : National Academy Pr., 1989. 749 p. : ill. **EH311**
  Discusses the complex relationship between dietary intake and chronic disease, and attempts to formulate dietary guidelines. Pt. 1 contains an introduction, definitions and methodology, Pt. 2 discusses evidence relating to chronic diseases, with chapters on individual dietary components, Pt. 3 describes the impact of dietary patterns on chronic diseases, with chapters on major diseases, and Pt. 4 provides an overall assessment, conclusions, and recommendations. Comprehensive index.   RC108.N38

National Research Council. Subcommittee on the Tenth Edition of the RDAs. Recommended dietary allowances. 10th ed. Wash. : National Academy Pr., 1989. 284 p.   **EH312**
  1st ed., 1943; 9th ed., 1980. Issuing body varies.
  Describes the physiological and biochemical bases for recommended dietary allowances of each specific nutrient. A table of recommended daily dietary allowances shows calories and nutrients tabulated by sex and by age categories. Includes lists of references.
                                TX551.N393

Sourcebook on food and nutrition. 3rd ed. Chicago : Marquis Academic Media, [1982]. 549 p. : ill.   **EH313**
  1st ed., 1978; 2nd ed., 1980.
  Contents: Pt. 1, Dietary directions for the 1980s; pt. 2, Nutrition from conception through adolescence; pt. 3, Adulthood into the golden years; pt. 4, Resources for further information.
  A compendium of dietary information, reprinted from various sources, reflecting important nutritional findings. Index. QP141.S567

Tables

Composition of foods : raw, processed, prepared / by the Nutrition Monitoring Div. Wash. : U.S. Dept. of Agriculture, Human Nutrition Information Service ; for sale by U.S. Govt. Print. Off., 1976–88. Pts. 1–21 (looseleaf). (Agriculture handbook, no. 8). (In progress).   **EH314**
  For annotation, see EJ220.   TX556.M5C68

PHARMACOLOGY

WHO drug information. v. 1, no. 1 (1987)– . Geneva : World Health Organization, c1987– . Four issues yearly.
                                EH315
  Provides an overview of topics relating to drug development and regulation that are of current relevance. Includes lists of proposed and recommended International Nonproprietary Names for Pharmaceutical Substances (INN) and changes to WHO's "Model list of essential drugs." Previously published as a supplement to *WHO chronicle.*

Guides

Andrews, Theodora. Guide to the literature of pharmacy and the pharmaceutical sciences. Littleton, Colo. : Libraries Unlimited, 1986. 383 p.   **EH316**
  A comprehensive bibliography of 958 entries covering the entire field of pharmacy and the pharmaceutical sciences. Annotations are descriptive and evaluative. Pt. 1 emphasizes reference works. Pt. 2, "Source material by subject area," lists standard treatises and textbooks in pharmacy practice, industrial and physical pharmacy, medicinal chemistry and pharmacognosy, pharmacology and toxicology, cosmetics, perfumes and flavors, and drug abuse. Pt. 3 covers computerized databases and provides a list of currently published periodicals.
                                Z6675.P5A56

Information sources in pharmaceuticals / W. R. Pickering, ed. London ; N.Y. : Bowker-Saur, c1990. 566 p. : ill. **EH317**
  Describes the pharmaceutical literature, including online databases, throughout the different stages of the pharmaceutical process. Considers the role of drug companies, relevant national associations, and the World Health Organization. Examines the "information scenario" in the U.S., Western Europe, Japan, Australia, South America, Africa, and China. Companion to *Information sources in the medical sciences* (EH5).   RS56.I54

Snow, Bonnie. Drug information : a guide to current resources. Chicago : Medical Library Association, c1989. 243 p.
EH318

Provides an introduction to a wide selection of relevant printed and online sources and discusses common problems in the provision of information concerning drugs. Background information on pharmacological terminology, legal and regulatory issues, and marketing and business data is given. Also included are a detailed contents listing, a keyword index, a glossary that defines pharmaceutical and information science terminology used in the text, and practicum exercises.
Z6675.P5S64

Bibliography

Andrews, Theodora. A bibliography on herbs, herbal medicine, "natural" foods, and unconventional medical treatment. Littleton, Colo. : Libraries Unlimited, 1982. 339 p.   **EH319**

Coverage includes a wide range of scientific and popular books on how to grow and use herbal plants for medicines, cosmetics, and foods, and books which challenge various medical practices and quackery. Critical annotations are provided for each book with specific comments on their strengths and weaknesses. Author and title index; subject index.
Z6665.H47A5

Cocaine : an annotated bibliography / Carlton E. Turner ... [et al.]. Jackson, Miss. : Research Institute of Pharmaceutical Sciences, Univ. of Mississippi, and Univ. Pr. of Mississippi, c1988. 2 v.
EH320

Vol. 1 is a two-part bibliography of the scientific literature on cocaine, including social and historical aspects of cocaine use, arranged alphabetically by author. Pre-1950 citations (1855–1949) lack annotations and are indexed by author only; 1950–1986 citations are annotated and indexed by both author and subject. Vol. 2 contains author and subject indexes.
Z6663.C63C63

Hefele, Bernhard. Drogenbibliographie : Verzeichnis der deutschsprachigen Literatur über Rauschmittel und Drogen von 1800 bis 1984 : mit einer Übersicht über internationale Bibliographien. München ; N.Y. : K.G. Saur, 1988. 2 v. (924 p.).   **EH321**

Covers German-language literature on drugs and drug usage. Includes literature of Germany to 1945 (German Reich), the Federal Republic of Germany, the German Democratic Republic, Switzerland, and Austria. Pt. 1 lists selected international drug bibliographies (349 annotated entries), including some report literature. Pt. 2 lists German-language literature (14,317 titles) on psychoactive drugs, drug usage and addiction and their medical, pharmacological, political, social, and legal aspects, emphasizing illegal drug use. Includes monographs, collected works, newspaper and magazine articles, dissertations, and *Habilitationsschriften*. Arranged alphabetically by author or year of publication for multiauthor works. Ten indexes, including author, key word, and broad subject.
RM300.Z99H44

Indexes; Abstract journals

International pharmaceutical abstracts. v. 1, no. 1 (Jan. 15, 1964)– . [Wash.] : Amer. Soc. of Hospital Pharmacists, [c1964]– . Semimonthly.   **EH322**

Now computer-produced. Signed abstracts in English. International in coverage. Author and subject index issued semiannually and annually. List of journals indexed appears annually in the Jan. 15 issue.
RS1.I63

Psychopharmacology abstracts / prep. by Medical Literature Inc. v. 1 (Jan. 1961)–19 (Apr. 1982). Chevy Chase, Md. : Nat. Inst. of Mental Health, 1961–83.   **EH323**

Superintendent of Documents classification: HE 20.8109/2.
Frequency varied.

Vol. 2, no. 7–v. 19, no. 4 issued by the Institute's National Clearinghouse for Mental Health Information.

"Designed to assist the Institute in meeting its obligation to foster and support laboratory and clinical research into the nature and causes of mental disorders and methods of treatment and prevention."—*Note*.

Abstracts are arranged in subject categories. Indexed by author and by subject.
RC475.P66

Encyclopedias

Bérdy, János. CRC handbook of antibiotic compounds / author, János Bérdy ; contributors, Adjoran [sic] Aszalos, Melvin Bostian, Karen L. McNitt. Boca Raton, Fla. : CRC Pr., [c1980–87]. 14 v. in 19 : ill.   **EH324**

Contents: v.1, Carbohydrate antibiotics; v.2, Macrocyclic lactone (lactam) antibiotics; v.3, Quinone and similar antibiotics; v.4, pt.1, Amino acid and peptide antibiotics; v.4, pt.2, Peptolide and macromolecular antibiotics; v.5, Heterocyclic antibiotics; v.6, Alicyclic, aromatic, and aliphatic antibiotics; v.7, Miscellaneous antibiotics with unknown chemical structure; v.8, pts.1–2, Antibiotics from higher forms of life: higher plants; v.9, Antibiotics from higher forms of life: lichens, algae, and animal organisms; v.10, General index; v.11, pts.1–2, Microbial metabolites; v.12, Antibiotics from higher forms of life.

Aims "to provide in a concise form ready access to information on important physical, chemical, and biological characteristics of the compounds."—*Pref*.
RS431.A6B47

Leung, Albert Y. Encyclopedia of common natural ingredients used in food, drugs, and cosmetics. N.Y. : Wiley, c1980. 409 p.   **EH325**

Provides data on 310 natural ingredients; excludes prescription drugs and medicinal herbs not readily available in commerce. Arrangement is by common name. Entries give Latin name, synonyms, general description, chemical composition, pharmacology or biological activities, uses, commercial preparations, and references. General, chemical indexes.
QD415.L48

Remington's pharmaceutical sciences. 13th ed. (1965)– . Easton, Pa. : Mack Publ., 1965– . Quinquennial.   **EH326**

18th ed., 1990. 1st–6th eds. had title: *The practice of pharmacy*; 7th–12th eds., *Remington's practice of pharmacy*.

More than 100 chapters are arranged in nine parts: pt. 1, Orientation; pt. 2, Pharmaceutics; pt. 3, Pharmaceutical chemistry; pt. 4, Testing and analysis; pt. 5, Radioisotopes in pharmacy and medicine; pt. 6, Pharmaceutical and medicinal agents; pt. 7, Biological products; pt. 8, Pharmaceutical preparations and their manufacture; pt. 9, Pharmaceutical practice; Index.
RS91.R4

Dictionaries

Dictionary of pharmacy / [ed. in chief, Julian H. Fincher]. Columbia, S.C. : Univ. of South Carolina Pr., c1986. 374 p.
EH327

Includes approximately 6,000 brief definitions, mainly from the pharmaceutical and pharmacological sciences, but also many from general medicine. Cross-references and 45 pages of appendixes.
RS51.D48

Elsevier's dictionary of pharmaceutical science and techniques : English, French, Italian, Spanish, German, Latin / comp. and arr. on English base by A. Sliosberg. N.Y. : Elsevier, 1968–80. 2 v.   **EH328**

Vol. 1, Pharmaceutical technology, lists 7,507 English terms with equivalents in the other four languages and indexes to the other languages. Vol. 2, Materia medica, deals particularly with substances of vegetable and animal origin used in the preparation of drugs for animals and humans. RS51.E48

Marler, E. E. J. Pharmacological and chemical synonyms : a collection of names of drugs, pesticides and other compounds drawn from the medical literature of the world. 9th ed. Amsterdam ; N. Y. : Elsevier, 1990. 562 p. **EH329**
1st ed., 1956; 8th ed., 1985.
A compilation of names used for drugs, pesticides, and other substances of pharmacological or biochemical interest. Names listed include nonproprietary (common) names, proprietary names and research code numbers. Arranged in an alphabetical list under proprietary name, followed by a list of synonyms, with cross-references from alternate names, trade names, chemical names, etc. Infrequently updated. RS51.M3

Negwer, Martin. Organic-chemical drugs and their synonyms : (an international survey). 6th rev. and enl. ed. N.Y. : VCH Publishers, c1987. 3 v. **EH330**
Rev. and enl. ed. and English translation of: *Organisch-chemische Arzneimittel und ihre Synonyma*, 5th ed.
This 1st English ed. includes "9,040 organo-chemical drugs which are chemically unified by molecular formula definition, and more than 80,000 synonyms."—*Pref.* Arrangement of drugs and their synonyms is "by the concept of incremental molecular formulas" (*Introd.*) in two columns per page. Entries include CAS Registry Number, structural formula, references, synonyms, and use. Group, CAS number, and synonym indexes. R551.N428

Steinbichler, Eveline. Lexikon für die Apothekenpraxis in sieben Sprachen. Frankfurt/Main : Govi-Verlag GmbH-Pharmazeutischer Verlag, [1963]. 474 p. **EH331**
A listing of pharmaceutical terms in seven languages: German, English, French, Spanish, Italian, Greek, and Russian. Arranged in five sections, one for each of the languages in the Roman alphabet, giving equivalent terms in the other six languages. Does not include definitions. RS51.S75

USAN and the USP dictionary of drug names. no. 1 (1961)– . Rockville, Md. : United States Pharmacopeial Convention, 1961– . Annual. **EH332**
Each issue is cumulative from 1961.
Cover title of 1993 ed. : *USAN 1994: 1961–1993 cumulative list.*
"The authorized list of established names for drugs in the United States of America...A compilation of the United States Adopted names (USAN) selected and released from June 15, 1961, through June 15, 1993, current USP and NF names for drugs, and other nonproprietary drug names."—*t.p.* Arranged alphabetically by generic, trade, or chemical name or drug code designated number. Entries give: USAN, year published as USAN, pronunciation, official compendium in which title occurs, molecular formula and weight, chemical names, CAS Registry Number(s), pharmacologic and/or therapeutic category, brand name, manufacturer, drug code designations, and graphic formula. Appendixes include listings of drugs in "Categories of pharmacologic activity," CAS Registry Numbers, molecular formulas, and names and addresses of U.S. drug companies and research institutes. RS55.U54

Handbooks

Blum, Kenneth. Handbook of abusable drugs. N.Y. : Gardner Pr., c1984. 721 p. : ill. **EH333**
For annotation, *see* CC134. RC564.B58

Dictionary of alkaloids / editorial board: G. A. Cordell ... [et al.]; comp. and ed. by I. W. Southon, J. Buckingham. London ; N.Y. : Chapman and Hall, 1989. 2 v. : ill. **EH334**
For annotation, *see* EE123. RS431.A53D53

Dictionary of antibiotics and related substances / ed. by B. W. Bycroft ; contributors, A. A. Higton, A. D. Roberts. London ; N.Y. : Chapman and Hall, 1988. 944 p. : ill. **EH335**
For annotation, *see* EE125. RS431.A6D53

Dictionary of drugs : chemical data, structures, and bibliographies / editors, J. Elks, C. R. Ganellin. London ; N.Y. : Chapman and Hall, 1990. 2 v. : ill. **EH336**
For annotation, *see* EE126. RS51.D479

Drug evaluations annual : DE / prep. by the Dept. of Drugs, Div. of Drugs and Toxicology, American Medical Association. 1991– . Chicago : American Medical Association, 1990– . Annual. **EH337**
Title varies: 1st–5th ed., 1971–83, called *AMA drug evaluations*; 6th ed., 1986, called *Drug evaluations*.
Also called *DE annual.*
Describes and evaluates most U.S. pharmaceuticals, including some investigational drugs. Organized by therapeutic category. Each chapter has a brief introduction followed by an evaluation for each drug with information on dosage, actions and uses, contraindications, adverse effects. Structural formula given for most single-entry drugs; selected list of further reading for each chapter. Indexed by drug name (generic, trademarks), indications, and adverse reactions.
RM300.D772

Drug facts and comparisons. 1982– . St. Louis : Facts and Comparisons Div., J.B. Lippincott, c1982– . Annual. **EH338**
Continues: *Facts and comparisons*, 1978–81. Also available as a loose-leaf text, kept up-to-date by monthly updates.
Provides comprehensive information on U.S. drugs. "Designed to provide a wide scope of drug information in a manner which facilitates comparisons among drugs. A comprehensive index, a detailed table of contents for each chapter and extensive cross referencing enables the reader to quickly locate needed information."—*Introd.* Organized by therapeutic drug classes, in 12 chapters. A typical entry includes action, indications, contraindications, warnings, precautions, adverse reactions, administration, and dosage. A "color locator" aids in identifying tablets and capsules. Drugs are arranged by dosage form, color, size, and shape. RM300.F33

Drug interaction facts. [1983]– . St. Louis : Facts and Comparison Division, Lippincott, [1983]– . Quarterly. **EH339**
Also available in bound ed., 1988– .
Comp. by MEDIPHOR (Monitoring and Evaluation of Drug Interactions by a Pharmacy Oriented Reporting System) Editorial Group, Division of Clinical Pharmacology, Stanford University School of Medicine.
"Attempts to present all drug-drug and drug-food interactions that have been reasonably well documented to occur in humans."—*Introd.* Drug interaction monographs are arranged alphabetically according to the principal drug affected. Each monograph has the following sections: interacting drugs (including generic and trade names), clinical significance; effects, mechanisms and management; and discussion, with primary literature references. Indexed by generic, class, and trade names. Clinically significant interactions are identified in the index.
RM302.D768

Drugs available abroad. 1991– . Detroit : Gale, c1991– . Annual. **EH340**
Subtitle: Guide to therapeutic drugs available and approved outside the U.S.
Lists more than 1,000 therapeutic drugs in use in Australia, Canada, Central America, South Africa, Western Europe, and elsewhere that have not been approved by the Food and Drug Administration, hence are not yet available in the U.S. Arranged alphabetically by generic name, entries include such information as countries where the drug is available, its release date, FDA approval status, and equivalent U.S. drug therapy. Indexes: drug action, clinical indications, manufacturer, country where used, drug name. Appendixes: directories of man-

ufacturers and regulatory authorities. Includes a survey of the drug approval process in various countries. Regular updates are planned.

RS51.D78

Drugs in pregnancy and lactation. [1st ed.]– . Baltimore : Williams & Wilkins, c1983– . Triennial.   **EH341**

Prep. by Gerald G. Briggs and others.

"This book was written to be used by the clinician who deals with pregnant patients [and] allows the clinician to have at his or her fingertips an up-to-date summary of available data bearing on specific drugs."—*Foreword.* Each drug includes fetal risk summary. Supplements (called *Update*) published between triennial editions.

RG627.6.D79D798

Duke, James A. CRC handbook of medicinal herbs. Boca Raton, Fla. : CRC Pr., 1985. 677 p. : ill.   **EH342**

Provides well-documented information for 365 species of plants having medicinal or folk medicinal uses. All entries include the scientific name and authority, the scientific name of the plant family, and one or two colloquial or common names. Most entries have four sections giving uses, folk medicinal applications, chemistry, and toxicity. Most plants are illustrated. Extensive tables, bibliography, and index.

QK99.A1D83

The essential guide to prescription drugs. [1977 ed.]– . N.Y. : Harper & Row, c1977– . Annual.   **EH343**

Publisher varies.

Frequency varies: irregular, 1977–84; annual, 1987– .

Arranged by generic drug name, giving dosage, side effects, adverse reactions, etc. There is a cross-index from brand-names to the generic names. Written for general readers. Glossary, bibliography, and index which also includes Canadian drug names.   RS51.E85

Handbook of nonprescription drugs. 1st ed. (Sept. 1967)– . Wash. : American Pharmaceutical Assoc., 1967– .   **EH344**

A compilation of facts on home remedies in 35 chapters with broad headings such as: Antacid products, Asthma products, Diabetes care products. Each chapter discusses the etiology of the condition; the anatomy, physiology, and pathophysiology of the affected systems; the signs and symptoms; the treatment and adjunctive measures; an evaluation of ingredients in over-the-counter products; and important patient and product considerations. Bibliography; index.   RM671.A1H34

The Merck index : an encyclopedia of chemicals, drugs, and biologicals / Susan Budavari, ed. 11th (centennial) ed. Rahway, N.J. : Merck, 1989. 1 v. (various pagings) : ill.   **EH345**

For annotation, *see* EE83.   RS51.M4

Ophthalmic drug facts : ODF. [1990]– . St. Louis : Facts and Comparisons Div., J.B. Lippincott, 1990– . Annual.

EH346

Preliminary issue dated 1989.

A comprehensive work that includes prescription and nonprescription products and intends "to provide reliable and objective ophthalmic drug information."—*Pref.* 12 chapters, organized according to therapeutic use, group comparable drugs to provide comparative information. Additional chapters treat dosage forms, routes of administration, systemic drugs, and investigational drugs. A cost index provides wholesale price ratios. Selected bibliographies; many cross-references. An index lists generic, brand, and group names, and many synonyms. Appendixes: Excipient glossary; Manufacturer index.

RE994.O64

Physicians' desk reference : PDR. 1947–. Rutherford, N.J. : Medical Economics, [1946–]. Annual.   **EH347**

Title varies: 1947–73 entitled *Physicians' desk reference to pharmaceutical specialties and biologicals.*

"Compendium of official, FDA-approved prescription drug labeling … [and] information on current indications and prescribing guidelines."—*Foreword.* Principal sections: (1) Alphabetical index by manufacturer's name (white pages); (2) Product name index (pink pages); (3) Product category index (blue pages), listing products by prescribing category; (4) Product identification section (gray pages), showing

more than 2,000 tablets and capsules in color and actual size; (5) Product information section (white pages), listing approximately 3,000 pharmaceuticals by manufacturer, giving full descriptions of composition, action, use, dosage, side effects, etc.; and (6) Diagnostic products information section (green pages), arranged alphabetically by manufacturer. Product descriptions have been provided and approved by the manufacturers.

New and revised product information is issued in periodic *Physicians desk reference supplements* (publ. in May and Sept.). A companion volume, *PDR guide to drug interactions, side effects, contraindications* 1993– , is cross-referenced by page number to *Physicians' desk reference, Physicians' desk reference for nonprescription drugs* (EH348), and *Physicians' desk reference for ophthalmology,* 1972– . Related works include: *Physicians' desk reference for radiology and nuclear medicine* (1971–1979/80) and *PDR family guide to prescription drugs* (1993).

•Machine-readable versions: *Physicians' desk reference (PDR)* [database] (Oradell, N.J. : Medical Economics Co.), available online, updated monthly; *PDR library on CD-ROM* [database], updated monthly. Also available on diskettes and magnetic tape. Current coverage.   RS75.P5

Physicians' desk reference for nonprescription drugs. 1st ed. (1980)– . Oradell, N.J. : Medical Economics, 1980– . Annual.   **EH348**

14th ed., 1993.

A companion to *Physicians' desk reference* (EH347).

The "purpose is to make available essential information on nonprescription drugs."—*Foreword.* Has product identification and product information sections. Indexed by manufacturer, product name, product category, and active ingredients.   RM671.A1P48

Physicians' genRx. 1993– . Smithtown, N.Y. : Data Pharmaceutica Inc., 1993– . Annual.   **EH349**

The official drug reference of FDA prescribing information and therapeutic equivalents. The main section lists product information, with entries arranged alphabetically by generic drug name and a keyword index. Also gives therapeutic equivalency rating, price information, directory of suppliers. Includes "top 100 selling drugs" and a list of certified regional poison control centers.   RS55.2.P48

Wee, Yeow Chin. An illustrated dictionary of Chinese medicinal herbs / Wee Yeow Chin and Hsuan Keng. Sebastopol, Calif. : CRCS Publications, 1992. 184 p. : col. ill.   **EH350**

Gives information on each plant, often with a color photograph, including usage other than in Chinese medicine. Plants are arranged in alphabetical order by generic names. Each entry lists botanical family, scientific name, Chinese name, and common name(s). Indexes of common and Chinese names.   RM666.H33W38

Yudofsky, Stuart C. What you need to know about psychiatric drugs / Stuart C. Yudofsky, Robert E. Hales, Tom Ferguson. N.Y. : Ballantine Books, 1992. 646 p. : ill.   **EH351**

Provides, in informal style and nontechnical language, comprehensive information on psychiatric drugs for the health consumer and an overview of different therapeutic options. Three major sections: (1) Basic information on psychiatric drugs and frequently asked questions; (2) Categories of psychiatric drugs (i.e., antidepressant drugs; sedatives and sleeping pills; antipsychotic drugs, etc.); (3) Individual drug listings. Drugs are arranged alphabetically by generic names, giving guidelines for users, benefits and risks, precautions, drug interactions, effects of overdose and long-term use, etc. Also mentions nondrug treatments where appropriate. Indexed.   RM315.Y83

Zimmerman, David R. Zimmerman's complete guide to nonprescription drugs. 2nd ed. Detroit : Gale, c1993. lix, 1125 p. : ill., map.   **EH352**

1st ed., 1983, had title: *The essential guide to nonprescription drugs* (N.Y. : Harper & Row. 886 p.).

Derived from "federally sponsored, decades-long review of nonprescription drugs … principal source is the many FDA reports that have been published in the *Federal register.*"—*p. xxviii.* Written for general readers. Arranged alphabetically by therapeutic categories such as cold and cough remedies, antihistamines, smoking deterrents, sunscreens, etc. Detailed table of contents; general index; symptoms index. Considered more useful than *Physician's desk reference for nonprescription drugs* (EH348). since various products for the same condition are compared and evaluated.   RM671.A1Z55

Dispensatories and pharmacopoeias

AHFS drug information. 1989– . Bethesda, Md. : American Society of Hospital Pharmacists, c1989– . Annual with quarterly supplements.   **EH353**

Supersedes: *American hospital formulary service* (1959–83, loose-leaf); *American hospital formulary service drug information* (1984–88).

"Prepared for the purpose of disseminating comprehensive, evaluative drug information."—*Pref.* Arrangement by pharmacologic-therapeutic classification. Within each class, arranged alphabetically by generic name. Gives comprehensive monograph for each drug including pertinent information such as administration, dosage, chemical stability, pharmacology, uses, and cautions, including drug interactions and interference with laboratory tests. Indexed for proprietary (trade) names, synonyms, and acronyms of drugs.   RS125.A562

American drug index. 1956– . Philadelphia : Lippincott, 1956– . Annual.   **EH354**

A listing of pharmaceuticals by generic, brand, and chemical name, with brief information as to manufacturer, forms, size, dosage, and use. The 37th ed. (1993) is in 13 sections. The major section, Monographs, is arranged alphabetically, with many cross-references. Other sections include common abbreviations used in medical orders, common systems of weight and measure, and container requirements for U.S.P. drugs.   RS355.A48

Blue book American druggist. 1987/88– . N.Y. : Hearst Corp., c1987– . Annual.   **EH355**

Supersedes: *American druggist price book* (1928–3?) and *American druggist blue book* (1938–87).

Drug products with prices, listed alphabetically by trade name. Includes a manufacturers' index.

British pharmacopoeia 1988 / publ. on the recommendation of the Medicines Commission pursuant to the Medicines Act 1968. [14th ed.]. London : H.M.S.O., 1988. 2 v. : ill.   **EH356**

Publ. continuously but irregularly since 1864.

Some vols. contain Addenda.

A compilation of monographs, alphabetically arranged, on drugs, preparations, etc., giving the official standard, description, dose, etc. Vol. 1 contains 2,100 monographs for medicinal and auxiliary substances; v. 2 comprises the formulary (substantially revised for this edition and contained in a section entitled "Formulated preparations"), which has sections on blood products, immunological products, radiopharmaceutical preparations, and surgical materials, and contains the index for both volumes.   RS141.3.B8

The extra pharmacopoeia / Martindale. 30th ed. / ed. by James E. F. Reynolds. London : Pharmaceutical Pr., 1993. 2363 p.   **EH357**

1st ed., 1883; 29th ed., 1989.

Comp. since 1933 by editorial staff of Royal Pharmaceutical Society of Great Britain.

1st–15th eds. (1883–1912) comp. by W. H. Martindale and W. W. Westcott.

Provides "concise unbiased information on the substances used in medicine and pharmacy … [with] a significant shift to more clinical emphasis …. Based on published information. It is not a book of standards."—*Pref.* International in scope, covering prescription and nonprescription drugs. In three parts: (1) Monographs on drugs and ancillary substances containing data on approximately 4,300 substances in 69 chapters; (2) Supplementary drugs and other substances, containing information on new and investigational drugs and obsolescent drugs

still of interest; (3) Preparations, with brief details of official and proprietary preparations. Includes a directory of 3,500 manufacturers. General index covers drugs and diseases.

•Machine-readable versions:

(1) *Martindale online* [database] (London : Royal Pharmaceutical Soc. of Great Britain). Corresponds to most recent edition of printed version; updated monthly.

(2) *Martindale : the extra pharmacopoeia* [database] (London : Royal Pharmaceutical Soc. of Great Britain). Available on CD-ROM; updated quarterly.   RS141.3.M4

The international pharmacopoeia = Pharmacopoeia internationalis. 3rd ed. Geneva : World Health Organization, 1979–88. 3 v. : ill. (In progress).   **EH358**

Title varies: 1st ed., 1951–59 called *Pharmacopoeia internationalis*; 2nd ed., 1967, called *Specifications for the quality control of pharmaceutical preparations*.

Contents: v. 1, General methods of analysis; v. 2–3, Quality specifications.

Constitutes "a collection of recommended specifications which, in accordance with the resolution of the Third World Health Assembly, are offered to serve as references so that national specifications can be established on a similar basis in any country."—*Pref.* The purpose is to give specifications for quality control of pharmaceutical preparations.

National drug code directory / prep. by Drug Listing Branch, Center for Drugs and Biologics. [1st ed.] (1969)– . Wash. : Food and Drug Administration, 1969– . Irregular.   **EH359**

8th ed., 1985. Updated between editions by supplements.

Four sections: Alphabetical index by product name; Numeric index of products by drug class; Numeric index of products by National Drug Code; Alphabetic index by short name (of the labeler/vendor). Includes the FDA approved new drug application numbers required since 1984 by the FDA's Drug Verification Compliance Program. Supplements list products that have been added, changed, or discontinued.   RS53.N35

The national formulary. Ed. 1 (1888)–14 (1975). Wash. : American Pharmaceutical Association, 1888–1975.   **EH360**

Title varies.

"The fundamental purpose … is to provide standards and specifications which can be used to evaluate the quality of pharmaceuticals so that the physician can prescribe drugs with assurance, the pharmacist can dispense drugs with reliability, and the patient can consume drugs with confidence."—*Pref.* The main section of monographs on drugs, chemicals, and preparations is arranged alphabetically by basic drug with specifications for preparation. This is followed by a section on general tests, processes, techniques, and apparatus; a section on reagents and test solutions; and a section of general information.

§ Continued by: *The United States pharmacopeia* (EH363).   RS141.2.N3

Pharmaceutical Society of Great Britain. Dept. of Pharmaceutical Sciences. The pharmaceutical codex. 11th ed. London : Pharmaceutical Pr., 1979. 1101 p. : ill.   **EH361**

1st ed., 1907. 10th ed., 1973, had title; *British pharmaceutical codex*.

12th ed. expected 1994.

Incorporates *British pharmaceutical codex*.

"Intended to be an encyclopedia of drug information for pharmacists and others who are engaged in work involving the preparation and use of medicines and medical preparations."—*Introd.* Entries are arranged alphabetically and preparations of drugs are appended to the appropriate drug entry. Indexed.   RS151.3.B75

The pharmacopoeia of the United States of America / by the authority of the medical societies and colleges. Ed. 1 (1820)–19 (1975). Easton, Pa. : Mack Print. Co., 1820–1975.   **EH362**

Some volumes have subtitle : The United States pharmacopoeia. Also called USP.

Imprint varies. Revised at approximate 5-year intervals. Two issued for 1830.

An official compendium of drug information, giving standards of purity and strength for each compound included.

Continued by *The United States pharmacopeia* (EH363).

RS141.2.P5

The United States pharmacopeia. 20th revision (1980)– . Rockville, Md. : U.S. Pharmacopeial Convention, c1979– . Irregular. **EH363**

Supersedes: *The pharmacopoeia of the United States of America* (EH362) and *The national formulary* (EH360).

Includes: *The national formulary*, 15th ed. (1980)– .

"In 1980 the scope of both the USP and NF changed, the Pharmacopeia being limited to drug substances and dosage forms, and the National Formulary ...to pharmaceutic ingredients"—*Pref., NF XVI.* An official compendium of drug information of the USPC, which is responsible for setting drug standards and specifications. Kept up-to-date between revisions by supplements.

•Machine-readable version: *USP ; NF : the official compendia of drug standards information on disk* [database]. Rockville, Md. : USPC. Includes most recent revision and its supplements.

RS141.2.P5

United States pharmacopoeia dispensing information : USP DI. 1980– . [Rockville, Md. : U.S. Pharmacopeial Convention, 1980]– . Annual. **EH364**

"Comprehensive collection of clinically relevant, established information about each drug...the result of a...nationwide consensus-generating system."—*Pref.* Vol. 1, Drug information for the health care professional, lists DI monographs in alphabetic order by chemical name, with information on use, pharmacology, precautions, side effects, dosage information, etc. The index includes established names, cross-references by brand names (U.S. and Canadian), and older nonproprietary names. Vol. 2, Advice for the patient, is written for consumers in nontechnical language. Both volumes contain numerous appendixes, including "precaution listings" (e.g., pregnancy, pediatrics, geriatrics, dental, athletes). Vol. 3, Approved drug product and legal requirements, provides information from the FDA "on therapeutic equivalence and other requirements relating to drug product selection, ... legal requirements for labeling, storage, packaging, and quality of drugs."—*Pref.*

Kept current by *USP DI update* (v. 1 [1980]– . Rockville, Md. : U.S. Pharmacopeial Convention. Bimonthly). RS141.2.U5U2

Unlisted drugs. v.1 (Jan. 1949)– . [Chatham, N.J. : Unlisted Drugs], 1949– . Monthly. **EH365**

Imprint varies.

Each monthly issue contains descriptions of 180 to 200 new drugs which are not yet recorded in standard sources. Also includes reviews of new books on drugs and other data of drug interest. Name and number indexes published annually. RS1.U55

History

Estes, J. Worth. Dictionary of protopharmacology : therapeutic practices, 1700–1850. Canton, Mass. : Science History Publ., 1990. 215 p. : ill. **EH366**

Provides definitions of drugs commonly prescribed by English-speaking physicians between approximately 1700 and 1850. Approximately 3,000 entries, including botanical drugs, chemicals, and mixtures and patent medicines. Many synonyms and cross-references.

RM36.E88

Griffenhagen, George B. Pharmacy museums and historical collections in the United States and Canada / by George Griffenhagen and Ernst W. Stieb. Madison, Wis. : American Inst. of the History of Pharmacy, 1988. 92 p. : ill. (American Institute of the History of Pharmacy. Publication, n.s., no. 11.).

EH367

Title varies: 1956, *Pharmacy museums*, by George Griffenhagen; 1972, *Pharmacy museums and historical collections on public view, U.S.A.*, by Sami K. Hamarneh; 1981, *Pharmacy museums and historical collections on public view in the United States and Canada*, by Sami K. Hamarneh and Ernst Stieb.

Museums are described and listed in alphabetical order by state or province and city. Includes sites of historical pharmacy markers. Name index. RS123.U6G75

Wootton, A. C. Chronicles of pharmacy. London : Macmillan, 1910. 2 v. : ill. **EH368**

Repr. : Boston : Milford House, [1971] (2 v. in 1) ; Tuckahoe, N.Y. : USV Pharmaceutical Corp, 1972.

In narrative form; describes the discovery and use of various drugs, medicines, and nostrums from ancient times through the 19th century. Includes some biographical material of famous apothecaries. Indexed.

PSYCHIATRY

Guides

Greenberg, Bette. How to find out in psychiatry. N.Y. : Pergamon, c1978. 113 p. **EH369**

Subtitle: A guide to sources of mental health information.

A bibliography arranged under broad headings, e.g., guides to libraries and the literature, primary sources, secondary sources, drug therapy, mental health statistics, etc. There is an appendix of classics in psychiatric literature. Indexed. Z6664.N5G69

Bibliography

Berlin, Irving Norman. Bibliography of child psychiatry and child mental health, with a selected list of films : an official publication of the Academy of Child Psychiatry. [2nd ed.]. N.Y. : Human Sciences Pr., c1976. 508 p. **EH370**

"An official publication of the Academy of Child Psychiatry."— *t.p.*

1st ed., 1963, had title: *Bibliography of child psychiatry*.

A topically arranged list of 4,257 citations, with asterisks marking the most important. Includes infant, child, and adolescent studies. Film titles also arranged by subject, with contents notes. Author and subject indexes. Z6671.5.B4

Core readings in psychiatry : an annotated guide to the literature / ed. by Michael H. Sacks, William H. Sledge, Phyllis Rubinton. N.Y. : Praeger Publ., 1984. 539 p. **EH371**

Presents 62 topical chapters by psychiatric specialists. "Core" is defined either as "classic in introducing a new concept, finding or methodology ... or as highly relevant to a current understanding of the topic area."—*Introd.* Critical annotations; essential works are starred. Author and subject indexes. RC454.C655

Favazza, Armando R. Anthropological and cross-cultural themes in mental health : an annotated bibliography, 1925– 1974 / Armando R. Favazza and Mary Oman. Columbia : Univ. of Missouri Pr., 1977. 386 p. (University of Missouri studies, v. 65). **EH372**

Includes more than 3,600 English-language periodical articles. Chronological arrangement, with author and subject indexes. The introduction provides a most interesting review of the cultural areas and specific themes included.

Continued by: Armando R. Favazza and Ahmed D. Faheem, *Themes in cultural psychiatry* (Columbia : Univ. of Missouri Pr., 1982).

194 p.). Cites 1,643 periodical articles and books. Non-English language journals, anthropological journals, and books have been added to this volume. Author listing; subject index.   RC455.4.E8F38

Menninger, Karl. A guide to psychiatric books in English. 3rd ed. N.Y. : Grune & Stratton, [1972]. 238 p. (Menninger Clinic monograph series, no. 7).   **EH373**

1st ed., 1950, and 2nd ed., 1956, had title: *A guide to psychiatric books.*

A checklist of English-language books on psychiatry and related fields arranged by topic; this edition does not include the series of reading lists for specific groups. Name index.   Z6664.N5M48

Tilton, James R. Annotated bibliography on childhood schizophrenia, 1955–1964 / James R. Tilton, Marian K. DeMyer, Lois Hendrickson Loew. N.Y. : Grune & Stratton, [1966]. 136 p.   **EH374**

Brings up-to-date W. Goldfarb and M. M. Dorsen's *Annotated bibliography of childhood schizophrenia* (N.Y. : Basic Books, 1956) which covered through 1954. Lists 346 English-language works classified by major themes: historical and general review articles; description and diagnosis; etiology; biochemical, neurological and physiological studies; family characteristics, treatment and care; and follow-up studies. Nearly all items are annotated. Author index.   Z6664.N5T5

Zukerman, Elyse. Changing directions in the treatment of women : a mental health bibliography. Rockville, Md. : National Institute of Mental Health, [1979]. 494 p.   **EH375**

A selected bibliography of 407 entries with detailed abstracts of journal articles, books, book chapters, and dissertations published mostly 1960–77, "with the objective of providing a helpful resource for the research, therapy, and women's communities and for individual women."—*Pref.* Author and subject indexes.   HQ1154.W6Z84

Library catalogs

Menninger Clinic (Topeka, Kansas). Library. Catalog of the Menninger Clinic Library, the Menninger Foundation .... Boston : G.K. Hall, 1971. 4 v. (1704 p.).   **EH376**

Contents: v. 1–3, Author-title catalog; v. 4, Subject catalog.

Photoreproduction of the catalog cards of a collection of about 30,000 volumes and 400 serials, with particular strength in psychiatry and clinical psychology, adjunctive therapy, psychiatric nursing, social work counseling, psychophysiology, and psychopharmacology.

———. *Catalog of the professional library of the Menninger Foundation. First supplement* (Boston : G.K. Hall, 1978. 2 v.).

Classification

ICD-10 : the ICD-10 classification of mental and behavioural disorders : clinical descriptions and diagnostics guidelines. Geneva : World Health Organization, 1992. 362 p.   **EH377**

Adopted by the World Health Organization, Jan. 1993.

Developed from chapter 5 of the *International statistical classification of diseases and related health problems* (EH56). "For each disorder, a description is provided of the main clinical features, and also of any important but less specific associated features."—*Introd.*   RC455.2.C4I343

Encyclopedias

Doctor, Ronald M. The encyclopedia of phobias, fears, and anxieties / Ronald M. Doctor and Ada P. Kahn. N.Y. : Facts on File, c1989. 487 p.   **EH378**

For annotation, *see* CD100.   RC535.D63

International encyclopedia of psychiatry, psychology, psychoanalysis, and neurology / ed. by Benjamin B. Wolman. N.Y. : Aesculapius Publ., 1977. 12 v. : ill.   **EH379**

For annotation, *see* CD23.   RC334.I57

Roesch, Roberta. The encyclopedia of depression. N.Y. : Facts on File, c1991. 263 p.   **EH380**

An alphabetic listing of entries that vary in length from 50 to 1,000 words and treat all aspects of depression. Appendixes include statistics, psychiatric drug information, and information sources (including selected treatment centers, self-help groups, publications, and an extensive bibliography). Numerous cross-references; subject index. Intended for general readers.   RC537.R63

Treatments of psychiatric disorders : a task force report of the American Psychiatric Association. Wash. : American Psychiatric Association, 1989. 4 v. (3068 p.).   **EH381**

Provides comprehensive descriptions for treatments of disorders, encompassing diverse orientations and treatment variables. Covers multiple approaches, including pharmacologic, psychodynamic, behavioral, cognitive, family, individual, and group treatments, recognizing evolving knowledge and preferred treatments as well as acceptable alternatives. More than 400 pages of references. Vol. 4 is a 250-page author-subject index. A cautionary statement emphasizes this should not serve as a standard of care. Useful for graduate research and health professionals.   RC480.T69

Dictionaries

Campbell, Robert Jean. Psychiatric dictionary. 6th ed. N.Y. : Oxford Univ. Pr., 1989. 811 p.   **EH382**

1st ed., 1940; 5th ed., 1981.

Continues the tradition of giving encyclopedic treatment to many terms [with] liberal use of cross-references."—*Pref.* Incorporates terms of the official *Diagnostic and statistical manual of mental disorders : DSM-III-R* (EH393) of the American Psychiatric Association, but also includes older terms if they are more familiar or continue to be widely used. Useful list of abbreviations.   RC437.H5

Kaplan, Harold I. Comprehensive glossary of psychiatry and psychology / Harold I. Kaplan, Benjamin J. Sadock ; senior contributing ed., Robert Cancro. Baltimore : Williams & Wilkins, c1991. 215 p. : col. ill.   **EH383**

Concise definitions of terms from the behavioral sciences, psychiatry, psychology, and social work, neurochemistry, neuroimmunology, and neurophysiology. Appendixes cover psychotherapeutic drugs used in psychiatry, and a list of commonly abused drugs. Includes a four-page "Psychotherapeutic drug identification guide."   RC437.K36

Lexicon of psychiatric and mental health terms. Geneva : World Health Organization ; Albany, N.Y. : WHO Publications Center, 1989. v. 1. (In progress).   **EH384**

"Designed for use in conjunction with Chapter V (Mental disorders) of the ninth revision of the *International classification of diseases* (ICD-9) [Wash. : U.S. Public Health Service, 1991. 3 v.] ... Many of the terms defined in this volume [v. 1] will be used ... in the ICD-10."—*Introd.* In three parts: (1) Terms used in psychiatric diagnosis; (2) Names for symptoms and signs; (3) Terms for concepts. Alphabetical index of all entries and synonyms.   RC436.5.L49

Stone, Evelyn M. American psychiatric glossary. 6th ed. Wash. : Amer. Psychiatric Pr., c1988. 143 p.   **EH385**

1st–5th ed., 1957–80, had title: *A psychiatric glossary.*

Brief definitions. This edition incorporates the revised nomenclature of *Diagnostic and statistical manual of mental disorders : DSM-III-R* (EH393) of the American Psychiatric Association. Diagnostic terms are cross-referenced from older nomenclatures. Includes valua-

ble lists of abbreviations, tables of commonly abused drugs, legal terms, psychological tests, research terms, and schools of psychiatry.
RC437.S76

Walrond-Skinner, Sue. A dictionary of psychotherapy. London ; Boston : Routledge & Kegan Paul, 1986. 379 p. **EH386**
Includes "many new ideas, forms and interventions that do not figure in older dictionaries ... less space has been devoted to classical concepts from the behavioural and psychoanalytic approaches."—*Pref.* For each term, gives definition and information concerning different usages or concepts; many items have brief bibliography. Includes biographical entries.
RC475.7.W35

Directories

American Psychiatric Association. Biographical directory. 1983– . Wash. : The Association, c1983– . **EH387**
At head of title: Fellows and members of the American Psychiatric Association.
Publisher varies. Title varies: 1941–1977, *Biographical directory of fellows and members of the American Psychiatric Association.*
Lists mostly American psychiatrists, and a few from other countries. Gives information on training, experience, specialty, publications, etc. Geographical index. Introductory material includes information on the development of the Association. Information is provided by members except for name, address, and initial membership year.
RC326.A56

Directory of mental health libraries and information centers / Barbara E. Epstein, ed. Wash. : Amer. Psychiatric Pr., [1984]. 297 p. **EH388**
Comp. under the auspices of the Assoc. of Mental Health Librarians.
Provides data on some 275 mental health library collections in the U.S. and Canada. Includes collection characteristics, services, publications, and access information. Arranged by state or province, then by city. Indexed by personnel, institution, and subject. Z675.M43D57

Directory of psychiatry residency training programs / American Association of Directors of Psychiatric Residency Training, American Medical Student Association, American Psychiatric Association. 1st ed.– . [Wash.] : American Psychiatric Assoc., 1982– . Irregular. **EH389**
Describes accredited residency programs in general and child psychiatry in both the U.S. and Canada. Arranged alphabetically by state, then by institution, with separate listings for general and child psychiatry programs. Canadian programs follow. Includes lists of joint programs and postgraduate fellowships, as well as requirements for residency training, certification, and training in Canada. An initial chapter discusses various types of psychiatric practice. RC459.5.U6D57

Gunn, John Charles. A directory of world psychiatry. [London : World Psychiatric Assoc., c1971]. 350 p. : maps.
EH390
An international directory for 89 countries of hospitals and institutions treating the mentally ill. Arranged by country. Each entry provides: brief description of the country's psychiatric services; list of the main public psychiatric hospitals; list of university departments which teach psychiatry; list of psychiatric journals published there; data on the national psychiatric associations. RC335.G85

Handbooks

American handbook of psychiatry / Silvano Arieti, ed. in chief. 2nd ed. N.Y. : Basic Books, 1974–81. 8 v. **EH391**
1st ed., 1959–66, 3 v.

Contents: v. 1, The foundation of psychiatry; v. 2, Child and adolescent psychiatry, sociocultural and community psychiatry; v. 3, Adult clinical psychiatry; v. 4, Organic disorders and psychosomatic medicine; v. 5, Treatment; v. 6, New psychiatric frontiers; v. 7, Advances and new directions; v. 8, Biological psychiatry.
A comprehensive, authoritative handbook. Name and subject indexes in each volume. Contains some dated material. RC435.A562

Comprehensive handbook of psychopathology / ed. by Henry E. Adams and Patricia B. Sutker. 2nd ed. N.Y. : Plenum, c1993. 864 p. : ill. **EH392**
1st ed., 1984.
"Resource textbook that covers both general and specific topics in psychopathology ... useful to researchers, practitioners, and graduate and other advanced students in the mental health professions."—*Pref.* In six main parts: Issues in psychopathology; Neurotic and psychotic disorders; Personality disorders; Disorders associated with social and situational problems; Disorders associated with physical trauma and medical illness; Disorders usually arising in specific life stages. Chapters by specialists focus on overviews of clinical description, research, and theories, with extensive references. Indexed. RC454.C636

Diagnostic and statistical manual of mental disorders : DSM-III-R. 3rd ed., rev. Wash. : American Psychiatric Assoc., 1987. 567 p. **EH393**
1st ed., 1952; 3rd ed., 1980.
The original publication attempted to establish a glossary for describing diagnoses. This edition, translated into 13 languages, is viewed by mental health researchers and clinicians as the accepted classification system for disorders. Contains all diagnostic criteria plus systematic descriptions of disorders, using a numerical code system. Includes an explanation of the code system and instructions for its use, descriptions of disorders, glossary, classification history, alphabetic and numeric listing of diagnoses and indexes of symptoms, diagnoses, and codes. Essential for mental health professionals. A 4th ed. is expected in 1994. RC455.2.C4D54

The Harvard guide to modern psychiatry / ed. by Armand M. Nicholi, Jr. Cambridge, Mass. : Belknap Pr. of Harvard Univ. Pr., 1978. 691 p. **EH394**
About 30 professors and subject specialists, most affiliated with Harvard University, have contributed to this guide which offers 31 signed chapters with bibliographic references. In six main sections: Examination and evaluation; Brain and behavior; Psychopathology; Treatment and management; Special populations; Psychiatry and society. Indexed. RC454.H36

Wolman, Benjamin B. Handbook of clinical psychology. N.Y. : McGraw-Hill, [1965]. 1596 p. : ill. **EH395**
Intended "to acquaint clinical psychologists and other professionals with the tremendous scope of research, experience, theory, and practice in this rapidly growing field."—*Pref.* Includes sections on research methods, theoretical foundations, diagnostic methods, clinical patterns, methods of treatment, and clinical psychology as a profession. Within each section chapters have been contributed by specialists, and extensive bibliographies are provided. Name and subject indexes. RC467.W6

History

Alexander, Franz. The history of psychiatry : an evaluation of psychiatric thought and practice from prehistoric times to the present / by Franz G. Alexander and Sheldon T. Selesnick. N.Y. : Harper & Row, [1966]. 471 p. : illus., ports. **EH396**
In four parts: The age of psychiatry, From the ancients through the modern era, The Freudian age, Recent developments. A comprehensive history of psychiatry, with chapter notes and extensive bibliography. Index. RC438.A39

Barton, Walter E. The history and influence of the American Psychiatric Association. Wash. : American Psychiatric Pr., c1987. 400 p., [16] p. of plates : ill., ports.   **EH397**

Follows "the development of psychiatry in America through the founding and growth of the American Psychiatric Association."—*Pref.*
          RC443.B35

Howells, John G. World history of psychiatry. London : Baillière Tindall ; N.Y. : Brunner/Mazel, 1975. 770 p. : ill., facsims., port.   **EH398**

Follows the development of psychiatry, exploring different eras, stages (primitive, rational, religious, somatic, harmonization) and regions, in the context of "cultural, economic, geographical, political and ecological factors."—*Introd.*   RC438.H67

Hunter, Richard Alfred. Three hundred years of psychiatry, 1535–1860 : a history presented in selected English texts / Richard Hunter, Ida Macalpine. London ; N.Y. : Oxford Univ. Pr., 1963. 1107 p. : ill., ports., facsims.   **EH399**

Not a systematic treatise, but an attempt "to present original sources and through them trace clinical and pathological observations, nosologies, theories, … [and] social and legal attitudes to mental illness. … It is intended to serve the dual purpose of a sourcebook of psychiatric history aiming at biographical and bibliographical accuracy."—*Introd.* Arranged by century, the book is built on extracts from original sources, which are introduced by explanatory notes discussing the topic historically and clinically and relating it to later developments. Extracts are arranged chronologically, each headed by the author's name, dates of birth and death, qualifications, and main offices.
          RC438.H84

Treatises

Comprehensive textbook of psychiatry/V / editors, Harold I. Kaplan, Benjamin J. Sadock. 5th ed. Baltimore : Williams & Wilkins, c1989. 2 v. (2158, 71 p.) : ill.   **EH400**

1st ed., 1967; 4th ed., 1985.

An encyclopedic work containing 192 sections written by 237 contributors that "constitutes the most thorough, complete, integrated, and revised book of record of clinical psychiatry … designed and used by psychiatrists, behavioral scientists, and all workers in the mental health field."—*Pref.* Substantially revised from the 4th ed. with closer integration between basic and clinical sciences, an expanded geriatric psychiatry section, and a new section on neuroscience. All described disorders are consistent with *Diagnostic and statistical manual of mental disorders : DSM-III-R* nosology (EH393). Bibliographic references accompany each section in 50 chapters. The volumes have identical subject indexes.   RC454.C637

Statistics

Mental health, United States. 1983– . Rockville, Md. : U.S. National Inst. of Mental Health, 1983– . Biennial.   **EH401**

[5th ed.], 1992.

Contains statistical reports and data on trends in mental health services, derived to a large extent from national surveys conducted by the Center for Mental Health Services and National Institute of Mental Health in collaboration with various major national, state, and professional associations.   RA790.6.M463

PUBLIC HEALTH

Guides

Health services : sources of information for research. Bethesda, Md. : National Library of Medicine, [1992]. 201 p.   **EH402**

Published as a result of NLM's expanded Health Services Research Information Program. "Developed to aid users and producers of health services research in accessing relevant literature and sources of information…especially geared toward the health services researcher who does not have ready access to an experienced librarian or other expert assistance in seeking and acquiring information…particularly valuable for researchers new to the field."—*Foreword.* Organized alphabetically by publication types, in broad categories. Author/organization index; title index.   Z6658.H44

Pease, Elizabeth Sue. Occupational safety and health : a sourcebook. N.Y. : Garland, 1985. 279 p. (Garland reference library of social science, v. 208).   **EH403**

An annotated bibliographic guide to about 500 English-language publications including audiovisuals, periodicals, reports, databases, statistical sources, and reference works published 1970–84. Also serves as a directory to government agencies, special interest groups, and private associations interested in this area. Provides text of the 1970 Occupational Safety and Health Act, as well as some relevant reprints. Indexed.   Z6675.I5P39

Bibliography

EPISOURCE : a guide to resources in epidemiology / ed. by Roger H. Bernier and Virginia M. Mason. Roswell, Ga. : Epidemiology Monitor, [c1991]. 1100 p.   **EH404**

A compilation of information sources, organized alphabetically by subject in 30 different categories, on individual products and services of interest to epidemiologists. International in scope, with English-language listings regardless of country of origin, but most sources are from the U.S. Includes reprints of selected items from *The epidemiology monitor.* No general index; coded index on back cover. Future editions are planned.

Rice, Mitchell F. Health of black Americans from post reconstruction to integration, 1871–1960 : an annotated bibliography of contemporary sources / comp. by Mitchell F. Rice and Woodrow Jones, Jr. N.Y. : Greenwood, 1990. 206 p. (Bibliographies and indexes in Afro-American and African studies, no. 26).   **EH405**

A comprehensive annotated bibliography of the literature on "the condition of blacks [including] … patterns of mortality, morbidity and utilization behaviors of blacks from slavery to the mid-20th century … " that aims to provide "a fuller understanding of the history of health care inequities in the U.S."—*Introd.* In three chapters: 1871–1919, 1920–50, 1951–60. Entries give full bibliographic information, and there are subject and author indexes.

§ A companion volume by the same compilers, *Black American health: an annotated bibliography* (N.Y. : Greenwood, 1987) treats the literature of the 1970s and 1980s.   RA448.5.N4R52

Walsh, Jim. Vital and health statistics series : an annotated checklist and index to the publications of the "rainbow series" / comp. by Jim Walsh and A. James Bothmer. N.Y. : Greenwood, 1991. 388 p. (Bibliographies and indexes in medical studies, no. 7).   **EH406**

The first report of U.S. National Health Survey (1958) in four series, A–D, and first report of the National Center for Health Statistics (1963) together with 18 additional series issued by the Center over the last 28 years, make up what medical librarians call the "Rainbow series." This index "lists, annotates, and indexes all the reports ... published from 1958 through March 1991."—*User guide.* Organized by series in numerical order. Author, title, and subject indexes.

Z7165.U5W27

World Health Organization. Publications of the World Health Organization. 1947/57– . Geneva : The Organization, 1957– . Quinquennial.   **EH407**
Title varies.
"Provides bibliographic and descriptive information for over 500 books published ...from 1986 to March 1990."—*Introd.* Also lists selected older titles, Includes titles published by WHO (Geneva), regional offices, and the International Agency for Research on Cancer (IARC). 50 subject categories, with entries listed alphabetically in each category.   Z6660.W57

Indexes; Abstract journals

Abstracts on hygiene and communicable diseases. v. 56 (1981)– . London : Bureau of Hygiene and Tropical Diseases, [1981]– . Monthly.   **EH408**
Continues: *Bulletin of hygiene* (v. 1 [1926]–v. 42 [1967]) and *Abstracts of hygiene* (v. 43 [1968]–v. 55 [1980]), assuming their volume numbering.
Selective and critical abstracts and reviews of world literature prepared by specialists on various aspects of community and environmental health, hygiene, and communicable diseases. Annual author and subject indexes.   RA421.L618

Encyclopedias

Encyclopaedia of occupational health and safety / technical ed., Luigi Parmeggiani. 3rd rev. ed. Geneva : International Labour Office, 1983. 2 v. : ill.   **EH409**
1st ed., 1930, had title: *Occupation and health*; 2nd ed., 1971–72. Sometimes cited as *ILO encyclopaedia of occupational health and safety.*
Consists of more than 1,000 signed articles with recent bibliographic references by international specialists. This latest edition has about 200 new articles on aspects of toxicology, occupational cancer, diseases of migrant workers, and institutions active in the field of occupational health. Most articles stress preventive safety and health measures. Appendixes; index.   RC963.3.E53

Dictionaries

A dictionary of epidemiology / ed. for the International Epidemiological Association by John M. Last. 2nd ed. N.Y. : Oxford Univ. Pr., 1988. 141 p. : ill.   **EH410**
1st ed., 1983.
Has a broad range of coverage including biostatistics, community and public health, demography, and microbiology. Definitions range from one word to short essays that incorporate tables, graphs, charts, mathematical formulas, and diagrams. The more common terms are defined with cross-references from their synonyms.   RA651.D53

Directories

National directory of drug abuse and alcoholism treatment and prevention programs. Rockville, Md. : Public Health Service, Substance Abuse and Mental Health Services Administration, [1993]. 523 p. (DHHS publication, no. [ADM] 89–1603).   **EH411**
Previous editions published at intervals.
Early eds. had title: *National directory of drug abuse and alcoholism treatment programs*. Name of issuing agency varies.
The directory is a source of information for treatment and prevention services in alcoholism and drug abuse. Arrangement is by state and city. Each entry gives address and telephone number and indicates the nature of the service program. A separate section lists Veterans Administration facilities and services by state.   HV5825.N323

National health directory. 1st ed. (1977)– . Gaithersburg, MD : Aspen Systems Corp., 1977– . Annual.   **EH412**
Imprint varies.
Ed., 1977– , John T. Grupenhoff.
"Contains the names, titles, addresses and telephone numbers of more than 11,500 key information sources on health programs and legislation."—*Pref.* Includes listings of key staff of standing committees and subcommittees of Congress and of state legislative committees that deal with health-related issues and legislation, and of officials of state, city and county health agencies; congressional district maps; organizational charts for agencies.   RA7.5.N37

Handbooks

Grad, Frank P. Public health law manual : a handbook on the legal aspects of public health administration and enforcement. 2nd ed. Wash. : American Public Health Assoc., 1990. 337 p.   **EH413**
Prep. under the joint sponsorship of the U.S. Public Health Service and the American Public Health Assoc.
1st ed., 1965, had title: *Public health manual : a handbook on the legal aspects of public health administration and enforcement.*
Intended for use by health officers and other public health administrators in planning, developing, and implementing public health programs. Deals with basic legal procedures in public health enforcement—restrictions of persons; permits, licenses, and registration; searches and inspections; embargo, seizure, etc.—and with legal administrative techniques of public health administration.

KF3775.Z9G7

Health care state rankings. 1st ed. (1993)– . Lawrence, Kan. : Morgan Quitno Corp., c1993– . Annual.   **EH414**
Data derived from federal and state government sources, and from professional and private organizations, are presented in tabular form. Tables are arranged in seven categories: Birth and reproductive health; Deaths; Facilities (hospitals, nursing homes, etc.); Finance; Incidence of disease; Personnel; Physical fitness. Index.

RA407.3.H423

Health information for international travel. 1974– . Atlanta, Ga. : Center for Disease Control : For sale by the U.S. Govt. Print. Off., [1974]– . Annual.   **EH415**
First published 1952. Title varies; issuing agency's name varies.
Provides up-to-date and comprehensive information on immunization requirements and recommendations for international travelers.

RA783.5.C45a

Roemer, Milton Irwin. National health systems of the world. N.Y. : Oxford Univ. Pr., 1991–1993. 2 v.   **EH416**

Vol. 1 consists of a comparative study and analysis of national health systems in 68 industrialized, middle-income, and very poor countries. Vol. 2 contains a cross-national analysis of the major health care issues within different systems.   RA393.R593

History

Rosen, George. A history of public health. Expanded ed. Baltimore : Johns Hopkins Univ. Pr., c1993. 535 p.   **EH417**
1st ed., 1958.
An eight-part history of public health from earliest times to the present. Includes: bibliography; list of memorable figures with brief biographical sketches; list of public health periodicals, arranged by country; list of worldwide public health societies and schools. Subject and author indexes.   RA424.R65

TOXICOLOGY

Guides

Wexler, Philip. Information resources in toxicology. 2nd ed. N.Y. : Elsevier, c1988. 510 p.   **EH418**
1st ed., 1982.
A basic, comprehensive guide to the major sources of information. Pt. 1 is devoted to U.S. resources, pt. 2 to international resources. Annotated entries are classified by subject and arranged by format (e.g., books, special documents, and journal articles). There is a section on governmental and nongovernmental organizations. Includes a brief history of toxicology. Indexed.   RA1193.4.W49

Bibliography

Toxic and hazardous materials : a sourcebook and guide to information sources / ed. by James K. Webster. N.Y. : Greenwood, 1987. 431 p. (Bibliographies and indexes in science and technology, no. 2).   **EH419**
"Interdisciplinary in scope and content. [12] chapters cover every aspect of the subject—from technical and engineering topics to legal matters to public policy concerns."—*Pref.* Chapter 1, "General sources of information," may be of special interest to librarians. Most material published 1980 onward. Index.   Z7914.S17T69

Indexes; Abstract journals

Pesticides abstracts. v.7, no.1 (Jan. 1974)– . [Wash. : U.S. Environmental Protection Agency, Off. of Pesticide Programs, Technical Service Div.], 1974– . Monthly, with annual index.   **EH420**
Continues: *Health aspects of pesticides : abstract bulletin* (1968–73).
Classed arrangement with author and subject indexes. Listings are drawn from more than 1,000 domestic and foreign journals.   RA1270.P4H4

•**TOXLINE** [database]. Bethesda, Md. : U.S. National Library of Medicine, Toxicology Information Program, 1965– .   **EH421**
Available online and on CD-ROM, updated monthly, and as part of *Pollution/toxicology CD-ROM.*

Provides information on the adverse effects of drugs and other chemicals. Composed of a number of subfiles with varying dates of coverage, most of which are also available individually in printed or machine-readable form: e.g., *Environmental mutagen information center file (EMIC), Environmental teratology information center file (ETIC), Pesticides abstracts* (1968–81), *Toxicity bibliography.* Almost all bibliographic records include abstracts, as well as CAS Registry Numbers.

Encyclopedias

Hodgson, Ernest. Dictionary of toxicology / Ernest Hodgson, Richard B. Mailman, Janice E. Chambers. N.Y. : Van Nostrand Reinhold, c1988. 395 p. : ill.   **EH422**
Designed as an introduction to the field for students and for scientists in other disciplines. Most entries relate directly to toxicology, but others provide background information that might be needed by toxicologists. Bibliography.   RA1211.H69

Handbooks

Dreisbach, Robert Hastings. Handbook of poisoning : prevention, diagnosis & treatment / Robert H. Dreisbach, William O. Robertson. 12th ed. Norwalk, Conn. : Appleton & Lange, 1987. 589 p. : ill.   **EH423**
1st ed., 1955; 11th ed., 1983.
Contents: 1, General considerations; 2, Agricultural poisons; 3, Industrial hazards; 4, Household hazards—cosmetics, food poisoning, miscellaneous chemicals; 5, Medicinal poisons; 6, Animal and plant hazards—reptiles, arachnids & insects, marine animals, plants.
Provides a "concise summary of the diagnosis and treatment of poisoning ... . Contains listings of more extensive sources of information about poisons, as well as selected references for specific poisons." *Pref.*   RA1211.D7

Gosselin, Robert E. Clinical toxicology of commercial products / Robert E. Gosselin, Roger P. Smith, Harold C. Hodge with the assistance of Jeanette E. Braddock. 5th ed. Baltimore, Md. : Williams & Wilkins, [1984]. 1 v., various pagings. : ill.   **EH424**
1st ed., 1957; 4th ed., 1976.
Intends "to assist the physician in dealing quickly and effectively with acute chemical poisonings, arising through misuse of commercial products. The book provides (a) a list of trade name products together with their ingredients, (b) addresses and telephone numbers of companies for use when descriptions are not available, (c) sample formulas of many types of products with an estimate of the toxicity of each formula, (d) toxicological information including an appraisal of toxicity of individual ingredients, (e) recommendations for treatment and supportive care. ... Over the years a second purpose of this reference manual has received increasing emphasis, namely to acquaint therapists and others with the pathophysiological mechanisms, induced by various poisons, insofar as they are understood." —*Pref.* Includes citations to sources of original toxicological information and references to medical and toxicological literature.   RA1211.G5

Handbook of toxicologic pathology / ed. by Wanda M. Haschek, Colin G. Rousseaux. San Diego, Calif. : Academic Pr., c1991. 1080 p. : ill.   **EH425**
In 26 chapters, this comprehensive text "deals systematically with organ-specific injury ... and evaluation of this injury."—*Pref.* A "repeatable generic outline" is used to structure chapters on the different organ systems (e.g., immune, nervous, endocrine). Includes chapters on the fetus and the effects of radiation and heat.   RA1199.4.A54H36

Plunkett, E. R. Handbook of industrial toxicology. 3rd ed. N.Y. : Chemical Publ. Co., c1987. 605 p.   **EH426**

1st ed., 1966; 2nd ed., 1976.

Intended as a "practical, quick reference guide for those who are actively involved in protecting the health of the worker."—*Pref.* Lists substances in alphabetical order under most common name, giving for each: synonyms, description, occupational exposure, threshold limit value, toxicity (route of entry, mode of action, signs and symptoms, diagnostic tests, treatment and disability), and preventive measures. Includes bibliography and subject index.   RA1229.P55

Sittig, Marshall. Handbook of toxic and hazardous chemicals and carcinogens. 3rd ed. Park Ridge, N.J. : Noyes Publ., 1991. 2 v. (1685 p.).   **EH427**

1st ed., 1981, had title: *Handbook of toxic and hazardous chemicals*; 2nd ed., 1985.

Presents concise chemical and safety information, giving for each substance: code number; DOT designation; synonyms; potential exposure; incompatibilities; permissible exposure limits and determination in water; routes of entry, harmful effects, symptoms, points of attack, medical surveillance, first aid, personal protective methods, and respirator selection; disposal method suggested; and references for, about, and to sources of more information.   RA1193.S58

Toxics A to Z : a guide to everyday pollution hazards / John Harte ... [et al.]. Berkeley : Univ. of California Pr., c1991. 479 p. : ill.   **EH428**

"This book originated with the conviction that people need reliable and easily understandable information about the most frequently encountered toxic dangers."—*Pref.* Toxins are included based on widespread exposure at levels known or suspected to be harmful, or because they are known to damage the environment. In two major sections: pt. 1 covers general issues, while pt. 2 contains specific information about individual toxins, arranged alphabetically. Entries include references. Glossary; lists of national hotlines; sources for home testing equipment; suggested further readings. Subject index.

RA1213.T76

EJ

Agricultural Sciences

AGRICULTURE

Guides

Guide to sources for agricultural and biological research / ed. by J. Richard Blanchard and Lois Farrell. Berkeley ; Los Angeles : Univ. of California Pr., [1981]. 735 p.   **EJ1**

"Sponsored by the United States Agricultural Library, United States Department of Agriculture, Beltsville, Maryland."—*t.p.*

An updating of Blanchard and Harold Ostvold's *Literature of agricultural research*, 1958.

Contents: (A) Agriculture and biology: general; (B) Plant sciences; (C) Crop protection; (D) Animal sciences; (E) Physical sciences; (F) Food science and nutrition; (G) Environmental sciences; (H) Social sciences; (I) Computerized data bases for bibliographic research.

"The purpose of this work is to describe and evaluate important sources of information for the fields of agriculture and biology with the major emphasis on agriculture with related subjects."—*Pref.* A guide to 5,700 sources organized by subject with subheadings by form. Almost all entries are annotated. An exceptional, indispensable guide.

Z5071.G83

Information sources in agriculture and food science / ed., G. P. Lilley. London ; Boston : Butterworths, 1981. 603 p.   **EJ2**

In two parts: (1) general topics (e.g., use of libraries, general abstracts and indexes, computerized bibliographic sources, statistical sources); (2) more specialized areas (food sciences, soils, farming, animal production, veterinary science). 18 contributors including the editor. Indexed. A new edition is in preparation.   S494.5.I47I53

The literature of agricultural engineering / ed. by Carl W. Hall and Wallace C. Olsen. Ithaca : Cornell Univ. Pr., 1992. 416 p. : ill.   **EJ3**

"Lists, analyzes, and summarizes the books and journals that have made important contributions to the evolution of the subject."—*Pref.* Includes the following lists; update of reference sources; recently initiated journals; historically important monographs, 1850–1950; core scholarly and professional journals; U.S. and Canadian trade and popular periodicals, 1850–1950; non-English historical monographs, 1850–1950; journals and annuals recorded from the source documents (590 titles, 497 cited only once).   S674.3.L58

The literature of soil science / ed. by Peter McDonald. Ithaca, N.Y. : Cornell Univ. Pr., 1994. 448 p.   **EJ4**

Contains qualitative and quantitative analysis of the literature as well as lists of core journals and monographs including: core list of 927 soils monographs; core journals and serials in soil science; recently started serials in soil science, 1983– ; catalog of major soil maps; reference sources update in soil science; core historical English language scholarly journals in soil science, 1850–1950; and core historical monograph lists, 1850–1950.   S590.45.L58

Morgan, Bryan. Keyguide to information sources in agricultural engineering. London ; N.Y. : Mansell, 1985. 209 p.   **EJ5**

In three parts: a survey of agricultural engineering and its literature, an annotated bibliography of sources of information, and organizational sources of information. International in scope; emphasis is on U.K. publications. Cross-references; index.   Z5074.E6M67

Olsen, Wallace C. Agricultural economics and rural sociology : the contemporary core literature / Wallace C. Olsen ; with contributions by Margot A. Bellamy and Bernard F. Stanton. Ithaca, N.Y. : Cornell Univ. Pr., 1991. 346 p.   **EJ6**

Aims to "provide assistance to persons engaged in several areas of library and literature collection management."—*Pref.* Contains qualitative and quantitative analysis of the literature as well as lists of core journals and monographs including: currently published core journals; primary numbered report series; core list of monographs for developed countries, 1950–88 (1,420 titles); core list of monographs for third world, 1950–88 (1,002 titles); monographs appearing in both monographs lists (543 titles); historically significant monographs; and the American Agricultural Economics Association "Classic books" list.   HD1415.O47

Turnbull, Deborah A. Keyguide to information sources in aquaculture. London ; N.Y. : Mansell, 1989. 137 p.   **EJ7**

"Collection of what are considered to be key references, databases, and organizations in aquaculture ... [citations provide information] on the type or resource, type of information it offers, and, by means of the source and organization directories, how to obtain it."—*Introd.* Contains an overview of aquaculture and its literature, annotated bibliographies of major reference sources including journals, newsletters, and databases, and descriptions of aquaculture libraries and organizations worldwide. Indexed.   Z5970.T87

United Nations. ACCIS guide to United Nations information sources on food and agriculture / comp. by the Advisory Committee for the Co-ordination of Information Systems (ACCIS). Rome : Food and Agriculture Organization of the United Nations, 1987. 124 p. (ACCIS guides to United Nations information sources, no. 1).   **EJ8**

Aims "to expand the existing Directory of United Nations Databases and Information Systems, by treating agricultural information sources in particular …. [Includes] specialised units, libraries, documentation centres, databases and publications. Over 120 sources are included from all organisations … that carry out activities in the areas of food and agriculture."—*Pref.* Sources are listed under the following topics: food and agriculture in general, plant production and protection, animal production and health, food and nutrition, land and water development and natural resources, economic and social development, trade and commodities, agro-industries and industrial development, fisheries and aquaculture, and statistics. Annexes include addresses of international organizations, addresses of database hosts, and national contact addresses. Contains indexes by subject, name of organization, publications, and systems of databases.   S494.5.I47U55

Bibliography

National Agricultural Library (U.S.). National Agricultural Library catalog. v.1 (Jan. 1966)–20 (1985). Totowa, N.J. : Rowman & Littlefield, 1966–1985. Monthly.   **EJ9**

Published as a supplement to *Dictionary catalog of the National Agricultural Library* (EJ13), to keep specialists and librarians informed of additions to the collection. By the time of cessation, monthly issues contained: the list of main entries organized by broad subject categories; indexes by specific subject headings, personal authors, corporate authors, and titles (indexes cumulated in June and December); and an alphabetical list of translations added to the collection during the previous month (also listed by category in the main entry section).

A quinquennial cumulation for 1966-70 appeared in 1973 in 4 v. (a names and subjects catalog like the work it supplements); v. 4 includes a cumulation of the translations sections. A cumulative index for 1971-75 appeared in 1978 in 2 v. (v.1, personal author, corporate author, and title index; v.2, subject index).

Periodicals

International union list of agricultural serials. Wallingford, U.K. : CAB International, c1990. 767 p.   **EJ10**

"Compilation of serials indexed in *AGRICOLA* [EJ14], *AGRIS* [EJ16 *note*], and *CAB abstracts* [EJ18] …. Gives details of 11,567 publications coming from 129 different countries, with titles in 53 languages."—*Foreword.* "The bibliographic data have been compiled from … the cataloging master file of serial records maintained by NAL … downloaded from OCLC … and manually input from data received from … CABI … and FAO … [It] shows only [records] relating to titles currently being indexed by CABI, FAO or NAL in 1988."—*Reader's guide.* Entries include language code for country of publication, ISSN, frequency, NAL call number (if held by NAL), one or more subject codes as used in *AGRICOLA*, and whether indexed in *AGRICOLA*, *AGRIS*, or *CAB abstracts*. Includes key to country codes, subject code index, and subject and country indexes.   Z5076

List of journals indexed in AGRICOLA. 1989– . [Beltsville, Md.] : U.S. National Agricultural Library, Technical Services Division, 1989– . Annual.   **EJ11**

The list represents the titles indexed for *AGRICOLA*. The main section is arranged alphabetically by full title and includes abbreviated index, NAL call number, ISSN number, place of publication and publisher, whether records in *AGRICOLA* contain abstracts, and if the indexing is cover-to-cover or selective. Includes abbreviated title list (most useful to identify citations from *Bibliography of agriculture*, EJ17, or *AGRICOLA*, EJ14), subject category list, and list of journals abstracted in *AGRICOLA*.   S493.L57

National Agricultural Library (U.S.). Serials currently received by the National Agricultural Library, 1975 : a keyword index. Beltsville, Md. : U.S. National Agricultural Library ; Wash. : for sale by U.S. Govt. Print. Off., 1976. 1333 p.   **EJ12**

Superintendent of Documents classification: A 17.18/2:Se6/975.

Includes "approximately 19,000 serials … defined as those for which the library has received at least one issue since January 1971."—*Introd.* In keyword-out-of-context (KWOC) format. Includes NAL's call number.   Z5073.U58

Library catalogs

National Agricultural Library (U.S.). Dictionary catalog of the National Agricultural Library, 1862–1965. N.Y. : Rowman and Littlefield, 1967–70. 73 v.   **EJ13**

Reproduces the main entry and subject listing for monographs, serials, and analytics for the works cataloged for the main collection of the National Agriculture Library and its Bee Culture and Beltsville branches. More than 1.5 million entries. Vol. 73 lists translations of articles.

Kept up-to-date by: *National Agricultural Library catalog* (EJ9).   Z5076.U63

Indexes; Abstract journals

•**AGRICOLA** : (AGRICultural OnLine Access) [database]. Beltsville, Md. : U.S. National Agricultural Library, 1970– .   **EJ14**

Available online, in CD-ROM, and on magnetic tape. Updated monthly.

Covers journal articles, monographs, reports, patents, dissertations, pamphlets, audiovisuals, software, and other materials. Includes publications by the U.S. Dept. of Agriculture, state agricultural experiment stations, cooperative extension services, land grant universities, the Food and Agricultural Organization of the U.N., and other government and international agencies. Books and other monographic materials are assigned LC subject headings. Since Jan. 1985, journal articles, monographs in series, chapters in books, and other documents are indexed using the *CAB thesaurus* (EJ36). The serials indexed are listed in *International union list of agricultural serials* (EJ10). Includes abstracts for approximately 400 publications as well as the documents input by the Food and Nutrition Information Center (FNIC).

Agricultural index : subject index to a selected list of agricultural periodicals and bulletins. v. 1 (1916/18)–18 (1962/64). N.Y. : H.W. Wilson, 1919–64.   **EJ15**

Published annually; cumulated triennially, 1916/18–1951/54, biennially, 1954/56–1962/64.

A detailed, alphabetical subject index to agricultural and related periodicals and to many reports, bulletins, and circulars of agricultural departments, experiment stations, etc. Most of the periodicals are in English, including American, British, and colonial publications, but a few journals in foreign languages are included.

Continued as *Biological & agricultural index* (EG10).   Z5073.A46

Agrindex. v. 1 (1975)– . [Rome] : AGRIS Coordinating Centre, 1975– .   **EJ16**

Available in separate English, French, and Spanish editions since January 1987.

Deals "with all fields of agriculture: plant and animal production, agricultural economics, rural development, forestry, fisheries, food and human nutrition, and auxiliary sciences when related to agriculture."—*How to consult Agrindex.* Covers journal articles, books, patents, maps, graphic charts, films, computer media, etc. Citations are contributed by 143 national centers (including the National Agricultural Library for the U. S.), 16 international centers, and eight regional centers, two of which contribute for nine countries that do not directly participate. Organized in three main sections. The introduction includes the list of participating centers, table of country and institution codes, table of language codes, AGLINET library network, and key to subdivisions within subject categories. The main entry section contains bibliographic references arranged by the subject categories listed in the table of contents and further organized by numeric code of geographic terms or commodities; entries include English title and complete bibliographic information, availability, AGROVOC descriptors, and abstracts if provided by report and patent number, and subject arranged alphabetically by AGROVOC descriptor.

•Machine-readable version: *International information system for the agricultural sciences and technology (AGRIS)* [database] (Rome : FAO, 1975–). Available online and on CD-ROM, updated monthly.

Z5073.A485

Bibliography of agriculture. v.1 (1942)– . Phoenix : Oryx, 1942– . Monthly with cumulated annual indexes.   **EJ17**

Subtitle: Data provided by National Agricultural Library, U.S. Department of Agriculture.

Publisher, title, and format vary.

A major index to agriculture and allied sciences. Compiled from the *AGRICOLA* database (EJ14). Since 1985, includes cataloging records previously published in *National Agricultural Library catalog* (EJ9). Since 1988, includes records provided by the National Agricultural Library Food and Nutrition Information Center which were previously published (including abstracts), in *Food and nutrition quarterly index* (Phoenix : Oryx, 1985–). Abstracts for these records and records from approximately 400 indexed materials are only available in AGRICOLA.

Sources covered include journal articles (about 2,000 titles are scanned yearly), pamphlets, government documents, special reports, proceedings, books, new serials, theses, patents, software, audiovisuals, and other materials. Current issues are divided into nine sections. The principal main entry section includes 20 main topics, each divided into subtopics. Another five sections list publications of the U.S. Department of Agriculture, the state agricultural experiment stations, the state agricultural extension services, the FAO, and translations; these entries are also included in the main entry section and are indexed from it. The last three sections are indexes: corporate author, personal author, and subject, all cumulated annually. Beginning 1985, subject index terms are derived from *CAB thesaurus* (EJ36).

Two supplements index literature not previously indexed: *1983 supplement* (Phoenix : Oryx, [1984]. 2 v. [3603 p.]), and *Transitional supplement 1985* (Phoenix : Oryx, [1985]. 2 v. [4625 p.]). A *Retrospective cumulation on microfiche, 1970–1978*, a full cumulation of citations and indexing on 458 microfiche (48x), was produced by Oryx in 1980.   Z5073.U55

•**CAB abstracts** [database]. Wallingford, Eng. : C.A.B. International, 1973– .   **EJ18**

Provides worldwide coverage of about 10,000 agricultural journals and monographs; contains all abstracts included in the abstracting journals published by CAB International. Available online and on CD-ROM, updated monthly. Indexed, like *AGRICOLA* (EJ14), using *CAB thesaurus* (EJ36). The serials indexed are listed in *International union list of agricultural serials* (EJ10).

C.A.B. International is producing CD-ROM databases that constitute subsets of *CAB abstracts*. *VETCD* contains 300,000 records and includes citations and abstracts from *Index veterinarius* (EJ103) and *Veterinary bulletin* (EJ105), 1972 to the present. *BEASTCD* compliments *VETCD* but covers the production side of animal science for the same period (e.g, *Animal breeding abstracts*, EJ102). *TREECD* includes *Forestry abstracts* (EJ175) from 1939 to the present as well as *Forest products abstracts* (1978–) and *Agroforestry abstracts* (1988–). *AGECONCD* covers economic and social aspects of agriculture, forestry, food, natural environment, rural development in developing countries; *CABPESTCD* covers crop protection; *CROPCD* covers field and forage crops and grasslands; *E-CD* covers environmental

degradation and conservation; *HORTCD* covrs horticulture' *PLANTGENECD* covers plant breeding, genetic resources, and biotechnology; and *SOILCD* covers soils, fertilizers, and land management. These CDs are updated annually.

CAB International. [Abstract journals]. Wallingford, Oxon, England : CAB International.   **EJ19**

Imprints vary.

Compiled from *CAB abstracts* (EJ18).

CAB International (formerly the Commonwealth Agricultural Bureaux), an international intergovernmental organization owned by 30 member governments, provides information for agriculture and allied disciplines, and publishes 24 main abstract journals (listed below), specialized abstract journals, and other printed and electronic products.

Together, the main abstract journals cover all aspects of the agricultural sciences and related areas of applied biology. Since 1984, all are indexed using *CAB thesaurus* (EJ36); before 1984, each publication used its own indexing system. As noted, some titles are treated elsewhere in the present *Guide.*

Agricultural engineering abstracts (1976–); *Animal breeding abstracts* (1933– . EJ102); *Dairy science abstracts* (1939–); *Field crop abstracts* (1948–); *Forest product abstracts* (1978–); *Forestry abstracts* (1939– . EJ175); *Grasslands and forage abstracts* (1931–); *Helminthological abstracts* (1939–); *Horticultural abstracts* (1931– . EJ230); *Index veterinarius* (1933– . EJ103); *Leisure, recreation and tourism abstracts* (1976–); *Nematological abstracts* (1939–); *Nutrition abstracts and reviews, A: Human and experimental* (1931– . *see* EH295); *Nutrition abstracts and reviews, B: Livestock feeds and feedings* (1931– . *see* EJ104); *Plant breeding abstracts* (1930–); *Review of agricultural entomology* (1990– . Formerly *Review of applied entomology : Series A: Agricultural; see* EG337); *Review of medical and veterinary entomology* (1990– . Formerly *Review of applied entomology : Series B: Medical and veterinary; see* EG337); *Review of medical and veterinary mycology* (1943–); *Review of plant pathology* (1922–); *Rural development abstracts* (1978–); *Soils and fertilizers abstracts* (1937–); *Veterinary bulletin* (1931– . EJ105); *Weed abstracts* (1952–); *World agricultural economics and rural sociology abstracts* (1959– . CH46).

CAB International also publishes a number of specialized abstract journals that treat such subjects as: crop physiology, irrigation and drainage, maize, ornamental horticulture, plant genetic resources, potatoes, poultry, seed, sugar industry, soybeans, and wheat, barley, and triticale. Other specialized journals contain news items and review papers: *Agbiotech news and information, Biocontrol news and information, Pig news and information,* and *Postharvest news and information.*

•CAB International abstract journals are available online, on CD-ROM, and on diskettes; see: *CAB abstracts* [database] (EJ18).

FAO documentation : Current bibliography = Documentation de la FAO. Bibliographie courante = Documentación de la FAO. Bibliografia corriente. 1972– . Rome : Food and Agriculture Organization of the United Nations, 1972– . Monthly with annual indexes.   **EJ20**

Title and frequency vary.

Continues: *FAO documentation. Current index,* 1967–71.

"Multilingual list of selected documents and publications produced by or on behalf of the Food and Agricultural Organization."— *Introd.* The main section, arranged by accession number, includes titles in the original language, complete bibliographic information, language code, index terms, and accession numbers of other language versions. Includes several indexes: author, subject and geographic (in English, French, and Spanish), project, and AGRIS/CARIS subject categories. Cumulations on COM microfiche are available from the David Lubin Memorial Library, FAO, which also supplies the full text of all documents listed in microfiche on a subscription basis.

Z5073.F2

Encyclopedias

The encyclopedia of natural insect & disease control : the most comprehensive guide to protecting plants—vegetables, fruits, flowers, trees, and lawns—without toxic chemicals / ed. by Roger B. Yepsen. Emmaus, Pa. : Rodale Pr., c1984. 490 p.   **EJ21**

Revised ed. of: *Organic plant protection*, 1976.

"[A] guide, arranged in encyclopedic form, to protecting plants from bugs, diseases, and the environment at large. It is addressed to gardeners, small-scale orchardists, and homeowners who wish to avoid using chemical toxins."—*Introd.* Includes appendix of insecticidal plants and detailed index.   SB974.E53

The encyclopedia of soil science / ed. by Rhodes W. Fairbridge and Charles W. Finkl, Jr. Stroudsburg, Pa. : Dowden, Hutchinson & Ross, 1979. Pt. 1. (Encyclopedia of earth sciences, v. 12).   **EJ22**

Contents: Pt. 1, Physics, chemistry, biology, fertility, and technology.

"Gives a comprehensive, alphabetical treatment of basic soil science."—*Pref.* The preface includes a list of texts and reference books, and a list of serial publications. Each entry includes references. Subject and author indexes.   S592.E52

McGraw-Hill encyclopedia of food, agriculture & nutrition / Daniel N. Lapedes, ed. in chief. N.Y. : McGraw-Hill, c1977. 732 p.   **EJ23**

"Designed to inform ... about all aspects of agriculture; the cultivation, harvesting, and processing of food crops; food manufacturing; and health and nutrition from the economic and political to the technological."—*Pref.* In two parts, the first containing five feature articles, the second 400 alphabetically arranged signed articles, cross-referenced and including further references. Some articles have been drawn from *McGraw-Hill encyclopedia of science & technology* (4th ed., 1977; *see* EA81) Compositions of selected foods are listed in an appendix. Indexed.   TX349.M2

Dictionaries

Dalal-Clayton, D. B. Black's agricultural dictionary. 2nd ed. London : A. & C. Black, 1985. 432 p. : ill.   **EJ24**

1st ed., 1981.

"Not only is the dictionary a complete coverage of the numerous terms used by farmers and agricultural scientists, but eighteen pages are devoted towards listing, and explaining, several hundred important abbreviations, acronyms and initials."—*Foreword.* "In this edition the facts have been updated and many entries have been expanded."—*Pref., 2nd ed.* Especially good for unusual British terms (e.g., "Batology, the study of brambles"). Many cross-references; British spelling.   S411.D245

Elsevier's dictionary of aquaculture : in six languages, English, French, Spanish, German, Italian, and Latin / comp. by Cheryl E. Marx. Amsterdam ; N.Y. : Elsevier, 1991. 454 p.   **EJ25**

Lists 4,553 terms in alphabetical order on English base with indexes in Latin, French, Spanish, German, and Italian.   SH201.E46

Elsevier's dictionary of soil mechanics in four languages : English/American, French, Dutch, and German / comp. and arr. by A. D. Visser. Amsterdam ; N.Y. : Elsevier, 1965. 359 p.   **EJ26**

English base with indexes from the other languages. More than 4,100 entries.   TA710.E45

English-Russian dictionary of agriculture / editors, V. G. Kozlovsky and N. G. Rakipov. Oxford ; N.Y. : Pergamon, 1985. 875 p.   **EJ27**

"Contains terminology on all aspects of agricultural science and agricultural production—agronomy, livestock rearing, the economics and organization of agricultural production, veterinary science, and the mechanisation and electrification of agriculture."—*Foreword.*   S411.E717

Fachwörterbuch : Landwirtschaft, Fortwirtschaft, Gartenbau : Deutsch-English, mit etwa 65,000 Wortstellen = Dictionary : agriculture, forestry, horticulture : German-English, with about 65,000 entries / ed. by Peter Mühle. Berlin : A. Hatier, c1993. 731 p.   **EJ28**

"Companion volume to the English-German edition previously published by Verlag Technik ... [Includes] the fundamental natural sciences ... names of species of useful plants and animals, beneficial animals and pests... farming terms ... relevant machinery and equipment, the vocabulary of animal husbandry and veterinary medicine ... forestry terms ... and the processing of agricultural produce, timber, etc."—*Pref.*   S411.F18

Haensch, Günther. Dictionary of agriculture : in six languages, German, English, French, Spanish, Italian, Russian : systematical and alphabetical / by Günther Haensch and Gisela Haberkamp de Anton. 5th completely rev. and enl. ed. Amsterdam ; N.Y. : Elsevier, 1986. 1264 p.   **EJ29**

1st ed., 1959, had title: *Wörterbuch der Landwirtschaft.*

The main part of the work lists terms in classified order on a German base, with consecutive numbering throughout. Alphabetical indexes in each language and of Latin names, refer by number to the classified section.   S411.H2613

Holliday, Paul. A dictionary of plant pathology. Cambridge ; N.Y. : Cambridge Univ. Pr., 1989. 369 p.   **EJ30**

Concerned with diseases of commercial crops, listing "the authoritative names of all important pathogens and many minor ones."—*Pref.* Besides definitions of terms, provides brief descriptions of each disease species, along with citations to major research papers. Common names of the diseases are listed under the name of the plant species they infect (e.g., "Cowpea chlorotic mottle"). Similarly, the plant species that each pathogen infects is listed beneath the pathogen name. Definitions of pathogen genera and species are very technical.   SB728.H65

Rakipov, N. G. Elsevier's dictionary of agriculture and food production : Russian-English / comp. by Nazib G. Rakipov and B. Geyer. Amsterdam ; N.Y. : Elsevier, 1994. 900 p.   **EJ31**

"Contains some 80,000 Russian terms and their English/American equivalents representing the modern level of knowledge in all fields of agriculture, agricultural science and food production."—*Pref.*   S411.R34

Schlebecker, John T. The many names of country people : an historical dictionary from the twelfth century onward. N.Y. : Greenwood, 1989. 325 p.   **EJ32**

"Dictionary... of the names of those country people... who are chiefly engaged in agricultural pursuits. All the names have been considered good English at some time or place."—*Pref.* Includes English, British, Canadian, Australian, New Zealander, South African, American, and West Indian names. Bibliography of dictionaries, linguistics, and history. Includes an index of all names.   S411.S34

Thesaurus of agricultural organisms, pests, weeds, and diseases / ed. by Derwent Publications Ltd., Literature Division with the assistance of CIBA-GEIGY SA. London ; N.Y. : Chapman and Hall, 1990. 2 v.   **EJ33**

An alphabetically arranged index with cross-references to the Latin names, keywords, and most frequently used synonyms and common names of weeds, pests and disease microorganisms. Includes also "extensive coverage of crop species ... a large number of non-target invertebrates, vertebrates, plants and microorganisms ... many of the organisms ... have been used or tested as biological control agents as well as crop species ... For each organism there is a MAIN ENTRY, consisting of an approved Latin name, followed by one or two HIGHER TAXA in parentheses."—*Pref.* Entries may also include Latin name synonyms and most frequently used common names in English, French, and German. Vol. 2 has a separate index of about 23,000 inverted species names (including main entries and synonyms).

Z695.1.A4T52

Williams, Gareth. Interdisciplinary dictionary of weed science : Dansk, Deutsch, English, Español, Français, Italiano, Nederlands, Portugues / ed. by G. H. Williams & W. van der Zweep. Wageningen [Netherlands] : Pudoc, 1990. 546 p.
EJ34

Contains 2,963 terms sequentially numbered on an English base and indexes in the other languages.　　　　SB611.W95

Thesauruses

Agricultural terms. 2nd ed. Phoenix : Oryx, 1978. 122 p.
EJ35

Subtitle: As used in the Bibliography of agriculture, from data provided by the National Agricultural Library, U.S. Department of Agriculture.

Lists about 37,000 terms. Useful for searching *Bibliography of agriculture* (EJ17) and *AGRICOLA* [database] (EJ14), 1978–84.

Z695.1.A4T54

CAB thesaurus. 1990 ed. Wallingford, U.K. : C.A.B. International, 1990. 2 v.　　　　　　　　　　　　　　**EJ36**

The basic source used in indexing the databases *AGRICOLA* (EJ14) and *CAB abstracts* (EJ18). Each entry is followed by a list, where appropriate, of nonpreferred, broader, narrower, and related terms. An excellent resource for those indexing agricultural literature; essential for those using *AGRICOLA* or *CAB abstracts*. Available both in printed form and on magnetic tape.　　　　Z699.5.A5T4

Commonwealth Agricultural Bureaux. CAB abstracts word list. Slough [Eng.] : Commonwealth Agricultural Bureaux, 1978. 120 p.　　　　　　　　　　　　　　　　　　**EJ37**

"A register of the principal terms used in the subject indexes of the CAB abstract journals and occurring in the descriptor field of the CAB ABSTRACTS database [EJ18]."—*Pref.* Indicates *see* and *see also* references. Useful for searching literature indexed between 1978 through 1983.　　　　　　　　　　　　　　Z695.1.A4C65

Organizational and biographical directories

Agricultural information resource centers : a world directory 1990 / Rita C. Fisher ... [et al.]. Urbana, Ill. : IAALD World Directory Working Group, 1990. 641 p.　　　**EJ38**

A directory of "3,971 information resource centers that have agriculture-related collections and/or information services. Agriculture is defined in the broadest sense ranging from production agriculture to basic research and including related sciences and social sciences."— *Introd.* Arranged by country, then by city and parent institution or, for Australia, Canada, U.S.S.R. and the U.S., by state, province, or Soviet Socialist Republic (SSR), then by city and parent institution. Indexes: country; city (for selected countries); institution (includes current, former, and variant names of the parent institutions); and subject. New edition scheduled for 1995.　　　　　　　S494.5.I47A47

Agricultural research centres : a world directory of organizations and programmes. 7th ed.– . Burnt Mill, Harlow, Essex, England : Longman ; Detroit : distr. by Gale, 1983– . Triennial.　　　　　　　　　　　　　　　　　**EJ39**

Subtitle: a world directory of organizations and programmes.

Continues: *Farming and mechanised agriculture*, 1st–4th eds. (1944/45–50); *Agricultural research index*, 5th–6th eds. (1970–78).

Issued in 2 v., 1983–88.

"Probably the most comprehensive listing of [agricultural] research and technology institutes worldwide .... [C]atalogues in excess of 5,000 laboratories or industrial companies active in all aspects of agricultural research including: agronomy, animal breeding & veterinary science, crop protection, environmental science, food technology, horticulture, natural resources, plant genetics."—*Introd. to 11th ed.* (1993). Arranged by country and then alphabetically in the language of the country. Entries indicate the size of the organization, major personnel, overview of research activities and programs, publications, and links with other organizations. Includes subject and organization indexes.　　　　　　　　　　　　　　　　　　S530.5.A33

Agriculture & veterinary sciences international who's who. 3rd ed. (1987)– . Harlow, Eng. : Longman ; Detroit : distr. by Gale, 1987– .　　　　　　　　　　　　　　　　**EJ40**

Continues: *Who's who in world agriculture*, 1979–85.

Subtitle: A biographical guide in the agricultural and veterinary sciences.

Issued in 2 pts.

"[P]rovides biographical details of about 7500 senior agricultural and veterinary scientists from over 100 countries ... Part one lists biographical profiles of scientists in alphabetical order of surname."— *Introd.* Pt. 2, country and subject index, lists the experts in each country for 13 subject areas: agricultural economics, agricultural engineering, animal production, botany, fisheries and aquaculture, food science and technology, forestry and forest products, horticulture, microbiology, oceanography, plant production, soil science, veterinary medicine, and zoology.

§ Companion volume to *Agricultural research centres* (EJ39).

S415.W48

Directory of American agriculture. v. 1 (1988)– . Wash. : Agricultural Resources & Communications, 1988– . Annual.
EJ41

Contains information on organizations, agencies, and others serving American agriculture. Contains two main sections (national and state organizations) and an appendix including U.S. Dept. of Agriculture agencies and state offices, state departments of agriculture, colleges of agriculture and land grant universities, farm credit system, commodity exchanges, farm broadcasters, farm networks, and agricultural information services. List of farm publications. Indexed.

Dyson, Lowell K. Farmers' organizations. Westport, Conn. : Greenwood, 1986. 383 p. (The Greenwood encyclopedia of American institutions, 10).　　　　　　　　　　　**EJ42**

Substantial histories of organizations of farm owners, tenants, and workers of the 19th and 20th centuries. Alphabetical arrangement; articles include bibliographies. Appendixes list organizations by state headquarters and provide names and dates of chief officers, as well as membership figures, for selected organizations. Index.　　HD1484.D97

Marti, Donald B. Historical directory of American agricultural fairs. N.Y. : Greenwood, 1986. 300 p.　　　　**EJ43**

"Surveys American fair history, describes 205 individual events, lists fairs ... in every state, briefly discusses sources of information and concludes with an index.—*Pref.* Events are included if announced for 1985. Descriptions include location, attendance, history, special attractions, address for further inquiry, and sources used for the entry.

S554.M37

U.S. agricultural groups : institutional profiles / ed. by William P. Browne and Allan J. Cigler. N.Y. : Greenwood, 1990. 274 p.　　　　　　　　　　　　　　　　　　**EJ44**

Intended "as a reference guide for those interested in the role of agricultural interests in American national politics"; provides "profiles of over 100 private organizations that are most likely to gain the greatest attention from those who observe, study, and participate in agriculture policy-making."—*Pref*. An additional list of about 100 major groups is provided as an appendix. Index to groups and persons mentioned in the text. HD9005.U19

World directory of pesticide control organisations / ed., George Ekstrom. Surrey, U.K. : British Crop Protection Council ; Cambridge, U.K. : Royal Society of Chemistry, Information Services, c1994. 423 p. : ill. **EJ45**

Contains directory information for 21 international organizations and programs (including name and relevant office addresses and contact numbers, aims/activities, and list of publications). Also includes for each of 158 countries, a list of responsible organizations involved in regulation and other activities concerning pesticides, Codex Alimetarius contact point, and Infoterra focal point (including name, address, telephone and fax numbers, and contact person if appropriate).

Handbooks

The agrochemicals handbook / [editors, Hamish Kidd and David R. James]. Cambridge, Eng. : Royal Society of Chemistry, c1991. 1 v. (loose-leaf) : ill. **EJ46**

"Consists principally of a large collection of individual datasheets on pesticide ingredient chemicals arranged in alphabetical order."—*p. 4*. Information includes chemical structure and chemical, physical, analytical, use, and toxicity data. Includes manufacturers' names and addresses, 15 biological activity lists, and chemical family, CAS Registry number, and names indexes.

•Machine-readable version: *Agrochemicals handbook* [database] (Cambridge : Royal Soc. of Chemistry, 1983–), available online, updated semiannually, and as part of *The pesticides disc* [database] (Cambridge : Royal Soc. of Chemistry), available on CD-ROM, current coverage updated semiannually.

CRC handbook of engineering in agriculture / ed., R. H. Brown. Boca Raton, Fla. : CRC Pr., 1988. 3 v. : ill. **EJ47**

Contents: v. 1, Crop production engineering; v. 2, Soil and water engineering; v. 3, Environmental systems engineering.

Each volume has its own index. S675.C73

CRC handbook of natural pesticides : methods / ed., N. Bhushan Mandava. Boca Raton, Fla. : CRC Pr., c1985–c1990. v. 1–5, pt. A; 6; in 7 : ill. **EJ48**

Contents: v. 1, Theory, practice, and detecting; v. 2, Isolation and identification; v. 3, Insect growth regulators (2 v.); v. 4, Pheromones (2 v.); v. 5, Microbial insecticides; pt. A: Entomogenous protozoa and fungi; v. 6, Insect attractants and repellents. SB951.145.N37C37

Crop protection chemicals reference : CPCR. 1st ed.– . N.Y. : Chemical and Pharmaceutical Pub. Corp., c1985– . **EJ49**

Contains the complete text of product labels arranged by manufacturer then brand name for about 500 products. Gives contents; patent number; EPA registry number; and safety, storage, and application information. Appendixes include general information on handling and storage of pesticides, storage and temperature requirements by product, DOT (Department of Transportation) information by product, and poison control centers and solid and hazardous waste agencies by state. Indexed by brand name, manufacturer, common and chemical name, product category, crop and non-crop use, and pest use. SB950.9.C76

Davidson, Ralph Howard. Insect pests of farm, garden, and orchard / Ralph H. Davidson, William F. Lyon. 8th ed. N.Y. : Wiley, c1987. 640 p. **EJ50**

Includes mites, spiders, snails, slugs, nematodes, symphylids, centipedes, millipedes, and sowbugs. Contains chapters on general en-

tomology (e.g., importance to humans; structure, physiology, and metamorphosis) followed by chapters on pests arranged by hosts. Descriptions of pests include references. Indexed. SB931.D38

Farm chemicals handbook. 1951– . [Willoughby, Ohio] : Meister Pub. Co., 1951?– . Annual. **EJ51**

Continues: *The American fertilizer handbook* (1908–50).

Main sections in the 1994 issue include: index listing alphabetically all products and services with cross-references; fertilizer dictionary; pesticide/biocontrol dictionary; regulatory file; environmental and safety; buyers guide; and company addresses. S633.A5

Handbook of pesticide toxicology / Wayland J. Hayes, Jr., Edward R. Laws, Jr., editors. San Diego, Calif. : Academic Pr., 1991. 3 v. **EJ52**

Contents: v. 1, General principles; v. 2–3, Classes of pesticides.

"The first volume … provides a detailed, fully documented overview of the general principles of toxicology, with special emphasis on [their] application … to pesticides. The second and third volumes provide a similar overview of the different classes of pesticides, with a separate section devoted to each of 256 compounds that have been studied in humans."—*Pref*. Indexed. RA1270.P4H36

Handbook of soils and climate in agriculture / ed. Victor J. Kilmer. Boca Raton, Fla. : CRC Pr., c1982. 445 p. **EJ53**

The aim is "to present in condensed form reliable information on soil science and climate as it relates to crop production."—*Pref*. Includes chapters on climate of the U.S. ; soil classifications; soil physics; soil chemistry; soil microbiology; soil organic matter; soil fertility, fertilizers, and plant nutrition; fertilizer sources and composition; lime, lime materials, and other soil amendments; soil and water management and conservation; and wind erosion. Each chapter contains a list of references. Glossary; index. S596.3.H36

Keys to soil taxonomy / by Soil Survey Staff, Agency for International Development, United States Department of Agriculture, Soil Management Support Services. 4th ed. Blacksburg, Va. : Virginia Polytechnic Institute and State Univ., 1990. 422 p. (SMSS technical monograph, no. 19). **EJ54**

"Provides the taxonomic keys required for the classification of a soil … and serves as a means of providing an up-to-date version of *Soil Taxonomy* [EJ63] that includes all revisions … that have been approved. It replaces the keys in *Soil Taxonomy*, but does not replace Agriculture handbook 436, which contains descriptive material, laboratory data, and chapters on other subjects."—*Foreword*. S592.16.K49

Lorenzi, Harri. Weeds of the United States and their control / Harri J. Lorenzi, Larry S. Jeffery. N.Y. : Van Nostrand Reinhold, c1987. 355 p., [34] p. of plates : ill. (some col.). **EJ55**

Describes and illustrates more than 300 plants. Each entry, on a separate page, provides the botanical description of a particular weed, describes its habitat, and suggests methods for its control. Each entry also includes a small-scale distribution map that gives a general indication where a specific weed may be found. Numbers preceding species name refer to illustrations in a color plates section. An introductory chapter describes weed identification and different kinds of weed control methods. Glossary of botanical terms; index. SB612.A2L67

Montgomery, John H. Agrochemicals desk reference : environmental data. Boca Raton, Fla. : Lewis Publ., c1993. 625 p. **EJ56**

"Designed to include, in one reference, all the information on widely used agrochemicals needed … in the protection and remediation of the groundwater environment … [B]ased on more than 740 references."—*Pref*. Contains data concerning more than 200 herbicides, insecticides, and fumigants commonly found in the groundwater environment. Includes EPA approved test methods and CAS, Registry of Toxic Effects of Chemical Substances (RTECS), empirical formula, and synonym indexes. TD428.A35.M66

MSDS reference for crop protection chemicals. MSDS 1st ed. (1988/89)– . N.Y. : Chemical and Pharmaceutical Pr., c1988– . Annual.   **EJ57**

Contains the complete text, supplied by the manufacturers, of the material safety data sheets of more than 500 products. Arranged by manufacturer, then brand name. Includes emergency phone number. Brand name cumulative index, manufacturer cumulative index, and common name index. Updated with bimonthly supplements.

SB952.5.M73

Nyvall, Robert F. Field crop diseases handbook. 2nd ed. N.Y. : Van Nostrand Reinhold, c1989. 817 p.   **EJ58**

"Includes information on approximately 1,200 diseases of 25 different plants."—*Pref.* For each plant, organizes diseases by causal organism (bacteria, fungi, mycoplasmas, nematoda, rickettsias, viroids, and viruses). Includes a bibliography with each chapter and a glossary. Index includes both common and scientific names of each disease.

SB731.N94

Official methods of analysis of the Association of Official Analytical Chemists. 11th ed. (1970)– . Wash. : The Association, c1970– . Quinquennial.   **EJ59**

Title and imprint vary. 15th ed., 1990, in 2 v. (1298 p.). Ed. 1–10, publ. 1920–65, by Association of Official Agricultural Chemists.

"Neither the 10th , 11th, 12th, 13th, or 14th editions should be destroyed upon appearance of the 15th edition. They contain surplus methods which are not reprinted."—*p.v.*

Contains more than 1,800 "methods for the analysis of foods, drugs, feeds, fertilizers, pesticides, water, or any other substances affecting public health and safety, economic protection of the consumer, or quality of the environment."—*p. xiii.* 1990 ed. in 2 v. : (1) Agricultural chemicals, contaminants, and drugs; (2) Food composition. CAS Registry Numbers are included where applicable. Has a section on preparation of standard solutions. Includes reference tables. Complete subject and method number indexes in each volume.

Supplemented annually by *Changes in official methods of analysis* (Wash. : A.O.A.C., 1946– ; repr. from *Journal of the Association of Official Analytical Chemists*); the purchase price includes five annual supplements.   S587.O38

Pesticide fact handbook / U.S. Environmental Protection Agency. Park Ridge, N.J. : Noyes, c1988–c1990. 2 v.   **EJ60**

"Contains 130 Pesticide Fact Sheets issued by the U.S. Environmental Protection Agency and announced in the Federal Register through December 1987. The Pesticide Fact Sheets include a description of the chemical use patterns and formulations, scientific findings, a summary of the Agency's regulatory position/rationale, and a summary of major data gaps ... [and] cover more than 550 trade-named pesticides."—*Foreword.* Organized alphabetically. Includes glossary; numerical listing; and common, generic, and trade-name indexes.

SB951.P396

The pesticide manual : a world compendium / ed., Charles R. Worthing, assoc. ed., Raymond J. Hance. 9th ed. Farnham, Surrey : British Crop Protection Council, 1991. 1141p. : ill.   **EJ61**

Lists pesticides in current use or under active development. It includes "chemicals and microbial agents used as active ingredients of products for the control of crop pests and diseases, animal ectoparasites and pests in public health. It also contains plant growth regulators, pest repellents, synergists, herbicide safeners and some timber preservatives."—*p. 1.* Also contains a list of superseded compounds. Arranged alphabetically by name (usually the ISO common name). Entries include entry number, molecular formula, chemical structure, nomenclature (including CAS Registry Numbers), development, properties, formulations, uses, toxicology, and analysis. Includes four indexes: CAS Registry Numbers, molecular formula, official manufacturers' code numbers, common or chemical names, and trademarks.

SB951.P434

Plant diseases of international importance / Uma S. Singh... [et al.]. Englewood Cliffs, N.J. : Prentice Hall, c1992. 4 v. : ill.   **EJ62**

Contents: v. 1, Diseases of cereals and pulses (22 diseases); v. 2, Diseases of vegetables and oil seed crops (19 diseases); v. 3, Diseases of fruit crops (19 diseases); v. 4, Diseases of sugar, forest, and plantation crops (18 diseases).

For each disease "history and distribution (including a disease distribution map), symptoms, etiology, and disease cycle are given, and control measures used in different countries have been combined into programs."—*Pref.*   SB731.P67

Soil taxonomy : a basic system of soil classification for making and interpreting soil surveys / Soil Survey Staff. Wash. : Soil Conservation Service, U.S. Dept. of Agriculture, 1975. 754 p., 6 leaves of plates : col. ill., map. (Agriculture handbook /United States Department of Agriculture, no. 436).   **EJ63**

"Gives the present status of the taxonomy being used to make and interpret soil maps in the United States and several other countries. It is the first publication of the complete system."—*Pref.* Chapter 21, "Relation to other soil taxonomies," relates its system to the French, Canadian, and Soviet taxonomies. Appendixes include terms used to describe soils, and tests of organic soil materials. Indexed.

See also *Keys to soil taxonomy* (EJ54).   S591.U5

The world's worst weeds : distribution and biology / LeRoy G. Holm ... [et al.]. Honolulu : publ. for the East-West Center by Univ. Pr. of Hawaii, c1977. 609p. : ill., maps.   **EJ64**

"An inventory of the principal weeds of the world's major crops."—*Pref.* Pt. 1 lists "the 18 most serious weeds in the approximate order in which they are troublesome to the world's agriculturalists" and another group of 58 of "the world's worst weeds." Entries include names, description with line drawing, biology and world distribution with map, and agricultural importance. Pt. 2 lists 18 major crops by common name including description, cultural requirements, major weeds, and maps indicating main production areas and most important weeds. Contains bibliographies of useful publications on weed distribution, identification, biology, and control; books and special publications on poisonous plants; and a general bibliography. Glossary; index.

SB611.W67

History

Bidwell, Percy Wells. History of agriculture in the northern United States, 1620–1860 / Percy Wells Bidwell ... and John I. Falconer .... Wash. : Carnegie Inst., 1925. 512 p. : ill. (Carnegie Institution of Washington, Pubn. no.358).   **EJ65**

Repr. N.Y. : Peter Smith, 1941.

A scholarly, well-documented work covering agriculture and agricultural economics in the northern states to the time of the Civil War. Includes a classified and critical bibliography with discussions of source materials, public and private records, books, periodicals, society publications, etc.; alphabetical index of authors; and statistical appendix.   S441.B5

Bowers, Douglas E. A list of references for the history of agriculture in the United States, 1790–1840. [Davis, Calif.] : Agricultural History Center, Univ. of Calif., Davis, [1969]. 141 p.   **EJ66**

Covers books, journal articles, and pamphlets. Organized mostly by regions and states. Contains also a general section and sections on several commodities and on slavery and free blacks, land, settlement, trade and transportation, agricultural journals, and agricultural societies, reformers, and technological changes. Author index.

Z5071.A1B786L

Chronological landmarks in American agriculture. Rev. version, Nov. 1990. Wash. : U.S. Dept. of Agriculture, Economics Research Service ; Rockville, Md. : ERS-NASS, 1990. 106 p. (Agriculture information bulletin, no. 425).   **EJ67**

Includes "key inventions, laws, changes in land policies, individuals, contributions, the development of institutions, and the introduction of new types of crops and livestock ... also notes on all commissioners, secretaries of agriculture, and agencies established in response to new programs in the U.S. Department of Agriculture."—*Introd.* Most events include a source for additional information. Name and subject index.   S21.A74

Gray, Lewis Cecil. History of agriculture in the southern United States to 1860 / Lewis Cecil Gray, assisted by Esther Katherine Thompson. Wash. : Carnegie Inst., 1933. 2 v. : ill. (Carnegie Institution of Washington, Pubn. no.430).   **EJ68**

Repr.: N.Y. : Peter Smith, 1941 and 1958.

A companion work to Percy Wells Bidwell, *History of agriculture in the northern United States, 1620–1860* (EJ65). Covers all phases of agriculture and its economics in the southern states up to the time of the Civil War. Well documented. Extensive bibliography, including references to books, periodicals, newspapers, and manuscripts.   S445.G8

Naftalin, Mortimer L. Historic books and manuscripts concerning general agriculture in the collection of the National Agricultural Library. Wash. : National Agricultural Library, U.S. Dept. of Agriculture, 1967. 94p. (National Agricultural Library. Library list, no. 86).   **EJ69**

An alphabetical author listing with full citations. Includes books published in Europe prior to 1800 and in the U.S. prior to 1830.

——————— Historic books and manuscripts concerning horticulture and forestry in the collection of the National Agricultural Library. Wash. : National Agricultural Library, U.S. Dept. of Agriculture, 1968. 106 p. (National Agricultural Library. Library list, no. 90).   **EJ70**

An alphabetical author list, with full citations, of pre-1800 European imprints and pre-1830 American imprints. Some selected later publications are also included.

Schapsmeier, Edward L. Encyclopedia of American agricultural history / Edward L. Schapsmeier, Frederick H. Schapsmeier. Westport, Conn. : Greenwood, 1975. 467 p.   **EJ71**

Aims "to provide a reference tool for the novice as well as the scholar ... [covering] information on all areas bearing on agricultural history." —*Pref.* Includes entries for terms, persons, events, organizations, publications, legislative acts, etc. Some bibliographic references. Includes a general index and a number of special indexes that group references topically.   S441.S36

Schlebecker, John T. Bibliography of books and pamphlets on the history of agriculture in the United States, 1607–1967. Santa Barbara, Calif. : ABC-Clio, 1969. 183 p.   **EJ72**

More than 2,000 items, listed alphabetically by author with index of subjects and titles. Some entries have brief annotations, some of which are critical.   Z5075.U5S28

Schor, Joel. A list of references for the history of black Americans in agriculture, 1619–1974 / comp. by Joel Schor and Cecil Harvey. Davis, Calif. : Agricultural History Center, Univ. of Calif., 1975. 116 p.   **EJ73**

Produced for the Agricultural History Program Area, Economic Research Service, U.S. Dept. of Agriculture, and the Agricultural History Center.

Covers books, journal articles, and pamphlets. "Printed manuscript guides and bibliographies are also included ... [as well as] some unpublished dissertations and mimeographed reports."—*Introd.* Sections include bibliographies and finding aids; general; slavery period, 1619–1865; reconstruction; the nadir, 1877–1914; inter-war years, 1919–40; World War II to 1952; Eisenhower to Nixon, 1952 to 1974; negro education; and black agricultural contributions. Author index.

An update, *A list of references for the history of black Americans in agriculture, 1619–1980*, was publ. 1981.   Z7164.L1S33

Reviews of research

•**Agrisearch** [database]. Norwood, Mass. : SilverPlatter International, 1992– .   **EJ74**

Available on CD-ROM, updated annually.

Contains five databases that provide access to worldwide research in progress in agriculture, food and nutrition:

Current research information system (CRIS), also available online, produced by the U.S. Dept. of Agriculture, provides information concerning ongoing or recently completed research projects sponsored or conducted primarily by USDA or state agricultural universities, and human nutrition research at federal agencies. Descriptions of each project include objectives, summary, progress report, and citations to publications.

SPAAR information system (SIS), produced by the World Bank's Special Program for African Agricultural Research.

Inventory of Canadian agri-food research (ICAR), produced by the Canadian Agricultural Research Council.

Australian rural research in progress (ARRIP), produced by the Australian Department of Primary Industries and Energy, CSIRO.

Permanent inventory of agricultural research projects (AGREP), produced by the European Economic Communities.

Atlases

World atlas of agriculture : under the aegis of the International Association of Agricultural Economists / Monographs ed. by the Committee for the World Atlas of Agriculture. Novara, Italy : Istituto Geografico de Agostini, [1969–76]. 4 v. : portfolio.   **EJ75**

Contents: v. 1, Europe, U.S.S.R., Asia Minor; v. 2, South and East Asia, Oceania; v. 3, Americas, v. 4, Africa.

Attempts to provide comparable data and cartographic illustration of agricultural and forestry resources, land utilization etc., of countries throughout the world. Country-by-country arrangement, with each country section contributed by one or more specialists and presented in five sections: (1) Physical environment and communications; (2) Population; (3) Exploitation of resources, ownership, and land tenure; (4) Land utilization, crops, and animal husbandry; (5) Agricultural economy. A bibliography is included for each country. A separate, looseleaf volume of "Land utilization and relief maps" (60 cm.) with plates, follows the arrangement of the text volumes.   G1046.J1W6

Statistics

1948–1985 world crop and livestock statistics : area, yield, and production of crops : production of livestock products = 1948–1985 statistiques mondiales des cultures et de l'acélevage : superficies, rendements et production des cultures : produits de l'acélevage. Rome : Food and Agriculture Organization of the United Nations, 1987. 760 p. (FAO processed statistics series, 1).   **EJ76**

Intends "to provide a comprehensive historical presentation of available data useful for socio-economic research... [I]ncludes statistics on the production of 237 agricultural commodities... culled from data covering 170 countries."—*Foreword.* Consists of 107 tables, 93 for crops and 14 for livestock products, giving area harvested, yield, and production as appropriate, for each country and year.   SB71.A16

Agricultural statistics / U.S. Dept. of Agriculture. 1936– . Wash. : The Department : for sale by U.S. Govt. Print. Off., 1936– . Annual.   **EJ77**

Superintendent of Documents classification: A 1.47: .
Imprint varies.

"Published each year to meet the diverse need for a reliable reference book on agricultural production, supplies, consumption, facilities, costs, and returns."—*Introd., 1993*. Consists of tables of data on the quantity and value of agricultural commodities of the U.S. and, in some cases, of foreign countries as well as farm resources, income, and expenses; taxes, insurance, credit, and cooperatives; stabilization and price-support programs; agricultural conservation and forestry; consumption and family living; fertilizers and pesticides; and other miscellaneous statistics. Tables generally limit the data to the last ten years. Includes a section on weights, measures, and conversion factors. Appendixes in the 1993 issue include: telephone contact list, tables deleted, and new tables. Indexed.   HD1751.A43

Census of agriculture. 1840– . Wash. : U.S. Bureau of the Census; for sale by U.S. Govt. Print. Off., 1840– . Quinquennial.   **EJ78**

Imprint varies; frequency varies.

Chiefly tables. "The first agriculture census was taken in 1840 as part of the sixth decennial census. From 1894 to 1950, an agricultural census was taken as part of the decennial census population. A mid-decade census was conducted in 1925, 1935, and 1945. From 1954 to 1974, the census of agriculture was taken for the years ending in 4 and 9. ...In 1976, Congress authorized the census of agriculture to be taken in 1978 and 1982 to [coincide]... with the economic censuses ... [establishing] the agriculture census on a 5-year cycle collecting data for the years ending in 2 and 7 ... The census of agriculture is the leading source of statistics about the Nation's agricultural production and the only source of consistent, comparable data at the country, State, and national levels."—*Introd., 1992*.

The 1992 census consists of three volumes: v. 1, National state, and county data, is published in parts (one volume for each state, one for the U.S. summary, and one each for Puerto Rico, Guam, and the Virgin Islands); v. 2, Subject series, consists of five parts: Agricultural atlas of the U.S., Coverage evaluation, Ranking of states, History, and Zip code tabulations of selected items from the 1992 and 1987 censuses of agriculture; v. 3, 1994 farm and ranch irrigation survey. Vol. 1 contains data on production and value of products sold; costs; number of farms and farm size and value; farm labor; livestock inventory and sales; crop production, yield, and gross value; etc.

•1987 census available on CD-ROM as : *1987 census of agriculture : v. 1, Geographic area series : State data files, county data files (including U.S. totals)* [database] (Wash. : U.S. Bureau of the Census), and as part of *Agricultural statistics* [database] (Wash., 1989).

FAO yearbook. Fertilizer. Rome : Food and Agriculture Organization of the United Nations, 1988– .   **EJ79**

In English, French, and Spanish.

Continues: *FAO fertilizer yearbook* (1978–86); *Annual fertilizer review* (1970–77); *Fertilizers: an annual review of world production, consumption, trade and prices* (1960–69); *An annual review of world production, consumption, and trade of fertilizers (1946–59)*.

Mostly tables. Contains data on production, trade, and consumption of nitrogen, phosphate, and potash fertilizers as well as rock phosphate, ammonia, and phosphoric acid in the world and by countries, continents, economic classes, and regions. Includes explanatory, tables, and country notes; classification of countries; list of countries, continents, economic classes, and regions; list of products; and exchange rates.   HD9483.A1F65

FAO yearbook. Production = FAO annuaire. Production. = FAO anuario. Producción. v. 41 (1987)– . Rome : Food and Agriculture Organization of the United Nations, 1988– . Annual.   **EJ80**

Continues: *Yearbook of food and agricultural statistics*, pt. 1 (1947–57); *Production yearbook* (1958–75); and *FAO production yearbook* (1976–86).

In English, French, and Spanish.

Mostly tables. in eight parts: (1) Land; (2) Population; (3) FAO indices of agricultural production; (4) Statistical summary; (5) Crops; (6) Livestock numbers and products; (7) Means of production; (8)

Prices. Includes symbols used; explanatory tables, country notes, classification of countries, and list of countries and continents.   HD1421.P76

FAO yearbook. Trade = FAO annuaire. Commerce = FAO anuario. Comercio. v. 41 (1987)– . Rome : Food and Agriculture Organization of the United Nations, 1988– . Annual.   **EJ81**

Continues: *Yearbook of food and agricultural statistics*, pt. 2 (1947–57); *Trade yearbook*, (1958–75); and *FAO trade yearbook* (1976–86).

Mostly tables. In four parts: (1) FAO regional index numbers of agricultural trade; (2) Trade in agricultural products; (3) Trade in agricultural requisites; (4) Value of agricultural trade, by countries. Includes explanatory tables and country notes; classification of countries; standard conversion factors; exchange rates; and list of countries, continents, economic classes, and regions.   HD9000.4.T7

The Knight-Ridder CRB commodity yearbook / Commodity Research Bureau, Knight-Ridder Financial Publishing. 1993– . N.Y. : Wiley, c1993– . Annual.   **EJ82**

For annotation, *see* CH433.   HF1041.C56

The state of food and agriculture : review and outlook. 1951– . Rome : Food and Agriculture Organization of the United Nations, 1951– . Annual.   **EJ83**

Title varies.

The main parts consist of a world review, regional review, and, since 1957, one or more special studies of problems of longer-term interest. A consistent feature of each issue since 1954 is the "Annex tables" which give statistics on agricultural, fishery, and forest products. Categories include volume of production, indexes of food production and agricultural production, and volume of exports and imports. Tables giving data by country include importance of agriculture in the economy, resources and their use in agriculture, and measures of output and productivity in agriculture. Also includes a list of acronyms and the titles of the previous special studies. The 1993 issue is supplemented by a computer diskette containing a "comprehensive set of annual statistical information ... [for] 153 countries and 12 country groups ... from the year 1961 to 1992."—*p. 303, 1993 issue*.   S401.U6A317

Statistical abstract of the United States. 1st no. (1878)– . Wash. : U.S. Bureau of the Census, 1879– . Annual.   **EJ84**

Includes sections on agriculture and forests and fisheries, with tables on farms, farm population; farm balance sheet, income; farm inputs, foreign trade; and crops, livestock. For complete annotation, *see* CG81.   HA202

U.S. Dept. of Agriculture

Bibliography

Handy, R. B. List by titles of publications of the United States Department of Agriculture from 1840 to June, 1901, inclusive / comp. and compared with the originals by R. B. Handy and Minna A. Cannon. Wash. : U.S. Dept. of Agriculture, Div. of Publications, 1902. 216 p. (*Its* Bulletin, no. 6).   **EJ85**

Organized by issuing agency, then name of series. Includes unnumbered series.

Continued by: Mabel Hunt Doyle, *List of publications of the United States Department of Agriculture from January, 1901, to December, 1925, inclusive* (Wash. : U.S. Dept. of Agriculture, 1927. 182 p. [*Its* Miscellaneous publ., no. 9]). Continued by 5-year supplements: Misc. publ. nos. 153, 1932 (1926/30); 252, 1936 (1931/35); 443, 1941 (1936/40); 611, 1946 (1941/45).

United States. Department of Agriculture. List of available publications of the United States Department of Agriculture. June 1, 1929– . Wash. : The Dept. : for sale by U.S. Govt. Print. Off., 1929– . Irregular. **EJ86**

Continues an established series of the same title, with variations in the name of the issuing agency. Includes subject and title indexes.

Z5075.U5U548

United States. Superintendent of Documents. List of publications of the Agricultural Department, 1862–1902, with analytical index. Wash. : U.S. Govt. Print. Off., 1904. 623 p. (Bibliography of United States public documents. Dept. list, no. 1). **EJ87**

The preface includes an "explanation of the method of classification for United States public documents, as it is now used in the Public Documents Library."—*p. 9.*

Arranged in tables according to the document classification. The author, title, and subject index refers to the classification number. The appendix, with its own subject index, lists 82 "reports originating in the agriculture department, but which were printed only as congressional documents."—*p. 615.* Z1223.A12

Zimmerman, Fred Lyon. Numerical list of current publications of the U.S. Dept. of Agriculture / comp. by comparison with the originals by Fred L. Zimmerman and Phyllis R. Read. Wash. : U.S. Dept. of Agriculture, 1941. 929 p. (Department of Agriculture. Miscellaneous publication, no. 450). **EJ88**

Under each number are listed the titles of the various USDA serial publications bearing that number.

Indexes

Greathouse, Charles H. Index to the yearbooks of the U.S. Department of Agriculture, 1894–1900. Wash. : U.S. Dept. of Agriculture, Div. of Publications, 1902. 196 p. (United States. Department of Agriculture. Division of Publications. Bulletin, no. 7). **EJ89**

Subject index. Updated in 1908, *Bulletin* no. 9 (1901–1905); 1913, *Bulletin* no. 10 (1906–1910); and 1922, (1911–1915). S21.A35

Thompson, George Fayette. Index to authors with titles of their publications appearing in the documents of the U.S. Dept. of Agriculture, 1841–1897. Wash. : U.S. Dept. of Agriculture, Div. of Publications, 1898. 303 p. (Department of Agriculture. Bulletin, no. 4). **EJ90**

Includes "synopsis only where it is necessary to explain what is not clearly shown in the title."—*Pref.*

————— Index to literature relating to animal industry in the publications of the Department of Agriculture, 1837–1898. Wash. : U.S. Dept. of Agriculture, Div. of Publications, 1900. 676 p. (United States. Department of Agriculture. Division of Publications. Bulletin, no. 5). **EJ91**

Author, geographic, and detailed subject index. Includes list of documents indexed. Z5074.L7U5

United States. Department of Agriculture. Division of Publications. Index to publications of the United States Department of Agriculture, 1901–40. Wash. : U.S. Govt. Print. Off., 1932–43. 4 v. **EJ92**

Contents: 1901–25 (1932. 2689 p.); 1926–30 (1935. 694 p.); 1931–35 (1937. 518 p.); 1936–40 (1943. 763 p.).

Comp. by Mary A. Bradley and Mabel G. Hunt.

Author and subject index to all the publications of the USDA for the period, except for the periodicals issued by USDA bureaus, but including *Journal of agricultural research* and *Official record.* For later years, see: *Bibliography of agriculture* (EJ17).

Other indexes to USDA publications:

United States. Department of Agriculture, *Index to the Annual reports of the U.S. Dept. of Agriculture for the years 1837 to 1893, inclusive* (Wash. : U.S. Govt. Print. Off., 1896. 252 p. [Div. of Publications. Bulletin 1]). A subject index.

—————. *Index to Farmers' bulletins no. 1–1750* (Wash. : U.S. Govt. Print. Off., 1920–41. 3 v.). An author and subject index.

—————. *Index to Department bulletins no. 1–1500*, by Mabel G. Hunt (Wash. : U.S. Govt. Print. Off., 1936. 384 p.). An author and subject index.

Miller, Ellen Kay, *Index to USDA Miscellaneous publications, no. 1–1479* (Bethesda, Md. : National Agricultural Library, 1980. 109 p.). Indexes documents published 1929–91. Consists of a title listing, document number listing, and index by subject.

—————. *Index to USDA Agricultural information bulletins, no. 1–649* (Beltsville, Md. : National Agricultural Library, [1992]. 50 p.). Indexes bulletins published 1949–92. Title listing, document number listing, index by subject.

—————. *USDA Agricultural handbooks no. 1–690* (Beltsville, Md. : National Agricultural Library, [1992]. 55 p.). Title listing, docu,ment number listing, index by subject.

—————. *Index to USDA Techhnical bulletins, no. 1–1802* (Beltsville, Md. : National Agricultural Library, [1993]. 120 p.). Indexes documents published 1927–92. Title listing, dicument number listing, subject index.

Reports of the statistician

Thompson, George Fayette. Synoptical index of the reports of the statistician, 1863 to 1894. Wash. : U.S. Dept. of Agriculture, Div. of Publications, 1897. 258 p. (*Its* Bulletin, no. 2). **EJ93**

Arranged by subject then by title of article in the report. Includes "synopsis of the article if it appears that one is necessary."—*Pref.*

S21.P9

Agricultural Experiment Stations

List of bulletins of the agricultural experiment stations in the United States …. Wash. : U.S. Govt. Print. Off., 1924–44. 12 v. **EJ94**

"A list of approximately 12,500 of the 17,500 or more publications of the State experiment stations (including those of Alaska and the insular possessions) from 1875 to 1920, inclusive."—*Pref.*

Continued by biennial supplements: Bulletin 1199, suppls. 1 (1921/22), 2 (1923/24), 3 (1925/26); Miscellaneous publications nos. 65 (1927/28), 128 (1929/1930), 181 (1931/32), 232 (1933/34), 294 (1935/36), 362 (1937/38), 459 (1939/40); Bibliographical bulletin no. 4 (1941/42). Beginning with suppl. 2, each update includes author and subject indexes.

United States. Office of Experiment Stations. Experiment station record. v. 1 (Sept. 1889)–v. 95 (1946). Wash. : U.S. Govt. Print. Off., 1890–1946. **EJ95**

Consists largely of abstracts of publications of the experiment stations of the USDA and of its various divisions. Earlier volumes are arranged by stations and divisions, later volumes by subject. Author and subject index to each volume.

Cumulative subject indexes were published in 1903 (v. 1 [1889]–12 [1901]. 671 p.); 1913 (v. 13 [1901]–25 [1911]. 1159 p.); 1926 (v. 26 [1912]–40 [1919]. 640 p.); 1931 (v. 41 [1919]–50 [1924]. 709 p.); 1932 (v. 51 [1924]–60 [1929]. 677 p.); 1937 (v. 61 [1929]–70 [1934]. 752 p.); 1949 (v. 71 [1934]–80 [1939]. 832 p.).

ANIMAL SCIENCE

Guides

Gibb, Mike. Keyguide to information sources in veterinary medicine. London ; N.Y. : Mansell, 1990. 459 p. : ill.   **EJ96**

Pt. 1, Survey of veterinary medicine and its literature, provides "a narrative survey of the kinds of information sources available with some discussion of their use in practice."—*Introd.* Pt. 2 consists of a bibliography of 1,782 entries with sections on general works, large animals, small animals, and specialties. Most entries contain brief annotations. Emphasis is on English-language works. Pt. 3, Directory of organizations, includes national veterinary associations, selected libraries, online databases and publishers. International in scope; index.
SF610.8.G53

Kerker, Ann E. Comparative & veterinary medicine : a guide to the resource literature / comp. by Ann E. Kerker and Henry T. Murphy. [Madison] : Univ. of Wisconsin Pr., [1973]. 308 p.   **EJ97**

Intended as "a selective guide to the recent literature for research workers and practitioners in comparative and veterinary medicine and in related biomedical disciplines which utilize animals as subjects."—*Pref.* In four sections: (1) Materials of general interest, including indexes and abstracting journals, reference works, handbooks, etc.; (2) Specific disciplines; (3) Veterinary medicine, subdivided by the various species of animals normally encountered in practice; and (4) Laboratory animals. Includes introductory notes to the sections and occasional annotations. Author index and list of conferences, congresses, symposia, and other meetings cited. Detailed subject index.

The literature of animal science and health / ed. by Wallace C. Olsen. Ithaca, N. Y. : Cornell Univ. Pr., 1993. 404 p.   **EJ98**

Covers literature related to "that part of agriculture concerned with animals used commercially for meat and other products."—*p. 18.* "The veterinary or clinical aspects of animal diseases are not included in the consideration of developed countries' literature, but are included in discussions of Third World Literature."—*p. 19.* Includes the following lists: core list of monographs, 1950–1990; core journals; journals inititated 1980– ; update of reference sources, "a supplement and complement to [*Guide to sources for agricultural and biological research*, 1981]; recently initiated journals; historically important monographs, 1860–1950; and historically important popular and trade periodicals, 1850–1950.
SF22.5.L58

Bibliography

Bibliography of reproduction : a classified monthly list of references compiled from the research literature. v. 1 (Jan. 1963)– . Cambridge, Eng. : Reproduction Research Information Service, 1963– . Monthly.   **EJ99**

Official publication of the Society for the Study of Fertility, the Society for the Study of Reproduction, the Australian Society for Reproductive Biology, and the Blair Bell Research Society.

Intends "to assist the study of reproductive biology and clinical science in vertebrates, including man."—*Inside front cover.* Sources include periodicals, abstracting services (i.e., *Animal breeding abstracts, Current contents, Index medicus, Index veterinarius*), books, and theses. Organized in sections by subject, with alphabetical guide to subject sections, author index, animal index (except man, mouse, and rat) and semiannual subject indexes.
Z6663.R4B58

Comben Collection. Historic books on veterinary science and animal husbandry / the Comben Collection in the Science Museum Library ; Pauline Dingley. London : H.M.S.O., 1992. 183 p. : ill., facsims.   **EJ100**

Contains 859 entries arranged in two sections: historic books and reference books. Cataloging is based on AACR2 (1988). Many entries include brief notes. Cross-references.

United States. Bureau of Animal Industry. Zoological Division. Index-catalogue of medical and veterinary zoology : authors. Wash. : U.S. Govt. Print. Off., 1932–52. 18 pts. in 12 v.   **EJ101**

At head of title: U.S. Dept. of Agriculture.

A revision and continuation of *Index-catalogue of medical and veterinary zoology—authors*, publ. 1902–12 as Bureau of Animal Industry *Bulletin* 39, under the authorship of Charles Wardell Stiles and Albert Hassall. The former author catalog has been incorporated in the present publication.

Kept up-to-date by supplements 1 (1953)–24 (1983).

Abstract journals

Animal breeding abstracts. v. 1 (Apr. 1933)– . [Farnham Royal : Commonwealth Agricultural Bureaux], 1934– . Monthly.   **EJ102**

Imprint varies. Published quarterly until Nov. 1977.

Compiled from *CAB abstracts* database (EJ18). Produced by the Division of Animal Production and Human Nutrition, CAB International (formerly Commonwealth Agricultural Bureaux).

Abstracts are arranged by species: livestock, horses, cattle, buffaloes, sheep, goats, pigs, furbearers, laboratory animals, other mammals, poultry and other breeds, and fishes and invertebrates in aquaculture. Includes also sections on general and theoretical genetics, reproduction, reports, conferences, and books. Cumulative annual author and subject indexes. The annual index contains a list of serial titles abstracted during that year.

•Available online and in CD-ROM as part of *CAB abstracts* database; also included in *BEASTCD* (*see* EJ18 *note*).   SF1.A63

Index veterinarius. v. 1 (Apr. 1933)– . Weybridge, Eng. : Commonwealth Bureau of Animal Health, 1933– . Monthly.   **EJ103**

Imprint varies. Frequency varies; quarterly through 1971. Comp. from *CAB abstracts* database (EJ18). Produced by the Division of Animal Health and Medical Parasitology of CAB International.

A subject and author index to the literature of veterinary and related sciences. Items are selected from some 3,500 serial publications and from books, annual reports, monographs, theses, and other non-serial publications from all over the world. All major items of veterinary literature are abstracted in *Veterinary bulletin* (EJ105) and listed in *Index veterinarius*, which also lists other items.   SF601.I52

Nutrition abstracts and reviews : Series B. Livestock feeds and feeding. v. 47 (Jan. 1977)– . Farnham Royal, Eng. : Commonwealth Agricultural Bureaux]. Monthly.   **EJ104**

Published with: *Nutrition abstracts and reviews. Series A: Human and experimental* (v. 47 [1977]–). Both parts split from and assumed the volume numbering of: *Nutrition abstracts and reviews* (EH295).

Imprint varies.

Compiled from *CAB abstracts* [database] (EJ18). Has sections for: Techniques, Technology, Feedingstuffs and feeds, Physiology and biochemistry. Author and subject indexes in each issue. Indexes cumulate annually; annual index has list of serial titles abstracted.
SF95.N867

The veterinary bulletin. v. 1 (Apr. 1931)– . Weybridge, Eng. : Commonwealth Agricultural Bureaux, 1932– . Monthly.   **EJ105**

Comp. from *CAB abstracts* database (EJ18). Produced by the Division of Animal Health and Medical Parasitology of CAB International. Continues *Tropical veterinary bulletin* (1912–30). Absorbed *Veterinary reviews* in 1962.

An international abstracting service in classed arrangement. Many issues include a review of a specific topic. Monthly and annual author and subject indexes.   SF601.V52

Veterinary update : clinical abstract service. [Small animals]. Vol. 29, no. 1 (Jan. 1988)– . Goleta, Calif. : American Veterinary Publications, 1988– . Monthly.   **EJ106**

Continues: *Modern veterinary practice, reference and data library* (1960–67); *International veterinary reference service* (1967–74); *Veterinary reference service* (1975–86); *Veterinary update: clinical abstract service (pet practice edition)* (1986–87).

"The material ... is selected for its clinical applications."—*How to use*. Abstracts are organized by clinical topics (e.g., alimentary system, diagnostic techniques and imaging, eye, nutrition, urinary system) and nonclinical topics (e.g., behavior and animal welfare, ethics and jurisprudence, insurance) and include title, summary sentence, abstract, species, authors, address of first author, and complete citation. Indexes include master index by topics, topics by species, summary sentences (by title including summary sentence), and author. Includes list of source journals.   SF607.M6

Veterinary update. Large animals. v. 33, no. 1 (Jan./Feb./Mar. 1992)– . Goleta, Calif. : American Veterinary Publ., c1992– . Quarterly.   **EJ107**

Frequency varies.

Title varies: 1960–67, *Modern veterinary practice : reference and data library*; 1967–74, *Veterinary reference service*; 1975–84, *Veterinary reference service : large animal edition*; 1986–87, *Veterinary update (large animal edition)*; 1987, split into *Veterinary update (equine edition)* and *Veterinary update (food animal edition)*; 1988–91, *Veterinary update (large animals [equine])* and *Veterinary update (large animals [food])*.

"Material is selected for its practical content ... for its clinical applications."—*Introd*. Abstracted articles are selected from more than 80 worldwide periodicals based on their utility. Some articles are not abstracted. Arranged by subject in two main sections: Clinical and Non-clinical. Covers horses, cattle, pigs, sheep and goats, and exotic animals. Includes subject, species, and author indexes. Also available on diskettes.   SF745.I5196

Encyclopedias

International encyclopedia of veterinary medicine / ed. in chief, Sir Thomas Dalling ... [et al.]. Edinburgh : Green ; London : Sweet & Maxwell, 1966. 5 v. : col. front., ill., plates, tables, diagrs.   **EJ108**

Aims to meet the "need for a comprehensive publication containing accurate information on subjects of veterinary interest and importance, provided in a concise form."—*Foreword*. Arranged by subjects in alphabetical order with many cross-references. Includes synonyms in French, German, and Spanish. Some articles list suggestions for further reading. Contains English index and French, German, and Spanish indexes to the main subjects.   [SF609]

Veterinary encyclopedia : diagnosis and treatment / ed. in chief: Kjeld Wamberg. Copenhagen : Medical Book Co., 1968. 4 v. (loose-leaf) : ill. (part col.).   **EJ109**

"An international reference book written for practitioners."—*Foreword*. Signed articles by leading veterinarians from all over the world. Contains general index and supplementary index including all amendments and addenda.   SF609.V395

Dictionaries

Association of American Feed Control Officials. Official publication. [s.l.] : Assoc. of American Feed Control Officials, 1977?– . Annual.   **EJ110**

Contains the list of official feed terms and the official names and definitions of feed ingredients as established by the Association. Includes the international feed name (IFN) number. Also includes sections on medicated feed labeling, drug assay limits, additives, and "Generally Recognized as Safe (GRAS)" substances.   SF97.A84

Black's veterinary dictionary / ed. by Geoffrey P. West. 17th ed. Lanham, Md. : Barnes & Noble, 1992. 660 p.   **EJ111**

1st ed., 1928; 4th–12th eds., 1957–77, publ. by Williams & Wilkins under title: *Encyclopedia of animal care*.

Gives comprehensive coverage of terms in veterinary medicine and animal husbandry, as well as the anatomy and physiology of domesticated animals. Includes "information on accidents, worldwide disease eradication campaigns, health promotion, the housing of animals, and pest control."—*Pref*. Includes references and cross-references.   SF609.B53

Concise veterinary dictionary / [consultant editors, Christopher M. Brown, D. A. Hogg, D. F. Kelly]. Oxford, [Eng.] ; N.Y. : Oxford Univ. Pr., 1988. 890 p. : ill.   **EJ112**

Covers "all the major fields in veterinary science .... For ... agricultural and veterinary students, veterinary assistants and practitioners, ... research workers ... in fields related to veterinary science."—*Pref*. Cross-references; line drawings.   SF609.C66

Dictionary of animal health terminology : in English, French, Spanish, German, and Latin / comp. by Office international des epizooties, Paris, France ; ed., Roy Mack. Amsterdam ; N.Y. : Elsevier, 1992. 426 p.   **EJ113**

Rev. ed. of the veterinary medicine portion of: *Dictionary of animal production terminology* (2nd ed., 1979).

The English section lists the equivalents in all other languages. Terms in other languages refer to the English section.   SF609.D55

Dictionary of animal production terminology : in English, French, Spanish, German, and Latin / comp. by European Association for Animal Production ; editors, Sophie Straszewska and Louis Ollivier. 2nd completely rev. and enl. ed. N.Y. : Elsevier, 1993. 656 p. (European Association for Animal Production publication, no. 60).   **EJ114**

1st ed., 1985, was a rev. ed. of *Vocabulary of animal husbandry terms*, publ. 1959.

"Includes terms specific to animal production as well as terms from related basic scientific disciplines, such as biochemistry, economics, genetics, nutrition, physiology, statistics, and computer science."—*p. xiii*. Includes only a limited number of terms relating to veterinary or dairy terminology. Contains a basic table consisting of blocks of words or phrases, each given in English, French, German, Spanish, and Latin (when appropriate), arranged in English alphabetical order and sequentially numbered. Indexes in French, German, Spanish, and Latin refer to the block number.   SF21

Dictionary of dairy terminology : in English, French, German, and Spanish / comp. by International Dairy Federation. Amsterdam ; N.Y. : Elsevier Scientific Pub. Co., 1983. 328 p.   **EJ115**

Lists 3,909 terms in alphabetical order on an English base with indexes in French, German, and Spanish. Does not cover names of cheeses.   SF229.D5

Hurnik, J. F. Dictionary of farm animal behaviour / J. F. Hurnik, A. B. Webster and P. B. Siegel. Guelph, Ontario : Univ. of Guelph, 1985. 176 p.   **EJ116**

The goal is "to provide a reference book for behavioural terminology and ethological concepts that is comprehensive yet comfortably sized ... [intended for] students of behaviour, animal scientists, veterinarians, and others who ... work with animals as a career or vocation."—*Introd*.   SF756.7.H87

Terminology

Mack, Roy. Veterinary subject headings : for use in Index Veterinarius and the Veterinary Bulletin. Farnham Royal, [Eng.] : Commonwealth Agricultural Bureaux, 1972. 70, 44 p.
EJ117

"To assist users of *Index Veterinarius* [EJ103] and *The Veterinary Bulletin* [EJ105] in literature retrieval, and to guide the staff of the Bureau in their indexing."—*Introd.* Subject headings or keywords are arranged in two separate lists: alphabetical and classified. Modeled on *Medical subject headings* (EH143). Useful for searching literature indexed between 1972 and 1978.   Z695.1.V4M3

Directories

American Veterinary Medical Association. Division of Membership and Field Services. AVMA directory. 1984– . Schaumburg, Ill. : Div. of Membership and Field Services, American Veterinary Medical Assoc., c1984– . Annual.
EJ118

Cover title for 1994: *Caring for animals.*
1st ed., 1956; 43rd ed., 1994. Frequency irregular until 1974.
Lists "AVMA members in the United States, Canada, and other countries and those nonmember veterinarians for whom data is available in AVMA records. The listings and statistics contained in the AVMA directory do not reflect the total veterinary population in the United States or any other country."—*Foreword.* Consists of three sections. The reference section contains information on AVMA organization and history; names and addresses of other veterinary and related associations, federal and state government agencies, and veterinary colleges; specialty boards and diplomates; model veterinary practice act; digests of state veterinary practice acts; state laws or regulations; directory of information sources; catalog of materials available from AVMA; and list of films and videotapes. The alphabetic section is arranged by veterinarian's name and indicates city, state, province, or country, spouse's name, and member status code. The geographic section is arranged by state, province, or country and gives name, address, telephone number and codes indicating professional activity, employer type, employment function, school and year of graduation, and member status.   SF611.A53

Compendium of veterinary products. 1st ed. (1991)– . Port Huron, Mich. : North American Compendiums Inc., c1991– .
EJ119

Aims "to make available to all professionals working in the animal health industry, a complete and concise reference text which will include veterinary products available in the USA ... pharmaceuticals registered by the FDA, biological products registered by the USDA, animal pesticides registered by the EPA, private label products with registrations as above, products sold exclusively to veterinarians, and registered products sold OTC."—*Editor's message.* The main section is arranged alphabetically by trade name. Includes biological charts (grouped by species and delineated by antigens) and withdrawal charts as well as alphabetical index of manufacturers (with address and list of products), therapeutic index, brandname/non-proprietary name index, and alphabetical index of products.

World veterinary directory / ed. by the World Veterinary Association in cooperation with the Food and Agriculture Organization of the United Nations (FAO), the World Health Organization (WHO), and the International Office of Epizootics (OIE). 1991– . Madrid : [The Association], 1991– .   **EJ120**

Contains data "from some 400 centres of veterinary education of university level existing in the world ... [as well as] more than 3,000 titles of video cassettes, films and other audiovisual aids, ... names and addresses of scientific, professional and private organizations and institutes, ... [and] veterinary journals."—*Foreword.* Arranged by country, giving for each: general data (i.e., total population, total num-

ber of veterinarians, number of veterinarians graduating each year, and animal population); descriptions of university teaching centers, including name, address, phone, fax and telex numbers, length of studies in years, number of teachers and students, restrictions, postgrade titles, and subjects of postgraduate studies; veterinary associations including name, address, and phone; and veterinary journals including title, address of publisher, and editor's name and phone.   SF775.W92

Handbooks

Ensminger, M. Eugene. Animal science. 9th ed. Danville, Ill. : Interstate Publishers, 1991. 1150 p. : ill.   **EJ121**

"Refers to the total store of knowledge relative to the breeding, feeding, care, and management of animals and marketing and processing of animals and their products, as gained through practical experience and research methods."—*Pref.* Contains general sections as well as sections on beef cattle, dairy cattle, sheep/goats, swine, poultry, horses, and rabbits/aquaculture. Each chapter includes a list of selected references. Includes numerous tables, drawings, and photographs as well as lists of breeds and breed magazines.   SF61.E5

——————— Feeds & nutrition / by M. E. Ensminger, J. E. Oldfield, W. W. Heinemann. 2nd ed. Clovis, Calif. : Ensminger Publ. Co., c1990. 1544 p. : ill. (some col.).   **EJ122**

Contains sections on nutrition, feeds, feeding (including chapters on feeding beef and dairy cattle, sheep, goats, swine, poultry, horses, rabbits, mink, and fish), and composition of feeds with numerous pictures, drawings, and tables. Includes glossaries of nutrition terms and feedstuffs, the last one indicating scientific name; description; place of origin, geographical adaptation, and cultural characteristics; importance/use; and other comments. Indexed.   SF95.E55

International feed descriptions, international feed names, and country feed names / L. E. Harris ... [et al.]. Logan : Utah State Univ., 1980. 769 p. : ill. (International Network of Feed Information Centers publication, no. 5).   **EJ123**

Prep. in conjunction with the USU International Feedstuffs Institute.

"Provides a list of International Feed Names to be used in scientific communications and describes the method of composing International Feed Descriptions and International Feed Names for other feeds."—*p. 1.*

Kirk, Robert Warren. Handbook of veterinary procedures & emergency treatment / Robert W. Kirk, Stephen I. Bistner, Richard B. Ford. 5th ed. Philadelphia : Saunders, 1990. 1016 p. : ill.   **EJ124**

1st ed., 1969; 4th ed., 1985.
"Compact reference text that provides rapid access to essential facts required in small animal practice today."—*Pref.* Sections include emergency care, patient evaluation and organ system examination, clinical signs, clinical procedures, interpretation of laboratory tests, and charts and tables. Emergency index inside front cover. Deals with domestic animals, almost exclusively the cat and dog. Indexed.   SF748.K57

The Merck veterinary manual : a handbook of diagnosis, therapy, and disease prevention and control for the veterinarian / Clarence M. Fraser, ed. ... [et al.]. 7th ed. Rahway, N.J. : Merck, 1991. 1832 p.   **EJ125**

1st ed., 1955; 6th ed., 1986.
Intends "to provide a concise and reliable source of information for those interested in the health and welfare of animals."—*Foreword.* Pt. 1 includes diseases of large and small animals and is arranged in sections by anatomical systems. Other parts include behavior; clinical values and procedures; fur, laboratory, and zoo animals; management, husbandry, and nutrition; pharmacology; diseases of poultry; toxicology; and zoonoses. Detailed index.

•Machine-readable version: *Merck veterinary manual* [database] (Rahway, N.J. : Merck Sharp & Dohme Research Laboratories). Available on CD-ROM, updated annually. Current CD-ROM provides text of most recent printed edition.   SF745.M4

National Research Council. Subcommittee on Feed Composition. Atlas of nutritional data on United States and Canadian feeds. Wash. : National Academy of Sciences, 1971 [c1972]. 772 p.   **EJ126**

Comp. by the Subcommitte on Feed Composition, Committee on Animal Nutrition, Agricultural Board, National Research Council, United States and Committee on Feed Composition, Research Branch, Department of Agriculture, Canada.

Contains names and analytical data on 6,152 feeds which have been used in North America. "Useful primarily for reference purposes."—*Pref.* Data is presented on both as-fed and dry basis. Includes data on digestible energy and metabolizable energy of feeds for cattle, horses, sheep, and swine and on metabolizable energy for feeds for poultry.   SF97.N284

Nutrient requirements of domestic animals. Wash. : National Academy Pr., 1944–1981. v. 1–15. (In progress).   **EJ127**

An unnumbered series of publications revised at intervals. Latest revisions: *Nutrient requirements of beef cattle* (6th rev. ed. 1984); *Cats* (rev. ed. 1986); *Coldwater fishes* (1981); *Dairy cattle* (6th rev. ed. 1988 [includes diskette]; *Dogs* (rev. ed. 1985); *Goats* (1981); *Horses* (5th rev. ed. 1989 [includes diskette]); *Laboratory animals* (3rd rev. ed. 1978); *Mink and foxes* (rev. ed. 1982); *Nonhuman primates* (1978); *Poultry* (8th rev. ed. 1984); *Rabbits* (2nd rev. ed. 1977); *Sheep* (6th rev. ed. 1985); *Swine* (9th rev. ed. 1988); *Warmwater fishes and shellfishes* (rev. ed. 1983).

Each number contains data on nutrient requirements of individual species and information on diets and feeding. All titles include bibliography and index.   SF95.N32

Quick reference to veterinary medicine / [ed. by] William R. Fenner ; with 27 additional contributors. 2nd ed. Philadelphia : J.B. Lippincott, c1991. 669 p. : ill.   **EJ128**

"Designed primarily for veterinarians in practice … helpful for senior veterinary students entering the small animal clinics."—*Pref.* Contains five parts: Clinical signs and client complaints, Systems disturbances, Laboratory abnormalities and principles of fluid management, Principles of fluid and electrolyte balance, and Physical and chemical injuries. Indexed.   SF771.Q53

The UFAW handbook on the care and management of laboratory animals / ed. by Trevor B. Poole ; editorial assistant, Ruth Robinson. 6th ed. London : Longman ; N.Y. : Churchill Livingstone, 1986. 933 p. : ill.   **EJ129**

1st ed., 1947; 5th ed., 1976.

[Sponsored by] Universities Federation for Animal Welfare.

Aims to provide "information which will encourage those keeping laboratory animals to adhere to the highest standards of care."—*Pref.* Contains three parts. Pt. 1, The laboratory animal, includes chapters on raising and defining laboratory animals, selection and supply of laboratory animals, animal production and breeding methods, nutrition and feeding, genetics, animals of defined microbiological status, and legislation. Pt. 2, Animal units, includes chapters on design, equipment, and environmental control of the animal house, hygiene in housing, transport, and safety. Pt. 3, Species kept in the laboratory, includes 45 chapters giving information on husbandry, feeding, breeding, common laboratory procedures, and disease control for mammals, birds, reptiles, amphibia, and fish. Indexed.   SF406.U55

United States-Canadian tables of feed composition : nutritional data for United States and Canadian feeds. 3rd revision. Wash. : National Academy Pr., 1982. 148 p.   **EJ130**

Comp. by the Subcommittee on Feed Composition, Committee on Animal Nutrition, Board on Agriculture and Renewable Resources, Commission on Natural Resources, National Research Council.

Contains "analytical data on more than 600 [selected] feeds … data are presented on 68 attributes (nutrients)."—*Pref.* Feed composi-tion tables include energy values, proximate analysis, plant cell wall constituents, and acid detergent fiber; mineral elements; vitamins, amino acids, fat and fatty acids; and mineral supplements. Data is expressed as as-fed and dry. Other tables include feed classes and weight-unit conversion factors.   SF97.U56

Veterinary pharmaceuticals & biologicals. 1980/81– . Media, Pa. : Harwal Publ. Co., c1980– . Biennial.   **EJ131**

Continues: *Comprehensive desk reference of veterinary pharmaceuticals and biologicals* (1976) and *The complete desk reference of veterinary pharmaceuticals & biologicals* (1978/79).

Product information is arranged in three main sections: pharmaceuticals and biologicals (including also parasiticides, fluids, and electrolytes), diets and nutritional supplements, and diagnostic aids and supplies. Each section is arranged alphabetically by name of manufacturer or distributor. Each product entry gives manufacturer's name, trade name, composition, indications of use, dose administration warnings, caution, and how supplied. Contains a list of recently discontinued products, and several appendixes including drug interactions, normal values, diagnostic laboratories, drug withdrawal time in food animals, and list of useful drugs and their appropriate doses. Indexed by company name, product name, product category/therapeutic classification, and active ingredients.   SF917.V49

Wolfenstine, Manfred R. The manual of brands and marks. Norman : Univ. of Oklahoma Pr., [1970]. 434 p. : ill.   **EJ132**

Contains chapters on the history of brands and branding, branding implements and methods, design of brands, federal and state government brands, marks, and brand registration. Includes glossary and 74 plates with more than 1,000 figures.   SF101.W64

Statistics

Animal health yearbook = Annuaire de la santé animale = Anuario de sanidad animal. 1959– . [Rome?] : FAO-OIE, c1960– . Annual.   **EJ133**

In English, French, and Spanish. Issued also in Chinese.

Continues: *FAO/OIE animal health yearbook* (1957–58) and *World livestock disease report* (1956).

Consists of tables containing information on diseases of mammals, birds, fish, and bees. Compiled from responses to questionnaires distributed by the Food and Agriculture Organization, World Health Organization, and International Office of Epizootics to veterinary services of member countries. Tables indicate for each disease: animal group, country, disease occurence, and control measures reported. The introduction and disease codes are also in Arabic, Russian, Chinese, and German.   SF600.F2

Domestic animals

Dolensek, Emil P. A practical guide to impractical pets / Emil P. Dolensek and Barbara Burn. N.Y. : Viking Pr., 1976. 382 p. : ill.   **EJ134**

Provides information on pets of various kinds: mammals, reptiles, birds, fishes, and insects. Contains sections on care and feeding, breeding, training, first aid, and humane ways of getting rid of pets. The first chapters organize pets into easy, difficult, and impossible pets. Includes reference charts arranged alphabetically, bibliographically, and index.   SF413.D58

Livestock

Ensminger, M. Eugene. The stockman's handbook. 7th ed. Danville, Ill. : Interstate Publishers, 1992. 1029 p. : ill. (some col.).   **EJ135**

"Correlates, and applies the art and science of livestock production, marketing, and processing relative to all species of four-footed animals."—*Pref.* Includes sections on animal behavior and environment, business aspects, breeding, feeding, buildings and equipment, animal health/disease prevention/parasite control, selecting and judging, fitting and showing, marketing, and law on the livestock farm. Also includes feed composition tables and a list of breeds and breed registry associations. SF61.E53

Mason, I. L. A world dictionary of livestock breeds, types and varieties. 3rd (rev.) ed. [Wallingford, Oxon, U.K.] : CAB International, 1988. 348 p. **EJ136**
"The aim of this dictionary is to list livestock names...to indicate which names are synonymous and to recommend one form for English use."—*Introd.* Indicates place of origin of breed, uses, relation to other breeds, breed characteristics, existence of breed society, and synonyms. Contains sections on asses, buffaloes, cattle, goats, horses, pigs, and sheep. SF61

Sambraus, Hans Hinrich. A colour atlas of livestock breeds. [London] : Wolfe, 1992. 272 p. : ill. (some col.). **EJ137**
Entries for cattle, sheep, goats, horses, donkeys, and pigs include color pictures, characteristics, distribution, uses, and breed history. Poultry and rabbits are covered only as species. Includes references. SF75.2S3613x

Cats

Carlson, Delbert G. Cat owner's home veterinary handbook / by Delbert G. Carlson and James M. Giffin. N.Y. : Howell Book House, c1983. 391 p. : ill. **EJ138**
Aims to "describe in the cat those signs and symptoms which will help you to arrive at a preliminary diagnosis ... [includes] the basics of health care and disease prevention for the young and the old."—*Introd.* Contains chapters on emergencies, diseases of various organs and systems, pregnancy and kittening, pediatrics, feeding and nutrition, feline behavior and training, geriatrics, and drugs and medications. Index of signs and symbols on inside cover. Appendix on normal physiological data. Indexed. SF985.C29

Henderson, G. N. The international encyclopedia of cats / ed. by G. N. Henderson and D. J. Coffey. N.Y. : McGraw-Hill, [1973]. 256 p. : ill. (part col.). **EJ139**
In dictionary format with numerous cross-references. SF442.2.H46

Necker, Claire. Four centuries of cat books : a bibliography, 1570–1970. Metuchen, N.J. : Scarecrow, 1972. 511 p. **EJ140**
Includes "all known separately published items in the English language (including translations) which deal exclusively or predominantly with cats ... [and] a selection of books covering Felidae."—*Introd.* Arranged by author. Contains title index and annotated subject index. Z5491.N43

Pond, Grace. The complete cat encyclopedia / ed. by Grace Pond ... [et al.]. N.Y. : Crown Publishers, [1972]. 384 p. : ill. (part. col.). **EJ141**
"Contains articles on all the breeds recognized in Britain or America."—*Editor's introd.* Breeds are grouped into long-hairs and short-hairs and then in alphabetical order. For each breed includes origin and subsequent history; special points of character, care, and show grooming; and a general description. Includes articles on anatomy, boarding, breeding, nutrition, diseases, evolution, and genetics. Contains glossary and bibliography. Indexed. SF442.2.P65

Dogs

Carlson, Delbert G. Dog owner's home veterinary handbook / by Delbert G. Carlson and James M. Giffin. N.Y. : Howell Book House, c1980. 364 p. : ill. **EJ142**
"Attempts to describe in the dog, signs and symptoms which will help the owner arrive at a preliminary diagnosis so he [sic] can weigh the severity of the problem."—*Introd.* First chapters cover emergencies, worms/intestinal parasites, and infectious diseases; the remaining 15 chapters are physiological—e.g., skin, ears, lungs. Index of signs and symptoms on inside cover. Appendix on normal physiological data. Indexed. Appendix: Normal physiology. SF991.C25

The complete dog book : the photograph, history, and official standard of every breed admitted to AKC registration, and the selection, training, breeding, care, and feeding of pure-bred dogs. 18th ed. N.Y. : Howell Book House, c1992. 672 p. : ill. **EJ143**
1st ed., 1929; 17th ed., 1985.
Official publication of the American Kennel Club.
Arranged by groups (sporting dogs, hounds, working dogs, terriers, toys, non-sporting dogs, and herding dogs), then by breeds. Includes a healthy dog section, glossary, and index. SF426.C66

Jones, E. Gwynne. A bibliography of the dog : books published in the English language, 1570–1965. London : Libr. Assoc., 1971. 431 p. **EJ144**
Includes 3,986 serially numbered entries in a classified arrangement. Includes the classification scheme, a names and title index, a subject index, and a chronological list of all works published up to 1850. "The subject index refers from generally accepted subject terms to points in the classification scheme where subjects will be found."—*Pref.* Z7997.D7J65

The new dog encyclopedia : completely rev. and expanded updating of the Henry P. Davis classic Modern dog encyclopedia. N.Y. : Galahad Books, [1974] c1970. 736 p. : ill. **EJ145**
For the "dog owner, breeder, fancier, trainer, trial or show enthusiast or handler, veterinarian or pet shop owner ... about dogs ... their feeding and handling, their health and training, their care and welfare."—*Foreword.* Indexed. SF426.D38

Wilcox, Bonnie. Atlas of dog breeds of the world / Bonnie Wilcox and Chris Walkowicz. Neptune, N.J. : T.F.H. Publ., c1989. 912 p. : col. ill. **EJ146**
Subsequent editions appear to be reprints.
Contains chapters on eight groups of dogs (flock guards, mastiffs, scent hounds or hounds, gun dogs, northern breeds, herding dogs, terriers, and southern dogs) describing general characteristics and historical evolution and including a complete listing of breeds in the group. The main section (Dogs of the world) is arranged alphabetically by breed name. Includes complete list of sources, contributors, and owners of the dogs portrayed as well as breed name. Cross-references, glossary and index. SF422.W55

FOOD SCIENCE

American Association of Cereal Chemists. Approved methods of the American Association of Cereal Chemists / comp. and pub. by the Approved Methods Committee. 8th ed. St. Paul, Minn : AACC, 1983– . 2 v. : ill. **EJ147**
Arranged by subject. Methods include definition, preparation, procedures, other pertinent information, and references. Indexed. TX557.A54

Food chemicals codex / Committee on Codex Specifications, Food and Nutrition Board, Division of Biological Sciences, Assembly of Life Sciences, National Research Council. 3rd ed. Wash. : Nat. Academy Pr., 1981. 735 p. : ill. **EJ148**
1st ed., 1966; 2nd ed., 1972.
The main section is an alphabetical listing of entries about food-grade chemicals. Entries include their description, requirements of purity and quality, tests for determining if the requirements are achieved, packaging and storage, labeling and functional use in foods. Other sections cover general test procedures for chemicals added directly to foods for some desired effect and substances which are used in processing that come into contact with food (e.g., extraction solvents or filter media). This edition includes specifications for ingredients which are usually considered foods but are also used as additives (e.g., dextrose and fructose). Index.
Kept up-to-date by supplements publ. 1983, 1986, 1992, 1993.
TP455.F66

Green, Syd. Keyguide to information sources in food science and technology. London ; N.Y. : Mansell, 1985. 231 p. **EJ149**
Pt. 1, Food science and technology and their literature, provides a narrative account of the major sources of information and the structure of this literature; pt. 2 is an annotated bibliography of sources of information; pt. 3, Directory of selected organizations, is international in scope. Detailed table of contents. Index of names, subjects, organizations, and geographic areas. TP370.5.G76

Abstract journals

Food science and technology abstracts. v. 1 (Jan. 1969)– [Shinfield, Eng.] : International Food Information Service. Monthly. **EJ150**
Compiled from *Food science and technology abstracts* database (below). "FSTA covers articles on the basic food sciences, food products and food processes published in more than 1600 journals in 40 languages, as well as information from patents, books, conference proceedings, legislative papers, etc."—*Inside front cover.* Organized by subject sections; each section is subdivided by topic and includes sections for standards and for legislation and patents. Author and subject indexes cumulate annually; the annual index contains a list of serial titles abstracted during the year.
•Machine-readable versions: *Food science and technology abstracts (FSTA)* [database] (Frankfurt am Main : International Food Information Service GmbH, 1969–), available online, updated monthly; and *FSTA : food science and technology abstracts* [database] (1969–), available on CD-ROM, updated quarterly.
§ See also: *The companion thesaurus to food science and technology abstracts* (EJ159).

Foods adlibra. v. 1 (Feb. 15, 1974)– . Louisville, Ky : K & M Publications. Semimonthly. **EJ151**
Contains information on food industry developments including new food products, food marketing, and research and development. Draws from periodicals; technical research journals; government publications; the *Federal register*; the *Official gazette*; and company, university, and association news releases. Entries include bibliographic information and short description. Includes list of publications cited on each issue.
•Machine-readable version: *FOODS ADLIBRA* [database] (Minneapolis, Minn. : FOODS ADLIBRA Publications, 1974–), available online, updated monthly.

Encyclopedias

Encyclopedia of food science / [ed. by] Martin S. Peterson, Arnold H. Johnson. Westport, Conn. : Avi Pub. Co., c1978. 1005 p. **EJ152**
Contains information about the constituents, attributes, and deteriorative factors that affect food. Also treats the methods and tools used in scientific investigations of modern requirements for nutritious, acceptable, and readily utilized foods. A separate section describes food science programs of selected countries. Glossary and index.
TP368.2.E6

Encyclopedia of food science and technology / Y. H. Hui, ed. in chief. N.Y. : Wiley, c1992. 4 v. **EJ153**
"Although this encyclopedia is designed for food scientists and technologists, it also contains information useful to food engineers, chemists, biologists, ingredient suppliers, and other professionals involved in the food chain."—*Pref.* Contains topics on basic and applied sciences; processing technology, engineering, and the unit operations; and food laws and regulations. Articles include bibliographies. Indexed. TP368.2.E62

Foods and food production encyclopedia / Douglas M. Considine, ed. in chief ; Glenn D. Considine, managing ed. N.Y. : Van Nostrand Reinhold, c1982. 2305 p. : ill. **EJ154**
Contains "1201 separate editorial entries, 2950 cross-reference headings, 1006 illustrations, 587 tables, [and] 7500 items in alphabetical index."—*A glance at this encyclopedia.* Covers food commodities, processes and processed foods, diseases and pests of plants and animals, control chemicals, land and soil-related topics, food ingredients and chemicals, biochemistry and nutrition, and scientific fundamentals. References follow most entries. Appendixes include: a table of additives and other food chemicals giving common names, functions, formulae, general characteristics, usual sources, and solubility; daily dietary information tables; and conversion tables. Index. TX349.F58

Johnson, Arnold H. Encyclopedia of food technology / [ed. by] Arnold H. Johnson, Martin S. Peterson. Westport, Conn. : Avi Pub. Co., 1974. 993 p. **EJ155**
Contains "275 subjects pertinent to food technology plus biographical coverage of men and women of historical importance in this field, awards to individuals in recognition of achievement in food technology ... and [other] information ... of general interest."—*Pref.* Indexed. TP368.2.J63

Dictionaries

Igoe, Robert S. Dictionary of food ingredients. 2nd ed. N.Y. : Van Nostrand Reinhold, c1989. 225 p. **EJ156**
1st ed., 1983.
Intended for those who work with foods. Each entry in the initial "Ingredients" section is defined according to functions, properties and applications; chemical formulations and usage levels are provided where applicable, and there are many cross-references. The second section, "Ingredients categories," groups principal ingredients and provides collective information, often in tabular form, on their properties and the relationship of their component ingredients. A final section reprints six parts of the Code of Federal Regulations, listing food ingredients and their U.S. approved status. An extensive bibliography is included. This edition includes additional ingredients and provides expanded information for ingredients previously listed. TX551.I26

Knight, John Barton. Knight's foodservice dictionary / John B. Knight ; ed. by Charles A. Salter. N.Y. : Van Nostrand Reinhold Co., c1987. 393 p. **EJ157**
"Brings together for the first time definitions from all aspects of the foodservice industry: basic terms, basic ingredients, cost controls, culinary arts, foodservice equipment, management information sys-

tems, menu analysis and development, nutrition, sanitation and safety, service and merchandisign, and bar management."—*Pref.*

TX905.K65

Light, N. D. Longman illustrated dictionary of food science : food, its components, nutrition, preparation and preservation. Beirut [Lebanon] : York Pr. ; Harlow, Essex : Longman, 1989. 184 p.   **EJ158**

"Contains over 1,200 words used in the food sciences ... arranged in groups under [24] main headings ... according to the meaning of the words to help ... obtain a broad understanding of the subject."—*How to use the dictionary.* Includes six appendixes and an alphabetical index of words.   TX349.L53

Thesauruses

The companion thesaurus to food science and technology abstracts / comp. by Linda Merryweather; assisted by Amanda Tomlinson ... [et al.]. Shinfield, Reading : International Food Information Service, 1992. 204 p.   **EJ159**

First publ. 1977.

Used to index materials in *FSTA* (EJ150) since Jan. 1993. "Contains 7375 terms of which 1142 are non-descriptors."—*Introd.* Terms are arranged alphabetically and may contain history note (HN); scope note (SN); broader (BT), narrower (NT), and related (RT) term(s); and use for (UF), USE, and synonyms. Includes list of information sources.

Directories

The directory of the canning, freezing, preserving industries. 1st ed. (1966/67)– . Westminster, Md. : E. E. Judge, c1966– . Biennial.   **EJ160**

Arranged in four sections: (1) Alphabetical, gives information about the companies, including cross-references to other related companies; (2) Geographical, a cross-referenced list arranged alphabetically by state or province; (3) Product, organized by product groups (e.g., fruits and berries, juices and drinks, meat and meat products, ethnic foods), with cross-references to every product from section 1; (4) Brand, an alphabetical list of processor-owned brands with the processor's name. Includes trade association list and detailed product index.

TX600.D55

Fenton, Thomas P. Food, hunger, agribusiness : a directory of resources / comp. and ed. by Thomas P. Fenton and Mary J. Heffron. Maryknoll, N.Y. : Oris Books, c1987. 131 p. **EJ161**

"The selections ... emphasize resources that stress the relationship of hunger to its political and economic origins."—*Foreword.* Contains chapters on organizations; books; periodicals; pamphlets and articles; audiovisuals; and catalogs, directories, guides, and curriculum and worship materials. Chapters include an annotated list, a supplementary list, and a list of information sources to locate more materials. Contains organizations, individuals, titles, geographical areas, and subject indexes.   Z7164.F7F46

Hui, Y. H. United States food laws, regulations, and standards. 2nd ed. N.Y. : Wiley, c1986. 2 v. : ill.   **EJ162**

1st ed., 1979.

Intends "to provide a basic understanding of the major food regulatory agencies in the U.S. and of the regulations they promulgate concerning food inspections, standards, specifications, and related matters."—*Pref.* Includes chapters on Advertisement (Federal Trade Commission, United States Postal Service), Agriculture (U.S. Dept. of Agriculture), Commerce (U.S. Dept of Commerce : National Bureau of Standards, National Marine Fisheries Service), Customs (U.S. Customs Service), Food (Food and Drug Administration), Food and transportation (Interstate Commerce Commission, U.S. Dept. of Agricul-

ture, and Food and Drug Administration), Food plant safety (Occupational Safety and Health Administration), and Trade associations. Includes index to both volumes in each one.   KF3875.H8

Thomas food industry register. 1990–1991 ed.– . N.Y. : Thomas Pub. Co., c1990– . Annual.   **EJ163**

Contains information on more than 40,000 U.S. and Canadian food industry companies. Published in 3 v. Vol. 1, Sales and distribution, includes supermarket chains, convenience stores, wholesalers/distributors, brokers/manufacturers, importers, exporters, warehouses, and transportation; arranged geographically by state and city. Vol. 2, Products, equipment, and services, is arranged alphabetically by product or service. Vol. 3, Company communication numbers, company description, key personnel, and size indicators. Includes also trademarks, brandnames, and private labels; trade associations; industry convention calendar; and a guide to government resources for the food industry.   HD9321.3.T5

Handbooks

Data sourcebook for food scientists and technologists / ed. by Y. H. Hui. N.Y. : VCH Publishers, c1991. 976 p. **EJ164**

"Provides domestic and foreign food scientists and technologists easy access to certain useful scientific, technical, and legal information."—*Pref.* In three parts: (A) Chemical and biological data; (B) Product categories data; (C) Safety, laws, and regulations. Index of topics, chemical names, food products, microorganisms, standards, definitions, and other similar categories; fish names are not included.

TX531.D37

Everything added to food in the United States / Center for Food Safety and Applied Nutrition, Division of Toxicological Review and Evaluation, U.S. Food and Drug Administration. Boca Raton, Fla. : C. K. Smoley, 1993. 149 p.   **EJ165**

"The information ... is derived from the files of the FDA. [Contains information on] 1755 regulated food additives, including direct, secondary direct, color and Generally Recognized as Safe (GRAS) additives ... [and] on 1167 additional such substances."—*p. 1.* Arranged alphabetically by mainterm (name of the chemical as recognized by the Center for Food Safety and Applied Nutrition of the FDA). Includes CAS Registry Number (or CAS-like number assigned by CFSAN) and regnum (regulation number(s) in Title 21 of the U.S. Code of Federal Regulations).   TX553.A3E94

Food industries manual / ed. by M. D. Ranken and R. C. Kill. 23rd ed. London ; N.Y. : Blackie Academic & Professional, 1993. 596 p.   **EJ166**

Published with the authority of the Leatherhead Food Research Association.

Contains 17 chapters (e.g., Meat and meat products; Dairy products; Cereals and cereal products; Snack foods; Storage, handling, and packaging), each arranged alphabetically with its own bibliography. Detailed index.   TP370.4.F65

Foodborne diseases / ed. by Dean O. Cliver. San Diego : Academic Pr., c1990. 395 p.   **EJ167**

The aim "has been to make essential information on food safety accessible."—*Pref.* Organized in five parts and 25 chapters: (1) Principles, (2) Intoxications, (3) Infections, (4) Illnesses linked to food, and (5) Prevention. Bibliography at the end of each chapter. Indexed.

QR201.F62F67

Handbook of food engineering / ed. by Dennis R. Heldman, Daryl B. Lund. N.Y. : M. Dekker, c1992. 756 p. : ill. (Food science and technology, 51).   **EJ168**

"Assembles essential information and data to be used by engineers involved in research, development, and operations in the food industry."—*Pref.* Organized in 14 chapters of traditional unit operations. Each chapter contains a list of references. Indexed.   TP370.4.H36

Hayes, George D. Food engineering data handbook. Harlow, Essex, England : Longman Scientific & Technical ; N.Y. : Wiley, 1987. 183 p.   **EJ169**

The aim is to provide "data related to food manufacture, in a convenient and accessible form."—*Pref.* Consists of five chapters: introduction, engineering data, chemical and physical properties of foods, food thermal data, and food processing, storage and packaging data. Indexed.   TP370.4.H39

Lewis, Richard J. Food additives handbook. N.Y. : Van Nostrand Reinhold, c1989. 592 p.   **EJ170**

In three sections. Section 1 includes two chapters: (1) Food additives: their regulatory status; their use by the food industry and (2) Indirect food additives. Section 2 lists in alphabetical order by substance "direct additives, indirect additives, packaging material components, pesticides added directly during food processing, pesticides remaining as residues on food, and selected animal drugs with residue limitations in finished foods."—*Pref.* Entries include the entry number, descriptive data (CAS Registry Numbers, molecular formula and weight, physical properties, synonyms), information relating to use in food, safety profiles, toxicity data, and references (CODEN, volume, page, and year). Section 3 includes four indexes (purpose served in food, food type, CAS number, and synonym) and a list by CODEN of complete bibliographic citations.   RA1270.F6L49

Sourcebooks

Ockerman, Herbert W. Food science sourcebook. 2nd ed. N.Y. : Van Nostrand Reinhold, c1991. 2 v.   **EJ171**

Rev. ed. of: *Source book for food scientists*, 1980.

In two parts. "Part 1 consists of dictionary terms and descriptions wherein the definition usually contains detailed information on the subject and, where feasible, some data concerning its use or properties ... the majority of these ... terms ... [contain] a reference to Part 2 ... Part 2 is composed of alphabetical sections containing food composition, properties, and general data ... [it is] a 'data book' of tables, figures, charts, formulas, etc."—*How to use.*   TX349.O3

FORESTRY

Bibliography

Fahl, Ronald J. North American forest and conservation history : a bibliography. Santa Barbara, Calif. : ABC-Clio, 1977. 408 p.   **EJ172**

Sponsored by Forest History Society, Inc.

A historical bibliography listing primary and secondary sources covering the exploitation, utilization, and appreciation of the forest and its resources. More than 8,000 annotated references, listed alphabetically, and indexed by subject. A companion to Richard C. Davis, *North American forest history* (EJ174).   Z5991.F33

Munns, Edward Norfolk. A selected bibliography of North American forestry. Wash. : U.S. Dept. of Agriculture : [For sale by U.S. Govt. Print. Off.], 1940. 1142 p. (U.S. Dept. of Agriculture. Miscellaneous publ., no. 364).   **EJ173**

Classified, with author index. Includes references to materials in books, periodicals, government bulletins, etc., published in the U.S., Canada, and Mexico prior to 1930.   Z5991.M91

Manuscripts; Archives

Davis, Richard C. North American forest history : a guide to archives and manuscripts in the United States and Canada. Santa Barbara, Calif. : ABC-Clio, 1977. 367 p.   **EJ174**

Sponsored by Forest History Society, Inc.

A guide to the 108 repositories in forest archives which were identified in 1956. Each of the 3,830 groups or collections of documents is numbered and arranged by state. Subject index is to entry number. A companion to Ronald J. Fahl's *North American forest and conservation history* (EJ172).   Z5991.D33

Abstract journals

Forestry abstracts. v. 1 (1939/40)– . Wallingford, Oxon, England : CAB International, 1940– . Monthly.   **EJ175**

Imprint varies. Frequency varies: 1939–72, quarterly.

Compiled from *CAB abstracts* [database] (EJ18). Covers the world literature on all aspects of forestry, including land use and conservation. Foreign titles are translated into English, and abstracts are in English. There are occasional review articles. Includes author and subject indexes cumulated annually. The annual index contains the list of serial titles abstracted during the year.   SD1.F66

Encyclopedias

Encyclopedia of American forest and conservation history / Richard C. Davis, ed. N.Y. : Macmillan ; London : Collier Macmillan, c1983. 2 v. (871 p.) : ill.   **EJ176**

"The goal ... has been to produce the standard, authoritative guide and reference to the history of forestry, conservation, forest industries, and other forest-related subjects in the United States."—*Pref.* Most articles are signed by one of the 203 contributors. Many articles include bibliographies. Appendixes include the national forests and parks of the U.S., a chronology of relevant federal legislation, a chronology of administrations, and an atlas. Indexed.   SD143.E53

Dictionaries

Corkhill, Thomas. The complete dictionary of wood. N.Y. : Stein and Day, 1980. 655 p. : ill.   **EJ177**

British ed. publ. 1948 under title: *A glossary of wood.*

Contains about 10,000 terms and more than 1,000 illustrations. Includes a list of geographical name changes and a table of conversion of unit measurements to the metric and U.S. systems.   TS804.C68

Elsevier's wood dictionary in seven languages : English/American, French, Spanish, Italian, Swedish, Dutch, and German / comp. and arranged on an English alphabetical base by W. Boerhave Beekman. Amsterdam ; N.Y. : Elsevier, 1964–68. 3 v. : ill., facsim., ports.   **EJ178**

Contents: v. 1, Commercial and botanical nomenclature of world-timbers; v. 2, Production, transport, trade; v. 3, Research, manufacture, utilization.

In v. 1, entries give the principal regions of the production of trees or wood and cite botanical numbers in a botanical species index. Vol. 2 contains a section of photographs and illustrations of figures and defects in wood. Vol. 3 has a section of illustrations of pests and parasites and wood constructions. Entries in v. 2–3 include subjects.   SD431.E4

James, N. D. G. An historical dictionary of forestry and woodland terms. Cambridge, Mass. : Blackwell, 1991. 235 p.
EJ179
Intends "to include only those [historical terms] which are concerned with woodlands, trees and forestry."—*Pref.* Includes numerous quotations from old forestry books, "intended to illustrate the use of a particular word or phrase ... [and] provide an insight into the practice and procedures of those days." Includes lists of references and a table of metric conversions.   SD179.J349

Linnard, William. Russian-English forestry and wood dictionary. Oxford : Commonwealth Agriculture Bureaux, 1966. 109 p.   **EJ180**
"Intended to meet the need for a practical Russian-English dictionary as an aid in reading, translating and abstracting Russian literature on forestry and the utilization of forest products."—*Introd.* Includes 7,000 terms.   SD1.C567

McCulloch, Walter Fraser. Woods words : a comprehensive dictionary of loggers terms. [Portland] : Oregon Historical Soc., 1958. 219 p.   **EJ181**
A glossary, with some longer explanations of some 4,000 words and phrases, used in the logging camps of the old Northwest.
PE3727.L8M3

Weck, Johannes. Dictionary of forestry in five languages : German, English, French, Spanish, Russian. Amsterdam ; N.Y. : Elsevier, 1966. 573 p.   **EJ182**
Arranged on a German base, with indexes from the other languages. Includes appendixes of tree species, and of animals and plants causing forest pests and diseases.   SD126.W35

Thesauruses

Terminology of forest science, technology, practice, and products : English-language version / authorized by the Joint FAO/IUFRO Committee on Forestry Bibliography and Terminology ; ed. by F. C. Ford-Robertson. Wash. : Soc. of American Foresters, 1983. 370 p. : ill. (The Multilingual forestry terminology series, no. 1).   **EJ183**
Second printing with addendum. 1st ed., 1971.
"Comprises 6,807 defined concepts, contained in over 5,150 main entries."—*Introd.* Entries are arranged alphabetically and include cross-references and related terms to show the relationships between words, alternative spellings and forms, context, region of currency, Universal Reference Number, and source of definition if taken intact. Appendixes include lists of sources, figures illustrating the vocabulary, families of connected terms, and abbreviations and other notations. Addendum 1 includes 181 new and revised entries.   SD126.J6

Directories

Directory of the wood products industry. 1993– . San Francisco : Miller Freeman Inc., c1992– . Annual.   **EJ184**
Continues *Directory of the forest products industry (DFPI)*, (1963–91), *Handbook and directory of the forest industries* (1958–61), and related titles publ. since 1910.
Contains sections on primary forest products, producers, wood treating, wholesalers, and secondary products manufacturers. Organized by industry sectors and/or state and city. Includes a buyers guide and a cross-reference section referring to the main chapter, state, and city. Indexed.   TS803.D5

Handbooks

Forestry handbook / ed. for the Society of American Foresters by Karl F. Wegner. 2nd ed. N.Y. : Wiley, c1984. 1335 p. : ill.   **EJ185**
1st ed., 1955.
Provides "a reference book of data and methods in all phases of forestry and allied fields [for] the practicing field forester."—*Pref.* Sections, written by specialists, include forest ecology, forest insect and disease management, fire management, timber measurements, timber inventory, silviculture, logging, outdoor recreation management, urban forestry, forest resource law, and safety. Bibliographies; index.
SD373.F58

Mohlenbrock, Robert H. The field guide to U.S. national forests. N.Y. : Congdon & Weed : Distr. by St. Martin's, c1984. 324 p. : ill., maps.   **EJ186**
A guide by region to 153 national forests. Entries include information on location, facilities and services, special attractions, activities, and wildlife. Indexed.   SD426.M64

Princes Risborough Laboratory. Handbook of hardwoods. 2nd ed. rev. / by R. H. Farmer. London : H.M.S.O., 1972. 243 p.   **EJ187**
1st ed., 1956.
Aims to "assist users of hardwoods to select the timbers best suited to their purposes and to process them in the most satisfactory manner."—*Introd.* Provides full descriptions of 117 hardwoods and briefer descriptions of an additional 103. Includes information on trees and numerical and other data on properties, processing, durability, preservation, and uses. Appendixes include a table summarizing data, table of types of saws, and kiln schedules. Indexed by botanical and trade names.   TA419.P76

Record, Samuel James. Timbers of the New World / by Samuel J. Record and Robert W. Hess. New Haven, Conn. : Yale Univ. Pr., 1943. 640 p. : ill.   **EJ188**
Repr.: N.Y. : Arno, 1972.
Also publ. London : H. Milford ; Oxford Univ. Pr., 1943.
A successor to Record and Clayton Mell's *Timbers of tropical America* (1924), containing more than twice the amount of material. Covers "the trees and larger shrubs of the entire Western Hemisphere, exclusive of the islands of the Pacific. Contains descriptions of the trees, tells where they grow and the sizes they attain, and attempts to evaluate their present and potential economic importance."—*Pref.* Arranged alphabetically by families and genera within two principal groups: gymnosperms and angiosperms. Includes lists of families classified with reference to special properties and uses of their bark, leaves, and timber. Index to scientific and common names.
SD434.R4

Rendle, Bernard John. World timbers. London : E. Benn ; Toronto : Univ. of Toronto Pr., 1969–1970. 3 v. : ill. (chiefly col.).   **EJ189**
Contents: v. 1, Europe and Africa; v. 2, North and South America, including Central America and the West Indies; v. 3, Asia and Australia and New Zealand.
During 1936–60 the journal *Wood* published a series on wood specimens and world timbers. Plates illustrating the grain of each type of wood have been selected from the series and reissued here in a more systematic arrangement, with revised and updated technical information (including notes on distribution and supply) to accompany each plate. Timbers were selected for economic importance or interest on the world market.   SD536.R4

Stoddard, Charles Hatch. Essentials of forestry practice / Charles H. Stoddard, Glenn M. Stoddard. 4th ed. N.Y. : Wiley, c1987. 407 p. : ill.   **EJ190**
Discusses "field practices and operations in timber growing, logging, protection, harvesting, and processing."—*Pref.* Appendixes include forest terminology, characteristics of important commercial tim-

ber species, principal federal, state, and private forestry organizations, bibliography (organized by chapters), and proposed metric equivalents for forestry. Indexed.   SD373.S79

Atlases

United States. Forest Service. Atlas of United States trees. Wash. : [U.S. Forest Service] : [for sale by U. S. Govt. Print. Off.], 1971–1981. 6 v. : maps. (U.S. Dept. of Agriculture. Miscellaneous publ., no. 1146 [etc.]).   **EJ191**

Superintendent of Documents classification: A 1.38l: .

Contents: v. 1, Conifers and important hardwoods, by E. L. Little, Jr.; v. 2, Alaska trees and common shrubs, by L. A. Viereck and E. L. Little, Jr.; v. 3, Minor western hardwoods, by E. L. Little, Jr.; v. 4, Minor eastern hardwoods, by E. L. Little, Jr.; v. 5, Florida, by E. L. Little, Jr.; v. 6, Supplement, by E. L. Little, Jr.

Each volume consists of maps with political boundaries to the county level showing the distribution of individual species. Indexes of common and scientific names in each volume.   S21.A46

Statistics

Forest products. 1987– . Rome : Food and Agriculture Organization of the United Nations, 1989– . Annual.   **EJ192**

Continues: *Yearbook of forest products*, 1967–86 and *Yearbook of forest products statistics*, 1947–66.

Title and text in English, French, and Spanish.

Tables on the quantity and value of the imported and exported forest products for most of the world's countries, with totals for the world and for various regions.   HD9750.4.Y4

HOME ECONOMICS

Bibliography

United States. Department of Agriculture. Home economics research report. no. 1 (April 1957)– . Wash. : The Department : for sale by U.S. Govt. Print. Off., [1957]– . Irregular.   **EJ193**

Covers clothing, fabrics, child development, nutrition, cooking, food storage, and family finance. Includes semitechnical and technical publications formerly issued as the Department's *Agricultural handbooks, Agriculture information bulletins, Miscellaneous publications*, and *Circulars*.   A321.9Ag8

Dissertations

American Home Economics Association. Titles of dissertations and theses completed in home economics. 1968/69– . Wash. : Assoc., 1970– . Annual.   **EJ194**

At head of title: Home economics research.

A classified listing with author index. Similar listings appeared in the *Journal of home economics*, 1964–69.

§ Beginning with v. 11 (1983) the *Home economics research journal* publishes an annual listing of titles by subject matter of theses and dissertations. The March 1983 issue lists titles of papers completed between Sept. 1, 1981 and Aug. 30, 1982. The journal also publishes scholarly articles on a variety of issues and research.   Z5775.A63

Home economics research abstracts. Wash. : Amer. Home Economics Assoc., 1967–78.   **EJ195**

Issued in 5 to 7 sections per year.

Contents (varies): 1, Family economics and home management; 2, Institution administration; 3, Textiles and clothing; 4, Art and housing, furnishings, and equipment; 5, Home economics communication and home economics education; 6, Family relations and child development; 7, Food and nutrition.

Each issue in the series is a compilation of abstracts of doctoral dissertations and master's theses from schools offering graduate programs in home economics.

United States. Agricultural Research Service. Titles of completed theses in home economics and related fields in colleges and universities of the United States. 1942/46–1961/62. Wash. : The Service, [1947?]–63.   **EJ196**

Title varies: 1942/46, *Completed theses in home economics and related fields in colleges and universities of the United States.*

Issued 1942/46–1951/52 by the Bureau of Human Nutrition and Home Economics; 1952/53–1961/62 by the Agricultural Research Service. Issued as U.S. Dept. of Agriculture, PA [Program aid], 1944/49–1961/62. Continued in *Journal of home economics.* 1964–69; currently continued by American Home Economics Association, *Titles of dissertations and theses completed in home economics* (EJ194).

A listing of master's and doctoral theses, arranged by subject with author index. "Intended to supplement the list 'Research in foods, human nutrition and home economics at the landgrant institutions' comp. annually by the Office of Experiment Stations... 1935/36–1955/56 and the list of 'Notes on research in home economics education' comp. in the Office of Education, 1934/36–1945. 6 v."—*Pref.*

§ The series, "Abstracts of doctoral theses related to home economics," formerly appearing in *Journal of home economics* has been discontinued, but the *Journal* continues to carry abstracts of selected articles of interest to home economics, together with notes on new books and audiovisual materials.

Indexes; Abstract journals

Fetterman, N. I. Index to research in home economics, 1972–1991 / Nelma I. Fetterman, Verna M. Lefebvre. 2nd ed. [Winnipeg] : authors, 1992. 449 p.   **EJ197**

1st ed., 1989.

Aims to help locate valuable work of home economics researchers difficult to identify through usual search strategies. Covers research reports in 1,290 articles published in 56 volumes of *Canadian home economics journal, Home economics research journal, Journal of consumer studies and home economics*, and *Journal of vocational home economics education* (v. 1–3 only). In four parts: a subject index, an author/title index, keyword-in-title index, and a complete bibliography. *Journal of home economics* was omitted because financial support was unavailable.   Z5775F48

History

American Home Economics Association. International Section. The international heritage of home economics in the United States : [75th annual meeting of the American Home Economics Association held in Anaheim, California, June, 1984] / Lela O'Toole, coordinating ed. [Wash.] : American Home Economics Assoc., 1988. 251 p. : ill.   **EJ198**

A history of the International Federation of Home Economics. Highlights home economics international activities through the efforts of home economists in the U.S. Biographical sketches of 24 early pioneers in international service. Descriptions of projects in India, Philippines, Ghana, Liberia, Brazil, and other foreign countries. Index.   TX5.A5

Brown, Marjorie M. Philosophical studies of home economics in the United States : our practical-intellectual heritage. East Lansing, Mich. : College of Human Ecology, Michigan State Univ., c1985. 2 v. (1101 p.).   **EJ199**

Vol. 1 "presents an overview of the philosophical studies and what they entail ... "; v. 2, "the history of home economics and theoretical conceptions ... ."—*Pref.* Extensive bibliography. Index.

TX23.B76

Du Vall, Nell. Domestic technology : a chronology of developments. Boston : G.K. Hall, 1988. 535 p.   **EJ200**

"Domestic or household technology ... includes all the tools, appliances, and services we use to maintain our homes, and our daily life-styles ... foods we eat, the tools and utensils we use, the clothes we buy, our homes and almost everything in them ... also includes some of the underlying structures and services including water supplies, waste disposal, and power."—*p. 2.* Topical chapters are followed by chronological tables noting major innovations and inventions. "Notes" section lists bibliographical references arranged by chapter. BCE and CE chronologies. Index.   TX15.D8

East, Marjorie. Home economics : past, present, and future. Boston : Allyn & Bacon, 1980. 292 p. : ill.   **EJ201**

"A book about home economics which examines its historical roots, its several definitions, its students and professionals, its potentials, and which asks many questions and answers a few."—*verso of t.p.* Offers a comprehensive survey of the field. Bibliography, p. 270–86; index.   TX145.E27

Pundt, Helen Marie. AHEA : a history of excellence. Wash. : American Home Economics Assoc., c1980. 396 p. : ill.

EJ202

A year-by-year synopsis and description of the annual meetings of the Association, 1909–69. (The preliminary meetings were hosted by Melvil and Anna Dewey). Includes summaries of government legislation affecting personal environment of individuals and families and biographical information of leaders in the profession;. Activities of the Association are assessed at 10-year intervals. Index.   TX1.A658P86

Food and cookery

Bibliography

Cook's index. v. 1– . Evanston, Ill. : John Gordon Burke Publisher, c1989– . Triennial.   **EJ203**

Vol. 1 has subtitle: an index of cookbooks and periodicals from 1975–1987.

Purpose: "to bring bibliographical control to the literature of cookery." The index "will be published every three years ... supplemented by the Cook's information service."—*Introd.* Provides author, title, and subject index to cookbooks and author and subject index to recipes located in standard cookery periodicals, selected women's periodicals, and a number of regional magazines around the U. S. Includes addresses for periodical sources.   Z5776.G2C59

Feret, Barbara L. Gastronomical and culinary literature : a survey and analysis of historically oriented collections in the U.S.A. Metuchen, N.J. : Scarecrow, 1979. 124 p.   **EJ204**

Aims "to survey, identify, and analyze important U.S. collections of printed materials on the culinary arts."—*Introd.* An introductory section reviews the nature and development of the literature of cookery and gastronomy in the Western world by country and by period, citing significant works. The section on collections offers information on the strengths and specialties of some 56 libraries and private collections, often citing specific early and rare works held. Includes a bibliography of culinary bibliographies, and one of secondary historical texts and references. Indexed.   Z5776.G2F47

Newman, Jacqueline M. Melting pot : an annotated bibliography and guide to food and nutrition information for ethnic groups in America. N.Y. : Garland, 1986. 194 p. (Garland reference library of social science, v. 351).   **EJ205**

In ten chapters, eight of which treat ethnic groups (African Americans, Hispanic Americans, Chinese Americans, Japanese Americans, other Asian Americans, Indian Americans, Middle Eastern Americans, and "mixed ethnic references"). East Europeans and Russians are omitted. Each chapter has three parts: an introduction, references (citations from medical, health, and nutrition journals) and "resources for recipes" (cookbooks). Chap. 1 provides an overview of American food preferences and nutritional habits, and chap. 10, tables of food compositions. No index.   Z7914.F63N48

Simon, André Louis. Bibliotheca gastronomica : a catalogue of books and documents on gastronomy. London : Wine and Food Soc., 1953. 196 p.   **EJ206**

"The production, taxation, distribution and consumption of food and drink, their use and abuse in all times and among all peoples."—*title page.* An annotated listing of 1,644 items, arranged alphabetically by author, with indexes by short title and by subject.

Z5776.G2S594b

Vicaire, Georges. Bibliographie gastronomique / introd. by André L. Simon. [2nd ed.]. London : Derek Verschoyle Academic and Bibliographical Publ., 1954. 972 col.   **EJ207**

Subtitle: A bibliography of books pertaining to food and drink and related subjects, from the beginning of printing to 1890.

Originally published: Paris, Rouquette, 1890.

An annotated bibliography of some 2,500 works pertaining to gastronomy. Titles are largely in French, but some are in other Western European languages. Annotations provide detailed bibliographic information and notes on content. Arranged alphabetically by author or by title when the work is anonymous. Title index.   Z5776.G2V5

Indexes

Torgeson, Kathryn W. The Garland recipe index / Kathryn W. Torgeson and Sylvia J. Weinstein. N.Y. : Garland, 1984. 314 p. (Garland reference library of the humanities, v. 414).

EJ208

An index to cookbooks, including basic, foreign, and ethnic, U.S. regional, and specialty (e.g., dietetic and vegetarian). Includes large quantity and illustrated cooking techniques. Recipes indexed by name, principal food ingredient, and cooking style.   Z5776.G2T67

Encyclopedias

Coyle, L. Patrick. The world encyclopedia of food. N.Y. : Facts on File, c1982. 790 p., [32] p. of plates : ill.   **EJ209**

About 4,000 entries in alphabetic arrangement. "Priority has been given to identification (including the scientific name), description, and discussions of where and how an item is eaten or drunk and what it tastes like."—*Introd.* Most entries treat individual items of food, but prepared foods (e.g., sausage, cheese, wine, bread, and sauces) are included. Most entries are brief, but some are lengthy, e.g., "Nutritive values of the edible part of foods" and "Wine and liquor terms." Bibliography; index.   TX349.C69

Foods & nutrition encyclopedia / Audrey H. Ensminger ... [et al.]. 2nd ed. Boca Raton, Fla. : CRC Pr., c1994. 2 v. (2415 p.) : ill. (some col.).   **EJ210**

1st ed., 1983.

A comprehensive encyclopedia covering all aspects of food and nutrition, and their relationship to health. Entries vary in length from brief definitions to articles several pages in length, with cross-references and footnotes ,or new or controversial topics. Many illustrations, with information presented in tabular form wherever possible. Food composition table; subject index.   TX349.F575

Montagné, Prosper. Larousse gastronomique : the new American edition of the world's greatest culinary encyclopedia / ed. by Jenifer Harvey Lang. N.Y. : Crown Publishers, 1988. 1193 p. : ill. (some col.).   **EJ211**

Translation of: *Nouveau Larousse gastronomique*, first publ. 1938.

Intends "to present an anthology of haute cuisine and recipes for home cooking ... to make readers more aware of the great classic dishes of other countries."—*Pref.* Articles are alphabetically arranged. Incorporates changes based on a growing interest in dietetics. New feature: recipes by leading contemporary chefs. Recipe index.

TX349.M613

Dictionaries

Mariani, John F. The dictionary of American food and drink. New Haven, Conn. : Ticknor & Fields, 1983. 477 p.   **EJ212**

Intends "to demonstrate both the array of American food, wine and drink and the way Americans speak of it, consume it, and have changed it over the centuries."—*Guide to the dictionary.* Attempts to gather "from A to Z the origins, changes, and current status of food and drink items, terms of culinary interest and slang." Frequently includes anecdotes and representative recipes. Index.   TX349.M26

Simon, André Louis. Dictionary of gastronomy / André L. Simon and Robin Howe. N.Y. : McGraw-Hill, [1970]. 400 p. : ill.   **EJ213**

Entries for foods, utensils, terms used in cookery, etc. Includes 64 color plates and numerous illustrations. Selected bibliography of nearly 200 items.   TX349.S53

Directories

Frank, Robyn C. The directory of food and nutrition information for professionals and consumers / ed. by Robyn C. Frank and Holly Berry Irving. 2nd ed. Phoenix : Oryx, 1992. 332 p.

EJ214

1st ed., 1984, had title: *Directory of food and nutrition information services and resources*, ed. by Robyn C. Frank.

Identifies sources of food and nutrition information, for both professionals and general readers. Divided into two major sections: pt. 1 includes organizations, academic programs, software and databases; pt. 2 is composed of annotated bibliographic entries for reference materials and journals, (including a list of cookbooks), and a listing of organizations that provide consumer information. The sections are separately indexed. Lists food- and nutrition-related museums and special collections.   TX353.D56

Handbooks

American Home Economics Association. Food and Nutrition Section. Handbook of food preparation. 9th ed. Dubuque, Iowa : Kendall/Hunt, c1993. 232 p.   **EJ215**

1st ed., 1946; 8th ed., 1980.

A classic for 47 years, greatly expanded and revised. Incorporates recent major federal legislation concerning nutrition labeling and education. Answers a broad spectrum of food-related questions. Topics include: description of properties, buying guides, recipe construction, cooking times, food preservation, high-altitude cooking, microwave cooking, using the slow cooker, international menus, weight and volume tables, servings per market unit. Index.   TX535.A5

Bowes, Anna De Planter. Bowes and Church's food values of portions commonly used. 16th ed. / rev. by Jean A. T. Pennington. Philadelphia : Lippincott, c1994. 483 p. : tables.

EJ216

Earlier editions by Anna De Planter Bowes and Helen Nichols Church.

Designed "to supply authoritative data on the nutritional values of foods in a form for quick and easy reference."–*Pref.* The main section provides tables of nutrient contents of foods; foods are arranged in 55 sections by food type. Includes discussion of brand name products, coversion tables, U.S. recommended daily allowances, and references for sources of food data. Bibliography, general index, and many supplementary tables, including a list of Latin names for plants and animals used in food. A classic work.   TX551.B64

Heath, Henry B. Source book of flavors. Westport, Conn. : Avi Publ., [1981]. 863 p. : ill.   **EJ217**

Updates Joseph Merory's *Food flavoring* (2nd ed., 1968).

Pt. 1, the major part of the book, contains chapters about the flavor industry; chemistry and chemists; research; materials (naturally occurring and synthetic); manufacturing (methods, test procedures, patents, classification, quality assurance, label regulations); chemistry of fragrances; food colorations; international regulations, and toxicology. Pt. 2 is an alphabetic bibliography of some 140 flavoring materials which occur naturally or as a result of processing. Includes references to research reports, articles, etc., dealing with the chemical composition of each. Pt. 3 covers flavoring formulations. Subject, bibliographical, and formulary indexes.   TP418.H43

McGee, Harold. The curious cook : more kitchen science and lore. San Francisco : North Point Pr., 1990. 339 p. : ill.

EJ218

Investigates what goes on in the kitchen, experimenting with various foods and ways of preparing them. Considers nutritional information. Connects scientific information with the fun of experimenting with foods. Illustrates the impact of cookery on biochemistry. Index.

TX651.M268

——————— On food and cooking. N.Y. : Scribner, c1984. 684 p. : ill.   **EJ219**

Subtitle: The science and lore of the kitchen.

Contents: pt. 1, Foods; pt. 2, Food and the body; pt. 3, The principles of cooking: a summary.

Explains the nature of foods, their composition and origin, and why the techniques employed in cooking work. Indexed.

TX651.M37

Tables

Composition of foods : raw, processed, prepared / by the Nutrition Monitoring Div. Wash. : U.S. Dept. of Agriculture, Human Nutrition Information Service ; for sale by U.S. Govt. Print. Off., 1976–88. Pts. 1–21 (looseleaf). (Agriculture handbook, no. 8). (In progress).   **EJ220**

Superintendent of Documents classification: A1.76:8-1 .

Preparing agency and publisher vary.

Contents: no. 8–1, Dairy and egg products; no. 8–2, Spices and herbs; no. 8–3, Baby foods; no. 8–4, Fats and oils; no. 8–5, Poultry products; no. 8–6, Soups, sauces, and gravies; no. 8–7, Sausages and luncheon meats; no. 8–8, Breakfast cereals; no. 8–9, Fruits and fruit juices; no. 8–10, Pork products; no. 8–11, Vegetables and vegetable products; no. 8–12, Nut and seed products; no. 8–13, Beef products; no. 8–14, Beverages; no. 8–15, Finfish and shellfist products; no. 8–17, Lamb, veal, and game products; no. 8–19, Snacks and sweets; no. 8–20, Cereal grains and pasta; no. 8–21, Fast foods. No. 8–18, Baked products, in preparation.

Kept up-to-date by annual supplements.

A major revision of USDA Handbook no. 8, "currently a basic source of food composition data in this country."—*Foreword.* "This revision... is being issued in sections so as to expedite release of data to the public. Each section contains a table of nutrient data for a major food group. The entire series will cover a wide range of food products."—*Pref.*   TX556.M5C68

Food and Agriculture Organization of the United Nations.
Food composition tables : updated annotated bibliography.
Rome : FAO, 1975. 181 p.   **EJ221**
    Title varies: 1965 ed. called *Review of food composition tables*;
1969 ed. called *Food composition tables : annotated bibliography*.
    International in scope; arranged by continent, then country. Includes information on techniques of gathering data, arrangement, portions analyzed, nutrients included, etc.

Cookbooks

Bulson, Christine. Current cookbooks : a selected list of methods and cuisines. Middletown, Conn. : Choice, 1990. 44 p.   **EJ222**
    A bibliography of 250 selected titles of current, basic, and in-print cookbooks published 1980–90. Categories are Reference, Classic, Basic American cuisine, Other cuisines, Cooking techniques, Books by chefs, Food writers or other famous people, Books without recipes. Aim: to provide "a manageable number from which a library or individual could develop a current basic collection of cookbooks."—*p. 5.* Includes a short history of cooking. Author and title indexes.
                                                      Z5776.G2B8

Shih, Tian-Chu. Health-related cookbooks : a bibliography. Metuchen, N.J. : Scarecrow, 1991. 401 p.   **EJ223**
    Brief annotations for English-language cookbooks from a wide variety of publishers. The majority of titles were published 1980–91, although for some subjects the inclusion date is 1970. Section 1 covers diets for specific diseases or disorders, section 2 those for general health. "Within each chapter, cookbooks are further subdivided according to the individual diet plants: high-fiber, high-complex-carbohydrate, high-calcium … and so on."—*Introd.* Provides detailed chapter outlines and a locator guide, which allows readers to locate cookbooks related to specific diets. Author, title, and keyword indexes; list of publishers and references.   Z6665.D53S54

Vassilian, Hamo B. Ethnic cookbooks and food marketplace : a complete bibliographic guide & directory to Armenian, Iranian, Afghan, Israeli, Middle Eastern, North African, and Greek foods in the U.S.A. & Canada. 2nd ed. Glendale, Calif. : Armenian Reference Books Co., 1991. 128 p. : ill.   **EJ224**
    Arranged in four parts: pt. 1, an alphabetical arrangement by author, title, and subject of 239 cookbooks in English; pt. 2, a guide to the food marketplace by specific categories, including bakeries, caterers, food manufacturers, grocers, night clubs, and restaurants; pt. 3, an index to business names; pt. 4, a geographical listing of the ethnic food marketplace for the U.S. and Canada.   TX725..M628E84

Wines

The companion to wine / ed. by Frank Prial, with Rosemary George and Michael Edwards. N.Y. : Prentice Hall General Reference, c1992. 365 p. : ill., maps (chiefly col.).   **EJ225**
    A sourcebook on wine and fruit-based spirits. Maps include locations of vintners. Directory, alphabetically organized, provides a selective gazetteer of wines, technical wine terms, grape types and certain wine growers throughout the world. Index.   TP548.C65

Johnson, Hugh. The world atlas of wine : a complete guide to the wines and spirits of the world. 3rd ed., enl. and completely rev. N.Y. : Simon and Schuster, 1985. 320 p. : ill., maps.
                                                      EJ226
    1st ed., 1971.

    Contents: Introduction, Choosing and serving wine, France, Germany, Southern and eastern Europe and the Mediterranean, The new world, Spirits.
    Describes the wines of specific parts of the world. Each area is accompanied by a map, generally detailed. Index; gazetteer.
                                                      TP548.J66

Lipinski, Robert A. The complete beverage dictionary / Robert A. Lipinski and Kathleen A. Lipinski. N.Y. : Van Nostrand Reinhold, c1992. 425 p.   **EJ227**
    More than 6,100 terms describing wines, spirits, beer, and nonalcoholic beverages. Serves as a quick resource "as well as providing much needed research and reference material with in-depth coverage. It encompasses international words and terms, label terminology, terms relating to the production, sale and service of beverages, slang, and geography, as well as origins of historical significance."—*Pref.*
                                                      TP503.L56

HORTICULTURE

Bibliography

Isaacson, Richard T. Gardening : a guide to the literature. N.Y. : Garland, 1985. 198 p.   **EJ228**
    "Lists materials (books, magazines, nursery and seed catalogs, etc.) that [the compiler] found to be of most use to gardeners."—*Introd.* Arranged by broad subject areas: reference works, landscape design, ornamental gardening plants, methods of growing and using plants, and gardening practices and plant problems. Also lists periodicals, seed and nursery catalogs (including reference sources), libraries, and book dealers. Under each section, titles are "arranged by the compiler's evaluation of their importance or effectiveness." Name, title, and subject indexes.   Z5996.A1I8

Indexes; Abstract journals

Clewis, Beth. The gardener's index : where to find information about gardens and garden plants. N.Y. : Neal-Schuman, 1993. 224 p.   **EJ229**
    A comprehensive index to a selected bibliography of 105 encyclopedias and dictionaries. The index includes approximately 10,000 species of plants arranged by botanical name. It provides other names as well as the code with pagination to the sources in the bibliography and includes cross-references from all other names. Contains an index to special plants and situations and a bibliography indicating the assigned code.   Z5996.A1C66

Horticultural abstracts. v. 1 (Mar. 1931)– . Wallingford, U.K. [etc.] : CAB International Information Services [etc.]. Monthly.   **EJ230**
    Frequency varies; quarterly, 1931–72. Publisher varies.
    Produced by the Division of Crop Production.
    Compiled from *CAB abstracts* [database] (EJ18). Sections include: General aspects of research and its applications; Temperate tree fruits and nuts; Small fruits; Viticulture; Vegetables, temperate, tropical and greenhouse; Ornamental plants; Minor temperate and tropical industrial crops; Subtropical fruit and plantation crops; Tropical fruit and plantation crops. Each issue includes author and subject indexes, cumulating annually. The annual index contains a list of serial titles abstracted.   SB1.H65

Encyclopedias

The American Horticultural Society encyclopedia of garden plants / ed. in chief, Christopher Brickell ; horticultural consultant, John Elsley. N.Y. : Macmillan, 1989. 608 p. : ill. **EJ231**

"Offers both amateur and professional horticulturists a wealth of theoretical and practical information on the potential garden value of … [over 8,000 plants], half of which are accompanied by excellent color photographs."—*Foreword*. Despite the title, the work, done under the editorship of the Royal Horticultural Society, has a marked bias toward European cultivars. American hardiness zones (some estimated) and American common names have been added. The plants are grouped systematically in the dictionary section, where their characteristics and cultivation are described, while in the catalog section they are arranged by size, color, and season of interest along with about 4,000 excellent color photographs. Covers ornamental plants and trees. The dictionary serves as an index to the catalog and there is a separate index to common names.   SB403.2.A46

The American Horticultural Society encyclopedia of gardening / ed. in chief, Christopher Brickell; ed. in chief, American Horticultural Society, Elvin McDonald; consulting ed. for Canada, Trevor Cole. London ; N.Y. : Dorling Kindersley, 1993. 648 p. : ill.   **EJ232**

Aims "to present in a clear, practical, and authoritative style all the information that gardeners need on how to design their gardens and cultivate, maintain, and increase plants of all types, whether they are ornamentals, fruits, or vegetables."—*Pref*. "The text is lavishly illustrated with full-color photographs and artworks showing design ideas, planting plans, and practical techniques."—*How to use this book*. Organized in two parts: Creating the garden, and Maintaining the garden. Most plants are referred to by botanical names, some (including fruits, herbs, and vegetables) by common names. Glossary of terms; comprehensive index including both common and botanical names for all mentioned plants.   SB450.95.A45

Everett, Thomas H. The New York Botanical Garden illustrated encyclopedia of horticulture. N.Y. : Garland, c1980–c1982. 10 v. (3601 p.) : ill. (some col.).   **EJ233**

Updates Liberty Hyde Bailey's *Standard cyclopedia of horticulture*, 1922 (various reprintings).

"A comprehensive description and evaluation of horticulture as it is known and practiced in the United States and Canada by amateurs and by professionals."–*Pref*. Attempts to describe the majority of genera known to be in cultivation. Follows the nomenclature adopted in *Hortus third* (EG147). Genera (approximately 3,500 items) and families are entered under Latin name with references from common name; vegetables, fruits, herbs, and ornamentals are entered under common name. Genus entries include pronunciation; synonymy; general characteristics (including number of species, natural geographic distribution, derivation of name, historical data, and uses); descriptions of species, hybrids, and varieties; and garden and landscape uses, cultivation, and pests and diseases. Includes definition and subject articles; each volume contains an organized listing of general subject entries. Numerous black-and-white photographs; some in color.   SB317.58.E94

Rodale's illustrated encyclopedia of herbs / Claire Kowalchik and William H. Hylton, editors. Emmaus, Pa. : Rodale Pr., c1987. 545 p. : ill.   **EJ234**

Contains entries for herbs and 16 general articles discussing uses of herbs (e.g., bathing, cooking, crafts, dyes, gardening, healing, lotions, scents, and teas) as well as definition, botany, dangers, growing, and history. Includes bibliography and index.   SB351.H5R58

Seymour, E. L. D. The Wise garden encyclopedia : a complete, practical, and convenient guide to every detail of gardening written for all U.S. climates, soils, seasons, and methods. N.Y. : Grosset & Dunlap, 1970. 1380 p. : ill.   **EJ235**

First publ. 1936 as: *The garden encyclopedia*. 1946 ed. had title *The new garden encyclopedia*.

Aims to present "in simple, practical, interesting and helpful form the information that will enable any person with a garden to get the most out of it."—*Foreword*. Follows *Hortus third* (EG147) as the authority for plant identity. Includes 61 halftone and 64 color illustrations.   SB45.S4

Wyman, Donald. Wyman's gardening encyclopedia. New expanded 2nd ed. N.Y. : Macmillan, c1986. 1221 p. : ill. **EJ236**

1st ed., 1971; rev. ed., 1977.

"[W]ritten by experienced gardeners, for gardeners. It contains many articles dealing with the growing of specialized groups of plants as well as brief descriptions of thousands of plants … [selected for their] ornamental or economic value … [Includes] most of the plants popularly known or grown … in all but the subtropical and tropical parts of the United States … [plants are] listed alphabetically with descriptions after the scientific names. Common names are cross-indexed. Exceptions are fruits and vegetables, which are listed and described according to their common names … [S]cientific names of plants … follow … the new International Code of Nomenclature for Cultivated Plants"—*Introd.*. The table of contents itemizes 59 major articles on horticultural practices and 52 lists of plants, experiment stations, societies, and display gardens.   SB450.95.W96

Dictionaries

Bagust, Harold. The gardener's dictionary of horticultural terms. London : Cassell ; N.Y. : Distr. by Sterling Publ. Co., 1992. 377 p. : ill.   **EJ237**

Provides "the enthusiastic gardener or student of horticulture with a basic guide through the labyrinth of technical terms in use today."—*Pref*. Numerous line drawings illustrate the entries, and appendixes include line drawings of leaf shapes, leaf margins, leaf tips, compound leaves, attachment of stem, foliage arrangement, leaf venation, forms of ovules, floral diagrams, types of corolla, forms of vegetative propagation, and budding and grafting methods.   SB450.95.B33

Bourke, D. O'D. French-English horticultural dictionary : with English-French index. [2nd ed.]. Oxford : C.A.B. International, 1989. 228 p.   **EJ238**

"The aim … is to make it possible for readers whose language is English … to discover the meaning of words … in horticultural literature written in the French languages"—*Pref*.   SB318

——————— Spanish-English horticultural dictionary : with English-Spanish index / by D. O'D. Bourke, L. Fanjul, A. J. Rendell-Dunn. 148 p. (CAB International Bureau of Horticulture and Plantation Crops. Technical communication, no. 36).   **EJ239**

The objective is "to make possible for anglophones to read … horticultural publications emanating from Hispanic countries."—*Pref*.   SB317.58.B6

Elsevier's dictionary of horticultural and plant production : in ten languages, English, Dutch, French, German, Danish, Swedish, Italian, Spanish, Portuguese, and Latin. Amsterdam [Netherlands] ; N.Y. : Elsevier : distr. by Elsevier Science Pub. Co., 1990. 817 p.   **EJ240**

Comp. under the auspices of the International Society for Horticultural Science, Wageningen, The Netherlands with the cooperation of the Ministry of Agriculture, Natural Management, and Fisheries, The Hague, The Netherlands.

Rev. ed. of: *Elsevier's dictionary of horticulture in nine languages*, 1970.

Covers traditional horticulture as well as tropical and subtropical horticulture, herbs and spices, landscaping, arable farming, and grasses. The basic list consists of 5,129 terms sequentially arranged on an English base, with indexes in the other nine languages. Includes a list of international organizations with acronyms.   SB45.E42

Hortus third : a concise dictionary of plants cultivated in the United States and Canada. N.Y. : Macmillan, [1976]. 1290 p. : ill.   **EJ241**

"Includes the description [uses, propagation, and cultivation] and correct botanical name with its author or authors for 281 families, 3,301 genera, and 20,397 species"—*Introd.* Includes index of common plant names. For complete annotation, *see* EG147.   SB45.H67

Index of garden plants / Mark Griffiths. Portland, Or. : Timber Pr., 1994. 1234 p. : ill.   **EJ242**

Derived from the Royal Horticultural Society's *Dictionary of gardening* (EG125).

"It has three aims: to list currently accepted botanical names, synonyms and popular names for some 60,000 plants in cultivation; to furnish each plant with a brief description; and to demystify the ways in which such names arise and sometimes change."—*Introd.*

Soule, James. Glossary for horticultural crops / sponsored by the American Society for Horticultural Science. N.Y. : Wiley, c1985. 898 p. : ill.   **EJ243**

Provides "ready access to technical terms over a broad spectrum of the plant and plant-related sciences."—*Pref.* In six main sections: Horticultural crops, Morphology and anatomy, Horticultural taxonomy and plant breeding, Horticultural physiology and crop ecology, Propagation, nursery handling, soils, crop production, and Postharvest handling and marketing. Line drawings; indexes of terms and crops.

SB317.58.S68

Directories

Barton, Barbara J. Gardening by mail : a source book : everything for the garden and gardener. 4th ed., updated and rev. Boston : Houghton Mifflin, 1994. 1 v. (various pagings) : ill.
                                                        EJ244

"A directory of mail-order resources for gardeners in the United States and Canada, including seed companies, nurseries, suppliers of all garden necessaries and ornaments, horticultural and plant societies, magazines, libraries, and a list of useful books on plants and gardening."—*t.p.*

Entries are annotated. Five indexes: Plant and seed sources, Geographical index of plant and seed sources, Products and services, Society index, and Magazines and newsletters by title.   SB450.943.B37

Horticultural research international : directory of horticultural research institutes and their activities in 63 countries / [organizing editors, H. H. van der Borg, M. Koning-van der Veen]. 4th ed. Wageningen : International Society for Horticultural Science, 1986. 903 p. : maps.   **EJ245**

1st ed., 1966; 3rd ed., 1981.

"The present edition covers some 16,650 scientists at 1,250 institutes in 63 countries."—*Pref.* Arranged alphabetically by country, some countries subdivided by regions and/or states or provinces. For each country includes a map indicating the horticultural research centers. For the U.S., cities are indicated in each regional map. For each country, region, state, or province, contains a survey of horticultural research and a list by cities of individual research institutes including address, name of head or contact person, and names of research workers and their projects or research interests as well as elevation in meters, rainfall in millimeters, hours of sunshine, and relative humidity. Indexes of places and research workers.

Handbooks

Dirr, Michael A. Manual of woody landscape plants : their identification, ornamental characteristics, culture, propagation and uses. 4th ed. Champaign, Ill. : Stipes Publ., 1990. 1007 p. : ill., maps.   **EJ246**

Covers 302 genera. Entries may contain a line drawing, identification characteristics, hardiness, culture, diseases and insects that affect it, landscape value, cultivars, propagation, related species (includes descriptions of other plants), and native habitat. Includes a bibliography, glossary of taxonomic terms, and scientific and common name indexes.   SB435.5.D57

———————— The reference manual of woody plant propagation : from seed to tissue culture : a practical working guide to the propagation of over 1100 species, varieties, and cultivars / by Michael A. Dirr and Charles W. Heuser, Jr. Athens, Ga. : Varsity Pr., c1987. 239 p. : ill.   **EJ247**

The main section lists plants alphabetically by scientific name. Entries describe the methods to propagate the plant including seeds, cuttings, grafting, and tissue culture. Contains chapters on each method. Bibliographies and scientific and common name indexes.

SB119.D57

Knott, James Edward. Knott's handbook for vegetable growers. 3rd ed. / Oscar A. Lorenz, Donald N. Maynard. N.Y. : Wiley, 1988. 456 p. : ill.   **EJ248**

"Ready reference for those concerned with vegetable crops."—*Pref.* Mainly tables. Comprehensive index.   SB321.K49

Wright, Michael. The complete handbook of garden plants / Michael Wright, assisted by Sue Minter and Brian Carter. N.Y. : Facts on File, 1984. 544 p. : col. ill., map.   **EJ249**

"Attempts … to provide … a comprehensive guide to all … decorative outdoor garden plants … and to give all the basic information needed to choose and grow such plants."—*Introd.* Organized by basic plant types, trees and shrubs, climbers, perennials, bulbs, rock plants, annuals and biennials, and water plants. Contains glossary and index.

SB407.W73

EK

Engineering

This section includes a selected list of reference works in the various branches of engineering. For libraries specializing in these fields, much more material will be needed, and the various guides to the literature of the subjects should be consulted. Current literature is of prime importance, and the indexes and abstract journals are essential as guides to this material. Most of the branches of engineering have handbooks and manuals which include data, charts, statistics, etc., useful to the practicing engineer. These handbooks are usually revised frequently to include new developments and practices. Dictionaries of technical terms, bilingual as well as those giving definitions in English, are much used in many libraries.

GENERAL WORKS

Guides

Engineering literature guides. no. 1– . Wash. : American Soc. for Engineering Education, Engineering Libraries Div., c1986– . Irregular.   **EK1**

Supersedes: *Guides to literature*, issued 1970–71 by the American Soc. for Engineering Education, Engineering School Libraries Div.

This series of brief, useful guides for engineering students includes: no. 1, *Selective guide to literature on computer engineering*, ed. by Margaret H. Bean; no. 2, *Selective guide to literature on mechanical engineering*, by Hugh Lockwood Franklin; no. 3, *Selective guide to literature on computer science*, by Rosemary Rousseau; no. 4, *Selective guide to literature on agricultural engineering*, by Gayla Staples Cloud; no. 5, *Selective guide to literature on engineering management*, by Jonathon Brown; no. 6, *Selective guide to literature on mining engineering*, by Charlotte A. Erdmann; no. 7, *Selective guide to literature on engineering geology*, by Cecilia P. Mullen; no. 8, *Selective guide to literature on software review sources*, ed. by Margaret H. Bean; no. 9, *Selective guide to literature on chemical engineering*, by Rosemary Rousseau; no. 12, *Selective guide to literature on artificial intelligence and expert systems*, by Julia Gelfand and Locke Morrisey; no. 13, *Union list of technical reports, standards, and patents in engineering libraries*, 2nd ed., by Rames A. Ruffner and Linda R. Musser; no. 14, *Selective guide to literature on advanced ceramics*, by Godlind Johnson; no. 15, *Selective guide to literature on telecommunications*, by Jill H. Powell; no. 16, *Selective guide to literature on composites*, by Steven Gass.

Information sources in engineering / ed., L. J. Anthony. 2nd ed. London ; Boston : Butterworths, 1985. 579 p. : ill.   **EK2**

Rev. ed. of *Use of engineering literature*, ed. by K. W. Mildren (London ; Boston : Butterworths, 1976).

The first ten chapters discuss primary sources (e.g., report literature, patents, standards, translations) and secondary sources (abstracts, indexes, bibliographies, online services). 18 subject fields are exam-

ined in detail, including: fluid mechanics, stress analysis, automotive engineering, electronics, computers, and public health engineering. Index of subjects, organizations, and information services.   T10.7.I54

Bibliography

Rink, Evald. Technical Americana : a checklist of technical publications printed before 1831. Millwood, N.Y. : Kraus Internat., [1981]. 776 p.   **EK3**

"Sponsored by the Eleutherian Mills Historical Library."—*t.p.*

A topically arranged checklist with chronological arrangement within topics. Only separately published works are included; articles in periodicals are omitted unless they were also issued separately. Entries include full bibliographic description, references to bibliographical sources, occasional annotations, and locations indicated by National Union Catalog abbreviations (a key to locations is provided). Section headings: 1, General works; 2, Technology; 3, Agriculture; 4, Crafts and trades; 5, Medical technology; 6, Military technology; 7, Civil engineering; 8, Mechanical engineering; 9, Manufacturing; 10, Mining and mineral production; 11, Sea transportation; 12, Inland transportation. Detailed index.   Z7912.R56

Library catalogs

Engineering Societies Library. Classed subject catalog. Boston : G. K. Hall, 1963. 12 v.   **EK4**

Reproduction of the catalog cards for the largest engineering library in the U.S. Arranged by modified Universal Decimal Classification.

§ The same publisher issued nine supplements (1964–73), and an *Index* (1963. 356 p.), as well as *Technology book guide* (1974; no more published), which may be considered a 10th supplement.

Later supplements issued as: New York Public Library. Research Libraries. *Bibliographic guide to technology* (EK5).

New York Public Library. Research Libraries. Bibliographic guide to technology. 1975– . Boston : G. K. Hall, 1976– . Annual.   **EK5**

Serves as a supplement to the Engineering Societies Library's *Classed subject catalog* (EK4) and its supplements.

Includes relevant publications cataloged during the year by the New York Public Library, with additional entries from Library of Congress MARC tapes and conference publications cataloged by the Engineering Societies Library.   Z5854.N48a

Indexes

Current technology index. v.1– . London : Libr. Assoc. ; Phoenix : Oryx, 1981– . Monthly, with annual cumulation.   **EK6**

Supersedes *British technology index*, 1962–80.

Covers "all branches of engineering and chemical technology, including the various manufacturing processes based on them. It also includes material on the pure sciences of man-made objects and industrial processes; the chemistry of individual substances; and instruments, irrespective of whether their application is in pure or applied science. CTI does not cover industrial economics, but articles of a mixed technical-economic character are included. From the management sphere, only material on physical and statistical techniques, such as work study, operations research and ergonomics, is included. In general, agriculture and medicine are omitted, but some borderline subjects are included."—*Introd.* Surveys about 400 British technical journals. Arranged alphabetically by subject; cross-references. Author index.

•Machine-readable versions: *Current technology index* (CTI) [database] (London : Bowker-Saur, 1981–), available online (updated monthly), and on CD-ROM as *CTI plus*, updated quarterly.
Z7913.B7

Engineering index. 1906– . N.Y. : Engineering Information, Inc., 1907– . Annual.   **EK7**

Publisher varies: 1907–19, Engineering Magazine; 1920–34, American Soc. of Mechanical Engineers; 1934–81, Engineering Index, Inc.; 1982– , Engineering Information, Inc.

An earlier series with the same title was published 1892–1906 in 4 v., covering the period 1884–1905, (v. 1, 1884–1891, had title *Descriptive index of current engineering literature*.) It indexed about 250 engineering and technical periodicals in English, French, German, Italian, Spanish, and Dutch—an alphabetical subject index with no author approach. Information given included author, title, brief digest or description of the article, length in number of words, periodical, and exact date but not volume or pages.

The present publication continues the earlier series, covering the same field but, for the years 1906–18, with a different arrangement, i.e., a classed subject index (rather than an alphabetical subject index) grouped in eight large classes: civil engineering, electrical engineering, industrial economy, marine and naval engineering, mechanical engineering, mining and metallurgy, railway engineering, street and electrical railways.

Beginning 1919, the form was changed to an alphabetical subject index, giving for each article exact reference to title, date, volume, and page of the periodical, and a brief digest. From 1928 on, an author index is included. From 1977, the annual volumes have included a list of serial publications covered, and since 1990 they have included a list of conference publications covered. Beginning in 1987 the annual volumes have also had a subject index, including both controlled vocabulary terms (in boldface) and free language terms and phrases (in lightface). International in scope, it now indexes and annotates selectively, on the basis of engineering significance, the literature appearing in over 2,700 serials, including regular professional and trade journals, and the publications of engineering societies, scientific and technical associations, universities, laboratories and research institutions, government departments and agencies, and industrial organizations. Papers of conferences, symposia, separate and nonserial publications of various kinds, and selected books are also covered.

Since Oct. 1962 monthly issues have appeared as *Engineering index monthly*, following the plan and layout of the annual volumes, each issue having an author index. The monthly issues are superseded by the annual volume.

•Available in machine-readable form as: *Compendex* [database] (N.Y.; Engineering Information, Inc., 1969–). Available online, updated monthly, and on CD-ROM as *COMPENDEX PLUS* (disks available for 1989– , including abstracts, updated quarterly). A related product for current awareness is *Ei Page One* [database] (N.Y. ; Engineering Information Inc.) which contains table of contents listings (no abstracts) for the most recent two years; however, it includes more journal articles and conference proceedings in each year than does *Compendex*. *Ei Page One* is also available online as a CD-ROM product.
Z5851.E62•

The Engineering index cumulative index. N.Y. : Engineering Information, Inc., [1979–91]. 45 v. (In progress).   **EK8**

Contents: 1973–77, 1978–81, 1982–84, 1985–87, 1988–90. Each set published in 9 v., arranged as follows: v. 1–3, Subject index; v. 4–7, Author index; v.8, Monthly number translation index; v. 9, Annual number translation index.

Each cumulation is an index to the contents of the *Engineering index annual* and *monthly* for the period covered. Commencing with the 1973 edition, abstracts in the *Annual* are numbered consecutively within each year, and this numbering differs from the numbering in the *Monthly;* the final volume in each set provides correlation between the numbering schemes.

Dictionaries

Ernst, Richard. Comprehensive dictionary of engineering and technology : with extensive treatment of the most modern techniques and processes. Cambridge, [Eng.] ; N.Y. : Cambridge Univ. Pr. ; Wiesbaden : Brandstetter, 1985. 2 v.   **EK9**

Based on the author's bilingual dictionaries of engineering and technology which previously appeared in separate French and English editions.

Added title page in French.

Contents: v. 1, French-English; v. 2, English-French.

"I have been careful to place each term strictly within its own specialized field. All branches of modern industry have been dealt with. ... Also included are farming, chemistry, electrical engineering, electronics, transport and commerce, space travel ... telecommunication; and finally ... data processing and microprocessors. Though 'Franglais' expressions have been included, they are marked as to be phased out and the correct French word is given."—*Pref.*   T10.E747

———————— Dictionary of engineering and technology : with extensive treatment of the most modern techniques and processes. 5th ed. N.Y. : Oxford Univ. Pr., [1985–89]. 2 v.   **EK10**

Added title page in German: *Wörterbuch der industriellen Technik*; some previous eds. under that title.

Contents: v. 1, German-English; v. 2, English–German.

An authoritative dictionary, covering major industrial, technical, and basic scientific disciplines.   T10.E76

Thesauruses

Ei thesaurus. 1st ed.– . Hoboken, N.J. : Engineering Information Inc., 1992– .   **EK11**

Also called: *Engineering information thesaurus*.

"Replaces the SHE (Subject headings for engineering) section of the 1990 *Ei vocabulary* and, effective January 1, 1993, serves as the indexing tool for the *Engineering index* [EK7] and the databases *Ei COMPENDEX*Plus, COMPENDEX, Ei engineering meetings* and other index products."—*Pref.*

Entries show other terms classed as BT (Broader Term), NT (Narrower Term), RT (Related Term), and UF (Used For); for terms that were not changed, the entry gives the entry date (DT) when the term was first used in indexing. Scope notes (SN) are provided when the meaning or usage may not be clear. Former *Ei vocabulary* terms are designated by an asterisk and the new term is given as a "USE" reference. Tables of Ei classification codes are included as an appendix.   ZTA145.E573

Institutional and biographical directories

Directory of engineering education institutions : Africa, Arab states, Asia, Latin America, and the Caribbean. 3rd ed. Paris : Unesco, 1986. 303 p. : ill.   **EK12**

1st ed., 1976; 2nd ed., 1981.

Title also in French.

Includes information about 781 degree-awarding institutions in 81 countries. Gives concise data about structure, number of students, and staff, plus types of specializations and research.   T165.D57

Who's who in engineering : a biographical dictionary of the engineering profession. 1922/23–1964. N.Y. : Lewis Historical Pub. Co., 1922–64.   **EK13**

Subtitle varies. Editions issued for 1922/23, 1925, 1931, 1937, 1941, 1948, 1954, 1959, 1964.

Standards for inclusion varied, but for many years required ten years of active practice with at least five years of responsibility in important engineering work, or ten years of teaching in engineering with at least five years of responsibility for major courses. Typical "who's who" entries. Contains a list of engineering and allied organizations, both national and regional; a list of professional fraternities and honor societies; and a list of professional publications, although inclusion of these, too, has varied. Geographical index.   TA139.W4

Who's who in engineering. 3rd ed.– . N.Y. : Amer. Assoc. of Engineering Societies, 1977– .   **EK14**
    8th ed., 1991, ed. by Gordon Davis.
    1st (1970) and 2nd (1973) eds. had title *Engineers of distinction.*
    Publisher formerly named Engineers Joint Council.
    Gives biographical data on engineers in the U. S. who have met stated criteria for inclusion. Also has a section on American and Canadian engineering societies. Includes a geographic index and an index to specialization.   TA139.E37

Who's who in technology / Amy L. Unterberger, ed. 6th ed. Detroit : Gale, c1989. 2 v.   **EK15**
    1st–4th eds., 1980–84, had title: *Who's who in technology today.*
    Contents: v. 1, Biographies; v. 2, Indexes.
    Publisher varies.
    Contains more than 38,000 entries for North Americans, with a separate obituary section listing persons from the 5th ed. who died between 1986 and 1988. Indexes: geographic; employer; technical discipline (corresponding to the general categories from the 5th ed.); expertise (with designations chosen by the biographees).   T39.W5

Handbooks

Eshbach, Ovid W. Eshbach's handbook of engineering fundamentals. 4th ed. / ed. by Byron D. Tapley; managing ed., Thurman R. Poston. N.Y. : Wiley, c1990. 1 v. (various pagings) : ill.   **EK16**
    1st ed., 1956. Previous eds. had title: *Handbook of engineering fundamentals.*
    Among the changes in this edition: a strong emphasis on computers and computer technology, including a new chapter on computers and computer science, and the incorporation of computer applications into other chapters; the chapter on aerodynamics and astrodynamics has been expanded to two separate chapters; the section on engineering economics has been substantially revised. Other additions include "the adoption of the international standard units throughout and the revision of the references to cite current literature."—*Pref.* Indexed.   TA151.E8

The McGraw-Hill handbook of essential engineering information and data / [ed. by] Ejup N. Ganić, Tyler G. Hicks. N.Y. : McGraw-Hill, c1991. 1 v. (various pagings).   **EK17**
    A practical book with numerous charts, tables, and diagrams. Much of the material was chosen from a number of specialized handbooks from the same publisher; information has been augmented and updated when necessary. Contains many worked-out examples.   TA151.M34

Standard handbook of engineering calculations. 2nd ed. / Tyler G. Hicks, ed.; S. David Hicks, coord. ed. N.Y. : McGraw-Hill, [1985]. 1 v., various pagings.   **EK18**
    1st ed., 1972.
    Presents step-by-step calculation procedures for solving problems met in engineering practice; separate sections for each branch of engineering. Indexed.   TA332.S73

Tuma, Jan J. Engineering mathematics handbook : definitions, theorems, formulas, tables. 3rd ed. N.Y. : McGraw-Hill, c1987. 498 p. : ill.   **EK19**
    1st ed., 1970; 2nd ed., 1979.

"A concise summary of the major tools of engineering mathematics."—*Pref.* In five parts: algebra and trigonometry, calculus, differential equations, numerical methods, and integrals. Bibliography; index.   TA332.T85

Biography

See also EK13 and EK15.

Great engineers and pioneers in technology / Roland Turner and Steven L. Goulden, eds. N.Y. : St. Martin's Pr., [1984]. v. 1 : ill.   **EK20**
    Contents: v. 1, From antiquity through the Industrial Revolution (488 p.). No more published?
    Entries are arranged alphabetically within topical sections; articles by experts include lists of further reading. Includes a glossary, a chronology of important engineering events, and a bibliographical essay. Indexed.   TA139.G7

Roysdon, Christine. American engineers of the nineteenth century : a biographical index / Christine Roysdon, Linda A. Khatri. N.Y. : Garland, 1978. 247 p. (Garland reference library of social science, v. 53).   **EK21**
    Entries include brief descriptions of the individuals with dates of birth and death, and references to biographical articles in engineering journals.   Z5851.R7

AERONAUTICAL AND SPACE ENGINEERING

Bibliography

Benton, Mildred Catherine. The literature of space science and exploration. Wash. : U.S. Naval Research Laboratory, 1958. 264 p. (U.S. Naval Research Laboratory, Bellevue, D.C. Bibliography, no. 13).   **EK22**
    2,274 numbered entries of "books, periodical articles, and research reports on the more scientific aspects of space exploration, both theoretical and applied."—*Introd.* Covers 1903–June 1958.
                    Z5064.S7B4

New York Public Library. History of aeronautics : a selected list of references to material in the New York Public Library / comp. by William B. Gamble. N.Y. : Libr., 1938. 325 p.   **EK23**
    Repr. from the New York Public Library *Bulletin*, Jan. 1936–Sept. 1937; reissued 1971.
    A classed list of more than 5,500 entries to books and periodical articles in many languages, with indexes of authors and subjects.
                    Z5063.N56

Ordway, Frederick I. Annotated bibliography of space science and technology, with an astronomical supplement : A history of astronautical book literature—1931 through 1961. [3rd ed.]. Wash. : Arfor Publ., [1962]. 77 p.   **EK24**
    1st ed., 1955, had title: *Specialized books on space flight and related disciplines.*
    Arranged chronologically by year of publication.   Z5064.A8O7

Periodicals

Library of Congress. Science and Technology Division. Aeronautical and space serial publications : a world list. Wash., 1962. 255 p.   **EK25**

A bibliography of 4,551 serial publications originating in 76 countries, but principally in the U.S., Germany, Great Britain, France, and Russia. Arrangement is alphabetical by country, then by title or issuing agency. Includes periodicals, documents, annuals, numbered monographic series, and other serial publications. Entries include title, issuing agency, place of publication, frequency, dates published, indication of title change or suspension, LC call number, and currency of publication. Alphabetical title index.

Supersedes *A checklist of aeronautical periodicals and serials in the Library of Congress* (1948).   Z5063.A2U64

Abstract journals

•**Aerospace database** [database]. N.Y. : American Institute of Aeronautics and Astronautics, 1962– .   **EK26**

Machine-readable version of *International aerospace abstracts* (Phillipsburg, N.J. : Technical Information Service, Amer. Inst. of Aeronautics and Astronautics, 1961–) and *Scientific and technical aerospace reports (STAR)* (United States. National Aeronautics and Space Administration. v. 1 [Jan. 8, 1963]–).

Available online, in CD-ROM and on magnetic tape; updated bimonthly.

Drawn from the worldwide literature on aerospace and related technology. The CD-ROM version provides coverage from the mid-1980s and is updated quarterly.

International aerospace abstracts. v. 1 (1961)– . Phillipsburg, N.J. : Technical Information Service, Amer. Inst. of Aeronautics and Astronautics, 1961– . Semimonthly.   **EK27**

Covers published literature in periodicals and books; meeting papers and conference proceedings issued by professional and academic organizations; and translations of journals and articles in the fields of aeronautics and space science and technology.

Covers published literature in periodicals and books; meeting papers and conference proceedings issued by professional and academic organizations; and translations of journals and articles in the fields of aeronautics and space science and technology.

Reports ("unpublished literature") are abstracted in *Scientific and technical aerospace reports* (EK28). These two services use the same subject categories and indexes, and thus "provide comprehensive access to the national and international unclassified report and published literature of current significance to aerospace science and technology."—*Introd., STAR v.1, no.1.* Indexes by subject, personal author, contract number, meeting paper and report number, and accession number. Indexes now cumulate semiannually and annually.

•Available online as part of *Aerospace database* (EK26).   TL500.I57•

United States. National Aeronautics and Space Administration. Scientific and technical aerospace reports : a semimonthly abstract journal with indexes. v. 1 (Jan. 8, 1963)– . Wash. : NASA, 1963– . Monthly, with cumulative annual indexes.   **EK28**

Supersedes *Technical publications announcements,* with the same scope and coverage.

STAR is a comprehensive abstracting and indexing journal covering current worldwide report literature on the science and technology of space and aeronautics. Publications abstracted include scientific and technical reports issued by NASA and its contractors, other U.S. Government agencies, corporations, universities, and research organizations throughout the world. Pertinent theses, translations, NASA-owned patents and patent applications, and other separates are also abstracted. Citations and abstracts are grouped in 76 subject categories, although accession numbers run in unbroken sequence through the

STAR issues, without regard to category assignment. Indexes by subject, personal author, corporate source, contract number, and report/accession number. Availability, whether hard copy or microfiche, and source are also given.

•Available online as one of the files in NASA RECON and as part of *Aerospace database* (EK26).

Dictionaries

Aviation/space dictionary / ed. by Larry Reithmaier. 7th ed. Blue Ridge Summit, Penn. : Aero, 1990. 461 p. : ill.   **EK29**

1st ed., 1940; 6th ed., 1980. Title and editors vary.

This edition includes terms from such fields as computer technology, geophysics, nucleonics, aviation and space technology, radar, electronics, and astronomy as well as selected terms from the basic sciences and mathematics. Contains more than a dozen short appendixes covering U.S. military engine designations; civil aircraft national registration markings; airport lighting and marking. Some plates and diagrams.   TL509.A8

Cambridge air and space dictionary / gen. ed. P.M.B. Walker. Cambridge ; N.Y. : Cambridge Univ. Pr., c1990. 216 p. : ill.   **EK30**

Published in the U.K. under title: *Chambers air and space dictionary.*

Offers more than 6,000 terms, emphasizing aeronautics, astronomy, space, and radar, but including some abbreviations and terms in engineering, physics, telecommunications, and acoustics. An unusual feature consists of 66 "special articles" enclosed in separate panels to allow a fuller description of such topics as cosmic rays, navigation systems, and planets. Alphabetical entries include symbols, abbreviations, phrases, and numerous *see* references. An appendix contains a table of specifications for jet fuels.   TL509.C35

Jane's aerospace dictionary / Bill Gunston. 3rd ed. Coulsdon, Surrey ; Alexandria, Va. : Jane's, 1988. 605 p.   **EK31**

1st ed., 1980.

Up-to-date and comprehensive. Fairly brief entries. Includes acronyms; cross-references.   TL509.G86

Directories

World aviation directory. v. 1– . Wash. : Ziff-Davis, 1940– . Biennial.   **EK32**

Title varies: 1940–51, *American aviation directory.* Publisher varies.

Subtitle varies: 1972/73, Listing aerospace companies and officials, covering the United States, Canada, and 160 countries in Europe, Central and South America, Africa and Middle East, Australasia and Asia.

Absorbed *World space directory,* 1966.

A directory of "executive, administrative and operating personnel of world-wide scheduled airlines, major aerospace manufacturers, component aerospace manufacturers and major subcontractors, distributors and aerospace equipment, U.S. airports—terminal and non-terminal, aviation repair stations and schools, aerospace publications, aerospace oriented organizations and government operations, etc."—*Publisher's description.* A buyer's guide to products and services and information on aerospace operations in foreign countries, publ. as a 2nd pt., 1986–89, published separately, 1990– . Personnel index.   TL512.A63

Handbooks

Johnson, Francis S. Satellite environment handbook. 2nd ed. Stanford : Stanford Univ. Pr., 1965. 193 p. : ill.   **EK33**
1st ed., 1961.
Chapters prepared by various authors present data in classed arrangement and include lists of references. "The major satellite-environment factors—the structure of the upper atmosphere and the ionosphere, penetrating-particle radiation, solar radiation, micrometeorites, radio noise, thermal radiation from Earth, and geomagnetism—are discussed, and existing data are evaluated."—*Pref., 1st ed.* This edition includes revisions and additions to the description of the satellite environment. Indexed.   QC879.5.J6

The RAE table of earth satellites, 1957–1989 / comp. at the Royal Aerospace Establishment, Farnborough, Hants, England by D. G. King-Hele … [et al.]. 4th ed. Farnborough, [Eng.] : Royal Aerospace Establishment, c1990. 1056 p. : ill.   **EK34**
First issued 1981, with coverage to 1980.
"A chronological list of the 3,196 launches of satellites and space vehicles between 1957 and the end of 1989, giving the name and international designation of each satellite and its associated rocket(s), with the date of launch, lifetime (actual or estimated), mass, shape, dimensions and at least one set of orbital parameters."—*t.p.* Indexed. A supplement for 1990–1991 was issued in 1992.   TL796.6.E2.R253

Yearbooks

Aerospace facts and figures / Aerospace Industries Association of America. Los Angeles : Aero Publishers, 1960– . Annual.   **EK35**
Comp. by Economic Data Service, Aerospace Research Center.
Includes sections for: Aerospace summary; Aircraft production; Missile programs; Space programs; Air transportation; Research and development; Foreign trade; Employment and finance. Data are drawn from both government and commercial sources.   TL501.A818

Aerospace year book. v. 1 (1919)–v. 48 (1970). Wash. : Amer. Aviation Publ., 1919–70.   **EK36**
Title varies: 1919–59, *The aircraft yearbook.* Publisher varies. Not published 1963–65.
Official publication of the Aerospace Industries Association of America, Inc.
Format and emphasis vary. Essentially a chronicle of the year's events, with particular attention to types of air- and spacecraft and their specifications. Contents of latest volumes have included a pictorial record of the year's highlights, plus information on the aerospace industry, government research and development, civil aviation, and a reference section containing specifications, performance, and other data on aerospace industry products and systems. Indexed.   TL501.A563

Jane's all the world's aircraft. 1909– . London : S. Low, 1909– . Annual.   **EK37**
Title varies: [v.1–2], *All the world's airships;* [v.3]–19, *All the world's aircraft.*
Offers illustrations, descriptions, and specifications of aircraft of various countries of the world including: airplanes, drones, sailplanes, airships, military missiles, research rockets, space vehicles, aero-engines. Arranged in sections by: Aircraft; Lighter than air; Aero engines, then alphabetically by country of manufacture. Separate indexes according to type of craft with entries for manufacturer and individual model name. Indexes include references to ten previous editions.   TL501.J3

AUTOMOTIVE ENGINEERING

Goodsell, Don. Dictionary of automotive engineering. London ; Boston : Butterworths ; Warrendale, Penn. : Society of Automotive Engineers, 1989. 182 p. : ill.   **EK38**
Includes brief definitions for more than 2,500 terms from both technical engineering and more informal vocabulary. Good cross-references.   TL9.G64

The new encyclopedia of motorcars, 1885 to the present. 1986 ed. N.Y. : Crescent Books : distr. by Crown, 1986. 688p. : ill.   **EK39**
1st–2d eds. 1968–73, had title: *The complete encyclopedia of motorcars, 1885 to the present.*
Entries in alphabetical sequence for all makes of automobiles from all periods and the world over. Attempts to include at least one illustration for every make of automobile.   TN15.N37

SAE glossary of automotive terms. 2nd ed. Warrendale, Penn. : Society of Automotive Engineers, c1992. 454 p.   **EK40**
1st ed., 1988, had title: *Glossary of automotive terms.*
Terms from automotive engineering and related fields, with definitions taken from SAE Standards, Recommended practices, and Information reports, as publ. in *SAE handbook* for 1992 (EK41).   TL9.S17

SAE handbook. 1926– . N.Y. : Soc. of Automotive Engineers, 1926– . Annual (slightly irregular).   **EK41**
Contents, 1993: v. 1, Materials; v. 2, Parts & components; v. 3, Engines, fuels, lubricants, emissions, & noise; v. 4, On-highway vehicles & off-highway machinery; Index.
A standard handbook presenting SAE standards, recommended practices, and information reports. Includes numerous charts and tables. Indexed.   TL151.S62

BIOTECHNOLOGY

Alston, Y. R. Biosciences : information sources and services / Y. R. Alston, J. Coombs. N.Y. : Stockton Pr., 1992. 407 p. : ill.   **EK42**
Contents: pt. 1, Development of information and technology, pt. 2, Organizations (international, government and national); pt. 3, Publications (e.g., journals, newsletters, directories, databases and abstracts); pt. 4, Services (computer software, consultants, culture collections, suppliers, and hosts and contact addreses); pt. 5, Indexes. Originated from *The international biotechnology directory* (N.Y. : Nature Pr., 1983), which it is meant to complement.
A directory, organized geographically, of organizations, information services (databases, abstracting services, journals, newsletters), societies, and companies. Listings of companies include products and areas of research. Indexes include a buyers' guide directory of products, research, and services.   QH303.2.A47

Atkinson, Bernard. Biochemical engineering and biotechnology handbook / Bernard Atkinson, Ferda Mavituna. 2nd ed. N.Y. : Stockton Pr., 1991. 1271 p. : ill.   **EK43**
1st ed., 1983.
Presents in 20 topical chapters a concise but thorough coverage of the science and technology of the production of useful materials through microbiological processes. Coverage includes microbiology and biochemistry as well as engineering factors in microbial reactors, mass and heat transfer, etc. Includes many tables and graphs, and references to the research literature. Indexed.   TP248.3.A853

The biotechnology directory. 3rd ed. (1986)– . N.Y. : Stockton Pr., 1986– . Annual.   **EK44**
Continues: *The international biotechnology directory,* ed. by J. Coombs (N.Y. : Nature Press, 1983).

Publisher varies: 1983–85, Nature Pr.; 1986– , Stockton Pr.

A directory, organized geographically, of organizations, information services (databases, abstracting services, journals, newsletters), societies, and companies. Listings of companies include products and areas of research. Indexes include a buyers' guide directory of products, research, and services.   TP248.3.I56

Coombs, J. Dictionary of biotechnology. 2nd ed. N.Y. : Stockton Pr., c1992. 364 p. : ill.   **EK45**

1st ed., 1986.

Most entries are brief paragraphs, a few are longer with tables, formulas, etc. Includes *see* references for acronyms.

§ Usefully complements John M. Walker and Michael Cox, *The language of biotechnology* (EK46).   TP248.16.C66

Walker, John M. The language of biotechnology : a dictionary of terms / John M. Walker and Michael Cox ; Allan Whitaker, contributor. Wash. : American Chemical Soc., 1988. 255 p. : ill.   **EK46**

Taking "biotechnology" to mean "the practical application of biological systems to the manufacturing and service industries and to the management of the environment," including "the wide spectrum of related disciplines that must come together to commercialize a biological process," the authors seek "to define routinely used specialized language in the various areas of biotechnology."—*Pref.* Definitions are usually of paragraph length; some illustrations and equations are used. Cross-references.   TP248.16.W35

CHEMICAL ENGINEERING

Bibliography

Bourton, Kathleen. Chemical and process engineering unit operations : a bibliographical guide / by Kay Bourton. N.Y. : IFI/Plenum, 1968. 534 p.   **EK47**

Presents "a selection from the chemical engineering literature which will be a guide to the available aids to searching and to those works which are likely to serve as the most productive sources for retrieval."—*Pref.* Nearly 4,600 entries in classed arrangement. Annotations; author and subject indexes.

§ Continued by: Martyn S. Ray, *Chemical engineering* (EK48).   Z7914.C4B6

Ray, Martyn S. Chemical engineering : bibliography (1967–1988). Park Ridge, N.J. : Noyes Publications, 1990. 887 p.   **EK48**

Continues *Chemical and process engineering unit operations*, by Kathleen Bourton (EK47).

Classed subject bibliography of about 20,000 references taken from 40 English-language journals. Within each category arrangement is by year, with citations listed alphabetically by author. No annotations. Subject index.

Abstract journals

See also *Chemical abstracts*, EE22.

•**Chemical engineering and biotechnology abstracts** : (CEABA) [database]. Cambridge, England : Royal Soc. of Chemistry, 1971– .   **EK49**

Available online, updated monthly.

Jointly produced by the Royal Society of Chemistry, DECHEMA, FIZ CHEMIE GmbH, and the Institution of Chemical Engineers, this database covers all aspects of chemical engineering and biotechnology from theoretical studies through plant operation, safety engineering, and related environmental areas. Six printed publications are derived

from the database: *Biotechnology : apparatus, plant, and equipment* (v. 7 [1991]–); *Current biotechnology* (v. 9 [1991]–); *Equipment, corrosion, and corrosion protection* (1991–); *Process and chemical engineering* (v. 10 [1991]–); *Safety, environmental protection, and analysis*; and *Theoretical chemical engineering* (v. 28 [1991]– . Through v. 27 [1990] called *Theoretical chemical engineering abstracts*).

Encyclopedias

Chemical technology : an encylopedic treatment : the economic application of modern technological developments. N.Y. : Barnes & Noble, [1968–75]. 8 v. : ill.   **EK50**

Some volumes issued under title *Materials and technology*.

"The economic application of modern technological developments, based upon a work originally devised by the late Dr. J. F. van Oss."—*t.p.*

Contents: v. 1, Air, water, inorganic chemicals and nucleonics; v. 2, Non-metallic ores, silicate industries, and solid mineral fuels; v. 3, Metals and ores; v. 4, Petroleum and organic chemicals; v. 5, Natural organic materials and related synthetic products; v. 6, Wood, paper, textiles, plastics and photographic materials; v. 7, Vegetable food products and luxuries; v. 8, Edible oils and fats, Animal products, Material resources, General index, Appendix—Recent developments in materials and technology.

Intended for general readers as well as for technologists, the work describes "the sources, manufacture, processing, and uses of both natural and synthetic materials."—*Pref.* A select bibliography accompanies each chapter.   TP200.M35

Encyclopedia of chemical technology / executive ed., Jacqueline I. Kroschwitz ; ed., Mary Howe-Grant. 4th ed. N.Y. : Wiley, c1991–94. 12 v. : ill. (some col.). (In progress). **EK51**

At head of title: Kirk-Othmer.

1st ed., 1947–56, ed. by Raymond E. Kirk and Donald F. Othmer.

Volumes of this new edition of this standard reference supersede the corresponding volumes of the 3rd ed. (EK52). Until the edition is completed and a cumulated index is issued, temporary cumulated indexes have been published for v. 1–4 and 5–8. Information from this ed. is used to update the data in the online version of the 3rd ed.

TP9.E685

Encyclopedia of chemical technology. 3rd ed. N.Y. : Wiley, [1978–84]. 24 v. : ill.   **EK52**

At head of title: Kirk-Othmer.

Editorial board: Herman F. Mark, Donald F. Othmer, Charles G. Overberger, and Glen T. Seaborg.

1st ed. (1947–56) ed. by Raymond E. Kirk and Donald F. Othmer; 2nd ed. (1963–72).

Articles in this standard reference are written by specialists, are signed, and include bibliographies. This edition uses SI as well as English units, and includes CAS Registry Numbers.

————. *Supplement volume.* Alcohol fuels to toxicology (N.Y. : Wiley, [1984]. 924 p.).

————. *Index to volumes 1–24 and supplement* (N.Y. : Wiley, [1984]. 1274 p.).

•Available in machine-readable form as: *Kirk-Othmer encyclopedia of chemical technology* [database] (N.Y. : Wiley, 1990). Available online and as CD-ROM.

Ullmann, Fritz. Ullmann's encyclopedia of industrial chemistry / executive ed. Wolfgang Gerhartz ... [et al.]. 5th, completely revised ed. Weinheim, Germany ; Deerfield Beach, Fla. : VCH, 1985–1994. 31 v. : ill. (In progress).   **EK53**

1st ed. (1914) through 4th ed. (1972–84) had title: *Ullmanns Enzyklopädie der technischen Chemie.* 4th ed. in 24 v. and index.

A European counterpart to the *Encyclopedia of chemical technology* (EK51), this standard reference work is now published for the first time in English. "The Encyclopedia is organized in two series. The 28 'A' volumes contain alphabetically arranged articles on chemicals, product groups, areas of application, processes, and technological concepts. Basic principles are treated in the eight volumes of the 'B' series, beginning with topics such as fluid dynamics or transport phenomena in the first volume, unit operations in the second and third, chemical reaction engineering and materials science in the fourth, analytical methods in volumes five and six, and environmental protection and plant safety in seven and eight. The plan is to publish three or four volumes each year. An annual cumulative index will provide easy access. ... Chemical Abstract Service Registry Numbers are given for all important chemicals. Nomenclature is consistent with IUPAC rules, and SI units are used."—*Pref.* Signed, authoritative articles contain substantial tabular data and extensive bibliographic references. Cross-references.   TP9.U57

Dictionaries

Noether, Dorit. Encyclopedic dictionary of chemical technology / by Dorit and Herman Noether. N.Y. : VCH, c1993. 297 p. : ill.   **EK54**

Brief entries, ranging from a sentence to a long paragraph, concentrate on chemical technology, industrial production, and uses of chemicals. Cross-referenced. Acronyms are listed in a separate section at the front.   TP9.N64

Handbooks

Cremer, Herbert W. Chemical engineering practice / under the general editorship of Herbert W. Cremer. Managing editor: Trefor Davies. N.Y. : Academic Pr., 1956–65. 12 v. : ill.
                    EK55

Contents: v. 1, General; v. 2, Solid state; v. 3, Solid systems; v. 4, Fluid state; v. 5–6, Fluid systems; v. 7, Heat transfer; v. 8, Chemical kinetics; v. 9, Design and construction; v. 10, Ancillary services; v. 11, Works design, layout, etc.; v. 12, Indexes.

Sections by specialists. Bibliographies.   TP155.C7

Industrial solvents handbook / ed. by Ernest W. Flick. 4th ed. Park Ridge, N.J. : Noyes Data Corp., c1991. 930 p. : ill.
                    EK56

1st ed., 1970; 3rd ed., 1985.

Contains extensive tables with basic data on physical properties of most solvents and on solubilities of a variety of materials in these solvents. Arranged by class of solvent, e.g., halogenated hydrocarbons, ethers, acids; contains phase diagrams for multicomponent systems. Sources of data are indicated.   TP247.5.I53

Perry's chemical engineers' handbook. 6th ed. / prep. by a staff of specialists under the editorial direction of late ed. Robert H. Perry ; ed., Don W. Green ; assistant ed., James O. Maloney. N.Y. : McGraw-Hill, c1984. 1 v. (various pagings) : 1846 ill.   **EK57**

1st–3rd eds., 1934–50, by John H. Perry. Previous eds. had title: *Chemical engineers' handbook*.

A standard handbook revised and updated; this edition uses both SI and U.S. customary units as much as possible and also includes conversion factors. Has contributions by 125 authorities in various engineering and scientific disciplines; sections include many tables, graphs, line drawings, literature references. Indexed.   TP151.P45

Riegel, Emil Raymond. Riegel's handbook of industrial chemistry. 9th ed. / ed. by James A. Kent. N.Y. : Van Nostrand Reinhold, c1992. 1288 p. : ill.   **EK58**

1st–5th eds., 1933–49, had title: *Industrial chemistry*; 6th ed., 1962, *Riegel's industrial chemistry*; 7th ed., 1974, *Handbook of industrial chemistry*. 8th ed., 1983.

"The aim of this book is to present in a single volume an up-to-date account of the chemistry and chemical engineering which underlie

major areas of the chemical process industry."—*Pref.* Contains 31 chapters by 50 specialist contributors. Chapters include tabular data, process diagrams, and bibliographic references. This edition adds topics such as waste minimization and safety considerations in chemical plant design and operation. Indexed.   TP145.R54

CIVIL ENGINEERING

General works

Handbooks

Civil engineering practice / ed. by Paul N. Cheremisinoff, Nicholas P. Cheremisinioff, Su Ling Cheng .... Lancaster, Penn. : Technomic Publ. Co., c1987–88. 5 v. : ill.   **EK59**

Contents: v. 1, Structures; v. 2, Hydraulics/mechanics; v. 3, Geotechnical/ocean engineering; v. 4, Surveying/transportation/energy/economics & government/computers; v. 5., Water resources/environmental.

A comprehensive treatise on the state of the art of civil engineering practice. Each volume includes signed technical articles, usually with extensive diagrams, tables, etc., as well as references to the technical literature. Volumes are separately indexed.   TA145.C58

Civil engineer's reference book / ed. by Leslie Spencer Blake ; with specialist contributors. 4th ed. London ; Boston : Butterworths, 1989. 1v. (various pagings) : ill.   **EK60**

1st–2nd eds., 1951–61, had title: *Civil engineering reference book*.

Chapters 1–10 discuss basic principles (e.g., strength of materials, engineering surveying, rock mechanics and rock engineering); chapters 11–44 give current design and construction practices (e.g., practical steel work, bridges, water supplies, offshore construction); chapter 45 treats units, conversion, and symbols. Includes references and bibliographies in all chapters except the last. Subject index.   TA151.C58

Standard handbook for civil engineers / Frederick S. Merritt, ed. 3rd ed. N.Y. : McGraw-Hill, 1983. 1 v. (various pagings) : ill.   **EK61**

1st ed., 1968.

Seeks to "provide in a single volume a compendium of the best of current civil engineering practices. ... Emphasis is on fundamental principles and their practical applications, with special attention to simplified procedures."—*Pref.* Signed contributions by specialists include tabular data, line drawings, references. Indexed.   TA151.S8

The surveying handbook / ed. by Russell C. Brinker, Roy Minnick. N.Y. : Van Nostrand Reinhold, c1987. 1270 p. : ill.
                    EK62

Chapters are illustrated with figures and tables, together with worked-out examples of calculations. Discusses surveys for land, mining, routes, construction, and public lands. Includes chapters on land litigation and courtroom techniques; also contains addresses of state registration agencies. Indexed.   TA555.S87

Biography

American Society of Civil Engineers. Committee on History and Heritage of American Civil Engineering. A biographical dictionary of American civil engineers. N.Y. : Society, 1972–91. v. 1–2. (American Society of Civil Engineers historical publication, no. 2). (In progress).   **EK63**

The first of a proposed series of biographical dictionaries based on information in the files of the Biographical Archive of American

Civil Engineers of the Smithsonian Institution. In two parts, the first containing biographical sketches of some 170 prominent civil engineers born before the Civil War; pt. 2 is a list of the names of civil engineers about whom the Archive has biographical information.

TA139.A53

Environment and environmental problems

General works

Bibliography

Anglemyer, Mary. The natural environment : an annotated bibliography on attitudes and values / comp. by Mary Anglemyer and Eleanor R. Seagraves. Wash. : Smithsonian Inst. Pr., 1984. 268 p.   **EK64**

A companion volume to the same compilers' *A search for environmental ethics* (EK65), this work has entries for 857 books, articles, proceedings, and reports, grouped by broad topics. Indexed.

Z7405.N38A52

—————— A search for environmental ethics : an initial bibliography. Wash. : Smithsonian Inst. Pr., 1980. 119 p.

EK65

"Comp. by Mary Anglemyer, Eleanor R. Seagraves, Catherine C. LeMaistre. Under the auspices of Rachel Carson Council, Inc. With an introduction by S. Dillon Ripley."—*t.p.*

An annotated alphabetical listing by author, editor, or title of 446 articles and books published since 1945, although principally in the 1970s. "The natural environment is the focal point of this bibliography. ... Works in science, philosophy, religion, education, literature, politics, and economics (wherever it touches on conservation-environmental values) are described."—*Pref.* Subject and name index.

Z7405.N38A53

Clark, Brian D. Environmental impact assessment : a bibliography with abstracts / by Brian D. Clark, Ronald Bisset, and Peter Wathern. N.Y. : Bowker, 1980. 516 p.   **EK66**

Contents: Aids to impact assessment; Critiques and reviews of environmental impact assessment; Environmental impact assessment and other aspects of planning; Environmental impact assessment in selected countries; Information sources.

Covers citations from a wide variety of sources; some entries lack abstracts. Indexed.   Z5863.I57C56

EIS : digests of environmental impact statements. v. 3, no. 7 (July 1979)– . Bethesda, Md. : Cambridge Scientific Abstracts, 1979– . Bimonthly.   **EK67**

Continues: *EIS : key to environmental impact statements* (v. 1 [Jan. 1977]–3, no. 6 [June 1979]. Wash. : Information Resources Pr., 197–79).

Frequency varies; 1977–88, monthly.

Available on microfiche.

Each monthly issue provides abstracts detailing the purpose, positive and negative aspects, legal mandates, and any prior references, for about 100 draft and final environmental impact statements. Arranged in 11 broad subject chapters; indexed by subject, legal instrument, geographical site, issuing agency, and EIS and EPA numbers.

EIS retrospective, covering the 1970–76 period, is available in a similar format (3 v.); also available on microfiche.

•Machine-readable version: *Digests of environmental impact statements* [database] (Bethesda, Md. : Cambridge Scientific Abstracts, 1970–). Available on CD-ROM, updated quarterly.

Z5863.E56E35

Selected water resources abstracts. v.1 (Jan. 1968)–v. 24, no. 12 (1991). [Springfield, Va. : National Technical Information Service], 1968–1991. Monthly with annual index.   **EK68**

For annotation, *see* EF129.   TC1.S45

United Nations. ACCIS guide to United Nations information sources on the environment / prepared by the Advisory Committee for the Co-ordination of Information Systems (ACCIS), in collaboration with the Programme Activity Centre of the International Environmental Information System (INFOTERRA PAC) of the United Nations Environment Programme (UNEP). N.Y. : United Nations, 1988. 141 p.   **EK69**

Separate sections describe: the organizations within the U.N., or related to it or any of its administrative units, that are concerned with the environment; environment-related directories produced by ACCIS or depository U.N. libraries; and, in a series of annexes at the end, addresses of national sources of U.N. environmental information and information about some U.N. online databases. Indexed.

TD169.5.U55

Indexes; Abstract journals

Environment abstracts. v.1 (Jan. 1971)– . [N.Y. : Environment Information Center, Inc.], 1971– . Monthly.   **EK70**

Publisher varies; 1988–93, N.Y. : Bowker; 1994– , Bethesda, Md. : Congressional Information Service.

Title varies. Vols. 1–3 were called *Environment information access* and published semimonthly.

An indexing and abstracting service covering both published and nonprint (e.g., radio and television programming, films and filmstrips) materials. Significant books, periodical articles (from scientific, scholarly, technical, and general publications), major conference proceedings, newspaper stories, and significant environmental entries from the *Federal register* are included. A classified "main entry section" provides a complete citation with abstract; this is followed by subject, industry, and author indexes. A calendar of conferences is included in each issue. Items designated by an asterisk may be purchased on microfiche, either singly or by subscription to one or more "main entry" categories.

Also available as *Environment index annual* in 2 v., of which the second is the index.

•Machine-readable version: *Enviroline* [database] (Bethesda, Md. : Congressional Information Service, 1971–). Available online (updated monthly) and on CD-ROM (updated quarterly).   Z7171.E59

Pollution abstracts. v.1, no.1 (May 1970)– . [Bethesda, Md. : Cambridge Scientific Abstracts, etc.], 1970– . Bimonthly.

EK71

Provides international coverage of technical literature on the environment. Covers air and water pollution, solid wastes, noise, pesticides, radiation, and general environmental quality. Includes books, technical journals, conference proceedings, papers, government reports, and limited-circulation documents. A permuted subject ("keytalpha") index and an author index. An annual cumulative index is available, but is not included in the yearly subscription.

•Machine-readable version: *Pollution abstracts* [database] (Bethesda, Md., 1970–). Available online (updated monthly) and on CD-ROM (updated quarterly).   TD172.P65

Dictionaries

Allaby, Michael. Dictionary of the environment. 3rd ed. N.Y. : New York Univ. Pr., 1989. 423 p.   **EK72**

1st ed., 1977; 2nd ed., 1983.

Extensively revised from the earlier ed. Lists acronyms, abbreviations, phrases, and some personal names and contains numerous cross-references. Some terms omitted from the 2nd ed. have been restored in the 3rd ed.   QH540.4.A44

Directories

Handbooks

Environmental protection directory / ed. by Thaddeus C. Trzyna, with the assistance of Sally R. Ogsberg. 2nd ed. Chicago : Marquis Academic Media, [1975]. 526 p.   **EK73**

Publ. for the Center for California Public Affairs.

1st ed. publ. 1973 as part of the *Directory of consumer protection and environmental agencies* (Orange, N.J. : Academic Media).

Subtitle: A comprehensive guide to environmental organizations in the United States and Canada.

A "User's guide" is arranged topically "to help readers identify organizations concerned with a specific area of interest, such as water quality or fish and wildlife."—*Introd.* Remainder of the text follows geographic arrangement. Subject, organization, personnel, and publication indexes.   TD171.E57

Gale environmental sourcebook. 1st ed.– . Detroit : Gale, c1992– . Biennial.   **EK74**

Designed as a "guide to the organizations, agencies, programs, publications and other resources that study, define, and report on the environment."—*Introd.* Lists scholarships and awards. Appendixes cover endangered and threatened wildlife and plants. Intended mainly for U.S. users. Indexed.

Katz, Linda Sobel. Environmental profiles : a global guide to projects and people / Linda Sobel Katz, Sarah Orrick, and Robert Honig ; foreword by Al Gore. N.Y. : Garland, 1993. 1083 p. : ill., maps. (Garland reference library of social science, v. 736).   **EK75**

A guide to organizations that combat environmental degradation. Entries are arranged by country, including for each a discussion of its geography and environmental problems and a list of organizations under the headings: Government, NGO (nongovernmental organizations), Private, and Universities. Organizations are listed in vernacular with an English translation. There is a list of abbreviations and acronyms, and an appendix that lists organizations by topic (e.g., Deforestation, Population planning). Index.

§ Complemented by: *World directory of environmental organizations* (EK77). See also *Who is who in service to the earth* (AL23).   GE1.K38

Pollution research index : a guide to world research in environmental pollution / ed. by Andrew I. Sors and David Coleman. 2nd ed. Harlow, Essex, Eng. : Francis Hodgson, 1979. 555 p.   **EK76**

1st ed., 1975.

Entries, arranged by country, include address, affiliation, director, scope of activity. Indexed.   TD178.5.P64

World directory of environmental organizations. 1973– . Claremont, Calif. : California Institute of Public Affairs [etc.], [1973]– . Irregular.   **EK77**

Issuing organization varies. Sometimes called *Sierra Club's world directory of environmental organizations*. Issued with the cooperation of the International Union for Conservation of Nature and Natural Resources.

Describes organizations concerned with resource management and environmental protection worldwide. Chapters group organizations by theme (e.g., Future studies, Mountains, Noise), region, country, and type (e.g., Intergovernmental, Non-governmental). A chapter on the U.N. outlines its six-year environmental program and describes the conservation activities of its agencies. Profiles include address, fax number, founding date, history, activities, and geographic areas of concern. Glossary of acronyms. Appendix of environmental directories and databases. Index of selected organizations and major programs.   S920.W67

Air pollution / ed. by Arthur C. Stern. 3rd ed. N.Y. : Academic Pr., 1986. 8 v. : ill.   **EK78**

Contents: v.1, Air pollutants, their transformation and transport; v.2, The effects of air pollution; v.3, Measuring, monitoring and surveillance of air pollution; v.4, Engineering control of air pollution; v.5, Air quality management; v. 6, Supplement to Air pollutants, their transformation, transport, and effects; v. 7, Supplement to Measurements, monitoring, surveillance, and engineering control; v. 8, Supplement to Management of air quality.

Revised and greatly expanded, with many new contributors represented. Each volume has its own subject index. Information in v. 1–5 revised and brought up to date in v. 6–8. Prefaces in v. 6–8 include charts showing how the supplements augment the corresponding chapters in the 2nd ed. (3 v., 1968) and the 3rd ed.   TD883.S83

Allegri, Theodore H. Handling and management of hazardous materials and wastes. N.Y. : Chapman and Hall, 1986. 458 p. : ill.   **EK79**

Discusses "the safe and legal handling of hazardous materials and waste from the manufacturer's plant through the storage, transportation and distribution channels to the user, and, ultimately, to the disposal of the product or waste materials."—*Pref.* Practices are based on U.S. laws and regulations. There are chapters on asbestos, polychlorinated biphenyls (PCBs), acid rain, oil spills, handling radioactive waste, the Code of Federal Regulations, Superfund, and Toxic Substances Control Act. Includes a glossary of terms and appendixes giving information about U.S. Environmental Protection Administration regional asbestos coordinators and state solid and hazardous waste agencies. Indexed.   T55.3.H3A45

Burchell, Robert W. The environmental impact handbook / Robert W. Burchell, David Listokin. [New Brunswick, N.J.] : Center for Urban Policy Research, [c1975]. 234 p. : ill. **EK80**

A guide for land-use planners when preparing environmental impact studies in accordance with the National Environment Policy Act of 1969. Gives detailed, comprehensive explanations of the content, format, responsibilities, recommended procedures, and review processes used in preparing environmental impact studies.   HC110.E5B87

Fortlage, Catharine A. Environmental assessment : a practical guide. Aldershot, Hants, England ; Brookfield, Vt. : Gower, c1990. 152 p. : ill.   **EK81**

For annotation, *see* BF284.   TD194.6.F67

Standard handbook of environmental engineering / [ed. by] Robert A. Corbitt. N.Y. : McGraw-Hill, c1990. 1281 p. : ill.   **EK82**

Although "oriented toward the needs of practicing environmental engineers," this work is also "intended to serve as a single-volume reference for other engineers, architects, planners, corporate managers, elected officials, lawyers, students, and others seeking insight into environmental engineering technology."—*Pref.* Six of the nine chapters (all by teams of authors) are longer than 100 pages: Environmental engineering; Air quality control; Water supply; wastewater disposal; Stormwater management; Solid waste; and Hazardous waste. Three shorter chapters describe Environmental legislation and regulations, Air and water quality standards, and Environmental assessment. Numerous tables and figures. SI and U.S. customary units are used throughout. Indexed.   TD145.S72

Verschueren, Karel. Handbook of environmental data on organic chemicals. 2nd ed. N.Y. : Van Nostrand Reinhold, 1983. 1310 p.   **EK83**

1st ed., 1977.

Presents information on physical and chemical properties, air pollution factors, water pollution factors, and biological effects, for organic compounds, mixtures, and preparations. Includes bibliographical references. Formula index.   TD196.O73V47

Statistics

Statistical record of the environment. [1st ed.]– . Detroit : Gale, c1992– . Irregular.   **EK84**
2nd ed., 1994.
Ten chapters, each with a prose introduction followed by numerous tables and graphics. Stresses U.S. information but gives some limited worldwide coverage. Data sources are listed in three appendixes. A keyword index covers topics as well as line items in the tables.
TD180.S73

Air pollution

Abstract journals

Air pollution abstracts. v. 1 (1969)–v. 7, no. 6 (June 1976). Research Triangle Park, N.C. : Air Pollution Technical Information Center, 1969–76.   **EK85**
Superintendent of Documents classification: EP 4.11: .
Imprint varies; issuing agency varies. Issued monthly.
Vol. 1–2[1], 1969–Jan. 1971, issued by the National Air Pollution Control Administration as *NAPCA abstracts bulletin*. Later issued by U.S. Environmental Protection Agency.
Classed arrangement with author and detailed subject indexes. International coverage. Titles of foreign-language items are given in English followed by the original title. Abstracts are in English. Some 7,000 periodicals were regularly scanned for pertinent material.
TD881.A44

Handbooks

Miller, E. Willard. Environmental hazards : air pollution : a handbook for reference / E. Willard Miller, Ruby M. Miller. Santa Barbara, Calif. : ABC-Clio, c1989. 250 p.   **EK86**
The principal sections are an annotated bibliography that lists some 400 works and an introduction that discusses various causes of air pollution. Contains a chronology of significant events, biographical sketches of major researchers, and a listing of relevant U.S. laws.
HC110.A4M55

Noise

Handbook of accoustical measurements and noise control / Cyril M. Harris, ed. in chief. 3rd ed. N.Y. : McGraw-Hill, c1991. 1 v. (various pagings) : ill.   **EK87**
1st ed., 1957, and 2nd ed., 1979, had title: *Handbook of noise control*. noise control.
Chapters by specialists include bibliographies. Indexed.
TD892.H32

Water resources and water pollution

Bibliography

Giefer, Gerald J. Sources of information in water resources : an annotated guide to printed materials. Port Washington, N.Y. : Water Information Center, [1976]. 290 p.   **EK88**
"This guide, compiled for the use of the student and researcher, cites and annotates over 1100 titles found useful for reference purposes in the water resources field. ... The emphasis here has been upon the literature of the United States."—*Pref.*   Z7935.G53

————— Water publications of state agencies / Gerald J. Giefer and David K. Todd. Port Washington, N.Y. : Water Information Center, [1972]. 319 p.   **EK89**
With the assistance of Mary Louise Quinn.
Subtitle: A bibliography of publications on water resources and their management published by the states of the United States.
"A listing of water resources publications issued by 335 state agencies in 50 states of the United States. Information is listed by state with publications grouped under the issuing agencies of each state."—*Pref.* Information on how to obtain publications is included.
A supplement for 1971–74, by Giefer and Todd with the assistance of Beverly Fish, was issued in 1976.

Ralston, Valerie Hunter. Water resources : a bibliographic guide to reference sources. Storrs : Univ. of Connecticut, 1975. 123 p. (University of Connecticut Library. Bibliography series, no. 2 ; Institute of Water Resources. Report, no. 23).   **EK90**
More than 400 entries arranged by type, e.g., guides, dictionaries, encyclopedias, handbooks, statistical sources, with author and keyword indexes. Many items are annotated.   TD224.C8A3

Water Resources Center Archives (Calif.). Dictionary catalog of the Water Resources Center Archives, University of California, Berkeley. Boston : G. K. Hall, 1970. 5 v.   **EK91**
An author-subject catalog reproducing the catalog cards for this collection of about 80,000 pieces, dealing with water as a natural resource, water utilization, municipal and industrial water-use problems, flood control, reclamation, waste disposal, water pollution, water law, etc. Emphasizes report literature.
—————. —————. *Supplement*, 1st–6th (Boston : G. K. Hall, 1970–78. 6 v. in 9). The supplements add more than 106,000 items. Only the 6th suppl. has title entries in addition to author-subject listings.   Z7935.C32

Dictionaries

Glossary : water and wastewater control engineering. 3rd ed. Wash. : Amer. Public Health Assoc., [1981]. 441 p.   **EK92**
"Prepared by joint editorial board representing American Public Health Association, American Society of Civil Engineers, American Water Works Association, Water Pollution Control Federation."—*t.p.*
1st ed., 1949, had title *Glossary: water and sewage control engineering*.
Includes relevant terms from chemistry and chemical engineering, and terms related to regulatory agency involvement, in addition to the terms from water and wastewater engineering. Cross-references.
TD9.G55

Directories

Library of Congress. National Referral Center for Science and Technology. A directory of information resources in the United States : water. [Wash. : U.S. Govt. Print. Off.], 1966. 248 p.   **EK93**
Lists more than 600 U.S. organizations and institutions engaged in research or in collecting data on water and water-related subjects. Focus is on fresh water, with oceanography excluded. Commercial, profit-making organizations are omitted. Subject index. Similar to the Center's directories for the physical sciences (1971) and for the social sciences (Rev. ed., 1973).   TD211.U5

Organization for Economic Cooperation and Development. Directorate for Scientific Affairs. Directory of water pollution research laboratories. [Paris] : Organization for Economic Co-operation and Development, Directorate for Scientific Affairs, Central Service for International Co-operation in Scientific Research, [1965]. 519 p.   **EK94**

A country-by-country listing of laboratories and institutions which regularly engage in research of general interest on the pollution of fresh water. Information includes address, name of director, notes on organization, personnel, special facilities and equipment, documentation service or publications issued, and research programs.

Handbooks

American Society for Testing and Materials. Committee D-19 on Water. Manual on water. 4th ed. Philadelphia : Amer. Soc. for Testing and Materials, [1978]. 472 p. : ill. (ASTM special technical publications, no. 442A).   **EK95**

1st–2nd eds. (1953–59) had title *Manual on industrial water and industrial waste water.*

"This manual is intended as a brief reference source of information on water. It will not replace an adequate library on the subject, but it does provide basic information for routine use and cites references to the technical literature, thus serving as a point of departure for more specific and detailed studies."—*Introd.* Provides general discussions of the nature, sources, treatment, analysis, and uses of water, particularly industrial water. Includes numerous tables and charts; reference tables and curves included in an appendix. Indexed.

————. *Supplement to Manual on water, 4th ed.* (Philadelphia : Amer. Soc. for Testing and Materials, [1983]. 47 p. [ASTM special technical pubn., no. 442A-S1]).

Includes new chapters on ion-selective electrodes and on membrane filtration.

Van der Leeden, Frits. The water encyclopedia / Frits van der Leeden, Fred L. Troise, David Keith Todd. 2nd ed. Chelsea, Mich. : Lewis Publishers, c1990. 808 p. : ill., maps.   **EK96**

1st ed., 1970.

This comprehensive statistical sourcebook on water and all its related aspects was compiled from a wide variety of governmental and private information sources. Substantially revised and expanded from the 1st ed. More than 700 tables, maps, charts, and diagrams are arranged in 11 chapters covering climate, hydrology, surface and ground water, water use, water quality, environmental problems, water management, water resources agencies, legislation, constants, and conversion factors. Subject index.   TD351.V36

Water and water pollution handbook / ed. by Leonard L. Ciaccio. N.Y. : Dekker, 1971–73. 4 v.   **EK97**

Consists of 32 chapters contributed by specialists, offering an interdisciplinary approach to water analysis and treatment. Bibliographies. Author index and subject index in v. 4.   TD380.W32

Water quality and treatment : a handbook of community water supplies / American Water Works Association ; Frederick W. Pontius, technical ed. 4th ed. N.Y. : McGraw-Hill, c1990. 1194 p. : ill.   **EK98**

1st ed., 1940, had title: *Manual of water quality and treatment.*

Each of the 18 chapters describes a specific water treatment process, whether standard or state-of-the-art. Bibliographies; numerous tables and figures.   TD430.W365

Statistics

Van der Leeden, Frits. Water resources of the world : selected statistics. Port Washington, N.Y. : Water Information Center, [1975]. 568 p. : ill.   **EK99**

A compilation and summary tabulation of worldwide water resources statistics. Presents data on the characteristics of major lakes, rivers, and reservoirs; desalination; hydrologic cycle, including glaciers and the oceans; water supplies in developing nations; and international water development and financing programs. The 578 tables and numerous maps and diagrams are arranged by continents. Detailed references.   GB661.V34

Hydaulic engineering and hydrodynamics

Bibliography

Kolupaila, Steponas. Bibliography of hydrometry. Notre Dame, Ind. : Univ. of Notre Dame Pr., 1961. 975 p.   **EK100**

A comprehensive, annotated bibliography of hydrometry—the science of measurement of water—including some 7,370 titles in more than 30 languages and from all periods. Titles are given in the original language, followed by a translation into English. Indexed.

Z5853.H9K6

Rowe, Robert Seaman. Bibliography of rivers and harbors and related fields in hydraulic engineering. Princeton, N.J. : Rivers and Harbors Section, Dept. of Civil Engineering, Princeton Univ., 1953. 407 p.   **EK101**

International in scope. Includes some 6,000 references to books and monographs. Omits periodical articles, abstracts, etc. Some entries annotated. Indexed.   Z5853.H9R6

Handbooks

Davis' handbook of applied hydraulics / Vincent J. Zipparro, ed. in chief ; Hans Hasen, co-ed. 4th ed. N.Y. : McGraw-Hill, c1993. 1 v. (various pagings) : ill.   **EK102**

1st ed. (1942)–3rd ed. (1969) had title: *Handbook of applied hydraulics,* Calvin Victor Davis, ed. in chief.

Consists of 28 sections written by practicing engineers. Sections include diagrams, equations, tabular material, bibliographic references, and in some cases lists of useful computer programs. Presents both basic principles and practical applications by means of examples drawn largely from the actual practice of hydraulic engineering, including dams, natural channels, reservoir hydraulics, etc.   TC145.D3

Structural engineering

Building design and construction handbook. 4th ed. / ed. by Frederick S. Merritt. N.Y. : McGraw-Hill, [1982]. 1 v. (various pagings) : ill.   **EK103**

1st ed., 1958. Previous eds. had title *Building construction handbook.*

Intended to offer information which would be most useful to those concerned with building design and construction, especially those who have to make decisions affecting building materials and construction methods. Sections by specialists; bibliographic references; index.   TH151.B825

Fire protection handbook / Arthur E. Cote, ed. in chief ; Jim L. Linville, managing ed. 17th ed. Quincy, Mass. : National Fire Protection Assoc., c1991. 1 v. (various pagings) : ill.

EK104

1st ed., 1896; 16th ed., 1986.

A single-source reference book on good fire protection and fire protection practices. Articles by specialists include bibliographies. Indexed.   TH9145.F523

Handbook of concrete engineering. 2nd ed. / ed. by Mark Fintel. N.Y. : Van Nostrand Reinhold, [1985]. 892 p. : ill.

EK105

1st ed., 1974.

"Contains up-to-date information on planning, design, analysis, and construction of engineered concrete structures ... to provide engineers, architects, contractors, and students of civil engineering and architecture with authoritative practical design information."—*Pref.* Design information based on the 1983 ACI (American Concrete Institute) Code. Chapters by specialists include equations, diagrams, bibliographic references. Indexed.   TA682.H36

Handbook of structural concrete / ed. by F. K. Kong ... [et al.]. N.Y. : McGraw-Hill, [1983]. 1 v. (various pagings) : ill.
                                                                          EK106
"Intended as an international reference work on the current state of the art and science of structural concrete ... the *Handbook* has been designed to meet the needs of practicing civil and structural engineers, consulting engineering and contracting firms, concrete materials producers and users, research institutes, universities and colleges."—*Pref.* Has sections on materials; design and analysis; construction; structures; practical considerations. Chapters by specialist authors include references. Indexed.   TA439.H275

Manual of steel construction : allowable stress design. 9th ed. Chicago : American Institute of Steel Construction, 1989. 1 v. (various pagings) : ill.   **EK107**
First publ. 1926 with title: *Steel construction*; 8th ed., 1980.
Treats one method of design; the companion title (EK108) offers a different design procedure. Arrangement in sections is continued from the 8th ed.; the section of "Miscellaneous data and mathematical tables" is repeated in the companion volume. Contains numerous tables, graphs, and worked examples expressed in U.S. customary units. Indexed.   TA684.A51

Manual of steel construction : load & resistance factor design. [Chicago] : American Institute of Steel Construction, c1986. 1 v. (various pagings) : ill.   **EK108**
Organization is similar to the companion title (EK107). Features graphs, tables, and solved problems; uses U.S customary units throughout. The section of "Miscellaneous data and mathematical tables" is printed in both volumes. Indexed.   TA684.L558

McMullan, Randall. Dictionary of building. N.Y. : Nichols Pub., c1988. 262 p. : ill.   **EK109**
Published in Great Britain as *Macmillan dictionary of building* (London : Macmillan, 1988).
Emphasizes the vocabulary of current building practice, as found in "modern specifications, technical standards, reports and product literature ... ."—*Pref.* Excludes classical terms not presently used and specialized "masonry and carpentry ... terms which deserve complete books of their own." Cross-references, *see also* references, and comparison references are ample, and distinctions are noted between British and American usage. Not illustrated, except for 11 pages of simple line drawings of some of the basics of construction.   TH9.M36

Means estimating handbook. Kingston, Mass. : R.S. Means Co., c1990. 905 p. : ill.   **EK110**
Senior editor: Jeffrey M. Goldman.
Directed primarily to architects, builders and engineers. Consists of 16 sections covering topics such as concrete, masonry, metals, mechanical, electrical, finishes, wood, and plastic. Each section is arranged similarly: a general overview; charts; tables and worked-out examples for estimating needed data; a check list of named items; and final reminders. Prices are omitted. Conversion tables and abbreviations appear in an appendix. Subject index.   TH435.M42

Merritt, Frederick S. Structural steel designers' handbook / Roger L. Brockenbrough, ed. ; Frederick S. Merritt, ed. N.Y. : McGraw-Hill, c1994. 1 v. (various pagings) : ill.   **EK111**
1st ed., 1972.
Extensive sections on properties of structural steels, general structural theory, building design, bridges. Chapters by specialists. Indexed.   TA684.M579

Stein, J. Stewart. Construction glossary : an encyclopedic reference and manual. N.Y. : Wiley, c1993. 1137 p.   **EK112**
1st ed., 1980.

A glossary arranged in 16 subject divisions, each with several subdivisions, within which definitions are listed alphabetically. Indexed.   TH9.S78

Structural engineering handbook / ed. by Edwin H. Gaylord, Jr., Charles N. Gaylord. 3rd ed. N.Y. : McGraw-Hill, c1990. 1 v. (various pagings) : ill.   **EK113**
1st ed., 1968; 2nd ed., 1979.
For the engineer, architect, and student of civil engineering and architecture. Contains 30 sections by 45 specialist contributors, covering a wide range of structures, design in various media, soil mechanics and foundations, etc. Includes bibliographic references, many worked-out examples. Indexed.   TA635.S77

Wood engineering handbook / Forest Products Laboratory. 2nd ed. Englewood Cliffs, N.J. : Prentice Hall, c1990. 1 v. (various pagings) : ill.   **EK114**
Rev. ed. of *Wood handbook*, 1974; 1st ed., 1940.
Chapters are written by specialists. Discusses woods of commercial importance in the U.S., including some imported varieties. Chapters cover commercial lumber, wood preservation, insulation board, plywood, and other applications. Illustrated with figures, tables, and photographs. A glossary precedes the subject index.   TA419.W78

Wood structural design data : a manual for architects, builders, engineers, and other concerned with wood construction. 1986 ed. Wash. : National Forest Products Assoc., c1986. 240 p. : ill.   **EK115**
1st ed., 1934. 1st–3rd eds. by National Lumber Manufacturers Assoc.
Includes tables, brief text, bibliography.   TA666.W64

Transportation engineering

Bibliography

King, Richard L. Airport noise pollution : a bibliography of its effects on people and property. Metuchen, N.J. : Scarecrow, 1973. 380 p.   **EK116**
More than 2,100 numbered items in six broad subject categories: environmental noise pollution; aircraft noise pollution; airport noise pollution; noise pollution and human health; noise pollution and property values; and control and abatement of noise pollution. Includes a directory of government, university and research, professional, civic, business, and international and foreign organizations concerned with noise pollution. Author and subject indexes.   Z5064.N6K55

Li, Shu-t'ien. Bibliography on airport engineering. [N.Y.] : Amer. Soc. of Civil Engineers, 1960. 170 p.   **EK117**
Subtitle: A compilation of free world literature numbering 2335 entries classified into 26 groups and arranged chronologically.
Each entry appears once; there are no cross-references. Period covered: 1938–59.   Z5064.A28L5

Abstract journals

Road abstracts. v. 1 (Feb. 1934)–v. 35 (Apr. 1968). London : Stat. Off., 1935–68.   **EK118**
Comp. by Dept. of Scientific and Industrial Research, Road Research Laboratory, London. Issued monthly.
Vols. 1–16 issued as supplements to the *Journal* of the Institution of Municipal Engineers.
Covers finance, planning, construction and materials, soil engineering, maintenance, traffic planning and theory, road users, accidents and safety measures, etc. Titles of foreign articles are translated into English with indication of original language.   TE1.R55

Transportation research abstracts. no. 1–142; v. 17, no. 7–v. 45. Wash. : [Highway Research Board], 1931–75.   **EK119**

Title varies: no. 1–v. 44, no. 6 called *Highway research abstracts.*

Published by the Highway Research Board of the National Research Council, National Academy of Sciences.

Absorbed by *Transportation research news* (1976–82, bimonthly), later *TR news* (1983–), with an "Abstracts" section at the end of each issue. Abstracts were discontinued after 1986.

———. *Index, 1931–1961* (Wash., 1963).

Includes English-language abstracts of journal articles, research reports, etc. The majority of publications are in English although there are a few in other languages. Volume numbering began with v. 17, no. 7, July 1947. Issued monthly from that date; previously publication was irregular. Annual subject index, 1962–75. Beginning 1937 the December issue was a "Synopsis" issue, containing abstracts of papers and reports scheduled for presentation at the annual meeting of the Highway Research Board. Each issue includes a list of new publications of the Board.   TE1.N462

Handbooks

Baker, Robert Fulton. Handbook of highway engineering. N.Y. : Van Nostrand Reinhold, [1975]. 894 p. : ill.   **EK120**
Repr.: Malabar, Fla. : Krieger Pub. Co., 1982.

"The purpose of this handbook is to provide a reference book of principles, processes and data for those interested in the application of technology to highway transportation."—*Pref.* Topical chapters by specialist authors include references. Indexed.   TE151.B24

Yearbooks

Jane's urban transport systems. v. 1 (1982)– . London : Jane's, 1982– . Annual (slightly irregular).   **EK121**
A listing, alphabetically by city, of urban transport systems. Includes address, telephone, administrators' names, statistical summaries of operations, and photographs. Also lists manufacturers of transport equipment, arranged by category, with data on models, contracts, etc., and illustrations. Includes a list of consultants. Indexed.

§ *See also* David Banister and Laurie Pickup, *Urban transport and planning* (BF269).   HE4211.J33

Statistics

Highway statistics. 1945– . Wash. : The Administration ; for sale by the U.S. Govt. Print. Off., 1947– . Annual.   **EK122**
Superintendent of Documents classification: TD 2.23: .

Previously issued by the Bureau of Public Roads and the Public Roads Administration, 1945–68.

Gives "statistical tabulations relating to highway transportation in three major areas: (1) highway use—the ownership and operation of motor vehicles; (2) highway finance—the receipts and expenditures for highways by public agencies; and (3) the highway plant—the extent, characteristics, and performance of the public highways, roads, and streets in the Nation."—*Introd., 1992.* Statistics for U.S. territories and for the Commonwealth of Puerto Rico are included in a separate section.

United States. Federal Highway Administration. Highway statistics : summary to 1985. Wash. : U.S. Govt. Print. Off., 1987. 260 p.   **EK123**
Provides a general historical summary of information dealing with highways, their use and financing, bringing together a comprehensive statistical review of highway development in the U.S. through 1985. Serves as background material for the annual *Highway statistics*

(EK122). Information supplements and in some instances supersedes similar data presented in other summaries covering to 1945, 1955, 1965, and 1975.   HE355.A3A535

ELECTRICAL AND ELECTRONIC ENGINEERING

General works

Guides

Ardis, Susan. A guide to the literature of electrical and electronics engineering / Susan B. Ardis ; ed. by Jean M. Poland. Littleton, Colo. : Libraries Unlimited, 1987. 190 p.   **EK124**
Cites the usual types of reference sources (handbooks, indexes, dictionaries, databases), together with more specialized categories such as patents, standards, data compilations, newsletters, and product literature. Entries give full bibliographic data and a short annotation. Subjects not covered are robotics, CAD/CAM, appliance repair, electrical wiring, and electrical construction. Author and title index.

Z5832.A83

Bibliography

Electronic properties of materials : a guide to the literature / ed. by H. Thayne Johnson. N.Y. : Plenum Pr., 1965–71. 3 v. in 6.   **EK125**
An extensive bibliography with coordinate index derived from the indexing project at the Electronic Properties Information Center, Hughes Aircraft Company, Culver City, California. Still useful although dated.   Z5838.M34E4

Mottelay, Paul Fleury. Bibliographical history of electricity and magnetism, chronologically arranged. London : Griffin, 1922. 673 p. : ill.   **EK126**
Subtitle: Researches into the domain of the early sciences, especially from the period of the revival of scholasticism, with biographical and other accounts of the most distinguished natural philosophers throughout the Middle Ages.

A chronological history with many bibliographical references. Indexed. Very important for the history of electricity.   QC507.M6

Shiers, George. Bibliography of the history of electronics. Metuchen, N.J. : Scarecrow, 1972. 323 p.   **EK127**
A classed bibliography of more than 1,800 items on historical aspects of electronics and telecommunications. Period covered: 1860 to the present. Most entries are annotated. Indexed.   Z5836.S54

Abstract journals

Science abstracts : Sec. B, Electrical & electronics abstracts. v. 1– . London : Inst. of Electrical Engineers, 1898– . Monthly, with semiannual author and subject indexes.

EK128
1898–1902 title reads: *Science abstracts. Physics and electrical engineering.* 1903–66, issued in two sections: A, Physics; B, Electrical engineering. Beginning with 1941, titles of sections changed to *Physics abstracts* and *Electrical engineering abstracts.* Title of Sec. B changed to *Electrical and electronics abstracts* beginning 1966. In Jan. 1967 the publication *Control abstracts* (later, *Computer and control abstracts,* EK162) was designated as Sec. C of *Science abstracts.*

Entries are arranged according to a subject classification listed on the back cover of each issue. Coverage is international and includes periodicals, reports, books, patents, dissertations, and conference papers. A complete list of periodicals is issued as a part of the semiannual author indexes. Author and subject indexes, plus several "small indexes"—bibliography index, book index, patent and report index, conference index. Now contains more than 40,000 abstracts a year.

Microfiche edition also issued.

Cumulative author and subject indexes: 1955–59; 1960–64; 1965–68; 1969–72; 1973–76; 1977–80; 1981–84; 1989–92.

•Machine-readable versions, online and on CD-ROM, are available as part of *INSPEC* (ED9).   Q1.S3

Encyclopedias

Encyclopedia of electronics / Stan Gibilisco, Neil Sclater. 2nd ed. Blue Ridge Summit, Pa. : TAB Professional and Reference Books, c1990. 960 p. : ill.   **EK129**

Descriptive entries treat electronics, electrical engineering, and some areas of computer science. Physical sciences, mathematics, and statistics are represented to a limited extent. Cross-references are plentiful; many line drawings and tables. Indexed.   TK7804.E47

Traister, John E. Encyclopedic dictionary of electronic terms / John E. Traister and Robert J. Traister. N.Y. : Prentice-Hall, 1984. 604 p. : ill.   **EK130**

"A quick reference source for serious comprehension of the basics involved in electronics."—*Pref.* Entries are relatively long and detailed.   TK7804.T7

Dictionaries

Institute of Electrical and Electronics Engineers. The new IEEE standard dictionary of electrical and electronics terms / Gediminas P. Kurpis, chair; Christopher J. Booth, ed. 5th ed. N.Y. : Inst. of Electrical and Electronics Engineers , 1993. 1619 p. : ill.   **EK131**

1st ed., 1972; 4th ed., 1988. Previous eds. had title: *IEEE standard dictionary of electrical and electronics terms.*

Definitions have been taken from IEEE standards, ANSI (American National Standards Institute) publications, and other sources. Following each definition, a number gives the source of the definition; unbracketed numbers designate IEEE standards, bracketed numbers refer to the "Sources" section at the back of the book. An appendix gives abstracts for all IEEE standards used. Obsolete and irrelevant terms have been eliminated from this edition. Acronyms and abbreviations are given in a section at the end (much reduced in size from the section in the previous edition). Cross-references.   TK9.I478

Jackson, Kenneth George. Dictionary of electrical engineering / Kenneth George Jackson and Raphael Feinberg. 2nd ed. London ; Boston : Butterworths, 1981. 350 p. : ill.   **EK132**

1st ed., 1965.
Brief entries. Cross-references.   TK9.J8

Modern dictionary of electronics / [by] Rudolf F. Graf. [6th ed.]. Indianapolis : Sams, 1984. 1152 p.   **EK133**

1st ed., 1962.
Brief definitions of several thousand terms. Additional sections: pronunciation guide for commonly mispronounced words; list of semiconductor symbols and abbreviations; schematic symbols.   TK7804.H6

Handbooks

American electricians' handbook / Terrell Croft, former ed. ; Wilford I. Summers, ed. 12th ed. N.Y. : McGraw-Hill, 1992. 1 v. (various pagings).   **EK134**

1st ed., 1913.
A standard handbook. Written to be in accordance with the latest ed. of the National Electrical Code. Indexed.   TK151.A47

The electrical engineering handbook / ed. in chief, Richard C. Dorf. Boca Raton : CRC Pr., c1993. 2662 p. : ill.   **EK135**

A compilation of chapters by academic authorities and engineers in industry that intends to provide comprehensive and up-to-date information on basic fields of electronics, circuits, and signal processing, and emerging fields of communications, digital devices, and biomedical engineering. Includes references. The final section includes a compilation of physical constants. Subject index, index of key equations.   TK145.E354

Electronics engineers' handbook / Donald G. Fink, ed., Donald Christiansen, ed. 3rd ed. N.Y. : McGraw-Hill, 1989. 1 v. (various pagings) : ill.   **EK136**

1st ed., 1975.
A companion volume to the *Standard handbook for electrical engineers*, (EK143), which is devoted primarily to techniques of electrical power engineering. This book, intended for electronics engineering, offers articles by specialists, oriented toward application rather than theory, and includes references. In this edition the section on computer-aided design includes a listing of CAD programs and languages; a new section covering standards and symbols has been added. Indexed.   TK7825.E34

Electronics engineer's reference book / ed. by F. F. Mazda ; with specialist contributors. 6th ed. London ; Boston : Butterworths, 1989. 1 v. (various pagings) : ill.   **EK137**

1st ed., 1958; 5th ed., 1983.
Emphasis on recent technologies, such as computer-aided design techniques, digital system analysis, local area networks. Indexed.   TK7825.E36

Fundamentals handbook of electrical and computer engineering / ed. by Sheldon S. L. Chang. N.Y. : Wiley, 1982. 3 v. : ill.   **EK138**

Contents: v.1, Circuits, fields, and electronics; v.2, Communication, control, devices, and systems; v.3, Computer hardware, software, and applications.

Chapters by experts give concise coverage of major areas in electrical and computer engineering, include bibliographic references. Volumes are separately indexed.   TK151.F86

Handbook of electronic tables and formulas / comp. and ed. by the Howard W. Sams Engineering Staff. 6th ed. Indianapolis : Sams, 1986. 265 p. : ill.   **EK139**

1st ed., 1959; 5th ed., 1979.
Covers electronics formulas and laws, constants and standards, symbols and codes, service and installation data, design data, mathematical tables and formulas, miscellaneous data.   TK7825.H378

Lighting handbook : reference & application / Mark S. Rea, ed. in chief. N.Y. : Illuminating Engineering Society of North America, c1993. 989 p. : ill.   **EK140**

Title varies: 5th–7th eds. called: *IES lighting handbook.*
1st ed., 1947. 6th–7th eds. publ. in 2 v., unnumbered: Reference volume; Applications volume.

Individual chapters of this standard reference handbook contain figures, tabular data, photographs, and references. Indexed.   TK4161.L5

Radar handbook / ed. in chief, Merrill I. Skolnik. 2nd. ed. N.Y. : McGraw-Hill, c1990. 1 v. (various pagings) : ill.   **EK141**

1st ed., 1970.

Chapters by specialists on major topics of interest in the field of radar. Designed for the person who "has a general knowledge of radar but is not necessarily an expert in the particular subject covered by the chapter."—*Pref.* Includes bibliographies.   TK6575.R262

Reference data for engineers : radio, electronics, computer, and communications. 8th ed. Indianapolis : H. W. Sams, c1993. 1 v. (various pagings) : ill.   **EK142**

1st–6th eds. 1943–75 had title: *Reference data for radio engineers.* 7th ed., 1985.

Originally a production of the International Telephone and Telegraph Corporation, this reference work has in recent editions obtained material from outside the ITT system. Includes a wide range of data, tables, definitions, and descriptions in separate chapters, with some bibliographic references.   TK6552.F4

Standard handbook for electrical engineers / Donald G. Fink and H. Wayne Beaty, eds. 13th ed. N.Y. : McGraw-Hill, 1993. 1 v. (various pagings) : ill.   **EK143**

1st ed., 1907.

A handbook oriented toward practical application, including the impact of economic considerations. Twenty-eight sections by practicing engineers include illustrations and tables of data appropriate to the detailed narrative information given; includes references. Indexed.   TK151.S83

Television and radio

The ARRL handbook for radio amateurs. Ed. 1 (1926)– . Newington, Conn. : American Radio Relay League, 1926– . Annual.   **EK144**

Eds. 1–61 (1926–84) had title: *Radio amateur's handbook*; eds. 62–67 (1985–90), *The ARRL handbook for the radio amateur.* Date of coverage often appears in title.

71st ed., 1994.

Chapters cover fundamentals and changing technology in the field and include many tables, circuit diagrams, photographs, and occasional references. Indexed.   TK6550.R18

Barton, David Knox. Handbook of radar measurement / David Knox Barton, Harold R. Ward. Englewood Cliffs, N.J. : Prentice-Hall, [1969]. 426 p. : ill.   **EK145**

Intends to present the results of studies of radar measurement "and to relate these results to design parameters of practical equipment."—*Pref.*   TK6580.B33

Freeman, Roger L. Reference manual for telecommunications engineering. 2nd ed. N.Y. : Wiley, 1993. 2308 p. : ill.   **EK146**

1st ed., 1985.

"The aim of this manual is to provide a central source of basic information that will have repeated application."—*Pref.* Divided into 29 subject areas; includes references and bibliographies. Many chapters have more text than the 1st ed. Indexed.   TK5102.5.F68

Middleton, Robert Gordon. Television service manual. 5th ed. / rev. by Joseph G. Barrile ; Rex Miller, consulting ed. Indianapolis : Audel, 1984. 470 p. : ill.   **EK147**

1st–2nd eds. (1951–61) had title: *Audels television service manual.* 1st–3rd eds. by E. P. Anderson.

Covers system and circuit theory, system standards, installation and maintenance procedures.   TK6642.A56

Television engineering handbook : featuring HDTV systems / K. Blair Benson, ed. Rev. ed. / rev. by Jerry C. Whitaker. N.Y. : McGraw-Hill, c1992. 1 v. (various pagings) : ill.   **EK148**

1st ed., 1986 (without subtitle) superseded *Television engineering handbook*, ed. by Donald G. Fink (1957).

Twenty-five signed chapters cover television technology including transmission, cable and satellite home distribution systems, electron optics, video tape recording, digital television, electronic editing, etc. Includes references. Indexed.   TK6642.T437

Weik, Martin H. Communications standard dictionary. 2nd ed. N.Y. : Van Nostrand Reinhold, c1989. 1219 p. : ill.   **EK149**

1st ed., 1983.

A comprehensive compilation of terms and definitions in the science and technology of communications. Words or terms used in definitions are italicized if they are themselves headwords. Cross-references.   TK5102.W437

COMPUTER SCIENCE

Guides

Hildebrandt, Darlene Myers. Computing information directory. 2nd ed. (1985)– . Federal Way, Wash. : Pedaro, c1985– . Annual.   **EK150**

Continues. *Computer science resources* (1981).

Imprint varies: 1990– , Colville, Wash.

An extensive guide to the computer science literature, providing bibliographic information at title or article level, depending on the focus of a particular section. Sections: Computing journals; University computing center newsletters; Books, biblios, special issues; Dictionaries and glossaries; Indexing and abstracting services; Software resources; Review resources; Hardware resources; Directories, encyclopedias, and handbooks; Computer languages; ACM SIG proceedings; Standards bibliography; Career and salary trends bibliography; Expansion to the Library of Congress Classification System; and Publishers' addresses. Detailed subject index.   Z5640.H54

Morrill, Chester. Computers and data processing : information sources. Detroit : Gale, [1969]. 275 p. (Management information guide, v. 15).   **EK151**

"An annotated guide to the literature, associations, and institutions concerned with input, throughout, and output of data."—*t. p.*. A classed, annotated listing of books, journal articles, and other information sources. Appendixes: directories of associations, manufacturers, periodicals, publishers, seminars, and personnel and placement firms. Author/editor, title, and subject indexes.   Z6654.C17M58

Pritchard, Alan. A guide to computer literature : an introductory survey of the sources of information. 2nd ed., rev. and expanded. London : Bingley, 1972. 194 p.   **EK152**

1st ed., 1969.

Describes the organization of the computer literature through 1972. Chapters discuss types of resources, including primary and secondary sources, hardware and software information sources, theses, and standards. Author and title index.   Z6654.C17P7

Bibliography

Artificial intelligence : bibliographic summaries of the select literature / Henry M. Rylko, compiling ed. Lawrence, Kan. : Report Store, c1984–85. 2 v.   **EK153**

Capsule reviews of monographs, conference proceedings, special issues of journals, series, and research reports are arranged alphabetically by personal or corporate author. Covers 1967–85. Entries include summary, contents listing, and bibliographical information. The two volumes are independently organized; each has author and subject index; v. 2 also includes a Guide to the subject index. A supplement, bound with v. 2, includes cumulative author, subject, and program indexes.　　　　　　Z7405.A7A77

The artificial intelligence compendium : abstracts and index to research on AI theory and applications, 1954–1987. N.Y. : Scientific DataLink, c1988. 5 v.　　　　　**EK154**
　　　1st ed., 1985, had title: *The Scientific DataLink index to artificial intelligence research, 1954–1984.*
　　　Contents: v. 1–2, Abstracts; v. 3, Author and title indexes; v. 4–5, Subject index.
　　　Provides abstracts to technical reports and dissertations from 24 research centers, both academic and industrial. Does not cover published articles. Organized by institution, then chronologically by report number.
　　　•Machine-readable version: *Artificial intelligence database of abstracts on CD-ROM* [database] (N.Y. : Professional and Technical Publishing, 1994–　). Available on CD-ROM, updated semiannually.
　　　　　　Q334.A77

Klimasauskas, Casimir C. The 1989 neuro-computing bibliography. 2nd ed. Cambridge, Mass. : MIT Pr., c1989. 624 p.　　　　　**EK155**
　　　1st ed., 1987, had title: *The 1987 annotated neuro-computing bibliography.*
　　　An extensive bibliography of journal articles, conference proceedings papers, and technical reports in a wide variety of fields that relate to neuro-computing. Full bibliographic citations are arranged alphabetically by first author with cross-references for additional authors. Title keyword index.　　　　　　Z5642.2.K57 1989

Stanford University. Computer science technical reports : selected holdings at Stanford University. Providence, R.I. : Amer. Mathematical Soc., c1992. 1160 p.　　　　　**EK156**
　　　Lists more than 36,000 technical reports issued by approximately 100 major computer science research institutions, both industrial and academic. Organized by institutions, then chronologically by report number. Entries include author, title, and date. Author index.
　　　•Available in machine-readable form as part of *MathSci* [database] (EB28).　　　　　　Z5640.S82

Wasserman, Philip D. NeuralSource : the bibliographic guide to artificial neural networks / Philip D. Wasserman and Roberta M. Oetzel. N.Y. : Van Nostrand Reinhold, c1990. 1014 p.　　　　　**EK157**
　　　A comprehensive listing of more than 4,200 journal articles, technical reports, and books published through 1989, representing the "bulk of published information on artificial neural networks." —*Pref.* Entries, arranged chronologically and then alphabetically by first author, include full bibliographic citations; more than half have brief abstracts. Author, publication, and keyword indexes. Periodic updates are planned.　　　　　　Z7405.A7W37

Youden, W. W. Computer literature bibliography. Wash. : U.S. National Bureau of Standards : For sale by the U.S. Govt. Print. Off., 1965–68. 2 v. (National Bureau of Standards miscellaneous publication, 266, 309).　　　　　**EK158**
　　　Repr. in 1 v. as: *Computer literature bibliography, 1946–1967* (N.Y. : Arno Pr., 1970).
　　　Contents: v. 1, 1946–63; v. 2, 1964–67.
　　　Vol. 1 indexes by source, title word, and author, all articles (more than 6,100) "published in 9 journals, 21 books, and over 100 proceedings."—*Introd. to v. 1.* Vol. 2 provides the same indexing for 5,200 articles "published in 17 journals, 20 books, and 43 conference proceedings."—*Introd. to v. 2.*　　　　　　QC100.U57

Indexes; Abstract journals

ACM guide to computing literature. 1977– . [N.Y.] : Assoc. for Computing Machinery, 1978– . Annual (slightly irregular).　　　　　**EK159**
　　　Continues in part: *Computing reviews : bibliography and subject index of current computing literature* (1975–76).
　　　Contains full bibliographic citations to books, journal articles, conference proceedings, technical reports, and theses in all fields of computer science and its applications. Also serves as an index to *Computing reviews* (EK166). Indexed by author, keyword, category (Computing reviews classification system) and proper noun subject (descriptors for specific names of hardware, languages, etc.). Also contains: Computing reviews reviewer index; Source index of publishers.
　　　•Machine-readable versions:
　　　(1) *MathSci* [database] (EB28).
　　　(2) *COMPUSCIENCE* [database] (EK161).
　　　(3) *Computing archive* [database] (EK165).　　　　QA75.7.A75

CompuMath citation index : CMCI. Philadelphia : Inst. for Scientific Information, 1981– . Semiannual.　　　　　**EK160**
　　　Frequency varies: annual, 1981–91.
　　　Indexes the international periodical literature in pure and applied mathematics, statistics and probability, mathematical methods for physical and social sciences, computer science and computer applications, control theory, and operations research. Provides full coverage for more than 440 journals and monographic series in mathematics and computer science, plus selective coverage for approximately 1,300 science, social science, and humanities journals. Each issue is divided into: Source index, Citation index, Permuterm index, Research front speciality index, and Corporate index. Includes Guide and list of source publications. A five-year cumulation has been published for 1976–80, a period not previously indexed.　　　　Z6653.C84

•**COMPUSCIENCE** [database]. Eggenstein-Leopoldshafen, Germany : FIZ Karlsruhe, 1972– .　　　　　**EK161**
　　　Available online, updated monthly.
　　　A cooperative project of the Association for Computing Machinery (ACM), the European Association of Theoretical Computer Science (EATCS), the Gesellschaft für Informatik (GI), and the Gesellschaft für Mathematik und Datenverarbeitung (GMD).
　　　Provides coverage of European and North American literature on computer science and technology and information processing, citing journal articles, conference papers, reports, theses, and preprints. Contains records from *ACM guide to computing literature* 1977– (EK159) and *Computing reviews* 1977– (EK166). Includes the computer science section of the database version of *Mathematics abstracts* 1972– (EB31).

Computer & control abstracts. v. 1 (1966)– . London : Inst. of Electrical Engineers, 1966– . Monthly, with semiannual author and subject indexes.　　　　　**EK162**
　　　Title varies: v. 1–3 (1966–68), *Control abstracts.* Beginning 1967, designated as *Science abstracts, Sec. C.*
　　　Issues for Jan. 1969– published in association with the Institute for Electrical & Electronics Engineers.
　　　Entries are arranged according to a subject classification listed in each issue. Provides international coverage for systems and control theory, computer technology and computer applications; includes periodicals, reports, dissertations, books, patents, and conference papers. A complete list of indexed periodicals is issued as part of the semiannual indexes; a supplementary list of periodicals is included in each issue. Author index in each issue; semiannual author and subject indexes.
　　　Cumulative author and subject indexes: 1966–68; 1969–72; 1973–76; 1977–80; 1981–84; 1985–88; 1989–92.
　　　•Machine-readable versions: *INSPEC* [database] (ED9) and on CD-ROM as part of *INSPEC ondisc* (ED9 *note*) and as part of *INSPEC electronics & computing* (ED9 *note*).　　　　QA76.C548

Computer abstracts. v. 1 (Oct. 1957)– . London : Technical Information Co., 1957– . Monthly.　　　　　**EK163**

Publisher and title vary: v. 1–2 (1957–58), *Bibliographical series. Computers* (London : Bureau of Technical Information); v. 3 (1959), *Computer bibliography* (London : Technical Information Co.).

Vols. for 1960–Mar. 1980 issued with: *Computer news.*

Offers abstracts of books, periodical articles, conference proceedings, U.S. government research reports, and patents in a classified arrangement. Monthly author and patent indexes; annual author, subject, and patent indexes. List of periodicals covered included with the annual indexes.   Z6654.C17C64

Computer literature index. v. 10, no. 1 (Apr. 1980)– . [Phoenix] : Applied Computer Research, 1980– . Quarterly, with annual cumulation.   **EK164**

Continues *Quarterly bibliography of computers and data processing* (EK168).

Indexes the literature in "computer-related trade publications, general business and management periodicals, and publications of computer and management-oriented professional societies and organizations."—*Guide to use.* Designed for computer professionals and individuals in computer-related fields. Presents an alphabetical subject arrangement of entries with brief abstracts; extensive cross-references. Issues include author and publisher indexes. Annual cumulation replaces quarterly issues; author and publisher indexes.   QA76.Q3

•**Computing archive** : bibliography and reviews from ACM [database]. N.Y. : ACM Pr., 1991– .   **EK165**

Available on CD-ROM, updated annually. Coverage began with 1982.

Corresponds to the printed versions of *ACM guide to computing literature* (EK159) and *Computing reviews* (EK166).

Computing reviews. v. 1 (1960)– . N.Y. : Assoc. for Computing Machinery, [1961]– . Monthly.   **EK166**

Frequency varies; bimonthly, 1960–67.

Provides a classified arrangement of extensive signed reviews of books, conference proceedings, and selected journal articles. Currently arranged by Computing reviews classification system within two sections: Books and proceedings and Nonbook literature. Most issues have indexes of authors and terms; recent volumes include annual cumulative author and reviewer indexes.

Indexed by:

(1) *Permuted (KWIC) index to Computing reviews* (1960–63).

(2) *Permuted and subject index to Computing reviews* (1964–65).

(3) *Comprehensive bibliography of computing literature : permuted and subject index to Computing reviews* (1966–67).

(4) *Bibliography of current computing literature* (1968–74).

(5) *Bibliography and subject index of current computing literature* (1975–76).

(6) *ACM guide to computing literature* (1977– ; EK159).

•Machine-readable versions:

(1) *MathSci* [database] (EB28).

(2) *COMPUSCIENCE* [database] (EK161).

(3) *Computing archive* [database] (EK165).   QA76.C5854

Microcomputer abstracts. v. 15, no. 1 (Mar. 1994)– . Santa Clara, Calif. : Microcomputer Information Services, 1980– . Quarterly.   **EK167**

Continues *Microcomputer index* (some issues called *Micro computer index*).

Indexes microcomputing-related articles; currently covers approximately 90 popular computing magazines. Entries include abstracts and are divided into seven sections: Articles, news and columns; Book reviews; Buyer and vendor guides; Hardware reviews; Product announcements; Program listings; and Software reviews. Includes author, company name, product name, compatible hardware and software, and subject indexes; annual cumulative indexes.

•Machine-readable version: *Microcomputer abstracts* [database], formerly *Microcomputer index* (Medford, N.J. : Learned Information, Inc., 1981–). Available online, updated monthly, and on CD-ROM (1989–), updated quarterly.   QA75.5.M5

Quarterly bibliography of computers and data processing. v. 1 (Apr. 1971)–9 (Jan. 1980). [Phoenix : Applied Computer Research], 1971–80. Quarterly, with annual cumulation.   **EK168**

Continued by *Computer literature index* (EK164).

Indexes books, periodical articles, and conference reports concerning computers and computer applications of interest to computer practitioners. Entries include brief abstracts and are arranged by subject with subject cross-references. Cumulated biennially for 1968–71, then annually 1972–80. Author index from 1973; list of publishers from 1972.   QA76.Q3

Encyclopedias

Concise encyclopedia of software engineering / editors, Derrick Morris, Boris Tamm. Oxford ; N.Y. : Pergamon, 1993. 400 p. : ill.   **EK169**

A comprehensive encyclopedia that covers all aspects of software engineering. "The content has been chosen to provide an introduction to the theory and techniques relevant to the software of a broad class of computer applications."—*Pref.* Designed for practicing software engineers and other professionals who need an overview of the field. Signed articles are detailed and understandable and include cross-references and bibliographies. Subject index.   QA76.758.C68

Encyclopedia of artificial intelligence / Stuart C. Shapiro, ed. in chief. 2nd ed. N.Y. : Wiley, c1992. 2 v. (1689 p.) : ill.   **EK170**

1st ed., 1987.

A comprehensive encyclopedia, written primarily for professionals. More than 450 alphabetically arranged, signed articles provide extensive, detailed treatment and contain bibliographies, many lengthy. Illustrations, some color plates, and cross-references. A detailed subject index helps offset the lack of a classified arrangement of the articles.   Q335.E53

Encyclopedia of computer science / editors, Anthony Ralston, Edwin D. Reilly ; Caryl Ann Dahlin, managing ed. 3rd ed. N.Y. : Van Nostrand Reinhold, 1993. 1558 p. : ill.   **EK171**

Title varies: 1st ed., 1976, *Encyclopedia of computer science*; 2nd ed., 1983, *Encyclopedia of computer science and engineering.*

Contains 605 articles, 174 new to this edition; in addition, many articles from the 2nd ed. have been extensively revised. Alphabetically arranged signed articles, written by 370 contributors, present definitions and basic information aimed at nonspecialists and include cross-references and bibliographies. Preceding the alphabetical entries is a classification that places all article titles in nine major subject categories, thereby serving as a broad subject index. Appendixes: Abbreviations and acronyms; Numerical tables; Computer science and engineering research journals; Universities offering the Ph.D. degree in computer science and/or computer engineering; Key high-level languages; Glossary of major terms in five languages; Timeline of significant computing milestones. Name and general index.   QA76.15.E48

Encyclopedia of computer science and technology / executive editors, Jack Belzer, Albert G. Holzman, Allen Kent. N.Y. : M. Dekker, [1975–43]. v. 1–30 : ill. (In progress).   **EK172**

Contents: v. 1–14, A–Z; v. 16, author and subject indexes to v. 1–15; v. 15 and v. 17 and after are supplements that continue the numbering of the main set.

Presents lengthy articles by specialists covering a wide range of topics (e.g., specific programming languages, corporations, leading figures, systems, mathematical and computational concepts, applications). Extensive bibliographies. Intended to be "scholarly and exhaustive, yet straightforward, so that most articles will be comprehensible to the newcomer and stimulating to the informed specialist as well." —*Pref.* Vols. 1–14 contain 277 articles, kept up-to-date by supplementary volumes.

§ Complemented by: *Encyclopedia of microcomputers* (EK173).
QA76.15.E5

Encyclopedia of microcomputers / executive editors, Allen Kent, James G. Williams ; administrative ed., Rosalind Kent. N.Y. : M. Dekker, c1988–94. v. 1–14 : ill. (In progress).
EK173

Contents: v. 1–14, Access methods—Productivity and Software maintenance.

Intended as a companion to *Encyclopedia of computer science and technology* (EK172), this set contains a "broad spectrum of microcomputer knowledge … aimed at the needs of microcomputer hardware specialists, programmers, systems analysts, engineers, operations researchers and mathematicians." —*Pref.* Comprehensive articles, written by specialists, include bibliographies.   QA76.15.E52

Macmillan encyclopedia of computers / Gary G. Bitter, ed. in chief. N.Y. : Macmillan : Maxwell Macmillan Internat., 1992. 2 v.   **EK174**

Designed to "provide an authoritative comprehensive work on all aspects of computers" (*Pref.*) and aimed at nonspecialists. Includes more than 200 well-written, signed articles, arranged alphabetically; most have bibliographies or further reading lists. Less comprehensive and technical than *Encyclopedia of computer science* (EK171). Appendixes list computing associations and various computer components/peripherals manufacturers. Subject index.   QA76.15.M33

Dictionaries

American national dictionary for information processing systems / developed by American National Standards Committee X3, Information Processing Systems. Homewood, Ill. : Dow Jones-Irwin, [1984]. 430 p. (Information processing systems technical report, X3/TR-1-82).   **EK175**

Defines terms in computing, data processing, information processing, and data communications for general readers; includes cross-references. "…based on the *American national directory for information processing* (X3/TR-1-77) and its predecessor, the *American national standard vocabulary for information processing* X3.12-1970."—*Foreword.*   QA76.15.A42

Cortada, James W. Historical dictionary of data processing. N.Y. : Greenwood, 1987. 3 v.   **EK176**

Contents: [v. 1], Biographies (321 p.); [v. 2], Technology (415 p.); [v. 3], Organizations (309 p.).

Provides "over 400 entries on all aspects of data processing, from the earliest to contemporary times."—*Pref.* Gives an overview of the history of data processing for general readers and functions as a reference source for specialists. The Biographies volume contains entries for more than 150 persons; concise articles provide basic biographical data as well as information on the individual's role in the history of data processing. The Technology volume includes entries for hardware, software, and special applications and projects. The Organizations volume includes entries for companies, societies, associations, laboratories, and government agencies of historical significance. Each volume provides brief bibliographies for each article, cross-references to entries in all three volumes, and a name/subject index.
QA76.15.C66

Covington, Michael A. Dictionary of computer terms / Michael Covington, Douglas Downing. 3rd ed. Hauppauge, N.Y. : Barron's, c1992. 364 p. : ill.   **EK177**

1st ed., 1986; 2nd ed., 1989.

A handy pocket-size dictionary that defines some 1,000 key terms; many entries have lengthy descriptions, examples, and tables or other illustrations. Covers a "wide range of topics, including hardware, software, programming concepts and languages, operating systems, electronics, logic circuits, history of computers, and specific models of personal computers."—*Pref.*   QA76.15.C68

Dictionary of computing. 3rd ed. Oxford ; N.Y. : Oxford Univ. Pr., 1990. 510 p. : ill.   **EK178**

1st ed., 1983; 2nd ed., 1987.
Gen. ed.: Valerie Illingworth.

Designed for students, professionals, and general readers involved with computing. Definitions for more than 4,500 terms are understandable and written by practitioners. Subject coverage is broad, ranging from algorithms and programming languages to information technology and legal aspects of computing. Illustrations and extensive cross-references.   QA76.15.D526

Freedman, Alan. The computer glossary : the complete illustrated desk reference. 6th ed. N.Y. : AMACOM, c1993. 574 p. : ill.   **EK179**

2nd ed., 1981; 5th ed., 1991.
Subtitle varies.

Presents concise, easy-to-understand definitions for more than 1,000 terms, both basic and advanced, with helpful illustrations and examples. Includes entries for acronyms, proprietary software and hardware, and computer companies. Some historical and biographical information available within definitions. Cross-references.

QA76.73.A8K38

Hordeski, Michael F. The illustrated dictionary of microcomputers. 3rd ed. Blue Ridge Summit, Pa. : TAB Professional and Reference Books, 1990. 442 p. : ill.   **EK180**

1st ed., 1978, had title: *The illustrated dictionary of microcomputer terminology*; 2nd ed., 1986.

Comprehensive and useful for anyone who works with microcomputers. Presents an alphabetical arrangement of more than 9,500 terms in all aspects of microcomputing, including software, hardware, desktop publishing, word processing, networking, and graphics. Definitions are clearly written and complemented by extensive illustrations.

TK7885.H67

IBM dictionary of computing / comp. and ed. by George McDaniel. 10th ed. N.Y. : McGraw-Hill, 1994. 758 p. : ill.
EK181

"Although this is the tenth edition … , it is the first edition to be made generally available to the public."—*Pref.* Formerly used as a "reference for IBM's technical writers, it has grown steadily in size, scope, and audience." This edition contains more than 22,000 entries; in addition to those related to IBM hardware and software, many are reprinted from various industry standards. Definitions are more technical than in Alan Freedman's *The computer glossary* (EK179).
QA76.15.I23

Latham, Roy. The dictionary of computer graphics technology and applications. N.Y. : Springer-Verlag, c1991. 160 p. : ill.
EK182

Designed for both novices and computer graphics professionals, this volume also contains terms from "allied technologies including image processing, electronics, general computing, video, hardware engineering, software management."—*Using this dictionary.* Entries have concise, relatively technical definitions; extensive cross-references lead to entries for synonyms, opposites, and related terms.
T385.L38

Longley, Dennis. Van Nostrand Reinhold dictionary of information technology / Dennis Longley and Michael Shain. 3rd ed. N.Y. : Van Nostrand Reinhold, c1989. 566 p. : ill. **EK183**

1st ed., 1982, had title: *Dictionary of information technology*; 2nd ed., 1986.

Designed to provide accurate, up-to-date definitions for terms in information technology. Contains some 7,800 entries (1,800 more than the 2nd ed.) with short and informative definitions, some illustrations, and extensive cross-references. Includes extended entries for a few important topics in the field, such as artificial intelligence, computer security, machine translation, and desktop publishing.   QA76.15.L63

Mercadal, Dennis. Dictionary of artificial intelligence. N.Y. : Van Nostrand Reinhold, c1990. 334 p.   **EK184**

Defines terms and concepts in artificial intelligence, robotics, expert systems, neural networks, and other related areas. Entries include examples, cross-references, and literature references. Has section on "Expert system shells/tools" and a list of references.   Q334.2.M47

Microsoft Press computer dictionary : the comprehensive standard for business, school, library, and home. 2nd ed. Redmond, Wash. : Microsoft Pr., c1994. 442 p. : ill.   **EK185**
1st ed., 1991.
Designed for all microcomputer users. Presents concise definitions in standard English for more than 5,000 computer-related terms and acronyms. Many entries include illustrations and cross-references.   QA76.15.M54

Rosenberg, Jerry Martin. Dictionary of artificial intelligence and robotics. N.Y. : Wiley, c1986. 203 p.   **EK186**
Useful for experts and general readers. Where multiple definitions occur for the same term the broadest definition is listed first. Contains abbreviations, acronyms, and symbols. Some noncurrent terms have been retained for historical reasons.   Q334.6.R67

Spencer, Donald D. Computer dictionary. 4th ed. Ormond Beach, Fla. : Camelot Publ. Co., c1993. 459 p. : ill.   **EK187**
1st ed., 1977; 3rd ed., 1992.
Presents concise, nontechnical definitions for more than 5,800 terms in computer science and allied fields, including artificial intelligence, expert systems, desktop publishing, electronics, and robotics. Designed for "anyone who is using or who wants to learn more about computers."—*Pref.* Includes short biographical entries for major computer personalities. Cross-references.   QA76.15.S64

——————————— Illustrated computer graphics dictionary. Ormond Beach, Fla. : Camelot Publ. Co., c1993. 305 p. : ill.   **EK188**
Provides brief, nontechnical definitions for more than 2,100 terms relating to processes, hardware, and software in the computer graphics field; contains many illustrations. Designed for computer graphic artists, computer science teachers and students, and others interested in computer graphics.   T385.S66

Tavaglione, David. Acronyms and abbreviations of computer technology and telecommunications. N.Y. : M. Dekker, c1993. 291 p.   **EK189**
Designed to "provide a ready reference for readers and writers of technical material to quickly look up familiar acronyms ... [and] provide a means of determining whether a newly proposed acronym is already in common use."—*Pref.* Entries include description and source of acronym; cross-references. Appendix of recommended references.   QA76.15.T38

Foreign terms

Bürger, Erich. Technical dictionary of data processing : computers, office machines / by Erich Bürger with the cooperation of Wolfgang Schuppe. Oxford ; N.Y. : Pergamon, [1970]. 1463 p.   **EK190**
Title also in German, French, and Russian.
Separate alphabetical section for each language. In each section corresponding equivalent terms in the other three languages appear in parallel columns.   QA76.15.B46

Ferber, Gene. English-Japanese, Japanese-English dictionary of computer and data-processing terms = Ei-Wa Wa-Ei konpyūta dēta shori yōgo jiten. Cambridge, Mass. : MIT Pr., c1989. 470 p.   **EK191**
Designed primarily for English-speaking engineers, computer professionals, and sales executives. In addition to the Japanese characters, both sections include romanized transcriptions of Japanese terms.   QA76.15.F47

Maslovskiĭ, E. K. Russko-anglo-nemetsko-frantsuzskiĭ slovar' po vychislitel'noĭ tekhnike : osnovnye terminy : 54,000 terminov / E. K. Maslovskiĭ, B. I. Zaĭchik, N. S. Skorokhod. Moscow : Russky Yazyk Publishers, 1990. 400 p.   **EK192**
Added title page: *Russian-English-German-French dictionary of computer science.*
Provides English, French, and German equivalents for Russian computer science terms. Main section is alphabetical by the Russian term; includes English, French, and German indexes.   QA76.15.M38

Müller, Dieter. Dictionary of microprocessor systems : in four languages, English, German, French, Russian / ed. by Dieter Müller. Amsterdam ; N.Y. : Elsevier, 1983. 312 p.   **EK193**
Designed "to make accessible to a broad range of interested parties the specialist vocabulary of microprocessor technology, computer technology and programming."—*Pref.* Lists about 10,000 English terms and their equivalents. German, French, and Russian indexes.   QA76.15.M85

Nania, Georges. Complete multilingual dictionary of computer terminology : English, French, Italian, Spanish, Portuguese. Lincolnwood, Ill. : Passport Books, c1984. 916 p.   **EK194**
Gives equivalents for "12,305 terms and phrases, of both general and technical nature ... in the fields of computer science, data processing, microcomputing, and data transmission."—*Introd.* Arranged by English term with French, Italian, Spanish, and Portuguese indexes.   QA76.15.N37

Vollnhals, Otto. A multilingual dictionary of artificial intelligence : English, German, French, Spanish, Italian. London ; N.Y. : Routledge, 1992. 423 p.   **EK195**
Gives foreign-language equivalents for English terms in a wide range of subjects comprising artificial intelligence, including expert systems, image processing, knowledge, linguistics, learning, logic, machine translation, neural networks, natural language processing, recognition, and robotics. Arranged by English term with German, French, Spanish, and Italian indexes.   Q334.2.V65

Wennrich, Peter. International dictionary of abbreviations and acronyms of electronics, electrical engineering, computer technology, and information processing = Internationales Verzeichnis der Abkürzungen und Akronyme der Elektronik, Elektrotechnik, Computertechnik und Informationsverarbeitung. München ; N.Y. : K.G. Saur, 1992. 2 v.   **EK196**
A comprehensive listing of approximately 90,000 abbreviations and acronyms in several interrelated technical fields. Most abbreviations and acronyms are for English terminology, but selected terms in Czech, Danish, Dutch, French, German, Hebrew, Hungarian, Italian, Latin, Polish, Portuguese, Spanish, and Swedish are included.   TK9.W38

Wittmann, Alfred. Dictionary of data processing : including applications in industry, administration, and business = Wörterbuch der Datenverarbeitung : mit Anwendungsgebieten in Industrie, Verwaltung, und Wirtschaft = Dictionnaire du traitement des données : et de son application dans l'industrie, l'administration, et l'économie / by Alfred Wittmann and Joithel Klos. 5th, rev. and enl. ed. Amsterdam ; N.Y. : Elsevier, 1987. 357 p.   **EK197**
1st ed., 1964, had title: *Dictionary of information processing*; 4th ed., 1984.
Lists some 6,000 English terms and acronyms with French and German equivalents. Terms are given broad subject codes. French and German indexes.   QA76.15.W57

Directories

The AI directory. 1990– . Menlo Park, Calif. : Amer. Assoc. for Artificial Intelligence, c1990– . Annual.   **EK198**

Continues: *American Association for Artificial Intelligence, Membership directory* (1985–89).

Vol. for 1992 not published.

1993/94 volume lists organizations related to the field of artificial intelligence, including associations, government agencies, manufacturers, publishers, universities, research and development firms, software companies. Also lists members, officials, and staff of three North American societies: American Association for Artificial Intelligence, Canadian Society for Computational Studies of Intelligence = Société canadienne pour l'étude et l'intelligence par ordinateur, and Sociedad Mexicana de Inteligencia Artificial.   Q334.A53a

Data sources : the comprehensive guide to the information processing industry : equipment, software, services, companies, and people. v. 1, no. 1 (Autumn 1981)– . N.Y. : Ziff-Davis Publ. Co., c1981– . Quarterly.   **EK199**

Subtitle varies; 1994 issues have: *The complete computer product book.*

Issues for 1994 contain more than 75,000 hardware and software product listings. Vol. 1 lists hardware and data communications products arranged by product categories and subcategories, then by company. Entries include technical specifications, warranty information, date, and price. Many sections have charts for easy product comparisons. Product name index, Company name index, and Manufacturer company profiles; Master index covers both volumes. Vol. 2 lists software packages arranged by type of application, then by company. Entries include product description, hardware requirements, systems and software compatibility, date, and price. Software package index, Company name index, and Software company profiles; Master index covers both volumes.   HD9696.C63U51592

Graduate assistantship directory in computing / Assoc. for Computing Machinery. 1993–94– . N.Y. : ACM Pr., 1993– . Annual.   **EK200**

Continues: *Graduate assistantship directory in the computer sciences* ([1st ed.], 1968–69–[24th ed.], 1992–93).

1993–94 edition presents information about 121 graduate programs in computer science in the U.S. and Canada. Lists degrees offered, faculty interest areas, departmental and university computing facilities, application requirements and deadlines, and type and quantity of financial assistance available.   QA76.27.G69

The software encyclopedia. 1985/86– . N.Y. : Bowker, c1985– .   **EK201**

Issued in 2 v.

1994 edition describes more than 21,000 microcomputer software packages. Entries in the Title index are arranged alphabetically and include title, subtitle, version, series, authors, grade level, release date, hardware compatibility, microprocessor type, operating system requirements, languages, memory requirements, publisher, cost, and a descriptive annotation. In the System compatibility/applications index, packages are organized by major operating systems, then by specific applications. Publishers index.   QA76.753.S67

Tölle, Wolfgang. Study and research guide in computer science : profiles of universities in the USA / W. Tölle, J. Yasner, M. Pieper. Berlin ; N.Y. : Springer-Verlag, c1993. 175 p.   **EK202**

A selective list of 39 university computer science departments in the U.S. Profiles provide basic departmental information, degree programs and requirements, graduate courses, faculty and their research areas, computing facilities, funding, special projects, and affiliated institutions. Also lists faculty alphabetically and by research area.   QA76.27.T64

Handbooks

Computer engineering handbook / C. H. Chen, ed. in chief. N.Y. : McGraw-Hill, c1992. 1 v. (various pagings) : ill.   **EK203**

Intended for computer engineering students and computer professionals; emphasizes "the basics and new developments in computer engineering."—*Pref.* Contains 20 chapters written by specialists; chapter bibliographies. Subject index.   TK7888.3.C652

The handbook of artificial intelligence / ed. by Avron Barr, Paul R. Cohen, and Edward A. Feigenbaum. Reading, Mass. : Addison-Wesley Pub. Co., c1989. 4 v. : ill.   **EK204**

Vols. 1–2 ed. by Avron Barr and Edward A. Feigenbaum; v. 3 ed. by Paul R. Cohen and Feigenbaum; v. 4 ed. by Barr, Cohen, and Feigenbaum.

Contains "short articles about AI concepts, techniques, and systems, grouped into chapters that correspond to the major subdivisions of the field."—*Introd.* Articles list references; each volume has its own bibliography. Vols. 1–2 have their own subject indexes; v. 3–4 have cumulated name and subject indexes.   Q335.H36

Handbook of theoretical computer science / ed., Jan van Leeuwen. Amsterdam ; N.Y. : Elsevier ; Cambridge, Mass. : MIT Pr., 1990. 2 v. : ill.   **EK205**

Contents: v. A, Algorithms and complexity; v. B, Formal models and semantics.

Designed to provide computer science professionals and students with an overview of the field of theoretical computer science, this handbook "attempts to offer an in-depth view of the field of Theoretical Computer Science as a whole, by a comprehensive exposition of the scientific advances in this area."—*Pref.* Presents 37 chapters, written by experts, with extensive bibliographies. Separate subject index in each volume.   QA76.H279

Henle, Richard A. Desktop computers : in perspective / Richard A. Henle, Boris W. Kuvshinoff ; ed., C. M. Kuvshinoff. N.Y. : Oxford Univ. Pr., 1992. 650 p. : ill.   **EK206**

A guide to desktop (i.e., personal) computer technology for all users: includes information on hardware, operating systems, networks and peripherals. Useful for increasing an individual's technical knowledge and computer management skills. Information is topically organized with an extensive subject index.   QA76.5.H4587

McGraw-Hill personal computer programming encyclopedia : languages and operating systems / William J. Birnes, ed. 2nd ed. N.Y. : McGraw-Hill, c1989. 752 p. : ill.   **EK207**

1st ed., 1985.

A topical arrangement of introductory and advanced articles on computer languages and systems for "the entire spectrum of endusers, from programming professionals to nontechnical hobbyists."—*Pref.* Sections include: Program design and architecture, Principles of effective programming, Special applications software, Microprocessor basics, High-level programming languages, Software command languages, Operating systems directory, Microcomputer systems hardware, and Major PC products: markets and specifications. Glossary, bibliography, and subject index.   QA76.6.M414

History

Bruemmer, Bruce. Resources for the history of computing : a guide to U.S. and Canadian records / by Bruce H. Bruemmer ; with the assistance of Thomas Traub and Celeste Brosenne. Minneapolis : Charles Babbage Inst. Center for the History of Information Processing, Univ. of Minnesota, 1987. 187 p.   **EK208**

A guide to manuscript and archival sources of interest to archivists and researchers in the field. Arranged by state or province, entries contain detailed information about special collections in academia and industry. Appendixes: Oral history collections; Selected readings in the history of computing; List of repositories. Name/subject index.   Z5640.B78

Cortada, James W. A bibliographic guide to the history of computing, computers, and the information processing industry. N.Y. : Greenwood, 1990. 644 p. (Bibliographies and indexes in science and technology, no. 6). **EK209**

Intended "to serve as a general introduction to the literature of the industry. Cast in historical terms, it provides an annotated list of published materials describing the history of the industry as well as items of importance to those interested in the general topic."—*Pref.* Organized in chapters with numerous subheadings by topic and historical period. Includes all entries in Cortada's *An annotated bibliography on the history of data processing* (1983). Z5640.C67

Yearbooks

Computer publishers & publications. 1984 ed.– . New Rochelle, N.Y. : Communications Trends, Inc., c1984– . Annual. **EK210**

Updated between editions by supplements.

A combined directory and yearbook, providing up-to-date information on computer literature. For use by "all who create, publish, distribute, purchase or advertise in computer publications."—*Introd.* The first chapter reviews trends in computer publishing. There are also: (1) a list of book publishers with basic directory information plus numbers of titles published and representative titles; (2) an index by type of publisher and location; (3) a list of periodicals with publishers, addresses, telephone, format, frequency, subscription and advertising rates, circulation, etc.; (4) index of periodicals by type, format, frequency, and computer coverage; (5) list of discontinued periodicals; (6) name and master indexes. Z286.C65C66

ENERGY

General works

Balachandran, Sarojini. Energy statistics : a guide to information sources. Detroit : Gale, 1980. 272 p. (Natural world information guide series, v.1). **EK211**

An expansion of *Energy statistics : a guide to sources* and *Energy statistics : an update* (Council of Planning Librarians. Exchange bibliography, nos. 1065 and 1247).

"The guide is divided into three major sections. The first contains a detailed alphabetical subject/keyword analysis of all recurring statistical data contained in some forty most used national and international energy serials. ... The second section ... gives full bibliographic descriptions of the sources analyzed in the earlier section. The rest of the book is an annotated guide to additional sources of statistical information on individual sources of energy."—*Introd.* Z5853.P83B25

Bibliography

McAninch, Sandra. Sun power : a bibliography of United States government documents on solar energy. Westport, Conn., Greenwood Pr., 1981. 944 p. **EK212**

An index to documents published through 1979, including documents on biomass, ocean, thermal, solar, and wind energy. Entries are arranged by broad subject area. Indexed by author, title, agency, accession number. Z5853.S63M28

Weber, R. David. Energy information guide. Santa Barbara, Calif. : ABC-Clio, 1982–84. 3 v. **EK213**

Contents: v. 1, General and alternative energy sources; v. 2, Nuclear and electric power; v. 3, Fossil fuels.

A guide to the reference literature of energy, with broad coverage including social, political, economic, and historical aspects as well as scientific and technical. Entries are annotated. Cross-references. Each volume has author, title, subject, and document number indexes. Z5853.P83W38

——————— Energy update : a guide to current reference literature. San Carlos, Calif. : Energy Information Pr., 1991. 455 p. **EK214**

Continues the author's *Energy information guide* (EK213).

Chapters cover environmental impact, energy in general, energy conservation, solar energy, other alternative energy, electric power, nuclear power, fossil fuels, coal, petroleum, and natural gas. Entries are annotated. Purposely omitted are: periodical titles from the earlier compilation if the title and format are unchanged; references written entirely in languages other than English; items dealing with areas outside the U.S. Separate indexes for authors, titles, subjects, and government publication numbers. Supplements are planned at four-year intervals.

Indexes; Abstract journals

United States. Department of Energy. Energy research abstracts. v. 1 (1976)– . Oak Ridge, Tenn. : Technical Information Center, 1976– . Semimonthly, with semiannual and annual indexes. **EK215**

Partially supersedes U.S. Atomic Energy Commission's *Nuclear science abstracts* (EK294). Supersedes U.S. Energy Research and Development, *ERDA research abstracts* (1975), nos.1–4 of which were titled *ERDA reports abstracts*. v.1–v.2, no.21 (1977) issued by the U.S. Energy Research and Development Administration as *ERDA energy research abstracts*.

"Provides abstracting and indexing coverage of all scientific and technical reports and patent applications originated by the U.S. Department of Energy, its laboratories, energy centers, and contractors, as well as theses and conference papers and proceedings issued by these organizations in report form ... ERA also covers other energy information prepared *in report form* by federal and state government organizations, foreign governments, and domestic and foreign universities and research organizations, *provided* that the full text of the document has been received by OSTI."—*[Note]*, 1994.

•Available online as part of *Energy science & technology* (Oak Ridge, Tenn. : U.S. Dept. of Energy, 1974–), which also includes information from *INIS atomindex* (1970–) and from *Coal abstracts* (1977–). Z5853.P83U533

Directories

Crowley, Maureen. Energy : sources of print and nonprint materials. N.Y. : Neal-Schuman, [1980]. 341 p. **EK216**

Offers descriptions of almost 800 organizations that are sources of information and publications on energy; arranged by category of organization. Indexed. HD9502.A2C76

Handbooks

Energy technology handbook / prep. by 142 specialists. Douglas M. Considine, ed in chief. N.Y. : McGraw-Hill, [1977]. 1 v. (various pagings) : ill. **EK217**

"This Handbook concentrates on those fundamental technologies which relate to energy sources, energy reserves, energy conversion, energy transportation and transmission, and to an extent limited both by time and space in the preparation of this volume, energy distribution, utilization, and the energy/environmental interface."—*Pref.* TJ163.9.E54

Handbook of energy systems engineering : production, and utilization / ed. by Leslie C. Wilbur. N.Y. : Wiley, c1985. 1775 p. : ill.   **EK218**
Consists of 18 chapters written by specialists. Discusses coal, nuclear, petroleum, and gas technology, hydroelectric and solar power, geothermal energy. Contains a chapter on guides to available codes, standards, and reference materials. Subject index.   TJ163.9.H35

Information sources in energy technology / ed., L.J. Anthony. London ; Boston : Butterworths, 1988. 324 p.   **EK219**
Sixteen chapters written by the editor and other specialists are presented in three parts: (1) Energy in general; (2) Fuel technology (combustion, steam and boiler plant ... electrical energy, energy conservation, energy and the environment); and (3) Specific energy sources (solid, liquid, and gaseous fuels, solar and geothermal energy, alternative energy sources). Extensive bibliographies with each chapter. Indexed.   TJ163.17.I54

Loftness, Robert L. Energy handbook. 2nd ed. N.Y. : Van Nostrand Reinhold, [1984]. 763 p. : ill.   **EK220**
1st ed., 1978.
Offers tabular data, including sources, and narrative information on a wide range of energy topics. Includes 16 chapters on topics such as consumption trends and projections, resources, costs, futures. Glossary; conversion factors; index.   TJ163.235.L64

Oak Ridge Associated Universities. Industrial energy use data book. N.Y. : Garland STPM Pr., 1980. 600 p. : ill.   **EK221**
"This document has been prepared for the U.S. Department of Energy to serve as a standard reference for government officials and other groups concerned with policy analysis. ... This data book is divided into three functional parts: Section I ... addresses facets of overall industrial energy use; Section II ... details energy use in the 13 most energy-intensive industrial sectors; Section III ... presents the important environmental, regional, and social parameters of industrial energy use."—*Introd.* Chapters by specialists contain extensive tabular data; references. Appendixes give conversion factors, price deflators, annotated bibliography, glossary. Indexed.   HD9502.U52O24

World energy and nuclear directory : organizations and research activities in atomic and non-atomic energy. 1st ed. (1990)– . Harlow, Essex : Longman ; Detroit : Distr. by Gale Research, 1990– . Irregular.   **EK222**
For annotation, *see* EK296.   TJ163.165.W66

Atlases

Cuff, David J. The United States energy atlas / David J. Cuff, William J. Young. 2nd ed. N.Y. : Macmillan ; London : Collier Macmillan, c1985. 387 p. : ill.   **EK223**
1st ed., 1980.
Arranged in three parts: pt. 1, Nonrenewable resources, and pt. 2, Renewable resources, are divided into chapters on various specific resources. Pt. 3 is an overview. Glossary of terms. Includes a chapter on ocean energy, and essays on such topics as the Strategic Petroleum Reserve and the importance of tax policy to wind power investments. Indexed.   TJ163.25.U6C83

HEATING AND REFRIGERATION

ASHRAE handbook. 1985– . Atlanta : American Society of Heating, Refrigerating and Air Conditioning Engineers, c1985– .   **EK224**

Issued in four sections: *Fundamentals* (1985–), *Refrigeration systems and applications* (1986–); *Heating, ventilating, and air-conditioning applications* (1991–), and *Heating, ventilating, and air-conditioning systems and equipment* (1992–). Each section issued (every four years) in two editions, Inch-pound and SI.
Continues in part: *ASHRAE handbook and product directory* (1973–80). Split 1981 into *ASHRAE handbook* and *ASHRAE product specification file*.
Most recent dates of issue for the four sections: *Fundamentals*, 1993; *Refrigeration*, 1990; *HVAC applications*, 1991; *HVAC systems and equipment*, 1992.   TH7015.A74

Handbook of air conditioning, heating, and ventilating. 3rd ed. / Eugene Stamper, ed. ; Richard L. Koral, consulting ed. N.Y. : Industrial Pr., [1979]. 1 v. (various pagings) : ill.
                                                       EK225
1st ed., 1959, by Clifford Strock.
A handbook for engineers, contractors, and other practitioners; presents tabular data, formulas, graphs, etc., for the solution of problems of design, installation, and operation. Includes bibliographic references. Detailed index.   TH7687.S76

Heat bibliography. 1948/52–1975. Edinburgh : Stat. Off., 1959–1975. Annual.   **EK226**
Prep. by the Heat Division, National Engineering Laboratory, East Kilbride, Scotland.
The first 3 v. of the series covered 1948–52, 1953–54, and 1955–56; beginning with the volume for 1957, issued annually.
Each annual includes only material *noted* in the National Engineering Library during that year and therefore contains some references to earlier papers. Most of the entries were obtained from abstracting and bibliographic journals, in which case the source is given along with indication of the presence of an abstract. Classed arrangement with subject, but no author, index.   Z5853.H27H4

International Institute of Refrigeration, Paris. Bibliographic guide to refrigeration, 1953–1968. Oxford : Pergamon, [1962–69]. 3 v.   **EK227**
Publisher varies. Title also in French, *Guide bibliographique du froid.*
Lists all documents abstracted in the *Bulletin* of the Institute during the 1953–68 period and gives the number of the abstract. Also includes lists of books received at the library of the Institute during the period covered and of the serials from which the abstracts were drawn. Classed arrangement with author and detailed subject indexes. The series ceased with v. 3, being supplanted from 1969 by an annual keyword index to the contents of the *Bulletin* and to the abstracts appearing therein.   Z7914.R33I5

INDUSTRIAL ENGINEERING

Handbook of human factors / [ed. by] Gavriel Salvendy. N.Y. : Wiley, c1987. 1874 p. : ill.   **EK228**
Gives "information about the effective design and use of systems requiring the interaction among human, machine (computer), and environment."—*Pref.* 68 chapters contributed by international specialists include bibliographies. General areas discussed include: human factors function; human factors fundamentals; functional analysis; job organization design; equipment and workplace design; environmental design; design for health and safety; design of selection and training systems; performance modeling; system evaluation; human factors in the design and use of computing systems; and selected applications of human factors in computer systems. Indexed.   TA166.H275

Handbook of industrial engineering / ed. by Gavriel Salvendy. 2nd ed. N.Y. : Wiley, 1991. 2780 p. : ill.   **EK229**
1st ed., 1982.
Contains 108 chapters organized in four main areas: Technology; Human dimensions; Planning, design, and control of operations; Quan-

titative methods for decision making. Chapters, by an international group of specialist authors, include references. Detailed index.
T56.23.H36

Handbook of industrial robotics / ed. by Shimon Y. Nof. N.Y. : Wiley, [1985]. 1358 p. : ill. **EK230**
Chapters by specialists include bibliographic references. Includes sections on robotic terms, organizations, manufacturers, and journals. Indexed. TS191.8.H36

Hunt, V. Daniel. Dictionary of advanced manufacturing technology. N.Y. : Elsevier, c1987. 431 p. : ill. **EK231**
A 52-page introduction is followed by brief definitions of terms (some accompanied by illustrations and photographs), including those relating to computer-aided design, manufacturing, process planning, robotics, machine vision, and communication and software interfaces. Also featured are directories of key organizations, a list of acronyms and abbreviations, a bibliography, and a directory of flexible manufacturing systems suppliers and users in the U.S. TS155.6.H85

International encyclopedia of robotics : applications and automation / Richard C. Dorf, ed. in chief ; Shimon Y. Nof, consulting ed. N.Y. : Wiley, c1988. 3 v. : ill. **EK232**
"... defines the discipline and the practice of robotics by bringing together the core of knowledge and practice from the field and all closely related fields. The *Encyclopedia* is written primarily for the professional who seeks to understand and use robots and automation."—*Pref.* Articles include bibliographies and cross-references. Indexed. TJ210.4.I57

Maynard's industrial engineering handbook / William K. Hodson, ed. in chief. 4th ed. N.Y. : McGraw-Hill, c1992. 1 v. (various pagings) : ill. **EK233**
1st–3rd ed., 1956–71, had title: *Industrial engineering handbook.*
Chapters by specialists are divided among sections on the industrial engineering function; industrial engineering in practice; methods engineering; work measurement techniques; work measurement application and control; incentive programs; manufacturing engineering; human factors, ergonomics, and human relations ; economics and controls; planning and control; quality control; use of computers; facilities and materials flow, mathematics and optimization techniques; special industry applications. Includes bibliographies; indexed. T56.M39

Tver, David R. Robotics sourcebook and dictionary / David R. Tver, Roger W. Bolz. N.Y. : Industrial Pr., [1983]. 258 p. : ill. **EK234**
Contents: pt. 1, Introduction and dictionary of types; pt. 2, Robotics dictionary of applications; pt. 3, Robotics glossary and computer-control terminology; pt. 4, Robotics manufacturers and typical specifications.
Covers "most of the key aspects of current industrial robots."—*Pref.* HD9696.R622T83

Waldman, Harry. Dictionary of robotics. N.Y. : Macmillan, [1985]. 303 p. **EK235**
More than 2,000 terms, including acronyms, names of some laboratories and manufacturers, and some individuals. Brief entries.
TJ210.4.W35

Woodson, Wesley E. Human factors design handbook : information and guidelines for the design of systems, facilities, equipment, and products for human use / Wesley E. Woodson, Barry Tillman, Peggy Tillman. 2nd ed. N.Y. : McGraw-Hill, 1992. 846 p. : ill. **EK236**
1st ed., 1981.
The division of sections into chapters (Systems; Subsystems design; Component and product design; Human factors data; Human engineering methods) is intended to relate to the steps according to which a design program usually progresses. A handbook for the designer and engineer. References. Indexed. TA166.W57

MECHANICAL ENGINEERING

General works

Dictionaries

Nayler, G. H. F. Dictionary of mechanical engineering. 3rd ed. London ; Boston : Butterworths, 1985. 394 p. **EK237**
1st ed., 1966; 2nd ed., 1975.
This edition contains more entries on engineering design and manufacture than the 2nd ed. Abbreviations, initialisms, and symbols occur at the beginning of the entries for each letter. Definitions generally are concise, with *see* and *see also* references. A few graphs and line drawings are used to enhance the brief definitions. Retains practically all the entries from preceding editions. TJ9.N28

Handbooks

Kent, William. Mechanical engineer's handbook / prep. by a staff of specialists. 12th ed. N.Y. : Wiley, 1950. 2 v. : ill. **EK238**
1st ed., 1895, entitled: *Mechanical engineer's pocket-book.*
Contents: v. 1, Design and production, ed. by Colin Carmichael; v. 2, Power, ed. by J. Kenneth Salisbury. TJ151.K4

Lubrication / ed. by M. J. Neale. Oxford; Boston : Butterworth-Heinemann, 1993. 138 p. : ill., maps. **EK239**
1st. ed. had title: *Tribology handbook* (N.Y. : Wiley ; London : butterworths, 1973. 1 v.).
This ed. is being issued as part of an unnumbered series, each volume called "A tribology handbook." Also published to date: *Bearings*, ed. by M. J. Neale (1993). Additional volumes, *Drives and seals* and *Component failure*, are expected 1994.
A series of handbooks for designers and engineers. Each volume offers topical chapters with practical information, much of it in graphical and tabular form. Volumes are separately indexed. TJ1075.N4

Marks' standard handbook for mechanical engineers. 9th ed. N.Y. : McGraw-Hill, 1987. **EK240**
Eugene A. Avallone, Theodore Baumeister III, editors.
Lionel S. Marks, ed. 1916–51.
1st–6th eds., 1916–58, had title: *Mechanical engineers' handbook.*
Also known as *Standard handbook for mechanical engineers.*
As the title suggests, a standard handbook, containing 100 chapters in 19 sections by specialist contributors, with illustrations and tabular data. Bibliographic references at beginnings of chapters. Uses dual units: International System (SI) and U.S. Customary System (USCS). Indexed. TJ151.S82

Mechanical components handbook / Robert O. Parmley, ed. in chief. N.Y. : McGraw-Hill, 1985. 1 v. (various pagings) : ill. **EK241**
Intends "to categorize, define, and discuss basic mechanical components used in current mechanical technology."—*Pref.* Chapters by specialists on topics such as gears and gearing, belts and pulleys, bearings, springs, retaining rings, etc. Indexed. TJ243.M43

Mechanical design and systems handbook. 2nd ed. / Harold A. Rothbart, ed. in chief. N.Y. : McGraw-Hill, 1985. 1 v. (various pagings). **EK242**
1st ed., 1964.
Chapters by specialist contributors include bibliographic references. This revised edition includes material on recent topics such as computer-aided design. Indexed. TJ230.M43

Mechanical engineers' handbook / ed. by Myer Kutz. N.Y. : Wiley, c1986. 2316 p. : ill.   **EK243**

Purposely omits mathematical tables. Stresses manufacturing engineering and research management, plus the traditional treatments of energy and power. Includes chapters on engineers' liability, patents, sources of mechanical engineering information, and online databases. Numerous charts, diagrams, tables, and graphs. Subject index.

§ Significantly supplements but does not totally supersede William Kent's *Mechanical engineer's handbook* (EK238).   TJ151.M395

Mechanical engineer's reference book / ed. by Edward H. Smith. 12th ed. London : Butterworths, [1994]. 1 v. (various pagings) : ill.   **EK244**

1st ed., 1946. 1st–10th eds. had title: *Newnes engineer's reference book.*

A standard handbook, British in origin. This ed. incorporates major revisions. Indexed.   TJ151.C335

Oberg, Erik. Machinery's handbook : a reference book for the mechanical engineer, designer, manufacturing engineer, draftsman, toolmaker, and machinist / by Erik Oberg ... [et al.] ; Robert E. Green, ed. 24th ed. N.Y. : Industrial Pr., c1992. 2543 p. : ill.   **EK245**

1st ed., 1914; 23rd ed., 1988.

Subtitle varies.

A standard handbook, frequently revised. Numerous charts, tables, line drawings, etc.

Shock and vibration handbook / ed. by Cyril M. Harris. 3rd ed. N.Y. : McGraw-Hill, c1988. 1 v. (various pagings) : ill.   **EK246**

1st ed., 1961 (3 v.); 2nd ed., 1976.

A comprehensive treatment prepared by 60 specialists, this edition includes 50% new or revised material. Worked examples of problems appear in many chapters. Included are chapters on packaging design and effects of shock and vibration on man. Subject index.
TA355.S5164

Standard handbook of machine design / editors in chief, Joseph E. Shigley, Charles R. Mischke. N.Y. : McGraw-Hill, c1986. 1 v. (various pagings) : ill.   **EK247**

Contains 47 chapters written by specialists. "Mathematical and statistical formulas and tabulations ... are not included in this handbook."—*Pref.* Indexed.   TJ230.S8235

Tool and manufacturing engineers handbook : a reference book for manufacturing engineers, managers, and technicians. 4th ed. / rev. under the supervision of the SME Publications Committee in cooperation with the SME Technical Divisions. Dearborn, Mich. : Society of Manufacturing Engineers, c1983–93. v. 1–7 : ill. (In progress).   **EK248**

1st–2nd eds. (1949–59) had title: *Tool engineers handbook*; Society previously called American Society of Tool Engineers (1st ed.), and American Society of Tool and Manufacturing Engineers (2nd ed.).

"Revised under the supervision of the SME Publications Committee in cooperation with the SME Technical Divisions"—*t.p.* Thomas J. Drozda, ed. in chief, v. 1; Charles Wick, ed. in chief, v. 2–4; Raymond F. Veilleux, staff ed., v. 5; Ramon Bakerjian, handbook ed., v. 6–7.

Contents: v. 1, Machining; v. 2, Forming; v. 3, Materials, finishing, and coating; v. 4, Quality control and assembly; v. 5, Manufacturing management; v. 6, Design for manufacturability; v. 7, Continuous improvement.

"The scope of this edition is multifaceted, offering a ready-reference source of authoritative manufacturing information for daily use by engineers, managers, and technicians, yet providing significant coverage of the fundamentals of manufacturing processes, equipment, and tooling for study by the novice engineer."—*Pref.* Chapters include tabular data, line drawings, references and bibliographies; many include a glossary of terms used in the subject covered. Each volume has its own index.   TS176.T63

Welding handbook. 8th ed. Miami, Fla. : American Welding Society, c1987–1991. v. 1–2 : ill. (some col.). (In progress).   **EK249**

1st ed., 1938; 7th ed., 1976–84 (5 v.).

Contents: v. 1, Welding technology, ed. by Leonard P. Conner; v. 2, Welding processes, ed. by R.L. O'Brien. To be complete in 3 vols.

Most chapters contain bibliographies as well as illustrations, drawings, and tables. Vol. 1 gives basic information (e.g., joining and cutting processes, physics of welding, welding metallurgy, residual stresses, distortion). Indexed.   TS227.W387

Biography

American Society of Mechanical Engineers. Mechanical engineers in America born prior to 1861 : a biographical dictionary / sponsored by the History and Heritage Committee. N.Y. : American Soc. of Mechanical Engineers, 1980. 330 p. : ports.
EK250

"The fundamental purpose of the *Dictionary* is to supply essential biographical data on a selected group of American mechanical engineers active from the late 18th to the early 20th century, both as a resource for scholars in the history of technology and to give mechanical engineers ... a basis for their conviction that the foundation of the profession is ... the engineers themselves."—*Pref.* Inspired by *Biographical dictionary of American civil engineers* (EK63), this work has a similar format. It is in two parts, the first being a list of 1,688 engineers identified in the biographical files of the Division of Mechanical & Civil Engineering, National Museum of History & Technology, Smithsonian Institution, with dates where known. The second part contains biographical sketches of 500 of these engineers; for 50 of the 500 a portrait is included.   TJ139.A47

Plant engineering and maintenance

Maintenance engineering handbook / Lindley R. Higgins, ed. in chief. 4th ed. N.Y. : McGraw-Hill, c1988. 1111 p. in various pagings : ill.   **EK251**

1st ed., 1957; 3rd ed., 1977.

Chapters by specialists. Indexed.   TS192.M335

Standard handbook of plant engineering / Robert C. Rosaler, ed. in chief. 2nd ed. N.Y. : McGraw-Hill, 1994. 1 v. (various pagings) : ill.   **EK252**

1st ed., 1983.

Chapters are grouped in four sections: Pt. A, The basic plant facility: construction, equipment, and maintenance; Pt. B, Plant operation equipment: selection and maintenance; Pt. C, The maintenance function: basic equipment and supplies; Pt. D, Supplementary technical data. Chapters by specialists include bibliographic references. Indexed.   TS184.S7

MINING ENGINEERING

Indexes; Abstract journals

Institution of Mining and Metallurgy (London). IMM abstracts : a survey of world literature on economic geology, mining, mineral dressing, extraction metallurgy [and] allied subjects. v.1– . London : Institution, 1950– . Bimonthly.
EK253

Subtitle varies.

Abstracts (many of them supplied by the authors) appear in classed arrangement according to Universal Decimal Classification. No index. Beginning with v. 35 (1985), accompanied by semiannual index.

• Machine-readable version: *IMMAGE* (London : Institution of Mining and Metallurgy, 1979–). Available online and on diskette, updated bimonthly.

Handbooks

SME mining engineering handbook / senior ed., Howard L. Hartman ; associate editors, Scott G. Britton ... [et al.]. Littleton, Colo. : Soc. for Mining, Metallurgy, amd Exploration, 1992. 2 v. : ill., maps. **EK254**

1st. ed., 1973.

Contributions from experts are in 25 sections divided into six parts; Pt. 1, Introduction; Pt. 2, Stages of mining; Pt. 3, Unit operations of mining; Pt. 4, Surface mining; Pt. 5, Underground mining; Pt. 6, Supplemental topics. A standard reference for mining engineers. Includes bibliographies. Indexed. TN145.S56.

ENGINEERING MATERIALS

General works

Guides

Materials data sources / comp. for the Materials Group, the Institution of Mechanical Engineers, and sponsored by the Institute of Metals ... [et al.]. London : Mechanical Engineering Publications Limited for the Institution of Mechanical Engineers, 1987. 111 p. **EK255**

Gen. ed., P.T. Houldcroft.

Lists sources of data rather than the data proper. In four main sections: Metals and alloys; Refractories, ceramics, glasses and hardmetals; Polymers and composites; and Timber. Within each section are listed published data (books and standards) and useful organizations. Chapters on databases and materials selectors, and higher educational establishments (U.K. universities and polytechnics) complete the volume. Appendixes: Addresses of standards organizations (an international listing); Joining and adhesive bonding consumables (with two entries). This edition "will be updated within two years."— *Foreword.* TA403.6M36

Bibliography

Mann, John Yeates. Bibliography on the fatigue of materials : components and structures. Oxford : Pergamon, [1970–90]. 4 v. **EK256**

"Published for and on behalf of the Royal Aeronautical Society (Fatigue Committee)."—*title page.*

Contents: v.1, 1838–1950; v.2, 1951–60; v.3, 1961–65; v. 4, 1966–69.

Entries give title of work in the language of publication, followed by translation into English. (In some cases—e.g., works written in Russian, Japanese, Chinese, or Polish—the title is given in English only, followed by a letter to indicate language of publication.) Arrangement is chronological by year of publication, then alphabetical by author. Author and subject indexes. Z5853.M38M35

Indexes; Abstract journals

American Society for Metals. Documentation Service. ASM review of metal literature : abstracts of the world's scientific, engineering and technical literature concerned with the production, properties, fabrication and applications of metals, their alloys and compounds. v.1 (1944)–24 (1967). Metals Park, Ohio : ASTM, 1945–67. Monthly. **EK257**

Subtitle varies.

Through 1964, cumulated into annual volumes with separate indexes. Changed format and classification notation with 1965. "Based on the decision to make RML completely compatible with and parallel to two new monthly abstract journals to be published by *Engineering Index* ... in the fields of plastics and electrical and electronics engineering ... will use interchangeable computer programs for generation of subject and author indexes."—*v.22, no.1.*

Merged with *Metallurgical abstracts*, Jan. 1968, to form *Metals abstracts* (EK260). TN1.A58

Engineered materials abstracts : EMA. Metals Park, Ohio : Materials Information, 198?– . Monthly. **EK258**

A companion publication to *Metals abstracts* (EK260), indexing the literature on polymers, ceramics, and composite materials as applied in an engineering environment.

• Machine-readable versions: *Engineered materials abstracts (EMA)* (1986–), available online, updated monthly, and as part of *DIALOG OnDisc : METADEX collection : metals, polymers, ceramics* (1985–), available on CD-ROM, updated quarterly. TA401.E47

Metallurgical abstracts (general and non-ferrous). Ser. 1 (1931–33); ser. 2 (1934–65); ser. 3, v. 1, pt. 1 (Jan. 1966)–v. 2, pr. 12 (1967). London : Inst. of Metals, 1931–67. Monthly. **EK259**

1931–33, issued monthly as a supplement to the *Journal* of the Institute of Metals.

A classified abstracting service of material in all languages. Titles of foreign articles are translated into English. Symbols denote papers describing results of original research and outstanding critical reviews. Also lists contents of symposia in book form, new journals, and book reviews. Monthly issues are without indexes, but name and subject indexes are published at the end of the year.

Merged with *ASM review of metal literature* in Jan. 1968 to form *Metals abstracts* (EK260).

Metals abstracts. v. 1, no. 1 (Jan. 1968)– . London : Metals Abstracts Trust, 1968– . Monthly. **EK260**

Published jointly by the Institute of Metals and the American Society for Metals, a result of the merger of the *Metallurgical abstracts* (EK259) and the *ASM review of metal literature* (EK257).

Covers all aspects of the science and practice of metallurgy and related fields. International coverage. Now provides abstracts from more than 1,400 journals. Classed arrangement with author index in each issue.

A companion publication, *Metals abstracts index* (v. 1, no. 1 [Jan. 1968]–), is issued simultaneously but mailed separately. It provides complete, computer-produced author and subject indexes to the abstracts. Annual cumulations of both abstracts and indexes are published.

Alloys index (v. 1, no. 1 [Jan. 1974]–), provides indexing by alloy composition to complement the general indexing in *Metals abstracts*; all papers found in *Alloys index* are also in *Metals abstracts*.

Steels alert (v. 3, no. 1 [Jan. 1985]– . Metals Park, Ohio : Metals Information, 1985–) began 1983 as *Steels supplement to Metals abstracts* and provides comprehensive international coverage of business aspects of the steel industry.

• Machine-readable versions: *METADEX* (Materials Park, Ohio : Materials Information, 1966–), available online, updated monthly. Includes *Metals abstracts*, *Alloys index*, and *Steels alert*. Also available on CD-ROM as *DIALOG OnDisc : METADEX collection : metals, polymers, ceramics* (1985–), updated quarterly. Includes citations from *Engineered materials abstracts* (EK258). TN1.M5153

Encyclopedias

Encyclopedia of materials science and engineering : Supplementary volume / ed., Robert W. Cahn ; senior advisory ed., Michael B. Bever. Oxford ; N.Y. : Pergamon Pr., 1988–1993. 3 v. (2229 p.) : ill.　　　　　　**EK261**

Each supplement contains some new articles as well as those which replace or update entries form the parent *Encyclopedia* (EK262). Numerous cross-references. Suppl. 2–3 cumulate the subject index and the systematic subject outline.　　TA402.E53

Encyclopedia of materials science and engineering / ed. in chief, Michael B. Bever. Oxford : Pergamon ; Cambridge, Mass. : MIT Pr., 1986. 8 v. : ill.　　　　**EK262**

Contents: v. 1–7, A–Z; v. 8, Systematic outline of the encyclopedia.

Although this work's 1,580 articles stress theory and practice, the treatment is not exhaustive. All the articles contain bibliographies, but indexes are found only in v.8, which also contains a systematic outline that readers should consult first. Indexes to authors of articles, cited authors, and acronyms, and an extensive subject index.　　TA402.E53

Dictionaries

American Society for Metals. ASM thesaurus of metallurgical terms : a vocabulary listing for use in indexing, storage, and retrieval of technical information in metallurgy. 3rd ed. Metals Park, Ohio : ASM, 1979. 176 p.　　　**EK263**

1st ed., 1968.
Revised by the ASM Metals Information Technical Advisory Committee.　　　　　　　　Z695.1.M55A5

ASM materials engineering dictionary / ed. by J.R. Davis. [Metals Park, Ohio] : ASM International, c1992. 555 p. : ill.　　　　　　　　　　　**EK264**

Provides definitions for about 7,500 terms drawn from several ASM handbooks (e.g., *ASM handbook* [EK269], *Engineered materials handbook* [EK274], *Metals handbook* [EK278]), revised and supplemented with new material. Some 64 key materials groups are treated in expanded "Technical briefs" rather than in short definitions. Cross-references. Includes an appendix of abbreviations and symbols.
TA402.A86

Malcolm, I. J. Dictionary of ceramic science and engineering. 2nd ed. N.Y. : Plenum, 1994. 384 p.　　　**EK265**

1st ed., 1984, by Loran S. O'Bannon.
"A reference book listing the words, terms, materials, processes, products, and some of the more prominent business terms that are important to the ceramic and related industries."—*Pref.* Brief definitions; listings for minerals and other compounds include some physical data (molecular weight, melting point, specific gravity). Cross-references. Includes bibliography.　　　　　　TP788.O2

Tottle, Charles Ronald. An encyclopaedia of metallurgy and materials. London : Metals Soc. ; Plymouth : Macdonald and Evans, 1984. 380 p. : ill.　　　　　**EK266**

Previous versions by Arthur Douglas Merriman had title: *A dictionary of metallurgy* (1958); *A concise encyclopaedia of metallurgy* (1965).

"Definitions have ... been tailored to the varying needs of potential readers, so that for the non-technical reader, the most likely terms of interest are tackled as simply as possible without causing confusion, but for the student, the more scientific aspects are given wider treatment, assuming prior understanding of physics, chemistry or engineering."—*Pref.* More a dictionary than an encyclopedia; a section of tables precedes the main part of the work, which consists mainly of brief definitions, though some are longer and some include tabular data. Cross-references.　　　　　　TN609.T677

Directories

Materials research centres : a world directory of organizations and programmes. 5th ed. Longman, 1993. 644 p.
EK267

The 5th ed. lists more than 3,300 research and technology institutes worldwide that are active in such aspects of materials science as chemical analysis, construction engineering, inorganic chemistry, and metallurgy. Entries are arranged alphabetically by country and include directory information, size, major personnel by name, overview of research activities, affiliations, products, annual expenditure, and publications. Trade associations are listed separately by country. Indexed by title of establishment and subject.

Handbooks

ASM engineered materials reference book / comp. by the editorial staff, Reference Publications, ASM International. Metals Park, Ohio : ASM International, c1989. 517 p. : ill.
EK268

Consists of tables and phase diagrams without text on "composites, ceramics, engineering or high-performance plastics, and electronic materials."—*Pref.* Appendixes: references; guide to general information sources; directory of composites laboratories and information centers; directory of composites manufacturers, suppliers, and services; international standards-issuing organizations; and universities with faculties in polymer science and in ceramics. No index.
TA403.4.A84

ASM handbook / prep. under the direction of the ASM International Handbook Committee. 10th ed. Materials Park, Ohio : ASM International, 1990–94. v. 1–18 : ill. (In progress).
EK269

Title varies: v. 1, *Metals handbook.*
1st ed., 1927; 9th ed., 1978–89 (EK278).
Contents: v. 1, Properties and selection—irons, steels, and high-performance alloys (1990); v. 2, Properties and selection—nonferrous alloys and special-purpose materials (1990); v. 3, Alloy phase diagrams (1992); v. 4, Heat treating (1991); v. 5, Surface engineering (1994); v. 6, Welding, brazing, and soldering (1993); v. 18, Friction, lubrication, and wear technology (1992).
An update of *Metals handbook* (EK278), volumes of which should be retained until superseded by a corresponding volume of this edition. This edition continues the thorough treatment of topics found in earlier versions. Each volume is indexed separately.　TA459.M43

ASM metals reference book / ed., Michael Bauccio. 3rd ed. Metals Park, Ohio : ASM International, 1993. 614 p. : ill.
EK270

1st ed., 1981; 2nd ed., 1983.
A quick source of data compiled from many sources, including *Metals handbook* (EK269). Data is presented largely in tabular form with some diagrams. Includes references. The first section is a glossary of metallurgical and metalworking terms.　　TA459.A78

Bansal, Narottam P. Handbook of glass properties / Narottam P. Bansal and R.H. Doremus. Orlando, Fla. : Academic Pr., 1986. 680 p. : ill.　　　　　　　　**EK271**

Tables and graphs predominate, with a minimum of text. Silicate glasses are treated more thoroughly than nonsilicate glasses. The authors have critically evaluated the literature relating to thermal, electrical, mechanical, transport, and other related properties for a variety of different glasses. Chapters contain extensive bibliographies; short subject index.　　　　　　　　TA450.B27

Brady, George S. Materials handbook : an encyclopedia for managers, technical professionals, purchasing and production managers, technicians, supervisors, and foremen / George S. Brady, Henry R. Clauser. 13th ed. N.Y. : McGraw Hill, c1991. 1 v. **EK272**
1st ed., 1929; 12th ed., 1986.
Covers more than 15,000 minerals, animal and plant substances, and commercial and engineering materials. Uses, production methods, and trade names are included for common items. Most entries are shorter than half a page. The special chapter on structure and properties of materials includes charts, tables, and a glossary of terms. Uses both SI and U.S. customary units. Subject index is very important because the main text has no cross-references. TA402.B73

Clauss, Francis Jacob. Engineer's guide to high-temperature materials. Reading, Mass. : Addison-Wesley, [1969]. 401 p. : ill. **EK273**
In three sections: (1) General background, defining "gross mechanical behavior of metals and alloys at elevated temperatures"; (2) Specific materials, in which "a number of specific materials are categorized according to their composition and structure"; (3) Special topics, which include "conditions of service that are more realistic than ideal laboratory conditions, as well as mathematical procedures for making the best use of limited laboratory tests."—*Pref.* Selected references; index. TA418.26.C55

Engineered materials handbook / prep. under the direction of the ASM International Handbook Committee ; Theodore J. Reinhart, technical chairman. Metals Park, Ohio : ASM International, c1987–1990. v. 1–4 : ill. (In progress). **EK274**
Contents: v. 1, Composites (1987); v. 2, Engineering plastics (1988); v. 3, Adhesives and sealants (1990); v. 4, Ceramics and glasses (1991).
Designed to be similar in comprehensiveness to the multivolume *Metals handbook* (9th ed., EK278; 10th ed., called *ASM handbook*, EK269). Engineered materials include composites, plastics, adhesives, sealants, ceramics, and glasses. Gives current and practical information for choosing, utilizing, and evaluating these materials; includes numerous charts and graphs. Each volume has its own subject index and a separate glossary of terms. TA403.E497

Handbook of corrosion data / ed. by Bruce D. Craig. Metals Park, Ohio : ASM International, c1989. 683 p. : ill. **EK275**
Designed to give users " a starting point to quickly and easily assess the recent literature on metals in corrosive environments."—*Pref.* In two parts: Corrosion of metals and alloys; Corrosion media. The latter category generally refers to specific compounds. Numerous charts and tables. TA462.H37

Lynch, Charles T. CRC handbook of materials science. Cleveland : CRC Pr., [1974–80]. 4 v. **EK276**
Contents: v. 1, General properties; v. 2, Metals, composites, and refractory materials; v. 3, Nonmetallic materials and applications; v. 4, Wood.
"It has been the goal of the CRC *Handbook of Materials Science* to provide a current and readily accessible guide to the physical properties of solid state and structural materials. ... Most of the information is in tabular format. ... This reference is particularly aimed at the nonexperts, or those who are experts in one field but seek information on materials in another."—*Pref.* Each volume indexed separately. TA403.4.L94

Materials handling handbook / ed. in chief, Raymond A. Kulwiec ; sponsored by The American Society of Mechanical Engineers and the International Material Management Society. 2nd ed. N.Y. : Wiley, [1985]. 1458 p. : ill. **EK277**
1st ed., 1958.
36 chapters by specialists include information under the topics of unit materials handling, bulk materials handling, transportation interface, and safety, environment, and human factors. Chapters include references. Indexed. TS180.M315

Metals handbook / prep. under the direction of the ASM Handbook Committee. 9th ed. Materials Park, Ohio : American Society for Metals, 1985–89. 17 v. : ill. **EK278**
1st ed., 1927.
Contents: v. 1, Properties and selection: irons, steels; v. 2, Properties and selection: nonferrous alloys and pure metals; v. 3, Properties and selection: stainless steels, tool materials and special-purpose metals; v. 4, Heat treating; v. 5, Surface cleaning, finishing, and coating; v. 6, Welding, brazing, and soldering; v. 7, Powder metallurgy; v. 8, Mechanical testing; v. 9, Metallography and microstructures; v. 10, Materials characterization; v. 11, Failure analysis and prevention; v. 12, Fractography; v. 13, Corrosion; v. 14, Forming and forging; v. 15, Casting; v. 16, Machining; v. 17, Nondestructive evaluation and quality control.
Vols. 14–17 prep. under the direction of the ASM International Handbook Committee.
An extremely comprehensive handbook, the work of a large number of contributors, each volume treating a different aspect of the subject in great detail. Contains bibliographical references, extensive tabular data, and illustrative material. Each volume is individually indexed.
§ Volumes on a particular topic should be kept available for reference consultation until superseded by the corresponding volumes of the 10th ed., now titled *ASM handbook* (EK269). TA459.M43

Parker, Earl Randall. Materials data book for engineers and scientists. N.Y. : McGraw-Hill, [1967]. 398 p. **EK279**
"The present book is primarily a collection of up-to-date tabulated data and is similar in form to the *Handbook of Chemistry and Physics* [now *CRC handbook of chemistry and physics*, EE70]. The descriptive matter ... is minimal; only information considered essential for interpretation and use of the tables has been included. Data on all the generally useful metals, alloys, ceramics, plastics, woods, and concretes have been included. In addition, sections on corrosion, welding, and suppliers' addresses have been added to guide engineers in the selection and procurement of materials."—*Pref.* TA403.4.P3

Ross, Robert Ballantyne. Metallic materials specification handbook. 4th ed. London ; N.Y. : Chapman & Hall, 1992. 830 p. **EK280**
1st ed., 1968, entitled: *Metallic materials*. 3rd ed., 1980.
Attempts to list comprehensively all known metallic material trade names, symbols, and specifications. Allows users to: identify chemical constituents and other properties of a material by trade name, specification, or symbol; obtain information on similar materials; find a specification, trade name, or symbol for a material for which mechanical and other properties have been identified. Divided into 118 sections according to the primary consitituent of the materials concerned. Indexed by name (trade name, specification, or symbol).
TA461.R67

Smithells, Colin J. Smithells metals reference book. 7th ed. / ed. by E. A. Brandes and G. B. Brook. Oxford ; Boston : Butterworth-Heinemann, 1992. 1 v. (various pagings) : ill. **EK281**
1st ed., 1949; 6th ed., 1983. 1st–5th eds. ed. by Colin J. Smithells.
A convenient summary, mostly in tabular form, of data relating to metallurgy; descriptive matter and diagrams (e.g., alloy phase diagrams) are included where appropriate. Includes references to sources of data. SI units are used throughout. Index. TN671.S55

Woldman's engineering alloys / ed. by John P. Frick. 7th ed. Materials Park, Ohio : ASM International, 1990. 1459 p. **EK282**
1st ed., 1936. 2nd–5th eds. had title: *Engineering alloys*. 6th ed., 1979.
Lists alloys from 23 countries under trade names, followed by the producer's name, alloy composition, properties and applications. In this edition obsolete alloys that were listed only by name in the 6th ed. now have complete entries and the designation "obsolete." Some 5,000 new alloys have been added and 12,000 entries revised. TA483.W64

Plastics

Comprehensive polymer science : the synthesis, characterization, reactions & applications of polymers / chairman of the editorial board, Sir Geoffrey Allen; deputy chairman of the editorial board, John C. Bevington. Oxford ; N.Y. : Pergamon Pr., 1989. 7 v. : ill.   **EK283**

    Contents: v. 1, Polymer characterization; v. 2, Polymer properties; v. 3, Chain reactions; v. 4, Chain polymerization II; v. 5, Step polymerization; v. 6, Polymer reactions; v. 7, Speciality polymers.

    Encyclopedic in scope, with signed, authoritative articles including tabular data and literature references. Vols. 1–6 have individual subject indexes, and v. 7 a cumulative subject index.

    ———. *Supplement* (Biennial. 1992–).   QD381.C66

Concise encyclopedia of polymer science and engineering / Jacqueline I. Kroschwitz, executive ed. N.Y. : Wiley, c1990. 1341 p. : ill.   **EK284**

    "Contains all of the subjects covered in the 17 main volumes and the supplement and index volumes of the ... 2nd edition of the Encyclopedia of polymer science and engineering"—*Pref.*

    Useful for smaller collections that lack the *Encyclopedia* (EK285).

Encyclopedia of polymer science and engineering / editorial board, Herman F. Mark ... [et al.] ; ed. in chief, Jacqueline I. Kroschwitz. 2nd ed. N.Y. : Wiley, c1985–90. 17 v., suppl. and index : ill.   **EK285**

    1st ed., 1964–77, (16 v. and 2 suppls.) had title: *Encyclopedia of polymer science and technology.*

    Contents: v. 1–17, A–Zwitterionic polymerization; Supplement (1989); Index (1990).

    Signed articles by specialist authors contain equations, graphs, tabular data, and extensive bibliographical references. Each volume begins with tables of conversion factors, abbreviations, and unit symbols. Coverage includes all aspects of polymer science (physics, chemistry, biology) and engineering. Cross-references. Index volume.   TP1087.E46

Handbook of plastics, elastomers, and composites / Charles A. Harper, ed. in chief. N.Y. : McGraw-Hill, c1992. 1 v. (various pagings) : ill.   **EK286**

    1st ed., 1975, had title: *Handbook of plastics and elastomers.*

    Signed chapters arranged by category of application or by type of material contain information on properties, testing, processing, and design considerations. Indexed.   TP1130.H36

Information sources in polymers and plastics / ed., R. T. Adkins. London ; N.Y. : Bowker-Saur, c1989. 313 p.   **EK287**

    The editor stresses international coverage of the topics, drawing chapter authors from industry, universities, and libraries. Pt. 1 treats specific categories such as serials, books, patents, theses, and online databases. Pt. 2 discusses individual subjects such as polymer structure and nomenclature, rubber coatings and adhesives, and new developments in polymers. Pt. 3 emphasizes national and regional sources. Indexed   Z5524.P7I54

Modern plastics encyclopedia. 1941– . N.Y. : McGraw-Hill, 1940– . Annual.   **EK288**

    Publisher varies.

    Title varies: 1941, *Modern plastics catalog*; 1942–45, *Plastics catalog*. Issued as part of the periodical *Modern plastics.*

    Now organized into: Industry overview; Raw materials; Additives; Primary processing; Components; Toolmaking; Auxiliary equipment; Fabricating and finishing; North American buyers' guide. Sections have narrative overviews, and where appropriate, extensive tabular information. The "Buyers' guide" includes a classified product index and an alphabetical list of suppliers with address, phone, and fax numbers.   TP986.A1M62

Polymer handbook / ed. by J. Brandrup, E. H. Immergut. 3rd ed. N.Y. : Wiley, c1989. 1 v. (various pagings) : ill.   **EK289**

    1st ed., 1966; 2nd ed., 1975.

    Brings together a vast amount of physical and chemical data on polymers. Uses data compilations of chapter length to summarize information for synthetic polymers, polysaccharides and derivatives, and oligomers; extensive bibliographies. Short subject index.   QD388.P65

SPI plastics engineering handbook of the Society of the Plastics Industry, Inc / ed. by Michael L. Berins. 5th ed. N.Y. : Van Nostrand Reinhold, c1991. 845 p. : ill.   **EK290**

    Title varies.

    1st ed., 1947; 4th ed., 1976, had title: *Plastics engineering handbook* .....

    Designed to be a state-of-the-art compilation. Chapters 1–3 include a glossary of terms and a description of classes of plastics. Chapters describe current types of processing (including machinery and equipment) as well as secondary processing methods. Contains numerous graphs, tables, line drawings, and photographs. Glossary terms are not listed in the subject index.   TP1130.S58

Whittington's dictionary of plastics / ed. by James F. Carley. 3rd ed. Lancaster, Pa. : Technomic Publ. Co., c1993. 568 p.   **EK291**

    1st ed., 1968, and 2nd ed., 1978, ed. by Lloyd R. Whittington.

    "Sponsored by the Society of Plastics Engineers, Inc."—*t.p.*

    Defines mainly terms in plastics technology. Most entries are one or two sentences, but some are fuller, and may contain equations, tables, etc. Includes abbreviations, with reference to the full form. Most numerical data given in SI units; conversion factors in an appendix.   T1110.W47

Wittfoht, Annemarie. Plastics technical dictionary : English-German, German-English. N.Y. : Macmillan, 1981. 3 v. : ill.   **EK292**

    Previous ed., 1961, in 2v.

    Also published in Germany with title *Kunststofftechnisches Wörterbuch* (München : Hanser, 1978–81. 3 v.). Both editions have title pages in the two languages.

    Contents: v. 1, Alphabetical dictionary, English-German (4th completely rev. ed.); v. 2, Alphabetical dictionary, German-English; v. 3, Reference volume, illustrated systematic groups E-G/G-E.

    Includes nomenclature used in processing, fabricating, molding, and welding.   TP1110.W534

NUCLEAR ENGINEERING

Abstract journals

INIS atomindex : an international abtracting service. v. 1– . Vienna : Internat. Atomic Energy Agency ; N.Y. : distr. by Unipub., 1970– . Semimonthly with semiannual indexes.   **EK293**

    Partially supersedes *Nuclear science abstracts* (EK294). Supersedes International Atomic Energy Agency, *List of references on nuclear energy* (Vienna, 1959–68).

    "INIS is a cooperative, decentralized information system set up by the International Atomic Energy Agency and its Member States. Its purpose is to construct a data base identifying publications relating to nuclear science and its peaceful applications."—*Introd.* Availability of the report literature is indicated; many of the reports are available on microfiche from INIS.

    •Machine-readable version: *International nuclear information system (INIS)* [database] (Vienna, 1970–). Available online, updated semimonthly, and as *INIS database on CD-ROM* [database], updated quarterly.   Z7144.N8I15

Nuclear science abstracts / United States Atomic Energy Commission. v. 1, no. 1 (July 15, 1948)–v. 33, no. 12 (June 30, 1976). Oak Ridge, Tenn. : Oak Ridge Directed Operations, Technical Information Division, [1948–1976]. Semimonthly.   **EK294**

Title varies.

Superseded the Commission's *Abstracts of declassified documents* and *Guide to published research on atomic energy*.

Subject, personal author, corporate author, and cumulative report indexes are available: v. 1–4, 1948–50; v. 5–10, 1951–56; v. 11–15, 1957–61; v. 16–20, 1962–66; v. 21–25, 1967–71.

Abstracts and indexes the nuclear science literature. "It covers scientific and technical reports of the U.S. Atomic Energy Commission and its contractors, other U.S. Government agencies, other governments, universities, and industrial and research organizations. In addition, books, conference proceedings, individual conference papers, patents, and journal literature on a worldwide basis are abstracted and indexed."—[*note*] 1975. In classed subject arrangement; the Jan. 15 issue includes additional information on scope and arrangement. Availability of all Commission reports is indicated. Titles of foreign-language articles are translated into English; abstracts are in English.

In governmental reorganization the U.S. Atomic Energy Commission was eliminated and its publication, *Nuclear science abstracts*, ceased. Some of the functions of the AEC were taken over by the new agency, U.S. Energy Research and Development Administration and, subsequently, by the U.S. Department of Energy. Much of the coverage of *NSA* was taken over by *Energy research abstracts* (EK215). *NSA* is also partially superseded by *INIS atomindex* (EK293).

•Machine-readable version: *Nuclear science abstracts* [database] (Oak Ridge, Tenn. : U.S. Dept. of Energy, Office of Scientific and Technical Information, 1948–76). Available online and on CD-ROM.
    QC770.U64

Dictionaries

Glossary of terms in nuclear science and technology / prep. by ANS-9, the American Nuclear Society Standards Subcommittee on Nuclear Terminology and Units ; Harry Alter, chairman. Rev. and updated. La Grange Park, Ill. : ANS, [1986]. 132 p.   **EK295**

1st ed., 1957, by the National Research Council Conference on Glossary of Terms in Nuclear Science and Technology, had title: *A glossary of terms in nuclear science and engineering*; 2nd ed., 1967, by the United States of America Standards Institute, had title: *USA standard glossary of terms in nuclear science and technology*; 3rd ed., 1976, by American Nuclear Society, had title: *American National Standard glossary of terms in nuclear science and technology*.

"A revision of N1.1–1976..."—*Introd.*   QC772.A43

Directories

World energy and nuclear directory : organizations and research activities in atomic and non-atomic energy. 1st ed. (1990)– . Harlow, Essex : Longman ; Detroit : Distr. by Gale Research, 1990– . Irregular.   **EK296**

Formed by the union of: *World nuclear directory* (Harlow : Longman ; Detroit : Gale, 1981–88) and *World energy directory* (2nd ed. Harlow : Longman ; Detroit : Gale, 1985).

Lists more than 2,500 industrial, academic, and noncommercial laboratories worldwide. The 2nd ed. includes trade associations and societies. Indexed by organization and subject.   TJ163.165.W66

Handbooks

Nuclear power plants worldwide. 1st ed.– . Detroit ; Wash. ; London : Gale, c1993– . Triennial.   **EK297**

Gives detailed information about 741 units at 310 sites, including facilities under construction, cancelled, or shut down. Contains maps of plant locations grouped by geographic area. Indexes: Technical problems (accidents or failures); Alphabetical (plants, organizations, and companies).   TK1194.N83

PETROLEUM ENGINEERING

Guides

Pearson, Barbara C. Guide to the petroleum reference literature / Barbara C. Pearson and Katherine B. Ellwood. Littleton, Colo. : Libraries Unlimited, 1987. 193 p.   **EK298**

Most chapters contain short annotated entries and full bibliographic information, but in the database chapter, one title is described per page. International sources are included. Although the emphasis is primarily on English-language material issued since 1978, some of the older "classic" titles have been listed also. Author/title index; subject index.   Z6972.P33

Bibliography

DeGolyer, Everette Lee. Bibliography on the petroleum industry / E. DeGolyer, Harold Vance. College Station, Tex., [1944]. 730 p. : ill. (School of Engineering, Texas Engineering Experiment Station. Bulletin, no. 83).   **EK299**

Combines a bibliography of some 12,000 items, compiled by DeGolyer, with the bibliography of the Petroleum Engineering Dept. at the A. & M. College of Texas, and a bibliography on the Air-Gas Lift prepared by S. F. Shaw. Arranged by a decimal classification devised by L. C. Uren of the University of California, with an alphabetical subject index.   Z6972.D4

Giddens, Paul H. The beginnings of the petroleum industry : sources and bibliography. Harrisburg, Penn. : Pennsylvania Historical Commission, 1941. 195 p. : ill.   **EK300**

In two parts: the first contains letters concerning the organization of the Pennsylvania Rock Oil Company of New York, the first petroleum company in the world; the second is a "Bibliography on the beginnings of the petroleum industry in 1871" (p. 87–172), arranged by form, e.g., atlases, books, bibliographies, pamphlets, periodical literature. Some annotations.   TN872.P4G5

Special Libraries Association. Petroleum Section. Committee on U.S. Sources of Petroleum and Natural Gas Statistics. U.S. sources of petroleum and natural gas statistics / comp. by Margaret M. Rocq. N.Y. : Special Libraries Assoc., 1961. 94 p.   **EK301**

An updating and expansion of Bradford A. Osborne's *An index to American petroleum statistics* (1943).

Indexes 231 publications. In three parts: the first lists trade journals, professional society, trade association, and company organs that are indexed; the second, the index, is an alphabetical list of products, plants, and other facilities, such as pipelines, wells, and refineries, keyed by number to the publications listed in the first part; and the third is a brief bibliography of statistical compilations not indexed in the second part, which include data on petroleum and natural gas. Only publications issued in the U.S. are indexed, but statistics about other countries are included.   Z6972.S65

Swanson, Edward Benjamin. A century of oil and gas in books : a descriptive bibliography. N.Y. : Appleton, [1960]. 214 p.   **EK302**
An annotated bibliography of books and monographs published in English from the mid-19th century to Aug. 1959. Arranged by topics, e.g., drilling and production, oil shales and shale oil, with sections on history and biography, reference works, general works, serials and periodicals. Author index.   Z6972.S9

Dictionaries

Agout, Marthe. Bibliographie des livres, thèses et conférences relatifs à l'industrie du pétrole. [Paris : Standard française de pétroles], 1949. 322 p. : ill.   **EK303**
A comprehensive, classified bibliography of 6,408 numbered items, based on the holdings of about 15 libraries and covering approximately 100 years from the start of the commercial development of petroleum in the mid-19th century. Scope is international; locations are given wherever possible; and sources of reference are indicated for items not seen. Subject and author indexes.

Boone, Lalia Phipps. The petroleum dictionary. Norman : Univ. of Oklahoma Pr., 1952. 338 p.   **EK304**
Gives definitions and sources of about 6,000 terms used in the oil industry, especially its colorful language. Bibliography, p. 333–8.
TN865.B6

Porter, Hollis Paine. Petroleum dictionary for office, field and factory. 4th ed. Houston, Tex. : Gulf Publ. Co., 1948. 326 p.   **EK305**
1st ed., 1930.
An enlarged edition of a standard work, now giving definitions for some 4,600 terms dealing with the prospecting, producing, and refining of petroleum. Definitions are generally brief, but some range to more than a page in length. Includes popular as well as technical terms.   TN865.P6

Tver, David F. The petroleum dictionary / David F. Tver, Richard W. Berry. N.Y. : Van Nostrand Reinhold, 1980. 374 p.   **EK306**
A combination dictionary-handbook that covers the petroleum industry and related fields (e.g., geology, geophysics, seismology, drilling, gas processes), and a detailed analysis of various refining operations and processes.   TN865.T83

Handbooks, yearbooks, etc.

Financial times oil and gas international year book. 1978/79– . London : [Financial Times], 1978– . Annual.   **EK307**
Continues: *Oil and petroleum yearbook* (1910–71); *Oil and petroleum international yearbook* (1972); *Oil and gas international yearbook* (also called *Skinner's oil and gas international yearbook*, 1973–78).
A worldwide directory of oil, gas, and kindred companies.

Petroleum engineering handbook / ed. in chief, Howard B. Bradley ; assoc. editors, Fred W. Gipson ... [et al.]. Richardson, Tex. : Society of Petroleum Engineers, c1987. 1 v. (various pagings) : ill.   **EK308**
Rev. ed. of: *Petroleum production handbook* (N.Y. : McGraw-Hill, 1962).
Contains 58 chapters covering all aspects of production engineering and reservoir engineering. Numerous charts and tables. Indexed.
TN870.P493

Index

Authors, editors, compilers, sponsoring bodies, titles, and subjects are interfiled in one alphabet. Authors print in roman, titles in italic, and subjects in boldface. Authors and titles mentioned in bibliographic notes or annotations are indexed as well as main entries. Entries for titles in machine-readable form are preceded by a bullet (•). Numbers precede alphabetic characters. Acronyms are not forced to the head of each letter but file as words. Names beginning "Mc" or "Mac" file separately as spelled. Entries beginning "U.S." have been regularized to "United States" but titles beginning "U.S." file as acronyms. "St." files as "Saint."

10 años de investigaciones sobre la mujer en Nicaragua 1976–1986, Diaz, Pamela, DB314
—— Pérez, Paola, DB314
10 eventful years, DA209
10 years of socio-economic development in the Lao People's Democratic Republic, CG409
The 100 best colleges for African-American students, Wilson, Erlene B., CB310
100 families of flowering plants, Hickey, Michael, EG176
100 libraries statistical survey 1985–86, AK95
100 noteworthy firsts in juvenile literature, AA245
120 years of American education, CB135
12,000 words, AC92
1500 modern Chinese novels and plays, Schyns, Joseph, BE1559
The 1890s, BE758
18th–19th reports containing all decisions to July 31, 1927, Canada. Board on Geographical Names, CL111
1928–1965 [i.e., Bin dokuz yüz yirmi sekiz, bin dokuz yüz altmışbeş] yılları arasında Türkiyede basılmış bibliyografyaların bibliyografyası, Başbuğoğlu, Filiz, AA68
1948–1985 world crop and livestock statistics, EJ76
The 1,978 international organizations founded since the Congress of Vienna, Union of International Associations, AL22
•*1987 census of agriculture,* EJ78
1989 directory of federally sponsored training materials, CB351
The 1989 neuro-computing bibliography, Klimasauskas, Casimir C., EK155
1990 census of population and housing, CH692
19th century art, Rosenblum, Robert, BF131
19th-century music, BJ189
19th century postage stamps of the United States, Brookman, Lester G., BG204
19th century sculpture, Janson, Horst Woldemar, BF393
—— Rheims, Maurice, BF393

20–seiki bunken yōran taikei, BE1580
200 Jahre Tageszeitung in Österreich, 1783–1983, AE44
200 years of the American circus, BH11
2000 books and more, Kaplan, Jonathan, BC515
20,000 years of fashion, Boucher, François, BG106
20th century American folk, self-taught, and outsider art, Sellen, Betty-Carol, BG27
20th-century literary movements index, BE55
20th century Spanish-American novel, Foster, David William, BE902
20th century theatre, Loney, Glenn Meredith, BH102

25 T'ang poets, Fung, Sydney S. K., BE1552
—— Lai, Shu Tim, BE1552
250 years of Afro-American art, Igoe, Lynn Moody, BF24

300 best buys in college education, CB291
300 most selective colleges, CB245
3200 revues et journaux arabes de 1800 à 1965, Ahmed-Bioud, Abdelghani, AD182

40 vjet Shqiperi socialiste, CG191
4000 books for secondary school libraries, AA342

50 biografías de figuras dominicanas, Clase, Pablo, AH154
50 years of recorded jazz, Bruyninckx, Walter, BJ307
500 early juveniles, AA245
5001 nights at the movies, Kael, Pauline, BH197
550 books on Buddhism, BC460
555 książek wydanych w okresie powojennym, Dąbrowska, Wanda, AA766

60 years of best sellers, 1895–1955, AA327
60 years of recorded jazz, BJ307
60 years of the Oscar, Osborne, Robert A., BH275
6,000 words, AC92

70 years of best sellers, 1895–1965, AA327
700 reproductions d'estampes des XIXᵉ et XXᵉ siècles pour servir de complément au 'Manuel', Delteil, Loÿs, BF377
75 yngre danske skonlitre reforfattere, Bryder, Margit, BE1119

80 years of best sellers, 1895–1975, Hackett, Alice Payne, AA327

9,000 words, AC92

The A. E. Nordenskiöld collection in the Helsinki University Library, Mickwitz, Ann-Mari, CL238
A. Ortelii Catalogus cartographorum, Bagrow, Leo, CL273
A pesquisa histórica do Brasil, Rodrigues, José Honório, DB340
An A to Z of the Middle East, Gresh, Alain, DE55
The A to Z of women's health, EH81
A to zax, Evans, Barbara Jean, AJ50
•*A-V online,* CB28, CB355
A–Z of astronomy, Moore, Patrick, EC36
A–Z of opera, Hamilton, Mary, BJ247
An A–Z of sailing terms, BK121
The A–Z of women's sexuality, Kahn, Ada P., CC282

Aa, Abraham Jacobus van der. *Biographisch woordenboek der Nederlanden,* AH269
AAA guide, American Anthropological Association, CE54
The AAAS science book list, Deason, Hilary J., EA27
AAAS science book list, 1978–1986, Montenegro, Valerie J., EA27
—— O'Connell, Susan M., EA27
—— Wolff, Kathryn, EA27
AAAS science book list supplement, Storey, Jill, EA27
—— Wolff, Kathryn, EA27
AAAS science books & films, EA34
AAAS science film catalog, EA25
AACR2, AK194, AK196
AAG directory of geographers, CL55
AAGE (Organization). *Anthropology of aging,* CC59, CE3
AALL directory and handbook, CK137
The AALS directory of law teachers, CK138
AAMC curriculum directory, EH163
AAMC directory of American medical education, EH163
Aarne, Antti Amatus. *The types of the folktale,* CF45, CF88
Aaron, Titus E. *Sexual harassment in the workplace,* CC555
Åarskatalog over norsk litteratur, AA761
Åastrand, Hans. *Sohlmans Musiklexikon,* BJ126
AATA, BF198
Aav, Yrjö. *Russian dictionaries,* AC696
ABA guide to foreign law firms, CK58
Abad de Santillán, Diego. *Gran enciclopedia argentina,* DB330
Abajian, James de T. *Blacks and their contributions to the American West,* CC360
—— *Blacks in selected newspapers, censuses and other sources,* AE105
Abasq, Joseph. *Dictionnaire breton,* AC234
Abate, Frank R. *Dictionary of borrowed words,* AC186
—— *Loanwords dictionary,* AC186
—— *Mottoes,* BE94
—— *Moving and relocation sourcebook,* CL73
—— *Omni gazetteer of the United States of America,* CL109
—— *Pronouncing dictionary of proper names,* AC109
Abbasid belles-lettres, Ashtiany, Julia, BE1546
Abbaye de Saint-André-lez-Bruges. *Saint Andrew Bible missal,* BC421
Abbink, J. *Ethiopian society and history,* DD154
Abbott, Anthony. *Publishers' trade list annual index,* AA436

Abbott, David. *The biographical dictionary of scientists*, EA173
—— *The biographical dictionary of scientists : astronomers*, EC63
—— *The biographical dictionary of scientists : biologists*, EG60
—— *The biographical dictionary of scientists : chemists*, EE100
—— *The biographical dictionary of scientists : mathematicians*, EB101
—— *The biographical dictionary of scientists : physicists*, ED54
Abbott, Maude E. *Classified and annotated bibliography of Sir William Osler's publications*, EH209
Abbott, Robert Tucker. *American seashells*, EG306
Abbrev, EH134
Abbreviations, Wall, C. Edward, AC46
Abbreviations dictionary, De Sola, Ralph, AC43, AC45
Abbreviations in Soviet publications, AC687
'Abbūd, Muḥammad Fatḥī. *Dalīl al-maṣādir al-iḥṣā'iyah fī al-bilād al-'Arabīyah*, CG374
ABC Chemie, EE26
The ABC-CLIO companion to the American labor movement, Taylor, Paul F., CH651
The ABC-CLIO companion to women in the workplace, Schneider, Dorothy, CC566, CH650
ABC for book-collectors, Carter, John, AA249
ABC News-Harris survey, CJ487
ABC of stage lighting, Reid, Francis, BH76
ABC pol sci, CJ17
•*ABC POL SCI on disc*, CJ17
'Abd al-Rahmān, 'Abd al-Jabbār. *Iraq*, DE190
Abdalian, Hamo. *Historical atlas of Armenia*, DC83
Abdeljaoued, Mohamed. *Répertoire de la presse et des publications périodiques tunisiennes*, AD179
Abdulahi Hassen. *Annotated bibliography on the population of Ethiopia*, CG329
Abdullah, Omanii. *Black playwrights, 1823–1977*, BE521
Abécasis, Armand. *Encyclopédie de la mystique juive*, BC550
Abecía, Valentín. *Adiciones á la Biblioteca boliviana de Gabriel René-Moreno*, AA500
Abegg, Margaret. *Apropos patterns for embroidery, lace and woven textiles*, BG152
Abel, Edward W. *Comprehensive organometallic chemistry*, EE120
Abel, Ernest L. *Alcohol and the elderly*, CC107
—— *A dictionary of drug abuse terms and terminology*, CC126
—— *Homocide*, CK246
—— *A marijuana dictionary*, CC127
Abélès, Marion. *Dictionnaire de l'ethnologie et de l'anthropologie*, CE38
ABELL, BD90, BE588
ABEPI, AH287
Abercrombie, M. *The Penguin dictionary of biology*, EG29
Abernathy, Peter L. *English novel explication*, BE675
ABHB, AA268, AK17
•*ABI/Inform*, CH32
Abidi, Sartaj A. *Social sciences in modern India*, CA28
Abingdon Bible handbook, Blair, Edward Payson, BC186
Abingdon dictionary of living religions, BC70
Abkoude, Johannes van. *Alphabetische naamlijst van boeken*, AA748
—— *Alphabetische naamlijst van fondsartikelen*, AA748
—— *Naamregister van de bekendste en meest in gebruik zynde Nederduitsche boeken*, AA748
Abler, Thomas S. *A Canadian Indian bibliography, 1960–1970*, CC472
ABMS compendium of certified medical specialists, EH164
Abonnenc, Émile. *Bibliographie de la Guyane Française*, DB377
Aboriginal place names and their meanings, Reed, A. W., CL218

Abortion, CC245, CC247, CC253
bibliography, CC246, CC251, CC256, CC259, EH31
biography, CC258
handbooks, CC249, CC252
statistics, CC247
Abortion, CC245
—— Costa, Marie, CC249
—— Flanders, Carl N., CC249, CC252
Abortion and family planning bibliography for [...], CC246
Abortion bibliography, CC246
The abortion debate in the United States and Canada, Muldoon, Maureen, CC256
Abortion factbook, CC247
Abortion services in the United States, each state & metropolitan area, CC247
Abraham, Gerald. *Concise Oxford history of music*, BJ136, BJ197
Abraham, Louis Arnold. *Abraham and Hawtrey's parliamentary dictionary*, CJ352
Abraham, Roy Clive. *Dictionary of modern Yoruba*, AC817
—— *Dictionary of the Hausa language*, AC808
—— *English-Somali dictionary*, AC724
—— *Somali-English dictionary*, AC724
Abraham and Hawtrey's parliamentary dictionary, Abraham, Louis Arnold, CJ352
Abrahams, Roger D. *Afro-American folk culture*, CF58
Abrahamsen, Adele A. *Child language*, BD62
Abramowicz, Dina. *Yiddish literature in English translation*, BE1079
Abramowitz, Milton. *Handbook of mathematical functions with formulas, graphs, and mathematical tables*, EB76
Abrams, Alan E. *Journalist biographies master index*, AE151
Abrams, Charles. *Language of cities*, BF277, CC293
Abrams, Irwin. *The Nobel Peace Prize and the laureates*, AL164
Abrams, Leslie E. *The history and practice of Japanese printmaking*, BF358
Abrams, M. H. *A glossary of literary terms*, BE73, BE83
—— *The Norton anthology of English literature*, BE619
Abrams, William B. *The Merck manual of geriatrics*, EH191
Abramson, Glenda. *Blackwell companion to Jewish culture*, BC552, DA177
ABREES, DC38
Abreu, Alzira Alves de. *Dicionário histórico-biográfico brasileiro, 1930–1983*, AH124, DB354
Abreu, Maria Isabel. *Latin American writers*, BE891
Abridged dictionary of the Ladin (or Romansch) language, AC665
Abridged index medicus, EH65
Abridged readers' guide to periodical literature, AD256
Abriss der deutschen Literaturgeschichte in Tabellen, Göres, Jörn, BE1252
—— Schmitt, Fritz, BE1252
The ABS guide to recent publications in the social and behavioral sciences, American Behavioral Scientist, CA9
Abse, Joan. *Art galleries of Britain and Ireland*, BF98
ABSEES, DC38, DC39, DC41
[Abstract journals], CAB International, EJ19
Abstract of British historical statistics, Mitchell, Brian R., CG234, CG235
Abstract of labour statistics of the United Kingdom, CH683
Abstract of statistics, CG125
Abstracting and indexing, Rowley, Jennifer E., AK215
Abstracts and index of articles, India (Republic). Parliament. House of the People, AD339, AF245
Abstracts and indexes in science and technology, Owen, Dolores B., EA76
Abstracts for social workers, CC45
Abstracts in anthropology, CE34

Abstracts in social gerontology, CC78
Abstracts of bacteriology, EG11
Abstracts of books, reports, and articles, India (Republic). Parliament. House of the People, AD339, AF245
Abstracts of dissertations approved for the Ph.D., M.Sc., and M.Litt. degrees in the University of Cambridge during the academical year, University of Cambridge, AG36
Abstracts of dissertations for the degree of doctor of philosophy, Oxford. University. Committee for Advanced Studies, AG34
Abstracts of health care management studies, EH69
Abstracts of hospital management studies, EH69
Abstracts of photographic science and engineering literature, Rochester Institute of Technology. Graphic Arts Research Center, BF332
—— Society of Photographic Scientists and Engineers, BF332
Abstracts of popular culture, AD257, CF41
Abstracts of Soviet and East European émigré periodical literature, DC30
Abstracts of technical studies in art and archaeology, BF198
Abstracts of theses in the field of speech, BE345
Abstracts of working papers in economics, CH33, CH40
•*Abstracts of working papers in economics (AWPE)*, CH33
Abstracts on criminology and penology, CK250
Abstracts on hygiene, EH79
Abstracts on hygiene and communicable diseases, EH79, EH408
Abstracts on rural development in the tropics, CC621
Abstracts, Russian and East European series, DC38
Abu-Zayed, Ziad. *The West Bank handbook*, CJ436
The abuse of elderly people, Pritchard, Jacki, CC100
Abuse of the elderly, CC55, CC92
Aby, Stephen H. *The IQ debate*, CB8, CC361
—— *Sociology*, CC1
Abyssinia to Zimbabwe, Kirchherr, Eugene C., CL155
Academia das Sciencias de Lisboa. *Bibliografia geral portuguesa*, AA772
Academia de Ciencias de Cuba. Instituto de Geografía. *Atlas regional del Caribe*, CL319
Academia Nacional de la Historia (Argentina). *Catálogo analítico de las publicaciones de la Academia Nacional de la Historia, 1903–1986*, DB323
Academia Portuguesa da História. *Guia da bibliografia histórica portuguesa*, DC485
Academia Republicii Populare Romîne. *Dicţionarul limbii romîne*, AC660
Academia Republicii Populare Romîne. Biblioteca. *Bibliografia literaturii romîne, 1948–1960*, BE1376
Academia Republicii Socialiste România. *Dicţionarul limbii române*, AC660
Academia Republicii Socialiste România. Biblioteca. *Bibliografia românească modernă, 1831–1918*, AA781
—— *Publicaţiunile periodice româneşti (ziare, gazete, reviste)*, AD140
Academia Republicii Socialiste România. Institutul de Lingvistică Bucureşti. *Dicţionar englez-român*, AC662
Academia Română, Bucharest. *Dicţionarul limbii române*, AC656, AC660
Academic achievement (by country or region)
United States, CB140
Academic American encyclopedia, AB2, AB25
•*Academic American encyclopedia on CD-ROM*, AB25
Academic costume, CB395, CB396
Academic degrees
statistics, CB341
Academic degrees (by country or region)
United States, CB252, CB253
Academic dress and insignia of the world, Smith, Hugh, CB396
Academic etiquette *see* **Academic protocol**

Academic heraldry in America, Sheard, Kevin, CB395

Academic international, AB2

Academic libraries in the United Kingdom and the Republic of Ireland, AK140

Academic library statistics, AK96, AK173

Academic Press dictionary of science and technology, EA84, EA93

Academic protocol, CB394

Academic writer's guide to periodicals, Birkos, Alexander S., AD26

Academic year abroad, CB242

Académie des inscriptions et belles-lettres (France). *Histoire littéraire de la France,* BE1171

Académie des Sciences (France). *Index biographique de l'Académie des Sciences du 22 décembre 1666 au 1ᵉʳ octobre 1978,* AH191

Académie française. *Dictionnaire de l'Académie française,* AC328

Académie royale des sciences, des lettres et des beaux-arts de Belgique. *Biographie nationale,* AH172, AH174, AH175, AH176

Académie royale des sciences d'outre-mer. *Biographie coloniale belge,* AH173

Academies *see* **Associations, societies, and academies**

Academies of art past and present, Pevsner, Nikolaus, BF257

Academy awards, Shale, Richard, BH275

The Academy Awards index, Shale, Richard, BH275

Academy of Motion Picture Arts and Sciences. *Annual index to motion picture credits,* BH203

Academy of Motion Picture Arts and Sciences. *Who wrote the movie and what else did he write?,* BH210

Academy of Natural Sciences of Philadelphia. *The birds of North America,* EG253

Academy of the Social Sciences in Australia. *The Southwest Pacific,* DF12

Acar, Lâmia. *1928–1965 [i.e., Bin dokuz yüz yirmi sekiz, bin dokuz yüz altmışbeş] yılları arasında Türkiyede basılmış bibliyografyaların bibliyografyası,* AA68

Acatos, Sylvio. *Ceramics and glass,* BG69

Accademia della Crusca (Florence). *Vocabolario degli Accademici della Crusca,* AC523

Accademia d'Italia. *Vocabolario della lingua italiana,* AC523

Accardi, Bernard. *Recent studies in myths and literature, 1970–1990,* BE29

Accepted dental remedies, EH262

Accepted dental therapeutics, EH262, EH263

Access, AD258, EA41, EE18

ACCESS ERIC, CB99

Access guide to foundations in peace, security, and international relations, CJ50

Access (Organization). *Search for security,* CJ50

Access quarterly, EA41, EE18

ACCESS resource guide, CJ690

Access: the index to literary magazines, AD258

Accessing early English books, 1641–1700, AA679

Accessions list, Brazil and Uruguay, Library of Congress. Library of Congress Office, Rio de Janeiro, AA511

Accessions list, Eastern and Southern Africa, Library of Congress. Library of Congress Office, Nairobi, Kenya, DD85

Accessions list, Indonesia, Malaysia, Singapore and Brunei, DE98

Accessions list, Middle East, Library of Congress. Library of Congress Office, Cairo, DE46

Accessions list, South Asia, Library of Congress. Library of Congress Office, New Delhi, DE79

Accessions list, Southeast Asia, Library of Congress. Library of Congress Office, Jakarta, DE98

Accidents, EH187

ACCIS. *ACCIS guide to United Nations information sources on food and agriculture,* EJ8

ACCIS guide to United Nations information sources on food and agriculture, United Nations, EJ8

ACCIS guide to United Nations information sources on the environment, United Nations, EK69

Accountant's desk handbook, Ameiss, Albert P., CH258

Accountants' handbook, CH257

Accountants' index, CH245, CH246

Accounting
  bibliography, CH245, CH246, CH247, CH248
    current, CH250
  databases, CH246
  dictionaries, CH252, CH253, CH254
  directories, CH255
  handbooks, CH220, CH251, CH257, CH258, CH260, CH261, CH262, CH263
  periodicals, CH249

•*Accounting & tax database*, CH246

Accounting & tax index, CH245, CH246

Accounting articles, Commerce Clearing House, CH250

Accounting desk book, Plank, Tom M., CH262

Accounting handbook, Siegel, Joel G., CH263

Accreditation Council for Graduate Medical Education (U.S.). *Graduate medical education directory,* EH160

Accredited institutions of postsecondary education, programs, candidates, CB246

Achêgas a um diccionario de pseudonymos, iniciaes, abreviaturas e obras anonymas de auctores brasileiros e de estrangeiros, sobre o Brasil ou no mesmo impressas, Barros Paiva, Tancredo de, AA157

Achenbaum, W. Andrew. *Social welfare in America,* CC32

Achour, Christiane. *Dictionnaire des oeuvres algériennes en langue française,* BE1523

Achtemeier, Paul J. *Harper's Bible dictionary,* BC139

Achtert, Walter S. *MLA handbook for writers of research papers,* AG2

———— *The MLA style manual,* AA317

Acker, Ally. *Reel women,* BH279

Ackerl, Isabella. *Österreichisches Personen Lexikon,* AH166

Ackerman, Hans Christoph. *Lexicon iconographicum mythologiae classicae,* BF188, CF23

Ackerman, Robert William. *An index of the Arthurian names in Middle English,* BE732

Ackroyd, Peter R. *Bible bibliography,* BC117

———— *Cambridge history of the Bible,* BC191

ACM guide to computing literature, EB28, EK159, EK161, EK165, EK166

Acocella, Nick. *Encyclopedia of major league baseball teams,* BK54

Acock, Alan C. *The influence of the family,* CC205

ACP basic statistics, CG45

ACP : statistical yearbook, CG45

Acquired immune deficiency syndrome *see* **AIDS (disease)**

Acquisitions and collection development in libraries, AK164, AK165, AK166, AK167, AK168, AK169, AK170

Acquisitions management and collection development in libraries, Magrill, Rose Mary, AK167

ACRL directory of curriculum materials centers, CB267

ACRL university library statistics, AK95, AK96

Acronyms *see* **Abbreviations**

Acronyms & abbreviations in astronomy, space sciences, & related fields, Heck, André, EC33

Acronyms and abbreviations of computer technology and telecommunications, Tavaglione, David, EK189

Acronyms and initialisms dictionary, AC42

Acronyms and initialisms in health care administration, EH129

Acronyms dictionary, AC42

Acronyms, initialisms & abbreviations dictionary, AC42

The ACS style guide, EE95

Acta philologica scandinavica, BD130

Acta sanctorum quotquot toto orbe coluntur, BC257, BC258, BC263

Action art, Gray, John, BF21

The activist's almanac, Walls, David, AL48

Actor guide to the talkies, Dimmitt, Richard Bertrand, BH205

Actor guide to the talkies, 1965 through 1974, Aros, Andrew A., BH205

Actors, BE467, BE663, BE667, BH116, BH123, BH124
  biography, BH286, BH288, BH289
  filmography, BH205, BH207, BH211, BH213, BH214, BH277

Actors' television credits 1950–1972, BH312

Acts of the Parliament of Canada, CK193

Ad $ summary, CH576

Adalekok Szabó Károly Régi magyar köyvtaar c. munkájának I–II kötetéhez, Sztripszky, Hiador, AA714

Adam, Antoine. *Littérature française,* BE1167

Adam, Frank. *The clans, septs, and regiments of the Scottish Highlands,* AJ125

Adam, Ingrid. *Meyers Handbuch über die Literatur,* BE187

Adamczyk, Alice J. *Black dance,* BH131

Adamec, Christine A. *The encyclopedia of adoption,* CC223

Adamec, Ludwig W. *A biographical dictionary of contemporary Afghanistan,* DE107

———— *First supplement to the Who's who of Afghanistan,* AH333

———— *Historical and political gazetteer of Afghanistan,* CL158

———— *Historical and political who's who of Afghanistan,* AH332

———— *Historical dictionary of Afghanistan,* DE108

———— *Historical gazetteer of Iran,* CL165

Adamec, Vladimír. *Kto je kto na Slovensku 1991?,* AH286

Adamescu, Gheorghe. *Contribuţiune la bibliografia românească,* BE1377

Adams, A. D. *Cruden's complete concordance of the Old and New Testaments,* BC165

Adams, Arthur E. *Atlas of Russian and East European history,* DC56

Adams, Catherine F. *Nutritive value of American foods in common units,* EH302

Adams, Charles J. *The encyclopedia of religion,* BC58

———— *A reader's guide to the great religions,* BC1

Adams, Henry E. *Comprehensive handbook of psychopathology,* EH392

Adams, J. N. *A bibliography of eighteenth century legal literature,* CK4

———— *A bibliography of nineteenth century legal literature,* CK5

Adams, J. R. R. *Northern Ireland newspapers, 1737–1987,* AE61

Adams, James Truslow. *Atlas of American history,* DB70

Adams, Michael. *The Middle East,* DE60

Adams, Ramon Frederick. *Burs under the saddle,* DB162, DB168

———— *More burs under the saddle,* DB162

———— *Rampaging herd,* DB162

———— *Six guns and saddle leather,* DB162

———— *Western words,* AC148

Adams, Roberta E. *Venezuelan history,* DB399

Adams, Thomas Randolph. *The American controversy,* DB84

———— *American independence,* DB85

Adamson, Lynda G. *Reference guide to historical fiction for children and young adults,* BE256

Aday, Ron H. *Crime and the elderly,* CC56

Addiction Research Foundation. *Alcohol use and world cultures,* CC113

Addis, Patricia K. *Through a woman's I,* BE508, CC485

Addis, William E. *A Catholic dictionary,* BC396

Address, forms of *see* **Etiquette**

Address list of public library authorities, AK147

Ade Ajayi, J. F. *Historical atlas of Africa,* DD65

Adelaide, Debra. *Australian women writers,* BE845, DF21

———— *Bibliography of Australian women's literature, 1795–1990,* BE845, DF21

Adeline, Jules. *The Adeline art dictionary,* BF81

—— Lexique des termes d'art, BF81
The Adeline art dictionary, Adeline, Jules, BF81
Adelman, George. Encyclopedia of neuroscience, EH87
—— Neuroscience year, EH87
Adelman, Irving. Contemporary novel, BE206
—— Modern drama, BE219
Adelung, Johann Christoph. Glossarium mediae et infimae latinitatis, AC587
Adey, David. Companion to South African English literature, BE1533
Adiciones á la Biblioteca boliviana de Gabriel René-Moreno, Abecía, Valentín, AA500
Adiciones y continuación de "La imprenta en Manila" de d. J. T. Medina, Pérez, Angel, AA928
Adkins, Cecil. Doctoral dissertations in musicology, BJ164
Adkins, Lesley. Handbook of life in ancient Rome, DA98
—— A thesaurus of British archaeology, DC309
Adkins, R. T. Information sources in polymers and plastics, EK287
Adkins, Roy A. A thesaurus of British archaeology, DC309
Adler, Anne G. Automation in libraries, AK190
Adler, Cyrus. Jewish encyclopedia, BC546
Adler, Elhanan. Mafteaḥ le-khitve-ēt be-'Ivrit, AD340
Adler, Joe anne. Women's colleges, CB247
Adler, Johann Anton. Elsevier's dictionary of criminal science in eight languages, CK258
Adler, Leo. Wasmuths Lexikon der Baukunst, BF239
Adler, Leonore Loeb. International handbook on gender roles, CC289
Adloff, R. People's Republic of the Congo, DD48
Administering grants, contracts, and funds, Bauer, David G., AL129
Administration and development in the Arab world, Jreisat, Jamil E., CJ468
Administration parisienne à la veille de la Révolution, DC151
Administration, personnel, buildings and equipment, Kohl, David F., AK174
Administrative agencies, CJ181
Administrative agencies (by country or region)
  United States
    acronyms, CJ125
    databases, AL80
    directories, AL80, CJ136, CJ146, CJ182
    encyclopedias, CJ120
    handbooks, CJ151
Administrative law, CK182
Administrators, AH77, CH101
Admirals of the new steel navy, Bradford, James C., CJ639
Admission requirements of American medical colleges, including Canada, EH163
Admission requirements of U.S. and Canadian dental schools, American Association of Dental Schools, EH259
Admussen, Richard L. Les petites revues littéraires, 1914–1939, BE1143
Ado, Anatoliĭ Vasil'vich. Novaia istoriia, DA174
Adolescence, CB10, CD106
  bibliography, CC205
  directories, CC48
  encyclopedias, CC159, CD83
  guides, CC141
  handbooks, CC169, CD84
Adolescence (by subject)
  sex and sexual behavior, CC142, CC168
  social conditions, CC174
Adolescent education, CB10
Adolescent pregnancy and parenthood, Zollar, Ann Creighton, CC220
Adolescent reproductive behaviour, CC248
Adolescent sexuality and pregnancy, CC168
Adolphe, H. Bibliography of Mauritius, (1502–1954), DD179
Adolphus, Lalit. Historical periodicals, DA14
Adomonis, Tadas. Lithuania, DC444
Adoption, CC228, CC231
  bibliography, CC215

directories, CC230
  encyclopedias, CC223
  handbooks, CC232
Adoption, Melina, Lois Ruskai, CC215
Adoption agencies, CC231
Adoption choices, Paul, Ellen, CC230
The adoption directory, CC228
ADP Brokerage Information Services Group. Symbol guide, CH315
Adresar pisaca Jugoslavije, BE1496
Adressbuch des Österreichischen Buchhandels, AA289
Adressbuch für den deutschsprachigen Buchhandel, AA289
Adriatico, Macario. Checklist of publications of the government of the Philippine Islands Sept. 1, 1900 to Dec. 31, 1917, AF258
Adult education
  bibliography, CB352, CB353, CB354
  biography, CB363
  databases, CB355, CB357
  dictionaries, CB356
  directories, CB256, CB357, CJ47
  encyclopedias, CB70
  guides, CB350
  handbooks, CB361, CB362
Adult education (by country or region)
  United States
    directories, CB300, CB359
The adult learner's guide to alternative and external degree programs, Sullivan, Eugene J., CB359
Adult literacy, French, Joyce N., CB352
Adult literacy/illiteracy in the United States, Costa, Marie, CB360
Advaita Vedānta up to Samkara and his pupils, Potter, Karl H., BB33
Advance bibliography of contents: political science & government, CJ17
Advance locator for Capitol Hill, CJ215
Advanced manufacturing technology, CH340, EK231
Advanced weapons systems, Champion, Brian, CJ604
Advances in librarianship, AK74
•Advertiser & agency red books plus, CH572, CH573, CH574
Advertising & press annual of Africa, AD177
Advertising & press annual of Southern Africa, AD177
Advertising and public relations, CC563
  bibliography, CH547, CH565
  biography, CH575
  databases, CH548, CH572, CH573, CH574
  dictionaries, CH549, CH550, CH570, CH571
    multilingual, CH552
  directories, CH555, CH566, CH567, CH572, CH573, CH574, CH575, CH601
  guides, CH546
  handbooks, CH568, CH569, CH587
  library resources, CH547
  statistics, CH576
Advertising and public relations (by country or region)
  Europe
    directories, CH553
    statistics, CH553
  Germany
    directories, AD103
  Great Britain
    dictionaries, CH551
  Netherlands
    directories, AD132, AE65
Advertising Research Foundation. ARF guidelines handbook, CH587
Advertising slogans of America, Sharp, Harold S., CH570
Advisory list of international educational travel and exchange programs, CB89
AEB, DA121
AECT Task Force on Definition and Terminology. Educational technology, CB171
Aeronautical and space engineering
  abstract journals, EK26, EK27, EK28
  bibliography, EK23, EK24
  databases, EK26, EK27, EK28

  dictionaries, CJ615, EK29, EK30
  periodicals, EK25
  yearbooks, EK36
Aeronautical and space serial publications, Library of Congress. Science and Technology Division, EK25
Aeronautics see **Aviation**
Aerospace agencies and organizations, D'Angelo, George V., CH480
•Aerospace database, EK26, EK27, EK28
Aerospace facts and figures, CH479, EK35
Aerospace industries, CH480
Aerospace Industries Association of America. Aerospace facts and figures, CH479, EK35
Aerospace Industries Association of America, Inc. Aerospace year book, EK36
Aerospace medicine and biology, EH70
Aerospace Research Center. Economic Data Service. Aerospace facts and figures, CH479, EK35
Aerospace technology centres, EC46, EF16
Aerospace year book, EK36
Aeschlimann, Erardo. Dictionnaire des miniaturistes du Moyen Âge et de la Renaissance dans les différentes contrées de l'Europe, BF310
Aesthetics
  bibliography, BF29
  encyclopedias, BB27
AF encyclopedia of textiles, BG155
Afanas'ev, M. D. Archives in Russia, DC557
AFB directory of services for blind and visually impaired persons in the United States and Canada, CC191
Afendras, Evangelos A. Le bilinguisme chez l'enfant et l'apprentissage d'une langue seconde, BD60
—— Child bilingualism and second language learning, BD60
Affirmative action and preferential admissions in higher education, Swanson, Kathryn, CB231
Affirmative action in higher education, Swanson, Kathryn, CB231
Afghanistan, DE109, DE111, DE112
  atlases, CL350
  biography, AH332, AH333, DE107
  gazetteers, CL158
  newspapers, AE90
Afghanistan (by subject)
  history, DE108
    bibliography, DE113, DE114
Afghanistan, Jones, Schuyler, DE111
—— Witherell, Julian W., DE114
AFI guide to college courses in film and television, BH263
Afolabi, M. O. President Idi Amin Dada of Uganda, a bibliography, DD240
Afre, S. A. Ashanti region of Ghana, DD161
Africa
  abstract journals, DD45
  atlases, CL337, CL342
  bibliography, AA847, DD12, DD18, DD20, DD118
    current, AA848, DD19, DD21, DD24
  bibliography of bibliography, AA70
  biography, AH312, AH314
  book reviews, DD46
  censuses, CG38, CG312
  congresses and meetings, DD8
  current surveys, DD59, DD60, DD62
  dissertations, DD31, DD32, DD33
  encyclopedias, DD48, DD49, DD50
  filmography, BH212, DD43
  gazetteers, CL155
  government publications, AF219
  guides, DD55, DD86
  handbooks, DD55, DD63
  indexes, DD44
  libraries, AK155
  library catalogs, DD34, DD35
  library resources, DD38
    directories, DD41
  museums
    directories, AL87
  newspapers, AE4, DD26
    bibliography, AE79

periodicals, AD169, AD170, DD27
    indexes, DD22
statistics, CG38, CG45, CG306
    bibliography, CG310, CG311, CG313
statistics, historical, CG309, CG375
Africa (by subject)
    anthropology and ethnology, CE101, CE102, CE103, CE105, CE106
    archaeology and ancient history
        atlases, DD64
    art, BG12
        bibliography, BF25, BF38, BG4, BG5
    children's literature, DD14
    costume and fashion, BG90, BG114
    economic conditions
        bibliography, CH189, DD6, DD25
        periodicals, DD61
    folklore and popular culture, CF90, CF91, CF92
    foreign relations, DC599
        bibliography, DD3
        directories, DD52
    history
        atlases, DD65
        bibliography, DD1, DD4, DD5, DD9, DD10, DD11, DD13, DD17, DD23, DD35
            current, DD24
        chronologies, DD56
        directories, DD36
        dissertations, DD29, DD30
        general histories, DD57
        guides, DD86
        library catalogs, DD23, DD34
        library resources, DD36, DD37
        manuscripts and archives, DD42
    law, CK225
    music, BF38, BJ217, BJ317, BJ330
    political leaders, CJ402
    politics and government, CE103, CJ397, CJ399, CJ400, CJ402, CJ403, CJ407
        bibliography, DD16
        registers, CJ398
    religion, BC33, BC221
    social conditions
        bibliography, DD25
    urbanization, CC300
    women, CC592, DD7
Africa, DD23
—— Fenton, Thomas P., DD93
—— McIlwaine, John, DD86
Africa bibliography, DD19
Africa, Central
    bibliography, DD111, DD141
    women, CC594
Africa contemporary record, DB294, DD59
Africa, East
    bibliography, DD107, DD108, DD109, DD110
        current, DD85
    periodicals
        indexes, DD92
Africa, East (by subject)
    women, CC593
Africa index, DD44
—— United Nations. Economic Commission for Africa. Library, DD25
Africa index to continental periodical literature, DD44
Africa journal, AH312
Africa, North
    bibliography, BC501, DD67, DD68, DD72, DD73, DE24, DE39, DE41
    biography, DE66
    dissertations, DD74, DE44
    encyclopedias, DD76
    filmography, DD71, DE34
    guides, DE21
    sourcebooks, DE64
    surveys, DD77
Africa, North (by subject)
    foreign relations, DE40
    history
        atlases, DE68
        bibliography, BC500, BC501, DD66, DD69, DD70, DD73, DE40

encyclopedias, DE54
    library resources, DE50
political parties, CJ405, CJ418
politics and government, CJ419
    biography, CJ417
religion, BC501, DD73
social conditions
    bibliography, DE26
women, CC594
Africa on film and videotape, 1960–1981, Wiley, David S., DD43
Africa orientale (Éritrea, Abissinia, Somalia) e colonialismo italiano, Stella, Gian Carlo, DD109
Africa research bulletin, DD60
Africa review, CH191, DD61
Africa, South of the Sahara
    bibliography, DD78, DD79, DD81, DD82, DD83, DD87, DD88, DD89, DD93
    biography, AH310, AH316, CJ404, CJ409
    book reviews, DD47
    directories, DD93
    handbooks, DD94, DD95
    library resources, DD39
    manuscripts, DD39
    periodicals
        indexes, DD91
    statistics, DD95
Africa, South of the Sahara (by subject)
    education, CB46
    foreign relations, DD96
    history, DD82
        bibliography, DD80, DD84
        library resources, DD39
    politics and government, CJ401
        biography, AH316, CJ404, CJ406, CJ409
    religion, BC34, BC35, BC497, DD90
Africa South of the Sahara, CJ94, DD94
—— Library of Congress. African Section, DD91
Africa, Southern
    atlases, CL345
    bibliography, DD12, DD114, DD117, DD118, DD124
        current, DD85
    biography, AH311, AH313, AH315
    gazetteers, CL345
    periodicals
        indexes, DD92
Africa, Southern (by subject)
    anthropology and ethnology, CE100
    church history
        bibliography, DD115
    foreign relations
        bibliography, DD112
    history
        bibliography, DD113, DD120
    place-names, CL156
    politics and government, CJ408
    women, CC593, DD123
Africa today, AH312
Africa today : an atlas of reproducible pages, DD65
Africa, West
    atlases, CL338
    bibliography, DD97, DD98, DD101, DD103
    directories, DD40
    library resources, DD40
    periodicals, AD176, DD104
Africa, West (by subject)
    economic conditions, DD100
    history
        archives, CG307, DD102, DD105
        bibliography, DD97, DD99, DD195
        manuscripts and archives, DD106
    women, CC594
Africa who's who, AH312
Africa yearbook and who's who, AH312
African abstracts, DD136
The African-American almanac, CC390
African-American art
    current surveys, BA1, BF44
African-American athletes, BK12, BK93
African-American authors, BE545
    bibliography, BE513, BE520, BE522, BE525, BE526, BE527, BE531, BE544

biography, BE518, BE532
    women authors
        bibliography, BE524
African American biographies, Hawkins, Walter L., CC397
African-American business leaders, Ingham, John N., CH100
African-American dance, BJ86
African-American education
    directories, CB303, CB304, CB310
    universities and colleges
        directories, CB307
        handbooks, CB307
The African American encyclopedia, CC385
African American generals and flag officers, Hawkins, Walter L., CJ643
African-American literature, BE530
    bibliography, BE511, BE512, BE513, BE514, BE515, BE517, BE519, BE522, BE525, BE526, BE527, BE528, BE529, BE533, BE535, BE542, BE544
    biobibliography, BE516
    biography, BE542
        indexes, BE543
    collections, BE541
    handbooks, BE539
    indexes, BE521, BE536, BE537, BE538
    library catalogs, BE523, BE1504, BJ86
    library resources, BE526
    women authors
        bibliography, BE534
African-American literature (by subject)
    history, BE540
African-American music
    bibliography, BJ15, BJ31, BJ212
    biography, BJ217
        bibliography, BJ220
        indexes, BJ225
    current surveys, BA1, BF44
    guides, BJ33
    library catalogs, BJ86, BJ95
African-American religion, BC33, BC56, BC216, BC374
African-American studies
    bibliography, CC364
    directories, DD53
    periodicals, AD26
African American women, CC614, CC623
    bibliography, BE534, CC376
    biography, AH67
    directories, CC545
African-American women (by occupation or profession)
    television, BH294
African American women, AH55
African American writers, BE542
African Americans
    archives, BC302, CC362, CC379
    atlases, CC399
    bibliography, BC302, CC311, CC360, CC362, CC365, CC369, CC370, CC374, CC375, CC379, CC380
    bibliography of bibliography, CC371, CC378
    biography, AH43, AH55, AH59, AH64, AH67, AH73, CC390, CC395, CC396, CC397, DB102
        bibliography, CC363
    book reviews, CC316
    chronologies, CC390
    directories, CC388, CC389
    encyclopedias, CC385, CC386, CC387
    filmography, BH270
    genealogy, AJ3
    guides, CC391
    handbooks, CC390, CC391
    indexes, AH41, CC383
    library catalogs, BC302, CC362, CC379, CC380, CC381
    library resources, CC382
    manuscripts; archives, CC382
    newspapers, AE15
        indexes, AE105
    periodicals
        indexes, AD274, CC384

quotations, BE115
statistics, CC400, CG83
yearbooks, CC394
African Americans (by occupation or profession)
agriculture, EJ73
architecture, BF251
artists, BF24, BF64, DB130
athletes, BK2
authors, BE516
business, CH100
bibliography, CH393
clergy, BC256
dance, BH131
drama, BE531
film, BH165, BH270
legislators, CJ231
mass media, CC398
medicine, EA183, EH217
military leaders, CJ643
musicians, BJ212, BJ217, BJ220, BJ225, DB130
nursing, EH281
performing arts, BH23
photographers, BF357
politics, CJ231
politics and government, CJ132
publishing, AA302
science, EA183, EH217
television, BH165, BH270, BH294
theater, BE531, BH83, BH109
African Americans (by subject)
aging, CC65
alcoholism, CC123
children and youth, CC369
bibliography, CC143
handbooks, CC140
communication, BE352
economic conditions, CC373
education, CB38
film portrayals, CC334
folklore and popular culture, CF58
health, EH405
history, CC392, CC395
chronology, CC393
intelligence, CB8, CC361
language, BD103
marriage and the family, CC206
mass media, CC398
names, AJ174
nationalism, CC367
politics and government, DB102
relations with Jews, CC366
slavery, CC377
social conditions, CC373
theater, BH109
universities and colleges, CB304
African Americans in film, BH227, CC611
African and African American studies, CC316
African archaeology, Ridinger, Robert B. Marks, DD13
African art, Stanley, Janet L., BF25
African Association of Science Editors. *Directory of scholarly journals published in Africa,* AD169
African authors, Herdeck, Donald E., BE1511
African Bibliographic Center. *Dictionary of Afro-Latin American civilization,* CC387
———— *Special bibliographic series,* DD21
African book publishing record, AA293, AA847, AK62, DD20
The African book world and press, AA293, AK62
African books in print, AA848
African dress, Eicher, Joanne Bubolz, BG90
African dress II, BG90
African governmental systems in static and changing conditions, Hertefelt, Marcel d', CE103
African historical demography, Gregory, Joel W., CG310
African historical dictionaries, DD48
African history and literatures, Harvard University. Library, BE1509
African history from oral sources, DD11
African history in maps, Kwamena-Poh, Michael, DD65
African international organisations, AF20

African international relations, DeLancey, Mark W., DD3
African language literatures, Gérard, Albert S., BE1501
African language materials in the Boston University Libraries, BD215
African language materials in the collection of Boston University's African Studies Library, Van Hoosen, Andrea M., BD215
African languages
bibliography, BD213, BD214, BD217, DD10
dictionaries
bibliography, AC191
handbooks, BD217
library catalogs, BD215, BD216
surveys, BE1501
see also **names of individual languages**
African law bibliography, Vanderlinden, Jacques, CK225
African libraries, Sitzman, Glenn L., AK155
African literature
bibliography, BE544, BE1503, BE1505, BE1507, BE1508, BE1511
biobibliography, BE1512
Caribbean authors, BE1517
encyclopedias, BE1510
library catalogs, BE523, BE1504, BE1509
surveys, BE1501
women authors
bibliography, BE1502
works in English, BE1506
works in French, BE1513, BE1518
bibliographies, BE1516
history, BE1514
works in Portuguese
bibliography, BE1519
African literature in French, Blair, Dorothy S., BE1514
African literatures in the 20th century, BE1510
African music, Gray, John, BJ317
The African National Congress of South Africa, Kagan, Alfred, DD214
African nationalist leaders in Rhodesia who's who, Cary, Robert, AH327
———— Mitchell, Diana., AH327
African newspapers available on positive microfilm, AE79, DD26
African newspapers currently received by American libraries, Shayne, Mette, AE79, DD26
African newspapers held by the Center for Research Libraries, AE79
African newspapers in selected American libraries, Library of Congress. Serial Division, AE79
African newspapers in the Library of Congress, AE79
———— Library of Congress. Serial and Government Publications Division, DD26
African newspapers on microfilm, AE79
———— McGee, M.D, AE79
African oral narratives, proverbs, riddles, poetry, and song, Scheub, Harold, CF92
The African political dictionary, Phillips, Claude S., CJ403
African political facts since 1945, Cook, Chris, CJ399
African population census reports, Pinfold, John R., CG313
The African slave trade and its suppression, Hogg, Peter C., DD5
African social psychology, Armer, Michael, CE101
African statistical yearbook, CG306
African studies, DD54
directories, DD53
periodicals
guides for authors, AD26
thesauruses, DD51
African studies abstracts, DD45
African Studies Association. *CAMP catalog,* DD81
———— *Guide to federal archives relating to Africa,* DD42
The African studies companion, Zell, Hans M., DD55

African studies information resources directory, DD36
———— Gosebrink, Jean E. Meeh, DD37, DD42
African studies thesaurus, Otchere, Freda E., DD51
African theatre, East, N. B., BE1503
African theology, Young, Josiah U., BC35, DD90
African women, Bullwinkle, Davis, CC592
Africana, Pélissier, René, DD12, DD118
Africana book reviews, 1885–1945, Easterbrook, David L., DD46
Africana catalogue of the Ibadan University Library, Ibadan, Nigeria, University of Ibadan. Library, DD195
The Africana conference paper index, Melville J. Herskovits Library of African Studies, DD8
Africana nova, AA874
Africana Publishing Company. *Liberia in maps,* CL342
Africana reference works, AA847, DD20
Africana serials in microform in the Library of Congress, Mullan, Anthony Páez, DD27
Africanderisms, Pettman, Charles, AC183
Afrika, DD49
Afrika Bibliographie, DD78
Afrika-Schrifttum, DD78
Afrikaans language
bibliography, BD132
dictionaries
bilingual
Afrikaans-English, AC197, AC198, AC199
Afrikaans literature, BE1536
bibliography, BD132
L'Afrique française du nord, France. État-major de l'armée, DD69
Afro-American artists, Cederholm, T. D., BF24
Afro-American cinematic experience, Hyatt, Marshall, CC334
Afro-American demography and urban issues, Obudho, Robert A., CC373
Afro-American fiction, 1853–1976, Margolies, Edward, BE525
Afro-American folk culture, Szwed, John F., CF58
Afro-American literature and culture since World War II, Peavy, Charles D., BE528
Afro-American nationalism, Herod, Agustina, CC367
The Afro-American novel, 1965–1975, Houston, Helen Ruth, BE522
Afro-American poetry and drama, 1760–1975, BE512, BE521
Afro-American religious music, Jackson, Irene V., BJ15
The Afro-American short story, Yancy, Preston M., BE538
Afro-American slang, AC128
Afro-American sources in Virginia, Plunkett, Michael, CC382
Afro-American women writers, 1746–1933, Shockley, Ann Allen, BE519
Afro-Americans *see* **African Americans**
Afro-Braziliana, Porter, Dorothy Burnett, CC475, DB347
Afro-Spanish American author, Jackson, Richard L., BE523, BE1504
Afshār, Īraj. *Kitābhā-ye Īrān,* AA905
After Hitler Germany, 1945–1963, Kehr, Helen, DC244
———— Wiener Library, London, DC244
Agbiotech news and information, EJ19
Agboli, Tilate. *Bibliographie sur la population et le développement au Togo,* CG364, DD237
•*AGECONCD,* EJ18
Agee, V. *Federal records,* AK112
———— *Manuscript Division, Library of Congress,* AK112
•*AgeLine,* CC79, CC84
Agency catalogue, AF185
Agency list of agencies in the U.S. and other countries, CH573
Agesthialingom, S. *A bibliography of Dravidian linguistics,* BD226
Ageton, Arthur Ainsley. *The naval officer's guide,* CJ635

Aggarwal, Narindar K. *A bibliography of studies on Hindi language and linguistics,* BD199
AGI yearbook, CL78
Aging, CC57
  bibliography, CC43, CC55, CC56, CC58, CC59, CC60, CC62, CC64, CC65, CC66, CC67, CC68, CC69, CC70, CC71, CC72, CC73, CC74, CC75, CC76, CC489, CE3
    current, CC78
  databases, CC79
  dictionaries, CC82
    multilingual, CC83
  directories, CC85, CC86, CC87, CC89, CC90, CE87
  encyclopedias, CC80, CC81
  guides, CC92
  handbooks, CC93, CC94, CC95, CC96, CC97, CC98, CC100, CC103, EH191
  library resources, CC88
  statistics, CC93, CC104, CC105, CC106, CG50, CG106
  terminology, CC84
Aging (by subject)
  alcohol and drug abuse, CC107
  crime, CC56
  drug abuse, CC121
  government policy, CC74
  legal rights, CC99
  political activity, CC91, CC102
  sex and sexual behavior, CC77
  volunteer workers, CC63
  women, CC61
  see also **Old age pensions**
Aging, CC57
Aging & cultural diversity, Strange, Heather, CC75
Aging with style and savvy, Donavin, Denise Perry, CC66
Ágnes, Kenyeres. *Magyar életrajzi lexikon,* AH249
Agnew, Swanzie. *Malawi in maps,* CL342
Agout, Marthe. *Bibliographie des livres, thèses et conférences relatifs à l'industrie du pétrole,* EK303
AGP, AF261
Agramont Virreira, Miriam. *Bibliografía de la mujer boliviana, 1920–1985,* DB335
Agrawal, Suren. *Indian periodicals in print, 1973,* AD190
Agrawal, Surendra P. *International guide to accounting journals,* CI1249
Ägren, Sven. *Svensk biografisk uppslagslitteratur,* AH295
•*AGREP,* EJ74
•*AGRICOLA,* EJ10, EJ11, EJ14, EJ17, EJ18, EJ35, EJ36
Agricultural chemicals, EJ49, EJ51, EJ57
  databases, EJ46
  handbooks, EJ46, EJ56
Agricultural dictionary, EJ24
Agricultural economics and rural sociology, Olsen, Wallace C., EJ6
Agricultural engineering abstracts, EJ19
Agricultural handbooks [Index], United States. Department of Agriculture, EJ92
Agricultural index, EG10, EJ15
Agricultural information bulletins [Index], United States. Department of Agriculture, EJ92
Agricultural information resource centers, EJ38
•*AGRIcultural OnLine Access (AGRICOLA),* EJ14
Agricultural pests, EJ21
  dictionaries, EJ30, EJ33
  handbooks, EG84, EJ335, EJ50, EJ55, EJ58
Agricultural research centres, EJ39, EJ40
Agricultural research index, EJ39
Agricultural Resources & Communications, Inc. *Directory of American agriculture,* EJ41
Agricultural statistics, EJ77, EJ78
Agricultural terms, EJ35
Agriculture
  abstract journals, EA72, EF118, EJ19
  atlases, EJ75
  bibliography, EA20, EJ9, EJ69, EJ73
  biography, EJ40
  chronologies, EJ67

  databases, EJ14, EJ16, EJ18, EJ74, EJ78
  dictionaries, EJ24, EJ29, EJ32, EJ33, EJ243
    bilingual
      English-Russian, EJ27
      German-English, EJ28
      Russian-English, EJ31
    multilingual, EJ26
  directories, EJ38, EJ39, EJ40, EJ41, EJ42, EJ43, EJ44
    bibliography, EA140, EH148
  encyclopedias, EJ22, EJ23, EJ71
  guides, EJ1, EJ2, EJ3, EJ5, EJ6, EJ8
  handbooks, EE84, EJ47, EJ53, EJ54, EJ59, EJ63
  indexes, EA73, EG10, EJ15, EJ16, EJ17, EJ20, EJ95
  library catalogs, EJ9, EJ13, EJ69
  periodicals, EJ10, EJ11, EJ12
  reviews of research, EJ74
  statistics, CG81, CH151, CH433, EJ76, EJ77, EJ78, EJ80, EJ81, EJ82, EJ83, EJ84
  thesauruses, EJ35, EJ36, EJ37
Agriculture (by country or region)
  Japan, EA48
  United States
    associations, EJ42
    bibliography, CC451
    history, EJ65, EJ68
Agriculture (by subject)
  economic aspects
    indexes, CH46
  history, EJ67, EJ71, EJ73
    bibliography, EJ66, EJ72
  see also **Aquaculture**
Agriculture & veterinary sciences international who's who, EJ40
Agrindex, EJ16
•*AGRIS,* EJ10, EJ16
•*Agrisearch,* EJ74
Agrochemicals desk reference, Montgomery, John H., EJ56
The agrochemicals handbook, EJ46
Agroforestry abstracts, EJ18
Aguayo Nayle, L. Rosa. *Archivo biográfico de España, Portugal e Iberoamérica,* AH287
Aguilar, Victoria. *Repertorio bibliográfico de las relaciones entre la península Ibérica y el Norte de África, siglos XV–XVI,* DD70
Aguilar Piñal, Francisco. *Bibliografía de autores españoles del siglo XVIII,* BE1431, DC499
———— *Bibliografía de estudios sobre Carlos III y su época,* DC499
Aguiló y Fustér, Mariano. *Catálogo de obras en lengua catalana impresas desde 1474 hasta 1860,* AA799
———— *Diccionari Aguiló,* AC246
Aguolu, Christian Chukwunedu. *Ghana in the humanities and social sciences, 1900–1971,* DD162
AIIA guide to the health care field, EH153
Aharoni, Yohanan. *The Macmillan Bible atlas,* BC197
AHEA, Pundt, Helen Marie, EJ202
Aherne, Consuelo Maria. *Encyclopedic dictionary of religion,* BC60
AHFS drug information, EH353
Åhlén, Bengt. *Svenskt författarlexikon, 1900–1940,* BE1480
Ahmed, Fatima Shalaby Sid. *Southern Sudan,* DD228
Ahmed, M. Rasheed. *The modern Persian dictionary (Persian-Urdu-English),* AC317
Ahmed-Bioud, Abdelghani. *3200 revues et journaux arabes de 1800 à 1965,* AD182
Ahnert, Heinz Jörg. *Deutsches Titelbuch 2,* BE1273
Ahokas, Jaakko. *A history of Finnish literature,* BE1126
Ahrendts, Jürgen. *Bibliographie zur alteuropäischen Religionsgeschichte,* BC6
Ahrens, Christian. *Lexikon Musikinstrumente,* BJ369
Ahrensfeld, Janet. *Special libraries,* AK181
The AI directory, EK198
Aide-mémoire de l'amateur et du professional, Monod, Lucien, BF382

AIDS (disease), CC550, CC570
  bibliography, EH20, EH21, EH29, EH71
  databases, EH72
  directories, EH20
  handbooks, EH170
  indexes, EH71
•*AIDS,* AF59
AIDS and women, Watstein, Sarah, EH29
AIDS bibliography, EH22, EH71
———— National Library of Medicine (U.S.), EH72
AIDS information resource directory, EH21
AIDS information sourcebook, EH170
Aids to geographical research, Platt, Elizabeth T., CL12
———— Wright, John Kirtland, CL4, CL12
•*AIDSLINE,* EH71, EH72
AIIM buying guide, AK247
Aikalaiskirja, AH189
Aikman, Lorna. *Foundation fundamentals,* AL137
Aimone, Alan Conrad. *A user's guide to the official records of the American Civil War,* DB106
Aimone, Barbara A. *A user's guide to the official records of the American Civil War,* DB106
Ainsworth, Geoffrey Clough. *Dictionary of the fungi,* EG184
———— *The fungi,* EG185
AIP 50th anniversary physics vade mecum, ED48
AIP style manual, American Institute of Physics, ED51
Air almanac, EC78
Air conditioning, EK224, EK225
The Air Force officer's guide, CJ627
Air forces, CJ579, CJ593, CJ649
The air officer's guide, CJ627
Air pollution
  abstract journals, EK85
  handbooks, EK78, EK86
Air pollution, EK78
Air pollution abstracts, EK85
Air Pollution Technical Information Center. *Air pollution abstracts,* EK85
Air transportation, Janiak, Jane M., CH444
Air University. Aerospace Studies Institute. *The United States Air Force dictionary,* CJ615
Air University Library index to military periodicals, CJ564
Air University periodical index, CJ564
Air wars and aircraft, Flintham, Victor, CJ593
The aircraft yearbook, EK36
The airline bibliography, Smith, Myron J., CH476
Airline industry, Leary, William M., CH383
Airline safety, Miletich, John J., CH475
Airlines
  bibliography, CH475, CH476
  statistics, CH473, CH477
Airplanes
  military, CJ577
  yearbooks, EK37
Airport noise pollution, King, Richard L., EK116
Airports, EK116, EK117
Aissing, Alena. *Russian dictionaries,* AC697
Aitchison, Jean. *Thesaurus construction,* AK218
Aitken, William Russell. *Scottish literature in English and Scots,* BE808
AIVF guide to international film and video festivals, BH265
A.J. Lohwater's Russian-English dictionary of the mathematical sciences, Lohwater, A. J., EB53
Akadémiai Kiadó. *Terminorum musicae index septem lingus redactus,* BJ159
Akadémiai kislexikon, AB58
Akademie der Wissenschaft der Berlin. Zentralinstitut für Sprachwissenschaft. *Wörterbuch der deutschen Gegenwartssprache,* AC412
Akademie der Wissenschaften der DDR. *Bibliographie bevölkerungswissenschaftlicher Literatur, 1945–1982,* CG227
———— *Jahresberichte für deutsche Geschichte,* DC218

Akademie der Wissenschaften der DDR.
Zentralinstitut für Sprachwissenschaft.
Etymologisches Wörterbuch des Deutschen,
AC427
Akademie der Wissenschaften in Göttingen.
Bibliographie der Runenkunde, BE1082
Akademie der Wissenschaften und der Literatur
(Germany). *Altfranzösisches Wörterbuch,* AC383
—— *Russisches geographisches Namenbuch,*
CL152
Akademie der Wissenschaften und der Literatur
(Germany). Kommission für Geschichte des
Altertums. *Bibliographie zur antiken Sklaverei,*
DA68
Akademie der Wissenschaften und der Literatur zu
Mainz. Kommission für Musikwissenschaft.
Handwörterbuch der musikalischen Terminologie,
BJ148
Akademie der Wissenschaften zu Göttingen. *Index
deutschsprachiger Zeitschriften, 1750–1815,*
AD316
Akademie für Raumforschung und Landesplanung
(Germany). *Handwörterbuch der Raumforschung
und Raumordnung,* BF276
Akademiia nauk SSSR. *Bibliographia studiorum
uralicorum, 1917–1987,* DC602
—— *Bibliograficheskiĭ ukazatel' literatury po
russkomu iāzykoznaniiu s 1825 po 1880 god,*
BD185
—— *Bibliografiia Türtsii, 1713–1917,* DC532
—— *Fiziko-geograficheskii atlas mira,* CL275
—— *Istoriki-slavisty SSSR,* DC54
—— *Nauchnye s'ezdy, konferentsii i
soveshchaniia v SSSR,* EA199
—— *Russkiĭ fol'klor,* CF83
—— *A scholars' guide to humanities and social
sciences in the Soviet successor states,* AL59,
DC593
—— *Social sciences in the USSR,* CA16
—— *Sovetskaia istoricheskaia entsiklopediia,*
DC569
Akademiia Nauk SSSR. Biblioteka. *Bibliografiia
izdaniĭ Akademii nauk SSSR,* AL55
—— *Bibliografiia trudov Instituta etnografiĭ im.
N. N. Miklukho-Maklaia, 1900–1962,* CE5
—— *Directory of libraries and information
centers of the academies of sciences of socialist
countries,* AK117
—— *Lingvisticheskie atlasy,* BD21
—— *Opisanie izdaniĭ, napechatannykh pri Petre
Pervom,* AA789
—— *Sovetskiĭ roman, ego teoriia i istoriia,*
BE1383
Akademiia nauk SSSR. Fundamental'naia biblioteka
obshchestvennykh nauk. *Istoriia SSSR,* DC548
—— *Sovetskoe literaturovedenie i kritika,* BE1384
—— *Sovetskoe slavianovedenie,* DC42
Akademiia Nauk SSSR. Institut Arkheologii.
Sovetskaia arkheologicheskaia literatura, DA71
Akademiia Nauk SSSR. Institut IAzykoznaniia.
Slovar' russkogo iazyka, AC666, AC674
Akademiia Nauk SSSR. Institut istori estestvoznaniia
tekhniki. *Russkaia tekhnicheskaia periodika
1800–1916,* EA52
Akademiia nauk SSSR. Institut istorii SSSR.
*Bibliografiia trudov po otechestvennomu
istochnikovedeniiu i spetsial'nym istoricheskim
distsiplinam izdannykh v XVIII v,* DC573
—— *Dvizhenie dekabristov,* DC577
Akademiia Nauk SSSR. Institut Russkogo Iazyka.
Slavianskoe iazykoznanie, BD183
—— *Slovar' sinonimov russkogo iazyka,* AC693
—— *Slovar' sovremennogo russkogo
literaturnogo iazyka,* AC667
—— *Slovari, izdannye v SSSR,* AC698
Akademiia nauk SSSR. Institut russkoi literatury.
Bibliografiia russkogo letopisaniia, DC576
—— *Istoriia russkoĭ literatury,* BE1417
—— *Istoriia russkoĭ literatury XIX veka,* BE1388
Akademiia Nauk SSSR. Institut Slavianovedeniia i
Balkanistiki. *Slavianovedenie v dorevoliutsionnoi
Rossii,* DC55

Akademiia Nauk URSR, Kiev. Biblioteka. *Knigi
grazhdanskoi pechati XVIII veka,* AA788
—— *Knigi pervoi chetverti XIX veka,* AA788,
AA842
Akademiia Nauk URSR, Kiev. Instytut
movoznavstva. *Ukrainsko-russkii slovar',* AC795
*Akademiska avhandlingar vid Sveriges universitet
och högskolor läsåren 1890/91–1909/10,* Nelson,
Axel Herman, AG42
*Akademiska avhandlingar vid Sveriges universitet
och högskolor läsåren 1910/11–1939/40,* Tuneld,
John, AG42
Akaishi, Tadashi. *Bibliography of New Testament
literature, 1900–1950,* BC118
Akdikmen, Resuhi. *Langenscheidt's standard
Turkish dictionary,* AC789
Akhmanovoĭ, O. S. *Russian-English dictionary,*
AC681
Akhromeev, S. F. *Sovetskaia voennaia
entsiklopediia,* CJ659
Akihiro, Satake. *Iwanami kogo jiten,* AC547
Akimov, V. M. *Russkie sovetskie pisateli-prozaiki,*
BE1393
Akimova, E. A. *Istoriia dorevoliutsionnoĭ Rossii v
dnevnikakh i vospominaniiakh,* DC579
Akiner, Shirin. *Islamic peoples of the Soviet Union,*
CC346
Akinyoto, Adetunji. *Who's who in science and
technology in Nigeria,* AH323, DD196
Akkadian language
  dictionaries
    bilingual
      Akkadian-English, AC200
      Akkadian-German, AC201, AC203
      Sumerian-German, AC202
Akkadisches Handwörterbuch, Soden, Wolfram von,
AC203
AKL, BF135
Akron-Summit County Public Library. *Science fair
project index, 1960–1972,* EA31
Aksenov, A. I. *Bibliografiia trudov po
otechestvennomu istochnikovedeniiu i spetsial'nym
istoricheskim distsiplinam izdannykh v XVIII v,*
DC573
al-Fihris al-musannaf li-majmū'at al-Sūdān,
Khartoum (Sudan). Jāmi'at al-Khartūm. al-
Maktabah, DD227
ALA filing rules, American Library Association.
Filing Committee, AK210
The ALA glossary of library and information science,
AK40
A.L.A. glossary of library terms, American Library
Association. Committee on Library Terminology,
AK40
—— Thompson, Elizabeth H., AK40
*ALA handbook of organization and membership
directory,* American Library Association, AK56
A.L.A. index, AD261, BE239
ALA-LC romanization tables, BD10
A.L.A. portrait index, BF65
ALA rules for filing catalog cards, AK210
ALA survey of librarian salaries, AK171
*ALA world encyclopedia of library and information
services,* AK39
*The ALA yearbook of library and information
services,* AK75
Alabama. [Laws, etc.]. *Code of Alabama, 1975,*
CK179
Alaev, É. B. *Geograficheskiĭ entsiklopedicheskiĭ
slovar',* CL88
Alain, Jean-Marc. *Thésaurus multilingue
international en administration publique,* CJ479
Alali, A. Odasuo. *Mass media sex and adolescent
values,* CC142
Alan Guttmacher Institute. *Abortion factbook,*
CC247
Alanne, Vieno Severi. *Suomalais-englantilainen
suursanakirja,* AC321
Alaska
  bibliography, DG3, DG5
Alaska. [Laws, etc.]. *Alaska statutes, 1962,* CK179
The Alaska Eskimos, Hippler, Arthur E., CC414
Alaska statutes, 1962, Alaska. [Laws, etc.], CK179

Alaska trees and common shrubs, Little, Elbert
Luther, EJ191
—— Viereck, Leslie A., EJ191
Alawar, Mohamed A. *A concise bibliography of
Northern Chad and Fezzan in Southern Libya,*
DD141
Alba C, Manuel María. *Cronología de los
gobernantes de Panamá, 1510–1967,* DB317
Albania, DC80
  bibliography, AA571, AA572
  gazetteers, CL129
  government publications, AF165
  periodicals
    indexes, AD301
  registers, CJ325
  statistics, CG191, CG192
Albania (by subject)
  archaeology and ancient history, DC81
  history
    bibliography, DC78, DC79
Albania. Drejtoria e Statistikës. *Vjetari statistikor i
Shqipërisë,* CG192
Albania, Bland, William B., DC78
Albanian-English and English-Albanian dictionary,
Drizari, Nelo, AC205
Albanian-English dictionary, Kici, Gasper, AC207
Albanian language
  dictionaries
    bilingual
      Albanian-English, AC205, AC207, AC208
      English-Albanian, AC206
Albanian literature, BE1093, BE1094
Albanie, une bibliographie historique, Daniel, Odile,
DC79
Albanien, Hetzer, Armin, DC80
Albérès, R. M. *Dictionnaire de littérature
contemporaine,* BE1150
Albert, E. *Biographisches Lexikon der
hervorragenden Ärzte aller Zeiten und Völker,*
EH222
Albert, Lorraine. *Guide bibliographique du
traducteur, rédacteur et terminologue,* BD88
Albert, Walter. *Detective and mystery fiction,* BE265
Albinski, Nan Bowman. *Directory of resources for
Australian studies in North America,* DF30
Albizúrez Palma, Francisco. *Diccionario de autores
guatemaltecos,* BE905
—— *Historia de la literatura guatemalteca,*
BE905
Alborg, Juan Luis. *Historia de la literatura española,*
BE1454
Albrecht, Günter. *Deutsches Schriftsteller Lexikon,*
BE1061
—— *Internationale Bibliographie zur Geschichte
der deutschen Literatur,* BE1213
—— *Lexikon deutschsprachiger Schriftsteller,*
BE1061
—— *Schriftsteller der DDR,* BE1061
Albrecht, Miguel A. *Databases & on-line data in
astronomy,* EC1
Albrecht, Otto Edwin. *A census of autograph music
manuscripts of European composers in American
libraries,* BJ51
Album musical, Kinsky, Georg, BJ199
Alcalay, Reuben. *Milon angli-'ivri shalem,* AC473
Alcaraz Varo, Enrique. *Diccionario de términos
judídicos,* CK55
Alchemy, Pritchard, Alan, EE14
Alcina Franch, José. *Bibliografía básica de
arqueología americana,* DB253
Alcohol and the elderly, Barnes, Grace M., CC107
Alcohol and the family, Barnes, Grace M., CC108
Alcohol and youth, Barnes, Grace M., CC109
The alcohol/drug abuse dictionary and encyclopedia,
Fay, John, CC128
Alcohol use and alcoholism, Page, Penny Booth,
CC119
Alcohol use and world cultures, Heath, Dwight B.,
CC113
Alcoholism and drug abuse, CC136
  bibliography, CC107, CC108, CC109, CC110,
  CC111, CC112, CC113, CC114, CC116, CC118,
  CC119, CC120, CC122, CC123

biography, CC138
dictionaries, CC128, CC129
directories, CC130, CC131, CC133, EH411
encyclopedias, CC125
handbooks, CC135
**treatment
  directories,** CC132
Alcover Sureda, Antonio Maria. *Diccionari català-valencià-balear,* AC247
•*ALD,* AK122
Aldcroft, Derek Howard. *Atlas of the world economy,* CH148
—— *Bibliography of European economic and social history,* DC1, DC272
Alden, John Eliot. *European Americana,* AA404
Alder, Daryl. *Sport on film and video,* BK36
Alderfer, Harold. *Bibliography of African government, 1950–66,* CJ397
Alderson, Anthony Dolphin. *The concise Oxford Turkish dictionary,* AC790
—— *The Oxford Turkish dictionary,* AC791
Alderson, Michael Rowland. *International mortality statistics,* CG46
Aldis, Harry Gidney. *List of books printed in Scotland before 1700,* AA678, AA695
Aldrich Chemical Company. *The Aldrich library of FT-IR spectra,* EE140
The Aldrich library of ^{13}C and ^{1}H FT NMR spectra, EE113
Aldrich library of FT-IR spectra, Pouchert, Charles J., ED43, EE140
Aldrich library of infrared spectra, EE140, EE141
Aldrich library of NMR spectra, EE113, ED43, EE142
Aleksakhina, I. V. *Russkie sovetskie pisateli—poêty,* BE1402
Aleksandrova, Zinaida Evgen'evna. *Slovar' sinonimov russkogo iazyka,* AC692
Aleksandrynas, Biržiška, Vaclovas, AH267
Alekseev, Dmitriĭ Ivanovich. *Slovar' sokrashcheniĭ russkogo iazyka,* AC685
Alekseev, M. N. *Anglo-russkiĭ geologicheskiĭ slovar',* EF89
Alekseev, P. M. *Statistika rechi, 1957–1985,* BD64
Alessio, Giovanni. *Dizionario etimologico italiano,* AC536
Aleut bibliography, Jones, Dorothy Miriam, CC414, CC418
  Wood, John R., CC414
Aleuts, CC418
Alexander, Ernest R. *Urban planning,* BF268
Alexander, Fran. *Multilingual dictionary of publishing, printing and bookselling,* AA275
Alexander, Franz. *The history of psychiatry,* EH396
Alexander, Gerard L. *Guide to atlases,* CL224
—— *Nicknames and sobriquets of U.S. cities, states and counties,* CL173, CL179
Alexander, Harriet Semmes. *American and British poetry,* BE488, BE693, BE710
Alexander, Michael. *St. Martin's anthologies of English literature,* BE618
Alexander, Miriam. *A bibliography of Israel,* DE191
Alexander, Robert Jackson. *Biographical dictionary of Latin American and Caribbean political leaders,* AH110, CJ306
Alexander, Yonah. *A bibliography of Israel,* DE191
—— *Terrorism,* CJ557
Alexander-Roberts, Colleen. *The essential adoption handbook,* CC232
Alexandrescu, Sorin. *Bibliografia literaturii romîne, 1948–1960,* BE1376
Alfavitnyi predmetno-imennoi ukazatel', AB88
Alfavitnyĭ sluzhebnyĭ katalog russkikh dorevoliutsionnykh gazet, 1703–1916, Gosudarstvennaia publichnaia biblioteka imeni M.E. Saltykova-Shchedrina. Gazetnyĭ otdel', AE69
Alfavitnyi ukazatel' imen, Morozov, P.O, AA790
Alford, Mark Hugh Tankerville. *Russian-English scientific and technical dictionary,* EA124
Alford, V. L. *Russian-English scientific and technical dictionary,* EA124
Algarin, Joanne P. *Japanese folk literature,* CF93

Algemene belgische persbond. *Annuaire officiel de la presse belge,* AD82
Algemene muziek encyclopedie, BJ127
Algeria
bibliography, AA849, BC501, DD18, DD67, DD73
biography, AH317, DD127
current surveys, DD62
encyclopedias, DD48
statistics, CG314
Algeria (by subject)
foreign relations, DD125
**history
  bibliography,** DD69, DD125, DD126
Algeria, Heggoy, A., DD48
—— Lawless, Richard I., DD18
—— Nelson, Harold D., DD62
Algerian literature, BE1515, BE1522, BE1523
Algerien-Bibliographie, Ruhe, Ernstpeter, DD126
Algulin, Ingemar. *History of Swedish literature,* BE1482
—— *Litteraturens historia i Sverige,* BE1482
Ali, Ahmed. *al-Qur'ān,* BC206
Alī, Kamāl Muḥammad. *Ph.D. Saudi dissertation abstracts,* AG57
Ali, Shaukat. *A comprehensive bibliography,* CJ443, DE241
Ali, Sheikh Rustum. *The peace and nuclear war dictionary,* CJ682, CJ683
—— *The presidential-congressional political dictionary,* CJ115
—— *The state and local government political dictionary,* CJ269
ALIAS, Australia's library, information, and archives services, AK161
Alibert, Louis. *Dictionnaire occitan-français d'après les parlers languedociens,* AC654
Alier Aixalà, Roger. *Diccionario de la zarzuela,* BJ260
Aligarh Muslim University. Dept. of History. Centre of Advanced Study. *An atlas of the Mughal Empire,* DE172
Aliko, Hysni. *English-Albanian dictionary,* AC207
ALISE Library and Information Science Education Statistics Committee. *Library and information science education statistical report,* AK68
Alisky, Marvin. *The foreign press,* AE141
Alison, Jennifer. *Directory of special collections in Australiana,* DF31
Alkala'i, Re'uven. *Milon angli-'ivri shalem,* AC473
Alkaloids, EE123, EH334
Alker, H. *Verzeichnis der an der Universität Wien approbierten Dissertationen,* AG23
Alker, Lisl. *Verzeichnis der an der Universität Wien approbierten Dissertationen,* AG23
Alkin, Marvin C. *Encyclopedia of educational research,* CB69
Alkire, Leland G. *Periodical title abbreviations,* AD23
—— *The writer's advisor,* BE11
All about old buildings, Maddex, Diane, BF265
All-American folk arts and crafts, Ketchum, William C., BG46
All-bank statistics, United States, 1896–1955, Board of Governors of the Federal Reserve System, CH292
All music guide, BJ374
All the monies of the world, Pick, Franz, BG182, CH286
—— Sédillot, René, BG182
All the world's aircraft, EK37
All the world's airships, EK37
All the world's fighting ships, CJ592
Allaby, Ailsa. *The concise Oxford dictionary of earth sciences,* EF14
Allaby, Michael. *The concise Oxford dictionary of botany,* EG124
—— *The concise Oxford dictionary of earth sciences,* EF14
—— *The concise Oxford dictionary of zoology,* EG227
—— *Dictionary of the environment,* EK72

—— *The Oxford dictionary of natural history,* EG78
Allaire, Jean Baptiste Arthur. *Dictionnaire biographique du clergé canadien-français,* AH91
Allan, Barbara. *Guide to information sources in alternative therapy,* EH1
—— *Medical information,* EH8
Allan, C. Wilfrid. *Collection of Chinese proverbs,* BE160
Allan, Elkan. *A guide to world cinema,* BH195
Allan, Graham A. *Handbook for research students in the social sciences,* CA2
Alland, Alexander. *Handbook of social and cultural anthropology,* CE58
Allard, Denise M. *Organizations master index,* AL20
Allardice, R. W. *A simplified dictionary of modern Samoan,* AC700
Allcock, John B. *Handbook of reconstruction in Eastern Europe and the Soviet Union,* CJ391
—— *New political parties of Eastern Europe and the Soviet Union,* CJ317
Allegri, Theodore H. *Handling and management of hazardous materials and wastes,* EK79
Allen, Anne. *Search for security,* AL121, CJ50
Allen, Charles. *The little magazine,* AD35
Allen, Charles Geoffry. *A manual of European languages for librarians,* AK46, AK50, BD11, BD17
Allen, Christopher. *The Peoples Republic of Benin,* DD129
Allen, Clabon Walter. *Astrophysical quantities,* EC48
Allen, Daniel. *Jazz,* BJ383
Allen, Frank H. *Molecular structures and dimensions,* EE139
Allen, G. G. *Guide to the availability of theses II,* AK224
Allen, Harold Byron. *Linguistics and English linguistics,* BD91
Allen, James Paul. *We the people,* CC358, DB74
Allen, Jelisaveta S. *Author index of Byzantine studies,* BF9, DA163
—— *Literature in various Byzantine disciplines, 1892–1977,* DA163
—— *Literature on Byzantine art, 1892–1967,* BF9, DA163
Allen, Louis. *Political scandals and causes célèbres since 1945,* CJ60
Allen, Peter S. *Archaeology on film,* DA62
Allen, R. E. *The concise Oxford dictionary of current English,* AC38
—— *The Oxford encyclopedic English dictionary,* AC40
Allen, Rebecca. *Southwest Native American arts and material culture,* BG9, CC422
Allen, Richard F. *Spanish American theatre,* BE897
—— *Teatro hispanoamericano,* BE897
Allen, Roger. *Modern Arabic literature,* BE1548
Allen, Sallie T. *The directory of black nursing faculty,* EH281
Allen, Thomas B. *World War II,* DA207
Allen, Walter Rechard. *Black American families, 1965–1984,* CC206
Allen, William Sidney. *Vox Graeca,* AC452
—— *Vox latina,* AC452, AC594
Allen County Public Library. Genealogy Dept. *Periodical source index,* AJ45
Allenbach, J. *Biblia patristica,* BC299
The Allende years, Williams, Lee H., DB360
Alley, Brian. *Biographical sources,* AH4
Alley, Robert S. *TV genres,* BH293
Allgayer, Wilhelm. *Dramenlexikon,* BE1261
Allgemeine Bücherkunde zur neueren deutschen Literaturgeschichte, Arnold, Robert Franz, BE1214
Allgemeine deutsche Biographie, AH202, AH210
Allgemeine Encyclopädie der Wissenschaften und Künste, AB47
Allgemeine Geschichtforschende Gesellschaft der Schweiz. *Bibliographie der Schweizergeschichte,* AH299, DC528

—— *Repertorium über die in Zeit- und Sammelschriften der Jahre 1812–1890 enthaltenen Aufsätze und Mitteilungen schweizergeschichtlichen Inhaltes,* AH300, DC523

Allgemeiner Bildniskatalog, Singer, Hans Wolfgang, BF68

Allgemeines Bücher-Lexikon, Heinsius, Wilhelm, AA644, AA646

Allgemeines europäisches Bücher-Lexicon, Georgi, Theophilus, AA92

Allgemeines Gelehrten-Lexikon, Jöcher, Christian Gottlieb, AH28

Allgemeines Künstlerlexikon, BF135

Allgemeines Lexikon der bildenden Künstler, Becker, Felix, BF135, BF147, BF149

—— Thieme, Ulrich, BF135, BF147, BF148, BF149

Allgemeines Lexikon der bildenden Künstler des XX. Jahrhunderts, Vollmer, Hans, BF135, BF148, BF149

Allibone, Samuel Austin. *A critical dictionary of English literature and British and American authors, living and deceased,* BE581, BE625

Allied health education directory, EH152

Allied medical education directory, EH152

Allin, Craig W. *International handbook of national parks and nature reserves,* BK125

Allis, Jeannette B. *West Indian literature,* BE968

Allison, Alexander W. *Norton anthology of poetry,* BE720

Allison, Antony Francis. *Catalogue of Catholic books in English printed abroad or secretly in England, 1558–1640,* BC388

—— *The contemporary printed literature of the English Counter-Reformation between 1558 and 1640,* BC388

—— *English translations from the Spanish and Portuguese to the year 1700,* BE1448

—— *Titles of English books (and of foreign books printed in England),* AA665

Allison, Brent. *Guide to U.S. map resources,* CL256

Alloway, David N. *Medical education in the United States,* EH13

Alloys
handbooks, EK280, EK282

Alloys index, EK260

Allusions, AC65, AC99, BE74, BE81, BE181
bibliography, BE16
dictionaries, BE86, BE716

Allusions—cultural, literary, biblical, and historical, AC65, BE74

Allworth, Edward. *Soviet Asia, bibliographies,* CC308

Alman, Miriam. *A guide to manuscripts relating to America in Great Britain and Ireland,* DB32

—— *Periodicals from Africa,* AD238, DD28

The almanac of American history, DB56

Almanac of American politics, CJ210, CJ361

Almanac of American presidents, CJ184

Almanac of American women in the 20th century, Clark, Judith Freeman, CC573

Almanac of British politics, Waller, Robert, CJ349, CJ361

Almanac of business and industrial financial ratios, CH418

The almanac of Canadian politics, CJ293

Almanac of China's foreign economic relations and trade, CH199

Almanac of federal PACs, CJ147

Almanac of higher education, CB329, CB336

Almanac of modern terrorism, Shafritz, Jay M., CJ555

Almanac of seapower, Navy League of the United States, CJ649

Almanac of the 50 states, Kane, Joseph Nathan, CG104

Almanac of the federal judiciary, CK139

The almanac of the unelected, CJ211

The almanac of transatlantic politics, 1991–92, Cossolotto, Matthew, CJ87

Almanach de Gotha, AJ75

Almanach des muses, BE1195

An almanack for the year of our Lord, AB109

Almanacs
bibliography, AB103, EC10

Almanacs of the United States, Drake, Milton, AB103, EC10

Almarcha Barbado, María Amparo. *Estadísticas básicas de España, 1900–1970,* CG281

Almindeligt Forfatter-Lexicon for kongeriget Danmark med tilhørende bilande, fra 1814 til 1840, Erslew, Thomas Hansen, BE1087, BE1117

Alonso Pedraz, Martin. *Enciclopedia del idioma,* AC726

Alphabetical arrangement of main entries from the shelf list, Union Theological Seminary (New York, N.Y.). Library, BC40

An alphabetical subject index and index encyclopaedia to periodical articles on religion, 1890–1899, Richardson, Ernest Cushing, BC47

Alphabetische naamlijst van boeken, Abkoude, Johannes van, AA748

—— Brinkman, Carel Leonhard, AA748, AA749

Alphabetische naamlijst van fondsartikelen, Abkoude, Johannes van, AA748

Alphabetischer Katalog, Institut für Zeitgeschichte, DA169

Alphabetischer Katalog 1501–1840, Bayerische Staatsbibliothek, AA117

Alphabets, AK46, AK50, BD11, BD12, BD14, BD17, BD18

Alred, Gerald J. *Business and technical writing,* CH428

ALS guide to Australian writers, 1963–90, Duwell, Martin, BE847

—— Hergenhan, Laurie, BE847

Alsop, Rachel. *German reunification,* CJ332

Alston, R. C. *A bibliography of the English language from the invention of printing to the year 1800,* BD97

—— *The British Library,* AK101

—— *A checklist of women writers, 1801–1900,* BE750

Alston, Sandra. *A bibliography of Canadiana,* DB188

Alston, Y. R. *Biosciences,* EK42

Alt-celtischer Sprachschatz, Holder, Alfred, AC252

Altamar, A. Curcio. *Evolución de la novela en Colombia,* BE948

Altaner, Berthold. *Patrologie,* BC300

Altbach, Philip G. *American students,* CB217

—— *International higher education,* CB238

—— *Student political activism,* CB326

—— *Student politics and higher education in the United States,* CB217

Alter, Robert. *The literary guide to the Bible,* BC176

Alteri, Charles F. *Modern poetry,* BE490

Alternative America, Gardner, Richard, AL44

An alternative directory of nongovernmental organizations in South Asia, AL15

The alternative guide to college degrees & non-traditional higher education, CB253

The alternative health guide, Inglis, Brian, EH186

Alternative Ireland directory, AL67

Alternative lifestyles, Selth, Jefferson P., CC2

Alternative medicine, EH186
bibliography, EH1

Alternative medicine, West, Ruth, EH30

Alternative press
directories, AL46
bibliography, AA280
indexes, AD259, AD279
union lists, AD221
see also **Underground press**

Alternative press index, AD221, AD259, AD279, CJ516

Alternative publications, AA280

Alternative service book of 1980, BC337

—— Church of England, BC335

Alternatives in classical logic, BB36

Alternatives in print, AA280

Altfranzösisches Wörterbuch, Tobler, Adolf, AC383

Althaus, Hans Peter. *Lexikon der Germanistischen Linguistik,* BD124

Althochdeutsches Wörterbuch, AC399

Altholz, Josef Lewis. *Victorian England, 1837–1901,* DC303, DC325

Altick, Richard Daniel. *The art of literary research,* BE1

—— *Guide to doctoral dissertations in Victorian literature, 1886–1958,* BE751

Altman, Edward I. *Handbook of financial markets and institutions,* CH234

Altman, Norman H. *CRC handbook of laboratory animal sciences,* EG235

Altman, Philip L. *Biology data book,* EG51

—— *Cell biology,* EG52

—— *Environmental biology,* EG50

—— *Handbook of circulation,* EG53

—— *Handbook of respiration,* EG53

—— *Respiration and circulation,* EG53

Altman, Roberta. *The cancer dictionary,* EH108

Altnordisches etymologisches Wörterbuch, Vries, Jan de, AC511

Altoma, Salih J. *Modern Arabic literature,* BE1545

Altsächsisches Wörterbuch, Holthausen, Ferdinand, AC404

Altschul, Michael. *Anglo-Norman England, 1066–1154,* DC303, DC307, DC308, DC319, DC320, DC331

Altshuler, Mordechai. *Russian publications on Jews and Judaism in the Soviet Union, 1917–1967,* BC535

Aluri, Rao. *A guide to U.S. government scientific and technical resources,* EA1

Alvar Ezquerra, A. *Bibliografía de los estudios clasicos en España,* DA95

Alvarez-Altman, Grace. *Spanish surnames in the Southwestern United States,* AJ187

Alvarez García, Teresa. *Collins Spanish-English, English-Spanish dictionary,* AC731

Alvarez Noguera, José Rogelio. *Enciclopedia de México,* DB244

Alves, Henrique L. *Bibliografía afro-brasileira,* CC475, DB347

Alvey, Christine E. *Conversion tables,* AK204

The Alyson almanac, CC287

Alzamora C., Lucia. *Ecuador, aspectos socio-económicos,* DB370

Alzheimer's disease, CC58

A.M. Best Company. *Best's flitcraft compend,* CH517

—— *Best's insurance reports,* CH518

—— *Key rating guide,* CH511

AMA drug evaluations, EH337

AMA handbook of poisonous and injurious plants, Lampe, Kenneth F., EG152

AMA management handbook, CH620

AMA stylebook, EH193

Aman, Mohammed M. *Arab periodicals and serials,* AD183

Amaniel, C. de. *Materiales de investigación,* AD329

Amann, Emile. *Dictionnaire de théologie catholique,* BC398

Amano, Keitaro. *Nihon shoshi no shoshi,* AA81

Amar Kaur Jasbir Singh. *Guide to source materials in the India Office Library and Records for the history of Tibet, Sikkim and Bhutan, 1765–1950,* DE12

Amateur astronomer's glossary, Moore, Patrick, EC36

Amati, Amato. *Dizionario corografico dell' Italia,* CL144

Amazon River region, DB321, DB322

Amazonas, Lee. *The film catalog,* BH191

Amazônia, DB321

Amazonía ecuatoriana, DB322

Amazons, bluestockings, and crones: a feminist dictionary, CC539

Ambert, Alba N. *Bilingual education and English as a second language,* CB30

Ambrasas, Kazys. *Tarybinių lietuvių rašytojų,* BE1325

Ambrose, David P. *Lesotho,* DD18, DD170

Ambrose-Grillet, Jeanne. *Glossary of transformational grammar,* BD46

Ameiss, Albert P. *Accountant's desk handbook,* CH258

America and World War I, Woodward, David R., DA197

America at the polls, CJ240, CJ243

America at the polls 2, McGillivray, Alice V., CJ240

America at war, 1941–1945, DA207

America : history and life, AH54, BC30, CC580, CJ499, CJ549, DA176, DB10, DB24, DB165, DB187

•*America, history and life on disc*, DB24

America in fiction, Coan, Otis Welton, BE470
—— Lillard, Robert Gordon, BE470

América Latina colonial, Monteiro, John M., DB259

America votes, CJ241, CJ254

American & British genealogy & heraldry, Filby, P. William, AJ28

American & Canadian doctoral dissertations & master's theses on Africa, 1886–1974, Sims, Michael, DD32

American Academy of Child Psychiatry. *Bibliography of child psychiatry and child mental health, with a selected list of films*, EH370

American actors, 1861–1910, Moyer, Ronald L., BH126

American actors and actresses, Archer, Stephen M., BH124

American Agricultural Economics Association. *Classic books*, EJ6

American Alliance for Health, Physical Education, Recreation and Dance. *Dance directory*, BH148
—— *Encyclopedia of physical education, fitness, and sports*, BK15

The American almanac of jobs and salaries, CH708

American and British genealogy & heraldry, AJ28

American and British literature, 1945–1975, Cooper, Barbara Eck, BE761
—— Somer, John L., BE414, BE761

American and British poetry, Alexander, Harriet Semmes, BE488, BE693, BE710

American and British theatrical biography, Wearing, J. P., BH129

American and Canadian doctoral dissertations and master's theses on Africa, 1974–1987, Kagan, Alfred, DD32
—— Larkin, Gregory V., DD32
—— Lauer, Joseph J., DD32

American and Canadian immigrant and ethnic folklore, Georges, Robert A., CF66

American and Canadian West, Smith, Dwight L., DB165

American and English genealogies in the Library of Congress, AJ32

American and English popular entertainment, Wilmeth, Don B., BH2

American Anthropological Association. *AAA guide*, CE54
—— *Films for anthropological teaching*, CE33
—— *Inventory of ethnological collections in museums of the United States and Canada*, CE88

American Antiquarian Society. *American engravers upon copper and steel*, BF386
—— *Bibliography of American imprints to 1901*, AA402
—— *Checklist of newspapers of the British Isles, 1665–1800, in the American Antiquarian Society*, AE56
—— *History and present condition of the newspaper and periodical press of the United States*, AE28
—— *Proceedings*, AA248, AE19, BE501

American Antiquarian Society. Library. *A dictionary catalog of American books pertaining to the 17th through 19th centuries*, AA401

American Arabic speaking community almanac, CC347

American architects 1, BF204

American architects 2, BF204

American architects directory, BF251

American architects from the Civil War to the First World War, Wodehouse, Lawrence, BF204

American architects from the First World War to the present, Wodehouse, Lawrence, BF204

American architectural books, Hitchcock, Henry Russell, BF217

American architecture since 1780, Whiffen, Marcus, BF252

American art
archives, BF58, BF59
bibliography, BF12, BF16, BF24, BF36
biography, BF151, BF152, BF153, BF154, BF155, BF157, BF386
dictionaries, BF82
encyclopedias, BG35
indexes, BF64

American art annual, BF102, BF153, BF157

American art auction catalogues, 1785–1942, Lancour, Harold, BF110, BF120

American art directory, BF102, BF157

American artists, Castagno, John, BF159

American Association for Artificial Intelligence. *Membership directory*, EK198

American Association for Higher Education. *Consortium directory*, CB266

American Association for Marriage and Family Therapy ethics casebook, CC233

American Association for State and Local History. *Local government records*, DB140
—— *National register of historic places, 1966–1991*, BF250
—— *Public works history in the United States*, DB19

American Association for the Advancement of Science. *The AAAS science book list*, EA27
—— *AAAS science film catalog*, EA25
—— *Science books & films*, EA34

American Association for the Advancement of Slavic Studies. *American bibliography of Slavic and East European studies*, DC39
—— *Current digest of the post-Soviet press*, AE68
—— *A guide to Yugoslav libraries and archives*, DC611

American Association of Architectural Bibliographers. *Papers*, BF205

American Association of Cereal Chemists. *Approved methods of the American Association of Cereal Chemists*, EJ147

American Association of Community and Junior Colleges. *Community college fact book*, CB337
—— *Community, technical, and junior college statistical yearbook*, CB338

American Association of Dental Schools. *Admission requirements of U.S. and Canadian dental schools*, EH259

American Association of Directors of Psychiatric Residency Training. *Directory of psychiatry residency training programs*, EH389

American Association of Law Libraries. *AALL directory and handbook*, CK137
—— *Biographical directory*, AK81
—— *Current law index*, CK22
—— *Foreign law*, CK3

American Association of Physical Anthropologists. *Yearbook of physical anthropology*, CE64

American Association of Political Consultants. *Political resource directory*, CJ141

American Association of Retired Persons. *AgeLine*, CC79
—— *Thesaurus of aging terminology*, CC84

American Association of School Administrators. *Who's who in educational administration*, CB183

American Association of Textile Chemists and Colorists. *Colour index*, ED63

The American atlas, Shanks, Thomas G., CL66

American authors, 1600–1900, BE203
—— Haycraft, Howard, BE449
—— Kunitz, Stanley Jasspon, BE449

American authors, 1795–1895, Foley, Patrick K., AA242

American authors and books, 1640 to the present day, Burke, William Jeremiah, BE432

American autobiography, 1945–1980, Bloom, Lynn Z., AH89, DB67
—— Briscoe, Mary Louise, AH89, BE507, DB66, DB67
—— Tobias, Barbara, AH89, DB67

American aviation directory, CH478, EK32

American badges and insignia, Kerrigan, Evans E., AL183

American Bankers Association. *Banking terminology*, CH270
—— *Statistical information on the financial services industry*, CH237

American Baptist Churches in the U.S.A. *Yearbook*, BC328

American Baptist Historical Society. *A Baptist bibliography*, BC326

American Baptist yearbook, BC328

American Bar Association. *Directory of lawyer referral services*, CK143
—— *The official guide to U.S. law schools*, CK154
—— *You and the law*, CK163

American Bar Association. Section of International Law and Practice. *Guide to foreign law firms*, CK58

American battle monuments, BF390
—— Nishiura, Elizabeth, CJ632

American Battle Monuments Commission. *American battle monuments*, BF390

American Behavioral Scientist. The ABS guide to recent publications in the social and behavioral sciences, CA9

The American bench, CK140

American Bible Society. *The book of a thousand tongues*, BC103
—— *The English Bible in America*, BC101

American Biblical Encyclopedia Society. *Encyclopedia of biblical interpretation*, BC182

American Bibliographical Center. *America : history and life*, DB24

American bibliography, Evans, Charles, AA403, AA405, AA407, AA408, AA410, BF223, BJ59, CL243, EH25
—— Shaw, Ralph R., AA417, AA418, CL243
—— Shoemaker, Richard H., AA418, CL243

American bibliography of Russian and East European studies, DC39

American bibliography of Slavic and East European studies, DC39

American biographical archive, AH56

American biographical index, Baillie, Laureen, AH56
—— Batty, Anthea, AH56

American Board of Medical Specialties. *The official ABMS directory of board certified medical specialists*, EH164

American book auction catalogues, 1713–1934, McKay, George Leslie, AA265

American book of days, Douglas, George W., AL147
—— Hatch, Jane M., AL147

American book-prices current, AA258

American book publishing record, AA424, AA440, AH3, BC16, BE244

American book publishing record, 1876–1949, AA97

American book publishing record cumulative, AA424

American book publishing record cumulative 1876–1949, AA420, AH2

American book publishing record cumulative 1950–1977, AA421

American book trade directory, AA281, AK33

American books, 1640–1940, Burke, William Jeremiah, BE432
—— Howe, Will David, BE432

American business climate & economic profiles, CH166

•*American business directory*, CH345

American Camping Association. *Guide to accredited camps*, BK110

American capitols, Hauck, Eldon, BF248

American catalogue ... 1876–1910, AA413

The American catalogue of books (original and reprints), published in the United States from Jan. 1861 to Jan. 1871, Kelly, James, AA415

American Catholic who's who, AH75, BC416

American ceramics before 1930, Weidner, Ruth Irwin, BG57

American chemical industry, Haynes, Williams, EE96

American Chemical Society. *Chemical research faculties,* EE56
—— *Chemical titles,* EE23
—— *College chemistry faculties,* EE57
—— *Directory of chemistry software,* EE58
—— *Handbook for authors of papers in American Chemical Society publications,* EE95
—— *The NBS tables of chemical thermodynamic properties,* EE94
—— *Nobel laureates in chemistry, 1901–1992,* AL166, EE103
—— *Reagent chemicals,* EE61
American Chemical Society. Chemical Abstracts Service. *Bibliographic guide for editors & authors,* EA38
—— *Chemical Abstracts Service source index,* EA41, EE18
—— *Ring systems handbook,* EE86
American Chemical Society. Committee on Professional Training. *Directory of graduate research,* EE59
American chemists and chemical engineers, EE99
American chronicle, Gordon, Lois G., DB135
American Civil War navies, Smith, Myron J., CJ609
The American clock, Distin, William H., BG84
American clocks and clockmakers, Drepperd, Carl William, BG84
American college dictionary, AC15
The American college president, 1636–1989, Sontz, Ann H. L., CB228
American college regalia, Sparks, Linda, CB397
The American college teacher, Astin, Alexander W., CB335
American Collegiate Service. *Handbook of world education,* CB327
American Committee on the History of the Second World War. *The Second World War,* DA201
American communal and utopian history, DB149
American communes, 1860–1960, Miller, Timothy, DB138
American communes to 1860, Dare, Philip N., DB138
American community, technical, and junior colleges, American Council on Education, CB248
American Comparative Literature Association. *Yearbook of comparative and general literature,* BE41
American composers, Ewen, David, BJ210
American composers today, BJ211
American Congress on Surveying and Mapping. *Polar regions atlas,* DG10
American congressional dictionary, CJ206
The American controversy, Adams, Thomas Randolph, DB84
American Correctional Association. *Directory, juvenile & adult correctional departments, institutions, agencies & paroling authorities,* CK261
—— *International directory of correctional administrations,* CK263
—— *National jail and adult detention directory,* CK265
—— *Probation and parole directory,* CK267
American costume, 1915–1970, O'Donnol, Shirley Miles, BH90
American Council for the Arts. *Money for visual artists,* AL120, BF105
American Council of Learned Societies. *Biographical dictionary of mathematicians,* EB100
—— *Census of medieval and Renaissance manuscripts in the United States and Canada,* AA212
—— *Codices latini antiquiores,* AA201
—— *Concise dictionary of scientific biography,* EA175
—— *Current digest of the post-Soviet press,* AE68
—— *Dictionary of American biography,* AH62
—— *Dictionary of scientific biography,* EA176
—— *Directory of constituent societies of the American Council of Learned Societies,* AL37
—— *East Central Europe,* DC33
—— *Kazakh-English dictionary,* AC561

—— *List of the serial publications of foreign governments, 1815–1931,* AF13
—— *Southeastern Europe,* DC59
American Council of Learned Societies. Committee on Musicology. *The history of music,* BJ109
American Council on Education. *Accredited institutions of postsecondary education, programs, candidates,* CB246
—— *American community, technical, and junior colleges,* CB248
—— *American universities and colleges,* CB248
—— *Community college fact book,* CB337
—— *Educational measurement,* CB150
—— *Fact book on higher education,* CB339
—— *Fact book on women in higher education,* CB344
—— *Guide to programs in nursing in four-year colleges and universities,* EH282
—— *A guide to the evaluation of educational experiences in the armed services,* CB361
—— *The "how to" grants manual,* AL130
—— *A rating of graduate programs,* CB348
American Council on Education. Office of Research. *The American freshman, national norms,* CB333
The American counties, Kane, Joseph Nathan, CL178
American country furniture, 1780–1875, Kovel, Ralph M., BG132
American decorations, United States. Adjutant General's Office, AL187
American defense annual, CJ636
American demographics, CH588
American Dental Association. *Accepted dental therapeutics,* EH262
—— *American dental directory,* EH260
—— *Dental abstracts,* EH248
—— *Dentist's desk reference,* EH263
—— *Index of the periodical dental literature published in the English language,* EH250
—— *Index to dental literature,* EH251
American Dental Association. Bureau of Library Services. *Basic dental reference works,* EH244
American Dental Association. Council on Dental Education. *Admission requirements of U.S. and Canadian dental schools,* EH259
American Dental Association specifications for dental materials, EH263
American dental directory, EH260
American dialect dictionary, Wentworth, Harold, AC154
American Dialect Society. *An American glossary,* AC153
—— *Dictionary of American regional English,* AC151
American dialects, Herman, Lewis, BH91
—— Herman, Marguerite Shalett, BH91
American diaries, Arksey, Laura, BE507, BE509, BE726, BE727, DB66
—— Pries, Nancy, BE509
—— Reed, Marcia, BE509
American diaries in manuscript, 1580–1954, Matthews, William, BE507, BE510, BE726, DB66
American dictionary of campaigns and elections, Young, Michael L., CJ121, CJ124
The American dictionary of economics, CH54
American directors, Coursodon, Jean-Pierre, BH290
—— Sauvage, Pierre, BH290
American directory of organized labor, CH660
American dissertations on foreign education, Parker, Franklin, CB24
American dissertations on the drama and the theatre, Litto, Fredric M., BH37
American doctoral dissertations, AG11, AG12, AG13
American doctoral dissertations on Africa 1886–1972, Bratton, Michael, DD32
—— Schneller, Anne, DD32
American Documentation Institute. *Annual review of information science and technology,* AK76
American drama
  African-American authors, BE512, BE513, BE521
    bibliography, BE520, BE531
  annuals, BE454

  bibliography, BE452, BE453, BE457, BE458, BE460, BE461, BE462, BE464, BE573, BE636, BE655
  biography, BE452
  criticism
    indexes, BE465
  directories, BH85
  indexes, BE463
  library catalogs, BE494
  reviews and criticism, BE457
  women authors
    bibliography, BE455, BE456, BE459
American drama (by subject)
  history, BE466, BE467, BE667
American drama, Bogard, Travis, BE467, BE667
—— Meserve, Walter J., BE467, BE667
—— Moody, Richard, BE467, BE667
American drama between the wars, Miller, Jordan Yale, BE466
American drama criticism, Dyson, Anne Jane, BE457
—— Eddleman, Floyd Eugene, BE232, BE457
—— Palmer, Helen H., BE457
American drama from the Colonial period through World War I, Richardson, Gary A., BE466
American drama to 1900, Meserve, Walter J., BE462
American drawing, Duomato, Lamia, BF297
American drug index, EH354
American druggist blue book, EH355
American druggist price book, EH355
American Economic Association. *Survey of members, including classification listings,* CH91
—— *Telephone directory of members,* CH91
American economic business history information sources, Lovett, Robert Woodbery, CH395
American economic history, Hutchinson, William Kenneth, CH172
American economic review, CH91
American educational catalog, AA431
American educational history, Sedlak, Michael W., CB33
American Educational Research Association. *Encyclopedia of educational research,* CB69
—— *Handbook of research on curriculum,* CB115
—— *Handbook of research on educational administration,* CB182
—— *Handbook of research on teaching,* CB117
—— *Review of research in education,* CB121
—— *Standards for educational and psychological testing,* CD76
American Educational Theatre Association. *Spanish plays in English translation,* BE1468
American educators' encyclopedia, Dejnozka, Edward L., CB65
American electricians' handbook, EK134
American engineers of the nineteenth century, Roysdon, Christine, EK21
American English, A dictionary of, AC150
American engravers upon copper and steel, Fielding, Mantle, BF386
—— Stauffer, David McNeely, BF386
American Enterprise Institute for Public Policy Research. *Evolution of the modern presidency,* CJ171
American entomologists, Mallis, Arnold, EG334
The American ephemeris and nautical almanac, EC78
American ethnic literatures, Peck, David R., BE511, BE546
American ethnic press, AD58
American export register, CH136
American families, CC234
American Federation of Arts. *Who's who in American art,* BF157
American Federation of Labor. *American Federation of Labor records,* CH624
American Federation of Labor records, American Federation of Labor, CH624
The American fertilizer handbook, EJ51
American fiction, BE484, BE485, BE486
  African-American authors, BE517, BE522, BE525

bibliography, BE254, BE468, BE470, BE472, BE473, BE474, BE475, BE476, BE477, BE478, BE479, BE480, BE481, BE482, BE564
biobibliography, BE469
criticism, BE471
history and criticism, BE473
indexes, BE483
reviews and criticism, BE471
American fiction, 1774–1850, Wright, Lyle Henry, BE482
American fiction, 1774–1910, BE482
American fiction, 1851–1875, Wright, Lyle Henry, BE482
American fiction, 1876–1900, Wright, Lyle Henry, BE482
American fiction, 1900–1950, Woodress, James Leslie, BE481
American fiction : an historical and critical survey, Quinn, Arthur Hobson, BE485
American fiction to 1900, Kirby, David K., BE478
American film-index, 1908–1915, Lauritzen, Einar, BH189
American film-index, 1916–1920, Lauritzen, Einar, BH189
——— Lundquist, Gunnar, BH189
The American film industry, Slide, Anthony, BH254, BH316, CH483
American Film Institute. *The American Film Institute catalog of motion pictures produced in the United States,* BH183
The American Film Institute catalog of motion pictures produced in the United States, American Film Institute, BH183
The American Film Institute guide to college courses in film and television, BH263
American first editions, AA242
American Fisheries Society. *The directory of North American fisheries and aquatic scientists,* EG48
American Fisheries Society. Committee on Names of Fishes. *A list of common and scientific names of fishes from the United States and Canada,* EG281
American folk architecture, Marshall, Howard W., BF213
American folk art, BG1
American Folklife Center. *Ethnic folklife dissertations from the United States and Canada, 1960–1980,* CF44
——— *Folklife sourcebook,* CF75
——— *Vernacular architecture in America,* BF213
American folklore, Flanagan, Cathleen C., CF64
American Folklore Society. *Afro-American folk culture,* CF58
——— *Folklore theses and dissertations in the United States,* CF43
——— *Membership directory and guide to the field,* CF55
American Forum for Global Education. *Who's doing what?,* AL50
American Foundation for AIDS Research. *Learning AIDS,* EH21
American Foundation for the Blind. *AFB directory of services for blind and visually impaired persons in the United States and Canada,* CC191
American foundations and their fields, AL112
American freshman, Astin, Alexander W., CB333
——— Dey, Eric L., CB333
——— Korn, William S., CB333
The American freshman, national norms, CB333
American genealogical-biographical index to American genealogical, biographical and local history materials, AJ35
American genealogical index, Rider, Fremont, AJ35
American Geographical Society of New York. *Antarctic map folio series,* CL369
——— *Atlas of the historical geography of the United States,* DB75
——— *A catalogue of early globes made prior to 1850 and conserved in the United States,* CL246
——— *Columbia Lippincott gazetteer of the world,* CL85
——— *Current geographical publications,* CL22
——— *A historical atlas of South Asia,* DE91

——— *Research catalogue of the American Geographical Society,* CL28
——— *Soviet geography,* CL275
American Geographical Society of New York. Map Dept. *Index to maps in books and periodicals,* CL225
American Geological Institute. *Bibliography and index of geology,* EF47
——— *Bibliography and index of geology exclusive of North America,* EF48
——— *Bibliography and index of micropaleontology,* EF234
——— *Bibliography of geoscience theses of the United States and Canada,* EF42
——— *Bibliography of theses written for advanced degrees in geology and related sciences at universities and colleges in the United States and Canada through 1957,* EF43
——— *Dictionary of geological terms,* EF72
——— *Directory of geoscience departments,* EF90
——— *Union list of geologic field trip guidebooks of North America,* EF93
American Geological Institute. Conference. (Duluth, 1959). *Geology and earth sciences sourcebook for elementary and secondary schools,* EF94
American geological literature, 1669 to 1850, Hazen, Robert M., EF32
American Geophysical Institute. *Geological reference file,* EF53
American Geophysical Union. *Annotated bibliography on hydrology (1951–54) and sedimentation (1950–54), United States and Canada,* EF126, EF127
——— *Bibliography of hydrology,* EF126
American given names, Stewart, George Rippey, AJ175
American glass, McKearin, George S., BG76
An American glossary, Thornton, Richard H., AC153
American governors and gubernatorial elections, 1775–1978, Glashan, Roy R., CJ291
American governors and gubernatorial elections, 1979–1987, Mullaney, Marie Marmo, CJ286, CJ291
American graphic design, Thomson, Ellen Mazur, BF369
American guide series, CL387
American handbook of psychiatry, EH391
The American heritage dictionary of Indo-European roots, AC47, AC51
The American heritage dictionary of science, Barnhart, Robert K., EA86
The American heritage dictionary of the English language, AB27, AC9, AC47, AC729
The American heritage illustrated encyclopedic dictionary, AC16
American heritage Larousse Spanish dictionary, AC729
The American heritage pictorial atlas of United States history, DB69
The American heritage Spanish dictionary. Spanish/ English, English/Spanish, AC729
The American heritage student's dictionary, AC21
American higher education, CB323
——— Olevnik, Peter P., CB215
American historians 1607–1865, DB65
American historians, 1866–1912, Wilson, Clyde W., DB65
American Historical Association. *Bibliography of British history,* DC270
——— *Bibliography of British history, 1851–1914,* DC330
——— *Bibliography of British history, Stuart period, 1603–1714,* DC315
——— *Doctoral dissertations in history,* DA16
——— *The eighteenth century, 1714–1789,* DC317
——— *Guide to historical literature,* DA1
——— *Guide to the study of United States history outside the U.S., 1945–1980,* DB17
——— *Public documents of the first fourteen Congresses, 1789–1817,* AF92
——— *Writings on American history,* DB23

American Historical Association. Committee for the Study of War Documents. *A catalogue of files and microfilms of the German Foreign Ministry archives, 1867–1920,* DC250, DC253
——— *Guide to captured German documents,* DC249
——— *Guides to German records microfilmed at Alexandria, Va,* DC254
——— *A list of archival references and data of documents from the archives of the German Foreign Ministry, 1867–1920,* DC251
American Historical Association. Institutional Services Program. *Directory of history departments and organizations in the United States and Canada,* DA27
——— *Grants, fellowships & prizes of interest to historians,* DA28
American historical fiction, Gerhardstein, Virginia Brokaw, BE470
American history atlas, Gilbert, Martin, DB72
The American history sourcebook, DB52
American Home Economics Association. *AHEA,* EJ202
——— *Titles of dissertations and theses completed in home economics,* EJ194, EJ196
American Home Economics Association. Food and Nutrition Section. *Handbook of food preparation,* EJ215
American Home Economics Association. International Section. *The international heritage of home economics in the United States,* EJ198
American homelessness, Hombs, Mary Ellen, CC202
American Horticultural Society. *North American horticulture,* EG155
The American Horticultural Society encyclopedia of garden plants, EG116, EJ231
The American Horticultural Society encyclopedia of gardening, EJ232
American Hospital Association. *Directory of health care professionals,* EH155
American Hospital Association. Resource Center. *Acronyms and initialisms in health care administration,* EH129
——— *Hospital administration terminology,* EH117
American Hospital Association guide to the health care field, EH153, EH155
American hospital formulary service, EH353
American hospital formulary service drug information, EH353
The American humanities index, AD260, BA2, BE499
American humor magazines and comic periodicals, AD28
American humorists, 1800–1950, Trachtenberg, Stanley, BE411
American hymns old and new, Hughes, Charles William, BC317
The American illustrated medical dictionary, EH97
American immigration history, DB41
American imprints, 1648–1797, in the Huntington Library, supplementing Evans' American bibliography, Henry E. Huntington Library and Art Gallery, AA407
American imprints inventory, Historical Records Survey, AA441
American imprints on art through 1865, Schimmelman, Janice Gayle, BF36
American independence, Adams, Thomas Randolph, DB85
American Indian and Alaska native newspapers and periodicals, AE16
——— Littlefield, Daniel F., CC424
American Indian and Eskimo authors, Hirschfelder, Arlene B., BE551
American Indian archival material, Chepesiuk, Ronald, CC427
American Indian Historical Society. *Index to literature on the American Indian,* CC416
The American Indian in graduate studies, Dockstader, Frederick J., CC425
The American Indian in short fiction, Beidler, Peter G., BE548

The American Indian index, Frazier, Gregory W., CC430

The American Indian language and literature, Marken, Jack W., BD242

American Indian literature, BE555

American Indian literatures, Ruoff, A. LaVonne Brown, BE553

American Indian novelists, Colonnese, Tom, BE550

American Indian painters, King, Jeanne Snodgrass, BF318

American Indian resource materials in the Western History Collections, University of Oklahoma, CC426

American Indian women, Bataille, Gretchen M., CC588

American insects, Arnett, Ross H., EG326

American Institute of Accountants. *Accountants' index*, CH245

American Institute of Architects. *Pro file*, BF251

American Institute of Architects. Committee on Historic Buildings. *Landmark yellow pages*, BF265

American Institute of Certified Planners. *Guide to graduate education in urban and regional planning*, BF282

American Institute of Certified Public Accountants. *Accountants' index*, CH245
—— *Specialized legal research*, CK119

American Institute of Islamic Studies. *An analytical guide to the bibliographies on Islam, Muhammad, and the Qur'an*, BC493
—— *Guide to reference books for Islamic studies*, BC494

American Institute of Parliamentarians. *Standard code of parliamentary procedure*, CJ458

American Institute of Physics. *AIP style manual*, ED51
—— *American Institute of Physics handbook*, ED32
—— *Directory of physics & astronomy staff members*, EC45, ED31
—— *Encyclopedia of applied physics*, ED14
—— *Graduate programs in physics, astronomy, and related fields*, ED29
—— *The NBS tables of chemical thermodynamic properties*, EE94
—— *A physicist's desk reference*, ED48
—— *Physics briefs*, ED10

American Institute of Physics handbook, American Institute of Physics, ED32

American Institute of Real Estate Appraisers. *Real estate appraisal bibliography, 1973–1980*, CH531

American Institute of the History of Pharmacy. *Pharmacy museums and historical collections in the United States and Canada*, EH367

American intelligence, 1775–1990, Petersen, Neal H., CJ544

American jewelry manufacturers, Rainwater, Dorothy T., BG89

American Jewish Archives. *Guide to the holdings of the American Jewish Archives*, BC538

American Jewish biographies, Polner, Murray, AH79

American Jewish Committee. *American Jewish year book*, BC563

American Jewish history, Gurock, Jeffrey S., BC523

The American-Jewish media directory, AE17

American Jewish year book, BC563

American Joint Committee on Horticultural Nomenclature. *Standardized plant names*, EG118

American journal of physical anthropology, CE64

American journal of psychology [indexes], CD15

American journalism, Mott, Frank Luther, AE145

American Journalism Historians Association. *Guide to sources in American journalism history*, AE144

American journalism history, Sloan, W. David, AE147

American jurisprudence 2d, CK132

American jurisprudence desk book, CK161

American jurisprudence legal forms, CK164

American jurisprudence pleading and practice forms, annotated, CK164

American Kennel Club. *The complete dog book*, EJ143

American labor history and comparative labor movements, McBrearty, James C., CH633

American labor union periodicals, Naas, Bernard G., CH635

American labor unions' constitutions and proceedings, Naas, Bernard G., CH636

American landscape architecture, BF294

The American language, Mencken, Henry Louis, BD107

The American law dictionary, Renstrom, Peter G., CK136

American leaders, 1789–1991, CJ153

American legislative leaders, 1850–1910, Ritter, Charles F., CJ289

American library and book trade annual, AK77

American library annual, AK77, AK122

American Library Association. *ALA handbook of organization and membership directory*, AK56
—— *The A.L.A. index*, BE239
—— *ALA-LC romanization tables*, BD10
—— *ALA survey of librarian salaries*, AK171
—— *The ALA yearbook of library and information services*, AK75
—— *American library laws*, AK172
—— *Anglo-American cataloguing rules*, AK194
—— *Blacks and their contributions to the American West*, CC360
—— *Canadian government publications*, AF152
—— *Directory of curriculum materials centers*, CB267
—— *Directory of library & information professionals*, AK88
—— *Find the law in the library*, CK116
—— *List of the serial publications of foreign governments, 1815–1931*, AF13
—— *Sources of library statistics, 1972–1982*, AK98
—— *Subject index to poetry for children and young people*, BE322
—— *World encyclopedia of library and information services*, AK39

American Library Association. Association for Library Service to Children. *Special collections in children's literature*, AK113

American Library Association. Association of College and Research Libraries. *Sourcebook for bibliographic instruction*, AK231

American Library Association. Business Reference Services Section. *Business serials of the U.S. government*, CH26

American Library Association. Collection Development Committee. *Guidelines for collection development*, AK164

American Library Association. Committee on Library Terminology. *A.L.A. glossary of library terms*, AK40

American Library Association. Committee on the Status of Women in Librarianship. *On account of sex*, AK14

American Library Association. Filing Committee. *ALA filing rules*, AK210

American Library Association. Government Documents Round Table. *The complete guide to citing government information resources*, AF69
—— *Directory of foreign document collections*, AF149
—— *Directory of government document collections & librarians*, AF86
—— *DttP. Documents to the people*, AF68
—— *Guide to official publications of foreign countries*, AF8

American Library Association. Library Instruction Round Table. *The LIRT library instruction handbook*, AK230

American Library Association. Library Technology Program. *Library technology reports*, AK177

American Library Association. Map and Geography Round Table. *Cartographic citations*, CL263

American Library Association. Office for Intellectual Freedom. *Intellectual freedom manual*, AK67

American Library Association. Reference and Adult Services Division. *United States of America national bibliographical services and related activities in 1965–1967*, AA21

American Library Association. State and Local Documents Task Force. *Guide to the publications of interstate agencies and authorities*, AF141
—— *State publications*, AF137

American Library Association. Task Force on Alternatives in Print. *Alternative publications*, AA280

American library directory, AK33, AK122, AK146, AK122

American library history, Davis, Donald G., AK71
—— Harris, Michael H., AK71
—— Young, Arthur P., AK27

American library laws, AK172

American library resources, Downs, Robert Bingham, AK103

American library resources cumulative index, 1870–1970, Keller, Clara D., AK103

American literary almanac, Rood, Karen L., BE437

American literary and drama reviews, Marks, Patricia, BE465

American literary annuals & gift books, 1825–1865, Thompson, Ralph, BE415

American literary magazines, BE420

American literary manuscripts, AH235
—— Robbins, John Albert, BE430

American literary publishing houses, 1638–1899, AA297

American literary publishing houses, 1900–1980, Dzwonkoski, Peter, AA297

American literary scholarship, BE403, BE404, BE418, BE468, BE513, BE589

American literature
  abstract journals, BE419
  African-American authors, BE519, BE526, BE528, BE532, BE537
    bibliography, BE515, BE527
    biography, BE518
  Asian-American authors, BE546
  bibliography, BD90, BE393, BE395, BE396, BE397, BE398, BE399, BE400, BE403, BE404, BE405, BE406, BE407, BE408, BE409, BE413, BE415, BE440, BE571, BE573, BE583, BE588
    current, BE418, BE589
  bibliography of bibliography, BE410
  biobibliography, BE201, BE581, BE584, BE608
  biography, BE443, BE444, BE445, BE446, BE447, BE448, BE449, BE578
    Catholic authors, BE446
  chronologies, BE436, BE437
  collections, BE441, BE442
  criticism, BE426, BE427, BE445, BE575, BE595
    bibliography, BE29
    collections, BE596, BE597, BE598, BE599
    indexes, BE465
  dissertations, BE423, BE424, BE425
  encyclopedias, BE431, BE433, BE435, BE608
  ethnic literature
    bibliography, BE511
  guidebooks, BE438
  guides, BE2, BE393, BE394, BE395, BE396, BE397, BE398, BE407, BE580
  handbooks, BE431, BE432, BE435, BE449
  history, BE439, BE440, BE576, BE577
  indexes, BE535
  Jewish authors
    handbooks, BE565
  library catalogs, BE406, BE583
  local and regional
    South, BE568
    West, BE579
  manuscripts and archives, BE429, BE430
  Mexican-American authors, BD172, BE560, BE1426
    bibliography, BE557, BE558
    biography, BE563
    guides, BE556
  periodicals, BE420, BE421, BE422
    indexes, BE409
  regional literature, BE573

Middle West, BE567
New England, BE416
South, BE518, BE571, BE574, BE578
    dissertations, BE569
    history, BE575
West, BE570, BE572
reviews of research, BE397, BE403, BE413, BE414, BE418
Spanish-American authors, BE890
women authors, BE399
    bibliography, BE401, BE412, BE534
    biobibliography, BE607
women writers, BE402
American literature (by period)
20th century
    criticism, BE428
American literature (by subject)
regional literature
    New England, BE516
    New England states
        history, BE577
    West
        history, BE576
see also African-American literature
American literature, Harvard University. Library, BE406
—— Leary, Lewis Gaston, BE397
American literature and language, Koster, Donald Nelson, BE407
American lobbyists directory, CJ130, CJ131
American Lutheran Church. Biographical directory of clergy, BC354
—— Lutheran book of worship, BC358
—— Yearbook, BC356
American magazine journalists, 1741–1850, AE148
American Management Association. Index to AMA resources of the seventies, 1970–1976, CH604
—— Management handbook, CH620
—— Ten-year index of AMA publications, CH604
American manufacturers directory, CH345
American Marketing Association. Greenbook, CH586
American mass-market magazines, AD29
American Mathematical Society. Assistantships and graduate fellowships in the mathematical sciences, EB58
—— Combined membership list of the American Mathematical Society, the Mathematical Association of America, and the Society for Industrial and Applied Mathematics, EB56
—— Computer science technical reports, EK156
—— Current mathematical publications, EB23
—— Index to translations selected by the American Mathematical Society, EB20
—— Mathematical reviews, EB27
—— Mathematical sciences professional directory, EB59
—— Mathematics into type, EB99
—— Selected tables in mathematical statistics, EB95
American Mathematical Society translations, EB20
American Medical Association. American Medical Association manual of style, EH193
—— Current medical information and terminology, EH96
—— Directory of physicians in the United States, EH157
—— Drug evaluations annual, EH337
—— Graduate medical education directory, EH160
—— Physicians' current procedural terminology, EH147
American Medical Association. Committee on Allied Health Education and Accreditation. Allied health education directory, EH152
The American Medical Association encyclopedia of medicine, EH80
The American Medical Association family medical guide, EH171
The American Medical Association handbook of first aid & emergency care, EH172
American Medical Association manual of style, EH193

American medical bibliography, 1639–1783, Guerra, Francisco, EH202
American medical directory, EH157
American medical imprints, 1820–1910, Cordasco, Francesco, EH12
American Medical Student Association. Directory of psychiatry residency training programs, EH389
American men & women of science, CA61, EA37, EA170, EA177
American Meteorological Society. Cumulated bibliography and index to Meteorological and geoastrophysical abstracts, EF143
—— Curricula in the atmospheric, oceanic, hydrologic, and related sciences, EF151
—— Glossary of meteorology, EF146
American Meteorological Society. Committee on the Compendium of Meteorology. Compendium of meteorology, EF152
American military biographies, CJ648
American military cemeteries, Holt, Dean W., BF390, CJ632
American Missionary Association. Author and added entry catalog of the American Missionary Association Archives, BC302, CC362
American Museum of Natural History. Bibliography and index of micropaleontology, EF234
—— A handbook of method in cultural anthropology, CE60
American Museum of Natural History. Library. Research catalog of the Library of the American Museum of Natural History. EG67
American music
    bibliography, BJ39, BJ46
        scores, BJ59
    periodicals
        indexes, BJ46
American music studies, Heintze, James R., BJ36
American musical theatre, Bordman, Gerald Martin, BJ259
American national dictionary for information processing systems, EK175
American national election studies data sourcebook, 1952–1986, Miller, Warren E., CJ255
American national standard for bibliographic references, American National Standards Institute, EA162
American National Standard glossary of terms in nuclear science and technology, American Nuclear Society, EK295
American national standards ... catalog, EA268
American National Standards Institute. American national dictionary for information processing systems, EK175
—— American national standard for bibliographic references, EA162
—— American national standards ... catalog, EA268
American Native Press Archives. Native American periodicals and newspapers, 1828–1982, AE16
American naval bibliography, Smith, Myron J., CJ609, CJ610
American naval fighting ships, CJ649
American naval history, Sweetman, Jack, DB60
American Navy, 1798–1860, Smith, Myron J., CJ609
American Navy, 1865–1918, Smith, Myron J., CJ609
American Navy, 1918–1941, Smith, Myron J., CJ609
American newspaper directory, AD51, AE23
American newspaper journalists, 1690–1872, AE149
American Newspaper Markets, Inc. Circulation, AE21
American newspapers, AE32
American newspapers, 1821–1936, AE18, AE19
American nicknames, Shankle, George Earlie, BE190
American notes and queries, BE168
—— Asterlund, B., BE168
—— Pilkington, Walter, BE168
The American novel, Gerstenberger, Donna Lorine, BE473
American Nuclear Society. American National Standard glossary of terms in nuclear science and technology, EK295

American Nuclear Society. Standards Committee. Subcommittee ANS-9. Glossary of terms in nuclear science and technology, EK295
American Numismatic Association. Library catalogue, BG177
American Numismatic Society. Library. Auction catalogue, BG177
—— Dictionary catalogue, BG177
American Nurses' Association. Facts about nursing, EH289
—— International nursing index, EH276
American nursing, EH287
American operas, Borroff, Edith, BJ234
American orators before 1900, BE346
American orators of the twentieth century, Duffy, Bernard K., BE346
—— Ryan, Halford R., BE346
American orders & societies and their decorations, AL178
American Oriental Society. The Sumerian dictionary of the University Museum of the University of Pennsylvania, AC204
American Ornithologists' Union. The birds of North America, EG253
American Ornithologists' Union. Committee on Classification and Nomenclature. Check-list of North American birds, EG255
American Osteopathic Association. Yearbook and directory of osteopathic physicians, EH154
American painting, Keaveney, Sydney Starr, BF297
American painting, history and interpretation, Barker, Virgil, BF309
American painting of the nineteenth century, Novak, Barbara, BF309
American passenger arrival records, Tepper, Michael, AJ25
American peace directory, CJ694
The American peace movement, Howlett, Charles F., CJ672
American peace writers, editors, and periodicals, Roberts, Nancy L., CJ701
American periodicals, 1741–1900, Heath, Trudy, AD272
—— Hoornstra, Jean, AD36, AD272
American periodicals, 1800–1850, AD36
American periodicals, 1850–1900, AD36
American periodicals, 18th century, AD36
American periodicals : series I, 1741–1800, AD273
American periodicals : series I, 1741–1900, AD272
American periodicals : series II, 1800–1850, AD38, AD272, AD273
American Pharmaceutical Association. Handbook of nonprescription drugs, EH344
American philatelic dictionary and Colonial and Revolutionary posts, Konwiser, Harry Myron, BG202
American philatelic periodicals, Smith, Chester M., BG199
American Philosophical Society. Library. Catalog of books in the American Philosophical Society Library, Philadelphia, Pennsylvania, EA225
—— Catalog of manuscripts in the American Philosophical Society Library, including the archival shelflist, EA226
American photographers, BF357
American Physical Society. Bulletin of the American Physical Society, EC45, ED31
American Phytopathological Society. A literature guide for the identification of plant pathogenic fungi, EG189
American place-names, Stewart, George Rippey, CL180
American plays printed 1714–1830, Hill, Frank Pierce, BE453, BE636
American playwrights since 1945, BE452
American poetry
20th century
    Bibliography., BE500
    African-American authors, BE512, BE536
        bibliography, BE533
    bibliography, BE487, BE489, BE490, BE492, BE493, BE495, BE496, BE700
    biobibliography, BE312, BE334

biography, BE333
criticism, BE312, BE492
indexes, BE499, BE501, BE502, BE536
library catalogs, BE494
musical settings, BJ272
periodicals, BE505
women authors
bibliography, BE708
American poetry (by subject)
history and criticism, BE488, BE491, BE497, .
BE503, BE504, BE693
American poetry 1609–1870, BE494, BE498
American poetry index, BE502
American poets, from the Puritans to the present,
Waggoner, Hyatt H., BE504
American political dictionary, Greenberg, Milton,
CJ122
—— Plano, Jack C., CJ122, CJ126
—— Whisker, James B., CJ123
American political leaders, O'Brien, Steven, CJ158
American political parties, Wynar, Lubomyr Roman,
CJ260
American Political Science Association.
Biographical directory, CJ154
—— *Graduate faculty and programs in political
science,* CJ49
—— *Guide to federal funding for social scientists,*
CA52
—— *Political science journal information,* CJ16
—— *Style manual for political science,* CJ4
—— *United States political science documents,*
CJ20
American political scientists, CJ155
American political terms, Sperber, Hans, CJ129
American political women, Stineman, Esther, CJ160
American popular illustration, Best, James J., BF372
American popular literature, BE434
American popular music, Booth, Mark W., BJ335
*American popular songs from the Revolutionary War
to the present,* Ewen, David, BJ277
American practical navigator, EC77
The American presidency, Davison, Kenneth E.,
CJ168
—— Goehlert, Robert, CJ170
—— Martin, Fenton S., CJ170, CJ172
The American presidents, Cohen, Norman S., CJ167
—— Goehlert, Robert, CJ167
—— Martin, Fenton S., CJ167, CJ173
American prints in the Library of Congress, Library
of Congress. Prints and Photographs Division,
BF365
An American profile, CJ484
—— Wood, Floris W., CC40
American Psychiatric Association. *American
psychiatric glossary,* EH385
—— *Biographical directory,* EH387
—— *Diagnostic and statistical manual of mental
disorders,* EH393
—— *Directory of psychiatry residency training
programs,* EH389
—— *The history and influence of the American
Psychiatric Association,* EH397
—— *Psychiatric dictionary,* EH382
American Psychiatric Association. Task Force on
Treatments of Psychiatric Disorders. *Treatments of
psychiatric disorders,* EH381
American psychiatric glossary, Stone, Evelyn M.,
EH385
American Psychological Association. *APA
membership register,* CD35
—— *Directory of the American Psychological
Association,* CD46
—— *Graduate study in psychology,* CD37
—— *Guide to research support,* CD36
—— *Journals in psychology,* CD13
—— *Library use,* CD5
—— *Membership register,* CD35
—— *PsycBOOKS,* CD16
—— *Psychological abstracts,* CD17
—— *Standards for educational and psychological
testing,* CD76
*American Psychological Association's guide to
research support,* CD36

American public administration, CJ463
American Public Health Association. *Glossary :
water and wastewater control engineering,* EK92
—— *Public health law manual,* EH413
—— *Standard methods for the examination of
water and wastewater,* EE62
American public opinion data, CJ485
American public opinion index, CJ485
American public school teacher, CB167
American Public Transit Association. *Transit fact
book,* CH454
American Radio Relay League. *The ARRL handbook
for radio amateurs,* EK144
American reference books annual, AA346, AA356,
AH1, AK8, AK80, CB1, EA53
American reformers, CC38
American regional theatre history to 1900, Larson,
Carl F. W., BH43
American register of exporters and importers,
CH136
American religion and philosophy, Sandeen, Ernest
Robert, BC31
American Renaissance in New England, Myerson,
Joel, BE577
American Research Center in Egypt. *An historical
bibliography of Egyptian prehistory,* DA122
The American Revolution, 1775–1783, DB92
—— Blanco, Richard L., DB93
American sacred music imprints, 1698–1810,
Britton, Allen Perdue, BJ68
American-Scandinavian Foundation. *A history of
Danish literature,* BE1118
American school law, CB154
American School of Classical Studies of Athens.
Catalogue, DC373
American screenwriters, BH280
American sculpture, Ekdahl, Janis, BF387
American seashells, Abbott, Robert Tucker, EG306
*American short fiction criticism and scholarship,
1959–1977,* Weixlmann, Joseph, BE479, BE548
American silversmiths and their marks IV, Ensko,
Stephen Guernsey Cook, BG144
American social change, CA35
American social leaders, McGuire, William, CA64
American Society for Clinical Pharmacology and
Therapeutics. *Drug evaluations annual,* EH337
American Society for Eighteenth-Century Studies.
The eighteenth century, BE36
American Society for Engineering Education.
Engineering Libraries Division. *Guides to
literature,* EK1
American Society for Horticultural Science.
Glossary for horticultural crops, EJ243
American Society for Information Science. *Annual
review of information science and technology,*
AK76
—— *ASIS handbook & directory,* AK57
—— *Directory of library & information
professionals,* AK88
American Society for Metals. *ASM metals reference
book,* EK270
—— *ASM thesaurus of metallurgical terms,*
EK263
American Society for Metals. Documentation
Service. *ASM review of metal literature,* EK257
American Society for Metals. Reference
Publications. *ASM engineered materials reference
book,* EK268
American Society for Psychical Research.
Parapsychology, CD131
American Society for Public Administration. *Public
administration in American society,* CJ475
American Society for Reformation Research. *Archiv
für Reformationsgeschichte,* DC25
American Society for Testing and Materials. *Annual
book of A.S.T.M. standards including tentative
standards,* EA269
—— *International directory of testing
laboratories,* EA215
American Society for Testing and Materials.
Committee D-19 on Water. *Manual on water,*
EK95

American Society for Theatre Research. *Directory of
doctoral programs in theatre studies in the U.S.A.
and Canada,* BH84
—— *International bibliography of theatre,* BH57
American Society of Civil Engineers. *Definitions of
surveying, mapping, and related terms,* EF123
American Society of Civil Engineers. Committee on
History and Heritage of American Civil
Engineering. *A biographical dictionary of
American civil engineers,* EK63, EK250
American Society of Composers, Authors and
Publishers. *ASCAP biographical dictionary,*
BJ201
—— *ASCAP index of performed compositions,*
BJ52
American Society of Heating, Refrigerating and Air-
Conditioning Engineers. *ASHRAE handbook,*
EK224
American Society of Hospital Pharmacists. *AHFS
drug information,* EH353
American Society of Indexers. *Indexing and
abstracting,* AK217
—— *Register of indexers,* AK214
American Society of International Law. *Basic
documents of international economic law,* CK112
—— *International legal materials,* CK114
American Society of Legislative Clerks &
Secretaries. *Mason's manual of legislative
procedure,* CJ456
American Society of Mammalogists. *Orders and
families of recent mammals of the world,* EG304
American Society of Mechanical Engineers.
Materials handling handbook, EK277
—— *Mechanical engineers in America born prior
to 1861,* EK250
American Society of Photogrammetry. *Manual of
photogrammetry,* EF18
—— *Manual of photographic interpretation,* EF18
American Sociological Association. Section on the
Sociology of World Conflicts. *Bibliography on
world conflict and peace,* CJ664
American song, Bloom, Ken, BJ258
American songwriters, Ewen, David, BJ271
American-South African relations, 1784–1980, Keto,
C. Tsehloane, DD218
American spirit in architecture, Hamlin, Talbott
Faulkner, BF256
The American stage to World War I, Wilmeth, Don
B., BH49
American state governors, 1776–1976, Kallenbach,
Joseph E., CJ286
American Statistical Association. *Current index to
statistics, applications, methods and theory,* CG15,
EB22
—— *Directory of members,* CG35, EB57
**American Statistical Association
directories,** CG35, EB57
American statistics index, AF62, CG69, CG96,
CG99
American students, Altbach, Philip G., CB217
*American studies and translations of contemporary
Italian poetry, 1945–1965,* Molinaro, Julius A.,
BE1317
American suburbs rating guide and fact book, Willis,
Alan, CL77
American surnames, Smith, Elsdon Coles, AJ186
American territorial governors, CJ287
American theatre, Bordman, Gerald Martin, BH97
American theatre companies, BH95
American theatre history, Taylor, Thomas J., BH48
American Theatre Wing. *The Tony Award,* BH93
American theatrical arts, Young, William C., BH6,
BH7
American theatrical periodicals, 1789–1967,
Stratman, Carl Joseph, BH36
American Theological Library Association. *ATLA
religion database on CD-ROM,* BC41
—— *Black holiness,* BC374
—— *Eastern Christianity,* BC446
—— *A guide to the study of the Pentecostal
movement,* BC375
—— *Index to book reviews in religion,* BC52,
BC53

—— *The New Testament apocrypha and pseudepigrapha*, BC107

—— *The Oxford Movement and its leaders*, BC214

—— *Politics and religion*, BC15

—— *Rediscovery of creation*, BC223, EG66

—— *Religion index one*, BC44

—— *Religion index two*, BC45

American thesaurus of slang, Berrey, Lester V., AC119

American third parties since the Civil War, Rockwood, D. Stephen, CJ259

American trade schools directory, CB295

American Transit Association. *Transit fact book*, CH454

American travelers to Mexico, 1821–1972, Cole, Garold, DB221

American Trucking Associations. Information Center. *Trucksource*, CH445

American Type Founders Company Library. *The history of printing from its beginnings to 1930*, AA299

American universities and colleges, CB240, CB248

—— Songe, Alice H., CB292

American University. Foreign area studies. *Area handbook series*, DD62

American University of Beirut. Economic Research Institute. *A selected and annotated bibliography of economic literature on the Arabic speaking countries of the Middle East*, CH193

American usage and style, Copperud, Roy H., AC69

American Veterinary Medical Association. Division of Membership and Field Services. *AVMA directory*, EJ118

American war medals and decorations, Kerrigan, Evans E., AL183

American war narratives, 1917–1918, Genthe, Charles V., DA197

American warplanes 1908–1988, Smith, Myron J., DA170

American Water Resources Association. *Hydata*, EF128

American Water Works Association. *Standard methods for the examination of water and wastewater*, EE62

—— *Water quality and treatment*, EK98

American Welding Society. *Welding handbook*, EK249

American wholesalers and distributors directory, CH346

American wit and humor
bibliography, BE411
periodicals, AD28

American women, AH88

American women, 1935–1940, AH57, AH88

American women and politics, Nelson, Barbara J., CC506

American women and the labor movement, 1825–1974, Soltow, Martha Jane, CC503, CC511

—— Wery, Mary K., CC503

American women and the U.S. armed forces, CJ612

American women artists, past and present, Tuft, Eleanor, BF16

American women civil rights activists, Hardy, Gayle J., CC577

American women dramatists of the twentieth century, Coven, Brenda, BE459

American women managers and administrators, Leavitt, Judith A., AH77, CH101

American women playwrights, 1900–1930, Bzowski, Frances Diodato, BE455

American women playwrights, 1964–1989, Gavin, Christy, BE459

American women sculptors, Rubenstein, Charlotte Streifer, BF400

American women writers, BE399, BE443, BE623

American women writers on Vietnam, Butler, Deborah A., BE417, DE278

American women's fiction, 1790–1870, White, Barbara Anne, BE480

American women's history, DB48

American women's magazines, Humphreys, Nancy K., AD37, CC522

American working class history, Neufeld, Maurice F., CH637

American writers, BE444, BE448, BE622

—— Unger, Leonard, BE201

American writers before 1800, BE445

American writers since 1900, Vinson, James, BE449

American writers to 1900, Vinson, James, BE449

The Americana annual, AB9

Americanisms, Mathews, Mitford McLeod, AC152

Americans of Jewish descent, Stern, Malcolm H., AJ66

Americas, DB6
bibliography, DB3
directories, CE86
statistics, CG38
bibliography, CG71, CG72

Americas (by subject)
art, BG12
censuses
handbooks, CG38
discovery and exploration
bibliography, DB22
sourcebooks, DB63
history
bibliography, AA404
library catalogs, DB1
statistics, CG70, DB7, DB290

America's best colleges, CB249

America's best money managers, CH311

America's black colleges, Bowman, J. Wilson, CB304

America's corporate families, CH347

America's corporate families and international affiliates, CH347

America's elderly, CC93

America's homeless, Burt, Martha R., CC200

America's new foundations, AL99

America's newest foundations, AL99

America's science museums, Danilov, Victor J., EA216

America's top-rated cities, CL69

America's white working-class women, Kennedy, Susan E., CC496

Amerika-Gedenkbibliothek/Berliner Zentralbibliothek. *Künstler der jungen Generation*, BF139

Amerindians of the Lesser Antilles, Myers, Robert A., CE80

Ameringer, Charles D. *Political parties of the Americas, 1980s to 1990s*, CJ97

Ames, John G. *Chronology and index of the Second World War 1938–1945*, DA209

—— *Comprehensive index, 1889–1893*, AF98

—— *Comprehensive index to the publications of the United States government, 1881–1893*, AF98

Ames, Kenneth L. *Decorative arts and household furnishings in America, 1650–1920*, BG117

—— *Material culture*, BG3

Amharic-English dictionary, Kane, Thomas Leiper, AC209

Amharic language
dictionaries
bilingual, AC209
Amharic-English, AC210
English-Amharic, AC211

Animal science
handbooks, EJ121

Amin, S. H. *Middle East legal systems*, CK227

Amin collection, Kleinschmidt, Harald, DD240

Amino acids, EE114

Amino acids and peptides, EE114, EE116

Amistad Research Center. *Author and added entry catalog of the American Missionary Association Archives*, BC302, CC362

Ammann, Daniel. *An index to dialect maps of Great Britain*, BD104

Ammer, Christine. *Fighting words*, CJ582

—— *The new A to Z of women's health*, EH81

Ammerman, David L. *Books about early America*, DB78

The Amnesty International report, CK109

Amo, Julian. *Anuario bibliográfico mexicano*, AA458

Amos, Ashley Crandell. *Old English word studies*, BD99

Amos, Linda K. *Guide to programs in nursing in four-year colleges and universities*, EH282

Amos, William. *Originals*, BE251, BE688

Amphibia-reptilia red data book, EG250

Amphibian species of the world, Frost, Darrel R., EG248

Amphibians and reptiles, EG245, EG246, EG247, EG248, EG249, EG250, EG251, EG252

Amptelike plekname in die Republiek van Suid-Afrika en in Suidwes-Afrika, goedgekeur tot 1 April 1977, CL156

Amtmann, Bernard. *Contributions to a dictionary of Canadian pseudonyms and anonymous works relating to Canada*, AA151

—— *Contributions to a short-title catalogue of Canadiana*, AA444

Amune, Stephen A. *Retrospective index to Nigerian doctoral dissertations and masters theses, 1895–1980*, AG48

The amusement park guide, O'Brien, Tim, BK126

The Amy Vanderbilt complete book of etiquette, Vanderbilt, Amy, AL158

An, Tai Sung. *North Korea*, CJ441, DE219

Un an de nouveautés, AA633

Analecta bollandiana, BC257, BC258

Analecta hymnica medii aevi, BC313

Analecta linguista, BD23

Analogy, Anttila, Raima, BD47

—— Brewer, Warren A., BD47

Analyses of nineteenth- and twentieth-century music, 1940–1985, Wenk, Arthur B., BJ113

Analysis of public policy, Robey, John S., CA11

Analyst's handbook, CH419

Analytic chemistry
nomenclature, EE35

Analytical abstracts, EE20

•*Analytical abstracts (AA)*, EE20

Analytical bibliography, 1961–1970, Vorlat, Emma, BD92

Analytical bibliography of international migration statistics, United Nations. Department of Economic and Social Affairs, CG12

Analytical bibliography of universal collected biography, Riches, Phyllis M., AH21

Analytical bibliography of writings on modern English morphology and syntax, 1877–1960, Scheurweghs, Gustave, BD92

Analytical chemistry, EE61

Analytical concordance to the Bible, Young, Robert, BC167

An analytical guide to the bibliographies on Islam, Muhammad, and the Qur'an, Geddes, Charles L., BC493

An analytical index to the ballad-entries (1557–1709) in the Registers of the Company of Stationers of London, Stationers' Company (London), BE634

An analytical index to the Book of Common Prayer and a brief account of its evolution, Pepper, George Wharton, BC348

Analytische Bibliographie der Gesamtregister schweizerischer Zeitschriften, Studer, Maja, AD330

Anarchism, Goehlert, Robert, CJ506

—— Herczeg, Claire, CJ506

Anarchisme, Fauvel-Rouif, Denise, CJ506

—— Gaillemin, Janine, CJ506

—— Richett, Diana, CJ506

—— Sowerwine-Mareschal, Marie-Aude, CJ506

Anarchist thinkers and thought, Nursey-Bray, Paul F., CJ506

Anatolian archaeology, Battersby, Harold R., DC531

Anatomy, BF123

Anatomy of wonder, BE276

Ancel, Jean. *Bibliography of the Jews in Romania*, DC493

Ancestry's guide to research, Cerny, Johni, AJ4

Ancestry's red book, AJ1

Anchor Bible, BC93

The Anchor Bible dictionary, BC125

The Anchor book of French quotations, BE127

The ancient arts of Western and Central Asia, Goldman, Bernard, BF3
Ancient Greek literature, Harvard University. Library, BE1029
Ancient history *see* **Archaeology and ancient history**
Ancient history, Harvard University. Library, DA65
Ancient history atlas, Banks, Arthur, DA117
—— Grant, Michael, DA117
Ancient Iran and Zoroastrianism in festschriften, Oxtoby, Willard Gurdon, BC575
Ancient writers, BE1012
—— Luce, T. James, BE201
Ancītis, Valdemars. *Piecos gados*, BE1320
Ancona, Paola d'. *Dictionnaire des miniaturistes du Moyen Âge et de la Renaissance dans les différentes contrées de l'Europe*, BF310
And so to bed, Havlice, Patricia Pate, BE507, BE726, DB66
Andereck, Paul A. *Computer genealogy*, AJ5
Andersen, Charles J. *Rating of graduate programs*, CB347, CB348
Andersen, Dines. *A critical Pali dictionary*, AC626
Andersen, Vilhelm. *Illustreret dansk Litteraturhistorie*, BE1121
Andersen, Hans Christian, BE1112
Anderson, A. Grant. *New Zealand in maps*, CL366
Anderson, Addell Austin. *Black theatre directory*, BH83
Anderson, Aksel. *Sveriges bibliografi, 1481–1600*, AA828
Anderson, Andy B. *Handbook of survey research*, CD63
Anderson, B. W. *Gems, their sources, descriptions, and identification*, EF180
Anderson, Beatrix. *Cassell's colloquial German*, AC437
Anderson, Benedict R. *Bibliography of Indonesian publications*, AD196
Anderson, Bernhard W. *The books of the Bible*, BC169
Anderson, Charles S. *Augsburg historical atlas of Christianity in the Middle Ages and Reformation*, BC287
Anderson, Donald K. *Guide to the records of the United States House of Representatives at the National Archives, 1789–1989*, CJ203
Anderson, E. Ruth. *Contemporary American composers*, BJ202
Anderson, Elliott. *The little magazine in America*, AD39
Anderson, Emily Ann. *English poetry, 1900–1950*, BE694
Anderson, Ewan W. *Atlas of world political flashpoints*, CJ72
Anderson, G. W. *Decade of Bible bibliography*, BC117
Anderson, George Lincoln. *Asian literature in English*, BE1542
Anderson, Gerald H. *Concise dictionary of the Christian world mission*, BC310
Anderson, Herbert Lawrence. *A physicist's desk reference*, ED48
Anderson, Ian Gibson. *Councils, committees, and boards*, AL65
Anderson, James. *The Harper dictionary of opera and operetta*, BJ247
Anderson, Janet A. *Women in the fine arts*, BF16
Anderson, Jay. *Living history sourcebook*, DB52
Anderson, John Parker. *The book of British topography*, DC347
Anderson, John Q. *Southwestern American literature*, BE570
Anderson, Kenneth. *Industrial medicine desk reference*, EH128
—— *Mosby's medical, nursing, and allied health dictionary*, EH102
Anderson, Lois E. *Mosby's medical, nursing, and allied health dictionary*, EH102
Anderson, Margaret. *Arabic materials in English translation*, DE45
Anderson, Martin. *Conscription*, CJ560

Anderson, Michael. *Crowell's handbook of contemporary drama*, BE230
Anderson, Nancy D. *French mathematical seminars*, EB7
—— *A guide to library service in mathematics*, EB1
Anderson, Ottilia C. *Index to festschriften in librarianship*, AK13
Anderson, Patricia J. *British literary publishing houses, 1820–1880*, AA297
—— *British literary publishing houses, 1881–1965*, AA297
Anderson, Peter J. *Research guide for undergraduates in political science*, CJ3
Anderson, Robert B. *Bibliography of early English law books*, CK212
Anderson, Robert Ralph. *Frühneuhochdeutsches Wörterbuch*, AC401
Anderson, Robert Roland. *Spanish American modernism*, BE872
Anderson, Ronald O. *Evaluation and educational technology*, CB168
Anderson, Sydney. *Orders and families of recent mammals of the world*, EG304
Anderson, Vicki. *Fiction sequels for readers 10–16*, BE246
Anderson, William. *The Scottish nation*, AH242
Anderson, William L. *Guide to Cherokee documents in foreign archives*, CC420
Anderson Imbert, Enrique. *Historia de la literatura hispanoamericana*, BE865
—— *Spanish-American literature*, BE865
Andersson, Per. *Pseudonymregister*, AA186
Andor, L. E. *The USSR and the Soviet bloc*, DD112, DD219
Andorra, DC82
Andorra, Taylor, Barry, DC82
Andors, Stephen. *Encyclopedia of China today*, DE141
Andover Theological Seminary. *The Congregationalism of the last 300 years, as seen in its literature*, BC383
Andrade, Marco. *Amazonía ecuatoriana*, DB322
Andrade, Vicente de Paula. *Ensayo bibliográfico mexicana del siglo XVII*, AA457
André, Jacques. *Dictionnaire étymologique de la langue latine*, AC579
Andre, Sam. *A pictorial history of boxing*, BK69
Andrea, Valerio. *Bibliotheca belgica*, AA580
Andreae, Daniel. *Illustrerad svensk ordbok*, AC761
Andréas, Bert. *Le manifeste communiste de Marx et Engels*, CJ497
Andreas, Willy. *Die grossen Deutschen*, AH208
Andreevskiĭ, I. E. *Entsiklopedicheskiĭ slovar'*, AB85
Andresen, Andreas. *Deutsche peintre-graveur*, BF382
—— *Die Monogrammisten und diejenigen bekannten und unbekannten Künstler aller Schulen*, BF160
Andresen, Carl. *Bibliographia Augustiniana*, BB60
Andresen, Harald. *Norsk biografisk oppslagsliteratur*, AH277
Andreucci, Franco. *Il movimento operaio italiano*, AH262
Andrew, Geoff. *Film Handbook*, BH290
—— *World film directors*, BH290
Andrews, Alice C. *The atlas of American higher education*, CB323
Andrews, Barry G. *Australian literature to 1900*, BE846
—— *The Oxford companion to Australian literature*, BE860
—— *The Oxford literary guide to Australia*, BE855
Andrews, Ethan Allen. *Harper's Latin dictionary*, AC574
Andrews, Eva L. *Subject index to poetry for children and young people*, BE322
Andrews, Frank. *Encyclopedia of recorded sound in the United States*, BJ392
Andrews, Henry Nathaniel. *Index of generic names of fossil plants, 1820–1965*, EF236
Andrews, John. *William Shakespeare*, BE785

Andrews, John A. *Keyguide to information sources on the international protection of human rights*, CK75
Andrews, Lorrin. *Dictionary of the Hawaiian language*, AC469
Andrews, Robert. *The Columbia dictionary of quotations*, BE97
—— *The concise Columbia dictionary of quotations*, BE98
Andrews, Theodora. *A bibliography on herbs, herbal medicine, "natural" foods, and unconventional medical treatment*, EH319
—— *Guide to the literature of pharmacy and the pharmaceutical sciences*, EH316
Andrews, William G. *International handbook of political science*, CJ54
Andrews, William L. *Southern literary culture, 1969–1975*, BE569
Andriot, Donna. *Guide to U.S. government publications*, AF80
—— *Guide to U.S. government statistics*, CG89
—— *Place guide*, CL110
—— *Population abstract of the United States*, CG76
Andriot, Jay. *Guide to U.S. government statistics*, CG89
Andriot, John L. *Guide to U.S. government publications*, AF80
—— *Guide to U.S. government serials and periodicals*, AF80
—— *Guide to U.S. government statistics*, CG89
—— *Township atlas of the United States*, CG76, CL297
Andriot, Laurie. *Guide to U.S. government statistics*, CG89
Andris-Michalaros, Aliki. *The Metropolitan Opera encyclopedia*, BJ250
Andrusyshen, C. H. *Ukrains'ko-anhliis'kyi slovnyk*, AC796
Andrzejewski, B. W. *Literatures in African languages*, BE1501
Aner, Ekkehard. *Grosser Atlas zur Weltgeschichte*, DA51
Angeles, Peter Adam. *Dictionary of philosophy*, BB37
—— *The HarperCollins dictionary of philosophy*, BB37
Angelova, Stefka. *Gŭrtsiĭa i bŭlgaro-grŭtskite otnosheniĭa v bŭlgarskata nauchna knizhnina, 1878–1980*, DC110
Angels to zeppelins, Lehnus, Donald J., BG198
Angelucci, Enzo. *The Rand McNally encyclopedia of military aircraft, 1914–1980*, CJ577
—— *World encyclopedia of civil aircraft*, CJ577
Angewandte Chemie, EE24
Anglemyer, Mary. *The natural environment*, EK64
—— *A search for environmental ethics*, EK65
Anglés, Higinio. *Diccionario de la música Labor*, BJ124
Angleško-slovenski in slovensko-angleški slovar, Komac, Daša, AC721
Angleško-slovenski slovar, Škerlj, Ružena, AC723
Anglia, BE419
Anglican Communion, BC333, BC334
see also **Church of England**
Anglicko-český geologický slovník, Zeman, Otakar, EF82
Anglicko-český technický slovník, EA106
Anglicko-slovenský slovník, Simko, Ján, AC719
Angliĭsko-bŭlgarski rechnik, Atanasova, Teodora, AC239
Angliski-latviska vārdnīca, Dravnieks, Jēkabs, AC597
Anglo-American cataloguing rules, AK194, AK195, AK196
Anglo-American first editions, Brussel, Isidore Rosenbaum, AA239
Anglo-American general encyclopedias, Walsh, S. Padraig, AB15
Anglo-amerikanische und deutsche Abkurzungen in Wissenschaft und Technik, Wennrich, Peter, EA98
Anglo-Irish literature, BE798
Anglo-Irish literature, BE797, BE798

Anglo-Jewish bibliography, 1937–1970, Goldschmidt-Lehmann, Ruth P., BC517

Anglo-Jewish bibliography, 1971–1990, Goldschmidt-Lehmann, Ruth P., BC517

———— Massil, Stephen W., BC517

———— Salinger, Peter Shmuel, BC517

Anglo-Latin literature, BE1049

Anglo-Norman dictionary, AC168

Anglo-Norman England, 1066–1154, Altschul, Michael, DC303, DC307, DC308, DC319, DC320, DC331

Anglo-Norman Text Society. *Anglo-Norman dictionary,* AC168

Anglo-russkiĭ astronomicheskiĭ slovar', EC38

Anglo-russkiĭ frazeologicheskiĭ slovar', Kunin, Aleksandr Vladimirovich, AC695

Anglo-russkiĭ geologicheskiĭ slovar', Timofeev, Petr Petrovich, EF89

Anglo-russkiĭ ĭadernyĭ slovar', Voskoboinik, David I., ED28

Anglo-russkiĭ politekhnicheskiĭ slovar', Chernukhin, Adol'f Efimovich, EA126

Anglo-Saxon and Celtic bibliography (450–1087), Bonser, Wilfrid, DC305

Anglo-Saxon dictionary, Bosworth, Joseph, AC171

Anglu-latviešu vārdnīca, AC596

Anglu-lietuviu kalbu žodynas, AC600, AC604

———— Laučka, A., AC604

———— Piesarkas, B., AC604

———— Stasiuleviciute, E., AC604

Angol-magyar keziszotar, Országh, László, AC496

Angol-magyar müszaki szotar, Katona, Lóránt, EA115

———— Klár, János, EA115

———— Nagy, Ernő, EA115

Angola
 anthropology and ethnology, CE104
 bibliography, DD18, DD114, DD128
 current surveys, DD62
 encyclopedias, DD48
 government publications
  bibliography, AF220
 statistics, CG315

Angola, Black, Richard, DD18

———— Broadhead, Susan H., DD48

———— Collelo, Thomas, DD62

———— Greenwood, Margaret Joan, DD128

———— Rodriguez de Areia, DD128

———— Somerville, Keith, DD128

Animal behavior *see* **Ethology**

Animal behavior abstracts, CD118, EG14

Animal breeding abstracts, EJ18, EJ19, EJ102

Animal health yearbook, EJ133

Animal identification, EG205

Animal life encyclopedia, Grzimek's, EG226

Animal rights, EG3

Animal science
 abstract journals, EJ102, EJ104, EJ105, EJ106, EJ107
 bibliography, EJ99, EJ100, EJ101
 catalogs, EJ119
 databases, EJ102, EJ125
 dictionaries, EJ111, EJ112, EJ116
  multilingual, EJ113, EJ114
 directories, EJ118, EJ119, EJ120
 encyclopedias, EJ108, EJ109
 guides, EJ96, EJ97, EJ98
 handbooks, EJ110, EJ122, EJ124, EJ125, EJ126, EJ127, EJ128, EJ129, EJ130, EJ131, EJ132
 indexes, EJ91, EJ103
 library catalogs, EJ100
 statistics, EJ133
 terminology, EJ123
 thesauruses, EJ117

Animal science, Ensminger, M. Eugene, EJ121

Animals
 illustrations, EG73

Animated TV specials, Woolery, George W., BH307

Animation, Hoffer, Thomas W., BH161

Aniskevich, N. P. *Slovar' geograficheskikh nazvaniĭ SSSR,* CL153

Anjos, Margarida dos. *Novo dicionário da língua portuguesa,* AC642

Ann, Martha. *Goddesses in world mythology,* BC62, CF2

Annalen der ältern deutschen Litteratur, Panzer, Georg Wolfgang Franz, AA639

Annales de géographie, CL23

Annales typographici ab artis inventae origine ad annum MD, Panzer, Georg Wolfgang Franz, AA226

Annals of American literature, 1602–1983, Ludwig, Richard M., BE436

Annals of Australian literature, Hooton, Joy W., BE851

Annals of Congress, AF127

Annals of English drama, BE648, BE661

Annals of English drama, 975–1700, Harbage, Alfred, BE660

Annals of English literature, 1475–1950, BE436, BE612, BE851

Annals of English verse, 1770–1835, Jackson, James Robert de Jager, BE707, BE708

Annals of opera, 1597–1940, Loewenberg, Alfred, BJ255

Annals of the American pulpit, Sprague, William Buell, BC255

Annals of the Metropolitan Opera Guild, BJ254

Annals of the New York stage, Odell, George Clinton Densmore, BH105

Annamalai, E. *Classified bibliography of linguistic dissertations on Indian languages,* BD225

L'année philologique, BE990, BE1003, BE1007

L'année psychologique, CD6

Anniversaries, AL143

Anniversaries and holidays, Gregory, Ruth W., AL146

Annotated and classified bibliography of Indian demography, Desai, Prasannavadan B., CG387

Annotated bibliographies of mineral deposits in Africa, Asia (exclusive of the USSR) and Australasia, Ridge, John Drew, EF175

Annotated bibliographies of mineral deposits in Europe, Ridge, John Drew, EF175

Annotated bibliographies of mineral deposits in the Western hemisphere, Ridge, John Drew, EF175

Annotated bibliography and index covering CPL bibliographies, Coatsworth, Patricia A., BF271

———— Hecimovich, James, BF271

———— Ravenhall, Mary, BF271

Annotated bibliography in religion and psychology, Meissner, William W., BC9

Annotated bibliography of Afghanistan, Hanifi, M. Jamil, DE110

An annotated bibliography of American Indian and Eskimo autobiographies, Brumble, H. David, BE549

An annotated bibliography of American literary periodicals, 1741–1850, Kribbs, Jayne K., BE422

Annotated bibliography of automation in libraries and information systems, MacCafferty, Maxine, AK190

Annotated bibliography of bibliographies on Indonesia, Kemp, Herman C., AA78, DE176

Annotated bibliography of bibliographies on selected government publications and supplementary guides to the Superintendent of Documents classification system, Body, Alexander C., AF78

An annotated bibliography of Byzantine sources in English translation, Hanawalt, Emily Albu, DA164

The annotated bibliography of Canada's major authors, BE819

Annotated bibliography of Canadian demography, Balakrishnan, T. R., CG116

———— Shiel, Suzanne, CG116

———— Wai, Lokky, CG116

An annotated bibliography of Chicano folklore from the Southwestern United States, Heisley, Michael, CF68

Annotated bibliography of child language and language disorders, BD63

Annotated bibliography of economic geology, EF21

An annotated bibliography of homosexuality, CC266

An annotated bibliography of Javanese folklore, Danandjaja, James, CF95

Annotated bibliography of library automation, Tinker, Lynne, AK190

Annotated bibliography of Mennonite writings on war and peace, 1930–1980, BC360

An annotated bibliography of North American doctoral dissertations on Old English language and literature, Pulsiano, Phillip, BD101, BE728, BE730

Annotated bibliography of Oceanic music and dance, McLean, Mervyn, BJ322

Annotated bibliography of Puerto Rican bibliographies, Fowlie-Flores, Fay, AA35, DB452

Annotated bibliography of quaternary shorelines, 1945–1964, Richards, Horace Gardiner, EF38

An annotated bibliography of research on Zambian women, DD246

An annotated bibliography of selected Chinese reference works, Teng, Ssu-yü, AA362, DE123

Annotated bibliography of social research in Pakistan, Bhatty, Khan Mohammad, DE240

Annotated bibliography of Southern American English, McMillan, James B., BD106

Annotated bibliography of space science and technology, with an astronomical supplement, Ordway, Frederick I., EK24

Annotated bibliography of technical and specialized dictionaries in Spanish-Spanish and Spanish-English, with commentary, Espinosa Elerick, María Luz, AC751

An annotated bibliography of texts on writing skills, BD95

An annotated bibliography of the Holy Roman Empire, Zophy, Jonathan W., DC12

An annotated bibliography of the languages of the Gilbert Islands, Ellice Islands and Nauru, Kunz, Egon F., BD235

An annotated bibliography of the Napoleonic era, Meyer, Jack Allen, DC193

An annotated bibliography of the novels of the Mexican Revolution of 1910–1917, Rutherford, John, BE916

An annotated bibliography of the Southwest Pacific and adjacent areas, DF1

Annotated bibliography of the visual arts of East Africa, Burt, Eugene C., BG5

An annotated bibliography of works on daily newspapers in Canada, 1914–1983, Sotiron, Minko, AE39

An annotated bibliography on adult day programs and dementia care, CC58

Annotated bibliography on childhood schizophrenia, 1955–1964, Tilton, James R., EH374

Annotated bibliography on hydrology (1951–54) and sedimentation (1950–54), United States and Canada, American Geophysical Union, EF126, EF127

Annotated bibliography on hydrology and sedimentation, Geological Survey (U.S.), EF126, EF127

An annotated bibliography on inner Asia, Lee, Don Y., DE75

Annotated bibliography on Puerto Rican materials and other sundry matters, Cardona, Luis A., DB451

An annotated bibliography on technical writing, editing, graphics, and publishing, 1950–1965, Society of Technical Writers and Publishers, EA164

Annotated bibliography on technical writing, editing, graphics, and publishing, 1966–80, Carlson, Helen V., EA164

Annotated bibliography on the economic history of India, CH194, DE153

Annotated bibliography on the history of data processing, Cortada, James W., EK209

Annotated bibliography on the population of Ethiopia, Abdulahi Hassen, CG329

An annotated bibliography on women, Ngcobo, Zipho G., DD229

Annotated bibliography on women in development in Asia and the Pacific, CC586

The annotated Book of Common Prayer, Church of England, BC336

Annotated catalogue of and guide to the publications of the Geological Survey Canada, 1845–1917, Ferrier, W. F., EF28

Annotated code of the public general laws of Maryland, Maryland. [Laws, etc.], CK179

Annotated critical bibliography of Augustan poetry, Nokes, David, BE711

An annotated critical bibliography of feminist criticism, Humm, Maggie, BE49

Annotated critical bibliography of Jacobean and Caroline comedy, Corbin, Peter, BE646

—— Sedge, Douglas, BE646

An annotated critical bibliography of modernism, Davies, Alistair, BE761

An annotated guide to current national bibliographies, Bell, Barbara L., AA388

An annotated guide to Philippine serials, Golay, Frank H., AD208

Annotated guide to Taiwan periodical literature, 1972, AD210

An annotated index of medieval women, Echols, Anne, CC575, DA149

An annotated journalism bibliography, 1958–1968, Price, Warren C., AE134

Annotated neuro-computing bibliography, EK155

Annotated statistical bibliography, CG432

Annotated world list of selected current geographical serials, Harris, Chauncy Dennison, CL24

Annuaire de la France protestante, Fédération protestante de France, BC323

L'annuaire de l'Afrique du Nord, DD68, DD77

Annuaire de statistique internationale des grandes villes, CG47

Annuaire démographique, CG49

Annuaire des cotes international, BF109

Annuaire des ventes de tableaux, dessins, aquarelles, pastels, gouaches, miniatures, Lang, L. Maurice, BF108

Annuaire diplomatique et consulaire de la République Française, AH200, CJ329

Annuaire européen, CJ313

Annuaire international de statistique, CG48

Annuaire international des beaux-arts, BF99

Annuaire international des ventes, BF109

Annuaire officiel de la presse belge, AD82, AE45

Annuaire protestant, BC323

Annuaire statistique, CG316, CG322, CG324, CG327, CG344, CG349, CG363

Annuaire statistique de Djibouti, CG326

Annuaire statistique de la Belgique, CG199

Annuaire statistique de la France, Institut national de la statistique et des études économiques (France), CG216

Annuaire statistique de la République populaire du Bénin, CG316

Annuaire statistique de la Société des Nations, League of Nations. Economic, Financial, and Transit Department, CG52

Annuaire statistique de la Tunisie, CG365

Annuaire statistique de l'Algérie, CG314

Annuaire statistique de l'Union française outre-mer, CG214

Annuaire statistique des territoires d'outre-mer, Institut national de la statistique et des études économiques, CG214

Annuaire statistique du Burkina Faso, CG319

Annuaire statistique du Dahomey, CG316 *

Annuaire statistique du Gabon, CG331

Annuaire statistique du Luxembourg, CG261

Annuaire statistique du Mali, CG342

Annuaire statistique du Maroc, CG346

Annuaire statistique du Tchad, CG323

Annuaire statistiques, CG320

Annual, Southern Baptist Convention, BC329

Annual abstract of statistics, CG125, CG264, CG350, CG442

—— Great Britain. Central Statistical Office, CG231

—— Iraq. Jihāz al-Markazī lil-Iḥsā', CG397

Annual abstract of statistics - Federation of Nigeria, Federal Office of Statistics, Nigeria. Federal Office of Statistics, CG350

Annual American catalog, 1886–1910, AA413

Annual bibliography of British and Irish history, DC281, DC282

Annual bibliography of Commonwealth literature, BE816

Annual bibliography of English language and literature, BD90, BE401, BE513, BE585, BE588, BE694

Annual bibliography of Indian archaeology, DE154

Annual bibliography of modern art, Museum of Modern Art (New York, N.Y.), BF55

Annual bibliography of Ontario history, DB212

Annual bibliography of Scottish literature, BE808

Annual bibliography of studies in Australian literature, BE847

Annual bibliography of the history of the printed book and libraries, AA268, AK17

Annual bibliography of Victorian studies, BE752

Annual book of A.S.T.M. standards including tentative standards, American Society for Testing and Materials, EA269

Annual bulletin of classical archaeology, DA96

Annual Canadian catalogue, AA448

The annual catalogue for the year, 1699–[March 25, 1704], AA676

Annual catalogue of Australian publications, AA941, AA942, AA944, AF261, DF23

Annual digest of statistics, CG345

Annual directory through press and advertising, AD103

Annual Egyptological bibliography, DA121

Annual fertilizer review, EJ79

Annual handbook : terms of admission to the colleges, CB261

Annual index of periodicals and photographs for 1890, AD286

Annual index to motion picture credits, BH203

Annual index to poetry in periodicals, BE502

Annual legal bibliography, Harvard Law School. Library, CK11

Annual library index, AD261, AD285

Annual list of consumer information, CH561

Annual literary index, AD261

Annual magazine subject index, 1907–49, AD262, AD270, BH55, CC384

The annual on terrorism, CJ552

Annual register, DA185

Annual register of grant support, AL100

Annual report—Indian Council of Social Science Research, CA45

Annual report of the Director for the twelve month period ending [...], United States. Administrative Office of the United States Courts, CK169

Annual report of the Registrar General, Northern Ireland. General Register Office, CG233, CG239

Annual report of the Registrar of Newspapers for India, AE88

Annual report on Latin American and Caribbean bibliographic activities, Seminar on the Acquisition of Latin American Library Materials, AA24

Annual report to Congress on the implementation of the Individuals with Disabilities Education Act, CB207

Annual reports [Index], United States. Department of Agriculture, EJ92

Annual review, BE35

Annual review of anthropology, CE21

Annual review of information science and technology, AK76

Annual review of psychology, CD44

Annual review of United Nations affairs, AF32

An annual review of world production, consumption, and trade of fertilizers, EJ79

Annual statistical abstract, CG408

Annual statistical bulletin, Swaziland. Central Statistical Office, CG360

Annual statistical bulletin, Malaysia, Malaysia. Jabatan Perangkaan, CG412

Annual statistical digest, CG178, CG180, CG354

—— Board of Governors of the Federal Reserve System, CH293

—— Central Bank of Barbados, CG167

Annual statistical yearbook (Amman, Jordan), CG405

Annual survey of American poetry, BE502

Annual survey of colleges, CB334

Annuario bibliografico di archaeologia, DA69

Annuario della stampa italiana, AD125

Annuario delle biblioteche italiane, AK149

Annuario di statistiche demografiche, CG258

Annuario pontificio, BC409

Annuario statistico italiano, CG255, CG257, CG258

Anonym– og Pseudonym-Lexikon for Danmark og Island til 1920 og Norge til 1814, Ehrencron-Müller, Holger, AA166

Anonymer og pseudonymer i den norske literatur 1678–1890, AA179

Anonymes 1501–1800 : état au 31 décembre 1986, Bibliothèque Nationale (France), AA101, AA613

Anonyms, Cushing, William, AA149

Anonyms and pseudonyms, AA148, AC43
  bibliography, AA145
  writers in English, AA147

Anonyms and pseudonyms (by country or region)
  Argentina, AA155, AA156
  Belgium, AA162, AA163
  Brazil, AA157
  Bulgaria, AA164
  Canada, AA151
  China, AA190
  Colombia, AA158
  Czechoslovakia, AA165
  Dominican Republic, AA159
  Estonia, AA167
  Flanders, AA178
  France, AA168, AA169
  Germany, AA170, AA171, AA172, AA173
  Great Britain, AA150
  Greece, AA174
  Hungary, AA175, AA176
  India, AA191, AA192
  international, AA146
  Italy, AA177
  Latin America, AA153, AA154
  Mexico, AA152
  Netherlands, AA178
  Norway, AA179
  Poland, AA180
  Portugal, AA181
  Romania, AA182
  Russia, AA183, AA184
  Scandinavia, AA166
  Spain, AA185
  Sweden, AA186, AA187
  Ukraine, AA188
  United States, AA150
  United States and Great Britain, AA149

Anonyms and pseudonyms (by language)
  Arabic, AA189
  Slovak, AA160
  Yiddish, AA161

ANQ, BE168

The Anschluss movement, 1918–1938, Low, Alfred D., DC88

Anschriften deutscher Verlage, AA286

Anselmo, António Joaquim. *Bibliografia das obras impressas em Portugal no século XVI,* AA773

Anshel, Mark H. *Dictionary of the sport and exercise sciences,* BK25

Anson, Christopher M. *Writing across the curriculum,* CB218

Ansted, A. *A dictionary of sea terms,* EC81

Ansteinsson, John. *English-Norwegian technical dictionary,* EA121

—— *Norsk-engelsk teknisk ordbok,* EA121

Antarctic
  atlases, CL369, CL370
  bibliography, DB214, DG1
  chronologies, DG9
  databases, DG1, DG2
  encyclopedias, DG8
  manuscripts and archives, DF15

Antarctic (by subject)
  discovery and exploration, DG6, DG9
  see also **Arctic**

Antarctic bibliography, DG1, DG2
—— Doumani, George A., DG1
—— Naval Photographic Interpretation Center, DG1
Antarctic map folio series, American Geographical Society of New York, CL369
Antarctica, Stewart, John, DG8
Ante-Nicene Christian library, BC293
Ante-Nicene Fathers, BC293
Antebellum black newspapers, Jacobs, Donald M., AE105
Anthologies of music, Murray, Sterling E., BJ116
Anthology of classical quotations, Harbottle, Thomas Benfield, BE144
Anthony, Henry B. *Dictionary catalog of the Harris collection of American poetry and plays, Brown University Library, Providence, Rhode Island,* BE494
Anthony, John B. *The gifted and talented,* CB184
Anthony, John W. *Handbook of mineralogy,* EF198
Anthony, L. J. *Information sources in energy technology,* EK219
—— *Information sources in engineering,* EK2
Anthony, Margaret M. *The gifted and talented,* CB184
Anthony memorial, Stockbridge, John Calvin, BE494
Anthropological and cross-cultural themes in mental health, Favazza, Armando R., EH372
Anthropological bibliographies, CE19
Anthropological bibliography of aboriginal Costa Rica, Lines, J. A., DB302
Anthropological bibliography of aboriginal El Salvador, Lines, J. A., DB302
Anthropological bibliography of aboriginal Guatemala, British Honduras, Lines, J. A., DB302
Anthropological bibliography of aboriginal Honduras, Lines, J. A., DB302
Anthropological bibliography of aboriginal Nicaragua, Lines, J. A., DB302
Anthropological bibliography of aboriginal Panama, Shook, E. W., DB302
Anthropological bibliography of Negro Africa, Wieschhoff, Heinrich Albert, CE105
An anthropological bibliography of South Asia, Fürer-Haimendorf, Elizabeth von, CE108
—— Kanitkar, Helen A., CE108
Anthropological fieldwork, Gravel, Pierre Bettez, CE11
Anthropological glossary, Pearson, Roger, CE50
Anthropological index to current periodicals in the Museum of Mankind Library, CE30, CE36
Anthropological literature, CE30, CE36
•*Anthropological literature on disc,* CE36
Anthropology and ethnology
  abstract journals, CE34
  atlases, CE70, CE71, CE72, CE73
  audiovisual materials, CE33
  bibliography, BD9, CC5, CE4, CE5, CE7, CE8, CE11, CE13, CE14, CE15, CE16, CE17, CE18, CE21, CE24, CE25, CE29, CE72, CE76, CE93, CE95, CL29, EA16, EB10, EC15, ED5, EE13, EF57, EF141, EF173, EF232, EG6, EG105, EG211, EG312, EH372
    current, CE34
  bibliography of bibliography, CE19
  biography, CE65, CE66, CE67, CE68, CE69, CE86, CE87
  book reviews, CE37
  classification, CE59, CE61
  congresses and meetings, CE6
  databases, CE8, CE36
  dictionaries, CE47, CE48, CE49, CE50, CE51
  directories, CE54, CE66, CE88, CE99
    Americas, CE86
  dissertations, CE27, CE28
  encyclopedias, CE38, CE39, CE40, CE41, CE42, CE44, CE45, CE46, CE48
  filmography, CE33
  grants-in-aid, CE55
  guides, CE1, CE2
  guides to records, CE32
  guides to research, CE57

  handbooks, CE56, CE58, CE59, CE60, CE61, CE62, CE116
  indexes, AD254, BB24, BE38, CE23, CE35, CE36
  library catalogs, CE22, CE29, CE30, CL29
  manuscripts and archives, CE31
  periodicals, CE26
  reviews of research, CE21
  serial publications, CE25
  terminology, CE53
  thesauruses, CE52
  yearbooks, CE21, CE64
Anthropology and ethnology (by country or region)
  Africa, CE101, CE102, CE103, CE105, CE106
  Africa, Southern, CE100
  Angola, CE104
  Asia, CE107
  Asia, South, CE108
  Asia, Southeast, CE108
  Asia, West, CE112
  Australia, CE113
  Caribbean, CE85
  Central America, CE75, CE79, CE82, CE89, CE90, DB302
  Europe, CE97, CE98
    bibliography, CE96
  India, CE110
  Latin America, CE78
    dictionaries, CC460
  Mexico, CE75, CE79, CE82, CE90
  Namibia, CE104
  North America, CE78
  Oceania, CE114, DF5
  Philippines, CE111
  Russia and the U.S.S.R., CE20
  South America, CE81, CE91
  West Indies, CE80
Anthropology in use, Van Willigen, John, CE18
Anthropology journals and serials, Williams, John T., CE26
Anthropology of aging, CC59, CE3
Anthropology of southern Africa in periodicals to 1950, CE100
The anthropology of war, Ferguson, R. Brian, CE10
The anthropology of Western Europe, Kuter, Lois, CE93
The anti-cult movement in America, Shupe, Anson D., BC32
Anti-Defamation League of B'nai B'rith. *American Jewish history,* BC523
—— *Bibliographical essays in medieval Jewish studies,* BC511
Anti-intervention, Doenecke, Justus D., CJ668
Anti-Semitism, BC508
Antibiotics, EE125, EH324, EH335
Antifaschistischer Widerstand und Klassenkampf, Goguel, Rudi, DC233
Antifeminism in American thought, Kinnard, Cynthia D., CC497
Antigua and Barbuda, CG164
Antigua and Barbuda. Ministry of Finance. Statistics Division. *Statistical yearbook,* CG164
Antigua statistical yearbook, CG164
Antiquarian catalogues of musical interest, Coover, James, BJ27
The antique buyer's dictionary of names, Coysh, Arthur Wilfred, BG50
Antique Collectors' Club. *The dictionary of British artists, 1880–1940,* BF316
—— *Pictorial dictionary of British 19th century furniture design,* BG120
Antique collector's guide, Benedictus, David, BG50
Antiques
  bibliography, BG36
  biography, BG50
  dictionaries, BG42, BG44
    multilingual, BG43
  encyclopedias, BG37, BG38, BG39, BG40, BG41
  handbooks, BG45
  prices, BG46, BG48, BG49
  restoration, BG45
  see also **Furniture**

Antiques and collectibles, Franklin, Linda Campbell, BG36
The antiques care & repair handbook, Jackson, Albert, BG45
Antisemitic propaganda, Singerman, Robert, BC508
Antisemitism, BC508
Antkiewicz, Susan. *Women and development in Zambia,* DD246
Antología de textos, citas, frases, modismos, y decires, Clarasó Daudí, Noel, BE148
Antonarakis, Stylianos E. *Mendelian inheritance in man,* EG342, EH189
Antonini, Rosalba. *Bibliografia dell'Italia antica,* DC417
Antônio, Irati. *Bibliografia da música brasileira,* BJ22
Antonio, Nicolás. *Bibliotheca hispana nova,* AA811
—— *Bibliotheca hispana vetus,* AA811
Antony, Arthur. *Guide to basic information sources in chemistry,* EE1
Antrobus, Frederick Ignatius. *History of the popes,* BC432
Anttila, Raima. *Analogy,* BD47
Anuario bibliográfico, Biblioteca Nacional de México, AA466
Anuario bibliográfico colombiano, AA527
Anuario bibliográfico colombiano "Rubén Pérez Ortiz", AA527
Anuario bibliográfico costarricense, AA477, AA480
Anuario bibliográfico cubano, AA559, AA562
Anuario bibliográfico de la República Argentina, AA494
Anuario bibliográfico dominicano, AA565
Anuario bibliográfico ecuatoriano, AA528, AA529, AA532
Anuario bibliográfico hondureño, AA486, AA489
Anuario bibliográfico mexicano, AA458, AA466
Anuario bibliográfico peruano, AA543
Anuario bibliográfico puertorriqueño, AA569
Anuario bibliográfico uruguayo, AA546, AA547
Anuario bibliográfico venezolano, AA548, AA549, AA552
Anuario de demografía, CG144
Anuario de estadística, 1963/68, Instituto Nacional de Estadística (Ecuador), CG155
Anuario de la prensa chilena, AA512
Anuario de la prensa española, AD151
Anuario demográfico de Cuba, CG168
Anuario español e hispano-americano del libro y de las artes gráficas con el Catálogo mundial del libro impreso en lengua española, AA821
Anuario estadístico, CG128, CG129, CG131
—— Argentine Republic. Dirección Nacional de Estadística y Censos, CG135
—— Dominican Republic. Dirección General de Estadística y Censos, CG172
Anuario estadístico de América Latina y el Caribe, CG120
Anuario estadístico de Chile, CG145
Anuario estadístico de Costa Rica, CG126
Anuario estadístico de Cuba, CG169
Anuario estadístico de España, CG280
Anuario estadístico de la República de Nicaragua, CG132
Anuario estadístico de la República del Paraguay, CG156
Anuario estadístico de los Estados Unidos Mexicanos, CG117
Anuario estadístico de Venezuela, CG162
Anuario estadístico del Paraguay, CG156
Anuario estadístico del Perú, CG157, DB389
Anuario estadístico, Uruguay, CG159
Anuário estatístico, CG277, CG315, CG335
Anuário estatístico de Angola, CG315
Anuário estatístico do Brasil, CG141
Anuario general de estadística, Colombia. Departamento Administrativo Nacional de Estadística, CG149
Anuario interamericano de derechos humanos, CK108
Anuarul cărții din Republica Populara Romînă, Bucharest (Romania). Biblioteca Centrală de Stat, AA783

Anuarul statistic al Romaniei, CG279
The Anugîtâ, BC92
Anwyl, Edward. *Geiriadur saesneg a chymraeg,* AC807
Anwyl, J. Bodvan. *Geiriadur saesneg a chymraeg,* AC807
Anzeiger für schweizerische Geschichte, AH299, DC528
Anzovin, Steven. *Facts about the states,* CG104
——— *Speeches of the American presidents,* CJ188
Aotearoa, AH379
APA membership register, American Psychological Association, CD35
APA publication manual, CD42
APAIS, Australian public affairs information service, CA23, DF22
Aparato bibliográfico de la historia general de Filipinas, Retana y Gamboa, Wenceslao Emilio, AA929
Apartheid, DD208, DD209
  bibliography, BE1534, DD216, DD217, DD220, DD224
Apel, Willi. *Harvard dictionary of music,* BJ153
Apelblat, Alexander. *Table of definite and indefinite integrals,* EB77
Apéndice a la Bibliografía guatemalteca, Figueroa Marroquín, Horacio, AA482
Aperçu de la démographie des divers pays du monde, CG48
API, BF207
Aplin, Graeme. *Australians : a historical dictionary,* DF37
——— *Australians : events and places,* DF37
Aplin, Richard. *A dictionary of contemporary France,* DC208
Apocrypha according to the Authorized Version, Pfeiffer, Robert H., BC94
Apocrypha of the Old Testament, BC94
Apocryphal New Testament, Elliot, J. K., BC94
——— James, Montague Rhodes, BC94
Apocryphal Old Testament, Sparks, H. F. D., BC94
Appalachian Consortium. *Bibliography of Southern Appalachia,* DB157
Appalachian State University. *Bibliography of Southern Appalachia,* DB157
Appel, Marsha E. *Illustration index,* BF60
Appendices ad Hainii-Copingeri Repertorivm bibliographicvm, Reichling, Dietrich, AA228
Apperley, Richard. *Pictorial guide to identifying Australian architecture,* BF208
Apperson, George Latimer. *English proverbs and proverbial phrases,* BE151
The Applause/best plays theater yearbook, BE454
Applause theatre world, BH111
Apple, Rima D. *The history of women and science, health, and technology,* EA231
——— *Women, health, and medicine in America,* EH198
Appleby, Barry Léon. *Elsevier's dictionary of commercial terms and phrases,* CH429
Appleton, George. *The Oxford book of prayer,* BC207
Appleton's cyclopaedia of American biography, AH58, AH62, AH65
Appleton's new Cuyás English-Spanish and Spanish-English dictionary, Cuyás, Arturo, AC732
Applied and decorative arts, Ehresmann, Donald L., BF2, BG2
Applied Anthropology Documentation Project. *Anthropology in use,* CE18
Applied arts
  bibliography
    current, BG11
  biography, AH213, BG32
  guides, BG2
Applied arts (by country or region)
  Africa
    bibliography, BG4
  United States
    bibliography, BG9, CC422
Applied mathematics, Handbook of, EB64, EB67
Applied mathematics series, EB78
——— National Bureau of Standards (U.S.), EB88

Applied science and technology index, CH37, EA67
Applied social sciences index & abstracts, CA24
Apponyi, Sándor. *Hungarica,* DC378
Appraisal, EA26
Approved lists of bacterial names, EG308
Approved methods of the American Association of Cereal Chemists, American Association of Cereal Chemists, EJ147
Apropos patterns for embroidery, lace and woven textiles, Abegg, Margaret, BG152
Apte, Vaman Shivaram. *The practical Sanskrit-English dictionary,* AC702
Apuntes para un catálogo de periódicos madrileños desde el año 1661 al 1870, Hartzenbusch, Eugenio, AE76
Apuntes para una bibliografía militar de México, 1536–1936, México. Comisión de Estudios Militares. Biblioteca del Ejército, DB230
Apuntes para una biblioteca de escritoras españolas, Serrano y Sanz, Manuel, BE1441
Aquaculture, EJ7, EJ25
  see also **Agriculture**
The aquarium encyclopedia, EG282
Aquatic sciences & fisheries abstracts, EG283
Arab American almanac, CC347
The Arab bulletin of publications, AA890
Arab Central Statistical Bureau. *al-Kitāb al-ihsa'i al-sanawi lil-bilād al-'Arabiyah,* CG372
Arab dissertation index, Kuwait University. Libraries Department, AG51
The Arab East, DD76
Arab Gulf states, Saliba, M., DE43
Arab Islamic bibliography, BC492, DE181
The Arab-Israeli conflict, DeVore, Ronald M., DE73
——— Gilbert, Martin, DE74
The Arab-Israeli conflict 1945–1971, DE72
Arab League Educational Cultural and Scientific Organization. *The Arab bulletin of publications,* AA890
Arab-Ogly, Édvard Arturovich. *Demograficheskiǐ éntsiklopedicheskiǐ slovar',* CG292
Arab periodicals and serials, Aman, Mohammed M., AD183
Arab regional organizations, Clements, Frank A., AF19
The Arab state of Zanzibar, Bennett, Norman Robert, DD250
Arab states
  atlases, CL349
  bibliography, AA890, DE28, DE29, DE43, DE45, DE238
  biography, AH328, AH329, AH330, AH331
  chronologies, CJ423, DE62
  dissertations, DE42
  encyclopedias, CJ424
  international organizations, AF19
  periodicals, AD182, AD183, AD184
  statistics, CG372, CG373
    bibliography, CG374
Arab states (by subject)
  corporations, CH409
  economic conditions, CH192, CH193
    bibliography, CJ468
  history
    bibliography, DD9
    statistics, CG373
  music, BJ38
  politics and government, CJ423, CJ424, DE62
  population, CG371
  public administration
    bibliography, CJ468
  social conditions, DE28
  women, CC610
The Arab West, DD76
Arab-world newspapers in the Library of Congress, Library of Congress, AE85
The Arab world, Turkey, and the Balkans, (1878–1914), McCarthy, Justin, CG373
Arabic biographical dictionaries, Auchterlonie, Paul, AH331
Arabic books published in Egypt in the nineteenth century, AA854

Arabic-English and English-Arabic dictionaries in the Library of Congress, Selim, George Dimitri, AC220
Arabic-English dictionary, AC224
Arabic-English dictionary of the modern Arabic of Egypt, Spiro, Socrates, AC221
Arabic-English lexicon, Lane, Edward William, AC218
Arabic/French/English dictionary, AC213
Arabic language
  bibliography, BD204
  dictionaries, AC225, EA104
    bibliography, AC220
    bilingual, AC216, AC222, AC224
      Arabic-English, AC214, AC215, AC218, AC221, AC223
      English-Arabic, AC217, AC219
    multilingual, AC213
  idioms and usage, AC219
Arabic linguistics, Bakalla, M. H., BD204
Arabic literature, BE1548
  bibliography, BE1545, BE1547, BE1549
Arabic literature (by subject)
  history, BE1546
Arabic literature to the end of the Umayyad period, Beeston, A. F. L., BE1546
Arabic materials in English translation, Anderson, Margaret, DE45
Arabic proverbs, Burckhardt, Johann Lewis, BE124
Arabische Musik in europäischen Sprachen, Krüger-Wust, Wilhelm J., BJ38
Arabisches Wörterbuch für die Schriftsprache der Gegenwart, AC222
Araji, Sharon. *A sourcebook on child sexual abuse,* CC167
An Aramaic bibliography, Fitzmyer, Joseph A., BD206
Aramaic language *see* **Hebrew language**
Arana Soto, Salvador. *Catálogo de poetas puertorriqueños,* BE980
——— *Diccionario geográfico de Puerto Rico,* CL126
Araoz Alfaro, Gregorio. *Diccionario biográfico colonial argentino,* AH119
Arap harfli süreli yayınlar toplu kataloğu, 1828–1928, AE78
Arata, Esther Spring. *Black American playwrights, 1800 to the present,* BE513
——— *Black American writers,* BE532
Araújo, Orestes. *Diccionario popular de historia de la República o. del Uruguay,* DB394
Araúz, Celestino Andrés. *Introducción al estudio de la historia de Panamá,* DB319
Araya Incera, Manuel E. *Materiales para la historia de las relaciones internacionales de Costa Rica,* DB305
ARBA, AA346
ARBA guide to biographical dictionaries, AH1
——— Wynar, Bohdan S., AH4
ARBA guide to education, CB1
ARBA guide to library science literature, 1970–1983, AK8, AK80
Arbeitsgemeinschaft Ostdeutscher Familienforscher. *Genealogical guide to German ancestors from East Germany and Eastern Europe,* AJ78
Arbeitsgemeinschaft Schweizer Familiennamen. *Familiennamenbuch der Schweiz,* AJ142
Arbeitsmaterialien zu einer Landesbibliographie, Albanien, Hetzer, Armin, DC80
Arbeláez A., María Soledad. *Bibliografía comentada sobre la mujer mexicana,* DB218
Arber, Edward. *Term catalogues, 1668–1709 A.D. with a number for Easter term, 1711 A.D,* AA675, AA676
——— *Transcript of the registers of the Company of Stationers of London, 1554–1640,* AA670, AA674, BE634, BE680
Arberry, Arthur J. *Cambridge history of Iran,* DE189
——— *Koran interpreted,* BC203, BC204
Arbingast, Stanley A. *Atlas of Central America,* CL312
——— *Atlas of Mexico,* CL310
Arbour, Roméo. *L'ère baroque en France,* BE1203

—— *Les revues littéraires éphémères paraissant à Paris entre 1900 et 1914,* AD90
Arceneaux, Cathann. *Key resources on student services,* CB224
ARCH. BF208
Archaeológgiai ertesitö, DC379
Archaeological atlas of the world, Whitehouse, David, DA89
Archaeological bibliography for Great Britain and Ireland, DC306
Archaeological encyclopedia of the Holy Land, BC192
Archaeological gazetteer of Afghanistan, DE109
Archaeological site index to radiocarbon dates for Great Britain and Ireland, Council for British Archaeology, DC306
Archaeological sites, BC193, DA78, DA82, DA88, DA89
  encyclopedias, BC196, DA105
Archaeology, Harvard University. Library, DA65
—— Heizer, Robert Fleming, DA60
Archaeology and ancient history
  abstract journals, BF33, BF198
  atlases, DA87, DA88, DA89, DA90, DA116
  bibliography, DA59, DA60, DA64, DA65, DA66, DA68, DA69, DA72, DC306
    current, DA71
  chronologies, DA83, DA84
  computer applications, BC188
  databases, BF198, DA70
  dictionaries, BF81, BF87, DA75, DA76
  dissertations, DA73
  encyclopedias, DA74, DA77, DA78, DA79, DA80
  festschriften, DA67
  general histories, DA85
  guides, DA59, DA60, DA61
  handbooks, DA81, DA82, DB54
  indexes, BG78
  library catalogs, CE22, DA63, DA65
  motion pictures, DA62
Archaeology and ancient history (by country or region)
  Africa, DD13
    atlases, DD64
  Africa, North, DD66
  Canada, CF84
  Central America, BF28
  China, BF40, BF85
  Egypt, DA121, DA122, DA123, DA125
  France, DC171, DC172
  Great Britain
    atlases, DC314
  Hungary, DC379
  India, DE154
  Iran, DE180
  Ireland, DC405
  Italy, DC417
    bibliography, BF13, BF14
  North America, DB49, DB214
  Palestine, BC192, BC194
  Peru, DB385
  Russia and the U.S.S.R., DA71
  Turkey, DC531
  United States, CE84, DB54
Archaeology and ancient history (by period)
  classical, BF71, BG176
  see also **Biblical archaeology**
Archaeology on film, Allen, Peter S., DA62
Archambault, Ariane. *The Facts on File English/ French visual dictionary,* AC338
Archäologische Bibliographie, DA69, DA70
Archer, John. *The literature of British domestic architecture, 1715–1842,* BF206
Archer, Stephen M. *American actors and actresses,* BH124
Archibald, E. H. H. *Dictionary of sea painters,* BF323
Archibald, Raymond Clare. *Guide to tables of Bessel functions,* EB73
Architectural Association (Great Britain). Library. *Periodicals, annuals and government serials held in the Architectural Association Library,* BF225

Architectural index, BF209
Architectural keywords, BF207
Architectural periodicals index, BF207, BF210, BF222, BF230
Architectural preservation and urban renovation, Tubesing, Richard L., BF267
Architectural preservation in the United States, 1941–1975, Tubesing, Richard L., BF267
Architectural Publication Society. *Dictionary of architecture,* BF232
•*Architectural publications index on disc,* BF207
Architectural treatises and building handbooks available in American libraries and bookstores through 1800, Schimmelman, Janice Gayle, BF223
Architecture
  bibliography, BF17, BF202, BF204, BF205, BF217, BF221, BF223, BF224, BF228, BF229
    current, BF45
  biography, BF236, BF244, BF258, BF259, BF260, BF261, BF262, BF263
  chronologies, DA36
  databases, BF94
  dictionaries, BF81, BF237, BF239, BF240, BF241, BF242, BF243, BF244, BF245, BF246, BF278, BG25
    multilingual, BF84, BF92
  directories, BF251
  encyclopedias, BF74, BF75, BF224, BF232, BF233, BF234, BF235, BF236, BF237, BF238, BF239, BF241, BF276
  filmography, BF247
  guides, BF1, BF7, BF201, BF202, BF203, BF204, CF19
  handbooks, BF195, BF252, BF253
  history, BF256
  indexes, BF207, BF208, BF210, BF212, BF218, BF222, BF231
  library catalogs, BF45, BF57
  library collections, BF212, BF228, BF230
  library resources, BF229
  periodicals, BF225, BF226
  quotations, BF95
  terminology, BF93, BF94
  yearbooks, BF264
Architecture (by country or region)
  Asia, West, BF243
  Australia, BF76, BF208
  Canada, BF210
    bibliography, BF31
  China
    dictionaries, BF88
  Europe, BF211, BF257
  France
    periodicals, BF46
  Great Britain, BF203, BF206, BF215, BF216, BF246, BF259, BF261
  Ireland, BF203
  Italy, BF231
    library catalogs, BF52
  Japan
    dictionaries, BF88
  United States, BF212, BF235, BF248, BF252, BF256
    dissertations, BF227
Architecture (by subject)
  history, BF253, BF254, BF255, BF257
  restoration and conservation, BF219, BF264, BF265, BF266, BF267
Architecture, Ehresmann, Donald L., BF2, BF202
Architecture and women, Doumato, Lamia, BF214, BF263
L'architecture dans les collections de périodiques de la Bibliothèque Forney, Bibliothèque Forney, BF225
•*Architecture database,* BF207
Architecture, domestic, BF206, BF241
Architecture on screen, BF247
Architecture through the ages, Hamlin, Talbott Faulkner, BF256
Archiv der Geschichte der Naturwissenschaften, EA245, EA247
Archiv für Reformationsgeschichte, DC25

Archive, AK137
Archive for Reformation history, DC25
Archive im deutschsprachigen Raum, AK137
Archive of Folk Song (U.S.). *Check-list of recorded songs in the English language in the Archive of American Folk Song to July, 1940,* BJ321, BJ327
Archive of Recorded Poetry and Literature (Library of Congress). *Literary recordings,* BE324
Archives
  administration, AK186, AK187
    bibliography, AK182
  dictionaries, AK42, AK184
    multilingual, AK183
  directories, AK185, DA175
  financial aids, BF104
  guides, AK188, DA175
  guides (by subject)
    Africa, DD38
    Africa, North, DD75
    art, BF59, BF118
    Asia, DD75, DE11, DF13
    Asia, West, DD75
    Latin America, DB272, DB275
    Oceania, DD75, DE11, DF13
    theater, BH54
    women, CC525
  periodicals, AK21
Archives (by country or region)
  Africa
    directories, AK154
  Canada
    directories, AK127
    guides to records, DB192
  Caribbean
    directories, AK130, DB278
  Europe
    directories, AK109, DC50
  German-speaking Europe
    directories, AK137
  Germany
    directories, AK139
  Great Britain, AJ98, AK145
  India, DE162
  Latin America
    directories, AK130, DB278
  Mexico, DB238
    directories, AK129
  New Zealand, AK163
  Norway, DC465
  Pakistan, DE239
  Panama, DB319
  Poland
    directories, AK152
  Russia, DC557
  United States, AA443
    guides, AK112
    library catalogs, BF58
  U.S.S.R., AK153, DC561
  Yugoslavia, DC611
  see also **Libraries; Manuscripts; Records management**
The archives, Szucs, Loretto Dennis, AJ24, DB37
Archives and libraries in a new Germany, Danyel, Jürgen, AK133, DC13, DC247
—— Kilton, Thomas, AK133, DC13
—— Welsch, Erwin K., AK133, AK139, DC13, DC247, DC390
Archives and libraries in France, Welsch, Erwin K., AK133, AK136, DC13, DC158, DC390
Archives and manuscript repositories in the USSR, Grimsted, Patricia Kennedy, AK153, DC561
Archives biographiques des pays du Benelux, AH270
Archives biographiques françaises, AH192
Archives de la Martinique, DB446
Archives de l'État dans les provinces (Belgium). *Het Rijksarchief in de provinciën,* DC107
Les archives du Ministère des relations extérieures depuis les origines, France. Ministère des relations extérieures. Archives et documentation, DC156
Archives du Sénégal. *Bibliographie du Sénégal,* AA872
—— *Guide des archives de l'Afrique occidentale française,* DD106

Archives in Russia, DC557, DC562

Archives nationales du Sénégal. *Bibliographie du Sénégal,* AA872

Archives nationales (France). *État des inventaires,* DC150

—— *État des inventaires des archives départementales, communales et hospitalières au 1er janvier 1983,* DC154

—— *État général des fonds,* DC151

—— *Guide des papiers des ministres et secrétaires d'État de 1871 à 1974,* DC152

—— *Guide des papiers privés d'époque révolutionnaire,* DC182

—— *Guide des recherches sur l'histoire des familles,* AJ85

—— *Guide des sources de l'histoire de l'Amérique latine et des Antilles dans les archives françaises,* DB272

—— *L'onomastique française,* CL188

—— *Les sources de l'histoire littéraire aux Archives Nationales,* BE1148

Archives New Zealand, Rogers, Frank, AK163

Archives of American Art. *Arts in America,* BF12

—— *The card catalog of the manuscript collections of the Archives of American Art,* BF58

—— *The card catalog of the oral history collections of the Archives of American Art,* BF59

—— *Collection of exhibition catalogs,* BF118

Archives of American art, McCoy, Garnett, BF58

Archivio biografico italiano, AH258

Archivio biografico italiano II, AH258

Archivio centrale dello Stato (Italy). *Bibliografia dell'Archivio centrale dello Stato, 1953–1978,* DC427

Archivo biográfico de España, Portugal e Iberoamérica, AH287

Archivo General de la Nación. *México,* DB238

Archivo Nacional de Historia (Ecuador). *Guía del Archivo Nacional de Historia,* DB373

Archivos del folklore chileno, CF71

Archivos quiteños, Escudero, Grecia Vasco de, DB373

Arco the right college, CB289

Arctic
  bibliography, DB214, DG3, DG4
  databases, DG2
  discovery and exploration, DG7
  guides, DG3
  see also **Antarctic**

•*Arctic & antarctic regions,* DG1, DG2

Arctic archaeology, Dekin, Albert A., DB214

Arctic bibliography, Arctic Institute of North America, DG4

Arctic exploration and development, c.500 B.C. to 1915, Holland, Clive, DG7

Arctic information and data, DG3

Arctic Institute of North America. *Arctic bibliography,* DG4

Arctic Research Consortium of the United States. Data and Information Resources Working Group. *Arctic information and data,* DG3

Ardagh, John. *Cultural atlas of France,* DC164

Ardayfio-Schandorf, Elizabeth. *Women in Ghana,* DD163

Ardenne, Manfred. *Tabellen zur angewandten Physik,* ED41

Ardis, Susan. *A guide to the literature of electrical and electronics engineering,* EK124

Ardissone, Elena. *Bibliografía de índices de publicaciones periódicas argentinas,* AD248

Area handbook for Ghana, Kaplan, Irving, DD62

Area handbook for Senegal, Nelson, Harold D., DD62

Area handbook for Sierra Leone, Kaplan, Irving, DD62

Area handbook for the Democratic Republic of the Congo (Congo Kinshasa), McDonald, Gordon C., DD62

Area handbook for the People's Republic of the Congo (Congo Brazzaville), McDonald, Gordon C., DD62

Area handbook for the United Republic of Cameroon, Nelson, Harold D., DD62

Area handbook series, DD62

Arellano, Jorge Eduardo. *Nicaraguan national bibliography, 1800–1978,* AA491

—— *Panorama de la literatura nicaragüense,* BE917

Arellano Moreno, Antonio. *Guía de historia de Venezuela,* DB403

Arem, Joel E. *Color encyclopedia of gemstones,* EF190

Arena, Héctor Luis. *Bibliografía general de la literatura latinoamericana,* BE869

Arents, Prosper. *Flemish writers translated (1830–1931),* BE1063

—— *De Vlaamse schrijvers in het Engels vertaald, 1481–1949,* BE1064

Arestis, Philip. *A biographical dictionary of dissenting economists,* CH92

ARF guidelines handbook, CH587

Argan, Giulio Carlo. *New discoveries and perspectives in the world of art,* BF73

Argentina
  atlases, CL314
  bibliography, AA469, AA494, AA495, AA496, AA497, AA498, DB324, DB328, DB329, DB332
    current, AA499
  bibliography of bibliography, AA26
  biography, AH117, AH118, AH119
    contemporary, AH120
  dissertations, AG18
  encyclopedias, DB330
  gazetteers, CL118, CL119
  government publications, AF159
  periodicals, AD70, AD71
  place-names, CL119
  statistics, CG135, CG136, CG137, DB331

Argentina (by subject)
  historiography, DB333
  history, DB326
    bibliography, DB323
    library resources, DB327
    statistics, CG137, DB331
  military history, DB325

Argentina. Dirección de Estadísticas de Salud. *Programa nacional de estadísticas de salud,* CG136

Argentina, Biggins, Alan, DB324

Argentina since independence, DB291

Argentine bibliography, Universidad de Buenos Aires, AA497

Argentine literature, Foster, David William, BE919

Argentine Republic. Dirección Nacional de Estadística y Censos. *Anuario estadístico,* CG135

Argentinian literature, BE918, BE919, BE920, BE921

Argueta, Mario R. *Diccionario de escritores hondureños,* BE906

Argument, Eisenberg, Abné M., BE369

Argumentation, Dause, Charles, BE371

—— Kay, Jack, BE371

—— Ziegelmueller, George, BE371

Argumentation and debate, Freeley, Austin J., BE371

—— Kruger, Arthur N., BE372

Argyle, Christopher. *Chronicle of the First World War,* DA198

Arias de Blois, Jorge. *Demografía guatemalteca, 1960–1976,* CG130

Arid regions, CL58, EF1, EF17

Arieti, Silvano. *American handbook of psychiatry,* EH391

Arizona. [Laws, etc.]. Arizona revised statutes, annotated, CK179

Arizona revised statutes, annotated, Arizona. [Laws, etc.], CK179

Arkansas. [Laws, etc.]. *Arkansas code of 1987 annotated,* CK179

Arkansas code of 1987 annotated, Arkansas. [Laws, etc.], CK179

Arkheologiia Belorussi, Korobushkina, Tat'iana Nikolaevna, DC98

Arkin, William M. *Research guide to current military and strategic affairs,* CJ559

Arksey, Laura. *American diaries,* BE507, BE509, BE726, BE727, DB66

ARL annual salary survey, Association of Research Libraries, AK173

ARL newsletter, AK173

ARL statistics, AK95, AK96

Arlott, John. *The Oxford companion to world sports and games,* BK20

Armarego, W. L. F. *Purification of laboratory chemicals,* EE85

Armbruster, Carl Hubert. *Dongolese Nubian, a lexicon,* AC623

Armbruster, Davis L. *Guide to the bibliographies of Russian literature,* BE1396

Armed forces
  abbreviations
    dictionaries, CJ588
  acronyms, CJ617
  atlases, CJ603
  bibliography, CJ546, CJ560, CJ564, CJ565, CJ566
  biography, AH26
  dictionaries, CJ578, CJ582, CJ585, CJ587
  encyclopedias, CJ571, CJ573, CJ574, CJ579
  guides, CJ559
  handbooks, CJ592, CJ597, CJ599
  indexes, CJ564
  periodicals, CJ567
  quotations, CJ591
  registers, AJ30
  yearbooks, CJ596, CJ601, CJ602

Armed forces (by country or region)
  United States
    biography, CJ642
  see also **Military history; Naval history; Naval warfare**

Armen, Garbis. *Historical atlas of Armenia,* DC83

Armengol, Lidia. *Materials per una bibliografia d'Andorra,* DC82

Armenia, DC83
  bibliography, DC85, DC86
  dissertations, DC84

Armenia, Nersessian, Vrej, DC85

Armenia and the Armenians in academic dissertations, Avakian, Anne M., DC84

Armenian American almanac, CC348

Armenian language
  dictionaries
    bilingual
      Armenian-English, AC226, AC227

Armenians
  bibliography, DC85

Armenians (by country or region)
  United States, CC348

The Armenians, DC85

Armer, Michael. *African social psychology,* CE101

Armies of the Crusades, Wise, Terence, CJ595

Armitage, Susan H. *Women in the West,* DB172

Armorial families, Fox-Davies, Arthur Charles, AJ152

Armorial général, Rietstap, Johannes Baptist, AJ160, AJ161

Armour, Robert A. *Film,* BH159

Arms, Thomas S. *World elections on file,* CJ88, CJ92

Arms and armour of the crusading era, 1050–1350, Nicolle, David, CJ575

Arms control and disarmament, CJ662

—— Burns, Richard Dean, CJ667, CJ673

Arms control and disarmament, defense and military, international security, and peace, Atkins, Stephen E., CJ663

Arms control and peace research
  abstracts, CJ681
  archives, CJ671
  bibliography, BC360, CJ662, CJ663, CJ665, CJ666, CJ667, CJ668, CJ669, CJ670, CJ672, CJ673, CJ675, CJ676, CJ677, CJ678, CJ679, CJ695
  bibliography of bibliography, CJ680
  biography, AL164, CJ700, CJ701
  classification, CJ688
  dictionaries, CJ687

directories, CJ50, CJ690, CJ691, CJ692, CJ693, CJ694, CJ695, CJ696
encyclopedias, CJ682, CJ683, CJ684, CJ685, CJ686
handbooks, CJ697, CJ701
quotations, CJ689
thesauruses, CJ688
yearbooks, CJ602, CJ698, CJ699
Arms control and peace research (by country or region)
Asia, East, CJ674
Oceania, CJ674
Pacific region, CJ674
Arms control, disarmament and military security dictionary, Elliot, Jeffrey M., CJ682, CJ683
—— Reginald, Robert, CJ682
Arms control fact book, Menos, Dennis, CJ697
Armstrong, F. H. *Bibliography of Canadian urban history*, DB210
Armstrong, George Henry. *Origin and meaning of place names in Canada*, CL181
Armstrong, Julia I. *The index of paintings sold in the British Isles during the nineteenth century*, BF302
Armstrong, Mary Willems. *The movie list book*, BH220
Armstrong, R. A. *Gaelic dictionary in two parts*, AC393
Armstrong, Richard B. *The movie list book*, BH220
Armstrong, Terry A. *A reader's Hebrew-English lexicon of the Old Testament*, BC133
Army dictionary and desk reference, Zurick, Timothy, CJ622
Army lineage series, CJ628
Army Military History Institute. *The era of the Civil War—1820–1876*, DB113
The Army officer's guide, CJ629
Army uniforms of World War I, Mollo, Andrew, CJ595
Armytage, George John. *Obituary prior to 1800*, AH237
Arnaldi, Francesco. *Latinitas italicae medii aevi inde ab a. CDLXXVI usque ad a. MXXII lexicon imperfectum cura et studio Francisci Arnaldi*, AC585
Arnason, H. Harvard. *History of modern art*, BF131
Arnaud, Etienne. *Répertoire de généalogies françaises imprimées*, AJ82
Arndt, Karl John Richard. *The German language press of the Americas*, AE1
Arndt, William. *A Greek-English lexicon of the New Testament and other early Christian literature*, AC453
Arnett, Mary E. *The naturalists' directory and almanac (international)*, EG80
Arnett, Ross H. *American insects*, EG326
—— *The naturalists' directory and almanac (international)*, EG80
Arngrímur Sigurðsson. *Íslenzk-ensk orðabók*, AC502
Arnheim, Johanna. *Swaziland*, DD232
Arnim, Max. *Internationale Personalbibliographie, 1800–1943*, AA19, AH14
Arnold, Alvin L. *The Arnold encyclopedia of real estate*, CH535
Arnold, C. A. *Rapport sur la paléobotanique dans le monde*, EG101
Arnold, Denis. *The new Oxford companion to music*, BJ142
Arnold, Frank. *Cinegraph*, BH281
Arnold, Guy. *Revolutionary and dissident movements*, CJ61
Arnold, Heinz Ludwig. *Kritisches Lexikon zur deutschsprachigen Gegenwartsliteratur*, BE1247
Arnold, Janet. *A handbook of costume*, BG104
Arnold, Louise. *The era of the Civil War—1820–1876*, DB113
Arnold, Peter. *A pictorial history of boxing*, BK69
Arnold, Robert Franz. *Allgemeine Bücherkunde zur neueren deutschen Literaturgeschichte*, BE1214
Arnold, Thomas. *A Catholic dictionary*, BC396
Arnold Arboretum. *A bibliography of eastern Asiatic botany*, EG106

The Arnold encyclopedia of real estate, Arnold, Alvin L., CH535
Arnott, James Fullarton. *English theatrical literature, 1559–1900*, BH38, BH40
Arntz, Helmut. *Bibliographie der Runenkunde*, BE1082
—— *Handbuch der runenkunde*, BE1082
Arntzen, Etta Mae. *Guide to the literature of art history*, BF1
Arocha, Jaime. *Bibliografía anotada y directorio de antropólogos colombianos*, CE88
Aronson, Eleanor J. *Report series codes dictionary*, EA65
Aronson, Elliot. *Handbook of social psychology*, CD97, CJ53
Aronson, Joseph. *The encyclopedia of furniture*, BG121
—— *New encyclopedia of furniture*, BG121
Aros, Andrew A. *Actor guide to the talkies, 1965 through 1974*, BH205
—— *Title guide to the talkies, 1964 through 1974*, BH217
—— *Title guide to the talkies, 1975 through 1984*, BH217
Arqueta, Mario. *Guía para el investigador de la historia colonial hondureña*, DB310
—— *Investigación y tendencias recientes de la historiografía hondureña*, DB310
Arranging and describing archives and manuscripts, Miller, Frederic M., AK188
Arrendondo, Horacio. *Bibliografía uruguaya*, AA545
Arneta, Rafael Alberto. *Historia de la literatura argentina*, BE918
Arriola Grande, F. Maurilio. *Diccionario literario del Perú*, BE954, BE957
Arrom, José Juan. *Historia de la literatura dramática cubana*, BE972
Arrubla, Mario. *Compendio de estadísticas históricas de Colombia*, CG151
Årsbibliografi över Sveriges offentliga publikationer, AF215, AF216
Arshem, James A. *Directory of patent depository libraries*, EA266
Årskatalog för Svenska bokhandeln, AA832
Art
abstract journals, BF33, BF34, BF42, BF43, BF198
audiovisual materials, BF96, BF195
bibliography, BF2, BF10, BF15, BF16, BF17, BF18, BF23, BF26, BF28, BF29, BF35, BF36, BF37, BF50, BF51, BF372
　current, BF41, BF43, BF45
biography, AH213, BF18, BF135, BF136, BF138, BF139, BF141, BF143, BF146, BF148, BF149, BF150, BF152, BF159
catalogs, BF113, BF119, BF120, BF196, BF197
chronologies, BF115, BF128, DA36
databases, BF33, BF34, BF43, BF94, BF198
dictionaries, BF71, BF81, BF83, BF87, BF90
　multilingual, BF84, BF92, BG43
directories, BF96, BF97, BF99, BF107
encyclopedias, BF69, BF73, BF74, BF75, BF77, BF78, BF79, BF80
grants-in-aid, BF106
guides, BF1, BF2, BF4, BF5, BF6, BF7, BF8, BF124, CF19
guides for authors, BF124
handbooks, BF78, BF115, BF124, BF304
indexes, BF11, BF19, BF120
laws, statutes, etc., BF122
library catalogs, BF45, BF53, BF54, BF55, BF56, BF57, BG14
library resources, BF110
museum publications, BF120
periodicals, BF47
　indexes, BF11
periodicals (by period)
　19th–20th centuries, BF19
quotations, BF95, BF145
reproductions, BF61, BF62, BF63, BF195, BF196, BF197

　indexes, BF60
sales, BF108, BF109, BF111, BF112, BF113
sourcebooks, BF196, BF197
symbols, BF171
terminology, BF86, BF91, BF93, BF94
Art (by country or region)
Africa
　bibliography, BF25, BF38, BG4, BG5
　library catalogs, BG4
Asia, BF3, BF35, BF126
Australia, BF76
Canada
　bibliography, BF31
　directories, BF102
Central America, BF28
China, BF40, BF85
　dictionaries, BF88
France
　archives, BF58
　manuscripts and archives, DC151
　periodicals, BF46
Germany, AH205, BF79
Great Britain, BF66, BF320
　directories, BF101, BF102
India, BF27, BF178, BF190, BF191
Italy
　bibliography, BF13, BF14
　library catalogs, BF52
Japan
　dictionaries, BF88
Latin America
　bibliography, BF22
　encyclopedias, BF70
Nepal, BF27
North America
　encyclopedias, BF70
Oceania
　bibliography, BG8
United States, BF12, BF16, BF36, BF152, BF320
　current surveys, BA1, BF44
　dictionaries, BF82
　directories, BF102, BF103
　exhibitions, BF118
Art (by period)
19th–20th centuries
　encyclopedias, BG19
19th century
　bibliography, BF32
　history, BF131
20th century, BF93
　handbooks, BF89
　history, BF131
　indexes, BF62
　library catalogs, BF55
medieval
　encyclopedias, BF72
pre-Columbian, BF28
Renaissance, BF37
　dictionaries, BF83
Art (by subject)
business management, BF39
Byzantine art
　bibliography, BF9
censorship, BF128
classical influences, BF189, CF24
collectors and collecting, BF121
computer art, BF374
foundations and philanthropic organizations, AL120, BF105
grants-in-aid, AL120, BF105
history, BF129, BF132, BF133
Jewish art, BF194
museum publications, BF49
restoration and conservation, BF199, BF200
Spanish-American art
　bibliography, BF20
symbolism, BF189, CF24
symbolism (by country or region)
　China, BF179

symbols and symbolism, BF163, BF165, BF166, BF167, BF168, BF169, BF172, BF173, BF174, BF176, BF177, BF180, BF181, BF182, BF184, BF185, BF187
   Buddhist, BF178
   Christian, BF298
   Hindu, BF190, BF191, BF192
   see also **Architecture; Painting; Sculpture**
•*ART,* BF94
Art & architecture thesaurus, BF94
Art & artists of South Africa, Berman, Esmé, BF142
Art : a history of painting, sculpture, architecture, Hartt, Frederick, BF132
Art and antiques dictionary, Müller, Christian, BG43
The art and archaeology of pre-Columbian Middle America, Kendall, Aubyn, BF28
Art and archaeology technical abstracts, BF198, DA69
Art and architecture in Canada, Lerner, Loren R., BF31
Art and architecture in the Western world, Garrison, J. J., BF129
   —— Robb, D. M., BF129
•*Art and architecture thesaurus,* BF94
Art and mythology, BF176
Art and psychology *see* **Psychology and art**
Art books, Freitag, Wolfgang M., BF18
   —— Lucas, Edna Louise, BF18
Art books, 1876–1949, BF10
Art books, 1950–1979, BF10
Art books 1980–1984, BF10
Art censorship, Clapp, Jane, BF128
Art, design, photo, BF42
Art exhibition catalogues, BF119
Art galleries of Britain and Ireland, Abse, Joan, BF98
Art in America, BF103
Art index, BF11, BF41, BF55, BF41
Art information, Jones, Lois Swan, BF4
Art Institute of Chicago. Ryerson Library. *The Burnham index to architectural literature,* BF212
   —— *Index to art periodicals,* BF11
Art law, Bresler, Judith, BF122
   —— Feldman, Franklin, BF122
   —— Lerner, Ralph E., BF122
Art law in a nutshell, DuBoff, Leonard D., BF122
•*Art literature international,* BF34, BF43
Art literature international (RILA), BF34
Art museums
   directories, BF99
   guidebooks, BF305, BF306
   handbooks, BF115
   library catalogs, BF53, BF54
   periodicals, BF49
Art museums (by country or region)
   Canada, BG68
   Japan, BF144
   North America, BG157
   United States, BG68
Art museums of America, AL90, BF116, EA217
The art museums of New England, AL90, BF116, EA217
Art museums of the world, Jackson, Virginia, BF115
The art of biography in 18th century England, Stauffer, Donald Alfred, AH239
Art of heraldry, Fox-Davies, Arthur Charles, AJ154
The art of literary research, Altick, Richard Daniel, BE1
The art of Oceania, Hanson, Louise, BG8
Art of picture research, Evans, Hilary, BF350
Art of pre-Columbian Mexico, Kendall, Aubyn, BF28
The art of the print, Eichenberg, Fritz, BF378
•*Art on film database,* BF96, BF327
Art on screen, BF96
•*Art on screen on CD-ROM,* BF96
Art prices current, BF108
Art research methods and resources, Jones, Lois Swan, BF4
Art sales from early in the eighteenth century to early in the twentieth century, Graves, Algernon, BF302
Art sales index, BF109
The art song, Seaton, Douglass, BJ273
Art terms and techniques, Mayer, Ralph, BF91

Art through the ages, BF129
Artbibliographies : current titles, BF42
Artbibliographies modern, BF42
Arte Chicano, Goldman, Shifra M., BF20, CC455
   —— Ybarra-Frausto, Tomás, CC455
The Arthur Andersen European Community sourcebook, AF22
Arthur D. Jenkins Library. *Rug and textile arts,* BG153
Arthurian bibliography, Pickford, Cedric Edward, BE338, BE339
Arthurian dictionary, Minary, Ruth, BE344
   —— Moorman, Charles, BE344
Arthurian encyclopedia, Lacy, Norris J., BE343
The Arthurian handbook, Lacy, Norris J., BE342
Arthurian legend and literature, Reiss, Edmund, BE340
Arthurian romances, BE342, BE343, BE344
   bibliography, BE338, BE339
   indexes, BE732, BE1165
Artibise, Alan F. J. *Bibliography of Canadian urban history,* DB210
   —— *Canada's urban past,* DB210
   —— *Western Canada since 1870,* DB211
Article clearinghouse, AD20
Articles of the Albanian press, AD301
Articles on American literature, 1900–1950, Leary, Lewis Gaston, BE408, BE473, BE826
Articles on American literature, 1950–1967, Bartholet, Carolyn, BE408
   —— Leary, Lewis Gaston, BE408
   —— Roth, Catharine, BE408
Articles on American literature, 1968–1975, Auchard, John, BE408
   —— Leary, Lewis Gaston, BE408
Articles on antiquity in festschriften, Rounds, Dorothy, DA67
Articles on the Middle East, 1947–1971, DE24
Articles on twentieth century literature, Pownall, David E., BE27, BE761
Articles on women writers, Schwartz, Narda Lacey, BE412
Artificial intelligence
   bibliography, EK153, EK154, EK157
   dictionaries, EK184, EK186
      multilingual, EK195
   directories, EK198
   encyclopedias, EK170
   handbooks, EK204
   indexes, EK154
   see also **Robotics**
Artificial intelligence, EK153, EK184
The artificial intelligence compendium, EK154
•*Artificial intelligence database of abstracts on CD-ROM,* EK154
Artificial languages, BD48, BD50
Artikler i bøger, AA605
Artinian, Vrej-Armen. *Historical atlas of Armenia,* DC83
Artist biographies master index, BF136, BG30
Artist issue, BJ385
Artists, BF16, BF18, BF143
   bibliography, BF145, BF363
   biography, BF141, BF147, BF148, BF149, BF156, BF317, BG34
   directories, BF140
   encyclopedias, BF135, BF137, BF148, BF149
   handbooks, BF123
   indexes, BF136
   quotations, BF145
Artists (by country or region)
   Australia, BF140
   Canada, BF314
   China, BF146, BF162
   Denmark, BF147
   Europe, BF322
      biography, BF139
   France
      biography, BF380
   Great Britain, BF150, BF323
      biography, BF316
   Japan, BF144, BF161
   Namibia, BF142

   South Africa, BF142
   Spain, BF147
   United States, BG27
      biography, BF155, BF157
Artists (by period)
   19th century, BF319
   20th century, BF138
      biography, BF139
      handbooks, BF89
Artists (by subject)
   occupational health, BF127
Artists and galleries of Australia, Germaine, Max, BF140
Artists' and illustrators' encyclopedia, Quick, John, BF91
Artists as illustrators, Castagno, James, BF372
The artist's complete health and safety guide, Rossol, Monona, BF127, BF304
The artists file, New York Public Library, BF141
Artist's handbook of materials and techniques, Mayer, Ralph, BF127, BF304
Artists in early Australia and their portraits, Buscombe, Eve, BF140
Artists in quotation, La Cour, Donna Ward, BF95
Artist's index to Stauffer's "American engravers", Gage, Thomas Hovey, BF386
Artist's market, BF346
Artists' marks, BF153, BF158, BF159, BF160, BF161, BF162, BF385, BG138, BG144
   guides, BG31
   handbooks, BG70, BG71
Artists' marks (by country or region)
   Asia, BG77
   Europe, BG77
   France, BG141
   Germany, BG142
   Great Britain, BG137, BG139, BG140, BG150
   United States, BG145, BG148, BG151
Artists' monograms and indiscernible signatures, Castagno, John, BF159
Artists of the "young generation", Bingel, Marie Agnes, BF139
   —— Hesse, Gritta, BF139
Artists on art, Goldwater, Robert, BF145
   —— Treves, Marco, BF145
Artists' signatures, BF137, BF153, BF158, BF159, BF160, BF161
ARTnews international directory of corporate art collections, BF97
Artola, Miguel. *Enciclopedia de historia de España,* DC513
The Artronix index, BF348
Arts & humanities citation index, BA3
•*Arts & humanities search,* BA3
Arts address book, BF102
Arts and civilization of black and African peoples, Okpaku, Joseph, DD58
   —— Oloruntimehin, Benjamin, DD58
   —— Opubor, Alfred, DD58
Arts and crafts movement, BG19
Arts and the world of business, Georgi, Charlotte, BF39
Arts in America, BF12
Arts management, Benedict, Stephen, BF39
Arts management in the '90s, Whittingham, Nik-ki, BF39
The arts of Africa, BF25, BG4
The arts of Central Africa, Biebuyck, Daniel P., BG5
Arts of the United States, Pierson, William Harvey, BF197
Arts of Zaire, Biebuyck, Daniel P., BG5
Artspeak, Atkins, Robert, BF93
Artspoke, Atkins, Robert, BF93
Aryal, Deepak Kumar. *SAARC women,* AH363
Aryan, K. C. *Encyclopedia of Indian art, references, symbols,* BF178
Aryan language *see* **Indo-European language**
Aryanpur, Manoochehr. *Farhang-i nuvin-i payvastah-i Fārsi-Ingilīsī va Ingilīsī-Fārsī,* AC313
Āryānpūr Kāshānī, ʿAbbās. *Farhang-i nuvin-i payvastah-i Fārsi-Ingilīsī va Ingilīsī-Fārsī,* AC313
   —— *The new unabridged English-Persian dictionary,* AC313

Arze, José Roberto. *Bibliografía de bibliografías bolivianas,* AA27
——— *Diccionario biográfico boliviano,* AH122
The A's and B's of academic scholarships, CB371
Asada, Sadao. *Japan and the world, 1853–1952,* DE201
Asakura, Haruhiko. *Jisho kaidai jiten,* AB72
Asamani, J. O. *Index Africanus,* DD1
Asante, Molefi K. *The historical and cultural atlas of African Americans,* CC399
Asbell, Milton B. *A bibliography of dentistry in America, 1790–1840,* EH264
ASCAP biographical dictionary, American Society of Composers, Authors and Publishers, BJ201
ASCAP index of performed compositions, American Society of Composers, Authors and Publishers, BJ52
Ascarelli, Fernanda. *La tipografia cinquecentina italiana,* AA305
Asch, Jürgen. *Taschenbuch der Zeitrechnung des deutschen mittelalters und der Neuzeit,* DC223
Aschehoug og Gyldendals store norske leksikon, AB73
Aschehougs konversasjonsleksikon, AB74
ASEAN, DE94
ASEEPL, DC30
Ash, Irene. *Industrial chemical thesaurus,* EE76
Ash, Lee. *A biographical directory of librarians in the United States and Canada,* AK83
——— *Subject collections,* AK100, AK119
Ash, Michael. *Industrial chemical thesaurus,* EE76
Ashanti region of Ghana, Afre, S. A., DD161
Ashby, Charlotte M. *Guide to cartographic records in the National Archives,* CL242
Ashcom, Benjamin Bowles. *Descriptive catalogue of the Spanish comedias sueltas in the Wayne State University Library and the private library of Professor B. B. Ashcom,* BE1472
Ashe, Arthur. *A hard road to glory,* BK12
Ashe, Geoffrey. *The Arthurian handbook,* BE342
'Ashe, traditional religion and healing in Sub-Saharan Africa and the diaspora, Gray, John, BC34
Asher, R. E. *Atlas of the world's languages,* BD20
——— *The encyclopedia of language and linguistics,* BD34
Ashford, Nigel. *A dictionary of conservative and libertarian thought,* CJ24
Ashley, Michael. *Science fiction, fantasy, and weird fiction magazines,* BE307
Ashley, Perry J. *American newspaper journalists, 1690–1872,* AE149
Ashliman, D. L. *A guide to folktales in the English language,* CF46
ASHRAE handbook, EK224
ASHRAE handbook and product directory, EK224
ASHRAE product specification file, EK224
Ashtiany, Julia. *Abbasid belles-lettres,* BE1546
Ashton, Julia F. *Index Islamicus, 1906–1955,* BC502
ASI microfiche library, CG96
Asia
 bibliography, DE1, DE4
  current, DE2, DE8
 bibliography of bibliography, AA73
 censuses
  handbooks, CG38
 directories, DE17
 dissertations, DE9
 guidebooks, CL388
 handbooks, DE16
 newspapers, AE4
 statistics, CG38, CG45, CG369, CG370, CG434
  bibliography, CG376
 statistics, historical, CG309, CG375
 yearbooks, CG369
Asia (by subject)
 art, BF3, BF35
 ceramics and glass, BG77
 costume and fashion, BG114
 economic conditions, CA53
  bibliography, CH202
 foreign relations (by country or region)
  Union of Soviet Socialist Republics, DC599

 United States, DE15
historiography, DE18
history
 bibliography, DE5
  current, DE2, DE8
  dissertations, DE10
 current surveys, DE19
 encyclopedias, DE14
 politics and government, CA53, CJ414, CJ416, CJ446
  biography, CJ415, DE20, DF20
 social conditions, CA53
 theater, BH31
 travel and tourism, CL373
Asia, Nunn, Godfrey Raymond, DE1
Asia and Oceania, DE11, DF13
Asia and Pacific, Fenton, Thomas P., DE17
Asia and Pacific review, CH191
Asia and the Pacific, DE16
Asia, case studies in the social sciences, CA53
Asia, Central, CC308
 see also **Asia, Northeast**
Asia, East
 encyclopedias, DE164
 library resources, DE106
Asia, East (by subject)
 coins, medals, currency, BG171
 history
  library resources, DE103, DE105
  politics and government, CJ422
Asia in Western and world history, CA53
Asia, Northeast, DE71, DE75
 see also **Asia, Central**
Asia Pacific, CH200
Asia Pacific handbook, Extel Financial Limited, CH358
Asia Society. *Encyclopedia of Asian history,* DE14
Asia, South
 archives, DE84, DE89
 atlases, CL347
 bibliography, DE77, DE78, DE81
 congresses and meetings, DE88
 encyclopedias, DE164
 library resources, DE12, DE13, DE88
Asia, South (by subject)
 anthropology and ethnology, CE108
 folklore and popular culture, CF97
 foreign relations, DE78
 geography, CL21
 history
  archives, DE89
  atlases, CL347, DE91
  bibliography, DE76, DE79, DE80, DE159
  encyclopedias, DE90
  library resources, DE82, DE83, DE85, DE86
  women, CC615
Asia, Southeast
 atlases, CL348
 bibliography, DE100
 guides, DE93
 history
  library resources, AE83
 library resources, DE12, DE13
 newspapers, AE82
 periodicals
  indexes, DE102
  union lists, AD186, AD216
Asia, Southeast (by subject)
 anthropology and ethnology, CE108
 history, DE92
  bibliography, DE94, DE95, DE97, DE98, DE99, DE200
  library resources, DE101
 politics and government, CJ421
 women, CC599
Asia, West
 atlases, DE74
 bibliography, DE24, DE25, DE30, DE39, DE41
  current, DE33, DE46
 bibliography of bibliography, BD211, DE31
 biography, DE66
 chronologies, DE63
 dissertations, DD74, DE44

filmography, DD71, DE34
 guides, DE21, DE22, DE23
 handbooks, DE58
 library catalogs, AA123, DE47, DE48
 periodicals, AD182, AD183, AD184
 sourcebooks, DE64, DE65
 union lists, AA123
Asia, West (by subject)
 anthropology and ethnology, CE112
 coins, medals, currency, BG174
 economic conditions, CH190, CH192
  bibliography, CH189
  yearbooks, CH191
 foreign relations, DE36
  Great Britain, DE37
  United States, DE3, DE40, DE56
 foreign relations (by country or region)
  Great Britain, DE38
  Union of Soviet Socialist Republics, DC599
 history
  abstract journals, DE52
  atlases, DE68, DE70, DE71
  bibliography, BC500, DE3, DE29, DE33, DE36, DE40
  encyclopedias, DE54, DE55, DE56
  handbooks, DE60
  indexes, DE53
  library catalogs, DE46
  library resources, DE50, DE51
  surveys, DE61
 law, CK227
 library resources, DE49
 political parties, CJ405, CJ418
 politics and government, CJ400, CJ419, CJ420, CJ436, DE57
  biography, CJ417
 social conditions
  bibliography, DE26
Asia yearbook, CG369
Asian-American journalism, Heiser, David, AE24
Asian-American literature, BE546
 bibliography, BE511
Asian-American literature (by subject)
 criticism, BE547
 history, BE547
Asian American literature, Cheung, King-Kok, BE546
 ——— Kim, Elaine H., BE547
Asian-American periodicals and newspapers, Hady, Maureen E., AE24
Asian American studies, Kim, Hyung-chan, BE546, CC407
Asian Americans, CC404, CC408
 bibliography, CC403, CC407, CC409
 book reviews, CC316
 directories, CC401
 encyclopedias, CC402
 library resources, CC405, CC411
 newspapers, AE24
 periodicals, AE24
 statistics, CC410, CG82
Asian Americans (by subject)
 history, CC402
 material culture, CC406
 women, CC614
Asian Americans information directory, AE24, CC401
Asian and Asian American studies, CC316
Asian company handbook, CH361
Asian literature in English, Anderson, George Lincoln, BE1542
Asian literatures
 bibliography, BE1542
 guides, BE1543, BE1544
Asian markets, CH375
Asian-Pacific economic literature, CH201
The Asian political dictionary, Ziring, Lawrence, CJ416
Asian recorder, DE19
Asian resources in American libraries, Yang, Teresa S., DE106
 ——— Yang, Winston L. Y., DE106

INDEX

Asian Studies Research Institute. *Modern Arabic literature*, BE1545
Asian theatre, BH31
Asian Wall Street journal [index], CH35
Asians (by country or region)
  Canada
    material culture, CC406
Asien-Bibliographie, DE2
Asimov, Isaac. *Asimov's biographical encyclopedia of science and technology*, EA171
——— *Asimov's chronology of science and discovery*, EA249, EA254
Asimov's biographical encyclopedia of science and technology, Asimov, Isaac, EA171
Asimov's chronology of science and discovery, Asimov, Isaac, EA249, EA254
ASIS handbook & directory, American Society for Information Science, AK57
Ask, Mihran Nicholas. *Who was who in journalism, 1925–1928*, AE153
Aslib. *British scientific and technical books*, EA13
——— *Index to theses with abstracts accepted for higher degrees by the universities of Great Britain and Ireland and the Council for National Academic Awards*, AG33
Aslib book guide, EA13, EA32
Aslib book list, EA13, EA32
Aslib directory of information sources in the United Kingdom, AK141
ASM engineered materials reference book, EK268
ASM handbook, EK264, EK269, EK274, EK278
ASM International. Handbook Committee. *ASM handbook*, EK269
——— *Engineered materials handbook*, EK274
——— *Metals handbook*, EK278
ASM materials engineering dictionary, EK264
ASM metals reference book, EK270
ASM review of metal literature, EK260
——— American Society for Metals. Documentation Service, EK257
ASM thesaurus of metallurgical terms, American Society for Metals, EK263
Aspects of medieval and renaissance music, BJ13
Aspects of the apartheid state, Kessel, Ineke van, DD217
The Aspen dictionary of health care administration, Goldstein, Arnold S., EH115
Aspen Institute guide to communication industry trends, CH496
Aspesi, Natalia. *Le donne italiane*, AH264
Asplin, P. W. A. *Medieval Ireland c.1170–1495*, DC392
A.Sp.Sc.R.O.W, EC44
Assassinations, CJ556
Assassinations and executions, Lentz, Harris M., CJ551
Assche, Hilda van. *Bibliografie van de Vlaamse tijdschriften*, AD303, BE1065, BE1066
Assembly of Life Sciences. Food and Nutrition Board. *Food chemicals codex*, EH306, EJ148
Assessment of quality in graduate education, Cartter, A. M., CB348
An assessment of research doctorate programs in the United States, National Academy of Sciences, CB347, CB348
ASSIA, CA24
Assistance and benefits information directory, AL101
Assistantships and graduate fellowships in the mathematical sciences, EB58
Associated Colleges of the Midwest. *Occasional paper*, DB302
Association for Anthropology and Gerontology. *Directory of anthropologists and anthropological research in aging*, CE87
——— *Topical bibliography*, CC59, CE3
Association for Asian Studies. *Bibliography of Asian studies*, DE8
——— *Chinese religion in Western languages*, BC37
——— *Cumulative bibliography of Asian studies, 1941–1965*, DE4
——— *South Asian library resources in North America*, DE87

Association for Asian Studies. Ming Biographical History Project Committee. *Dictionary of Ming biography, 1368–1644*, AH336
Association for Computing Machinery. *ACM guide to computing literature*, EK159
——— *Computing archive*, EK165
——— *Computing reviews*, EK166
——— *Graduate assistantship directory in computing*, EK200
Association for Documentary Editing. *A guide to documentary editing*, AA320
Association for Education in Journalism. *Journalism abstracts*, AE137
Association for Educational and Training Technology. *International yearbook of educational and training technology*, CB175
Association for Educational Communications and Technology. *Educational media and technology yearbook*, CB177
——— *Educational technology*, CB171
Association for Geographic Information. *Geographic information*, CL78
The Association for Geographic Information yearbook, CL78
Association for Gerontology in Higher Education. *National directory of educational programs in gerontology and geriatrics*, CC86
Association for Information and Image Management. *Buying guide*, AK247
——— *Glossary of imaging technology*, AK246
——— *Introduction to micrographics*, AK251
Association for Investment Management and Research. *Standards of practice handbook*, CH317
Association for Library and Information Science Education. *Directory of the Association for Library and Information Science Education*, AK58
——— *Library and information science education statistical report*, AK68
Association for Population/Family Planning Libraries and Information Centers, International. *National population censuses, 1945–1976*, CG7
Association for Supervision and Curriculum Development. *Only the best*, CB176
Association for the Bibliography of History (U.S.). *Bibliographical foundations of French historical studies*, DC162
Association for the Study of Animal Behaviour. *Animal behavior abstracts*, CD118
Association for the Study of Australian Literature. *The Oxford literary guide to Australia*, BE855
Association for the Study of Jewish Languages. *Yiddish literary and linguistic periodicals and miscellanies*, BE1081
Association générale de la presse belge. *Annuaire officiel de la presse belge*, AD82
Association meeting planners & conference/convention directors, AL25
Association of American Feed Control Officials. *Official publication*, EJ110
Association of American Geographers. *Guide to programs of geography in the United States and Canada*, CL55
Association of American Law Schools. *The AALS directory of law teachers*, CK138
——— *The official guide to U.S. law schools*, CK154
Association of American Library Schools. *Directory of the Association for Library and Information Science Education*, AK58
Association of American Medical Colleges. *Medical school admission requirements, United States and Canada*, EH163
Association of American Railroads. *Railroad facts*, CH462
Association of Arab-American University Graduates. *The Palestine question*, DE244
Association of Australian Philanthropic Trusts. *Philanthropic trusts in Australia*, AL127
Association of Borderlands Scholars. *Borderlands sourcebook*, DB164
Association of British Theological and Philosophical Libraries. *Religious bibliographies in serial literature*, BC50

Association of College and Research Libraries. *Books for college libraries*, AA335
——— *Choice*, AA336
Association of College and Research Libraries. Education and Behavioral Sciences Section. *Directory of curriculum materials centers*, CB267
Association of College and Research Libraries. Education-related Government Publications Subcommittee. *State education documents*, CB106
Association of College and Research Libraries. Western European Specialists Section. *Women's studies in Western Europe*, CC626
Association of College and Research Libraries. Women's Studies Discussion Group. *Women's studies in Western Europe*, CC626
Association of Collegiate Schools of Planning (U.S.). *Guide to graduate education in urban and regional planning*, BF282
Association of Commonwealth Universities. *Commonwealth universities yearbook*, CB319
Association of Independent Video and Filmmakers. *The guide to international film and video festivals*, BH265
Association of Indian Universities. *Indian dissertation abstracts*, CA21
Association of Mental Health Librarians. *Directory of mental health libraries and information centers*, EH388
Association of Official Analytical Chemists. *Official methods of analysis of the Association of Official Analytical Chemists*, EE84, EJ59
Association of Research Libraries. *American doctoral dissertations*, AG11
——— *ARL annual salary survey*, AK173
——— *ARL statistics*, AK96
Association of Research Libraries. Office of Management Studies. *Preservation planning program*, AK238
Association of Specialized and Cooperative Library Agencies. *A deafness collection*, CC187
Association of Theatrical Artists and Craftsmen. *The New York theatrical sourcebook*, BH86
Association of Universities of the British Commonwealth. *Commonwealth universities yearbook*, CB319
Association periodicals, AD50
Associations Canada, AL51
Associations, societies, and academies
  abbreviations, AL11, AL14
  bibliography, AL12
  directories, AL19, AL20, AL24, AL25, AL37, AL44, EA201
  directories and handbooks, AL50
  directories and handbooks (by country or region)
    Canada, AL34
    Mexico, AL34
    United States, AL34
  indexes, AL20
  periodicals, AD50
    indexes, BE31, EA21, EC17, ED6, EE15, EG98, EG213, EH68
Associations, societies, and academies (by country or region)
  Asia, South
    directories, AL15
  Australia, AL72
  Canada, AL51
    directories, AL52
  China, EA148
  Europe
    directories, CH183
  Europe, Eastern
    directories, AL58
  former Soviet republics
    directories, AL59, AL60, DC593
    publications, AL55
  France, AL61, DC213
    publications, EA208
  Germany, AL64
    directories, AL62, AL63
    publications, AL63

Great Britain
  directories, AL66
  international, CA48
    directories, AL13, AL16
Italy, AL68
  history, AL69
Pacific Rim, EA146
Poland, AL70, AL71
Russia
  directories, AL56
Socialist states
  directories, AK117
United States
  databases, AL41
  directories, AL17, AL35, AL41, AL42, AL43, AL45, AL46, AL47, AL49, AL178, CH670, DE210, EA198
  encyclopedias, AL83
  publications, AL38
Uruguay, AL53
U.S.S.R.
  directories, AL57
  publications, AL55
Associations, societies, and academies (by subject)
  environment and environmental problems, EK77
  history, DA27
  library and information science, AK55
  religion, BC80
  science
    directories, EA200
    publications, EA208
Associations yellow book, CH350
Associazione italiana editori. *Catalogo degli editori italiani,* AA291
L'associazionismo operaio in Italia (1870–1900) nelle raccolte della Biblioteca nazionale centrale di Firenze, Dolci, Fabrizio, DC428
Assyrian dictionary, AC200
—— University of Chicago. Oriental Institute, AC204
Ast, Friedrich. *Lexicon Platonicum,* BB52
Aster, Sidney. *British foreign policy 1918–1945,* DC326
Asterlund, B. *American notes and queries,* BE168
Astin, Alexander W. *The American college teacher,* CB335
—— *American freshman,* CB333
Astle, Melvin J. *CRC handbook of data on organic compounds,* EE149
ASTM standards, EA269
Astone, Nicholas A. *Criminal justice vocabulary,* CK257
Astorquia, Madeline. *Guide des sources de l'histoire des États-Unis dans les archives françaises,* DB31
Astronautics
  bibliography, EC3, EK22, EK24
  dictionaries, EK29, EK30, EK31
  handbooks, CH479, EK33, EK35
  periodicals, EK25
  yearbooks, EK36
Astronomers
  directories, EC45, ED31
The astronomer's sourcebook, Gibson, Bob, EC50
Astronomical algorithms, Meeus, Jean, EC55
The astronomical almanac for the year 1981– , EC78, EC79
Astronomical catalogues, 1951–75, Collins, Mike J., EC8
Astronomical ephemeris, EC78
Astronomical formulae for calculators, Meeus, Jean, EC55
Astronomical phenomena, EC78
L'astronomie et les astronomes, Collard, Auguste, EC6
Astronomischer Jahresbericht, EC14, EC22, EC23
Astronomy
  abstract journals, EC22, EC23
  atlases, EC31, EC64, EC65, EC67
  bibliography, CE14, EA16, EB10, EC2, EC3, EC4, EC6, EC8, EC11, EC13, EC14, EC15, EC18, EC22, ED5, EE13, EF57, EF141, EF173, EF232, EG6, EG105, EG211, EG312

  early works to 1800, BE31, EA21, EC17, ED6, EE15, EG98, EG213, EH68
  biography, EC63
  computer applications, EC55
  databases, EC23
    bibliography, EC1
  dictionaries, EA90, EC32, EC34, EC35, EC36, EC37
    abbreviations, EC33
    bilingual
      Chinese-English, EC39, EC40
      Russian-English, EC38
    multilingual, EC41, EC42
  directories, EC44, EC45, EC46, EC50, ED29, ED31, EF16
  encyclopedias, EC24, EC25, EC26, EC28, EC29, EC30, EC31, ED17, EF145
  eponyms, EC37
  formulas, EC55
  guides, EC2, EC3, EC4
  handbooks, EC50, EC53, EC56, EC57, EC58, EC79
  indexes, EC23
  observers' manuals, EC51, EC56, EC57, EC70, EC71, EC75
  periodicals, EC21, EC43
  sourcebooks, EC62
  tables, EA155
Astronomy (by country or region)
  the Americas, EC60
    bibliography, EC7
Astronomy (by period)
  to 1800
    bibliography, EC12
Astronomy (by subject)
  history, EC59, EC60, EC61
    bibliography, BE31, EA21, EC5, EC9, EC13, EC14, EC16, EC17, EC20, ED6, EE15, EG98, EG213, EH68
  museums, EC47
  study and teaching
    bibliography, EC19
  see also **Planets; Stars**
Astronomy and astronautics, Lusis, Andy, EC3
Astronomy and astrophysics, Kemp, D. Alasdair, EC2, EC18
Astronomy and astrophysics abstracts, EC18, EC22, EC23
The astronomy and astrophysics encyclopedia, EC24
Astronomy data book, Robinson, J. Hedley, EC56
Astronomy Education Materials Network (West Virginia University). *Astronomy education materials resource guide,* EC19
Astronomy education materials resource guide, Sunal, Dennis W., EC19
Astronomy, space sciences, and related organizations of the world, EC33, EC44
Astrophysical data, Lang, Kenneth R., EC53
Astrophysical formulae, Lang, Kenneth R., EC54, ED45
Astrophysical journal, EC34
Astrophysical quantities, Allen, Clabon Walter, EC48
Astrophysics
  abstract journals, EC23, EF143
  bibliography, EC2, EC4, EC18
  databases, EC23
  dictionaries, EA90, EC32, EC35
    multilingual, EC41
  directories, EC44, EC46, EF16
  encyclopedias, EC24, EC25, EC26, EC28, EC29, EC30, ED17
  handbooks, EC48, EC53, EC54, EC58, ED45
  indexes, EC23
  periodicals, EC21
  sourcebooks, EC62
Astrophysics (by subject)
  history, EC59
    bibliography, EC9
Astrophysics and twentieth-century astronomy to 1950, Gingerich, Owen, EC59
Atanasova, Teodora. *Angliĭsko-bŭlgarski rechnik,* AC239

—— *Bŭlgarski-angliĭsko rechnik,* AC239
Atatürk, Kemal, DC531, DC533
Atatürk kaynakçasi, Senalp. Leman, DC533
Atatürk ve devrimleri tarihi bibliyografyasi, Gökman, Muzaffer, DC533
Ateneo de Manila University. *Philippine retrospective national bibliography, 1523–1699,* AA926
Athens, DA106
Atiya, Aziz Suryal. *The Coptic encyclopedia,* BC452
—— *The crusade,* DA167
—— *Crusade, commerce and culture,* DA167
—— *A history of eastern Christianity,* BC443
Atiyeh, George Nicholas. *The contemporary Middle East, 1948–1973,* DE25
—— *The Near East national union list,* AA123
Atkins, Beryl T. *Collins-Robert French-English, English-French dictionary,* AC335
—— *Collins Robert French-English, English-French dictionary, unabridged,* AC336
Atkins, Peter Joseph. *The directories of London, 1677–1977,* AL1, AL7, CH366, CH381
Atkins, Robert. *Artspeak,* BF93
—— *Artspoke,* BF93
Atkins, Stephen E. *Arms control and disarmament, defense and military, international security, and peace,* CJ663
—— *Terrorism,* CJ548
Atkinson, Alan. *Atlas of the British Empire,* DC346
—— *Australians 1838,* DF37
Atkinson, Bernard. *Biochemical engineering and biotechnology handbook,* EK43
Atkinson, Frank. *Dictionary of literary pseudonyms,* AA147
Atkinson, Richard C. *Stevens' handbook of experimental psychology,* CD114
Atkinson, Steven D. *Women online,* CC571
•*ATLA religion database on CD-ROM,* BC41, BC44, BC45, BC52, BC53
ATLA religion index select bibliographies, BC446
Atlanta constitution and journal [index], AE104
Atlanta constitution [index], AE112
Atlanta journal [index], AE112
Atlante enciclopedico degli aerei militari del mondo dal 1914 a oggi, CJ577
Atlante internazionale del Touring Club Italiano, Touring Club Italiano, CL294
Atlantic Canadian imprints, 1801–1820, Fleming, Patricia, DB182
Atlantic Ocean, King, H. G. R., DA8
Atlantic provinces, Morley, W. F. E., DB213
Atlantic provinces checklist, DB213
Atlas Antarktiki, Sovetskaia antarkticheskaia ekspeditsiia, CL370
Atlas Belfrum, DC165
Atlas buying guide, Kister, Kenneth F., CL221
Atlas censal de Bolivia, Instituto Nacional de Estadística (Bolivia), CL315
Atlas ČSSR, Geodetický a kartografický podnik v Praze, CL323
Atlas cultural de México, DB248
Atlas de Colombia, Instituto Geográfico "Agustín Codazzi", CL317
Atlas de Cuba, CL320
Atlas de España y Portugal, CL331, CL333
Atlas de France, CL327
Atlas de géographie historique de la France et de la Gaule, Sinclair, Stéphane, DC166
Atlas de la Côte d'Ivoire, Vennetier, Pierre, CL339
Atlas de la Haute-Volta, Péron, Yves, CL339
Atlas de la Nouvelle-France, Trudel, Marcel, DB208
Atlas de la Republique du Zaire, Laclavère, Georges, CL339
Atlas de la République Islamique du Mauritanie, Laclavère, Georges, CL339
—— Toupet, Charles, CL339
Atlas de la République Unie du Cameroun, Laclavère, Georges, CL339
Atlas de la Révolution française, DC190
Atlas de Portugal, Girão, Aristides de Amorim, CL332
Atlas de Togo, Gu-Konu, Yema E., CL339
Atlas de Tunisie, Fakhfakh, Mohamed, CL339

Atlas de Venezuela, CL318
Atlas del desarrollo territorial de la Argentina, Randle, Patricio H., CL314
Atlas demográfico de Cuba, Comité Estatal de Estadísticas, CL320
Atlas démographique du Maroc, CG347
Atlas départemental, CL328
Atlas des départements français d'outre-mer, Centre d'Études de Géographie Tropicale, CL276
Atlas des diasporas, Chaliand, Gérard, DA188
Atlas des peuples d'Europe centrale, Sellier, André, DC57
Atlas do Brasil Globo, Ira, Rudolf, CL316
Atlas du Luxembourg, Luxembourg. Ministère de l'éducation nationale, CL330
Atlas du Mali, Traoré, Mamadou, CL339
Atlas du monde chrétien, BC289
Atlas du Niger, Bernus, Edmond, CL339
—— Hamidou, Sidikou A., CL339
Atlas du Rwanda, CL344
Atlas estadístico de Costa Rica, no. 2, Sánchez Chinchilla, Luis Angel, CL313
Atlas for anthropology, Spencer, Robert F., CE73
Atlas hierarchicus, Emmerich, Heinrich, BC420
Atlas histórico de México, Florescano, Enrique, DB248
—— Moreno Toscano, Alejandra, DB248
Atlas historique, DC165
Atlas historique de la France, DC166
Atlas historique de la musique, BJ198
Atlas historique des routes de France, Reverdy, Georges, DC167
Atlas historique et culturel de France, DC164
Atlas historique et culturel de las Russie et de monde slav, Kovalevsky, Pierre, DC572
Atlas historyczny Polski, DC482
Les atlas Jeune Afrique, CL339
Aṭlas Karṭa le-toldot 'Am Yiśra'el ba-zeman he-ḥadash, DA190
Aṭlas Karṭa le-toldot 'am Yiśra'el bi-Yeme ha-benayim, DA159
Atlas nacional de España, CL334
L'atlas national du Canada, CL307
The atlas of Africa, Institut géographique national (France), CL337
Atlas of African history, Fage, John D., DD65
Atlas of African prehistory, Clark, John Desmond, DD64
The atlas of American higher education, Fonseca, James W., CB323
Atlas of American history, DB70
—— Ferrell, Robert H., DB71
Atlas of American Indian affairs, Prucha, Francis Paul, CC440
Atlas of American sport, Rooney, John F., BK22
Atlas of American women, Shortridge, Barbara G., DB74
Atlas of America's ethnic diversity, CC358
Atlas of ancient Egypt, Baines, John, DA126
An atlas of Anglo-Saxon England, Hill, David, DC312
Atlas of Australian resources, Australia. Division of National Mapping, CL364
Atlas of British history, Freeman-Grenville, Greville Stewart Parker, DC301
—— Gilbert, Martin, DC301
Atlas of British overseas expansion, Porter, A.N, DC346
The atlas of British politics, Waller, Robert, CJ349
Atlas of British social and economic history since c. 1700, DC299
Atlas of Central America, CL312
Atlas of China, Hsieh, Chiao-min, CL353
Atlas of classical archaeology, DA116
Atlas of classical history, DA117
Atlas of communism, CJ525
Atlas of congressional roll calls, Historical Records Survey, CJ237
Atlas of continental displacement, Owen, H.G, EF112
Atlas of dog breeds of the world, Wilcox, Bonnie, EJ146
Atlas of early American history, DB96

Atlas of economic mineral deposits, Dixon, Colin J., EF196
An atlas of English literature, Goode, Clement Tyson, BE627
Atlas of European architecture, Sachar, Brian, BF253
Atlas of Finland, CL326
An atlas of functions, Spanier, Jerome, EB68
Atlas of Great Lakes Indian history, CC438
An atlas of India, CL356
Atlas of industrializing Britain 1780–1914, DC300
An atlas of international migration, Segal, Aaron, CC359
Atlas of invertebrate reproduction and development, Conn, David Bruce, EG231
An atlas of Irish history, Edwards, Ruth Dudley, DC416
Atlas of Israel, Israel. Agaf ha-medidot, CL357
—— Israel. Mahleket ha-Medidot, CL358
Atlas of Kenya, CL341
Atlas of landforms, EF109
Atlas of mankind, CE70
Atlas of maritime history, Lloyd, Christopher, DA56
—— Natkiel, Richard, DA56
Atlas of medieval Jewish history, Beinart, Haim, DA159
Atlas of Mesopotamia, Beek, Martinus Adrianus, DA86, DE67
Atlas of Mexico, CL310
Atlas of modern Jewish history, Friesel, Evyatar, DA190
Atlas of modern world history, Heater, Derek, DA189
—— Middleton, Haydn, DA189
Atlas of naval warfare, Pemsel, Helmut, CJ600
Atlas of Nazi Germany, Freeman, Michael J., DC263
The atlas of Nepal in the modern world, Sill, Michael, CL359
An atlas of New France, DB208
Atlas of nutritional data on United States and Canadian feeds, National Research Council. Subcommittee on Feed Composition, EJ126
Atlas of ore minerals, Picot, Paul, EF203
Atlas of Pakistan, Survey of Pakistan, CL360
The atlas of past worlds, Manley, John, DA87
Atlas of prehistoric Britain, Manley, John, DC314
Atlas of religious change in America, 1952–1971, Halvorson, Peter L., BC85
Atlas of religious change in America, 1971–1980, Halvorson, Peter L., BC85
—— Newman, William M., BC85
An atlas of Roman Britain, Jones, Barri, DC313
Atlas of Russia and the Soviet Union, Milner-Gulland, R. R., DC572
Atlas of Russian and East European history, Adams, Arthur E., DC56
—— Matley, Ian M., DC56
—— McCagg, William O., DC56
Atlas of Russian history, Chew, Allen F., DC571
—— Gilbert, Martin, DC571
Atlas of South Asia, Dutt, Ashok K., CL347
Atlas of South-east Asia, CL348
Atlas of the 1990 census, Mattson, Mark T., CG109, CL303
Atlas of the American Revolution, Nebenzahl, Kenneth, DB97
Atlas of the Arab world, Dempsey, Michael W., CL349
Atlas of the Bible, Grollenberg, Luc H., BC198
Atlas of the British Empire, DC346
Atlas of the classical world, Heyden, A. A. M. van der, DA120
The atlas of the Crusades, Riley-Smith, Jonathan Simon Christopher, DA160
Atlas of the early Christian world, Meer, Frederik van der, BC290
Atlas of the English civil war, DC324
Atlas of the Greek and Roman world in antiquity, DA118
Atlas of the Greek world, Levi, Peter, DA119
Atlas of the historical geography of the Holy Land, Smith, George Adam, BC202

Atlas of the historical geography of the United States, Paullin, Charles Oscar, DB69, DB75
Atlas of the Holocaust, DA223
—— Gilbert, Martin, DA223
Atlas of the Islamic world since 1500, Robinson, Francis, DE71
Atlas of the Jewish world, DeLange, N. R. M., DA52, DE193
Atlas of the Middle East, Karta (Firm), DE70
Atlas of the moon, Rükl, Antonín, EC68
An atlas of the Mughal Empire, Habib, Irfan, DE172
Atlas of the North American Indian, Waldman, Carl, CC441
Atlas of the Philippines, Hendry, Robert S., CL362
Atlas of the Renaissance, DA158
Atlas of the Republic of China, CL352
Atlas of the Roman world, Cornell, Tim, DA119
Atlas of the South Pacific, CL367
Atlas of the Third World, CJ96
Atlas of the Union of South Africa, Talbot, A. M., CL346
Atlas of the universe, Moore, Patrick, EC67
Atlas of the world, CL285, CL287
Atlas of the world economy, Freeman, Michael J., CH148
Atlas of the world's languages, BD20
Atlas of twentieth century world history, Dockrill, Michael L., DA189
Atlas of United States trees, United States. Forest Service, EJ191
Atlas of world cultures, Murdock, George Peter, CE71, CE72
—— Price, David H., CE72
Atlas of world history, DA49, DA54
Atlas of world political flashpoints, Anderson, Ewan W., CJ72
Atlas of world population history, McEvedy, Colin, CG44
Atlas over Danmark, CL324
Atlas över Sverige, Svenska Sällskapet för Antropologi och Geografi, CL335
Atlas regional andino, Instituto Geográfico "Agustín Codazzi", CL317
Atlas regional del Caribe, CL319
Atlas regional pacifico, Instituto Geográfico "Agustín Codazzi", CL317
Atlas Republiky Československé, Česká Akademie Věd a Umeadní, Prague, CL322
Atlas to the Topographical dictionaries of England and Wales, Lewis, Samuel, CL137, CL206
Atlas van de antieke wereld, DA120
Atlas van de Bijbel, Grollenberg, Luc H., BC198
Aṭlas Yiśra'el. Atlas of Israel, CL357
Atlas zur deutschen Zeitgeschichte, 1918–1968, Hilgemann, Werner, DC264
Atlas zur Kirchengeschichte, BC288
Atlases
　bibliography, CL224, CL226, CL228, CL231, CL239, CL243, CL252, CL254, CL255, CL269
　　current, CL248
　directories, CL269
　general, CL65, CL275, CL277, CL278, CL279, CL280, CL281, CL283, CL284, CL285, CL286, CL287, CL288, CL289, CL291, CL292, CL293, CL294, CL295
　guides, CL221, CL223
　guides to records, CL242
　handbooks, CL264, CL265, CL266
　historical, CL282, DA49, DA53, DA54, DA55, DA57, DA126
　　Africa, DD65
　　American Revolution, DB96, DB97
　　Canada, DB76, DB207, DB208
　　Civil War, DB77, DB123
　　classical studies, DA116, DA117, DA118
　　France, DC165, DC167
　　Germany, DC264
　　Great Britain, DC300
　　Greece, DA119
　　India, DE172
　　Judaism, DA52, DA159, DE193
　　maritime history, DA56
　　military history, DA50

Native Americans, CC-38
Palestine, BC202
Rome, DA119
Russia and the U.S.S.R., DC571
United States, CJ258, DB69, DB73, DB75, DB76
library catalogs, CL254
library collections, CL237, CL255
Atlases (by country or region)
Ukraine, DC544
United States
immigration, CC358
Western states, DB176
Atlases (by subject)
agriculture, EJ75
anthropology, CE70, CE71, CE72, CE73
archaeology, DA87
armed forces, CJ603
Bible, BC197, BC198, BC199, BC200, BC201, BC202
geology, EF113, EF115
Holocaust, DA223
languages, BD20, BD21
linguistic
bibliography, BD104
migration, CC359
oceans, EF225
population, CG44
religion, BC384
women, CC581, CC582
see also Maps
The atomic papers, Burns, Grant, CJ665, CJ666
Atterbury, Paul. *Dictionary of Minton,* BG73
——— *The history of porcelain,* BG73
Attic black-figure vase-painters, Beazley, John Davidson, BF324
Attic red-figure vase-painters, Beazley, John Davidson, BF324
Attig, John C. *The works of John Locke,* BB71
Attinger, V. *Dictionnaire géographique de la Suisse,* CL150
Attitudes toward education, 1969–1988, CB137
Attributs et symboles dans l'art profane, 1450–1600, Tervarent, Guy de, BF171
Attwater, Donald. *A Catholic dictionary,* BC406
——— *Catholic Eastern churches,* BC444
——— *The Christian churches of the East,* BC444
——— *A dictionary of saints,* BC262
——— *Dissident Eastern churches,* BC444
——— *Lives of the saints,* BC263
Aubert, R. *Dictionnaire d'histoire et de géographie ecclésiastiques,* BC412
Aubin, Paul. *Bibliographie de l'histoire du Québec et du Canada,* DB178
Aublet, Robert. *Nouveau guide de généalogie,* AJ83
Auboyer, Jeannine. *Grammaire des formes et des styles,* BF35
——— *Oriental art,* BF35, BF126
Aubry, Marie-Christine. *Djibouti,* DD147
Auchard, John. *American literature,* BE397
——— *Articles on American literature, 1968–1975,* BE408
Aucher, Paschal. *A dictionary, English and Armenian,* AC226
Auchterlonie, Paul. *Arabic biographical dictionaries,* AH331
——— *Union catalogue of Arabic serials and newspapers in British libraries,* AE84
Auctarium bibliotheca hagiographica graeca, Halkin, François Halkin, BC259
Auction catalogue, American Numismatic Society. Library, BG177
Auction Index, Inc. *Leonard's annual price index of art auctions,* BF111
Auction records, AA258, AA259, AA260, AA261, AA262, AA263, AA264, AA265
indexes, BF348
Auction records (by subject)
art, BF108, BF109, BF110, BF111, BF112, BF113
photography, BF356
Audels television service manual, EK147

Auderska, Halina. *Maly słownik języka polskiego,* AC630
The audio dictionary, White, Glenn D., BJ393
Audio video market place, AA379
Audiocassette & compact disc finder, CB28
Audiovisual equipment, AK43
Audiovisual market place, AA379
Audiovisual materials, AA379, AA382, AA383
bibliography, AA381, BF48, EA25
catalogs, AA384, AA385
databases, CB28
handbooks, AK248
library catalogs, AA107
reviews, AA386, AA387
yearbooks, CB177
Audiovisual materials, AA107
——— Library of Congress, AA381
Auditing
directories, CH256
handbooks, CH259
Audouze, Jean. *The Cambridge atlas of astronomy,* EC65
Audubon Society. *Field guide to North American …,* EG81
The Audubon Society encyclopedia of North American birds, Terres, John K., EG277
Audubon Society field guide series, EG81
The Audubon Society field guide to North American fossils, Thompson, Ida, EF251
Audubon wildlife report, EG87
Auer, Michel. *Encyclopédie internationale des photographes de 1839 à nos jours,* BF353
Auer, Michèle. *Encyclopédie internationale des photographes de 1839 à nos jours,* BF353
Auerbach, Hellmuth. *Bibliographie zur Zeitgeschichte, 1953–1989,* DA169
Aufricht, Hans. *Guide to League of Nations publications,* AF27
Augarde, Tony. *Oxford dictionary of modern quotations,* BE113
Auger, Charles P. *Information sources in patents,* EA261
Augsburg historical atlas of Christianity in the Middle Ages and Reformation, Anderson, Charles S., BC287
August, Eugene R. *Men's studies,* CC267
Augustine, Saint, BB60, BB65
Augustinian bibliography, 1970–1980, Miethe, Terry L., BB65
Augustino, Diane K. *Alcohol and the family,* CC108
Aukerian, Haroutiun. *A dictionary, English and Armenian,* AC226
Auld, Douglas A. L. *The American dictionary of economics,* CH54
Aulestia, Gorka. *Basque-English dictionary,* AC230
——— *English-Basque dictionary,* AC231
Auraria Library (Denver, Colo.). *A bibliography of Vietnamese magazines, newspapers and newsletters published in the United States and other countries,* AD211
Aurenche, Olivier. *Dictionnaire illustré multilingue de l'architecture du Proche Orient ancien,* BF243
Aurenhammer, Hans. *Lexikon der christlichen Ikonographie,* BF184
The Aurum film encyclopedia, BH224
Ausgewählte Bibliographie zur Vorgeschichte von Mitteleuropa, Hachmann, Rolf, DC6
Ausgewählte Bibliographien und Bibliothekskatalog zur russischen Sozialgesichte (1861–1917), Schmidt, Christoph, DC581
Austeda, Franz. *Lexikon der Philosophie,* BB38
Austin, Anne L. *A history of nursing, from ancient to modern times,* EH286
Austin, Bruce A. *The film audience,* BH162
Austin, Erik W. *Political facts of the United States since 1789,* CJ148, DB53
Austin, Robert B. *Early American medical imprints,* EH12, EH25
Austin, Roland. *Tercentenary handlist of English & Welsh newspapers, magazines & reviews,* AE59
Austral English, AC179
——— Morris, Edward Ellis, AC180
Australasian dictionary, AC179

Australasian religion index, BC42
Australia
archives, AK161
associations, AL72
atlases, CL364
bibliography, AA941, AA942, DF25, DF26, DF27, DF29
current, AA943, AA944, DF23
bibliography of bibliography, AA84, AA85
biography, AH371, AH372, AH373, AH374, CJ415, DE20, DF20, DF40
contemporary, AH375
dissertations, AG59
encyclopedias, DF33
government publications, AF261, AF263
bibliography, AF266
guides, AF264, AF265
handbooks, AF262
guides, AA84
library resources, AK104, AK161, AK162, DF11, DF30, DF32
manuscripts and archives, DF15, DF32
newspapers
union lists, AE99
periodicals, AD213, AD214
indexes, AD346
place-names, CL218
statistics, CG435, CG436, CJ448, DF33, DF36
bibliography, CG376, CG437, CG438
yearbooks, CG436
Australia (by subject)
anthropology and ethnology, CE113
artists, BF140
economic conditions
bibliography, CH202
folklore and popular culture, CF99
foundations and philanthropic organizations, AL127
history, DF37, DF38, DF39
bibliography, DF26, DF27
encyclopedias, DF33
handbooks, DF34
law, CK233, CK235
military history, DF35
music, BJ28
politics and government, CJ415, CJ447, CJ448, CJ449, CJ450, DE20, DF20, DF36
population, CG435
religion, BC42
social and behavioral sciences
indexes, CA23, DF22
social conditions, DF33
Australia. Department of Immigration and Ethnic Affairs. *Australia's population trends and prospects,* CG435
Australia. Division of National Mapping. *Atlas of Australian resources,* CL364
Australia. Kepars, I., DF27
Australia 1788–1988: a Bicentennial History (Project). *Checklist of nineteenth century Australian colonial statistical sources,* CG437
Australian aboriginals
bibliography, DF28
Australian and New Zealand library resources, Downs, Robert Bingham, AK104
Australian and New Zealand Theological Library Association. *Australasian religion index,* BC42
Australian architectural periodicals index, BF208
Australian architectural serials, 1870–1983, Fung, Stanislaus, BF208
——— Luscombe, Desley, BF208
Australian artists' index, McDonald, Jan, BF140
Australian bibliography, Borchardt, D. H., AA84, CG438
Australian bibliography and bibliographical services, Commonwealth National Library (Canberra). Australian Bibliographical Centre, AA85
Australian books in print, AA943
Australian Bureau of Statistics. *Catalogue of publications,* CG438
——— *Year book, Australia,* CG436

The Australian concise Oxford dictionary of current English, AC177
Australian Council for Educational Research. *Philanthropic trusts in Australia,* AL127
Australian dictionary of biography, AH371, AH372, DF40
Australian education index, CB57
Australian government directory, CJ447
Australian government publications, AF261
Australian Government Publishing Service. *New Commonwealth government books from AGPS,* AF266
Australian legal directory, CK233
Australian literary criticism, 1945–1988, Ross, Robert L., BE856
Australian literary pseudonyms, Nesbitt, Bruce, AA193
Australian literary studies, BE847, BE854
Australian literature, BE851
  bibliography, BE847, BE853, BE856, BE857, BE858
  biobibliography, BE845, BE848, BE859, DF21
  biography, BE853
  ethnic authors
    bibliography, DF24
  guidebooks, BE855
  guides, BE846, BE852
  handbooks, BE855, BE860
  history, BE854
  history and criticism, BE856
  indexes, BE849
Australian literature (by subject)
  history, BE850
Australian literature, Lock, Fred, BE852
  ——— Miller, Edmund Morris, BE853
Australian literature to 1900, Andrews, Barry G., BE846
Australian national bibliography, AA941, AA944, CA23, DF22, DF23
Australian national bibliography, 1901–1950, AA942
The Australian national dictionary, AC178
Australian National University. *Manuscripts in the British Isles relating to Australia, New Zealand, and the Pacific,* DF15
Australian National University. National Centre for Development Studies. *Asian-Pacific economic literature,* CH201
Australian National University. Pacific Manuscripts Bureau. *Complete annotated catalogue PMB manuscript series microfilms PMB 1–1030,* DF14
  ——— *Where the whalers went,* DF9
Australian National University. Research School of Pacific Studies. *The Southwest Pacific,* DF12
Australian official publications, AF262
  ——— Coxon, Howard, AF264
The Australian people, DF33
Australian periodicals in print, AD214, AE99
Australian public affairs information service, CA23, DF22
Australian rare books, 1788–1900, Wantrup, Jonathan, DF29
•*Australian rural research in progress,* EJ74
Australian serials in print, AD214
The Australian short story, 1940–1980, Torre, Stephen, BE858
Australian Society for Sports History. *The Oxford companion to Australian sport,* BK27
Australian Sports Commission. *The Oxford companion to Australian sport,* BK27
Australian women writers, Adelaide, Debra, BE845, DF21
Australian words and their origins, AC178
Australian writers, Blake, Leslie James, BE848
Australians, DF37
Australians 1838, Atkinson, Alan, DF37
  ——— Aveling, Marian, DF37
Australians 1888, Davison, Graeme, DF37
  ——— McCarty, J. W., DF37
  ——— McLeary, Ailsa, DF37
Australians 1938, Douglas, Louise, DF37
  ——— Gammage, Bill, DF37
  ——— Spearritt, Peter, DF37

Australians : a guide to sources, Borchardt, D. H., DF37
  ——— Crittenden, Victor, DF37
Australians : a historical atlas, Camm, J. C. R., DF37
  ——— McQuilton, John, DF37
  ——— Plumb, Trevor W., DF37
Australians : a historical dictionary, Aplin, Graeme, DF37
  ——— Foster, S. G., DF37
  ——— McKernan, Michael, DF37
Australians : events and places, Aplin, Graeme, DF37
  ——— Foster, S. G., DF37
  ——— McKernan, Michael, DF37
Australians from 1939, Curthoys, Ann, DF37
  ——— Martin, A. W., DF37
  ——— Rowse, Tim, DF37
Australians : historical statistics, Vamplew, Wray, DF37
Australians : the guide and index, DF37
Australians to 1788, Mulvaney, D. J., DF37
  ——— White, J. Peter, DF37
Australia's library, information, and archives services, AK161
Australia's population trends and prospects, CG435
Australia's writers, Smith, Graeme Kinross, BE848
Austria
  bibliography, AA573, AA574, DC91
    current, AA575
  bibliography of bibliography, AA36
  biography, AH166, AH167, AH168, AH169, AH170, DC95
    contemporary, AH171, AH213
  dissertations, AG22, AG23
  encyclopedias, DC96
  guides, DC93
  newspapers, AE44
    directories, AD81
  periodicals
    directories, AD81
  place-names, CL184
  statistics, CG193, CG194, CG195, CG196, CG197, CG198
Austria (by subject)
  censuses, CG196
  foreign relations
    bibliography, DC87
  history, DC92, DC97
    bibliography, DC88, DC89, DC90, DC91, DC94
  law, CK206
  politics and government, CJ326
    directories, CJ327
    encyclopedias, CJ334
  social conditions
    statistics, CG197
Austria, Salt, Denys, DC91
Austrian historical bibliography, DC94
Austrian literature, BE1059
  bibliography, BE1055, BE1096
  biobibliography, BE1057, BE1060, BE1095
  women authors
    biobibliography, BE1062
Austronesian languages, BD232
Auswahlbibliographie zum Studium der anglistischen Sprachwissenschaft, Höhlein, Helga, BD91
Authentic decor, Thornton, Peter, BG133
Author and added entry catalog of the American Missionary Association Archives, Amistad Research Center, BC302, CC362
Author and subject catalogues of the Tozzer Library, Tozzer Library, CE22, CE30, CE36
Author biographies master index, BE196, BE387
Author catalog, New York Academy of Medicine. Library, EH50
Author catalog of the Peruvian Collection, National Library of Peru, AA544
Author index of Byzantine studies, Allen, Jelisaveta S., BF9, DA163
  ——— Dumbarton Oaks. Center for Byzantine Studies, DA163

Author index to Psychological index, 1894–1935, and Psychological abstracts, 1927–1958, CD17
  ——— Columbia University. Libraries. Psychology Library, CD18
An author index to selected British 'little magazines,' 1930–1939, Bloomfield, Barry Cambray, AD263
Author newsletters and journals, Patterson, Margaret C., BE43
An author, title, and subject check list of Smithsonian Institution publications relating to anthropology, Miller, Mamie Ruth Tanquist, CE16
Author-title catalog, John Crerar Library, EA17
Author-title catalog of the Department Library, United States. Department of Health, Education, and Welfare. Library, CB35
Author-title index to Joseph Sabin's Dictionary of books relating to America, Molnar, John Edgar, AA409
Authors
  biobibliography, AH42, BE198
  indexes, BE197
  periodicals, BE43
Authors (by country or region)
  Canada
    biography, BE451
  Commonwealth of Nations
    biography, BE817
  Greece
    indexes, BE1031
  United States, BE450
    bibliography, BE435
    biography, BE432, BE433, BE435, BE451
    guidebooks, BE438
Authors (by period)
  classical, BE1026
    biography, BE1025
Authors, Combs, Richard E., BE206
  ——— Owen, Nancy R., BE206
Author's & writer's who's who, Martell, Edward, BE211
Authors' and printers' dictionary, AA277
Author's and writer's who's who, Pine, E. G., BE211
Authors: critical & biographical references, Combs, Richard E., BE197
Author's guide to journals in psychology, psychiatry and social work, Markle, Allen, CD14
  ——— Rinn, Roger C., CD14
Author's guide to journals in the behavioral sciences, Wang, Alvin Yafu, CD14
An author's guide to social work journals, Mendelsohn, Henry N., CC41
Authors of plant names, EG119
Authors of Wales today, Handley-Taylor, Geoffrey, BE812
Authorship
  bibliography, BE11
  congresses and meetings, BE171
  directories, BE174, BE175, BE176
Die Autobiographien zur deutschen Literatur, Kunst und Musik, 1900–1965, Bode, Ingrid, AH205
Autobiographies
  dictionaries, BE217
Autobiographies (by country or region)
  United States
    bibliography, AH89, DB67
Autobiographies (by subject)
  African Americans, CC363
  Native Americans, BE549
  women, BE508, CC485
The autobiography of the working class, Burnett, John, CH679
Automation in libraries, AK209
  bibliography, AK19, AK190
  directories, AK191
Automation in libraries, AK19, AK190
Automobile industry, 1896–1920, May, George S., CH383
Automobile industry, 1920–1980, May, George S., CH383
Automobiles, EK39, EK40
  handbooks, EK455
  statistics, CH456
Automotive engineering, EK38

handbooks, EK41

Die Autoren und Bücher des literarischen Expressionismus, Raabe, Paul, BE1230

Autorenlexikon der Gegenwart, Kutzbach, Karl August, BE1054

Autorenlexikon deutschsprachiger Literatur des 20. Jahrhunderts, BE1054

Autrand, Françoise. *Histoire médiévale en France,* DC168

Auty, Robert. *An introduction to Russian language and literature,* BD186, BE1382

—— *Lexikon des Mittelalters,* DA150

Avakian, Anne M. *Armenia and the Armenians in academic dissertations,* DC84

Avallone, Eugene A. *Marks' standard handbook for mechanical engineers,* EK240

Avalos, Francisco. *The Mexican legal system,* CK196

Avance del anuario, CG280

Avant-garde choral music, May, James D., BJ292

Avanzi, Giannetto. *La bibliografia italiana,* AA52

Avec les "Guides bleues" à travers la France et le monde, Hachette. (firm, publishers, Paris), CL375

Aveling, Marian. *Australians 1838,* DF37

Aveni, Anthony F. *Native American astronomy,* EC60

—— *A selected bibliography on Native American astronomy,* EC7

Averley, G. *A bibliography of eighteenth century legal literature,* CK4

Avery, Barbara Brower. *Guide to sources of professional ethics,* AL9

Avery, Catherine B. *Appleton's new Cuyás English-Spanish and Spanish-English dictionary,* AC732

—— *The new Appleton dictionary of the English and Portuguese languages,* AC647

—— *New Century dictionary of the English language,* AC11

—— *The new Century handbook of classical geography,* CL104

Avery Architectural and Fine Arts Library. *Avery index to architectural periodicals,* BF209

—— *Avery obituary index of architects,* BF258

—— *Catalog of the Avery Memorial Architectural Library of Columbia University,* BF228

Avery index to architectural periodicals, BF212, BF258

—— Avery Architectural and Fine Arts Library, BF209

Avery obituary index of architects, BF258

Aves, EG270

—— Vincent, Jack, EG278

Avhandlingar ock program utgivna vid svenska ock finska akademier ock skolor under aren 1855–1890, Josephson, Aksel Gustav Salomon, AG42

Avi-Yonah, Michael. *Encyclopedia of archaeological excavations in the Holy Land,* BC194

—— *Illustrated encyclopaedia of the classical world,* DA100

—— *The Macmillan Bible atlas,* BC197

Aviation
abbreviations, CH474
bibliography, CH475
dictionaries, CH474, EK31
directories, CH478, EK32
handbooks, CH479, EK35
statistics, CH477

Aviation medicine
bibliography, EH70
indexes, EH70

Aviation/space dictionary, EK29

Avicenne, Paul. *Bibliographic services throughout the world,* AA16

Avilés, Jorge. *Thésaurus multilingue international en administration publique,* CJ479

Avilova, N. S. *Bibliograficheskiĭ ukazatel' literatury po russkomu iazykoznaniiu s 1825 po 1880 god,* BD185

Aviñoa, Xosé. *Diccionario de la zarzuela,* BJ260

Aviram, Joseph. *The new encyclopedia of archaeological excavations in the Holy Land,* BC194

Avis, Walter S. *Dictionary of Canadianisms on historical principles,* AC158

—— *Writings on Canadian English, 1792–1987,* BD105

Avis-kronik-index, AD308, AD309, AE119

•*AVLINE,* EH42, EH43, EH44, EH71, EH72

AVMA directory, American Veterinary Medical Association. Division of Membership and Field Services, EJ118

Avnimelech, Moshe A. *Bibliography of Levant geology,* EF22

Avondale to Zimbabwe, Smith, Robert C., CL157

Avtobiografii sovetskikh litovskikh pisateleĭ, BE1325

Avviamento allo studio critico delle lettere italiane, Mazzoni, Guido, BE1289

Award movies, Pickard, Roy, BH274

Award winning films, Mowrey, Peter C., BH274

Awards see **Prizes and awards**

Awards, honors, and prizes, AL161, AL162, BE180

Awards of honour, Jocelyn, Arthur, AL182

Awn, Peter. *The Columbia encyclopedia,* AB6

•*AWPE,* CH33

Axelrod, Herbert R. *Encyclopedia of tropical fishes,* EG284

—— *Handbook of tropical aquarium fishes,* EG285

Axelsen, Jens. *Dansk-engelsk Ordbog,* AC287

—— *The standard Danish-English, English-Danish dictionary,* AC289

Ayala Poveda, Fernando. *Manual de literatura colombiana,* BE943

Ayensu, Edward S. *Endangered and threatened plants of the United States,* EG145

Ayer, Joseph Cullen. *A source book for ancient church history,* BC281

Ayer directory, AD51, AE23

Ayer directory of publications, AD51, AE23

Ayers, Jerry B. *Teacher education program evaluation,* CB158

Ayto, John. *The Longman register of new words,* AC93

—— *The Oxford dictionary of modern slang,* AC131

Ayuso de Vicente, María Victoria. *Diccionario de términos literarios,* BE75

Azadovskiĭ, M.K. *Sibirskaia sovetskaia entsiklopediia,* DC604

Azevedo, Carmo. *Bibliography of Goa and the Portuguese in India,* DE161

Azevedo, Mario. *Mozambique,* DD48

Aztecs, AH100
bibliography, CC477

The Aztecs, Welch, Thomas L., CC477

Azzi Vitalleschi, Giustiniano degli. *Saggio di bibliografia araldica italiana,* AJ139

Azzolina, David S. *Tale type- and motif-indexes,* CF47

B. H. Blackwell, Ltd. *Classical hand-list,* BE1004

B-P-H, Hunt Botanical Library, EG111

Baa, Enid M. *Theses on Caribbean topics, 1778–1968,* DB411

Baatz, Charles Albert. *The psychological foundations of education,* CD88

Baatz, Olga K. *The psychological foundations of education,* CD88

Babchuk, Nicholas. *Fraternal organizations,* AL36

Babco, Eleanor L. *Professional women and minorities,* CH686

Babichev, F. S. *Ukrainskaia Sovetskaia Sotsialisticheskaia Respublika,* DC545

Babiĭ, B. M. *Ukrainskaia Sovetskaia Sotsialisticheskaia Respublika,* DC545

Babiniotis, George. *Bibliographical bulletin of the Greek language,* BD135

Babula, William. *Shakespeare in production, 1935–1978,* BE792

Babuscio, Jack. *European political facts, 1648–1789,* CJ314

The Babylonian Talmud, BC181

Babylonisch-assyrisches Glossar, Bezold, Carl, AC201

Bach, Adolf. *Deutsche Namenkunde,* AJ192, CL189

Bach, Daniel. *Le Nigeria contemporain,* DD194

Bach, Giovanni. *The history of the Scandinavian literatures,* BE1084

Bach, Kathryn F. *Romance linguistics and the romance languages,* BD149

Bacharach, Jere L. *A Middle East studies handbook,* DE58

—— *Near East studies handbook,* DE58

Bachiller y Morales, Antonio. *Catálogo de libros y folletos publicados en Cuba,* AA560

Bachkatov, Nina. *Russia and the commonwealth A to Z,* DC597

Bächtold-Stäubli, Hanns. *Handwörterbuch des deutschen Aberglaubens,* CF86

The Back Stage theater guide, BH62

Background notes, CJ64, CJ185

Backgrounds to Restoration and eighteenth-century English literature, Spector, Robert Donald, BE747

Backhaus, Karl-Otto. *Wörterbuch Kristallografie,* EF116

Backstage handbook, Carter, Paul, BH89

Bacon, E. D. *Catalogue of the philatelic library of the Earl of Crawford,* BG201

Bacon, Gershon C. *The Jews in Poland and Russia,* DC34

Bacon, Jean C. *Poole's index : date and volume key,* AD281

Bacteriology, EG308, EG309, EG310, EG311, EG313
bibliography, CE14, EA16, EB10, EC15, ED5, EE13, EF57, EF141, EF173, EF232, EG6, EG105, EG211, EG312

Badawi, El-Said M. *A dictionary of Egyptian Arabic,* AC216

Badawi, Muhammad M. *Early Arabic drama,* BE1546

—— *Modern Arabic drama in Egypt,* BE1546

—— *Modern Arabic literature,* BE1546

—— *Short history of modern Arabic literature,* BE1546

Badger, George Percy. *English-Arabic lexicon,* AC212

Baechler, Lea. *African American writers,* BE542

—— *Modern American women writers,* BE448

Baeck, Godehard. *Handbuch der deutschsprachigen ethnologie,* CF99

Baedeker's handbook(s) for travellers, Greenwood Press, CL389

Baedeker's Reisehandbucher 1828–1945, Hinrichsen, Alex, CL389

Baer, Beverly. *Cities of the world,* CL57

Baer, Eleanora A. *Titles in series,* AA95

Baer, Elizabeth. *The Fowler architectural collection of the Johns Hopkins University,* BF229

Baer, Florence E. *Folklore and literature of the British Isles,* CF80

Baer, George W. *International organizations, 1918–1945,* AF1

Baert, A. G. C. *Van Goor's aardrijkskundig woordenboek van Nederland,* CL146

Baez, Vincente. *La gran enciclopedia de Puerto Rico,* DB454

Bagnall, Austin Graham. *New Zealand national bibliography to the year 1960,* AA946, DF42

Bagossy, Lászlo. *Encyclopaedia Hungarica,* AB59

Bagrow, Leo. *A. Ortelii Catalogus cartographorum,* CL273

Bagust, Harold. *The gardener's dictionary of horticultural terms,* EJ237

Bahamas, DB416
bibliography, DB417
dictionaries, AC161
guides to records, DB418
statistics, CG165, CG166

Bahamas. Department of Statistics. *Statistical abstract,* CG166

—— *Vital statistics report,* CG165

The Bahamas, Boultbee, Paul G., DB416

Bahamas index, DB416

Bahamas index and yearbook, DB416

Bahlow, Hans. *Deutsches Namenlexikon,* AJ193

—— *Deutschlands geographische Namenwelt,* CL190

——— *Unsere Vornamen im Wandel der Jahrhunderte,* AJ167

Bahn, Paul G. *Collins dictionary of archaeology,* DA76

Bahr, Stephen J. *Family research,* CC237

Bahrain
  bibliography, DE115
  statistics, CG377

Bahrain. Maktab al-Iḥṣā. *Statistical abstract,* CG377

Bahrain, Unwin, P. T. H., DE115

Baiculescu, George. *Publicaţiunile periodice româneşti (ziare, gazete, reviste),* AD140

Baigell, Matthew. *Dictionary of American art,* BF82

Bailar, J. C. *Comprehensive inorganic chemistry,* EE108

Bailey, Claudia Jean. *A guide to reference and bibliography for theatre research,* BH30

Bailey, Dorothy. *An etymological dictionary of chemistry and mineralogy,* EF181

Bailey, Ethel Zoe. *Hortus third,* EG147, EJ241

Bailey, Hamilton. *Bailey and Bishop's notable names in medicine and surgery,* EH220

——— *Notable names in medicine and surgery,* EH220

Bailey, J. P. *Intercontinental migration to Latin America,* CC309

Bailey, Joyce Waddell. *Handbook of Latin American art,* BF22

Bailey, Kenneth C. *An etymological dictionary of chemistry and mineralogy,* EF181

Bailey, Lavern. *Women of distinction in Jamaica,* AH156

Bailey, Liberty Hyde. *Hortus third,* EG147, EJ241

——— *Manual of cultivated plants most commonly grown in the continental United States and Canada,* EG167

——— *Standard cyclopedia of horticulture,* EJ233

Bailey, Lloyd R. *Word of God,* BC94

Bailey, Richard W. *Early modern English,* AC29

——— *English stylistics,* BE374

Bailey, Roger B. *Guide to Chinese poetry and drama,* BE1557

Bailey, Susan F. *Women and the British empire,* CC587

Bailey, Victory B. *Understanding United States foreign trade data,* CH155

Bailey, William G. *The encyclopedia of police science,* CK252

——— *Guide to popular U.S. government publications,* AF77

——— *Human longevity from antiquity to the modern lab,* CC60

Bailey and Bishop's notable names in medicine and surgery, Bailey, Hamilton, EH220

Bailie, J. M. *Hamlyn dictionary of dates and anniversaries,* AL143

Baillie, Granville Hugh. *Clocks and watches,* BG80

——— *Watchmakers and clockmakers of the world,* BG88

Baillie, Laureen. *American biographical archive,* AH56

——— *American biographical index,* AH56

——— *British biographical archive,* AH224

——— *The catalogue of printed music in the British Library to 1980,* BJ53

Baillière's abbreviations in medicine, Steen, Edwin Benzel, EH135

Bailly, René. *Dictionnaire des synonymes de la langue française,* AC359

Bailly-Herzberg, Janine. *Dictionnaire de l'estampe en France, 1830–1950,* BF380

Baily, Dee. *A checklist of music bibliographies and indexes in progress and unpublished,* BJ23

Bain, George Sayers. *Bibliography of British industrial relations,* CH625, CH638

——— *Bibliography of British industrial relations, 1971–1979,* CH625

Bain, Richard C. *Convention decisions and voting records,* CJ263

Bain, Robert. *Contemporary fiction writers of the South,* BE568

——— *Fifty Southern writers after 1900,* BE571

——— *Fifty Southern writers before 1900,* BE571

——— *Southern writers,* BE578

Baines, John. *Atlas of ancient Egypt,* DA126

Bainton, A. J. C. *Comedias sueltas in Cambridge University Library,* BE1461

——— *Edward M. Wilson collection of comedias sueltas in Cambridge University Library,* BE1461

Bainton, Roland Herbert. *Bibliography of the continental Reformation,* DC26

Bair, Frank E. *Cancer sourcebook,* EH173

——— *The weather almanac,* EF156

Baird, Donald. *English novel, 1578–1956,* BE206, BE671, BE675

Baird, Keith E. *Names from Africa,* AJ168

Baird's manual of American college fraternities, CB398

Bajec, Anton. *Slovar slovenskega knjižnega jezika,* AC720

Bajot, Édouard. *Encyclopédie du meuble du XVᵉ siècle jusqu'à nos jours,* BG122

Bajpai, Shiva G. *A historical atlas of South Asia,* DE91

Bak, János M. *Medieval narrative sources,* DA135

Bakalla, M. H. *Arabic linguistics,* BD204

——— *Bibliography of Arabic linguistics,* BD204

Baker, B. B. *Glossary of oceanographic terms,* EF220

Baker, Brian L. *Encyclopedia of legal information sources,* CK124

Baker, Daniel B. *Explorers and discoverers of the world,* CL81

——— *Political quotations,* CJ45

Baker, Edward Cecil. *Guide to records in the Leeward Islands,* DB419, DB444, DB460

——— *Guide to records in the Windward Islands,* DB419, DB444, DB460

Baker, Ernest Albert. *Guide to historical fiction,* BE250

——— *Guide to the best fiction, English and American,* BE240

——— *The history of the English novel,* BE691

Baker, Melvin. *Bibliography of Canadian urban history,* DB210

Baker, Michael John. *Dictionary of marketing and advertising,* CH549

Baker, Nancy L. *A research guide for undergraduate students,* BE2, BE396

Baker, Philip. *International guide to African studies research,* DD54

Baker, Richard A. *The United States Senate,* CJ197

Baker, Robert A. *Catalogue of Renaissance philosophers (1350–1650),* BB70

Baker, Robert Fulton. *Handbook of highway engineering,* EK120

Baker, Sheridan. *Harper handbook to literature,* BE84

Baker, Susan P. *The injury fact book,* EH187

Baker, Sylva. *Endangered vertebrates,* EG206

Baker, Theodore. *Baker's biographical dictionary of musicians,* BJ203, BJ219

Baker encyclopedia of psychology, CD19

Baker Library. *Harvard Business School core collection,* CH7

——— *Studies in enterprise,* CH389, CH390

Bakerjian, Ramon. *Tool and manufacturing engineers handbook,* EK248

Baker's biographical dictionary of musicians, Baker, Theodore, BJ203, BJ219

Baker's dictionary of Christian ethics, Henry, Carl F. H., BC241

Bakhmeteff Archive of Russian and East European History and Culture. *Russia in the twentieth century,* DC558

Bakish, David. *Afro-American fiction, 1853–1976,* BE525

Bako, Elemer. *Finland and the Finns,* DC136

——— *Hungarian abbreviations,* AC497

Bal, Willy. *Bibliographie sélective de linguistique romane et française,* BD150

——— *Guide bibliographique de linguistique romane,* BD150

Bala, Vehbi. *Historia e letërsisë shqiptare,* BE1094

Balaban, Robin Mayper. *Directory of internships, work experience programs, and on-the-job training opportunities,* CB364, CH695

Balachandran, M. *Encyclopedia of business information sources : Europe,* CH329

——— *A guide to statistical sources in money, banking, and finance,* CH290

——— *Regional statistics,* CG91

Balachandran, Sarojini. *Decision making,* CH605

——— *Energy statistics,* EK211

Balakrishnan, N. *The chronological annotated bibliography of order statistics,* EB9

Balakrishnan, T. R. *Annotated bibliography of Canadian demography,* CG116

Balan, Alexsandar Teodorov. *Bŭlgarski tulkoven rechnik, s ogled kŭm narodnite govori,* AC241

Balance of payments statistics, CH238

Balance of payments yearbook, CH238

Balanchine, George. *Balanchine's complete stories of the great ballets,* BH150

Balanchine's complete stories of the great ballets, Balanchine, George, BH150

Balanchine's new complete stories of the great ballets, BH150

Balandier, Georges. *Dictionary of Black African civilization,* CE106

Balard, Michel. *Bibliographie de l'histoire médiévale en France (1965–1990),* DC168

Balášová, Olga. *Bibliografie české literární vědy, 1945–1955,* BE1104

Balazs, Etienne. *A Sung bibliography,* DE135

Balázs, János. *A magyar nyelv értelmező szótára,* AC493

Balázs, Péter. *Guide to the archives of Hungary,* DC386

Balbo, Michael P. *Illustrated dental terminology,* EH256

Baldazzi, Anna. *Contributo a una bibliografia del futurismo letterario italiano,* BE1291

Baldensperger, Fernand. *Bibliography of comparative literature,* BE12, BE13, BE41

——— *La littérature comparée,* BE13

Balderston, Daniel. *The Latin American short story,* BE903

Baldinger, Kurt. *Dictionnaire étymologique de l'ancien français,* AC346

——— *Introduction aux dictionnaires les plus importants pour l'histoire du français,* AC387

Baldner, R. W. *Bibliography of the seventeenth-century novel in France,* BE1190

Baldrige, Letitia. *The Amy Vanderbilt complete book of etiquette,* AL158

——— *Letitia Baldrige's complete guide to the new manners for the 90's,* AL152

Baldwin, Claudia. *Nigerian literature,* BE1530

Baldwin, James Mark. *Dictionary of philosophy and psychology,* BB26

Baldwin, Robert. *College football records,* BK73

Baleyte, Jean. *Dictionnaire économique et juridique,* CK48

——— *Dictionnaire juridique,* CK48

Balfour, Edward Green. *Cyclopædia of India and of eastern and southern Asia, commercial, industrial, and scientific,* DE164

Bali en lombok, Liefrinck, Frederick Albert, DE178

Balima, Mildred Grimes. *Botswana, Lesotho, and Swaziland,* AF218

Balkan languages, BD202

Balkan military history, Jessup, John E., DC60

Balkans
  bibliography, DC58, DC61, DC62, DC64, DC66, DC114, DC536
  dissertations, DC67
  guides, DC59
  handbooks, DC68
  library catalogs, DC45, DC49
  statistics, CG373

Balkans (by subject)
  foreign relations, DC62, DC114
  history
    bibliography, DC60, DC65
    manuscripts and archives, DC63
    statistics, CG373

Balkema, John B. *Aging*, CC57

Balkin, Richard. *A writer's guide to book publishing*, AA295

Ball, John. *Bibliography of theatre history in Canada*, BH39

Ball, P. W. *Flora Europaea*, EG170

Ball, Robert Hamilton. *Theatre language*, BH77

Ball, Ronald G. *Uniforms of the world*, CJ595

Ball, Sarah. *The directory of international sources of business information*, CH1

Ball, Warwick. *Catalogue des sites archéologiques d'Afghanistan*, DE109

Ballad scholarship, Richmond, W. Edson, BE633

Ballads
  bibliography, BE630, BE631, BE632, BE633, BE634, BJ314
  indexes, BE634

Ballads (by country or region)
  England
    texts, BE632
  Latin America, BE878
  Scotland
    texts, BE632

Ballantyne, James. *Researcher's guide to British film & television collections*, BH181

Ballantyne, Lygia Maria F. C. *Haitian publications*, AA566

Ballentyne, Denis William George. *A dictionary of named effects and laws in chemistry, physics, and mathematics*, EA85

Ballet
  annuals, BH155
  dictionaries, BH145, BH146
  encyclopedias, BH140, BH141, BH142, BH143, BH144, BJ252
  handbooks, BH150, BH151, BH154
  indexes, BH138
  plot summaries, BH138, BH150, BH151
  see also **Dance**

Ballet, Terry, Walter, BH154

Ballet annual, BH155

Ballet guide, Terry, Walter, BH154

Ballet plot index, Studwell, William E., BH138

Balley, A. W. *Stratigraphic atlas of North America and Central America*, EF113

Ballinger, Jack T. *Chemical technician's ready reference handbook*, EE87

Ballou, Hubbard. *Photographic literature*, BF326

Ballou, Robert O. *The Bible of the world*, BC91

Ballou, Stephen Vaughan. *Form and style*, AG1

Ballparks of North America, Benson, Michael, BK51

The ballplayers, BK48, BK52

Balski, Grzegorz. *Directory of Eastern European film-makers and films, 1945–1991*, BH212

Balteau, J. *Dictionnaire de biographie française*, AH194

Baltic drama, BE989

Baltic languages, BD194

Baltic languages, BD194

Baltic literatures, BE989

Baltic region
  bibliography, DC70
  handbooks, DC69

Baltic region (by subject)
  history, DC137

The Baltic states, DC69
  ——— Smith, Inese A., DC70

Baltsan, Hayim. *Webster's new World Hebrew dictionary*, AC474

Baltušis, Juozas. *Tarybų Lietuvos rašytojai*, BE1325

Balys, John P. *Lithuanian periodicals in American libraries*, AD220

Balz, Horst Robert. *Exegetical dictionary of the New Testament*, BC137
  ——— *Theologische Realenzyklopädie*, BC69

Bamberger, Bernard Jacob. *The Torah*, BC184

Bamberger, Richard. *Österreich-Lexikon*, DC96

Bamford, Lawrence Von. *Design resources*, BF201

Banco Central del Ecuador. *Boletín anuario – Banco Central del Ecuador*, CG152

Banco Nacional Ultramarino, Lourenço Marques. Centro de Documentação e Informação. *Catálogo dos livros sobre Moçambique existentes no CDI do Banco em Lourenço Marques*, DD183

Bancroft Library. *Catalog of printed books*, DB163
  ——— *Index to printed maps*, CL250, DB163

Band music, BJ294

Bandecchi, Pedro Brasil. *Dicionário de história do Brasil*, DB353

Bander, Edward J. *Medical legal dictionary*, EH267

Bandinelli, Ranuccio Bianchi. *Enciclopedia dell'arte antica, classica e orientale*, BF71

Bandmann, Günter. *Lexikon der christlichen Ikonographie*, BF184

Bane, Adele F. *The leisure literature*, BK5

Banerjea, Jitendra Nath. *The development of Hindu iconography*, BF190

Banerjee, D. L. *A bibliography of Indology*, CE109

Banerjee, Satya Ranjan. *Chhotelal Jain's Jaina bibliography*, BC507

Bang, Jorgen. *Gyldendals tibinds leksikon*, AB33

Bangla Desh, Satyaprakash, DE116

Bangladesh, DE116, DE117
  atlases, CL351
  bibliography, AA891
  biography, AH334, AH335
  statistics, CG378

Bangladesh (by subject)
  history
    encyclopedias, DE90
  see also **Pakistan**

Bangladesh in maps, CL351

Bangladesh national bibliography, AA891

Banham, Martin. *Cambridge guide to Asian theatre*, BH66
  ——— *The Cambridge guide to world theatre*, BH67

Banister, David. *Urban transport and planning*, BF269, CK451, EK121

Bank, David. *British biographical archive*, AH224
  ——— *British biographical index*, AH224

Bank quarterly, CH291

The bankers' almanac, CH275

Bankers' guide to foreign currency, CH285

The bankers' handbook, CH282

Bankers magazine (Boston). *The Thorndike encyclopedia of banking and financial tables*, CH269

Banki, Ivan S. *Dictionary of administration and management*, CH612

Banking *see* **Finance and banking**

Banking and finance, 1913–1989, Schweikart, Larry E., CH265, CH383

Banking and finance to 1913, CH265, CH383

Banking and monetary statistics, Board of Governors of the Federal Reserve System, CH292, CH293

Banking in the U.S, Deuss, Jean, CH283

Banking law journal (Boston). *The Thorndike encyclopedia of banking and financial tables*, CH269

Banking terminology, CH270

Banks, Arthur. *Ancient history atlas*, DA117
  ——— *The Dent atlas of Jewish history*, DA52, DE193
  ——— *A world atlas of military history*, DA50

Banks, Jennifer. *Options for replacing and reformatting deteriorated materials*, AK238

Banks, Margaret A. *Banks on using a law library*, CK195

Banks, Olive. *The biographical dictionary of British feminists*, AH218

Banks, Paul Noble. *A selective bibliography on the conservation of research library materials*, AK237

Banks on using a law library, Banks, Margaret A., CK195

Bannānukrom hāeng chāt, AA939

Banner, János. *Bibliographia archaeologica hungarica, 1793–1943*, DC379

Bannock, G. *Penguin dictionary of economics*, CH54

Bansal, Narottam P. *Handbook of glass properties*, EK271

The Bantam great outdoors guide to the United States and Canada, Landi, Val, BK107

Bantaş, Andrei. *Dicţionar de buzunar englez-român, român-englez*, AC663
  ——— *Dicţionar englez-român*, AC663
  ——— *Dicţionar român-englez*, AC663

Banton, Michael. *Dictionary of race and ethnic relations*, CC341

Banuazizi, Ali. *Social stratification in the Middle East and North Africa*, DE26

Banville, Christian de. *Bibliographie centrafricaine*, DD139

Ban'yu hyakka dai-jiten, AB68

A Baptist bibliography, Starr, Edward Caryl, BC326
  ——— Whitley, William Thomas, BC327

Baptist Union of Great Britain and Ireland. *A Baptist bibliography*, BC327

Baptists, BC326, BC327
  directories, BC328
  encyclopedias, BC325
  yearbooks, BC328, BC329

Bar, Adam. *Słownik pseudonimów i kryptonimów pisarzy polskich oraz Polski dotyczących*, AA180

Barac, Antun. *Jugoslavenska književnost*, BE1497

Barachino, Maria. *Periodici italiani, 1968–1981*, AD128

Baranowski, Henryk. *Bibliografia kopernikowska*, EC5

Barashenkov, V. M. *Bibliografiĭa periodicheskikh izdaniĭ Rossii 1901–1916*, AD142

Barashkova, V. S. *Dvizhenie dekabristov*, DC577

Baratier, Édouard. *Atlas historique*, DC165

Baratte-Eno Belinga, Thérèse. *Bibliographie des auteurs africains de langue française*, BE1513
  ——— *Écrivains, cinéastes et artistes camerounais*, BE1525

Baravykas, Vaclovas. *Anglų-lietuvių kalbų žodynas*, AC600

Barba, Enrique M. *Catálogo analítico de las publicaciones de la Academia Nacional de la Historia, 1903–1986*, DB323

Barbados, DB419, DB421
  bibliography, AA557
  sourcebooks, DB420
  statistics, CG167

Barbados (by subject)
  history, DB420

Barbados, Potter, Robert B., DB421

Barber, Edwin Atlee. *Ceramic collectors' glossary*, BG63

Barber, Eric Arthur. *A Greek-English lexicon*, AC444

Barbier, Ant.-Alex. *Les supercheries littéraires dévoilées*, AA169

Barbier, Frédéric. *Bibliographie de l'histoire de France*, DC142

Barbier, Jean. *Atlas départemental*, CL328

Barbosa Machado, Diogo. *Bibliotheca lusitana historica, critica, e cronologica*, AA774

Barbour, K. Michael. *Nigeria in maps*, CL342

Barbour, Roger William. *Turtles of the world*, EG247

Barcala de Moyano, Graciela G. *Catálogo analítico de las publicaciones de la Academia Nacional de la Historia, 1903–1986*, DB323

Barciela López, Carlos. *Estadísticas históricas de España*, CG282

Barclay, H. M. *Abraham and Hawtrey's parliamentary dictionary*, CJ352

Bárczi, Géza. *A magyar nyelv értelmező szótára*, AC493

Bardales, Alejandro. *Perú, las provincias en cifras, 1876–1981*, CG158

Barden, Judith. *Directory of British and Irish law libraries*, CK213

Bardhan, Gail P. *The history and art of glass*, BG53

Bardis, Panos Demetrios. *Dictionary of quotations in sociology*, CC22

Bardouille, Raj. *Research on Zambian women in retrospect and prospect*, DD246

Bardsley, Charles W. *Dictionary of English and Welsh surnames*, AJ184

Baretta-Bekker, J. G. *Encyclopedia of marine sciences*, EF219

Barin, Ihsan. *Thermochemical data of pure substances*, EE63

Barkas, J. L. *Friendship*, CC3

Barker, Christine R. *The Arthurian bibliography*, BE339

Barker, Nicolas. *ABC for book-collectors*, AA249

Barker, Robert L. *The social work dictionary*, CC47

Barker, Virgil. *American painting, history and interpretation*, BF309

Barkhudarov, S. G. *Slovar' russkogo iazyka XI-XVII vv*, AC673

Barkley, William D. *Seed identification manual*, EG154

Barlow, Diane. *Moving and relocation sourcebook*, CL73

Barlow, Harold. *A dictionary of musical themes*, BJ228, BJ229
———— *A dictionary of opera and song themes*, BJ229

Barlow, Richard G. *The fifth directory of periodicals publishing articles on American and English language and literature, criticism and theory, film, American studies, poetry and fiction*, BE170

Barman, Jean. *Contemporary Canadian childhood and youth*, CC152
———— *History of Canadian childhood and youth*, CC153

Barman, Thomas E. *Enzyme handbook*, EG314

Barnadas, Josep M. *Introducción a los estudios bolivianos contemporáneos, 1960–1984*, DB334

Barnard, Henry. *Pamphlets in American history*, CH641, DB20

Barnard, Nicholas. *Living with decorative textiles*, BG158

Barnard, Stephen. *Encyclopedia of rock*, BJ345

Barnes, A. C. *Chinese-English glossary of mineral names*, EF182

Barnes, Grace M. *Alcohol and the elderly*, CC107
———— *Alcohol and the family*, CC108
———— *Alcohol and youth*, CC109

Barnes, P. M. *Steinberg's dictionary of British history*, DC293

Barnes, Thomas Charles. *Northern New Spain*, DB249

Barnet, Sylvan. *Short guide to writing about art*, BF124

Barnett, Patricia J. *Guide to indexing and cataloging with the Art & architecture thesaurus*, BF94

Barnhart, Clarence Lewis. *American college dictionary*, AC15
———— *The Barnhart dictionary of new English since 1963*, AC95
———— *New Century cyclopedia of names*, AH29, BE209
———— *Scott, Foresman advanced dictionary*, AC23
———— *Scott, Foresman beginning dictionary*, AC24
———— *Scott, Foresman intermediate dictionary*, AC25

Barnhart, David K. *Barnhart dictionary companion-index*, AC94

Barnhart, Robert K. *The American heritage dictionary of science*, EA86
———— *The Barnhart dictionary of etymology*, AC48
———— *The Barnhart dictionary of new English since 1963*, AC95

The Barnhart dictionary companion, AC94

Barnhart dictionary companion-index, Barnhart, David K., AC94

The Barnhart dictionary of etymology, AC48

The Barnhart dictionary of new English since 1963, AC95

Barnouw, Erik. *International encyclopedia of communications*, CH482

Barockthemen, Pigler, Andor, BF172

Baron, John H. *Chamber music*, BJ269

Baron, Joseph L. *A treasury of Jewish quotations*, BE121

Baron, Salo Wittmayer. *A social and religious history of the Jews*, BC561

Baroque art, BF172

Baroque literature
    bibliography, BE1203, BE1217, BE1234
    library catalogs, BE1234

Barquero, Sara Luisa. *Gobernantes de Nicaragua*, DB313

Barr, Avron. *The handbook of artificial intelligence*, EK204

Barr, Larry J. *Libraries in American periodicals before 1876*, AK9

Barr, Rebecca. *Handbook of reading research*, CB114

Barraclough, E. M. C. *Flags of the world*, AL190

Barraclough, Geoffrey. *The Times atlas of world history*, DA58

Barranger, Milly S. *Notable women in the American theatre*, BH118

Barrau-Dihigo, Louis. *Manuel de l'hispanisant*, AA67, AA801, AH290, BE1435

Barreiro, Fernando. *Organizaciones no gubernamentales de Uruguay*, AL53

Barrenechea, Enrique. *Adiciones á la Biblioteca boliviana de Gabriel René-Moreno*, AA500

Barrère, Albert. *Dictionary of slang, jargon & cant*, AC118

Barrett, David B. *World Christian encyclopedia*, BC233, BC292

Barrett, Jacqueline K. *Encyclopedia of women's associations worldwide*, AL18

Barrett, Jane R. *Bibliography of works on Canadian foreign relations, 1976–1980*, DB186
———— *Bibliography of works on Canadian foreign relations, 1981–1985*, DB186

Barrett, P. R. *The printing of mathematics*, EB97

Barrett, Paul H. *A concordance to Darwin's Origin of species, first edition*, EG68

Barrett, Thomas M. *North American horticulture*, EG155

Barriga López, Franklin. *Diccionario de la literatura ecuatoriana*, BE950

Barriga López, Leonardo. *Diccionario de la literatura ecuatoriana*, BE950

Barrile, Joseph G. *Television service manual*, EK147

Barrios y Barrios, Catalina. *Historia de la literatura guatemalteca*, BE905

Barron, Neil. *Anatomy of wonder*, BE276
———— *Fantasy literature*, BE277
———— *Horror literature*, BE278

Barron's 300 best buys in college education, Solórzano, Lucia, CB291

Barron's business and financial weekly, AE115

Barron's complete college financing guide, CB376

Barron's Educational Series, Inc. *Barron's profiles of American colleges*, CB250

Barron's finance & investment handbook, Downes, John, CH233

Barron's guide to law schools, CK154

Barron's index, AE115, CH45

Barron's profiles of American colleges, CB250

Barron's top 50, CB251

Barros Paiva, Tancredo de. *Achêgas a um diccionario de pseudonymos, iniciaes, abreviaturas e obras anonymas de auctores brasileiros e de estrangeiros, sobre o Brasil ou no mesmo impressas*, AA157

Barroso, Gustavo. *Pequeno dicionário brasileiro da língua portuguêsa*, AC643

Barroux, M. *Dictionnaire de biographie française*, AH194

Barrow, Geoffrey Battiscombe. *Genealogists guide*, AJ109

Barrow, John Graves. *A bibliography of bibliographies in religion*, BC4

Barrow, Margaret. *Women, 1870–1928*, CC524

Barrow, Robin. *A critical dictionary of educational concepts*, CB72

Barrows, Floyd D. *A dictionary of obituaries of modern British radicals*, AH219

Barry, Inviolata. *A complete index of the Summa theologica of St. Thomas Aquinas*, BB62
———— *A lexicon of St. Thomas Aquinas based on the Summa theologica and selected passages of his other works*, BB63

Barry, Randall K. *ALA-LC romanization tables*, BD10

Bart, Pauline. *The student sociologist's handbook*, CC23

Barteczko, Ewa. *Polskie wydawnictwa informacyjne, 1945–1981*, AA347

Bartel, Horst. *Sachwörterbuch der Geschichte Deutschlands und der deutschen Arbeiterbewegung*, DC257

Bartel, Klaus J. *German literary history, 1777–1835*, BE1254

Bartelski, Lesław M. *Polscy pisarze współczesni*, BE1345

Bartelt, Chuck. *Variety obituaries*, BH25

Barth, Else M. *Women philosophers*, BB4

Barth, Hans. *Bibliographie der schweizer Geschichte enthaltend die selbständig erschienenen Druckwerke zur Geschichte der Schweiz bis Ende 1912*, AH298, AH299, DC522, DC528
———— *Repertorium über die in Zeit- und Sammelschriften der Jahre 1812–1890 enthaltenen Aufsätze und Mitteilungen schweizergeschichtlichen Inhaltes*, AH300, DC523

Bartholet, Carolyn. *Articles on American literature, 1950–1967*, BE408

Bartholomew, John. *The Times atlas of the world*, CL292

Bartholomew gazetteer of Britain, CL135

Bartholomew gazetteer of places in Britain, CL135

Bartis, Peter. *Folklife sourcebook*, CF75

Bartke, Wolfgang. *Biographical dictionary and analysis of China's party leadership, 1922–1988*, CJ425
———— *Chinaköpfe*, AH337
———— *China's new party leadership*, CJ426
———— *Who's who in the People's Republic of China*, AH344, CJ426, CJ428

Bartl, Gerda. *Bestandskatalog der Bibliothek des Südost-Instituts München*, DC65

Bartlett, John. *Familiar quotations*, BE99

Bartlett, John Russell. *Bibliotheca americana*, DB1

Bartlett, Roger. *Eighteenth century Russia*, DC574

Bartley, Numan V. *Southern elections*, CJ290

Bartley, Russell H. *Soviet historians on Latin America*, DB260

Bartolotta, Francesco. *Governi d'Italia, 1848–1961*, CJ380

Barton, Barbara J. *Gardening by mail*, EJ244

Barton, David Knox. *Handbook of radar measurement*, EK145

Barton, Derek. *Comprehensive organic chemistry*, EE118

Barton, John P. *An ounce of prevention*, AK243

Barton, Judith S. *Guide to the Bureau of Applied Social Research*, CA12

Barton, Lela Viola. *Bibliography of seeds*, EG99

Barton, Walter E. *The history and influence of the American Psychiatric Association*, EH397

Bartsch, Adam von. *The illustrated Bartsch*, BF381
———— *Peintre graveur*, BF381, BF382

Bartsch, Hans-Jochen. *Handbook of mathematical formulas*, EB61

Bartz, Bettina. *World guide to libraries*, AK121

Barwick, Margaret M. *A guide to centres of international lending and copying*, AK223

Barzun, Jacques. *A catalogue of crime*, BE266
———— *Modern American usage*, AC71
———— *The modern researcher*, DA3

Bas-Canada, Ouellet, R., DB203

Basadre, Jorge. *Introducción a las bases documentales para la historia de la República del Perú*, DB381

Basart, Ann Phillips. *Writing about music*, BJ99

Başbuğoğlu, Filiz. *1928–1965 [i.e., Bin dokuz yüz yirmi sekiz, bin dokuz yüz altmışbeş] yılları arasında Türkiyede basılmış bibliyografyaların bibliyografyası*, AA68

•*Base audiart*, BF327

Baseball, BK9, BK48, BK51, BK52, BK53, BK54, BK55, BK57, BK58, BK59, BK60, BK61, BK62
    encyclopedias, BK49
    quotations, BK50

Baseball, Smith, Myron J., BK60

The baseball encyclopedia, BK48, BK49, BK62

Baseball guide, BK61

Baseball guide and record book, BK61
Baseball official guide, BK61
Baseball's greatest quotations, BK50
Baseline (Firm). *The encyclopedia of film*, BH283
Basford, Terry K. *Near-death experiences*, CC177
Bashkina, Nina N. *The United States and Russia*, DB64
A basic bibliography for the study of Semitic languages, BD203
Basic books in the mass media, AE131
The basic business library, CH8
A basic classical and operatic recordings collection for libraries, Rosenberg, Kenyon C., BJ381
Basic classical and operatic recordings collection on compact discs for libraries, Rosenberg, Kenyon C., BJ381
Basic dental reference works, Kowitz, Aletha, EH244
Basic documents of international economic law, CK112
Basic documents of international environmental law, Hohmann, Harald, CK91
Basic documents on human rights, Brownlie, Ian, CK113
Basic facts and figures, CB145
Basic geographical library, Church, Martha, CL17
—— Huke, Robert E., CL17
—— Winters, Harold A., CL17
Basic international bibliography of archive administration, AK182
Basic Japanese-English dictionary, AC551
Basic laboratory and industrial chemicals, EE64
Basic literature in policy studies, Nagel, Stuart S., CJ12
Basic literature on Austrian law, CK206
Basic literature on law, CK211
Basic map of Finland, Finland. Maanmittaushallitus, CL325
A basic music library, BJ24
Basic research methods for librarians, Powell, Ronald R., AK7
Basic Russian publications, Horecky, Paul Louis, DC550
Basic statistics for fifteen European countries, CG182
Basic statistics of the community, CG182
Basic technical writing, Weisman, Herman M., EA163
Baskerville, David. *Music business handbook & career guide*, BJ179
Basket making, BG159
Basketball, BK64, BK65, BK66, BK67
 biography, BK63
The basketball bible, BK64
Basketball biographies, Taragano, Martin, BK67
Basketball resource guide, Krause, Jerry V., BK64
Baskin, Ellen. *Enser's filmed books and plays*, BH215
Basler, Otto. *Deutsches Fremdwörterbuch*, AC409
Basler, Roy P. *Guide to the study of the United States of America*, DB13
Basque-English dictionary, Aulestia, Gorka, AC230
Basque language
 dictionaries
  bilingual, AC230, AC231
   Basque-French, AC229
   Spanish-Basque, AC228
Basque region
 periodicals, AD158
Basques, CC465
Bass, Bernard M. *Bass & Stogdill's handbook of leadership*, CD126, CH608
Bass & Stogdill's handbook of leadership, Bass, Bernard M., CD126, CH608
Bassa, Ramon. *Llibres [sic] editats à Mallorca (1939–1972)*, AA743
Bassan, Fernande. *French language and literature*, BD156, BE1130
Basseches, Bruno. *A bibliography of Brazilian bibliographies*, AA28
Bassett, Charles. *Political parties & elections in the United States*, CJ262
Bassett, John Earl. *Harlem in review*, BE514

Bassett, T. D. Seymour. *Socialism and American life*, CJ527
Basso, Alberto. *Dizionario enciclopedico universale della musica e dei musicisti : il lessico*, BJ130
—— *Dizionario enciclopedico universale della musica e dei musicisti : le biografie*, BJ131
Basutoland, Groen, Julie te, DD169
Basutoland bibliography, Shaskolsky, D. L., DD169
Bataille, Gretchen M. *American Indian women*, CC588
—— *Images of American Indians on film*, CC334
Batalden, Sandra K. *The newly independent states of Eurasia*, DC598
Batalden, Stephen K. *The newly independent states of Eurasia*, DC598
Bataviaasch Genootschap van Kunsten en Wetenschappen. *Proeve eener Ned*, DE174
Batchelor, R. E. *Using French synonyms*, AC360
Bate, John Drew. *New English-Hindustani dictionary*, AC489
Bateman, Harry. *Guide to tables of Bessel functions*, EB73
—— *Higher transcendental functions*, EB79
Bateman Manuscript Project. *Higher transcendental functions*, EB79, EB80
—— *Tables of integral transforms*, EB80
Bateman New Zealand encyclopedia, DF43
Bates, Ralph Samuel. *Scientific societies in the United States*, EA198
Bates, Robert Latimer. *Dictionary of geological terms*, EF72
—— *Glossary of geology*, EF70, EF71, EF72
Bateson, Frederick Wilse. *Cambridge bibliography of English literature*, BE582, BE585
—— *A guide to English and American literature*, BE580
Batey, Charles. *The printing of mathematics*, EB97
Batho, V. A. *Scotland in the nineteenth century*, DC359
Batiste, Angel. *Japanese-African relations*, DD3
—— *Liberia during the Tolbert era*, DD172
Batlle, Monica. *Materials per una bibliografia d'Andorra*, DC82
Batschelet, Margaret. *Early American scientific and technical literature*, EA227
The Batsford companion to medieval England, Saul, Nigel, DC311
The Batsford dictionary of drama, BH78
Battaglia, Salvatore. *Grande dizionario della lingua italiana*, AC524
Battaini, P. *La nuova Italia*, CL145
Battersby, Harold R. *Anatolian archaeology*, DC531
Battie, David. *Sotheby's concise encyclopedia of glass*, BG61
—— *Sotheby's concise encyclopedia of porcelain*, BG62
Battisti, Carlo. *Dizionario etimologico italiano*, AC536
Battle, Carl W. *Legal-wise*, CK164
Battle of Antietam and the Maryland Campaign of 1862, Hartwig, D. Scott, DA170
Battle of Jutland, Rasor, Eugene L., DA170
Battle of Pearl Harbor, Smith, Myron J., DA170
Battledress, Schick, I. T., CJ595
Battlefield atlas of the Civil War, Symonds, Craig L., DB123
Battles, DA22, DA24, DB118
 atlases, DA50
 bibliography, DA170
 encyclopedias, DA20, DA21, DA25
Battles of Coral Sea and Midway, May–June 1942, Smith, Myron J., DA170
Batts, John Stuart. *British manuscript diaries of the nineteenth century*, BE724, DC327
Batts, Michael S. *The bibliography of German literature*, BE1215
—— *History of histories of German literature, 1835–1914*, BE1254
Batty, Anthea. *American biographical index*, AH56
Batty, Linda. *Retrospective index to film periodicals, 1930–1971*, BH231
Bauab, Heloísa Helena. *Bibliografia da música brasileira*, BJ22

Bauccio, Michael. *ASM metals reference book*, EK270
Baudicour, Prosper de. *Peintre-graveur français continué*, BF377
Baudot, Marcel. *Encyclopédie de la guerre 1939–1945*, DA208
—— *Historical encyclopedia of World War II*, DA208
Baudouin de Courtenay, J. *Tolkovyi slovar' zhivogo velikorusskago iazyka*, AC668
Baudrillart, Alfred. *Dictionnaire d'histoire et de géographie ecclésiastiques*, BC412
Bauer, David G. *Administering grants, contracts, and funds*, AL129
—— *Complete grants sourcebook for higher education*, AL130, CB372
—— *Complete grants sourcebook for nursing and health*, AL130
—— *The "how to" grants manual*, AL130
Bauer, Johannes B. *Encyclopedia of biblical theology*, BC126, BC130
Bauer, K. Jack. *United States Navy and Marine Corps bases, domestic*, CJ626
Bauer, N. *Wörterbuch der Münzkunde*, BG181
Bauer, Walter. *Greichisch-deutsches Wörterbuch zu den Schriften des Neuen Testament und der übrigen urchristlichen Literatur*, AC453
Bauer, Wolfgang. *Lexikon der Symbole*, CF11
Bauer-Arndt-Gingrich Greek lexicon, AC453
Bauer encyclopedia of biblical theology, BC130
Bauerhorst, Kurt. *Bibliographie der Stoff- und Motivgeschichte der deutschen Literatur*, BE1231
Baugh, Albert Croll. *A history of the English language*, BD98
—— *A literary history of England*, BE615
Baughman, Ernest Warren. *Type and motif-index of the folktales of England and North America*, CF48
Baughman, Judith. *Bibliography of American fiction, 1919–1988*, BE468
Baughn, William Hubert. *The bankers' handbook*, CH282
Baum, David W. *Color theory*, BF125, ED59
Bauman, Richard. *Folklore, cultural performances, and popular entertainments*, CF56
Baumann, Dorothea. *Analecta hymnica medii aevi*, BC313
Baumann, Lotte. *Enzyklopädie des Märchens*, CF50
Baumbach, Lydia. *Studies in Mycenaean inscriptions and dialect, 1965–1978*, BD139
Baume, Louis J. *A lexicon of English dental terms*, EH257
Baumeister, Theodore. *Marks' standard handbook for mechanical engineers*, EK240
Baumgarten, Rolf. *Bibliography of Irish linguistics and literature, 1942–71*, BD178
Baumgartner, Konrad. *Lexikon für Theologie und Kirche*, BC63
Baumgartner, Walter. *Dictionary of the Aramaic parts of the Old Testament in English and German*, AC482
—— *Hebräisches und aramäisches Lexikon zum Alten Testament*, AC481, AC482
Baumhögger, Goswin. *Simbabwe, Geschichte, Politik, Wirtschaft, Gesellschaft*, DD251
—— *Zimbabwe, history, politics, economics, society*, DD251
Baur, Frank. *Geschiedenis van de letterkunde der Nederlanden*, BE1326
Bausch, Judith Lola. *Sky and telescope cumulative index*, EC43
Bausinger, Hermann. *Enzyklopädie des Märchens*, CF50
Bautz, Friedrich Wilhelm. *Biographisch-bibliographisches Kirchenlexikon*, BC253
Bavier, Richard. *The study of Judaism*, BC521
Bawden, Liz-Anne. *The Oxford companion to film*, BH253
Baxter, Angus. *In search of your British & Irish roots*, AJ2, AJ96
—— *In search of your Canadian roots*, AJ2
—— *In search of your European roots*, AJ2
—— *In search of your German roots*, AJ2, AJ90
Baxter, Colin F. *Normandy campaign, 1944*, DA170

Baxter, Herbert. *Phytochemical dictionary*, EG161

Baxter, James Houston. *Medieval Latin word-list from British and Irish sources*, AC589

Baxter, Pam M. *Library use*, CD5
——— *Psychology*, CD1

Baxter, R. E. *Penguin dictionary of economics*, CH54

Bay, Jens Christian. *Bibliographies of botany*, EG88

Bayerische Akademie der Wissenschaften. *Mittellateinisches Wörterbuch bis zum ausgehenden 13. [i.e. dreizehnten] Jahrhundert*, AC591

Bayerische Akademie der Wissenschaften. Historische Kommission. *Neue deutsche Biographie*, AH210

Bayerische Staatsbibliothek. *Alphabetischer Katalog 1501–1840*, AA117
——— *Catalogue of music periodicals*, BJ100
——— *Katalog der Musikdrucke*, BJ91
——— *Katalog der Musikzeitschriften*, BJ100

Bayerischer Schulbuch-Verlag. *Grosser historischer Weltatlas*, DA53

Bayitch, S. A. *Latin America and the Caribbean*, DB257

Baylen, Joseph O. *Biographical dictionary of modern British radicals*, AH219, AH221

Bayley, Stephen. *The Conran directory of design*, BG130

Bayly, C. A. *Atlas of the British Empire*, DC346
——— *The new Cambridge history of India*, DE169

Baym, Nina. *The Norton anthology of American literature*, BE442

Bayne, Pauline S. *A basic music library*, BJ24

Bazin, Germain. *Concise history of world sculpture*, BF392
——— *The history of world sculpture*, BF392
——— *Kindlers Malerei Lexikon*, BF317

Bažnt, Zdeněk. *Anglicko-český technický slovník*, EA106
——— *Česko-anglický technický slovník*, EA106

BB, AA42

BBB, AA506, AK18

BBC English dictionary, AC35

BBC pronouncing dictionary of British names, AC102

BBC world service glossary of current affairs, CJ36

BBHS, BD66

BBP. Monografias, AA778

BBP. Publicações em série, AD138

BDZ, AD313

Beach, Edward Latimer. *Naval terms dictionary*, CJ618

Beach, Goodwin B. *Follett world-wide Latin dictionary*, AC576

Beach, Mark. *A bibliographic guide to American colleges and universities*, CB219

Beach, William W. *United States congressional districts*, CJ239

Beacham, Walton. *Beacham's guide to key lobbyists*, CJ131
——— *Beacham's marketing reference*, CH579
——— *Research guide to biography and criticism*, BE7

Beacham's guide to key lobbyists, CJ131

Beacham's marketing reference, CH579

Beaches, EF4

Beacon book of quotations by women, Maggio, Rosalie, BE111

Beadle, M. *Consolidated index to Flora Europaea*, EG170

Beal, Greg. *The American Film Institute guide to college courses in film and television*, BH263

Beal, Peter. *Index of English literary manuscripts*, BE603

Beale, Helen Purdy. *Bibliography of plant viruses and index to research*, EG89

Beale, Joseph Henry. *Bibliography of early English law books*, CK212

Beale, Paul. *Concise dictionary of slang and unconventional English*, AC132
——— *A dictionary of slang and unconventional English*, AC132

Beale, Walter H. *Old and Middle English poetry to 1500*, BE695

Beall, Karen F. *American prints in the Library of Congress*, BF365

Beals, Alan R. *Sources of information in the social sciences*, CA8

Bean, R. *International labour statistics*, CH684

Bear, John. *Bear's guide to earning college degrees non-traditionally*, CB252, CB253
——— *College degrees by mail*, CB252

Beard, Charles. *A dictionary of English costume [900–1900]*, BG99

Beard, Geoffrey. *Dictionary of English furniture makers, 1660–1840*, BG135

Beard, Joseph J. *Specialized legal research*, CK119

Beard, Joseph W. *Teacher attitudes*, CB159
——— *Teacher effectiveness*, CB160

Beard, Robert. *Bibliography of morphology, 1960–1985*, BD43

Bearings, EK239

Bearings, Neale, Michael John, EK239

Bearman, P. J. *The encyclopaedia of Islam*, BC503

Bear's guide to earning college degrees non-traditionally, Bear, John, CB252, CB253

Beasley, David R. *How to use a research library*, AK4

Beasley, Jerry C. *A check list of prose fiction published in England, 1740–1749*, BE669, BE681
——— *English fiction, 1660–1800*, BE670

Beasley, W. G. *Historical writing on the peoples of Asia*, DE18

•*BEASTCD*, EJ18, EJ102

Beattie, Judith. *Directory of Canadian archives*, AK127

Beatty, Betty. *Short dictionary of architecture*, BF244

Beaty, H. Wayne. *Standard handbook for electrical engineers*, EK143

Beaubien, Anne K. *Learning the library*, AK229

Beaudiquez, Marcelle. *Bibliographic services throughout the world*, AA16
——— *Inventaire général des bibliographies nationales rétrospectives*, AA395

Beaujean, A. *Dictionnaire de la langue française*, AC332

Beaulieu, André. *Les journaux de Québec de 1764 à 1964*, AD59
——— *Quebec*, DB213
——— *Répertoire des publications gouvernementales du Québec de 1867 à 1964*, AF155

Beaumarchais, Jean-Pierre de. *Chronologie de la littérature française*, BE1152
——— *Dictionnaire des littératures de langue française*, BE1149

Beaumont, Cyril William. *Bibliography of dancing*, BH133
——— *A bibliography of the dance collection of Doris Niles and Serge Leslie*, BH133
——— *Complete book of ballets*, BH151

Beaumont, Jane. *Bibliography of works on Canadian foreign relations, 1976–1980*, DB186
——— *Bibliography of works on Canadian foreign relations, 1981–1985*, DB186

Beaumont, Roger A. *Special operations and elite units 1939–1988*, CJ608

Beautiful thoughts from Greek authors, Ramage, Craufurd Tait, BE138

Beautiful thoughts from Latin authors, Ramage, Craufurd Tait, BE145

Beautrix, Pierre. *Bibliographie du bouddhisme*, BC461
——— *Bibliographie du bouddhisme Zen*, BC462

Beaver, Frank E. *Dictionary of film terms*, BH256

Beaver, Paul. *Encyclopaedia of the modern Royal Navy*, CJ652

Beazley, John Davidson. *Attic black-figure vase-painters*, BF324
——— *Attic red-figure vase-painters*, BF324

Beazley addenda, Burn, Lucilla, BF324
——— Carpenter, Thomas H., BF324
——— Mannack, Thomas, BF324
——— Mendonça, Melanie, BF324

Beazley Archive. *Attic red-figure vase-painters*, BF324

Bębenek, Stanisław. *Bibliografia literatury tłumaczonej na język polski*, BE1347

Beccaro, Felice del. *Guida allo studio della letteratura italiana*, BE1288

Becco, Horacio Jorge. *Bibliografía de bibliografías literarias argentinas*, BE919
——— *Bibliografía de bibliografías venezolanas*, BE961
——— *Diccionario de literatura hispanoamericana*, BE888
——— *Fuentes para el estudio de la literatura venezolana*, BE961

Becela, Lidia. *Kto jest kim w Polsce*, AH281

Bech, Sv. Cedergreen. *Dansk biografisk leksikon*, AH183

Bechtle, Thomas C. *Dissertations in philosophy accepted at American universities, 1861–1975*, BB15

Beck, Diemut. *Verzeichnis der Zeitschriften in der Bibliothek der Römisch-Germanischen Kommission*, BE1008

Beck, Leland E. *The Constitution of the United States of America*, CK173

Beck, Richard. *History of Icelandic poets, 1800–1940*, BE1285

Beck, Warren A. *Historical atlas of the American West*, DB176

Beck, Wolfgang. *Autorenlexikon deutschsprachiger Literatur des 20. Jahrhunderts*, BE1054

Becker, Charlotte B. *The encyclopedia of ethics*, BB32

Becker, E. Lovell. *International dictionary of medicine and biology*, EG38, EH100

Becker, Felix. *Allgemeines Lexikon der bildenden Künstler*, BF135, BF147, BF148, BF149

Becker, Gerhard. *Historische Forschungen in der DDR 1960–1970*, DC217
——— *Historische Forschungen in der DDR 1970–1980*, DC217

Becker, H. *UdSSR : Enzyklopädie der Union der Sozialistischen Sowjetrepubliken*, AB83

Becker, Lawrence G. *The encyclopedia of ethics*, BB32

Becker, Robert H. *The plains & the Rockies*, DB168

Becket, Henry S. A. *The dictionary of espionage*, CJ534

Beckman, Erik. *Criminal justice dictionary*, CK257

Beckson, Karl E. *Literary terms*, BE76
——— *Reader's guide to literary terms*, BE76

Bédé, Jean-Albert. *Columbia dictionary of modern European literature*, BE60

Bedevian, Armenag K. *Illustrated polyglottic dictionary of plant names in Latin, Arabic, Armenian, English, French, German, Italian and Turkish languages*, EG141

Bedier, Joseph. *Littérature française*, BE1167

Bedrossian, Matthias. *New dictionary*, AC226

Bedürftig, Friedemann. *The encyclopedia of the Third Reich*, DC255
——— *Grosse Lexikon des Dritten Reiches*, DC255

Beebe, Linda. *Professional writing for the human services*, CC54

Beeching, Cyril Leslie. *Dictionary of dates*, AL143, DA34
——— *A dictionary of eponyms*, AC49

Beede, Benjamin R. *Military and strategic policy*, CJ98

Beek, Martinus Adrianus. *Atlas of Mesopotamia*, DA86, DE67

Beekman, Anton Albert. *Lijst der aardrijkskundige namen van Nederland*, CL147

Beene, Wayne. *A dictionary of Iraqi Arabic*, AC214

Beer, Colin. *A dictionary of ethology*, CD121

Beere, Carole A. *Gender roles*, CC556, CC557
——— *Sex and gender issues*, CC557
——— *Women and women's issues*, CC556, CC557

Beers, Henry Putney. *Bibliographies in American history*, DB9
——— *Confederacy*, DB114
——— *The French and British in the Old Northwest*, DB26

—— *French and Spanish records of Louisiana*, DB26

—— *French in North America*, DB26

—— *Guide to federal archives relating to the Civil War*, DB116

—— *Guide to the archives of the government of the Confederate States of America*, DB114

—— *Spanish & Mexican records of the American Southwest*, DB26, DB171

Beeson, Paul B. *The Oxford companion to medicine*, EH88

Beeston, A. F. L. *Arabic literature to the end of the Umayyad period*, BE1546

Beeton, Douglas Ridley. *A dictionary of English usage in Southern Africa*, AC181

—— *A pilot bibliography of South African English literature (from the beginnings to 1971)*, BE1538

Befolkning, CG213

Befolkningens bevægelser, CG209

Befolkningsförändringar, CG285

Befolkningsstatistik, CG183, CG285

Befolkningsstatistikk, CG268

Begescu, George. *Essai d'une notice biobibliographique sur la question d'Orient*, DC59

The beginnings of the petroleum industry, Giddens, Paul H., EK300

Begley, Donal F. *Irish genealogy*, AJ134

Beharrell, H. *Printed maps in the atlases of Great Britain and Ireland*, CL228

Behavior science notes, CE97

Behavioral sciences *see* **Social and behavioral sciences**

Behavioural biology abstracts. Section A: Animal behaviour, CD118

Behm, Carl. *Eighteenth century British novel and its background*, BE670

Behnke, Jacqlynn. *The Aldrich library of ¹³C and ¹H FT NMR spectra*, EE113

Behrens, Heinrich. *Datensammlungen in der Physik*, ED4

Behrens, Hermann. *The Sumerian dictionary of the University Museum of the University of Pennsylvania*, AC204

Behrmann, Lilly-Ralou. *Bibliographie zur Aussenpolitik der Republik Österreich seit 1945*, DC87

Beidler, Peter G. *The American Indian in short fiction*, BE548

Beierle, John. *Lappa ethnographic bibliography*, CE94

Beigel, Hugo G. *The Adeline art dictionary*, BF81

Beijing Foreign Languages Institute. *The pinyin Chinese-English dictionary*, AC267

Beilstein, Friedrich. *Handbuch der organischen Chemie*, EA41, ED43, EE18, EE115, EE132

Beilstein, EE115

•*Beilstein current facts in chemistry*, EE115

Beilstein guide, Weissbach, Oskar, EE115

Beilstein handbook of organic chemistry, EE115

•*Beilstein online*, EE115

Beilstein's index, Giese, Friedo, EE132

Beinart, Haim. *Atlas of medieval Jewish history*, DA159

Beinecke Rare Book and Manuscript Library. *Catalog of the Yale collection of Western Americana*, DB170

Beirne, Piers. *Comparative criminology*, CK243

Beit-Hallahmi, Benjamin. *Psychoanalysis and religion*, BC5

Bekker-Nielsen, Hans. *Old Norse-Icelandic studies*, BD129, BE1083, DA138

Beknopt handboek tot de geschiedenis der Nederlandse letterkunde, Knuvelder, Gerard Petrus Maria, BE1330

Bektaev, K. B. *Statistika rechi, 1957–1985*, BD64

Béla, Dezsényi. *A magyar sajtó bibliográfiája, 1945–1954*, AD120

Belarus
  manuscripts and archives, AK153, DC561
Belarus (by subject)
  archaeology
    bibliography, DC98

Belarusian language
  bibliography, BD185

Belaynesh, Michael. *The dictionary of Ethiopian biography*, AH318

Belcher, Jane C. *From idea to funded project*, AL92

Belder, J. de. *Bibliographie de l'histoire de Belgique*, DC99

Belgian literature
  biobibliography, BE1098, BE1099, BE1100, BE1101, BE1102, BE1328
Belgian literature (by subject)
  history, BE1097, BE1334
  see also **Walloon literature**

Belgian National Committee for Astronomy. *Bibliography of astronomy, 1881–1898, on microfilm*, EC14

Belgica typographica, 1541–1600, Cockx-Indestege, Elly, AA578

Belgische bibliografie, AA582

Belgische koloniale biografie, AH173

Belgium
  archives, DC106, DC107
  bibliography, AA576, AA577, AA578, AA579, AA580, AA581, AH174, DC103, DC105, DC456
    current, AA582
    early, AA745
  biography, AH172, AH173, AH175, AH176, AH270
    bibliography, AH178
    contemporary, AH177
  encyclopedias, DC108, DC109
  gazetteers, CL130
  government publications
    bibliography, AF229
  guides to records, DC106, DC107
  newspapers, AE45
    directories, AD82
  periodicals
    bibliographies, AD84
    directories, AD82, AD83, AD84, AD85, AD131
    indexes, AD302, AD303, BE1066
  place-names, CL210
  statistics, CG199, CG200
Belgium (by subject)
  archaeology and ancient history, DC175
  history, DC99, DC104, DC459
    archives, AK133, DC13
    bibliography, DC100, DC101

Belgium, Riley, Raymond Charles, DC101

Belikov, Evgenii Fedorovich. *Bibliograficheskii ukazatel' geodezicheskoi literatury za 40 let 1917–1956*, EF23

Belize, DB303
  statistics, CG125

Belize. Central Statistical Office. *Abstract of statistics*, CG125

Belize, Woodward, Ralph Lee, DB303

Belknap, Sara Yancey. *Guide to dance periodicals*, BH136

—— *Guide to the musical arts*, BH8

—— *Guide to the performing arts*, BH8

Bell, Alice. *National prison directory*, CK266

Bell, Barbara L. *An annotated guide to current national bibliographies*, AA388

Bell, C. Ritchie. *A synonymized checklist of the vascular flora of the United States, Canada, and Greenland*, EG132

Bell, Charles Alfred. *English-Tibetan colloquial dictionary*, AC781

—— *Manual of colloquial Tibetan*, AC781

Bell, David Scott. *Biographical dictionary of French political leaders since 1870*, CJ328

—— *Communist and Marxist parties of the world*, CJ526

Bell, Doris L. *Contemporary art trends, 1960–1980*, BF93

Bell, George K. A. *Documents on Christian unity*, BC283

Bell, Herbert W. *How to get your book published*, AA296

Bell, Inglis Freeman. *English novel, 1578–1956*, BE206, BE671, BE675

—— *On Canadian literature, 1806–1960*, BE826

Bell, James. *New and comprehensive gazetteer of England and Wales*, AJ113

Bell, James B. *Searching for your ancestors*, AJ7

Bell, Marion V. *Poole's index : date and volume key*, AD281

Bell, Maureen. *A biographical dictionary of English women writers, 1580–1720*, BE620

Bell, Robert E. *Dictionary of classical mythology*, CF26

—— *Place-names in classical mythology*, CF21

—— *Women of classical mythology*, CF22

Bell, S. Peter. *Dissertations on British history, 1815–1914*, DC334

Bell, Simon. *Women in rural development in Kenya, Tanzania and Zimbabwe*, DD165, DD235, DD253

Bell & Howell newspaper indexes, AE104

Bell & Howell transdex, AF109

[Bell & Howell/UMI newspaper indexes], AE104, AE109

Bell & Howell's index to the Christian Science monitor, AE106

Bell & Howell's newspaper index to the Christian Science monitor, AE106

Bellack, Alan S. *The clinical psychology handbook*, CD103

Bellamy, Joyce M. *Dictionary of labour biography*, AH220

Bellamy, Margot A. *Agricultural economics and rural sociology*, EJ6

Bellanger, Claude. *Histoire générale de la presse française*, AE52

Bellardo, Lewis J. *A glossary for archivists, manuscript curators, and records managers*, AK184, AK188

Bellardo, Lynn Lady. *A glossary for archivists, manuscript curators, and records managers*, AK184, AK188

Belle, Gilbert van. *Johannine bibliography 1966–1985*, BC105

Bellen, Heinz. *Bibliographie zur antiken Sklaverei*, DA68

Belles lettres, Mullaney, Janet Palmer, CC534

Belli, Melvin M. *Everybody's guide to the law*, CK159

Bellini, Bernardo. *Dizionario della lingua italiana*, AC524

Bellmann, Renate. *Handbuch der Bibliothekswissenschaft*, AK38

Belloni, Lanfranco. *The history of modern physics*, ED52

Beloch, Israel. *Dicionário histórico-biográfico brasileiro, 1930–1983*, AH124, DB354

Belorussia *see* **Belarus**

Belousova, L. S. *Rare plants of the world*, EG156

Beltrán B., Arlette. *Compendio estadístico del Perú, 1900–1990*, CG157, DB389

Beltrán Bernal, Trinidad. *Bibliografía histórica del Estado de México*, DB217

Belzer, Jack. *Encyclopedia of computer science and technology*, EK172

Bemis, Samuel Flagg. *Guide to the diplomatic history of the United States, 1775–1921*, DB15

Ben-Yehuda, Eliezer. *Milon ha-lashon ha-ivrit*, AC470

Bénac, Henri. *Dictionnaire des synonymes, conforme au dictionnaire de l'Académie française*, AC361

Bender, Arnold E. *Dictionary of nutrition and food technology*, EH301

Bendiner, Elmer. *Biographical dictionary of medicine*, EH221

Bendiner, Jessica. *Biographical dictionary of medicine*, EH221

Benecke, Georg Friedrich. *Mittelhochdeutsches Wörterbuch*, AC406

Benedek, Marcell. *Magyar irodalmi lexikon*, BE1275

Benedetto, Robert. *Guide to the manuscript collections of the Presbyterian Church, U.S.*, BC376

Benedict, Friedrich. *Orbis Latinus*, CL103

Benedict, Stephen. *Arts management*, BF39

Benedictus, David. *Antique collector's guide*, BG50

Benelux nations (by subject)
  law, CK202
  literature
    guidebooks, BE982
Beneš, Karel. *Anglicko-český geologický slovník,* EF82
Benét, William Rose. *Reader's encyclopedia,* BE58
Benét's reader's encyclopedia, BE58, BE431
Benét's reader's encyclopedia of American literature, BE431
Benewick, Robert. *The Routledge dictionary of twentieth-century political thinkers,* CJ69
Bénézit, Emmanuel. *Dictionnaire critique et documentaire des peintres, sculpteurs, dessinateurs et graveurs de tous les temps et de tous les pays,* BF137
Bengali language
  dictionaries
    bilingual
      English-Bengali, AC232
  etymology
    dictionaries, AC233
Bengtson, Hermann. *Grosser historischer Weltatlas. Erläuterungen,* DA53
  —— *Introduction to ancient history,* DA59
Benham, William Gurney. *Benham's book of quotations, proverbs, and household words,* BE100
Benham's book of quotations, proverbs, and household words, Benham, William Gurney, BE100
Benin
  bibliography, AA850, DD129
  encyclopedias, DD48
  government publications
    bibliography, AF230
  statistics, CG316
Benin, Decalo, S., DD48
Benin literature
  works in French, BE1524
Benina, M. A. *Russkaia khudozhestvennaia literatura i literaturovedenie,* BE1396
Benítez, Luis G. *Breve historia de grandes hombres,* AH138
Benjacob, Isaac. *Ozar ha-sepharim,* BC509
Benjamin, Bernard. *Population statistics,* CG236
Benjamin, Ludy T. *A history of American psychology in notes and news, 1883–1945,* CD15
Benmaman, Virginia. *Bilingual dictionary of criminal justice terms (English/Spanish),* CK256
Benner, David G. *Baker encyclopedia of psychology,* CD19
Bennett, George. *Seychelles,* DD18
Bennett, Gillian. *Contemporary legend,* CF37
Bennett, H. *Concise chemical and technical dictionary,* EE34
Bennett, J. D. *Bibliography of British industrial relations, 1971–1979,* CH625
Bennett, James R. *Bibliography of stylistics and related criticism, 1967–83,* BE374
Bennett, Kenneth A. *Centers for training in physical anthropology,* CE88
Bennett, Norman Robert. *The Arab state of Zanzibar,* DD250
Bennett, Pramila Ramgulam. *Mauritius,* DD18
Bennett, Scott. *Victorian periodicals,* AD113
Bennett, Tess. *Developing individualized family support plans,* CC235
Bennie, W. G. *A new concise Xhosa-English dictionary,* AC810
Bennington, James L. *Saunders dictionary & encyclopedia of laboratory medicine and technology,* EH109
Benn's media, AD1, AE2, AE4
Benn's media directory, AD1, AE2
Benn's press directory, AD1, AE2
Benoit, France. *Greenland since 1979,* DC376
Bensen, Clark H. *Committees in the U.S. Congress, 1947–1992,* CJ217
Benson, Adolph Burnett. *The history of the Scandinavian literatures,* BE1084
Benson, Eugene. *Oxford companion to Canadian theatre,* BE833, BH73

Benson, Hazel B. *The dying child,* CC178
Benson, K. Blair. *Television engineering handbook,* EK148
Benson, Michael. *Ballparks of North America,* BK51
Benson, Morton. *Dictionary of Russian personal names,* AJ203
  —— *Englesko-srpskohrvatski rečnik,* AC710
  —— *An English-SerboCroatian dictionary,* AC710
  —— *SerboCroatian-English dictionary,* AC710
  —— *Srpskohrvatski-engleski rečnik,* AC710
Benson, Peter L. *Private schools in the United States,* CB136
Benson Latin American Collection. *Catalog of the Nettie Lee Benson Latin American Collection,* DB265, DB270
  —— *Handbook of Latin American studies,* BE874, DB266
Benson Latin American Collection serials list, DB270
Bentivogli, Bruno. *IUPI,* BE1316
Bentley, Elizabeth Petty. *County courthouse book,* AJ51
  —— *Directory of family associations,* AJ52
  —— *The genealogist's address book,* AJ53
Bentley, G. Carter. *Ethnicity and nationality,* CC310
Bentley, Gerald Eades. *The Jacobean and Caroline stage,* BE663
Bentley, Harry Clark. *Bibliography of works on accounting by American authors,* CH247
Benton, Josiah Henry. *The Book of Common Prayer and books connected with its origin and growth,* BC338
Benton, Mildred Catherine. *The literature of space science and exploration,* EK22
Benton, Rita. *Directory of music research libraries,* BJ169
Benvenisti, Meron. *West Bank data project,* CJ436
  —— *The West Bank handbook,* CJ436
Benyuch, O. *Anglu-latviešu vārdnica,* AC596
Benz, Wolfgang. *Biographisches Lexikon zur Weimarer Republik,* DC261
Beraldi, Henri. *Graveurs du XIXᵉ siècle,* BF377
Bérard, Michèle. *Encyclopedia of modern art auction prices,* BF108
Berbers
  bibliography, DD68
Berck, Peter. *Economists' mathematical manual,* CH84
Berckelaers, Ferdinand Louis. *Dictionary of abstract painting,* BF300
Bercovitch, Sacvan. *Cambridge history of American literature,* BE439
Bercuson, David Jay. *The Collins dictionary of Canadian history,* DB197
Bérdy, János. *CRC handbook of antibiotic compounds,* EH324
Berei, Andor. *Uj magyar lexikon,* AB61
Berens, John F. *Criminal justice documents,* CK244
Berent, Irwin M. *Jewish genealogy,* AJ146
Berer, Marge. *Women and HIV/AIDS,* CC570
Berg, Dieter. *Deutschlands Geschichtsquellen im Mittelalter vom Tode Kaiser Heinrichs V. bis zum Ende des Interregnum,* DC228
Berg, Hans van den. *Material bibliográfico para el estudio de las aymaras, callawayas, chipayas, urus,* CE74
Berg, Steven L. *Jewish alcoholism and drug addiction,* CC110
Bergan, Ronald. *The Holt foreign film guide,* BH194
Bergdoll, Barry. *Encyclopaedia of 20th-century architecture,* BF233
Berger, Adolf. *Encyclopedic dictionary of Roman law,* CK52
Berger, Arthur S. *The encyclopedia of parapsychology and psychical research,* CD133
Berger, Bruno. *Deutsches Literatur-Lexikon,* BE1246
Berger, Dieter. *Deutsche Namenkunde,* AJ192, CL189
Berger, Elsbeth. *Lateinisches etymologisches Wörterbuch,* AC584

Berger, Joyce. *The encyclopedia of parapsychology and psychical research,* CD133
Berger, Marilyn. *Urban planning,* BF268
Berger, Rebehak. *Directory of internships, work experience programs, and on-the-job training opportunities,* CB364, CH695
Berger, Sidney E. *Medieval English drama,* BE635
Berger, Thomas L. *An index of characters in English printed drama to the Restoration,* BE658
  —— *Which Shakespeare?,* BE765
Bergeron, Barbara. *Variety obituaries,* BH25
Bergeron, Chantal. *Répertoire bibliographique de textes de présentation générale et d'analyse d'oeuvres musicales canadiennes (1900–1980),* BJ41
Bergeron, Claude. *Index des périodiques d'architecture canadiens, 1940–1980,* BF210
Bergerson, Peter J. *Ethics and public policy,* CJ6
Bergey, D. H. *Manual of determinative bacteriology,* EG309
Bergey's manual of systematic bacteriology, EG309
Berghe, Louis van den. *Bibliographie analytique de l'archéologie de l'Iran ancien,* DE180
Bergheim, Laura. *The map catalog,* CL266
Bergin, Thomas Goddard. *Encyclopedia of the Renaissance,* DA146
  —— *A history of Italian literature,* BE1308
Bergman, Hannah E. *A catalogue of comedias sueltas in The New York Public Library,* BE1459
Bergmann, Eckhart. *Lexikon der Kunst,* BF75
Bergquist, G. William. *Three centuries of English and American plays, a checklist,* BE453, BE636
Bergsten, Bebe. *Early motion pictures,* BH190
Bergstrom, Len V. *Women and society,* CC510
Bériel, Marie-Magdeleine. *Complé à la Bibliographie du Tchad,* DD140
Berins, Michael L. *SPI plastics engineering handbook of the Society of the Plastics Industry, Inc,* EK290
Beristain de Souza, José Mariano. *Biblioteca hispano americana septentrional,* AA459, AH99
Berita bibliografi, AA901, AA902, AA903, AA904
Berita bulanan, AA902, AA904
Berita Idayu bibliografi, AA903
Berkhout, Carl T. *Medieval heresies,* BC210
Berkova, P. N. *Obshchie bibliografi russkikh knig grazhdanskoĭ pechati, 1708–1955,* AA63
Berkow, Robert. *The Merck manual of geriatrics,* EH191
Berkowitz, David Sandler. *Bibliotheca bibliographica incunabula,* AA217
Berkowitz, Freda Pastor. *Popular titles and subtitles of musical compositions,* BJ173
Berkowitz, Luci. *Thesaurus Linguae Graecae canon of Greek authors and works,* AC443, BE1036
Berlage, Jean. *Répertoire de la presse du Congo Belge (1884–1958) et du Ruanda-Urundi (1920–1958) … ,* AD171
Berleant-Schiller, Riva. *Montserrat,* DB447
Berlin, Charles. *Index to festschriften in Jewish studies,* BC510
Berlin, Howard M. *The handbook of financial market indexes, averages, and indicators,* CH232
Berlin, Irving Norman. *Bibliography of child psychiatry and child mental health, with a selected list of films,* EH370
Berlin. Japan-Institut. *Bibliographischer Alt-Japan-Katalog, 1542–1853,* DE195
Berliner Titeldruke, Preussische Staatsbibliothek, AA121
Berman, Esmé. *Art & artists of South Africa,* BF142
Berman, Larry. *Evolution of the modern presidency,* CJ171
Bermerkungen und Korrekturen zum Lexikon der Ägyptologie, Westendorf, Wolfhart, DA125
Bermuda, DB422
  bibliography, AA558
Bermuda national bibliography, AA558
Bernal, Ignacio. *Bibliografía de arqueología y etnografía,* CE75
Bernal Villa, Segundo. *Guía bibliográfica de Colombia de interés para el antropólogo,* DB363

Bernard, Annick. *Guide de l'utilisateur des catalogues des livres imprimés de la Bibliothèque Nationale*, AA100

Bernard, Gildas. *Les familles protestantes en France*, AJ84

—— *Guide des recherches sur l'histoire des familles*, AJ85

Bernard, H. Russell. *Research methods in cultural anthropology*, CE56

Bernard, Madeleine. *Répertoire de manuscrits mediévaux contenant des notations musicales*, BJ55

Bernardini, Nicola. *Guida della stampa periodica italiana*, AE64

Bernardo, Gabriel Adriano. *Bibliography of Philippine bibliographies, 1593–1961*, AA82

—— *A critical and annotated bibliography of Philippine, Indonesian and other Malayan folk-lore*, CF94

—— *Philippine retrospective national bibliography, 1523–1699*, AA926

Bernath, Mathias. *Historische Bücherkunde Südosteuropa*, DC58

Berndt, Judy. *Rural sociology*, CC4

Bernet, Charles. *Dictionnaire du français parlé*, AC353

Bernet de Rodrigues, Josefina. *Harrap's diccionario de expresiones idiomáticas*, AC745

Berney, K.A. *Contemporary dramatists*, BE223

Berney, Mary F. *Teacher education program evaluation*, CB158

Bernhard, Judith. *International handbook of early childhood education*, CB119

Bernhardt, Rudolf. *Encyclopedia of public international law*, CK100

Bernice Pauahi Bishop Museum. Library. *Dictionary catalog of the Library*, CE115, DF10

Bernier, Bernard A. *Popular names of U.S. government reports*, AF101

Bernier, Roger H. *EPISOURCE*, EH404

Bernot, Denise. *Bibliographie birmane, années 1950 1960*, DE119

Bernsdorf, Wilhelm. *Internationales Soziologenlexikon*, CA63

Bernshtein, S. B. *Slavianskoe iazykoznanie*, BD183

Bernstein, Elizabeth. *Peace resource book*, CJ694

Bernstein, Georg Heinrich. *Thesaurus syriacus*, AC773

Bernstein, Kenneth. *Music lover's Europe*, BH193

Bernstein, Theodore Menline. *Bernstein's reverse dictionary*, AC136

Bernstein's reverse dictionary, Bernstein, Theodore Menline, AC136

Bernus, Edmond. *Atlas du Niger*, CL339

Berque, Jacques. *Bibliographie de la culture arabe contemporaine*, DE28

Berrey, Lester V. *American thesaurus of slang*, AC119

Berrian, Brenda F. *Bibliography of African women writers and journalists*, BE1502

—— *Bibliography of women writers from the Caribbean 1831–1986*, BE971

Berring, Robert C. *Finding the law*, CK115

—— *How to find the law*, CK115

Berry, Dorothea M. *A bibliographic guide to educational research*, CB2

Berry, L. *Tanzania in maps*, CL342

Berry, Margaret. *Chinese classic novels*, BE1562

Berry, Richard W. *The petroleum dictionary*, EK306

Bershas, Henry N. *The Wayne State University collection of comedias sueltas*, BE1472

Bertaud, Jean Paul. *Dictionnaire historique de la Révolution française*, DC184

Bertaud du Chazaud, Henri. *Dictionnaire des synonymes*, AC362

Bertelson, Lionel. *La presse d'information*, AE45

Berthand, Pierre Louis. *Bibliographie occitane*, BE1370

Berthelot, André. *La grande encyclopédie*, AB44

Berthold, Lothar. *Wer war wer, DDR*, AH216

Berthold, Werner. *Exil-Literatur 1933–1945*, BE1232

Bertin, Jacques. *The Harper atlas of world history*, DA54

Berton, Peter Alexander Menquez. *Contemporary China*, AA362, DE123

Bertrand, Verna. *Index to statistics and probability*, EB30

Beruf und Arbeit in deutscher Erzählung, Schmitt, Franz Anselm, BE1269

Berwick, Sam. *Who's who in Fiji*, AH376

Besancon, Robert Martin. *The encyclopedia of physics*, ED12

Besch, Werner. *Dialektologie*, BD126, BD127

—— *Sprachgeschichte*, BD125

Besemer, Susan P. *From museums, galleries, and studios*, BF48

Besford, Pat. *Encyclopedia of swimming*, BK100

Bessel functions, Kirk, A., EB94

—— Olver, F. W. J., EB94

—— Young, A., EB94

Bessette, Peg. *Sports fan's connection*, BK37

Bessinger, Jess Balsor. *A short dictionary of Anglo-Saxon poetry in a normalized early West-Saxon orthography*, AC169

Besson, Alain. *Thornton's medical books, libraries, and collectors*, EH28

Bessy, Maurice. *Dictionnaire du cinéma et de la télévision*, BH247

Best, James J. *American popular illustration*, BF372

Best, Richard I. *Bibliography of Irish philology and manuscript literature*, BD178

The best American poetry, BE505

Best American short stories, BE483, BE486

Best books for children, AA337

—— Wolff, Kathryn, EA34

Best business schools, CB255, CH76

Best dictionaries for adults and young people, AC2

Best encyclopedias, Kister, Kenneth F., AB1

The best lawyers in America, CK141

Best plays, BE454

The best plays of [...], BE454, BE463

Best reference books, 1986–1990, AA348

Best resumes for scientists and engineers, Lewis, Adele Beatrice, EA151

Best science and technology reference books for young people, Malinowsky, H. Robert, EA29

Best science books & A-V materials for children, Montenegro, Valerie J., EA34

—— O'Connell, Susan M., EA34

—— Wolff, Kathryn, EA34

Best science films, filmstrips, and videocassettes for children, Wolff, Kathryn, EA34

Best-sellers, AA327

Best short stories and the Yearbook of the American short story, BE486

Bestandsaufnahme der Literatur und Forschungen in der Bundesrepublik Deutschland sowie der EG-Veröffentlichungen zum Thema der politischen und wirtschaftlichen Beziehungen zwischen der Türkei und Westeuropa seit 1973, Esen, Erol, DC539

Bestandskatalog der Bibliothek des Südost-Instituts München, Südost-Institut München. Bibliothek, DC65

Besterman, Theodore. *Medicine*, EH9

—— *A world bibliography of African bibliographies*, AA70

—— *A world bibliography of bibliographies*, AA14, AA70, AA73, EH9

—— *A world bibliography of Oriental bibliographies*, AA73

Bestor, George Clinton. *City planning bibliography*, BF270

Best's flitcraft compend, CH517

Best's insurance reports, CH518

Best's key rating guide, CH511

Beta mathematics handbook, Råde, Lennart, EB92

Bethell, Leslie. *The Cambridge history of Latin America*, DB291

BETI, CB50, CB57

Bettelheim, Anton. *Biographisches Jahrbuch und deutscher Nekrolog, 1896–1913*, AH204

Betteridge, Harold T. *Cassell's German-English, English-German dictionary*, AC414

—— *New Cassell's German dictionary*, AC414

Betts, Douglas A. *Chess*, BK134

Betz, Louis Paul. *La littérature comparée*, BE13

Beugnot, Bernard. *Manuel bibliographique des études littéraires*, BE1128

Bevan, A. W. R. *Catalogue of meteorites*, EF207

Bevan, Amanda. *Tracing your ancestors in the Public Record Office*, AJ97

Bevan, John. *Index and finding list to Joseph Gillow's Bibliographical dictionary of the English Catholics*, AH228

Bevans, Charles I. *Treaties and other international agreements of the United States of America, 1776–1949*, CK94

—— *United States treaties and other international agreements*, CK95

Bever, Michael B. *Concise encyclopedia of medical & dental materials*, EH176

—— *Encyclopedia of materials science and engineering*, EK261, EK262

Beverages, EJ227

dictionaries, EJ212

Beveraggi-Allende, Walter. *Appleton's new Cuyás English-Spanish and Spanish-English dictionary*, AC732

Bevezetés a magyar történelem forrásaiba és irodalmába, Kosáry, Domokos G., DC382

Bevis, Richard W. *Bibliotheca cisorientalia*, DE27

Bevölkerung und Erwerbstätigkeit, CG220

Bevölkerungsbewegung in der Schweiz, Switzerland. Eidgenössisches Statistisches Amt, CG289

Beyer, Edvard. *Norges litteratur historie*, BE1337

Beyer, Erich. *Wörterbuch der Sportwissenschaft*, BK29

Beyer, Harald. *A history of Norwegian literature*, BE1338

—— *Norsk littertur historie*, BE1338

Beyer, Klaus G. *Glass*, BG75

Beyer, William H. *CRC handbook of tables for probability and statistics*, EB81

Beyerly, Elizabeth. *Public international law*, CK76

Beyond safaris, Danaher, Kevin, DD52

Beyond the dictionary in German, AC437

Beyreuther, Erich. *The new international dictionary of New Testament theology*, BC148

Bezold, Adele. *Babylonisch-assyrisches Glossar*, AC201

Bezold, Carl. *Babylonisch-assyrisches Glossar*, AC201

Bezzel, Irmgard. *Verzeichnis der im deutschen Sprachbereich erschienenen Drucke des XVI. Jahrhunderts*, AA640

The BFI companion to the Western, BH245

BFI film and television handbook, BH264

BHA, BF33, BF34, BF43

Bhagavad-Gītā, Kapoor, Jagdish Chander, BC483

The Bhagavadgîtâ, BC92

Bhan, Susheela. *Terrorism*, CJ550

Bhargava's standard illustrated dictionary of the English language (Anglo-Hindi ed.), Pathak, Ram Chandra, AC486

Bhargava's standard illustrated dictionary of the Hindi language, AC486

Bhatia, Mohan. *Canadian provincial government publications*, AF155

Bhatnagar, K. P. *Elsevier's dictionary of geosciences*, EF86

Bhattacharya, Ram Shankar. *Encyclopedia of Indian philosophies*, BB33

—— *Sāmkhya*, BB33

Bhattacharya, S. K. *Elsevier's dictionary of geosciences*, EF86

Bhattacharyya, Benoytosh. *The Indian Buddhist iconography*, BF178

Bhatty, Khan Mohammad. *Annotated bibliography of social research in Pakistan*, DE240

BHI, AD264

Bhutan

statistics, CG379

Bhutan (by subject)

history

encyclopedias, DE90

library resources, DE86

Bhutan. Central Statistical Office. *Statistical yearbook of Bhutan*, CG379
Bhutan, Dogra, R. C., DE118
Biagi, Adele. *The Follett Zanichelli Italian dictionary*, AC533
Bianco, David. *Heat wave*, BJ352
——— *Who's new wave in music*, BJ352
Bianu, Ioan. *Bibliografia românească veche, 1508–1830*, AA780
——— *Publicațiunile periodice românești (ziare, gazete, reviste)*, AD140
Biard, J. D. *The concise Oxford French dictionary*, AC337
The bias-free word finder, AC77
Bibeltheologisches Wörterbuch, BC130
Bible, BC93
  abstract journals, BC120, BC123, BC124
  Apocrypha, BC94, BC107, BC158
  atlases, BC197, BC198, BC199, BC200, BC201, BC202
  bibliography, AA102, BC96, BC97, BC98, BC99, BC100, BC103, BC104, BC105, BC108, BC109, BC110, BC111, BC112, BC113, BC114, BC115, BC116, BC117, BC118, BC120, BC121, BC220
    current, BC123, BC124
    reference works, BC217
  commentaries, BC163, BC168, BC169, BC170, BC171, BC172, BC173, BC174, BC175, BC176, BC177, BC178, BC179, BC180, BC182
  computer applications, BC188
  concordances, BC157, BC158, BC159, BC160, BC161, BC162, BC164, BC165, BC166, BC167
  dictionaries, AC456, AC475, BC71, BC128, BC133, BC134, BC135, BC136, BC137, BC138, BC139, BC141, BC142, BC143, BC144, BC145, BC146, BC147, BC148, BC149, BC150, BC152, BC160, BC193, BC195
    Hebrew, BC151
    pronunciation, BC140
  encyclopedias, BC125, BC126, BC127, BC130, BC131, BC132, BC189
  guides, BC187
  handbooks, BC185, BC186, BC187, BC189, BC190
  Hebrew Bible
    commentaries, BC181, BC183, BC184
    encyclopedias, BC129
  history, BC191
  indexes, BC119, BC121, BC122
  language
    Greek, BD140
  library catalogs, AA102, BC96
  Old Testament
    language, AC482
  quotations, BC154, BC155, BC156
  translations, BC97, BD9
    New International Version, BC201
  versions, BC94, BC97
    American Revised, BC94
    American Standard, BC94
    Authorized, BC94
    bibliography, AA113, BC95, BC101, BC102, BC103
    Confraternity, BC94
    dictionaries, BC153
    Douay, BC94
    Douay-Rheims, BC94
    Jerusalem, BC94
    King James, BC94
    Moffatt, BC94
    New American, BC94
    New American Standard, BC94
    New English, BC94
    New International, BC94
    Revised, BC94
  versions (by language)
    African languages, BC99
    English, BC100, BC101
    French, BC98
Bible (by subject)
  art
    indexes, BF298

law
  bibliography, CK241
The Bible almanac, BC185
The Bible and modern literary criticism, Powell, Mark Allan, BC115
Bible bibliography, Ackroyd, Peter R., BC117
Bible book, Hort, Erasmus, BC108
Bible commentary, BC172
The Bible commentary for today, BC179
La Bible de Jerusalem, BC94
Bible dictionary, BC139
Bible in literature, BC115, BE609
The Bible of the world, BC91
Bible pronunciation guide, BC140
The Bible word book, Bridges, Ronald, BC135
Biblia patristica, BC299
Biblica, BC119
Biblical archaeology, BC109, BC192, BC193, BC194, BC195
  dictionaries, BC142
  encyclopedias, BC196
Biblical bibliography, BC113
A biblical law bibliography, Welch, John W., CK241
Biblical quotations, BC154
The Biblical world, Pfeiffer, Charles F., BC196
Bibligrafía sobre la mujer, DB218
Biblio, AA625, AA626, AA627, AA628, AA629
BiblioData (Firm). *Fulltext sources online*, AD271
Bibliografi e arkeologjisë dhe historisë së lashtë të shqipërisë, Jubani, Bep, DC81
Bibliografi nasional Indonesia, Kantor Bibliografi Nasional (Indonesia), AA904
——— *Projek Perpustakaan Nasional*, AA902
Bibliografi negara Malaysia, AA921
Bibliografi over Danmarks offentlige publikationer, AA605, AF166
Bibliografi over moderne dansk rigssprog, 1850–1978, Hansen, Erik, BD131
Bibliografi over Norges offentlige publikasjoner, AF213
Bibliografi til Norges historie, DC463
La bibliografia, Fumagalli, Giuseppe, AA51, AA54
Bibliografía actual del Caribe, AA554
Bibliografía afro-brasileira, Alves, Henrique L., CC475, DB347
Bibliografía Afrovenezolana, Ramos Guédez, José Marcial, CC476
Bibliografia analitică a periodicelor românești, Lupu, Ioan, AD324
Bibliografía anotada de obras de referencia sobre Centroamérica y Panamá en el campo de las ciencias sociales, Garst, Rachel, DB298
Bibliografia anotada multidisciplinar sobre população desenvolvimento em Moçambique, DD182
Bibliografía anotada y directorio de antropólogos colombianos, Arocha, Jaime, CE88
——— Friedemann, Nina S. de, CE88
Bibliografía antropológica para el estudio de los pueblos indígenas en el Caribe, Sued Badillo, Jalil, CE85
Bibliografía argentina, Universidad de Buenos Aires, AA497, DB324
Bibliografía argentina de artes y letras, AA498
Bibliografía básica de arqueología americana, Alcina Franch, José, DB253
Bibliografia bibliografii i nauki o ksiazce, AA57
Bibliografia bibliografii polskich, AA57
Bibliografia bibliografiĭ polskich, 1951–1960, Sawoniak, Henryk, AA60
Bibliografia bibliografiĭ polskich, 1961–1970, Bienkowa, Maria Barbara, AA60
——— Eychlerowa, Barbara, AA60
Bibliografia bibliografij polskich, Hahn, Wiktor, AA60
Bibliografia bibliografij polskich do 1950 roku, Hahn, Wiktor, AA59
Bibliografía biográfica mexicana, Iguíniz, Juan Bautista, AH109
Bibliografía bogotana, Posada, Eduardo, AA526
Bibliografía boliviana, AA501, AA502
Bibliografia bras, AA510
Bibliografia brasileira, AA507, AA510

Bibliografia brasileira do período colonial, Moraes, Rubens Borba de, AA508
Bibliografia brasileira mensal, AA507
Uma bibliografia brasiliense, AA28
Bibliografía catalana, Givanel Mas, Juan, AD153
Bibliografía chilena, AA512, AA513
——— Montt, Luis, AA517
Bibliografía colombiana, AA523
——— Laverde Amaya, Isidoro, AA524
Bibliografía colombiana de viajes, Giraldo Jaramillo, Gabriel, DB366
Bibliografía colonial, Fontán Lobé, Juan, DD4
Bibliografía comentada sobre la mujer mexicana, DB218
Bibliografía crítica de la nueva estilística, aplicada a las literaturas románicas, Hatzfeld, Helmut, BE1072
Bibliografía cubana, AA559, AA564
Bibliografía cubana del siglo XIX, Trelles y Govín, Carlos Manuel, AA563
Bibliografía cubana del siglo XX, Trelles y Govín, Carlos Manuel, AA563, AA564
Bibliografia czasopism i wydawnictw zbiorowych, AD133
Bibliografia czasopism polskich wydanych poza granicami Kraju od września 1939 roku, Kowalik, Jan, AD135
Bibliografia da dramaturgia brasileira, BE923
Bibliografia da literatura portuguêsa, Moisés, Massaud, BE1367
Bibliografia da música brasileira, Antônio, Irati, BJ22
Bibliografia das obras impressas em Portugal no século XVI, Anselmo, António Joaquim, AA773
Bibliografía de arqueología y etnografía, Bernal, Ignacio, CE75
Bibliografía de autores españoles del siglo XVIII, Aguilar Piñal, Francisco, BE1431, DC499
Bibliografía de bibliografías argentinas, 1807–1970, Geoghegan, Abel Rodolfo, AA26
Bibliografía de bibliografías bolivianas, Siles Guevara, Juan, AA27
Bibliografía de bibliografías chilenas, Elgueta de Ochsenius, Herminia, AA514
——— Laval, Ramón Arminio, AA514
Bibliografía de bibliografías colombianas, Giraldo Jaramillo, Gabriel, AA29
Bibliografía de bibliografías individuales, Bohdziewicz, Jorge C., DB332
Bibliografía de bibliografías literarias argentinas, Becco, Horacio Jorge, BE919
Bibliografía de bibliografías sobre la literatura venezolana en las bibliotecas de Madrid, Paris y Londres, Cardozo, Lubio, AA32
Bibliografía de bibliografías uruguayas, Musso Ambrosi, Luis Alberto, AA31
Bibliografía de bibliografías venezolanas, Becco, Horacio Jorge, BE961
Bibliografia de dramaturgia brasileira, BE923
Bibliografía de escritores hispanoamericanos, 1609–1974, Flores, Angel, BE871
Bibliografía de estudios sobre Carlos III y su época, Aguilar Piñal, Francisco, DC499
Bibliografía de historia económica y social de México, López Rosado, Diego H., DB229
Bibliografía de índices de publicaciones periódicas argentinas, Ardissone, Elena, AD248
Bibliografía de la arqueología guatemalteca, Laporte Molina, Juan Pedro, DB308
Bibliografía de la bibliografía dominicana, Florén Lozano, Luis, AA34
Bibliografía de la crítica literaria venezolana, 1847–1977, Lovera De-Sola, Roberto J., BE965
Bibliografía de la imprenta en Guatemala, Reyes Monroy, José Luis, AA481
Bibliografía de la imprenta en Santiago de Chile desde sus orígenes hasta febrero de 1817, Medina, José Toribio, AA516
Bibliografía de la Inquisición, BC272
Bibliografía de la lengua valenciana. ..., Ribelles Comín, José, AA819
Bibliografía de la lingüística española, Serís, Homero, BD169, BE1438

Bibliografía de la literatura ecuatoriana, Gutierrez, Rene L., BE950
────── Welch, Thomas L., BE950
Bibliografía de la literatura hispánica, Simón Díaz, José, BE1439
Bibliografía de la literatura paraguaya, Welch, Thomas L., BE953
Bibliografía de la literatura picaresca, Laurenti, Joseph L., BE1475
Bibliografía de la literatura uruguaya, Welch, Thomas L., BE960
Bibliografía de la mujer boliviana, 1920–1985, DB335
Bibliografía de la novela en Colombia, Porras Collantes, Ernesto, BE948
Bibliografía de la poesía colombiana, Orjuela, Héctor H., BE944, BE948
Bibliografía de la poesía española del siglo XIX (1801–1850), Rokiski Lázaro, Gloria, BE1479
Bibliografía de la primera imprenta de Buenos Aires desde su fundación hasta el año 1810 inclusive ..., Gutiérrez, Juan María, AA496
Bibliografía de la Revolución de Mayo, 1810–1828, Fúrlong Cárdiff, Guillermo, DB326
Bibliografía de la revolución mexicana, Ramos, Roberto, DB232, DB233
Bibliografía de las Islas Malvinas, Torre Revello, José, DB376
Bibliografía de libros y folletos, 1958–1960, Herrera, Carmen D. de, AA493
Bibliografía de libros y folletos publicados en Nicaragua (en 1942, o antes según fecha de publicación), Biblioteca Americana de Nicaragua, AA490
Bibliografía de linguística portuguesa, BD164
Bibliografía de los cancioneros castellanos del siglo XV y repertorio de sus generos poeticos, Knapp, Lothar, BE1477
────── Steunou, Jacqueline, BE1477
Bibliografía de los estudios clasicos en España, Alvar Ezquerra, A., DA95
────── Sociedad Española de Estudios Clásicos, DA95
Bibliografía de novelistas de la revolución Mexicana, Moore, Ernest, BE916
Bibliografía de teatro puertorriqueño, González, Nilda, BE979
Bibliografía de tesis peruanos sobre indigenismo y ciencias sociales, Muñoz de Linares, Elba, DB384
Bibliografía de trabajos publicados en Nicaragua, González, Graciela, AA490
Bibliografía de viajeros a la Argentina, Santos Gómez, Susana, DB329
Bibliografía degli studi italiani sulla Cecoslovacchia (1918–1978), Wildová Tosi, Alena, DC127
Bibliografía del arte en España, BF13
Bibliografía del cuento mexicano, Leal, Luis, BE912
Bibliografía del cuento venezolano, Larrazábal Henríquez, Osvaldo, BE964
Bibliografía del Emperador Carlos V, Cadenas y Vicent, Vicente de, DC501
Bibliografía del folklore chileno, 1952–1965, Dannemann Rothstein, Manuel, CF71
Bibliografía del folklore de Guatemala, 1892–1980, CF59
Bibliografía del folklore mexicano, Boggs, Ralph Steele, CF61
Bibliografía del folklore peruano, Pan American Institute of Geography and History. Comisíon de Historia. Committee on Folklore, CF70
Bibliografía del libro d'arte italiano, BF13
Bibliografía del Poder Legislativo desde sus comienzos hasta el ano 1965, Musso Ambrosi, Luis Alberto, AF162
Bibliografía del proceso chileno 1970–1973, Garritón, Manuel A., DB360
────── Hola, Eugenia, DB360
Bibliografía del siglo XIX, Burgo, Jaime del, DC500
Bibliografía del socialismo e del movimento operaio italiano, Ente per la Storia del Socialismo e del Movimento Operaio Italiano, CH628
Bibliografía del teatro colombiano, Orjuela, Héctor H., BE945, BE948

Bibliografía del teatro ecuatoriano, 1900–1982, Luzuriaga, Gerardo, BE951
Bibliografía del teatro en México, Monterde, Francisco, BE914
Bibliografía del teatro hispanoamericano contemporaneo (1900–1980), Toro, Fernando de, BE900
Bibliografía del teatro mexicano del siglo XX, Lamb, Ruth S., BE914
Bibliografía del teatro venezolano, Rojas Uzcátegui, José de la Cruz, BE966
Bibliografía della linguistica italiana, Hall, Robert Anderson, BD161
Bibliografía della miniatura, Donati, Lamberto, BF311
Bibliografía della stampa periodica operaia e socialista italiana, 1860–1926, Istituto Giangiacomo Feltrinelli (Milan), CH657
Bibliografía dell'Archivio centrale dello Stato, 1953–1978, DC427
Bibliografía delle opere demografiche in lingua italiana (1930–1965), Golini, Antonio, CG4
Bibliografía delle opere demografiche italiane (1966–1972), Caselli, Graziella, CG4
────── Golini, Antonio, CG4
Bibliografía dell'Italia antica, Antonini, Rosalba, DC417
Bibliografía di bibliografie, Bosco, Giovanna, AA50
Bibliografía do conto brasileiro, Gomes, Celuta Moreira, BE931
Bibliografía do folclore brasileiro, Colonelli, Cristina Argenton, CF63
Bibliografía do pensamento político republicano (1879/1980), Fonseca, Edson Nery da, DB341
────── Mendes, Evelyse Maria Freire, DB341
Bibliografía ecuatoriana, AA528
Bibliografía ecuatoriana, 1534–1809, Espinosa Cordero, Nicolás, AA530
Bibliografía en extranjero de demósgrafos franceses, CG218
Bibliografía española, AA822, AA825, AD159
Bibliografía española de las Islas Filipinas (1523–1810), Medina, José Toribio, AA927
Bibliografía etiopica ... , Fumagalli, Giuseppe, DD156
Bibliografía etiopica in continuazione alla "Bibliografía etiopica" di G. Fumagalli, Zanutto, Silvio, DD156
Bibliografía etnologica de Mocambique (das origens a 1954), Rita-Ferreira, A., DD184
Bibliografía folclórica, CF60
Bibliografía general de Chile, Biblioteca Nacional (Chile), AA514
────── Vaisse, Emilio, AA514
Bibliografía general de la literatura hispanoamericana, Leguizamón, Julio A., BE877
Bibliografía general de la literatura latinoamericana, BE869
Bibliografía general de temblores y terremotos, Montessus de Ballore, Fernand, *Comte de,* EF261
Bibliografía general del desarrollo económico de México 1500–1976, DB219
Bibliografía general española e hispanoamericana, AA822
Bibliografía geral de Moçambique, Costa, Mario Augusto da, DD184
Bibliografía geral portuguesa, Academia das Sciencias de Lisboa, AA772
Bibliografía guatemalteca, AA481, AA482
────── Valenzuela, Gilberto, AA481
────── Valenzuela Reyna, Gilberto, AA481
────── Villacorta Calderon, José Antonio, AA485
Bibliografía guatemalteca de los siglos XVII y XVIII, O'Ryan, Jan Enrique, AA481
Bibliografía hispánica, AA822, AA826
Bibliografía hispano-latina clásica, Menéndez y Pelayo, Marcelino, BE1043
Bibliografía hispanoamericana y filipina, Hilton, Sylvia L., BE876, DE248
Bibliografía histórica de España e Hispanoamérica, DC509
Bibliografía histórica del Estado de México, Beltrán Bernal, Trinidad, DB217

Bibliografía historii Polski, Polska Akademia Nauk. Instytut Historii, DC473
Bibliografía historii polskiej ... , DC477
Bibliografía historiographical la cuestion Malvinar, Etchepareborda, Roberto, DB374
Bibliografía historyi polskiej, Finkel, Ludwik, DC473
Bibliografía hondureña, García, Miguel Angel, AA486, AA489
Bibliografía hrvatska, Kukuljevic-Sakcinski, Ivan, AA843
Bibliografía ibérica del siglo XV, Haebler, Konrad, AA817
Bibliografía indígena andina peruana (1900–1968), Martínez, Héctor, DB383
Bibliografía indigenista de México y Centroamerica (1850–1950), Parra, Manuel Germán, CE82
Bibliografía inorečových novín a časopisov na Slovensku do roku 1918, Potemra, Michal, AE47
Bibliografía istorica a României, DC494
Bibliografía italiana, AA725, AA732
────── Istituto nazionale per le relazioni culturali con l'estero, AA52
Bibliografía italiana di storia e studi militari, 1960–1984, DC418
Bibliografía italo-ebraica (1848–1977), Romano, Giorgio, BC530
Bibliografía jurídica de América Latina, 1810–1965, Villalón Galdames, Alberto, CK199
Bibliografía kombëtare e librit që botohet në RPS të Shqipërisë, AA571
Bibliografía kombëtare e Republikës Popullore Socialiste të Shqipërisë : Artikujt e periodikut shqip, AD301
Bibliografía kombëtare e Republikës Popullore të Shqipërisë : Artikujt e periodikut shqip, AD301
Bibliografía kombëtare e RPS të Shqupërisë, AD301
Bibliografía kopernikowska, Baranowski, Henryk, EC5
Bibliografía lingüística de la República Mexicana, Marino Flores, Anselmo, BD241
Bibliografía literaturii romîne, 1948–1960, Academia Republicii Populare Romîne. Biblioteca, BE1376
Bibliografía literatury polskiej, BE1346, BE1350
Bibliografía literatury polskiej okresu odrodzenia, Polska Akademia Nauk. Instytut Badań Literackich, BE1357
Bibliografía literatury tłumaczonej na język polski, BE1347
Bibliografía mexicana, AA465, AA466
Bibliografía mexicana del siglo XVI, García Icazbalceta, Joaquín, AA460
Bibliografía mexicana del siglo XVIII, León, Nicolás, AA462
Bibliografía missionaria, BC303
Bibliografía nacional, Biblioteca Nacional (Peru), AA538
Bibliografía nacional de Nicaragua, 1800–1978, AA491
Bibliografía nacional de Nicaragua, 1979–1989, AA491
Bibliografía nacional paraguaya, AA534
Bibliografía Naționala România, AA783
Bibliografía nazionale italiana, AA727, AA732, AA736
Bibliografía nazionale italiana. Pubblicazione mensile, AA726
Bibliografía onomastyki polskiej, Taszycki, Witold, CL211
Bibliografía opracowań demograficznych z lat 1976–1991, Groblewska, Celina, CG273
Bibliografía panameña, Biblioteca Nacional (Panama), AA492
Bibliografía paraguaya, Biblioteca Nacional (Paraguay), AA535
────── Fernandez-Caballero, Marianne, AA536
Bibliografía patagónica y de las tierras australes, Matijevic, Nicolás, DB328
Bibliografía, periodicelor din Republica Populara Romîna (1957–1962), AD323
Bibliografía peruana, AA543

Bibliografia písomníctva slovenského na sposob slovníka od najstarších čias do konca r. 1900, Rizner, L'udovít Vladimir, AA598

Bibliografia polska, AA768

——— Estreicher, Karol Józef Teofil, AA762, AA765

Bibliografia polska 1901–1939, AA765

Bibliografia polska XIX stulecia, Estreicher, Karol Józef Teofil, AA762, AA763

Bibliografia polskiego písmiennictwa demograficznego 1945–1975, CG272

Bibliografia polskiej, Bieńkowski, Wiesław, DC473

Bibliografia prasy polskeij, 1944–1948, Polska Akademia Nauk. Pracownia Historii Czasopiśmiennictwa Polskiego XIX–XX Wieku, AE66

Bibliografia prasy polskiej, 1944–1948, Polska Akademia Nauk. Pracownia Historii Czasopiśmiennictwa Polskiego XIX–XX Wieku, AD137

Bibliografía puertorriqueña (1492–1930), Pedreira, Antonio Salvador, DB453

Bibliografía puertorriqueña de fuentes para investigaciones sociales, 1930–1945, Bird, Augusto, DB453

Bibliografía razonada y anotada de las obras maestras de la picaresca española, Ricapito, J. V., BE1476

Bibliografía regional y local de España, Simón Díaz, José, DC508

Bibliografia Republicii Populare Romîne, AD323

Bibliografia Republicii Socialiste România, AA783, AD323

Bibliografia româna-ungara, Veress, Endre, AA782

Bibliografia românească modernă, 1831–1918, AA780, AA781

Bibliografia românească veche, 1508–1830, AA781

——— Bianu, Ioan, AA780

Bibliografia României, AA783

Bibliografia selectiva da língua portuguesa, Ferreira, José de Azevedo, BD164

Bibliografía selectiva de las culturas indígenas de América, Comas, Juan, CE78

Bibliografía selectiva sobra desarrollo rural en Bolivia, Hernandez, Margarita, DB338

——— Uribe, Maruja, DB338

Bibliografía selectiva sobre desarrollo rural en el Ecuador, Uribe, Maruja, DB372

Bibliografia slovenskej kniznej tvorby, AA591

Bibliografía slovenského písomníctva do knock XIX, Misianik, Jan, AA598

Bibliografía slovenských novín a časopisov do roku 1918, Potemra, Michal, AE47

Bibliografía sobre el español de América, 1920–1986, Solé, Carlos A., BD175

Bibliografía sobre el español del Caribe hispánico, BD174

Bibliografía sobre la mujer en el Ecuador, Rosero, Rocío, DB371

Bibliografía sobre relaciones internacionales y política exterior de Chile, 1964–1980, Portales, Carlos, DB359

Bibliografía social, económica y política del Ecuador, Ecuador. Junta Nacional de Planificatión y Coordinación Económica. Sección de Investigaciones Sociales, DB370

Bibliografía socioeconómica de Nicaragua, Gutiérrez, G., DB316

Bibliografia somala, Carboni, Fabio, DD206

Bibliografia storica nazionale, DC425

Bibliografia storico internazionale, 1940–1947, Palumbo, Pier Fausto, DA12

Bibliografía temática de estudios sobre el teatro español antiguo, McCready, Warren T., BE1466

Bibliografía tlačí vydaných na Slovensku do roku 1700, Čaplovič, Ján, AA595

Bibliografía uruguaya, AA547

——— Arrendondo, Horacio, AA545

Bibliografía venezolana, AA548, AA549, AA552

Bibliografia wydawnictw ciągłych, AD133

Bibliografia wydawnictw Głownego Urzędu Statystycznego, Poland. Głowny Urząd Statystyczny, CG274

Bibliograficheskiĭ ukazatel' geodezicheskoĭ literatury za 40 let 1917–1956, Belikov, Evgeniĭ Fedorovich, EF23

Bibliograficheskiĭ ukazatel' literatury po russkomu ĭazykoznaniiu s 1825 po 1880 god, Institut iazykoznaniia (Akademiia nauk SSSR), BD185

Bibliograficky katalog, AA592

Bibliograficky katalog. České knihy, AA600

Bibliograficky katalog Československé Republiky, AA593, AA594

Bibliograficky katalog ČSFR, AG25

Bibliograficky katalog ČSRF, AA600

Bibliograficky katalog ČSSR, AA594, AD307

Bibliograficky katalog slovenskej kniznej tvorby, AA591

Bibliografie české historie za rok 1904–41, DC122

Bibliografie české literárni vědy, 1945–1955, Balášová, Olga, BE1104

Bibliografie československé historie za rok 1955–65, DC122

Bibliografie československé statistiky a demografie, CG205

Bibliografie déjin Československa, DC122

Bibliografie del ventennio, Istituto nazionale per le relazioni culturali con l'estero, AA53

Bibliografie der geschiedenis van Nederland, Buck, Hendrik de, DC451

Bibliografie der ungarischin nationalen und internationalen Literatur, Kertbeny, Károly Mária, DC378

Bibliografie van Afrikaanse boeke, Nienaber, Petrus Johannes, AA875

Bibliografie van de geschiedenis van België, DC99, DC104

Bibliografie van de literaire tijdschriften in Vlaanderen en Nederland, AD303, BE1066

Bibliografie van de stedengeschiedenis van Nederland, Herwijnen, G. van, DC453

Bibliografie van de Vlaamse tijdschriften, Assche, Hilda van, AD303, BE1066

——— Roemans, Robert, AD303, BE1065, BE1066

Bibliografie van in Nederland verschenen officiële en semiofficiële uitgaven, AF212

Bibliografie van in Nederland verschenen officiële uitgaven bij rijksoverheid en provinciale besturen, AF212

Bibliografie van Nederlandse proefschriften, AG38

Bibliografie van vertalingen van Noord- en Zuidnederlandse werken, Raan, E. van, AA138, DC450

Bibliografiia bibliografiĭ po iazykoznaniiu, Gosudarstvennaia biblioteka SSSR imeni V.I. Lenina, BD6

Bibliografiia izdaniĭ Akademii nauk, Rossĭskaia Akademiia Nauk. Biblioteka, AL55

Bibliografiia izdaniĭ Akademii nauk SSSR, Akademiia Nauk SSSR. Biblioteka, AL55

Bibliografiia na bŭlgarskata bibliografiia, AA37, AA39

Bibliografiia na bŭlgarskata bibliografiia, 1852–1944, AA38

Bibliografiia na bŭlgarskata bibliografiia, 1944–1969, Petkova, Zornitsa Malcheva, AA38, AA39

Bibliografiia periodicheskikh izdaniĭ Rossii 1901–1916, Gosudarstvennaia publichnaia biblioteka imeni M.E. Saltykova-Shchedrina, AD142

Bibliografiia po problemam narudonaseleniiu, CG298, CG299

Bibliografiia russkogo letopisaniia, Dmitrieva, Rufina Petrovna, DC576

Bibliografiia sovetskikh russkikh rabot po literature XI–XVII vv. za 1917–1957 gg, Droblenkova, Nadezhda Feotitovna, BE1386

Bibliografiia sovetskoĭ bibliografii, AA61

Bibliografiia stran Afriki i Arabskogo Vostoka, Miliavskaia, S. L., DD9

Bibliografiia trudov Instituta etnografiĭ im. N. N. Miklukho-Maklaia, 1900–1962, Bunakova, O. V., CE5

Bibliografiia trudov po otechestvennomu istochnikovedeniiu i spetsial'nym istoricheskim distsiplinam izdannykh v XVIII v, DC573

Bibliografiia Tŭrtsii, 1713–1917, DC532

Bibliografiia v pomoshch' nauchnoĭ rabote, Kirpicheva, Iraida Konstantinova, AA65

Bibliografija Jugoslavije, AA845, AA846, AD167, AD332

Bibliografija jugoslovenske periodike, AD167

Bibliografija jugoslovenskih bibliografija, 1945–55, Savez društava bibliotekara FNRJ, AA69

Bibliografija rasprava, članaka i književnih radova, Jugoslavenski leksikografski zavod, AD333

Bibliografija rasprava, članaka i književnih radova u časopisima Narodne Republike Hrvatske za godunu, AD306

Bibliografija rasprava i članaka, AD333

Bibliografio de internacia lingvo, Stojan, Petro E., BD50

Bibliografskii iztochnitsi za istoriiata na Turtsiia i Bulgariia, Mikhov, Nikola V., DC537

Le bibliographe moderne, AA10

Bibliographer's manual of English literature, Lowndes, William Thomas, AA663, AA694

Bibliographi shqipe, Kastrati, Jup, AA572

Bibliographia Aethiopica, Lockot, Hans Wilhelm, DD157

Bibliographia anastatica, AA393

Bibliographia antiqua, Forbes, Robert James, EA229

Bibliographia archaeologica hungarica, 1793–1943, Banner, János, DC379

Bibliographia asiatica, DE2

Bibliographia Augustiniana, Andresen, Carl, BB60

Bibliographia brasiliana, Moraes, Rubens Borba de, DB346

Bibliographia Cartesiana, Sebba, Gregor, BB72, BB76

Bibliographia cartographica, CL227, CL247

Bibliographia Catholica Americana, Finotti, Joseph Maria, BC392

Bibliographia dramatica et dramaticorum, Meyer, Reinhart, BE1266

Bibliographia geodaetica, EF121

Bibliographia Hungariae, AA709, DC379

Bibliographia hungarica, 1921-1944, AA710

Bibliographia huntiana, EG111

Bibliographia indicum, lexicorum et concordantiarum auctorum Latinorum, Quellet, Henri, BE1044

Bibliographia liturgica, Johnson, Matthew, BC267

——— Weale, William Henry James, BC429

Bibliographia medica, EH60

Bibliographia musicologica, BJ8

Bibliographia neerlandica, AA138, DC450

Bibliographia onomastica helvetica, Hubschmid, Johannes, CL212

Bibliographia patristica, BC295

Bibliographia patristica. Supplementum, Sieben, H. J., BC295

Bibliographia polonica XV ac XVI ss, Wierzbowski, Teodor, AA764

Bibliographia primatologica, Ruch, Theodore Cedric, EG214

Bibliographia studiorum uralicorum, 1917–1987, DC602

Bibliographia tōn Hellēnikōn bibliographiōn, 1791–1947, Phousaras, G. I., AA47

Bibliographia zoologica, EG216

Bibliographic annual in speech communication, BE353

The bibliographic control of official publications, AF2

Bibliographic guide for editors & authors, BioSciences Information Service of Biological Abstracts, EA38

Bibliographic guide for translators, writers and terminologists, BD88

A bibliographic guide to American colleges and universities, Beach, Mark, CB219

Bibliographic guide to anthropology and archaeology, CE22, CE30

Bibliographic guide to art and architecture, BF57

——— New York Public Library. Art and Architecture Division, BF45

Bibliographic guide to black studies, Schomburg Center for Research in Black Culture, CC380, CC381

Bibliographic guide to dance, New York Public Library. Dance collection, BH135

Bibliographic guide to education, CB6, CB9

A bibliographic guide to educational research, Berry, Dorothea M., CB2

Bibliographic guide to government publications— foreign, AF10
——— New York Public Library. Research Libraries, AF83, AF148

Bibliographic guide to government publications— U.S, AF10, AF83

Bibliographic guide to Iran, DE181

Bibliographic guide to Latin American studies, DB265, DB270

Bibliographic guide to maps and atlases, CL248, CL255

Bibliographic guide to microform publications, AA128

Bibliographic guide to Middle Eastern studies, DE41

Bibliographic guide to music, New York Public Library. Music Division, BJ50, BJ88

Bibliographic guide to North American history, DB5, DB25, DB179

Bibliographic guide to psychology, CD7

Bibliographic guide to refrigeration, 1953–1968, International Institute of Refrigeration, Paris, EK227

Bibliographic guide to Soviet and East European studies, DC40
——— New York Public Library. Research Libraries, DC45

A bibliographic guide to Spanish diplomatic history, 1460–1977, Cortada, James W., DC502

Bibliographic guide to studies on the status of women, CC589

Bibliographic guide to technology, New York Public Library. Research Libraries, EK4, EK5

A bibliographic guide to the history of computing, computers, and the information processing industry, Cortada, James W., EK209

A bibliographic guide to the literature of professional school psychology (1890–1985), CD89

Bibliographic guide to theatre arts, New York Public Library. Research Libraries, BH33

Bibliographic handbooks, Conference on British Studies, DC308, DC319, DC320, DC325, DC331

Bibliographic index, AA15, BE476, BE587

The bibliographic instruction-course handbook, Wheeler, Helen Rippier, AK232

Bibliographic services throughout the world, AA16, AA21

Bibliographica hungarica, AA716

Bibliographical account of English theatrical literature, Lowe, Robert W., BH38

Bibliographical bulletin of the Greek language, BD135

Bibliographical catalogue of privately printed books, Martin, John, AA693, AA694

A bibliographical check list of North and Middle American Indian linguistics in the Edward E. Ayer Collection, Edward E. Ayer Collection, BD237

A bibliographical companion, Stokes, Roy Bishop, AA11

Bibliographical dictionary of the English Catholics, AH228

Bibliographical essays in medieval Jewish studies, BC511

Bibliographical foundations of French historical studies, DC162

A bibliographical guide to African-American women writers, Jordan, Casper LeRoy, BE524

A bibliographical guide to black studies programs in the United States, Davis, Lenwood G., CC364

A bibliographical guide to colonialism in sub-Saharan Africa, Duignan, Peter, DD82

A bibliographical guide to Danish literature, Mitchell, Phillip Marshall, BE1120

Bibliographical guide to materials on American Spanish, Nichols, Madaline W., BD175

A bibliographical guide to Midwestern literature, BE567

A bibliographical guide to Old Frisian studies, Bremmer, Rolf H., BD133

A bibliographical guide to Spanish American literature, Rela, Walter, BE868

A bibliographical guide to the history of Indian-white relations in the United States, Prucha, Francis Paul, CC423

A bibliographical guide to the history of the British Empire, 1748–1776, Gipson, Lawrence Henry, DC341

A bibliographical guide to the Romance languages and literatures, Palfrey, Thomas Rossman, BD152, BE1073

A bibliographical guide to the Russian language, Unbegaun, Boris Ottokar, BD188

A bibliographical guide to the study of Chinese language and linguistics, Kim, T. W., BD218

A bibliographical guide to the study of Southern literature, Rubin, Louis Decimus, BE574

Bibliographical guide to the study of the literature of the U.S.A., Gohdes, Clarence Louis Frank, BE395, BE397

A bibliographical guide to the study of Western American literature, BE572
——— Etulain, Richard W., BE570

Bibliographical handbook of American music, Krummel, Donald William, BJ39

Bibliographical handbook on law and public administration, CK15

Bibliographical handbooks, Conference on British Studies, DC303, DC307

The bibliographical history of anonyma and pseudonyma, Taylor, Archer, AA145

Bibliographical history of electricity and magnetism, chronologically arranged, Mottelay, Paul Fleury, EK126

Bibliographical introduction to nationalism, Pinson, Koppel, CJ9

Bibliographical inventory of the early music in the Newberry Library, Chicago, Illinois, Newberry Library, BJ96

A bibliographical list of plays in the French language, 1700–1789, Brenner, Clarence Dietz, BE1177

Bibliographical series. Computers, Bureau of Technical Information (London), EK163

Bibliographical services throughout the world, AA16

Bibliographical Society (London). [*Dictionaries of printers and booksellers in England, Scotland and Ireland*], AA306
——— *Hand-lists of books printed by London printers, 1501–1556*, AA666

Bibliographical Society of America. *American newspapers, 1821–1936*, AE18
——— *Bibliography of American literature*, BE400
——— *A dictionary of books relating to America, from its discovery to the present time*, AA409

Bibliographical Society of Canada. *Bibliography of Canadian bibliographies*, AA22

Bibliographical Society of the Philippines. *Checklist of Philippine government publications, 1917–1949*, AF258

Bibliographie albanaise, Legrand, Emile Louis Jean, AA572

Bibliographie algérienne, Maynadies, Michel, DD125

Bibliographie américaniste, linguistique amérindienne, Pottier, Bernard, BD239

Bibliographie analytique de l'Afrique antique, DD66

Bibliographie analytique de l'archéologie de l'Iran ancien, Berghe, Louis van den, DE180

Bibliographie analytique des biographies collectives imprimées de la France contemporaine, Fierro, Alfred, AH196

Bibliographie analytique des langues parlées en Afrique subsaharienne, 1970–1980, BD213

Bibliographie analytique des revues littéraires de Suisse romande, Hayoz, Chantal, BE1489

Bibliographie annotée sur la population du Rwanda, Hategekimana, Grégoire, CG352, DD197

Bibliographie annuelle de l'histoire de France du cinquième siècle à 1939, DC148

Bibliographie annuelle de Madagascar, AA863, AA864, AA865, DD175

Bibliographie annuelle des travaux historiques et archéologiques publiés par les sociétés savantes de la France, Gandilhon, René, DC213

Bibliographie astronomique, Lalande, Joseph Jérôme le Français de, EC16

Bibliographie balkanique 1920–1938, Savadjian, Léon, DC59

Bibliographie bevölkerungswissenschaftlicher Aufsätze und Kurzartikel im damaligen Deutschen Reich erschienener sozialwissenschaftlicher und erbbiologischer Fachzeitschriften zwischen 1900 und ca. 1945, Thieme, Frank, CG229

Bibliographie bevölkerungswissenschaftlicher Literatur, 1945–1982, CG227

Bibliographie biblique, Langevin, Paul-Emile, BC113

Bibliographie birmane, années 1950–1960, Bernot, Denise, DE119

Bibliographie bouddhique, BC463, BC469

Bibliographie brésilienne, Garraux, Anatole Louis, DB346

Bibliographie cartographique internationale, CL226

Bibliographie centrafricaine, Banville, Christian de, DD139

Bibliographie critique de la nouvelle de langue française (1940–1985), Godenne, René, BE1188

Bibliographie critique des mémoires sur la Révolution écrits ou traduits en français, Fierro, Alfred, DC180

Bibliographie critique du roman canadien-français, 1837–1900, Hayne, David M., BE842

Bibliographie de Belgique, AA582, AD302

Bibliographie de civilisation de l'Inde contemporaine, Chambard, Jean-Luc, DE155

Bibliographie de la Côte d'Ivoire, AA852
——— Janvier, Geneviève, DD146

Bibliographie de la critique de la littérature québécoise dans les revues des XIXe et XXe siécles, Cantin, Pierre, BE838
——— Harrington, Normand, BE838
——— Hudon, Jean-Paul, BE838

Bibliographie de la critique de la littérature québécoise et canadienne-française dans les revues canadiennes, Dionne, René, BE838

Bibliographie de la culture arabe contemporaine, DE28

Bibliographie de la France, AA625, AA626, AA629, AF168

Bibliographie de la France—Biblio, AA625, AA627, AA629, AA633, AA634, AA636

Bibliographie de la France. Bulletin du livre, AA636

Bibliographie de la France. Livres, AA627

Bibliographie de la Guyane Française, Abonnenc, Émile, DB377

Bibliographie de la langue latine, 1880–1948, Cousin, Jean, BD143

Bibliographie de la littérature "algérienne" des Français, Déjeux, Jean, BE1522

Bibliographie de la littérature française, 1930–1939 … complément à Bibliographie de H. P. Thieme, Dreher, Silpelitt, BE1209
——— Rolli, Madeline, BE1209

Bibliographie de la littérature française, 1940–1949 … complément à Bibliographie de H. P. Thieme, Drevet, Marguerite L., BE1209

Bibliographie de la littérature française de 1800 à 1930, Thieme, Hugo Paul, BE1137, BE1209

Bibliographie de la littérature française du dix-huitième siècle …, Cioranescu, Alexandre, BE1206

Bibliographie de la littérature française du dix-septième siècle, Cioranescu, Alexandre, BE1205

Bibliographie de la littérature française du Moyen Âge à nos jours, BE1140

Bibliographie de la littérature française du seizième siècle, Cioranescu, Alexandre, BE1204

Bibliographie de la littérature japonaise contemporaine, Bonneau, Georges, BE1580

Bibliographie de la littérature latine, Herescu, Niculae I., BE1040

Bibliographie de la littérature "marocaine" des Français, 1875–1983, Dugas, Guy, BE1529

Bibliographie de la littérature "tunisienne" des Français, 1881–1980, Dugas, Guy, BE1539

Bibliographie de la Martinique, Jardel, Jean Pierre, DB445

Bibliographie de la philosophie, BB12

Bibliographie de la presse classique, 1600–1789, Sgard, Jean, AD79

Bibliographie de la presse française politique et d'information générale, 1865–1944, Bibliothèque Nationale (France). Département des Périodiques, AD92, AE50

Bibliographie de la RDD, DD147

Bibliographie de la réforme, 1450–1648, Commission Internationale d'Histoire Ecclésiastique Comparée, DC27

Bibliographie de la Révolution française, 1940–1988, DC176

Bibliographie de l'Afrique occidentale française, Joucla, Edmond A., DD101

Bibliographie de l'Afrique sud-saharienne, sciences humaines et sociales, DD79

Bibliographie de l'Algérie, AA849

Bibliographie de l'Angola, Borchardt, Paul, DD128

Bibliographie de l'antiquité classique, 1896–1914, Lambrino, Scarlat, BE1001

Bibliographie de l'art des jardins, Ganay, Ernest, BF286

Bibliographie de l'histoire de Belgique, DC99, DC104

———— Pirenne, Henri, DC100, DC451

Bibliographie de l'histoire de France, Barbier, Frédéric, DC142

Bibliographie de l'histoire du Québec et du Canada, Aubin, Paul, DB178

Bibliographie de l'histoire médiévale en France (1965–1990), DC168

Bibliographie de Madagascar, Grandidier, Guillaume, AA863, AA865, DD175

Bibliographie de Tahiti et de la Polynésie française, O'Reilly, Patrick, DF51

Bibliographie d'éditions originales et rares d'auteurs français des XVᵉ, XVIᵉ, XVIIᵉ et XVIIIᵉ siècles contenant environ 6000 facsimilés de titres et de gravures, Tchemerzine, Avenir, AA621

Bibliographie der amtlichen westdeutschen Statistik, 1945–1951, Deutsche Statistische Gesellschaft, CG228

Bibliographie der archäologischen Konservierungstechnik, Gaudel, Paul, DA64

Bibliographie der Autobiographien, Jessen, Jens Christian, AH214

Bibliographie der Bibliographien, AA42, AA43, AA44

Bibliographie der Bibliographien zur slavischen Sprachwissenschaft, Schaller, Helmut Wilhelm, BD182

Bibliographie der Buch- und Bibliotheksgeschichte, AK18

Bibliographie der deutschen Bibliographien, AA42, AA43, AA44, AA45

Bibliographie der deutschen Literaturwissenschaft, BE1141

Bibliographie der deutschen Sprach- und Literaturwissenschaft, BD116, BE1235

Bibliographie der deutschen Zeitschriftenliteratur, AA364, AD253, AD255, AD313, AE122

Bibliographie der Deutschsprachigen Arabistik und Islamkunde, DE29

Bibliographie der deutschsprachigen Hochschulschriften zur Theaterwissenschaft von 1885 bis 1952, Schwanbeck, Gisela, BE235

Bibliographie der deutschsprachigen Lyrikanthologien, 1840–1914, Häntzschel, Günter, BE1272

Bibliographie der Dissertationen über Judentum und jüdische Persönlichkeiten…, Bihl, Wolfdieter, BC529

Bibliographie der ehemaligen preussischen Ostprovinzen, Rister, Herbert, DC474

Bibliographie der Filmbibliographien = Bibliography of film bibliographies, Wulff, Hans Jürgen, BH173

Bibliographie der französischen Literaturwissenschaft, BE1141

Bibliographie der fremdsprachigen Zeitschriftenliteratur, AA364, AD253, AD255

Bibliographie der germanistischen Zeitschriften, Diesch, Carl Hermann, AD99

Bibliographie der Hispanistik in der Bundesrepublik Deutschland, Österreich und der deutschsprachigen Schweiz, Heydenreich, Titus, BD167

Bibliographie der Kameralwissenschaften, Humpert, Magdalene, CH336

Bibliographie der literarwissenschaftlichen Slawistik, Wytrzens, Günther, BE1078

Bibliographie der lokalen Alternativpresse, Rösch-Sondermann, Hermann, AD102

Bibliographie der Middelnederlandsche taal– en letterkunde, Petit, Louis David, BE1335

Bibliographie der Musikbuchreihen 1886–1990, Walther, Hermann, BJ9, BJ45

Bibliographie der Namenforschung in Österreich, Zwanziger, Ronald, CL184

Bibliographie der nationalen Bibliographien, Domay, Friedrich, AA391

Bibliographie der nordischen Philologie, BD130

Bibliographie der österreichischen Drucke des XV. und XVI. Jahrhunderts, Langer, Eduard, AA573

Bibliographie der Personalbibliographien zur deutschen Gegenwartsliteratur, Stoll, Christoph, BE1221

———— Wiesner, Herbert, BE1221

———— Živsa, Irena, BE1221

Bibliographie der Photographie deutschsprachige Publikationen der Jahre 1839–1984, Heidtmann, Frank, BF329

Bibliographie der Rezensionen, AA364, AA373

Bibliographie der Runeninschriften nach Fundorten, Krause, Wolfgang, BE1082

———— Skandinavischen Seminar der Wissenschaften der Universität Göttingen, BE1082

Bibliographie der Runenkunde, Arntz, Helmut, BE1082

Bibliographie der russischen Autoren und anonymen Werke, Wytrzens, Günther, BE1078

Bibliographie der schweizer Geschichte enthaltend die selbständig erschienenen Druckwerke zur Geschichte der Schweiz bis Ende 1912, Barth, Hans, AH298, AH299, DC522, DC528

Bibliographie der schweizer Presse, Blaser, Fritz, AE77

Bibliographie der Schweizergeschichte, AH298, AH299, DC522, DC528

Bibliographie der schweizerischen Amtsdruckschriften, AF217

Bibliographie der Sozialwissenschaften, CH9

Bibliographie der Städtegeschichte der Schweiz, Guyer, Paul, DC524

Bibliographie der Stoff- und Motivgeschichte der deutschen Literatur, Bauerhorst, Kurt, BE1231

Bibliographie der Troubadours, Pillet, Alfred, BE1374

Bibliographie der Übersetzungen deutschsprachiger Werke, AA139, AA142

Bibliographie der uralischen Sprachwissenschaft 1830–1970, BD208

Bibliographie der versteckten Bibliographien, AA43

———— Deutsche Bücherei (Germany), AA45

Bibliographie der Wirtschaftswissenschaften, CH9

Bibliographie der Zeitschriften des deutschen Sprachgebietes bis 1900, Kirchner, Joachim, AD100

Bibliographie des articles de périodiques allemands, anglais, français et italiens sur la Turquie et la Bulgarie, Mikhov, Nikola V., DC538

Bibliographie des auteurs africains de langue française, Baratte-Eno Belinga, Thérèse, BE1513

Bibliographie des auteurs modernes de langue française (1801–1975), Talvart, Hector, BE1208

Bibliographie des chansonniers français, Raynaud, Gaston, BE1200

Bibliographie des chansons de geste, BE1199

Bibliographie des deutschen rechts in englischer und deutscher sprache, German Association of Comparative law, CK211

Bibliographie des dictionnaires patois galloromans (1550–1967), Wartburg, Walther von, AC390

Bibliographie des écrivains français de Belgique, 1881–1960, Culot, Jean-Marie, BE1099

Bibliographie des études créoles languages et littétures, Chaudenson, Robert, BD55

———— Hazael-Massieux, Marie-Christine, BD55

———— Valdman, Albert, BD55

Bibliographie des impressions espagnoles des Pays-Bas Méridionaux, Peeters-Fontainas, Jean F., AA747

Bibliographie des Juifs en France, Blumenkranz, Bernhard, BC527

Bibliographie des livres, thèses et conférences relatifs à l'industrie du pétrole, Agout, Marthe, EK303

Bibliographie des manuscrits littéraires en ancien provençal, Brunel, Clovis, BE1369

Bibliographie des Musikschrifttums, BJ47

Bibliographie des oeuvres de Leibniz, Ravier, Emile, BB75

Bibliographie des ouvrages arabes ou relatifs aux arabes publiés dans l'Europe chrétienne de 1810 à 1885, Chauvin, Victor, BE1547

Bibliographie des poètes provençaux des XIVᵉ et XVᵉ siècles, Zufferey, François, BE1374

Bibliographie des principales éditions originales d'écrivains français du XVᵉ aux XVIIIᵉ siècle, Le Petit, Jules, AA617

Bibliographie des principales publications editées dans l'Empire japonais, BE1580

Bibliographie des publications officielles suisses, AF217

Bibliographie des recueils collectifs de poésies du XVIᵉ siècle, Lachèvre, Frédéric, BE1193

Bibliographie des recueils collectifs de poésies publiés de 1597 à 1700 … , Lachèvre, Frédéric, BE1193, BE1194

Bibliographie des régions du Sénégal, Porgès, Laurence, DD202

Bibliographie des répertoires nationaux de périodiques en cours, Duprat, Gabrielle, AD8

Bibliographie des revues et journaux littéraires des XIXᵉ et XXᵉ siècles, Place, Jean-Michel, AD96, BE1144

Bibliographie des revues et périodiques d'art parus en France de 1746 à 1914, Lebel, Gustave, BF46

Bibliographie des romans et nouvelles en prose française antérieurs à 1500, Woledge, Brian, BE1202

Bibliographie des schweizerischen Rechts, CK224

Bibliographie des Socialismus und Communismus, Stammhammer, Josef, CJ510

Bibliographie des travaux publiés de 1866 à 1897 sur l'histoire de la France de 1500 à 1789, Saulnier, Eugène, DC173

Bibliographie des travaux publiés de 1866 à 1897 sur l'histoire de la France depuis 1789, Caron, Pierre, DC198

Bibliographie des travaux scientifiques, Deniker, Joseph, EA208

Bibliographie d'études balkaniques, DC66

Bibliographie deutscher Übersetzungen aus dem Französischen, 1700–1948 … , Fromm, Hans, AA143

Bibliographie deutschsprachiger bevölkerungswissenschaftlicher Literatur, 1978–1984, Gärtner, Karla, CG3, CG221

Bibliographie deutschsprachiger Sowjetunion-Reiseberichte, -Reportagen und -Bildbände, 1917–1990, Metzger, Wolfgang, DC588

Bibliographie d'histoire des villes de France, Dollinger, Philippe, DC212, DC265

———— Guenée, Simonne, DC265

———— Wolff, Philippe, DC265

Bibliographie d'histoire littéraire française, BE1141

Bibliographie d'histoire luxembourgeoise, DC446

Bibliographie du Bénin, AA850

Bibliographie du bouddhisme, Beautrix, Pierre, BC461

Bibliographie du bouddhisme Zen, Beautrix, Pierre, BC462

Bibliographie du Burundi, Witherell, Julian W., DD135

Bibliographie du Cameroun, Dippold, Max F., DD136

Bibliographie du Congo, 1880–1895, Wauters, Alphonse Jules, DD15, DD245

Bibliographie du Congo Belge et du Ruanda-Urundi, Heyse, Théodore, AA871, DD135, DD198, DD244

Bibliographie du genre romanesque français, 1751– 1800, Martin, Angus, BE1191

Bibliographie du Katanga, Walraet, Marcel, DD15, DD245

Bibliographie du Laos, Lafont, Pierre-Bernard, DE222, DE223

Bibliographie du meuble (mobilier civil français), Viaux, Jacqueline, BG118

Bibliographie du Népal, DE234

Bibliographie du roman canadien-français, 1900– 1950, Drolet, Antonio, BE842

Bibliographie du Sénégal, AA872

Bibliographie du Shintô et des sectes shintôistes, Herbert, Jean, BC568

Bibliographie du Tchad, DD140

Bibliographie du théâtre profane français des XVe et XVIe siècles, Lewicka, Halina, BE1183

Bibliographie du Zaire, AA884

Bibliographie économique, juridique et sociale de l'Égypte moderne, (1798–1916), Maunier, René, DD149

Bibliographie en langue française d'histoire du droit, DC149

Bibliographie ethnographique de l'Afrique sud-saharienne, DD79

Bibliographie ethnographique du Congo Belge et des régions avoisinantes, DD79

Bibliographie ethnographique du Congo et des régions avoisinantes, DD79

Bibliographie française de demographie 1975–1984, CG218

—— Lunazzi, Marie Claude, CG217

Bibliographie franco-portugaise, Coutinho, Bernardo Xavier da Costa, DC184

Bibliographie französischer Dissertationen zur deutschsprachigen Literatur, 1885–1975, Gabel, Gernot U., BE1237

Bibliographie fremdsprachiger Germanica, AA142

Bibliographie Friedensforschung und Friedenspolitik, CJ676

Bibliographie Friedrich der Grosse, 1786–1986, Henning, Herzeleide, DC234

Bibliographie gastronomique, Vicaire, Georges, EJ207

Bibliographie généalogique, héraldique et nobiliaire de la France, Saffroy, Gaston, AJ87

Bibliographie générale de la Haute-Volta, 1956– 1965, Izard, Françoise, DD133

Bibliographie générale de l'astronomie jusqu'en 1880, Houzeau, Jean Charles, EC6, EC13, EC14

—— Lancaster, Albert, EC6, EC14

Bibliographie generale des études de population au Cameroun, Gubry, Patrick, DD138

Bibliographie générale des ouvrages publiés ou illustrés en Suisse et à l'étranger de 1475 à 1914 par des écrivains et des artistes suisses, Lonchamp, Frédéric Charles, AA834

Bibliographie générale des travaux historiques et archéologiques publiés par les sociétés savantes de la France, Lasteyrie du Saillant, Robert Charles, DC213, EA208

Bibliographie générale des travaux palethnologiques et archéologiques (époques préhistorique, protohistorique et gallo-romaine). France … , Montandon, Raoul, DC171

Bibliographie générale du costume et de la mode, Colas, René, BG91

Bibliographie générale du Mali, Institut Fondamental d'Afrique Noire, DD97

Bibliographie générale du Mali (anciens Soudan Français et Haut-Sénégal-Niger), Brasseur, Paule Marion, DD97

Bibliographie générale et méthodique d'Haiti, Duvivier, Ulrick, AA566, AA567

Bibliographie géographique, CL23

Bibliographie géographique internationale, AD254, BB24, BE38, CE23, CL6, CL23

Bibliographie hellénique, Legrand, Emile Louis Jean, AA701, AA702, AA703, AA704

Bibliographie hellénique du dix-huitième siècle, Pernot, Hubert, AA703

—— Petit, Louis, AA703

Bibliographie hispanique, BE1432

Bibliographie hispanique extra-péninsulaire, Vaganay, Hugues, AA810

Bibliographie historique et critique de la presse périodique française, Hatin, Louis Eugène, AD92, AD95, AE50

Bibliographie historique sur la Tunisie, 1881–1955, Tunisia. Maktabah al-Qawmīyah, DD238

Bibliographie historischer Zeitschriften, 1939–1951, Kramm, Heinrich, DA14

Bibliographie internationale de l'humanisme et de la renaissance, DA140

Bibliographie internationale des travaux historiques publiés dans les volumes de "Mélanges", International Committee of Historical Sciences, DA6

Bibliographie internationale d'histoire militaire, DA170

Bibliographie internationale, retrospective (1950– 1983) et partiellement commentée sur la planification des transports urbains, Merlin, Pierre, BF272

Bibliographie internationale sur le bilinguisme, BD61

Bibliographie ionienne, Legrand, Emile Louis Jean, AA703

—— Pernot, Hubert, AA703

Bibliographie juridique suisse, CK224

Bibliographie juristischer Festschriften und Festschriftenbeiträge, CK6

Bibliographie linguistique de l'ancien occitan (1960–1982), Klingebiel, Kathryn, BD177

Bibliographie linguistique des années 1939/47, BD25

Bibliographie linguistique du Canada français, Dulong, Gaston, DD162

Bibliographie Linguistischer Literatur, BD1

Bibliographie littéraire de la Republique du Zaïre, 1931–1972, Kadima-Nzuji Mukala, BE1540

Bibliographie luxembourgeoise, AA742

—— Blum, Martin, AA742

Bibliographie marocaine, 1923–1933, Cenival, Pierre de, DD180

Bibliographie méthodique, analytique et critique de la Nouvelle-Calédonie, O'Reilly, Patrick, DF41

Bibliographie méthodique, analytique et critique de la Nouvelle-Calédonie, 1955–1982, Pisier, George, DF41

Bibliographie méthodique, analytique et critique des Nouvelles-Hébrides, O'Reilly, Patrick, DF52

Bibliographie méthodique et critique de la littérature algérienne de langue française, 1945–1977, Déjeux, Jean, BE1522

Bibliographie musikalischer thematischer Werkverzeichnisse, Wettstein, Hermann, BJ232

Bibliographie nationale, AA576

Bibliographie nationale de la Tunisie, AA882

Bibliographie nationale de Madagascar, AA863, AA864

Bibliographie nationale de Madagascar, 1956–1963, Fontvieille, Jean Roger, AA863, AA865

Bibliographie nationale. Dictionnaire des écrivains belges et catalogue de leurs publications, 1830– 80, BE1099

Bibliographie nationale française, AA627, AF168, BJ78

Bibliographie nationale française. Livres, AA634

Bibliographie nationale française. Musique, BJ78

Bibliographie nationale marocaine, AA867

Bibliographie numismatique, Grierson, Philip, BG172

Bibliographie numismatique: supplément : ordres et decorations, Suetens, Ivo, BG172

Bibliographie occitane, Berthand, Pierre Louis, BE1370

Bibliographie österreichischer Bibliographien, Sammelbiographien und Nachschlagewerke, Stock, Karl F., AA36

Bibliographie relative à la Nouvelle-France, Messier, Jean-Jacques, DB215

Bibliographie rétrospective des périodiques français de littérature musicale, 1870–1954, Thoumin, Jean-Adrien, BJ105

Bibliographie sélective de linguistique romane et française, BD150

Bibliographie sélective sur l'organisation internationale, 1885–1964, Speeckaert, Georges Patrick, AF21

Bibliographie sélective, terminologie et disciplines connexes, Felber, H., BD58

—— Rondeau, G., BD58

Bibliographie signalétique du latin des chrétiens, Sanders, Gabriel, BD146

Bibliographie sommaire de l'Almanach des muses (1765–1833), Lachèvre, Frédéric, BE1195

Bibliographie sommaire des chansonniers provençaux (manuscrits et éditions) … , Jeanroy, Alfred, BE1371

Bibliographie sommaire du Canada français, 1854– 1954, Martin, Gérard, AA449

Bibliographie Sprache und Literatur, BD2

Bibliographie stratigraphisch wichtiger mikropaläontologischer Publikationen von etwa 1830 bis 1958 mit Kurzreferaten, Hiltermann, Heinrich, EF231

Bibliographie suisse de statistique et d'économie politique, CG287

Bibliographie sur la planification des transports urbains, BF272

Bibliographie sur la population et le développement au Togo, CG364, DD237

Bibliographie sur les villes nouvelles françaises et étrangères, Merlin, Pierre, BF273

Bibliographie Thomiste, Destrez, J., BB61

—— Mandonnet, Pierre Félix, BB61, BB66

Bibliographie universelle de sécurité sociale, CH498

Bibliographie unselbständiger Literatur-Linguistik, Suchan, Elke, BD1

Bibliographie van de moderne Vlaamsche literatuur, 1893–1930, Roemans, Robert, AD303, BE1066

Bibliographie van den Vlaamschen taalstrijd, Coopman, Theophiel, AA579

Bibliographie védique, Renou, Louis, BC484

Bibliographie over Japan, 1906–[1943], Nachod, Oskar, DE204

Bibliographie zu den Handschriften vom Toten Meer, Burchard, Christoph, BC106

Bibliographie zu Kunst und Kunstgeschichte, BF13

Bibliographie zu Politik und Gesellschaft der Dominikanischen Republik, Grabendorff, Wolf, DB434

Bibliographie zum deutschen Liberalismus, Hess, Jürgen C., DC235

Bibliographie zum Nationalismus, Schnabel, Thomas, CJ9

—— Winkler, Heinrich, CJ9

Bibliographie zur Afghanistan-Literatur 1960–1987, Nursai, Ata M., DE113

Bibliographie zur alteuropäischen Religionsgeschichte, BC6

Bibliographie zur antiken Sklaverei, Vogt, Joseph, DA68

Bibliographie zur Architektur im 19 Jahrhundert, BF211

Bibliographie zur Aussenpolitik der Republik Österreich seit 1945, Behrmann, Lilly-Ralou, DC87

Bibliographie zur Aussprache des Latein, Steitz, Lothar, BD144

Bibliographie zur Balkanphilologie, Schaller, Helmut Wilhelm, BD202

Bibliographie zur Bevölkerungsforschung in Österreich, 1945–1978, CG193

Bibliographie zur deutschen Geschichte im Zeitalter der Glaubensspaltung 1517–1585, Schottenloher, Karl, DC226, DC227

Bibliographie zur deutschen Grammatik, Eisenberg, Peter, BD117

Bibliographie zur deutschen historischen Städteforschung, Schröder, Brigitte, BF274, DC266

Bibliographie zur deutschen Lyrik nach 1945, Paulus, Rolf, BE1272

────── Steuler, Ursula, BE1272

Bibliographie zur Geschichte der deutschen Arbeiterbewegung, CH626

Bibliographie zur Geschichte der deutschen Arbeiterbewegung, 1914–1945, Klotzbach, Kurt, CH626

Bibliographie zur Geschichte der deutschen Arbeiterbewegung, sozialistischen und kommunistischen Bewegung von den Anfängen bis 1863, Dowe, Dieter, CH627

Bibliographie zur Geschichte der deutschen Arbeiterschaft und Arbeiterbewegung 1863 bis 1914, CH626

────── Ritter, Gerhard A., CH627

────── Tenfelde, Klaus, CH627

Bibliographie zur Geschichte der Juden in der Schweiz, Kaufmann, Uri R., DC525

Bibliographie zur Geschichte der Judenfrage, Eichstädt, Volkmar, BC528

Bibliographie zur Geschichte der Kreuzzüge, Mayer, Hans Eberhard, DA168

Bibliographie zur Geschichte der Städte Österreichs, Rausch, Wilhelm, DC90

Bibliographie zur Geschichte Kaiser Friedrichs II. und der letzten Staufer, Willemsen, Carl Arnold, DC229

Bibliographie zur Geschichte Luxemburgs, DC446

Bibliographie zur Geschichte und Landeskunde der Böhmischen Länder von den Anfängen bis 1948, Jilek, Heinrich, DC125

Bibliographie zur Grammatik der deutschen Dialekte, Wiesinger, Peter, BD126, BD127

Bibliographie zur Heraldik, Henning, Eckart, AJ156

Bibliographie zur Kunstgeschichte des 19. Jahrhunderts, Lietzmann, Hilda, BF32

────── Prause, Marianne, BF32

Bibliographie zur lateinischen Wortforschung, BD142

Bibliographie zur oberösterreichischen Geschichte, 1891–1926, Strassmayr, Eduard, DC92

Bibliographie zur österreichischen Zeitgeschichte, 1918–1985, Malina, Peter, DC89

Bibliographie zur osteuropäischen Geschichte, Meyer, Klaus, DC37

────── Schmidt, Christian D., DC37

Bibliographie zur russischen Sprache, Schaller, Helmut Wilhelm, BD187

Bibliographie zur Städtegeschichte Deutschlands, Keyser, Erich, DC265

Bibliographie zur Transformationsgrammatik, Krenn, Herwig, BD45

Bibliographie zur Zeitgeschichte, 1953–1989, DA169

Bibliographie zur Zeitgeschichte und zum Zweiten Weltkreig für die Jahre 1945–50, Herre, Franz, DA169

Bibliographie zur Zeitgeschrifte, 1953–1989, Institue für Zeitgeschichte, DA169

Bibliographien zum deutschen Schrifttum der Jahre 1939–1950, Widmann, Hans, AA46

Bibliographies, Krummel, Donald William, AA5

Bibliographies analytiques sur l'Afrique centrale, DD243

Bibliographies and indexes in Afro-American and African studies, BE536

Bibliographies for African studies, 1970–1986, Scheven, Yvette, DD88, DD190

Bibliographies in American history, Beers, Henry Putney, DB9

Bibliographies internationales de la doctrine juridique africaine, Vanderlinden, Jacques, CK225

Bibliographies of battles and leaders, DA170

Bibliographies of botany, Bay, Jens Christian, EG88

Bibliographies of Mon-Khmer and Tai linguistics, Shorto, H. L., BD230

Bibliographies of New England history, DB152

Bibliographies of studies in Victorian literature for the thirteen years 1932–1944, BE753

Bibliographies of the languages of the North American Indians, Pilling, J. C., BD240

Bibliographies of the presidents of the United States, CJ167

Bibliographies on South African political history, CJ410, DD213

Bibliographies on the Australian aborigine, Thawley, John, DF28

Bibliographische Berichte, AA17

Bibliographische Einführung in das Studium der slavischen Literaturen, Wytrzens, Günther, BE1078

Bibliographische Einführungen in das Studium der Philosophie, BB5

Bibliographischer Alt-Japan-Katalog, 1542–1853, Berlin. Japan-Institut, DE195

Bibliographischer Wegweiser der philosophischen Literatur, Totok, Wilhelm, BB9

Bibliographisches Beiblatt, BC225

Bibliographisches Bulletin der Schweiz, AA839

Bibliographisches Handbuch der Barockliteratur, Dünnhaupt, Gerhard, BE1217

Bibliographisches Handbuch der deutschen Literaturwissenschaft, 1945–1969, Köttelwesch, Clemens, BE1228

Bibliographisches Handbuch der Rechts– und Verwaltungswissenschaften, Lansky, Ralph, CK15

Bibliographisches Handbuch der Sprachwörterbücher, Zaunmüller, Wolfram, AC196

Bibliographisches Handbuch der Turkologie, Hazai, György, BD211, DE31

Bibliographisches Handbuch des deutschen Schrifttums, Körner, Josef, BE1227

Bibliographisches Handbuch zur Sprachinhaltsforschung, Gipper, Helmut, BD22

Bibliographisches Institut (Mannheim, Germany). Meyers Handbuch über die Literatur, BE187

────── *The Oxford-Duden pictorial Serbo-Croat & English dictionary,* AC714

Bibliography

  bibliography, AA14, AA15, AA16, AA17, AA18, AA19, AA20, AA90, AH14

  dictionaries, AA11

  guides, AA1, AA2, AA3, AA4, AA5, AA6, AA7, AA8, AA9, AA10, AA12, AA13

  library catalogs, AA18

  national and trade, AA388, AA389, AA390, AA391, AA395

    bibliography, AA392, AA394, AA396, AA397, AA472

    periodicals, AA18, AA89

  universal, AA88, AA89, AA90, AA91, AA92, AA93, AA94, AA129

Bibliography and bibliography periodicals, Harvard University. Library, AA18

Bibliography and catalogue of the fossil vertebrata of North America, Hay, Oliver Perry, EF230, EF233

Bibliography and index of English verse in manuscript, 1501–1558, Ringler, Susan J., BE714

────── Ringler, William A., BE714

────── Rudick, Michael, BE714

Bibliography and index of English verse printed 1476–1558, Ringler, William A., BE714

Bibliography and index of geology, EF44, EF47, EF48, EF49, EF53, EF73

Bibliography and index of geology exclusive of North America, EF47, EF48, EF53

Bibliography and index of mainland Southeast Asian languages and linguistics, Huffman, Franklin E., BD228

Bibliography and index of micropaleontology, EF234

Bibliography and reel index, Research Publications, inc, CG93

Bibliography and research manual of the history of mathematics, May, Kenneth Ownsworth, EB8, EB14

Bibliography and subject index of current computing literature, EK166

Bibliography de documents et rapports sur les pays de Sahel, 1977–85, DD103

Bibliography for social science research on Tanzania, Hundsdörfer, Volkhard, DD235

────── Küper, Wolfgang, DD235

A bibliography for the study of African politics, CJ397

Bibliography for the study of magazines, Schacht, John H., AD41

Bibliography, historical and bibliothecal, Vitale, Philip H., AA13

Bibliography in the history of women in the progressive era, Papachristou, Judith, CC508

Bibliography-index to current U.S. JPRS translations, AF102, AF108, AF109

A bibliography of 17th century German imprints in Denmark and the duchies of Schleswig-Holstein, Mitchell, Phillip Marshall, AA602

Bibliography of aesthetics and of the philosophy of the fine arts, 1900–1932, Hammond, William Alexander, BF29

A bibliography of Afghanistan, McLachlan, Keith Stanley, DE112

Bibliography of African anthropology, Hambly, Wilfrid Dyson, CE102

Bibliography of African art, Gaskin, L. J. P., BG4

────── International African Institute, BF25, BG4

Bibliography of African government, 1950–66, Alderfer, Harold, CJ397

Bibliography of African languages, Meier, Wilma, BD214

Bibliography of African oral narratives, CF92

Bibliography of African women writers and journalists, Berrian, Brenda F., BE1502

Bibliography of agriculture, EJ11, EJ17, EJ35, EJ92

A bibliography of American autobiographies, AH89, DB67

────── Kaplan, Louis, BE507, CC485, DB66

A bibliography of American children's books printed prior to 1821, Welch, D'Alté Aldridge, AA248

A bibliography of American county histories, Filby, P. William, DB139

Bibliography of American directories through 1860, Spear, Dorothea N., AL8, CH401

A bibliography of American doctoral dissertations in classical studies and related fields, Thompson, Lawrence Sidney, BE1009, DA97

A bibliography of American educational history, CB29

Bibliography of American fiction, 1919–1988, BE468, BE472

Bibliography of American folk art for the year, BG10

Bibliography of American historical societies, Griffin, Appleton Prentiss Clark, AD262

Bibliography of American hymnals, Ellinwood, Leonard, BC315

────── Lockwood, Elizabeth, BC315

Bibliography of American imprints to 1901, AA402

Bibliography of American literature, Blanck, Jacob Nathaniel, BE400, BE405

Bibliography of American natural history, Meisel, Max, EG71

Bibliography of American newspapers, 1690–1820, AE19

Bibliography of American publications on East Central Europe, 1945–1967, Byrnes, Robert Francis, DC39

A bibliography of American studies on the French Renaissance, (1500–1600), Will, Samuel F., BE1207

Bibliography of Anabaptism, 1520–1630, Hillerbrand, Hans J., BC362

A bibliography of Anglo-Welsh literature, 1900–1965, Jones, Brynmor, BE813

Bibliography of anthropology of India, Ray, Shyamal Kumar, CE110

A bibliography of applied numismatics in the fields of Greek and Roman archaeology and the fine arts, Vermeule, Cornelius Clarkson, BG176

Bibliography of Arabic linguistics, Bakalla, M. H., BD204

Bibliography of arms control verification, Scrivener, David, CJ679

Bibliography of Asian studies, DE8, DE196

Bibliography of astronomy, 1881–1898, on microfilm, International Astronomical Union, EC14

Bibliography of astronomy, 1970–1979, Martin, Sarah S., EC2

—— Seal, Robert A., EC2, EC18

Bibliography of Australia, Ferguson, John Alexander, AA942, DF26

Bibliography of Australian art, Hanks, Elizabeth Finn, BF76

A bibliography of Australian multicultural writers, DF24

Bibliography of Australian music, Crisp, Deborah, BJ28

Bibliography of Australian women's literature, 1795–1990, Adelaide, Debra, BE845, DF21

Bibliography of Bali, Stuart-Fox, David J., DE178

Bibliography of bibliographies in American literature, Nilon, Charles H., BE410

A bibliography of bibliographies in religion, Barrow, John Graves, BC4

Bibliography of bibliographies of the languages of the world, Troike, Rudolph C., BD3, BD8

A bibliography of bibliographies on India, Kalia, D. R., AA75

A bibliography of bibliographies on Malaysia, Ding, Choo Ming, DE227

A bibliography of bibliographies on patristics, Stewardson, Jerry L., BC298

Bibliography of bioethics, EH237, EH238

A bibliography of birds, Strong, Reuben Myron, EG276

Bibliography of black music, De Lerma, Dominique-René, BJ31

Bibliography of books and articles on Liberia as edited in German speaking countries since 1960, Kappel, Robert, DD173

—— Korte, Werner, DD173

Bibliography of books and pamphlets on the history of agriculture in the United States, 1607–1967, Schlebecker, John T., EJ72

Bibliography of books in Polish or relating to Poland published outside Poland since Sept. 1st, 1939, Polish University College (London, England), AA767

A bibliography of Brazilian bibliographies, Basseches, Bruno, AA28

Bibliography of British and American travel in Italy to 1860, Pine-Coffin, R. S., DC424

Bibliography of British and Irish municipal history, Martin, Geoffrey Haward, DC348

—— McIntyre, Sylvia, DC348

A bibliography of British business histories, Goodall, Francis, CH391

Bibliography of British economic and social history, Chaloner, William Henry, DC1, DC272

—— Richardson, R. C., DC1

Bibliography of British gardens, Desmond, Ray, BF285

Bibliography of British history, DC270, DC304, DC317, DC329, DC330

Bibliography of British history (1700–1715) with special reference to the reign of Queen Anne, Morgan, William Thomas, DC316

Bibliography of British history, 1789–1851, Brown, Lucy M., DC328

Bibliography of British history, 1851–1914, Hanham, Harold John, DC330

Bibliography of British history, Stuart period, 1603–1714, Davies, Godfrey, DC315

Bibliography of British history, Tudor period, 1485–1603, Read, Conyers, DC318

Bibliography of British industrial relations, Bain, George Sayers, CH625, CH638

—— Woolven, Gillian B., CH638

Bibliography of British industrial relations, 1971–1979, Bain, George Sayers, CH625

—— Bennett, J. D., CH625

A bibliography of British military history, from the Roman invasions to the Restoration, 1660, Bruce, A. P. C., DC271

A bibliography of British municipal history, Gross, Charles, DC348

Bibliography of British newspapers, AE55

A bibliography of British railway history, Ottley, George, CH461

A bibliography of Cameroon, DeLancey, Mark W., DD136

Bibliography of Canadian bibliographies, Lochhead, Douglas, AA22

A bibliography of Canadian demography, Stone, Martha, CG116

A bibliography of Canadian folklore in English, Fowke, Edith F., CF65

A bibliography of Canadian imprints, 1751–1800, Tremaine, Marie, AA453

A bibliography of Canadian theatre history, 1583–1975, BH39

Bibliography of Canadian urban history, Armstrong, F. H., DB210

—— Artibise, Alan F. J., DB210

—— Baker, Melvin, DB210

A bibliography of Canadiana, Toronto Public Libraries, DB188

Bibliography of Canadiana published in Great Britain, 1519–1763, Morley, W. F. E., DB188

—— Waldon, Freda Farrell, DB188

A bibliography of Caribbean migration and Caribbean immigrant communities, Brana-Shute, Rosemary, CE77

The bibliography of cartography, Library of Congress. Geography and Map Division, CL253

A bibliography of Celtic-Latin literature, 400–1200, Lapidge, Michael, BE1042

Bibliography of census publications in India, India. Office of the Registrar General, CG391

A bibliography of Ceylon, Goonetileke, H. A. I., DE259

Bibliography of child psychiatry and child mental health, with a selected list of films, Berlin, Irving Norman, EH370

Bibliography of Chinese academic serials, pre-1949, Tung, Julia, AD189

A bibliography of Christian philosophy and contemporary issues, McLean, George F., BC218

A bibliography of comedias sueltas in the University of Toronto library, University of Toronto. Library, BE1471

Bibliography of comparative literature, Baldensperger, Fernand, BE12, BE13, BE41

—— Friederich, Werner P., BE13, BE41

Bibliography of computer-aided language learning, Stevens, Vance, BD73

—— Sussex, Roland, BD73

—— Tuman, Walter Vladimir, BD73

Bibliography of congressional geology, Pestana, Harold R., EF37

Bibliography of contemporary African-American literature, Burnett, Elsie, BE527

The bibliography of contemporary American fiction, 1945–1988, McPheron, William, BE476

The bibliography of contemporary American poetry, 1945–1985, McPheron, William, BE495

A bibliography of contemporary linguistic research, Gazdar, Gerald, BD4

Bibliography of costume, Hiler, Hilaire, BG92

Bibliography of creative African writing, Dressler, Claus Peter, BE1531

—— Jahn, Janheinz, BE1505, BE1512, BE1531

Bibliography of cricket, BK71

—— Padwick, E. W., BK71

Bibliography of critical Arthurian literature for the years 1922–1929, Parry, John J., BE339

Bibliography of critical Arthurian literature for the years 1930–1935, Parry, John J., BE339

—— Schlauch, Margaret A., BE339

A bibliography of criticism of contemporary Chicano literature, Eger, Ernestina N., BE557

Bibliography of cultivated trees and shrubs hardy in the cooler temperate regions of the Northern Hemisphere, Rehder, Alfred, EG204

Bibliography of current computing literature, EK166

Bibliography of dancing, Beaumont, Cyril William, BH133

—— Magriel, Paul David, BH134

Bibliography of Danish law, CK207

Bibliography of Danish literature in translation, 1950–1980, Schroeder, Carol L., BE1112

A bibliography of David Hume and of Scottish philosophy from Francis Hutcheson to Lord Balfour, Jessop, Thomas Edmund, BB74

A bibliography of dentistry in America, 1790–1840, Asbell, Milton B., EH264

A bibliography of design in Britain, 1851–1970, Coulson, Anthony J., BG6

Bibliography of discographies, BJ383

Bibliography of dissertations in classical studies, Thompson, Lawrence Sidney, BE1009, DA97

Bibliography of dissertations in geography, 1901 to 1969, Browning, Clyde Eugene, CL26

Bibliography of doctoral dissertations, AG52, CA21

A bibliography of doctoral dissertations accepted by Indian universities, 1857–1970, Inter-University Board of India and Ceylon, AG52

A bibliography of doctoral dissertations in television and radio, Sparks, Kenneth R., BH296

Bibliography of doctoral dissertations in the humanities and the social sciences submitted to Israeli universities, AG53, CA20

Bibliography of doctoral dissertations relating to American architectural history, 1897–1991, Goode, James M., BF227

A bibliography of Dravidian linguistics, Agesthialingom, S., BD226

A bibliography of Dutch publications on the Middle East and Islam 1945–1981, Groot, Alexander H. de, DE30

Bibliography of Dutch seventeenth century political thought, Klashorst, G. O. van de, DC455

Bibliography of early American architecture, Roos, Frank John, BF204, BF221

Bibliography of early English law books, Beale, Joseph Henry, CK212

Bibliography of early secular American music (18th century), Sonneck, Oscar George Theodore, BJ64, BJ68

A bibliography of eastern Asiatic botany, Merrill, Elmer Drew, EG106

Bibliography of economic geology, EF50

A bibliography of eighteenth century legal literature, Adams, J. N., CK4

A bibliography of encyclopedias and dictionaries dealing with military, naval and maritime affairs, 1577–1971, Craig, Hardin, Jr, CJ561

Bibliography of English corantos and periodical newsbooks, 1620–1642, Dahl, Folke, AE56

A bibliography of English history to 1485, DC304

A bibliography of English poetical miscellanies, 1521–1750, Case, Arthur Ellicott, BE699, BE705

Bibliography of English printed drama to the Restoration, Greg, Walter Wilson, BE658, BE663

Bibliography of English printed tragedy, 1565–1900, Stratman, Carl Joseph, BE654

Bibliography of English translations from medieval sources, Evans, Austin Patterson, DA164

—— Farrar, Clarissa Palmer, BE45, DA164

Bibliography of English translations from medieval sources, 1943–1967, Ferguson, Mary Anne Heyward, BE45, DA164

A bibliography of Ethiopian bibliographies, 1932–1972, Girma Makonnen, AA71

A bibliography of etiquette books published in America before 1900, Bobbitt, Mary Reed, AL149

A bibliography of Etruscan culture and archaeology, 1498–1981, Fay, George Emory, CA423

Bibliography of European economic and social history, Aldcroft, Derek Howard, DC1, DC272

—— Rodger, Richard, DC272

A bibliography of Fiji, Tonga, and Rotuma, Snow, Philip A., DF7

Bibliography of film bibliographies, BH173

A bibliography of finance, Brealey, Richard A., CH224
—— Masui, Mitsuzō, CH207
Bibliography of Finnish periodicals, 1782–1955, AD89
Bibliography of Finnish periodicals, 1956–1977, AD89
A bibliography of fishes, Dean, Bashford, EG286
Bibliography of fossil vertebrates, EF237
—— Camp, Charles Lewis, EF228, EF230
—— Vanderhoof, V. L., EF230
Bibliography of fossil vertebrates exclusive of North America, 1509–1927, Romer, Alfred Sherwood, EF233
Bibliography of French Bibles, Chambers, Bettye Thomas, BC98
Bibliography of French-Canadian poetry, Fraser, Ian Forbes, BE839
A bibliography of French plays on microcards, Thompson, Lawrence Sidney, BE1185
Bibliography of French seventeenth century studies, Modern Language Association of America. French III, BE1138
A bibliography of geographic thought, CL5
Bibliography of geography, Harris, Chauncy Dennison, CL12
Bibliography of geoscience theses of the United States and Canada, EF42
Bibliography of German culture in America to 1940, Pochmann, Henry August, CC329, CC330
Bibliography of German-language photographic publications, 1839–1984, BF329
Bibliography of German law in English and German, CK211
The bibliography of German literature, Batts, Michael S., BE1215
Bibliography of Germany studies, 1945–1971, Hersch, Gisela, DC238
Bibliography of Ghana, 1930–1961, Johnson, Albert Frederick, AA859, DD162
Bibliography of Goa and the Portuguese in India, Scholberg, Henry, DE161
A bibliography of Hispanic dictionaries, Fabbri, Maurizio, AC752
Bibliography of historical works issued in the United Kingdom, University of London. Institute of Historical Research, DA12
The bibliography of human behavior, Caton, Hiram, CA10, CD8
Bibliography of Hungarian dictionaries, 1410–1963, Halasz de Beky, I. L., AC500
Bibliography of hydrology, American Geophysical Union, EF126
Bibliography of hydrometry, Kolupaila, Steponas, EK100
Bibliography of Indian art, history & archaeology, Jagdish Chandra, BF27
A bibliography of Indian bibliographies, 1961–1980, Kochukoshy, K. K., AA76
A bibliography of Indian English, Central Institute of English and Foreign Languages, Hyderabad, BE1563
A bibliography of Indian folk literature, Handoo, Jawaharlal, CF96
Bibliography of Indian philosophies, BB18
A bibliography of Indology, Kanitkar, J. M., CE109
Bibliography of Indonesian publications, Anderson, Benedict R., AD196
Bibliography of industrial relations in the railroad industry, Morris, James Oliver, CH460
A bibliography of insurance history, Nelli, Humbert O., CH504
Bibliography of International Geographic Congresses, 1871–1976, Kish, George, CL15
A bibliography of Iran, Nawabi, Y. M., BD195, DE186
A bibliography of Irish ethnology and folk tradition, Danaher, Kevin, CF81
Bibliography of Irish history, National Library of Ireland, DC397
Bibliography of Irish linguistics and literature, 1942–71, Baumgarten, Rolf, BD178

Bibliography of Irish philology and manuscript literature, Best, Richard I., BD178
Bibliography of Irish philology and of printed Irish literature, National Library of Ireland, BD178
A bibliography of Israel, Alexander, Yonah, DE191
Bibliography of Israel law in English and other European languages, Wegner, Judith Romney, CK231
Bibliography of Israeli law in European languages, Sanilevici, Renée, CK231
Bibliography of Israeli politics, Mahler, Gregory S., CJ438
Bibliography of Italian linguistics, BD161
A bibliography of jazz, Merriam, Alan P., BJ305
Bibliography of Jewish art, Mayer, Leo Ary, BF194
Bibliography of Jewish bibliographies, Shunami, Shlomo, BC519
Bibliography of Jewish music, Sendrey, Alfred, BJ19
Bibliography of Jewish numismatics, Mayer, Leo Ary, BF194, BG174
Bibliography of landscape architecture, environmental design, and planning, Powell, Antoinette Paris, BF288
Bibliography of Latin American and Caribbean bibliographies, 1985–1989, Loroña, Lionel V., AA24
Bibliography of Latin American bibliographies, Cordeiro, Daniel Raposo, AA24
—— Gropp, Arthur Eric, AA24, AA25
Bibliography of Latin American bibliographies, 1975–1979, Piedracueva, Haydée, AA24
Bibliography of Latin American bibliographies, 1980–1984, Loroña, Lionel V., AA24
A bibliography of Latin American bibliographies published in periodicals, Gropp, Arthur Eric, AA25
Bibliography of Latin American folklore, Boggs, Ralph Steele, CF61
A bibliography of Latin American theater criticism, 1940–1974, Lyday, Leon F., BE899
Bibliography of Latvian publications published outside Latvia, AA739
Bibliography of law and economics, CK7
Bibliography of law and journalism, Swindler, William F., AE135
Bibliography of legal festschriften, CK6
Bibliography of Levant geology, Avnimelech, Moshe A., EF22
A bibliography of librarianship, Burton, Margaret, AK11
Bibliography of library economy, Cannons, Harry George Turner, AK9, AK12
A bibliography of literary contributions to Nigerian periodicals, 1946–1972, Lindfors, Bernth, BE1531
Bibliography of literary criticism, BE22
A bibliography of Malawi, Brown, Edward E., DD176
Bibliography of Malay and Arabic periodicals published in the Straits Settlements and peninsular Malay states 1876–1941, Roff, William R., AD205
Bibliography of Malaysia & Singapore, Karni, Rahadi S., DE229, DE255
The bibliography of marketing research methods, Dickinson, John R., CH577
A bibliography of master's theses in geography, Stuart, Merrill M., CL27
Bibliography of mathematical logic, EB15
Bibliography of mathematical works printed in America through 1850, Karpinski, Louis Charles, EB11
A bibliography of Mauritian government publications, 1955–1978, Deerpalsingh, S., AF234, DD179
Bibliography of Mauritius, (1502–1954), Mauritius. Archives Dept, DD179
A bibliography of medical and biomedical biography, Morton, Leslie Thomas, EH219
Bibliography of medical reviews, EH64, EH66
Bibliography of medieval drama, Stratman, Carl Joseph, BE237, BE635
A bibliography of Melanesian bibliographies, Filer, Colin, AA77

Bibliography of meteorology, United States. Army. Signal Corps, EF142
Bibliography of Mexican American history, Meier, Matt S., CC448
A bibliography of middle Scots poets, Geddie, William, BE810
A bibliography of military name lists from pre-1675 to 1900, Horowitz, Lois, AJ30
A bibliography of modern British novelists, Stanton, Robert J., BE685
Bibliography of modern Hebrew literature in English translation, Goell, Yohai, BE1575
Bibliography of modern Hebrew literature in translation, Goell, Yohai, BE1576
Bibliography of modern Icelandic literature in translation, Mitchell, Phillip Marshall, BE1287
Bibliography of modern Indian art, Ghose, D. C., BF27
A bibliography of modern Irish and Anglo-Irish literature, Kersnowski, Frank L., BE804
Bibliography of Monaco, Handley-Taylor, Geoffrey, DC449
Bibliography of mono- and multilingual dictionaries and glossaries of technical terms used in geography, as well as in related natural and social sciences, Meynen, Emil, CL53
Bibliography of morphology, 1960–1985, Beard, Robert, BD43
Bibliography of Moslem numismatics, India excepted, Mayer, Leo Ary, BG174
The bibliography of museum and art gallery publications and audiovisual aids in Great Britain and Ireland, 1977–80, BF48
Bibliography of music dictionaries, Coover, James B., BJ12
Bibliography of musical literature, BJ8
Bibliography of national filmographies, Gebauer, Dorothea, BH164
•*Bibliography of native North Americans on disc*, CC412
Bibliography of Nepal, DE235
Bibliography of Nepalese art, Jagdish Chandra, BF27
A bibliography of Nepalese languages and linguistics, BD227
A bibliography of Netherlandic dictionaries, Claes, Frans M., AC300
Bibliography of new religious movements in primal societies, Turner, Harold W., BC19
Bibliography of New Testament literature, 1900–1950, Akaishi, Tadashi, BC118
—— Bowman, John Wick, BC118
—— San Francisco Theological Seminary, San Anselmo, Calif. Department of New Testament Literature. Graduate Seminar in New Testament, BC118
A bibliography of New Zealand bibliographies, New Zealand Library Association, AA87
A bibliography of nineteenth century legal literature, Adams, J. N., CK5
Bibliography of non-periodical literature on Sierra Leone, 1925–1966, Zell, Hans M., DD205
Bibliography of North American dissertations on Old English, BD101, BE730
Bibliography of North American folklore and folksong, Haywood, Charles, CF64, CF67
Bibliography of North American geology, EF36, EF48, EF49, EF53
Bibliography of novels related to American frontier and colonial history, Van Derhoof, Jack Warner, BE470
A bibliography of numismatic books printed before 1800, Lipsius, Johann Gottfried, BG173
A bibliography of nursing literature, Thompson, Alice M. C., EH273
Bibliography of Oceanic linguistics, Klieneberger, H. R., BD232
Bibliography of official statistical yearbooks and bulletins, Westfall, Gloria, CG14
Bibliography of old Catalan texts, Concheff, Beatrice Jorgensen, BE1433
A bibliography of old French lyrics, Linker, Robert White, BE1200

Bibliography of old Norse-Icelandic romances, Kalinke, Marianne E., BE1090

Bibliography of Old Norse-Islandic studies, BD129, BE1083

Bibliography of Old Spanish texts, BE1433

Bibliography of Ontario history, 1867–1976, Bishop, Olga B., DB212

Bibliography of Pacific/Asian American materials in the Library of Congress, Yu, Elena S. H., CC411

Bibliography of periodical articles relating to the South Pacific, DF2

Bibliography of periodical literature in musicology and allied fields, Daugherty, D. H., BJ109
—— Ellinwood, Leonard, BJ109
—— Hill, Richard S., BJ109

Bibliography of periodicals of Russia, 1901–1916, AD142

Bibliography of Persia, AA905

Bibliography of Persian books from 921 to 1921, AA907

Bibliography of Philippine bibliographies, 1593– 1961, Bernardo, Gabriel Adriano, AA82

Bibliography of Philippine bibliographies, 1962– 1985, Jacinto, Yolanda E., AA82
—— Orbase, Lily O., AA82

A bibliography of philosophical bibliographies, Guerry, Herbert, BB11

Bibliography of philosophy, Rand, Benjamin, BB26

Bibliography of picaresque literature, Laurenti, Joseph L., BE1475

A bibliography of pidgin and creole languages, Reinecke, John E., BD55

Bibliography of place-name literature, Sealock, Richard B., CL177

Bibliography of plant viruses and index to research, Beale, Helen Purdy, EG89

Bibliography of Polish dictionaries, Lewanski, Richard Casimir, AC193

Bibliography of Polish serials, AD133

Bibliography of population literature in the Arab world, CG371

Bibliography of poverty and related topics in Costa Rica, Carvajal, Manuel J., DB304

A bibliography of pre-independence Zambia, Rau, William E., DD248, DD249

A bibliography of pre-Islamic Persia, Pearson, J. D., DE187

A bibliography of presidential commissions, committees, councils, panels, and task forces, 1961–1972, Tollefson, Alan M., AF132

A bibliography of printing, with notes and illustrations, Bigmore, Edward Clements, AA266

Bibliography of proceedings of international meetings, AL33

Bibliography of publications issued by Unesco or under its auspices, United Nations Educational, Scientific and Cultural Organization, AF60

Bibliography of publications of the Academy of Sciences of the USSR, AL55

A bibliography of publications on Old English literature to the end of 1972, Greenfield, Stanley B., BE728

Bibliography of publications on the New Zealand Maori and the Moriori of the Chatham Islands, Taylor, Clyde Romer Hughes, DF8

Bibliography of published articles on American Presbyterianism, 1901–1980, Parker, Harold M., BC377

A bibliography of published works on Irish foreign relations, 1921–1978, Maguire, Maria, DC396

A bibliography of recent literature on Macedonian, Serbo-Croatian, and Slovene languages, Lenček, Rado L., BD189

Bibliography of regional statistical handbooks in the U.S.S.R, CG300

Bibliography of religion in the South, Lippy, Charles H., BC29

Bibliography of reports arising out of meetings held by international organizations, Tew, Eyvind S., AL33

Bibliography of reproduction, EJ99

Bibliography of research in Japanese literature, BE1583

Bibliography of research projects reports, United States. Work Projects Administration, AA443

Bibliography of research studies in music education, 1932–1948, Larson, W. S., BJ164

Bibliography of rhetoric and public address, BE349

Bibliography of rivers and harbors and related fields in hydraulic engineering, Rowe, Robert Seaman, EK101

Bibliography of Roman drama and poetry and ancient fiction, BE1038

Bibliography of Russian and East European history, DC37

Bibliography of Russian émigré literature, 1918– 1968, Foster, Ludmilla A., BE1390

Bibliography of Russian literature in English translation to 1900, Line, Maurice B., BE1409

Bibliography of Russian literature in English translation to 1945, BE1409

A bibliography of Sanskrit language and literature, Satyaprakash, BD198

A bibliography of Scandinavian dictionaries, Haugen, Eva Lund, AC190

A bibliography of Scandinavian languages and linguistics, 1900–1970, Haugen, Einar, BD130

Bibliography of Scandinavian linguistics, BD130

Bibliography of scientific and industrial reports, EA64

Bibliography of Scotland, AA696

Bibliography of Scriptures in African languages, Coldham, Geraldine Elizabeth, BC95, BC99

Bibliography of seeds, Barton, Lela Viola, EG99

Bibliography of semiotics, 1975–1985, Eschbach, Achim, BD53

A bibliography of Shinto in Western languages, Kato, Genchi, BC570

Bibliography of Sierra Leone, Luke, Harry, DD205

A bibliography of Sierra Leone, 1925–1967, Williams, Geoffrey J., DD205

A bibliography of sixteenth-century Italian verse collections in the University of Toronto Library, University of Toronto. Library, BE1318

A bibliography of skaldic studies, Hollander, Lee Milton, BE1089

A bibliography of Slavic dictionaries, Lewanski, Richard Casimir, AC193

A bibliography of Slavic mythology, Kulikowski, Mark, CF34

Bibliography of society, ethics, and the life sciences, Sollitto, Sharmon, EH237
—— Veach, Robert M., EH237

A bibliography of songsters printed in America before 1821, Lowens, Irving, BJ280

Bibliography of sources on Yugoslavia, Matulic, Rusko, DC609

Bibliography of South African history, Liebenberg, B. J., DD223
—— Smith, K. W., DD223
—— Spies, S. B., DD223

A bibliography of South Asian folklore, Kirkland, Edwin Capers, CF97

The bibliography of South Asian periodicals, AD215

Bibliography of Southern Appalachia, Ross, Charlotte T., DB157

Bibliography of Soviet statistical handbooks, 1956 to 1991, Heleniak, Timothy E., CG300

A bibliography of Spanish-American writers, BE871

A bibliography of Spanish plays on microcards, Thompson, Lawrence Sidney, BE1470

Bibliography of stained glass, Evans, David, BG51

A bibliography of state bibliographies, 1970–1982, Parish, David W., AF143

Bibliography of statistical bibliographies, Lancaster, Henry Oliver, EB13

Bibliography of statistical literature, Kendall, Maurice George, EB12

A bibliography of studies and translations of modern Chinese literature, 1918–1942, Gibbs, Donald A., BE1553

A bibliography of studies on Hindi language and linguistics, Aggarwal, Narindar K., BD199

Bibliography of stylistics and related criticism, 1967–83, Bennett, James R., BE374

Bibliography of the American theatre, excluding New York City, Stratman, Carl Joseph, BH43, BH46

A bibliography of the Anglo-Egyptian Sudan, Hill, Richard Leslie, DD226

A bibliography of the architecture, arts, and crafts of Islam to 1st Jan. 1960, Creswell, Keppel Archibald Cameron, BF17

A bibliography of the arts of Africa, Western, Dominique Coulet, BF38, BG4

A bibliography of the Australian aborigines and the native peoples of Torres Strait to 1959, Greenway, John, CE113

Bibliography of the Blackfoot, Dempsey, Hugh A., CC420
—— Moir, Lindsay, CC420

Bibliography of the British Army, Bruce, A. P. C., DC271

Bibliography of the Catawba, Blumer, Thomas J., CC420

Bibliography of the Chickasaw, Hoyt, Anne Kelley, CC420

Bibliography of the Chinese language, Yang, Teresa S., BD221
—— Yang, Winston L. Y., BD221

A bibliography of the collective biography of Spanish America, Toro, Josefina de, AH113

Bibliography of the Communist International (1919–1979), Kahan, Vilém, CJ503, CJ511

Bibliography of the Communist problem in the United States, Fund for the Republic, New York, CJ507

Bibliography of the continental Reformation, Bainton, Roland Herbert, DC26

A bibliography of the dance collection of Doris Niles and Serge Leslie, Leslie, Serge, BH133

Bibliography of the Dead Sea Scrolls, 1948–1957, La Sor, William Sanford, BC112

A bibliography of the dog, Jones, E. Gwynne, EJ144

A bibliography of the English language from the invention of printing to the year 1800, Alston, R. C., BD97

A bibliography of the English printed drama to the Restoration, Greg, Walter Wilson, BE643

Bibliography of the English-speaking Caribbean, DB405

Bibliography of the Finnish newspapers, 1771–1963, AE49

Bibliography of the Gold Coast, Cardinall, Allan Wolsey, DD98, DD162

Bibliography of the history of art, BF33, BF34, BF43

Bibliography of the history of British art, BF13

Bibliography of the history of electronics, Shiers, George, EK127

Bibliography of the history of medicine, EH2, EH199

Bibliography of the history of medicine of the United States and Canada, 1939–1960, Miller, Genevieve, EH204

Bibliography of the history of technology, Ferguson, Eugene S., EA228

A bibliography of the history of Wales, Jones, Philip Henry, DC370

A bibliography of the Hungarian Revolution, 1956, Halász de Beky, I. L., DC380

Bibliography of the International Congresses of Philosophy, Geldsetzer, Lutz, BB17

Bibliography of the International Court of Justice, International Court of Justice, CK110

A bibliography of the Iran-Iraq borderland, McLachlan, Keith Stanley, DE35

Bibliography of the Japanese Empire, DE204
—— Wenckstern, Friedrich von, DE204

Bibliography of the Jews in Romania, Ancel, Jean, DC493

Bibliography of the languages of native California, Bright, William, CC420

A bibliography of the literature on British and Irish labour law, Hepple, B. A., CH677

A bibliography of the literature on North American climates of the past 13,000 years, Grayson, Donald K., EF161

Bibliography of the literature relating to New Zealand, Hocken, T. M., AA946, DF42*

Bibliography of the literature translated into Polish, BE1347

Bibliography of the Negro in Africa and America, Work, Monroe Nathan, CC368

A bibliography of the novel and short story in French from the beginning of printing till 1600, De Jongh, William Frederick Jekel, BE1187

Bibliography of the Osage, Wilson, Terry P., CC420

Bibliography of the peace movement before 1899, Meulen, Jacob ter, CJ675

Bibliography of the peoples and cultures of mainland Southeast Asia, Dotson, Lillian Ota, DE119
——— Embree, John Fee, DE119

A bibliography of the periodical literature on the Acts of the Apostles, 1962–1984, Mills, Watson E., BC114

A bibliography of the philosophy of science, 1945–1981, Blackwell, Richard J., EA11

A bibliography of the philosophy of technology, Mitcham, Carl, EA18

Bibliography of the Prairie Provinces to 1953, Peel, Bruce Braden, DB213, DB216

Bibliography of the Reform, 1450–1648, Commission Internationale d'Histoire Ecclésiastique Comparée. British Sub-Commission, DC27

Bibliography of the registers (printed) of the universities, inns of court, colleges and schools of Great Britain and Ireland, Hart, Hester E. R., AH234

A bibliography of the research in tissue culture, Murray, Margaret Ransome, EG7

A bibliography of the romance and related forms in Spanish America, Simmons, Merle Edwin, BE878

Bibliography of the Scottish national movement (1844–1973), Fraser, Kenneth C., CJ375

Bibliography of the sequence novel, Kerr, Elizabeth Margaret, BE255

Bibliography of the seventeenth-century novel in France, Baldner, R. W., BE1190
——— Williams, R. C., BE1190

Bibliography of the Sioux, Hoover, Herbert T., CC420
——— Marken, Jack W., CC420

Bibliography of the Sudan, 1938–1958, el Nasri, Abdel Rahman, DD226

Bibliography of the Summer Institute of Linguistics, Wares, Alan Campbell, BD9

Bibliography of the Summer Institute of Linguistics, Philippines, 1953–1984, Cook, Marjorie, BD233

Bibliography of the writings, general, special and periodical, forming the literature of philately, Crawford, James Ludovic Lindsay, BG201

Bibliography of the Wycliffe Bible Translators, Wares, Alan Campbell, BD9

Bibliography of theatre history in Canada, Ball, John, BH39

A bibliography of theatre technology, Howard, John T., BH50

A bibliography of theses & dissertations in broadcasting, 1920–1973, Kittross, John M., BH295

A bibliography of theses and dissertations on Portuguese topics completed in the United States and Canada, 1861–1983, Kettenring, N. Ernest, DC491

A bibliography of theses and dissertations on the subject of film, 1916–1979, Fielding, Raymond, BH176

Bibliography of theses in geology, 1958–63, Chronic, Halka, EF43, EF44
——— Chronic, John, EF43, EF44

Bibliography of theses in geology, 1964, Ward, Dederick C., EF44

Bibliography of theses in geology, 1965–66, O'Callaghan, T. C., EF44

Bibliography of theses written for advanced degrees in geology and related sciences at universities and colleges in the United States and Canada through 1957, Chronic, John, EF43

Bibliography of Tibetan studies, DE268

Bibliography of tourism and travel research studies, reports, and articles, Goeldner, Charles R., CL374

Bibliography of translations from Russian scientific and technical literature, EA62

Bibliography of translations from the Japanese into western languages from the 16th century to 1912, Inada, Hide Ikehara, BE1584

Bibliography of Ukrainian literature in English and French, Piaseckyj, Oksana, BE1494

A bibliography of unfinished books in the English language, with annotations, Corns, Albert Reginald, AA662

A bibliography of U.S. newspaper bibliographies, Pluge, John, AE29

Bibliography of vertebrate paleontology and related subjects, EF50, EF227

A bibliography of Vietnamese magazines, newspapers and newsletters published in the United States and other countries, Pham, Henry Thuoc V., AD211

Bibliography of Wales, National Library of Wales, AA698, AD290, DC370

A bibliography of West African life and literature, Saint-Andre-Utudjian, Eliane, BE1507

Bibliography of Western European-Latin American relations, Wolf, Ulrike, DB264

Bibliography of women & literature, Boos, Florence Saunders, BE401

Bibliography of women writers from the Caribbean 1831–1986, Berrian, Brenda F., BE971

A bibliography of word formations in the Germanic languages, Seymour, Richard K., BD115

Bibliography of works about life-writing, BE213

A bibliography of works in English on early Russian history to 1800, Crowther, Peter A., DC575

Bibliography of works on accounting by American authors, Bentley, Harry Clark, CH247

Bibliography of works on Canadian foreign relations, 1945–1970, Page, Donald M., DB186

Bibliography of works on Canadian foreign relations, 1971–1975, Page, Donald M., DB186

Bibliography of works on Canadian foreign relations, 1976–1980, Barrett, Jane R., DB186
——— Beaumont, Jane, DB186

Bibliography of works on Canadian foreign relations, 1981–1985, Barrett, Jane R., DB186
——— Beaumont, Jane, DB186
——— Broadhead, Lee-Anne, DB186

Bibliography of works published in Nicaragua, González, Graciela, AA490

A bibliography of writings about New Zealand music published to the end of 1983, Harvey, D. R., BJ35

A bibliography of writings for the history of the English language, Fisiak, Jacek, BD100

Bibliography of writings on the English language from the beginning of printing to the end of 1922, Kennedy, Arthur Garfield, BD102

A bibliography of writings on varieties of English, 1965–1983, Viereck, Wolfgang, BD108

Bibliography of Yiddish books on the catastrophe and heroism, DA215

Bibliography of Zambiana theses and dissertations, 1930s–1989, Mwanza, Ilse, AG50, DD247

Bibliography on airport engineering, Li, Shu-t'ien, EK117

A bibliography on Bechuanaland, Mohome, Paulus, DD132

Bibliography on Buddhism, Hanayama, Shinsho, BC469

Bibliography on Cyprus, Coufoudakis, Evangelos, DC120

Bibliography on Eritrea, DD153

A bibliography on Far Eastern numismatology and a coin index, Coole, Arthur Braddan, BG171

A bibliography on foreign and comparative law, CK8

Bibliography on French and foreign new towns, Merlin, Pierre, BF273

Bibliography on geographic thought, 1950–1982, Wheeler, James O., CL5

Bibliography on Haiti, Lawless, Robert, DB441

A bibliography on herbs, herbal medicine, "natural" foods, and unconventional medical treatment, Andrews, Theodora, EH319

A bibliography on historical organization practices, Rath, Frederick L., BF117

Bibliography on Holocaust literature, Edelheit, Abraham J., DA215

A bibliography on Japanese Buddhism, BC464

Bibliography on Kenya, Webster, John B., DD108, DD165, DD167

Bibliography on Lesotho, Mohome, Paulus, DD169
——— Webster, John B., DD169

A bibliography on Liberia, Holsoe, Svend E., DD173

A bibliography on meteorites, Brown, Harrison Scott, EF206

Bibliography on peace research and peaceful international relations, Müller-Brettel, Marianne, CJ676

Bibliography on portraiture, Heppner, Irene, BF23

Bibliography on racism, Center for Minority Group Mental Health Programs (U.S.), CC314

A bibliography on South American economic affairs, Jones, Tom Bard, CH179

Bibliography on Soviet intelligence and security services, Rocca, Raymond G., CJ545

Bibliography on Sudan international relations, El-Fadil, Amal Eisa, DD228
——— Wawa, Yosa H., DD228

Bibliography on Swaziland, Mohome, Paulus, DD232
——— Webster, John B., DD232

A bibliography on temples of the ancient Near East and Mediterranean world, Parry, Donald W., BF220

Bibliography on the colonial Germans of North America, Meynen, Emil, CC330

Bibliography on the fatigue of materials, Mann, John Yeates, EK256

A bibliography on the foreign relations of the Republic of Turkey, 1919–1967, and brief biographies of Turkish statesmen, Tamkoç, Metin, DC539

Bibliography on the petroleum industry, DeGolyer, Everette Lee, EK299

Bibliography on the society, culture, and political economy of post-independence Botswana, Kerven, Carol, DD131

Bibliography on Uralic studies, DC602

Bibliography on urban transport planning, BF272

Bibliography on urbanization in India, 1947–1976, Bose, Ashish, CC305

A bibliography on vernacular architecture, Hall, Robert de Zouche, BF215

Bibliography on world conflict and peace, Boulding, Elise, CJ664

Bibliography : Pakistan government and administration, 1970–1981, Khan, Mohamed Jameelur Rehman, CJ443, DE241

Biblioteca Americana de Nicaragua. *Bibliografía de libros y folletos publicados en Nicaragua (en 1942, o antes según fecha de publicación),* AA490

Biblioteca boliviana, René-Moreno, Gabriel, AA500, AA505

Biblioteca Centrală de Stat a Republicii Socialiste România. *Bibliografia Republicii Socialiste România,* AD323

Biblioteca Centrală Universitară Bucureşti. *Literatura română,* BE1378

Biblioteca Centrală Universitară Bucureşti Serviciul de Inormare şi Documentare. *Teze de doctorat,* AG40

Biblioteca cientifica cubana, Trelles y Govín, Carlos Manuel, AA563

Biblioteca de autores españoles, desde la formación del lenguaje hasta nuestros días, BE1441

Biblioteca geográfica cubana, Trelles y Govín, Carlos Manuel, AA563

Biblioteca hispano-americana (1493–1810), Medina, José Toribio, AA470

Biblioteca hispano americana septentrional, Beristain de Souza, José Mariano, AA459, AH99

Biblioteca hispano-chilena (1523–1817), Medina, José Toribio, AA516

Biblioteca histórica cubana, Trelles y Govín, Carlos Manuel, AA563

Biblioteca histórica de la filología castellana, Viñaza, Cipriano Muñoz y Manzano, BD170

Biblioteca Nacional (Brazil). *Bibliografia brasileira,* AA510

Biblioteca Nacional (Chile). *Bibliografía general de Chile,* AA514

——— *Impresos chilenos, 1776–1818,* AA514

Biblioteca Nacional (Costa Rica). *Boletín bibliográfico,* AA477

Biblioteca Nacional de Honduras. *Anuario bibliográfico hondureño,* AA486

Biblioteca Nacional de Lisboa. *Subsidios para a bibliografia da história local portuguêsa,* DC483

Biblioteca Nacional de México. *Anuario bibliográfico,* AA466

——— *Impresos mexicanos del siglo XVI (incunables americanos) en la Biblioteca Nacional de México, el Museo Nacional y el Archivo General de la Nación,* AA464

Biblioteca Nacional Instituto Bibliográfico Mexicano. *Bibliografía mexicana,* AA465

Biblioteca Nacional (Panama). *Bibliografía panameña,* AA492

Biblioteca Nacional (Paraguay). *Bibliografía paraguaya,* AA535

Biblioteca Nacional (Peru). *Anuario bibliográfico peruano,* AA543

——— *Bibliografía nacional,* AA538

——— *Catalogo de autores de la colección peruana,* AA544

Biblioteca Nacional Rubén Darío. *Nicaraguan national bibliography, 1800–1978,* AA491

Biblioteca Nacional (Spain). *Catálogo colectivo de obras impresas en los siglos XVI al XVIII existentes en las bibliotecas españolas,* AA812

——— *Catálogo de obras iberoamericanas y filipinas de la Biblioteca Nacional de Madrid,* DB268, DE245

——— *Catalogo general de incunables en bibliotecas españolas,* AA229

——— *Catálogo general de libros impresos, hasta 1981,* AA105

——— *Publicaciones periódicas existentes en la Biblioteca Nacional,* AD152

Biblioteca nazionale centrale. *Bollettino delle pubblicazioni italiane,* AA736

Biblioteca nazionale centrale di Firenze. *L'associazionismo operaio in Italia (1870–1900) nelle raccolte della Biblioteca nazionale centrale di Firenze,* DC428

——— *Bibliografia italiana,* AA725

——— *Bollettino delle pubblicazioni italiane ricevute per diritto di stampa,* AA726, AA727

——— *Catalogo cumulativo 1886–1957,* AA727

——— *Catalogo cumulativo stampa dalla Biblioteca nazionale centrale de firenze,* AD128

Biblioteca peruana, AA539

Bibliotecha danica og Dansk bogfortegnelse, Ehrencron-Müller, Holger, AA601

Biblioteka Jagiellońska. *Katalog czasopism polskich Biblioteki Jagiellońskiej,* AD134

Biblioteka Kombëtare (Albania). Sektori i Bibliografisë. *Bibliografia kombëtare e librit që botohet në RPS të Shqipërisë,* AA571

——— *Bibliografia kombëtare e RPS të Shqipërisë,* AD301

Biblioteka Kombëtare e Republikës Popullore të Shqiprise, AA571

Biblioteka Narodowa (Poland). *Polska prasa konspiracyjna (1939–1945) i powstania warszawskiego w zbiorach Biblioteki Narodowej,* AE66

Biblioteka Narodowa (Poland). Instytut Bibliograficzny. *Bibliografia wydawnictw ciągłych,* AD133

Biblioteki i tsentry informatsii akademiĭ nauk sotsialisticheskikh stran, AK117

Bibliotekscentralen (Denmark). *Dansk bogfortegnelse [for aarene] …,* AA606

Bibliotheca alchemica et chemica, Duveen, Denis I., EE11, EE12, EE17

Bibliotheca americana, Brown, John Carter, DB1

——— John Carter Brown Library, DB1

——— Roorbach, Orville Augustus, AA416, AA418

——— Sabin, Joseph, AA409

Bibliotheca americana vetustissima, Harrisse, Henry, DB3

Bibliotheca americana vetustissima : últimas adiciones, Sanz, Carlos, DB3

Bibliotheca anglo-judaica, Jacobs, Joseph, BC517

——— Wolf, Lucien, BC517

Bibliotheca annua, AA676

Bibliotheca anti-Quakeriana, Smith, Joseph, BC352

Bibliotheca belgica, AA577

——— Foppens, Jean François, AA580

Bibliotheca bibliographica historiae sanctae inquisitionis, Vekene, Emil van der, BC272

Bibliotheca bibliographica incunabula, Berkowitz, David Sandler, AA217

Bibliotheca bibliographica italica, Fumagalli, Giuseppe, AA51

——— Ottino, Giuseppe, AA51, AA54

Bibliotheca bibliographica nova, AA10

Bibliotheca britannica, Watt, Robert, AA664, BE581

Bibliotheca canadensis, Morgan, Henry James, AA450

Bibliotheca cartographica, CL227, CL232, CL247

Bibliotheca celtica, AA698, DC370

——— National Library of Wales, AD290

Bibliotheca chemica, Ferguson, John, EE11

——— Royal College of Science and Technology (Glasgow, Scotland). Andersonian Library, EE16

Bibliotheca cisorientalia, Bevis, Richard W., DE27

Bibliotheca danica, AA601, AA607

——— Bruun, Henry, DC131

Bibliotheca entomologica, EG331

Bibliotheca Estoniae historica, 1877–1917, Blumfeldt, Evald, DC134

Bibliotheca gastronomica, Simon, André Louis, EJ206

Bibliotheca geographica, CL6

Bibliotheca graeca, Fabricius, Johann Albert, BE993

Bibliotheca graeca et latina à l'usage des professeurs des humanités gréco-latines, Ooteghem, Jules van, BE1005

Bibliotheca hagiographica graeca, BC259

Bibliotheca hagiographica latina antiquae et mediae aetatis, BC259

Bibliotheca hagiographica orientalis, BC259

Bibliotheca Hertziana, Max-Planck Institut. *Kataloge der Bibliotheca Hertziana in Rom (Max-Planck-Institut),* BF52

Bibliotheca hispana, AA823

——— Casalbón, R., AA811

——— Pellicer, J. A., AA811

——— Sánchez, T. A., AA811

Bibliotheca hispana nova, Antonio, Nicolás, AA811

Bibliotheca hispana vetus, Antonio, Nicolás, AA811

Bibliotheca historica italo-judaica, Milano, Attilio, BC530

Bibliotheca historica medii aevi, Potthast, August, DA136

Bibliotheca historico-militaris, Pohler, Johann, CJ562

Bibliotheca historico-naturalis, Engelmann, Wilhelm, EG209

Bibliotheca indosinica, Cordier, Henri, DE96, DE119

Bibliotheca japonica, Cordier, Henri, DE195, DE198

Bibliotheca latina, mediae et infimae aetatis, Fabricius, Johann Albert, BE993

——— Mansi, Giovanni Domenico, BE993

——— Schöttgen, Christian, BE993

Bibliotheca lexicologiae Medii Aevi, Tremblay, Florent A., BD147

Bibliotheca Lindesiana, Crawford, James Ludovic Lindsay, BE631, BG201

Bibliotheca lusitana historica, critica, e cronologica, Barbosa Machado, Diogo, AA774

Bibliotheca missionum, BC304

Bibliotheca norvegica, AA757

Bibliotheca numaria, Lipsius, Johann Gottfried, BG173

Bibliotheca orientalis, Friederici, Karl, DE7

——— Zenker, Julius Theodor, DE7

Bibliotheca Osleriana, Osler, William, EH206

Bibliotheca philologica classica, BE991, BE1007

Bibliotheca Quakeristica, Smith, Joseph, BC352

Bibliotheca sanctorum, BC260

Bibliotheca scriptorum classicorum, Engelmann, Wilhelm, BE991, BE992, BE1001

Bibliotheca scriptorum classicorum et graecorum et latinorum, Klussmann, Rudolf, BE991, BE992, BE1001

Bibliotheca sinica, Cordier, Henri, DE127, DE129, DE137, DE138

Bibliotheca symbolica ecclesiae universalis, Schaff, Philip, BC311

Bibliotheca zoologica, EG216

——— Carus, J. Victor, EG209

——— Engelmann, Wilhelm, EG209

——— Taschenberg, O., EG209

The bibliotheck, BE808

Bibliotheek van Nederlandsche pamfletten, Muller, Frederik, AA752

Bibliothek des Johann Gottfried Herder-Instituts, Marburg/Lahn, Germany, Johann Gottfried Herder-Institut, Marburg. Bibliothek, DC44

Bibliothek für Zeitgeschichte. *Bibliothek für Zeitgeschichte—Weltskreisgsbücherei, Stuttgart,* DA169

Bibliothek für Zeitgeschichte—Weltskreisgsbücherei, Stuttgart, Bibliothek für Zeitgeschichte, DA169

Bibliothèque de documentation internationale contemporaine (France). *L'emigration russe,* AD300

Bibliothèque de la Construction moderne, BF237

Bibliothèque de la Sorbonne. *Inventaire des thèses de doctorat soutenues devant les universités françaises,* EA55

Bibliothèque dramatique de Monsieur de Soleinne, Soleinne, Martineau de, BE1184

Bibliothèque dramatique de Pont de Vesle, Lacroix, Paul, BE1184

Bibliothèque Forney. *L'architecture dans les collections de périodiques de la Bibliothèque Forney,* BF225

——— *Catalogue matières,* BG14

Bibliothèque Nationale (France). *Anonymes 1501–1800 : état au 31 décembre 1986,* AA101, AA613

——— *Bibliographie nationale française,* AF168

——— *Bibliographie nationale française. Livres,* AA634

——— *Bibliographie nationale française. Musique,* BJ78

——— *Catalogue des périodiques clandestins diffusés en France de 1939 à 1945,* AD91

——— *Catalogue général des livres imprimés,* AA101, AA613, BC400

——— *Catalogue général des périodiques du début du XVIIᵉ siècle à 1959,* AE52

——— *Les catalogues imprimés de la Bibliothèque Nationale,* AA202

——— *Inventaire du fonds français,* BF377

——— *Library guide for Brazilian studies,* DB351

——— *Les publications en série éditées au Sénégal, 1856–1982,* AD176, DD104

Bibliothèque Nationale (France). Département des Imprimés. *Catalogue de l'histoire de France,* DC143

——— *Catalogue de l'histoire de la révolution française,* DC177

——— *Catalogue des dissertations et écrits académiques provenant des échanges avec les universités étrangères et reçus par la Bibliothèque Nationale, 1882–1924,* AG8

Bibliothèque Nationale (France). Département des Périodiques. *Bibliographie de la presse française politique et d'information générale, 1865–1944,* AD92, AE50

——— *Catalogue collectif des périodiques du début du XVIIᵉ siècle à 1939,* AD231, AD232

——— *Périodiques slaves en caracatères cyrilliques,* AD231

——— *Périodiques slaves en caractères cyrilliques,* AD232

——— *Répertoire collectif des quotidiens et hebdomadaires,* AE51

——— *Répertoire de la presse et des publications périodiques françaises, 1977/1978,* AD97

—— *Répertoire national des annuaires français, 1958–1968,* AD93

Bibliothèque Nationale (France). Office général du livre. *Bibliographie nationale française. Livres,* AA634

—— *Bibliographie nationale française. Musique,* BJ78

Bibliothèque nationale (Luxembourg). *Bibliographie d'histoire luxembourgeoise,* DC446

Bibliothèque Nationale (Madagascar). *Bibliographie nationale de Madagascar,* AA864

Bibliothèque Nationale (Malagasy Republic). *Bibliographie nationale de Madagascar,* AA864

Bibliothèque Royale de Belgique. *Catalogue collectif belge et luxembourgeois des périodiques étrangers en cours de publication,* AD230

Bibliothèque universitaire de Tananarive. *Bibliographie nationale de Madagascar,* AA864

Bibliothèques et archives, Chauleur, André, AK135

Bibliothèques et musées des arts du spectacle dans le monde, BH5

Les bibliothèques françoises de La Croix du Maine et de Du Verdier, La Croix du Maine, François Grudé, AA616

Bibliyografyah le-toldot ha-Yehudim be-Romanyah, DC493

Bibliyografyah shel ʻalvodot dokṭor be-madaʻe ha-ruaḥ yeha-ḥevrah she-nikhtevu be-universiṭaʼot Yiśraʼel, Ilsar, Nira, AG53, CA20

al-Bibliyūghrāfiyā al-qawmīyah al-Tūnisīyah. al-Dawrīyāt al-ʻArabīyah, AD180

al-Bibliyūghrāfiyā al-waṭanīyah al-Maghrabīyah, AA867

al-Bibliyūghrāfiyā al-waṭanīyah al-Sūrīyah, AA936

al-Bibliyūghrāfiyā al-waṭanīyah al-Sūrīyah al-rājiʻah, Maktabat al-Asad (Damascus, Syria), AA937

Bibliyūghrāfiyā al-watanīyah al Urdunīyah, AA919

Bibliyūghrāfiyah al-ʻArabīyah al-Lībīyah, AA862

Bibliyūghrāfiyah al-Waṭanīyah al-ʻArabīyah al-Lībīyah, AA862

al-Bibliyūghrāfiyah al-waṭanīyah al-ʻIrāqīyah, AA908

Bibliyūghrāfiyah al-Watanīyah al-lībīyah, AA862

Bibljografija nazzjonali taʼ Malta, AA744

Biblograf, S.A. *Vox: new college Spanish and English dictionary,* AC741

The bicentennial guide to the American Revolution, Stember, Sol, DB95

Bickerman, Elias Joseph. *Chronology of the ancient world,* DA110

Bickley, Francis. *A guide to the reports on collections of manuscripts of private families, corporations and institutions in Great Britain and Ireland,* DC285

The bicyclist's sourcebook, Leccese, Michael, BK72

Bidwell, Percy Wells. *History of agriculture in the northern United States, 1620–1860,* EJ65, EJ68

Bidwell, Robin. *Bidwell's guide to government ministers,* CJ398

—— *Guide to African ministers,* CJ398

Bidwell's guide to government ministers, Bidwell, Robin, CJ398

Biebel, Susan C. *Library of Congress filing rules,* AK211

Bieber, Doris M. *Dictionary of legal abbreviations used in American law books,* CK42

Bieber, León Enrique. *Katalog der Quellen zur Geschichte Mexikos in der Bundesrepublik Deutschland, 1521–1945,* DB239

Bieber's dictionary of legal abbreviations, Prince, Mary Miles, CK42

Biebuyck, Daniel P. *The arts of Central Africa,* BG5

—— *Arts of Zaire,* BG5

Biedermann, Hans. *Dictionary of symbolism,* BF163

Biegel, David E. *Social networks and mental health,* CC29

—— *Social support networks,* CC29

Bielefelder Katalog Klassik, BJ386

Bien, Günther. *Historisches Wörterbuch der Philosophie,* BB40

Bienkowa, Maria Barbara. *Bibliografia bibliografii polskich, 1961–1970,* AA60

Bieńkowski, Wiesław. *Bibliografia historii Polski,* DC473

—— *Bibliografia polskiej,* DC473

Biennial review of anthropology, CE21

Biennial survey of education, United States. Office of Education, CB146

Bier, Robert A. *Geologic reference sources,* EF20

Bierley, Paul E. *The heritage encyclopedia of band music,* BJ294

Biesiekierski, Mieczysław. *Répertoire des thèses concernant les études slaves,* DC555

Bietenhard, Hans. *The new international dictionary of New Testament theology,* BC148

The big book of buttons, Hughes, Elizabeth, BG105

The big book of halls of fame in the United States and Canada, BK32

Big broadcast, 1920–1950, Buxton, Frank, BH311

—— Owen, Bill, BH311

Big business directory, CH345

Big gifts, Williams, M. Jane, AL141

Big powers and the German question 1941–1990, Doerr, Juergen C., DC231

Biggerstaff, Knight. *An annotated bibliography of selected Chinese reference works,* AA362, DE123

Biggins, Alan. *Argentina,* DB324

Biggs, Bruce. *The complete English-Maori dictionary,* AC608

Biggs, Frederick M. *Sources of Anglo-Saxon literary culture,* BE731

Bigler-Marschall, Ingrid. *Deutsches Theater-Lexikon,* BH113

Bigmore, Edward Clements. *A bibliography of printing, with notes and illustrations,* AA266

Bihalji-Merin, Oto. *World encyclopedia of naive art,* BF315

Bihiku, Koço. *History of Albanian literature,* BE1094

Bihl, Wolfdieter. *Bibliographie der Dissertationen über Judentum und jüdische Persönlichkeiten...,* BC529

Bijbelse encyclopedie, BC136

Bilancia, Philip R. *Dictionary of Chinese law and government,* CK47

Bilboul, Roger R. *Retrospective index to theses of Great Britain and Ireland, 1716–1950,* AG35

Bilderatlas zur Geschichte der deutschen Nationallitteratur, Könnecke, Gustav, BE1257

Bilets'kyi, O. I. *Ukrains'ki pys'mennyky,* BE1495

Bilgray, Albert. *Index to Jewish festschriften,* BC510

Bilingual dictionary of criminal justice terms (English/Spanish), Benmaman, Virginia, CK256

Bilingual dictionary of dental terms, Freiberg, Marcos A., EH254

Bilingual education, CB30
  abstracts, CB62
  databases, CB40, CB41

Bilingual education and English as a second language, CB30

Bilingualism
  bibliography, BD60, BD61

Le bilinguisme chez l'enfant et l'apprentissage d'une langue seconde, Afendras, Evangelos A., BD60

Billet, Fernand. *Chemical dictionary,* EE47

Billiards, BK68

Billick, David J. *Lexical studies of medieval Spanish texts,* BD165

Billings, Bruce H. *American Institute of Physics handbook,* ED32

Billion dollar directory, CH347

Bills, Garland D. *Spanish and English of United States Hispanos,* BD176

Billy, George J. *Shipping,* CH444

Bilodid, I. K. *Slovnyk ukrains'koi movy,* AC798

Bin dokuz yüz yirmi sekiz, bin dokuz yüz altmışbeş yılları arasında Türkiyede basılmış bibliyografyalarm bibliyografyası, AA68

Binder, Wolfgang. *Partial autobiographies,* BE563

Bingel, Marie Agnes. *Artists of the "young generation",* BF139

—— *Künstler der jungen Generation,* BF139

Bingham, Jane M. *Writers for children,* BE392

Binns, Margaret. *Sierra Leone,* DD18

Binns, Tony. *Sierra Leone,* DD18

Binstock, Robert H. *Handbook of aging and the social sciences,* CC97

Bio-base, AH8, AH9

Bio-bibliografia boliviana, AA501, AA502

Bio-bibliografía eclesiástica mexicana (1821–1943), Valverde Tellez, Emeterio, AH104

Bio-bibliographies in music, BJ221

Bio-bibliographisches Handbuch zur Sprachwissenschaft des 18. Jahrhunderts, BD66

Bio-bibliographisches Literaturlexikon Osterreichs, Giebisch, Hans, BE1095

Bio-bibliographisches Verzeichnis jüdischer Doktoren im 17. und 18. Jahrhundert, Komorowski, Manfred, EH223

Bio-bibliographisches Verzeichnis von Universitäts-u. Hochschuldrucken (Dissertationen) vom Ausgang des 16. bis Ende des 19. Jahrhunderts, Mundt, Hermann, AG32

A bio-bibliography for the history of the biochemical sciences since 1800, Fruton, Joseph S., EG319

A biobibliographical handbook of Bulgarian authors, BE1103

Biobibliography of British mathematics and its applications, Wallis, R. V., EB19

A biobibliography of native American writers, 1772–1924, Littlefield, Daniel F., BE551, CC420

—— Parins, James W., CC420

•*BioBusiness,* EG9

Biochemical engineering and biotechnology handbook, Atkinson, Bernard, EK43

Biochemistry, EG314, EG315, EG316, EG317, EG318, EG320, EG321, EG322, EG323, EG324, EG325
  bibliography, EG319
  biography, EG319
  handbooks, CD122

Biochemistry (by subject)
  history, EG319

Biochemistry abstracts : amino-acid, peptide, and protein, EG14

Biochemistry abstracts : biological membranes, EG14

Biochemistry abstracts : nucleic acids, EG14

Biochemists' handbook, Long, Cyril, EG322

Biocontrol news and information, EJ19

Bioethics, EH239
  bibliography, EH237, EH242
  databases, EH238
  dictionaries, EH240
  encyclopedias, EH241

Bioethics, Goldstein, Doris M., EH242

Bioethics reporter, EH239

Bioethics thesaurus, EH237, EH238

•*BIOETHICSLINE,* EH237, EH238

BioExpress, EG13

Biofeedback, Butler, Francine, CD115

Biográf Szerkesztőség. *Magyar ki kicsoda 1990,* AH253

Biografia italica, Manzoni, Cesare, AH266

Biografias de la literatura boliviana, Guzman, Augusto, BE922

Biografias de la nueva literatura boliviana, Guzman, Augusto, BE922

Biografías de Mexicanos distinguidos, Sosa, Francisco, AH103

Biografías politicos Mexicanos, 1935–1988, Camp, Roderic Ai, AH106, CJ305

Biografías puertorriqueñas, Rosa-Nieves, Cesáreo, AH161

Biografisch archief van de Benelux, AH270

Biografisch woordenboek van Nederland, AH271

Biografiske artikler i norske tidsskrifter, 1931–35, AD322

Biografiske artikler i norske tidsskrifter, AD321, AH274

Biografiske tidsskriftartikler, Houmøller, Sven, AD309, AD310

Biogramy uczonych polskich, AH278

Biographia Nigeriana, Orimoloye, S. A., AH322

Biographic dictionary of Chinese communism, 1921–1965, Klein, Donald W., CJ429

The biographic register, United States. Department of State, CJ143

Biographical and bibliographical dictionary of the Italian humanists and of the world of classical scholarship in Italy, 1300–1800, Cosenza, Mario Emilio, BE1310

Biographical and historical index of American Indians and persons involved in Indian affairs, United States. Department of the Interior. Library, CC436

Biographical annals of the civil government of the United States, Lanman, Charles, CJ140

Biographical archive of the Benelux countries, AH270

Biographical books, 1876–1949, AH2

Biographical books, 1950–1980, AH3

Biographical dictionaries and related works, Slocum, Robert B., AH4, AH6

Biographical dictionaries master index, AH9

Biographical dictionary and analysis of China's party leadership, 1922–1988, Bartke, Wolfgang, CJ425

A biographical dictionary of actors, actresses, musicians, dancers, managers & other stage personnel in London, 1660–1800, Highfill, Philip H., BH112

Biographical dictionary of Afro-American and African musicians, Southern, Eileen, BJ217

Biographical dictionary of American architects (deceased), Withey, Henry F., BF263

Biographical dictionary of American business leaders, Ingham, John N., CH98, CH99

A biographical dictionary of American civil engineers, American Society of Civil Engineers. Committee on History and Heritage of American Civil Engineering, EK63, EK250

Biographical dictionary of American educators, CB130

A biographical dictionary of American geography in the twentieth century, Dunbar, Gary S., CL80

Biographical dictionary of American journalism, AE150

Biographical dictionary of American labor, CH678

Biographical dictionary of American labor leaders, CH678

Biographical dictionary of American mayors, 1820–1980, CJ285

Biographical dictionary of American science, Elliott, Clark A., EA177, EA192

Biographical dictionary of American sports, BK13, BK21

Biographical dictionary of American sports : baseball, BK52

Biographical dictionary of American sports : basketball and other indoor sports, BK63

Biographical dictionary of American sports : football, BK74

Biographical dictionary of American sports : outdoor sports, BK14

A biographical dictionary of ancient Egypt, David, A. Rosalie, DA124

Biographical dictionary of Australian librarians, AK82

Biographical dictionary of British architects, 1600–1840, Colvin, Howard Montagu, BF216, BF259

The biographical dictionary of British feminists, Banks, Olive, AH218

Biographical dictionary of British women, AH227

A biographical dictionary of contemporary Afghanistan, Adamec, Ludwig W., DE107

Biographical dictionary of contemporary Catholic American writing, BE446

Biographical dictionary of dance, Cohen-Stratyner, Barbara N., BH158

A biographical dictionary of dissenting economists, Arestis, Philip, CH92

Biographical dictionary of dissidents in the Soviet Union, 1956–1975, AH303

A biographical dictionary of English women writers, 1580–1720, BE620

A biographical dictionary of film, Thomson, David, BH287

Biographical dictionary of French political leaders since 1870, CJ328

Biographical dictionary of geography, Larkin, Robert P., CL83

Biographical dictionary of Hispanic literature in the United States, Kanellos, Nicolás, BE562

Biographical dictionary of internationalists, Kuehl, Warren F., CJ66, CJ700

A biographical dictionary of Irish writers, BE799

Biographical dictionary of Japanese art, Tazawa, Yutaka, BF144

Biographical dictionary of Japanese literature, BE1579

Biographical dictionary of Latin American and Caribbean political leaders, AH110, AH111, CJ306, CJ310

Biographical dictionary of Latin American historians and historiography, Thomas, Jack Ray, DB296

Biographical dictionary of Marxism, CJ531

—— Gorman, Robert A., CJ532

Biographical dictionary of mathematicians, EB100

Biographical dictionary of medallists, Forrer, Leonard, BG186

Biographical dictionary of medallists by L. Forrer: index, Martin, J. S., BG186

Biographical dictionary of medicine, Bendiner, Jessica, EH221

Biographical dictionary of modern British radicals, AH221

—— Baylen, Joseph O., AH219

—— Gossman, Norbert J., AH219

Biographical dictionary of modern peace leaders, CJ700

—— Josephson, Harold, CJ66, CJ686

Biographical dictionary of neo-Marxism, CJ532

—— Gorman, Robert A., CJ531

Biographical dictionary of North American classicists, Briggs, Ward W., BE1024, DA113

Biographical dictionary of Republican China, AH338

Biographical dictionary of Russian/Soviet composers, BJ204

A biographical dictionary of scenographers, 500 B.C. to 1900 A.D, Lacy, Robin Thurlow, BH114

Biographical dictionary of science fiction and fantasy artists, Weinberg, Robert E., BE303, BF372

A biographical dictionary of scientists, EA172, EA173

The biographical dictionary of scientists : astronomers, EC63

The biographical dictionary of scientists : biologists, EG60

The biographical dictionary of scientists : chemists, EE100

The biographical dictionary of scientists : mathematicians, EB101

The biographical dictionary of scientists : physicists, ED54

Biographical dictionary of social welfare in America, CC39

Biographical dictionary of the American left, CJ156

A biographical dictionary of the Anglo-Egyptian Sudan, AH326

A biographical dictionary of the British colonial governor, Kirk-Greene, A. H. M., CJ402

A biographical dictionary of the Byzantine Empire, Nicol, Donald MacGillivray, DA165

Biographical dictionary of the cinema, Thomson, David, BH287

Biographical dictionary of the Comintern, Lazić, Branko M., CJ533

Biographical dictionary of the Confederacy, Wakelyn, Jon L., AH71

A biographical dictionary of the extreme right since 1890, Rees, Philip, CJ68

A biographical dictionary of the former Soviet Union, Vronskaya, Jeanne, AH179

The biographical dictionary of the Middle East, Shimoni, Yaacov, DE66

Biographical dictionary of the Soviet Union, 1917–1988, Vronskaya, Jeanne, AH163, AH179

A biographical dictionary of the Sudan, Hill, Richard Leslie, AH326

Biographical dictionary of wax modellers, Pyke, E. J., BF396

Biographical dictionary of women artists in Europe and America since 1850, Dunford, Penny, BF152

Biographical dictionary of World War I, Herwig, Holger H., DA199

—— Heyman, Neil M., DA199

Biographical directory, American Association of Law Libraries, AK81

—— American Political Science Association, CJ154

—— American Psychiatric Association, EH387

Biographical directory of American colonial and Revolutionary governors, 1607–1789, Raimo, John W., CJ288

Biographical directory of American territorial governors, McMullin, Thomas A., CJ287

Biographical directory of anthropologists born before 1920, CE65

Biographical directory of clergy, BC354

A biographical directory of librarians in the United States and Canada, AK83, AK93

Biographical directory of national librarians, Carroll, Frances Laverne, AK84

Biographical directory of Negro ministers, Williams, Ethel L., BC256

Biographical directory of the Council of Economic Advisers, Council of Economic Advisers (U.S.), CH95

Biographical directory of the governors of the United States, Mullaney, Marie Marmo, CJ288

—— Raimo, John W., CJ288

—— Sobel, Robert, CJ288

Biographical directory of the United States Congress, 1774–1989, CJ212, CJ222, CJ230, CJ231, CJ233, CJ239

—— United States. Congress, CJ232, CJ212

Biographical directory of the United States executive branch, 1774–1989, CJ189

Biographical encyclopaedia and who's who of the American theatre, Rigdon, Walter, BH117

Biographical encyclopedia of Pakistan, AH365

Biographical encyclopedia of science and technology, EA171

A biographical encyclopedia of scientists, EA174

A biographical handbook of education, Nauman, Ann Keith, CB132

Biographical index to American science, Elliott, Clark A., EA192

Biographical key—names of birds of the world—to authors and those commemorated, Wynne, Owen E., EG280

Biographical memoirs, National Academy of Sciences, EA188, EH219

Biographical memoirs of fellows of the Royal Society, Royal Society (Great Britain), EA182, EA189, EH219

Biographical notices of graduates of Yale College, Dexter, Franklin Bowditch, AH61

—— Yale University, AH61

A biographical register, 1788–1939, Gibbney, H. J., AH372

A biographical register of the Commonwealth Parliament, 1901–1972, Rydon, Joan, CJ450

Biographical register of the Confederate Congress, Warner, Ezra J., DB121

—— Yates, Buck, DB121

Biographical register of the officers and graduates of the U.S. Military Academy at West Point, N.Y, Cullum, George Washington, CJ640

Biographical Research Institute, Pakistan. *Biographical encyclopedia of Pakistan,* AH365

Biographical sketches of graduates of Harvard University, AH70

Biographical sketches of the graduates of Yale college, Dexter, Franklin Bowditch, AH61

Biographical sketches of those who attended Harvard College with bibliographical and other notes, Sibley, John Langdon, AH70

Biographical sources, Cimbala, Diane J., AH4

Biographie belge d'outre-mer, AH173

Biographie coloniale belge, Académie royale des sciences d'outre-mer, AH173

Biographie nationale, Académie royale des sciences, des lettres et des beaux-arts de Belgique, AH172, AH174, AH175, AH176
Biographie nationale du pays de Luxembourg depuis ses origines jusqu'à nos jours, AH268
Biographie universelle ancienne et moderne, AH22
Biographie universelle (Michaud) ancienne et moderne, AH22
———— Michaud, Joseph François, AH31
———— Michaud, Louis Gabriel, AH31
Biographies of British women, Sweeney, Patricia E., AH240
Biographies of creative artists, Stievater, Susan M., BF138
Biographisch-bibliographisches Kirchenlexikon, Bautz, Friedrich Wilhelm, BC253
Biographisch-bibliographisches Quellen-Lexikon der Musiker und Musikgelehrten der christlichen Zeitrechnung bis zur Mitte des neunzehnten Jahrhunderts, Eitner, Robert, BJ57
Biographisch-literarisches Handwörterbuch zur Geschichte der exakten Wissenschaften, Poggendorff, Johann Christian, EA181
Biographisch woordenboek der Nederlanden, Aa, Abraham Jacobus van der, AH269
Biographisch woordenboek der Noord– en Zuidnederlandsche letterkunde, Frederiks, Johannes Godefridus, BE1328
Biographischer Katalog, Institut für Zeitgeschichte, DA169
Biographisches Archiv der Benelux-Länder (BAB), AH270
Biographisches Handbuch der deutschsprachigen Emigration nach 1933, AH203
Biographisches Handbuch der Reichstage, CJ333
Biographisches Jahrbuch für Altertumskunde, BE1023
Biographisches Jahrbuch und deutscher Nekrolog, 1896–1913, AH202, AH204
Biographisches Lexikon, Pagel, Julius Leopold, EH222
Biographisches Lexikon der hervorragenden Ärzte aller Zeiten und Völker, EH222
Biographisches Lexikon der hervorragenden Ärzte der letzten 50 Jahre, Fischer, Isidor, EH222
Biographisches Lexikon des Kaiserthums Oesterreich, Wurzbach, Constantin, AH169, AH170, AH247
Biographisches Lexikon zur Geschichte der böhmischen Länder, AH181
Biographisches Lexikon zur Geschichte Südosteuropas, AH23
Biographisches Lexikon zur Geschichtswissenschaft in Deutschland, Österreich und der Schweiz, Weber, Wolfgang, DC225
Biographisches Lexikon zur Weimarer Republik, DC261
Biographisches Wörterbuch zur deutschen Geschichte, Franz, Günther, DC222
———— Rössler, Hellmuth, AH215, DC222
Biography
  bibliography, AH1, AH2, AH3, AH4, AH5, AH6, AH7, BE213, BE214, BE215, BE216
  book reviews, AH1
  criticism
    bibliography, AH7, BE216
  dictionaries, BE217
  filmography, BH226
  guides, BE214
  indexes, AA19, AE108, AH8, AH9, AH10, AH11, AH13, AH14, AH15, AH16, AH17, AH18, AH20, AH21, AH32, AH33, AH34, AH40, AH41
  periodicals, BE213
Biography (by country or region)
  Africa, North, DE66
  Asia, West, DE66
  Bolivia, DB337
  Bulgaria, DC115
  Canada, AA450
  Chile, DB362
  Dominican Republic, AH153
  Europe, Southeast, AH23
  European Communities, AF23

France
  government officials, AH200, CJ329
  Germany, DC261
  Great Britain, CJ360
  international, AE108, AH22, AH23, AH24, AH25, AH27, AH28, AH29, AH30, AH31, AH32, AH33, AH34, AH35, AH36, AH37, AH38, AH50, AL170, BE209
    blacks, AH43, CC396
    contemporary, AH42, AH44, AH45, AH47, AH48, AH49, AH51, AH52, BE198
    indexes, AH19
  Mexico, AH106, CJ305
  Namibia, DD189
  South Africa, CJ412, DD212
Biography (by occupation or profession)
  actors, BH112, BH115, BH116, BH117, BH118, BH119, BH122, BH123, BH124, BH126, BH127, BH128, BH129
  agriculture, EJ40
  anthropologists, CE65
  architecture, BF204, BF258, BF260, BF262, BF263
  artists, AH335, BF142, BF148, BF149, BF151, BF153, BF154, BF155, BF156, BF157, BF314, BF316, BF317, BF318, BF323, BF386, BG34
  artists (by country or region)
    Denmark, BF147
    Spain, BF147
  astronomers, EC63
  authors, BE451
    Bangladesh, AH335
    Hungarian, AH247, AH250, BE1282
  biologists, EG60
  book trade, AA310
  business, CH96, CH387
  cartographers, CL272
  chemists, AL174, EE105
  clock and watchmakers, BG89
  dancers, BH158
  designers, BG22, BG29
  economists, CH92, CH103, CH104
  education, CB131, CB133, CB134
  engineers, EK13
  espionage, CJ539
  film, BH213, BH248, BH250, BH251, BH266, BH267, BH279, BH280, BH281, BH282, BH283, BH284, BH285, BH286, BH287, BH288, BH289, BH290, BH291
  geographers, CL80, CL82, CL83, CL272, CL274
  government officials, CJ143
  government officials (by country or region)
    France, DC211
    Italy, CJ381
  historians, DA47, DB65, DB68, DB296, DC54, DC55, DC225
  international relations, CJ66
  labor leaders, AH220, CH678
  law librarians, AK81
  librarians, AK82, AK83, AK84, AK85, AK86, AK89, AK91, AK93
  linguists, BD6, BD34, BD66, BD69, BD70, BD128
  medicine, EH221
  military leaders, AH26, CJ638, CJ643, CJ647
    France, AH195
    United States, CJ639
  musicians, BC314, BJ207, BJ215, BJ221
  oceanographers, EF218
  Peace Corps, CJ702
  philosophers, BB37
  photographers, BF354
  physicists, AL175, ED56
  political activists, CC38, DD127
  political leaders, CJ65, CJ67, CJ71, CJ533, DB102
    Namibia, DD189
  political leaders (by country or region)
    Africa, North, CJ417
    Africa, South of the Sahara, AH316, CJ404, CJ406, CJ409
    Asia, CJ415, DE20, DF20
    Asia, West, CJ417

    Australia, CJ415, DE20, DF20
    Equatorial Guinea, DD152
    Europe, AH162
    France, CJ328
    Germany, CJ333
    Great Britain, CJ348, CJ362, DC340
    India, CJ432
    Oceania, CJ415, DE20, DF20
    Pacific Rim countries, CJ415, DE20, DF20
    United States, CJ153
    Nicaragua, DB313
  political scientists, CJ154, CJ155
  politicians, DC262
  printing, AA310
  psychologists, CD46, CD48, CD52, CD62
  religious leaders, BC82, BC83, BC84, BC253, BC254, BC255, BC256, BC263, BC265, BC418, BC419
  screenwriters, BH280
  social and behavioral sciences, CA62
  sociologists, CA63
  television, BH267, BH319, BH320
  theater, BH114, BH117, BH118, BH121, BH122, BH128, BH129
  theater personnel, BH120, BH127
  veterinarians, EJ40
Biography (by period)
  medieval and Renaissance
    bibliography, DA130
Biography (by subject)
  adult education, CB363
  advertising and public relations, CH575
  African Americans, CC397
  education, CB130, CB132
  folk art, BG33, BG35
  Japanese literature, BE1579
  Jews, BC553
  Judaism, BC566
  psychology, CD49, CD50, CD55
  Russian authors, BE1424
  United Nations, AF42
  United States. Congress, CJ212, CJ232
  women, AH25, AH37, CC258, CC576, CC580
Biography, BE213, BE217
———— Rollyson, Carl E., BE215
Biography and genealogy master index, AH8, AH9, BF136, CH94
Biography catalogue of the Library of the Royal Commonwealth Society, Royal Commonwealth Society. Library, AH238
———— Simpson, Donald H., DC344
Biography index, AA625, AH10
BioLaw, EH239
Biological & agricultural index, EG10, EJ15, EG10
Biological & biomedical measurement systems, EH82
Biological abstracts, EG11, EG13, EG18, EG11
•*Biological abstracts on compact disc,* EG11
Biological abstracts/RRM, EG12, EG13, EG18
Biological and agricultural index, EG10, EJ15
Biological nomenclature, Jeffrey, Charles, EG42
Biological sciences
  abstract journals, EG11, EG12, EG16, EG17
  bibliography, CE14, EA16, EA20, EB10, EC15, ED5, EE13, EF57, EF141, EF173, EF232, EG6, EG7, EG8, EG105, EG211, EG312
    current, EA35
  biography, EG29
  classification, EG28, EG46
  databases, EG9, EG11, EG13, EG14, EG15
  dictionaries, EG30, EG31, EG32, EG34, EG35, EG36, EG37, EG38, EG40, EG41, EG42, EG43, EG44, EG45, EH100, EK46
    bilingual
      French-English, EH141
  directories, EG48, EG49
  encyclopedias, EG19, EG20, EG23, EG24, EG25, EG26
  guides, EG1, EG2, EG5, EJ1
  handbooks, EG50, EG51, EG52, EG53, EG54, EG55
  indexes, EG10, EG18
  statistics, EG61

style manuals, EA223, EG57, EG58
Biological sciences (by country or region)
   Great Britain
      directories, EG47
Biological sciences (by subject)
   history, EG59
   see also Botany; Zoology
The biologist's handbook of pronunciations, Jaeger, Edmund Carroll, EG40
Biology data book, Altman, Philip L., EG51
Biomedical engineering, EH82, EH86
   encyclopedias, EH89
   handbooks, EH181, EH182
Biometric Society. Directory of members, CG35, EB57
Biometric Society
   directories, CG35, EB57
Biometrika tables for statisticians, Pearson, Egon Sharpe, EB90
Biophysics
   encyclopedias, EH89
   tables, EA155
Bioresearch index, EG12
Biosciences, Alston, Y. R., EK42
BioSciences Information Service of Biological Abstracts. Bibliographic guide for editors & authors, EA38
BIOSIS, EA41, EE18, EG18
•BIOSIS previews, EG11, EG12, EG13
BIOSIS previews/RN, EG13
Biot, Édouard Constant. Dictionnaire des villes chinoises, CL160
Biotechnology, EK43, EK44, EK45, EK46
   directories, EK42
Biotechnology, EK49
The biotechnology directory, EK42, EK44
Biotechnology research abstracts, EG14
BIP, AA425
Birch, Alan. Research material for Hong Kong studies, DE150
Birch, Carol L. Unity in diversity, CJ111
Birchfield, Mary Eva. The complete reference guide to United Nations sales publications, 1946–1978, AF30
—— Consolidated catalog of League of Nations publications, offered for sale, AF28
Bird, Augusto. Bibliografía puertorriqueña de fuentes para investigaciones sociales, 1930–1945, DB453
Bird, Keith W. German naval history, DC214
The birder's handbook, Ehrlich, Paul R., EG258
Birds, EG255, EG256, EG257, EG258, EG260, EG261, EG262, EG263, EG266, EG267, EG268, EG270, EG271, EG272, EG273, EG274, EG276, EG277, EG278, EG279, EG280
   classification, EG269
   distribution, EG275
   encyclopedias, EG254, EG264
   nomenclature, EG265
   periodicals, EG253
   taxonomy, EG275
Birds (by country or region)
   North America, EG259
Birds, Miller, Melanie Ann, EG268
Birds in jeopardy, Ehrlich, Paul R., EG259
The birds of North America, EG253
—— Robbins, Chandler S., EG274
Birkhead, T. R. The Cambridge encyclopedia of ornithology, EG254
Birkin, Stanley J. Job satisfaction and motivation, CD125
Birkos, Alexander S. Academic writer's guide to periodicals, AD26
Birmingham Shakespeare Library. A Shakespeare bibliography, BE770
Birnbach, Lisa. Lisa Birnbach's new and improved college book, CB254
Birnbaum, Max. Comparative guide to American colleges for students, parents, and counselors, CB265
Birnbaum, Philip. A book of Jewish concepts, BC557
Birnes, William J. McGraw-Hill personal computer programming encyclopedia, EK207

Birney, Alice L. The literary lives of Jesus, BC211
Birren, James E. Handbook of the psychology of aging, CC97
Birth defects, EH91
Birth of Botswana, Morton, Fred, DD132
—— Ramsay, Jeff, DD132
Biržiška, Vaclovas. Aleksandrynas, AH267
—— Lietuvių bibliografija [1517–1910], BE1322
Bisby, Guy Richard. Dictionary of the fungi, EG184
Bisengimana, Etienne. Femmes et enfants au Burundi, DD134
Bishko, C. Julian. Medieval studies, DA131
Bishop, Cynthia. Science fair project index, 1960–1972, EA31
Bishop, David. Handbook of medical library practice, EH4
Bishop, Jackie. BBC world service glossary of current affairs, CJ36
Bishop, Olga B. Bibliography of Ontario history, 1867–1976, DB212
—— Canadian official publications, AF150
—— Ontario since 1867, DB212
—— Publications of the government of Ontario, 1867–1900, AF155
—— Publications of the government of the Province of Canada, 1841–1867, AF155
—— Publications of the governments of Nova Scotia, Prince Edward Island, New Brunswick, 1758–1952, AF155
Bishop, Robert. The American clock, BG84
Bishop, W. J. Notable names in medicine and surgery, EH220
Bishop, William Warner. A checklist of American copies of "Short-title catalogue" books, AA667, AA671
Bishops see Popes, cardinals, bishops
BISNIS bulletin, CH497
Bissainthe, Max. Dictionnaire de bibliographie haïtienne, AA566
Bisselle, Walter C. East European peasantries, CE96
Bisset, Ronald. Environmental impact assessment, EK66
Bistner, Stephen I. Handbook of veterinary procedures & emergency treatment, EJ124
Bits & bytes review, BC188
Bits, bytes & biblical studies, Hughes, John J., BC188
Bittel, Lester Robert. Handbook for professional managers, CH622
Bittel, Muriel Albers. Handbook for professional managers, CH622
Bitter, Gary G. Macmillan encyclopedia of computers, EK174
Bitterworth's international law directory, CK61
Bitton, Davis. Guide to Mormon diaries & autobiographies, BC368
Bjerg, Hans Christian. Dansk marinehistorisk bibliografi, 1500–1975, DC130
Bjerke, Lucie. English-Norwegian dictionary, AC618
Bjerkoe, Ethel Hall. The cabinetmakers of America, BG134
Bjerkoe, John Arthur. The cabinetmakers of America, BG134
Bjørner, Susanne. Newspapers online, AE113
Blachère, Régis. Dictionnaire arabe-français-anglais, AC213
Black, Arthur Davenport. Index of the periodical dental literature published in the English language, EH250
Black, C. Atlas of the Renaissance, DA158
Black, David. The Macmillan atlas of rugs & carpets, BG169
Black, Dorothy M. Guide to lists of master's theses, AG14
Black, George, F. Ethiopia & Amharica, DD158
Black, George Fraser. The surnames of Scotland, AJ205
Black, Henry Campbell. Black's law dictionary, CK33
Black, J. L. Origins, evolution, and nature of the Cold War, CJ7

—— Soviet perception of Canada, 1917–1987, DB180
—— Soviet perception of Canada, 1945–1987, DB180
Black, Karen L. A biobibliographical handbook of Bulgarian authors, BE1103
Black, Matthew. Peake's commentary on the Bible, BC168
Black, Richard. Angola, DD18
Black, Robert Dionysius Collison. A catalogue of pamphlets on economic subjects published between 1750 and 1900 and now housed in Irish libraries, CH10
Black access, Newman, Richard, CC371
Black adolescence, CC143
Black Africa, Klíma, Vladimír, BE1501
—— Morrison, Donald George, DD95
Black African literature in English, Lindfors, Bernth, BE1506
Black African traditional religions and philosophy, Ofori, Patrick E., BC34, BC497
The black aged in the United States, Davis, Lenwood G., CC65
Black alcohol abuse and alcoholism, Watts, Thomas D., CC123
Black American families, 1965–1984, CC206
Black American fiction, Fairbanks, Carol, BE517
Black American health, Jones, Woodrow, EH405
—— Rice, Mitchell F., EH405
Black American literature forum, BJ298
Black American playwrights, 1800 to the present, Arata, Esther Spring, BE513
Black American poets and dramatists, Bloom, Harold, BE512
Black American women in literature, Glikin, Ronda, BE519
Black American writers, BE515
—— Rush, Theressa Gunnels, BE532
Black American writers, 1773–1949, Matthews, Geraldine O., BE526
Black Americans in autobiography, Brignano, Russell Carl, CC363
Black Americans in Congress, 1870–1989, CJ212
—— Ragsdale, Bruce A., CJ231
Black Americans information directory, AE15, CC388
The black artist in America, Thomison, Dennis, BF64
Black artists in the United States, Davis, Lenwood G., BF24
—— Sim, Janet, BF24
Black arts annual, BA1, BF44
Black athletes in the United States, Davis, Lenwood G., BK2
Black authors, Newby, James Edward, BE527
Black biographical dictionaries, 1790–1950, AH59
Black biography, 1790–1950, Burkett, Nancy H., AH59
—— Burkett, Randall K., AH59
—— Gates, Henry Louis, AH59
Black book publishers in the United States, Joyce, Donald F., AA302
Black business and economics, Hill, George H., CH393
Black child development in America, 1927–1977, Myers, Hector F., CC369
Black children and American institutions, Washington, Valora, CC140
Black dance, Adamczyk, Alice J., BH131
Black elected officials, CJ132
Black English, Johnson, James P., BD103
—— Leffall, Dolores, BD103
The black family in the United States, Davis, Lenwood G., CC365
Black genealogy, Blockson, Charles L., AJ3
Black holiness, Jones, Charles Edwin, BC374
Black image on the American stage, Hatch, James Vernon, BE520, BH109
Black immigration and ethnicity in the United States, CC311
Black index, Newman, Richard, CC384
Black-Jewish relations in the United States, 1752–1984, Davis, Lenwood G., CC366

Black leaders of the nineteenth century, CC395
Black list, AE15
Black literature, 1827–1940, BE535
Black literature, 1827–1940 index on CD-ROM, BE535
Black media in America, Hill, George H., CC398
Black music, BJ344
Black music and musicians in The new Grove dictionary of American music and The new Harvard dictionary of music, De Lerma, Dominique-René, BJ225
Black music biography, Floyd, Samuel A., BJ220
Black music in the United States, Floyd, Samuel A., BJ33
Black names in America, Puckett, Newbell Niles, AJ174
Black newspaper collection, AE15
Black newspapers index, AE104, AE105
Black Olympian medalists, Page, James A., BK93
Black Periodical Literature Project. *Black literature, 1827–1940*, BE535
Black photographers, 1840–1940, Willis-Thomas, Deborah, BF357
Black playwrights, 1823–1977, Hatch, James Vernon, BE521, BE530
Black plots & black characters, Southgate, Robert L., BE539
Black poets of the United States, Wagner, Jean, BE533
Black press handbook, AE15
The black press periodical directory, AE15
The black resource guide, CC389
Black rhetoric, Glenn, Robert W., BE352
Black slavery in the Americas, Smith, John David, CC377
The black student's guide to college success, CB303
Black studies *see* **African-American studies; African studies**
Black theatre and performance, Gray, John, BH32
Black theatre directory, BH83
Black Theatre Network. *Black theatre directory*, BH83
Black theology, Evans, James H., BC216
Black-white racial attitudes, Obudho, Constance E., CC372
The black who's who of Southern Africa today, AH313
Black women in television, Hill, George H., BH294
—— Johnson, Chas Floyd, BH294
—— Raglin, Lorraine, BH294
Black writers in New England, Clark, Edward, BE516
Blackburn, Clare. *Improving health and welfare work with families in poverty*, CC51
Blackburn, G. Meredith. *Index to children's poetry*, BE376
—— *Index to poetry for children and young people*, BE376
Blackburn, Lorraine A. *Index to children's poetry*, BE376
Blacker-Wood Library of Zoology and Ornithology. *A dictionary catalogue of the Blacker-Wood library ...*, EG207
Blackey, Robert. *Revolutions and revolutionists*, CJ75
Blackfoot dictionary of stems, roots, and affixes, Frantz, Donald, AC717
Blackfoot language *see* **Siksika language**
Blackman, Michelle. *LLBA user's reference manual*, BD31
Blackman, Murray. *Guide to Jewish themes in American fiction, 1940–1980*, BE564
Blackmore, A. S. G. *An index of composers*, BJ205
Blackmore, Ruth Matteson. *Cumulative index to the annual catalogues of Her Majesty's Stationery Office publications, 1922–1972*, AF184
Blacks
  biography, AH43, CC396
Blacks (by country or region)
  Brazil, CC475, DB347
  see also **African Americans**
Black's agricultural dictionary, Dalal-Clayton, D. B., EJ24

Blacks and their contributions to the American West, Abajian, James de T., CC360
Blacks in American films and television, Bogel, Donald, BH227
—— Bogle, Donald, BH270
Blacks in classical music, Gray, John, BJ212
Blacks in film and television, Gray, John, BH165
Blacks in science and medicine, Sammons, Vivian O., EA183, EH217
Blacks in selected newspapers, censuses and other sources, Abajian, James de T., AE105
Black's law dictionary, CK38
—— Black, Henry Campbell, CK33
Black's medical dictionary, EH92
Blacks on television, Hill, George H., BH294
Black's veterinary dictionary, EJ111
Blackstock, Paul W. *Intelligence, espionage, counterespionage, and covert operations*, CJ535
Blackwelder, Richard Eliot. *Guide to the taxonomic literature of vertebrates*, EG208
Blackwell, Richard J. *A bibliography of the philosophy of science, 1945–1981*, EA11
The Blackwell biographical dictionary of British political life in the twentieth century, CJ348, DC340
The Blackwell companion to Jewish culture, DA177
—— Abramson, Glenda, BC552
The Blackwell companion to the Enlightenment, BE749, DC19
The Blackwell dictionary of historians, DA46
The Blackwell dictionary of Judaica, Cohn-Sherbok, Dan, BC553
The Blackwell dictionary of twentieth-century social thought, CA30
The Blackwell encyclopaedia of political institutions, CJ21
The Blackwell encyclopaedia of political science, CJ21
The Blackwell encyclopaedia of political thought, CJ21, CJ22
The Blackwell encyclopedia of industrial archaeology, CH47, DA178
The Blackwell encyclopedia of modern Christian thought, BC229
The Blackwell encyclopedia of the American Revolution, DB93
The Blackwell encyclopedia of the Russian Revolution, DC594, DC595
Bladlisten, AD80
Blahynky, Milana. *Čeští spisovatelé 20*, BE1105
Blaiklock, Edward M. *The new international dictionary of biblical archaeology*, BC195
Blain, Virginia. *The feminist companion to literature in English*, BE607, BE623
Blair, Claude. *The complete encyclopedia of arms & weapons*, CJ569
Blair, Dorothy S. *African literature in French*, BE1514
—— *Senegalese literature*, BE1532
Blair, Edward Payson. *Abingdon Bible handbook*, BC186
—— *The illustrated Bible handbook*, BC186
Blair, Emma Helen. *The Philippine Islands, 1493–1898*, DE246
Blair, Karen J. *The history of American women's voluntary organizations, 1810–1960*, CC486
Blair, Michael. *Thesaurus of sociological indexing terms*, CC20
Blaise, Albert. *Dictionnaire latin-français des auteurs chrétiens*, AC581, AC586
—— *Dictionnaire latin-français des auteurs du moyen-age*, AC586
Blake, David. *Periodicals from Africa*, AD238, DD28
Blake, Fay M. *Verbis non factis*, CJ242
Blake, G. Noel. *Chisholm's handbook of commercial geography*, CL67
Blake, Gerald Henry. *The Cambridge atlas of the Middle East and North Africa*, DE68
Blake, John Ballard. *Medical reference works, 1679–1966*, EH2

—— *Short title catalogue of eighteenth century printed books in the National Library of Medicine*, EH24
Blake, Judith. *Western European censuses, 1960*, CG186
Blake, Leslie James. *Australian writers*, BE848
Blake, Leslie Spencer. *Civil engineer's reference book*, EK60
Blake, N. F. *The index of Middle English prose*, BE733
—— *Index of printed Middle English prose*, BE733
Blake, Sidney Fay. *Geographical guide to floras of the world*, EG100
Blake, William, BJ70
Blake set to music, Fitch, Donald, BJ70
Blakely, Pamela A. R. *Directory of visual anthropology*, CE88
Blakely, Thomas D. *Directory of visual anthropology*, CE88
Blakemore, Colin. *Handbook of psychobiology*, CD122
Blakemore, Frances. *Who's who in modern Japanese prints*, BF358
Blakemore, Harold. *The Cambridge encyclopedia of Latin America and the Caribbean*, DB281
—— *Chile*, DB358
Blakiston's Gould medical dictionary, EH93
Blamires, Harry. *Guide to twentieth century literature in English*, BE764
Blanc, Brigitte. *Atlas de España y Portugal*, CL331, CL333
Blancare, Roberto. *Diccionario biográfico y histórico de la Revolución Mexicana en el Estado de México*, DB242
Blanchard, J. Richard. *Guide to sources for agricultural and biological research*, EJ1
—— *Literature of agricultural research*, EJ1
Blanck, Jacob Nathaniel. *Bibliography of American literature*, BE400, BE405
—— *Merle Johnson's American first editions*, AA242, BE405
Blanco, Richard L. *The American Revolution, 1775–1783*, DB92, DB93
—— *The War of the American Revolution*, DB86
Blanco-González, Manuel. *New revised Velázquez Spanish and English dictionary*, AC740
Bland, William B. *Albania*, DC78
Blandford, Linda A. *Supreme Court of the United States, 1789–1980*, CK183
Blank, Thomas O. *Topics in gerontology*, CC76
Blanke, Richard. *Eastern European national minorities, 1919–1980*, CE92
Blankenship, Frank J. *The Prentice Hall real estate investor's encyclopedia*, CH532
Blankner, Frederika. *The history of the Scandinavian literatures*, BE1084
Blanpain, R. *International encyclopaedia for labour law and industrial relations*, CK29
Blaser, Fritz. *Bibliographie der schweizer Presse*, AE77
Blasi, Anthony J. *Issues in the sociology of religion*, BC7
—— *The sociology of religion*, BC7
Blasio, Mary-Ann. *New day/New Deal*, DB128
Blass, Birgit A. *Provisional survey of materials for the study of neglected languages*, BD71
Blatt, Franz. *Novum glossarium mediae latinitatis*, AC593
Blättel, Harry. *International dictionary miniature painters, porcelain painters, silhouettists*, BF311
Blaudin de Thé, Bernard. *Essai de bibliographie du Sahara français et des régions avoisinantes*, DD67
Blaug, Mark. *Great economists before Keynes*, CH93
—— *Great economists since Keynes*, CH93
—— *Who's who in economics*, CH104
Blaustein, Albert P. *Constitutions of dependencies and special sovereignties*, CK72
—— *Constitutions of the countries of the world*, CK72
Blaustein, Eric P. *Constitutions of dependencies and special sovereignties*, CK72

Blauvelt, Euan. *Sources of African and Middle-Eastern economic information*, CH189
—— *Sources of Asian/Pacific economic information*, CH202
—— *Sources of European economic information*, CH185
Blazer, A. S. *Sovetskoe literaturovedenie i kritika*, BE1384
Blazer, Anna M. *Index of generic names of fossil plants, 1966–1973*, EF236
BLC to 1975, AA102, BC96
Bleaney, C. H. *Lebanon*, DE225
Bledsoe, Robert L. *The international law dictionary*, CK101
Bleiberg, Germán. *Diccionario de historia de España*, DC512
—— *Diccionario de literatura Española*, BE1070, BE1451
—— *Dictionary of the literature of the Iberian peninsula*, BE1070
Bleiler, Everett Franklin. *The guide to supernatural fiction*, BE279, BE280
—— *Science-fiction, the early years*, BE280
—— *Science fiction writers*, BE303
—— *Supernatural fiction writers*, BE303
Blensly, Douglas L. *Accounting desk book*, CH262
Bles, Arthur de. *How to distinguish the saints in art by their costumes, symbols and attributes*, BF180
Blessing, Patrick J. *The Irish in America*, CC312
Bletzer, June G. *The Donning international encyclopedic psychic dictionary*, CD135
Blevins, Winfred. *Dictionary of the American West*, AC149
Bleznick, Donald W. *A sourcebook for Hispanic literature and language*, BD172, BE1426
Blindness and the blind
  collections (by subject)
    music, BJ171
  directories, CC191
  encyclopedias, EH90
  library resources, CC196, CL258
Blinn, Hansjürgen. *Informationshandbuch Deutsche Literaturwissenschaft*, BE1055
Bibliographic classification, Bliss, Henry Evelyn, AK198
Bibliographie de la France Biblio, AA626
Blishen, Edward. *Encyclopedia of education*, CB67
Bliss, Alan Joseph. *A dictionary of foreign words and phrases in current English*, AC184
Bliss, Anne M. *Zambia*, DD18
Bliss, Henry Evelyn. *Bibliographic classification*, AK198
Bliss, John William Michael. *Canadian history in documents, 1763–1966*, DB205
Bliss bibliographic classification, AK198
BLL, BD1
BLL conference index, 1964–1973, British Library. Lending Division, AL26, EA206
Bloch, Oscar. *Dictionnaire étymologique de la langue française*, AC347
Bloch, R. Howard. *A new history of French literature*, BE1174
Block, Andrew. *English novel, 1740–1850*, BE681
Block, B. Peter. *Inorganic chemical nomenclature*, EE107
Block, Eleanor S. *Communication and the mass media*, AE130
Block, Walter. *Lexicon of economic thought*, CH48
Blockson, Charles L. *Black genealogy*, AJ3
Blodgett, Richard E. *Photographs*, BF352
Blogie, Jeanne. *Répertoire des catalogues de ventes de livres imprimés*, AA259
Blok, P. J. *Nieuw Nederlandsch biografisch woordenboek*, AH272
Blom, H. W. *Bibliography of Dutch seventeenth century political thought*, DC455
Blöndal, Björg Thorláksson. *Íslandsk-dansk ordbog*, AC506
Blond's encyclopaedia of education, CB67
Bloom, Harold. *Black American poets and dramatists*, BE512
—— *The critical perspective*, BE596

—— *The new Moulton's library of literary criticism*, BE599, BE600
—— *Twentieth-century American literature*, BE428
—— *Twentieth-century British literature*, BE601
Bloom, Ken. *American song*, BJ258
—— *Broadway*, BH63
Bloom, Lynn Z. *American autobiography, 1945–1980*, AH89, DB67
Bloom, Valerie. *Conscription*, CJ560
Bloomberg, Marty. *Jewish holocaust*, DA214
Bloomfield, Barry Cambray. *An author index to selected British 'little magazines,' 1930–1939*, AD263
—— *Theses on Asia accepted by universities in the United Kingdom and Ireland, 1877–1964*, DE9
Bloomfield, Gerald T. *New Zealand*, CG439
Bloomfield, Maurice. *A Vedic concordance*, BC489
Bloomfield, Valerie. *Commonwealth elections, 1945–1970*, CJ371
—— *Resources for Australian and New Zealand studies*, DF11
Bloomsbury dictionary of opera and operetta, BJ247
Bloomsbury dictionary of phrase & allusion, Rees, Nigel, BE86
Bloomsbury dictionary of quotations, BE101
Bloomsbury foreign film guide, BH194
The Bloomsbury group, Markert, Lawrence W., BE762
Bloomsbury guide to English literature, BE611
—— Wynne-Davies, Marion, BE611
Bloomsbury theatre guide, BH62
Bloss, Ingeborg. *Zeitschriftenverzeichnis Moderner Orient*, AD184
Bloxom, Marguerite D. *Pickaxe and pencil*, DB124
BLS publications, 1886–1971, United States. Bureau of Labor Statistics, CH639
Blue book, CJ140
Blue book American druggist, EH355
The blue book of college athletics for senior, junior & community colleges, BK33
The bluebook, CK66
The blues, Hart, Mary L., BJ337
Blues music
  bibliography, BJ337
  discography
    bibliography, BJ384
Blues who's who, Harris, Sheldon, BJ354
Blum, Daniel C. *A pictorial history of the American theatre, 1860–1985*, BH96
—— *Screen world*, BH268
Blum, Eleanor. *Mass media bibliography*, AE131
Blum, Fred. *Music monographs in series*, BJ9, BJ10, BJ45
Blum, Kenneth. *Handbook of abusable drugs*, CC134, EH333
Blum, Laurie. *The complete guide to getting a grant*, AL131
—— *Free money for [education]*, CB90, CB373
—— *Free money for foreign study*, CB90, CB373
Blum, Martin. *Bibliographie luxembourgeoise*, AA742
Blume, Clemens. *Analecta hymnica medii aevi*, BC313
Blumenkranz, Bernhard. *Bibliographie des Juifs en France*, BC527
Blumer, Thomas J. *Bibliography of the Catawba*, CC420
Blumfeldt, Evald. *Bibliotheca Estoniae historica, 1877–1917*, DC134
Blumhofer, Edith Waldvogel. *Twentieth-century evangelicalism*, BC212
Blunt, John Henry. *The annotated Book of Common Prayer*, BC336
Blyth, Dale A. *Philosophy, policies and programs for early adolescent education*, CB10
B'nai B'rith. Anti-defamation League. *The study of Judaism*, BC521
BNA's directory of state and federal courts, judges, and clerks, CK156
BNB, AA689
Board and card games, BK127, BK128, BK129

Board of Geographic Names (United States). *Bibliography of geography*, CL12
Board of Governors of the Federal Reserve System. *All-bank statistics, United States, 1896–1955*, CH292
—— *Annual statistical digest*, CH293
—— *Banking and monetary statistics*, CH292, CH293
—— *Federal reserve bulletin*, CH241
Boas, Ralph Philip. *A.J. Lohwater's Russian-English dictionary of the mathematical sciences*, EB53
Boasberg, Sarah S. *Historic landscape directory*, BF293
Boase, Frederic. *Modern English biography*, AH222, AH230
Boast, Carol. *Subject compilations of state laws*, CK181
Boatner, Mark Mayo. *Civil War dictionary*, DB118
—— *Encyclopedia of the American Revolution*, DB92
Boban, Vjekoslav. *The Oxford-Duden pictorial Serbo-Croat & English dictionary*, AC714
Bobb, F. Scott. *Zaire*, DD48
Bobbitt, Mary Reed. *A bibliography of etiquette books published in America before 1900*, AL149
Bober, Phyllis Pray. *Renaissance artists & antique sculpture*, BF391
Boberg, Folke. *Mongolian-English dictionary*, AC612
Bobev, Bobi. *Krat'uk spravochnik po istoriia na Bŭlgariia*, DC119
Bobillier, Marie. *Diccionario de la música, histórico y técnico*, BJ146
Bobinski, George S. *Dictionary of American library biography*, AK86
Bobrowski, Ryszard. *Contemporary photographers*, BF355
Bocabeille, Jean-Marc. *Dictionnaire des abréviations et acronymes scientifiques, techniques, médicaux, économiques, juridiques*, EA96
Bocchetta, Vittore E. *Follett world-wide Latin dictionary*, AC576
Bochenski, I. M. *Bibliographische Einführungen in das Studium der Philosophie*, BB5
Bock, Hans-Michael. *Cinegraph*, BH281
Boczek, Boleslaw Adam. *The international law dictionary*, CK101
Bodart, Roger. *Guide littéraire de la Belgique, de la Hollande, et du Luxembourg*, BE982
Bodders yn de Fryske striid, Wumkes, G. A., BE1068
Bode, Ingrid. *Die Autobiographien zur deutschen Literatur, Kunst und Musik, 1900–1965*, AH205
Bodelsen, Carl Adolf. *Dansk-engelsk Ordbog*, AC287
Bodensieck, Julius. *The encyclopedia of the Lutheran church*, BC355
Bodi, Leslie. *Image of a continent*, DF25
Bødker, Laurits. *Folk literature (Germanic)*, CE49, CF87
Bodleian Library. *A catalogue of English newspapers and periodicals in the Bodleian Library, 1622–1800*, AD104
—— *Catalogus dissertationum academicarum*, AG9
—— *Catalogus librorum impressorum Bibliothecae Bodleianae in Academia Oxoniensi. …*, AA119
—— *Index to the early printed books in the British Museum*, AA227
Bodman, Herbert L. *Women in the Muslim world*, CC590
Bodurgil, Abraham. *Kemal Atatürk*, DC533
—— *Turkey—politics and government*, DC533
Body, Alexander C. *Annotated bibliography of bibliographies on selected government publications and supplementary guides to the Superintendent of Documents classification system*, AF78
Body movement and nonverbal communication, Davis, Martha, CD116
—— Skupien, Janet, CD116
Boeder, Robert P. *Malawi*, DD18

Boehm, Eric H. *Historical abstracts, 1775–1945,* DA176
—— *Historical periodicals,* DA14
—— *Historical periodicals directory,* DA14
Boehm, Randolph. *American Federation of Labor records,* CH624
Boer, S. P. de. *Biographical dictionary of dissidents in the Soviet Union, 1956–1975,* AH303
Boerhave Beekman, W. *Elsevier's wood dictionary in seven languages,* EJ178
Boëthius, Bertil. *Svenskt biografiskt lexikon,* AH293
Boff, Kenneth R. *Handbook of perception and human performance,* CD113
Bogadek, Francis Aloysius. *New English-Croatian and Croatian-English dictionary,* AC711
Bogard, Travis. *American drama,* BE467, BE667
Bogdanor, Vernon. *The Blackwell encyclopaedia of political institutions,* CJ21
Bogdanov, Ivan. *Rechnik na bŭlgarskite psevdonimi,* AA164
Bogel, Donald. *Blacks in American films and television,* BH227
Bögel, Hellmuth. *A collector's guide to minerals and gemstones,* EF191
Boger, H. Batterson. *The dictionary of antiques and the decorative arts,* BG42
Boger, Louise Ade. *The complete guide to furniture styles,* BG131
—— *The dictionary of antiques and the decorative arts,* BG42
—— *Dictionary of world pottery and porcelain,* BG42
Boggs, Ralph Steele. *Bibliografía del folklore mexicano,* CF61
—— *Bibliography of Latin American folklore,* CF61
—— *Tentative dictionary of medieval Spanish,* AC749
Boghen, Jeannine. *Catalogue de l'histoire de France,* DC143
Bogle, Donald. *Blacks in American films and television,* BH270
Bogotá. Biblioteca Nacional. *Catálogo de todos los periódicos que existen desde su fundación hasta el año de 1935, inclusive,* AD73
Bogue, Donald J. *The population of the United States,* CG73
Bogus, Ronald J. *The complete rhyming dictionary and poet's craft book,* AC116
Bohatta, Hanns. *Bibliographia liturgica,* BC429
—— *Deutsches Anonymen-Lexikon,* AA170
—— *Deutsches Pseudonymen-Lexikon,* AA171
Bohdziewicz, Jorge C. *Bibliografía de bibliografías individuales,* DB332
Bohle, Bruce. *The international cyclopedia of music and musicians,* BJ137
Bohman, Nils. *Svenska män och kvinnor,* AH292
Böhmer, Elizabeth W. *Left-radical movements in South Africa and Namibia 1900–1981,* DD113
Bohn, H. G. *Bibliographer's manual of English literature,* AA663
Böhtlingk, Otto von. *Sanskrit-Wörterbuch,* AC703
—— *Sanskrit-Wörterbuch in kürzerer Fassung,* AC704
Boia, Lucian. *Great historians from antiquity to 1800,* DA48
Boĭadzhiev, Simeon. *Rechnik na bŭlgarskiia ezik,* AC242
Boisacq, Émile. *Dictionnaire étymologique de la langue grecque,* AC449
Boisdeffre, Pierre de. *Dictionnaire de littérature contemporaine,* BE1150
—— *Histoire de la littérature de langue française des années 1930 aux années 1980,* BE1168
—— *Histoire vivante de la littérature d'aujourd'hui,* BE1168
Boisvert, Lionel. *Dictionnaire du français québécois,* AC385
Bokszczanin, Maria. *A history of Polish literature,* BE1352
Bold, Alan Norman. *Longman dictionary of poets,* BE333
—— *Scotland,* BE809

—— *True characters,* BE251
—— *Who was really who in fiction,* BE251
Boldis, Josef. *Directory of libraries and information centers of the academies of sciences of socialist countries,* AK117
Boletim bibliográfico brasileiro, AA506
Boletim bibliográfico da Biblioteca Nacional, AA510
Boletim de bibliografia portuguesa, AA770, AA778
Boletim de bibliografia portuguesa. Documentos não textuais, AA778
Boletim de bibliografia portuguesa. Monografias, AA770, AA778, AD138
Boletim de bibliografia portuguesa. Publicações em série, AA778, AD138
Boletín anuario – Banco Central del Ecuador, Banco Central del Ecuador, CG152
Boletín bibliográfico, AA473
—— Biblioteca Nacional (Costa Rica), AA477
—— Universidad de San Marcos (Lima). Biblioteca, AA541
Boletín bibliográfico argentino, AA495
Boletín bibliográfico CERLALC, AA473
Boletín bibliográfico de antropología americana, CE76
Boletín bibliográfico dominicano, AA565
Boletín bibliográfico mexicano, AA467
Boletín bibliográfico nacional, AA495
Boletín estadístico de la OEA, CG121
Boletín ISBN, Venezuela, AA553
Bolivia
atlases, CL315
bibliography, AA500, AA501, AA502, AA503, AA504, AA505, DB334, DB338
bibliography of bibliography, AA27
biography, AH122, AH123
directories, CG139
dissertations, AG19
encyclopedias, DB337
gazetteers, CL120
government publications, AF159
statistics, CG138, CG139, CG140
Bolivia (by subject)
ethnic groups, CE74
foreign relations, DB336
history, DB279, DB334
bibliography, DB338
women, DB335
Bolivia, Yeager, Gertrude Matyoka, DB338
Bolivia en cifras, CG138
Bolivian literature
biobibliography, BE922
history, BE922
Bolkhovitinov, N. N. *Russia and the United States,* DC559
Bollandists. *Acta sanctorum quotquot toto orbe coluntur,* BC257
—— *Analecta bollandiana,* BC258
—— *Bibliotheca hagiographica graeca,* BC259
Bollandus, Joannes. *Acta sanctorum quotquot toto orbe coluntur,* BC257
Bollard, John K. *Pronouncing dictionary of proper names,* AC109
Boller, Paul F. *They never said it,* BE90
Bollettino del Servizio per il diritto d'autore e diritti connessi, AA736
Bollettino delle pubblicazioni italiane, Biblioteca nazionale centrale, AA736
Bollettino delle pubblicazioni italiane ricevute per diritto di stampa, Biblioteca nazionale centrale di Firenze, AA726, AA727
Bollettino delle pubblicazioni italiane ricevute pre diritto di stampa, AA725
Bollettino dell'emigrazione, CC318
Bollettino dell'Ufficio della proprieta letteraria, artistica e scientifica, AA736
Bollier, John A. *The literature of theology,* BC209
Bologne, Jean-Claude. *Les grandes allusions,* BE128
Bol'shaia sovetskaia entsiklopediia, AB82, AB83, AB84, AB87
Bol'shaia sovetskaia entsiklopediia. Ezhegodnik, AB91
Bol'shoĭ anglo-russkiĭ slovar', AC675

Bolton, Charles Knowles. *Bolton's American armory,* AJ147
Bolton, Geoffrey Curgenven. *The Oxford history of Australia,* DF39
Bolton, Henry Carrington. *Catalogue of scientific and technical periodicals, 1665–1895,* EA39, EA42
—— *A select bibliography of chemistry, 1492–1892,* EE10, EE11
Bolton, Phyllis L. *German-English science dictionary,* EA111
Bolton, Whitney French. *A history of Anglo-Latin literature, 597–1066,* BE1049
Bolton's American armory, Bolton, Charles Knowles, AJ147
Bolz, Roger W. *Robotics sourcebook and dictionary,* EK234
Bompiani, Valentino. *Dizionario letterario Bompiani delle opere e dei personaggi di tutti i tempi e di tutte le letterature,* BE63
Bonacker, Wilhelm. *Kartenmacher aller Länder und Zeiten,* CL272
Bond, Cynthia D. *The pen is ours,* BE534
Bond, John James. *Handy-book of rules and tables for verifying dates with the Christian Era,* EC83
Bond, Mary E. *Canadian directories, 1790–1987,* DB200
Bond, Maurice F. *Dictionary of English church history,* BC332
—— *Guide to the records of Parliament,* AF175
Bond, Otto Ferdinand. *The University of Chicago Spanish dictionary,* AC739
Bond, Richmond Pugh. *Studies of British newspapers and periodicals from their beginning to 1800,* AD109, AE60
Bond, W. H. *Census of medieval and Renaissance manuscripts in the United States and Canada,* AA212
Bond guide, CH313
Bondanella, Julia Conway. *Dictionary of Italian literature,* BE1298
Bondanella, Peter. *Dictionary of Italian literature,* BE1298
Bonded passengers to America, Coldham, Peter Wilson, AJ61
Bonds, Ray. *The illustrated encyclopedia of the strategy, tactics and weapons of Russian military power,* CJ656
Bone, Sheila. *Osborn's concise law dictionary,* CK34
Bonecki, Henryk. *Encyklopedia powszechna PWN,* AB76
Bonenfant, Jean-Charles. *Répertoire des publications gouvernementales du Québec de 1867 à 1964,* AF155
Bonét-Maury, Géo. *Parlementaires français,* AH200, CJ329
Bongard, David L. *The Harper encyclopedia of military biography,* AH26
Boni, Albert. *Photographic literature,* BF326
Bonin, Serge. *Atlas de la Révolution française,* DC190
Bonitz, Hermann. *Index Aristotelicus,* BB53
Bonnard, Jean. *Lexique de l'ancien français,* AC378
Bonnardel, Régine. *The atlas of Africa,* CL337
Bonneau, Georges. *Bibliographie de la littérature japonaise contemporaine,* BE1580
Bonneau, Richard. *Écrivains, cinéastes et artistes ivoiriens,* BE1527
Bonnefous, Raymonde. *Guide littéraire de la France,* BE1166
Bonnefoy, Claude. *Dictionnaire de littérature française contemporaine,* BE1151
Bonnefoy, Yves. *Mythologies,* CF7
Bonner Durchmusterung (BD), Universitäts-Sternwarte zu Bonn, EC75
Bonner Durchmusterung : Südliche Teil (SBD), EC75
Bonnerjea, Biren. *Index to Bulletins 1–100 of the Bureau of American Ethnology,* CE83
Bonser, Wilfrid. *Anglo-Saxon and Celtic bibliography (450–1087),* DC305
—— *A prehistoric bibliography,* DC305

—— *Proverb literature,* BE162

—— *Romano-British bibliography, 55 B.C.–A.D. 449,* DC305

Bonte, Pierre. *Dictionnaire de l'ethnologie et de l'anthropologie,* CE38

Book-auction records, AA260

Book catalogue of the Library of the Royal Society, Royal Society (Great Britain). Library, EA23

Book collecting
    bibliography, AA238, AA239, AA240, AA241, AA242, AA243, AA244
    dictionaries, AA249
    guides, AA237

The book collector's guide, Ricci, Seymour de, AA244

The book collector's handbook of values, Bradley, Van Allen, AA237

Book illustration, BF372, EG92
    bibliography, BF333
    encyclopedias, BF72

The book in America, Lehmann-Haupt, Hellmut, AA303

Book industry and trade
    bibliography, AK18, EA240
    dictionaries, AK42

Book industry and trade (by country or region)
    German-speaking countries
        directories, AA289

Book industry register, AA282, BE172

Book industry telephone directory, AA282, BE172

Book list, Society for Old Testament Study, BC117

The book of a thousand tongues, North, Eric McCoy, BC103

The book of British topography, Anderson, John Parker, DC347

Book of buildings, Reid, Richard, BF253

The book of calendars, EC84

The book of classical music lists, Kupferberg, Herbert, BJ176

Book of Common Prayer, BC335, BC336

—— Church of England, BC337, BC348

—— Episcopal Church, BC348

The Book of Common Prayer among the nations of the world, Muss-Arnolt, William, BC339

The Book of Common Prayer and administration of the sacraments and other rites and ceremonies of the church, Episcopal Church, BC347
    Protestant Episcopal Church in the U.S.A, BC349

The Book of Common Prayer and books connected with its origin and growth, Benton, Josiah Henry, BC338

The book of costume, Davenport, Millia, BG108

Book of crests of the families of Great Britain and Ireland, Fairbairn, James, AJ151

Book of days, Chambers, Robert, AL142

The book of dignities … , Haydn, Joseph Timothy, AJ155

The book of European light opera, Ewen, David, BJ236

A book of French quotations, BE127

The book of garden design, Brookes, John, BF295

Book of Jewish books, Frank, Ruth S., BC518

—— Wollheim, William, BC518

A book of Jewish concepts, Birnbaum, Philip, BC557

The book of knowledge, AB20

A book of Latin quotations, Guterman, Norbert, BE143

The book of lists, AB108

The Book of Mormon, BC371

The book of New Zealand women, AH377, DF46

The book of orders and decorations, Měřička, Václav, AL184

The book of orders of knighthood and decorations of honour of all nations, Burke, John Bernard, AL179

The book of predictions, AB108

The book of public arms, Fox-Davies, Arthur Charles, AJ153

The book of saints, BC261

The book of the epic, Guerber, H.A, BE341

Book of the states, CJ271, CJ272, CJ278

Book of vital world statistics, CG58

The book of women's firsts, Read, Phyllis J., CC579

The book of world-famous music, Fuld, James J., BJ231

The book of world rankings, CG51

Book-prices current, AA261

Book printing in Britain and America, Brenni, Vito Joseph, AA267

Book publishers directory, AA284

Book review digest, AA365, AA422, AA430, AD285, EA54, AA365

Book review index, AA366, AA368

Book reviews, AA346, AA365, AA367
    indexes, AA364, AA366, AA368, AA369, AA370, AA371, AA372, AA373, BA7
    periodicals, AA330, AA334, AA336, AA738
    reference books, AA348, AA357

Book reviews (by period)
    18th century
        indexes, BE748

Book reviews (by subject)
    ethnic groups, CC316
    geography, CL34
    religion, BC41, BC51, BC52, BC53

Book selection, AA326
    children and young adults, AA338, AA340
    children and young people, AA337, AA339, AA342, AA343
    colleges
        current, AA336
    colleges and universities, AA335
    elementary schools, AA341
    guides, AA325, AA327, AA329
        current, AA330
        Great Britain, AA331
        Italian, AA334, AA738
    public libraries, AA325, AA328
    reference books, AA86, AA347, AA348, AA350, AA352, AA353, AA354, AA356, AA357, AA358, AA359, AA360, AA361, AA363, AF268, EA10
        Japanese, AA355
        Latin America, AA349
        Russian, AA351
    reviews, AA330, AA357
    secondary schools, AA344, AA345

Book selection (by subject)
    Judaism, BC516

Book subscription lists, Book Subscriptions List Project, AA298

Book Subscriptions List Project. *Book subscription lists,* AA298

Bookbuyer's reference book, AA943

Booker, Karen M. *Languages of the aboriginal southeast,* CC420

Booklist, AA330, AA357

The bookman's glossary, AA271

Bookman's guide to Americana, Heard, J. Norman, AA240

Bookman's manual, AA329

Bookman's price index, AA262

Books
    auction records, AA259
    bibliography, AA326

Books about early America, Ammerman, David L., DB78

Books about Malawi, Malawi National Library Service, DD177

Books and periodicals online, AD2, AD6

Books and plays in films, 1896–1915, Gifford, Denis, BH219

Books and printing, Ulrich, Carolyn F., AA269

Books at Brown, Brown University, BE498

Books for college libraries, AA335

Books for public libraries, AA325

Books for secondary school libraries, National Association of Independent Schools. Ad Hoc Library Committee, AA342

Books from Israel, AA910

Books from Pakistan, AA923, AA924

Books from Pakistan published during the decade of reforms, 1958–1968, National Book Centre of Pakistan, AA924

Books in print, AA425, AA426, AA432, AA436, AA438, BE244, CB158, EA36, EA37, EH23

Books in print of the United Nations system, AF46

•*Books in print plus,* AA425, AA426, AA432, AA438

Books in psychology, CD10

Books in series, AA96, AA97

Books in series, 1876–1949, AA96, AA97

Books in series in the United States, AA96

Books in the Hirsch Library, with supplementary list of music, British Museum. Department of Printed Books. Hirsch Library, BJ85, BJ87

Books of India, AA896

The books of the Bible, BC169

Books on art, Lucas, Edna Louise, BF18

Books on Buddhism, BC460

—— Yoo, Yushin, BC475

Books on communism and the communist countries, Vigor, Peter Hast, CJ514

Books on demand, AA398

Books on Soviet Russia, Grierson, Philip, BE1409

Books on the Netherlands in foreign languages, 1940–57, Mollema, M. P., AA138, DC450

Books out-of-print, AA427

Books published in Australia, AA944, DF23

Books, their care and repair, Greenfield, Jane, AK240

The bookseller, AA684, AA688, AA690

Booksellers and bookselling, AA310

Bookseller's reference book, AA943

Boomgaarden, Wesley L. *Staff training and user awareness in preservation management,* AK238

Boone, Ellen. *HAER checklist,* BF219

Boone, Lalia Phipps. *The petroleum dictionary,* EK304

Boor, Helmut Anton Wilhelm de. *Geschichte der deutschen Literatur von den Anfängen bis zur Gegenwart,* BE1255

Boorkman, Jo Anne. *Introduction to reference sources in the health sciences,* EH6

Boorman, Howard L. *Biographical dictionary of Republican China,* AH338

Boos, Florence Saunders. *Bibliography of women & literature,* BE401

Booth, Alan R. *Swaziland,* DD231

Booth, Barbara. *Thesaurus of sociological indexing terms,* CC20

Booth, Christopher J. *The new IEEE standard dictionary of electrical and electronics terms,* EK131

Booth, Mark W. *American popular music,* BJ335

Booth, Vernon. *Communicating in science,* EA157

Bopp, Mary S. *Research in dance,* BH130

Bopp, Richard E. *Reference and information services,* AK235

Borchardt, C. F. A. *South African theological bibliography,* BC49

Borchardt, D. H. *Australian bibliography,* AA84, CG438

—— *Australian official publications,* AF262

—— *Australians : a guide to sources,* DF37

—— *Guide to the availability of theses,* AK224

—— *How to find out in psychology,* CD2

Borchardt, Paul. *Bibliographie de l'Angola,* DD128

Borchling, Conrad. *Niederdeutsche bibliographie,* AA637

Borck, Karin. *Sowjetische Forschungen zur Geschichte der deutsch-russischen Beziehungen von den Anfängen bis 1949,* DC237

Borden, Arthur R. *A comprehensive Old-English dictionary,* AC170

The border guide, DB250

Borderlands sourcebook, DB164

BorderLine, Valk, Barbara G., CC452, DB167

Bordley, James. *Two centuries of American medicine, 1776–1976,* EH211

Bordman, Gerald Martin. *American musical theatre,* BJ259

—— *American theatre,* BH97

—— *Concise Oxford companion to the American theatre,* BH64

—— *The Oxford companion to American theatre,* BH64, BH65

Borel, Maurice. *Dictionnaire géographique de la Suisse,* CL150

Borenstein, Audrey. *Older women in 20th-century America*, CC61

Borg, H. H. van der. *Horticultural research international*, EJ245

Borgatta, Edgar F. *Encyclopedia of sociology*, CC15

Borgatta, Marie L. *Encyclopedia of sociology*, CC15

Bork, Inge. *The Wuerttemberg emigration index*, AJ46

Borklund, Carl W. *U.S. defense and military fact book*, CJ630

Borklund, Elmer. *Contemporary literary critics*, BE212, BE426, BE595

Borland, Anne. *The Foundation Center's user-friendly guide*, AL91

Born, Lester K. *British manuscripts project*, AA133

Börner, Rudolf. *Minerals, rocks, and gemstones*, EF192

———— *Welcher Stein ist das?*, EF192

Bornschier, Volker. *Comparative world data*, CG40

Borras y Bemejo, Tomás. *Diccionario de sabiduría*, BE147

Borremans, Raymond. *Le grand dictionnaire encyclopédique de la Côte d'Ivoire*, DD145

Borroff, Edith. *American operas*, BJ234

Borroni Salvadori, Fabia. *"Il Cicognara"*, BF14

Borsdorf, Wolfgang. *Fachwörterbuch, Chemie und chemische Technik*, EE50

Bort, Barry D. *Guide to Japanese prose*, BE1587

Boschi, Caio César. *Roteiro sumário dos arquivos portugueses de interesse para o pesquisador da história do Brasil*, DB350

Bosco, Giovanna. *Bibliografia di bibliografie*, AA50

Bosco, Umberto. *Repertorio bibliografico della letteratura italiana*, BE1295

Bose, Ashish. *Bibliography on urbanization in India, 1947–1976*, CC305

Bose, Shankar. *Elections in India*, CJ435

———— *State elections in India*, CJ435

Boškov, Zivojin. *Jugoslovenski književni leksikon*, BE1498

———— *Leksikon pisaca Jugoslavije*, BE1498

Bosl, Karl. *Biographisches Wörterbuch zur deutschen Geschichte*, AH215

Bosman, Daniël Brink. *Tweetalige woordeboek*, AC197

Bosnich, Victor W. *Congressional voting guide*, CJ213

Bosoni, Anthony J. *Legal resource directory*, CK144

Bossuat, Marie-Louise. *Bibliographie des répertoires nationaux de périodiques en cours*, AD8

Bossuat, Robert. *Manuel bibliographique de la littérature française du Moyen Âge*, BE1198

Bostock, John Knight. *A handbook on Old High German literature*, BE1256

Bostock, Kate. *The mathematical practitioners of Hanoverian England, 1714–1840*, EB102

Boston, Ray. *The newspaper press in Britain*, AE58

The Boston composers project, BJ67

Boston Conference on South Asian Library Resources in North America (1974). *South Asian library resources in North America*, DE87

Boston globe [index], AE104, AE112

Boston Public Library. *Dictionary catalog of the music collection*, BJ84

Boston Public Library. Ticknor Collection. *Catalogue of the Spanish library and of the Portuguese books bequeathed by George Ticknor*, AA800

•*Boston Spa conferences*, AL26, EA206

Boston University. Libraries. *Catalog of African government documents*, AF219

Boston University. School of Education. *Appraisal*, EA26

Boston Women's Health Book Collective. *The new our bodies, ourselves*, CC564

———— *Ourselves, growing older*, CC95, CC564

Boswick, Storm. *Guide to the universities of Europe*, CB318

Bosworth, Joseph. *Anglo-Saxon dictionary*, AC171

Botanical abstracts, EG11

Botanical bibliographies, Swift, Lloyd H., EG94

Botanical chemistry, EG161

Botanical gardens, AL88

Botanical Latin, Stearn, William T., EG143

Botanicheskiĭ slovar', Davydov, Nikolai Nikolaevich, EG142

Botanico-Periodicum-Huntianum, EG111

Die botanische Buchillustration, Nissen, Claus, EG92

Botanisches Zentralblatt, EG112

Botany

  abstract journals, EG112

  bibliography, CE14, EA16, EB10, EC15, ED5, EE13, EF57, EF141, EF173, EF232, EG6, EG88, EG89, EG91, EG92, EG93, EG94, EG105, EG211, EG312

  bibliography (by period)

    early, BE31, EA21, EC17, ED6, EE15, EG95, EG96, EG97, EG98, EG213, EH68

    modern, EG99, EG100, EG101, EG102, EG103, EG104, EG106, EG107, EG108, EG109, EG110

  biography, EG165

  classification, EG93, EG126, EG129, EG130, EG136

  dictionaries, EG116, EG121, EG122, EG123, EG124, EG126, EG127, EG128, EG129, EG130, EG131, EG132, EG133, EG134, EG135, EG136, EG137, EG138, EG140, EG147, EJ231, EJ241

    multilingual, EG141, EG142, EG143, EG144

  directories, EG118, EG120, EG145, EG146, EG148, EG149, EG150, EG151, EG152, EG153, EG154

  encyclopedias, EG116, EG117, EJ231

  eponyms, EG119

  guides, EG90

  handbooks, EG159, EG162, EG163, EG164

  indexes, EG113, EG114, EG115

  nomenclature, EG119, EG139

  periodicals, EG111

  research methods, EG151, EG152

Botany (by country or region)

  Europe, EG169, EG170

  North America

    treatises, EG171

  see also **Plants**

Bothamley, Jennifer. *Dictionary of theories*, CA31

Bothmer, A. James. *Vital and health statistics series*, CG100, EH406

Botswana

  bibliography, AA851, DD18, DD117, DD131, DD132

  encyclopedias, DD48

  government publications

    bibliography, AF218

  indexes, DD130

  statistics, CG317, CG318

Botswana (by subject)

  status of women, DD122, DD171

Botswana. Central Statistics Office. *Statistical abstract*, CG317

———— *Statistical bulletin*, CG318

Botswana, CG317

———— Morton, Fred, DD48

———— Murray, Andrew, DD48

———— Ramsay, Jeff, DD48

———— Wiseman, John A., DD18

Botswana, Lesotho, and Swaziland, Balima, Mildred Grimes, AF218

Botswana's environment, Henderson, Francine I., DD130

———— Opschoor, Johannes, DD130

Böttcher, Kurt. *Geflügelte Worte*, BE136

———— *Lexikon deutschsprachiger Schriftsteller*, BE1061

Botterweck, G. Johannes. *Theologisches Wörterbuch zum Alten Testament*, AC475, BC134

Bottle, R. T. *Information sources in chemistry*, EE3

———— *Use of biological literature*, EG2

Bottomore, T. B. *The Blackwell dictionary of twentieth-century social thought*, CA30

———— *A dictionary of Marxist thought*, CJ519

Bötze, Albrecht. *Babylonisch-assyrisches Glossar*, AC201

Boubounelle, Nicole. *Atlas départemental*, CL328

Boucher, Carl O. *Current clinical dental terminology*, EH252

Boucher, François. *20,000 years of fashion*, BG106

Boucher, Virginia. *Interlibrary loan practices handbook*, AK225

Boucher's current clinical dental terminology, EH252

Bouckaert, Boudewijn. *Bibliography of law and economics*, CK7

Boudon, Raymond. *A critical dictionary of sociology*, CC17

Bouillet, Catherine. *Littérature annotée littérature orale d'Afrique noire*, CF91

Boulanger, Grégoire. *Écrivaines et écrivains d'aujourd'hui: Suisse*, BE1490

———— *Schriftstellerinnen und Schriftsteller der Gegenwart: Schweiz*, BE1490

Boulanger, Norman. *Theatre backstage from A to Z*, BH76, BH80

———— *Theatre lighting from A to Z*, BH76

Boulding, Elise. *Bibliography on world conflict and peace*, CJ664

Boulnois, L. *Bibliographie du Népal*, DE234

Boultbee, Paul G. *The Bahamas*, DB416

———— *Turks and Caicos Islands*, DB417

Boundaries of parliamentary constituencies, 1885–1972, Craig, Fred W. S., CJ356

Boundaries of the United States and the several states, Van Zandt, Franklin K., CL76

Bourdin, Jean-François. *Bibliographie analytique des langues parlées en Afrique subsaharienne, 1970–1980*, BD213

Boureau, Édouard. *Rapport sur la paléobotanique dans le monde*, EG101

Bourgeois, Joanne. *The encyclopedia of sedimentology*, EF64

Bourke, D. O'D. *French-English horticultural dictionary*, EJ238

———— *Spanish-English horticultural dictionary*, EJ239

Bourke, Vernon J. *Thomistic bibliography, 1920–1940*, BB61, BB66, BB68

———— *Thomistic bibliography, 1940–1978*, BB68

Bourloton, Edgar. *Dictionnaire des parlementaires français*, AH200, CJ329, DC211

Bourne, Edward Gaylord. *The Philippine Islands, 1493–1898*, DE246

Bourommavong, Sing. *Lao-English dictionary*, AC569

Bourque, Amanda S. *Historical dictionary of the Third French Republic, 1870–1940*, DC207

Bourricaud, François. *A critical dictionary of sociology*, CC17

Bourton, Kathleen. *Chemical and process engineering unit operations*, EK47, EK48

Bouscarle, Marie-Elisabeth. *Les publications en série éditées au Sénégal, 1856–1982*, AD176, DD104

Bousser, Marcel. *Bibliographie marocaine, 1923–1933*, DD180

Boussinot, Roger. *Encyclopédie du cinéma*, BH247

Boutell, Charles. *Boutell's heraldry*, AJ148

———— *English heraldry*, AJ148

———— *Manual of heraldry*, AJ148

Boutell's heraldry, Boutell, Charles, AJ148

Boutier, Robert H. *État des inventaires des archives départementales, communales et hospitalières au 1er janvier 1983*, DC154

Bouty, Michel. *Dictionnaire des oeuvres et des thèmes de la littérature française*, BE1152

Bövarsson, Árni. *Íslenzk orðabók, handa skólum og almenningi*, AC505

Bover, Jaume. *Llibres [sic] editats à Mallorca (1939–1972)*, AA743

Bowden, Henry Warner. *Dictionary of American religious biography*, BC82

Bowden, John. *The Westminster dictionary of Christian theology*, BC243

Bowden, Sara R. *Understanding United States foreign trade data*, CH155

Bowder, Diana. *Who was who in the Greek world, 776 BC–30 BC*, DA114, DA115

———— *Who was who in the Roman world, 753 BC–AD 476*, DA114, DA115

Bowditch, James L. *A primer on organizational behavior,* CH602

Bowditch, Nathaniel. *American practical navigator,* EC77

Bowe, Forrest. *French literature in early American translation,* BE1146
—— *List of additions and corrections to Early Catholic Americana,* BC392

Bowen, Russell J. *Scholar's guide to intelligence literature,* CJ538

Bowers, Douglas E. *A list of references for the history of agriculture in the United States, 1790–1840,* EJ66

Bowers, Fredson Thayer. *A check list of English plays, 1641–1700,* BE657
—— *Principles of bibliographical description,* AA1

Bowers, Michael. *North American fighting uniforms,* CJ634

Bowers, Q. David. *Encyclopedia of automatic musical instruments,* BJ366

Bowes, Anna De Planter. *Bowes and Church's food values of portions commonly used,* EH303, EJ216

Bowes, D. R. *The encyclopedia of igneous and metamorphic petrology,* EF253

Bowes and Church's food values of portions commonly used, Bowes, Anna De Planter, EH303, EJ216

Bowhunter's encyclopedia, Schuh, Dwight R., BK117

Bowker, Howard F. *A bibliography on Far Eastern numismatology and a coin index,* BG171
—— *Numismatic bibliography of the Far East,* BG171

Bowker, Richard Rogers. *Publications of societies,* AL38

The Bowker annual library and book trade almanac, AK33, AK77

Bowker international serials database update, AD19

Bowker-Saur who's who in South African politics, CJ412, DD212

Bowker serials bibliography supplement, AD19

Bowker's law books and serials in print, CK18

Bowles, Stephen E. *Index to critical film reviews in British and American film periodicals,* BH243
—— *Index to critical reviews of books about film,* BH243

Bowman, J. Wilson. *America's black colleges,* CB304

Bowman, James S. *Ethics, government, and public policy,* CJ462
—— *Gubernatorial and presidential transitions,* CJ99

Bowman, John S. *Civil War almanac,* DB118

Bowman, John Wick. *Bibliography of New Testament literature, 1900–1950,* BC118

Bowman, Larry W. *Mauritius,* DD179

Bowman, M. J. *Multilateral treaties,* CK84

Bowman, Mary Ann. *Library and information science journals and serials,* AK20
—— *Western mysticism,* BC8

Bowman, Steven. *Greece in the 1940s,* DC372

Bowman, Walter Parker. *Theatre language,* BH77

Bowring, Richard John. *The Cambridge encyclopedia of Japan,* DE207

Bowser, Kathryn. *The guide to international film and video festivals,* BH265

Boxing, BK69, BK70

Boxshall, Geoffrey A. *The Cambridge illustrated dictionary of natural history,* EG75
—— *A dictionary of ecology, evolution and systematics,* EG65, EG75

Boyan, Norman J. *Handbook of research on educational administration,* CB182

Boyce, Byrl N. *Minority groups and housing,* CH529

Boyce, Charles. *Dictionary of furniture,* BG125
—— *Shakespeare A to Z,* BE783

Boyce, Gray Cowan. *Literature of medieval history, 1930–1975,* DA134

Boyce, Mary. *History of Zoroastrianism,* BC574
—— *Textual sources for the study of Zoroastrianism,* BC576
—— *Zoroastrians,* BC574, BC576

Boyd, Anne Morris. *United States government publications,* AF70

Boyd, Margaret Ann. *The crafts supply sourcebook,* BK140

Boyden, Karen. *Encyclopedia of medical organizations and agencies,* EH159

Boyer, Carl. *Index to genealogical periodicals,* AJ42

Boyer, Mildred Vinson. *The Texas collection of comedias sueltas,* BE1460

Boyer, Rick. *Places rated almanac,* CL74, CL75

Boyer, Robert D. *Realism in European theatre and drama, 1870–1920,* BE218

Boykin, James H. *The real estate handbook,* CH543

Boylan, Henry. *A dictionary of Irish biography,* AH255

Boyle, Gertrude M. *A bibliography of Canadiana,* DB188

Boyle, L. *Medieval Latin palaeography,* DA138

Boys, Richard C. *Finding-list of English poetical miscellanies 1700–48 in selected American libraries,* BE699

BPi Media Services. *News bureau contacts,* AE128

BPR annual cumulative, AA424

BPR cumulative, AA424

Brabec, Jiří. *Slovník českých spisovatelů,* BE1111

Bracken, James K. *Communication and the mass media,* AE130
—— *Reference works in British and American literature,* BE393, BE396, BE398, BE763

Brackman, Barbara. *Encyclopedia of pieced quilt patterns,* BG163

Braddock, David L. *The state of the states in developmental disabilities,* CC199

Bradford, James C. *Admirals of the new steel navy,* CJ639
—— *Captains of the old steam navy,* CJ639
—— *Command under sail,* CJ639

Bradford, Thomas Lindsley. *Homeopathic bibliography of the United States, from the year 1825 to the year 1891, inclusive,* EH200

Bradford, William C. *An index of characters in English printed drama to the Restoration,* BE658

Bradford's directory of marketing research agencies and management consultants in the United States and the world, CH583

Bradley, Diarmuid. *Collins Spanish-English, English-Spanish dictionary,* AC738

Bradley, Henry. *A Middle-English dictionary,* AC176

Bradley, Howard B. *Petroleum engineering handbook,* EK308

Bradley, J. E. S. *Chinese-English glossary of mineral names,* EF182

Bradley, John William. *A dictionary of miniaturists, illuminators, calligraphers, and copyists,* BF311

Bradley, Martin B. *Churches and church membership in the United States, 1990,* BC86

Bradley, Mary A. *Index to publications of the United States Department of Agriculture, 1901–40,* EJ92

Bradley, Susan. *Archives biographiques françaises,* AH192

Bradley, Van Allen. *The book collector's handbook of values,* AA237
—— *New gold in your attic,* AA237

Bradshaw, David N. *World photography sources,* BF347

Bradshaw, Peter. *Historical dictionary of Hong Kong & Macau,* DE151

Brady, Anna. *Union list of film periodicals,* BH174
—— *Women in Ireland,* CC591, DC393

Brady, Anne M. *A biographical dictionary of Irish writers,* BE799

Brady, Darlene. *Stained glass,* BG51

Brady, George S. *Materials handbook,* EK272

Braeuer, Walter. *Handbuch zur Geschichte der Volkswirtschaftslehre,* CH11

Bragadir, Sabine. *Dictionnaire des 10,000 dirigeants politiques français,* CJ328

Braganti, Nancy L. *European customs and manners,* CL388

Braham, Randolph L. *The Hungarian Jewish catastrophe,* DA213

Braille music collections, International directory of, BJ171

Brailow, David. *Dictionary of British literary characters,* BE688

Brain, BD78, CD117

Brana-Shute, Rosemary. *A bibliography of Caribbean migration and Caribbean immigrant communities,* CE77

Branca, Vittore. *Dizionario critico della letteratura italiana,* BE1299

Branch, Don. *New Zealand in maps,* CL366

Branch, Katherine. *Sourcebook for bibliographic instruction,* AK231

Branch, M. C. *Comprehensive urban planning,* BF270

Branciard, Michel. *Dictionnaire économique et social,* CH55

Brand, Joan. *A dictionary, English and Armenian,* AC226

Brand, Ronald A. *Basic documents of international economic law,* CK112

Brandell, Gunnar. *Svensk litteratur 1870–1970,* BE1481

Branden, F. J. van den. *Biographisch woordenboek der Noord– en Zuidnederlandsche letterkunde,* BE1328

Brandes, Eric A. *Smithells metals reference book,* EK281

Brandis, Tilo. *Nachlässe in den Bibliotheken der Bundesrepublik Deutschland,* DC248

Brandon, James R. *Asian theatre,* BH31
—— *Cambridge guide to Asian theatre,* BH66
—— *An international dictionary of theatre language,* BH79

Brandon, S. G. F. *Dictionary of comparative religion,* BC72

Brandrup, J. *Polymer handbook,* EK289

Brands and their companies, CH348

Brandstetter, Josef Leopold. *Repertorium über die in Zeit- und Sammelschriften der Jahre 1812–1890 enthaltenen Aufsätze und Mitteilungen schweizergeschichtlichen Inhaltes,* AH298, AH300, DC522, DC523

Brandt, Leo. *Bibliographisches Handbuch zur Sprachinhaltsforschung,* BD22

Branford, Jean. *A dictionary of South African English,* AC182

Brang, Karin. *Kommentierte Bibliographie zur slavischen Soziolinguistik,* BD180

Brang, Peter. *Kommentierte Bibliographie zur slavischen Soziolinguistik,* BD180

Branham automobile reference book, CH455

Brasch, Ila Wales. *A comprehensive annotated bibliography of American Black English,* BD103

Brasch, Walter M. *A comprehensive annotated bibliography of American Black English,* BD103

Brasil, Assis. *Dicionário prático de literatura brasileira,* BE924

Brasil A/Z, DB352

Brasseur, Paule Marion. *Bibliographie générale du Mali (anciens Soudan Français et Haut-Sénégal-Niger),* DD97
—— *Sources bibliographiques de l'Afrique de l'Ouest et de l'Afrique equatoriale d'expression française,* DD40

Brassey's battles, Laffin, John, DA25

Brassey's multilingual military dictionary, CJ583

Brassey's Soviet and communist quotations, CJ524

Braswell, Laurel Nichols. *The index of Middle English prose,* BE733
—— *Western manuscripts from classical antiquity to the Renaissance,* AA198

Bratkowsky, Joan Gloria. *Yiddish linguistics,* BD134

Bratton, Michael. *American doctoral dissertations on Africa 1886–1972,* DD32

Bräuer, Herbert. *Russisches geographisches Namenbuch,* CL152

Brauer, Jerald C. *Westminster dictionary of church history,* BC244

Braun, Molly. *Atlas of the North American Indian,* CC441

Braun, Wilhelm. *Etymologisches Wörterbuch des Deutschen,* AC427

Brauneck, Manfred. *Autorenlexikon deutschsprachiger Literatur des 20. Jahrhunderts,* BE1054

Braunfels, Wolfgang. *Lexikon der christlichen Ikonographie,* BF184

Braunmuller, A. R. *The Cambridge companion to English Renaissance drama,* BE659

Brawer, Moshe. *Atlas of the Middle East,* DE70

Brazil, Mary Jo. *Building library collections on aging,* CC62

Brazil
  atlases, CL316
  bibliography, AA506, AA507, AA509, AA510, DB321, DB345, DB346
    current, AA511
    historical, AA508
  bibliography of bibliography, AA28
  biography, AH124, AH125, AH126, DB354
    contemporary, AH127
  dissertations, AG20
  encyclopedias, DB352
  gazetteers, CL121, CL122
  government publications, AF159, AF160
  library resources, DB351
  periodicals
    bibliographies, AD72
    directories, AD72
  statistics, CG141, CG142, CG143, DB356

Brazil (by subject)
  economic conditions, DB348
    statistics, CG143
  ethnic groups, CC475, DB347
  folklore and popular culture
    bibliography, CF60, CF63
  foreign relations, DB349
  historiography, DB339, DB340, DB357
  history, DB353, DB357
    archives, DB350
    bibliography, DB341, DB344
    library resources, DB349
    statistics, CG143, DB356
  military history, DB355
  music, BJ22, BJ132
  place-names, CL183
  politics and government, DB342
  social conditions, DB343, DB345, DB348
    statistics, CG143

Brazil. Ministério da Educação e Cultura. Secretaria Geral. *Catálogo do banco de teses,* AG20

Brazil, Bryant, Solena V., DB341
—— Ludwig, Armin K., DB356

Brazil, 1822–1930, Levine, Robert M., DB345

Brazil and its radical left, Chilcote, Ronald H., DB342

Brazil : empire and republic, 1822–1930, DB291

Brazil in reference books, 1965–1989, Hartness, Ann, DB344

Brazil since 1930, Levine, Robert M., DB345

Brazilian drama
  bibliography, BE923
  dictionaries, BE932

Brazilian fiction
  bibliography, BE931

Brazilian literature
  bibliography, BD163, BE879, BE925, BE926, BE930, BE936, BE937, BE1362, BE1363
  biobibliography, BE924, BE934, BE936
  dictionaries, BE935
  encyclopedias, BE928, BE929, BE1366
  guides, BD163, BE926, BE1362

Brazilian literature (by subject)
  history, BE927

Brazilian literature, Foster, David William, BE925, BE930

Brazilian poetry
  biobibliography, BE933

Brazilian serial documents, Lombardi, Mary, AF160

Brazol, Demetrio. *Dictionary of meteorological and related terms,* EF150

Breakthroughs, Parkinson, Claire L., EA254

Brealey, Richard A. *A bibliography of finance,* CH224

Breban, Vasile. *Dicţionar general al limbii române,* AC657

Brebner, Lilias W. *German-English mathematical vocabulary,* EB51

Brechenmacher, Josef Karlmann. *Etymologisches Wörterbuch der deutschen Familiennamen,* AJ194

Brecher, George. *Saunders dictionary & encyclopedia of laboratory medicine and technology,* EH109

Brednich, Rolf Wilhelm. *Enzyklopädie des Märchens,* CF50

Bredsdorff, Elias. *Danish literature in English translation,* BE1112

Breed, Paul Francis. *Dramatic criticism index,* BE219
—— *Songs in collections,* BJ284

Breen, Walter H. *Encyclopedia of United States silver & gold commemorative coins, 1892–1954,* BG193
—— *Walter Breen's complete encyclopedia of U.S. and colonial coins,* BG193

Bréhier, Émile. *Histoire de la philosophie … ,* BB46
—— *History of philosophy,* BB46

Breitenberg, Maureen A. *Directory of international and regional organizations conducting standards-related activities,* EA271

Brekle, Herbert E. *Bio-bibliographisches Handbuch zur Sprachwissenschaft des 18. Jahrhunderts,* BD66

Brelin, Christa. *Fund your way through college,* CB383

Bremmer, Rolf H. *A bibliographical guide to Old Frisian studies,* BD133

Bremser, Martha. *International dictionary of ballet,* BH142

Bremt, F. van den. *Historical atlas of music,* BJ198

Brendon, J. A. *Dictionary of British history,* DC293

Brenet, Michel. *Dictionnaire pratique et historique de la musique,* BJ146

Brenford, Robert J. *A bibliography of jazz,* BJ305

Brennan, James F. *History and systems of psychology,* CD53

Brennan, Shawn. *Resourceful woman,* CC558

Brennan, Stephen J. *Basketball resource guide,* BK64

Brenner, Clarence Dietz. *A bibliographical list of plays in the French language, 1700–1789,* BE1177

Brenner, Morris. *Handbook of applied mathematics,* EB64

Brenni, Vito Joseph. *Book printing in Britain and America,* AA267

Bresler, Judith. *Art law,* BF122

Bressett, Kenneth. *A guide book of United States coins,* BG195

Bretherick, L. *Bretherick's handbook of reactive chemical hazards,* EE65

Bretherick's handbook of reactive chemical hazards, Bretherick, L., EE65

Brethren churches, BC330

The Brethren encyclopedia, BC330

Breton, Émile. *Dictionnaire des cinéastes,* BH285
—— *Dictionnaire des films,* BH200

Breton language
  dictionaries, AC236, AC237, AC238
  bilingual
    Breton-French, AC234

Brett, Lewis E. *Appleton's new Cuyás English-Spanish and Spanish-English dictionary,* AC732

Brett, Simon. *Faber book of parodies,* BE723

Brett, Vanessa. *Phaidon guide to pewter,* BG149
—— *The Sotheby's directory of silver, 1600–1940,* BG143

Breuille, Jean-Philippe. *Dictionnaire de la sculpture,* BF389

Breul, Karl. *Cassell's German-English, English-German dictionary,* AC414

Breve diccionario etimológico de la lengua castellana, Corominas, Joan, AC742

Breve historia de grandes hombres, Benítez, Luis G., AH138

Breviate of parliamentary papers, 1900–1916, Ford, Grace, AF196
—— Ford, Percy, AF196

Breviate of parliamentary papers, 1917–1939, Ford, Grace, AF196
—— Ford, Percy, AF196

Brewer, Annie M. *Dictionaries, encyclopedias, and other word-related books,* AC189

Brewer, David Josiah. *World's best orations,* BE347

Brewer, Deborah J. *ARBA guide to education,* CB1

Brewer, Ebenezer Cobham. *Brewer's dictionary of phrase and fable,* BE181
—— *Reader's handbook of famous names in fiction, allusions, references, proverbs, plots, stories, and poems,* BE181

Brewer, James Gordon. *The literature of geography,* CL1

Brewer, Mary. *Concise encyclopedia of biochemistry,* EG316

Brewer, Warren A. *Analogy,* BD47

Brewer's dictionary of phrase and fable, AC91
—— Brewer, Ebenezer Cobham, BE181

Brewster, K. G. *New Century dictionary of the English language,* AC11

Brewton, John Edmund. *Index to children's poetry,* BE376
—— *Index to poetry for children and young people,* BE376

Brewton, Sara Westbrook. *Index to children's poetry,* BE376
—— *Index to poetry for children and young people,* BE376

Brey Mariño, María. *Catálogo de los manuscritos poéticos castellanos existentes en la Biblioteca de The Hispanic Society of America (siglos XV, XVI y XVII),* BE1465, BE1478

Briamonte, Nino. *Saggio di bibliografia sui problemi storici, teorici e pratici della traduzione,* BD86

Brian Rust's guide to discography, Rust, Brian A. L., BJ382

Bricault, Giselle C. *Major companies of the Arab world,* CH409

Brice, F. F. *The new layman's Bible commentary in one volume,* BC179

Brice, William C. *An historical atlas of Islam,* DE69

Bricka, Carl Frederik. *Dansk biografisk leksikon,* AH183

Brickell, Christopher. *The American Horticultural Society encyclopedia of garden plants,* EG116, EJ231
—— *The American Horticultural Society encyclopedia of gardening,* EJ232

Bricker, Victoria Reifler. *Handbook of Middle American Indians,* CE89

Brickey, Wayne E. *A catalogue of theses and dissertations concerning the Church of Jesus Christ of Latter-Day Saints, Mormonism and Utah,* BC369

Brickman, William W. *A bibliography of American educational history,* CB29
—— *The Jewish community in America,* BC522
—— *Russian and Soviet education, 1731–1989,* CB45

Bridge, F. R. *Hapsburg monarchy, 1804–1918,* DC95

Bridge, BK130

Bridgers, F. E. *Guide to genealogical records in the National Archives,* AJ15

Bridges, Ronald. *The Bible word book,* BC135

Bridges to knowledge in political science, Kalvelage, Carl, CJ3

Bridgman, Jon. *German Africa,* DD80

Bridson, Gavin D. R. *Plant, animal & anatomical illustration in art & science,* EA220
—— *Printmaking & picture printing,* BF359

Brief glossary of Buddhist terms, March, Arthur Charles, BC477

A brief guide to centres of international lending and photocopying, AK223

A brief history of entomology, Osborn, Herbert, EG336

Brief introduction to the use of Beilstein's Handbuch der organischen Chemie, Huntress, Ernest Hamlin, EE115

Brieger, Gert H. *Nobel prize winners,* AH30, AL170

Brierley, P. W. *UK Christian handbook,* BC251

Brigance, W. N. *A history and criticism of American public address*, BE365
Briggs, Asa. *The Longman encyclopedia*, AB11
Briggs, Charles Augustus. *The international critical commentary on the Holy Scriptures of the Old and New Testaments*, BC173
——— *The new Brown, Driver, Briggs, Gesenius Hebrew and English lexicon*, AC476, BC133
Briggs, Geoffrey. *The Cambridge photographic atlas of the planets*, EC64
Briggs, Gerald G. *Drugs in pregnancy and lactation*, EH341
Briggs, Katharine Mary. *British folktales*, CF88
——— *A dictionary of British folktales in the English language*, CF88
Briggs, Martin Shaw. *Everyman's concise encyclopedia of architecture*, BF244
Briggs, Ward W. *Biographical dictionary of North American classicists*, BE1024, DA113
——— *Classical scholarship*, BE1024, DA113
Brigham, Clarence Saunders. *American book auction catalogues, 1713–1934*, AA265
——— *History and bibliography of American newspapers, 1690–1820*, AE19, AE26
Brigham Young University. College of Religious Instruction. *A catalogue of theses and dissertations concerning the Church of Jesus Christ of Latter-Day Saints, Mormonism and Utah*, BC369
Brigham Young University. Institute for Polynesian Studies. *Who's who in Oceania, 1980–1981*, AH385
Brigham Young University. Library. *Mormons in the Pacific*, BC370
Brigham Young University–Hawaii Campus. Library. *Mormons in the Pacific*, BC370
Bright, Charles D. *Historical dictionary of the U.S. Air Force*, CJ614
Bright, William. *Bibliography of the languages of native California*, CC420
——— *International encyclopedia of linguistics*, BD35
Brignano, Russell Carl. *Black Americans in autobiography*, CC363
Brimmer, Brenda. *A guide to the use of United Nations documents*, AF31
Bring, Samuel Ebbe. *Itineraria svecana*, DC519
Brinker, Russell C. *The surveying handbook*, EK62
Brinker-Gabler, Gisela. *Lexikon deutschsprachiger Schriftstellerinnen, 1800–1945*, BE1056
Brinkman, Carel Leonhard. *Alphabetische naamlijst van boeken*, AA748, AA749
——— *Brinkman's cumulatieve catalogus van boeken*, AA756
Brinkman's catalogus van boeken en tijdschriften, AA749, AA753, AA754, AA756
Brinkman's cumulatieve catalogus van boeken, AA753
——— Brinkman, Carel Leonhard, AA756
Brinkman's titel-catalogus, AA754
Brinson, H. F. *Engineered materials handbook*, EK274
Briquet, Charles Moïse. *Filigranes*, AA255, AA256
Briquet, Marie. *Musique dans les congrès internationaux, 1835–1939*, BJ20
The Briquet album, AA255
Briscoe, Mary Louise. *American autobiography, 1945–1980*, AH89, BE507, DB66, DB67
Brisebois, Madeleine. *Vocabulaire de technologie éducative et de formation*, CB172
Briseño, Ramón. *Estadística bibliográfica de la literatura chilena*, AA515
Brisman, Shimeon. *Jewish research literature*, BC512
Bristol, Roger Pattrell. *American bibliography*, AA405
——— *Supplement to Charles Evans' American bibliography*, AA403
Britain, CJ346
Britain & the world, 1815–1986, Weigall, David, DC338
Britain, an official handbook, CJ346
Britain and Europe during [year], CJ337
Britain and Europe since 1945, CJ337

Britain and Palestine, 1914–1948, Jones, Philip, DE243
Britain in the Middle East, 1921–1956, Ponko, Vincent, DE38
Britain votes, Craig, Fred W. S., CJ364, CJ365
Britain's elusive empire in the Middle East, 1900–1921, Olson, William J., DE37
Britain's theatrical periodicals, 1920–1967, Stratman, Carl Joseph, BH36
Britannica book of English usage, AC66
The Britannica book of the year, AB12, DA209
•*Britannica CD*, AB12
•*Britannica electronic index*, AB12
•*Britannica electronic index on CD-ROM*, AB12
The Britannica encyclopedia of American art, BF82
•*Britannica instant research system*, AB12
Britannica junior, AB17
Britannica yearbook of science and the future, EA169
British *see* **Britons**
British abstracts, EE21
British abstracts of medical sciences, EG17
British abstracts. Pt. C, Analysis and apparatus, EE20
British Academy. *Dictionary of medieval Latin from British sources*, AC588
——— *Revised medieval Latin word-list from British and Irish sources*, AC589
——— *Summary guide to Corpus vasorum antiquorum*, BG78
The British alternative theatre directory, BH87
British and American utopian literature, 1516–1985, Sargent, Lyman Tower, BE684
British and Foreign Bible Society. Library. *Historical catalogue of the printed editions of Holy Scripture in the library of the British and Foreign Bible Society*, BC95, BC99, BC100
British and Irish architectural history, Kamen, Ruth H., BF203
British and Irish Association of Law Librarians. *Directory of British and Irish law libraries*, CK213
British and Irish biographies, 1840–1940, AH223
British and Irish library resources, Downs, Robert Bingham, AK144
British archaeological abstracts, DC306
British archaeological bibliography, DC306
British architects, 1840–1976, Wodehouse, Lawrence, BF204, BF239
British architectural books and writers, 1556–1785, Harris, Eileen, BF216
British Architectural Library. *Architectural periodicals index*, BF207
——— *Directory of British architects, 1834–1900*, BF259
British archives, Foster, Janet, AJ98, AK145
British Association for American Studies. *A guide to manuscripts relating to America in Great Britain and Ireland*, DB32
British Association for Mycenaean Studies. *Studies in Mycenaean inscriptions and dialect, 1965–1978*, BD139
British Association for the Advancement of Science. *Mathematical tables*, EB82, EB94
British Association for the Advancement of Science. Research Committee. *A glossary of geographical terms*, CL42
British Association of Slavonic and East European Studies. *Abstracts, Russian and East European series*, DC38
The British atlas of historic towns, DC354
British authors before 1800, BE203
——— Kunitz, Stanley Jasspon, BE624
British authors of the 19th century, BE203, BE625
British autobiographies, Matthews, William, AH236, BE727
British biographical archive, AH223, AH224
British biographical index, Bank, David, AH224
——— Esposito, Anthony, AH224
British book news, AA331
British books in print, AA691
British Broadcasting Corporation. *BBC English dictionary*, AC35

——— *BBC world service glossary of current affairs*, CJ36
British Broadcasting Corporation. Central Music Library. *[Catalogues]*, BJ92
The British Burma gazetteer, Spearman, Horace Ralph, CL159
British catalogue of music, BJ53, BJ79
British catalogue of music, 1957–1985, BJ25, BJ53, BJ79
British Colour Council. *The British Colour Council dictionary of colour standards*, ED58
The British Colour Council dictionary of colour standards, British Colour Council, ED58
British command papers, McBride, Elizabeth A., AF195, AF206
British Committee of Historic Towns. *Historic towns*, DC354
British Council. *Public administration*, CJ473
British Council. English Language & Literature Division. *Language teaching*, BD74, CB58
British Crop Protection Council. *The pesticide manual*, EJ61
British diaries, Matthews, William, BE724, BE726, BE727, DC327
British directories, Shaw, Gareth, AL1, AL7, CH366, CH381
——— Tipper, Allison, AL1, AL7, CH366, CH381
British drama, Nicoll, Allardyce, BE666
——— Trewin, J. C., BE666
British East Africa, 1856–1963, Ofcansky, Thomas P., DD108
British economic and social history, DC272
British education index, CB50, CB57, CB81
British education thesaurus, CB50, CB57, CB81
British education theses index, CB50, CB57
British elections and parties yearbook, CJ363
British electoral facts, 1832–1987, Craig, Fred W. S., CJ364, CJ365
The British electorate 1963–1987, Crewe, Ivor, CJ367
British Empire and Commonwealth
  bibliography, DC291
    periodicals, DC343
  biography, AH230
    bibliography, AH238
  library catalogs, DC342
  manuscripts and archives, DB412, DB413
British Empire and Commonwealth (by subject)
  history
    atlases, DC346
    library catalogs, DC344
    manuscripts and archives, DC341
  politics and government, CJ372
The British Empire in the Victorian press, 1832–1867, Palmegiano, Eugenia M., DC343
British English, A to Zed, Schur, Norman W., AC83
The British establishment, 1760–1784, Valentine, Alan Chester, AH229
British fiction
  bibliography, BE254
British fiction, 1750–1770, Raven, James, BE681
British film actors' credits, 1895–1987, Palmer, Scott, BH211
The British film catalogue, 1895–1985, Gifford, Denis, BH186
British Film Institute. *The BFI companion to the Western*, BH245
——— *BFI film and television handbook*, BH264
——— *Pre-cinema history*, BH166
British Film Institute. Library. *Catalogue of the book library of the British Film Institute*, BH163
——— *Film index international*, BH185
British folktales, Briggs, Katharine Mary, CF88
British Food Manufacturing Industries Research Association. *Food industries manual*, EJ166
British foreign policy 1918–1945, Aster, Sidney, DC326
British gardeners, Hadfield, Miles, BF285
British general election manifestos, 1959–1987, CJ350
British government publications, Richard, Stephen, AF193

British historical facts, Cook, Chris, DC323
———— Keith, Brendan, DC323
———— Stevenson, John, DC323
British historical statistics, Mitchell, Brian R., CG234, CG235
British history, 1945–1987, Catterall, Peter, DC329
British humanities index, AD264, AD289, BA6
British imperial calendar and civil service list, CJ340
The British labour movement to 1970, Smith, Harold, CH638
British labour statistics, Great Britain. Department of Employment and Productivity, CH683
British librarianship and information science, AK78
British librarianship and information work, AK78
British Library. *The British Library,* AK101
———— *British Library general catalogue of printed books, 1976 to 1982,* AA102, BC96
———— *British Library general catalogue of printed books, 1982 to 1985,* AA102, BC96
———— *British Library general catalogue of printed books, 1986 to 1987,* AA102, BC96
———— *British Library general catalogue of printed books, 1988 to 1989,* AA102, BC96
———— *The British Library general catalogue of printed books to 1975,* AA102, BC96
———— *British Library general subject catalog, 1971–1975,* AA104
———— *British Library general subject catalog, 1975–1985,* AA104
———— *British Library general subject catalogue, 1986 to 1990,* AA104
———— *Catalogue of books from the Low Countries 1601–1621 in the British Library,* AA750
———— *Catalogue of books printed in Spain and of Spanish books printed elsewhere in Europe before 1601, now in the British Library,* AA468, AA813
———— *Catalogue of cartographic materials in the British Library, 1975–1988,* CL251
———— *Catalogue of seventeenth century Italian books in the British Library,* AA728
———— *Catalogue of the Crawford library of philatelic literature at the British Library,* BG201
———— *The eighteenth century short title catalogue 1990,* AA681
———— *A guide to Latin American and Caribbean census material,* CG122
———— *Modern British and American private presses, 1850–1965,* AA238
———— *The South Asia and Burma retrospective bibliography (SABREB),* AA889
British Library, AK10
British Library. Bibliographic Services Division. *British education index,* CB50
———— *Serials in the British Library,* AD116
British Library. Department of Manuscripts. *Catalogue of dated and datable manuscripts, c.700–1600 in the Department of Manuscripts, the British Library,* AA203
———— *Index of manuscripts in the British Library,* AA204
British Library. Department of Printed Books. *Subject index of modern books acquired, 1961–1970,* AA104
British Library. Department of Printed Books. Burney Collection. *Early English newspapers,* AE57
British Library. Document Supply Centre. *Index of conference proceedings,* AL26, EA206
British Library. Lending Division. *BLL conference index, 1964–1973,* AL26, EA206
———— *Current British journals,* AD115
———— *Current research in Britain,* BA8, CA46, EA138, EG47
———— *Index of conference proceedings received,* AL26, EA206
———— *Japanese journals in English,* EA50
———— *Microform research collections at the British Library Lending Division,* AA129
British Library. Music Division. *Catalogue of printed music in the British Library to 1980,* BJ25, BJ53
British Library. National Sound Archive. *Oral history,* DC332

British Library. Newspaper Library, Colindale. *Catalogue of the Newspaper Library, Colindale,* AE56
British Library. Official Publications Library. *Check list of British official serial publications,* AF181
British Library. Reference Division. *Catalogue of books and periodicals on Estonia in the British Library Reference Division,* DC135
———— *Check list of British official serial publications,* AF181
British Library. Research and Development Dept. *Complete list of reports published by the British Library R&D Department,* AK10
British Library. Science, Technology, and Industry. *Guide to libraries in Western Europe,* AK132
The British Library, British Library, AK101
British Library general catalogue of printed books, 1976 to 1982, British Library, AA102, BC96
British Library general catalogue of printed books, 1982 to 1985, British Library, AA102, BC96
British Library general catalogue of printed books, 1986 to 1987, British Library, AA102, BC96
British Library general catalogue of printed books, 1988 to 1989, British Library, AA102, BC96
The British Library general catalogue of printed books to 1975, British Library, AA102, BC96
British Library general subject catalog, 1971–1975, British Library, AA104
British Library general subject catalog, 1975–1985, British Library, AA104
British Library general subject catalogue, 1986 to 1990, British Library, AA104
British library history, AK70
British Library of Political and Economic Science. *International bibliography of economics,* CH43
———— *London bibliography of the social sciences,* CA13
———— *Sources in British political history, 1900–1951,* DC335
British library resources, AK144
British literary bibliography, BE587
British literary magazines, BE590
British literary publishing houses, 1820–1880, Anderson, Patricia J., AA297
———— Rose, Jonathan, AA297
British literary publishing houses, 1881–1965, Anderson, Patricia J., AA297
———— Rose, Jonathan, AA297
British Malaya, Heussler, Robert, DE228
British manuscript diaries of the nineteenth century, Batts, John Stuart, BE724, DC327
British manuscripts project, Library of Congress. Processing Department, AA133
British medical dictionary, MacNalty, Arthur Salusbury, EH94
British military history, Jordan, Gerald, DC277
British Museum. *The book of British topography,* DC347
———— *Catalog of books printed in the XVth century,* AA231
———— *General catalogue of printed books,* AL12, BE456
———— *Newspapers published in Great Britain and Ireland, 1801–1900,* AD114
———— *Short-title catalogues of Portuguese books and of Spanish-American books printed before 1601,* AA775
British Museum. Department of Manuscripts. *Catalogue of additions to the manuscripts,* BE637, BE644
———— *Catalogue of manuscript music in the British Museum,* BJ93
———— *The catalogues of the manuscript collections,* AA205
———— *Handlist of music manuscripts acquired 1908–67,* BJ93
British Museum. Department of Oriental Printed Books and Manuscripts. *Catalogue of Syriac printed books and related literature in the British Museum,* BD205

British Museum. Department of Printed Books. *Catalogue of books in the library of the British Museum printed in England, Scotland, and Ireland, and of books in English printed abroad to the year 1640,* AA668
———— *Catalogue of books printed in the XVth century now in the British Museum,* AA219, AA639
———— *Catalogue of printed books,* AD4
———— *Catalogue of printed books : Academies,* AL12
———— *Catalogue of printed music published between 1487 and 1800 now in the British Museum,* BJ54
———— *A catalogue of the works of Linnaeus (and publications more immediately relating thereto) preserved in the libraries of the British Museum (Bloomsbury) and the British Museum (Natural History) (South Kensington),* EG102
———— *General catalogue of printed books,* AA103, AA615, AA661, AD3, AD4, BE707
———— *An index to the authors (other than Linnaeus) mentioned in the Catalogue … ,* EG103
———— *Index to the early printed books in the British Museum,* AA227
———— *Short-title catalogue of books printed in France and of French books printed in other countries from 1470 to 1600, now in the British Museum,* AA615
———— *Short-title catalogue of books printed in Italy and of Italian books printed in other countries from 1465 to 1600, now in the British Museum,* AA728, AA729, AA735
———— *Short-title catalogue of books printed in Spain and of Spanish books printed elsewhere in Europe before 1601, now in the British Museum,* AA813, AA816
———— *Short-title catalogue of books printed in the German-speaking countries and German books printed in other countries from 1455 to 1600, now in the British Museum,* AA638
———— *Short-title catalogue of books printed in the Netherlands and Belgium and of Dutch and Flemish books printed in other countries from 1470 to 1600, now in the British Museum,* AA745
———— *Short title catalogue of French books, 1601–1700,* AA615
———— *Short-title catalogue of Portuguese books printed before 1601, now in the British Museum,* AA468, AA775
———— *Short-title catalogues of Portuguese books and of Spanish-American books printed before 1601, now in the British Museum,* AA468
———— *Short-title catalogues of Spanish, Spanish-American and Portuguese books printed before 1601 in the British Museum,* AA468
———— *Subject index of the modern works added to the library, 1881–1900,* AA94, AA104
British Museum. Department of Printed Books. Hirsch Library. *Books in the Hirsch Library, with supplementary list of music,* BJ85, BJ87
———— *Music in the Hirsch Library,* BJ85, BJ87, BJ94
British Museum. Department of Printed Books. Thomason Collection. *Catalogue of the pamphlets, books, newspapers, and manuscripts relating to the Civil War, the Commonwealth, and Restoration collected by George Thomason, 1640–1661,* AA677
British Museum. Dept. of Manuscripts. *Catalogue of romances in the Department of Manuscripts in the British Museum,* BE335
British Museum. Map Room. *Catalogue of printed maps, charts and plans,* CL251
British Museum. State Paper Room. *Check list of British official serial publications,* AF181
British Museum (Natural History). *Catalogue of meteorites,* EF207
British Museum (Natural History). Library. *Catalogue of the books, manuscripts, maps and drawings in the British Museum (Natural History),* EA12

—— *Serial publications in the British Museum (Natural History) Library*, EA40

British national bibliography, AA103, AA150, AA661, AA689, AD3, BJ79

•*British national bibliography on CD-ROM*, AA689

British natural history books, 1495–1900, Freeman, Richard Broke, EG69

British naval history since 1815, Rasor, Eugene L., DC333

British newspapers and periodicals, 1632–1800, Stewart, Powell, AE56

British newspapers and periodicals, 1641–1700, Nelson, Carolyn, AA412, AA683, AD107

—— Seccombe, Matthew, AA412, AA683

British novel, Wiley, Paul L., BE682

British official films in the Second World War, Pronay, Nicholas, DA204

—— Thorpe, Frances, DA204

British paperbacks in print, AA685

British parliamentary constituencies, Crewe, Ivor, CJ368

British parliamentary election results, Craig, Fred W. S., CJ356, CJ364, CJ365, CJ366

British parliamentary election results, 1832–1885, Craig, Fred W. S., CJ365

British parliamentary papers, AF205

British periodicals & newspapers, 1789–1832, AE58

—— Ward, William Smith, AD108

British pharmaceutical codex, EH361

British pharmacopoeia 1988, EH356

British Pharmacopoeia Commission. *British pharmacopoeia 1988*, EH356

British poetry and the American Revolution, Kallich, Martin, BE709

British political facts, Butler, David, CJ373

British political facts, 1900–1985, Butler, David, CJ347, DC339

British Politics Group research register, CJ342

British Record Society. *An index to the biographical and obituary notices in the Gentleman's magazine, 1731–1780*, AH241

British Science Guild. *Catalogue of British scientific and technical books*, EA13

British scientific and technical books, EA13, EA32

British self-taught, Schur, Norman W., AC83

British sound films, Quinlan, David, BH186

British sources of information, Jackson, Paul, DC278

British standard glossary of dental terms, EH253

British Standards Institution. *Universal decimal classification*, AK205

British Standards Intitution. *BSI standards catalogue*, EA270

British technology index, AD289, BA6, EK6

British theatre, Cavanagh, John, BH38, BH40

British theatre directory, BH87

The British traditional ballad in North America, Coffin, Tristram Potter, BE630

British union-catalogue of early music printed before the year 1801, BJ54

British union-catalogue of periodicals, AD114, AD116, AD236, AD237, EA46

British Universities Film & Video Council. *Researcher's guide to British film & television collections*, BH181

British voter, Kinnear, Michael, CJ349, CJ369

British women writers, BE621

British women's diaries, Huff, Cynthia, BE724, DC327

British writers, BE448, BE622

—— Scott-Kilvert, Ian, BE201

British writing on disarmament from 1914–1978, Lloyd, Lorna, CJ673

Britons (by country or region)
 Canada
  manuscripts and archives, CC332
 United States, AJ63
  manuscripts and archives, CC332

Britten, Frederick James. *Britten's old clocks and watches and their makers*, BG85

Britten, James. *Dictionary of English plant-names*, EG120

Britten's old clocks and watches and their makers, Britten, Frederick James, BG85

Britton, Allen Perdue. *American sacred music imprints, 1698–1810*, BJ68

Britton, N. L. *The new Britton and Brown illustrated flora of the northeastern United States and adjacent Canada*, EG173

Britton, Scott G. *SME mining engineering handbook*, EK254

Brix, Michel. *Guide bibliographique des études d'histoire de la littérature française*, BE1128

The broadcast communications dictionary, CH484

Broadcast research definitions, CH485

The broadcaster's dictionary, McDonald, James R., BH318

Broadcasting
 dictionaries, BH260, CH485
 see also **Mass media; Radio; Television**

Broadcasting & cable market place, CH489

Broadcasting & cable yearbook, CH489

Broadcasting cablecasting yearbook, CH489

The broadcasting yearbook, CH489

Broadhead, Lee-Anne. *Bibliography of works on Canadian foreign relations, 1981–1985*, DB186

Broadhead, Susan H. *Angola*, DD48

The Broadman Bible commentary, BC170

Broadway, Bloom, Ken, BH63

Broadway musicals, show by show, Green, Stanley, BJ264

Broadway on record, Lynch, Richard Chigley, BJ361

Brock, George W. *American Association for Marriage and Family Therapy ethics casebook*, CC233

The Brock bibliography of published Canadian plays in English, 1766–1978, BE820

Brockelmann, Carl. *Geschichte der arabischen Literatur*, BE1549

—— *Lexicon syriacum*, AC771

Brockenbrough, Roger L. *Structural steel designers' handbook*, EK111

Der Brockhaus, AB49, AB85, AB89

Brockhaus ABC Biochemie. Concise encyclopedia biochemistry, EE26

Brockhaus ABC Biochemie, EG315, EG316

Brockhaus ABC Chemie, EE26

Brockhaus Enzyklopädie, AB48, AB49

Brockhaus' Konversations-Lexikon, AB49

Brockhaus picture dictionary, AC648

Brockhaus Riemann Musiklexikon, BJ128

Brockhaus Wahrig, AC400

Brockman, William S. *Music*, BJ1

Brockmeyer, Norbert. *Bibliographie zur antiken Sklaverei*, DA68

Brodeur, Léo A. *Guide bibliographique des thèses littéraires canadiennes de 1921 à 1976*, BE831

—— *Répertoire des thèses littéraires canadiennes de 1921 à 1976*, BE44

Brodman, Estelle. *The development of medical bibliography*, EH10

Brody, Elaine. *The music guide to Austria and Germany*, BJ190

—— *Music guide to Belgium, Luxembourg, Holland and Switzerland*, BJ190

—— *Music guide to Great Britain*, BJ190

—— *Music guide to Italy*, BJ190

Brody, Jules. *A critical bibliography of French literature*, BE1131

Broeckaert, Jan. *Bibliographie van den Vlaamschen taalstrijd*, AA579

Broeckx, J. L. *Flandria nostra*, DC109

Brogan, Marianne C. *The ACS style guide*, EE95

Brogan, Martha L. *Research guide to libraries and archives in the Low Countries*, AK133, DC13

Brogan, Terry V. F. *English versification, 1570–1980*, BE311, BE696

—— *The new Princeton encyclopedia of poetry and poetics*, BE329, BE696

—— *Verseform*, BE311

Bromell, Anne. *Tracing family history in New Zealand*, AJ145

Bromiley, Geoffrey William. *The international standard Bible encyclopedia*, BC131

—— *Theological dictionary of the New Testament*, AC456, BC143

Bromlei, ÎU. V. *Slavianovedenie v SSSR*, DC54

Bromley, David G. *The anti-cult movement in America*, BC32

Bromley, John. *The clockmakers' library*, BG81

Bromwich, R. *Medieval Celtic literature*, DA138

Brøndsted, Mogens. *Nordens litteratur*, BE1091

Bronne by die studie van Afrikaanse prosawerke, Senekal, Jan, BE1536

Bronnegids by die studie van die Afrikaanse taal en letterkunde, Nienaber, Petrus Johannes, BD132

Bronnegids vir toponimie en topologie, Raper, P. E., CL217

Bronner, Edwin. *The encyclopedia of the American theatre, 1900–1975*, BH98

Bronner, Simon J. *American folk art*, BG1

Bronshteĭn, I. N. *Handbook of mathematics*, EB62

Bronson, Bertrand Harris. *Traditional tunes of the Child ballads*, BE632, BJ314

Brook, Barry S. *Thematic catalogues in music*, BJ230

Brook, Claire. *The music guide to Austria and Germany*, BJ190

—— *Music guide to Belgium, Luxembourg, Holland and Switzerland*, BJ190

—— *Music guide to Great Britain*, BJ190

—— *Music guide to Italy*, BJ190

Brook, G. B. *Smithells metals reference book*, EK281

Brooke, Iris. *Western European costume, 13th to 17th century, and its relation to the theatre*, BG107

—— *Western European costume and its relation to the theatre*, BG107

Brooke, John. *The House of Commons, 1715–1754*, CJ360

—— *House of Commons, 1754–1790*, CJ354

Brooke, Michael. *The Cambridge encyclopedia of ornithology*, EG254

—— *Handbook of international trade*, CH137

Brooke-Little, John Philip. *Boutell's heraldry*, AJ148

—— *A complete guide to heraldry*, AJ154

—— *An heraldic alphabet*, AJ162

Brookes, John. *The book of garden design*, BF295

—— *Garden book*, BF295

—— *Garden styles*, BF295

Brookhart, Edward. *Music in American higher education*, BJ26

Brookings Institution. *Government publications and their use*, AF76

Brooklyn College. Theatre Research Data Center. *International bibliography of theatre*, BH57

Brooklyn Public Library. *Business rankings annual*, CH402

Brookman, Lester G. *19th century postage stamps of the United States*, BG204

—— *The United States postage stamps of the 19th century*, BG204

Brooks, Constance. *Disaster preparedness*, AK238

Brooks, David. *Disease data book*, EH178

Brooks, Phillip Coolidge. *Research in archives*, DB27

Brooks, Richard A. *A critical bibliography of French literature*, BE1131

Brooks, Tim. *The complete directory to prime time network TV shows, 1946–present*, BH299

—— *The complete directory to prime time TV stars, 1946–present*, BH320

Brooks-Gunn, Jeanne. *Encyclopedia of adolescence*, CC159, CD83

Brosenne, Celeste. *Resources for the history of computing*, EK208

Bross, Donald C. *The new child protection team handbook*, CC172

Brosse, Jacques. *Dizionario letterario Bompiani delle opere e dei personaggi di tutti i tempi e di tutte le letterature*, BE63

Brosseau, John P. *Foreign language, area, and other international studies*, BD76

Brostrøm, Torben. *Danske Digtere i det 20. arhundrede*, BE1115

Brotherton Library. *Catalogue of the Romany collection*, CC479

Brottman, May. *The LIRT library instruction handbook*, AK230

Broughton, Bradford B. *Dictionary of medieval knighthood and chivalry,* DA147

Broughton, J. Mills. *Bibliographic classification,* AK198

Broughton, Vanda. *Bibliographic classification,* AK198

Brower, Carol. *The permanence and care of color photographs,* BF351

Brower, Keith H. *Contemporary Latin American fiction,* BE901

Brown, Addison. *The new Britton and Brown illustrated flora of the northeastern United States and adjacent Canada,* EG173

Brown, Barbara E. *Canadian business and economics,* CH175

Brown, Carleton Fairchild. *The index of Middle English verse,* BE697, BE714
—— *Register of Middle English religious and didactic verse,* BE697, BE698

Brown, Caroline M. *Abortion,* CC252

Brown, Catherine L. *A bibliography of geographic thought,* CL5
—— *The urban South,* DB154

Brown, Charles N. *Science fiction, fantasy & horror,* BE300

Brown, Christopher C. *English prose and criticism, 1900–1950,* BE760

Brown, Christopher M. *Concise veterinary dictionary,* EJ112

Brown, Clifton F. *Ethiopian perspectives,* DD155
—— *The Howard University bibliography of African and Afro-American religious studies,* BC33

Brown, Deming. *Soviet Russian literature since Stalin,* BE1421

Brown, Edward E. *A bibliography of Malawi,* DD176

Brown, Enid. *Suriname and the Netherlands Antilles,* DB390

Brown, Francis. *The new Brown, Driver, Briggs, Gesenius Hebrew and English lexicon,* AC476, BC133

Brown, Fred. *Virology,* EG345

Brown, Gene. *Handbook of American-Jewish literature,* BE565

Brown, Harrison Scott. *A bibliography on meteorites,* EF206

Brown, John Carter. *Bibliotheca americana,* DB1

Brown, John H. *The Russian Empire and the Soviet Union,* AK106, DC560

Brown, K. R. *Library, documentation, and archives serials,* AK21

Brown, Karl. *Guide to the reference collections of the New York Public Library,* AK115
—— *Union lists of serials,* AD219

Brown, Langdon. *Shakespeare around the globe,* BE792

Brown, Les. *Les Brown's encyclopedia of television,* BH313

Brown, Lucy M. *Bibliography of British history, 1789–1851,* DC328

Brown, Marjorie M. *Philosophical studies of home economics in the United States,* EJ199

Brown, Michelle P. *A guide to western historical scripts from antiquity to 1600,* AA213

Brown, Peter. *World list of scientific periodicals published in the years 1900–1960,* EA46

Brown, R. C. *Confederation to 1949,* DB205

Brown, R. H. *CRC handbook of engineering in agriculture,* EJ47

Brown, Rae Linda. *Music, printed and manuscript, in the James Weldon Johnson Memorial Collection of Negro Arts and Letters,* BJ95

Brown, Raymond Edward. *The new Jerome biblical commentary,* BC178

Brown, Reginald F. *La novela española, 1700–1850,* BE1473

Brown, Richard D. *The encyclopedia of New England,* DB153

Brown, Robert K. *New Greek-English interlinear New Testament,* BC94

Brown, Russell K. *Fallen in battle,* CJ637

Brown, Samuel R. *Finding the source in sociology and anthropology,* CC5, CE4

Brown, Stephen James. *A guide to books on Ireland,* BE800
—— *Ireland in fiction,* BE800

Brown, Steven D. *Handbook of counseling psychology,* CD105

Brown, William Edward. *History of eighteenth-century Russian literature,* BE1418
—— *A history of Russian literature of the romantic period,* BE1418
—— *History of seventeenth-century Russian literature,* BE1418

Brown, William Holmes. *Deschler's precedents of the United States House of Representatives,* CJ224

The brown book, BF265

Brown, Driver, Briggs, Gesenius Hebrew and English lexicon, AC476

Brown University. *Books at Brown,* BE498

Browne, Cynthia E. *State constitutional conventions from independence to the completion of the present Union, 1776–1959,* CK174

Browne, E. J. *Dictionary of the history of science,* EA246

Browne, Edgardo. *Table of isotopes,* ED46
—— *Table of radioactive isotopes,* ED42

Browne, Edward Granville. *A literary history of Persia,* BE1572

Browne, N. E. *A.L.A. portrait index,* BF65

Browne, Turner. *Macmillan biographical encyclopedia of photographic artists & innovators,* BF354

Browne, William Paul. *U.S. agricultural groups,* EJ44

Browning, Clyde Eugene. *Bibliography of dissertations in geography, 1901 to 1969,* CL26

Browning, David Clayton. *Everyman's dictionary of literary biography,* BE625

Brownlie, Ian. *Basic documents on human rights,* CK113

Brownson, Anna L. *Judicial staff directory,* CK149

Brownson, Charles Bruce. *Judicial staff directory,* CK149

Brownstone, David M. *Dictionary of 20th-century history,* DA179, DA181
—— *The dictionary of publishing,* AA272
—— *The parent's desk reference,* CC238
—— *The women's desk reference,* CC562

Brubaker, Robert L. *Contemporary issues criticism,* CA62

Bruccoli, Arlyn. *Dictionary of British literary characters,* BE688

Bruccoli, Matthew Joseph. *Bibliography of American fiction, 1919–1988,* BE468
—— *First printings of American authors,* BE405

Bruce, A. P. C. *A bibliography of British military history, from the Roman invasions to the Restoration, 1660,* DC271
—— *Bibliography of the British Army,* DC271
—— *Illustrated companion to the First World War,* DA199

Bruce, Colin R. *Standard catalog of world coins,* BG188
—— *Standard catalog of world paper money,* BG189

Bruce, F. F. *History of the Bible in English,* BC191

Bruce, George. *Dictionary of battles,* DA22

Bruce-Mitford, Miranda. *World directory of minorities,* CC345

Bruce-Novoa, Juan D. *Chicano authors,* BE561
—— *The Heath anthology of American literature,* BE441

Brucher, Roger. *Bibliographie des écrivains français de Belgique, 1881–1960,* BE1099

Brückner, Alexander. *Słownik etymologiczny języka polskiego,* AC638

Brueckner, John H. *Brueckner's French contextuary,* AC364

Brueckner's French contextuary, Brueckner, John H., AC364

Bruemmer, Bruce. *Resources for the history of computing,* EK208

Brüggemeier, Monika. *Transfer and interference in language,* BD80

Bruggencate, Karel ten. *Engels woordenboek,* AC296

Bruguière, Michel. *Guide du chercheur pour la période 1789–1815,* DC153

Bruhn, John G. *Handbook of clinical sociology,* CC25
—— *Medical sociology,* CC6, EH11
—— *Social support and health,* CC31

Bruhn, Peter. *Gesamtverzeichnis russischer und sowjetischer Periodika und Serienwerke,* AD234
—— *Russika und Sowjetika unter den deutschsprachigen Hochschulschriften, 1961–1973,* DC553

Bruijning, C. F. A. *Encyclopedie van Suriname,* DB391

Brumbaugh, Robert S. *The Plato manuscripts,* BB59

Brumble, H. David. *An annotated bibliography of American Indian and Eskimo autobiographies,* BE549

Brümmer, Franz. *Lexikon der deutschen Dichter und Prosaisten vom Beginn des 19. Jahrhunderts bis zur Gegenwart,* BE1057

Brummitt, R. K. *Authors of plant names,* EG119

Brun, Christian F. *Maps and charts published in America before 1800,* CL245

Brun, Christophe. *Dictionnaire des maréchaux de France,* AH195

Brune, Lester H. *Chronological history of United States foreign relations,* DB57

Brüne, Stefan. *Die französische Afrikapolitik,* DD2

Brunei
history, DE99
statistics, CG380

Brunei. Statistics Division. *Brunei Darussalam statistical yearbook,* CG380

Brunei Darussalam statistical yearbook, CG380

Brunel, Clovis. *Bibliographie des manuscrits littéraires en ancien provençal,* BE1369

Brunel, Ghislain. *Guide de l'utilisateur des Inventaires des Archives nationales,* DC150

Brunel, Pierre. *Companion to literary myths,* CF3

Brunet, Gustave. *Dictionnaire des ouvrages anonymes [de Barbier],* AA168
—— *Imprimeurs imaginaires et libraires supposés,* AA194
—— *Table générale des noms réels,* AA169

Brunet, Jacques Charles. *Manuel du libraire et de l'amateur de livres,* AA88, AA632, CL101

Brunholzl, Franz. *Geschichte der lateinischen Literatur des Mittelalters,* BE1050, BE1051, BE1052

Brunkow, Robert deV. *Religion and society in North America,* BC30, DB10

Brunnings, Florence E. *Folk song index,* BJ315

Bruno, Frank Joe. *Dictionary of key words in psychology,* CD27

Bruntjen, Scott. *A checklist of American imprints,* AA414

Brunvand, Jan Harold. *Folklore,* CF36

Brush, Stephen G. *The history of geophysics and meteorology,* EF97
—— *The history of modern physics,* ED52

Brussel, Isidore Rosenbaum. *Anglo-American first editions,* AA239

Brussell, Eugene E. *Dictionary of quotable definitions,* BE122
—— *Webster's new World dictionary of quotable definitions,* BE122

Bruton, Eric. *Clocks and watches, 1400–1900,* BG86
—— *Dictionary of clocks and watches,* BG86
—— *The history of clocks and watches,* BG86

Bruun, Bertel. *Birds of North America,* EG274

Bruun, Christian Walther. *Bibliotheca danica,* AA601

Bruun, Henry. *Bibliotheca danica,* DC131

Bruyn, G. W. *Handbook of clinical neurology,* EH183

Bruyninckx, Walter. *50 years of recorded jazz,* BJ307
—— *Jazz,* BJ307
—— *Modern jazz,* BJ307
—— *Progressive jazz,* BJ307
—— *[Sixty years of recorded jazz],* BJ307

—— *Traditional jazz,* BJ307

Bryan, Bonita J. Orosz. *The Brock bibliography of published Canadian plays in English, 1766–1978,* BE820

Bryan, Carter R. *The foreign press,* AE141

Bryan, George B. *Stage deaths,* BH127

—— *Stage lives,* BH128

Bryan, Gordon. *Scottish nationalism and cultural identity in the twentieth century,* CJ375

Bryan, Harrison. *ALIAS, Australia's library, information, and archives services,* AK161

Bryan, Michael. *Bryan's dictionary of painters and engravers,* BF312

Bryan's dictionary of painters and engravers, Bryan, Michael, BF312

Bryant, D. *A history and criticism of American public address,* BE365

Bryant, Keith L. *Railroads in the age of regulation, 1900–1980,* CH383

Bryant, Margaret M. *Current American usage,* AC67

Bryant, Shasta M.*Selective bibliography of bibliographies of Hispanic American literature. Latin American literary authors,* BE881

Bryant, Solena V. *Brazil,* DB341

Brychkov, ĪŪ. A. *Integrals and series,* EB91

Bryden, John Rennie. *An index of Gregorian chant,* BJ290

Bryder, Margit. *75 yngre danske skonlitter re forfattere,* BE1119

Bryer, Jackson R. *American women writers,* BE399

—— *Black American writers,* BE515

—— *Sixteen modern American authors,* BE413

Bryfogle, R. Charles. *City in print,* CC294

Bryfonski, Dedria. *Contemporary issues criticism,* CA62

Bryson, Thomas A. *United States/Middle East diplomatic relations, 1784–1978,* DE3

Brzezinski, Mary Jo. *Employee benefit plans,* CH507

BSB-AK 1501–1840, AA117

BSB-Musik, BJ91

BSB-MuZ, BJ100

BSI catalogue, EA270

BSI standards catalogue, EA270

BTN black theatre directory, BH83

Buch, Günther. *Namen und Daten wichtiger Personen der DDR,* AH217

Buchanan, Daniel Crump. *Japanese proverbs and sayings,* BE152

Buchanan, Mary. *Educators' desk reference for special learning problems,* CB205

Buchanan, William W. *Cumulative subject index to the Monthly catalog of United States government publications, 1900–1971,* AF103, AF111

Buchanan-Brown, John. *Cassell's encyclopaedia of world literature,* BE59

Bucharest (Romania). Biblioteca Centrală de Stat. *Anuarul cărții din Republica Populara Romînă,* AA783

Buchberger, Michael. *Lexikon für Theologie und Kirche,* BC63

Der Buchdruck im 15. Jahrhundert, Corsten, Severin, AA300

Büchel, K. H. *Erweiterungs-und Folgebände zur vierten Auflage,* EE138

Bücherkunde für Germanisten, Hansel, Johannes, BE1211

Buchhandels-Adressbuch für die Bundesrepublik Deutschland, AA289

Buchholz, Peter. *Bibliographie zur alteuropäischen Religionsgeschichte,* BC6

Büchler, Edeltrud. *Deutsche Sprache im Reformationszeitalter,* BD122

Büchmann, Georg. *Geflügelte Worte,* BE135

Buchwald, Wolfgang. *Tusculum-Lexicon,* BE1026

Buck, Carl Darling. *A dictionary of selected synonyms in the principal Indo-European languages,* AC512

Buck, Hendrik de. *Bibliografie der geschiedenis van Nederland,* DC451

Buck, Stuart H. *Tibetan-English dictionary,* AC782

Buckingham, John. *Dictionary of alkaloids,* EE123, EH334

—— *Gardner's chemical synonyms and trade names,* EE39

Buckland, Charles Edward. *Dictionary of Indian biography,* AH349

Buckland, William R. *Dictionary of statistical terms,* CG25, EB43

Buckley, Mary L. *Color theory,* BF125, ED59

Buckley, Peter. *Handbook of international trade,* CH137

Bud Collins' modern encyclopedia of tennis, BK101

Budapest. Országos Széchényi Könyvtár. *A magyar sajtó bibliográfiája, 1945–1954,* AD120

Budavari, Susan. *The Merck index,* EE83, EH345

Budd, John. *Eight Scandinavian novelists,* BE1085

Buddhadatta, Ambalangoda Polvattē. *Concise Pali-English dictionary,* AC624

—— *English-Pali dictionary,* AC624

Buddhica, BC463

Buddhism, BC455, BC456, BC458, BC464, BC467, BC471, BF178

bibliography, BB20, BC37, BC460, BC461, BC462, BC463, BC465, BC466, BC468, BC469, BC470, BC472, BC473, BC474, BC475

collections, BC92

dictionaries, BC477, BC478, BC479, BC480

encyclopedias, BB31, BC57, BC476

indexes, BC459

philosophy, BB20, BC470

sacred books, BC468

sacred writings, BC457

Buddhism, Satyaprakash, BC473

—— Yoo, Yushin, BC459

Buddhist America, BC455

The Buddhist handbook, Snelling, John, BC458

Buddhist Mâhâyana texts, BC92

Buddhist scriptures, Conze, Edward, BC466

Buddhist Society (London, England). *A popular dictionary of Buddhism,* BC477

A Buddhist students' manual, BC477

Buddhist suttas, BC92

Der buddhistische Kanon, Grönbold, Günter, BC468

Budeit, Janice L. *Early English newspapers,* AE57

Budge, Ernest Alfred Thompson Wallis. *An Egyptian hieroglyphic dictionary,* AC301

Budget of the U.S. government, CH244

Budurowycz, Bohdan. *Slavic and East European resources in Canadian academic and research libraries,* DC46

Budzyk, Kazimierz. *Bibliografia literatury polskiej,* BE1346

Buenker, John D. *Historical dictionary of the Progressive Era, 1890–1920,* DB132

—— *Immigration and ethnicity,* CC313

—— *Multiculturalism in the United States,* CC353

—— *Progressive reform,* DB125

Bufkin, E. C. *Foreign literary prizes,* BE177

Buganov, V. I. *Bibliografiia trudov po otechestvennomu istochnikovedeniiu i spetsial'nym istoricheskim distsiplinam izdannykh v XVIII v,* DC573

Bugher, Wilmer. *The Phi Delta Kappa Gallup polls of attitudes toward education, 1969–1988,* CB137

Buhle, Mari Jo. *Encyclopedia of the American left,* DB129

—— *Women and the American left,* CC487

Buhle, Paul. *Encyclopedia of the American left,* DB129

Bühler, Curt Ferdinand. *The fifteenth-century book,* AA236

Building a Judaica library collection, Lubetski, Edith, BC516

Building an American pedigree, AJ27

Building construction, EK103, EK115

dictionaries, EK109, EK112

handbooks, EK110

Building construction handbook, EK103

Building design and construction handbook, EK103

Building library collections on aging, Brazil, Mary Jo, CC62

Buildings

bibliography, BF223

dictionaries, BF240, BF242

directories, BF283

encyclopedias, BF238

restoration and conservation, BF265

Buildings of Alaska, Hoagland, Alison K., BF254

Buildings of Iowa, Gebhard, David, BF254

—— Mansheim, Gerald, BF254

Buildings of Michigan, Eckert, Kathryn Bishop, BF254

Buildings of the District of Columbia, Lee, Antoinette J., BF254

—— Scott, Pamela, BF254

Buildings of the United States, BF254

Buisman, M. *Populaire prozaschrijvers van 1600 tot 1815,* BE1327

Buja, Maureen E. *Italian Renaissance poetry,* BE1316

Bujas, Željko. *Englesko-hrvatski ili srpski rječnik,* AC713

—— *Hrvatsko ili srpasko engleski rječnik,* AC713

—— *Hrvatsko ili srpsko-engleski enciklopedijski rječnik,* AC712

Bukharina, N. I. *Bol'shaia sovetskaia entsiklopediia,* AB84

Buku rasmi tahunan Malaysia, CG413

Buku tahunan perangkaan Malaysia, CG412

BUL-L, BD1

Bulas, Kazimierz. *Kościuszko Foundation dictionary,* AC634

Buletinul bibliografic, AD323

Bulgaria

bibliography, AA583, AA584, AA585, AA586, AA587, AA588, DC62, DC112, DC113, DC114

current, AA589

bibliography of bibliography, AA37, AA38, AA39

biography, DC115

dissertations, AG24

encyclopedias, DC119

government publications, AF165

manuscripts and archives, DC117

newspapers, AE46

periodicals, AD86, AD87

indexes, AD304, AD305

registers, CJ325

statistics, CG201, DC538

Bulgaria (by subject)

foreign relations, DC62, DC110, DC114

historiography, DC118

history, DC115, DC537, DC538

archives, DC117

bibliography, DC111, DC112, DC116

Bulgaria, Crampton, R. J., DC112

—— Library of Congress. Slavic and Central European Division, DC112

—— Pundeff, Marin V., DC112

Bulgaria in the Balkans, DC62, DC114

Bulgarian abbreviations, Library of Congress. Slavic and Central European Division, AC243

Bulgarian-English dictionary, AC239

Bulgarian language

abbreviations, AC243

bibliography, BD191

dictionaries, AC240, AC241, AC242

bilingual

Bulgarian-English, AC239

English., EA105

Bulgarian literature, BE1103

Bulgarian national bibliography, AE46

Bulgarian national bibliography. Series 5. Articles from Bulgarian journals and collections, AD305

Bŭlgariia na balkanite, 1944–1974, Lazarov, Mikhail, DC62, DC114

Bŭlgarska akademiia na naukite. *Bŭlgariia na balkanite, 1944–1974,* DC62, DC114

—— *Entsiklopediia Bŭlgariia,* DC119

Bŭlgarska Akademiia na Naukite. Institut Bŭlgarski Ezik. *Bŭlgarski etimologichen rechnik,* AC240

Bŭlgarska akademiia na naukite. Institut za balkanistika "Liudmila Zhivkova". *Gŭrtsiia i bŭlgaro-grŭtskite otnosheniia v bŭlgarskata nauchna knizhnina, 1878–1980,* DC110

Bŭlgarska vŭzrozhdenska knizhnina, Narodna biblioteka "Kiril i Metodii", AA584

Bŭlgarskata Akademiĩa na Naukite. *Rechnik na suvremennais bulgarski ezik*, AC242

Bŭlgarskata Akademiĩa na Naukite, Sofia. Institut za Istoriĩa. *Bŭlgarskata istoricheska nauka*, DC111

Bŭlgarskata istoricheska nauka, DC111

Bŭlgarski-angliĭsko rechnik, AC239

Bŭlgarski bibliografski institut Elin Pelin. *Letopis na periodichniĩa pechat*, AD304

Bŭlgarski disertatsii, AG24

Bŭlgarski etimologichen rechnik, AC240

Bŭlgarski gramofonni plochi, AA589

Bŭlgarski istoricheski arkhiv. *Obzor na arkhivnite fondove, kolektsii i edinichni postŭpleniĩa, sŭkhraĩavani v Bŭlgarski istoricheski arkhiv*, DC117

Bŭlgarski istoritsi, Cholov, Petur, DC118

Bŭlgarski knigi, 1878–1944, Narodna biblioteka "Kiril i Metodii", AA585

Bŭlgarski knigopis, AA583, AA589

Bulgarski knigopis, Ser. 2 : Sluzhebni izdaniĩa disertatsii, AG24

Bŭlgarski knigopis za sto godini, 1806–1905, Teodorov-Balan, Aleksandŭr, AA588

Bŭlgarski periodichen pechat, AA589, AD86

Bŭlgarski periodichen pechat 1844–1944, AD87

Bŭlgarski periodichen pechat, 1944–1969, Spasova, Mariia Vladimorova, AD87

Bŭlgarski tulkoven rechnik, s ogled kŭm narodnite govori, Mladenov, Stefan, AC241

Bull, C. Neil. *The older volunteer*, CC63

Bull, Edvard. *Norsk biografisk leksikon*, AH275

Bull, Francis. *Norsk literaturhistorie*, BE1339

Bull, Storm. *Index to biographies of contemporary composers*, BJ224

Bullard, Roger Aubrey. *Mercer dictionary of the Bible*, BC146

Bulletin, National Museum of Canada, EF31

—— New York Public Library, AA265, AL149, BF110, EK23

Bulletin analytique, AD254, BB24, BE38, CE23, EA72, EF118

Bulletin analytique de bibliographie hellénique, AA706

Bulletin bibliographique de la Société internationale arthurienne, International Arthurian Society, BE338, BE339

Bulletin bibliographique de la Société Rencesvals, Société Rencesvals, BE1201

Bulletin bibliographique des Archives du Sénégal, AA872

Bulletin critique du livre français, AA332

Bulletin de l'Institut Pasteur, Institut Pasteur, EG311

Bulletin de statistique, CG174

Bulletin de statistique. Supplément annuel, CG351

Bulletin des sommaires, AD302

Bulletin Du Cange, AC585

Bulletin du livre, AA636

Bulletin mensuel de statistique, CG363

Bulletin mensuel des articles de fond parus les revues belges, AD302

Bulletin of bibliography, AA89, AA90, BH55

Bulletin of labour statistics, CH691

Bulletin of reprints, AA393

Bulletin of the American Physical Society, American Physical Society, EC45, ED31

Bulletin of the Institute of Historical Research. Theses supplement, DC284

Bulletin signalétique, AD254, BB24, BD24, BE38, CE23, EA72, EF118

Bulletin signalétique 526 : art et archéologie, BF33

Bulletin signalétique de bibliographie hellénique, AA706

Bulletin signalétique d'information administrative, AF171

Bulletins trimestriel de statistique, CG174

Bulletins of the U.S. Bureau of Labor and the U.S. Bureau of Labor Statistics, 1895–1919, CH639, CH644

Bullock, Orin M. *Restoration manual*, BF265

Bullough, Bonnie. *Human sexuality*, CC278

—— *Nursing*, EH285

Bullough, Geoffrey. *Narrative and dramatic sources of Shakespeare*, BE786

Bullough, Vern L. *American nursing*, EH287

—— *An annotated bibliography of homosexuality*, CC266

—— *Human sexuality*, CC278

—— *Nursing*, EH285

Bullwinkle, Davis. *African women*, CC592

—— *Women of eastern and southern Africa*, CC593

—— *Women of northern, western, and central Africa*, CC594

The bully pulpit, CJ180

Bulmer, Martin. *Directory of social research organisations in the United Kingdom*, AL66, CA56

Bulson, Christine. *Current cookbooks*, EJ222

Bultman, Scott. *All music guide*, BJ374

Bunakova, O. V. *Bibliografiĩa trudov Instituta etnografiĩ im. N. N. Miklukho-Maklaiĩa, 1900–1962*, CE5

Bunch, Bryan H. *The timetables of science*, EA252, EA254

—— *The timetables of technology*, EA250

Bundesanzeiger, CG223

Bundy, Alan. *Directory of Australian academic and research libraries*, AK162

Bundy, Carol. *The African book world and press*, AA293, AK62

—— *A new reader's guide to African literature*, BE1508

Bundy, Judith. *Directory of Australian academic and research libraries*, AK162

Bundy, Mary Lee. *National prison directory*, CK266

Bunes Ibarra, Miguel Angel de. *Repertorio bibliográfico de las relaciones entre la península Ibérica y el Norte de África, siglos XV–XVI*, DD70

Bunge, Frederica M. *Indian Ocean: five island countries*, DD62

—— *Oceania, a regional study*, DF19

Bungei nenkan, Nihon Bungeika Kyōkai hen, BE1583

Bunjes, Werner E. *German-English, English-German dictionary for physicians*, EH140

Bunjes, Werner Ernst. *Medical and pharmaceutical dictionary*, EH136

Bunson, Margaret. *The encyclopedia of ancient Egypt*, DA123

Buonincontro, Pasquale. *La presenza delle Romania in Italia nel secolo XX*, DC495

Buono, Anthony F. *A primer on organizational behavior*, CH602

Buranelli, Nan. *Spy/counterspy*, CJ536, CJ540

Buranelli, Vincent. *Spy/counterspy*, CJ536, CJ540

Burbank, Richard. *Twentieth century music*, BJ186

Burbidge, Robert B. *Dictionary of British flower, fruit, and still life painters*, BF323

Burchard, Christoph. *Bibliographie zu den Handschriften vom Toten Meer*, BC106

Burchell, Robert W. *The environmental impact handbook*, EK80

Burchfield, R. W. *Oxford dictionary of English etymology*, AC58

—— *A supplement to the Oxford English dictionary*, AC34

Burckel, Nicholas C. *Immigration and ethnicity*, CC313

—— *Progressive reform*, DB125

Burckhardt, Johann Lewis. *Arabic proverbs*, BE124

Burdett, Anita L. P. *Manuscripts and government records in the United Kingdom and Ireland relating to Canada*, DB196

—— *Summary guide to the archive and manuscript collections relevant to the former British colonial territories in the United Kingdom for the Joint Copyists Standing Committee of the Commonwealth Archivists' Association*, DC345

Burdett's official intelligence, CH327

Bureau of Mines (U.S.). *Minerals yearbook*, EF200

Bureau of National Affairs. *Directory of U.S. labor organizations*, CH663

—— *Labor relations yearbook*, CH673

Bureau of Railway Economics. *Railway economics*, CH458

Bureau of Technical Information (London). *Bibliographical series. Computers*, EK163

Bureau of the Census catalog, CG90

Bureau of the Census catalog and guide, CG86

Bureau of the Census catalog of publications, 1790–1972, CG86

Bureau of the Census catalog of publications, 1946–1972, CG93

The bureaucratic state, Miewald, Robert D., CJ76

Burge, David A. *Patent and trademark tactics and practice*, EA257

Bürger, Erich. *Dictionary of information science*, AK41

—— *Technical dictionary of data processing*, EK190

Burger, Konrad. *Ludwig Hain's Repertorium bibliographicum*, AA221

—— *Ludwig Hain's Repertorium bibliographicum : Register*, AA223

—— *Supplement zu Hain und Panzer*, AA220, AA223

Burgess, Michael. *Reference guide to science fiction, fantasy, and horror*, BE281, BE291

Bürgisser, Max. *Etymologisches Wörterbuch der deutschen Sprache*, AC428

Burgo, Jaime del. *Bibliografía del siglo XIX*, DC500

Burguière, André. *Dictionnaire des sciences historiques*, DA42

Burgunker, Mark E. *Russian-English dictionary of earth sciences*, EF87

Burington, Richard Stevens. *Handbook of mathematical tables and formulas*, EB63, EB83

—— *Handbook of probability and statistics, with tables*, EB63, EB83

Burke, A. M. *Key to the ancient parish registers of England and Wales*, AJ112

Burke, James Henry. *80 years of best sellers, 1895–1975*, AA327

Burke, John Bernard. *The book of orders of knighthood and decorations of honour of all nations*, AL179

—— *Burke's genealogical and heraldic history of the peerage, baronetage, and knightage*, AJ114

—— *Genealogical and heraldic history of the colonial gentry*, AJ115

—— *Genealogical history of the dormant, abeyant, forfeited, and extinct peerages of the British Empire*, AJ116

—— *The general armory of England, Scotland, Ireland, and Wales*, AJ149

Burke, John Gordon. *Access*, AD258

—— *Guide to ecology information and organizations*, EG62

—— *Index to the Sporting news*, BK9

Burke, John McDonald. *Jowitt's dictionary of English law*, CK38

Burke, Patrick. *The nuclear weapons world*, CJ597

Burke, Robert E. *New era and the New Deal, 1920–1940*, DB128

Burke, William Jeremiah. *American authors and books, 1640 to the present day*, BE432

—— *American books, 1640–1940*, BE432

Burke's distinguished families of America, AJ58

Burke's family index, AJ150

Burke's genealogical and heraldic history of the peerage, baronetage, and knightage, Burke, John Bernard, AJ114

Burke's Irish family records, AJ131

Burke's landed gentry of Ireland, AJ131

Burke's presidential families of the United States of America, AJ59

Burke's royal families of the world, AJ76

Burkett, Nancy H. *Black biography, 1790–1950*, AH59

Burkett, Randall K. *Black biography, 1790–1950*, AH59

Burkina Faso, DD133
    atlases, CL339
    encyclopedias, DD48
    government publications
        bibliography, AF230
    statistics, CG319

Burland, C. A. *Man, myth & magic*, BC64

Burling, William J. *Checklist of new plays and entertainments on the London stage, 1700–1737,* BH101

Burma, DE121
    bibliography, AA889, DE119
    gazetteers, CL159
    manuscripts, DE163

Burma (by subject)
    history
        guides, DE120

Burma, Herbert, Patricia M., DE121
———— Shulman, Frank Joseph, DE120

Burma, a study guide, DE120

A Burmese-English dictionary, Stewart, John Alexander, AC245

Burmese language
    dictionaries
        bilingual
            Burmese-English, AC244, AC245

Burmov, Aleksandŭr K. *Bŭlgarska vŭzrozhdenska knizhnina,* AA584

Burn, Barbara. *A practical guide to impractical pets,* EJ134

Burn, Lucilla. *Beazley addenda,* BF324

Burn, Richard. *Imperial gazetteer of India,* CL164

Burnashev, Ėlgizar Ĭusupovich. *Bibliografiîa po problemam narodonaseleniîa,* CG298
———— *Literatura o narodonaselenii,* CG298, CG299

Burnell, A. C. *Hobson-Jobson,* AC162

Burnet, Charles. *Table des pièces de théâtre décrites dans le catalogue de la bibliothèque de M. de Soleinne,* BE1184

Burnett, Collins W. *Higher education literature,* CB232

Burnett, Elsie. *Bibliography of contemporary African-American literature,* BE527

Burnett, John. *The autobiography of the working class,* CH679

Burnette, Charles. *Directory to industrial design in the United States,* BG26

Burnham, Dorothy K. *United States & Canada,* BG157
———— *Warp & weft,* BG154

Burnham, Linda. *Women of color,* CC545

Burnham, Robert. *Burnham's celestial handbook,* EC70

Burnham, Walter Dean. *Presidential ballots, 1836–1892,* CJ243

The Burnham index to architectural literature, BF212

Burnham Library of Architecture. *The Burnham index to architectural literature,* BF212

Burnham's celestial handbook, Burnham, Robert, EC70

Burnim, Kalman A. *A biographical dictionary of actors, actresses, musicians, dancers, managers & other stage personnel in London, 1660–1800,* BH112

Burnout, CD124

Burns, Grant. *The atomic papers,* CJ665, CJ666
———— *The nuclear present,* CJ666

Burns, J. H. *The Cambridge history of medieval political thought c.350–c.1450,* CJ23
———— *Cambridge history of political thought, 1450–1700,* CJ23

Burns, James. *New Zealand novels and novelists, 1861–1979,* BE861

Burns, Richard Dean. *Arms control and disarmament,* CJ667, CJ673
———— *Encyclopedia of arms control and disarmament,* CJ684
———— *Guide to American foreign relations since 1700,* DB15
———— *Vietnam conflict,* DE95
———— *The wars in Vietnam, Cambodia and Laos, 1945–1982,* DE95

Burns, Shannon. *An annotated bibliography of texts on writing skills,* BD95

Burns Indiana statutes annotated, Indiana. [Laws, etc.], CK179

Burns Mantle best plays, BE454

The Burns Mantle theater yearbook, BE454

Buros, Oscar Krisen. *The mental measurements yearbook,* CD69
———— *Personality tests and reviews,* CD69

Buros Institute of Mental Measurements. *The mental measurements yearbook,* CD69
———— *Tests in print III,* CD73

Burr, Charlotte A. *World philosophy,* BB10

Burr, John R. *Handbook of world philosophy,* BB10, BB81
———— *World philosophy,* BB10

Burr, Nelson Rollin. *A critical bibliography of religion in America,* BC27, BC31
———— *Religion in American life,* BC27

Burrage, Walter L. *Dictionary of American medical biography,* EH229

Burrelle's Hispanic media directory, AE31

Burrington, Douglas. *East Germany,* DC243

Burrow, Thomas. *A Dravidian etymological dictionary,* AC291

Burrows, Sandra. *Checklist of indexes to Canadian newspapers,* AE117

Burs under the saddle, Adams, Ramon Frederick, DB162, DB168

Bursian, Conrad. *Jahresbericht über die Fortschritte der klassischen Altertumswissenschaft,* BE1023

Bursian's Jahresberricht, BE992

Burt, Eugene C. *Annotated bibliography of the visual arts of East Africa,* BG5
———— *Erotic art,* BF15
———— *Ethnoart,* BG13
———— *Ethnoarts index,* BG12
———— *Serials guide to ethnoart,* BG13

Burt, Martha R. *America's homeless,* CC200

Burton, Dennis A. *Guide to manuscripts in the presidential libraries,* AJ24, AK102, CJ176, DB37

Burton, Dolores M. *English stylistics,* BE374

Burton, John A. *The Collins guide to the rare mammals of the world,* EG289

Burton, Margaret. *A bibliography of librarianship,* AK11

Burton, Maurice. *Systematic dictionary of mammals of the world,* EG290

Burton, Vivien G. *The Collins guide to the rare mammals of the world,* EG289

Burton, William C. *Legal thesaurus,* CK56

Burundi
    bibliography, DD18, DD111, DD135, DD244
    encyclopedias, DD48
    government publications
        bibliography, AF229
    periodicals, AD171
    statistics, CG320

Burundi (by subject)
    status of women, DD134

Burundi, Daniels, Morna, DD18
———— Weinstein, Warren, DD48

Burunova, Nina Mikhallovna. *A guide to mathematical tables,* EB74

Burwell, Helen P. *The Burwell directory of information brokers,* AK59

The Burwell directory of information brokers, AK59

Bury, J. B. *Cambridge mediaeval history,* DA157

Bus lines
    timetables, CL395

Busa, Roberto. *Sancti Thomae Aquinatis Opera omnia,* BB64

Busby, Douglas L. *A reader's Hebrew-English lexicon of the Old Testament,* BC133

Buschman, Isabel. *Handweaving,* BG158

Buscombe, Edward. *The BFI companion to the Western,* BH245

Buscombe, Eve. *Artists in early Australia and their portraits,* BF140

Buse, Dieter K. *German nationalism,* DC231

Bush, Geneva L. *Finding the source of medical information,* EH3

Bush, Gregory Wallace. *Campaign speeches of American presidential candidates, 1948–1984,* CJ244

Bush, Louise K. *The history and art of glass,* BG53

Bushey, Galen. *Prayer book concordance,* BC347

Bushnell, Brooks. *Directors and their films,* BH188, BH204

Bushnell, G. H. *Dictionary of the printers and booksellers who were at work in England, Scotland and Ireland from 1726 to 1775; those in Scotland,* AA306

Bushnell, Vivian C. *Antarctic map folio series,* CL369

Business
    bibliography, CH2, CH7, CH12, CH329, CH330, CH332, CH333, CH336
    biography, AH77, AH80, CH94, CH101, CH387
    book reviews, CH13
    business services, CH333
    chronologies, CH399
    databases, CH32, CH34, CH35, CH36, CH37, CH338, CH387, CH423, CH426
        guides, CH6
    dictionaries, CH56, CH57, CH63, CH274, CH342, CH344
        bilingual
            French-English, AC343, CH61
        German, CH67
        multilingual, CH58, CH429
    directories, AL8, CH401
        bibliography, AL4
    eponyms, CH386
    guides, CH1, CH2, CH4, CH5, CH8, CH330, CH332, CH334
    handbooks, CH4, CH334, CH378
    indexes, CH32, CH35, CH36, CH37
    library catalogs, CH7
    periodicals, AD34, CH25, CH26, CH29, CH78
        directories, CH27
    quotations, CH72, CH73, CH74, CH75
    statistics, CH378, CH418, CH421, CH425

Business (by country or region)
    Canada, AE118, CH38
        bibliography, CH390
        guides, CH175
    Europe
        directories, CH410, CH413
        periodicals, CH335
        statistics, CH593
    Europe, Eastern
        directories, CH412
    Great Britain
        biography, CH96
        directories, CH82
    India
        guides, CH196
    Japan
        guides, CH204
    Scotland
        biography, CH97
    United States
        bibliography, CH206, CH390
        biography, CH98, CH99, CH100
        history, CH383

Business (by subject)
    history, CH382, CH399
        bibliography, CH389, CH395
    minority ownership, CH364
    ownership by women, CH364
    see also **Corporations; International business enterprises; Small business**

•*Business America on CD-ROM,* CH345

Business and economics books, 1876–1983, CH12

Business and Professional Women's Foundation. *A women's thesaurus,* CC543

Business and technical writing, Alred, Gerald J., CH428

•*Business ASAP,* CH35

Business biographies and company histories, Harvard University. Graduate School of Business Administration. Baker Library, CH389

Business biography master index, CH94

Business collection, CH35

•*Business dateline,* CH34

Business dictionary, Eichborn, Reinhart von, CH67

Business education, CB51, CB255, CH76, CH81

Business education index, CB51

Business ethics, CH317
    bibliography, CH565

Business forecasting, CH423, CH426

Business history collection, Dallas Public Library. Business and Technology Division, CH382

Business history of the world, Robinson, Richard, CH399

•*Business index,* CH35, CH338

•*Business index on InfoTrac,* CH35

Business information, Lavin, Michael R., CH4

Business information sources, Daniells, Lorna M., CH2

Business journals of the United States, CH25

Business Library (Brooklyn Public Library). *Business rankings and salaries index,* CH402

Business library review, CH13

Business management *see* **Management**

Business mathematics, CH220

•*Business Newsbank plus,* CH36

Business One Irwin business and investment almanac, CH378

The Business One Irwin investor's handbook, CH318

Business online, Scanlan, Jean M., CH6

Business periodicals global, CH32

Business periodicals index, CH37, EA67, CH37

Business publications rates and data, CH601

Business rankings and salaries index, Business Library (Brooklyn Public Library), CH402

Business rankings annual, CH402

Business ratios, CH418, CH421, CH424

Business schools, CB255, CH76

Business serials of the U.S. government, CH26

Business statistics, CH420

Business statistics, CH420, CH425

Business surveys, CH598

A Business week guide, Byrne, John A., CB255, CH76

Business week (New York, N.Y.). *A Business week guide,* CB255, CH76

Business week's guide to the best business schools, CB255, CH76

Businessmen *see* **Executives**

Businesswomen *see* **Executives**

Bussho kaisetsu daijiten, BC465

Bustamante, Jorge A. *México—Estados Unidos,* DB220

Busto Duthurburu, José Antonio del. *Diccionario histórico biográfico de los conquistadores del Perú,* AH140, DB387

Butcher, David. *Official publications in Britain,* AF176

Butcher, Judith. *Copy-editing,* AA318

Butler, Alan. *A New Guinea bibliography,* DF48

Butler, Alban. *A dictionary of saints,* BC262
—— *Lives of the saints,* BC262, BC263

Butler, Audrey. *Everyman's dictionary of dates,* DA30

Butler, David. *British political facts,* CJ373
—— *British political facts, 1900–1985,* CJ347, DC339
—— *Compendium of Indian elections,* CJ431
—— *India decides,* CJ431

Butler, Deborah A. *American women writers on Vietnam,* BE417, DE278

Butler, Francine. *Biofeedback,* CD115

Butler, Francis J. *Foundation guide for religious grant seekers,* BC78

Butler, Gareth. *British political facts, 1900–1985,* CJ347, DC339

Butler, Inge. *A New Guinea bibliography,* DF48

Butler, Ruth Lapham. *Checklist of manuscripts in the Edward E. Ayer collection,* DB6

Butler's lives of the saints, Walsh, Michael J., BC263

Butorin, Pavel. *Dictionary of development,* CH120

Butt, Irene. *Bibliographie Sprache und Literatur,* BD2

Butt, Suhail. *International dictionary of architects and architecture,* BF236

The butterflies of North America, Howe, William H., EG332

Butterworth, Neil. *A dictionary of American composers,* BJ206

Butterworth's law directory, CK221

Butterworths legal research guide, Holborn, Guy, CK218

Butterworths medical dictionary, EH94

Butterworths Spanish/English legal dictionary, Cabanellas, Guillermo, CK55
—— Hoague, Eleanor C., CK55

Buttlar, Lois. *Education,* CB3

Buttons, BG105

Buttress's world guide to abbreviations of organizations, Swinbank, Jean C. M., AL14

Buttrick, George Arthur. *The interpreter's dictionary of the Bible,* BC132

Buxton, Frank. *Big broadcast, 1920–1950,* BH311

Buying guide, Association for Information and Image Management, AK247

BV, AA549

Bycroft, B. W. *Dictionary of antibiotics and related substances,* EE125, EH335

Byerly, Greg. *Incest, the last taboo,* CC218

Bygdén, Anders Leonard. *Svenskt anonym– och pseudonym-lexikon,* AA187

Bykova, Tat'iâna Aleksandrovna. *Dopolneniîâ i prilozheniîâ,* AA789
—— *Opisanie izdaniĭ, napechatannykh pri Petre Pervom,* AA789

Bynagle, Hans E. *Philosophy,* BB1

Bynum, W. F. *Dictionary of the history of science,* EA246

Byrne, F. J. *A new history of Ireland,* DC413

Byrne, John A. *A Business week guide,* CB255, CH76

Byrne, Mary. *Eureka!,* AC50

Byrne, Pamela R. *Women in North America,* CC580
—— *Women in the Third World,* CC595

Byrne, Sherry. *Collection maintenance and improvement,* AK238

Byrnes, Rita M. *Uganda,* DD62

Byrnes, Robert Francis. *Bibliography of American publications on East Central Europe, 1945–1967,* DC39

Y Bywgraffiadur Cymreig hyd 1940, AH245

Byzantine art, BF9, BF80

Byzantine coins, Grierson, Philip, BG172

Byzantine Empire, DA165

Byzantine Library serials list, Dumbarton Oaks. Center for Byzantine Studies, DA162

Byzantine studies, DA161, DA166
  bibliography, DA162
    current, DA163
    translations, DA164
  library catalogs, DA162
  periodicals, DA162

Byzantinische Zeitschrift, BF9, DA163

Byzantinoslavica, DA163

Byzantium, Diehl, Charles, DA161

Byzanz, Dölger, Franz Joseph, DA161

Bzowska, Maria. *Materiały do bibliografii dziennikarstwa i prasy w Polsce, w latach 1944–1954,* AE67

Bzowski, Frances Diodato. *American women playwrights, 1900–1930,* BE455

C. S. Hammond & Company. *Historical atlas,* DA57

C. F. Whistling's Handbuch, BJ60

•*CA file,* EE22

•*CA surveyor,* EE22

•*CAB abstracts,* CH46, EJ10, EJ18, EJ19, EJ36, EJ37, EJ102, EJ103, EJ104, EJ105, EJ175, EJ230

CAB abstracts word list, Commonwealth Agricultural Bureaux, EJ37

CAB International. *[Abstract journals],* EJ19
—— *Animal breeding abstracts,* EJ102
—— *Forestry abstracts,* EJ175
—— *Horticultural abstracts,* EJ230
—— *International union list of agricultural serials,* EJ10
—— *Review of agricultural entomology,* EG337
—— *Spanish-English horticultural dictionary,* EJ239
—— *The veterinary bulletin,* EJ105
—— *World agricultural economics and rural sociology abstracts,* CH46
—— *A world dictionary of livestock breeds, types and varieties,* EJ136

CAB thesaurus, EJ14, EJ17, EJ18, EJ19, EJ36

Cabala, BC520

Cabanellas, Guillermo. *Butterworths Spanish/English legal dictionary,* CK55

Cabeen, David Clark. *A critical bibliography of French literature,* BE1131

Cabeen, Richard McP. *Standard handbook of stamp collecting,* BG203

Cabell, David W. E. *Cabell's directory of publishing opportunities in business and economics,* CH27

Cabello-Argandoña, Roberto. *The Chicana,* CC444, CC596

Cabell's directory of publishing opportunities in business and economics, Cabell, David W. E., CH27

Cabell's directory of publishing opportunities in education, CB20

Cabinet officers, CJ189

The cabinetmakers of America, Bjerkoe, Ethel Hall, BG134

Cable, Frances. *Memorable film characters,* BH276

Cable, Thomas. *Companion to Baugh & Cable's History of the English language,* BD98
—— *A history of the English language,* BD98

Cable television, CH493

Cabourdin, Guy. *Lexique historique de la France d'ancien régime,* DC174

•*CABPESTCD,* EJ18

Cabral, António Carlos Pereira. *Dicionário de nomes geográficos de Moçambique,* CL215

Cabrol, Fernand. *Dictionnaire d'archéologie chrétienne et de liturgie,* BC246

Cáceres Romero, Adolfo. *Diccionario de la literatura boliviana,* BE922

CACI, Inc. *The sourcebook of zip code demographics,* CH600

CAD, AC200

Caden, Tom Scott. *What a bunch of characters!,* BH277

Cadenas y Vicent, Vicente de. *Bibliografía del Emperador Carlos V,* DC501

Caenegem, R. C. van. *Guide to the sources of medieval history,* DA127

Caes, Lucien. *Collectio bibliographica operum ad ius romanum pertinentium,* BE1037

Caetano, Marcelo. *Guia da bibliografia histórica portuguesa,* DC485

Çağdaş Türkiye, Tuğlaci, Pars, DC531

Cahalan, James M. *Modern Irish literature and culture,* BE801

Cahen, Claude. *Introduction to the history of the Muslim East,* BC500

Cahiers de civilisation médiévale, DA141

Cahiers du monde russe et soviétique, DC41

Cahill, James Francis. *Index of early Chinese painters and paintings,* BF146, BF313

Cahn, R. W. *Concise encyclopedia of medical & dental materials,* EH176
—— *Encyclopedia of materials science and engineering,* EK261

Cahner, Max. *Diccionari etimològic i complementari de la llengua catalana,* AC248

Caiden, Gerald E. *American public administration,* CJ463
—— *International handbook of the ombudsman,* CJ55

Cailleux, André. *Dictionnaire des racines scientifiques,* EA87

Cairnduff, Maureen. *Who's who in Ireland,* AH257

Cairns, Earle E. *Wycliffe biographical dictionary of the church,* BC254

Cajías, Lupe. *Las relaciones de Bolivia, Chile y Perú,* DB336

Calabi, Silvio. *The illustrated encyclopedia of fly-fishing,* BK114

Calasibetta, Charlotte Mankey. *Fairchild's dictionary of fashion,* BG98

Calcagno, Francisco. *Diccionario biográfico cubano,* AH150

Calcified tissue abstracts, EG14

Caldas Aulete, F. J. *Diccionario contemporâneo da língua portugueza,* AC641

Calder, William M. *Classical scholarship,* BE1024, DA113

—— *An introductory bibliography to the history of classical scholarship chiefly in the XIXth and XXth centuries*, DA92

Calderini, Simonetta. *Mauritania*, DD18

Caldwell, Ronald J. *Era of Napoleon*, DC178, DC191

—— *The era of the French Revolution*, DC178, DC191

—— *The history of the Episcopal Church in America, 1607–1991*, BC343

Caldwell, Sandra M. *The history of the Episcopal Church in America, 1607–1991*, BC343

Caldwell-Wood, Naomi. *Checklist of bibliographies appearing in the Bulletin of bibliography 1897–1987*, AA90

Calédoniens, O'Reilly, Patrick, AH382

A calendar of American poetry in the colonial newspapers and magazines and in the major English magazines through 1765, Lemay, J. A. Leo, BE501

Calendar of creative man, Paxton, John, DA36

Calendar of English Renaissance drama, 1558–1642, Kawachi, Yoshiko, BE661

Calendar of literary facts, Rogal, Samuel J., BE192, BE437

A calendar of the principal ecclesiastical dignitaries in England and Wales, BC331

Calendars, EC83, EC84, EC85, EC87, EC88

California. [Laws, etc.]. *West's annotated California codes*, CK179

California Institute of Public Affairs. *World directory of environmental organizations*, EK77

California State Library. *Catalogue of Mexican pamphlets in the Sutro collection (1623–[1888])*, DB235

California State University, Los Angeles. Latin American Studies Center. *Latin American women writers in English translation*, BE883

Călinescu, George. *Istoria literaturii române dela origini până in prezent*, BE1379

Calinger, Ronald S. *The dictionary of 20th-century world politics*, CJ33

Calisher, Charles H. *Stedman's ICTV virus words*, EG347

Call, Jerry. *Census-catalogue of manuscript sources of polyphonic music, 1400–1550*, BJ69

Callaham, Ludmilla Ignatiev. *Russian-English chemical and polytechnical dictionary*, EE53

Callahan, Edward William. *List of officers of the Navy of the United States and of the Marine Corps from 1775 to 1900*, CJ638

The calligraphers' dictionary, Folsom, Rose, BF370

Calligraphy, BF370

Callot, Olivier. *Dictionnaire illustré multilingue de l'architecture du Proche Orient ancien*, BF243

Calsat, Jean-Henri. *Vocabulaire international des termes d'urbanisme et d'architecture*, BF278

Calvert, Peter. *Political and economic encyclopaedia of South America and the Caribbean*, DB283

Calvet, J. *Histoire de la littérature française*, BE1170

Calvi, Emilio. *Bibliotheca bibliographica italica*, AA54

Camarillo, Albert. *Mexican Americans in urban society*, CC445

Cambodia, DE122

Cambodia, Zaleha Tamby, DE122

Cambodian-English dictionary, AC562, AC564

Cambodian language *see* **Khmer language**

Cambrian bibliography, Rowlands, William, AA700

Cambridge air and space dictionary, EK30

Cambridge ancient history, DA85

The Cambridge atlas of astronomy, EC65

The Cambridge atlas of the Middle East and North Africa, DE54, DE68

Cambridge bibliography of English literature, BE582, BE707

—— Bateson, Frederick Wilse, BE585

Cambridge biographical dictionary, AH24

The Cambridge companion to English Renaissance drama, BE659

The Cambridge companion to Shakespeare studies, BE784

Cambridge dictionary of science and technology, EA88

Cambridge-Eichborn German dictionary, Eichborn, Reinhart von, CH67

The Cambridge encyclopaedia of astronomy, EC25

The Cambridge encyclopedia, AB3

The Cambridge encyclopedia of Africa, DD50

The Cambridge encyclopedia of archaeology, DA74

Cambridge encyclopedia of Australia, Hambrick, Susan, DF33

The Cambridge encyclopedia of China, DE140

The Cambridge encyclopedia of earth sciences, EF3

The Cambridge encyclopedia of India, Pakistan, Bangladesh, Sri Lanka, Nepal, Bhutan, and the Maldives, DE90

The Cambridge encyclopedia of Japan, DE207

The Cambridge encyclopedia of language, Crystal, David, BD32, BD37

The Cambridge encyclopedia of Latin America and the Caribbean, DB281

The Cambridge encyclopedia of ornithology, EG254

The Cambridge encyclopedia of the Middle East and North Africa, DE54, DE68

Cambridge guide to American theatre, BH65

Cambridge guide to Asian theatre, BH66

Cambridge guide to English literature, Stapleton, Michael, BE608

The Cambridge guide to literature in English, BE608

Cambridge guide to the museums of Britain and Ireland, Hudson, Kenneth, BF98

—— Nicholls, Ann, BF98

The Cambridge guide to the museums of Europe, Hudson, Kenneth, BF98

The Cambridge guide to theatre, BH67

The Cambridge guide to world theatre, BH65, BH66, BH67

The Cambridge handbook for editors, authors, and publishers, AA318

Cambridge handbook of American literature, Salzman, Jack, BE431

The Cambridge handbook of contemporary China, Mackerras, Colin, DE148

The Cambridge historical encyclopedia of Great Britain and Ireland, DC289

—— Haigh, Christopher, DC293

The Cambridge history of Africa, DD57

Cambridge history of American literature, BE440

—— Bercovitch, Sacvan, BE439

—— Patell, Cyrus R. K., BE439

—— Trent, William Peterfield, BE439

The Cambridge history of Arabic literature, BE1546

Cambridge history of China, DE146

The Cambridge history of classical literature, BE1020, BE1052

Cambridge history of English literature, Waller, A.R, BE617

—— Ward, A. W., BE617

Cambridge history of India, DE169

Cambridge history of Iran, DE189

The Cambridge history of Japan, DE194

The Cambridge history of Judaism, BC562

The Cambridge history of Latin America, DB291

The Cambridge history of medieval political thought c.350–c.1450, CJ23

Cambridge history of political thought, 1450–1700, Burns, J. H., CJ23

—— Goldie, Mark, CJ23

The Cambridge history of Renaissance philosophy, BB69

The Cambridge history of Russian literature, BE1419

The Cambridge history of Southeast Asia, DE92

Cambridge history of the Bible, BC191

The Cambridge illustrated dictionary of British heritage, DC290

The Cambridge illustrated dictionary of natural history, Lincoln, Roger J., EG75

Cambridge International Reference on Current Affairs, Ltd. *World development directory*, CH134

The Cambridge Italian dictionary, AC535

—— Reynolds, Barbara, AC529, AC534

Cambridge mediaeval history, DA157

The Cambridge photographic atlas of the planets, Briggs, Geoffrey, EC64

Cambridge Scientific Abstracts, Inc. *CSA life sciences collection*, EG14

Cambridge South Asian archive, University of Cambridge. Centre for South Asian Studies, DE89

•*Cambridge structural database*, EE139

Cambridge University Library. *Comedias sueltas in Cambridge University Library*, BE1461

—— *Early English printed books in the University Library, 1475–1640*, AA669

The Cambridge world history of human disease, EH212

Cameo C., Miguel. *Bibliografía indígena andina peruana (1900–1968)*, DB383

Cameron, Angus. *Old English word studies*, BD99

Cameron, Elisabeth. *Encyclopedia of pottery & porcelain, 1800–1960*, BG58

Cameron, James. *EC legal systems*, CK204

—— *EFTA legal systems*, CK204

Cameron, John. *International handbook of education systems*, CB125

Cameron, Kenneth. *English place-names*, CL192

Cameron, Lucille W. *Labor and industrial relations journals and serials*, CH659

Cameroon
  atlases, CL339
  bibliography, DD18, DD136, DD138
  biobibliography, BE1525
  current surveys, DD62
  encyclopedias, DD48, DD137
  government publications
    bibliography, AF224, AF229
    statistics, CG321

Cameroon. Dept. of Statistics and National Accounts. *Note annuelle de statistique*, CG321

Cameroon, DeLancey, Mark W., DD18, DD48, DD138

—— Mokeba, H. Mbella, DD48

—— Schraeder, Peter J., DD18, DD138

Cameroonian literature, BE1525
  bibliography, BE1526

Camm, J. C. R. *Australians : a historical atlas*, DF37

Camp, Charles Lewis. *Bibliography of fossil vertebrates*, EF228, EF230

—— *The plains & the Rockies*, DB168

Camp, Roderic A. *Biografías políticos Mexicanos, 1935–1988*, AH106, CJ305

—— *Mexican political biographies, 1884–1935*, AH106, CJ305

—— *Who's who in Mexico today*, AH107

CAMP catalog, Cooperative Africana Microform Project, DD81

Campaign funds, CJ249

Campaign funds (by country or region)
  United States, CJ247, CJ248

Campaign speeches of American presidential candidates, 1948–1984, CJ244

Campbell, Alistair. *Anglo-Saxon dictionary*, AC171

Campbell, Bruce. *A dictionary of birds*, EG257

Campbell, Colin. *Canadian political facts, 1945–1976*, CJ294

Campbell, Dorothy W. *Index to black American writers in collective biographies*, BE543

Campbell, Enid Mona. *Legal research*, CK235

Campbell, George L. *Compendiums of the world's languages*, BD12

Campbell, Georgetta Merritt. *Extant collections of early black newspapers*, AE15, AE105

Campbell, James Edward. *Pottery and ceramics*, BG51

Campbell, James Oscar. *Reader's encyclopedia of Shakespeare*, BE783

Campbell, Joan. *European labor unions*, CH665

Campbell, Malcolm. *The Random House international encyclopedia of golf*, BK81

Campbell, N. J. M. *Conway's all the world's fighting ships, 1947–1982*, CJ592

Campbell, Paul J. *Women of mathematics*, EB104

Campbell, Paul R. *Detailed statistics on the population of South Africa by race and urban/rural residence, 1950 to 2010*, CG356

—— *Detailed statistics on the urban and rural population of Pakistan, 1950 to 2010,* CG415
Campbell, R. D. *Dictionary of aviation,* CH474
Campbell, Robert Jean. *Psychiatric dictionary,* EH382
Campbell, Thomas J. *Encyclopedia of minerals,* EF186
Campbell, William Giles. *Form and style,* AG1
Campbell-Kease, John. *Companion to local history research,* DC351
Campground directory, BK111
Camphausen, Rufus C. *The encyclopedic dictionary of erotic wisdom,* CC279
Camping, BK107, BK111
    directories, BK110
Campos, Agostinho de. *História da literatura portuguesa ilustrada,* BE1365
Campus-free college degrees, CB256
Camus, Raoul F. *National tune index,* BJ288
Canada. *Revised statutes of Canada, 1985,* CK193
Canada
    almanacs, CG111
    archives, DB193
        guides, CC525
    associations, AL51, AL52
    atlases, CL307, CL308, DB208
        handbooks, CL309
    bibliography, AA444, AA445, AA446, AA447, AA448, AA449, AA450, AA452, AA453, DB180, DB181, DB183, DB184, DB188
        current, AA454, AA455, AA456
        pamphlets, AA451
    bibliography of bibliography, AA22
    biography, AA450, AH91, AH92, AH93, AH94, AH95, AH96, AH98
        contemporary, AH76, AH97
        indexes, AH54
    current surveys, DB204
    directories, DB201
        bibliography, DB200
    dissertations, AG17
    encyclopedias, DB198
    gazetteers, CL112, CL113
    government publications, AF150, AF151, AF152
        bibliography, AF154, CJ303
        collections, AF156, DB206
        indexes, AF153
        provinces, AF155
    guides, DB177
    handbooks, DB202
    library resources, AK128, DB199
    manuscripts and archives, DB192, DB194
    newspapers, AE39, AE117
        databases, AE118, CH38
        indexes, AE118, CH38
        union lists, AE38
    periodicals, AD59, AD60
        directories, AD55
        indexes, AD293, AD312
    quotations, BE102
    statistics, CG110, CG111, CG112, CG113, DB209
        bibliography, CG114
    statistics (by subject)
        ethnic groups, CC410, CC442, CC471, CG82, CG84, CG85
    statutes, CK193
Canada (by subject)
    archaeology and ancient history, CE84
    armed forces, CJ650
    art and architecture, BF31
    children and youth, CC152, CC153
    economic conditions
        bibliography, CH176
        encyclopedias, CH48
        guides, CH175
    elections, CJ295
    ethnic groups
        dissertations, CF44
        literature, BE828
    folklore and popular culture, CF65, CF66, CF73, CF75

foreign relations
    bibliography, DB186
    Caribbean, DB261
    Latin America, DB261
foundations and philanthropic organizations, AL125
French language, AC386
history
    atlases, DB76, DB207, DB208
    bibliography, DB24, DB25, DB177, DB178, DB179, DB187, DB188, DB189, DB190, DB191, DB210
    diaries and letters, DB185
    encyclopedias, DB82, DB197
    general histories, DB203
    guides to records, DB196
    library catalogs, BE825
    manuscripts and archives, DB194, DB195
    regional and local, DB212, DB213, DB214, DB216
        bibliography, DB211, DB215
    registers, CJ299
    resources, DB193
    sourcebooks, AF156, DB206
    sources, DB205
    statistics, CG113, DB209
immigration
    bibliography, CC311
languages
    bibliography, BD105
    English, AC158
law, CK35
    directories, CK194
    guides, CK195
marketing
    statistics, CH595
nationalsim, CJ301
place-names, CL111, CL113, CL176, CL177, CL181, CL182
politics and government, CJ293, CJ294, CJ297, CJ298, CJ299, CJ300, CJ302, CJ304, CJ515, DB204
    bibliography, AF154, CJ303
    handbooks, CJ295
population
    bibliography, CG116
public administration
    bibliography, CJ465
religion, BC30, BC59, BC270
    directories, BC324
    yearbooks, BC324
statistics and demography
    bibliography, CG115, CG116
textiles, BG157
theater, BH73
travel and tourism, CL372
treaties, CK97
Canada. Board on Geographical Names. *18th–19th reports containing all decisions to July 31, 1927,* CL111
Canada. Census Division. *A bibliography of Canadian demography,* CG116
Canada. Department of Agriculture. Committee on Feed Composition. *Atlas of nutritional data on United States and Canadian feeds,* EJ126
Canada. Department of External Affairs. Treaty Section. *Treaties in force for Canada,* CK97
Canada. Energy, Mines and Resources Canada. *The national atlas of Canada,* CL307, CL308
Canada. Geographical Branch. *Gazetteer of Canada,* CL112
Canada. Labour Data Branch. *Directory of labour organizations in Canada,* CH662
—— *Répertoire des organisations de travailleurs au Canada,* CH662
Canada. Parliament, CJ296
Canada. Public Archives. *Register of post-graduate dissertations in progress in history and related subjects,* DB191
Canada. Surveys and Mapping Branch. *Gazetteer of Canada,* CL112
Canada, DB202
—— Ingles, Ernest Boyce, DB183

Canada atlas toponymique, CL308
Canada gazette, CK193
Canada gazetteer atlas, CL308
Canada Institute for Scientific and Technical Information. *Union list of scientific serials in Canadian libraries,* EA45
Canada-Latin American Resource Centre. *Canada's relations with Latin America and the Caribbean, 1970–1990,* DB261
Canada legal directory, CK194
Canada since 1867, DB187
Canada votes, Scarrow, Howard A., CJ298
Canada votes, 1935–1988, Feigert, Frank B., CJ293, CJ298
Canada year book, CG110
Canada's playwrights, BE821
Canada's relations with Latin America and the Caribbean, 1970–1990, Phillips, Gillian, DB261
Canada's urban past, Artibise, Alan F. J., DB210
Canadian almanac and directory, CG111
Canadian architectural periodicals index, BF210
Canadian Architectural Records Survey. *Index des périodiques d'architecture canadiens, 1940–1980,* BF210
Canadian Association of Latin American and Caribbean Studies. *Canada's relations with Latin America and the Caribbean, 1970–1990,* DB261
Canadian astronomical handbook, EC57
Canadian Bibliographic Centre (Ottawa). *Canadian graduate theses in the humanities and social sciences, 1921–1946,* AG17
Canadian Board on Geographical Names. *Gazetteer of Canada,* CL112
Canadian book review annual, AA367
Canadian books in print, AA454, AA455
Canadian books in print : author and title indexes, AA455
Canadian books in print : subject index, AA454
Canadian business and economics, CH175
Canadian business index, AE118, CH38
Canadian business periodicals index, AE118, CH38
Canadian catalogue of books, AA456
Canadian catalogue of books, 1791–1897, Haight, Willet Ricketson, AA448
Canadian catalogue of books published in Canada, about Canada, AA445
The Canadian centenary series, DB203
Canadian Centre for Architecture. *Index des périodiques d'architecture canadiens, 1940–1980,* BF210
Canadian Centre for Philanthropy. *A Canadian directory to foundations,* AL125
Canadian Chamber of Commerce. *Organization of the government of Canada,* CJ304
Canadian Council for Research in Education. *Canadian education index,* CB52
Canadian crime statistics. Uniform crime reports for the United States, CK270
Canadian diaries and autobiographies, Matthews, William, BE726, DB185
Canadian directories, 1790–1987, National Library of Canada, DB200
A Canadian directory to foundations, AL125
Canadian drama
    bibliography, BE820
    biobibliography, BE821
    encyclopedias, BE833
    French authors
        handbooks, BE843
    library catalogs, BE494
•*Canadian Dun's market identifiers,* CH363
Canadian Education Association. *Canadian education index,* CB52
Canadian education index, CB52, CB57
The Canadian encyclopedia, DB198
Canadian essay and literature index, BE822
Canadian essays and collections index, BE822
Canadian ethnic groups bibliography, Gregorovich, Andrew, CC474
Canadian feature film index, 1913–1985, Turner, D. John, BH192
The Canadian feminist periodical index, CC527, CC541

Canadian feminist thesaurus, CC527, CC541
Canadian fiction
  bibliography, BE823, BE824, BE835
  biobibliography, BE819
Canadian fiction, Fee, Margery, BE823, BE824
Canadian government publications, Higgins, Marion
  Villiers, AF152
Canadian government publications : catalogue,
  AF153
Canadian Government Publishing Centre. *Education
  in Canada*, CB42
*Canadian graduate theses in the humanities and
  social sciences, 1921–1946*, Canadian
  Bibliographic Centre (Ottawa), AG17
Canadian guide to uniform legal citation, CK66
Canadian historical documents series, DB205
Canadian historical review, DB191
Canadian history and literature, Harvard University.
  Library, BE825
Canadian history in documents, 1763–1966, Bliss,
  John William Michael, DB205
Canadian Hospital Association. *Canadian hospital
  directory*, EH165
Canadian hospital directory, EH165
Canadian index, AE118, CH38
*Canadian index to periodicals and documentary
  films*, AD293
A Canadian Indian bibliography, 1960–1970, Abler,
  Thomas S., CC472
Canadian Institute of International Affairs. *A
  bibliography of the Hungarian Revolution, 1956*,
  DC380
Canadian Institute of Ukrainian Studies. *Galicia*,
  DC35
The Canadian law list, CK194
Canadian life and health insurance facts, CH525
Canadian literary landmarks, Colombo, John
  Robert, BE829
Canadian literary periodicals index, McQuarrie,
  Jane, BE822
——— Ripley, Gordon, BE822
Canadian literature
  bibliography, BE826, BE828, BE830, BE844
  biobibliography, BE819, BE834, BE836
  dissertations, BE831
  encyclopedias, BE431, BE833
  guidebooks, BE829
  handbooks, BE431
  indexes, BE822
  library catalogs, BE825
  manuscripts
    library catalogs, BE832
  works in French
    bibliography, BE838
    encyclopedias, BE837
Canadian literature (by subject)
  history, BE826, BE840
Canadian literature, BE826
——— Gabel, Gernot U., BE831
Canadian literature index, BE822
Canadian local histories to 1950, DB213
Canadian magazine index, AE118, CH38
Canadian medical directory, EH166
Canadian men and women of the time, Morgan,
  Henry James, AH98
The Canadian military experience, 1867–1983,
  Cooke, O. A., CJ650
Canadian Museum Association. *Directory of
  Canadian museums and related institutions*, AL90,
  BF116, EA217
Canadian musical works 1900–1980, BJ41
Canadian news facts, DB204
Canadian news index, AE118, CH38
•*Canadian NewsDisc*, AE118, CH38
Canadian official publications, Bishop, Olga B.,
  AF150
Canadian parliamentary companion, CJ295
Canadian parliamentary guide, CJ295
Canadian parliamentary handbook, CJ296
Canadian party platforms, 1867–1968, Carrigan, D.
  Owen, CJ297
Canadian Peace Research Institute. *Peace research
  abstracts journal*, CJ681

Canadian periodical index, AD293
Canadian periodicals index, 1920–1937, Heggie,
  Grace F., AD293
Canadian Permanent Committee on Geographical
  Names. *Gazetteer of Canada*, CL112
Canadian poetry
  biobibliography, BE819
  indexes, BE827
  library catalogs, BE494
  works in French
    bibliography, BE839
Canadian political facts, 1945–1976, Campbell,
  Colin, CJ294
Canadian political parties, 1867–1968, Heggie,
  Grace F., CJ300
Canadian provincial government publications,
  Bhatia, Mohan, AF155
Canadian public administration : bibliography,
  Grasham, W. E., CJ465
Canadian quotations, BE102
Canadian quotations and phrases, BE104
Canadian reference sources, Ryder, Dorothy E.,
  AA456
Canadian review of comparative literature, BE32
Canadian review of Hungarian studies, DC380
Canadian review of studies in nationalism, CJ8, CJ9,
  DC64
Canadian serials directory, AD60
Canadian Society for Computational Studies of
  Intelligence. *The AI directory*, EK198
Canadian statistics index, CG112
Canadian studies, Jones, Linda M., DB184
Canadian studies on Hungarians, 1886–1986, Miska,
  John P., DC384
Canadian theses, National Library of Canada, AG17
Canadian translations, AA140
Canadian treaty calendar, Wiktor, Christian L.,
  CK97
Canadian who's who, AH97, AH98
Canadian who's who index, 1898–1984, McMann,
  Evelyn de R., AH98
Canadian Women's Indexing Group. *The Canadian
  feminist periodical index*, CC527
——— *The Canadian feminist thesaurus*, CC541
The Canadian women's movement, 1960–1990,
  CC525
Canadian Women's Movement Archives. *The
  Canadian women's movement, 1960–1990*, CC525
Canadian writers, Sylvestre, Guy, BE844
Canadian writers and their works: fiction series,
  David, Jack, BE819
——— Lecker, Robert, BE819
——— Quigley, Ellen, BE819
Canadian writers and their works: poetry series,
  Davis, Jack, BE819
——— Lecker, Robert, BE819
——— Quigley, Ellen, BE819
Canadiana, AA445, AA456, AD293
Canadiana, 1867–1900, AA446
Canal Zone. Library-Museum, Balboa Heights.
  *Subject catalog of the special Panama Collection
  of the Canal Zone Library-Museum*, DB318
Cancer, EH173
  bibliography, EH26
  databases, EH73
  dictionaries, EH108
  periodicals, EH38
The cancer dictionary, Altman, Roberta, EH108
Cancer journals and serials, Vaillancourt, Pauline
  M., EH38
Cancer sourcebook, EH173
Cancer therapy abstracts, EH73
•*CANCERLIT*, EH72, EH73
El cancionero del siglo XV, c. 1360–1520, BE1477
Cancro, Robert. *Comprehensive glossary of
  psychiatry and psychology*, EH383
Canfield, D. Lincoln. *The University of Chicago
  Spanish dictionary*, AC739
Cankar, Izidor. *Slovenski biografski leksikon*, AH309
Cankarjeva Založba. *The Oxford-Duden pictorial
  Serbo-Croat & English dictionary*, AC714
Canlit bibliographic series, DC384

Cann, Marjorie Mitchell,. *Cann's keys to better
  meetings*, CJ452
——— *Point of order*, CJ452
Cannabis, CC127
Canney, Margaret. *Catalogue of the Goldsmiths'
  Library of Economic Literature*, CH15
Cannistraro, Philip V. *Historical dictionary of fascist
  Italy*, DC433
Cannon, Carl L. *Journalism*, AE135, AE136
Cannon, John Ashton. *The Blackwell dictionary of
  historians*, DA46
Cannon, Minna A. *List by titles of publications of the
  United States Department of Agriculture from
  1840 to June, 1901, inclusive*, EJ85
Cannons, Harry George Turner. *Bibliography of
  library economy*, AK9, AK12
*Cannons' bibliography of library economy, 1876–
  1920*, Jordan, Anne Harwell, AK12
——— Jordan, Melbourne, AK12
Cannon's precedents, CJ224
Cann's keys to better meetings, Cann, Marjorie
  Mitchell,, CJ452
Canon law, CK237, CK238
Canon law abstracts, CK237
Canon Law Society of America. *The code of canon
  law*, CK238
Cantin, Pierre. *Bibliographie de la critique de la
  littérature québécoise dans les revues des XIXe et
  XXe siécles*, BE838
——— *Bibliographie de la critique de la littérature
  québécoise et canadienne-française dans les
  revues canadiennes*, BE838
Cantonese dictionary, Huang, Parker Po-fei, AC264
The Cantonese speaker's dictionary, Cowles, Roy T.,
  AC260
Cantor, Aviva. *The Jewish woman, 1900–1985*,
  CC597
Cantor, George. *Historic black landmarks*, BF248
——— *Historic landmarks of black America*, BF248,
  CC391
Cantor, Milton. *Documents of American history*,
  DB62
Cantrell, Karen. *Funding for anthropological
  research*, CE55
——— *Funding for museums, archives, and special
  collections*, BF104
Cantwell, John D. *The Second World War*, DA204,
  DC286
Cape Verde
  bibliography, DD18, DD114
  encyclopedias, DD48
  government publications
    bibliography, AF220
Cape Verde, Halter, Marilyn, DD48
——— Lobban, Richard A., DD48
——— Shaw, Caroline S., DD18
Capek, Mary Ellen S. *Women's thesaurus*, CC542,
  CC543, CC623
Capelan, Tor. *Finsk biografisk handbok*, AH186
Capell, Arthur. *A new Fijian dictionary*, AC319
Capie, Forrest. *Directory of economic institutions*,
  CH77
Capitals of the world, CL86
Caplan, H. H. *The classified directory of artists'
  signatures, symbols & monograms*, BF158
Caplan, Perri. *Namibia handbook and political who's
  who*, DD189
Čaplovič, Ján. *Bibliografia tlačí vydaných na
  Slovensku do roku 1700*, AA595
Cappelens Musikkleksikon, BJ126
Cappelens store engelsk-norsk ordbok, AC619
Cappeller, C. *A Sanskrit-English dictionary*, AC706
Cappelli, Adriano. *Cronologia, cronografia e
  calendario perpetuo*, EC85
Cappon, Lester J. *Atlas of early American history*,
  DB96
Caprile, Jean-Pierre. *Bibliographie analytique des
  langues parlées en Afrique subsaharienne, 1970–
  1980*, BD213
Captains of the old steam navy, Bradford, James C.,
  CJ639

Carabillo, Toni. *Feminist chronicles, 1953–1993*, CC572

Caratini, Roger. *Dictionnaire des personnages de la Révolution*, AH193

—— *La force des faibles*, CE47

Carbohydrates, EE114, EE116

Carboni, Fabio. *Bibliografia somala*, DD206

Carbonnel, Isabelle. *Guide de l'utilisateur des Inventaires des Archives nationales*, DC150

Carcinogenesis abstracts, EH73

Carcinogenically active chemicals, Lewis, Richard J., EE80

Card, Josefina J. *Handbook of adolescent sexuality and pregnancy*, CC168

The card catalog of the manuscript collections of the Archives of American Art, Archives of American Art, BF58

The card catalog of the oral history collections of the Archives of American Art, Archives of American Art, BF59

Cardenas, Francisco José. *Handbook of Latin American studies*, BE874, DB266

Cardenas, Maria Elena. *Handbook of Latin American studies*, BE874, DB266

Cárdenas Ramírez, Julio. *Diccionario biográfico de Venezuela*, AH146

Cardenas y Vicent, Vicente de. *Índice nobiliario español*, AJ140

Cardim, Ismael. *Dicionário inglês-português*, AC645

Cardinale, Susan. *Women and the literature of the seventeenth century*, BE740

Cardinall, Allan Wolsey. *Bibliography of the Gold Coast*, DD98, DD162

Cardinals *see* Popes, cardinals, bishops

Cardona, Luis A. *Annotated bibliography on Puerto Rican materials and other sundry matters*, DB451

Cardona Grisález, Guillermo. *Para un estudío sobre la violencia en Columbia*, DB364

Cardozo, Lubio. *Bibliografía de bibliografías sobre la literatura venezolana en las bibliotecas de Madrid, Paris y Londres*, AA32

—— *Bibliografía del teatro venezolano*, BE966

Career advancement for women in the federal service, Ross, Lynn C., CJ109

Career America, CH696

The career guide, CH694

Career information center, CB211

•*Career options*, CB213

Careers *see* Occupations

Careers Research and Advisory Centre (Cambridge, England). *The students' guide to graduate studies in the UK*, CB321

Cargas, Harry J. *The Holocaust*, DA214

Cargill, Jennifer S. *Biographical sources*, AH4

Caribbean
    atlases, CL319
    bibliography, AA472, AA554, AA555, AA556, DB404, DB405, DB406, DB407, DB408
    bibliography of bibliography, AA33
    biography, AH110, AH148, AH149, CJ306
    directories, DB288
    dissertations, CA22, DB411
    encyclopedias, CC387, DB281
    guides, DB251
    handbooks, DB295
    manuscripts and archives, DB412, DB413
    newspapers, AE41
    statistics, CG38, CG45, CG120, CG163
        periodicals, CG121
    yearbooks, DB294

Caribbean (by subject)
    anthropology and ethnology, CE85
    censuses, CG122
        handbooks, CG38
    economic conditions, DB410
    foreign relations
        Canada, DB261
    history, DB259
        guides to records, DB273, DB274
        library catalogs, DB269, DC344
        manuscripts and archives, DB301, DB414
    languages, BD174
    law, CK200

migration
    bibliography, CE77
    politics and government, AH110, CJ306, CJ311
    encyclopedias, DB283

The Caribbean, Hughes, Roger, DB406

Caribbean acquisitions, University of Florida. Libraries. Catalog Dept, AA556

Caribbean basin databook, DB293

Caribbean Community. *The CARICOM bibliography*, AA555

Caribbean fiction
    women authors
        bibliography, BE971

Caribbean literature
    bibliography, BE544, BE870, BE968, BE981
    biobibliography, BE969, BE970
    Indian Ocean authors, BE1517
    library catalogs, BE523, BE1504

Caribbean women novelists, Paravisini-Gebert, Lizabeth, BE971

Caribbean writers, BE969

Caribbean year book, CG163

Caribbeana 1900–1965, DB405

The CARICOM bibliography, AA555, DB405

CARINDEX : social sciences, DB405

Caring for animals, EJ118

Caring for kids with special needs, CC163

Carl Gregor, *Duke of Mecklenburg. International jazz bibliography*, BJ297

Carlberg, Berthold. *Stieler's atlas of modern geography*, CL291

Carlen, Claudia. *The papal encyclicals*, BC434

—— *Papal pronouncements*, BC433

Carleton, R. Milton. *Index to common names of herbaceous plants*, EG121

Carley, James F. *Whittington's dictionary of plastics*, EK291

Carlier, Robert. *Dictionnaire des citations françaises et étrangères*, BE129

Carlisle, Richard. *The illustrated encyclopedia of mankind*, CE42

Carlos, Pere. *Llibres [sic] editats à Mallorca (1939–1972)*, AA743

Carlos V, DC501

Carlsbergfondet (Copenhagen, Denmark). *Dansk historisk bibliografi*, DC131

—— *Forfatterlexikon omfattende Danmark, Norge og Island indtil 1814*, BE1087

Carlson, Delbert G. *Cat owner's home veterinary handbook*, EJ138

—— *Dog owner's home veterinary handbook*, EJ142

Carlson, Helen V. *An annotated bibliography on technical writing, editing, graphics, and publishing, 1950–1965*, EA164

—— *Annotated bibliography on technical writing, editing, graphics, and publishing, 1966–80*, EA164

Carlton, Robert G. *Newspapers of east central and southeastern Europe in the Library of Congress*, AE43

Carman, Harry James. *Guide to the principal sources for American civilization, 1800–1900, in the city of New York*, DB79, DB98

Carmichael, Colin. *Mechanical engineer's handbook*, EK238

Carmichael, D. R. *Accountants' handbook*, CH257

Carmichael, Leonard. *Manual of child psychology*, CD85

Carmichael, Robert S. *Handbook of physical properties of rocks*, EF254

Carnandet, Jean Baptiste. *Acta sanctorum quotquot toto orbe coluntur*, BC257

Carnegie Commission on Higher Education. *A statistical portrait of higher education*, CB340

Carnegie Foundation for the Advancement of Teaching. *A classification of institutions of higher education*, CB322

—— *The condition of teaching*, CB165

Carnegie Institution of Washington. *Codices latini antiquiores*, AA201

—— *Guides to manuscript materials for the history of the United States*, DB28, DB32

Carnegie Institution of Washington. Division of Historical Research. *Atlas of the historical geography of the United States*, DB75

Carnegie Library of Pittsburgh. Science and Technology Department. *Science and technology desk reference*, EA153

Carnegie Library of Pittsburgh. Technology Department. *Technical book review index*, EA54

Carnell, Hilary. *Oxford literary guide to the British Isles*, BE614

Carner, Gary. *Jazz performers*, BJ298

Carnes, Pack. *Fable scholarship*, CF38

Carnoy, Albert Joseph. *Dictionnaire étymologique des noms grecs de plantes*, EG122

—— *Dictionnaire étymologique du proto-indo-européen*, AC513

Carocci, Sandro. *Bibliografia dell'Archivio centrale dello Stato, 1953–1978*, DC427

Carolina Population Center. *Population/family planning thesaurus*, CC254

Caroline drama, Fordyce, Rachel, BE642

Carolson, Maria. *Dictionary of Russian literature since 1917*, BE1412

Caron, Gilbert. *Guide du chercheur en histoire canadienne*, DB177

Caron, Pierre. *Bibliographie des travaux publiés de 1866 à 1897 sur l'histoire de la France depuis 1789*, DC198

—— *Répertoire des périodiques de langue française, philosophiques, historiques, philologiques et juridiques*, AD94

—— *Répertoire des sociétés françaises de sciences philosophiques, historiques, philologiques et juridiques*, AL61

Caron-Houle, Françoise. *Guide to the reports of the Public Archives of Canada, 1872–1972*, DB193

Carozzi, Albert V. *A history of geology*, EF100

Carozzi, Carlo. *Congo Brazzaville*, DD143

Carozzi, Marguerite. *A history of geology*, EF100

Carpeaux, Otto Maria. *Pequena bibliografia crítica da literatura brasileira*, BE925

Carpenter, Allan. *The encyclopedia of the Central West*, DB173

—— *Encyclopedia of the Far West*, DB173

—— *The encyclopedia of the Midwest*, DB160

Carpenter, C. L. *Guide to New Zealand information sources*, AA86, AF268

Carpenter, Carole Henderson. *A bibliography of Canadian folklore in English*, CF65

Carpenter, Charles A. *Modern British drama*, BE638

—— *Modern drama scholarship and criticism, 1966–1980*, BE220, BE638

Carpenter, Edwin. *Collins-Robert French-English, English-French dictionary*, AC335

Carpenter, Humphrey. *The Oxford companion to children's literature*, BE377

Carpenter, Joel A. *Twentieth-century evangelicalism*, BC212

Carpenter, John Richard. *An ecological glossary*, EG123

Carpenter, Pierre. *Glossarium mediae et infimae latinitatis*, AC587

Carpenter, Thomas H. *Beazley addenda*, BF324

—— *Summary guide to Corpus vasorum antiquorum*, BG78

Carper, James C. *Religious colleges and universities in America*, CB223

—— *Religious schools in America*, CB37

Carr, Cyril F. *A reader's Hebrew-English lexicon of the Old Testament*, BC133

Carr, Ian. *Jazz*, BJ299

Carr, John Charles. *Sex differences and learning*, CB7

Carradice, Ian. *The coin atlas*, BG182

Carrasquillo, Angela. *Hispanic children and youth in the United States*, CC461

Carratelli, Giovanni Pugliese. *Enciclopedia dell'arte antica, classica e orientale*, BF71

Carrera, Blanca. *Demografía en el Ecuador*, CG153

Carrera, Gustavo Luis. *Bibliografía del cuento venezolano*, BE964

Carrera, Michael. *The language of sex*, CC280

Carrera Andrade, Jorge. *Bibliografía general de la literatura latinoamericana,* BE869

Carrera Damas, Germán. *Venezuelan history,* DB399

Carreras, Albert. *Estadísticas históricas de España,* CG282

Carreras i Martí, Joan. *Diccionari de la llengua catalana,* AC249

Carrigan, D. Owen. *Canadian party platforms, 1867–1968,* CJ297

Carrington, David K. *Map collections in the United States and Canada,* CL259

Carroll, Berenice A. *Peace and war,* CJ680

Carroll, Frances Laverne. *Biographical directory of national librarians,* AK84

Carroll, M. J. *Key to League of Nations documents,* AF28

Carroll, Mark. *Records of the presidency,* CJ174

Carruth, Gorton. *Encyclopedia of American facts and dates,* DA29, DB58
—— *The encyclopedia of world facts and dates,* DA29
—— *The Oxford illustrated literary guide to the United States,* BE438

Carskadon, Mary A. *Encyclopedia of sleep and dreaming,* CD111

Carson, Anne. *Feminist spirituality and the feminine divine,* BC10
—— *Goddesses & wise women,* BC10

Carson, Edward. *Guide to the records of the Bahamas,* DB418

Carson, Emmett Devon. *The charitable appeals fact book,* AL132

Carson, Patricia. *Guides to materials for West African history in European archives,* DD105

Carstens, Henry. *Bibliographie der Troubadours,* BE1374

Carta (Jerusalem). *The Macmillan Bible atlas,* BC197

Cartano, Tony. *Dictionnaire de littérature française contemporaine,* BE1151

Carter, Boyd George. *Las revistas literarias de Hispano-américa,* BE882

Carter, Brian. *The complete handbook of garden plants,* EJ249

Carter, Craig. *Daguerreotypes,* BK53
—— *Pro football guide,* BK79

Carter, Deborah J. *Community college fact book,* CB337

Carter, Gwendolyn. *From protest to challenge,* CJ413

Carter, Jared. *A writer's guide to book publishing,* AA295

Carter, John. *ABC for book-collectors,* AA249

Carter, Paul. *Backstage handbook,* BH89

Carter, Robert L. *Dictionary of dermatologic terms,* EH111

Carter, Sarah. *Women's studies,* CC480

Carter G. Woodson Institute series in Black studies. *Afro-American sources in Virginia,* CC382

Cartographic citations, Clark, Suzanne M., CL263

Cartographic materials, CL252

Cartographical innovations, CL262

Cartography
bibliography, CL226, CL227, CL232, CL236, CL247, CL251, CL255
biography, CL272, CL273, CL274
dictionaries, CL52
directories, CL260
guides, CL220, CL222, CL240
guides to records, CL257
handbooks, CL262
library collections, CL242, CL253, CL255
style manuals, CL263
yearbooks, CL270, CL271

Cartography (by country or region)
United States, CL244

Carton, François. *Dictionnaire de sigles nationaux et internationaux,* AC345

Carton, Jean. *Dictionnaire de sigles nationaux et internationaux,* AC345

Cartoons, AE127

Cartter, A. M. *Assessment of quality in graduate education,* CB348

Carty, James. *Bibliography of Irish history,* DC397

Carus, J. Victor. *Bibliotheca zoologica,* EG209

Carvajal, Manuel J. *Bibliography of poverty and related topics in Costa Rica,* DB304

Carver, Terrell. *Atlas of communism,* CJ525
—— *A Marx dictionary,* CJ518

Cary, Mary Flagler. *The Mary Flagler Cary music collection,* BJ89

Cary, Robert. *African nationalist leaders in Rhodesia who's who,* AH327

Cary, Tristram. *Dictionary of musical technology,* BJ310

•*CAS ONLINE,* EE6

CAS source index, EA41, EE18

Casalbón, R. *Bibliotheca hispana,* AA811

Casares, Julio. *Diccionario histórico de la lengua española,* AC728

Casares y Sánchez, Julio. *Diccionario ideológico de la lengua española,* AC747

Casas de Barrán, Alicia. *Uruguay,* DB396

Case, Arthur Ellicott. *A bibliography of English poetical miscellanies, 1521–1750,* BE699, BE705

Case, Lynn M. *The new guide to the diplomatic archives of Western Europe,* DC18

Case, Margaret H. *South Asian history, 1750–1950,* DE76

Caselli, Graziella. *Bibliografia delle opere demografiche italiane (1966–1972),* CG4

Casey, Magdalen. *Catalogue of pamphlets in the Public Archives of Canada, with index,* AA451

Cash, Caleb George. *A contribution to the bibliography of Scottish topography,* DC360

Cash for college, McKee, Cynthia Ruiz, CB384

Cashin, James A. *Cashin's handbook for auditors,* CH259

Cashin's handbook for auditors, CH259

Cashman, Norine D. *Slide buyers' guide,* BF195

Cashmore, Ernest Ellis. *Dictionary of race and ethnic relations,* CC341

Caskey, Jefferson D. *Index to poetry in popular periodicals,* BE499

•*CASPAR,* CB257

Casper, Dale E. *Urban America examined,* CC295

Cass, James. *Comparative guide to American colleges for students, parents, and counselors,* CB265

Cassata, Mary B. *Television,* BH292

Cassell & the Publishers' Association directory of publishing, AA290

Cassell's colloquial German, Anderson, Beatrix, AC437

Cassell's Dutch dictionary, AC297

Cassell's encyclopaedia of literature, Steinberg, Sigfrid H., BE59

Cassell's encyclopaedia of world literature, BE59

Cassell's Engels-Nederlands, Nederlands-Engels woordenboek, AC297

Cassell's English-Dutch, Dutch-English dictionary, AC297

Cassell's French-English, English-French dictionary, AC342

Cassell's German-English, English-German dictionary, Betteridge, Harold T., AC414

Cassell's Italian-English, English-Italian dictionary, AC528

Cassell's Latin dictionary, AC575

Cassell's modern guide to synonyms & related words, AC139

Cassell's new English-Croatian and Croatian-English dictionary, AC711

Cassell's new Latin dictionary, AC575

Cassell's Spanish-English English-Spanish dictionary, AC730

Cassels, Alan. *Italian foreign policy, 1918–1945,* DC419

Cassel's directory of publishing in Great Britain, the Commonwealth, and Ireland, AA290

CASSI, EA41, EE18

CASSI keyword-out-of-context index, 1907–1989, EA41, EE18

CASSI KWOC, EA41, EE18

Cassiday, Bruce. *Modern mystery, fantasy, and science fiction writers,* BE293

Cassidy, Daniel J. *Graduate scholarship directory,* CB374
—— *International scholarship directory,* CB374
—— *Scholarship book,* CB374

Cassidy, Frederic Gomes. *Dictionary of American regional English,* AC151
—— *Dictionary of Jamaican English,* AC157

Cassin, Barbara. *Dictionary of eye terminology,* EH110

Cassin-Scott, Jack. *Costumes and settings for staging historical plays,* BH90

Cassis, A. F. *The twentieth-century English novel,* BE672

A cast of thousands, Corey, Melinda, BH205

Castagno, James. *Artists as illustrators,* BF372

Castagno, John. *American artists,* BF159
—— *Artists' monograms and indiscernible signatures,* BF159
—— *European artists,* BF159

Castagno, Margaret. *Somalia,* DD48

Castel, Jacqueline R. *Practical guide to Canadian legal research,* CK195

Castellarium Anglicanum, King, David James Cathcart, BF206

Castello-Cortes, Ian. *The Economist atlas,* CH147

Castelot, André. *Dictionnaire d'histoire de France Perrin,* DC160

Castiglioni, Arturo. *A history of medicine,* EH213

Castilla's Spanish and English technical dictionary, EA131

Castillo, Carlos. *The University of Chicago Spanish dictionary,* AC739

Castillo, Homero. *Historia bibliográfica de la novela chilena,* BE938

Castillo-Speed, Lillian. *The Chicana studies index,* CC454, CC528

Castleman, Riva. *Contemporary prints,* BF376
—— *Prints of the twentieth century,* BF376

Castro Arroyo, María de los Angeles. *Los primeros pasos,* DB450

Castronovo, Valerio. *Storia della stampa italiana,* AE64

Casucci, Costanzo. *Bibliografia dell'Archivio centrale dello Stato, 1953–1978,* DC427

Caswell, Lucy Shelton. *Guide to sources in American journalism history,* AE144

Cat owner's home veterinary handbook, Carlson, Delbert G., EJ138

Catalan language
dictionaries, AC246, AC247, AC249, AC250, AC251
etymology, AC248
festschriften, BD166, BE1436

Catalan literature
encyclopedias, BE1450
festschriften, BD166, BE1436
women authors
biobibliography, BE1444

Catalog, Library of the Marine Biological Laboratory and the Woods Hole Oceanographic Institution, EF209
—— National Library of Medicine (U.S.), EH48

Catalog of African government documents, Boston University. Libraries, AF219

Catalog of American antiques, Ketchum, William C., BG46

Catalog of American national standards, EA268

Catalog of biographies, New York Academy of Medicine. Library, EH224

Catalog of books in the American Philosophical Society Library, Philadelphia, Pennsylvania, American Philosophical Society. Library, EA225

Catalog of books printed in the XVth century, British Museum, AA231

A catalog of books represented by Library of Congress printed cards issued to July 31, 1942, AA113, BC102
—— Library of Congress, AA106

Catalog of cards for printed music, 1953–1972, BJ63

The catalog of catalogs III, Palder, Edward L., CH556

Catalog of copyright entries, Library of Congress. Copyright Office, AA433, BE461, BH193, BJ81

Catalog of copyright entries. Fourth series. Part two, serials and periodicals, AD28

Catalog of current law titles, CK19, CK120

Catalog of federal domestic assistance, AL108, AL110, BA9, AH167, CH169

A catalog of files and microfilms of the German Foreign Ministry archives, 1920–1945, United States. Department of State. Historical Office, DC253

Catalog of government publications, New York Public Library. Research Libraries, AF83

Catalog of government publications in the Research Libraries, AF148, AF10

Catalog of Landscape Records in the United States (Project). *Historic landscape directory*, BF293

Catalog of little magazines, University of Wisconsin-Madison. Libraries, AD46

Catalog of manuscripts in the American Philosophical Society Library, including the archival shelflist, American Philosophical Society. Library, EA226

Catalog of manuscripts of the Folger Shakespeare Library, Washington, D.C, Folger Shakespeare Library, BE737

A catalog of modern world coins, 1850–1964, Yeoman, Richard S., BG192

Catalog of museum publications & media, BF48

Catalog of national historic landmarks, BF248

Catalog of new foreign and international law titles, CK19, CK120

A catalog of phonorecordings of music and oral data held by the Archives of Traditional Music, Indiana University. Archives of Traditional Music, BJ328

Catalog of printed books, Bancroft Library, DB163

Catalog of printed books of the Folger Shakespeare Library, Washington, D.C, Folger Shakespeare Library, BE737

Catalog of publications, 1930–35, League of Nations, AF28

Catalog of significant earthquakes, Dunbar, Paul K., EF260

—— Lockridge, Patricia A., EF260

—— Whiteside, Lowell S., EF260

Catalog of significant earthquakes, 2000 b.c.–1979, including quantitative casualties and damage, Ganse, Robert A., EF260

Catalog of the African collection, Northwestern University. Library, DD34

Catalog of the Avery Memorial Architectural Library of Columbia University, Avery Architectural and Fine Arts Library, BF228

Catalog of the book and serials collections of the Friends Historical Library of Swarthmore College, Friends Historical Library of Swarthmore College, BC350

Catalog of the Cooper-Hewitt Museum of Design Library of the Smithsonian Institution Libraries, Cooper-Hewitt Museum. Library, BG15

Catalog of the Cuban and Caribbean Library, University of Miami, Coral Gables, Florida, University of Miami. Cuban and Caribbean Library, DB408

Catalog of the E. Azalia Hackley memorial collection of Negro music, dance, and drama, Detroit Public Library, BJ86

Catalog of the Foreign Relations Library, Inc., New York, Foreign Relations Library, DA171

A catalog of the Greenlee collection, Newberry Library, DC489

Catalog of the Latin-American collection, University of Florida. Libraries, DB269

—— University of Texas at Austin. Library. Latin American Collection, DB265, DB270

Catalog of the Latin American Library of the Tulane University Library, New Orleans, Tulane University. Latin American Library, DB269

Catalog of the Library, Museum of Modern Art (New York, N.Y.). Library, BF55

Catalog of the Library of the French Biblical and Archeological School, Jerusalem, Israel, BC109

Catalog of the Library of the National Museum of African Art branch of the Smithsonian Institution Libraries, National Museum of African Art, BG4

Catalog of the Melville J. Herskovits Library of African Studies, Northwestern University Library and Africana in selected libraries, Evanston, Ill, Melville J. Herskovits Library of African Studies, DD34

Catalog of the Menninger Clinic Library, the Menninger Foundation … , Menninger Clinic (Topeka, Kansas). Library, EH376

Catalog of the Modern Greek collection, University of Cincinnati. Library, DC375

Catalog of the National Taiwan University theses and dissertations, AG58

Catalog of the Nettie Lee Benson Latin American Collection, Benson Latin American Collection, DB265, DB270

Catalog of the parliamentary papers of southern Rhodesia and Rhodesia, 1954–1970, Wilding, Norman W., AF242

Catalog of the professional library of the Menninger Foundation, Menninger Clinic (Topeka, Kansas), EH376

Catalog of the public documents of Congress and of other departments of the government of the United States for the period March 4, 1893–Dec. 31, 1940, United States. Superintendent of Documents, AF87, AF88, AF98, AF103, AF110

Catalog of the Robert Goldwater Library, the Metropolitan Museum of Art, Metropolitan Museum of Art (New York, N.Y.). Robert Goldwater Library, BF54

—— Robert Goldwater Library, BF54

Catalog of the Rübel Asiatic Research Collection, Harvard University. Fine Arts Library. Rübel Asiatic Research Collection, BF53

—— Rübel Asiatic Research Collection, BF53

Catalog of the Shakespeare collection, Folger Shakespeare Library, BE771

Catalog of the Sierra Leone collection, Fourah Bay College Library, University of Sierra Leone, Freetown, Sierra Leone. Fourah Bay College. Library, DD204

Catalog of the South Pacific collection, University of California, Santa Cruz. University Library, CE115, DF10

Catalog of the Tamiment Institute Library of New York University, Tamiment Library, CH642

Catalog of the theatre and drama collections, New York Public Library. Research Libraries, BH33

Catalog of the Transportation Center Library, Northwestern University … , Northwestern University. Transportation Center. Library, CH443

Catalog of the type specimens of invertebrate fossils, Purnell, Louis R., EF241

Catalog of the United States Geological Survey Library, United States. Geological Survey. Library, EF46

Catalog of the William B. Greenlee collection, Welsh, Doris Varner, DC489

Catalog of the Yale collection of Western Americana, Yale University. Library, DB170

Catalog of United States census publications, CG86

Catalog of United States census publications, 1790–1945, CG93

—— Dubester, Henry J., CG86

—— Library of Congress. Census Library Project, CG90

A catalog of United States government produced audiovisual materials, AA382

The catalog of world antiques, Ketchum, William C., BG46

Catalog to manuscripts at the National Anthropological Archives, Department of Anthropology, National Museum of Natural History, Smithsonian Institution, Washington, D.C, National Anthropological Archives, CE31

Cataloging, AK195, AK197, AK209

codes (by country or region)

United States, AK194, AK196

Cataloging service bulletin, AK195, AK197, BD10

Cataloging service bulletin index, Olson, Nancy, AK195

Catálogo analítico de las publicaciones de la Academia Nacional de la Historia, 1903–1986, Academia Nacional de la Historia (Argentina), DB323

Catálogo bibliográfico y crítico de las comedias anunciadas en los periódicos de Madrid desde 1661 hasta 1819, Coe, Ada May, BE1462

Catálogo colectivo de obras impresas en los siglos XVI al XVIII existentes en las bibliotecas españolas, Biblioteca Nacional (Spain), AA812

Catálogo colectivo de publicaciones periódicas en bibliotecas españolas, Spain. Dirección General de Archivos y Bibliotecas, AD241

Catálogo colectivo de publicaciones periódicas existentes en bibliotecas de la República Mexicana, Velásquez Gallardo, Pablo, AD229

Catálogo colectivo del patrimonio bibliográfico español, AA814, AA815

Catalogo collettivo nazionale delle pubblicazioni periodiche, AD239

Catalogo cumulativo 1886–1957, Biblioteca nazionale centrale di Firenze, AA727

Catalogo cumulativo stampa dalla Biblioteca nazionale centrale de firenze, Biblioteca nazionale centrale di Firenze, AD128

Catálogo de autores de la colección peruana, Biblioteca Nacional (Peru), AA544

Catálogo de autores teatrales del siglo XVIII, Herrera Navarro, Jerónimo, BE1464

Catálogo de autores y obras anonimas de la Biblioteca Nacional de Madrid, AA105

Catálogo de la bibliografía boliviana, Costa de la Torre, Arturo, AA503

Catálogo de la biblioteca de Salvá, Salvá y Pérez, Vicente, AA805, AA807

Catálogo de las lenguas de América del Sur, Tovar, Antonio, BD243

Catálogo de las publicaciones periódicas madrileñas existentes en la Hemeroteca Municipal de Madrid, 1661–1930, Hemeroteca Municipal de Madrid, AD154, AE76

Catálogo de las tesis doctorales manuscritas en la Universidad de Madrid, Universidad de Madrid, AG41

Catálogo de libros y folletos publicados en Cuba, Bachiller y Morales, Antonio, AA560

Catálogo de los manuscritos poéticos castellanos existentes en la Biblioteca de The Hispanic Society of America (siglos XV, XVI y XVII), Brey Mariño, Maria, BE1465

—— Rodriguez Moñino, Antonio R., BE1465, BE1478

Catálogo de manuscritos de América existentes en la Biblioteca Nacional, Paz, Julín, DB268, DE245

Catálogo de nombres geográficos del Perú, CL125

Catálogo de novelas y novelistas españoles del siglo XIX, Ferreras, Juan Ignacio, BE1474

Catálogo de obras en lengua catalana impresas desde 1474 hasta 1860, Aguiló y Fustér, Mariano, AA799

Catálogo de obras iberoamericanas y filipinas de la Biblioteca Nacional de Madrid, Biblioteca Nacional (Spain), DB268, DE245

Catálogo de periódicos sudamericanos existentes en la Biblioteca Pública de la Universidad (1791–1861), Universidad Nacional de La Plata. Biblioteca, AD69

Catálogo de poetas puertorriqueños, Arana Soto, Salvador, BE980

Catálogo de publicaciones oficiales, 1840–1977, Instituto Autónomo Biblioteca Nacional. Sección de Publicaciones Oficiales, AF163

Catálogo de publicaciones periódicas mexicanas, Mendoza-López, Margarita, AD62

Catálogo de publicaciones periódicas vascas de los siglos XIX y XX, Ruiz de Gauna, Adolfo, AD158

Catálogo de revistas españolas, Instituto de Cultura Hispánica (Spain). Departamento de Información, AD156

Catálogo de seudónimos, anagramas, iniciales y otros alias usados por escritores mexicanos y extranjeros que han publicado en México, Ruiz Castañeda, María del Carmen, AA152

Catálogo de tesis sobre historia de México, DB237

Catálogo de todos los periódicos que existen desde su fundación hasta el año de 1935, inclusive, Bogotá. Biblioteca Nacional, AD73

Catalogo degli editori italiani, AA291

Catalogo dei libri in commercio, AA737

Catalogo dei periodici italiani, AD130

Catalogo della stampa periodica della Biblioteche dell' Istituto Nazionale per la Storia del Movimento di Liberazione in Italia e degli Istituti associati, 1900/1975, Istituto Nazionale per la Storia del Movimento di Liberazione in Italia, DC426

Catálogo descriptivo de la gran colección de comedias escogidas que consta de cuarenta y ocho volúmenes, impresos de 1652 a 1704, Cotarelo y Mori, Emilio, BE1463

Catálogo descriptivo del material del Archivo de Indias referente a la historia de Bolivia, Vázquez Machicado, José, DB338

Catálogo do banco de teses, AG20

Catálogo dos livros disponíveis, AA779

Catálogo dos livros sobre Moçambique existentes no CDI do Banco em Lourenção Marques, Banco Nacional Ultramarino, Lourenço Marques. Centro de Documentação e Informação, DD183

Catalogo general de incunables en bibliotecas españolas, Biblioteca Nacional (Spain), AA229

Catálogo general de la librería española, 1931–1950, AA824

Catálogo general de la librería española e hispanoamericana, 1901-30, AA824

Catálogo general de libros, folletos y revistas, Guatemala. Tipografía Nacional, AA483

Catálogo general de libros impresos, hasta 1981, Biblioteca Nacional (Spain), AA105

Catalogo generale della libreria italiana, 1847–99, Pagliaini, Attilio, AA727, AA730, AA734

Catálogo-índice de la poesía cancioneril del siglo XV, Dutton, Brian, BE1477

Catalogo metodico degli scritti contenuti nelle pubblicazioni periodiche italiane e straniere, Italy. Parlamento. Camera dei Deputati. Biblioteca, AD318

Catálogo y noticias de los literators, AA459, AH99

Catalogs of the Library of the State Historical Society of Wisconsin, CH641

Catalogue, Gennadius Library, DC373
———— Harvard University. Museum of Comparative Zoology. Library, EG210
———— London Library, AA120
———— National Indian Law Library, CK127

Catalogue and index of contributions to North American geology, 1732–1891, Darton, Nelson Horatio, EF26

Catalogue bibliographique des ventes publiques, AA263

Catalogue checklist of English prose fiction, 1750–1800, Orr, Leonard, BE681

Catalogue collectif belge et luxembourgeois des périodiques étrangers en cours de publication, Bibliothèque Royale de Belgique, AD230

Catalogue collectif des journaux quotidiens d'information générale publiés en France métropolitaine de 1957 à 1961, AE51

*Catalogue collectif des périodiques du début du XVII*ᵉ* siècle à 1939*, Bibliothèque Nationale (France). Département des Périodiques, AD231, AD232

Catalogue collectif des publications scientifiques dans les bibliothèques canadiennes, EA45

Catalogue de la Bibliothèque de l'École biblique et archéologique française, École biblique et archéologique française (Jerusalem). Bibliothèque, BC109

Catalogue de la bibliothèque de M. Ricardo Heredia, Heredia y Livermore, Ricardo, AA802, AA805

Catalogue de la Bibliothèque Nationale suisse, AA838, AH301

Catalogue de la Bibliothèque Nationale Suisse á Berne, Schweizerische Landesbibliothek, AA837

Catalogue de la musique imprimée avant 1800, Lesure, François, BJ72, BJ73

Catalogue de la musique imprimée avant 1801, Guillo, Laurent, BJ72

Le catalogue de l'édition française, AA635

Catalogue de l'histoire de France, Bibliothèque Nationale (France). Département des Imprimés, DC143

Catalogue de l'histoire de la révolution française, Bibliothèque Nationale (France). Département des Imprimés, DC147

Catalogue des bibliographies géologiques, Margerie, Emmanuel de, EF34, EF35

Catalogue des dissertations et écrits académiques provenant des échanges avec les universités étrangères et reçus par la Bibliothèque Nationale, 1882–1924, Bibliothèque Nationale (France). Département des Imprimés, AG8

Catalogue des éditions de la Suisse romande, Jullien, Alexandre, AA836
———— Société des Libraires et Éditeurs de la Suisse Romande, AA836

Catalogue des films français de long métrage, Chirat, Raymond, BH184

Catalogue des livres imprimés au quinzième siècle des bibliothèques de Belgique, Polain, Louis, AA235

Catalogue des ouvrages de langue francaise publiés en Suisse, Jullien, Alexandre, AA836
———— Société des Libraires et Éditeurs de la Suisse Romande, AA836

Catalogue des périodiques clandestins diffusés en France de 1939 à 1945, Bibliothèque Nationale (France), AD91

Catalogue des périodiques d'Afrique noire francophone (1858–1962) conservés à l'IFAN, Thomassery, Marguerite, AD170

Catalogue des sites archéologiques d'Afghanistan, Ball, Warwick, DE109

Catalogue des thèses de doctorat ès sciences naturelles, soutenues à Paris de 1891 à 1954, Lavaud, Suzanne, EA56

Catalogue des thèses de doctorat soutenues devant les universités françaises, AG26, AG27, EA55

Catalogue des thèses de sciences soutenues en France de 1810 à 1890 inclusivement, Maire, Albert, EA56, EA57

Catalogue des thèses et écrits académiques, AG27

Catalogue du fonds "Iles de l'océan Indien", Safla, Roucaya, DD203
———— Université de la Réunion, DD203

Catalogue général de la librairie française, 1840–1925, Lorenz, Otto Henri, AA628, AA630, AA632, BC400

Catalogue général de l'édition musicale en France, Pierreuse, Bernard, BJ76

Catalogue général des incunables des bibliothèques publiques de France, Pellechet, Marie Léontine Catherine, AA234

Catalogue général des livres imprimés, Bibliothèque Nationale (France), AA101, AA163, BC400

Catalogue général des ouvrages en langue française, 1926–1929, AA628

*Catalogue général des périodiques du début du XVII*ᵉ* siècle à 1959*, Bibliothèque Nationale (France), AE52

Catalogue matières, Bibliothèque Forney, BG14

Catalogue of 18th-century symphonies, BJ295

Catalogue of additions to the manuscripts, British Museum. Department of Manuscripts, BE637, BE644

A catalogue of American watermarks, 1690–1835, Gravell, Thomas L., AA257

A catalogue of audio and video collections of Holocaust testimony, Ringelheim, Joan Miriam, DA220

Catalogue of books and pamphlets unrecorded in Oscar Wegelin's Early American poetry, 1650–1820, Stoddard, Roger E., BE498

Catalogue of books and periodicals on Estonia in the British Library Reference Division, British Library. Reference Division, DC135

Catalogue of books from the Low Countries 1601–1621 in the British Library, British Library, AA750

Catalogue of books in English on Japan, 1945–1981, DE196, DE197

Catalogue of books in the library of the British Museum printed in England, Scotland, and Ireland, and of books in English printed abroad to the year 1640, British Museum. Department of Printed Books, AA668

Catalogue of books on Japan translated from the Japanese into English, 1945–1981, DE197

Catalogue of books printed for private circulation, Dobell, Bertram, AA693

Catalogue of books printed in Spain and of Spanish books printed elsewhere in Europe before 1601, now in the British Library, British Library, AA468, AA813

Catalogue of books printed in the XVth century now in the British Museum, British Museum. Department of Printed Books, AA219, AA639

Catalogue of books relating to the discovery and early history of North and South America, Church, Elihu Dwight, DB2

Catalogue of botanical books in the collection of Rachel McMasters Miller Hunt, Hunt, Rachel McMasters Miller, EG95

Catalogue of British drawings for architecture, decoration, sculpture and landscape gardening, Harris, John, BF230

A catalogue of British family histories, Thomson, Theodore Radford, AJ110

Catalogue of British official publications not published by HMSO, AF180

Catalogue of British scientific and technical books, British Science Guild, EA13
———— Shaw, Daphne, EA13

Catalogue of cartographic materials in the British Library, 1975–1988, British Library, CL251

Catalogue of Catholic books in English printed abroad or secretly in England, 1558–1640, Allison, Antony Francis, BC388
———— Rogers, D. M., BC388

A catalogue of comedias sueltas in The New York Public Library, Bergman, Hannah E., BE1459

A catalogue of crime, Barzun, Jacques, BE266

Catalogue of dated and datable manuscripts, c.700–1600 in the Department of Manuscripts, the British Library, British Library. Department of Manuscripts, AA203

Catalogue of early Dublin-printed books, 1601 to 1700, Dix, Ernest Reginald McClintock, AA678, AA721

A catalogue of early globes made prior to 1850 and conserved in the United States, Yonge, Ena L., CL246

Catalogue of English Bible translations, Chamberlin, William J., BC94, BC97, BC100

A catalogue of English books printed before 1801 held by the University Library at Göttingen, Jefcoate, Graham, AA682

A catalogue of English newspapers and periodicals in the Bodleian Library, 1622–1800, Bodleian Library, AD104

Catalogue of European printed books, India Office Library, DE158

A catalogue of files and microfilms of the German Foreign Ministry archives, 1867–1920, American Historical Association. Committee for the Study of War Documents, DC250, DC253

Catalogue of Foraminifera, EF238

Catalogue of government publications, 1956–71, AF190

Catalogue of Hebrew books, Harvard University. Library, BC537

Catalogue of incunabula and manuscripts in the Army Medical Library, Schullian, Dorothy, EH24
———— Sommer, Francis E., EH24

Catalogue of incunabula and sixteenth century books in the National Library of Medicine, Krivatsy, Peter, EH24

Catalogue of index Foramenifera, Ellis, Brooks Fleming, EF238, EF239
———— Messina, Angelina R., EF238

Catalogue of Indonesian serials [Jakarta], AD194

Catalogue of Italian books, 1465–1600, AA729

Catalogue of Italian plays, 1500–1700, in the library of the University of Toronto, Corrigan, Beatrice, BE1314
—— University of Toronto. Library, BE1314
Catalogue of manuscript music in the British Museum, British Museum. Department of Manuscripts, BJ93
Catalogue of manuscripts containing Anglo-Saxon, Ker, Neil Ripley, BE604
Catalogue of meteorites, Graham, A. L., EF207
Catalogue of Mexican pamphlets in the Sutro collection (1623–[1888]), Sutro Library, DB235
Catalogue of music periodicals, Bayerische Staatsbibliothek, BJ100
Catalogue of official publications of the Parliament and government of Canada, AF153
Catalogue of opera librettos printed before 1800, Library of Congress. Music Division, BJ239
Catalogue of Ostracoda, Ellis, Brooks Fleming, EF239
Catalogue of pamphlets in the Public Archives of Canada, with index, Public Archives Canada, AA451
A catalogue of pamphlets on economic subjects published between 1750 and 1900 and now housed in Irish libraries, Black, Robert Dionysius Collison, CH10
Catalogue of papers printed by order of the House of Commons from the year 1731 to 1800, in the custody of the Clerk of the Journals, Great Britain. Parliament. House of Commons, AF197
Catalogue of parliamentary reports and a breviate of their contents, AF196, AF198
Catalogue of periodicals in Polish or relating to Poland and other Slavonic countries, published outside Poland since September 1st, 1939, Polish Library (London, England), AD136
A catalogue of persons named in German heroic literature (700–1600), including named animals and objects and ethnic names, Gillespie, George T., BE1245
Catalogue of printed books, British Museum. Department of Printed Books, AD4
Catalogue of printed books : Academies, British Museum. Department of Printed Books, AL12
A catalogue of printed books in the Wellcome Historical Medical Library, Wellcome Historical Medical Library, EH210
Catalogue of printed maps, charts and plans, British Museum. Map Room, CL251
Catalogue of printed music in the British Library to 1980, British Library. Music Library, BJ25, BJ53
Catalogue of printed music published between 1487 and 1800 now in the British Museum, British Museum. Department of Printed Books, BJ54
—— Squire, W. Barclay, BJ54
Catalogue of publications, Australian Bureau of Statistics, CG438
Catalogue of publications issued and in preparation 1928–1966, Irish Manuscript Commission, DC403
Catalogue of published bibliographies in geology, 1896–1920 ... , Mathews, Edward Bennett, EF35
A catalogue of rare books, pamphlets, and journals on business and economics in the Krannert Library special collection, 1500–1870, Krannert Library, CH19
Catalogue of Renaissance philosophers (1350–1650), Riedl, John Orth, BB70
Catalogue of romances in the Department of Manuscripts in the British Museum, British Museum. Dept. of Manuscripts, BE335
Catalogue of Runic literature, Hermannsson, Halldór, AA717, BE1284
Catalogue of scientific and technical periodicals, 1665–1895, Bolton, Henry Carrington, EA39, EA42
Catalogue of scientific papers, Royal Society (Great Britain). Library, BE31, EA21, EC17, ED6, EE15, EG98, EG213, EH68

Catalogue of scientific papers, 1800–1900, Royal Society (Great Britain), CE14, EA16, EA22, EB10, EB16, EC15, ED5, ED7, EE13, EF57, EF141, EF173, EF232, EG6, EG105, EG211, EG312
Catalogue of seventeenth century Italian books in the British Library, British Library, AA728
A catalogue of seventeenth century printed books in the National Library of Medicine, National Library of Medicine (U.S.), EH24
Catalogue of sixteenth century printed books in the National Library of Medicine, Durling, Richard J., EH24
Catalogue of statistical materials of developing countries, CG8
Catalogue of Syriac printed books and related literature in the British Museum, British Museum. Department of Oriental Printed Books and Manuscripts, BD205
Catalogue of the active volcanoes of the world, International Volcanological Association, EF264
Catalogue of the American books in the library of the British Museum at Christmas MDCCCLVI, Stevens, Henry, AA419
Catalogue of the Arabic manuscripts preserved in the University Library, Ibadan, Nigeria, Kensdale, W. E. N., DD195
Catalogue of the book library of the British Film Institute, British Film Institute. Library, BH163
Catalogue of the books, manuscripts, maps and drawings in the British Museum (Natural History), British Museum (Natural History). Library, EA12
Catalogue of the C. M. Doke collection on African languages in the Library of the University of Rhodesia, University of Rhodesia. Library, BD216
Catalogue of the Colonial Office Library, London, DC274
—— Great Britain. Colonial Office. Library, DC342
Catalogue of the Crawford library of philatelic literature at the British Library, British Library, BG201
A catalogue of the Epstean collection on the history and science of photography and its applications especially to the graphic arts, Columbia University. Libraries, BF336
Catalogue of the Everett D. Graff Collection of Western Americana, Storm, Colton, DB6
A catalogue of the fifteenth-century printed books in the Harvard University Library, Harvard University. Library, AA224
Catalogue of the Foreign Office Library, 1926–1968, Great Britain. Foreign Office. Library, DA171, DC274
Catalogue of the Frederick W. and Carrie S. Beinecke collection of Western Americana, Goddard, Jeanne M., DB170
—— Hanna, Archibald, DB170
—— Kritzler, Charles, DB170
Catalogue of the Goldsmiths' Library of Economic Literature, Canney, Margaret, CH15
—— Knott, David, CH15
Catalogue of the government of Pakistan publications, Pakistan, AF254, AF255
Catalogue of the Icelandic collection, University of Leeds. Library, AA717, BE1284
Catalogue of the Icelandic collection bequeathed by Willard Fiske, Cornell University. Library, AA717, BE1284
Catalogue of the Larpent plays in the Huntington Library, BE637
—— Henry E. Huntington Library and Art Gallery, BE644
Catalogue of the Library, Geological Society of London, EF45
Catalogue of the Library of the British Museum (Natural History), EA12
Catalogue of the Library of the Graduate School of Design, Frances L. Loeb Library, BF228
Catalogue of the McAlpin collection of British history and theology, Union Theological Seminary (New York, N.Y.). Library, BC227, DC321

Catalogue of the Newspaper Library, Colindale, British Library. Newspaper Library, Colindale, AE56
Catalogue of the pamphlets, books, newspapers, and manuscripts relating to the Civil War, the Commonwealth, and Restoration collected by George Thomason, 1640–1661, British Museum. Department of Printed Books. Thomason Collection, AA677
Catalogue of the parliamentary papers of Southern Rhodesia, 1899–1953, Passmore, Gloria C., DD176
—— Willson, Francis Michael Glenn, AF242, DD176
Catalogue of the parliamentary papers of Southern Rhodesia and Rhodesia, 1954–1970, and the Federation of Rhodesia and Nyasaland, 1954–1963, Wilding, Norman W., AF241, DD176
Catalogue of the philatelic library of the Earl of Crawford, Crawford, James Ludovic Lindsay, BG201
Catalogue of the printed books in the Library of the Foreign Office, London, DC274
Catalogue of the publications of Scottish historical and kindred clubs and societies, Matheson, Cyril, DC275, DC281, DC361, DC362
Catalogue of the publications of Scottish historical and kindred clubs and societies and of the volumes relative to Scottish history issued by His Majesty's Stationery Office, 1780–1908, with a subject-index, Terry, Charles Sanford, DC275
Catalogue of the publications of Scottish historical and kindred clubs and societies and of the volumes relative to Scottish history issued by His Majesty's Stationery Office, 1780–1908, with a subject-index, Terry, Charles Sanford, DC281
Catalogue of the publications of Scottish historical and kindred clubs and societies and of the volumes relative to Scottish history issued by His Majesty's Stationery Office, 1780–1908, with a subject-index, Terry, Charles Sanford, DC361
Catalogue of the publications of Scottish historical and kindred clubs and societies and of the volumes relative to Scottish history issued by His Majesty's Stationery Office, 1780–1908, with a subject-index, Terry, Charles Sanford, DC362
Catalogue of the Romany collection, Brotherton Library, CC479
Catalogue of the Royal Institute of British Architects Library, Royal Institute of British Architects. Library, BF230
Catalogue of the Spanish library and of the Portuguese books bequeathed by George Ticknor, Boston Public Library. Ticknor Collection, AA800
•*Catalogue of the United Kingdom official publications,* AF182
A catalogue of the works of Linnaeus (and publications more immediately relating thereto) preserved in the libraries of the British Museum (Bloomsbury) and the British Museum (Natural History) (South Kensington), British Museum. Department of Printed Books, EG102
A catalogue of the works of Linnaeus issued in commemoration of the 250th anniversary of the birthday of Carolus Linnaeus, 1707–1778, Sandbergs Bokhandel, Stockholm, EG109
Catalogue of the world's most popular coins, Reinfeld, Fred, BG191
Catalogue of theses and dissertations accepted for degrees by the South African universities, Robinson, Anthony Meredith Lewin, AG49
A catalogue of theses and dissertations concerning the Church of Jesus Christ of Latter-Day Saints, Mormonism and Utah, Brigham Young University. College of Religious Instruction, BC369
Catalogue : with data upon cognate items in other Harvard libraries, Kress Library of Business and Economics, CH15
[Catalogues], British Broadcasting Corporation. Central Music Library, BJ92

Catalogues and indexes of British government publications, 1920–1970, Great Britain. Stationery Office, AF183

Les catalogues imprimés de la Bibliothèque Nationale, Bibliothèque Nationale (France), AA202

The catalogues of the manuscript collections, British Museum. Department of Manuscripts, AA205

Catalogus dari buku-buku jang diterbitkan di Indonesia, AA901, AA902

Catalogus der Friesche taal- en letterkunde en overige Friesche geschriften, Provinciale Bibliotheek van Friesland, BE1067

Catalogus dissertationum academicarum, Bodleian Library, AG9

Catalogus librorum impressorum Bibliothecae Bodleianae in Academia Oxoniensi. ..., Bodleian Library, AA119

Catalogus translationum et commentariorum, Kristeller, Paul Oskar, BE999

Catalogus van academische geschriften in Nederland verschenen, Rijksuniversiteit te Utrecht. Bibliotheek, AG38

Catalogus van Belgische en Luxemburgse periodieken, AD83, AD131

Catalogus van Belgische en Luxemburgse tijdschriften, AD83, AD131

Catalogus van boeken en tijdschriften uit in Ned. Oost-Indië, AA901

Catalogus van de pamfletten-verzameling, Koninklijke Bibliotheek (Netherlands), AA751

Catanese, Anthony James. *Urban planning,* BF268

Cates, Jo A. *Journalism,* AE29, AE130, AE132

Catholic almanac, BC415

Catholic biblical encyclopedia, BC126

Catholic Church. *Lectionary for Mass,* BC422

―――― *The liturgy of the hours,* BC423

―――― *The sacramentary,* BC424

―――― *Saint Andrew Bible missal,* BC421

Catholic Church. Codex Juris Canonici (1983). *The code of canon law,* CK238

Catholic Church. Curia Romana. *Annuario pontificio,* BC409

Catholic Church. Liturgy and ritual. *Lectionary for Mass,* BC424

―――― *The rites of the Catholic Church,* BC425

Catholic Church. Martyrology. *The Roman martyrology,* BC426

Catholic Church. Pope. *The papal encyclicals,* BC434

The Catholic church in America, Vollmar, Edward R., BC393

Catholic colleges and universities, CB305

Catholic commentary, Orchard, Bernard, BC177

A Catholic dictionary, BC406

―――― Addis, William E., BC396

Catholic directory, BC411

The Catholic directory of England and Wales, BC410

Catholic Eastern churches, Attwater, Donald, BC444

The Catholic encyclopaedic dictionary, BC406

Catholic encyclopedia, BC397, BC401, BC404, BC437

The Catholic left in Latin America, Dahlin, Therrin C., DB255

Catholic Library Association. *The guide to Catholic literature,* BC390

The Catholic novel, Menendez, Albert J., BE258

Catholic peace tradition, Musto, Ronald G., CJ677

Catholic periodical and literature index, AD265, AD266, BC390, BC394, BC395, BC437

Catholic periodical index, AD265, AD266, BC390, BC394, BC395

Catholic press directory, AE33

Catholic reference books, BC391

Catholic religious orders, Kapsner, Oliver Leonard, BC440

Catholic school education in the United States, Grant, Mary A., CB36

Catholic serials of the nineteenth century in the United States, Willging, Eugene Paul, AD227

Catholic University of America. *New Catholic encyclopedia,* BC401

Catholic who's who, AH225, BC417

Catholicism in early modern history, BC413

―――― O'Malley, John W., DC28

Catholics *see* **Roman Catholic Church**

•*CATLINE,* EH46, EH49, EH71, EH72

Caton, Hiram. *The bibliography of human behavior,* CA10, CD8

Cats, EJ138, EJ139, EJ140, EJ141

Catterall, Peter. *British history, 1945–1987,* DC329

Cattermole Tally, Frances. *Guide to the gods,* BC62

Catton, Bruce. *Centennial history of the Civil War,* DB120

Caune, Andris. *Latvijas PSR arheologija, 1940–1974,* DC434

Caune, C. *Latvijas PSR arheologija, 1940–1974,* DC434

Cauwenbergh, Ét. *Dictionnaire d'histoire et de géographie ecclésiastiques,* BC412

Cavalcade, BE541

Cavallera, Ferdinand. *Dictionnaire de spiritualité,* BC54

Cavallo, Maria Lucia. *Periodici italiani 1914–1919,* DC426

Cavanagh, John. *British theatre,* BH38, BH40

Cavendish, Richard. *Man, myth & magic,* BC64

Cavinato, Joseph L. *Transportation-logistics dictionary,* CH448

Caviness, Madeline Harrison. *Stained glass before 1540,* BG52

―――― *Stained glass before 1700 in American collections,* BG52

Cawker, Ruth. *Canadian fiction,* BE823, BE824

Cayrou, Gaston. *Le français classique,* AC374

Cayton, Mary Kupiec. *Encyclopedia of American social history,* DB46

Cazottes, Gisèle. *Presse périodique madrilène entre 1871–1885,* AE76

CBE style manual, Council of Biology Editors. CBE Style Manual Committee, EG57

CBEL, BE585

CBI, AA422, AA430

CBR Consulting Services. *Directory of telefacsimile sites in North American libraries,* AK60

CCCA : Current contents Afrika, DD22

CCCC bibliography of composition and rhetoric, BE348

―――― Conference on College Composition and Communication, BE348

CCH accounting articles, CH250

CCLM literary magazine directory, Coordinating Council of Literary Magazines (U.S.), AD49

•*CD CoreWorks,* BE319

•*CD: Education,* CB52

•*CD/private plus,* CH373

•*CD-ROM databases,* AK206

•*CD-ROM index to House of Commons parliamentary papers,* AF203

CD-ROMs in print, AK207

CDA/Wiesenberger mutual funds update, CH308

CDI, AG12

•*CDMARC,* AK220

•*CEABA,* EK49

Ceballos, Jorge. *Bibliografía general del desarrollo económico de México 1500–1976,* DB219

Cecchi, Emilio. *Storia della letteratura italiana,* BE1303

Cecić, Ivo. *Hrvatski biografski leksikon,* AH307

CEDDS, CG103

Cedergreen Bech, Svend. *Dansk biografisk leksikon,* AH183

Cederholm, T. D. *Afro-American artists,* BF24

Cejador y Frauca, Julio. *Historia de la lengua y literatura castellana,* BE1455

CELADE (Organization). *Resúmenes sobre población en América Latina,* CG123

Celestial handbook, EC70

•*CELEX,* CK203

Cell biology, Altman, Philip L., EG52

Cellard, Jacques. *Dictionnaire du français non conventionnel,* AC354

Celluloid wars, Curley, Stephen J., CJ608

―――― Wetta, Frank Joseph, CJ608

Celtic language
dictionaries, AC252
faculty
directories, BD93

Celtic literature
faculty
directories, BD93

Celtic myth and legend, CF18

Celts
mythology, CF17, CF18

Cenival, Pierre de. *Bibliographie marocaine, 1923–1933,* DD180

Censimento delle edizioni italiane del XVI secolo, AA731

Censored, AL46

Censorship, AK67

Censorship (by subject)
art, BF128

Censorship and Hollywood's Hispanic image, Richard, Alfred Charles, BH230

Census 1981, CL136, CL206

Census and you, CG86

Census catalog and guide, United States. Bureau of the Census, CG86

Census-catalogue of manuscript sources of polyphonic music, 1400–1550, BJ69

Census of agriculture, EJ78

Census of Antique Works of Art Known to Renaissance Artists at the Warburg Institute of the University of London, University of London. Warburg Institute, BF391

A census of autograph music manuscripts of European composers in American libraries, Albrecht, Otto Edwin, BJ51

A census of British newspapers and periodicals, 1620–1800, AE56

―――― Crane, Ronald Salmon, AD106

Census of housing, CH692

―――― United States. Bureau of the Census, CH545

Census of India, 1971, CG391

Census of medieval and Renaissance manuscripts in the United States and Canada, Ricci, Seymour de, AA212

Census of modern Greek literature, Philippides, Dia Mary L., BE1274

Census of population and housing, CH692

Census of pre-nineteenth-century Italian paintings in North American public collections, Fredericksen, Burton B., BF325

Census publications, catalog and subject guide, CG86

Censuses
bibliography, CG6, CG7, CG9, CG11, CG13

Censuses (by country or region)
Africa
bibliography, CG38, CG312
Asia
bibliography, CG38
Caribbean
bibliography, CG122
Europe, Western, CG186, CG188
India, CG391
Latin America
bibliography, CG122
United States
atlases, AJ26, CL306
bibliography, CG93
guides, CG93
indexes, AJ20, CG98
U.S.S.R.
bibliography, CG300

Cent portes du Proche-orient, Gresh, Alain, DE55

Centennial history of the Civil War, Catton, Bruce, DB120

The centennial of the United States Military Academy at West Point, New York, 1802–1902, United States Military Academy, CJ611

Center for Academic Publications Japan. *Current contents of academic journals in Japan,* AD341

Center for Applied Linguistics. *Graduate theses and dissertations in English as a second language,* BD109

—— *A survey of materials for the study of the uncommonly taught languages*, BD71
Center for Applied Linguistics. Library. *Dictionary catalog of the Library of the Center for Applied Linguistics, Washington, D.C*, BD29
Center for Arts Administration. *For more information*, BF39
Center for Computer Assisted Research in the Humanities. *Computing in musicology*, BJ167
Center for Demographic Studies (U.S.). *Social indicators III*, CG78
Center for Disease Control. *Health information for international travel*, EH415
Center for Food Safety and Applied Nutrition. *Everything added to food in the United States*, EJ165
Center for International Business Cycle Research. *International economic indicators*, CH109
Center for International Financial Analysis and Research. *CIFAR's global company handbook*, CH405
Center for International Research (U.S.). *Detailed statistics on the population of Israel by ethnic and religious group and urban and rural residence, 1950 to 2010*, CG399
—— *Detailed statistics on the urban and rural population of Indonesia, 1950 to 2010*, CG395
—— *Detailed statistics on the urban and rural population of Pakistan, 1950 to 2010*, CG415
—— *Detailed statistics on the urban and rural population of the Philippines, 1950 to 2010*, CG418
Center for Mental Health Services. *Mental health, United States*, EH401
Center for Minority Group Mental Health Programs (U.S.). *Bibliography on racism*, CC314
Center for Reformation Research. *Catholicism in early modern history*, BC413
Center for Research Libraries. *CAMP catalog*, DD81
—— *A checklist of Southeast Asian newspapers and other research materials in microform held by the Center for Research Libraries*, AE82
—— *Foreign newspapers held by the Center for Research Libraries*, AE3
—— *SAMP catalog*, DE77
—— *Southeast Asia microforms project resources*, AE83
—— *Soviet serials currently received at the Center for Research Libraries*, AD141
—— *Union list of little magazines*, AD224
Center for Responsive Politics (Washington, D. C.). *The price of admission*, CJ249
Center for Socialist History (Berkeley, Calif.). *The Marx-Engels cyclopedia*, CJ520
Center for the American Women and Politics (Eagleton Institute of Politics). *The political participation of women in the United States*, CC512
—— *Women and American politics*, CC512
Center for the Study of Language and Information. *Natural language processing in the 1980s*, BD64
Center for the Study of Southern Culture. *Encyclopedia of Southern culture*, DB158
Center for Women Policy Studies. *The guide to resources on women and AIDS*, CC550
Centers for training in physical anthropology, Bennett, Kenneth A., CE88
—— Osborne, Richard H., CE88
Centner, C. *Geigy scientific tables*, EA154
Central African Republic
  atlases, CL339
  bibliography, DD18, DD139
  encyclopedias, DD48
  government publications
    bibliography, AF229
  statistics, CG322
Central African Republic, Kalck, Pierre, DD18, DD48
Central America
  associations
    directories, AL35
  atlases, CL312
  bibliography, DB302, DB408

directories, CE79
handbooks, DB295
statistics
  bibliography, CG71, CG72
Central America (by subject)
  anthropology and ethnology, CE75, CE79, CE89, CE90
  art, BF28
  foreign relations, DB300
  history
    bibliography, CE75, DB298, DB299
    library catalogs, DB163, DB269
    manuscripts and archives, DB301, DB414
  native languages, BD237, BD239
  politics and government, CJ311
Central America in the nineteenth and twentieth centuries, Grieb, Kenneth J., DB299
Central America newspak, DB293
Central America Resource Center (Austin, Tex.). *Directory of Central America organizations*, AL35
Central America since independence, DB291
Central American literature
  bibliography, BE870
Central Bank of Barbados. *Annual statistical digest*, CG167
—— *Economic and financial statistics*, CG167
Central Eurasia military-naval encyclopedia, Daly, John C. K., CJ657
Central European economic history from Waterloo to OPEC, 1815–1975, Hacken, Richard D., DC7
Central Institute of English and Foreign Languages, Hyderabad. *A bibliography of Indian English*, BE1563
Central Institute of Indian Languages. *A bibliography of Indian folk literature*, CF96
—— *Classified state bibliography of linguistic research on Indian languages*, BD224
—— *Dissertations in Indian linguistics and on Indian languages*, BD225
Central Intelligence Agency (U.S.). *Polar regions atlas*, DG10
Central Library of Trinidad and Tobago. *Trinidad and Tobago national bibliography*, AA570
Central Pacific campaign, 1943–1944, Controvich, James T., DA170
Central State University (Wilberforce, Ohio). Hallie Q. Brown Library. *Index to black periodicals*, AD274
Centrale catalogus van periodieken en seriewerken in Nederlandse bibliotheken (CCP), Koninklijke Bibliotheek (Netherlands), AD240
Centralna Biblioteka Statystyczna im. Stefana Szulca. *Bibliografia wydawnictw Głownego Urzędu Statystycznego*, CG274
Centralna Biblioteka Statystyczna (Poland). *Bibliografia polskiego piśmiennictwa demograficznego 1945–1975*, CG272
Centre d'analyse et de documentation patristiques (France). *Biblia patristica*, BC299
Centre de documentation sciences humaines (France). *Ecodoc*, CH39
Centre de données de Strasbourg. *Astronomy, space sciences and related organizations of the world*, EC44
Centre de recherche pour un trésor de la langue française. *Trésor de la langue française*, AC331
Centre de recherches et d'études sur les sociétés méditerranéennes. *Bibliographie de la littérature "marocaine" des Français, 1875–1983*, BE1529
—— *Bibliographie de la littérature "tunisienne" des Français, 1881–1980*, BE1539
Centre des archives diplomatiques de Nantes (France). *Papiers du Consulat de France á Alger*, DD125
Centre d'Études de Géographie Tropicale. *Atlas des départements français d'outre-mer*, CL276
Centre d'etudes des manuscrits. *Scriptorium*, AA200
Centre for Information on Language Teaching. *A language-teaching bibliography*, BD72
Centre for Information on Language Teaching and Research. *Language teaching*, BD74, CB58
Centre International d'Étude des Textiles Anciens. *Vocabulary of technical terms*, BG154

Centre national de la recherche scientifique (France). *Albanie, une bibliographie historique*, DC79
—— *Bibliographie annuelle de l'histoire de France du cinquième siècle à 1939*, DC148
—— *Bibliographie cartographique internationale*, CL226
—— *Guide des centres de documentation en histoire ouvrière et sociale*, DC157
—— *Guide des sources de l'histoire des congrégations féminines françaises de vie active*, BC442
—— *Répertoire de manuscrits mediévaux contenant des notations musicales*, BJ55
—— *World translations index*, EA63
Centre on Transnational Corporations (United Nations). *Transnational business information*, CH117
Centro Brasileiro de Estudos Demograficos. *Registro civil do Brasil*, CG142
Centro de Documentación en Población y Desarrollo (Bolivia). *Directorio boliviano en población y desarrollo*, CG139
Centro di Studi Filosofici di Gallarate. *Enciclopedia filosofica*, BB30
Centro italiano di studi sull'alto Medioevo. *Medioevo latino*, DA144
Centro lessicografico Sansoni. *Inglese-italiano, italiano-inglese*, AC531
Centro Mexicano de Escritores. *Catálogo de publicaciones periódicas mexicanas*, AD62
Centro nazionale d'informazioni bibliografiche (Italy). *Indice generale degli incunaboli delle biblioteche d'Italia*, AA233
Centro nazionale per il catalogo unico delle biblioteche italiane e per le informazioni bibliografiche. *Bibliografia nazionale italiana. Pubblicazione mensile*, AA726
Centro Paraguayo de Documentación Social. *Las migraciones en America Latina*, CC315
Centro Regional para el Fomento del Libro en America Latina y el Caribe. *Editoriales, distribuidoras y librerías*, AA285
Century cyclopedia of names, AH29, BE209
Century dictionary and cyclopedia, AC11, AH29, BE209
A century of doctorates, National Research Council. Board on Human-Resource Data and Analysis, CB342
Century of musicals in black and white, Peterson, Bernard L., BE531
A century of oil and gas in books, Swanson, Edward Benjamin, EK302
Century of population growth, United States. Bureau of the Census, CG90
A century of serial publications in psychology, 1850–1950, Osier, Donald V., CD12
Century of the English book trade ... 1457–1557, Duff, Gordon E., AA306
Ceramic collectors' glossary, Barber, Edwin Atlee, BG63
The ceramic, furniture, and silver collectors' glossary, BG63
Ceramic literature, Solon, Louis Marc Emmanuel, BG55
Ceramics, Nelson, Glenn C., BG65
Ceramics and glass
  bibliography, BG52, BG53, BG55
  catalogs, BG78
  collections, BG52, BG68
  dictionaries, BG42, BG63, BG64, BG65, BG66, BG67, EK265
  encyclopedias, BG58, BG59
  guides, BG51
  handbooks, BG70, BG72, EK271
  indexes, BG53
  prices, BG69
Ceramics and glass (by country or region)
  Asia, BG77
  China, BG79
  Europe, BG77
    history, BG74
  Great Britain, BG60
  United States, BG57

bibliography, BG54, BG56
handbooks, BG71
history, BG76
Ceramics and glass (by subject)
history, BG61, BG62, BG73, BG75
Ceramics and glass, BG69
Černý, Jaroslav. *Coptic etymological dictionary,*
AC272
Černý, Jochen. *Wer war wer, DDR,* AH216
Cerny, Johni. *Ancestry's guide to research,* AJ4
—— *The library,* AJ14
—— *The source,* AJ23
*Certification and preparation of educational
personnel in the United States,* CB163
Cesbron, Fabien. *World directory of mineralogists,*
EF189
Česká Akademie Věd a Umeadní, Prague. *Atlas
Republiky Československé,* CL322
Česká Akademie Věd a Umĕni. Třída 3. *Příruční
slovník jazyka českého,* AC276
Česká literární bibliografie, 1945–1966, Kunc,
Jaroslav, BE1109
Česká literatura 1785–1985, Mĕštan, Antonín,
BE1106
České disertace a autoreferáty, AG25
Česko-anglický slovník, Poldauf, Ivan, AC280
Česko-anglický technický slovník, Bažnt, Zdenĕk,
EA106
Československá akademie věd. Ústav pro českou
literaturu. *Dĕjiny, české literatury,* BE1106
Československá Akademie Věd. Ústav pro Jazyk
Český. *Slovník spisovného jazyka českého,* AC277
Československá demografická společnost. *National
population bibliography of Czechoslovakia,
1945–1977,* CG207
Český statistický úřad. *Statistická ročenka České a
Slovenské federativní republiky,* CG208
Céspedes, Mario. *Gran diccionario de Chile,* DB362
Céspedes de Reynaga, Alicia. *Bibliografía de tesis
peruanos sobre indigenismo y ciencias sociales,*
DB384
Čeští spisovatelé 19. a počátku 20. století, BE1105
Čeští spisovatelé 20, Blahynky, Milana, BE1105
Cevallos, Elena E. *Puerto Rico,* DB451
Cevasco, G. A. *The 1890s,* BE758
Ceylon *see* **Sri Lanka**
Ceylon national bibliography, AA934, AA935
CFR, CK182
Chabrán, Richard. *Chicano periodical index,* AD267,
CC156
Chad
bibliography, DD140
current surveys, DD62
encyclopedias, DD48
government publications
bibliography, AF224, AF229
statistics, CG323
Chad (by subject)
history
bibliography, DD141
Chad. Direction de la statistique, des études
économiques et démographiques. *Tchad relance
économique en chiffres,* CG323
Chad, Collelo, Thomas, DD62
—— Decalo, S., DD48
Chadwick, Alena F. *Herbs,* EG110
Chadwick, Bruce A. *Statistical handbook on the
American family,* CG107
Chadwick, Owen. *Popes and European revolution,*
BC278
Chadwick Healey Paris. *Catalogue de l'histoire de
France,* DC143
Chadzingwa, M. M. *Women in development in
Southern Africa,* DD122, DD171
Chafetz, Morris E. *Encyclopedia of alcoholism,*
CC124, CC125
Chaff, Sandra L. *Women in medicine,* EH32
Chaffers, William. *Collector's handbook of marks
and monograms on pottery and porcelain,* BG77
—— *Hall marks on gold and silver plate,* BG139
—— *Marks & monograms on European and
Oriental pottery and porcelain,* BG77
—— *New keramic gallery,* BG77

Chajes, Saul. *Thesaurus pseudonymorum quae in
litteratura hebraica et judaeo-germanica
inveniuntur,* AA161
Chakalov, G. *Elsevier's dictionary of science and
technology,* EA125
Chaker, Salem. *Une décennie d'études berbères
(1980-1990),* DD68
Chalcraft, Anthony. *Walford's guide to reference
material,* AA363
Chalfant, H. Paul. *Social and behavioral aspects of
female alcoholism,* CC111
—— *Sociology of poverty in the United States,*
CC260
Chaliand, Gérard. *Atlas des diasporas,* DA188
—— *A strategic atlas,* CJ73
Chall, Leo P. *Sociological abstracts,* CC13
Chall, Miriam. *LLBA user's reference manual,* BD31
Challinor, John. *Challinor's dictionary of geology,*
EF71
—— *Dictionary of geology,* EF71
—— *The history of British geology,* EF98
Challinor's dictionary of geology, Challinor, John,
EF71
Chaloner, William Henry. *Bibliography of British
economic and social history,* DC1, DC272
Chambard, Jean-Luc. *Bibliographie de civilisation de
l'Inde contemporaine,* DE155
Chamber music, BJ270
Chamber music, Baron, John H., BJ269
Chamber music catalogue, BJ92
Chamber of Commerce of the United States of
America. *Foreign commerce handbook,* CH141
Chamberlain, Bobby J. *Portuguese language and
Luso-Brazilian literature,* BD163, BE926, BE1362
Chamberlain, Greg. *The dictionary of contemporary
politics of Central America and the Caribbean,*
CJ311
—— *The dictionary of contemporary politics of
South America,* CJ312
Chamberlin, Mary Walls. *Guide to art reference
books,* BF1
Chamberlin, Willard Joseph. *Entomological
nomenclature and literature,* EG327
Chamberlin, William J. *Catalogue of English Bible
translations,* BC94, BC97, BC100
Chambers, Bettye Thomas. *Bibliography of French
Bibles,* BC98
Chambers, D. S. *Guides to materials for West
African history in European archives,* DD105
Chambers, Edmund Kerchever. *Elizabethan stage,*
BE663, BE664, BE665
—— *The mediaeval stage,* BE664
—— *William Shakespeare,* BE664, BE665
Chambers, Frances. *France,* DC144
—— *Guyana,* DB378
—— *Haiti,* DB438
—— *Trinidad and Tobago,* DB458
Chambers, Janice E. *Dictionary of toxicology,*
EH422
Chambers, Kevin. *Travelers' guide to Asian customs
& manners,* CL388
Chambers, Robert. *Book of days,* AL142
—— *Lives of illustrious and distinguished
Scotsman,* AH243
Chambers 20th century dictionary, AC36
Chambers air and space dictionary, EK30
Chambers biographical dictionary, AH24
Chambers biology dictionary, EG30
Chambers dictionary of political biography, CJ65
Chambers earth sciences dictionary, EF13
Chambers English dictionary, AC36
Chambers/Murray Latin-English dictionary, Smith,
William, AC578
Chambers of commerce, CH133
Chambers science and technology dictionary, EA88
—— Walker, Peter M. B., EF13
Chambers Scottish biographical dictionary, AH243
Chambers world gazetteer, CL84
Chambers's encyclopaedia, AB4
Chambers's technical dictionary, EA88
*Chambers's twentieth century dictionary of the
English language,* AC36

*Chambers's world gazetteer and geographical
dictionary,* CL84
Chametzky, Jules. *Handbook of American-Jewish
literature,* BE565
Champagne, Duane. *The Native North American
almanac,* CC434
Champion, Brian. *Advanced weapons systems,* CJ604
Champion, Edouard. *Comédie-Française, 1927–37,*
BE1179
Champion, Larry S. *The essential Shakespeare,*
BE766
Champion, Sara. *A dictionary of terms and
techniques in archaeology,* DA75
Champion, Selwyn Gurney. *The eleven religions and
their proverbial lore,* BC89
—— *Racial proverbs,* BE153
Champlin, John Denison. *Cyclopedia of painters and
paintings,* BF299, BF312
Chan, Betty. *Sports and physical education,* BK3
Chan, F. Gilbert. *Nationalism in East Asia,* CJ422
Chan, Lois Mai. *Immroth's guide to the Library of
Congress classification,* AK199
—— *Library of Congress subject headings,*
AK219, AK220
Chan, Wing-tsit. *Guide to Chinese philosophy,* BB19
Chanda, K. L. *Women in development in Southern
Africa,* DD122, DD171
Chandler, David G. *Dictionary of battles,* DA24
—— *Dictionary of the Napoleonic wars,* DC197
Chandler, Michael John. *A guide to records in
Barbados,* DB419, DB444, DB460
Chandler, Ralph C. *The constitutional law
dictionary,* CK129
—— *The public administration dictionary,* CJ477,
CJ478
Chandler, Tertius. *Four thousand years of urban
growth,* CC296
—— *Three thousand years of urban growth,*
CC296
Chang, Ch'i-yün. *National atlas of China,* CL352
Chang, Fang-hua. *Checklist of Chinese local
histories,* DE131
Chang, Henry C. *A bibliography of presidential
commissions, committees, councils, panels, and
task forces, 1961–1972,* AF132
Chang, Sheldon S. L. *Fundamentals handbook of
electrical and computer engineering,* EK138
Chang, Sung-Un. *A Korean-English dictionary,*
AC565
Changes in official methods of analysis, EE84, EJ59
Changing directions in the treatment of women,
Zukerman, Elyse, EH375
Chanin, Leah F. *Specialized legal research,* CK119
Channels, Upjohn, Richard, AL60
Channing, Edward. *Guide to the study and reading of
American history,* DB13
Chansons de geste
bibliography, BE1199
dictionaries, BE1164
Chant, Christopher. *The handbook of British
regiments,* CJ651
Chant, Stuart R. *Popular encyclopedia of plants,*
EG179
Chantraine, Pierre. *Dictionnaire étymologique de la
langue grecque,* AC450
Chantreau, Sophie. *Dictionnaire des expressions et
locutions,* AC371
Chants, BJ290
Chao, Shih-li. *Jen k'ou hsüeh Ying Han Han Ying fen
lei tz'u hui,* CG34
Chapancev, Jurij Vladimirovič. *Dictionary of
microprocessor systems,* EK193
Chapin Metz, Helen. *Egypt,* DD62
—— *Nigeria,* DD62
—— *Somalia,* DD62
—— *Sudan,* DD62
—— *Zaire,* DD62
Chaplin, James Patrick. *Dictionary of psychology,*
CD28
Chapman, Anne. *Feminist resources for schools and
colleges,* CC481
Chapman, Dorothy Hilton. *Index to black poetry,*
BE536, BE537

—— *Index to poetry by black American women,* BE536, BE537

Chapman, Karen J. *Commodities price locator,* CH430

—— *Investment statistics locator,* CH324

Chapman, Michael D. *British catalogue of music, 1957–1985,* BJ25

Chapman, Mike. *Encyclopedia of American wrestling,* BK105

Chapman, R. W. *Annals of English literature, 1475–1950,* BE612

Chapman, Robert L. *New dictionary of American slang,* AC120

—— *Roget's international thesaurus,* AC144

Chapman and Hall. *HEILBRON,* EE133

Chappell, V. C. *Twenty-five years of Descartes scholarship, 1960–1984,* BB72

Characters in 19th-century literature, Howes, Kelly King, BE184

Characters in 20th-century literature, Harris, Laurie Lanzen, BE184

Characters in film, BH276, BH277, BH278

Characters in literature, BE71, BE184, BE186, BE188, BE189, BE344, BE381, BE484, BE688, BE1245, BE1269
   dictionaries, BE251
   indexes, BE251

Characters in performing arts, BH21, BH205, BH220, BH222
   indexes, BE658

Chardans, Jean-Louis. *Dictionnaire du cinéma et de la télévision,* BH247

Charen, Thelma. *MEDLARS indexing manual,* EA162

The charitable appeals fact book, Carson, Emmett Devon, AL132

Charitable organizations of the U.S, AL102

Charité, J. *Biografisch woordenboek van Nederland,* AH271

Charlemagne, BE983

Charles, Jill. *Directory of theatre training programs,* BH84

Charles, Sydney Robinson. *A handbook of music and music literature in sets and series,* BJ10, BJ45

Charles Brockden Brown, Parker, Patricia L., BE478

Charles Sturt University. Centre for Information Studies. *Australasian religion index,* BC42

Charles Szladits' guide to foreign legal materials, Kearley, Timothy, CK210

Charlesworth, James H. *Graphic concordance to the Dead Sea scrolls,* BC556

—— *New Testament Apocrypha and pseudepigrapha,* BC94, BC107

—— *Old Testament pseudepigrapha,* BC94

Charlier, Gustave. *Histoire illustrée des lettres françaises de Belgique,* BE1097

Charlton, D. G. *France,* DC159

Charlton, James. *The ballplayers,* BK48

Charno, Steven M. *Latin American newspapers in United States libraries,* AE12, AE40

Charpentreau, Jacques. *Dictionnaire des poètes et de la poésie,* BE1197

Chart of ratifications, CK113

Chart of the nuclides, ED38

Charvet, P. E. *A literary history of France,* BE1173

Chase, Gilbert. *Guide to Latin American music,* BJ11

—— *A guide to the music of Latin America,* BJ11

Chase, Helen M. *Chase's annual events,* DA182

Chase, William D. *Chase's annual events,* DA182

Chase's annual events, DA182

Chase's calendar of annual events, DA182

Chater, A. O. *Flora Europaea,* EG170

Chatham, James R. *Dissertations in Hispanic languages and literatures,* BE1446

—— *Western European dissertations on the Hispanic and Luso-Brazilian languages and literatures,* BE1446

Chatterjee, Amitabha. *Dictionary of Indian pseudonyms,* AA191

Chatzēdēmos, Athanasios D. *Hellēnikē vivliographia,* AA702

Chaucer : *a bibliographical introduction,* Leyerle, John, DA138

—— Quick, Anne, DA138

Chaudenson, Robert. *Bibliographie des études créoles languages et littétures,* BD55

Chaudhuri, Brahma. *Comprehensive bibliography of Victorian studies, 1970–1984,* BE752

—— *Cumulated index to reviews of books on Victorian studies, 1975–1989,* BE752

—— *Cumulative bibliography of Victorian studies, 1970–1984,* BE752

—— *Cumulative bibliography of Victorian studies, 1976–1980,* BE752

—— *Cumulative bibliography of Victorian studies, 1985–1989,* BE752

Chauleau, Liliane. *Guide des Archives de la Martinique,* DB446

Chauleur, André. *Bibliothèques et archives,* AK135

Chaundy, Theodore W. *The printing of mathematics,* EB97

Chauveau-Rabut, Jacqueline. *Bibliographie des auteurs africains de langue française,* BE1513

Chauvin, Victor. *Bibliographie des ouvrages arabes ou relatifs aux arabes publiés dans l'Europe chrétienne de 1810 à 1885,* BE1547

Chavda, P. *Who's who, Indian personages,* AH354

•*CHCD dictionary of inorganic compounds on CD-ROM,* EE109

•*CHCD dictionary of organic compounds on CD-ROM,* EE127

A check list of American 18th century newspapers in the Library of Congress, AE20

Check list of British official serial publications, AF181

A check list of Canadian imprints, 1900–1925, Tod, Dorothea D., AA452

A check list of courtesy books in the Newberry Library, Newberry Library, AL151

A check list of cumulative indexes to individual periodicals in the New York Public Library, New York Public Library, AD252

A check list of English plays, 1641–1700, Woodward, Gertrude Loop, BE657

Check list of English prose fiction, 1700–1739, McBurney, William Harlin, BE669, BE678, BE681

Check list of foreign missionary agencies in the United States, BC308

A check list of foreign newspapers in the Library of Congress, Library of Congress. Periodical Division, AE10

Check list of native and naturalized trees of the United States (including Alaska), Little, Elbert Luther, EG197

Check-list of North American birds, EG255

A check list of prose fiction published in England, 1740–1749, Beasley, Jerry C., BE669, BE681

Check-list of recorded songs in the English language in the Archive of American Folk Song to July, 1940, Archive of Folk Song (U.S.), BJ321, BJ327

A check list of selected material on Samoa, Pereira, Janet Aileen, DF54

Check-list of works of British authors printed abroad in languages other than English, to 1641, Shaaber, Matthias Adam, AA673

Checkland, S. G. *Dictionary of Scottish business biography, 1860–1960,* CH97

Checklist of additions to Evans' American bibliography in the Rare Book Division of the New York Public Library, New York Public Library. Rare Book Division, AA408

A checklist of aeronautical periodicals and serials in the Library of Congress, EK25

A checklist of American copies of "Short-title catalogue" books, Bishop, William Warner, AA667, AA671

A checklist of American imprints, AA414, AA418

Checklist of American imprints for 1820–1829, Shoemaker, Richard H., AA418

Checklist of Asian periodicals and newspapers, 1884–1978, AE82

Checklist of bibliographies appearing in the Bulletin of bibliography 1897–1987, AA90

Checklist of British parliamentary papers in the Irish University Press 1000-volume series, 1801–1899, Irish University Press, AF204

Checklist of Canadian literature and background materials, 1628–1960, Watters, Reginald Eyre, BE826

Checklist of Chinese local histories, Chang, Fang-hua, DE131

Checklist of exchange materials, AF257

Checklist of French political pamphlets 1560–1653 in the Newberry Library, Newberry Library, DC169

—— Welsh, Doris Varner, DC169

Checklist of indexes to Canadian newspapers, Burrows, Sandra, AE117

A checklist of Indonesian serials in the Cornell University Library (1945–1970), Thung, Yvonne, AD196

Checklist of manuscripts in the Edward E. Ayer collection, Butler, Ruth Lapham, DB6

A checklist of monographs and periodicals on the Japanese colonial empire, Hoover Institution on War, Revolution and Peace. East Asian Collection, DE199

A checklist of music bibliographies and indexes in progress and unpublished, Baily, Dee, BJ23

Checklist of new plays and entertainments on the London stage, 1700–1737, Burling, William J., BH101

A checklist of newspapers in New Zealand libraries 1938–1959, AE100

Checklist of newspapers of the British Isles, 1665–1800, in the American Antiquarian Society, American Antiquarian Society, AE56

Checklist of nineteenth century Australian colonial statistical sources, CG437

A checklist of painters, c.1200–1976, represented in the Witt Library, Courtauld Institute of Art, London, Witt Library, BF322

Checklist of Philippine government documents, 1950, Library of Congress, AF258

Checklist of Philippine government publications, AF257

Checklist of Philippine government publications, 1917–1949, Bibliographical Society of the Philippines, AF258

—— Rebadavia, Consolacion B., AF258

A checklist of printed materials relating to French-Canadian literature, 1763–1968, University of British Columbia. Library, BE844

Checklist of publications of the government of the Philippine Islands Sept. 1, 1900 to Dec. 31, 1917, Manila (Philippines). National Library. Legislative Reference Division, AF258

A checklist of published instrumental music by Japanese composers, Matsushita, Hitoshi, BJ74

Checklist of rare Filipiniana serials (1811–1944), National Library (Philippines). Filipiniana and Asia Division, AD209

A checklist of Southeast Asian newspapers and other research materials in microform held by the Center for Research Libraries, Center for Research Libraries, AE82

—— Doeppers, Daniel F., AE83

Checklist of southeast Asian serials, AE82

Checklist of the world's birds, Gruson, Edward S., EG261

Checklist of thematic catalogues, Music Library Association, BJ230

Checklist of United Nations documents, 1946–49, United Nations. Dag Hammarskjöld Library, AF52

Checklist of United States public documents, 1789–1909, AF90, AF129

—— United States. Superintendent of Documents, AF99

Checklist of United States public documents, 1789–1976, Lester, Daniel W., AF95

A checklist of women writers, 1801–1900, Alston, R. C., BE750

Cheetham, Samuel. *Dictionary of Christian antiquities,* BC246, BC249

•*Chem sources,* EE66

Chem sources Europe, EE66

Chem sources international, EE66
Chem sources U.S.A, EE66
Chemia et res metallica, BE31, EA21, EC17, ED6, EE15, EG98, EG213, EH68
Chemical abstracts, EA41, EE4, EE6, EE18, EE22, EE24, EE115
Chemical Abstracts Service source index, EA41, EE18, EA41, EE18
Chemical age directory and who's who, EE55
The chemical age yearbook, EE55
Chemical and process engineering unit operations, Bourton, Kathleen, EK47, EK48
Chemical dictionary, EE40
—— Fouchier, Jean, EE47
Chemical elements, EE30, EE73
Chemical engineering
 bibliography, EK47, EK48
 catalogs, EE76
 databases, EK49
 dictionaries, EK54
 encyclopedias, EE144, EK50, EK51, EK52, EK53
 handbooks, EK55, EK56, EK57, EK58
 research centers
  directories, EK267
Chemical engineering, Ray, Martyn S., EK47, EK48
•*Chemical engineering and biotechnology abstracts,* EK49
Chemical engineering practice, Cremer, Herbert W., EK55
Chemical engineers' handbook, EK57
Chemical formulary, EA277
Chemical guide to the United States, Noyes Data Corporation, EE60
Chemical Heritage Foundation. *Nobel laureates in chemistry, 1901–1992,* AL166, EE103
Chemical industry
 dictionaries, EK54
 directories, EE60
 encyclopedias, EE27, EE144, EK50
Chemical industry (by country or region)
 Europe
  directories, EE55
Chemical industry (by subject)
 history, EE96, EE97
Chemical industry directory, EE55
Chemical industry directory and who's who, EE55
Chemical industry Europe, EE55
Chemical information, Wolman, Yecheskel, EE9
Chemical information sources, Wiggins, Gary, EE8
Chemical literature, 1700–1860, Cole, William A., EE11
Chemical, medical, and pharmaceutical books printed before 1800, in the collections of the University of Wisconsin Libraries, University of Wisconsin-Madison. Libraries, EE17
Chemical names and synonyms, EE42
Chemical publications, Mellon, Melvin Guy, EE5, EE115
Chemical reactions, EE69, EE137, EE145
Chemical research faculties, EE56
Chemical Rubber Company. *Basic laboratory and industrial chemicals,* EE64
—— *CRC handbook of chemistry and physics,* EE70
—— *CRC handbook of laboratory safety,* EE88
—— *CRC handbook of laser science and technology,* EC49, ED34
—— *CRC handbook of mathematical sciences,* EB84
—— *CRC handbook of microbiology,* EG54
—— *CRC handbook of tables for probability and statistics,* EB81
—— *Handbook of food additives,* EH304
Chemical Society (Great Britain). *Analytical abstracts,* EE20
—— *Index of reviews in organic chemistry,* EE134
Chemical solutions, Welcher, Frank Johnson, EE92
Chemical synonyms and trade names, Gardner, William, EE39
Chemical technician's ready reference handbook, Ballinger, Jack T., EE87
—— Shugar, Gershon J., EE87
Chemical technology, EK50

Chemical titles, EE23
Chemicals
 catalogs, EE39, EE76
 dictionaries, EE42, EE72
 handbooks, EE64, EE66
 indexes, EH144
 safety measures, EE65, EE78
Chemicals (by subject)
 purification, EE85
Chemie Lexikon, EE32
Chemisches Zentralblatt, EA41, EE18, EE19, EE24, EE122
Chemistry
 abstract journals, EE20, EE21, EE22, EE24
 bibliography, EE14
  early works to 1800, BE31, EA21, EC17, ED6, EE10, EE11, EE12, EE15, EE16, EE17, EG98, EG213, EH68
 biography, AL165, AL166, AL171, EE99, EE100, EE101, EE102, EE103, EE104
 computer programs, EE58
 databases, EE20, EE22, EE66
 dictionaries, EA90, EE29, EE34, EE36, EE37, EE38, EE40, EE41, EE42, EE44, EE46, EF181
  bilingual
   French-English, EE48
   German-English, EE49, EE50, EE51, EE52
   Russian-English, EE53, EE54
  multilingual, EE47
 directories, EE57, EE59
 encyclopedias, EE25, EE26, EE31, EE32, EE33, EE43
 eponyms, EA85
 guides, EE1, EE2, EE3, EE4, EE5, EE6, EE7, EE8, EE9
 handbooks, EA149, EE39, EE61, EE63, EE64, EE65, EE66, EE68, EE70, EE73, EE74, EE77, EE78, EE81, EE83, EE84, EE86, EE87, EE89, EE90, EH345, EJ59
 indexes, BE31, EA21, EC17, ED6, EE15, EE23, EG98, EG213, EH68
 laboratory manuals, EE75
 library catalogs, EE12, EE16, EE17
 periodicals, EA41, EE18, EE19
 prizes and awards, AL165, AL166, AL171, AL174, EE102, EE103, EE104, EE105
 style manuals, EE95
 tables, EA154, EA155, EA156, ED43, ED44, EE93
Chemistry (by subject)
 history, EE14, EE37, EE96, EE97, EE98
  bibliography, BE31, EA21, EC17, ED6, EE10, EE11, EE12, EE15, EE16, EE17, EG98, EG213, EH68
 tests and reagents, EE92
 see also **Biochemistry; Coordination chemistry; Geochemistry; Surface chemistry**
Chemistry, Nobelstiftelsen, AL171, AL174, EE104, EE105
Chemistry, analytic, EE82
 encyclopedias, EE27
 handbooks, EE124
Chemistry, inorganic, EE107, EE108, EE111
 databases, EE109, EE110
 encyclopedias, EE110
 handbooks, EE91, EE109
 nomenclature, EE112
Chemistry, organic, EE117, EE118, EE119, EE120, EE131, EE138, EE145
 bibliography, EE115, EE122, EE143
 databases, EE127, EE133, EE149
 dictionaries, EE146
 encyclopedias, EE115, EE144
 handbooks, EE91, EE121, EE123, EE125, EE126, EE127, EE128, EE129, EE130, EE148, EE149, EE150, EH334, EH335, EH336
 indexes, EE134, EE135
 nomenclature, EE132, EE136
 reviews of research, EE134, EE135
 tables, EE147, EE151
 see also **Organic compounds**
Chemists, EE100, EE101
The chemist's companion, Gordon, Arnold J., EE74

Chemist's ready reference handbook, Shugar, Gershon J., EE87
Chemoreception abstracts, EG14
Chen, C. H. *Computer engineering handbook,* EK203
Chen, Ching-chih. *Scientific and technical information sources,* EA2
Chen, Janey. *A practical English-Chinese pronouncing dictionary,* AC257
Chen, Nai-ruenn. *Chinese economic statistics,* CG381
Chenchabi, Hédi. *Langues, cultures et éducation au Maghreb,* DD72
Cheney, Christopher Robert. *Handbook of dates for students of English history,* DC295
Cheng, James K. M. *China,* AA74
Cheng, Peter. *China,* DE126
Cheng, Su Ling. *Civil engineering practice,* EK59
Chennells, A. J. *Rhodesian literature in English,* BE1541
Chenu, M. D. *Bibliographie thomiste,* BB66
Chepesiuk, Ronald. *American Indian archival material,* CC427
Chercheurs et curieux, BE185
Cheremisinoff, Nicholas P. *Civil engineering practice,* EK59
Cheremisinoff, Paul N. *Civil engineering practice,* EK59
Cherepakhov, Matvei Samoilovich. *Russkaia periodicheskaia pechat',* AD146
Cherkaoui, Aziz. *Langues, cultures et éducation au Maghreb,* DD72
Cherkesi, E. *Georgian-English dictionary,* AC397
Cherman, T. P. *Bibliografiia Tiurtsii, 1713–1917,* DC532
Cherniss, H. F. *Plato,* BB55
Chernov, G. *Anglu-latviešu vārdnīca,* AC596
Chernow, Barbara Ann. *The Columbia encyclopedia,* AB6
Cherns, J. J. *Official publishing,* AF3
Chernukhin, Adol'f Efimovich. *Anglo-russkiĭ politekhnicheskiĭ slovar',* EA126
Cherow O'Leary, Renée. *The state-by-state guide to women's legal rights,* CK162
Cherry, Virginia R. *Public administration research guide,* CJ459, CJ460
Chertoff, Mordecai. *A bibliography of Israel,* DE191
Chervel, André. *Les grammaires françaises, 1800–1914,* BD157
Chesko, L. A. *Slovar' sinonimov russkogo iazyka,* AC692
Chesneau, Roger. *Conway's all the world's fighting ships, 1947–1982,* CJ592
Chess, BK131, BK132, BK133, BK134, BK135
Chess, Betts, Douglas A., BK134
—— Lusis, Andy, BK134
The chess encyclopedia, Divinsky, N. J., BK131
Chester, David T. *Profile of teachers in the U.S.—1990,* CB166
Chettiar, A. Chidambaranatha. *English-Tamil dictionary,* AC775
Cheung, King-Kok. *Asian American literature,* BE546
Chevalier, Cyr Ulysse Joseph. *Répertoire des sources historiques du Moyen Âge,* AH11, DA130
Chevalier, Jean. *Dictionnaire des symboles,* CF4
Chevalier, Tracy. *Contemporary poets,* BE212, BE334
—— *Contemporary world writers,* BE199
—— *Twentieth-century children's writers,* BE391
Chevalley, Abel. *The concise Oxford French dictionary,* AC337
Chew, Allen F. *Atlas of Russian history,* DC571
Chhotelal Jain's Jaina bibliography, Jain, Chhotelal, BC507
Chi, Wen-shun. *Chinese-English dictionary of contemporary usage,* AC258
Chi à?, AH259
Chi l'ha detto?, Fumagalli, Giuseppe, BE139
Chi scrive, BE1309
Chiang, T. *Chinese studies research methodology,* DE125

Chiang, Win-Shin S. *Legal bibliography index*, CK17

Chiarmonte, Paula L. *Women artists in the United States*, BF16, BF152

Chicago Assyrian dictionary, AC200

Chicago Board of Trade. Education and Marketing Services Department. *Commodity trading manual*, CH440

Chicago guide to preparing electronic manuscripts, University of Chicago Press, AA324

The Chicago manual of style, AA319, AG1, BJ189

Chicago tribune [index], AE104, AE112

The Chicana, Cabello-Argandoña, Roberto, CC444, CC596

The Chicana studies index, CC454, CC528

Chicano anthology index, CC455

—— García-Ayvens, Francisco, CC457

Chicano authors, Bruce-Novoa, Juan D., BE561

•*Chicano database*, AD267, CC455, CC456

Chicano index, AD267, CC455, CC456

Chicano literature, BE556

—— Tatum, Charles M., BE560

Chicano periodical index, AD267, CC455, CC456

Chicano Periodical Indexing Project. *Chicano periodical index*, AD267, CC456

Chicano perspectives in literature, Lomeli, Francisco A., BE558

—— Urioste, Donaldo, BE558

Chicano scholars and writers, Martínez, Julio A., BE562

Chicano thesaurus, BF20

Chickering, Robert B. *How to register a copyright and protect your creative work*, AA312

Chief elements used in English place-names, Mawer, A., CL201

Chiefs of state and cabinet members of foreign governments, CJ64, CJ83

Chielens, Edward E. *American literary magazines*, BE420

—— *Literary journal in America, 1900–1950*, BE421

—— *Literary journal in America to 1900*, BE420, BE421, BE590

Chien, David. *Lexicography in China*, AC269

Chien, Shu. *Handbook of bioengineering*, EH181

Chijs, Jacobus Anne van der. *Proeve eener Ned*, DE174

Chilcote, Ronald H. *Brazil and its radical left*, DB342

—— *Cuba, 1953–1978*, DB423

—— *Revolution and structural change in Latin America*, DB254

Child, Francis James. *The English and Scottish popular ballads*, BE632, BJ314

Child, Heather. *Christian symbols, ancient & modern*, BF182

Child abuse, CC167
  bibliography, CC144, CC185
  databases, CC156, CC161
  dictionaries, CC160
  directories, CC36
  encyclopedias, CC158
  handbooks, CC171, CC172
  thesauruses, CC161

Child abuse, Layman, Richard, CC171

•*Child abuse and neglect and family violence*, CC156, CC161

Child abuse and neglect and family violence thesaurus, CC156, CC161

Child bilingualism and second language learning, BD60

—— Afendras, Evangelos A., BD60

—— Pianarosa, Albertina, BD60

Child care, CC170

Child care crisis, Reeves, Diane Lindsey, CC173

Child development
  bibliography, CC147, CC151

Child development abstracts and bibliography, CC157, CD81

Child language
  bibliography, BD60, BD62, BD63

Child language, Abrahamsen, Adele A., BD62

Child molestation, De Young, Mary, CC144

Child protection team handbook, Schmitt, Barton D., CC172

Child Welfare League of America. *CWLA's guide to adoption agencies*, CC231

Childbearing, CC225

CHILDES/BIB, Higginson, Roy, BD63

Childhood information resources, Woodbury, Marda, CC139, CC141, CD77, CD80

Children and adjustment to divorce, Nofsinger, Mary M., CC216

Children and youth
  abstract journals, CB194, CC157, CD81, CD92
  associations
    directories, AL40
  atlases, CC175
  bibliography, CC145, CC148, CC149, CC150, CC155, CC178, CC205, CC216, CC248, CC369, CD78, CD79
  directories, CC131, CC164, CC165, CC461
  guides, CC139, CC141, CD77, CD80
  handbooks, CC149, CC154, CC166, CC173, CC238, CD85
  quotations, CC162
  statistics, CC175, CC250

Children and youth (by country or region)
  Canada, CC152, CC153

Children and youth (by subject)
  alcoholism, CC109
  disabilities and the disabled, CC163
  economic conditions, CC176
  health care, CC176
  history, CC166
  mental health
    bibliography, EH370
  mental illness, CC163
  sex and sexual behavior, CC142
  social conditions, CC174, CC176
  social work, CC172
  treatment
    directories, CC132

Children, culture, and ethnicity, Slonim, Maureen, CC151

Children in historical and comparative perspective, CC166

Children of alcoholics, Page, Penny Booth, CC120

Children, youth, and family services, CC48

Children's authors and illustrators, Nakamura, Joyce, BE387

Children's book review index, AA368

Children's books in print, AA428

Children's books in the Rare Book Division of the Library of Congress, Library of Congress. Rare Book Division, AA246

Children's books on Africa and their authors, Schmidt, Nancy J., DD14

Children's Britannica, AB17

Children's catalog, AA338

Children's costume in England ..., Cunnington, Cecil Willett, BG99

Children's literature
  abstract journals, AA339
  bibliography, AA337, AA340, AA428, BE379, BE386, CB191
  biobibliography, BE384, BE388, BE389, BE391, BE392
  biography
    indexes, BE387
  book reviews, AA368, BE378
  directories, BE380
  handbooks, BE377, BE381, BE382, BE383, BE385
  historical, AA245, AA246, AA247, AA248
  indexes, BE322, BE376, BE390
  library resources, AK113
  periodicals, AD30
    indexes, AD268
  prizes and awards, AA343, BE388

Children's literature (by country or region)
  United States
    periodicals, AD30

Children's literature (by subject)
  Africa, DD14
  history, BE385

see also **Nursery rhymes**

Children's literature abstracts, AA339

Children's Literature Association (U.S.). *The Phoenix Award of the Children's Literature Association, 1985–1989*, BE388

Children's literature review, BE378

Children's magazine guide, AD268

Children's periodicals of the United States, AD30

Children's Science Book Review Committee. *Appraisal*, EA26

Children's song index, Cushing, Helen Grant, BJ283

Children's television, Woolery, George W., BH307

Childress, James F. *BioLaw*, EH239

—— *The Westminster dictionary of Christian ethics*, BC241

Childs, James Bennett. *German Federal Republic official publications, 1949–1957*, AF173

—— *Government document bibliography in the United States and elsewhere*, AF11

Chile
  archives, DB361
  bibliography, AA512, AA513, AA514, AA515, AA516, AA517, AA518, AA519, AA520
    current, AA521, AA522
  biography, AH128, AH129, AH130, AH131, DB362
    contemporary, AH132
  encyclopedias, DB362
  government publications, AF159, AF161
  library resources, DB361
  statistics, CG144, CG145, CG146, CG147, CG148

Chile (by subject)
  folklore and popular culture, CF71
  foreign relations, DB336, DB359
  history, DB279
    bibliography, DB358, DB360
    statistics, CG148
  politics and government
    bibliography, DB360

Chile. Instituto Nacional de Estadísticas. *Compendio estadístico*, CG147

Chile. Servicio Nacional de Estadística y Censos. *Anuario estadístico de Chile*, CG145

Chile, Blakemore, Harold, DB358

Chile, series estadísticas, CG146

Chile since independence, DB291

Chilean literature, BE938, BE939, BE940, BE941
  bibliography, BE942
  biography, BE942

Chilean literature, Foster, David William, BE940

Chilvers, Ian. *The Oxford dictionary of art*, BF90

Chin, Hsien-tseng. *The five thousand dictionary*, AC262

China
  atlases, CG385, CL352, CL353, CL354, CL355
  bibliography, AA892, AA893, AA894, AA895, DE125, DE127, DE129, DE130, DE138
  bibliography of bibliography, AA74
  biography, AH336, AH337, AH338, AH339, AH340, AH341, AH342, AH343
    bibliography, AH347
    contemporary, AH344, AH345, AH346, CJ426
  directories, CJ428
  encyclopedias, DE140, DE141
  gazetteers, CL160, CL161, CL162
  government publications, AF243
  guides, AA362, DE123, DE124
  handbooks, CG382, DE145
  library resources, DE131
  newspapers, AD187, AE86, AE87
    union lists, AE96
  periodicals, AD187, AD188, AD189
  research methods, DE124, DE125
  sourcebooks, DE149
  statistics, CG381, CG382, CG383, CG384, CG385, DE145

China (by subject)
  archaeology and ancient history, BF85
  art, BF40, BF85, BF162
  artists, BF146
  ceramics and glass, BG79
  commerce, CH199

demography, CG34
economic conditions, CH199
  statistics, CG381, CH203
education, CB47
foreign economic relations, CH199
government officials, CJ425, CJ426, CJ430
historiography, DE128
history, CJ425, DE147
  bibliography, DE126, DE127, DE128, DE132,
    DE134, DE135, DE137
  dictionaries, DE144
  encyclopedias, DE140, DE142, DE143
  general histories, DE146, DE148
  indexes, DE139
  regional and local, DE131
law
  bibliography, CK228
music, BJ18
painting, BF313
place-names, CL93, CL162
political activity, DE136
politics and government, CJ425, CJ428, CJ429,
  CJ430, DE147
religion, BC37, BC38
teaching aids, DE133
women, CC619
  see also Taiwan
China. Kuo Chia T'ung Chi Chü. China trade and
  price statistics, CH203
China, Cheng, Peter, DE126
—— Posner, Arlene, DE133
—— Sive, Mary Robinson, DE133
—— Tsien, Tsuen-Hsuin, AA74
China after Mao, DE132
China directory in pinyin and Chinese, CJ427
China facts & figures annual, CG382
China in Western literature, Yüan, T'ung-li, BF40,
  DE127, DE129, DE138
China nach Mao, Müller, Meike, DE132
China statistical abstract, CG383
China Statistical Information and Consultancy
  Service Centre. China trade and price statistics,
  CH203
China statistical yearbook, CG384
China trade and price statistics, CH203
Chinaköpfe, Bartke, Wolfgang, AH337
China's new party leadership, Bartke, Wolfgang,
  CJ426
Chinese-American calendar for the 102 Chinese
  years commencing Jan. 24, 1849, and ending Feb.
  5, 1951, Welch, Windon Chandler, EC88
Chinese art and archaeology, BF85
A Chinese biographical dictionary, Giles, Herbert
  Allen, AH339
Chinese characters, Wieger, Leon, AC255
Chinese classic novels, Berry, Margaret, BE1562
Chinese classics, Legge, James, BE1555
Chinese cooperative catalog, AA111, AA892
Chinese dialectology, Yang, Paul Fu-mien, BD219,
  BD220, BD221
Chinese dictionaries, AC270
Chinese economic statistics, Chen, Nai-ruenn,
  CG381
Chinese-English and English-Chinese dictionaries in
  the Library of Congress, Library of Congress,
  AC271
Chinese-English dictionary, Giles, Herbert Allen,
  AC263
—— Mathews, Robert Henry, AC266
Chinese-English dictionary of contemporary usage,
  Chi, Wen-shun, AC258
Chinese-English dictionary of modern usage, Lin,
  Yutang, AC265
Chinese-English, English-Chinese astronomical
  dictionary, Chiu, Hong-yee, EC40
Chinese-English glossary of astro-science terms,
  EC39
Chinese-English glossary of mineral names, Bradley,
  J. E. S., EF182
Chinese-English glossary of the mathematical
  sciences, DeFrancis, John, EB48

Chinese-English Translation Assistance Group.
  Chinese-English glossary of astro-science terms,
  EC39
Chinese fiction, Li, Tien-Yi, BE1556
Chinese historiography on the Revolution of 1911,
  Hsieh, Winston, DE128
Chinese history, DE139
The Chinese in California, Hansen, Gladys C.,
  CC405
Chinese Inland Mission. Mathews' Chinese-English
  dictionary, AC266
Chinese language
  bibliography, AC269, BD218, BD220, BD221
  dialects
    bibliography, BD219
  dictionaries, AC253, AC254, AC255, AC256,
    BC480
    bibliography, AC269, AC270, AC271
    bilingual, AC263
      Chinese-English, AC258, AC259, AC260,
      AC261, AC262, AC264, AC265, AC266,
      AC267, AC268
      English-Chinese, AC257
      idioms and usage, AC258
      visual, AC259
  idioms and usage, AC265
Chinese lexicology and lexicography, Yang, Paul
  Fu-mien, BD220
Chinese linguistics, Yang, Paul Fu-mien, BD219,
  BD220, BD221
Chinese literature
  bibliography, BE1553, BE1556, BE1557,
    BE1558, BE1561, BE1562
  biography, BE1559
  collections, BE1555
  encyclopedias, BE1554
  guides, BE1562
  surveys, BE1560
  translations, BE1552, BE1553
Chinese literature (by subject)
  history, BE1559
Chinese local histories, University of Chicago. Far
  Eastern Library, DE131
Chinese music, Lieberman, Fredric, BJ18
Chinese national bibliography, AA938
Chinese newspapers in the Library of Congress,
  Library of Congress, AE87
Chinese painting, Sirén, Osvald, BF313
Chinese paintings in Chinese publications, Laing,
  Ellen Johnston, BF313
Chinese periodicals in the Library of Congress,
  Library of Congress, AD188
Chinese philosophy, BB19
Chinese religion, Seaman, Gary, BC37
—— Thompson, Laurence G., BC37
Chinese religion in Western languages, Thompson,
  Laurence G., BC37
Chinese studies, Wolff, Ernest, DE125
Chinese studies research methodology, Chiang, T.,
  DE125
—— Herbert, P. A., DE125
Chipman, John H. Index to top-hit tunes, 1900–1950,
  BJ282
Chipman, Kathe. Print index, BF367
Chirat, Henri. Dictionnaire latin-français des auteurs
  chrétiens, AC581
Chirat, Raymond. Catalogue des films français de
  long métrage, BH184
Chiropractic, EH197
Chiropractic, Wardwell, Walter I., EH197
Chisholm, L. J. Units of weight and measure, AL196
Chisholm's handbook of commercial geography,
  Stamp, L. Dudley, CL43, CL67
Chismore, W. Dale. A classification of educational
  subject matter, CB111
Chitambar, Jashwant Rao. The new royal dictionary,
  AC488
Chitambo, A. M. Women in Zambia, DD246
Chittenden, Betsy. Preserving historic landscapes,
  BF287, BF293
Chitty, Mary Glen. Federal information sources in
  health and medicine, EH41

Chiu, Hong-yee. Chinese-English, English-Chinese
  astronomical dictionary, EC40
Chivalry, DA147
Chizhakovskiĭ, V. A. Statistika rechi, 1957–1985,
  BD64
Chlebowski, Bronisław. Słownik geograficzny
  Królestwa polskiego i innych krajów słowiańskich,
  CL148
Chmurski, A. M. La Pologne en France, BE1354
Cho, Sung Yoon. Introductions to research in
  foreign law: Japan, CK232
Choay, Françoise. Dictionnaire de l'urbanisme et de
  l'aménagement, BF273
Choe, Hye Yun. Index to historic preservation
  periodicals, BF218
Choice, AA336
Choice (Chicago, Ill.). Choice ethnic studies reviews,
  CC316
Choice ethnic studies reviews, CC316
Chojnacki, Stanisław. The dictionary of Ethiopian
  biography, AH318
Cholakova, Kristalina. Rechnik na bŭlgarskiia ezik,
  AC242
Cholov, Petur. Bŭlgarski istoritsi, DC118
Chonchol, Maria Edy. Guide bibliographique du
  Mozambique, DD183
Choose the right word, AC139
Chopra, Prabha. Encyclopaedia of India, DE165
Chopra, Pran Nath. Encyclopaedia of India, DE165
Choquette, Diane. New religious movements in the
  United States and Canada, BC28
Choral and opera catalogue, BJ92
Choral music, BJ291, BJ292
Chorherr, Edith. Bibliographie der Zeitschriften des
  deutschen Sprachgebietes bis 1900, AD100
Choudhury, N. C. Bibliography of anthropology of
  India, CE110
Chouémi, Moustafa. Dictionnaire arabe-français-
  anglais, AC213
Chouliarakēs, Michaēl G. Statistikē vivliographia
  peri Hellados, 1821–1971, CG242
Chow, Ven Te. Handbook of applied hydrology,
  EF137, EF139
Chrissanthaki, Thana. World index of economic
  forecasts, CH122
Christ, Karl. Römische Geschichte, eine
  Bibliographie, DA94
Christ, Wilhelm von. Geschichte der griechischen
  Literatur, BE1035
Christ-Janer, Albert. American hymns old and new,
  BC317
Christaller, Johann Gottlieb. Dictionary of the Asante
  and Fante language, called Tshi (Twi), AC794
Christensen, Clay Benjamin. Research on language
  teaching, BD75
Christian annual, BC386
Christian antiquities, BC222, BC248, BC249,
  BC274, BC275
  atlases, BC290
  dictionaries, BC247
  encyclopedias, BC246
The Christian churches of the East, Attwater,
  Donald, BC444
Christian communication, Soukup, Paul A., BC224
Christian ethics, BC241
Christian literature
  bibliography, BE5
Christian literature (by period)
  medieval, 500-1500, BE5
Christian periodical index, BC43
Christian religion
  bibliography, BC12, BC17, BC209, BC212,
    BC214, BC216, BC218, BC220, BC221, BC224,
    BC225, BC226, BC227, BC259, BC374, BC375,
    DC321
    reference works, BC217
  biography, BC82, BC83, BC253, BC254, BC255,
    BC256, BC257, BC258, BC259, BC260, BC261,
    BC262, BC263, BC264, BC265, BC266
  Christian antiquities, BC275
  dictionaries, BC234, BC236, BC237, BC238,
    BC240, BC241, BC242, BC243, BC245, BC268,
    BC554

encyclopedias, BC54, BC63, BC67, BC69, BC229, BC231, BC232, BC233, BC239, BC241, BC244, BC292
  guides, BC12, BC209
  statistics, BC233, BC292
Christian religion (by country or region)
  Africa, Southern
    bibliography, DD115
  Canada, BC270
  China, BC305
  Ireland
    directories, BC251
  United Kingdom
    directories, BC251
  United States, BC235, BC270
Christian religion (by subject)
  church history and expansion, BC210, BC234, BC236, BC240, BC270, BC272, BC273, BC276, BC277, BC278, BC279, BC280, BC443, BC444
    atlases, BC85, BC287, BC288, BC289, BC290
    bibliography, BC121, DA132
    dictionaries, BC244
    sourcebooks, BC281, BC283, BC284, BC285, BC286, BC436
    statistics, BC291
  costume, BC312
  creeds, BC311
  environment and environmental problems, BC223, EG66
  history, BC280
    bibliography, BC271
  hymnology, BC313, BC316, BC318, BC319, BC320, BC321
    indexes, BC315
  liturgy and ritual, BC268, BC269
  missions, BC305, BC306, BC307
    bibliography, BC303, BC304
    encyclopedias, BC310
    handbooks, BC308
    library resources, BC309
  patrology, BC293, BC294, BC300, BC301
    bibliography, BC295, BC298
    handbooks, BC296
  symbols and symbolism, BC208, BF181, BF182, BF184, BF185, BF187, BF298
Christian Science monitor [index], AE104, AE106, AE112
Christian symbols, ancient & modern, Child, Heather, BF182
———— Colles, Dorothy, BF182
Christian theology *see* **Theology**
Christian theology, BC243
Christianity in China, BC305
Christianity in tropical Africa, Ofori, Patrick E., BC221, BC497
Christiansen, Carla E. *Scholar's guide to intelligence literature,* CJ538
Christiansen, Donald. *Electronics engineers' handbook,* EK136
Christianson, Elin. *Special libraries,* AK181
Christie, Ian R. *Bibliography of British history, 1789–1851,* DC328
Christie's guide to collecting, BF121
Christmann, Hans Helmut. *Altfranzösisches Wörterbuch,* AC383
Christmas, Brian. *The dictionary of genealogy,* AJ111
Christmas carols, Studwell, William E., BJ274
Christo, Doris H. *National directory of education libraries and collections,* CB94
Christophory, Jules. *Luxembourg,* DC447
Christy, Francis Jr. *Trends in natural resource commodities,* CH441
Chromec, Břetislav. *Místopisný slovník Československé republiky,* CL131
Chronic, Halka. *Bibliography of theses in geology, 1958–63,* EF43, EF44
———— *Bibliography of theses written for advanced degrees in geology and related sciences at universities and colleges in the United States and Canada through 1957,* EF43
Chronic, John. *Bibliography of theses in geology, 1958–63,* EF43, EF44

———— *Bibliography of theses written for advanced degrees in geology and related sciences at universities and colleges in the United States and Canada through 1957,* EF43
The chronicle of higher education almanac, CB336
Chronicle of the First World War, Gray, Randal, DA198
Chronicles of pharmacy, Wootton, A. C., EH368
Chronicles of the age of chivalry, Hallam, Elizabeth M., DC310
Chronicles of the Wars of the Roses, Hallam, Elizabeth M., DC310
Chronik deutscher Zeitgeschichte, Overesch, Manfred, DC260
Die Chronik Österreichs, Kleindel, Walter, DC97
The chronological annotated bibliography of order statistics, Harter, H. Leon, EB9
The chronological atlas of World War II, Pitt, Barrie, DA211
Chronological history of United States foreign relations, Brune, Lester H., DB57
Chronological landmarks in American agriculture, EJ67
Chronological list, Roberts, Brian, DG9
Chronological list of Antarctic expeditions and related historical events, Headland, Robert, DG9
Chronological list of prose fiction in English printed in England and other countries, 1475–1640, O'Dell, Sterg, BE679, BE680
A chronological outline of American literature, Rogal, Samuel J., BE437
A chronological outline of British literature, Rogal, Samuel J., BE613
A chronological outline of world theatre, Meserve, Walter J., BH94
Chronological table of Japanese art, Yamasaki, Shigehisa, BF88
Chronological table of statutes, CK214
Chronological tables of American newspapers, 1690–1820, Lathem, Edward Connery, AE26
Chronologie de la littérature française, Beaumarchais, Jean-Pierre de, BE1152
———— Couty, Daniel, BE1152
———— Ferreyrolles, Gérard, BE1152
Chronologie générale de l'histoire du Zaïre, Mwanyimi-Mbonba, Mandjumba, DD15, DD245
De chronologie van de middeleeuwen en de moderne tijden in de Nederlanden, Strubbe, Egied I., DC460
Chronologies in Old World archaeology, DA83
Chronologisches Verzeichnis französischer Grammatiken, Stengel, Edmund, BD157
Chronology, AL143, DA29, EC86
  tables, EC83, EC84, EC85, EC87
A chronology and fact book of the United Nations, AF32
Chronology and index of the Second World War 1938–1945, Ames, John G., DA209
———— Royal Institute of International Affairs, DA209
Chronology of African-American history, Hornsby, Alton, CC393
Chronology of African history, Freeman-Grenville, Greville Stewart Parker, DD56
A chronology of conflict and resolution, 1945–1985, Jessup, John E., CJ63
Chronology of culture, DA36
A chronology of geological thinking from antiquity to 1899, Thompson, Susan J., EF104
A chronology of Irish history since 1500, Doherty, J. E., DC412
A chronology of Islamic history, 570–1000 CE, Rahman, H. U., DE63
Chronology of science and discovery, EA249
Chronology of the ancient world, Bickerman, Elias Joseph, DA110
Chronology of the expanding world, 1492–1762, Williams, Neville, DA184
Chronology of the medieval world, 800 to 1491, Storey, R. L., DA156, DA184
Chronology of the modern world, 1793–1965, Williams, Neville, DA184

A chronology of the United Nations, 1941–1958, AF32
Chronology of western architecture, Yarwood, Doreen, BF253
Chronology of world events, 1972–1989, Weilant, Edward, CJ484
Chronology of world history, Freeman-Grenville, Greville Stewart Parker, DA32
Chüan kuo hsin shu mu, AA893
Ch'üan kuo po shuo shih lun wen mu lu, AG58
Chubb, Basil. *A source book of Irish government,* CJ378
Chubb, Thomas. *Printed maps in the atlases of Great Britain and Ireland,* CL228
Chubinashvili, D. *Russian-Georgian dictionary,* AC397
Chuguev, Vladimir. *A biographical dictionary of the former Soviet Union,* AH179
Chujoy, Anatole. *The dance encyclopedia,* BH139
Chuks-orji, Ogonna. *Names from Africa,* AJ168
Chumas, Sophie. *Directory of United States standardization activities,* EA276
Chun, Ki-Taek. *Measures for psychological assessment,* CD67
Chung-hua min kuo ch'u pan t'u shu mu lu, AA938
Chung-kuo pao k'an ta ch'üan, AD187
Chung-kuo shih hsüeh lun wên yin tê, Yu, Ping-Kuen, DE139
Chung-kuo ta pai ko chuan shu, AB29
Chung-kuo tù shu kuan ming lu, AK156
Church, Elihu Dwight. *Catalogue of books relating to the discovery and early history of North and South America,* DB2
Church, Helen Nichols. *Bowes and Church's food values of portions commonly used,* EH303, EJ216
Church, Martha. *Basic geographical library,* CL17
Church, Olga Maranjian. *American nursing,* EH287
Church and state, BC15
Church and state (by country or region)
  Europe, East and Southeast
    bibliography, BC213, DC31
  United States
    bibliography, DB10
Church and state in America, DB10
Church and state in postwar eastern Europe, BC213, DC31
Church in Wales, BC334
Church music
  encyclopedias, BC322, BJ155
Church of England. *The alternative service book of 1980,* BC335
———— *The annotated Book of Common Prayer,* BC336
———— *The Book of Common Prayer,* BC337, BC348
Church of England
  directories, BC334
  history, BC331, BC332
  service books, BC335, BC336, BC337, BC338, BC339
  sourcebooks, BC284
  yearbooks, BC333
  see also **Anglican Communion**
Church of England. General Synod. *The Church of England year book,* BC333
The Church of England year book, Church of England. General Synod, BC333
Church of Ireland, BC334, BC338, BC340
Church of Jesus Christ of Latter-Day Saints. *Holdings of the University of Utah on Utah and the Church of Jesus Christ of Latter-Day Saints,* BC373
Church of Jesus Christ of Latter-Day Saints. Family History Library. *The library,* AJ14
Church of Jesus Christ of Latter-Day Saints. Historical Dept. *Mormons in the Pacific,* BC370
Church of Scotland, BC338, BC341, BC342
Church symbolism, Webber, Frederick Roth, BF187
Church vestments, Norris, Herbert, BC312
Churches & church membership in the United States, Johnson, Douglas W., BC85, BC87

Churches and church membership in the United States, BC87
———— National Council of the Churches of Christ in the U.S.A. Bureau of Research and Survey, BC85, BC88
Churches and church membership in the United States, 1990, BC86
Churchill's illustrated medical dictionary, EH95
The churchman's almanac, BC346
Churchman's year book and American church almanac, BC346
Čhyžhevskyj, Dmytro. *History of Ukrainian literature,* BE1493
•*CIA world factbook,* CL68
Ciaccio, Leonard L. *Water and water pollution handbook,* EK97
Cianciolo, Patricia Jean. *Picture books for children,* AA340
Ciba-Geigy, S.A. *Thesaurus of agricultural organisms, pests, weeds, and diseases,* EJ33
Cibbarelli, Pamela R. *Directory of library automation software, systems, and services,* AK191
"Il Cicognara", Borroni Salvadori, Fabia, BF14
CIC's school directory, Curriculum Information Center, CB96
Cieślakiewicz, Jadwiga. *Polska prasa konspiracyjna (1939–1945) i powstania warszawskiego w zbiorach Biblioteki Narodowej,* AE66
CIFAR's global company handbook, CH405
Cigler, Allan J. *U.S. agricultural groups,* EJ44
CIJE, AK28, CB54, CB56, CD90, CD91
CIJE : cumulated author index, 1969–1984, AK28, CB54, CD90
•*CIJE OnDisc,* AK28, CB54, CD90
Cimbala, Diane J. *Biographical sources,* AH4
CINAHL, EH274, EH275
CINAHL subject headings, EH280
Cinegraph, BH281
Cinema *see* **Film**
Cinema, BH246
Cinema booklist, Rehrauer, George, BH170
Cinema sequels and remakes, Nowlan, Gwendolyn Wright, BH222
———— Nowlan, Robert A., BH222
Cinematographers
   filmography, BH206, BH207, BH208
Cinematographers, production designers, costume designers and film editors guide, BH207
Cinti, Decio. *Dizionario dei sinònimi e dei contrari,* AC540
CIO and industrial unionism in America, CH624
Cioranescu, Alexandre. *Bibliographie de la littérature française du dix-huitième siècle ...,* BE1206
———— *Bibliographie de la littérature française du dix-septième siècle,* BE1205
———— *Bibliographie de la littérature française du seizième siècle,* BE1204
Cirac Estopañan, Sebastian. *Sintesis bibliografica de filologia griega,* BD136
CIRCA Ltd. *Political and economic encyclopaedia of Western Europe,* CJ319
CIRCA Research & Reference Information Limited. *Political parties of Asia and the Pacific,* CJ446
Circular of information concerning census publications, 1790–1916, CG90
Circulation, AE21
Circum-Mediterranean peasantry, Sweet, Louise Elizabeth, CE97
Circus, BH11
   bibliography, BH4
Circus and allied arts, Toole-Stott, Raymond, BH4
Cirker, Blanche. *Dictionary of American portraits,* BF65
Cirker, Hayward. *Dictionary of American portraits,* BF65
Cirlot, Juan Eduardo. *A dictionary of symbols,* BF164
•*CIS,* AF118
CIS annual, AF126
———— Congressional Information Service, AF125
•*CIS cumulative database,* CG15, EB22

•*CIS extended database,* CG15, EB22
CIS foreign gazetteers [of the] USBGN, CL87
CIS index to presidential executive orders & proclamations, AF128
CIS/index to publications of the United States Congress, AF119, AF126
CIS/index to publications of the U.S. Congress, AF124, AF125
CIS index to unpublished U.S. House of Representatives committee hearings, 1833–1936, AF118, AF121
CIS index to unpublished U.S. Senate committee hearings, AF118, AF122
CIS index to U.S. executive branch documents, 1789–1909, AF99, AF129
CIS index to U.S. Senate executive documents & reports, AF117, AF118
CIS U.S. congressional committee hearings index, Congressional Information Service, AF123
CIS U.S. congressional committee hearings index, 1833–1969, AF118
CIS U.S. congressional committee prints index from the earliest publications through 1969, AF118, AF124
CIS U.S. serial set index, AF88, AF90, AF118, AF87
•*CitaDel,* AD296
Les citations françaises, Guerlac, Othon Goepp, BE131
CITE II, EA60
Cities
   abstract journals, CC304
   bibliography, CC294, CC295, DB145
   biography, CJ285
   encyclopedias, CL64
   government publications, AF147
   handbooks, CC299, CL57, CL70, CL73, CL74, CL75
   maps
      bibliography, CL234
   quotations, CC297
   sourcebooks, CG55
   statistics, CC296, CG47, CG56, CH166, CL69, CL75
Cities (by country or region)
   Austria, DC90
   Canada, DB210
   Denmark, DC132
   Europe, DC2
   France, BF273, DC212
   Germany, BF274, DC265, DC266
   Great Britain, DC353
   India, DC305
   Netherlands
      history, DC453
   Scandinavia, DC72
   Switzerland, DC524
   United States
      bibliography, DB148
      statistics, CG74, CG75, CG79
Cities (by subject)
   economic conditions, CH166, CL72
   see also **Urbanization**
Cities and churches, Hartley, Loyde H., DB10
Cities and towns in American history, Young, Arthur P., DB148
The cities and towns of China, Playfair, George M. H., CL160
Cities of opportunity, Marlin, John Tepper, CL72
Cities of the United States, CL70
Cities of the world, CL57
Cities supplement, CG75
The city, Clapp, James A., CC297
City directories of the United States, AL8, CH401
City finances, CG74
City government finances, CG74
City in print, Bryfogle, R. Charles, CC294
The city-manager directory, CJ279
City manager yearbook, CJ279
City of London from prehistoric times to c.1520, Lobel, Mary D., DC354
City planning, CC293, CC302, CC303
   bibliography, BF269, BF270, BF271, BF274, BF275, BF288, DC266

   dictionaries, BF277, BF278
   directories, BF279, BF280, BF281, BF282
   encyclopedias, BF276
   guides, BF268
   indexes, BF275
   library resources, BF281
City planning (by country or region)
   France, BF273
   Great Britain
      handbooks, BF284, EK81
   United States
      directories, BF283
   see also **Urbanization**
City planning bibliography, Bestor, George Clinton, BF270
Civil aviation statistics of the world, CH473
Civil engineering
   biography, EK63
   dictionaries, EF76
   handbooks, EK59, EK60, EK61
Civil engineering practice, EK59
Civil engineering reference book, EK60
Civil engineer's reference book, EK60
Civil rights, CC392
   biography, CC577
Civil rights (by country or region)
   United States
      directories, CK147
Civil service reform, Dillman, David L., CJ100
The civil service year book, CJ340
Civil War almanac, Bowman, John S., DB118
Civil War battlefield guide, Kennedy, Frances H., DB118
Civil War books, Nevins, Allan, DB111
The Civil War day by day, Long, Everette Beach, DB120
Civil War dictionary, Boatner, Mark Mayo, DB118
Civil War eyewitnesses, Cole, Garold, DB107
Civil War manuscripts, Library of Congress. Manuscript Division, DB115
Civil War maps, Library of Congress. Geography and Map Division, CL301, DB122
Civil War naval chronology, 1861–1865, United States. Naval History Division, DB120
Civil War novels, Menendez, Albert J., BE477, DB107
Civil War unit histories, DB109
Civil war years, Denny, Robert E., DB120
Civilization of the ancient Mediterranean, DA98
CJPI, CK249
Claes, Frans M. *A bibliography of Netherlandic dictionaries,* AC300
Clagett, Helen Lord. *Guide to the law and legal literature of Mexico,* CK197
———— *A revised guide to the law and legal literature of Mexico,* CK197
Claghorn, Charles E. *Naval officers of the American Revolution,* CJ639
Claghorn, Charles Eugene. *Women composers & hymnists,* BC314, BJ207
Claiborne, Robert. *The roots of English,* AC51
Clain-Stefanelli, Elvira Eliza. *Numismatic bibliography,* BG170
———— *Select numismatic bibliography,* BG170
Clair, Jeffrey M. *The influence of the family,* CC205
Clancy, Paul R. *The Congress dictionary,* CJ205
Články v českých časopisech, AD307
Clans and tartans, AJ125, AJ126
The clans, septs, and regiments of the Scottish Highlands, Adam, Frank, AJ125
Clapham, A. R. *Flora of the British Isles,* EG168
Clapham, Christopher. *A concise dictionary of mathematics,* EB38
Clapp, James A. *The city,* CC297
Clapp, Jane. *Art censorship,* BF128
———— *Museum publications,* AL86, EF24, EF25
———— *Sculpture index,* BF367, BF388
Clarasó Daudí, Noel. *Antología de textos, citas, frases, modismos, y decires,* BE148
Clardy, Andrea. *Words to the wise,* CC559
Clareson, Thomas D. *Science fiction criticism,* BE301, BE310

—— *Science fiction in America, 1870s–1930s,* BE301

Claretie, Jules. *La Comédie-Française de 1680 à 1900,* BE1179

Clark, Alan J. *Book catalogue of the Library of the Royal Society,* EA23

Clark, Andrew. *Hey's mineral index,* EF182, EF193

Clark, Anne B. *Biographic dictionary of Chinese communism, 1921–1965,* CJ429

Clark, Audrey N. *Chisholm's handbook of commercial geography,* CL67

—— *A glossary of geographical terms,* CL42

—— *Longman dictionary of geography,* CL43

Clark, Brian D. *Environmental impact assessment,* EK66

Clark, Burton R. *The encyclopedia of higher education,* CB236

Clark, Charles Manning Hope. *A history of Australia,* DF38

Clark, David Sanders. *Index to maps of the American Revolution in books and periodicals illustrating the Revolutionary War and other events of the period 1763–1789,* DB87

Clark, Edward. *Black writers in New England,* BE516

Clark, George. *Oxford history of England,* DC296

Clark, George Lindenberg. *The encyclopedia of microscopy,* EG19

Clark, Gladys L. H. *Dublin stage, 1720–1745,* BH101

Clark, Gregory R. *Words of the Vietnam War,* AC121, DE279

Clark, J. Bunker. *American operas,* BJ234

Clark, Jeffrey. *North American Indian language materials, 1890–1965,* BD240

Clark, John Desmond. *Atlas of African prehistory,* DD64

Clark, John Owen Edward. *Word perfect,* AC68

Clark, Judith Freeman. *Almanac of American women in the 20th century,* CC573

—— *The encyclopedia of child abuse,* CC158

Clark, Mary Virginia. *Medical reference works, 1679–1966,* EH2

Clark, P. F. *A dictionary of ecology, evolution and systematics,* EG65, EG75

Clark, Randall. *American screenwriters,* BH280

Clark, Robin E. *The encyclopedia of child abuse,* CC158

Clark, Suzanne M. *Cartographic citations,* CL263

Clark, Sydney P. *Handbook of physical constants,* EF96

Clark, Thomas Dionysius. *Travels in the new South,* DB108, DB155

—— *Travels in the old South,* DB108, DB155

Clark, Thomas L. *The dictionary of gambling & gaming,* BK136

Clark, Virginia. *Books for college libraries,* AA335

Clark, William S. *A field guide to hawks,* EG256

Clarke, David E. *German Africa,* DD80

Clarke, Ignatius Frederick. *Tale of the future,* BE282

Clarke, Jack A. *Modern French literature and language,* BD158, BE1134

Clarke, John I. *Sierra Leone in maps,* CL342

Clarke, Joseph F. *Pseudonyms,* AA148

Clarke, Mary. *The encyclopedia of dance & ballet,* BH141

Clarke, Prescott. *A research guide to China-coast newspapers, 1822–1911,* AE86

Clarke, Roger A. *Soviet economic facts, 1917–81,* CH181

Clarkson, Kenneth W. *Economics sourcebook of government statistics,* CH171

Clase, Pablo. *50 biografías de figuras dominicanas,* AH154

Clason, W. E. *Dictionary of pure and applied physics,* ED25

—— *Elsevier's dictionary of cinema, sound, and music, in six languages,* BH257

—— *Elsevier's lexicon of international and national units,* AL198

Clasper, James W. *Guide to the holdings of the American Jewish Archives,* BC538

Class/brand $, CH576

Classed subject catalog, Engineering Societies Library, EK4, EK5

Classen, Lynda Corey. *Finder's guide to prints and drawings in the Smithsonian Institution,* BF365

Classic books, American Agricultural Economics Association, EJ6

Classic mineral localities of the world, Scalisi, Philip, EF205

Classic myths in English literature and in art, Gayley, Charles Mills, CF25

Classical and foreign quotations, King, William Francis Henry, BE93

Classical and medieval literature criticism, BE46

Classical catalogue, BJ387

Classical Chinese fiction, Yang, Winston L. Y., BE1562

Classical dictionary, Room, Adrian, CF29

A classical dictionary of Hindu mythology and religion, geography, history, and literature, Dowson, John, BC486

Classical drama, BE1016, BE1017

The classical epic, Sienkewicz, Thomas J., BE1006

Classical geography, CL104

Classical Greek and Roman drama, Forman, Robert J., BE995

Classical hand-list, Nairn, John Arbuthnot, BE1004

Classical literature, BE716
   bibliography, BE990, BE991, BE992, BE995, BE997, BE998, BE1001, BE1003, BE1004, BE1005, BE1006, BE1007, DA93
   biography, BE1025
   collections, BE1002
   criticism, BE46, BE996, BE1012
      bibliography, BE29
   dictionaries, BE1026
      abbreviations, BE1019
   encyclopedias, BE1014, BE1015, DA104
   handbooks, BE1014, BE1015
   library catalogs, BE998
   library resources, BE1008
   periodicals
      bibliography, BE1008
   reviews of research, BE994
   surveys, BE1003
   translations, BE1002, BE1010, BE1011, BE1028

Classical literature (by subject)
   drama
      handbooks, BE1016, BE1017
   history, BE1020, BE1022

Classical music
   bibliography, BJ231
   discography, BJ377, BJ378
      bibliography, BJ384

Classical music, 1925–1975, Gibson, Gerald D., BJ383

—— Gray, Michael H., BJ383

Classical music discographies, 1976–1988, Gray, Michael H., BJ383

Classical mythology, Peradotto, John Joseph, CF20

Classical mythology, Crowell's handbook of, CF25

Classical philology
   bibliography, BE998, BE1003
   biography, BE1023
   library catalogs, BE998

Classical scholarship, BE1024, DA113

—— Halton, Thomas P., BE997, DA93

Classical sculpture, Hanfmann, George M. A., BF393

Classical studies
   atlases, DA116, DA117, DA118, DA119, DA120
   bibliography, BE991, BE997, BE998, BE1001, BE1004, DA92, DA93, DA94, DA95
      current, DA96
   biography, BE1023, BE1024, DA113, DA114, DA115
   chronologies, DA110, DA111, DA112
   dictionaries
      abbreviations, BE1019
   dissertations, BE1009, DA97
   encyclopedias, DA98, DA99, DA100, DA101, DA103, DA104, DA105
   general histories, BE1021, DA107
   guides, DA91

   handbooks, DA102, DA106, DA108, DA109
   library catalogs, BE998
   reviews of research, BE994

Classical studies (by subject)
   art, BF71, BF391
   history, BE1022
   war, CJ580

Classical studies, Harvard University. Library, BE998

The Classical world, BE1027, BE1038

The Classical world bibliography of Greek drama and poetry, BE1027, BE1038

The Classical world bibliography of Roman drama and poetry and ancient fiction, BE1027, BE1038

Classicial Association (Great Britain). Council. *The year's work in classical studies,* BE1007

The classics in translation, Smith, F. Seymour, BE1011

Classification
   bibliography, AK201
   schedules, AK198, AK199, AK200, AK202, AK204, AK205

Classification, Library of Congress. Subject Cataloging Division, AK202

Classification and index of the world's languages, Voegelin, Charles, BD16

—— Voegelin, Florence, BD16

A classification of educational subject matter, Chismore, W. Dale, CB111

A classification of igneous rocks and glossary of terms, International Union of Geological Sciences. Subcommission on the Systematics of Igneous Rocks, EF255

A classification of institutions of higher education, CB232

Classified and annotated bibliography of Sir William Osler's publications, Abbott, Maude E., EH209

A classified bibliography of lexical and grammatical studies on the language of the Septuagint, Tov, Emanuel, BD140

Classified bibliography of linguistic dissertations on Indian languages, Sakuntala Sharma, J., BD225

Classified bibliography of literature on the Acts of the Apostles, Mattill, Andrew J., BC122

—— Mattill, Mary B., BC122

Classified bibliography of the finds in the desert of Judah, Jongeling, Bastiaan, BC112

A classified bibliography of the periodical literature of the trans-Mississippi West (1811-1957), Winther, Oscar Osburn, DB169

Classified catalog of the ecumenical movement, World Council of Churches. Library, BC273

The classified catalogue of the Sudan collection in the University of Khartoum Library, DD227

The classified directory of artists' signatures, symbols & monograms, Caplan, H. H., BF158

Classified state bibliography of linguistic research on Indian languages, Geetha, K. R., BD224

Clauser, Henry R. *Materials handbook,* EK272

Clauss, Carl. *Die Monogrammisten und diejenigen bekannten und unbekannten Künstler aller Schulen,* BF160

Clauss, Francis Jacob. *Engineer's guide to high-temperature materials,* EK273

Claussen, Bruno. *Niederdeutsche bibliographie,* AA637

Claussen, Martin Paul. *Descriptive catalog of maps published by Congress,* CL229

Clavis apocryphorum Novi Testamenti, Geerard, Maurice, BC107

Clavis mediaevalis, Meyer, Otto, DA151

Clavis Patrum Graecorum, Geerard, Maurice, BC297

Clavis patrum latinorum, Dekkers, Eligius, BC296

Clavis scriptorum Graecorum at Latinorum, LaRue, Rodrigue, BD147

Clavreuil, Gérard. *Littératures nationales d'écriture française,* BE1517

Claxton, J. H. *Serial bibliographies for medieval studies,* DA137

Clayman, Charles B. *The American Medical Association encyclopedia of medicine,* EH80

Clayton, Henry Helms. *World weather records*, EF168

Clayton, Michael. *The collector's dictionary of the silver and gold of Great Britain and North America*, BG136

Clayton, Thompson. *A handbook of wrestling terms and holds*, BK106

CLC, BE47

Cleare, John. *The world guide to mountains and mountaineering*, BK118

Clearinghouse on Child Abuse and Neglect Information. *Child abuse and neglect and family violence*, CC156

——— *Child abuse and neglect and family violence thesaurus*, CC161

Clearinghouse on Family Violence Information. *Child abuse and neglect and family violence thesaurus*, CC161

Cleary, James W. *Rhetoric and public address*, BE349

Cleasby, Richard. *An Icelandic-English dictionary*, AC503, AC509

Cleeve, Brian Talbot. *A biographical dictionary of Irish writers*, BE799

——— *Dictionary of Irish writers*, BE799

Cleevely, R. J. *World palaeontological collections*, EF244

Clegg, H. A. *World medical periodicals*, EH40

Clem, Ralph S. *Research guide to the Russian and Soviet censuses*, CG302

Clément, Joseph R. A. M. *Essai de bibliographie du Ruanda-Urundi*, DD135

——— *Essai de bibliographie Ruanda-Urundi*, AA871

Clement, Joseph R.A.M. *Essai de bibliographie du Ruanda-Urundi*, DD198

Clement, Russell T. *Mormons in the Pacific*, BC370

——— *Who's who in Oceania, 1980–1981*, AH385

Clemente, Mark N. *The marketing glossary*, CH580

Clements, Frank A. *Arab regional organizations*, AF19

——— *Kuwait*, DE220

——— *Oman*, DE237

——— *Saudi Arabia*, DE252

——— *United Arab Emirates*, DE270

Clements, John. *Clements' encyclopedia of world government*, CJ94

——— *Encyclopedia of world government*, CJ94

——— *Taylor's encyclopedia of government officials, federal and state*, CJ133

Clements, Patricia. *The feminist companion to literature in English*, BE607

Clements, William M. *Native American folklore, 1879–1979*, CF62

Clements' encyclopedia of world government, Clements, John, CJ94

Clendenning, Philip. *Eighteenth century Russia*, DC574

Clennett, Margaret A. *Keyguide to information sources in dentistry*, EH243

Clerical directory, BC334

Clerical directory of the Protestant Episcopal church in the United States of America, BC344

Cleveland, Ana D. *Introduction to indexing and abstracting*, AK212

Cleveland, Donald B. *Introduction to indexing and abstracting*, AK212

Clewis, Beth. *The gardener's index*, EJ229

——— *Index to illustrations of animals and plants*, EA220, EG73

Clifford, Anne. *Reference and online services handbook*, AK236

Clifford, Denis. *A legal guide for lesbian and gay couples*, CC288

Clifford Vaughan, F. *Glossary of economics, including Soviet terminology*, CH65

Clifford Vaughan, Michalina. *Glossary of economics, including Soviet terminology*, CH65

Clifton, Merritt. *Those who were there*, DE100

Climate Analysis Center. *Daily weather maps*, EF169

Climate normals for the U.S. (base: 1951–80), EF157

Climates of the states, EF158

Climatic atlas of the United States, Visher, Stephen Sargent, EF170

Climatological data, EF159, EF160

Climatology, EF167
  bibliography, EF162
  charts, diagrams, etc., EF164
  compendiums, EF163, EF164
  encyclopedias, EF144
  statistics, EF168
  tables, EF166

Climatology (by country or region)
  North America, EF161
  United States, EF157, EF159, EF160
    atlases, EF170
    compendiums, EF156
    maps, EF169
    states, EF158

Clinch, Peter. *Using a law library*, CK218

Cline, Cheryl. *Women's diaries, journals, and letters*, BE508, BE725

Cline, David. *Dictionary of visual science*, EH113

Cline, Gloria Stark. *Index to criticisms of British and American poetry*, BE710

Cline, Marjorie W. *Scholar's guide to intelligence literature*, CJ538

Cline, Ruth K. J. *Focus on families*, CC236

Clinical guide to laboratory tests, EH174

Clinical psychology, CD106, EH395
  dictionaries, CD102
  encyclopedias, CD99, CD100, EH378
  handbooks, CD103, CD104

The clinical psychology handbook, CD103

Clinical sociology, CC6, CC25, EH11

Clinical toxicology of commercial products, Gosselin, Robert E., EH424

The clinician's handbook, Meyer, Robert G., CD106

CLIO, AA730

Clissold, Peter. *A dictionary of sea terms*, EC81

Cliver, Dean O. *Foodborne diseases*, EJ167

Cloak and dagger fiction, Smith, Myron J., BE271

The clockmakers' library, Worshipful Company of Clockmakers (London), BG81

Clocks and watches, BG86
  bibliography, BG80
  biography, BG88
  dictionaries
    multilingual, BG82
    library catalogs, BG81
    United States, BG84, BG89

Clocks and watches (by subject)
  history, BG85, BG87

Clocks and watches, Baillie, Granville Hugh, BG80

——— Clutton, Cecil, BG81

——— Daniels, George, BG81

——— Worshipful Company of Clockmakers (London), BG81

Clocks and watches, 1400–1900, Bruton, Eric, BG86

Clodfelter, Micheal. *Warfare and armed conflicts*, CJ568

Clogg, Mary Jo. *Greece*, DC371

Clogg, Richard. *Greece*, DC371

Cloonan, Michele. *Collection conservation*, AK238

Clough, Eric A. *A short-title catalogue arranged geographically of books printed and distributed by printers, publishers and booksellers in the English provincial towns and in Scotland and Ireland up to and including the year 1700*, AA678

Clough, Francis F. *The world's encyclopaedia of recorded music*, BJ375

Clubb, Jerome M. *Political facts of the United States since 1789*, CJ148, DB53

Clubb, Louise George. *Italian plays (1500–1700) in the Folger Library*, BE1314

Clubbe, John. *The English romantic poets*, BE702, BE984

Clute, John. *The encyclopedia of science fiction*, BE286

——— *Science fiction encyclopedia*, BE286

Clutton, Cecil. *Britten's old clocks and watches and their makers*, BG85

——— *Clocks and watches*, BG81

CMCI, EB21, EK160

CMIT, EH96

CMLC, BE46

Coal abstracts, EK215

Coan, Otis Welton. *America in fiction*, BE470

Coast and Geodetic Survey. *Definitions of terms used in geodetic and other surveys*, EF122

Coastal and maritime archaeology, Kerber, Jordan E., DA66

Coasts, EF4

Coates, Donald Robert. *The Facts on File dictionary of geology and geophysics*, EF75

Coatsworth, Patricia A. *Annotated bibliography and index covering CPL bibliographies*, BF271

——— *Directory of planning and urban affairs libraries in the United States and Canada, 1990*, BF281

Cobb, David A. *Guide to U.S. map resources*, CL256

Cobb, Richard Charles. *French Revolution documents*, DC189

Cobb, Sidney. *Measures for psychological assessment*, CD67

Cobbett, Walter Wilson. *Cyclopedic survey of chamber music*, BJ270

Cobbett, William. *Parliamentary history of England from the earliest period to the year 1803*, AF208

Coblans, Herbert. *Use of physics literature*, ED1

Cobos de Belchite, *Barón* de. *Índice nobiliario español*, AJ140

Cocaine, EH320

Cochran, Doris Mabel. *The new field book of reptiles and amphibians*, EG245

Cochran, Moncrieff. *International handbook of child care policies and programs*, CC170

Cochrane, John. *Union list of higher degree theses of the unversities of New Zealand*, AG60

Cockfield, W. E. *Index to reports of Geological Survey of Canada from 1927–50*, EF31

Cockton, Peter. *Subject catalogue of the House of Commons Parliamentary papers, 1801–1900*, AF194

Cockx, A. *Catalogue collectif belge et luxembourgeois des périodiques étrangers en cours de publication*, AD230

Cockx-Indestege, Elly. *Belgica typographica, 1541–1600*, AA578

Cocozzoli, Gary. *German-American history and life*, CC324

Code name directory, CJ586

Code name directory, US, CJ586

Code of Alabama, 1975, Alabama. [Laws, etc.], CK179

The code of canon law, CK238

Code of canon law in English translation, CK238

Code of federal regulations, AF67, CJ136, CK182

Code of laws of South Carolina, 1976, South Carolina. [Laws, etc.], CK179

Code of Virginia, 1950, Virginia. [Laws, etc.], CK179

Codes of professional responsibility, CH85, CK64, CK160, EH175

Codes of professional standards, Public Relations Society of America, CH565

Codices latini antiquiores, AA201

Codification of presidential proclamations and executive orders, United States. President, AF134

Codlin, Ellen M. *Aslib directory of information sources in the United Kingdom*, AK141

Cody, Sue A. *Political science*, CJ4

Coe, Ada May. *Catálogo bibliográfico y crítico de las comedias anunciadas en los periódicos de Madrid desde 1661 hasta 1819*, BE1462

Coelho, Jacinto do Prado. *Dicionário de literatura*, BE1363

Coenen, Lothar. *The new international dictionary of New Testament theology*, BC148

Coetzee, J. C. *South African newspapers on microfilm*, AE80

Coetzer, P. W. *Bibliographies on South African political history*, CJ410, DD213

Coffey, David J. *The international encyclopedia of cats*, EJ139

Coffin, Tristram Potter. *The British traditional ballad in North America*, BE630

—— *The folklore of American holidays*, AL144

Coffman, Jerry L. *Earthquake history of the United States*, EF262

—— *Seismicity of the United States, 1568–1989 (revised)*, EF262

Cofrestri plwyf Cymru = Parish registers of Wales, Williams, C. J., AJ130

Cogar, William B. *Dictionary of admirals of the U.S. Navy*, CJ639

Coger, Dalvan M. *Semper ex Africa*, DD84

Coggins, John. *Political parties of the Americas and the Caribbean*, CJ97

Coggins, R. J. *A dictionary of Biblical interpretation*, BC127

Cognition and intelligence, CD114
  handbooks, CD113

Cohen, Aaron I. *International discography of women composers*, BJ376

—— *International encyclopedia of women composers*, BJ208

Cohen, Arthur A. *Handbook of Christian theology*, BC252

Cohen, Arthur M. *Key resources on community colleges*, CB224

Cohen, Barbara E. *America's homeless*, CC200

Cohen, Chester G. *Shtetl finder*, CL127

Cohen, Hennig. *The folklore of American holidays*, AL144

Cohen, J. M. *The new Penguin dictionary of quotations*, BE110

—— *Penguin dictionary of quotations*, BE110

Cohen, Jeffrey J. *Handbook of school-based interventions*, CB212

Cohen, M. J. *The new Penguin dictionary of quotations*, BE110

—— *Penguin dictionary of quotations*, BE110

Cohen, Marcel. *Dictionaire du français vivant*, AC327

—— *Langues du monde*, BD12

Cohen, Morris L. *Finding the law*, CK115

—— *How to find the law*, CK115, CK122

—— *Legal research in a nutshell*, CK115

Cohen, Myron L. *Asia, case studies in the social sciences*, CA53

Cohen, Nathan M. *Library science dissertations, 1925–60*, AK26

Cohen, Norman S. *The American presidents*, CJ167

Cohen, Paul R. *The handbook of artificial intelligence*, EK204

Cohen, Richard M. *Sports encyclopedia*, BK48, BK58, BK65

Cohen, Ronald. *A handbook of method in cultural anthropology*, CE60

Cohen, Selma Jeanne. *Dictionary of modern ballet*, BH140

Cohen, Sidney. *The encyclopedia of drug abuse*, CC124

Cohen, Susan Sarah. *Antisemitism*, BC508

Cohen, Yitshak Yosef. *Jewish publications in the Soviet Union, 1917–1960*, BC535

Cohen-Stratyner, Barbara N. *Biographical dictionary of dance*, BH158

—— *Popular music, 1900–1919*, BJ333

Cohen Stuart, Bertie A. *Women in the Caribbean*, DB404

Cohn, Arthur. *Recorded classical music*, BJ377

Cohn-Sherbok, Dan. *The Blackwell dictionary of Judaica*, BC553

The coin atlas, Cribb, Joe, BG182

Coins, BG185

Coins and medals, Grierson, Philip, BG172

Coins, medals, currency, BG189
  auction records, BG172, BG177
  bibliography, BF194, BG170, BG172, BG173, BG176
    current, BG175
  biography, BG186
  catalogs, BG187, BG188, BG191, BG192
  dictionaries, BG178, BG180, BG181
    multilingual, BG179
  encyclopedias, BG178
  handbooks, BG182, BG183, BG184, CH285
  Latin inscriptions, BG183

  library catalogs, BG177
  periodicals, BG175
Coins, medals, currency (by country or region)
  Asia, East, BG171
  Great Britain
    catalogs, BG190
  Islamic states, BG174
  United States
    catalogs, BG194, BG195, BG196, BG197
    encyclopedias, BG193
Coins, medals, currency (by subject)
  history, BG185

Coins of England and the United Kingdom, Purvey, P. Frank, BG190

Cokayne, George Edward. *Complete baronetage*, AJ118

—— *The complete peerage*, AJ117

Colaianni, Lois Ann. *Handbook of medical library practice*, EH4

Colas, René. *Bibliographie générale du costume et de la mode*, BG91

Colbeck, Marjorie. *A bibliography of Canadiana*, DB188

Colby, Anita Y. *Dictionary of educational acronyms, abbreviations, and initialisms*, CB78

Colby, Robert W. *The encyclopedia of technical market indicators*, CH300

Colby, Vineta. *European authors, 1000–1900*, BE204

—— *World authors, 1975–1980*, BE205

—— *World authors, 1980–1985*, BE205

•*COLD*, DG2

•*Cold regions data base*, DG2

Cold War, CJ7

Coldham, Geraldine Elizabeth. *Bibliography of Scriptures in African languages*, BC95, BC99

Coldham, Peter Wilson. *Bonded passengers to America*, AJ61

—— *The complete book of emigrants*, AJ60

—— *The complete book of emigrants in bondage, 1614–1775*, AJ61

—— *English convicts in colonial America*, AJ61

Cole, Garold. *American travelers to Mexico, 1821–1972*, DB221

—— *Civil War eyewitnesses*, DB107

—— *Travels in America from the voyages of discovery to the present*, DB11

Cole, George Watson. *Catalogue of books relating to the discovery and early history of North and South America*, DB2

Cole, Maud D. *Checklist of additions to Evans' American bibliography in the Rare Book Division of the New York Public Library*, AA408

Cole, Sylvia. *Facts on File dictionary of classical, biblical, and literary allusions*, BE86

—— *Facts on File dictionary of twentieth-century allusions*, BE86

Cole, Trevor. *The American Horticultural Society encyclopedia of gardening*, EJ232

Cole, W. Owen. *A popular dictionary of Sikhism*, BC572

Cole, William A. *Chemical literature, 1700–1860*, EE11

The Cole Library of early medicine and zoology, University of Reading. Library, EH53

Colección Atlas cultural, DB248

Coleccíon de índices de publicaciones periódicas, AD327

Colee, C. M. *Union list of Victorian serials*, AD222

Coleman, Arthur. *Drama criticism*, BE221

—— *Epic and romance criticism*, BE336

Coleman, David. *Pollution research index*, EK76

Coleman, Earle Jerome. *Magic*, CF39

Coleman, James R. *Public administration desk book*, CJ460

Coleman, Kathleen. *Guide to French poetry explication*, BE1192

Coleman, Marion Moore. *Polish literature in English translation*, BE1348

Coleman, Rex. *An index to Japanese law*, CK232

Coles, Catherine M. *Nigerian women in development*, CC598, DD191

Coletta, Paolo Enrico. *United States Navy and Marine Corps bases, domestic*, CJ626

Colin, Jean-Paul. *Dictionnaire de l'argot*, AC355

—— *Dictionnaire des difficultés du français*, AC365

Colindres O., Ramiro. *Enciclopedia histórica de Honduras*, DB311

Colket, M. D. *Guide to genealogical records in the National Archives*, AJ15

Coll, Edna. *Indice informativo de la novela hispanoamericana*, BE902

Collaer, Paul. *Historical atlas of music*, BJ198

Collar, N. J. *Threatened birds of Africa and related islands*, EG278

—— *Threatened birds of the Americas*, EG278

Collard, Auguste. *L'astronomie et les astronomes*, EC6

Collazo, Javier L. *Encyclopedic dictionary of technical terms*, EA132

Collea, Beth A. *A selected bibliography on Native American astronomy*, EC7

Collected editions, historical sets, and monuments of music, Hill, George R., BJ58

—— Stephens, Norris L., BJ58

Collecting American pewter, Ebert, Katherine, BG151

Collecting miniatures, Foskett, Daphne, BF303

Collectio bibliographica operum ad ius romanum pertinentium, Caes, Lucien, BE1037

Collection conservation, Cloonan, Michele, AK238

—— DeCandido, Robert, AK238

Collection maintenance and improvement, Byrne, Sherry, AK238

Collection of Chinese proverbs, Scarborough, William, BE160

Collection of exhibition catalogs, Archives of American Art, BF118

Collections toward a bibliography of Congregationalism, BC383

Collective biography of Spanish America, AH113

Collective nouns and group terms, AC85

Collectors Club (New York, N.Y.). Library. *Philately*, BG200

The collector's complete dictionary of American antiques, Phipps, Frances, BG39

The collector's dictionary of the silver and gold of Great Britain and North America, Clayton, Michael, BG136

Collector's encyclopedia, BG40

The collectors' encyclopedia of antiques, Phillips, Phoebe, BG38

A collector's guide to minerals and gemstones, Bögel, Hellmuth, EF191

Collectors' guide to nineteenth-century photographs, Welling, William, BF352

Collector's guide to the American musical theatre, Hummel, David, BJ258

Collector's handbook of marks and monograms on pottery and porcelain, Chaffers, William, BG77

College admissions, Sparks, Linda, CB230

College Art Association of America. *Index of twentieth century artists*, BF156

—— *Répertoire international de la littérature de l'art*, BF34

College blue book, CB258

The college blue book : occupational education, CB297

The college blue book : scholarships, fellowships, grants, and loans, CB393

College chemistry faculties, EE57

The college cost book, College Entrance Examination Board. College Scholarship Service, CB259, CB375

College degrees by mail, Bear, John, CB252

College English Association. *Good reading*, AA326

College Entrance Examination Board. *Annual survey of colleges*, CB334

—— *College explorer*, CB260

—— *The college handbook*, CB261

—— *The college handbook for transfer students*, CB262

—— *The college handbook. Foreign student supplement*, CB316

—— *Index of majors and graduate degrees,* CB273

College Entrance Examination Board. College Scholarship Service. *The college cost book,* CB259, CB375

•*College explorer,* CB260

College financing guide, CB376

The college football bibliography, BK75

College football encyclopedia, Ours, Robert M., BK78

College football records, Baldwin, Robert, BK73

College graduates
  biography, AH61, AH70

College guide for the learning disabled, CB314

The college handbook, CB261, CB316

The college handbook for transfer students, CB262

The college handbook. Foreign student supplement, CB316

College majors, Lederman, Ellen, CB275

The college media directory, CB263

College money handbook, CB386

College Music Society. *First performances in America to 1900,* BJ175

College presidency, 1900–1960, Eells, Walter C., CB228

—— Hollis, Ernest V., CB228

College Research Group of Concord, Massachusetts. *300 most selective colleges,* CB245

—— *The right college,* CB289

College student personnel abstracts, CB234

College students
  directories, CB332
  publications, CB263
  statistics, CB333
  travel and tourism, CB93

College students (by subject)
  political activity, CB217, CB326

The college student's guide to transferring schools, Wilcha, Jennifer, CB294

College teachers *see* **Universities and colleges (by subject)—faculty**

Colleges *see* **Universities and colleges**

Collegiate dictionary of zoology, Pennak, Robert William, EG230

Collegium Carolinum (Munich, Germany). *Biographisches Lexikon zur Geschichte der böhmischen Länder,* AH181

Collelo, Thomas. *Angola,* DD62

—— *Chad,* DD62

Colles, Dorothy. *Christian symbols, ancient & modern,* BF182

Collier, James. *Literature relating to New Zealand,* AA946, DF42

Collier, Simon. *The Cambridge encyclopedia of Latin America and the Caribbean,* DB281

Collier's encyclopedia, AB5

Collijn, Isak. *Sveriges bibliografi, 1600-talet,* AA828

—— *Sveriges bibliografi intill år 1600,* AA828

Collinder, Bjorn. *Fenno-Ugric vocabulary,* AC326

Collinge, J. M. *Office-holders in modern Britain,* CJ344

Collinge, N. E. *An encyclopaedia of language,* BD33

Collins, Bud. *Bud Collins' modern encyclopedia of tennis,* BK101

Collins, David Norman. *Siberia and the Soviet Far East,* DC603

Collins, Emily C. *Handbook of instructional resources and references for teaching the gifted,* CB186

Collins, Henry Hill. *Harper & Row's complete field guide to North American wildlife,* EG82

Collins, James T. *An Indonesian-English dictionary,* AC517

Collins, Martin. *The history of geophysics and meteorology,* EF97

Collins, Mary. *The new dictionary of theology,* BC407

Collins, Mary Ellen. *Education journals and serials,* CB21

Collins, Mike J. *Astronomical catalogues, 1951–75,* EC8

Collins, N. Mark. *The IUCN invertebrate red data book,* EG234

Collins, P. M. *Carbohydrates,* EE116

Collins, Pamela. *Contemporary composers,* BJ209

Collins atlas of twentieth century world history, Dockrill, Michael L., DA189

Collins concise Spanish-English, English-Spanish dictionary, AC731, AC738

Collins dictionary of archaeology, DA76

The Collins dictionary of Canadian history, Bercuson, David Jay, DB197

Collins dictionary of economics, CH62

Collins dictionary of the English language, AC37

Collins encyclopedia of antiques, BG40

Collins English dictionary, AC37

Collins German-English, English-German dictionary, AC415

Collins guide to mushrooms and toadstools, Lange, Morten, EG187

The Collins guide to the rare mammals of the world, Burton, John A., EG289

Collins-Robert French-English, English-French dictionary, AC335

Collins Robert French-English, English-French dictionary, unabridged, AC336

Collins Spanish-English, English-Spanish dictionary, AC730, AC731

—— Smith, Colin, AC738

Collison, Mary. *Dictionary of foreign quotations,* BE91

Collison, Robert L. *Bibliographic services throughout the world,* AA16

—— *Kenya,* DD18

—— *Uganda,* DD18

Collison, Robert Lewis. *Dictionaries of English and foreign languages,* AC1

—— *Dictionary of foreign quotations,* BE91

—— *Hamlyn dictionary of dates and anniversaries,* AL143, DA34

—— *Newnes dictionary of dates,* AL143

Colloids, EE45

Collotti, Enzo. *Die Kommunistische Partei Deutschlands, 1918–1933,* CJ498

Colombia, DB365
  atlases, CL317
  bibliography, AA523, AA525, AA526, DB363, DB364, DB366
    current, AA527
  bibliography of bibliography, AA29
  biobibliography, AA524
  biography, AH133, AH134
  gazetteers, CL123
  government publications, AF159
  periodicals, AD73
  statistics, CG149, CG150, CG151

Colombia (by subject)
  history, DB367, DB368
  statistics, CG151

Colombia. Departamento Administrativo Nacional de Estadística. *Anuario general de estadística.* CG149

Colombia. Departamento Administrativo Nacional de Estadística. *Estadísticas históricas,* CG151

Colombia, Davis, Robert H., DB365

Colombia estadística, CG150

Colombian literature, BE943, BE944, BE947, BE949
  bibliography, BE945, BE946, BE948
  guides, BE946

Colombo, John Robert. *Canadian literary landmarks,* BE829

—— *Colombo's Canadian quotations,* BE102

—— *New Canadian quotations,* BE102

Colombo's Canadian quotations, Colombo, John Robert, BE102

Colonelli, Cristina Argenton. *Bibliografia do folclore brasileiro,* CF63

Colonial and Revolutionary posts, BG202

Colonial Brazil, DB291

Colonial British Caribbean newspapers, Pactor, Howard S., AE41

Colonial clergy and the colonial churches of New England, Weis, Frederick Lewis, BC255

Colonial clergy of Maryland, Delaware and Georgia, Weis, Frederick Lewis, BC255

Colonial clergy of the Middle Colonies, Weis, Frederick Lewis, BC255

Colonial clergy of Virginia, North Carolina, and South Carolina, Weis, Frederick Lewis, BC255

Colonial governors from the fifteenth century to the present, Henige, David P., CJ85

Colonial Latin America, DB291

Colonial Spanish America, DB291

Colonialism in Africa, 1870–1960, Duignan, Peter, DD82

Colonnese, Tom. *American Indian novelists,* BE550

Color, BF125, ED58, ED59, ED60, ED61, ED62, ED63, ED64

Color, Kelly, Kenneth L., ED60

The color compendium, Hope, Augustine, BF125, ED59

The color dictionary of flowers and plants for home and garden, Hay, Roy, EG175

Color encyclopedia of gemstones, Arem, Joel E., EF190

Color science, Wyszecki, Günter, ED64

Color standards and color nomenclature, Ridgway, Robert, ED62

Color theory, Baum, David W., BF125, ED59

—— Buckley, Mary L., BF125, ED59

Color-universal language and dictionary of names, Kelly, Kenneth L., ED60

Colorado. [Laws, etc.]. *West's Colorado revised statutes annotated,* CK179

Colored minorities in Great Britain, Madan, Raj, CC326

A colour atlas of livestock breeds, Sambraus, Hans Hinrich, EJ137

Colour index, Society of Dyers and Colourists, ED63

Coloured minorities in Britain, Sivanandan, Ambalavaner, CC326

Columbia dictionary of European political history since 1914, DC20

Columbia dictionary of modern European literature, BE60

The Columbia dictionary of political biography, CJ65

Columbia dictionary of quotations, AB27

—— Andrews, Robert, BE97

The Columbia encyclopedia, AB6, AB7

The Columbia encyclopedia of nutrition, EH296

Columbia Granger's dictionary to poetry quotations, Hazen, Edith P., BE315

Columbia Granger's guide to poetry anthologies, Crain, Esther, BE315

—— Katz, Linda Sternberg, BE315

—— Katz, William, BE315

Columbia Granger's index to poetry, BE314, BE316, BE317, BE319, BE827, BJ289

—— Hazen, Edith P., BE315

•*Columbia Granger's world of poetry on CD-ROM,* BE315

The Columbia history of American poetry, BE503

The Columbia history of British poetry, BE717

The Columbia history of the American novel, BE485

Columbia law review, CK66

Columbia Lippincott gazetteer of the world, CL85, CL96

Columbia literary history of the United States, BE439, BE554

Columbia University. Avery Architectural and Fine Arts Library. *Avery index to architectural periodicals,* BF209

—— *Avery obituary index of architects,* BF258

—— *Catalog of the Avery Memorial Architectural Library of Columbia University,* BF228

Columbia University. Bureau of Applied Social Research. *Guide to the Bureau of Applied Social Research,* CA12

Columbia University. Center for International Business Cycle Research. *International economic indicators,* CH109

Columbia University. Center for Population and Family Health. *International encyclopedia of population,* CG19

Columbia University. Committee on Oriental Studies. *A guide to Oriental classics,* BE1543

Columbia University. Getty Art History Information Program. *Avery index to architectural periodicals*, BF209

Columbia University. Institute of Human Nutrition. *The Columbia encyclopedia of nutrition*, EH296

Columbia University. Legislative Drafting Research Fund. *Constitutions of the United States, national and state*, CK170

Columbia University. Libraries. *A catalogue of the Epstean collection on the history and science of photography and its applications especially to the graphic arts*, BF336

—— *The history of printing from its beginnings to 1930*, AA299

Columbia University. Libraries. Psychology Library. *Author index to Psychological index, 1894–1935, and Psychological abstracts, 1927–1958*, CD18

Columbia University. Rare Book and Manuscript Library. *Russia in the twentieth century*, DC558

Columbia University. Teachers College. *The world year book of education*, CB129

Columbia University. Teachers College. Library. *Dictionary catalog of the Teachers College Library*, CB6, CB9

Columbia University Press. *Columbia Lippincott gazetteer of the world*, CL85

Columbus Memorial Library. *The Aztecs*, CC477

—— *The Incas*, CC478

—— *Pan American book shelf*, AA471

Columbus Memorial Library (Washington, D.C.). *Index to Latin American periodical literature, 1929–1960*, AD295

—— *Índice general de publicaciones periódicas latino-americanas*, AD298

Colvin, Howard Montagu. *Biographical dictionary of British architects, 1600–1840*, BF216, BF259

Colvin, L. G. *Senegal*, DD48

Colwell, Richard. *Handbook of research on music teaching and learning*, CB116

Colwell, Robert N. *Manual of remote sensing*, EF18

Colwell, Stella. *Dictionary of genealogical sources in the Public Record Office*, DC286

Comaromi, John P. *Dewey decimal classification and relative index*, AK200

Comas, Juan. *Bibliografía selectiva de las culturas indígenas de América*, CE78

—— *Historia y bibliografía de los congresos internacionales de ciencias antropológicas, 1865–1954*, CE6

Comben Collection. *Historic books on veterinary science and animal husbandry*, EJ100

Combined membership list of the American Mathematical Society, the Mathematical Association of America, and the Society for Industrial and Applied Mathematics, American Mathematical Society, EB56

The combined new Persian-English and English-Persian dictionary, AC313

Combined retrospective index set to journals in history, 1838–1974, DA4

The combined retrospective index set to journals in political science, 1886–1974, CJ18

Combined retrospective index set to journals in sociology, 1895–1974, CC12

Combined retrospective index to book reviews in humanities journals, 1802–1974, AA369, BA7

Combined retrospective index to book reviews in scholarly journals, 1886–1974, AA369

Combs, Richard E. *Authors*, BE206

—— *Authors: critical & biographical references*, BE197

COMECON data, CH182

COMECON foreign trade data, CH182

Comedians, BH24, BH284

Comedias nuevas escogidos de los mejores ingenios de España, BE1463

Comedias sueltas, BE1459, BE1460, BE1461, BE1471, BE1472

Comedias sueltas in Cambridge University Library, Cambridge University Library, BE1461

The Comédie Française, 1680–1701, Lancaster, Henry Carrington, BE1180

Comédie-Française, 1680 à 1920, Joannidès, A., BE1179

Comédie-Française, 1927–37, Champion, Edouard, BE1179

La Comédie-Française de 1680 à 1900, Joannidès, A., BE1179

Comedy, BH252

Comets, EC52

    bibliography, EC11

Comets, Kronk, Gary W., EC52

Comfort, Philip W. *New Greek-English interlinear New Testament*, BC94

Comic books and strips, CF72, CF76

Comic books and strips, Scott, Randall W., CF72

Comissiong, Barbara. *The English-speaking Caribbean*, AA33

Comitas, Lambros. *Complete Caribbeana*, DB423, DB440

—— *Complete Caribbeana, 1900–1975*, DB404, DB405

Comité Estatal de Estadísticas. *Atlas demográfico de Cuba*, CL320

Comité Français de Sciences Historiques. *Bibliographie annuelle de l'histoire de France du cinquième siècle à 1939*, DC148

Comité Mexicano de Ciencias Históricas. *Catálogo de tesis sobre historia de México*, DB237

Comité national français de géographie. *Atlas de France*, CL327

—— *Bibliographie cartographique internationale*, CL226

Commager, Henry Steele. *Documents of American history*, DB62

Command under sail, Bradford, James C., CJ639

●*Commdisc Telefax worldwide*, CH490

●*Commdisc Telex Teletex worldwide*, CH490

Commedia dell'arte, BE1315

Commedia dell'arte, Heck, Thomas F., BE1315

Commentary of the Lutheran book of worship, Pfatteicher, Philip H., BC358

Commentary on the American prayer book, Hatchett, Marion, BC347

Commentary on the Bible, Peake, Arthur Samuel, BC168

Commentary on the documents of Vatican II, BC435

A commentary on the medical writings of Rudolf Virchow, Rather, L. J., EH207

Commerce

    dictionaries

        bilingual

            Portuguese-English, CH127, CH128

        multilingual, CH429

    directories, CH491

        bibliography, CH83

    guides, CH1

    handbooks, CL67

    handbooks, manuals, etc., CH138

    statistics, CH149

Commerce (by country or region)

    Great Britain

        directories, AL1, CH82, CH381

    London

        directories, AL1, CH381

Commerce Clearing House. *AALL directory and handbook*, CK137

—— *Accounting articles*, CH250

Commerce yearbook, CH152

Commercial atlas and marketing guide, CL304

Commercial catalogs *see* **Trade catalogs**

Commercial law, CK165

    digests and collections, CK68

Commission Internationale d'Histoire Ecclésiastique Comparée. *Bibliographie de la réforme, 1450–1648*, DC27

Commission Internationale d'Histoire Ecclésiastique Comparée. British Sub-Commission. *Bibliography of the Reform, 1450–1648*, DC27

Commission of the European Communities. *Directory of higher education institutions*, CB239

—— *Thesaurus guide*, AK216

Commission on Accreditation of Service Experiences. *A guide to the evaluation of educational experiences in the armed services*, CB361

Commission on Professionals in Science and Technology. *Professional women and minorities*, CH686

Commission on the History of Geographical Thought. *Bibliography of International Geographic Congresses, 1871–1976*, CL15

Commission on the Humanities and Social Sciences. *Guide to research and scholarship in Hungary*, DC389

Commission on the Nomenclature of Inorganic Chemistry. *Nomenclature of inorganic chemistry*, EE112

Committee for a New England Bibliography. *Bibliographies of New England history*, DB152

Committee for the World Atlas of Agriculture. *World atlas of agriculture*, EJ75

Committee on College Reading. *Good reading*, AA326

Committee on Institutional Cooperation. *Women scholars in women's studies*, CC552

Committee on Latin America. *Literature with language, art and music*, AD64

Committees in the U.S. Congress, 1947–1992, Nelson, Garrison, CJ217

Commodities, CH435, CH439

    bibliography, CH431, CH434

    dictionaries, CH437

    guides, CH440

    handbooks, CL67

    markets

        directories, CH216, CH436

    prices, CH430, CH432

    statistics, CH433, CH438, CH441, EJ82

Commodities futures trading, Nicholas, David, CH435

Commodities price locator, Chapman, Karen J., CH430

Commodity futures trading, CH431

Commodity prices, Friedman, Catherine, CH432

Commodity Research Bureau (New York, N.Y.). *The Knight-Ridder CRB commodity yearbook*, CH433, EJ82

Commodity trade statistics, CH157

Commodity trading manual, CH440

Commodity yearbook, CH433, EJ82

Common knowledge, Grote, David, BE81

The common-sense guide to American colleges, CB264

Common stock newspaper abbreviations and trading symbols, Jarrell, Howard R., CH210

Common weeds of the United States, EG181

Commons, John Rogers. *Documentary history of American industrial society*, CH675

—— *History of labour in the United States*, CH675

Commonwealth

    bibliography

        national and trade, AA389, AA390

    newspapers, AE7

Commonwealth (by subject)

    law, CK14

Commonwealth Agricultural Bureaux. *[Abstract journals]*, EJ19

—— *Animal breeding abstracts*, EJ102

—— *CAB abstracts word list*, EJ37

—— *CAB thesaurus*, EJ36

—— *Forestry abstracts*, EJ175

—— *French-English horticultural dictionary*, EJ238

—— *Nutrition abstracts and reviews*, EH295, EJ104

—— *Spanish-English horticultural dictionary*, EJ239

—— *Veterinary subject headings*, EJ117

Commonwealth Archivists' Association. Joint Copyists Standing Committee. *Summary guide to the archive and manuscript collections relevant to the former British colonial territories in the United Kingdom for the Joint Copyists Standing Committee of the Commonwealth Archivists' Association*, DC345

Commonwealth Bureau of Agricultural Economics. *World agricultural economics and rural sociology abstracts*, CH46

Commonwealth Bureau of Nutrition. *Nutrition abstracts and reviews*, EJ104

Commonwealth Bureaux of Nutrition. *Nutrition abstracts and reviews*, EH295

Commonwealth Caribbean legal literature, Newton, Velma, CK200

Commonwealth elections, 1945–1970, Bloomfield, Valerie, CJ371

Commonwealth government directory, CJ447

Commonwealth literature
  bibliography, BE816
  bibliography (by period)
    20th century, BE815
  criticism, BE817
  encyclopedias, BE608
  periodicals
    bibliography, BE818
  women authors
    bibliography, BE750
    biobibliography, BE607

Commonwealth literature, Walsh, William, BE817
Commonwealth literature periodicals, Warwick, Ronald, BE818
Commonwealth national bibliographies, AA389, AA390

Commonwealth National Library (Australia). *APAIS, Australian public affairs information service*, CA23, DF22

Commonwealth National Library (Canberra). Australian Bibliographical Centre. *Australian bibliography and bibliographical services*, AA85

Commonwealth of Australia directory, CJ447

Commonwealth of Independent States
  population, CG202

Commonwealth political facts, Cook, Chris, CJ373
Commonwealth Relations Office year book, CJ341
Commonwealth retrospective national bibliographies, AA389, AA390

Commonwealth Secretariat. *Commonwealth retrospective national bibliographies*, AA390

Commonwealth sources in British official records, DC345

Commonwealth universities yearbook, CB240, CB319

The Commonwealth yearbook, CJ372
Communes, DB138, DB149
Communicable diseases, EH408
Communicating in science, Booth, Vernon, EA157
Communication
  bibliography, BD84, CC495
  dictionaries, CH486, CH488
  directories, CH491
  encyclopedias, CH482
  guides, AE130

Communication (by subject)
  religion, BC224

Communication and the mass media, Block, Eleanor S., AE130

The communication handbook, DeVito, Joseph A., CH486

Communications standard dictionary, Weik, Martin H., EK149

Communicative disorders, EH122

Communism and anti-communism in the United States, Haynes, John Earl, CJ502

Communism and Christianity, BC213, DC31

Communism and socialism
  atlases, CJ525
  bibliography, CH634, CJ497, CJ499, CJ501, CJ503, CJ510, CJ511, CJ513, CJ514, CJ517
  biography, CJ531, CJ532, CJ533
  dictionaries, CJ523
  encyclopedias, CJ519, CJ521, CJ522, DB129
  handbooks, CJ525, CJ526
  periodicals, CH657
    indexes, CJ516
  quotations, CJ524
  yearbooks, CJ530

Communism and socialism (by country or region)
  Brazil, DB342
  Canada, CJ515
  China, CJ429
  Germany, CJ498
  India, CJ508
  Italy, CH628
  Japan, CJ512
  Korea, North, CJ442
  United States, CJ502, CJ507, CJ527
  Vietnam, CJ445

Communism and socialism (by subject)
  history
    handbooks, CJ529

Communism in Latin America, Dennis, M. Wayne, CJ513
—— Lauerhass, Ludwig, CJ513
—— Sable, Martin Howard, CJ513

Communism in the United States, Seidman, Joel Isaac, CJ507
Communism in the world since 1945, CJ499
Communist and Marxist parties of the world, CJ526
Communist bloc and the free world, CJ596
Communist bloc and the western alliances, CJ596
Communist International and its front organizations, Sworakowski, Witold S., CJ503, CJ511

Communist states, CJ528
  bibliography, CJ514
  biography, AH47

Communist states (by subject)
  economic conditions
    statistics, CH182

Communists, AH47

Community and junior colleges
  directories, CB261, CB268, CB272, CB298
  statistics, CB338, CB343

Community and junior colleges (by country or region)
  United States
    directories, CB296

Community college fact book, CB337

Community colleges
  statistics, CB337

Community languages, Horvath, Barbara M., BD83
Community publication advertising source, CH601
Community resource tie line, AL123, CC35
Community resources directory, AL123, CC35
Community, technical, and junior college statistical yearbook, CB338

The Comoro Islands, Newitt, M. D. D., DD142
Comoros, DD142
  bibliography, DD121
  government publications
    bibliography, AF222

Compact Cambridge life sciences, EG14
The compact right college, CB289
•*CompactMATH*, EB31
Companies and their brands, Wood, Donna, CH348
The companion thesaurus to food science and technology abstracts, EJ159
—— Merryweather, Linda, EJ150
A companion to aesthetics, BB27
Companion to animal behaviour, CD120
A companion to Arber, Greg, Walter Wilson, AA670
Companion to Baugh & Cable's History of the English language, Cable, Thomas, BD98
Companion to Chinese history, O'Neill, Hugh B., DE143
A companion to epistemology, BB28
Companion to Gaelic Scotland, Thomson, Derick S., DC363
Companion to Greek studies, Whibley, Leonard, DA108, DA109
A companion to Irish history, DC413
Companion to Irish history, 1603–1921, Newman, P. R., DC408
Companion to Latin studies, Sandys, John Edwin, DA108, DA109

Companion to literary myths, CF3
Companion to local history research, Campbell-Kease, John, DC351
Companion to neo-Latin studies, IJsewijn, Jozef, BE1041
Companion to Russian history, Paxton, John, DC567
A companion to Scottish culture, DC363
Companion to Scottish history, Donnachie, Ian L., DC365
Companion to Scottish literature, Royle, Trevor, BE811
Companion to Shakespeare studies, Granville-Barker, Harley, BE784
—— Harrison, G. B., BE784
Companion to South African English literature, BE1533
Companion to the French Revolution, Paxton, John, DC187
Companion to the history of modern science, EA255
Companion to the Industrial Revolution, Lines, Clifford John, DC336
A companion to the medieval theatre, BE222
The companion to wine, EJ225
Company/brand $, CH576
•*Company intelligence*, CH373
Company of Military Historians. *Military uniforms in America*, CJ634
Comparative & veterinary medicine, Kerker, Ann E., EJ97
Comparative criminology, Beirne, Piers, CK243
Comparative dictionary of Ge'ez (Classical Ethiopic), Leslau, Wolf, AC312
A comparative dictionary of Indo-Aryan languages, Turner, Ralph Lilley, AC516
Comparative guide to American colleges for students, parents, and counselors, CB265

Comparative literature, BE17, BE182, BE1043
  bibliography, BE12, BE13, BE18, BE21, BE32, BE33
    current, BE41
  indexes, BE32

Comparative literature (by country or region)
  Italy
    bibliography, BE1442
  Spain
    bibliography, BE1442

Comparative public administration, Heady, Ferrel, CJ467
—— Huddleston, Mark W., CJ467
—— Stoke, Sybil, CJ467
—— University of Michigan. Institute of Public Administration, CJ467
Comparative reading, Hladczuk, John, CB48
Comparative world data, Müller, Georg P., CG40
Comparisons of distance, size, area, volume, mass, weight, density, energy, temperature, time, speed and number throughout the universe, Diagram Group, EA150
•*Compendex*, EK7, EK11
•*COMPENDEX PLUS*, EK7
Compendio de estadísticas históricas de Colombia, Urrutia Montoya, Miguel, CG151
Compendio estadístico, CG147
Compendio estadístico del Perú, 1900–1990, Beltrán B., Arlette, CG157
—— Portocarrero S., Felipe, CG157, DB389
—— Romero Pinillos, María Elena, CG157
Compendio statistico italiano, CG255
Compendious Syriac dictionary, Payne Smith, J., AC773
—— Payne Smith, Robert, AC773
Compendium of American public opinion, Gilbert, Dennis A., CJ488
Compendium of analytical nomenclature, EE35
A compendium of biographical literature on deceased entomologists, Gilbert, Pamela, EG329
Compendium of chemical terminology, EE36
Compendium of hazardous chemicals in schools and colleges, EE67, EE72
Compendium of Indian elections, Butler, David, CJ431
—— Lahiri, Ashok, CJ431
—— Roy, Prannot, CJ431

Compendium of Irish biography, Webb, Alfred John, AH255

Compendium of meteorology, American Meteorological Society. Committee on the Compendium of Meteorology, EF152

Compendium of national urban mass transportation statistics, CH452

Compendium of the war of the rebellion, Dyer, Frederick Henry, DB119

Compendium of veterinary products, EJ119

Compendiums of the world's languages, Campbell, George L., BD12

Competitive colleges, CB284

Compilation of Chinese dictionaries, Hixson, S., AC270

—— Mathias, James, AC270

Compilation of graduate theses prepared in the Philippines, Philippines. National Science Development Board, AG56

A compilation of the messages and papers of the Presidents, United States. President, AF135

Complé à la Bibliographie du Tchad, Bériel, Marie-Magdeleine, DD140

Complément au Dictionnaire généalogique Tanguay, Leboeuf, J. Arthur, AJ73

A complement to genealogies in the Library of Congress, Kaminkow, Marion J., AJ31, AJ32

The complete actors' television credits, 1948–1988, Parish, James Robert, BH312

Complete and systematic concordance to the works of Shakespeare, Spevack, Marvin, BE776, BE777, BE778

Complete annotated catalogue PMB manuscript series microfilms PMB 1–1030, Australian National University. Pacific Manuscripts Bureau, DF14

Complete annotated resource guide to black American art, Holmes, Oakley N., BF24

Complete baronetage, Cokayne, George Edward, AJ117

The complete beverage dictionary, Lipinski, Robert A., EJ227

Complete Bible, Goodspeed, Edgar J., BC94

—— Powis Smith, J. M., BC94

Complete book of ballets, Beaumont, Cyril William, BH151

The complete book of emigrants, Coldham, Peter Wilson, AJ60

The complete book of emigrants in bondage, 1614–1775, Coldham, Peter Wilson, AJ61

The complete book of Jewish observance, Trepp, Leo, BC560

The complete book of light opera, Lubbock, Mark Hugh, BJ241

Complete book of the American musical theater, Ewen, David, BJ261

The complete book of the Olympics, Wallechinsky, David, BK94

The complete book of the Winter Olympics, Wallechinsky, David, BK95

Complete Caribbeana, Comitas, Lambros, DB423, DB440

Complete Caribbeana, 1900–1975, Comitas, Lambros, DB404, DB405

The complete cat encyclopedia, Pond, Grace, EJ141

A complete checklist of the birds of the world, Howard, Richard, EG263

The complete color encyclopedia of antiques, BG37

Complete concordance of the Revised Standard Version Bible, BC158

A complete concordance to the American Standard Version of the Holy Bible, Hazard, Marshall Custiss, BC160

The complete concordance to the Bible : New King James version, BC164

The complete desk reference of veterinary pharmaceuticals & biologicals, EJ131

A complete dictionary of ancient and modern Hebrew, AC470

Complete dictionary of English and Hebrew first names, Kolatch, Alfred J., AJ171, AJ172

Complete dictionary of furniture, Gloag, John, BG126

The complete dictionary of television and film, Ensign, Lynne Naylor, BH317

The complete dictionary of wood, Corkhill, Thomas, EJ177

The complete directory for people with disabilities, CC192

The complete directory for people with learning disabilities, CB200, CC193

The complete directory of large print books & serials, AA429

The complete directory to prime time network TV shows, 1946–present, Brooks, Tim, BH299

The complete directory to prime time TV stars, 1946–present, Brooks, Tim, BH320

The complete dog book, EJ143

The complete economic and demographic data source, CG103

The complete encyclopedia of arms & weapons, CJ569, CJ581

The complete encyclopedia of hockey, BK86

The complete English-Hebrew dictionary, AC473

The complete English-Maori dictionary, Biggs, Bruce, AC608

A complete English-Persian dictionary, Wollaston, Arthur Naylor, AC318

The complete entertainment discography, from 1897 to 1942, Rust, Brian A. L., BJ343

The complete enyclopedia of popular music and jazz, 1900–1950, Kinkle, Roger D., BJ349

Complete field guide to North American wildlife, EG82

The complete film dictionary, Konigsberg, Ira, BH258

Complete grants sourcebook for higher education, Bauer, David G., AL130, CB372

Complete grants sourcebook for nursing and health, Bauer, David G., AL130

The complete guide to America's national parks, BK124

Complete guide to citing government documents, Garner, Diane L., AF69

—— Smith, Diane H., AF69

The complete guide to citing government information resources, Garner, Diane L., AF69

The complete guide to corporate fund raising, AL133

The complete guide to furniture styles, Boger, Louise Ade, BG131

The complete guide to getting a grant, Blum, Laurie, AL131

The complete guide to graduate school admission, Keith-Spiegel, Patricia, CD38

A complete guide to heraldry, Fox-Davies, Arthur Charles, AJ154

Complete guide to investment information, CH320

Complete guide to medical tests, Griffith, H. Winter, EH180

The complete guide to modern dance, McDonagh, Don, BH152

Complete guide to the new manners for the 90's, AL152

The complete Haitiana, Laguerre, Michel S., DB440

The complete handbook of garden plants, Wright, Michael, EJ249

The complete Hebrew-English dictionary, AC473

Complete index for the six volumes of Wild flowers of the United States, Pennington, Lee, EG180

A complete index of the Summa theologica of St. Thomas Aquinas, Deferrari, Roy Joseph, BB62

Complete list of reports published by the British Library R&D Department, British Library. Research and Development Dept, AK10

Complete multilingual dictionary of advertising, marketing and communications, Paetzel, Hans W., CH552

Complete multilingual dictionary of computer terminology, Nania, Georges, EK194

Complete office handbook, CH87

The complete opera book, BJ237

The complete peerage, Cokayne, George Edward, AJ118

Complete punctuation thesaurus of the English language, AC110

The complete reference guide to United Nations sales publications, 1946–1978, Birchfield, Mary Eva, AF30

The complete rhyming dictionary and poet's craft book, Wood, Clement, AC116

Complete secretary's handbook, De Vries, Mary Ann, CH86

Complete stories of the great ballets, BH150

The complete trees of North America, Elias, Thomas, EG194

Complete walker 3, BK113

The complete walker III, Fletcher, Colin, BK113

The complete Welsh-English, English-Welsh dictionary, AC805

The complete words of Wall Street, Pessin, Allan H., CH212

The completely illustrated atlas of reptiles and amphibians for the terrarium, Obst, Fritz Jürgen, EG252

Composers, BJ211, BJ271
  bibliography, BJ212, BJ221
  biography, BJ208
    indexes, BJ224
  chronologies, BJ205
  discography
    indexes, BJ227
  filmography, BH207
  indexes, BJ205, BJ226
Composers (by country or region)
  Israel, BJ65
  Russia, BJ204
  United States
    bibliography, BJ202
    biography, BJ206, BJ210
  U.S.S.R., BJ204

Composers of today, BJ211

Composers on record, Greene, Frank, BJ227

Composers since 1900, Ewen, David, BJ211

Composite index for CRC handbooks, EA149

Composite materials, EK286

Composition of foods, EH302, EH314, EJ220

The composition of leading organs of the CPSU (1952–1982), Kraus, Herwig, CJ394

A comprehensive annotated bibliography of American Black English, Brasch, Ila Wales, BD103

A comprehensive bibliography, Jones, Garth N., CJ443, DE241

Comprehensive bibliography for the study of American minorities, Miller, W. C., BE546

A comprehensive bibliography of American constitutional and legal history, 1896–1979, Hall, Kermit, CK125

Comprehensive bibliography of computing literature, EK166

A comprehensive bibliography of English-Canadian short stories, 1950–1983, Weiss, Allan Barry, BE835

Comprehensive bibliography of modern African religious movements, Mitchell, Robert Cameron, BC19

—— Turner, Harold W., BC19

A comprehensive bibliography of music for film and television, Wescott, Steven D., BJ364

A comprehensive bibliography of pragmatics, Nuyts, Jan, BD65

Comprehensive bibliography of the peoples of Namibia (South West Africa) and Southwestern Angola, CE104

Comprehensive bibliography of Victorian studies, 1970–1984, Chaudhuri, Brahma, BE752

A comprehensive bibliography of Yugoslav literature in English, 1593–1980, Mihailovich, Vasa D., BE1499

A comprehensive bibliography on American sign language, Federlin, Tom, BD49

The comprehensive catalog of U.S. paper money, Hessler, Gene, BG196

Comprehensive coordination chemistry, EE68

Comprehensive desk reference of veterinary pharmaceuticals and biologicals, EJ131

A comprehensive dictionary, Armenian-English, Kouyoumdjian, Mesrob G., AC227

Comprehensive dictionary of engineering and technology, Ernst, Richard, EA109, EK9
Comprehensive dictionary of idioms, English-Armenian, Kouyoumdjian, Mesrob G., AC227
Comprehensive dictionary of physical chemistry, EE25
Comprehensive dissertation index, BE424, BE425
Comprehensive dissertation index, 1861–1972, AG12
•*Comprehensive dissertation index online,* AG13
A comprehensive English-Hindi dictionary of governmental and educational words and phrases, Raghu Vira, AC487
Comprehensive English-Swedish dictionary, Santesson, Rudolf, AC769
A comprehensive etymological dictionary of the English language, Klein, Ernest David, AC56
A comprehensive etymological dictionary of the Hebrew language for readers of English, Klein, Ernest David, AC471
Comprehensive glossary of psychiatry and psychology, Kaplan, Harold I., EH383
Comprehensive handbook of psychopathology, EH392
A comprehensive handbook of the United Nations, AF33
Comprehensive heterocyclic chemistry, EE117
Comprehensive index, 1889–1893, Ames, John G., AF98
Comprehensive index to architectural periodicals, 1956–1970, BF222
Comprehensive index to English-language little magazines, 1890–1970, Sader, Marion, AD263, AD287, BE420, BE500
Comprehensive index to the publications of the United States government, 1881–1893, United States. Department of the Interior. Division of Documents, AF98
Comprehensive inorganic chemistry, EE108
A comprehensive Old-English dictionary, Borden, Arthur R., AC170
Comprehensive organic chemistry, EE118, EE119
Comprehensive organic synthesis, EE119
Comprehensive organometallic chemistry, EE120
Comprehensive polymer science, EK283
A comprehensive survey of Persian bibliographies in the world, AA80
Comprehensive textbook of psychiatry/V, EH400
A comprehensive treatise on inorganic and theoretical chemistry, Mellor, Joseph William, EE111
Comprehensive urban planning, Branch, M. C., BF270
Compressed Russian, Zalucky, Henry K., AC690
Compton, Carolyn. *A guide to 85 tests for special education,* CB189
Compton yearbook, AB18
Compton's dictionary of the natural sciences, EG76
Compton's encyclopedia and fact-index, AB18, AB23
•*Compton's multimedia encyclopedia,* AB18, AB23
CompuMath citation index, EB21, EK160
•*COMPUSCIENCE,* EK159, EK161, EK166
•*COMPUSTAT,* CH313
Computational linguistics, BD64
Computer & control abstracts, ED9, EK162
Computer abstracts, EK163
•*Computer aided science policy & research database system,* CB257
Computer and control abstracts, EK128
Computer applications in music, Davis, Deta S., BJ30
Computer art, BF374
The computer artist's handbook, Schwartz, Lillian, BF374
Computer assisted instruction, EH272
bibliography, BD73
Computer bibliography, EK163
Computer dictionary, Spencer, Donald D., EK187
Computer engineering handbook, EK203
Computer genealogy, AJ5
The computer glossary, Freedman, Alan, EK179, EK181

Computer graphics, EK182
dictionaries, EK188
Computer hardware, EK199
Computer industry
directories, EK199, EK201
Computer literature bibliography, Youden, W. W., EK158
Computer literature bibliography, 1946–1967, EK158
Computer literature index, EK164, EK168
Computer methods for literary research, Oakman, Robert L., BE6
Computer music, BJ167, BJ313
bibliography, BJ30
Computer news, EK163
Computer programming, EK207
Computer publishers & publications, EK210
Computer-readable data bases, AK208
Computer science
abbreviations, EK196
bibliography, EK150, EK152, EK210
courses of study
directories, EK200, EK202
databases, EB28
dictionaries, EK131, EK183
encyclopedias, EK171, EK172
faculty
directories, EK202
financial aids, EB58, EK200
guides, EK150, EK152
handbooks, EK138, EK142, EK205, EK207, EK210
indexes, EB21, EK160
yearbooks, EK210
see also **Electrical and electronic engineering**
Computer science resources, Hildebrandt, Darlene Myers, EK150
Computer science technical reports, Stanford University, EK156
Computer software, EH272
catalogs, EK199, EK201
directories, EE58
Computer software (by subject)
education, CB176
Computers
abbreviations, EK189
abstract journals, EK162, EK163, EK166
acronyms, EK189
bibliography, EK151, EK156, EK158, EK163
databases, EK159, EK161, EK165, EK166
dictionaries, AK43, EK175, EK177, EK178, EK179, EK180, EK181, EK185, EK187
bilingual
Japanese-English, EK191
multilingual, EK190, EK192, EK193, EK194, EK197
encyclopedias, EK174
handbooks, EK203, EK205
handbooks of usage, BF374
indexes, EK158, EK159, EK161, EK164, EK168
Computers (by subject)
history
bibliography, EK208, EK209
see also **Data processing; Microcomputers**
Computers and data processing, Morrill, Chester, EK151
Computers and literature, Rudall, Brian H., BE8
•*Computing archive,* EK159, EK165, EK166
Computing in musicology, BJ167
Computing information directory, Hildebrandt, Darlene Myers, EK150
Computing reviews, EB28, EK159, EK161, EK165, EK166
Comrie, Bernard. *The world's major languages,* BD19
Comstock, Helen. *Concise encyclopaedia of American antiques,* BG37
———— *Concise encyclopedia of American antiques,* BG41
Concert and opera conductors, Cowden, Robert H., BJ219
Concert and opera singers, Cowden, Robert H., BJ219

Concheff, Beatrice Jorgensen. *Bibliography of old Catalan texts,* BE1433
Conciliorum oecumenicorum decreta, BC436
The concise AACR2, 1988 revision, Gorman, Michael, AK196
Concise Amharic dictionary, Leslau, Wolf, AC210
Concise Anglo-Saxon dictionary, Hall, John Richard Clark, AC173
Concise atlas of the universe, Moore, Patrick, EC67
A concise bibliography of ancient Greek literature, Kessels, A. H. M., BE1030
Concise bibliography of Greek language and literature, Kessels, A. H. M., BE1030
———— Verdenius, W. J., BE1030
A concise bibliography of Northern Chad and Fezzan in Southern Libya, DD141
A concise biographical dictionary of singers, BJ214
Concise Bulgarian-English technical dictionary, EA105
A concise Cambodian-English dictionary, Jacob, Judith M., AC564
Concise Cambridge bibliography of English literature, 600–1950, Watson, George, BE603
Concise Cambridge history of English literature, Sampson, George, BE617
Concise Cambridge Italian dictionary, Reynolds, Barbara, AC529, AC535
Concise chemical and technical dictionary, Bennett, H., EE34
The concise Columbia dictionary of quotations, Andrews, Robert, BE98
The concise Columbia encyclopedia, AB7, AB11, AB27
Concise Coptic-English lexicon, Smith, Richard, AC273
Concise dictionary of American biography, AH60, DB43
The concise dictionary of American Jewish biography, BC565
A concise dictionary of astronomy, Mitton, Jacqueline, EC35
A concise dictionary of business, CH56
Concise dictionary of classical mythology, Kershaw, Stephen, CF27
The concise dictionary of early Christianity, Kelly, Joseph F., BC247
Concise dictionary of Eastern religion, Winternitz, Moriz, BC92
A concise dictionary of Indian philosophy, Grimes, John A., BB39
Concise dictionary of Irish biography, Crone, John Smyth, AH255, AH256
Concise dictionary of Japanese history, Hunter, Janet, DE211
A concise dictionary of law, CK34
The concise dictionary of management, Statt, David A., CH616
A concise dictionary of mathematics, Clapham, Christopher, EB38
A concise dictionary of Middle Egyptian, Faulkner, Raymond O., AC304
A concise dictionary of modern place-names in Great Britain and Ireland, Room, Adrian, CL200, CL209
The concise dictionary of national biography, AH226
A concise dictionary of old Icelandic, Zoëga, Geir Tómasson, AC509
Concise dictionary of Old Russian, AC671
Concise dictionary of physics and related subjects, Thewlis, James, ED24
Concise dictionary of scientific biography, EA175
Concise dictionary of slang and unconventional English, Beale, Paul, AC132
———— Partridge, Eric, AC132
Concise dictionary of Soviet terminology, institutions, and abbreviations, Crowe, Barry, AC686
Concise dictionary of the Christian world mission, Neill, Stephen Charles, BC310
A concise dictionary of the Persian language, Palmer, Edward H., AC316

Concise encyclopaedia of American antiques, Comstock, Helen, BG37

Concise encyclopaedia of antiques, Connoisseur, BG37

Concise encyclopaedia of Arabic civilization, Ronart, Stephan, DD76

Concise encyclopaedia of metallurgy, Merriman, Arthur Douglas, EK266

A concise encyclopaedia of the Italian Renaissance, DC430

Concise encyclopedia biochemistry, EG315
———— Brockhaus ABC Biochemie, EE26

Concise encyclopedia chemistry, EE26

Concise encyclopedia of American antiques, Comstock, Helen, BG41

A concise encyclopedia of antiques, Wills, Geoffrey, BG41

Concise encyclopedia of archaeology, Cottrell, Leonard, DA77

Concise encyclopedia of biochemistry, EG316

Concise encyclopedia of biological & biomedical measurement systems, EH82

Concise encyclopedia of industrial relations, Marsh, Arthur Ivor, CH649

Concise encyclopedia of interior design, Dizik, A. Allen, BG130

The concise encyclopedia of Islam, Glasse, Cyril, BC504

Concise encyclopedia of mathematics, EB69

Concise encyclopedia of medical & dental materials, EH176

Concise encyclopedia of polymer science and engineering, EK284

Concise encyclopedia of software engineering, EK169

Concise encyclopedia of special education, CB195, CB196

Concise encyclopedia of the sciences, EA91

A concise English-Hungarian dictionary, Országh, László, AC496

A concise English-Mongolian dictionary, Hangin, John G., AC613

A concise English-Swahili dictionary, Snoxall, R. A., AC759

Concise etymological dictionary of the English language, Skeat, Walter William, AC62

A concise etymological Sanskrit dictionary, AC708

Concise Hebrew and Arabic lexicon of the Old Testament, Holladay, William Lee, AC481

Concise history of bronzes, Savage, George, BF396

Concise history of costume, Laver, James, BG109

Concise history of German literature to 1900, Vivian, Kim, BE1259

Concise history of modern painting, Read, Herbert Edward, BF307

Concise history of world sculpture, Bazin, Germain, BF392

A concise Hungarian-English dictionary, Magay, Tamás, AC495

Concise Icelandic-English dictionary, AC508

Concise illustrated dental dictionary, Harty, F. J., EH255

A concise Kaffir-English dictionary, AC810

Concise Māori dictionary, Reed, A. W., AC609

The concise McGraw-Hill dictionary of modern economics, CH70

Concise Oxford companion to English literature, Drabble, Margaret, BE610
———— Stringer, Jenny, BE610

Concise Oxford companion to the American theatre, Bordman, Gerald Martin, BH64

Concise Oxford companion to the theatre, Found, Peter, BH74
———— Hartnoll, Phyllis, BH74

The concise Oxford dictionary of ballet, Koegler, Horst, BH143

The concise Oxford dictionary of botany, EG124

The concise Oxford dictionary of current English, AC38, AC197, AC337, AC683
———— Sykes, J. B., AC177

The concise Oxford dictionary of earth sciences, EF14

The concise Oxford dictionary of English etymology, AC52

Concise Oxford dictionary of English place-names, Ekwall, Eilert, CL193

Concise Oxford dictionary of French literature, Reid, Joyce M. H., BE1158

The concise Oxford dictionary of geography, Mayhew, Susan, CL48

The concise Oxford dictionary of literary terms, BE73

A concise Oxford dictionary of mathematics, EB38

Concise Oxford dictionary of music, Kennedy, Michael, BJ138
———— Scholes, Percy A., BJ138

The concise Oxford dictionary of opera, Rosenthal, Harold D., BJ253

Concise Oxford dictionary of proverbs, Simpson, J. A., BE159
———— Speake, Jennifer, BE159

The concise Oxford dictionary of zoology, EG124, EG227

Concise Oxford English-Arabic dictionary of current usage, Doniach, N. S., AC219

The concise Oxford French dictionary, AC337

Concise Oxford history of music, Abraham, Gerald, BJ136, BJ197

The concise Oxford Turkish dictionary, Alderson, Anthony Dolphin, AC790

Concise Pali-English dictionary, Buddhadatta, Ambalangoda Polvatte, AC624

A concise pronouncing dictionary of British and American English, Lewis, Jack Windsor, AC98

Concise science dictionary, EA89

The concise Scots dictionary, AC163

Concise Spanish and English dictionary, AC734

Concise theological dictionary, BC408

Concise veterinary dictionary, EJ112

Concordance de la Bible, Nouveau Testament, BC161

A concordance of the Qur'an, Kassis, Hanna E., BC203

A concordance to Darwin's Origin of species, first edition, EG68

A concordance to Eddic poetry, Kellogg, Robert, BE1286

Concordance to hymns, BC319

Concordance to Middle English metrical romances, Saito, Toshio, BE736

Concordance to the American Book of Common Prayer, Huggett, Milton, BC348

A concordance to the Apocrypha/Deuterocanonical books, BC158

Concordance to the works of St. Anselm, Evans, G. R., BB64

Concordia cyclopedia, BC359

Concrete construction, EK105, EK106

Concrete poetry, McCullough, Kathleen, BE313

Conde, Roberto Cortés. *Latin America,* CH180

Condensed chemical dictionary, EE41

The condition of education, CB138

The condition of teaching, CB165

Conditions of work and quality of working life, CH661

Condon, Edward Uhler. *Handbook of physics,* ED33

Conetta, Carl. *Peace resource book,* CJ694

The Confederacy, DB117
———— Beers, Henry Putney, DB114

Confederate imprints, Parrish, T. Michael, DB112

Confederate research sources, Neagles, James C., AJ16

Confederate States of America, CJ292

Confederation of American Indians. *Indian reservations,* CC431

Confederation to 1949, Brown, R. C., DB205
———— Prang, M. E., DB205

Conference on British Studies. *Bibliographic handbooks,* DC308, DC319, DC320, DC325, DC331
———— *Bibliographical handbooks,* DC303, DC307

Conference on College Composition and Communication. *CCCC bibliography of composition and rhetoric,* BE348

Conference papers index, EA207

•*Conference proceedings index,* AL26, EA206

Confucianism
  collections, BC92

Congo
  atlases, CL339
  bibliography, DD18, DD144
  current surveys, DD62
  encyclopedias, DC108, DD48
  government publications
      bibliography, AF224, AF229
  periodicals, AD171
  statistics, CG324
  see also **Zaire**

Congo, Fegley, Randall, DD18

Congo Brazzaville, Carozzi, Carlo, DD143

Congrat-Butlar, Stefan. *Translation & translators,* BD87

Congregate care by county, CC85

The Congregational two hundred, 1530–1948, Peel, Albert, BC385

Congregational yearbook, BC386

The Congregationalism of the last 300 years, as seen in its literature, Dexter, Henry Martyn, BC383

The Congregationalists, Youngs, J. William T., BC387

Les congrès internationaux de 1681 à 1899, Union of International Associations, AL31

Les congrès internationaux de 1900 à 1919, AL31

Congress & defense, CJ223

Congress A to Z, CJ179, CJ204

Congress and defense, CJ223

Congress and law-making, Goehlert, Robert, CJ195

Congress and the nation, CJ207, CJ214

The Congress dictionary, Dickson, Paul, CJ205

Congresses and meetings, EA211
  bibliography, AL27, AL30, AL33, EA209, EA210, EA212
  databases, AL28, BK34, CH554, EA210
  directories, AL25, AL28, BK34, CH554, EA203, EA204, EA205
  indexes, AL26, AL29, EA202, EA206, EA207
  publications
      bibliography, AL26, EA206
      databases, AL26, EA206
  union lists, AL30

Congresses and meetings (by country or region)
U.S.S.R.
  bibliography, EA199

Congresses and meetings (by subject)
  Africa, DD8
  authorship, BE171
  philosophy, BB17
  see also **International congresses**

Congressional and gubernatorial primaries, McGillivray, Alice V., CJ254

Congressional committees, 1789–1982, Stubbs, Walter, CJ219

Congressional directories, CJ222

Congressional directory, CJ221

Congressional district atlas, United States. Bureau of the Census, CJ238

Congressional districts in the 1990s, CJ234

Congressional globe, AF127

Congressional Information Service. *CIS/annual,* AF125
———— *CIS index to presidential executive orders & proclamations,* AF128
———— *CIS/index to publications of the United States Congress,* AF126
———— *CIS index to unpublished U.S. House of Representatives committee hearings, 1833–1936,* AF121
———— *CIS index to unpublished U.S. Senate committee hearings,* AF122
———— *CIS index to U.S. executive branch documents, 1789–1909,* AF129
———— *CIS index to U.S. Senate executive documents & reports,* AF117
———— *CIS U.S. congressional committee hearings index,* AF123
———— *CIS U.S. congressional committee prints index from the earliest publications through 1969,* AF124

——— *CIS U.S. serial set index*, AF87
——— *Congressional masterfile 1*, AF118
——— *Foreign gazetteers [of the] U.S. Board on Geographic Names*, CL87
——— *State constitutional conventions from independence to the completion of the present Union, 1776–1959*, CK174
——— *Statistical reference index*, CG99
——— *U.S. government periodicals index*, AD291, AF115
•*Congressional masterfile 1*, AF87, AF117, AF118, AF121, AF122, AF123, AF124
•*Congressional masterfile 2*, AF119, AF126
The Congressional Medal of Honor, AL180, AL187
Congressional practice and procedure, Tiefer, Charles, CJ225
Congressional publications, AF120, CJ200
Congressional publications and proceedings, Zwirn, Jerrold, AF120, CJ200
Congressional Quarterly almanac, CJ207, CJ208
Congressional Quarterly, inc. *America at the polls*, CJ240
——— *America votes*, CJ241
——— *Congress A to Z*, CJ204
——— *Congress and the nation*, CJ207
——— *Congressional districts in the 1990s*, CJ234
——— *Congressional Quarterly weekly report*, CJ209
——— *Congressional Quarterly's guide to Congress*, CJ193
——— *Congressional Quarterly's politics in America*, CJ214
——— *The directory of congressional voting scores and interest group ratings*, CJ218
——— *Handbook of campaign spending*, CJ247
——— *Historic documents*, DB137
——— *Members of Congress since 1789*, CJ230
——— *National party conventions, 1831–1988*, CJ265
——— *Open secrets*, CJ248
——— *Presidency A to Z*, CJ178, CJ179
——— *Presidential elections since 1789*, CJ250
——— *Public interest profiles*, CJ142
——— *Vital statistics on Congress*, CJ229
Congressional quarterly Washington alert, AF64
Congressional Quarterly weekly report, AF64, CJ209
Congressional Quarterly's American congressional dictionary, Kravitz, Walter, CJ206
Congressional Quarterly's guide to 1990 congressional redistricting, CJ235
Congressional Quarterly's guide to Congress, CJ193
Congressional Quarterly's guide to the presidency, CJ164
Congressional Quarterly's guide to the U. S. Constitution, Mitchell, Ralph, CK173
Congressional Quarterly's guide to the U.S. Supreme Court, Witt, Elder, CK192
Congressional Quarterly's guide to U.S. elections, CJ245, CJ250
Congressional Quarterly's politics in America, CJ214
Congressional record, AF67
——— United States. Congress, AF64, AF127, CJ217
Congressional staff directory, CJ137, CJ211, CJ215, CK149
•*Congressional staff directory on disk*, CJ215
Congressional voting guide, Bosnich, Victor W., CJ213
Congressional yellow book, CH350, CJ216, CJ220
Conibear, Shirley A. *First aid manual for chemical accidents*, EE78
Conifers and important hardwoods, Little, Elbert Luther, EJ191
Conio, Gérard. *Dictionnaire fondamental du français littéraire*, BE1156
Conjuring, CF39
Conklin, Harold C. *Folk classification*, CE7
Conlon, Pierre M. *Le siècle des lumières*, AA622
Conn, David Bruce. *Atlas of invertebrate reproduction and development*, EG231
Conn, Howard F. *Current therapy*, EH177

Connaissance du Gabon, Darkowska-Nidzgorska, Olenka, DD159
Connecticut. [Laws, etc.]. *Connecticut general statutes annotated*, CK179
Connecticut general statutes annotated, Connecticut. [Laws, etc.], CK179
Connell, Royal W. *Naval ceremonies, customs, and traditions*, CJ633
Connelly, Owen. *Historical dictionary of Napoleonic France, 1799–1815*, DC197
Connelly, Robert. *The motion picture guide*, BH199
Connelly, Thomas Lawrence. *Almanac of American presidents*, CJ184
Connoisseur. *Concise encyclopaedia of antiques*, BG37
The Connoisseur complete color encyclopedia of antiques, BG37
The connoisseur's complete period guide to houses, BG41
Connolly, J. D. *Dictionary of terpenoids*, EE121
Connolly, Norma C. *Bilingual dictionary of criminal justice terms (English/Spanish)*, CK256
Connolly, S. J. *The public record*, DC401
Connor, Billie M. *Ottemiller's index to plays in collections*, BE231
Connor, Leonard P. *Welding handbook*, EK249
Connors, Martin. *The Olympics factbook*, BK92
——— *VideoHound's golden movie retriever*, BH202
Connotillo, Barbara Cahn. *Specialized study options U.S.A*, CB317
Conn's current therapy, EH177
Conolly, Leonard W. *English drama and theatre, 1800–1900*, BE639
——— *Oxford companion to Canadian theatre*, BE833, BH73
Conover, Helen F. *Current national bibliographies*, AA397
——— *Guide to research and reference works on sub-Saharan Africa*, DD83
——— *Nigerian official publications, 1869–1959*, AF235
——— *Official publications of British East Africa*, AF223, DD108
——— *Official publications of French West Africa*, AF230
——— *Official publications of Somaliland, 1941–1959*, AF237, DD207
Conquest, John. *Trouble is their business*, BE267
The Conran directory of design, BG130
Conron, Brandon. *Canadian writers*, BE834
Conroy, Thomas F. *Markets of the U.S. for business planners*, CH598
Consciousness, CD108
Conscription, Anderson, Martin, CJ560
Conseil international de la langue française. *Vocabulaire d'astronomie*, EC42
Consejo Latinoamericano de Ciencias Sociales. *Latin America*, CH180
Consejo Latinoamericano de Ciencias Sociales. Grupo de Trabajo de Migraciones Internas. *Las migraciones en America Latina*, CC315
CONSER, AD15
Conservation, EG79
abstract journals, BF198
Conservation (by subject)
history, EJ176
Conservation directory, EG79
Conservation treatment procedures, Dyal, Carole, AK242
——— Morrow, Carolyn Clark, AK242
Conservatism, CJ117, CJ152
bibliography, CJ111, CJ112
dictionaries, CJ24
directories, CJ80
periodicals, AD45, AD54
see also **Right and left (Political science)**
Conservative Judaism in America, Nadell, Pamela S., BC559
Considine, Douglas M. *Energy technology handbook*, EK217
——— *Foods and food production encyclopedia*, EJ154

——— *Van Nostrand Reinhold encyclopedia of chemistry*, EE33
——— *Van Nostrand's scientific encyclopedia*, EA83
Considine, Glenn D. *Foods and food production encyclopedia*, EJ154
——— *Van Nostrand Reinhold encyclopedia of chemistry*, EE33
Considine, Tim. *The language of sport*, BK24
Consiglio nazionale delle ricerche (Italy). *Periodici italiani scientifici, tecnici e di cultura generale*, AD126
Consolidated bibliography of county histories in fifty states in 1961, Peterson, Clarence S., DB139
Consolidated catalog of League of Nations publications, offered for sale, Birchfield, Mary Eva, AF28
The consolidated catalog to the Index of American design, BG17
Consolidated index of translations into English, National Translations Center (U.S.), EA60
Consolidated index of translations into English II, EA60
Consolidated index to Flora Europaea, Beadle, M., EG170
——— Halliday, G., EG170
Consolidated index to government publications, Great Britain. Stationery Office, AF189
Consolidated indexes, Raper, Richard, DC296
Consolidated list of government publications, 1923–50, AF190
Consolidated list of parliamentary and Stationery Office publications, 1922, AF190
Consolidated list of United Nations document series symbols, AF53
Consolidated treaties & international agreements, CK92
The consolidated treaty series, CK85
Consortium directory, CB266
Consortium for the Study of Intelligence. *Bibliography on Soviet intelligence and security services*, CJ545
Consortium of College and University Media Centers. *Educational film & video locator of the Consortium of College and University Media Centers and R. R. Bowker*, AA380, CB31
Consortium on Peace Research. *Bibliography on world conflict and peace*, CJ664
Constable, G. *Medieval monasticism*, DA139
Constantinides, George C. *Intelligence and espionage*, CJ537
Constitution, Jefferson's manual and rules of the House of Representatives of the United States, United States. Congress. House, CJ226
Constitution of the United States, Reams, Bernard D., CK172
——— Yoak, Stuart D., CK172
The Constitution of the United States of America, United States. Constitution, CK173
The Constitution of the United States of America, as amended, CK173
The constitutional law dictionary, Chandler, Ralph C., CK129
Constitutions
collections, AF18, CK72, CK73
Constitutions (by country or region)
United States, CK130, CK170
bibliography, CK125
encyclopedias, CK185
sourcebooks, CK171, CK172
states, CK170, CK174, CK175
Constitutions of dependencies and special sovereignties, Blaustein, Albert P., CK72
——— Blaustein, Eric P., CK72
Constitutions of nations, Peaslee, Amos Jenkins, CK73
Constitutions of the countries of the world, Blaustein, Albert P., CK72
Constitutions of the states, Reams, Bernard D., CK175
——— Yoak, Stuart D., CK175
Constitutions of the United States, national and state, CK170

Construction glossary, Stein, J. Stewart, EK112
Construction index, BF209
Consultants and consulting directories, AK176, CH617, CH619
   see also **Political consultants**
Consultants and consulting organizations, CH617
Consultants and consulting organizations directory, CH617
Consultants Bureau Enterprises. *Russian-English physics dictionary,* ED27
Consultants directory, CH619
Consumer and Food Economics Institute (U.S.). *Composition of foods,* EH314, EJ220
Consumer Eastern Europe, CH591
Consumer Europe, CH591
Consumer goods statistics, CH597
Consumer guide, CK163
Consumer health, EH27, EH80, EH171, EH344
   databases, CH558, EH57
   handbooks, EH178
   indexes, CH558, EH57
Consumer health & nutrition index, CH558, EH57
The consumer health information source book, Rees, Alan M., EH27
Consumer information catalog, CH561
Consumer law, CK135, CK159, CK163
Consumer magazine & agri-media source, CH601
Consumer medicine, EH343
Consumer Nutrition Center (U.S.). *Composition of foods,* EH314, EJ220
Consumer protection, CH559, CH563, CH564
   handbooks, CH561
Consumer protection manual, Eiler, Andrew, CH563
Consumer Reports Books. *The facts about drug use,* CC136
Consumer sourcebook, CH559
Consumerism
   handbooks, CH559, CH561
   indexes, CH560
Consumers index to product evaluations and information sources, CH558, CH560, EH57
Consumers reference disc, CH558, EH57
Consumer's resource handbook, CH561
Contag, Victoria. *Seals of Chinese painters and collectors of the Ming and Ch'ing periods,* BF162, BF313
Conteanu, Ion. *Dicţionarul explicativ al limbii române,* AC659
Contemporary African music, BJ330
Contemporary American business leaders, Ingham, John N., CH99
Contemporary American composers, Anderson, E. Ruth, BJ202
Contemporary American poetry, Davis, Lloyd M., BE487
Contemporary American women sculptors, Watson-Jones, Virginia, BF152, BF400
Contemporary approaches to moral education, Leming, James S., CB15
Contemporary architects, BF260
Contemporary art and artists, Parry, Pamela Jeffcott, BF62
Contemporary art documentation and fine arts libraries, Keaveney, Sydney Starr, BF297
Contemporary art trends, 1960–1980, Bell, Doris L., BF93
Contemporary artists, BF138, BF260
——— Emmanuel, Muriel, BF138
Contemporary authors, AH42, BE198, BE296, BE890, BH22, AH42, BE198
Contemporary authors autobiographical series, AH42, BE198
Contemporary authors bibliographical series, AH42, BE198
Contemporary authors. New revision series, Evory, Ann, AH42, BE198
Contemporary authors. Permanent series, Kinsman, Clare D., AH42, BE198
Contemporary black American playwrights and their plays, BE531
——— Peterson, Bernard L., BE521, BE530
Contemporary black biography, AH43, CC396

Contemporary Canadian childhood and youth, Sutherland, Neil, CC152
Contemporary Canadian politics, Mahler, Gregory S., CJ302
Contemporary Chilean literature in the University Library at Berkeley, University of California, Berkeley. Library, BE942
Contemporary China, Berton, Peter Alexander Menquez, AA362, DE123
——— Wu, Eugene, AA362, DE123
Contemporary Chinese novels and short stories, 1949–1974, Tsai, Meishi, BE1561
Contemporary composers, BJ209
Contemporary critical theory, Marshall, Donald G., BE23
Contemporary designers, BF260, BG29
Contemporary dramatists, BE223
——— Kirkpatrick, D. L., BE212
Contemporary fiction writers of the South, BE568
Contemporary foreign language writers, BE199
Contemporary gay American novelists, BE469
——— Nelson, Emmanuel S., BE402
Contemporary graphic artists, BF260, BF383
Contemporary Indian literature : a symposium, BE1566
Contemporary Indonesian-English dictionary, Schmidgall Tellings, A. Ed, AC518
The contemporary Islamic revival, Haddad, Yvonne Yazbeck, BC496
Contemporary issues criticism, CA62
Contemporary Latin American fiction, Brower, Keith H., BE901
Contemporary legend, Bennett, Gillian, CF37
Contemporary lesbian writers of the United States, BE402
——— Knight, Denise D., BE469
——— Pollack, Sandra, BE469
Contemporary literary criticism, BE47, BE50, BE54, CA62
Contemporary literary critics, Borklund, Elmer, BE212, BE426, BE595
Contemporary masterworks, BF69, BF138
The contemporary Middle East, 1948–1973, Atiyeh, George Nicholas, DE25
Contemporary Native American literature, Jacobsen, Angeline, BE551
Contemporary novel, Adelman, Irving, BE206
——— Dworkin, Rita, BE206
Contemporary novelists, BE252
——— Henderson, Lesley, BE212
Contemporary photographers, BF355
Contemporary poetry in America and England, 1950–1975, Gingerich, Martin E., BE490
Contemporary poets, BE334
——— Chevalier, Tracy, BE212
Contemporary poets, dramatists, essayists, and novelists of the South, BE568
Contemporary popular music, BJ344
The contemporary printed literature of the English Counter-Reformation between 1558 and 1640, Allison, Antony Francis, BC388
Contemporary printed sources for British and Irish economic history, 1701–1750, Hanson, Laurence William, CH187
Contemporary prints, Castleman, Riva, BF376
Contemporary quotations, Simpson, James Beasley, BE118
Contemporary Russian literature, 1881–1925, Mirskii, D. S., BE1420
Contemporary science fiction authors, BE296
Contemporary Spanish American poets, Sefamí, Jacobo, BE904
Contemporary subject headings for urban affairs, Urban Documents Program, BF277
Contemporary theatre, film, and television, BH22, BH122
Contemporary theology, Steiner, Urban J., BC220
The contemporary thesaurus of social science terms and synonyms, Knapp, Sara D., CA43
Contemporary Turkish writers, Mitler, Louis, BE1491
Contemporary world writers, BE199
Contemporary writers of Japan, BE1581

Contento, William. *Index to crime and mystery anthologies,* BE268
——— *Index to science fiction anthologies and collections,* BE283, BE300
——— *Science fiction, fantasy & horror,* BE300
Contents of contemporary mathematical journals and new publications, EB23
Contents pages in education, CB53
Contests, CB86
Contests for students, CB86
Continental drift, EF112
The Continental novel, Kearney, E. I., BE257
Continuing education (by country or region)
   United States
      directories, CB359
The continuity of American poetry, Pearce, Roy Harvey, BE504
The Continuum dictionary of women's biography, AH25
Contreras, Jackeline. *Bibliografía sobre la mujer en el Ecuador,* DB371
Contribución a una bibliografía general de la poesía venezolana en el siglo XX, Sambrano Urdaneta, Oscar, BE967
A contribution to the bibliography of Scottish topography, Mitchell, Arthur, DC360
Contribution to the national bibliography of Rwanda, 1965–1970, Lévesque, Albert, AA871, DD198
Contributions to a bibliography of Australia and the South Sea Islands, Robert, Willem Carel Hendrik, DF1
Contributions to a dictionary of Canadian pseudonyms and anonymous works relating to Canada, Amtmann, Bernard, AA151
Contributions to a dictionary of the Irish language, Royal Irish Academy (Dublin), AC519
Contributions to a short-title catalogue of Canadiana, Amtmann, Bernard, AA444
Contributions to Irish lexicography, Meyer, Kuno, AC519
Contributions to North American ethnology, United States. Department of the Interior, CE83
Contributions to the history of American geology, Merrill, George Perkins, EF102
Contributions to the history of geology, La Rocque, Aurèle, EF101
Contribuţiune la bibliografia românească, Adamescu, Gheorghe, BE1377
Contributo a una bibliografia del futurismo letterario italiano, BE1291
Contributors' index to the Dictionary of national biography, 1885–1901, Fenwick, Gillian, AH226
Control abstracts, EK128
Control theory, EK162
Controversial issues in librarianship, Herring, Mark Youngblood, AK15
Controvich, James T. *Central Pacific campaign, 1943–1944,* DA170
——— *United States Army unit histories,* CJ628
Convention decisions and voting records, Bain, Richard C., CJ263
Convention on the rights of the child, CC176
Conversion tables, Scott, Mona L., AK204
Convestion equivalents in international trade, AL199
Conway, H. McKinley. *The weather handbook,* EF166
Conway, Jill K. *The female experience in eighteenth- and nineteenth-century America,* CC488
Conway's all the world's fighting ships, 1947–1982, CJ592
Conze, Edward. *Buddhist scriptures,* BC466
Coogan, Michael David. *The Oxford companion to the Bible,* BC189
Cook, Barrie. *The coin atlas,* BG182
Cook, Charles. *The essential guide to hiking in the United States,* BK112
Cook, Chris. *African political facts since 1945,* CJ399
——— *British historical facts,* DC323
——— *Commonwealth political facts,* CJ373
——— *Dictionary of historical terms,* DA41
——— *English historical facts, 1485–1603,* DC323
——— *European political facts, 1648–1789,* CJ314

—— *The Facts on File world political almanac,* CJ86

—— *Longman handbook of modern British history, 1714–1987,* DC21, DC294

—— *The Longman handbook of modern European history, 1763–1985,* DC21

—— *Macmillan dictionary of historical terms,* DA41

—— *Sources in British political history, 1900–1951,* DC17, DC335

—— *Sources in European political history,* DC17

Cook, David. *Classic mineral localities of the world,* EF205

Cook, Dorothy Elizabeth. *Costume index,* BG94, BH51

—— *Short story index,* BE260, BE262

Cook, Elizabeth. *550 books on Buddhism,* BC460

Cook, John. *A guide to commonwealth government information sources,* AF263

Cook, Marjorie. *Bibliography of the Summer Institute of Linguistics, Philippines, 1953–1984,* BD233

Cook, Michael L. *Monthly murders,* BE269

—— *Mystery, detective, and espionage fiction,* BE269

—— *Mystery, detective, and espionage magazines,* BE270

Cook, Ramsey. *The Canadian centenary series,* DB203

Cook, Samantha. *International dictionary of films and filmmakers,* BH250

Cook, T. D. *Stratigraphic atlas of North America and Central America,* EF113

Cook, Terry. *Historical records of the government of Canada,* DB192

Cookbooks
  bibliography, EH290, EH294, EJ214, EJ222, EJ223, EJ224
  indexes, EJ208

Cooke, Jacob Ernest. *Encyclopedia of the North American colonies,* DB83

Cooke, Melinda W. *Oceania, a regional study,* DF19

Cooke, O. A. *The Canadian military experience, 1867–1983,* CJ650

Cookery
  bibliography, EJ203, EJ204, EJ205, EJ206, EJ207
  dictionaries, EJ212, EJ213
  encyclopedias, EJ209
  handbooks, EH302, EH303, EH313, EJ215, EJ216, EJ217, EJ218, EJ219
  library resources, EJ204
  see also **Cookbooks; Food**

Cook's index, EJ203

Coole, Arthur Braddan. *A bibliography on Far Eastern numismatology and a coin index,* BG171

—— *Encyclopedia of Chinese coins,* BG171

Cooley, C. Earl. *Encyclopedia of world travel,* CL380

Coolhaas, Willem Philippus. *A critical survey of studies on Dutch colonial history,* DC452

Cooling, B. Franklin. *The era of the Civil War—1820–1876,* DB113

Coolman, Jacqueline. *The complete reference guide to United Nations sales publications, 1946–1978,* AF30

Coombs, J. *Biosciences,* EK42

—— *Dictionary of biotechnology,* EK45

—— *International biotechnology directory,* EK44

Cooper, A. M. *Alcohol use and world cultures,* CC113

Cooper, B. Lee. *Literature of rock II, 1979–1983,* BJ338

—— *A resource guide to themes in contemporary American song lyrics, 1950–1985,* BJ316

—— *Rockabilly,* BJ336

Cooper, Barbara Eck. *American and British literature, 1945–1975,* BE414, BE761

Cooper, David E. *A companion to aesthetics,* BB27

Cooper, David Edwin. *International bibliography of discographies,* BJ384

Cooper, Gayle. *A checklist of American imprints,* AA414

—— *Checklist of American imprints for 1820–1829,* AA418

Cooper, Jeremy. *Keyguide to information sources in public interest law,* CK9

Cooper, Jerry. *Militia and the national guard in America since colonial times,* CJ608

Cooper, M. Frances. *Checklist of American imprints for 1820–1829,* AA418

Cooper, Richard. *A dictionary of British ships and seamen,* CJ653

Cooper, Stephen. *ESL theses and dissertations, 1979–80,* BD109

—— *Graduate theses and dissertations in English as a second language,* BD109

Cooper, William W. *Kohler's dictionary for accountants,* CH252

Cooper-Hewitt Museum. Library. *Catalog of the Cooper-Hewitt Museum of Design Library of the Smithsonian Institution Libraries,* BG15

Cooperative Africana Microform Project. *CAMP catalog,* DD81

Cooperative Institutional Research Program. *The American freshman, national norms,* CB333

Cooperative learning, CB11

Coopers & Lybrand (International). *International accounting summaries,* CH261

Coopman, Theophiel. *Bibliographie van den Vlaamschen taalstrijd,* AA579

Coordinating Council of Literary Magazines (U.S.). *CCLM literary magazine directory,* AD49

Coordination chemistry, EE68

Coover, James. *Antiquarian catalogues of musical interest,* BJ27

—— *Musical instrument collections,* BJ367

Coover, James B. *Bibliography of music dictionaries,* BJ12

—— *Music lexicography,* BJ12

Copeland, J. Isaac. *The old South,* DB156

Coper, Ingrid. *Russisches geographisches Namenbuch,* CL152

Copernicus, Nicolaus, EC5

Copinger, Walter Arthur. *Supplement to Hain's Repertorium bibliographicum,* AA222, AA223, AA228

Copley, Eric James. *Guide to Referativnyi zhurnal,* EA73

Coppa, Frank J. *Dictionary of modern Italian history,* DC420, DC431

  Modern Italian history, DC420, DC431

Coppe, Paul. *Dictionnaire bio-bibliographique des littérateurs d'expression wallonne, 1622 à 1950,* BE1098

Copper, John Franklin. *Historical dictionary of Taiwan,* DE263

Copperud, Roy H. *American usage and style,* AC69

A Coptic bibliography, Kammerer, Winifred, BC454, BE1521

Coptic dictionary, Crum, Walter Ewing, AC272, AC273

The Coptic encyclopedia, BC452

Coptic etymological dictionary, Černý, Jaroslav, AC272

Coptic language
  bibliography, BC454, BE1521
  dictionaries
    bilingual
      Coptic and English, AC273
      Coptic-English, AC272
    etymology, AC272

Coptic literature, BC453, BE1520
  bibliography, BC454, BE1521

Copts, BC452

Copy-editing, Butcher, Judith, AA318

Copy preparation, AA277, AA317, AA318, AA319, AA320, AA321, AA322, AA324, EA159
  see also **Style manuals**

Copyright, AA312, AA313, AA315, AA316
  collections, CK67
  digests and collections, CK68
  encyclopedias, CK134
  handbooks, AA314

Copyright (by subject)
  music, BJ81

The copyright book, Strong, William S., AA316

The copyright handbook, Fishman, Stephen, AA314

—— Johnston, Donald F., AA315

Copyright laws and treaties of the world, AA313, CK67

Copyright publications, AA949

—— New Zealand. General Assembly. Library, AA947

Corbeil, Jean Claude. *The Facts on File English/Chinese visual dictionary,* AC259

—— *The Facts on File English/French visual dictionary,* AC338

Corbin, John. *Find the law in the library,* CK116

Corbin, John Boyd. *Acquisitions management and collection development in libraries,* AK167

—— *An index of state geological survey publications issued in series,* EF25

Corbin, Peter. *Annotated critical bibliography of Jacobean and Caroline comedy,* BE646

Corbin, Solange. *Répertoire de manuscrits médiévaux contenant des notations musicales,* BJ55

Corbitt, Robert A. *Standard handbook of environmental engineering,* EK82

Cordasco, Francesco. *American medical imprints, 1820–1910,* EH12

—— *A bibliography of American educational history,* CB29

—— *Dictionary of American immigration history,* DB41

—— *Homeopathy in the United States,* EH200

—— *Italian American experience,* CC317

—— *Italian Americans,* CC317

—— *The Italian emigration to the United States, 1880–1930,* CC318

—— *Italians in the United States,* CC317

—— *Medical education in the United States,* EH13

—— *The new American immigration,* CC319

—— *Puerto Ricans and other minority groups in the continental United States,* CC446

Cordasco, Michael Vaughn. *The Italian emigration to the United States, 1880–1930,* CC318

Cordeiro, Daniel Raposo. *Bibliography of Latin American bibliographies,* AA24

Cordell, Dennis D. *African historical demography,* CG310

Cordell, Geoffrey A. *Dictionary of alkaloids,* EE123, EH334

Cordell, Helen. *Laos,* DE221

Cordier, Henri. *Bibliotheca indosinica,* DE96, DE119

—— *Bibliotheca japonica,* DE195, DE198

—— *Bibliotheca sinica,* DE127, DE129, DE137, DE138

—— *L'imprimerie sino-européenne en Chine,* AA894

Cordingley, Audrey. *A check list of Canadian imprints, 1900–1925,* AA452

Cordoba Durchmusterung (CoD), Universidad Nacional de Córdoba, EC75

Córdova, Dardon. *Índice bibliográfico guatemalteco,* AA484

Core list of books and journals in education, O'Brien, Nancy P., CB16

Core list of books and journals in science and technology, Powell, Russell H., EA19

Core readings in psychiatry, EH371

CoreFiche, BE319

Coren, Robert W. *Guide to the records of the United States House of Representatives at the National Archives, 1789–1989,* CJ203

Corey, Melinda. *A cast of thousands,* BH205

Coriden, James A. *The code of canon law,* CK238

Corkhill, Thomas. *The complete dictionary of wood,* EJ177

—— *Glossary of wood,* EJ177

Corkill, David. *Ecuador,* DB369

Corley, Dawn. *New day/New Deal,* DB128

Corley, Nora Teresa. *Travel in Canada,* CL372

Cormack, Lesley B. *International directory of Renaissance and Reformation associations and institutes*, DA153

Cornejo A., Manuel. *Publicaciones oficiales de Chile, 1973–1983*, AF161

Cornell, G. A. *Index of twentieth century artists*, BF156

Cornell, James. *The great international disaster book*, DA19

Cornell, Tim. *Atlas of the Roman world*, DA119

Cornell University. Library. *Catalogue of the Icelandic collection bequeathed by Willard Fiske*, AA717, BE1284

Cornell University. New York State School of Industrial and Labor Relations. Library. *Library catalog*, CH640

Cornell University. Southeast Asia Program. *Studies on Vietnamese language and literature*, BD231, BE1601

Corning Museum of Glass. *Glass collections in museums in the United States and Canada*, BG68
—— *Guide to trade catalogs from the Corning Museum of Glass*, BG53
—— *The history and art of glass*, BG53

Cornish, Graham P. *Religious periodicals directory*, BC23

Cornish language
  dictionaries, AC275
    bilingual
      English-Cornish, AC274

Corns, Albert Reginald. *A bibliography of unfinished books in the English language, with annotations*, AA662

Corns, Thomas N. *Computers and literature*, BE8

Cornucopia, Facciola, Stephen, EG157

Corominas, Joan. *Breve diccionario etimológico de la lengua castellana*, AC742
—— *Diccionari etimològic i complementari de la llengua catalana*, AC248
—— *Diccionario crítico etimológico de la lengua castellana*, AC742

The corporate 1000, CH350

Corporate 500, AL121

•*Corporate affiliations plus*, CH228, CH351

Corporate and foundation givers, AL107

Corporate and foundation grants, AL103

Corporate art collections, BF97

The corporate contributions handbook, AL134

Corporate eponymy, Room, Adrian, CH386

The corporate finance bluebook, CH228, CH351

The corporate finance sourcebook, CH229

Corporate foundation profiles, AL104

Corporate fund raising, AL133

Corporate giving directory, AL105

Corporate giving yellow pages, AL106

Corporate magazines of the United States, CH28

Corporate museums, galleries, and visitor centers, Danilov, Victor J., BF97, BF114

•*Corporate technology database*, CH349

Corporate technology directory, CH349, EA37

Corporate yellow book, CH350

Corporations
  databases, CH306, CH309, CH351, CH363, CH369, CH411
  directories, CH228, CH306, CH309, CH316, CH348, CH351, CH360, CH363, CH369, CH404, CH405, CH406, CH411
  guides, CH331
  handbooks, CH331
  indexes, CH337
  periodicals, CH28

Corporations (by country or region)
  Arab nations
    directories, CH409
  Asia
    directories, CH358
    handbooks, CH375
  Asia, West
    directories, CH409
  Australia
    directories, CH358
  Canada
    databases, CH313

  directories, CH313
  ownership, CH353
  Europe, CH337
    directories, CH362, CH413
    handbooks, CH375
    rankings, CH402
  Europe, Eastern
    directories, CH412
  European Communities
    directories, CH376
  Germany
    bibliography, CH392
  Great Britain
    directories, AL7, CH366, CH414
    history, CH391, CH398
  Japan
    directories, CH361, CH408
  Latin America
    handbooks, CH375
  Pacific Rim
    directories, CH361
  United States
    bibliography, CH397
    biography, CH385
    charitable contributions, AL105
    databases, CH313, CH367, CH373
    directories, AL84, CH313, CH347, CH350, CH352, CH355, CH357, CH367, CH373, CH385, CH566, CH698
    ownership, CH353
    rankings, CH402

Corporations (by subject)
  art collections, BF97
  charitable contributions, AL105, AL109, AL134
  collections
    directories, BF114
  history, CH382, CH394
    bibliography, CH389, CH397
  philanthropy
    directories, AL106
  public assistance programs, AL104
  see also **Multinational corporations**

Corporations, nonprofit, AL10, CH365, CH615

•*Corptech*, EA37

Corpus der altdeutschen Originalurkunden bis zum Jahr 1300, AC413

Corpus dictionary of Western churches, BC234

Corpus juris secundum, CK132

Corpus vasorum antiquorum, BG78

Corpus vitrearum checklist, BG52

Corpus Vitrearum Medii Aevi, BG78

Correct form, AL159

Corrections and additions to the Dictionary of national biography, AH226

Correlation index, Special Libraries Council of Philadelphia and Vicinity, EA66

Correlation index of technical reports (AD-PB reports), United States. Department of Commerce. Office of Technical Services, EA77

Correns, C. W. *Handbook of geochemistry*, EF19

Correspondence schools, CB103, CB252, CB277, CB358

Corrigan, Beatrice. *Catalogue of Italian plays, 1500–1700, in the library of the University of Toronto*, BE1314

Corris, John J. *Encyclopedia of world travel*, CL380

Corrosion and anticorrosives, EK275

Corsi, Pietro. *Information sources in the history of science and medicine*, EA224

Corsini, Raymond J. *Encyclopedia of psychology*, CD21

Corsten, Severin. *Der Buchdruck im 15. Jahrhundert*, AA300
—— *Lexikon des gesamten Buchwesens*, AA270

Corswant, Willy. *A dictionary of life in Bible times*, BC193
—— *Dictionnaire d'archéologie biblique*, BC193

Cortada, James W. *Annotated bibliography on the history of data processing*, EK209
—— *A bibliographic guide to Spanish diplomatic history, 1460–1977*, DC502

—— *A bibliographic guide to the history of computing, computers, and the information processing industry*, EK209
—— *Historical dictionary of data processing*, EK176
—— *Historical dictionary of the Spanish Civil War 1936–1939*, DC514, DC517

Cortelazzo, Manlio. *Dizionario etimologico della lingua italiana*, AC537

Cortelyou, Catherine. *Directory of transportation libraries and information centers in North America*, CH449
—— *Urban transportation*, CH444

Cortés, Eladio. *Dictionary of Mexican literature*, BE908

Cortina, Lynn Ellen Rice. *Spanish-American women writers*, BE896

Corvalán, Graciela N. V. *Latin American women writers in English translation*, BE883

Corwin, Charles E. *Manual of the Reformed Church in America*, BC380

Cosenza, Mario Emilio. *Biographical and bibliographical dictionary of the Italian humanists and of the world of classical scholarship in Italy, 1300–1800*, BE1310

Cosgrove, Art. *A new history of Ireland*, DC413

Cosío Villegas, Daniel. *Cuestiones internacionales de México*, DB222

Cosmetics, EH325

Cosminsky, Sheila. *Traditional medicine*, CE12, EH185

Cosmology
  encyclopedias, EC27

Cosmopolitan world atlas, CL288

Cossolotto, Matthew. *The almanac of transatlantic politics, 1991–92*, CJ87

Cost of living, CH111

Costa, Agenor. *Dicionário de sinônimos e locuções da língua portuguêsa*, AC652

Costa, Joseph J. *Abuse of the elderly*, CC92

Costa, Marie. *Abortion*, CC249
—— *Adult literacy/illiteracy in the United States*, CB360

Costa, Mario Augusto da. *Bibliografia geral de Moçambique*, DD184

Costa de la Torre, Arturo. *Catálogo de la bibliografía boliviana*, AA503

Costa Rica
  atlases, CL313
  bibliography, AA477, AA478, AA479, DB305
  biography, AH114, AH115
  encyclopedias, AH114
  government publications, AF159
  statistics, CG126, CG126, CG127

Costa Rica. Dirección General de Estadística y Censos. *Atlas estadístico de Costa Rica, no. 2*, CL313
—— *Diez años de estadística vital, 1978–1987*, CG127

Costa Rica, Stansifer, Charles L., DB305

Costinescu, Mariana. *Dicţionarul limbii române literare vechi, 1640–1780*, AC658

Costume, Lister, Margot, BG110

Costume and fashion, BG95
  bibliography, BG91, BG92, BH51
  biography, BG115, BG116
  chronologies, BG108
  collections
    directories, BG103
  dictionaries, BG98, BG100, BG101
  encyclopedias, BG96, BG102
  handbooks, BG104
  indexes, BG94
  library catalogs, BG93
  theatrical, BH51, BH90, BH120

Costume and fashion (by country or region)
  Africa
    bibliography, BG90
  Europe, BG107
  Great Britain
    dictionaries, BG99
  United States, BG111

Costume and fashion (by period)
  20th century, BG115, BG116
    encyclopedias, BG97
Costume and fashion (by subject)
  history, BG106, BG109, BG110, BG112, BG113,
    BG114
Costume and fashion, Laver, James, BG109
———— Norris, Herbert, BC312
Costume and fashion in film, BH169
Costume design on Broadway, Owen, Bobbi, BH120
Costume designers
  filmography, BH208
Costume for births, marriages & deaths, Cunnington,
  Cecil Willett, BG99
Costume historique, Racinet, A., BG96
Costume index, Cook, Dorothy Elizabeth, BH51
———— Monro, Isabel Stevenson, BG94, BH51
Costume of the western world, Yarwood, Doreen,
  BG102
Costumes and settings for staging historical plays,
  Cassin-Scott, Jack, BH90
Cotarelo y Mori, Emilio. *Catálogo descriptivo de la
  gran colección de comedias escogidas que consta
  de cuarenta y ocho volúmenes, impresos de 1652 a
  1704,* BE1463
———— *Teatro español,* BE1463
Cote, Arthur E. *Fire protection handbook,* EK104
Cote des tableaux, Lang, L. Maurice, BF108
Côte d'Ivoire, DD145
  atlases, CL339
  bibliography, AA852, DD146
  current surveys, DD62
  encyclopedias, DD48
  government publications
    bibliography, AF230
  statistics, CG325
Côte d'Ivoire, Handloff, Robert E., DD62
La Côte d'Ivoire en chiffres, CG325
Côte d'Ivoire literature, BE1527
Cote internationale des livres et manuscrits,
  Matterlin, O., AA263
Coteanu, Ion. *Dicţionarul limbii române,* AC660
Cotter, Michael. *Vietnam,* DE271
Cotterell, Howard Herschel. *Old pewter,* BG150
———— *Pewter down the ages,* BG150
Cottineau, L. H. *Répertoire topo-bibliographique des
  abbayes et prieurés,* BC438
Cottle, Basil. *The Penguin dictionary of surnames,*
  AJ182
Cottle, Simon. *Sotheby's concise encyclopedia of
  glass,* BG61
Cotton, James Sutherland. *Imperial gazetteer of
  India,* CL164
Cottrell, Leonard. *Concise encyclopedia of
  archaeology,* DA77
Cottrell, P. L. *Events,* DA183
Cottrill, Tim. *Science fiction and fantasy series and
  sequels,* BE284
Coufoudakis, Evangelos. *Bibliography on Cyprus,*
  DC120
Coughlan, Margaret N. *Folklore from Africa to the
  United States,* CF90
Cougny, Gaston. *Dictionnaire des parlementaires
  français,* AH200, CJ329, DC211
Coulomb wave functions, Curtis, A. R., EB94
Coulon, Virginia. *A new reader's guide to African
  literature,* BE1508
Coulson, Anthony J. *A bibliography of design in
  Britain, 1851–1970,* BG6
Coulson, Jessie. *Oxford illustrated dictionary,* AC41
———— *The shorter Oxford English dictionary on
  historical principles,* AC31
Coulson, John. *The saints,* BC266
Coulter, Ellis Merton. *Travels in the Confederate
  states,* DB108, DB155
Council for British Archaeology. *Archaeological site
  index to radiocarbon dates for Great Britain and
  Ireland,* DC306
Council for Exceptional Children. *Exceptional child
  education resources,* CB194, CD92
Council for Interinstitutional Leadership. *Consortium
  directory,* CB266

Council of Arab Economic Unity. *al-Kitāb al-iḥṣā'ī
  al-sanawī lil-bilād al-'Arabīyah,* CG372
Council of Biology Editors. CBE Style Manual
  Committee. *CBE style manual,* EG57
Council of Biology Editors. Scientific Illustration
  Committee. *Illustrating science,* EA221
Council of Chief State School Officers. *Directory of
  state education agencies,* CB98
Council of Economic Advisers (U.S.). *Biographical
  directory of the Council of Economic Advisers,*
  CH95
———— *Economic indicators,* CH168
———— *Economic report of the President transmitted
  to the Congress,* CH174
Council of Europe. *Annuaire européen,* CJ313
———— *Judicial organisation in Europe,* CK201
Council of Graduate Schools in the United States.
  *The official GRE/CGS directory of graduate
  programs,* CB301
Council of Literary Magazines and Presses.
  Directory of literary magazines, AD49
*Council of Ministers of the Socialist Republic of
  Vietnam,* United States. Central Intelligence
  Agency, CJ325
Council of Planning Librarians. *Directory of
  planning and urban affairs libraries in the United
  States and Canada, 1990,* BF281
———— *Exchange bibliography,* BF267, BF271
———— *Urban planning,* BF268
Council of Societies for the Study of Religion.
  *Directory of departments and programs of
  religious studies in North America,* BC77
———— *Religious studies review,* BC26
Council of State Governments. *Interstate compacts
  and agencies,* AF141
———— *The book of the states,* CJ278
———— *State government research checklist,* AF145
Council of Urban Boards of Education. *Survey of
  public education in the nation's urban school
  districts,* CB143
Council on Foreign Relations. *Catalog of the Foreign
  Relations Library, Inc., New York,* DA171
———— *Political handbook of the world,* CJ95
Council on Foundations. *The corporate contributions
  handbook,* AL134
———— *Evaluation for foundations,* AL135
Council on Graduate Studies in Religion. *Doctoral
  dissertations in the field of religion, 1940–1952,*
  BC26
Council on International Educational Exchange.
  Work, study, travel abroad, CB93
Council on Postsecondary Accreditation. *Accredited
  institutions of postsecondary education, programs,
  candidates,* CB246
Council on Standards for International Educational
  Travel (U.S.). *Advisory list of international
  educational travel and exchange programs,* CB89
Councils, committees, and boards, Anderson, Ian
  Gibson, AL65
Councils of ministers in India, 1947–1982, Kohli, A.
  B., CJ433
Counseling, CD105
  handbooks, CB212
Counter-Reformation, BC388
Coutinho, Eduardo de Faria. *A literatura no Brasil,*
  BE927
Countries and islands of the world, Wilcocks, Julie,
  CL98
Countries of the world and their leaders yearbook,
  CJ64
Country house described, Holmes, Michael, BF206
The Country life international dictionary of clocks,
  BG87
Country profile, CH112
Country report, CH112
Country reports on human rights practices, United
  States. Department of State, CK109
●*County & city data book,* CG75
County and city data book, CG75, CG81, EJ84
County boundaries, 1788–1980, CL300
County business patterns, CH600
County courthouse book, Bentley, Elizabeth Petty,
  AJ51

County databook, CG75
County executive directory, CJ274
Couper, A. D. *The Times atlas and encyclopedia of
  the sea,* EF225
Couper, William James. *The Edinburgh periodical
  press,* AD105
Couprie, L. D. *Iconclass,* BF175
Coursodon, Jean-Pierre. *American directors,* BH290
Court-hand restored, Wright, Andrew, AA215
Courteault, Henri. *État des inventaires des archives
  départementales, communales et hospitalières au
  1er janvier 1983,* DC154
Courtés J. *Semiotics and language,* BD52
Courthope, William John. *A history of English
  poetry,* BE718
Courtney, E. *A handbook of Latin literature,* BE1048
Courts (by country or region)
  Canada
    directories, CK156, CK194
  Europe, CK201
  Great Britain
    directories, CK216
  United States
    databases, CK149
    directories, CK140, CK149, CK155, CK156
Cousin, Jean. *Bibliographie de la langue latine,
  1880–1948,* BD143
Cousin, John W. *Short biographical dictionary of
  English literature,* BE625
Cousins, Norman. *March's thesaurus and dictionary
  of the English language,* AC141
Coutinho, Afrânio. *Enciclopédia de literatura
  brasileira,* BE929
———— *A literatura no Brasil,* BE927
Coutinho, Bernardo Xavier da Costa. *Bibliographie
  franco-portugaise,* DC484
Coutts, Brian E. *Reference sources in history,* DA2
Couty, Daniel. *Chronologie de la littérature
  française,* BE1152
———— *Dictionnaire des littératures de langue
  française,* BE1149
Coven, Brenda. *American women dramatists of the
  twentieth century,* BE459
The cover story index, 1960–1991, AD269
Covert, Nadine. *Architecture on screen,* BF247
———— *Art on screen,* BF96
Covington, Michael A. *Dictionary of computer
  terms,* EK177
Covington, Paula Hattox. *Indexed journals,* AD248
———— *Latin America and the Caribbean,* DB251
Cowan, Henry J. *Dictionary of architectural and
  building technology,* BF240
Cowan, Ian Borthwick. *Medieval religious houses,
  Scotland,* BC441
Cowan, J. Milton. *A dictionary of modern written
  Arabic,* AC222
Cowan, Richard S. *Taxonomic literature,* EG93
Cowan, Samuel Tertius. *A dictionary of microbial
  taxonomy,* EG31
Coward, Harold G. *Philosophy of the grammarians,*
  BB33
Cowden, Robert H. *Concert and opera conductors,*
  BJ219
———— *Concert and opera singers,* BJ219
Cowen, Robert. *International handbook of education
  systems,* CB125
Cowie, Alexander. *Rise of the American novel,*
  BE485
Cowie, Anthony Paul. *Oxford dictionary of current
  idiomatic English,* AC80
Cowie, Peter. *Variety international film guide,*
  BH269
Cowles, Roy T. *The Cantonese speaker's dictionary,*
  AC260
Cox, Barbara G. *HAPI,* AD296
Cox, Edward Franklin. *State and national voting in
  federal elections, 1910–1970,* CJ253
Cox, Edward Godfrey. *A reference guide to the
  literature of travel,* CL7
Cox, Jane. *Tracing your ancestors in the Public
  Record Office,* AJ97
Cox, Michael. *Language of biotechnology,* EK45,
  EK46

Cox, Richard William. *Sport in Britain*, BK1
Cox, Susan M. *Early English newspapers*, AE57
Coxe, A. Cleveland. *Ante-Nicene Fathers*, BC293
Coxon, Howard. *Australian official publications*, AF264
Coyle, Jean M. *Families and aging*, CC64
—— *Women and aging*, CC489
Coyle, L. Patrick. *The world encyclopedia of food*, EJ209
Coyle, Martin. *Encyclopedia of literature and criticism*, BE65
Coysh, Arthur Wilfred. *The antique buyer's dictionary of names*, BG50
CPCR, EJ49
•*CPI*, AL26, EA206
CPL bibliography, BF271
CPM, BJ53
•*CPM plus*, BJ53
CPT, EH147
•*CQ member profiles*, CJ214
CQ researcher, AF64
CQ weekly report, CJ209
CQ's guide to 1990 congressional redistricting, CJ235
•*CQ's Washington alert*, AF64
Crabb, George. *Crabb's English synonyms*, AC137
Crabb's English synonyms, Crabb, George, AC137
Crabtree, Phillip. *Sourcebook for research in music*, BJ2
Craddock, Jerry R. *Spanish and English of United States Hispanos*, BD176
Craeybeckx, A. S. H. *Elsevier's dictionary of photography in three languages*, BF342
The craft of public history, DB12
Crafts, BK139, BK140
   bibliography, BF17
   encyclopedias, BK138
   see also **Quilts; Weaving**
Crafts index for young people, Pilger, Mary Anne, BK139
The crafts supply sourcebook, Boyd, Margaret Ann, BK140
Cragg, Dan. *A dictionary of soldier talk*, CJ616
—— *Guide to military installations*, CJ623
Craig, Bruce D. *Handbook of corrosion data*, EK275
Craig, Fred W. S. *Boundaries of parliamentary constituencies, 1885–1972*, CJ356
—— *Britain votes*, CJ364, CJ365
—— *British electoral facts, 1832–1987*, CJ364, CJ365
—— *British general election manifestos, 1959–1987*, CJ350
—— *British parliamentary election results*, CJ356, CJ364, CJ365, CJ366
—— *British parliamentary election results, 1832–1885*, CJ365
—— *Minor parties at British parliamentary elections, 1885–1974*, CJ366
Craig, Hardin, Jr. *A bibliography of encyclopedias and dictionaries dealing with military, naval and maritime affairs, 1577–1971*, CJ561
Craig, Robert D. *Dictionary of Polynesian mythology*, CF32
—— *Historical dictionary of Oceania*, DF17
—— *Historical dictionary of Polynesia*, DF16
—— *Who's who in Oceania, 1980–1981*, AH385
Craighead's international business, travel, and relocation guide to … countries, CH621
Craigie, William Alexander. *Dictionary of American English on historical principles*, AC30, AC150, AC152
—— *Dictionary of the older Scottish tongue*, AC30, AC163, AC164
—— *An Icelandic-English dictionary*, AC503
Craik, T. W. *The Revels history of drama in English*, BE467, BE667
Crain, Esther. *Columbia Granger's guide to poetry anthologies*, BE315
Craker, Lyle E. *Herbs*, EG110
Cramp, Stanley. *Handbook of the birds of Europe, the Middle East and North Africa*, EG262
Crampton, R. J. *Bulgaria*, DC112
Crampton, W. G. *Flags of the world*, AL190

Crandall, Marjorie. *Confederate imprints*, DB112
Crandall, Ruth. *Index to economic history essays in festschriften, 1900–1950*, CH20
Crane, Evan Jay. *A guide to the literature of chemistry*, EE2
Crane, Ronald Salmon. *Census of British newspapers and periodicals, 1620–1800*, AD106
—— *English literature, 1660–1800*, BE743
Cranmer-Byng, Alison. *Canada's playwrights*, BE821
Cranz, F. Edward. *A microfilm corpus of the indexes to printed catalogues of Latin manuscripts before 1600 A.D.*, AA208
—— *A microfilm corpus of unpublished inventories of Latin manuscripts through 1600 A.D.*, AA209
Craven, Robert R. *Symphony orchestras of the United States*, BJ296
—— *Symphony orchestras of the world*, BJ296
Craven, Thomas. *The new royal dictionary*, AC488
Craven, Toni. *Harper's Bible pronunciation guide*, BC140
Crawford, Anne. *The Europa biographical dictionary of British women*, AH227
Crawford, Elizabeth D. *Fourth book of junior authors & illustrators*, BE384
Crawford, James Ludovic Lindsay. *Bibliography of the writings, general, special and periodical, forming the literature of philately*, BG201
—— *Bibliotheca Lindesiana*, BE631, BG201
—— *Catalogue of the philatelic library of the Earl of Crawford*, BG201
Crawford, Phyllis. *Song index*, BJ289
Crawford, Richard. *American sacred music imprints, 1698–1810*, BJ68
Crawford, Tad. *Legal guide for the visual artist*, BF122
Crawford, Walt. *Technical standards*, AK65
CRB, BA8, CA46, EA138, EG47
CRB commodity yearbook, CH433, EJ82
CRC handbook of antibiotic compounds, Bérdy, János, EH324
CRC handbook of bimolecular and termolecular gas reactions, EE69
CRC handbook of chemistry and physics, EA149, EE70, EK279
CRC handbook of data on organic compounds, Astle, Melvin J., EE149
—— Weast, Robert C., EE149
CRC handbook of engineering in agriculture, EJ47
CRC handbook of food additives, EH304
CRC handbook of laboratory animal sciences, Melby, Edward C., EG235
CRC handbook of laboratory safety, EE71
—— Steere, Norman V., EE88
CRC handbook of laser science and technology, EC49, ED34
CRC handbook of lasers, Pressley, Robert J., EC49, ED34
CRC handbook of materials science, Lynch, Charles T., EK276
CRC handbook of mathematical sciences, EB84
CRC handbook of medicinal herbs, Duke, James A., EH342
CRC handbook of microbiology, EG54
—— Laskin, Allen I., EG56
—— Lechevalier, Hubert A., EG56
CRC handbook of natural pesticides, EJ48
CRC handbook of tables for organic compound identification, Rappoport, Zvi, EE151
CRC handbook of tables for probability and statistics, Beyer, William H., EB81
CRC standard mathematical tables and formulae, EB84
Creating a legend, Moran, John B., CJ607
Creationism
   bibliography, BC223, EG66
Creative Canada, AH92
Creative literature of Trinidad and Tobago, Wharton-Lake, Beverly D., BE981
Credit manual of commercial laws for …, CK165
Credit unions, CH279
Creditweek international ratings guide, CH321

Creedman, Theodore S. *Historical dictionary of Costa Rica*, AH114
The creeds of Christendom, BC311
Creel, Austin B. *Guide to Indian philosophy*, BB21
Creighton, D. G. *The Canadian centenary series*, DB203
Cremer, Herbert W. *Chemical engineering practice*, EK55
Cremerius, Johannes. *Literatur und Sexualität*, BE26
Creole languages, BD55
   bibliography, BD159
Crescent dictionary of mathematics, Karush, William, EB42
Creswell, Keppel Archibald Cameron. *A bibliography of the architecture, arts, and crafts of Islam to 1st Jan. 1960*, BF17
Creth, Sheila D. *Personnel administration in libraries*, AK178
Crewe, Ivor. *The British electorate 1963–1987*, CJ367
—— *British parliamentary constituencies*, CJ368
Cribb, Joe. *The coin atlas*, BG182
Cribb, Robert B. *Historical dictionary of Indonesia*, DE173
Crick, Bernard R. *A guide to manuscripts relating to America in Great Britain and Ireland*, DB32
Cricket, BK71
Cricket Society. *A bibliography of cricket*, BK71
Crim, Keith. *Abingdon dictionary of living religions*, BC70
—— *The interpreter's dictionary of the Bible*, BC132
Crimando, William. *Staff training*, CH713
Crime and delinquency literature, CK248
Crime and the elderly, Aday, Ron H., CC56
Crime dictionary, De Sola, Ralph, CK257
Crime fiction criticism, Johnson, Julia, BE265
—— Johnson, Timothy W., BE265
Crime fiction II, Hubin, Allen J., BE271
Crime in the United States, CK270
Criminal intelligence and security intelligence, Farson, Anthony Stuart, CK245
Criminal justice abstracts, CK248
Criminal justice dictionary, Beckman, Erik, CK257
Criminal justice documents, Berens, John F., CK244
Criminal justice periodical index, CK249
Criminal Justice Research Center. *Sourcebook of criminal justice statistics*, CK269
Criminal justice research in libraries, Lutzker, Marilyn, CK242
Criminal justice vocabulary, Astone, Nicholas A., CK257
—— Martin, Julian A., CK257
Criminal statistics England and Wales, CK270
Criminologica Foundation. *Criminology, penology, and police science abstracts*, CK250
Criminology
   abstract journals, CK248, CK250
   bibliography, CC56, CK243, CK245, CK246
   dictionaries, CK254, CK257, CK259, CK260
      bilingual
         Spanish-English, CK256
      multilingual, CK258
   directories, CK262, CK264, CK268
   encyclopedias, CK251, CK252, CK253, CK254
   guides, CK242, CK244
   indexes, CK249
   statistics, CK269, CK270
Criminology (by country or region)
   United States, CC37
   see also **Police**
Criminology & penology abstracts, CK250
Criminology, penology, and police science abstracts, CK250
C.R.I.S., CC12, CJ18, DA4, EJ74
Crisp, Deborah. *Bibliography of Australian music*, BJ28
Crispell, Diane. *The insider's guide to demographic know-how*, CH588
Critchley, Macdonald. *Butterworths medical dictionary*, EH94
Critical analyses in English renaissance drama, Salomon, Brownell, BE653

A critical and annotated bibliography of Philippine, Indonesian and other Malayan folk-lore, Bernardo, Gabriel Adriano, CF94
Critical bibliography of building conservation, Smith, John F., BF206
Critical bibliography of ecumenical literature, Lescrauwaet, Josephus F., BC276
A critical bibliography of French literature, BE1131, BE1205
A critical bibliography of German literature in English translation, 1481–1927, Morgan, Bayard Quincy, BE1239
A critical bibliography of religion in America, Burr, Nelson Rollin, BC27, BC31
Critical bibliography of the history and philosophy of science, EA256
Critical bibliography of the history of science and its cultural influences, EA241
Critical bibliography of the new stylistics applied to the Romance languages, Hatzfeld, Helmut, BE1072
A critical bibliography of writings on Judaism, Griffiths, David B., BC514
A critical dictionary of educational concepts, Barrow, Robin, CB72
A critical dictionary of English literature and British and American authors, living and deceased, Allibone, Samuel Austin, BE581, BE625
A critical dictionary of sociology, Boudon, Raymond, CC17
A critical dictionary of the French Revolution, DC183
Critical guide to Catholic reference books, McCabe, James Patrick, BC12, BC13, BC391, BC437
The critical index, Gerlach, John C., BH233
•*Critical inventory of films on art,* BF327
A critical Pali dictionary, Trenckner, Vilhelm, AC626
The critical perspective, BE596
Critical review of books in religion, BC51
Critical reviews of books about film, BH243
Critical survey of literary theory, BE48
—— Magill, Frank Northen, BE426, BE595
Critical survey of long fiction, BE241
Critical survey of long fiction : foreign language series, Magill, Frank Northen, BE241
Critical survey of mystery and detective fiction, Magill, Frank Northen, BE275
Critical survey of poetry, BE312
Critical survey of poetry : Foreign language series, Magill, Frank Northen, BE312
Critical survey of short fiction, BE261, BE479
A critical survey of studies on Dutch colonial history, Coolhaas, Willem Philippus, DC452
The critical temper, BE427, BE597
Critical terms for literary study, BE61
Critical terms for science fiction and fantasy, Wolfe, Gary K., BE309
Critical writings on Commonwealth literatures, New, William H., BE816
Criticism
  bibliography, BE23
  dictionaries, BE85
  encyclopedias, BE68
Critics' theatre reviews, BH58
Critique, CK109
Crittenden, Victor. *Australians : a guide to sources,* DF37
CRLIS, AK29
Croatia
  bibliography, DC608
Croatia and the Croatians, Prpič, George J., DC608
Croatian or Serbian-English dictionary, AC713
Croatoserbian-English encyclopedic dictionary, AC712
Crockford's clerical directory, BC334
Cröert, Wilhelm. *Handwörterbuch der griechischen Sprache,* AC445
Croft, L. R. *Handbook of protein sequence analysis,* EG317
Croft, P. J. *Index of English literary manuscripts,* BE603

Croft, Terrell. *American electricians' handbook,* EK134
Crofton, Ian. *A dictionary of art quotations,* BF95
—— *A dictionary of musical quotations,* BJ162
Croiset, Alfred. *Histoire de la littérature grecque,* BE1033
Croiset, Maurice. *Histoire de la littérature grecque,* BE1033
Crompton, Paul. *A dictionary of the martial arts,* BK89
Crone, John Smyth. *Concise dictionary of Irish biography,* AH255, AH256
Croner, U. H. E. *Reference book for world traders,* CH138
Croner's world register of trade directories, CH83
Cronin, Gloria L. *Jewish American fiction writers,* BE564, BE566
Cronjé, Ulrich Jerome. *Groot woordeboek,* AC198
Cronologia, cronografia e calendario perpetuo, Cappelli, Adriano, EC85
Cronología de los gobernantes de Panamá, 1510–1967, Alba C, Manuel María, DB317
Cronon, Edmund David. *Second World War and the atomic age, 1940–1973,* DA170
Crooke, William. *Hobson-Jobson,* AC162
Croom, Emily Anne. *Unpuzzling your past,* AJ6
Crop protection chemicals reference, EJ49
•*CROPCD,* EJ18
Crosby, Cynthia A. *Malawi,* DD48
Crosby, Everett U. *Medieval studies,* DA131
Cross, Anthony Glenn. *Eighteenth century Russian literature, culture and thought,* BE1385
Cross, F. L. *The Oxford dictionary of the Christian church,* BC240
Cross, K. E. *History of the church in southern Africa,* DD115
Cross-border links, AL34
•*Cross-cultural CD,* CE8
A cross-cultural summary, Textor, Robert B., CE62
Cross index title guide to classical music, Pallay, Steven G., BJ178
Cross index title guide to opera and operetta, Pallay, Steven G., BJ178
Cross-index to the geological illustration of Canada, Faessler, Carl, EF27
Cross-reference index of hazardous chemicals, synonyms, and CAS registry numbers, EE72
Crosse, Gordon. *Dictionary of English church history,* BC332
Crossman, Frederic S. *Judson concordance to hymns,* BC319
Crouch, Archie R. *Christianity in China,* BC305
Croucher, Murlin. *Slavic studies,* DC29
Crow, Paul A. *Ecumenical movement in bibliographical outline,* BC276
Crowder, Michael. *The Cambridge encyclopedia of Africa,* DD50
—— *Historical atlas of Africa,* DD65
Crowe, Barry. *Concise dictionary of Soviet terminology, institutions, and abbreviations,* AC686
Crowe, Deborah. *Science fair project index, 1960–1972,* EA31
Crowell's handbook of classical drama, Hathorn, Richmond Yancey, BE1017
Crowell's handbook of classical literature, Feder, Lillian, BE1015
Crowell's handbook of classical mythology, Tripp, Edward, CF25
Crowell's handbook of contemporary drama, Anderson, Michael, BE230
Crowell's handbook of Elizabethan & Stuart literature, Ruoff, James E., BE739
Crowley, Edward L. *Party and government officials of the Soviet Union, 1917–1967,* CJ393
—— *Who was who in the USSR,* AH304
Crowley, F. K. *Australians,* DF37
Crowley, Maureen. *Energy,* EK216
The Crown guide to the world's great plays, from ancient Greece to modern times, Shipley, Joseph Twadell, BE236
Crowther, Peter A. *A bibliography of works in English on early Russian history to 1800,* DC575

Croze, Marcel. *Tableaux démographiques,* CG215
Crozier, Michel. *Mouvements ouvriers et socialistes,* CH634
Cruden, Alexander. *Cruden's complete concordance of the Old and New Testaments,* BC165
Cruden's complete concordance of the Old and New Testaments, Adams, A. D., BC165
—— Cruden, Alexander, BC165
—— Irwin, C. H., BC165
—— Waters, S. A., BC165
Cruikshank, Margaret. *Lesbian studies,* CC272
Crum, Margaret. *First-line index of English poetry, 1500–1800,* BE704
Crum, Walter Ewing. *Coptic dictionary,* AC272, AC273
Crumb, Lawrence N. *The Oxford Movement and its leaders,* BC214
The crusade, Atiya, Aziz Suryal, DA167
Crusade, commerce and culture, Atiya, Aziz Suryal, DA167
Crusades, CJ575, DA160, DA167
  bibliography, DA168
Crusades, Mayer, Hans Eberhard, DA168
Cruz, Anabel. *Organizaciones no gubernamentales de Uruguay,* AL53
Cruz-Meléndez, Josefina. *Mexican autobiography,* AH105
Crystal, David. *The Cambridge encyclopedia,* AB3
—— *The Cambridge encyclopedia of language,* BD32, BD37
—— *Dictionary of linguistics and phonetics,* BD35, BD36, BD37
—— *Encyclopedic dictionary of language and languages,* BD35, BD37
—— *First dictionary of linguistics and phonetics,* BD36
Crystal structures, Wyckoff, Ralph W. G., EF120
Crystallographic Data Centre. *Molecular structures and dimensions,* EE139
Crystallography, EE89
  abstract journals, EF178
  bibliography, EF174
  dictionaries
    multilingual, EF116
  directories, EF119
  tables, EF117, EF120
•*CSA life sciences collection,* EF214, EG14
•*CSD,* EE139
Csida, June Bundy. *Feminist chronicles, 1953–1993,* CC572
•*CTI plus,* EK6
Cuadernos bibliográficos, BE1434
Cuadra, Carlos A. *Annual review of information science and technology,* AK76
Cuba
  atlases, CL320
  bibliography, AA559, AA560, AA561, AA562, AA563, DB408
    current, AA564
  bibliography of bibliography, AA396
  biography, AH150, AH151, AH152
  encyclopedias, DB424
  government publications, AF159
  periodicals, AD74, AD75
  registers, CJ325
  statistics, CG168, CG169, CG170, CG171, DB428
Cuba (by subject)
  historiography, DB425
  history
    bibliography, DB423, DB426, DB429, DB430, DB431
    manuscripts and archives, DB427
    statistics, CG171, DB428
Cuba, Pérez, Louis A., DB426
—— Schroeder, Susan, CG171, DB428
Cuba, 1953–1978, Chilcote, Ronald H., DB423
Cuba : a short history, DB291
Cuba en la mano, DB424
Cuban drama
  bibliography, BE972
Cuban drama (by subject)
  history, BE972

Cuban exile periodicals at the University of Miami Library, Varona, Esperanza Bravo de, AD47, CC458

Cuban literature
    bibliography, BE975
    biobibliography, BE973, BE974, BE976
    dictionaries, BE973, BE974
Cuban literature (by subject)
    history, BE977
Cuban literature, Foster, David William, BE975
Cuban periodicals in the University of Pittsburgh libraries, University of Pittsburgh. University Libraries, AD75
The Cuban revolution, Suchlicki, Jaime, DB431
The Cuban revolutionary war, 1953–1958, Pérez, Louis A., DB430
Cubans (by country or region)
    United States
        bibliography, CC447
        directories, CC462
        handbooks, CC466
        library resources, AD47, CC458
        periodicals, AD47, CC458
Cubans in the United States, MacCorkle, Lyn, CC447
Cubism and twentieth-century art, Rosenblum, Robert, BF307
Cuddon, John A. *A dictionary of literary terms and literary theory,* BE77
Cuento mexicano index, Hoffman, Herbert H., BE912
Cuesta, Luisa. *Catálogo de obras iberoamericanas y filipinas de la Biblioteca Nacional de Madrid,* DB268, DE245
Cuesta, Modesta. *Catálogo de obras iberoamericanas y filipinas de la Biblioteca Nacional de Madrid,* DB268, DE245
Cuestiones internacionales de México, Cosío Villegas, Daniel, DB222
Cuff, David J. *The United States energy atlas,* EK223
Cull, Peter. *The sourcebook of medical illustration,* EH236
Cullen, Clara. *Writings on Irish history,* DC399
Culliver, Concetta C. *Female criminality,* CC37
Cullum, George Washington. *Biographical register of the officers and graduates of the U.S. Military Academy at West Point, N.Y,* CJ640
Cully, Iris V. *A guide to biblical resources,* BC108
Cully, Kendig Brubaker. *A guide to biblical resources,* BC108
Culme, John. *The directory of gold & silversmiths, jewellers, and allied traders, 1838–1914,* BG137, BG140
Culot, Jean-Marie. *Bibliographie des écrivains français de Belgique, 1881–1960,* BE1099
Cults, BC28
    bibliography, BC32
La cultura española medieval, Vera, Francisco, BE1443
Cultural anthropology, Kibbee, Josephine Z., CE1, CE2
Cultural anthropology of the Middle East, Strijp, Ruud, CE112
Cultural atlas of France, Ardagh, John, DC164
Cultural atlas of Russia and the Soviet Union, Milner-Gulland, R. R., DC572
Cultural diversity, CC75, DF24
    associations, AL50
A cultural encyclopedia of the 1850s in America, Gale, Robert L., DB103
Cuming, G. J. *The world's encyclopaedia of recorded music,* BJ375
Cumming, Robert. *Christie's guide to collecting,* BF121
Cummings, Gary. *A New Guinea bibliography,* DF48
Cummings, Paul. *Dictionary of contemporary American artists,* BF151
Cumulated bibliography and index to Meteorological and geoastrophysical abstracts, American Meteorological Society, EF143
Cumulated dramatic index, 1909–1949, BH55
Cumulated fiction index, BE242

Cumulated index medicus, EH35, EH64, EH66
Cumulated index to reviews of books on Victorian studies, 1975–1989, Chaudhuri, Brahma, BE752
Cumulated indexes to the public papers of the Presidents of the United States, AD262
Cumulated magazine subject index, AD262
Cumulated magazine subject index, 1907–1949, AD270
Cumulative author index for Poole's index to periodical literature, 1802–1906, Wall, Edward, AD282
Cumulative author index to Psychological abstracts, 1959/63–1981/83, CD17
Cumulative bibliography of African studies ... author catalogue, International African Institute, DD23
Cumulative bibliography of African studies ... classified catalogue, International African Institute, DD23
Cumulative bibliography of Asian studies, 1941–1965, DE4
Cumulative bibliography of Victorian studies, 1970–1984, Chaudhuri, Brahma, BE752
Cumulative bibliography of Victorian studies, 1976–1980, Chaudhuri, Brahma, BE752
Cumulative bibliography of Victorian studies, 1985–1989, Chaudhuri, Brahma, BE752
Cumulative book index, AA422, AA423, AA430, AA422, AA430
Cumulative index, AD285
Cumulative index of hospital literature, 1945–1977, EH74, EH77
Cumulative index to English translations, 1948–1968, AA141
Cumulative index to Hickcox's monthly catalog of United States government publications, 1885–1894, Kanely, Edna A., AF93
Cumulative index to journals in education, CB158, CB194, CD92
Cumulative index to nursing & allied health literature, EH274, EH275, EH277, EH280
Cumulative index to nursing literature, EH274, EH277
Cumulative index to the annual catalogues of Her Majesty's Stationery Office publications, 1922–1972, Great Britain. Stationery Office, AF184
A cumulative index to the Biographical dictionary of American sports, Porter, David L., BK21
Cumulative microform reviews, AA137
Cumulative subject guide to U.S. government bibliographies, 1924–1973, Kanely, Edna A., AF81
Cumulative subject index to the Monthly catalog of United States government publications, 1895–1899, Kanely, Edna A., AF94, AF103
Cumulative subject index to the Monthly catalog of United States government publications, 1900–1971, AF103
———— Buchanan, William W., AF111
———— Kanely, Edna A., AF111
Cumulative title index to United States public documents, 1789–1976, Lester, Daniel W., AF96
Cuneo, Michael W. *Issues in the sociology of religion,* BC7
———— *The sociology of religion,* BC7
Cunningham, Phyllis M. *Handbook of adult and continuing education,* CB362
———— *The independent learners' sourcebook,* CB350
Cunnington, Cecil Willett. *Children's costume in England ...,* BG99
———— *Costume for births, marriages & deaths,* BG99
———— *A dictionary of English costume [900–1900],* BG99
———— *Occupational costume in England ...,* BG99
Cunnington, Phillis. *A dictionary of English costume [900–1900],* BG99
Cure, Karen. *The travel catalogue,* CL371
Cureton, Thomas K. *Encyclopedia of physical education, fitness, and sports,* BK15
The curious cook, McGee, Harold, EJ218
Curl, James Stevens. *Encyclopedia of architectural terms,* BF241

———— *English architecture,* BF241
Curley, Arthur. *Modern Romance literatures,* BE1069
Curley, Dorothy Nyren. *Modern American literature,* BE427, BE598, BE600, BE1069
———— *Modern Romance literatures,* BE1069
Curley, Stephen J. *Celluloid wars,* CJ608
Curran, Allen H. *Atlas of landforms,* EF109
Curran, Barbara A. *The lawyer statistical report,* CK167
Currency *see* **Coins, medals, currency**
Current, Richard Nelson. *Encyclopedia of the Confederacy,* DB117
Current American usage, Bryant, Margaret M., AC67
Current anthropology, CE66
Current Australian serials, AD214
Current awareness in biological sciences, EG16, EG17, EG15
Current bibliographic directory of the arts & sciences, EA137
Current bibliographic survey of national defense, CJ566
Current bibliographies in medicine, EH14, EH22
Current bibliography, BE754
Current bibliography in the history of technology, EA228, EA242
A current bibliography of vernacular architecture, BF215
A current bibliography on African affairs, DD21
Current bibliography on life-writing, BE213
Current biography, AH15, AH44
Current biography yearbook, AH44
Current biotechnology, EK49
Current British directories, AL2
Current British journals, AD115
Current Caribbean bibliography, AA554
Current Central American–U.S. relations, Nordquist, Joan, DB300
Current clinical dental terminology, Boucher, Carl O., EH252
Current coins of the world, BG192
Current contents, CA17, EA68, EA75
Current contents address directory, EA137
Current contents address directory : social sciences/arts & humanities, EA137
Current contents Africa, DD22
Current contents Linguistik, BD23
Current contents of academic journals in Japan, AD341
•*Current contents on CD-ROM : Agriculture, biology & environmental sciences,* CA17, EA68
•*Current contents on CD-ROM : Clinical medicine,* CA17, EA68
•*Current contents on CD-ROM : Life sciences,* CA17, EA68
•*Current contents on CD-ROM : Physical, chemical & earth sciences,* CA17, EA68
•*Current contents on diskette,* CA17, EA68
•*Current contents search,* CA17, EA68
Current cookbooks, Bulson, Christine, EJ222
Current diagnosis & treatment, EH83
Current digest of the post-Soviet press, AE68
Current digest of the Soviet press, AE68
Current European directories, Henderson, George P., AL5
Current geographical publications, CL22, CL28
Current guide to the contents of the Public Record Office, DC286
Current index to journals in education, AK28, AK35, BE348, CB1, CB54, CB56, CB61, CB83, CD90, CD91
Current index to statistics, applications, methods and theory, CG15, EB22, EB28
Current Indian periodicals in English, Gidwani, N. N., AD191, AD193
———— Navalani, K., AD193
Current Indonesian studies in the Netherlands, DE179
Current issues resource builder, Smallwood, Carol, CA50

Current Japanese serials in the humanities and social sciences received in American libraries, Indiana University. Libraries, AD223

Current law index, CK22, CK26, CK27

Current leaders of nations, CJ65

Current legal forms, with tax analysis, Johnson, Mark H., CK164

——— Rabkin, Jacob, CK164

Current list of medical literature, EH62, EH63

Current list of publications, AF253

Current literature in traffic and transportation, CH443

Current literature in transportation, CH443

Current literature on aging, CC78

Current literature on general medical practice, EH76

Current literature on health services, EH76

Current mathematical publications, EB23, EB28

Current medical diagnosis and treatment, EH83

Current medical information and terminology, EH96

Current military & political literature, CJ565

Current military literature, CJ565

Current national bibliographies, Library of Congress. General Reference and Bibliography Division, AA397

Current national bibliographies of Latin America, Zimmerman, Irene, AA472

Current national bibliography of New Zealand books & pamphlets, AD347

Current national bibliography of New Zealand books and pamphlets published in [1950–65], AA949

Current population reports, CG97

Current primate references, EG291

Current procedural terminology, EH147

Current programs, EA207

Current research in Britain, BA8, CA46, EA138, EG47, EA138

Current research in French studies at universities & polytechnics in the United Kingdom & Ireland, BE1142

Current research in library & information science, AK29

•*Current research information system,* EJ74

Current Slavic, Baltic and East European periodical and newspaper titles in the Slavic and Baltic Division, the Periodicals Division, and the branch libraries of the New York Public Library, Davis, Robert H., AE42

Current sociology, CC11

Current Swedish periodicals, AD161

Current technology index, EK6

Current therapy, Conn, Howard F., EH177

Current treaty index, CK96

Current trends in linguistics, Sebeok, Thomas Albert, BD137, BD238

Current work in the history of medicine, EH199, EH218

——— Wellcome Historical Medical Library, EH54

Current world affairs, CJ566

Currer-Briggs, Noel. *Worldwide family history,* AJ2

Currey, L. W. *Research guide to science fiction studies,* BE281

——— *Science fiction and fantasy authors,* BE285

Curricula in the atmospheric, oceanic, hydrologic, and related sciences, EF151

Curriculum Information Center. *CIC's school directory,* CB96

Curry, Hayden. *A legal guide for lesbian and gay couples,* CC288

Curthoys, Ann. *Australians from 1939,* DF37

Curtis, A. R. *Coulomb wave functions,* EB94

Curtis, Laurence. *World atlas of geology and mineral deposits,* EF110

Curtis, Melissa C. *The Bible and modern literary criticism,* BC115

Curzon, Leslie B. *Dictionary of law,* CK34

Cushing, Helen Grant. *Bibliography of costume,* BG92

——— *Children's song index,* BJ283

——— *Nineteenth century readers' guide to periodical literature, 1890–1899,* AD280

Cushing, William. *Anonyms,* AA149

——— *Initials and pseudonyms,* AA149

Cushion, John Patrick. *Handbook of pottery and porcelain marks,* BG70

——— *Pocket book of British ceramic marks,* BG70

Cushman, Clare. *The Supreme Court justices,* CK189

Custom house guide, CH146

Cutchin, D. A. *Guide to public administration,* CJ461

Cuthbert, Eleanora Isabel. *Index of Australian and New Zealand poetry,* BE849

Cuthbert, John A. *Vernacular architecture in America,* BF213

Cutler, John L. *The index of Middle English verse,* BE697

Cutolo, Vicente Osvaldo. *Diccionario de alfónimos y seudónimos de la Argentina (1800–1930),* AA155

——— *Nuevo diccionario biografico argentino (1750–1930),* AH117

Cutter, Charles. *Judaica reference sources,* BC513

Cuyás, Arturo. *Appleton's new Cuyás English-Spanish and Spanish-English dictionary,* AC732

CVA, BG78

CVMA, BG78

CWLA's guide to adoption agencies, Posner, Julia L., CC231

Cycling, BK72

Cyclopaedia of American literature, Duyckinck, Evert Augustus, BE433

Cyclopaedia of costume, Planché, J. R., BG96

The cyclopaedia of fraternities, Stevens, Albert Clark, AL77

Cyclopædia of India and of eastern and southern Asia, commercial, industrial, and scientific, Balfour, Edward Green, DE164

Cyclopedia of American biography, AH58

Cyclopedia of American medical biography, Kelly, Howard Atwood, EH229

A cyclopedia of education, Monroe, Paul, CB71

Cyclopedia of literary characters, Magill, Frank Northen, BE186, BE688

Cyclopedia of literary characters II, BE186

Cyclopedia of painters and paintings, Champlin, John Denison, BF299, BF312

——— Perkins, Charles C., BF312

Cyclopedia of world authors, Magill, Frank Northen, BE208

Cyclopedia of world authors II, Magill, Frank Northen, BE208

Cyclopedic survey of chamber music, Cobbett, Walter Wilson, BJ270

Cylke, Frank Kurt. *International directory of tactile map collections,* CL258

Cypress, Sandra Messinger. *Women authors of modern Hispanic South America,* BE896

Cyprus, DC121

bibliography, DC120

current, AA590

statistics, CG203, CG204

Cyprus (by subject)

history

bibliography, DC374

Cyprus. Financial Secretary's Office. Statistics Section. *Statistical abstract,* CG203

Cyprus, Kitromilides, Paschalis, DC120

Cyprus (Turkish republic of northern Cyprus, 1983–). *Statistical yearbook,* CG204

Cyr, Helen W. *A filmography of the Third World,* BH221

——— *Filmography of the Third World, 1976–1983,* BH221

——— *Third World in film and video,* BH221

Cyrillic union catalog, Library of Congress, AA784, AA785

Czachowska, Jadwiga. *Przewodnik polonisty,* AA58

Czachowski, Kasimierz. *Najnowsza twórczość literacka, 1935–37,* BE1349

——— *Obraz współczesnej literatury polskiej, 1884–[1934],* BE1349

Czachowskiej, Jadwigi. *Słownik współczesnych pisarzy polskich,* BE1351

Czapliński, Władysław. *The historical atlas of Poland,* DC482

Czarnecka, J. *555 książek wydanych w okresie powojennym,* AA766

Czarra, Fred R. *Guide to historical reading,* BE256

Czech and Slovak abbreviations, Library of Congress. Slavic and Central European Division, AC282

Czech and Slovak literature in English, Kovtun, George J., BE1108

Czech-English dictionary, AC280

Czech-English technical dictionary, EA106

Czech language

abbreviations, AC282

dictionaries, AC276, AC277, AC278

bilingual

Czech-English, AC280, AC281

English-Czech, AC279

etymology, AC283

Czech literature, Novak, Arne, BE1106

Czechoslovak contribution to world culture, Rechcígl, Miloslan, BE1106

Czechoslovak Republic. Komise pro knihopisn y soupis českých a slovenských tiskú až do konce XVIII. století. *Knihopis československých tiskú,* AA596

Czechoslovakia

atlases, CL322, CL323

bibliography, AA591, AA592, AA593, AA594, AA595, AA596, AA597, AA598, AA599, AA600, DC123, DC126, DC127

biography, AH181

encyclopedias, DC129

gazetteers, CL131

government publications, AF165

guides, DC93

historiography, DC124

library resources, DC128

newspapers, AE47

periodicals, AD88

indexes, AD307

registers, CJ325

statistics, CG205, CG206, CG207, CG208

Czechoslovakia (by subject)

demography, CG205

history, DC122

bibliography, DC125, DC126

statistics, CG206

Czechoslovakia. Federální statistický úřad. *Statistická ročenka České a Slovenske federativní republiky,* CG208

Czechoslovakia, Short, David, DC126

——— Sturm, Rudolf, DC126

Czechoslovakia, 1968–1969, Hejzlar, Zdeněk, DC123

Czechoslovakian literature, BE1106, BE1107

bibliography, BE1104, BE1109

biobibliography, BE1105, BE1110, BE1111

translations, BE1108

Czechs (by country or region)

United States

bibliography, CC323

Czechs and Slovaks in North America, Jerabek, Esther, CC323

Czerni, Sergiusz. *Słownik naukowo-techniczny polsko-angielski,* EA122

Czigány, Lóránt. *The Oxford history of Hungarian literature from the earliest times to the present,* BE1276

Czigány, Magda. *Hungarian literature in English translation published in Great Britain 1830–1968,* BE1280

Członkowie Polskiej Akademii Nauk, Krzyzanowska, Jadwiga, AH280

D & B Europe. *Duns Europa,* CH411

The Da Capo guide to contemporary African music, Graham, Ronnie, BJ330

Da Graça, John V. *Heads of state and government,* CJ84

daai, BG11

Dabla, Sewanou. *Guide de litterature africaine (de langue francaise),* BE1516

Dąbrowska, Wanda. *555 książek wydanych w okresie powojennym,* AA766

Dabundo, Laura Susan. *The encyclopedia of romanticism,* BE759

Dachs, Herbert. *Handbuch des politischen Systems Österreichs*, CJ326

Dadzie, E. W. *Directory of archives, libraries and schools of librarianship in Africa*, AK154

Daemmrich, Horst S. *Themes & motifs in western literature*, BE182

Daemmrich, Ingrid. *Themes & motifs in western literature*, BE182

Daftar karya bibliografi Indonesia, AA79

Daftar majalah Indonesia yang telah mempunyai ISSN, Zulkarjono, Maesarah, AD197

Dag Hammarskjöld Library. *Index to proceedings of the Security Council*, AF38

—— *Index to proceedings of the Trusteeship Council*, AF39

Dāghir, Yūsuf As'ad. *Mu'jam al-asmā' al-musta 'ārah wa-aṣhābihā lā siyyama fi al-adab al-'Arabī al-hadīth*, AA189

—— *Qāmūs al-siḥāfah al-Lubnānīyah, 1858– 1974 : wa-huwa mujam yua/a1rrif wa-yu rrikh lil-ṣuḥuf wa-al-dawrīyāt al-latī aṣdarahā al-Lubnāniyūn fi Lubnān wa-al-khārij*, AE91

Daglish, Robert. *Russko-angliiskii slovar'*, AC680

Daguerreotypes, BK53

Daguerreotypes of great stars of baseball, MacFarlane, Paul, BK53

Dagytė, Emilija. *Tarybų Lietuvos rašytojai : biobibliografinis*, BE1325

Dahl, Folke. *Bibliography of English corantos and periodical newsbooks, 1620–1642*, AE56

Dahl, Henry S. *Dahl's law dictionary*, CK55

—— *Diccionario juridico*, CK55

Dahl, Svend. *Dansk biografisk leksikon*, AH183

—— *Dansk skønlitteraert forfatterleksikon, 1900– 1950*, BE1114

Dahl, Torsten. *Svenska män och kvinnor*, AH292

Dahl, Willy. *Norges litteratur*, BE1337

—— *Nytt norsk forfatterleksikon*, BE1340

Dahlberg, Ingetraut. *International classification and indexing bibliography*, AK201

Dahlerup, Verner. *Ordbog over det danske sprog*, AC285

Dahlhaus, Carl. *Brockhaus Riemann Musiklexikon*, BJ128

—— *Pipers Enzyklopädie des Musiktheaters*, BJ252

—— *Riemann musik Lexikon*, BJ125

Dahlin, Caryl Ann. *Encyclopedia of computer science*, EK171

Dahlin, Therrin C. *The Catholic left in Latin America*, DB255

Dahlke, Günther. *Internationale Bibliographie zur Geschichte der deutschen Literatur*, BE1213

Dahlmann, Friedrich Christoph. *Dahlmann-Waitz Quellenkunde der deutschen Geschichte*, DC215, DC226

Dahlmann-Waitz Quellenkunde der deutschen Geschichte, Dahlmann, Friedrich Christoph, DC215, DC226

—— Waitz, Georg, DC226

Dahl's law dictionary, Dahl, Henry S., CK55

Dahmus, Joseph. *Dictionary of medieval civilization*, DA152

DAI, AG13

Dai-genkai, Ōtsuki, Fumihiko, AC549

Dai-hyakka jiten, AB70

Dai-Nihon hakushiroku, AH357

Dai-Nihon hyakka jiten, AB69

Daiches, David. *A companion to Scottish culture*, DC363

Daijiten, AC545

Daijiten desuku, AB69

Dailey, Kazuko. *Library buildings consultants list*, AK176

Daily, Jay Elwood. *Encyclopedia of library and information science*, AK36

Daily stock price record, CH313

Daily weather maps, Climate Analysis Center, EF169

Daims, Diva. *Novels in English by women, 1891– 1920*, BE474, BE480, BE750

—— *Toward a feminist tradition*, BE474

Daintith, John. *A biographical encyclopedia of scientists*, EA174

—— *Bloomsbury dictionary of quotations*, BE101

—— *The Facts on File dictionary of chemistry*, EE38

—— *The Facts on File dictionary of physics*, ED18

Dairiki, Janis M. *Table of isotopes*, ED46

Dairy science abstracts, EJ19

Dairying, EJ115

Daisne, Johan. *Dictionnaire filmographique de la littérature mondiale*, BH216

—— *Filmographic dictionary of world literature*, BH216

Dakov, Todor. *Krat'uk spravochnik po istoriǐa na Bŭlgariǐa*, DC119

Dal', Vladimir Ivanovich. *Tolkovyi slovar' zhivogo velikorusskago ǐazyka*, AC668

Dalal-Clayton, D. B. *Black's agricultural dictionary*, EJ24

Dalbiac, Lilian. *Dictionary of quotations (German)*, BE134

Dalbiac, P. H. *Dictionary of quotations (French and Italian)*, BE132

Dalby, David. *Language map of Africa and the adjacent islands*, BD217

—— *A thesaurus of African languages*, BD217

Dale, Doris Cruger. *A directory of oral history tapes of librarians in the United States and Canada*, AK85

Dale, Edgar. *The educator's quotebook*, CB84

Dale, Laura. *Parapsychology*, CD131

Dale, Peter. *Directory of library and information organizations in the United Kingdom*, AK142

—— *Guide to libraries in Western Europe*, AK132

D'Aleo, Richard J. *FEDfind*, AF71

Dalhousie Ocean Studies Programme. *Marine affairs bibliography*, CK81

Dalīl al-dawrīyāt al-ṣādirah bi-al-bilād al-Tūnisīyah, Ḥamdān, Muḥammad, AD181

Dalīl al-jarā'id wa-al-majallāt al-'Irāqīyah, 1869– 1978, Ibrāhīm, Zāhidah, AE91

Dalīl al-maṣādir al-iḥṣā' iyah fi al-bilād al-'Arabīyah, 'Abbūd, Muḥammad Fatḥī, CG374

Dalīl al-matbuat al-miṣriyah, 1940–1956, AA854

Dalīl al-risālāt al-'Arabīyah, Jāmi̇at al-Kuwayt. Qism al-Tawthīq, AG51

Dall, C. H. *Genealogical notes and errata to Savage's Genealogical dictionary*, AJ65

Dallas Public Library. Business and Technology Division. *Business history collection*, CH382

Dallet, Sylvie. *Filmographie mondiale de la Révolution française*, DC179

Dalling, Thomas. *International encyclopedia of veterinary medicine*, EJ108

Daly, Elaine L. *Sports ethics in America*, BK4

Daly, John C. K. *Central Eurasia military-naval encyclopedia*, CJ657

Daly, M. W. *Sudan*, DD18

Dam, Esther. *Bibliography of periodical articles relating to the South Pacific*, DF2

Damien, Yvonne M. *Anthropological bibliographies*, CE19

Dampierre, Jacques de. *Les publications officielles des pouvoirs publics*, AF169

Damschroder, David. *Music theory from Zarlino to Schenker*, BJ29

Dana, Edward Salisbury. *The system of mineralogy of James Dwight Dana and Edward Salisbury Dana, Yale University, 1837–1892*, EF194

Dana, Henry Wadsworth Longfellow. *Handbook on Soviet drama*, BE1410

Dana, James Dwight. *The system of mineralogy of James Dwight Dana and Edward Salisbury Dana, Yale University, 1837–1892*, EF194

Danaher, Kevin. *Beyond safaris*, DD52

—— *A bibliography of Irish ethnology and folk tradition*, CF81

Danandjaja, James. *An annotated bibliography of Javanese folklore*, CF95

Dance, Daryl Cumber. *Fifty Caribbean writers*, BE970

Dance
annuals, BH155, BH156, BH157
bibliography, BH131, BH132, BH133, BH134, BH135
biography, BH158
databases, BH135
dictionaries, BH145, BH146, BH147
directories, BH18, BH148, BH149, BH157
encyclopedias, BH139, BH140, BH141, BH142, BH143, BH144
filmography, BH149
guides, BH130
handbooks, BH150, BH152, BH153, BH154
indexes, BH136, BH137
library catalogs, BH135
periodicals, BJ104
plot summaries, BH154
Dance (by country or region)
Africa
bibliography, BF38
see also **Ballet**
Dance, Forbes, Fred R., BH132
Dance directory, BH148
The dance encyclopedia, Chujoy, Anatole, BH139
Dance film and video guide, BH149
Dance Films Association. *Dance film and video guide*, BH149
The dance handbook, Robertson, Allen, BH153
Dance magazine annual, BH18
Dance magazine college guide, BH148
•*Dance on disc*, BH135
Dance world, BH156
Dancy, Jonathan. *A companion to epistemology*, BB28
Dandekar, Ramchandra Narayan. *Vedic bibliography*, BC484
D'Andrea, Anna. *Il secondo dopoguerra in Italia, 1945–1960*, DC421
Dane, Jean. *How to use a law library*, CK218
Dang, Shu-leung. *Research guide to English translation of Chinese verse*, BE1552
D'Angelo, George V. *Aerospace agencies and organizations*, CH480
Dangerous properties of industrial materials, Sax, N. Irving, EE79, EE80
Dangerous sky, Wilson, Eunice, DA170
D'Angiolini, Piero. *Guida generale degli archivi di Stato italiani*, AK150, DC429
Dania Polyglotta, AA604, AA605
Daničić, úrua. *Rječnik hrvatskoga ili srpskoga jezika*, AC709
Daniel, Glyn. *Illustrated encyclopedia of archaeology*, DA77
Daniel, Howard. *Encyclopedia of themes and subjects in painting*, BF165
Daniel, Odile. *Albanie, une bibliographie historique*, DC79
Daniel Blum's screen world, BH268
Daniells, Lorna M. *Business information sources*, CH2
—— *Studies in enterprise*, CH389, CH390
Daniels, Belinda S. *Black athletes in the United States*, BK2
Daniels, George. *Clocks and watches*, BG81
Daniels, Gilbert S. *Manual of cultivated broad-leaved trees & shrubs*, EG196
Daniels, Judith M. *The concise dictionary of American Jewish biography*, BC565
Daniels, Mary. *French literature in early American translation*, BE1146
Daniels, Morna. *Burundi*, DD18
Danilewicz Zielińska, Maria. *Catalogue of periodicals in Polish or relating to Poland and other Slavonic countries, published outside Poland since September 1st, 1939*, AD136
Danilov, Victor J. *America's science museums*, EA216
—— *Corporate museums, galleries, and visitor centers*, BF97, BF114
Danish language
bibliography, BD131
dictionaries, AC285, AC286

bilingual
Danish-English, AC289
English-Danish, AC288
etymology, AC290
Danish literature
bibliography, BE1114, BE1116, BE1119, BE1120, BE1122
biography, BE1114, BE1115, BE1117, BE1122
translations, BE1112
Danish literature (by subject)
history, BE1113, BE1118, BE1121
Danish literature in English translation, Bredsdorff, Elias, BE1112
The Danish national bibliography, AD308, AE119
The Danish national bibliography. Books, AA605
Danker, Frederick. *A Greek-English lexicon of the New Testament and other early Christian literature*, AC453
Danky, James Philip. *Asian-American periodicals and newspapers*, AE24
—— *Hispanic Americans in the United States*, AE31
—— *Native American periodicals and newspapers, 1828–1982*, AE16
—— *Undergrounds*, AD221
—— *Women's periodicals and newspapers from the 18th century to 1981*, AD48, AE25
Danmark, Trap, Jens Peter, CL132
Dann, Graham. *Barbados*, DB421
Dannemann Rothstein, Manuel. *Bibliografía del folklore chileno, 1952–1965*, CF71
Danova, Nadia Khristova. *Gŭrtsiia i bŭlgaro-grŭtskite otnosheniia v bŭlgarskata nauchna knizhnina, 1878–1980*, DC110
Dansk anmeldelsesindeks, AA605
Dansk artikelindeks, AD308, AD309, AE119
Dansk artikelindeks. Aviser og tidsskrifter, AA605
Dansk Bibliografi, 1482–1550, 1551–1600, Nielsen, Lauritz Martin, AA603
Dansk billedfortegnelse, AA605
Dansk biografisk leksikon, AH183
Dansk bogfortegnelse, AA604, AA605, AA606, AD308, AE119, AF166
Dansk bogfortegnelse [for aarene] ..., AA601, AA605, AA606, AA607, AA718
Dansk-engelsk Ordbog, Axelsen, Jens, AC287
Dansk forfatterleksikon, Woel, Cai Mogens, BE1122
Dansk historisk Bibliografi, AH185
—— Erichsen, Balder, DC131
Dansk juridisk bibliografi, CK207
Dansk litteraturhistorie, BE1113, BE1121
Dansk lydfortegnelse, AA605
Dansk marinehistorisk bibliografi, 1500–1975, Bjerg, Hans Christian, DC130
Dansk musikfortegnelse, AA605
Dansk periodicafortegnelse, AA605
Dansk personalhistorisk bibliografi, Erichsen, Balder, AH185
Dansk skønlitteraert forfatterleksikon, 1900–1950, BE1114
Dansk sprogrøgtslitteratur 1900–1955, Jacobsen, Henrik Galberg, BD131
Dansk Tidsskrift-Index, AD308, AD309, AD310, AE119, AH185
Danske blandede Tidsskrifter, 1855–1912, Thomsen, Svend, AD310
Danske bogmarked, AA605
Danske Digtere i det 20. arhundrede, BE1115
Danske grammofonplader og kassetteband, AA605
Danske historiske forening. *Dansk historisk bibliografi*, DC131
Danske klassikere, Lindtner, Niels Christian, BE1119
Danske sprog- og litteraturselskab. *Ordbog over det danske sprog*, AC285
Dansmark statistik. *Statistisk årbog*, CG210
Danstrup, John. *Kulturhistorisk Leksikon for nordisk Middelalder fra Vikingetid til Reformationstid*, DC75, DC76
Dantaitė, A. *Anglų-lietuvių kalbų žodynas*, AC600
Danton, Joseph Periam. *Index to festschriften in librarianship*, AK13

—— *Index to festschriften in librarianship, 1967–1975*, AK13
Dantsig, B. M. *Bibliografiia Türtsii, 1713–1917*, DC532
Danyel, Jürgen. *Archives and libraries in a new Germany*, AK133, AK139, DC13, DC247
Danz, Alexander. *Le peintre graveur*, BF382
Dār al-Kutub al-Qaṭarīyah. *Qāʾimat al-intāj al-fikrī al-Qaṭarī li-ʿām*, AA932
Dār al-Kutub al-Qawmīyah (Tunisia). *Récapitulation des périodiques officiels parus en Tunisie de 1881 à 1955*, AF239
DAR patriot index, Daughters of the American Revolution, AJ36
Darby, William. *Masters of lens and light*, BH206
Darch, Colin. *Mozambique*, DD18
—— *Russian writings on Tanganyika, Zanzibar, and Tanzania*, DD107
—— *A Soviet view of Africa*, DD107, DD147, DD207
—— *Soviet view of Arica*, DD158
—— *Tanzania*, DD18
Dare, Philip N. *American communes to 1860*, DB138
•*DARE*, AF59
Daremberg, Charles Victor. *Dictionnaire des antiquités grecques et romaines d'après les textes et les monuments*, DA99
Darkowska-Nidzgorska, Olenka. *Connaissance du Gabon*, DD159
Darley, Gillian. *Dictionary of ornament*, BG23
Darling, Louise. *Handbook of medical library practice*, EH4
Darling, Pamela W. *Preservation planning program*, AK238
Darlow, T. H. *Historical catalogue of the printed editions of Holy Scripture in the library of the British and Foreign Bible Society*, BC95, BC99, BC100
Darmesteter, Arsène. *Dictionnaire général de la langue française*, AC330
Darmstaedter, Ludwig. *Handbuch zur Geschichte der Naturwissenschaften und der Technik ...*, EA251
Darnay, Arsen. *Economic indicators handbook*, CH107
Darnay, Arsen J. *Manufacturing USA*, CH422
—— *Statistical record of older Americans*, CC105
Darnay, Brigitte T. *Life sciences organizations and agencies directory*, EG49
Darrell, R. D. *Gramophone Shop encyclopedia of recorded music*, BJ375
The Dartnell personnel administration handbook, CH712
Darton, Michael. *Modern concordance to the New Testament*, BC161
Darton, Nelson Horatio. *Catalogue and index of contributions to North American geology, 1732–1891*, EF26
Darwin, Charles, EG68, EG70
Das, Sarat Chandra. *A Tibetan-English dictionary with Sanskrit synonyms*, AC783
Data for biochemical research, EG318
Data for elementary-particle physics, ED49
The data game, Maier, Mark, CA54
Data on serial publications of Vietnam, AD212
Data processing
abstract journals, EK166
bibliography, EK151, EK158
biography, EK176
dictionaries, EK175, EK176, EK177, EK178, EK179, EK187
bilingual
Japanese-English, EK191
multilingual, EK190, EK192, EK194, EK197
indexes, EB21, EK159, EK160, EK164, EK168
Data processing (by subject)
history, EK176
bibliography, EK208, EK209
Data sourcebook for food scientists and technologists, EJ164
Data sources, EK199
Data user news, CG86

DataBase Publishing (Hong Kong). *Who's who in Hong Kong*, AH348
Databases
bibliography, AF107
congresses and meetings, AL28, BK34, CH554, EA210
directories, AD2, AF65, AF104, AK206, AK207, AK208
Databases (by subject)
accounting, CH246
administrative law, CK182
adult education, CB355, CB357
advertising and public relations, CH548, CH572, CH573, CH574
aeronautical and space engineering, EK26, EK27, EK28
aging, CC79
agriculture, EJ14, EJ16, EJ18, EJ46, EJ74, EJ78
AIDS (disease), EH72
animal science, EJ102, EJ125
Antarctic, DG1
anthropology and ethnology, CE8, CE36
archaeology and ancient history, BF198, DA70
architecture, BF94
armed forces, CJ223
art, BF33, BF34, BF42, BF43, BF94, BF198, BG12
associations, AL41
astronomy, EC1, EC23
audiovisual materials, EH42
bilingual education, CB40, CB41
bioethics, EH238
biography, AH42, BE198
biological sciences, EG9, EG11, EG13, EG14, EG15
biotechnology, EK49
business, CH6, CH32, CH34, CH35, CH36, CH37, CH306, CH337, CH338, CH345, CH363, CH367, CH373, CH411, CH423, CH426
cancer, EH73
chemical engineering, EK49
chemistry, EE20, EE22, EE66, EE93, EE109, EE127, EE133, EE139
chemistry, inorganic, EE110
chemistry, organic, EE149
child abuse, CC156, CC161
computer science, EB28
computers, EK159, EK161, EK165, EK166, EK167
congresses and meetings, AL26, EA206
congressional committee hearings, AF118
consumer health, CH558, EH57
corporations, CH309, CH313, CH369
courts
directories, CK149
dance, BH135
dentistry, EH67
directories, AL3
economic development, CH119
economics, CH32, CH40, CH41, CH42, CH150
education, AK28, CB17, CB28, CB54, CB55, CB56, CB57, CB95, CB151, CB283, CB302, CD68, CD90, CD91
directories, CB147
financial aid, CB100
education, higher, CB257, CB308
electrical and electronic engineering, ED9
encyclopedias, AB2, AB10, AB13, AB18, AB22, AB23, AB24, AB25, AB26, AB27, AB28, AB56
energy, EK215
engineering, EA67, EK6, EK7
English language, AC33
environment and environmental problems, EK67, EK70, EK71
ethnic press, AE107, CC339
European communities, AF25
family violence, CC156
fellowships and scholarships, CB387
film, BH185, BH234, BH240, BH297
finance and banking, CH299
financial aid, CB388
folklore and popular culture, CF49
food science, EJ150, EJ151

foreign relations, CJ185
foundations and philanthropic organizations, AL122
geographical names and terms, CL108
geography, CL30, CL68, CL111, EF51
geology, EF50, EF53
government publications, AF104
government publications (by country or region)
 Great Britain, AF182, AF203
 United States, AD291, AF105, AF106, AF111, AF115
grants-in-aid, AL110
Great Britain
 bibliography, AA689
Greek literature, AC443, BE1036
health care, EH75
high technology industries, CH349
history of science, EA241, EA242
humanities, BA3, BA5
industries, CH337
information services, EH158
insurance, CH506
international law, CK112
international trade, CH118, CH119, CH497
laboratories, EA213, EA214
Latin America, BE874, DB266
Latinos, CC455
law, CK22, CK26
legislation, AF64, AF67, CJ209
library and information science, AK28, AK29, AK30, AK31, AK32, AK33, AK88, CB54, CD90
linguistics, BD31
management, CH610
manufacturing industries, CH345
marketing, CH548, CH578
marriage and the family, CC221
materials, EK258
mathematical statistics, EB28
mathematics, EB28, EB31
medicine, EA37, EA70, EH37, EH42, EH46, EH58, EH67
meteorology, EF143
mining and metallurgical engineering, EK253
music, BJ53, BJ108, BJ111
mutual funds, CH326
Native Americans, CC412
navigation, EC78
newspapers, AE106, AE111, AE112, AE113, AE118, CH38
nuclear engineering, EK293
nuclear physics, EK294
nursing, EH67, EH275
oceanography, EF214
periodical indexes, AD272, AD273, AD278, AD284, AD285, AD335
periodicals, AD15, AD18, AD19, AE118, CH38, EH37
 directories, AD6
 indexes, AD296
pharmacology, EH58, EH357
philosophy, BB25
physics, ED9, ED10, ED11
poetry, BE315, BE319, BE320, BE715
polar regions, DG2, DG5
political science, CA3, CJ17, CJ20, CJ161, CJ210, CJ223, CL68
politics and government, CJ17, CJ137, CJ151, CJ161, CJ210, CJ214, CJ223
population, CC257, CG17, EH78
printing and publishing, AA282, AK33, BE172
psychology, CB151, CD16, CD17, CD68, CD69
public opinion, CJ485, CJ491, CJ494
recorded music, BJ380
religion, BC41, BC46
science, EA36, EA37, EA69, EA70, EA75
social and behavioral sciences, CA3, CA25, CA27
special education, CB194, CD92
sports and games, BK11, BK44
standards, EA272
student aid, BD390
subject headings, AK220
technology, EA36, EA37, EA67

television, BH297
tests and measurements, CB151, CD68, CD69
thermochemistry, EE93
toxicology, EH421
trademarks, CH348
treaties, CK92
United Nations, AF43
 publications, AF40
United States
 bibliography, AA426
 government agencies, AL80
United States. Congress, AF119, CJ209, CJ215
universities and colleges, CB260
vocational guidance, CB210, CB213
water resources, EF131
women's studies
 guides, CC571

Databases & on-line data in astronomy, EC1
DataMap, CG16
Daten der griechischen und römischen Geschichte, Lauffer, Siegfried, DA111
Daten deutscher Dichtung, Frenzel, Elisabeth, BE1252
—— Frenzel, Herbert, BE1252
Daten zu deutschen Geschichte, Hellwig, Gerhard, DC223
Datensammlungen in der Physik, ED4
Datos para la bibliografía boliviana. 1. sección, Gutiérrez, José Rosendo, AA504
Datta, Amaresh. Encyclopaedia of Indian literature, BE1565
Dauben, Joseph Warren. The history of mathematics from antiquity to the present, EB8
Daubenas, Joseph. Baltic drama, BE989
Daugherty, D. H. Bibliography of periodical literature in musicology and allied fields, BJ109
Daughters of the American Revolution. DAR patriot index, AJ36
Daum, Edmund. A dictionary of Russian verbs, AC669
Dause, Charles. Argumentation, BE371
Dauzat, Albert. Dictionnaire étymologique de la langue française, AC348
—— Dictionnaire étymologique des noms de famille et prénoms de France, AJ189
—— Dictionnaire étymologique des noms de lieux en France, CL185
—— Dictionnaire étymologique des noms de rivières et de montagnes en France, CL186
—— Nouveau dictionnaire étymologique et historique, AC348
Davau, Maurice. Dictionaire du français vivant, AC327
Davenport, Millia. The book of costume, BG108
Davey, Gwenda Beed. The Oxford companion to Australian folklore, CF99
David, A. Rosalie. A biographical dictionary of ancient Egypt, DA124
David, Antony E. A biographical dictionary of ancient Egypt, DA124
David, Jack. The annotated bibliography of Canada's major authors, BE819
—— Canadian writers and their works: fiction series, BE819
David, Zdeněk V. Scholars' guide to Washington, D.C. for cartography and remote sensing imagery, CL257
—— Scholars' guide to Washington, D.C. for southwest European studies, DC15
Davids, W. Rhys. Pali-English dictionary, AC625
Davidson, Cathy N. The Columbia history of the American novel, BE485
Davidson, Francis. The new Bible commentary, revised, BC171
Davidson, Henry A. Handbook of parliamentary procedure, CJ453
Davidson, James. Dictionary of Protestant church music, BC322, BJ155
Davidson, Judith A. Sport on film and video, BK36
Davidson, Linda Kay. Pilgrimage in the Middle Ages, DA132
Davidson, Martha. Arts of the United States, BF197

—— A list of published translations from Chinese into English, French and German ... , BE1552
Davidson, Ralph Howard. Insect pests of farm, garden, and orchard, EJ50
Davie, W. J. An historical atlas of Scotland, c.400–c.1600, DC367
Davies, Adriana. Middle Ages to the early Georgians, BF66
—— Twentieth century : historical figures born before 1900, BF66
Davies, Alistair. An annotated critical bibliography of modernism, BE761
Davies, D. Hywel. Zambia in maps, CL342
Davies, Godfrey. Bibliography of British history, Stuart period, 1603–1714, DC315
Davies, Hugh. Répertoire international des musiques électroacoustiques, BJ311
Davies, J. S. Amino acids and peptides, EE114
Davies, John Gordon. The new Westminster dictionary of liturgy and worship, BC268
Davies, Leslie. Harper dictionary of economics, CH62
Davies, M. J. A bibliography of nineteenth century legal literature, CK5
Davies, Robert H. The struggle for South Africa, DD208
Davies, Stephen. A dictionary of conservative and libertarian thought, CJ24
Davies, Thomas Lewis Owen. Supplementary English glossary, AC97
Davies, Trefor. Chemical engineering practice, EK55
Davies, William David. The Cambridge history of Judaism, BC562
Davies, William Llewellyn. Y Bywgraffiadur Cymreig hyd 1940, AH245
Davis, Arthur Paul. The new cavalcade, BE541
Davis, Bob J. Information sources in transportation, material management, and physical distribution, CH442
Davis, Calvin Victor. Handbook of applied hydraulics, EK102
Davis, Clive M. Sexuality-related measures, CC292
Davis, Deta S. Computer applications in music, BJ30
Davis, Donald G. American library history, AK71
—— ARBA guide to library science literature, 1970–1983, AK8
—— Encyclopedia of library history, AK72
Davis, Elisabeth B. Guide to information sources in the botanical sciences, EG90
—— Using the biological literature, EG1
Davis, Gwenn. Drama by women to 1900, BE456
—— Personal writings by women to 1900, BE508
—— Poetry by women to 1900, BE489
Davis, Henry P. Modern dog encyclopedia, EJ145
Davis, J. C. Bancroft. United States reports, CK190
Davis, J. R. ASM materials engineering dictionary, EK264
Davis, Jack. Canadian writers and their works: poetry series, BE819
Davis, John D. Westminster dictionary of the Bible, BC138
Davis, Lenwood G. A bibliographical guide to black studies programs in the United States, CC364
—— The black aged in the United States, CC65
—— Black artists in the United States, BF24
—— Black athletes in the United States, BK2
—— The black family in the United States, CC365
—— Black-Jewish relations in the United States, 1752–1984, CC366
Davis, Lloyd M. Contemporary American poetry, BE487
Davis, Lynne. Fact book on women in higher education, CB344
Davis, Martha. Body movement and nonverbal communication, CD116
—— Understanding body movement, CD116
Davis, Nanette J. Prostitution, CC291
—— Women and deviance, CC490
Davis, Richard C. Encyclopedia of American forest and conservation history, EJ176
—— North American forest history, EJ172, EJ174
Davis, Robert H. Colombia, DB365

—— *Current Slavic, Baltic and East European periodical and newspaper titles in the Slavic and Baltic Division, the Periodicals Division, and the branch libraries of the New York Public Library,* AE42

Davis, Sandra L. *Sexuality-related measures,* CC292

Davis, Stephen D. *Plants in danger,* EG162

Davis, William Edmund. *Resource guide to special education,* CB203

The Davis book of medical abbreviations, Mitchell-Hatton, Sarah Lu, EH133

Davis' handbook of applied hydraulics, EK102

Davison, Graeme. *Australians 1888,* DF37

Davison, Kenneth E. *The American presidency,* CJ168

Davydov, Nikolai Nikolaevich. *Botanicheskii slovar',* EG142

Davydova, A. G. *Literatura o narodonaselenii,* CG298, CG299

Dawes, Benjamin. *A hundred years of biology,* EG59

The dawn and twilight of Zoroastrianism, Zaehner, Robert Charles, BC577

Dawn to the west, Keene, Donald, BE1582

Dawson, Joseph G. *Dictionary of American military biography,* CJ641, CJ648

—— *Late 19th century U.S. Army, 1865–1898,* CJ608

Dawson, Rex M. C. *Data for biochemical research,* EG318

Day, A. Colin. *Roget's thesaurus of the Bible,* BC157

Day, Alan. *Walford's guide to reference material,* AA363

Day, Alan Edwin. *Discovery and exploration,* CL35

—— *England,* DC273

—— *History,* DC291

—— *Search for the Northwest Passage,* DB181

Day, Alan J. *Peace movements of the world,* CJ693

—— *Political parties of the world,* CJ77

—— *A world record of major conflict areas,* CJ57

Day, Arthur Grove. *Modern Australian prose, 1901–1975,* BE846

Day, Cyrus Lawrence. *English song-books, 1651–1702,* BJ275

Day, David. *The antiques care & repair handbook,* BG45

Day, Donald B. *Index to the science fiction magazines, 1926–1950,* BE294

Day, John. *Oxford Bible atlas,* BC200

Day, Neil. *The British electorate 1963–1987,* CJ367

Day, Peter D. *The liturgical dictionary of Eastern Christianity,* BC445

Day, Robert A. *How to write & publish a scientific paper,* EA158

Day care, Watkins, Kathleen Pullan, CC154

Day care centers, CC58

Dāyirat al-ma'ārif-i Fārsī, AB38

Dayton, William A. *Standardized plant names,* EG118

DDR drama Handbuch, 1945–1985, BE1265

DDR Handbuch, CJ330

DE annual, EH337

De Bary, William Theodore. *A guide to Oriental classics,* BE1543

De Bhaldraithe, Tomás. *English-Irish dictionary,* AC520

De Bray, R. G. A. *Guide to the Slavonic languages,* BD181

De Breffny, Brian. *Ireland,* DC407

De Brou, David. *Documenting Canada,* AF156, DB206

De Conde, Alexander. *Encyclopedia of American foreign policy,* DB43

De Felice, Emidio. *Dizionario dei cognomi italiani,* AJ198

De Franchis, Francesco. *Dizionario giuridico,* CK50

De Francisci, Giovanni. *Dictionary of medical syndromes,* EH120

De Gámez, Tana. *Simon and Schuster's international dictionary,* AC737

De George, Richard T. *Philosopher's guide to sources, research tools, professional life and related fields,* BB1, BB2

De Gorog, Ralph Paul. *Lexique français moderne-ancien français,* AC375

De Jongh, William Frederik Jekel. *A bibliography of the novel and short story in French from the beginning of printing till 1600,* BE1187

De Kock, W. J. *Dictionary of South African biography,* AH325

De Koster, Lester. *Vocabulary of communism,* CJ522

De la Croix, Horst. *Gardner's art through the ages,* BF129

De Laura, David J. *Victorian prose,* BE984

De Lerma, Dominique-René. *Bibliography of black music,* BJ31

—— *Black music and musicians in The new Grove dictionary of American music and The new Harvard dictionary of music,* BJ225

de Luise, Alexandra A. *Historical bibliography of art museum serials from the United States and Canada,* BF49

De Mello Vianna, Fernando. *Webster's new World children's dictionary,* AC27

De Montreville, Doris. *Fourth book of junior authors & illustrators,* BE384

—— *Third book of junior authors,* BE384

De Sanctis, Francesco. *History of Italian literature,* BE1304

—— *Storia della letteratura italiana,* BE1304

De Silva, Chandra Richard. *Sri Lanka since independence,* DE258

De Silva, Daya. *The Portuguese in Asia,* DE5

—— *Sri Lanka (Ceylon) since independence (1948–1974),* DE258

—— *Sri Lanka since independence,* DE258

De Sola, Ralph. *Abbreviations dictionary,* AC43, AC45

—— *Crime dictionary,* CK257

—— *International conversion tables,* AL199

De Stricker, Ulla. *Business online,* CH6

De Vries, Louis. *Dictionary of chemistry and chemical engineering,* EE49

—— *Dictionary of pure and applied physics,* ED25

—— *German-English science dictionary,* EA111

De Vries, Mary Ann. *Complete secretary's handbook,* CH86

—— *New Robert's rules of order,* CJ457

De Winter, Patrick M. *European decorative arts, 1400–1600,* BG7

De Young, Mary. *Child molestation,* CC144

—— *Incest,* CC207

Deacon, Richard. *Spyclopaedia,* CJ540

Dead Sea Scrolls, BC106, BC109, BC112, BC187, BC556

The Dead Sea Scrolls, Fitzmyer, Joseph A., BC187

DEAF, AC346

Deafness and the deaf, CC189

bibliography, CC187

encyclopedias, CC188

A deafness collection, Ritter, Audrey L., CC187

Deak, Étienne. *Dictionnaire d'américanismes,* AC339

—— *Grand dictionnaire d'américanismes,* AC339

De'ak, Gloria. *Guide to research and scholarship in Hungary,* DC389

Deak, Simone. *Grand dictionnaire d'américanismes,* AC339

Deakin University. Centre for Studies in Literary Education. *A bibliography of Australian multicultural writers,* DF24

Deal, Angela G. *Enabling and empowering families,* CC235

Deal, Ernest L. *A dictionary of soldier talk,* CJ616

Dean, Bashford. *A bibliography of fishes,* EG286

Dean, John Aurie. *Chemist's ready reference handbook,* EE87

—— *Handbook of organic chemistry,* EE148

—— *Lange's handbook of chemistry,* EE77

Deane, Phyllis. *Abstract of British historical statistics,* CG234

Deane, Seamus. *Short history of Irish literature,* BE803

Dear, Ian. *An A–Z of sailing terms,* BK121

—— *Oxford English,* BD96

Dearing, Vinton A. *Transfer vectors for Poole's Index to periodical literature,* AD281

Dearman, John Andrew. *Harper's Bible pronunciation guide,* BC140

Deason, Hilary J. *The AAAS science book list,* EA27

Death and dying

bibliography, CC177, CC178, CC179, CC180, CC181

encyclopedias, CC182, CC183

handbooks, CC184

Death and dying, Southard, Samuel, CC181

Death education, CC179

Debate index, BE368

—— Dunlap, Joseph R., BE368

—— Kuhn, Martin A., BE368

Debate index supplement, Johnsen, Julia E., BE368

The debater's guide, Ericson, Jon M., BE370

Debates and proceedings in the Congress of the United States, AF127

Debates and proceedings of the British parliaments, Jones, David Lewis, AF209

Debating

bibliography, BE372

handbooks, BE369, BE370, BE371, BE373

indexes, BE368

Debets, N. P. *Slovari, izdannye v SSSR,* AC698

Debrett's correct form, Montague-Smith, Patrick W., AL159

Debrett's etiquette and modern manners, AL153

Debrett's handbook of Australia and New Zealand, AH373

Debrett's peerage and baronetage, AJ119

Debrett's peerage, baronetage, knightage, and companionage, AJ119

Debrett's Peerage Ltd. *Debrett's correct form,* AL159

—— *Debrett's etiquette and modern manners,* AL153

Debus, Allen G. *The complete entertainment discography, from 1897 to 1942,* BJ343

Decade of Bible bibliography, Anderson, G. W., BC117

A decade of Ethiopian languages publications, 1959–1969, Solomon Gebre Christos, AA857

Decade of Gallup polls of attitudes toward education, 1969–1978, Elam, Stanley M., CB137

Decalo, S. *Benin,* DD48

—— *Chad,* DD48

—— *Niger,* DD48

—— *Togo,* DD48

Decamp, David. *A bibliography of pidgin and creole languages,* BD55

Decan, Rik. *Wie is wie in Vlaanderen, 1989–1993,* AH177

DeCandido, Robert. *Collection conservation,* AK238

Decaux, Alain. *Dictionnaire d'histoire de France Perrin,* DC160

Une décennie d'études berbères (1980-1990), Chaker, Salem, DD68

DeCharms, Désirée. *Songs in collections,* BJ284

DECHEMA. *Chemical engineering and biotechnology abstracts,* EK49

Dechert, Hans W. *Transfer and interference in language,* BD80

Decision making, Balachandran, Sarojini, CH605

Decisions on geographic names in the United States, United States Board on Geographic Names, CL174, CL175

Decorative arts, BG23

bibliography, BG12

biography, BG34

collections, BG28

dictionaries, BG21, BG24, BG42

encyclopedias, BG20

library catalogs, BG15

Decorative arts (by country or region)

Europe

bibliography, BG7

Oceania

bibliography, BG8

United States, BG18, BG117

directories, BG28

indexes, BG16, BG17

library catalogs, BG16
Decorative arts (by period)
19th–20th centuries
encyclopedias, BG19
Decorative arts and household furnishings in America, 1650–1920, BG117
DeCoste, F. C. *Feminist legal literature*, CK10
Decrees of the ecumenical councils, BC436
Deebel, W. R. *Glossary of oceanographic terms*, EF220
Deep-sea research. Part B : Oceanographic literature review, EF215
Deer, William Alexander. *Rock-forming minerals*, EF195
Deering, Dorothy. *The Waterloo directory of Victorian periodicals, 1824–1900*, AD114
Deerpalsingh, S. *A bibliography of Mauritian government publications, 1955–1978*, AF234, DD179
Deeson, Eric. *The Facts on File dictionary of physics*, ED18
Defense Activity for Non-Traditional Education Support (Government Agency : U.S.). *A guide to the evaluation of educational experiences in the armed services*, CB361
Defense Marketing Services, Inc. *International code name directory*, CJ586
Deferrari, Roy Joseph. *A complete index of the Summa theologica of St. Thomas Aquinas*, BB62
—— *A lexicon of St. Thomas Aquinas based on the Summa theologica and selected passages of his other works*, BB63
DeFilipps, Robert A. *Endangered and threatened plants of the United States*, EG145
Definitions of surveying, mapping, and related terms, American Society of Civil Engineers, EF123
Definitions of terms used in geodetic and other surveys, Coast and Geodetic Survey, EF122
—— Mitchell, H.C, EF123
DeFrancis, John. *Chinese-English glossary of the mathematical sciences*, EB48
Degener, Hermann August Ludwig. *Wer ist wer?*, AH211
Degeners Wer ist's?, AH211
Degenhardt, Henry W. *Maritime affairs—a world handbook*, CH466
—— *Political dissent*, CJ61
—— *Revolutionary and dissident movements*, CJ61
—— *Treaties and alliances of the world*, CK107
DeGolyer, Everette Lee. *Bibliography on the petroleum industry*, EK299
Dei, Oleksii Ivanovych. *Slovnyk ukrains'kykh psevdonimiv ta kriptonimiv (XVI–XX st.)*, AA188
Deĭateli revoliutsionnogo dvizheniia v Rossii, AH283
Deichmanske Bibliotek, Oslo. *Register til en del norske tidsskrifter*, AD321, AH274
Deighton, Lee C. *Encyclopedia of education*, CB68
Deimel, Anton. *Šumerisches Lexikon*, AC202
Déjeux, Jean. *Bibliographie de la littérature "algérienne" des Français*, BE1522
—— *Bibliographie méthodique et critique de la littérature algérienne de langue française, 1945–1977*, BE1522
—— *Dictionnaire des auteurs maghrebins de langue française*, BE1515
Dejevsky, Nikolai J. *Cultural atlas of Russia and the Soviet Union*, DC572
Dějiny, české literatury, BE1106
Dejnozka, Edward L. *American educators' encyclopedia*, CB65
—— *Educational administration glossary*, CB181
Dekin, Albert A. *Arctic archaeology*, DB214
Dekkers, Eligius. *Clavis patrum latinorum*, BC296
Del Cervo, Diane M. *International population census publications*, CG9
Del Tutto Palma, L. *Bibliografia dell'Italia antica*, DC417
DeLancey, Mark W. *African international relations*, DD3
—— *A bibliography of Cameroon*, DD136
—— *Cameroon*, DD18, DD48, DD138

—— *Handbook of political science research on sub-Saharan Africa*, CJ401
—— *Historical dictionary of international organizations in sub-Saharan Africa*, DD6
—— *Nigeria*, DD192
—— *Somalia*, DD18
DeLancey, Virginia H. *A bibliography of Cameroon*, DD136
Delaney, John J. *Dictionary of American Catholic biography*, BC418
—— *Dictionary of Catholic biography*, BC419
—— *Dictionary of saints*, BC264
DeLange, N. R. M. *Atlas of the Jewish world*, DA52, DE193
Delano, Isaac O. *A dictionary of Yoruba monosyllabic verbs*, AC818
—— *Modern dictionary of Yoruba usage*, AC818
Delaunay, Daniel. *Demografía en el Ecuador*, CG153
DeLaura, David J. *Victorian prose*, BE686, BE703, BE755
DeLaurier, Nancy. *Slide buyers' guide*, BF195
Delaware. [Laws, etc.]. *Delaware code annotated*, CK179
Delaware code annotated, Delaware. [Laws, etc.], CK179
Delecourt, Jules Victor. *Dictionnaire des anonymes et pseudonymes, XVᵉ siècle–1900*, AA162
—— *Essai d'un dictionnaire des ouvrages anonymes et pseudonymes publiés en Belgique au XIVᵉ siècle et principalement depuis 1830*, AA162
Deletant, Andrea. *Romania*, DC496
Deletant, Dennis. *Romania*, DC496
Delisle, Jean. *Guide bibliographique du traducteur, rédacteur et terminologue*, BD88
Delivering government services, Murin, William F., CJ471
Dell, David. *Guide to Hindu religion*, BC481
Della Corte, Francesco. *Dizionario degli scrittori greci e latini*, BE1013
Della Peruta, Franco. *Bibliografia della stampa periodica operaia e socialista italiana, 1860–1926*, CH657
Dellenbach, M. Carolyn. *Guide to the holdings of the American Jewish Archives*, BC538
DeLoach, Charles. *The quotable Shakespeare*, BE774
Delorme, Robert. *Latin America*, DB256
Delpar, Helen. *The discoverers*, CL36
Delson, Eric. *Encyclopedia of human evolution and prehistory*, CE40
Delteil, Löys. *700 reproductions d'estampes des XIXᵉ et XXᵉ siècles pour servir de complément au 'Manuel'*, BF377
—— *Manuel de l'amateur d'estampes au XVIIIᵉ siècle*, BF377
—— *Manuel de l'amateur d'estampes des XIXᵉ et XXᵉ siècles*, BF377
—— *Peintre-graveur illustré*, BF377
Deltion hellēnikēs bibliographias, AA707
Deltion vivliographias tēs Hellēnikēs glōssēs, BD135
Deltour, F. *Notice sur le doctorat ès lettres suivie du Catalogue et de l'analyse des thèses françaises et latines admises par les facultés des lettres depuis 1810*, AG29
Delury, George E. *World encyclopedia of political systems & parties*, CJ77
Delves, Peter J. *Encyclopedia of immunology*, EG21, EH85
Dēmadēs, K. A. *Valkanikē vivliographia*, DC66
DeMars, Jo. *Final choices*, CC184
Demchik, V. Carol. *Astronomy education materials resource guide*, EC19
Dement'ev, A. G. *Istoriia russkoĭ sovetskoĭ literatury, 1917–1965*, BE1417
—— *Russkaia periodicheskaia pechat'*, AD146
Dēmētrakos, Dēmētrios B. *Mega lexikon tēs Hellēnikēs glōssēs*, AC460
Demetrio y Radaza, Francisco. *A critical and annotated bibliography of Philippine, Indonesian and other Malayan folk-lore*, CF94
Demetrius, James K. *Greek scholarship in Spain and Latin America*, DA95

DeMiller, Anna L. *Linguistics*, BD3, BD8
Demise of the Soviet Union, Kavass, Igor I., CK223
Demografía, CG144
Demografía en el Ecuador, Delaunay, Daniel, CG153
Demografía en el Ecuador, una bibliografia, CG153
Demografía guatemalteca, 1960–1976, Arias de Blois, Jorge, CG130
Demográfiai évkönyv, CG245
Demograficheskiĭ ėntsiklopedicheskiĭ slovar', CG292
Demografska statistika, CG303
Demographic research in japan, 1955–70, Matsumoto, Y. Scott, CG404
Demographic review of the Maltese Islands, CG265
Demographic statistics, CG175, CG183
Demographic yearbook, CG49, CG202
Demographics USA, CH592
Demographisches Jahrbuch Österreichs, CG194
Demography, urbanization, and spatial planning in Kenya, Obudho, Robert A., DD166
Demougin, Jacques. *Dictionnaire de la littérature française et francophone*, BE1160
—— *Dictionnaire historique, thématique et technique des littératures*, BE62, BE1160
Dempsey, Hugh A. *Bibliography of the Blackfoot*, CC420
Dempsey, Michael W. *Atlas of the Arab world*, CL349
Dempsey, Patrick E. *Panoramic maps of cities in the United States and Canada*, CL234
DeMyer, Marian K. *Annotated bibliography on childhood schizophrenia, 1955–1964*, EH374
Denecke, Ludwig. *Nachlässe in den Bibliotheken der Bundesrepublik Deutschland*, DC248
Deniker, Joseph. *Bibliographie des travaux scientifiques*, EA208
Denisova, L. V. *Rare plants of the world*, EG156
Denizeau, Claude. *Dictionnaire arabe-français-anglais*, AC213
Denmark
atlases, CL324
bibliography, AA605
19th–20th centuries, AA606, AA607
early, AA601, AA602, AA603
bibliography (by period)
19th and 20th centuries, AA604
bibliography of bibliography, AA40
biography, AH164, AH183, DC131
bibliography, AH185
contemporary, AH184
gazetteers, CL132
government publications, AF166
periodicals
indexes, AD308, AD309, AD310, AE119
statistics, CG209, CG210
Denmark (by subject)
history, DC72, DC130, DC131, DC132
bibliography, DC133
law
bibliography, CK207
Denmark. Statistiske departement. *Statistisk àrbog*, CG210
Denmark, Miller, Kenneth E., DC133
Dennen, J. van der. *The bibliography of human behavior*, CA10, CD8
Dennett, Herbert. *Guide to modern versions of the New Testament*, BC94
Denning, Margaret B. *A handbook of American diplomacy*, CJ150
Dennis, Deborah Ellis. *Suburbia*, CC307
Dennis, M. Wayne. *Communism in Latin America*, CJ513
Dennis, Marguerite J. *Dollars for scholars*, CB376
Denny, Robert E. *Civil war years*, DB120
Dent, David W. *Handbook of political science research on Latin America*, CJ307
The Dent atlas of American history, Gilbert, Martin, DB72
The Dent atlas of Jewish history, Gilbert, Martin, DA52, DE193
Dent atlas of the Holocaust, DA223
The Dent dictionary of fictional characters, BE189
Dental abstracts, EH248, EH249

Dental bibliography, New York Academy of Medicine. Library, EH245
Dental schools (by country or region)
  Canada, EH259
  United States, EH259
Dental terminology, EH256
Denti, Renzo. *Dizionario tecnico italiano-inglese, inglese-italiano,* EA116
Dentistry
  abstract journals, EH248, EH249
  bibliography, EH23, EH243, EH244, EH245
  databases, EH67
  dictionaries, EH252, EH253, EH255, EH256, EH258
    bilingual
      Spanish-English, EH254
      multilingual, EH256, EH257
  directories, EH260, EH261
  encyclopedias, EH176
  guides, EH243, EH244
  handbooks, EH262, EH263
  indexes, EH250, EH251
  periodicals, EH246, EH247
Dentistry (by country or region)
  United States
    history, EH264
Dentistry (by subject)
  history, EH264, EH265, EH266
Dentistry journals and serials, Kowitz, Aletha, EH246
Dentists
  directories, EH260, EH261
Dentist's desk reference, EH262, EH263
The dentists register, EH261
Denver Folklore Center. *The folk music sourcebook,* BJ324
Denver post [index], AE104
Department bulletins [Index], United States. Department of Agriculture, EJ92
Department of Defense dictionary of military and associated terms, CJ584, CJ585
The Department of State and American diplomacy, Goehlert, Robert, CJ169
Departments, academic *see* **Universities and colleges—departments**
DePew, John N. *Library, media, and archival preservation glossary,* AK239
    A library, media, and archival preservation handbook, AK239
Deposit bulletin of Iraqi publications. AA908
Depression, EH380
I deputati e senatori del … Parlamento republicano, CJ381
Derdak, Thomas. *International directory of company histories,* CH394
Derieux, Emmanuel. *Presse quotidienne française,* AE52
Derivan, William J. *Prevention education,* CC112
A derivational dictionary of Latvian, Metuzāle-Kangere, Baiba, AC598
Derks, Scott. *The value of a dollar,* CH111
Derksen, Charlotte. *Union list of geologic field trip guidebooks of North America,* EF93
Derksen, Walther. *Index litteraturae entomologicae,* EG328
Derkx, Jo. *Suriname,* DB393
Dermatology, EH111
Dermer, Joseph. *The complete guide to corporate fund raising,* AL133
Dermineur, Bernard. *Catalogue général des ouvrages en langue française, 1926–1929,* AA628
Derry, Charles. *Film book bibliography, 1940–1975,* BH170
Derry, Duncan R. *World atlas of geology and mineral deposits,* EF110
Deruguine, T. *Dictionary of Russian geographical names,* CL154
Dervaes, Claudine. *The travel dictionary,* CL381
Derwent Publications Ltd. *Thesaurus of agricultural organisms, pests, weeds, and diseases,* EJ33
Desai, Prasannavadan B. *Annotated and classified bibliography of Indian demography,* CG387

Deśapāṇḍe, Bhāratī. *Modern English-Gujarati dictionary,* AC468
    Universal English-Gujarati dictionary, AC468
Deśapāṇḍe, Pāṇḍuraṅga Ganeśa. *Modern English-Gujarati dictionary,* AC468
    Universal English-Gujarati dictionary, AC468
Descartes, René, BB72, BB76
Descartes and his philosophy, Sebba, Gregor, BB76
Deschamps, Pierre. *Dictionnaire de géographie ancienne et moderne,* CL101
Descharmes, René. *Bibliographie des travaux scientifiques,* EA208
Deschler, Lewis. *Deschler's precedents of the United States House of Representatives,* CJ224
    Deschler's rules of order, CJ454
Deschler-Brown precedents of the United States House of Representatives, CJ224
Deschler's precedents of the United States House of Representatives, Deschler, Lewis, CJ224
Deschler's rules of order, Deschler, Lewis, CJ454
Descours-Gatin, Chantal. *Guide de recherches sur le Vietnam,* DE272
Descriptive atlas of New Zealand, McLintock, Alexander H., CL365
A descriptive atlas of the Pacific islands, Kennedy, Thomas Fillans, CL368
A descriptive bibliography of art music by Israeli composers, Tischler, Alice, BJ65
A descriptive bibliography of the most important books in the English language relating to the art & history of engraving and the collecting of prints, with supplement and index, Levis, Howard Coppuck, BF361
Descriptive catalog of maps published by Congress, Claussen, Martin Paul, CL229
Descriptive catalog of the history of economics collection, (1850–1930), University of Kansas. Libraries, CH24
Descriptive catalogue of Friends' books, Smith, Joseph, BC353
A descriptive catalogue of the bibliographies of 20th century British poets, novelists, and dramatists, Mellown, Elgin W., BE763
A descriptive catalogue of the government publications of the United States, Sept. 5, 1774–March 4, 1881, Poore, Benjamin Perley, AF97, AF98
Descriptive catalogue of the Spanish comedias sueltas in the Wayne State University Library and the private library of Professor B. B. Ashcom, Ashcom, Benjamin Bowles, BE1472
A descriptive checklist of book catalogues separately printed in America, 1693–1800, Winans, Robert B., AA99, BF223
A descriptive dictionary and atlas of sexology, CC281
Descriptive index of current engineering literature, EK7
A descriptive list of United Nations reference documents on Namibia (1946–1978), Evborokhai, A. O., DD186
A descriptive petrography of the igneous rocks, Johannsen, Albert, EF256
Deserts *see* **Arid regions**
Deserts of the world, CL58, EF17
Desgraves, Louis. *Répertoire bibliographique des livres imprimés en France au XVIIIe siècle,* AA620, AA623
Design
  abstract journals, BF42
  bibliography
    current, BF41, BG11
  biography, BG22, BG32
  collections, BG28
  dictionaries, BG22, BG23, BG24, BG25
  guides, BG2
  library catalogs, BG15
Design (by country or region)
  Great Britain
    bibliography, BG6
  United States, BG18

  directories, BG28
Design (by period)
  20th century
    biography, BG29
Design (by subject)
  symbols and symbolism, BF177
  see also **Industrial design**
Design & applied arts index, BG11, BG32
Design and applied arts periodicals, BG11
Design index, BG11
Design international, BG32
Design resources, Bamford, Lawrence Von, BF201
Designers international index, BG11
    Jagger, Janette, BG32
Designing and conducting survey research, Rea, Louis M., CA58
Desk encyclopedia of intellectual property, CK134
Desk reference for neuroanatomy, Lockard, Isabel,, EH119
Desk reference for neuroscience, Lockard, Isabel, EH119
Deskbook encyclopedia of American school law, CB154
Desktop computers, Henle, Richard A., EK206
Deslandes, Gaston. *Dictionnaire étymologique des noms de rivières et de montagnes en France,* CL186
Deslandres, Yvonne. *20,000 years of fashion,* BG106
Desmond, Ray. *Bibliography of British gardens,* BF285
    Dictionary of British and Irish botanists and horticulturists including plant collectors and botanical artists, BF285, EG165
Desplaces, Eugène Ernest. *Biographie universelle (Michaud) ancienne et moderne,* AH22
Dessaint, Alain Y. *Minorities of Southwest China,* CE107
Dessalegn Rahmato. *Short guide to the study of Ethiopia,* DD156
Destrez, J. *Bibliographie Thomiste,* BB61, BB66
Destructive and useful insects, Metcalf, Robert Lee, EG84, EG335
Detailed statistics on the population of Israel by ethnic and religious group and urban and rural residence, 1950 to 2010, Roof, Michael K., CG399
Detailed statistics on the population of South Africa by race and urban/rural residence, 1950 to 2010, Johnson, Peter D., CG356
Detailed statistics on the urban and rural population of Cuba, 1950 to 2010, Rowe, Patricia M., CG170
Detailed statistics on the urban and rural population of Indonesia, 1950 to 2010, Way, Peter O., CG395, CG415
Detailed statistics on the urban and rural population of Mexico, 1950 to 2010, Rowe, Patricia M., CG119
Detailed statistics on the urban and rural population of Pakistan, 1950 to 2010, Finch, Glenda, CG415
Detailed statistics on the urban and rural population of the Philippines, 1950 to 2010, Kinsella, Kevin G., CG418
Detailed statistics on the urban and rural population of Turkey, 1950 to 2000, Spitler, James F., CG291
Detectionary, Lachman, Marvin, BE267
    Penzler, Otto, BE267
    Steinbrunner, Chris, BE267
Detective and mystery fiction
  bibliography, BE265, BE266, BE269, BE271, BE273, BE274
  biobibliography, BE272, BE275
  criticism, BE293
  dictionaries, BE267
  handbooks, BE274
  indexes, BE268, BE269
  periodicals, BE270
Detective and mystery fiction, Albert, Walter, BE265
Detemmerman, Jacques. *Bibliographie des écrivains français de Belgique, 1881–1960,* BE1099
Deth, Jan W. van. *Dutch parliamentary election studies data source book, 1971–1989,* CJ383
Detroit news [index], AE104

Detroit Public Library. *Catalog of the E. Azalia Hackley memorial collection of Negro music, dance, and drama,* BJ86

Detroit Public Library. Career and Employment Information Center. *Job hunter's sourcebook,* CH702

Detti, Tommaso. *Il movimento operaio italiano,* AH262

Detwiler, Donald S. *West Germany,* DC232

Deubert, K. *Guide to the availability of theses II,* AK224

Deuring, M. *Encyklopädie der mathematischen Wissenschaften mit Einschluss ihrer Anwendungen,* EB36

Deuss, Jean. *Banking in the U.S,* CH283

Deutch, Yvonne. *The illustrated encyclopedia of mankind,* CE42

—— *Man, myth & magic,* BC64

Deutsch, Babette. *Poetry handbook,* BE326

Deutsch, Karl Wolfgang. *Interdisciplinary bibliography on nationalism, 1935–1953,* CJ9

—— *Nationalism and national development,* CJ9

Deutsch-Englisches, Englisches-Deutsches Wörterbuch für Aerzte, Lejeune, Fritz, EH136

Deutsche Akademie der Wissenschaften zu Berlin. *Mittellateinisches Wörterbuch bis zum ausgehenden 13. [i.e. dreizehnten] Jahrhundert,* AC591

Deutsche Bibliographie, AA333, AA647

Deutsche Bibliographie. Fünfjahres-Verzeichnis, AA650

Deutsche Bibliographie. Halbjahres-Verzeichnis, AA651, AA658

Deutsche Bibliographie. Hochschulschriften-Verzeichnis, AA657, AA659, AG30

Deutsche Bibliographie : Wöchentliches Verzeichnis, AA651, AA652, AA653, AA659

Deutsche Bibliographie. Wöchentliches Verzeichnis. Neuerscheinungen Sofortdienst (CIP), AA653

Deutsche Bibliographie : Zeitschriften Verzeichnis, AA650, AD98

Deutsche Bibliothek (Frankfurt am Main). *Deutsche Bibliographie,* AA333

—— *Deutsche Bibliographie. Halbjahres-Verzeichnis,* AA651

Deutsche Bibliothek (Frankfurt am Main, Germany). *Deutsche Bibliographie. Zeitschriften-Verzeichnis,* AD98

—— *Deutsche Nationalbibliographie und Bibliographie der im Ausland erschienenen deutschsprachigen Veröffentlichungen,* AA657, AA658, AA659, AG30

Deutsche Bibliothekskataloge im 19. Jahrhundert, AA118

Deutsche Bücherei. *Monatliches Verzeichnis der reichsdeutschen amtlichen Druckschriften,* AF174

Deutsche Bücherei (Germany). *Bibliographie der versteckten Bibliographien,* AA45

Deutsche Chemische Gesellschaft. *Literatur Register der organischen Chemie,* EE122, EE143

—— *System der organischen Verbindungen,* EE115

Deutsche Dichterhandschriften von 1400 bis 1900, Frels, Wilhelm, BE1242

Deutsche Dissertationen über Afrika, Köhler, Jochen, DD30

Deutsche Exil Literatur, 1933 1945, Sternfeld, Wilhelm, BE1232

Deutsche Forschungsgemeinschaft. *Verzeichnis ausgewählter wissenschaftlicher Zeitschriften des Auslandes,* AD5

Deutsche Forschungsgemeinschaft. Südosteuropa-Arbeitskreis. *Südosteuropa-Handbuch,* DC68

Deutsche Geschichte in deutscher Erzahlung, Luther, Arthur, BE1267

Deutsche Geschichtswissenschaft im zweiten Weltkrieg, Holtzmann, Walter, DC218

Deutsche Gesellschaft für Kartographie. *Bibliographia cartographica,* CL247

—— *Bibliotheca cartographica,* CL227

Deutsche literarische Zeitschriften, 1880–1945, Dietzel, Thomas, AD76, AD77

Die Deutsche Literatur, BE1216

Die deutsche Literatur des Mittelalters, Stammler, Wolfgang, BE1253

Deutsche Literaturgeschichte in Tabellen, Schmitt, Fritz, BE1252

Deutsche Literaturwissenschaft, BE1055

Deutsche Morgenländische Gesellschaft. *Wörterbuch der klassischen arabischen Sprache,* AC225

Deutsche Musikbibliographie, BJ80

Deutsche Namenkunde, Bach, Adolf, AJ192, CL189

—— Gottschald, Max, AJ195

Deutsche Nationalbibliographie, AA647, AA653, AA654, AA656, AA658, AA659

•*Deutsche Nationalbibliographie DNB aktuelle,* AA657, AG30

Deutsche Nationalbibliographie und Bibliographie, AA651

Deutsche Nationalbibliographie und Bibliographie der im Ausland erschienenen deutschsprachigen Veröffentlichungen, AA139, AA142, AA650, AA652, AA655, AA657, AA658, AA659, AG30, BJ48

Deutsche peintre-graveur, Andresen, Andreas, BF382

Die deutsche Photoliteratur 1839–1978, BF329

Deutsche Physikalische Gesellschaft. *Physics briefs,* ED10

Deutsche rechtsbibliographie, CK211

Deutsche Schriftsteller der Gegenwart, Lennartz, Franz, BE1258

Deutsche Schriftsteller des 20. Jahrhunderts im Spiegel der Kritik, Lennartz, Franz, BE1258

Deutsche Shakespeare-Gesellschaft. *Shakespeare Jahrbuch,* BE779

Deutsche sozialistische Literatur, 1918–1945, Melzwig, Brigitte, BE1229, BE1249

Deutsche Sprache, BD124

Deutsche Sprache im Reformationszeitalter, Pasiersbky, Fritz, BD122

Deutsche Statistische Gesellschaft. *Bibliographie der amtlichen westdeutschen Statistik, 1945–1951,* CG228

Deutsche Wirtschaftsarchive, DC245

Deutsche Wörterbücher, Kühn, Peter, AC425

Der deutsche Wortschatz nach Sachgruppen, Dornseiff, Franz, AC432

Deutsche Zeitungsbestände in Bibliotheken und Archiven, Hagelweide, Gert, AE53

Deutschen Bücherei. *Jahresverzeichnis der deutschen Hochschulschriften 1885–1973,* BE594

Deutschen Chemischen Gesellschaft. *Handbuch der organischen Chemie,* EE115

Deutschen Exilpresse 1933–1945, AD101

Die deutschen Inkunabeldrucker, Geldner, Ferdinand, AA307

Deutschen Literatur-Zeitschriften, 1815–1850, Estermann, Alfred Adolph, AD77

Die deutschen Literatur-Zeitschriften, 1850–1880, Estermann, Alfred Adolph, AD77

Deutschen Literatur-Zeitschriften, 1850–1880, Estermann, Alfred Adolph, AD76

Deutscher biographischer index, Koch, Hans-Albrecht, AH206

—— Koch, Uta, AH206

—— Koller, Angelika, AH206

Deutscher Gesamtkatalog, AA121, AA122

Deutscher Wortschatz, Lemmer, Manfred, AC426

—— Wehrle, Hugo, AC435

Deutsches Anonymen-Lexikon, Holzmann, Michael, AA170

Deutsches Archäologisches Institut. *Archäologische Bibliographie,* DA69

—— *DYABOLA,* DA70

—— *Pictorial dictionary of ancient Athens,* DA106

—— *Pictorial dictionary of ancient Rome,* DA102

Deutsches Archäologisches Institut. Römische Abteilung. Bibliothek. *Kataloge der Bibliothek des Deutschen Archäologischen Instituts, Rom,* DA63

—— *Subject catalogue of the Library of the German Archaeological Institute at Rome,* DA63

Deutsches Archiv für Erforschung des Mittelalters, DA142

Deutsches Archiv für Geschichte des Mittelalters. *Deutsches Archiv für Erforschung des Mittelalters,* DA142

Deutsches biographisches Archiv, AH202, AH206

Deutsches biographisches Jahrbuch, AH202, AH204, AH207

Deutsches Bücherverzeichnis, AA647, AA655, AA656

Deutsches Fremdwörterbuch, Schulz, Hans, AC409

Deutsches land in deutscher Erzahlung, Luther, Arthur, BE1267

Deutsches Literatur-Lexikon, Kosch, Wilhelm, BE1246

Deutsches Literaturarchiv (Germany). *Deutsche literarische Zeitschriften, 1880–1945,* AD76

Deutsches Namenlexikon, Bahlow, Hans, AJ193

Deutsches Pseudonymen-Lexikon, Holzmann, Michael, AA171

Deutsches Schriftsteller Lexikon, Albrecht, Günter, BE1061

Deutsches Theater-Lexikon, Kosch, Wilhelm, BH113

Deutsches Titelbuch, Schneider, Max, BE1273

Deutsches Titelbuch 2, Ahnert, Heinz Jörg, BE1273

Deutsches Übersee-Institut. Referat Afrika. *Integrationsbestrebungen in Afrika,* DD6

Deutsches Übersee-Institut. Übersee-Dokumentation. *Integrationsbestrebungen in Afrika,* DD6

Deutsches Wörterbuch, Grimm, Jakob Ludwig Karl, AC402

—— Mackensen, Lutz, AC439

—— Paul, Hermann, AC407

—— Wahrig, Gerhard, AC411

Deutschlands geographische Namenwelt, Bahlow, Hans, CL190

Deutschlands Geschichtsquellen im Mittelalter, Holtzmann, Robert, DC228

Deutschlands Geschichtsquellen im Mittelalter bis zur mitte des dreizehnten Jahrhunderts, Wattenbach, Wilhelm, DC228

Deutschlands Geschichtsquellen im Mittelalter seit der Mitte des 13. Jahrhunderts, Lorenz, Ottokar, DC228

Deutschlands Geschichtsquellen im Mittelalter vom Tode Kaiser Heinrichs V. bis zum Ende des Interregnum, Berg, Dieter, DC228

—— Schmale, Franz-Josef, DC228

—— Schmale-Ott, Irene, DC228

Deutschsprachige Dissertationen zur alten Geschichte, 1844–1978, Drexhage, Hans-Joachim, DA73

Die deutschsprachige Presse der Amerikas, AE1

Deutschsprachige Verlage, Deutschland, Österreich, Schweiz, sowie Anschriften weiterer ausländischer Verlage mit deutschen Auslieferungen, AA286

Deutschsprachige Schriftstellerinnen des 18. und 19. Jahrhunderts, Friedrichs, Elisabeth, BE1243

Dev, Ashu Tosh. *Students' favourite dictionary, English-to-Bengali & English,* AC232

Developing collections of U.S. government publications, Hernon, Peter, AF72

Developing countries, CJ28

  abstract journals, CH44

  atlases, CJ96

  bibliography, CJ669, DA11

    national and trade, AA392

  dictionaries, CJ39

  economic conditions, CH120

  encyclopedias, CJ27

  filmography, BH221, CC611

Developing countries (by subject)

  economic conditions, CC264, CH142

    statistics, CH161

  law, CK16

  public administration, CJ483

  statistics and demography

    directories, CG36

Developing individualized family support plans, Bennett, Tess, CC235

Developing skills in proposal writing, Hall, Mary S., AL92

Development aid, CH130

The development directory, CH113

The development of Hindu iconography, Banerjea, Jitendra Nath, BF190

The development of medical bibliography, Brodman, Estelle, EH10

Development review and outlook, CH544

Developmental psychology
abstract journals, CC157, CD81
encyclopedias, CD82
guides, CD80
handbooks, CD84, CD85, CD86, CD87

Developments and research on aging, CC94

DeVenney, David P. *Early American choral music*, BJ291
⸻ *Nineteenth-century American choral music*, BJ291

Devine, Elizabeth. *European customs and manners*, CL388
⸻ *Travelers' guide to African customs & manners*, CL388
⸻ *Travelers' guide to Latin American customs and manners*, CL388
⸻ *Travelers' guide to Middle Eastern and North African customs and manners*, CL388

Devine, Mary Elizabeth. *Restoration and eighteenth century theatre research*, BH47

Devisch, M. *National population bibliography of Flanders, 1945–1983*, CG200

DeVito, Joseph A. *The communication handbook*, CH486

Devlet Istatistik Enstitüsü (Turkey). *Türkiye istatistik yilligi*, CG290

Devlin, Robert James. *Dictionary of the Russian Revolution*, DC595

DeVore, Ronald M. *The Arab-Israeli conflict*, DE73

DeVorkin, David H. *The history of modern astronomy and astrophysics*, EC9

Devoto, Giacomo. *Nouvo vocabolario illustrato della lingua italiana*, AC525
⸻ *Vocabolario illustrato della lingua italiana*, AC525

Devriès, Anik. *Dictionnaire des éditeurs de musique française*, BJ180

DeVries, Louis. *English-German technical and engineering dictionary*, EA112
⸻ *French-English science and technology dictionary*, EA107
⸻ *French-English science dictionary for students in agricultural, biological, and physical sciences*, EA107
⸻ *German-English technical and engineering dictionary*, EA112

Dewar, Daniel. *Dictionary of the Gaelic language*, AC395

Dewdney, John C. *The Cambridge atlas of the Middle East and North Africa*, DE68
⸻ *The U.S.S.R. in maps*, CL336

Dewey, Donald. *Encyclopedia of major league baseball teams*, BK54

Dewey, Melvil. *Dewey decimal classification and relative index*, AK200

Dewey, Patrick R. *Fan club directory*, AL39

Dewey decimal classification and relative index, Dewey, Melvil, AK200

Dewhirst, D. W. *Bibliographie générale de l'astronomie jusqu'en 1880*, EC13

DeWhitt, Benjamin L. *A guide to pre-federal records in the National Archives*, DB81

DeWitt, Donald L. *American Indian resource materials in the Western History Collections, University of Oklahoma*, CC426
⸻ *Guides to archives and manuscript collections in the United States*, DB29

Dexter, Franklin Bowditch. *Biographical notices of graduates of Yale College*, AH61
⸻ *Biographical sketches of the graduates of Yale college*, AH61

Dexter, Henry Martyn. *The Congregationalism of the last 300 years, as seen in its literature*, BC383

Dexter, O. P. *Genealogical cross index of ... the Genealogical dictionary of James Savage*, AJ65

Dey, Eric L. *The American college teacher*, CB335
⸻ *American freshman*, CB333

Dezsényi, Béla. *A magyar hirlapirodalom elsö százada, 1705–1805*, AD121

Dézsi, Lajos. *Hungarica*, DC378

DFPI, EJ184

The Dhammapada, BC92

Dhondt, Jan. *Instruments biographiques pour l'histoire contemporaine de la Belgique*, AH178

Di Berardino, Angelo. *Encyclopedia of the early church*, BC275
⸻ *Patrology*, BC301

Di Roma, Edward. *A numerical finding list of British command papers published 1833–1961/62*, AF195, AF201, AF206

Diabina, N. I. *Sovetskaia bolgaristika*, DC113

Diagnostic and statistical manual of mental disorders, EH382, EH385, EH393, EH400

Diagnostic imaging, EH188

Diagram Group. *Comparisons of distance, size, area, volume, mass, weight, density, energy, temperature, time, speed and number throughout the universe*, EA150
⸻ *Rules of the game*, BK46
⸻ *Weapons*, CJ569, CJ581

Diakov, V. A. *Slavianovedenie v dorevoliutsionnoi Rossii*, DC55
⸻ *Slavianovedenie v SSSR*, DC54

Diakun, Nadia Odette. *Ucrainica at the University of Toronto Library*, DC546

Dial in, AK209

Dialectología hispánica y geografía lingüística en los estudios locales (1920–1984). Viudas Camarasa, Antonio, DD173

La dialectologie, Pop, Sever, BD57

Dialectology, BD57
handbooks, BD126

Dialektologie, BD126
⸻ Besch, Werner, BD127

●*DIALOG OnDisc*, CB50, CB52, CB56, CD91, EK260

●*Dialog OnDisc ERIC*, CB57

●*Dialog OnDisc international ERIC*, CB57

●*DIALOG OnDisc : METADEX collection*, EK258

●*DIALOG OnDisc : Philosopher's index*, BB25

●*DIALOG OnDisc Standard & Poor's corporations*, CH367

Diamant, Lincoln. *The broadcast communications dictionary*, CH484

Diamond, Harold J. *Music analyses*, BJ106
⸻ *Music criticism*, BJ107

Diana, Joan P. *Pro-choice/pro-life*, CC251

Diaries and letters
bibliography, BE726

Diaries and letters (by country or region)
Canada, DB185
Great Britain
bibliography, BE724, BE727, DC327
United States, BE507, BE510, DB66

Diaries and letters (by subject)
women, BE509

Diario de Barcelona (1792–1929) [index], AE126

Diaz, Albert James. *Guide to reprints*, AA393

Diaz, Pamela. *10 años de investigaciones sobre la mujer en Nicaragua 1976–1986*, DB314

Díaz Plaja, Guillermo. *Historia de la literatura espanola*, BE1456
⸻ *Historia general de las literaturas hispánicas*, BE1456

Díaz Polanco, Héctor. *Directorio de antropólogos latinoamericanos, México*, CE86

DiCanio, Margaret. *The encyclopedia of marriage, divorce, and the family*, CC224
⸻ *The encyclopedia of violence*, CC33

Diccionari Aguiló, Aguiló y Fúster, Mariano, AC246

Diccionari biogràfic, AH288

Diccionari català-valencià-balear, Alcover Sureda, Antonio Maria, AC247

Diccionari de la literatura catalana, BE1450

Diccionari de la llengua catalana, AC249

Diccionari de la llengua catalana ab la correspondència castellana, AC250

Diccionari enciclopèdic de la llengua catalana amb la correspondència castellana, AC250

Diccionari etimològic i complementari de la llengua catalana, Corominas, Joan, AC248

Diccionari general de la llengua catalana, Fabra, Pompeu, AC251

Diccionari manual de la llengua catalana, Fabra, Pompeu, AC251

Diccionario argentino de seudónimos, Tesler, Mario, AA156

Diccionario bibliográfica-histórico de los antiguos reinos, provincais, ciudades, villas, iglesias y santuarios de España, Muñoz y Romero, Tomás, DC512

Diccionario bibliographico brasileiro, Sacramento Blake, Augusto Victorino Alves do, AA509

Diccionario bio-bibliographico brasileiro, Segadas Machado-Guimarães, Argeu de, AH126

Diccionario biobibliográfico de escritores contemporaneos de México, Lara Valdez, Josefina, BE907

Diccionario biográfico boliviano, Arze, José Roberto, AH122

Diccionario biográfico colonial argentino, Udaondo, Enrique, AH119

Diccionario biográfico colonial de Chile, Medina, José Toribio, AH131

Diccionario biográfico cubano, AH152
⸻ Calcagno, Francisco, AH150
⸻ Peraza Sarausa, Fermín, AH150, AH151

Diccionario biográfico de Chile, AH132
⸻ Figueroa, Pedro Pablo, AH128

Diccionario biográfico de estranjeros en Chile, Figueroa, Pedro Pablo, AH129

Diccionario biográfico de historia antigua de Méjico, García Granados, Rafael, AH100

Diccionario biográfico de la mujer en el Uruguay, AH143, DB395

Diccionario biográfico de mujeres argentinas, Sosa de Newton, Lily, AH118

Diccionario biográfico de Venezuela, AH146

Diccionario biográfico del Ecuador, Pérez Marchant, Braulio, AH135
⸻ Pérez Pimentel, Rodolfo, AH136

Diccionario biográfico ecuatoriano, AH137

Diccionario biográfico-histórico dominicano, 1821–1930, Martínez, Rufino, AH153

Diccionario biográfico mexicano, Peral, Miguel Angel, AH102

Diccionario biográfico y bibliográfico de Colombia, Ospina, Joaquín, AH133

Diccionario biográfico y histórico de la Revolución Mexicana en el Estado de México, Blancare, Roberto, DB242

Diccionario contemporâneo da língua portugueza, Caldas Aulete, F. J., AC641

Diccionario crítico etimológico de la lengua castellana, Corominas, Joan, AC742

Diccionario de alfónimos y seudónimos de la Argentina (1800–1930), Cutolo, Vicente Osvaldo, AA155

Diccionario de anónimos y seudónimos hispanoamericanos, Medina, José Toribio, AA153

Diccionario de autores guatemaltecos, Albizúrez Palma, Francisco, BE905

Diccionario de autores hondureños, González, José, BE906

Diccionario de autores iberoamericanos, Shimose, Pedro, BE888

Diccionario de autores teatrales argentinos, 1950–1990, Zayas de Lima, Perla, BE921

Diccionario de autores teatrales uruguayos & breve historia del teatro uruguayo, Rela, Walter, BE959

Diccionario de escritores colombianos, Sánchez López, Luis María, BE949

Diccionario de escritores hondureños, Argueta, Mario R., BE906

Diccionario de escritores mexicanos, Ocampo, Aurora M., BE915

Diccionario de escritores mexicanos, siglo XX, BE907

Diccionario de escritores uruguayos, Rela, Walter, BE959

Diccionario de expresiones idiomáticas, AC745

Diccionario de frases de los autores clásicos españoles, Mir y Noguera, Juan, BE150
Diccionario de historia de España, DC512
Diccionario de historia de Venezuela, DB402
Diccionario de hombres y mujeres ilustres de Puerto Rico y de hechos históricos, Reynal, Vicente, AH160
Diccionario de la historia de Colombia, Gómez Aristizábal, Horacio, DB368
Diccionario de la lengua castellana, AC727
Diccionario de la lengua española, AC727
Diccionario de la literatura boliviana, Ortega, José, BE922
Diccionario de la literatura chilena, Szmulewicz, Efraín, BE941
Diccionario de la literatura cubana, BE973
Diccionario de la literatura ecuatoriana, Barriga López, Franklin, BE950
Diccionario de la literatura latinoamericana, Pan American Union. Division of Philosophy and Letters, BE892
Diccionario de la música cubana, Orovio, Helio, BJ154
Diccionario de la música, histórico y técnico, Bobillier, Marie, BJ146
Diccionario de la música Labor, Pena, Joaquín, BJ124
Diccionario de la zarzuela, BJ260
Diccionario de literatura española, BE1451
—— Bleiberg, Germán, BE1070
—— Marías, Julián, BE1070
Diccionario de literatura española e hispanoamericana, Gullón, Ricardo, BE1451
Diccionario de literatura hispanoamericana, Becco, Horacio Jorge, BE888
Diccionario de literatura puertorriqueña, Rivera de Alvarez, Josefina, BE980
Diccionario de literatura uruguaya, BE958
Diccionario de sabiduría, Borras y Bemejo, Tomás, BE147
Diccionario de seudónimos literarios españoles, con algunas iniciales, Rogers, Paul Patrick, AA185
Diccionario de seudónimos y escritores Iberoamericanos, Sáenz, Gerardo, AA154
Diccionario de símbolos tradicionales, BF164
Diccionario de términos científicos y técnicos, EA133
Diccionario de términos judídicos, Alcaraz Varo, Enriqué, CK55
—— Hughes, Brian, CK55
Diccionario de términos literarios, Ayuso de Vicente, María Victoria, BE75
Diccionario de términos médicos, inglés-español, español-inglés, Ruiz Torres, Francisco, EH142
Diccionario de uso del español, Moliner, María, AC746
El diccionario del español chicano, Galván, Roberto A., AC754
El diccionario del español de Tejas, AC754
Diccionario del español medieval, Müller, Bodo, AC750
Diccionario enciclopédico abreviado, AB92
Diccionario enciclopédico de México, Musacchio, Humberto, DB246
Diccionario enciclopédico ilustrado y crítico de los hombres de España, Esperabé Arteaga, Enrique, AH289
Diccionario enciclopédico Salvat universal, AB96
Diccionario etimológico español e hispánico, García de Diego, Vicente, AC743
Diccionario general de bibliografía española, Hidalgo, Dionisio, AA803
Diccionario general de la literatura venezolana, BE962
Diccionario general español-inglés [y English-Spanish], García-Pelayo y Gross, Ramón, AC733
Diccionario geográfico argentino, Latzina, Francisco, CL118
Diccionario geográfico boliviano, Gonzales M., René, CL120
Diccionario geográfico de Colombia, CL123
Diccionario geográfico de El Salvador, Instituto Geográfico Nacional (El Salvador), CL115

Diccionario geográfico de España, CL149
Diccionario geográfico de Guatemala, CL116
Diccionario geográfico de Honduras, Instituto Geográfico National (Honduras), CL117
Diccionario geográfico de Puerto Rico, Arana Soto, Salvador, CL126
Diccionario geográfico general de Bolivia, CL120
Diccionario histórico bibliográfico comentado de Puerto Rico, Hostos, Adolfo de, DB455
Diccionario histórico biográfico de los conquistadores del Perú, Busto Duthurburu, José Antonio del, AH140, DB387
Diccionario histórico-biográfico del Perú, Mendiburu, Manuel de, AH141
Diccionario histórico, biográfico y bibliográfico de Chile, Figueroa, Virgilio, AH130
Diccionario histórico de Chile, Fuentes, Jordi, DB362
Diccionario histórico de la lengua española, Real Academia Española, AC726, AC728
Diccionario histórico del México contemporáneo, 1900–1982, Nieto López, J. de Jesús, DB247
Diccionario histórico dominicano, Rutinel Domínguez, Ulises, DB436
Diccionario histórico-enciclopédico de la República de El Salvador, García, Miguel Angel, AH116, DB306
Diccionario histórico y biográfico de Chile, AH130
Diccionario histórico y biográfico de la Revolución Mexicana, DB242
Diccionario histórico y biográfico del Perú, siglos XV–XX, AH140, DB387
Diccionario ideológico de la lengua española, Casares y Sánchez, Julio, AC747
Diccionario ilustrado de frases célebres y citas literarias, Vega, Vicente, BE96
Diccionario inglés-español, español-inglés, Martínez Amador, Emilio M., AC735
Diccionario jurídico, Dahl, Henry S., CK55
Diccionario jurídico español/inglés Butterworths, CK55
Diccionario legal Español-Inglés/Inglés-Español, CK55
Diccionario literario del Perú, Arriola Grande, F. Maurilio, BE954, BE957
Diccionario manual de literatura peruana y materias afines, Romero de Valle, Emilia, BE957
Diccionario manual de sinónimos y antónimos, AC748
Diccionario matemático, García Rodríguez, Mariano, EB54
Diccionario Oxford de literatura española e hispanoamericana, Ward, Philip, BE1452
—— Zayas, Gabriela, BE1452
Diccionario político, histórico, cultural, Lora, Guillermo, DB337
Diccionario popular de historia de la República o. del Uruguay, Araújo, Orestes, DB394
Diccionario Porrúa de historia, biografía y geografía de México, DB243
Diccionario Porrúa de la lengua española, Raluy Poudevida, Antonio, AC755
Diccionario Salvat, AB96
Diccionario temático de antropología, CE47
Diccionario uruguayo de biografías, 1810–1940, Fernández Saldaña, José María, AH144
Dichter, Harry. *Handbook of American sheet music,* BJ56
—— *Handbook of early American sheet music, 1768–1889,* BJ56
Dicionário bibliográfico portuguêz, Silva, Innocencio Francisco da, AA777
Dicionário biobibliográfico de historiadores, geógrafos e antropólogos brasileiros, DB353
Dicionário contemporâneo da língua portuguesa Caldas Aulete, AC641
Dicionário cronológico de autores portugueses, BE1364
Dicionário da terra e da gente do Brasil, Souza, Bernardino José de, CL183
Dicionário das batalhas brasileiras, Donato, Hernâni, DB355

Dicionário das literaturas portuguesa, galega e brasileira, BE1363
Dicionário de geografia do Brasil, CL121, CL122
Dicionário de história do Brasil, DB353
Dicionário de literatura, Coelho, Jacinto do Prado, BE1363
Dicionário de literatura portuguêsa e brasileira, Luft, Celso Pedro, BE1366
Dicionário de nomes geográficos de Moçambique, Cabral, António Carlos Pereira, CL215
Dicionário de poetas contemporâneos, Igreja, Francisco, BE933
Dicionário de sinónimos, Nascentes, Antenor, AC653
Dicionário de sinónimos e locuções da língua portuguêsa, Costa, Agenor, AC652
Dicionário de termos técnicos inglês-português, EA123
Dicionário etimológico da língua portuguesa, AC651
Dicionário etimológico de nomes e sobrenomes, Guérios, Rosário Farâni Mansur, AJ202
Dicionário geográfico brasileiro, CL122
Dicionário histórico-biográfico brasileiro, 1930–1983, AH124, DB354
Dicionário histórico e literário do teatro no Brasil, Gonçalves, Augusto de Freitas Lopes, BE932
Dicionário inglês-português, AC645
—— Ferreira, Julio Albino, AC646
Dicionário jurídico português-inglês, inglês-português, Mello, Maria Chaves de, CK54
Dicionário literário brasileiro, Menezes, Raimundo de, BE934
Dicionário português-inglês, AC646
Dicionário prático de literatura brasileira, Brasil, Assis, BE924
Dick, Esther A. *A glossary of mycology,* EG138
Dick, Trevor J. O. *Economic history of Canada,* CH176
Dicke, Karen. *Bibliography of tourism and travel research studies, reports, and articles,* CL374
Dickey, Lynn E. *Composition of foods,* EH314, EJ220
Dickinson, A. T. *Dickinson's American historical fiction,* BE470
Dickinson, Alis. *Doctoral dissertations in musicology,* BJ164
Dickinson, Fidelia. *Greek and Roman authors,* BE996
Dickinson, John R. *The bibliography of marketing research methods,* CH577
Dickinson, William Crofts. *A source book of Scottish history,* DC366
Dickinson's American historical fiction, Dickinson, A. T., BE470
Dicks, G. R. *Sources of world financial and banking information,* CH221
Dickson, Bruce J. *A research guide to central party and government meetings in China, 1949–1986,* DE147
Dickson, Erica. *Research guide to biography and criticism,* BE7
Dickson, Lance E. *Legal bibliography index,* CK17
Dickson, Paul. *Baseball's greatest quotations,* BK50
—— *The Congress dictionary,* CJ205
—— *The Dickson baseball dictionary,* BK55
—— *Timelines,* DB134
—— *The Worth book of softball,* BK56
Dickson, Roy. *The directory of Caribbean personalities in Britain and North America,* AH148
The Dickson baseball dictionary, Dickson, Paul, BK55
Dickstein, Ruth. *Women in LC's terms,* CC542
Dictionaire du français vivant, Davau, Maurice, AC327
Dicţionar al limbii române contemporane, AC657
Dicţionar de buzunar englez-român, român-englez, Bantaş, Andrei, AC663
Dictionar de istorie veche a Românie, Pippidi, D.M, DC498

Dictionar de pseudonime, alonime [sic], anagrame, asteronime, criptonime ale scriitorilor si publicistilor români, Straje, Mihail, AA182

Dicţionar englez-român, AC662
—— Bantaš, Andrei, AC663
—— Levitchi, Leon, AC663

Dicţionar general al limbii române, Breban, Vasile, AC657

Dicţionar român-englez, Leviţchi, Leon, AC663

**Dictionaries
bibliography,** AC1, AC189, AC192, AC196, BD71, EA95

Dictionaries, encyclopedias, and other word-related books, AC189

Dictionaries of English and foreign languages, Collison, Robert Lewis, AC1

Dictionaries of foreign languages, AC1

[Dictionaries of printers and booksellers in England, Scotland and Ireland], Bibliographical Society (London), AA306

Dictionarium bibliothecarii practicum, Pipics, Zoltán, AK48

Dicţionarul explicativ al limbii române, AC659

Dicţionarul limbii române, AC660
—— Academia Română, Bucharest, AC656

Dicţionarul limbii române : (DLR), AC656

Dicţionarul limbii române literare vechi, 1640–1780, Costinescu, Mariana, AC658

Dicţionarul limbii romîne literare contemporane, AC661

Dicţionarul limbii romîne moderne, AC661

Dicţionarul literaturii romane de la origini pina la 1900, BE1380

Dictionary and encyclopedia of laboratory medicine and technology, EH109

Dictionary and handbook of nuclear medicine and clinical imaging, Iturralde, Mario P., EH188

Dictionary catalog, New York Public Library. Art and Architecture Division, BF45, BF57
—— Schomburg Collection of Negro Literature and History, CC381

A dictionary catalog of American books pertaining to the 17th through 19th centuries, American Antiquarian Society. Library, AA401

Dictionary catalog of the Arthur B. Spingarn collection of Negro authors, Howard University. Library, BE523, BE1504

Dictionary catalog of the Dance Collection, New York Public Library. Dance Collection, BH33, BH135

Dictionary catalog of the Edward E. Ayer collection of Americana and American Indians in the Newberry Library, Newberry Library, DB6

Dictionary catalog of the Harris collection of American poetry and plays, Brown University Library, Providence, Rhode Island, John Carter Brown Library, BE494

Dictionary catalog of the history of the Americas, New York Public Library. Reference Department, DB5, DB25, DB179

Dictionary catalog of the Jesse E. Moorland Collection of Negro Life and History, Howard University Library, Washington, D.C, Howard University. Libraries. Moorland Foundation, CC379

Dictionary catalog of the Jewish collection, New York Public Library. Reference Department, BC540

Dictionary catalog of the Klau Library, Cincinnati, Hebrew Union College—Jewish Institute of Religion. Library, BC539

Dictionary catalog of the Library, Bernice Pauahi Bishop Museum. Library, CE115, DF10
—— Freer Gallery of Art, BF53

Dictionary catalog of the Library of the Center for Applied Linguistics, Washington, D.C, Center for Applied Linguistics. Library, BD29

Dictionary catalog of the Local History and Genealogy Division, New York Public Library. Local History and Genealogy Division, DB25, DB179

Dictionary catalog of the Map Division, New York Public Library, CL248
—— New York Public Library. Map Division, CL255

Dictionary catalog of the Missionary Research Library, New York, Missionary Research Library (New York, N.Y.), BC309

Dictionary catalog of the music collection, Boston Public Library, BJ84
—— New York Public Library. Research Libraries, BJ50, BJ88

Dictionary catalog of the National Agricultural Library, EJ9

Dictionary catalog of the National Agricultural Library, 1862–1965, National Agricultural Library (U.S.), EJ13

Dictionary catalog of the Prints Division, New York Public Library. Prints Division, BF366

Dictionary catalog of the Research Libraries, New York Public Library. Research Libraries, AF83

Dictionary catalog of the Research Libraries of the New York Public Library, New York Public Library. Research Libraries, BC540, DC45

Dictionary catalog of the Research Libraries of the New York Public Library, 1911–1971, New York Public Library. Reference Department, DB5
—— New York Public Library. Research Libraries, AA116

Dictionary catalog of the Slavonic collection, New York Public Library. Slavonic Division, DC45

Dictionary catalog of the Teachers College Library, Columbia University. Teachers College. Library, CB6, CB9

Dictionary catalog of the theatre and drama collections, 1974, BH33

Dictionary catalog of the Water Resources Center Archives, University of California, Berkeley, Water Resources Center Archives (Calif.), EK91

Dictionary catalogue, American Numismatic Society. Library, BG177

A dictionary catalogue of the Blacker-Wood library …, Blacker-Wood Library of Zoology and Ornithology, EG207

Dictionary catalogue of the Byzantine collection of the Dumbarton Oaks Research Library, Washington, D.C. Dumbarton Oaks, DA162

A dictionary, English and Armenian, Aukerian, Haroutiun, AC226

Dictionary, English and Sanskrit, Monier-Williams, Monier, AC706

Dictionary, English-French, French-English, of medical & biological terms, EH141

Dictionary for accountants, CH252

Dictionary for business & finance, Terry, John V., CH274

Dictionary of 16th and 17th century British painters, Waterhouse, Ellis, BF323

Dictionary of 19th century antiques and later objets d'art, Savage, George, BG44

Dictionary of 20th-century design, Pile, John F., BG130

Dictionary of 20th-century history, Brownstone, David M., DA179, DA181
—— Franck, Irene M., DA181

The dictionary of 20th-century world politics, Shafritz, Jay M., CJ33

Dictionary of abbreviations, AC45

Dictionary of abbreviations in medical sciences, Heister, Rolf, EH131

Dictionary of abstract painting, Berckelaers, Ferdinand Louis, BF300
—— Seuphor, Michel, BF300

Dictionary of accounting terms, Siegel, Joel G., CH254

The dictionary of acronyms and abbreviations in applied linguistics and language learning, Jung, Heidrun, BD40

Dictionary of actors and of other persons associated with the public representation of plays in England before 1642, Nungezer, Edwin, BH119

Dictionary of administration and management, Banki, Ivan S., CH612

Dictionary of admirals of the U.S. Navy, Cogar, William B., CJ639

Dictionary of advanced manufacturing technology, Hunt, V. Daniel, CH340, EK231

Dictionary of advertising, CH571
—— Jefkins, Frank William, CH551

Dictionary of advertising and direct mail terms, Imber, Jane, CH550

Dictionary of advertising terms, Urdang, Laurence, CH571

Dictionary of African biography, AH314, DD15, DD158, DD245

Dictionary of African historical biography, Lipschutz, Mark R., AH310

Dictionary of Afro-American slang, Major, Clarence, AC128

Dictionary of Afro-American slavery, CC386

Dictionary of Afro-Latin American civilization, Nuñez, Benjamin, CC387

Dictionary of agriculture, Haensch, Günther, EJ29

Dictionary of Albanian literature, Elsie, Robert, BE1093

Dictionary of alkaloids, EE123, EH334

Dictionary of altitudes in the United States, Gannett, Henry, CL71

Dictionary of American and British euphemisms, Holder, R. W., AC125

Dictionary of American art, Baigell, Matthew, BF82

Dictionary of American biography, AH56, AH58, AH60, AH62, AH65, AH66, DB40, DB43

Dictionary of American Catholic biography, Delaney, John J., BC418

Dictionary of American children's fiction, 1859–1959, Helbig, Alethea, BE382

The dictionary of American clock & watch makers, Sposato, Kenneth A., BG89

Dictionary of American communal and utopian history, Fogarty, Robert S., DB149

A dictionary of American composers, Butterworth, Neil, BJ206

Dictionary of American conservatism, Filler, Louis, CJ24, CJ117

Dictionary of American diplomatic history, Findling, John E., CJ118, CJ119, CJ150

Dictionary of American English, AC30

Dictionary of American English on historical principles, Craigie, William Alexander, AC30, AC150, AC152

Dictionary of American-English usage, Nicholson, Margaret, AC71

Dictionary of American family names, AJ186

The dictionary of American food and drink, Mariani, John F., EJ212

Dictionary of American foreign affairs, Flanders, Carl N., CJ150
—— Flanders, Stephen A., CJ119, CJ150

Dictionary of American history, DB40, DB70

Dictionary of American hymnology, BC315

Dictionary of American immigration history, DB41

Dictionary of American legal usage, CK39

Dictionary of American library biography, AK86

Dictionary of American literary characters, BE484, BE688

Dictionary of American medical biography, EH228, EH288
—— Kelly, Howard Atwood, EH229

Dictionary of American military biography, CJ641
—— Dawson, Joseph G., CJ648
—— Spiller, Roger J., CJ648
—— Williams, T. Harry, CJ648

Dictionary of American naval fighting ships, CJ649

Dictionary of American Negro biography, Logan, Rayford W., AH64

Dictionary of American nursing biography, EH228, EH288

Dictionary of American painters, sculptors & engravers, Opitz, Glenn B., BF154

Dictionary of American politics, Smith, Edward Conrad, CJ128

Dictionary of American portraits, Cirker, Blanche, BF65
—— Cirker, Hayward, BF65

A dictionary of American proverbs, BE154

Dictionary of American proverbs and proverbial phrases, 1820–1880, Taylor, Archer, BE165
—— Whiting, Bartlett Jere, BE165
Dictionary of American regional English, AC151
Dictionary of American religious biography, Bowden, Henry Warner, BC82
Dictionary of American sculptors, Opitz, Glenn B., BF398
Dictionary of American slang, Flexner, Stuart Berg, AC120
—— Wentworth, Harold, AC120, AC135
A dictionary of American social change, Filler, Louis, CA35
Dictionary of American temperance biography, Lender, Mark Edward, CC138
A dictionary of Americanisms on historical principles, Mathews, Mitford McLeod, AC152
Dictionary of analytical reagents, EE123, EE124, EH334
Dictionary of ancient Near Eastern architecture, Leick, Gwendolyn, BF243
Dictionary of Anglo-American law, CK51
Dictionary of animal health terminology, EJ113
Dictionary of animal production terminology, EJ113, EJ114
Dictionary of anonymous and pseudonymous English literature, Halkett, Samuel, AA150
Dictionary of anonymous and pseudonymous publications in the English language, Horden, John, AA150
Dictionary of anthropology, CE48
—— Winick, Charles, CE50, CE51
Dictionary of antibiotics and related substances, EE123, EE125, EH334, EH335
Dictionary of antiques, Savage, George, BG44
The dictionary of antiques and the decorative arts, Boger, Louise Ade, BG42
Dictionary of applied chemistry, EE46
Dictionary of applied geology, Nelson, Archibald, EF76
Dictionary of applied physics, Glazebrook, Richard, ED13
Dictionary of archaic and provincial words, Halliwell-Philips, James Orchard, AC97
Dictionary of architectural and building technology, Cowan, Henry J., BF240
Dictionary of architecture, Architectural Publication Society, BF232
Dictionary of architecture & construction, BF242
—— Harris, Cyril M., BF245
Dictionary of architecture and building, Sturgis, Russell, BF238
Dictionary of archival terminology, AK183
Dictionary of art and artists, Murray, Linda, BF78
—— Murray, Peter, BF78
A dictionary of art quotations, BF95
Dictionary of artificial intelligence, Mercadal, Dennis, EK184
Dictionary of artificial intelligence and robotics, Rosenberg, Jerry Martin, EK186
Dictionary of artists in America, 1564–1860, BF155
Dictionary of Asian American history, CC402
Dictionary of astronomical names, Room, Adrian, EC37
A dictionary of Austral English, Morris, Edward Ellis, AC179
Dictionary of Australian artists, Kerr, Joan, BF140
A dictionary of Australian colloquialisms, Wilkes, G. A., AC180
A dictionary of Australian military history, Grant, Ian, DF35
Dictionary of automotive engineering, Goodsell, Don, EK38
Dictionary of aviation, Hall, R. J., CH474
Dictionary of Bahamian English, Holm, John A., AC161
A dictionary of ballet, Wilson, George Buckley, BH144
A dictionary of ballet terms, Kersley, Leo, BH146
Dictionary of banking, Rosenberg, Jerry Martin, CH273
Dictionary of banking terms, Fitch, Thomas P., CH272

Dictionary of battles, Chandler, David G., DA24
—— Eggenberger, David, DA21
—— Harbottle, Thomas Benfield, DA22
Dictionary of behavioral science, CD29
The dictionary of bias-free usage, Maggio, Rosalie, AC77
The dictionary of Bible and religion, BC71
A dictionary of Biblical interpretation, BC127
Dictionary of biblical theology, Léon-Dufour, Xavier, BC144
A dictionary of biblical tradition in English literature, BE609
Dictionary of bibliographic abbreviations found in the scholarship of classical studies and related disciplines, Wellington, Jean Susorney, BE1019
Dictionary of biochemistry, Stenesh, J., EG324
Dictionary of biochemistry and molecular biology, Stenesh, J., EG324
The dictionary of biographical quotation of British and American subjects, BE103
Dictionary of biographical reference, Phillips, Lawrence Barnett, AH20
Dictionary of biological terms, EG43
Dictionary of biology, Steen, Edwin Benzel, EG45
Dictionary of biomedical acronyms and abbreviations, Dupayrat, Jacques, EH130
Dictionary of biotechnology, Coombs, J., EK45
A dictionary of birds, EG257
—— Newton, Alfred, EG257
Dictionary of Black African civilization, CE106
A dictionary of book history, Feather, John, AA274
Dictionary of books relating to America, from its discovery to the present time, Sabin, Joseph, AA404, AA409, AA411
Dictionary of borrowed words, Abate, Frank R., AC186
—— Urdang, Laurence, AC186
A dictionary of botany, Little, R. John, EG134
—— Usher, George, EG140
Dictionary of Brazilian literature, BE928
The dictionary of British and American homophones, Williams, Stephen N., AC89
A dictionary of British and American women writers, 1660–1800, BE447
—— Todd, Janet M., BE621
Dictionary of British and Irish botanists and horticulturists including plant collectors and botanical artists, Desmond, Ray, BF285, EG165
Dictionary of British artists, 1760–1893, Graves, A., BF316
The dictionary of British artists, 1880–1940, Johnson, Jane, BF316
Dictionary of British artists, working 1900–1950, Waters, Grant M., BF316
Dictionary of British book illustrators and caricaturists, 1800–1914, Houfe, Simon, BF323
Dictionary of British children's fiction, Helbig, Alethea, BE383
Dictionary of British equestrian artists, Mitchell, Sally, BF323
Dictionary of British flower, fruit, and still life painters, Burbidge, Robert B., BF323
A dictionary of British folktales in the English language, Briggs, Katharine Mary, CF88
Dictionary of British history, Brendon, J. A., DC293
Dictionary of British literary characters, BE484, BE688
Dictionary of British marine painters, Wilson, Arnold, BF323
Dictionary of British military painters, Wilson, Arnold, BF323
Dictionary of British miniature painters, Foskett, Daphne, BF303
Dictionary of British portraiture, BF66
Dictionary of British sculptors, 1660–1851, Gunnis, Rupert, BF394
A dictionary of British ships and seamen, Uden, Grant, CJ653
Dictionary of British sporting painters, Pavière, Sidney H., BF323
Dictionary of British steel engravers, Hunnisett, Basil, BF359

A dictionary of British surnames, Reaney, Percy Hide, AJ184, AJ185
Dictionary of British women writers, Todd, Janet M., BE621
Dictionary of building, McMullan, Randall, EK109
Dictionary of business and management, Rosenberg, Jerry Martin, CH344
Dictionary of business biography, CH96
A dictionary of business quotations, CH72
Dictionary of Canadian artists, McDonald, Colin S., BF314
Dictionary of Canadian biography, AH93, AH94
The dictionary of Canadian law, Dukelow, Daphne A., CK35
The dictionary of Canadian quotations and phrases, BE104
Dictionary of Canadianisms on historical principles, AC158
Dictionary of Catholic biography, Delaney, John J., BC419
The dictionary of cell biology, EG32
—— Dow, J. A. T., EG341
—— Lackie, J. M., EG341
Dictionary of Celtic myth and legend, Green, Miranda J., CF18
Dictionary of Celtic mythology, Ellis, Peter Berresford, CF17
Dictionary of ceramic science and engineering, Malcolm, I. J., EK265
Dictionary of changes in meaning, Room, Adrian, AC82
The dictionary of chemical names, Flood, Walter Edgar, EE29
Dictionary of chemical names and synonyms, Howard, Philip H., EE42
Dictionary of chemistry, EE38
—— Sharp, D. W. A., EE44
Dictionary of chemistry and chemical engineering, De Vries, Louis, EE49
Dictionary of chemistry and chemical technology. English-German, EE50
The dictionary of Chicano Spanish, AC754
Dictionary of Chinese and Japanese art, Munsterberg, Hugo, BF88
A dictionary of Chinese Buddhist terms, Soothill, William Edward, BC480
Dictionary of Chinese history, Dillon, Michael, DE144
Dictionary of Chinese law and government, Bilancia, Philip R., CK47
Dictionary of Christ and the Gospels, Hastings, James, BC128
Dictionary of Christian antiquities, Cheetham, Samuel, BC246, BC249
—— Smith, William, BC246, BC249
Dictionary of Christian biography, Smith, William, BC249
Dictionary of Christian biography and literature to the end of the sixth century A.D, Piercy, William C., BC249
—— Wace, Henry, BC249
Dictionary of Christian ethics, Macquarrie, John, BC241
Dictionary of Christian lore and legend, Metford, J. C. J., BC238
Dictionary of Christian spirituality, BC242
Dictionary of Christian theology, Richardson, Alan, BC243
Dictionary of Christianity in America, BC235
Dictionary of church history, BC244
A dictionary of classical and contemporary English, AC217
Dictionary of classical mythology, Bell, Robert E., CF26
—— Grimal, Pierre, CF27
A dictionary of classical reference in English poetry, Smith, Eric, BE716
Dictionary of clocks and watches, Bruton, Eric, BG86
Dictionary of coin names, Room, Adrian, BG180
Dictionary of collective nouns and group terms, Sparkes, Ivan George, AC85

A dictionary of colonial American printers' ornaments and illustrations, Reilly, Elizabeth Carroll, AA252

Dictionary of color, Maerz, Aloys John, ED61

A dictionary of colorful Italian idioms, Pekelis, Carla, AC544

Dictionary of commercial, financial and legal terms, Herbst, Robert, CK44

Dictionary of comparative religion, BC72

The dictionary of computer graphics technology and applications, Latham, Roy, EK182

Dictionary of computer terms, Covington, Michael A., EK177

Dictionary of computing, EK178

Dictionary of concepts in cultural anthropology, Winthrop, Robert H., CE46

Dictionary of concepts in general psychology, Popplestone, John A., CD26

Dictionary of concepts in history, Ritter, Harry, DA45

Dictionary of concepts in human geography, Larkin, Robert P., CL38

Dictionary of concepts in literary criticism and theory, Harris, Wendell V., BE82

Dictionary of concepts in physical anthropology, Stevenson, Joan C., CE45

Dictionary of concepts in physical geography, Huber, Thomas Patrick, CL37

Dictionary of concepts in recreation and leisure studies, Smith, Stephen L. J., BK109

Dictionary of concepts in the philosophy of science, Durbin, Paul T., EA78

Dictionary of concepts on American politics, Whisker, James B., CJ123

A dictionary of conservative and libertarian thought, CJ24

Dictionary of contemporary American artists, Cummings, Paul, BF151

A dictionary of contemporary American usage, Evans, Bergen, AC70

Dictionary of contemporary Brazilian authors, Foster, David William, BE891

Dictionary of contemporary English, AC39

A dictionary of contemporary France, Aplin, Richard, DC208

Dictionary of contemporary Latin American authors, Foster, David William, BE891

Dictionary of contemporary music, Vinton, John, BJ143

Dictionary of contemporary photography, Stroebel, Leslie D., BF343

The dictionary of contemporary politics of Central America and the Caribbean, Gunson, Phil, CJ311

The dictionary of contemporary politics of South America, Gunson, Phil, CJ312

The dictionary of contemporary politics of southern Africa, Williams, Gwyneth, CJ408

The dictionary of costume, Wilcox, Ruth Turner, BG101

Dictionary of country furniture, Filbee, Marjorie, BG132

Dictionary of crime, CK254

Dictionary of criminal justice, Rush, George E., CK257

A dictionary of critical theory, Orr, Leonard, BE85

Dictionary of crystallography, EF116

Dictionary of dairy terminology, EJ115

Dictionary of data processing, Wittmann, Alfred, EK197

Dictionary of dates, Beeching, Cyril Leslie, AL143, DA34

Dictionary of dates and universal information relating to all ages and nations, Haydn, Joseph Timothy, DA33

The dictionary of demography, Pressat, Roland, CG30

Dictionary of demography : biographies, Petersen, William, CG43

Dictionary of demography : multilingual glossary, Petersen, William, CG28

Dictionary of demography : terms, concepts, and institutions, Petersen, William, CG29

Dictionary of dermatologic terms, EH111
—— Carter, Robert L., EH111

Dictionary of development, CH120

Dictionary of developmental and educational psychology, CD22, CD82

A dictionary of drug abuse terms and terminology, Abel, Ernest L., CC126

Dictionary of drugs, EE123, EE126, EH334, EH336

Dictionary of early English, Shipley, Joseph Twadell, AC100

A dictionary of early music, Roche, Jerome, BJ157

A dictionary of early Zhou Chinese, Schuessler, Axel, AC268

Dictionary of earth sciences, Michel, Jean-Pierre, EF84

Dictionary of ecology, evolution and systematics, Boxshall, Geoffrey A., EG75
—— Clark, P. F., EG75
—— Lincoln, Roger J., EG65, EG75

Dictionary of economic plants, Uphof, Johannes Cornelis Theodorus, EG164

A dictionary of economic quotations, CH73

Dictionary of economics, Rutherford, Donald, CH64

A dictionary of economics and commerce, Hanson, John Lloyd, CH57

A dictionary of education, CB73
—— Good, Carter V., CB75
—— Rowntree, Derek, CB79

Dictionary of educational acronyms, abbreviations, and initialisms, Palmer, James C., CB78

Dictionary of effects and phenomena in physics, Schubert, Joachim, ED23

A dictionary of Egyptian Arabic, Hinds, Martin, AC216

Dictionary of Egyptian civilization, Posener, Georges, DA123
—— Sauneron, Serge, DA123
—— Yoyotte, Jean, DA123

Dictionary of electrical engineering, Jackson, Kenneth George, EK132

Dictionary of electronic and computer music technology, Dobson, Richard, BJ310

Dictionary of engineering and technology, Ernst, Richard, EA114, EK10

Dictionary of English and Welsh surnames, Bardsley, Charles W., AJ184

Dictionary of English church history, Ollard, Sidney Leslie, BC332

A dictionary of English costume [900–1900], Cunnington, Cecil Willett, BG99

Dictionary of English domestic architecture, Osborne, Arthur Leslie, BF241

Dictionary of English furniture, from the Middle Ages to the late Georgian period, Macquoid, Percy, BG123

Dictionary of English furniture makers, 1660–1840, BG135

Dictionary of English law, CK38

A dictionary of English place names, Mills, A. D., CL198

Dictionary of English plant-names, Britten, James, EG120

A dictionary of English usage in Southern Africa, Beeton, Douglas Ridley, AC181

A dictionary of English weights and measures from Anglo-Saxon times to the nineteenth century, AL201

Dictionary of environmental hydrogeology, EF132

A dictionary of epidemiology, EH410

A dictionary of eponyms, Beeching, Cyril Leslie, AC49

The dictionary of espionage, Becket, Henry S. A., CJ534
—— Dobson, Christopher, CJ540
—— Payne, Ronald, CJ540

The dictionary of Ethiopian biography, AH318

Dictionary of ethnology and animal learning, CD22

A dictionary of ethology, Immelmann, Klaus, CD121

The dictionary of ethology and animal learning, CD119

Dictionary of eye terminology, Cassin, Barbara, EH110

Dictionary of farm animal behaviour, Hurnik, J. F., EJ116

The dictionary of feminist theory, Humm, Maggie, CC538

Dictionary of fictional characters, Freeman, William, BE188
—— Seymour-Smith, Martin, BE188, BE189
—— Urquhart, Fred, BE188

Dictionary of film makers, Sadoul, Georges, BH285

Dictionary of film terms, Beaver, Frank E., BH256

Dictionary of films, Sadoul, Georges, BH200

Dictionary of finance and investment terms, Downes, John, CH209

Dictionary of financial terms in English, German, Spanish, French, Italian, and Dutch, CH214

A dictionary of folk artists in Canada, BG30

Dictionary of folk artists in Canada from the 17th century to the present, McKendry, Blake, BF314, BG33

Dictionary of food ingredients, Igoe, Robert S., EH307, EJ156

Dictionary of Forces' slang, Partridge, Eric, AC132

Dictionary of foreign phrases and abbreviations, Guinagh, Kevin, AC185

Dictionary of foreign quotations, Collison, Robert Lewis, BE91

Dictionary of foreign terms, Mawson, Christopher Orlando Sylvester, AC187
—— Pei, Mario Andrew, AC188

A dictionary of foreign words and phrases in current English, Bliss, Alan Joseph, AC184

Dictionary of forestry in five languages, Weck, Johannes, EJ182

Dictionary of furniture, BG125

The dictionary of gambling & gaming, Clark, Thomas L., BK136

Dictionary of gardening, EG125, EJ242

Dictionary of gastronomy, Simon, André Louis, EJ213

Dictionary of gemmology, Read, Peter G., EF185

Dictionary of gems and gemology, Shipley, Robert Morrill, EF187

Dictionary of genealogical sources in the Public Record Office, Colwell, Stella, DC286

The dictionary of genealogy, FitzHugh, Terrick V. H., AJ111

A dictionary of genetics, King, Robert C., EG339, EG341
—— Stansfield, William D., EG341

Dictionary of genetics & cell biology, Maclean, Norman, EG341

Dictionary of genetics, including terms used in cytology, animal breeding and evolution, Knight, Robert L., EG340

A dictionary of geography, Monkhouse, Francis John, CL49, CL50

Dictionary of geological terms, EF72

Dictionary of geology, Challinor, John, EF71

Dictionary of geosciences, EF85

Dictionary of German history, 1806–1945, Fest, Wilfried, DC256

Dictionary of German synonyms, Farrell, Ralph Barstow, AC433

Dictionary of gerontology, Harris, Diana K., CC82

Dictionary of given names, with origins and meanings, Loughead, Flora Haines Apponyi, AJ173

Dictionary of gods and goddesses, devils and demons, Lurker, Manfred, CF12

A dictionary of Greek and Roman geography, Smith, William, CL105

A dictionary of Greek Orthodoxy, Patrinacos, Nicon D., BC451

Dictionary of health care administration, EH115

Dictionary of Hinduism, Stutley, James, BC488
—— Stutley, Margaret, BC488

Dictionary of historic documents, Kohn, George C., DA23

The dictionary of historic nicknames, Sifakis, Carl, AJ180

A dictionary of historic records of Tanzania (1497–1982), Makaidi, Emmanuel J. E., DD234

Dictionary of historical terms, Cook, Chris, DA41

INDEX

Dictionary of hospitality, travel, and tourism, Metelka, Charles J., CL382

Dictionary of human geography, CL44

A dictionary of hymnology, Julian, John, BC318, BC320

Dictionary of immunology, EG33
——— Rosen, Fred S., EH124

Dictionary of Indian biography, Buckland, Charles Edward, AH349

Dictionary of Indian philosophical concepts, Singh, B. N., BB39

Dictionary of Indian pseudonyms, Chatterjee, Amitabha, AA191

Dictionary of industrial relations, CH649, CH654

Dictionary of information science, Bürger, Erich, AK41

Dictionary of information science and technology, Watters, Carolyn, AK44

Dictionary of inorganic compounds, EE109

Dictionary of instructional technology, Ellington, Henry, CB173

Dictionary of insurance and risk prevention, Elsevier Science Publishers, CH508

Dictionary of insurance terms, Rubin, Harvey W., CH509

The dictionary of interior design, Pegler, Martin, BG127

Dictionary of international & comparative law, Fox, James R., CK102

Dictionary of international economics, Kohls, Siegfried, CH126

Dictionary of international relations terms, CJ37
——— United States. Department of State, CJ37

Dictionary of international trade, Rosenberg, Jerry Martin, CH124

Dictionary of investing, Rosenberg, Jerry Martin, CH302

A dictionary of Iraqi Arabic, AC214

A dictionary of Irish archaeology, Flanagan, Laurence, DC405

A dictionary of Irish biography, Boylan, Henry, AH255

Dictionary of Irish history since 1800, Doherty, J. E., DC412
——— Hickey, D. J., DC406, DC412

Dictionary of Irish literature, BE802

A dictionary of Irish mythology, Ellis, Peter Berresford, CF30

Dictionary of Irish writers, Cleeve, Brian Talbot, BE799

Dictionary of Italian literature, BE1298

Dictionary of Jamaican English, Cassidy, Frederic Gomes, AC157

A dictionary of Japanese art terms, bilingual, BF88

A dictionary of Japanese artists, Roberts, Laurance P., BF144

Dictionary of Japanese Buddhist terms, Inagaki, Hisao, BC478
——— O'Neill, Patrick Geoffrey, BC478

Dictionary of jargon, Green, Jonathon, AC123

Dictionary of Jesus and the Gospels, BC128

Dictionary of jewellery and watchmaking, BG82

Dictionary of Jewish lore and legend, Unterman, Alan, BC555, CF54

A dictionary of Jewish names and their history, Kaganoff, Benzion C., AJ200

A dictionary of Jewish Palestinian Aramaic of the Byzantine period, Sokoloff, Michael, AC472

Dictionary of key words in psychology, Bruno, Frank Joe, CD27

Dictionary of labor-management relations, CH654

Dictionary of labour biography, Bellamy, Joyce M., AH220

A dictionary of landscape, Goulty, George A., BF291

A dictionary of landscape architecture, Morrow, Baker H., BF292

A dictionary of Late Egyptian, AC302

Dictionary of Latin American racial and ethnic terminology, Stephens, Thomas M., CC460

Dictionary of law, Curzon, Leslie B., CK34

Dictionary of legal abbreviations used in American law books, Bieber, Doris M., CK42

Dictionary of legal and commercial terms, Romain, Alfred, CK49

Dictionary of legal, commercial and political terms, CK49

Dictionary of legal quotations, James, Simon, CK57
——— Stebbins, Chantal, CK57

Dictionary of legal terms, Gifis, Steven H., CK37

Dictionary of library and educational technology, Rosenberg, Kenyon C., AK43

Dictionary of library and information science, Keitz, Saiedeh von, AK47

A dictionary of life in Bible times, Corswant, Willy, BC193

Dictionary of life sciences, EG34

Dictionary of linguistics and phonetics, Crystal, David, BD35, BD36, BD37

Dictionary of literary biography, AA297, BE200, BE411, BE426, BE452, BE566, BE577, BE595

Dictionary of literary biography documentary series, BE200

Dictionary of literary biography yearbook, BE200

Dictionary of literary devices, Dupriez, Bernard Marie, BE78, BE356
——— Halsall, Albert W., BE356

Dictionary of literary pseudonyms, Atkinson, Frank, AA147

A dictionary of literary quotations, Stephens, Meic, BE119

Dictionary of literary-rhetorical conventions of the English Renaissance, Donker, Marjorie, BE351

A dictionary of literary terms, BE77

A dictionary of literary terms and literary theory, Cuddon, John A., BE77

Dictionary of literary themes and motifs, BE183

Dictionary of literature in the English language from 1940–1970, Myers, Robin, BE584

A dictionary of literature in the English language, from Chaucer to 1940, Myers, Robin, BE584

Dictionary of liturgical terms, Pfatteicher, Philip H., BC268

Dictionary of liturgy, Lang, Jovian, BC427

A dictionary of liturgy & worship, BC268

Dictionary of logical terms and symbols, Greenstein, Carol Horn, EA92

A dictionary of Maori place names, Reed, A. W., CL219

The dictionary of marketing, Ostrow, Rona, CH581

Dictionary of marketing and advertising, Baker, Michael John, CH549

Dictionary of marketing research, Van Minden, Jack J. R., CH582

A dictionary of Marxist thought, CJ519

Dictionary of mathematical sciences, Herland, Leo Joseph, EB50

Dictionary of mathematics, Eisenreich, Günther, EB47
——— Glenn, J. A., EB38, EB39
——— Littler, G. H., EB38

Dictionary of mechanical engineering, Nayler, G. H. F., EK237

Dictionary of medical acronyms and abbreviations, Jablonski, Stanley, EH132

A dictionary of medical and surgical syndromes, Gibson, John, EH114

Dictionary of medical eponyms, Firkin, Barry G., EH99

Dictionary of medical ethics, EH240

The dictionary of medical folklore, Rinzler, Carol Ann, CF52

Dictionary of medical syndromes, Magalini, Sergio I., EH120

Dictionary of medicine, EH137, EH138

Dictionary of medieval civilization, Dahmus, Joseph, DA152

Dictionary of medieval knighthood and chivalry, Broughton, Bradford B., DA147

Dictionary of medieval Latin from British sources, Latham, Ronald Edward, AC588

A dictionary of medieval romance and romance writers, Spence, Lewis, BE344

Dictionary of mental handicap, Lindsey, Mary P., CC190

Dictionary of metallurgy, Merriman, Arthur Douglas, EK266

Dictionary of meteorological and related terms, Brazol, Demetrio, EF150

Dictionary of Mexican American history, Meier, Matt S., CC468

A dictionary of Mexican American proverbs, Glazer, Mark, CC459

Dictionary of Mexican literature, BE908

A dictionary of microbial taxonomy, Cowan, Samuel Tertius, EG31

Dictionary of microbiology, Jacobs, Morris B., EG39

Dictionary of microbiology and molecular biology, Singleton, Paul, EG27

Dictionary of microprocessor systems, Müller, Dieter, EK193

Dictionary of military and naval quotations, Heinl, Robert, CJ591

Dictionary of military and technological abbreviations and acronyms, Pretz, Bernhard, CJ588

Dictionary of military, defense contractor & troop slang acronyms, Gutzman, Philip C., CJ617

Dictionary of military quotations, Royle, Trevor, CJ591

Dictionary of military terms, Dupuy, Trevor Nevitt, CJ585

Dictionary of Ming biography, 1368–1644, Association for Asian Studies. Ming Biographical History Project Committee, AH336

A dictionary of miniaturists, illuminators, calligraphers, and copyists, Bradley, John William, BF311

Dictionary of mining and mineralogy, EF183

A dictionary of mining, mineral, and related terms, Thrush, Paul W., EF188

Dictionary of Minton, Atterbury, Paul, BG73

Dictionary of modern American usage, Horwill, Herbert William, AC76

Dictionary of modern ballet, BH140

Dictionary of modern colloquial French, Hérail, René James, AC357

Dictionary of modern critical terms, Fowler, Roger, BE73

A dictionary of modern defence and strategy, CJ578

The dictionary of modern economics, CH59

Dictionary of modern English usage, Fowler, Henry Watson, AC71, AC72

Dictionary of modern French idioms, Gerber, Barbara L., AC368

Dictionary of modern French literature, Dolbow, Sandra W., BE1155

A dictionary of modern German prose usage, Eggeling, Hans F., AC438

A dictionary of modern Indian history, 1707–1947, Mehra, Parshotam, DE168

Dictionary of modern Italian history, DC431
——— Coppa, Frank J., DC420

A dictionary of modern legal usage, Garner, Bryan A., CK36

The dictionary of modern medicine, Segen, J. C., EH103

Dictionary of modern painting, BF300

Dictionary of modern political ideologies, CJ25

A dictionary of modern politics, Robertson, David, CJ31

Dictionary of modern sculpture, BF397

Dictionary of modern theological German, Ziefle, Helmut W., BC153

The dictionary of modern war, Luttwak, Edward, CJ573

A dictionary of modern written Arabic, Wehr, Hans, AC222

Dictionary of modern Yoruba, Abraham, Roy Clive, AC817

Dictionary of mottos, Pine, L. G., BE94

A dictionary of musical quotations, Crofton, Ian, BJ162

Dictionary of musical technology, Cary, Tristram, BJ310

A dictionary of musical themes, Barlow, Harold, BJ228, BJ229
——— Morgenstern, Sam, BJ229

A dictionary of named effects and laws in chemistry, physics, and mathematics, Ballentyne, Denis William George, EA85

Dictionary of national biography, AH32, AH62, AH194, AH222, AH224, AH226, AH228, AH229, AH230, AH231, AH237, AH245, AH371, CJ355, DF40

—— Sen, Siba Pada, AH350, AH351

Dictionary of Native American mythology, Gill, Sam D., CF16

Dictionary of naval abbreviations, Wedertz, Bill, CJ618, CJ621

A dictionary of neuropsychology, Goodwin, Diana M., CD102

The dictionary of New Zealand biography, AH378, DF47

—— Scholefield, Guy Hardy, AH380

Dictionary of Newfoundland English, AC159

Dictionary of nineteenth-century American artists in Italy, 1760–1914, Soria, Regina, BF319

Dictionary of non-Christian religions, Parrinder, Edward Geoffrey, BC75

Dictionary of northern mythology, Simek, Rudolf, CF35

Dictionary of numismatic names, Frey, Albert Romer, BG179

Dictionary of nutrition and food technology, Bender, Arnold E., EH301

A dictionary of obituaries of modern British radicals, Barrows, Floyd D., AH219

A dictionary of obscenity, taboo & euphemism, McDonald, James, AC130

Dictionary of obstetrics and gynecology, EH112

Dictionary of occupational titles, CB209, CH693

Dictionary of Old English, AC172, BD99

A dictionary of opera and song themes, Barlow, Harold, BJ229

Dictionary of optometry, Millodot, Michel, EH121

Dictionary of organic compounds, EE109, EE123, EE127, EE128, EE133, EH334

Dictionary of organometallic compounds, EE123, EE128, EE133, EH334

Dictionary of organophosphorus compounds, EE123, EE129, EH334

Dictionary of Oriental quotations (Arabic and Persian), Field, Claud, BE124

Dictionary of ornament, Lewis, Philippa, BG23

Dictionary of painters and engravers, BF312

Dictionary of Parisian music publishers, 1700–1950, Hopkinson, Cecil, BJ181

Dictionary of personal finance, Siegel, Joel G., CH213

Dictionary of personality and social psychology, CD22, CD95

Dictionary of personnel management and labor relations, CH711

Dictionary of petrology, Tomkeieff, S.I, EF259

Dictionary of pharmacy, EH327

Dictionary of Philippine biography, Manuel, E. Arsenio, AH367

Dictionary of philosophy, Angeles, Peter Adam, BB37

Dictionary of philosophy and psychology, Baldwin, James Mark, BB26

Dictionary of physics, ED18

Dictionary of physics and allied sciences, ED26

Dictionary of physiological and clinical psychology, CD22, CD99

Dictionary of pictorial subjects from classical literature, Preston, Percy, BF189, CF24

Dictionary of plant names, Gerth van Wijk, H. L., EG127

A dictionary of plant pathology, Holliday, Paul, EJ30

The dictionary of Polish pronunciation, AC640

Dictionary of political analysis, Plano, Jack C., CJ40, CJ41

—— Riggs, Robert E., CJ40

—— Robin, Helenan S., CJ40

Dictionary of political parties and organizations in Russia, Pribylovskiĭ, Vladimir, CJ386

Dictionary of political quotations, CJ44

—— Stewart, Robert, CJ45

The dictionary of political quotations on Ireland, 1886–1987, O'Clery, Conor, CJ377, DC409

A dictionary of political thought, Scruton, Roger, CJ32

Dictionary of politics, Elliott, Florence, CJ33

—— Laqueur, Walter, CJ33

Dictionary of polling, Young, Michael L., CJ496

Dictionary of Polynesian mythology, Craig, Robert D., CF32

Dictionary of popular phrases, Rees, Nigel, BE86

Dictionary of Prince Edward Island English, AC160

Dictionary of printers and booksellers in England, Scotland and Ireland and of foreign printers of English books, 1557–1640, McKerrow, R. B., AA306

Dictionary of problem words and expressions, Shaw, Harry, AC84

Dictionary of pronunciation, Lass, Abraham Harold, AC107

—— Noory, Samuel, AC108

Dictionary of proper names and places in the Bible, Odelain, O., BC149

Dictionary of Protestant church music, Davidson, James, BC322, BJ155

Dictionary of protopharmacology, Estes, J. Worth, EH366

Dictionary of pseudonmys [sic] in Indian literature, Virendra Kumar, AA192

Dictionary of pseudonyms and pennames, AA147

Dictionary of psychology, Chaplin, James Patrick, CD28

A dictionary of psychotherapy, Walrond-Skinner, Sue, EH386

Dictionary of public administration, CJ478

The dictionary of publishing, Brownstone, David M., AA272

Dictionary of pure and applied physics, De Vries, Louis, ED25

Dictionary of quotable definitions, Brussell, Eugene E., BE122

Dictionary of quotations, Evans, Bergen, BE120

Dictionary of quotations (classical), Harbottle, Thomas Benfield, BE144

Dictionary of quotations (French and Italian), Harbottle, Thomas Benfield, BE132

Dictionary of quotations (German), Dalbiac, Lilian, BE134

Dictionary of quotations in geography, Wheeler, James O., CL51

Dictionary of quotations in sociology, Bardis, Panos Demetrios, CC22

Dictionary of Qur'ānic terms and concepts, Mir, Mustansir, BC205

Dictionary of race and ethnic relations, Cashmore, Ernest Ellis, CC341

A dictionary of reading and related terms, CB74

The dictionary of real estate appraisal, CH533

Dictionary of religion and philosophy, MacGregor, Geddes, BC74

Dictionary of report series codes, Special Libraries Association, EA65

Dictionary of robotics, Waldman, Harry, EK235

Dictionary of rocks, Mitchell, Richard Scott, EF257

Dictionary of Russian abbreviations, Scheitz, Edgar, AC689

Dictionary of Russian geographical names, Deruguine, T., CL154

—— Volostnova, M. B., CL154

Dictionary of Russian historical terms from the eleventh century to 1917, Pushkarev, Sergei Germanovich, DC584

A dictionary of Russian idioms and colloquialisms, Jaszczun, Wasyl, AC694

Dictionary of Russian literature since 1917, Kasack, Wolfgang, BE1412

Dictionary of Russian personal names, Benson, Morton, AJ203

Dictionary of Russian technical and scientific abbreviations, Zalucky, Henry K., EA129

A dictionary of Russian verbs, Daum, Edmund, AC669

A dictionary of saints, Butler, Alban, BC262

—— Delaney, John J., BC264

Dictionary of Scandinavian literature, BE1086

Dictionary of science and technology, EA84, EA88

—— Dorian, Angelo Francis, EA108, EA113

Dictionary of science and technology : French-English, Dorian, Angelo Francis, EA108

Dictionary of science and technology : German-English, Dorian, Angelo Francis, EA113

Dictionary of scientific and technical terminology, EA100

Dictionary of scientific biography, EA175, EA176, EB100, EH219

A dictionary of scientific bird names, Jobling, James A., EG265

A dictionary of scientific units, Jerrard, Harold George, ED19

Dictionary of Scottish business biography, 1860–1960, CH97

A dictionary of Scottish emigrants to the U.S.A, Whyte, Donald, AJ69

A dictionary of Scottish history, Donaldson, Gordon, DC364

The dictionary of sculptors in bronze, BF396

The dictionary of SDI, Waldman, Harry, CJ620

Dictionary of sea painters, Archibald, E. H. H., BF323

A dictionary of sea terms, Ansted, A., EC81

Dictionary of secret and other societies, Preuss, Arthur, AL75, AL76

A dictionary of selected synonyms in the principal Indo-European languages, Buck, Carl Darling, AC512

Dictionary of sexual slang, Richter, Alan, CC283

A dictionary of signatures & monograms of American artists, Falk, Peter H., BF153

Dictionary of slang and its analogues, AC122

A dictionary of slang and unconventional English, Partridge, Eric, AC132

Dictionary of slang, jargon & cant, Barrère, Albert, AC118

A dictionary of social science methods, Miller, P. McC, CA39

A dictionary of soldier talk, Elting, John Robert, CJ616

Dictionary of South African biography, AH325

A dictionary of South African English, Branford, Jean, AC182

The dictionary of South African painters and sculptors, including Namibia, Ogilvie, Grania, BF142

Dictionary of special education and rehabilitation, Vergason, Glenn A., CB199

Dictionary of spoken Chinese, AC261

Dictionary of sport science, BK29

Dictionary of sports quotations, BK30

Dictionary of statistical terms, Buckland, William R., CG25, EB43

—— Kendall, Maurice George, CG25, EB43

—— Marriott, F. H. C., CG25, EB43

Dictionary of statistics, Mulhall, Michael George, CG53

Dictionary of statistics and methodology, Vogt, W. Paul, CG33

Dictionary of steroids, EE123, EE130, EH334

A dictionary of stylistics, Wales, Katie, BE375

Dictionary of subjects and symbols in art, Hall, James, BF167

A dictionary of superstitions, CF53

A dictionary of surnames, Hanks, Patrick, AJ183

Dictionary of symbolism, Biedermann, Hans, BF163

A dictionary of symbols, Cirlot, Juan Eduardo, BF164

—— Liungman, Carl G., BF170

Dictionary of symbols and imagery, Vries, Ad de, BF174

A dictionary of technical and scientific terms : English-Italian, Italian-English, EA117

Dictionary of technical terms, English-Arabic, EA104

A dictionary of terms and techniques in archaeology, Champion, Sara, DA75

Dictionary of terms in art, Fairholt, F. W., BF81

Dictionary of terms in music, BJ147

Dictionary of terpenoids, EE123, EH334
——— Connolly, J. D., EE121
Dictionary of the African left, Ray, Donald Iain, CJ407
Dictionary of the American West, Blevins, Winfred, AC149
Dictionary of the Aramaic parts of the Old Testament in English and German, Baumgartner, Walter, AC482
Dictionary of the Asante and Fante language, called Tshi (Twi), Christaller, Johann Gottlieb, AC794
Dictionary of the Bible, Hastings, James, BC141
The dictionary of the biological sciences, Gray, Peter, EG37
Dictionary of the black theatre, Woll, Allen L., BH109
A dictionary of the characters and proper names in the works of Shakespeare, Stokes, Francis Griffin, BE789
Dictionary of the Czech literary language, AC277
Dictionary of the dance, Raffé, Walter George, BH147
A dictionary of the Eastern Orthodox church, Langford-James, Richard Lloyd, BC449
Dictionary of the ecumenical movement, BC230
Dictionary of the environment, Allaby, Michael, EK72
Dictionary of the flowering plants and ferns, Willis, John Christopher, EG117, EG182
Dictionary of the fungi, Ainsworth, Geoffrey Clough, EG184
Dictionary of the Gaelic language, MacLeod, Norman, AC395
Dictionary of the graphic arts industry, AA273
Dictionary of the Grebo language, Wilson, J. L., AC441
Dictionary of the Hausa language, Abraham, Roy Clive, AC808
Dictionary of the Hawaiian language, Andrews, Lorrin, AC469
——— Parker, Henry H., AC469
A dictionary of the Hebrew Old Testament in English and German, AC482
Dictionary of the history of ideas, BB29
Dictionary of the history of science, Bynum, W. F., EA246
Dictionary of the Irish language, Royal Irish Academy (Dublin), AC519
A dictionary of the Jewish-Christian dialogue, BC554
Dictionary of the literature of the Iberian peninsula, BE1070
Dictionary of the Lithuanian and English languages, AC601
A dictionary of the Maori language, Williams, Herbert William, AC610
A dictionary of the martial arts, Frederic, Louis, BK89
Dictionary of the Middle Ages, DA148
Dictionary of the Napoleonic wars, Chandler, David G., DC197
A dictionary of the natural environment, Monkhouse, Francis John, CL50
Dictionary of the New Testament, Léon-Dufour, Xavier, BC145
Dictionary of the New Zealand language, Williams, William, AC610
Dictionary of the older Scottish tongue, Craigie, William Alexander, AC30, AC163, AC164
Dictionary of the physical sciences, Emiliani, Cesare, EA90
Dictionary of the printers and booksellers who were at work in England, Scotland and Ireland from 1726 to 1775; those in England, Plomer, H. R., AA306
Dictionary of the printers and booksellers who were at work in England, Scotland and Ireland from 1726 to 1775; those in Ireland, Dix, Ernest Reginald McClintock, AA306
Dictionary of the printers and booksellers who were at work in England, Scotland and Ireland from 1726 to 1775; those in Scotland, Bushnell, G. H., AA306

Dictionary of the printers who were at work in England, Scotland and Ireland, from 1641 to 1667, Plomer, H. R., AA306
Dictionary of the proverbs in England in the sixteenth and seventeenth centuries, Tilley, Morris Palmer, BE159, BE166
Dictionary of the Russian Revolution, DC594, DC595
Dictionary of the sport and exercise sciences, BK25
Dictionary of the stabilized and enriched Assyrian language and English, AC772
Dictionary of the Swahili language, Krapf, Johann Ludwig, AC756
Dictionary of the Targumim, the Talmud Babli and Yerushalmi, and the Midrashic literature, Jastrow, Marcus, AC479
Dictionary of the Third Reich, Shaw, Warren, DC259
——— Taylor, James, DC259
Dictionary of the underworld, British and American, Partridge, Eric, AC132
Dictionary of the Vietnam War, DE279
Dictionary of theatrical terms, Granville, Wilfred, BH77
Dictionary of theology, Rahner, Karl, BC408
Dictionary of theoretical concepts in biology, Roe, Keith E., EG44
Dictionary of theories, CA31
Dictionary of Third World terms, Hadjor, Kofi Buenor, CJ27
Dictionary of tools used in the woodworking and allied trades, c. 1700–1970, Salaman, R. A., BG128
Dictionary of tourism, Metelka, Charles J., CL382
Dictionary of toxicology, Hodgson, Ernest, EH422
Dictionary of trade name origins, Room, Adrian, CH343
Dictionary of translated names and titles, Room, Adrian, BE87
Dictionary of twentieth-centry music, Vinton, John, BJ145
Dictionary of twentieth-century Cuban literature, BE974
A dictionary of twentieth century history, Teed, Peter, DA181
Dictionary of twentieth-century social thought, CA30
Dictionary of twentieth-century world politics, CJ33
Dictionary of uncommon words, AC79
Dictionary of United States military terms for joint usage, CJ584
A dictionary of universal biography of all ages and of all peoples, Hyamson, Albert Montefiore, AH13
Dictionary of Urdū, classical Hindi and English, Platts, John Thompson, AC485, AC801
A dictionary of usage and style, AC69
Dictionary of Victorian engravers, print publishers and their works, Engen, Rodney K., BF323
Dictionary of Victorian painters, Wood, Christopher, BF323
Dictionary of Victorian wood engravers, Engen, Rodney K., BF323, BF359
Dictionary of visual science, EH113
A dictionary of vocal themes, BJ229
Dictionary of war quotations, Wintle, Justin, CJ591
Dictionary of wars, Kohn, George C., DA24
Dictionary of watercolour painters, 1750–1900, Fisher, Stanley W., BF316
A dictionary of weights and measures for the British Isles, Zupko, Ronald Edward, AL201
The dictionary of Welsh biography down to 1940, AH245
Dictionary of Western church music, Poultney, David, BC322, BJ155
The dictionary of Western sculptors in bronze, Mackay, James A., BF396
Dictionary of women artists, Petteys, Chris, BF143, BF152
Dictionary of women artists of Australia, Germaine, Max, BF140
Dictionary of woodworking tools c. 1700–1970, and tools of allied trades, Walker, Philip, BG128
Dictionary of word and phrase origins, Morris, Mary, AC57
——— Morris, William, AC57

A dictionary of words about alcohol, Keller, Mark, CC129
The dictionary of world politics, Evans, Graham, CJ26
Dictionary of world pottery and porcelain, Boger, Louise Ade, BG42
A dictionary of Yoruba monosyllabic verbs, Delano, Isaac O., AC818
A dictionary of zoology, Leftwich, A. W., EG229
Dictionnaire abrégé des imprimeurs/éditeurs français du seizième siècle, Muller, Jean, AA309
Dictionnaire alphabétique et analogique de la langue française, Robert, Paul, AC329, AC334
Dictionnaire arabe-français-anglais, Blachère, Régis, AC213
Dictionnaire archéologique de la France, DC175
Dictionnaire archéologique de la Gaule, époque celtique, France. Commission de la topographie des Gaules, DC175
Dictionnaire basque-français et français-basque, Lhande, Pierre, AC229
Dictionnaire bio-bibliographique des littérateurs d'expression wallonne, 1622 à 1950, Coppe, Paul, BE1098
Dictionnaire biographique de militants nationalistes algériens, Stora, Benjamin, DD127
Dictionnaire biographique des artistes contemporains, 1910–1930, Édouard-Joseph, René, BF139
Dictionnaire biographique des comédiens français du XVIIᵉ siècle, Mongrédien, Georges, BH115
Dictionnaire biographique des dédecins en France au Moyen Âge, Wickersheimer, Ernest, EH226
Dictionnaire biographique des sciences, des lettres et des arts en Belgique, Seyn, Eugène de, AH176
Dictionnaire biographique du Canada, AH93
Dictionnaire biographique du clergé canadien-français, Allaire, Jean Baptiste Arthur, AH91
Dictionnaire Bordas de littérature française et francophone, Lemáitre, Henri, BE1160
Dictionnaire breton, AC234
Dictionnaire chronologique du vocabulaire français, Kesselring, Wilhelm, AC382
Dictionnaire commercial et financier, Servotte, Jozef V., CH129
Dictionnaire complet de la langue hebraique ancienne et moderne, AC470
Dictionnaire critique de la révolution française, DC183
Dictionnaire critique de la sociologie, CC17
Dictionnaire critique et documentaire des peintres, sculpteurs, dessinateurs et graveurs de tous les temps et de tous les pays, Bénézit, Emmanuel, BF137
Dictionnaire d'américanismes, Deak, Étienne, AC339
Dictionnaire d'ancien français, Grandsaignes d'Hauterive, Robert, AC379
Dictionnaire d'archéologie biblique, Corswant, Willy, BC193
Dictionnaire d'archéologie chrétienne et de liturgie, Cabrol, Fernand, BC246
Dictionnaire de bibliographie haïtienne, Bissainthe, Max, AA566
Dictionnaire de biographie française, AH194
Dictionnaire de démographie, Pressat, Roland, CG30
Dictionnaire de géographie ancienne et moderne, Deschamps, Pierre, CL101
Dictionnaire de géologie, Foucault, Alain, EF83
Dictionnaire de la Bible, Vigouroux, Fulcran Grégoire, BC152
Dictionnaire de la géographie, CL45
Dictionnaire de la langue française, Littré, Émile, AC332
Dictionnaire de la langue française du seizième siècle, Huguet, Edmond Eugène Auguste, AC382
Dictionnaire de la littérature française et francophone, Demougin, Jacques, BE1160
Dictionnaire de la musique, BJ129, BJ136
Dictionnaire de la mythologie grecque et romaine, Grimal, Pierre, CF27

Dictionnaire de la noblesse ... de la France ..., La Chesnaye-Desbois, François Alexandre Aubert de, AJ86

Dictionnaire de la noblesse française, Sereville, Etienne de, AJ88

Dictionnaire de la préhistoire, DA78

Dictionnaire de la sculpture, BF389

Dictionnaire de la sculpture moderne, BF397

Dictionnaire de l'Académie française, AC328

Dictionnaire de l'ancien français, Greimas, Algirdas Julien, AC380

Dictionnaire de l'ancienne langue française, Godefroy, Frédéric Eugène, AC346, AC384

Dictionnaire de l'ancienne langue française, et de tous ses dialectes, du IXᵉ au XVᵉ siècle, Godefroy, Frédéric Eugène, AC378

Dictionnaire de l'argot, Colin, Jean-Paul, AC355

Dictionnaire de l'estampe en France, 1830–1950, Bailly-Herzberg, Janine, BF380

Dictionnaire de l'ethnologie et de l'anthropologie, CE38

Dictionnaire de littérature contemporaine, Boisdeffre, Pierre de, BE1150

Dictionnaire de littérature française contemporaine, Bonnefoy, Claude, BE1151

Dictionnaire de l'urbanisme et de l'aménagement, Choay, Françoise, BF273

—— Merlin, Pierre, BF273

Dictionnaire de poétique et de rhétorique, Morier, Henri, BE327

Dictionnaire de sigles nationaux et internationaux, Carton, Jean, AC345

Dictionnaire de sociologie, CA32

Dictionnaire de spiritualité, BC54

Dictionnaire de théologie catholique, BC398

Dictionnaire des 10,000 dirigeants politiques français, Bragadir, Sabine, CJ328

—— Dioudonnat, Pierre-Marie, CJ328

Dictionnaire des abréviations et acronymes scientifiques, techniques, médicaux, économiques, juridiques, Murith, Jean, EA96

Dictionnaire des anonymes et pseudonymes, XVᵉ siècle–1900, Delecourt, Jules Victor, AA162

Dictionnaire des antiquités grecques et romaines d'après les textes et les monuments, Daremberg, Charles Victor, DA99

Dictionnaire des artistes de langue française en Amérique du nord, Karel, David, BF314

Dictionnaire des attributs, allégories, emblèmes et symboles, Seyn, Eugène de, BF173

Dictionnaire des auteurs de langue française en Amérique du Nord, Hamel, Réginald, BE841

Dictionnaire des auteurs maghrebins de langue française, Déjeux, Jean, BE1515

Dictionnaire des canadianismes, Dulong, Gaston, AC386

Dictionnaire des cinéastes, Breton, Émile, BH285

Dictionnaire des citations françaises, Oster Soussouev, Pierre, BE133

Dictionnaire des citations françaises et étrangères, BE129

Dictionnaire des civilisations africaines, CE106

Dictionnaire des comédiens français (ceux d'hier), Lyonnet, Henry, BH115

Dictionnaire des conventionnels, Kuscinski, August, AH198

Dictionnaire des critiques littéraires, Le Sage, Laurent, BE1159

Dictionnaire des difficultés du français, Colin, Jean-Paul, AC365

Dictionnaire des difficultés grammaticales et lexicologiques, AC370

Dictionnaire des écrivains belges, Seyn, Eugène de, AH176

Dictionnaire des écrivains belges, bio-bibliographie, Seyn, Eugène de, BE1102

Dictionnaire des écrivains belges et catalogue de leurs publications, 1830–80, AA576

Dictionnaire des ecrivains français, Malignon, Jean, BE1162

Dictionnaire des écrivains québécois contemporains, Légaré, Yves, BE841

Dictionnaire des éditeurs de musique française, Devriès, Anik, BJ180

Dictionnaire des expressions et locutions, Rey, Alain, AC371

Dictionnaire des films, Breton, Émile, BH200

Dictionnaire des illustrateurs, Osterwalder, Marcus, BF384

Dictionnaire des lettres françaises, BE1153

Dictionnaire des littératures de langue française, Beaumarchais, Jean-Pierre de, BE1149

Dictionnaire des maréchaux de France, AH195

Dictionnaire des miniaturistes du Moyen Âge et de la Renaissance dans les différentes contrées de l'Europe, Aeschlimann, Erardo, BF310

Dictionnaire des ministres de 1789 à 1989, DC211

—— Yvert, Benoît, CJ328

Dictionnaire des mots contemporains, Gilbert, Pierre, AC373

Dictionnaire des mots nouveaux, Gilbert, Pierre., AC373

Dictionnaire des mots sauvages (écrivains des XIXᵉ et XXᵉ siècles), Rheims, Maurice, AC358

Dictionnaire des mythes littéraires, CF3

Dictionnaire des mythologies et des religions des sociétés traditionnelles et du monde antique, CF7

Dictionnaire des noms propres de la Bible, BC149

Dictionnaire des oeuvres algériennes en langue française, BE1523

Dictionnaire des oeuvres contemporaines de tous les pays, BE63

Dictionnaire des oeuvres de tous les temps et de tous les pays, BE63

Dictionnaire des oeuvres et des thèmes de la littérature française, Bouty, Michel, BE1152

Dictionnaire des oeuvres littéraires du Québec, BE837

Dictionnaire des œuvres littéraires négro-africaines de langue française des origines à 1978, BE1516

Dictionnaire des ouvrages anonymes [de Barbier], Brunet, Gustave, AA168

Dictionnaire des parlementaires français, Bourloton, Edgar, DC211

—— Cougny, Gaston, DC211

—— Jolly, Jean, AH200, CJ329

—— Robert, Adolphe, AH200, CJ329, DC211

Dictionnaire des personnages de la Révolution, Caratini, Roger, AH193

Dictionnaire des personnages du cinéma, Horvilleur, Gilles, BH220

Dictionnaire des personnages littéraires et dramatiques de tous les temps et de tous les pays, BE63

Dictionnaire des philosophes antiques, BB54

Dictionnaire des poètes et de la poésie, Charpentreau, Jacques, BE1197

—— Jean, Georges, BE1197

Dictionnaire des proverbes et dictons de France, Dournon, Jean-Yves, BE130

Dictionnaire des racines scientifiques, Cailleux, André, EA87

Dictionnaire des sciences économiques, CH66

Dictionnaire des sciences historiques, DA42

Dictionnaire des sculpteurs de l'antiquité, Lami, Stanislas, BF395

Dictionnaire des sculpteurs de l'école française ..., Lami, Stanislas, BF395

Dictionnaire des sociétés secrètes en Occident, Mariel, Pierre, AL75

Dictionnaire des symboles, CF4

Dictionnaire des synonymes, Bertaud du Chazaud, Henri, AC362

Dictionnaire des synonymes, conforme au dictionnaire de l'Académie française, Bénac, Henri, AC361

Dictionnaire des synonymes de la langue française, Bailly, René, AC359

Dictionnaire des villes chinoises, Biot, Édouard Constant, CL160

Dictionnaire d'histoire de France Perrin, DC160

Dictionnaire d'histoire et de géographie ecclésiastiques, Baudrillart, Alfred, BC412

Dictionnaire d'orthographe et des difficultés du français, Dournon, Jean-Yves, AC366

Dictionnaire du ballet moderne, BH140

Dictionnaire du bon français, AC369

Dictionnaire du cinéma, BH247

—— Tulard, Jean, BH288

Dictionnaire du cinéma et de la télévision, Bessy, Maurice, BH247

—— Chardans, Jean-Louis, BH247

Dictionnaire du français classique, Dubois, Jean, AC376

Dictionnaire du français contemporain, Dubois, Jean, AC372

Dictionnaire du français contemporain illustré, AC372

Dictionnaire du français non conventionnel, Cellard, Jacques, AC354

Dictionnaire du français parlé, Bernet, Charles, AC353

Dictionnaire du français québécois, AC385

Dictionnaire du moyen français, Greimas, Algirdas Julien, AC381

Dictionnaire économique et juridique, CK48

Dictionnaire économique et social, Branciard, Michel, CH55

Dictionnaire encyclopédique des sciences du langage, BD38

Dictionnaire étymologique de la langue française, Bloch, Oscar, AC347

—— Dauzat, Albert, AC348

Dictionnaire étymologique de la langue grecque, Boisacq, Émile, AC449

—— Chantraine, Pierre, AC450

Dictionnaire etymologique de la langue latine, Ernout, Alfred, AC579

Dictionnaire etymologique de l'ancien français, AC387

—— Baldinger, Kurt, AC346

Dictionnaire étymologique des noms de famille et prénoms de France, Dauzat, Albert, AJ189

Dictionnaire étymologique des noms de lieux en France, Dauzat, Albert, CL185

Dictionnaire étymologique des noms de rivières et de montagnes en France, Dauzat, Albert, CL186

Dictionnaire étymologique des noms grecs de plantes, Carnoy, Albert Joseph, EG122

Dictionnaire étymologique du breton moyen, Ernault, Émile, AC235

Dictionnaire étymologique du français, Picoche, Jacqueline, AC351

Dictionnaire étymologique du proto-indo-européen, Carnoy, Albert Joseph, AC513

Dictionnaire filmographique de la littérature mondiale, Daisne, Johan, BH216

Dictionnaire fondamental du français littéraire, Forest, Philippe, BE1156

Dictionnaire français-anglais, anglais-français des termes médicaux et biologiques, Lépine, Pierre, EH141

Dictionnaire française breton, Hermon, Roparz, AC237

Dictionnaire française et anglais de terminologie mathématique, Lyle, William David, EB49

Dictionnaire généalogique des familles canadiennes, Tanguay, Cyprien, AJ71, AJ73

Dictionnaire généalogique des familles du Québec ..., Jetté, René, AJ71

Dictionnaire général de biographie, histoire, littérature, [etc.], Le Jeune, Jean Marie, DB198

Dictionnaire général de la langue française, Hatzfeld, Adolphe, AC330

Dictionnaire général des sciences humaines, Thinès, Georges, CA42

Dictionnaire géographique de la Suisse, AH296, DC529

—— Knapp, Charles, CL150

Dictionnaire géographique et administratif de la France, Joanne, Paul Bénigne, CL133

Dictionnaire historique de la langue française, AC349

Dictionnaire historique de la Révolution française, DC184

Dictionnaire historique des argots français, Esnault, Gaston, AC355, AC356

Dictionnaire historique des Canadiens et des Métis français de l'Ouest, Morice, Adrien Gabriel, AH95

Dictionnaire historique du breton, Hemon, Roparz, AC237

Dictionnaire historique du Japon, DE208

Dictionnaire historique et biographique de la Révolution et de l'Empire, Robinet, J. F. E., DC185

Dictionnaire historique et biographique de la Suisse, AH296, DC529

Dictionnaire historique et géographique des communes belges, Seyn, Eugène de, CL130

Dictionnaire historique, thématique et technique des littératures, BE62

—— Demougin, Jacques, BE1160

Dictionnaire illustré multilingue de l'architecture du Proche Orient ancien, BF243

Dictionnaire international des termes littéraires, Escarpit, Robert, BE88

Dictionnaire juridique, Baleyte, Jean, CK48

—— Quemner, Th. A., CK48

Dictionnaire juridique et economique, Doucet, Michel, CK48

Dictionnaire latin-français des auteurs chrétiens, Blaise, Albert, AC581, AC586

Dictionnaire latin-français des auteurs du moyen-age, Blaise, Albert, AC586

Dictionnaire : littérature française contemporaine, Garcin, Jérôme, BE1151

Dictionnaire Napoléon, DC195

Dictionnaire occitan-français d'après les parlers languedociens, Alibert, Louis, AC654

Dictionnaire polyglotte des termes d'art et d'archéologie, Réau, Louis, BF92

Dictionnaire pratique et historique de la musique, Brenet, Michel, BJ146

Dictionnaire raisonné de l'architecture françcaise du XIe au XVIe siècle, Viollet-le-Duc, Eugène Emmanuel, BF237

Dictionnaire raisonné du mobilier français de l'époque carlovingienne à la Renaissance, Viollet-Le-Duc, Eugène Emmanuel, BG124

Dictionnaire topographique de la France comprenant les noms de lieu anciens et modernes, CL187

Dictionnaire universel de l'art et des artistes, BF77

Dictionnaire universel des noms propres, alphabétique et analogique, Rey, Alain, AJ191

—— Rey-Debove, Josette, AJ191

Dictionnaire universel des poids et mesures, Doursther, Horace, AL197

Dicziunari scurznieu da la lingua ladina, Velleman, Antoine, AC665

Diderot, D. *Encyclopédie*, AB41

Diderot, AB41

Didik, Frank X. *Eastern European business directory*, CH412

Diederich, Nils. *Wahlstatistik in Deutschland*, CJ336

Diehl, Charles. *Byzantium*, DA161

Diehl, Katharine Smith. *Hymns and tunes*, BC316

Diesch, Carl. *Grundriss zur Geschichte der deutschen Dichtung aus den Quellen*, BE1218

Diesch, Carl Hermann. *Bibliographie der germanistischen Zeitschriften*, AD99

Diet *see* **Nutrition**

Diet and health, National Research Council. Committee on Diet and Health, EH311

Dietl, Clara-Erika. *Wörterbuch für Recht, Wirtschaft und Politik*, CK49

Dietzel, Thomas. *Deutsche literarische Zeitschriften, 1880–1945*, AD76, AD77

Diez años de estadística vital, 1978–1987, CG127

Differential equations, EB70

Digest of commercial laws of the world, CK68

Digest of data on persons with disabilities, Ficke, Robert C., CB206, CC198

Digest of education statistics, CB139

Digest of intellectual property laws of the world, CK68

Digest of statistics, CG179

Digest of statistics for Northern Ireland, CG240

•*Digests of environmental impact statements*, EK67

Diglossia, Fernández, Mauro, BD81

dii, BG32

Dijkstra, Waling. *Friesch woordenboek*, AC391

Dillman, August. *Lexicon linguae Aethiopicae*, AC311

Dillman, David L. *Civil service reform*, CJ100

Dillmann, August. *Lexicon linguae Aethiopicae cum indice Latino*, AC310

Dillon, Kenneth J. *Scholars' guide to Washington, D.C. for Central and East European studies*, DC14

Dillon, Michael. *Dictionary of Chinese history*, DE144

DILSI, NZ, Szentirmay, Paul, AK63

Dimensions : a journal of Holocaust studies, DA216

Dimensions of the independent sector, AL139

Dimitrov, Théodore Delchev. *World bibliography of international documentation*, AF7

Dimmitt, Richard Bertrand. *Actor guide to the talkies*, BH205

—— *A title guide to the talkies*, BH217

Dindinger, P. Johannes. *Bibliotheca missionum*, BC304

Dindorf, Ludwig August. *Thēsauros tēs hellēnikēs glōssēs*, AC442

Dindorf, Wilhelm. *Thēsauros tēs hellēnikēs glōssēs*, AC442

Diner, Hasia R. *Women and urban society*, CC298

Ding, Choo Ming. *A bibliography of bibliographies on Malaysia*, DE227

Dingley, Pauline. *Historic books on veterinary science and animal husbandry*, EJ100

Dingwall, William Orr. *Language and the brain*, BD78, CD117

Dinneen, Patrick Stephen. *Irish-English dictionary*, AC521

Dinosaurs
  bibliography, EF229

Dinosaurs, Fleury, Bruce E., EF229

Dinstel, Marion. *List of French doctoral dissertations on Africa, 1884–1961*, DD29

Dionne, Narcisse Eutrope. *Inventaire chronologique …*, AA447

Dionne, René. *Bibliographie de la critique de la littérature québecoise et canadienne-française dans les revues canadiennes*, BE838

Dioudonnat, Pierre-Marie. *Dictionnaire des 10,000 dirigeants politiques français*, CJ328

Diplomacy
  handbooks, AL155

Diplomacy (by country or region)
  Europe, CJ316, DC10
  United States
    bibliography, CJ169
    handbooks, CJ150

Diplomacy in the Near and Middle East, DE64

The diplomatic service list, CJ341

Diplomatics, AA213

Diplomats, CJ70, CJ81

Diplomats (by country or region)
  Great Britain
    directories, CJ341
  United States, CJ183
    encyclopedias, CJ118

Dippold, Max F. *Bibliographie du Cameroun*, DD136

Dirección General de Estadística y Censos (Ecuador). *Síntesis estadística del Ecuador*, CG154

Direct-line distances—international edition, Fitzpatrick, Gary L., CL59

Direct-line distances—United States edition, Fitzpatrick, Gary L., CL60

Direct mail terms, CH550

Direct marketing list source, CH601

The direct marketing market place, CH584

Direction des archives de France. Services d'archives départementaux et communaux. *État des inventaires des archives départementales, communales et hospitalières au 1er janvier 1983*, DC154

Direction des Musées de France. *Films and videos on photography*, BF327

Direction of trade statistics, CH149

Directories
  bibliography, AL3, AL4, AL8, CH401

Directories (by country or region)
  Europe
    bibliography, AL5
  Great Britain
    bibliography, AL2

Directories in print, AL3

•*Directories in print (DIP)*, AL3

The directories of London, 1677–1977, Atkins, Peter Joseph, AL1, AL7, CH366, CH381

Directories of photographers, Rudisill, Richard, BF345

Directorio boliviano en población y desarrollo, CG139

Directorio de antropólogos latinoamericanos, México, Díaz Polanco, Héctor, CE86

Directorio de instituciones y organismos relacionados con la etnografía, CE99

Directorio de organizaciones indígenas de América, AL54

Directorio de publicaciones periódicas mexicanas, AD61

Directorio de revistas y periódicos de Cuba, AD74

Directorio latinoamericano, DB285

Directors and their films, Bushnell, Brooks, BH188, BH204

Directory, AK53

Directory, African American Architects, BF251

Directory for exceptional children, CB201

Directory, Japanese-affiliated companies in USA & Canada, CH353

Directory, juvenile & adult correctional departments, institutions, agencies & paroling authorities, CK261

Directory of accredited allied medical education programs, EH152

Directory of African and African-American studies in the United States, DD53

Directory of African film-makers and films, Shiri, Keith, BH212

Directory of African museums, AL87

Directory of Albanian officials, CJ325

Directory of American agriculture, EJ41

The directory of American Jewish institutions, AH83

Directory of American libraries with genealogy or local history collections, Filby, P. William, AJ54

Directory of American philosophers, BB44

Directory of American poets and fiction writers, BE451

Directory of American research and technology, EA37, EA213

Directory of American scholars, AH76

Directory of American silver, pewter, and silver plate, Kovel, Ralph M., BG145

—— Kovel, Terry H., BG145

Directory of American youth organizations, AL40

Directory of anthropological resources in New York City libraries, Reed, Monica, CE88

Directory of anthropologists and anthropological research in aging, CE87

Directory of approved allied medical education programs, EH152

Directory of archives and manuscript repositories in the United States, DB30

Directory of archives, libraries and schools of librarianship in Africa, Dadzie, E. W., AK154

—— Strickland, J. T., AK154

Directory of associations in Canada, AL51, AL52

Directory of Australian academic and research libraries, AK162

Directory of Australian academic libraries, AK162

Directory of Australian associations, AL72

Directory of bankruptcy attorneys, CK142

The directory of black nursing faculty, Allen, Sallie T., EH281

Directory of blacks in the performing arts, Mapp, Edward, BH23

Directory of bodies concerned with urban and regional research, BF279

The directory of British alternative periodicals, 1965–1974, Noyce, John L., AD111

Directory of British and Irish law libraries, CK213

Directory of British architects, 1834–1900, British Architectural Library, BF259

—— Felstead, Alison, BF259

Directory of British associations & associations in Ireland, AL65, AL66

Directory of British official publications, Richard, Stephen, AF178

Directory of British photographic collections, National Photographic Record, BF344

—— Wall, John, BF344

The directory of business information resources, CH78

The directory of business to business catalogs, CH562

Directory of Canadian archives, AK127

Directory of Canadian museums and related institutions, Canadian Museum Association, AL90, BF116, EA217

Directory of Canadian records and manuscript repositories, AK127

Directory of Canadian theatre archives, McCallum, Heather, BH54

Directory of Canadianists, DB201

The directory of Caribbean personalities in Britain and North America, AH148

Directory of Catholic colleges and universities, CB305

Directory of Central America organizations, AL35

Directory of chemistry software, EE58

Directory of Chinese libraries, AK156

Directory of Chinese officials and organizations, CJ428

—— United States. Central Intelligence Agency, CJ427

Directory of Chinese scientific and educational officials, CJ428

Directory of college facilities and services for people with disabilities, CB311

Directory of college facilities and services for the handicapped, CB311

Directory of community legislation in force and other acts of the community institutions, CK203

Directory of computer assisted research in musicology, BJ167

The directory of congressional voting scores and interest group ratings, Sharp, J. Michael, CJ218

Directory of conservative and libertarian serials, publishers, and freelance markets, Murphy, Dennis D., AD54

Directory of constituent societies of the American Council of Learned Societies, American Council of Learned Societies, AL37

Directory of consumer protection and environmental agencies, EK73

Directory of corporate affiliations, CH351

The directory of corporate and foundation givers, AL107

Directory of corporate counsel, CK142

Directory of criminal justice information sources, CK262

Directory of current Latin American periodicals, AD67

Directory of curriculum materials centers, CB267

Directory of departments and programs of religious studies in North America, BC77

Directory of development research and training institutes in Europe, AL79

Directory of directories, AL3

Directory of doctoral programs in theatre studies in the U.S.A. and Canada, American Society for Theatre Research, BH84

Directory of documentation, libraries and archives services in Africa, AK154

Directory of Eastern European film-makers and films, 1945–1991, Balski, Grzegorz, BH212

Directory of economic institutions, Capie, Forrest, CH77

Directory of education studies in Canada, CB52

Directory of educational contests for students K–12, Long, Kim, CB86

Directory of educational documentation and information services, CB87

Directory of educational research institutions, CB88

Directory of educational software for nursing, EH272

Directory of engineering education institutions, EK12

Directory of environmental attorneys, CK142

The directory of ethnic professionals in LIS (library and information science), AK87

Directory of European associations, AL16

Directory of European banking and financial associations, CH276

Directory of European business, CH410

Directory of European industrial and trade associations, AL16

Directory of European political scientists, CJ46

Directory of European professional & learned societies, AL16

Directory of executive recruiters, CH618

Directory of family associations, Bentley, Elizabeth Petty, AJ52

Directory of federal laboratory & technology resources, EA214

Directory of federal libraries, Evinger, William R., AK124

Directory of federal statistical data files, CG101, CG102

Directory of federal technology resources, EA214

Directory of federally sponsored training materials, CB351

The directory of fee-based information services, AK59

Directory of financial aids for minorities, CB377

Directory of financial aids for women, CB378, CC546

Directory of fine art representatives & corporations collecting art, BF97

The directory of food and nutrition information for professionals and consumers, Frank, Robyn C., EH290, EJ214

Directory of food and nutrition information services and resources, Frank, Robyn C., EH290, EJ214

Directory of foreign document collections, Turner, Carol A., AF149

Directory of foreign firms operating in the United States, CH352

Directory of foreign investment in the U.S., CH538

Directory of foreign trade organizations in Eastern Europe, CH131

Directory of geoscience departments, EF90

The directory of gold & silversmiths, jewellers, and allied traders, 1838–1914, Culme, John, BG137, BG140

Directory of government document collections & librarians, AF86

Directory of graduate medical education programs, EH160

Directory of graduate programs, CB301

Directory of graduate research, EE56, EE59

Directory of grants for organizations serving people with disabilities, CC194

Directory of grants in the humanities, AL108, BA9

Directory of health care professionals, EH155

Directory of higher education institutions, CB239

Directory of historic American theatres, Frick, John W., BH110

—— League of Historic American Theatres, BH110

—— Ward, Carlton, BH110

Directory of history departments and organizations in the United States and Canada, DA27

Directory of human settlements management and development training institutions in developing countries, United Nations Centre for Human Settlements, BF279

Directory of industry data sources, CH328

Directory of information and library services in New Zealand, AK63

Directory of information resources in housing and urban development, BF280

A directory of information resources in the United States, Library of Congress. National Referral Center for Science and Technology, EK93

•*Directory of information resources online*, EH158

Directory of information sources in Japan, 1986, AK159

Directory of institutional photocopying services, AK244

Directory of intellectual property attorneys, CK142

Directory of international and regional organizations conducting standards-related activities, EA271

Directory of international corporate giving in America, AL109

Directory of international corporate giving in America and abroad, AL109

Directory of international periodicals and newsletters on the built environment, Gretes, Frances C., BF226

The directory of international sources of business information, Ball, Sarah, CH1

Directory of internships, work experience programs, and on-the-job training opportunities, CB364, CH695

Directory of investment managers, CH311

Directory of investment research, CH312

Directory of Iranian officials, United States. Central Intelligence Agency. Directorate of Intelligence, CJ325

A directory of Iranian periodicals, AD198

Directory of Irish archives, DC400

—— Helferty, Seamus, AJ133

Directory of Japanese-affiliated companies in the USA & Canada, CH353

Directory of Japanese scientific periodicals, EA48

Directory of Japanese technical resources in the United States, EA139

Directory of labour organizations in Canada, CH662

Directory of law teachers, CK138

Directory of lawyer referral services, CK143

Directory of leading private companies, CH351

Directory of leading U.S. accounting firms, CH255

Directory of legal aid and defender offices in the United States, CK144

Directory of libraries and information centers of the academies of sciences of socialist countries, AK117

Directory of libraries and special collections on Eastern Europe and the USSR, Lockwood, Crosby, DC51

Directory of libraries and special collections on Latin America and the West Indies, Hallewell, Laurence, AK111

—— Naylor, Bernard, AK111

—— Steele, Colin, AK111

Directory of library & information professionals, AK83, AK88

Directory of library and information organizations in the United Kingdom, AK142

Directory of library automation software, systems, and services, AK191

Directory of library reprographic services, AK244

Directory of library resources for the blind and physically handicapped, CC196

Directory of literary magazines, AD49

Directory of litigation attorneys, CK142

Directory of little magazines, AD12

The directory of mail order catalogs, CH562

Directory of medical and health care libraries in the United Kingdom and Republic of Ireland, EH167

Directory of medical libraries belonging to the Medical Library Association, AK52

Directory of medical specialists, EH164

Directory of members, American Statistical Association, CG35, EB57

—— History of Science Society, EA248

—— Special Libraries Association, AK61

Directory of mental health libraries and information centers, EH388

Directory of meteorite collections and meteorite research, Unesco, EF208

Directory of military bases in the U.S, CJ624

—— Evinger, William R., CJ623

Directory of multinationals, CH354

The directory of museums & living displays, Hudson, Kenneth, AL88

Directory of museums in Africa, AL87

Directory of music faculties in American colleges and universities, BJ168

Directory of music faculties in colleges and universities, U.S. and Canada, BJ168

Directory of music research libraries, BJ77, BJ169

Directory of national information sources on disabilities, CC195

Directory of national information sources on handicapping conditions and related services, CC195

Directory of national unions and employee associations, United States. Bureau of labor Statistics, CH663

Directory of new and emerging foundations, AL112

Directory of newspaper libraries in the U.S. and Canada, Parch, Grace D., AE30

Directory of non-governmental environment and development organisations in OECD member countries, CH114

The directory of North American fisheries and aquatic scientists, EG48

Directory of nursing homes, EH156

Directory of official publications in Scotland, AF12

Directory of officials and organizations in China, 1968–1983, Lamb, Malcolm, CJ430

Directory of officials of Czechoslovak Socialist Republic, United States. Central Intelligence Agency. National Foreign Assessment Center, CJ325

Directory of officials of the Bulgarian People's Republic. *Directory of Albanian officials,* CJ325

Directory of officials of the German Democratic Republic, United States. Central Intelligence Agency, CJ325

Directory of officials of the Hungarian People's Republic, United States. Central Intelligence Agency. National Foreign Assessment Center, CJ325

Directory of officials of the People's Socialist Republic of Albania, United States. Central Intelligence Agency, CJ325

Directory of officials of the Polish People's Republic, CJ325

Directory of officials of the Republic of Cuba, United States. Central Intelligence Agency. National Foreign Assessment Center, CJ325

Directory of officials of the Socialist Federal Republic of Yugoslavia, United States. Central Intelligence Agency, CJ325

Directory of officials of the Socialist Republic of Romania, National Foreign Assessment Center, CJ325

Directory of officials of the Socialist Republic of Vietnam, United States. Central Intelligence Agency. National Foreign Assessment Center, CJ325

Directory of online databases, AK208

Directory of oral history collections, Smith, Allen, DB36

A directory of oral history tapes of librarians in the United States and Canada, Dale, Doris Cruger, AK85

Directory of organizations and individuals professionally engaged in governmental research and related activities, Governmental Research Association (U.S.), CJ48

Directory of osteopathic physicians, EH154

Directory of overseas schools, International Schools Services, CB91

Directory of paleontologists of the world, International Paleontological Association, EF245

Directory of patent depository libraries, Phillips, John B., EA266

Directory of periodicals online, AD2, AD6

Directory of periodicals published by international organizations, Union of International Associations, AD21

Directory of periodicals published in India, 1991, Susheel Kaur, AD193

Directory of periodicals publishing articles on English and American literature and language, BE170

Directory of philanthropic trusts, AL128

A directory of philanthropic trusts in New Zealand, Fieldhouse, Arthur E., AL128

Directory of physicians in the United States, EH157

Directory of physicists from developing countries, ED30

Directory of physics & astronomy faculties in North American colleges & universities, EC45, ED31

Directory of physics & astronomy staff members, EC45, ED31

Directory of planning and urban affairs libraries in the United States and Canada, 1990, BF281

Directory of political newsletters, CJ101

Directory of political periodicals, CJ101

Directory of popular culture collections, CF73

Directory of portable databases, AK208

Directory of postsecondary institutions, CB268

Directory of practicing anthropologists, Drake, H. Max, CE88

Directory of practicing anthropologists, Drake, Ann M., CE88

—— Karlish, Roger D., CE88

Directory of psychiatry residency training programs, EH389

Directory of public elementary and secondary education agencies, CB97

A directory of public vocational-technical schools and institutes in the U.S.A, CB296

Directory of published proceedings. Series SEMT, AL27, EA209

Directory of published proceedings. Series SSH, AL27

Directory of publishers and booksellers in India, AA294

Directory of publishing, AA287, AA290

Directory of publishing opportunities in accounting, economics and finance, CH27

Directory of publishing opportunities in business and economics, CH27

Directory of publishing opportunities in education, CB20

Directory of publishing opportunities in journals and periodicals, AD27

Directory of publishing opportunities in management and marketing, CH27

Directory of publishing. United Kingdom, Commonwealth and overseas, AA290

Directory of railway officials & yearbook, CH463

A directory of rare book and special collections in the United Kingdom and the Republic of Ireland, AK143

The directory of real estate investors, CH540

Directory of registered investment advisors, CH305

Directory of registered lobbyists and lobbyist legislation, CJ130

Directory of religious organizations in the United States, Melton, J. Gordon, BC80

Directory of research grants, AL108, AL110, BA9

Directory of residential treatment facilities for emotionally handicapped children and youth, Sherman, Barbara Smiley, CC165

Directory of resources for Australian studies in North America, Albinski, Nan Bowman, DF30

Directory of Roman Catholic newspapers on microfilm, University of Notre Dame. Library, AE33

Directory of Russian MPs, CJ385

Directory of Scandinavian studies in North America, DC77

Directory of scholarly journals published in Africa, AD169

Directory of scientific directories, EA140, EH148

Directory of scientific research institutes in the People's Republic of China, Swannack-Nunn, Susan, EA148

Directory of Scots banished to the American plantations, 1650–1775, Dobson, David, AJ62

Directory of Scottish newspapers, Ferguson, Joan P. S., AE62

Directory of Scottish settlers in North America, 1625–1825, Dobson, David, AJ62

Directory of selected national testing programs, CD74

Directory of social research organisations in the United Kingdom, CA56

—— Bulmer, Martin, AL66

—— Schwerzel, Marleen, AL66

—— Sykes, Wendy, AL66

Directory of South Asian library resources in the UK and the Republic of Ireland, DE82

Directory of Soviet officials, United States. Central Intelligence Agency, CJ325

Directory of special and research libraries in India, AK157

Directory of special collections in Australiana, DF31

Directory of special collections in Western Europe, AK131

Directory of special libraries and information centers, AK123, AK126

Directory of special programs for minority group members, CC343

Directory of state court clerks & county courthouses, CK156

Directory of state education agencies, CB98

Directory of statisticians, CG35, EB57

Directory of surveys in developing countries, Lloyd, Cynthia B., CG36

Directory of technical and scientific directories, EA140, EH148

Directory of telefacsimile sites in libraries in the United States and Canada, AK60

Directory of telefacsimile sites in North American libraries, AK60

Directory of the American Baptist Churches in the U.S.A, BC328

Directory of the American left, CJ139

Directory of the American Psychological Association, American Psychological Association, CD46

Directory of the American theater, 1894–1971, Guernsey, Otis L., BE454, BE463

Directory of the Association for Library and Information Science Education, Association for Library and Information Science Education, AK58

The directory of the canning, freezing, preserving industries, EJ160

Directory of the college student press in America, CB263

Directory of the forest products industry, EJ184

Directory of the Medical Library Association, AK52

Directory of the wood products industry, EJ184

Directory of theatre resources, Howard, Diana, BH53

Directory of theatre training programs, Charles, Jill, BH84

Directory of Third World women's publications, CC547

Directory of transportation libraries and information centers in North America, CH449

Directory of undergraduate political science faculty, CJ49

Directory of United Nations databases and information systems, AF43

Directory of United Nations documentary and archival sources, Hajnal, Peter I., AF45

Directory of United Nations serial publications, AF47

Directory of United States exporters, CH132

Directory of United States government periodicals and subscription publications, AF112

Directory of United States import concerns, CH132

Directory of United States importers, CH132

Directory of United States standardization activities, Chumas, Sophie, EA276

Directory of university research bureaus and institutes, AL82, EA147

Directory of unpublished experimental mental measures, Goldman, Bert A., CD75

A directory of urban public transportation service, CH450

Directory of U.S. government datafiles for mainframes and microcomputers, AF104

Directory of U.S. labor organizations, CH663

Directory of visual anthropology, Blakely, Pamela A. R., CE88

—— Blakely, Thomas D., CE88

Directory of Washington rep. esentatives of American associations and industry, CJ144
Directory of water pollution research laboratories, Organization for Economic Cooperation and Development. Directorate for Scientific Affairs, EK94
A directory of women's media, AE25, CC549
Directory of women's studies programs & library resources, CC548
Directory of world futures and options, Robertson, M. J. M., CH436
Directory of world Jewish press and publications, AD7, AE6
Directory of world museums, Hudson, Kenneth, AL88
A directory of world psychiatry, Gunn, John Charles, EH390
Directory of world stock exchanges, CH215
Directory on European training institutions in the fields of bilateral and multilateral diplomacy, public administration and management, economic and social development, CJ47
Directory, state education agencies, CB98
Directory to industrial design in the United States, Burnette, Charles, BG26
Dirkschnieder, Edmund. *Deutsche Sprache im Reformationszeitalter,* BD122
•*DIRLINE,* EH158
Dirr, Michael A. *Manual of woody landscape plants,* EJ246
———— *The reference manual of woody plant propagation,* EJ247
Disabilities and the disabled, BK40, CC189
  bibliography, CC185, CC186, CC187
  directories, CB199, CB311, CC163, CC191, CC192, CC195, CC197
  encyclopedias, CC188
  grants-in-aid, CC194
  guidebooks, CL384
  handbooks, CC199, CC235
  library resources, CC196
  statistics, CB206, CC198
Disabilities and the disabled (by subject)
  education, CB156, CB202, CB207
    directories, CB201
  law, CB156
    see also **Blindness and the blind; Deafness and the deaf; Learning disabled**
Disability, sexuality, and abuse, CC185
Disarmament *see* **Arms control and peace research**
Disarmament terminology, CJ687
Disaster preparedness, Brooks, Constance, AK238
Disasters, DA19
Disciunari rumantsch grischen, Società Retorumantscha, AC664
•*DISCLOSURE database,* CH306
•*Disclosure/Worldscope global,* CH306
The discoverers, CL36
Discovery and exploration, CL35, DB63, DC486
  bibliography, DB181
  biography, CL81
  encyclopedias, CL36
Discovery and exploration (by country or region)
  North America, DB2, DB4, DB5
  South America, DB2, DB4, DB5
Discovery and exploration, Day, Alan Edwin, CL35
Discrimination
  bibliography, CC30, CH529
Discrimination and prejudice, CC30
Disease and destiny, Gilbert, Judson Bennett, EH16
Disease and diseases, EH311
  bibliography, EH16
  classification, EH55, EH56
  dictionaries, EH118
  handbooks, EJ167
Disease and diseases (by subject)
  history, EH212
Disease data book, Fry, John D., EH178
Diseases of trees and shrubs, Sinclair, Wayne A., EG203
Dispatch, CJ185
Dispatch supplements, CJ185

Dispute Resolution Program directory, CK145
Dissension in the House of Commons, Norton, Philip, CJ359
Dissertation abstracts international, AG11, AG12, AG13, AG16, BE348, BE424, BE425, BF227, BJ164, CB152, CB158, DB24
•*Dissertation abstracts ondisc,* AG13
•*Dissertation abstracts online,* AG13
Dissertation title index, BC26
Dissertations
  abstract journals, AG13
  bibliography, AG11, AG12, CB23
  bibliography of bibliography, AG7, AK224
  indexes, CB152
  manuals, AG1, AG2, AG3, AG4, AG5, AG6
Dissertations (by country or region)
  Arab states, AG51
  Argentina, AG18
  Australia
    bibliography, AG59
  Austria, AG23
    bibliography, AG22
  Bolivia, AG19
  Brazil
    bibliography, AG20
  Bulgaria, AG24
  Canada, BE44, BE831, DB191
    bibliography, AG17
  Europe
    bibliography, AG21
  Former Soviet republics, AG46
  France, AG26, BE1237, EA55, EA56, EA57
    bibliography, AG27, AG28, AG29
  Germany, AA657, AG30, BD155, BE235, BE594, BE1071
    bibliography, AG31, AG32
  Great Britain, AG33, BE1142, BE1237, CA22, CC337
    bibliography, AG34, AG35, AG36
  Hungary, AG37
  India, BD197
    bibliography, AG52
  international
    abstract journals, AG13
    bibliography, AG8, AG9, AG10, AG12
  Ireland, AG33, BE1142, CC337
    bibliography, AG35
  Israel, AG53, CA20
  Japan, AG54
  Netherlands, AG38
  New Zealand, AG60
  Nigeria, AG47, AG48
  Philippines, AA931, AG55, AG56
  Poland, AG39
  Romania, AG40
  Russia, AG45, AG46
  Saudi Arabia, AG57
  South Africa, AG49
  Spain, AG41
  Sweden, AG42
  Switzerland, AG43
  Taiwan, AG58
  Turkey, AG44
  Union of Soviet Socialist Republics, AG45
  United States
    abstract journals, AG13
    bibliography, AG11, AG12, CB26, CB233
  Zambia, AG50, DD247
Dissertations (by subject)
  Africa, DD29, DD30, DD31, DD32, DD33
  Africa, North, DD74, DE44
  American literature, BE423, BE424, BE425, BE569
  anthropology and ethnology, CE27, CE28
  Arab states, DE42, DE43
  archaeology and ancient history, DA73
  architecture, BF227
  Armenia, DC84
  Asia, DE9
  Asia, West, DD74, DE44
  Balkans, DC67
  Belgium, DC105
  Canada, DB184, DB190, DB191

  Caribbean, DB411
  chemistry, EE10
  cities, DB148
  classical studies, BE1009, DA97
  Costa Rica, DB305
  drama, BE235, BH37
  earth sciences, EF42
  education, CB24, CB26, CB152, CB233
  engineering, EA58
  English as a second language, BD109
  English language, BE594
    Old English, BD101, BE730
  English literature, BE424, BE593, BE594, BE751
    Old English, BD101, BE730
  ethnic groups, CC337, CF44
  film, BH176
  folk art, BG13
  folklore and popular culture, CF43, CF44
  French literature, BE1142, BE1145
  geography, CL26, CL27
  geology, EF43, EF44
  German literature, BE1237
  Germany, DC219
  Great Britain, CH295, DC283, DC334
  history, DA17, DC284
  history and area studies, CA22, DA16, DA18
  home economics, EJ194, EJ195, EJ196
  humanities, AG53, CA20
  immigration, CC337
  Indian languages, BD225
  Ireland, CH295, DC283, DC334
  Irish literature, BE797
  Islam, DD74, DE42, DE44
  journalism, AE137
  Judaism, BC529
  labor and industrial relations, CH295, DC283
  labor history, CH295, DC283
  languages, linguistics, philology, BD2, BE44
  Latin America, DB267, DC510
  library and information science, AK23, AK24, AK25, AK26
  literature, BE44, BE831
  medieval history, DA145
  Mexico, DB237
  Mormons, BC369
  music, BJ164, BJ165, BJ166
  Native Americans, CC425
  philosophy, BB15, BB16
  physics, ED8
  Poland, DC478
  Portugal, DB267, DC491, DC510
  radio, BH295, BH296
  religion, BC26
  Romance languages, BD155, BE1071
  Romance literatures, BD155, BE1071
  Russia and the U.S.S.R., DC553, DC554
  Russian literature, BE1408
  Sanskrit language, BD197
  Scandinavia, DC73
  science, EA55, EA56, EA57, EA58
  science fiction, BE281
  Slavic languages, BE1408
  social and behavioral sciences, AG53, CA20, CA21, CA22
  Southern states, BE569
  Spain, DB267, DC510
  Spanish-American literature, BE1446
  Spanish literature, BE1446
  speech, BE345, BE350, BE353
  television, BH295, BH296
  theater, BH37
  Turkey, DC541
  Venezuela, DB400
    see also **Masters theses; Theses and term papers**
Dissertations and theses on Venezuelan topics, 1900–1985, Sullivan, William M., DB400
Dissertations in American literature, 1891–1966, Woodress, James Leslie, BE425
Dissertations in English and American literature, Gabel, Gernot U., BE423
———— McNamee, Lawrence F., BE424

Dissertations in Hispanic languages and literatures, Chatham, James R., BE1446

Dissertations in history, Kuehl, Warren F., DA18

Dissertations in Indian linguistics and on Indian languages, Central Institute of Indian Languages, BD225

—— Sharada, B. A., BD225

Dissertations in philosophy accepted at American universities, 1861–1975, Bechtle, Thomas C., BB15

Dissertations in physics, Marckworth, M. Lois, ED8

Dissertations on British history, 1815–1914, Bell, S. Peter, DC334

Dissertations on Iberian and Latin American history, Hanson, Carl A., DB267, DC510

Dissident Eastern churches, Attwater, Donald, BC444

Distance tables, CL59, CL60

Distances between ports, CH471

Distances between United States ports, CH472

Distin, William H. *The American clock,* BG84

Distinguished families of America, AJ58

Distribution and taxonomy of birds of the world, Sibley, Charles Gald, EG275

District of Columbia. [Laws, etc.]. *District of Columbia code, annotated,* CK179

District of Columbia code, annotated, District of Columbia. [Laws, etc.], CK179

Ditmars, Raymond Lee. *The reptiles of North America,* EG246

Dittmann, I. E. *Almindeligt Forfatter-Lexicon for kongeriget Danmark med tilhørende bilande, fra 1814 til 1840,* BE1117

Divale, William Tulio. *Warfare in primitive societies,* CE9, CE10

Divekar, V. D. *Annotated bibliography on the economic history of India,* CH194, DE153

Divinsky, N. J. *The chess encyclopedia,* BK131

Divorce
  bibliography, CC216
  encyclopedias, CC224
  see also **Marriage and the family**

Divry, George C. *Divry's modern English-Greek and Greek-English desk dictionary = Meizon neōteron Angloellēnikon kai Hellēnoanglikon lexikon,* AC463

Divry's modern English-Greek and Greek-English desk dictionary = Meizon neōteron Angloellēnikon kai Hellēnoanglikon lexikon, Divry, George C., AC463

Dix, Ernest Reginald McClintock. *Catalogue of early Dublin-printed books, 1601 to 1700,* AA678, AA721

—— *Dictionary of the printers and booksellers who were at work in England, Scotland and Ireland from 1726 to 1775; those in Ireland,* AA306

Dix années de bibliographie classique, Marouzeau, Jules, BE990, BE1001, BE1003

Dix ans de recherche universitaire française sur le monde arabe et islamique de 1968–69 à 1979, DE42

Dixen, Diana. *Local newspapers & periodicals of the nineteenth century,* AE56

Dixon, Bernard. *The encyclopedic dictionary of science,* EA91

Dixon, Colin J. *Atlas of economic mineral deposits,* EF196

Dixon, Diana. *The nineteenth-century periodical press in Britain,* AD110

Dixon, Judith M. *International directory of tactile map collections,* CL258

Dixon, Penelope. *Mothers and mothering,* CC208

Dizik, A. Allen. *Concise encyclopedia of interior design,* BG130

Dizionario autori italiani contemporanei, BE1311

Dizionario bio-bibliografico dei bibliotecari e bibliofili italiani dal sec. XIV al XIX, Frati, Carlo, AK90

Dizionario biografico degli Italiani, AH260

Dizionario commerciale, Motta, Giuseppe, CH127

Dizionario corografico dell' Italia, CL145

—— Amati, Amato, CL144

Dizionario critico della letteratura francese, BE1154

Dizionario critico della letteratura italiana, BE1299

Dizionario degli istituti di perfezione, BC439

Dizionario degli scrittori greci e latini, BE1013

Dizionario degli scrittori italiani d'oggi, BE1311

Dizionario dei cognomi italiani, De Felice, Emidio, AJ198

Dizionario dei luoghi di stampa falsi, inventati o supposti in opere di autori e traduttori italiani, Parenti, Marino, AA195

Dizionario dei proverbi italiani, Schwamenthal, Riccardo, BE161

Dizionario dei sinònimi e dei contrari, Cinti, Decio, AC540

—— Giocondi, Michele, AC542

Dizionario della lingua italiana, Bellini, Bernardo, AC524

—— Tommaseo, Nicholò, AC524

Dizionario della politica italiana, Pallotta, Gino, CJ382

Dizionario delle lingue italiana e inglese, AC531

Dizionario delle scrittrici italiane contemporanee (arte, lettere, scienze), Gastaldi, Mario, BE1313

Dizionario di citazioni, Spagnol, Elena, BE141

Dizionario di citazioni latine ed italiane, Finzi, Giuseppe, BE142

Dizionario di opere anonime e pseudonime di scrittori italiani, Melzi, Gaetano, AA177

Dizionario di sociologia e antropologia culturale, CE47

Dizionario enciclopedico della letteratura italiana, BE1300

Dizionario enciclopedico di architettura e urbanistica, BF276

Dizionario enciclopedico italiano, AB62

Dizionario enciclopedico universale della musica e dei musicisti : il lessico, BJ130

Dizionario enciclopedico universale della musica e dei musicisti : le biografie, BJ131

Dizionario etimologico della lingua italiana, Cortelazzo, Manlio, AC537

Dizionario etimologico italiano, Battisti, Carlo, AC536

Dizionario etimologico sardo, Wagner, M. L., AC538

Dizionario Garzanti dei sinonimi e dei contrari, AC541

Dizionario generale degli autori italiani contemporanei, BE1301

Dizionario giuridico, De Franchis, Francesco, CK50

Dizionario inglese/italiano, italiano-inglese, AC529, AC532, AC533

Dizionario letterario Bompiani degli autori di tutti i tempi e di tutte le letterature, BE63

Dizionario letterario Bompiani delle opere e dei personaggi di tutti i tempi e di tutte le letterature, BE63, BE64

Dizionario patristico e di antichità cristiane, BC275

Dizionario politico e parlamentare italiano, Pallotta, Gino, CJ382

Dizionario storico della letteratura italiana, Turri, Vittorio, BE1302

Dizionario tecnico, inglese-italiano, italiano-inglese, Marolli, Giorgio, EA118

Dizionario tecnico italiano-inglese, inglese-italiano, Denti, Renzo, EA116

Dizionario tecnico scientifico illustrato, Gatto, Simon, EA117

Dizionario universale della letteratura contemporanea, BE64

Djambatan Uitgeversbedrijf, N.V., Amsterdam. *Atlas of South-east Asia,* CL348

Djibouti
  bibliography, DD18, DD107, DD147
  statistics, CG326

Djibouti, Aubry, Marie-Christine, DD147

—— Schraeder, Peter J., DD18

Dlamini, Sipho. *The struggle for South Africa,* DD208

DLB, BE200

DLIP, AK88

DLR, AC660

Dmitrieva, Rufina Petrovna. *Bibliografiia russkogo letopisaniia,* DC576

DMS code name handbook, CJ586

Doane, Gilbert Harry. *Searching for your ancestors,* AJ7

Dobell, Bertram. *Catalogue of books printed for private circulation,* AA693

Dobkin, David S. *The birder's handbook,* EG258

—— *Birds in jeopardy,* EG259

Doblado, J. M. *English-French-Spanish-Russian systematic glossary of the terminology of statistical methods,* CG27

Dobles Segreda, Luis. *Indice bibliográfico de Costa Rica,* AA478

Dobrée, Bonamy. *The Oxford history of English literature,* BE617

Dobson, Christopher. *Dictionary of espionage,* CJ540

—— *Who's who in espionage,* CJ540

Dobson, David. *Directory of Scots banished to the American plantations, 1650–1775,* AJ62

—— *Directory of Scottish settlers in North America, 1625–1825,* AJ62

Dobson, Michael W. *The new cosmopolitan world atlas,* CL288

Dobson, Richard. *Dictionary of electronic and computer music technology,* BJ310

Doc : documentazione, AL68

Doc Italia, AL68

Docherty, James C. *Historical dictionary of Australia,* DF34

Dock, Lavinia L. *Short history of nursing,* EH286

Dockrill, Michael L. *Atlas of twentieth century world history,* DA189

—— *Collins atlas of twentieth century world history,* DA189

Dockstader, Alice W. *The American Indian in graduate studies,* CC425

Dockstader, Frederick J. *The American Indian in graduate studies,* CC425

—— *Great North American Indians,* AH63

—— *Labors of love,* BG156

—— *Weaving arts of the North American Indian,* BG156

DOCPAL Resúmenes de población en América Latina, CG123

Doctor, Ronald M. *The encyclopedia of phobias, fears, and anxieties,* CD100, EH378

Doctoral dissertations and masters theses regarding Polish subjects, 1900–1985, Wielewinski, Bernard, DC478

Doctoral dissertations in history, DA16

Doctoral dissertations in history and the social sciences on Latin America and the Caribbean accepted by universities in the United Kingdom, 1920–1972, Zubatsky, David S., CA22

Doctoral dissertations in musicology, Adkins, Cecil, BJ164

Doctoral dissertations in speech, BE350

Doctoral dissertations in the field of religion, 1940–1952, Council on Graduate Studies in Religion, BC26

Doctoral research on Canada and Canadians, 1884–1983, Dossick, Jesse John, DB190

Doctoral research on Russia and the Soviet Union, Dossick, Jesse John, BE1408, DC554

Document catalog, AF87, AF88, AF98, AF110

Documentaçao Amazônica, DB321

Documentary history of American industrial society, Commons, John Rogers, CH675

Documentary history of faith and order, 1963–1993, BC282

Documentary history of the faith and order movement 1927–1963, Vischer, Lukas, BC282

Documentary history of the modern civil rights movement, CC392

Documentary sources of Philippine history, DE247

Documentatieblad, DD45

Documentatio geographica, CL8

Documentation abstracts, AK30

Documentation abstracts and information science abstracts, AK30

Documentation—bibliographic references—content, form and structure, International Organization for Standardization, EA162

Documentation bibliographique sur le Burundi, Rodegem, F. M., DD135

Documentation économique, CH39

Documentation in the social sciences, CE24

The documentation of the European Communities, Thomson, Ian, AF26

Documentation sur le Rwanda, Rwanda. Ministère du plan. Centre de documentation, DD198

Documenting Canada, AF156, DB206

Documentos relativos a la independencia de Norteamérica existentes en archivos españoles, DB61

Documents du Minutier central des notaires de Paris, Jurgens, Madeleine, DC151

Documents illustrative of English church history, comp. from original sources, Gee, Henry, BC284

Documents illustrative of the continental Reformation, Kidd, Beresford James, BC285

Documents illustrative of the history of the church, Kidd, Beresford James, BC285

Documents inedits sur les artistes français du dix-huitième siècle, Wildenstein, Daniel, DC151

Documents of American Catholic history, Ellis, John Tracy, BC414

Documents of American history, DB62

Documents of international organisations, AF7

Documents of Vatican II, Vatican Council (2nd : 1962–1965), BC437

Documents on Christian unity, BC283

Documents on the International Court of Justice, Rosenne, Shabtai, CK110

Documents to the people, AF68

Dodd, Janet S. *The ACS style guide,* EE95

Doderer, Klaus. *Lexikon der Kinder- und Jugendliteratur,* BE385

Dodge, Meredith D. *Historical dictionary of modern Spain, 1700–1988,* DC514

Dod's parliamentary companion, CJ343, CJ357, CJ362

Dodson, Suzanne Cates. *Microform research collections,* AA130

Doebler, Raymond E. *Table of isotopes,* ED46

Doenecke, Justus D. *Anti-intervention,* CJ668

Doeppers, Daniel F. *A checklist of Southeast Asian newspapers and other research materials in microform held by the Center for Research Libraries,* AE82, AE83

Doerr, Juergen C. *Big powers and the German question 1941–1990,* DC231

—— *German nationalism,* DC231

Doescher, Rex A. *Directory of paleontologists of the world,* EF245

Doezema, Linda Pegman. *Dutch Americans,* CC320

Dog owner's home veterinary handbook, Carlson, Delbert G., EJ142

Doggett, JoElla. *Seventeenth-century American poetry,* BE497

Dogra, R. C. *Bhutan,* DE118

Dogs, EJ142, EJ143, EJ145, EJ146
  bibliography, EJ144

Doherty, J. E. *A chronology of Irish history since 1500,* DC412

—— *A dictionary of Irish history since 1800,* DC406, DC412

Döhring, Sieghart. *Pipers Enzyklopädie des Musiktheaters,* BJ252

Doi, Mary L. *Pacific/Asian American research,* CC403

Doig, Alison G. *Bibliography of statistical literature,* EB12

Doke, Clement Martyn. *English-Zulu Zulu-English dictionary,* AC819

Doke Collection on African Languages, University of Rhodesia. *Catalogue of the C. M. Doke collection on African languages in the Library of the University of Rhodesia,* BD216

Dokumentation zur Raumentwicklung, CL8

Dolan, Eleanor F. *Mature woman in America,* CC61

Dolan, John. *Handbook of church history,* BC277

—— *History of the church,* BC277

Dolbow, Sandra W. *Dictionary of modern French literature,* BE1155

Dolby, J. L. *The statistics cumindex,* EB24

Dolch, Walther. *Bibliographie der österreichischen Drucke des XV. und XVI. Jahrhunderts,* AA573

Dolci, Fabrizio. *L'associazionismo operaio in Italia (1870–1900) nelle raccolte della Biblioteca nazionale centrale di Firenze,* DC428

Dolcini, Carlo. *Guida allo studio della storia medievale,* DA128

Doll, Howard D. *Oral interpretation of literature,* BE14

Dollarhide, William. *Map guide to the U.S. federal censuses, 1790–1920,* AJ26, CL306

Dollars for scholars, Dennis, Marguerite J., CB376

Dolléans, Édouard. *Mouvements ouvriers et socialistes,* CH634

Dollinger, Philippe. *Bibliographie d'histoire des villes de France,* DC212, DC265

Domandi, Agnes Körner. *Modern German literature,* BE1058

Domay, Friedrich. *Bibliographie der nationalen Bibliographien,* AA391

Domestic animals, EJ121, EJ135, EJ136, EJ137
  handbooks, EJ134

Domestic society in medieval Europe, Sheehan, Michael M., DC11

Domestic technology, Du Vall, Nell, EJ200

Domestic violence, Nordquist, Joan, CC217

Dominica, DB432

Dominica, Myers, Robert A., DB432

Dominican Republic
  bibliography, AA565
  bibliography of bibliography, AA34
  biography, AH153
    contemporary, AH154, AH155
  encyclopedias, DB435
  government publications, AF159
  statistics, CG172, CG173
Dominican Republic (by subject)
  history, AH153, DB433
    encyclopedias, DB436
  politics and government
    bibliography, DB434

Dominican Republic. Dirección General de Estadística y Censos. *Anuario estadístico,* CG172

—— *República Dominicana en cifras,* CG173

Dominican Republic, Schoenhals, Kai P., DB433

Dominion Bureau of Statistics catalogue, CG115

Domschke, Eliane. *The handbook of national population censuses : Africa and Asia,* CG38

Donadio, Stephen. *The New York Public Library book of twentieth century American quotations,* BE112

Donald, Elsie Burch. *Debrett's etiquette and modern manners,* AL153

Donaldson, David. *Etymological dictionary of the Scottish language,* AC165

Donaldson, Gordon. *A dictionary of Scottish history,* DC364

—— *A source book of Scottish history,* DC366

Donaldson, James. *Ante-Nicene Fathers,* BC293

Donati, Lamberto. *Bibliografia della miniatura,* BF311

Donato, Hernâni. *Dicionário das batalhas brasileiras,* DB355

Donavin, Denise Perry. *Aging with style and savvy,* CC66

Doney, Willis. *Twenty-five years of Descartes scholarship, 1960–1984,* BB72

Dongolese Nubian, a lexicon, Armbruster, Carl Hubert, AC623

Doniach, N. S. *Concise Oxford English-Arabic dictionary of current usage,* AC219

—— *The Oxford English-Arabic dictionary of current usage,* AC219

Doniger, Wendy. *Mythologies,* CF7

Donker, Marjorie. *Dictionary of literary-rhetorical conventions of the English Renaissance,* BE351

Donlan, Walter. *The Classical world bibliography of Greek drama and poetry,* BE1027

Donnachie, Ian L. *Companion to Scottish history,* DC365

Le donne italiane, AH264

The Donning international encyclopedic psychic dictionary, CD135, CD136

Donohue, Joseph. *English drama of the nineteenth century,* BE640

Donovan, Jerry J. *Western European censuses, 1960,* CG186

Donovan, Maureen. *Korean and Japanese women,* CC609

Donow, Herbert S. *The sonnet in England and America,* BE700

Donson, Theodore B. *Prints and the print market,* BF375

Donzel, E. van. *The encyclopaedia of Islam,* BC503

Doorninck, Jan Izaak van. *Vermomde en naamlooze schrijvers,* AA178

Dopolneniĭa i prilozheniĭa, Bykova, Tat'iana Aleksandrovna, AA789

Dopolneniĭa, razyskivaemye izdaniĭa utocheneniĭa, Sikorskii, N. M., AA791

Doran, Lawrence R. *Atlas of the Philippines,* CL362

Doremus, R. H. *Handbook of glass properties,* EK271

Doress-Worters, Paula Brown. *Ourselves, growing older,* CC95, CC564

Dorf, Richard C. *The electrical engineering handbook,* EK135

—— *International encyclopedia of robotics,* EK232

Dorian, Angelo Francis. *Dictionary of science and technology,* EA108, EA113

—— *Dictionary of science and technology : French-English,* EA108

—— *Dictionary of science and technology : German-English,* EA113

—— *Elsevier's dictionary of mining and mineralogy,* EF183

—— *Elsevier's encyclopaedic dictionary of medicine,* EH139

Doris, Lillian. *Complete secretary's handbook,* CH86

Dority, G. Kim. *Best reference books, 1986–1990,* AA348

Dorland, W. A. Newman. *Dorland's illustrated medical dictionary,* EH97

Dorland's illustrated medical dictionary, EH97, EH269

Dorling, Alison Rosemary. *Use of mathematical literature,* EB6

Dornbusch, Charles Emil. *Histories, personal narratives,* CJ628

—— *Military bibliography of the Civil War,* DB109

—— *Unit histories of the United States Air Forces,* CJ628

Dorner, Helen. *A dictionary of English usage in Southern Africa,* AC181

Dornette, William H. L. *Illustrated Stedman's medical dictionary,* EH270

Dornseiff, Franz. *Der deutsche Wortschatz nach Sachgruppen,* AC432

Doro, Marion E. *Rhodesia/Zimbabwe,* DD251

Doronin, I. P. *Istoriĭa SSSR,* DC548

Doroszewski, Witold. *Słownik języka polskiego,* AC632

Dorr, Steven R. *Scholars' guide to Washington, D.C. for Middle Eastern studies,* DE49

Dörries, Wilhelm von. *Botanisches Zentralblatt,* EG112

Dorsen, Marilyn M. *Annotated bibliography on childhood schizophrenia, 1955–1964,* EH374

Dorsey dictionary of American government and politics, Shafritz, Jay M., CJ122

Dorson, Richard M. *Handbook of American folklore,* CF77

Dosky, J. S. *Media equipment,* AK43

Dosoudil, Ilse. *Grundliteratur zum österreichischen Recht,* CK206

Dossick, Jesse John. *Doctoral research on Canada and Canadians, 1884–1983,* DB190

—— *Doctoral research on Russia and the Soviet Union,* BE1408, DC554

Dotson, Lillian Ota. *Bibliography of the peoples and cultures of mainland Southeast Asia,* DE119

Dotti, Ugo. *Storia della letteratura italiana,* BE1305

Doty, Richard G. *The Macmillan encyclopedic dictionary of numismatics,* BG178

Dotzauer, Winfried. *Das Zeitalter der Glaubensspaltung (1500–1618),* DC226

Doubleday, Nelson. *Encyclopedia of world travel,* CL380

The Doubleday dictionary for home, school, and office, AC138

The Doubleday Roget's thesaurus in dictionary form, AC138

Doucet, Michel. *Dictionnaire juridique et economique,* CK48

Doughan, David. *Feminist periodicals, 1855–1984,* CC521

Dougherty, James J. *Writings on American history,* DB23

—— *Writings on American history, 1962–1973,* DB23

Doughty, Harold R. *Guide to American graduate schools,* CB299

Douglas, David C. *English historical documents,* DC297

Douglas, George W. *American book of days,* AL147

Douglas, James Dixon. *New Bible dictionary,* BC147

—— *New international dictionary of the Christian church,* BC148, BC236

Douglas, Louise. *Australians 1938,* DF37

Doumani, George A. *Antarctic bibliography,* DG1

Doumato, Lamia. *Architecture and women,* BF214, BF263

Dournon, Jean-Yves. *Dictionnaire des proverbes et dictons de France,* BE130

—— *Dictionnaire d'orthographe et des difficultés du français,* AC366

—— *Le grand dictionnaire des citations françaises,* BE130

Doursther, Horace. *Dictionnaire universel des poids et mesures,* AL197

Dow, J. A. T. *The dictionary of cell biology,* EG32, EG341

Dow, Susan L. *State document checklists,* AF140

The Dow Jones averages, 1885–1990, CH325

The Dow Jones investor's handbook, CH318

Dow Jones-Irwin. *The Irwin business and investment almanac,* CH378

Dow Jones-Irwin business almanac, CH378

Dow Jones-Irwin business and investment almanac, CH378

Dow Jones-Irwin guide to franchises, Norback, Craig T., CH359

—— Norback, Peter G., CH359

Dowe, Dieter. *Bibliographie zur Geschichte der deutschen Arbeiterbewegung, sozialistischen und kommunistischen Bewegung von den Anfängen bis 1863,* CH627

Downes, Andrew S. *Economic literature on the Commonwealth Caribbean,* DB410

Downes, John. *Barron's finance & investment handbook,* CH233

—— *Dictionary of finance and investment terms,* CH209

Downey, Michael. *The new dictionary of Catholic spirituality,* BC402

Downing, Douglas. *Dictionary of computer terms,* EK177

Downing, Theodore E. *Human rights and anthropology,* CE13

Downs, Elizabeth C. *British and Irish library resources,* AK144

Downs, Robert Bingham. *American library resources,* AK103

—— *Australian and New Zealand library resources,* AK104

—— *British and Irish library resources,* AK144

Dowson, John. *A classical dictionary of Hindu mythology and religion, geography, history, and literature,* BC486

Dox, Ida. *Melloni's illustrated medical dictionary,* EH98

Doyle, A. I. *A finding-list of English books to 1640 in libraries in the British Isles (excluding the national libraries and the libraries of Oxford and Cambridge),* AA672

Doyle, Brian. *The who's who of children's literature,* BE379

Doyle, Francis R. *Searching the law, the states,* CK121

Doyle, Mabel Hunt. *List of publications of the United States Department of Agriculture from January, 1901, to December, 1925, inclusive,* EJ85

Draaijer, Gera E. *The handbook of national population censuses : Africa and Asia,* CG38

Drabble, Margaret. *Concise Oxford companion to English literature,* BE610

—— *The Oxford companion to English literature,* BE610

Drabek, Anne Gordon. *The politics of African and Middle Eastern states,* CJ400

Drachkovitch, Milorad M. *Biographical dictionary of the Comintern,* CJ533

The dragon's almanac, Wintle, Justin, BE167

Drake, Ann M. *Directory of practicing anthropologists,* CE88

Drake, Ellen T. *Geologists and ideas,* EF99

Drake, Greg. *Index to American photographic collections,* BF344

Drake, H. Max. *Directory of practicing anthopologists,* CE88

Drake, Maurice. *Saints and their emblems,* BF181

Drake, Milton. *Almanacs of the United States,* AB103, EC10

Drake, Wilfred. *Saints and their emblems,* BF181

Drama
  bibliography, BE218, BE225, BE226, BE227, BE236, BE238, BE461, BE1178, BH34, BH40
    dissertations, BH37
  biography, BE223
  criticism
    bibliography, BE219, BE220, BE221, BE224, BE232
      biobibliography, BE224
    collections, BE229
  dictionaries, BH77, BH78, BH82
  discography, BH56
  dissertations, BE235
  encyclopedias, BE230, BH62, BH64, BH70, BH71, BH72
  indexes, BE226, BE227, BE228, BE231, BE233, BE234, BE238, BH55
  library catalogs, BH33
  translations (by language)
    French, BE1178
Drama (by period)
  medieval
    bibliography, BE237
    encyclopedias, BE222
  see also **Theater**

Drama A to Z, Vaughn, Jack A., BH82

Drama by women to 1900, BE489

—— Davis, Gwenn, BE456

Drama criticism, BE224, BE325

—— Coleman, Arthur, BE221

The drama dictionary, Hodgson, Terry, BH78

The drama of German expressionism, Hill, Claude, BE1264

Drama scholars' index to plays and filmscripts, Samples, Gordon, BH168

Drama und Theater des deutschen Barock, Gabel, Gernot U., BE1262

Dramatic books and plays (in English), BH55

Dramatic compositions copyrighted in the United States, Library of Congress. Copyright Office, BE461

Dramatic criticism index, Breed, Paul Francis, BE219

Dramatic index for 1909–49, BH55

Dramatic music (class M 1500, 1510, 1520), Library of Congress. Music Division, BJ240

Dramatic re-visions, Steadman, Susan M., BH34

Dramatic texts and records of Britain, Lancashire, Ian, BE662

Dramatic texts and records of Britain to 1558, BE662

Dramatik trykt pä svenska 1914–1962, Uppsala. Universitet. Litteraturvetenskapliga institutionen. Avdelningen för dramaforskning, BE1484

Dramatists (by country or region)
  United States, BE452

Dramatists sourcebook, BH85

Dramenlexikon, Allgayer, Wilhelm, BE1261

Drandakēs, Paulos. *Megalē hellēnikē enkyklopaideia,* AB54

Draper, Hal. *The Marx-Engels cyclopedia,* CJ520

Draper, Larry W. *A Mormon bibliography, 1830–1930,* BC372

A Dravidian etymological dictionary, Burrow, Thomas, AC291

Dravidian languages
  bibliography, BD226
  dictionaries
    bilingual, AC291

Dravidian languages and literatures, Rajannan, Busnagi, BD226

Dravnieks, Jēkabs. *Angliski-latviska vārdnīca,* AC597

The dream, Parsifal-Charles, Nancy, CD109

Dreams, CD109, CD111

Dreher, Silpelitt. *Bibliographie de la littérature française, 1930–1939 ... complément à Bibliographie de H. P. Thieme,* BE1209

Dreisbach, Robert Hastings. *Handbook of poisoning,* EH423

Drenikoff, Iván. *Impresos venezolanos del siglo XIX,* AA550

Drepperd, Carl William. *American clocks and clockmakers,* BG84

Dresley, Susan. *General transportation,* CH444

Dresser, Peter D. *Scientific and technical organizations and agencies directory,* EA200

Dressler, Claus Peter. *Bibliography of creative African writing,* BE1505, BE1531

Dressler, Hermigild. *Introduction to medieval Latin studies,* BD145

Dreves, Guido Maria. *Analecta hymnica medii aevi,* BC313

Drevet, Marguerite L. *Bibliographie de la littérature française, 1940–1949 ... complément à Bibliographie de H. P. Thieme,* BE1209

Drew, Bernard A. *Motion picture series and sequels,* BH222

Drew, Roger Michael. *CRC handbook of bimolecular and termolecular gas reactions,* EE69

Drewry, Gavin. *Information sources in politics and political science,* CJ2

Drexel, John. *Facts on File encyclopedia of the 20th century,* DA180

Drexhage, Hans-Joachim. *Deutschsprachige Dissertationen zur alten Geschichte, 1844–1978,* DA73

Dreyfus, F. Camille. *La grande encyclopédie,* AB44

Dreyfus, Michel. *Guide des centres de documentation en histoire ouvrière et sociale,* DC157

Dreyfuss, Henry. *Symbol sourcebook,* BF166

Driessen, E. J. *Biographical dictionary of dissidents in the Soviet Union, 1956–1975,* AH303

Drini, Faik. *Bibliografi e arkeologjisë dhe historisë së lashtë të shqipërisë,* DC81

Driscoll, Walter G. *Handbook of optics,* ED37

Driver, Edwin D. *World population policy,* CG1

Driver, S. R. *The new Brown, Driver, Briggs, Gesenius Hebrew and English lexicon,* AC476, BC133

Driver, Samuel Rolles. *The international critical commentary on the Holy Scriptures of the Old and New Testaments,* BC173

Drizari, Nelo. *Albanian-English and English-Albanian dictionary,* AC205

Droblenkova, Nadezhda Feotitovna. *Bibliografiĩa sovetskikh russkikh rabot po literature XI–XVII vv. za 1917–1957 gg*, BE1386

Drogenbibliographie, Hefele, Bernhard, EH321

Droit de la mer, CK79

Drolet, Antonio. *Bibliographie du roman canadien-français, 1900–1950*, BE842

Drone, Jeanette Marie. *Index to opera, operetta and musical comedy synopses in collections and periodicals*, BJ245

Drosdowski, Günther. *Das Grosse Wörterbuch der deutschen Sprache in 6 Bänden*, AC403

Drost, Harry. *The world's news media*, AE143

Drost, Jerome. *Themes and settings in fiction*, BE253

Droste, Kathleen. *Super LCCS*, AK202

Droulers, Eug. *Dictionnaire des attributs, allégories, emblèmes et symboles*, BF173

Drozda, Tom. *Tool and manufacturing engineers handbook*, EK248

Druesedow, John E. *Library research guide to music*, BJ3

Drug abuse, CC136
    bibliography, CC112, CC115, CC117, CC121, CC122
    dictionaries, CC126, CC128
    directories, CC130, CC133, EH411
    encyclopedias, CC124
    handbooks, CC134, CC137, EH333
    see also **Alcoholism and drug abuse**

Drug abuse and the elderly, Ruben, Douglas H., CC121

Drug abuse in society, Woods, Geraldine, CC137

Drug, alcohol, and other addictions, CC130

Drug evaluations, EH337

Drug evaluations annual, EH337

Drug facts and comparisons, EH338

Drug industry, EH355

Drug information, Snow, Bonnie, EH318

Drug interaction facts, EH339

Drugs
    bibliography, EH317, EH318, EH321
    catalogs, EH347, EH349, EH353, EH355, EH359, EH362
    dictionaries, EH329, EH330, EH332
    guides, EH318
    handbooks, EE126, EH336, EH337, EH338, EH340, EH341, EH343, EH344, EH348, EH352
    indexes, EH354, EH359
    ingredients, EH325
    interactions, EH339
    nomenclature, EH332
    periodicals, EH315, EH365
    see also **Cocaine; Pharmacology; Psychotropic drugs**

Drugs available abroad, EH340

Drugs in pregnancy and lactation, EH341

Drury, Francis K. W. *Drury's guide to best plays*, BE225

Drury's guide to best plays, Drury, Francis K. W., BE225

Drvodelić, Milan. *Englesko-hrvatski ili srpski rječnik*, AC713

—— *Hrvatsko ili srpasko engleski rječnik*, AC713

DSM-III-R, EH393

DSp, BC54

DttP, AF68

DttP. Documents to the people, AF68

DTV-Wörterbuch zur Publizistik, AE140

Du Bois-Reymond, Renáe. *Handbuch zur Geschichte der Naturwissenschaften und der Technik …*, EA251

Du Cange, Charles Du Fresne. *Glossarium ad scriptores mediæ & infimæ graecitatis*, AC454

—— *Glossarium mediae et infimae latinitatis*, AC587, AC592, AC593

Du Sahara à Timor, Pélissier, René, DD12, DD118

Du Vall, Nell. *Domestic technology*, EJ200

Du Verdier, Antoine. *Les bibliothèques françoises de La Croix du Maine et de Du Verdier*, AA616

Duarte i Montserrat, Carles. *Diccionari etimològic i complementari de la llengua catalana*, AC248

Dubbeld, Catherine E. *Reflecting apartheid*, BE1534

Dubester, Henry J. *Catalog of United States census publications, 1790–1945*, CG86, CG90

—— *National censuses and vital statistics in Europe, 1918–1939*, CG188

—— *Population censuses and other official demographic statistics of Africa (not including British Africa)*, CG312

—— *Population censuses and other official demographic statistics of British Africa*, CG312

—— *State censuses*, CG90

Dubiez, F. J. *Populaire prozaschrijvers van 1600 tot 1815*, BE1327

Dubin, Michael J. *United States congressional districts*, CJ239

Dublin stage, 1720–1745, Clark, Gladys L. H., BH101

—— Greene, John C., BH101

DuBoff, Leonard D. *Art law in a nutshell*, BF122

Dubois, Jean. *Dictionnaire du français classique*, AC376

—— *Dictionnaire du français contemporain*, AC372

—— *Nouveau dictionnaire étymologique et historique*, AC348

Dubois, Marguerite Marie. *Larousse modern French-English [English-French] dictionary*, AC341

Dubois, Michel. *French and international acronyms & initialisms dictionary*, AC345

Dubois, William R. *English and American stage productions*, BH42

Dubreuil, Lorraine. *World directory of map collections*, CL261

Duby, Georges. *Atlas historique*, DC165

Duchein, Michel. *Basic international bibliography of archive administration*, AK182

Duchesne, Alain. *L'obsolète*, AC377

Duckles, Vincent Harris. *Music reference and research materials*, BJ4, BJ5

Ducrot, Oswald. *Encyclopedic dictionary of the sciences of language*, BD38

Duda, Frederick. *Personnel administration in libraries*, AK178

Duden, AC403

Duden, das grosse Wörterbuch der deutschen Sprache in acht Bänden, AC403

Duden, deutsches Universal-Wörterbuch, AC403

Dudenradaktion (Bibliographisches Institut) *The Oxford-Duden pictorial German-English dictionary*, AC420

Dudenredaktion (Bibliographisches Institut). *The Oxford-Duden German dictionary*, AC419

Dudenredaktion (Bibliographisches Institut). Wissenschaftlicher Rat. *Das Grosse Wörterbuch der deutschen Sprache in 6 Bänden*, AC403

Duensing, Edward. *America's elderly*, CC93

Duff, A. M. *Literary history of Rome from the origins to the close of the golden age*, BE1052

Duff, Gordon E. *Century of the English book trade … 1457–1557*, AA306

Duff, J. Wight. *Literary history of Rome from the origins to the close of the golden age*, BE1052

Duffy, Bernard K. *American orators before 1900*, BE346

—— *American orators of the twentieth century*, BE346

Duffy, Susan. *The political left in the American theatre of the 1930's*, BH41

Dufourcq, Norbert. *Larousse de la musique*, BJ120

Dugan, Robert E. *Public administration desk book*, CJ460

Dugas, Guy. *Bibliographie de la littérature "marocaine" des Français, 1875–1983*, BE1529

—— *Bibliographie de la littérature "tunisienne" des Français, 1881–1980*, BE1539

Duggan, Margaret M. *English literature and backgrounds, 1660–1700*, BE742

Duggan, Mary Kay Conyers. *Italian music incunabula*, BJ32

Dühmert, Anneliese. *Von wem ist das Gedicht?*, BE1270

Duignan, Peter. *A bibliographical guide to colonialism in sub-Saharan Africa*, DD82

—— *Colonialism in Africa, 1870–1960*, DD82

—— *Guide to research and reference works on sub-Saharan Africa*, DD83

—— *Handbook of American resources for African studies*, DD36, DD37

Duiker, William J. *Historical dictionary of Vietnam*, DE273

Duke, James A. *CRC handbook of medicinal herbs*, EH342

Duke, Maurice. *American women writers*, BE399

—— *Black American writers*, BE515

Duke Biederman, Susan. *Art law*, BF122

Dukelow, Daphne A. *The dictionary of Canadian law*, CK35

Dulbecco, Renato. *Encyclopedia of human biology*, EG20

Dulichenko, A. D. *Mezhdunarodnye vspomogatel'nye iazyki*, BD48

Dulong, Gaston. *Bibliographie linguistique du Canada français*, BD162

—— *Dictionnaire des canadianismes*, AC386

Duman, Hasan. *İstanbul kütüphaneleri Arap harfli süreli yayınlar toplu kataloğu, 1828–1928*, AE78

Dumbarton Oaks. *Dictionary catalogue of the Byzantine collection of the Dumbarton Oaks Research Library, Washington, D.C*, DA162

—— *The Oxford dictionary of Byzantium*, DA166

Dumbarton Oaks. Center for Byzantine Studies. *Author index of Byzantine studies*, DA163

—— *Byzantine Library serials list*, DA162

Dumbleton, C. W. *Russian-English biological dictionary*, EG35

Dümotz, Irmtraud. *Lexikon der Symbole*, CF11

Dumouchel, J. Robert. *Government assistance almanac*, CH169

Dumuis, Henriette. *French sculptors of the 17th and 18th centuries*, BF399

Dun & Bradstreet middle market directory, CH363

Dun & Bradstreet million dollar directory, CH363

Dun & Bradstreet reference book of corporate managements, CH385

Dun & Bradstreet's exporters' encyclopaedia, CH139

Dunbar, Gary S. *A biographical dictionary of American geography in the twentieth century*, CL80

—— *The history of modern geography*, CL9

—— *Modern geography*, CL39

Dunbar, Paul K. *Catalog of significant earthquakes*, EF260

Duncan, A. S. *Dictionary of medical ethics*, EH240

Duncan, Andrea. *Tracing your ancestors in the Public Record Office*, AJ97

Duncan, Evan M. *Principal officers of the Department of State and United States chiefs of mission, 1778–1990*, CJ183

Duncan, Robert. *The Warwick guide to British labour periodicals, 1790–1970*, CH655

Dundes, Alan. *Folklore theses and dissertations in the United States*, CF43

Dunford, Penny. *Biographical dictionary of women artists in Europe and America since 1850*, BF152

Dunhouse, Mary Beth. *International directory of children's literature*, BE380

Dunkin, Michael J. *International encyclopedia of teaching and teacher education*, CB70

Dunkling, Leslie. *Everyman's dictionary of first names*, AJ169

Dunlap, Joseph R. *Debate index*, BE368

Dunmore-Leiber, Leslie. *Book review digest*, AA365

Dunn, Charles William. *A Burmese-English dictionary*, AC245

Dunn, D. Elwood. *Liberia*, DD48

Dunn, Maryjane. *Pilgrimage in the Middle Ages*, DA132

Dunn, Richard J. *The English novel*, BE674

Dunn, Richard Minta. *European political facts, 1648–1789*, CJ314

Dunn, Robert. *Chinese-English and English-Chinese dictionaries in the Library of Congress*, AC271

Dunnette, Marvin D. *Handbook of industrial and organizational psychology*, CD127

Dünnhaupt, Gerhard. *Bibliographisches Handbuch der Barockliteratur*, BE1217

Dunning, John. *Tune in yesterday*, BH308

•*Dun's business locator*, CH363

Dun's business rankings, CH355

Dun's consultants directory, CH619

Dun's directory of service companies, CH356

•*Dun's electronic directory of education*, CB95

Dun's employment opportunities directory, CH694

Duns Europa, CH411

•*Dun's market identifiers*, CH363

Dun's Marketing Services. *America's corporate families*, CH347

—— *The career guide*, CH694

•*Dun's million dollar disc*, CH363

Dunst, Carl J. *Enabling and empowering families*, CC235

Dunstan, G. R. *Dictionary of medical ethics*, EH240

Duomato, Lamia. *American drawing*, BF297

Dupayrat, Jacques. *Dictionary of biomedical acronyms and abbreviations*, EH130

Dupois, Diane L. *Cities of the United States*, CL70

Duprat, Gabrielle. *Bibliographie des répertoires nationaux de périodiques en cours*, AD8

DuPre, Flint O. *U.S. Air Force biographical dictionary*, CJ642

Dupré, P. *Encyclopédie du bon français dans l'usage contemporain*, AC367

Dupré, Paul. *Encyclopédie des citations*, BE92

Dupriez, Bernard Marie. *Dictionary of literary devices*, BE78, BE356

Dupuis, Diane L. *The Olympics factbook*, BK92

Dupuy, Richard Ernest. *The Harper encyclopedia of military history*, DA20

Dupuy, Trevor Nevitt. *Dictionary of military terms*, CJ585

—— *The Harper encyclopedia of military biography*, AH26

—— *The Harper encyclopedia of military history*, DA20

—— *International military and defense encyclopedia*, CJ571

—— *People & events of the American Revolution*, DB94

Durán Cerda, Julio. *Repertorio del teatro chileno*, BE939

Durand, Micheline. *Gran diccionario moderno*, AC733

Durant, Lucius. *Day care*, CC154

Durbin, Paul T. *Dictionary of concepts in the philosophy of science*, EA78

—— *A guide to the culture of science, technology, and medicine*, EA15

Durga Das Pvt. Ltd. *Eminent Indians who was who, 1900–1980, also annual diary of events*, AH350

Durham, Weldon B. *American theatre companies*, BH95

DuRietz, Rolf E. *Swedish imprints, 1731–1833*, AA829

Durlacher, Jennifer. *Sources of African and Middle-Eastern economic information*, CH189

—— *Sources of Asian/Pacific economic information*, CH202

—— *Sources of European economic information*, CH185

Durling, Richard J. *Catalogue of sixteenth century printed books in the National Library of Medicine*, EH24

Durón, Jorge Fidel. *Índice de la bibliografía hondureña*, AA487

—— *Repertorio bibliográfico hondureño*, AA488

Duru, Jeannine. *Inventaire des archives de la Tunisie*, DD69

Dusenbury, Carolyn. *Sourcebook for bibliographic instruction*, AK231

Dutch
emigration
registers, AJ67

Dutch (by country or region)
United States
bibliography, CC320
registers, AJ68

Dutch Americans, Doezema, Linda Pegman, CC320

Dutch and Flemish etchings, engravings and woodcuts, ca.1450–1700, Hollstein, F. W. H., BF382

Dutch colonial history, DC452

Dutch East Indies *see* **Indonesia**

Dutch East Indies. Centraal Kantoor voor de Statistiek. *Statistisch jaaroverzicht van Nederlandsch-Indie*, CG394

Dutch emigrants to the United States, South Africa, South America, and Southeast Asia, 1835–1880, Swierenga, Robert P., AJ67

Dutch fiction
bibliography, BE1327

Dutch immigrants in U.S. ship passenger manifests, 1820–1880, Swierenga, Robert P., AJ68

Dutch language
bibliography, BD128, BE1335
dictionaries, AC292, AC293
bibliography, AC300
bilingual
Dutch-English, AC296, AC297, AC298
early, AC294, AC295
etymology, AC299

Dutch literature
bibliography, BE1329, BE1335
biobibliography, BE1328, BE1331, BE1332, BE1333

Dutch literature (by subject)
history, BE1326, BE1330, BE1334, BE1336

Dutch parliamentary election studies data source book, 1971–1989, Deth, Jan W. van, CJ383

Dutch social science data, 1962–1992, CA51

Dutch theses, AG38

Dutcher, George M. *Guide to historical literature*, DA1

Dutt, Ashok K. *Atlas of South Asia*, CL347

Dutton, Brian. *El cancionero del siglo XV, c. 1360–1520*, BE1477

—— *Catálogo-índice de la poesía cancioneril del siglo XV*, BE1477

Dutton, Geoffrey. *Literature of Australia*, BE854

Duursma, E. K. *Encyclopedia of marine sciences*, EF219

Duval, Paul-Marie. *Gaule jusqu'au milieu de Vᵉ siècle*, DC147

Duveen, Denis I. *Bibliotheca alchemica et chemica*, EE11, EE12, EE17

Duverger, Jozef. *Nationaal biografisch woordenboek*, AH174

Duvivier, Ulrick. *Bibliographie générale et méthodique d'Haiti*, AA566, AA567

Duwell, Martin. *ALS guide to Australian writers, 1963–90*, BE847

Duxbury, Janell R. *Rockin' the classics and classicizin' the rock*, BJ378

Duyckinck, Evert Augustus. *Cyclopaedia of American literature*, BE433

Duyckinck, G. L. *Cyclopaedia of American literature*, BE433

Dvizhenie dekabristov, DC577

Dwelly, Edward. *The illustrated Gaelic-English dictionary*, AC393

Dwight, Pamela. *Landmark yellow pages*, BF265

DWM : a directory of women's media, AE25, CC549

Dworkin, Rita. *Contemporary novel*, BE206

—— *Modern drama*, BE219

Dworkin, Steven Norman. *Lexical studies of medieval Spanish texts*, BD165

DWPI, EJ184

Dwyer, Joseph D. *Russia, the Soviet Union, and Eastern Europe*, DC49

—— *Slovenes in the United States and Canada*, CC321, CC473

•*DYABOLA*, DA63, DA69, DA70

Dyal, Carole. *Conservation treatment procedures*, AK242

Dyck, Cornelius J. *Annotated bibliography of Mennonite writings on war and peace, 1930–1980*, BC360

—— *The Mennonite encyclopedia*, BC361

Dyck, Joachim. *Rhetorik, Topik, Argumentation*, BE372

Dyer, Frederick Henry. *Compendium of the war of the rebellion*, DB119

The dying child, Benson, Hazel B., CC178

Dying, death, and grief, Simpson, Michael A., CC180

Dykes, Jeff. *American guide series*, CL387

The dynamics of world power, DB136

Dynasties of the world, Morby, John E., CJ78

Dynes, Patrick S. *Program evaluation*, CJ464

Dynes, Wayne R. *Encyclopedia of homosexuality*, CC277

—— *Homosexuality*, CC268

Dyos, G. T. *Electrical resistivity handbook*, ED35

Dyserinck, Hugo. *Internationale bibliographie zu Geschichte und Theorie der Komparatistik*, BE18

Dyson, A. E. *The English novel*, BE673

—— *English poetry*, BE701

Dyson, Anne Jane. *American drama criticism*, BE457

—— *English novel explication*, BE671, BE675

—— *European drama criticism, 1900–1975*, BE232

Dyson, Lowell K. *Farmers' organizations*, EJ42

Dziak, John J. *Bibliography on Soviet intelligence and security services*, CJ545

Dzieje literatury polskiej od początków do czasów najnowszych, BE1352

Dzwonkoski, Peter. *American literary publishing houses, 1638–1899*, AA297

—— *American literary publishing houses, 1900–1980*, AA297

E. Azalia Hackley memorial collection, BJ86

•*E-CD*, EJ18

Eager, Alan R. *A guide to Irish bibliographical material*, AA49

Eagle, Dorothy. *The Oxford illustrated literary guide to Great Britain and Ireland*, BE614

—— *Oxford literary guide to Great Britain and Ireland*, BE614

—— *Oxford literary guide to the British Isles*, BE614

Eagle, Selwyn. *Library resources in London and South East England*, AK148

Eagle Walking Turtle. *Indian America*, CC429

Eagles, Brenda M. *The blues*, BJ337

Eagles, Donald Munroe. *The almanac of Canadian politics*, CJ293

Eagleson, Mary. *Concise encyclopedia biochemistry*, EG315

—— *Concise encyclopedia chemistry*, EE26

Eagleson, Robert D. *A Shakespeare glossary*, BE772

Eakins, Rosemary. *Picture sources UK*, BF349

Eakle, Arlene. *Ancestry's guide to research*, AJ4

—— *The source*, AJ23

Eales, Nellie B. *The Cole Library of early medicine and zoology*, EH53

Eames, Wilberforce. *A dictionary of books relating to America, from its discovery to the present time*, AA409

Earhart, H. Byron. *The new religions of Japan*, BC36

Earls, Irene. *Renaissance art*, BF83

Early American children's books, Rosenbach, Abraham Simon Wolf, AA247

Early American choral music, DeVenney, David P., BJ291

Early American fiction, Parker, Patricia L., BE478

Early American imprints, AA410, BF223

Early American imprints, 1639–1800, Readex Corporation, BJ59

Early American medical imprints, Austin, Robert B., EH12

—— National Library of Medicine (U.S.), EH25

Early American music, Heintze, James R., BJ36

Early American newspapers, 1704–1820, AE19

Early American plays, 1714–1830, Wegelin, Oscar, BE453, BE636

Early American poetry, Wegelin, Oscar, BE498

Early American proverbs and proverbial phrases, Whiting, Bartlett Jere, BE165

Early American scientific and technical literature, Batschelet, Margaret, EA227

Early American sheet music : its lure and its lore, BJ56

Early American silver, Fales, Martha Gandy, BG144

Early and rare books, AA218, AA220, AA221, AA226, AA227, AA228, AA231, AA233, AA235, AK143
  bibliography, BC104
  facsmilies and reproductions, AA134
  union lists, AA225, AA229, AA230
Early and rare books (by country or region)
  Australia, DF29

Early Arabic drama, Badawī, Muhammad M., BE1546

Early black American playwrights and dramatic writers, Peterson, Bernard L., BE531

Early Catholic Americana, Parsons, Wilfrid, BC392

Early childhood education, CB66, CB119

The early church, Robinson, Thomas A., BC222

Early English books, AA679

Early English books, 1641–1700, AA679

Early English drama, Everyman to 1580, White, D. Jerry, BE656

Early english fiction, BE678

Early English hymns, Parks, Edna D., BC320

Early English manuscripts in facsimile, BE602

Early English newspapers, Cox, Susan M., AE57

Early English printed books in the University Library, 1475–1640, Cambridge University Library, AA669

Early English stages, 1300–1600, Wickham, Glynne William Gladstone, BE664

Early history of Ireland : ecclesiastical, DC395

Early midwestern travel narratives, Hubach, Robert Rogers, DB161

Early modern English, AC29

Early modern English lexicography, Schäfer, Jürgen, AC7

Early motion pictures, Library of Congress. Motion Picture, Broadcasting, and Recorded Sound Division, BH190

Early painters and engravers in Canada, Harper, J. Russell, BF314

Early paper money of America, Newman, Eric P., BG194

Earth and astronomical sciences research centres, EC46, EF16

Earth, astronomical, and aerospace science research centres, EC46, EF16

Earth book world atlas, Esselte kartor (Firm), CL277

Earth satellites, 1957–1989, EK34

Earth scale art, Havlice, Patricia Pate, BF136

Earth sciences
  bibliography, EF47, EF48, EF59, EF103
    current, EF56
  dictionaries, EF13, EF14, EF15
    bilingual
      French-English, EF84
      Russian-English, EF86
      multilingual, EC41
  directories, EC46, EF16, EF92, EF222
  encyclopedias, EF3, EF5, EF6, EF12, EF61
  guides, EF2
  indexes, EF48, EF50
Earth sciences (by country or region)
  Canada
    dissertations, EF42
  North America
    bibliography, EF49
  United States
    dissertations, EF42
  see also **Geology**

The earth sciences, Porter, Roy, EF103

Earthquake history of the United States, Coffman, Jerry L., EF262
—— United States Coast and Geodetic Survey, EF262

Earthquakes, EF260, EF263
  bibliography, EF261
Earthquakes (by country or region)
  United States, EF262
  see also **Seismology**

E.A.S.A. register, Husmann, Gaby, CE99
—— Husmann, Rolf, CE99

Easson, David E. *Medieval religious houses, Scotland,* BC441

East, Marjorie. *Home economics,* EJ201

East, N. B. *African theatre,* BE1503

East, Roger. *Communist and Marxist parties of the world,* CJ526
—— *Political parties of Africa and the Middle East,* CJ405, CJ418
—— *World development directory,* CH134

East Africa High Commission. *Official publications of British East Africa,* AF223

East African Common Services Organization. *East African community,* AF221
—— *Uganda,* AF240

East African Community. *East African community,* AF221

East African community, Howell, John Bruce, AF221

East African High Commission. *East African community,* AF221

East and Southeast Asian material culture in North America, Haseltine, Patricia, CC406

East Asia, Nunn, Godfrey Raymond, DE1

East Asian resources in American libraries, Yang, Teresa S., DE106

East Central and Southeast Europe, AK105, DC47

East Central Europe, Horecky, Paul Louis, DC33, DC59

East European accessions index, Library of Congress. Processing Department, AA793

The East European Newspaper Collection of the Slavic and Baltic Division, the New York Public Library, Estafy, George D., AE42

East European peasantries, Sanders, Irwin Taylor, CE96

East European research index, EA141

East European studies
  bibliography, DC41
  periodicals
    guides for authors, AD26

East Germany, Wallace, Ian, DC243

East-West Center. *The world's worst weeds,* EJ64

Faster, Gerry. *American biographical archive,* AH56

Easterbrook, David L. *Africana book reviews, 1885–1945,* DD46

Easterbrook, Ian. *The travellers, Canada to 1900,* DB189

Easterling, P. E. *Greek literature,* BE1020

Eastern Christianity, BC446

Eastern churches, DC443, DC444, DC445, DC446
  dictionaries, BC449, BC451
  liturgy and ritual, BC448, BC450
  yearbooks, BC447

Eastern definitions, Rice, Edward, BC76

Eastern Europe and Russia/Soviet Union, Lewanski, Richard Casimir, AK109, DC50

Eastern Europe and the Commonwealth of Independent States, CJ94

Eastern European business directory, CH412

Eastern European national minorities, 1919–1980, Horak, Stephan M., CE92

Eastern Michigan University. Center of Educational Resources. *Index to black American literary anthologies,* BE537

Eastin, Roy B. *Government publications and their use,* AF76

Eastlick, John T. *Library management,* AK174

Eastman, C. R. *A bibliography of fishes,* EG286

Eastman, Mary Huse. *Index to fairy tales, myths and legends,* BE243

Eaton, Helen S. *Appleton's new Cuyás English-Spanish and Spanish-English dictionary,* AC732

Eaton, Quaintance. *Opera production,* BJ235

Eatwell, John. *The new Palgrave,* CH52
—— *The new Palgrave dictionary of money & finance,* CH268

Ebeling, Erich. *Reallexikon der Assyriologie, unter Mitwirkung zahlreicher Fachgelehrter,* DA80

Eberhard, G. *Handbuch der Astrophysik,* EC28

Eberhardt, George M. *The whole library handbook 2,* AK69

Eberlins Bladliste, AD80

Ebert, Katherine. *Collecting American pewter,* BG151

Ebert, Max. *Reallexikon der Vorgeschichte,* DA82

Ebin, F. E. *Velikaia Oktīabr'skaīa sotsialisticheskaīa revoliutsīīa v proizvedenīīakh sovetskikh pisateleī,* BE1399

EC legal systems, Sheridan, Maurice, CK204

•*ECER,* CB194, CD92

Echard, William E. *Foreign policy of the French Second Empire,* DC199
—— *Historical dictionary of the French Second Empire, 1852–1870,* DC206

Echemendia, Otto R. *Marketing information,* CH546

Echols, Anne. *An annotated index of medieval women,* CC575, DA149

Echols, John M. *A checklist of Indonesian serials in the Cornell University Library (1945–1970),* AD196
—— *English-Indonesian dictionary,* AC517
—— *An Indonesian-English dictionary,* AC517

Eckert, Kathryn Bishop. *Buildings of Michigan,* BF254

Eckstein, Richard M. *Directory of grants for organizations serving people with disabilities,* CC194

Ecodoc, CH39

École biblique et archéologique française (Jerusalem). Bibliothèque. *Catalogue de la Bibliothèque de l'École biblique et archéologique française,* BC109

École des Hautes Études en Sciences Sociales. *Revue bibliographique de Sinologie,* DE134

École des hautes études en sciences sociales. Centre d'Études Africaines. *Répertoire des thèses africanistes françaises,* DD31

Ecole française de Rome. *Bibliographie analytique de l'Afrique antique,* DD66

Ecole nationale supérieure des beaux-arts (France). *Fonds parisiens d'archives de l'architecture,* BF225

École Pratique des Hautes Études (France). Section des sciences économiques et sociales. *Revue bibliographique de Sinologie,* DE134

École pratique des hautes-études (France). Section des sciences historiques et philologiques. *Répertoire de manuscrits mediévaux contenant des notations musicales,* BJ55

Ecological abstracts, CL30, EF51, EG63

An ecological glossary, Carpenter, John Richard, EG123

Ecology, EG62, EG63, EG64
  associations, AL23
  bibliography, CA15
  directories, CA15

Ecology abstracts, EG14

•*ECONBASE,* CH150

•*Econlit,* CH33, CH40, CH42

The economic almanac for ... , CH106

Economic and financial statistics, Central Bank of Barbados, CG167

Economic and legal dictionary, CK48

Economic arithmetic, Palmer, Stanley H., CH188

Economic books, CH14

The Economic Community of West African States (ECOWAS), Irele, Modupeola, DD100

Economic development, CH162
  abstract journals, CH44
  associations
    directories, CH114
  bibliography, CH23
  databases, CH119
  dictionaries, CH120, CH121
    multilingual, CH125
  directories, CH113, CH120, CH130, CH134
  handbooks, CH142, CH666
  indexes, CH119
  international organizations, CH134
  periodicals, CH112, CH164
  statistics, CH160, CH161, CH163
  yearbooks, CH112
Economic development (by country or region)
  Pacific Rim, CH201
Economic forecasting, CH162, CH163
  databases, CH150
  directories, CH122

Economic forecasting (by country or region)
  United States
    handbooks, CG103
    statistics, CG105, CH110
Economic geology, EF196
  abstract journals, EK253
  bibliography, EF21
  encyclopedias, EF62
Economic history
  bibliography, CH10, CH24
  library catalogs, CH24
  statistics, CH106
Economic history (by country or region)
  Arab States, CH193
  Canada, CH176
  Caribbean and Islands of the Western Atlantic,
    CH178
  Great Britain, CH187, CH188
  India
    bibliography, CH197
  Ireland, CH187
  Latin America, CH178, CH180
  Mexico, CH178
  United States, CH172
    encyclopedias, CH49, DB42
Economic history of Canada, Dick, Trevor J. O.,
  CH176
Economic history of India, CH194, DE153
•Economic index, CH42
Economic indicators, CG41, CH108, CH158,
  CH159, CH162
  databases, CH150
  handbooks, CH109
  statistics, CH154
Economic indicators (by country or region)
  United States, CH107, CH168, CH170, CH171
    handbooks, CH236
Economic indicators, CH168
Economic indicators handbook, CH107
Economic interdependence in southern Africa,
  1961–1989, Schoeman, Elna, DD116
The economic library of Jacob H. Hollander,
  Hollander, Jacob Harry, CH17
•Economic literature index, CH40
Economic literature of Latin America, Harvard
  University. Bureau for Economic Research in
  Latin America, CH178
Economic literature on the Commonwealth
  Caribbean, Wilkinson, Audine, DB410
Economic report, CH164
Economic report of the President transmitted to the
  Congress, United States. President, CH174
Economic statistics, 1900–1983, CH158
Economic statistics yearbook, Han'guk Ŭnhaeng.
  Chosabu, CG407
Economic times, BC473
Economically active population estimates and
  projections, 1950–2025, CH680
Economics
  abbreviations, EA96
  abstracts, CH39
  atlases, CH147, CH148
  bibliography, CG287, CH9, CH10, CH11, CH14,
    CH15, CH16, CH17, CH18, CH19, CH20, CH21,
    CH30, CH31, CH33, CH336, CK7
    current, CH39, CH41, CH43
  bibliography of bibliographies, CA14
  biographies, CH52
  biography, AL167, CH11, CH91, CH92, CH93,
    CH95, CH102, CH104
  book reviews, CH13, CH42
  databases, CH32, CH40, CH41, CH42, CH150
  dictionaries, CH54, CH55, CH57, CH59, CH60,
    CH62, CH63, CH64, CH66, CH68, CH70
    German, CH67
    polyglot, CH65, CH69
    Russian-English, CH71
  directories, CH77, CH80
  encyclopedias, CH48, CH50, CH51, CH52,
    CH53, CH268
  guides, CH3, CH18
  handbooks, CH84, CH89
  indexes, CH32, CH40, CH42

library catalogs, CH16, CH17, CH19
  periodicals, CH16, CH30, CH31
    directories, CH27
  quotations, CH73, CH75
  statistics, CH158, CH188
  terminology, CH43
  union lists, CH10
Economics (by country or region)
  Canada, AE118, CH38
  India
    guides, CH196
    indexes, CH195
  Islamic countries
    bibliography, CH190
Economics (by subject)
  history
    bibliography, CH15
  study and teaching
    directories, CH79
Economics America, Inc. The right guide, CJ80
Economics and business, CH13
Economics and economics periodicals, Harvard
  University. Library, CH16
Economics and finance : index to periodical articles,
  1947–1971, CH119
Economics dictionary, Moffat, Donald W., CH60
Economics journals and serials, Sichel, Beatrice,
  CH31
Economics of education, Psacharopoulos, George,
  CB70
Economics sourcebook of government statistics,
  Hoel, Arline Alchian, CH171
Economics working papers bibliography, CH41
Economies of the German-speaking countries of
  Europe, Krewson, Margrit B., DC9
———— Lindner, Stephan H., DC9
The Economist atlas, CH147
The Economist atlas of the new Europe, CL321
The Economist book of vital world statistics, CG58
Economist Books. The Economist atlas, CH147
Economist guide to business numeracy, Stuteley,
  Richard, CH89
The Economist guide to weights and measures,
  AL200
Economist Intelligence Unit (Great Britain). Country
  report, CH112
Economist (London, England). The Columbia
  dictionary of political biography, CJ65
The Economist measurement guide and reckoner,
  AL200
The Economist numbers guide, CH89
Economist Publications (Firm). Directory of world
  stock exchanges, CH215
———— The world in figures, CG61
Economists
  biography, CH103
Economists' mathematical manual, Berck, Peter,
  CH84
The economy of the U.S.S.R, CH186
Écrivaines et écrivains d'aujourd'hui: Suisse,
  Boulanger, Grégoire, BE1490
Les écrivains belges contemporains de langue
  française, 1800–1946, Hanlet, Camille, BE1101
Écrivains canadiens, BE834
Écrivains, cinéastes et artistes camerounais,
  Baratte-Eno Belinga, Thérèse, BE1525
Écrivains, cinéastes et artistes ivoiriens, Bonncau,
  Richard, BE1527
Écrivains d'aujourd'hui, 1940–1960, Pingaud,
  Bernard, BE1150
Ecuador
  bibliography, AA528, AA529, AA530, AA531,
    AA532, DB322, DB370, DB372
  biography, AH135, AH136
    contemporary, AH137
  gazetteers, CL124
  government publications, AF159
  manuscripts and archives, DB373
  statistics, CG152, CG153, CG154, CG155
Ecuador (by subject)
  history, DB279
    bibliography, DB369
  social and behavioral sciences, DB370

women, DB371
Ecuador. Junta Nacional de Planificatión y
  Coordinación Económica. Sección de
  Investigaciones Sociales. Bibliografía social,
  económica y política del Ecuador, DB370
Ecuador, Corkill, David, DB369
Ecuador, aspectos socio-económicos, Alzamora C.,
  Lucia, DB370
Ecuador : bibliografía analítica, AA529, AA532
Ecuadorian literature, BE950, BE951, BE952
Ecumenical movement in bibliographical outline,
  Crow, Paul A., BC276
Ecumenism, BC230, BC273, BC276, BC283
  sourcebooks, BC282
Eda Kuhn Loeb Music Library. Music in Harvard
  libraries, BJ90
Edda, Kuhn, Hans, BE1286
———— Neckel, Gustav, BE1286
Eddas, BE1286
Eddleman, Floyd Eugene. American drama criticism,
  BE232, BE457
Eddukvæði, Jónsson, Guðni, BE1286
Ede, David. Guide to Islam, BC495
Edelheit, Abraham J. Bibliography on Holocaust
  literature, DA215
———— The rise and fall of the Soviet Union, DC589
———— A world in turmoil, DA222
Edelheit, Hershel. Bibliography on Holocaust
  literature, DA215
———— The rise and fall of the Soviet Union, DC589
———— A world in turmoil, DA222
Federal reserve bulletin, CH293
Edgar, Neal L. A history and bibliography of
  American magazines, 1810–1820, AD31
———— Travel in Asia, CL373
Edgerton, William B. Columbia dictionary of modern
  European literature, BE60
Ediafric, La Documentation africaine (Firm). Les
  élites algériennes, AH317
Edible plants, EG157
Edición nacional de las obras completas de
  Menéndez Pelayo, González Palencia, Angel,
  BE1043
Ediff, Sonia. The Tony Award, BH93
Edimages (Firm). Atlas historique de la France,
  DC166
Edin vek kultura na Bŭlgariĭa, otrazena v
  memoarnata literatura, DC115
Edinburgh Bibliographical Society. List of books
  printed in Scotland before 1700, AA695
The Edinburgh periodical press, Couper, William
  James, AD105
Les editeurs et diffuseurs de langue française,
  AA288
Editing see Copy preparation
Éditions Jeune Afrique. Grand atlas du continent
  africain, CL337
Editor & publisher. Market guide, CH585
Editor and publisher. Editor and publisher
  international yearbook, AE22
Editor and publisher international yearbook, AE22
Editorial cartoons see Cartoons
Editorial Research Service. Guide to the American
  left, CJ139
Editoriales, distribuidoras y librerías, AA285
Editorials, AE127
  see also Journalism
Editorials on file, AE127
Le edizioni italiane del XVI secolo, AA124, AA731
Edmonds, Cecil John. A Kurdish-English dictionary,
  AC568
Edmonds, Richard L. Macau, DE226
Edmunds, R. David. Kinsmen through time, CC420
Edmundson, Ronald Stanley. Dictionary of
  organophosphorus compounds, EE129
•EDOL, CB95
Édouard-Joseph, René. Dictionnaire biographique
  des artistes contemporains, 1910–1930, BF139
Edridge, Sally. Solomon Islands bibliography to
  1980, DF50
Educating the gifted, Greenlaw, M. Jean, CB185
Education
  abbreviations, CB78

abstract journals, AK35, CB59, CB61, CB179
acronyms, CB78
bibliography, CB6, CB9, CB12, CB13, CB16, CB44, CB47
  current, CB7
  periodicals, AK35, CB61
biography, CB130, CB131, CB132, CB133, CB134, CB183
book reviews, CB1
classification, CB111
computer software, CB176
databases, AK28, CB17, CB52, CB54, CB55, CB56, CB57, CB95, CB147, CB151, CB283, CD68, CD90, CD91
  subject headings, CB82
dictionaries, CB72, CB73, CB75, CB76, CB77, CB78, CB79, CB80
directories, CB88, CB95, CB100, CB108, CB325
  bibliography, CB101
directories (by country or region)
  international, CB87
dissertations, CB24
encyclopedias, CB65, CB67, CB68, CB69, CB70, CB71, CB127
free materials, CB13
government publications, CB106
guides, CB1, CB2, CB3, CB5
guides for authors, CB20
handbooks, CB112, CB117, CB122, CB126, CB127, CB258
indexes, AK28, AK35, CB51, CB52, CB54, CB55, CB61, CB64, CB153, CD90
information centers, CB99
library catalogs, CB6, CB9, CB35
library resources, CB94, CB267
periodicals, CB21, CB22, CB178
  bibliography, CB20
  indexes, CB50, CB53, CB55, CB64
quotations, CB84, CB85
research, CB113, CB121
research methods, CB4
reviews of research, CB121
statistics, CB135, CB138, CB139, CB142, CB143, CB144, CB145, CB146, CB147, CB148, CB149, CB258
subject headings, CB82
surveys, CB137
terminology, CB83
thesauruses, CB81, CB83
yearbooks, CB122, CB128, CB129
Education (by country or region)
Africa South of the Sahara, CB46
Canada, CB42, CB52
China, CB47
England, CB44
  dictionaries, CB76
Great Britain
  periodicals
    indexes, CB50
international
  directories, CB89, CB91, CB92, CB93
  handbooks, CB124, CB125
Latin America
  bibliography, CB43
Russia
  bibliography, CB45
United States, CB33, CB38
  bibliography, CB29
  directories, CB97, CB98, CB102, CB104
  encyclopedias, CB65
  handbooks, CB123
  statistics, CB144
Wales, CB44
Education (by subject)
associations, societies, and academies
  directories, CB241
curricula, CB115
ethnic attitudes, CB18
financial aid
  databases, CB100
  directories, CB100
gifted children, CB184

history
  bibliography, CB33
law and legislation, CB154, CB157
mathematics, CB116
music, CB116
public opinion, CB137
research
  bibliography
    periodicals, AK35, CB61
sexism, CB18
social and behavioral sciences, CB116
tests and measurements, CB150, CB151, CB152, CD68
  directories, CD74
see also Adolescent education; Adult education; Intercultural education; Physical education; Religious education; Remedial education; Special education
Education, Buttlar, Lois, CB3
Education, adult
  bibliography, CB351
Education and anthropology, Rosenstiel, Annette, CE17
Education and religion see Religion and education
Education au Canada, CB42
Education, comparative, CB127, CB238
  handbooks, CB327
Education directory : colleges & universities, CB268
Education directory : public school systems, CB97
Education for older adult learning, Greenberg, Reva M , CB353
Education Funding Research Council. Guide to federal funding for education, CB380
Education, higher
  abstract journals, CB234
  bibliography, CB217, CB219, CB221, CB222, CB224, CB229, CB232
  databases, CB302, CB308
  directories, CB248, CB250, CB256, CB261, CB265, CB272, CB276, CB286, CB288, CB290, CB294, CB295, CB301, CB305, CB308, CB313, CB332, CB346, CB347, CB348, CH81
    United States, CB280
  encyclopedias, CB236, CB237, CB238
  fellowships and scholarships, CB383
  guides to research, CB216
  handbooks, CB327, CB328
  indexes, CB234, CB235
  rankings, CB345
  statistics, CB336, CB339, CB340, CB341, CB342, CB347, CB348
    databases, CB257
  yearbooks, CB329, CB339
Education, higher (by country or region)
British Commonwealth
  directories, CB319
Canada
  directories, CB274, CB302
Europe, CB239
  directories, CB318, CB320
Great Britain, CB235, CB324
international, CB238
  directories, AL13, CB240, CB241, CB244
United States, CB217, CB219
  atlases, CB323
  bibliography, CB225, CB226
  directories, CB104, CB246, CB248, CB252, CB253, CB255, CB264, CB268, CB271, CB273, CB274, CB275, CB278, CB281, CB282, CB284, CB285, CB288, CB289, CB291, CB296, CB298, CB299, CB300, CB302, CB304, CB330, CH76
  dissertations, CB26, CB233
  guides, CB215
  history, CB26, CB233
  statistics, CB323, CB334, CB343, CB344
Education, higher (by subject)
city planning, BF282
fellowships and scholarships, CB259, CB371, CB375, CB389
finance, CB222
regional planning, BF282
religion, BC79

teachers and teaching
  directories, CB331
  surveys, CB335
Education in Canada, Finley, E. Gault, CB42
Education in England and Wales, Parker, Franklin, CB44
Education in Latin America, Lauerhass, Ludwig, CB43
Education in Sub-Saharan Africa, Urch, George E. F., CB46
Education in the People's Republic of China, past and present, Parker, Franklin, CB47
Education index, CB1, CB55, CB157
Education indicators, CB138
Education journals and serials, Collins, Mary Ellen, CB21
Education literature, 1907–1932, CB12
Education News Service. Only the best, CB176
Education of the black adult in the United States, McGee, Leo, CB38
Education, preschool, CB66
  handbooks, CB119
Education, primary, CB66
  directories, CB96, CB105
  handbooks, CB119
Education, primary (by subject)
  teaching aids, CB14
Education, secondary
  directories, CB96
Education Systems, Inc. The FCLD learning disabilities resource guide, CB202
Educational administration
  biography, CB183
  dictionaries, CB181
  directories, CB98
  handbooks, CB182
  periodicals, CB178
Educational administration abstracts, CB179
Educational administration glossary, Dejnozka, Edward L., CB181
Educational and training courses, CB357
Educational contests for students k-12, CB86
•Educational database, CB95
•Educational directory online, CB95
Educational equity, CB18
Educational evaluation
  bibliography, CB168
Educational events, CB357
Educational film & video locator of the Consortium of College and University Media Centers and R. R. Bowker, AA380, CB31
Educational law see School law
Educational measurement, CB150
Educational media and technology yearbook, CB177
Educational media yearbook, CB177
Educational psychology
  abstract journals, CB194, CD92
  bibliography, CD88, CD89
  encyclopedias, CD82
  handbooks, CD93, CD94
  tests and measurements, CD93
Educational rankings annual, CB345
Educational research, methodology, and measurement, Keeves, John P., CB70
Educational Research Service (Arlington, Va.). Kindergarten programs and practices in public schools, CB141
Educational Resources Information Center. Resources in education, AK35, CB61
Educational Resources Information Center (U.S.). Current index to journals in education, AK28, CB54, CD90
——— ERIC, CB56, CD91
——— Thesaurus of ERIC descriptors, CB83
Educational sociology, CB63
Educational technology
  abstract journals, CB169
  bibliography, CB168
  dictionaries, CB172, CB173, CB174
  directories, CB175
  encyclopedias, CB70, CB170
  terminology, CB171
  yearbooks, CB177

Educational technology, AECT Task Force on Definition and Terminology, CB171

Educational technology abstracts, CB169

Educational Testing Service. *Index to ETS research series, 1948–1991,* CB153

────── *The official GRE/CGS directory of graduate programs,* CB301

────── *Tests in microfiche,* CB151, CD68

────── *Trends in academic progress,* CB140

Educational Testing Service. Test Collection. *Directory of selected national testing programs,* CD74

────── *The ETS Test Collection catalog,* CB151, CD68

The educator's desk reference (EDR), Freed, Melvyn N., CB4

Educators' desk reference for special learning problems, Weller, Carol, CB205

The educator's encyclopedia of school law, Gatti, Daniel Jon, CB155

Educators guide to free audio and video materials, CB13

Educators guide to free curriculum materials, CB13

Educators guide to free films, CB13

Educators guide to free filmstrips, CB13

Educators guide to free guidance materials, CB13

Educators guide to free health, physical education and recreation materials, CB13

Educators guide to free [materials], CA50, CB13

Educators guide to free social studies materials, CB13

The educator's quotebook, Dale, Edgar, CB84

Educator's resource guide to special education, CB203

Eduskunnan kirjasto (Finland). *Valtion virallisjulkaisut,* AF167

•*EDVENT,* CB357

The Edward Deming Andrews Memorial Shaker Collection, Henry Francis du Pont Winterthur Museum, BC381

Edward E. Ayer Collection. *A bibliographical check list of North and Middle American Indian linguistics in the Edward E. Ayer Collection,* BD237

────── *Dictionary catalog of the Edward E. Ayer collection of Americana and American Indians in the Newberry Library,* DB6

Edward Fry Library of International Law. *London bibliography of the social sciences,* CA13

Edward M. Wilson collection of comedias sueltas in Cambridge University Library, Bainton, A. J. C., BE1461

Edwardian architecture, Gray, Alexander Stuart, BF259

Edwards, A. S. G. *The index of Middle English prose,* BE733

────── *Index of printed Middle English prose,* BE733

────── *Middle English prose,* BE735

Edwards, Alistair. *A new dictionary of political analysis,* CJ40

Edwards, Clive D. *John Gloag's dictionary of furniture,* BG126

Edwards, Gary. *International guide to nineteenth-century photographers and their works,* BF356

Edwards, George C. *Studying the presidency,* CJ166

Edwards, Helen. *A bibliography of finance,* CH224

Edwards, J. Michele. *Literature for voices in combination with electronic and tape music,* BJ276

Edwards, John. *The Irish language,* BD179

Edwards, Marcia A. *Nomenclator zoologicus,* EG244

Edwards, Michael. *The companion to wine,* EJ225

Edwards, Paul. *Encyclopedia of philosophy,* BB34

Edwards, Paul M. *General Matthew B. Ridgeway,* DA170

────── *Inchon Landing, Korea, 1950,* DA170

────── *Pusan perimeter, Korea, 1950,* DA170

Edwards, R. Dudley. *Sources for early modern Irish history, 1534–1641,* DC410

Edwards, Ralph. *Dictionary of English furniture, from the Middle Ages to the late Georgian period,* BG123

────── *Shorter dictionary of English furniture,* BG123

Edwards, Ruth Dudley. *An atlas of Irish history,* DC416

Edwards, Willie M. *Gerontology,* CC67

The Edwin A. Fleischer Collection of Orchestral Music, Philadelphia Free Library, BJ98

Edzard, Dietz Otto. *Reallexikon der Assyriologie, unter Mitwirkung zahlreicher Fachgelehrter,* DA80

Eeckaute, Denise. *Thesaurus des institutions de l'ancienne Russie,* DC584

Eells, Walter C. *College presidency, 1900–1960,* CB228

Een, JoAnn Delores. *Women and society,* CC510

Eenoo, Romain van. *Bibliographie de l'histoire de Belgique,* DC99

The Eerdmans analytical concordance to the Revised Standard Version of the Bible, Whitaker, Richard E., BC166

The Eerdmans Bible commentary, BC171

The Eerdmans Bible dictionary, BC136

Eerste Nederlandse systematisch ingerichte encyclopaedie, AB36

Eesti-inglise sõnaraamat, Saagpakk, Paul Friidrih, AC307

────── Silvet, J., AC308

Eesti keele mõisteline sõnaraamat, Saareste, Andrus Kustas, AC306

Eesti kirjandus, BE1125

Eesti kirjandus võõrkeeltes, Mauer, Mare, BE1124

Eesti kirjanduse ajalugu, Sõgel, Endel, BE1125

Eesti kirjanduse biograafiline leksikon, BE1123

Eesti pseudonüümide leksikon, Kahu, Meelik, AA167

Eesti-saksa sõnaraamat kolmas muutmatu trük teisest, dr. Jakob Hurt'i poolt redigeeritud väljaandest, Wiedemann, F. J., AC309

────── Wiedemann, Ferdinand Johann, AC306

Efemérides biográficas (defunciones-nacimientos), Mestre Ghigliazza, Manuel, AH101

Efimov, Oleg P. *Russian-English dictionary of mathematics,* EB52

Efron, Vera. *A dictionary of words about alcohol,* CC129

EFTA legal systems, Cameron, James, CK204

────── Sheridan, Maurice, CK204

Egan, David R. *Russian autocrats from Ivan the Great to the fall of the Romanov dynasty,* DC578

Egan, Melinda A. *Russian autocrats from Ivan the Great to the fall of the Romanov dynasty,* DC578

Egbert, Donald Drew. *Socialism and American life,* CJ527

Egbert, Lawrence Deems. *Multilingual law dictionary : English-Français-Español-Deutsch,* CK46

Egberts, A. *Late reviews AEB, 1947–1984,* DA121

Eger, Ernestina N. *A bibliography of criticism of contemporary Chicano literature,* BE557

Egerod, Søren. *Postwar Japanese women writers,* BE1595

Egge, Marion F. *The American Indian in short fiction,* BE548

Eggebrecht, Hans Heinrich. *Brockhaus Riemann Musiklexikon,* BJ128

────── *Handwörterbuch der musikalischen Terminologie,* BJ148

Eggeling, Hans F. *A dictionary of modern German prose usage,* AC438

Eggenberger, David. *Dictionary of battles,* DA21

────── *An encyclopedia of battles,* DA21, DA25

Egger, Carl. *Lexicon nominum virorum et mulierum,* AJ170

Eggers, Hans. *Deutscher Wortschatz,* AC435

Egli, Johann Jacob. *Nomina geographica,* CL170

Egorov, V. N. *Mezhdunarodnye otnosheniia,* DC586

Egret, Daniel. *Databases & on-line data in astronomy,* EC1

Egypt, DA124

bibliography, AA853, AA854, DD18, DD148, DD149, DE32

current surveys, DD62

encyclopedias, DD48

statistics, CG327, CG328

Egypt (by subject)

archaeology and ancient history, DA121, DA122, DA123, DA125

atlases, DA126

religion, BC452

Egypt, Chapin Metz, Helen, DD62

────── Makar, Ragai N., DD18

────── Wucher King, J., DD48

An Egyptian hieroglyphic dictionary, Budge, Ernest Alfred Thompson Wallis, AC301

Egyptian language

dictionaries, AC301

bilingual, AC304

Egyptian-German, AC303

English-Egyptian, AC302

Egyptian publications bulletin, AA853

The Egyptian who's who, AH330

Ehlers, Eckart. *Iran,* DE182

────── *Orbis geographicus,* CL56

Ehrenberg, Ralph E. *Scholars' guide to Washington, D.C. for cartography and remote sensing imagery,* CL257

Ehrencron-Müller, Holger. *Anonym– og Pseudonym-Lexikon for Danmark og Island til 1920 og Norge til 1814,* AA166

────── *Bibliotecha danica og Dansk bogfortegnelse,* AA601

────── *Forfatterlexikon omfattende Danmark, Norge og Island indtil 1814,* BE1087, BE1117

────── *Forfatterlexikon omfattende Danmark, Norge og Island indtil 1819,* BE1341

────── *Stikordsregister til den danske Skønlitteratur. 1841/1908–1909/40,* AA607

Ehresmann, Donald L. *Applied and decorative arts,* BF2, BG2

────── *Architecture,* BF2, BF202

────── *Fine arts,* BF2

Ehrich, Robert W. *Chronologies in Old World archaeology,* DA83

Ehrlich, Eugene H. *The Harper dictionary of foreign terms,* AC187

────── *Mene, Mene, Tekel,* BC155

────── *NBC handbook of pronunciation,* AC103, AC108

────── *Oxford American dictionary,* AC18

────── *The Oxford illustrated literary guide to the United States,* BE438

Ehrlich, Paul R. *The birder's handbook,* EG258

────── *Birds in jeopardy,* EG259

Ei-Beihō jiten, CK51

•*Ei COMPENDEX*Plus,* EK11

•*Ei engineering meetings,* EK11

Ei Page One, EK7

Ei thesaurus, EK11

Ei vocabulary, EK11

Eichborn, Reinhart von. *Business dictionary,* CH67

────── *Cambridge-Eichborn German dictionary,* CH67

────── *Spezialwörterbuch für Handel und Wirtschaft,* CH67

Eichelberger, Clayton L. *A guide to critical reviews of United States fiction, 1870–1910,* BE471

Eichelberger, Ursula. *Zitatenlexikon,* BE137

Eichenberg, Fritz. *The art of the print,* BF378

────── *Lithography and silkscreen,* BF378

Eicher, Joanne Bubolz. *African dress,* BG90

Eichholz, Alice. *Ancestry's red book,* AJ1

Eichler, Margrit. *Nonsexist research methods,* CC560

Eichler, Monika. *Bibliographie Sprache und Literatur,* BD2

Eichstädt, Volkmar. *Bibliographie zur Geschichte der Judenfrage,* BC528

Eigen, Lewis D. *The Macmillan dictionary of political quotations,* CJ44, CJ45

Eight American authors, BE399, BE403, BE404, BE413, BE572

Eight Scandinavian novelists, Budd, John, BE1085

The eighteen-nineties, BE758

The eighteenth century, AA681, BE36, BE743

The eighteenth century, 1714–1789, Pargellis, Stanley, DC317

Eighteenth century British and Irish promptbooks, Langhans, Edward A., BH42
Eighteenth-century British books, AA680
Eighteenth century British novel and its background, Behm, Carl, BE670
—— Hahn, H. George, BE670
Eighteenth-century English literary studies, Glock, Waldo Sumner, BE745
The eighteenth-century Gothic novel, McNutt, Dan J., BE292
An eighteenth-century musical chronicle, Hall, Charles J., BJ187
Eighteenth century Russia, Clendenning, Philip, DC574
Eighteenth century Russian literature, culture and thought, Cross, Anthony Glenn, BE1385
Eighteenth century short title catalogue, AA402, AA680
The eighteenth century short title catalogue 1990, AA681
Eiland, Murray L. *Oriental rugs,* BG165
Eiler, Andrew. *Consumer protection manual,* CH563
Eĭmontova, R. G. *Dvizhenie dekabristov,* DC577
—— *Istoriña istoricheskoĭ nauki v SSSR,* DC570
Einarsson, Stefan. *History of Iceland prose writers, 1800–1940,* BE1285
—— *A history of Icelandic literature,* BE1285
Einführung in das Studium der mittelalterlichen Geschichte, Quirin, Heinz, DA135
Einführung in die alte Geschichte, DA59
Einstein, Daniel. *Special edition,* BH300
Fis, Arlene L. *Legal looseleafs in print,* CK122
—— *Legal newsletters in print,* CK123
EIS, EK67
EIS : key to environmental impact statements, EK67
Eisaguirre, Lynne. *Sexual harassment,* CC561
Eisen, Sydney. *Victorian science and religion,* BC215
Eisenberg, Abné M. *Argument,* BE369
Eisenberg, Alex. *Skønlitteratur i danske Tidsskrifter 1943–1962,* BE1116
Eisenberg, Peter. *Bibliographie zur deutschen Grammatik,* BD117
Eisenbichler, Konrad. *International directory of Renaissance and Reformation associations and institutes,* DA153
Eisenreich, Gunther. *Dictionary of mathematics,* EB47
Eisler, Rudolf. *Wörterbuch der philosophischen Begriffe,* BB40
Eisner, Gilbert M. *Melloni's illustrated medical dictionary,* EH98
Eitinger, Leo. *Psychological and medical effects of concentration camps and religious persecution on survivors of the Holocaust,* DA215
Eitner, Kurt. *Nigeria,* DD193
Eitner, Robert. *Biographisch-bibliographisches Quellen-Lexikon der Musiker und Musikgelehrten der christlichen Zeitrechnung bis zur Mitte des neunzehnten Jahrhunderts,* BJ57
Eiyaku Nihon kankei hobun tosho mokuroku, DE197
Ekdahl, Janis. *American sculpture,* BF387
Ekistic index of periodicals, BF275
EKL, BC232
Eklund, Jon. *The incompleat chymist,* EE37
Ekmanis, Rolfs. *Latvian literature under the Soviets, 1940–1975,* BE1319
Ekonomika SSSR, Sivolgin, Vladimir Epifanovich, CH22
Ekpaideutikē Hellēnikē enkyklopaideia, AB53
Eksteen, Louis Cornelis. *Groot woordeboek,* AC198
Ekwall, Eilert. *Concise Oxford dictionary of English place-names,* CL193
—— *English river names,* CL194
El-Fadil, Amal Eisa. *Bibliography on Sudan international relations,* DD228
—— *Southern Sudan,* DD228
El-Hi textbooks in print, AA431
el Nasri, Abdel Rahman. *Bibliography of the Sudan, 1938–1958,* DD226
El Salvador, DB307
  biography, AH116, DB306
  gazetteers, CL115

government publications, AF159
statistics, CG128
El Salvador (by subject)
  history, AH116, DB306
El Salvador. Dirección General de Estadística y Censos. *Anuario estadístico,* CG128
El Salvador, Woodward, Ralph Lee, DB307
El-Singaby, Talaat. *La République Démocratique du Soudan,* DD225
Elam, Stanley M. *Decade of Gallup polls of attitudes toward education, 1969–1978,* CB137
Elastomers, EK286
Elazar, Daniel Judah. *Federal systems of the world,* CJ51
Elbert, Samuel H. *Hawaiian dictionary,* AC469
Elcano, Barrett. *Nursing,* EH285
Elder neglect and abuse, Johnson, Tanya F., CC71
The elderly in America, Nordquist, Joan, CC72
Eldridge, Hope T. *The materials of demography,* CG2
The election data book, CJ246
Election Data Services. *The election data book,* CJ246
Election index, CJ215
Election results directory, CJ271
Election statistics
  handbooks, CJ92
Election statistics (by country or region)
  Canada, CJ298
  Great Britain, CJ361, CJ364, CJ365
  India, CJ435
  Ireland, CJ379
  United States, CJ241, CJ246
    directories, CJ271
Elections, CJ89
  handbooks, CJ88, CJ92
Elections (by country or region)
  British Empire and Commonwealth, CJ371
  Canada, CJ293
  Germany, West
    statistics, CJ335
  Great Britain, CJ350, CJ365, CJ366
  Netherlands, CJ383
  United States, CJ192, CJ251
    bibliography, CJ103, CJ105
    campaigns, CJ244
    encyclopedias, CJ121, CJ124, CJ262
    history, CJ242, CJ252
    state and local government, CJ291
    statistics, CJ240, CJ243, CJ245, CJ250, CJ253, CJ254, CJ255, CJ256
  see also **Primary elections**
Elections in India, Singh, V. B., CJ435
Elections, Public Opinion and Parties in Britain (Political Studies Association of the United Kingdom). *British elections and parties yearbook,* CJ363
Elections Research Center. *America votes,* CJ241
Elections Research Center. Governmental Affairs Institute. *America at the polls,* CJ240
Elections since 1945, CJ88
The electoral politics dictionary, Renstrom, Peter G., CJ121, CJ124
Electrical & electronics abstracts, ED9, ED11
Electrical and electronic engineering
  abbreviations, EK196
  abstract journals, EK128
  bibliography, EK125, EK127
  databases, ED9
  dictionaries, EK131, EK132, EK133
  encyclopedias, EK129, EK130
  guides, EK124
  handbooks, EK134, EK135, EK136, EK137, EK138, EK139, EK143
  see also **Computer science; Radio; Television**
Electrical engineering abstracts, EK128
The electrical engineering handbook, EK135
Electrical resistivity handbook, ED35
Electricity, EK126
Electronic data processing *see* **Data processing**
•*Electronic directory of education,* CB95
•*Electronic encyclopedia,* AB25
Electronic music, BJ276, BJ310, BJ311, BJ313

handbooks, BJ312
Electronic music, Schwartz, Elliott Shelling, BJ312
Electronic music dictionary, Tomlyn, Bo, BJ313
Electronic properties of materials, EK125
Electronics, EK127
  encyclopedias, EK129, EK130
  handbooks, EK139, EK142
Electronics engineers' handbook, EK136
Electronics engineer's reference book, EK137
Elekronenphysik, Ionenphysik und Übermikroskopie, ED41
The elementary school library collection, AA341
The elements, Emsley, J., EE73
Éléments de bibliographie sur l'histoire des institutions et des faits sociaux, 987–1875, Lepointe, Gabriel, DC149
Elements of bibliography, Harmon, Robert B., AA4
Elements of classical logic, BB36
Elements of Hindu iconography, Gopinātha Rāu, T. A., BF191
Elements of style, Strunk, William, CA55
—— White, E. B., CA55
Elenchus bibliographicus, BC119
Elenchus bibliographicus biblicus of Biblica, BC119
Elenchus of Biblica, BC119
Elenco del libro svizzero, AA835
Eleuterio-Comer, Susan K. *Irish American material culture,* CC312, DC402
Eleutherian Mills Historical Library. *Technical Americana,* EA237, EK3
The eleven religions and their proverbial lore, Champion, Selwyn Gurney, BC89
Eleven years of Bible bibliography, Rowley, H. H., BC117
Eley, Stephen. *A bibliography of cricket,* BK71
Elgueta de Ochsenius, Herminia. *Bibliografía de bibliografías chilenas,* AA514
ELH, a journal of English literary history, BE40
Eliade, Mircea. *Encyclopedia of religion,* BC55, BC58
Elias, Edward E. *Elias' modern dictionary, English-Arabic,* AC215
Elias, Elias Antoon. *Elias' modern dictionary, English-Arabic,* AC215
Elias, Stephen. *Legal research,* CK117
Elias, Thomas. *The complete trees of North America,* EG194
Elias' modern dictionary, English-Arabic, Elias, Elias Antoon, AC215
Les élites algériennes, AH317
Les elites sénégalaises, DD200
Elizabethan bibliographies [concise bibliographies], Tannenbaum, Samuel A., BE741
Elizabethan stage, Chambers, Edmund Kerchever, BE663, BE664, BE665
Elizabethan translations from the Italian, Scott, Mary Augusta, BE1297
Elizondo, Carlos L. *Research guide to Costa Rica,* DB304
Elkhadem, Saad. *York dictionary of English-French-German-Spanish literary terms and their origin,* BE88
Elkin, Judith Laikin. *Latin American Jewish studies,* BC526
Elkins, Aubrey Christian. *The Romantic movement bibliography, 1936–1970,* BE40, BE754
Elkjaer, Kjeld. *Skønlitteratur i danske Tidsskrifter, 1913-1942,* BE1116
Elks, J. *Dictionary of drugs,* EE126, EH336
Eller, William. *Comparative reading,* CB48
—— *General issues in literacy/illiteracy,* CB49
—— *International handbook of reading education,* CB120
—— *Literacy/illiteracy in the world,* CB49
Ellington, Henry. *Dictionary of instructional technology,* CB173
Ellinwood, Leonard. *Bibliography of American hymnals,* BC315
—— *Bibliography of periodical literature in musicology and allied fields,* BJ109
—— *Dictionary of American hymnology,* BC315
Elliot, J. K. *Apocryphal New Testament,* BC94

Elliot, Jeffrey M. *Arms control, disarmament and military security dictionary*, CJ682, CJ683
—— *The presidential-congressional political dictionary*, CJ115
—— *The state and local government political dictionary*, CJ269
Elliot, Stephen P. *Reference guide to the United States Supreme Court*, CK192
Elliott, Clark A. *Biographical dictionary of American science*, EA177, EA192
—— *Biographical index to American science*, EA192
Elliott, David L. *Textbooks in school and society*, CB19
Elliott, Emory. *The Columbia history of the American novel*, BE485
—— *Columbia literary history of the United States*, BE439
Elliott, Florence. *Dictionary of politics*, CJ33
Elliott, Jacqueline D. *Pacific law bibliography*, CK234
Elliott, Wendy L. *The library*, AJ14
Elliott, Sydney. *Northern Ireland : a political directory, 1966–88*, CJ374
Ellis, Brooks Fleming. *Catalogue of Foraminifera*, EF238
—— *Catalogue of index Foraminifera*, EF238, EF239
—— *Catalogue of Ostracoda*, EF239
Ellis, Harold. *Bailey and Bishop's notable names in medicine and surgery*, EH220
Ellis, Jack C. *Film book bibliography, 1940–1975*, BH170
Ellis, James. *English drama of the nineteenth century*, BE639, BE640
Ellis, Jessie Croft. *Index to illustrations*, BF60
—— *Nature and its applications*, BF60
—— *Travel through pictures*, BF60
Ellis, John. *The World War II databook*, DA205
Ellis, John Tracy. *Documents of American Catholic history*, BC414
—— *A guide to American Catholic history*, BC389
Ellis, Linda. *Laboratory techniques in archaeology*, DA64
Ellis, Peter Berresford. *Dictionary of Celtic mythology*, CF17
—— *A dictionary of Irish mythology*, CF30
Ellison, H. L. *The new layman's Bible commentary in one volume*, BC179
Ellison, John William. *Nelson's complete concordance of the Revised Standard Version Bible*, BC158
Elliston, Frederick. *Ethics, government, and public policy*, CJ462
Ellmann, Richard. *The Norton anthology of modern poetry*, BE332, BE506
Ellsworth, Dianne J. *The role of women in librarianship, 1876–1976*, AK73
Ellwood, Katherine B. *Guide to the petroleum reference literature*, EK298
Elman, Robert. *The hunter's field guide to the game birds and animals of North America*, BK115
Elmendorf, G. E. *Nicaraguan national bibliography, 1800–1978*, AA491
Elmer, Emma Osterman. *Checklist of publications of the government of the Philippine Islands Sept. 1, 1900 to Dec. 31, 1917*, AF258
Elmes, Gregory A. *The historical atlas of state power in Congress, 1790–1990*, CJ236, CJ237, CJ258, CJ292, DB73
Elnicki, Susan E. *Fund raiser's guide to human service funding*, AL117
Elphick, Richard. *Southern African history before 1900*, DD120, DD223
Elsbree, John J. *Dictionary of library and educational technology*, AK43
Elsevier Science Publishers. *Dictionary of insurance and risk prevention*, CH508
Elsevier's banking dictionary in seven languages, CH271
Elsevier's concise Spanish etymological dictionary, Gómez de Silva, Guido, AC744

Elsevier's dictionary of agriculture and food production, Rakipov, N. G., EJ31
Elsevier's dictionary of aquaculture, EJ25
Elsevier's dictionary of chemistry, Macura, Paul, EE54
Elsevier's dictionary of cinema, sound, and music, in six languages, Clason, W. E., BH257
Elsevier's dictionary of commercial terms and phrases, Appleby, Barry Léon, CH429
Elsevier's dictionary of criminal science in eight languages, CK258
Elsevier's dictionary of environmental hydrogeology, EF132
Elsevier's dictionary of financial terms in English, German, Spanish, French, Italian, and Dutch, CH214
Elsevier's dictionary of geosciences, Bhatnagar, K. P., EF86
Elsevier's dictionary of glaciology in four languages, EF125
Elsevier's dictionary of horticultural and plant production, EJ240
Elsevier's dictionary of horticulture in nine languages, EJ240
Elsevier's dictionary of hydrogeology in three languages, EF132
Elsevier's dictionary of hydrology and water quality management, Tuin, J. D. van der, EF136
Elsevier's dictionary of insurance and risk prevention, Lucca, J. L. de, CH508
Elsevier's dictionary of jewellery and watchmaking, Forget, Carl, BG82
Elsevier's dictionary of mining and mineralogy, Dorian, Angelo Francis, EF183
Elsevier's dictionary of pharmaceutical science and techniques in five languages, EH328
Elsevier's dictionary of photography in three languages, BF342
Elsevier's dictionary of physical planning, Logie, Gordon, BF277
Elsevier's dictionary of science and technology, Chakalov, G., EA125
Elsevier's dictionary of soil mechanics in four languages, EJ26
Elsevier's dictionary of technology, Thomann, Arthur E., EA134
Elsevier's encyclopaedic dictionary of medicine, Dorian, Angelo Francis, EH139
Elsevier's lexicon of international and national units, AL198
Elsevier's Russian-English dictionary, Macura, Paul, AC677, EA127
Elsevier's wood dictionary in seven languages, EJ178
Elsey, Barry. *International biography of adult education*, CB363
Elsie, Robert. *Dictionary of Albanian literature*, BE1093
Elsley, John. *The American Horticultural Society encyclopedia of garden plants*, EG116, EJ231
Elster, Ludwig. *Wörterbuch der Volkswirtschaft*, CH68
Elting, John Robert. *A dictionary of soldier talk*, CJ616
—— *Military uniforms in America*, CJ634
Elwell-Sutton, L. P. *Bibliographic guide to Iran*, DE181
Emanoil, Mary. *Assistance and benefits information directory*, AL101
Emanuel, Shirley P. *International directory of braille music collections*, BJ171
•*EMBASE*, EH34, EH58, EH59
EMBASE list of journals abstracted, EH58
EMBASE list of journals indexed, EH34
Emblemata, Henkel, Arthur, BF168
Embree, Ainslie Thomas. *Encyclopedia of Asian history*, DE14
—— *A guide to Oriental classics*, BE1543
Embree, John Fee. *Bibliography of the peoples and cultures of mainland Southeast Asia*, DE119
Embrey, Peter G. *A manual of new mineral names, 1892–1978*, EF184
Emde, Fritz. *Tafeln höherer Funktionen*, EB76

Emeneau, Murray Barnson. *A Dravidian etymological dictionary*, AC291
—— *A union list of printed Indic texts and translations in American libraries*, BE1564
An emerging entertainment, Meserve, Walter J., BE466
Emerson, James C. *Emerson's directory of leading U.S. accounting firms*, CH255
Emerson, O. B. *Southern literary culture*, BE569
Emerson's directory of leading U.S. accounting firms, CH255
Emerton, Bruce. *American college regalia*, CB397
Emery, H. G. *New Century dictionary of the English language*, AC11
Emigration, CC359
  see also **Immigration; Migration**
L'emigration russe, AD300
L'émigration russe en Europe, Ossorguine-Bakounine, Tatiana, AD218
Emigré literature, AD47, CC458
  bibliography, AA586
  indexes, AD300
  union lists, AD218
  see also **Exiled authors**
Emiliani, Cesare. *Dictionary of the physical sciences*, EA90
Emily Post's etiquette, Post, Emily, AL156
Emin, Irving. *Russian-English physics dictionary*, ED27
Eminent Chinese of the Ch'ing period (1644–1912), Library of Congress. Orientalia Division, AH338, AH339, AH340
Eminent Indians who was who, 1900–1980, also annual diary of events, AH350
Emmanuel, Muriel. *Contemporary artists*, BF138
Emmens, Carol A. *Short stories on film and video*, BH218
Emmerich, Heinrich. *Atlas hierarchicus*, BC420
Emmett, Kathleen. *Perception*, CD107
Emmons, Glenroy. *Spanish literature, 1500–1700*, BE1437
Emmons, Marilyn C. *Spanish literature, 1500–1700*, BE1437
Emotionally disturbed children, CC165
Empire State College. Learning Resources Center. *Innovative graduate programs directory*, CB300
Employee benefit plans, CH507
Employee fringe benefits, CH500, CH503, CH505, CH507
Employees
  training, CB364, CH695, CH713, CH717
Employers' organizations of the world, CH664
Employment
  dictionaries
    multilingual, CH653
  statistics, CH644, CH681, CH682, CH685, CH689
Employment (by country or region)
  United States
    statistics, CH687
Employment and earnings, CH681, CH682, CH685
Employment, hours and earnings, states and areas, CH681
Employment, hours and earnings, United States, CH682
Employment relations abstracts, CH646
La Empress periodistica en España, AE76
Emrich, Amy Lynn. *Scientific and technical organizations and agencies directory*, EA200
Emsley, J. *The elements*, EE73
Enabling and empowering families, Deal, Angela G., CC235
—— Dunst, Carl J., CC235
—— Trivette, Carol M., CC235
•*Encarta*, AB10, AB24
•*Encarta multimedia encyclopedia*, AB24
Enciclopedia, AB63
Enciclopedia biografica e bibliografica "Italiana", AH261
Enciclopedia cattolica, BC399
Enciclopédia da música brasileira, BJ132
Enciclopedia de historia de España, DC513

Enciclopedia de la literatura argentina, Orgambide, Pedro G., BE920

Enciclopédia de literatura brasileira, BE929

Enciclopedia de México, DB244

Enciclopedia de orientación bibliográfica, AA91

Enciclopedia del arte en América, BF70

Enciclopedia del idioma, Alonso Pedraz, Martin, AC726

Enciclopedia del novecento, AB64

Enciclopedia della musica, BJ133

Enciclopedia dell'antifascismo e della Resistenza ..., DC432

Enciclopedia dell'arte antica, classica e orientale, BF71, BF72

Enciclopedia dell'arte medievale, BF72

Enciclopedia dello spettacolo, BH10

Enciclopedia dominicana, DB435

Enciclopedia Einaudi, AB63

Enciclopedia europea, AB65

Enciclopedia filosofica, BB30

Enciclopedia hispanica, AB93

Enciclopedia histórica de Honduras, DB311

Enciclopedia ilustrada del Perú, Tauro, Alberto, DB388

Enciclopedia istoriografiei româneşti, DC497

Enciclopedia italiana, BH10

Enciclopedia italiana di scienze, lettere ed arti, AB64, AB66

Enciclopédia Mirador internacional, AB79

Enciclopedia ragionata delle armi, CJ569

Enciclopedia Românlel, DC498

Enciclopedia storico-nobiliare italiana, Spreti, Vittorio, AJ139

Enciclopedia universal ilustrada europeo-americana, AB94

Enciclopedia universale dell' arte, BF73

Enciclopedia yucatanense, DB245

Enciklopedija jugoslavije, DC612

Enciklopēdiskā vārdnīca, DC435

Encyclopaedia Africana, AH314

Encyclopaedia biblica, BC129

Encyclopaedia Britannica. 10 eventful years, DA209

—— *Enciclopedia hispanica,* AB93

—— *Yearbook of science and the future,* EA169

Encyclopaedia Britannica, AB8, AB12, AC66

Encyclopaedia Britannica do Brasil Publicações Ltda. *Enciclopédia Mirador internacional,* AB79

Encyclopaedia hebraica, AB57

Encyclopaedia Hungarica, AB59

Encyclopædia Iranica, DE188

Encyclopaedia Judaica, BC546, DC493

Encyclopaedia of 20th-century architecture, BF233

Encyclopaedia of band music, BJ294

Encyclopaedia of British porcelain manufacturers, Godden, Geoffrey A., BG60

Encyclopaedia of Buddhism, BC476

The encyclopaedia of chess, Sunnucks, Anne, BK135

The encyclopaedia of educational media communications and technology, CB170

Encyclopaedia of food science, food technology, and nutrition, EH297

Encyclopaedia of heraldry, AJ149

Encyclopaedia of India, Chopra, Pran Nath, DE165

An encyclopaedia of Indian archaeology, DE166

Encyclopaedia of Indian culture, Saletore, Rajaram Narayan, DE170

Encyclopaedia of Indian literature, BE1565

—— Garg, Gaṅgā Rām, BE1565

Encyclopaedia of Indian medicine, EH84

The encyclopaedia of Islam, BC503, BC505, DE69

An encyclopaedia of language, BD33

Encyclopaedia of librarianship, Landau, Thomas, AK37

Encyclopaedia of mathematics, EB33

An encyclopaedia of metallurgy and materials, Tottle, Charles Ronald, EK266

An encyclopaedia of Napoleon's Europe, Palmer, Alan, DC22

Encyclopaedia of New Zealand, DF43

Encyclopaedia of occupational health and safety, EH409

Encyclopaedia of oil painting, Palmer, Frederick, BF304

An encyclopaedia of Parliament, Wilding, Norman W., CJ353

Encyclopaedia of psychic science, Fodor, Nandor, CD134

Encyclopaedia of religion and ethics, BC55

—— Hastings, James, BC58

Encyclopaedia of the modern British Army, Gander, Terry, CJ652

Encyclopaedia of the modern Royal Air Force, Gander, Terry, CJ652

Encyclopaedia of the modern Royal Navy, Beaver, Paul, CJ652

Encyclopaedia of the musical film, Green, Stanley, BJ358

Encyclopaedia of the musical theatre, Green, Stanley, BJ263, BJ358

Encyclopaedia of the Second World War, Hogg, Ian V., DA206

Encyclopaedia of the social sciences, CA33, CA36, CA44

The encyclopaedia of the solid earth sciences, EF61

Encyclopaedia of world costume, Yarwood, Doreen, BG102

Encyclopaedia of world Hindi literature, Garg, Gaṅgā Rām, BE1565

Encyclopaedia universalis, AB40

Encyclopædia Universalis (Firm). *Le grand atlas des littératures,* BE67

Encyclopaedic dictionary of heraldry, Franklyn, Julian, AJ162, AJ163

—— Tanner, John, AJ162

Encyclopaedic dictionary of photography, Woodbury, Walter E., BF340

Encyclopaedic dictionary of physics, ED13

An encyclopaedic dictionary of Sanskrit on historical principles, AC705

Encyclopedia Americana, AB9

Encyclopedia and dictionary of medicine, nursing, and allied health, Miller, Benjamin Frank, EH279

Encyclopedia Canadiana, Pearson, Kenneth H., DB198

Encyclopedia Heibonsha, AB70

Encyclopedia Judaica, BC546, DC493

Encyclopedia Lituanica, DC441

Encyclopedia of accounting systems, CH251

Encyclopedia of adolescence, CC159, CD83

The encyclopedia of adoption, Adamec, Christine A., CC223

Encyclopedia of African American religions, BC56

The encyclopedia of aging, CC80

The encyclopedia of aging and the elderly, Roy, Frederick Hampton, CC81

Encyclopedia of alcoholism, Chafetz, Morris E., CC124

—— Evans, Glen, CC124

—— O'Brien, Robert, CC125

Encyclopedia of American agricultural history, Schapsmeier, Edward L., EJ71

Encyclopedia of American architecture, Hunt, William Dudley, BF235

Encyclopedia of American associations, AL41

Encyclopedia of American biography, Garraty, John Arthur, AH60

—— Sternstein, Jerome L., AH60

Encyclopedia of American business history and biography, CH383

The encyclopedia of American comics, CF76

Encyclopedia of American crime, Sifakis, Carl, CK254

Encyclopedia of American economic history, CH49, DB42

Encyclopedia of American facts and dates, Carruth, Gorton, DA29, DB58

Encyclopedia of American film comedy, Langman, Larry, BH252

Encyclopedia of American foreign policy, DB43

Encyclopedia of American forest and conservation history, EJ176

Encyclopedia of American history, DB44

Encyclopedia of American humorists, Gale, Steven H., BE411

The encyclopedia of American intelligence and espionage, O'Toole, G. J. A., CJ541

The encyclopedia of American journalism, Paneth, Donald, AE138

Encyclopedia of American political history, CH49, DB42, DB45

Encyclopedia of American religions, Melton, J. Gordon, BC65, BC66

Encyclopedia of American school law, CB154

Encyclopedia of American silver manufacturers, Rainwater, Dorothy T., BG148

Encyclopedia of American social history, DB46

Encyclopedia of American wrestling, Chapman, Mike, BK105

The encyclopedia of ancient Egypt, Bunson, Margaret, DA123

Encyclopedia of animal care, EJ111

Encyclopedia of anthropology, CE39, CE50

The encyclopedia of applied geology, EF5, EF62, EF63

Encyclopedia of applied physics, ED14

Encyclopedia of archaeological excavations in the Holy Land, Avi-Yonah, Michael, BC194

Encyclopedia of architectural technology, Guedes, Pedro, BF234

Encyclopedia of architectural terms, Curl, James Stevens, BF241

Encyclopedia of architecture, BF234

Encyclopedia of architecture, historical, theoretical, and practical, Gwilt, Joseph, BF232

Encyclopedia of arms control and disarmament, CJ684

Encyclopedia of artificial intelligence, EK170

The encyclopedia of arts and crafts, BG19

Encyclopedia of Asian history, DE14

Encyclopedia of assassinations, Sifakis, Carl, CJ556

Encyclopedia of associations, AL41, EH159, AL41

Encyclopedia of associations. Association periodicals, AD50, AL41

Encyclopedia of associations. International organizations, AL17, AL41

Encyclopedia of associations. Regional, state, and local organizations, AL41, AL42, AL47

Encyclopedia of astronomy and astrophysics, EC26

The encyclopedia of atmospheric sciences and astrogeology, EF5

—— Fairbridge, Rhodes Whitmore, EF145

Encyclopedia of Australian art, McCulloch, Alan, BF76, BF140

Encyclopedia of automatic musical instruments, Bowers, Q. David, BJ366

Encyclopedia of banking & finance, Munn, Glenn G., CH267

Encyclopedia of banking and financial tables, CH269

An encyclopedia of battles, Eggenberger, David, DA21, DA25

The encyclopedia of beaches and coastal environments, EF4, EF5

Encyclopedia of biblical interpretation, Kasher, Menachem Mendel, BC182

Encyclopedia of biblical theology, BC130

—— Bauer, Johannes B., BC126

The encyclopedia of biochemistry, Williams, Roger John, EG325

Encyclopedia of bioethics, EH241

The encyclopedia of birds, EG260

Encyclopedia of blindness and vision impairment, Paul, T. Otis, CC189

—— Sardegna, Jill, CC189, EH90

Encyclopedia of boxing, Odd, Gilbert E., BK70

Encyclopedia of Britain, Gascoigne, Bamber, DC292

Encyclopedia of British pottery and porcelain marks, Godden, Geoffrey A., BG60

An encyclopedia of British women writers, BE623

—— Schlueter, June, BE621

—— Schlueter, Paul, BE621

Encyclopedia of business information sources, CH329

Encyclopedia of business information sources : Europe, Balachandran, M., CH329

The encyclopedia of careers and vocational guidance, CB209

Encyclopedia of chemical technology, EK51, EK52, EK53

Encyclopedia of chemistry, EE33

The encyclopedia of child abuse, Clark, Robin E., CC158
Encyclopedia of childbearing, CC225
Encyclopedia of China today, DE141
Encyclopedia of Chinese coins, Coole, Arthur Braddan, BG171
Encyclopedia of Chinese symbolism and art motives, Williams, Charles Alfred Speed, BF179
The encyclopedia of climatology, EF5, EF144
The encyclopedia of colonial and revolutionary America, DB82
Encyclopedia of common natural ingredients used in food, drugs, and cosmetics, Leung, Albert Y., EH325
Encyclopedia of community planning and environmental management, Schultz, Marilyn Spigel, CC302
Encyclopedia of comparative education and national systems of education, Postlethwaite, T. Neville, CB70
Encyclopedia of computer science, EK171, EK174
Encyclopedia of computer science and engineering, EK171
Encyclopedia of computer science and technology, EK172, EK173
Encyclopedia of consumer brands, CH564
Encyclopedia of contemporary knowledge, AB69
Encyclopedia of contemporary literary theory, BE79
Encyclopedia of cosmology, EC27
The encyclopedia of crafts, BK138
Encyclopedia of crime and justice, CK251
The encyclopedia of dance & ballet, BH141
The encyclopedia of deafness and hearing disorders, Turkington, Carol, CC189
Encyclopedia of death, CC182
The encyclopedia of depression, Roesch, Roberta, EH380
The encyclopedia of drug abuse, Evans, Glen, CC124
Encyclopedia of early childhood education, CB66
Encyclopedia of early Christianity, BC274
Encyclopedia of earth sciences, EF5
———— Fairbridge, Rhodes Whitmore, EF12
Encyclopedia of earth system science, EF6
The encyclopedia of Eastern philosophy and religion, BB31, BC57, BC479
Encyclopedia of economics, CH50, CH51
Encyclopedia of education, CB67, CB68
Encyclopedia of educational research, CB69
Encyclopedia of electronics, EK129
Encyclopedia of espionage, Seth, Ronald, CJ540
The encyclopedia of ethics, BB32
The encyclopedia of evolution, Milner, Richard, EG26
Encyclopedia of fashion, O'Hara, Georgina, BG98
Encyclopedia of feminism, Tuttle, Lisa, CC535
The encyclopedia of field and general geology, EF5, EF63
The encyclopedia of film, Monaco, James, BH283
The encyclopedia of folk, country, & western music, Stambler, Irwin, BJ326
Encyclopedia of food science, EJ152
Encyclopedia of food science and technology, EJ153
Encyclopedia of food technology, Johnson, Arnold H., EJ155
Encyclopedia of frontier biography, Thrapp, Dan L., DB175
The encyclopedia of furniture, Aronson, Joseph, BG121
Encyclopedia of gambling, Sifakis, Carl, BK137
The encyclopedia of genetic disorders and birth defects, Wynbrandt, James, EH91
The encyclopedia of geochemistry and environmental sciences, EF5
———— Fairbridge, Rhodes Whitmore, EF67
Encyclopedia of geographic information sources, CH329
The encyclopedia of geomorphology, EF5, EF7
Encyclopedia of German-American genealogical research, Smith, Anna Piszczan-Czaja, AJ90
———— Smith, Clifford Neal, AJ22, AJ90
The encyclopedia of glass, BG59
Encyclopedia of government and politics, CJ52

Encyclopedia of governmental advisory organizations, CJ134
Encyclopedia of health information sources, EH15
The encyclopedia of higher education, CB236
Encyclopedia of homosexuality, CC277
Encyclopedia of human behavior, CD20
Encyclopedia of human biology, EG20
Encyclopedia of human evolution and prehistory, CE40, DA78
Encyclopedia of human rights, CK99
The encyclopedia of igneous and metamorphic petrology, EF5, EF253
Encyclopedia of immunology, EG21, EH85
Encyclopedia of Indian art, references, symbols, Aryan, K. C., BF178
Encyclopedia of Indian philosophies, BB18, BB33
Encyclopedia of industrial chemical analysis, EE27
Encyclopedia of information systems and services, AK192
Encyclopedia of investments, CH301
The encyclopedia of jazz, Feather, Leonard G., BJ300
Encyclopedia of jazz in the seventies, Feather, Leonard G., BJ300
———— Gitler, Ira, BJ300
Encyclopedia of jazz in the sixties, Feather, Leonard G., BJ300
Encyclopedia of Jewish concepts, BC557
The encyclopedia of Judaism, BC547
The encyclopedia of language and linguistics, BD34, BD35
Encyclopedia of learning and memory, CD110
Encyclopedia of legal information sources, CK124
Encyclopedia of library and information science, AK36
Encyclopedia of library history, AK72
Encyclopedia of literature and criticism, BE65
Encyclopedia of living artists in America, BF151
Encyclopedia of major league baseball teams, Dewey, Donald, BK54
The encyclopedia of mammals, EG292
The encyclopedia of management, CH611
The encyclopedia of marine resources, Firth, Frank E., EF217
Encyclopedia of marine sciences, EF219
The encyclopedia of marriage, divorce, and the family, DiCanio, Margaret, CC224
Encyclopedia of materials science and engineering, EH176, EK261, EK262
Encyclopedia of medical devices and instrumentation, EH86
Encyclopedia of medical history, McGrew, Roderick E., EH195
Encyclopedia of medical organizations and agencies, EH159
Encyclopedia of medical sources, Kelly, Emerson Crosby, EH203
Encyclopedia of microbiology, EG22
Encyclopedia of microcomputers, EK172, EK173
The encyclopedia of microscopy, Clark, George Lindenberg, EG19
The encyclopedia of microscopy and microtechnique, Gray, Peter, EG23
The encyclopedia of mineralogy, EF5, EF179
Encyclopedia of minerals, Roberts, Willard Lincoln, EF186
Encyclopedia of modern art auction prices, Bérard, Michèle, BF108
Encyclopedia of modern murder, Seaman, Donald, CK254
———— Wilson, Colin, CK254
Encyclopedia of modern physics, ED15
The encyclopedia of modern war, Parkinson, Roger, CJ576
Encyclopedia of Mormonism, BC371
Encyclopedia of mortgage & real estate finance, CH534
Encyclopedia of mountaineering, Unsworth, Walter, BK120
Encyclopedia of murder, Pitman, Patricia, CK254
———— Wilson, Colin, CK254
Encyclopedia of music in Canada, BJ134

Encyclopedia of mystery and detection, Penzler, Otto, BE267
———— Steinbrunner, Chris, BE267
Encyclopedia of Napoleon's Europe, Palmer, Alan, DC197
Encyclopedia of nationalism, Snyder, Louis Leo, CJ34
The encyclopedia of Native American religions, Hirschfelder, Arlene B., BC567
The encyclopedia of natural insect & disease control, EJ21
Encyclopedia of neuroscience, EH87
The encyclopedia of New England, DB153
The encyclopedia of North American sports history, Hickok, Ralph, BK16
Encyclopedia of occultism, Spence, Lewis, CD134
Encyclopedia of occultism & parapsychology, CD134
The encyclopedia of oceanography, EF5
———— Fairbridge, Rhodes Whitmore, EF216
Encyclopedia of pacifism, Huxley, Aldous, CJ685
The encyclopedia of paleontology, EF5, EF235
The encyclopedia of parapsychology and psychical research, Berger, Arthur S., CD133
Encyclopedia of philosophy, BB34
The encyclopedia of phobias, fears, and anxieties, Doctor, Ronald M., CD100, EH378
Encyclopedia of photography, International Center of Photography, BF341
Encyclopedia of physical education, fitness, and sports, BK15
Encyclopedia of physical science and technology, EA79, EC26, ED14, ED15, EF6
Encyclopedia of physical science and technology yearbook, EA165
Encyclopedia of physical sciences and engineering information sources, EA14
Encyclopedia of physics, EC29, ED16, ED17
———— Besancon, Robert Martin, ED12
Encyclopedia of pieced quilt patterns, Brackman, Barbara, BG163
Encyclopedia of poetry and poetics, BE329
The encyclopedia of police science, CK252
Encyclopedia of policy studies, CA34
Encyclopedia of polymer science and engineering, EK284, EK285
Encyclopedia of polymer science and technology, EK285
Encyclopedia of pop, rock & soul, Stambler, Irwin, BJ351
Encyclopedia of popular music, BJ347
Encyclopedia of pottery & porcelain, 1800–1960, Cameron, Elisabeth, BG58
Encyclopedia of professional management, CH622
Encyclopedia of psychology, CD21
Encyclopedia of public affairs information sources, CA1
Encyclopedia of public international law, CK100
An encyclopedia of quotations about music, BJ163
Encyclopedia of recorded sound in the United States, BJ392
Encyclopedia of religion, BC51, BC58
———— Eliade, Mircea, BC55
Encyclopedia of rock, BJ345
Encyclopedia of rock music on film, Sandahl, Linda J., BJ363
The encyclopedia of romanticism, BE759
Encyclopedia of Russian history, Paxton, John, DC567
Encyclopedia of sailing, BK122
Encyclopedia of school administration & supervision, CB180
The encyclopedia of science fiction, BE286
Encyclopedia of science fiction and fantasy through 1968, Tuck, Donald H., BE286
Encyclopedia of security management, CK253
The encyclopedia of sedimentology, EF5, EF64
Encyclopedia of senior citizens information sources, CC96
Encyclopedia of sleep and dreaming, CD111
Encyclopedia of social work, CC46
Encyclopedia of sociology, CC14, CC15
The encyclopedia of soil science, EF5, EJ22

The encyclopedia of solid earth geophysics, EF5, EF65

Encyclopedia of Southern Baptists, BC325

Encyclopedia of Southern culture, DB158

The encyclopedia of Southern history, DB159

Encyclopedia of special education, CB196

—— Mann, Lester, CB195

—— Reynolds, Cecil R., CB195

The encyclopedia of sports, Menke, Frank Grant, BK17

Encyclopedia of statistical sciences, EB34

The encyclopedia of structural geology and plate tectonics, EF5, EF66

The encyclopedia of suicide, Evans, Glen, CC183

Encyclopedia of swimming, Besford, Pat, BK100

The encyclopedia of technical market indicators, Colby, Robert W., CH300

Encyclopedia of telecommunications, CH481

Encyclopedia of television, BH313

—— Terrace, Vincent, BH306

The encyclopedia of television, cable, and video, Reed, Robert M., BH315

Encyclopedia of terrorism and political violence, Thackrah, John Richard, CJ558

Encyclopedia of textiles, BG155

—— Jerde, Judith, BG155

Encyclopedia of textiles, fibers, and nonwoven fabrics, Grayson, Martin, BG155

Encyclopedia of the American Constitution, CK130

Encyclopedia of the American judicial system, CK131

Encyclopedia of the American left, DB129

Encyclopedia of the American legislative system, CJ116

Encyclopedia of the American presidency, CJ178

Encyclopedia of the American religious experience, BC59

Encyclopedia of the American Revolution, Boatner, Mark Mayo, DB92

The encyclopedia of the American theatre, 1900–1975, Bronner, Edwin, BH98

The encyclopedia of the biological sciences, Gray, Peter, EG24, EG37

The encyclopedia of the Central West, Carpenter, Allan, DB173

Encyclopedia of the chemical elements, Hampel, Clifford A., EE30

Encyclopedia of the Confederacy, DB117

Encyclopedia of the early church, BC275

Encyclopedia of the Far West, Carpenter, Allan, DB173

Encyclopedia of the First World, Kurian, George Thomas, CJ28

Encyclopedia of the Jewish religion, Werblowsky, R. J. Zwi, BC547

—— Wigoder, Geoffrey, BC547

The encyclopedia of the Lutheran church, Bodensieck, Julius, BC355

The encyclopedia of the Midwest, Carpenter, Allan, DB160

Encyclopedia of the New York stage, 1920–1930, Leiter, Samuel L., BH98, BH100

Encyclopedia of the North American colonies, DB83

Encyclopedia of the opera, BJ248

Encyclopedia of the Renaissance, Bergin, Thomas Goddard, DA146

Encyclopedia of the Second World, Karch, John J., CJ28

—— Kurian, George Thomas, CJ28

Encyclopedia of the social sciences, CA36, CA44

The encyclopedia of the Third Reich, DC255

—— Snyder, Louis Leo, DC258, DC259

The encyclopedia of the Third World, Kurian, George Thomas, CJ28, CJ35, CJ39, CJ96

The encyclopedia of the United Nations and international agreements, Osmańszyk, Edmund Jan, AF41

Encyclopedia of the world's air forces, Taylor, Michael John Haddrick, CJ579

Encyclopedia of theater music, Lewine, Richard, BJ267

—— Simon, Alfred, BJ267

Encyclopedia of themes and subjects in painting, Daniel, Howard, BF165

Encyclopedia of theology, BC231

Encyclopedia of third parties in the United States, Kruschke, Earl R., CJ261

Encyclopedia of tropical fishes, Axelrod, Herbert R., EG284

Encyclopedia of twentieth-century American folk art and artists, BG35

Encyclopedia of twentieth-century architecture, BF233

Encyclopedia of twentieth-century journalists, Taft, William H., AE152

Encyclopedia of Ukraine, DC543

Encyclopedia of United States silver & gold commemorative coins, 1892–1954, Breen, Walter H., BG193

—— Swiatek, Anthony, BG193

Encyclopedia of U.S. marks on pottery, porcelain & clay, BG71

The encyclopedia of Victoriana, BG40

The encyclopedia of violence, DiCanio, Margaret, CC33

Encyclopedia of women's associations worldwide, AL18

Encyclopedia of world architecture, Steirlin, Henri, BF253

Encyclopedia of world art, BF73, BF77

Encyclopedia of world crime, CK254

Encyclopedia of world cultures, CE41, CE44

The encyclopedia of world facts and dates, Carruth, Gorton, DA29

Encyclopedia of world government, Clements, John, CJ94

Encyclopedia of world literature in the 20th century, BE66, BE1510

The encyclopedia of world Methodism, BC363

The encyclopedia of world regional geology, EF5

—— Fairbridge, Rhodes Whitmore, EF68

The encyclopedia of world theater, BH68

Encyclopedia of world travel, CL380

Encyclopedia of Zionism and Israel, BC548

Encyclopedia Talmudica, BC549, CK239

Encyclopedia USA, DB47

Encyclopedias

American and English, AB2, AB3, AB4, AB5, AB6, AB7, AB8, AB9, AB10, AB11, AB12, AB13, AB14

bibliography, AB15

juvenile, AB17, AB18, AB19, AB22

juvenile, AB20

Brazilian, AB80, AB81

Chinese, AB29

Czech, AB30, AB31, AB32

Danish, AB33, AB34, AB35

databases, AB2, AB13, AB18, AB22, AB23, AB24, AB25, AB26, AB27, AB28, AB56

Dutch, AB36, AB37

electronic, AB23, AB24, AB25, AB26, AB27, AB28

Finnish, AB39

French, AB40, AB41, AB42, AB43, AB44, AB45, AB46

German, AB47, AB48, AB49, AB50, AB51, AB52

Greek, AB53, AB54, AB55

guides, AB1

Hebrew, AB56, AB57

Hungarian, AB58, AB59, AB60, AB61

indexes, AB16

Iranian, AB38

Italian, AB62, AB63, AB64, AB65, AB66, AB67

Japanese, AB68, AB69, AB70

bibliography, AB72

juvenile, AB21

Norwegian, AB73, AB74, AB75

Polish, AB76, AB77, AB78

Portuguese, AB79, AB80, AB81

reviews, AB1

Russian, AB82, AB83, AB84, AB85, AB86, AB88, AB89

annuals, AB91

bibliography, AB90

translations, AB87

Spanish, AB92, AB93, AB94, AB95, AB96

Swedish, AB97, AB98, AB99

Swiss, AB100, DC530

Turkish, AB101, AB102

Encyclopedic dictionary of accounting and finance, Shim, Jae K., CH253

Encyclopedic dictionary of chemical technology, Noether, Dorit, EK54

Encyclopedic dictionary of electronic terms, Traister, John E., EK130

The encyclopedic dictionary of erotic wisdom, Camphausen, Rufus C., CC279

Encyclopedic dictionary of language and languages, Crystal, David, BD35, BD37

An encyclopedic dictionary of Marxism, socialism and communism, Wilczynski, Jozef, CJ522

Encyclopedic dictionary of mathematics, EB35

The encyclopedic dictionary of physical geography, CL46

The encyclopedic dictionary of psychology, CD22

—— Harré, Rom, CD82, CD95, CD99, CD119

—— Lamb, Roger, CD82, CD95, CD99, CD119

Encyclopedic dictionary of religion, BC60

Encyclopedic dictionary of Roman law, Berger, Adolf, CK52

The encyclopedic dictionary of science, EA91

Encyclopedic dictionary of semiotics, BD52

The encyclopedic dictionary of sociology, CC18

Encyclopedic dictionary of sports medicine, Tver, David F., EH127

Encyclopedic dictionary of technical terms, Collazo, Javier L., EA132

Encyclopedic dictionary of the sciences of language, Ducrot, Oswald, BD38

Encyclopedic dictionary of yoga, Feuerstein, Georg, BC487

Encyclopedic directory of ethnic newspapers and periodicals in the United States, Wynar, Lubomyr Roman, AE34

An encyclopedic outline of Masonic, Hermetic, Qabbalistic, and Rosicrucian symbolical philosophy, Hall, Manly Palmer, AL73, AL75

Encyclopédie, AB41

Encyclopédie de la guerre 1939–1945, Baudot, Marcel, DA208

Encyclopédie de la musique, BJ117, BJ120

Encyclopédie de la mystique juive, BC550

L'Encyclopédie de la République unie du Cameroun, DD137

Encyclopédie de l'architecture et de la construction, Planat, Paul Amédée, BF237

Encyclopédie de l'utopie, des voyages extraordinaires, et de la science fiction, Versins, Pierre, BE308

Encyclopédie de l'utopie et de la science fiction, BE308

Encyclopédie des citations, BE92

Encyclopédie des gaz, EE28

Encyclopédie des musiques sacrées, BJ118

Encyclopédie du bon français dans l'usage contemporain, Dupré, P., AC367

Encyclopédie du cinéma, Boussinot, Roger, BH247

Encyclopédie du meuble du XVᵉ siècle jusqu'à nos jours, Bajot, Édouard, BG122

Encyclopédie internationale des photographes, BF353

Encyclopédie internationale des photographes de 1839 à nos jours, Auer, Michèle, BF353

Encyclopédie philosophique universelle, BB35

Encyclopédie polonaise, DC480

Encyclopédie théologique, Migne, Jacques Paul, BC400

Encyclopedie van de Geschiedenis der Middeleeuwen, DA127

Encyclopedie van de Nederlandse Antillen, DB448

Encyclopedie van Suriname, DB391

Encyklopädie der mathematischen Wissenschaften mit Einschluss ihrer Anwendungen, EB36

Encyklopedia języka polskiego, BD192

Encyklopedia powszechna PWN, AB76

Encyklopédia slovenská, DC129

Encyklopédia slovenských spisovateľov, BE1425

Encyklopedia wiedzy o języku polskim, BD192
Encyklopedja pow-szechna z ilustracjami i mapami, AB77
Endangered and threatened plants of the United States, Ayensu, Edward S., EG145
Endangered birds of the world, Vincent, Jack, EG278
Endangered species, EG145, EG156, EG162, EG206, EG237, EG259, EG270, EG278
   see also **Wildlife**
Endangered vertebrates, Baker, Sylva, EG206
Endocrinology abstracts, EG14
Energy, EK218
  abstract journals, EK215
  atlases, EK223
  bibliography, EK213, EK214, EK216, EK219
  databases, EK215
  directories, EK222, EK296
  guides, EK216
  handbooks, EK217, EK220, EK221
  statistics
    bibliography, EK211
Energy, Crowley, Maureen, EK216, AF59
Energy handbook, Loftness, Robert L., EK220
Energy information guide, Weber, R. David, EK213, EK214
Energy research abstracts, EK294
  —— United States. Department of Energy, EK215
Energy statistics, Balachandran, Sarojini, EK211
Energy technology handbook, EK217
Energy update, Weber, R. David, EK214
Engelbarts, Rudolf. *Librarian authors,* AK89
Engelbrecht, Elmarie. *Bronne by die studie van Afrikaanse prosawerke,* BE1536
Engeldinger, Eugene A. *Black American fiction,* BE517
  —— *Spouse abuse,* CC209
Engeli, Christian. *Modern urban history research in Europe, USA, and Japan,* CC299
Engelmann, Wilhelm. *Bibliotheca historico-naturalis,* EG209
  —— *Bibliotheca scriptorum classicorum,* BE991, BE992, BE1001
  —— *Bibliotheca zoologica,* EG209
Engels, Odilo. *Series episcoporum ecclesiae catholicae,* BC430
Engels, Friedrich, CJ497, CJ500, CJ520, CJ523
Engels woordenboek, Bruggencate, Karel ten, AC296
Engelsk-dansk ordbog, Kjaerulff Nielsen, Bernhard, AC288
Engelsk-norsk ordbok, AC619, AC620
Engelsk-svensk ordbok, Kärre, Karl, AC765
Engelsk-svensk teknisk ordbok, Engström, Einar, EA135
Engelstad, Irene. *Norsk kvinnelitteraturhistorie,* BE1344
Engelstoft, Povl. *Danmark,* CL132
  —— *Dansk biografisk leksikon,* AH183
  —— *Hagerups Illustrerede Konversations Leksikon,* AB34
Engen, Rodney K. *Dictionary of Victorian engravers, print publishers and their works,* BF323
  —— *Dictionary of Victorian wood engravers,* BF323, BF359
Engineered materials abstracts, EK258, EK260
•*Engineered materials abstracts (EMA),* EK258
Engineered materials handbook, EK264, EK274
Engineering
  abbreviations, EA98, EA99
  abstract journals, EA72, EF118
    bibliography, EA76
  bibliography, EA14, EA20, EA237, EK3, EK4, EK5
    current, EA35, EA36
  biography, EA20, EK21
  book reviews
    indexes, EA54
  congresses and meetings, AL26, EA203, EA204, EA205, EA206, EA209
    indexes, EA207
  databases, EA67, EA75, EK6, EK7

dictionaries, EA84, EA88
  bilingual
    French-English, EA109, EK9
    German-English, EA112, EA114, EK10
    Japanese-English, EA119
    Russian-English, EA130
    Spanish-English, EA133
  multilingual, EA102
directories, EA145, EK13
  bibliography, EA140, EH148
dissertations, EA58
encyclopedias, EA79, EA81, EA83
guides, EA1, EA2, EA3, EA4, EA5, EA6, EA7, EB3, ED2, EK1, EK2
handbooks, EA149, EA153, EK16, EK17, EK18, EK19
  bibliography, EA152
indexes, EA67, EA74, EA75, EK6, EK7, EK8
  bibliography, EA76
institutional and biographical directories, EK15
library catalogs, EK4, EK5
periodicals, EA38, EA39, EA43, EA44
  bibliography, EA41, EE18
  early works to 1800, EA243
  union lists, EA45
reference books, EA10
tables, EA155, EA156
thesauruses, EK11
yearbooks, EA165, EA167
Engineering (by country or region)
  Europe
    directories, EA142
  Japan
    periodicals, EA48, EA50
Engineering (by period)
  early works to 1800
    bibliography, EA227
  see also **Chemical engineering; Electrical and electronic engineering; Human engineering; Industrial engineering; Mechanical engineering; Nuclear engineering; Plant engineering and maintenance; Production engineering; Structural engineering; Technology; Transportation engineering**
Engineering alloys, EK282
Engineering index, EA41, EE18, EK7, EK11
The Engineering index cumulative index, EK8
Engineering Index, Inc. *Bibliographic guide for editors & authors,* EA38
Engineering literature guides, EK1
Engineering mathematics handbook, Tuma, Jan J., EK19
Engineering schools
  directories, EK12
Engineering Societies Library. *Classed subject catalog,* EK4, EK5
Engineers, EK20
  biography, EA172, EA179, EA190, EK13, EK14
  directories, EA137, EK14
Engineers (by country or region)
  Canada
    biography, EA185
  United States, EK21
    biography, EA184, EA185
Engineer's guide to high-temperature materials, Clauss, Francis Jacob, EK273
England
  atlases, CL137
  gazetteers, CL137, CL138
  place-names, CL193
England (by subject)
  education, CB44
    dictionaries, CB76
  folklore and popular culture, CF85
  history, CC624
  place-names, CL136, CL192, CL201
England, Day, Alan Edwin, DC273
Englanti-suomi suursanakirja, Hurme, Raija, AC322
Englantilais-suomalainen koulusanakirja, Wuolle, Aino, AC325
Englantilais-suomalainen sanakirja, Tuomikoski, Aune, AC324

Englantilais-suomalais-englantilainen yleiskielen käyttösanakirja, Särkkä, Heikki, AC323
Englefield, Dermot. *Information sources in politics and political science,* CJ2
Englesko-hrvatski ili srpski rječnik, Drvodelić, Milan, AC713
Englesko-srpskohrvatski rečnik, Benson, Morton, AC710
English, Richard A. *Black American families, 1965–1984,* CC206
English-Albanian dictionary, Kici, Gasper, AC207
  —— Mann, Stuart Edward, AC208
English-Amharic context dictionary, Leslau, Wolf, AC209, AC211
English and American drama of the nineteenth century, BE640
English and American plays of the nineteenth century, BE464
English and American stage productions, Dubois, William R., BH42
English and American studies in German, BE419
The English and Scottish popular ballads, BE632
  —— Child, Francis James, BJ314
  —— Kittredge, George Lyman, BE632
  —— Sargent, Helen Child, BE632
English-Arabic and Arabic-English dictionary, Wortabet, John, AC223
English-Arabic lexicon, Badger, George Percy, AC212
English Arabic vocabulary of the modern and colloquial Arabic of Egypt, Spiro, Socrates, AC221
English architecture, Curl, James Stevens, BF241
English as a second language, CB30
  bibliography, BD110
  dissertations, BD109
  handbooks, BD111
English Association. *The year's work in English studies,* BE589
English ayres, Swanekamp, Joan, BJ275
English-Basque dictionary, Aulestia, Gorka, AC231
English Bible from KJV to NIV, Lewis, Jack Pearl, BC94
English Bible in America, Hills, Margaret Thorndike, BC94, BC97, BC101
English biography before 1700, Stauffer, Donald Alfred, AH239
English-Bulgarian dictionary, AC239
English-Canadian literature to 1900, Moyles, R. G., BE830
English catalogue of books, AA686
English-Chinese and Chinese-English glossary of demography, CG34
English-Chinese dictionary of furniture industry, Li Chung, BG125
An English-classical dictionary for the use of taxonomists, Woods, Robert S., EG46
English convicts in colonial America, Coldham, Peter Wilson, AJ61
An English-Cornish dictionary, Nance, Robert Morton, AC274
English-Croatian and Croatian-English dictionary, AC711
English-Croatian or Serbian dictionary, AC713
English-Czech and Czech-English dictionary, AC281
English-Czech dictionary, Hais, Karel, AC279
English-Czech technical dictionary, EA106
English dialect dictionary, Wright, Joseph, AC156
English Dialect Society. *Dictionary of English plant-names,* EG120
  —— *English dialect dictionary,* AC156
The English dictionary from Cawdrey to Johnson, 1604–1755, Starnes, DeWitt Talmage, AC8
English drama
  (by period)
    18th century, BH47
    medieval
      bibliography, BE635
    Restoration, BH47

bibliography, BE453, BE460, BE635, BE636, BE637, BE638, BE639, BE640, BE641, BE642, BE643, BE644, BE645, BE646, BE647, BE648, BE649, BE650, BE651, BE652, BE653, BE654, BE655, BE656, BE657, BE659, BE661, BH42
  chronologies, BE660, BE661
  handbooks, BE659
  indexes, BE662
  women authors
    bibliography, BE456
English drama (by subject)
  history, BE467, BE659, BE663, BE664, BE665, BE666, BE667
English drama, 1660–1800, Link, Frederick M., BE647
English drama, 1900–1930, Nicoll, Allardyce, BE666
English drama 1900–1950, Mikail, E. H., BE638
English drama and theatre, 1800–1900, Conolly, Leonard W., BE639
English drama, excluding Shakespeare, BE641
English drama of the nineteenth century, Ellis, James, BE639, BE640
English drama to 1660 excluding Shakespeare, Penninger, Frieda Elaine, BE652
English English, Schur, Norman W., AC83
English-Estonian dictionary, AC308
English fiction
  bibliography, BE474, BE668, BE669, BE670, BE671, BE672, BE673, BE674, BE675, BE678, BE679, BE680, BE681, BE682, BE685, BE686, BE687, BE690
  biobibliography, BE689
  chronologies, BE679, BE681
  encyclopedias, BE689
  regional
    bibliography, BE677
  reviews of research, BE668, BE673, BE686
English fiction (by period)
  19th century, BE689, BE690
    bibliography, BE683
  20th century, BE685
  to 1660
    bibliography, BE676
English fiction (by subject)
  criticism, BE692
  history, BE692
English fiction, 1660–1800, Beasley, Jerry C., BE670
English fiction, 1900–1950, Rice, Thomas Jackson, BE682
English fiction of the eighteenth century, 1700–1789, Probyn, Clive, BE691
English-Finnish dictionary, AC324
English-Finnish-English general dictionary, AC323
English-Finnish general dictionary, AC322
English-French-Spanish-Russian manual of the terminology of public international law (law of peace) and international organizations, Paenson, Isaac, CK103
English-French-Spanish-Russian manual of the terminology of the law of armed conflicts and of international humanitarian organizations, Paenson, Isaac, CK104
English-French-Spanish-Russian systematic glossary of the terminology of statistical methods, Paenson, Isaac, CG27
English/French visual dictionary, AC338
English-Georgian dictionary, Gvardzhaladze, Tamara, AC398
English-German technical and engineering dictionary, DeVries, Louis, EA112
——— Herrmann, Theo M., EA112
English goldsmiths and their marks, Jackson, Charles, BG138
English Gothic, Spector, Robert Donald, BE292
English-Greek dictionary, Woodhouse, Sidney Chawner, AC448
An English-Hausa dictionary, Newman, Roxana Ma, AC811
English-Hebrew dictionary, Kaufman, Judah, AC480
English heraldry, Boutell, Charles, AJ148
English historical documents, DC297

English historical facts, 1485–1603, Powell, Ken, DC323
English historical poetry, 1476–1603, Gutierrez, Nancy A., BE714
English-Hungarian technical dictionary, Nagy, Ernő, EA115
English-Indonesian dictionary, Echols, John M., AC517
——— Shadily, Hassan, AC517
English-Irish dictionary, De Bhaldraithe, Tomás, AC520
English-Japanese, Japanese-English dictionary of computer and data-processing terms, Ferber, Gene, EK191
English-Khmer dictionary, Huffman, Franklin E., AC563
English language
  abbreviations, AC42, AC44, AC45, AC46
    dictionaries, AC43
  Americanisms, AC83, AC88, AC106, AC152
  bibliography, BD91, BE407
    current, BD90, BE588, BE589
  composition, CB218
    bibliography, BD95, BE348, BE364
  dialects
    African-American, BD103
    American, BD107
      southern states, BD106
    bibliography, BD108
    Canadian, BD105
    Great Britain
      atlases, DD104
  dictionaries, AC29, AC36, AC79
    abridged, AC31, AC35, AC41
      American, AC15, AC16, AC17, AC18, AC19, AC20
      English, AC37, AC38, AC39, AC40
    American
      juvenile, AC21, AC22, AC26, AC27
    Anglo-Norman, AC168
    Anglo-Saxon, AC172, AC173, AC174
    bibliography, AC2, AC3, AC4, AC5, AC6, AC7, AC8
    eponyms, AC49
    etymology, AC47, AC48, AC51, AC52, AC53, AC55, AC56, AC57, AC58, AC59, AC60, AC62, AC63, AC64, AC82
    foreign words and phrases, AC185, AC186, AC187, AC188
    juvenile, AC23, AC24, AC25, AC28
    Middle English, AC175, AC176
    obscene words, AC130, AC133
    pronunciation, AC105, AC108
      American, AC106
    regional and dialect, BH91
      American, AC148, AC149, AC150, AC151, AC152, AC153, AC154, AC155
      Anglo-Indian, AC162
      Anglo-Saxon, AC169, AC170
      Australian, AC177, AC178, AC179, AC180
      Bahamian, AC161
      Canadian, AC158, AC159, AC160
      Commonwealth, AC157, AC158
      English, AC156
      Jamaica, AC157
      Scottish, AC163, AC166, AC167
      South Africa, AC181, AC183
      South African, AC182
    unabridged, AC32
      American, AC9, AC10, AC11, AC12, AC13, AC14
      databases, AC33
      English, AC30, AC33, AC34
  dictionaries (by period)
    Anglo-Saxon, AC171
  dissertations, BE594
  encyclopedias, BD94
  etymology, AC100
    dictionaries, AC50, AC54, AC61
  euphemisms, AC125, AC127, AC130, AC133
    dictionaries, AC134
  faculty
    directories, BD93

  figures of speech, BE89
  glossaries, vocabularies, etc, CC540
  grammar
    bibliography, BD114
    handbooks, BD94
    history, BD98
      bibliography, BD97, BD100
  homonyms, AC75
  homophones, AC89
  idioms and usage, AC66, AC67, AC68, AC69, AC70, AC71, AC72, AC73, AC74, AC76, AC77, AC80, AC81, AC83, AC84, AC85, AC86, AC87, AC88, AC89, AC90
    dictionaries, AC78
    indexes, AC91
  morphology
    bibliography, BD92
  new words, AC92, AC93, AC94, AC95, AC96
  obscene words
    dictionaries, CJ616
  obsolete and provincial words, AC97, AC99, AC100, AC101, BC135
  periodicals, BE170
  pronunciation, AC75, AC98, AC102, AC103, AC107, BH91
    dictionaries, AC104, AC109
  punctuation, AC110, AC111, AC112
  regional and dialect
    India
      bibliography, BE1563
  rhymes, AC113, AC114, AC116, AC117
  slang, AC123, AC125, AC130, AC131, AC132, AC133, CC283
    dictionaries, AC118, AC119, AC120, AC121, AC122, AC124, AC127, AC128, AC129, AC134, CC284, CJ616
      American, AC126, AC135
  social aspects, CC540
  southern states
    bibliography, BD106
  style manuals, BD96
    bibliography, BD95
  synonyms and antonyms, AC74, AC136, AC137, AC138, AC139, AC140, AC141, AC142, AC143, AC144, AC145, AC146, AC147
  syntax
    bibliography, BD92
  teaching, CB118
  usage, CA55
    handbooks, BD96
  variation
    bibliography, BD108
    encyclopedias, BD94
  versification
    bibliography, BE696
English language (by country or region)
  United States, BE407
English language (by period)
  Middle English
    bibliography, BD102
  Old English
    bibliography, BD99, BD102
    dissertations, BD101, BE730
    periodicals, BE729
English language and orientation programs in the United States, CB161, CB269
English-language dictionaries, 1604–1900, O'Neill, Robert Keating, AC6
English language equivalent editions of foreign language serials, Gremling, Richard C., AD9
English language notes, BE40
English language publications from Pakistan, AA924
English-Latvian dictionary, AC596
English legal history, Hines, W. D., CK217
The English literary journal to 1900, White, Robert B., BE592
English literary journals, 1900–1950, Stanton, Michael N., BE591
English literature
  abstract journals, BE419
  atlases, BE628

bibliography, BE393, BE396, BE398, BE583, BE585, BE586, BE611, BE760, BE813, BE816
  current, BD90, BE588, BE589
bibliography (by period)
  20th century, BE815
bibliography of bibliography, BE587
biobibliography, BE201, BE581, BE584, BE608, BE622, BE626
biography, BE447, BE624, BE625
book reviews
  indexes, BE744
chronologies, BE612, BE613
collections, BE618, BE619
criticism, BE426, BE595
  bibliography, BE29, BE760
  collections, BE596, BE597, BE598, BE599, BE600, BE601
  dissertations, BE424, BE593, BE594
encyclopedias, BE608, BE610, BE611, BE758
faculty
  directories, BD93
gazetteers, BE628, BE629
guidebooks, BE614, BE627, BE628, BE629
guides, BE2, BE393, BE396, BE398, BE580
handbooks, BE764
library catalogs, BE583
manuscripts, BE602
  catalogs, BE604
  indexes, BE603
  union lists, BE605
manuscripts and archives, BE429
periodicals, BE590, BE591, BE592
women authors
  bibliography, BE401, BE412, BE740, BE750
  biobibliography, BE607, BE620, BE621, BE623
English literature (by country or region)
Commonwealth
  biography, BE817
English literature (by period)
16th–17th centuries
  handbooks, BE739
19th century
  bibliography, BE752, BE753, BE754, BE756
  book reviews, BE757
  dissertations, BE751
  guides, BE755
  manuscripts and archives., BE606
20th century, BE764
  bibliography, BE762
  bibliography of bibliography, BE763
  reviews of research, BE414
Middle English
  bibliography, BE733, BE734, BE735, BE736
  indexes, BE733
  manuscripts, BE733, BE735
  reviews of research, BE734
Old and Middle English
  bibliography, BE1082
Old English, BE604
  bibliography, BE728, BE731
  dissertations, BD101, BE730
  manuscripts, BE731
  periodicals, BE729
Restoration and 18th century
  bibliography, BE742, BE743, BE745, BE746, BE747
  book reviews, BE744, BE748
  to 1660
    bibliography, BE676, BE738, BE740, BE741
    library catalogs, BE737
Victorian period
  musical settings, BJ278, BJ279
English literature (by subject)
  history, BE615, BE616, BE617
  musical settings, BJ278, BJ279
  World Wars, DA194
English literature, Harvard University. Library, BE583
English literature, 1660–1800, BE743
English literature and backgrounds, 1660–1700, Duggan, Margaret M., BE742
English-Lithuanian dictionary, AC600, AC604

English local history handlist, DC353
English mediaeval architects, Harvey, John Hooper, BF261
English-modern Greek and modern Greek-English dictionary, Kykkōtēs, Hierotheos, AC464
English-Norwegian dictionary, Bjerke, Lucie, AC618
  —— Kirkeby, Willy, AC620
English-Norwegian technical dictionary, Ansteinsson, John, EA121
  —— Reiersen, Olav, EA121
The English novel, BE674
  —— Dyson, A. E., BE673
English novel, 1578–1956, Baird, Donald, BE206, BE675
  —— Bell, Inglis Freeman, BE206, BE671, BE675
English novel, 1740–1850, Block, Andrew, BE681
English novel, a panorama, Stevenson, Lionel, BE691
English novel explication, BE675
  —— Dyson, Anne Jane, BE671
  —— Palmer, Helen H., BE671
English novel in the magazines, 1740–1815, Mayo, Robert Donald, BE669
English-Old English, Old English-English dictionary, Jember, Gregory K., AC174
English-Pali dictionary, Buddhadatta, Ambalangoda Polvattē, AC624
English place-name elements, Smith, Albert Hugh, CL201
English Place-Name Society. *Concise Oxford dictionary of English place-names,* CL193
  —— *English place-name elements,* CL201
  —— *[Survey of English place-names],* CL195
English place names, CL198
  —— Cameron, Kenneth, CL192
English poetry
  bibliography, BE489, BE490, BE694, BE695, BE698, BE699, BE700, BE701, BE702, BE703, BE704, BE705, BE706, BE707, BE709, BE710, BE711, BE713, BE714
  biobibliography, BE312, BE334
  biography, BE333
  chronologies, BE707
  collections, BE720
  criticism, BE312
  databases, BE715
  indexes, BE697, BE704, BE714, BE715
  manuscripts, BE697, BE704, BE714
  reviews of research, BE701, BE702, BE703
  women authors
    bibliography, BE708
English poetry (by period)
  18th–19th centuries, BE702
  19th century, BE703, BE706, BE713
  20th century, BE334, BE719
  Middle English, BE695, BE697, BE698
  Old English, BE695
English poetry (by subject)
  classical influences, BE716
  history, BE717, BE718, BE719
  history and criticism, BE488, BE693
  versification
    bibliography, BE696
  see also **Ballads**
English poetry, BE701, BE715
English poetry, 1660–1800, Mell, Donald C., BE711
English poetry, 1900–1950, Anderson, Emily Ann, BE694
English poetry of the First World War, Reilly, Catherine W., BE712
English poetry of the Second World War, Reilly, Catherine W., BE712
English-Polish dictionary of science and technology, EA122
English prepositional idioms, Wood, Frederick Thomas, AC90
An English pronouncing dictionary, AC105
English prose and criticism, 1900–1950, Brown, Christopher C., BE760
English prose and criticism in the nineteenth century, Hoeveler, Diane Long, BE755
  —— Wilson, Harris W., BE755

English prose fiction, 1558–1700, Salzman, Paul, BE679, BE680, BE692
English prose fiction, 1600–1700, Mish, Charles Carroll, BE679, BE680
English prose, prose fiction, and criticism to 1660, Heninger, S. K., BE738
English Renaissance prose fiction, 1500–1660, Harner, James L., BE676
English Renaissance theatre history, Stevens, David, BH45
English river names, Ekwall, Eilert, CL194
English romantic poetry, 1800–1835, Reiman, Donald H., BE713
The English romantic poets, BE702
  —— Clubbe, John, BE984
  —— Jordan, Frank, BE984
English romantic poets and essayists, Houtchens, Carolyn Washburn, BE702, BE984
  —— Houtchens, Lawrence Huston, BE702, BE984
English-Russian astronomical dictionary, EC38
English-Russian dictionary, Müller, Vladimir Karlovich, AC679
English-Russian dictionary of agriculture, EJ27
English-Russian dictionary of applied geophysics, EF88
English-Russian dictionary of geology, EF89
English-Russian nuclear dictionary, ED28
English-Russian phraseological dictionary, AC695
English-Russian polytechnical dictionary, EA126
English-Russian, Russian-English dictionary, Katzner, Kenneth, AC676
An English-SerboCroatian dictionary, Benson, Morton, AC710
English short title catalogue, AA681
English silver coinage from 1649, Rayner, P. Alan, BG190
English-Slovene and Slovene-English dictionary, Komac, Daša, AC721
English-Slovene dictionary, AC723
English-Somali dictionary, Abraham, Roy Clive, AC724
English song-books, 1651–1702, Day, Cyrus Lawrence, BJ275
The English-speaking Caribbean, Jordan, Alma, AA33
English stylistics, Bailey, Richard W., BE374
English-Swahili dictionary, Madan, Arthur Cornwallis, AC756
English-Swedish dictionary, AC765
English-Swedish Swedish-English dictionary, Petti, Vincent, AC766
English-Swedish technical dictionary, Engström, Einar, EA135
English synonyms, AC137
English-Tamil dictionary, AC775
English-Teaching Information Centre (London). *A language-teaching bibliography,* BD72
English theatrical literature, 1559–1900, Arnott, James Fullarton, BH38, BH40
  —— Robinson, John William, BH40
English-Tibetan colloquial dictionary, Bell, Charles Alfred, AC781
English-Tibetan dictionary of modern Tibetan, Goldstein, Melvyn C., AC784
English to English and Urdu dictionary, AC799
English translations from the Greek, Foster, Finley Melville Kendall, BE1028
English translations from the Spanish, 1484–1943, Pane, Remigio Ugo, BE1447
English translations from the Spanish and Portuguese to the year 1700, Allison, Antony Francis, BE1448
English-Turkish dictionary, İz, Fahir, AC790
English usage in Southern Africa, AC181
English verse, 1701–1750, Foxon, David Fairweather, BE705
English versification, 1570–1980, Brogan, Terry V. F., BE311, BE696
English-Xhosa dictionary, Fischer, A., AC809

English-Yiddish [Yiddish-English] dictionary, Harkavy, Alexander, AC815
English-Zulu Zulu-English dictionary, Doke, Clement Martyn, AC819
Engström, Einar. *Engelsk-svensk teknisk ordbok,* EA135
——— *English-Swedish technical dictionary,* EA135
——— *Svensk-engelsk teknisk ordbok,* EA135
——— *Swedish-English technical dictionary,* EA135
Enlightenment, AA622
  encyclopedias, BE749, DC19
Ensayo bibliográfico del periodo colonial de México, López Cervantes, Gonzalo, DB228
Ensayo bibliográfico mexicana del siglo XVII, Andrade, Vicente de Paula, AA457
Ensayo de bibliografía cubana de los siglos XVII y XVIII, Trelles y Govín, Carlos Manuel, AA563
Ensayo de un diccionario de la literatura, Sáinz de Robles, Federico Carlos, BE70
Ensayo de un repertorio bibliográfico venezolano, Villasana, Angel Raúl, AA551
Ensayo de una bibliografía de bibliografías mexicanas, Millares Carlo, Agustín, AA23
Enser, A. G. S. *Filmed books and plays,* BH215
——— *A subject bibliography of the First World War,* DA193
——— *Subject bibliography of the Second World War,* DA193, DA200
Enser's filmed books and plays, Baskin, Ellen, BH215
Ensign, Lynne Naylor. *The complete dictionary of television and film,* BH317
Ensign, Marie S. *Historical periodicals directory,* DA14
Ensk-Íslensk orðabók, Sören Sörensen, AC507
Ensko, Stephen Guernsey Cook. *American silversmiths and their marks IV,* BG144
Enslen, Richard A. *The constitutional law dictionary,* CK129
Ensminger, Audrey. *Foods & nutrition encyclopedia,* EH298, EJ210
Ensminger, M. Eugene. *Animal science,* EJ121
——— *Feeds & nutrition,* EJ122
——— *The stockman's handbook,* EJ135
Ente per la Storia del Socialismo e del Movimento Operaio Italiano. *Bibliografia del socialismo e del movimento operaio italiano,* CH628
Entertainment *see* **Popular entertainment**
Entin, Paula B. *Public library catalog,* AA328, BF245
Entomological nomenclature and literature, Chamberlin, Willard Joseph, EG327
Entomology, EG326, EG327, EG328, EG329, EG331, EG332, EG333, EG334, EG336, EG337, EG338
  guides, EG330
  handbooks, EG84, EG335
Entomology, Gilbert, Pamela, EG330
Entomology abstracts, EG14
Entsiklopedicheskiĭ muzykal'nyĭ slovar', BJ119
Entsiklopedicheskiĭ slovar', AB85, AB86, AB89
Entsiklopediia Bŭlgariia, DC119
ha-Entsiklopedyah ha-'ivrit, AB57
ha-Entsiklopedyah ha-Yiśre'elit ha-kelalit, AB56
Entsiklopedyah Talmudit, BC549, CK239
Entsikopediyah mikra'it, BC129
Entsyklopediia ukraïnoznavstva, DC543
Entwhisle, Barbara. *Nigerian women in development,* CC598, DD191
Die Entwicklung der Bevölkerungsforschung in Österreich nach dem Zweiten Weltkrieg, CG193
Entwistle, Noel James. *Handbook of educational ideas and practices,* CB112
•*Enviroline,* EK70
Environment abstracts, EK70
Environment and environmental problems, CH357
  abstract journals, EK67, EK70, EK71
  associations
    directories, CH114
  bibliography, EK64, EK65, EK66
  databases, EK67, EK70, EK71
  dictionaries, EK72

  directories, EK69, EK73, EK74, EK75, EK76, EK77
  encyclopedias, EF67
  handbooks, EH428, EK79, EK80, EK82, EK83
  laws, etc., CK91
  statistics, EK84
Environment and environmental problems (by country or region)
  Great Britain
    handbooks, BF284, EK81
Environment and environmental problems (by subject)
  religious aspects, BC223, EG66
  see also **Air pollution**
Environment information access, EK70
Environmental assessment, Fortlage, Catharine A., BF284, EK81
Environmental biology, Altman, Philip L., EG50
Environmental Data Service (U.S.). *Climatological data,* EF160
Environmental hazards, Miller, E. Willard, EK86
Environmental health, EH17
Environmental Hydrology Corporation. *Hydata,* EF128
Environmental impact assessment, Clark, Brian D., EK66
The environmental impact handbook, Burchell, Robert W., EK80
Environmental industries marketplace, CH357
Environmental mutagen information center file, EH421
Environmental policy, CC302
Environmental profiles, Katz, Linda Sobel, EK75
Environmental protection directory, EK73
Environmental teratology information center file, EH421
Enzyklopädie der Union der Sozialistischen Sowjetrepubliken, Wawilor, S. I., AB84
Enzyklopädie des Märchens, CF50
Enzyklopädie des Musiktheaters, BJ252
Enzyme handbook, Barman, Thomas E., EG314
Enzyme nomenclature 1984, International Union of Biochemistry. Nomenclature Committee, EG321
EPAIS, CA1
Epic and romance criticism, Coleman, Arthur, BE336
Epic poetry, BE341
  bibliography, BE336, BE1006, BE1199, BE1201
Epidemiology, EH212
  bibliography, EH404
  dictionaries, EH410
  directories, EH404
The epidemiology monitor, EH404
Episcopal Church. *Book of common prayer,* BC348
——— *The Book of Common Prayer and administration of the sacraments and other rites and ceremonies of the church,* BC347
Episcopal Church, BC344
  Book of Common Prayer, BC338, BC339, BC348, BC349
  dictionaries, BC345
  yearbooks, BC346
  see also **Anglican Communion**
The Episcopal church annual, BC346
Episcopal clerical directory, BC344
The Episcopalian's dictionary, Harper, Howard V., BC345
EPISOURCE, EH404
Epistemology, BB28
Eponymous syndromes, National Library of Medicine (U.S.). Index Section, EH118
Eponyms, AC43, AC49, AC55, AC59
  biobibliography, EH203
  dictionaries, EA85, EH99
Eponyms (by subject)
  botany, EG119
  business, CH386
  chemistry, EE137
  medicine, EH118, EH123, EH203, EH220
  ophthalmology, EH126
  psychology, CD33
  see also **Named effects**
Eponyms dictionaries index, AC53

Eponyms in psychology, Zusne, Leonard, CD33
Les épopées françaises, Gautier, Léon, BE1199
Epstein, Barbara E. *Directory of mental health libraries and information centers,* EH388
Epstein, Catherine. *A past renewed,* DA47
Epstein, Edward. *A catalogue of the Epstean collection on the history and science of photography and its applications especially to the graphic arts,* BF336
Epstein, Fritz T. *Guide to captured German documents,* DC249
Epstein, Isidore. *The Babylonian Talmud,* BC181
——— *Encyclopedia Talmudica,* BC549, CK239
Epstein, Lee. *Public interest law,* CK9
——— *Public interest law groups,* CK153
Epstein, Rosalie K. *BLS publications, 1886–1971,* CH639
Eqtedar, Reza. *A directory of Iranian periodicals,* AD198
Equal rights amendment, Equal Rights Amendment Project, CC491
——— Feinberg, Renee, CC491
Equal Rights Amendment Project. *Equal rights amendment,* CC491
Equatorial Guinea
  bibliography, DD18, DD150
  encyclopedias, DD151
  government publications
    bibliography, AF227
Equatorial Guinea (by subject)
  politics and government, DD152
Equatorial Guinea, Fegley, Randall, DD18
——— Liniger-Goumaz, Max, DD48
Equipment, corrosion, and corrosion protection, EK49
Era of Napoleon, Caldwell, Ronald J., DC178, DC191
The era of the Civil War—1820–1876, United States. Army. Military History Institute, DB113
The era of the French Revolution, Caldwell, Ronald J., DC178, DC191
Eraut, Michael. *International encyclopedia of educational technology,* CB70
Erbse, Hartmut. *Lexikon des frühgriechischen Epos,* AC447
Ercilasun, Ahmet B. *Karşılaşrmalı Türk lehçeleri sözlüğü,* AC788
Erdei, Ferenc. *Information Hungary,* DC388
Erdélyi, Arthur. *Higher transcendental functions,* EB79
——— *Tables of integral transforms,* EB80
Erdman, David V. *The Romantic movement bibliography, 1936–1970,* BE40
Erdmann, Kurt. *Oriental carpets,* BG166
——— *Seven hundred years of oriental carpets,* BG166
——— *Siebenhundert Jahre Orientteppich,* BG166
L'ère baroque en France, Arbour, Roméo, BE1203
Eren, Hasan. *Türkçe sözlük,* AC787
Ergänzungsband zu den Mitteilungen des Oberösterreichischen Landesarchiv, DC92
•*ERIC,* AK28, CB54, CB56, CB83, CD90, CD91
ERIC Clearinghouse for Junior Colleges. *Dictionary of educational acronyms, abbreviations, and initialisms,* CB78
ERIC Clearinghouse on Languages and Linguistics. *ESL theses and dissertations, 1979–80,* BD109
——— *Graduate theses and dissertations in English as a second language,* BD109
ERIC directory of education-related information centers, CB99
ERIC identifier authority list, CB82
•*ERIC on SilverPlatter,* CB56, CD91
•*ERIC retrospective files,* CB56, CD91
ERIC RIE cumulative index, AK35, CB61
Erichsen, Balder. *Dansk historisk bibliografi,* DC131
——— *Dansk personalhistorisk bibliografi,* AH185
Erickson, Eston Everett. *A bibliography of publications on Old English literature to the end of 1972,* BE728
Erickson, Hal. *Syndicated television,* BH301
Erickson, Judith B. *Directory of American youth organizations,* AL40

Erickson, Ronald E. *Infrared band handbook*, EE90
Erickson, Rosemary. *The futures markets dictionary*, CH437
Ericson, Jon M. *The debater's guide*, BE370
Eriksen, Tore Linné. *The political economy of Namibia*, DD185
Erisman, Fred. *Fifty Western writers*, BE572
Eritrea
  bibliography, DD109, DD153
Erixon, Sigurd Emanuel. *International dictionary of regional European ethnology and folklore*, CE49
Erklärung der Abkürzungen auf Münzen der neueren Zeit, des Mittelalters und des Altertums, sowie auf Denkmünzen und münzartigen Zeichen, Schlickeysen, F. W. A., BG184
Erlen, Jonathon. *The history of the health care sciences and health care, 1700–1980*, EH201
Erlewine, Michael. *All music guide*, BJ374
Erman, Adolf. *Wörterbuch der aegyptischen Sprache*, AC303
Ermisse, Gerard. *Guide du lecteur*, DC150
Ernault, É. *Grand dictionnaire français-breton*, AC238
Ernault, Émile. *Dictionnaire étymologique du breton moyen*, AC235
—— *Études grammaticales sur les langues celtiques*, AC236
—— *Glossaire moyen-breton*, AC236
Ernout, Alfred. *Dictionnaire étymologique de la langue latine*, AC579
Ernst, Carl H. *Turtles of the world*, EG247
Ernst, Charles A. S. *Alcohol and the elderly*, CC107
Ernst, Petra. *Neues Handbuch der deutschen Gegenwartsliteratur seit 1945*, BE1250
Ernst, Richard. *Comprehensive dictionary of engineering and technology*, EA109, EK9
—— *Dictionary of engineering and technology*, EA114, EK10
Erotic art, BF15
Erotic art, Burt, Eugene C., BF15
Erotic poetry, BE1194
Errores y omisiones del Diccionario de anónimos y seudónimos hispaoanoamericanos de José Toribio de Medina, Victoria, Ricardo, AA153
Ersch, J. S. *Allgemeine Encyclopädie der Wissenschaften und Künste*, AB47
Ersch und Gruber Encyclopädie, AB47
Erslew, Thomas Hansen. *Almindeligt Forfatter-Lexicon for kongeriget Danmark med tilhørende bilande, fra 1814 til 1840*, BE1087, BE1117
Erstausgaben deutscher Dichtung, Wilpert, Gero von, BE1233
Ertle, Katherine. *Science fair project index, 1960–1972*, EA31
Erweiterungs-und Folgebände zur vierten Auflage, Büchel, K. H., EE138
Escarpit, Robert. *Dictionnaire international des termes littéraires*, BE88
Eschbach, Achim. *Bibliography of semiotics, 1975–1985*, BD53
—— *Semiotik-Bibliographie I*, BD53
—— *Zeichen, Text, Bedeutung*, BD53
Eschbach-Szabó, Viktoria. *Bibliography of semiotics, 1975–1985*, BD53
Escritoras españolas del siglo XIX, Simón Palmer, María del Carmen, BE1441
Escritores de la diáspora cubana, Maratos, Daniel C., BE976
Escudero, Grecia Vasco de. *Archivos quiteños*, DB373
Esdaile, Arundell James Kennedy. *Esdaile's manual of bibliography*, AA2
—— *List of English tales and prose romances printed before 1740*, BE337, BE679
—— *National libraries of the world*, AK118
—— *Student's manual of bibliography*, AA2
Esdaile's manual of bibliography, Esdaile, Arundell James Kennedy, AA2

Esen, Erol. *Bestandsaufnahme der Literatur und Forschungen in der Bundesrepublik Deutschland sowie der EG-Veröffentlichungen zum Thema der politischen und wirtschaftlichen Beziehungen zwischen der Türkei und Westeuropa seit 1973*, DC539
Eshbach, Ovid W. *Eshbach's handbook of engineering fundamentals*, EK16
Eshbach's handbook of engineering fundamentals, Eshbach, Ovid W., EK16
Eshelby, Yvonne. *Sheppard's international directory of print and map sellers*, CL260
Eskenasy, Victor. *Bibliography of the Jews in Romania*, DC493
Eski harfli Türkçe yayınlar toplu kataloğu, AE78
Eskimo acculturation, Hippler, Arthur E., CC414
Eskimos see **Native Americans**
Eskind, Andrew H. *Index to American photographic collections*, BF344
ESL theses and dissertations, 1979–80, Cooper, Stephen, BD109
—— ERIC Clearinghouse on Languages and Linguistics, BD109
Esnault, Gaston. *Dictionnaire historique des argots français*, AC355, AC356
Espasa, AB94
Espenshade, Edward Bowman. *Goode's world atlas*, CL278
Esperabé Arteaga, Enrique. *Diccionario enciclopédico ilustrado y crítico de los hombres de España*, AH289
Esperanto see **Artificial languages**
Espinosa, Tomás. *Teatro mexicano del siglo XX, 1900–1986*, BE913
Espinosa Cordero, Nicolás. *Bibliografía ecuatoriana, 1534–1809*, AA530
—— *Estudios literarios y bibliográficos*, AA530
Espinosa Elerick, María Luz. *Annotated bibliography of technical and specialized dictionaries in Spanish-Spanish and Spanish-English, with commentary*, AC751
Espionage
  bibliography, CJ535, CJ537, CJ545, CJ546
  biography, CJ539
  dictionaries, CJ534
  encyclopedias, CJ536, CJ540
Espionage (by country or region)
  United States, CJ541, CJ544, CJ547
Esposito, Anthony. *British biographical archive*, AH224
—— *British biographical index*, AH224
Esposito, John L. *The contemporary Islamic revival*, BC496
Esposito, Vincent J. *The West Point atlas of American wars*, DB77
—— *West Point atlas of the Civil War*, DB77
Espy, Willard R. *Words to rhyme with*, AC113
Esquire's encyclopedia of 20th century men's fashions, Gale, William, BG115
—— Schoffler, O. E., BG97, BG115
ESSA libraries holdings in oceanography and marine meteorology, 1710–1967, United States. Environmental Science Services Administration, EF213
Essai de bibliographie canadienne, Gagnon, Philéas, DB182
Essai de bibliographic critique de stylistique française et romane (1955–1960), Hatzfeld, Helmut, BE1072
—— LeHir, Yves, BE1072
Essai de bibliographie du Ruanda-Urundi, Clément, Joseph R. A. M., DD135
—— Clement, Joseph R.A.M, DD198
Essai de bibliographie du Sahara français et des régions avoisinantes, Blaudin de Thé, Bernard, DD67
Essai de bibliographie Jaina, Guérinot, Armand Albert, BC506
Essai de bibliographie Ruanda-Urundi, Clément, Joseph R. A. M., AA871
Essai de bibliographie sélective et annotée sur l'Islam maghrébin contemporain, Shinar, Pessah, BC501, DD73

Essai de terminologie musicale, Vannes, René, BJ161
Essai de toponymie, Jaccard, Henri, CL213
Essai d'un dictionnaire des ouvrages anonymes et pseudonymes publiés en Belgique au XIVe siècle et principalement depuis 1830, Delecourt, Jules Victor, AA162
Essai d'une bibliographie générale du théâtre, Filippi, Joseph de, BE1184
Essai d'une notice biobibliographique sur la question d'Orient, Begescu, George, DC59
Essay and general literature index, AH12, BA4, BE37, BE239
Essays
  indexes, AH12, BA4, BE37, BE239
Essays on ancient Near Eastern literature, Hallo, William W., BC184
Esselte kartor (Firm). *Earth book world atlas*, CL277
Esselte Map Service. *The Economist atlas*, CH147
The essential adoption handbook, Alexander-Roberts, Colleen, CC232
Essential English-Vietnamese dictionary, Nguyên, Dình-Hòa, AC803
The essential guide to hiking in the United States, Cook, Charles, BK112
The essential guide to prescription drugs, EH343
The essential jazz records, Harrison, Max, BJ308
The essential Shakespeare, Champion, Larry S., BE766
Essentials of forestry practice, Stoddard, Charles Hatch, EJ190
Esslin, Martin. *The encyclopedia of world theater*, BH68
Estadística bibliográfica de la literatura chilena, Briseño, Ramón, AA515
Estadística panamena, Panama. Dirección de Estadística y Censo, CG133
Estadísticas básicas de España, 1900–1970, CG281
Estadísticas históricas, Colombia. Departamento Administrativo Nacional de Estadística, CG151
Estadísticas históricas argentinas (comparadas), Vázquez-Presedo, Vicente, CG137, DB331
Estadísticas históricas de España, CG282
Estadísticas históricas de México, CG118
Estadísticas históricas de Uruguay, 1850–1930, Rial Roade, Juan, CG160
Estadísticas vitales, Uruguay. Dirección General de Estadística y Censos, CG161
Estadisticas vitales y de salud, CG136
Estafy, George D. *The East European Newspaper Collection of the Slavic and Baltic Division, the New York Public Library*, AE42
Estatísticas demográficas, CG278
Estatísticas do registro civil, CG142
Estatísticas históricas do Brasil, CG143
ESTC, AA680, AA681
ESTC (Project). *The eighteenth century short title catalogue 1990*, AA681
Estell, Kenneth. *The African-American almanac*, CC390
Estermann, Alfred Adolph. *Deutschen Literatur-Zeitschriften, 1815–1850*, AD77
—— *Die deutschen Literatur-Zeitschriften, 1850–1880*, AD77
—— *Deutschen Literatur-Zeitschriften, 1850–1880*, AD76
Estes, J. Worth. *Dictionary of protopharmacology*, EH366
Estes, Kenneth W. *The Marine officer's guide*, CJ631
Esthetics see **Aesthetics**
Estienne, Henri. *Thēsauros tēs hellēnikēs glōssēs*, AC442
Estimating handbook, EK110
Estnisch-deutsches wörterbuch, AC309
Estonia, DC135
  bibliography, AA608, DC70, DC134
  manuscripts and archives, AK153, DC561
Estonian-English dictionary, AC307, AC308
Estonian language
  dictionaries, AC305, AC306
    bilingual
      Estonian-English, AC307, AC308

Estonian-German, AC309
Estonian literature, BE1123
  biobibliography, BE1125
  handbooks, BE989
  translations, BE1124
Estonian literature (by subject)
  history, BE1125
Estonian literature, Nirk, Endel, BE1125
Estonian literature in foreign languages, BE1124
Estonian literature in the early 1970s, Mallene,
  Endel, BE1125
Estonskaiā khudozhestvennaiā litertura, Kivi,
  Osvald, BE1124
Estrada, Dardo. *Historia y bibliografía de la*
  imprenta en Montevideo, 1810–1865, AA545
Estrada, James. *Library buildings consultants list,*
  AK176
Estratificación y movilidad social en el Uruguay,
  Latin American Center for Research in the Social
  Sciences, DB397
Estreicher, Karol Józef Teofil. *Bibliografia polska,*
  AA762, AA765
  ——— *Bibliografia polska XIX stulecia,* AA762,
  AA763
Estudio bibliográfico de los archivos venzolanos y
  extranjeros de interés para la historia de
  Venezuela, Millares Carlo, Agustín, DB398
Estudios literarios y bibliográficos, Espinosa
  Cordero, Nicolás, AA530
État de la population, CG48
État des inventaires, Archives nationales (France),
  DC150
État des inventaires des archives départementales,
  communales et hospitalières au 1er janvier 1983,
  DC154
État général des fonds, Archives nationales (France),
  DC151
État général des inventaires des archives
  diplomatiques, France. Ministère des affaires
  étrangères, DC155
Etchepareborda, Roberto. *Bibliografía*
  historiographical la cuestion Malvinar, DB374
  ——— *Historiografía militar argentina,* DB325
Ethics
  dictionaries, BC241
  encyclopedias, BB32
  see also **Bioethics; Medical ethics; Political**
    ethics; Professional ethics
Ethics and public policy, Bergerson, Peter J., CJ6
Ethics and the professor, Herring, Mark
  Youngblood, CB220
Ethics, government, and public policy, CJ462
Ethiopia
  atlases, CL340
  bibliography, AA855, AA856, AA857, DD107,
    DD109, DD154, DD155, DD157, DD158
  bibliography of bibliography, AA71
  biography, AH318
  current surveys, DD62
  encyclopedias, DD48
  statistics, CG330
Ethiopia (by subject)
  population, CG329
  religion, BC452
Ethiopia, Nelson, Harold D., DD62
  ——— Paulos Milkias., DD158
Ethiopia & Amharica, Black, George, F., DD158
Ethiopia and Eritrea, Prouty, Chris, DD48
  ——— Rosenfield, Eugene, DD48
Ethiopia statistical abstract, CG330
Ethiopian incunabula, Wright, Stephen G., AA856
Ethiopian languages
  dictionaries, AC311
    bilingual
      English-Ethiopian, AC312
      Ethiopian-Latin, AC310
    etymology, AC312
Ethiopian Mapping Agency. Geography Division.
  National atlas of Ethiopia, CL340
Ethiopian perspectives, Brown, Clifton F., DD155
Ethiopian publications, AA855, AA856
  ——— Höjer, Christianne, AA856
Ethiopian society and history, Abbink, J., DD154

Ethnic and native Canadian literature, Miska, John
  P., BE828
Ethnic and native Canadian literature 1850–1979,
  BE828
Ethnic and racial images in American film and
  television, Woll, Allen L., CC334
Ethnic attitudes, CC372
Ethnic conflict and human rights in Sri Lanka,
  Rupesinghe, Kumar, DE260
Ethnic cookbooks and food marketplace, Vassilian,
  Hamo B., EJ224
Ethnic folklife dissertations from the United States
  and Canada, 1960–1980, Kerst, Catherine Hiebert,
  CF44
Ethnic genealogy, AJ8
Ethnic groups
  abstract journals, CC340
  atlases, CC358
  bibliography, CC151, CC310, CC313, CC625
    periodicals, CC336
  directories, CC344, CC345
  dissertations, CC337
  encyclopedias, CC341, CC342
  filmography, CC611
  grants-in-aid, CB381
  handbooks, CC343
  library resources, AK116
  manuscripts and archives, CC356
Ethnic groups (by country or region)
  Asia, Central
    bibliography of bibliography, CC308
  Brazil, CC475, DB347
  Canada, CC474
    literature, BE828
  Great Britain, CC326
    encyclopedias, CC341
  Mexico
    bibliography, DB223
  Sri Lanka, DE260
  Union of Soviet Socialist Republics, CC346
  United States, CC68, CC353, CC404, CC467
    bibliography, CC316, CC446
    book reviews, CC316
    Chicanas, CC444, CC596
    genealogy, AJ8
    handbooks, CC354
    universities and colleges, CB308
  Venezuela, CC476
Ethnic groups (by occupation or profession)
  librarians, AK87
Ethnic groups (by subject)
  alcohol and drug abuse, CC122
  education, higher, CB309
  fellowships and scholarships, CB377
  food and cookery, EJ205
  housing
    bibliography, CH529
  music, BJ329
Ethnic groups and employment
  directories, CH364
  statistics, CH686
Ethnic music on records, Spottswood, Richard K.,
  BJ329
•*Ethnic newswatch,* AE107, CC339
Ethnic periodicals, CC336
Ethnic periodicals in contemporary America, Ireland,
  Sandra L. Jones, AD52
Ethnic press, AD32, AD52, AD58, AE1, AE6, AE8,
  AE15, AE16, AE24, AE31, AE34
  databases, AE107, CC339
  indexes, AE105
Ethnic press (by subject)
  history, AA302
  see also **Newspapers; Periodicals**
The ethnic press in the United States, AD32
  ——— Miller, Sally M., AE34
Ethnic theater, BH32
Ethnicity and aging, CC68
Ethnicity and nationality, Bentley, G. Carter, CC310
Ethnikē Statistikē Hypēresia tēs Hellados. *Statistikē*
  epetēris tēs Hellados, CG243
Ethnoart, Burt, Eugene C., BG13
Ethnoarts index, BG12, BG13, BG12

Ethnoarts index supplemental publication, BG12
Ethnographic atlas, Murdock, George Peter, CE62,
  CE71
Ethnographic bibliography of North America,
  Murdock, George Peter, CC412, CC419
  ——— O'Leary, Timothy J., CC412
Ethnographic bibliography of South America,
  O'Leary, Timothy J., CE81
Ethnohistory, CE57
Ethnologue, BD13
Ethnology *see* **Anthropology and ethnology**
Ethnomusicology, BJ319, BJ329
  bibliography, BJ323, BJ325
  dictionaries, BJ318
  discography, BJ328
  guides, BJ323
Ethnomusicology, Kunst, Jaap, BJ319
Ethnomusicology research, Schuursma, Ann
  Briegleb, BJ325
Ethology, CD119, CD123
  abstract journals, CD118
  dictionaries, CD121
  encyclopedias, CD120
Etimologicheskiĭ slovar' russkogo iāzyka, Larina, B.
  A., AC691
  ——— Trubacheva, O. N., AC691
  ——— Vasmer, Max, AC691
Etiquette, AL152
  bibliography, AL149, AL150, AL151
  handbooks, AL153, AL154, AL155, AL156,
    AL157, AL158, AL159, AL160
Etiquette, AL158
  ——— Hodges, Deborah Robertson, AL150
Etiquette and modern manners, AL153
Etiquette in society, in business, in politics, and at
  home, AL156
Etnografiia, Titova, Zoia Dmitrievna, CE20
Etruscans
  bibliography, DC423
•*ETS Test Collection,* CB151, CD68
The ETS Test Collection catalog, CB151, CD68
Ettlinger, Amrei. *Russian literature, theatre, and art,*
  BE1409
Ettre, Leslie S. *Encyclopedia of industrial chemical*
  analysis, EE27
L'étude des auteurs classiques latins aux XIe et XIIe
  siècles, Munk Olsen, B., BE1045
Etudes africaines en Europe, DD54
Études grammaticales sur les langues celtiques,
  Ernault, Émile, AC236
Études historiques hongroises 1990, Glatz, Ferenc,
  DC389
Etulain, Richard W. *A bibliographical guide to the*
  study of Western American literature, BE570
  ——— *Fifty Western writers,* BE572
An etymological dictionary of Bengali, c.1000–1800
  A.D, Sen, Sukumar, AC233
An etymological dictionary of chemistry and
  mineralogy, Bailey, Dorothy, EF181
Etymological dictionary of modern English,
  Weekley, Ernest, AC64
Etymological dictionary of the English language,
  Skeat, Walter William, AC58, AC62
Etymological dictionary of the Scottish language,
  Jamieson, John, AC165
Etymologický slovník jazyka českého, Machek,
  Václav, AC284
Etymologisch woordenboek der Nederlandsche taal,
  AC299
Etymologisches Wörterbuch der deutschen
  Familiennamen, Brechenmacher, Josef Karlmann,
  AJ194
Etymologisches Wörterbuch der deutschen Sprache,
  Kluge, Friedrich, AC428
Etymologisches Wörterbuch der französischen
  Sprache, Gamillscheg, Ernst, AC350
Etymologisches Wörterbuch des Altindoarischen,
  Mayrhofer, Manfred, AC707
Etymologisches Wörterbuch des Deutschen, AC427
Etymologisk ordbog over det norske og det danske
  sprog, AC290
Eubanks, Cecil L. *Karl Marx and Friedrich Engels,*
  CJ500

Eubel, Konrad. *Hierarchia catholica medii aevi*, BC430

Eureka!, Byrne, Mary, AC50

Euro who's who, AF23

Eurofi (UK) Limited. *Development aid*, CH130

Euromoney. *Asia Pacific*, CH200

Euromonitor. *The European directory of trade and business journals*, CH335

Euromonitor Publications Limited. *European directory of trade and business associations*, CH183

The Europa biographical dictionary of British women, AH227

Europa Publications Limited. *The Europa world year book*, CJ94

The Europa world year book, CJ28, CJ35, CJ81, CJ88, CJ94

Europa year book, CJ94

Europaeiske ordner i farver, Hieronymussen, Poul Ohm, AL181

Europäische Stammtafeln, AJ77

Europe
  archives, DC18
  atlases, CL321
  biography, AH53, AH162
  directories
    bibliography, AL5
  guidebooks, CL388
  guides to records, DC14, DC15, DC16, DC18
  library resources, AK119, DC14, DC15, DC16
  library resources (by subject)
    Latin America, AK111
    West Indies, AK111
  newspapers, AE4
  statistics, CG182, CG183, CG184
    bibliography, CG185
Europe (by subject)
  anthropology and ethnology, CE97, CE98
  associations
    directories, CH183
  ceramics and glass, BG77
  cities, DC2
  decorative arts
    bibliography, BG7
  economic conditions, DC7
    bibliography, CH185
    history, DC1
  foreign relations, CJ316, DB286, DC10
  foreign relations (by country or region)
    Latin America, DB264
  history
    archives, DC17
    bibliography, DC1, DC3, DC6, DC7, DC9, DC11, DC191
    biography, AH162
    chronologies, DC224
    encyclopedias, DC20, DC23
  history (by period)
    Napoleonic era, DC22
  overseas territories (by country or region)
    North America, DB83
  politics and government, CJ313, CJ314
    archives, DC17
    bibliography, CJ321
    biography, CJ324
    directories, CJ324
    encyclopedias, CJ322
    sourcebooks, CJ315
  social conditions
    history, DC1
Europe, DC2
—— Theodoratus, Robert J., CE98
Europe : a thematic atlas, CL321
Europe, Eastern
  abstract journals, DC30, DC38
  archives, AK109, DC50
  associations, AL58
  atlases, DC56, DC57
  bibliography, DC32, DC39, DC41, DC58, DC555, DC558
    current, DC43
  bibliography of bibliography, AA396
  biography, AH163

encyclopedias, DC53
gazetteers, CL152
guides, DC29, DC33, DC59
handbooks, DC68
library catalogs, DC44, DC45, DC49
library resources, AK105, DC46, DC47
newspapers, AE43
Europe, Eastern (by subject)
  costume and fashion, BG114
  economic conditions
    encyclopedias, DC52
    statistics, CH182
  ethnic groups
    bibliography, CE92
  foreign relations, DC36
  history
    bibliography, DC37
    encyclopedias, DC52
  politics and government, CJ317, CJ390, CJ391
    encyclopedias, CJ396, DC52
    sourcebooks, CJ315
  see also **Ukraine**
Europe in figures, CG184
Europe in transition, Ferguson, Chris D., DC3
Europe transformed, CJ315
Europe, Western
  government publications, AF164
  library resources, AK132
  newspapers, AE8
  statistics, CG186, CG188, CG189, DC24
    bibliography, CG187
Europe, Western (by subject)
  economic conditions
    encyclopedias, CJ319
  politics and government, CJ323
    encyclopedias, CJ319
    handbooks, CJ87
European advertising, marketing, and media data, CH553
European American elderly, Guttmann, David, CC69
European Americana, AA404
European and American carpets and rugs, Faraday, Cornelia Bateman, BG167
European artists, Castagno, John, BF159
European Association for Animal Production. *Dictionary of animal production terminology*, EJ114
European authors, 1000–1900, BE203
—— Kunitz, Stanley Jasspon, BE204
European Bank for Reconstruction and Development. *A study of the Soviet economy*, CH186
European bibliography of Soviet, East European and Slavonic studies, DC41
European biographical directory, AH53
European business rankings, CH402
European business services directory, CH413
European ceramic art, from the end of the Middle Ages to about 1815, Honey, William Bowyer, BG74
European Communities
  bibliography, AF24
  biography, AF23, AH53
  directories, AF23
  handbooks, AF22, CH376
  publications, AF22, AF26
    databases, AF25
    indexes, AF25
  statistics, CG182, CG183, CG184, CG185
  yearbooks, CH184
European Communities (by subject)
  law, CK203, CK204
    encyclopedias, CK205
  politics and government, CJ320, CJ337
European Communities, Paxton, John, AF24
The European Communities encyclopedia and directory, CJ94
European composers today, BJ211
European Consortium for Political Research. Central Services. *Directory of European political scientists*, CJ46
European consultants directory, CH617

European customs and manners, Braganti, Nancy L., CL388
European decorative arts, 1400–1600, De Winter, Patrick M., BG7
European directory of non-official statistical sources, CG185
European directory of trade and business associations, CH183
The European directory of trade and business journals, CH335
European drama criticism, 1900–1975, Palmer, Helen H., BE232
•*European Dun's market identifiers*, CH363
European economic and social history, 1450–1789, Taylor, Barry, DC1
European faculty directory, CB320
European Free Trade Association. *Legal systems*, CK204
The European garden flora, EG169
European gardens, Vercelloni, Virgilio, BF295
European historical statistics, 1750–1975, CG189, DC24
European Institute of Education and Social Policy. Office for Cooperation in Education. *Directory of higher education institutions*, CB239
European integration *see* **European Communities**
European labor unions, CH665
European-language writing in sub-Saharan Africa, Gérard, Albert S., BE1501
European-Latin American relations, DB286
European legal journals index, CK28
European literature
  biobibliography, BE201, BE202
  biography, BE202
  criticism
    bibliography, BE257
  encyclopedias, BE988
European literature (by period)
  16th century
    bibliography, BE987
  Renaissance
    bibliography, BE28, BE985, BE987
European manuscript sources of the American Revolution, Koenig, William J., DB90
European market share reporter, Newman, Oksana, CH596
European marketing data and statistics, CH593
European markets, CH375
The European political dictionary, Rossi, Ernest E., CJ322
European political facts, 1648–1789, Babuscio, Jack, CJ314
European political parties, Henig, Stanley, CJ320
—— Pinder, John, CJ320
European political scientists, CJ46
European research centres, EA141
European research index, EA141
European Society for the History of Photography. *Photohistorica*, BF332
European sources of scientific and technical information, EA142
European Translations Centre. *World translations index*, EA63
European Union *see* **European Communities**
European wholesalers and distributors directory, CH346
The European women's almanac, Snyder, Paula, CC569
European writers, BE201
European yearbook, CJ313
Europeans (by country or region)
  United States, CC69
Evaluation and educational technology, Tennyson, Robert D., CB168
Evaluation for foundations, Council on Foundations, AL135
Evaluation resource handbook, Udinsky, B. Flavian, CD65
Evangelical and Reformed Church. *Year book of the Evangelical and Reformed Church*, BC386
Evangelical Lutheran Church in America. *Biographical directory of clergy*, BC354
—— *Yearbook*, BC356

Evangelical Lutheran Church of Canada. *Lutheran book of worship*, BC358

Evangelicalism, BC43, BC212

Evangelisches Kirchenlexikon, BC232

Evans, Austin Patterson. *Bibliography of English translations from medieval sources*, BE45, DA164

Evans, Barbara Jean. *A to zax*, AJ50
———— *The new A to Zax*, AJ50

Evans, Bergen. *A dictionary of contemporary American usage*, AC70
———— *Dictionary of quotations*, BE120

Evans, C. F. *Cambridge history of the Bible*, BC191

Evans, Charles. *American bibliography*, AA403, AA405, AA407, AA408, AA410, BF223, BJ59, CL243, EH25

Evans, Cornelia. *A dictionary of contemporary American usage*, AC70

Evans, D. Silvan. *Cambrian bibliography*, AA700

Evans, David. *Bibliography of stained glass*, BG51

Evans, G. Blakemore. *Riverside Shakespeare*, BE772, BE774, BE777, BE778

Evans, G. Edward. *North American Indian language materials, 1890–1965*, BD240

Evans, G. R. *Concordance to the works of St. Anselm*, BB64

Evans, Glen. *Encyclopedia of alcoholism*, CC124, CC125
———— *The encyclopedia of drug abuse*, CC124
———— *The encyclopedia of suicide*, CC183

Evans, Graham. *The dictionary of world politics*, CJ26

Evans, H. Meurig. *Y geiriadur mawr*, AC805

Evans, Hilary. *Art of picture research*, BF350
———— *Picture researcher's handbook*, BF349
———— *Practical picture research*, BF350

Evans, Ivan H. *Steinberg's dictionary of British history*, DC293

Evans, Ivor H. *Brewer's dictionary of phrase and fable*, BE181

Evans, James H. *Black theology*, BC216

Evans, Karen. *A bibliography of Canadiana*, DB188

Evans, Mary. *Picture researcher's handbook*, BF349

Evans, Patricia Russell. *Supreme Court of the United States, 1789–1980*, CK183

Evans, Patrick. *Penguin history of New Zealand literature*, BE863

Evans, Rand B. *The great psychologists*, CD62

Evborokhai, A. O. *A descriptive list of United Nations reference documents on Namibia (1946 1978)*, DD186

Eveleth, F. H. *The Judson Burmese-English dictionary*, AC244

Even, Pascal. *Guide des sources de l'histoire du Brésil aux archives du Ministère français des affaires étrangères*, DB349
———— *Papiers du Consulat de France à Alger*, DD125

Event line, AL28, BK34, CH554

●*EventLine*, AL28, BK34, CH554

Events, DA183

Everett, Craig A. *Family therapy glossary*, CC226

Everett, James L. *Inventor's handbook*, EA258

Everett, Thomas H. *The New York Botanical Garden illustrated encyclopedia of horticulture*, EJ233

Everitt, Alastair. *The left in Britain*, CJ509
———— *The underground and alternative press in Britain*, AD112

Everton, George B. *Handy book for genealogists*, AJ1, AJ9

Everton, Louise Mathews. *The handy book for genealogists*, AJ9

Everybody's guide to the law, Belli, Melvin M., CK159

The Everyman companion to East European literature, BE988

Everyman's concise encyclopedia of architecture, Briggs, Martin Shaw, BF244

Everyman's dictionary of abbreviations, Paxton, John, AC45

Everyman's dictionary of dates, DA30

Everyman's dictionary of European writers, Hargreaves-Mawdsley, William Norman, BE202

Everyman's dictionary of first names, Dunkling, Leslie, AJ169

Everyman's dictionary of literary biography, Browning, David Clayton, BE625

Everyman's dictionary of non-classical mythology, CF14

Everyman's dictionary of nonclassical mythology, Sykes, Egerton, CF13

Everyman's dictionary of pictorial art, Gaunt, William, BF301

Everyman's English pronouncing dictionary, Jones, Daniel, AC105

Everyman's United Nations, AF44

Everyone's United Nations, AF44

Everything added to food in the United States, EJ165

Evgen'eva, A. P. *Slovar' sinonimov russkogo iazyka*, AC693

Evinger, William R. *Directory of federal libraries*, AK124
———— *Directory of military bases in the U.S*, CJ623, CJ624
———— *Federal statistical data bases*, CG102
———— *Guide to federal government acronyms*, CJ125

Evleth, Donna. *France under the German occupation, 1940–1944*, DC200

Evola, Niccoló Domenico. *Origini e dottrina del fascismo*, DC422

Evolución de la novela en Colombia, Altamar, A. Curcio, BE948

Evolution, BC215, EG65
encyclopedias, CE40, EG26

Evolution of English lexicography, Murray, James Augustus Henry, AC5

Evolution of modern sculpture, Hammacher, A. M., BF393

Evolution of the modern presidency, Greenstein, Fred I., CJ171

The evolving Constitution, Lieberman, Jethro Koller, CK185

Evory, Ann. *Contemporary authors. New revision series*, AH42, BE198

Evriviades, Marios L. *Cyprus*, DC120

Ewedemi, Soga. *A bibliography of insurance history*, CH504

Ewen, David. *American composers*, BJ210
———— *American popular songs from the Revolutionary War to the present*, BJ277
———— *American songwriters*, BJ271
———— *The book of European light opera*, BJ236
———— *The complete book of light opera*, BJ241
———— *Complete book of the American musical theater*, BJ261
———— *Composers since 1900*, BJ211
———— *New complete book of the American musical theater*, BJ261
———— *The new encyclopedia of the opera*, BJ248
———— *Popular American composers from revolutionary times to the present*, BJ271

Exceptional child education abstracts, CB194, CD92

Exceptional child education resources, CB194, CD92, CB194, CD92

Exceptional human experience, CD132

Excerpta criminologica, CK250

Excerpta Indonesica, DE179

Excerpta medica, EH58, EH59

Excerpta medica : list of journals abstracted, EH34

Exchange bibliography, Council of Planning Librarians, BF267, BF271

Executive advisory bodies, CJ134

The executive branch of the U.S. government, Goehlert, Robert, CJ170

Executive departments, CJ151, CJ181, CJ182

Executive recruiters, CH618

Executive register of the United States, 1789–1902, Mosher, R. B., CJ140

Executives
biography
bibliography, CH389
training
directories, CH718

Executives (by country or region)
Scotland
biography, CH97
United States
biography, CH98, CH99
directories, CH350

The executive's book of quotations, CH74

Exegetical bibliography of the New Testament, Wagner, Günter, BC114, BC118

Exegetical dictionary of the New Testament, AC456, BC137, BC143

Exegetisches Wörterbuch zum Neuen Testament, BC137

Exercise, BK25, BK39

Exhaustive concordance of the Bible, Strong, James, BC151, BC159, BC165

Exhibitions
bibliography, BF118
current, BF34, BF43
directories, CH557

Exil-Literatur 1933–1945, Berthold, Werner, BE1232

Exiled authors, AA739, BE207, BE976, BE1232
see also **Emigré literature**

Exotica, series 4 international, Graf, Alfred Byrd, EG158

Experiment station record, United States. Department of Agriculture, EJ95
———— United States. Office of Experiment Stations, EJ95

Explanatory supplement to the Astronomical almanac, EC79

The exploration of South America, Goodman, Edward J., CL11

Explorers and discoverers of the world, CL81

Export documentation handbook, CH139

Export yellow pages, CH497

Exporters' encyclopaedia, CH139

Exporter's guide to federal resources for small business, CH140

Exports and exporting
handbooks, CH140

Exports and exporting (by country or region)
United States
databases, CH497
directories, CH136
handbooks, CH139
statistics, CH497

L'Express, DC208

Expressionism, BE1264
bibliography, BE1223, BE1230

Extant collections of early black newspapers, Campbell, Georgetta Merritt, AE15, AE105

The Extel Financial Asia Pacific handbook, CH358

Extel Financial Limited. *Asia Pacific handbook*, CH358

Extensions of classical logic, BB36

External public debt, CH161

The extra pharmacopoeia, EH357

Extracto estadístico del Peru, CG157

Extranjeros en México, 1821–1990, DB223

Extrapolation, BE310

Eychlerowa, Barbara. *Bibliografia bibliografii polskich, 1961–1970*, AA60

Eyll, Klara van. *Deutsche Wirtschaftsarchive*, DC245

Ezhegodnik knigi SSSR, AA795, AA796

Ezhegodnik periodicheskikh izdanii SSSR, AD150

Ezhegodnik knigi Gosudarstvennaia TSentral'noi knizhnoi palaty RSFSR, AA795

F. A. Brockhaus Verlag Leipzig. *Entsiklopedicheskii slovar'*, AB85
———— *Novyi entsiklopedicheskii slovar'*, AB89
———— *Der Sprach-Brockhaus*, AC410

F & S index United States, CH337

F&S index Europe, CH337

F&S index international, CH337

F&S index United States, CH337

Fabbri, Maurizio. *A bibliography of Hispanic dictionaries*, AC752

Faber, Edward. *Nobel prize winners in chemistry, 1901–1961*, AL171, EE104

Faber book of art anecdotes, Lucie-Smith, Edward, BF95

Faber book of parodies, Brett, Simon, BE723

The Faber companion to 20th-century popular music, Hardy, Phil, BJ348

The Faber dictionary of euphemisms, Holder, R. W., AC125

Faber du Faur, Curt von. *German Baroque literature*, BE1234

Fabian, Bernhard. *A catalogue of English books printed before 1801 held by the University Library at Göttingen*, AA682

—— *Deutsches biographisches Archiv*, AH206

Fabiano, Emily. *Core list of books and journals in education*, CB16

—— *Index to tests used in educational dissertations*, CB152

Fable scholarship, Carnes, Pack, CF38

Fabozzi, Frank J. *The handbook of economic and financial measures*, CH170

—— *Handbook of financial markets*, CH218

Fabra, Pompeu. *Diccionari Aguiló*, AC246

—— *Diccionari general de la llengua catalana*, AC251

—— *Diccionari manual de la llengua catalana*, AC251

Fabre, Genevieve. *Afro-American poetry and drama, 1760–1975*, BE512

Fabricius, Johann Albert. *Bibliotheca graeca*, BE993

—— *Bibliotheca latina, mediae et infimae aetatis*, BE993

Facciola, Stephen. *Cornucopia*, EG157

Face of the nation, 1987, Fanshel, David, CC46

—— Lutz, Mary E., CC46

—— Rosen, Sumner M., CC46

Faces in the news, Hoffman, Herbert H., BF65

Fachgelehrten, Stefan. *Series episcoporum ecclesiae catholicae*, BC430

Fachwörterbuch, Chemie und chemische Technik, EE50

Fachwörterbuch : Landwirtschaft, Fortwirtschaft, Gartenbau, EJ28

Faclair gàidhlig le dealbhan, MacDonald, Ewen, AC393

Facsimile transmission, AK60

directories, CH490

Fact book on aging, Vierck, Elizabeth, CC106

Fact book on higher education, CB339

Fact book on women in higher education, Touchton, Judith G., CB344

Fact books and compendiums, AB104, AB105, AB107, AB108, AB109, AB110

The facts about drug use, Stimmel, Barry, CC136

Facts about nursing, EH289

Facts about the presidents, Kane, Joseph Nathan, CJ190

Facts about the states, Anzovin, Steven, CG104

—— Podell, Janet, CG104

Facts and comparisons, EH338

Facts and figures on government finance, Tax Foundation, CH244

Facts on file, AE127, DA186, DB204

Facts on File bibliography of American fiction, 1866–1918, BE472

The Facts on File dictionary of archaeology, DA79

The Facts on File dictionary of astronomy, EC32, EC35

The Facts on File dictionary of biology, EG36

The Facts on File dictionary of chemistry, EE38

Facts on File dictionary of classical, biblical, and literary allusions, Cole, Sylvia, BE86

—— Lass, Abraham Harold, BE86

The Facts on File dictionary of design and designers, Jervis, Simon, BG22

The Facts on File dictionary of education, Shafritz, Jay M., CB80

The Facts on File dictionary of European history, 1485–1789, Williams, E. Neville, DC23

The Facts on File dictionary of film and broadcast terms, Penney, Edmund F., BH260

The Facts on File dictionary of first names, AJ169

The Facts on File dictionary of geology and geophysics, Lapidus, Dorothy Farris, EF75

The Facts on File dictionary of military science, Shafritz, Jay M., CJ589

The Facts on File dictionary of nonprofit organization management, Ott, J. Steven, AL10, CH615

The Facts on File dictionary of personnel management and labor relations, Shafritz, Jay M., CH711

The Facts on File dictionary of physics, ED18

The Facts on File dictionary of public administration, Shafritz, Jay M., CJ478

The Facts on File dictionary of religions, BC73

The Facts on File dictionary of the theatre, BH69

Facts on File dictionary of twentieth-century allusions, Cole, Sylvia, BE86

—— Lass, Abraham Harold, BE86

Facts on File encyclopedia of the 20th century, DA180

The Facts on File encyclopedia of word and phrase origins, Hendrickson, Robert, AC54

The Facts on File encyclopedia of world mythology and legend, Mercatante, Anthony S., CF5

The Facts on File English/Chinese visual dictionary, Corbeil, Jean Claude, AC259

The Facts on File English/French visual dictionary, Corbeil, Jean Claude, AC338

Facts on File, Inc. *The Facts on File dictionary of geology and geophysics*, EF75

—— *The Facts on File dictionary of public administration*, CJ478

—— *Historical maps on file*, CL282, DA55

—— *Maps on file*, CL281

—— *State maps on file*, CL302

—— *World elections on file*, CJ92

•*Facts on File news digest CD-ROM*, DA186

The Facts on File scientific yearbook, EA166

The Facts on File world political almanac, Cook, Chris, CJ86

Faculté des lettres de Paris. Institut d'histoire de la Révolution française. *Répertoire des travaux universitaires inédits sur la période révolutionnaire*, DC181

Faculty directory of higher education, CB330

Faculty white pages, CB330

Fads and fallacies in the name of science, Gardner, Martin, EA80

Færøsk bogfortegnelse, AA605

Faessler, Carl. *Cross-index to the geological illustration of Canada*, EF27

Fagan, Thomas K. *A bibliographic guide to the literature of professional school psychology (1890–1985)*, CD89

Fage, J. D. *The Cambridge history of Africa*, DD57

—— *A guide to original sources for precolonial western Africa published in European languages*, DD99

Fage, John D. *Atlas of African history*, DD65

Faheem, Ahmed D. *Themes in cultural psychiatry*, EH372

Fahl, Ronald J. *North American forest and conservation history*, EJ172, EJ174

Fahlbusch, Erwin. *Evangelisches Kirchenlexikon*, BC232

Faider, Paul. *Répertoire des index et lexiques d'auteurs latins*, BE1031, BE1044

Fairbairn, James. *Book of crests of the families of Great Britain and Ireland*, AJ151

Fairbairn's crests, AJ151

Fairbank, John K. *Cambridge history of China*, DE146

Fairbanks, Carol. *Black American fiction*, BE517

Fairbridge, Rhodes Whitmore. *Annotated bibliography of quaternary shorelines, 1945–1964*, EF38

—— *Dictionary of earth sciences*, EF84

—— *The encyclopedia of atmospheric sciences and astrogeology*, EF145

—— *The encyclopedia of climatology*, EF144

—— *Encyclopedia of earth sciences*, EF5, EF12

—— *The encyclopedia of geochemistry and environmental sciences*, EF67

—— *The encyclopedia of geomorphology*, EF7

—— *The encyclopedia of oceanography*, EF216

—— *The encyclopedia of paleontology*, EF235

—— *The encyclopedia of sedimentology*, EF64

—— *The encyclopedia of soil science*, EJ22

—— *The encyclopedia of world regional geology*, EF68

Fairchild, Halford H. *Discrimination and prejudice*, CC30

Fairchild's dictionary of fashion, Calasibetta, Charlotte Mankey, BG98

Fairchild's dictionary of textiles, Wingate, I.B, BG98

Fairfield, Sheila. *Calendar of creative man*, DA36

Fairholt, F. W. *Dictionary of terms in art*, BF81

Fairpo, C. Gavin. *Heinemann dental dictionary*, EH253

Fairpo, Jenifer E. H. *Heinemann dental dictionary*, EH253

Fairs, AL148

directories, EJ43

Fairweather, Digby. *Jazz*, BJ299

Fairy tales, BE243

Fajcsek, Magda. *Magyarországi irodalom idegen nyelven*, BE1280

Fakes and forgeries in the fine arts, Reisner, Robert George, BF30

Fakhfakh, Mohamed. *Atlas de Tunisie*, CL339

Faking it, Koobatian, James, BF30

Falassi, Alessandro. *Italian folklore*, CF82

Falciola, Kristine. *Conditions of work and quality of working life*, CH661

Falconer, John I. *History of agriculture in the northern United States, 1620–1860*, EJ65

Fales, Martha Gandy. *Early American silver*, BG144

Falk, Byron A. *Personal name index to "The New York times index," 1851–1974*, AE108

Falk, Hjalmar Sejersted. *Norwegisch-dänisches etymologisches Wörterbuch*, AC290

Falk, Joyce Duncan. *Searching America : history and life*, DB24

Falk, Peter H. *Dictionary of signatures & monograms of American artists*, BF153

—— *Who was who in American art*, BF153

Falk, Peter Hastings. *Print price index*, BF371

Falk, Valerie R. *Personal name index to "The New York times index," 1851–1974*, AE108

Falkland Islands, DB374, DB376

bibliography, DB375

Falkland/Malvinas Islands, Mundo Lo, Sara de, DB376

Falklands/Malvinas campaign, Rasor, Eugene L., DA170, DB375

The Falklands War, Orgill, Andrew, DB375

Falkowska, Hanna. *Polska prasa konspiracyjna (1939–1945) i powstania warszawskiego w zbiorach Biblioteki Narodowej*, AE66

Falkus, Malcolm E. *Historical atlas of Britain*, DC302

Falla, P. S. *Oxford English-Russian dictionary*, AC683

Fallen in battle, Brown, Russell K., CJ637

Fallon, S. W. *New English-Hindustani dictionary*, AC489

—— *New Hindustani-English dictionary*, AC489

Fallon, William K. *AMA management handbook*, CH620

Die falschen und fingirten Druckorte, Weller, Emil Ottokar, AA196

Familiar quotations, Bartlett, John, BE99

Familiar quotations from Greek authors, Ramage, Craufurd Tait, BE138

Familiar quotations from Latin authors, Ramage, Craufurd Tait, BE145

Familiengeschichtliche Bibliographie, AJ91

Familiennamenbuch der Schweiz, AJ142

Families and aging, Coyle, Jean M., CC64

Families in transition, Sadler, Judith DeBoard, CC219

Les familles protestantes en France, Bernard, Gildas, AJ84

Family *see* **Marriage and the family**

Family associations, AJ52

Family history and local history in England, Hey, David, AJ102

Family index, AJ150
Family legal guide, CK135
Family planning *see* **Population planning**
Family planning and child survival programs as assessed in 1991, CC250
Family planning perspectives, CC247
Family research, CC237
•*Family resources database*, CC221
Family studies abstracts, CC222
Family therapy, CC210
——— Sauber, S. Richard, CC227
Family therapy glossary, CC226
Family violence, CC92, CC209, CC211, CC240, CC517
  bibliography, CC217
  databases, CC156
  thesauruses, CC161
The famine immigrants, AJ37
Famous actors and actresses on the American stage, Young, William C., BH123
Famous American playhouses, Young, William C., BH110, BH123
Famous American women, CC576
Famous first facts, Kane, Joseph Nathan, AB106
Famularo, Joseph J. *Handbook of human resources administration*, CH719
Fan, Kok-sim. *Women in Southeast Asia*, CC599
Fan club directory, Dewey, Patrick R., AL39
Fandel, Nancy A. *National directory of arts & education support by business corporations*, AL121, BA10
Fang, Anna J. *International guide to library and information science education*, AK54
——— *World guide to library, archive, and information science associations*, AK55
Fang, Josephine Riss. *International guide to library and information science education*, AK54
——— *World guide to library, archive, and information science associations*, AK55
Fanjul, L. *Spanish-English horticultural dictionary*, EJ239
Fanshel, David. *Face of the nation, 1987*, CC46
Fantasy for children, Lynn, Ruth Nadelman, BE386
Fantasy literature, BE277
Fantasy literature for children and young adults, Lynn, Ruth Nadelman, BE386
Fante language *see* **Twi language**
FAO documentation, EJ20
FAO documentation. Current index, EJ20
FAO fertilizer yearbook, EJ79
FAO/OIE animal health yearbook, EJ133
FAO production yearbook, EJ80
FAO trade yearbook, CH151, EJ81
FAO yearbook. Fertilizer, EJ79
FAO yearbook. Production, EJ80
FAO yearbook. Trade, CH151, EJ81
The Far East and Australasia, CJ94
Far Eastern bibliography, DE8
Far Eastern economic review yearbook, CG369
Far Eastern quarterly, DE8
Faraday, Cornelia Bateman. *European and American carpets and rugs*, BG167
Faragher, John Mack. *The encyclopedia of colonial and revolutionary America*, DB82
Farazmand, Ali. *Handbook of comparative and development public administration*, CJ480
Farber, Bernard E. *A teacher's treasury of quotations*, CB85
Farber, Eduard. *Great chemists*, EE101
——— *Nobel prize winners in chemistry, 1901–1961*, AL165, EE102
Farber, Evan Ira. *The combined retrospective index set to journals in political science, 1886–1974*, CJ18
——— *Combined retrospective index to book reviews in humanities journals, 1802–1974*, BA7
——— *Combined retrospective index to book reviews in scholarly journals, 1886–1974*, AA369
——— *C.R.I.S*, CC12, DA4
Farberow, Norman L. *The encyclopedia of suicide*, CC183
Farenholtz, Brigitte. *Manual para las relaciones Europeo-Latinoamericanas*, DB286

Farey series of order 1025, Neville, E. H., EB94
Farhang-i jadīd-i Inglīlisī Fārsī, AC313
Farhang-i kitābhā–yi Fārsī, Mudabbirī, Maḥmūd, AA907
Farhang-i nuvin-i payvastah-i Fārsi-Ingilīsī va Ingilisī-Fārsī, Aryanpur, Manoochehr, AC313
——— Āryānpūr Kāshānī, 'Abbās, AC313
Faries, Cynthia. *The social sciences*, CA7
Faris, Robert E. L. *Handbook of modern sociology*, CC27
Farkas, Andres. *Opera and concert singers*, BJ219
Farm chemicals handbook, EJ51
Farmer, David Hugh. *The Oxford dictionary of saints*, BC265
Farmer, John Stephen. *Slang and its analogues, past and present*, AC122
——— *Vocabula amatoria*, AC122
Farmer, Robert Harvey. *Handbook of hardwoods*, EJ187
Farmers' bulletins [Index], United States. Department of Agriculture, EJ92
Farmers' organizations, Dyson, Lowell K., EJ42
Farming and mechanised agriculture, EJ39
Faroe Islands
  statistics, CG210
Farouk-Sluglett, Marion. *Tuttle guide to the Middle East*, DE23
Farr, David F. *Fungi on plants and plant products in the United States*, EG186
Farr, Dennis. *The Oxford dictionary of art*, BF90
Farr, Ellen R. *Index nominum genericorum (plantarum)*, EG129
Farragher, Leslie E. *The anthropology of war*, CE10
Farran, Clarissa Palmer. *Bibliography of English translations from medieval sources*, BE45, DA164
Farrar, Robert Henry. *An index to the biographical and obituary notices in the Gentleman's magazine, 1731–1780*, AH241
Farrell, Lois. *Guide to sources for agricultural and biological research*, EJ1
Farrell, Ralph Barstow. *Dictionary of German synonyms*, AC433
Farrell, T. *Electrical resistivity handbook*, ED35
Farrell-Beck, Jane. *The history of costume*, BG112
Farrier, Susan E. *The medieval Charlemagne legend*, BE983
Farsi language
  dictionaries
    bilingual, AC313, AC314, AC316, AC318
      English-Farsi, AC315
    multilingual, AC317
Farson, Anthony Stuart. *Criminal intelligence and security intelligence*, CK245
Fascism, DC432
  bibliography, DC422
Fascism (by country or region)
  Europe, CJ321
  Great Britain, CJ339
  Italy, DC433
    biography, AH263
Fascism and pre-fascism in Europe, 1890–1945, Rees, Philip, CJ321
Fascism in Britain, Rees, Philip, CJ339
Fashion *see* **Costume and fashion**
The fashion dictionary, Picken, Mary (Brooks), BG100
The fashion guide : international designer directory, BG98
Fashion in the western world, 1500–1900, Yarwood, Doreen, BG102
Fasman, Gerald D. *Handbook of biochemistry and molecular biology*, EG320
Fassig, Oliver. *Bibliography of meteorology*, EF142
Fast, Timothy. *The women's atlas of the United States*, CC581
Fasti archeologici, DA96
Fasti ecclesiae Anglicanae, Le Neve, John, BC331
Fasti ecclesiae Scoticanae, Scott, Hew, BC342
Fatherhood U.S.A, Klinman, Debra G., CC242
Faugères, Arlette. *Répertoire des historiens français pour la période moderne et contemporaine*, DC163

Faulhaber, Charles. *Bibliography of Old Spanish texts*, BE1433
Faulhaber, Uwe K. *German literature*, BE1210
Faulkner, Raymond O. *A concise dictionary of Middle Egyptian*, AC304
Faull, Sandra K. *Cumulative title index to United States public documents, 1789–1976*, AF96
Fauquet, C. *Stedman's ICTV virus words*, EG347
Faust, Langdon Lynne. *American women writers*, BE443
Faust, Patricia L. *Historical times illustrated encyclopedia of the Civil War*, DB118
Fauvel-Rouif, Denise. *Anarchisme*, CJ506
Faux amis, AC340
Favazza, Armando R. *Anthropological and cross-cultural themes in mental health*, EH372
——— *Themes in cultural psychiatry*, EH372
Faverty, Frederic Everett. *Victorian poets*, BE686, BE703, BE706, BE755, BE984
Favier, Jean. *État des inventaires*, DC150
——— *État général des fonds*, DC151
Favre, Léopold. *Glossarium mediae et infimae latinitatis*, AC587
Fax Post international, CH490
Fay, A. H. *Glossary of the mining and mineral industry*, EF188
Fay, George Emory. *A bibliography of Etruscan culture and archaeology, 1498–1981*, DC423
Fay, Gordon S. *The rockhound's manual*, EF197
Fay, John. *The alcohol/drug abuse dictionary and encyclopedia*, CC128
——— *The police dictionary and encyclopedia*, CK259
Fay, John J. *Encyclopedia of security management*, CK253
Fayard, Jean-François. *Histoire et dictionnaire de la Révolution française*, DC188
Faye, C. U. *Census of medieval and Renaissance manuscripts in the United States and Canada*, AA212
The FCLD learning disabilities resource guide, CB202
Feather, John. *A dictionary of book history*, AA274
Feather, Leonard G. *The encyclopedia of jazz*, BJ300
——— *Encyclopedia of jazz in the seventies*, BJ300
——— *Encyclopedia of jazz in the sixties*, BJ300
Featherly, Henry Ira. *Taxonomic terminology of the higher plants*, EG126
Fed in print, CH264
Fed in print : Business and banking topics, CH264
Fedden, Robin. *The National Trust guide*, BF249
Fedele, Pietro. *Grande dizionario enciclopedico UTET*, AB67
Feder, Lillian. *Crowell's handbook of classical literature*, BE1015
——— *The Meridian handbook of classical literature*, BE1015
•*Federal assistance programs retrieval system*, CH167
Federal career directory, CH696
Federal Computer Products Center. *Directory of U.S. government datafiles for mainframes and microcomputers*, AF104
Federal copyright records, 1790–1800, AA406
Federal Council year book, BC324
The federal data base finder, AF65
Federal Deposit Insurance Corporation. Division of Research and Statistics. *Historical statistics on banking*, CH294
Federal Document Retrieval, Inc. *Directory of periodicals online*, AD6
Federal executive directory, CJ135
Federal executive directory annual, CJ135
Federal funding for education, CB380
•*Federal information exchange*, CB100
Federal information sources in health and medicine, Chitty, Mary Glen, EH41
Federal laboratory & technology resources, EA214
The federal legal directory, Hermann, R. L., CK146
Federal public policy on aging since 1960, Oriol, William E., CC74
Federal records, Agee, V., AK112
Federal regional executive directory, CJ135

Federal regional yellow book, CH350, CJ181
Federal register, AF64, AF67, CJ136, CJ151, CK182
The federal register : what it is and how to use it, CK182
Federal regulatory directory, CJ136
Federal Republic of Germany, Price, Arnold Hereward, DC232
Federal Reserve Bank reviews, selected subjects, CH264
Federal reserve bulletin, CH241
Federal royal commissions in Canada, 1867–1966, Henderson, George Fletcher, AF151
Federal staff directory, CJ137, CJ162, CJ215, CK149
Federal-state court directory, CK156
Federal/state executive directory, CJ135, CJ275
Federal statistical data bases, Evinger, William R., CG102
Federal systems of the world, Elazar, Daniel Judah, CJ51
Federal tax research, Richmond, Gail Levin, CK119
Federal Writers' Project. *American guide series,* CL387
Federal yellow book, CH350, CJ182
Federally sponsored training materials, CB351
Fédération Dentaire Internationale. *A lexicon of English dental terms,* EH257
Fédération des sociétés françaises de sciences philosophiques, historiques, philologiques et juridiques. *Répertoire des périodiques de langue française, philosophiques, historiques, philologiques et juridiques,* AD94
Fédération internationale des instituts d'études médiévales. *Répertoire international des médiévistes,* DA154
Fédération internationale des sociétés et instituts pour l'étude de la Renaissance. *Bibliographie internationale de l'humanisme et de la renaissance,* DA140
Federation of American Societies for Experimental Biology. *Environmental biology,* EG50
—— *Respiration and circulation,* EG53
Federation of Indian Publishers. *Directory of publishers and booksellers in India,* AA294
Fédération protestante de France. *Annuaire de la France protestante,* BC323
Federazione Nazionale tra le Associazioni Giornalistiche Italiane. *Annuario della stampa italiana,* AD125
Federlin, Tom. *A comprehensive bibliography on American sign language,* BD49
FEDfind, D'Aleo, Richard J., AF71
Fediushina, L. M. *Russkaia khudozhestvennaia literatura i literaturovedenie,* BE1396
•*FEDIX,* CB100
Fedorova, Rimma Maksimovna. *A guide to mathematical tables,* EB74
•*FedWorld Gateway,* AF105
Fee, Margery. *Canadian fiction,* BE823, BE824
Fee-based information services, AK59
Feeds & nutrition, Ensminger, M. Eugene, EJ122
Fegley, Randall. *Congo,* DD18
—— *Equatorial Guinea,* DD18
—— *Rwanda,* DD18
Fehlauer, Michael. *DDR Handbuch,* CJ330
Feigen de Roca, Elisabeth. *Historiografía Argentina 1930–1970,* DB333
Feigenbaum, Edward A. *The handbook of artificial intelligence,* EK204
Feigert, Frank B. *Canada votes, 1935–1988,* CJ293, CJ298
Feinberg, Raphael. *Dictionary of electrical engineering,* EK132
Feinberg, Renee. *The Equal Rights Amendment,* CC491
—— *The feminization of poverty in the United States,* CC261
Feingold, Marie. *Scholarships, fellowships, and loans,* CB392
Feingold, S. Norman. *Scholarships, fellowships, and loans,* CB392

Feist, Sigmund,. *Vergleichendes Wörterbuch der gotischen Sprache,* AC440
Feistritzer, C. Emily. *Profile of teachers in the U.S.—1990,* CB166
Fekete, Márton. *Prominent Hungarians,* AH252
Feki, Habib. *3200 revues et journaux arabes de 1800 à 1965,* AD182
Felber, H. *Bibliographie sélective, terminologie et disciplines connexes,* BD58
Feldman, Franklin. *Art law,* BF122
Feldman, Lynne B. *African-American business leaders,* CH100
—— *Contemporary American business leaders,* CH99
Feldman, Paula R. *The wordworthy computer,* BE3
Felipe Herrera Library. *Index of periodical articles on the economics of Latin America,* CH177
Feliú Cruz, Guillermo. *Historia de las fuentes de la bilbiografía chilena,* DB358
—— *Viajes relativos a Chile,* DB358
Fellhauer, Ruth. *550 books on Buddhism,* BC460
Fellinger, Imogen. *Periodica musicalia (1789–1830),* BJ114
—— *Verzeichnis der Musikzeitschriften des 19. Jahrhunderts,* BJ101, BJ114
Fellmann, Jerome D. *International list of geographical serials,* CL25
—— *Union list of geographical serials,* CL25
Fellowships and scholarships, CB365, CB366, CB369, CB370, CB371, CB372, CB376, CB377, CB381, CB382, CB386, CB392, CB393, DA28
  databases, CB100, CB387, CB388, CB390
  directories, AL114, CB367, CB374, CB384, CB389
Fellowships and scholarships (by country or region)
  United States, CB259, CB375
Fellowships and scholarships (by subject)
  computer science, EK200
  education, CB379, CB387
  foreign study, CB90, CB373
  mathematics, EB58
  sports and games, CB391
  women, CB378, CC546
  see also **Prizes and awards**
Felstead, Alison. *Directory of British architects, 1834–1900,* BF259
Felzenberg, Alvin S. *Evolution of the modern presidency,* CJ171
Fem decennier av nittonhundratalet, Linder, Erik Hjalmar, BE1485
Female criminality, CC37
The female experience in eighteenth- and nineteenth-century America, Conway, Jill K., CC488
Feminism, CC499
  bibliography, BH34, CC208, CC261, CC263, CC276, CC491, CC497, CC498, CC504, CC507, CC514, CC516, CK10
    current, CC519, CC520
  chronologies, CC572
  dictionaries, CC538, CC539
  directories, CC554
  encyclopedias, CC535
  guides, CC481, CC483
  guides for authors, CC559
  handbooks, CC558, CC568
  newspapers, AE25
  periodicals, AE25, CC518, CC559
    indexes, CC521
Feminism (by country or region)
  Canada
    archives, CC525
    indexes, CC527
    thesauruses, CC541
Feminism (by subject)
  history, CC484
  see also **Women**
Feminism and women's issues, Watson, G. Llewellyn, CC514
Feminist bookstore news, CC518

Feminist chronicles, 1953–1993, Carabillo, Toni, CC572
Feminist chronicles of the 20th century, CC572
Feminist collections, CC519
The feminist companion to literature in English, Blain, Virginia, BE607, BE623
Feminist criticism, BE49, BE1133
A feminist dictionary, Kramarae, Cheris, CC539
Feminist legal literature, DeCoste, F. C., CK10
Feminist literary criticism, Frost, Wendy, BE49
The feminist movement, Nordquist, Joan, CC507
Feminist newspapers, 1970–1980, AE25
Feminist periodicals, 1855–1984, Doughan, David, CC521
Feminist research methods, Miller, Connie, CC504
Feminist resources for schools and colleges, Chapman, Anne, CC481
Feminist spirituality and the feminine divine, Carson, Anne, BC10
Feminists, AH218
Feminists, pornography & the law, Sellen, Betty-Carol, CC276
The feminization of poverty, Nordquist, Joan, CC263
The feminization of poverty in the United States, Feinberg, Renee, CC261
Femmes, Weitz, Margaret Collins, CC620
Femmes et enfants au Burundi, Pabanel, Jean-Pierre, DD134
Fenaroli, Giovanni. *Fenaroli's handbook of flavor ingredients,* EH305
Fenaroli's handbook of flavor ingredients, Fenaroli, Giovanni, EH305
Fenn, Courtenay Hughes. *The five thousand dictionary,* AC262
Fenner, Susan W. *Professional Secretaries International complete office handbook,* CH87
Fenner, Terrence W. *Inventor's handbook,* EA258
Fenner, William R. *Quick reference to veterinary medicine,* EJ128
Fennia, Finland. Maanmittaushallitus, CL325
•*Fennica CD-ROM,* AA612
Fenno-Ugric vocabulary, Collinder, Bjorn, AC326
Fenster, Valmai Kirkham. *Guide to American literature,* BE394
Fenstermaker, John J. *The art of literary research,* BE1
Fenton, Jill Rubinson. *Women writers, from page to screen,* BH215
Fenton, Thomas P. *Africa,* DD93
—— *Asia and Pacific,* DE17
—— *Food, hunger, agribusiness,* EJ161
—— *Middle East,* DE21
—— *Third World resource directory,* DD93, DE17, DE21
—— *Third World resource directory, 1994–1995,* DA11
—— *Third World struggle for peace with justice,* CJ669
—— *Transnational corporations and labor,* CH666
—— *Women in the Third World,* CC600
Fenwick, Gillian. *Contributors' index to the Dictionary of national biography, 1885–1901,* AH226
Fenwick, M. J. *Writers of the Caribbean and Central America,* BE870
Feofanov, Dmitry. *Biographical dictionary of Russian/Soviet composers,* BJ204
Ferber, Gene. *English-Japanese, Japanese-English dictionary of computer and data-processing terms,* EK191
Ferber, Marianne A. *Women and work, paid and unpaid,* CH629
Ferdico, John N. *Ferdico's criminal law and justice dictionary,* CK260
Ferdico's criminal law and justice dictionary, Ferdico, John N., CK260
Feret, Barbara L. *Gastronomical and culinary literature,* EJ204
Ferguson, Chris D. *Europe in transition,* DC3
Ferguson, Ed. *Zanzibar under colonial rule,* DD250
Ferguson, Eugene S. *Bibliography of the history of technology,* EA228

Ferguson, Everett. *Encyclopedia of early Christianity*, BC274

Ferguson, F. S. *A short-title catalogue of books printed in England, Scotland, & Ireland and of English books printed abroad, 1475–1640*, AA671

Ferguson, George Wells. *Signs & symbols in Christian art*, BF182

Ferguson, Joan P. S. *Directory of Scottish newspapers*, AE62

—— *Scottish family histories*, AJ121

Ferguson, John. *Bibliotheca chemica*, EE11, EE16

—— *An illustrated encyclopaedia of mysticism and the mystery religions*, BC61

Ferguson, John Alexander. *Bibliography of Australia*, AA942, DF26

Ferguson, Mary. *Scottish Gaelic union catalogue*, AA697

Ferguson, Mary Anne Heyward. *Bibliography of English translations from medieval sources, 1943–1967*, BE45, DA164

Ferguson, R. Brian. *The anthropology of war*, CE10

Ferguson, Sinclair B. *New dictionary of theology*, BC239

Ferguson, T. J. *A Zuni atlas*, CC439

Ferguson, Tom. *What you need to know about psychiatric drugs*, EH351

Fernald, Anne Conway. *Business online*, CH6

Fernald, Merritt Lyndon. *Gray's manual of botany*, EG159

Fernández, Mauro. *Diglossia*, BD81

Fernández-Caballero, Carlos F. S. *The Paraguayan bibliography*, AA536

Fernandez-Caballero, Marianne. *Bibliografía paraguaya*, AA536

—— *The Paraguayan bibliography*, AA536

Fernández de Zamora, Rosa María. *Las publicaciones oficiales de México*, AF157

Fernández Saldaña, José María. *Diccionario uruguayo de biografías, 1810–1940*, AH144

Fernández-Shaw, Carlos M. *The Hispanic presence in North America from 1492 to today*, CC464

Fernelius, W. Conard. *Inorganic chemical nomenclature*, EE107

Ferns, EG166

Ferns and allied plants, Tryon, Rolla M., EG166

Ferozsons English to English and Urdu dictionary, AC799

Ferozsons Urdu-English dictionary, AC800

Ferrall, Eleanor. *Criminal justice research in libraries*, CK242

Ferrar, H. *The concise Oxford French dictionary*, AC337

Ferrara, Lawrence. *A guide to research in music education*, BJ6

Ferrari, Corinna. *Top symbols and trademarks of the world*, CH370

Ferrari, Luigi. *Onomasticon*, BE1312

Ferré, John P. *Public relations & ethics*, CH565

Ferré, Régine. *Répertoire des historiens français pour la période moderne et contemporaine*, DC163

Ferreira, Aurélio Buarque de Holanda. *Novo dicionário da língua portuguesa*, AC642

—— *Pequeno dicionário brasileiro da língua portuguêsa*, AC643

Ferreira, José de Azevedo. *Bibliografia selectiva da língua portuguesa*, BD164

Ferreira, Julio Albino. *Dicionário inglês-português*, AC646

Ferreira, Manuel. *A new bibliography of the lusophone literatures of Africa*, BE1519

Ferreira Sobral, Eduardo F. *Publicaciones periódicas argentinas, 1781–1969*, AD70

Ferreiro, Alberto. *The Visigoths in Gaul and Spain, A.D. 418–711*, DC4

Ferrell, Robert H. *Atlas of American history*, DB71

Ferrer, Maxima M. *Union list of serials of government agency libraries of the Philippines*, AD244

Ferreras, Juan Ignacio. *Catálogo de novelas y novelistas españoles del siglo XIX*, BE1474

Ferres, John H. *Modern Commonwealth literature*, BE815

Ferreyrolles, Gérard. *Chronologie de la littérature française*, BE1152

Ferrier, Dorothy J. *Annotated catalogue of and guide to the publications of the Geological Survey Canada, 1845–1917*, EF28

Ferrier, W. F. *Annotated catalogue of and guide to the publications of the Geological Survey Canada, 1845–1917*, EF28

Ferris, William R. *Encyclopedia of Southern culture*, DB158

Ferrua, Antonio. *Note al Thesaurus linguae latinae*, AC571, BE1047

Fertig, Barbara C. *Folklife sourcebook*, CF75

Fertility modification thesaurus, International Institute for the Study of Human Reproduction, CC254

Fertilizers, EJ51, EJ79

Fertilizers, EJ79

Fest, Wilfried. *Dictionary of German history, 1806–1945*, DC256

Festivals, AL145, AL148, CF57

Festivals (by subject)
 film, BH265
 music, BJ193, BJ195, BJ196
 video, BH265

Festschriften
 bibliography, AA125, AA126

Festschriften (by country or region)
 Sweden
  bibliography, AA127

Festschriften (by subect)
 law, CK6

Festschriften (by subject)
 ancient history, DA67
 art, BF51
 art history, BF50
 Catalan literature, BD166, BE1436
 economics, CH20
 French language, BD158, BE1134
 French literature, BD158, BE1134
 Germanic languages, BD112
 history and area studies, DA6
 Iberian language and literature, BD166, BE1436
 Italian language, BD160, BE1293
 Italian literature, BD160, BE1293
 Jewish studies, BC510
 library and information science, AK13
 medieval studies, DA139
 music, BJ13
 Portuguese literature, BD166, BE1436
 religion, BC14, BC121
 Spanish literature, BD166, BE1436

Festschriften in art history, 1960–1975, Lincoln, Betty Woelk, BF50, BF51

Fetterman, N. I. *Index to research in home economics, 1972–1991*, EJ197

Fetzer, Mary. *Introduction to United States government information sources*, AF73, AF120, CJ200

Feuereisen, Fritz. *Die Presse in Afrika*, AE4

—— *Presse in Asien und Ozeanien*, AE4

—— *Presse in Europa*, AE4

—— *Presse in Lateinamerika*, AE4

Feuerstein, Georg. *Encyclopedic dictionary of yoga*, BC487

Feuerwerker, Albert. *Cambridge history of China*, DE146

Fey, Harold E. *A history of the ecumenical movement*, BC276

FIAF. *Bibliography of national filmographies*, BH164

—— *Glossary of filmographic terms*, BH257

—— *International directory of cinematographers, set- and costume designers in film*, BH208

—— *International directory of film and TV documentation centres*, BH179

—— *International index to film periodicals*, BH234

Fichas para el anuario bibliografico colombiano, AA523

Fichero bibliográfico hispanoamericano, AA474

Fichier augustinien, Institut des Études Augustiniennes, BB65

Ficke, Robert C. *Digest of data on persons with disabilities*, CB206, CC198

Fickenscher, W. *UdSSR : Enzyklopädie der Union der Sozialistischen Sowjetrepubliken*, AB83

Fiction
 bibliography, BE240, BE242, BE244, BE245, BE246, BE248, BE250, BE258, BE259
 bibliography of bibliography, BE253
 biobibliography, BE241, BE247, BE249, BE252
 criticism, BE264
  bibliography, BE257
  collections, BE263
 indexes, BE243, BE264
 sequence novels
  bibliography, BE255

Fiction (by country or region)
 Europe
  bibliography, BE986

Fiction (by language)
 English
  bibliography, BE254
 see also **Detective and mystery fiction; Fairy tales; Historical fiction; Science fiction, fantasy, and Gothic literature; Short stories**

Fiction, 1876–1983, BE244

Fiction catalog, BE245

Fiction index, BE242

Fiction narrative en prose au XVIIème siècle, Lever, Maurice, BE1187, BE1190

Fiction sequels for readers 10–16, Anderson, Vicki, BE246

Fictitious imprints, AA194, AA195, AA196

Fidel, Estelle A. *Play index*, BE234

Fidler, Linda M. *International music journals*, BJ102

Fieg, Eugene C. *Religion journals and serials*, BC23

Field, C. W. *National index of parish registers*, AJ107

Field, Carolyn W. *Special collections in children's literature*, AK113

—— *Subject collections in children's literature*, AK113

Field, Claud. *Dictionary of Oriental quotations (Arabic and Persian)*, BE124

—— *A learner's dictionary of Arabic and Persian quotations*, BE124

Field, John. *Place-names of Great Britain and Ireland*, CL196, CL209

Field, Norman S. *League of Nations & United Nations monthly list of selected articles*, CH23

Field crop abstracts, EJ19

Field crop diseases handbook, Nyvall, Robert F., EJ58

Field guide to American architecture, Rifkind, Carole, BF252

Field guide to American houses, McAlester, Lee, BF252

—— McAlester, Virginia, BF252

A field guide to hawks, Clark, William S., EG256

Field guide to North American ... , Audubon Society, EG81

A field guide to rocks and minerals, Pough, Frederick H., EF204

A field guide to the birds, Peterson, Roger Tory, EG272

Field guide to the study of American literature, Kolb, Harold H., BE397

The field guide to U.S. national forests, Mohlenbrock, Robert H., EJ186

A field guide to western mushrooms, Smith, Alexander Hanchett, EG190

Fieldhouse, Arthur E. *A directory of philanthropic trusts in New Zealand*, AL128

Fieldiana : anthropology, CE102

Fielding, Mantle. *American engravers upon copper and steel*, BF386

—— *Mantle Fielding's dictionary of American painters, sculptors & engravers*, BF154

Fielding, Raymond. *A bibliography of theses and dissertations on the subject of film, 1916–1979*, BH176

Fierro, Alfred. *Bibliographie analytique des biographies collectives imprimées de la France contemporaine,* AH196
—— *Bibliographie critique des mémoires sur la Révolution écrits ou traduits en français,* DC180
—— *Bibliographie de la Révolution française, 1940–1988,* DC176
—— *Histoire et dictionnaire de la Révolution française,* DC188
Fieser, Louis Frederick. *Fieser and Fieser's reagents for organic synthesis,* EE131
Fieser, Mary. *Fieser and Fieser's reagents for organic synthesis,* EE131
Fieser and Fieser's reagents for organic synthesis, Fieser, Louis Frederick, EE131
Fifteen American authors before 1900, BE399, BE404
Fifteen modern American authors, BE413
The fifteenth-century book, Bühler, Curt Ferdinand, AA236
Fifth book of junior authors & illustrators, Holtze, Sally Holmes, BE384
The fifth directory of periodicals publishing articles on American and English language and literature, criticism and theory, film, American studies, poetry and fiction, Barlow, Richard G., BE170
Fifth international directory of anthropologists, CE66
Fifty Caribbean writers, BE970
Fifty Southern writers after 1900, BE568, BE578
—— Bain, Robert, BE571
—— Flora, Joseph M., BE571
Fifty Southern writers before 1900, BE568, BE571, BE578
Fifty Western writers, BE570, BE572
Fifty years (and twelve) of classical scholarship, BE994
Fifty years of best sellers, 1895–1945, AA327
Fifty years of classical scholarship, Platnauer, Maurice, BE994
Fifty years of Hume scholarship, Hall, Roland, BB73
Fifty years of television, Terrace, Vincent, BH299
Figatner, ÏU. ÏU. *Velikaĭa Oktiabr'skaĭa sotsialisticheskaĭa revoliutsiĭa,* DC601
Fighters for independence, White, J. Todd, DB89
Fighting words, Ammer, Christine, CJ582
Figueras, Myriam. *Travel accounts and descriptions of Latin America and the Caribbean, 1800–1920,* DB263, DB409
Figueroa, Pedro Pablo. *Diccionario biográfico de Chile,* AH128
—— *Diccionario biográfico de estranjeros en Chile,* AH129
Figueroa, Virgilio. *Diccionario histórico, biográfico y bibliográfico de Chile,* AH130
Figueroa Marroquín, Horacio. *Apéndice a la Bibliografía guatemalteca,* AA482
al-Fihris al-waṭanī lil-maṭbūāt al-'Irāqīyah, AA908
Fiji
  bibliography, AA945, DF7
  biography, AH376
Fiji national bibliography, AA945
Fijian language
  dictionaries
    bilingual
      Fijian-English, AC319
Filatov, V. P. *Russko-angliĭskiĭ slovar' obshchestvenno-politicheskoĭ leksiki,* CA40
Filbee, Marjorie. *Dictionary of country furniture,* BG132
Filby, P. William. *American & British genealogy & heraldry,* AJ28
—— *A bibliography of American county histories,* DB139
—— *Directory of American libraries with genealogy or local history collections,* AJ54
—— *Germans to America,* AJ40, AJ64
—— *Italians to America,* AJ64
—— *Passenger and immigration lists bibliography, 1538–1900,* AJ29
—— *Passenger and immigration lists index,* AJ44
—— *Who's who in genealogy & heraldry,* AJ56

Fildes, Robert. *World index of economic forecasts,* CH122
Filer, Colin. *A bibliography of Melanesian bibliographies,* AA77
Filigranes, Briquet, Charles Moïse, AA255, AA256
Filin, Fedot Petrovich. *Slovar' russkikh narodnykh govorov,* AC670
—— *Slovar' russkogo iazyka XI-XVII vv,* AC673
Filing and indexing, AK210, AK211
Filing arrangement in the Library of Congress catalogs, AK211
Filing rules for the dictionary catalogs in the Library of Congress, AK211
Filipiniana union catalog, AA930
Filipinos overseas, Saito, Shiro, CC409
Filippelli, Ronald L. *Labor conflict in the United States,* CH647
Filippi, Joseph de. *Essai d'une bibliographie générale du théâtre,* BE1184
Filler, Louis. *Dictionary of American conservatism,* CJ24, CJ117
—— *A dictionary of American social change,* CA35
Filler, Louise. *Progressivism and muckraking,* DB125
Film
  adaptations, BH20, BH215, BH216, BH217, BH218, BH219
  annuals, BH238, BH268, BH269
  bibliography, BH162, BH163, BH164, BH165, BH166, BH167, BH169, BH170, BH172, BH177
  bibliography of bibliography, BH173
  biography, BH22, BH185, BH213, BH266, BH279, BH282, BH283, BH284, BH285, BH286, BH287, BH288, BH289, BH290
    indexes, BH291
  catalogs, BH183, BH184, BH185, BH188, BH190, BH191, BH193, BH204, BH303
    bibliography, BH164
  catalogs and filmography, BH189, BH203
  databases, BH185, BH234, BH240, BH297
  dictionaries, BH256, BH258, BH259, BH260, BH261, BH317
    multilingual, BH257
  directories, BH263, BH265, BH266, BH267
  dissertations, BH176
  encyclopedias, BH245, BH246, BH247, BH248, BH249, BH250, BH251, BH252, BH253, BH254, BH255
  guides, BH159, BH160, BH161, BH194, BH195, BH196, BH197, BH198, BH199, BH200, BH201, BH202
  handbooks, BH270, BH272
  indexes, AA380, BH231, BH232, BH233, BH234, BH235, CB31
  library catalogs, AA107, BH163, BH190, BH191
  library resources, BH178, BH179, BH180, BH181, BH182
  periodicals, BH175
    union lists, BH174
  prizes and awards, BH273, BH274, BH275
  quotations, BH262
  reviews
    indexes, BH61
  reviews and criticism, BH236, BH237, BH238, BH239, BH240, BH241, BH242
    indexes, BH243, BH244
  themes and genres, BH220, BH222, BH223, BH224, BH225, BH228, BH245
Film (by country or region)
  Africa, BH165
  Africa, South of the Sahara
    bibliography, BH171
  Canada
    catalogs, BH192
  developing countries
    filmography, BH221
  Europe, Eastern
    handbooks, BH271
  German-speaking countries, BH281
  Germany
    catalogs, BH187

Great Britain
  catalogs, BH186
  directories, BH264
U.S.S.R.
  handbooks, BH271
Film (by subject)
  Africa, DD43
  African Americans, BH227
  archaeology, DA62
  art, BF96
  biography, BH226
  costume, BH169
  homosexuality, BH229
  Latinos and Latinas, BH230
  treatment of minorities, CC334
  women
    filmography, CC513
Film, Armour, Robert A., BH159
Film actors guide, BH207
Film and broadcast terms, BH260
Film and literature, BH215, BH217, BH219
  bibliography, BH177, BH216
Film and television, BH236
Film and television handbook, BH264
Film and Television Study Center. *Motion pictures, television and radio,* BH180
Film and video finder, CB28
Film and video resources about Africa, University of Illinois Film Center, DD43
Film as literature, literature as film, Ross, Harris, BH177
The film audience, Austin, Bruce A., BH162
Film book bibliography, 1940–1975, Derry, Charles, BH170
—— Ellis, Jack C., BH170
—— Kern, Sharon, BH170
Film Canadiana, AA456
The film catalog, Museum of Modern Art (New York, N.Y.), BH191
—— United States. Public Health Service, EH45
Film composers guide, BH207
Film costume, Prichard, Susan Perez, BH169
Film directors, BH207, BH305
The film encyclopedia, Katz, Ephraim, BH251
The film handbook, BH290
—— Andrew, Geoff, BH290
The film index, BH235
—— Writers' Program (New York, N.Y.), BH172
•*Film index international,* BH185
Film literature index, BH232
Film music, Limbacher, James L., BJ360
Film noir, Silver, Alain, BH224
—— Ward, Elizabeth, BH224
Film producers and directors
  biography, BH288, BH289
  filmography, BH188, BH204, BH205, BH207, BH209, BH214, BH290
Film producers and directors (by country or region)
  Africa
    filmography, BH212
Film producers, studios, agents, and casting directors guide, BH207
Film review annual, BH237
Film review index, BH244
Film study, Manchel, Frank, BH167
Film, television, and stage music on phonograph records, Harris, Steve, BJ359
Film, television, and video periodicals, Loughney, Katharine, BH175
Film theaters, BH35
Film writers guide, BH207
Filmed books and plays, Enser, A. G. S., BH215
Filmer, Alison J. *Harrap's book of film directors and their films,* BH204
Filmgoer's and video viewer's companion, BH249
Filmlexicon degli autori e delle opere, BH248
Filmmakers dictionary, Singleton, Ralph S., BH261
Filmographic dictionary of world literature, Daisne, Johan, BH216
Filmographie mondiale de la Révolution française, Dallet, Sylvie, DC179

A filmography of the Third World, Cyr, Helen W., BH221

Filmography of the Third World, 1976–1983, Cyr, Helen W., BH221

Films
  preservation, BF351

Films (by subject)
  architecture, BF247

Films and other materials for projection, Library of Congress, AA107, AA381

Films and videos on photography, BF96, BF327

Films by genre, López, Daniel, BH228

Films for anthropological teaching, Heider, Karl G., CE33

Films for, by, and about women, Sullivan, Kaye, CC513

Films in the sciences, McRae, Madelyn A., EA34
  —— Newman, Michele M., EA34

Films of the Holocaust, Skirball, Sheba F., DA221

Films on art, BF96

Filmscripts
  bibliography, BH168
  catalogs, BH163

Filmstrip & slide set finder, CB28

Filov, V. A. *Svodnyi katalog knig na inostrannykh iazikakh, izdannykh v Rossii v XVII veke, 1701–1800*, AA791

Filson, Lawrence E. *The legislative drafter's desk reference*, CJ194

Filtcraft compendium, CH517

Final choices, Norrgard, Lee E., CC184

Finance and banking
  bibliography, CH206, CH207, CH221, CH224, CH283
  biography, CH105, CH265, CH289
  databases, CH299
  dictionaries, CH63, CH123, CH209, CH212, CH227, CH270, CH272, CH273, CH274
    multilingual, CH214, CH271
  directories, CH222, CH228, CH229, CH230, CH231, CH275, CH277, CH278, CH280, CH281, CH289, CH360, CH388, CH524, CH539
  encyclopedias, CH211, CH226, CH265, CH266, CH267, CH268
  handbooks, CH218, CH230, CH233, CH234, CH235, CH282, CH319, CH322, CH323
  indexes, CH225, CH264
  periodicals, CH205
  statistics, CH222, CH223, CH237, CH241, CH290, CH292, CH293, CH388, CH524, CH539
  tables, CH269

Finance and banking (by country or region)
  Europe
    directories, CH276
  United States
    statistics, CH291, CH294

Finance and investment handbook, CH233

Finance, insurance, & real estate USA, CH222, CH388, CH524, CH539

Finance literature index, CH225

Financial aid for research and creative activities abroad, CB366

Financial aid for research, study, travel and other activities abroad, CB366

Financial aid for study and training abroad, Schlachter, Gail Ann, CB366
  —— Weber, R. David, CB366

Financial aids for higher education, Keeslar, Oreon, CB382

Financial Analysts Federation. *Standards of practice handbook*, CH317

The financial analyst's handbook, CH319

Financial journals and serials, Fisher, William Harvey, CH205

Financial market indexes, averages, and indicators, CH232

Financial mathematics handbook, Muksian, Robert, CH220

Financial post, AE118, CH38

Financial statistics of cities, CG74

Financial statistics of states, CG80

Financial times, AE118, CH38

Financial times (London). *Financial times oil and gas international year book*, EK307
  —— *Financial times world hotel directory*, CL393
  —— *The Financial times world insurance yearbook*, CH512

Financial times of Canada [index], CH35

Financial times oil and gas international year book, EK307

Financial times world hotel directory, CL393

The Financial times world insurance yearbook, CH512

Financial yellow book, CH350

Financing foreign operations, CH217

The financing of American higher education, Quay, Richard H., CB226

Finch, Glenda. *Detailed statistics on the urban and rural population of Pakistan, 1950 to 2010*, CG415

Finch, M. H. J. *Uruguay*, DB396

Fincher, Julian H. *Dictionary of pharmacy*, EH327

Find the law in the library, Corbin, John, CK116

Finders' guide to decorative arts in the Smithsonian Institution, Smithsonian Institution, BG28

Finder's guide to prints and drawings in the Smithsonian Institution, Classen, Lynda Corey, BF365

FINDex, CH578

Finding answers in science and technology, Primack, Alice Lefler, EA7

Finding-list of English books to 1640 in libraries in the British Isles (excluding the national libraries and the libraries of Oxford and Cambridge), Ramage, David, AA671, AA672

Finding-list of English poetical miscellanies 1700–48 in selected American libraries, Boys, Richard C., BE699

Finding our fathers, Rottenberg, Dan, AJ21

Finding the law, Berring, Robert C., CK115
  —— Cohen, Morris L., CK115
  —— Olson, Kent C., CK115

Finding the source in sociology and anthropology, Brown, Samuel R., CC5, CE4

Finding the source of medical information, EH3

Findlay, Allan M. *Tunisia*, DD18

Findlay, Anne M. *Morocco*, DD18

Findlay, James A. *Modern Latin American art*, BF22

Findling, John E. *Dictionary of American diplomatic history*, CJ118, CJ119, CJ150
  —— *Statesmen who changed the world*, CJ70

Fine, Bernard D. *Glossary of psychoanalytic terms and concepts*, CD30
  —— *Psychoanalytic terms and concepts*, CD30

Fine, Morris. *Israel-Diaspora relations*, DA7

Fine art reproductions of old & modern masters, New York Graphic Society, BF196

Fine arts see **Architecture; Art**

Fine arts, Ehresmann, Donald L., BF2

Fine arts periodicals, Robinson, Doris, BF47

Fine print references, Ludman, Joan, BF362

Fine prints, Shapiro, Cecile, BF375

Fingerit, Efim Markovich. *Gazetnyi mir Sovetskogo Soiuza, 1917–1970 gg*, AE73
  —— *Russkaia periodicheskaia pechat'*, AD146

Fink, Clinton F. *Peace and war*, CJ680

Fink, Donald G. *Electronics engineers' handbook*, EK136
  —— *Standard handbook for electrical engineers*, EK143
  —— *Television engineering handbook*, EK148

Fink, Gary M. *Biographical dictionary of American labor*, CH678
  —— *Labor unions*, CH648
  —— *State labor proceedings*, CH630

Fink, John W. *Indices to American literary annuals and gift books, 1825–1865*, BE415

Fink, Peter E. *The new dictionary of sacramental worship*, BC427

Fink, Robert. *The language of twentieth century music*, BJ149

Finke, Horst-Dieter. *Bibliographischer Wegweiser der philosophischen Literatur*, BB9

Finkel, Asher J. *The American Medical Association family medical guide*, EH171

Finkel, Ludwik. *Bibliografia historyi polskiej*, DC473

Finkelhor, David. *A sourcebook on child sexual abuse*, CC167

Finkelstein, Louis. *The Cambridge history of Judaism*, BC562

Finkl, Charles W. *The encyclopedia of applied geology*, EF62
  —— *The encyclopedia of field and general geology*, EF63
  —— *The encyclopedia of soil science*, EJ22

Finland
  atlases, CL325, CL326
  bibliography, AA609, AA610, AA611, DC136, DC139, DC140
    current, AA612
  bibliography of bibliography, AA41
  biography, AH164, AH186, AH187, AH188
    bibliography, AH295
    contemporary, AH189, AH190
  government publications, AF167
  newspapers, AE49
  periodicals, AD89
    indexes, AD311
  statistics, CG212, CG213

Finland (by subject)
  history, DC72, DC137
    bibliography, DC141
  manuscripts and archives, DC138
  population, CG211

Finland. Maanmittaushallitus. *Basic map of Finland*, CL325
  —— *Fennia*, CL325
  —— *Finland in maps*, CL325
  —— *Road map of Finland*, CL325

Finland, Screen, J. E. O., DC140

Finland and the Finns, Bako, Elemer, DC136

Finland in maps, Finland. Maanmittaushallitus, CL325

Finland—sources of information, Ruokonen, Kyllikki, DC139

Finlandianska tidskriftsartiklar, nyhetsindex, AD311

Finlands bibliografiska litteratur, Grönroos, Henrik, AA41

Finlands litteratur, AA612

Finley, E. Gault. *Education in Canada*, CB42

Finley, M. I. *Atlas of classical archaeology*, DA116

Finneran, Richard J. *Anglo-Irish literature*, BE798
  —— *Recent research on Anglo-Irish writers*, BE798

Finnish and Baltic history and literatures, Harvard University. Library, DC137

Finnish-English general dictionary, AC321

Finnish language
  dictionaries, AC320
    bilingual
      English-Finnish, AC322, AC324
      Finnish-English, AC321, AC323, AC325

Finnish literature, DC137
  biobibliography, BE1127

Finnish literature (by subject)
  history, BE1126

The Finnish national bibliography, AA612

Finno-Ugric languages, BD208
  dictionaries, AC326

Finot, Enrique. *Historia de la literatura boliviana*, BE922

Finotti, Joseph Maria. *Bibliographia Catholica Americana*, BC392

Finsk biografisk handbok, AH186

Finson, Shelley Davis. *Women and religion*, BC10

Fintel, Mark. *Handbook of concrete engineering*, EK105

Finzi, Giuseppe. *Dizionario di citazioni latine ed italiane*, BE142

Fire insurance maps in the Library of Congress, Library of Congress. Geography and Map Division. Reference and Bibliography Section, CL235

Fire music, Gray, John, BJ301

Fire prevention, EK104

Fire protection handbook, EK104

FIRE USA, CH222, CH388, CH524, CH539

Firestone, Richard B. *Table of radioactive isotopes*, ED42

Firkin, Barry G. *Dictionary of medical eponyms*, EH99

Firkins, Ina Ten Eyck. *Index to plays, 1800–1926*, BE226

———— *Index to short stories*, BE260

First 100 years of American geology, Merrill, George Perkins, EF102

First aid, EE78, EH172

First aid manual for chemical accidents, Lefèvre, M. J., EE78

First American Jewish families, Stern, Malcolm H., AJ66

The first century of New England verse, Jantz, Harold Stein, BE492

The first demographic portraits of Russia, 1951–1990, CG293

First dictionary of linguistics and phonetics, Crystal, David, BD36

First District Dental Society of the State of New York. *Dental bibliography*, EH245

First editions, AA239, AA242

First editions (by language)
German, BE1233

First facts of American labor, CH676

The first Gothics, Frank, Frederick S., BE288

First-line index of English poetry, 1500–1800, BE704

First performances in America to 1900, Johnson, Harold Earle, BJ175

First person female American, Rhodes, Carolyn H., BE508

First printings of American authors, BE405

First proofs of the Universal catalogue of books on art, National Art Library (Great Britain), BF56

First stop, Ryan, Joe, AB16

First supplement to the Who's who of Afghanistan, Adamec, Ludwig W., AH333

The FirstBook of demographics for the republics of the former Soviet Union, CG293

The FirstBook of demographics for the republics of the former Soviet Union, 1951–1990, CG294

•*FirstPortraitsPlus*, CG293

Firth, Frank E. *The encyclopedia of marine resources*, EF27

Firth, Margaret A. *Handbook of scientific and technical awards in the United States and Canada, 1900–1952*, EA197

Fischbeck, Helmut J. *Formulas, facts, and constants for students and professionals in engineering, chemistry, and physics*, ED36

Fischbeck, Kurt. *Formulas, facts, and constants for students and professionals in engineering, chemistry, and physics*, ED36

Fischel, Jack. *Jewish-American history and culture*, BC551

Fischer, A. *English-Xhosa dictionary*, AC809

Fischer, Andreas. *An index to dialect maps of Great Britain*, BD104

Fischer, August. *Wörterbuch der klassischen arabischen Sprache*, AC225

Fischer, Claus A. *Wahlhandbuch für die Bundesrepublik Deutschland*, CJ335

Fischer, Dennis. *Horror film directors, 1931–1990*, BH290

Fischer, Gayle V. *Journal of women's history guide to periodical literature*, CC529

Fischer, Isidor. *Biographisches Lexikon der hervorragenden Ärzte der letzten 50 Jahre*, EH222

Fischer, Jango. *Diccionario bibliographico brasileiro*, AA509

Fischer, Manfred S. *Internationale bibliographie zu Geschichte und Theorie der Komparatistik*, BE18

Fischer, Wolfram. *Charles Szladits' guide to foreign legal materials*, CK210

Fischer-Galati, Stephen A. *Rumania*, DC496

Fischer-Schreiber, Ingrid. *The encyclopedia of Eastern philosophy and religion*, BB31, BC57

Fischgrund, Tom. *Barron's top 50*, CB251

Fischler, Shirley Walton. *The hockey encyclopedia*, BK87

Fischler, Stan. *The hockey encyclopedia*, BK87

Fischler's hockey encyclopedia, BK87

Fiscina, Salvatore F. *A sourcebook for research in law and medicine*, EH268

Fish, Beverly. *Water publications of state agencies*, EK89

Fish, Marian C. *Handbook of school-based interventions*, CB212

Fisher, Benjamin Franklin. *The Gothic's Gothic*, BE287

Fisher, Carol A. *A bibliography of Malawi*, DD176

Fisher, Harold A. *The world's great dailies*, AE133

Fisher, James C. *Encyclopedia of school administration & supervision*, CB180

Fisher, John Hurt. *The medieval literature of Western Europe*, BE984

Fisher, John Robert. *Peru*, DB382

Fisher, Kim N. *On the screen*, BH160

Fisher, Lois H. *A literary gazetteer of England*, BE629

Fisher, Louis. *Encyclopedia of the American presidency*, CJ178

Fisher, Margery Turner. *Who's who in children's books*, BE381

Fisher, Mary L. *Guide to state legislative and administrative materials*, CJ267

Fisher, Morris. *Provinces and provincial capitals of the world*, CL86

Fisher, Ralph T. *Dictionary of Russian historical terms from the eleventh century to 1917*, DC584

Fisher, Rita C. *Agricultural information resource centers*, EJ38

Fisher, Ronald A. *Statistical tables for biological, agricultural and medical research*, EG61

Fisher, Stanley W. *Dictionary of watercolour painters, 1750–1900*, BF316

Fisher, William Harvey. *Business journals of the United States*, CH25

———— *Financial journals and serials*, CH205

Fishes, EG281, EG282, EG283, EG284, EG285, EG286, EG287, EG288

Fishes of the world, Wheeler, Alwyne C., EG288

Fishing *see* **Hunting and fishing**

Fishman, Stephen. *The copyright handbook*, AA314

Fisiak, Jacek. *A bibliography of writings for the history of the English language*, BD100

Fiske, Edward B. *The Fiske guide to colleges*, CB270

Fiske, John. *Appleton's cyclopaedia of American biography*, AH58

The Fiske guide to colleges, CB270

Fitch, Donald. *Blake set to music*, BJ70

Fitch, Jennifer M. *Earth and astronomical sciences research centres*, EC46, EF16

Fitch, Thomas P. *Dictionary of banking terms*, CH272

Fitness, BK39
bibliography, BK5
encyclopedias, BK15

Fitter, Maisie. *The Penguin dictionary of British natural history*, EG77

Fitter, Richard Sidney Richmond. *The Penguin dictionary of British natural history*, EG77

Fitton, Robert A. *Leadership*, CJ590

Fitzgerald, Gerald. *Annals of the Metropolitan Opera Guild*, BJ254

Fitzgerald, L. S. *The Continental novel*, BE257

Fitzgerald, Wilma. *Ocelli nominum*, AA197

FitzHugh, Terrick V. H. *The dictionary of genealogy*, AJ111

Fitzmyer, Joseph A. *An Aramaic bibliography*, BD206

———— *The Dead Sea Scrolls*, BC187

———— *Introductory bibliography for the study of scripture*, BC13, BC110

———— *The new Jerome biblical commentary*, BC178

Fitzpatrick, André Jude. *Irish historical statistics*, CG253

Fitzpatrick, Gary L. *Direct-line distances—international edition*, CL59

———— *Direct-line distances—United States edition*, CL60

———— *International time tables*, EC86

Fitzpatrick, Sheila. *A researcher's guide to sources on Soviet social history in the 1930s*, DC592

Fitzsimmons, Richard. *Pro-choice/pro-life*, CC251

Five hundred early juveniles, AA245

Five hundred fifty books on Buddhism, BC460

Five kingdoms, Margulis, Lynn, EG341

Five thousand and one nights at the movies, BH197

The five thousand dictionary, Fenn, Courtenay Hughes, AC262

Five years' work in librarianship, AK78

Fiziko-geograficheskii atlas mira, Akademiiā nauk SSSR, CL275

Fjalor anglisht-shqip, AC206

Fjioka, Keisuke. *Intā Puresu-ban kagaku gijutsu 35–mango daijiten*, EA119

FLA theses, Library Association. Library, AK24

Flackes, William D. *Northern Ireland : a political directory, 1966–88*, CJ374

Flags, AL190, AL191, AL192, AL193, AL194, AL195, DB151

Flags and arms across the world, Smith, Whitney, AL193

Flags of the world, AL190

Flags through the ages and across the world, Smith, Whitney, AL193, AL194

Flaisher, 'Karniyah. *Mafteaḥ le-khitve-ʿet be-' Ivrit*, AD340

Flake, Chad J. *A Mormon bibliography, 1830–1930*, BC372

Flanagan, Cathleen C. *American folklore*, CF64

Flanagan, John T. *American folklore*, CF64

Flanagan, Laurence. *A dictionary of Irish archaeology*, DC405

Flanders, Carl N. *Abortion*, CC249, CC252

———— *Dictionary of American foreign affairs*, CJ119, CJ150

Flanders, Stephen A. *Dictionary of American foreign affairs*, CJ119, CJ150

Flanders, DC109
periodicals
indexes, AD303, BE1066
statistics, CG200

Flandria nostra, Broeckx, J. L., DC109

Flannery, Austin P. *Documents of Vatican II*, BC437

Flanz, G. H. *Constitutions of the countries of the world*, CK72

Flasche, Hans. *Romance languages and literatures as presented in German doctoral dissertations, 1885–1950*, BD155, BE1071

———— *Die Sprachen und Literaturen der Romanen im Spiegel der deutschen Universitätsschriften, 1885–1950*, BD155, BE1071

Flavor, EH305, EJ217

Fleischer, Hagen. *Greece in the 1940s*, DC372

Fleischer, Nat. *A pictorial history of boxing*, BK69

Fleischer, Wolfgang. *Deutsche Sprache*, BD124

Fleischmann, Wolfgang Bernard. *Encyclopedia of world literature in the 20th century*, BE66

Fleming, Ian. *Comprehensive organic synthesis*, EE119

Fleming, John. *The Penguin dictionary of architecture*, BF244

———— *The Penguin dictionary of decorative arts*, BG21

———— *Visual arts*, BF132

———— *World history of art*, BF132

Fleming, Patricia. *Atlantic Canadian imprints, 1801–1820*, DB182

Flemish literature, AD303, BE1063, BE1064, BE1066

Flemish literature (by subject)
history, BE1334

Flemish writers translated (1830–1931), Arents, Prosper, BE1063

Flemming, Peter A. *Terrorism, 1980–1987*, CJ552

Fletcher, Alan. *Guide to tables of elliptic functions*, EB73

———— *An index of mathematical tables*, EB72

Fletcher, Andrew J. *The Merck manual of geriatrics*, EH191

Fletcher, Banister. *History of architecture*, BF255

———— *Sir Banister Fletcher's A history of architecture*, BF255

Fletcher, Colin. *The complete walker III*, BK113

———— *New complete walker*, BK113

Fletcher, James E. *Broadcast research definitions*, CH485

Fletcher, John. *Information sources in economics*, CH3

Fletcher, Katy. *Spy fiction*, BE272

Fletcher, Marilyn P. *Reader's guide to twentieth-century science fiction*, BE295

Fletcher, Marvin. *Peacetime army, 1900–1941*, CJ608

Fletcher, Richard A. *Who's who in Roman Britain and Anglo-Saxon England*, DC298

Fletcher, William Isaac. *The A.L.A. index*, BE239
——— *Poole's index to periodical literature, 1802–81*, AD282

Fletcher-Janzen, Elaine. *Concise encyclopedia of special education*, CB195

Fletcher School of Law and Diplomacy. *Leftwing social movements in Japan*, CJ512

Fleurent, C. H. A. *World medical periodicals*, EH40

Fleury, Bruce E. *Dinosaurs*, EF229

Flexner, Stuart Berg. *Dictionary of American slang*, AC120, AC135
——— *March's thesaurus and dictionary of the English language*, AC141
——— *The Random House dictionary of the English language*, AC12
——— *The Random House thesaurus*, AC143

Flick, Ernest W. *Industrial solvents handbook*, EK56

Flieger, Wilhelm. *World population growth and aging*, CG50

Fling, Robert Michael. *A basic music library*, BJ24

Flint, W. P. *Destructive and useful insects*, EG84, EG335

Flintham, Victor. *Air wars and aircraft*, CJ593

Flood, James. *Handbook of research on teaching the English language arts*, CB118

Flood, Walter Edgar. *The dictionary of chemical names*, EE29
——— *Origins of chemical names*, EE29

•*Floppy almanac*, EC78

Flora, Francesco. *Storia della letteratura italiana*, BE1306

Flora, Joseph M. *Contemporary fiction writers of the South*, BE568
——— *Fifty Southern writers after 1900*, BE571
——— *Fifty Southern writers before 1900*, BE571
——— *Southern writers*, BE578

Flora, EG167, EG173, EG174, EG175, EG176, EG177, EG178, EG179, EG180, EG181, EG182, EG183

Flora (by country or region)
Europe, EG169, EG170
Great Britain, EG168
North America
treatises, EG171

Flora Europaea, EG170, EG178

Flora of North America, EG171

Flora of the British Isles, Clapham, A. R., EG168

Florén Lozano, Luis. *Bibliografía de la bibliografía dominicana*, AA34

Flores, Angel. *Bibliografía de escritores hispanoamericanos, 1609–1974*, BE871
——— *Spanish American authors*, BE889

Flores, Arturo A. *Foreign law*, CK3

Flores Silva, Eusebio. *Atlas estadístico de Costa Rica, no. 2*, CL313

Flores Villela, Carlos Arturo. *México, la cultura, el arte y la vida cotidiana*, DB224

Florescano, Enrique. *Atlas histórico de México*, DB248
——— *Catálogo de tesis sobre historia de México*, DB237

Florida. [Laws, etc.]. *West's Florida statutes annotated*, CK179

Florida, Little, Elbert Luther, EJ191

Floristic regions of the world, Takhtadzhîân, A. L., EG163

Flou, Karel de. *Woordenboek der toponymie van Westelijk Vlaanderen, Vlaamsch Artesië, het Land van den Hoek*, CL210

Flower, John. *Atlas of classical archaeology*, DA116

Flowering plants of the world, EG172

Flowers of Europe, Polunin, Oleg, EG178

Floyd, Dale E. *World bibliography of armed land conflict from Waterloo to World War I*, DA170

Floyd, Samuel A. *Black music biography*, BJ220
——— *Black music in the United States*, BJ33

Flüchter, Wilfried. *Bibliographie zur alteuropäischen Religionsgeschichte*, BC6

Fluehr-Lobban, Carolyn. *Sudan*, DD48

Flugge, S. *Handbuch der Physik*, EC29, ED17

Fluid dynamics
handbooks, ED39

Fluk, Louise R. *Jews in the Soviet Union*, BC534

Flutre, Fernand. *Table des noms propres avec toutes leurs variantes*, BE1163

Flynn, Francis. *Gerontology*, CC67

Flynt, Dorothy S. *Southern poor whites*, CC262

Flynt, J. Wayne. *Southern poor whites*, CC262

The Fo-sho-hing-tsan-king, BC92

Foakes, R. A. *Routledge history of English poetry*, BE718

Focal dictionary of photographic technologies, Spencer, Douglas Arthur, BF340

Focal encyclopedia of photography, BF340

Focus Japan II, AL43, DE210

Focus on Buddhism, McDermott, Robert A., BC472

Focus on families, Cline, Ruth K. J., CC236

Focus on Hinduism, McDermott, Robert A., BC481
——— Smith, H. Daniel, BC481

Focus on teens in trouble, Sander, Daryl, CC174

Focus, uppslagsbok, AB97

Fodor, Nandor. *Encyclopaedia of psychic science*, CD134

Fogarty, Robert S. *Dictionary of American communal and utopian history*, DB149

Fogg, G. E. *A history of Antarctic science*, DG6

Foitzik, Jan. *Biographisches Handbuch der deutschsprachigen Emigration nach 1933*, AH203

Foix, Pierre. *Dictionnaire basque-français et français-basque*, AC229

Földrajzi nevek etimológiai szótára, Kiss, Lajos, CL207

Folena, Gianfranco. *Novissimo dizionario della lingua italiana*, AC526

Foley, Patrick K. *American authors, 1795–1895*, AA242

Folger Shakespeare Library. *Catalog of manuscripts of the Folger Shakespeare Library, Washington, D.C*, BE737
——— *Catalog of printed books of the Folger Shakespeare Library, Washington, D.C*, BE737
——— *Catalog of the Shakespeare collection*, BE771
——— *Shakespeare quarterly*, BE780

Folk and festival costume of the world, Wilcox, Ruth Turner, BG101

Folk and popular culture (by country or region)
South America, CF74

Folk architecture, BF215, BG3

Folk art
bibliography, BG12
current, BG10
biography
indexes, BG30
databases, BG12
dissertations, BG13
guides, BG1

Folk art (by country or region)
Africa, BG13
Americas, BG13
Canada
biography, BG33
Latin America, BF70
Oceania, BG13
United States, BG18
biography, BG35
directories, BG27
encyclopedias, BG35
indexes, BG17

Folk art, McKendry, Blake, BG33

Folk artists biographical index, BG30

Folk classification, Conklin, Harold C., CE7

Folk costumes from East Europe, Africa, and Asia, Tilke, Max, BG114

Folk costumes of the world in colour, Harrold, Robert, BG95

Folk literature (by country or region)
Africa, CF91
Ireland, CF89

Folk literature (Germanic), Bødker, Laurits, CE49, CF87

Folk literature of South American Indians, Wilbert, Johannes, CF74

Folk medicine, EH342
bibliography, EH319
encyclopedias, CF52

Folk music, BJ319
bibliography, BJ14, BJ231, BJ314, BJ322, CF67
biography, BJ326
dictionaries, BJ318
discography, BJ328, BJ329
encyclopedias, BJ326
handbooks, BJ324
indexes, BJ315
library catalogs, BJ321, BJ327, BJ328, CF85

Folk music (by country or region)
Oceania, BJ322
United States, BJ320
see also **Ballads; Ethnomusicology; Popular music**

Folk music, Library of Congress. Music Division, BJ321

The folk music sourcebook, Sandberg, Larry, BJ324

Folk song index, Brunnings, Florence E., BJ315

Folkemengden etter alder og ekteskapelig status, CG268

Folklife sourcebook, Bartis, Peter, CF75

Folklore, Brunvand, Jan Harold, CF36

Folklore and folklife, Steinfirst, Susan, CF40

Folklore and literature of the British Isles, Baer, Florence E., CF80

Folklore and popular culture
bibliography, CF37, CF38, CF39, CF40, CF46, CF47, CF62, CF64, CF65, CF66, CF67, CF68, CF69, CF70, CF71, CF90, CF92
current, CF42
databases, CF49
dictionaries, CE49, CF51
directories, CF55, CF75
dissertations, CF43, CF44
encyclopedias, CF50, CF51, CF52, CF86, CF87, CF88
guides, BH2, CF36
handbooks, CF56, CF77, CF78
indexes, AD257, CF41
library catalogs, CF85
library resources, CF73
thematic indexes, CF45, CF46, CF47, CF48, CF49

Folklore and popular culture (by country or region)
Africa, CF90, CF91, CF92
Americas, CF58
Asia, South, CF97
Australia, CF99
Brazil, CF60, CF63
Canada, CF65, CF66, CF73, CF75
Chile, CF71
England, CF85
France, DC209
German-speaking countries, CF87
Germany, CF86
Great Britain, CF88
bibliography, CF80
Greece
bibliography, BD141
Guatemala, CF59
India, CF96
Indonesia, CF94, CF95
Ireland, CF81, CF89
Italy, CF82
Japan, CF93, CF98
Java, CF95
Latin America, CF61, DB289
bibliography, BE878
Malaysia, CF94
Mexico, CF61

North America, CF64, CF67
Peru, CF70
Philippines, CF94
Russia and the U.S.S.R., CF83
South America, CF69
United States, CF66, CF68, CF73, CF75, CF77, CF78, CF90
West Indies, CF90
Folklore and popular culture (by subject)
  ethnic groups
    Jews, CF84
    Jewish, BC555, CF54
Folklore, cultural performances, and popular entertainments, CF56
Folklore from Africa to the United States, Coughlan, Margaret N., CF90
The folklore of American holidays, AL144
The folklore of world holidays, AL145, CF57
Folklore theses and dissertations in the United States, Dundes, Alan, CF43
Folkmängd, CG285
Folksingers and folksongs in America, Lawless, Ray McKinley, BJ320
Folktales in the English language, A guide to, CF46
Follett, Wilson. *Modern American usage,* AC71
Follett world-wide Latin dictionary, Levine, Edwin B., AC576
The Follett Zanichelli Italian dictionary, Ragazzini, Giuseppe, AC533
Folman, Wanda. *Bibliografia polskiego písmiennictwa demograficznego 1945–1975,* CG272
Folsom, Rose. *The calligraphers' dictionary,* BF370
Folter, Siegrun H. *Private libraries of musicians and musicologists,* BJ34
Fomin, Aleksandr Grigor'evich. *Putevoditel' po bibliografii, biobibliografii, istoriografii, khronologii i entsiklopedii literatury,* BE1389
Foncin, M. *Bibliographie cartographique internationale,* CL226
Fondation Custodia. *Répertoire des catalogues de ventes publiques,* BF112
Fonds parisiens d'archives de l'architecture, Ecole nationale supérieure des beaux-arts (France), BF225
—— Ruyssen, Geneviève, BF225
Foner, Eric. *Freedom's lawmakers,* DB102
Foner, Philip S. *First facts of American labor,* CH676
Fonseca, Edson Nery da. *Bibliografia do pensamento político republicano (1879/1980),* DB341
Fonseca, James W. *The atlas of American higher education,* CB323
Fonseca, Martinho Augusto Ferreira da. *Subsídios para um diccionario de pseudonymos, iniciaes e obras anonymas de escriptores portuguezes, contribuição para o estudo da litteratura portugueza,* AA181
Fontaine, Judith M. *Scholar's guide to intelligence literature,* CJ538
Fontán Lobé, Juan. *Bibliografía colonial,* DD4
Fontvieille, Jean Roger. *Bibliographie nationale de Madagascar, 1956–1963,* AA863, AA865
Food
  bibliography, EH291, EH293, EJ203, EJ204, EJ205, EJ206, EJ207
  dictionaries, EH301, EJ212, EJ213
    bilingual
      Russian-English, EJ31
  encyclopedias, EJ209
  handbooks, EH290, EH302, EH303, EH307, EH313, EJ156, EJ214, EJ215, EJ216, EJ217, EJ218, EJ219
  ingredients, EH325
  library resources, EJ204
  tables, EH308, EH314, EJ220
  see also **Cookbooks; Cookery; Natural foods; Nutrition**
Food additives, EH304
Food additives handbook, Lewis, Richard J., EJ170
Food and agriculture legislation, Food and Agriculture Organization of the United Nations, CK69

Food and Agriculture Organization of the United Nations. *1948–1985 world crop and livestock statistics,* EJ76
—— *ACCIS guide to United Nations information sources on food and agriculture,* EJ8
—— *FAO documentation,* EJ20
—— *FAO yearbook. Fertilizer,* EJ79
—— *FAO yearbook. Production,* EJ80
—— *FAO yearbook. Trade,* CH151, EJ81
—— *Food and agriculture legislation,* CK69
—— *Food composition tables,* EH292, EJ221
—— *Forest products,* EJ192
—— *International directory of marine scientists,* EF221
—— *The state of food and agriculture,* EJ83
—— *World demographic estimates and projections, 1950-2025,* CG59
Food and cookery, EJ211
  encyclopedias, EH298, EJ210
Food and nutrition information guide, Szilard, Paula, EH291
Food and nutrition quarterly index, EJ17
Food chemicals codex, EH306, EJ148
Food composition tables, Food and Agriculture Organization of the United Nations, EH292, EJ221
Food engineering data handbook, Hayes, George D., EJ169
Food flavoring, Merory, Joseph, EJ217
Food, hunger, agribusiness, Fenton, Thomas P., EJ161
Food industries manual, EJ166
Food science
  abstract journals, EH295, EJ150, EJ151
  databases, EJ150, EJ151
  dictionaries, EJ157
  directories, EJ160, EJ162, EJ163
  encyclopedias, EH297, EH325, EJ152, EJ153, EJ154, EJ155
  guides, EJ149
  handbooks, EH304, EH306, EH307, EJ147, EJ148, EJ156, EJ164, EJ165, EJ166, EJ167, EJ168, EJ169, EJ170
  sourcebooks, EJ171, EJ217
  thesauruses, EJ159
Food science and technology abstracts, EJ150, EJ159, EJ150
Food science sourcebook, Ockerman, Herbert W., EJ171
Food supply
  bibliography, EJ161
  directories, EJ161
  statistics, CH151, EJ81
Food values of portions commonly used, EH303, EJ216
Foodborne diseases, EJ167
Foods & nutrition encyclopedia, EH298, EJ210
Foods adlibra, EJ151
Foods and food production encyclopedia, EJ154
Foodservice dictionary, EJ157
Foos, Donald D. *How libraries must comply with the Americans with Disabilities Act (ADA),* AK66
Footage 89, BH178
Footage 91, Prelinger, Richard, BH178
Football, BK73, BK76, BK77, BK78, BK79
  bibliography, BK75, BK80
  biography, BK74
Foppens, Jean François. *Bibliotheca belgica,* AA580
For more information, Center for Arts Administration, BF39
—— Hample, Henry S., BF39
Foraminifera, EF238
Foray, C. P. *Sierra Leone,* DD48
Forbes, Fred R. *Dance,* BH132
Forbes, Harriette M. *New England diaries, 1602–1800,* BE507, DB66
Forbes, Robert James. *Bibliographia antiqua,* EA229
La force des faibles, Caratini, Roger, CE47
Ford, Boris. *Guide for readers to the new Pelican guide to English literature,* BE616
—— *The new Pelican guide to English literature,* BE616
Ford, Charles A. *Compton's dictionary of the natural sciences,* EG76

Ford, George H. *Victorian fiction,* BE668, BE686, BE984
Ford, Grace. *Breviate of parliamentary papers, 1900–1916,* AF196
—— *Breviate of parliamentary papers, 1917–1939,* AF196
—— *A guide to parliamentary papers,* AF177
—— *Select list of British parliamentary papers, 1833–1899,* AF196
—— *A select list of reports of inquiries of the Irish Dáil and Senate, 1922–72,* CJ376
Ford, Jeremiah D. M. *Tentative bibliography of Brazilian belles-lettres,* BE937
Ford, Percy. *Breviate of parliamentary papers, 1900–1916,* AF196
—— *Breviate of parliamentary papers, 1917–1939,* AF196
—— *A guide to parliamentary papers,* AF177
—— *Select list of British parliamentary papers, 1833–1899,* AF196
—— *Select list of British parliamentary papers, 1955–1964,* AF196
—— *A select list of reports of inquiries of the Irish Dáil and Senate, 1922–72,* CJ376
Ford, Richard A. *The chemist's companion,* EE74
Ford, Richard B. *Handbook of veterinary procedures & emergency treatment,* EJ124
Ford list of British parliamentary papers, 1965–1974, Marshallsay, Diana, AF196
—— Smith, J. H., AF196
Ford-Robertson, F. C. *Terminology of forest science, technology, practice, and products,* EJ183
Fordyce, Rachel. *Caroline drama,* BE642
Foreign and Commonwealth Office, accessions to the Library, May 1971–June 1977, Great Britain. Foreign and Commonwealth Office. Library, DC342
Foreign area studies, DD62
Foreign Broadcast Information Service daily reports, AF106
Foreign Broadcast Information Service daily reports electronic index, AF106
Foreign commerce handbook, CH141
Foreign commerce yearbook, CH152
Foreign dialects, Herman, Lewis, BH91
Foreign gazetteers [of the] U.S. Board on Geographic Names, CL87
Foreign gazetteers USBGN, CL87
Foreign investment, CH307, CJ11
Foreign investment (by country or region)
  United States
    directories, CH538
Foreign investment in the U.S, CH538
Foreign language, area, and other international studies, Petrov, Julia A., BD76
Foreign language index, CA25
Foreign law, Reynolds, Thomas H., CK3
Foreign literary prizes, Bufkin, E. C., BE177
Foreign newspaper and gazette report, AE5
Foreign newspaper report, AE5
Foreign newspapers held by the Center for Research Libraries, Center for Research Libraries, AE3
Foreign newspapers in the Library of Congress, AE10
Foreign Office list and diplomatic and consular year book, CJ341
Foreign policy of the French Second Empire, Echard, William E., DC199
The foreign press, Merrill, John Calhoun, AE141
Foreign Relations Library. *Catalog of the Foreign Relations Library, Inc., New York,* DA171
Foreign ships in Micronesia, Hezel, Francis X., DF9
Foreign student supplement, CB316
Foreign students, CB316
  grants-in-aid, CB379
Foreign students (by country or region)
  United States
    directories, CB317
Foreign study, CB366, CB369, CB370
  directories, CB89, CB91, CB92, CB93, CB242, CB244
  fellowships and scholarships, CB90, CB373
  grants-in-aid, CB90, CB373

handbooks, CB243
Foreign trade
  directories, CH132
  handbooks, CH137, CH143, CH145
Foreign trade (by country or region)
  Europe, Eastern
    directories, CH131
  see also **International business enterprises**
•*Foreign traders index*, CH118, CH497
Forest, Philippe. *Dictionnaire fondamental du français littéraire*, BE1156
Forest History Society. *North American forest and conservation history*, EJ172
—— *North American forest history*, EJ174
Forest product abstracts, EJ19
Forest products, EJ192
Forest products abstracts, EJ18
Forest Products Laboratory (U.S.). *Wood engineering handbook*, EK114
Forestry
  abstract journals, EJ175
  bibliography, EJ70, EJ172
  dictionaries, EJ177, EJ178, EJ179
    bilingual
      German-English, EJ28
      Russian-English, EJ180
    multilingual, EJ182
  directories, EJ184
  encyclopedias, EJ176
  handbooks, EJ185, EJ187, EJ188, EJ189, EJ190
  manuscripts and archives, EJ174
  statistics, EJ192
  thesauruses, EJ183
Forestry (by country or region)
  North America
    bibliography, EJ173
  United States
    atlases, EJ191
    dictionaries, EJ181
    guidebooks, EJ186
    handbooks, EJ186
    history, EJ176
Forestry (by subject)
  history, EJ172
  see also **Wood**
Forestry abstracts, DD136, EJ18, EJ19, EJ175
Forestry handbook, EJ185
Forfatterlexikon omfattende Danmark, Norge og Island indtil 1814, Ehrencron-Müller, Holger, BE1087, BE1117
Forfatterlexikon omfattende Danmark, Norge og Island indtil 1814, Ehrencron-Müller, Holger, BE1341
Forgeries
  art, BF30
  literature, BF30
Forget, Carl. *Elsevier's dictionary of jewellery and watchmaking*, BG82
Forjaz de Sampaio, Albino. *História da literatura portuguesa ilustrada*, BE1365
Form and style, Campbell, William Giles, AG1
Forman, Robert J. *Classical Greek and Roman drama*, BE995
Former Soviet republics
  abstract journals, DC38
  associations, AL60
  bibliography, DC591
  biography, AH179, AH180
  dissertations, AG46
  encyclopedias, DC597
  handbooks, DC598, DC600
  newspapers
    translations, AE68
  population
    statistics, CG294
  statistics, CG297
Former Soviet republics (by subject)
  history
    library resources, DC556
  politics and government, CJ317, CJ391
Formíggini, Angelo Fortunato. *Chi à?*, AH259
Forms and functions of twentieth-century architecture, Hamlin, Talbott Faulkner, BF256

Forms of address, AL159, AL160
Formulas and recipes, EA277, EA278, EA279
Formulas, facts, and constants for students and professionals in engineering, chemistry, and physics, Fischbeck, Helmut J., ED36
Formulas, methods, tips, and data for home and workshop, Swezey, Kenneth M., EA279
Forrer, Leonard. *Biographical dictionary of medallists*, BG186
Forrest, J. *Republic of Guinea-Bissau*, DD48
Forsdyke, Lionel. *A descriptive atlas of the Pacific islands*, CL368
Forst, Vladimír. *Slovník české literatury 1970–1981*, BE1105
Forster, Antonia. *Index to book reviews in England, 1749–1774*, BE744, BE748
Forster, Merlin H. *An index to Mexican literary periodicals*, BE909
—— *Vanguardism in Latin American literature*, BE872
Forstner, Lorne J. *The Romantic movement bibliography, 1936–1970*, BE40, BE754
Forsythe, William E. *Smithsonian physical tables*, ED50
Fortes, Amyr Borges. *Atlas do Brasil Globo*, CL316
Fortescue, G. K. *Subject index of the modern works added to the library, 1881–1900*, AA104
Forthcoming books, AA426, AA432
Fortin, Marcel. *Guide de la littérature québécoise*, BE844
Fortlage, Catharine A. *Environmental assessment*, BF284, EK81
Fortschritte der Physik, ED10
Fortschritte der Technik, EA74
The Fortune encyclopedia of economics, CH50
Fortunoff Video Archive for Holocaust Testimonies. *Guide to Yale University Holocaust video testimonies*, DA220
Forty years of screen credits, 1929–1969, Weaver, John T., BH214
Forty years of socialist Albania, CG191
Forum for Scientific Excellence, Inc. *Compendium of hazardous chemicals in schools and colleges*, EE67
—— *Cross-reference index of hazardous chemicals, synonyms, and CAS registry numbers*, EE72
Fosberg, Frances Raymond. *Island bibliographies*, EG108
Foskett, Daphne. *Collecting miniatures*, BF303
—— *Dictionary of British miniature painters*, BF303
—— *Miniatures*, BF303
Fossil indexes, EF230, EF238, EF239, EF240, EF241, EF242, EF243
Fossilium catalogus, EF240
Fossilium catalogus. Animalia, EF252
Fossils, EF248
  collections, EF244
  field guides, EF250, EF251
Fossils in America, Ransom, Jay Ellis, EF250
Foster, David William. *20th century Spanish-American novel*, BE902
—— *Argentine literature*, BE919
—— *Brazilian literature*, BE925, BE930
—— *Chilean literature*, BE940
—— *Cuban literature*, BE975
—— *Dictionary of contemporary Brazilian authors*, BE891
—— *Dictionary of contemporary Latin American authors*, BE891
—— *Handbook of Latin American literature*, BE866
—— *Latin American gay and lesbian narrative*, BE402
—— *Manual of Hispanic bibliography*, BE1427
—— *Mexican literature*, BE910
—— *Modern Latin American literature*, BE887
—— *Peruvian literature*, BE955
—— *Puerto Rican literature*, BE978
—— *Research guide to Argentine literature*, BE919
—— *Research on language teaching*, BD75

Foster, Dennis L. *The rating guide to franchises*, CH403
Foster, Donald H. *Sourcebook for research in music*, BJ2
Foster, Finley Melville Kendall. *English translations from the Greek*, BE1028
Foster, Janet. *British archives*, AJ98, AK145
Foster, Joseph. *Members of Parliament, Scotland*, CJ354
Foster, Leslie A. *Marine affairs bibliography*, CK81
Foster, Ludmilla A. *Bibliography of Russian émigré literature, 1918–1968*, BE1390
Foster, Lynn. *Subject compilations of state laws*, CK181
Foster, Mamie Marie Booth. *Southern black creative writers, 1829–1953*, BE518
Foster, Merlin H. *Vanguardism in Latin American literature*, BE936
Foster, S. G. *Australians : a historical dictionary*, DF37
—— *Australians : events and places*, DF37
Foster, Virginia Ramos. *Manual of Hispanic bibliography*, BE1427
—— *Modern Latin American literature*, BE887
—— *Research guide to Argentine literature*, BE919
Foster, William. *Guide to the India Office records 1600–1858*, DE83
Fóti, Istvánné. *Statisztikai adatforrások*, CG246
Foucault, Alain. *Dictionnaire de géologie*, EF83
Fouchier, Jean. *Chemical dictionary*, EE47
Foulché-Delbosc, Raymond. *Manuel de l'hispanisant*, AA67, AA801, AH290, BE1435
Found, Peter. *Concise Oxford companion to the theatre*, BH74
The Foundation 1000, AL111
Foundation Center. *Corporate foundation profiles*, AL104
—— *The Foundation 1000*, AL111
—— *The Foundation Center's user-friendly guide*, AL91
—— *The foundation directory*, AL112
—— *Foundation fundamentals*, AL137
—— *The foundation grants index*, AL113
—— *Foundation grants to individuals*, AL114
—— *Foundations today*, AL136
—— *Guide to U.S. foundations, their trustees, officers, and donors*, AL119
—— *The literature of the nonprofit sector*, AL94
—— *National directory of corporate giving*, AL121
—— *National guide to foundation funding in higher education*, CB365
—— *National guide to funding for libraries and information services*, AK64
Foundation Center national data book, AL119
The Foundation Center source book profiles, AL111
The Foundation Center's user-friendly guide, AL91
The foundation directory, AL107, AL112
Foundation for Children with Learning Disabilities (U.S.). *The FCLD learning disabilities resource guide*, CB202
Foundation for Independent Video and Film. *The guide to international film and video festivals*, BH265
Foundation for Public Affairs. *Public interest profiles*, CJ142
Foundation fundamentals, Margolin, Judith B., AL137
Foundation funding in higher education, CB365
The foundation grants index, AL113
Foundation grants index quarterly, AL113
Foundation grants to individuals, AL114
Foundation guide for religious grant seekers, BC78
The Foundation one thousand, AL111
Foundation profiles, Hague Club, The, AL96
Foundation reporter, AL115
Foundations, AL116
Foundations and philanthropic organizations
  bibliography
    current, AL94
  databases, AL122

directories, AL98, AL101, AL106, AL111, AL112, AL113, AL114, AL115, AL119, AL122, AL124, CJ50
   handbooks, AL92, AL136, AL137, AL139
   indexes, AL95
   statistics, AL139
Foundations and philanthropic organizations (by country or region)
   Australia, AL127
   Canada, AL125
   international
      directories, AL96, AL97
   Japan, AL126
   New Zealand, AL128
   United States, AL100
      directories, AL93, AL99, AL102, AL103, AL104, AL105, AL107, AL110, AL121, BA10
      history, AL116
Foundations and philanthropic organizations (by subject)
   education, CB365
   religion, BC78
   see also **Grants-in-aid; Philanthropists**
Foundations of architecture, Viollet-le-Duc, Eugène Emmanuel, BF237
Foundations of moral education, Leming, James S., CB15
Foundations of students' learning, Marjoribanks, Kevin, CB70
Foundations today, AL136
The founders' constitution, CK171
The founders of geology, Geikie, Archibald, EF106
Four centuries of cat books, Necker, Claire, EJ140
Four decades of international social security research, CH499
Four Gothic kings, Hallam, Elizabeth M., DC310
Four thousand years of urban growth, Chandler, Tertius, CC296
Four-year colleges, CB271
Fournier, Robert L. *Illustrated dictionary of pottery form,* BG64
—— *Illustrated dictionary of practical pottery,* BG64
Fourth book of junior authors & illustrators, Crawford, Elizabeth D., BE384
—— De Montreville, Doris, BE384
Fourth directory of periodicals publishing articles on English and American literature and language, Gerstenberger, Donna Lorine, BE170
—— Hendrick, George, BE170
Fowells, H. A. *Silvics of forest trees of the United States,* EG202
Fowke, Edith F. *A bibliography of Canadian folklore in English,* CF65
Fowler, F. G. *The concise Oxford dictionary of current English,* AC38
Fowler, Henry Watson. *The concise Oxford dictionary of current English,* AC38
—— *Dictionary of modern English usage,* AC71, AC72
—— *The shorter Oxford English dictionary on historical principles,* AC31
Fowler, Laurence Hall. *The Fowler architectural collection of the Johns Hopkins University,* BF229
Fowler, Roger. *Dictionary of modern critical terms,* BE73
The Fowler architectural collection of the Johns Hopkins University, Johns Hopkins University, BF229
Fowlie-Flores, Fay. *Annotated bibliography of Puerto Rican bibliographies,* AA35, DB452
—— *Index to Puerto Rican collective biography,* AH159
Fox, Anthony D. *The British electorate 1963–1987,* CJ367
—— *British parliamentary constituencies,* CJ368
Fox, Charles. *The essential jazz records,* BJ308
Fox, Daniel M. *Nobel laureates in medicine or physiology,* AL169, EH216
Fox, Gerald. *Three thousand years of urban growth,* CC296
Fox, James R. *Dictionary of international & comparative law,* CK102

Fox-Davies, Arthur Charles. *Armorial families,* AJ152
—— *Art of heraldry,* AJ154
—— *Book of crests of the families of Great Britain and Ireland,* AJ151
—— *The book of public arms,* AJ153
—— *A complete guide to heraldry,* AJ154
Foxon, David Fairweather. *English verse, 1701–1750,* BE705
Fraenkel, Annie. *Bibliographie zur Geschichte der Juden in der Schweiz,* DC525
Fraenkel, Ernst. *Litauisches etymologisches Wörterbuch,* AC605
Fraenkel, Josef. *Jewish press of the world,* AD7, AE6
Fraenkel-Conrat, Heinz. *The viruses,* EG344
Fraire, Osvaldo A. *Diccionario biográfico de la mujer en el Uruguay,* AH143, DB395
—— *Quién es quién en el Uruguay,* AH145
Frame by frame, Klotman, Phyllis Rauch, BH227
Frampton, Kenneth. *Modern architure,* BF257
Le français classique, Cayrou, Gaston, AC374
France. *Journal officiel de la République française,* AF170
France
   atlases, CL327, CL328, CL329, DC164
   bibliography, AA101, AA613, AA614, AA615, AA635, DC144
      18th century, AA623, AA624
      19th-20th centuries, AA625, AA626, AA627, AA628, AA629, AA630, AA631, AA632
      current, AA633, AA634, AA636
      early, AA616, AA617, AA618, AA619, AA620, AA621
   biography, AH191, AH192, AH193, AH194, AH195, AH197, AH198, AH199, AH200, AH321, CJ329
      bibliography, AH196
      contemporary, AH201
   dissertations, AG28, AG29
   gazetteers, CL133
   government publications, AF168, AF169, AF170, AF171, AF172
   handbooks, DC159
   library catalogs, AA100
   library resources, AK135, AK136, DC158
   manuscripts and archives (by subject)
      United States, DB31
   newspapers, AE52
      indexes, AE120, AE121
   periodicals, AD90, AD91, AD92, AD93, AD94, AD95, AD96, AD97, AE50, AE52, BE1143, BE1144
      bibliography, AE51
      indexes, AD312
   place-names, CL187, CL188
   statistics, CG214, CG215, CG216, CG218, CG219
France (by subject)
   archaeology and ancient history, DC171
      bibliography, DC172
      encyclopedias, DC175
   art
      periodicals, BF46
   cities, DC212
   economic conditions, DC153
   folklore and popular culture, DC209
   foreign relations, DB349, DC199, DC201, DC203, DD125
      archives, DC155
      manuscripts and archives, DC156
   furniture, BG118, BG124
   government officials, AH200, CJ329, DC152
      biography, DC211
   historiography, DC162
   history
      atlases, DC165, DC166, DC167, DC190
      bibliography, DC143, DC147, DC148, DC149, DC200
      dissertations, DC181
      chronologies, DC161
      diaries and letters, DC180
      encyclopedias, DC160

      guides, DC142
      library catalogs, DC202
      manuscripts and archives, DB26, DC150, DC151, DC154, DC157, DC162
      regional and local, BF273, DC212
   history (by period)
      French Revolution, DC177, DC186, DC187
         biography, AH193
      Napoleonic era, DC22, DC191, DC193, DC194
      since 1789, DC153, DC195, DC197, DC198, DC199, DC204, DC205, DC206, DC207
      to 1789, DC4, DC168, DC174
      to1789
         bibliography, DC173
   law, DC149
      guides, CK209
   laws
      bibliography, CK208
   military history, DC145, DC192, DC196
      bibliography, DC146
   music, BJ76, BJ180
   overseas territories
      atlases, CL276
      government publications, AF228, AF237
         bibliography, AF222, AF224, AF229
      statistics, CG214
   place-names, CL185, CL186
   politics and government
      biography, CJ328
      dictionaries, DC208
      library resources, DC169
      manuscripts and archives, DC152
   population, CG215
   social conditions
      bibliography, DC149
   statistics and demography, CG217
France. Armée. Service historique. *L'Afrique française du nord,* DD69
France. Comité des Travaux Historiques et Scientifiques. *Dictionnaire topographique de la France comprenant les noms de lieu anciens et modernes,* CL187
France. Commission de coordination de la documentation administrative. *Répertoire des publications officielles (séries et périodiques),* AF171
France. Commission de la topographie des Gaules. *Dictionnaire archéologique de la Gaule, époque celtique,* DC175
France. Direction des bibliothèques, des musées et de l'information scientifique et technique. *Inventaire des thèses de doctorat soutenues devant les universités françaises,* EA55
France. Direction générale des enseignements supérieurs et de la recherche. *Inventaire des thèses de doctorat soutenues devant les universités françaises,* EA55
France. État-major de l'armée. *L'Afrique française du nord,* DD69
France. Ministère de la France d'outre-mer. Service des statistique. *Annuaire statistique de l'Union française outre-mer,* CG214
France. Ministère des affaires étrangères. *État général des inventaires des archives diplomatiques,* DC155
France. Ministère des affaires étrangères. Archives. *Guide des sources de l'histoire du Brésil aux archives du Ministère français des affaires étrangères,* DB349
France. Ministère des relations extérieures. Archives et documentation. *Les archives du Ministère des relations extérieures depuis les origines,* DC156
France. Statistique générale. *Annuaire statistique de la France,* CG216
France, Chambers, Frances, DC144
—— Charlton, D. G., DC159
France-Allemagne, relations internationes et interdépendances bilatérales, Menyesch, Dieter, DC201
La France contemporaine, 1946–1990, Guillaume, Sylvie, DC210
La France littéraire, Quérard, Joseph Marie, AA624, AA631

France révolutionnaire et impériale, Monglond, André, DC176
France under the German occupation, 1940–1944, Evleth, Donna, DC200
Frances L. Loeb Library. *Catalogue of the Library of the Graduate School of Design*, BF228
Franchise company data, CH359
Franchise opportunities handbook, CH359, CH403
Franchises, CH403, CH407
   directories, CH359
Francis, Henry G. *The official encyclopedia of bridge*, BK130
Francis, R. D. *How to find out in psychology*, CD2
•*FRANCIS*, AD254, BB24, BE38, CE23, CH39
FRANCIS. Bibliographie géographique internationale, CL23
FRANCIS. Bulletin signalétique, AD254, BB24, BD24, BE38, CE23, EA72, EF118
FRANCIS. Bulletin signalétique 526 : art et archéologie, BF33
Franciscan almanac, BC415
La francité canadienne, Sabourin, Conrad, BD162
Franck, Irene M. *Dictionary of 20th-century history*, DA179, DA181
—— *The dictionary of publishing*, AA272
—— *The parent's desk reference*, CC238
—— *The women's desk reference*, CC562
Franck, Johannes. *Franck's Etymologisch woordenboek der Nederlandsche taal*, AC299
Franck's Etymologisch woordenboek der Nederlandsche taal, Franck, Johannes, AC299
Franco, Jean. *Introduccion a la literatura hispanoamericana*, BE865
—— *Introduction to Spanish-American literature*, BE865
Franco-Judaica, Szajkowski, Zosa, BC533
Francoeur, Robert T. *A descriptive dictionary and atlas of sexology*, CC281
Francomano, Claire A. *Mendelian inheritance in man*, EG342, EH189
Franda, Marcus F. *The Seychelles*, DD203
Frank, Frederick S. *The first Gothics*, BE288
—— *Gothic fiction*, BE289
—— *Guide into the Gothic*, BE289
—— *Through the pale door*, BE288
Frank, Joseph. *Hobbled Pegasus*, BE699
Frank, Robyn C. *The directory of food and nutrition information for professionals and consumers*, EH290, EJ214
—— *Directory of food and nutrition information services and resources*, EH290, EJ214
Frank, Ruth S. *Book of Jewish books*, BC518
Franke, Hermann. *Lexikon der Physik*, ED20
Frankel, Linda. *The student sociologist's handbook*, CC23
Frankel, Max. *Tables for identification of organic compounds*, EE151
Frankish church, Wallace-Hadrill, John Michael, BC278
Franklin, Benjamin. *Dictionary of American literary characters*, BE484
Franklin, Linda Campbell. *Antiques and collectibles*, BG36
Franklyn, Julian. *Encyclopaedic dictionary of heraldry*, AJ162, AJ163
Frantskevich, Valentina N. *Gosudarstvennaia bibliografiia SSSR*, AA792
—— *Gosudarstvennaia bibliografiia SSSR : Spravochnik*, AA794, AA796
Frantz, Donald. *Blackfoot dictionary of stems, roots, and affixes*, AC717
Franz, Günther. *Biographisches Wörterbuch zur deutschen Geschichte*, AH215, DC222
—— *Sachwörterbuch zur deutschen Geschichte*, DC222
Franzosa, Susan Douglas. *Integrating women's studies into the curriculum*, CC492
Die französische Afrikapolitik, Brüne, Stefan, DD2
Französisches etymologisches Wörterbuch, Wartburg, Walther von, AC346, AC350, AC352, AC387, AC538
Fraser, Clarence M. *The Merck veterinary manual*, EJ125

Fraser, Donald. *A dictionary of musical quotations*, BJ162
Fraser, Ian Forbes. *Bibliography of French-Canadian poetry*, BE839
Fraser, Janet. *Canadian literature index*, BE822
Fraser, Kenneth C. *Bibliography of the Scottish national movement (1844–1973)*, CJ375
Fraser, Robert. *The world financial system*, CH226
Fraser, T G. *The Middle East, 1914–1979*, DE65
Fraser-Lu, Sylvia. *Handwoven textiles of South-East Asia*, BG158
Frasier, Jane. *Women composers*, BJ376
Fraternal organizations, Schmidt, Alvin J., AL36
Fraternities *see* **Secret societies**
Frati, Carlo. *Dizionario bio-bibliografico dei bibliotecari e bibliofili italiani dal sec. XIV al XIX*, AK90
Frauen und Erster Weltkrieg in England, DA194
Frautschi, Richard. *Bibliographie du genre romanesque français, 1751–1800*, BE1191
Frauwallner, Erich. *Die Weltliteratur*, BE72
Frayser, Suzanne G. *Studies in human sexuality*, CC269
Frazer, Ruth F. *Eastern Christianity*, BC446
—— *Politics and religion*, BC15
Frazier, Gregory W. *The American Indian index*, CC430
Frazier, Patrick. *Portrait index of North American Indians in published collections*, BF67, CC435
Frederic, Louis. *A dictionary of the martial arts*, BK89
Frederick, Richard G. *Dictionary of theoretical concepts in biology*, EG44
Frederick II, 1215–1250, DC229
Frederick II, King of Prussia, DC234
Fredericks, Marcel A. *Second steps in sociology*, CC24
Fredericksen, Burton B. *Census of pre-nineteenth-century Italian paintings in North American public collections*, BF325
—— *The index of paintings sold in the British Isles during the nineteenth century*, BF302
Frederiks, Johannes Godefridus. *Biographisch woordenboek der Noord– en Zuidnederlandsche letterkunde*, BE1328
Frederiksen, Elke. *Women writers of Germany, Austria, and Switzerland*, BE1062
Fredland, Richard A. *A guide to African international organisations*, AF20
Fredriksen, John C. *Free trade and sailors' rights*, CJ605
—— *Shield of republic, sword of empire*, CJ605
Free money for [education], Blum, Laurie, CB90, CB373
Free money for foreign study, Blum, Laurie, CB90, CB373
Free resource builder for librarians and teachers, Smallwood, Carol, CA50
Free trade and sailors' rights, Fredriksen, John C., CJ605
Free voices in Russian literature, 1950s–1980s, Stevanovic, Bosiljka, BE1407
—— Sumerkin, Alexander, BE1407
—— Wertsman, Vladimir, BE1407
Freed, Melvyn N. *The educator's desk reference (EDR)*, CB4
Freedman, Alan. *The computer glossary*, EK179, EK181
Freedman, David Noel. *The Anchor Bible dictionary*, BC125
Freedman, Deborah A. *The technical editor's and secretary's desk guide*, EA159
Freedman, George. *The technical editor's and secretary's desk guide*, EA159
Freedman, Harry. *Encyclopedia of biblical interpretation*, BC182
—— *Encyclopedia Talmudica*, BC549, CK239
Freedman, Lawrence. *Europe transformed*, CJ315
Freedman, Robert L. *Human food uses*, EH293
Freedom in the world, CK109
Freedom's lawmakers, Foner, Eric, DB102
Freedson, Patty. *Dictionary of the sport and exercise sciences*, BK25

Freeley, Austin J. *Argumentation and debate*, BE371
Freeman, Michael J. *Atlas of Nazi Germany*, DC263
—— *Atlas of the world economy*, CH148
Freeman, Morton S. *A handbook of problem words & phrases*, AC73
—— *Wordwatcher's guide to good writing & grammar*, AC73
Freeman, Richard Broke. *British natural history books, 1495–1900*, EG69
—— *The works of Charles Darwin*, EG70
Freeman, Roger L. *Reference manual for telecommunications engineering*, EK146
Freeman, Ronald E. *Bibliographies of studies in Victorian literature for the thirteen years 1932–1944*, BE753
Freeman, Samuel. *Historical dictionary of the Spanish Empire, 1402–1975*, DC515
Freeman, Thomas Walter. *Geographers*, CL82
Freeman, William. *Dictionary of fictional characters*, BE188, BE189
Freeman-Grenville, Greville Stewart Parker. *Atlas of British history*, DC301
—— *Chronology of African history*, DD56
—— *Chronology of world history*, DA32
—— *New atlas of African history*, DD65
Freemon, Frank R. *Microbes and minie balls*, DB110
Freer Gallery of Art. *Dictionary catalog of the library*, BF53
Freetown, Sierra Leone. Fourah Bay College. Library. *Catalog of the Sierra Leone collection, Fourah Bay College Library, University of Sierra Leone*, DD204
Frei, Karl. *Die schweizerische Bundesversammlung, 1848–1920*, CJ388
Freiberg, Marcos A. *Bilingual dictionary of dental terms*, EH254
Freiberger, W. F. *International dictionary of applied mathematics*, EB40
Freidel, Frank B. *Harvard guide to American history*, DB13
Freimann, A. *Judaica*, BC532
Freiser, Henry. *Compendium of analytical nomenclature*, EE35
Freitag, Anton. *The twentieth century atlas of the Christian world*, BC289
Freitag, Ruth S. *Halley's comet*, EC11
—— *Union lists of serials*, AD219
Freitag, Wolfgang M. *Art books*, BF18
Freis, Wilhelm. *Deutsche Dichterhandschriften von 1400 bis 1900*, BE1242
French, Hollis. *Silver collectors' glossary and a list of early American silversmiths and their marks*, BG63, BG144
French, John R. P. *Measures for psychological assessment*, CD67
French, Joyce N. *Adult literacy*, CB352
French, Tom. *The SCOLMA directory of libraries and special collections on Africa in the United Kingdom and Western Europe*, DD41
French, Warren. *Reference guide to American literature*, BE449
French, William P. *Afro-American poetry and drama, 1760–1975*, BE512
French (by country or region)
   United States, DB26
French 17, BE1138
The French and British in the Old Northwest, Beers, Henry Putney, DB26
French and English business dictionary, National Textbook Co, AC343, CH61
French and English dictionary of mathematical vocabulary, EB49
French and English science dictionary, EA110
French and Indian War, DB80
French and international acronyms & initialisms dictionary, Dubois, Michel, AC345
French and Spanish records of Louisiana, Beers, Henry Putney, DB26
French Army bibliography, DC146
French books in print, AA635
French-Canadian literature
   bibliography, BE838, BE839, BE842, BE844
   biobibliography, BE841

encyclopedias, BE837
handbooks, BE843
French-Canadian literature (by subject)
history, BE840
French colonial Africa, Westfall, Gloria, AF228
French consuls in the United States, Monell, G. E.,
DB31
———— Nasatir, A. P., DB31
French dictionaries, Klaar, R. M., AC388
French drama
bibliography, BE1177, BE1179, BE1180,
BE1181, BE1183, BE1184, BE1185, BE1186
French drama (by period)
17th–18th centuries, BE1180
17th century, BE1181
French drama (by subject)
history, BE1179, BE1182
French-English dictionary for chemists, Patterson,
Austin McDowell, EE48
French-English horticultural dictionary, Bourke, D.
O'D, EJ238
French-English science and technology dictionary,
DeVries, Louis, EA107
*French-English science dictionary for students in
agricultural, biological, and physical sciences,*
DeVries, Louis, EA107
French feminist criticism, Gelfand, Elissa D.,
BE1133
French fiction
bibliography, BE1187, BE1188, BE1189,
BE1190, BE1191, BE1202
French foreign policy, 1918–1945, Young, Robert J.,
DC203
*French, German, and Swiss university dissertations
on twentieth century Turkey,* Suzuki, Peter T.,
DC541
French Guiana, DB377
atlases, CL276
French in North America, Beers, Henry Putney,
DB26
French language
abbreviations, AC345
bibliography, BD150, BD156, BD158, BE1130,
BE1134
dictionaries, AC327, AC328, AC329, AC330,
AC331, AC332, AC333, AC334, AC339, AC372
abridged
bilingual, AC341
bibliography, AC387, AC388, AC389, AC390
bilingual
French-English, AC335, AC336, AC337,
AC338, AC340, AC342
etymology, AC330, AC348, AC349, AC351
idioms and usage, AC366
new words, AC373
regional and dialect, AC385, AC386
slang, AC353, AC355
visual, AC344
etymology
dictionaries, AC346, AC347, AC350, AC352
festschriften, BD158, BE1134
grammar
bibliography, BD157
guides, BE1129
idioms and usage, AC354, AC360, AC364,
AC365, AC367, AC368, AC369, AC370, AC371
obsolete and provincial words, AC377
regional and dialect
Canadian, BD162
Louisiana, BD159
slang, AC339
dictionaries, AC354, AC356, AC358
bilingual, AC357
synonyms and antonyms, AC359, AC360,
AC361, AC362, AC363
French language (by period)
old–17th century
dictionaries, AC374, AC375, AC376, AC377,
AC378, AC379, AC380, AC381, AC382,
AC384
bilingual, AC383
French language and literature, Bassan, Fernande,
BD156, BE1130

French language dissertations in music, BJ166
French literature
African authors, BE1517
bibliography, BD156, BE983, BE1130, BE1131,
BE1132, BE1135, BE1137, BE1138, BE1141,
BE1208, BE1209, BE1529
current, BE1140
bibliography of bibliography, BE1136
biobibliography, BE1162, BE1168, BE1208
biography, BE1150, BE1151, BE1153, BE1154
chronologies, BE1152, BE1162
criticism
biobibliography, BE1159
collections, BE1147
dictionaries, BE1152, BE1156
dissertations, BE1142, BE1145
encyclopedias, BE1149, BE1153, BE1154,
BE1155, BE1158, BE1160, BE1161
festschriften, BD158, BE1134
guidebooks, BE1166
guides, BE1129
bibliography, BE1128
handbooks, BE1158
library catalogs, BE1135
manuscripts, BE1148
plot summaries, BE1152
reviews of research, BE1139
translations
bibliography, BE1146
women authors
Biobibliography, BE1157
French literature (by period)
16th–17th centuries
bibliography, BE1203
16th–18th centuries
bibliography, BE1138
16th century
bibliography, BE1204, BE1207
17th century
bibliography, BE1205
18th century
bibliography, BE1206
19th–20th centuries
bibliography, BE1132
19th–20th centuries
bibliography, BE1188
19th–20th centuries
bibliography, BE1209
Baroque
bibliography, BE1203
medieval
bibliography, BE1198, BE1199, BE1202
dictionaries, BE1164
French literature (by subject)
history, BE1167, BE1168, BE1169, BE1170,
BE1171, BE1172, BE1173, BE1174, BE1175,
BE1176
French literature, Harvard University. Library,
BE1135
———— Kempton, Richard, BE1136
French literature in early American translation,
Bowe, Forrest, BE1146
French mathematical seminars, Anderson, Nancy D.,
EB7
French military history, 1661–1799, Ross, Steven T.,
DC146
French official publications, Westfall, Gloria,
AF170, AF172
French periodical index, AD312
French poetry
bibliography, BE1192, BE1193, BE1196
biobibliography, BE1194
biography, BE1197
criticism
collections, BE1196
indexes, BE1195
French poetry (by period)
medieval
bibliography, BE1200
French poetry (by subject)
history, BE1197
French policy in Africa, DD2

French political pamphlets, 1547–1648, Lindsay,
Robert O., DC169
French régime, Nish, C., DB205
French Revolution
atlases, DC190
bibliography, DC176, DC177, DC178, DC180,
DC181
encyclopedias, DC183, DC184, DC186
filmography, DC179
handbooks, DC187, DC188
manuscripts and archives, DC182
sourcebooks, DC189
The French Revolution, Jones, Colin, DC187
French Revolution documents, Roberts, John Morris,
DC189
French sculptors of the 17th and 18th centuries,
Souchal, François, BF399
French Second Empire, 1852–1870, DC206
French-speaking central Africa, Witherell, Julian W.,
AF229
French-speaking West Africa, Witherell, Julian W.,
AF230
*French tragedy in the reign of Louis XVI and the
early years of the French Revolution, 1774–1792,*
Lancaster, Henry Carrington, BE1182
*French tragedy in the time of Louis XV and Voltaire,
1715–1774,* Lancaster, Henry Carrington, BE1182
French VI bibliography, BE1132
French VII bibliography, BE1132
French weights and measures before the Revolution,
Zupko, Ronald Edward, AL202
French women writers, BE1157
French XX bibliography, BE1132, BE1370
Frenzel, Elisabeth. *Daten deutscher Dichtung,*
BE1252
———— *Motive der Weltliteratur,* BE80
Frenzel, Herbert. *Daten deutscher Dichtung,* BE1252
Fresh-water invertebrates of the United States,
Pennak, Robert William, EG241
Freudenthal, Juan R. *Index to anthologies of Latin
American literature in English translation,* BE884
Freudenthal, Patricia M. *Index to anthologies of
Latin American literature in English translation,*
BE884
Freund, William. *Harper's Latin dictionary,* AC574
Frey, Albert Romer. *Dictionary of numismatic
names,* BG179
Frey, Linda. *Women in Western European history,*
DC5
Frey, Marsha. *Women in Western European history,*
DC5
Frey, Richard L. *The new complete Hoyle,* BK128
Frey, Robert L. *Railroads in the nineteenth century,*
CH383
Frick, John P. *Woldman's engineering alloys,* EK282
Frick, John W. *Directory of historic American
theatres,* BH110
———— *Theatrical directors,* BH121
Frick Art Reference Library. *Frick Art Reference
Library sales catalogue index,* BF113
———— *Guide to the Frick Art Reference Library
sales catalogue index,* BF113
———— *Original index to art periodicals,* BF19
———— *Spanish artists from the fourth to the
twentieth century,* BF147
Frick Art Reference Library sales catalogue index,
Frick Art Reference Library, BF113
Frickx, Robert. *Lettres françaises de Belgique,*
BE1100
Fried, Jerome. *Funk and Wagnalls standard
dictionary of folklore, mythology and legend,*
CF51
Fried, Lewis. *Handbook of American-Jewish
literature,* BE565
Friedberg, Arthur L. *A catalog of modern world
coins, 1850–1964,* BG192
Friedberg, Ira S. *A catalog of modern world coins,
1850–1964,* BG192
———— *Gold coins of the world,* BG187
Friedberg, Robert. *Gold coins of the world,* BG187
———— *Paper money of the United States,* BG194
Friedemann, Nina S. de. *Bibliografía anotada y
directorio de antropólogos colombianos,* CE88

Frieden, Pierre. *Bibliographie luxembourgeoise*, AA742

Friederich, Werner P. *Bibliography of comparative literature*, BE12, BE13, BE41

Friederici, Karl. *Bibliotheca orientalis*, DE7

Friedman, Catherine. *Commodity prices*, CH432

Friedman, Francine. *Yugoslavia*, DC606

Friedman, Jack P. *Encyclopedia of investments*, CH301

Friedman, Jennifer Adler. *Women's colleges*, CB247

Friedman, Julian R. *Human rights*, CK77

Friedman, Leon. *Justices of the United States Supreme Court, 1789–1969*, CK189

Friedman, Leslie. *Sex role stereotyping in the mass media*, CC270

Friedman, Norman. *Conway's all the world's fighting ships, 1947–1982*, CJ592

Friedman, Saul S. *Holocaust literature*, DA217

Friedrich, Gerhard. *Theological dictionary of the New Testament*, AC456, BC143

Friedrich der Grosse, Bibliographie, DC234

Friedrich Reinhold Kreutzwaldi nimeline Eeste NSV Riiklik Raamatukogu (Tallinn). *Nõukogude Eesti raamat, 1940–1954*, AA608

Friedrichs, Elisabeth. *Deutschsprachigen Schriftstellerinnen des 18, und 19. Jahrhunderts*, BE1243

—— *Literarische Lokalgrössen 1700–1900*, BE1243

Friedrichs Ballettlexikon von A–Z, BH143

Friedrichs Theaterlexikon, Gröning, Karl, BH68

—— Kliess, Werner, BH68

Friedrichsen, G. W. S. *Oxford dictionary of English etymology*, AC58

—— *The shorter Oxford English dictionary on historical principles*, AC31

Friends directory, Friends World Committee for Consultation. Section of the Americas, BC351

Friends Historical Library of Swarthmore College. *Catalog of the book and serials collections of the Friends Historical Library of Swarthmore College*, BC350

Friends, Society of, BC350, BC351, BC352, BC353

Friends World Committee for Consultation. Section of the Americas. *Friends directory*, BC351

Friendship, Barkas, J. L., CC3

Friesch woordenboek, Dijkstra, Waling, AC391

Friesel, Evyatar. *Atlas of modern Jewish history*, DA190

Friesenhahn, Heinz. *Land und Leute in deutscher Erzählung*, BE1267

Friesian language
bibliography, BD133
dictionaries, AC391
bilingual
Friesian-Dutch, AC392

Friesian literature, BE1067, BE1068

Friis, Herman R. *Descriptive catalog of maps published by Congress*, CL229

Frings, Theodor. *Althochdeutsches Wörterbuch*, AC399

Frisk, Hjalmar. *Griechisches etymologisches Wörterbuch*, AC450, AC451

Fritsch, Lilian de A. *Processo de modernização do Brasil, 1850–1930*, DB348

Fritz, Sara. *Handbook of campaign spending*, CJ247

Fritze, Ronald H. *Historical dictionary of Tudor England, 1485–1603*, DC322

—— *Reference sources in history*, DA2

Fritzner, Johan. *Ordbog over det gamle norsk sprog*, AC504

Frodin, D. G. *Guide to standard floras of the world*, EG91

Froehlich, Fritz E. *The Froehlich/Kent encyclopedia of telecommunications*, CH481

Froehlich, Hildegard C. *Research in music education*, BJ6

The Froehlich/Kent encyclopedia of telecommunications, CH481

Froelke, Ruth. *The Wuerttemberg emigration index*, AJ46

Frohn, Axel. *Guide to inventories and finding aids of German archives at the German Historical Institute, Washington, D.C*, DC246

From Brown to Boston, Jones, Leon, CB32

From CA to CAS ONLINE, Schulz, Hedda, EE6

From day to day, Johnson, David E., DA34

From Erasmus to Tolstoy, Meulen, Jacob ter, CJ675

From generation to generation, Kurzweil, Arthur, AJ13

From idea to funded project, Belcher, Jane C., AL92

—— Jacobsen, Julia M., AL92

From museums, galleries, and studios, Besemer, Susan P., BF48

From protest to challenge, Carter, Gwendolyn, CJ413

—— Karis, Thomas, CJ413

From radical left to extreme right, Skidmore, Gail, AD45

From real life to reel life, Karsten, Eileen, BH226

From Weimar to Hitler, Wiener Library, London, DC244

Fromberg, Doris Pronin. *Encyclopedia of early childhood education*, CB66

Fromm, Hans. *Bibliographie deutscher Übersetzungen aus dem Französischen, 1700–1948 ...*, AA143

Frongia, Guido. *Guida alla letteratura su Wittgenstein*, BB80

—— *Wittgenstein*, BB80

Frontier and pioneer life, DB68, DB165, DB168, DB175
encyclopedias, CC433, DB174

The frontier experience, DB165

—— Tuska, Jon, BE570

Frontiers, CC454, CC528

Froschl, Merle. *Feminist resources for schools and colleges*, CC481

—— *Resources for educational equity*, CB18

Frost, Darrel R. *Amphibian species of the world*, EG248

Frost, Elizabeth. *The bully pulpit*, CJ180

—— *Quotable lawyer*, CK57

Frost, Pandora Kerr. *Chambers English dictionary*, AC36

Frost, Wendy. *Feminist literary criticism*, BE49

Frühneuhochdeutsches Wörterbuch, AC401

Frumin, Alan S. *Riddick's Senate procedure*, CJ227

Frumkin, Norman. *Guide to economic indicators*, CH108

Fruton, Joseph S. *A bio-bibliography for the history of the biochemical sciences since 1800*, EG319

Fry, Donald K. *Norse sagas translated into English*, BE1088

Fry, Gerald. *The international development dictionary*, CH121

—— *Pacific Basin and Oceania*, DF3

Fry, John D. *Disease data book*, EH178

—— *The health care data source book*, EH179

Fry, Ron. *Black genealogy*, AJ3

Fryde, E. B. *Handbook of British chronology*, BE612, DC295

Frye, Keith. *The encyclopedia of mineralogy*, EF179

Frye, Northrop. *Harper handbook to literature*, BE84

Fryer, Deborah J. *The Columbia Granger's index to poetry*, BE315

Frysk Academy. *Lysts Frysk wirdboek*, AC392

Frysk wurdboek, AC392

FSTA, EJ159, EJ150

Fu, Charles Wei-Hsün. *Guide to Chinese philosophy*, BB19

Fuchs, Rudolf Herman. *Iconclass*, BF175

Fucilla, Joseph Guerin. *A bibliographical guide to the Romance languages and literatures*, BD152, BE1073

—— *Our Italian surnames*, AJ199

—— *Saggistica letteraria italiana*, BE1292

—— *Universal author repertoire of Italian essay literature*, BE1292

Fuentes, Jordi. *Diccionario histórico de Chile*, DB362

Fuentes de la historia contemporánea de México, González y González, Luis, DB226

—— Ross, Stanley Robert, DB234

Fuentes de la historia española e hispanoamericana, Sánchez Alonso, Benito, DC506

Fuentes generales para el studio de la literatura colombiana, Orjuela, Héctor H., BE946

Fuentes para el estudio de la literatura uruguaya, Rela, Walter, BE959

Fuentes para el estudio de la literatura venezolana, Becco, Horacio Jorge, BE961

Fuentes para el estudio de la nueva literatura brasileña, de las vanguardias a hoy, Rela, Walter, BE936

Fuentes para el estudio del Perú, Lostaunau Rubio, Gabriel, AA30

Fuentes para la historia de Ibero-América : Escandinavia, Mörner, M., DB275

Füher durch die Quellen zur Geschichte Lateinamerikas in der Bundesrepublic Deutschland, Hauschild-Thiessen, R., DB275

Fujie-Winter, Kimiko. *Kan-Ei jukugo ribāsu jiten*, AC558

Fujioka, Jerry Y. *The Japanese in Hawaii*, CC408

Fukuda, Naomi. *Survey of Japanese collections in the United States*, DE206

Fukui, Haruhiro. *Political parties of Asia and the Pacific*, CJ414, CJ446

Fuld, James J. *The book of world-famous music*, BJ231

Fulford, Margaret. *The Canadian women's movement, 1960–1990*, CC525

Fullard, Harold. *Muir's historical atlas*, DA57

Fuller, Clifford. *London bibliography of the social sciences*, CA13

Fuller, Edmund. *Thesaurus of book digests*, BE193

Fuller, Graham. *The illustrated who's who of the cinema*, BH282

Fuller, John P. *A manual of new mineral names, 1892–1978*, EF184

Fuller, Muriel. *More junior authors*, BE384

Fuller, Reginald Cuthbert. *A new Catholic commentary on Holy Scripture*, BC177

Fuller Theological Seminary. Library. *Bibliography of the Dead Sea Scrolls, 1948–1957*, BC112

Fulltext sources online, AD271, AE113

Fulton, Len. *International directory of little magazines & small presses*, AD12

Fulton, Richard D. *Union list of Victorian serials*, AD222

Fumagalli, Giuseppe. *La bibliografia*, AA51, AA54

—— *Bibliografia etiopica ...*, DD156

—— *Bibliotheca bibliographica italica*, AA51, AA54

—— *Chi l'ha detto?*, BE139

—— *Lexicon typographicum Italiae*, AA301

Funck-Brentano, Christian. *Bibliographie marocaine, 1923–1933*, DD180

Functions (mathematics), EB76
handbooks, EB68
tables, EB79, EB80

Fund for Assistance to Private Education. *Philippine atlas*, CL361

Fund for the Republic, New York. *Bibliography of the Communist problem in the United States*, CJ507

Fund raiser's guide to human service funding, AL117

Fund raiser's guide to private fortunes, AL118

Fund raising, AL132
guides, AL93, AL117, AL138
handbooks, AL91, AL133, AL137
manuals, AL130, AL131
United States, AL141

Fund raising (by country or region)
United States
guides, AL129, AL140

Fund raising (by subject)
universities and colleges, CB227

Fund your way through college, Kirby, Debra M., CB383

Fundação Carlos Chagas. *Mulher brasileira*, DB343

Fundação Instituto Brasileiro de Geografia e Estatística. *Estatísticas históricas do Brasil*, CG143

Fundação Instituto Brasileiro de Geografia e Estatística. Departamento de Estatísticas de População e Sociais. *Estatísticas do registro civil,* CG142

Fundamental formulas of physics, Menzel, Donald Howard, ED47

Fundamentalist churches, BC43

Fundamental'naîa biblioteka obshchestvennykh nauk. (Akademiîa nauk SSSR). *Istoriîa SSSR,* DC548

Fundamental'naîa biblioteka obshchestvennykh nauk (Akademiîa nauk SSSR). *Nauchnye s'ezdy, konferentsii i soveshchaniîa v SSSR,* EA199

Fundamentals handbook of electrical and computer engineering, EK138

Fundamentals of legal research, Jacobstein, J. Myron, CK118, CK122

Fundamentals of musical composition, Schoenberg, Arnold, BJ29

Funding for anthropological research, Cantrell, Karen, CE55

Funding for museums, archives, and special collections, BF104

Funding for U.S. study, CB379

Fünfjahrs-Katalog der im deutschen Buchhandel erschienenen Bücher, Hinrichs, firm, publishers (Leipzig), AA655

Fünfjahrs-Katalog der im deutschen Buchhandel erschienenen Bücher, Zeitschriften, Landkarten, etc. , AA641

Fung, Stanislaus. *Australian architectural serials, 1870–1983,* BF208

Fung, Sydney S. K. *25 T'ang poets,* BE1552

Fungi, EG184, EG185, EG186, EG187, EG188, EG189, EG190, EG191, EG192

The fungi, Ainsworth, Geoffrey Clough, EG185

Fungi on plants and plant products in the United States, EG186

Funk, Arthur L. *Selected bibliography of books on the Second World War … ,* DA201

Funk, Arthur Layton. *The Second World War,* DA201

Funk & Wagnalls modern guide to synonyms and related words, Hayakawa, Samuel Ichiyé, AC139

Funk & Wagnalls new encyclopedia, AB10, AB24, AB26

Funk & Wagnalls new international dictionary of the English language, AC10

Funk & Wagnalls new standard dictionary, AC10

Funk & Wagnalls standard college dictionary, AC136

Funk and Wagnalls standard dictionary of folklore, mythology and legend, CF51

Fürer-Haimendorf, Elizabeth von. *An anthropological bibliography of South Asia,* CE108

Furet, François. *A critical dictionary of the French Revolution,* DC183

Furia, Thomas E. *CRC handbook of food additives,* EH304

Furlani, Silvio. *Archivio biografico italiano,* AH258

Fúrlong Cárdiff, Guillermo. *Bibliografía de la Revolución de Mayo, 1810–1828,* DB326

—— *Historia y bibliografía de las primeras imprentas rioplatenses, 1700–1850,* AA469

Furness, Konstantin Z. *Bulgarian abbreviations,* AC243

Furniture
  bibliography, BG126
  dictionaries, BG21, BG125, BG126
  directories, BG130
  encyclopedias, BG121, BG122, BG129
Furniture (by country or region)
  France, BG118, BG124
  Great Britain, BG120, BG123
    bibliography, BG135
  United States, BG119, BG132
    biography, BG134
Furniture (by subject)
  history, BG131
Furniture collectors' glossary, Lockwood, L. V., BG63

Furniture History Society. *Dictionary of English furniture makers, 1660–1840,* BG135

Furniture treasury (mostly of American origin), Nutting, Wallace, BG119

Furr, A. Keith. *CRC handbook of laboratory safety,* EE71

Fürstenau, Eugênio. *Novo dicionário de termos técnicos inglês-português,* EA123

Fürstentum Liechtenstein, DC439

Furtado, Ken. *Gay and lesbian American plays,* BE458

Furtaw, Julia. *VideoHound's golden movie retriever,* BH202

Fusco, Enrico M. *Scrittori e idee : dizionario critico della letteratura italiana,* BE1302

Futrell, Allan W. *Language of the underworld,* AC129

Fütterer, Dietmar. *Transfer and interference in language,* BD80

The future of Coptic studies, BC453, BE1520

Futures *see* **Commodities**

The futures markets dictionary, Steinbeck, George, CH437

Futurism
  bibliography, BE1291

Fyfe, Janet. *History journals and serials,* DA13

Gaar, Emil. *Clavis patrum latinorum,* BC296

Gabaccia, Donna R. *Immigrant women in the United States,* CC601

Gabbay, Dov. *Handbook of philosophical logic,* BB36

Gabel, Gernot U. *Bibliographie franzosischer Dissertationen zur deutschsprachigen Literatur, 1885–1975,* BE1237

—— *Canadian literature,* BE831

—— *Dissertations in English and American literature,* BE423

—— *Drama und Theater des deutschen Barock,* BE1262

—— *Leibniz,* BB75

—— *Litterature française,* BE1145

—— *Répertoire bibliographique des thèses françaises (1885–1975) concernant la littérature française des origines à nos jours,* BE1145

—— *Theses on Germany accepted for higher degrees by the universities of Great Britain and Ireland, 1900–1975,* DC219

Gabel, Gisela R. *Dissertations in English and American literature,* BE423

—— *Litterature française,* BE1145

—— *Theses on Germany accepted for higher degrees by the universities of Great Britain and Ireland, 1900–1975,* DC219

Gabon
  bibliography, DD18, DD159
  encyclopedias, DD48
  government publications
    bibliography, AF224, AF229
    statistics, CG331
Gabon (by subject)
  bibliography, DD159
Gabon, Gardinier, David E., DD18, DD48

Gabriel, Michael. *Micrographics, 1900–1977,* AK245

Gabrieli, Giuseppe. *Manuale di bibliografia musulmana,* BC492

Gacs, Ute. *Women anthropologists,* CE69

Gadan, Francis. *Dictionary of modern ballet,* BH140

Gaehde, Christa M. *Guide to the collecting and care of original prints,* BF379

Gaelic dictionary in two parts, Armstrong, R. A., AC393

Gaelic language
  dictionaries, AC393
    bilingual
      Gaelic-English, AC395
    etymology, AC394
    pronunciation, AC394
Gaer de Sabulsky, Alicia. *Historiografía Argentina 1930–1970,* DB333

Gage, Thomas Hovey. *Artist's index to Stauffer's "American engravers",* BF386

Gage, William W. *Provisional survey of materials for the study of neglected languages,* BD71

Gagnon, Philéas. *Essai de bibliographie canadienne,* DB182

Gailey, H. A. *Gambia,* DD48

Gaillemin, Janine. *Anarchisme,* CJ506

Gaina sûtras, BC92

Gajdos, Martina von. *Leben und Arbeit von Frauen, Frauenforschung und Frauenbewegung in Afrika,* DD7

Gajewski, Jerzy. *Medical risks,* EH233

Gakken kokugo daijiten, AC546

Gakovich, Robert P. *Serbs in the United States and Canada,* CC321, CC473

Galand, Lionel. *Langue et littérature berbéres,* DD68

Gale, Robert L. *A cultural encyclopedia of the 1850s in America,* DB103

—— *The gay nineties in America,* DB104

Gale, Steven H. *Encyclopedia of American humorists,* BE411

Gale, William. *Esquire's encyclopedia of 20th century men's fashions,* BG97, BG115

Gale directory of databases, AK208

Gale directory of publications, AD51, AE23

Gale directory of publications and broadcast media, AD51, AE23

Gale environmental sourcebook, EK74

Gale Research, inc. *American wholesalers and distributors directory,* CH346

—— *Asian Americans information directory,* CC401

—— *Awards, honors, and prizes,* AL161

—— *Black Americans information directory,* CC388

—— *Classical and medieval literature criticism,* BE46

—— *Directory of foreign investment in the U.S. ,* CH538

—— *Encyclopedia of associations,* AL41

—— *Encyclopedia of associations. International organizations,* AL17

—— *Environmental industries marketplace,* CH357

—— *Faculty white pages,* CB330

—— *Information industry directory,* AK192

—— *Job seeker's guide to private and public companies,* CH698

—— *Law and legal information directory,* CK150

—— *Library of Congress and national union catalog author lists, 1942–1962,* AA111

—— *Literature criticism from 1400 to 1800,* BE50

—— *Organizations master index,* AL20

—— *Personnel executives contactbook,* CH715

—— *Religious leaders of America,* BC83

—— *Telecommunications directory,* CH492

—— *Training and development organizations directory,* CH718

—— *Twentieth-century literary criticism,* BE54

—— *Vocational careers sourcebook,* CB214

—— *Women's information directory,* CC553

—— *World trade resources guide,* CH135

Galerstein, Carolyn L. *Women writers of Spain,* BE1444

Galicia, Magocsi, Paul R., DC35

Galishoff, Stuart. *Dictionary of American medical biography,* EH228

Gall, Ernst. *Reallexikon zur deutschen Kunstgeschichte,* BF79

Gall, Francis. *Diccionario geográfico de Guatemala,* CL116

Gall, Susan B. *Statistical record of Asian Americans,* CC410, CG82

Gall, Timothy L. *Statistical record of Asian Americans,* CC410, CG82

Gallaudet College. *Gallaudet encyclopedia of deaf people and deafness,* CC188

Gallaudet encyclopedia of deaf people and deafness, CC188

Galle, Marc. *Guide littéraire de la Belgique, de la Hollande, et du Luxembourg,* BE982

Gallegan literature, BE1363

Gallet-Guerne, Danielle. *Les sources de l'histoire littéraire aux Archives Nationales,* BE1148

Galli, Rosemary E. *Guinea-Bissau*, DD18
Gallia typographica, Lepreux, Georges, AA308
Gallico, Alison. *Directory of special collections in Western Europe*, AK131
Galling, Kurt. *Die Religion in Geschichte und Gegenwart*, BC68
Gallup, George Horace. *Gallup international public opinion polls, Great Britain, 1937–1975*, CJ486
—— *The Gallup poll*, CJ487
—— *The international Gallup polls*, CJ490
—— *The Phi Delta Kappa Gallup polls of attitudes toward education, 1969–1988*, CB137
The Gallup international public opinion polls, France, 1939, 1944–1975, CJ486
Gallup international public opinion polls, Great Britain, 1937–1975, Gallup, George Horace, CJ486
The Gallup poll, CJ487
The Gallup poll monthly, CJ487
Gallup polls of attitudes toward education, 1969–1984, CB137
Gallup polls of attitudes toward education, 1969–1988, CB137
The Gallup report, CJ487
Gal'perin, Il'ia Romanovich. *Bol'shoĭ anglo-russkiĭ slovar'*, AC675
Galván, Roberto A. *El diccionario del español chicano*, AC754
Galvin, Herman. *The Yiddish dictionary sourcebook*, AC813
Gambia, Gailey, H. A., DD48
—— Gamble, David P., DD18
Gambia national bibliography, AA858
Gambia, The
  bibliography, AA858, DD18, DD160
  encyclopedias, DD48
  government publications
    bibliography, AF225
Gamble, David P. *Gambia*, DD18
—— *A general bibliography of the Gambia, up to 31 December 1977*, DD160
Gamble, William B. *History of aeronautics*, EK23
Gambling, BK136, BK137
The games treasury, Mohr, Merilyn Simonds, BK18
Gamillscheg, Ernst. *Etymologisches Wörterbuch der französischen Sprache*, AC350
Gamma, Karl. *The handbook of skiing*, BK96
Gammage, Bill. *Australians 1938*, DF37
Gammond, Peter. *The Oxford companion to popular music*, BJ346
Ganay, Ernest. *Bibliographie de l'art des jardins*, BF286
Ganda language
  dictionaries
    bilingual
      Ganda-English, AC396
Gander, Terry. *Encyclopaedia of the modern British Army*, CJ652
—— *Encyclopaedia of the modern Royal Air Force*, CJ652
Gandhi, H. N. D. *Indian periodicals in print, 1973*, AD190
Gandilhon, René. *Bibliographie annuelle des travaux historiques et archéologiques publiés par les sociétés savantes de la France*, DC213
Ganellin, C. R. *Dictionary of drugs*, EE126, EH336
Ganić, Ejup N. *The McGraw-Hill handbook of essential engineering information and data*, EK17
Ganly, John. *Serials for libraries*, AA374
Gann, Lewis H. *A bibliographical guide to colonialism in sub-Saharan Africa*, DD82
Gannett, Henry. *Dictionary of altitudes in the United States*, CL71
Gans-Ruedin, E. *Great book of Oriental carpets*, BG165
Ganschow, Gerhard. *Bibliographie der uralischen Sprachwissenschaft 1830–1970*, BD208
Ganse, Robert A. *Catalog of significant earthquakes, 2000 b.c.–1979, including quantitative casualties and damage*, EF260
Ganshoff, F. L. *Guide to the sources of medieval history*, DA127
Ganz, Arthur F. *Literary terms*, BE76

—— *Reader's guide to literary terms*, BE76
Gänzl, Kurt. *Gänzl's book of the musical theatre*, BJ262
Gänzl's book of the musical theatre, Gänzl, Kurt, BJ262
Garber, Linda. *Lesbian sources*, CC271
García, Barbara M. *The University of Chicago Spanish dictionary*, AC739
Garcia, F. L. *Encyclopedia of banking & finance*, CH267
García, Gervasio Luis. *Los primeros pasos*, DB450
Garcia, Marina. *Diccionario de la literatura cubana*, BE973
García, Miguel Angel. *Bibliografía hondureña*, AA486, AA489
—— *Diccionario histórico-enciclopédico de la República de El Salvador*, AH116, DB306
García-Arenal, Mercedes. *Repertorio bibliográfico de las relaciones entre la península Ibérica y el Norte de África, siglos XV–XVI*, DD70
García-Ayvens, Francisco. *Chicano anthology index*, CC457
—— *Chicano periodical index*, AD267, CC456
García Craviotto, Francisco. *Catalogo general de incunables en bibliotecas españolas*, AA229
García de Diego, Carmen. *Diccionario etimológico español e hispánico*, AC743
García de Diego, Vicente. *Diccionario etimológico español e hispánico*, AC743
García de Paredes, Angel. *Cassell's Spanish-English English-Spanish dictionary*, AC730
García Durán, Juan. *La guerra civil española, fuentes*, DC516
García Gallarín, Consuelo. *Diccionario de términos literarios*, BE75
García García, Rosa María. *Ensayo bibliográfico del periodo colonial de México*, DB228
García Granados, Rafael. *Diccionario biográfico de historia antigua de Méjico*, AH100
García Icazbalceta, Joaquín. *Bibliografía mexicana del siglo XVI*, AA460
García-Pelayo y Gross, Ramón. *Diccionario general español-inglés [y English-Spanish]*, AC733
—— *Gran diccionario moderno*, AC733
García Rodríguez, Mariano. *Diccionario matemático*, EB54
Garcin, Jérôme. *Dictionnaire : littérature française contemporaine*, BE1151
Garden book, Brookes, John, BF295
The garden encyclopedia, EJ235
Garden literature, BF289
Garden styles, Brookes, John, BF295
The gardener's dictionary of horticultural terms, Bagust, Harold, EJ237
The gardener's index, Clewis, Beth, EJ229
Gardening
  bibliography, EJ228
  dictionaries, EJ242
  directories, EJ244
  encyclopedias, EG125, EJ232, EJ235, EJ236
  handbooks, EJ248, EJ249
  indexes, BF289, EJ229
  see also **Horticulture; Weeds**
Gardening, Isaacson, Richard T., EJ228
Gardening by mail, Barton, Barbara J., EJ244
Gardens
  bibliography, BF285, BF286
  encyclopedias, BF290
  guidebooks, BF296
  handbooks, BF295
Gardiner, Robert. *Conway's all the world's fighting ships, 1947–1982*, CJ592
Gardinier, David E. *Gabon*, DD18, DD48
Gardner, David E. *Genealogical research in England and Wales*, AJ99
Gardner, Helen. *Gardner's art through the ages*, BF129
Gardner, Helen Louise. *The new Oxford book of English verse, 1250–1950*, BE720
Gardner, James L. *Zen Buddhism*, BC467
Gardner, Katherine Ann. *The Library of Congress main reading room reference collection subject catalog*, AA350

Gardner, Martin. *Fads and fallacies in the name of science*, EA80
—— *In the name of science*, EA80
Gardner, Richard. *Alternative America*, AL44
Gardner, Robert L. *Tax research techniques*, CK119
Gardner, Sheldon. *The women of psychology*, CD51, CD52
Gardner, William. *Chemical synonyms and trade names*, EE39
Gardner's art through the ages, Gardner, Helen, BF129
Gardner's chemical synonyms and trade names, EE39
Garfield, Eugene. *Transliterated dictionary of the Russian language*, AC682, EA128
Garg, Gaṅgā Rām. *Encyclopaedia of Indian literature*, BE1565
—— *Encyclopaedia of world Hindi literature*, BE1565
—— *International encyclopaedia of Indian literature*, BE1565
Garland, Henry B. *The Oxford companion to German literature*, BE1244
Garland, Mary. *The Oxford companion to German literature*, BE1244
Garland composer resource manuals, BJ221
The Garland recipe index, Torgeson, Kathryn W., EJ208
The Garland Shakespeare bibliographies, BE767
Garlant, Julia. *Latin American bibliography*, DB252
Garmonsway, George Norman. *Penguin dictionary of English*, AC461
Garner, Bryan A. *A dictionary of modern legal usage*, CK36
Garner, Diane L. *Complete guide to citing government documents*, AF69
—— *The complete guide to citing government information resources*, AF69
Garoogian, Rhoda. *America's top-rated cities*, CL69
Garraty, John Arthur. *Encyclopedia of American biography*, AH60
—— *The nature of biography*, BE214
Garraux, Anatole Louis. *Bibliographie brésilienne*, DB346
Garreaud, Lelia. *Gran diccionario de Chile*, DB362
Garrison, Fielding Hudson. *Introduction to the history of medicine*, EH213, EH214
—— *Medical bibliography (Garrison and Morton)*, EH205
Garrison, J. J. *Art and architecture in the Western world*, BF129
Garrison, Robert H. *The nutrition desk reference*, EH299
Garritón, Manuel A. *Bibliografía del proceso chileno 1970–1973*, DB360
Garst, Rachel. *Bibliografía anotada de obras de referencia sobre Centroamérica y Panamá en el campo de las ciencias sociales*, DB298
Gartenberg, Jon. *The film catalog*, BH191
—— *Glossary of filmographic terms*, BH257
Gartner, Hans. *Paulys Realencyclopadie der classischen Altertumswissenschaft : Register der Nachträge und Supplemente*, DA104
Gärtner, Karla. *Bibliographie deutschsprachiger bevölkerungswissenschaftlicher Literatur, 1978–1984*, CG3, CG221
Gartner, Robert. *The national parks fishing guide*, BK116
Garwood, Alfred N. *Almanac of the 50 states*, CG104
—— *Regional differences in America*, CG77, DB150
Garza, Hedda. *The Watergate investigation index*, CJ113
Garzanti comprehensive Italian-English, English-Italian dictionary, AC532
Gascoigne, Bamber. *Encyclopedia of Britain*, DC292
—— *How to identify prints*, BF373
Gascoigne, Robert Mortimer. *A historical catalogue of scientific periodicals, 1665–1900*, EA42
—— *Historical catalogue of scientists and scientific books*, EA42, EA193

Gasero, Russell L. *Historical directory of the Reformed Church in America, 1628–1992,* BC380

Gases, EE28, EE69

Gaskell, Philip. *A new introduction to bibliography,* AA3, EE11

Gaskin, L. J. P. *A bibliography of African art,* BF25, BG4

Gassler, Robert Scott. *Bibliography on world conflict and peace,* CJ664

Gassmann, Günther. *Documentary history of faith and order, 1963–1993,* BC282

Gassner, John. *The reader's encyclopedia of world drama,* BH70

Gastaldi, Mario. *Dizionario delle scrittrici italiane contemporanee (arte, lettere, scienze),* BE1313

Gasteazoro, Carlos Manuel. *Introducción al estudio de la historia de Panamá,* DB319

Gasteazoro, Raul A. *West's Spanish-English/ English-Spanish law dictionary,* CK55

Gastronomical and culinary literature, Feret, Barbara L., EJ204

Gastrow, Shelagh. *Who's who in South African politics,* CJ412, DD212

Gates, Henry Louis. *Black biography, 1790–1950,* AH59

—— *Black literature, 1827–1940,* BE535

Gates, Jean Key. *Guide to the use of libraries and information sources,* AK3

Gateway Japan (Organization). *Focus Japan II,* AL43, DE210

GATT international trade, CH156

Gatti, Daniel Jon. *The educator's encyclopedia of school law,* CB155

Gatti, Richard D. *The educator's encyclopedia of school law,* CB155

Gatto, Simon. *Dizionario tecnico scientifico illustrato,* EA117

Gauchat, Patrick. *Hierarchia catholica medii aevi,* BC430

Gauci, Sarah. *Bibliographies on the Australian aborigine,* DF28

Gaudel, Paul. *Bibliographie der archäologischen Konservierungstechnik,* DA64

Gaudet, Franceen. *Checklist of indexes to Canadian newspapers,* AE117

Gaule jusqu'au milieu de Ve siècle, Duval, Paul-Marie, DC147

Gaunt, William. *Everyman's dictionary of pictorial art,* BF301

Gaur, Albertine. *South Asian studies,* DE88

Gaustad, Edwin Scott. *Historical atlas of religion in America,* BC85

Gaute, J. H. H. *New murderers' who's who,* CK254

Gauthier, Joseph D. *French XX bibliography,* BE1370

Gautier, Léon. *Les épopées françaises,* BE1199

Gavault, Paul. *Les livres de l'enfance du XVe au XIXe siècle,* AA245

Gavin, Christy. *American women playwrights, 1964–1989,* BE459

Gavrilenko, N. V. *Gosudarstvennye (natsional'nye) bibliograficheskie ukazateli sotsialisticheskikh stran,* AA396

Gay, William. *The nuclear arms race,* CJ670

Gay and lesbian American plays, Furtado, Ken, BE458

The gay, lesbian, and bisexual students' guide to colleges, universities, and graduate schools, Sherrill, Jan-Mitchell, CB290

The gay nineties in America, Gale, Robert L., DB104

Gayley, Charles Mills. *Classic myths in English literature and in art,* CF25

Gaylord, Charles N. *Structural engineering handbook,* EK113

Gaylord, Edwin Henry. *Structural engineering handbook,* EK113

Gays and lesbians in mainstream cinema, Parish, James Robert, BH229

Gazdar, Gerald. *A bibliography of contemporary linguistic research,* BD4

—— *Natural language processing in the 1980s,* BD64

Gazetnyi mir Sovetskogo Soiuza, 1917–1970 gg, Kuznetsov, Ivan Vasil'evich, AE73

Gazette des beaux-arts, BF46

Gazette nationale, ou Moniteur universel, AF170

Gazetteer, United States. Defense Mapping Agency, CL95

—— United States Board on Geographic Names, CL87

Gazetteer of Afghanistan, CL158

A gazetteer of Albania, Permanent Committee on Geographical Names for British Official Use, CL129

Gazetteer of Burma, CL159

Gazetteer of Canada, CL112

Gazetteer of China, Tien, H. C., CL161

Gazetteer of conventional names, CL87

The gazetteer of England, Mason, Oliver, CL138

A gazetteer of Greece, Permanent Committee on Geographical Names for British Official Use, CL142

Gazetteer of India, CL163, CL164

A gazetteer of Japanese place names in characters and in Rōmaji script giving latitudes and longitudes, Gerr, Stanley, CL166

Gazetteer of Persia, CL165

Gazetteer of Scotland, CL140

Gazetteer of the British Isles, CL135

Gazetteer of the Japanese Empire, United States. Hydrographic Office, CL167

Gazetteer of the People's Republic of China, United States. Defense Mapping Agency, CL162

Gazetteer of the United States of America, CL109

Gazetteer of undersea feature names, 1987, CL171

Gazetteers, CL65, CL84, CL85, CL86, CL87, CL88, CL89, CL90, CL92, CL94, CL96, CL97, CL98

bibliography, CL100

Gazetteers (by period)

ancient and medieval, CL101, CL102, CL103, CL104, CL105

see also **Geographical names and terms; subheading Gazetteers under names of countries**

Gazetteers and glossaries of geographical names of the member-countries of the United Nations and the agencies in relationship with the United Nations, Meynen, Emil, CL100

Gazzaniga, Michael S. *Handbook of psychobiology,* CD122

•*GDB,* EG342, EH189

GDEL, AB42

Geahigan, Priscilla Cheng. *American business climate & economic profiles,* CH166

—— *Business serials of the U.S. government,* CH26

—— *U.S. and Canadian businesses, 1955 to 1987,* CH389, CH390

Gealt, Adelheid M. *Looking at art,* BF115

Gebauer, Dorothea. *Bibliography of national filmographies,* BH164

Gebbie Press house directory, AD57

Geber, Halina. *A history of Polish literature,* BE1352

Gebhard, David. *Buildings of Iowa,* BF254

Gebhardt, Bruno. *Handbuch der deutschen Geschichte,* DC220

Gebiet und Bevölkerung, CG220

Geddes, Charles L. *An analytical guide to the bibliographies on Islam, Muhammad, and the Qur'an,* BC493

—— *Guide to reference books for Islamic studies,* BC494

Geddie, William. *A bibliography of middle Scots poets,* BE810

Gedeon, Borsa. *Régi magyarországi nyomtatványok, 1473–1600,* AA713

Gee, Henry. *Documents illustrative of English church history, comp. from original sources,* BC284

Geelan, P. J. M. *The Times atlas of China,* CL354

Geelen, J. van. *Lexicon van de moderne Nederlandse literatuur,* BE1333

Geer, Gary. *Dictionary of American literary characters,* BE484

Geerard, Maurice. *Clavis apocryphorum Novi Testamenti,* BC107

—— *Clavis Patrum Graecorum,* BC297

Geerts, Guido. *Groot woordenboek der Nederlandse taal,* AC292

Geest, Gerrit de. *Bibliography of law and economics,* CK7

Geetha, K. R. *Classified state bibliography of linguistic research on Indian languages,* BD224

Geflügelte Worte, BE135, BE136

Gehart, Alois. *Statistik in Österreich, 1918–1938,* CG195

Gehman, Henry Snyder. *The new Westminster dictionary of the Bible,* BC138

Gehring, Wes D. *Handbook of American film genres,* BH223

Geib, M. Margaret. *Atlas of South Asia,* CL347

Geigy scientific tables, EA154

Geikie, Archibald. *The founders of geology,* EF106

Geils, Peter. *Gesamtverzeichnis des deutschsprachigen Schrifttums (GV), 1700–1910,* AA643

Y geiriadur mawr, Evans, H. Meurig, AC805

Geiriadur Prifysgol Cymru, AC806

Geiriadur saesneg a chymraeg, Spurrell, William, AC807

Geisenderfer, R. D. *Glossary of oceanographic terms,* EF220

Geist, Christopher D. *Directory of popular culture collections,* CF73

Das geistige Ungarn, Jásznigi, Alexander, AH248

Gelb, Ignace J. *Assyrian dictionary,* AC200

Gelbert, Doug. *Sports halls of fame,* BK35

Geldner, Ferdinand. *Die deutschen Inkunabeldrucker,* AA307

Geldsetzer, Lutz. *Bibliography of the International Congresses of Philosophy,* BB17

Geldzahler, Annette. *Lisa Birnbach's new and improved college book,* CB254

Gelfand, Elissa D. *French feminist criticism,* BE1133

Gel'fand, V. S. *Naselenie SSSR za 50 let, 1941–1990,* CG295

Gellert, Charles Lawrence. *Holocaust, Israel and the Jews,* DA221

Gellert, Walter. *The VNR concise encyclopedia of mathematics,* EB69

Gelling, Margaret. *The names of towns and cities in Britain,* CL197

Gemmyō, Ono. *Bussho kaisetsu daijiten,* BC465

Gemology, Sinkankas, John, EF176

Gems, EF180, EF185, EF187, EF191, EF192

bibliography, EF176

handbooks, EF190

Gems, their sources, descriptions, and identification, Webster, Robert, EF180

Gendai Nihon shippitsusha daijiten, BE1581

Gender roles, Beere, Carole A., CC556, CC557

Gendron, Francis. *Dictionnaire historique de la Révolution française,* DC184

—— *Filmographie mondiale de la Révolution française,* DC179

Gendron, Jean-Denis. *Dictionnaire étymologique de l'ancien français,* AC346

Genealogical abstracts of Revolutionary War pension files, AJ38

Genealogical and heraldic history of the colonial gentry, Burke, John Bernard, AJ115

Genealogical and heraldic history of the landed gentry, AJ58

Genealogical and local history books in print, Yantis, Netti Schreiner, AJ34

Genealogical books in print, AJ34

Genealogical cross index of … the Genealogical dictionary of James Savage, Dexter, O. P., AJ65

A genealogical dictionary of the first settlers of New England, Savage, James, AJ65

A genealogical gazetteer of England, Smith, Frank, AJ112

Genealogical guide, Whitmore, John Beach, AJ109

Genealogical guide to German ancestors from East Germany and Eastern Europe, AJ78

Genealogical handbook of German research, Jensen, Larry O., AJ90, AJ92

Genealogical historical guide to Latin America, Platt, Lyman De, AJ74

Genealogical history of the dormant, abeyant, forfeited, and extinct peerages of the British Empire, Burke, John Bernard, AJ116

Genealogical libraries
  directories, AJ54

Genealogical manuscripts in British libraries, Kaminkow, Marion J., AJ108

Genealogical notes and errata to Savage's Genealogical dictionary, Dall, C. H., AJ65

Genealogical periodical annual index, AJ39

Genealogical research, AJ10

Genealogical research in England and Wales, Gardner, David E., AJ99

Genealogical research in Israel, AJ143

Genealogical resources in English repositories, Moulton, Joy Wade, AJ104

Genealogies cataloged by the Library of Congress since 1986, AJ32

Genealogies in the Library of Congress, AJ31
  —— Library of Congress, AJ32

Genealogisches Handbuch des Adels, AJ75, AJ79

The genealogist's address book, Bentley, Elizabeth Petty, AJ53

Genealogists guide, Barrow, Geoffrey Battiscombe, AJ109
  —— Marshall, George William, AJ109

Genealogist's handbook for Atlantic Canada research, AJ70

Genealogy
  associations
    Canada, AJ55
    directories, AJ52
    United States, AJ55
  bibliography, AJ31, AJ32
    current, AJ34
  biography, AJ56
  computer applications, AJ5
  dictionaries, AJ50, AJ111
  directories, AJ53
  guides, AJ2, AJ7, AJ11, AJ17, AJ19, AJ101, DB143
  guides to records, AJ12, AJ14
  indexes, AJ35, AJ39, AJ42, AJ45, AJ47
  library resources, AJ14, AJ54
  periodicals, AJ33
  registers, AJ81

Genealogy (by country or region)
  Australia, AJ144
  Canada, AJ70, AJ71, AJ72, AJ73
  Europe, AJ75
    registers, AJ76, AJ77, AJ79, AJ80
    tables, AJ77
  Europe, Eastern
    guides to records, AJ78
  France, AJ88
    bibliography, AJ82, AJ87
    guides, AJ83
    guides to records, AJ84, AJ85
    registers, AJ86, AJ89
  Germany, AJ40, AJ93
    bibliography, AJ91
    guides, AJ90
    guides to records, AJ78
    handbooks, AJ92, AJ95
    registers, AJ94
  Great Britain, AJ63
    atlases, AJ113
    bibliography, AJ28, AJ109, AJ110
    compendiums, AJ114, AJ115, AJ116, AJ117, AJ118, AJ119
    gazetteers, AJ112
    guides, AJ96, AJ97, AJ102, AJ105, AJ106
    guides to records, AJ99, AJ104, AJ107
    indexes, AJ107, AJ113
    manuscripts, AJ108
    registers, AJ150, AJ155
  Ireland, AJ37, AJ134, AJ135
    guides, AJ96, AJ132
    guides to records, AJ136, AJ137, AJ138
    atlases, AJ137
    registers, AJ131

Israel
  guides, AJ143
Italy, AJ64, AJ139
Latin American
  guides, AJ74
New Zealand, AJ145
Scotland
  bibliography, AJ121
  guides, AJ122, AJ123, AJ124
Spain, AJ140
  guides, AJ141
Sweden, AJ43
United States, AJ44, AJ61, AJ65
  bibliography, AJ28
  directories, AJ51
  guides, AJ4, AJ6, AJ9, AJ10, AJ11, AJ16, AJ17, AJ22, AJ23, AJ27, AJ93, DB143
  guides to records, AJ1, AJ12, AJ15
  indexes, AJ36, AJ38, AJ41, AJ48
  registers, AJ25, AJ58
Wales, AJ128, AJ129
  guides to records, AJ127, AJ130

Genealogy for librarians, Harvey, Richard, AJ19, AJ101

Genealogy in Ontario, Merriman, Brenda Dougall, AJ72

General Agreement on Tariffs and Trade. *International trade*, CH156

General alphabetical index to the bills, reports, estimates, accounts and papers printed by order of the House of Commons and to the papers presented by command, 1801–1948/49, Great Britain. Parliament. House of Commons, AF199

General alphabetical index to the town lands and towns, parishes, and baronies of Ireland, AJ137

A general analytical bibliography of the regional novelists of the British Isles, 1800–1950, Leclaire, Lucien, BE677

General and applied linguistics, BD7

The general armory of England, Scotland, Ireland, and Wales, Burke, John Bernard, AJ149

General armory two, Humphery-Smith, Cecil R., AJ149
  —— Morant, Alfred, AJ149

General bibliography of astronomy to the year 1880, EC13

A general bibliography of the Gambia, up to 31 December 1977, Gamble, David P., DD160

General catalog of music publishing in France, Pierreuse, Bernard, BJ76

General catalogue of printed books, British Museum, AL12, BE456
  —— British Museum. Department of Printed Books, AA103, AA615, AA661, AD3, AD4, BE707

General censuses and vital statistics in the Americas, Library of Congress. Census Library Project, CG72

General Douglas MacArthur, 1880–1964, Rasor, Eugene L., DA170

General ethnological concepts, Hultkrantz, Åke, CE49

General guide to the India Office Records, India Office Library and Records, DE12, DE83
  —— Moir, Martin, DE12

General history of Africa, DD58

The general history of astronomy, EC59

General illustrated armorial, Rolland, H., AJ160
  —— Rolland, V., AJ160

General index to sessional papers printed by order of the House of Lords or presented by special command, Great Britain. Parliament. House of Lords, AF202

General index to the names and subject matter of the Sacred books of the East, Winternitz, Moriz, BC92

General inventory, Public Archives of Canada, DB194

General issues in literacy/illiteracy, Hladczuk, John, CB49

General laws of Rhode Island, 1956, Rhode Island. [Laws, etc.], CK179

General Matthew B. Ridgeway, Edwards, Paul M., DA170

General minutes of the annual conferences of the United Methodist Church, United Methodist Church (U.S.), BC365

General science index, EA69

General social survey, National Opinion Research Center, CC40

General statutes of North Carolina, North Carolina. [Laws, etc.], CK179

General Telephone & Electronics Corporation. Financial Services Division. *Symbol guide*, CH315

General transportation, Dresley, Susan, CH444
  —— Pearlstein, Toby, CH444

General world atlases in print, 1972–1973, Walsh, S. Padraig, CL223

Generalregister der Zeitschrift für Krystallographie und Mineralogie, EF174

Generals in blue, Warner, Ezra J., DB121

Generals in gray, Warner, Ezra J., DB121

Generative grammar *see* **Transformational grammar**

Genetic disorders, EH91

Genetic disorders and birth defects, EH91

Genetics, EG339, EG340, EG341, EG342, EH189
  dictionaries, EG343

Genetics abstracts, EG14

Genetisches und cytogenetisches Wörterbuch, EG343

Genicot, Léopold. *Vingt ans de recherche historique en Belgique, 1969–1988*, DC102

Genkai, AC549

Genkina, Esfir Borisovna. *Sovetskaia strana v period vosstanovleniia narodnogo khoziaistva, 1921–1925 gg*, DC590

Gennadius Library. *Catalogue*, DC373
  —— *Voyages and travels in Greece, the Near East and adjacent regions made previous to the year 1801*, DE47
  —— *Voyages and travels in the Near East made during the XIX century*, DE48

●*Genome data base*, EG342, EH189

Genre fiction, BE248

Genreflecting, Rosenberg, Betty, BE248

Genthe, Charles V. *American war narratives, 1919?–1918*, DA197

Gentleman's magazine biographical and obituary notices, 1781–1819, Nangle, Benjamin Christie, AH241

Gentz, William H. *The dictionary of Bible and religion*, BC71

Geo abstracts, CL18, CL31, CL32

Geo-data, Kurian, George Thomas, CL90

●*GeoArchive*, EF50, EF56, EF227

●*GEOBASE*, CH44, CL30, EF51, EF52, EF177, EG63

Geochemistry, EF19
  abstract journals, EF178
  encyclopedias, EF67

Geodesy
  bibliography, EF23, EF121
  dictionaries, EF122, EF123
    multilingual, EF124

Geodetic glossary, EF122

Geodetický a kartografický podnik v Praze. *Atlas ČSSR*, CL323

Geoghegan, Abel Rodolfo. *Bibliografía de bibliografías argentinas, 1807–1970*, AA26
  —— *Bibliografía de la Revolución de Mayo, 1810–1828*, DB326
  —— *Obras de referencia de América Latina*, AA349

Geografía basica del Ecuador, CG153

Geograficheskiĭ entsiklopedicheskiĭ slovar', CL88

Geografiska Sällskapet i Finland, Helsingfors. *Suomen kartasto*, CL326

Geographers, CL82

Geographic information, CL78

Geographic names & the federal government, Library of Congress. Geography and Map Division, CL99

●*Geographic names information system (GNIS)*, CL108

Geographical abstracts, CL32, EG63

Geographical abstracts. Human geography, CL30, CL31, EF51

Geographical abstracts. Physical geography, CL30, CL32, EF51

A geographical bibliography for American college libraries, CL10

———— Lewthwaite, Gordon Rowland, CL17

A geographical bibliography for American libraries, CL10

Geographical features in Canada named for surveyors, Jolicoeur, T., CL112

Geographical guide to floras of the world, Blake, Sidney Fay, EG100

Geographical names and terms, CL40, CL47, CL52, CL93, CL95, CL100, CL110, CL170, CL172, CL173, CL174, CL175, CL207, CL267
  bibliography, CL99
  databases, CL108
  dictionaries
    multilingual, CL91
Geographical names and terms (by period)
  medieval and Renaissance
    bibliography, DA130
Geographical names and terms (by subject)
  mythology, CF21
  see also **Gazetteers**

Géographie politique, Sanguin, André Louis, CL20

Geographische-Kartogrtaphisches Institut Meyer. *Meyers grosser Weltatlas*, CL283

Geography
  abstract journals, CL31, CL32
  bibliography, CE29, CL4, CL5, CL6, CL7, CL8, CL9, CL10, CL12, CL14, CL15, CL16, CL17, CL18, CL19, CL20, CL29, CL251, EF47
    current, CL22
    dissertations, CL26
  biography, CL80, CL81, CL82, CL83, CL272, CL273, CL274
  book reviews, CL34
  databases, CL30, EF51
  dictionaries, CL42, CL43, CL44, CL45, CL48, CL49, CL50, CL51, CL52, CL89, CL97
    bibliography, CL53
    Russian, CL154
  directories, CL55, CL56
  dissertations, CL26, CL27
  encyclopedias, CL35, CL36, CL37, CL38, CL39, CL40, CL41, CL46, CL47
  guides, CL1, CL2, CL3, CL4, CL12
  handbooks, CL67, CL68, CL76, CL262
  indexes, CL23, CL33
  library catalogs, CE29, CL28, CL29
  library collections, CL253
  periodicals, CL24, CL25
    indexes, CL8
  quotations, CL54
  yearbooks, CL78, CL79, CL270
Geography (by country or region)
  Russia and the U.S.S.R.
    guides, CL13
  Union of Soviet Socialist Republics
    bibliography, CL151
  United States
    handbooks, CL71

Geography and anthropology, Harvard University. Library, CE29, CL29

Geography and earth sciences publications, Van Balen, John, CL34

Geologic literature on North America, 1785–1918, Nickles, John Milton, EF36

Geologic names of North America, Wilson, Druid, EF77

Geologic reference sources, Ward, Dederick C., EF20

Geological abstracts, CL30, EF51, EF52

Geological atlas of Western and Central Europe, Ziegler, Peter A., EF115

Geological dictionary, Zylka, Romauld, EF81

Geological nomenclature, Nederlands Geologisch Mijnbouwkundig Genootschap, EF80

•*Geological reference file*, EF49, EF53, EF54, EF234

•*Geological reference file (GeoRef)*, EF47, EF48

Geological Society of America. *Annotated bibliography of economic geology*, EF21

———— *Bibliography and index of geology*, EF47

———— *Bibliography and index of geology exclusive of North America*, EF48

———— *Bibliography of theses in geology, 1964*, EF44

———— *Handbook of physical constants*, EF96

———— *Memorials*, EF107

Geological Society of London. *Catalogue of the Library*, EF45

Geological Society of London. Library. *List of geological literature added to the Geological Society's library, [July 1894]–1934*, EF45

Geological Survey of Canada. *Annotated catalogue of and guide to the publications of the Geological Survey Canada, 1845–1917*, EF28

———— *Index of publications of the Geological Survey of Canada, 1845–1958*, EF29

———— *Index to publications*, EF30

———— *Index to reports of Geological Survey of Canada from 1927–50*, EF31

———— *Publications of the Geological Survey of Canada, 1917–1952*, EF33

Geological Survey (U.S.). *Annotated bibliography on hydrology and sedimentation*, EF126, EF127

———— *Bibliography of North American geology*, EF49

———— *Geophysical abstracts*, EF54

———— *Guide to USGS geologic and hydrologic maps*, CL249, EF111

———— *The national atlas of the United States of America*, CL298

———— *The national gazetteer of the United States of America*, CL108

———— *Selected water resources abstracts*, EF129, EK68

———— *Worldwide directory of national earth-science agencies and related international organizations*, EF92

Geologisches Zentralblatt, EF55

Geologisches Zentralblatt. Abt. A, Geologie, EF55

Geologisches Zentralblatt. Abt. B, Palaeontologisches Zentralblatt, EF55

Geologists and ideas, EF99

Geologists and the history of geology, Sarjeant, William A. S., EF108

Geology
  abstract
    journals, EF52
  abstract journals, EF55, EF58, EF60, EF178
  atlases, EF110, EF112
  bibliography, AL86, CE14, EA16, EB10, EC15, ED5, EE13, EF20, EF24, EF34, EF45, EF46, EF48, EF57, EF59, EF103, EF141, EF173, EF232, EG6, EG105, EG211, EG312
    current, EF56
  bibliography of bibliography, EF35
  biobibliography, EF252
  biography, EF101, EF107, EF108
  chronologies, EF104
  databases, EF50, EF53
  dictionaries, EA90, EF13, EF70, EF71, EF72, EF74, EF75, EF76
    bilingual
      English-Czech, EF82
      English-Russian, EF89
      German-English, EF85
      Russian-English, EF87
    French, EF83
    multilingual, EF78, EF79, EF81
    polyglot, EF80
  dissertations, EF43, EF44
  encyclopedias, EF61, EF62, EF63, EF68, EF69
  guidebooks
    bibliography, EF93
  guides, EF20
  handbooks, EF94
  indexes, EF47, EF48, EF50
  library catalogs, EF45, EF46
  maps, CL249, EF111
  nomenclature, EF74
  periodicals, EF40, EF41

  tables, EF96
  thesauruses, EF73
Geology (by country or region)
  Asia, West
    bibliography, EF22
  Canada
    bibliography, EF28, EF29, EF30, EF31, EF33
    indexes, EF27, EF31
    maps, EF30
  Europe
    atlases, EF115
  Great Britain
    bibliography, EF98
  North America
    atlases, EF113
    bibliography, EF26, EF36, EF49
    history, EF99
    indexes, EF49
  United States
    bibliography, EF32, EF37, EF39
    nomenclature, EF77
    state publications, EF25
Geology (by subject)
  history, EF98, EF100, EF101, EF102, EF105, EF106, EF108
    bibliography, EF103
  study and teaching
    Canada, EF90
    Mexico, EF90
    United States, EF90
  see also **Economic geology; Plate tectonics**

Geology and earth sciences sourcebook for elementary and secondary schools, American Geological Institute. Conference. (Duluth, 1959), EF94

Geology, stratigraphic, EF95

Geology, stratigraphic (by country or region)
  North America
    atlases, EF113

Geology, structural, EF66

Geomorphology, EF114
  atlases, EF109
  encyclopedias, EF7

Geophysical abstracts, EF53

———— Geological Survey (U.S.), EF54

Geophysical directory, EF91

Geophysics
  abstract journals, EF143
  abstracts, EF54
  dictionaries, EF11, EF75
    bilingual
      English-Russian, EF88
    multilingual, EF78
  directories, EF91
  encyclopedias, EF11, EF65
  handbooks, EF155
  tables, EA155, EF96
Geophysics (by subject)
  history
    bibliography, EF97
  study and teaching, EF151

Geopolitical crisis, CJ72

•*GeoRef*, EF40, EF42, EF49, EF53, EF54, EF73, EF234

GeoRef serials list, EF40

GeoRef thesaurus and guide to indexing, EF42, EF53, EF73

Georg, Karl. *Karl Georgs Schlagwort-katalog*, AA642

Georg Westermann Verlag. *Grosser Atlas zur Weltgeschichte*, DA51

———— *Westermann Lexikon der Geographie*, CL40

Georgakas, Dan. *Encyclopedia of the American left*, DB129

George, J. David. *Marine life*, EG224

George, Jennifer J. *Marine life*, EG224

George, John H. *They never said it*, BE90

George, Linda K. *Handbook of aging and the social sciences*, CC97

George, Mary W. *Learning the library*, AK229

George, Pierre. *Dictionnaire de la géographie*, CL45

George, Rosemary. *The companion to wine*, EJ225

George, Tracey E. *Public interest law*, CK9

George Kleine collection of early motion pictures in the Library of Congress, Library of Congress. Motion Picture, Broadcasting, and Recorded Sound Division, BH190

The George Washington journal of international law and economics, CK74

Georges, Christopher J. *The Harvard independent insider's guide to prep schools,* CB108

Georges, Robert A. *American and Canadian immigrant and ethnic folklore,* CF66

Georgescu, Magdalena. *Dicționarul limbii române literare vechi, 1640–1780,* AC658

Georgetown University. Library. *Scholar's guide to intelligence literature,* CJ538

Georgi, Charlotte. *Arts and the world of business,* BF39

Georgi, Theophilus. *Allgemeines europäisches Bücher-Lexicon,* AA92

Georgia. [Laws, etc.]. *Official code of Georgia annotated,* CK179

Georgia State University. College of Business Administration. Business Publishing Division. *Marketing information,* CH546

Georgia State University. Library. Insurance History Collection. *A bibliography of insurance history,* CH504

Georgian-English dictionary, Cherkesi, E., AC397

Georgian language
  dictionaries
    bilingual
      English-Georgian, AC398
      Georgian-English, AC397

Georgiev, Vladimir Ivanov. *Bŭlgarski etimologichen rechnik,* AC240

—— *Entsiklopediia Bŭlgariia,* DC119

Georgy, Ursula. *From CA to CAS ONLINE,* EE6

Geoscience abstracts, EF44

Geoscience documentation, EF50

Geoscience Information Society. Guidebooks Committee. *Union list of geologic field trip guidebooks of North America,* EF93

Geostatistical glossary and multilingual dictionary, EF78

Geotitles, EF50, EF56

Geotitles weekly, EF56

Gephart, Ronald M. *Revolutionary America, 1763–1789,* DB88

GER, AB95

Geraghty & Miller's groundwater bibliography, Van der Leeden, Frits, EF130

Gerarchia cattolica, BC409

Gérard, Albert S. *African language literatures,* BE1501

—— *European-language writing in sub-Saharan Africa,* BE1501

Gerasimov, Innokentiĭ Petrovich. *Fiziko-geograficheskiĭ atlas mira,* CL275

Gerasimova, IŪ. Ivanovna. *Lichnye arkhivnye fondy v gosudarstvennykh kranilishchakh SSSR,* DC565

Gerber, Barbara L. *Dictionary of modern French idioms,* AC368

Gerboth, Walter. *An index to musical festschriften and similar publications,* BJ13

Gerdts, William H. *The National Museum of American Art's index to American art exhibition catalogues,* BF120

Gerhan, David R. *A retrospective bibliography of American demographic history from colonial times to 1983,* CG92, DB14

Gerhard, Peter. *A guide to the historical geography of New Spain,* DB225

—— *North frontier of New Spain,* DB225

—— *Southeast frontier of New Spain,* DB225

Gerhardstein, Virginia Brokaw. *American historical fiction,* BE470

Gerhart, Eugene C. *Quote it!,* CK57

—— *Quote it II,* CK57

Gerhatz, Wolfgang. *Ullmann's encyclopedia of industrial chemistry,* EK53

Geriadur istorel ar brezhoneg, Hemon, Roparz, AC237

Gericke, Hannelore. *Wiener Musikalienhandel von 1700 bis 1778,* BJ181

Gérin, Paul. *Bibliographie de l'histoire de Belgique,* DC99

Gering, Hugo. *Vollständiges Wörterbuch zu den Liedern der Edda,* BE1286

Gerlach, Arch C. *The national atlas of the United States of America,* CL298

Gerlach, Gudrun. *Verzeichnis vor- und frühgeschichtlicher Bibliographien,* DC6

Gerlach, John C. *The critical index,* BH233

Gerlach, Lana. *The critical index,* BH233

Germain, Claire M. *Germain's transnational law research,* CK1

—— *Guide to foreign legal materials,* CK208

—— *Guide to foreign legal materials : French,* CK202

Germain, Jean. *Bibliographie sélective de linguistique romane et française,* BD150

—— *Guide bibliographique de linguistique romane,* BD150

Germaine, Max. *Artists and galleries of Australia,* BF140

—— *Dictionary of women artists of Australia,* BF140

Germain's transnational law research, Germain, Claire M., CK1

German Africa, Bridgman, Jon, DD80

German-American history and life, Keresztesi, Michael, CC324

German-American names, Jones, George Fenwick, AJ196

German-American relations and German culture in America, Schultz, Arthur R., CC330

German Association of Comparative law. *Bibliographie des deutschen rechts in englischer und deutscher sprache,* CK211

German Baroque literature, Yale University. Library. Yale Collection of German Literature, BE1234

German biographical archive, AH206

German books in print, AA660

German chemical abbreviations, Wohlauer, Gabriele E. M., EE52

German drama, BE1261, BE1262
  bibliography, BE1264, BE1266
  biobibliography, BE1265
  encyclopedias, BE1263
German drama (by subject)
  history, BE1263

German-English-Chinese polytechnical dictionary, Lü, Wen-chảo, EA101

A German-English dictionary for chemists, EE51

German-English, English-German dictionary for physicians, Lejeune, Fritz, EH136, EH140

German-English mathematical vocabulary, MacIntyre, Sheila, EB51

German-English science dictionary, De Vries, Louis, EA111

German-English technical and engineering dictionary, DeVries, Louis, EA112

German engravings, etchings and woodcuts, ca.1400–1700, Hollstein, F. W. H., BF382

German Federal Republic official publications, 1949–1957, Childs, James Bennett, AF173

German fiction, BE1267, BE1268, BE1269

German foreign policy, 1918-1945, Kimmich, Christoph M., DC237

German Historical Institute (Washington, D.C.). *Guide to inventories and finding aids of German archives at the German Historical Institute, Washington, D.C,* DC246

German immigrants, Zimmerman, Gary J., AJ40, AJ49

German institutions, AL62

German Jewry, Wiener Library, London, BC541

German language
  bibliography, BD116, BD118, BD119, BD120, BD121, BD123, BE1224, BE1225, BE1226, BE1235
  dialects
    bibliography, BD127
    handbooks, BD126

  dictionaries, AC399, AC400, AC401, AC402, AC403, AC404, AC405, AC406, AC407, AC408, AC409, AC411, AC412, AC413
    abridged, AC410
    bibliography, AC425, AC426
    bilingual
      English-German, AC418
      German, AC438
      German-English, AC414, AC415, AC416, AC417, AC419, AC420, AC421, AC422, AC423, AC424
    idioms and usage, AC437, AC439
    visual, AC420
  encyclopedias, BD124
  etymology
    dictionaries, AC427, AC428
  grammar
    bibliography, BD117
  guides, BE1211
  new words
    dictionaries, AC436
  slang
    dictionaries, AC429, AC430, AC431
  synonyms and antonyms, AC432, AC433, AC435
    dictionaries, AC434

German language (by period)
  16th-17th centuries
    bibliography, BD122
German language (by subject)
  history, BD125

German language and literature, University of London. Institute of Germanic Studies, BD123

German-language press, AE1

The German language press of the Americas, AE53

—— Arndt, Karl John Richard, AE1

•*German language publications on Russia/USSR/CIS,* DC41

German literary history, 1777–1835, Bartel, Klaus J., BE1254

German literature, BE1245
  bibliography, BD116, BD118, BD119, BD120, BD121, BD123, BE1055, BE1211, BE1212, BE1215, BE1218, BE1219, BE1220, BE1222, BE1223, BE1224, BE1225, BE1226, BE1227, BE1228, BE1229, BE1233, BE1235, BE1246, BE1248, BE1250, BE1251
    current, BE1236
  bibliography of bibliography, BE1221
  biobibliography, BE1054, BE1057, BE1059, BE1060, BE1061, BE1216, BE1247, BE1248, BE1258, BE1260
  biography, BE1061, BE1220, BE1243, BE1246
    bibliography, AH205
  chronologies, BE1252
  criticism
    collections, BE1058
  dictionaries, BE1249
  dissertations, BE1237
  encyclopedias, BE1246, BE1251
  guides, BE1210, BE1211, BE1212
  handbooks, BE1244, BE1252
  indexes, BE1273
  library catalogs, BE1222
  manuscripts, BE1242
  translations, AA142, BE1238, BE1239, BE1240, BE1241
  women authors
    biobibliography, BE1056, BE1062
    biography, BE1243

German literature (by period)
  16th–18th centuries
    bibliography, BE1234
    library catalogs, BE1234
  17th century
    bibliography, BE1217
  1933–45
    biobibliography, BE1232
  medieval
    bibliography, BE1253
    biography, BE1253
German literature (by subject)
  Expressionism, BE1230

history, BE1250, BE1255, BE1256, BE1259, BE1260
  bibliography, BE1213, BE1214, BE1219, BE1254
history and criticism, BE1247
themes, motifs, BE1231
German literature, Faulhaber, Uwe K., BE1210
——— Harvard University. Library, BE1222
German literature in American magazines, 1846 to 1880, Haertel, Martin Henry, BE1238, BE1240
German literature in American magazines prior to 1846, Goodnight, Scott Holland, BE1238, BE1240
German literature in British magazines, 1750–1810, Hohlfeld, A. R., BE1238
——— Morton, Bayard Quincy, BE1238
German literature in British magazines, 1750–1860, Morgan, Bayard Quincy, BE1240
German literature in English translation, O'Neill, Patrick, BE1241
German military history, 1648–1982, Showalter, Dennis E., DC240
German nationalism, Buse, Dieter K., DC231
German naval history, Bird, Keith W., DC214
German newspapers in libraries and archives, AE53
German poetry, BE1270, BE1271, BE1272
  indexes, BE1273
German reunification, Osmond, Jonathan, CJ332
The German-speaking countries of Europe, Krewson, Margrit B., DC9
German stage, 1767–1890, Richel, Veronica C., BE1261
German studies
  bibliography, DC238
  guides, BE1212
Germanic and its dialects, Markey, Thomas L., BD113
Germanic languages
  bibliography, BD112, BD115
  dialects
    bibliography, BD113
    biobibliography, BD113
  grammar
    bibliography, BD114
The Germanic press of Europe, Iben, Icko, AE8
Germanistik, BE1236
Germanistik in Festschriften von den Anfängen (1877) bis 1973, BD112
Germans
  emigration
    registers, AJ46
Germans (by country or region)
  Africa
    bibliography, DD80
  Australia, DF25
  Canada
    handbooks, CC352
  United States, AJ22, AJ49, AJ93, CC330, DC9
    bibliography, CC324, CC329
    biography, DA47
    handbooks, CC352
    manuscripts; archives, CC324
    registers, AJ40
The Germans, Noelle-Neumann, Elisabeth, CJ493
The Germans after World War II, Paul, Barbara Dotts, DC239
Germans to America, AJ40, AJ49
——— Filby, P. William, AJ64
——— Glazier, Ira A., AJ64
Germany
  archives, DC245
  bibliography, AA333, DC230
    18th–19th centuries, AA641, AA642, AA643, AA644, AA645, AA646
    20th century, AA647, AA648, AA649, AA651
      Frankfurt-am-Main, AA652, AA653
      Leipzig, AA654, AA655, AA656
    current, AA657, AA658, AA659, AA660, AG30
    dissertations, DC219
    early, AA637, AA638, AA639, AA640
    Frankfurt am Main, AA650
  bibliography of bibliography, AA42, AA43, AA44, AA45, AA46

biography, AH202, AH203, AH204, AH206, AH207, AH208, AH209, AH210, AH215, AH216, DC261
  bibliography, AH214
  contemporary, AH211, AH212, AH213
dissertations, AA657, AG30, AG31, AG32
gazetteers, CL134
government publications, AF174
guides to records, DC245
history and area studies
  library resources, DC216
library catalogs, AA117
  bibliography, AA118
newspapers, AE53
  directories, AD103
  indexes, AE122, AE123
periodicals, AD76, AD77, AD102
  bibliography, AD99, AD100, AD101
  directories, AD98, AD103
  indexes, AD313, AD314, AD315
place-names, AJ192, CL189, CL190, CL191
registers, CJ325
statistics, CG222, CG224, CG225, CG226
  bibliography, CG223, CG228
translations
  bibliography, AA139
Germany (by subject)
  cities, DC265
  economic history
    bibliography, CH336
  election statistics, CJ336
  folklore and popular culture, CF86
  foreign relations, DC201, DC237
    archives and manuscripts, DC251
  government officials, CJ331
  history, DC220, DC221, DC222
    archives, DC247
    archives and manuscripts, DC248, DC249, DC250, DC251, DC252, DC254
    atlases, DC263, DC264
    bibliography, DC88, DC200, DC215, DC218, DC229, DC234, DC236, DC238, DC239, DC241, DC242
    chronologies, DC224, DC260
    chronology, DC223
    encyclopedias, DC255, DC256, DC257, DC258, DC259
    guides to records, DC246, DC247, DC248, DC249, DC250, DC251, DC252, DC254
    handbooks, DC237, DC260
    library catalogs, DC244
    oral history, BF274, DC266
    to 1600, DC228
  history (by period)
    20th century, DC261
  law, CK210
    bibliography, CK211
  military history, DC240
  photography, BF329
  politics and government, CJ331, CJ333, CJ336, CJ498, DC262
    bibliography, DC231, DC235
    encyclopedias, CJ334
    handbooks, CJ332
    history, DC257
  population, CG3, CG220, CG221, CG227, CG229
  statistics and demography, CG227
Germany. Bundesanstalt für Landeskunde. Bibliotheca cartographica, CL227
Germany. Bundestag, CJ331
Germany. Institut Für Landeskunde. Bibliotheca cartographica, CL227
Germany. Statistisches Bundesamt. Statistisches Jahrbuch der Deutschen Demokratischen Republik, CG224
Germany. Statistisches Reichsamt. Statistisches Handbuch von Deutschland, 1928–1944, CG222
Germany, East
  bibliography, DC243
    20th century, DC267
  biography, AH216, AH217
  government publications, AF165

Germany, East (by subject)
  history, DC267
  politics and government, CJ330
Germany (East). Staatliche Zentralverwaltung für Statistik. Statistisches Jahrbuch der Deutschen Demokratischen Republik, CG224
Germany (Federal Republic). Bundesanstalt für Landeskunde und Raumforschung. Documentatio geographica, CL8
Germany (Territory under Allied Occupation, 1945–1955 : U.S. Zone). Statistisches Handbuch von Deutschland, 1928–1944, CG222
Germany, West
  bibliography, DC232
  election statistics, CJ335
  government publications, AF173
Germany, West (by subject)
  history, DC217
    bibliography, DC232
Germany (West). Statistisches Bundesamt. Bevölkerung und Erwerbstätigkeit, CG220
——— *Statistisches Jahrbuch für die Bundesrepublik Deutschland,* CG226
——— *Veröffentlichungsverzeichnis,* CG223
Gernsheim, Alison. *History of photography,* BF328
——— *Origins of photography,* BF328
Gernsheim, Helmut. *History of photography,* BF328
——— *Incunabula of British photographic literature,* BF328
——— *Origins of photography,* BF328
——— *Rise of photography,* BF328
Geron, Leonard. *Who's who in Russia and the new states,* AH180
Gerontological social work, Parham, Iris A., CC43
Gerontology *see* Aging
Gerontology, Edwards, Willie M., CC67
Gerontology and geriatrics libraries and collections in the United States and Canada, Post, Joyce A., CC88
Gerould, Daniel. *Polish plays in translation,* BE1361
Gerow, Edwin. *Guide to Indian philosophy,* BB21
Gerr, Stanley. *A gazetteer of Japanese place names in characters and in Rōmaji script giving latitudes and longitudes,* CL166
Gerritsen, J. *Engels woordenboek,* AC296
Gershanek, Sinai. *Who was who in journalism, 1925–1928,* AE153
Gershman, Michael. *Total baseball,* BK62
Gerstein, Maurice J. *Dictionary of microbiology,* EG39
Gerstenberger, Donna Lorine. *The American novel,* BE473
——— *Fourth directory of periodicals publishing articles on English and American literature and language,* BE170
Gerstle, Gary. *American political leaders,* CJ158
Gerteiny, A. G. *Mauritania,* DD48
Gerth van Wijk, H. L. *Dictionary of plant names,* EG127
Gertzel, Cherry J. *Uganda, an annotated bibliography of source materials,* DD239
Gervais, Raymond. *African historical demography,* CG310
Gesamentlike katalogus van proefskrifte en verhandelinge van die Suid-Afrikaanse universiteite, AG49
——— Malan, Stephanus I., AG49
Gesamtinhaltsverzeichnis der wissenschaftlichen Zeitschriften der Universitäten und Hochschulen der Deutschen Demokratischen Republik, AD314
Gesamtkatalog der preussischen Bibliotheken, AA122
Gesamtkatalog der Wiegendrucke, AA230, AA231, AA233
Gesamtverzeichnis ausländischer Zeitschriften und Serien 1939–1958, AD235
Gesamtverzeichnis der ausländischen Zeitschriften (GAZ), AD235
Gesamtverzeichnis des deutschsprachigen Schrifttums ausserhalb des Buchhandels (GVB), 1966–1980, AA648
Gesamtverzeichnis des deutschsprachigen Schrifttums (GV), 1700–1910, AA643

Gesamtverzeichnis des deutschsprachigen Schrifttums (GV); 1911–1965, AA647

Gesamtverzeichnis deutschsprachiger Hochschulschriften (GVH), 1966–1980, AG10

Gesamtverzeichnis österreichischer Dissertationen, AG22

Gesamtverzeichnis russischer und sowjetischer Periodika und Serienwerke, Bruhn, Peter, AD234

Gesamtworterbuch der alt- und neuhebraischen sprache, AC470

Geschichte der arabischen Literatur, Brockelmann, Carl, BE1549

Geschichte der byzantinischen Literatur von Justinian bis zum Ende des Oströmischen Reiches, Krumbacher, Karl, DA163

Geschichte der deutschen Literatur, Scherer, Wilhelm, BE1227
—— Walzel, Oskar, BE1227

Geschichte der deutschen Literatur von den Anfängen bis zur Gegenwart, Boor, Helmut Anton Wilhelm de, BE1255
—— Gysi, Klaus, BE1255

Die Geschichte der deutschen Passagierschiffahrt, Kludas, Arnold, AJ93

Geschichte der deutschen Presse, Lindemann, Margot, AE54

Geschichte der deutschsprachigen Literatur seit 1945, Schnell, Ralf, BE1260

Geschichte der estnischen Literatur, Jänes, Henno, BE1125

Geschichte der Geologie und Paläontologie bis Ende des 19. Jahrhunderts, Zittel, Karl Alfred von, EF105

Geschichte der griechischen Literatur, Christ, Wilhelm von, BE1035
—— Lesky, Albin, BE1034
—— Schmid, Wilhelm, BE1035

Geschichte der indischen Litteratur, Winternitz, Moriz, BE1571

Geschichte der jugoslavischen Literaturen von den Anfängen bis zur Gegenwart, BE1497

Geschichte der Kreuzzüge, Mayer, Hans Eberhard, DA168

Geschichte der lateinischen Literatur des Mittelalters, Brunholzl, Franz, BE1050, BE1051, BE1052
—— Manitius, Maximilianus, BE1050, BE1051, BE1052

Geschichte der mongolischen Literatur, Heissig, Walther, BE1597

Geschichte der Musik, BJ136

Geschichte der Musik in Bildern, Kinsky, Georg, BJ199

Geschichte der Päpiste, Pastor, Ludwig, BC432

Geschichte der Philologie, Wilamowitz-Moellendorff, Ulrich von, BE1021, DA107

Geschichte der römischen Literatur, Teuffel, Wilhelm Sigismund, BE1053

Geschichte der römischen Literatur bis zum Gesetzgebungswerk des Kaisers Justinian, Schanz, Martin, BE1052

Geschichte der slowenischen Literatur, Slodnjak, Anton, BE1497

Geschichte der tschechischen Literatur im 19. und 20. Jahrhundert, Měšťan, Antonín, BE1106

Geschichte des arabischen Schrifttums, Sezgin, Fuat, BE1549

Geschichte und Bibliographie der astronomischen Literatur in Deutschland zur Zeit der Renaissance, Zinner, Ernst, EC20

Geschiedenis van de letterkunde der Nederlanden, Baur, Frank, BE1326

Geschiedkundige atlas van Nederland, DC462

Gesellschaft für Deutsche Philologie in Berlin. *Jahresbericht über die Erscheinungen auf dem Gebiete der germanischen Philologie,* BD119

Gesellschaft für Erdkunde zu Berlin. *Bibliotheca geographica,* CL6

Gesellschaft für Information und Dokumentation. *Thesaurus guide,* AK216

Gesellschaft für Unternehmensgeschichte. *Deutsche Wirtschaftsarchive,* DC245

Gesenius, Friedrich Heinrich Wilhelm. *Hebräisches und aramäisches Handwörterbuch über das Alte Testament …* , AC477

Gesenius, Wilhelm. *Hebräisch-deutsches Handwörterbuch,* AC476

Geshikhte fun der literatur bay Yidn, Zinberg, Israel, BE1578

Gesualdo, Vicente. *Enciclopedia del arte en América,* BF70

Gesuga, Angelica Wanjinu. *Swahili-English dictionary,* AC758

Getting a grant in the 1990s, Lefferts, Robert, AL92

Getting funded, Hall, Mary S., AL92

Getty Art History Information Program. *Art & architecture thesaurus,* BF94
—— *Avery index to architectural periodicals,* BF209
—— *Bibliography of the history of art,* BF43
—— *The index of paintings sold in the British Isles during the nineteenth century,* BF302

Getty Conservation Institute. *Art and archaeology technical abstracts,* BF198

Geuljans, Robert. *Bibliographie des dictionnaires patois galloromans (1550–1967),* AC390

Geuss, Herbert. *Dahlmann-Waitz Quellenkunde der deutschen Geschichte,* DC215

Geyer, B. *Elsevier's dictionary of agriculture and food production,* EJ31

Geyer, Douglas W. *Index to book reviews in religion,* BC52

Geyser, O. *Bibliographies on South African political history,* CJ410, DD213

•*GFDB,* EE110

•*GFI,* EE110

Ghana
bibliography, AA859, AA860, DD18, DD162
biography, AH319
current surveys, DD62
encyclopedias, AH319, DD48
government publications
bibliography, AF231
statistics, CG334

Ghana (by subject)
history
bibliography, DD161, DD162
population, CG333
status of women
bibliography, DD163

Ghana. Central Bureau of Statistics. *Statistical hand book of the Republic of Ghana,* CG332
—— *Statistical year book,* CG334

Ghana, McFarland, D. M., DD48
—— Myers, Robert A., DD18
—— Witherell, Julian W., AF231

Ghana in the humanities and social sciences, 1900–1971, Aguolu, Christian Chukwunedu, DD162

Ghana national bibliography, AA859

Ghana national bibliography bi-monthly, AA860

Ghana who's who, AH319

Ghanaian literature, BE1528

Ghanaian literatures, BE1528

Ghandi, H. N. D. *Indian periodicals in print, 1973,* AE88

Ghani, Sirūs. *Iran and the West,* DE183

Ghatage, Amrit Madhav. *An encyclopaedic dictionary of Sanskrit on historical principles,* AC705

Ghisalberti, Alberto Maria. *Dizionario biografico degli Italiani,* AH260

Gholston, H. D. *German chemical abbreviations,* EE52

Ghorayshi, Parvin. *The sociology of work,* CC7

Ghose, D. C. *Bibliography of modern Indian art,* BF27

Ghosh, Amalananda. *An encyclopaedia of Indian archaeology,* DE166

Ghosh, J. G. *Annals of English literature, 1475–1950,* BE612

Ghost walks, Sampson, Henry T., BH109

Ghūshah, Zakī Rātib. *Administration and development in the Arab world,* CJ468

Gianakos, Larry James. *Television drama series programming,* BH302

Gibaldi, Joseph. *Introduction to scholarship in modern languages and literatures,* BE4
—— *MLA handbook for writers of research papers,* AG2
—— *The MLA style manual,* AA317

Gibb, Hamilton Alexander Rosskeen. *The encyclopaedia of Islam,* BC503
—— *Shorter encyclopaedia of Islam,* BC505

Gibb, Mike. *Keyguide to information sources in veterinary medicine,* EJ96

Gibbney, H. J. *A biographical register, 1788–1939,* AH372

Gibbons, E. F. *Almanac of modern terrorism,* CJ555

Gibbons, S. R. *Handbook of modern history,* DA179

Gibbs, Donald A. *A bibliography of studies and translations of modern Chinese literature, 1918–1942,* BE1553

Gibian, George. *Soviet Russian literature in English,* BE1391

Gibilisco, Stan. *Encyclopedia of electronics,* EK129

Gibney, Frank. *Britannica book of English usage,* AC66

Gibraltar, DC269
statistics, CG230

Gibraltar, Shields, Graham J., DC269

Gibraltar abstract of statistics, CG230

A Gibraltar bibliography, Green, Muriel M., DC268

Gibson, Anne. *The women's atlas of the United States,* CC581

Gibson, Bob. *The astronomer's sourcebook,* EC50

Gibson, Gerald D. *Classical music, 1925–1975,* BJ383

Gibson, Haldo. *Svensk slangordbok,* AC760

Gibson, Jeremy Sumner Wycherley. *Record offices,* AJ100

Gibson, John. *A dictionary of medical and surgical syndromes,* EH114

Gibson, M. J. *United States of America national bibliographical services and related activities in 1965–1967,* AA21

Gibson, Mary Jane. *Portuguese Africa,* AF220, DD114, DD184

Gibson, Mary Jo Storey. *International glossary of social gerontology,* CC83

Gibson, Robert W. *Japanese scientific and technical literature,* EA49

Giddens, Paul H. *The beginnings of the petroleum industry,* EK300

Giddings, Robert. *True characters,* BE251
—— *Who was really who in fiction,* BE251

Gidwani, N. N. *Current Indian periodicals in English,* AD191, AD193
—— *A guide to reference materials on India,* DE156

Giebisch, Hans. *Bio-bibliographisches Literaturlexikon Osterreichs,* BE1095

Giebsich, Hans. *Die Weltliteratur,* BE72

Giefer, Gerald J. *Sources of information in water resources,* EK88
—— *Water publications of state agencies,* EK89

Giese, Friedo. *Beilstein's index,* EE132

Gieysztorowa, Irena. *The historical atlas of Poland,* DC482

Giffin, James M. *Cat owner's home veterinary handbook,* EJ138
—— *Dog owner's home veterinary handbook,* EJ142

Gifford, Charles S. *American educators' encyclopedia,* CB65

Gifford, Denis. *Books and plays in films, 1896–1915,* BH219
—— *The British film catalogue, 1895–1985,* BH186
—— *Illustrated who's who in British films,* BH211

Gifford, Prosser. *Transfer of power in Africa,* DD4

Gifis, Steven H. *Dictionary of legal terms,* CK37
—— *Law dictionary,* CK37

Gifted & talented information resources, Wicker, Gerald L., CB188

The gifted and talented, Anthony, John B., CB184

Gifted and talented information resources, CB188

Gifted children, CB184, CB185, CB188
bibliography, CB187

Gifted children (by subject)
  education, CB186
Gifted, talented, and creative young people, Stein, Morris Isaac, CB187
Gifts and exchange manual, Lane, Alfred H., AK166
Gilbert, Alan D. *Australians*, DF37
Gilbert, Anne. *The British Library*, AK101
Gilbert, Christopher. *Dictionary of English furniture makers, 1660–1840*, BG135
Gilbert, Dennis A. *Compendium of American public opinion*, CJ488
Gilbert, Judson Bennett. *Disease and destiny*, EH16
Gilbert, Martin. *American history atlas*, DB72
—— *The Arab-Israeli conflict*, DE74
—— *Atlas of British history*, DC301
—— *Atlas of Russian history*, DC571
—— *Atlas of the Holocaust*, DA223
—— *The Dent atlas of American history*, DB72
—— *The Dent atlas of Jewish history*, DA52, DE193
—— *Russian history atlas*, DC571
Gilbert, Pamela. *A compendium of biographical literature on deceased entomologists*, EG329
—— *Entomology*, EG330
Gilbert, Pierre. *Dictionnaire des mots contemporains*, AC373
—— *Dictionnaire des mots nouveaux*, AC373
Gilbert, Sandra M. *Norton anthology of literature by women*, BE619
Gilbert, Victor Francis. *Immigrants, minorities and race relations*, CC337
—— *Labour and social history theses*, CH295, DC283
Gilchrist, Alan. *Thesaurus construction*, AK218
Giles, Herbert Allen. *A Chinese biographical dictionary*, AH339
—— *Chinese-English dictionary*, AC263
Gilgen, Albert R. *International handbook of psychology*, CD45
Gilgen, Carol K. *International handbook of psychology*, CD45
Giliarevskii, R. S. *Languages identification guide*, BD14, BD18
Gilissen, John. *Introduction bibliographique à l'histoire du droit et à l'ethnologie juridique*, CK12
Gill, Kay. *Assistance and benefits information directory*, AL101
—— *State government research directory*, CJ280
Gill, Sam D. *Dictionary of Native American mythology*, CF16
Gillespie, George T. *A catalogue of persons named in German heroic literature (700–1600), including named animals and objects and ethnic names*, BE1245
Gillespie, John Thomas. *Best books for children*, AA337
Gillett, Charles Ripley. *Catalogue of the McAlpin collection of British history and theology*, BC227, DC321
Gillie, Christopher. *Longman companion to English literature*, BE611
Gillingham, John. *Historical atlas of Britain*, DC302
Gillis, Irvin Van Gorder. *Supplementary index to Giles' "Chinese biographical dictionary"*, AH339
Gillispie, Charles Coulston. *Dictionary of scientific biography*, EA176
Gillow, Joseph. *A literary and biographical history*, AH228
Gillum, Gary P. *The Catholic left in Latin America*, DB255
Gilmore, George William. *New Schaff-Herzog encyclopedia of religious knowledge*, BC67
Gilmore, William J. *Psychohistorical inquiry*, DA5, DA43
Gilreath, James. *Federal copyright records, 1790–1800*, AA406
Gimson, A. C. *Everyman's English pronouncing dictionary*, AC105
Ginger, Ann Fagan. *Human rights organizations and periodicals directory*, CK147
Gingerich, Martin E. *Contemporary poetry in America and England, 1950–1975*, BE490

Gingerich, Owen. *Astrophysics and twentieth-century astronomy to 1950*, EC59
—— *Source book in astronomy and astrophysics, 1900–1975*, EC62
Gingrich, Felix Wilbur. *A Greek-English lexicon of the New Testament and other early Christian literature*, AC453
—— *Shorter lexicon of the Greek New Testament*, AC453
Ginsberg, Leon H. *Encyclopedia of social work*, CC46
—— *Social work almanac*, CC52
Ginzel, Friedrich Karl. *Handbuch der mathematischen und technischen Chronologie*, EC87
Giocondi, Michele. *Dizionario dei sinonimi e dei contrari*, AC542
Giornale della libreria, AA725, AA732
Gipper, Helmut. *Bibliographisches Handbuch zur Sprachinhaltsforschung*, BD22
Gipson, Carolyn Renee. *The McGraw-Hill dictionary of international trade and finance*, CH123
Gipson, Fred W. *Petroleum engineering handbook*, EK308
Gipson, Lawrence Henry. *A bibliographical guide to the history of the British Empire, 1748–1776*, DC341
—— *Guide to manuscripts relating to the history of the British Empire, 1748–1776*, DC341
Giraldo Jaramillo, Gabriel. *Bibliografía colombiana de viajes*, DB366
—— *Bibliografía de bibliografías colombianas*, AA29
Girão, Aristides de Amorim. *Atlas de Portugal*, CL332
Girard, Denis. *New Cassell's French dictionary*, AC342
Giraud, Jeanne. *Manuel de bibliographie littéraire pour les XVIᵉ, XVIIᵉ et XVIIIᵉ siècles français*, BE1209
—— *Manuel de bibliographie littéraire pour les XVIᵉ, XVIIᵉ et XVIIIᵉ siècles français, 1921–1935*, BE1137
Girke, Wolfgang. *Handbibliographie zur neueren Linguistik in Osteuropa*, BD5
Girma Makonnen. *A bibliography of Ethiopian bibliographies, 1932–1972*, AA71
Girodet, Jean. *Pièges et difficultées de la langue française*, AC369
•*GIS*, CB210
The GIS guide to four-year colleges, CB271
Gisbert, Teresa. *Iconografía y mitos indígenas en el arte*, BF70
Gisler, Jean-Robert. *Lexicon iconographicum mythologiae classicae*, BF188, CF23
Gitisetan, Dariush. *Iran, politics and government under the Pahlavis*, DE184
Gitler, Ira. *Encyclopedia of jazz in the seventies*, BJ300
Giuseppi, M. S. *Guide to the manuscripts preserved in the Public Record Office*, DC286
Givanel Mas, Juan. *Bibliografía catalana*, AD153
The giver's guide, Mackey, Philip English, AL93
Gkinēs, Dēmētrios S. *Hellēnikē bibliographia, 1800–1863*, AA701
GLA, BF84
Glaciology
  dictionaries
    multilingual, EF125
Gladkova, T. L. *L'emigration russe*, AD300
Gladstone, Joan M. *Russian literature, theatre, and art*, BE1409
Gladstone, W. E. *An analytical index to the Book of Common Prayer and a brief account of its evolution*, BC348
Glannon, Ann M. *Kits, games, and manipulatives for the elementary school classroom*, CB14
Glanze, Walter D. *Mosby's medical, nursing, and allied health dictionary*, EH102
Glanzman, George S. *An introductory bibliography for the study of scripture*, BC110
Glare, P. G. W. *Oxford Latin dictionary*, AC577
Glareanus, Henricus. *Isagoge in musicen*, BJ29

Glashan, Roy R. *American governors and gubernatorial elections, 1775–1978*, CJ291
Glass *see* **Ceramics and glass**
Glass, Kämpfer, Fritz, BG75
Glass collections in museums in the United States and Canada, BG68
Glasse, Cyril. *The concise encyclopedia of Islam*, BC504
Glatz, Ferenc. *Études historiques hongroises 1990*, DC389
Glauser, Beat. *New bibliography of writings on varieties of English*, BD108
Glavatskikh, G. A. *Istoriĩa dorevoliũtsionnoĩ Rossii v dnevnikakh i vospominaniĩakh*, DC579
—— *Istoriĩa SSSR*, DC549
—— *Spravochnik po istorii dorevoliũtsionnoi Rossii*, DC582
Glavnoe upravianie geodezii i kartografii. *Atlas Antarktiki*, CL370
Glavnoe upravlenie geodezii i kartografii. *Fiziko-geograficheskii atlas mira*, CL275
Glazebrook, Richard. *Dictionary of applied physics*, ED13
Glazer, Mark. *A dictionary of Mexican American proverbs*, CC459
Glazier, Ira A. *The famine immigrants*, AJ37
—— *Germans to America*, AJ40, AJ64
—— *Italians to America*, AJ64
Glazier, Jack D. *Qualitative research in information management*, AK7
Glazier, Stephen. *Random House word menu*, AC74
Gleason, Henry Allan. *The new Britton and Brown illustrated flora of the northeastern United States and adjacent Canada*, EG173
Glen, Duncan. *Poetry of the Scots*, BE810
Glendale Adventist Medical Center. *Cumulative index to nursing & allied health literature*, EH274
—— *Nursing & allied health (CINAHL)*, EH275
—— *Nursing & allied health (CINAHL) … subject heading list*, EH280
Glenn, J. A. *Dictionary of mathematics*, EB38, EB39
Glenn, James R. *Guide to the National Anthropological Archives, Smithsonian Institution*, CE32
Glenn, Robert W. *Black rhetoric*, BE352
—— *The Haymarket affair*, DB99
Gli editori italiani, AA291
Glickman, Harvey. *Political leaders of contemporary Africa south of the Sahara*, AH316, CJ404, CJ406, CJ409
Glikin, Ronda. *Black American women in literature*, BE519
Glimpses of India, Riddick, John F., DE159
Glixon, David M. *Allusions—cultural, literary, biblical, and historical*, AC65, BE74
Gloag, John. *Complete dictionary of furniture*, BG126
—— *Guide to Western architecture*, BF256
—— *John Gloag's dictionary of furniture*, BG126
—— *Short dictionary of furniture*, BG126
Global company handbook, CH405
Global estimates and projections of population by sex and age, CG65
Global guide to international education, CB102
Global terrorism, CJ549
Global trade, CH146
Globes, CL246
Glock, Waldo Sumner. *Eighteenth-century English literary studies*, BE745
Glockner, Herman. *Hegel-Lexikon*, BB79
Glorieux, Geneviève. *Belgica typographica, 1541–1600*, AA578
Glosario de términos de tecnologia de la educación, CB174
Glosario de términos literarios, Turaiev, S., BE906
Glossaire des termes de technologie éducative, CB174
Glossaire moyen-breton, Ernault, Émile, AC236
Glossaries, Permanent Committee on Geographical Names for British Official Use, CL267
Glossariĩ terminov po tekhnologii obrazovaniĩa, CB174

Glossarium ad scriptores mediæ & infimæ graecitatis, Du Cange, Charles Du Fresne, AC454
Glossarium artis, BF84, BF278
Glossarium mediae et infimae latinitatis, Du Cange, Charles Du Fresne, AC587, AC592, AC593
A glossary for archivists, manuscript curators, and records managers, AK184
—— Bellardo, Lewis J., AK188
—— Bellardo, Lynn Lady, AK188
Glossary for horticultural crops, Soule, James, EJ243
A glossary of American technical linguistic usage, 1925–1950, Hamp, Eric P., BD39
Glossary of art, architecture & design since 1945, Walker, John Albert, BF93
Glossary of astronomy and astrophysics, Hopkins, Jeanne, EC34
Glossary of automotive terms, EK40
Glossary of botanic terms with their derivation and accent, Jackson, Benjamin Daydon, EG131
A glossary of Chinese art and archaeology, Hansford, S. Howard, BF85
A glossary of contemporary literary theory, Hawthorn, Jeremy, BE83
Glossary of economics, including Soviet terminology, Clifford Vaughan, F., CH65
Glossary of educational technology terms, CB174
Glossary of employment and industry, Logie, Gordon, CH653
A glossary of entomology, EG338
Glossary of filmographic terms, Gartenberg, Jon, BH257
Glossary of financial terms, Horn, S. F., CH214
Glossary of genetics, Rieger, Rigomar, EG343
Glossary of genetics and cytogenetics, Rieger, Rigomar, EG343
Glossary of geographical names in six languages, Lana, Gabriella, CL91
Glossary of geographical terms, CL43
—— British Association for the Advancement of Science. Research Committee, CL42
Glossary of geology, Bates, Robert Latimer, EF70, EF71, EF72
—— Jackson, Julia A., EF71, EF72
Glossary of graphic signs and symbols, BF177
Glossary of hydrology, EF133
—— Lo, Shuh-shiaw, EF134
Glossary of imaging technology, AK246
Glossary of later Latin to 600 A.D., Souter, Alexander, AC583
A glossary of literary terms, Abrams, M. H., BE73, BE83
Glossary of mapping, charting, and geodetic terms, United States. Defense Mapping Agency. Topographic Center, CL52
Glossary of meteorology, EF146
Glossary of micrographics, National Micrographics Association, AK246
A glossary of mycology, Snell, Walter Henry, EG138
Glossary of numismatic terms in English, French, German, Italian, Swedish, Salton, Mark W., BG179
Glossary of oceanographic terms, United States. Naval Oceanographic Office, EF220
Glossary of population and housing, Logie, Gordon, CG24
Glossary of psychoanalytic terms and concepts, Fine, Bernard D., CD30
—— Moore, Burness E., CD30
Glossary of Russian abbreviations and acronyms, EA129
—— Library of Congress. Aerospace Technology Division, AC688
A glossary of Spanish literary composition, Redfern, James, BE1453
A glossary of special education, CB197
Glossary of succulent plant terms, Marshall, William Taylor, EG135
Glossary of terms in nuclear science and engineering, National Research Council Conference on Glossary of Terms in Nuclear Science and Technology, EK295

Glossary of terms in nuclear science and technology, EK295
Glossary of terms used in British heraldry, Gough, H., AJ164
A glossary of terms used in heraldry, Parker, James, AJ164
Glossary of the mining and mineral industry, Fay, A. H., EF188
Glossary of the Third World, Kurian, George Thomas, CJ39
Glossary of transformational grammar, Ambrose-Grillet, Jeanne, BD46
Glossary of transport, Logie, Gordon, CH446
Glossary of Tudor and Stuart words, especially from the dramatists, Skeat, Walter William, AC101
Glossary of U.S. government vocabulary, Whisker, James B., CJ123
Glossary of wood, Corkhill, Thomas, EJ177
Glossary of words, phrases, names, and allusions in the works of English authors, particularly of Shakespeare and his contemporaries, Nares, Robert, AC99
A glossary of Zen terms, Inagaki, Hisao, BC478
Glossary : water and wastewater control engineering, EK92
Glossolalia, BC18
Głowiński, Michał. *Słownik terminów literackich,* BE1359
Gluski, Jerzy. *Proverbs,* BE155
Glynn, Prudence. *In fashion: dress in the twentieth century,* BG115
Gmelin, Leopold. *Handbuch der anorganischen Chemie,* EE110
Gmelin, EE110
•*Gmelin factual database,* EE110
•*Gmelin formula index,* EE110
Gmelin handbook of inorganic chemistry, EE110
Gmelins Handbuch der anorganischen Chemie, EE110
Gnielinski, Stefan. *Liberia in maps,* CL342
Gnirss, Christa. *Internationale Bibliographie der Reprints,* AA399
GNIS, CL108
Goa, DE161
Gobernantes de Nicaragua, Barquero, Sara Luisa, DD313
Goble, Alan. *The international film index, 1895–1990,* BH188
Godbolt, Shane. *Information sources in the medical sciences,* EH5
Godbout, Archange. *Nos ancêtres au XVIIᵉ siècle,* AJ71
Goddard, Carolyn E. *On the trail of the UCC,* BC384
Goddard, Jeanne M. *Catalogue of the Frederick W. and Carrie S. Beinecke collection of Western Americana,* DB170
Goddard, Stephen. *A guide to information sources in the geographical sciences,* CL2
Godden, Geoffrey A. *Encyclopaedia of British porcelain manufacturers,* BG60
—— *Encyclopedia of British pottery and porcelain marks,* BG60
—— *Godden's guide to European porcelain,* BG60
Godden's guide to European porcelain, Godden, Geoffrey A., BG60
Goddesses & wise women, Carson, Anne, BC10
Goddesses in world mythology, Ann, Martha, BC62, CF2
—— Imel, Dorothy, BC62
Gode, P. K. *The practical Sanskrit-English dictionary,* AC702
Godefroy, Frédéric Eugéne. *Dictionnaire de l'ancienne langue française,* AC346, AC384
—— *Dictionnaire de l'ancienne langue française, et de tous ses dialectes, du IXᵉ au XVᵉ siècle,* AC378
—— *Histoire de la littérature française depuis le 16ᵉ siècle jusqu'à nos jours,* BE1169
—— *Lexique de l'ancien français,* AC375, AC378
Godenne, René. *Bibliographie critique de la nouvelle de langue française (1940–1985),* BE1188

Gods and heroes, Harnsberger, Caroline Thomas, CF28
Godshalk, William. *The Garland Shakespeare bibliographies,* BE767
Goebel, Ulrich. *Frühneuhochdeutsches Wörterbuch,* AC401
Goedeke, Karl. *Grundriss zur Geschichte der deutschen Dichtung aus den Quellen,* BE1096, BE1218, BE1227
Goehlert, Robert. *American presidency,* CJ170, CJ172
—— *American presidents,* CJ167, CJ173
—— *Anarchism,* CJ506
—— *Congress and law-making,* CJ195
—— *The Department of State and American diplomacy,* CJ169
—— *The executive branch of the U.S. government,* CJ170
—— *How to research the Supreme Court,* CK186
—— *The Parliament of Great Britain,* CJ351
—— *Policy analysis and management,* CA11
—— *Political science journal information,* CJ16
—— *The presidency,* CJ165
—— *State legislatures,* CJ268
—— *The United States Congress,* CJ198
—— *The U.S. Supreme Court,* CK186
Goehring, James E. *The Eerdmans analytical concordance to the Revised Standard Version of the Bible,* BC166
Goeldner, Charles R. *Bibliography of tourism and travel research studies, reports, and articles,* CL374
Goell, Yohai. *Bibliography of modern Hebrew literature in English translation,* BE1575
—— *Bibliography of modern Hebrew literature in translation,* BE1576
Goers, Sue. *Goers guide to parliamentary procedure,* CJ452
Goers guide to parliamentary procedure, Goers, Sue, CJ452
Goetsch, Lori A. *On account of sex,* AK14
Goetze, Edmund. *Grundriss zur Geschichte der deutschen Dichtung aus den Quellen,* BE1218
Goetzfridt, Nicholas J. *Micronesia, 1975–1987,* CE114, DF5
Goff, Frederick Richmond. *Incunabula in American libraries,* AA231
Goff, Penrith B. *German literature,* BE1210
Goguel, Rudi. *Antifaschistischer Widerstand und Klassenkampf,* DC233
Gohau, Gabriel. *Histoire de la géologie,* EF100
—— *A history of geology,* EF100
Gohdes, Clarence Louis Frank. *Bibliographical guide to the study of the literature of the U.S.A.,* BE395, BE397
—— *Literature and theater of the states and regions of the U.S.A,* BE573
Goić, Cedomil. *Historia y crítica de la literatura hispanoamericana,* BE894
Goin, Coleman J. *The new field book of reptiles and amphibians,* EG245
Going places, Hayes, Gregory, CL390
Gokhale Institute of Politics and Economics. *Annotated bibliography on the economic history of India,* CH194, DE153
Gökman, Muzaffer. *Atatürk ve devrimleri tarihi bibliyografyasi,* DC533
Golany, Gideon. *New-town planning,* BF273
Golay, Andre. *Harrap's book of film directors and their films,* BH204
Golay, Frank H. *An annotated guide to Philippine serials,* AD208
Gold, David L. *A dictionary of surnames,* AJ183
Gold, Edgar. *Maritime affairs—a world handbook,* CH466
Gold, Victor. *Compendium of chemical terminology,* EE36
Gold and silver plate dictionaries, BG136
Gold and silver plate (by country or region)
France, BG141
Germany, BG142
Great Britain, BG137, BG139, BG140

Gold coins of the world, Friedberg, Robert, BG187
Goldberg, Isaac. *Bibliography of modern Hebrew literature in translation,* BE1576
Goldberg, Lana. *The Jewish student's guide to American colleges,* CB306
Goldberg, Lee. *The Jewish student's guide to American colleges,* CB306
Goldberg, Nathan. *New functional Hebrew-English, English-Hebrew dictionary,* AC478
Golden, Herbert Hershel. *Modern French literature and language,* BD158, BE1134
—— *Modern Iberian language and literature,* BD166, BE1436
—— *Modern Italian language and literature,* BD160, BE1293
Golden, Richard L. *Sir William Osler,* EH209
Golden, Robert Dorne. *Pru's standard Thai-English dictionary,* AC779
Golden movie retriever, BH202
Goldfarb, S. F. *Inside the law schools,* CK154
Goldfarb, William. *Annotated bibliography on childhood schizophrenia, 1955–1964,* EH374
Goldfiem, Jacques de. *Personnalités chinoises d'aujourd'hui,* AH345
Goldfinger, Eliot. *Human anatomy for artists,* BF123
Goldie, Mark. *Cambridge history of political thought, 1450–1700,* CJ23
Golding, Alfred S. *Bibliothèques et musées des arts du spectacle dans le monde,* BH5
Goldman, Bernard. *The ancient arts of Western and Central Asia,* BF3
—— *Reading and writing in the arts,* BF124
Goldman, Bert A. *Directory of unpublished experimental mental measures,* CD75
Goldman, Bram J. *Deserts of the world,* CL58, EF17
Goldman, Jeffrey M. *Means estimating handbook,* EK110
Goldman, Paul. *Looking at prints, drawing and watercolours,* BF373
Goldman, Perry M. *The United States congressional directories, 1789–1840,* CJ222
Goldman, Shifra M. *Arte Chicano,* BF20, CC455
Goldschmidt-Lehmann, Ruth P. *Anglo-Jewish bibliography, 1937–1970,* BC517
—— *Anglo-Jewish bibliography, 1971–1990,* BC517
—— *Nova bibliotheca anglo-judaica,* BC517
Der goldschmiede Merkzeichen, Rosenberg, Marc, BG142
Goldsmith, Valentine Fernande. *Short title catalogue of French books, 1601–1700,* AA615
—— *A short title catalogue of Spanish and Portuguese books, 1601–1700, in the Library of the British Museum (The British Library—Reference Division),* AA816
—— *Titles of English books (and of foreign books printed in England),* AA665
Goldsmiths'-Kress Library of Economic Literature, CH15
Goldsmiths' Library of Economic Literature. *Goldsmiths'-Kress Library of Economic Literature,* CH15
—— *London bibliography of the social sciences,* CA13
Goldstein, Arnold S. *The Aspen dictionary of health care administration,* EH115
Goldstein, Doris M. *Bioethics,* EH242
Goldstein, Franz. *Monogram-Lexikon,* BF160
Goldstein, Melvyn C. *English-Tibetan dictionary of modern Tibetan,* AC784
—— *Tibetan-English dictionary of modern Tibetan,* AC785
Goldstein, Seth. *Encyclopedia of world travel,* CL380
Goldstein, Wallace L. *Teaching English as a second language,* BD110
Goldstucker, Jac L. *Marketing information,* CH546
Goldwater, Robert. *Artists on art,* BF145
Goldwater, Walter. *Radical periodicals in America, 1890–1950,* AD33
Goldwork, BG138
Golf, BK81, BK82, BK83, BK84, BK85
Golf course directory and guide, BK85

Golf magazine's encyclopedia of golf, BK82
Golf playoffs, Marrandette, David G., BK83
Golikova, G. N. *Velikaĩa Oktiabr'skaĩa sotsialisticheskaĩa revoliutsiĩa,* DC601
Golini, Antonio. *Bibliografia delle opere demografiche in lingua italiana (1930–1965),* CG4
—— *Bibliografia delle opere demografiche italiane (1966–1972),* CG4
Golowin, Sergius. *Lexikon der Symbole,* CF11
Golubeva, O. D. *Literaturno-khudozhestvennye al'manakhi i sborniki,* BE1406
Golubevoĭ, O. D. *Bibliografiĩa periodicheskikh izdaniĩ Rossii 1901–1916,* AD142
Gombocz, Zoltán. *Magyar etymologiai szótár,* AC498
Gomer, Eva. *Prisma's Swedish-English and English-Swedish dictionary,* AC767
Gomes, Celuta Moreira. *Bibliografía do conto brasileiro,* BE931
—— *O conto brasileiro e sua crítica,* BE931
Gómez Aristizábal, Horacio. *Diccionario de la historia de Colombia,* DB368
Gómez de Silva, Guido. *Elsevier's concise Spanish etymological dictionary,* AC744
Gómez F., Héctor. *Publicaciones oficiales de Chile, 1973–1983,* AF161
Gómez-Quiñones, Juan. *The Chicana,* CC444, CC596
Gomme, George Laurence. *Index of archaeological papers, 1665–1890,* DC275
Gonçalves, Augusto de Freitas Lopes. *Dicionário histórico e literário do teatro no Brasil,* BE932
Gonda, Jan. *A history of Indian literature,* BE1566
Gondolf, Edward W. *Research on men who batter,* CC211
Gonzales, Sylvia Alicia. *Hispanic American voluntary organizations,* CC462
Gonzales M., René. *Diccionario geográfico boliviano,* CL120
Gonzalez, Andrew. *A preliminary annotated bibliography of Pilipino linguistics (1604–1976),* BD234
González, Graciela. *Bibliografía de trabajos publicados en Nicaragua,* AA490
—— *Bibliography of works published in Nicaragua,* AA490
González, José. *Diccionario de autores hondureños,* BE906
González, Juan B. *Research guide to Costa Rica,* DB304
González, Nilda. *Bibliografía de teatro puertorriqueño,* BE979
Gonzalez, Pierre-Gabriel. *Le livre d'or des noms de famille,* AJ190
González, Silvino M. *Apuntes para una bibliografía militar de México, 1536–1936,* DB230
González de Cossio, Francisco. *Imprenta en México, 1553–1820,* AA461
—— *La imprenta en México, 1594–1820,* AA461
González Ollé, Fernando. *Manual bibliográfico de estudios españoles,* DC503
González Palencia, Angel. *Edición nacional de las obras completas de Menéndez Pelayo,* BE1043
González Peña, Carlos. *Historia de la literatura mexicana desde los origines hasta nuestros dias,* BE911
—— *History of Mexican literature,* BE911
González y González, Luis. *Fuentes de la historia contemporánea de México,* DB226
Gooch, Anthony. *Cassell's Spanish-English English-Spanish dictionary,* AC730
Gooch, Bryan N. S. *Musical settings of early and mid-Victorian literature,* BJ278, BJ279
—— *Musical settings of late Victorian and modern British literature,* BJ279
—— *A Shakespeare music catalogue,* BJ71
Good, Carter V. *Dictionary of education,* CB75
Good reading, AA326
Goodall, Francis. *A bibliography of British business histories,* CH391
Goode, Clement Tyson. *An atlas of English literature,* BE627
Goode, J. Paul. *Goode's world atlas,* CL278

Goode, James M. *Bibliography of doctoral dissertations relating to American architectural history, 1897–1991,* BF227
Goode, Patrick. *The Oxford companion to gardens,* BF290
Goode, Stephen H. *Index to Commonwealth little magazines,* AD275
—— *Population and the population explosion,* CG5
Goodenberger, Jennifer. *Subject guide to classical instrumental music,* BJ293
Goode's world atlas, CL295
—— Goode, J. Paul, CL278
Goodfriend, Joyce D. *The published diaries and letters of American women,* BE509
Goodman, Barbara A. *GeoRef thesaurus and guide to indexing,* EF73
Goodman, Edward J. *The exploration of South America,* CL11
Goodman, Jordan Elliot. *Barron's finance & investment handbook,* CH233
—— *Dictionary of finance and investment terms,* CH209
Goodnight, Scott Holland. *German literature in American magazines prior to 1846,* BE1238, BE1240
Goodrich, L. Carrington. *Dictionary of Ming biography, 1368–1644,* AH336
Goodrick, Edward W. *The NIV exhaustive concordance,* BC159
Goodsell, Don. *Dictionary of automotive engineering,* EK38
Goodspeed, Edgar J. *Complete Bible,* BC94
Goodwin, Diana M. *A dictionary of neuropsychology,* CD102
Goodwin, John. *Concise dictionary of the Christian world mission,* BC310
Goodwin, R. A. *March's thesaurus and dictionary of the English language,* AC141
Goolsby, Thomas W. *A guide to research in music education,* BJ6
Goonetileke, H. A. I. *A bibliography of Ceylon,* DE259
Gopinātha Rāu, T. A. *Elements of Hindu iconography,* BF191
Goralski, Robert. *World War II almanac, 1931–1945,* DA210
Gorbachev's law, Kavass, Igor I., CK223
Gordijn, W. *Encyclopedie van Suriname,* DB391
Gordon, Alan. *American chronicle,* DB135
Gordon, Arnold J. *The chemist's companion,* EE74
Gordon, Lois G. *American chronicle,* DB135
Gordon, Loraine. *Lesotho,* DD169
Gordon, Peter. *A guide to English educational terms,* CB76
Gordon, R. B. *A list of books on the history of science, January 1911,* EA235
Gordon, Robert S. *Union list of manuscripts in Canadian repositories,* DB195
Gordon, W. Terrence. *Semantics,* BD51
Gordon's print price annual, BF371
Göres, Jörn. *Abriss der deutschen Literaturgeschichte in Tabellen,* BE1252
Goring, Rosemary. *Cambridge biographical dictionary,* AH24
—— *Chambers Scottish biographical dictionary,* AH243
Görlach, Manfred. *A bibliography of writings on varieties of English, 1965–1983,* BD108
—— *New bibliography of writings on varieties of English,* BD108
Gorlin, Rena A. *Codes of professional responsibility,* CH85, CK64, CK160, EH175
Gorman, G. E. *Black theology,* BC216
—— *Church and state in postwar eastern Europe,* BC213, DC31
—— *Death and dying,* CC181
—— *Guide to current national bibliographies in the Third World,* AA392
—— *The South African novel in English since 1950,* BE1535
—— *Theological and religious reference materials,* BC217

Gorman, Lyn. *Theological and religious reference materials*, BC217

Gorman, Michael. *Anglo-American cataloguing rules*, AK194

—— *The concise AACR2, 1988 revision*, AK196

Gorman, Robert A. *Biographical dictionary of Marxism*, CJ532

—— *Biographical dictionary of neo-Marxism*, CJ531

Gorn, Elliott J. *Encyclopedia of American social history*, DB46

Görner, Herbert. *Synonymwörterbuch*, AC434

Görög, Veronika. *Littérature annotée littérature orale d'Afrique noire*, CF91

—— *Litterature orale d'Afrique Noire*, CF91

Görres-Gesellschaft. *Staatslexikon*, CJ334

Gorshkov, Sergei Georgievich. *World ocean atlas*, CL296, EF226

Górska, Joanna. *Bibliografia polskiego písmiennictwa demograficznego 1945–1975*, CG272

—— *Bibliografia wydawnictw Głównego Urzędu Statystycznego*, CG274

Gorton, Richard A. *Encyclopedia of school administration & supervision*, CB180

Gorvin, Ian. *Elections since 1945*, CJ88

Gorzny, Willi. *Biografisch archief van de Benelux*, AH270

—— *Deutsches biographisches Archiv*, AH206

—— *Gesamtverzeichnis des deutschsprachigen Schrifttums (GV), 1700–1910*, AA643

—— *Gesamtverzeichnis deutschsprachiger Hochschulschriften (GVH), 1966–1980*, AG10

—— *Neue Folge bis zur Mitte des 20. Jahrhunderts*, AH206

—— *Zeitungs-Index*, AE123

Gosebrink, Jean E. Meeh. *African studies information resources directory*, DD36, DD37, DD42

Gosling, William. *Everyman's dictionary of first names*, AJ169

Gosman, I. G. *Slovar' sokrashchenii russkogo iazyka*, AC685

Gosnell, Charles Francis. *Spanish personal names*, AJ206

The Gospel of Mark, BC111

Goss, Charles. *London directories, 1677–1855*, AL1, CH381

Gosselin, Robert E. *Clinical toxicology of commercial products*, EH424

Gossman, Norbert J. *Biographical dictionary of modern British radicals*, AH219, AH221

Gössman, P. Felix. *Šumerisches Lexikon*, AC202

Gosudarstvennaia bibliografiia SSSR, Gracheva, Iia Borisovna, AA792

Gosudarstvennaia bibliografiia SSSR : Spravochnik, Frantskevich, Valentina N., AA794, AA796

—— Gracheva, Iia Borisovna, AA794, AA796

Gosudarstvennaia biblioteka SSSR imeni V.I. Lenina. *Bibliografiia bibliografii po iazykoznaniiu*, BD6

—— *Informatsionnyi ukazatel' bibliograficheskikh spiskov i kartotek, sostavlennykh bibliotekami Sovetskogo Soiuza*, AA64

—— *Istoriia SSSR*, DC549

—— *Katalog doktorskikh i kandidatskikh dissertatsii, postupivshikh v Gosudarstvennuiu biblioteku SSSR imeni V. I. Lenina*, AG45

—— *Russkie pisateli vtoroi poloviny XIX nachala XX vv. (do 1917 goda)*, BE1392

—— *Svodnyi ukazatel' bibliograficheskikh spiskov i kartotek, sostavlennykh bibliotekami Sovetskogo Soiuza. Obshchestvennye nauki. Khudozhestvennaia literatura*, AA62

—— *Velikaia Oktiabr'skaia sotsialisticheskaia revoliutsiia v proizvedeniiakh sovetskikh pisatelei*, BE1399

Gosudarstvennaia biblioteka SSSR imeni V.I. Lenina. Informatsionno-bibliograficheskii otdel. *Ekonomika SSSR*, CH22

Gosudarstvennaia publichnaia biblioteka imeni M.E. Saltykova-Shchedrina. *Bibliografiia periodicheskikh izdanii Rossii 1901–1916*, AD142

—— *Obshchie bibliografi russkikh knig grazhdanskoi pechati, 1708–1955*, AA63, AA796, AD143

—— *Obshchie bibliografii russkikh periodicheskikh izdanii, 1703–1954, i materialy po statistike russkoi periodicheskoi pechati*, AD143

—— *Opisanie izdanii, napechatannykh pri Petre Pervom*, AA789, AA791

—— *Russkie anonimnye i podpisannye psevdonimami proizvedeniia pechati*, AA183

—— *Russkie sovetskie pisateli-prozaiki*, BE1393

Gosudarstvennaia publichnaia biblioteka imeni M.E. Saltykova-Shchedrina. Gazetnyi otdel'. *Alfavitnyi sluzhebnyi katalog russkikh dorevoliutsionnykh gazet, 1703–1916*, AE69

—— *Volnaia russkaia pechat'*, AE69

Gosudarstvennaia publichnaia istoricheskaia biblioteka RSFSR. *Istoriia istoricheskoi nauki v SSSR*, DC570

—— *Sovetskaia strana v period vosstanovleniia narodnogo khoziaistva, 1921–1925 gg*, DC590

Gosudarstvennaia registratsionno-uchetnaia bibliografiia v SSSR, AA792

Gosudarstvennye (natsional'nye) bibliograficheskie ukazateli sotsialisticheskikh stran, Kuznetsova, T. R., AA396

Gosudarstvennyi komitet SSSR po delam izdatel'stv, poligrafii i knizhnoi torgovli. *Letopis' periodicheskikh i prodolzhaiushchikhsia izdanii. Biulleteni*, AE74

A Gothic bibliography, Summers, Montague, BE302

A Gothic etymological dictionary, Lehmann, Winfred Philipp, AC440

Gothic fiction, Frank, Frederick S., BE289

Gothic language, AC440

The Gothic's Gothic, Fisher, Benjamin Franklin, BE287

Gottesman, Roberta. *The music lover's guide to Europe*, BJ193

Gotthold, Donald W. *Indian Ocean*, DE6

Gotthold, Julia J. *Indian Ocean*, DD18, DE6

Gottleher, Timothy T. *A concordance to Darwin's Origin of species, first edition*, EG68

Gottschald, Max. *Deutsche Namenkunde*, AJ195

Gottsegen, Abby J. *Humanistic psychology*, CD56

Gottsegen, Gloria Behar. *Humanistic psychology*, CD56

Goudie, Andrew. *The encyclopedic dictionary of physical geography*, CL46

—— *The student's companion to geography*, CL3

Gough, H. *Glossary of terms used in British heraldry*, AJ164

Gouke, Mary Noel. *One-parent children, the growing minority*, CC145

Goulart, Ron. *The encyclopedia of American comics*, CF76

Gould, George M. *Medical dictionary*, EH93

Gould, Robert F. *American chemists and chemical engineers*, EE99

Goulden, Steven L. *Great engineers and pioneers in technology*, EK20

Goulet, Richard. *Dictionnaire des philosophes antiques*, BB54

Goulty, George A. *A dictionary of landscape*, BF291

Gourman, Jack. *Gourman report*, CB346

Gourman report, CB345, CB346

Gove, Philip Babcock. *Webster's third new international dictionary of the English language, unabridged*, AC14

Governi d'Italia, 1848–1961, Bartolotta, Francesco, CJ380

Government Affairs Institute. *America votes*, CJ241

Government agencies, EA200

Government agencies, CJ120

Government and politics, CJ52

Government and politics in Bangladesh, Zafarullah, Habib Mohammad, DE117

Government Archives Division, National Archives of Canada, DB192

Government archives in South Asia, Low, Donald Anthony, DE84

Government assistance almanac, CH169

Government books in print, AF244

The government directory of addresses and telephone numbers, CJ138

Government document bibliography in the United States and elsewhere, Childs, James Bennett, AF11

•*Government documents catalog service*, AF111

Government finance statistics yearbook, CH242

Government information quarterly, AF14

Government of Canada publications, AF153

Government of India publications, Singh, Mohinder, AF247

The government of Northern Ireland, 1922–72, Maltby, Arthur, AF210

Government officials, CJ181, CJ182

  biography, CJ157, CJ161, CJ162

  directories, AL49, CJ135

  regional and local directories, CJ276

Government officials (by country or region)

  Africa

    registers, CJ398

  France, DC152

  Germany, CJ333

  Great Britain, CJ344, CJ345, CJ354, CJ362

  India, CJ433

  Russia and the U.S.S.R., CJ385

  Scotland, CJ354

  Union of Soviet Socialist Republics, CJ393, CJ394

  United States

    biography, CJ143

    directories, CJ133, CJ140, CJ271, CJ275

    state and local government, CJ273

Government periodicals and subscription services, AF116

Government publications

  bibliography, AF8, AF10, AF11, AF13, AF83

  catalogs and indexes

    databases, AD291, AF111, AF115

  Great Britain, AF176

  guides, AF2, AF3, AF6, AF8, AF11, AF61, AF62, CK244

  libraries, AF61

  library catalogs, AF10, AF83

  library resources, AF86, AF149

  periodicals, AF14, AF15

  style manuals, AF69

  union lists, AF13

Government publications (by subject)

  education, CB106

Government publications, Great Britain. Stationery Office, AF186, AF187, AF190

—— Palic, Vladimir M., AF11

Government publications and their use, Schmeckebier, Laurence Frederick, AF76

Government publications : catalogue, 1954–55, AF190

Government publications : consolidated list, 1951–53, AF190

•*Government publications index on INFOTRAC*, AF111

Government publications monthly list, Great Britain. Stationery Office, AF186, AF187

Government publications of India, Singh, Mohinder, AF248

Government publications of Papua New Guinea, AF269

Government publications review, AF15

Government reference books, AF74, AF79, AF84

Government reference serials, Schwarzkopf, LeRoy C., AF79, AF84

Government reports announcements, EA64

Government reports announcements & index, EA64

Government reports annual index, EA64

Government reports index, EA64

Government research centers directory, AL80

Government research directory, AL80, AL81, CJ280

Government Research Service. *Directory of political periodicals*, CJ101

—— *State legislative sourcebook*, CJ281

Government-wide index, EA64

Governmental Research Association (U.S.). *Directory of organizations and individuals professionally engaged in governmental research and related activities,* CJ48

Governors, CJ85, CJ210, CJ286, CJ287, CJ291
   bibliography, CJ99

Gowan, Susan Jean. *Portuguese-speaking Africa 1900–1979,* DD114, DD184

Gowers, Ernest. *Dictionary of modern English usage,* AC72

Goyer, Doreen S. *The handbook of national population censuses : Africa and Asia,* CG38
   —— *International population census bibliography,* CG6
   —— *International population census bibliography, revision and update, 1945–1977,* CG13
   —— *National population censuses, 1945–1976,* CG7

Gözaydın, Nevzat. *Türkçe sözlük,* AC787

Gozdecka-Sanford, Adriana. *Poland,* DC475

Gozmany, László. *Seven-language thesaurus of European animals,* EG225

•*GPO monthly catalog,* AF111

•*GPO on SilverPlatter,* AF111

G.R.A. directory, CJ48

Grabendorff, Wolf. *Bibliographie zu Politik und Gesellschaft der Dominikanischen Republik,* DB434

Grabois, Arveh. *Illustrated encyclopedia of medieval civilization,* DA152

Gracheva, Iıa Borisovna. *Gosudarstvennaıa bibliografiıa SSSR,* AA792
   —— *Gosudarstvennaıa bibliografiıa SSSR : Spravochnik,* AA794, AA796

Grad, Anton. *Veliki angleško-slovenski slovar,* AC721

Grad, Frank P. *Public health law manual,* EH413

Gradshtein, Izrail Solomonovich. *Table of integrals, series, and products,* EB85

Graduate assistantship directory in computing, EK200

Graduate faculty and programs in political science, CJ49

Graduate medical education directory, EH160

Graduate programs in physics, astronomy, and related fields, American Institute of Physics, ED29

Graduate Record Examinations Board. *The official GRE/CGS directory of graduate programs,* CB301

Graduate research, Smith, Robert V., EA8

Graduate scholarship book, CB374

Graduate scholarship directory, Cassidy, Daniel J., CB374

Graduate studies in economics, CH79

Graduate study in psychology, CD37, CD38

Graduate theses, BE353
   —— Orta Doğu Teknik Üniversitesi (Ankara, Turkey), AG44

Graduate theses and dissertations in English as a second language, Cooper, Stephen, BD109

Graef, Hilda C. *Patrology,* BC300

Graf, Alfred Byrd. *Exotica, series 4 international,* EG158
   —— *Hortica,* EG174

Graf, Rudolf F. *Modern dictionary of electronics,* EK133

Graff, Carol. *The dictionary of South African painters and sculptors, including Namibia,* BF142

Graff, Henry F. *The modern researcher,* DA3
   —— *The presidents,* CJ191

Graham, A. L. *Catalogue of meteorites,* EF207

Graham, Hugh Davis. *Southern elections,* CJ290

Graham, Joe Stanley. *Hispanic-American material culture,* CC465

Graham, John. *The literature of chess,* BK132

Graham, John W. *The U.S. Securities and Exchange Commission,* CH296

Graham, Ronnie. *The Da Capo guide to contemporary African music,* BJ330

Grainger, Thomas H. *A guide to the history of bacteriology,* EG310

Grambs, Jean Dresden. *Sex differences and learning,* CB7

Graml, Hermann. *Biographisches Lexikon zur Weimarer Republik,* DC261

Grammaire des formes et des styles, BF126
   —— Auboyer, Jeannine, BF35

Les grammaires françaises, 1800–1914, Chervel, André, BD157

Grammar, BD19
   handbooks, BD12
   see also **Transformational grammar**

Gramophone classical catalogue, BJ387

Gramophone compact disc…guide, BJ387

Gramophone Shop encyclopedia of recorded music, Darrell, R. D., BJ375

Gran diccionario de Chile, Céspedes, Mario, DB362

Gran diccionario moderno, García-Pelayo y Gross, Ramón, AC733

Gran enciclopedia argentina, DB330

La gran enciclopedia de Puerto Rico, DB454

Gran enciclopedia Rialp, AB95

Gran secreto de la carta de Colón, Sanz, Carlos, DB3

Granatstein, J. L. *The Collins dictionary of Canadian history,* DB197
   —— *A reader's guide to Canadian history,* DB187

Grand allusions, Webber, Elizabeth, BE81

Grand armorial de France, Jougla de Morenas, Henri, AJ158

Grand atlas de la France, Sélection du Reader's Digest. S.A.R.L, CL329

Le grand atlas de l'archéologie, DA90

Le grand atlas de l'architecture mondiale, BF253

Grand atlas de l'astronomie, EC65

Le grand atlas des littératures, BE67

Grand atlas du continent africain, Éditions Jeune Afrique, CL337

Grand dictionnaire d'américanismes, Deak, Étienne, AC339

Le grand dictionnaire des citations françaises, Dournon, Jean-Yves, BE130

Le grand dictionnaire encyclopédique de la Côte d'Ivoire, Borremans, Raymond, DD145

Grand dictionnaire encyclopédique Larousse, AB42

Grand dictionnaire français-breton, Vallée, François, AC238

Grand dictionnaire universel du XIXᵉ siècle, Larousse, Pierre, AB42, AB46

Grand Larousse de la langue française, AC329

Grand Larousse encyclopédique en dix volumes, AB42, AB43

Grandchamp-Tupula, Mariette. *Vocabulaire de technologie éducative et de formation,* CB172

Grande dicionário da língua portuguesa, Moraes Silva, António de, AC644

Grande dizionario, AC532

Grande dizionario della lingua italiana, Battaglia, Salvatore, AC524

Grande dizionario enciclopedico UTET, AB67

Grande enciclopédia portuguesa e brasileira, AB80

La grande encyclopédie, AB42, AB44, AB45

Grande encyclopédie de la Belgique et du Congo, DC108

La grande encyclopédie du Maroc, DD181

Les grandes allusions, Bologne, Jean-Claude, BE128

Grandidier, Guillaume. *Bibliographie de Madagascar,* AA863, AA865, DD175

Grandpré, Pierre de. *Histoire de la littérature française du Québec,* BE840

Les grands hommes d'état de l'histoire de France, Maurepas, Arnaud de, AH199

Grandsaignes d'Hauterive, Robert. *Dictionnaire d'ancien français,* AC379

Granger, Edith. *The Columbia Granger's index to poetry,* BE315

Granger Book Co. *Index to poetry in periodicals, American poetic renaissance, 1915–1919,* BE500

Granger's index to poetry, BE315, BE316, BJ289

Granić, Gordana. *Adresar pisaca Jugoslavije,* BE1496

Grant, Claire. *Grant & Hackh's chemical dictionary,* EE40

Grant, Eric G. *Scotland,* DC357

Grant, Frederick C. *Dictionary of the Bible,* BC141

Grant, Gail. *Technical manual and dictionary of classical ballet,* BH145

Grant, George C. *The directory of ethnic professionals in LIS (library and information science),* AK87

Grant, Ian. *A dictionary of Australian military history,* DF35

Grant, John P. *Parry and Grant encyclopaedic dictionary of international law,* CK105

Grant, Mary A. *Catholic school education in the United States,* CB36

Grant, Michael. *Ancient history atlas,* DA117
   —— *Civilization of the ancient Mediterranean,* DA98
   —— *Greek and Latin authors, 800 B.C.–A.D. 1000,* BE1025
   —— *A guide to the ancient world,* CL102
   —— *Roman emperors,* DA115

Grant, Roger L. *Grant & Hackh's chemical dictionary,* EE40

Grant, Steven A. *The Russian Empire and the Soviet Union,* AK106, DC560
   —— *Scholars' guide to Washington, D.C. for Russian, Central Eurasian, and Baltic studies,* DC556

Grant, William. *Scottish national dictionary,* AC166

Grant & Hackh's chemical dictionary, Hackh, Ingo W. D., EE40

Grant data quarterly, AL100

Grant update! for Guide to federal funding for education, CB380

•*GRANTS,* AL108, AL110, BA9

Grants, fellowships & prizes of interest to historians, DA28

Grants for graduate study, CB389

Grants-in-aid, CB365, CB366, CB372, CB381, CB382, CB386, CB393
   databases, AL110
   directories, AL101, AL103, AL107, AL108, AL110, AL111, AL112, AL113, AL119, BA9, CB367, CB374, CB380, CB389
   handbooks, AL91, AL135, AL137
   manuals, AL92, AL130, AL131

Grants-in-aid (by country or region)
   Canada, AL125
   United States, AL100, CH167, CH169

Grants-in-aid (by subject)
   anthropology and ethnology, CE55
   archives, BF104
   art, AL120, BF104, BF105, BF106
   disabilities and the disabled, CC194
   education, AL114, CB370, CB379

Grants in aid (by subject)
   education, CB387

Grants-in-aid (by subject)
   education, CB392
   foreign study, CB90, CB369, CB373
   history, DA28
   humanities, AL108, BA9
   libraries, AK64
   museums, BF104
   psychology, CD36
   publishing, BA11
   social and behavioral sciences, CA52
   women, CB378, CC546
   see also **Fellowships and scholarships; Foundations and philanthropic organizations**

Grants register, CB367

GRANTS subject authority guide, AL110

Grantseeker's guide to resources, AL91

Granville, Wilfred. *Dictionary of theatrical terms,* BH77

Granville-Barker, Harley. *Companion to Shakespeare studies,* BE784

Graphic arts, BF177, BF371, BF383
   biography, BF312, BF376, BF382, BF384, BF386
   catalogs, BF365
   dictionaries
     multilingual, AA273
   encyclopedias, BF369
   exhibitions, BF368

indexes, BF68, BF368
library catalogs, BF366
terminology, BF91
Graphic arts (by country or region)
Canada, BF314
France, BF377
Japan, BF358
Graphic arts (by subject)
history, BF376, BF378, BF381, BF382
Graphic arts encyclopedia, Stevenson, George A., BF369
Graphic concordance to the Dead Sea scrolls, Charlesworth, James H., BC556
Graphics, design and printing terms, BF369
Grapow, Hermann. *Wörterbuch der aegyptischen Sprache,* AC303
Grasham, W. E. *Canadian public administration : bibliography,* CJ465
Grass roots music, BJ344
Grässe, Johann Georg Theodor. *Orbis Latinus,* CL103
—— *Trésor de livres rares et précieux,* AA88
Grassé, Pierre-P. *Traité de zoologie,* EG242
Grasselli, Jeanette G. *Handbook of data on organic compounds,* EE149
Grassi, Gaetano. *Guida agli archivi della resistenze,* DC426
Grassi, Giovanna. *Union catalogue of printed books of 15th, 16th and 17th centuries in European astronomical observatories,* EC12
Grasslands and forage abstracts, EJ19
Gratch, Bonnie. *Sports and physical education,* BK3
Graulich, Paul. *Guide to foreign legal materials,* CK202
Graur, Alexandru. *Dicţionarul limbii române,* AC660
Gravel, Pierre Bettez. *Anthropological fieldwork,* CE11
Gravell, Thomas L. *A catalogue of American watermarks, 1690–1835,* AA257
Gravelle, Susan. *Worker benefits, industrial welfare in America, 1900–1935,* CH505
Graves, A. *Dictionary of British artists, 1760–1893,* BF316
Graves, Algernon. *Art sales from early in the eighteenth century to early in the twentieth century,* BF302
Graves, Carol. *Archaeology,* DA60
Graves, Diane J. *Biographical sources,* AH4
Graves, Edgar B. *A bibliography of English history to 1485,* DC304
Graves, Robert. *New Larousse encyclopedia of mythology,* CF8
Gravesteijn, J. *Multilingual thesaurus of geosciences,* EF79
Graveurs du XIXᵉ siècle, Beraldi, Henri, BF377
Gravimetric and celestial geodesy, Mueller, Ivan Istvan, EF123
Gray, Alexander Stuart. *Edwardian architecture,* BF259
Gray, Asa. *Gray's manual of botany,* EG159
Gray, Beverly Ann. *Japanese-African relations,* DD3
—— *Liberia during the Tolbert era,* DD172
—— *Uganda,* AF240, DD240
Gray, Cecile G. *The Bible and modern literary criticism,* BC115
Gray, Dwight E. *American Institute of Physics handbook,* ED32
Gray, Edward. *New revised Velázquez Spanish and English dictionary,* AC740
Gray, John. *Action art,* BF21
—— *African music,* BJ317
—— *'Ashe, traditional religion and healing in Sub-Saharan Africa and the diaspora,* BC34
—— *Black theatre and performance,* BH32
—— *Blacks in classical music,* BJ212
—— *Blacks in film and television,* BH165
—— *Fire music,* BJ301
Gray, John Milner. *History of Zanzibar, from the Middle Ages to 1856,* DD250
Gray, Lewis Cecil. *History of agriculture in the southern United States to 1860,* EJ68
Gray, Louis H. *Encyclopaedia of religion and ethics,* BC55

Gray, Michael H. *Classical music, 1925–1975,* BJ383
—— *Classical music discographies, 1976–1988,* BJ383
—— *Popular music,* BJ383
Gray, Peter. *The dictionary of the biological sciences,* EG37
—— *The encyclopedia of microscopy and microtechnique,* EG23
—— *The encyclopedia of the biological sciences,* EG24, EG37
Gray, Randal. *Chronicle of the First World War,* DA198
—— *Conway's all the world's fighting ships, 1947–1982,* CJ592
Gray, Richard. *Guides to materials for West African history in European archives,* DD105
Gray's manual of botany, Gray, Asa, EG159
Grayson, Donald K. *A bibliography of the literature on North American climates of the past 13,000 years,* EF161
Grayson, Martin. *Encyclopedia of textiles, fibers, and nonwoven fabrics,* BG155
Grazda, Edward E. *Handbook of applied mathematics,* EB64
Grazhdanskaia voina i voennaia interventsiia v SSSR, DC596
GRE/CGS directory of graduate programs, CB301
The great all-time baseball record book, Reichler, Joseph L., BK59
Great architecture of the world, Norwich, John Julius, BF233
Great book of Oriental carpets, Gans-Ruedin, E., BG165
Great botanical gardens of the world, Hyams, Edward, EG148
Great Britain
archives
directories, AJ100
associations
directories, AL65
atlases, CJ349
bibliography, CL228
bibliography, AA103, AA661, AA662, AA663, AA664, AD3, DC273, DC278
17–18th centuries, AA677
17th-18th centuries, AA412
17th–18th centuries, AA675, AA676, AA678, AA679, AA680
17th-18th centuries, AA681, AA682, AA683
19th-20th centuries, AA684
19th-20th centuries, AA686
19th-20th centuries, AA687
20th century, AA685
before 1640, AA665, AA666, AA667, AA668, AA669, AA670, AA671, AA672, AA673, AA674
current, AA684, AA688, AA689, AA690, AA691, AA692
privately printed books, AA693, AA694
biography, AH218, AH219, AH220, AH221, AH222, AH223, AH224, AH225, AH226, AH227, AH228, AH229, AH230, AH231, AH232, AJ120, BC417, CJ348, CJ355, DC340
bibliography, AH234, AH235, AH236, AH238, AH239, AH240
contemporary, AH233
indexes, AH237, AH241
databases, AA689
directories, DC278
bibliography, AL2
dissertations, AG33, AG34, AG35, AG36
encyclopedias, DC292
gazetteers, CL135, CL139, CL140, CL141, CL206
government agencies
directories, AL65
government publications, AF178, AF179, AF192
bibliography, AF181
catalogs, AF188
catalogs and indexes, AF186, AF187
databases, AF182
guides, AF175, AF176, AF177

indexes, AF180, AF182, AF183, AF184, AF185, AF189, AF190, AF191, AF193
parliamentary debates, AF175, AF209
indexes, AF196, AF208
parliamentary papers, AF204, AF205, AF206, AF207
guides, AF177
indexes, AF194, AF195, AF197, AF198, AF199, AF200, AF201, AF202, AF203
guides to records, DC285, DC286
library catalogs, AA103, AA661, AD3
bibliography, AK144
library resources, AE14, AK142, AK144, AK148, DE50, DE51, DE82, DE83, DE86, DE105
periodicals, AD199
manuscripts and archives, DC285
newspapers, AD104, AE57, AE59
bibliography, AD106, AD107, AD108, AD109, AE56, AE58, AE60
directories, AD118
indexes, AE124
regional and local, AE55
periodicals, AD104
bibliography, AD105, AD106, AD107, AD108, AD109, AD110, AD111, AD112, AE60
directories, AD114, AD115, AD116, AD118
guides, AD113, AD117
history, AD113
indexes, AD287, AD292
place-names, CL193, CL195, CL203
statistics, CG231, CG233, CG235, DC323
bibliography, CG236, CG237, CG238
statutes, CK214
Great Britain (by subject)
archaeology and ancient history, DC306, DC309
atlases, DC313, DC314
armed forces, CJ651
encyclopedias, CJ652
history, CJ653
art, BF101, BF150
British Empire and Commonwealth
elections, CJ371
yearbooks, CJ372
censuses, CL136
ceramics and glass, BG60
city planning, BF284, EK81
corporations
history, CH391
design
bibliography, BG6
economic conditions, CH187, CH188, DC272
atlases, DC299, DC300
history, DC336
statistics, CG235
election statistics, CJ364, CJ365, CJ368
elections, CJ358, CJ363, CJ366, CJ367
environment and environmental problems, BF284, EK81
ethnic groups
bibliography, CC326
folklore and popular culture, CF80
foreign relations, DC63
Asia, West, DE37, DE38
guides, DC326
handbooks, DC338
library catalogs, DC342
Palestine, DE243
furniture, BG120, BG123
government officials, CJ344, CJ345
directories, CJ341
history, DC296
archives, AJ98, AK145
atlases, DC299, DC300, DC301, DC302, DC312, DC313, DC324, DC346, DC354
bibliography, CC607, CK217, DA171, DC270, DC272, DC274, DC275, DC276, DC279, DC281, DC282, DC291, DC303, DC304, DC305, DC307, DC308, DC315, DC320, DC325, DC328, DC330, DC332
20th century, DC331
biography, DC298

British Empire and Commonwealth, DC345, DE228
  chronologies, DC295
  dissertations, CH295, DC283, DC334
  encyclopedias, DC20, DC289, DC293, DC310, DC322
  guides to records, DA204, DC288, DC350
  handbooks, DC290, DC294, DC323
  library catalogs, BC227, DC321, DC342, DC344, DC347
  manuscripts and archives, DC285, DC287
  regional, DC352
  regional and local, DC349, DC353
    bibliography, DC348
    guides, DC351
    guides to records, DC350
  sourcebooks, DC280, DC297
  statistics, CG235
history (by period)
  16th-17th centuries
    atlases, DC324
  16th century, DC505
  18th-19th centuries, BE606, DC316, DC317, DC330, DC336, DC337
  19th century, BE758
  20th century, DC329
  early
    atlases, DC314
  medieval, DC311
  Tudor period, DC318
immigration
  bibliography, CC311
insurance, CH514
international relations
  bibliography, DC274
law, CK2, CK218
  bibliography, CK220
  directories, CK216
  encyclopedias, CK215
  guides, CK219
metalwork, BG150
military history, DC271, DC277
  guides to records, AJ103
naval history, DC333, DC505
navies, CJ653
oral history, DC332
overseas territories
  government publications, AF218, AF221, AF225, AF235, AF237
    bibliography, AF222, AF231, AF232, AF240
overseas territories (by country or region)
  Asia, South, DE89
  North America, DB82
photography, BF328
place-names, CL136, CL192, CL194, CL196, CL197, CL198, CL199, CL200, CL201, CL204, CL205
political leaders
  biography, CJ402
political parties, CJ363
politics and government, CJ338, CJ367, CJ372, CJ509
  18th-19th centuries, DC323
  archives and manuscripts, DC335
  atlases, CJ349
  bibliography, CJ337, CJ339, CJ351
  biography, CJ348, CJ360, DC340
  directories, CJ342, CJ343, CJ354
  elections, CJ369
  handbooks, CJ346, CJ347, CJ356, CJ358, CJ361, DC339
  local government, CJ370
  voting records, CJ359
  yearbooks, CJ340
population, CG232
  bibliography, CG236
religion, BC215
  library catalogs, BC227, DC321
social conditions, DC272
  atlases, DC299, DC300
  dissertations, CH295, DC283
  statistics, CG235

statistics and demography, CG232
  treaties, CK98
  women, CC607
Great Britain. Board of Trade. *Statistical abstract for the United Kingdom*, CG231
Great Britain. Cabinet Office. *The civil service year book*, CJ340
Great Britain. Central Office of Information. *Britain*, CJ346
Great Britain. Central Statistical Office. *Annual abstract of statistics*, CG231
—— *Guide to official statistics*, CG237
Great Britain. Colonial Office. Library. *Catalogue of the Colonial Office Library, London*, DC342
Great Britain. Department of Employment and Productivity. *British labour statistics*, CH683
Great Britain. Department of Health and Social Security Library. *Health service abstracts*, EH76
Great Britain. Department of Science and Art. *First proofs of the Universal catalogue of books on art*, BF56
Great Britain. Department of Scientific and Industrial Research. *LLU translations bulletin*, EA61
—— *Translated contents lists of Russian periodicals*, EA59
Great Britain. Department of Technical Co-operation. Library. *Public administration*, CJ473
Great Britain. Foreign and Commonwealth Office. *The Commonwealth yearbook*, CJ372
—— *The diplomatic service list*, CJ341
Great Britain. Foreign and Commonwealth Office. Library. *Foreign and Commonwealth Office, accessions to the Library, May 1971–June 1977*, DC342
Great Britain. Foreign Office. Library. *Catalogue of the Foreign Office Library, 1926–1968*, DA171, DC274
Great Britain. General Register Office (Scotland). *Guide to the public records of Scotland deposited in H. M. General Register House, Edinburgh*, DC358
Great Britain. Historical Manuscripts Commission. *A guide to the reports on collections of manuscripts of private families, corporations and institutions in Great Britain and Ireland*, DC285
Great Britain. India Office. *Imperial gazetteer of India*, CL164
Great Britain. [Laws, etc.]. *Halsbury's statutes of England and Wales*, CK214
Great Britain. Medicines Commission. *British pharmacopoeia 1988*, EH356
Great Britain. Meteorological Office. *Meteorological glossary*, EF147
Great Britain. Ministry of Overseas Development. Library. *Catalogue of the Colonial Office Library, London*, DC342
—— *Public administration*, CJ473
Great Britain. Nautical Almanac Office. *Explanatory supplement to the Astronomical almanac*, EC79
Great Britain. Office of Population Censuses and Surveys. *Census 1981*, CL136
—— *Population trends*, CG232
—— *The Registrar General's statistical review of England and Wales*, CG233
—— *Statistical review of England and Wales*, CG233
Great Britain. Overseas Development Administration. Library. *Public administration*, CJ473
Great Britain. Parliament. *Checklist of British parliamentary papers in the Irish University Press 1000-volume series, 1801–1899*, AF204
—— *Irish University Press series of British parliamentary papers*, AF205
—— *Parliamentary debates*, AF208
Great Britain. Parliament, CJ358, CJ363, CJ367, CJ368
  bibliography, CJ351
  biography, AH231, CJ355, CJ362
  encyclopedias, CJ352
  handbooks, CJ353, CJ356, CJ357, CJ361
Great Britain. Parliament (by subject)
  history, AH231, CJ355

Great Britain. Parliament. Committee on History of Parliament. *History of Parliament, 1439–1509*, AH231, CJ355
Great Britain. Parliament. House of Commons. *Catalogue of papers printed by order of the House of Commons from the year 1731 to 1800, in the custody of the Clerk of the Journals*, AF197
—— *Catalogue of parliamentary reports and a breviate of their contents*, AF198
—— *Debates and proceedings of the British parliaments*, AF209
—— *Dissension in the House of Commons*, CJ359
—— *General alphabetical index to the bills, reports, estimates, accounts and papers printed by order of the House of Commons and to the papers presented by command, 1801–1948/49*, AF199
—— *The House of Commons, 1715–1754*, CJ360
—— *House of Commons sessional papers of the eighteenth century*, AF200
—— *Index to House of Commons parliamentary papers*, AF203
—— *List of the bills, reports, estimates, and accounts and papers printed by order of the House of Commons and of the papers presented by command ...*, AF201
—— *Members of Parliament ...*, CJ354
—— *Serial publications in the British parliamentary papers, 1900–1968*, AF207
Great Britain. Parliament. House of Lords. *General index to sessional papers printed by order of the House of Lords or presented by special command*, AF202
Great Britain. Parliament. House of Lords. Record Office. *Guide to the records of Parliament*, AF175
Great Britain. Public Record Office. *Guide to documents and manuscripts in Great Britain relating to the Kingdom of Hungary from the earliest times to 1800*, DC387
—— *Guide to the contents of the Public Record Office*, DC286
—— *Irish history from 1700*, DC404
—— *List of British diplomatic records for Balkan history, 1879–1905*, DC63
—— *Maps and plans in the Public Record Office*, CL230
—— *Printing for Parliament, 1641–1700*, AF188
—— *The Second World War*, DA204
Great Britain. Royal Commission on Historical Manuscripts. *Catalogue of the publications of Scottish historical and kindred clubs and societies and of the volumes relative to Scottish history issued by His Majesty's Stationery Office, 1780–1908, with a subject-index*, DC362
—— *A guide to the reports on collections of manuscripts of private families, corporations and institutions in Great Britain and Ireland*, DC285
—— *Guides to sources for British history based on the National Register of Archives*, DC287
—— *The manuscript papers of British scientists, 1600–1940*, EA244
—— *Record repositories in Great Britain*, DC288
Great Britain. Stationery Office. *Catalogue of the publications of Scottish historical and kindred clubs and societies and of the volumes relative to Scottish history issued by His Majesty's Stationery Office, 1780–1908, with a subject-index*, DC362
—— *Catalogue of the United Kingdom official publications*, AF182
—— *Catalogues and indexes of British government publications, 1920–1970*, AF183
—— *Consolidated index to government publications*, AF189
—— *Cumulative index to the annual catalogues of Her Majesty's Stationery Office publications, 1922–1972*, AF184
—— *Government publications*, AF186, AF187, AF190
—— *Government publications monthly list*, AF186, AF187
—— *HMSO agency catalogue*, AF185
—— *HMSO annual catalogue*, AF186
—— *International organisations catalogue*, AF185

—— *The sale catalogues of British government publications, 1836–1921,* AF191
Great Britain. War Office. General Staff. Geographical Section. *Short glossaries,* CL267
Great chemists, Farber, Eduard, EE101
The great depression, DB128
Great economists before Keynes, Blaug, Mark, CH93
Great economists since Keynes, Blaug, Mark, CH93
Great engineers and pioneers in technology, EK20
The great English-Polish dictionary, AC635
The great English-Slovene dictionary, AC721
Great historians from antiquity to 1800, DA48
Great index of biographical reference, AH20
The great international disaster book, Cornell, James, DA19
The great movie stars, Shipman, David, BH286
Great North American Indians, Dockstader, Frederick J., AH63
Great outdoors guide to the United States and Canada, BK107
The great Polish-English dictionary, supplemented, AC635
The great psychologists, Watson, Robert Irving, CD62
The great song thesaurus, Lax, Roger, BJ286
Great Soviet encyclopedia, AB82, AB87, DC566
The great stage stars, Morley, Sheridan, BH116
Great writers of the English language, BE626
Greathouse, Charles H. *Index to the yearbooks of the U.S. Department of Agriculture, 1894–1900,* EJ89
Greaves, Cecilia. *Segundo catalog de tesis sobre historia de México,* DB237
Grébaut, Sylvain. *Supplément au Lexicon linguae Aethiopicae … (1865) et édition du lexique de Juste d'Urbin (1850–1855),* AC311
A Grebo-English dictionary, Innes, Gordon, AC441
Grebo language
    dictionaries, AC441
Grechko, A. A. *Sovetskaia voennaia entsiklopediia,* CJ659
Greece
    bibliography, AA701, AA702, AA703, AA704, AA705, BD136, BD138, DC110, DC371, DC372
        current, AA706, AA707, AA708
    bibliography of bibliography, AA47
    biography, AH246
    gazetteers, CL142
    library catalogs, DC373, DC375
    statistics, CG242, CG243, CG244
Greece (by subject)
    art, BF324
    foreign relations, DC110
    history, DC373
        atlases, DA119
        bibliography, DC374
        biography, DA114
        handbooks, DA109
        statistics, CG242
Greece, Clogg, Mary Jo, DC371
Greece and Cyprus since 1920, Richter, Heinz A., DC374
Greece in the 1940s, DC372
—— Fleischer, Hagen, DC372
Greek, Householder, Fred W., BD137
Greek and Latin authors, 800 B.C.–A.D. 1000, BE203
—— Grant, Michael, BE1025
Greek and Latin in scientific terminology, Nybakken, Oscar Edward, EA94
The Greek and Latin literatures, Parks, George B., BE1010
Greek and Latin palaeography, AA216, BE1018
Greek and Roman authors, Gwinup, Thomas, BE996
Greek and Roman chronology, Samuel, Alan Edouard, DA112
Greek and Roman sport, Matz, David, BK26
Greek bibliography, AA707
Greek drama
    bibliography, BE995
A Greek-English lexicon, Liddell, Henry George, AC444, AC445, AC450, AC457
—— Scott, Robert, AC445, AC450, AC457
Greek-English lexicon of the New Testament, AC455

A Greek-English lexicon of the New Testament and other early Christian literature, Arndt, William, AC453
Greek language
    biblical
        bibliography, BD140
    bibliography, BD135, BD136, BD138, BE1030
    dictionaries, AC442, AC456, BC143
        bilingual, AC444, AC448
            German, AC445
            Greek-German, AC446, AC447
        Christian and medieval, AC453, AC454, AC455, AC457, AC458, AC459
        etymology, AC449, AC450, AC451
        pronunciation, AC452
    Modern Greek
        bibliography, BD141
        dictionaries, AC460, AC462
            bilingual, AC461, AC463, AC464, AC465, AC466, AC467
    Mycenaean
        bibliography, BD139
Greek language (by subject)
    history
        handbooks, BD137
    study and teaching
        handbooks, BD137
Greek lexicon of the Roman and Byzantine periods, Sophocles, Evangelinus Apostolides, AC459
Greek literature
    bibliography, AC443, BD138, BE1005, BE1027, BE1030, BE1036
    biobibliography, BE201
    biography, BE1025
    collections, BE1002
        databases, AC443, BE1036
    criticism, BE996
    encyclopedias, BE1013
    handbook, BE1032
    indexes, BE1031
    library catalogs, BE1029
    translations, BE1002, BE1010, BE1028
        Spanish, BE1043
Greek literature (by period)
    medieval
        biobibliography, BE993
    modern, BE1274
Greek literature (by subject)
    drama
        handbooks, BE1017
        history, BE1020, BE1033, BE1034, BE1035
Greek literature, Easterling, P. E., BE1020
—— Knox, B. M. W., BE1020
Greek national bibliography, AA708
Greek Orthodox Archdiocese of North and South America. *Yearbook,* BC447
Greek philosophical terms, Peters, Francis Edwards, BB42
Greek scholarship in Spain and Latin America, Demetrius, James K., DA95
Greely, A. W. *Bibliography of meteorology,* EF142
Greely, Adolphus Washington. *Public documents of the first fourteen Congresses, 1789–1817,* AF92
Green, David Bonnell. *Keats, Shelley, Byron, Hunt, and their circles,* BE754
Green, Don W. *Perry's chemical engineers' handbook,* EK57
Green, Dorothy. *A history of Australian literature,* BE850
Green, Fletcher M. *The old South,* DB156
Green, Henry Mackenzie. *A history of Australian literature,* BE850
Green, Joel B. *Dictionary of Jesus and the Gospels,* BC128
Green, Jonathon. *Dictionary of jargon,* AC123
—— *Newspeak,* AC123
Green, Laura R. *Money for artists,* AL120, BF105
Green, Marguerite. *Peace archives,* CJ671
Green, Melvin M. *Glossary of genetics,* EG343
Green, Miranda J. *Dictionary of Celtic myth and legend,* CF18
Green, Morton. *Bibliography of fossil vertebrates,* EF228

Green, Muriel M. *A Gibraltar bibliography,* DC268
Green, Philip. *The Routledge dictionary of twentieth-century political thinkers,* CJ69
Green, Rayna. *Native American women,* CC602
Green, Richard D. *Index to composer bibliographies,* BJ226
Green, Robert E. *Machinery's handbook,* EK245
Green, Stanley. *Broadway musicals, show by show,* BJ264
—— *Encyclopaedia of the musical film,* BJ358
—— *Encyclopaedia of the musical theatre,* BJ263, BJ358
—— *The world of musical comedy,* BJ265
Green, Syd. *Keyguide to information sources in food science and technology,* EJ149
Green, Thomas J. *The code of canon law,* CK238
Green, William C. *Soviet nuclear weapons policy,* CJ654
The green book, EH160
Green cathedrals, Lowry, Philip J., BK51, BK57
Greenaway, G. W. *English historical documents,* DC297
Greenbaum, Alfred Abraham. *Russian publications on Jews and Judaism in the Soviet Union, 1917–1967,* BC535
—— *Yiddish literary and linguistic periodicals and miscellanies,* BE1081
Greenberg, Bette. *How to find out in psychiatry,* EH369
Greenberg, Martin Harry. *Index to crime and mystery anthologies,* BE268
    Science fiction and fantasy series and sequels, BE284
Greenberg, Milton. *American political dictionary,* CJ122, CJ126
Greenberg, Reva M. *Education for older adult learning,* CB353
Greenbook, CH586
Greenburg, Martin H. *International terrorism,* CJ550
Greene, Albert G. *Dictionary catalog of the Harris collection of American poetry and plays, Brown University Library, Providence, Rhode Island,* BE494
Greene, Evarts Boutell. *A guide to the principal sources for early American history (1600–1800) in the city of New York,* DB79, DB98
Greene, Frank. *Composers on record,* BJ227
Greene, Jack P. *The Blackwell encyclopedia of the American Revolution,* DB93
—— *Encyclopedia of American political history,* DB45
Greene, John C. *Dublin stage, 1720–1745,* BH101
Greenfield, Edward. *Penguin guide to compact discs,* BJ379
—— *Penguin guide to compact discs and cassettes yearbook,* BJ379
Greenfield, Gerald Michael. *Latin American labor organizations,* CH667
Greenfield, Harry I. *The handbook of economic and financial measures,* CH170
Greenfield, Jane. *Books, their care and repair,* AK240
Greenfield, John R. *Dictionary of British literary characters,* BE688
Greenfield, Stanley B. *A bibliography of publications on Old English literature to the end of 1972,* BE728
Greenfield, Stanley R. *Who's who in the United Nations and related agencies,* AF42
Greenfieldt, John. *Fiction catalog,* BE245
—— *Play index,* BE234
Greenhalgh, Susan. *Jen k'ou hsüeh Ying Han Han Ying fen lei tz'u hui,* CG34
Greenland
    bibliography, DC376, DC377
    statistics, CG210
Greenland, Miller, Kenneth E., DC377
Greenland since 1979, DC376
Greenlaw, M. Jean. *Educating the gifted,* CB185
Greenleaf, Richard E. *Research in Mexican history,* DB240
Greenlee, William Brooks. *A catalog of the Greenlee collection,* DC489

Greenslade, S. L. *Cambridge history of the Bible*, BC191

Greenstein, Carol Horn. *Dictionary of logical terms and symbols*, EA92

Greenstein, Edward L. *The timetables of Jewish history*, DA31

Greenstein, Fred I. *Evolution of the modern presidency*, CJ171
—— *Handbook of political science*, CJ53

Greenwald, Douglas. *McGraw-Hill dictionary of modern economics*, CH70
—— *The McGraw-Hill encyclopedia of economics*, CH51

Greenway, Diana E. *Fasti ecclesiae Anglicanae*, BC331

Greenway, John. *Bibliography of the Australian aborigines and the native peoples of Torres Strait to 1959*, CE113

Greenwood, Joseph Arthur. *Guide to tables in mathematical statistics*, EB73

Greenwood, Margaret Joan. *Angola*, DD128

Greenwood, Val D. *The researcher's guide to American genealogy*, AJ11

Greenwood Press. *Baedeker's handbook(s) for travellers*, CL389

Greer, Roger C. *Illustration index*, BF60

Greet, William Cabell. *War words*, AC104
—— *World words*, AC104

Greeves, Lydia. *The National Trust guide*, BF249

Grefsheim, Suzanne. *Encyclopedia of health information sources*, EH15

Greg, Walter Wilson. *Bibliography of English printed drama to the Restoration*, BE658, BE663
—— *A bibliography of the English printed drama to the Restoration*, BE643
—— *A companion to Arber*, AA670

Gregor, Bernd. *Etymologisches Wörterbuch der deutschen Sprache*, AC428

Gregor, Carl. *International bibliography of jazz books*, BJ297

Gregor, Joseph. *Der Schauspielführer*, BE1263

Gregorovich, Andrew. *Canadian ethnic groups bibliography*, CC474

Gregory, Derek. *Dictionary of human geography*, CL44

Gregory, Hugh. *Soul music A–Z*, BJ353

Gregory, Joel W. *African historical demography*, CG310

Gregory, Joseph T. *Bibliography of fossil vertebrates*, EF237

Gregory, Richard L. *The Oxford companion to the mind*, CD25

Gregory, Ruth W. *Anniversaries and holidays*, AL146

Gregory, Winifred. *American newspapers, 1821–1936*, AE18
—— *International congresses and conferences, 1840–1937*, AL30
—— *List of the serial publications of foreign governments, 1815–1931*, AF13

Greichisch-deutsches Wörterbuch zu den Schriften des Neuen Testament und der übrigen urchristlichen Literatur, Bauer, Walter, AC453

Greimas, Algirdas Julien. *Dictionnaire de l'ancien français*, AC380
—— *Dictionnaire du moyen français*, AC381
—— *Semiotics and language*, BD52

Grekoff, George V. *Thai-English student's dictionary*, AC777

Gremling, Richard C. *English language equivalent editions of foreign language serials*, AD9

Grenada, DB437

Grenada, Schoenhals, Kai P., DB437

Grenham, John. *Tracing your Irish ancestors*, AJ132

Grente, Georges. *Dictionnaire des lettres françaises*, BE1153

Grenz, Wolfgang. *Manual para las relaciones Europeo-Latinoamericanas*, DB286

Gresh, Alain. *An A to Z of the Middle East*, DE55
—— *Cent portes du Proche-orient*, DE55

Gresswell, R. Kay. *Standard encyclopedia of the world's rivers and lakes*, CL61, CL62, CL63, EF8, EF9, EF10

Gretes, Frances C. *Directory of international periodicals and newsletters on the built environment*, BF226

Greulich, Walter. *Encyclopedia of applied physics*, ED14

Greuter, W. *International code of botanical nomenclature*, EG130

Greutzner, A. *The dictionary of British artists, 1880–1940*, BF316

Gribenski, Jean. *Thèses de doctorat en langue française relatives à la musique*, BJ166

Gribetz, Judah. *The timetables of Jewish history*, DA31

Grieb, Kenneth J. *Central America in the nineteenth and twentieth centuries*, DB299
—— *Research guide to Central America and the Caribbean*, DB301, DB414

Griechisches etymologisches Wörterbuch, Frisk, Hjalmar, AC450, AC451

Griera y Gaja, Antonio. *Vocabolario vasco*, AC228

Grierson, Philip. *Bibliographie numismatique*, BG172
—— *Books on Soviet Russia*, BE1409
—— *Byzantine coins*, BG172
—— *Coins and medals*, BG172
—— *Numismatics*, BG172

Griffenhagen, George B. *Pharmacy museums*, EH367
—— *Pharmacy museums and historical collections in the United States and Canada*, EH367

Griffin, Appleton Prentiss Clark. *Bibliography of American historical societies*, AD262

Griffin, Charles Carroll. *Latin America*, DB257

Griffin, Grace Gardner. *Guide to manuscripts relating to American history in British depositories reproduced for the Division of Manuscripts of the Library of Congress*, DB32
—— *Guide to the diplomatic history of the United States, 1775–1921*, DB15

Griffin, John R. *Dictionary of visual science*, EH113

Griffin, Lloyd W. *Modern French literature and language*, BD158, BE1134

Griffin, P. J. *Index to publications*, EF30

Griffith, H. Winter. *Complete guide to medical tests*, EH180

Griffith, Jerry. *Proposal planning and writing*, AL138

Griffiths, David B. *A critical bibliography of writings on Judaism*, BC514

Griffiths, Mark. *Dictionary of gardening*, EG125
—— *Index of garden plants*, EJ242

Griffiths, Paul. *The Thames and Hudson encyclopaedia of 20th-century music*, BJ135

Griffiths, Peter. *A bibliography of cricket*, BK71

Griffiths, Trevor R. *The Back Stage theater guide*, BH62

Grigor'ev, A. A. *Kratkaia geograficheskaia éntsiklopediia*, CL89

Grigorova, Aleksandra. *Gŭrtsiia i bŭlgaro-grŭtskite otnosheniia v bŭlgarskata nauchna knizhnina, 1878–1980*, DC110

The Grihya-sûtras, BC92

Grim, Ronald E. *Historical geography of the United States*, CL106, CL107

Grimal, Pierre. *The dictionary of classical mythology*, CF27
—— *Dictionnaire de la mythologie grecque et romaine*, CF27

Grimann, Jutta. *Antifaschistischer Widerstand und Klassenkampf*, DC233

Grimes, Janet. *Novels in English by women, 1891–1920*, BE474, BE480, BE750
—— *Toward a feminist tradition*, BE474

Grimes, John A. *A concise dictionary of Indian philosophy*, BB39

Grimm, Jakob Ludwig Karl. *Deutsches Wörterbuch*, AC402

Grimm, Wilhelm. *Deutsches Wörterbuch*, AC402

Grimsted, Patricia Kennedy. *Archives and manuscript repositories in the USSR*, AK153, DC561
—— *Archives in Russia*, DC557

—— *A handbook for archival research in the USSR*, DC562

Grimwade, Arthur. *London goldsmiths 1697–1837*, BG140

Grimwood-Jones, Diana. *Arab Islamic bibliography*, BC492
—— *Middle East and Islam*, DE22

Grinstein, Alexander. *The index of psychoanalytic writings*, CD9

Grinstein, Louise S. *Mathematical book review index, 1800–1940*, EB32
—— *Women in chemistry and physics*, EA187, ED57, EE106
—— *Women of mathematics*, EB104

Grismer, Raymond Leonard. *New bibliography of the literatures of Spain and Spanish America*, BE873
—— *A reference index to twelve thousand Spanish American authors*, BE873

Grisoli, Angelo. *Guide to foreign legal materials*, CK222
—— *Guide to foreign legal materials : Italian*, CK202

Gritsch, Eric W. *Bibliography of the continental Reformation*, DC26

Gröber, Gustav. *Grundriss der romanischen Philologie*, BD148

Groblewska, Celina. *Bibliografia opracowań demograficznych z lat 1976–1991*, CG273

Groce, George C. *The New-York Historical Society dictionary of artists in America, 1564–1860*, BF155

Groden, Michael. *The Johns Hopkins guide to literary theory and criticism*, BE68

De groei van ons wereldbeeld, EC61

Groen, Julie te. *Basutoland*, DD169

Grogan, Denis Joseph. *Science and technology*, EA3

Grolandsk bogfortegnelse, AA605

Grolier, Éric de. *Directory of documentation, libraries and archives services in Africa*, AK154

Grolier academic encyclopedia, AB2

Grolier Club. *One hundred books famous in science*, EA232

Grolier international encyclopedia, AB2

•*Grolier master encyclopedia index*, AB9, AB20

•*Grolier multimedia encyclopedia*, AB2, AB25

Grollenberg, Luc H. *Atlas of the Bible*, BC198
—— *Atlas van de Bijbel*, BC198

Grollig, F. X. *Serial publications in anthropology*, CE25

Gromyko, Anatolii Andreevich. *Afrika*, DD49

Grönbold, Günter. *Der buddhistische Kanon*, BC468

Gröning, Karl. *Friedrichs Theaterlexikon*, BH68

Grønlandsk avis- og tidsskrift-index, AA605

Grönroos, Henrik. *Finlands bibliografiska litteratur*, AA41

Groom, A. J. R. *International relations*, CJ10
—— *International relations theory*, CJ10

Groombridge, Brian. *The IUCN amphibia-reptilia red data book*, EG250

Groos, Arthur. *Medieval Christian literary imagery*, BE5

Groot, Alexander H. de. *A bibliography of Dutch publications on the Middle East and Islam 1945–1981*, DE30

Groot literair citatenboek van Nederlandse en Vlaamse auteurs uit de 19e en 20e eeuw, BE125

Groot woordeboek, Kritzinger, Matthys Stefanus Benjamin, AC198

Groot woordenboek der Nederlandse taal, Geerts, Guido, AC292

Gropp, Arthur Eric. *A bibliography of Latin American bibliographies*, AA24, AA25
—— *A bibliography of Latin American bibliographies published in periodicals*, AA25
—— *Union list of Latin American newspapers in libraries in the United States*, AE40

Gropp, Dorothy M. *Mature woman in America*, CC61

Gross, Charles. *A bibliography of British municipal history*, DC348
—— *Sources and literature of English history from the earliest times to about 1485*, DC304

Gross, Dorothy-Ellen. *From real life to reel life*, BH226

Gross, Ernie. *This day in American history*, DB59

Gross, Helmut. *Fachwörterbuch, Chemie und chemische Technik*, EE50

Gross family collection, BF193

Grosse, Siegfried. *Die Rezeption mittelalterlicher deutscher Dichtung*, BE1271

Der grosse Brockhaus, AB37, AB49

Das grosse Buch der Österreicher, Kleindel, Walter, AH167

Grosse deutsche Wörterbuch, Wahrig, Gerhard, AC411

Der grosse Eichborn, CH67

Das grosse Fachwörterbuch für Kunst und Antiquitäten, BG43

Der Grosse Herder, AB50

Grosse jüdische National-Biographie, Wininger, Salomon, BC566

Das Grosse Lexikon der Musik, BJ136

Grosse Lexikon des Dritten Reiches, Bedürftig, Friedemann, DC255

―――― Zentner, Christian, DC255

Grosse Österreicher, AH168

Das Grosse Wörterbuch der deutschen Sprache in 6 Bänden, AC403

Die grossen Deutschen, AH208

Grosser Atlas zur Weltgeschichte, Georg Westermann Verlag, DA51

Grosser historischer Weltatlas, DA53

Grosser historischer Weltatlas. Erläuterungen, Bengtson, Hermann, DA53

Grosses deutsches Ortsbuch, Bundesrepublik Deutschland, CL134

Grosses Sängerlexikon, Kutsch, K. J., BJ214

Grosses vollständiges Universal-Lexikon aller Wissenschaften und Künste, AB51

Grossman, Jorge. *Índice general de publicaciones periódicas latino-americanas*, AD298

Grossmann, Rudolf. *Historia y problemas de la literatura latinoamericana*, BE895

Grosvenor, Gilbert. *Insignia and decorations of the United States armed forces*, AL185

Grote, David. *Common knowledge*, BE81

Grote Winkler Prins encyclopedie in 26 delen, AB37

Grotefend, Hermann. *Taschenbuch der Zeitrechnung des deutschen Mittelalters und der Neuzeit*, DC223

―――― *Zeitrechnung des deutschen Mittelalters und der Neuzeit*, DC223

Grothusen, Klaus-Detlev. *Südosteuropa-Handbuch*, DC68

Grotpeter, John J. *Swaziland*, DD48

―――― *Zambia*, DD48

Ground water, EF130

Groundwater bibliography, EF130

Grout, Abel Joel. *Mosses with a hand-lens*, EG193

Grouws, Douglas A. *Handbook of research on mathematics teaching and learning*, CB116

Grove, George. *Grove's dictionary of music and musicians*, BJ141

Grove, Grenville. *Engelsk-svensk ordbok*, AC765

Grover, Mark L. *The Catholic left in Latin America*, DB255

Groves, Donald G. *Ocean world encyclopedia*, EF218

Grove's dictionary of music and musicians, Grove, George, BJ141

Grow, Michael. *Scholars' guide to Washington, D.C. for Latin American and Caribbean studies*, DB273

Growth of world industry, United Nations. Statistical Office, CH427

Groyser verterbukh fun der Yidisher shprakh, AC812

Groznova, N. A. *Sovetskiĭ roman, ego teoriĭa i istoriĭa*, BE1383

Gruber, Ellen J. *Stepfamilies*, CC212

Gruber, J. G. *Allgemeine Encyclopädie der Wissenschaften und Künste*, AB47

Gruber, Robert. *American women and the U.S. armed forces*, CJ612

Grun, Bernard. *The timetables of history*, DA32

Gründer, Karlfried. *Historisches Wörterbuch der Philosophie*, BB40

Grundliteratur Recht, Lansky, Ralph, CK206, CK211

Grundliteratur zum österreichischen Recht, Dosoudil, Ilse, CK206

Grundmann, Herbert. *Handbuch der deutschen Geschichte*, DC220

Grundriss der germanischen Philologie unter Mitwirkung zahlreicher Fachgelehrter, Paul, Hermann, AJ192, CL189

Grundriss der Geschichte der Philosophie, Ueberweg, Friedrich, BB50

Grundriss der romanischen Philologie, BD148

―――― Gröber, Gustav, BD148

Grundriss zur Geschichte der deutschen Dichtung aus den Quellen, Goedeke, Karl, BE1096, BE1218, BE1227

Grundy, Isobel. *The feminist companion to literature in English*, BE607

Grunendahl, Reinhold. *Hochschulschriften zu Süd– und Südostasien*, DE10

Gruner, Erich. *Schweizerische Bundesversamlung, 1920–1968*, CJ388

―――― *Die schweizerische Bundesversammlung, 1848–1920*, CJ388

Grunts, Marita V. *The Baltic states*, DC70

Grupenhoff, John T. *National health directory*, EH412

Gruson, Edward S. *Checklist of the world's birds*, EG261

Grzegorczykowej, Renaty. *Indeks a tergo do Słownika jezyka polskiego*, AC632

Grzeszczuk, Stanisław. *Katalog czasopism polskich Biblioteki Jagiellońskiej*, AD134

Grzimek, Bernhard. *Grzimek's animal life encyclopedia*, EG226

―――― *Grzimek's encyclopedia of ecology*, EG64

―――― *Grzimek's encyclopedia of evolution*, EG74

―――― *Grzimek's encyclopedia of mammals*, EG293

Grzimek's animal life encyclopedia, EG64, EG293

―――― Grzimek, Bernhard, EG226

Grzimek's encyclopedia of ecology, EG64

Grzimek's encyclopedia of evolution, EG74

Grzimek's encyclopedia of mammals, EG293

GTE Telenet Information Services. *Symbol guide*, CH315

Gu-Konu, Yema E. *Atlas de Togo*, CL339

Guadeloupe
  atlases, CL276

Gual, Ramon. *Materials per una bibliografia d'Andorra*, DC82

Guardian (Boston). *Extant collections of early black newspapers*, AE15

The Guardian index, AE124

Guardian weekly [index], AE124

Guatemala
  bibliography, AA481, AA482, AA483, AA484, AA485, DB308, DB309
  gazetteers, CL116
  government publications, AF159
  statistics, CG129

Guatemala (by subject)
  folklore and popular culture bibliography, CF59
  statistics and demography, CG130

Guatemala. Dirección General de Estadística. *Anuario estadístico*, CG129

Guatemala. Museo nacional. *Bibliografía guatemalteca*, AA485

Guatemala. Tipografía Nacional. *Catálogo general de libros, folletos y revistas*, AA483

Guatemala, Woodward, Ralph Lee, DB309

Guatemala en cifras, CG129

Guatemalan literature, BE905

Gubar, Susan. *Norton anthology of literature by women*, BE619

Gubernatorial and presidential transitions, Bowman, James S., CJ99

Gubry, Patrick. *Bibliographie generale des études de population au Cameroun*, DD138

Güçlü, Meral. *Turkey*, DC534

Gudbranur Vigfússon. *An Icelandic-English dictionary*, AC503

Guedes, Pedro. *Encyclopedia of architectural technology*, BF234

Guedes, Peônia Viana. *Dicionário inglês-português*, AC645

Güemes, Cecilio. *Adiciones y continuación de "La imprenta en Manila" de d. J. T. Medina*, AA928

Guenée, Simonne. *Bibliographie d'histoire des villes de France*, DC212, DC265

Guenther, Franz. *Handbook of philosophical logic*, BB36

Guenther, Nancy Anderman. *United States Supreme Court decisions*, CK184

Guerber, H.A. *The book of the epic*, BE341

Guercio, Francis Michael. *Cassell's Italian-English, English-Italian dictionary*, AC528

Guerini, Vincenzo. *A history of dentistry from the most ancient times until the end of the eighteenth century*, EH265

Guérinot, Armand Albert. *Essai de bibliographie Jaina*, BC506

Guérios, Rosário Farâni Mansur. *Dicionário etimológico de nomes e sobrenomes*, AJ202

Guerlac, Othon Goepp. *Les citations françaises*, BE131

Guernsey, Otis L. *The best plays of [...]*, BE454

―――― *Directory of the American theater, 1894–1971*, BE454, BE463

Guerra, Francisco. *American medical bibliography, 1639–1783*, EH202

La guerra civil española, fuentes, García Durán, Juan, DC516

Guerrilla and terrorist organisations, Janke, Peter, CJ61

―――― Sim, Richard, CJ61

Guerry, Herbert. *A bibliography of philosophical bibliographies*, BB11

Gugitz, Gustav. *Bio-bibliographisches Literaturlexikon Osterreichs*, BE1095

Gühring, Adolf. *Erstausgaben deutscher Dichtung*, BE1233

Guía a las reseñas de libros de y sobre Hispanoamérica, AA370

Guía bibliográfica de Colombia de interés para el antropólogo, Bernal Villa, Segundo, DB363

Guía bibliográfica de la literatura hispano-americana desde siglo XIX hasta 1970, Rela, Walter, BE868

Guía bibliográfica para el estudio del folklore chileno, Pereira Salas, Eugenio, CF71

Guia da bibliografia histórica portuguesa, DC485

Guía de archivos y bibliotecas, AK129

Guia de história de la República Portuguesa, Marques, António Henrique R. de Oliveira, DC487

Guía de historia de Venezuela, Arellano Moreno, Antonio, DB403

Guia de história dos Descobrimentos e expansão portuguesa, Marques, Alfredo Pinheiro, DC486

Guía de la documentación diplomática británica sobre Ecuador, Mora, Enrique Ayala, DB373

Guía de las fuentes en el Archivo General de Indias para el estudio de la administración virreinal española en México y en el Perú, 1535–1700, Hanke, Lewis, DB276

Guía de las fuentes en hispanoamérica para el estudio de la administración virreinal española en México y en el Perú, 1535–1700, Hanke, Lewis, DB276

Guía de los archivos estatales españoles, Spain. Subdirección General de Archivos, DC511

Guía de los archivos nacionales de America latina y el Caribe, AK130, DB277

Guía de publicaciones periódicas de universidades latinoamericanas, Levi, Nadia, AD65

Guia de publicações seriadas brasileiras, AD72

Guía del archivo histórico, Peru. Archivo General de la Nación, DB386

Guía del Archivo Nacional de Historia, Archivo Nacional de Historia (Ecuador), DB373

Guia do estudante de história medieval portuguesa, Marques, António Henrique R. de Oliveira, DC488

Guía genealógico-histórica de Latinamérica, Platt, Lyman De, AJ74

Guía nacional de tesis, AG19

Guía para el estudio de la historia de Venezuela, Lovera De-Sola, Roberto J., DB398

Guía para el investigador de la historia colonial hondureña, Arqueta, Mario, DB310

Guia preliminar de fontes para a história de Brasília, DB350

Guia preliminar de fontes para a história do Brasil, DB350

Guibert, Joseph de. *Dictionnaire de spiritualité*, BC54

Guida agli archivi della resistenze, Grassi, Gaetano, DC426

Guida alla letteratura su Wittgenstein, Frongia, Guido, BB80

Guida alle bandiere di tutto il mondo, Talocci, Mauro, AL195

Guida allo studio della letteratura italiana, Beccaro, Felice del, BE1288

Guida allo studio della storia delle matematiche, Loria, Gino, EB2

Guida allo studio della storia medievale, Dolcini, Carlo, DA128

Guida della stampa periodica italiana, Bernardini, Nicola, AE64

Guida generale degli archivi di Stato italiani, AK150, DC429

Guidance
  bibliography, CB208, CH707
  see also **Occupational education**

Guidance Information System. *The GIS guide to four-year colleges*, CB271

•*The guidance information system*, CB210

Guide annuaire á travers la presse et la publicité, AD103

Guide bibliographique de linguistique romane, Bal, Willy, BD150

———— Germain, Jean, BD150

Guide bibliographique des études d'histoire de la littérature française, Brix, Michel, BE1128

Guide bibliographique des thèses littéraires canadiennes de 1921 à 1976, Naaman, Antoine, BE831

Guide bibliographique du froid, EK227

Guide bibliographique du Mozambique, Chonchol, Maria Edy, DD183

Guide bibliographique du traducteur, rédacteur et terminologue, Delisle, Jean, BD88

A guide book of United States coins, BG195

Guide de la littérature québécoise, Fortin, Marcel, BE844

———— Lamonde, Yvan, BE844

———— Richard, François, BE844

Guide de l'étudiant en histoire du Zaïre, Vellut, Jean Luc, DD15, DD245

Guide de litterature africaine (de langue francaise), Dabla, Sewanou, BE1516

———— Merand, Patrick, BE1516

Guide de l'utilisateur des catalogues des livres imprimés de la Bibliothèque Nationale, Bernard, Annick, AA100

Guide de l'utilisateur des Inventaires des Archives nationales, Brunel, Ghislain, DC150

———— Carbonnel, Isabelle, DC150

Guide de recherches sur le Vietnam, Descours-Gatin, Chantal, DE272

Guide delle fonti per la Storia dell'America latina esistenti in Italia, Lodolini, E., DB275

Guide delle fonti per storia dell'America Latina negli archivi della Santa Sede e negli archivi ecclesiastici d'Italia, Pásztor, L., DB275

Guide des Archives de la Martinique, Martinique. Archives, DB446

Guide des archives de l'Afrique occidentale française, M'baye, Saliou, DD106

Guide des centres de documentation en histoire ouvrière et sociale, DC157

Guide des papiers des ministres et secrétaires d'État de 1871 à 1974, Archives nationales (France), DC152

Guide des papiers privés d'époque révolutionnaire, Archives nationales (France), DC182

Guide des périodiques parus en Tunisie, AD181

Guide des recherches sur l'histoire des familles, Bernard, Gildas, AJ85

Guide des sources de l'histoire de l'Amérique latine et des Antilles dans les archives françaises, Archives nationales (France), DB272

Guide des sources de l'histoire des congrégations féminines françaises de vie active, Molette, Charles, BC442

Guide des sources de l'histoire des États-Unis dans les archives françaises, DB31

Guide des sources de l'histoire du Brésil aux archives du Ministère français des affaires étrangères, France. Ministère des affaires étrangères. Archives, DB349

Guide du chercheur en histoire canadienne, DB177

Guide du chercheur pour la période 1789–1815, Bruguière, Michel, DC153

Guide du lecteur, Ermisse, Gerard, DC150

Guide for readers to the new Pelican guide to English literature, Ford, Boris, BE616

Guide for the care and use of laboratory animals, Institute of Laboratory Animal Resources. Committee on Care and Use of Laboratory Animals, EG295

A guide for the study of British Caribbean history, 1763–1834, Ragatz, Lowell Joseph, DB407

Guide littéraire de la Belgique, de la Hollande, et du Luxembourg, Bodart, Roger, BE982

Guide littéraire de la France, BE1166

Guide Mont Blanc des prix et concours littéraires, Labes, Bertrand, BE177

Guide parlementaire canadien, CJ295

A guide to 85 tests for special education, Compton, Carolyn, CB189

A guide to academic protocol, Gunn, Mary Kemper, CB394

Guide to accredited camps, BK110

A guide to African international organisations, Fredland, Richard A., AF20

Guide to African ministers, Bidwell, Robin, CJ398

A guide to American Catholic history, Ellis, John Tracy, BC389

Guide to American directories, AL4

Guide to American educational directories, CB101

A guide to American film directors, Langman, Larry, BH209

Guide to American foreign relations since 1700, DB15

Guide to American graduate schools, Doughty, Harold R., CB299

Guide to American Indian documents in the Congressional serial set, 1817–1899, Johnson, Steven L., CC417

The guide to American law, CK132

Guide to American literature, Fenster, Valmai Kirkham, BE394

Guide to American literature and its backgrounds since 1890, Jones, Howard Mumford, BE395

———— Ludwig, Richard M., BE395

Guide to American poetry explication, BE488, BE491, BE693, BE710, BE1192

A guide to American screenwriters, Langman, Larry, BH210

A guide to American trade catalogs, 1744–1900, Romaine, Lawrence B., CH400

Guide to archival sources for French-American art history in the Archives of American Art, BF58

Guide to archives and manuscripts in the United States, Hamer, Philip M., CC332, DB30

———— United States. National Historical Publications Commission, CC332, DB30

Guide to art reference books, Chamberlin, Mary Walls, BF1

Guide to artifacts of colonial America, Noël Hume, Ivor, DB54

Guide to atlases, Alexander, Gerard L., CL224

A guide to Australian economic and social statistics, Hagger, A. J., CG438

Guide to basic information sources in chemistry, Antony, Arthur, EE1

Guide to basic information sources in the visual arts, Muehsam, Gerd, BF6

Guide to best plays, BE225

A guide to biblical resources, Cully, Iris V., BC108

A guide to books on Ireland, Brown, Stephen James, BE800

A guide to British government publications, Rodgers, Frank, AF179

Guide to British poetry explication, BE488, BE693, BE1192

———— Martinez, Joseph G. R., BE491, BE695, BE1192

———— Martinez, Nancy C., BE491, BE695, BE710, BE1192

Guide to Buddhist philosophy, Inada, Kenneth K., BB20, BC470, BC472

Guide to Buddhist religion, Reynolds, Frank E., BB20, BC470, BC472

Guide to business history, Larson, Henrietta Melia, CH395

Guide to Canadian ministries since confederation, July 1, 1867–February 1, 1982, CJ299

Guide to captured German documents, Weinberg, Gerhard L., DC249

Guide to cartographic records in the National Archives, AK114, DB38

———— United States. National Archives and Records Service, CL242

The guide to Catholic literature, AD265, BC390, BC394

A guide to centres of international lending and copying, Barwick, Margaret M., AK223

Guide to Cherokee documents in foreign archives, Anderson, William L., CC420

———— Lewis, James A., CC420

Guide to Cherokee documents in the northeastern United States, Kutsche, Paul, CC420

Guide to Chinese philosophy, Fu, Charles Wei-Hsün, BB19

Guide to Chinese poetry and drama, Bailey, Roger B., BE1557

———— Lynn, Richard John, BE1557

Guide to Chinese prose, Paper, Jordan D., BE1558

Guide to Chinese religion, Yu, David C., BC38

A guide to Civil War maps in the National Archives, CL299

Guide to collections of manuscripts relating to Australia, DF32

Guide to college courses in film and television, BH263

A guide to colleges for learning disabled students, CB312

Guide to colleges for the learning disabled, CB313

A guide to Commonwealth government departments and authorities, CJ447

A guide to commonwealth government information sources, Cook, John, AF263

A guide to computer literature, Pritchard, Alan, EK152

Guide to Congress, CJ193

Guide to corporate giving in the arts 4, AL121

A guide to critical reviews, Salem, James M., BH61

A guide to critical reviews of United States fiction, 1870–1910, Eichelberger, Clayton L., BE471

A guide to Cuban collections in the United States, Pérez, Louis A., DB427

Guide to current British journals, AD115

Guide to current British periodicals in the humanities and social sciences, AD117

A guide to current Latin American periodicals, Zimmerman, Irene, AD68

Guide to current Malaysian serials, Harris, L. J., AD203

Guide to current national bibliographies in the Third World, Gorman, G. E., AA392

Guide to current official statistics, CG238

Guide to dance in film, Parker, David L., BH149

———— Siegel, Esther, BH149

Guide to dance periodicals, BH8, BH136

A guide to Danish bibliography, Munch-Petersen, Erland, AA40

Guide to dental materials and devices, EH263

Guide to departments of anthropology, CE54

Guide to departments of geography in the United States and Canada, CL55

Guide to doctoral dissertations in Victorian literature, 1886–1958, Altick, Richard Daniel, BE751

A guide to documentary editing, Kline, Mary-Jo, AA320

Guide to documents and manuscripts in Great Britain relating to the Kingdom of Hungary from the earliest times to 1800, Kurucz, György, DC387

Guide to documents and manuscripts in the United Kingdom relating to Russia and the Soviet Union, Hartley, Janet M., DC563

A guide to Dutch bibliographies, Library of Congress. Netherlands Studies Unit, AA56

Guide to earning college degrees non-traditionally, CB253

A guide to East Asian collections in North America, Lee, Thomas H., AK108, DE104

A guide to Eastern literatures, Lang, David Marshall, BE1544

Guide to ecology information and organizations, Burke, John Gordon, EG62

Guide to economic indicators, Frumkin, Norman, CH108

A guide to eighty five tests for special education, CB189

A guide to English and American literature, Bateson, Frederick Wilse, BE580

A guide to English educational terms, Gordon, Peter, CB76

Guide to English Renaissance literature, 1500–1600, Wynne-Davies, Marion, BE611

Guide to European company information, CH376

A guide to European financial centres, Hay, Tony, CH276

Guide to European sources of technical information, EA142

Guide to excruciatingly correct behavior, AL154

Guide to exhibited artists, BF119

A guide to fairs and festivals in the United States, Shemanski, Frances, AL148

A guide to federal archives relating to Africa, South, Aloha, DD36, DD38, DD42

Guide to federal archives relating to the Civil War, Munden, Kenneth White, DB116

Guide to federal funding for education, CB380

Guide to federal funding for social scientists, CA52

Guide to federal government acronyms, CJ125

Guide to festschriften, New York Public Library. Research Libraries, AA126

A guide to films about the Pacific Islands, Hamnett, Judith D., DF4

Guide to films on apartheid and the southern African region, Media Network, DD43

Guide to fitness and motor performance tests, BK39

A guide to folktales in the English language, Ashliman, D. L., CF46

A guide to foreign language courses and dictionaries, Walford, Albert John, AC195

Guide to foreign law firms, CK58

Guide to foreign legal materials, CK202
—— Grisoli, Angelo, CK222
—— Szladits, Charles, CK208, CK210

Guide to foreign legal materials : French, Germain, Claire M., CK202
—— Szladits, Charles, CK202

Guide to foreign legal materials : Italian, Grisoli, Angelo, CK202

Guide to foreign trade statistics, CH153

A guide to fossils, Mayr, Helmut, EF248

Guide to foundations and granting agencies, AL125

Guide to French literature, Levi, Anthony, BE1161

Guide to French poetry explication, Coleman, Kathleen, BE1192

Guide to genealogical records in the National Archives, Bridgers, F. E., AJ15
—— Colket, M. D., AJ15

Guide to genealogical research in the National Archives, National Archives and Records Service, AJ15

Guide to geographical bibliographies and reference works in Russian or on the Soviet Union, Harris, Chauncy Dennison, CL13

A guide to Germanic reference grammars, McKay, John C., BD114

Guide to government information, AF267

A guide to government monographs, reports, and research works, Kenya National Archives, AF233

The guide to government publications in Australia, Harrington, Michael, AF265

Guide to graduate departments of anthropology, CE54

Guide to graduate education in urban and regional planning, BF282

Guide to graduate study in economics, agricultural economics, public administration, and doctoral programs in business administration in the United States and Canada, CH79

Guide to graduate study in political science, CJ49

Guide to great plays, Shipley, Joseph Twadell, BE236

Guide to Hindu religion, Dell, David, BC481

Guide to historic and significant gardens of America, Nicholls, Robert P., BF296
—— Ray, Mary Helen, BF296

Guide to historic preservation, historical agencies, and museum practices, BF117

Guide to historical cartography, LeGear, Clara E., CL240
—— Library of Congress. Map Division, CL240

Guide to historical fiction, Baker, Ernest Albert, BE230

A guide to historical fiction for the use of schools, libraries, and the general reader, Irwin, Leonard Bertram, BE256

Guide to historical literature, American Historical Association, DA1
—— Dutcher, George M., DA1

Guide to historical reading, Czarra, Fred R., BE256

Guide to hydrological practices, EF138

Guide to indexing and cataloging with the Art & architecture thesaurus, Barnett, Patricia J., BF94
—— Petersen, Toni, BF94

Guide to Indian periodical literature, AD337

Guide to Indian philosophy, Potter, Karl H., BB21

A guide to Indonesian serials (1945–1965) in the Cornell University Library, AD196

Guide to information sources in alternative therapy, Allan, Barbara, EH1

A guide to information sources in mining, minerals, and geosciences, Kaplan, Stuart R., EF171

Guide to information sources in the botanical sciences, Davis, Elisabeth B., EG90

A guide to information sources in the geographical sciences, CL2

Guide to international education in the United States, CB102

The guide to international film and video festivals, Bowser, Kathryn, BH265

Guide to international legal research, CK74

A guide to international music congress reports in musicology, 1900–1975, Tyrrell, John, BJ20

Guide to inventories and finding aids of German archives at the German Historical Institute, Washington, D.C, Frohn, Axel, DC246

A guide to Irish bibliographical material, Eager, Alan R., AA49

Guide to Irish mythology, Smyth, Daragh, CF30, CF31

A guide to Irish parish registers, Mitchell, Brian, AJ136

Guide to Irish surnames, AJ197

Guide to Islam, BC495

Guide to Italian libraries and archives, Lewanski, Rudolf J., AK133, AK151, DC13

Guide to Japanese drama, Pronko, Leonard Cabell, BE1592

Guide to Japanese poetry, Rimer, J. Thomas, BE1593

Guide to Japanese prose, Marks, Alfred H., BE1587

Guide to Japanese reference books, Nihon no Sankō Tosho Henshū Iinkai, AA355

Guide to Jewish art, Kaniel, Michael, BF194

A guide to Jewish genealogical research in Israel, Sack, Sallyann Amdur, AJ143

Guide to Jewish religious practice, Klein, Isaac, BC560

Guide to Jewish themes in American fiction, 1940–1980, Blackman, Murray, BE564

A guide to journals in psychology and education, Loke, Wing Hong, CB22

A guide to Latin American and Caribbean census material, CG122

Guide to Latin American music, Chase, Gilbert, BJ11

Guide to Latin American pamphlets from the Yale University Library, Yale University. Library, DB271

Guide to League of Nations publications, Aufricht, Hans, AF27

Guide to libraries in Central and Eastern Europe, DC48

Guide to libraries in Western Europe, AK132

Guide to library research in public administration, Simpson, Anthony E., CJ459

Guide to library research methods, Mann, Thomas, AK6

A guide to library service in mathematics, EB1

Guide to lists of master's theses, Black, Dorothy M., AG14

A guide to literary criticism and research, Stevens, Bonnie Klomp, BE9

Guide to literary manuscripts in the Huntington Library, Henry E. Huntington Library and Art Gallery, BF429

Guide to Malay periodicals, Roff, William R., AD205

A guide to manuscript collections in the history of psychology and related areas, Sokal, Michael M., CD58

Guide to manuscript sources for the history of Latin America and the Caribbean, DC345

Guide to manuscript sources for the history of Latin America and the Caribbean in the British Isles, DB274

A guide to manuscript sources in United States and West Indian depositories relating to the British West Indies during the era of the American Revolution, Tyson, George F., DB415

Guide to manuscripts and documents in the British Isles relating to Africa, Matthews, Noel, DC345, DD38, DD39
—— Pearson, J. D., DC345, DD38, DD39
—— Wainwright, M. Doreen, DC345, DD38, DD39

A guide to manuscripts and documents in the British Isles relating to South and South-East Asia, Pearson, J. D., DE12

A guide to manuscripts and documents in the British Isles relating to the Far East, Matthews, Noel, DE105

Guide to manuscripts and documents in the British Isles relating to the Middle East and North Africa, Matthews, Noel, DD38, DE50
—— Pearson, J. D., DD38
—— Wainwright, M. Doreen, DD38

Guide to manuscripts in the presidential libraries, Burton, Dennis A., AJ24, AK102, CJ176, DB37

A guide to manuscripts relating to America in Great Britain and Ireland, DB32

Guide to manuscripts relating to American history in British depositories reproduced for the Division of Manuscripts of the Library of Congress, Griffin, Grace Gardner, DB32

Guide to manuscripts relating to the history of the British Empire, 1748–1776, Gipson, Lawrence Henry, DC341

Guide to materials on Latin America in the National Archives, AK114, DB38
—— Harrison, John P., DB280

Guide to materials on Latin America in the National Archives of the United States, United States. National Archives and Records Service, DB280

A guide to mathematical tables, Lebedev, Aleksandr Vasil'evich, EB74

Guide to meteorological instruments and methods of observation, EF153

Guide to microforms in print, AA131
Guide to microforms in print. Author, title, AA131
Guide to military installations, Cragg, Dan, CJ623
Guide to MLA documentation, Trimmer, Joseph, AG2
Guide to modern defense and strategy, Robertson, David, CJ578
Guide to modern versions of the New Testament, Dennett, Herbert, BC94
Guide to Mormon diaries & autobiographies, Bitton, Davis, BC368
Guide to mushrooms & toadstools, Lange, Morten, EG187
Guide to music festivals in America, BJ195
Guide to musical America, Gusikoff, Lynne, BJ191
Guide to New Zealand information sources, AA86, AF268
Guide to non-federal archives and manuscripts in the United States relating to Africa, South, Aloha, DD36, DD42
Guide to non-traditional college degrees, CB253
Guide to Nordic bibliography, DC71
A guide to North American bird clubs, Rickert, Jon E., EG273
A guide to official gazettes and their contents, Roberts, John E., AF6
Guide to official industrial property publications, EA267
Guide to official publications of foreign countries, AF8
Guide to official statistics, CG390
—— Great Britain. Central Statistical Office, CG237
A guide to Oriental classics, BE1543
A guide to original sources for precolonial western Africa published in European languages, Fage, J. D., DD99
A guide to parliamentary papers, Ford, Percy, AF177
A guide to periodical articles about Botswana, 1965–80, Henderson, Francine I., DD130
Guide to periodical literature, CC529
A guide to periodical publications and newspapers of Pakistan, Moid, A., AD207
Guide to Polish libraries and archives, Lewanski, Richard Casimir, AK152
Guide to popular U.S. government publications, Bailey, William G., AF77
—— Schwarzkopf, LeRoy C., AF77
A guide to pre-federal records in the National Archives, Wehmann, Howard H., DB81
Guide to prehistoric ruins of the Southwest, Oppelt, Norman T., BG54
Guide to preservation literature, Massey, James C., BF219
Guide to private fortunes, AL118
Guide to programs in geography in the United States and Canada, CL26
Guide to programs in nursing in four-year colleges and universities, EH282
Guide to programs of geography in the United States and Canada, CL55
A guide to psychiatric books in English, Menninger, Karl, EH373
Guide to public administration, Cutchin, D. A., CJ461
A guide to publications of the Executive branch, O'Hara, Frederic J., AF131
A guide to published library catalogs, Nelson, Bonnie R., AA98
A guide to records in Barbados, Chandler, Michael John, DB419, DB444, DB460
Guide to records in the Leeward Islands, Baker, Edward Cecil, DB419, DB444, DB460
Guide to records in the Windward Islands, Baker, Edward Cecil, DB419, DB444, DB460
Guide to Referativnyi zhurnal, Copley, Eric James, EA73
A guide to reference and bibliography for theatre research, Bailey, Claudia Jean, BH30
Guide to reference books for Islamic studies, Geddes, Charles L., BC494
Guide to reference material, AA363

Guide to reference materials in political science, Wynar, Lubomyr Roman, CJ1
A guide to reference materials on India, DE156
A guide to reference materials on Southeast Asia, Johnson, Donald Clay, DE93
Guide to reference works for the study of the Spanish language and literature and Spanish American literature, Woodbridge, Hensley Charles, BD171, BE1430
Guide to reprints, AA393
Guide to research and reference works on sub-Saharan Africa, Duignan, Peter, DD83
Guide to research and scholarship in Hungary, DC389
A guide to research collections of former members of the United States House of Representatives, 1789–1987, AJ24, CJ201, DB37
Guide to research collections of former United States senators, 1789–1982, AJ24, CJ201, CJ202, DB37
Guide to research collections of the New York Public Library, Williams, Sam P., AK115
Guide to research in American library history, Harris, Michael H., AK27
Guide to research in classicial art and mythology, Van Keuren, Frances Dodds, BF7, CF19
A guide to research in gerontology, Zito, Dorothea R., CC103
A guide to research in music education, Phelps, Roger P., BJ6
Guide to research support, American Psychological Association, CD36
Guide to resources and services, Inter-university Consortium for Political and Social Research, CA3
The guide to resources on women and AIDS, CC550
Guide to Restoration and Augustan literature, Simmonds, Eva, BE611
A guide to reviews of books from and about Hispanic America, AA370
A guide to romance reference grammars, McKay, John C., BD151
Guide to romantic literature, 1780–1830, Ward, Geoff, BE611
Guide to Russian reference books, Maichel, Karol, AA351, AB86
Guide to schools and departments of religion and seminaries in the United States and Canada, BC79
Guide to selected diplomatic archives of South America, Seckinger, Ron L., AK130, DB278
A guide to serial bibliographies for modern literatures, Wortman, William A., BE34
Guide to social science resources in women's studies, Oakes, Elizabeth H., CA5
A guide to source materials for the study of Barbados history, 1627–1834, Handler, Jerome S., DB420
Guide to source materials in the India Office Library and Records for the history of Tibet, Sikkim and Bhutan, 1765–1950, Amar Kaur Jasbir Singh, DE12
—— Singh, Amar Kaur Jasbir, DE86
Guide to sources for agricultural and biological research, EJ1, EJ98
Guide to sources in American journalism history, AE32, AE144
A guide to sources of educational information, Woodbury, Marda, CB5
Guide to sources of professional ethics, Avery, Barbara Brower, AL9
Guide to South African reference books, Musiker, Reuben, AA353
Guide to special issues and indexes of periodicals, AD34, CH29
Guide to standard floras of the world, Frodin, D. G., EG91
Guide to state legislative and administrative materials, Fisher, Mary L., CJ267
Guide to state legislative materials, CJ267
Guide to statistical materials produced by governments and associations in the United States, Stratford, Juri, CG95
A guide to statistical methods and to the pertinent literature, Sachs, Lothar, EB17

A guide to statistical sources in money, banking, and finance, Balachandran, M., CH290
Guide to Statistics Canada data on women, CG114
The guide to supernatural fiction, Bleiler, Everett Franklin, BE279, BE280
Guide to Swedish-American archival and manuscript sources in the United States, CC338
Guide to tables in mathematical statistics, Greenwood, Joseph Arthur, EB73
Guide to tables in the theory of numbers, Lehmer, Derrick H., EB73
—— Lehmer, Derrick Henry, EB75
Guide to tables of Bessel functions, Archibald, Raymond Clare, EB73
—— Bateman, Harry, EB73
Guide to tables of elliptic functions, Fletcher, Alan, EB73
Guide to technical services resources, AK228
Guide to the American ethnic press, Wynar, Lubomyr Roman, AD58
Guide to the American left, CJ139
Guide to the American occult, CD137
Guide to the American right, CJ139
—— Wilcox, Laird M., CJ80
A guide to the ancient world, Grant, Michael, CL102
Guide to the archive groups, collections, and single documents preserved in the Archives of Bulgarian History, DC117
Guide to the archives of Hungary, DC386
Guide to the archives of the government of the Confederate States of America, Beers, Henry Putney, DB114
Guide to the art of Latin America, Smith, Robert Chester, BF22
—— Wilder, Elizabeth, BF22
Guide to the arts of the Americas, Johnson, Harmer, BF70
Guide to the availability of theses, Borchardt, D. H., AK224
Guide to the availability of theses II, Allen, G. G., AK224
—— Deubert, K., AK224
Guide to the best business schools, CB255, CH76
Guide to the best fiction, English and American, Baker, Ernest Albert, BE240
Guide to the best historical novels and tales, Nield, Jonathan, BE250
Guide to the bibliographies of Russian literature, Armbruster, Davis L., BE1396
—— Zenkovsky, Serge A., BE1396
Guide to the bibliography of astronomy, 1881–1989, on microfilm, Sykes, J. B., EC14
Guide to the Bureau of Applied Social Research, CA12
Guide to the collecting and care of original prints, Gaehde, Christa M., BF379
—— Zigrosser, Carl, BF379
Guide to the collections in the Hoover Institution archives relating to Imperial Russia, the Russian revolutions and civil war, and the first emigration, Hoover Institution on War, Revolution, and Peace, DC564
Guide to the contents of the Public Record Office, Great Britain. Public Record Office, DC286
A guide to the culture of science, technology, and medicine, EA15
Guide to the diplomatic history of the United States, 1775–1921, Bemis, Samuel Flagg, DB15
—— Griffin, Grace Gardner, DB15
A guide to the evaluation of educational experiences in the armed services, CB361
Guide to the flags of the world, Talocci, Mauro, AL195
The guide to the foundations of public administration, Martin, Daniel, CJ469
Guide to the Frick Art Reference Library sales catalogue index, Frick Art Reference Library, BF113
Guide to the gods, Leach, Marjorie, BC62
Guide to the Gothic, Frank, Frederick S., BE289
Guide to the Hebrew press, Kressel, Getzel, AD14

Guide to the historical and archaeological publications of societies in England and Wales, 1903–1933, Mullins, Edward Lindsay Carson, DC275, DC279, DC281

A guide to the historical geography of New Spain, Gerhard, Peter, DB225

Guide to the historical publications of the societies of England and Wales, DC275

A guide to the history of bacteriology, Grainger, Thomas H., EG310

Guide to the history of cartography, Ristow, Walter William, CL240

Guide to the history of psychology, Lawry, John D., CD55

Guide to the history of science, EA248
—— Sarton, George, EA239, EG8

Guide to the holdings of the American Jewish Archives, Hebrew Union College—Jewish Institute of Religion. American Jewish Archives, BC538

Guide to the Hoover Institution archives, Palm, Charles G., DA172
—— Reed, Dale, DA172

Guide to the House of Commons, CJ358

Guide to the identification and acquisition of Canadian government publications, Pross, Catherine A., AF155

Guide to the incomparable New York times index, Morse, Grant W., AE110

Guide to the India Office records 1600–1858, Foster, William, DE83

Guide to the languages of the world, Ruhlen, Merritt, BD16

Guide to the law and legal literature of Mexico, Clagett, Helen Lord, CK197
—— Vance, John T., CK197

Guide to the Library of Congress classification, Immroth, John Philip, AK199

Guide to the literature of art history, Arntzen, Etta Mae, BF1

A guide to the literature of astronomy, Seal, Robert A., EC4

Guide to the literature of botany, Jackson, Benjamin Daydon, EG96

A guide to the literature of chemistry, Crane, Evan Jay, EE2

A guide to the literature of electrical and electronics engineering, Ardis, Susan, EK124

Guide to the literature of mathematics and physics including related works on engineering science, Parke, Nathan Grier, EB3, ED2

Guide to the literature of pharmacy and the pharmaceutical sciences, Andrews, Theodora, EH316

A guide to the literature of tennis, Lumpkin, Angela, BK102

Guide to the literature of the life sciences, EG5

Guide to the literature of the zoological sciences, EG5

Guide to the manuscript collection of the Tamiment Library, CH642

Guide to the manuscript collections of the Bancroft Library, Hammond, George P., DB163
—— Morgan, Dale L., DB163

Guide to the manuscript collections of the Presbyterian Church, U.S., Benedetto, Robert, BC376

Guide to the manuscript sources for the history of Latin America and the Caribbean in the British Isles, Walne, Peter, DB275

Guide to the manuscripts and documents in the British Isles relating to Africa, Pearson, J. D., DD105

Guide to the manuscripts preserved in the Public Record Office, Giuseppi, M. S., DC286

A guide to the microfilm collection of early state records, Library of Congress, DB141

Guide to the microfilm edition of International population census publication, 1945–1967, Research Publications, inc, CG9

A guide to the microfilm edition of International population census publications, 1945–1967, Research Publications, inc, CG11

Guide to the Middle East, DE23

A guide to the music of Latin America, Chase, Gilbert, BJ11

Guide to the musical arts, Belknap, Sara Yancey, BH8

Guide to the national and provincial directories of England and Wales, excluding London, published before 1856, Norton, Jane Elizabeth, AL1, AL7, CH366, CH381

Guide to the National Anthropological Archives, Smithsonian Institution, National Anthropological Archives, CE32

Guide to the National Archives of the United States, United States. National Archives and Records Administration, AK114, DB38

A guide to the official publications of the other American republics, Library of Congress, AF159

Guide to the performing arts, BH8, BH136

Guide to the petroleum reference literature, Pearson, Barbara C., EK298

Guide to the photographic collections at the Smithsonian Institution, BF365

Guide to the Presidential advisory commissions, 1973–1984, Zink, Steven D., AF132, CJ186

Guide to the principal sources for American civilization, 1800–1900, in the city of New York, Carman, Harry James, DB79, DB98
—— Thompson, Arthur W., DB79

A guide to the principal sources for early American history (1600–1800) in the city of New York, Greene, Evarts Boutell, DB79, DB98

Guide to the public records of Scotland deposited in H. M. General Register House, Edinburgh, Great Britain. General Register Office (Scotland), DC358

Guide to the publications of interstate agencies and authorities, AF141

Guide to the records deposited in the Public Record Office of Ireland, Wood, Herbert, DC401

Guide to the records in the National Archives, AK114, DB38

A guide to the records of Bermuda, Rowe, Helen, DB422

Guide to the records of Parliament, Bond, Maurice F., AF175

Guide to the records of the Bahamas, Saunders, D. Gail, DB418

Guide to the records of the United States House of Representatives at the National Archives, 1789–1989, United States. National Archives and Records Administration, CJ203, CJ212

Guide to the records of the United States Senate at the National Archives, United States. National Archives and Records Administration, CJ203

Guide to the records of the United States Senate at the National Archives, 1789–1989, United States. National Archives and Records Administration, CJ212

Guide to the reference collections of the New York Public Library, Brown, Karl, AK115

Guide to the reports of the Public Archives of Canada, 1872–1972, Public Archives Canada, DB193

Guide to the reports of the Royal Commission on Historical Manuscripts, 1911–1957, Hall, A. C. S., DC285

A guide to the reports on collections of manuscripts of private families, corporations and institutions in Great Britain and Ireland, Great Britain. Historical Manuscripts Commission, DC285

Guide to the republics of the former Soviet Union, Twining, David Thomas, DC600

Guide to the research collections of former U.S. representatives, CJ212

Guide to the research collections of former U.S. senators, 1789–1989, CJ212

Guide to the Slavonic languages, De Bray, R. G. A., BD181

Guide to the sources of Asian history, DE162

Guide to the sources of Asian history. 8. Pakistan, DE239

A guide to the sources of British military history, Higham, Robin D. S., DC277

Guide to the sources of medieval history, Caenegem, R. C. van, DA127

Guide to the sources of the history of nations, DD58

Guide to the sources of the history of the nations, DB275, DD38, DE162, DE239

Guide to the sources of the history of the nations : B. Africa, DD105

Guide to the sources of United States military history, DB16

Guide to the Soviet navy, CJ658

Guide to the special collections of prints and photographs in the Library of Congress, BF365

Guide to the study and reading of American history, Channing, Edward, DB13
—— Hart, Albert B., DB13
—— Turner, Frederick J., DB13

A guide to the study of medieval history, Paetow, Louis John, DA134, DA135

A guide to the study of the Pentecostal movement, Jones, Charles Edwin, BC375

Guide to the study of the United States of America, Basler, Roy P., DB13
—— Library of Congress. General Reference and Bibliography Division, DB13
—— McCrum, Blanche P., DB13
—— Mugridge, Donald H., DB13
—— Orr, Oliver H., DB13

Guide to the study of United States history outside the U.S., 1945–1980, DB17

Guide to the study of United States imprints, Tanselle, George Thomas, AA400

Guide to the taxonomic literature of vertebrates, Blackwelder, Richard Eliot, EG208

Guide to the United States treaties in force, CK93

Guide to the universities of Europe, Boswick, Storm, CB318

Guide to the use of libraries and information sources, Gates, Jean Key, AK3

A guide to the use of United Nations documents, Brimmer, Brenda, AF31

A guide to the world's languages, Ruhlen, Merritt, BD16

Guide to the writings of pioneer Latinoamericanists of the United States, Sable, Martin Howard, DB296

Guide to the year's work in Victorian poetry, BE703, BE706

Guide to the year's work in Victorian poetry and prose, Tobias, Richard C., BE755

Guide to theses and dissertations, Reynolds, Michael M., AF12

A guide to tracing the history of a business, Orbell, John, CH398

Guide to trade catalogs from the Corning Museum of Glass, Corning Museum of Glass, BG53

Guide to twentieth century literature in English, Blamires, Harry, BE764

Guide to Unesco, Hajnal, Peter I., AF58

Guide to United Nations organization, documentation & publishing for students, researchers, librarians, Hajnal, Peter I., AF34

Guide to United States government maps : geologic and hydrologic maps, CL249, EF111

Guide to U.S. foundations, their trustees, officers, and donors, AL119

Guide to U.S. government publications, AF80

A guide to U.S. government scientific and technical resources, Aluri, Rao, EA1

Guide to U.S. government serials and periodicals, Andriot, John L., AF80

Guide to U.S. government statistics, CG89

Guide to U.S. map resources, Cobb, David A., CL256

A guide to usage for writers and students in the social sciences, Runkel, Philip Julian, CA55

Guide to USGS geologic and hydrologic maps, CL249, EF111

Guide to Western architecture, Gloag, John, BF256

A guide to western historical scripts from antiquity to 1600, Brown, Michelle P., AA213

Guide to Western manuscripts and documents in the British Isles relating to South and South East Asia, Matthews, Noel, DE12
—— Wainwright, M. D., DE12, DE13
Guide to women's art organizations, Navaretta, Cynthia, BF102
A guide to world cinema, BH195
The guide to world equity markets, CH307
The guide to writers conferences, BE171
Guide to Yale University Holocaust video testimonies, Fortunoff Video Archive for Holocaust Testimonies, DA220
A guide to Yugoslav libraries and archives, Jovanovič, Slobodan, DC611
Guidebooks, CL371
   bibliography, CL375, CL389, CL390, CL391, CL392
Guidelines for collection development, American Library Association. Collection Development Committee, AK164
Guidelines for college and university archives, Society of American Archivists, AK186
Les Guides bleues, CL375
Guides des sources de l'histoire d'Amérique Latine conservées en Belgique, Liagre, L., DB275
Guides to archives and manuscript collections in the United States, DeWitt, Donald L., DB29
Guides to European diplomatic history research and research materials, DC586
Guides to German records microfilmed at Alexandria, Va, DC246
—— United States. National Archives and Records Service, DC254
Guides to Library of Congress subject headings and classification on peace and international conflict resolution, CJ688
Guides to literature, American Society for Engineering Education. Engineering Libraries Division, EK1
Guides to manuscript materials for the history of the United States, Carnegie Institution of Washington, DB28, DB32
Guides to materials for West African history in European archives, DD105
Guides to sources for British history based on the National Register of Archives, DC287
Guides to the sources for the history of nations, DE11, DF13
Guides to the sources for the history of the nations, DB272, DD42
Guides to the sources for the history of the nations : 3rd series, North Africa, Asia, and Oceania, DD38, DD75
Guides to the sources in the Netherlands for the history of Latin America, Roessingh, M. P. H., DB275
Guilbert, Louis. *Grand Larousse de la langue française,* AC329
The Guild handbook of scientific illustration, EA222
Guild of Natural Science Illustrators (U.S.). *The Guild handbook of scientific illustration,* EA222
Guillaume, Sylvie. *La France contemporaine, 1946–1990,* DC210
Guillo, Laurent. *Catalogue de la musique imprimée avant 1801,* BJ72
Guimarães, Argeu. *Diccionario bio-bibliographico brasileiro,* AH126
Guinagh, Kevin. *Dictionary of foreign phrases and abbreviations,* AC185
—— *I am happy to present,* BE357
Guinea
   encyclopedias, DD48
Guinea-Bissau
   bibliography, DD18, DD114
   encyclopedias, DD48
   statistics, CG335
Guinea-Bissau. Direcção-Geral de Estatística. *Anuário estatístico,* CG335
Guinea-Bissau, Galli, Rosemary E., DD18
Guinea ecuatorial, Liniger-Goumaz, Max, DD150
Guinea (Republic of Guinea/Conakry), O'Toole, Thomas E., DD48

La Guinée équatoriale, Liniger-Goumaz, Max, DD151
Guinness book of records, AB104
•*Guinness book of records on CD-ROM,* AB104
The Guinness book of sports records, BK42
Guinness book of superlatives, AB104
The Guinness encyclopedia of popular music, BJ347
Guirand, Félix. *Mythologie générale,* CF8
Gujarati language
   dictionaries, AC468
Guldan, Ernst. *Kataloge der Bibliotheca Hertziana in Rom (Max-Planck-Institut),* BF52
Gulick, Charles Adams. *History and theories of working-class movements,* CH631
Gullón, Ricardo. *Diccionario de literatura española e hispanoamericana,* BE1451
Gulsoy, Joseph. *Diccionari etimològic i complementari de la llengua catalana,* AC248
Gulyás, Pál. *Magyar írói álnév lexikon,* AA175, AA176
—— *Magyar írók,* AH247, AH250, BE1282
Gumuchian et compagnie, booksellers, Paris. *Les livres de l'enfance du XV⁰ au XIX⁰ siècle,* AA245
Gunasingam, S. *Directory of South Asian library resources in the UK and the Republic of Ireland,* DE82
Gunderson, Nels L. *Pension funds,* CH500
Gunev, Sneja. *A bibliography of Australian multicultural writers,* DF24
Gunn, James. *New encyclopedia of science fiction,* BE286
Gunn, John Charles. *A directory of world psychiatry,* EH390
Gunn, Mary Kemper. *A guide to academic protocol,* CB394
Gunnis, Rupert. *Dictionary of British sculptors, 1660–1851,* BF394
Gunson, Phil. *The dictionary of contemporary politics of Central America and the Caribbean,* CJ311
—— *The dictionary of contemporary politics of South America,* CJ312
Gunston, Bill. *The illustrated encyclopedia of rockets and missiles,* CJ570
—— *Jane's aerospace dictionary,* EK31
Günümüz Türkiyesinde kim kimdir, AH302
Gupta, Brijen K. *India,* DE157
—— *India in English fiction, 1800–1970,* BE1568
Gupta, H. *Representations of primes by quadratic forms,* EB94
Guralnik, David Bernard. *Webster's new World dictionary of American English,* AC20
Gurevich, Miron M. *Opisanie izdanii, napechatannykh pri Petre Pervom,* AA789
Gurlitt, Wilibald. *Riemann musik Lexikon,* BJ125
Gurlt, Ernst. *Biographisches Lexikon der hervorragenden Ärzte aller Zeiten und Völker,* EH222
Gurock, Jeffrey S. *American Jewish history,* BC523
Gŭrtsiia i bŭlgaro-grŭtskite otnosheniia v bŭlgarskata nauchna knizhnina, 1878–1980, Angelova, Stefka, DC110
Gusev, B. V. *English-Russian dictionary of applied geophysics,* EF88
Guseva, G. Z. *Russkie anonimnye i podpisannye psevdonimami proizvedeniia pechati,* AA183
Gusikoff, Lynne. *Guide to musical America,* BJ191
Gusovius, Alexander. *Bibliographie zur deutschen Grammatik,* BD117
Gustafson, Alrik. *A history of Swedish literature,* BE1482
Güterbock, Hans Gustav. *The Hittite dictionary of the Oriental Institute of the University of Chicago,* AC491
Guterman, Norbert. *The Anchor book of French quotations,* BE127
—— *A book of Latin quotations,* BE143
Guth, DeLloyd J. *Late-medieval England, 1377–1485,* DC303, DC307
Guðnason, Jón. *Islenzkar æviskrár frá lannámstímum til ársloka 1965,* AH254
Guthrie, Donald. *The new Bible commentary, revised,* BC171

Guthrie, Paul. *Scandinavian biographical archive,* AH164
Gutiérrez, G. *Bibliografía socioeconómica de Nicaragua,* DB316
Gutiérrez, José Rosendo. *Datos para la bibliografía boliviana. 1. sección,* AA504
Gutiérrez, Juan María. *Bibliografía de la primera imprenta de Buenos Aires desde su fundación hasta el año 1810 inclusive ...,* AA496
Gutiérrez, Margo. *The border guide,* DB250
Gutierrez, Nancy A. *English historical poetry, 1476–1603,* BE714
Gutiérrez, René L. *The Aztecs,* CC477
—— *Bibliografía de la literatura ecuatoriana,* BE950
—— *Bibliografía de la literatura paraguaya,* BE953
—— *The Incas,* CC478, DB385
Gutkin, Terry B. *The handbook of school psychology,* CD94
Gutter life and language in the early "street" literature of England, Henke, James T., AC124
Guttmann, David. *European American elderly,* CC69
Gutzman, Philip C. *Dictionary of military, defense contractor & troop slang acronyms,* CJ617
Guy, Henry A. *Women of distinction in Jamaica,* AH156
Guy, Patricia A. *Women's poetry index,* BE314
Guyana, DB378
   bibliography, AA533
Guyana, Chambers, Frances, DB378
Guyanese national bibliography, AA533
Guyer, Paul. *Bibliographie der Städtegeschichte der Schweiz,* DC524
Guzeeva, Irina Andreevna. *Istoriia SSSR,* DC549
Guzman, Augusto. *Biografías de la literatura boliviana,* BE922
—— *Biografías de la nueva literatura boliviana,* BE922
GV, AA643
Gvardzhaladze, Isidore. *English-Georgian dictionary,* AC398
Gvardzhaladze, Tamara. *English-Georgian dictionary,* AC398
GVH, AG10
Gwilt, Joseph. *Encyclopedia of architecture, historical, theoretical, and practical,* BF232
Gwinup, Thomas. *Greek and Roman authors,* BE996
Gwynn, Aubrey Osborn. *Medieval religious houses, Ireland,* BC441
Gyldendals tibinds leksikon, AB33
Gypsies see **Peripatetics**
Gysi, Klaus. *Geschichte der deutschen Literatur von den Anfängen bis zur Gegenwart,* BE1255

Haack, Hermann. *Stieler's atlas of modern geography,* CL291
Haag, Enid E. *Research guide for studies in infancy and childhood,* CC139, CD77, CD80
Haan, David Bierens de. *Nouvelles tables d'intégrales définies,* EB86
Haar, John M. *The military in imperial history,* DC145
Haas, Marilyn L. *Indians of North America,* CC413
Haas, Mary Rosamond. *Thai-English student's dictionary,* AC777
Haas, Verena. *Bibliographie zur Architektur im 19 Jahrhundert,* BF211
Haase, Carl. *The records of German history in German and certain other record offices,* DC247
Haase, Ynez D. *Historical atlas of the American West,* DB176
Haber, Barbara. *Women in America,* CC493
Haberkamp de Antón, Gisela. *Dictionary of agriculture,* EJ29
Haberling, W. *Biographisches Lexikon der hervorragenden Ärzte aller Zeiten und Völker,* EH222
Haberman, Frederick W. *Rhetoric and public address,* BE349
Haberman, Martin. *Handbook of research on teacher education,* CB162
Habib, Irfan. *An atlas of the Mughal Empire,* DE172

HABS/HAER, BF219

Die Habsburger, DC95

Hachette. (firm, publishers, Paris). *Avec les "Guides bleues" à travers la France et le monde*, CL375

Hachmann, Rolf. *Ausgewählte Bibliographie zur Vorgeschichte von Mitteleuropa*, DC6

Hachmann, Rolf. *Verzeichnis vor- und frühgeschichtlicher Bibliographien. Ausgewählte Bibliographie zur Vorgeschichte von Mitteleuropa*, DC6

Hacken, Richard D. *Central European economic history from Waterloo to OPEC, 1815–1975*, DC7

Hackett, Alice Payne. *80 years of best sellers, 1895–1975*, AA327

Hackett, Amy. *The encyclopedia of the Third Reich*, DC255

Hackett, Janet M. *Index to book reviews in religion*, BC52

Hackett, Jeremiah. *Medieval philosophers*, BB67

Hackh, Ingo W. D. *Grant & Hackh's chemical dictionary*, EE40

Hackland, Brian. *The dictionary of contemporary politics of southern Africa*, CJ408

Hadamitzky, Wolfgang. *Kan-Ei jukugo ribāsu jiten*, AC558

Hadas, Moses. *History of Latin literature*, BE1052

Hadcock, Richard Neville. *Medieval religious houses, England and Wales*, BC441

Haddad, Yvonne Yazbeck. *The contemporary Islamic revival*, BC496

Hadas, Moses. *History of Greek literature*, BE1034

Hadfield, Miles. *British gardeners*, BF285

Hadfield, Susan. *Australian literary pseudonyms*, AA193

Hadjor, Kofi Buenor. *Dictionary of Third World terms*, CJ27

Hady, Maureen E. *Asian-American periodicals and newspapers*, AE24

—— *Native American periodicals and newspapers, 1828–1982*, AE16

—— *Women's periodicals and newspapers from the 18th century to 1981*, AD48, AE25

Haeberli, André. *Human protein data*, EG160

Haebler, Konrad. *Bibliografía ibérica del siglo XV*, AA817

Haenisch, Wolf. *Bibliographie von Japan, 1906– [1943]*, DE204

Haensch, Gunther. *Dictionary of agriculture*, EJ29

HAER checklist, Boone, Ellen, BF219

—— Keyes, Alice, BF219

Haerinck, E. *Bibliographie analytique de l'archéologie de l'Iran ancien*, DE180

Haering, Hermann. *Dahlmann-Waitz Quellenkunde der deutschen Geschichte*, DC215

Haeringen, Coenraad Bernardus van. *Franck's Etymologisch woordenboek der Nederlandsche taal*, AC299

—— *Netherlandic language research*, BD128

Haertel, Geneva D. *International encyclopedia of educational evaluation*, CB70

Haertel, Martin Henry. *German literature in American magazines, 1846 to 1880*, BE1238, BE1240

Haftmann, Werner. *Painting in the twentieth century*, BF307

Hagberg Wright, C. T. *Catalogue*, AA120

Hagelweide, Gert. *Deutsche Zeitungsbestände in Bibliotheken und Archiven*, AE53

Hagen, Ordean. *Who done it?*, BE271

Hagen, Waltraud. *Handbuch der Editionen*, BE1220

Hagerups Illustrerede Konversations Leksikon, AB34

Hagger, A. J. *A guide to Australian economic and social statistics*, CG438

Hagiography *see* **Saints**

Hagström, Tore. *Svensk litteraturhistorisk bibliografi intill år 1900*, BE1483

Hague, Lois. *The sourcebook of medical illustration*, EH236

Hague Club, The. *Foundation profiles*, AL96

Hahn, H. George. *Eighteenth century British novel and its background*, BE670

Hahn, Theo. *International tables for crystallography*, EF117

Hahn, Wiktor. *Bibliografia bibliografij polskich*, AA60

—— *Bibliografia bibliografij polskich do 1950 roku*, AA59

Hahner, June Edith. *Recent research on women in Brazil*, DB343

Haig, Judith Giblin. *Dictionary of American literary characters*, BE484

Haigh, Christopher. *The Cambridge historical encyclopedia of Great Britain and Ireland*, DC289, DC293

Haight, Timothy R. *The mass media*, CH496

Haight, Willet Ricketson. *Canadian catalogue of books, 1791–1897*, AA448

Hain, Ludwig Friedrich Theodor. *Repertorim bibliographicum*, AA222, AA227, AA230, AA231, AA233

—— *Repertorium bibliographicum*, AA223, AA228

Haines, David W. *Refugee resettlement in the United States*, CC322

—— *Refugees in the United States*, CC354

Haines, Gerald K. *A reference guide to United States Department of State special files*, CJ177

Hairston, Maxine. *Scott, Foresman handbook for writers*, BD96

Hais, Karel. *English-Czech dictionary*, AC279

—— *Velký anglicko-český slovník*, AC279

Haiti, DB438, DB440, DB441

bibliography, AA566, AA567, DB439

government publications, AF159

statistics, CG174

Haiti, DB439

—— Chambers, Frances, DB438

—— Lawless, Robert, DB441

Haitian publications, Ballantyne, Lygia Maria F. C., AA566

Haitiana 1971–1975, Manigat, Max, AA566

Haitsma Mulier, E. O. G. *Bibliography of Dutch seventeenth century political thought*, DC455

—— *Repertorium van geschiedschrijvers in Nederland, 1500–1800*, DC461

Hajko, Vladimír. *Encyklopédia slovenska*, DC129

Hajnal, Peter I. *Directory of United Nations documentary and archival sources*, AF45

—— *Guide to Unesco*, AF58

—— *Guide to United Nations organization, documentation & publishing for students, researchers, librarians*, AF34

—— *International information*, AF4

Häkli, Esko. *Bibliographia studiorum uralicorum, 1917–1987*, DC602

Halachmi, Arie. *Public sector productivity*, CJ466

Halasz de Beky, I. L. *Bibliography of Hungarian dictionaries, 1410–1963*, AC500

—— *A bibliography of the Hungarian Revolution, 1956*, DC380

—— *Medieval Hungarian historians*, DC380

Halbjahresverzeichnis der im deutschen Buchhandel erschienen Bücher, Zeitschriften und Landkarten, AA641

Halbjahrsverzeichnis der im deutschen Buchhandel erschienenen Bücher, Zeitschriften und Landkarten, AA656

Haldar, A. K. *Research methodology in social science in India*, CA59

Hale, Frederick. *American religion and philosophy*, BC31

Hale, J. R. *A concise encyclopaedia of the Italian Renaissance*, DC430

Hale, Linda Louise. *Contemporary Canadian childhood and youth*, CC152

—— *History of Canadian childhood and youth*, CC153

Hale, Linton. *Human rights organizations and periodicals directory*, CK147

Hales, Robert E. *What you need to know about psychiatric drugs*, EH351

Halevy, Shoshana Dyamont. *Ha-Sefarim ha-ivriyim she-nidpesu bi-Yerushalayim ... 1841–1891*, AA909

Haley, John. *An index to Japanese law*, CK232

Half a century of Russian serials, 1917–1968, Schatoff, Michael, AD78

Half a century of Soviet serials, 1917–1968, Smits, Rudolf, AD147

Haliburton, Gordon. *Lesotho*, DD48

Halkett, Samuel. *Dictionary of anonymous and pseudonymous English literature*, AA150

Halkin, François Halkin. *Auctarium bibliotheca hagiographica graeca*, BC259

—— *Novum auctarium bibliotheca hagiographica graeca*, BC259

Hall, A. C. S. *Guide to the reports of the Royal Commission on Historical Manuscripts, 1911–1957*, DC285

Hall, Blaine H. *Jewish American fiction writers*, BE564

Hall, Carl W. *The literature of agricultural engineering*, EJ3

Hall, Charles J. *An eighteenth-century musical chronicle*, BJ187

—— *A Nineteenth-century musical chronicle*, BJ187

—— *A Twentieth-century musical chronicle*, BJ187

Hall, D. G. E. *Atlas of South-east Asia*, CL348

—— *Historical writing on the peoples of Asia*, DE18

Hall, E. *Index to reports of Geological Survey of Canada from 1927–50*, EF31

Hall, Eugene Raymond. *The mammals of North America*, EG294

Hall, Halbert W. *Science fiction and fantasy book review index, 1980–1984*, BE290

—— *Science fiction and fantasy reference index, 1878–1985*, BE290

—— *Science fiction and fantasy reference index, 1985–1991*, BE299

—— *Science fiction and fantasy research index*, BE299

—— *Science fiction book review index*, BE290, BE299

—— *Science fiction book review index, 1974–1979*, BE290

—— *Science fiction magazines*, BE307

Hall, James. *Dictionary of subjects and symbols in art*, BF167

Hall, Jo Anne. *Black American families, 1965–1984*, CC206

Hall, Joan Houston. *Dictionary of American regional English*, AC151

Hall, John Richard Clark. *Concise Anglo-Saxon dictionary*, AC173

Hall, John W. *The Cambridge history of Japan*, DE194

Hall, Kermit. *A comprehensive bibliography of American constitutional and legal history, 1896–1979*, CK125

—— *The Oxford companion to the Supreme Court of the United States*, CK187

Hall, Louise McG. *Medieval and Renaissance studies*, DA128

Hall, Manly Palmer. *An encyclopedic outline of Masonic, Hermetic, Qabbalistic, and Rosicrucian symbolical philosophy*, AL73, AL75

Hall, Mary S. *Developing skills in proposal writing*, AL92

—— *Getting funded*, AL92

Hall, R. J. *Dictionary of aviation*, CH474

Hall, Rachel. *Iconographic index to New Testament subjects represented in photographs and slides of paintings in the visual collections, Fine Arts Library, Harvard University*, BF298

Hall, Robert Anderson. *Bibliografia della linguistica italiana*, BD161

Hall, Robert de Zouche. *A bibliography on vernacular architecture*, BF215

Hall, Roland. *Fifty years of Hume scholarship*, BB73

Hall marks on gold and silver plate, Chaffers, William, BG139

Hallam, Elizabeth M. *Chronicles of the age of chivalry*, DC310

—— *Chronicles of the Wars of the Roses*, DC310

—— *Four Gothic kings*, DC310
—— *Plantagenet chronicles*, DC310
—— *The Plantagenet encyclopedia*, DC310
—— *Wars of the Roses*, DC310
Halldórsson, Halldór. *Íslandsk-dansk ordbog*, AC506
Halleron, Trish A. *Learning AIDS*, EH21
Hallewell, L. *Literature with language, art and music*, AD64
Hallewell, Laurence. *Directory of libraries and special collections on Latin America and the West Indies*, AK111
Halley's comet, Freitag, Ruth S., EC11
Hallgarth, Susan A. *DWM : a directory of women's media*, CC549
Halliday, Ernest. *Shakespeare companion*, BE783
Halliday, G. *Consolidated index to Flora Europaea*, EG170
Halliwell, Leslie. *Halliwell's film guide*, BH196
—— *Halliwell's filmgoer's and video viewer's companion*, BH249
—— *Halliwell's television companion*, BH314
Halliwell-Philips, James Orchard. *Dictionary of archaic and provincial words*, AC97
—— *Glossary of words, phrases, names, and allusions in the works of English authors, particularly of Shakespeare and his contemporaries*, AC99
Halliwell's film guide, BH196, BH249
Halliwell's filmgoer's and video viewer's companion, BH220
—— Halliwell, Leslie, BH249
Halliwell's teleguide, BH314
Halliwell's television companion, Halliwell, Leslie, BH314
Hallo, William W. *Essays on ancient Near Eastern literature*, BC184
Halls of fame, BK35
Halls of fame in the United States and Canada, BK32
Halperin, Michael. *International business information*, CH5
Halpern, Jana. *Materiały do bibliografii dziennikarstwa i prasy w Polsce, w latach 1944–1954*, AE67
Halsall, Albert W. *Dictionary of literary devices*, BE78, BE356
Halsbury's laws of England, CK215
Halsbury's statutes of England and Wales, Great Britain. [Laws, etc.], CK214
Halsey, William D. *New Century cyclopedia of names*, AH29, BE209
Halstead, Bruce W. *Poisonous and venomous marine animals of the world*, EG239
Halstead, D. Kent. *Higher education*, CB221
Halstead, John P. *Modern European imperialism*, DC8
Halter, Marilyn. *Cape Verde*, DD48
Haltod, Mattai. *Mongolian-English dictionary*, AC615
Halton, Thomas P. *Classical scholarship*, BE997, DA93
Halverson, Marvin. *Handbook of Christian theology*, BC252
Halvorsen, Jens Braage. *Norsk forfatter-lexikon, 1814–1880*, BE1087, BE1341
Halvorson, Peter L. *Atlas of religious change in America, 1952–1971*, BC85
—— *Atlas of religious change in America, 1971–1980*, BC85
Ham, F. Gerald. *Selecting and appraising archives and manuscripts*, AK188
Hamann, Brigitte. *Die Habsburger*, DC95
Hamarneh, Sami Khalaf. *Pharmacy museums and historical collections on public view in the United States and Canada*, EH367
—— *Pharmacy museums and historical collections on public view, U.S.A*, EH367
Hambly, Wilfrid Dyson. *Bibliography of African anthropology*, CE102
—— *Source book for African anthropology*, CE102
Hambrick, Susan. *Cambridge encyclopedia of Australia*, DF33

Hamburgisches Welt-Wirtschafts-Archiv. *Verzeichnis der Fest- und Denkschriften von Unternehmungen und Organisationen der Wirtschaft im Hamburgisches Welt-Wirtschafts-Archiv*, CH392
Ḥamdān, Muḥammad. *Dalīl al-dawrīyāt al-ṣādirah bi-al-bilād al-Tūnisīyah*, AD181
Hamel, Réginald. *Dictionnaire des auteurs de langue française en Amérique du Nord*, BE841
Hamelin, Jean. *Les journaux de Québec de 1764 à 1964*, AD59
—— *Répertoire des publications gouvernementales du Québec de 1867 à 1964*, AF155
Hamelsdorf, Ora. *The Jewish woman, 1900–1985*, CC597
Hamer, Frank. *The potter's dictionary of materials and techniques*, BG65
Hamer, Janet. *The potter's dictionary of materials and techniques*, BG65
Hamer, Philip M. *Guide to archives and manuscripts in the United States*, CC332, DB30
Hamidou, Sidikou A. *Atlas du Niger*, CL339
Hamilton, Chris J. *Entomology*, EG330
Hamilton, David. *The Metropolitan Opera encyclopedia*, BJ250
—— *Thames and Hudson manual of pottery and ceramics*, BG65
Hamilton, David A. *Ballet plot index*, BH138
—— *Opera plot index*, BJ246
Hamilton, Edith. *Mythology*, CF1
Hamilton, Mary. *A–Z of opera*, BJ247
Hamilton, R. W. *Oxford Bible atlas*, BC200
Hamilton, Robert M. *The dictionary of Canadian quotations and phrases*, BE104
Hamilton, Sheila. *Dictionary of Scottish business biography, 1860–1960*, CH97
Hamilton, Walter. *Parodies of the works of English and American authors*, BE722
Hamilton, William B. *The Macmillan book of Canadian place names*, CL181
Hamilton-Edwards, Gerald Kenneth Savery. *In search of Scottish ancestry*, AJ122
Hamlin, Talbott Faulkner. *American spirit in architecture*, BF256
—— *Architecture through the ages*, BF256
—— *Forms and functions of twentieth-century architecture*, BF256
Hamlyn dictionary of dates and anniversaries, Collison, Robert Lewis, AL143, DA34
The Hamlyn encyclopedia of golf, Morrison, Ian, BK84
Hamm, Charles. *Census-catalogue of manuscript sources of polyphonic music, 1400–1550*, BJ69
Hammacher, A. M. *Evolution of modern sculpture*, BF393
—— *Modern sculpture*, BF393
Hammer, Tad Bentley. *International film prizes*, BH273
Hammerman, Gay M. *People & events of the American Revolution*, DB94
Hammond, Eugene A. *The medical practitioners in medieval England*, EH226
Hammond, George P. *Guide to the manuscript collections of the Bancroft Library*, DB163
Hammond, Muriel E. *British union-catalogue of periodicals*, AD236
Hammond, N. G. L. *Atlas of the Greek and Roman world in antiquity*, DA118
—— *Oxford classical dictionary*, DA103
Hammond, Thomas Taylor. *Soviet foreign relations and world communism*, CJ501
Hammond, William Alexander. *Bibliography of aesthetics and of the philosophy of the fine arts, 1900–1932*, BF29
Hammond atlas of the world, AB26
Hammond Barnhart dictionary of science, EA86
Hammond Inc. *Hammond world atlases*, CL279
Hammond past worlds, DA88
Hammond world atlases, Hammond Inc, CL279
Hamnett, Judith D. *A guide to films about the Pacific Islands*, DF4

Hamp, Eric P. *A glossary of American technical linguistic usage, 1925–1950*, BD39
Hampel, Clifford A. *Encyclopedia of the chemical elements*, EE30
Hample, Henry S. *For more information*, BF39
Hamrick, Lillian A. *A guide to the microfilm collection of early state records*, DB141
Han yü ta tz'u tien, AC253
Han yü ta tz'u tien pien che wei yüan hui. Han yü ta tz'u tien, AC253
Han yü ta tz'u tien pien tsuan ch'u. Han yü ta tz'u tien, AC253
Hanawalt, Emily Albu. *An annotated bibliography of Byzantine sources in English translation*, DA164
Hanayama, Shinsho. *Bibliography on Buddhism*, BC469
Hance, R. J. *The pesticide manual*, EJ61
Hancock, Ian F. *International English usage*, AC86
Hand, Raymond. *NBC handbook of pronunciation*, AC103, AC108
Hand-list of books relating to the classics and classical antiquity, Nairn, John Arbuthnot, BE1004
A hand-list of Irish newspapers, 1685–1750, Munter, Robert LaVerne, AE63
Hand-lists of books printed by London printers, 1501–1556, Bibliographical Society, London, AA666
Handbibliographie der Linguistik in Osteuropa, BD5
Handbibliographie zur neueren Linguistik in Osteuropa, Girke, Wolfgang, BD5
Handbibliographie zur slavistischen und allgemeinen Lingusitik in Osteuropa, BD5
Handboek tot de geschiedenis der Nederlandse letterkunde, Knuvelder, Gerard Petrus Maria, BE1330
Handboek van de Nederlandse pers en publiciteit, AD132, AE65
Handbook and directory of the forest industries, EJ184
Handbook for AACR2 1988 revision, Maxwell, Margaret, AK194
Handbook for academic authors, Luey, Beth, AA321
A handbook for archival research in the USSR, Grimsted, Patricia Kennedy, DC562
Handbook for assessing and treating addictive disorders, CC135
Handbook for auditors, CH259
Handbook for authors of papers in American Chemical Society publications, American Chemical Society, EE95
Handbook for biblical studies, Turner, Nicholas, BC190
Handbook for professional managers, CH622
Handbook for research in American history, Prucha, Francis Paul, DB8
Handbook for research students in the social sciences, CA2
Handbook for vegetable growers, EJ248
Handbook, member churches, BC250
Handbook of abusable drugs, Blum, Kenneth, CC134, EH333
Handbook of accounting and auditing, CH260
Handbook of accoustical measurements and noise control, EK87
Handbook of adolescent psychology, CD84
Handbook of adolescent sexuality and pregnancy, CC168
Handbook of adult and continuing education, CB362
Handbook of adult education, CB362
Handbook of African names, Madubuike, Ihechukwu, AJ174, AJ188
Handbook of aging and the social sciences, CC97
Handbook of air conditioning, heating, and ventilating, EK225
Handbook of American business history, CH396
A handbook of American diplomacy, Sweeney, Jerry K., CJ150
Handbook of American film genres, BH223
Handbook of American folklore, CF77
Handbook of American-Jewish literature, BE565
A handbook of American operatic premières, 1731–1962, Mattfeld, Julius, BJ256

Handbook of American popular culture, BE434, CF78

Handbook of American popular literature, BE434, CF78

Handbook of American resources for African studies, Duignan, Peter, DD36, DD37

Handbook of American sheet music, Dichter, Harry, BJ56

Handbook of American women's history, DB48

Handbook of analytical chemistry, Meites, Louis, ed, EE82

Handbook of applied hydraulics, Davis, Calvin Victor, EK102

Handbook of applied hydrology, Chow, Ven Te, EF137, EF139

Handbook of applied mathematics, Grazda, Edward E., EB64

—— Pearson, Carl E., ed, EB67

Handbook of applied meteorology, EF154

Handbook of applied psycholinguistics, BD79

The handbook of artificial intelligence, EK204

Handbook of biblical criticism, Soulen, Richard N., BC190

Handbook of bibliographies on law in the developing countries, CK16

Handbook of bimolecular and termolecular gas reactions, EE69

Handbook of biochemistry and molecular biology, EG320

Handbook of bioengineering, EH181

A handbook of biological illustration, Zweifel, Frances W., EA223, EG58

Handbook of biomedical engineering, EH182

Handbook of British chronology, DC295

—— Fryde, E. B., BE612

—— Powicke, Frederick Maurice, BE612

The handbook of British regiments, Chant, Christopher, CJ651

Handbook of business information, Strauss, Diane Wheeler, CH334

Handbook of campaign spending, Fritz, Sara, CJ247

Handbook of chemistry, EE77

Handbook of chemistry and physics, EE70, EK279

Handbook of child psychology, CD85

A handbook of Chinese ceramics, Valenstein, Suzanne G., BG79

Handbook of Christian symbols and stories of the saints as illustrated in art, Waters, Clara (Erskine) Clement, BF176

Handbook of Christian theology, Cohen, Arthur A., BC252

—— Halverson, Marvin, BC252

Handbook of church history, Jedin, Hubert, BC277

Handbook of circulation, Altman, Philip L., EG53

A handbook of classical drama, Harsh, Philip Whaley, BE1016, BE1017

Handbook of clinical neurology, EH183

The handbook of clinical psychology, CD104

—— Wolman, Benjamin B., EH395

Handbook of clinical sociology, CC25

Handbook of commercial geography, CL67

Handbook of comparative and development public administration, CJ480

Handbook of concrete engineering, EK105

Handbook of contemporary developments in world sociology, CC26

The handbook of corporate finance, CH234

Handbook of corrosion data, EK275

A handbook of costume, Arnold, Janet, BG104

Handbook of counseling psychology, CD105

Handbook of data on organic compounds, EE149

Handbook of dates for students of English history, Cheney, Christopher Robert, DC295

Handbook of denominations in the United States, Mead, Frank Spencer, BC65

Handbook of developmental psychology, CD86

Handbook of differential equations, Zwillinger, Daniel, EB70, EB71

Handbook of early American sheet music, 1768–1889, Dichter, Harry, BJ56

Handbook of East German drama, 1945–1985, Lederer, Herbert, BE1265

The handbook of economic and financial measures, CH170

Handbook of economic statistics, CH154

Handbook of educational ideas and practices, CB112

Handbook of electronic tables and formulas, EK139

Handbook of Elizabethan and Stuart literature, BE739

Handbook of energy systems engineering, EK218

Handbook of engineering fundamentals, EK16

Handbook of English and Celtic studies in the United Kingdom and Republic of Ireland, BD93

Handbook of environmental data on organic chemicals, Verschueren, Karel, EK83

Handbook of ethological methods, Lehner, Philip N., CD123

Handbook of experimental psychology, Stevens, S. S., CD114

Handbook of family measurement techniques, CC239

Handbook of family violence, CC240

The handbook of financial market indexes, averages, and indicators, Berlin, Howard M., CH232

Handbook of financial markets, CH218

Handbook of financial markets and institutions, CH234

Handbook of first aid & emergency care, EH172

Handbook of fluid dynamics, Streeter, Victor Lyle, ED39

Handbook of food additives, Chemical Rubber Company, EH304

Handbook of food engineering, EJ168

Handbook of food preparation, American Home Economics Association. Food and Nutrition Section, EJ215

Handbook of French popular culture, DC209

Handbook of general psychology, Wolman, Benjamin B., CD41

Handbook of geochemistry, Wedepohl, Karl Hans, EF19

Handbook of geographical nicknames, Sharp, Harold S., CL173

Handbook of geophysics and space environments, United States. Air Force. Geophysics Laboratory, EF155

Handbook of geophysics for Air Force designers, EF155

Handbook of glass properties, Bansal, Narottam P., EK271

Handbook of Greek and Latin palaeography, Thompson, Edward Maunde, AA216, BE1018

A handbook of Greek literature, Rose, Herbert Jennings, BE1032

Handbook of hardwoods, Princes Risborough Laboratory, EJ187

Handbook of highway engineering, Baker, Robert Fulton, EK120

Handbook of human factors, EK228

Handbook of human intelligence, CD112

Handbook of human resources administration, CH719

Handbook of hydrology, EF139

Handbook of industrial and organizational psychology, CD127

Handbook of industrial chemistry, EK58

Handbook of industrial engineering, EK229

Handbook of industrial robotics, EK230

Handbook of industrial toxicology, Plunkett, E. R., EH426

Handbook of infant development, CD87

Handbook of information sources and research strategies in public administration, Rock, Mary G., CJ459

Handbook of instructional resources and references for teaching the gifted, Karnes, Frances A., CB186

Handbook of integration, Zwillinger, Daniel, EB71

Handbook of international economic statistics, CH154

Handbook of international trade, Brooke, Michael, CH137

Handbook of international trade and development statistics, United Nations Conference on Trade and Development, CH160

Handbook of Irish folklore, O'Súilleabháin, Seán, CF81

Handbook of Korea, DE217

Handbook of labor statistics, United States. Bureau of Labor Statistics, CH687

Handbook of laser science and technology, EC49, ED34

A handbook of Latin American & Caribbean national archives, Nauman, Ann Keith, AK130, DB278

Handbook of Latin American art, BF22

Handbook of Latin American literature, BE866

Handbook of Latin American popular culture, DB289

Handbook of Latin American studies, BE874, BF22, CJ307, DB266

A handbook of Latin literature, Rose, Herbert Jennings, BE1048

Handbook of leadership, Stogdill, Ralph Melvin, CD126, CH608

Handbook of legendary and mythological art, Waters, Clara Erskine Clement, BF176

Handbook of life in ancient Rome, Adkins, Lesley, DA98

Handbook of literary research, Miller, R. H., BE2

A handbook of living primates, Napier, John Russell, EG301

Handbook of major Soviet nationalities, CC349

Handbook of marine science, EF223

Handbook of marriage and the family, CC241

Handbook of materials science, EK276

Handbook of mathematical formulas, Bartsch, Hans-Jochen, EB61

Handbook of mathematical functions with formulas, graphs, and mathematical tables, Abramowitz, Milton, EB76

Handbook of mathematical sciences, EB84

Handbook of mathematical tables and formulas, Burington, Richard Stevens, EB63, EB83

Handbook of mathematics, Bronshteĭn, I. N., EB62

Handbook of medical library practice, EH4

Handbook of medicinal herbs, EH342

A handbook of method in cultural anthropology, Naroll, Raoul, CE60

Handbook of Middle American Indians, CE89

Handbook of mineralogy, EF198

Handbook of modern finance, CH235

Handbook of modern history, Gibbons, S. R., DA179

Handbook of modern personnel management, CH719

Handbook of modern sociology, Faris, Robert E. L., CC27

Handbook of monolayers, Mingotaud, Anne-Françoise, EE150

A handbook of music and music literature in sets and series, Charles, Sydney Robinson, BJ10, BJ45

Handbook of national development plans, CH142

The handbook of national population censuses : Africa and Asia, Domschke, Eliane, CG38

Handbook of nations, CL68

Handbook of neurochemistry, EH184

Handbook of noise control, EK87

The handbook of non-violence, Seeley, Robert A., CJ685

Handbook of nonprescription drugs, EH344

Handbook of North American birds, Palmer, Ralph S., EG271

Handbook of North American Indians, CC432

—— Smithsonian Institution, CC419

—— Sturtevant, William C., CC419

Handbook of old-time radio, Swartz, Jon David, BH310

Handbook of optics, ED37

Handbook of organic chemistry, Dean, John Aurie, EE148

Handbook of organizational behavior, CD128

Handbook of paleontological techniques, Kummel, Bernhard, EF247

Handbook of paleozoology, Kuhn-Schnyder, Emil, EF246

Handbook of parapsychology, CD138

Handbook of parliamentary procedure, Davidson, Henry A., CJ453

Handbook of perception and human performance, CD113

Handbook of personality, CD96
Handbook of pesticide toxicology, EJ52
Handbook of philosophical logic, BB36
Handbook of physical calculations, Tuma, Jan J., ED40
Handbook of physical constants, Clark, Sydney P., EF96
Handbook of physical properties of rocks, EF254
Handbook of physics, Condon, Edward Uhler, ED33
Handbook of plastics, elastomers, and composites, EK286
Handbook of poisoning, Dreisbach, Robert Hastings, EH423
Handbook of poisons, EH423
Handbook of political science, Greenstein, Fred I., CJ53
Handbook of political science research on Latin America, CJ307
Handbook of political science research on sub-Saharan Africa, CJ401
Handbook of political science research on the USSR and Eastern Europe, CJ390
Handbook of pottery and porcelain marks, Cushion, John Patrick, BG70
Handbook of private schools, CB107
Handbook of probability and statistics, with tables, Burington, Richard Stevens, EB63, EB83
——— May, Donald Curtis, EB83
A handbook of problem words & phrases, Freeman, Morton S., AC73
Handbook of protein sequence analysis, Croft, L. R., EG317
Handbook of protein sequences, EG317
Handbook of psychobiology, Gazzaniga, Michael S., CD122
Handbook of psychological and educational assessment of children, CD93
Handbook of public administration, CJ481, CJ482
The handbook of qualitative research in education, CB113
Handbook of radar measurement, Barton, David Knox, EK145
Handbook of reactive chemical hazards, EE65
Handbook of reading research, CB114
Handbook of reconstruction in Eastern Europe and the Soviet Union, CJ391
Handbook of research and quantitative methods in psychology, CD64
Handbook of research design and social measurement, Miller, Delbert Charles, CA57
Handbook of research on curriculum, CB115
Handbook of research on educational administration, CB182
Handbook of research on mathematics teaching and learning, Grouws, Douglas A., CB116
——— National Council of Teachers of Mathematics, CB116
Handbook of research on music teaching and learning, Colwell, Richard, CB116
——— Music Educators National Conference, CB116
Handbook of research on social studies teaching and learning, CB116
Handbook of research on teacher education, CB162
Handbook of research on teaching, CB117
Handbook of research on teaching the English language arts, CB118
Handbook of respiration, Altman, Philip L., EG53
Handbook of Russian literature, BE1411
Handbook of school-based interventions, Cohen, Jeffrey J., CB212
The handbook of school psychology, CD94
Handbook of scientific and technical awards in the United States and Canada, 1900–1952, Special Libraries Association. Science-Technology Division, EA197
Handbook of secret organizations, Whalen, William Joseph, AL78
Handbook of semiotics, Nöth, Winfried, BD54
The handbook of skiing, Gamma, Karl, BK96
Handbook of small business data, CH377
Handbook of social and cultural anthropology, Honigmann, John J., CE58

Handbook of social psychology, CD97
——— Aronson, Elliot, CJ53
——— Lindzey, Gardner, CJ53
Handbook of social services for Asian and Pacific islanders, CC404
Handbook of sociology, CC27
Handbook of soils and climate in agriculture, EJ53
Handbook of South American Indians, Steward, Julian Haynes, CE91
Handbook of Soviet and East European films and filmmakers, BH271
Handbook of space astronomy and astrophysics, Zombeck, Martin V., EC58
Handbook of special education, CB204
The handbook of state legislative leaders, CJ272
Handbook of statistics, EB65
Handbook of structural concrete, EK106
Handbook of survey research, CD63
Handbook of symbols in Christian art, Sill, Gertrude Grace, BF182
Handbook of tables for organic compound identification, EE151
Handbook of tables for probability and statistics, EB81
Handbook of the American frontier, Heard, J. Norman, CC433
Handbook of the biology of aging, Rowe, John W., CC97
——— Schneider, Edward L., CC97
Handbook of the birds of Europe, the Middle East and North Africa, EG262
Handbook of the churches, BC324
Handbook of the foreign press, Merrill, John Calhoun, AE141
Handbook of the German exile press, AD101
Handbook of the psychology of aging, Birren, James E., CC97
——— Schaie, K. Warner, CC97
Handbook of the trees of the northern states and Canada east of the Rocky Mountains, Hough, Romeyn Beck, EG195
A handbook of theological terms, Harvey, Van Austin, BC237
Handbook of theoretical computer science, EK205
Handbook of toxic and hazardous chemicals, EH427
Handbook of toxic and hazardous chemicals and carcinogens, Sittig, Marshall, EH427
Handbook of toxicologic pathology, EH425
Handbook of tropical aquarium fishes, Axelrod, Herbert R., EG285
Handbook of United States economic and financial indicators, O'Hara, Frederick M., CH236
Handbook of veterinary procedures & emergency treatment, Kirk, Robert Warren, EJ124
Handbook of vitamins, Machlin, Lawrence J., EH309
Handbook of vocational psychology, CD129
Handbook of world education, CB327
Handbook of world philosophy, BB81
——— Burr, John R., BB10
Handbook of world salt resources, Lefond, Stanley J., EF199
The handbook of world stock and commodity exchanges, CH216
A handbook of wrestling terms and holds, Clayton, Thompson, BK106
Handbook of writing for the mathematical sciences, Higham, N. J., EB98
Handbook on international migration, CC350
A handbook on Old High German literature, Bostock, John Knight, BE1256
Handbook on South Eastern Europe, DC68
Handbook on Soviet drama, Dana, Henry Wadsworth Longfellow, BE1410
Handbook on the international exchange of publications, United Nations Educational, Scientific and Cultural Organization, AK169
Handbook to county bibliography, Humphreys, Arthur Lee, DC349
Handbook to English romanticism, Raimond, Jean, BE759
——— Watson, J. R., BE759
Handbook to literature, Harmon, William, BE83
——— Holman, C. Hugh, BE76, BE83, BE84

Handbook to sixteenth-century rhetoric, Sonnino, Lee A., BE351
Handbooks and tables in science and technology, Powell, Russell H., EA152
Handbooks to the modern world, DE60
Handbuch der Altertumswissenschaft, Müller, I. P. E., DA81
Handbuch der anorganischen Chemie, Gmelin, Leopold, EE110
Handbuch der Archaeologie, DA81
——— Hausmann, Ulrich, DA81
Handbuch der Astrophysik, EC28
Handbuch der Bibliographie, Schneider, Georg, AA9
Handbuch der Bibliographien zum Recht der Entwicklungsländer, Lansky, Ralph, CK15, CK16
Handbuch der bibliographischen Nachschlagewerke, Totok, Wilhelm, AA12
Handbuch der Bibliotheken Bundesrepublik Deutschland, Österreich, Schweiz, AK138
Handbuch der Bibliothekswissenschaft, Milkau, Fritz, AK38
Handbuch der deutschen Exilpresse 1933–1945, Maas, Lieselotte, AD101
Handbuch der deutschen Gegenwartsliteratur, Kunisch, Hermann, BE1248, BE1250
Handbuch der deutschen Geschichte, Gebhardt, Bruno, DC220
Handbuch der deutschen Literaturgeschichte, BE1219
Handbuch der deutschsprachigen ethnologie, Baeck, Godehard, CE99
——— Husmann, Rolf, CE99
Handbuch der Editionen, BE1220
Handbuch der Geschichte der Philosophie, Totok, Wilhelm, BB49
Handbuch der Geschichte Österreich-Ungarns, DC93
Handbuch der Geschichte Österreichs und seiner Nachbarländer Böhmen und Ungarn, Uhlirz, Karl, DC93
Handbuch der internationalen Dokumentation und Information, AK121
Handbuch der Islam-Literatur, Pfannmüller, Gustav, BC498
Handbuch der Kirchengeschichte, BC277
Handbuch der mathematischen und technischen Chronologie, Ginzel, Friedrich Karl, EC87
Handbuch der Monogramme in der europäischen Graphik vom 15. bis zum 18. Jahrhundert, Prein, Wolfgang, BF385
Handbuch der musikalischen Literatur, BJ60, BJ80
Handbuch der organischen Chemie, Beilstein, Friedrich, EA41, ED43, EE18, EE115, EE132
Handbuch der Physik, EC29, ED17
Handbuch der runenkunde, Arntz, Helmut, BE1082
Handbuch der russischen und sowjetischen Bibliographien, AA65
Handbuch der Semiotik, BD54
Handbuch der türkischen Sprachwissenschaft, BD212
Handbuch der Vorgeschichte, Müller-Karpe, Hermann, DA82
Handbuch der Zoologie, EG232
Handbuch des politischen Systems Österreichs, CJ326
Handbuch Österreichs Presse, Werbung, Graphik, AD81
Handbuch über die Literatur, BE187
Handbuch zur Geschichte der Naturwissenschaften und der Technik ..., Darmstaedter, Ludwig, EA251
Handbuch zur Geschichte der Volkswirtschaftslehre, Braeuer, Walter, CH11
Handel's national directory for the performing arts, BH13
Handicapped see **Disabilities and the disabled**
Handicapped funding directory, CC194
Handige woordeboek : Afrikaans-Engels, Kritzinger, Matthys Stefanus Benjamin, AC198
Handke, Kwiryna. *Przewodnik po jezykoznawstwie polskim*, BD193
Handler, Jerome S. *A guide to source materials for the study of Barbados history, 1627–1834*, DB420

—— *Supplement to a guide to source materials for the study of Barbados history, 1627–1834*, DB420
Handley-Taylor, Geoffrey. *Authors of Wales today*, BE812
—— *Bibliography of Monaco*, DC449
Handlin, Oscar. *Harvard guide to American history*, DB13
Handling and management of hazardous materials and wastes, Allegri, Theodore H., EK79
Handlist of music manuscripts acquired 1908–67, British Museum. Department of Manuscripts, BJ93
—— Willetts, Pamela Jean, BJ93
Handlist of newspapers, 1620–1920, AE59
A handlist of rhetorical terms, Lanham, Richard A., BE356
Handloff, Robert E. *Côte d'Ivoire*, DD62
—— *Mauritania*, DD62
Handoo, Jawaharlal. *A bibliography of Indian folk literature*, CF96
Handweaving, Buschman, Isabel, BG158
Handwörterbuch der griechischen Sprache, Passow, Franz, AC445
Handwörterbuch der musikalischen Terminologie, Eggebrecht, Hans Heinrich, BJ148
Handwörterbuch der Raumforschung und Raumordnung, Akademie für Raumforschung und Landesplanung (Germany), BF276
Handwörterbuch der Staatswissenschaften, CH68
Handwörterbuch des deutschen Aberglaubens, Bächtold-Stäubli, Hanns, CF86
Handwoven textiles of South-East Asia, Fraser-Lu, Sylvia, BG158
Handwriting, AA213
The handwriting of English documents, Hector, Leonard Charles, AA214
Handy, Lowell K. *Index to book reviews in religion*, BC52
Handy, R. B. *List by titles of publications of the United States Department of Agriculture from 1840 to June, 1901, inclusive*, EJ85
Handy, Robert T. *History of the churches in the United States and Canada*, BC278
Handy book for genealogists, Everton, George B., AJ1, AJ9
Handy book of rules and tables for verifying dates with the Christian Era, Bond, John James, EC83
Handy dictionary : English-Afrikaans, Kritzinger, Matthys Stefanus Benjamin, AC198
Haney, Wayne S. *Rockabilly*, BJ336
Hanfmann, George M. A. *Classical sculpture*, BF393
Hangin, John G. *A concise English-Mongolian dictionary*, AC613
—— *A modern Mongolian-English dictionary*, AC614
Han'guk sŏmok, AA920
Han'guk t'onggye yŏn'gam, CG406
Han'guk Ūnhaeng. Chosabu. Economic statistics yearbook, CG407
Hanham, Harold John. *Bibliography of British history, 1851–1914*, DC330
Hanhloser, Hans R. *Glossarium artis*, BF84
Hanifi, M. Jamil. *Annotated bibliography of Afghanistan*, DE110
Hanke, Lewis. *Guía de las fuentes en el Archivo General de Indias para el estudio de la administración virreinal española en México y en el Perú, 1535–1700*, DB276
—— *Guía de las fuentes en hispanoamérica para el estudio de la administración virreinal española en México y en el Perú, 1535–1700*, DB276
—— *Guide to the study of United States history outside the U.S., 1945–1980*, DB17
Hanks, Elizabeth Finn. *Bibliography of Australian art*, BF76
Hanks, Patrick. *A dictionary of surnames*, AJ183
Hanle, Adolf. *Meyers grosser Weltatlas*, CL283
Hanlet, Camille. *Les écrivains belges contemporains de langue française, 1800–1946*, BE1101
Hanley, Louise. *An American glossary*, AC153
Hanna, Archibald. *Catalogue of the Frederick W. and Carrie S. Beinecke collection of Western Americana*, DB170

—— *A mirror for the nation*, BE475
Hanna, Ralph. *The index of Middle English prose*, BE733
Hannam, Harry. *The SCOLMA directory of libraries and special collections on Africa in the United Kingdom and Western Europe*, DD41
Hannan, M. *Standard Shona dictionary*, AC716
Hannes, J. *Bibliographie de l'histoire de Belgique*, DC99
Hannesson, Jóhann S. *Ensk-Íslensk orðabók*, AC507
Hannich-Bode, Ingrid. *Die Autobiographien zur deutschen Literatur, Kunst und Musik, 1900–1965*, AH205
—— *Die Autoren und Bücher des literarischen Expressionismus*, BE1230
—— *Germanistik in Festschriften von den Anfängen (1877) bis 1973*, BD112
Hannick, J.-M. *Introduction aux études classiques*, DA91
Hannigan, Francis J. *Standard index of short stories, 1900–1914*, BE262
Hansard's catalogue and breviate, AF198
Hansard's parliamentary debates, AF208
Hanse, Joseph. *Histoire illustrée des lettres françaises de Belgique*, BE1097
—— *Nouveau dictionnaire des difficultés du français moderne*, AC370
Hansel, Johannes. *Bücherkunde für Germanisten*, BE1211
—— *Personalbibliographie zur deutschen Literaturgeschichte*, BE1221
Hansen, Eldon R. *A table of series and products*, EB87
Hansen, Erik. *Bibliografi over moderne dansk rigssprog, 1850–1978*, BD131
Hansen, Gladys C. *The Chinese in California*, CC405
Hansen, Peter. *Illustreret dansk litteraturhistorie*, BE1121
Hansford, S. Howard. *A glossary of Chinese art and archaeology*, BF85
Hanson, Carl A. *Dissertations on Iberian and Latin American history*, DB267, DC510
Hanson, F. Allan. *The art of Oceania*, BG8
Hanson, John Lloyd. *A dictionary of economics and commerce*, CH57
Hanson, Laurence William. *Contemporary printed sources for British and Irish economic history, 1701–1750*, CH187
Hanson, Louise. *The art of Oceania*, BG8
Hanson, Patricia King. *Film review index*, BH244
—— *Magill's bibliography of literary criticism*, BE22
—— *Magill's survey of cinema*, BH239
—— *Sourcebook for the performing arts*, BH17
Hanson, Stephen L. *Film review index*, BH244
—— *Magill's bibliography of literary criticism*, BE22
—— *Magill's survey of cinema*, BH239
—— *Sourcebook for the performing arts*, BH17
Häntzschel, Günter. *Bibliographie der deutschsprachigen Lyrikanthologien, 1840–1914*, BE1272
Hapgood, Isabel Florence. *Service book of the Holy Orthodox-Catholic Apostolic church*, BC450
HAPI, AA24, AD296, BE874, DB266
Hapsburg, House of, DC95
Hapsburg monarchy, 1804–1918, Bridge, F. R., DC95
Harap, Louis. *Handbook of American-Jewish literature*, BE565
Harasztos, Barbara. *Guide to research and scholarship in Hungary*, DC389
Harbage, Alfred. *Annals of English drama, 975–1700*, BE660
Harbert, Earl N. *Fifteen American authors before 1900*, BE404
Harborne, J. B. *Phytochemical dictionary*, EG161
Harbors, CH472
  bibliography, EK101
  handbooks, CH469
Harbottle, Thomas Benfield. *Anthology of classical quotations*, BE144

—— *Dictionary of battles*, DA22
—— *Dictionary of quotations (classical)*, BE144
—— *Dictionary of quotations (French and Italian)*, BE132
—— *Paladin dictionary of battles*, DA22
Harbrace college handbook, BD96
A hard road to glory, Ashe, Arthur, BK12
Harder, Kelsie B. *A dictionary of American proverbs*, BE154
—— *Illustrated dictionary of place names, United States and Canada*, CL176, CL182
Harderwijk, Karel Johan Reinier van. *Biographisch woordenboek der Nederlanden*, AH269
Harding, Keith A. *Venomous snakes of the world*, EG249
Hardison, O. B. *Princeton handbook of poetic terms*, BE329
Hardner, Margaret. *Nigerian women in development*, CC598, DD191
Harduf, David Mendel. *Harduf's transliterated Yiddish-English dictionary*, AC814
—— *Transliterated English-Yiddish dictionary*, AC814
—— *Transliterated Yiddish-English dictionary = Transliterirṭer Yidish-Englisher verṭerbukh*, AC814
Harduf's transliterated Yiddish-English dictionary, Harduf, David Mendel, AC814
Hardwick, Michael. *A literary atlas & gazetteer of the British Isles*, BE628
Hardy, Gayle J. *American women civil rights activists*, CC577
Hardy, Joan E. *Information sources in the earth sciences*, EF2
Hardy, Phil. *Encyclopedia of rock*, BJ345
—— *The Faber companion to 20th-century popular music*, BJ348
—— *Horror*, BH224
—— *Science fiction*, BH224
—— *The Western*, BH224
Hardy, Thomas Duffus. *Fasti ecclesiae Anglicanae*, BC331
Hardy, William John. *Documents illustrative of English church history, comp. from original sources*, BC284
Hare, John. *Dictionnaire des auteurs de langue française en Amérique du Nord*, BE841
Harewood, George Henry Hubert Lascelles. *Kobbé's complete opera book*, BJ237
Hargreaves-Mawdsley, William Norman. *Everyman's dictionary of European writers*, BE202
Harkanyi, Katalin. *The natural sciences and American scientists in the revolutionary era*, EA230
Harkavy, Alexander. *English-Yiddish [Yiddish-English] dictionary*, AC815
—— *Yiddish-English dictionary*, AC815
Harkins, William E. *Dějiny české literatury*, BE1106
Harlem in review, Bassett, John Earl, BE514
The Harlem Renaissance, DB130
—— Kellner, Bruce, BE529
—— Perry, Margaret, BE529
Harlem Renaissance and beyond, Roses, Lorraine Elena, BE529, BE545
Harling, Robert. *Studio dictionary of design and decoration*, BG25
Harlow, Geoffrey. *Early English manuscripts in facsimile*, BE602
Harmon, Lindsey R. *A century of doctorates*, CB342
Harmon, Maurice. *Short history of Anglo-Irish literature from its origins to the present day*, BE803
Harmon, Nolan B. *The encyclopedia of world Methodism*, BC363
Harmon, Robert B. *Elements of bibliography*, AA4
—— *Political science*, CJ1
—— *Political science bibliographies*, CJ14
Harmon, William. *Handbook to literature*, BE83, BE84
Harmonized tariff schedule of the United States, CH155

Harned, Frederic T. *Handbook of major Soviet nationalities*, CC349

Harner, James L. *English Renaissance prose fiction, 1500–1660*, BE676
—— *Literary research guide*, BE393, BE396, BE398, BE400
—— *MLA directory of scholarly presses in language and literature*, BE173

Harnsberger, Caroline Thomas. *Gods and heroes*, CF28

Harper, Charles A. *Handbook of plastics, elastomers, and composites*, EK286

Harper, Howard V. *The Episcopalian's dictionary*, BC345

Harper, J. Russell. *Early painters and engravers in Canada*, BF314
—— *Painting in Canada*, BF314

Harper, Pat Callbeck. *Public opinion polling*, CJ491

Harper & Row, Publishers. *Harper dictionary of contemporary usage*, AC78

Harper & Row's complete field guide to North American wildlife, Collins, Henry Hill, EG82
—— Ransom, Jay Ellis, EG86

The Harper atlas of the Bible, BC199

The Harper atlas of world history, DA54

Harper concise atlas of the Bible, Pritchard, James Bennett, BC199

Harper dictionary of contemporary usage, Morris, William, AC78

Harper dictionary of economics, Pass, Christopher, CH62

The Harper dictionary of foreign terms, Mawson, Christopher Orlando Sylvester, AC187

The Harper dictionary of opera and operetta, Anderson, James, BJ247

The Harper encyclopedia of military biography, Dupuy, Trevor Nevitt, AH26

The Harper encyclopedia of military history, Dupuy, Richard Ernest, DA20

Harper encyclopedia of the modern world, Irwin, Graham W., DA180
—— Morris, Richard B., DA180

Harper handbook to literature, Baker, Sheridan, BE84
—— Frye, Northrop, BE84
—— Perkins, George, BE84

The HarperCollins dictionary of American government and politics, Shafritz, Jay M., CJ122, CJ205

HarperCollins dictionary of art terms and techniques, Mayer, Ralph, BF91

HarperCollins dictionary of astronomy and space science, Moore, Dianne F., EC35

The HarperCollins dictionary of philosophy, Angeles, Peter Adam, BB37

HarperCollins dictionary of sociology, Jary, David, CC19

Harper's Bible commentary, BC172

Harper's Bible dictionary, BC139, BC172

Harper's Bible pronunciation guide, BC140

Harper's dictionary of Hinduism, Stutley, Margaret, BC488

Harper's Latin dictionary, Andrews, Ethan Allen, AC574

Harper's topical concordance, Joy, Charles Rhind, BC157

Harrap's book of film directors and their films, Filmer, Alison J., BH204
—— Golay, Andre, BH204

Harrap's concise German and English dictionary, AC416

Harrap's concise Spanish and English dictionary, AC734

Harrap's diccionario de expresiones idiomáticas, AC745

Harrap's dictionary of idioms : English-Spanish/ Spanish-English, AC745

Harrap's five language business dictionary, CH58

Harrap's French and English science dictionary, EA110

Harrap's standard German and English dictionary, Jones, Trevor, AC421

Harré, Rom. *The dictionary of developmental and educational psychology*, CD82
—— *The dictionary of ethology and animal learning*, CD119
—— *The dictionary of personality and social psychology*, CD95
—— *The dictionary of physiological and clinical psychology*, CD99
—— *The encyclopedic dictionary of psychology*, CD22, CD82, CD95, CD99, CD119

Harriet, Maurice. *Dictionnaire basque-français et français-basque*, AC229

Harrington, Denis J. *The Pro Football Hall of Fame*, BK76

Harrington, Michael. *The guide to government publications in Australia*, AF265

Harrington, Normand. *Bibliographie de la critique de la littérature québécoise dans les revues des XIXe et XXe siécles*, BE838

Harris, Caleb Fiske. *Dictionary catalog of the Harris collection of American poetry and plays, Brown University Library, Providence, Rhode Island*, BE494

Harris, Chauncy Dennison. *Annotated world list of selected current geographical serials*, CL24
—— *Bibliography of geography*, CL12
—— *A geographical bibliography for American libraries*, CL10
—— *Guide to geographical bibliographies and reference works in Russian or on the Soviet Union*, CL13
—— *International list of geographical serials*, CL25
—— *Union list of geographical serials*, CL25

Harris, Cyril M. *Dictionary of architecture & construction*, BF242, BF245
—— *Handbook of accoustical measurements and noise control*, EK87
—— *Historic architecture sourcebook*, BF245
—— *Shock and vibration handbook*, EK246

Harris, D. J. *Multilateral treaties*, CK84

Harris, Diana K. *Dictionary of gerontology*, CC82
—— *Sociology of aging*, CC70

Harris, Eileen. *British architectural books and writers, 1556–1785*, BF216

Harris, Janie Miller. *A bibliographical guide to black studies programs in the United States*, CC364

Harris, John. *Catalogue of British drawings for architecture, decoration, sculpture and landscape gardening*, BF230
—— *Illustrated dictionary of architecture, 800–1914*, BF246

Harris, L. J. *Guide to current Malaysian serials*, AD203

Harris, Laura A. *The real estate industry*, CH530

Harris, Laurie Lanzen. *Characters in 20th-century literature*, BE184
—— *Shakespearean criticism*, BE769
—— *Twentieth-century literary movements index*, BE55

Harris, Lorin E. *International feed descriptions, international feed names, and country feed names*, EJ123

Harris, Marcia. *Black child development in America, 1927–1977*, CC369

Harris, Michael H. *American library history*, AK71
—— *Guide to research in American library history*, AK27

Harris, N. D. C. *Dictionary of instructional technology*, CB173

Harris, Paul. *The New Zealand politics source book*, CJ451

Harris, R. Laird. *Theological wordbook of the Old Testament*, BC151

Harris, Richard Colebrook. *Historical atlas of Canada*, DB207

Harris, Richard Hough. *Modern drama in America and England, 1950–1970*, BE460, BE638

Harris, Seymour Edwin. *A statistical portrait of higher education*, CB340

Harris, Sheldon. *Blues who's who*, BJ354

Harris, Steve. *Film, television, and stage music on phonograph records*, BJ359

Harris, Theodore Lester. *A dictionary of reading and related terms*, CB74

Harris, Wendell V. *Dictionary of concepts in literary criticism and theory*, BE82

The Harris collection of American poetry and plays, BE494

The Harris poll, CJ487

The Harris survey, CJ487

Harrison, Charles Hampton. *Public schools USA*, CB148

Harrison, Elaine P. *Index to reviews, symposia volumes and monographs in organic chemistry*, EE135

Harrison, Frederick W. *Microscopic anatomy of invertebrates*, EG236

Harrison, G. B. *Companion to Shakespeare studies*, BE784

Harrison, Harriet. *Bibliography of national filmographies*, BH164

Harrison, Ira E. *Traditional medicine*, CE12, EH185

Harrison, John P. *Guide to materials on Latin America in the National Archives*, DB280
—— *Guide to materials on Latin America in the National Archives of the United States*, DB280

Harrison, Max. *The essential jazz records*, BJ308

Harrison, R. K. *The new international dictionary of biblical archaeology*, BC195

Harrison, Royden John. *The Warwick guide to British labour periodicals, 1790–1970*, CH655

Harrisse, Henry. *Bibliotheca americana vetustissima*, DB3

Harrod's librarians glossary, AK42

Harrold, Ann. *Academic libraries in the United Kingdom and the Republic of Ireland*, AK140

Harrold, Robert. *Folk costumes of the world in colour*, BG95

Harry Frank Guggenheim Foundation. *The anthropology of war*, CE10

Harryman, Elizabeth. *Terminology of communication disorders*, EH122

Harsh, Philip Whaley. *A handbook of classical drama*, BE1016, BE1017

Hart, Albert B. *Guide to the study and reading of American history*, DB13

Hart, Don Vorhis. *Thailand*, AA83

Hart, E. Richard. *A Zuni atlas*, CC439

Hart, Hester E. R. *Bibliography of the registers (printed) of the universities, inns of court, colleges and schools of Great Britain and Ireland*, AH234

Hart, James David. *Oxford companion to American literature*, BE431, BE435

Hart, Mary L. *The blues*, BJ337

Hartdegen, Stephen J. *Nelson's complete concordance of the New American Bible*, BC162

Harte, John. *Toxics A to Z*, EH428

Harter, H. Leon. *The chronological annotated bibliography of order statistics*, EB9

Hartgrove, J. Dane. *Russia and the United States*, DC559

Hartigan, Maureen. *The history of the Irish in Britain*, DC276

Harting, Emille C. *Literary tour guide to the United States : Northeast*, BE438

Hartley, H. O. *Biometrika tables for statisticians*, EB90
—— *Guide to tables in mathematical statistics*, EB73

Hartley, Janet M. *Guide to documents and manuscripts in the United Kingdom relating to Russia and the Soviet Union*, DC563
—— *Study of Russian history from British archival sources*, DC563

Hartley, Katherine. *Guide to the performing arts*, BH8

Hartley, Loyde H. *Cities and churches*, DB10

Hartley, Robert A. *Keats, Shelley, Byron, Hunt, and their circles*, BE754

Hartman, A. *Repertorium op de literatuur betreffende de Nederlandsche koloniën*, DE175

Hartman, Donald K. *Themes and settings in fiction*, BE253

Hartman, Howard L. *SME mining engineering handbook*, EK254

Hartman, Stephen. *Dictionary of personal finance,* CH213

Hartman, Susan. *How to register a copyright and protect your creative work,* AA312

Hartmann, Benedikt. *Hebräisches und aramäisches Lexikon zum Alten Testament,* AC481, AC482

Hartness, Ann. *Brazil in reference books, 1965–1989,* DB344

Hartnoll, Phyllis. *Concise Oxford companion to the theatre,* BH74

—— *The Oxford companion to the theatre,* BH74

Hartridge, Anne. *Rhodesia national bibliography, 1890 to 1930,* AA886

Hartt, Frederick. *Art : a history of painting, sculpture, architecture,* BF132

Hartung, Albert E. *A manual of the writings in Middle English, 1050–1500,* BE734

Hartwig, D. Scott. *Battle of Antietam and the Maryland Campaign of 1862,* DA170

Harty, F. J. *Concise illustrated dental dictionary,* EH255

Hartzenbusch, Eugenio. *Apuntes para un catálogo de periódicos madrileños desde el año 1661 al 1870,* AE76

Harvard Business School core collection, Baker Library, CH7

Harvard concordance to Shakespeare, Spevack, Marvin, BE776, BE778

Harvard dictionary of music, Apel, Willi, BJ153

Harvard encyclopedia of American ethnic groups, CC342

Harvard guide to American history, Freidel, Frank B., DB13

—— Handlin, Oscar, DB13

The Harvard guide to modern psychiatry, EH394

The Harvard independent insider's guide to prep schools, CB108

Harvard Law Review Association. *The bluebook,* CK66

Harvard Law School. Library. *Annual legal bibliography,* CK11

     The Harvard legal bibliography, 1961–1981, CK11

The Harvard legal bibliography, 1961–1981, Harvard Law School. Library, CK11

The Harvard list of books in psychology, Harvard University, CD10

Harvard list of books on art, Lucas, Edna Louise, BF18

The Harvard outline and reading lists for Oriental art, Rowland, Benjamin, BF35

Harvard Ukrainian Research Institute. *Galicia,* DC35

Harvard University. *The Harvard list of books in psychology,* CD10

Harvard University. Bureau for Economic Research in Latin America. *Economic literature of Latin America,* CH178

Harvard University. East Asian Research Center. *A research guide to China-coast newspapers, 1822–1911,* AE86

Harvard University. Fine Arts Library. *Iconographic index to New Testament subjects represented in photographs and slides of paintings in the visual collections, Fine Arts Library, Harvard University,* BF298

Harvard University. Fine Arts Library. Rübel Asiatic Research Collection. *Catalog of the Rübel Asiatic Research Collection,* BF53

Harvard University. Graduate School of Business Administration. *Harvard Business School core collection,* CH7

Harvard University. Graduate School of Business Administration. Baker Library. *Business biographies and company histories,* CH389

Harvard University. Graduate School of Design. *Catalog of the Avery Memorial Architectural Library of Columbia University,* BF228

Harvard University. Library. *African history and literatures,* BE1509

—— *American literature,* BE406

—— *Ancient Greek literature,* BE1029

—— *Ancient history,* DA65

—— *Archaeology,* DA65

—— *Bibliography and bibliography periodicals,* AA18

—— *Canadian history and literature,* BE825

—— *Catalogue of Hebrew books,* BC537

—— *A catalogue of the fifteenth-century printed books in the Harvard University Library,* AA224

—— *Classical studies,* BE998

—— *Economics and economics periodicals,* CH16

—— *English literature,* BE583

—— *Finnish and Baltic history and literatures,* DC137

—— *French literature,* BE1135

—— *Geography and anthropology,* CE29, CL29

—— *German literature,* BE1222

—— *Hungarian history and literature,* BE1277

—— *Italian history and literature,* BE1294

—— *Judaica,* BC537

—— *The Kilgour collection of Russian literature, 1750–1920,* BE1394

—— *Latin America and Latin American periodicals,* DB270

—— *Latin American literature,* BE875

—— *Latin literature,* BE1039

—— *Literature : general and comparative,* BE15

—— *Periodical classes,* AD10

—— *Philosophy and psychology,* BB6, CD11

—— *Russian history since 1917,* DC585

—— *Twentieth century Russian literature,* BE1395

—— *Widener Library shelflist,* AA115

Harvard University. Museum of Comparative Zoology. Library. *Catalogue,* EG210

Harvard University. Peabody Museum of Archaeology and Ethnology. Library. *Author and subject catalogues of the Tozzer Library,* CE30

Harvard University. Program on Nonviolent Sanctions in Conflict and Defense. *Political terrorism,* CJ554

Harvard University. W.E.B. Du Bois Institute for Afro-American Research. *Black biographical dictionaries, 1790–1950,* AH59

Harvard-Yenching Institute. *A bibliography of eastern Asiatic botany,* EG106

—— *Mathews' Chinese-English dictionary,* AC266

Harvard-Yenching Library. *Chung-kuo shih hsueh lun wên yin tê,* DE139

Harvester/Primary social sources, CJ509

Harvey, Anthony P. *Information sources in the earth sciences,* EF2

Harvey, Cecil. *A list of references for the history of black Americans in agriculture, 1619–1974,* EJ73

Harvey, D. R. *A bibliography of writings about New Zealand music published to the end of 1983,* BJ35

—— *Union list of New Zealand newspapers before 1940,* AE100

Harvey, Joan M. *Statistics Africa,* CG311

—— *Statistics America,* CG71

—— *Statistics Asia & Australasia,* CG376

—— *Statistics Europe,* CG187

—— *Walford's guide to current British periodicals in the humanities and social sciences,* AD117

—— *Walford's guide to reference material,* AA363

Harvey, John Hooper. *English mediaeval architects,* BF261

—— *Sources for the history of houses,* BF206

Harvey, Paul. *The Oxford companion to classical literature,* BE1014

—— *The Oxford companion to English literature,* BE610

—— *The Oxford companion to French literature,* BE1158

Harvey, Richard. *Genealogy for librarians,* AJ19, AJ101

Harvey, Van Austin. *A handbook of theological terms,* BC237

Harwell, Richard Barksdale. *More Confederate imprints,* DB112

Harzig, Christiane. *The immigrant labor press in North America, 1840s–1970s,* CH656

Haschek, Wanda M. *Handbook of toxicologic pathology,* EH425

Hase, Charles Benoît. *Thēsauros tēs hellēnikēs glōssēs,* AC442

Haselbauer, Kathleen J. *A research guide to the health sciences,* EH17

Haselgrove, C. B. *Tables of the Riemann Zeta function,* EB94

Haseltine, Patricia. *East and Southeast Asian material culture in North America,* CC406

Hasen, Hans. *Davis' handbook of applied hydraulics,* EK102

Haskell, Daniel C. *A check list of cumulative indexes to individual periodicals in the New York Public Library,* AD252

—— *Provençal literature and language including the local history of southern France,* BE1373

—— *Union lists of serials,* AD219

Haskins, Arthur L-F. *Manual bibliográfico de cancioneros y romanceros,* BE1478

Haslam, Malcolm. *Marks and monograms of the modern movement, 1875–1930,* BG31

Hassal, Albert. *Index-catalogue of medical and veterinary zoology—authors,* EJ101

Hassan, Hanafi. *3200 revues et journaux arabes de 1800 à 1965,* AD182

Hasse, H. *Encyklopädie der mathematischen Wissenschaften mit Einschluss ihrer Anwendungen,* EB36

Hastings, James. *Dictionary of Christ and the Gospels,* BC128

—— *Dictionary of the Bible,* BC141

—— *Encyclopaedia of religion and ethics,* BC55, BC58

Hastings, Max. *Oxford book of military anecdotes,* CJ591

Hastings Center. Institute of Society, Ethics, and the Life Sciences. *Bibliography of bioethics,* EH237

Hatch, James Vernon. *Black image on the American stage,* BE520, BH109

—— *Black playwrights, 1823–1977,* BE521, BE530

Hatch, Jane M. *The American book of days,* AL147

Hatch, Warren L. *Selective guide to climatic data sources,* EF162

Hatcher, John. *History of British pewter,* BG150

Hatchett, Marion. *Commentary on the American prayer book,* BC347

Hate crimes, CC357

Hategekimana, Grégoire. *Bibliographie annotée sur la population du Rwanda,* CG352, DD197

—— *Recueil des études et ouvrages ayant trait à la femme rwandaise,* DD199

—— *Sources bibliographiques des états de l'ancien domaine colonial belge d'Afrique centrale,* DD111

Hatfield, Debora. *Survey of materials for the study of uncommonly taught languages,* BD71

Hathorn, Richmond Yancey. *Crowell's handbook of classical drama,* BE1017

Hathway, D. E. *Harrap's French and English science dictionary,* EA110

Hatin, Louis Eugène. *Bibliographie historique et critique de la presse périodique française,* AD92, AD95, AE50

Hatje, Gerd. *Encyclopaedia of 20th-century architecture,* BF233

—— *Knaurs Lexikon der modernen Architektur,* BF233

Hatje-Lexikon der Architaektur des 20. Jahrhunderts, BF233

Hattaway, Michael. *The Cambridge companion to English Renaissance drama,* BE659

Hatten tojō koku no tōkei shiryō mokuroku, CG8

Hatzfeld, Adolphe. *Dictionnaire général de la langue française,* AC330

Hatzfeld, Helmut. *Bibliografía crítica de la nueva estilística, aplicada a las literaturas románicas,* BE1072

—— *Critical bibliography of the new stylistics applied to the Romance languages,* BE1072

—— *Essai de bibliographie critique de stylistique française et romane (1955–1960),* BE1072

Hatzfeld, Herta. *Catholic serials of the nineteenth century in the United States*, AD227

Haubrich, William S. *Medical meanings*, EH116

Hauck, Albert. *Realencyklopädie für protestantische Theologie und Kirche*, BC67, BC69

Hauck, Eldon. *American capitols*, BF248

Hauck, Philomena. *Sourcebook on Canadian women*, CC603

Hauff, Nils Selmer. *Stikords-katalog over norsk literatur, 1883–1907*, AA758

Haugen, Einar. *A bibliography of Scandinavian languages and linguistics, 1900–1970*, BD130
——— *A history of Norwegian literature*, BE1338
——— *Norwegian English dictionary*, AC621

Haugen, Eva Lund. *A bibliography of Scandinavian dictionaries*, AC190

Haugse, Vera Lucia Oliveira de Araujo. *Education in Latin America*, CB43

Haukaas, Kaare. *Norwegian literary biography, 1956–1970*, BE1343

Haun, Harry. *The movie quote book*, BH262

Haupenthal, Reinhard. *Bibliografio de internacia lingvo*, BD50

Haupt, Arthur. *The Population Reference Bureau's population handbook*, CG39

Hausa language *see* Xhosa language

Hauschild-Thiessen, R. *Füher durch die Quellen zur Geschichte Lateinamerikas in der Bundesrepubulic Deutschland*, DB275

Hauser, Arnold. *The social history of art*, BF130

Hausmann, Ulrich. *Handbuch der Archaeologie*, DA81

Haussig, Hans Wilhelm. *Wörterbuch der Mythologie*, CF10

Hauswedell, Marianne H. *An annotated guide to Philippine serials*, AD208

Havel, Rudolf. *Slovník českých spisovatelů*, BE1105

Havers, Wilhelm. *Indogermanische Chronik*, BD201

Havighurst, Alfred F. *Modern England, 1901–1984*, DC303, DC331

Havlice, Patricia Pate. *And so to bed*, BE507, BE726, DB66
——— *Earth scale art*, BF136
——— *Index to American author bibliographies*, BE476, BE495
——— *Index to artistic biography*, BF136
——— *Popular song index*, BJ285

Hawaii, CC408

Hawaii. [Laws, etc.]. *Hawaii revised statutes annotated*, CK179

Hawaii revised statutes annotated, Hawaii. [Laws, etc.], CK179

Hawaiian dictionary, Pukui, Mary Kawena, AC469

Hawaiian language
dictionaries
bilingual
English and Hawaiian, AC469

Hawaiians, CC325

The Hawaiians, Kittelson, David J., CC325

Hawbaker, A. Craig. *Industry and company information*, CH330

Hawelek, Alice. *Periodica chemica*, EE19

Hawes, Joseph M. *American families*, CC234
——— *Children in historical and comparative perspective*, CC166

Hawkesworth, M. E. *Encyclopedia of government and politics*, CJ52

Hawkins, Joyce. *The Oxford encyclopedic English dictionary*, AC40

Hawkins, Walter L. *African American biographies*, CC397
——— *African American generals and flag officers*, CJ643

Hawkins-Dady, Mark. *International dictionary of theatre*, BH71

Hawks, eagles & falcons of North America, Johnsgard, Paul A., EG266

Hawley, Gessner Goodrich. *Hawley's condensed chemical dictionary*, EE41

Hawley's condensed chemical dictionary, EE41

Hawthorn, Jeremy. *A glossary of contemporary literary theory*, BE83

Hawtrey, Stephen Charles. *Abraham and Hawtrey's parliamentary dictionary*, CJ352

Hay, Michael. *The strategy handbook*, CH613

Hay, Oliver Perry. *Bibliography and catalogue of the fossil vertebrata of North America*, EF230, EF233
——— *Second bibliography and catalogue of fossil vertebrata of North America*, EF230

Hay, Roy. *The color dictionary of flowers and plants for home and garden*, EG175

Hay, Tony. *A guide to European financial centres*, CH276

Hayakawa, Samuel Ichiyé. *Funk & Wagnalls modern guide to synonyms and related words*, AC139

Haycraft, Howard. *American authors, 1600–1900*, BE449
——— *British authors before 1800*, BE624
——— *British authors of the 19th century*, BE625
——— *The junior book of authors*, BE384
——— *Twentieth century authors*, BE205

Haydn, Hiram. *Thesaurus of book digests*, BE193

Haydn, Joseph Timothy. *The book of dignities ...* , AJ155
——— *Dictionary of dates and universal information relating to all ages and nations*, DA33

Hayes, George D. *Food engineering data handbook*, EJ169

Hayes, Grace P. *Dictionary of military terms*, CJ585

Hayes, Gregory. *Going places*, CL390

Hayes, Nicky. *A student's dictionary of psychology*, CD31, CD32

Hayes, Richard J. *Manuscript sources for the history of Irish civilisation*, DC403
——— *Sources for the history of Irish civilisation*, DC394

Hayes, Wayland J. *Handbook of pesticide toxicology*, EJ52

The Haymarket affair, Glenn, Robert W., DB99

Hayne, David M. *Bibliographie critique du roman canadien-français, 1837–1900*, BE842

Haynes, John Earl. *Communism and anti-communism in the United States*, CJ502

Haynes, Williams. *American chemical industry*, EE96

Hayoz, Chantal. *Bibliographie analytique des revues littéraires de Suisse romande*, BE1489

Haythornthwaite, J. A. *Scotland in the nineteenth century*, DC359

Haythornthwaite, Philip J. *The Napoleonic source book*, DC196

Hayward, Arthur Lawrence. *Cassell's Italian-English, English-Italian dictionary*, AC528

Hayward, Diane. *The official encyclopedia of bridge*, BK130

Haywood, Charles. *Bibliography of North American folklore and folksong*, CF64, CF67
——— *A Shakespeare music catalogue*, BJ71

Hayyim, Sulaymān. *The larger English-Persian dictionary*, AC314
——— *New Persian-English dictionary*, AC314
——— *Shorter Persian-English dictionary*, AC314

Hazael-Massieux, Marie-Christine. *Bibliographie des études créoles languages et littétures*, BD55

Hazai, György. *Bibliographisches Handbuch der Turkologie*, BD211, DE31
——— *Handbuch der türkischen Sprachwissenschaft*, BD212
——— *Sovietico Turcica*, BD210

Hazard, Marshall Custiss. *A complete concordance to the American Standard Version of the Holy Bible*, BC160

Hazard, Paul. *Littérature française*, BE1167

Hazardous chemical desk reference, Lewis, Richard J., EE79

Hazardous substances, EE65, EE71, EE75, EE78, EE79, EE80, EE88, EK79
bibliography, EH419
compendiums, EE67
dictionaries, EE72
handbooks, EH427

Hazards in the chemical laboratory, EE75

Hazell's guide to the judiciary and the courts, with the Holborn Law Society's bar list, CK216

Hazen, Edith P. *Columbia Granger's dictionary to poetry quotations*, BE315
——— *The Columbia Granger's index to poetry*, BE315

Hazen, Margaret H. *American geological literature, 1669 to 1850*, EF32

Hazen, Robert M. *American geological literature, 1669 to 1850*, EF32

Hazewinkel, Michiel. *Encyclopaedia of mathematics*, EB33

Hazlep, William L. *Atlas of Central America*, CL312

Hazon, Mario. *Il nuovo dizionario Hazon Garzanti*, AC532

HCIA directory of health care professionals, EH155

Headicar, Bertie Mason. *London bibliography of the social sciences*, CA13

Headlam, Freya. *Intercontinental migration to Latin America*, CC309

Headland, Robert. *Chronological list of Antarctic expeditions and related historical events*, DG9

Headley, Robert K. *Cambodian-English dictionary*, AC562

Heads of state, CJ65, CJ70, CJ78, CJ84, CJ91, CJ318
biography, CC578
directories, CJ82, CJ83
genealogy, AJ76
registers, CJ83

Heads of state (by country or region)
Africa, CJ402
registers, CJ398
France, AH199

Heads of state and government, Da Graça, John V., CJ84

Heady, Ferrel. *Comparative public administration*, CJ467

Heal, Ambrose. *London furniture makers from the Restoration to the Victorian era, 1660–1840*, BG135
——— *London goldsmiths, 1200–1800*, BG140

Healey, Antonette. *Dictionary of Old English*, AC172

•*HEALTH*, EH77

Health affairs information guide series, EH18

Health aspects of pesticides, EH420

Health care
abstract journals, EH69, EH76
bibliography, EH18, EH402
databases, EH75
dictionaries, EH115, EH125
directories, EH153
guides, EH402
handbooks, EH179, EH416
indexes, EH74, EH77, EH274
statistics, CG100, EH232, EH406
compendiums, EH234

Health care (by country or region)
United States
states, EH414

The health care data source book, Fry, John D., EH179

Health care state rankings, EH414

Health care terms, Slee, Vergil N., EH125

Health information for international travel, EH415

Health Insurance Association of America. *Source book of health insurance data*, CH527

Health Insurance Institute (New York, N.Y.). *Source book of health insurance data*, CH527

Health media review index, EH43

Health of black Americans from post reconstruction to integration, 1871–1960, Rice, Mitchell F., EH405

Health planning and administration, EH36, EH72, EH75, EH77, EH276

Health-related cookbooks, Shih, Tian-Chu, EH294, EJ223

Health science books, 1876–1982, EH19

Health sciences *see* Medicine

Health service abstracts, EH76

Health services, EH402

Health statistics, Weise, Frieda O., EH235

Health statistics report (Wellington, N.Z.), CG440

Health, United States, EH232

Heaney, Henry J. *Buttress's world guide to abbreviations of organizations,* AL14

Heard, Alexander. *Southern primaries and elections, 1920–1949,* CJ290

Heard, J. Norman. *Bookman's guide to Americana,* AA240

—— *Handbook of the American frontier,* CC433

Heard Museum. Library. *Native American artists directory,* BF318

Heat bibliography, EK226

Heat wave, Bianco, David, BJ352

Heater, Derek. *Atlas of modern world history,* DA189

Heath, Dwight B. *Alcohol use and world cultures,* CC113

Heath, Henry B. *Source book of flavors,* EJ217

Heath, Jeffrey. *Profiles in Canadian literature,* BE819

Heath, Trudy. *American periodicals, 1741–1900,* AD36, AD272

—— *Index to American periodicals of the 1700's and 1800's,* AD273

The Heath anthology of American literature, BE332, BE441, BE506, BE555

Heating and refrigeration
  bibliography, EK226, EK227
  handbooks, EK224, EK225

Heaton, Tim B. *Statistical handbook on the American family,* CG107

Hebáková, Olga. *Historická statistická ročenka ČSSR,* CG206

Hebel, Udo J. *Intertextuality, allusion, and quotation,* BE16

Hébert, John R. *Panoramic maps of cities in the United States and Canada,* CL234

Heberth, Alfred. *Neue Wörter,* AC436

Hebräisch-deutsches Handwörterbuch, Gesenius, Wilhelm, AC476

Hebräisches und aramäisches Handwörterbuch über das Alte Testament ... , Gesenius, Friedrich Heinrich Wilhelm, AC477

Hebräisches und aramäisches Lexikon zum Alten Testament, Baumgartner, Walter, AC482

—— Hartmann, Benedikt, AC482

—— Koehler, Ludwig Hugo, AC481

—— Kutscher, E. Y., AC482

Hebrew and English lexicon, AC476

Hebrew-character title catalog of the Jewish collection, New York Public Library. Research Libraries, BC540

Hebrew language, BD206
  bibliography, BD207
  dictionaries, AC470, AC471, AC472, AC475, BC134
    bilingual, AC478, AC484
      English-Hebrew, AC480
      Hebrew-English, AC473, AC474, AC476, AC479, AC481, AC483
      Hebrew-German, AC477, AC481
    multilingual, AC482

Hebrew literature, BE1578
  bibliography, BE1575
  translations, BE1576

Hebrew literature (by subject)
  history, BE1577
  see also **Yiddish literature**

Hebrew Union College—Jewish Institute of Religion. American Jewish Archives. *Guide to the holdings of the American Jewish Archives,* BC538

Hebrew Union College—Jewish Institute of Religion. American Jewish Periodical Center. *Jewish newspapers and periodicals on microfilm available at the American Jewish Periodical Center,* AD11

Hebrew Union College—Jewish Institute of Religion. Center for the Study of the American Jewish Experience. *Judaica Americana,* BC525

Hebrew Union College—Jewish Institute of Religion. Library. *Dictionary catalog of the Klau Library, Cincinnati,* BC539

Hebrew University. *2000 books and more,* BC515

Hebrew University. Museum of Jewish Antiquities. *Encyclopaedia biblica,* BC129

Hébridais, O'Reilly, Patrick, AH383, DF52

Hecht, Ann. *Pre-cinema history,* BH166

Hecht, Hermann. *Pre-cinema history,* BH166

Hecimovich, James. *Annotated bibliography and index covering CPL bibliographies,* BF271

Heck, André. *Acronyms & abbreviations in astronomy, space sciences, & related fields,* EC33

Heck, Jean Louis. *Finance literature index,* CH225

Heck, Thomas F. *Commedia dell'arte,* BE1315

Hecker, Helen. *Travel for the disabled,* CL384

Heckethorn, Charles William. *The secret societies of all ages and countries ... ,* AL74

Hector, Leonard Charles. *The handwriting of English documents,* AA214

Hedberg, Hollis D. *International stratigraphic guide,* EF95

Hedges, Jane T. *Dictionary of Russian literature since 1917,* BE1412

Hedlund, Mary F. *Atlas of the early Christian world,* BC290

Heestermans, Hans. *Groot woordenboek der Nederlandse taal,* AC292

Hefele, Bernhard. *Drogenbibliographie,* EH321

—— *Jazz-bibliography,* BJ302

Heffron, Mary J. *Africa,* DD93

—— *Asia and Pacific,* DE17

—— *Food, hunger, agribusiness,* EJ161

—— *Middle East,* DE21

—— *Third World resource directory,* DD93, DE17, DE21

—— *Third World resource directory, 1994–1995,* DA11

—— *Third World struggle for peace with justice,* CJ669

—— *Transnational corporations and labor,* CH666

—— *Women in the Third World,* CC600

Heflin, Woodford Agee. *The United States Air Force dictionary,* CJ615

Hegel, Georg Wilhelm Friedrich, BB79

Hegel bibliography, Steinhauer, Kurt, BB79

Hegel-Lexikon, Glockner, Herman, BB79

Heggie, Grace F. *Canadian periodicals index, 1920–1937,* AD293

—— *Canadian political parties, 1867–1968,* CJ300

Heggoy, A. Algeria, DD48

Heggoy, Alf Andrew. *The military in imperial history,* DC145

Heginbotham, Erland. *Focus Japan II,* AL43, DE210

Heibonsha dai-hyakka jiten, AB70

Heidegger, Martin, BB82

Heidelberger Akademie der Wissenschaften. *Diccionario del español medieval,* AC750

Heider, Karl G. *Films for anthropological teaching,* CE33

Heidtmann, Frank. *Bibliographie der Photographie deutschsprachige Publikationen der Jahre 1839–1984,* BF329

Heikinheimo, Ilmari. *Suomen elämäkerrasto,* AH187

Heikkilä, Marjatta. *Suomen tieteellisten Kirjastojen opas,* AK134

Heilbron, J. L. *Literature on the history of physics in the 20th century,* ED52, ED53

•HEILBRON, EE109, EE121, EE123, EE124, EE125, EE126, EE127, EE128, EE129, EE133, EH334, EH335, EH336

Heilig, Gerhard. *The population of Indonesia,* CG392

Heilinger, Rudolf. *Bibliographie österreichischer Bibliographien, Sammelbiographien und Nachschlagewerke,* AA36

—— *Personalbibliographien österreichischer Dichter und Schriftsteller,* BE1096

Heim, Kathleen M. *On account of sex,* AK14, AK73

—— *The role of women in librarianship, 1876–1976,* AK73

Heimpel, Hermann. *Dahlmann-Waitz Quellenkunde der deutschen Geschichte,* DC215

—— *Die grossen Deutschen,* AH208

Heine, Heinrich, BJ75

Heine in der Musik, Metzner, Günter, BJ75

Heinekamp, Albert. *Leibniz-Bibliographie,* BB75

Heinemann, W. W. *Feeds & nutrition,* EJ122

Heinemann dental dictionary, Fairpo, Jenifer E. H., EH253

Heinemann modern dictionary for dental students, EH253

Heinl, Robert. *Dictionary of military and naval quotations,* CJ591

Heinl, Robert Debs. *The Marine officer's guide,* CJ631

Heinrich, Amy Vladeck. *A guide to Oriental classics,* BE1543

Hein's United States treaties and other international agreements—current microfiche service, CK92

•*Hein's United States treaty index on CD-ROM,* CK96

Heinsius, Wilhelm. *Allgemeines Bücher-Lexikon,* AA644, AA646

Heintschel, Donald E. *The code of canon law,* CK238

Heintz, William F. *The Chinese in California,* CC405

Heintze, James R. *American music studies,* BJ36

—— *Early American music,* BJ36

Heinzel, E. *Lexikon historischer Ereignisse und Personen in Kunst, Literatur und Musik,* AH27

—— *Die Weltliteratur,* BE72

Heise, Jon O. *Travel guidebooks in review,* CL392

Heisley, Michael. *An annotated bibliography of Chicano folklore from the Southwestern United States,* CF68

Heissig, Walther. *Geschichte der mongolischen Literatur,* BE1597

Heister, Rolf. *Dictionary of abbreviations in medical sciences,* EH131

Heitman, Francis Bernard. *Historical register and dictionary of the United States Army from its organization, Sept. 29, 1789, to March 2, 1903,* CJ644, CJ646

—— *Historical register of officers of the Continental Army during the war of the Revolution, April 1775 to Dec. 1783,* CJ645

Heizer, Robert Fleming. *Archaeology,* DA60

Hejzlar, Zdeněk. *Czechoslovakia, 1968–1969,* DC123

Helander, Brock. *The rock who's who,* BJ342

Helbig, Alethea. *Dictionary of American children's fiction, 1859–1959,* BE382

—— *Dictionary of British children's fiction,* BE383

—— *The Phoenix Award of the Children's Literature Association, 1985–1989,* BE388

Helck, Wolfgang. *Lexikon der Ägyptologie,* DA125

Held, John. *Mail art,* BF360

Heldman, Dennis R. *Handbook of food engineering,* EJ168

Heleniak, Timothy E. *Bibliography of Soviet statistical handbooks, 1956 to 1991,* CG300

Helfenstein, Ulrich. *Bibliographie internationale des travaux historiques publiés dans les volumes de "Mélanges",* DA6

Helferty, Seamus. *Directory of Irish archives,* AJ133, DC400

Hélias, Pierre Jakez. *Dictionnaire breton,* AC234

Hellebust, Lynn. *State reference publications,* AF146, CJ284

Hellemans, Alexander. *The timetables of science,* EA252, EA254

—— *The timetables of technology,* EA250

Hellēnikē bibliographia, Politēs, Nikolaos G., AA705

Hellēnikē bibliographia, 1800–1863, Gkinēs, Dēmētrios S., AA701

Hellēnikē vivliographia, AA708

—— Ladas, Geōrgios G., AA702

—— Papadopoulos, Thōmas I., AA704

Heller, Joseph. *Annalen der ältern deutschen Litteratur,* AA639

Heller, Robert L. *Geology and earth sciences sourcebook for elementary and secondary schools,* EF94

Hellman, Ronald G. *Tinker guide to Latin American and Caribbean policy and scholarly resources in metropolitan New York,* DB288

Hellner, Nancy. *Gay and lesbian American plays*, BE458

Hellquist, Elof. *Svensk etymologisk ordbok*, AC770

Hellwege, K. H. *Landolt-Börnstein Zahlenwerte und Funktionen aus Naturwissenschaften und Technik*, EA155

Hellwig, Gerhard. *Daten zu deutschen Geschichte*, DC223

Helmcke, J. G. *Handbuch der Zoologie*, EG232

Helminthological abstracts, EJ19

Helmstadter, Sarah. *Dictionary of political parties and organizations in Russia*, CJ386

Helps for students of history, DC353

Helsingin yliopisto. Kehitysmaainstituutti. *Rural development in Tanzania*, DD236

Helt, Marie E. *West German cinema, 1985–1990*, BH187

—— *West German cinema since 1945*, BH187

Helt, Richard C. *West German cinema, 1985–1990*, BH187

—— *West German cinema since 1945*, BH187

Heltzel, Virgil B. *A check list of courtesy books in the Newberry Library*, AL151

Hemerografía venezolana, 1890–1930, Hirshbein, Cesia Ziona, BE963

Hemeroteca Municipal de Madrid. *Catálogo de las publicaciones periódicas madrileñas existentes en la Hemeroteca Municipal de Madrid, 1661–1930*, AD154, AE76

Hemon, Roparz. *Dictionnaire historique du breton*, AC237

—— *Geriadur istorel ar brezhoneg*, AC237

Henchy, Judith A. N. *Laos*, DE222, DE223

Henchy, Monica. *Writings on Irish history*, DC399

Henderson, D. M. *International directory of botanical gardens*, EG146

Henderson, David, R. *The Fortune encyclopedia of economics*, CH50

Henderson, Francine I. *Botswana's environment*, DD130

—— *A guide to periodical articles about Botswana, 1965–80*, DD130

—— *Women in Botswana*, DD122, DD171

Henderson, G. N. *The international encyclopedia of cats*, EJ139

Henderson, George Fletcher. *Federal royal commissions in Canada, 1867–1966*, AF151

Henderson, George P. *Current European directories*, AL5

Henderson, Helene. *Science tracer bullets*, EA35

—— *Twentieth-century literary movements index*, BE55

Henderson, Isabella Ferguson. *Henderson's dictionary of biological terms*, EG43

Henderson, Lesley. *Contemporary novelists*, BE212, BE252

—— *Twentieth-century crime and mystery writers*, BE275

—— *Twentieth-century romance and historical writers*, BE212, BE249

Henderson, Richard. *Encyclopedia of sailing*, BK122

Henderson, Virginia. *Nursing studies index*, EH278

Henderson's dictionary of biological terms, Henderson, Isabella Ferguson, EG43

—— Lawrence, Eleanor, EG43

Hendrick, George. *The American novel*, BE473

—— *Fourth directory of periodicals publishing articles on English and American literature and language*, BE170

Hendrickson, Robert. *The Facts on File encyclopedia of word and phrase origins*, AC54

—— *Human words*, AC55

Hendrickx, Jean-Pierre. *Répertoire des mémoires de licence et des thèses de doctorat présentés dans les départements d'histoire contemporaine des universités belges*, DC105

Hendriksen, Hans. *A critical Pali dictionary*, AC626

Hendrix, Melvin K. *An international bibliography of African lexicons*, AC191

Hendry, Robert S. *Atlas of the Philippines*, CL362

Henig, Stanley. *European political parties*, CJ320

—— *Political parties in the European Community*, CJ320

Henige, David P. *Colonial governors from the fifteenth century to the present*, CJ85

—— *Serial bibliographies and abstracts in history*, DA13

—— *Works in African history*, DD47

Heninger, S. K. *English prose, prose fiction, and criticism to 1660*, BE738

Henke, James T. *Gutter life and language in the early "street" literature of England*, AC124

Henkel, Arthur. *Emblemata*, BF168

Henle, Richard A. *Desktop computers*, EK206

Henley, Nancy. *Language and sex*, BD82

—— *Language, gender, and society*, BD82, BD84, CC495

—— *She said / he said*, BD82

Henley, William Ernest. *Slang and its analogues, past and present*, AC122

Henley's twentieth century book of formulas, processes and trade secrets, Hiscox, Gardner Dexter, EA278

Henne, Helmut. *Deutsches Wörterbuch*, AC407

—— *Lexikon der Germanistischen Linguistik*, BD124

Hennessee, Don A. *Nineteenth-century American drama*, BE464, BE640

—— *Women in music*, BJ222

Henning, Charles. *Wit and wisdom of politics*, CJ45

Henning, Eckart. *Bibliographie Friedrich der Grosse, 1786–1986*, DC234

—— *Bibliographie zur Heraldik*, AJ156

—— *Taschenbuch für Familiengeschichtsforschung*, AJ95

Henning, Herzeleide. *Bibliographie Friedrich der Grosse, 1786–1986*, DC234

Henrion, R. *Collectio bibliographica operum ad ius romanum pertinentium*, BE1037

Henry, Carl F. H. *Baker's dictionary of Christian ethics*, BC241

Henry, Dawn. *DWM : a directory of women's media*, CC549

Henry E. Huntington Library and Art Gallery. *American imprints, 1648–1797, in the Huntington Library, supplementing Evans' American bibliography*, AA407

—— *Catalogue of books relating to the discovery and early history of North and South America*, DB2

—— *Catalogue of the Larpent plays in the Huntington Library*, BE644

—— *Guide to literary manuscripts in the Huntington Library*, BE429

Henry Francis du Pont Winterthur Museum. *The Edward Deming Andrews Memorial Shaker Collection*, BC381

Henry Francis du Pont Winterthur Museum. Libraries. *The Winterthur Museum Libraries collection of printed books and periodicals*, BG16

Henry Harrissee, Sanz, Carlos, DB3

Henry Holt encyclopedia of word and phrase origins, AC54

Henry Sweet Society for the History of Linguistic Ideas. *Renaissance linguistics archive, 1350–1700*, BD67

Henschel, G. A. Louis. *Glossarium mediae et infimae latinitatis*, AC587

Henschenius, Godefridus. *Acta sanctorum quotquot toto orbe coluntur*, BC257

Henshaw, Richard. *The world encyclopedia of soccer*, BK98

Henslin, James M. *Homelessness*, CC201

HEP higher education directory, CB272

Hepple, B. A. *A bibliography of the literature on British and Irish labour law*, CH677

—— *Labour law in Great Britain and Ireland to 1978*, CH677

Heppner, Irene. *Bibliography on portraiture*, BF23

Hepworth, Philip. *Select biographical sources*, AH235

Hérail, René James. *Dictionary of modern colloquial French*, AC357

Herald, Earl Stannard. *Living fishes of the world*, EG287

An heraldic alphabet, Brooke-Little, John Philip, AJ162

Heraldry, AJ147, AJ148, AJ149, AJ151, AJ152, AJ153, AJ154, AJ157, AJ158, AJ159, AJ160, AJ161

bibliography, AJ156

dictionaries, AJ162, AJ163, AJ164, BF81

multilingual, AJ165

Heraldry of the royal families of Europe, AJ159

Heralds of promise, Meserve, Walter J., BE466

Héraucourt, Will. *The new Wildhagen German dictionary*, AC424

Herbert, Arthur Sumner. *Historical catalogue of printed editions of the English Bible, 1525–1961*, BC95, BC97, BC100

Herbert, J. A. *Catalogue of romances in the Department of Manuscripts in the British Museum*, BE335

Herbert, Jean. *Bibliographie du Shintô et des sectes shintôistes*, BC568

Herbert, Miranda C. *Biography and genealogy master index*, AH9

—— *Performing arts biography master index*, BH28

Herbert, P. A. *Chinese studies research methodology*, DE125

Herbert, Patricia. *South-East Asia*, BD229, BD236, BE1550

Herbert, Patricia M. *Burma*, DE121

Herbert, W. J. *Dictionary of immunology*, EG33

Herbs, EG110, EH342, EH350

bibliography, EH319

encyclopedias, EJ234

Herbs, Simon, James E., EG110

Herbst, Robert. *Dictionary of commercial, financial and legal terms*, CK44

Herczeg, Claire. *Anarchism*, CJ506

Herdeck, Donald E. *African authors*, BE1511

—— *Caribbean writers*, BE969

Herders Konversationslexikon, AB50

Heredia y Livermore, Ricardo. *Catalogue de la bibliothèque de M. Ricardo Heredia*, AA802, AA805

Herescu, Niculae I. *Bibliographie de la littérature latine*, BE1040

Heresy, BC210

Hergenham, Laurie. *Penguin new literary history of Australia*, BE854

Hergenhan, Laurie. *ALS guide to Australian writers, 1963–90*, BE847

The heritage encyclopedia of band music, Rehrig, William H., BJ294

Herland, Leo Joseph. *Dictionary of mathematical sciences*, EB50

Herman, Kali. *Women in particular*, AH90

Herman, Lewis. *American dialects*, BH91

—— *Foreign dialects*, BH91

Herman, Marguerite Shalett. *American dialects*, BH91

—— *Foreign dialects*, BH91

Hermann, Dan. *United States congressional districts*, CJ239

Hermann, R. L. *The federal legal directory*, CK146

Hermann, Ursula. *Deutsches Wörterbuch*, AC411

Hermannsson, Halldór. *Catalogue of Runic literature*, AA717, BE1284

—— *Catalogue of the Icelandic collection bequeathed by Willard Fiske*, AA717, BE1284

Hermon, Roparz. *Dictionnaire française breton*, AC237

—— *Nouveau dictionnaire breton*, AC237

Hermon Dunlap Smith Center for the History of Cartography. *Historical atlas and chronology of county boundaries, 1788–1980*, CL300

Hernandez, Margarita. *Bibliografía selectiva sobra desarrollo rural en Bolivia*, DB338

—— *Bibliografía selectiva sobre desarrollo rural en el Ecuador*, DB372

Hernández, Ricardo. *Cross-border links*, AL34

Hernon, Peter. *Developing collections of U.S. government publications*, AF72

Herod, Agustina. *Afro-American nationalism*, CC367

Herod, Charles C. *Afro-American nationalism*, CC367

Herre, Franz. *Bibliographie zur Zeitgeschichte und zum Zweiten Weltkrieg für die Jahre 1945–50*, DA169

Herrera, Carmen D. de. *Bibliografía de libros y folletos, 1958–1960*, AA493

Herrera, Diane. *Puerto Ricans and other minority groups in the continental United States*, CC446
—— *Puerto Ricans in the United States*, CC446

Herrera Durán, Patricia. *The Chicana*, CC444, CC596

Herrera Gómez, Néstor. *Apuntes para una bibliografía militar de México, 1536–1936*, DB230

Herrera Huerta, Juan Manuel. *México*, DB238

Herrera Navarro, Jerónimo. *Catálogo de autores teatrales del siglo XVIII*, BE1464

Herrero Mediavilla, Victor. *Archivo biográfico de España, Portugal e Iberoamérica*, AH287

Herrick, A.B. *Tanzania*, DD62

Herrick, Marvin Theodore. *Italian plays, 1500–1700 in the University of Illinois library*, BE1314

Herring, Kenneth Lee. *American Psychological Association's guide to research support*, CD36

Herring, Mark Youngblood. *Controversial issues in librarianship*, AK15
—— *Ethics and the professor*, CB220

Herrmann, Elisabeth. *Bibliographie zur antiken Sklaverei*, DA68

Herrmann, Theo M. *English-German technical and engineering dictionary*, EA112
—— *German-English technical and engineering dictionary*, EA112

Herron, Nancy L. *The leisure literature*, BK5
—— *Social sciences*, CA4, CA7

Hersch, Gisela. *Bibliography of Germany studies, 1945–1971*, DC238

Hersch, Ruth K. *An annotated bibliography on technical writing, editing, graphics, and publishing, 1950–1965*, EA164

Hersen, Michel. *The clinical psychology handbook*, CD103
—— *Handbook of adolescent psychology*, CD84

Herstein, Sheila R. *Belize*, DB303
—— *Brazil*, DB341
—— *Nicaragua*, DB316
—— *Panama*, DB320
—— *Puerto Rico*, DB451

Herstory, AE25

Hertefelt, Marcel d'. *African governmental systems in static and changing conditions*, CE103
—— *Société, culture et histoire du Rwanda*, DD198

Hertz, J. H. *The Pentateuch and Haftorahs*, BC183

Hervouet, Yves. *A Sung bibliography*, DE135

Herwig, Holger H. *Biographical dictionary of World War I*, DA199

Herwijnen, G. van. *Bibliografie van de stedengeschiedenis van Nederland*, DC453

Herz, Alexandra. *World guide to library, archive, and information science associations*, AK55

Herzenberg, Caroline L. *Women scientists from antiquity to the present*, EA194

Herzog, Johann Jakob. *Realencyklopädie für protestantische Theologie und Kirche*, BC67, BC69

Heseltine, Harry. *Annals of Australian literature*, BE851

Heseltine, Janet E. *The Oxford companion to French literature*, BE1158

Heskes, Irene. *The resource book of Jewish music*, BJ37

Hespéris, DD180

Hess, Jürgen C. *Bibliographie zum deutschen Liberalismus*, DC235

Hess, Robert K. *The educator's desk reference (EDR)*, CB4

Hess, Robert L. *Semper ex Africa*, DD84

Hess, Robert W. *Timbers of the New World*, EJ188

Hesse, Gritta. *Artists of the "young generation"*, BF139
—— *Künstler der jungen Generation*, BF139

Hessler, Gene. *The comprehensive catalog of U.S. paper money*, BG196

Hester, Thomas R. *Archaeology*, DA60

Hetherington, Norriss S. *Encyclopedia of cosmology*, EC27

Hethitisches Worterbuch, Kammenhuber, Annelies, AC491

Hetzer, Armin. *Albanien*, DC80
—— *Arbeitsmaterialien zu einer Landesbibliographie, Albanien*, DC80

Heuer, W. C. *Stratigraphic atlas of North America and Central America*, EF113

Heuser, Charles W. Jr. *The reference manual of woody plant propagation*, EJ247

Heuss, Theodor. *Die grossen Deutschen*, AH208

Heussler, Robert. *British Malaya*, DE228

Hewes, Gordon Winant. *Language origins*, BD56

Hewitt, Arthur Reginald. *Union list of Commonwealth newspapers in London, Oxford and Cambridge*, AE7

Hewitt, George. *Companion to Scottish history*, DC365

Hewitt, Helen-Jo J. *A Gothic etymological dictionary*, AC440

Hewlett, John F. *Keyguide to information sources in paramedical sciences*, EH7

Hewlett-Woodmere Public Library. *Index to art reproductions in books*, BF60

Hewson, Colin. *Theses on Africa, 1976–1988*, DD33

Hey, D. H. *Kingzett's chemical encyclopaedia*, EE31

Hey, David. *Family history and local history in England*, AJ102

Hey, Max H. *Index of mineral species & varieties arranged chemically*, EF193

Heyde, William A. *A Tibetan-English dictionary with Sanskrit synonyms*, AC783

Heyden, A. A. M. van der. *Atlas of the classical world*, DA120
—— *Shorter atlas of the classical world*, DA120

Heydenreich, Ludwig Heinrich. *Reallexikon zur deutschen Kunstgeschichte*, BF79

Heydenreich, Titus. *Bibliographie der Hispanistik in der Bundesrepublik Deutschland, Österreich und der deutschsprachigen Schweiz*, BD167

Heyel, Carl. *The encyclopedia of management*, CH611

Heyer, Anna Harriet. *Historical sets, collected editions, and monuments of music*, BJ10, BJ58

Heyman, Neil M. *Biographical dictionary of World War I*, DA199

Hey's mineral index, Clark, Andrew, EF182, EF193

Heyse, Micheline. *Bibliographie de l'histoire de Belgique*, DC99

Heyse, Théodore. *Bibliographie du Congo Belge et du Ruanda-Urundi*, AA871, DD135, DD198, DD244

Heywood, Vernon H. *Flowering plants of the world*, EG172
—— *Popular encyclopedia of plants*, EG179

Hezel, Francis X. *Foreign ships in Micronesia*, DF9

Hiatt, Robert M. *Library of Congress rule interpretations*, AK197

Hibbard, Addison. *A handbook to literature*, BE84

Hickcox, J. H. *United States government publications*, AF93, AF100

Hicken, Mandy. *Enser's filmed books and plays*, BH215
—— *Now read on*, BE254

Hicken, Marilyn E. *Sequels*, BE246, BE255

Hickey, D. J. *A chronology of Irish history since 1500*, DC412
—— *A dictionary of Irish history since 1800*, DC406, DC412

Hickey, John T. *Vietnam War bibliography*, DE276

Hickey, Michael. *100 families of flowering plants*, EG176

Hickman, C. J. *The Penguin dictionary of biology*, EG29

Hickman, Mary J. *The history of the Irish in Britain*, DC276

Hickok, Ralph. *The encyclopedia of North American sports history*, BK16

Hicks, Benjamin E. *Plots and characters in classic French fiction*, BE1152

Hicks, David S. *Standard handbook of engineering calculations*, EK18

Hicks, Michael A. *Who's who in late medieval England*, DC298

Hicks, Tyler G. *The McGraw-Hill handbook of essential engineering information and data*, EK17
—— *Standard handbook of engineering calculations*, EK18

Hidalgo, Dionisio. *Diccionario general de bibliografía española*, AA803

Hidaru, Alula. *Short guide to the study of Ethiopia*, DD156

Hidden research resources in the German collections of the Library of Congress, Krewson, Margrit B., DC216

Hiemstra, L. W. *Tweetalige woordeboek*, AC197

Hierarchia catholica medii aevi, BC430

Hieronymussen, Poul Ohm. *Europaeiske ordner i farver*, AL181
—— *Orders, medals and decorations of Britain and Europe in colour*, AL181

Higbee, Joan Florence. *Scholars' guide to Washington, D.C. for southwest European studies*, DC15

Higginbotham, Don. *Atlas of the American Revolution*, DB97

Higgins, James. *A history of Peruvian literature*, BE956

Higgins, Lindley R. *Maintenance engineering handbook*, EK251

Higgins, Marion Villiers. *Canadian government publications*, AF152

Higgins, Ruby D. *The black student's guide to college success*, CB303

Higginson, Roy. *CHILDES/BIB*, BD63

High Commission territories, 1909–1964, Parsons, Neil Quentin, DD170
—— Parsons, Quentin Neil, DD117, DD232

High interest easy reading, National Council of Teachers of English. Committee to Revise High Interest-Easy Reading, CB191

High/low handbook, CB190

High Middle Ages in England, 1154–1377, Wilkinson, Bertie, DC303, DC308

High technology industries, CH349

Higham, N. J. *Handbook of writing for the mathematical sciences*, ED98

Higham, Robin D. S. *A guide to the sources of British military history*, DC277
—— *Guide to the sources of United States military history*, DB16
—— *Historical dictionary of the U.S. Air Force*, CJ614

Higher education, CB221

Higher education abstracts, CB234

Higher education directory, CB272

Higher education finance, Hines, Edward R., CB222

Higher education in American life, 1636–1986, Young, Arthur P., CB26, CB233

Higher education in the European community, CB239

Higher education literature, White, Jane N., CB232

Higher education opportunities for minorities and women, annotated selections, CB381

Higher education planning, CB221

Higher Education Publications, Inc. *HEP higher education directory*, CB272

Higher Education Research Institute (Los Angeles, Calif.). *The American college teacher*, CB335

Higher transcendental functions, Bateman Manuscript Project, EB79, EB80

Highfill, Philip H. *A biographical dictionary of actors, actresses, musicians, dancers, managers & other stage personnel in London, 1660–1800*, BH112

Highway research abstracts, EK119

Highway statistics, EK122
—— United States. Federal Highway Administration, EK123

Highways see **Roads**

Highways, Krummes, Daniel C., CH444

Higton, A. A. *Dictionary of antibiotics and related substances,* EE125, EH335
Hiking, BK112, BK113
Hiking in the United States, BK112
Hildebrand, Bengt. *Svenska män och kvinnor,* AH292
Hildebrandt, Darlene Myers. *Computer science resources,* EK150
—— *Computing information directory,* EK150
Hildenbrand, William F. *Guide to research collections of former United States senators, 1789–1982,* CJ202
Hildesheimer, Ernest. *Atlas historique,* DC165
Hildesheimer, Françoise. *Guide des papiers privés d'époque révolutionnaire,* DC182
Hildreth, W. Bartley. *Handbook of public administration,* CJ482
Hiler, Hilaire. *Bibliography of costume,* BG92
Hiler, Meyer. *Bibliography of costume,* BG92
Hilgemann, Werner. *Atlas zur deutschen Zeitgeschichte, 1918–1968,* DC264
Hill, Ann. *Visual dictionary of art,* BF78
Hill, Arthur W. *Index londinensis to illustrations of flowering plants, ferns and fern allies,* EG104
Hill, C. P. *Who's who in Stuart England,* DC298
Hill, Claude. *The drama of German expressionism,* BE1264
Hill, David. *An atlas of Anglo-Saxon England,* DC312
Hill, Dennis Auburn. *Icelandic libraries and archives,* DC390
—— *Norwegian local history,* DC469
Hill, Donald. *A finding-list of English books to 1640 in libraries in the British Isles (excluding the national libraries and the libraries of Oxford and Cambridge),* AA672
Hill, Donna. *Third book of junior authors,* BE384
Hill, F. J. *National libraries of the world,* AK118
Hill, Frank Pierce. *American plays printed 1714–1830,* BE453, BE636
Hill, George H. *A bibliographical guide to black studies programs in the United States,* CC364
—— *Black business and economics,* CH393
—— *Black media in America,* CC398
—— *Black women in television,* BH294
—— *Blacks on television,* BH294
Hill, George R. *Collected editions, historical sets, and monuments of music,* BJ58
Hill, Holly. *The encyclopedia of the New York stage, 1920–1930,* BH100
Hill, Howard B. *Guide to foreign law firms,* CK58
Hill, James A. *The American Medical Association handbook of first aid & emergency care,* EH172
Hill, Joan. *Comparative criminology,* CK243
Hill, L. R. *A dictionary of microbial taxonomy,* EG31
Hill, Marnesba D. *Escritores de la diáspora cubana,* BE976
—— *Puerto Rican authors,* BE980
Hill, Quentin M. *A classification of educational subject matter,* CB111
Hill, R. A. *Dictionary of steroids,* EE130
—— *Dictionary of terpenoids,* EE121
Hill, Richard Leslie. *A bibliography of the Anglo-Egyptian Sudan,* DD226
—— *A biographical dictionary of the Sudan,* AH326
Hill, Richard S. *Bibliography of periodical literature in musicology and allied fields,* BJ109
Hill, Susan. *Profile of education doctorates,* CB341
Hill, Sylvia Saverson. *Blacks on television,* BH294
Hill, Thomas D. *Sources of Anglo-Saxon literary culture,* BE731
Hillerbrand, Hans J. *Bibliography of Anabaptism, 1520–1630,* BC362
Hillner, Kenneth P. *History and systems of modern psychology,* CD54
Hills, Margaret Thorndike. *English Bible in America,* BC94, BC97, BC101
Hills, P. J. *A dictionary of education,* CB73
Hills of faraway, Waggoner, Diana, BE304
Hillyard, Simon. *International directory of legal aid,* CK59
Hillyer, N. *New Bible dictionary,* BC147

Hiltbrunner, Otto. *Bibliographie zur lateinischen Wortforschung,* BD142
Hiltermann, Heinrich. *Bibliographie stratigraphisch wichtiger mikropaläontologischer Publikationen von etwa 1830 bis 1958 mit Kurzreferaten,* EF231
Hilton, Clifford L. *Encyclopedia of industrial chemical analysis,* EE27
Hilton, Ruth B. *An index to early music in selected anthologies,* BJ115
Hilton, Sylvia L. *Bibliografía hispanoamericana y filipina,* BE876, DE248
Himalayas, DE86
Himelstein, Shmuel. *The Jewish primer,* BC558
Hindi language
   bibliography, BD199
   dictionaries
      bilingual, AC486, AC487
         Hindi-English, AC485
      multilingual, AC801
Hinding, Andrea. *Women's history sources,* BC228, CC526, DB39, DB172
Hinds, Harold E. *Handbook of Latin American popular culture,* DB289
Hinds, Martin. *A dictionary of Egyptian Arabic,* AC216
Hinds' precedents, CJ224
Hindu world, Walker, George Benjamin, BC485
Hinduism, BF190, BF191, BF192
   bibliography, BC481, BC482, BC483, BC484
   collections, BC92
   dictionaries, BC76, BC486, BC487, BC488
   encyclopedias, BB31, BC57, BC485
   indexes, BC490
Hinduism (by subject)
   sacred books, BC484, BC489
Hindustani classical music, BJ156
Hindustani language
   dictionaries
      bilingual, AC488
         Hindustani-English, AC489
Hines, Edward R. *Higher education finance,* CB222
Hines, W. D. *English legal history,* CK271
—— *Keyguide to information sources on the international protection of human rights,* CK75
Hinnells, John R. *The Facts on File dictionary of religions,* BC73
Hinojosa, Ida Navarro. *New revised Velázquez Spanish and English dictionary,* AC740
Hinrichs, firm, publishers (Leipzig). *Fünfjahrs-Katalog der im deutschen Buchhandel erschienenen Bücher,* AA655
—— *Fünfjahrs-Katalog der im deutschen Buchhandel erschienenen Bücher, Zeitschriften, Landkarten, etc.,* AA641
—— *Halbjahrsverzeichnis der im deutschen Buchhandel erschienenen Bücher, Zeitschriften und Landkarten,* AA656
—— *Supplement zu Heinsius', Hinrichs' und Kaysers Bücher-Lexikon … ,* AA646
Hinrichs' Halbjahrs-Katalog, AA656
Hinrichsen, Alex. *Baedeker's Reisehandbucher 1828–1945,* CL389
Hinter, N. Ray. *Children in historical and comparative perspective,* CC166
Hinton, Frances. *The Continuum dictionary of women's biography,* AH25
Hinton, Harold C. *The People's Republic of China, 1949–1979,* DE149
Hippler, Arthur E. *The Alaska Eskimos,* CC414
—— *Eskimo acculturation,* CC414
—— *Subarctic Athabascans,* CC414
Hiribarren, Martin. *Dictionnaire basque-français et français-basque,* AC229
Hirose, Nobuko. *Japanese art signatures,* BF161
Hirsch, August. *Biographisches Lexikon der hervorragenden Ärzte aller Zeiten und Völker,* EH222
Hirsch, Elisabeth S. *Problems of early childhood,* CC146
Hirsch, K. A. *Handbook of mathematics,* EB62
—— *The VNR concise encyclopedia of mathematics,* EB69

Hirsch, Paul. *Katalog der Musikbibliothek Paul Hirsch, Frankfurt am Main,* BJ85, BJ87, BJ94
Hirsch, Robert O. *Political campaign communication,* CJ103
Hirschfeld, Al. *The best plays of […],* BE454
Hirschfelder, Arlene B. *American Indian and Eskimo authors,* BE551
—— *The encyclopedia of Native American religions,* BC567
Hirshbein, Cesia Ziona. *Hemerografía venezolana, 1890–1930,* BE963
Hirshfeld, Alan. *Sky catalogue 2000.0,* EC72
Hirvonen, Maija. *Suomen kirjailijat, 1945–1980,* BE1127
Hisamatsu, Sen'ichi. *Biographical dictionary of Japanese literature,* BE1579
Hiscox, Gardner Dexter. *Henley's twentieth century book of formulas, processes and trade secrets,* EA278
Hise, Richard T. *Beacham's marketing reference,* CH579
The Hispanic almanac, CC466
The Hispanic-American almanac, CC467
Hispanic American historical review, DB296
Hispanic-American material culture, Graham, Joe Stanley, CC465
Hispanic American periodicals index, AA24, AD296, BE874, DB266
Hispanic American voluntary organizations, Gonzales, Sylvia Alicia, CC462
Hispanic Americans in the United States, State Historical Society of Wisconsin. Library, AE31
Hispanic Americans information directory, 1950–1991, AE31
Hispanic children and youth in the United States, Carrasquillo, Angela, CC461
Hispanic first names, Woods, Richard D., AJ178
The Hispanic image on the silver screen, Richard, Alfred Charles, BH230
Hispanic media & market sources, CH601
Hispanic media, USA, AE31
Hispanic Policy Development Project. *The Hispanic almanac,* CC466
The Hispanic presence in North America from 1492 to today, Fernández-Shaw, Carlos M., CC464
Hispanic resource directory, AE31, CC463
Hispanic Society of America. *Manuel de l'hispanisant,* AA67, AA801, AH290, BE1435
—— *Printed books, 1468–1700, in the Hispanic Society of America,* AA818
Hispanic Society of America. Library. *Catálogo de los manuscritos poéticos castellanos existentes en la Biblioteca de The Hispanic Society of America (siglos XV, XVI y XVII),* BE1478
—— *Spanish drama of the Golden Age,* BE1465
Hispanic writers, BE890
•*HISTLINE,* EH199
Histoire de la géologie, Gohau, Gabriel, EF100
Histoire de la langue et de la littérature française des origines à 1900, Petit de Julleville, Louis, BE1175
Histoire de la littérature canadienne-française, Tougas, Gerard, BE840
Histoire de la littérature de langue française des années 1930 aux années 1980, Boisdeffre, Pierre de, BE1168
Histoire de la littérature française, BE1170
—— Lanson, Gustave, BE1172
Histoire de la littérature française depuis le 16ᵉ siècle jusqu'à nos jours, Godefroy, Frédéric Eugène, BE1169
Histoire de la littérature française du Québec, Grandpré, Pierre de, BE840
Histoire de la littérature grecque, Croiset, Alfred, BE1033
Histoire de la littérature tchèque, Jelinek, Hanus, BE1107
Histoire de la Nouvelle-France, Trudel, Marcel, DB203
Histoire de la philosophie … , Bréhier, Émile, BB46
Histoire de la poésie française, Sabatier, Robert, BE1197
Histoire de l'art au XVIe siècle, 1540–1600, DC151

Histoire de l'humanité, DA54
Histoire des bibliothèques françaises, AK107
Histoire des institutions et des faits sociaux de la France, Lepointe, Gabriel, DC149
Histoire du Burundi, Mworoha, Emile, DD135
Histoire du costume en Occident, BG106
Histoire et dictionnaire de la Révolution française, Tulard, Jean, DC188
Histoire générale de la presse française, AE52
Histoire illustré de la littérature française, Lanson, Gustave, BE1172
Histoire illustrée des lettres françaises de Belgique, Charlier, Gustave, BE1097
Histoire littéraire de la France, BE1171
Histoire médiévale en France, Autrand, Françoise, DC168
Histoire mondiale de l'art, BF134
Histoire vivante de la littérature d'aujourd'hui, Boisdeffre, Pierre de, BE1168
Historia bibliográfica de la novela chilena, Castillo, Homero, BE938
História da história do Brasil, Rodrigues, José Honório, DB357
História da literatura portuguêsa, Saraiva, António José, BE1368
História da literatura portuguesa ilustrada, Forjaz de Sampaio, Albino, BE1365
Historia de la historiografía española, Sánchez Alonso, Benito, DC506
Historia de la lengua y literatura castellana, Cejador y Frauca, Julio, BE1455
Historia de la literatura argentina, Arrieta, Rafael Alberto, BE918
Historia de la literatura boliviana, Finot, Enrique, BE922
Historia de la literatura colombiana, Ortega Torres, José Joaquin, BE947
Historia de la literatura cubana, Remos y Rubio, Juan Nepomuceno José, BE977
Historia de la literatura dramática cubana, Arrom, José Juan, BE972
Historia de la literatura española, Alborg, Juan Luis, BE1454
——— Díaz Plaja, Guillermo, BE1456
——— Valbuena Prat, Angel, BE1457
Historia de la literatura guatemalteca, Albizúrez Palma, Francisco, BE905
Historia de la literatura hispanoamericana, Anderson Imbert, Enrique, BE965
——— Leguizamón, Julio A., BE877
Historia de la literatura mexicana, Monterde, Francisco, BE1456
Historia de la literatura mexicana desde los origines hasta nuestros dias, González Peña, Carlos, BE911
Historia de las fuentes de la bilbiografía chilena, Feliú Cruz, Guillermo, DB358
Historia del arte, BF134
Historia e letërsisë shqiptare, BE1094
Historia general de las literaturas hispánicas, Díaz Plaja, Guillermo, BE1456
Historia y bibliografía de la imprenta en el antiguo vireinato del Río de la Plata, Medina, José Toribio, AA470
Historia y bibliografía de la imprenta en Montevideo, 1810–1865, Estrada, Dardo, AA545
Historia y bibliografía de las primeras imprentas rioplatenses, 1700–1850, AA469
Historia y bibliografía de los congresos internacionales de ciencias antropológicas, 1865–1954, Comas, Juan, CE6
Historia y crítica de la literatura española, Rico, Francisco, BE894
Historia y crítica de la literatura hispanoamericana, Goić, Cedomil, BE894
Historia y problemas de la literatura latinoamericana, Grossmann, Rudolf, BE895
Historians, DA46, DA48
biography, DA47, DB296
directories, DA27
Historians (by country or region)
Austria, DC225
Bulgaria, DC118

France, DC163
Germany, DC225
Netherlands, DC461
Switzerland, DC225
United States
biography, DB65
Historian's handbook, Poulton, Helen, DA2
Historians of the American frontier, DB68
Historic America, Peatross, C. Ford, BF219
——— Stamm, Alice, BF219
Historic American Buildings Survey. *Historic American Buildings Survey/Historic American Engineering Record,* BF219
Historic American Buildings Survey/Historic American Engineering Record, Massey, James C., BF219
Historic American Engineering Record. *Historic American Buildings Survey/Historic American Engineering Record,* BF219
Historic architecture sourcebook, BF245
Historic black landmarks, Cantor, George, BF248
Historic books and manuscripts concerning general agriculture in the collection of the National Agricultural Library, Naftalin, Mortimer L., EJ69
Historic books and manuscripts concerning horticulture and forestry in the collection of the National Agricultural Library, Naftalin, Mortimer L., EJ70
Historic books on veterinary science and animal husbandry, Comben Collection, EJ100
Historic documents, DB137
Historic documents on presidential elections, CJ187
Historic documents on the presidency, 1776–1989, CJ187
Historic dress in America 1607–1800, McClellan, Elisabeth, BG111
Historic dress in America 1800–1870, McClellan, Elisabeth, BG111
Historic landmarks of black America, Cantor, George, BF248, CC391
Historic landscape directory, BF293
Historic preservation, Markowitz, Arnold L., BF266
Historic preservation periodicals, Mulligan, Allison Smith, BF218
The historic preservation yearbook, BF264
Historic sites, BF219
bibliography, BF117
directories, AL88, BF248, BF250, BF265
United States
guidebooks, CC574
Historic sites (by country or region)
Canada, CC352
Great Britain, BF249
United States, BF294, CC352, CC391
Southwestern states, BG54
Historic sites (by subject)
restoration and conservation, BF117, BF218, BF264, BF266, BF267, BF287, BF293
Historic towns, DC354
Historic Towns Trust. *Historic towns,* DC354
Historic U.S. court cases, 1690–1990, Johnson, John W., CK133
Historical abstracts, AH19, CJ499, CJ549, DA176, DC241, DE36
Historical abstracts, 1775–1945, Boehm, Eric H., DA176
Historical accounting literature, Institute of Chartered Accountants in England and Wales, London. Library, CH248
An historical Albanian-English dictionary, Mann, Stuart Edward, AC208
The historical and cultural atlas of African Americans, Asante, Molefi K., CC399
Historical and cultural dictionary of India, Kurian, George Thomas, DE167
Historical and cultural dictionary of Thailand, Smith, Harold Eugene, DE266
Historical and political gazetteer of Afghanistan, India. Army. General Staff Branch, CL158
Historical and political who's who of Afghanistan, Adamec, Ludwig W., AH332
Historical archaeology, Noël Hume, Ivor, DB54
Historical atlas, Shepherd, William Robert, DA57

Historical atlas and chronology of county boundaries, 1788–1980, CL300
Historical atlas of Africa, DD65
Historical atlas of Armenia, Armen, Garbis, DC83
Historical atlas of Britain, DC302
Historical atlas of Canada, DB207
——— Kerr, Donald Gordon Grady, DB207
Historical atlas of East Central Europe, Magocsi, Paul R., DC56
An historical atlas of Islam, DE69
Historical atlas of music, Collaer, Paul, BJ198
The historical atlas of Poland, DC482
Historical atlas of political parties in the United States Congress, 1789–1989, Martis, Kenneth C., CJ236, CJ237, CJ258, CJ292, DB73
Historical atlas of religion in America, Gaustad, Edwin Scott, BC85
An historical atlas of Scotland, c.400–c.1600, DC367
A historical atlas of South Asia, DE91
Historical atlas of state power in Congress, 1790–1990, Elmes, Gregory A., CJ237, CJ258, CJ292, DB73
——— Martis, Kenneth C., CJ236, CJ237, CJ258, CJ292, DB73
Historical atlas of the American West, Beck, Warren A., DB176
The historical atlas of the Congresses of the Confederate States of America, 1861–1865, Martis, Kenneth C., CJ292
Historical atlas of the United States, Lord, Clifford L., DB69
——— Lord, Elizabeth H., DB69
——— National Geographic Society, DB74
Historical atlas of United States congressional districts, 1789–1983, Martis, Kenneth C., CJ236, CJ237, CJ258, CJ292, DB73
Historical bibliography of art museum serials from the United States and Canada, Klos, Sheila M., BF49
An historical bibliography of Egyptian prehistory, Weeks, Kent R., DA122
Historical catalogue of printed editions of the English Bible, 1525–1961, Herbert, Arthur Sumner, BC95, BC97, BC100
A historical catalogue of scientific periodicals, 1665–1900, Gascoigne, Robert Mortimer, EA42
Historical catalogue of scientists and scientific books, Gascoigne, Robert Mortimer, EA42, EA193
Historical catalogue of the printed editions of Holy Scripture in the library of the British and Foreign Bible Society, British and Foreign Bible Society. Library, BC95, BC99, BC100
——— Darlow, T. H., BC99, BC100
——— Moule, H. F., BC99, BC100
Historical dictionary of Afghanistan, Adamec, Ludwig W., DE108
A historical dictionary of American industrial language, CH339
Historical dictionary of Australia, Docherty, James C., DF34
Historical dictionary of Buddhism, Prebish, Charles S., BC456
Historical dictionary of Costa Rica, Creedman, Theodore S., AH114
Historical dictionary of data processing, Cortada, James W., EK176
Historical dictionary of fascist Italy, DC433
An historical dictionary of forestry and woodland terms, James, N. D. G., EJ179
Historical dictionary of France from the 1815 restoration to the Second Empire, DC197, DC204
An historical dictionary of German figurative usage, Spalding, Keith, AC423
Historical dictionary of Hong Kong & Macau, Roberts, Elfed Vaughan, DE151
Historical dictionary of Indonesia, Cribb, Robert B., DE173
Historical dictionary of international organizations in sub-Saharan Africa, DeLancey, Mark W., DD6
——— Mays, Terry M., DD6
Historical dictionary of Israel, Reich, Bernard, DE192

Historical dictionary of Laos, Stuart-Fox, Martin, DE224

Historical dictionary of Malaysia, Kaur, Amarjit, DE230

Historical dictionary of modern Spain, 1700–1988, DC514

Historical dictionary of Napoleonic France, 1799–1815, DC185, DC195, DC197, DC204

Historical dictionary of North American archaeology, DB49

Historical dictionary of Oceania, DF17

Historical dictionary of Papua New Guinea, Turner, Ann, DF49

Historical dictionary of Polynesia, Craig, Robert D., DF16

Historical dictionary of Portugal, Wheeler, Douglas L., DC492

Historical dictionary of Reconstruction, Trefousse, Hans Louis, DB105

Historical dictionary of revolutionary China, 1839–1976, DE142

Historical dictionary of Saudi Arabia, Peterson, John, DE253

Historical dictionary of Singapore, Mulliner, K., DE256

Historical dictionary of Taiwan, Copper, John Franklin, DE263

Historical dictionary of the 1920s, Olson, James Stuart, DB133

Historical dictionary of the French Fourth and Fifth Republics, 1946–1991, DC205

Historical dictionary of the French Revolution, 1789–1799, DC185, DC197, DC204

Historical dictionary of the French Second Empire, 1852–1870, DC199, DC206

Historical dictionary of the International Monetary Fund, Humphreys, Norman K., DF239

Historical dictionary of the Korean War, DE215

Historical dictionary of the New Deal, DB131

Historical dictionary of the Progressive Era, 1890–1920, DB132

Historical dictionary of the Republic of Korea, Nahm, Andrew C., DE216

Historical dictionary of the Spanish Civil War, 1936–1939, DC517

—— Cortada, James W., DC514

Historical dictionary of the Spanish Empire, 1402–1975, DC515

Historical dictionary of the Third French Republic, 1870–1940, DC207

Historical dictionary of the U.S. Air Force, CJ614

Historical dictionary of Tudor England, 1485–1603, DC322

Historical dictionary of Vietnam, Duiker, William J., DE273

Historical directory of American agricultural fairs, Marti, Donald B., EJ43

Historical directory of the Reformed Church in America, 1628–1992, Gasero, Russell L., BC380

Historical directory of trade unions, Marsh, Arthur Ivor, CH668

Historical documentary editions, DB18

The historical encyclopedia of costumes, Racinet, A., BG96

Historical encyclopedia of World War II, Baudot, Marcel, DA208

Historical fiction, BE470, BE475, BF477
  bibliography, BE250, BE256

Historical fiction, Logasa, Hannah, BE256

Historical gazetteer of Iran, Adamec, Ludwig W., CL165

Historical geography of the United States, Grim, Ronald E., CL106, CL107

—— McManis, Douglas R., CL106, CL107

Historical journal of film, radio, and television, BH176

Historical journals, Steiner, Dale R., DA15

Historical maps on file, Martin Greenwald Associates, CL282, DA55

Historical periodicals, Adolphus, Lalit, DA14

—— Boehm, Eric H., DA14

Historical periodicals directory, DA14

Historical records of the government of Canada, Cook, Terry, DB192

—— Wright, Glenn T., DB192

Historical Records Survey. *American imprints inventory*, AA441

—— *Atlas of congressional roll calls*, CJ237

Historical register and dictionary of the United States Army from its organization, Sept. 29, 1789, to March 2, 1903, Heitman, Francis Bernard, CJ644, CJ646

Historical register of officers of the Continental Army during the war of the Revolution, April 1775 to Dec. 1783, Heitman, Francis Bernard, CJ645

Historical research for university degrees in the United Kingdom, DC284

—— University of London. Institute of Historical Research, DA17

Historical rhetoric, BE354

—— Horner, Winifred Bryan, BE361

Historical sets, collected editions, and monuments of music, Heyer, Anna Harriet, BJ10, BJ58

Historical sources in Costa Rica, Jenkins, Richard J., DB305

Historical statistics of Canada, CG113, DB209

Historical statistics of Chile, Mamalakis, Markos, CG148

Historical statistics of the United States, CG113, DB209

—— United States. Bureau of the Census, CG87

—— United States. Congress. House, CG87

Historical statistics on banking, CH294

Historical tables, 58 BC–AD 1990, Steinberg, Sigfrid H., DA38

Historical tables on population, marriages and deaths 1911–1976, CG270

Historical times illustrated encyclopedia of the Civil War, DB118

Historical writing on the peoples of Asia, University of London. School of Oriental and African Studies, DE18

Historically black colleges and universities fact book, CB307

Historická statistická ročenka ČSSR, CG206

Les historiens français de la période moderne et contemporaine, DC163

Histories, personal narratives, Dornbusch, Charles Emil, CJ628

Historiografía Argentina 1930–1970, Feigen de Roca, Elisabeth, DB333

—— Gaer de Sabulsky, Alicia, DB333

Historiografía argentina, 1958–1988, DB333

Historiografía argentina contemporánea, Tanzi, Héctor José, DB333

Historiografía de Cuba, Pérez Cabrera, José Manuel, DB425

Historiografía militar argentina, Etchepareborda, Roberto, DB325

Historiografía y bibliografía de la emancipación del Nuevo Reino de Granada, Ocampo López, Javier, DB367

Historiografie v Československu, 1970–1980, DC124

Historiographia linguistica, BD59

Historiography, Stephens, Lester D., DA44

Historiography and historical method, DA3, DA43
  bibliography, DA44, DC102
  biography, DA46, DA48
  dictionaries, DA45
    bilingual
      Russian-English, DC584

Historiography and historical method (by country or region)
  Argentina, DB333
  Belgium, DC102
  France, DA42

Latin America, DB260
Netherlands, DC461

Historiography in the Revolution, Pérez, Louis A., DB429

Historisch-biographisches Lexikon der Schweiz, AH296, DC529

Historisch-geographisches Wörterbuch des deutschen Mittelalters, Oesterley, Hermann, CL191

Historische Bücherkunde Südosteuropa, DC58

Historische Forschungen in der DDR 1960–1970, Becker, Gerhard, DC217

Historische Forschungen in der DDR 1970–1980, Becker, Gerhard, DC217

Historisches Wörterbuch der Philosophie, BB40

Historisk bibliografi, DC463

Historisk tidsskrift, DC521

Historisk tidsskrift, Oslo, DC463

Historiske tabeller over folkemengde, giftermål og dødsfall 1911–1976, Norway. Statistisk sentralbyrå, CG270

History, Day, Alan Edwin, DC291

History and area studies
  abstract journals, DA176
  atlases, CL282, DA49, DA51, DA52, DA53, DA54, DA55, DA57, DA58, DE193
  bibliography, BE31, BE256, DA5, DA6, DA7, DA8, DA9, DA10, EA21, EC17, ED6, EE15, EG98, EG213, EH68
    current, DA12
  biography, DA48
  chronologies, DA29, DA30, DA32, DA33, DA34, DA36, DA37, DA38, DA39, DA40, DC224
  dictionaries, DA41
  dissertations, DA17, DA18, DB191, DC284
  encyclopedias, DA19, DA26, DA35, DC569
  festschriften, DA6
  financial aids, DA28
  guides, DA1, DA2
  guides for writers, DA15
  guides to research, CE57
  indexes, DA9, DA176
  library catalogs, DA172
  library resources, DA10
  periodicals, DA13, DA14, DA15
    indexes, DA4
  research
    Ireland, DC410
  sourcebooks, DA23
History and area studies (by period)
  Byzantine studies, DA161, DA162, DA163, DA164, DA166
  medieval and Renaissance
    atlases, DA159
    bibliography, DA130, DA131, DA133, DA134, DA135, DA136, DA137, DA138, DC11
      current, DA140, DA141, DA142, DA143, DA144
    chronologies, DA155, DA156
    dictionaries, DA151
    directories, DA154
    dissertations, DA145
    encyclopedias, DA146, DA147, DA148, DA150, DA152
    festschriften, DA139
    general histories, DA157
    guides, DA127, DA128, DA129, DA131, DA134
    handbooks, DA155
    periodicals, DA137
  modern
    atlases, DA188, DA189
    bibliography, CC299, DA169, DA174
    chronologies, DA182, DA183, DA184, DA209
    current surveys, DA185, DA186, DA187
    encyclopedias, DA179, DA180, DA181

History and area studies (by subject)
  Jewish history, DA7
The history and art of glass, Corning Museum of Glass, BG53
A history and bibliography of American magazines, 1800–1810, Lewis, Benjamin Morgan, AD38
A history and bibliography of American magazines, 1810–1820, Edgar, Neal L., AD31
History and bibliography of American newspapers, 1690–1820, Brigham, Clarence Saunders, AE19, AE26
A history and criticism of American public address, Speech Association of America, BE365
History and growth of the United States census, United States. Bureau of Labor, CG90
The history and influence of the American Psychiatric Association, Barton, Walter E., EH397
The history and practice of Japanese printmaking, Abrams, Leslie E., BF358
History and present condition of the newspaper and periodical press of the United States, North, Simon Newton Dexter, AE21, AE28
History and systems of modern psychology, Hillner, Kenneth P., CD54
History and systems of psychology, Brennan, James F., CD53
History and theories of working-class movements, Gulick, Charles Adams, CH631
History (archaeology, history, history of art, music, religion, and church), 1945–1983, Mäelo, Meemo, DC135
History journals and serials, Fyfe, Janet, DA13
History of aeronautics, New York Public Library, EK23
History of Afro-American literature, Jackson, Blyden, BE533, BE540
History of agriculture in the northern United States, 1620–1860, Bidwell, Percy Wells, EJ65, EJ68
History of agriculture in the southern United States to 1860, Gray, Lewis Cecil, EJ68
History of Albanian literature, Bihiku, Koço, BE1094
History of American ceramics, Strong, Susan R., BG54, BG56
History of American costume, 1607–1870, McClellan, Elisabeth, BG111
History of American literature, Marshall, Walker, BE449
History of American magazines, Mott, Frank Luther, AD30, AD40
History of American painting, Isham, Samuel, BF309
History of American pewter, Montgomery, Charles F., BG151
A history of American psychology in notes and news, 1883–1945, CD15
The history of American women's voluntary organizations, 1810–1960, Blair, Karen J., CC486
History of Anglo-Latin literature, Rigg, A. G., BE1049
A history of Anglo-Latin literature, 597–1066, Bolton, Whitney French, BE1049
A history of Antarctic science, Fogg, G. E., DG6
The history of anthropology, Kemper, Robert V., CE15
History of architecture, Fletcher, Banister, BF255
History of art, Janson, Horst Woldemar, BF132
History of art for young people, Janson, Anthony F., BF132
—— Janson, Horst Woldemar, BF132
A history of astronomy, Pannekoek, Antonie, EC61
A history of Australia, Clark, Charles Manning Hope, DF38
A history of Australian literature, Green, Henry Mackenzie, BE850
A history of book publishing in the United States, Tebbel, John William, AA304
The history of British geology, Challinor, John, EF98
History of British pewter, Hatcher, John, BG150
History of building types, Pevsner, Nikolaus, BF257
A history of Canada, DB203
—— Smith, Dwight L., DB187

History of Canadian childhood and youth, Sutherland, Neil, CC153
The history of cancer, Olson, James Stuart, EH26
The history of chemical technology, Multhauf, Robert P., EE97
A history of chemistry, Partington, James Riddick, EE98
History of Christian names, Yonge, Charlotte Mary, AJ179
History of classical scholarship, Lloyd-Jones, Hugh, BE1021, DA107
—— Sandys, John Edwin, BE1022, BE1024, DA113
—— Wilamowitz-Moellendorff, Ulrich von, BE1021, DA107
History of classical scholarship from 1300 to 1850, Pfeiffer, Rudolf, BE1021, DA107
History of classical scholarship from the beginnings to the end of the Hellenistic age, Pfeiffer, Rudolf, BE1021, BE1024, DA107, DA113
The history of clocks and watches, Bruton, Eric, BG86
The history of costume, Payne, Blanche, BG112
A history of costume in the West, BG106
A history of Danish literature, BE1118
—— Mitchell, Phillip Marshall, BE1118
A history of dentistry from the most ancient times until the end of the eighteenth century, Guerini, Vincenzo, EH265
A history of eastern Christianity, Atiya, Aziz Suryal, BC443
History of economic analysis, Hutchinson, William Kenneth, CH18
History of eighteenth-century Russian literature, Brown, William Edward, BE1418
History of English drama, 1660–1900, Nicoll, Allardyce, BE453, BE636, BE666
A history of English poetry, Courthope, William John, BE718
History of European and American sculpture from the early Christian period to the present day, Post, Chandler Rathfon, BF393
History of Far Eastern art, Lee, Sherman E., BF132
A history of Finnish literature, Ahokas, Jaakko, BE1126
History of French-Canadian literature, Tougas, Gerard, BE840
History of French dramatic literature in the 17th century, Lancaster, Henry Carrington, BE1181, BE1182
A history of geology, Gohau, Gabriel, EF100
History of geology and palaeontology to the end of the nineteenth century, Zittel, Karl Alfred von, EF105
The history of geophysics and meteorology, Brush, Stephen G., EF97
A history of German literature, Robertson, John George, BE1259
History of glass, Klein, Dan, BG75
—— Lloyd, Ward, BG75
History of Greek literature, Hades, Moses, BE1034
—— Lesky, Albin, BE1034
—— Levi, Peter, BE1034
A history of hand-made lace, Jackson, Emily, BG160
History of Hispanic theatre in the United States, Kanellos, Nicolas, BE560
History of histories of German literature, 1835–1914, Batts, Michael S., BE1254
History of Hungarian literature, Klaniczay, Tibor, BE1276
—— Nemeskurty, Istvan, BE1276
History of Hungary and the Hungarians, 1848–1971, Telek, J., DC385
History of Iceland prose writers, 1800–1940, Einarsson, Stefan, BE1285
A history of Icelandic literature, Einarsson, Stefan, BE1285
History of Icelandic poets, 1800–1940, Beck, Richard, BE1285
History of ideas, BB29, EF100
The history of ideas, Tobey, Jeremy L., BB22
The history of imperial China, Wilkinson, Endymion, DE124

A history of Indian literature, BE1566
—— Winternitz, Moriz, BE1571
History of Irish civilisation, DC394
History of Italian literature, De Sanctis, Francesco, BE1304
—— Wilkins, Ernest Hatch, BE1308
History of Japanese literature, Konishi, Jin'ichi, BE1582
—— Miner, Earl Roy, BE1582
A history of Jewish costume, Rubens, Alfred, BG113
A history of Jewish literature, Waxman, Meyer, BE1577
—— Zinberg, Israel, BE1578
History of labour in the United States, Commons, John Rogers, CH675
History of lace, Palliser, Bury, BG160
History of Latin literature, Hadas, Moses, BE1052
The history of mathematics from antiquity to the present, Dauben, Joseph Warren, EB8
History of medicine see **Medicine (by subject)— history**
A history of medicine, Castiglioni, Arturo, EH213
History of medicine in the United States, Packard, Francis Randolph, EH215
History of Mexican literature, González Peña, Carlos, BE911
History of modern art, Arnason, H. Harvard, BF131
—— Wheeler, Daniel, BF131
The history of modern astronomy and astrophysics, DeVorkin, David H., EC9
A history of modern criticism, Wellek, René, BE57, DC426, DE595
History of modern Ethiopia, Zewde, Bahru, DD154
The history of modern geography, Dunbar, Gary S., CL9
The history of modern physics, Brush, Stephen G., ED52
A history of modern poetry, Perkins, David, BE719
The history of music, Krohn, Ernst Christopher, BJ109
—— Wood, David A., BJ90
A history of music in pictures, Kinsky, Georg, BJ199
The history of musical instruments, Sachs, Curt, BJ373
A history of Norwegian literature, BE1342
  Beyer, Harald, BE1338
History of nursing, Nutting, M. Adelaide, EH286
A history of nursing, from ancient to modern times, Stewart, Isabel Maitland, EH286
History of Parliament, CJ360
History of Parliament, 1439–1509, Wedgwood, Josiah Clement, AH231, CJ354, CJ355
A history of Persian literature, BE1572
A history of Peruvian literature, Higgins, James, BE956
History of philosophy, Bréhier, Émile, BB46
—— Thomas, Joseph, BB46
History of photography, Gernsheim, Alison, BF328
—— Gernsheim, Helmut, BF328
—— Roosens, Laurent, BF334
A history of Polish literature, Krzyżanowski, Julian, BE1352
—— Miłosz, Czesław, BE1356
The history of porcelain, BG73
The history of printing from its beginnings to 1930, Columbia University. Libraries, AA299
The history of psychiatry, Alexander, Franz, EH396
History of psychology, Viney, Wayne, CD57
The history of psychology and the behavioral sciences, Watson, Robert Irving, CD60
A history of psychology in autobiography, CD47
A history of public health, Rosen, George, EH417
History of Roman literature, Teuffel, Wilhelm Sigismund, BE1052, BE1053
A history of Russian literature from the earliest times to the death of Dostoevsky (1881), Mirskii, D. S., BE1420
A history of Russian literature of the romantic period, Brown, William Edward, BE1418
A history of Scandinavian literature, 1870–1980, Rossel, Sven Hakon, BE1092
History of science see **Science (by subject)— history**

The history of science and technology in the United States, Rothenberg, Marc, EA238
History of Science Society. *Critical bibliography of the history of science and its cultural influences*, EA241
———— *Directory of members*, EA248
———— *Guide to the history of science*, EA248
History of seventeenth-century Russian literature, Brown, William Edward, BE1418
History of South Africa, Thompson, Leonard Monteath, DD211
The history of Southern literature, BE575
History of Spanish literature, Monterde, Francisco, BE1456
The history of surgery in the United States, 1775–1900, Rutkow, Ira M., EH196
History of Swaziland, Matsebula, J. S. M., DD231
History of Swedish literature, Algulin, Ingemar, BE1482
———— Gustafson, Alrik, BE1482
History of Tanzania, Kimambo, I. N., DD235
———— Temu, A. J., DD235
History of technology see **Technology (by subject)—history**
History of the American drama from the beginnings to the Civil War, Quinn, Arthur Hobson, BE466
History of the American drama from the Civil War to the present day, Quinn, Arthur Hobson, BE466
History of the Bible in English, Bruce, F. F., BC191
History of the Christian church, Schaff, Philip, BC280
History of the church, Dolan, John, BC277
———— Jedin, Hubert, BC277
History of the church in southern Africa, Hofmeyr, J. W., DD115
History of the Church of Ireland, Phillips, Walter Alison, BC340
History of the churches in the United States and Canada, Handy, Robert T., BC278
A history of the ecumenical movement, BC276
A history of the English language, Baugh, Albert Croll, BD98
The history of the English novel, Baker, Ernest Albert, BE691
The history of the Episcopal Church in America, 1607–1991, Caldwell, Sandra M., BC343
A history of the expansion of Christianity, Latourette, Kenneth Scott, BC306
History of the family and kinship, CC213
The history of the health care sciences and health care, 1700–1980, Erlen, Jonathon, EH201
The history of the Irish in Britain, Hartigan, Maureen, DC276
History of the Irish newspaper, 1685–1760, Munter, Robert LaVerne, AE63
History of the life sciences, Smit, Pieter, EG8
History of the Newbery and Caldecott medals, Smith, Irene, AA343
History of the popes, Antrobus, Frederick Ignatius, BC432
———— Pastor, Ludwig, BC432
The history of the Scandinavian literatures, Blankner, Frederika, BE1084
History of Ukrainian literature, Chyžhevskyj, Dmytro, BE1493
History of urban and regional planning, Sutcliffe, Anthony, BF270, CC303
History of wages in the United States from colonial times to 1928, United States. Bureau of Statistics, CH689
A history of war at sea, Pemsel, Helmut, CJ600
History of Western sculpture, Pope-Hennessy, John, BF393
History of women, AH37
The history of women and science, health, and technology, EA231
A history of women philosophers, BB47
History of world art, Upjohn, Everard Miller, BF134
The history of world sculpture, Bazin, Germain, BF392
A history of Yiddish literature, Liptzin, Solomon, BE1080
History of Yugoslav literature, BE1497

History of Zanzibar, from the Middle Ages to 1856, Gray, John Milner, DD250
History of Zoroastrianism, Boyce, Mary, BC574
History theses, 1901–70, Jacobs, Phyllis M., DA17, DC284
History theses, 1971–80, Horn, Joyce M., DA17, DC284
Hit parade, Tyler, Don, BJ334
Hitchcock, H. Wiley. *The new Grove dictionary of American music*, BJ140
Hitchcock, Henry Russell. *American architectural books*, BF217
Hitt, Deborah S. *Selected bibliography of the Dominican Republic*, DB434
The Hittite dictionary of the Oriental Institute of the University of Chicago, University of Chicago. Oriental Institute, AC491
Hittite etymological dictionary, Puhvel, Jaan, AC490
Hittite language
  dictionaries
    bilingual, AC491
  etymology
    bilingual, AC490
Hixon, Donald L. *Music in early America*, BJ59
———— *Nineteenth-century American drama*, BE464, BE640
———— *Women in music*, BJ222
Hixson, S. *Compilation of Chinese dictionaries*, AC270
HLAA, BF22
Hladczuk, John. *Comparative reading*, CB48
———— *General issues in literacy/illiteracy*, CB49
———— *International handbook of reading education*, CB120
———— *Literacy/illiteracy in the world*, CB49
Hladczuk, Sharon. *General issues in literacy/illiteracy*, CB49
———— *Literacy/illiteracy in the world*, CB49
HMSO agency catalogue, Great Britain. Stationery Office, AF185
HMSO annual catalogue, AF186, AF187, AF190
HMSO monthly catalogue, AF186, AF187, AF190
Ho, Allan Benedict. *Biographical dictionary of Russian/Soviet composers*, BJ204
Ho, K. M. *Annotated guide to Taiwan periodical literature, 1972*, AD210
Ho, Pung. *Research guide to English translation of Chinese verse*, BE1552
Hoad, Linda. *Literary manuscripts at the National Library of Canada*, BE832
Hoad, T. F. *The concise Oxford dictionary of English etymology*, AC52
Hoadley, Steve. *The New Zealand foreign affairs handbook*, DF44
———— *The South Pacific foreign affairs handbook*, DF18
Hoagland, Alison K. *Buildings of Alaska*, BF254
Hoague, Eleanor C. *Butterworths Spanish/English legal dictionary*, CK55
Hoare, Alfred. *Italian dictionary*, AC534
Hoà's essential English-Vietnamese dictionary, AC803
Hobbie, Margaret. *Italian American material culture*, CC351
———— *Museums, sites, and collections of Germanic culture in North America*, CC352
Hobbled Pegasus, Frank, Joseph, BE699
Hobbs, James B. *Homophones and homographs*, AC75
Hobday, Charles. *Communist and Marxist parties of the world*, CJ526
Hobson, Burton. *Catalogue of the world's most popular coins*, BG191
———— *Illustrated encyclopedia of world coins*, BG178
Hobson-Jobson, Yule, Henry, AC162
Hochman, Stanley. *French-English science and technology dictionary*, EA107
———— *McGraw-Hill encyclopedia of world drama*, BH72
Hochmuth, M. K. *A history and criticism of American public address*, BE365

Hochschulschriften zu Schwarz-Afrika, Maurer, Barbara, DD30
———— Schwarz, Klaus, DD30
Hochschulschriften zu Süd– und Südostasien, Grunendahl, Reinhold, DE10
Hochschulschriften zur Geschichte und Kultur des Mittelalters 1939 bis 1972/74, Monumenta Germaniae Historica, DA145
Hochstadt, Jenny. *African language materials in the Boston University Libraries*, BD215
Hocken, T. M. *Bibliography of the literature relating to New Zealand*, AA946, DF42
Hockey, BK86, BK87, BK88
The hockey encyclopedia, Fischler, Stan, BK87
Hocks, Paul. *Index zu deutschen Zeitschriften der Jahre 1773–1830*, AD315
Hodek, Břetislav. *Velký anglicko-český slovník*, AC279
Hodes, Franz. *Internationale Personalbibliographie, 1800–1943*, AA19, AH14
Hodge, Harold C. *Clinical toxicology of commercial products*, EH424
Hodges, Daniel. *Who gets grants/who gives grants*, AL124
Hodges, Deborah Robertson. *Etiquette*, AL150
Hodges, Elaine R. S. *The Guild handbook of scientific illustration*, EA222
Hodges, Flavia. *A dictionary of surnames*, AJ183
Hodges, John Cunyus. *Harbrace college handbook*, BD96
Hodges, Richard E. *A dictionary of reading and related terms*, CB74
Hodges, T. *Western Sahara*, DD48
Hodges' Harbrace college handbook, BD96
Hodgkiss, Alan G. *A literary atlas & gazetteer of the British Isles*, BE628
Hodgson, Ernest. *Dictionary of toxicology*, EH422
Hodgson, Godfrey. *The United States*, DB55
Hodgson, Julian. *Music titles in translation*, BJ174
Hodgson, Terry. *The drama dictionary*, BH78
Hödl, Günther. *Österreichische historische Bibliographie*, DC94
Hødnebø, Finn. *Ordbog over det gamle norsk sprog*, AC504
Hodnett, Grey. *Leaders of the Soviet Republics, 1955–1972*, CJ392
Hodoş, Nerva. *Bibliografia românească veche, 1508–1830*, AA780
———— *Publicaţiunile periodice româneşti (ziare, gazete, reviste)*, AD140
Hodous, Lewis. *A dictionary of Chinese Buddhist terms*, BC480
Hodson, Sue. *Guide to literary manuscripts in the Huntington Library*, BE429
Hodson, William K. *Maynard's industrial engineering handbook*, EK233
Hoe, Robert. *The heritage encyclopedia of band music*, BJ294
Hoefer, Jean Chrétien Ferdinand. *Nouvelle biographie générale depuis les temps plus reculés jusqu'à nos jours*, AH31
———— *Nouvelle biographie universelle ancienne et moderne*, AH22
Hoefte, Rosemarijn. *A bibliography of Caribbean migration and Caribbean immigrant communities*, CE77
———— *Suriname*, DB392
Hoel, Arline Alchian. *Economics sourcebook of government statistics*, CH171
Hoerder, Dirk. *The immigrant labor press in North America, 1840s–1970s*, CH656
Hoeveler, Diane Long. *English prose and criticism in the nineteenth century*, BE755
Hof- und Staatshandbuch, CJ327
Hoffer, Thomas W. *Animation*, BH161
Hoffman, Andrea C. *Kits, games, and manipulatives for the elementary school classroom*, CB14
Hoffman, Catherine. *The consumer health information source book*, EH27
Hoffman, Frederick John. *The little magazine*, AD35, AD39
Hoffman, Herbert H. *Cuento mexicano index*, BE912
———— *Faces in the news*, BF65

—— *Hoffman's index to poetry,* BE316

—— *International index to recorded poetry,* BE323

—— *Latin American play index,* BE898

—— *Recorded plays,* BH56

Hoffman, Rita Ludwig. *International index to recorded poetry,* BE323

Hoffmann, Frank W. *The literature of rock, 1954–1978,* BJ338

—— *Literature of rock II, 1979–1983,* BJ338

Hoffman's index to poetry, Hoffman, Herbert H., BE316

Hoffmeister, Elizabeth R. *The Department of State and American diplomacy,* CJ169

Hoffmeister, Johannes. *Wörterbuch der philosophischen Begriffe,* BB43

Hoffnar, Celeste R. *Footage 89,* BH178

Hoffner, Harry A. *The Hittite dictionary of the Oriental Institute of the University of Chicago,* AC491

Hofmann, Hanns Hubert. *Biographisches Wörterbuch zur deutschen Geschichte,* AH215

Hofmann, J. B. *Lateinisches etymologisches Wörterbuch,* AC584

Hofmann, Theodore. *Index of English literary manuscripts,* BE603

Hofmann, Winfried. *Geflügelte Worte,* BE135

Hofmann Cortesi, Livio. *I segreti dell'inglese,* AC530

Hofmeister, Adolf. *Hofmeisters Handbuch der Musikliteratur,* BJ60

Hofmeisters Handbuch der Musikliteratur, BJ60

Hofmeisters Jahresverzeichnis, BJ16

Hofmeisters Musikalisch-literarischer Monatsbericht, BJ80

Hofmeyr, J. W. *History of the church in southern Africa,* DD115

Hofstetter, Eleanore O. *The twentieth-century German novel,* BE1268

Hofstetter, Henry William. *Dictionary of visual science,* EH113

Hogan, Edmund. *Onomasticon goedelicum locorum et tribuum Hiberniae et Scotiae,* CL202, CL208

Hogan, Robert. *Dictionary of Irish literature,* BE802

Hogan, Sharon A. *Learning the library,* AK229

Hogg, D. A. *Concise veterinary dictionary,* EJ112

Hogg, Ian V. *Encyclopaedia of the Second World War,* DA206

Hogg, Peter C. *The African slave trade and its suppression,* DD5

Hoggart, Richard. *Oxford illustrated encyclopedia of peoples and cultures,* CE44

Höhlein, Helga. *Auswahlbibliographie zum Studium der anglistischen Sprachwissenschaft,* BD91

Hohlfeld, A. R. *German literature in British magazines, 1750–1810,* BE1238

—— *German literature in British magazines, 1750–1860,* BE1240

Hohlweg, Armin. *Tusculum-Lexicon,* BE1026

Hohmann, Harald. *Basic documents of international environmental law,* CK91

Höjer, Christianne. *Ethiopian publications,* AA856

Hola, Eugenia. *Bibliografía del proceso chileno 1970–1973,* DB360

Holberg, Ludwig. *Forfatterlexikon omfattende Danmark, Norge og Island indtil 1814,* BE1087

Holborn, Guy. *Butterworths legal research guide,* CK218

Holborn Law Society. *Hazell's guide to the judiciary and the courts, with the Holborn Law Society's bar list,* CK216

Holbrook, William Collar. *A bibliographical guide to the Romance languages and literatures,* BD152, BE1073

Holden, Amanda. *The Viking opera guide,* BJ244

Holden, Edward Singleton. *The centennial of the United States Military Academy at West Point, New York, 1802–1902,* CJ611

Hol'denberh, Lev Izraïlevych. *Ukraïns'ka radians'ka literaturna bibliohrafiia,* BE1492

Holder, Alfred. *Alt-celtischer Sprachschatz,* AC252

Holder, R. W. *Dictionary of American and British euphemisms,* AC125

—— *The Faber dictionary of euphemisms,* AC125

Holdings of the newspapers and periodicals, National Archives of Pakistan, AE97

Holdings of the University of Utah on Utah and the Church of Jesus Christ of Latter-Day Saints, University of Utah. Libraries, BC373

Holdsworth, Mary. *Soviet African studies, 1918–59,* DD112

Holidays, AL142, AL144, AL145, AL146, AL147, CF57, DA182

Holladay, William Lee. *Concise Hebrew and Arabic lexicon of the Old Testament,* AC481

Holland, Barron. *Popular Hinduism and Hindu mythology,* BC482

Holland, Clive. *Arctic exploration and development, c.500 B.C. to 1915,* DG7

Holland, Robert. *Dictionary of English plant-names,* EG120

Holland. Rijksbureau voor Kunsthistorische en Ikonografische Documentatie. *Répertoire des catalogues de ventes publiques,* BF112

Hollander, Jacob Harry. *The economic library of Jacob H. Hollander,* CH17

Hollander, John. *The Oxford anthology of English literature,* BE618

Hollander, Joyce P. *Worldwide directory of national earth-science agencies and related international organizations,* EF92

Hollander, Lee Milton. *A bibliography of skaldic studies,* BE1089

Hollander, Zander. *Bud Collins' modern encyclopedia of tennis,* BK101

—— *The complete encyclopedia of hockey,* BK86

Holler, Frederick L. *Information sources of political science,* CJ1

Holley, E. Jens. *Religion and the American experience, 1620–1900,* DB10

Holli, Melvin G. *Biographical dictionary of American mayors, 1820–1980,* CJ285

Holliday, Paul. *A dictionary of plant pathology,* EJ30

Hollier, Denis. *A new history of French literature,* BE1174

Hollier, Elisabeth. *Dictionnaire des citations françaises,* BE133

Hollingsworth, Paul. *Medieval narrative sources,* DA135

Hollis, D. *Animal identification,* EG205

Hollis, Ernest V. *College presidency, 1900–1960,* CB228

Holloway, Merlyn. *Steel engravings in nineteenth century British topographical books,* BF359

Hollstein, F. W. H. *Dutch and Flemish etchings, engravings and woodcuts, ca.1450–1700,* BF382

—— *German engravings, etchings and woodcuts, ca.1400–1700,* BF382

The Hollywood reporter book of box office hits, Sackett, Susan, BH272

Holm, John A. *Dictionary of Bahamian English,* AC161

Holm, LeRoy G. *The world's worst weeds,* EJ64

Holm-Olsen, Ludvig. *Norges litteratur historie,* BE1337

Holman, C. Hugh. *Handbook to literature,* BE76, BE83, BE84

Holmes, Brian. *International handbook of education systems,* CB125

Holmes, Frederic Lawrence. *Dictionary of scientific biography,* EA176

Holmes, Lowell Don. *Samoan Islands bibliography,* DF53

Holmes, Marjorie C. *Publications of the government of British Columbia, 1871–1947,* AF155

Holmes, Michael. *Country house described,* BF206

Holmes, Oakley N. *Complete annotated resource guide to black American art,* BF24

Holmes, Peter. *Who's who in Tudor England,* DC298

Holmesland, Arthur. *Aschehougs konversasjonsleksikon,* AB74

Holocaust, CL128

atlases, DA223

bibliography, CK80, DA203, DA213, DA214, DA215, DA216, DA217, DA219, DA220, DC244

chronologies, DA222

filmography, DA216, DA220, DA221

The Holocaust, DA216

—— Cargas, Harry J., DA214

The Holocaust : catalog of publications and audio-visual materials, 1988–1990, DA216

Holocaust in books and films, Klein, Dennis B., DA216

—— Muffs, Judith Herschlag, DA216

Holocaust, Israel and the Jews, Gellert, Charles Lawrence, DA221

Holocaust literature, DA217

Holocaust studies, Sable, Martin Howard, DA216

Holoman, D. Kern. *Writing about music,* BJ189

Hols, Edith. *Metaphor II,* BD47

Holsoe, Svend E. *A bibliography on Liberia,* DD173

—— *Liberia,* DD48

Holst, Peter. *Dansk litteraturhistorie,* BE1113

Holt, Anne D. *History of Parliament, 1439–1509,* AH231, CJ355

Holt, Constance Wall. *Welsh women,* DC368

Holt, Dean W. *American military cemeteries,* BF390, CJ632

Holt, John. *Guide to Buddhist religion,* BC472

Holt, John G. *Bergey's manual of systematic bacteriology,* EG309

Holt, Linda Hughey. *The A–Z of women's sexuality,* CC282

Holt, P. M. *Historical writing on the peoples of Asia,* DE18

The Holt foreign film guide, Bergan, Ronald, BH194

Holthausen, Ferdinand. *Altsächsisches Wörterbuch,* AC404

Holtje, Stephen. *The ballplayers,* BK48

Holtom, Daniel Clarence. *The national faith of Japan,* BC569

Holtsmark, A. *Norsk literaturhistorie,* BE1339

Holtus, Günter. *Lexikon der Romanistischen Linguistik,* BD148

Holtz, Barry W. *The Schocken guide to Jewish books,* BC518

Holtz, Walter. *Lexikon der Münzabkürzungen mit geschichtlich-geographischen Erläuterungen,* BG183

Holtze, Sally Holmes. *Fifth book of junior authors & illustrators,* BE384

—— *Sixth book of junior authors & illustrators,* BE384

Holtzmann, Robert. *Deutschlands Geschichtsquellen im Mittelalter,* DC228

Holtzmann, Walter. *Deutsche Geschichtswissenschaft im zweiten Weltkrieg,* DC218

Holub, Josef. *Stručný etymologický slovník jazyka českého se zvláštním zřetelem k slovům kulturním a cizím,* AC283

The Holy Bible, BC94

Holy Roman Empire, DC12, DC501

Holy Roman Empire, Zophy, Jonathan W., DC12

Holzer, Marc. *Public administration research guide,* CJ459, CJ460

—— *Public sector productivity,* CJ466

Holzman, Albert George. *Encyclopedia of computer science and technology,* EK172

Holzmann, Michael. *Deutsches Anonymen-Lexikon,* AA170

—— *Deutsches Pseudonymen-Lexikon,* AA171

Hombs, Mary Ellen. *American homelessness,* CC202

The home book of Bible quotations, Stevenson, Burton Egbert, BC156

The home book of proverbs, maxims and familiar phrases, Stevenson, Burton Egbert, BE163

Home book of quotations, classical and modern, Stevenson, Burton Egbert, BE95, BE120, BE163

Home book of Shakespeare quotations, Stevenson, Burton Egbert, BE775

Home economics, EJ201

bibliography, EJ193

dissertations, EJ194, EJ195, EJ196

indexes, EJ197

Home economics (by subject)

history, EJ198, EJ199, EJ200, EJ202

Home economics, East, Marjorie, EJ201

Home economics research, EJ194

Home economics research abstracts, EJ195
Home economics research report, United States. Department of Agriculture, EJ193
The homeless in America, Nordquist, Joan, CC204
Homelessness, Henslin, James M., CC201
Homelessness and the homeless
  bibliography, CC201, CC204
  handbooks, CC202
  statistics, CC200, CC203
Homelessness in the United States, CC203
Homeopathic bibliography of the United States, from the year 1825 to the year 1891, inclusive, Bradford, Thomas Lindsley, EH200
Homeopathy in the United States, Cordasco, Francesco, EH200
Homicide, Jerath, Bal K., CK246
Hommes et destins, AH197, AH321
Homocide, Abel, Ernest L., CK246
Homolové, Květy. *Čeští spisovatelé 19. a počátku 20. století,* BE1105
Homophones and homographs, Hobbs, James B., AC75
The homosexual and society, Ridinger, Robert B. Marks, CC274
Homosexuality, CC266
  bibliography, CC268, CC274
  biography, BE469
  book reviews, CC265
  dictionaries, CC284
  drama, BE458
  encyclopedias, CC277
  handbooks, CC287
  periodicals, CC285
Homosexuality (by subject)
  legal rights, CC288
  see also **Lesbianism**
Homosexuality, Dynes, Wayne R., CC268
Homosexuals (by subject)
  education
    directories, CB290
Honduran literature, BE906
Honduras
  bibliography, AA486, AA487, AA488, AA489, DB312
  gazetteers, CL117
  government publications, AF159
  statistics, CG131
Honduras (by subject)
  history, DB310
    encyclopedias, DB311
Honduras. Dirección General de Estadística y Censos. *Anuario estadístico,* CG131
Honduras, Howard-Reguindin, Pamela F., DB312
Honegger, Marc. *Dictionnaire de la musique,* BJ129
  —— *Das Grosse Lexikon der Musik,* BJ136
Honegger, R. E. *The IUCN amphibia-reptilia red data book,* EG250
Honey, William Bowyer. *European ceramic art, from the end of the Middle Ages to about 1815,* BG74
  —— *Handbook of pottery and porcelain marks,* BG70
Hong Kong
  biography, AH348
  encyclopedias, DE151
  statistics, CG386
Hong Kong (by subject)
  history
    bibliography, DE152
    general histories, DE148
    guides, DE150
Hong Kong. Census and Statistics Department. *Hong Kong annual digest of statistics,* CG386
Hong Kong, Scott, Ian, DE152
Hong Kong annual digest of statistics, CG386
Hong Kong union catalogue, Rydings, H. Anthony, DE150
Honig, Alice S. *Prosocial development in children,* CC147
Honig, Robert. *Environmental profiles,* EK75
Honigmann, John J. *Handbook of social and cultural anthropology,* CE58

Honigsblum, Bonnie Birtwistle. *A manual for writers of term papers, theses, and dissertations,* AG6
Honour, Hugh. *The Penguin dictionary of architecture,* BF244
  —— *The Penguin dictionary of decorative arts,* BG21
  —— *Visual arts,* BF132
  —— *World history of art,* BF132
Honourable Society of Cymmrodorion (London, England). *Y Bywgraffiadur Cymreig hyd 1940,* AH245
Hony, H. C. *The Oxford Turkish dictionary,* AC791
  —— *Turkish-English dictionary,* AC790
Hood, Albert B. *Key resources on student services,* CB224
Hood, Jennings. *American orders & societies and their decorations,* AL178
Hoogvelt, Ankie M. M. *Multinational enterprise,* CH341
Hook, Brian. *The Cambridge encyclopedia of China,* DE140
Hooper, David. *The Oxford companion to chess,* BK133
Hoopes, Laura L. Mays. *Magill's survey of science. Life science series,* EG25
Hoops, Johannes. *Reallexikon der germanischen Altertumskundes,* DC230
Hoornstra, Jean. *American periodicals, 1741–1900,* AD36, AD272
  —— *Index to American periodicals of the 1700's,* AD272
  —— *Index to American periodicals of the 1700's and 1800's,* AD273
Hooton, Joy W. *Annals of Australian literature,* BE851
  —— *The Oxford companion to Australian literature,* BE860
Hoover, Herbert T. *Bibliography of the Sioux,* CC420
Hoover Institution on War, Revolution, and Peace. *A catalog of files and microfilms of the German Foreign Ministry archives, 1920–1945,* DC253
  —— *Guide to the collections in the Hoover Institution archives relating to Imperial Russia, the Russian revolutions and civil war, and the first emigration,* DC564
  —— *The library catalogs of the Hoover Institution on War, Revolution, and Peace, Stanford University,* DA172
  —— *Peronism and the three Perons,* DB327
  —— *Russia, the Soviet Union, and Eastern Europe,* DC49
  —— *Soviet and Russian newspapers at the Hoover Institution,* AE70
  —— *Women in the First and Second World Wars,* DA192
  —— *Yearbook on international communist affairs,* CJ530
Hoover Institution on War, Revolution, and Peace. East Asian Collection. *Bibliography of Chinese academic serials, pre-1949,* AD189
  —— *A checklist of monographs and periodicals on the Japanese colonial empire,* DE199
Hoover's handbook of American business, CH360
Hoover's handbook of emerging companies, CH360
Hoover's handbook of world business, CH360
Hoover's handbook : profiles of over 500 major corporations, CH360
Hoover's masterlist of major U.S. companies, CH360
Hooykaas, J. C. *Repertorium op de koloniale litteratuur,* DE175
Hope, Anne. *Guide to inventories and finding aids of German archives at the German Historical Institute, Washington, D.C,* DC246
Hope, Augustine. *The color compendium,* BF125, ED59
Hopke, William E. *The encyclopedia of careers and vocational guidance,* CB209
Hopkins, Charity. *An index of British treaties, 1101–1968,* CK98
Hopkins, Jeanne. *Glossary of astronomy and astrophysics,* EC34
Hopkins, Karen A. *A deafness collection,* CC187

Hopkins, Stephen T. *Research guide to the arid lands of the world,* EF1
Hopkins, Vincent C. *Catholic encyclopedia,* BC397
Hopkinson, Cecil. *Dictionary of Parisian music publishers, 1700–1950,* BJ181
Hopple, Gerald W. *United States intelligence,* CJ547
Hopwood, A. Tindell. *Nomenclator zoologicus,* EG244
Hopwood, Derek. *Arab Islamic bibliography,* BC492
Hora, F. Bayard. *Collins guide to mushrooms and toadstools,* EG187
  —— *Oxford encyclopedia of trees of the world,* EG198
Horak, Stephan M. *Eastern European national minorities, 1919–1980,* CE92
  —— *Russia, the USSR, and Eastern Europe,* DC32
  —— *Soviet Union and Eastern Europe,* DC32
Horblit, Harrison D. *One hundred books famous in science,* EA232
Horden, John. *Dictionary of anonymous and pseudonymous publications in the English language,* AA150
  —— *Index of English literary manuscripts,* BE603
Hordeski, Michael F. *Illustrated dictionary of microcomputer terminology,* EK180
  —— *The illustrated dictionary of microcomputers,* EK180
Horecky, Paul Louis. *Basic Russian publications,* DC550
  —— *Czech and Slovak abbreviations,* AC282
  —— *East Central and Southeast Europe,* AK105, DC47
  —— *East Central Europe,* DC33, DC59
  —— *Newspapers of the Soviet Union in the Library of Congress,* AE75
  —— *Russia and the Soviet Union,* DC550
  —— *Russian, Ukrainian, and Belorussian newspapers, 1917–1953,* AE71, AE75
  —— *Southeastern Europe,* DC33, DC59
Horn, David. *The literature of American music in books and folk music collections,* BJ14
Horn, Joyce M. *Fasti ecclesiae Anglicanae,* BC331
  —— *History theses, 1971–80,* DA17, DC284
Horn, Judy. *Directory of government document collections & librarians,* AF86
Horn, Maurice. *Contemporary graphic artists,* BF383
Horn, Pierre L. *Handbook of French popular culture,* DC209
Horn, S. F. *Glossary of financial terms,* CH214
Horn, Walther. *Index litteraturae entomologicae,* EG331
Horn-Monval, Madeleine. *Répertoire bibliographique des traductions et adaptations françaises du théâtre étranger du XVᵉ siècle à nos jours,* BE1178
Horne, Elinor McCullough Clark. *Javanese-English dictionary,* AC559
Horner, Winifred Bryan. *Historical rhetoric,* BE354, BE361
Hornsby, Alton. *Chronology of African-American history,* CC393
Hornung, Clarence Pearson. *Treasury of American design,* BG18
Horowitz, Lois. *A bibliography of military name lists from pre-1675 to 1900,* AJ30
Horrigan, William James. *The American Film Institute guide to college courses in film and television,* BH263
Horror, Hardy, Phil, BH224
Horror fiction
  bibliography, BE276, BE278, BE281
  biography, BE303
  book reviews, BE298
  guides, BE276, BE278
  indexes, BE283
Horror film directors, 1931-1990, Fischer, Dennis, BH290
Horror literature, BE278
Horstman, Raymond. *Dutch parliamentary election studies data source book, 1971–1989,* CJ383
Hort, Erasmus. *Bible book,* BC108

•*HORTCD*, EJ18
Hortica, Graf, Alfred Byrd, EG174
Horticultural abstracts, EJ230
Horticultural research international, EJ245
Horticulture
  abstract journals, EJ230
  bibliography, EJ70, EJ228, EJ229
  dictionaries, EG147, EJ237, EJ241, EJ242
    bilingual
      French-English, EJ238
      German-English, EJ28
      Spanish-English, EJ239
    multilingual, EJ240
  directories, EG155, EJ244, EJ245
  encyclopedias, BF290, EG116, EG125, EJ231,
    EJ233
  handbooks, EG157, EJ246, EJ247, EJ248, EJ249
  indexes, BF289, EJ229
  see also **Gardening**
Horton, Carrell Peterson. *Statistical record of black
  America*, CC400, CG83
Horton, John J. *Iceland*, DC391
——— *Yugoslavia*, DC607
Hortus third, EG147, EJ233, EJ235, EJ241
Horvath, Barbara M. *Community languages*, BD83
Horvath, Laszlo. *Peronism and the three Perons*,
  DB327
Horvilleur, Gilles. *Dictionnaire des personnages du
  cinéma*, BH220
Horward, Donald D. *Napoleonic military history*,
  DC192
Horwill, Herbert William. *Dictionary of modern
  American usage*, AC76
Horwitz, William. *Official methods of analysis of the
  Association of Official Analytical Chemists*, EE84,
  EJ59
Hosamut hāēng Chat (Bangkok). *Bannānukrom
  hāēng chāt*, AA939
Hosius, Carl. *Geschichte der römischen Literatur bis
  zum Gesetzgebungswerk des Kaisers Justinian*,
  BE1052
Hoskin, Michael A. *The general history of
  astronomy*, EC59
Hospers, J. H. *A basic bibliography for the study of
  Semitic languages*, BD203
Hospital abstracts, EH76
Hospital administration terminology, EH117, EH129
Hospital literature index, EH74, EH75, EH77
Hospital statistics, EH153
Hospitals
  abstract journals, EH69, EH76
  acronyms, EH129
  dictionaries, EH115, EH117
  directories, EH153
  indexes, EH74, EH77
  staff, EH155
Hospitals (by country or region)
  Canada
    directories, EH165
  Great Britain
    directories, EH168
Hostos, Adolfo de. *Diccionario histórico
  bibliográfico comentado de Puerto Rico*, DB455
——— *Tesauro de datos históricos*, DB456
Hot topics, AD278
Hotaling, Edward R. *Shakespeare and the musical
  stage*, BE790
Hotel & motel red book, CL394
Hotel red book, CL394
Hotels, CL393
  directories, CL394
Hotten, John Camden. *The original lists of persons of
  quality, emigrants, religious exiles, political rebels
  … and others who went from Great Britain to the
  American plantations*, AJ63
Hottentot (Khoekhoen) place names, Nienaber,
  Grabriel Stefanus, CL216
Houaiss, Antônio. *Dicionário inglês-português*,
  AC645
——— *The new Appleton dictionary of the English
  and Portuguese languages*, AC647
Houben, Josef. *Methoden der organischen Chemie
  (Houben-Weyl)*, EE138

Houben-Weyl Methoden der Organischen Chemie,
  EE138
Houbová, Bohumila. *Historiografie v
  Československu, 1970–1980*, DC124
Houck, Carter. *The quilt encyclopedia illustrated*,
  BG163
Houdek, Frank G. *Law for the layman*, CK126
Houfe, Simon. *Dictionary of British book illustrators
  and caricaturists, 1800–1914*, BF323
Hough, Romeyn Beck. *Handbook of the trees of the
  northern states and Canada east of the Rocky
  Mountains*, EG195
Houghton, David D. *Handbook of applied
  meteorology*, EF154
Houghton, Walter Edwards. *The Wellesley index to
  Victorian periodicals, 1824–1900*, AD292
Houghton Library. *Music in Harvard libraries*, BJ90
Houkes, John M. *A catalogue of rare books,
  pamphlets, and journals on business and
  economics in the Krannert Library special
  collection, 1500–1870*, CH19
Houldcroft, P. T. *Materials data sources*, EK255
Houlden, J. L. *A dictionary of Biblical interpretation*,
  BC127
Houle, Cyril Orvin. *The literature of adult education*,
  CB354
Houlette, Forrest. *Nineteenth-century rhetoric*,
  BE355
Houm, Philip. *Norsk litteraturhistorie*, BE1339
Houmøller, Sven. *Biografiske tidskriftartikler*,
  AD309, AD310
Hourani, Albert Habib. *The Cambridge encyclopedia
  of the Middle East and North Africa*, DE54
House, Jonathan M. *Military intelligence, 1870–
  1991*, CJ608
House, Richard. *Radical geography*, CL18
House and garden dictionary, BG25
House of Commons, CJ358
House of Commons, 1715–1754, Sedgwick, Romney,
  CJ354, CJ360
House of Commons, 1754–1790, Brooke, John,
  CJ354
——— Namier, Lewis Bernstein, CJ354
•*House of Commons parliamentary papers CD-ROM
  index*, AF203
*House of Commons sessional papers of the
  eighteenth century*, Great Britain. Parliament.
  House of Commons, AF200
Household economic studies, CG97
Householder, Fred W. *Greek*, BD137
Housing
  bibliography, CH529
  directories, BF280
  statistics, CH545
  see also **Real estate**
Housing construction statistics, 1889 to 1964, United
  States. Bureau of the Census, CH545
Houston, Helen Ruth. *The Afro-American novel,
  1965–1975*, BE522
Houston, W. Robert. *Handbook of research on
  teacher education*, CB162
Houston post [index], AE104
Houtchens, Carolyn Washburn. *English romantic
  poets and essayists*, BE702, BE984
Houtchens, Lawrence Huston. *English romantic
  poets and essayists*, BE702, BE984
Houzeau, Jean Charles. *Bibliographie générale de
  l'astronomie jusqu'en 1880*, EC6, EC13, EC14
Hove, Julien van. *Répertoire des périodiques
  paraissant en Belgique*, AD84
Hovestreydt, W. *Late reviews AEB, 1947–1984*,
  DA121
Hovland, Michael A. *Musical settings of American
  poetry*, BJ272
*How libraries must comply with the Americans with
  Disabilities Act (ADA)*, AK66
How prints look, Ivins, William Mills, BF373
*How to distinguish the saints in art by their
  costumes, symbols and attributes*, Bles, Arthur de,
  BF180
How to find chemical information, Maizell, Robert
  E., EE4

How to find information about AIDS, Huber, Jeffrey
  T., EH20
How to find information about companies, CH331
How to find out in mathematics, Pemberton, John E.,
  EB4
How to find out in psychiatry, Greenberg, Bette,
  EH369
How to find out in psychology, Borchardt, D. H.,
  CD2
How to find the law, Cohen, Morris L., CK115,
  CK122
How to get your book published, Bell, Herbert W.,
  AA296
The "how to" grants manual, Bauer, David G.,
  AL130
How to identify old maps and globes, Lister,
  Raymond, CL222
How to identify prints, Gascoigne, Bamber, BF373
*How to locate anyone who is or has been in the
  military*, Johnson, Richard S., CJ625
*How to register a copyright and protect your
  creative work*, Chickering, Robert B., AA312
How to research the Supreme Court, Goehlert,
  Robert, CK186
——— Martin, Fenton S., CK186
How to use a law library, Dane, Jean, CK218
——— Thomas, Philip A., CK218
How to use a research library, Beasley, David R.,
  AK4
How to write & publish a scientific paper, Day,
  Robert A., EA158
*How to write and publish papers in the medical
  sciences*, Huth, Edward J., EH194
Howard, Diana. *Directory of theatre resources*,
  BH53
——— *London theatres and music halls, 1850–1950*,
  BH99
Howard, Edrice. *Specialized study options U.S.A*,
  CB317
Howard, John T. *A bibliography of theatre
  technology*, BH50
Howard, Neale E. *The telescope handbook and star
  atlas*, EC51
Howard, Patsy C. *Theses in American literature,
  1896–1971*, BE425
——— *Theses in English literature, 1894–1970*,
  BE593
Howard, Philip H. *Dictionary of chemical names and
  synonyms*, EE42
Howard, Richard. *A complete checklist of the birds of
  the world*, EG263
Howard-Hill, Trevor Howard. *Index to British
  literary bibliography*, BE587, BE763
——— *Oxford Shakespeare concordances*, BE776
Howard-Reguindin, Pamela F. *Honduras*, DB312
Howard University. Libraries. Moorland Foundation.
  *Dictionary catalog of the Jesse E. Moorland
  Collection of Negro Life and History, Howard
  University Library, Washington, D.C*, CC379
Howard University. Library. *Dictionary catalog of
  the Arthur B. Spingarn collection of Negro
  authors*, BE523, BE1504
*The Howard University bibliography of African and
  Afro-American religious studies*, Williams, Ethel
  L., BC33
Howard W. Sams & Co. *Handbook of electronic
  tables and formulas*, EK139
Howard-Williams, Jeremy. *The sailing dictionary*,
  BK123
Howarth, Helen E. *A source book in astronomy*,
  EC62
Howatson, M. C. *The Oxford companion to classical
  literature*, BE1014
Howe, George Frederick. *Guide to historical
  literature*, DA1
Howe, Marshall A. *Mosses with a hand-lens*, EG193
Howe, Robin. *Dictionary of gastronomy*, EJ213
Howe, Will David. *American authors and books,
  1640 to the present day*, BE432
——— *American books, 1640–1940*, BE432
Howe, William H. *The butterflies of North America*,
  EG332

Howe-Grant, Mary. *Encyclopedia of chemical technology,* EK51

Howell, John Bruce. *East African community,* AF221
—— *Kenya,* AF232, DD167
—— *Tanganyika African National Union,* DD233

Howells, John G. *A reference companion to the history of abnormal psychology,* CD101
—— *World history of psychiatry,* EH398

Howes, Durwood. *American women, 1935–1940,* AH57

Howes, Kelly King. *Characters in 19th-century literature,* BE184

Howes, Wright. *U.S.iana, 1650–1950,* AA241

Howie, R. A. *Rock-forming minerals,* EF195

Howlett, Charles F. *The American peace movement,* CJ672

Howlett, D. R. *Dictionary of medieval Latin from British sources,* AC588

Howley, G. C. D. *The new layman's Bible commentary in one volume,* BC179

Howorth, Lisa N. *The blues,* BJ337

Hoxie, Frederick E. *Native Americans,* CC415

Hoy, Helen. *Modern English-Canadian prose,* BE830

Hoy, Suellen M. *Public works history in the United States,* DB19

Hoyle, Edmond. *The new complete Hoyle,* BK128

Hoyle's rules of games, Morehead, Alfred H., BK128

Hoyos Villanueva, Luis H. *Enciclopedia yucatanense,* DB245

Hoyt, Anne Kelley. *Bibliography of the Chickasaw,* CC420

Hoyt, Jehiel Keeler. *Hoyt's new cyclopedia of practical quotations,* BE105

Hoyt's new cyclopedia of practical quotations, Hoyt, Jehiel Keeler, BE105

Hrvatski biografski leksikon, AH307

Hrvatsko ili srpasko engleski rječnik, Bujas, Željko, AC713
—— Drvodelić, Milan, AC713

Hrvatsko ili srpsko-engleski enciklopedijski rječnik, Bujas, Željko, AC712

Hsia, Ronald. *Gazetteer of China,* CL161

Hsieh, Chiao-min. *Atlas of China,* CL353

Hsieh, Wan-jo. *Chung-kuo tù shu kuan ming lu,* AK156

Hsieh, Winston. *Chinese historiography on the Revolution of 1911,* DE128
—— *Modern Chinese society,* DE130

Hsu, David H. G. *Chinese periodicals in the Library of Congress,* AD188

Huang, Han-chu. *Chinese newspapers in the Library of Congress,* AE87
—— *Chinese periodicals in the Library of Congress,* AD188

Huang, Parker Po-fei. *Cantonese dictionary,* AC264

Huannou, Adrien. *La littérature béninoise de langue française,* BE1524

Hubach, Robert Rogers. *Early midwestern travel narratives,* DB161

Hubbard, Linda S. *Publishers directory,* AA284

Hubbard, Monica M. *Cities of the world,* CL57

Hubbell, Jay B. *South in American literature, 1607–1900,* BE575

Hubbell's legal directory, CK151

Huber, A. *Deutsches Wörterbuch,* AC402

Huber, Jeffrey T. *How to find information about AIDS,* EH20

Huber, Kristina R. *Women in Japanese society,* CC604

Huber, Thomas Patrick. *Dictionary of concepts in physical geography,* CL37

Hubert, Marilyn L. *Lexicon of new formal geologic names of the United States, 1976–1980,* EF77
—— *Lexicon of new formal geologic names of the United States, 1981–1985,* EF77

Hubin, Allen J. *Crime fiction II,* BE271

Hubschmid, Johannes. *Bibliographia onomastica helvetica,* CL212

Huck, Burkhardt J. *Informationshandbuch internationale Beziehungen und Länderkunde,* DA173

HUD USER. *Directory of information resources in housing and urban development,* BF280

Huddleston, Mark W. *Comparative public administration,* CJ467

Hudon, Jean-Paul. *Bibliographie de la critique de la littérature québécoise dans les revues des XIXe et XXe siécles,* BE838

Hudson, Grace L. *Monaco,* DC449

Hudson, Judith. *Women online,* CC571

Hudson, Kenneth. *Cambridge guide to the museums of Britain and Ireland,* BF98
—— *The Cambridge guide to the museums of Europe,* BF98
—— *The directory of museums & living displays,* AL88
—— *Directory of world museums,* AL88

Hudson, Margaret F. *Elder neglect and abuse,* CC71

Hudson's newsletter directory, AE35

Hudson's subscription newsletter directory, AE35

Hue, Pascal. *Senegal,* DD201

Huellmantel, Michael B. *European business services directory,* CH413

Huenefeld, Irene Pennington. *International directory of historical clothing,* BG103

Huff, Cynthia. *British women's diaries,* BE724, DC327

Huffman, Franklin E. *Bibliography and index of mainland Southeast Asian languages and linguistics,* BD228
—— *English-Khmer dictionary,* AC563

Hüfner, Klaus. *The United Nations system, international bibliography,* AF35
—— *Zwanzig Jähre Vereinte Nationen … 1945–1965,* AF35

Hügel, Hans-Otto. *Deutsche literarische Zeitschriften, 1880–1945,* AD76

Huggett, Milton. *Concordance to the American Book of Common Prayer,* BC348

Hughes, Andrew. *Medieval music,* DA138

Hughes, Brian. *Diccionario de términos judídicos,* CK55

Hughes, Charles William. *American hymns old and new,* BC317

Hughes, David G. *An index of Gregorian chant,* BJ290

Hughes, Elizabeth. *The big book of buttons,* BG105

Hughes, Heather. *Women in Southern Africa,* DD123

Hughes, John J. *Bits, bytes & biblical studies,* BC188

Hughes, Maria. *Guide to libraries in Central and Eastern Europe,* DC48

Hughes, Roger. *The Caribbean,* DB406

Hughes-Hughes, Augustus. *Catalogue of manuscript music in the British Museum,* BJ93

Huguet, Edmond Eugène Auguste. *Dictionnaire de la langue française du seizième siècle,* AC382

Hui, Y. H. *Data sourcebook for food scientists and technologists,* EJ164
—— *Encyclopedia of food science and technology,* EJ153
—— *United States food laws, regulations, and standards,* EJ162

Huke, Robert E. *Basic geographical library,* CL17

Hulbert, James Root. *Dictionary of American English on historical principles,* AC150

Hulbert, Mark. *The Hulbert guide to financial newsletters,* CH297

Hulbert Financial Digest. The Hulbert guide to financial newsletters, CH297

The Hulbert guide to financial newsletters, Hulbert, Mark, CH297

Hules, Virginia T. *French feminist criticism,* BE1133

Hulet, Claude L. *Latin American poetry in English translation,* BE885
—— *Latin American prose in English translation,* BE885

Hull, Roger. *Virology,* EG345

Hulme, F. Edward. *Flags of the world,* AL190

Huls, Mary Ellen. *United States government documents on women, 1800–1990,* AF66, CC494

Hultkrantz, Åke. *General ethnological concepts,* CE49

Human anatomy for artists, Goldfinger, Eliot, BF123

Human behavior, CA10, CD8, CD20

Human biology, Encyclopedia of, EG20

Human engineering
handbooks, EK228, EK236

Human evolution and prehistory, CE40

Human factors design handbook, Woodson, Wesley E., EK236

Human food uses, Freedman, Robert L., EH293

Human longevity from antiquity to the modern lab, Bailey, William G., CC60

Human protein data, EG160

Human Relations Area Files, Inc. *Annotated bibliography of Afghanistan,* DE110
—— *Atlas of world cultures,* CE72
—— *Cross-cultural CD,* CE8
—— *The Indian city,* CC305
—— *Introduction to library research in anthropology,* CE2
—— *Lapps ethnographic bibliography,* CE94
—— *Minorities of Southwest China,* CE107
—— *Outline of cultural materials,* CE61
—— *Outline of world cultures,* CE59

Human resource management in libraries, Rubin, Richard, AK178

Human resources *see* **Personnel management**

The human resources glossary, Tracey, William R., CH714

Human rights
annuals, CK108
bibliography, CC333, CK75, CK77
directories, CC345, CK75
encyclopedias, CK99
sourcebooks, CK113
surveys, CK109

Human rights (by country or region)
Sri Lanka, DE260
United States
directories, CK147

Human rights, CK113
—— Friedman, Julian R., CK77
—— Martin, J. Paul, CK77
—— Sherman, Marc I., CK77

Human rights and anthropology, CE13

Human rights bibliography, CK77

Human rights in developing countries, CK109

Human rights organizations and periodicals directory, CK147

Human rights : sixty major global instruments, Langley, Winston E., CK113

Human rights : status of international instruments, CK113

Human rights watch world report, CK109

Human services professionals, CC50

Human sexuality, CC278

Human words, Hendrickson, Robert, AC55

Humana, Charles. *World human rights guide,* CK109

Humanism
bibliography, BE20, DA140

Humanism (by country or region)
Italy, BE1310

Humanistic psychology, Gottsegen, Gloria Behar, CD56

Humanistica Lovaniensia, BE1041

Humanities
abstract journals, AD254, BB24, BE38, CE23
bibliography, BE20
book reviews, BA7
congresses and meetings
bibliography, AL27
indexes, AL29
databases, BA3
directories
Great Britain, BA8
dissertations, AG53, CA20
encyclopedias, CA31
financial aids, AL108, BA9
indexes, AD254, AD260, AD264, AD288, BA2, BA3, BB24, BE38, CE23
periodicals
databases, BA5
guides, AD117
indexes, BA5
reviews of research, BA8

Humanities (by country or region)
  Hungary, DC389
Humanities and social sciences in the Soviet Union, AL59, DC593
Humanities index, AD288, BA5, BE260, BE499, CA29, BA5
Humanities Research Council of Canada. *Union list of manuscripts in Canadian repositories*, DB195
Humash Torah Shelemath, Kasher, Menachem Mendel, BC182
Hume, Robert Ernest. *Treasure house of the living religions*, BC90
Hume, David, BB73, BB74
Humm, Maggie. *An annotated critical bibliography of feminist criticism*, BE49
———— *The dictionary of feminist theory*, CC538
Hummel, Arthur W. *Eminent Chinese of the Ch'ing period (1644–1912)*, AH340
Hummel, David. *Collector's guide to the American musical theatre*, BJ258
Humor, AD28, CF79
Humor in America, CF79
Humor in American literature, Nilsen, Don Lee Fred, BE411
Humpert, Magdalene. *Bibliographie der Kameralwissenschaften*, CH336
Humphery-Smith, Cecil R. *General armory two*, AJ149
———— *The Phillimore atlas and index of parish registers*, AJ113
Humphreys, Arthur Lee. *Handbook to county bibliography*, DC349
Humphreys, Christmas. *A popular dictionary of Buddhism*, BC47
Humphreys, Nancy K. *American women's magazines*, AD37, CC522
Humphreys, Norman K. *Historical dictionary of the International Monetary Fund*, CH239
Humphreys, R. A. *Latin American history*, DB257
Humphries, Charles. *Music publishing in the British Isles from the beginning until the middle of the nineteenth century*, BJ181, BJ184
Hümübottor, Franz. *Biographisches Lexikon der hervorragenden Ärzte aller Zeiten und Völker*, EH222
Hundert, Gershon David. *The Jews in Poland and Russia*, DC34
———— *Polish Jewish history*, DC34
A hundred eminent Congregationalists, BC383
A hundred years of biology, Dawes, Benjamin, EG59
Hundsdörfer, Volkhard. *Bibliography for social science research on Tanzania*, DD235
Hungarian abbreviations, Library of Congress. Slavic and Central European Division, AC497
Hungarian authors, Tezla, Albert, BE1283
Hungarian-English technical dictionary, Nagy, Ernő, EA115
Hungarian historiography, DC380
Hungarian history and literature, Harvard University. Library, BE1277
The Hungarian Jewish catastrophe, Braham, Randolph L., DA213
Hungarian language
  abbreviations, AC497
  bibliography, BD208
  dictionaries, AC492, AC493, AC494
    bibliography, AC500
    bilingual
      English-Hungarian, AC496
      Hungarian-English, AC495
    etymology
      dictionaries, AC498, AC499
Hungarian literature
  bibliography, BE1277, BE1278, BE1279
  biobibliography, BE1283
  dictionaries, BE1275
  indexes, BE1278
  library catalogs, BE1277
  translations, BE1280
Hungarian literature (by subject)
  history, BE1276, BE1281

Hungarian literature in English translation published in Great Britain 1830–1968, Czigány, Magda, BE1280
Hungarian Revolution in perspective, Wagner, Francis S., DC380
Hungarian statistical yearbook, CG247
Hungarians in America, Szy, Tibor, AH251
Hungarians in the United States and Canada, Szeplaki, Joseph, CC321, CC473
Hungarica, Apponyi, Sándor, DC378
Hungary
  bibliography, AA709, AA710, AA711, AA712, AA713, AA714, DC378, DC381, DC384
    current, AA715, AA716
  bibliography of bibliography, AA48
  biography, AH247, AH248, AH249, AH250, AH251, AH252, AH253, BE1282
  dissertations, AG37
  encyclopedias, AB59
  government publications, AF165
  guides, DC93, DC389
  handbooks, DC388
  library catalogs, BE1277
  manuscripts and archives, DC386
  newspapers, AD121, AD123
  periodicals, AD120, AD121, AD122, AD123
    indexes, AD317
  registers, CJ325
  statistics, CG245, CG246, CG247, CG248
Hungary (by subject)
  archaeology and ancient history, DC379
  history, DC378, DC380, DC385
    bibliography, DC382, DC383
    guides to records, DC387
    manuscripts and archives, DC387
  place-names, CL207
  population, CG248
Hungary. Központi Statisztikai Hivatal. *Statisztikai évkönyv*, CG247
———— *Statisztikai szótár*, CG21
———— *Time series of historical statistics 1867–1992*, CG248
Hungary. Központi Statisztikai Hivatal. Könyvtár és Dokumentációs Szolgálat. *Statisztikai adatforrások*, CG246
Hungary, Kabdebó, Thomas, DC381
Hungary's literature in translation, BE1280
Hunnisett, Basil. *Dictionary of British steel engravers*, BF339
Hunt, Candida. *The encyclopedic dictionary of science*, EA91
Hunt, G. N. S. *Oxford Bible atlas*, BC200
Hunt, Howard F. *Encyclopedic dictionary of sports medicine*, EH127
Hunt, Lee M. *Ocean world encyclopedia*, EF218
Hunt, Mabel G. *Index to Department bulletins no. 1–1500*, EJ92
———— *Index to publications of the United States Department of Agriculture, 1901–40*, EJ92
Hunt, R. N. Carew. *Books on communism and the communist countries*, CJ514
Hunt, Rachel McMasters Miller. *Catalogue of botanical books in the collection of Rachel McMasters Miller Hunt*, EG95
Hunt, Thomas C. *Catholic school education in the United States*, CB36
———— *Religious colleges and universities in America*, CB223
———— *Religious schools in America*, CB37
Hunt, V. Daniel. *Dictionary of advanced manufacturing technology*, CH340, EK231
Hunt, William Dudley. *Encyclopedia of American architecture*, BF235
Hunt Botanical Library. *B-P-H*, EG111
Hunt Institute for Botanical Documentation. *Plant, animal & anatomical illustration in art & science*, EA220
Hunter, David E. *Encyclopedia of anthropology*, CE39
Hunter, Janet. *Concise dictionary of Japanese history*, DE211

Hunter, John E. *Inventory of ethnological collections in museums of the United States and Canada*, CE88
Hunter, Joy W. *Health media review index*, EH43
Hunter, Richard Alfred. *Three hundred years of psychiatry, 1535–1860*, EH399
Hunter, Rosemary. *The Oxford literary guide to Australia*, BE855
Hunter, Sam. *Modern art*, BF131
Hunter, William Wilson. *Imperial gazetteer of India*, CL164
The hunter's field guide to the game birds and animals of North America, Elman, Robert, BK115
Hunting and fishing, BK114, BK115, BK116, BK117
Huntress, Ernest Hamlin. *Brief introduction to the use of Beilstein's Handbuch der organischen Chemie*, EE115
Hurault, J. *Bibliographie de la Guyane Française*, DB377
Hurewitz, Jacob Coleman. *The Middle East and North Africa in world politics*, DE64
Hurme, Raija. *Englanti-suomi suursanakirja*, AC322
Hurmie, J. F. *Dictionary of farm animal behaviour*, EJ116
Hurrelmann, Klaus. *International handbook of adolescence*, CC169
Hurst, Paul. *International handbook of education systems*, CB125
Hurt, Charlie Deuel. *Information sources in science and technology*, EA4
Hurt, Jakob. *Eesti-saksa sõnaraamat kolmas muutmatu trük teisest, dr. Jakob Hurt'i poolt redigeeritud väljaandest*, AC309
Hurt, Michael. *The mathematical practitioners of Hanoverian England, 1714–1840*, EB102
Hurt, Susan. *The mathematical practitioners of Hanoverian England, 1714–1840*, EB102
Hury, Carlo. *Luxembourg*, DC447
———— *Luxemburgensia*, AA55
Husa, Karl. *Bibliographie zur Bevölkerungsforschung in Österreich, 1945–1978*, CG193
Husband, Janet. *Sequels*, BE255
Husband, Jonathan F. *Sequels*, BE255
Huschke, Ralph E. *Glossary of meteorology*, EF146
Husén, Torsten. *The international encyclopedia of education*, CB70
Husmann, Gaby. *E.A.S.A. register*, CE99
Husmann, Rolf. *E.A.S.A. register*, CE99
———— *Handbuch der deutschsprachigen ethnologie*, CE99
Hussain, Asaf. *Islamic movements in Egypt, Pakistan and Iran*, DE32
Husselman, Elinor Mullet. *A Coptic bibliography*, BC454, BE1521
Hussey, Joan Mervyn. *Orthodox church in Byzantine Empire*, BC278
Hussey, Maurice. *Longman companion to twentieth century literature*, BE764
The Hussite movement and the reformation in Bohemia, Moravia and Slovakia (1350–1650), Zeman, Jarold K., DC128
Hutchinson, J. A. *The concise Oxford French dictionary*, AC337
Hutchinson, William Kenneth. *American economic history*, CH172
———— *History of economic analysis*, CH18
Hutchison, Robert. *Catalogue of meteorites*, EF207
Hutera, Donald. *The dance handbook*, BH153
Huth, Edward J. *How to write and publish papers in the medical sciences*, EH194
———— *Medical style and format*, EH194
Hutton, Patrick H. *Historical dictionary of the Third French Republic, 1870–1940*, DC207
Huws, Gwilym. *Wales*, DC369
Huxley, Aldous. *Encyclopedia of pacifism*, CJ685
Huxley, Anthony Julian. *Dictionary of gardening*, EG125
———— *Standard encyclopedia of the world's mountains*, CL61, CL62, CL63, EF8, EF9, EF10
———— *Standard encyclopedia of the world's oceans and islands*, CL61, CL62, CL63, EF8, EF9, EF10

——— *Standard encyclopedia of the world's rivers and lakes*, CL61, CL62, CL63, EF8, EF9, EF10
Hvem er hvem?, AH276
Hyams, Edward. *Great botanical gardens of the world*, EG148
Hyamson, Albert Montefiore. *A dictionary of universal biography of all ages and of all peoples*, AH13
Hyatt, Marshall. *Afro-American cinematic experience*, CC334
Hydata, EF128
Hyde, Douglas. *A literary history of Ireland from earliest times to the present day*, BE803
Hydraulic engineering and hydrodynamics bibliography, EK101
   handbooks, EK102
Hydro-index, EF128
Hydrodynamics *see* **Hydraulic engineering and hydrodynamics**
Hydrology
   bibliography, EF126, EF127, EF128, EF130
   dictionaries, EF134
      multilingual, EF132, EF133, EF135, EF136
   handbooks, EF137, EF138, EF139
   maps, CL249, EF111
Hydrology (by subject)
   study and teaching, EF151
Hydrometry, EK100
Hylton, William H. *Rodale's illustrated encyclopedia of herbs*, EJ234
Hyman, Charles J. *Dictionary of physics and allied sciences*, ED26
Hyman, Libbie Henrietta. *The invertebrates*, EG240
Hymn Society of America. *Dictionary of American hymnology*, BC315
Hymn Society of Great Britain and Ireland. *Hymns and tunes indexed by first lines, tune names, and metres, compiled from current English hymnbooks*, BC321
Hymns and hymnology, BC313, BC316, BC317, BC318, BC319, BC320, BC321, BC358
   bibliography, BC315
   indexes, BC315
Hymns and tunes, Diehl, Katharine Smith, BC316
Hymns and tunes indexed by first lines, tune names, and metres, compiled from current English hymnbooks, Perry, David W., BC321
Hymns of the Atharva-veda, BC92

I am happy to present, Lyle, Guy Redvers, BE357
IAC magazine index, AD278
Iacono, Bruno. *Dictionnaire de sigles nationaux et internationaux*, AC345
ÌAmpol'skii, I. M. *Entsiklopedicheskiĭ muzykal'nyĭ slovar'*, BJ119
Iasbez, Liliana. *Glossary of geographical names in six languages*, CL91
IASLIC (Association). *Directory of special and research libraries in India*, AK157
IATG, Schwertner, Siegfried M., BC25
Iatrides, John O. *Greece in the 1940s*, DC372
•*IAUDOC*, AF59
•*IBEDOCS*, AF59
Iben, Icko. *The Germanic press of Europe*, AE8
Iberian languages
   bibliography, BD167
   festschriften, BD166, BE1436
Iberian literatures
   bibliography, BD167
   festschriften, BD166, BE1436
Ibero-American Institute, Prussian Cultural Heritage Foundation. *Catalog of the Latin-American collection*, DB269
•*IBISCUS*, DD201
IBM dictionary of computing, EK181
IBN, AA910
——— Lobies, Jean-Pierre, AH16
I.B.R., AA373
Ibrāhīm, Zāhidah. *Dalīl al-jarā'id wa-al-majallāt al-'Irāqiyah, 1869–1978*, AE91
Ibrahim-Hilmy, *Prince*. *The literature of Egypt and the Soudan, from the earliest times to the year 1885 [i.e., 1887] inclusive*, DD148

IBRR, BC52
IBT, BH57
IBZ, AD255, DE33
•*IBZ CD-ROM*, AD255
•*ICAR*, EJ74
Icart, Roger. *Catalogue des films français de long métrage*, BH184
The ICBP/IUCN red data book, EG278
ICC, BC173
ICCROM. *International index of conservation research*, BF199
ICD-10, EH56, EH377
ICD-9, EH384
ICD-9–CM, EH55
Iceland
   bibliography, AA718, AA719, DC391
      current, AA720
   biography, AH164, AH254
   library resources, DC390
   manuscripts and archives, DC390
   statistics, CG249
Iceland (by subject)
   population, CG250
Iceland. Hagstofa. *Mannfjöldaskýrslur arin 1971–80*, CG250
Iceland, Horton, John J., DC391
Icelandic-English dictionary, AC502
——— Cleasby, Richard, AC503, AC509
Icelandic language
   bibliography, BD129, BE1083
   dictionaries, AC504, AC505, AC507
      bilingual, AC503
      Danish-Icelandic, AC506
      Icelandic-Danish, AC506
      Icelandic-English, AC502, AC508, AC509
   etymology
      dictionaries, AC510, AC511
Icelandic libraries and archives, Hill, Dennis Auburn, DC390
Icelandic literature
   bibliography, BD129, BE1083, BE1090
   library catalogs, AA717, BE1284
   translations, BE1088, BE1287
Icelandic literature (by subject)
   history, BE1285
The Icelandic national bibliography, AA720
Icelandic poetry
   concordances, BE1286
ICIB, AK201
•*ICOMMOS*, AF59
Iconclass, Waal, H. van de, BF175
Iconclass indexes : Italian prints, BF175
Iconografia rinascimentale italiana, Zappella, Giuseppina, BF72
Iconografía y mitos indígenas en el arte, Gisbert, Teresa, BF70
Iconographic index to New Testament subjects represented in photographs and slides of paintings in the visual collections, Fine Arts Library, Harvard University, Roberts, Helene E., BF175, BF298
Iconographic index to Old Testament subjects, Roberts, Helene E., BF175, BF298
Iconographic index to Stanislas Lami's Dictionnaire des sculpteurs de l'Ecole française au dix-neuvième siècle, Janson, Horst Woldemar, BF395
Iconographical index of Hebrew illuminated manuscripts, BF193
Iconographie de l'art chrétien, Réau, Louis, BF185
Iconographie de l'art profane au Moyen-Âge et à la Renaissance, et la décoration des demeures, Marle, Raimond van, BF171
Iconography *see* **Symbols and symbolism**
Iconography of Christian art, Seligman, Janet, BF186
Iconography of the saints in Italian painting from its beginnings to the early XVIth century, Kaftal, George, BF183
ICP encyclopedia of photography, BF341
ICPSR. *Guide to resources and services*, CA3
ICSSR research projects, 1969–1987, CA47
Idaho. [Laws, etc.]. *Idaho code*, CK179
Idaho code, Idaho. [Laws, etc.], CK179

Identifying American architecture, BF252
Identifying Australian architecture, BF208
Idioms and phrases index, AC91
Idlin, Ralph. *Dictionary of physics and allied sciences*, ED26
Idrizi, Frida. *Fjalor anglisht-shqip*, AC206
IEEE standard dictionary of electrical and electronics terms, EK131
IES lighting handbook, EK140
IFLA directory, AK53
IFLA International Office for UBC. *Commonwealth national bibliographies*, AA389
——— *Commonwealth retrospective national bibliographies*, AA390
IFLA Office for International Lending. *A guide to centres of international lending and copying*, AK223
Igaku yakugaku hen, AD342
Igbo, Welmers, Beatrice F., AC501
Igbo language
   dictionaries, AC501
Iglesias de Souza, Luis. *El teatro lírico español*, BJ266
Igoe, Lynn Moody. *250 years of Afro-American art*, BF24
Igoe, Robert S. *Dictionary of food ingredients*, EH307, EJ156
Igreja, Francisco. *Dicionário de poetas contemporâneos*, BE933
Iguíniz, Juan Bautista. *Bibliografía biográfica mexicana*, AH109
Ihme, Heinrich. *Deutsches biographisches Jahrbuch*, AH207
Ihrie, Maureen. *Dictionary of the literature of the Iberian peninsula*, BE1070
•*IHS international standards & specifications*, EA272
IIC abstracts, BF198
IIS microfiche library, CG69
IJBF, AA125
Ijiri, Yuji. *Kohler's dictionary for accountants*, CH252
IJsewijn, Jozef. *Companion to neo-Latin studies*, BE1041
Ikonographie der christlichen kunst, Künstle, Karl, BF186
——— Schiller, Gertrud, BF186
Ilardo, Joseph A. *Argument*, BE369
Iles du sud-ouest de l'océan Indien, Safla, Roucaya, DD142, DD175
——— Université de la Réunion. Service commun de la documentation, DD121, DD142, DD175, DD179
Iles du sud-ouest de l'océn Indien, Safla, Roucaya, DD179
Illies, Joachim. *Grzimek's encyclopedia of ecology*, EG64
Illingworth, Valerie. *Dictionary of computing*, EK178
——— *The Facts on File dictionary of astronomy*, EC32
Illinois. [Laws, etc.]. *West's Smith-Hurd Illinois compiled statutes annotated*, CK179
Illuminating Engineering Society of North America. *Lighting handbook*, EK140
The illustrated Bartsch, Bartsch, Adam von, BF381
Illustrated Bible dictionary, BC147
The illustrated Bible handbook, Blair, Edward Payson, BC186
An illustrated bio-bibliography of black photographers, 1940–1988, Willis-Thomas, Deborah, BF357
Illustrated companion to the First World War, Bruce, A. P. C., DA199
Illustrated computer graphics dictionary, Spencer, Donald D., EK188
Illustrated dental terminology, EH256
Illustrated dictionary & concordance of the Bible, BC142
Illustrated dictionary of architecture, 800–1914, Lever, Jill, BF246
An illustrated dictionary of art and archaeology, Mollett, John William, BF87

An illustrated dictionary of ceramics, Savage, George, BG67

An illustrated dictionary of Chinese medicinal herbs, Wee, Yeow Chin, EH350

Illustrated dictionary of dentistry, Jablonski, Stanley, EH258

Illustrated dictionary of eponymic syndromes and diseases and their synonyms, Jablonski, Stanley, EH118

An illustrated dictionary of glass, Newman, Harold, BG66

An illustrated dictionary of Hindu iconography, Stutley, Margaret, BF192

Illustrated dictionary of historic architecture, BF245

An illustrated dictionary of jewellery, Mason, Anita, BG82

An illustrated dictionary of jewelry, Newman, Harold, BG83, BG146

Illustrated dictionary of microcomputer terminology, Hordeski, Michael F., EK180

The illustrated dictionary of microcomputers, Hordeski, Michael F., EK180

An illustrated dictionary of ornament, Stafford, Maureen, BG24

Illustrated dictionary of place names, United States and Canada, Harder, Kelsie B., CL176, CL182

Illustrated dictionary of pottery form, Fournier, Robert L., BG64

Illustrated dictionary of practical pottery, Fournier, Robert L., BG64

An illustrated dictionary of silverware, Newman, Harold, BG146

An illustrated encyclopaedia of mysticism and the mystery religions, Ferguson, John, BC61

Illustrated encyclopaedia of the classical world, DA100

Illustrated encyclopedia of archaeology, Daniel, Glyn, DA77

Illustrated encyclopedia of architects and architecture, Sharp, Dennis, BF224

The illustrated encyclopedia of billiards, Shamos, Michael Ian, BK68

The illustrated encyclopedia of birds, EG264

Illustrated encyclopedia of film character actors, Quinlan, David, BH284

The illustrated encyclopedia of fly-fishing, Calabi, Silvio, BK114

The illustrated encyclopedia of mankind, CE42

Illustrated encyclopedia of medieval civilization, Grabois, Aryeh, DA152

The illustrated encyclopedia of rockets and missiles, Gunston, Bill, CJ570

The illustrated encyclopedia of the securities industry, Pessin, Allan H., CH211

The illustrated encyclopedia of the strategy, tactics and weapons of Russian military power, Menaul, Stewart, CJ656

The illustrated encyclopedia of the strategy, tactics, and weapons of the Soviet War machine, CJ656

The illustrated encyclopedia of the universe, Lewis, Richard S., EC31

Illustrated encyclopedia of world coins, Hobson, Burton, BG178

—— Obojski, Robert, BG178

The illustrated Gaelic-English dictionary, Dwelly, Edward, AC393

Illustrated glossary of architecture, BF246

Illustrated guide to film directors, Quinlan, David, BH290

Illustrated guide to the textile collections in United States and Canadian museums, BG157

An illustrated history of those frills and furbelows of fashion which have come to be known as: accessories of dress, Lester, Katherine Morris, BG110

Illustrated medical dictionary, EH98

Illustrated polyglottic dictionary of plant names in Latin, Arabic, Armenian, English, French, German, Italian and Turkish languages, Bedevian, Armenag K., EG141

Illustrated Stedman's medical dictionary, Stedman, Thomas Lathrop, EH270

Illustrated who's who in British films, Gifford, Denis, BH211

The illustrated who's who of the cinema, BH282

Illustrating science, Council of Biology Editors. Scientific Illustration Committee, EA221

Illustration catalog, New York Academy of Medicine. Library, EH51

Illustration index, BF60

Illustrators, BE384, BF372
  biography, BF384
  indexes, BE387

Illustrerad svensk litteraturhistoria, Schuck, Henrik, BE1485

—— Warburg, Karl, BE1485

Illustrerad svensk ordbok, AC761

Illustreret dansk litteraturhistorie, Hansen, Peter, BE1121

—— Petersen, Carl Sophus, BE1121

Illustreret norsk konversations-leksikon, AB74

Illustriertes Lexikon der deutschen Umgangssprache, Küpper, Heinz, AC429

ILO encyclopaedia of occupational health and safety, EH409

ILO thesaurus 1991, International Labour Office, CH652

Ilsar, Nira. *Bibliyografyah shel 'a1 vodot doktor bemada'e ha-ruah yeha-hevrah she-nikhtevu be-universita'ot Yiśra'el,* AG53, CA20

Iltis, J. C. *Government archives in South Asia,* DE84

Imaeda, Yoshiro. *Bibliography of Tibetan studies,* DE268

The image makers, Miles, William, CJ106

Image of a continent, Bodi, Leslie, DF25

The image of older adults in the media, Nuessel, Frank H., CC73

The image of the black in Western art, BF64

Images of American Indians on film, Bataille, Gretchen M., CC334

—— Silet, Charles L. P., CC334

Imaginary people, Pringle, David, BE188

Imaging abstracts, Royal Photographic Society of Great Britain, BF332

Imber, Jane. *Dictionary of advertising and direct mail terms,* CH550

Imbs, Paul. *Trésor de la langue française,* AC331

Imel, Dorothy. *Goddesses in world mythology,* BC62, CF2

IMF glossary, CH125

IMG, AE9

IMM abstracts, Institution of Mining and Metallurgy (London), EK253

•*IMMAGE,* EK253

Immelmann, Klaus. *A dictionary of ethology,* CD121

—— *Wörterbuch der Verhaltensforschung,* CD121

Immergut, E. H. *Polymer handbook,* EK289

The immigrant labor press in North America, 1840s–1970s, Hoerder, Dirk, CH656

Immigrant women in the United States, Gabaccia, Donna R., CC601

Immigrants (by country or region)
  Australia, DF33

Immigrants from Great Britain and Ireland, Lester, DeeGee, DC402

—— Weaver, Jack W., CC332, DC402

Immigrants from the German-speaking countries of Europe, Krewson, Margrit B., DC9

Immigrants, minorities and race relations, Gilbert, Victor Francis, CC337

Immigration, AJ49
  bibliography, CC311, CC313, CC319
  dissertations, CC337
  encyclopedias, CC342
  handbooks, CC350
  manuscripts and archives, CC332

Immigration (by country or region)
  Canada, DB41
  United States, DB41
    bibliography, CC601
    directories, CC34
    periodicals, CH656

Immigration and ethnicity, Buenker, John D., CC313

Immigration History Research Center. *Serbs in the United States and Canada,* CC321, CC473

The Immigration History Research Center, University of Minnesota. Immigration History Research Center, CC356

Immroth, John Philip. *Guide to the Library of Congress classification,* AK199

Immroth's guide to the Library of Congress classification, Chan, Lois Mai, AK199

Immunology, EG21, EH85
  dictionaries, EG33, EH124
  guides, EG4

Immunology, Nicholas, Robin, EG4

Immunology abstracts, EG14

Imperato, Eleanor M. *Mali,* CG343

Imperato, Pascal J. *Mali,* CG343, DD48

Imperial Chemical Industries. Plastics Division. *Index of reviews in organic chemistry,* EE134

Imperial gazetteer of India, CL163, CL164

Imperial Russian Historical Society. *Russkiĭ biograficheskiĭ slovar' …,* AH284

Imperialism, DC8

Impex reference catalogue of Indian books, AA896

•*IMPL online,* CC221

Imprenta en Arequipa, el Cuzco, Trujillo y otros pueblos del Perú durante las campañas de la independencia (1820–1825), Medina, José Toribio, AA540

La imprenta en Bogotá (1739–1821), Medina, José Toribio, AA525

Imprenta en Cartagena de las Indias (1809–1820), Medina, José Toribio, AA525

La imprenta en Filipinas, Retana y Gamboa, Wenceslao Emilio, AA929

Imprenta en Guadalajara de México (1793–1821), Medina, José Toribio, AA463

Imprenta en Guatemala, 1660–1821, Medina, José Toribio, AA481

La imprenta en la Habana (1707–1810), Medina, José Toribio, AA561

Imprenta en la Puebla de Los Angeles (1640–1821), Medina, José Toribio, AA463

La imprenta en Lima (1584–1824), Medina, José Toribio, AA540

La imprenta en Málaga, Llordén, Andrés, AA804

Imprenta en Manila, Medina, José Toribio, AA928

Imprenta en Manila desde sus orígenes hasta 1810, Medina, José Toribio, AA927

Imprenta en Mérida de Yucatán (1813–21), Medina, José Toribio, AA463

—— Suárez, Victor M., AA463

La imprenta en México (1539–1821), Medina, José Toribio, AA461

Imprenta en México, 1553–1820, González de Cossio, Francisco, AA461

La imprenta en México, 1594–1820, González de Cossio, Francisco, AA461

Imprenta en Oaxaca (1720–1820), Medina, José Toribio, AA463

La imprenta en Quito (1760–1818), Medina, José Toribio, AA531

Imprenta en Veracruz (1794–1821), Medina, José Toribio, AA463

Impresos chilenos, 1776–1818, Biblioteca Nacional (Chile), AA514

Impresos del siglo XVII, Simón Díaz, José, AA808

Impresos localizados (siglos XV–XVII), Simón Díaz, José, DC508

Impresos mexicanos del siglo XVI (incunables americanos) en la Biblioteca Nacional de México, el Museo Nacional y el Archivo General de la Nación, Valtón, Emilio, AA464

Impresos peruanos, Vargas Ugarte, Rubén, AA542

Impresos venezolanos del siglo XIX, Drenikoff, Iván, AA550

L'imprimerie sino-européenne en Chine, Cordier, Henri, AA894

Imprimeurs & libraires parisiens du XVIe siècle, Renouard, Philippe, AA310

Imprimeurs imaginaires et libraires supposés, Brunet, Gustave, AA194

Improving health and welfare work with families in poverty, Blackburn, Clare, CC51

Imps, Paul. *Trésor de la langue française,* AC331

IMS … Ayer directory of publications, AD51, AE23

IMS directory of publications, AD51, AE23
In black and white, Spradling, Mary Mace, AH41
In fashion: dress in the twentieth century, Glynn, Prudence, BG115
In pursuit of the past, Porter, Frank W., CC420
In search of enemies, Stockwell, John, DD128
In search of Scottish ancestry, Hamilton-Edwards, Gerald Kenneth Savery, AJ122
In search of the "Forlorn hope", Kitzmiller, John M., AJ103
In search of your British & Irish roots, Baxter, Angus, AJ2, AJ96
In search of your Canadian roots, Baxter, Angus, AJ2
In search of your European roots, Baxter, Angus, AJ2
In search of your German roots, Baxter, Angus, AJ2, AJ90
In the name of science, Gardner, Martin, EA80
In-vitro fertilization clinics, Partridge-Brown, Mary, CC229
Inada, Hide Ikehara. *Bibliography of translations from the Japanese into western languages from the 16th century to 1912,* BE1584
Inada, Kenneth K. *Guide to Buddhist philosophy,* BB20, BC470, BC472
Inagaki, Hisao. *Dictionary of Japanese Buddhist terms,* BC478
────── *A glossary of Zen terms,* BC478
Inaugural addresses of the Presidents of the United States, 1789–1989, CJ212
Incas
  bibliography, CC478
Incas, Gutiérrez, René L., DB385
────── Welch, Thomas L., CC478, DB385
Incest, CC218
  bibliography, CC207
Incest, De Young, Mary, CC207
Incest, the last taboo, Rubin, Richard, CC218
Inchon Landing, Korea, 1950, Edwards, Paul M., DA170
Incipitario unificato della poesia italiana, BE1316
Income, CH689
The incompleat chymist, Eklund, Jon, EE37
Incunabula, AA220, AA221, AA226, AA307
  bibliography, AA219, AA222, AA223, AA227, AA228, EH33
  guides, AA217, AA218
  library catalogs, AA224
  union lists, AA229, AA230, AA231, AA232, AA233, AA234, AA235
Incunabula (by subject)
  history, AA236
  medicine, EH24
Incunabula and Americana, 1450–1800, Stillwell, Margaret Bingham, AA218
Incunabula in American libraries, Goff, Frederick Richmond, AA231
Incunabula in Dutch libraries, AA232
Incunabula of British photographic literature, Gernsheim, Helmut, BF328
Incunabula scientifica et medica, Klebs, Arnold Carl, EH33
Indeks a tergo do Słownika języka polskiego, Grzegorczykowej, Renaty, AC632
────── Puzininy, Jadwigi, AC632
Indeks majalah Malaysia, AD343
The independence of Latin America, DB291
The independent learners' sourcebook, Smith, Robert McCaughan, CB350
Independent schools, CB110
Independent Sector (Firm). *Nonprofit almanac,* AL139
Independent study, CB350
Independent study catalog, CB358
Independent Zambia, Williams, Geoffrey J., DD249
Index, Wall Street journal, AE115
Index Africanus, Asamani, J. O., DD1
Index analytique d'articles de periodiques de langue francaise, AD294
The index and abstract directory, AD249
Index and directory of industry standards, EA272

Index and finding list of serials published in the British Isles, 1789–1832, Ward, William Smith, AD108
Index and finding list to Joseph Gillow's Bibliographical dictionary of the English Catholics, Bevan, John, AH228
Index Aristotelicus, Bonitz, Hermann, BB53
Index Aureliensis, AA225
Index bio-bibliographicus notorum hominum, AH16
Index biographique de l'Académie des Sciences du 22 décembre 1666 au 1er octobre 1978, Académie des Sciences (France), AH191
Index-catalogue of medical and veterinary zoology, United States. Bureau of Animal Industry. Zoological Division, EJ101
Index-catalogue of medical and veterinary zoology—authors, Hassal, Albert, EJ101
────── Stiles, Charles Wardell, EJ101
Index-catalogue of the library of the Surgeon General's Office, United States Army (Army Medical Library), authors and subjects, National Library of Medicine (U.S.), EH10, EH16, EH47
Index de périodiques canadiens, AD293
Index der zahnärztlichen Zeitschriften der Welt, Schmidt, Hans Joachim, EH247
Index des périodiques d'architecture canadiens, 1940–1980, Bergeron, Claude, BF210
Index deutschsprachiger Zeitschriften, 1750–1815, AD316
An index-dictionary of Chinese artists, collectors, and connoisseurs with character identification by modified stroke count, Seymour, Nancy N., BF146
Index/directory of women's media, CC549
Index Expressionismus, BE1223
Index fossils of North America, Shimer, Hervey Woodburn, EF242
Index-gazetteer of the world, Times, London, CL94
Index herbariorum, Lanjouw, Joseph, EG153
Index hortensis, Trehane, Piers, EG139
Index India, AD338
Index Islamicus, BC499
Index Islamicus, 1906–1955, University of London. School of Oriental and African Studies. Library, BC502
Index kewensis, EG104, EG128
Index kewensis supplementum, EG128
Index litteraturae entomologicae, Derksen, Walther, EG328
────── Horn, Walther, EG331
Index londinensis to illustrations of flowering plants, ferns and fern allies, EG104, EG128
Index medicus, EH14, EH16, EH22, EH35, EH60, EH61, EH62, EH63, EH64, EH65, EH66, EH67, EH118, EH251, EH276
Index nominum genericorum (plantarum), EG129
The index of African social science periodical articles, DD44
Index of all reports issued by bureaus of labor statistics in the United States prior to March 1902, United States. Bureau of Labor, CH644
Index of American design. Treasury of American design, BG18
Index of American design, BG17
Index of American periodical verse, BE499
Index of American print exhibitions, 1785–1940, Wilson, Raymond L., BF120
Index of American print exhibitions, 1882–1940, Wilson, Raymond L., BF368
Index of archaeological papers, 1665–1890, Gomme, George Laurence, DC275
Index of art sales catalogs, 1981–1985, BF113
An index of articles on Armenian studies in Western journals, Nersessian, Vrej, DC86
Index of articles on Jewish studies, BC544
Index of articles on the New Testament and the early church published in festschriften, Metzger, Bruce Manning, BC121
Index of articles relative to Jewish history and literature published in periodicals, from 1665 to 1900, Schwab, Moïse, BC545
Index of artists : international, Mallett, Daniel Trowbridge, BF136

Index of Australian and New Zealand poetry, Cuthbert, Eleanora Isabel, BE849
Index of Bibliographie zur Transformationsgrammatik, Knoop, Ulrich, BD45
────── Kohrt, Manfred, BD45
────── Küper, Christopher, BD45
An index of British treaties, 1101–1968, Parry, Clive, CK98
An index of characters in English printed drama to the Restoration, Berger, Thomas L., BE658
Index of chemical and physical data, ED43
Index of college majors, CB250
An index of composers, Blackmore, A. S. G., BJ205
Index of conference proceedings, British Library. Document Supply Centre, AL26, EA206
Index of conference proceedings received, British Library. Lending Division, AL26, EA206
Index of early Chinese painters and paintings, Cahill, James Francis, BF146, BF313
Index of economic articles, CH40
Index of economic articles in journals and collective volumes, CH40, CH42
Index of economic journals, CH42
Index of English literary manuscripts, BE603
Index of garden plants, EJ242
Index of generic names of fossil plants, 1820–1965, Andrews, Henry Nathaniel, EF236
Index of generic names of fossil plants, 1966–1973, Blazer, Anna M., EF236
Index of generic names of fossil plants, 1974–1978, Watt, Arthur Dwight, EF236
An index of Gregorian chant, Bryden, John Rennie, BJ290
Index of Indian economic journals, 1916–1965, Rath, Vimal, CH195
Index of Jewish art, BF193
Index of majors and graduate degrees, CB273
Index of manuscripts in the British Library, British Library. Department of Manuscripts, AA204
Index of mathematical papers, EB25, EB27
An index of mathematical tables, Fletcher, Alan, EB72
An index of mediaeval studies published in festschriften, 1865–1946, Williams, Harry Franklin, DA139
Index of microfilmed records of the German Foreign Ministry and the Reich's Chancellery covering the Weimar period, deposited at the National Archives, Schwändt, Ernst, DC252
The index of Middle English prose, BE733
Index of Middle English verse, BE733
────── Brown, Carleton Fairchild, BE697, BE714
────── Robbins, Rossell Hope, BE714
Index of mineral species & varieties arranged chemically, Hey, Max H., EF193
Index of NLM serial titles, EH37
The index of paintings sold in the British Isles during the nineteenth century, BF302
Index of patents issued from the United States Patent and Trademark Office, EA259, EA264
Index of periodical articles on the economics of Latin America, Felipe Herrera Library, CH177
Index of post-1937 European manuscript accessions, India Office Library, DE163
Index of printed Middle English prose, Blake, N. F., BE733
────── Edwards, A. S. G., BE733
────── Lewis, R. E., BE733
Index of proper names in French Arthurian prose romances, West, G. D., BE1165
An index of proper names in French Arthurian verse romances, 1150–1300, West, G. D., BE1165
The index of psychoanalytic writings, Grinstein, Alexander, CD9
Index of publications of the Geological Survey of Canada, 1845–1958, Geological Survey of Canada, EF29
Index of reviews in organic chemistry, EE134
Index of Revolutionary War pension applications in the National Archives, National Genealogical Society, AJ38
Index of selected publications of the Rand Corporation, CA26

An index of state geological survey publications issued in series, Corbin, John Boyd, EF25

An index of the Arthurian names in Middle English, Ackerman, Robert William, BE732

Index of the periodical dental literature published in the English language, EH250, EH251

Index of themes and motifs in twelfth-century French Arthurian poetry, Ruck, Elaine H., BE1165

Index of trademarks issued from the United States Patent and Trademark Office, EA260

Index of twentieth century artists, BF156

Index psychoanalyticus 1893–1926, Rickman, John, CD9

Index scriptorum novus mediae latinitatis, AC593

Index sinicus, Lust, John, DE129, DE138

Index Society, London. *An index to the biographical and obituary notices in the Gentleman's magazine, 1731–1780*, AH241

Index Society, New York. *The index of Middle English verse*, BE697

Index Thomisticus, BB64

Index to 16mm educational films, AA383

Index to 35mm educational filmstrips, AA383

Index to 8mm motion cartridges, AA383

Index to Afro-American reference resources, Stevenson, Rosemary M., CC378

Index to AMA resources of the seventies, 1970–1976, American Management Association, CH604

Index to American author bibliographies, Havlice, Patricia Pate, BE476, BE495

Index to American botanical literature, Torrey Botanical Club, EG115

Index to American genealogies, AJ41

Index to American little magazines, AD276

Index to American periodicals of the 1700's, AD272

Index to American periodicals of the 1700's and 1800's, Heath, Trudy, AD273
—— Hoornstra, Jean, AD273, AD272, AD273

Index to American periodicals of the 1800's, AD273

Index to American photographic collections, BF344

Index to American women speakers, 1828–1978, Manning, Beverley, BE358, CC530

Index to anthologies of Latin American literature in English translation, Freudenthal, Juan R., BE884

An index to Aristotle in English translation, Organ, Troy Wilson, BB57

Index to art periodicals, Art Institute of Chicago. Ryerson Library, BF11

Index to art reproductions in books, Hewlett-Woodmere Public Library, BF60

Index to articles on photography, BF330

Index to artistic biography, Havlice, Patricia Pate, BF136

Index to Australasian taxonomic literature, EG113

Index to Australian book reviews, AA371

Index to authors with titles of their publications appearing in the documents of the U.S. Dept. of Agriculture, 1841–1897, Thompson, George Fayette, EJ90

Index to Best American short stories and O. Henry prize stories, White, Ray Lewis, BE483

Index to biographies of contemporary composers, Bull, Storm, BJ224

Index to black American literary anthologies, Kallenbach, Jessamine S., BE537

Index to black American writers in collective biographies, Campbell, Dorothy W., BE543

Index to black periodicals, AD274

Index to black poetry, Chapman, Dorothy Hilton, BE536, BE537

Index to book reviews in England, 1749–1774, Forster, Antonia, BE744, BE748

Index to book reviews in religion, BC41, BC44, BC52, BC53

Index to book reviews in the humanities, AA372

Index to British literary bibliography, Howard-Hill, Trevor Howard, BE587, BE763

Index to Bulletins 1–100 of the Bureau of American Ethnology, Smithsonian Institution. Bureau of American Ethnology, CE83

Index to Canadian legal literature, CK23

Index to Canadian legal periodical literature, CK23

Index to Canadian poetry in English, McQuarrie, Jane, BE827

Index to card games, BK127

Index to characters in the performing arts, Sharp, Harold S., BH21

Index to children's plays in collections, 1975–1984, Trefny, Beverly Robin, BE390

Index to children's poetry, Blackburn, G. Meredith, BE376
—— Blackburn, Lorraine A., BE376
—— Brewton, John Edmund, BE376

Index to common names of herbaceous plants, Carleton, R. Milton, EG121

Index to Commonwealth little magazines, AD275

Index to composer bibliographies, Green, Richard D., BJ226

Index to crime and mystery anthologies, Contento, William, BE268

Index to critical film reviews in British and American film periodicals, Bowles, Stephen E., BH243

Index to critical reviews of books about film, Bowles, Stephen E., BH243

Index to criticisms of British and American poetry, Cline, Gloria Stark, BE710

Index to current Malaysian, Singapore and Brunei periodicals, AD345

Index to current periodicals received in the Library of the Royal Anthropological Institute, Royal Anthropological Institute of Great Britain and Ireland, CE35

Index to current urban documents, AF147

Index to dance periodicals, BH137

Index to dental literature, EH67, EH250, EH251

Index to dental periodical literature in the English language, EH251

Index to Department bulletins no. 1–1500, Hunt, Mabel G., EJ92

An index to dialect maps of Great Britain, Fischer, Andreas, BD104

An index to early music in selected anthologies, Hilton, Ruth B., BJ115

Index to economic history essays in festschriften, 1900–1950, Schleiffer, Hedwig, CH20

Index to educational audio tapes, AA383

Index to educational overhead transparancies, AA383

Index to educational records, AA383

Index to educational slides, AA383

Index to educational videotapes, AA383

Index to environmental studies (multimedia), AA383

Index to ETS research report series, 1948–1991, Saretsky, Gary D., CB153

Index to ETS research series, 1948–1991, CB153

Index to European taxonomic literature, EG113, EG114

Index to fairy tales, 1949–1972, Ireland, Norma Olin, BE243

Index to fairy tales, myths and legends, Eastman, Mary Huse, BE243

Index to festschriften in Jewish studies, Berlin, Charles, BC510

Index to festschriften in librarianship, Danton, Joseph Periam, AK13

Index to festschriften in librarianship, 1967–1975, Danton, Joseph Periam, AK13
—— Pulis, Jane F., AK13

Index to Finnish periodicals, 1959–1981, AD311

Index to foreign legal periodicals, CK11, CK24, CK27

Index to full length plays, 1895 to 1925, Thomson, Ruth Gibbons, BE238

Index to full length plays, 1926 to 1944, Thomson, Ruth Gibbons, BE238

Index to full length plays, 1944 to 1964, Ireland, Norma Olin, BE238

Index to genealogical periodical literature, Sperry, Kip, AJ47

Index to genealogical periodicals, Jacobus, Donald Lines, AJ42

Index to health and safety education (multimedia), AA383

Index to Hebrew periodicals, AD340

Index to historic preservation periodicals, BF218

•*Index to House of Commons parliamentary papers*, AF203

Index to illustrations, Ellis, Jessie Croft, BF60

Index to illustrations of animals and plants, Clewis, Beth, EA220, EG73

Index to illustrations of living things outside North America, Munz, Lucile Thompson, EA220, EG72
—— Slauson, Nedra G., EA220

Index to illustrations of the natural world, Slauson, Nedra G., EA220
—— Thompson, John W., EA220, EG72, EG73

Index to Indian economic journals, CH195

Index to Indian periodical literature, AD337

The index to international economics, development and finance, CH119

Index to international public opinion, CJ489, CJ490

Index to international statistics, CG69

Index to Italian architecture, Teague, Edward H., BF231

An index to Japanese law, Coleman, Rex, CK232

Index to Jewish festschriften, Bilgray, Albert, BC510
—— Marcus, Jacob Rader, BC510

Index to Jewish periodicals, BC542

Index to labor articles, CH643

Index to labor periodicals, CH643

Index to Latin American periodical literature, 1929–1960, AD296
—— Columbus Memorial Library (Washington, D.C.), AD295

Index to Latin American periodicals : humanities and social sciences, AD298

Index to legal citations and abbreviations, Raistrick, Donald, CK42, CK43

Index to legal periodical literature, CK25

Index to legal periodicals, CK11, CK26, CK27, CK26

Index to literature on race relations in South Africa, 1910–1975, Potgieter, Pieter Jacobus Johannes Stephanus, DD220

Index to literature on the American Indian, CC416

Index to literature relating to animal industry in the publications of the Department of Agriculture, 1837–1898, Thompson, George Fayette, EJ91

Index to little magazines, AD276

Index to maps in books and periodicals, American Geographical Society of New York. Map Dept, CL225

Index to maps of the American Revolution in books and periodicals illustrating the Revolutionary War and other events of the period 1763–1789, Clark, David Sanders, DB87

An index to Mexican literary periodicals, Forster, Merlin H., BE909

An index to microform collections, AA132

An index to musical festschriften and similar publications, Gerboth, Walter, BJ13

Index to New Zealand periodicals, AD347

Index to Nigeriana in selected periodicals, AD334

Index to old wars pension files, 1815–1926, White, Virgil D., AJ48

An index to one-act plays, Logasa, Hannah, BE228

Index to opera, operetta and musical comedy synopses in collections and periodicals, Drone, Jeanette Marie, BJ245

Index to periodical articles, Royal Institute of International Affairs Library, DA171

Index to periodical articles by and about blacks, AD274

Index to periodical articles related to law, CK27

Index to periodical articles relating to Singapore, Malaysia, Brunei, ASEAN, AD336

Index to periodical literature on Christ and the Gospels, Metzger, Bruce Manning, BC122

Index to periodicals, AD346
—— Mitchell Library, Sydney, AD346

Index to personal names in the National union catalog of manuscript collections, 1959–1984, Ostroff, Harriet, DB34

Index to Philippine periodicals, AD344

Index to Philippine plays, 1923–1983, Mata, Maria Nena R., BE1598

Index to plays, 1800–1926, Firkins, Ina Ten Eyck, BE226

Index to plays in collections, BE231
Index to plays in periodicals, Keller, Dean H., BE227
Index to poetry, BE315
Index to poetry by black American women, Chapman, Dorothy Hilton, BE536, BE537
Index to poetry for children and young people, Blackburn, G. Meredith, BE376
—— Brewton, John Edmund, BE376
—— Brewton, Sara Westbrook, BE376
Index to poetry in periodicals, American poetic renaissance, 1915–1919, BE500
Index to poetry in popular periodicals, Caskey, Jefferson D., BE499
Index to printed maps, Bancroft Library, CL250, DB163
Index to proceedings of the Economic and Social Council, AF36
Index to proceedings of the General Assembly, AF37
Index to proceedings of the Security Council, AF38
Index to proceedings of the Trusteeship Council, AF39
Index to producers and distributors, AA383
Index to psychology (multimedia), AA383
Index to publications, Geological Survey of Canada, EF30
Index to publications of the United States Department of Agriculture, 1901–40, United States. Department of Agriculture. Division of Publications, EJ92
Index to Puerto Rican collective biography, Fowlie-Flores, Fay, AH159
Index to record and tape reviews, BJ390
Index to record reviews, BJ391
Index to religious periodical literature, BC44, BC52
Index to reports of Geological Survey of Canada from 1927–50, Geological Survey of Canada, EF31
Index to reproductions of American paintings, Monro, Isabel Stevenson, BF61, BF63
—— Monro, Kate M., BF63
Index to reproductions of American paintings appearing in more than 400 books, mostly published since 1960, Moure, Nancy Dustin Wall, BF61
—— Smith, Lyn Wall, BF61, BF63
Index to reproductions of European paintings, Monro, Isabel Stevenson, BF61
—— Monro, Kate M., BF61
Index to reproductions of paintings by twentieth century Chinese artists, Laing, Ellen Johnston, BF313
Index to research in home economics, 1972–1991, Fetterman, N. I., EJ197
Index to reviews, symposia volumes and monographs in organic chemistry, EE135
Index to science fiction anthologies and collections, Contento, William, BE283, BE300
Index to science fiction anthologies and collections, 1977–1983, BE283
Index to scientific and technical proceedings, EA210
An index to scientific articles on American Jewish history, Marcus, Jacob Rader, BC543
Index to scientific book contents, EA70
Index to scientific reviews, EA71
Index to scientists, Ireland, Norma Olin, AH15
Index to scientists of the world from ancient to modern times, Ireland, Norma Olin, EA195
Index to selected Nigerian periodicals, AD334
Index to short stories, Firkins, Ina Ten Eyck, BE260
Index to social sciences and humanities proceedings, AL29
Index to song books, Leigh, Robert, BJ287
Index to South African periodicals, AD335
Index to Southeast Asian journals, 1960–1974, Johnson, Donald Clay, DE102
Index to Spanish American collective biography, Mundo Lo, Sara de, AH112
Index to statistics and probability, EB28
—— Tukey, John Wilder, EB30
Index to subjects and corporate names in the National union catalog of manuscript collections, 1959–1984, DB34

Index to tests used in educational dissertations, Fabiano, Emily, CB152
An index to the authors (other than Linnaeus) mentioned in the Catalogue …, British Museum. Department of Printed Books, EG103
An index to the biographical and obituary notices in the Gentleman's magazine, 1731–1780, Farrar, Robert Henry, AH241
Index to the Biographical dictionary of medallists, Martin, J. S., BG186
Index to the Christian Science monitor, AE106
Index to the early printed books in the British Museum, Proctor, Robert, AA219, AA227
Index … to The Elizabethan stage…, White, Beatrice, BE665
Index to the English catalogue of books, AA686
•*Index to the Foreign Broadcast Information Service (FBIS) daily reports*, AF106
Index to the London stage, 1660–1800, Schneider, Ben Ross, BH101
Index to the papers relating to Scotland, Terry, Charles Sanford, DC362
Index to the periodical literature of the world, AD286
Index to the portraits in Odell's Annals of the New York stage, BH105
Index to The proverb, Taylor, Archer, BE164
Index to the science fiction magazines, 1926–1950, Day, Donald B., BE294
Index to the science fiction magazines, 1966–1970, BE294
Index to the Sporting news, Burke, John Gordon, BK9
Index to the statutes, CK214
Index to the supplements and suppl. volumes of Pauly-Wissowa's R.E, Murphy, John P., DA104
Index to the Times, AE125
Index to The Tower Commission report, Sanchez, James, CJ114
Index to the Wilson authors series, BE203
Index to the yearbooks of the U.S. Department of Agriculture, 1894–1900, Greathouse, Charles H., EJ89
•*Index to theses*, AG33
Index to theses accepted for higher degrees by the universities of Great Britain and Ireland, AG33, DA17
Index to theses accepted for higher degrees by the universities of Great Britain and Ireland and the Council for National Academic Awards, AG33
Index to theses with abstracts accepted for higher degrees by the universities of Great Britain and Ireland and the Council for National Academic Awards, AG33, AG35
Index to top-hit tunes, 1900–1950, Chipman, John H., BJ282
Index to transdex, AF109
Index to translations selected by the American Mathematical Society, American Mathematical Society, EB20
•*Index to United Nations documents and publications*, AF40
Index to U.S. government periodicals, AD277
Index to USDA Agricultural information bulletins no. 1–649, Miller, Ellen Kay, EJ92
Index to USDA Miscellaneous publications no. 1–1479, Miller, Ellen Kay, EJ92
Index to USDA Technical bulletins no. 1–1802, Miller, Ellen Kay, EJ92
Index to vocational and technical education (multimedia), AA383
Index to War of 1812 pension files, White, Virgil D., AJ48
Index to women of the world from ancient to modern times, Ireland, Norma Olin, AH15
Index translationum, AA144
Index veterinarius, EJ18, EJ19, EJ103, EJ117
Index zu deutschen Zeitschriften der Jahre 1773–1830, Hocks, Paul, AD315
Indexed journals, Covington, Paula Hattox, AD248
Indexed periodicals, Marconi, Joseph V., AD251

Indexes in the Newspaper and Current Periodicals Room, Library of Congress. Serial and Government Publications Division. Newspaper Section, AE101
—— Pluge, John, AE101
Indexes to all editions of Brown-Driver-Briggs Hebrew lexicon, Robinson, Maurice Arthur, AC476
Indexing, AK213
  bibliography, AK201, AK217
  directories, AK214
  handbooks, AK212, AK215
Indexing and abstracting, Wellisch, Hans H., AK217
Indexing and abstracting in theory and practice, Lancaster, F. Wilfrid, AK213
India
  abstract journals, AD339
  archives, DE162
  atlases, CL356
  bibliography, AA897, DE77, DE155, DE156, DE158
    current, AA896, AA898, AA899, AA900
  bibliography of bibliography, AA75, AA76
  biography, AH349, AH351, AH352
    contemporary, AH353, AH354
  chronology, DE171
  dissertations, AG52, CA21
  encyclopedias, DE164, DE165, DE166, DE167, DE168
  gazetteers, CL163, CL164
  government publications, AF244, AF245, AF247, AF248, AF249
    periodicals, AF246
  library catalogs, DE158, DE163
  manuscripts, DE163
  newspapers, AD190, AE88
  periodicals, AD190, AD191, AD192, AD193
    indexes, AD337, AD338, AD339
  research centers
    directories, CA45
  statistics, CG388, CG389
    bibliography, CG390, CG391
India (by subject)
  anthropology and ethnology, CE109, CE110
  archaeology, DE154, DE166
  art, BF27, BF178
  cities, CC305
  economic conditions
    atlases, CH198
    bibliography, CH194, CH197, DE153
    guides, CH196
    periodicals
      indexes, CH195
  elections, CJ431
  folklore and popular culture, CF96
  foreign relations, DC599, DE160
  history, DE169
    atlases, DE172
    bibliography, DE154, DE157, DE159, DE161
    encyclopedias, DE90, DE168, DE170
  languages
    bibliography, BD224
    dissertations, BD225
  law
    bibliography, CK229
  music, BJ156
  politics and government, CJ432, CJ433, CJ434, CJ435, CJ508
  population, CG387
  social and behavioral sciences, CA6
  social conditions, DE170
    atlases, CH198
  women, CC612
India. Army. General Staff Branch. *Historical and political gazetteer of Afghanistan*, CL158
India. Central Statistical Organisation. *Guide to official statistics*, CG390
—— *Statistical abstract, India*, CG389
India. Office of the Registrar. *Vital statistics of India*, CG388
India. Office of the Registrar General. *Bibliography of census publications in India*, CG391
India. Parliament. Lok Sabha. *Who's who*, CJ432

India. Parliament. Lok Sabha. Secretariat. *Who's who*, CJ432
India. Parliament. Rajya Sabha. *Who's who*, CJ432
India, Gupta, Brijen K., DE157
India and the Soviet Union, Roy, A., DC599
India decides, Butler, David, CJ431
India in English fiction, 1800–1970, Gupta, Brijen K., BE1568
India information sources, economics and business, Ruokonen, Kyllikki, CH196
India Office Library. *Catalogue of European printed books*, DE158
——— *Index of post-1937 European manuscript accessions*, DE163
India Office Library and Records. *General guide to the India Office Records*, DE12, DE83
——— *A guide to source materials in the India Office Library and Records for the history of Tibet, Sikkim and Bhutan 1765–1950*, DE86
——— *Press in India*, AE88
India (Republic). Central Gazetteers Unit. *Gazetteer of India*, CL163
India (Republic). Ministry of Information and Broadcasting. *Press in India*, AE88
India (Republic). Office of the Registrar of Newspapers. *Press in India*, AE88
India (Republic). Parliament. House of the People. *Abstracts and index of articles*, AD339, AF245
——— *Abstracts of books, reports, and articles*, AD339, AF245
India since the advent of the British, Sharma, Jagdish Saran, DE171
India who's who, AH353
Indian America, Eagle Walking Turtle, CC429
Indian anthropology, Kanitkar, J. M., CE109
Indian book industry, AA898
Indian books, AA896
Indian books in print, AA899
The Indian Buddhist iconography, Bhattacharyya, Benoytosh, BF178
The Indian city, Van Willigen, John, CC305
Indian Council of Social Science Research. *Annotated and classified bibliography of Indian demography*, CG387
——— *Annotated bibliography on the economic history of India*, CH194, DE153
——— *Annual report—Indian Council of Social Science Research*, CA45
——— *ICSSR research projects, 1969–1987*, CA47
——— *Indian dissertation abstracts*, CA21
——— *Survey of research in economic and social history of India*, CH197
Indian dissertation abstracts, CA21
Indian fiction in English, Spencer, Dorothy Mary, BE1567
Indian government and politics, Rana, Mahendra Singh, CJ434
Indian legal materials, Jain, Hem Chandra, CK229
Indian library directory, AK158
Indian literature
  bibliography, BE1563, BE1564, BE1568
  biobibliography, BE1570
  encyclopedias, BE1565
  translations, BE1564, BE1567
  works in English
    bibliography, BE1567, BE1568
    history, BE1569
Indian literature (by subject)
  history, BE1566, BE1571
Indian literature in English, Walsh, William, BE1569
Indian literature in English, 1827–1979, Joshi, Irene M., BE1542
——— Singh, Amritjit, BE1542, BE1567
——— Verma, Rajiva, BE1542
Indian medicine, EH84
Indian metaphysics and epistemology, Potter, Karl H., BB33
Indian national bibliography, AA76, AA896, AA897, AA900
Indian Ocean, DE6
  bibliography, DD18
  current surveys, DD62

Indian Ocean, Gotthold, Julia J., DD18, DE6
Indian Ocean: five island countries, Bunge, Frederica M., DD62
Indian periodicals, AD191
Indian periodicals in print, 1973, Gandhi, H. N. D., AD190
——— Ghandi, H. N. D., AE88
Indian reference sources, Sharma, H. D., AA360
Indian reservations, CC431
Indian review, CA28
Indian socialism, Sharma, Jagdish Saran, CJ508
Indian-white relations in the United States, Prucha, Francis Paul, CC423
Indian writing in English, Srinivasa Iyengar, K. R., BE1569
Indiana. [Laws, etc.]. *Burns Indiana statutes annotated*, CK179
The Indiana companion to traditional Chinese literature, BE1554
Indiana University. *Yearbook of comparative and general literature*, BE41
Indiana University. Archives of Traditional Music. *A catalog of phonorecordings of music and oral data held by the Archives of Traditional Music*, BJ328
Indiana University. Center on Philanthropy. *Philanthropic studies index*, AL95
Indiana University. Libraries. *Current Japanese serials in the humanities and social sciences received in American libraries*, AD223
——— *Union list of little magazines*, AD224
Indiana University. Research Center in Anthropology, Folklore, and Linguistics. *A bibliography of South Asian folklore*, CF97
Indiana University. Research Institute for Inner Asian Studies. *Ottoman Turkish writers*, BE1491
Indiana University Latin American Studies Program. *Brazilian serial documents*, AF160
Indians of North America, Haas, Marilyn L., CC413
Indians of Texas, Tate, Michael L., CC420
Indic literature *see* **Indian literature**
Indice bibliográfico de Costa Rica, Dobles Segreda, Luis, AA478
Índice bibliográfico guatemalteco, AA484
Indice biográfico de España, Portugal e Iberoamérica, AH287
Indice biografico italiano, AH258
Índice de artículos de publicaciones periódicas en el área de ciencias sociales y humanidades, AD297
Índice de la bibliografía hondureña, Durón, Jorge Fidel, AA487
Indice español de humanidades, AD328
Índice general de publicaciones periódicas latino americanas, AD295, AD298
Indice generale degli incunaboli delle biblioteche d'Italia, AA233
Índice histórico español, DC509
Indice informativo de la novela hispanoamericana, Coll, Edna, BE902
Índice nobiliario español, Instituto Internacional de Genealogía y Heráldica, AJ140
Índice para facilitar el manejo y consulta de los catálogos de Salvá y Heredia, Molina Navarro, Gabriel, AA802, AA805, AA807
Indice toponímico de la República del Ecuador, Instituto Geográfico Militar (Ecuador), CL124
Indices to American literary annuals and gift books, 1825–1865, Fink, John W., BE415
——— Kirkham, E. Bruce, BE415
Indigenous architecture worldwide, Wodehouse, Lawrence, BF204
Indigenous art *see* **Folk art**
Indigenous peoples, CE63
Indigenous peoples (by country or region)
  Latin America, AL54
Indigenous world, CE63
Indisch verslag, CG394
The individual investor's guide to investment publications, CH298
Individuals with Disabilities Education Act, CB207
——— Lantzy, M. Louise, CB156
Indo-Aryan languages, AC516
An Indo-European comparative dictionary, Mann, Stuart Edward, AC514

Indo-European language
  bibliography
    current, BD201
  dictionaries, AC512, AC516
    etymology, AC514
  etymology, AC513, AC515
Indo-European roots, AC47
Indo-U.S. relations, 1947–1988, Saha, Santosh C., DE160
Indochina, DE96
Indogermanische Chronik, BD201
Indogermanisches etymologisches Wörterbuch, Pokorny, Julius, AC515
Indonesia
  bibliography, AA901, AA902, DE174, DE175, DE177, DE178
    current, AA903, AA904, DE179
  bibliography of bibliography, AA78, AA79, DE176
  newspapers, AD195, AE89
  periodicals, AD194, AD195, AD196, AD197
  statistics, CG393, CG394
    statistics, vital, CG395
Indonesia (by subject)
  folklore and popular culture, CF94, CF95
  history, DE173
    bibliography, DE99, DE175, DE179
  law, CK230
  population
    bibliography, CG392
    population forecasting, CG395
Indonesia. Biro Pusat Statistik. *Statistik Indonesia*, CG393
Indonesia, Tairas, J. N. B., AA79
An Indonesian-English dictionary, Echols, John M., AC517
Indonesian language
  dictionaries
    bilingual
      Indonesian-English, AC517, AC518
Indonesian law 1949–1989, CK230
Indonesian newspapers, Nunn, Godfrey Raymond, AE89
Indonesian serials, 1942–1950, in Yogyakarta libraries, Reid, Anthony, AD195
Industrial accidents, EH78
Industrial and organizational psychology
  handbooks, CD127, CD129
Industrial archaeology, CH47, DA178
Industrial arts index, CH37, EA67
Industrial chemical thesaurus, EE76
Industrial chemistry, EK58
Industrial design
  guides, BF201
Industrial design (by country or region)
  United States
    directories, BG26
Industrial energy use data book, Oak Ridge Associated Universities, EK221
Industrial engineering, EK229, EK233
Industrial engineering handbook, EK233
Industrial medicine desk reference, Tver, David F., EH128
Industrial relations *see* **Labor and industrial relations**
Industrial research, EA213
Industrial research in the United Kingdom, EA143
Industrial research laboratories of the United States, EA213
Industrial Revolution, DC336
Industrial safety, EH409
Industrial solvents handbook, EK56
Industries
  annuals, CH384
  biography, CH105
  classification, CH379
  dictionaries, CH339
    multilingual, CH653
  periodicals, CH78
  statistics, CH424, CH427
  surveys, CH417

Industries (by country or region)
  Canada
    bibliography, CH328
  Europe, CH184
  Europe, Western
    bibliography, CH328
  Great Britain
    manuscripts and archives, DC287
  United States
    bibliography, CH328
    handbooks, CH380, CH415
Industries (by subject)
  history, CH399
  see also **Aerospace industries**
Industry and company information, Hawbaker, A. Craig, CH330
Industry and development, CH384
Industry norms and key business ratios, CH421
Industry surveys, CH417
Infancy
  bibliography, CC148, CD78
  guides, CC139, CD77
Infancy, Scheffler, Hannah Nuba, CC148, CD78
The influence of the family, Acock, Alan C., CC205
Info Globe. *Directory of periodicals online,* AD6
•*Infopedia,* AB10, AB26, AB27, AB110, AC87, AH38
InfoPLACE (Career information center).
  Professional careers sourcebook, CB208, CH707
  —— *Vocational careers sourcebook,* CB214
Information Access Company. *Predicasts F&S index United States,* CH337
Information China, DE145
•*Information finder,* AB22, AB28, AC28
Information Handling Services. *Index and directory of industry standards,* EA272
Information Hungary, Erdei, Ferenc, DC388
Information industry directory, AK192
Information management sourcebook, AK247
Information Mongolia, DE232
Information networks, CH487
Information on music, Marco, Guy A., BJ5
Information please almanac, atlas and yearbook, AB105
The Information please sports almanac, BK43
Information resources in housing and urban development, BF280
Information resources in the arts, Shipley, Lloyd W., BF107
Information resources in toxicology, Wexler, Philip, EH418
Information Resources Inc. *The marketing fact book,* CH597
Information review on crime and delinquency, CK248
Information science see **Library and information science**
Information science
  abbreviations, EK196
  annuals, AK76
Information science abstracts, AK30
Information services
  databases, EH158
  directories, AK59, AK192, EH158
Information services (by country or region)
  Europe, EA142
Information Services on Latin America. *ISLA,* DB293
Information sources in advertising history, Pollay, Richard W., CH547
Information sources in agriculture and food science, EJ2
Information sources in cartography, CL220
Information sources in chemistry, EE3
Information sources in economics, CH3
Information sources in energy technology, EK219
Information sources in engineering, EK2
Information sources in law, CK219
Information sources in patents, EA261
Information sources in pharmaceuticals, EH5, EH317
Information sources in physics, ED1

Information sources in politics and political science, CJ2
Information sources in polymers and plastics, EK287
Information sources in science and technology, Hurt, Charlie Deuel, EA4
—— Parker, C. C., EA6
Information sources in sport and leisure, Shoebridge, Michele, BK8
Information sources in the earth sciences, EF2
Information sources in the history of science and medicine, EA224
Information sources in the life sciences, EG2
Information sources in the medical sciences, EH5
—— Pickering, W. R., EH317
Information sources in transportation, material management, and physical distribution, Davis, Bob J., CH442
Information sources of political science, Holler, Frederick L., CJ1
Informations bibliographique marocaines, AA867
Informationshandbuch Deutsche Literaturwissenschaft, Blinn, Hansjürgen, BE1055
Informationshandbuch internationale Beziehungen und Länderkunde, Huck, Burkhardt J., DA173
Informator nauki polskiej, AL70
Informatsionnyĭ ukazatel' bibliograficheskikh spiskov i kartotek, sostavlennykh bibliotekami Sovetskogo Soĭuza, AA62, AA64
Infoterm. *International bibliography of terminological literature,* BD58
Infrared band handbook, Szymanski, Herman A., EE90
Infrared spectroscopy, EE90, EE140
  tables, EE141
Inge, M. Thomas. *American women writers,* BE399
—— *Black American writers,* BE515
—— *Handbook of American popular culture,* CF78
—— *Handbook of American popular literature,* BE434
Ingham, John N. *African-American business leaders,* CH100
—— *Biographical dictionary of American business leaders,* CH98, CH99
—— *Contemporary American business leaders,* CH99
Ingles, Ernest Boyce. *Canada,* DB183
Inglese-italiano, italiano-inglese, AC531
Inglis, Brian. *The alternative health guide,* EH186
Inglis, Kenneth Stanley. *Australians,* DF37
Inglise-Eesti sonaraamat, Silvet, J., AC308
Ingram, John Van Ness. *A check list of American 18th century newspapers in the Library of Congress,* AE20
Ingram, Kenneth E. *Jamaica,* DB442
—— *Manuscripts relating to Commonwealth Caribbean countries in United States and Canadian repositories,* DB412
—— *Sources for West Indian studies,* DB413
—— *Sources of Jamaican history, 1655–1838,* DB443
•*INIS,* EK293
INIS atomindex, EK215, EK293, EK294
•*INIS database on CD-ROM,* EK293
Initialisms see **Abbreviations**
Initials and pseudonyms, Cushing, William, AA149
The injury fact book, EH187
Inland water transportation, Roy, Mary L., CH444
Innes, Gordon. *A Grebo-English dictionary,* AC441
—— *A Mende-English dictionary,* AC611
Innes, Malcolm R. *Scots heraldry,* AJ157
Innes, Thomas. *The clans, septs, and regiments of the Scottish Highlands,* AJ125
—— *Scots heraldry,* AJ157
—— *The tartans of the clans and families of Scotland,* AJ126
Innis, Pauline B. *Protocol,* AL155
Innovative graduate programs directory, CB300
Inönü ansiklopedisi, AB101
Inorganic chemical nomenclature, Block, B. Peter, EE107
Inquisition, BC272

Insect pests of farm, garden, and orchard, Davidson, Ralph Howard, EJ50
Insects see **Entomology**
Insects that feed on trees and shrubs, Johnson, Warren T., EG333
Inside Japanese support, AL126
Inside the law schools, Goldfarb, S. F., CK154
Inside the legislature, CJ272
Inside U.S. business, Mattera, Philip, CH415
The insider's guide to demographic know-how, Crispell, Diane, CH588
Insider's guide to prep schools, CB108
The insiders' guide to the colleges, CB274
Insignia and decorations of the United States armed forces, National Geographic Society, AL185
•*INSPEC,* ED9, ED11, EK128, EK162
•*INSPEC electronics & computing,* ED9, EK162
•*INSPEC ondisc,* ED9, EK162
•*INSPEC physics,* ED9
Institue für Zeitgeschichte. *Bibliographie zur Zeitgeschrifte, 1953–1989,* DA169
Institum Bialik Procurationi Iudaicae pro Israel (Jewish Agency). *Encyclopaedia biblica,* BC129
Institut Afriki (Akademiia nauk SSSR). *Izuchenie kul'tury i iazykov narodov Afriki v Sovetskom Soiuze,* DD10
Institut de l'information scientifique et technique (France). *Bibliography of the history of art,* BF43
—— *PASCAL. v. 4, Sciences de la terre,* EF59
Institut de recherche et d'histoire des textes (France). *Répertoire international des médiévistes,* DA154
Institut des Études Augustiniennes. *Fichier augustinien,* BB65
Institut etnografii im. N.N. Miklukho-Maklaia. *Bibliografiia trudov Instituta etnografiĭ im. N. N. Miklukho-Maklaia, 1900–1962,* CE5
Institut Fondamental d'Afrique Noire. *Bibliographie générale du Mali,* DD97
—— *West African international atlas,* CL338
Institut français de presse et des sciences de l'information. Section d'histoire. *Tables du journal Le temps,* AE121
Institut für Demoskopie Allensbach. *The Germans,* CJ493
Institut für Deutsche Sprache. *Deutsches Fremdwörterbuch,* AC409
Institut für Landeskunde. *Documentatio geographica,* CL8
Institut für Zeitgeschichte. *Alphabetischer Katalog,* DA169
—— *Biographischer Katalog,* DA169
—— *Biographisches Handbuch der deutschsprachigen Emigration nach 1933,* AH203
Institut géographique national (France). *The atlas of Africa,* CL337
Institut haïtien de statistique et d'informatique. *Bulletin de statistique,* CG174
Institut iazykoznaniia (Akademiia nauk SSSR). *Bibliograficheskiĭ ukazatel' literatury po russkomu iazykoznaniiu s 1825 po 1880 god,* BD185
Institut istorii (Akademiia nauk SSSR). *Istoriia istoricheskoĭ nauki v SSSR,* DC570
Institut national de la language française. *Trésor de la langue française,* AC331
Institut national de la statistique et de la démographie. *Annuaire statistique du Burkina Faso,* CG319
Institut National de la Statistique et de l'Analyse Économique. *Annuaire statistique,* CG316
Institut national de la statistique et des études économiques. *Annuaire statistique des territoires d'outre-mer,* CG214
—— *Tableaux démographiques,* CG215
Institut national de la statistique et des études économiques (France). *Annuaire statistique de la France,* CG216
—— *La situation démographique,* CG219
Institut national de recherche pédagogique (France). Service d'histoire de l'éducation. *Les grammaires françaises, 1800–1914,* BD157
Institut national de statistique (Belgium). *Annuaire statistique de la Belgique,* CG199

Institut national d'études démographiques. *Tableaux démographiques*, CG215

Institut nauchnoĭ informatsii po obshchestvennym naukam (Rossiĭskaĭa akademiĭa nauk). *Novaĭa otechestvennaĭa i inostrannaĭa literatura po obshchestvennym naukam. Slavĭanovedenie i balkanistika*, DC43

Institut Pasteur. *Bulletin de l'Institut Pasteur*, EG311

Institut pour Journalistes de Belgique. *La presse d'information*, AE45

Institut russkogo ĬAzyka (Akademiĭa nauk SSSR). *Slovar' russkogo ĭazyka XI-XVII vv*, AC673

Institut russkogo ĬAzyka (Akademiĭa nauk SSSR). Slovarnyĭ sektor. *Slovar' russkikh narodnykh govorov*, AC670

Institut russkoĭ litertury (Pushkinskiĭ dom). *Russkiĭ fol'klor*, CF83

Institut voennoĭ istorii. *Sovetskaĭa voennaĭa entsiklopediĭa*, CJ659

Inštitut za slovenski jezik (Slovenska akademija znanosti in umetnosti). *Slovar slovenskega knjižnega jezika*, AC720

Institut zur Erforschung der UdSSR. *Party and government officials of the Soviet Union, 1917–1967*, CJ393

—— *Who was who in the USSR*, AH304

Institute for Antiquity and Christianity. *The Eerdmans analytical concordance to the Revised Standard Version of the Bible*, BC166

Institute for Defense and Disarmament Studies (U.S.). *Peace resource book*, CJ694

Institute for European-Latin American Relations. *Bibliography of Western European-Latin American relations*, DB264

—— *Manual para las relaciones Europeo-Latinoamericanas*, DB286

Institute for Policy Studies. *Research guide to current military and strategic affairs*, CJ559

Institute for Scientific Information. *CompuMath citation index*, EB21, EK160

—— *Current contents*, CA17, EA68

—— *Current contents address directory*, EA137

—— *Nursing citation index*, EH276

—— *SCI JCR*, EA136

—— *Science citation index*, EA75

Institute for Social Research. Survey Research Center. *Measures for psychological assessment*, CD67

Institute for Strategic Studies (London, England). *The military balance*, CJ596

Institute for the Development of Indian Law. *Guide to American Indian documents in the Congressional serial set, 1817–1899*, CC417

Institute for the Study of the USSR. *Prominent personalities in the USSR*, AH304

Institute of Asian Affairs (Hamburg, Germany). *Who's who in the People's Republic of China*, AH344

Institute of Chartered Accountants in England and Wales, London. Library. *Historical accounting literature*, CH248

Institute of Early American History and Culture. *Money and exchange in Europe and America, 1600–1775*, CH284

Institute of Electrical and Electronics Engineers. *The new IEEE standard dictionary of electrical and electronics terms*, EK131

Institute of International Education (New York, N.Y.). *Academic year abroad*, CB242

—— *English language and orientation programs in the United States*, CB161, CB269

—— *Funding for U.S. study*, DB379

Institute of Jamaica, Kingston. *Jamaican national bibliography, 1964–1974*, AA568

Institute of Laboratory Animal Resources. Committee on Care and Use of Laboratory Animals. *Guide for the care and use of laboratory animals*, EG295

Institute of Mathematical Statistics. *Current index to statistics, applications, methods and theory*, CG15, EB22

—— *Directory of members*, CG35, EB57

—— *Selected tables in mathematical statistics*, EB95

Institute of Mathematical Statistics directories, CG35, EB57

Institute of Mennonite Studies (Elkhart, Ind.). *Annotated bibliography of Mennonite writings on war and peace, 1930–1980*, BC360

—— *Mennonite bibliography, 1631–1961*, BC362

Institute of Metals. *Materials data sources*, EK255

Institute of Public Administration of Canada. *Canadian public administration : bibliography*, CJ465

Institute of Race Relations (London). *Sage race relations abstracts*, CC340

Institute of Scientific Information in the Social Sciences. *A scholars' guide to humanities and social sciences in the Soviet successor states*, AL59, DC593

Institute of Social and Economic Research. *The Alaska Eskimos*, CC414

Institute of Southeast Asian Studies. *ASEAN*, DE94

—— *Laos*, DE223

The Institutes of Vishnu, BC92

Instituti i Gjuhësisë dhe i Letërsisë (Akademia Shkencave e RPS të Shqipërisë). *Historia e letërsisë shqiptare*, BE1094

Institution of Electrical Engineers. *INSPEC*, ED9

—— *Science abstracts*, ED11

Institution of Mechanical Engineers (Great Britain). *Materials data sources*, EK255

Institution of Mining and Metallurgy (London). *IMM abstracts*, EK253

Institution of Municipal Engineers (Great Britain). *Road abstracts*, EK118

Institutional advancement, CB227

Institutions of higher education, Sparks, Linda, CB229

Instituto Autónomo Biblioteca Nacional. Sección de Publicaciones Oficiales. *Catálogo de publicaciones oficiales, 1840–1977*, AF163

Instituto Bibliográfico Hispánico. *Revistas españolas, 1973-1978*, AD155

Instituto Brasileiro de Estatística. *Anuário estatístico do Brasil*, CG141

Instituto Brasileiro de Informação em Ciência e Tecnologia. *Guia de publicações seriadas brasileiras*, AD72

Instituto Cubano de Geodésia y Cartografía. *Atlas de Cuba*, CL320

Instituto de Conservación y Restauración de Bienes Culturales (Spain). *Directorio de instituciones y organismos relacionados con la etnografía*, CE99

Instituto de Cultura Hispánica (Spain). Departamento de Información. *Catálogo de revistas españolas*, AD156

Instituto de Investigaciones Literarias Zonzalo Picón Febres. *Diccionario general de la literatura venezolana*, BE962

Instituto Geográfico "Agustín Codazzi". *Atlas de Colombia*, CL317

—— *Atlas regional andino*, CL317

—— *Atlas regional pacifico*, CL317

—— *Diccionario geográfico de Colombia*, CL123

Instituto geografico De Agostini. *La nazione operante*, AH263

Instituto Geográfico Militar (Argentina). *Toponimia de la República Argentina*, CL119

Instituto Geográfico Militar (Ecuador). *Indice toponímico de la República del Ecuador*, CL124

Instituto Geográfico Nacional (El Salvador). *Diccionario geográfico de El Salvador*, CL115

Instituto Geográfico Nacional (Spain). *Atlas nacional de España*, CL334

Instituto Geográfico National (Honduras). *Diccionario geográfico de Honduras*, CL117

Instituto Geográfico y Catastral (Spain). *Atlas nacional de España*, CL334

Instituto Indigenista Peruano. *Bibliografía de tesis peruanos sobre indigenismo y ciencias sociales*, DB384

Instituto Internacional de Genealogía y Heráldica. *Índice nobiliario español*, AJ140

Instituto Mexicano del Seguro Social. *El territorio mexicano*, CL311

Instituto "Miguel de Cervantes". *Bibliografía de autores españoles del siglo XVIII*, BE1431

Instituto Nacional de Antropología e Historia (Mexico). *Atlas cultural de México*, DB248

—— *Estadísticas históricas de México*, CG118

Instituto Nacional de Estadística (Bolivia). *Atlas censal de Bolivia*, CL315

—— *Bolivia en cifras*, CG138

—— *Resumen estadístico*, CG140

Instituto Nacional de Estadística (Ecuador). *Anuario de estadística, 1963/68*, CG155

Instituto Nacional de Estadística, Geografía e Informática (Mexico). *Anuario estadístico de los Estados Unidos Mexicanos*, CG117

—— *Estadísticas históricas de México*, CG118

Instituto Nacional de Estadística (Guatemala). *Anuario estadístico*, CG129

Instituto Nacional de Estadística (Spain). *Movimiento natural de la población española*, CG284

—— *Zona de protectorado y de los territorios de soberanía de España en el norte de Africa*, CG283, CG348

Instituto Nacional de Estadística y Censos (Ecuador). *Serie estadística*, CG155

Instituto Nacional de Estadísticas (Chile). *Anuario de demografía*, CG144

—— *Chile, series estadísticas*, CG146

Instituto Nacional de Estatística (Portugal). *Anuário estatístico*, CG277

Instituto Nacional de Estudios Históricos de la Revolución Mexicana. *Diccionario histórico y biográfico de la Revolución Mexicana*, DB242

Instituto Nacional del Libro Español. *Quién es quién en las letras españolas*, BE1458

Instituto Nacional Indigenista (Mexico). *Bibliografía indigenista de México y Centroamerica (1850–1950)*, CE82

Instituto nazionale di statistica. *Sommario storico di statistiche sulla popolazione*, CG257

Instituto Panamericano de Geografía e Historia. *Boletín bibliográfico de antropología americana*, CE76

Instituto Panamericano de Geografía e Historia. Comisión de Historia. *Bibliografía del folklore peruano*, CF70

Instituto Português do Livro. *Dicionário cronológico de autores portugueses*, BE1364

Instituto Profesional de Santiago. Escuela de Bibliotecología y Documentación. *Publicaciones oficiales de Chile, 1973–1983*, AF161

Instituto Storico Italiano per il Medio Evo. *Repertorium fontium historiae medii aevi*, DA136

Instituto Tecnológico Autónomo de México. *Las publicaciones periódicas mexicanas*, AD63

Instituut Kern (Rijksuniversiteit te Leiden). *Annual bibliography of Indian archaeology*, DE154

Instructional technology, CB173

Instrumental music, BJ293

Instruments biographiques pour l'histoire contemporaine de la Belgique, Dhondt, Jan, AH178

Instrumentum bibliograpicum Neolatinum, BE1041

Instytut Badan Literackich, Polska Akademia Nauk. *Bibliografia literatury polskiej*, BE1346

Instytut Historii (Polska Akademia Nauk). *Polski słownik biograficzny*, AH279

Insurance
annuals, CH513
bibliography, CH504, CH522
current, CH501
biography, CH523
databases, CH506
dictionaries, CH509, CH510
multilingual, CH508
directories, CH222, CH388, CH512, CH513, CH515, CH516, CH524, CH539
indexes, CH506
library catalogs, CH502, CH504
manuals, CH512

statistics, CH222, CH388, CH511, CH517, CH518, CH521, CH524, CH525, CH527, CH528, CH539
yearbooks, CH521
Insurance (by country or region)
Great Britain
statistics, CH514
Insurance almanac, CH513, CH523
Insurance and employee benefits literature, CH501
Insurance book reviews, CH501
Insurance dictionary, Thomsett, Michael C., CH510
Insurance directory and year book, CH514
Insurance facts, CH525
The insurance industry, Weiner, Alan R., CH522
Insurance literature, CH501
Insurance periodicals index, CH506
Insurance Society of New York. Library. *Life insurance catalog of the Library of the Insurance Society of New York,* CH502
Insurance year book, CH521
Intā Puresu-ban kagaku gijutsu 35–mango daijiten, EA119
Integrals
tables, EB77, EB85, EB86, EB91
Integrals and series, Prudnikov, Anatoliĭ Platonovich, EB91
Integraly i riady, EB91
Integrating women's studies into the curriculum, Franzosa, Susan Douglas, CC492
Integration efforts in Africa, DD6
Integrationsbestrebungen in Afrika, Kersebaum, Andrea, DD6
Intellect, CB8, CC361, CD112
Intellectual freedom manual, AK67
Intelligence and espionage, Constantinides, George C., CJ537
Intelligence, espionage, counterespionage, and covert operations, Blackstock, Paul W., CJ535
Intelligence service, CJ539
bibliography, CJ535, CJ537, CJ538, CK245
periodicals, CJ543
Intelligence service (by country or region)
United States, CJ541, CJ544, CJ547
U.S.S.R., CJ542
bibliography, CJ545
see also **Espionage**
InTer, CJ552
Inter-American Commission on Human Rights. *Anuario interamericano de derechos humanos,* CK108
Inter-American Court of Human Rights. *Anuario interamericano de derechos humanos,* CK108
Inter-American review of bibliography, AA476
Inter-American Statistical Institute. *Statistical vocabulary,* CG22
Inter-American treaties and conventions, Organization of American States. General Secretariat, CK88
Inter-Lutheran Commission on Worship. *Lutheran book of worship,* BC358
Inter Press dictionary of science and engineering, EA119
Inter-territorial Language (Swahili) Committee to the East African Dependencies. *A standard English-Swahili dictionary,* AC756
—— *Standard Swahili-English dictionary,* AC756
Inter-University Board of India and Ceylon. *A bibliography of doctoral dissertations accepted by Indian universities, 1857–1970,* AG52
Inter-University Consortium for Political and Social Research. *Congressional Quarterly's guide to U.S. elections,* CJ245
—— *Guide to resources and services,* CA3
—— *Transnational terrorism,* CJ553
Intercity bus lines, McHenry, Renée E., CH444
Intercontinental migration to Latin America, Bailey, J. P., CC309
Intercultural education, CB102
Interdisciplinary bibliography on nationalism, 1935–1953, Deutsch, Karl Wolfgang, CJ9
Interdisciplinary dictionary of weed science, Williams, Gareth, EJ34

Interdisciplinary glossary on child abuse and neglect, CC160
InterDok directory of published proceedings, AL27, EA209
Intergovernmental Maritime Consultative Organization. *International code of signals,* EC80
Interior design
dictionaries, BG127
directories, BG130
indexes, BG14
library catalogs, BG14
Interior design (by subject)
history, BG133
Interlibrary loan, AK223, AK224, AK225, AK227
Interlibrary loan (by country or region)
Canada, AK226
Interlibrary loan policies directory, Morris, Leslie R., AK227
Interlibrary loan policies in Canada, AK226
Interlibrary loan practices handbook, Boucher, Virginia, AK225
Interlibrary loan procedures, Thomson, S. K., AK225
Interlibrary loan services manual. Directory of interlibrary loan, AK226
Interlibrary loan services manual. Envoy index, AK226
L'intermédiaire des chercheurs et curieux, BE185
—— Valynseele, Joseph, BE185
The intermediate world atlas [Hammond], AB27
International abstracts of biological sciences, EG16, EG17
International accounting summaries, CH261
International aerospace abstracts, EK26, EK27
International affairs directory of organizations, CJ690
International African bibliography, DD23
International African bibliography, 1973–1978, Pearson, J. D., DD23
International African Institute. *Africa bibliography,* DD19
—— *A bibliography of African art,* BF25, BG4
—— *Cumulative bibliography of African studies … author catalogue,* DD23
—— *Cumulative bibliography of African studies … classified catalogue,* DD23
—— *International African bibliography,* DD23
—— *International guide to African studies research,* DD54
International Air Transport Association. *World air transport statistics,* CH477
The international almanac of electoral history, Mackie, Thomas T., CJ89
International and regional politics in the Middle East and North Africa, Schulz, Ann, CJ419
International annual bibliography of festschriften, AA125
International annual bibliography South West Asia, DE33
International antiques price guide, BG48
International armed conflict since 1945, Tillema, Herbert K., CJ563
International Art Alliance. *ARTnews international directory of corporate art collections,* BF97
International art price annual, BF109
International Arthurian Society. *Bulletin bibliographique de la Société internationale arthurienne,* BE338, BE339
International Association for Classical Archaeology. *Fasti archeologici,* DA96
International Association for Mathematical Geology. Committee on Geostatistics. *Geostatistical glossary and multilingual dictionary,* EF78
International Association for the History of Glass. American National Committee. *Glass collections in museums in the United States and Canada,* BG68
International Association of Agricultural Economists. *World atlas of agriculture,* EJ75
International Association of Agricultural Librarians and Documentalists. *Agricultural information resource centers,* EJ38

International Association of Egyptologists. *Annual Egyptological bibliography,* DA121
International Association of Libraries and Museums of the Performing Arts. *International bibliography of theatre,* BH57
International Association of Music Libraries. *Terminorum musicae index septem lingus redactus,* BJ159
International Association of Music Libraries. Commission of Research Libraries. *Directory of music research libraries,* BJ169
International Association of Music Libraries, Archives, and Documentation Centres. *Répertoire international de la presse musicale,* BJ112
International Association of Schools of Social Work. *World guide to social work education,* CC49
International Association of Universities. *International handbook of universities and other institutions of higher education,* CB240
—— *World list of universities,* CB241
International Astronomical Union. *Bibliography of astronomy, 1881–1898, on microfilm,* EC14
—— *A bibliography of astronomy, 1970–1979,* EC18
—— *The general history of astronomy,* EC59
The international atlas, Shanks, Thomas G., CL65
International atlas of West Africa, CL338
International auction records, BF109
International auxiliary languages, BD48
International Bank for Reconstruction and Development. *IntlEc CD-ROM,* CH119
—— *Women and development,* CC606, CH115
—— *World atlas of the child,* CC175
—— *World debt tables,* CH161
—— *World development report,* CH162
—— *World population projections,* CG64
—— *World tables,* CG66
International Bank for Reconstruction and Development. Socio-Economic Data Division. *Social indicators of development,* CG41, CH159
International Bar Association. *International directory of legal aid,* CK59
International bibliography, AF9
An international bibliography of African lexicons, Hendrix, Melvin K., AC191
International bibliography of book reviews of scholarly literature, AA373
An international bibliography of computer-assisted language learning with annotations in German, Jung, Udo O. H., BD73
International bibliography of dictionaries, AC192, EA95
International bibliography of directories and guides to archival repositories, Vázquez de Parga, Margarita, DA175
International bibliography of discographies, Cooper, David Edwin, BJ384
International bibliography of economics, CA13, CE52, CH43
International bibliography of festschriften from the beginnings until 1979, AA125
International bibliography of historical articles in festschriften and miscellanies, DA6
International bibliography of historical sciences, DA12, DC425
International bibliography of jazz books, Gregor, Carl, BJ297
International bibliography of Jewish history and thought, Kaplan, Jonathan, DA7
International bibliography of periodical literature covering all fields of knowledge, AD255
International bibliography of political science, CA13, CE52, CJ15, CJ43
International bibliography of research in marriage and the family, CC221
International bibliography of social and cultural anthropology, CA13, CE24, CE52
International bibliography of sociology, CA13, CC8, CC21, CE52
International bibliography of specialized dictionaries, AC192, EA95
International bibliography of terminological literature, BD58

International bibliography of the history of religions, BC11, BC48
International bibliography of the social sciences, CA13, CE24, CE52, CH43, CJ15
International bibliography of theatre, BH57
International bibliography of translations, AA144
International bibliography of urban history, DC72
—— Svenska Stadshistoriska Institut, DC132
International bibliography on bilingualism, Mackey, William Francis, BD61
International biographical dictionary of Central European emigrés, AH203
International biography of adult education, CB363
International biotechnology directory, EK42
—— Coombs, J., EK44
International books in print, AA394
International Botanical Congress (*14th : 1987 : Berlin, Germany*). *International code of botanical nomenclature,* EG130
International brands and their companies, Wood, Donna, CH348
International Bureau of Education. *Directory of educational documentation and information services,* CB87
—— *Directory of educational research institutions,* CB88
—— *International yearbook of education,* CB128
The international business dictionary and reference, Presner, Lewis A., CH63
International business enterprises, CH217, CH337, CH666
  bibliography, CH117
  dictionaries, CH341
  directories, CH354
  guides, CH5, CH117
International business enterprises (by subject)
  law, CK70
  see also **Multinational corporations**
International business handbook, CH143
International business information, Pagell, Ruth A., CH5
International Business Machines Corporation. *IBM dictionary of computing,* EK181
International Cartographic Association. *Cartographic innovations,* CL262
—— *International yearbook of cartography,* CL270
—— *National and regional atlases,* CL239
International catalogue of scientific literature, CE14, EA16, EA22, EB10, EB16, EC15, ED5, ED7, EE13, EF57, EF141, EF173, EF177, EF232, EG6, EG105, EG211, EG220, EG312
International Center of Photography. *Encyclopedia of photography,* BF341
International centers for research on women, CC551
International Centre for Parliamentary Documentation. *Parliaments of the world,* CJ90
International Centre for Settlement of Investment Disputes. *Investment laws of the world,* CK70
International Centre for the Study of the Preservation and the Restoration of Cultural Property. *International index of conservation research,* BF199
International Centre for Theoretical Physics. *Directory of physicists from developing countries,* ED30
International City/County Management Association. *The municipal year book,* CJ279
International Civil Aviation Organization. *Civil aviation statistics of the world,* CH473
International classification and indexing bibliography, AK201
International classification of diseases, EH384
The International classification of diseases, 9th revision, clinical modification, EH55
International code name directory, CJ586
International code of botanical nomenclature, International Botanical Congress (*14th : 1987 : Berlin, Germany*), EG130
International code of signals, EC80
International code of zoological nomenclature, EG228
International CODEN directory, EA47

International Commission for the History of Towns. *Europe,* DC2
—— *Historic towns,* DC354
International Commission of Historical Sciences. *Bibliographie d'histoire des villes de France,* DC212
International Commission of Military History. *Neue Forschungen zum Ersten Weltkrieg,* DA195
International Commission on English in the Liturgy. *The liturgy of the hours,* BC423
International Commission on Folk Arts and Folklore. *International dictionary of regional European ethnology and folklore,* CE49
—— *Internationale Volkskundliche Bibliographie,* CF42
International Committee for Social Science Information and Documentation. *International bibliography of economics,* CH43
—— *International bibliography of political science,* CJ15
—— *International bibliography of social and cultural anthropology,* CE24
—— *Thematic list of descriptors—anthropology,* CE52
—— *Thematic list of descriptors—political science,* CJ43
—— *Thematic list of descriptors—sociology,* CC21
International Committee for Social Sciences Documentation. *International bibliography of sociology,* CC8
International Committee for Soviet and East European Studies. *European bibliography of Soviet, East European and Slavonic studies,* DC41
International Committee for the History of the Second World War. *Neue Forschungen zum Ersten Weltkrieg,* DA195
International Committee of Historical Sciences. *Bibliographie internationale des travaux historiques publiés dans les volumes de "Mélanges",* DA6
—— *International bibliography of historical sciences,* DA12
International Committee of Historical Sciences. Comité Argentino. *Historiografía argentina, 1958–1988,* DB333
International Committee of Historical Sciences. Commission of the History of Historiography. *Great historians from antiquity to 1800,* DA48
International Committee on English in the Liturgy. *Lectionary for Mass,* BC422
—— *The rites of the Catholic Church,* BC425
—— *The sacramentary,* BC424
International Committee on Taxonomy of Viruses. *Stedman's ICTV virus words,* EG347
International Committee on the History of Art. *Glossarium artis,* BF84
International companies and their brands, Wood, Donna, CH348
International Conference on Education. *International yearbook of education,* CB128
International Congress of Anthropological and Ethnological Sciences. *International bibliography of social and cultural anthropology,* CE24
International Congress of Historical Sciences. *Bŭlgarskata istoricheska nauka,* DC111
—— *La Pologne au XIIIᵉ Congrès International des Sciences Historiques à Moscou,* DC472
—— *The Second World War,* DA201
International Congress of Philosophy. *Bibliography of the International Congresses of Philosophy,* BB17
International congresses
  bibliography, AL33
  chronologies, AL31
International congresses, 1681 to 1899, AL31
International congresses and conferences, 1840–1937, AL30
International contemporary arts directory, Morgan, Ann Lee, BF102
—— Naylor, Colin, BF102
International conversion tables, Naft, Stephen, AL199

International corporate giving in America, AL109
International corporate yellow book, CH350
International Council for Bird Preservation. *The illustrated encyclopedia of birds,* EG264
—— *Rare birds of the world,* EG270
—— *Threatened birds of the Americas,* EG278
International Council for Canadian Studies. *Canadian studies,* DB184
—— *Répertoire international des études canadiennes,* DB201
International Council for Philosophy and Humanistic Studies. *Bibliographie internationale de l'humanisme et de la renaissance,* DA140
—— *Linguistic bibliography for the year [...] and supplement for the years [...],* BD25
International Council of Museums. *International directory of musical instrument collections,* BJ368
International Council of Scientific and Technical Information. *Multilingual thesaurus of geosciences,* EF79
International Council of Scientific Unions. Abstracting Board. *International serials catalogue,* EA43
International Council on Archives. *Dictionary of archival terminology,* AK183
—— *Guide to manuscript sources for the history of Latin America and the Caribbean in the British Isles,* DB274
—— *Guide to the sources of Asian history,* DE162
—— *Guide to the sources of Asian history. 8. Pakistan,* DE239
—— *Guide to the sources of the history of the nations,* DD38
—— *Guides to the sources for the history of the nations : 3rd series, North Africa, Asia and Oceania,* DD75
—— *International directory of archives,* AK185
—— *Modern archives administration and records management,* AK187
International Court of Justice. *Bibliography of the International Court of Justice,* CK110
—— *Yearbook,* CK110
International crime statistics, International Criminal Police Organization (Interpol), CK270
International Criminal Police Organization (Interpol). *International crime statistics,* CK270
The international critical commentary on the Holy Scriptures of the Old and New Testaments, BC173
International critical tables of numerical data, physics, chemistry and technology, National Research Council, EA156
International Culture Institute (Hong Kong). *Who's who in Japan,* AH359
International current awareness services, CC8
International current awareness services : political science and related disciplines, CJ15
The international cyclopedia of music and musicians, BJ137
International Dairy Federation. *Dictionary of dairy terminology,* EJ115
International Defence and Aid Fund. Research Information and Publicity Dept. *Namibia,* DD188
International Demographic Data Center (U.S.). *Detailed statistics on the population of South Africa by race and urban/rural residence, 1950 to 2010,* CG356
—— *Detailed statistics on the urban and rural population of Mexico, 1950 to 2010,* CG119
—— *Detailed statistics on the urban and rural population of Turkey, 1950 to 2000,* CG291
International Dental Federation. *A lexicon of English dental terms,* EH257
International development abstracts, CH44, CL30, EF51, EG63
The international development dictionary, Fry, Gerald, CH121
International Development Information Network. *Directory of development research and training institutes in Europe,* AL79
International dictionary miniature painters, porcelain painters, silhouettists, Blättel, Harry, BF311

The international dictionary of 20th-century biography, Vernoff, Edward, AH49

International dictionary of abbreviations and acronyms of electronics, electrical engineering, computer technology, and information processing, Wennrich, Peter, EK196

An international dictionary of adult and continuing education, Jarvis, Peter, CB356

International dictionary of anthropologists, CE67

International dictionary of applied mathematics, EB40

International dictionary of architects and architecture, BF236

International dictionary of art and artists, BF236

International dictionary of ballet, BH142

International dictionary of clocks, BG87

International dictionary of education, Page, G. Terry, CB77

International dictionary of films and filmmakers, BH250

International dictionary of geophysics, EF11

International dictionary of management, Johannsen, Hano, CH614

International dictionary of medicine and biology, EG38, EH100

International dictionary of opera, BJ249

The international dictionary of psychology, Sutherland, N. S., CD32

International dictionary of regional European ethnology and folklore, CE49, CF87

International dictionary of the securities industry, Valentine, Stuart P., CH304

International dictionary of theatre, BH71

An international dictionary of theatre language, BH79

The international dictionary of women workers in the decorative arts, Prather-Moses, Alice Irma, BG34

The international dictionary of women's biography, AH25

International digest of health legislation, CK69

International directory of anthropologists, CE66

International directory of archives, AK185, DA175

International directory of arts, BF99

International directory of astronomical associations and societies, EC44

International directory of botanical gardens, Henderson, D. M., EG146

International directory of braille music collections, Thorin, Suzanne E., BJ171

An international directory of building research organizations, BF283

International directory of Canadian studies, DB201

International directory of children's literature, Dunhouse, Mary Beth, BE380

International directory of cinematographers, set- and costume designers in film, BH208

International directory of company histories, CH394

International directory of corporate affiliations, CH351

International directory of correctional administrations, CK263

International directory of exhibiting artists, BF119

International directory of film and TV documentation centres, BH179

International directory of gay and lesbian periodicals, Malinowsky, H. Robert, CC285

International directory of historical clothing, Huenefeld, Irene Pennington, BG103

International directory of legal aid, CK59

International directory of little magazines & small presses, AD12

International directory of marine scientists, EF221

International directory of marketing research companies and services, CH586

International directory of marketing research houses and services, CH586

International directory of medievalists, DA154

International directory of musical instrument collections, BJ368

International directory of philosophy and philosophers, BB45

International directory of professional astronomical institutions, EC44

International directory of psychologists, exclusive of the U.S.A, CD48

International directory of psychology, Wolman, Benjamin B., CD39, CD45

International directory of Renaissance and Reformation associations and institutes, Eisenbichler, Konrad, DA153

International directory of tactile map collections, CL258

International directory of testing laboratories, EA215

International directory of youth bodies, CC164

International discography of women composers, Cohen, Aaron I., BJ376

International doctoral dissertations in musicology, BJ164

International documents review, AF55

•*International Dun's market identifiers*, CH363

International economic indicators, Columbia University. Center for International Business Cycle Research, CH109
—— Moore, Geoffrey Hoyt, CH109

International economic institutions, Meerhaeghe, Marcel Alfons Gilbert van, CH80

International economic law, Kunig, Philip, CK112
—— Lau, Niels, CK112
—— Meng, Werner, CK112

•*International economic law documents*, CK112

International education in the United States, CB102

International electronic music catalog, BJ311

International encyclopaedia for labour law and industrial relations, CK29

International encyclopaedia of Indian literature, Garg, Gaṅgā Rām, BE1565

International encyclopaedia of laws, CK29

International encyclopedia of abbreviations and acronyms of organizations, Wennrich, Peter, AL11

The international encyclopedia of astronomy, EC30

The international encyclopedia of cats, Henderson, G. N., EJ139

International encyclopedia of communications, CF56, CH482

International encyclopedia of comparative law, CK30

International encyclopedia of curriculum, Lewy, Arieh, CB70

The international encyclopedia of education, CB70
—— Walberg, Herbert J., CB70

International encyclopedia of educational evaluation, Haertel, Geneva D., CB70

International encyclopedia of educational technology, Eraut, Michael, CB70

International encyclopedia of foundations, AL97

The international encyclopedia of hard rock & heavy metal, Jasper, Tony, BJ355

The international encyclopedia of higher education, CB237

International encyclopedia of learned societies and academies, AL19

International encyclopedia of linguistics, BD34, BD35

International encyclopedia of population, CG19

International encyclopedia of psychiatry, psychology, psychoanalysis, and neurology, CD23, EH379

International encyclopedia of robotics, EK232

International encyclopedia of sociology, CC16

International encyclopedia of statistics, CG19, CG20, EB37

International encyclopedia of teaching and teacher education, Dunkin, Michael J., CB70

International encyclopedia of the social sciences, CA33, CA36, CA44, CG19

International encyclopedia of veterinary medicine, EJ108

International encyclopedia of women composers, Cohen, Aaron I., BJ208

International English usage, Todd, Loreto, AC86

International Environmental Information System (United Nations Environment Programme). Programme Activity Centre. *ACCIS guide to United Nations information sources on the environment*, EK69

International environmental law, Weiss, Edith Brown, CK91

International Epidemiological Association. *A dictionary of epidemiology*, EH410

•*International ERIC*, CB50, CB52, CB57, CB81

International facsimile directory, CH490

International Federation for Documentation. *Library, documentation, and archives serials*, AK21

International Federation for Housing and Planning. *International glossary of technical terms used in housing and town planning*, BF278

International Federation for Modern Languages and Literature. *Répertoire chronologique des littératures modernes*, BE17

International Federation for Theatre Research. *International bibliography of theatre*, BH57

International Federation of Film Archives. *Bibliography of national filmographies*, BH164
—— *Glossary of filmographic terms*, BH257
—— *International directory of cinematographers, set- and costume designers in film*, BH208
—— *International directory of film and TV documentation centres*, BH179
—— *International index to film periodicals*, BH234

International Federation of Home Economics, EJ198

International Federation of Library Associations. *Annual bibliography of the history of the printed book and libraries*, AA268, AK17
—— *Répertoire des associations de bibliothécaires membres de la Fédération internationale*, AK53

International Federation of Library Associations and Institutions. *Directory*, AK53
—— *Inventaire général des bibliographies nationales rétrospectives*, AA395
—— *Librarianship in Japan*, AK160
—— *World guide to library, archive, and information science associations*, AK55

International Federation of Library Associations and Institutions. Section of Geography and Map Libraries. *World directory of map collections*, CL261

International Federation of Library Associations and Institutions. Section of Libraries for the Blind. *International directory of tactile map collections*, CL258

International Federation of Library Associations and Institutions. Section of University Libraries and other General Research Libraries. *Guide to the availability of theses*, AK224

International feed descriptions, international feed names, and country feed names, EJ123

International film guide, BH269, BJ192

The international film index, 1895–1990, BH188, BH204

International film industry, Slide, Anthony, BH254

International film prizes, Hammer, Tad Bentley, BH273

International film, radio, and television journals, BH175

•*International filmarchive CD-ROM*, BH234, BH297

International finance, CH217, CH242
statistics, CH238, CH240

International Finance Corporation. *World tables*, CG66

The international financial law review 1000, CK60

International financial statistics, CH240

International financial statistics yearbook, CH240

International folklore and folklife bibliography, CF42

International folklore bibliography, CF42

International Food Information Service. *The companion thesaurus to food science and technology abstracts*, EJ159
—— *Food science and technology abstracts*, EJ150

The international foundation directory, AL97, AL98
The international Gallup polls, CJ490
The international geographic encyclopedia and atlas, CL47
International Geographical Congress. *Bibliography of International Geographic Congresses, 1871–1976,* CL15
International Geographical Union. *Bibliographie cartographique internationale,* CL226
────── *Bibliography of International Geographic Congresses, 1871–1976,* CL15
────── *Bibliography of mono- and multilingual dictionaries and glossaries of technical terms used in geography, as well as in related natural and social sciences,* CL53
────── *Geographers,* CL82
────── *Orbis geographicus,* CL56
International Geological Congress. *Catalogue des bibliographies géologiques,* EF34
International Geological Congress. Commission de stratigraphie. *Lexique stratigraphique international,* EF74
International GIS sourcebook, CL79
International glossary of abbreviations for theology and related subjects, BC25
International glossary of hydrology, EF133
International glossary of social gerontology, CC83
International glossary of technical terms used in housing and town planning, International Federation for Housing and Planning, BF278
────── Spiwak, H. J., BF278
International governmental organizations, Peaslee, Amos Jenkins, AF18
International guide to accounting journals, Spiceland, J. David, CH249
International guide to African studies research, DD54
International guide to electoral statistics, CJ89
International guide to library and information science education, AK54
International guide to library, archival, and information science associations, AK55
International guide to nineteenth-century photographers and their works, Edwards, Gary, BF356
International guide to official industrial property publications, Rimmer, Brenda M., EA267
International guide to qualifications in education, CB324
International handbook of adolescence, CC169
International handbook of child care policies and programs, CC170
International handbook of early childhood education, CB119
International handbook of education systems, CB125
International handbook of national parks and nature reserves, BK125
International handbook of political science, CJ54
International handbook of psychology, CD45
International handbook of reading education, CB120
International handbook of the ombudsman, CJ55
International handbook of universities and other institutions of higher education, CB240
International handbook of women's education, CB126
International handbook on abortion, CC253
International handbook on aging, CC94
International handbook on gender roles, CC289
The international heritage of home economics in the United States, American Home Economics Association. International Section, EJ198
International higher education, CB238
International historical statistics, Mitchell, Brian R., CG70, DB7, DB290
International historical statistics, Africa and Asia, CG70, DB7, DB290, CG309, CG375
International historical statistics, Europe, CG70, CG309, CG375, DB7, DB290
International historical statistics, Europe, 1750–1988, Mitchell, Brian R., CG189, DC24
International historical statistics, the Americas 1750–1988, CG70, DB7, DB290

International historical statistics : the Americas and Australasia, CG70, CG309, CG375, DB7, DB290
International imaging source book, AK248
International index, AD288, AD289, BA6
International index of conservation research, BF199
International index to film periodicals, BH234, BH297
International index to periodicals, AD253
International index to recorded poetry, Hoffman, Herbert H., BE323
International index to television periodicals, BH234, BH297
International information, AF4
•*International information system for the agricultural sciences and technology,* EJ16
International insider, CH289
International Institute for Conservation of Historic and Artistic Works. *Art and archaeology technical abstracts,* BF198
International Institute for Strategic Studies. *The military balance,* CJ596
────── *Strategic survey,* CJ601
International Institute for the Study of Human Reproduction. *Fertility modification thesaurus,* CC254
International Institute for the Study of Human Reproduction. Center for Population and Family Health. *International encyclopedia of population,* CG19
International Institute of Philosophy. *International directory of philosophy and philosophers,* BB45
International Institute of Refrigeration, Paris. *Bibliographic guide to refrigeration, 1953–1968,* EK227
International institutions and international organization, Speeckaert, Georges Patrick, AF21
International inventory of musical sources, BJ77, BJ169
International ISBN Agency. *Publishers' international ISBN directory,* AA279
International ISBN publishers' directory, AA279
International jazz bibliography, Carl Gregor, *Duke of Mecklenburg,* BJ297
International jobs, Kocher, Eric, CH699
International journal of abstracts, EB29
International journal of abstracts, statistical theory and method, EB12
International Labour Office. *Economically active population estimates and projections, 1950–2025,* CH680
────── *Encyclopaedia of occupational health and safety,* EH409
────── *ILO thesaurus 1991,* CH652
────── *Labour information,* CH632
────── *Labour law documents,* CK69
────── *Poverty in developing countries,* CC264
────── *World labour report,* CH690
────── *Year-book of labour statistics,* CH691
International Labour Organisation. *World demographic estimates and projections, 1950–2025,* CG59
International labour statistics, CH684
International law
  annuals, CK111
  bibliography, CK76, CK78, CK81, CK82
    current, CK19
  collections, CK112, CK114
  databases, CK112
  dictionaries, CK101, CK102, CK105
    multilingual, CK45, CK103, CK104
  directories, CK106
  encyclopedias, CK100
  guides, CK1, CK74, CK76
  indexes, CK24
The international law dictionary, Bledsoe, Robert L., CK101
────── Lindbergh, Ernest, CK45
International law digest, CK71
The international law list, CK61
International law of the sea, Papadakis, Nikos, CK79
International law of the sea and marine affairs, CK79
International legal books in print, CK20

International legal materials, CK114
International list of geographical serials, Harris, Chauncy Dennison, CL25
International literary market place, AA278, AK33
International marketing data and statistics, CH593
International Material Management Society. *Materials handling handbook,* EK277
International Mathematical Union. *World directory of mathematicians,* EB60
International media guide, AE9
International medical who's who, EH150
International medieval bibliography, DA143
International meteorological vocabulary, World Meteorological Organization, EF148
International microforms in print, AA131
International micrographics source book, AK248
International military and defense encyclopedia, CJ571
The international military encyclopedia, CJ572
International Mineralogical Association. *World directory of mineralogists,* EF189
International Monetary Fund. *Balance of payments statistics,* CH238
────── *IMF glossary,* CH125
────── *International financial statistics yearbook,* CH240
────── *IntlEc CD-ROM,* CH119
────── *Occasional paper,* CH163
────── *A study of the Soviet economy,* CH186
────── *Women and development,* CC606, CH115
International Monetary Fund, CH239
International Monetary Fund. Government Finance Statistics Division. *Government finance statistics yearbook,* CH242
The International Monetary Fund, Salda, Anne C. M., AF57
International mortality statistics, Alderson, Michael Rowland, CG46
International motion picture almanac, BH266
International Museum of Photography at George Eastman House. *Index to American photographic collections,* BF344
International Museum of Photography at George Eastman House. Library. *Library catalog of the International Museum of Photography at George Eastman House,* BF337
International music & opera guide, BJ192
International music guide, BJ192
International music journals, BJ102
International Musicological Society. *Doctoral dissertations in musicology,* BJ164
────── *Répertoire international de la presse musicale,* BJ112
────── *Terminorum musicae index septem lingus redactus,* BJ159
International Network of Feed Information Centers. *International feed descriptions, international feed names, and country feed names,* EJ123
International Nietzsche bibliography, Reichert, Herbert William, BB78
•*International nuclear information system (INIS),* EK293
International nursing index, EH67, EH276
International Office of Epizooties. *Dictionary of animal health terminology,* EJ113
International organisations and overseas agencies publications, AF185
International organisations catalogue, AF185
────── Great Britain. Stationery Office, AF185
International organisations publications, AF185
International organization and integration, AF17
International Organization for Standardization. *Documentation—bibliographic references—content, form and structure,* EA162
────── *ISO catalogue,* EA273
International Organization of Palaeobotany. *Rapport sur la paléobotanique dans le monde,* EG101
International organizations
  archives, AF1
  bibliography, AF7, AF19
    periodicals., AD21
  biography, AH50
  chronologies, AL22

collections, AF17, AF18
directories, AF16, AL21, AL24, CA48, CH80, CH134, CJ82, EA201
publications, AF1, AF2, AF3, AF5, AF7, AF9, AF11, AF148
  guides, AF4
  library resources, AF12
statistics
  indexes, CG69
yearbooks, AF16
International organizations (by region)
Africa, DD6
  directories, AF20
  publications, AF20
International organizations (by subject)
history, AL22
International organizations, Schiavone, Giuseppe, AL21
International organizations, 1918–1945, Baer, George W., AF1
International Paleontological Association. *Directory of paleontologists of the world*, EF245
The international peace directory, CJ691
International pharmaceutical abstracts, EH322
The international pharmacopoeia, EH358
International philosophical bibliography, BB13
International Phonetic Alphabet, BD15
International photography index, BF330
International planning glossaries, Logie, Gordon, BF277
International political science abstracts, CJ19
International Political Science Association. *International political science abstracts*, CJ19
International population census bibliography, CG93
  —— Goyer, Doreen S., CG6
  —— University of Texas at Austin. Population Research Center, CG9, CG11, CG13
International population census bibliography, revision and update, 1945–1977, Goyer, Doreen S., CG13
International population census publications, CG9, CG11
International Pragmatics Association. *A comprehensive bibliography of pragmatics*, BD65
International proverb scholarship, Mieder, Wolfgang, BE156, BE158
International Reading Association. *A dictionary of reading and related terms*, CB74
  —— *Handbook of research on teaching the English language arts*, CB118
International red series, AH171, AH212, AH213, AH282, AH291
International Refugee Integration Resource Centre. *Refugee abstracts*, CK83
International register of nobility, AJ80
International register of research on British politics, CJ342
The international registry of who's who, AH127
International relations, CJ70
  bibliography, CJ10, CJ566, DA171
  biography, CJ66
  dictionaries, CJ37
  encyclopedias, AF41, CJ30
  guides, DA173
International relations, CJ10
International relations dictionary, CJ37
  —— Plano, Jack C., CJ30
The international relations of Eastern Europe, Remington, Robin Alison, DC36
International relations of South Asia, 1947–1980, Kozicki, Richard J., DE78
International relations theory, Groom, A. J. R., CJ10
  —— Mitchell, Christopher, CJ10
International Repertory of Music Literature. *RILM abstracts of music literature*, BJ108
  —— *Thèses de doctorat en langue française relatives à la musique*, BJ166
International repertory of the literature of art, BF34
International Research and Exchanges Board. *Guide to research and scholarship in Hungary*, DC389
  —— *A handbook for archival research in the USSR*, DC562
International research centers directory, AL81

International review of biblical studies, BC120
International scholarship directory, Cassidy, Daniel J., CB374
International Schools Services. *Directory of overseas schools*, CB91
International scientist's directory, EG80
International serials catalogue, EA38
  —— International Council of Scientific Unions. Abstracting Board, EA43
International shipping and shipbuilding directory, CH464
International Social Security Association. *Bibliographie universelle de sécurité sociale*, CH498
International Society for Ethnology and Folklore. *Internationale Volkskundliche Bibliographie*, CF42
International Society for Horticultural Science. *Elsevier's dictionary of horticultural and plant production*, EJ240
International Sociological Association. *Current sociology*, CC11
  —— *International bibliography of sociology*, CC8
The international standard Bible encyclopedia, BC131
International Standard Book Numbers, AA279
International statistical classification of diseases and related health problems, EH56, EH377
International Statistical Institute. *Bibliography of statistical bibliographies*, EB13
  —— *A dictionary of statistical terms*, CG25, EB43
  —— *Revue de l'institut, international de statistique*, EB13
  —— *Statistical theory and method abstracts*, EB29
International Statistical Institute. Permanent Office. *Annuaire de statistique internationale des grandes villes*, CG47
  —— *Annuaire international de statistique*, CG48
International statistical review, EB13
International Statistical Union. *Statistique internationale des grandes villes*, CG56
International statistical year-book, CG52
International statistical yearbook of large towns, CG47
International statistics of large towns, CG56
The International Stock Exchange official yearbook, CH327
International stratigraphic guide, International Union of Geological Sciences. International Subcommission on Stratigraphic Classification, EF95
International subscription agents, Wilkas, Lenore, AK170
International tables for crystallography, EF117
International tables for X-ray crystallography, EF117
International television & video almanac, BH319
International television almanac, BH319
International terrorism, Greenburg, Martin H., CJ550
  —— Lakos, Amos, CJ550
  —— Norton, Augustus R., CJ550
International terrorism : attributes of terrorist events (ITERATE), CJ553
International terrorism in the 1980s, Mickolus, Edward F., CJ553
  —— Murdock, Jean M., CJ553
  —— Sandler, Todd, CJ553
The international thesaurus of quotations, Tripp, Rhoda Thomas, BE95
International time tables, Fitzpatrick, Gary L., EC86
International title abbreviations of periodicals, newspapers, important handbooks, dictionaries, laws, etc., AD22
International trade
  annuals, CH152
  bibliography, CH140
  databases, CH118, CH119, CH497
  dictionaries, CH123, CH124
    bilingual
      Portuguese-English, CH127, CH128
    multilingual, CH125, CH126, CH129

  directories, CH135, CH136, CH165, CH414
  guides, CH135
  handbooks, CH141, CH144, CH146
  handbooks, manuals, etc., CH138
  indexes, CH119
  periodicals, CH156
  statistics, CH149, CH153, CH154, CH157, CH160
International trade, CH156
International trade names company index, CH348
International trade names dictionary, CH348
International trade statistics, CH157
International trade statistics yearbook, CH157
International Translations Centre. *Translations journals*, AD25
  —— *World translations index*, EA63
International travel, business and relocation directory, CH621
International Union for Conservation of Nature and Natural Resources. *Red data book*, EG149, EG234, EG250, EG278, EG296
  —— *World directory of environmental organizations*, EK77
International Union for the Scientific Study of Population. *The materials of demography*, CG2
  —— *National population bibliography of Czechoslovakia, 1945–1977*, CG207
  —— *National population bibliography of Finland*, CG211
  —— *National population bibliography of Flanders, 1945–1983*, CG200
  —— *National population bibliography of Norway, 1945–1977*, CG269
  —— *Non-national bibliography of French demographers*, CG218
  —— *al-Qāmūs al-dimūghrāfi al-thulāthī*, CG31
International union list of agricultural serials, EJ10, EJ14, EJ18
International Union of Biochemistry. Nomenclature Committee. *Enzyme nomenclature 1984*, EG321
International Union of Crystallography. *International tables for crystallography*, EF117
  —— *Molecular structures and dimensions*, EE139
  —— *World directory of crystallographers and of other scientists employing crystallographic methods*, EF119
International Union of Geological Sciences. *Multilingual thesaurus of geosciences*, EF79
International Union of Geological Sciences. International Subcommission on Stratigraphic Classification. *International stratigraphic guide*, EF95
International Union of Geological Sciences. Subcommission on the Systematics of Igneous Rocks. *A classification of igneous rocks and glossary of terms*, EF255
International Union of Local Authorities. *Annuaire de statistique internationale des grandes villes*, CG47
  —— *Statistique internationale des grandes villes*, CG56
International Union of Psychological Science. *International directory of psychologists, exclusive of the U.S.A*, CD48
International Union of Pure and Applied Chemistry. *Compendium of chemical terminology*, EE36
International Union of Pure and Applied Chemistry. Analytical Chemistry Division. *Compendium of analytical nomenclature*, EE35
International Union of Pure and Applied Chemistry. Commission on the Nomenclature of Organic Chemistry. *Nomenclature of organic chemistry*, EE136
International Union of the History and Philosophy of Science. *The general history of astronomy*, EC59
International veterinary reference service, EJ106
International vital records handbook, Kemp, Thomas Jay, AJ12
An international vocabulary of technical theatre terms in eight languages, Rae, Kenneth, BH81
International vocabulary of town planning and architecture, BF278

International Volcanological Association. *Catalogue of the active volcanoes of the world*, EF264
International who's who, AH45, AH46, AH51
International who's who in music and musicians' directory, BJ213
The international who's who of the Arab world, AH328
The international who's who of women, AH46
International Work Group for Indigenous Affairs. *Indigenous world*, CE63
International year book and statemen's who's who, CJ65
International Year of the Child, 1979. *World atlas of the child*, CC175
International yearbook of cartography, CL270
International yearbook of education, CB128
International yearbook of educational and instructional technology, CB175
International yearbook of educational and training technology, CB175
International zoo yearbook, EG233
Internationale Bibliographie der Festschriften von den Anfängen bis 1979, Leistner, Otto, AA125
Internationale Bibliographie der Kunstwissenschaft, BF26
Internationale Bibliographie der Reprints, AA399
Internationale Bibliographie der Rezensionen wissenschaftlicher Literatur, AA364, AA373
Internationale Bibliographie der Zeitschriftenliteratur aus allen Gebieten des Wissens, AA373, AD253, AD255, AD313
Internationale bibliographie zu Geschichte und Theorie der Komparatistik, BE18
Internationale Bibliographie zur Geschichte der deutschen Literatur, Albrecht, Günter, BE1213
Internationale economische betrekkingen en instellingen, Meerhaeghe, Marcel Alfons Gilbert van, CH80
Internationale germanistische Bibliographie, Koch, Hans-Albrecht, BD116, BE1235
—— Koch, Uta, BD116, BE1235
Internationale Jahresbibliographie der Festschriften, AA125
Internationale Jahresbibliographie Südwestasien, DE33
Internationale Musical-Bibliographie, Tischler, Gerhard, BJ268
—— Wildbihler, Hubert, BJ268
Internationale ökumenische Bibliographie, BC273
Internationale patristische bibliographie, BC295
Internationale Personalbibliographie, 1800–1943, AA19, AH14
Internationale Tabellen zur Bestimmung von Kristallstrukturen, EF117
Internationale Titelabkürzungen von Zeitschriften, Zeitungen, wichtigen Handbüchern, Wörterbüchern, Gesetzen usw, AD22
Internationale Volkskundliche Bibliographie, CF42
Internationale Zeitschriftenschau für Bibelwissenschaft und Grenzgebiete, BC120
Internationalen Institut für Missionswissenschaftliche. *Bibliotheca missionum*, BC304
Internationales Abkürzungsverzeichnis für Theologie und Grenzgebiete, BC25
Internationales Bibliotheks-Handbuch, AK121
Internationales ISBN-Verlagsverzeichnis, AA279
Internationales Kunst-Adressbuch, BF99
Internationales Soziologenlexikon, CA63
Internationales Verlagssadressbuch, AA279
Internationales Wörterbuch der Abkürzungen von Organisationen, Spillner, Paul, AL11
Internet world. *Internet world's On Internet*, CH495
Internet world's On Internet, CH495
Internships, CB364, CB368, CH695, CH697
directories, AL6, CB385
Internships, CB368, CH697
Interpretation of diagnostic tests, Wallach, Jacques B., EH192
Interpreter's Bible, BC174
The interpreter's dictionary of the Bible, BC125, BC132

Interpreter's one-volume commentary on the Bible, BC175
Interstate agencies and authorities, AF141
Interstate compacts and agencies, Council of State Governments, AF141
Intertextuality, BE16
Intertextuality, allusion, and quotation, Hebel, Udo J., BE16
Interviews and conversations with 20th-century authors writing in English, Vrana, Stan A., BE450
•*IntlEc CD-ROM*, CH119
Intner, Sheila S. *Guide to technical services resources*, AK228
Introdução ao estudo da história do Brasil, Lacombe, Américo Jacobina, DB339
Introduccion a la literatura hispanoamericana, Franco, Jean, BE865
Introducción a las bases documentales para la historia de la República del Perú, Basadre, Jorge, DB381
Introducción a los estudios bolivianos contemporáneos, 1960–1984, Barnadas, Josep M., DB334
Introducción a una bibliografía general de la arqueología del Perú, 1860–1988, Ravines, Rogger, DB385
Introducción al estudio de la historia de Panamá, Gasteazoro, Carlos Manuel, DB319
Introduction aux dictionnaires les plus importants pour l'histoire du français, Baldinger, Kurt, AC387
Introduction aux études classiques, Poucet, Jacques, DA91
Introduction bibliographique à l'histoire du droit et à l'ethnologie juridique, CK12
Introduction to ancient history, Bengtson, Hermann, DA59
Introduction to bibliography for literary students, McKerrow, R. B., AA3
Introduction to classical scholarship, McGuire, Martin, BE997, DA93
An introduction to Greek and Latin palaeography, Thompson, Edward Maunde, AA216, BE1018
Introduction to indexing and abstracting, Cleveland, Donald B., AK212
An introduction to Japanese government publications, Kuroki, Tsutomu, AF251
Introduction to library research in anthropology, Weeks, John M., CE2
Introduction to library research in German studies, Richardson, Larry L., BE1212
Introduction to library research in women's studies, Searing, Susan E., CC483
Introduction to medieval Latin studies, McGuire, Martin Rawson Patrick, BD145
Introduction to micrographics, Vilhauer, Jerry, AK251
An introduction to Persian literature, Levy, Reuben, BE1573
Introduction to reference sources in the health sciences, EH6
Introduction to reference work, Katz, William A., AK233, AK235
An introduction to Russian language and literature, BD186, BE1382
Introduction to scholarship in modern languages and literatures, BE4
Introduction to Soviet national bibliography, Lorković, Tanja, AA792, AD150
—— Whitby, Thomas Joseph, AA792, AA794, AD150
Introduction to Spanish-American literature, Franco, Jean, BE865
An introduction to the history of dentistry, Weinberger, Bernhard Wolf, EH266
Introduction to the history of medicine, Garrison, Fielding Hudson, EH213, EH214
Introduction to the history of science, Sarton, George, EA256
Introduction to the history of the Muslim East, Sauvaget, Jean, BC500
An introduction to the literature of vertebrate zoology, Wood, Casey Albert, EG215

Introduction to United States government information sources, Fetzer, Mary, AF120, CJ200
—— Morehead, Joe, AF73, AF120, CJ200
Introduction to United States public documents, Morehead, Joe, AF73
Introductions to research in foreign law : Israel, Levush, Ruth, CK231
Introductions to research in foreign law: Japan, Cho, Sung Yoon, CK232
Introductory bibliography for the study of scripture, Fitzmyer, Joseph A., BC13, BC110
An introductory bibliography to the history of classical scholarship chiefly in the XIXth and XXth centuries, Calder, William M., DA92
Introductory bibliography to the study of Hungarian literature, Tezla, Albert, BE1278, BE1283
Inuit, CC414
Inuit artists, BF318
Inventaire chronologique … , Dionne, Narcisse Eutrope, AA447
Inventaire chronologique des éditions parisiennes du XVIᵉ siècle … d'après les manuscrits de Philippe Renouard, Moreau, Brigitte, AA618
Inventaire des archives de la Tunisie, Duru, Jeannine, DD69
—— Nicot, Jean, DD69
Inventaire des périodiques de sciences sociales et d'humanités posse'abdent les bibliothèques canadiennes, AD228
Inventaire des périodiques étrangers et des publications en série étrangères reçus en France par les bibliothèques et les organismes de documentation en 1965, AD233
Inventaire des périodiques étrangers reçus en France, AD233
Inventaire des thèses de doctorat soutenues devant les universités françaises, AG27, EA55
Inventaire du fonds français, Bibliothèque Nationale (France), BF377
Inventaire général des bibliographies nationales rétrospectives, AA395
Inventaire selectif des services d'information et de documentation en sciences sociales, CA49
Inventario selectivo de servicios de informaci on y documentaci on en ciencias sociales, CA49
Inventing and patenting sourcebook, Levy, Richard C., EA262
Inventions, EA249, EA253, EA258, EA262
Inventor's handbook, Fenner, Terrence W., EA258
Inventory of American Paintings Executed Before 1914 (Project). *The National Museum of American Art's index to American art exhibition catalogues*, BF120
•*Inventory of Canadian agri-food research*, EJ74
Inventory of ethnological collections in museums of the United States and Canada, Hunter, John E., CE88
Inventory of geographical research on desert environments, University of Arizona. Office of Arid Lands Research, CL58, EF17
Inventory of longitudinal research on childhood and adolescence, Verdonik, Frederick, CA60
Inventory of longitudinal studies in the social sciences, Young, Copeland H., CA60
Inventory of longitudinal studies of middle and old age, Migdall, Susan, CA60
Inventory of marriage and family literature, CC221
Inventory of published letters to and from physicists, 1900–1950, Wheaton, Bruce R., ED53
Inventory of the records of the National Arts Club, 1898–1960, Stover, Catherine, BF58
Invertebrates, EG231, EG236
fossil indexes, EF243
The invertebrates, Hyman, Libbie Henrietta, EG240
•*Investext*, CH299
Investigación y tendencias recientes de la historiografía hondureña, Arqueta, Mario, DB310
Investigations of proverbs, proverbial expressions, quotations and cliches, Mieder, Wolfgang, BE156
Investigators' guide to sources of information, CH206
Investing, licensing & trading conditions abroad, CH144

Investment, CH301
  abbreviations, CH315
  bibliography, CH297
  databases, CH309
  dictionaries, CH209, CH212, CH227, CH300, CH302, CH303
    multilingual, CH304
  directories, CH229, CH231, CH305, CH306, CH308, CH309, CH311, CH312, CH313, CH316
  encyclopedias, CH211
  guides, CH320
  handbooks, CH218, CH232, CH233, CH318, CH319, CH320, CH322, CH378
  periodicals, CH298
  ratings, CH321
  statistics, CH223, CH325
    indexes, CH324
Investment (by subject)
  law, CK70
Investment and securities dictionary, Thomsett, Michael C., CH303
Investment companies, CH308
Investment companies yearbook, CH308
Investment laws of the world, CK70
Investment statistics locator, Chapman, Karen J., CH324
Investor's dictionary, Rosenberg, Jerry Martin, CH302
The investor's guide to stock quotations and other financial listings, Warfield, Gerald, CH323
Invisible poets, Sherman, Joan R., BE533
Ionescu, Alexandru Sadi. *Publicaţiunile periodice româneşti (ziare, gazete, reviste),* AD140
Ionov, E. P. *Pisateli Moskvy,* BE1422
Iordan, Iorgu. *Dicţionarul limbii române,* AC660
Iowa. [Laws, etc.]. *Iowa code annotated,* CK179
Iowa code annotated, Iowa. [Laws, etc.], CK179
•*IPI,* CH506
The IQ debate, Aby, Stephen H., CB8, CC361
Iqtidār, Riẓā. *A directory of Iranian periodicals,* AD198
Ira, Rudolf. *Atlas do Brasil Globo,* CL316
Iran
  bibliography, AA905, AA906, AA907, BD195, DE32, DE182, DE186
  bibliography of bibliography, AA80
  biography, AH355
  chronologies, CJ423, DE62
  encyclopedias, DE188
  gazetteers, CL165
  guides, DE181
  newspapers, AD199, AE90
  periodicals, AD198, AD199
  registers, CJ325
  statistics, CG396
Iran (by subject)
  archaeology
    bibliography, DE180
  foreign relations, CJ114
  history, DE187
    bibliography, DE35, DE180, DE181, DE183, DE185
    general histories, DE189
  politics and government, CJ423, DE62
    bibliography, DE184
  religion, BC575
Iran, Ehlers, Eckart, DE182
——— Navabpour, Reza, DE185
Iran and the West, Ghanī, Sīrūs, DE183
Iran-Contra Affair, CJ114
Iran-Contra hearings summary report, CJ114
Iran, Iraq, and the Arabian Peninsula, CJ423, DE62
Iran, politics and government under the Pahlavis, Gitisetan, Dariush, DE184
Iran statistical yearbook, CG396
Iran who's who, AH355
Iranian languages
  bibliography, BD195, BD196, DE186
  see also **Farsi language**
Iranian literature
  biobibliography, BE1574
Iranian literature (by subject)
  history, BE1572, BE1573

Iraq
  atlases, DA86, DE67
  bibliography, AA908
  chronologies, CJ423, DE62
  newspapers, AE91
  periodicals, AE91
  registers, CJ325
  statistics, CG397
Iraq (by subject)
  history
    bibliography, DE35, DE190
  politics and government, CJ423, DE62
Iraq. Jihāz al-Markazī lil-Iḥṣā'. *Annual abstract of statistics,* CG397
Iraq, 'Abd al-Rahmān, 'Abd al-Jabbār, DE190
Iraqi national bibliography, AA908
Ireland, Norma Olin. *Index to fairy tales, 1949–1972,* BE243
——— *Index to full length plays, 1944 to 1964,* BE238
——— *Index to scientists,* AH15
——— *Index to scientists of the world from ancient to modern times,* EA195
——— *Index to women of the world from ancient to modern times,* AH15
Ireland, Sandra L. Jones. *Ethnic periodicals in contemporary America,* AD52
Ireland
  archives
    directories, AJ133
  atlases, DC416
  bibliography, AA721, AA722
    current, AA723, AA724
  bibliography of bibliography, AA49
  biography, AH223, AH255, AH256
    bibliography, AH234
    contemporary, AH257
  dissertations, AG33
  encyclopedias, DC407
  gazetteers, CL143
  government publications, AF211
  guides to records, DC404
  library catalogs
    bibliography, AK144
  library resources, AK144, DC402, DE51, DE82, DE105
  manuscripts and archives, DC395, DC400, DC402
  newspapers, AD124, AE63
  periodicals, AD124
  statistics, CG251, CG252, CG253, CG254
Ireland (by subject)
  applied arts, DC407
  archaeology and ancient history, DC306, DC405
  economic conditions, CH187
    statistics, CG254
  elections, CJ379
  folklore and popular culture, CF81
  foreign relations
    bibliography, DC396
  genealogy, AJ132
  historiography, DC414
  history, DC392, DC395, DC408, DC411, DC413
    19th century, AF192
    atlases, DC416
    bibliography, DC282, DC397, DC398, DC399
    chronology, DC412
    dissertations, CH295, DC283
    encyclopedias, DC289, DC406
    indexes, DC394
    library catalogs, DC347
    library resources, DC403
    manuscripts and archives, DC403, DC404
    quotations, CJ377, DC409
    regional and local, DC349
    sourcebooks, DC415
    statistics, CG253
  place-names, CL196, CL200, CL209
  politics and government, CJ376, CJ377, CJ378, CJ379, DC409
  religion, BC251
  social conditions, AL67, DC407
    dissertations, CH295, DC283

  women, CC591, DC393
Ireland. Central Statistics Office. *Ireland statistical abstract,* CG252
——— *Report on vital statistics,* CG251
——— *Tuarascáil ar staidreamh beatha,* CG251
Ireland. Department of Health. *Tuarascáil ar staidreamh beatha,* CG251
Ireland. Public Record Office. *Irish history from 1700,* DC404
——— *The public record,* DC401
Ireland. State Paper Office. *The public record,* DC401
Ireland, DC407
Ireland in fiction, Brown, Stephen James, BE800
Ireland in literature, BE800
Ireland in the nineteenth century, Maltby, Arthur, AF192
Ireland, Northern
  bibliography, DC355, DC356
  government publications., AF210
  newspapers, AE61
  statistics, CG240, CG241
Ireland, Northern (by subject)
  history
    sourcebooks, DC415
  politics and government, CJ374
  population, CG239
Ireland statistical abstract, CG252
Irele, Modupeola. *The Economic Community of West African States (ECOWAS),* DD100
Iribas, Juan L. *New revised Velázquez Spanish and English dictionary,* AC740
Irick, Robert L. *Annotated guide to Taiwan periodical literature, 1972,* AD210
IRIDE, Zappella, Giuseppina, BF72
Irish (by country or region)
  Canada
    bibliography, CC327
    manuscripts and archives, CC332
  United States, AJ37, DC402
    bibliography, CC327
    manuscripts and archives, CC332
The Irish-American experience, Metress, Seamus P., CC327
Irish American material culture, Eleuterio-Comer, Susan K., CC312, DC402
Irish Americans
  guides, CC312
Irish Americans (by subject)
  history
    guides, CC312
Irish books in print & Leabhair Gaeilge i gCló, AA723
Irish Committee of Historical Sciences. *Irish historiography, 1936–70,* DC414
——— *Writings on Irish history,* DC399
Irish Dáil and Senate, 1922–72, CJ376
Irish drama
  bibliography, BH42
Irish economic and social history, DC399
Irish economic statistics, Kirwan, Frank, CG254
Irish-English dictionary, Dinneen, Patrick Stephen, AC521
Irish families, MacLysaght, Edward, AJ135, AJ197
Irish genealogy, AJ134
Irish historical documents since 1800, DC415
Irish historical statistics, CG253
Irish historical studies, DC399
Irish historiography, 1936–70, Moody, T. W., DC414
Irish history from 1700, Prochaska, Alice, DC404
The Irish in America, Blessing, Patrick J., CC312
Irish in Britain, DC276
Irish in British History Group. *The history of the Irish in Britain,* DC276
Irish language
  bibliography, BD178, BD179
  dictionaries, AC519
    bilingual
      Irish-English, AC520, AC521
      etymology, AC522
The Irish language, Edwards, John, BD179

Irish literature
bibliography, BD178, BE800, BE802, BE804, BE806
biography, BE799, BE802
chronologies, BE801
criticism
   collections, BE805
dissertations
   bibliography, BE797
guides, BE806
history, BE803
reviews of research, BE798
Irish literature, 1800–1875, McKenna, Brian, BE806
Irish Manuscript Commission. *Catalogue of publications issued and in preparation 1928–1966,* DC403
Irish official publications, Maltby, Arthur, AF211
Irish poetry
bibliography, BE807
biography, BE807
Irish publishing record, AA724
Irish records, Ryan, James G., AJ138
Irish Republic, Shannon, Michael Owen, DC398
Irish research, Lester, DeeGee, CC312, CC332, DC402
Irish University Press. *Checklist of British parliamentary papers in the Irish University Press 1000-volume series, 1801–1899,* AF204
Irish University Press series of British parliamentary papers, AF205
Iron and steel construction, EK111
Iron and steel in the nineteenth century, Paskoff, Paul F., CH383
Iron and steel industry in the 20th century, Seely, Bruce E., CH383
Irregular serials and annuals, AD13, AD17, AD18
Irving, Holly Berry. *The directory of food and nutrition information for professionals and consumers,* EH290, EJ214
Irving, Robert. *Pictorial guide to identifying Australian architecture,* BF208
Irwin, Barbara I. *Bibliography of Ontario history, 1867–1976,* DB212
Irwin, C. H. *Cruden's complete concordance of the Old and New Testaments,* BC165
Irwin, Graham W. *Harper encyclopedia of the modern world,* DA180
Irwin, Leonard Bertram. *A guide to historical fiction for the use of schools, libraries, and the general reader,* BE256
Irwin, Robert. *Contemporary American poetry,* BE487
—— *The McGraw-Hill real estate handbook,* CH542
The Irwin business and investment almanac, CH378
Isaac, Frank. *Index to the early printed books in the British Museum,* AA227
Isaacman, Allen F. *Mozambique,* DD184
Isaacman, Barbara. *Mozambique,* DD184
Isaacs, Alan. *The Cambridge illustrated dictionary of British heritage,* DC290
—— *Multilingual dictionary of publishing, printing and bookselling,* AA275
Isaacs, Katherine M. *Pronouncing dictionary of proper names,* AC109
Isaacson, Richard T. *Gardening,* EJ228
Isagoge in musicen, Glareanus, Henricus, BJ29
Isaksen, Judith A. *Sexual harassment in the workplace,* CC555
ISAP, AD335
The ISCC-NBS method of designating colors and a dictionary of color names, ED60
Iscla Rovira, Luis. *Spanish proverbs,* BE149
Iseki, Kurō. *Dai-Nihon hakushiroku,* AH357
Isham, Samuel. *History of American painting,* BF309
Işik, M. Asif. *Türk arkeoloji dergisis makaleler bibliografyasi,* DC531
Isis, EA241, EA248, EA256, EH199
Isis cumulative bibliography, EA233, ED52
Isis cumulative bibliography, 1966–1975, Neu, John, EA233
Isis cumulative bibliography, 1975–1985, Neu, John, EA233

ISIS Women's International Information and Communication Service. *Women in development,* CC622
•*ISISDIF,* AF59
ISLA, DB293
Islam, M. Aminul. *Bangladesh in maps,* CL351
Islam, BC491, BC498
bibliographies, BC496
bibliography, BC492, BC493, BC494, BC495, BC497, BC499, BC500, BC501, BC502, DD73, DE29, DE30, DE32
collections, BC92
dictionaries, BC76
dissertations, DD74, DE42, DE44
encyclopedias, BC503, BC504, BC505, CE43
handbooks, CC346
Islam (by country or region)
Africa, North, BC501, DD73
Islam (by subject)
history, DE63, DE187
   atlases, DE69
sacred books, BC204, BC206
Islam in Africa south of the Sahara, Ofori, Patrick E., BC497
Islam in North America, BC491
Islam in sub-Saharan Africa, Zoghby, Samir M., BC497
Islamic art
bibliography, BF17
Islamic economics, Khan, Muhammad Akram, CH190
Islamic movements in Egypt, Pakistan and Iran, Hussain, Asaf, DE32
Islamic peoples of the Soviet Union, Akiner, Shirin, CC346
Islamic states, DE71
encyclopedias, DD76
   see also **Arab states**
The Islamic world since 1500, DE71
Island bibliographies, Sachet, Marie-Hélène, EG108
Islandica, AA717, BE1284
Isländisches etymologisches Wörterbuch, Jóhannesson, Alexander, AC510
Islandkatalog der Universitäts-bibliothek Kiel und der Universitäts– und Stadtbibliothek Köln, Universität Kiel. Bibliothek, AA719
Islands, CL63, EF10
Islands of the Indian Ocean
bibliography, DD121, DD142, DD175
Islandsk bogfortegnelse, AA605, AA606, AA718
Íslandsk-dansk ordbog, Sigfús Blöndal, AC506
Islas Malvinas, DB374
Íslensk-dönsk orðabók, AC506
Íslensk-ensk orðabók, Sverrir Hólmarsson, AC508
Íslenzk bókaskrá, AA720
Íslenzk-ensk orðabók, Arngrímur Sigurðsson, AC502
Íslenzk orðabók, handa skólum og almenningi, AC505
Íslenzkar æviskrár frá landnámstímum til ársloka 1940, Ólason, Páll Eggert, AH254
Íslenzkar æviskrár frá lannámstímum til ársloka 1965, Guðnason, Jón, AH254
—— Ólafur Þ. Kristjánsson, AH254
ISO catalogue, International Organization for Standardization, EA273
Iso tietosanakirja, AB39
Isotopes, ED42, ED46
Israel, Fred L. *Justices of the United States Supreme Court, 1789–1969,* CK189
Israël, Guy. *The Cambridge atlas of astronomy,* EC65
Israel
atlases, CL357, CL358, DE74
bibliography, AA909, DE191, DE244
   current, AA910, AA911, AA912
biography, AH356
encyclopedias, BC548, DE192
government publications, AF250
newspapers, AE92
periodicals, AD200
   indexes, AD340
statistics, CG398, CG400

   statistics, vital, CG399
Israel (by subject)
history
   encyclopedias, DE192
law
   bibliography, CK231
music, BJ65
politics and government, CJ436, CJ437, CJ438, CJ439
population forecasting, CG399
   see also **Arab-Israeli conflict; Palestine; Zionism**
Israel. Agaf ha-medidot. *Atlas of Israel,* CL357
Israel. Central Bureau of Statistics. *Statistical abstract of Israel,* CG398
Israel. Ganzakh ha medina yeha-sifriyah. *Israel government publications,* AF250
Israel. ha-Lishkah ha-Merkazit li-Statistiskah. *Statistical abstract of Israel,* CG398
Israel. Lishkat ha-'itonut ha-memshaltit. *Newspapers and periodicals appearing in Israel,* AE92
Israel. Mahleket ha-Medidot. *Atlas of Israel,* CL358
Israel book news, AA910
Israel book world, AA910
Israel-Diaspora relations, Fine, Morris, DA7
Israel government publications, AF250
Israel government year-book, CJ437
Israel legal bibliography in European languages, Livneh, Ernest, CK231
Israeli books in print, AA911
Israeli general encyclopedia, AB56
Israeli periodicals & serials in English & other European languages, Tronik, Ruth, AD200
ISS directory of overseas schools, CB91
ISSN, publicações periódicas brasileiras, AD72
Issues in the sociology of religion, Blasi, Anthony J., BC7
—— Cuneo, Michael W., BC7
İstanbul kütüphaneleri Arap harfli süreli yayımlar toplu kataloğu, 1828–1928, Duman, Hasan, AE78
Istavn, Csahók. *Time series of historical statistics 1867–1992,* CG248
Istituto centrale di statistica (Italy). *Sommario di statistiche storiche, 1926–1985,* CG256
Istituto centrale per il catalogo unico delle biblioteche italiane e per le informazioni bibliografiche. *Bibliografia nazionale italiana. Pubblicazione mensile,* AA726
—— *Le edizioni italiane del XVI secolo,* AA731
—— *Periodici italiani, 1886–1957,* AD128
Istituto di studi rinascimentali (Ferrara, Italy). *Renaissance linguistics archive, 1350–1700,* BD67
Istituto Giangiacomo Feltrinelli (Milan). *Bibliografia della stampa periodica operaia e socialista italiana, 1860–1926,* CH657
Istituto Nazionale per la Storia del Movimento di Liberazione in Italia. *Catalogo della stampa periodica della Biblioteche dell' Istituto Nazionale per la Storia del Movimento di Liberazione in Italia e degli Istituti associati, 1900/1975,* DC426
Istituto nazionale per le relazioni culturali con l'estero. *La bibliografia italiana,* AA52
—— *Bibliografie del ventennio,* AA53
Istituto patristico Augustinianum. *Encyclopedia of the early church,* BC275
Istochniki slovaria russkikh pisatelei, Vengerov, Semen Afanas'evich, BE1424
Istoria literaturii române dela origini până în prezent, Călinescu, George, BE1379
Istoria literaturii romîne, BE1381
Istoriia dorevoliutsionnoĭ Rossii v dnevnikakh i vospominaniiakh, DC579
Istoriia istoricheskoĭ nauki v SSSR, Gosudarstvennaia publichnaia istoricheskaia biblioteka RSFSR, DC570
Istoriia latyshskoi literatury, BE1319
Istoriia russkoĭ bibliografii nachala XX veka, Zdobnov, Nikolai Vasilevich, AA66
Istoriia russkoĭ literatury, Akademiia Nauk SSSR. Institut Russkoĭ Literatury, BE1417
Istoriia russkoĭ literatury kontsa XIX nachala XX veka : bibliograficheskiĭ ukazatel, BE1388

Istoriia russkoĭ literatury XIX veka, Akademiia Nauk SSSR. Institut Russkoĭ Literatury, BE1388
Istoriia russkoĭ literatury XVIII veka, Stennik, ĬU. V., BE1386
—— Stepanov, V. P., BE1386, BE1387
Istoriia russkoĭ sovetskoĭ literatury, 1917–1965, Dement'ev, A. G., BE1417
Istoriia srednikh vekov, DA133
Istoriia SSSR, Fundamental'naia biblioteka obshchestvennykh nauk. (Akademiia nauk SSSR), DC548
—— Glavatskikh, G. A., DC549
Istoriia ukraïns'koï literatury, BE1493
Istoriia ukraïns'koï literatury vid pochatkiv do doby realizmu, Tschiżewskij, Dmitrij, BE1493
Istoriiata na Bŭlgariia v memoarnata literatura, Petrova, Ivanka Apostolova, DC115
Istoriki-slavisty SSSR, DC54
•*ISTP search,* EA210
ISTP&B search, EA70
ITA, Leistner, Otto, AD22, BE1019
Italian American experience, Cordasco, Francesco, CC317
Italian American material culture, Hobbie, Margaret, CC351
Italian Americans, CC351
Italian Americans, Cordasco, Francesco, CC317
Italian biographical archive II, AH258
Italian biographical index, AH258
Italian books and periodicals, AA334, AA738
Italian books in print, AA737
Italian dictionary, AC533
—— Hoare, Alfred, AC534
Italian drama
  bibliography, BE1314, BE1315
  library catalogs, BE1314
The Italian emigration to the United States, 1880–1930, Cordasco, Francesco, CC318
Italian folklore, Falassi, Alessandro, CF82
Italian foreign policy, 1918–1945, Cassels, Alan, DC419
Italian history and literature, Harvard University. Library, BE1294
Italian language
  bibliography, BD161
  dictionaries, AC523, AC524, AC525, AC526, AC527
    bilingual, AC528
      English-Italian, AC530, AC533
      Italian-English, AC529, AC531, AC532, AC534, AC535
    etymology, AC536
      dictionaries, AC537, AC538, AC539
    festschriften, BD160, BE1293
    idioms and usage, AC544
    synonyms and antonyms, AC540, AC541, AC542, AC543
Italian literature
  bibliography, BD160, BE1292, BE1293, BE1295, BE1296, BE1299, BE1305, BE1442
  biobibliography, BE1300, BE1301, BE1302, BE1309, BE1310, BE1311
  biography, BE1309, BE1311
    indexes, BE1312
  encyclopedias, BE1298, BE1299, BE1300
  festschriften, BD160, BE1293
  guides, BE1288, BE1289, BE1290
  library catalogs, BE1294
  translations, BE1297
  women authors
    biobibliography, BE1313
Italian literature (by subject)
  futurism
    bibliography, BE1291
  history, BE1303, BE1304, BE1305, BE1306, BE1307, BE1308
Italian music incunabula, Duggan, Mary Kay Conyers, BJ32
Italian plays (1500–1700) in the Folger Library, Clubb, Louise George, BE1314
Italian plays, 1500–1700 in the University of Illinois library, Herrick, Marvin Theodore, BE1314

Italian poetry
  bibliography, BE1318
  indexes, BE1316
  library catalogs, BE1318
  translations, BE1317
Italian Renaissance poetry, Buja, Maureen E., BE1316
Italian translations in America, Shields, Nancy Catchings, BE1297
Italians (by country or region)
  United States, AJ64
    bibliography, CC317, CC318
    guides, CC317
Italians in the United States, Cordasco, Francesco, CC317
Italians to America, AJ64
Italy
  bibliography, AA124, AA725, AA727, AA728, AA729, AA730, AA732, AA733, AA734, AA735, DC425
    current, AA334, AA726, AA736, AA737, AA738
  bibliography (by period)
    16th century, AA731
  bibliography of bibliography, AA50, AA51, AA52, AA53, AA54
  biography, AH258, AH259, AH260, AH261, AH262, AH263, AH264
    bibliography, AH266
    contemporary, AH265
  encyclopedias, DC430
  gazetteers, CL144, CL145
  library resources, AK151
  newspapers, AD125, AE64
  periodicals, AD125, AD126, AD127, AD128, AD129
    current, AD130
    indexes, AD318, AD319
  statistics, CG255, CG256, CG257, CG258
Italy (by subject)
  archaeology and ancient history, BF14, DC423
  architecture, BF52
  art, BF13, BF14, BF52
  economic conditions, DC421
  emigration
    bibliography, CC318
  Fascism, DC433
  folklore and popular culture, CF82
  foreign relations
    bibliography, DC419
  history, DC430, DC431, DC432
    bibliography, DC417, DC419, DC420, DC427
    library catalogs, BE1294
    manuscripts and archives, AK150, DC427, DC429
  law
    guides, CK222
  military history, DC418
  overseas territories
    government publications, AF237
  politics and government, CJ381, CJ382, DC422, DC433
    library resources, DC426
    registers, CJ380
  social conditions, DC421
  trade unions, DC428
  travelers' accounts, DC424
Italy. Istituto Centrale di Statistica. *Annuario statistico italiano,* CG255
Italy. Parlamento. Camera dei Deputati. Biblioteca. *Catalogo metodico degli scritti contenuti nelle pubblicazioni periodiche italiane e straniere,* AD318
Italy. Provveditorato Generale dello Stato. *Pubblicazioni edite dallo stato o col suo concorso,* AD319
Iter Italicum, Kristeller, Paul Oskar, AA206
•*ITERATE 2,* CJ553
•*ITERATE 3,* CJ552
Iterson, P. D. J. van. *De Rijksarchieven in Nederland,* DC458
Itineraria Norvegica, DC468
Itineraria svecana, Bring, Samuel Ebbe, DC519

Ito, Jujiro. *Japanese-English dictionary of legal terms, with supplement,* CK51
Itō, Kiyosi. *Encyclopedic dictionary of mathematics,* EB35
Iturralde, Mario P. *Dictionary and handbook of nuclear medicine and clinical imaging,* EH188
'Ityôpyā, òāmatoawi yastātistiks maṣḥét, CG330
The IUCN amphibia-reptilia red data book, EG250
The IUCN invertebrate red data book, EG234
The IUCN mammal red data book, EG296
The IUCN plant red data book, EG149
IUPI, BE1316
ĬUzhnoslavianskie iazyki, Mozhaeva, Inessa Evgen'evna, BD191
Ivamy, E. R. Hardy. *Mozley and Whiteley's law dictionary,* CK34
Ivan, Franz. *200 Jahre Tageszeitung in Österreich, 1783–1983,* AE44
Ivanchev, Dimitur P. *Bŭlgarski periodichen pechat 1844–1944,* AD87
Iverson, Cheryl. *American Medical Association manual of style,* EH193
Ivins, William Mills. *How prints look,* BF373
Ivory Coast *see* **Côte d'Ivoire**
Ivory Coast, Mundt, Robert J., DD48
Iwanami Ei-Wa daijiten, Nakajima, Fumio, AC555
Iwanami kogo jiten, AC547
Iwanami sūgaku jiten, EB35
Iwasaki, Ikuo. *Japan and Southeast Asia,* DE97, DE200
Iwaschkin, Roman. *Popular music,* BJ339
IWGIA yearbook, CE63
İz, Fahir. *The concise Oxford Turkish dictionary,* AC790
—— *English-Turkish dictionary,* AC790
—— *The Oxford Turkish dictionary,* AC791
Izady, Mehrdad R. *The Kurds,* DE59
Izard, Françoise. *Bibliographie générale de la Haute-Volta, 1956–1965,* DD133
Izard, Michel. *Dictionnaire de l'ethnologie et de l'anthropologie,* CE38
Izdatel'stvo "Sovetskaia ėntsiklopediia." Nauchno-redaktsionnyĭ sovet. *Demograficheskiĭ ėntsiklopedicheskiĭ slovar',* CG292
Izhevskaia, M. G. *Slovari, izdannye v SSSR,* AC698
Izuchenie kul'tury i iazykov narodov Afriki v Sovetskom Soiuze, Miliavskaia, S. L., DD10
Izvestiia [index], AE68

J. Paul Getty Trust. *Art & architecture thesaurus,* BF94
—— *Répertoire des catalogues de ventes publiques,* BF112
J. R. McKenzie Trust. Board. *A directory of philanthropic trusts in New Zealand,* AL128
J. R. O'Dwyer Company. *O'Dwyer's directory of corporate communications,* CH555
—— *O'Dwyer's directory of public relations firms,* CH567
Jaarcijfers voor Nederlanden, CG266, CG267, CG394
Jabłońska, Barbara. *Catalogue of periodicals in Polish or relating to Poland and other Slavonic countries, published outside Poland since September 1st, 1939,* AD136
Jablonski, David. *The encyclopedia of paleontology,* EF235
Jablonski, Stanley. *Dictionary of medical acronyms and abbreviations,* EH132
—— *Illustrated dictionary of dentistry,* EH258
—— *Illustrated dictionary of eponymic syndromes and diseases and their synonyms,* EH118
—— *Jablonski's dictionary of syndromes and eponymic diseases,* EH118
Jablonski's dictionary of syndromes and eponymic diseases, Jablonski, Stanley, EH118
The Jacaranda dictionary and grammar of Melanesian Pidgin, Mihalic, Francis, AC628
Jaccard, Henri. *Essai de toponymie,* CL213
Jachnow, Helmut. *Handbibliographie zur neueren Linguistik in Osteuropa,* BD5
Jacinto, Yolanda E. *Bibliography of Philippine bibliographies, 1962–1985,* AA82

Jackman, Michael. *The Macmillan book of business and economic quotations*, CH75

Jackson, Albert. *The antiques care & repair handbook*, BG45

Jackson, Benjamin Daydon. *Glossary of botanic terms with their derivation and accent*, EG131
—— *Guide to the literature of botany*, EG96

Jackson, Blyden. *History of Afro-American literature*, BE533, BE540

Jackson, Byron M. *The public policy dictionary*, CJ38

Jackson, Charles. *English goldsmiths and their marks*, BG138

Jackson, Ellen. *Subject guide to major United States publications*, AF63

Jackson, Emily. *A history of hand-made lace*, BG160
—— *Old handmade lace*, BG160

Jackson, George D. *Dictionary of the Russian Revolution*, DC595

Jackson, Guida. *Women who ruled*, CC578

Jackson, Irene V. *Afro-American religious music*, BJ15

Jackson, James Robert de Jager. *Annals of English verse, 1770–1835*, BE707, BE708
—— *Poetry of the Romantic period*, BE718
—— *Romantic poetry by women*, BE708

Jackson, Julia A. *Dictionary of geological terms*, EF72
—— *Glossary of geology*, EF70, EF71, EF72

Jackson, K. David. *Vanguardism in Latin American literature*, BE872, BE936

Jackson, Kenneth George. *Dictionary of electrical engineering*, EK132

Jackson, Kenneth T. *Atlas of American history*, DB70

Jackson, Miles M. *Pacific Island studies*, DF6

Jackson, Paul. *British sources of information*, DC278

Jackson, Philip W. *Handbook of research on curriculum*, CB115

Jackson, R. D. *Textile arts index, 1950–1987*, BG153

Jackson, Radway. *Visual index of artists' signatures and monograms*, BF158

Jackson, Richard. *The literature of American music in books and folk music collections*, BJ14

Jackson, Richard L. *Afro-Spanish American author*, BE523, BE1504

Jackson, Samuel Macauley. *New Schaff-Herzog encyclopedia of religious knowledge*, BC67

Jackson, Virginia. *Art museums of the world*, BF115

Jackson, W. T. H. *European writers*, BE201

Jackson, William A. *A short-title catalogue of books printed in England, Scotland, & Ireland and of English books printed abroad, 1475–1640*, AA671

Jackson, William Vernon. *Library guide for Brazilian studies*, DB351
—— *Resources for Brazilian studies at the Bibliothèque nationale*, DB351

Jackson's silver & gold marks of England, Scotland & Ireland, BG138

Jacob, André. *Encyclopédie philosophique universelle*, BB35

Jacob, Herbert. *Allgemeine Bücherkunde zur neueren deutschen Literaturgeschichte*, BE1214

Jacob, Judith M. *Bibliographies of Mon-Khmer and Tai linguistics*, BD230
—— *A concise Cambodian-English dictionary*, AC564

Jacob, Kathryn Allamong. *Biographical directory of the United States Congress, 1774–1989*, CJ232
—— *Guide to research collections of former United States senators, 1789–1982*, CJ202

Jacob, Udo. *The completely illustrated atlas of reptiles and amphibians for the terrarium*, EG252

The Jacobean and Caroline stage, Bentley, Gerald Eades, BE663

Jacobs, Donald M. *Antebellum black newspapers*, AE105

Jacobs, Francis. *Western European political parties*, CJ323

Jacobs, Joseph. *Bibliotheca anglo-judaica*, BC517

Jacobs, Morris B. *Dictionary of microbiology*, EG39

Jacobs, Phyllis M. *History theses, 1901–70*, DA17, DC284

Jacobsen, A. *Painting and bronze price guide*, BF111

Jacobsen, Angeline. *Contemporary Native American literature*, BE551

Jacobsen, Henrik Galberg. *Dansk sprogrøgtslitteratur 1900–1955*, BD131

Jacobsen, Julia M. *From idea to funded project*, AL92

Jacobsen, Lis. *Kulturhistorisk Leksikon for nordisk Middelalder fra Vikingetid til Reformationstid*, DC75, DC76
—— *Nudansk ordbog*, AC286

Jacobsen, Lotte. *Dansk juridisk bibliografi*, CK207

Jacobsen, Niels Kingo. *Atlas over Danmark*, CL324

Jacobsen's painting and bronze price guide, BF111

Jacobstein, Bennett. *American suburbs rating guide and fact book*, CL77

Jacobstein, J. Myron. *Fundamentals of legal research*, CK118, CK122
—— *Index to periodical articles related to law*, CK27
—— *Legal research illustrated*, CK118

Jacobus, Donald Lines. *Index to genealogical periodicals*, AJ42

Jacobus, John M. *Modern art*, BF131

Jacolev, Leon. *German-English science dictionary*, EA111

Jacquemet, G. *Dictionnaire de sociologie*, CA32

Jaderstrom, Susan. *Professional Secretaries International complete office handbook*, CH87

Jadhav, Chandrakant Ganpatrao. *Bibliography of census publications in India*, CG391

Jaeger, Edmund Carroll. *The biologist's handbook of pronunciations*, EG40
—— *A source-book of biological names and terms*, EG41

Jaffa, Herbert C. *Modern Australian poetry, 1920–1970*, BE846

Jagdish Chandra. *Bibliography of Indian art, history & archaeology*, BF27
—— *Bibliography of Nepalese art*, BF27

Jagger, Janette. *Designers international index*, BG32

Jagodziński, Zdzisław. *Bibliography of books in Polish or relating to Poland published outside Poland since Sept. 1st, 1939*, AA767

Jahmin, J. *Indonesian serials, 1942–1950, in Yogyakarta libraries*, AD195

Jahn, Janheinz. *Bibliography of creative African writing*, BE1505, BE1512, BE1531
—— *Who's who in African literature*, BE1512

Jahnke, Eugen. *Tafeln höherer Funktionen*, EB76

Jahrbuch der Auktionspreise für Bücher und Autographen, AA264

Jahrbuch der Bücherpreise, AA264

Jahrbuch der Deutschen Shakespeare-Gesellschaft, BE779

Jahrbuch der historischen Forschung in der Bundesrepublik Deutschland, DC217

Jahrbuch für Antike und Christentum, BC248

Jahrbuch über die Fortschritte der Mathematik, EB26

Jahresbericht für deutsche Sprache und Literatur, BD118, BD119, BD120, BE1225, BE1226

Jahresbericht über die Erscheinungen auf dem Gebiete der germanischen Philologie, BD118, BD119, BE1226

Jahresbericht über die Fortschritte der klassischen Altertumswissenschaft, BE992
—— Bursian, Conrad, BE1023

Jahresbericht über die wissenschaftlichen Erscheinungen auf dem Gebiete der neueren deutschen Literatur, BD118, BD120, BD121, BE1224, BE1225, BE1226

Jahresberichte der Geschichtswissenschaft, DC218

Jahresberichte für deutsche Geschichte, DC218

Jahresberichte für neuere deutsche Literaturgeschichte, BD121, BE1224

Jahresverzeichnis der deutschen Hochschulschriften 1885–1973, Deutschen Bücherei, BE594

Jahresverzeichnis der deutschen Musikalien und Musikschriften, BJ16, BJ49, BJ80

Jahresverzeichnis der Hochschulschriften der DDR, der BRD, und Westberlins, AG31

Jahresverzeichnis der Musikalien und Musikschriften, BJ16, BJ49

Jahresverzeichnis der schweizerischen Hochschulschriften, AG43

Jahresverzeichnis der Verlagsschriften, AA656

Jahresverzeichnis des deutschen Schrifttums, AA656

Jain, Chhotelal. *Chhotelal Jain's Jaina bibliography*, BC507

Jain, Hem Chandra. *Indian legal materials*, CK229

Jain, M. K. *A bibliography of bibliographies on India*, AA75

Jaina bibliography, BC507

Jainism, BC506, BC507
  collections, BC92

Jakovsky, Anatole. *Peintres naïfs*, BF315

JALA, DD24, DD34

Jamaica
  bibliography, AA568, DB442
  biography, AH156, AH157, AH158
  statistics, CG175, CG176, CG177
Jamaica (by subject)
  history
    bibliography, DB442, DB443
  languages
    English, AC157

Jamaica. Central Planning and Development Division. *Statistical yearbook of Jamaica*, CG177

Jamaica. Department of Statistics. *Statistical abstract*, CG176
—— *Statistical yearbook of Jamaica*, CG177

Jamaica, Ingram, Kenneth E., DB442

The Jamaica directory of personalities, AH157

Jamaican accessions, AA568

Jamaican national bibliography, AA568, DB442

Jamaican national bibliography, 1964–1974, Institute of Jamaica, Kingston, AA568

Jamail, Milton H. *United States-Mexico border*, DB250

James, A. M. *VNR index of chemical and physical data*, ED43

James, C. V. *Information China*, DE145

James, David E. *The encyclopedia of solid earth geophysics*, EF65

James, David R. *The agrochemicals handbook*, EJ46

James, Edward T. *Notable American women*, AH66

James, Glenn. *Mathematics dictionary*, EB41

James, Laylin K. *Nobel laureates in chemistry, 1901–1992*, AL162, EE103

James, Montague Rhodes. *Apocryphal New Testament*, BC94

James, N. D. G. *An historical dictionary of forestry and woodland terms*, EJ179

James, Richard S. *International music journals*, BJ102

James, Robert C. *Mathematics dictionary*, EB41

James, Simon. *A dictionary of business quotations*, CH72
—— *A dictionary of economic quotations*, CH73
—— *Dictionary of legal quotations*, CK57

James, Theodore E. *Aristotle dictionary*, BB51

James, Thurston. *The what, where, when of theater props*, BH92

James Ford Bell Library. *The James Ford Bell Library*, DB4
—— *Jesuit relations and other Americana in the library of James Ford Bell*, DB4

The James Ford Bell Library, James Ford Bell Library, DB4

James Weldon Johnson Memorial Collection of Negro Arts and Letters. *Music, printed and manuscript, in the James Weldon Johnson Memorial Collection of Negro Arts and Letters*, BJ95

Jāmiát al-Kuwayt. Qism al-Tawthīq. *Dalīl al-risālāt al-'Arabiyah*, AG51

Jamieson, John. *Etymological dictionary of the Scottish language*, AC165

Jamieson's dictionary of the Scottish language, Johnstone, J., AC165
—— Longmuir, John, AC165
—— Metcalfe, W. M., AC165

Jamison, A. Leland. *Religion in American life*, BC27

Jamison, Robert. *Rhetorik, Topik, Argumentation*, BE372

JANAF thermochemical tables, EE63, EE93

Jane, Fred T. *Jane's fighting ships*, CJ594

Jänes, Henno. *Geschichte der estnischen Literatur*, BE1125

Jane's aerospace dictionary, EK31

Jane's air-launched weapons, CJ570

Jane's all the world's aircraft, EK37

Jane's armour and artillery, CJ594

Jane's defence glossary, CJ587

Jane's fighting ships, CJ592, CJ594

Jane's military communications, CJ594

Jane's underwater warfare systems, CJ594

Jane's urban transport systems, CH451, EK121

Jane's world railways, CH459

Janhuhn, Herbert. *Reallexikon der germanischen Altertumskundes*, DC230

Janiak, Jane M. *Air transportation*, CH444

Janke, Peter. *Guerrilla and terrorist organisations*, CJ61

Janosik, Robert J. *Encyclopedia of the American judicial system*, CK131

Jansen, Henrik M. *A select bibliography of Danish works on the history of towns published 1960–1976*, DC132

Janson, Anthony F. *History of art*, BF132
——— *History of art for young people*, BF132

Janson, Dora Jane. *Key monuments of the history of art*, BF132

Janson, Horst Woldemar. *19th century sculpture*, BF393
——— *History of art*, BF132
——— *History of art for young people*, BF132
——— *Iconographic index to Stanislas Lami's Dictionnaire des sculpteurs de l'Ecole française au dix-neuvième siècle*, BF395
——— *Key monuments of the history of art*, BF132

Janssen, Jozef M. A. *Annual Egyptological bibliography*, DA121

Jantz, Harold Stein. *The first century of New England verse*, BE492
——— *German Baroque literature*, BE1234

Janvier, Geneviève. *Bibliographie de la Côte d'Ivoire*, DD146

Janzing, Grażyna. *Library, documentation, and archives serials*, AK21

Jao, Y. C. *Research material for Hong Kong studies*, DE150

Japan
associations
directories, AL43, DE210
bibliography, AA913, AA914, AA915, DE195, DE198, DE204
current, AA916, AA917, AA918
bibliography of bibliography, AA81
biography, AH357, AH358, AH359, CJ440
dissertations, AG54
encyclopedias, AB71, DE207, DE209
gazetteers, CL166, CL167
government publications, AF251
bibliography, AF252
union lists, AF252
indexes, AD341
library resources, DE199
library resources (by country or region)
United States, DE206
newspapers, AD202
bibliography, AE94
catalogs, AE94
directories, AE93, AE95
union lists, AE96
periodicals, AD201, AD202
indexes, AD342
statistics, CG23, CG401, CG402, CG403
Japan (by subject)
art, BF161, BF358
biography, BF144
corporations
directories, CH361
economic conditions
bibliography, CH204
folklore and popular culture, CF93, CF98

foreign relations
bibliography, DE201
history, DE194, DE199
bibliography, DE97, DE196, DE197, DE200, DE202, DE205
encyclopedias, DE208
handbooks, DE211
translations into English, DE197
investment, CH353
law, CK232
music, BJ44, BJ74
place-names, CL166, CL167
politics and government, CJ440, CJ512
population, CG404
religion, BC36, BC307, BC569

Japan. Kōseishō. Tōkei Jōhōbu. *Jinkō dōtai tōkei*, CG401

Japan, Shulman, Frank Joseph, DE205

Japan : an illustrated encyclopedia, Kōdansha, AB71, DE209

Japan and Southeast Asia, Iwasaki, Ikuo, DE97, DE200

Japan and the world, 1853–1952, DE201

A Japan bibliography of bibliographies, AA81

The Japan biographical encyclopedia and who's who, AH358

Japan company directory, CH361

Japan company handbook, CH361

Japan Foundation. *Catalogue of books in English on Japan, 1945–1981*, DE196
——— *Catalogue of books on Japan translated from the Japanese into English, 1945–1981*, DE197

Japan Library Association. *Librarianship in Japan*, AK160

Japan/MARC shomei choshamei sakuin, AA916

Japan P.E.N. Club. *Japanese literature in European languages*, BE1584

Japan P.E.N Club. *Japanese literature in foreign languages, 1945–1990*, BE1584

Japan reading guide, DE196

Japan, sources of economic and business information, Ruokonen, Kyllikki, CH204

Japan statistical yearbook, CG402

Japan trade directory, CH408

Japanese-affiliated companies in the USA & Canada, CH353

Japanese-African relations, Batiste, Angel, DD3
——— Gray, Beverly Ann, DD3

Japanese American Research Center (JARC). *The Japanese in Hawaii*, CC408

Japanese Americans, CC408

Japanese art signatures, Self, James, BF144, BF161

Japanese character dictionary with compound lookup, AC558

Japanese drama, BE1592

Japanese-English dictionary of legal terms, with supplement, Ito, Jujiro, CK51

Japanese/English English/Japanese glossary of scientific and technical terms, Tung, Louise Watanabe, EA120

Japanese folk literature, Algarin, Joanne P., CF93

The Japanese in Hawaii, Matsuda, Mitsugu, CC408

Japanese journals in English, Science Reference Library (British Library), EA50

Japanese language
abbreviations, AC548
bibliography, BD222, BE1596
dictionaries, AC545, AC546, AC547, AC548, AC549, AC550
bilingual, AC557
English-Japanese, AC555
Japanese-English, AC551, AC552, AC553, AC554, AC558

Japanese law in Western languages, Scheer, Matthias K., CK232

Japanese literature, BE1594
bibliography, BD222, BE1580, BE1583, BE1587, BE1590, BE1592, BE1593, BE1596
biobibliography, BE1581, BE1585
biography, BE1579
encyclopedias, BE1589, BE1591
handbooks, BE1588
translations, BE1584

women authors
biobibliography, BE1595
translations, BE1586
Japanese literature (by subject)
history, BE1582

Japanese literature in European languages, Japan P.E.N. Club, BE1584

Japanese literature in foreign languages, 1945–1990, Japan P.E.N Club, BE1584

Japanese museums, Roberts, Laurance P., BF144

Japanese music, Tsuge, Gen'ichi, BJ44

Japanese names, O'Neill, Patrick Geoffrey, AC556

Japanese national bibliography, AA916

Japanese national government publications in the Library of Congress, Library of Congress, AF252

Japanese newspaper annual, AD202

Japanese periodicals
indexes, AD341

Japanese periodicals and newspapers in Western languages, Nunn, Godfrey Raymond, AD217

Japanese poetry
translations, BE1593

Japanese press, AE93

Japanese proverbs and sayings, Buchanan, Daniel Crump, BE152

Japanese scientific and technical literature, Gibson, Robert W., EA49

Japanese studies from pre-history to 1990, DE202

Japanese women writers in English translation, Mamola, Claire Zebroski, BE1586

Japanisches Recht in westlichen Sprachen, Scheer, Matthias K., CK232

Japan's high technology, Talbot, Dawn E., EA9

Japonica, AB69

Jaques, Harry Edwin. *Pictured-key nature series*, EG83

Jaques Cattell Press. *ASCAP biographical dictionary*, BJ201
——— *The big book of halls of fame in the United States and Canada*, BK32

Jarā'id wa-al-majallāt al.'Irāqīyah, 1869–1978, AE91

Jarboe, Betty. *Obituaries*, AH5

Jardel, Jean Pierre. *Bibliographie de la Martinique*, DB445

Jarrard, Mary E. W. *Women speaking*, BD84, CC495

Jarrell, Howard R. *Common stock newspaper abbreviations and trading symbols*, CH210

Jarrick, Inez. *Southern African history before 1900*, DD120, DD223

Jarvis, Peter. *An international dictionary of adult and continuing education*, CB356

Jary, David. *HarperCollins dictionary of sociology*, CC19

Jary, Julia. *HarperCollins dictionary of sociology*, CC19

Jaryc, Marc. *Répertoire des périodiques de langue française, philosophiques, historiques, philologiques et juridiques*, AD94
——— *Répertoire des sociétés françaises de sciences philosophiques, historiques, philologiques et juridiques*, AL61

Jarzyńska, Joanna. *Polskie wydawnictwa informacyjne, 1945–1981*, AA347

Jäschke, Heinrich August. *Tibetan-English dictionary*, AC786

Jáslan, Janina. *Wiedza Powszechna compact Polish and English dictionary*, AC633

Jason, Philip K. *Nineteenth century American poetry*, BE493
——— *Vietnam War in literature*, BE417, DE278

Jasper, Tony. *The international encyclopedia of hard rock & heavy metal*, BJ355

Jassem, Wiktor. *Wielki słownik angielsko-polski*, AC635
——— *Wielki słownik polsko-angielski*, AC635

Jastrow, Marcus. *Dictionary of the Targumim, the Talmud Babli and Yerushalmi, and the Midrashic literature*, AC479

Jaszczun, Wasyl. *A dictionary of Russian idioms and colloquialisms*, AC694

Jásznigi, Alexander. *Das geistige Ungarn*, AH248

Jauralde Pou, Pablo. *Manual de investigación literaria*, BE1428
Javanese-English dictionary, Horne, Elinor McCullough Clark, AC559
Javanese language, AC559
  see also **Kawi language**
Javelin Associates. *Federally sponsored training materials*, CB351
Jayawardene, S. A. *Reference books for the historian of science*, EA234
Jazz, BJ304, BJ306, BJ362
  bibliography, BJ297, BJ301, BJ302, BJ305
  biography, BJ299
    bibliography, BJ298
  discography, BJ307, BJ308, BJ309
    bibliography, BJ384
  encyclopedias, BJ300, BJ349
  handbooks, BJ299
  indexes, BJ303
Jazz, BJ344
——— Allen, Daniel, BJ383
——— Bruyninckx, Walter, BJ307
——— Carr, Ian, BJ299
Jazz-bibliography, Hefele, Bernhard, BJ302
Jazz in the movies, Meeker, David, BJ362
Jazz index, BJ303
Jazz performers, Carner, Gary, BJ298
Jazz records, 1897–1942, Rust, Brian A. L., BJ309
Jean, Georges. *Dictionnaire des poètes et de la poésie*, BE1197
Jean Sauvaget's introduction to the history of the Muslim East, BC500
Jeanroy, Alfred. *Bibliographie sommaire des chansonniers provençaux (manuscrits et éditions) …*, BE1371
——— *La poésie lyrique des troubadours*, BE1372
Jedin, Hubert. *Atlas zur Kirchengeschichte*, BC288
——— *Handbook of church history*, BC277
——— *History of the church*, BC277
Jefcoate, Graham. *A catalogue of English books printed before 1801 held by the University Library at Göttingen*, AA682
Jeffares, Norman. *St. Martin's anthologies of English literature*, BE618
Jefferson's manual, CJ226
Jeffery, Larry S. *Weeds of the United States and their control*, EJ55
Jeffrey, Alan. *Table of integrals, series, and products*, EB85
Jeffrey, Charles. *Biological nomenclature*, EG42
Jeffrey, David L. *A dictionary of biblical tradition in English literature*, BE609
Jeffries, Stephen. *Image of a continent*, DF25
Jefkins, Frank William. *Dictionary of advertising*, CH551
Jegede, Oluremi. *Nigerian legal bibliography*, CK226
Jēgers, Benjamins. *Latviešu trimdas izdevumu bibliografija, 1940–1960*, AA739
Jelaludin Ahmed. *Annotated bibliography on the population of Ethiopia*, CG329
Jelavich, Charles. *Opis na starite pechatani bulgarski knigi, 1802–1877 g*, AA587
Jelinek, Hanus. *Histoire de la littérature tchèque*, BE1107
Jelks, Edward B. *Historical dictionary of North American archaeology*, DB49
Jelks, Juliet C. *Historical dictionary of North American archaeology*, DB49
Jellicoe, Geoffrey. *The Oxford companion to gardens*, BF290
Jellicoe, Susan. *The Oxford companion to gardens*, BF290
Jember, Gregory K. *English-Old English, Old English-English dictionary*, AC174
Jen, Hseo-chin. *Chinese newspapers in the Library of Congress*, AE87
Jen k'ou hsüeh Ying Han Han Ying fen lei tz'u hui, Yeh, Hsiu-shu, CG34
Jenkins, David Lloyd. *Union list of theses of the University of New Zealand, 1910–1954*, AG60
Jenkins, Jean L. *International directory of musical instrument collections*, BJ368

Jenkins, Martin. *The IUCN mammal red data book*, EG296
Jenkins, Richard J. *Historical sources in Costa Rica*, DB305
Jenkins, Robert Thomas. *Y Bywgraffiadur Cymreig hyd 1940*, AH245
Jenkins, William Sumner. *A guide to the microfilm collection of early state records*, DB141
Jenner, Philip N. *Southeast Asian literatures in translation*, BE1542
Jens, Walter. *Kindlers neues Literatur Lexikon*, BE69
Jensen, Larry O. *Genealogical handbook of German research*, AJ90, AJ92
Jerabek, Esther. *Czechs and Slovaks in North America*, CC323
Jerath, Bal K. *Homicide*, CK246
Jerath, Rajinder. *Homicide*, CK246
Jerde, Judith. *Encyclopedia of textiles*, BG155
Jeremy, David J. *Dictionary of business biography*, CH96
The Jerome biblical commentary, BC178
Jerrard, Harold George. *A dictionary of scientific units*, ED19
Jerusalem Bible, BC94, BC149
Jerusalem Center for Public Affairs. *Federal systems of the world*, CJ51
Jervis, Simon. *The Facts on File dictionary of design and designers*, BG22
Jesse E. Moorland Collection of Negro Life and History, CC379
Jessen, Jens Christian. *Bibliographie der Autobiographien*, AH214
Jessop, Thomas Edmund. *A bibliography of David Hume and of Scottish philosophy from Francis Hutcheson to Lord Balfour*, BB74
Jessup, John E. *Balkan military history*, DC60
——— *A chronology of conflict and resolution, 1945–1985*, CJ63
Jesuit relations and other Americana in the library of James Ford Bell, James Ford Bell Library, DB4
Jesus Christ
  biography, BC211
  dictionaries, BC128
  indexes, BC122
Jesus Christ in literature, BC211
Jetté, René. *Dictionnaire généalogique des familles du Québec …*, AJ71
Jeudy, Colette. *Les manuscrits classiques latins des bibliothèques publiques de France*, AA211
Jewelry, EF180
  dictionaries, BG82, BG83
    multilingual, BG82
Jewish alcoholism and drug addiction, Berg, Steven L., CC110
Jewish American fiction writers, Cronin, Gloria L., BE564, BE566
Jewish-American history and culture, BC551
Jewish and Hebrew onomastics, Singerman, Robert, AJ201
Jewish art, BF193
  bibliography, BF194
Jewish autobiographies and biographies, Zubatsky, David S., AH39
Jewish-Christian relations, Shermis, Michael, BC17
The Jewish community in America, Brickman, William W., BC522
Jewish culture, DA177
Jewish encyclopedia, Adler, Cyrus, BC546
——— Singer, Isidore, BC546
Jewish film directory, BH225
Jewish folklore, Yassif, Eli, CF84
Jewish genealogy, Zubatsky, David S., AJ146
Jewish heritage in America, Karkhanis, Sharad, BC524
Jewish Historical Society of England. *Magna bibliotheca anglo-judaica*, BC517
Jewish history, DA31
  atlases, DA159, DA190
Jewish history atlas, DA52, DE193
Jewish holocaust, Bloomberg, Marty, DA214
Jewish iconography, Rubens, Alfred, BG113

Jewish immigrants of the Nazi period in the USA, DA218, DB126
Jewish law, BC549, CK239, CK240
  bibliography, CK241
Jewish law, Schonbert, David, CK240
——— Weisbard, Phyllis Holman, CK240
Jewish law annual, CK241
Jewish life in the Middle Ages, Metzger, Mendel, BG113
——— Metzger, Thérèse, BG113
Jewish literature, BE564, BE1578
  guides, BE566
Jewish literature (by country or region)
  United States
    handbooks, BE565
Jewish literature (by subject)
  history, BE1577
Jewish lore and legend, BC555, CF54
Jewish music, BJ37
  bibliography, BJ19
Jewish mysticism, Spector, Sheila, BC520
Jewish newspapers, AE6
  bibliography, AD7, AD11, AD14
Jewish newspapers (by country or region)
  United States, AE17
Jewish newspapers and periodicals on microfilm available at the American Jewish Periodical Center, Hebrew Union College—Jewish Institute of Religion. American Jewish Periodical Center, AD11
Jewish periodicals, AE6
  bibliography, AD7, AD11, AD14, AD16
Jewish periodicals (by country or region)
  United States, AE17
Jewish-Polish coexistence, 1772–1939, Lerski, Jerzy J., DC471
Jewish press and publications, AD7
Jewish press of the world, Fraenkel, Josef, AD7, AE6
The Jewish primer, Himelstein, Shmuel, BC558
Jewish Publication Society of America. *American Jewish year book*, BC563
——— *The Torah*, BC184
Jewish publications in the Soviet Union, 1917–1960, Kohen, Yitshak Yosef, BC535
Jewish research literature, Brisman, Shimeon, BC512
Jewish serials of the world, Singerman, Robert, AD16
Jewish students, CB306
The Jewish student's guide to American colleges, Goldberg, Lee, CB306
Jewish time line encyclopedia, Kantor, Máttis, DA31
The Jewish woman, 1900–1985, Cantor, Aviva, CC597
Jewish writers of North America, Nadel, Ira Bruce, BE566
Jewish year book, BC564
Jews
  biography, AH39, AH52, AH203, AH356, BC553
  encyclopedias, DA177
  genealogy, AJ13, AJ21, AJ143, AJ146
Jews (by country or region)
  Caribbean, BC526
  Europe, CL128
  Europe, Central, BC541
  Europe, Eastern, CL127
  France, BC527, BC533
  Germany, BC532, BC541
  Great Britain, BC517
  Italy, BC530
  Latin America, BC526
  Lithuania, CC355
  Poland, DC34, DC471
  Portugal, BC531
  Russia, DC34
    bibliography, BC535
  Spain, BC531
  Switzerland, DC525
  United States, BC522, BC524, BC525, BC565, DA218, DB126
    bibliography, BC523, CC366
    biography, AH79, AH83

encyclopedias, BC551
handbooks, BC559
indexes, BC543
library resources, BC538
registers, AJ66
yearbooks, BC563
U.S.S.R., BC534, BC536, DC34, DC587
bibliography, BC535
Jews (by occupation or profession)
physicians, EH223
Jews (by subject)
alcoholism and drug abuse, CC110
biography, BC566
costume, BG113
folklore
bibliography, BD134
folklore and popular culture, CF84
history, DA31
atlases, DA52, DE193
languages
bibliography, BD154
see also Holocaust
Jews in film, BH225
The Jews in Poland and Russia, Hundert, Gershon David, DC34
Jews in Romania, DC493
Jews in Spain and Portugal, Singerman, Robert, BC531
Jews in the Soviet Union, Fluk, Louise R., BC534
Języki bałtyckie, Kubicka, Weronika, BD194
Językoznawstwo polonistyczne, Paryl, Władysław, BD193
Jien, AC550
Jilek, Heinrich. Bibliographie zur Geschichte und Landeskunde der Böhmischen Länder von den Anfängen bis 1948, DC125
Jimbun shakai hen, AD342
Jiménez Moreno, Wigberto. Bibliografía indigenista de México y Centroamerica (1850–1950), CE82
Jinkō dōtai tōkei, Japan. Kōseishō. Tōkei Jōhōbu, CG401
Jinkō jiten, CG23
Jinrong, Wu. The pinyin Chinese-English dictionary, AC267
Jirin, Shōzaburo, Kanazawa, AC548
Jisho kaidai jiten, Sogō, Masaki, AB72
Jiten jiten sōgo mokuroku, AB72
JNRC, AA922
Joan of Arc in history, literature, and film, Margolis, Nadia, DC170
Joanne, Paul Bénigne. Dictionnaire géographique et administratif de la France, CL133
Joannidès, A. Comédie-Française, 1680 à 1920, BE1179
—— La Comédie-Française de 1680 à 1900, BE1179
Job hunter's sourcebook, CH702
Job satisfaction and motivation, Walsh, Ruth M., CD125
Job seeker's guide to private and public companies, CH698
Jobling, James A. A dictionary of scientific bird names, EG265
Jobs '93, Petras, Kathryn, CH705
Jobs rated almanac, Krantz, Les, CH703
Jocelyn, Arthur. Awards of honour, AL182
Jöcher, Christian Gottlieb. Allgemeines Gelehrten-Lexikon, AH28
Jochums, Gabriele. Bibliographie zur Heraldik, AJ156
Jockin-La Bastide, J. A. Cassell's English-Dutch, Dutch-English dictionary, AC297
—— Kramers' Engels woordenboek, AC298
Jodice, David A. Political risk assessment, CJ11
Joekes, Rosemary. The National Trust guide, BF249
Joel, Susan. Women factory workers in less developed countries, CC605
Joffe, Judah Achilles. Groyser verterbukh fun der Yidisher shprakh, AC812
Joginder Singh. Indian library directory, AK158
Johan, Zdenek. Atlas of ore minerals, EF203
Johann, Sara Lee. Sourcebook on pornography, CC290

Johann Gottfried Herder-Institut, Marburg. Bibliothek. Bibliothek des Johann Gottfried Herder-Instituts, Marburg/Lahn, Germany, DC44
Jóhann S. Hannesson. Ensk-Íslensk orðabók, AC507
Johannesburg (South Africa). Public Library. Southern African material in anthologies of English literature in the Strange Library of Africana, BE1537
Jóhannesson, Alexander. Isländisches etymologisches Wörterbuch, AC510
Johannine bibliography 1966–1985, Belle, Gilbert van, BC105
Johannsen, Albert. A descriptive petrography of the igneous rocks, EF256
Johannsen, Hano. International dictionary of management, CH614
Johansen, Elaine. Political corruption, CJ102
Johanson, Cynthia J. 20th century American folk, self-taught, and outsider art, BG27
Johansson, Eve. Official publications of Western Europe, AF164
Johansson, Warren. Encyclopedia of homosexuality, CC277
John Bartholomew and Son, Ltd. Bartholomew gazetteer of places in Britain, CL135
—— Chambers world gazetteer, CL84
—— The New York times atlas of the world, CL285
—— The Times atlas of China, CL354
John Carter Brown Library. Bibliotheca americana, DB1
—— Dictionary catalog of the Harris collection of American poetry and plays, Brown University Library, Providence, Rhode Island, BE494
—— European Americana, AA404
John Crerar Library. Author-title catalog, EA17
—— A list of books on the history of science, January 1911, EA235
John Gloag's dictionary of furniture, Gloag, John, BG126
John Locke, a reference guide, Yolton, Jean S., BB77
John Willis' screen world, BH268
John Work Garrett Library. The Fowler architectural collection of the Johns Hopkins University, BF229
Johnpoll, Bernard K. Biographical dictionary of the American left, CJ156
The Johns Hopkins guide to literary theory and criticism, BE68
Johns Hopkins University. The Fowler architectural collection of the Johns Hopkins University, BF229
Johns Hopkins University. Population Information Program. POPLINE, CC257, CG17, EH78
Johnsen, Arne Odd. Norsk militarhistorisk bibliografi, DC464
Johnsen, Julia E. Debate index supplement, BE368
Johnsgard, Paul A. Hawks, eagles & falcons of North America, EG266
Johnson, A. F. Dictionary of anonymous and pseudonymous English literature, AA150
—— Short-title catalogue of books printed in the Netherlands and Belgium and of Dutch and Flemish books printed in other countries from 1470 to 1600, now in the British Museum, AA745
Johnson, Albert Frederick. Bibliography of Ghana, 1930–1961, AA859, DD162
Johnson, Alexandra F. Records of early English drama, BE662
Johnson, Alvin Saunders. Encyclopaedia of the social sciences, CA33
Johnson, Arnold H. Encyclopedia of food science, EJ152
—— Encyclopedia of food technology, EJ155
Johnson, Barnabas D. Almanac of the federal judiciary, CK139
Johnson, Burges. New rhyming dictionary and poets' handbook, AC114
Johnson, Charles. Medieval Latin word-list from British and Irish sources, AC589
Johnson, Chas Floyd. Black women in television, BH294
Johnson, Claudia D. Nineteenth-century theatrical memoirs, BH125

Johnson, Curt. Dictionary of military terms, CJ585
—— The Harper encyclopedia of military biography, AH26
Johnson, David E. From day to day, DA34
Johnson, Donald Bruce. National party platforms, CJ257
Johnson, Donald Clay. A guide to reference materials on Southeast Asia, DE93
—— Index to Southeast Asian journals, 1960–1974, DE102
Johnson, Dora E. Provisional survey of materials for the study of neglected languages, BD71
—— A survey of materials for the study of the uncommonly taught languages, BD71
Johnson, Douglas W. Churches & church membership in the United States, BC85, BC87
Johnson, Douglas W. J. Biographical dictionary of French political leaders since 1870, CJ328
Johnson, Elden. Atlas for anthropology, CE73
Johnson, Francis S. Satellite environment handbook, EK33
Johnson, Frederick. A standard English-Swahili dictionary, AC756
Johnson, Gordon. The new Cambridge history of India, DE169
Johnson, H. Thayne. Electronic properties of materials, EK125
Johnson, Harmer. Guide to the arts of the Americas, BF70
Johnson, Harold Earle. First performances in America to 1900, BJ175
Johnson, Hugh. The world atlas of wine, EJ226
Johnson, Jackie. Library resources in Britain for the study of Eastern Europe and the former U.S.S.R, DC51
Johnson, James P. Black English, BD103
Johnson, Jane. The dictionary of British artists, 1880–1940, BF316
Johnson, Janet Buttolph. Political science research methods, CJ56
Johnson, John W. Historic U.S. court cases, 1690–1990, CK133
Johnson, Jonathan K. The relations of literature and science, BE30
Johnson, Julia. Crime fiction criticism, BE265
Johnson, M. L. The Penguin dictionary of biology, EG29
Johnson, Mallveen Roy. Who's who in Sierra Leone, AH324
Johnson, Mark H. Current legal forms, with tax analysis, CK164
Johnson, Matthew. Bibliographia liturgica, BC267
Johnson, Merle DeVore. Merle Johnson's American first editions, AA242, BE405
Johnson, Norman Lloyd. Encyclopedia of statistical sciences, EB34
Johnson, Peggy. Guide to technical services resources, AK228
Johnson, Peter D. Detailed statistics on the population of South Africa by race and urban/rural residence, 1950 to 2010, CG356
Johnson, R. Benjamin. The black resource guide, CC389
Johnson, Richard S. How to locate anyone who is or has been in the military, CJ625
Johnson, Steven L. Guide to American Indian documents in the Congressional serial set, 1817–1899, CC417
Johnson, Tanya F. Elder neglect and abuse, CC71
Johnson, Timothy W. Crime fiction criticism, BE265
Johnson, Vernon E. Nineteenth-century theatrical memoirs, BH125
Johnson, Warren T. Diseases of trees and shrubs, EG203
—— Insects that feed on trees and shrubs, EG333
Johnson, William A. Thesaurus Linguae Graecae canon of Greek authors and works, AC443, BE1036
Johnson, William S. International photography index, BF330
—— Nineteenth-century photography, BF331
Johnson, Willis L. Directory of special programs for minority group members, CC343

Johnston, A. G. *Index of publications of the Geological Survey of Canada, 1845–1958,* EF29

Johnston, Donald F. *Copyright handbook,* AA315

Johnston, Grahame. *Annals of Australian literature,* BE851

Johnston, James B. *The place-names of Scotland,* CL203

Johnston, Marjorie. *Bibliography of the registers (printed) of the universities, inns of court, colleges and schools of Great Britain and Ireland,* AH234

Johnston, Marliss. *A directory of public vocational-technical schools and institutes in the U.S.A,* CB296

Johnston, R. J. *Dictionary of human geography,* CL44

Johnston, Robert H. *Soviet foreign policy, 1918–1945,* DC586

Johnston & Bacon. *Johnston's gazetteer of Scotland,* CL140

Johnstone, I. J. *Zimbabwean political material published in exile, 1959–1980,* DD252

Johnstone, J. *Jamieson's dictionary of the Scottish language,* AC165

Johnston's gazetteer of Scotland, Johnston & Bacon, CL140

Joint acquisitions list of Africana, DD24, DD34

Joint Bank-Fund Library. *IntlEc CD-ROM,* CH119
—— *Women and development,* CC606, CH115

Joint Center for Political Studies. *Black elected officials,* CJ132
—— *The charitable appeals fact book,* AL132

Joint Committee on Centemporary China. *Modern Chinese society,* DE130

Joint Committee on Latin American Studies. *Latin America,* CH180

Joint Committee on the Union List of Serials. *New serial titles,* AD225

Joint documentary projects, Yad Vashem Martyrs' and Heroes Memorial Authority, Jerusalem, DA219

Joint FAO/IUFRO Committee on Forestry Bibliography and Terminology. *Terminology of forest science, technology, practice, and products,* EJ183

Joint Steering Committee for Revision of AACR. *Anglo American cataloguing rules,* AK194

Joksimovic, Milan. *Jugoslovenski savremenici,* AH308

Jolicoeur, T. *Geographical features in Canada named for surveyors,* CL112

Jolly, Claude. *Histoire des bibliothèques françaises,* AK107

Jolly, Jean. *Dictionnaire des parlementaires français,* AH200, CJ329

Jolobe, J. R. R. *A new concise Xhosa-English dictionary,* AC810

The Jonathan David dictionary of first names, Kolatch, Alfred J., AJ172

Jones, Barri. *An atlas of Roman Britain,* DC313

Jones, Brynmor. *A bibliography of Anglo-Welsh literature, 1900–1965,* BE813

Jones, C. Eugene. *A dictionary of botany,* EG134

Jones, C. Lee. *Library, media, and archival preservation glossary,* AK239

Jones, Cecil K. *A bibliography of Latin American bibliographies,* AA24

Jones, Charles Edwin. *Black holiness,* BC374
—— *A guide to the study of the Pentecostal movement,* BC375

Jones, Cheslyn. *The study of liturgy,* BC269

Jones, Colin. *Cultural atlas of France,* DC164
—— *The French Revolution,* DC187

Jones, Daniel. *Everyman's English pronouncing dictionary,* AC105

Jones, David Lewis. *British and Irish biographies, 1840–1940,* AH223
—— *Debates and proceedings of the British parliaments,* AF209
—— *Paraguay,* DB379

Jones, David R. *Military-naval encyclopedia of religions in Russia and the Soviet Union,* DC566
—— *The military-naval encyclopedia of Russia and the Soviet Union,* CJ657

Jones, Donald G. *Sports ethics in America,* BK4

Jones, Dorothy Miriam. *Aleut bibliography,* CC414, CC418

Jones, Douglas E. *Research guide to the arid lands of the world,* EF1

Jones, E. Gwynne. *A bibliography of the dog,* EJ144

Jones, Errol D. *Latin American military history,* DB258

Jones, Garth N. *A comprehensive bibliography,* CJ443, DE241

Jones, George Fenwick. *German-American names,* AJ196

Jones, H. G. *Second abstract of British historical statistics,* CG234, CG235

Jones, Helen Gertrude (Dudenbostel). *United States of America national bibliographical services and related activities in 1965–1967,* AA21

Jones, Henry Stuart. *A Greek-English lexicon,* AC444

Jones, Holway R. *City planning bibliography,* BF270

Jones, Houston Gwynne. *Local government records,* DB140

Jones, Howard Mumford. *Guide to American literature and its backgrounds since 1890,* BE395

Jones, J. Knox. *Orders and families of recent mammals of the world,* EG304

Jones, Jeffery A. *Sports and recreation for the disabled,* BK40

Jones, Johanna. *New Zealand fiction,* BE861

Jones, Joseph. *New Zealand fiction,* BE861

Jones, Leon. *From Brown to Boston,* CB32

Jones, Linda M. *Canadian studies,* DB184

Jones, Lois Swan. *Art information,* BF4
—— *Art research methods and resources,* BF4

Jones, Michael Owen. *Guide to the gods,* BC62

Jones, Peter d'A. *Biographical dictionary of American mayors, 1820–1980,* CJ285

Jones, Philip. *Britain and Palestine, 1914–1948,* DE243

Jones, Philip Henry. *A bibliography of the history of Wales,* DC370

Jones, Richard. *Atlas of world population history,* CG44

Jones, Schuyler. *Afghanistan,* DE111

Jones, Silas Paul. *A list of French prose fiction from 1700 to 1750,* BE1189, BE1191

Jones, Tom Bard. *A bibliography on South American economic affairs,* CH179

Jones, Trevor. *Harrap's standard German and English dictionary,* AC421
—— *The Oxford-Harrap standard German-English dictionary,* AC421

Jones, William McKendrey. *The present state of scholarship in sixteenth-century literature,* BE987

Jones, Willis Knapp. *Latin American writers in English translation,* BE885

Jones, Woodrow. *Black American health,* EH405
—— *Health of black Americans from post reconstruction to integration, 1871–1960,* EH405

Jong, Dirk de. *Het vrije boek in onvrije tijd,* BE1329

Jong, Frits J. de. *Quadrilingual economics dictionary,* CH69

Jongeling, Bastiaan. *Classified bibliography of the finds in the desert of Judah,* BC112

Jongman, A. J. *Political terrorism,* CJ554

Jónsson, Finnur. *Lexicon poeticum antiquæ linguæ septentrionalis,* BE1286

Jónsson, Guðni. *Eddukvæði,* BE1286

Jordan, Alma. *The English-speaking Caribbean,* AA33

Jordan, Anne Harwell. *Cannons' bibliography of library economy, 1876–1920,* AK12

Jordan, Casper LeRoy. *A bibliographical guide to African-American women writers,* BE524

Jordan, Frank. *The English romantic poets,* BE702, BE984

Jordan, Gerald. *British military history,* DC277

Jordan, Melbourne. *Cannons' bibliography of library economy, 1876–1920,* AK12

Jordan, William M. *Geologists and ideas,* EF99

Jordan
bibliography, AA919
statistics, CG405

Jordan (by subject)
history
bibliography, DE212

Jordan. Dāʾirat al-Iḥṣaʾat al-ʾAmmah. *Statistical yearbook,* CG405

Jordan, Seccombe, Ian J., DE212

The Jordanian national bibliography, AA919

Jorgensen, Jan Jelmert. *Uganda,* DD239

Jorgensen, Janice. *Encyclopedia of consumer brands,* CH564

Jose, Jim. *Anarchist thinkers and thought,* CJ506

Joseph, Tanya. *Political parties of Africa and the Middle East,* CJ405, CJ418

Joseph, William A. *The Oxford companion to politics of the world,* CJ29

Josephson, A. G. S. *A list of books on the history of science, January 1911,* EA235

Josephson, Aksel Gustav Salomon. *Avhandlingar ock program utgivna vid svenska ock finska akademier ock skolor under aren 1855–1890,* AG42

Josephson, Harold. *Biographical dictionary of modern peace leaders,* CJ66, CJ686, CJ700

Joshi, Irene M. *Indian literature in English, 1827–1979,* BE1542, BE1567

Joslyn, Richard. *Political science research methods,* CJ56

Jost, Jean E. *Ten Middle English Arthurian romances,* BE736

Joucla, Edmond A. *Bibliographie de l'Afrique occidentale française,* DD101

Jouette, André. *Toute l'histoire par les dates et les documents,* DC161

Jougla de Morenas, Henri. *Grand armorial de France,* AJ158

Journal asiatique, BC506

Journal of agricultural research, EJ92

Journal of applied psychology [indexes], CD15

Journal of Commonwealth literature, BE816

Journal of economic literature, CH40, CH42, CH195

Journal of family history, CC213

Journal of futures markets, CH431

Journal of government information, AF15

Journal of home economics, EJ194, EJ196

Journal of marketing, CH589

Journal of modern literature, BE35, BE761

Journal of philosophy, psychology and scientific method [indexes], CD15

Journal of physical and chemical reference data, EE93

Journal of religion in Africa, BC19

Journal of research in music education, BJ164

Journal of the Association of Official Analytical Chemists, EE84, EJ59

Journal of the fantastic in the arts, BE310

Journal of the Nepal Research Centre, AA922

Journal of women's history, CC529

Journal of women's history guide to periodical literature, Fischer, Gayle V., CC529

Journal officiel de la République française, France, AF170

Journal officiel de l'Empire Français, AF170

Journalism
bibliography, AE131, AE132, AE134, AE135, AE136
biography, AE148, AE149, AE150, AE151, AE152, AE153
dictionaries, AE139, AE140
directories, AE143
dissertations, AE137
editorials, AE127
encyclopedias, AE138
guides, AE132

Journalism (by country or region)
Belgium, AD82
Italy, AD125
Japan, AE93
Poland
bibliography, AE67
United States, AE144, AE150
history, AE145

Journalism (by subject)
history, AE141, AE144, AE145, AE146, AE147

Journalism, Cannon, Carl L., AE135, AE136
—— Cates, Jo A., AE29, AE130, AE132
Journalism abstracts, AE137
Journalism quarterly, AE137
Journalist biographies master index, AE151
The journalist's bookshelf, Wolseley, Roland Edgar, AE136
Journals in psychology, CB22, CD13
Journals in translation, AD25
Les journaux de Québec de 1764 à 1964, Beaulieu, André, AD59
Journaux français, 1944–1956, AE51
Jovanovič, Slobodan. *A guide to Yugoslav libraries and archives,* DC611
Jowitt, William Allen Jowitt. *Jowitt's dictionary of English law,* CK38
Jowitt's dictionary of English law, Jowitt, William Allen Jowitt, CK38
Joy, Charles Rhind. *Harper's topical concordance,* BC157
Joyce, Beverly A. *Drama by women to 1900,* BE456
—— *Personal writings by women to 1900,* BE508
—— *Poetry by women to 1900,* BE489
Joyce, Donald F. *Black book publishers in the United States,* AA302
Joyce, Joyce Ann. *The new cavalcade,* BE541
Joyce, Patrick W. *Origin and history of Irish names of places,* CL209
József, Juhász. *Magyar értelmező kéziszótár,* AC492
Jreisat, Jamil E. *Administration and development in the Arab world,* CJ468
Jubani, Bep. *Bibliografi e arkeologjisë dhe historisë së lashtë të shqipërisë,* DC81
Jubb, Annemarie. *Indonesian serials, 1942–1950, in Yogyakarta libraries,* AD195
Judaica, Freimann, A., BC532
—— Harvard University. Library, BC537
Judaica Americana, Singerman, Robert, BC525
Judaica reference sources, Cutter, Charles, BC513
Judaism
  bibliography, BC17, BC509, BC510, BC511, BC512, BC513, BC514, BC515, BC516, BC517, BC518, BC519, BC520, BC521, BC522, BC523, BC524, BC525, BC526, BC527, BC528, BC530, BC531, BC532, BC533, BC534, BC535
  biography, BC565
  dictionaries, BC553, BC554, BC555, CF54
  dissertations, BC529
  encyclopedias, BC546, BC547, BC548, BC549, BC550, BC551, BC552, BC554, CK239
  guides, BC518
  handbooks, BC557, BC558, BC559, BC560
  history, BC561, BC562
  indexes, BC542, BC543, BC544, BC545
  library catalogs, BC537, BC539, BC540, BC541
  library resources, BC528
  manuscripts and archives, BC538
  periodicals
    indexes, BC542, BC545
  reference books, BC512
  statistics, BC564
  yearbooks, BC563, BC564
Judaism (by subject)
  folklore and popular culture, BC555, CF54
  history
    bibliography, DA7
  see also **Israel**
Judaistische Bibliographie, Kisch, Guido, BC529
Judd, Deane B. *Color,* ED60
Judeo-Romance linguistics, Wexler, Paul, BD154
Judges
  directories, CK158
Judges (by country or region)
  Canada
    directories, CK156
  United States
    biography, CK140, CK148
    directories, CK139, CK140, CK149, CK156
Judges of the United States, Judicial Conference of the United States. Bicentennial Committee, CK148
Judicial Conference of the United States. Bicentennial Committee. *Judges of the United States,* CK148

Judicial organisation in Europe, Council of Europe, CK201
Judicial staff directory, CJ137, CJ215, CK149
Judit, Fejér. *A magyar sajtó bibliográfiája, 1945–1954,* AD120
Judkins, David. *Study abroad,* CB243
Judson, Adoniram. *The Judson Burmese-English dictionary,* AC244, AC245
The Judson Burmese-English dictionary, Judson, Adoniram, AC244, AC245
Judson concordance to hymns, McDormand, Thomas Bruce, BC319
Jugoslavenska akademija znanosti i umjetnosti. *Rječnik hrvatskoga ili srpskoga jezika,* AC709
Jugoslavenska književnost, Barac, Antun, BE1497
Jugoslavenski bibligrafski institut. *Bibliografija Jugoslavije,* AA846
Jugoslavenski leksikografski zavod. *Bibliografija rasprava, članaka i književnih radova,* AD333
Jugoslavenska bibliografija, AA845
Jugoslovenski bibliografski institut. *Bibliografija Jugoslavije,* AD332
Jugoslovenski casopisi (izbor), AD168
Jugoslovenski književni leksikon, Boškov, Zivojin, BE1498
—— Milisavac, Zivan, BE1498
Jugoslovenski savremenici, AH308
Juhněviča, I. *Anglu-latviešu vārdnica,* AC596
Julian, John. *A dictionary of hymnology,* BC318, BC320
Julien, Germain. *Canadian public administration : bibliography,* CJ465
Jullien, Alexandre. *Catalogue des éditions de la Suisse romande,* AA836
—— *Catalogue des ouvrages de langue francaise publiés en Suisse,* AA836
Jung, Heidrun. *The dictionary of acronyms and abbreviations in applied linguistics and language learning,* BD40
Jung, Kurt Michael. *Weltgeschichte in einem Griff,* DC224
—— *Weltgeschichte in Stichworten,* DC224
Jung, Udo O. H. *The dictionary of acronyms and abbreviations in applied linguistics and language learning,* BD40
—— *An international bibliography of computer-assisted language learning with annotations in German,* BD73
Jung, Václav. *Slovník anglicko-česky,* AC279
Junge, Ewald. *World coin encyclopedia,* BG178
Jungian literary criticism, 1920–1980, Meurs, Jos van, BE24
The junior book of authors, Kunitz, Stanley Jasspon, BE384
Junior high school library catalog, AA344
—— Yaakov, Juliette, AA345
Jupp, James. *The Australian people,* DF33
Jurgens, Madeleine. *Documents du Minutier central des notaires de Paris,* DC151
—— *Ronsard et ses amis,* DC151
Juridiske literaturhenvisninger, Lund, Torben, CK207
Jursa, Adeolph. *Handbook of geophysics and space environments,* EF155
Jussen, Virginia M. *Lexicon of new formal geologic names of the United States, 1976–1980,* EF77
Justice, Keith L. *Science fiction, fantasy, and horror reference,* BE291
Justices of the United States Supreme Court, 1789–1969, Friedman, Leon, CK189
—— Israel, Fred L., CK189
Justus, Douglas R. *Research guide to science fiction studies,* BE281
Juvenile and adult correctional departments, institutions, agencies and paroling authorities, United States and Canada, CK261
Juvenile delinquency, CC174
Juvigny, Rigoley de. *Les bibliothèques françoises de La Croix du Maine et de Du Verdier,* AA616
•*J+W Commdisc,* CH490
J+W telefax international, CH490

The K & W guide to colleges for the learning disabled, Kravets, Marybeth, CB313
Kaarna, Väinö. *Suomen sanomalehdistön bibliografia, 1771–1963,* AE49
Kabdebó, Thomas. *Hungary,* DC381
Kadetsky, Jill. *Current biography,* AH44
Kadima-Nzuji Mukala. *Bibliographie des auteurs africains de langue française,* BE1513
—— *Bibliographie litteraire de la Republique du Zaïre, 1931–1972,* BE1540
Kadish, Sanford H. *Encyclopedia of crime and justice,* CK251
Kadushkina, N. V. *Istoriia SSSR,* DC549
Kaegbein, Paul. *Bibliotheca Estoniae historica, 1877–1917,* DC134
—— *Deutsche Bibliothekskataloge im 19. Jahrhundert,* AA118
Kael, Pauline. *5001 nights at the movies,* BH197
Kaftal, George. *Iconography of the saints in Italian painting from its beginnings to the early XVIth century,* BF183
—— *Saints in Italian art,* BF183
Kagaku gijutsu hen, AD342
Kagan, Alfred. *The African National Congress of South Africa,* DD214
—— *American & Canadian doctoral dissertations & master's theses on Africa, 1886–1974,* DD32
—— *American and Canadian doctoral dissertations and master's theses on Africa, 1974–1987,* DD32
—— *Reference service for publications of intergovernmental organizations,* AF5
Kaganoff, Benzion C. *A dictionary of Jewish names and their history,* AJ200
Kahan, Vilém. *Bibliography of the Communist International (1919–1979),* CJ503, CJ511
Kahl, Willi. *Repertorium der Musikwissenschaft,* BJ17
Kahn, Ada P. *The A–Z of women's sexuality,* CC282
—— *The encyclopedia of phobias, fears, and anxieties,* CD100, EH378
Kahn, Tamar Joy. *Bibliography of bioethics,* EH237
Kahu, Meelik. *Eesti pseudonüümide leksikon,* AA167
Kaid, Lynda Lee. *Political campaign communication,* CJ103
The Kaiser index to black resources, 1948–1986, CC383
Kakodker, Archana Ashok. *Bibliography of Goa and the Portuguese in India,* DE161
Kalck, Pierre. *Central African Republic,* DD18, DD48
Kalia, D. R. *A bibliography of bibliographies on India,* AA75
Kalinke, Marianne E. *Bibliography of old Norse-Icelandic romances,* BE1090
Kallenbach, Jessamine S. *American state governors, 1776–1976,* CJ286
—— *Index to black American literary anthologies,* BE537
Kallenbach, Joseph E. *American state governors, 1776–1976,* CJ286
Kalley, Jacqueline Audrey. *Pressure on Pretoria,* DD215
—— *South Africa under apartheid,* DD216
—— *South Africa's foreign relations, 1980–1984,* DD221
—— *South Africa's road to change, 1987–1990,* DD216
Kallich, Martin. *British poetry and the American Revolution,* BE709
Kallmann, Helmut. *Encyclopedia of music in Canada,* BJ134
Kallsen, Margarita. *Paraguay … años de bibliografía,* AA537
Kalmbacher, George. *The color dictionary of flowers and plants for home and garden,* EG175
Kalnyn, I︠A︡. *Istoriia latyshskoi literatury,* BE1319
Kaloeva, I. A. *Sovetskaia bolgaristika,* DC113
—— *Sovetskoe slavi︠a︡novedenie,* DC42
Kalvelage, Carl. *Bridges to knowledge in political science,* CJ3

—— *Research guide for undergraduates in political science*, CJ3

—— *Research guide in political science*, CJ3

Kamazi, Joséphine. *Femmes et enfants au Burundi*, DD134

Kamen, Ruth H. *British and Irish architectural history*, BF203

Kamenetskaia, R. V. *Bibliografiia trudov Instituta etnografii im. N. N. Miklukho-Maklaia, 1900–1962*, CE5

Kaminkow, Marion J. *A complement to genealogies in the Library of Congress*, AJ31, AJ32

—— *Genealogical manuscripts in British libraries*, AJ108

—— *Genealogies in the Library of Congress*, AJ32

—— *United States local histories in the Library of Congress*, DB142

Kammenhuber, Annelies. *Hethitisches Wörterbuch*, AC491

Kammerer, Winifred. *A Coptic bibliography*, BC454, BE1521

Kamp, Jim. *Notable Hispanic American women*, AH78

Kämper-Jensen, Heidrun. *Deutsches Wörterbuch*, AC407

Kämpfer, Fritz. *Glass*, BG75

Kamphaus, Randy W. *Handbook of psychological and educational assessment of children*, CD93

Kamus Indonesia-Inggris, AC517

Kamus Inggris-Indonesia, AC517

Kan-Ei jukugo ribāsu jiten, Spahn, Mark, AC558

Kandel', Boris L'vovich. *Russkaia khudozhestvennaia literatura i literaturovedenie*, BE1396

Kandidátusi és doktori disszertációk katalógusa, AG37

Kane, John D. H. *The United States Navy and Coast Guard, 1946–1983*, CJ610

Kane, Joseph Nathan. *Almanac of the 50 states*, CG104

—— *The American counties*, CL178

—— *Facts about the presidents*, CJ190

—— *Famous first facts*, AB106

—— *Nicknames and sobriquets of U.S. cities, states and counties*, CL173, CL179

Kane, Thomas Leiper. *Amharic-English dictionary*, AC209

Kane, Thomas T. *The Population Reference Bureau's population handbook*, CG39

Kanellos, Nicolás. *Biographical dictionary of Hispanic literature in the United States*, BE562

—— *The Hispanic-American almanac*, CC467

—— *History of Hispanic theatre in the United States*, BE560

Kanely, Edna A. *Cumulative index to Hickcox's monthly catalog of United States government publications, 1885–1894*, AF93

—— *Cumulative subject guide to U.S. government bibliographies, 1924–1973*, AF81

—— *Cumulative subject index to the Monthly catalog of United States government publications, 1895–1899*, AF94, AF103

—— *Cumulative subject index to the Monthly catalog of United States government publications, 1900–1971*, AF103, AF111

Kaniel, Michael. *Guide to Jewish art*, BF194

Kanikova, S. I. *Reader's encyclopedia of Eastern European literature*, BE988

Kanitkar, Helen A. *Anthropological bibliography of South Asia*, CE108

Kanitkar, J. M. *A bibliography of Indology*, CE109

—— *Indian anthropology*, CE109

Kanka, August Gerald. *Poland*, DC470

Kanner, Barbara. *Women in English social history, 1800–1914*, CC607

—— *The women of England from Anglo-Saxon times to the present*, CC624

Kansallinen elämäkerrasto, AH188

Kansas. [Laws, etc.]. *Kansas statutes annotated*, CK179

Kansas statutes annotated, Kansas. [Laws, etc.], CK179

Kantautas, Adam. *A Lithuanian bibliography*, DC442

Kantautas, Filomena. *A Lithuanian bibliography*, DC442

Kantor, Máttis. *Jewish time line encyclopedia*, DA31

Kantor Bibliografi Nasional (Indonesia). *Bibliografi nasional Indonesia*, AA904

Kantowicz, Edward R. *Historical dictionary of the Progressive Era, 1890–1920*, DB132

Kapches, Mima. *A preliminary bibliography of early man in eastern North America, 1839–1973*, CE84

Kapel, David E. *American educators' encyclopedia*, CB65

Kapel, Marilyn B. *American educators' encyclopedia*, CB65

Kaplan, Frederic M. *Encyclopedia of China today*, DE141

Kaplan, Harold I. *Comprehensive glossary of psychiatry and psychology*, EH383

—— *Comprehensive textbook of psychiatry/V*, EH400

Kaplan, Irving. *Area handbook for Ghana*, DD62

—— *Area handbook for Sierra Leone*, DD62

—— *Kenya*, DD62

—— *Zambia*, DD62

Kaplan, Jonathan. *2000 books and more*, BC515

—— *International bibliography of Jewish history and thought*, DA7

Kaplan, Justin. *Familiar quotations*, BE99

Kaplan, Kristine. *ERIC directory of education-related information centers*, CB99

Kaplan, Louis. *A bibliography of American autobiographies*, AH89, BE507, CC485, DB66, DB67

Kaplan, Mike. *Variety's directory of major U.S. show business awards*, BH19

—— *Variety's who's who in show business*, BH26

Kaplan, Stuart R. *A guide to information sources in mining, minerals, and geosciences*, EF171

Kaplan, Wendy. *The encyclopedia of arts and crafts*, BG19

Kapoor, Jagdish Chander. *Bhagavad-Gītā*, BC483

Kappel, Robert. *Bibliography of books and articles on Liberia as edited in German speaking countries since 1960*, DD173

Kapsner, Oliver Leonard. *Catholic religious orders*, BC440

Kapteyn, P. J. G. *International organization and integration*, AF17

Karaś, Mieczysław. *Słownik wymowy polskiej PWN*, AC640

Karasik, Theodore. *Post-Soviet archives*, DC557

Karch, John J. *Encyclopedia of the Second World*, CJ28

Karel, David. *Dictionnaire des artistes de langue française en Amérique du nord*, BF314

Kāretu, T. S. *Concise Māori dictionary*, AC609

Karg-Gasterstädt, Elisabeth. *Althochdeutsches Wörterbuch*, AC399

Kargas, Nicholas A. *Accountant's desk handbook*, CH258

Karia, Bhupendra. *The Artronix index*, BF348

Karis, Thomas. *From protest to challenge*, CJ413

Karkhanis, Sharad. *Jewish heritage in America*, BC524

Karl Baedeker (Firm). *Baedeker's handbook(s) for travellers*, CL389

Karl Georgs Schlagwort-katalog, Georg, Karl, AA642

Karl Marx and Friedrich Engels, Eubanks, Cecil L., CJ500

Karlish, Roger D. *Directory of practicing anthropologists*, CE88

Karmī, Ḥasan Sa'īd. *al-Mughni al-akbar*, AC217

Karnes, Elizabeth Leuder. *Philosophy, policies and programs for early adolescent education*, CB10

Karnes, Frances A. *Handbook of instructional resources and references for teaching the gifted*, CB186

Karney, Robyn. *The Holt foreign film guide*, BH194

—— *Who's who in Hollywood*, BH289

Karni, Rahadi S. *Bibliography of Malaysia & Singapore*, DE229, DE255

Karp, Rashelle S. *The basic business library*, CH8

Karpel, Bernard. *Arts in America*, BF12

Karpinski, Louis Charles. *Bibliography of mathematical works printed in America through 1850*, EB11

Kärre, Karl. *Engelsk-svensk ordbok*, AC765

Karrow, Robert W. *Mapmakers of the sixteenth century and their maps*, CL273

Karşılaşrmalı Türk lehçeleri sözlüğü, AC788

Karst, Kenneth L. *Encyclopedia of the American Constitution*, CK130

Karsten, Eileen. *From real life to reel life*, BH226

Karṭa (Firm). *Atlas of medieval Jewish history*, DA159

—— *Atlas of the Middle East*, DE70

—— *The Macmillan Bible atlas*, BC197

Kartenmacher aller Länder und Zeiten, Bonacker, Wilhelm, CL272

Kartesz, John T. *A synonymized checklist of the vascular flora of the United States, Canada, and Greenland*, EG132

Kartesz, Rosemarie. *A synonymized checklist of the vascular flora of the United States, Canada, and Greenland*, EG132

Kartograficheskaia letopis', CL231

Kartographie 1943–1954, Kosack, Hans-Peter, CL227, CL232

—— Meine, Karl-Heinz, CL227

Karush, William. *Crescent dictionary of mathematics*, EB42

—— *Webster's new World dictionary of mathematics*, EB42

Karve, C. G. *The practical Sanskrit-English dictionary*, AC702

Kasack, Wolfgang. *Dictionary of Russian literature since 1917*, BE1412

Kasher, Menachem Mendel. *Encyclopedia of biblical interpretation*, BC182

—— *Humash Torah Shelemath*, BC182

Kaske, Robert Earl. *Medieval Christian literary imagery*, BE5, DA138

Kasper, Walter. *Lexikon für Theologie und Kirche*, BC63

Kassam, Shirin G. F. *A bibliography on Kenya*, DD167

Kassen, Vivian Loeb. *Encyclopedia of community planning and environmental management*, CC302

Kassis, Hanna E. *A concordance of the Qur'an*, BC203

Kastenbaum, Beatrice. *Encyclopedia of death*, CC182

Kastenbaum, Robert. *Encyclopedia of death*, CC182

Kastrati, Jup. *Bibliographi shqipe*, AA572

Katalog czasopism polskich Biblioteki Jagiellońskiej, Biblioteka Jagiellońska, AD134

Katalog der Freiherrlich von Lipperheide'schen Kostümbibliothek, Lipperheide, Franz Joseph, BG93

Katalog der Judaica und Hebraica, Stadtbibliothek Frankfurt am Main, BC532

Katalog der Lipperheideschen Kostümbibliothek, Kunstbibliothek (Berlin, Germany), BG93

—— Nienholdt, Eva, BG93

—— Wagner-Neumann, Gretel, BG93

Katalog der Musikbibliothek Paul Hirsch, Frankfurt am Main, Hirsch, Paul, BJ85, BJ87, BJ94

Katalog der Musikdrucke, Bayerische Staatsbibliothek, BJ91

Katalog der Musikzeitschriften, Bayerische Staatsbibliothek, BJ100

Katalog der Quellen zur Geschichte Mexikos in der Bundesrepublik Deutschland, 1521–1945, Bieber, León Enrique, DB239

Katalog der Schweizer Presse, AD165

Katalog der Schweizerische Landesbibliothek Bern, Schweizerische Landesbibliothek, AA838, AH301

Katalog der Schweizerischen Landesbibliothek, AA835

Katalog doktorskikh i kandidatskikh dissertatsiĭ, postupivshikh v Gosudarstvennuiu biblioteku SSSR imeni V. I. Lenina, Gosudarstvennaia biblioteka SSSR imeni V.I. Lenina, AG45

Katalog kandidatskikh i doktorskikh dissertatsiĭ, AG45

Katalog majalah terbitan Indonesia, Perpustakaan Nasional (Indonesia), AD194

Katalog rozpraw doktorskich i habilitacyjnych, AG39

Katalog slovákumových kníh Knižnice, Matica Slovenská, Turčiansky sv. Martin. Knižnica, AA597

Katalog surat kabar, Perpustakaan Nasional (Indonesia), AE89

Kataloge der Bibliotheca Hertziana in Rom (Max-Planck-Institut), Bibliotheca Hertziana, Max-Planck-Institut, BF52

Kataloge der Bibliothek des Deutschen Archaeologischen Instituts, Rom, Deutsches Archäologisches Institut. Römische Abteilung. Bibliothek, DA63

Katalogus surat-karab, lokeksi Perpustakaan Museum pusat 1810–1973, AE89

Katayen, Lelia. *Russian-English dictionary of musical terms,* BJ150

Kato, Genchi. *A bibliography of Shinto in Western languages,* BC570

Katona, Lóránt. *Angol-magyar müszaki szótár,* EA115

—— *Magyar-angol müszaki szótár,* EA115

Katritzky, Alan R. *Comprehensive heterocyclic chemistry,* EE117

Katz, Bernard. *The travellers, Canada to 1900,* DB189

Katz, Bernard S. *Biographical directory of the Council of Economic Advisers,* CH95

—— *Nobel laureates in economic sciences,* AL167, CH102

Katz, Doris B. *Guide to special issues and indexes of periodicals,* AD34, CH29

Katz, Dorothy Dittmer. *Biology data book,* EG51

—— *Cell biology,* EG52

—— *Environmental biology,* EG50

—— *Respiration and circulation,* EG53

Katz, Dovid. *The Blackwell companion to Jewish culture,* DA177

Katz, Ellen L. *Socrates,* BB56

Katz, Ephraim. *The film encyclopedia,* BH251

Katz, Linda Sobel. *Environmental profiles,* EK75

Katz, Linda Sternberg. *Columbia Granger's guide to poetry anthologies,* BE315

—— *Magazines for libraries,* AA375

Katz, Richard S. *Party organisations,* CJ58

Katz, William. *Columbia Granger's guide to poetry anthologies,* BE315

Katz, William A. *Introduction to reference work,* AK233, AK235

—— *Magazines for libraries,* AA375

—— *Reference and online services handbook,* AK236

Katz, Zev. *Handbook of major Soviet nationalities,* CC349

Katzinger, Willibald. *Bibliographie zur Geschichte der Städte Österreichs,* DC90

Katzner, Kenneth. *English-Russian, Russian-English dictionary,* AC676

Kaufman, Isaak Mikhailovich. *Russkie biograficheskie i biobibliograficheskie slovari,* AH305

—— *Russkie entsiklopediĭ,* AB86, AB90

—— *Terminologicheskie slovari,* AC699

Kaufman, Judah. *English-Hebrew dictionary,* AC480

—— *Milon angli-ivri,* AC480

Kaufman, Lloyd. *Handbook of perception and human performance,* CD113

Kaufman, Martin. *Dictionary of American medical biography,* EH228

—— *Dictionary of American nursing biography,* EH288

Kaufman, Stephen A. *An Aramaic bibliography,* BD206

Kaufmann, Uri R. *Bibliographie zur Geschichte der Juden in der Schweiz,* DC525

Kaufmann, Walter. *Selected musical terms of non-Western cultures,* BJ318

Kaul, H. K. *Travels in South Asia,* CL376

Kaur, Amarjit. *Historical dictionary of Malaysia,* DE230

Kavass, Igor I. *Demise of the Soviet Union,* CK223

—— *Gorbachev's law,* CK223

—— *Soviet law in English,* CK223

—— *United States treaty index,* CK96

—— *World dictionary of legal abbreviations,* CK41, CK42

Kavenik, Frances M. *Handbook of American women's history,* DB48

Kawachi, Yoshiko. *Calendar of English Renaissance drama, 1558–1642,* BE661

Kawi language, AC560

Kay, Ian. *Jane's defence glossary,* CJ587

Kay, Jack. *Argumentation,* BE371

Kay, Robert S. *Handbook of accounting and auditing,* CH260

Kaye, Frederick Benjamin. *Census of British newspapers and periodicals, 1620–1800,* AD106

Kaye, G. W. C. *Tables of physical and chemical constants and some mathematical functions,* ED44

Kayser, Christian Gottlob. *Vollst ändiges Bücher-Lexikon,* AA646

—— *Vollständiges Bücher-Lexikon,* AA655

—— *Vollständiges Bücher-Lexikon, 1750–1910,* AA645

Kazakh-English dictionary, Shnitnikov, Boris Nikolayevich, AC561

Kazakh language, AC561

Kazdin, Alan E. *The clinical psychology handbook,* CD103

Kazhdan, A. P. *The Oxford dictionary of Byzantium,* DA166

Kdo je kdo, AH182

Kealey, Linda. *The female experience in eighteenth- and nineteenth-century America,* CC488

Keane, Claire Brackman. *Encyclopedia and dictionary of medicine, nursing, and allied health,* EH279

Keane, Teresa Mary. *Dictionnaire du moyen français,* AC381

Kearey, Philip. *The encyclopaedia of the solid earth sciences,* EF61

Kearley, Timothy. *Charles Szladits' guide to foreign legal materials,* CK210

Kearney, E. I. *The Continental novel,* BE257

Keats, Shelley, Bryon, Hunt, and their circles, Wilson, Edwin Graves, BE754

Keats, Shelley, Byron, Hunt, and their circles, Green, David Bonnell, BE754

—— Hartley, Robert A., BE754

Keats-Shelley journal, BE702, BE754

Keaveney, Sydney Starr. *American painting,* BF297

—— *Contemporary art documentation and fine arts libraries,* BF297

Keckeissen, Rita G. *Bibliography of American folk art for the year,* BG10

Keeble, N. H. *Handbook of English and Celtic studies in the United Kingdom and Republic of Ireland,* BD93

Keegan, Elizabeth A. *Index to AMA resources of the seventies, 1970–1976,* CH604

Keegan, John. *Rand McNally encyclopedia of World War II,* DA206

—— *The Times atlas of the Second World War,* DA212

—— *World armies,* CJ599

Keele, Harold M. *Foundations,* AL116

Keeler, Maggie. *Vernacular architecture in America,* BF213

Keeler, Mary Frear. *Bibliography of British history, Stuart period, 1603–1714,* DC315

Keeling, Denis F. *British library history,* AK70

Keene, Donald. *Dawn to the west,* BE1582

—— *Nihon bungakushi, Kindai, gendai hen,* BE1582

Keene, James A. *Planning, equipping, and staffing a document reprographic service,* AK249

Keeping score, Limbacher, James L., BJ360

—— Wright, H. Stephen, BJ360

Keesey, Ray E. *Modern parliamentary procedure,* CJ455

Keesing's contemporary archives, CJ693, DA187

Keesing's record of world events, CJ61, CJ693, DA187

Keeslar, Oreon. *Financial aids for higher education,* CB382

Keeves, John P. *Educational research, methodology, and measurement,* CB70

Kehde, Ned. *Access,* AD258

Kehr, Helen. *After Hitler Germany, 1945–1963,* DC244

—— *German Jewry,* BC541

—— *The Nazi era, 1919–1945,* DC236

—— *Persecution and resistance under the Nazis,* DC244

—— *Prejudice : racist-religious-nationalist,* BC541

Keijzer, Anne J. de. *China,* DE133

Keith, Arthur B. *Vedic index of names and subjects,* BC490

Keith, Brendan. *British historical facts,* DC323

Keith, Jone M. *Women and deviance,* CC490

Keith, Robert G. *New Iberian world,* DB292

Keith-Spiegel, Patricia. *The complete guide to graduate school admission,* CD38

Keitz, Saiedeh von. *Dictionary of library and information science,* AK47

Keitz, Wolfgang von. *Dictionary of library and information science,* AK47

Keldysh, IUriĭ Vsevolodovich. *Muzykal'naia entsiklopediia,* BJ123

Keller, Clara D. *American library resources cumulative index, 1870–1970,* AK103

Keller, Dean H. *Index to plays in periodicals,* BE227

Keller, Fernand. *Encyclopédie des citations,* BE92

Keller, Hans-Erich. *Bibliographie des dictionnaires patois galloromans (1550–1967),* AC390

Keller, Helen Rex. *Reader's digest of books,* BE193

Keller, James. *Family therapy glossary,* CC226

Keller, Kate Van Winkle. *National tune index microfiche,* BJ288

Keller, Mark. *A dictionary of words about alcohol,* CC129

Keller, Michael A. *Music reference and research materials,* BJ4, BJ5

Kellman, Herbert. *Census-catalogue of manuscript sources of polyphonic music, 1400–1550,* BJ69

Kellner, Bruce. *Harlem Renaissance,* BE529, DB130

Kellner-Heinkele, Barbara. *Bibliographisches Handbuch der Turkologie,* BD211, DE31

Kellner, Irwin. *Dictionary of banking terms,* CH272

Kellogg, Robert. *A concordance to Eddic poetry,* BE1286

Kellogg, Robert L. *Medieval studies,* DA131

Kelly, Bernice M. *Nigerian artists,* BF142

Kelly, D. F. *Concise veterinary dictionary,* EJ112

Kelly, David H. *American students,* CB217

—— *Women's education in the Third World,* CB27

Kelly, Emerson Crosby. *Encyclopedia of medical sources,* EH203

Kelly, Gail Paradise. *International handbook of women's education,* CB126

—— *Women's education in the Third World,* CB27

Kelly, Howard Atwood. *Cyclopedia of American medical biography,* EH229

—— *Dictionary of American medical biography,* EH229

Kelly, J. N. D. *The Oxford dictionary of Popes,* BC431

Kelly, James. *The American catalogue of books (original and reprints), published in the United States from Jan. 1861 to Jan. 1871,* AA415

Kelly, James R. *Encyclopedia of public affairs information sources,* CA1

Kelly, Joseph F. *The concise dictionary of early Christianity,* BC247

Kelly, Kenneth L. *Color,* ED60

—— *Color-universal language and dictionary of names,* ED60

Kelly, Leo J. *Dictionary of special education and rehabilitation,* CB199

Kelly, Matthew A. *Labor and industrial relations,* CH672

Kelly, R. Gordon. *Children's periodicals of the United States,* AD30

Kelly's, CH414
Kelly's business directory, CH414
Kelly's handbook to the titled, landed, and official classes, AJ119, AJ120
Kelly's manufacturers and merchants directory, CH414
Kelsall, Denis. New Zealand in maps, CL366
Kelsey, J. Horace. Standardized plant names, EG118
Kemal Atatürk, Bodurgil, Abraham, DC533
Kemény, György. Magyarország időszaki sajtója, 1911–töl 1920–ig, AD122
Kemmer, Elizabeth Jane. Violence in the family, CC214
Kemp, D. Alasdair. Astronomy and astrophysics, EC2, EC18
Kemp, Herman C. Annotated bibliography of bibliographies on Indonesia, AA78, DE176
Kemp, Peter Kemp. An A–Z of sailing terms, BK121
Kemp, T. J. Comprehensive dictionary of physical chemistry, EE25
Kemp, Thomas Jay. International vital records handbook, AJ12
Kempcke, Günter. Synonymwörterbuch, AC434
Kempenaer, A. de. Vermomde Nederlandsche en Vlaamsche schrijvers, AA178
Kemper, Robert V. The history of anthropology, CE15
Kemps film, TV & video yearbook, BH267
Kempton, Richard. French literature, BE1136
Kendall, Alan. Who's who in non-classical mythology, CF14
Kendall, Aubyn. The art and archaeology of pre-Columbian Middle America, BF28
—— Art of pre-Columbian Mexico, BF28
Kendall, Katherine A. Social casework. Cumulative index, 1920–1989, CC44
—— World guide to social work education, CC49
Kendall, Maurice George. Bibliography of statistical literature, EB12
—— Dictionary of statistical terms, CG25, EB43
Keng, Hsuan. An illustrated dictionary of Chinese medicinal herbs, EH350
Kenin, Richard. The dictionary of biographical quotation of British and American subjects, BE103
Kenkyūsha's new English-Japanese dictionary, Koine, Yoshio, AC553
Kenkyūsha's new Japanese-English dictionary, Masuda, Koh, AC554
Kennan Institute for Advanced Russian Studies. A handbook for archival research in the USSR, DC562
—— A scholars' guide to humanities and social sciences in the Soviet successor states, AL59, DC593
—— Scholars' guide to Washington, D.C. for Russian, Central Eurasian, and Baltic studies, DC556
—— Soviet research institutes project, AL85
Kennard, Olga. Molecular structures and dimensions, EE139
Kennedy, Arthur Garfield. Bibliography of writings on the English language from the beginning of printing to the end of 1922, BD102
Kennedy, DayAnn M. Science & technology in fact and fiction, EA28
Kennedy, Frances H. Civil War battlefield guide, DB118
Kennedy, James. Dictionary of anonymous and pseudonymous English literature, AA150
Kennedy, James R. Library research guide to religion and theology, BC2
Kennedy, Michael. Concise Oxford dictionary of music, BJ138
—— The Oxford dictionary of music, BJ138
Kennedy, Susan E. America's white working-class women, CC496
Kennedy, Thomas Fillans. A descriptive atlas of the Pacific islands, CL368
Kennedy Institute. Center for Bioethics. Bibliography of bioethics, EH237
Kenney, E. J. Latin literature, BE1020
Kenney, James Francis. Sources for the early history of Ireland, DC395

Kennington, Donald. The literature of jazz, BJ304
Kennon, Donald R. The speakers of the U.S. House of Representatives, CJ199
Kensdale, W. E. N. Catalogue of the Arabic manuscripts preserved in the University Library, Ibadan, Nigeria, DD195
Kent, Allen. Encyclopedia of computer science and technology, EK172
—— Encyclopedia of library and information science, AK36
—— Encyclopedia of microcomputers, EK173
—— The Froehlich/Kent encyclopedia of telecommunications, CH481
Kent, George O. A catalog of files and microfilms of the German Foreign Ministry archives, 1920–1945, DC253
Kent, James A. Riegel's handbook of industrial chemistry, EK58
Kent, Rosalind. Encyclopedia of microcomputers, EK173
Kent, Ruth K. The language of journalism, AE139
Kent, Ruth Kimball. Webster's new World dictionary of synonyms, AC147
Kent, William. Mechanical engineer's handbook, EK238, EK243
Kentucky. [Laws, etc.]. Kentucky revised statutes, annotated, CK179
Kentucky revised statutes, annotated, Kentucky. [Laws, etc.], CK179
Kenya
atlases, CL341
bibliography, AA861, DD18, DD167
biography, AH320
current surveys, DD62
encyclopedias, DD48
government publications, AF221, AF223, AF233, DD167
bibliography, AF232
handbooks, DD164
periodicals, AD172
statistics, CG336
Kenya (by subject)
economic conditions, DD166
history, DD166
population, CG337
social conditions, DD166
bibliography, DD165
women, DD168
Kenya. Central Bureau of Statistics. Statistical abstract, CG336
Kenya. Ministry of Information and Broadcasting. Kenya, DD164
Kenya, DD164
—— Collison, Robert L., DD18
—— Howell, John Bruce, AF232, DD167
—— Kaplan, Irving, DD62
—— Ogot, B. A., DD48
Kenya in the social sciences, Norgaard, Ole, DD165
Kenya National Archives. A guide to government monographs, reports, and research works, AF233
Kenya national bibliography, AA861
Kenya National Library Service. National Reference & Bibliographic Dept. Kenya population, CG337
Kenya population, CG337
Kenya statistical digest, CG336
Kenyan periodicals directory, AD172
Kenyon, John A. Mission handbook, BC308
Kenyon, John Samuel. A pronouncing dictionary of American English, AC106
Kenyon, Nicholas. The Viking opera guide, BJ244
Kepars, I. Australia, DF27
Kepple, Robert J. Reference works for theological research, BC12, BC13
Ker, A. M. Mexican government publications, AF157
Ker, Neil Ripley. Catalogue of manuscripts containing Anglo-Saxon, BE604
—— Medieval manuscripts in British libraries, AA199
Kerber, Jordan E. Coastal and maritime archaeology, DA66
Keresztesi, Michael. German-American history and life, CC324

Kerker, Ann E. Comparative & veterinary medicine, EJ97
Kermode, Frank. The literary guide to the Bible, BC176
—— The Oxford anthology of English literature, BE618
Kern, Robert W. Historical dictionary of modern Spain, 1700–1988, DC514
Kern, Sharon. Film book bibliography, 1940–1975, BH170
Kernchen, Dagmar. Handbuch der bibliographischen Nachschlagewerke, AA12
Kernchen, Hans-Jürgen. Handbuch der bibliographischen Nachschlagewerke, AA12
Kernfeld, Barry Dean. The new Grove dictionary of jazz, BJ306
Kernig, C. D. Marxism, communism and Western society, CJ521
Keroher, Grace C. Lexicon of geologic names of the United States for 1936–1960, EF77
—— Lexicon of geologic names of the United States for 1961–1967, EF77
Kerr, Allen D. Lao-English dictionary, AC569
Kerr, Donald Gordon Grady. Historical atlas of Canada, DB207
Kerr, Elizabeth Margaret. Bibliography of the sequence novel, BE255
Kerr, J. Alistair. CRC handbook of bimolecular and termolecular gas reactions, EE69
Kerr, Joan. Dictionary of Australian artists, BF140
Kerrigan, Evans E. American badges and insignia, AL183
—— American war medals and decorations, AL183
Kersebaum, Andrea. Integrationsbestrebungen in Afrika, DD6
Kersey, Ethel M. Women philosophers, BB48
Kershaw, Stephen. Concise dictionary of classical mythology, CF27
Kersley, Leo. A dictionary of ballet terms, BH146
Kersnowski, Frank L. A bibliography of modern Irish and Anglo-Irish literature, BE804
Kerst, Catherine Hiebert. Ethnic folklife dissertations from the United States and Canada, 1960–1980, CF44
Kertbeny, Károly Mária. Bibliografie der ungarischin nationalen und internationalen Literatur, DC378
Kerven, Carol. Bibliography on the society, culture, and political economy of post-independence Botswana, DD131
Kesavan, B. S. Indian national bibliography, AA900
—— National bibliography of Indian literature, 1901–1953, AA897
Kesler, Jackson. Theatrical costume, BH51
Kessel, Ineke van. Aspects of the apartheid state, DD217
Kessel, Lorraine. Atlas of British history, DC301
Kesselring, Wilhelm. Dictionnaire chronologique du vocabulaire français, AC382
Kessels, A. H. M. A concise bibliography of ancient Greek literature, BE1030
—— Concise bibliography of Greek language and literature, BE1030
Kessler, Eckhard. The Cambridge history of Renaissance philosophy, BB69
Kessler, Peter. Beacham's guide to key lobbyists, CJ131
Kestenbaum, Ray. The American-Jewish media directory, AE17
Ketchum, William C. All-American folk arts and crafts, BG46
—— Catalog of American antiques, BG46
—— The catalog of world antiques, BG46
Keto, C. Tsehloane. American-South African relations, 1784–1980, DD218
Kettenring, N. Ernest. A bibliography of theses and dissertations on Portuguese topics completed in the United States and Canada, 1861–1983, DC491
Ketz, Louise Bilebof. Dictionary of American history, DB40
Keutner, Herbert. Sculpture, BF393

Key, Jack D. *Medicine, literature & eponyms*, EH123

Key monuments of the history of art, Janson, Dora Jane, BF132

—— Janson, Horst Woldemar, BF132

Key officers at U.S. foreign service posts, CJ185

Key rating guide, A.M. Best Company, CH511

Key resources on community colleges, Cohen, Arthur M., CB224

—— Palmer, James C., CB224

—— Zwemer, Diane K., CB224

Key resources on higher education governance, management, and leadership, Mets, Lisa A., CB224

—— Patterson, Marvin W., CB224

Key resources on institutional advancement, Rowland, A. Westley, CB224, CB227

Key resources on student services, Arceneaux, Cathann, CB224

—— Hood, Albert B., CB224

Key resources on teaching, learning, curriculum, and faculty development, Menges, Robert J., CB224

Key sources in comparative and world literature, Thompson, George A., BE33

Key to League of Nations documents, Carroll, M. J., AF28

Key to the ancient parish registers of England and Wales, Burke, A. M., AJ112

Keyes, Alice. *HAER checklist*, BF219

Keyes, Ralph. *"Nice guys finish seventh"*, BE106

Keyfitz, Nathan. *World population growth and aging*, CG50

Keyguide to information sources in agricultural engineering, Morgan, Bryan, EJ5

Keyguide to information sources in animal rights, Magel, Charles R., EG3

Keyguide to information sources in aquaculture, Turnbull, Deborah A., EJ7

Keyguide to information sources in archaeology, Woodhead, Peter, BF8, DA61

Keyguide to information sources in dentistry, Clennett, Margaret A., EH243

Keyguide to information sources in food science and technology, Green, Syd, EJ149

Keyguide to information sources in museum studies, Woodhead, Peter, BF8

Keyguide to information sources in paramedical sciences, EH7

Keyguide to information sources in public interest law, Cooper, Jeremy, CK9

Keyguide to information sources in veterinary medicine, Gibb, Mike, EJ96

Keyguide to information sources on the international protection of human rights, Andrews, John A., CK75

Keyguide veterinary medicine, EJ96

Keys to soil taxonomy, EJ54, EJ63

Keyser, Daniel J. *Test critiques*, CD71

—— *Tests*, CD72

Keyser, Erich. *Bibliographie zur Städtegeschichte Deutschlands*, DC265

Keysers Lexikon der Pflanzen, EG133

Keywords and concepts, Ranade, Ashok D., BJ156

Khairallah, Shereen. *Lebanon*, DE225

Khan, Khan Tahawar Ali. *Biographical encyclopedia of Pakistan*, AH365

Khan, Mohamed Jameelur Rehman. *Bibliography : Pakistan government and administration, 1970–1981*, CJ443, DE241

Khan, Muhammad Akram. *Islamic economics*, CH190

Kharasch, Norman. *Index to reviews, symposia volumes and monographs in organic chemistry*, EE135

Kharbas, Datta S. *India*, DE157

Kharlakova, Ivanka. *Bŭlgarski-angliĭsko rechnik*, AC239

Khartoum (Sudan). Jāmiʿat al-Khartūm. al-Maktabah. *al-Fihris al-musannaf li-majmūʿat al-Sūdān*, DD227

Khaṭīb, Ahmad Shafiq. *A new dictionary of scientific and technical terms*, EA103

Khatri, Linda A. *American engineers of the nineteenth century*, EK21

Khizānah al-ʿAmmah lil-Kutub wa-al-Wathāʾiq. *al-Bibliyūghrāfiyā al-waṭanīyah al-Maghrabīyah*, AA867

Khmer language
  dictionaries
    bilingual
      English-Khmer, AC563
      Khmer-English, AC562, AC564

Khrenova, L. S. *Bibliograficheskiĭ ukazatel' geodezicheskoĭ literatury za 40 let 1917–1956*, EF23

Khromov, S. S. *Grazhdanskaia voina i voennaia interventsiia v SSSR*, DC596

Khudozhestvennaia literatura narodov SSSR v perevodakh na russkiĭ iazyk, Startsev, Ivan Ivanovich, BE1405

Khudozhestvennaia literatura, russkaia i perevodnaia, Matsuev, Nikolai Ivanovich, BE1397

—— Natsuev, N. I., BE1398

Kiadja az Országos Széchényi Könyvtár. *Magyar nemzeti bibliográfia*, AA712

Kibbee, Josephine Z. *Cultural anthropology*, CE1, CE2

Kici, Gasper. *Albanian-English dictionary*, AC207

—— *English-Albanian dictionary*, AC207

Kida, Jun'ichiro. *Gendai Nihon shippitsusha daijiten*, BE1581

Kidd, Beresford James. *Documents illustrative of the continental Reformation*, BC285

—— *Documents illustrative of the history of the church*, BC285

Kidd, Hamish. *The agrochemicals handbook*, EJ46

Kidd, John. *Jungian literary criticism, 1920–1980*, BE24

Kidney, Walter C. *Twentieth century American nicknames*, AJ181

Kidron, Michael. *The new state of the world atlas*, CL280

—— *The war atlas*, CJ603

—— *Women in the world*, CC582

Kiell, Norman. *Psychiatry and psychology in the visual arts and aesthetics*, BF29

—— *Psychoanalysis, psychology, and literature*, BE19, BE25, BE26, BF29

Kiernan, Thomas P. *Aristotle dictionary*, BB51

Kies, Cosette N. *The occult in the western world*, CD130

Kiessling, Emil. *Wörterbuch der griechischen Papyrusurkunden*, AC446

Kiger, Anne Fox. *Acronyms and initialisms in health care administration*, EH129

—— *Hospital administration terminology*, EH117

Kiger, Joseph Charles. *Foundations*, AL116

—— *International encyclopedia of foundations*, AL97

—— *International encyclopedia of learned societies and academies*, AL19

—— *Research institutions and learned societies*, AL83

Kilgour, Heather. *Bibliography of the Summer Institute of Linguistics, Philippines, 1953–1984*, BD233

The Kilgour collection of Russian literature, 1750–1920, Harvard University. Library, BE1394

Kilian, Jansie. *South African theological bibliography*, BC49

Kill, R. C. *Food industries manual*, EJ166

Killen, Linda. *Versailles and after*, DB127

Killian, Johnny H. *The Constitution of the United States of America*, CK173

Killingray, David. *African political facts since 1945*, CJ399

Killingsworth, Charles C. *Trade union publications*, CH658

Kilmer, Victor J. *Handbook of soils and climate in agriculture*, EJ53

Kilmurray, Elaine. *Later Georgians and early Victorians*, BF66

—— *Victorians : historical figures born between 1800 and 1860*, BF66

Kilton, Thomas. *Archives and libraries in a new Germany*, AK133, AK139, DC13

Kim, C. I. Eugene. *The Asian political dictionary*, CJ416

Kim, David U. *Policies of publishers*, AK165

Kim, Elaine H. *Asian American literature*, BE547

Kim, Han-Kyo. *Studies on Korea*, DE214

Kim, Hong N. *Scholars' guide to Washington, D.C. for East Asian studies*, DE103

Kim, Hyung-chan. *Asian American studies*, BE546, CC407

—— *Dictionary of Asian American history*, CC402

Kim, T. W. *A bibliographical guide to the study of Chinese language and linguistics*, BD218

Kimambo, I. N. *History of Tanzania*, DD235

Kimble, Gregory A. *Portraits of pioneers in psychology*, CD50

Kime's international law directory, CK61

Kimmich, Christoph M. *German foreign policy, 1918–1945*, DC237

Kinauer, Rudolf. *Lexikon geographischer Bildbände*, CL14

Kinder, A. Gordon. *Spanish Protestants and reformers in the sixteenth century*, DC504

Kindergarten
  statistics, CB141

Kindergarten programs and practices in public schools, CB141

Kindlam, M. *Õigekeelsuse sõnaraamat*, AC305

Kindlers Literatur Lexikon, BE69

Kindlers Malerei Lexikon, BF317

Kindlers neues Literatur Lexikon, BE69

King, Anita. *Quotations in black*, BE115

King, Archdale Arthur. *The rites of Eastern Christendom*, BC448

King, Clive John. *100 families of flowering plants*, EG176

King, David. *Special libraries*, AK181

King, David James Cathcart. *Castellarium Anglicanum*, BF206

King, F. P. *Historical dictionary of Oceania*, DF17

King, Frank H. H. *A research guide to China-coast newspapers, 1822–1911*, AE86

King, H. G. R. *Atlantic Ocean*, DA8

King, Jeanne Snodgrass. *American Indian painters*, BF318

King, K. C. *A handbook on Old High German literature*, BE1256

King, Kimball. *Twenty modern British playwrights*, BE645

King, Norman D. *Ryukyu Islands*, DE203

King, Peter. *The Netherlands*, DC454

King, Richard L. *Airport noise pollution*, EK116

King, Robert C. *A dictionary of genetics*, EG339, EG341

King, Shirley V. *Japanese journals in English*, EA50

King, Warren B. *Rare birds of the world*, EG270

King, William Francis Henry. *Classical and foreign quotations*, BE93

King Edward's Hopital Fund for London. *A bibliography of nursing literature*, EH273

King-Hele, Desmond G. *The RAE table of earth satellites, 1957–1989*, EK34

Kingoro, Maeda. *Iwanami kogo jiten*, AC547

Kings and rulers *see* **Heads of state**

Kingsbury, John Merriam. *Poisonous plants of the United States and Canada*, EG150

Kingsbury, Stewart A. *A dictionary of American proverbs*, BE154

Kingsley, Anne. *A bibliography on South American economic affairs*, CH179

Kingsmill, Allison. *Old English word studies*, BD99

Kingzett, Charles Thomas. *Kingzett's chemical encyclopaedia*, EE31

Kingzett's chemical encyclopaedia, Kingzett, Charles Thomas, EE31

Kinkle, Roger D. *The complete encyclopedia of popular music and jazz, 1900–1950*, BJ349

Kinloch, Graham Charles. *Social stratification*, CC9

Kinnard, Cynthia D. *Antifeminism in American thought*, CC497

Kinnear, Michael. *British voter*, CJ349, CJ369

Kinnell, Susan K. *Communism in the world since 1945,* CJ499
—— *People in history,* AH54
—— *Searching America : history and life,* DB24
—— *Women in North America,* CC580
Kinney, A. J. *The Air Force officer's guide,* CJ627
Kinsella, Kevin G. *Detailed statistics on the urban and rural population of the Philippines, 1950 to 2010,* CG418
Kinsky, Georg. *Album musical,* BJ199
—— *Geschichte der Musik in Bildern,* BJ199
—— *A history of music in pictures,* BJ199
Kinsley, James. *Oxford book of ballads,* BE632
Kinsman, Clare D. *Contemporary authors. Permanent series,* AH42, BE198
Kinsmen through time, Edmunds, R. David, CC420
Kinton, Jack F. *Leaders in anthropology,* CE68
Kinzie, Mary. *The little magazine in America,* AD39
Kiple, Kenneth F. *The Cambridge world history of human disease,* EH212
Kirby, David K. *American fiction to 1900,* BE478
Kirby, Debra M. *Fund your way through college,* CB383
Kirby, Ronald F. *Kirby's guide to fitness and motor performance tests,* BK39
Kirby-Smith, H. T. *U.S. observatories,* EC47
Kirby's guide to fitness and motor performance tests, Kirby, Ronald F., BK39
Kirchenlateinisches Wörterbuch, Sleumer, Albert, AC582
Kirchheimer, Jean-Georges. *Voyageurs francophones en Amérique hispanique au cours du XIX* siècles,* DB263, DB409
Kirchherr, Eugene C. *Abyssinia to Zimbabwe,* CL155
—— *Place names of Africa, 1935–1986,* CL155
Kirchner, Joachim. *Bibliographie der Zeitschriften des deutschen Sprachgebietes bis 1900,* AD100
—— *Lexikon des Buchwesens,* AA270
Kirishitan bunko, Laures, John, BC307
Kirjath sepher, AA912
Kirk, A. *Bessel functions,* EB94
Kirk, John Foster. *A critical dictionary of English literature and British and American authors, living and deceased,* BE581
Kirk, Raymond E. *Encyclopedia of chemical technology,* EK51, EK52
Kirk, Robert Warren. *Handbook of veterinary procedures & emergency treatment,* EJ124
Kirk Greene, A. H. M. *A biographical dictionary of the British colonial governor,* CJ402
Kirk-Greene, C. W. E. *NTC's dictionary of faux amis,* AC340
•*Kirk-Othmer encyclopedia of chemical technology,* EK52
Kirkby, John. *The atlas of Nepal in the modern world,* CL359
Kirkeby, Willy. *English-Norwegian dictionary,* AC620
Kirkham, E. Bruce. *Indices to American literary annuals and gift books, 1825–1865,* BE415
Kirkland, Edwin Capers. *A bibliography of South Asian folklore,* CF97
Kirkpatrick, D. L. *Contemporary dramatists,* BE212
—— *Reference guide to American literature,* BE449
—— *Reference guide to English literature,* BE626
—— *Twentieth-century children's writers,* BE212, BE391
—— *Twentieth-century romance and historical writers,* BE249
Kirkpatrick, Diane. *Gardner's art through the ages,* BF129
Kirkpatrick, Leonard Henry. *Holdings of the University of Utah on Utah and the Church of Jesus Christ of Latter-Day Saints,* BC373
Kirpalani, V. H. *International business handbook,* CH143
Kirpicheva, Iraida Konstantinova. *Bibliografiía v pomoshch' nauchnoĭ rabote,* AA65
Kirschbaum, Engelbert. *Lexikon der christlichen Ikonographie,* BF184
Kirschstein, Bettina. *Wörterbuch der mittelhochdeutschen Urkundensprache,* AC413

Kirwan, Frank. *Irish economic statistics,* CG254
Kirwin, W. J. *Dictionary of Newfoundland English,* AC159
Kisch, Guido. *Judaistische Bibliographie,* BC529
—— *Schriften zur Geschichte der Juden,* BC529
Kiseleva, N. P. *Knigi kirillovskoĭ pechati, izdannye v Moskve v XVI-XVII vekakh,* AA787
Kish, George. *Bibliography of International Geographic Congresses, 1871–1976,* CL15
Kishindo, G. W. P. *Women in development in Southern Africa,* DD122, DD171
Kiso Nihongo gakushū jiten, AC551
Kiss, Lajos. *Földrajzi nevek etimológiai szótára,* CL207
Kissinger, Warren S. *Lives of Jesus,* BC211
Kister, Kenneth F. *Atlas buying guide,* CL221
—— *Best encyclopedias,* AB1
—— *Kister's atlas buying guide,* CL221
—— *Kister's best dictionaries for adults & young people,* AC2, AC3
—— *Kister's best encyclopedias,* AB1
—— *Kister's concise guide to best encyclopedias,* AB1
Kister's atlas buying guide, Kister, Kenneth F., CL221
Kister's best dictionaries for adults & young people, Kister, Kenneth F., AC2, AC3
Kister's best encyclopedias, Kister, Kenneth F., AB1
Kister's concise guide to best encyclopedias, Kister, Kenneth F., AB1
al-Kitāb al-iḥṣā'ī al sanawī, Saudi Arabia. Maṣlaḥat al-Iḥṣā'at al-'Āmah, CG421
al-Kitāb al-iḥṣa'ī al-sanawī lil-bilād al-'Arabīyah, CG372
Kitābhā-ye Īrān, AA905
Kitābkhānah-i Millī-i Īrān. *Kitābshināsī-i millī,* AA906
Kitābshināsī-i millī, Kitābkhānah-i Millī-i Īrān, AA906
Kitromilides, Paschalis. *Cyprus,* DC120
Kits, games, and manipulatives for the elementary school classroom, Hoffman, Andrea C., CB14
Kittel, Gerhard. *Theological dictionary of the New Testament,* AC456, BC137, BC143
Kittelson, David J. *The Hawaiians,* CC325
Kittredge, George Lyman. *English and Scottish popular ballads,* BE632
Kittross, John M. *A bibliography of theses & dissertations in broadcasting, 1920–1973,* BH295
Kitzinger, Rachel. *Civilization of the ancient Mediterranean,* DA98
Kitzmiller, John M. *In search of the "Forlorn hope",* AJ103
Kivi, Osvald. *Estonskaíā khudozhestvennaíā litertura,* BE1124
Kiyohara, Michiko. *A checklist of monographs and periodicals on the Japanese colonial empire,* DE199
Kjaerulff Nielsen, Bernhard. *Engelsk-dansk ordbog,* AC288
Klaar, R. M. *French dictionaries,* AC388
Kladas, S. *Statistikē en Helladi,* CG242
Klaniczay, Tibor. *History of Hungarian literature,* BE1276
Klapp, Friedrich-Albert. *Bibliographie der französischen Literaturwissenschaft,* BE1141
Klapp, Otto. *Bibliographie der französischen Literaturwissenschaft,* BE1141
Klapp-Lehrmann, Astrid. *Bibliographie der französischen Literaturwissenschaft,* BE1141
Klappenbach, Ruth. *Wörterbuch der deutschen Gegenwartssprache,* AC412
Klár, János. *Angol-magyar műszaki szótár,* EA115
—— *Magyar-angol műszaki szótár,* EA115
Klashorst, G. O. van de. *Bibliography of Dutch seventeenth century political thought,* DC455
Klassen, A. J. *Mennonite bibliography, 1631–1961,* BC362
Klau Library (Cincinnati). *Dictionary catalog of the Klau Library, Cincinnati,* BC539
Klauser, Renate. *Clavis mediaevalis,* DA151
Klauser, Theodor. *Reallexikon für Antike und Christentum,* BC248

Klausewitz, Wolfgang. *Grzimek's encyclopedia of ecology,* EG64
Klebs, Arnold Carl. *Incunabula scientifica et medica,* EH33
Kleckner, Simone-Marie. *Public international law and international organization,* CK78
Kleczek, Josip. *Space sciences dictionary,* EC41
Kleczková, Helena. *Space sciences dictionary,* EC41
Klehr, Harvey. *Biographical dictionary of the American left,* CJ156
Klein, Barry T. *Reference encyclopedia of American psychology and psychiatry,* CD3
—— *Reference encyclopedia of the American Indian,* CC428
Klein, Bernard. *Guide to American directories,* AL4
Klein, Dan. *History of glass,* BG75
Klein, Deana T. *Research methods in plant science,* EG151
Klein, Dennis B. *Holocaust in books and films,* DA216
Klein, Donald W. *Biographic dictionary of Chinese communism, 1921–1965,* CJ429
Klein, Ernest David. *A comprehensive etymological dictionary of the English language,* AC56
—— *A comprehensive etymological dictionary of the Hebrew language for readers of English,* AC471
Klein, Ewan. *A bibliography of contemporary linguistic research,* BD4
Klein, George. *The Soviet and East European political dictionary,* CJ396
Klein, Isaac. *Guide to Jewish religious practice,* BC560
Klein, Jean-Rene. *Bibliographie sélective de linguistique romane et française,* BD150
Klein, Leonard, S. *Encyclopedia of world literature in the 20th century,* BE66
Klein, Richard M. *Research methods in plant science,* EG151
Kleinbauer, W. Eugene. *Research guide to the history of Western art,* BF5
Kleindel, Walter. *Die Chronik Österreichs,* DC97
—— *Das grosse Buch der Österreicher,* AH167
Der kleine Pauly, DA101, DA104
Kleines deutsches dramalexikon, Lehmann, Jakob, BE1263
Kleines theologisches Wörterbuch, BC408
Kleines Wörterbuch der Philosophie, BB38
Kleinschmidt, Harald. *Amin collection,* DD240
Klemanski, John S. *The urban politics dictionary,* CJ42
Klemming, G. E. *Sveriges bibliografi, 1481–1600,* AA828
—— *Sveriges, dramatiska litteratur till och med 1875,* BE1484
Klenicki, Leon. *A dictionary of the Jewish-Christian dialogue,* BC554
Klesney, S. P. *Nomenclature of organic chemistry,* EE136
Klētniece, A. *Anglu-latviešu vārdnīca,* AC596
Klettner, Edgar. *Atlas do Brasil Globo,* CL316
KLG, BE1247
Klieneberger, H. R. *Bibliography of Oceanic linguistics,* BD232
Kliess, Werner. *Friedrichs Theaterlexikon,* BH68
Klíma, Vladimír. *Black Africa,* BE1501
Klimasauskas, Casimir C. *The 1989 neuro-computing bibliography,* EK155
Klinck, Carl Frederick. *Canadian writers,* BE834
—— *Literary history of Canada,* BE826
Kline, Jacob. *Handbook of biomedical engineering,* EH182
Kline, Mary-Jo. *A guide to documentary editing,* AA320
Kline, Victoria. *Last lines,* BE317
Klingebiel, Kathryn. *Bibliographie linguistique de l'ancien occitan (1960–1982),* BD177
Klinger, András. *Time series of historical statistics 1867–1992,* CG248
Klinisches Wörterbuch, Pschyrembel, Willibald, EH112
Klinman, Debra G. *Fatherhood U.S.A,* CC242

Kloesel, Christian J. W. *English novel explication*, BE675

Klos, Joithel. *Dictionary of data processing*, EK197

Klos, Sheila M. *Historical bibliography of art museum serials from the United States and Canada*, BF49

Klose, A. *Languages of the world*, BD13
—— *Sprachen der Welt*, BD13

Klose, Olaf. *Islandkatalog der Universitäts-bibliothek Kiel und der Universitäts– und Stadtbibliothek Köln*, AA719

Kloth, Karen. *A catalogue of English books printed before 1801 held by the University Library at Göttingen*, AA682

Klotman, Phyllis Rauch. *Frame by frame*, BH227

Klotzbach, Kurt. *Bibliographie zur Geschichte der deutschen Arbeiterbewegung, 1914–1945*, CH626

Kludas, Arnold. *Die Geschichte der deutschen Passagierschiffahrt*, AJ93

Kluge, Friedrich. *Etymologisches Wörterbuch der deutschen Sprache*, AC428

Klussmann, Rudolf. *Bibliotheca scriptorum classicorum et graecorum et latinorum*, BE991, BE992, BE1001

Knapp, Charles. *Dictionnaire géographique de la Suisse*, CL150

Knapp, Lothar. *Bibliografia de los cancioneros castellanos del siglo XV y repertorio de sus generos poeticos*, BE1477

Knapp, Sara D. *The contemporary thesaurus of social science terms and synonyms*, CA43

Knapp, Wilfrid. *The politics of African and Middle Eastern states*, CJ400

Knapton, Robyn Eileen. *The complete dictionary of television and film*, BH317

Knaster, Meri. *Women in Spanish America*, CC608, CC617, DB262

Knaurs Lexicon der Symbole, BF163

Knaurs Lexikon der modernen Architektur, Hatje, Gerd, BF233
—— Pehnt, Wolfgang, BF233

Knepper, Joachim. *Fachwörterbuch, Chemie und chemische Technik*, EE50

Kneschke, Ernst Heinrich. *Neues allgemeines deutsches Adels-Lexicon im Vereine mit mehreren Historikern*, AJ94

Knevel, P. *Repertorium van geschiedschrijvers in Nederland, 1500–1800*, DC461

Knevitt, Charles. *Perspectives*, BF95

Knight, Denise D. *Contemporary lesbian writers of the United States*, BE402, BE469

Knight, John Barton. *Knight's foodservice dictionary*, EJ157

Knight, Robert L. *Dictionary of genetics, including terms used in cytology, animal breeding and evolution*, EG340

The Knight-Ridder CRB commodity yearbook, CH433, EJ82

Knight-Ridder (Firm). *The Knight-Ridder CRB commodity yearbook*, CH433, EJ82

Knights and knighthood, DA147

Knight's foodservice dictionary, Knight, John Barton, EJ157

Knigi grazhdanskoi pechati XVIII veka, Akademiia Nauk URSR, Kiev. Biblioteka, AA788

Knigi kirillovskoi pechati, izdannye v Moskve v XVI-XVII vekakh, Zernova, Antonina S., AA787

Knigi pervoi chetverti XIX veka, Akademiia Nauk URSR, Kiev. Biblioteka, AA788, AA842

Knihopis československých tisků, Czechoslovak Republic. Komise pro knihopisn y soupis českých a slovenských tisků až do konce XVIII. století, AA596

Kniker, Charles R. *Religious schools in America*, CB37

Knizhnaia letopis', AA795, AA796

Knizhnaia letopis' : avtoreferaty dissertatsiĭ, AG46

Književna zajednica Novog Sada. *Adresar pisaca Jugoslavije*, BE1496

Knobloch, Johann. *Sprachwissenschaftliches Wörterbuch*, BD41

Knoop, Ulrich. *Index of Bibliographie zur Transformationsgrammatik*, BD45

Knospe, Horst. *Internationales Soziologenlexikon*, CA63

Knötel, Herbert. *Uniforms of the world*, CJ595, CJ634

Knötel, Richard. *Uniforms of the world*, CJ595, CJ634

Knott, David. *Catalogue of the Goldsmiths' Library of Economic Literature*, CH15

Knott, James Edward. *Knott's handbook for vegetable growers*, EJ248

Knott, Thomas Albert. *A pronouncing dictionary of American English*, AC106

Knott's handbook for vegetable growers, Knott, James Edward, EJ248

Know Africa, AH312

Knowledge, theory of see **Epistemology**

Knowles, Asa S. *The international encyclopedia of higher education*, CB237

Knowles, David. *Medieval religious houses, England and Wales*, BC441
—— *Religious houses of medieval England*, BC441

Knox, B. M. W. *Greek literature*, BE1020

Knox, Kathleen. *The feminization of poverty in the United States*, CC261

Knox-Davies, Laetitia. *Russian and Soviet perspectives on South Africa*, DD219

Knudsen, Trygve. *Norsk riksmålsordbok*, AC617
—— *Ordbog over det gamle norsk sprog*, AC504

Knuttel, W. P. C. *Catalogus van de pamfletten-verzameling*, AA751

Knuvelder, Gerard Petrus Maria. *Beknopt handboek tot de geschiedenis der Nederlandse letterkunde*, BE1330
—— *Handboek tot de geschiedenis der Nederlandse letterkunde*, BE1330

Knygos lietuvių kalba, AA741

Knyžhkova palata Ukraïns'koi RSR. *Periodychni vydannia URSR, 1917–1960*, AE72
—— *Periodychni vydannia URSU, 1918–1950*, AD166

Ko je ko u Jugoslaviji, AH308

Ko kui ma te kaupapa, AH377, DF46

Kobbé, Gustav. *Kobbé's complete opera book*, BJ237, BJ241

Kobbé's complete opera book, BJ262
—— Kobbé, Gustav, BJ237, BJ241

Kobylika, Joseph F. *Public interest law*, CK9

Koch, Hans-Albrecht. *Deutscher biographischer index*, AH206
—— *Internationale germanistische Bibliographie*, BD116, BE1235

Koch, Uta. *Deutscher biographischer index*, AH206
—— *Internationale germanistische Bibliographie*, BD116, BE1235

Kocher, Eric. *International jobs*, CH699

Kochukoshy, K. K. *A bibliography of Indian bibliographies, 1961–1980*, AA76

Kōdansha. *Japan : an illustrated encyclopedia*, AB71, DE209

Kodansha encyclopedia of Japan, AB71, DE209

Kodansha's compact Kanji guide, AC552

Kodin Suuri tietosanakirja, AB39

Koegler, Horst. *The concise Oxford dictionary of ballet*, BH143

Koehl, Stuart L. *The dictionary of modern war*, CJ573

Koehler, Barbara. *Encyclopedia of senior citizens information sources*, CC96

Koehler, Ludwig Hugo. *Hebräisches und aramäisches Lexikon zum Alten Testament*, AC481
—— *Lexicon in Veteris Testamenti libros*, AC482

Koeneman, Joyce. *Railroads*, CH444

Koenig, William J. *European manuscript sources of the American Revolution*, DB90
—— *The two World Wars*, DA191

Koeppe, Richard P. *The Facts on File dictionary of education*, CB80

Koerner, E. F. K. *Western histories of linguistic thought*, BD59

Kogan, Maurice. *Encyclopedia of government and politics*, CJ52

Koh, Hesung Chun. *Korean and Japanese women*, CC609

Kohen, Yitshak Yosef. *Jewish publications in the Soviet Union, 1917–1960*, BC535

Kohl, Benjamin G. *Renaissance humanism, 1300–1550*, BE20

Kohl, David F. *Administration, personnel, buildings and equipment*, AK174

Kohl, Rhiana. *Fatherhood U.S.A*, CC242

Kohlenberger, John R. *The NIV exhaustive concordance*, BC159
—— *NIV interlinear Hebrew-English New Testament*, BC94

Kohler, Eric Louis. *Kohler's dictionary for accountants*, CH252

Köhler, Jochen. *Deutsche Dissertationen über Afrika*, DD30

Kohler's dictionary for accountants, Kohler, Eric Louis, CH252

Kohli, A. B. *Councils of ministers in India, 1947–1982*, CJ433

Kohls, Siegfried. *Dictionary of international economics*, CH126

Kohlschmidt, Werner. *Reallexikon der deutschen Literaturgeschichte*, BE1251

Kohlschütter, A. *Handbuch der Astrophysik*, EC28

Kohn, George C. *Dictionary of historic documents*, DA23
—— *Dictionary of wars*, DA24
—— *Twentieth century American nicknames*, AJ181

Kohn, Michael H. *The Shambhala dictionary of Buddhism and Zen*, BC479

Kohrt, Manfred. *Index of Bibliographie zur Transformationsgrammatik*, BD45

Kohut, David R. *Women authors of modern Hispanic South America*, BE896

Køie, Tove. *Kunstnerleksikon*, BF147

al-Kōil dictionnaire arabe-français-anglais, AC213

Koine, Yoshio. *Kenkyūsha's new English-Japanese dictionary*, AC553

Kōjien, Shinmura, Izuru, AC550

Kōjirin, AC548

Kokich, George J. V. *A bibliography of Canadian demography*, CG116

Kokubungaku nenkan, BE1583

Kokuritsu Kokkai Toshokan (Japan). *Zen nihon shuppanbutsu so-mokuroku*, AA916

Kokuritsu Kokkai Toshokan (Japan). Chikuji Kankōbutsubu. *Zenkoku maikuro shinbun shozō ichiran*, AE96

Kokuritsu Kokkai Toshokan (Japan). Etsuranbu. *Kokuritsu Kokkai Toshokan shozo shinbun moruroku*, AE94

Kokuritsu Kokkai Toshokan shozo Gaikoku chikuji kankobutsu mokuroku, AE94

Kokuritsu Kokkai Toshokan shozo kokunai chikuji kankobutsu mokuroku, AE94

Kokuritsu Kokkai Toshokan shozo shinbun moruroku, Kokuritsu Kokkai Toshokan (Japan). Etsuranbu, AE94

Kokusai Bunka Kaikan (Tokyo, Japan). *A dictionary of Japanese artists*, BF144

Kokusai Bunka Kaikan (Tokyo, Japan). Toshoshitsu. *Modern Japanese literature in translation*, BE1584

Kokusai Kōryū Kikin. *Basic Japanese-English dictionary*, AC551
—— *Catalogue of books on Japan translated from the Japanese into English, 1945–1981*, DE197

Kokusho kaidai, Samura, Hachiro, AA915

Kokusho sōmokuroku, AA913

Kolarz, Walter. *Books on communism and the communist countries*, CJ514

Kolatch, Alfred J. *Complete dictionary of English and Hebrew first names*, AJ171, AJ172
—— *The Jonathan David dictionary of first names*, AJ172

Kolb, Harold H. *Field guide to the study of American literature*, BE397

Kolesnik, Eugene M. *Conway's all the world's fighting ships, 1947–1982*, CJ592

Kolin, Philip C. *American playwrights since 1945*, BE452

Koller, Angelika. *Deutscher biographischer index*, AH206

Kolosova, E. V. *Lichnye arkhivnye fondy v gosudarstvennykh kranilishchakh SSSR*, DC565

Kolov, S. P. *Pisateli Moskvy*, BE1422

Kolumbić, Nikica. *Hrvatski biografski leksikon*, AH307

Kolupaila, Steponas. *Bibliography of hydrometry*, EK100

Kom, Ambroise. *Dictionnaire des œuvres littéraires négro-africaines de langue française des origines à 1978*, BE1516

Komac, Daša. *Angleško-slovenski in slovensko-angleški slovar*, AC721

—— *English-Slovene and Slovene-English dictionary*, AC721

Kömives, Wilma. *Bestandskatalog der Bibliothek des Südost-Instituts München*, DC65

Kommentierte Bibliographie zur slavischen Soziolinguistik, Brang, Peter, BD180

Kommission zur Erforschung der Geschichte der Reformation und Gegenreformation. *Bibliographie zur deutschen Geschichte im Zeitalter der Glaubensspaltung 1517–1585*, DC227

Die Kommunistische Partei Deutschlands, 1918–1933, Collotti, Enzo, CJ498

Komonchak, Joseph A. *The new dictionary of theology*, BC407

Komorn, Jean. *Dictionnaire des racines scientifiques*, EA87

Komorowski, Manfred. *Bio-bibliographisches Verzeichnis jüdischer Doktoren im 17. und 18. Jahrhundert*, EH223

Kondakov, I. P. *Svodnyi katalog russkoĭ knigi grazhdanskoi pechati XVIII veka, 1725–1800*, AA791

Koner, Wilhelm. *Repertorium über die vom Jahre 1800 bis zum Jahre 1850 in Akademischen Abhandlungen, Gesellschaftsschriften und wissenschaftlichen Journalen auf dem Gebiete der Geschichte und ihrer Hülfswissenschaften erschienenen Aufsätze*, DA9

Kong, F. K. *Handbook of structural concrete*, EK106

Konigsberg, Ira. *The complete film dictionary*, BH258

Koning-van der Veen, M. *Horticultural research international*, EJ245

Koninklijk Instituut voor de Tropen. Information & Documentation. *Women and development*, CC621

Koninklijk Instituut voor Taal–, Land– en Volkenkunde (Netherlands). Adeling Documentatie Modern Indonesie. *Excerpta Indonesica*, DE179

Koninklijk Nederlands Aardrijkskundig Genootschap. *Lijst der aardrijkskundige namen van Nederland*, CL147

Koninklijke Bibliotheek (Netherlands). *Catalogus van de pamfletten-verzameling*, AA751

—— *Centrale catalogus van periodieken en seriewerken in Nederlandse bibliotheken (CCP)*, AD240

—— *Nederlandse bibliografie 1801–1832*, AA755

Koninklijke Vlaamse Academiën van Belgie. *Nationaal biografisch woordenboek*, AH174

Konishi, Jin'ichi. *History of Japanese literature*, BE1582

—— *Nihon bungei shi*, BE1582

Konn, Tania. *Soviet studies guide*, DC591

Könnecke, Gustav. *Bilderatlas zur Geschichte der deutschen Nationallitteratur*, BE1257

Konopczyński, Władysław. *Polski słownik biograficzny*, AH279

Kontsevich, L. R. *Linguistique coréenne*, BD223

Konuš, Joseph James. *Slovak-English phraseological dictionary*, AC718

Konversasjonsleksikon, AB74

Konwiser, Harry Myron. *American philatelic dictionary and Colonial and Revolutionary posts*, BG202

Könyvtáros gyakorlati szótára, Pipics, Zoltán, AK48

Koobatian, James. *Faking it*, BF30

Kooten, G. van. *Cassell's English-Dutch, Dutch-English dictionary*, AC297

—— *Kramers' Engels woordenboek*, AC298

Kooyman, Mary. *Historical dictionary of Laos*, DE224

Kopal, Zdeněk. *A new photographic atlas of the moon*, EC66

—— *Photographic atlas of the moon*, EC66

Kopech, Gertrude. *A bibliography of the research in tissue culture*, EG7

Köppen, Elke. *Movimientos sociales en México (1968–1987)*, DB227

Koral, Richard L. *Handbook of air conditioning, heating, and ventilating*, EK225

Koran, BC206, BC493
concordances, BC203
dictionaries, BC205

The Koran interpreted, BC204
—— Arberry, Arthur J., BC203

Koray, Enver. *Türkiye tarih yayinlari bibliyografyasi*, DC535

Korbut, Gabrjel. *Literatura polska od początków do wojny światowej*, BE1346, BE1350, BE1351

Korea
bibliography, AA920
handbooks, DE217
newspapers
union lists, AE96
registers, CJ325
statistics, CG406, CG407

Korea (by subject)
economic conditions, CG407
history, DE216
bibliography, DE213, DE214
guides, DE214
handbooks, DE218

Korea, North (by subject)
politics and government, CJ441, CJ442, DE219

Korea statistical yearbook, CG406

Korean and Japanese women, Koh, Hesung Chun, CC609

Korean Communism, 1945–1980, Suh, Dae-Sook, CJ442

A Korean-English dictionary, Martin, Samuel Elmo, AC565

Korean language
bibliography, BD223
dictionaries
bilingual
English-Korean, AC566
Korean-English, AC565

Korean national bibliography, AA920

Korean War, DE215
bibliography, DE213
handbooks, DE218

The Korean War, McFarland, Keith D., DE213

Korean War almanac, Summers, Harry G., DE218

Koritz, Marian. *Dissertations in American literature, 1891–1966*, BE425

Kormúth, Dezider. *Slovník slovenských pseudonymov 1919–1944*, AA160

Korn, Granino Arthur. *Mathematical handbook for scientists and engineers*, EB66

Korn, Theresa M. *Mathematical handbook for scientists and engineers*, EB66

Korn, William S. *The American college teacher*, CB335

—— *American freshman*, CB333

Korndorf, I. I. *Istoriia srednikh vekov*, DA133

—— *Novaia istoriia*, DA174

Körner, Josef. *Bibliographisches Handbuch des deutschen Schrifttums*, BE1227

Kornick, Rebecca Hodell. *Recent American opera*, BJ238

Kornicki, Peter F. *The Cambridge encyclopedia of Japan*, DE207

Kornrumpf, Hans-Jürgen. *Osmanische Bibliographie mit Besonderer Berücksichtigung der Türkei in Europa*, DC61, DC536

Kornrumpf, Jutta. *Osmanische Bibliographie mit Besonderer Berücksichtigung der Türkei in Europa*, DC61, DC536

Korobushkina, Tat'iana Nikolaevna. *Arkheologiia Belorussi*, DC98

Korsch, Boris. *Religion in the Soviet Union*, BC39

—— *Soviet publications on Judaism, Zionism, and the State of Israel, 1984–1989*, BC536, BC587

Korte, Werner. *Bibliography of books and articles on Liberia as edited in German speaking countries since 1960*, DD173

Kortner, Olaf. *Aschehoug og Gyldendals store norske leksikon*, AB73

Korzeniewska, Ewa. *Bibliografia literatury polskiej*, BE1346

—— *Słownik współczesnych pisarzy polskich*, BE1350, BE1351

Kósa, Géza Attila. *Biographical dictionary of Australian librarians*, AK82

Kosack, Hans-Peter. *Kartographie 1943–1954*, CL227, CL232

Kosáry, Domokos G. *Bevezetés a magyar történelem forrásaiba és irodalmába*, DC382

Kosch, Wilhelm. *Deutsches Literatur-Lexikon*, BE1246

—— *Deutsches Theater-Lexikon*, BH113

Koschnick, Wolfgang J. *Standard dictionary of the social sciences*, CA38

Kościuszko Foundation dictionary, AC634

Kossmann, F. K. H. *Nieuw Nederlandsch biografisch woordenboek*, AH272

Koster, C. J. *British union-catalogue of periodicals*, AD237

Koster, Donald Nelson. *American literature and language*, BE407

Köster, Rudolf. *Das Grosse Wörterbuch der deutschen Sprache in 6 Bänden*, AC403

Kőszegi, Michael A. *Islam in North America*, BC491

—— *Religious information sources*, BC13

Koszyk, Kurt. *Geschichte der deutschen Presse*, AE54

—— *Wörterbuch zur Publizistik*, AE140

Kotel'nikova, L. A. *Sovetskaia strana v period vosstanovleniia narodnogo khoziaistva, 1921–1925 gg*, DC590

Kotliakov, Vladimir Mikhaĭlovich. *Elsevier's dictionary of glaciology in four languages*, EF125

Kotnik, Janko. *Slovene-English dictionary*, AC722
—— *Slovensko-angleški slovar*, AC722

Kottak, Conrad Phillip. *Madagascar : society and history*, DD175

Köttelwesch, Clemens. *Bibliographisches Handbuch der deutschen Literaturwissenschaft, 1945–1969*, BE1228

Kotz, Samuel. *Encyclopedia of statistical sciences*, EB34

Koubek, Josef. *National population bibliography of Czechoslovakia, 1945–1977*, CG207

Kouri, Mary K. *Volunteerism and older adults*, CC98

Kouyoumdjian, Mesrob G. *A comprehensive dictionary, Armenian-English*, AC227

—— *Comprehensive dictionary of idioms, English-Armenian*, AC227

—— *Practical dictionary for adults*, AC227

Kovačević, Krešimir. *Leksikon jugoslavenske muzike*, BJ151

—— *Muzicka enciklopedija*, BJ151

Kovacs, Gabor. *Annotated bibliography of bibliographies on selected government publications and supplementary guides to the Superintendent of Documents classification system*, AF78

Kovacs, Ruth. *National guide to foundation funding in higher education*, CB365

—— *National guide to funding for libraries and information services*, AK64

—— *Who gets grants/who gives grants*, AL124

Kovalevsky, Pierre. *Atlas historique et culturel de las Russie et de monde slav*, DC572

Kovel, Ralph M. *American country furniture, 1780–1875*, BG132

—— *Directory of American silver, pewter, and silver plate*, BG145

—— *Kovels' American silver marks*, BG145

—— *The Kovels' antiques & collectibles price list*, BG47

—— *Kovel's new dictionary of marks*, BG71

Kovel, Terry H. *American country furniture, 1780–1875*, BG132

—— *Directory of American silver, pewter, and silver plate*, BG145

—— *Kovels' American silver marks*, BG145

—— *The Kovels' antiques & collectibles price list*, BG47

—— *Kovel's new dictionary of marks*, BG71

Kovels' American silver marks, Kovel, Ralph M., BG145

The Kovels' antiques & collectibles price list, Kovel, Ralph M., BG47

Kovel's new dictionary of marks, Kovel, Ralph M., BG71

—— Kovel, Terry H., BG71

Kovtun, George J. *Czech and Slovak literature in English*, BE1108

Kowalchik, Claire. *Rodale's illustrated encyclopedia of herbs*, EJ234

Kowalczyk, Georg. *Wasmuths Lexikon der Baukunst*, BF239

Kowalenki, Władisława. *Słownik starożytności słowiańskich*, DC53

Kowalik, Jan. *Bibliografia czasopism polskich wydanych poza granicami Kraju od września 1939 roku*, AD135

Kowitz, Aletha. *Basic dental reference works*, EH244

—— *Dentistry journals and serials*, EH246

Kozicki, Richard J. *International relations of South Asia, 1947–1980*, DE78

Kozlova, A. I. *Periodychni vydannīā URSR, 1917–1960*, AE72

Kozlovskiĭ, Vasiliĭ G. *English-Russian dictionary of agriculture*, EJ27

Kozono, Hitoshi. *A bibliography on Far Eastern numismatology and a coin index*, BG171

Krak, Ove Holger. *Kraks blå bog*, AH184

Kraks blå bog, AH184

Krallert, Gertrud. *Historische Bücherkunde Südosteuropa*, DC58

Kramarae, Cheris. *A feminist dictionary*, CC539

—— *Language, gender, and society*, BD82, BD84, CC495

Kramer, Alex A. *Sokrashchenīā v sovetskikh izdanīākh*, AC687

Kramer, Daniel J. *An introductory bibliography to the history of classical scholarship chiefly in the XIXth and XXth centuries*, DA92

Kramer, Elaine Fialka. *Modern American literature*, BE427, BE1069

Krämer, Hildegard. *Brockhaus Wahrig*, AC400

Kramer, Leonie. *The Oxford history of Australian literature*, BE854

Kramer, Maurice. *Modern American literature*, BE427, BE1069

Kramers, J. H. *Shorter encyclopaedia of Islam*, BC505

Kramers, Jacob. *Kramers' Engels woordenboek*, AC297, AC298

Kramers' Engels woordenboek, Jockin-La Bastide, J. A., AC298

—— Kramers, Jacob, AC297, AC298

Kramm, Heinrich. *Bibliographie historischer Zeitschriften, 1939–1951*, DA14

Krannert Library. *A catalogue of rare books, pamphlets, and journals on business and economics in the Krannert Library special collection, 1500–1870*, CH19

Krantz, Les. *Jobs rated almanac*, CH703

Kranz, Walter. *The Principality of Liechtenstein*, DC439

Krapf, Johann Ludwig. *Dictionary of the Swahili language*, AC756

Krarup, Alfred. *Dansk historisk bibliografi*, DC131

—— *Dansk personalhistorisk bibliografi*, AH185

Krasilovsky, M. William. *This business of music*, BJ185

Krathwohl, David R. *Methods of educational and social science research*, CC28

—— *Social and behavioral science research*, CC28

Kratkaīā geograficheskaīā ēntsiklopedīīā, CL89

Kratkaīā literaturnaīā entsiklopedīīā, BE1413

Kratkii slovar' drevnerusskogo īāzyka (XI–XVII vekov), Lunt, Horace Gray, AC671

Kratŭk bŭlgarsko-angliĭski politekhnicheski rechnik, EA105

Krat'uk spravochnik po istoriīā na Bŭlgariīā, Bobev, Bobi, DC119

—— Dakov, Todor, DC119

—— Matanov, Kristo, DC119

Kratz, Charles E. *Library personnel consultants list*, AK176

Krauch, Helmut. *Organic name reactions*, EE137

Kraus, David H. *East Central and Southeast Europe*, AK105, DC47

Kraus, Herwig. *The composition of leading organs of the CPSU (1952–1982)*, CJ394

Krause, Chester L. *Standard catalog of U.S. paper money*, BG197

—— *Standard catalog of world coins*, BG188

Krause, Gerhard. *Theologische Realenzyklopädie*, BC69

Krause, Jerry V. *Basketball resource guide*, BK64

Krause, Wolfgang. *Bibliographie der Runeninschriften nach Fundorten*, BE1082

Krauss, Harriet P. *Old master print references*, BF363

Krautz, Alfred. *International directory of cinematographers, set- and costume designers in film*, BH208

Kravchenko, H. O. *Periodychni vydannīā URSU, 1918–1950*, AD166

Kravets, Marybeth. *The K & W guide to colleges for the learning disabled*, CB313

Kravitz, Walter. *Congressional Quarterly's American congressional dictionary*, CJ206

Krawiec, T. S. *The psychologists*, CD49

Kraye, Jill. *The Cambridge history of Renaissance philosophy*, BB69

Kreider, Barbara A. *Index to children's plays in collections, 1975–1984*, BE390

Kreiswirth, Martin. *The Johns Hopkins guide to literary theory and criticism*, BE68

Krell, Robert. *Psychological and medical effects of concentration camps and religious persecution on survivors of the Holocaust*, DA215

Krendel, R. N. *Russkie pisateli vtoroi poloviny XIX nachala XX vv. (do 1917 goda)*, BE1392

Krenn, Herwig. *Bibliographie zur Transformationsgrammatik*, BD45

Kresheck, Janet. *Terminology of communication disorders*, EH122

Kress Library of Business and Economics. *Catalogue : with data upon cognate items in other Harvard libraries*, CH15

Kressel, Getzel. *Guide to the Hebrew press*, AD14

Krett, J. N. *Ukraïns'ko-anhliïs'kyi slovnyk*, AC796

Krewson, Margrit B. *Economies of the German-speaking countries of Europe*, DC9

—— *The German-speaking countries of Europe*, DC9

—— *Hidden research resources in the German collections of the Library of Congress*, DC216

—— *Immigrants from the German-speaking countries of Europe*, DC9

—— *Netherlands*, DC456

—— *The Netherlands and Northern Belgium*, DC456

Kribbs, Jayne K. *An annotated bibliography of American literary periodicals, 1741–1850*, BE422

Krichmar, Albert. *The women's movement in the seventies*, CC498

—— *The women's rights movement in the United States, 1848–1970*, CC499

Kridl, Manfred. *Literatura polska na tle rozwoju kultury*, BE1352

—— *Survey of Polish literature and culture*, BE1352

Krieg, Michael O. *Mehr nicht erschienen*, AA93

Krieg, Noel R. *Bergey's manual of systematic bacteriology*, EG309

Krieger, Joel. *The Oxford companion to politics of the world*, CJ29

Krishnaiah, P. R. *Handbook of statistics*, EB65

Kristeller, Paul Oskar. *Catalogus translationum et commentariorum*, BE999

—— *Iter Italicum*, AA206

—— *Latin manuscript books before 1600*, AA202, AA205, AA207, AA208, BE1000

—— *A microfilm corpus of the indexes to printed catalogues of Latin manuscripts before 1600 A.D*, AA208

—— *A microfilm corpus of unpublished inventories of Latin manuscripts through 1600 A.D*, AA209

Kritisch lexicon van de Nederlandstalige literatuur na 1945, BE1331

Kritisches Lexikon zur deutschsprachigen Gegenwartsliteratur, BE1247

Kritzinger, Matthys Stefanus Benjamin. *Groot woordeboek*, AC198

—— *Handige woordeboek : Afrikaans-Engels*, AC198

—— *Handy dictionary : English-Afrikaans*, AC198

Kritzler, Charles. *Catalogue of the Frederick W. and Carrie S. Beinecke collection of Western Americana*, DB170

Krivatsy, Peter. *Catalogue of incunbula and sixteenth century books in the National Library of Medicine*, EH24

—— *A catalogue of seventeenth century printed books in the National Library of Medicine*, EH24

Krleža, Miroslav. *Enciklopedija jugoslavije*, DC612

Kroe, P. Elaine. *Profile of education doctorates*, CB341

Kroff, Alexander Y. *Modern French literature and language*, BD158, BE1134

Krogstad, Jineen. *El cancionero del siglo XV, c. 1360–1520*, BE1477

Kroha, Tyll. *Lexikon der Numismatik*, BG181

Krohn, Ernst Christopher. *The history of music*, BJ109

Krol, John. *Older Americans information directory*, CC87

—— *Telecommunications directory*, CH492

Kroll, Wilhelm. *Paulys Real-Encyclopädie der classischen Altertumswissenschaft*, DA104

Kronenberg, M. E. *Nederlandsche bibliographie van 1500 tot 1540*, AA746

Kronick, David A. *Scientific and technical periodicals of the seventeenth and eighteenth centuries*, EA243

Kronk, Gary W. *Comets*, EC52

Kroschwitz, Jacqueline I. *Concise encyclopedia of polymer science and engineering*, EK284

—— *Encyclopedia of chemical technology*, EK51

—— *Encyclopedia of polymer science and engineering*, EK285

Krueger, John R. *A modern Mongolian-English dictionary*, AC614

Krug, Samuel E. *Psychware*, CD40

—— *Psychware sourcebook*, CD40

Kruger, Arthur N. *Argumentation and debate*, BE372

Kruger, Gustav. *Geschichte der römischen Literatur bis zum Gesetzgebungswerk des Kaisers Justinian*, BE1052

Krüger-Wust, Wilhelm J. *Arabische Musik in europäischen Sprachen*, BJ38

Kruk, Leonard B. *Professional Secretaries International complete office handbook*, CH87

Krumbacher, Karl. *Geschichte der byzantinischen Literatur von Justinian bis zum Ende des Oströmischen Reiches*, DA163

Krumbhaar, E. B. *A history of medicine*, EH213

Krummel, Donald William. *Bibliographical handbook of American music*, BJ39

—— *Bibliographical inventory of the early music in the Newberry Library, Chicago, Illinois*, BJ96

—— *Bibliographies*, AA5

—— *A librarian's collacon*, AK51

—— *The literature of music bibliography*, BJ40

—— *Music printing and publishing*, BJ183

—— *Resources of American music history*, BJ170

Krummes, Daniel C. *Highways*, CH444

—— *Sources of information in transportation,* CH444

Kruschke, Earl R. *Encyclopedia of third parties in the United States,* CJ261

—— *The public policy dictionary,* CJ38

Kruskal, William H. *International encyclopedia of statistics,* CG20, EB37

Krüssmann, Gerd. *Manual of cultivated broad-leaved trees & shrubs,* EG196

Kruyskamp, C. H. A. *Woordenboek der nederlandsche taal,* AC293

Kruzas, Anthony Thomas. *Medical and health information directory,* EH162

Krynski, Szymon. *A dictionary of Russian idioms and colloquialisms,* AC694

Krzyzanowska, Jadwiga. *Członkowie Polskiej Akademii Nauk,* AH280

Krzyżanowski, Julian. *A history of Polish literature,* BE1352

—— *Literatura polska,* BE1353

Kto je kto na Slovensku 1991?, AH286

Kto jest kim w Polsce, AH281

Ku, Min-chaun. *A comprehensive handbook of the United Nations,* AF33

Ku Klux Klan
encyclopedias, DB50

The Ku Klux Klan, Newton, Michael, DB50

Kubicka, Weronika. *Języki bałtyckie,* BD194

Kubiíovych, Volodymyr. *Encyclopedia of Ukraine,* DC543

Kucher, Sylvia. *Bibliographie der deutschsprachigen Lyrikanthologien, 1840–1914,* BE1272

Kudelásek, Miloslav. *Historiografie v Československu, 1970–1980,* DC124

Kuehl, Warren F. *Biographical dictionary of internationalists,* CJ66, CJ700

—— *Dissertations in history,* DA18

Kuhn, Annette. *Women in film,* BH255

Kuhn, Hans. *Edda,* BE1286

Kuhn, Martin A. *Debate index,* BE368

Kühn, Peter. *Deutsche Wörterbücher,* AC425

Kuhn, Sherman M. *Middle English dictionary,* AC175

Kuhn-Schnyder, Emil. *Handbook of paleozoology,* EF246

Kuibysheva, V. V. *Bol'shaía sovetskaía entsiklopediía,* AB84

Kuipers, B. R. *Encyclopedia of marine sciences,* EF219

Kujoth, Jean Spealman. *Subject guide to periodical indexes and review indexes,* AD250

Kuka kukin on, AH189, AH190

Kükenthal, Willy. *Handbuch der Zoologie,* EG232

Kukuljevic-Sakcinski, Ivan. *Bibliografia hrvatska,* AA843

Kukushkina, E. I. *Bibliografiía bibliografiĭ po iazykoznaniíu,* BD6

Kuldkepp, E. *Nõukogude Eesti raamat, 1955–1965,* AA608

Kulikowski, Mark. *A bibliography of Slavic mythology,* CF34

Kulkarni, V. Y. *National bibliography of Indian literature, 1901–1953,* AA897

Kullerud, Gunnar. *A bibliography on meteorites,* EF206

Kullman, Colby H. *Theatre companies of the world,* BH106

Kuløy, Hallvard Kåre. *Bibliography of Tibetan studies,* DE268

Kultermann, Udo. *New paintings,* BF307

Kulturfahrplan, Stein, Werner, DA32

Kulturhistorisk Leksikon for nordisk Middelalder fra Vikingetid til Reformationstid, DC75

—— Danstrup, John, DC76

—— Jacobsen, Lis, DC76

Kulturrådet (Sweden). *Nationalencyklopedin,* AB98

Kulwiec, Raymond A. *Materials handling handbook,* EK277

Kummel, Bernhard. *Handbook of paleontological techniques,* EF247

Kümmerly + Frey. *Peters atlas of the world,* CL287

Kunc, Jaroslav. *Česká literární bibliografie, 1945–1966,* BE1109

—— *Slovník českých spisovatelů beletristů, 1945–1956,* BE1110

—— *Slovník soudobých českých spisovatelů,* BE1110

Kungliga biblioteket (Sweden). Bibliografiska institutet. *Svensk bokforteckning,* AA832

Kungnip chungang Tosŏgwan (Seoul, Korea). *Taehan Min'guk ch'ulp'anmul ch'ongmongnok,* AA920

Kunig, Philip. *International economic law,* CK112

Kunin, Aleksandr Vladimirovich. *Anglo-russkiĭ frazeologicheskiĭ slovar',* AC695

Kunisch, Hermann. *Handbuch der deutschen Gegenwartsliteratur,* BE1248, BE1250

—— *Lexikon der deutschprachigen Gegenwartsliteratur,* BE1250

—— *Neues Handbuch der deutschen Gegenwartsliteratur seit 1945,* BE1250

Kunitz, Stanley Jasspon. *American authors, 1600–1900,* BE449

—— *British authors before 1800,* BE624

—— *British authors of the 19th century,* BE625

—— *European authors, 1000–1900,* BE204

—— *The junior book of authors,* BE384

—— *Twentieth century authors,* BE205

Kunkel, Barbara K. *Japanese scientific and technical literature,* EA49

Kunst, Jaap. *Ethnomusicology,* BJ319

—— *Musicologica,* BJ319

Kunstbibliothek (Berlin, Germany). *Katalog der Lipperheideschen Kostümbibliothek,* BG93

Kunstgeschichte in Festschriften, Rave, Paul Ortwin, BF50, BF51

Künstle, Karl. *Ikonographie der christlichen kunst,* BF186

Künstler der jungen Generation, Hesse, Gritta, BF139

Künstler Lexikon, BF148

Künstlerlexikon des XX. Jahrhunderts, BF149

Die Kunstliteratur, BF37

Kunstnerleksikon, Køie, Tove, BF147

—— Malmqvist, Ole, BF147

Kunststofftechnisches Wörterbuch, Wittfoht, Annemarie, EK292

Kuntz, Joseph M. *Poetry explication,* BE491, BE710, BE1192

Kunz, Egon F. *An annotated bibliography of the languages of the Gilbert Islands, Ellice Islands and Nauru,* DD235

Kunz, Jeffrey R. M. *The American Medical Association family medical guide,* EH171

Kunz, Werner. *Organic name reactions,* EE137

Kuo, Thomas C. *East Asian resources in American libraries,* DE106

Kuo li chung yang t'u shu kuan (China). *Chung-hua min kuo ch'u pan t'u shu mu lu,* AA938

Kuo li T'ai-wan ta hsöueh po shu shih lun wen mu lu, AG58

Küp, Karl. *Books and printing,* AA269

Kuper, Adam. *The social science encyclopedia,* CA37

Küper, Christopher. *Index of Bibliographie zur Transformationsgrammatik,* BD45

Kuper, Jessica. *A lexicon of psychology, psychiatry, and psychoanalysis,* CD24

—— *The social science encyclopedia,* CA37

Küper, Wolfgang. *Bibliography for social science research on Tanzania,* DD235

Kupferberg, Herbert. *The book of classical music lists,* BJ176

Küpper, Heinz. *Illustriertes Lexikon der deutschen Umgangssprache,* AC429

—— *Pons Wörterbuch der deutschen Umgangssprache,* AC430

Kurath, Hans. *Middle English dictionary,* AC175, AC176

A Kurdish-English dictionary, McCarus, Ernest Nasseph, AC567

—— Wahby, Taufiq, AC568

Kurdish language
dictionaries
bilingual
Kurdish-English, AC567, AC568

The Kurds, Izady, Mehrdad R., DE59

Kurian, George Thomas. *Encyclopedia of the First World,* CJ28

—— *Encyclopedia of the Second World,* CJ28

—— *The encyclopedia of the Third World,* CJ28, CJ35, CJ39, CJ96

—— *Geo-data,* CL90

—— *Glossary of the Third World,* CJ39

—— *Historical and cultural dictionary of India,* DE167

—— *The new book of world rankings,* CG51

—— *Sourcebook of global statistics,* CG10

—— *World education encyclopedia,* CB127

—— *World encyclopedia of cities,* CL64

—— *World encyclopedia of police forces and penal systems,* CK255

—— *World press encyclopedia,* AE142

Kurikka, Jussi. *Suomen aikakauslehdistön bibliografia 1782–1955,* AD89

Kurland, Philip B. *The founders' constitution,* CK171

Kuroki, Tsutomu. *An introduction to Japanese government publications,* AF251

Kurpis, Gediminas P. *The new IEEE standard dictionary of electrical and electronics terms,* EK131

Kurrens idõszaki kiadványok, AD123

Kürschner Nekrolog, 1901–1935, BE1059

Kürschner Nekrolog, 1936–1970, Schuder, Werner, BE1059

Kürschners deutscher Gelehrten-Kalender, AH209, BE1060

Kürschners deutscher Literatur-Kalender, AH209, BE1059, BE1060

Kürschners Deutscher Reichstag, CJ331

Kürschners Volkshandbuch Deutscher Bundestag, CJ331

Kurtz, L. S. *Tanzania,* DD48

Kurucz, György. *Guide to documents and manuscripts in Great Britain relating to the Kingdom of Hungary from the earliest times to 1800,* DC387

Kurz, Otto. *La letteratura artistica,* BF37

Kurze Quellenkunde des west-europäischen Mittelalters, DA127

Kurzes Verzeichnis sämmtlicher in Deutschland und den angrenzenden Landern gedruckter Musikalien, BJ16

Kurzgefasstes etymologisches Wörterbuch des Altindischen, Mayrhofer, Manfred, AC707, AC708

Kurzweil, Arthur. *From generation to generation,* AJ13

Kuscinski, August. *Dictionnaire des conventionnels,* AH198

Kushner, Gilbert. *Human rights and anthropology,* CE13

Kusin, Vladimir. *Czechoslovakia, 1968–1969,* DC123

Kuter, Lois. *The anthropology of Western Europe,* CE93

Kutsch, K. J. *Grosses Sängerlexikon,* BJ214

Kutsche, Paul. *Guide to Cherokee documents in the northeastern United States,* CC420

Kutscher, E. Y. *Hebräisches und aramäisches Lexikon zum Alten Testament,* AC481, AC482

al-Kutub al-'Arabīyah allati nushirat fī Miṣr fi al-qarn al-tāsi' 'ashar, Nuṣayr, 'Āydah Ibrāhīm, AA854

Kutz, Myer. *Mechanical engineers' handbook,* EK243

Kutzbach, Karl August. *Autorenlexikon der Gegenwart,* BE1054

Kuvshinoff, Boris W. *Desktop computers,* EK206

Kuvshinoff, C. M. *Desktop computers,* EK206

Kuwait
statistics, CG408

Kuwait (by subject)
history
bibliography, DE220

Kuwait, Clements, Frank A., DE220

Kuwait University. Libraries Department. *Arab dissertation index,* AG51

Kuznetsov, Ivan Vasil'evich. *Gazetnyi mir Sovetskogo Soiuza, 1917–1970 gg*, AE73

Kuznetsova, I. V. *Liudi russkoĭ nauki*, EA178

Kuznetsova, M. I. *Velikaia Oktiabr'skaia sotsialisticheskaia revoliutsiia*, DC601

Kuznetsova, T. R. *Gosudarstvennye (natsional'nye) bibliograficheskie ukazateli sotsialisticheskikh stran*, AA396

Kvasil, Bohumil. *Malá československá encyklopedie*, AB30

Kvavik, Robert B. *Directory of Scandinavian studies in North America*, DC77

Kwafo-Akoto, Kate O. *Women in Ghana*, DD163

Kwamena-Poh, Michael. *African history in maps*, DD65

KWIC index of international standards, EA273

Kyes, Robert L. *Germanic and its dialects*, BD113

Kykkōtēs, Hierotheos. *English-modern Greek and modern Greek-English dictionary*, AC464

Kyle, Hedi. *Library materials preservation manual*, AK241

Kypriakē vivliographia, AA590

Kyriakidēs, Stilpōs P. *Hellēnikē bibliographia*, AA705

Kyrychenko, I. M. *Ukrainsko-russkii slovar'*, AC795

Kyryliuk, IE. P. *Istoriia ukraïns'koï literatury*, BE1493

Kyvig, David E. *New day/New Deal*, DB128

La Beau, Dennis. *Theatre, film, and television biographies master index*, BH28

La Brie, Henry. *Survey of black newspapers in America*, AE15

La Chesnaye-Desbois, François Alexandre Aubert de. *Dictionnaire de la noblesse ... de la France ...*, AJ86

La Cour, Donna Ward. *Artists in quotation*, BF95

La Croix du Maine, François Grudé. *Les bibliothèques françoises de La Croix du Maine et de Du Verdier*, AA616

La Moureyre-Gavoty, Françoise de. *French sculptors of the 17th and 18th centuries*, BF399

La Point, Velma. *Black children and American institutions*, CC140

La Roche, Nancy. *Synonym finder*, AC140

La Rocque, Aurèle. *Contributions to the history of geology*, EF101

La Sor, William Sanford. *Bibliography of the Dead Sea Scrolls, 1948–1957*, BC112

Laak, Ursula. *Bibliographie zur Zeitgeschichte, 1953–1989*, DA169

Laan, Kornelis ter. *Van Goor's aardrijkskundig woordenboek van Nederland*, CL146

Labandeira Fernández, Amancio. *Bibliografía hispanoamericana y filipina*, BE876, DE248

L'Abate, Luciano. *Family therapy*, CC227

Labes, Bertrand. *Guide Mont Blanc des prix et concours littéraires*, BE177

LABFAX series, EG55

LaBlanc, Michael L. *The world encyclopedia of soccer*, BK98

Labor and industrial relations
  abstract journals, CH646
  annuals, CH673
  bibliography, CH460, CH632, CH634, CH640
  chronologies, CH673
  dictionaries, CH654
  directories, CH661
  encyclopedias, CC566, CH650, CK29
  handbooks, CH666, CH672, CH674
  indexes, CH643
  library catalogs, CH640, CH641, CH642
  manuscripts, CH642
  periodicals, CH656, CH659, CH688
  statistics, CH644, CH680, CH681, CH682, CH684, CH685, CH688, CH689, CH690, CH691
    bibliography, CH639
  thesauruses, CH652
Labor and industrial relations (by country or region)
  Germany
    bibliography, CH626, CH627

Great Britain
  bibliography, CH625, CH638, CH679
  biography, CH679
  dissertations, CH295, DC283
  encyclopedias, CH649
  statistics, CH683
Ireland
  dissertations, CH295, DC283
Italy, CH628
  periodicals, CH657
United States, CH647
  bibliography, CH633, CH637
  history, CH651, CH675, CH676
  statistics, CH687
Labor and industrial relations (by subject)
  history, DB99
  see also **Trade unions**
Labor and industrial relations, Kelly, Matthew A., CH672
Labor and industrial relations journals and serials, Vocino, Michael C., CH659
Labor conflict in the United States, CH647
Labor fact book, Labor Research Association (U.S.), CH674
Labor force statistics derived from the Current population survey, CH685
Labor law (by country or region)
  Great Britain, CH677
  Ireland, CH677
Labor-personnel index, CH646
Labor relations reporter, CH673
Labor relations yearbook, CH673
Labor Research Association (U.S.). *Labor fact book,* CH674
Labor union periodicals, CH624, CH635
Labor unions *see* **Trade unions**
Labor unions, CH648
Laboratories
  databases, EA213, EA214
  directories, EA213, EA214, EA215
  handbooks, EE71, EE88
Laboratories (by country or region)
  Pacific Rim, EA146
Laboratory animals, EG235, EG295, EJ129
Laboratory handbook of toxic agents, EE75
Laboratory medicine, EH109
Laboratory safety, EE71, EE88
Laboratory techniques in archaeology, Ellis, Linda, DA64
•*LABORDOC,* CH652
Labors of love, Dockstader, Frederick J., BG156
Labour and social history theses, Gilbert, Victor Francis, CH295, DC283
Labour force estimates and projections, 1950–2000, CH680
Labour force projections, 1965–1985, CH680
Labour information, CH632
Labour law documents, International Labour Office, CK69
Labour law in Great Britain and Ireland to 1978, Hepple, B. A., CH677
Labour statistics, CH691
Labudy, Gerarda. *Słownik starożytności słowiańskich,* DC53
Laby, T. H. *Tables of physical and chemical constants and some mathematical functions,* ED44
Labys, Walter C. *Primary commodity markets and models,* CH434
Lace
  bibliography, BG162
  dictionaries
    multilingual, BG162
  handbooks, BG161, BG162
Lace (by subject)
  history, BG152, BG160
Lace and lace-making, Powys, Marian, BG161
Lace guide for makers and collectors, Whiting, Gertrude, BG162
Lachèvre, Frédéric. *Bibliographie des recueils collectifs de poésies du XVIᵉ siècle,* BE1193
—— *Bibliographie des recueils collectifs de poésies publiés de 1597 à 1700 ... ,* BE1193, BE1194

—— *Bibliographie sommaire de l'Almanach des muses (1765–1833),* BE1195
—— *Recueils collectifs de poésies libres et satiriques publiés depuis 1600 ... ,* BE1194
Lachman, Marvin. *Detectionary,* BE267
Lachmann, Richard. *The encyclopedic dictionary of sociology,* CC18
Lachs, John. *Marxist philosophy,* CJ504
Lack, Elizabeth. *A dictionary of birds,* EG257
Lack, Jean. *Who owns what in world banking,* CH281
Lackie, J. M. *The dictionary of cell biology,* EG32, EG341
Laclavère, Georges. *Atlas de la Republique du Zaire,* CL339
—— *Atlas de la République Islamique du Mauritanie,* CL339
—— *Atlas de la République Unie du Cameroun,* CL339
Lacombe, Américo Jacobina. *Introdução ao estudo da história do Brasil,* DB339
Lacroix, Paul. *Bibliothèque dramatique de Pont de Vesle,* BE1184
Lactation, EH341
Lacy, Norris J. *Arthurian encyclopedia,* BE343
—— *The Arthurian handbook,* BE342
—— *The new Arthurian encyclopedia,* BE343
Lacy, Robin Thurlow. *A biographical dictionary of scenographers, 500 B.C. to 1900 A.D,* BH114
Ladas, Geōrgios G. *Hellēnikē vivliographia,* AA702
Ladenson, Alex. *American library laws,* AK172
Ładogórski, Tadeusz. *The historical atlas of Poland,* DC482
Ladusaw, William A. *Phonetic symbol guide,* BD10, BD15
Lael, Richard L. *Versailles and after,* DB127
Laffin, John. *Brassey's battles,* DA25
Laffont, Robert. *Dizionario letterario Bompiani delle opere e dei personaggi di tutti i tempi e di tutte le letterature,* BE63
Laffont-Bompiani, BE63
Lafon, Michel. *Bibliographie analytique des langues parlées en Afrique subsaharienne, 1970–1980,* BD213
Lafond, Mireille. *Recueil de theses africanistes, droit et science politique 1967–1984,* DD29
Lafont, Pierre-Bernard. *Bibliographie du Laos,* DE222, DE223
LaFrance, David G. *Latin American military history,* DB258
Lafrance, Yvon. *Les présocratiques,* BB58
Lagane, René. *Dictionnaire du français classique,* AC376
—— *Grand Larousse de la langue française,* AC329
Lagardère, Laure. *L'architecture dans les collections de périodiques de la Bibliothèque Forney,* BF225
Laguerre, Michel S. *The complete Haitiana,* DB440
Lahiri, Ashok. *Compendium of Indian elections,* CJ431
—— *India decides,* CJ431
Lai, Shu Tim. *25 T'ang poets,* BE1552
Laing, Dave. *Encyclopedia of rock,* BJ345
—— *The Faber companion to 20th-century popular music,* BJ348
Laing, Ellen Johnston. *Chinese paintings in Chinese publications,* BF313
—— *Index to reproductions of paintings by twentieth century Chinese artists,* BF313
Laing, John. *Dictionary of anonymous and pseudonymous English literature,* AA150
Laing, William E. *Newspaper indexes in the Newspaper and Current Periodical Room,* AE102
Laird, Betty A. *A Soviet lexicon,* CJ395
Laird, Roy D. *A Soviet lexicon,* CJ395
Laitin, David D. *Somalia,* DD207
Lajha, Abel. *Handbook of neurochemistry,* EH184
Lake, Carlton. *Dictionary of modern painting,* BF300
Lake, Celinda C. *Public opinion polling,* CJ491
Lakes, CL61, EF8
Lakos, Amos. *International terrorism,* CJ550
—— *Terrorism 1980–1990,* CJ550

Lakshminarasimha Moorty, C. *Reasearch [sic] trends in Sanskrit*, BD197

Lal, Jagdish. *Indian periodicals in print, 1973*, AD190

Lal, Manohar. *India information sources, economics and business*, CH196

Lal, Monan. *Encyclopaedia of Indian literature*, BE1565

Lalande, André. *Vocabulaire technique et critique de la philosophie*, BB41

Lalande, Joseph Jérôme le Français de. *Bibliographie astronomique*, EC16

Lalis, Anthony. *Lietuviškos ir angliškos kalbu žodynas*, AC601

Lallemand, Maurice. *Dictionaire du français vivant*, AC327

Lamar, Howard R. *The reader's encyclopedia of the American West*, DB174

Lamarche, Rolande. *La francité canadienne*, BD162

Lamb, Andrew. *Gänzl's book of the musical theatre*, BJ262

Lamb, Connie. *Jewish American fiction writers*, BE564

Lamb, J. A. *Fasti ecclesiae Scoticanae*, BC342

Lamb, Malcolm. *Directory of officials and organizations in China, 1968–1983*, CJ430

Lamb, Roger. *The dictionary of developmental and educational psychology*, CD82

—— *The dictionary of ethology and animal learning*, CD119

—— *The dictionary of personality and social psychology*, CD95

—— *The dictionary of physiology and clinical psychology*, CD99

—— *The encyclopedic dictionary of psychology*, CD22, CD82, CD95, CD99, CD119

Lamb, Ruth S. *Bibliografía del teatro mexicano del siglo XX*, BE914

—— *Mexican theatre of the twentieth century*, BE914

Lambda book report, CC265

Lambert, Monique. *Répertoire national des annuaires français, 1958–1968*, AD93

Lambert, Ronald D. *The sociology of contemporary Quebec nationalism*, CJ301

Lambert, Sheila. *House of Commons sessional papers of the eighteenth century*, AF200

—— *Printing for Parliament, 1641–1700*, AF188

Lambert's worldwide government directory, CJ82

Lambin, Petr Petrovich. *Russkaia istoricheskaia bibliografiia 1855–64*, DC580

Lambrecht, Kalman. *Palaeontologi*, EF252

Lambrino, Scarlat. *Bibliographie de l'antiquité classique, 1896–1914*, BE1001

Lame, Danielle de. *Société, culture et histoire du Rwanda*, DD198

Lami, Stanislas. *Dictionnaire des sculpteurs de l'antiquité*, BF395

—— *Dictionnaire des sculpteurs de l'école française ...*, BF395

Lämmert, Eberhard. *Handbuch der deutschen Exilpresse 1933–1945*, AD101

Lamonde, Yvan. *Guide de la littérature québécoise*, BE844

Lamothe, Ruth. *Guide to programs in nursing in four-year colleges and universities*, EH282

Lampe, David. *Cities of opportunity*, CL72

Lampe, Geoffrey William Hugo. *Cambridge history of the Bible*, BC191

—— *A patristic Greek lexicon*, AC457

Lampe, Kenneth F. *AMA handbook of poisonous and injurious plants*, EG152

Lana, Gabriella. *Glossary of geographical names in six languages*, CL91

Lancashire, Ian. *Dramatic texts and records of Britain*, BE662

Lancaster, Albert. *Bibliographie générale de l'astronomie jusqu'en 1880*, EC6, EC13, EC14

Lancaster, F. Wilfrid. *Indexing and abstracting in theory and practice*, AK213

Lancaster, Henry Carrington. *The Comédie Française, 1680–1701*, BE1180

—— *French tragedy in the reign of Louis XVI and the early years of the French Revolution, 1774–1792*, BE1182

—— *French tragedy in the time of Louis XV and Voltaire, 1715–1774*, BE1182

—— *History of French dramatic literature in the 17th century*, BE1181, BE1182

—— *Sunset*, BE1182

Lancaster, Henry Oliver. *Bibliography of statistical bibliographies*, EB13

Lancaster, Lewis. *Buddhist scriptures*, BC466

Lancaster, Michael. *The Oxford companion to gardens*, BF290

Lancour, Harold. *American art auction catalogues, 1785–1942*, BF110, BF120

—— *Encyclopedia of library and information science*, AK36

Land und Leute in deutscher Erzählung, Luther, Arthur, BE1267

Landau, Sidney I. *The Doubleday Roget's thesaurus in dictionary form*, AC138

—— *International dictionary of medicine and biology*, EG38, EH100

Landau, Thomas. *Encyclopaedia of librarianship*, AK37

Landes, William-Alan. *Western European costume, 13th to 17th century, and its relation to the theatre*, BG107

Landeskunde DDR, Sperling, Walter, DC267

Landforms *see* **Geomorphology**

Landi, Val. *The Bantam great outdoors guide to the United States and Canada*, BK107

Landis, Dennis Channing. *European Americana*, AA404

Landmark yellow pages, BF265

Landolt, Hans Heinrich. *Zahlenwerte und Funktionen aus Physik, Chemie, Astronomie, Geophysik und Technik*, EA155

Landolt-Börnstein Zahlenwerte und Funktionen aus Naturwissenschaften und Technik, Hellwege, K. H., EA155

Landon, Grelun. *The encyclopedia of folk, country, & western music*, BJ326

Landsberg, Helmut E. *The history of geophysics and meteorology*, EF97

—— *World survey of climatology*, EF167

Landscape architecture
bibliography, BF286, BF288
biography, BF294
dictionaries, BF291, BF292
encyclopedias, BF290, BF292
handbooks, BF295
indexes, BF289

Landscape architecture (by subject)
restoration and conservation, BF287, BF293

Landscape vocabulary, Marsh, Warner L., BF292

Landsford, Edwin M. *The encyclopedia of biochemistry*, EG325

Landshagir, CG249

Landy, Eugene E. *The underground dictionary*, AC126

Lane, Alfred H. *Gifts and exchange manual*, AK166

Lane, Carol McCrory. *Modern Irish literature*, BE805

Lane, Denis. *Modern British literature*, BE600

—— *Modern Irish literature*, BE805

Lane, Dermot A. *The new dictionary of theology*, BC407

Lane, Edward William. *Arabic-English lexicon*, AC218

Lane, Judy. *International directory of legal aid*, CK59

Lane, Margaret T. *Selecting and organizing state government publications*, AF138

—— *State publications*, AF137

—— *State publications and depository libraries*, AF139

Lane, Nancy D. *A guide to commonwealth government information sources*, AF263

Lane, W. C. *A.L.A. portrait index*, BF65

Lane-Poole, Stanley. *Arabic-English lexicon*, AC218

Lang, David Marshall. *A guide to Eastern literatures*, BE1544

Lang, Helmut W. *200 Jahre Tageszeitung in Österreich, 1783–1983*, AE44

Lang, Jenifer Harvey. *Larousse gastronomique*, EJ211

Lang, Jovian. *Dictionary of liturgy*, BC427

Lang, Jovian P. *Reference sources for small and medium-sized libraries*, AA358

Lang, Kenneth R. *Astrophysical data*, EC53

—— *Astrophysical formulae*, EC54, ED45

—— *Source book in astronomy and astrophysics, 1900–1975*, EC62

Lang, L. Maurice. *Annuaire des ventes de tableaux, dessins, aquarelles, pastels, gouaches, miniatures*, BF108

—— *Cote des tableaux*, BF108

Lang, Valerie. *Bibliographic classification*, AK198

Langdon, Robert. *Thar she went*, DF9

—— *Where the whalers went*, DF9

Lange, Dagmar. *Women and the First World War in England*, DA194

Lange, Morten. *Collins guide to mushrooms and toadstools*, EG187

—— *Guide to mushrooms & toadstools*, EG187

Lange, Norbert Adolph. *Lange's handbook of chemistry*, EE77

Langenscheidt's condensed Muret-Sanders German dictionary, AC417

Langenscheidt's new Muret-Sanders encyclopedic dictionary of the English and German languages, AC417, AC418

Langenscheidt's standard Turkish dictionary, Akdikmen, Resuhi, AC789

Langer, Eduard. *Bibliographie der österreichischen Drucke des XV. und XVI. Jahrhunderts*, AA573

Langer, William Leonard. *The new illustrated encyclopedia of world history*, DA35

Lange's handbook of chemistry, Lange, Norbert Adolph, EE77

Langevin, Paul-Emile. *Bibliographie biblique*, BC113

Langford, Eugenia. *Biographical and historical index of American Indians and persons involved in Indian affairs*, CC436

Langford-James, Richard Lloyd. *A dictionary of the Eastern Orthodox church*, BC449

Langhans, Edward A. *A biographical dictionary of actors, actresses, musicians, dancers, managers & other stage personnel in London, 1660–1800*, BH112

—— *Eighteenth century British and Irish promptbooks*, BH42

—— *An international dictionary of theatre language*, BH79

Langley, Winston E. *Human rights : sixty major global instruments*, CK113

Langlois, Claude. *Atlas de la Révolution française*, DC190

Langlois, Ernest. *Table des noms propres de toute nature compris dans les chansons de geste imprimées*, BE1164

Langmaid, Janet. *The Nazi era, 1919–1945*, DC236

Langman, Larry. *Encyclopedia of American film comedy*, BH252

—— *A guide to American film directors*, BH209

—— *A guide to American screenwriters*, BH210

—— *Writers on the American screen*, BH215

Langosch, Karl. *Die deutsche Literatur des Mittelalters*, BE1253

Langstaff, Eleanor De Selms. *Panama*, DB320

Langton, John. *Atlas of industrializing Britain 1780–1914*, DC300

Language and language behavior abstracts, BD31

Language and literature of the Anglo-Saxon nations as presented in German doctoral dissertations, 1885–1950, Mummendey, Richard, BD155, BE594, BE1071

Language and sex, Henley, Nancy, BD82

—— Thorne, Barrie, BD82

Language and the brain, Dingwall, William Orr, BD78, CD117

Language arts, CB118

Language, gender, and society, Henley, Nancy, BD82, BD84, CC495
———— Kramarae, Cheris, BD82, BD84, CC495
———— Thorne, Barrie, BD82, BD84, CC495
Language map of Africa and the adjacent islands, Dalby, David, BD217
The language of American popular entertainment, Wilmeth, Don B., BH12
Language of biotechnology, Cox, Michael, EK45
———— Walker, John M., EK45, EK46
Language of cities, Abrams, Charles, BF277, CC293
The language of colloid and interface science, Schramm, Laurier Lincoln, EE45
Language of fashion, Picken, Mary (Brooks), BG100
The language of journalism, Kent, Ruth K., AE139
The language of real estate, Reilly, John W., CH536
The language of sex, Carrera, Michael, CC280
The language of sport, Considine, Tim, BK24
The language of the foreign book trade, Orne, Jerrold, AA276
Language of the underworld, Maurer, David W., AC129
The language of twentieth century music, Fink, Robert, BJ149
The language of visual effects, McAlister, Micheal J., BH259
Language origins, Hewes, Gordon Winant, BD56
Language teaching, CB118
  abstract journals, BD74, CB58
  abstracts, CB62
  bibliography, BD72, BD75
  dictionaries, BD77
Language teaching, BD74, CB58
Language teaching & linguistics, BD74, CB58
Language-teaching abstracts, BD74, CB58
A language-teaching bibliography, Centre for Information on Language Teaching, BD72
Language transfer, BD80
Languages
  abbreviations, BD40
  abstract journals, BD31
  atlases, BD20
    bibliography, BD21
  bibliography, AC195, BD2, BD6, BD22, BD26, BE39
    current, BD1, BD23, BD24, BD25, BD27, BD28
  bibliography of bibliography, BD8
  classification, BD16, BD19
  dialects, BD13, BD57
  dictionaries, BD37
    multilingual, BD42
  encyclopedias, BD32, BD33, BD34, BD35
  handbooks, AK50, BD12, BD13, BD17
Languages (by country or region)
  Asia
    dictionaries, AC194
  Europe, AK46, BD11
    bibliography, BD85
  The Americas
    bibliography, BD175
Languages (by subject)
  acquisition
    bibliography, BD62, BD63
  history, BD19
  identification, BD14
  origins, BD56
  phonetic transcription, BD15
  sex differences
    bibliography, BD82, BD84, CC495
  social aspects, BD19
  study and teaching
    bibliography, BD71, BD73, BD76
  transliteration, BD10
  writing systems, AK50, BD12, BD14, BD17, BD18
Languages identification guide, Giliarevskii, R. S., BD14, BD18
Languages of the aboriginal southeast, Booker, Karen M., CC420
Languages of the world, Klose, A., BD13
The languages of the world, ancient and modern, Wemyss, Stanley, BD18

Langue et littérature berbéres, Galand, Lionel, DD68
Langues, cultures et éducation au Maghreb, Moatassime, Ahmed, DD72
Langues du monde, Cohen, Marcel, BD12
———— Meillet, Antoine, BD12
Lanham, Richard A. *A handlist of rhetorical terms,* BE356
Lanjouw, Joseph. *Index herbariorum,* EG153
Lankutis, Jonas. *Tarybų Lietuvos rašytojai,* BE1325
Lanman, Charles. *Biographical annals of the civil government of the United States,* CJ140
Lansky, Ralph. *Bibliographisches Handbuch der Rechts– und Verwaltungswissenschaften,* CK15
———— *Grundliteratur Recht,* CK206, CK211
———— *Handbuch der Bibliographien zum Recht der Entwicklungsländer,* CK15, CK16
Lanson, Gustave. *Histoire de la littérature française,* BE1172
———— *Histoire illustré de la littérature française,* BE1172
———— *Manual illustré de la litterature française,* BE1172
———— *Manuel bibliographique de la littérature française moderne, XVIᵉ, XVIIᵉ, XVIIIᵉ, et XIXᵉ siècles,* BE1137
Lantzy, M. Louise. *The Individuals with Disabilities Education Act,* CB156
Lao-English dictionary, Kerr, Allen D., AC569
Lao language, AC569
Laos, DE222, DE223
  bibliography, DE221
  encyclopedias, DE224
  statistics, CG409
Laos (by subject)
  history
    bibliography, DE221
    encyclopedias, DE224
Laos, Cordell, Helen, DE221
———— Henchy, Judith A. N., DE222
———— Sage, William W., DE222, DE223
Lapedes, Daniel N. *Diccionario de términos científicos y técnicos,* EA133
———— *McGraw-Hill encyclopedia of food, agriculture & nutrition,* EJ23
Lapidge, Michael. *A bibliography of Celtic-Latin literature, 400–1200,* BE1042
Lapidus, Dorothy Farris. *The Facts on File dictionary of geology and geophysics,* EF75
Laporte Molina, Juan Pedro. *Bibliografía de la arqueología guatemalteca,* DB308
Lappish language, AC570
Lappisk (samisk) ordbok, Nielsen, Konrad, AC570
Lapps ethnographic bibliography, O'Leary, Timothy J., CE94
Lapuente, Felipe-Antonio. *Diccionario de seudónimos literarios españoles, con algunas iniciales,* AA185
Laqueur, Walter. *Dictionary of politics,* CJ33
Lara Valdez, Josefina. *Diccionario biobibliográfico de escritores contemporaneos de México,* BE907
Lardet, Pierre. *Renaissance linguistics archive, 1350–1700,* BD67
Larence's dealer print prices 1992, BF371
Large print books and serials, AA429
The larger English-Persian dictionary, Hayyim, Sulaymān, AC314
Larina, B. A. *Etimologicheskiĭ slovar' russkogo iazyka,* AC691
Larkin, Colin. *The Guinness encyclopedia of popular music,* BJ347
Larkin, Gregory V. *American and Canadian doctoral dissertations and master's theses on Africa, 1974–1987,* DD32
Larkin, Robert P. *Biographical dictionary of geography,* CL83
———— *Dictionary of concepts in human geography,* CL38
———— *Dictionary of concepts in physical geography,* CL37
LaRoche, Nancy. *Picturesque expressions,* AC81
Larousse, Pierre. *Grand dictionnaire universel du XIXᵉ siècle,* AB42, AB46
———— *Petit Larousse illustré, 1990,* AC333

Larousse cultural, Brasil A/Z, DB352
Larousse de la musique, BJ117, BJ120
Larousse des citations françaises et étrangères, BE129
Larousse dictionnaire du français contemporain, AC372
Larousse du XXᵉ siècle, AB43
Larousse encyclopedia of animal life, EG302
Larousse encyclopedia of mythology, CF8
Larousse (Firm). *Grand Larousse de la langue française,* AC329
Larousse gastronomique, Montagné, Prosper, EJ211
Larousse modern French-English [English-French] dictionary, AC341
Larrazábal Henríquez, Osvaldo. *Bibliografía del cuento venezolano,* BE964
Larrucea de Tovar, Consuelo. *Catálogo de las lenguas de América del Sur,* BD243
Larsen, John C. *Researcher's guide to archives and regional history sources,* DB35
Larsgaard, Mary Lynette. *Cartographic citations,* CL263
———— *Map librarianship,* CL264
Larson, Carl F. W. *American regional theatre history to 1900,* BH43
Larson, Gerald James. *Sāmkhya,* BB33
Larson, Henrietta Melia. *Guide to business history,* CH395
Larson, Jeanne. *Seeds of peace,* CJ689
Larson, W. S. *Bibliography of research studies in music education, 1932–1948,* BJ164
LaRue, C. Steven. *International dictionary of opera,* BJ249
LaRue, Jan. *The symphony,* BJ295
LaRue, Rodrigue. *Clavis scriptorum Graecorum at Latinorum,* BD147
Lasers
  handbooks, EC49, ED34
Láska, Václav Jan. *Atlas Republiky Československé,* CL322
Laskin, Allen I. *CRC handbook of microbiology,* EG54, EG56
Laskin, Emily J. *The American Film Institute guide to college courses in film and television,* BH263
Lass, Abraham Harold. *Dictionary of pronunciation,* AC107
———— *Facts on File dictionary of classical, biblical, and literary allusions,* BE86
———— *Facts on File dictionary of twentieth-century allusions,* BE86
Lass, Betty. *Dictionary of pronunciation,* AC107
Last, John M. *A dictionary of epidemiology,* EH410
Last, Rex. *The Arthurian bibliography,* BE339
Last lines, Kline, Victoria, BE317
The last word, CC544
Lasteyrie du Saillant, Robert Charles. *Bibliographie générale des travaux historiques et archéologiques publiés par les sociétés savantes de la France,* DC213, EA208
Laszlo, Ervin. *World encyclopedia of peace,* CJ686
Latchman, Omeela K. *Practical guide to Canadian legal research,* CK195
Late 19th century U.S. Army, 1865–1898, Dawson, Joseph G., CJ608
Late Georgian and Regency England, 1760–1837, Smith, Robert A., DC303, DC320
Late-medieval England, 1377–1485, Guth, DeLloyd J., DC303, DC307
Late reviews AEB, 1947–1984, Egberts, A., DA121
———— Hovestreydt, W., DA121
———— Nederlands Instituut voor het Nabije Oosten, DA121
———— Zonhoven, L. M. J., DA121
Lateinamerikanische Autoren, Reichardt, Dieter, BE893
Lateinisches etymologisches Wörterbuch, Walde, Alois, AC584
Later American plays, 1831–1900, Roden, Robert F., BE464
Later Georgians and early Victorians, Kilmurray, Elaine, BF66
The later Jacobean and Caroline dramatists, Logan, Terence P., BE651

Latham, Alison. *The Norton/Grove concise encyclopedia of music,* BJ143
Latham, Ronald Edward. *Dictionary of medieval Latin from British sources,* AC588
—— *Revised medieval Latin word-list from British and Irish sources,* AC589
Latham, Roy. *The dictionary of computer graphics technology and applications,* EK182
Lathem, Edward Connery. *Chronological tables of American newspapers, 1690–1820,* AE26
Lathrop, Lorin Andrews. *Rhymers' lexicon,* AC115
Lathrop, Mary Lou. *Lathrop report on newspaper indexes,* AE101
Lathrop, Norman W. *Lathrop report on newspaper indexes,* AE101
Lathrop report on newspaper indexes, AE102
—— Lathrop, Mary Lou, AE101
—— Lathrop, Norman W., AE101
Latin America
　abstract journals, AD248
　archives, DB280
　bibliography, AA468, AA469, AA470, AA471, BE874, BE876, DB266, DB268, DE245, DE248
　　current, AA473, AA474, AA475, AA476
　bibliography of bibliography, AA24, AA25
　biobibliography, BE896
　biography, AH110, AH111, AH287, CJ306, CJ310, DB296
　　bibliography, AH112, AH113
　　indexes, AH112
　databases, BE874, DB266
　directories, DB285, DB288, DB295
　dissertations, CA22
　encyclopedias, DB281, DB282
　government publications
　　bibliography, AF159
　　periodicals, AF158
　guides, DB251, DB257
　guides to records, DB275, DB277, DB280
　handbooks, DB295
　library catalogs, DB270
　library resources, AK111
　newspapers, AE4
　　union lists., AE40
　periodicals, AD64, AD65, AD67, AD68, AF158
　　databases, AD296
　　indexes, AD295, AD296, AD297, AD298, AD299
　　　bibliography, AD248
　sourcebooks, DB277, DB292, DB293
　statistics, CG38, CG120, CG124
　　bibliography, CG71, CG72
　　periodicals, CG121
　surveys, DB293
　yearbooks, DB294
Latin America (by subject)
　anthropology and ethnology, CE78
　archaeology and ancient history
　　bibliography, DB253
　art, BF22, BF70
　censuses, CG122
　　handbooks, CG38
　economic conditions
　　bibliography, DB256
　　indexes, CH177
　economic history, CH180
　ethnic attitudes
　　encyclopedias, CC387
　folklore and popular culture, DB289
　　bibliography, CF61
　foreign relations, DB286
　foreign relations (by country or region)
　　Canada, DB261
　　Europe, DB264
　　United States, DB284
　historiography, DB296
　history, DB259
　　atlases, DB297
　　bibliography, BE876, DB252, DB271, DC506, DC509, DE248
　　dissertations, DB267, DC510
　　guides to records, DB61, DB273, DB274
　　library catalogs, DB269

　sourcebooks, DB291
　immigration
　　bibliography, CC309
　law, CK198
　　bibliography, CK199
　migration
　　bibliography, CC315
　military history
　　bibliography, DB258
　politics and government, AH110, CJ306, CJ307, CJ308, CJ309
　　bibliography, DB254, DB255, DB256
　　biography, AH111, CJ310
　　encyclopedias, DB283
　population
　　abstract journals, CG123
　social conditions
　　bibliography, DB256
　women, CC608
Latin America, CH180
—— Delorme, Robert, DB256
—— Griffin, Charles Carroll, DB257
—— Plano, Jack C., CJ311, CJ312
—— Rossi, Ernest E., CJ309, CJ311, CJ312
Latin America and Caribbean contemporary record, DB294
Latin America and Caribbean review, CH191
Latin America and Latin American periodicals, Harvard University. Library, DB270
Latin America and the Caribbean, DB251
—— Bayitch, S. A., DB257
Latin America : economy and society, 1870–1930, DB291
Latin America in Soviet writings, Okinshevich, Leo, DB260
Latin America in the nineteenth century, Wilgus, Alva Curtis, DB263, DB409
Latin America since 1930, DB291
Latin America weekly report, DB293
Latin American and Caribbean official statistical serials on microfiche, CG154
Latin American Bibliographic Foundation (Redlands, Calif.). *Nicaraguan national bibliography, 1800–1978,* AA491
Latin American bibliography, Garlant, Julia, DB252
Latin American Center for Research in the Social Sciences. *Estratificación y movilidad social en el Uruguay,* DB397
Latin American directory, DB285
Latin American drama
　biobibliography, BE899
　indexes, BE898
Latin American fiction, BE902
Latin American gay and lesbian narrative, Foster, David William, BE402
Latin American historical dictionaries, DB282
Latin American history, Humphreys, R. A., DB257
—— Lombardi, Cathryn L., DB297
Latin American Jewish studies, Elkin, Judith Laikin, BC526
Latin American Jewry, Sable, Martin Howard, BC526
Latin American labor organizations, CH667
Latin American literary authors, Zubatsky, David S., BE881, BE1445
Latin American literature
　bibliography, BE868, BE869, BE872, BE874, BE875, BE876, BE901, BE903, DB266, DE248
　bibliography of bibliography, BE881
　biobibliography, BE888, BE889, BE892, BE893
　biography, BE891
　criticism, BE887
　encyclopedias, BE431
　guides, BE867, BE1429
　handbooks, BE431, BE866
　library catalogs, BE875
　translations, BE885, BE886, BE893
　　bibliography, BE1074
　　indexes, BE884
　women authors
　　translations, BE883
Latin American literature (by subject)
　history, BE867, BE895, BE1429

Latin American literature, Harvard University. Library, BE875
Latin American literature in English translation, Shaw, Bradley A., BE886
Latin American markets, CH375
Latin American Marxism, Vanden, Harry E., CJ513
Latin American military history, DB258
Latin American monitor, DB293
Latin American newspapers in United States libraries, AE40
—— Charno, Steven M., AE12
Latin American pamphlets from the Yale University Library, DB271
Latin American play index, Hoffman, Herbert H., BE898
Latin American poetry, BE885
Latin American poetry in English translation, Hulet, Claude L., BE885
Latin American political dictionary, Plano, Jack C., CJ309
—— Rossi, Ernest E., CJ309
Latin American political movements, Ó Maoláin, Ciarán, CJ97
Latin American popular culture, DB289
Latin American population abstracts, CG123
•*Latin American Population Documentation System,* CG123
Latin American prose in English translation, Hulet, Claude L., BE885
Latin American racial and ethnic terminology, CC460
Latin American regional reports, DB293
Latin American research review, DB319, DB343, DB358
Latin American revolutionaries, Radu, Michael, CJ308
Latin American serial documents, AF158
Latin American serials list, University of Texas at Austin. Library. Latin American Collection, DB270
The Latin American short story, BE903
Latin American studies, DB252, DB260
　atlases, DB297
　bibliography, DB265
　biography, DB287
　directories, DB287
　periodicals
　　guides for authors, AD26
Latin American studies, DB252, AD296, BE874, DB266
Latin American studies in the non-Western world and Eastern Europe, Sable, Martin Howard, DB260
Latin American women writers in English translation, Corvalán, Graciela N. V., BE883
Latin American writers, BE891
Latin American writers in English translation, Jones, Willis Knapp, BE885
A latin dictionary, AC574
Latin drama
　bibliography, BE995
Latin language
　bibliography, BD142, BD143, BD150
　dictionaries, AC571, AC572, AC573, BE1047
　　bibliography, AC595
　　bilingual, AC574, AC576, AC577, AC578
　　　English, AC575
　　Christian and medieval, AC454
　　early Christian era, AC581, AC582, AC583
　　etymology, AC584
　　medieval, AC585, AC586, AC587, AC588, AC589, AC590, AC591, AC592, AC593
　　pronunciation, AC594
　　Syriac, AC771
　etymology, AC580
　　dictionaries, AC579
　medieval
　　bibliography, BD145, BD146, BD147
　pronunciation
　　bibliography, BD144
Latin literature
　bibliography, AA207, BE999, BE1000, BE1005, BE1037, BE1038, BE1040, BE1041, BE1044, BE1045, BE1053

biography, BE1025
Celtic authors
  bibliography, BE1042
collections, BE1002
encyclopedias, BE1013
handbooks, AA207, BE999, BE1000, BE1041,
  BE1048
library catalogs, BE1039
translations, BE1002, BE1010
  Spanish, BE1043
Latin literature (by country or region)
  England, BE1049
Latin literature (by period)
  medieval, BE1049, BE1050, BE1051
    bibliography, BE1042
    biobibliography, BE993
Latin literature (by subject)
  criticism, BE996
  history, BE1020, BE1050, BE1051, BE1052,
    BE1053
  influence studies, BE1043
Latin literature, Harvard University. Library,
  BE1039
——— Kenney, E. J., BE1020
Latin manuscript books before 1600, Kristeller, Paul
  Oskar, AA202, AA205, AA207, AA208, BE1000
Latin poetry
  indexes, BE1046
Latin words & phrases for lawyers, CK53
Latinas, CC614, CC617, DB262
  biography, AH78
  indexes, CC454, CC528
Latinas of the Americas, Stoner, K. Lynn, CC617,
  DB262
*Latinitas italicae medii aevi inde ab a. CDLXXVI
  usque ad a. MXXII lexicon imperfectum cura et
  studio Francisci Arnaldi,* Arnaldi, Francesco,
  AC585
Latino literature, BE560
  bibliography, BE511, BE557, BE558, BE559
  biography, BE561, BE562, BE563
  guides, BE556
Latino studies, CC316
Latinos, CC467
  bibliography, AD47, CC444, CC449, CC453,
    CC458, CC596
  biography, AH81, BE562, CC470
  book reviews, CC316
  databases, CC455
  dictionaries, CC460
  directories, CC461, CC462, CC463
  handbooks, CC466
  indexes, AD267, CC456
  newspapers, AE31
  periodicals, AE31
    indexes, AD267, CC456
  statistics, CC471, CG84
Latinos (by subject)
  art, BF20
  folklore and popular culture, CF68
  historic sites
    guides, CC464
  history, CC448, CC468
  language, BD176
  material culture, CC465
  names, AJ178, AJ187
  proverbs, CC459
Latourette, Kenneth Scott. *Atlas zur
  Kirchengeschichte,* BC288
——— *A history of the expansion of Christianity,*
  BC306
Latvia, DC434, DC437
  bibliography, AA739, DC70
  encyclopedias, DC435, DC436
  manuscripts and archives, AK153, DC561
Latvia, Ozols, Selma Aleksandra, DC437
Latvian-English dictionary, AC599
Latvian language
  bibliography, BD194
  dictionaries, AC598
    bilingual
      English-Latvian, AC596, AC597
      Latvian-English, AC598, AC599

Latvian literature, BE1319, BE1320, BE1321
  handbooks, BE989
Latvian literature under the Soviets, 1940–1975,
  Ekmanis, Rolfs, BE1319
Latviešu-anglu vārdnīca, Turkina, Eiženija, AC599
Latviešu pirmspadomju literatūra, BE1320
Latviešu trimdas izdevumu bibliografija, 1940–1960,
  Jēgers, Benjamins, AA739
Latvijas PSR arheologija, 1940–1974, Caune,
  Andris, DC434
Latvijas PSR mazā enciklopēdija, DC436
Latzina, Francisco. *Diccionario geográfico
  argentino,* CL118
Lau, Niels. *International economic law,* CK112
Laučka, A. *Anglų-lietuvių kalbų žodynas,* AC600,
  AC604
Lauer, Joseph J. *American and Canadian doctoral
  dissertations and master's theses on Africa,
  1974–1987,* DD32
Lauerhass, Ludwig. *Communism in Latin America,*
  CJ513
——— *Education in Latin America,* CB43
Lauffer, Siegfried. *Daten der griechischen und
  römischen Geschichte,* DA111
Laughlin, Ledlie Irwin. *Pewter in America,* BG151
Laundy, Philip. *An encyclopaedia of Parliament,*
  CJ353
Launonen, Hannu. *Suomen kirjailijat 1917-1944,*
  BE1127
——— *Suomen kirjailijat, 1945–1970,* BE1127
Laurenti, Joseph L. *Bibliografía de la literatura
  picaresca,* BE1475
——— *Bibliography of picaresque literature,*
  BE1475
Laures, John. *Kirishitan bunko,* BC307
Laurich, Robert Anthony. *AIDS and women,* EH29
Laurie Blum's free money for private schools, CB90,
  CB93
Lauritzen, Einar. *American film-index, 1908–1915,*
  BH189
——— *American film-index, 1916–1920,* BH189
Lauter, Paul. *The Heath anthology of American
  literature,* BE441
Lauther, Howard. *Lauther's complete punctuation
  thesaurus of the English language,* AC110
*Lauther's complete punctuation thesaurus of the
  English language,* Lauther, Howard, AC110
Laval, Ramón Arminio. *Bibliografía de bibliografías
  chilenas,* AA514
Lavaud, Suzanne. *Catalogue des thèses de doctorat
  ès sciences naturelles, soutenues à Paris de 1891
  à 1954,* EA56
Laver, James. *Concise history of costume,* BG109
——— *Costume and fashion,* BG109
Laverde Amaya, Isidoro. *Bibliografía colombiana,*
  AA524
Lavin, Michael R. *Business information,* CH4
Lavine, Irvin. *Scientific and technical abbreviations,
  signs and symbols,* EA99
Law, Derek G. *Royal Navy in World War Two,*
  DA200
Law
  abbreviations, CK42, CK43, EA96
  bibliography, CK4, CK5, CK7, CK8, CK11,
    CK12, CK13, CK20, CK21, CK122, CK126,
    CK212
    current, CK18, CK19, CK120
  bibliography of bibliography, CK15, CK16,
    CK17
  collections, CK69, CK71
  databases, CK22, CK26
  dictionaries, CK33, CK34, CK36, CK37, CK38,
    CK39, CK40, CK61
    abbreviations, CK41
    bilingual
      Chinese-English, CK47
      English-Japanese, CK51
      French-English, CK48
      German-English, CK49
      Italian-English, CK50
      Latin-English, CK53
      Portuguese-English, CK54
      Spanish-English, CK55

  multilingual, CK41, CK44, CK46
  directories, CK58, CK58
  encyclopedias, CK29, CK30, CK31, CK32
  festschriften, CK6
  guides, CK1, CK2, CK3, CK115, CK117
  handbooks, CK65
  indexes, CK22, CK24, CK25, CK26, CK27,
    CK28
  library catalogs, CK11
  quotations, CK57
  style manuals, CK66
  thesauruses, CK56
Law (by country or region)
  Africa
    bibliography, CK225
  Asia, West, CK227
  Australia, CK235
  Austria
    bibliography, CK206
  Benelux nations, CK202
  Canada
    dictionaries, CK35
    guides, CK195
    indexes, CK23
  Caribbean
    bibliography, CK200
  China, CK228
  Commonwealth, CK14
    bibliography, CK20
  Denmark
    bibliography, CK207
  Europe, Western
    bibliography, CK20
  European Communities, CK203, CK204
  France, CK208
    guides, CK209
  Germany, CK210
    bibliography, CK211
  Great Britain
    bibliography, CK20, CK217, CK220
    dictionaries, CK34, CK38
    encyclopedias, CK215
    guides, CK2, CK218, CK219
  India, CK229
  Indonesia, CK230
  Israel, CK231
  Italy
    guides, CK222
  Japan
    bibliography, CK232
  Latin America, CK198
    bibliography, CK199
  Mexico, CK197
    bibliography, CK196
  Nigeria, CK226
  Oceania, CK234, CK236
  Russia and the U.S.S.R., CK223
  Switzerland, CK224
  United States
    bibliography, CK122, CK124, CK125, CK126,
      CK128
      current, CK18, CK120
      periodicals, CK123
    collections, CK165, CK166
    directories, CK150
    encyclopedias, CK129, CK131, CK132,
      CK133, CK135, CK136
    formbooks, CK164
    guides, CK115, CK116, CK118, CK119
    handbooks, CK159, CK161, CK163
    states, CK181
      bibliography, CK121
    statistics, CK168, CK169, CK269
    statutes
      states, CK179
Law (by subject)
  history
    bibliography, CK12
  libraries and library resources, AK172
  see also **Commercial law; International law;**
    Labor law; Maritime law
Law and art, BF122

Law and judicial systems of nations, World Peace Through Law Center, CK65
Law and legal information directory, CK150
Law books, 1876–1981, CK13
Law books in print, Triffin, Nicholas, CK21
Law books published, CK21
Law Council of Australia. *Australian legal directory,* CK233
Law dictionary, CK50
—— Gifis, Steven H., CK37
Law dictionary for nonlawyers, Oran, Daniel, CK40
Law dictionary, Portuguese-English, English-Portuguese, CK54
Law, educational *see* **School law**
Law firms yellow book, CH350
Law for the layman, Houdek, Frank G., CK126
Law in Japan, CK232
Law information, CK18
Law information update, CK18
The law librarian's professional desk reference and diary, CK161
Law libraries, CK2
  biography, AK81
  directories, CK137, CK213
Law Library Microform Consortium. *The Harvard legal bibliography, 1961–1981,* CK11
Law, medicine & health care, Ziegenfuss, James T., EH271
The law of the sea, CK79
Law, school *see* **School law**
Law School Admission Council. *The official guide to U.S. law schools,* CK154
Law School Admission Services (U.S.). *The official guide to U.S. law schools,* CK154
Law schools
  directories, CK63, CK106, CK138
Law schools (by country or region)
  United States
    directories, CK154
Lawless, Ilona Maria. *Haiti,* DB441
Lawless, Ray McKinley. *Folksingers and folksongs in America,* BJ320
Lawless, Richard I. *Algeria,* DD18
—— *Morocco,* DD18
—— *Tunisia,* DD18
Lawless, Robert. *Bibliography on Haiti,* DB441
—— *Haiti,* DB441
Lawrence, Alberta. *Who's who among living authors of older nations,* BE211
Lawrence, Eleanor. *Henderson's dictionary of biological terms,* EG43
Lawrence, George H. M. *B-P-H,* EG111
Lawrence, Robert M. *Strategic Defense Initiative,* CJ606
Lawry, John D. *Guide to the history of psychology,* CD55
Laws, Edward R. *Handbook of pesticide toxicology,* EJ52
The laws of England, CK215
The laws of Manu, BC92
Laws of Puerto Rico annotated, Puerto Rico. [Laws, etc.], CK179
The laws of Scotland, CK215
Lawson, Alan. *Australian literature,* BE852
Lawson, Edward. *Encyclopedia of human rights,* CK99
Lawton, Denis. *A guide to English educational terms,* CB76
Lawton, Henry. *Psychohistorian's handbook,* DA5, DA43
Lawyer referral services, CK143
The lawyer statistical report, Curran, Barbara A., CK167
Lawyers
  directories, CK60, CK62, CK158
Lawyers (by country or region)
  Australia
    directories, CK233
  Canada
    directories, CK194
  Great Britain
    directories, CK216, CK221

United States
  directories, CK141, CK142, CK151, CK152, CK155
  statistics, CK167
The lawyer's almanac, CK161
Lawyer's diary and desk reference, CK161
Lawyers' law books, Raistrick, Donald, CK220
Lawyer's monthly catalog, CK120
Lax, Roger. *The great song thesaurus,* BJ286
Laying down the law, Morris, Gwen, CK235
Layman, Richard. *Child abuse,* CC171
Laymon, Charles M. *Interpreter's one-volume commentary on the Bible,* BC175
Layton, Robert. *The Penguin guide to compact discs and cassettes,* BJ379
Lazar, Yisrael. *ha-Milion he-ḥadash,* AC483
Lazarov, Mikhail. *Bŭlgariia na balkanite, 1944–1974,* DC62, DC114
Lazarus, John. *Opera handbook,* BJ247
Lazić, Branko M. *Biographical dictionary of the Comintern,* CJ533
Lazio, Carole. *Archaeology on film,* DA62
LC classification, additions and changes, Library of Congress. Subject Cataloging Division, AK202
LC classification outline, Library of Congress. Office for Subject Cataloging Policy, AK202
•*LC MARC,* AK220
•*LC MARC : GPO monthly catalog,* AF111
LC science tracer bullet, Library of Congress. Science and Technology Division. Reference Section, EA35
LCJC : Liste collective des Journaux canadiens, AE38
LCSH, AK220
Le Fanu, William Richard. *Lives of the fellows of the Royal College of Surgeons of England, 1930–1951,* EH230
Le Jeune, Jean Marie. *Dictionnaire général de biographie, histoire, littérature, [etc.],* DB198
Le Maitre, R. W. *A classification of igneous rocks and glossary of terms,* EF255
Le Neve, John. *Fasti ecclesiae Anglicanae,* BC331
Le Page, R. B. *Dictionary of Jamaican English,* AC157
Le Petit, Jules. *Bibliographie des principales éditions originales d'écrivains français du XVe aux XVIIIe siècle,* BE558
Le Roux, J. H. *Bibliographies on South African political history,* CJ410, DD213
Le Roux, R. *Grand dictionnaire français-breton,* AC238
Le Sage, Laurent. *Dictionnaire des critiques littéraires,* BE1159
LEA : librarians, editors, authors, AA471
Leab, Daniel J. *American working class history,* CH637
Leabhair Gaeilge i gCló, AA723
Leach, Chris. *The psychologist's companion,* CD43
Leach, Maria. *Funk and Wagnalls standard dictionary of folklore, mythology and legend,* CF51
Leach, Marjorie. *Guide to the gods,* BC62
Leach, Steven G. *Libraries in American periodicals before 1876,* AK9
Leacy, F. H. *Historical statistics of Canada,* CG113, DB209
Leadenham, Carol A. *Guide to the collections in the Hoover Institution archives relating to Imperial Russia, the Russian revolutions and civil war, and the first emigration,* DC564
Leaders in anthropology, Kinton, Jack F., CE68
Leaders in education, CB131
Leaders of Malaya, AH362, AH369
Leaders of the Soviet Republics, 1955–1972, Hodnett, Grey, CJ392
Leaders of twentieth-century China, Wu, Eugene, AH347
Leadership, CD126
Leadership, CJ590
Leadership abstracts and bibliography, 1904 to 1974, Stogdill, Ralph Melvin, CH608
Leaffloor, Lorne B. *Publications of the Geological Survey of Canada, 1917–1952,* EF33

League of Historic American Theatres. *Directory of historic American theatres,* BH110
League of Nations. *Catalog of publications, 1930–35,* AF28
—— *Treaty series,* CK85, CK86, CK89, CK90
League of Nations
  bibliography, AF27
  publications, AF27, AF28, AF29
  yearbooks, CG52
League of Nations. Economic, Financial, and Transit Department. *Annuaire statistique de la Société des Nations,* CG52
League of Nations & United Nations monthly list of selected articles, United Nations Library (Geneva), CH23
League of Nations documents, 1919–1946, Reno, Edward A., AF29
Leal, Luis. *Bibliografía del cuento mexicano,* BE912
—— *Literatura Chicana,* BE558
A learner's dictionary of Arabic and Persian quotations, Field, Claud, BE124
Learning, CD110, CD114
Learning AIDS, EH21
Learning disabilities resource guide, CB202
Learning disabled, CB207
  bibliography, CB190, CB193
  directories, CB200, CB313, CC193
  handbooks, CB205
Learning disabled (by subject)
  education, CB202
  education, higher, CB312, CB313, CB314, CB315
Learning disabled, CB315
Learning the library, Beaubien, Anne K., AK229
Learning to look, Taylor, Joshua Charles, BF124
Learning to teach, AK231
The learning traveler, CB242, CB244
Leary, Lewis Gaston. *American literature,* BE397
—— *Articles on American literature, 1900–1950,* BE408, BE473, BE826
—— *Articles on American literature, 1950–1967,* BE408
—— *Articles on American literature, 1968–1975,* BE408
—— *Reference guide to American literature,* BE449
Leary, William M. *Airline industry,* CH383
Leavitt, Judith A. *American women managers and administrators,* AH77, CH101
—— *Women in administration and management,* CH606
—— *Women in management,* CH606
Leavitt, Sturgis Elleno. *Revistas hispanoamericanas,* AD299
Lebanon
  bibliography, DE225
  biography, AH360
  statistics, CG410
Lebanon. Mudīriyat al-Iḥṣā' al-Markazī. *al-Majmū'ah al-iḥṣa'iyah al-Lubnānīyah,* CG410
Lebanon, Bleaney, C. H., DE225
Lebed, Andreĭ I. *Party and government officials of the Soviet Union, 1917–1967,* CJ393
—— *Who was who in the USSR,* AH304
Lebedev, Aleksandr Vasil'evich. *A guide to mathematical tables,* EB74
Lebedev-Polianskii, P. I. *Literaturnaia entsiklopediia,* BE1414
Lebel, Gustave. *Bibliographie des revues et périodiques d'art parus en France de 1746 à 1914,* BF46
Leben und Arbeit von Frauen, Frauenforschung und Frauenbewegung in Afrika, Maurer, Margarete, DD7
Leboeuf, J. Arthur. *Complément au Dictionnaire généalogique Tanguay,* AJ73
Leccese, Michael. *The bicyclist's sourcebook,* BK72
Lechevalier, Hubert A. *CRC handbook of microbiology,* EG54, EG56
Lecker, Robert. *The annotated bibliography of Canada's major authors,* BE819
—— *Canadian writers and their works: fiction series,* BE819

—— *Canadian writers and their works: poetry series*, BE819

Leclaire, Lucien. *A general analytical bibliography of the regional novelists of the British Isles, 1800–1950*, BE677

Leclère, Christian. *Dictionnaire de l'argot*, AC355

Leclerq, Henri. *Dictionnaire d'archéologie chrétienne et de liturgie*, BC246

LeCompte, Margaret Diane. *The handbook of qualitative research in education*, CB113

Lectionary for Mass, Catholic Church, BC422

—— Catholic Church. Liturgy and ritual, BC424

Lectionary of music, Slonimsky, Nicolas, BJ158

Lectuur-Repertorium, BE1332

Lederberg, Joshua. *Encyclopedia of microbiology*, EG22

Lederer, Charles Michael. *Table of isotopes*, ED42, ED46

Lederer, Herbert. *Handbook of East German drama, 1945–1985*, BE1265

Lederman, Ellen. *College majors*, CB275

Lee, Antoinette J. *Buildings of the District of Columbia*, BF254

Lee, Cuthbert. *Portrait register*, BF65

Lee, David R. *Women and geography*, CL16

Lee, Don Y. *An annotated bibliography on inner Asia*, DE75

Lee, Joel M. *Who's who in library and information services*, AK93

Lee, Joseph. *Irish historiography, 1936–70*, DC414

Lee, Lauren K. *The elementary school library collection*, AA341

Lee, Mien-min. *The Facts on File English/Chinese visual dictionary*, AC259

Lee, R. Alton. *Encyclopedia USA*, DB47

Lee, Sherman E. *History of Far Eastern art*, BF132

Lee, Sidney. *Dictionary of national biography*, AH226

Lee, Tanya H. *-ologies & -isms*, AC79

Lee, Thomas H. *A guide to East Asian collections in North America*, AK108, DE104

Lee, Wei-chin. *Taiwan*, DE264

Lee, Yang Ha. *A Korean-English dictionary*, AC565

Leech, Clifford. *The Revels history of drama in English*, BE467, BE667

Leeds University Romany catalogue, CC479

Lees, Stephen. *Who's who of British Members of Parliament*, CJ362

Leeuwen, Jan van. *Handbook of theoretical computer science*, EK205

Leeward Islands, DB444

Lefebvre, Verna M. *Index to research in home economics, 1972–1991*, EJ197

Lefèvre, M. J. *First aid manual for chemical accidents*, EE78

Leffall, Dolores. *Black English*, BD103

Lefferts, Robert. *Getting a grant in the 1990s*, AL92

Lefond, Stanley J. *Handbook of world salt resources*, EF199

The left in Britain, Spiers, John, CJ509

Left in Britain during 1973 and 1974, Pidduck, William, CJ509

The left index, CJ516

Left-radical movements in South Africa and Namibia 1900–1981, Böhmer, Elizabeth W., DD113

Leftwich, A. W. *A dictionary of zoology*, EG229

Leftwing social movements in Japan, Uyehara, Cecil H., CJ512

The legal 500, CK221

Legal aid
  directories, CK59, CK144

Legal bibliography index, CK17

A legal bibliography of the British Commonwealth of Nations, CK14

Legal deposit bulletin, AA853

A legal guide for lesbian and gay couples, Curry, Hayden, CC288

Legal guide for the visual artist, Crawford, Tad, BF122

Legal issues and older adults, Millman, Linda Josephson, CC99

Legal journals index, CK28

Legal literature and conditions affecting legal publishing in the Commonwealth Caribbean, Newton, Velma, CK200

Legal looseleafs in print, Eis, Arlene L., CK122

Legal newsletters in print, Eis, Arlene L., CK123

Legal research, CK235

—— Elias, Stephen, CK117

Legal research guide, CK218

Legal research handbook, MacEllvan, Douglass T., CK195

Legal research illustrated, Jacobstein, J. Myron, CK118

—— Mersky, Roy M., CK118

Legal research in a nutshell, Cohen, Morris L., CK115

—— Olson, Kent C., CK115

The legal researcher's desk reference, CK161

Legal resource directory, Bosoni, Anthony J., CK144

•*Legal resource index*, CK22

Legal systems, European Free Trade Association, CK204

Legal thesaurus, Burton, William C., CK56

Legal-wise, Battle, Carl W., CK164

•*LegalTrac on InfoTrac*, CK22

Légaré, Yves. *Dictionnaire des écrivains québécois contemporains*, BE841

LeGear, Clara E. *Guide to historical cartography*, CL240

LeGear, Clara Egli. *United States atlases*, CL237

Leggat, Portia. *Union list of of architectural records in Canadian public collections*, BF210

Legge, James. *Chinese classics*, BE1555

•*Legi-Slate*, AF67

Legislation
  databases, AF64, AF67
  guides, CJ195
  periodicals, CJ207, CJ208, CJ209
Legislation (by country or region)
  United States
    guides, CJ194, CJ196
Legislation (by subject)
  state and local government, CJ281
Legislative bodies (by country or region)
  United States, CJ116

The legislative drafter's desk reference, Filson, Lawrence E., CJ194

Legislators, CJ210
  archives, CJ201, CJ202
  biography, CJ157, CJ212, CJ214, CJ221, CJ230, CJ232
  directories, CJ214, CJ221, CJ222, CJ272

Legrand, Emile Louis Jean. *Bibliographie albanaise*, AA572

—— *Bibliographie hellénique*, AA701, AA702, AA703, AA704

—— *Bibliographie ionienne*, AA703

Leguay, Thierry. *L'obsolète*, AC377

Leguizamón, Julio A. *Bibliografía general de la literatura hispanoamericana*, BE877

—— *Historia de la literatura hispanoamericana*, BE877

Legum, Colin. *Middle East contemporary survey*, DE61

LeHir, Yves. *Essai de bibliographie critique de stylistique française et romane (1955–1960)*, BE1072

Lehmann, Jakob. *Kleines deutsches dramalexikon*, BE1263

Lehmann, Stephen. *Women's studies in Western Europe*, CC626

Lehmann, Winfred Philipp. *A Gothic etymological dictionary*, AC440

Lehmann-Haupt, Hellmut. *The book in America*, AA303

Lehmer, Derrick H. *Guide to tables in the theory of numbers*, EB73

Lehmer, Derrick Henry. *Guide to tables in the theory of numbers*, EB75

Lehner, Ernst. *Symbols, signs and signets*, BF169

Lehner, Lois. *Lehner's encyclopedia of U.S. marks on pottery, porcelain & clay*, BG71

Lehner, Philip N. *Handbook of ethological methods*, CD123

Lehner's encyclopedia of U.S. marks on pottery, porcelain & clay, Lehner, Lois, BG71

Lehnus, Donald J. *Angels to zeppelins*, BG198

Lehra-Spławińskiego, Tadeusza. *Słownik starożytności słowiańskich*, DC53

LEI, AC538

Leibniz, Gottfried Wilhelm, BB75

Leibniz, Gabel, Gernot U., BB75

Leibniz-Bibliographie, BB75

Leich, Harold M. *Russian imperial government serials on microfilm in the Library of Congress*, AD144, AF214

Leick, Gwendolyn. *Dictionary of ancient Near Eastern architecture*, BF243

Leiden Afrika-Studiecentrum. *African studies abstracts*, DD45

Leider, Morris. *A dictionary of dermatologic terms*, EH111

Leigh, Carol. *Southern African material in anthologies of English literature in the Strange Library of Africana*, BE1537

Leigh, G. J. *Nomenclature of inorganic chemistry*, EE112

Leigh, Robert. *Index to song books*, BJ287

Leighton, Philip D. *Planning academic and research library buildings*, AK175

Leininger, Phillip. *Benét's reader's encyclopedia of American literature*, BE431

Leistner, Otto. *Internationale Bibliographie der Festschriften von den Anfängen bis 1979*, AA125

—— *ITA*, AD22, BE1019

Leisure, BK109
  bibliography, BK5, BK8

The leisure literature, BK5

Leisure, recreation and tourism abstracts, EJ19

Leitenberg, Milton. *Vietnam conflict*, DE95

—— *The wars in Vietnam, Cambodia and Laos, 1945–1982*, DE95

Leiter, Richard A. *National survey of state laws*, CK180

Leiter, Samuel L. *Encyclopedia of the New York stage, 1920–1930*, BH98, BH100

—— *Shakespeare around the globe*, BE792

Die leitfaden für Presse und Werbung, AD103

Leitzmann, Johan Jakob. *Schriften über Münzkunde*, BG173

Lejeune, Fritz. *Deutsch-Englisches, Englisches-Deutsches Wörterbuch für Aerzte*, EH136

—— *German-English, English-German dictionary for physicians*, EH136, EH140

Leksikon jugoslavenske muzike, BJ151

Leksikon pisaca Jugoslavije, BE1498

Leksikon pseudonymorum Estonicorum, AA167

Leksikon Yehudah ye-Shomron, CJ436

Leland, Charles Godfrey. *Dictionary of slang, jargon & cant*, AC118

Lem, G. A. C. van der. *Repertorium van geschiedschrijvers in Nederland, 1500–1800*, DC461

LeMaistre, Catherine C. *A search for environmental ethics*, EK65

Lemáitre, Henri. *Dictionnaire Bordas de littérature française et francophone*, BE1160

Lemay, J. A. Leo. *A bibliographical guide to the study of Southern literature*, BE574

—— *A calendar of American poetry in the colonial newspapers and magazines and in the major English magazines through 1765*, BE501

Leming, James S. *Contemporary approaches to moral education*, CB15

—— *Foundations of moral education*, CB15

Lemire, Maurice. *Dictionnaire des oeuvres littéraires du Québec*, BE837

Lemke, Robert F. *Standard catalog of U.S. paper money*, BG197

Lemmer, Manfred. *Deutscher Wortschatz*, AC426

Lemoine, Bertrand. *Revues d'architecture et de construction en France au XIX siècle*, BF46

Lempereur, Agnès. *Dictionnaire général des sciences humaines*, CA42

Łempicka, Zofia. *Maly słownik języka polskiego*, AC630

Lenček, Rado L. *A bibliography of recent literature on Macedonian, Serbo-Croatian, and Slovene languages*, BD189

Lender, Mark Edward. *Dictionary of American temperance biography*, CC138

Lengenfelder, Helga. *Handbuch der Bibliotheken Bundesrepublik Deutschland, Österreich, Schweiz*, AK138

—— *International bibliography of specialized dictionaries*, AC192, EA95

—— *World guide to libraries*, AK121

Leningrad. Publichnaia Biblioteka. *Russkie sovetskie pisateli-prozaiki*, BE1393

Lennartz, Franz. *Deutsche Schriftsteller der Gegenwart*, BE1258

—— *Deutsche Schriftsteller des 20. Jahrhunderts im Speigel der Kritik*, BE1258

Lenski, Wolfgang. *[Omega]—bibliography of mathematical logic*, EB15

Lent, John A. *Malaysian studies*, DE231

—— *Women and mass communications*, CC500

Lent, Robert W. *Handbook of counseling psychology*, CD105

Lentricchia, Frank. *Critical terms for literary study*, BE61

Lentz, Harris M. *Assassinations and executions*, CJ551

Leo, John R. *Guide to American poetry explication*, BE491

Leo Rosten's treasury of Jewish quotations, Rosten, Leo, BE121

León, Juan. *Demografía en el Ecuador*, CG153

León, Manuel Darío de. *Diccionario histórico dominicano*, DB436

León, Nicolás. *Bibliografía mexicana del siglo XVIII*, AA462

Léon-Dufour, Xavier. *Dictionary of biblical theology*, BC144

—— *Dictionary of the New Testament*, BC145

Leonard, Harold. *The film index*, BH172

Leonard, Robin. *A legal guide for lesbian and gay couples*, CC288

Leonard, Ruth S. *Bibliography of works on accounting by American authors*, CH247

Leonard, Steve. *Electronic music dictionary*, BJ313

Leonard, William Torbert. *Theatre*, BH20

Leonard Maltin's movie and video guide, Maltin, Leonard, BH198

Leonard Maltin's TV movies and video guide, BH198

Leonardi, Claudio. *Medioevo latino*, DA144

Leonard's annual price index of art auctions, BF111

Leonard's annual price index of prints, posters & photographs, BF371

LePage, Jane Weiner. *Women composers, conductors, and musicians of the twentieth century*, BC314, BJ207, BJ215

Lépine, Pierre. *Dictionnaire français-anglais, anglais-français des termes médicaux et biologiques*, EH141

Lepointe, Gabriel. *Bibliographie en langue française d'histoire du droit*, DC149

—— *Éléments de bibliographie sur l'histoire des institutions et des faits sociaux, 987–1875*, DC149

—— *Histoire des institutions et des faits sociaux de la France*, DC149

Lepreux, Georges. *Gallia typographica*, AA308

Lerminier, Georges. *Littérature française*, BE1167

Lerner, Loren R. *Art and architecture in Canada*, BF31

Lerner, Ralph. *The founders' constitution*, CK171

Lerner, Ralph E. *Art law*, BF122

Lerner, Richard M. *Encyclopedia of adolescence*, CC159, CD83

Lerner, Rita G. *Encyclopedia of physics*, ED16

Leroi-Gourhan, André. *Dictionnaire de la préhistoire*, DA78

Lerond, Alain. *Dictionnaire du français classique*, AC376

Lerski, Halina T. *Jewish-Polish coexistence, 1772–1939*, DC471

Lerski, Jerzy J. *Jewish-Polish coexistence, 1772–1939*, DC471

Les Brown's encyclopedia of television, Brown, Les, BH313

Lesbian and gay couples, CC288

Lesbian periodicals index, Potter, Clare, CC271, CC286

Lesbian sources, Garber, Linda, CC271

Lesbian studies, CC272

Lesbianism, CC272, CC273
  bibliography, CC268, CC271, CC274
  book reviews, CC265
  directories, CB290
  encyclopedias, CC277
  periodicals, CC285, CC559
    indexes, CC271, CC286
  see also **Homosexuality**

Lesbianism, Maggiore, Dolores J., CC273

Lesbians
  biography, BE402

Lescrauwaet, Josephus F. *Critical bibliography of ecumenical literature*, BC276

Lesko, Barbara S. *A dictionary of Late Egyptian*, AC302

Lesko, Leonard H. *A dictionary of Late Egyptian*, AC302

Lesko, Matthew. *The federal data base finder*, AF65

Lesky, Albin. *Geschichte der Griechischen literatur*, BE1034

—— *A history of Greek literature*, BE1034

Leslau, Wolf. *Comparative dictionary of Ge'ez (Classical Ethiopic)*, AC312

—— *Concise Amharic dictionary*, AC210

—— *English-Amharic context dictionary*, AC209, AC211

Leslie, Serge. *A bibliography of the dance collection of Doris Niles and Serge Leslie*, BH133

Lesly, Philip. *Lesly's handbook of public relations and communications*, CH568

Lesly's handbook of public relations and communications, CH568

Lesly's public relations handbook, CH568

Lesothana, DD170

Lesotho
  bibliography, DD18, DD117, DD169, DD170
  encyclopedias, DD48
  government publications
    bibliography, AF218
  statistics, CG338

Lesotho (by subject)
  status of women, DD122, DD171

Lesotho. Bureau of Statistics. *Lesotho statistical yearbook*, CG338

Lesotho, Ambrose, David P., DD18, DD170

—— Gordon, Loraine, DD169

—— Haliburton, Gordon, DD48

—— Willet, Shelagh M., DD18, DD170

Lesotho statistical yearbook, CG338

Lesser, Charles H. *Fighters for independence*, DB89

Lesser, Stephen O. *American screenwriters*, BH280

Lessico etimologico italiano, Pfister, Max, AC538

Lessing, Ferdinand D. *Mongolian-English dictionary*, AC615

Lester, Daniel W. *Checklist of United States public documents, 1789–1976*, AF95

—— *Cumulative title index to United States public documents, 1789–1976*, AF96

Lester, DeeGee. *Immigrants from Great Britain and Ireland*, CC332, DC402

—— *Irish research*, CC312, CC332, DC402

Lester, Katherine Morris. *An illustrated history of those frills and furbelows of fashion which have come to be known as: accessories of dress*, BG110

Lester, Lorraine E. *Cumulative title index to United States public documents, 1789–1976*, AF96

Lester, Marilyn A. *Checklist of United States public documents, 1789–1976*, AF95

Lester, Marion. *The big book of buttons*, BG105

Lester-Massman, Elli. *Women, race, and ethnicity*, CC625

Lesure, François. *Catalogue de la musique imprimée avant 1800*, BJ72, BJ73

—— *Dictionnaire des éditeurs de musique française*, BJ180

Letitia Baldrige's complete guide to the new manners for the 90's, Baldrige, Letitia, AL152

Letopis' avtoreferatov dissertatsiĭ, AA796, AG46

Letopis' gazetnykh stateĭ, AE103

Letopis na periodichnaia pechat, AA589

Letopis na periodichnia pechat, AD304, AD305, AE46

Letopis na statiite ot bŭlgarskite spisaniia i sbronitsi, AD304

Letopis na statiite ot bŭlgarskite spisaniia i sbornitsi, AD305

Letopis na statiite ot bulgarskite vestnitsi, AD304, AE46

Letopis' periodicheskikh i prodolzhaiushchikhsia izdanii, AD150

Letopis' periodicheskikh i prodolzhaiushchikhsia izdanii. Biulleteni, AE74

Letopis' periodicheskikh i prodolzhaiushchikhsia izdanii. Sborniki, AD149, AE74

Letopis' periodicheskikh izdaniĭ SSSR, AD150, AE74

Letopis' zhurnal'nykh stateĭ, AD325

La letteratura artistica, Schlosser, Julius, Ritter von, BF37

Lettish language *see* **Latvian language**

Lettres françaises de Belgique, Frickx, Robert, BE1100

Leuchtmann, Horst. *Dictionary of terms in music*, BJ147

—— *Terminorum musicae index septem lingus redactus*, BJ159

Leumann, E. *A Sanskrit-English dictionary*, AC706

Leung, Albert Y. *Encyclopedia of common natural ingredients used in food, drugs, and cosmetics*, EH325

Leung, Pak-wah. *Historical dictionary of revolutionary China, 1839–1976*, DE142

Leussink, Jan A. *Index nominum genericorum (plantarum)*, EG129

Lev, Yvonne. *Encyclopedia of senior citizens information sources*, CC96

Levarie, Siegmund. *Musical morphology*, BJ152

Leveille, Gilbert A. *Nutrients in foods*, EH308

Lever, Christopher. *Naturalized birds of the world*, EG267

—— *Naturalized mammals of the world*, EG297

Lever, Jill. *Illustrated dictionary of architecture, 800–1914*, BF246

Lever, Maurice. *Fiction narrative en prose au XVIIème siècle*, BE1187, BE1190

Levernier, James A. *American writers before 1800*, BE445

Lévesque, Albert. *Contribution to the national bibliography of Rwanda, 1965–1970*, AA871, DD198

Levey, Judith S. *Macmillan dictionary for children*, AC22

Levi, Anthony. *Guide to French literature*, BE1161

Levi, Jeffrey. *The combined retrospective index set to journals in political science, 1886–1974*, CJ18

Levi, Nadia. *Guía de publicaciones periódicas de universidades latinoamericanas*, AD65

Levi, Peter. *Atlas of the Greek world*, DA119

—— *History of Greek literature*, BE1034

Levina, R. Sh. *Sovetskaia arkheologicheskaia literatura*, DA71

Levine, Edwin B. *Follett world-wide Latin dictionary*, AC576

Levine, Evyatar. *Political dictionary of the Middle East in the twentieth century*, CJ424, CJ439

Levine, Mortimer. *Tudor England, 1485–1603*, DC303

Levine, Nancy D. *The older volunteer*, CC63

Levine, Paula L. *Medical sociology*, CC6, EH11

Levine, Robert M. *Brazil, 1822–1930*, DB345

—— *Brazil since 1930*, DB345

Levine, Stephen I. *The New Zealand politics source book*, CJ451

Levine, Sumner N. *The financial analyst's handbook*, CH319

Levinkind, Susan. *Legal research*, CK117

Levinson, David. *Encyclopedia of world cultures*, CE41

Levinson, Louis. *Medical risks*, EH233

Levis, Howard Coppuck. *A descriptive bibliography of the most important books in the English language relating to the art & history of engraving and the collecting of prints, with supplement and index*, BF361

Levison, Wilhelm. *Vorzeit und Karolinger*, DC228

Levitchi, Leon. *Dicţionar englez-român*, AC663
—— *Dicţionar român-englez*, AC663

Leviton, Alan E. *Reptiles and amphibians of North America*, EG251

Levitt, John L. *Handbook for assessing and treating addictive disorders*, CC135

Levush, Ruth. *Introductions to research in foreign law : Israel*, CK231

Levy, Emil. *Petit dictionnaire provençal-français*, AC655

Levy, Ernst. *Musical morphology*, BJ152

Levy, John F. *Cashin's handbook for auditors*, CH259

Levy, Leonard Williams. *Encyclopedia of the American Constitution*, CK130
—— *Encyclopedia of the American presidency*, CJ178

Levy, Margot. *Dictionary of gardening*, EG125

Lévy, Monique. *Bibliographie des Juifs en France*, BC527

Levy, Peter B. *Documentary history of the modern civil rights movement*, CC392

Levy, Raphael. *Répertoire des lexiques du vieux français*, AC389

Levy, Reuben. *An introduction to Persian literature*, BE1573

Levy, Richard C. *Inventing and patenting sourcebook*, EA262

Lew, Edward A. *Medical risks*, EH233

Lewanski, Richard Casimir. *Bibliography of Polish dictionaries*, AC193
—— *A bibliography of Slavic dictionaries*, AC193
—— *Eastern Europe and Russia/Soviet Union*, AK109, DC50
—— *Guide to Polish libraries and archives*, AK152
—— *Poland*, DC475
—— *The Slavic literatures*, BE1075
—— *Subject collections in European libraries*, AK119

Lewanski, Rudolf J. *Guide to Italian libraries and archives*, AK133, AK151, DC13

Lewell, John. *Modern Japanese novelists*, BE1585

Lewicka, Halina. *Bibliographie du théâtre profane français des XVe et XVIe siècles*, BE1183

Lewin, Albert E. *The thesaurus of slang*, AC127

Lewin, Esther. *The thesaurus of slang*, AC127

Lewin, Evans. *Subject catalogue of the Library of the Royal Empire Society, formerly Royal Colonial Institute*, DC344

Lewine, Richard. *Encyclopedia of theater music*, BJ267
—— *Songs of the American theater*, BJ267
—— *Songs of the theater*, BJ267

Lewis, Adele Beatrice. *Best resumes for scientists and engineers*, EA151

Lewis, Benjamin Morgan. *A history and bibliography of American magazines, 1800–1810*, AD38

Lewis, Bernard. *Historical writing on the peoples of Asia*, DE18

Lewis, Charlton T. *Harper's Latin dictionary*, AC574

Lewis, D. S. *Political parties of Asia and the Pacific*, CJ414, CJ446
—— *Political parties of the Americas and the Caribbean*, CJ97

Lewis, George Griffin. *The practical book of Oriental rugs*, BG168

Lewis, H. A. G. *The Times atlas of the moon*, EC69

Lewis, I. M. *Modern history of Somalia*, DD207

Lewis, Jack Pearl. *English Bible from KJV to NIV*, BC94

Lewis, Jack Windsor. *A concise pronouncing dictionary of British and American English*, AC98

Lewis, James A. *Guide to Cherokee documents in foreign archives*, CC420

Lewis, John Rodney. *Uncertain judgement*, CK80, DA203

Lewis, Philippa. *Dictionary of ornament*, BG23

Lewis, R. E. *Index of printed Middle English prose*, BE733

Lewis, Richard J. *Carcinogenically active chemicals*, EE80
—— *Food additives handbook*, EJ170
—— *Hawley's condensed chemical dictionary*, EE41
—— *Hazardous chemical desk reference*, EE79
—— *Reproductively active chemicals*, EE80
—— *Sax's dangerous properties of industrial materials*, EE79, EE80

Lewis, Richard S. *The illustrated encyclopedia of the universe*, EC31

Lewis, Robert E. *Middle English dictionary*, AC175

Lewis, Samuel. *Atlas to the Topographical dictionaries of England and Wales*, CL137, CL206
—— *Topographical dictionary of England*, CL137
—— *Topographical dictionary of Ireland*, CL143
—— *Topographical dictionary of Scotland*, CL141
—— *Topographical dictionary of Wales*, CL206

Lewis, Shelby. *Women in Lesotho*, DD122, DD171

Lewis and Short, AC574

Lewthwaite, Gordon Rowland. *A geographical bibliography for American college libraries*, CL17

Lewy, Arieh. *International encyclopedia of curriculum*, CB70

Lewytzkyj, Borys. *Who's who in the socialist countries*, AH47, AH306
—— *Who's who in the Soviet Union*, AH306

Lexer, Matthias von. *Matthias Lexers Mittelhochdeutsches Taschenwörterbuch*, AC405
—— *Mittelhochdeutsches Handwörterbuch*, AC405

Lexical studies of medieval Spanish texts, Dworkin, Steven Norman, BD165

Lexicographical Centre for Canadian English. *Dictionary of Canadianisms on historical principles*, AC158

Lexicography in China, Chien, David, AC269

Lexicon academicum, Zürcher, Josef, BB52

Lexicon Cornu-Britannicum, Williams, Robert, AC275

Lexicón histórico-documental de Puerto Rico (1912–1899), Rosa Martínez, Luis de la, DB455

Lexicon iconographicum mythologiae classicae, BF188, CF23

Lexicon in Veteris Testamenti libros, Koehler, Ludwig Hugo, AC482

Lexicon latinitatis medii aevi, AC586

Lexicon linguae Aethiopicae, Dillman, August, AC311

Lexicon linguae Aethiopicae cum indice Latino, Dillmann, August, AC310

Lexicon manuale ad scriptores mediae et infimae latinitatis, Maigne d'Arnis, W. H., AC590

Lexicon nominum virorum et mulierum, Egger, Carl, AJ170

A lexicon of ancient Latin etymologies, Maltby, Robert, AC580

Lexicon of economic thought, Block, Walter, CH48

A lexicon of English dental terms, International Dental Federation, EH257

Lexicon of geologic names of the United States, Wilmarth, Mary Grace, EF77

Lexicon of geologic names of the United States for 1936–1960, Keroher, Grace C., EF77
—— Luttrell, Gwendolyn W., EF77

Lexicon of geologic names of the United States for 1961–1967, Keroher, Grace C., EF77

Lexicon of new formal geologic names of the United States, 1976–1980, Hubert, Marilyn L., EF77
—— Jussen, Virginia M., EF77
—— Luttrell, Gwendolyn W., EF77

Lexicon of new formal geologic names of the United States, 1981–1985, Hubert, Marilyn L., EF77
—— Luttrell, Gwendolyn W., EF77
—— Murdock, Cunthia R., EF77

Lexicon of psychiatric and mental health terms, EH384

A lexicon of psychology, psychiatry, and psychoanalysis, CD24

A lexicon of St. Thomas Aquinas based on the Summa theologica and selected passages of his other works, Deferrari, Roy Joseph, BB63

Lexicon Platonicum, Ast, Friedrich, BB52

Lexicon poeticum antiquæ linguæ septentrionalis, Jónsson, Finnur, BE1286

Lexicon pseudonymorum hungaricum, AA175, AA176

Lexicon syriacum, Brockelmann, Carl, AC771

Lexicon typographicum Italiae, Fumagalli, Giuseppe, AA301

Lexicon universal encyclopedia, AB2

Lexicon van de moderne Nederlandse literatuur, BE1333

Lexikon der Ägyptologie, DA125

Lexikon der baukunst, BF239

Lexikon der christlichen Ikonographie, BF184
—— Aurenhammer, Hans, BF184

Lexikon der deutschen Dichter und Prosaisten vom Beginn des 19. Jahrhunderts bis zur Gegenwart, Brümmer, Franz, BE1057

Lexikon der deutschen Geschichte, DC221

Lexikon der deutschprachigen Gegenwartsliteratur, Kunisch, Hermann, BE1250

Lexikon der deutschsprachigen Gegenwartsliteratur, Weisner, Herbert, BE1248, BE1250

Lexikon der germanischen Mythologie, CF35

Lexikon der Germanistischen Linguistik, Althaus, Hans Peter, BD124
—— Henne, Helmut, BD124
—— Wiegand, Herbert Ernst, BD124

Lexikon der Geschichte der Naturwissenschaften, EA245, EA247

Lexikon der Geschichte Russlands, DC583

Lexikon der Götter und Dämonen, CF12

Lexikon der Kinder- und Jugendliteratur, BE385

Lexikon der Kohlenstoff-Verbindungen, Richter, Max Moritz, EE122, EE143

Lexikon der Kunst, BF74, BF75

Lexikon der Liturgie, Podhradsky, Gerhard, BC428

Lexikon der Münzabkürzungen mit geschlichtlich-geographischen Erläuterungen, Holtz, Walter, BG183

Lexikon der Numismatik, Kroha, Tyll, BG181

Lexikon der östlichen Weisheitslehren, BB31, BC57

Lexikon der Philosophie, Austeda, Franz, BB38

Lexikon der Physik, ED20

Lexikon der Romanistischen Linguistik, BD148

Lexikon der russischen Literatur ab 1917, BE1412

Lexikon der russischen Literatur des 20. Jahrhunderts, BE1412

Lexikon der Schweizer Literaturen, BE1490

Lexikon der Symbole, Bauer, Wolfgang, CF11

Lexikon der Terraristik und Herpetologie, EG252

Lexikon der Weltliteratur, Wilpert, Gero von, BE72

Lexikon der Weltliteratur im 20. Jahrhundert, BE66

Lexikon des Buchwesens, Kirchner, Joachim, AA270

Lexikon des frühgriechischen Epos, Snell, Bruno, AC447

Lexikon des gesamten Buchwesens, AA270

Lexikon des Mittelalters, DA150

Lexikon deutschsprachiger Schriftsteller, BE1061

Lexikon deutschsprachiger Schriftstellerinnen, 1800–1945, Brinker-Gabler, Gisela, BE1056

Lexikon für die Apothekenpraxis in sieben Sprachen, Steinbichler, Eveline, EH331

Lexikon für Theologie und Kirche, BC63, BC231

Lexikon geographischer Bildbände, Kinauer, Rudolf, CL14

Lexikon Hellenikes Orthodoxias, BC451

Lexikon historischer Ereignisse und Personen in Kunst, Literatur und Musik, Heinzel, E., AH27

Lexikon Musikinstrumente, BJ369

Lexikon Neas Hellēnikēs glōssēs, AC462

Lexikon sozialistischer deutscher Literatur, von den Anfängen bis 1945, BE1229, BE1249
Lexikon tēs Hellēnikēs glōssēs, AC462
Lexique de l'ancien français, Bonnard, Jean, AC378
—— Godefroy, Frédéric Eugène, AC375, AC378
—— Salmon, Amédée, AC378
Lexique démographique trilingue, CG31
Lexique des termes d'art, Adeline, Jules, BF81
Lexique étymologique de l'irlandais ancien, Vendryes, Joseph, AC522
Lexique français moderne-ancien français, De Gorog, Ralph Paul, AC375
Lexique historique de la France d'ancien régime, Cabourdin, Guy, DC174
Lexique stratigraphique international, International Geological Congress. Commission de stratigraphie, EF74
•*LEXIS,* CK179
Ley, Gerd de. *Groot literair citatenboek van Nederlandse en Vlaamse auteurs uit de 19e en 20e eeuw,* BE125
—— *Modern citatenboek,* BE126
—— *Standaard modern citatenboek,* BE126
Ley, Ralph. *The drama of German expressionism,* BE1264
Leyerle, John. *Chaucer : a bibliographical introduction,* DA138
Leyh, Georg. *Handbuch der Bibliothekswissenschaft,* AK38
Lhamsüren, B. *Information Mongolia,* DE232
Lhande, Pierre. *Dictionnaire basque français et français-basque,* AC229
Lhéritier, Andrée. *Manuel de bibliographie,* AA6
Li, Christine. *The political participation of women in the United States,* CC512
Li, Hong-Chan. *Social work education,* CC42
Li, Peter. *Classical Chinese fiction,* BE1562
—— *Modern Chinese fiction,* BE1562
Li, Shu-t'ien. *Bibliography on airport engineering,* EK117
Li, Tien-Yi. *Chinese fiction,* BE1556
Li, Tze-chung. *Social science reference sources,* CA4
Li, Yun-chen. *A bibliography of studies and translations of modern Chinese literature, 1918–1942,* BE1553
Li Chung. *English-Chinese dictionary of furniture industry,* BG125
Liagre, L. *Guides des sources de l'histoire d'Amérique Latine conservées en Belgique,* DB275
Liber, George. *Nonconformity and dissent in the Ukrainian SSR, 1955–1975,* CJ389
Liberalism
dictionaries, CJ24
Liberation theologies, Musto, Ronald G., BC219
Liberia
atlases, CL342
current surveys, DD62
encyclopedias, DD48
statistics, CG339
Liberia (by subject)
history
bibliography, DD172
Liberia. Ministry of Planning and Economic Affairs. *Statistical bulletin of Liberia,* CG339
Liberia, Dunn, D. Elwood, DD48
—— Holsoe, Svend E., DD48
—— Nelson, Harold D., DD62
Liberia during the Tolbert era, Gray, Beverly Ann, DD172
Liberia in maps, Gnielinski, Stefan, CL342
Libertarianism
bibliography, CJ111, CJ112
periodicals, AD54
Liberty's women, McHenry, Robert, CC576
Librairie française, AA629
Librarian authors, Engelbarts, Rudolf, AK89
Librarians
bibliography, AK89
biography, AK83, AK84
directories, AF86, AK87, AK92
salaries, AK171, AK173, AK179

Librarians (by country or region)
Australia, AK82
Great Britain, AK91
Italy, AK90
New Zealand, AK94
A librarian's collacon, Krummel, Donald William, AK51
Librarians' glossary, AK42
Librarians of Institutes of Education (Great Britain). *British education index,* CB50
Librarian's practical dictionary in twenty-two languages, Pipics, Zoltán, AK48
Librarianship and information work worldwide, AK79
Librarianship in Japan, AK160
Libraries
databases, AK33
directories, AK118, AK120
facsimile transmission, AK60
financial aids, AK64
guides, AK3, AK6
handbooks, AK69
quotations, AK51
statistics, AK98
Libraries (by country or region)
Africa, AK155
directories, AK154
Australia, AK104
directories, AK162
encyclopedias, AK161
Austria
directories, AK138
Belgium, AK133, DC13
directories, AD230
Canada, AK100, AK128, DB199
directories, AK123
China
directories, AK156
Europe
directories, AK109, AK119, DC50
Europe, Central
directories, DC48
Europe, Eastern
directories, DC48
Europe, Western
directories, AK131, AK132
Finland
directories, AK134
France
directories, AK135, AK136, DC158
history, AK107
Germany
directories, AK138, AK139
union lists, AA122
Great Britain, AJ98, AK140, AK141, AK143, AK145, AK147
directories, AK142, AK146, AK148
history
bibliography, AK70
statistics, AK97
India, AK158
directories, AK157
international
directories, AK121
Ireland, AK143, AK147
directories, AK146
Italy
directories, AK149, AK151
Japan, AK160
directories, AK159
Luxembourg, AK133, DC13
directories, AD230
Mexico
directories, AK129
Netherlands, AK133, DC13
New Zealand, AK104
directories, AK63
Poland
directories, AK152
Socialist states
directories, AK117
Switzerland
directories, AK138

United States, AK100, AK103, AK125
directories, AK122, AK123, AK126
history, AK27
dissertations, AK27
Yugoslavia, DC611
Libraries (by subject)
architecture, AK175
disaster prevention, AK243
history
bibliography, AK71
planning, AK180
transportation
directories, CH449
see also **Archives; Art libraries; Genealogical libraries; Medical libraries; Presidential libraries; Public libraries; Research libraries; Scientific libraries; Technical libraries; University and college libraries**
Libraries and archives in France, Welsch, Erwin K., AK136, DC158
Libraries and archives in Germany, Welsch, Erwin K., AK139
Libraries and special collections on Latin America and the Caribbean, Macdonald, Roger, AK111
Libraries and the disabled, AK66
The libraries directory, AK146
Libraries in American periodicals before 1876, Barr, Larry J., AK9
Libraries in colleges of further and higher education in the UK, AK140
Libraries in the United Kingdom and the Republic of Ireland, AK147
Libraries, information centers and databases in science and technology, EA144
Libraries, museums and art galleries year book, AK146
Libraries year book, AK146
The library, AJ14
Library & information science abstracts, AK31, AK34
Library administration, AK7, AK174, AK176, AK178
Library Administration and Management Association. *Library management consultants list,* AK176
Library and documentation journals, AK21
Library and information science
abbreviations, AK45
abstract journals, AK29, AK30, AK31, AK34
annuals, AK74, AK79, AK80
bibliography, AA268, AK1, AK8, AK9, AK11, AK12, AK13, AK15, AK17, AK18, AK78
biography, AK85, AK86, AK87, AK88, AK89, AK93
book reviews, AK80
databases, AK28, AK29, AK30, AK32, AK88, CB54, CD90
dictionaries, AA270, AK40, AK42, AK43, AK44, EK183
bilingual
German-English, AK47
multilingual, AK41, AK48, AK49
directories, AK52, AK55, AK122
Canada, AK58
international, AK53, AK121
U.S., AK58
dissertations, AK23, AK24, AK25, AK26
encyclopedias, AK36, AK37, AK38, AK39, EK171
guides, AK2
guides for authors, AK22
indexes, AK28, AK32, AK35, CB54, CB61, CD90
periodicals, AK20, AK21, AK22
research methods, AK5, AK7
standards, AK65
yearbooks, AK75, AK77, AK78
Library and information science (by country or region)
China
bibliography, AK16
international
directories, AK54

United States
  directories, AK56, AK57
Library and information science (by subject)
  censorship, AK67
  history
    encyclopedias, AK72
  status of women, AK14
•*Library and information science abstracts*, AK29, AK31
Library and information science annual, AK26, AK80
Library and information science education statistical report, AK68
Library and information science in China, Wei, Karen T., AK16
Library and information science journals and serials, Bowman, Mary Ann, AK20
Library and information service today, AK75
Library and information studies in the United Kingdom and Ireland, 1950–1974, AK23, AK24
Library and Information Technology Association. *Telecommunications and networking glossary*, CH487
Library-Anthropology Resource Group. *Anthropological bibliographies*, CE19
—— *Biographical directory of anthropologists born before 1920*, CE65
—— *International dictionary of anthropologists*, CE67
Library Association. *A bibliography of Anglo-Welsh literature, 1900–1965*, BE813
—— *British librarianship and information work*, AK78
—— *Walford's guide to current British periodicals in the humanities and social sciences*, AD117
—— *Walford's guide to reference material*, AA363
Library Association. Library. *FLA theses*, AK24
Library Association. Library History Group. *British library history*, AK70
Library Association. Medical, Health and Welfare Libraries Group. *Directory of medical and health care libraries in the United Kingdom and Republic of Ireland*, EH167
Library Association. Northern Ireland Branch. *Northern Ireland newspapers, 1737–1987*, AE61
Library Association. Rare Books Group. *A directory of rare book and special collections in the United Kingdom and the Republic of Ireland*, AK143
Library Association. Reference, Special, and Information Section. *Bibliography of British newspapers*, AE55
—— *British government publications*, AF193
Library Association of Australia. *Directory of special collections in Australiana*, DF31
Library buildings consultants list, Dailey, Kazuko, AK176
—— Estrada, James, AK176
Library catalog, Cornell University. New York State School of Industrial and Labor Relations. Library, CH640
Library catalog of the Conservation Center, New York University, Institute of Fine Arts, New York University. Institute of Fine Arts. Conservation Center, BF200
Library catalog of the International Museum of Photography at George Eastman House, International Museum of Photography at George Eastman House. Library, BF337
Library catalog of the Metropolitan Museum of Art, Metropolitan Museum of Art (New York, N.Y.). Library, BF54
Library catalogs, AA101, AA102, AA104, AA108, AA114, AA115, AA116, AA119, AA120, AA121, AA122, AA124, AA613, BC96
  bibliography, AA98, AA99
Library catalogs (by country or region)
  France, AA100
  Germany, AA117
  Spain, AA105
  United States, AA106, AA110, AA111, AA112, AA113, BC102

The library catalogs of the Hoover Institution on War, Revolution, and Peace, Stanford University, Hoover Institution on War, Revolution and Peace, DA172
Library catalogue, American Numismatic Association, BG177
—— University of London. School of Oriental and African Studies. Library, DD35
Library data collection handbook, AK5
Library, documentation, and archives serials, Janzing, Grażyna, AK21
Library education
  directories, AK54, AK58
  statistics, AK68
Library fax directory, AK60
Library guide for Brazilian studies, Jackson, William Vernon, DB351
Library hi tech bibliography, AK19
Library Information and Research Service. *The Middle East*, DE52
Library instruction, AK3, AK6, AK193, AK229, AK231
  handbooks, AK230, AK232
Library instruction handbook, AK230
Library literature, AK12, AK32
Library management, Eastlick, John T., AK174
—— Steuart, Robert D., AK174
Library management consultants list, AK176
Library materials preservation manual, Kyle, Hedi, AK241
Library, media, and archival preservation glossary, DePew, John N., AK239
—— Jones, C. Lee, AK239
A library, media, and archival preservation handbook, DePew, John N., AK239
Library of Congress. *Africana serials in microform in the Library of Congress*, DD27
—— *ALA-LC romanization tables*, BD10
—— *Antarctic bibliography*, DG1
—— *Arab-world newspapers in the Library of Congress*, AE85
—— *Arabic-English and English-Arabic dictionaries in the Library of Congress*, AC220
—— *Audiovisual materials*, AA381
—— *Bibliographic guide to microform publications*, AA128
—— *Bibliography of Pacific/Asian American materials in the Library of Congress*, CC411
—— *A catalog of books represented by Library of Congress printed cards issued to July 31, 1942*, AA106
—— *Checklist of Philippine government documents, 1950*, AF258
—— *Chinese cooperative catalog*, AA892
—— *Chinese-English and English-Chinese dictionaries in the Library of Congress*, AC271
—— *Chinese newspapers in the Library of Congress*, AE87
—— *Chinese periodicals in the Library of Congress*, AD188
—— *Cyrillic union catalog*, AA784, AA785
—— *Dictionary catalog of the Teachers College Library*, CB6
—— *East African community*, AF221
—— *Films and other materials for projection*, AA107, AA381
—— *Genealogies in the Library of Congress*, AJ32
—— *A guide to the microfilm collection of early state records*, DB141
—— *A guide to the music of Latin America*, BJ11
—— *A guide to the official publications of the other American republics*, AF159
—— *Hidden research resources in the German collections of the Library of Congress*, DC216
—— *Japanese national government publications in the Library of Congress*, AF252
—— *Library of Congress catalog*, AA107, BJ61, CL252
—— *Library of Congress catalog : music and phonorecords*, BJ62
—— *The Library of Congress main reading room reference collection subject catalog*, AA350

—— *Libya, 1969–1989, an American perspective*, DD174
—— *Main catalog of the Library of Congress*, AA108
—— *Manuscript sources in the Library of Congress for research on the American Revolution*, DB91
—— *Maps and atlases*, CL252
—— *Maps and charts of North America and the West Indies, 1750–1789*, CL233
—— *Monographic series*, AA109
—— *National union catalog*, AA111
—— *National union catalog of manuscript collections*, DB34
—— *The Negro in the United States*, CC374
—— *Negro newspapers on microfilm*, AE15
—— *The Netherlands and Northern Belgium*, DC456
—— *New serial titles*, AD225
—— *Newspapers of the Soviet Union in the Library of Congress*, AE43, AE75
—— *The Republic of Turkey*, DC540
—— *Revolutionary America, 1763–1789*, DB88
—— *Russian imperial government serials on microfilm in the Library of Congress*, AD144, AF214
—— *Southeast Asia*, AD185
—— *Special collections in the Library of Congress*, AK110
—— *Subject catalog*, AA111
—— *United States local histories in the Library of Congress*, DB142
—— *Vernacular architecture in America*, BF213
Library of Congress. Aerospace Technology Division. *Glossary of Russian abbreviations and acronyms*, AC688
Library of Congress. African and Middle Eastern Division. *The Near East national union list*, AA123
Library of Congress. African Section. *Africa south of the Sahara*, DD91
—— *Botswana, Lesotho, and Swaziland*, AF218
—— *French-speaking central Africa*, AF229
—— *French-speaking West Africa*, AF230
—— *Kenya*, AF232
—— *Madagascar and adjacent islands*, AF222, DD175
—— *Nigeria*, AF235, AF236
—— *Official publications of British East Africa*, AF223, DD108
—— *Official publications of French Equatorial Africa*, AF224
—— *Official publications of Sierra Leone and Gambia*, AF225
—— *Official publications of Somaliland, 1941–1959*, AF237
—— *Portuguese Africa*, AF220
—— *The Rhodesias and Nyasaland*, AF226
—— *Spanish-speaking Africa*, AF227
—— *Tanganyika African National Union*, DD233
—— *Uganda*, AF240
—— *U.S. imprints on Sub-Saharan Africa*, DD89
Library of Congress. Arms Control and Disarmament Bibliography Section. *Arms control and disarmament*, CJ662
Library of Congress. Catalog Management and Publication Division. *Newspapers in microform*, AE13, AE27
Library of Congress. Catalog Publication Division. *Slavic Cyrillic union catalog of pre-1956 imprints*, AA784, AA785
Library of Congress. Cataloging Distribution Service. *Library of Congress rule interpretations*, AK197
—— *The music catalog*, BJ82
—— *New serial titles*, AD225
Library of Congress. Cataloging Policy and Support Office. *Library of Congress subject headings*, AK219, AK220, CC542, CJ688
Library of Congress. Census Library Project. *Catalog of United States census publications, 1790–1945*, CG90

———— *General censuses and vital statistics in the Americas,* CG72

———— *National censuses and vital statistics in Europe, 1918–1939,* CG188

———— *Population censuses and other official demographic statistics of Africa (not including British Africa),* CG312

———— *Population censuses and other official demographic statistics of British Africa,* CG312

Library of Congress. Congressional Research Service. *The Constitution of the United States of America,* CK173

———— *Major studies & issue briefs of the Congressional Research Service,* AF82

———— *Respectfully quoted,* BE116

Library of Congress. Copyright Office. *Catalog of copyright entries,* AA433, BE461, BH193, BJ81

———— *Dramatic compositions copyrighted in the United States,* BE461

Library of Congress. Cyrillic Bibliographic Project. *Serial publications of the Soviet Union, 1939–1957,* AD147

Library of Congress. Descriptive Cataloging Division. *National union catalog of manuscript collections,* DB34

Library of Congress. Division of Manuscripts. *A guide to manuscripts relating to America in Great Britain and Ireland,* DB32

Library of Congress. European Division. *Czech and Slovak literature in English,* BE1108

———— *Russian imperial government serials on microfilm in the Library of Congress,* AD144, AF214

Library of Congress. Exchange and Gift Division. *Monthly checklist of state publications,* AF142

Library of Congress. General Reference and Bibliography Division. *Current national bibliographies,* AA397

———— *French-speaking West Africa,* AF230

———— *Guide to the study of the United States of America,* DB13

———— *Official publications of Somaliland, 1941–1959,* AF237

———— *Union lists of serials,* AD219

Library of Congress. Geography and Map Division. *The bibliography of cartography,* CL253

———— *Civil War maps,* CL301, DB122

———— *Geographic names & the federal government,* CL99

———— *Guide to the history of cartography,* CL240

———— *Panoramic maps of Anglo-American cities,* CL234

———— *Panoramic maps of cities in the United States and Canada,* CL234

Library of Congress. Geography and Map Division. Reference and Bibliography Section. *Fire insurance maps in the Library of Congress,* CL235

Library of Congress. Hispanic Division. *Handbook of Latin American studies,* BE874, DB266

———— *National directory of Latin Americanists,* DB287

Library of Congress. Hispanic Foundation. *Latin America,* DB257

Library of Congress. Law Library. *The People's Republic of China,* CK228

Library of Congress. Library of Congress Office, Cairo. *Accessions list, Middle East,* DE46

Library of Congress. Library of Congress Office, Jakarta. *Accessions list, Southeast Asia,* DE98

Library of Congress. Library of Congress Office, Nairobi, Kenya. *Accessions list, Eastern and Southern Africa,* DD85

———— *Quarterly index to periodical literature, Eastern and Southern Africa,* DD92

Library of Congress. Library of Congress Office, New Delhi. *Accessions list, South Asia,* DE79

Library of Congress. Library of Congress Office, Rio de Janeiro. *Accessions list, Brazil and Uruguay,* AA511

Library of Congress. Manuscript Division. *Civil War manuscripts,* DB115

Library of Congress. Manuscripts Section. *National union catalog of manuscript collections,* DB30, DB34

Library of Congress. Map Division. *Guide to historical cartography,* CL240

———— *A list of geographical atlases in the Library of Congress, with bibliographical notes,* CL254

———— *List of maps of America in the Library … preceded by a list of works relating to cartography,* CL236

———— *United States atlases,* CL237

Library of Congress. Motion Picture, Broadcasting, and Recorded Sound Division. *Early motion pictures,* BH190

———— *George Kleine collection of early motion pictures in the Library of Congress,* BH190

Library of Congress. Music Division. *Catalogue of opera librettos printed before 1800,* BJ239

———— *Dramatic music (class M 1500, 1510, 1520),* BJ240

———— *Folk music,* BJ321

Library of Congress. National Library Service for the Blind and Physically Handicapped. *International directory of braille music collections,* BJ171

———— *International directory of tactile map collections,* CL258

———— *Library resources for the blind & physically handicapped,* CC196

Library of Congress. National Preservation Program Office. *National preservation news,* AE5

Library of Congress. National Referral Center for Science and Technology. *A directory of information resources in the United States,* EK93

Library of Congress. Near East Section. *Kemal Atatürk,* DC533

Library of Congress. Netherlands Studies Unit. *A guide to Dutch bibliographies,* AA56

Library of Congress. Office for Descriptive Cataloging. *Library of Congress rule interpretations,* AK197

Library of Congress. Office for Subject Cataloging Policy. *LC classification outline,* AK202

———— *Library of Congress subject headings,* AK220

———— *Subject cataloging manual,* AK221

Library of Congress. Orientalia Division. *Eminent Chinese of the Ch'ing period (1644–1912),* AII338, AII339, AH340

———— *Southern Asia accessions list,* DE79

Library of Congress. Periodical Division. *A check list of American 18th century newspapers in the Library of Congress,* AE20

———— *A check list of foreign newspapers in the Library of Congress,* AE10

Library of Congress. Poetry Office. *Literary recordings,* BE324

Library of Congress. Preservation Microfilming Office. *Russian imperial government serials on microfilm in the Library of Congress,* AD144, AF214

Library of Congress. Prints and Photographs Division. *American prints in the Library of Congress,* BF365

Library of Congress. Processing Department. *British manuscripts project,* AA133

———— *East European accessions index,* AA793

———— *Monthly index of Russian accessions,* AA793

Library of Congress. Rare Book Division. *Children's books in the Rare Book Division of the Library of Congress,* AA246

Library of Congress. Reference Department. *Soviet geography,* CL151

Library of Congress. Science and Technology Division. *Aeronautical and space serial publications,* EK25

———— *Arctic & antarctic regions,* DG2

———— *Scientific and technical serial publications of the Soviet Union, 1945–1960,* EA51

Library of Congress. Science and Technology Division. Reference Section. *LC science tracer bullet,* EA35

Library of Congress. Serial and Government Publications Division. *African newspapers in the Library of Congress,* DD26

———— *A bibliography of U.S. newspaper bibliographies,* AE29

———— *Newspapers received currently in the Library of Congress,* AE11, AE75

———— *Popular names of U.S. government reports,* AF101

Library of Congress. Serial and Government Publications Division. Newspaper Section. *Indexes in the Newspaper and Current Periodicals Room,* AE101

———— *Newspaper indexes in the Newspaper and Current Periodical Room,* AE102

Library of Congress. Serial Division. *African newspapers in selected American libraries,* AE79

———— *A check list of American 18th century newspapers in the Library of Congress,* AE20

———— *Latin American newspapers in United States libraries,* AE40

———— *Postwar foreign newspapers,* AE12

Library of Congress. Serial Record Division. *New serial titles,* AD225

Library of Congress. Slavic and Central European Division. *Bulgaria,* DC112

———— *Bulgarian abbreviations,* AC243

———— *Czech and Slovak abbreviations,* AC282

———— *Hungarian abbreviations,* AC497

———— *Newspapers of east central and southeastern Europe in the Library of Congress,* AE43

———— *Polish abbreviations,* AC636

———— *Romania,* DC496

———— *Russian, Ukrainian, and Belorussian newspapers, 1917–1953,* AE71, AE75

———— *Yugoslav abbreviations,* AC715

———— *Yugoslav history,* DC609

Library of Congress. Subject Cataloging Division. *Classification,* AK202

———— *LC classification, additions and changes,* AK202

———— *Subject cataloging manual,* AK219, AK220

The Library of Congress, Neagles, James C., AJ17, DB143

Library of Congress and national union catalog author lists, 1942 1962, Gale Research, inc, AA111

Library of Congress author catalog, AA106

Library of congress author catalog, 1948–52, AA107

Library of Congress catalog, Library of Congress, AA107, BJ61, CL252

Library of Congress catalog. Books: subjects, AA110

Library of Congress catalog : music and phonorecords, BJ63, BJ62

The Library of Congress catalogs, AA111

Library of Congress filing rules, Rather, John Carson, AK211

The Library of Congress main reading room reference collection subject catalog, Library of Congress, AA350

Library of Congress rule interpretations, AK197

Library of Congress subject headings, Chan, Lois Mai, AK219, AK220

———— Library of Congress. Cataloging Policy and Support Office, AK219, AK220, CC542, CJ688

Library of literary criticism of English and American authors, Moulton, Charles Wells, BE427, BE597, BE598, BE599, BE600

Library of literary criticism of English and American authors through the beginning of the twentieth century, Moulton, Charles Wells, BE598

———— Tucker, Martin, BE598

Library of the Marine Biological Laboratory and the Woods Hole Oceanographic Institution. *Catalog,* EF209

Library periodicals, AK22

Library personnel consultants list, Kratz, Charles E., AK176

•*Library reference plus,* AA281, AA282, AK33, AK77, AK122, BE172

Library research guide to music, Druesedow, John E., BJ3

Library research guide to religion and theology, Kennedy, James R., BC2

Library research models, Mann, Thomas, AK6

Library resources for the blind & physically handicapped, CC196

Library resources in Britain for the study of Eastern Europe and the former U.S.S.R, Walker, Gregory, DC51

Library resources in London and South East England, Taylor, L. J., AK148

Library science *see* **Library and information science**

Library science abstracts, AK31, AK34

Library science annual, AK80

Library science dissertations, 1925–1972, Schlachter, Gail Ann, AK26

Library science dissertations, 1925–60, Cohen, Nathan M., AK26

Library science dissertations, 1973–1981, Schlachter, Gail Ann, AK26

———— Thomison, Dennis, AK26

Library science research, 1974–1979, Magnotti, Shirley, AK25

Library service for genealogists, Parker, J. Carlyle, AJ19

Library technology reports, AK177

Library use, Reed, Jeffrey G., CD5

Libres editats à Mallorca (1939–1972), AA743

I libretti italiani a stampa dalle origini al 1800, Sartori, Claudio, BJ243

LiBretto, Ellen V. *High/low handbook,* CB190

Libri e riviste d'Italia, AA334, AA738

Libri Walliae, Rees, Eiluned, AA699

El libro chileno en venta, AA521

Il libro dei mille savi, Palazzi, Fernando, BE140

Il libro delle citazioni, Spagnol, Elena, BE141

El libro español, AA822, AA826

Libros argentinos. ISBN, AA499

Libros chilenos ISBN, AA522

Libros disponíveis, acttualizacão e adenda, AA779

Libros en venta en Hispanoamérica y España, AA475

Libros españoles en venta ISBN, AA827

Libros españoles ISBN, AA827

Libros y folletos publicados en Costa Rica durante los años 1830–1849, Lines, J. A., AA479

Libya

  bibliography, BC501, DD18, DD73

  current surveys, DD62

  encyclopedias, DD48

  statistics, CG340

Libya (by subject)

  foreign relations

    bibliography, DD174

  history

    bibliography, DD174

Libya. Maṣlaḥat al-Iḥṣa' wa-al-Taʿdād. *Majmuʿah al-iḥṣā'iyah,* CG340

Libya, Nelson, Harold D., DD62

———— St. John, Ronald Bruce, DD18, DD48

Libya, 1969–1989, an American perspective, Witherell, Julian W., DD174

Libyan national bibliography, AA862

Lichnye arkhivnye fondy v gosudarstvennykh kranilishchakh SSSR, Soviet Union. Glavnoe arkhivnoe upravlenie, DC565

Licht, Fred. *Sculpture, 19th & 20th centuries,* BF393

Lichtenstein, Nelson. *Political profiles,* CJ159

Liddell, Henry George. *A Greek-English lexicon,* AC444, AC445, AC450, AC457

Liddle, Barry. *Dictionary of sports quotations,* BK30

Lide, David R. *Basic laboratory and industrial chemicals,* EE64

Lidman, Mark J. *Studies in Jacobean drama, 1973–1984,* BE646, BE648

Liebenberg, B. J. *Bibliography of South African history,* DD223

Lieber, Gothild. *An international bibliography of computer-assisted language learning with annotations in German,* BD73

Lieberman, Fredric. *Chinese music,* BJ18

Lieberman, Jethro Koller. *The evolving Constitution,* CK185

Lieberman, Susan. *Memorable film characters,* BH276

Lieberthal, Kenneth. *A research guide to central party and government meetings in China, 1949–1986,* DE147

Liebscher, Herbert. *Handbook of mathematical formulas,* EB61

Liechtenstein, DC439, DC440

  bibliography, AA740, DC438

  biography, AH297

  statistics, CG259, CG260

Liechtenstein. Amt für Volkswirtschaft. *Statistisches Jahrbuch,* CG259

———— *Zivilstandsstatistik,* CG260

Liechtenstein, Meier, Regula A., DC438

Liechtensteinische Bibliographie, AA740

Liechtensteinische Bibliographie 1960–1973, Roeckle, Heidi, DC440

Liefrinck, Frederick Albert. *Bali en lombok,* DE178

Liesner, Thelma. *One hundred years of economic statistics,* CH158

Lietuviškai angliškas žodynas, Peteraitis, Vilius, AC603

Lietuviškoji tarybiné enciklopedija, DC443

Lietuviškos ir angliškos kalbu žodynas, Lalis, Anthony, AC601

Lietuvių-anglų kalbų žodynas, Piesarskas, Bronius, AC604

Lietuvių bibliografija [1517–1910], Biržiška, Vaclovas, BE1322

Lietuvių kalbos ir literatūros institutas (Lietuvos TSR Mokslų akademija). *Tarybinis lietuvių literatūros mokslas ir kritika apie literatūrini palikimą, 1944–1958,* BE1321

Lietuviu literaturos mosklas ir kritika, BE1321

Lietuvių rašytojai, BE1323

Lietuvos TSR Mokslų Akademija. Lietuvių Kalbos ir Literatūros Institutas. *Tarybiné lietuvių literatūra ir kritika,* BE1324

———— *Tarybinis lietuvių literatūros mokslas ir kritika apie literatūrini palikimą, 1944–1958,* BE1321

Lietzmann, Hans. *Reallexikon für Antike und Christentum,* BC248

Lietzmann, Hilda. *Bibliographie zur Kunstgeschichte des 19. Jahrhunderts,* BF32

Life, Page West. *Sir Thomas Malory and the Morte Darthur,* BE340

Life expectancy, EH233

Life insurance catalog of the Library of the Insurance Society of New York, Insurance Society of New York. Library, CH502

Life insurance fact book, CH525

Life sciences organizations and agencies directory, EG49

Life-writing, Winslow, Donald J., BE217

Lifelong education for adults, Titmus, Colin J., CB70

The lifestyle market analyst, CH594

Lifestyle marketplanner, CH594

Light, Margot. *International relations,* CJ10

Light, N. D. *Longman illustrated dictionary of food science,* EJ158

Lighting, EK140

Lighting design on Broadway, Owen, Bobbi, BH120

Lighting handbook, EK140

Lightman, Bernard V. *Victorian science and religion,* BC215

Liinamaa, Matti. *Suomen tieteellisten Kirjastojen opas,* AK134

Lijst der aardrijkskundige namen van Nederland, CL146, CL147

Likhachev, D. S. *Russkie pisateli,* BE1423

Lilien, Steven B. *Accountants' handbook,* CH257

Lillard, Robert Gordon. *America in fiction,* BE470

Lilley, George P. *Information sources in agriculture and food science,* EJ2

Lillian Roxon's rock encyclopedia, Roxon, Lillian, BJ357

Lilly, Jerry. *The martial arts,* BK91

Lim, Patricia Pui Huen. *ASEAN,* DE94

———— *The Malay world of Southeast Asia,* DE99

Lim, Shirley. *Reading the literatures of Asian America,* BE547

Lima, Hildebrando de. *Pequeno dicionário brasileiro da língua portuguêsa,* AC643

Limaye, Mohan R. *Business and technical writing,* CH428

Limbacher, James L. *Film music,* BJ360

———— *Keeping score,* BJ360

LIMC, BF188, CF23

Lin, Chien. *Bibliography of Pacific/Asian American materials in the Library of Congress,* CC411

———— *Pacific/Asian American research,* CC403

Lin, Yutang. *Chinese-English dictionary of modern usage,* AC265

Lincoln, Betty Woelk. *Festschriften in art history, 1960–1975,* BF50, BF51

Lincoln, Roger J. *The Cambridge illustrated dictionary of natural history,* EG75

———— *A dictionary of ecology, evolution and systematics,* EG65, EG75

Lind, Henry C. *United States reports,* CK190

Linda Hall Library. *Serials holdings in the Linda Hall Library [as of April 30] 1989,* EA44

Lindau, Gustav. *Thesaurus litteraturae mycologicae et lichenologicae ratione habita praecipue omnium quae adhuc scripta sunt de mycologia applicata quem congesserunt,* EG188

Lindbergh, Ernest. *International law dictionary,* CK45

Lindemann, Erika. *Longman bibliography of composition and rhetoric,* BE348

Lindemann, Margot. *Geschichte der deutschen Presse,* AE54

Linden, Albert Vander. *Historical atlas of music,* BJ198

Linder, Erik Hjalmar. *Fem decennier av nittonhundratalet,* BE1485

Linder, Robert Dean. *Dictionary of Christianity in America,* BC235

Lindfors, Bernth. *A bibliography of literary contributions to Nigerian periodicals, 1946–1972,* BE1531

———— *Black African literature in English,* BE1506

Lindner, Stephan H. *Economies of the German-speaking countries of Europe,* DC9

Lindow, John. *Scandinavian mythology,* CF33

Lindsay, Robert O. *French political pamphlets, 1547–1648,* DC169

Lindsey, Anne H. *A synonymized checklist of the vascular flora of the United States, Canada, and Greenland,* EG132

Lindsey, Mary P. *Dictionary of mental handicap,* CC190

Lindtner, Niels Christian. *Danske klassikere,* BE1119

Lindzey, Gardner. *Handbook of social psychology,* CD97, CJ53

Line, Maurice B. *Bibliography of Russian literature in English translation to 1900,* BE1409

———— *Librarianship and information work worldwide,* AK79

Lines, Clifford John. *Companion to the Industrial Revolution,* DC336

Lines, J. A. *Anthropological bibliography of aboriginal Costa Rica,* DB302

———— *Anthropological bibliography of aboriginal El Salvador,* DB302

———— *Anthropological bibliography of aboriginal Guatemala, British Honduras,* DB302

———— *Anthropological bibliography of aboriginal Honduras,* DB302

———— *Anthropological bibliography of aboriginal Nicaragua,* DB302

———— *Libros y folletos publicados en Costa Rica durante los años 1830–1849,* AA479

Lines of succession, Louda, Jiří, AJ159

Ling, Amy. *Reading the literatures of Asian America,* BE547

Ling, Sum Ngai. *Historical dictionary of Hong Kong & Macau,* DE151

Lingenfelter, Judith. *Sports and physical education,* BK3

Lingerfelt, Barbara V. *Developing individualized family support plans,* CC235

Lingle, Virginia A. *How to find information about AIDS,* EH20

Lingrës, Nikolaos. *Penguin-Hellenews anglo-hellēnikon lexikon,* AC461

Linguistic atlases, BD21

Linguistic bibliography for the year [...] and supplement for the years [...], BD25
—— Permanent International Committee of Linguists, BD149

Linguistic change, BD68

Linguistic geography, BD21

Linguistics
  abbreviations, BD40
  abstract journals, BD30, BD31
  atlases, BD20
  bibliography, BD2, BD3, BD4, BD6, BD7, BD9, BD22, BD43, BD44, BD204
    current, BD1, BD23, BD24, BD25, BD27, BD28
  biography, BD6, BD34, BD66, BD69, BD70
  databases, BD31
  dictionaries, BD36, BD37, BD38, BD39, BD41, BD77
    multilingual, BD42
  encyclopedias, BD32, BD33, BD34, BD35
  guides, BD3
  library catalogs, BD29
  periodicals, BE42
  statistical methods
    bibliography, BD64

Linguistics (by country or region)
  Europe, Eastern
    bibliography, BD5
  France, BE1129
  USSR
    bibliography, BD5, BD7

Linguistics (by subject)
  history, BD70
    bibliography, BD59, BD67, BD69
    biobibliography, BD66
  see also Sociolinguistics

Linguistics, DeMiller, Anna L., BD3, BD8

Linguistics abstracts, BD30

Linguistics and English linguistics, Allen, Harold Byron, BD91

Linguistics and language behavior abstracts, BD31

Linguistique coréenne, Lucas, Alain, BD223

Linguistische Bibliographie, 1963–1965, BD5

Lingvisticheskie atlasy, Sukhachev, N. L., BD21

Liniger-Goumaz, Max. *Equatorial Guinea,* DD48
—— *Guinea ecuatorial,* DD150
—— *La Guinée équatoriale,* DD151
—— *Who's who de la dictature de Guinée équatoriale,* DD152

Link, Frederick M. *English drama, 1660–1800,* BE647

Linke, William F. *Solubilities, inorganic and metal organic compounds,* EE81

Linker, Robert White. *A bibliography of old French lyrics,* BE1200

Linn, Robert L. *Educational measurement,* CB150

Linnard, William. *Russian-English forestry and wood dictionary,* EJ180

Linnström, Hjalmar. *Svenskt boklexikon, 1830–65,* AA830, AA831

Linton, David. *The newspaper press in Britain,* AE58

Linville, Jim L. *Fire protection handbook,* EK104

Lipinski, Kathleen A. *The complete beverage dictionary,* EJ227

Lipinski, Robert A. *The complete beverage dictionary,* EJ227

Lipp, Martin R. *Medical landmarks USA,* EH161

Lipper Analytical Services, Inc. *Standard & Poor's/ Lipper mutual fund profiles,* CH314

Lipper mutual fund profiles, CH314

Lipperheide, Franz Joseph. *Katalog der Freiherrlich von Lipperheide'schen Kostümbibliothek,* BG93

The Lippincott manual of nursing practice, Suddarth, Doris Smith, EH284

Lippincott's biographical dictionary, AH36

Lippincott's new gazetteer, CL85

Lippy, Charles H. *Bibliography of religion in the South,* BC29
—— *Encyclopedia of the American religious experience,* BC59
—— *Religious periodicals of the United States,* BC24

Lipschutz, Mark R. *Dictionary of African historical biography,* AH310

Lipsius, Johann Gottfried. *A bibliography of numismatic books printed before 1800,* BG173
—— *Bibliotheca numaria,* BG173

Lipstadt, Helene. *Revues d'architecture et de construction en France au XIX siècle,* BF46

Liptzin, Solomon. *A history of Yiddish literature,* BE1080

The LIRT library instruction handbook, AK230

•*LISA,* AK31

Lisa Birnbach's new and improved college book, Birnbach, Lisa, CB254

•*LISA plus,* AK29

Lisäyksiä Fredrik Wilhelm Pippingin bibliografiaan Luettelo suomeksi präntätyistä kirjoista, AA609, AA610

Lisboa, Eugénio. *Dicionário cronológico de autores portugueses,* BE1364

Liscio, Mary Ann. *A guide to colleges for learning disabled students,* CB312

Lisovskiĭ, Nikolai Mikhailovich. *Russkaĭa periodicheskaĭa pechat' 1703–1900 gg,* AD145

Lissens, R. F. *Winkler Prins encyclopedie van Vlaanderen,* DC109

List, Barbara A. *Milestones in science and technology,* EA253

List and Index Society. *Printing for Parliament, 1641–1700,* AF188

List by titles of publications of the United States Department of Agriculture from 1840 to June, 1901, inclusive, Handy, R. B., EJ85

List of additions and corrections to Early Catholic Americana, Bowe, Forrest, BC392

List of architectural books available in America before the Revolution, Park, Helen, BF223

A list of archival references and data of documents from the archives of the German Foreign Ministry, 1867–1920, American Historical Association Committee for the Study of War Documents, DC251

List of available publications of the United States Department of Agriculture, United States. Department of Agriculture, EJ86

A list of books on the history of science, January 1911, John Crerar Library, EA235

List of books printed 1601–1700, in the Library, Penney, Clara Louisa, AA818

List of books printed before 1601 in the Library of the Hispanic Society of America, Penney, Clara Louisa, AA818

List of books printed in Scotland before 1700, Aldis, Harry Gidney, AA678, AA695

List of British diplomatic records for Balkan history, 1879–1905, DC63

List of bulletins of the agricultural experiment stations in the United States ..., EJ94

List of clandestine periodicals of World War II, Muzzy, Adrienne Florence, AD18

A list of common and scientific names of fishes from the United States and Canada, American Fisheries Society. Committee on Names of Fishes, EG281

List of dental periodicals, EH247

List of doctoral dissertations in history in progress or recently completed in the United States, 1909–1970/73, DA16

List of English editions and translations of Greek and Latin classics printed before 1641, Palmer, Henrietta, BE1028

List of English tales and prose romances printed before 1740, Esdaile, Arundell James Kennedy, BE337, BE679

List of French doctoral dissertations on Africa, 1884–1961, Dinstel, Marion, DD29

A list of French prose fiction from 1700 to 1750, Jones, Silas Paul, BE1189, BE1191

A list of geographical atlases in the Library of Congress, with bibliographical notes, Library of Congress. Map Division, CL254

List of geological literature added to the Geological Society's library, [July 1894]–1934, Geological Society of London. Library, EF45

List of journals indexed in AGRICOLA, EJ11

List of journals indexed in Index medicus, EH35, EH37, EH65, EH66

List of journals with abbreviations used in the Catalogue as references, CE14, EA16, EB10, EC15, ED5, EE13, EF57, EF141, EF173, EF232, EG6, EG105, EG211, EG312

List of maps of America in the Library ... preceded by a list of works relating to cartography, Library of Congress. Map Division, CL236

List of named glaciological features in Canada, Stevenson, C. F., CL112

A list of New Zealand books in print, AA948

List of officers of the army of the United States from 1779–1900, Powell, William Henry, CJ646

List of officers of the army of the United States from 1779 to 1900, Powell, William Henry, CJ644

List of officers of the Navy of the United States and of the Marine Corps from 1775 to 1900, Callahan, Edward William, CJ638

List of Philippine government publications, 1945–1958, University of the Philippines. Institute of Public Administration. Library, AF259

List of publications deposited in the library, National Archives of Rhodesia, AA887

List of publications deposited in the Library of the National Archives, 1965–66, National Archives of Malawi, AA866

List of publications deposited under the terms of the Industrial and Commercial Property (Protection) Act, 1927, National Library of Ireland, AA722

List of publications of the Agricultural Department, 1862–1902, with analytical index, United States. Superintendent of Documents, EJ87

List of publications of the Bureau of American Ethnology, CE83

List of publications of the United States Department of Agriculture from January, 1901, to December, 1925, inclusive, Doyle, Mabel Hunt, EJ85

A list of published translations from Chinese into English, French and German ... , Davidson, Martha, BE1552

A list of references for the history of agriculture in the United States, 1790–1840, Bowers, Douglas E., EJ66

A list of references for the history of black Americans in agriculture, 1619–1974, Schor, Joel, EJ73

List of references on nuclear energy, EK293

List of serial publications in the British Museum (Natural History) Library, EA40

List of serials indexed for online users, EH36, EH37, EH67, EH75

A list of South African newspapers, 1800–1982, with library holdings, AE81

List of the bills, reports, estimates, and accounts and papers printed by order of the House of Commons and of the papers presented by command ... , Great Britain. Parliament. House of Commons, AF201

List of the serial publications of foreign governments, 1815–1931, AF13

List of United Nations document series symbols, United Nations. Dag Hammarskjöld Library, AF53

Liste collective des journaux canadiens, AE38

Liste mensuelle d'articles sélectionnés, CH23

Liste mondiale des périodiques spécialisés dans les sciences sociales, AD66, CA18

Liste mondiale des universités, CB241

Lister, Margot. *Costume,* BG110

Lister, Raymond. *How to identify old maps and globes,* CL222
—— *Prints and printmaking,* BF359

Listokin, David. *The environmental impact handbook,* EK80

Liston, Linda L. *The weather handbook,* EF166

LISU annual library statistics, AK97

Litauisches etymologisches Wörterbuch, Fraenkel, Ernst, AC605
Literacy, CB120
   bibliography, CB49, CB352
   handbooks, CB360
   see also **Reading**
Literacy/illiteracy in the world, Eller, William, CB49
   ——— Hladczuk, John, CB49
   ——— Hladczuk, Sharon, CB49
Literarische Lokalgrössen 1700–1900, Friedrichs, Elisabeth, BE1243
A literary and biographical history, Gillow, Joseph, AH228
Literary and library prizes, BE178
A literary atlas & gazetteer of the British Isles, Hardwick, Michael, BE628
Literary Britain, Morley, Frank, BE628
Literary characters *see* **Characters in literature**
Literary-critical approaches to the Bible, Minor, Mark, BC115
Literary criticism and authors' biographies, BE206
Literary criticism index, Weiner, Alan R., BE56
Literary exile in the twentieth century, BE207
A literary gazetteer of England, Fisher, Lois H., BE629
The literary guide to the Bible, BC176
Literary history of Canada, Klinck, Carl Frederick, BE826
A literary history of England, Baugh, Albert Croll, BE615
A literary history of France, BE1173
Literary history of Ireland, Power, Patrick C., BE803
A literary history of Ireland from earliest times to the present day, Hyde, Douglas, BE803
A literary history of New England, Westbrook, Perry D., BE577
A literary history of Persia, Browne, Edward Granville, BE1572
Literary history of Rome from the origins to the close of the golden age, Duff, A. M., BE1052
   ——— Duff, J. Wight, BE1052
A literary history of the American West, BE576
Literary history of the Arabs, Nicholson, Reynold A., BE1546
Literary history of the United States, BE440
   ——— Spiller, Robert E., BE439
Literary index to American magazines, 1815–1865, Wells, Daniel A., BE420
Literary journal in America, 1900–1950, Chielens, Edward E., BE421
Literary journal in America to 1900, Chielens, Edward E., BE420, BE421, BE590
The literary lives of Jesus, Birney, Alice L., BC211
Literary manuscripts at the National Library of Canada, National Library of Canada, BE832
Literary market place, AA282, AA284, AA290, AA379, AD53, AK33, BE172
Literary motifs, BE182, BE183
   dictionaries, BE80
Literary prizes and their winners, BE178
Literary recordings, Library of Congress. Poetry Office, BE324
Literary research, BE6
Literary research guide, Harner, James L., BE393, BE396, BE398, BE400
   ——— Patterson, Margaret C., BE396
Literary research newsletter, BE6
Literary reviews in British periodicals, 1789–1797, Ward, William Smith, BE748
Literary reviews in British periodicals, 1798–1820, Ward, William Smith, BE757
Literary reviews in British periodicals, 1821–1826, Ward, William Smith, BE757
Literary terms, Beckson, Karl E., BE76
Literary tour guide to the United States : Northeast, Harting, Emilie C., BE438
Literary tour guide to the United States : South and Southwest, Stein, Rita, BE438
Literary tour guide to the United States : West and Midwest, Stein, Rita, BE438
Literary writings in America, BE409
Literatur-Kalender, BE1060

Literatur Register der organischen Chemie, Deutsche Chemische Gesellschaft, EE122, EE143
Literatur und Sexualität, Cremerius, Johannes, BE26
Literatur zur deutschsprachigen Presse, AE53
Literatura Chicana, Trujillo, Roberto G., BE558
Literatura colombiana, Nuñnez Segura, José, BE947
Literatura ecuatoriana, 1830–1980, Rodríguez Castelo, Hernán, BE952
A literatura hispano-americana no Brasil, 1877–1944, Wogan, Daniel S., BE879
Literatura hispanoamericana, Valbuena Briones, Angel, BE1457
A literatura no Brasil, Coutinho, Afrânio, BE927
Literatura o narodonaselenii, Burnashev, Ėlgizar Ĩusupovich, CG298
   ——— Davydova, A. G., CG298, CG299
   ——— Valenteĭ, D. I., CG298
Literatura polska, BE1353
Literatura polska na tle rozwoju kultury, Kridl, Manfred, BE1352
Literatura polska od początków do wojny światowej, Korbut, Gabrjel, BE1346, BE1350, BE1351
Literatura română, Biblioteca Centrală Universitară Bucureşti, BE1378
Literatura uruguaya, Rela, Walter, BE958, BE959
Literaturarchivgesellschaft in Berlin. *Jahresbericht über die wissenschaftlichen Erscheinungen auf dem Gebiete der neueren deutschen Literatur,* BD120, BE1225
Literature
   bibliography, BD26, BE7, BE15, BE16, BE17, BE18, BE21, BE23, BE28, BE33, BE35, BE36, BE39, BE187, BE199, BE200, BE985, BE987
   bibliography of bibliography, BE34
   biobibliography, AH42, BE198, BE201, BE208
   biographies of authors, BE187, BE199
   biography, AH42, AH213, BE7, BE198, BE205, BE208, BE211, BE212
      databases, AH42, BE198
      indexes, BE196, BE197, BE203, BE206
   chronologies, BE17, DA36
   chronology, BE192
   computer applications, BE6
   criticism, BE46, BE47, BE48, BE49, BE50, BE53, BE54, BE61
      African-American writers, BE51
      bibliography, BE29, BE52, BE57
      black writers, BE51
      dictionaries, BE85
      encyclopedias, BE65
      history, BE57
      indexes, BE56, BE197
   dictionaries, BE73, BE75, BE76, BE77, BE78, BE80, BE82, BE83, BE84, BE86, BE330
      bilingual
         English-Spanish, BE1453
      multilingual, BE87, BE88
   digests, BE193, BE195
      indexes, BE194
   dissertations, BE44, BE831
   encyclopedias, BE58, BE59, BE60, BE62, BE63, BE64, BE66, BE67, BE68, BE69, BE70, BE71, BE72, BE79, BE80
   guides, BE7, BE9
   handbooks, BE181, BE182, BE186, BE187
   indexes, AD254, BB24, BE38, BE55, CE23
   manuscripts, BE10
   notes and queries, BE168, BE169, BE185
   periodicals, AD49, BE34, BE42, BE170
   plot summaries
      indexes, BE194
   prizes and awards, AL168, BE177, BE178, BE179, BE210
   research methods, BE1, BE4, BE7, BE9, BE10
   reviews of research, BE4
   terminology, BE61
   translations
      bibliography, BD89
Literature (by country or region)
   Africa, Southern, BE1537
   Africa, West
      bibliography, BE1507

   Europe, Eastern
      encyclopedias, BE988
Literature (by period)
   18th century
      bibliography, BE36
   19th century
      criticism, BE54
   20th century
      bibliography, BE26, BE27
      criticism, BE54
   medieval
      bibliography, BE338
      manuscripts, BE335
Literature (by subject)
   computer applications, BE3, BE8
   criticism
      bibliography, BE22
   history
      bibliography, BE1214
   influence studies, BE191
   oral interpretation, BE14
   plot summaries, BE186
Literature and film, Welch, Jeffrey Egan, BH177
Literature and medicine, EH123
Literature and psychology *see* **Psychology and literature**
Literature and science
   bibliography, BE30
Literature and theater of the states and regions of the U.S.A, Gohdes, Clarence Louis Frank, BE573
Literature Bureau (Zimbabwe). *Standard Shona dictionary,* AC716
Literature criticism from 1400 to 1800, BE50
Literature for voices in combination with electronic and tape music, Edwards, J. Michele, BJ276
Literature : general and comparative, Harvard University. Library, BE15
A literature guide for identifying mushrooms, Watling, Roy, EG192
A literature guide for the identification of plant pathogenic fungi, Rossman, Amy Y., EG189
Literature in various Byzantine disciplines, 1892–1977, Allen, Jelisaveta S., DA163
   ——— Ševčenko, Ihor, DA163
The literature matrix of chemistry, Skolnik, Herman, EE7
The literature of adult education, Houle, Cyril Orvin, CB354
The literature of agricultural engineering, EJ3
Literature of agricultural research, Blanchard, J. Richard, EJ1
   ——— Ostvold, Harold, EJ1
The literature of American music in books and folk music collections, Horn, David, BJ14
The literature of animal science and health, EJ98
Literature of Australia, Dutton, Geoffrey, BE854
The literature of British domestic architecture, 1715–1842, Archer, John, BF206
The literature of chess, Graham, John, BK132
The literature of Egypt and the Soudan, from the earliest times to the year 1885 [i.e., 1887] inclusive, Ibrahim-Hilmy, *Prince,* DD148
The literature of fantasy, Schlobin, Roger C., BE297
The literature of geography, Brewer, James Gordon, CL1
The literature of jazz, Kennington, Donald, BJ304
The literature of journalism, Price, Warren C., AE135, AE136
Literature of medieval history, 1930–1975, Boyce, Gray Cowan, DA134
The literature of mineralogy, O'Donoghue, Michael, EF172
The literature of music bibliography, Krummel, Donald William, BJ40
The literature of rock, 1954–1978, Hoffmann, Frank W., BJ338
Literature of rock II, 1979–1983, Cooper, B. Lee, BJ338
   ——— Hoffmann, Frank W., BJ338
The literature of soil science, EJ4
The literature of space science and exploration, Benton, Mildred Catherine, EK22

The literature of Spain in English translation, Rudder, Robert S., BE1448

The literature of terrorism, Mickolus, Edward F., CJ552

Literature of the Low Countries, Meijer, Reinder P., BE1334

The literature of the nonprofit sector, AL94, AL95

Literature of the Renaissance, BE985

The literature of theology, Bollier, John A., BC209

Literature on Byzantine art, 1892–1967, Allen, Jelisaveta S., BF9, DA163

Literature on modern art, BF42

Literature on the history of physics in the 20th century, Heilbron, J. L., ED52, ED53

—— Wheaton, Bruce R., ED52

Literature relating to New Zealand, Collier, James, AA946, DF42

Literature search, EH22

—— National Library of Medicine (U.S.), EH14, EH71

Literature with language, art and music, Committee on Latin America, AD64

Literatures in African languages, Andrzejewski, B. W., BE1501

Literaturnaia entsiklopediia, BE1414

Literaturno-khudozhestvennye al'manakhi i sborniki, BE1404

—— Vsesoiuznaia Knizhnaia Palata, BE1406

Literaturpsychologie, 1945–1987, Pfeiffer, Joachim, BE26

Lithography and silkscreen, Eichenberg, Fritz, BF378

Lithuania
  bibliography, DC70, DC445
  biography, AH267
  encyclopedias, DC441, DC443, DC444
  library resources, DC442, DC445
  manuscripts and archives, AK153, DC561
Lithuania (by subject)
  history, CC355
Lithuania, DC444

A Lithuanian bibliography, Kantautas, Adam, DC442

Lithuanian-English dictionary, AC604

—— Svecevicius, Bronius, AC604

Lithuanian Jewish communities, Schoenburg, Nancy, CC355

Lithuanian language
  bibliography, BD194
  dictionaries
    bilingual, AC601
      English-Lithuanian, AC600
      Lithuanian-English, AC603, AC604
      Lithuanian-German, AC602
    etymology
      dictionaries, AC605
Lithuanian literature
  bibliography, BE1322, BE1324
  biobibliography, BE1323, BE1325
  handbooks, BE989

Lithuanian periodicals in American libraries, Balys, John P., AD220

Lithuanian Research and Studies Center (Chicago, Ill.). Lituanica collections in European research libraries, DC445

Litman, Theodor J. *Sociology of medicine and health care,* CC6, EH11

Litteraturblatt für orientalische Philologie, DE7

Littérature annotée littérature orale d'Afrique noire, Görög, Veronika, CF91

La littérature artistique, BF37

La littérature béninoise de langue française, Huannou, Adrien, BE1524

La littérature comparée, Betz, Louis Paul, BE13

Littérature française, Adam, Antoine, BE1167

—— Gabel, Gernot U., BE1145

—— Gabel, Gisela R., BE1145

—— Pichois, Claude, BE1176

La littérature française contemporaine, 1827–49, Quérard, Joseph Marie, AA631

La littérature occitane du Moyen Age, Taylor, Robert Allen, BE1375, DA138

Littérature orale d'Afrique Noire, Görög, Veronika, CF91

Litteraturens historia i Sverige, Algulin, Ingemar, BE1482

—— Olsson, Bernt, BE1482

Littératures nationales d'écriture française, Rouch, Alain, BE1517

Little, Brooks. *Methodist union catalog,* BC364

Little, Elbert Luther. *Alaska trees and common shrubs,* EJ191

—— *Check list of native and naturalized trees of the United States (including Alaska),* EG197

—— *Conifers and important hardwoods,* EJ191

—— *Florida,* EJ191

—— *Minor eastern hardwoods,* EJ191

—— *Minor western hardwoods,* EJ191

Little, R. John. *A dictionary of botany,* EG134

Little, William. *The shorter Oxford English dictionary on historical principles,* AC31

The Little, Brown guide to writing research papers, Meyer, Michael, AG4

The little magazine, Hoffman, Frederick John, AD35, AD39

The little magazine in America, AD39

Little magazines, AD35, AD39, AD46, AD49
  bibliography, AD12, BE1143
  indexes, AD260, AD276, BA2
  union lists, AD224
Little magazines (by country or region)
  Commonwealth
    indexes, AD275
  France
    bibliographies, AD90
  Great Britain
    indexes, AD263, AD275

Littlefield, Daniel F. *American Indian and Alaska native newspapers and periodicals,* CC424

—— *A biobibliography of native American writers, 1772–1924,* BE551, CC420

Littler, G. H. *Dictionary of mathematics,* EB38, EB39

Litto, Fredric M. *American dissertations on the drama and the theatre,* BH37

Littré, Émile. *Dictionnaire de la langue française,* AC332

Lituanica collections in European research libraries, Šešplaukis, Alfonsas, DC445

Liturgia horarum, BC423

The liturgical dictionary of Eastern Christianity, Day, Peter D., BC447

Liturgical psalter, BC335

Liturgischen Lexikons, Sleumer, Albert, AC582

Liturgy and ritual, BC267, BC358, BC423, BC424, BC427
  bibliography, BC220, BC269
  dictionaries, BC268, BC428
  encyclopedias, BC246

Liturgy and worship, BC268

The liturgy of the hours, Catholic Church, BC423

Litwack, Leon F. *Black leaders of the nineteenth century,* CC395

Litz, A. Walton. *African American writers,* BE542

—— *Modern American women writers,* BE448

Liudi russkoi nauki, EA178

Liungman, Carl G. *Dictionary of symbols,* BF170

—— *Symboler,* BF170

Liutova, Ksenia. *Bibliographie des répertoires nationaux de périodiques en cours,* AD8

The lively arts information directory, BH14

Livermore, Mary A. *A woman of the century,* AH74

Lives of illustrious and distinguished Scotsman, Chambers, Robert, AH243

Lives of Jesus, Kissinger, Warren S., BC211

Lives of the fellows, EH231

Lives of the fellows of the Royal College of Surgeons of England, 1930–1951, Le Fanu, William Richard, EH230

—— Power, D'Arcy, EH230

Lives of the fellows of the Royal College of Surgeons of England, 1952–1964, Robinson, R. H. O. B., EH230

Lives of the fellows of the Royal College of Surgeons of England, 1965–1973, Ross, James Patterson, EH230

The lives of the popes in the early Middle Ages, Mann, Horace Kinder, BC432

Lives of the popes in the Middle Ages, Mann, Horace Kinder, BC432

Lives of the saints, Butler, Alban, BC262, BC263

Livestock, EJ122, EJ135, EJ136, EJ137

Livestock brands, EJ132

Livestock feeds, EJ110, EJ123, EJ126, EJ130

The living church annual, BC346

Living fishes of the world, Herald, Earl Stannard, EG287

Living history sourcebook, Anderson, Jay, DB52

Living with decorative textiles, Barnard, Nicholas, BG158

Livingston, Alan. *Thames and Hudson encyclopaedia of graphic design and designers,* BF369

Livingston, Isabella. *Thames and Hudson encyclopaedia of graphic design and designers,* BF369

Livingston College. *A syllabus of comparative literature,* BE21

Livingstone, E. A. *The Oxford dictionary of the Christian church,* BC240

Livingstone, Matthew. *Guide to the public records of Scotland deposited in H. M. General Register House, Edinburgh,* DC358

Livneh, Ernest. *Israel legal bibliography in European languages,* CK231

Le livre d'or des noms de famille, Gonzalez, Pierre-Gabriel, AJ190

Les livres de l'année, AA629

Les livres de l'année—Biblio, AA625, AA629

Les livres de l'enfance du XVe au XIXe siècle, Gumuchian et compagnie, booksellers, Paris, AA245

Les livres disponibles, AA635

Les livres du mois, AA636

Les livres du trimestre, AA636

Livres-hebdo, AA627, AA633, AA636

Livros antigos portuguezes, 1489–1600, Manuel II, King of Portugal, AA776

Livros de Portugal, AA771

Livros disponíveis, AA779

LLBA, BD31

LLBA user's reference manual, Blackman, Michelle, BD31

—— Chall, Miriam, BD31

Llebot, Amaya. *Bibliografía del cuento venezolano,* BE964

Llibres [sic] editats à Mallorca (1939–1972), Bassa, Ramon, AA743

Llordén, Andrés. *La imprenta en Málaga,* AA804

Lloshi, Xhevat. *Fjalor anglisht-shqip,* AC206

Lloyd, Ann. *The illustrated who's who of the cinema,* BH282

Lloyd, Christopher. *Atlas of maritime history,* DA56

Lloyd, Cynthia B. *Directory of surveys in developing countries,* CG36

Lloyd, John Edward. *Y Bywgraffiadur Cymreig hyd 1940,* AH245

Lloyd, Lorna. *British writing on disarmament from 1914–1978,* CJ673

Lloyd, Susan M. *Roget's thesaurus of English words and phrases,* AC145

Lloyd, Ward. *History of glass,* BG75

Lloyd-Jones, Hugh. *History of classical scholarship,* BE1021, DA107

Lloyd's clerical directory, BC344

Lloyd's maritime directory, CH464

Lloyd's ports of the world, CH464

Lloyd's register of ships, CH465

LLU translations bulletin, Great Britain. Department of Scientific and Industrial Research, EA61

Llyfregell Genedlaethol Cymru. *Llyfryddiaeth Cymru,* AA698, AD290, DC370

Llyfryddiaeth Cymru, Llyfregell Genedlaethol Cymru, AA698, AD290, DC370

LMP, AA282, BE172

Lo, Chu-feng. *Han yü ta tz'u tien,* AC253

Lo, Shuh-shiaw. *Glossary of hydrology,* EF134

Loanwords dictionary, AC186

Lobb, Michael L. *Native American youth and alcohol,* CC114

Lobban, Richard A. *Cape Verde,* DD48
——— *Republic of Guinea-Bissau,* DD48
——— *Sudan,* DD48

The lobbying handbook, CJ149

Lobbyists, CJ149
directories, CJ130, CJ131, CJ142, CJ144
see also **Pressure groups**

Lobel, Mary D. *City of London from prehistoric times to c.1520,* DC354
——— *Historic towns,* DC354

Lobies, Jean-Pierre. *IBN,* AH16

Local government records, Jones, Houston Gwynne, DB140

The local historian's encyclopedia, Richardson, John, AJ105

Local newspapers & periodicals of the nineteenth century, Dixen, Diana, AE56

Local record sources in print and in progress, DC353

Locating the printed source materials for United States history, McMurtrie, Douglas Crawford, AA442

Location register of twentieth-century English literary manuscripts and letters, BE605

Lochar, Ruth. *World guide to libraries,* AK121

Lochhead, Douglas. *Bibliography of Canadian bibliographies,* AA22

Lock, Fred. *Australian literature,* BE852

Lockard, Isabel,. *Desk reference for neuroanatomy,* EH119
——— *Desk reference for neuroscience,* EH119

Locke, Lawrence F. *Proposals that work,* EA160

Locke, John, BB71, BB77

Lockhart, Charles. *American political scientists,* CJ155

Lockot, Hans Wilhelm. *Bibliographia Aethiopica,* DD157

Lockridge, Patricia A. *Catalog of significant earthquakes,* EF260

Lockwood, Crosby. *Directory of libraries and special collections on Eastern Europe and the USSR,* DC51

Lockwood, Elizabeth. *Bibliography of American hymnals,* BC315

Lockwood, John Francis. *Chambers/Murray Latin-English dictionary,* AC578

Lockwood, L. V. *Furniture collectors' glossary,* BG63

Lockwood, Sharon Burdge. *Ghana,* AF231
——— *Nigeria,* AF235, AF236

Lodolini, E. *Guide delle fonti per la Storia dell'America latina esistenti in Italia,* DB275

Löe, Heinz. *Vorzeit und Karolinger,* DC228

Loe, Mary. *The LIRT library instruction handbook,* AK230

Loeb, Catherine. *Women's studies,* CC501

Loeb, James. *Loeb classical library,* BE1002

Loeb classical library, BE1002

Loetscher, Lefferts Augustine. *Twentieth century encyclopedia of religious knowledge,* BC67

Loew, Lois Hendrickson. *Annotated bibliography on childhood schizophrenia, 1955–1964,* EH374

Loewenberg, Alfred. *Annals of opera, 1597–1940,* BJ255

Loewenthal, Rudolf. *The Turkic languages and literatures of Central Asia,* BD209

Löfgren, Ake. *SADCC literature and literature on SADCC,* DD116

Lofthouse, Andrea. *Who's who of Australian women,* AH374

Loftness, Robert L. *Energy handbook,* EK220

Log-books, DF9

Logan, R. G. *Information sources in law,* CK219

Logan, Rayford W. *Dictionary of American Negro biography,* AH64

Logan, Terence P. *The later Jacobean and Caroline dramatists,* BE651
——— *The new intellectuals,* BE650
——— *The popular school,* BE649
——— *The predecessors of Shakespeare,* BE648

——— *Studies in Jacobean drama, 1973–1984,* BE646

Logarithmetica Britannica, Thompson, Alexander John, EB96

Logarithms, EB96

Logasa, Hannah. *Historical fiction,* BE256
——— *An index to one-act plays,* BE228

Logic, BB36

Logie, Gordon. *Elsevier's dictionary of physical planning,* BF277
——— *Glossary of employment and industry,* CH653
——— *Glossary of population and housing,* CG24
——— *Glossary of transport,* CH446
——— *International planning glossaries,* BF277

Logos : monografías y síntesis bibliográfica de filología griega por Sebastian Cirac Estopañan, BD136

Logue, Dennis E. *Handbook of modern finance,* CH235

Lohwater, A. J. *A.J. Lohwater's Russian-English dictionary of the mathematical sciences,* EB53

Loke, Wing Hong. *A guide to journals in psychology and education,* CB22

Lola, Judith A. *Union list of astronomy serials,* EC21

LOMA, BF42

Lombardi, Cathryn L. *Latin American history,* DB297

Lombardi, John V. *Latin American history,* DB297
——— *Venezuelan history,* DB399

Lombardi, Mary. *Brazilian serial documents,* AF160

Lomelí, Francisco A. *Chicano literature,* BE556
——— *Chicano perspectives in literature,* BE558

Lommatzsch, Erhard. *Altfranzösisches Wörterbuch,* AC383

Lomský, Josef. *Soupis periodik geologickych ved,* EF41

Lonchamp, Frédéric Charles. *Bibliographie générale des ouvrages publiés ou illustrés en Suisse et à l'étranger de 1475 à 1914 par des écrivains et des artistes suisses,* AA834

London, Barbara. *The photograph collector's guide,* BF352

London, DC354

London. Commonwealth Institute. Working Party on Library Holdings of Commonwealth Literature. *Commonwealth literature periodicals,* BE818

London Assay Office. *The directory of gold & silversmiths, jewellers, and allied traders, 1838–1914,* BG137

London bibliography of the social sciences, CA13, CE24, CH43, CJ15

London directories, 1677–1855, Goss, Charles, AL1, CH381

London furniture makers from the Restoration to the Victorian era, 1660–1840, Heal, Ambrose, BG135

London goldsmiths, 1200–1800, Heal, Ambrose, BG140

London goldsmiths 1697–1837, Grimwade, Arthur, BG140

London Library. *Catalogue,* AA120

London School of Economics. *Dictionary of business biography,* CH96

London School of Economics and Political Science. *London bibliography of the social sciences,* CA13

The London stage, 1660–1800, BE453, BE636, BH101

The London stage, 1890–1899, Wearing, J. P., BH108

London theatre index, BH60

London theatre record, BH60

London theatres and music halls, 1850–1950, Howard, Diana, BH99

London Times index, AE125

Loney, Glenn Meredith. *20th century theatre,* BH102

Long, Barbara. *The Civil War day by day,* DB120

Long, Cyril. *Biochemists' handbook,* EG322

Long, Everette Beach. *The Civil War day by day,* DB120

Long, John H. *Historical atlas and chronology of county boundaries, 1788–1980,* CL300

Long, Karen. *Population/family planning thesaurus,* CC254

Long, Kim. *Directory of educational contests for students K–12,* CB86

Long, Odean. *A Shakespeare music catalogue,* BJ71

Long term economic growth, United States. Bureau of Economic Analysis, CH173

Longley, Dennis. *Van Nostrand Reinhold dictionary of information technology,* EK183

Longman bibliography of composition and rhetoric, Lindemann, Erika, BE348

Longman companion to English literature, Gillie, Christopher, BE611

The Longman companion to the French Revolution, DC187

Longman companion to twentieth century literature, Ward, A. C., BE764

Longman companion to Victorian fiction, Sutherland, John, BE689

Longman dictionary and handbook of poetry, BE328

Longman dictionary of contemporary English, AC39

Longman dictionary of geography, Clark, Audrey N., CL43

Longman dictionary of language teaching and applied linguistics, Richards, Jack C., BD77

The Longman dictionary of poetic terms, Myers, Jack Elliott, BE328

Longman dictionary of poets, Bold, Alan Norman, BE333

The Longman encyclopedia, AB11

Longman guide to Shakespeare's characters, McLeish, Kenneth, BE788

Longman guide to world science and technology, EA145

Longman handbook of modern British history, 1714–1987, Cook, Chris, DC21, DC294
——— Stevenson, John, DC21

The Longman handbook of modern European history, 1763–1985, Cook, Chris, DC21

Longman illustrated dictionary of food science, Light, N. D., EJ158

The Longman register of new words, Ayto, John, AC93

Longman synonym dictionary, AC140

Longmuir, John. *Etymological dictionary of the Scottish language,* AC165
——— *Jamieson's dictionary of the Scottish language,* AC165

Looking at art, Gealt, Adelheid M., BF115

Looking at prints, drawing and watercolours, Goldman, Paul, BF373

Loomes, Brian. *Watchmakers and clockmakers of the world,* BG88

Loomis, Laird. *A bibliography of modern Irish and Anglo-Irish literature,* BE804

Loone, Nigolas. *Bibliotheca Estoniae historica, 1877–1917,* DC134

Looney, Anna. *Middle Scots poets,* BE810

Loos, Scott Robert. *Bilingual dictionary of criminal justice terms (English/Spanish),* CK256

Lopes, Óscar. *História da literatura portuguêsa,* BE1368

Lopes Viera, Afonso. *História da literatura portuguesa ilustrada,* BE1365

López, Daniel. *Films by genre,* BH228

López Cervantes, Gonzalo. *Ensayo bibliográfico del periodo colonial de México,* DB228

López Rosado, Diego H. *Bibliografía de historia económica y social de México,* DB229

Lopos, George J. *Peterson's guide to certificate programs at American colleges and universities,* CB285

Lora, Guillermo. *Diccionario político, histórico, cultural,* DB337

Lora y Bolivia, DB337

Loránd, Benkö. *A magyar nyelv történeti-etimológiai szótára,* AC499

Lord, Clifford L. *Historical atlas of the United States,* DB69

Lord, Elizabeth H. *Historical atlas of the United States,* DB69

Lord, M. P. *Macmillan dictionary of physics,* ED21
——— *VNR index of chemical and physical data,* ED43

Lorentowicz, Jan. *La Pologne en France,* BE1354

Lorenz, Egon. *Wörterbuch für Recht, Wirtschaft und Politik,* CK49

Lorenz, Oscar A. *Knott's handbook for vegetable growers,* EJ248

Lorenz, Otto Henri. *Catalogue général de la librairie française, 1840–1925,* AA628, AA630, AA632, BC400

Lorenz, Ottokar. *Deutschlands Geschichtsquellen im Mittelalter seit der Mitte des 13. Jahrhunderts,* DC228

Lorenzi, Harri. *Weeds of the United States and their control,* EJ55

Lorenzini, Jean A. *Medical phrase index,* EH101

Loria, Gino. *Guida allo studio della storia delle matematiche,* EB2

Loring, Andrew. *Rhymers' lexicon,* AC115

Lorković, Tanja. *Introduction to Soviet national bibliography,* AA792, AA794, AD150

Loroña, Lionel V. *Bibliography of Latin American and Caribbean bibliographies, 1985–1989,* AA24

—— *Bibliography of Latin American bibliographies, 1980–1984,* AA24

Lorsch, Jay William. *Handbook of organizational behavior,* CD128

Łoś, Leon. *Słownik polskich towarzystw naukowych,* AL71

Los Angeles times [index], AE104, AE112

Lösch, Friedrich. *Tables of higher functions,* EB76

Lossky, Nicolas. *Dictionary of the ecumenical movement,* BC230

Lostaunau Rubio, Gabriel. *Fuentes para el estudio del Perú,* AA30

Loth, Bernard. *Tables générales,* BC398

Loth, Roman. *Przewodnik polonisty,* AA58

Lottes, Wolfgang. *The contemporary printed literature of the English Counter-Reformation between 1558 and 1640,* BC388

Louda, Jiří. *Lines of succession,* AJ159

Louder, Dean R. *This remarkable continent,* DB76

Loughborough University of Technology. Library and Information Statistics Unit. *LISU annual library statistics,* AK97

Loughead, Flora Haines Apponyi. *Dictionary of given names, with origins and meanings,* AJ173

Lougheed, W. C. *Writings on Canadian English, 1976–1987,* BD105

Loughney, Katharine. *Film, television, and video periodicals,* BH175

Loughridge, Brendan. *Which dictionary?,* AC3

Louis, W. R. *Transfer of power in Africa,* DD4

Louis L. Snyder's historical guide to World War II, Snyder, Louis L., DA208

Louisiana
manuscripts and archives, DB26

Louisiana (by subject)
French language, BD159

Louisiana. [Laws, etc.]. *West's Louisiana statutes annotated,* CK179

Louisiana French, Oukada, Larbi, BD159

Lounsbury, Warren C. *Theatre backstage from A to Z,* BH76, BH80

—— *Theatre lighting from A to Z,* BH76

Louw, J. P. *Greek-English lexicon of the New Testament,* AC455

Lovatt, Edwin A. *Dictionary of modern colloquial French,* AC357

Lovejoy's college guide, CB276

Lovejoy's college guide for the learning disabled, CB314

Lovell Johns, ltd. *The Economist atlas,* CH147

Lovera De-Sola, Roberto J. *Bibliografía de la crítica literaria venezolana, 1847–1977,* BE965

—— *Guía para el estudio de la historia de Venezuela,* DB398

Lovering, Cynthia. *Government Archives Division,* DB192

Lovett, D. R. *A dictionary of named effects and laws in chemistry, physics, and mathematics,* EA85

Lovett, Robert Woodberry. *American economic business history information sources,* CH395

Lovette, Leland Pearson. *Naval ceremonies, customs, and traditions,* CJ633

Lovi, George. *Uranometria 2000.0,* EC75

Loving, Elizabeth. *Picture sources UK,* BF349

Low, Alfred D. *The Anschluss movement, 1918–1938,* DC88

Low, Donald Anthony. *Government archives in South Asia,* DE84

Low, Sampson. *English catalogue of books,* AA686

Lowe, David W. *The official World Wildlife Fund guide to endangered species of North America,* EG237

Lowe, E. A. *Codices latini antiquiores,* AA201

Lowe, Robert W. *Bibliographical account of English theatrical literature,* BH38

Lowens, Irving. *American sacred music imprints, 1698–1810,* BJ68

—— *A bibliography of songsters printed in America before 1821,* BJ280

Lowenstein, Amy C. *The Middle East,* DE52

Lower, Dorothy M. *Passenger and immigration lists bibliography, 1538–1900,* AJ29

Lowery, Roger C. *Political science,* CJ4

Lowes, Bryan. *Harper dictionary of economics,* CH62

Lowitt, Richard. *New era and the New Deal, 1920–1940,* DB128

Lowndes, William Thomas. *Bibliographer's manual of English literature,* AA663, AA694

Lowrey, Burling. *Twentieth century parody, American and British,* BE723

Lowry, Philip J. *Green cathedrals,* BK51, BK57

Loyn, H. R. *The Middle Ages,* DA152

Lozano, Eduardo. *Cuban periodicals in the University of Pittsburgh libraries,* AD75

Lü, Wen-chảo. *German-English-Chinese polytechnic dictionary,* EA101

—— *Te Ying Han tsung ho kỏ chi ta tzủ tien,* EA101

Lübben, August. *Mittelniederdeutsches Handwörterbuch,* AC408

—— *Mittelniederdeutsches Wörterbuch,* AC408

Lubbock, Mark Hugh. *The complete book of light opera,* BJ241

Lubeck & Lubeck's who's who in Costa Rica, AH115

Lubell, Cecil. *United States & Canada,* BG157

Lubetski, Edith. *Building a Judaica library collection,* BC516

Lubetski, Meir. *Building a Judaica library collection,* BC516

Lubin, Bernard. *Family therapy,* CC210

Lubitz, Petra. *Trotskyist serials bibliography 1927–1991,* CJ517

Lubitz, Wolfgang. *Trotsky bibliography,* CJ505

—— *Trotskyist serials bibliography 1927–1991,* CJ517

Lubrication, EK239

Lubrication, EK239

Lucas, Alain. *Linguistique coréenne,* BD223

Lucas, Caroline. *Population/family planning thesaurus,* CC254

Lucas, Edna Louise. *Art books,* BF18

—— *Books on art,* BF18

—— *Harvard list of books on art,* BF18

Lucas, Gren. *The IUCN plant red data book,* EG149

Lucca, J. L. de. *Elsevier's dictionary of insurance and risk prevention,* CH508

Luce, T. James. *Ancient writers,* BE201, BE1012

Luchsinger, Arlene E. *Smith's guide to the literature of the life sciences,* EG5

Lucie-Smith, Edward. *Faber book of art anecdotes,* BF95

—— *The Thames and Hudson dictionary of art terms,* BF86

Lucio, Troy. *A Zuni atlas,* CC439

Luckert, Yelena. *Soviet Jewish history, 1917–1991,* BC536, DC587

Ludendorff, H. *Handbuch der Astrophysik,* EC28

Ludlow, Daniel H. *Encyclopedia of Mormonism,* BC371

Ludlow, Nicholas H. *Directory of scientific research institutes in the People's Republic of China,* EA148

Ludman, Joan. *Fine print references,* BF362

—— *Fine prints,* BF375

—— *Old master print references,* BF363

Ludman, Mark D. *The encyclopedia of genetic disorders and birth defects,* EH91

Ludovici, Carl Günther. *Grosses vollständiges Universal-Lexikon aller Wissenschaften und Künste,* AB51

Lüdtke, Gerhard. *Kürschner Nekrolog, 1901–1935,* BE1059

—— *Kürschners deutscher Literatur-Kalender,* BE1060

Ludwig, Armin K. *Brazil,* DB356

Ludwig, Karola. *Lexikon deutschsprachiger Schriftstellerinnen, 1800–1945,* BE1056

Ludwig, Richard M. *Annals of American literature, 1602–1983,* BE436

—— *Guide to American literature and its backgrounds since 1890,* BE395

Ludwig Hain's Repertorium bibliographicum, Burger, Konrad, AA221

Ludwig Hain's Repertorium bibliographicum : Register, Burger, Konrad, AA223

Luebking, Sandra Hargreaves. *The archives,* AJ24, DB37

Lueker, Erwin L. *Lutheran cyclopedia,* BC359

Luettelo suomeksi präntätyistä kirjoista, kuin myös muutamista muista teoksista, joissa löytyy joku kirjoitus suomen, kielellä, tahi joku johdatus sitä tuntemaan, Pipping, Fredrik Wilhelm, AA609, AA610

Luey, Beth. *Handbook for academic authors,* AA321

—— *Publication grants for writers & publishers,* BA11

Luft, Celso Pedro. *Dicionário de literatura portuguêsa e brasileira,* BE1366

Luganda-English dictionary, Snoxall, R. A., AC396

Lugt, Frits. *Répertoire des catalogues de ventes publiques,* BF112, BF302

Luke, Harry. *Bibliography of Sierra Leone,* DD205

Lukman, Franc Ksaver. *Slovenski biografski leksikon,* AH309

Lulat, Y. G.-M. *U.S. relations with South Africa,* DD218

Luling, Virginia. *Somali-English dictionary,* AC725

Lumas, Susan. *The dictionary of genealogy,* AJ111

Lumpkin, Angela. *A guide to the literature of tennis,* BK102

Luna Kan, Francisco. *Enciclopedia yucatanense,* DB245

Lunazzi, Marie-Claude. *Bibliographie française de démographie, 1975–1984,* CG217

—— *Non-national bibliography of French demographers,* CG218

Lund, Daryl B. *Handbook of food engineering,* EJ168

Lund, Roger D. *Restoration and early eighteenth-century English literature, 1660–1740,* BE746

Lund, Torben. *Juridiske literaturhenvisninger,* CK207

Lundqvist, Gunnar. *American film-index, 1908–1915,* BH189

—— *American film-index, 1916–1920,* BH189

Lunds universitet. Litteraturhistoriska institutionen. *Svensk litteraturhistorisk bibliografi,* BE1487

Lundstedt, Bernhard Wilhelm. *Sveriges periodiska litteratur,* AD160

Lung, Rita Gaston. *The senior movement,* CC102

Lunsford, Ronald F. *Research in composition and rhetoric,* BE364

Lunt, Horace Gray. *Kratkii slovar' drevnerusskogo iazyka (XI–XVII vekov),* AC671

—— *Short vocabulary of Old Russian,* AC671

Lupu, Ioan. *Bibliografia analitică a periodicelor românești,* AD324

Luque de Sánchez, Dolores. *Los primeros pasos,* DB450

Luquiens, Frederick Bliss. *Spanish American literature in the Yale University Library,* BE880

Lure, IA. S. *Bibliografiia russkogo letopisaniia,* DC576

Lurker, Manfred. *Dictionary of gods and goddesses, devils and demons,* CF12

Luscombe, Desley. *Australian architectural serials, 1870–1983,* BF208

Lusis, Andy. *Astronomy and astronautics*, EC3
—— *Chess*, BK134
Lust, John. *Index sinicus*, DE129, DE138
—— *Western books on China published up to 1850 in the Library of the School of Oriental and African Studies, University of London*, DE137
Luther, Arthur. *Deutsche Geschichte in deutscher Erzahlung*, BE1267
—— *Deutsches land in deutscher Erzahlung*, BE1267
—— *Land und Leute in deutscher Erzählung*, BE1267
Luther, Wilhelm Martin. *Repertorium der Musikwissenschaft*, BJ17
Lutheran annual, BC357
Lutheran book of worship, BC358
Lutheran Church in America. *Lutheran book of worship*, BC358
—— *Yearbook*, BC356
Lutheran Church–Missouri Synod. *Lutheran book of worship*, BC358
—— *Statistical yearbook*, BC357
Lutheran cyclopedia, BC359
Lutheran World Federation. *The encyclopedia of the Lutheran church*, BC355
Lutherans, BC354, BC355, BC356, BC357, BC358, BC359
Lutjens, Sheryl. *Cuba, 1953–1978*, DB423
Lütolf, Max. *Analecta hymnica medii aevi*, BC313
Luttrell, Gwendolyn W. *Lexicon of geologic names of the United States for 1936–1960*, EF77
—— *Lexicon of new formal geologic names of the United States, 1976–1980*, EF77
—— *Lexicon of new formal geologic names of the United States, 1981–1985*, EF77
Luttwak, Edward. *The dictionary of modern war*, CJ573
Lutz, Liselotte. *Lexikon des Mittelalters*, DA150
Lutz, Mary E. *Face of the nation, 1987*, CC46
Lutzker, Marilyn. *Criminal justice research in libraries*, CK242
Luxembourg
atlases, CL330
bibliography, AA742, DC447
bibliography of bibliography, AA55
biography, AH268, AH270
periodicals
directories, AD83, AD131
statistics, CG261, CG262, CG263
Luxembourg (by subject)
economic conditions, CG263
history, DC446
archives, AK133, DC13
Luxembourg. Ministère de l'éducation nationale. *Atlas du Luxembourg*, CL330
Luxembourg. Service central de la statistique et des études économiques. *Annuaire statistique du Luxembourg*, CG261
—— *Statistiques du mouvement de la population*, CG262
—— *Statistiques historiques*, CG263
Luxembourg, Hury, Carlo, DC447
Luxemburgensia, Hury, Carlo, AA55
Luxon, S. G. *Hazards in the chemical laboratory*, EE75
Luzuriaga, Gerardo. *Bibliografía del teatro ecuatoriano, 1900–1982*, BE951
Lyday, Leon F. *A bibliography of Latin American theater criticism, 1940–1974*, BE899
Lydon, James G. *Struggle for empire*, DB80
Lyer, Stanislav. *Stručny etymologický slovník jazyka českého se zvláštním zřetelem k slovům kulturním a cizím*, AC283
Lyle, Guy Redvers. *I am happy to present*, BE357
Lyle, William David. *Dictionnaire française et anglais de terminologie mathématique*, EB49
The Lyle official antiques review, BG48
Lynch, Charles T. *CRC handbook of materials science*, EK247
Lynch, Mary Jo. *Library data collection handbook*, AK5
—— *Sources of library statistics, 1972–1982*, AK98

Lynch, Richard Chigley. *Broadway on record*, BJ361
—— *Movie musicals on record*, BJ361
Lynch, Samuel W. *Evaluation resource handbook*, CD65
Lynn, Richard John. *Guide to Chinese poetry and drama*, BE1557
Lynn, Ruth Nadelman. *Fantasy for children*, BE386
—— *Fantasy literature for children and young adults*, BE386
Lyon, Howard H. *Diseases of trees and shrubs*, EG203
—— *Insects that feed on trees and shrubs*, EG333
Lyon, Randy. *The encyclopedia of the Midwest*, DB160
Lyon, William F. *Insect pests of farm, garden, and orchard*, EJ50
Lyonnet, Henry. *Dictionnaire des comédiens français (ceux d'hier)*, BH115
Lysts Frysk wirdboek, Frysk Academy, AC392

Ma, Wendy Yu. *Travel in Asia*, CL373
Maas, Lieselotte. *Handbuch der deutschen Exilpresse 1933–1945*, AD101
Mabberley, D. J. *The plant-book*, EG117
Macalpine, Ida. *Three hundred years of psychiatry, 1535–1860*, EH399
MacAlpine, Neil. *Pronouncing Gaelic dictionary*, AC394
Macao
encyclopedias, DE151
Macao (by subject)
history
bibliography, DE226
Macartney, Frederick Thomas Bennett. *Australian literature*, BE853
Macau, Edmonds, Richard L., DE226
MacCafferty, Maxine. *Annotated bibliography of automation in libraries and information systems*, AK190
MacCann, Richard Dyer. *The new film index*, BH235
Macchi, Vladimiro. *Inglese-italiano, italiano-inglese*, AC531
MacCorkle, Lyn. *Cubans in the United States*, CC447
MacDonagh, Oliver. *Australians*, DF37
Macdonald, Charlotte. *The book of New Zealand women*, AH377, DF46
MacDonald, Christine. *Publications of the governments of the Northwest Territories, 1876–1905 and of the Province of Saskatchewan, 1905–1952*, AF155
Macdonald, David. *The encyclopedia of mammals*, EG292
Macdonald, Donald Farquhar Macleod. *Fasti ecclesiae Scoticanae*, BC342
Macdonald, Dwight. *Parodies*, BE723
MacDonald, Ewen. *Faclair gàidhlig le dealbhan*, AC393
MacDonald, Linda Brew. *Teaching technologies in libraries*, AK193
MacDonald, Margaret Read. *The folklore of world holidays*, AL145, CF57
Macdonald, Roger. *Libraries and special collections on Latin America and the Caribbean*, AK111
Macdonald, Teresa. *Union catalogue of the serial publications of the Indian government, 1858–1947, held in libraries in Britain*, AF246
Macdonnell, Arthur Anthony. *Vedic index of names and subjects*, BC490
Macedonian language
bibliography, BD189, BD190, BD191
MacEllvan, Douglass T. *Legal research handbook*, CK195
MacFarlane, Paul. *Daguerreotypes of great stars of baseball*, BK53
MacFarquhar, Roderick. *Cambridge history of China*, DE146
MacGregor, Geddes. *Dictionary of religion and philosophy*, BC74
Macgregor, Malcolm B. *The sources and literature of Scottish church history*, BC341
Machabey, Armand. *Larousse de la musique*, BJ120

MacHale, Carlos F. *Vox: new college Spanish and English dictionary*, AC741
Machalka-Felser, Rautgundis. *Bibliographie zur Geschichte der Städte Österreichs*, DC90
Machamer, Peter K. *Perception*, CD107
Machek, Václav. *Etymologický slovník jazyka českého*, AC284
Machinery, EK247
Machinery's handbook, Oberg, Erik, EK245
Machlin, Lawrence J. *Handbook of vitamins*, EH309
Machovec, George S. *Telecommunications and networking glossary*, CH487
Macintyre, Clement. *Political Australia*, CJ448, DF36
Macintyre, J. E. *Dictionary of inorganic compounds*, EE109
MacIntyre, Sheila. *German-English mathematical vocabulary*, EB51
Maciuszko, Jerzy J. *The Polish short story in English*, BE1355
Mack, Roy. *Dictionary of animal health terminology*, EJ113
—— *Veterinary subject headings*, EJ117
Mack, William P. *Naval ceremonies, customs, and traditions*, CJ633
—— *The naval officer's guide*, CJ635
Mackay, Duncan. *The New York times atlas of the world*, CL285
—— *The world atlas of revolutions*, CJ74
Mackay, James A. *The dictionary of Western sculptors in bronze*, BF396
Mackensen, Lutz. *Deutsches Wörterbuch*, AC439
Mackenzie, Graham. *Librarianship and information work worldwide*, AK79
Mackenzie, Leslie. *The directory of business information resources*, CH78
Mackenzie, William Cook. *Scottish place-names*, CL204
Mackerras, Colin. *The Cambridge handbook of contemporary China*, DE148
Mackey, Philip English. *The giver's guide*, AL93
Mackey, Robert. *Bibliography of the philosophy of technology*, EA18
Mackey, William Francis. *International bibliography on bilingualism*, BD61
Mackie, Thomas T. *The international almanac of electoral history*, CJ89
Mackin, R. *Oxford dictionary of current idiomatic English*, AC80
Mackler, Tasha. *Murder … by category*, BE273
Macksey, Kenneth. *The Penguin encyclopedia of modern warfare*, CJ574
Maclagan, Michael. *Lines of succession*, AJ159
Maclean, Donald. *Typographia Scoto-Gadelica*, AA697
Maclean, Norman. *Dictionary of genetics & cell biology*, EG341
Maclennan, Malcolm. *A pronouncing and etymological dictionary of the Gaelic language*, AC394
Macleod, Iseabail. *Scoor-oot*, AC167
Macleod, M. S. G. *A finding-list of English books to 1640 in libraries in the British Isles (excluding the national libraries and the libraries of Oxford and Cambridge)*, AA672
MacLeod, Norman. *Dictionary of the Gaelic language*, AC395
Maclin, Alice. *Reference guide to English*, BD111
MacLysaght, Edward. *Irish families*, AJ135, AJ197
—— *More Irish families*, AJ135
—— *Surnames of Ireland*, AJ197
MacMillan, Dougald. *Catalogue of the Larpent plays in the Huntington Library*, BE644
The Macmillan atlas of rugs & carpets, BG169
Macmillan atlas of the Holocaust, DA223
The Macmillan Bible atlas, Aharoni, Yohanan, BC197
Macmillan biographical encyclopedia of photographic artists & innovators, Browne, Turner, BF354
The Macmillan book of business and economic quotations, CH75

The Macmillan book of Canadian place names,
Hamilton, William B., CL181
*The Macmillan book of proverbs, maxims and
famous phrases,* BE163
———— Stevenson, Burton Egbert, BE163
Macmillan book of social science quotations, CA36,
CA44
The Macmillan companion to Scottish literature,
BE811
Macmillan concise dictionary of world history,
Wetterau, Bruce, DA26
Macmillan dictionary for children, AC22
Macmillan dictionary of archaeology, DA79
Macmillan dictionary of astronomy, EC32
*Macmillan dictionary of British and European
history since 1914,* DC20
The Macmillan dictionary of Canadian biography,
AH94
Macmillan dictionary of historical terms, Cook,
Chris, DA41
The Macmillan dictionary of Italian literature,
BE1298
Macmillan dictionary of marketing & advertising,
CH549
Macmillan dictionary of physics, Lord, M. P., ED21
The Macmillan dictionary of political quotations,
Eigen, Lewis D., CJ44, CJ45
———— Siegel, Jonathan P., CJ45
The Macmillan dictionary of quotations, BE107
The Macmillan dictionary of women's biography,
AI125
*Macmillan directory of international advertisers and
agencies,* CH574
Macmillan encyclopedia of architects, BF224,
BF234, BF236, BF262
*Macmillan encyclopedia of architecture and
technological change,* BF234
Macmillan encyclopedia of computers, EK174
*The Macmillan encyclopedic dictionary of
numismatics,* Doty, Richard G., BG178
The Macmillan film bibliography, Rehrauer, George,
BH170
The Macmillan guide to correspondence study,
CB103, CB277
Macmillan illustrated animal encyclopedia, EG298
Macmillan school dictionary, AC22
The Macmillan student encyclopedia of sociology,
CC16
MacNalty, Arthur Salusbury. *British medical
dictionary,* EH94
Macnamara, Eve. *Women in Zimbabwe,* DD253
MacNelly, Jeff. *The World almanac of presidential
campaigns,* CJ251
MacNicholas, John. *Twentieth-century American
dramatists,* BE452
MacPherson, Lillian. *Feminist legal literature,* CK10
Macquarrie, John. *Dictionary of Christian ethics,*
BC241
———— *The Westminster dictionary of Christian
ethics,* BC241
MacQuilty, William. *Great botanical gardens of the
world,* EG148
Macquoid, Percy. *Dictionary of English furniture,
from the Middle Ages to the late Georgian period,*
BG123
Macrae, R. *Encyclopaedia of food science, food
technology, and nutrition,* EH297
MacTaggart, Hazel I. *Publications of the government
of Ontario, 1901–1955,* AF155
———— *Publications of the government of Ontario,
1956–1971,* AF155
Macura, Paul. *Elsevier's dictionary of chemistry,*
EE54
———— *Elsevier's Russian-English dictionary,*
AC677, EA127
MacWhinney, Brian. *CHILDES/BIB,* BD63
Madagascar
  bibliography, AA863, AA864, AA865, DD175
  biography, AH197, AH321
  **government publications
    bibliography,** AF222

Madagascar and adjacent islands, Library of
Congress. African Section, AF222, DD175
———— Witherell, Julian W., DD175
Madagascar : society and history, Kottak, Conrad
Phillip, DD175
Madan, Arthur Cornwallis. *English-Swahili
dictionary,* AC756
———— *Swahili-English dictionary,* AC756
Madan, Falconer. *Oxford books,* AA678
Madan, Raj. *Colored minorities in Great Britain,*
CC326
Madden, Lionel. *The nineteenth-century periodical
press in Britain,* AD110
———— *Primary sources for Victorian studies,*
BE606
Maddex, Diane. *All about old buildings,* BF265
Maddox, George L. *The encyclopedia of aging,*
CC80
Maddox, Robert Franklin. *America and World War I,*
DA197
Madeira Islands, CG278
Madejowa, Marla. *Słownik wymowy polskiej PWN,*
AC640
Madison Center for Educational Affairs. *The
common-sense guide to American colleges,* CB264
Madrid newspapers, 1661–1870, Sinclair, Alison,
AE76
Madsen, David. *Successful dissertations and theses,*
AG3
Madsen, Mona. *Guide to Nordic bibliography,* DC71
Madubuike, Ihechukwu. *Handbook of African names,*
AJ174, AJ188
Madurowicz-Urbańskiej, Heleny. *Bibliografia
historii Polski,* DC473
Mäelo, Meemo. *History (archaeology, history,
history of art, music, religion, and church), 1945–
1983,* DC135
Maerz, Aloys John. *Dictionary of color,* ED61
Mafai, Miriam. *Le donne italiane,* AH264
Mafia encyclopedia, Sifakis, Carl, CK254
Mafteah le-khitve-èt be-'Ivrit, AD340
Magalhaes, Erasmo d'Almeida. *Dicionário de
geografia do Brasil,* CL121
Magalini, Sabina C. *Dictionary of medical
syndromes,* EH120
Magalini, Sergio I. *Dictionary of medical syndromes,*
EH120
Magay, Tamás. *A concise English-Hungarian
dictionary,* AC496
———— *A concise Hungarian-English dictionary,*
AC495
•*Magazine ASAP,* AD278
Magazine index, AD278
•*Magazine index/plus,* AD278
Magazine industry market place, AD53
Magazine subject index, AD262
Magazines, Paine, Fred K., AD41
Magazines for children, Richardson, Selma K.,
AA376, AA377
Magazines for libraries, AA375
Magazines for young adults, Richardson, Selma K.,
AA377
Magazines of the American South, Riley, Sam G.,
AD44
Magel, Charles R. *Keyguide to information sources
in animal rights,* EG3
Maggio, Rosalie. *Beacon book of quotations by
women,* BE111
———— *The dictionary of bias-free usage,* AC77
Maggiore, Dolores J. *Lesbianism,* CC273
Maghreb see Africa, North
Magic see Conjuring
Magic, Coleman, Earle Jerome, CF39
Magill, Frank Northen. *Critical survey of literary
theory,* BE48, BE426, BE595
———— *Critical survey of long fiction,* BE241
———— *Critical survey of long fiction : foreign
language series,* BE241
———— *Critical survey of mystery and detective
fiction,* BE275
———— *Critical survey of poetry,* BE312
———— *Critical survey of poetry : Foreign language
series,* BE312

———— *Critical survey of short fiction,* BE261,
BE479
———— *Cyclopedia of literary characters,* BE186,
BE688
———— *Cyclopedia of world authors,* BE208
———— *Cyclopedia of world authors II,* BE208
———— *Magill's bibliography of literary criticism,*
BE22
———— *Magill's cinema annual,* BH238
———— *Magill's quotations in context,* BE108
———— *Magill's survey of cinema,* BH239
———— *Magill's survey of cinema : foreign language
films,* BH239
———— *Magill's survey of cinema : silent films,*
BH239
———— *Magill's survey of science. Earth science
series,* EF12
———— *Magill's survey of science. Life science
series,* EG25
———— *The Nobel Prize winners,* AL173, EH225
———— *Nobel Prize winners : chemistry,* AL166,
AL171, EE103, EE104
———— *The Nobel Prize winners : physics,* AL172,
ED55
———— *Survey of modern fantasy literature,* BE304
———— *Survey of science fiction literature,* BE305
———— *Survey of social science,* CH53
Magill's bibliography of literary criticism, Magill,
Frank Northen, BE22
Magill's cinema annual, BH238, BH240
Magill's quotations in context, Magill, Frank
Northen, BE108
Magill's survey of cinema, BH238, BH239, BH240
Magill's survey of cinema : foreign language films,
Magill, Frank Northen, BH239
Magill's survey of cinema : silent films, Magill,
Frank Northen, BH239
Magill's survey of science. Earth science series,
EF12
Magill's survey of science. Life science series, EG25
Magini, Lorenzo. *Nouvo vocabolario illustrato della
lingua italiana,* AC525
Magna bibliotheca anglo-judaica, Roth, Cecil,
BC517
Magnago Lampugnani, Vittorio. *Encyclopaedia of
20th-century architecture,* BF233
Magner, Thomas F. *Soviet dissertations for advanced
degrees in Russian literature and Slavic
linguistics, 1934–1962,* BE1408
Magnotti, Shirley. *Library science research, 1974–
1979,* AK25
———— *Master's theses in library science, 1960–
1969,* AK25
———— *Master's theses in library science, 1970–74,*
AK25
Magnusson, Magnus. *Cambridge biographical
dictionary,* AH24
Magocsi, Paul R. *Galicia,* DC35
———— *Historical atlas of East Central Europe,*
DC56
———— *Ucrainica at the University of Toronto
Library,* DC546
———— *Ukraine, a historical atlas,* DC544
Magon, Leopold. *Grundriss zur Geschichte der
deutschen Dichtung aus den Quellen,* BE1218
Magraw, Daniel Barstow. *International
environmental law,* CK91
Magriel, Paul David. *A bibliography of dancing,*
BH134
Magrill, Rose Mary. *Acquisitions management and
collection development in libraries,* AK167
Magubane, Bernard. *Political economy of race and
class in South Africa,* DD211
Maguire, Maria. *A bibliography of published works
on Irish foreign relations, 1921–1978,* DC396
Magyar-angol kéziszótár, Országh, László, AC495
Magyar-angol műszaki szótár, EA115
A magyar bibliográfiák bibliográfiája, AA48
Magyar életrajzi lexikon, AH249
Magyar értelmező kéziszótár, AC492
Magyar etymologiai szótár, Gombocz, Zoltán,
AC498
Magyar folyóiratok repertóriuma, AD317

A magyar hirlapirodalom elsö százada, 1705–1805, Dezsényi, Béla, AD121

Magyar irodalmi lexikon, Benedek, Marcell, BE1275

A Magyar irodalom és irodalomtudomány bibliográfiája, BE1278

Magyar irodalom története, Sötér, Istvan, BE1281

A Magyar irodalomtörténet bibliográfiája, BE1279

Magyar irodalomtörténete, Pintér, Jenö, BE1281

Magyar írói álnév lexikon, Gulyás, Pál, AA175, AA176

—— Sz. Debreczeni, Kornélia, AA176

Magyar írók, Gulyás, Pál, AH247

—— Szinnyei, József, AH247, AH250, BE1282

Magyar ki kicsoda 1990, AH253

Magyar könyvészet, AA710, AA712, AA715, AA716

Magyar könyvészet, 1712/1860–1911/20, AA709

Magyar könyvészet, 1921–1944, AA710

Magyar könyvészet, 1945–60, AA711

Magyar nemzeti bibliográfia, AA711, AA712, AA715, AA716, AD317

Magyar nemzeti bibliográfia. Időszaki kiadványok bibliográfiája, AD123

Magyar nemzeti bibliográfia. Könyvek bibliográfiája, AA712, AA716

A magyar nyelv értelmező szótára, AC493

A magyar nyelv történeti-etimológiai szótára, AC499

Magyar-nyelvtörténeti szótár a legrégibb nyelvemlékektöl a nyelvújításig, Szarvas, Gábor, AC494

A magyar sajtó bibliográfiája, 1945–1954, Budapest. Országos Széchényi Könyvtár, AD120

Magyar statisztikai évkönyv, CG247

Magyar Todományos Akadémia. Nyelvtodományi Intézet. *Magyar értelmező kéziszótár*, AC492

Magyar történeti bibliográfia, 1825–1867, Magyar Tudományos Akadémia. Történettudományi Intézet, DC383

Magyar Tudományos Akadémia. *A Magyar irodalomtörténet bibliográfiája*, BE1279

Magyar Tudományos Akadémia. Kézirattár. *A Magyar Tudományos Akadémia Könyvtára Kézirattárának katalógusai*, AG37

Magyar Tudományos Akadémia. Nyelvtudományi Intézet. *A magyar nyelv értelmező szótára*, AC493

Magyar Tudományos Akadémia. Történettudományi Intézet. *Bevezetés a magyar történelem forrásaiba és irodalmába*, DC382

—— *Magyar történeti bibliográfia, 1825–1867*, DC383

Magyar Tudományos Akadémia, Budapest. *Régi magyarországi nyomtatványok, 1473–1600*, AA713

A Magyar Tudományos Akadémia Könyvtára Kézirattárának katalógusai, Magyar Tudományos Akadémia. Kézirattár, AG37

Magyarország időszaki sajtója, 1911–töl 1920–ig, Kemény, György, AD122

Magyarországi irodalom idegen nyelven, BE1280

Ma'had al-Idārah al-'Āmmah (Riyadh, Saudi Arabia). Markaz al-Wathā'iq. Qism al-Maṭbū'āt al-Rasmīyah. *al-Maṭbū'āt al-rasmīyah fī al-Mamlakah al-'Arabīyah al-al-Sa'ūdīyah*, AF260

Ma'had al-Takhṭiṭ al-Qawmī (Egypt). *Dalīl al-maṣādir al-iḥṣā' iyah fī al-bilād al-'Arabīyah*, CG374

Maher, William J. *The management of college and university archives*, AK186

Mahler, Gregory S. *Bibliography of Israeli politics*, CJ438

—— *Contemporary Canadian politics*, CJ302

Mahler, Jane Gaston. *History of world art*, BF134

Mahmud, Shabana. *Urdu language and literature*, BD200

Mahmud, Zamurad. *Pakistani serials*, AD206

Mahmud ul-Hassan. *Pakistani serials*, AD206

Mahoney, Dennis J. *Encyclopedia of the American Constitution*, CK130

Mahoney, M. H. *Women in espionage*, CJ539

Mahrenholz Wolff, Barbara. *Music manuscripts at Harvard*, BJ90

Maichel, Karol. *Guide to Russian reference books*, AA351, AB86

—— *Soviet and Russian newspapers at the Hoover Institution*, AE70

Maidment, David R. *Handbook of hydrology*, EF139

Maier, Mark. *The data game*, CA54

Maier-Bruck, Franz. *Österreich-Lexikon*, DC96

Maigne d'Arnis, W. H. *Lexicon manuale ad scriptores mediae et infimae latinitatis*, AC590

Maikovich, Andrew J. *Sports quotations*, BK31

Mail art, Held, John, BF360

Mail-order business directories, CH556, CH562

Maillard, Robert. *Dictionary of modern ballet*, BH140

—— *Dictionary of modern painting*, BF300

—— *New dictionary of modern sculpture*, BF397

—— *Nouveau dictionnaire de la sculpture moderne*, BF397

Maillet, Lise. *Provincial royal commissions and commissions of inquiry, 1867–1982*, AF154, CJ303

Mailman, Richard B. *Dictionary of toxicology*, EH422

Main catalog of the Library of Congress, Library of Congress, AA108

Maine. [Laws, etc.]. *Maine revised statutes annotated*, CK179

Maine revised statutes annotated, Maine. [Laws, etc.], CK179

Maini, Roberti. *Catalogo dei periodici italiani*, AD130

Mainiero, Lina. *American women writers*, BE443

Maintenance engineering handbook, EK251

Mair, Peter. *Party organisations*, CJ58

Maire, Albert. *Catalogue des thèses de sciences soutenues en France de 1810 à 1890 inclusivement*, EA56, EA57

—— *Répertoire alphabétique des thèses de doctorat ès lettres des universités françaises, 1810–1900*, AG28

Maisel, Louis Sandy. *Political parties & elections in the United States*, CJ262

Maison des sciences de l'homme. 3200 revues et journaux arabes de 1800 à 1965, AD182

Maison Européenne de la Photographie. *Encyclopédie internationale des photographes de 1839 à nos jours*, BF353

Maizell, Robert E. *How to find chemical information*, EE4

Majava, Altti. *National population bibliography of Finland*, CG211

Majerowa, Halina. *Bibliographie du théâtre profane français des XVe et XVIe siècles*, BE1183

al-Majmū al-iḥṣāīya, Syria. Wizārat al-Takhtīt al-Qawmī. Mudīriyat al-Iḥṣā, CG428

Majmu'ah al-iḥṣā'iyah, Libya. Maṣlaḥat al-Iḥṣa' wa-al-Ta'dād, CG340

al-Majmū'ah al-iḥṣa'īyah al-Lubnānīyah, CG410

Al-Majmūāh al-iḥṣāīyah al-sanawīyah, CG377, CG408

Majolo Molinari, Olga. *La stampa periodica romana dell' Ottocento*, AD127

Major, Clarence. *Dictionary of Afro-American slang*, AC128

Major business organisations of Eastern Europe and the Soviet Union, CH362, CH409

Major companies of Europe, CH362, CH409

Major companies of the Arab world, CH362, CH409

Major companies of the Far East and Australasia, CH362, CH409

Major libraries of the world, Steele, Colin, AK120

Major modern dramatists, BE229

Major political events in Indo-China, 1945–1990, Sagar, D. J., CJ421

Major political events in Iran, Iraq, and the Arabian Peninsula, 1945–1990, Mostyn, Trevor, CJ423, DE62

Major political events in South Africa, 1948–1990, Riley, Eileen, CJ411, DD210

Major Soviet nationalities, CC349

Major studies & issue briefs of the Congressional Research Service, AF82

Mak, Alice W. *Philippine newspapers*, AE98

Makaidi, Emmanuel J. E. *A dictionary of historic records of Tanzania (1497–1982)*, DD234

Makar, Ragai N. *Egypt*, DD18

Makarenko, Vladimir A. *A preliminary annotated bibliography of Pilipino linguistics (1604–1976)*, BD234

Makaryk, Irena R. *Encyclopedia of contemporary literary theory*, BE79

Makers of modern Africa, AH312

Makhlouf, Katia. *Perú, las provincias en cifras, 1876–1981*, CG158

Makinson, Larry. *Open secrets*, CJ248

—— *The price of admission*, CJ249

Makower, Joel. *The American history sourcebook*, DB52

—— *The map catalog*, CL266

Makowski, Colleen Lahan. *Quilting, 1915–1983*, BG164

Maktabat al-Asad (Damascus, Syria). *al-Bibliyūghrāfiyā al-waṭanīyah al-Sūrīyah al-rāji'ah*, AA937

Malá československá encyklopedie, AB30

Malaîã sovetskaîã entsiklopediîã, AB88

Malalasekera, G. P. *Encyclopaedia of Buddhism*, BC476

Malan, Jacques P. *South African music encyclopedia*, BJ144

Malan, Stephanus I. *Gesamentlike katalogus van proefskrifte en verhandelinge van die Suid-Afrikaanse universiteite*, AG49

—— *Union catalogue of theses and dissertations of the South African universities, 1942–1958*, AG49

Malatesta, Edward. *St. John's Gospel, 1920–1965*, BC105

Malawi
    atlases, CL342
    bibliography, AA866, DD18, DD176, DD177
    current surveys, DD62
    encyclopedias, DD48
    government publications, AF226, AF241
    statistics, CG341

Malawi (by subject)
    status of women, DD122, DD171

Malawi. National Statistical Office. *Malaŵi statistical yearbook*, CG341

Malawi, Boeder, Robert P., DD18

—— Crosby, Cynthia A., DD48

—— Msiska, Augustine W.C, DD176

—— Nelson, Harold D., DD62

Malawi in maps, Agnew, Swanzie, CL342

—— Stubbs, Michael, CL342

Malawi national bibliography, National Archives of Malawi, AA866

Malawi National Library Service. *Books about Malawi*, DD177

Malaŵi statistical yearbook, CG341

Malay, Armando. *Atlas of the Philippines*, CL362

Malay-English dictionary (romanised), Wilkinson, Richard James, AC606

Malay language
    dictionaries, AC606
    bilingual
        Malay-English, AC607

The Malay world of Southeast Asia, Lim, Patricia Pui Huen, DE99

Malayo-Polynesian languages, BD232, BD235

Malaysia, DE228, DE231
    bibliography, AA921, DE229, DE255
    bibliography of bibliography, DE227
    biography, AH361, AH362, AH369
    government publications, AF253
    handbooks, DE230
    periodicals, AD203, AD204, AD205
        indexes, AD343
    statistics, CG412, CG413

Malaysia (by subject)
    folklore and popular culture, CF94
    history
        bibliography, DE99

Malaysia. Jabatan Cetak Kerajaan (Sabah). *Senarai penerbitan-penerbitan lengkap*, AF253

Malaysia. Jabatan Perangkaan. *Annual statistical bulletin, Malaysia,* CG412
Malaysia official yearbook, CG413
Malaysia yearbook of statistics, CG412
Malaysian current serials, AD204
Malaysian national bibliography, AA921
Malaysian studies, DE231
Malaysian who's who, AH361
Malclès, Louise-Noëlle. *Manuel de bibliographie,* AA6
—— *Sources du travail bibliographique,* AA6, AA12, AA352
Malcolm, I. J. *Dictionary of ceramic science and engineering,* EK265
Malcolm, Jacqueline. *New Zealand in maps,* CL366
Maldives, CG411, DE90
Maldives. Ministry of Planning and Development. *Statistical year book of Maldives,* CG411
Maldonis, Alfonsas. *Tarybų Lietuvos rašytojai,* BE1325
Malec, Karel. *Soupis bibliografí novin a časopisů, vydávaných na území Československé republiky,* AD88
Málek, Jaromír. *Atlas of ancient Egypt,* DA126
Malerei im 20. Jahrhundert, BF307
Malerei Lexikon, BF317
Maletta, Héctor. *Perú, las provincias en cifras, 1876–1981,* CG158
Mali
  atlases, CL339
  encyclopedias, DD48
  government publications
    bibliography, AF230
  statistics, CG342, CG343
Mali. Direction nationale de la statistique et de l'informatique. *Annuaire statistique du Mali,* CG342
Mali, Imperato, Pascal J., CG343, DD48
Malige-Klappenbach, H. *Wörterbuch der deutschen Gegenwartssprache,* AC412
Malignon, Jean. *Dictionnaire des ecrivains français,* BE1162
Malina, Peter. *Bibliographie zur österreichischen Zeitgeschichte, 1918–1985,* DC89
Malindkaĭâ, B. A. *Obshchee i prikladnoe ûzykoznuniye,* BD7
Malinowsky, H. Robert. *AIDS information sourcebook,* EI1170
—— *Best science and technology reference books for young people,* EA29
—— *International directory of gay and lesbian periodicals,* CC285
—— *Reference sources in science, engineering, medicine, and agriculture,* EA5
—— *Science and engineering literature,* EA4, EA5
—— *Science and technology annual reference review,* EA53
Malla, Khadga Man. *Bibliography of Nepal,* DE235
Mallene, Endel. *Estonian literature in the early 1970s,* BE1125
Mallett, Daniel Trowbridge. *Index of artists : international,* BF136
Malley, Elaine. *Spanish-American literature,* BE865
Mallis, Arnold. *American entomologists,* EG334
Mallon, Bill. *The Olympics,* BK6
Mallorca, AA743
Malmqvist, N. G. D. *A selective guide to Chinese literature, 1900–1949,* BE1560
Malmqvist, Ole. *Kunstnerleksikon,* BF147
Malmström, Rosa. *Svensk festskriftsbibliografi, åren 1936–1960,* AA127
Malone, Thomas F. *Compendium of meteorology,* EF152
Maloney, James O. *Perry's chemical engineers' handbook,* EK57
Malonis, Jane A. *Encyclopedia of women's associations worldwide,* AL18
Malony, H. Newton. *Psychology and theology in Western thought, 1672–1965,* BC20, CD59
Malpezzi, Frances M. *Native American folklore, 1879–1979,* CF62
Malta, DC448

  bibliography, AA744
  statistics, CG264, CG265
Malta. Central Office of Statistics. *Annual abstract of statistics,* CG264
—— *Demographic review of the Maltese Islands,* CG265
Malta, Thackrah, John Richard, DC448
Malta national bibliography, AA744
Maltby, Arthur. *The government of Northern Ireland, 1922–72,* AF210
—— *Ireland in the nineteenth century,* AF192
—— *Irish official publications,* AF211
Maltby, Jean. *Ireland in the nineteenth century,* AF192
Maltby, Robert. *A lexicon of ancient Latin etymologies,* AC580
Maltby, William S. *Reformation Europe,* DC28
Maltin, Leonard. *Leonard Maltin's movie and video guide,* BH198
Malvinas *see* **Falkland Islands**
Mały słownik historii Polski, Sienkiewicz, Witold, DC481
Mały słownik języka polskiego, Skorupka, Stanisław, AC630
Mamalakis, Markos. *Historical statistics of Chile,* CG148
Mamdani, Mahmood. *Politics and class formation in Uganda,* DD239
Mammal species of the world, EG299
Mammals, EG289, EG290, EG291, EG292, EG293, EG294, EG296, EG297, EG298, EG299, EG300, EG301, EG302, EG303, EG304, EG305
The mammals, Morris, Desmond, EG300
The mammals of North America, Hall, Eugene Raymond, EG294
Mammals of the world, EG303
Mamola, Claire Zebroski. *Japanese women writers in English translation,* BE1586
Man, myth & magic, BC64
Manac'h, Bérénice. *France-Allemagne, relations internationes et interdépendances bilatérales,* DC201
Management
  bibliography, CH604, CH605, CH608, CH609
  biography, AH77, CH101
  congress and meetings, AL32
  databases, CH338, CH610
  dictionaries, CH344, CH612, CH614, CH616
  directories, CH618, CH716
  encyclopedias, CH611
  handbooks, CH620, CH622
  see also **Personnel management; Public administration**
•*Management contents,* CH610
Management handbook, American Management Association, CH620
The management of college and university archives, Maher, William J., AK186
Management of government information resources in libraries, AF61
Management strategy, CH613
Managing a library binding program, Merrill-Oldham, Jan, AK238
Managing archival and manuscript repositories, Nolte, William, AK188
—— Wilsted, Thomas, AK188
Managing the special library, White, Herbert S., AK181
Manceron, Anne. *La Révolution française,* DC186
Manceron, Claude. *La Révolution française,* DC186
Manchel, Frank. *Film study,* BH167
Manchester, Phyllis Winifred. *The dance encyclopedia,* BH139
Mandava, N. Bhushan. *CRC handbook of natural pesticides,* EJ48
Mander, Raymond. *Theatres of London,* BH99
Mander-Jones, Phyllis. *Manuscripts in the British Isles relating to Australia, New Zealand and the Pacific,* DF11, DF15
Mandonnet, Pierre Félix. *Bibliographie Thomiste,* BB61, BB66
Mangan, Elizabeth Unger. *Geographic names & the federal government,* CL99

Mangenot, E. *Dictionnaire de théologie catholique,* BC398
Mangrum, Charles T. *Peterson's guide to colleges with programs for learning-disabled students,* CB315
Manheim, Jarol B. *DataMap,* CG16
—— *Political violence in the United States, 1875–1974,* CJ104
Manheim, Ralph. *Painting in the twentieth century,* BF307
Manhold, John H. *Illustrated dental terminology,* EH256
Le manifeste communiste de Marx et Engels, Andréas, Bert, CJ497
Manigat, Max. *Haitiana 1971–1975,* AA566
Manila (Philippines). National Library. Legislative Reference Division. *Checklist of publications of the government of the Philippine Islands Sept. 1, 1900 to Dec. 31, 1917,* AF258
Manion, Judith. *A research guide to Congress,* CJ196
Maniruzzaman Miah, M. *Bangladesh in maps,* CL351
Manitius, Maximilianus. *Geschichte der lateinischen Literatur des Mittelalters,* BE1050, BE1051, BE1052
Manley, John. *The atlas of past worlds,* DA87
—— *Atlas of prehistoric Britain,* DC314
Mann, Horace Kinder. *The lives of the popes in the early Middle Ages,* BC432
—— *Lives of the popes in the Middle Ages,* BC432
Mann, John Yeates. *Bibliography on the fatigue of materials,* EK256
Mann, Lester. *Encyclopedia of special education,* CB195, CB196
Mann, Margaret. *Complete list of reports published by the British Library R&D Department,* AK10
Mann, Michael. *International encyclopedia of sociology,* CC16
—— *A thesaurus of African languages,* BD217
Mann, Stuart Edward. *English-Albanian dictionary,* AC208
—— *An historical Albanian-English dictionary,* AC208
—— *An Indo-European comparative dictionary,* AC514
Mann, Thomas. *Guide to library research methods,* AK6
—— *Library research models,* AK6
Mann, Thomas L. *Biographical directory of anthropologists born before 1920,* CE65
Mannack, Thomas. *Beazley addenda,* BF324
Mannfjöldaskýrslur arin 1971–80, CG250
Manning, Beverley. *Index to American women speakers, 1828–1978,* BE358, CC530
—— *We shall be heard,* BE358, CC530
Mansell, W. E. *Tables of natural and common logarithms to 110 decimals,* EB94
Mansheim, Gerald. *Buildings of Iowa,* BF254
Mansi, Giovanni Domenico. *Bibliotheca latina, mediae et infimae aetatis,* BE993
Mantecón, José Ignacio. *Ensayo de una bibliografía de bibliografías mexicanas,* AA23
Mantegna, Anne G. *Guide to federal funding for social scientists,* CA52
Manthy, Robert S. *Natural resource commodities—a century of statistics,* CH441
Mantle Fielding's dictionary of American painters, sculptors & engravers, Fielding, Mantle, BF154
Manual bibliográfico de cancioneros y romanceros, Haskins, Arthur L-F, BE1478
—— Rodríguez Moñino, Antonio R., BE1478
Manual bibliográfico de estudios españoles, González Ollé, Fernando, DC503
Manual de bibliografía de la literatura española, Serís, Homero, BE1438
—— Simón Díaz, José, BE1440
Manual de fuentes de información, Sabor, Josefa Emilia, AA349
Manual de investigación literaria, Jauralde Pou, Pablo, BE1428
Manual de literatura colombiana, Ayala Poveda, Fernando, BE943

Manual de literatura española, Pedraza Jiménez, Felipe B., BE867, BE1429

Manual de literature hispanoamericana, Pedraza Jiménez, Felipe B., BE867, BE1429

Manual del librero hispano-americano, Palau y Dulcet, Antonio, AA806

Manual for authors and editors, EH193

A manual for writers of term papers, theses, and dissertations, Turabian, Kate L., AG6

Manual gráfico-descriptivo del bibliófilo hispano-americano (1475–1850), Vindel, Francisco, AA820

Manual illustré de la litterature française, Lanson, Gustave, BE1172

——— Tuffrau, Paul, BE1172

Manual of American college fraternities, CB398

The manual of brands and marks, Wolfenstine, Manfred R., EJ132

A manual of Canadian literature, AA450

Manual of child psychology, Carmichael, Leonard, CD85

Manual of colloquial Tibetan, Bell, Charles Alfred, AC781

Manual of color aerial photography, EF18

Manual of cultivated broad-leaved trees & shrubs, Krüssmann, Gerd, EG196

Manual of cultivated plants most commonly grown in the continental United States and Canada, Bailey, Liberty Hyde, EG167

Manual of cultivated trees and shrubs, EG204

Manual of cultivated trees and shrubs hardy in North America, Rehder, Alfred, EG200

Manual of determinative bacteriology, Bergey, D. H., EG309

A manual of European languages for librarians, Allen, Charles Geoffry, AK46, AK50, BD11, BD17

Manual of federal geographic data products, CL265

Manual of foreign languages for the use of librarians, bibliographers, research workers, editors, translators, and printers, Von Ostermann, Georg Frederick, AK46, AK50, BD11, BD17

Manual of heraldry, Boutell, Charles, AJ148

Manual of Hispanic bibliography, Foster, David William, BE1427

Manual of industrial and miscellaneous securities, CH309

Manual of law librarianship, CK2

Manual of legislative procedure, CJ456

Manual of monograms in European graphic arts from the 15th to the 18th centuries, BF385

A manual of new mineral names, 1892–1978, EF184

A manual of Old English prose, Quinn, Karen Jane, BE731

Manual of photogrammetry, American Society of Photogrammetry, EF18

Manual of photographic interpretation, American Society of Photogrammetry, EF18

Manual of remote sensing, EF18

Manual of steel construction, EK107, EK108

Manual of style, University of Chicago Press, AA319

Manual of the international statistical classification of diseases, injuries and causes of death, EH56

Manual of the Reformed Church in America, Corwin, Charles E., BC380

Manual of the terminology of the law of armed conflicts and of international humanitarian organizations, CK104

Manual of the writings in Middle English, 1050–1400, Wells, John Edwin, BE734, BE736

A manual of the writings in Middle English, 1050–1500, BE734

Manual of universal history, Ploetz, Karl Julius, DA35

Manual of water quality and treatment, EK98

Manual of woody landscape plants, Dirr, Michael A., EJ246

Manual on certification and preparation of educational personnel in the United States, CB163

Manual on industrial water and industrial waste water, EK95

Manual on water, American Society for Testing and Materials. Committee D-19 on Water, EK95

Manual para las relaciones Europeo-Latinoamericanas, DB286

Manuale bibliograficocritico per lo studio della letteratura italiana, BE1290

Manuale critico-bibliografico per lo studio della letteratura italiana, Puppo, Mario, BE1290

Manuale di bibliografia musulmana, Gabrieli, Giuseppe, BC492

Manuel, E. Arsenio. *Dictionary of Philippine biography*, AH367

Manuel, Esperanza V. *Philippine literature in English*, BE1599

Manuel analytique et critique de bibliographie générale de l'histoire suisse, Santschy, Jean-Louis, DC527

Manuel bibliographique de la littérature française du Moyen Âge, Bossuat, Robert, BE1198

Manuel bibliographique de la littérature française moderne, XVIᵉ, XVIIᵉ, XVIIIᵉ, et XIXᵉ siècles, Lanson, Gustave, BE1137

Manuel bibliographique des études littéraires, Beugnot, Bernard, BE1128

Manuel bibliographique des sciences sociales et économiques, Maunier, René, CA14

Manuel de bibliografía de la literatura española, Serís, Homero, BD169

Manuel de bibliographie, Malclès, Louise-Noëlle, AA6

Manuel de bibliographie biographique et d'iconographie des femmes célèbres, Ungherini, Aglauro, AH37

Manuel de bibliographie générale, Stein, Henri, AA10

Manuel de bibliographie littéraire pour les XVIᵉ, XVIIᵉ et XVIIIᵉ siècles français, Giraud, Jeanne, BE1209

Manuel de bibliographie littéraire pour les XVIᵉ, XVIIᵉ et XVIIIᵉ siècles français, 1921–1935, Giraud, Jeanne, BE1137

Manuel de l'amateur de livres du XIXᵉ siècle, 1801–1893, Vicaire, Georges, AA632

Manuel de l'amateur d'estampes au XVIIIᵉ siècle, Delteil, Löys, BF377

Manuel de l'amateur d'estampes des XIXᵉ et XXᵉ siècles, Delteil, Löys, BF377

Manuel de l'hispanisant, Foulché-Delbosc, Raymond, AA67, AA801, AH290, BE1435

Manuel du libraire et de l'amateur de livres, Brunet, Jacques Charles, AA88, AA632, CL101

Manuel II, *King of Portugal. Livros antigos portuguezes, 1489–1600*, AA776

Manufacturing, CH396

Manufacturing industries
  bibliography, CH396
  databases, CH345
  directories, CH345
  handbooks, CH623, EK248

Manufacturing industries (by country or region)
  United States
    handbooks, CH380
    statistics, CH422

Manufacturing, retail, service, and wholesale industries
  dictionaries, CH340, EK231

Manufacturing USA, CH422

Manuila, Alexandre. *International dictionary of medicine and biology*, EG38, EH100

Manuscript catalog of the American Jewish Archives, BC538

Manuscript catalogue of the Library of the Royal Commonwealth Society, Simpson, Donald H., DC344

Manuscript Division, Library of Congress, Agee, V., AK112

The manuscript papers of British scientists, 1600–1940, EA244

Manuscript sources for the history of Irish civilisation, National Library of Ireland, DC403

Manuscript sources in the Library of Congress for research on the American Revolution, Library of Congress, DB91

Manuscripts
  ancient, medieval, and Renaissance
    bibliography, AA198, AA199, AA200, AA207, AA210, BE1000, BE1042, BE1045
    catalogs, AA201, AA202, AA203, AA205, AA207, AA210, BE1000
      bibliography, AA209
      indexes, AA204
  diplomatics, handwriting, and scripts, AA214, AA215, AA216, BE1018
  facsimiles and reproductions, AA133, AA134
  guides, AA197, AA198
  union lists, AA206, AA211, AA212
  guides, AK188
  guides (by subject)
    English literature, BE603, BE605
    history (by country or region)
      United States, DB90
    history of science, EA226
    literature, BE10
      English, BE602
    Mexico, DB241
    performing arts, BH7
    science and technology, EA244

Manuscripts (by country or region)
  Canada, BE832
    guides, DB194
  France, DC157
  Great Britain, AA199, BE604, BE605, BE724, DC327
    library catalogs, BE637
  Mexico, DB241
  New Zealand, AK163
  Panama, DB319
  United States, DB27
    guides, AK112
  U.S.S.R., AK153, DC561
  see also **Archives**

Manuscripts and government records in the United Kingdom and Ireland relating to Canada, Wilson, Bruce, DB196

Manuscripts in the British Isles relating to Australia, New Zealand and the Pacific, Mander-Jones, Phyllis, DF11, DF15

Manuscripts relating to Commonwealth Caribbean countries in United States and Canadian repositories, Ingram, Kenneth E., DB412

Les manuscrits classiques latins des bibliothèques publiques de France, Jeudy, Colette, AA211

The many names of country people, Schlebecker, John T., EJ32

Manzoni, Cesare. *Biografia italica*, AH266

Mao, Nathan K. *Classical Chinese fiction*, BE1562

——— *Modern Chinese fiction*, BE1562

Maori and Pacific films from New Zealand 1901–1984, New Zealand Film Archive, DF4

Maori language
  dictionaries, AC179
    bilingual, AC610
      English-Maori, AC608
      Maori-English, AC609

Maori place names and their meanings, CL219

The map catalog, CL266

Map collections, CL242, CL251, CL255, CL256, CL257, CL258, CL261, CL264

Map collections (by country or region)
  Canada, CL234
    directories, CL259
  Finland, CL238
  Great Britain, CL230
  North America, CL233, CL235
  United States, CL234, CL236, CL250
    directories, CL259

Map collections in the United States and Canada, CL259

Map guide to the U.S. federal censuses, 1790–1920, Thorndale, William, AJ26, CL306

Map librarianship, Larsgaard, Mary Lynette, CL264

Map Library (British Library). *Catalogue of printed maps, charts and plans*, CL251

Mapetia, E. R. M. *Women in Lesotho*, DD122, DD171

Mapmakers of the sixteenth century and their maps, Karrow, Robert W., CL273

Mapp, Edward. *Directory of blacks in the performing arts*, BH23

The mapping of the world, Shirley, Rodney W., CL241

Mapping the Transmississippi West, 1540–1861, Wheat, Carl Irving, CL244

Maps
  bibliography, CL226, CL229, CL241, CL245, CL250, CL255
    current, CL248
  directories, CL260
  guides, CL222
  handbooks, CL264, CL265
  indexes, CL225
  see also **Atlases**

Maps and atlases, Library of Congress, CL252

Maps and charts of North America and the West Indies, 1750–1789, Library of Congress, CL233

Maps and charts published in America before 1800, Wheat, James Clements, CL245

Maps and plans in the Public Record Office, Great Britain. Public Record Office, CL230

Maps contained in the publications of the American bibliography, 1639–1819, Walsh, Jim, CL243

Maps for America, Thompson, Morris Mordecai, CL268

The maps of Canada, Nicholson, Norman Leon, CL309

Maps on file, CL281

Maquet, Jacques. *Dictionary of Black African civilization*, CE106

Maram, Sheldon L. *Latin American labor organizations*, CH667

Maran, Stephen P. *The astronomy and astrophysics encyclopedia*, EC24

Maratos, Daniel C. *Escritores de la diáspora cubana*, BE976

Marburger index : photographic documentation of art in Germany, BF175

Marcan, Peter. *Poetry themes*, BE318

March, Arthur Charles. *Brief glossary of Buddhist terms*, BC477

March, Francis Andrew. *March's thesaurus and dictionary of the English language*, AC141

March, Ivan. *The Penguin guide to compact discs and cassettes*, BJ379

Marchal, Paul. *Catalogue de l'histoire de France*, DC143

Marcheteau, Michel. *NTC's French and English business dictionary*, AC343, CH61

March's thesaurus and dictionary of the English language, March, Francis Andrew, AC141

Marckworth, M. Lois. *Dissertations in physics*, ED8

Marco, Guy A. *Encyclopedia of recorded sound in the United States*, BJ392
  —— *Information on music*, BJ5
  —— *Opera*, BJ242

Marconi, Joseph V. *Indexed periodicals*, AD251

Marconi's international register, CH491

Marcus, Harold G. *Modern history of Ethiopia and the horn of Africa*, DD158

Marcus, Jacob Rader. *The concise dictionary of American Jewish biography*, BC565
  —— *Index to Jewish festschriften*, BC510
  —— *An index to scientific articles on American Jewish history*, BC543

Marcuse, Michael J. *Reference guide for English studies*, BE393, BE396, BE398

Marcuse, Sibyl. *Musical instruments*, BJ370

Marder, Joan V. *British education thesaurus*, CB81

Marder, Stephen. *A supplementary Russian-English dictionary*, AC678

Marechal, Yvon. *Répertoire pratique des périodiques [belges] édités en langue française*, AD85

Margadant, Steven Willem Floris. *Twintigduizend citaten, aphorismen en spreekwoorden*, BE126

Margaret Sanger and the birth control movement, Moore, Gloria, CC255

Margerie, Emmanuel de. *Catalogue des bibliographies géologiques*, EF34, EF35

Margolies, Edward. *Afro-American fiction, 1853–1976*, BE525

Margolin, Judith B. *The Foundation Center's user-friendly guide*, AL91
  —— *Foundation fundamentals*, AL137

Margoliouth, D. S. *Thesaurus syriacus*, AC773

Margoliouth, J. P. *Thesaurus syriacus*, AC773

Margolis, Joseph. *A companion to aesthetics*, BB27

Margolis, Nadia. *Joan of Arc in history, literature, and film*, DC170

Margulis, Lynn. *Five kingdoms*, EG341

Mariani, John F. *The dictionary of American food and drink*, EJ212

Marías, Julián. *Diccionario de literatura Española*, BE1070, BE1451

Marichev, O. I. *Integrals and series*, EB91

Mariel, Pierre. *Dictionnaire des sociétés secrètes en Occident*, AL75

A marijuana dictionary, Abel, Ernest L., CC127

Marill, Alvin H. *More theatre*, BH20
  —— *Movies made for television*, BH303

Marine affairs bibliography, CK81

Marine biology
  abstract journals, EF214
  biography, EF221
  directories, EF222
  library catalogs, EF209

Marine biotechnology abstracts, EG14

The marine encyclopaedic dictionary, Sullivan, Eric, CH468

Marine engineering, EF214

Marine life, George, J. David, EG224

The Marine officer's guide, Estes, Kenneth W., CJ631

Marine sciences, EF219

Marino Flores, Anselmo. *Bibliografía lingüística de la República Mexicana*, BD241

Maritime affairs—a world handbook, CH466

Maritime history, DA56

Maritime law
  bibliography, CK79, CK81
  handbooks, CH466

Maritime services directory, CH467

Marjoribanks, Kevin. *Foundations of students' learning*, CB70

Mark, H. F. *Encyclopedia of polymer science and engineering*, EK285

Mark, Yudel. *Groyser verterbukh fun der Yidisher shprakh*, AC812

Markaz-i Āmār-i Īrān. *Sālnāmah-i āmārī-i … kishvar*, CG396

Marken, Jack W. *The American Indian language and literature*, BD242
  —— *Bibliography of the Sioux*, CC420

Markert, Lawrence W. *The Bloomsbury group*, BE762

Market Data Retrieval. *CIC's school directory*, CB96

Market guide, Editor & publisher, CH585

Market profiles, CH544

Market research handbook, CH595

Market share reporter, CH596

Market Statistics (firm). *Demographics USA*, CH592

Marketing, CC563
  bibliography, CH577, CH578
  databases, CH548, CH578
  dictionaries, CH549, CH580, CH581, CH582
    multilingual, CH552
  directories, CH116, CH562, CH583, CH584, CH585, CH586
  encyclopedias, CH579
  guides, CH546
  handbooks, CH588
  indexes, CH589
  statistics, CH592, CH594, CH596, CH597, CH599, CH600

Marketing (by country or region)
  Canada
    statistics, CH595
  Europe, CH596
    directories, CH553
    periodicals, CH335
    statistics, CH593

  Europe, Eastern
    statistics, CH591
  Great Britain
    dictionaries, CH551
  United States, CH598

The marketing fact book, CH597

The marketing glossary, Clemente, Mark N., CH580

Marketing information, CH546

Marketing mix promodata, AD177

Markets of the U.S. for business planners, CH598

Markey, Kay. *The Neal-Schuman index to card games*, BK127

Markey, Thomas L. *Germanic and its dialects*, BD113

Markham, Christopher Alexander. *Hall marks on gold and silver plate*, BG139

Markle, Allen. *Author's guide to journals in psychology, psychiatry and social work*, CD14

Marklund, Kari. *Nationalencyklopedin*, AB98

Markmann, Sigrid. *Women and the First World War in England*, DA194

Markov, A. S. *Dictionary of scientific and technical terminology*, EA100

Markowitz, Arnold L. *Historic preservation*, BF266

Markowitz, Harvey. *Native Americans*, CC415

Marks, Alfred. *Bibliographie zur oberösterreichischen Geschichte, 1891–1926*, DC92

Marks, Alfred H. *Guide to Japanese prose*, BE1587

Marks, Claude. *World artists, 1950–1980*, BF138
  —— *World artists, 1980–1990*, BF138

Marks, Lionel S. *Marks' standard handbook for mechanical engineers*, EK240

Marks, Patricia. *American literary and drama reviews*, BE465

Marks & monograms on European and Oriental pottery and porcelain, Chaffers, William, BG77

Marks and monograms of the modern movement, 1875–1930, Haslam, Malcolm, BG31

Marks' standard handbook for mechanical engineers, EK240

Marle, Raimond van. *Iconographie de l'art profane au Moyen-Âge et à la Renaissance, et la décoration des demeures*, BF171

Marler, E. E. J. *Pharmacological and chemical synonyms*, EH329

Marlin, John Tepper. *Cities of opportunity*, CL72

Marolli, Giorgio. *Dizionario tecnico, inglese-italiano, italiano inglese*, EA118

Marouzeau, Jules. *Bibliographie de la littérature latine*, BE1040
  —— *Dix années de bibliographie classique*, BE990, BE1001, BE1003

Marovelli, Piero. *Dizionario dei sinonimi e dei contrari*, AC542

Marovitz, Sanford E. *Bibliographical guide to the study of the literature of the U.S.A.*, BE395

Marques, Alfredo Pinheiro. *Guia de história dos Descobrimentos e expansão portuguesa*, DC186

Marques, António Henrique R. de Oliveira. *Guia de história de la República Portuguesa*, DC487
  —— *Guia do estudante de história medieval portuguesa*, DC488

Marques des imprimeurs et libraires en France au XVᵉ siècle, Polain, Louis, AA251

Marques typographiques, Silvestre, Louis Catherine, AA251, AA254

Marquette, Catherine M. *Directory of surveys in developing countries*, CG36

Márquez Acevedo, Sergio. *Catálogo de seudónimos, anagramas, iniciales y otros alias usados por escritores mexicanos y extranjeros que han publicado en México*, AA152

Marquis Who's Who, Inc. *Who's who in entertainment*, BH27

Marquis Who's Who index to Who's Who books, AH40

Marr, David G. *Vietnam*, DE274

Marr, Eleanor B. *A guide to the literature of chemistry*, EE2

Marrandette, David G. *Golf playoffs*, BK83

Marriage and the family, CC236
  abstract journals, CC222

bibliography, CC64, CC108, CC155, CC205, CC206, CC207, CC210, CC212, CC213, CC214, CC215, CC216, CC217, CC219, CC221, CC228, CC365
  databases, CC221
  dictionaries, CC226, CC227
  directories, CC229
  encyclopedias, CC224
  handbooks, CC231, CC233, CC234, CC235, CC241
  reviews of research, CC237
  statistics, CC244
  tests and measurements, CC239
Marriage and the family (by country or region)
  United States
    statistics, CG107
Marriage and the family (by subject)
  legal rights, CC243
  social conditions, CC51
  see also **Children and youth; Divorce; Parents**
Marriott, F. H. C. *A dictionary of statistical terms,* CG25, EB43
Marrou, Henri. *Dictionnaire d'archéologie chrétienne et de liturgie,* BC246
Marsden, Peter H. *Auswahlbibliographie zum Studium der anglistischen Sprachwissenschaft,* BD91
Marsden, Ruth A. *Peintres naïfs,* BF315
Marsh, Arthur Ivor. *Concise encyclopedia of industrial relations,* CH649
—— *Historical directory of trade unions,* CH668
—— *Trade union handbook,* CH669
Marsh, Earle. *The complete directory to prime time network TV shows, 1946–present,* BH299
Marsh, Elsie Agnes Gillespie. *The economic library of Jacob H. Hollander,* CH17
Marsh, James H. *The Canadian encyclopedia,* DB198
Marsh, Warner L. *Landscape vocabulary,* BF292
Marshall, Alan R. *International dictionary of education,* CB77
Marshall, Alfred. *NASB interlinear Greek-English New Testament,* BC94
Marshall, Donald G. *Contemporary critical theory,* BE23
Marshall, George William. *The genealogist's guide,* AJ109
Marshall, Howard W. *American folk architecture,* BF213
Marshall, I. Howard. *Dictionary of Jesus and the Gospels,* BC128
Marshall, Joan K. *Serials for libraries,* AA374
Marshall, M. J. *Union list of higher degree theses in Australian university libraries,* AG59
Marshall, Mac. *Micronesia, 1944–1974,* CE114, DF5
Marshall, Marion B. *Public finance,* CH219
Marshall, Walker. *History of American literature,* BE449
Marshall, William Taylor. *Glossary of succulent plant terms,* EG135
Marshall Cavendish Corporation. *The illustrated encyclopedia of mankind,* CE42
The Marshall Cavendish illustrated encyclopedia of World War I, DA199
Marshallsay, Diana. *Ford list of British parliamentary papers, 1965–1974,* AF196
—— *Select list of British parliamentary papers, 1955–1964,* AF196
Martell, Edward. *Author's & writer's who's who,* BE211
Marti, Donald B. *Historical directory of American agricultural fairs,* EJ43
Marti, Hanspeter. *Philosophische Dissertationen deutscher Universitäten 1660–1750,* BB16
Marti, James. *The new book of world rankings,* CG51
Marti, Karin. *Philosophische Dissertationen deutscher Universitäten 1660–1750,* BB16
Martial arts, BK89, BK90, BK91
The martial arts, Nelson, Randy F., BK91
Martial arts encyclopedia, BK90
Martin, A. W. *Australians from 1939,* DF37

Martin, Alexander Campbell. *Seed identification manual,* EG154
Martin, André. *Bibliographie des travaux publiés de 1866 à 1897 sur l'histoire de la France de 1500 à 1789,* DC173
—— *Catalogue de l'histoire de la révolution française,* DC177
Martin, Angus. *Bibliographie du genre romanesque français, 1751–1800,* BE1191
Martin, Charles Trice. *The record interpreter,* AA215
Martin, Daniel. *The guide to the foundations of public administration,* CJ469
Martin, Dennis D. *The Mennonite encyclopedia,* BC361
Martin, Elizabeth A. *A concise dictionary of law,* CK34
—— *Dictionary of life sciences,* EG34
—— *Multilingual dictionary of publishing, printing and bookselling,* AA275
Martin, F. X. *A new history of Ireland,* DC413
Martin, Fenton S. *American presidency,* CJ170, CJ172
—— *American presidents,* CJ167, CJ173
—— *Congress and law-making,* CJ195
—— *How to research the Supreme Court,* CK186
—— *The Parliament of Great Britain,* CJ351
—— *Policy analysis and management,* CA11
—— *Political science journal information,* CJ16
—— *The presidency,* CJ165
—— *The U.S. Supreme Court,* CK186
Martin, Galen R. *The international development dictionary,* CH121
Martin, Geoffrey Haward. *Bibliography of British and Irish municipal history,* DC348
Martin, Gérard. *Bibliographie sommaire du Canada français, 1854–1954,* AA449
Martin, J. Paul. *Human rights,* CK77
Martin, J. S. *Biographical dictionary of medallists by L. Forrer: index,* BG186
—— *Index to the Biographical dictionary of medallists,* BG186
Martin, Jochen. *Atlas zur Kirchengeschichte,* BC288
Martin, John. *Bibliographical catalogue of privately printed books,* AA693, AA694
Martin, Judith. *Miss Manners' guide to excruciatingly correct behavior,* AL154
Martin, Julian A. *Criminal justice vocabulary,* CK257
Martin, M. Marlene. *Ethnographic bibliography of North America,* CC419
Martin, Mick. *Video movie guide,* BH202
Martin, Priscilla Clark. *A Portuguese-English dictionary,* AC650
Martin, Samuel Elmo. *A Korean-English dictionary,* AC565
Martin, Sarah S. *Bibliography of astronomy, 1970–1979,* EC2, EC18
Martin Gordon Inc. *Gordon's print price annual,* BF371
Martin Greenwald Associates. *Historical maps on file,* CL282, DA55
—— *State maps on file,* CL302
Martin Heidegger, Sass, Hans-Martin, BB82
Martindale, Don. *Handbook of contemporary developments in world sociology,* CC26
Martindale, William. *The extra pharmacopoeia,* EH357
Martindale-Hubbell bar register of preeminent lawyers, CK151
Martindale-Hubbell international law digest, CK71
Martindale-Hubbell international law directory, CK62
Martindale-Hubbell law digest, CK71, CK166
Martindale-Hubbell law directory, CK71, CK151, CK166, CK221, CK151
•*Martindale online,* EH357
•*Martindale : the extra pharmacopoeia,* EH357
Martindale's American law directory, CK151
Martinello, Gilda. *Railroads,* CH444
Martínez, Héctor. *Bibliografía indígena andina peruana (1900–1968),* DB383

Martinez, Joseph G. R. *Guide to British poetry explication,* BE491, BE695, BE710, BE1192
Martínez, Julio A. *Chicano literature,* BE556
—— *Chicano scholars and writers,* BE562
—— *Dictionary of twentieth-century Cuban literature,* BE974
Martínez, Luis F. *Research guide to Costa Rica,* DB304
Martinez, Nancy C. *Guide to British poetry explication,* BE491, BE695, BE710, BE1192
—— *Poetry explication,* BE491, BE710, BE1192
Martínez, Rufino. *Diccionario biográfico-histórico dominicano, 1821–1930,* AH153
Martínez Amador, Emilio M. *Diccionario inglés-español, español-inglés,* AC735
Martínez de Cartay, Beatriz. *Catálogo de publicaciones oficiales, 1840–1977,* AF163
Martínez Kleiser, Luis. *Refranero general, ideológico español,* BE149
Marting, Diane E. *Spanish American women writers,* BE896
—— *Women writers of Spanish America,* BE896
Martinique, DB445, DB446
  atlases, CL276
Martinique. Archives. *Guide des Archives de la Martinique,* DB446
Martis, Kenneth C. *Historical atlas of political parties in the United States Congress, 1789–1989,* CJ236, CJ237, CJ258, CJ292, DB73
—— *The historical atlas of state power in Congress, 1790–1990,* CJ236, CJ237, CJ258, CJ292, DB73
—— *The historical atlas of the Congresses of the Confederate States of America, 1861–1865,* CJ292
—— *Historical atlas of United States congressional districts, 1789–1983,* CJ236, CJ237, CJ258, CJ292, DB73
Maruţa, Silvia. *Teze de doctorat,* AG40
Marvel, Mary K. *Program evaluation,* CJ464
Marx, Cheryl E. *Elsevier's dictionary of aquaculture,* EJ25
Marx, Gerhard. *Jahresbericht für deutsche Sprache und Literatur,* BD118, BE1226
Marx, Karl, CJ497, CJ500, CJ520, CJ523
A Marx dictionary, Carver, Terrell, CJ518
The Marx-Engels cyclopedia, Draper, Hal, CJ520
Marx-Engels dictionary, Russell, James, CJ523
Marxism, CJ528
  bibliography, CJ504, CJ513
  encyclopedias, CJ518, CJ519, CJ521, CJ522
  handbooks, CJ526
Marxism, CJ531
Marxism, communism and Western society, CJ521
Marxist governments, CJ528
Marxist philosophy, Lachs, John, CJ504
Mary, Geo T. *Afrika-Schrifttum,* DD78
Mary, Blessed Virgin, Saint, BC403
The Mary Flagler Cary music collection, Pierpont Morgan Library, BJ89
Maryland. [Laws, etc.]. *Annotated code of the public general laws of Maryland,* CK179
Mas-Latrie, Louis, Comte de. *Trésor de chronologie d'histoire et de géographie pour l'étude et l'emploi des documents du moyen âge,* DA155
Masanov, I︠U︡riĭ Ivanovich. *Slovar' psevdonimov russkikh pisateleĭ, uchenykh i obshchestvennykh dei︠a︡teleĭ,* AA184
—— *Teorii︠a︡ i praktika bibliografii,* AA7
—— *Ukazateli soderzhanii︠a︡ russkikh zhurnalov i prodolzhai︠u︡shchikhsi︠a︡ izdaniĭ 1755–1970 gg,* AD326
Masanov, Ivan Filippovich. *Slovar' psevdonimov russkikh pisateleĭ, uchenykh i obshchestvennykh dei︠a︡teleĭ,* AA183, AA184
Masarykův slovník naučný, AB31
Mascarenhas, Ophelia. *Women in Tanzania,* DD235
Mashikhin, Evgeniĭ Aleksandrovich. *Statisticheskie publikat︠s︡ii v SSSR,* CG301
Mashkova, Marii︠a︡ Vasil'evna. *Istorii︠a︡ russkoĭ bibliografii nachala XX veka,* AA66
—— *Obshchie bibliografii russkikh periodicheskikh izdaniĭ, 1703–1954, i materialy po statistike russkoĭ periodicheskoĭ pechati,* AD143

Maslova, L. M. *Istoriĭa SSSR*, DC549

Maslovskiĭ, E. K. *Russko-anglo-nemetsko-frantsuzskiĭ slovar' po vychislitel'noĭ tekhnike*, EK192

Mason, Anita. *An illustrated dictionary of jewellery*, BG82

Mason, C. M. *Cyclopedic survey of chamber music*, BJ270

Mason, Francis. *Balanchine's complete stories of the great ballets*, BH150

Mason, I. L. *A world dictionary of livestock breeds, types and varieties*, EJ136

Mason, Lauris. *Fine print references*, BF362

────── *Fine prints*, BF375

────── *Old master print references*, BF363

Mason, Oliver. *Bartholomew gazetteer of places in Britain*, CL135

────── *The gazetteer of England*, CL138

Mason, Paul. *Mason's manual of legislative procedure*, CJ456

Mason, Tim. *Atlas of Nazi Germany*, DC263

Mason, Virginia M. *EPISOURCE*, EH404

Mason's manual of legislative procedure, Mason, Paul, CJ456

Mass-market magazines, American, AD29

Mass media
  bibliography, AE131, CC73, CC398, CC500
  dictionaries, CH488
  directories, AD51, AE23
  encyclopedias, CH482
  guides, AE130
  statistics, CH496, CH599

Mass media (by country or region)
  Europe
    directories, AD1, AE2
  Germany
    directories, AD103
  Great Britain
    directories, AD1, AE2
  international
    directories, AD1, AE2
  Netherlands
    directories, AD132, AE65
  United States
    directories, CB263
  see also **Press**; **Radio**; **Television**

The mass media, Sterling, Christopher H., CH196

Mass media bibliography, Blum, Eleanor, AE131

Mass media sex and adolescent values, Alah, A. Odasuo, CC142

Mass murder, Newton, Michael, CK246

Mass transportation, CH450
  see also **Urban transportation**

Massachusetts. [Laws, etc.]. *Massachusetts general laws annotated*, CK179

Massachusetts general laws annotated, Massachusetts. [Laws, etc.], CK179

Massenkeil, Günther. *Das Grosse Lexikon der Musik*, BJ136

Massey, James C. *Guide to preservation literature*, BF219

────── *Historic American Buildings Survey/Historic American Engineering Record*, BF219

────── *Readings in historic preservation*, BF219

Massicotte, Micheline. *Dictionnaire du français québécois*, AC385

Massil, Stephen W. *Anglo-Jewish bibliography, 1971–1990*, BC517

Massot i Muntaner, Josep. *Diccionari de la literatura catalana*, BE1450

Master index to Directory of corporate affiliations, CH351

Master index to poetry, BE319

Master index to subject encyclopedias, AB16

Masterplots cyclopedia of literary characters, BE186

Masterplots literary annual, BE186

Masters abstracts international, AG13, AG15, AG16

Masters of lens and light, Darby, William, BH206

Masters theses
  abstract journals, AG15, AG16
  bibliography, AG14

Masters theses (by country or region)
  Australia
    bibliography, AG59

Master's theses directories, CB23

Masters' theses in anthropology, McDonald, David Roark, CE27

Master's theses in library science, 1960–1969, Magnotti, Shirley, AK25

Master's theses in library science, 1970–74, Magnotti, Shirley, AK25

Masters theses in the pure and applied sciences accepted by colleges and universities of the United States and Canada, EA58

Masterson, James R. *Writings on American history, 1962–1973*, DB23

Masterworks of Asian literature in comparative perspective, Miller, Barbara Stoler, CA53

Masuda, Koh. *Kenkyūsha's new Japanese-English dictionary*, AC554

Masui, Mitsuzō. *A bibliography of finance*, CH207

Mata, F. X. *Diccionario de la zarzuela*, BJ260

Mata, Maria Nena R. *Index to Philippine plays, 1923–1983*, BE1598

Matanov, Kristo. *Krat'uk spravochnik po istoriĭa na Bŭlgariĭa*, DC119

al-Maṭbūʿāt al-rasmīyah fī al-Mamlakah al-ʿArabīyah al-al-Saʿūdīyah, Maʿhad al-Idārah al-ʿĀmmah (Riyadh, Saudi Arabia). Markaz al-Wathāʾiq. Qism al-Maṭbūʿāt al-Rasmīyah, AF260

Matejic, Mateja. *A biobibliographical handbook of Bulgarian authors*, BE1103

────── *A comprehensive bibliography of Yugoslav literature in English, 1593–1980*, BE1499

Matematicheskaĭa ėntsiklopediĭa, EB33

Material bibliográfico para el estudio de las aymaras, callawayas, chipayas, urus, Berg, Hans van den, CE74

Material culture
  bibliography, BG9, CC422
  directories, CC465
  guides, BG3

Material culture (by country or region)
  United States, BG117, CC351
  see also **Folk art**

Material culture, BG3

Materialen zur Quellenkunde der Kunstgeschichte, BF37

Materiales de investigación, Tortajada, A., AD329

Materiales para la historia de las relaciones internacionales de Costa Rica, Araya Incera, Manuel E., DB305

Materials
  abstract journals, EK258
  bibliography, EK125
  databases, EK258
  dictionaries, EK264, EK266
  encyclopedias, EK261, EK262
  guides, EK255
  handbooks, EK248, EK268, EK272, EK273, EK274, EK276, EK277, EK279
  research centers
    directories, EK267

Materials (by subject)
  fatigue
    bibliography, EK256

Materials and strategies for the education of trainable mentally retarded learners, White, James P., CB193

Materials and technology, EK50

Materials data book for engineers and scientists, Parker, Earl Randall, EK279

Materials data sources, EK255

Materials for the study of politics and government in the Dominican Republic, 1930–1966, Wiarda, Howard J., DB434

Materials handbook, Brady, George S., EK272

Materials handling handbook, EK277

The materials of demography, Eldridge, Hope T., CG2

Materials per una bibliografia d'Andorra, Armengol, Lidia, DC82

────── Batlle, Monica, DC82

────── Gual, Ramon, DC82

Materials research centres, EK267

Materials safety data sheets reference for crop protection chemicals, EJ57

Materials science and engineering, EK262

Materiały do bibliografii dziennikarstwa i prasy w Polsce, w latach 1944–1954, "Prasa," Robotnicza Spółdzielnia Wydawnicza, Warsaw. Zakład Badań Prasoznawczych, AE67

•*MATH*, EB31

Math equals, Perl, T., EB104

Mathematical Association of America. *Combined membership list of the American Mathematical Society, the Mathematical Association of America, and the Society for Industrial and Applied Mathematics*, EB56

────── *Mathematical reviews*, EB27

Mathematical book review index, 1800–1940, Grinstein, Louise S., EB32

Mathematical handbook for scientists and engineers, Korn, Granino Arthur, EB66

Mathematical logic, EA92
  bibliography, EB15

The mathematical practitioners of Hanoverian England, 1714–1840, Taylor, Eva Germaine Rimington, EB102

Mathematical practitioners of Tudor and Stuart England, Taylor, Eva Germaine Rimington, EB102, EB103

Mathematical reviews, EB7, EB15, EB23, EB27, EB28, EB31

Mathematical sciences administrative directory, EB59

Mathematical sciences professional directory, EB59

Mathematical scientist, EB13

Mathematical Society of Japan (Nihon Sūgakkai). *Encyclopedic dictionary of mathematics*, EB35

Mathematical statistics
  abstract journals, EB29
  bibliography, EB12, EB13, EB17
  databases, EB28
  dictionaries, CG32, EB45
  encyclopedias, EB34
  financial aids, EB58
  handbooks, EB63, EB65, EB81
  indexes, CG15, EB21, EB22, EB24, EB30, EK160
  tables, EB81, EB90, EB93, EB95
    bibliography, EB73
    indexes, EB73

Mathematical tables, British Association for the Advancement of Science, EB82, EB94

────── Mathematical Tables Project, EB88

Mathematical tables and other aids to computation, EB73, EB89

Mathematical Tables Project. *[Mathematical tables]*, EB88

Mathematical tables series, EB74

Mathematicians, EB19, EB100, EB101, EB102, EB103, EB104
  directories, EB56, EB60

Mathematics
  abstract journals, EB26, EB27, EB31
  bibliography, CE14, EA16, EA22, EB8, EB10, EB11, EB14, EB16, EB18, EB19, EC15, ED5, ED7, EE13, EF57, EF141, EF173, EF232, EG6, EG105, EG211, EG312
  biography, EB14, EB100, EB101, EB102, EB103, EB104
  book reviews, EB32
  chronologies, EA254
  congresses and meetings
    meetings, EB7
  databases, EB28, EB31
  dictionaries, CG25, CG32, EB38, EB39, EB41, EB42, EB43, EB45, EB46
    bilingual
      Chinese-English, EB48
      French-English, EB49
      German-English, EB50, EB51
      Russian-English, EB52, EB53
      Spanish-English, EB54
    German, EB44
    multilingual, EB40, EB47

directories, EB59
education, CB116
encyclopedias, EB33, EB34, EB35, EB36
eponyms, EA85
financial aids, EB58
formulas, EB61
guides, EB1, EB2, EB3, EB4, EB5, EB6, ED2
guides for authors, EB98, EB99
handbooks, EA149, EB61, EB62, EB63, EB64, EB66, EB67, EB68, EB69, EB70, EB71, EK18, EK19
indexes, EB20, EB21, EB23, EB25, EB27, EK160
quotations, EB55
style manuals, EB98, EB99
tables, EB76, EB77, EB78, EB79, EB80, EB82, EB83, EB84, EB85, EB86, EB87, EB88, EB89, EB91, EB92, EB94, EB96
  bibliography, EB72, EB75
  indexes, EB74
translations
  indexes, EB20
Mathematics (by subject)
history, EB102, EB103
  bibliography, EB2, EB8, EB14
Mathematics abstracts, EB31, EK161
Mathematics dictionary, James, Robert C., EB41
Mathematics into type, Swanson, Ellen, EB99
Mathematics of computation, EB89
Mathematische Formeln, EB61
Mathematisches Wörterbuch mit Einbeziehung der theoretischen Physik, Naas, Josef, EB44
Mather, Frank Jewett. *Western European painting of the Renaissance,* BF308
Matheson, Ann. *Scottish Gaelic union catalogue,* AA697
Matheson, Cyril. *Catalogue of the publications of Scottish historical and kindred clubs and societies,* DC275, DC281, DC361, DC362
Mathews, Edward Bennett. *Catalogue of published bibliographies in geology, 1896–1920 … ,* EF35
Mathews, J. Chesley. *Eight American authors,* BE403
Mathews, Mitford McLeod. *Americanisms,* AC152
—— *A dictionary of Americanisms on historical principles,* AC152
—— *A survey of English dictionaries,* AC4
Mathews, Robert Henry. *Chinese-English dictionary,* AC266
—— *Mathews' Chinese-English dictionary,* AC266
Mathews' Chinese-English dictionary, Mathews, Robert Henry, AC266
•*MATHFILE,* EB28
Mathias, James. *Chinese dictionaries,* AC270
—— *Compilation of Chinese dictionaries,* AC270
Mathies, M. Lorraine. *Scholarships, fellowships, grants, and loans,* CB393
Mathis, B. Claude. *Key resources on teaching, learning, curriculum, and faculty development,* CB224
•*MathSci,* CG15, EB22, EB23, EB27, EB28, EB30, EK156, EK159, EK166
•*MathSci disc,* EB28
Matica Slovenská, Turčiansky sv. Martin. Knižnica. *Katalog slovákumových knih Knižnice,* AA597
Matijevic, Nicolás. *Bibliografía patagónica y de las tierras australes,* DB328
Matijevic, Olga H. de. *Bibliografía patagónica y de las tierras australes,* DB328
Matko, Dubravko J. I. *Soviet economic facts, 1917–81,* CH181
Matlaw, Myron. *Modern world drama,* BE230
Matley, Ian M. *Atlas of Russian and East European history,* DC56
—— *Historical atlas of East Central Europe,* DC56
Matos, Antonio. *Guía a las reseñas de libros de y sobre Hispanoamérica,* AA370
Matray, James Irving. *Historical dictionary of the Korean War,* DE215
Matricardi, Paolo. *The Rand McNally encyclopedia of military aircraft, 1914–1980,* CJ577
Matsebula, J. S. M. *History of Swaziland,* DD231

Matsuda, Mitsugu. *The Japanese in Hawaii,* CC408
Matsuev, Nikolai Ivanovich. *Khudozhestvennaĩa literatura, russkaĩa i perevodnaĩa,* BE1397
Matsumoto, Y. Scott. *Demographic research in japan, 1955–70,* CG404
Matsushita, Hitoshi. *A checklist of published instrumental music by Japanese composers,* BJ74
Mattas, Linda L. *Only the best,* CB176
Mattera, Philip. *Inside U.S. business,* CH415
Matterlin, O. *Catalogue bibliographique des ventes publiques,* AA263
—— *Cote internationale des livres et manuscrits,* AA263
Mattfeld, Julius. *A handbook of American operatic premières, 1731–1962,* BJ256
—— *Variety music cavalcade, 1620–1969,* BJ331
Matthews, Catherine J. *Criminal intelligence and security intelligence,* CK245
Matthews, Geoffrey J. *Historical atlas of Canada,* DB207
—— *Historical atlas of East Central Europe,* DC56
—— *Ukraine, a historical atlas,* DC544
Matthews, Geraldine O. *Black American writers, 1773–1949,* BE526
Matthews, John. *Atlas of the Roman world,* DA119
Matthews, John R. *The official World Wildlife Fund guide to endangered species of North America,* EG237
Matthews, Noel. *Guide to manuscripts and documents in the British Isles relating to Africa,* DC345, DD38, DD39
—— *A guide to manuscripts and documents in the British Isles relating to the Far East,* DE105
—— *Guide to manuscripts and documents in the British Isles relating to the Middle East and North Africa,* DD38, DE50
—— *Guide to Western manuscripts and documents in the British Isles relating to South and South East Asia,* DE12, DE13
—— *Guides to materials for West African history in European archives,* DD105
Matthews, William. *American diaries in manuscript, 1580–1954,* BE507, BE510, BE726, DB66
—— *British autobiographies,* AH236, BE727
—— *British diaries,* BE724, BE726, BE727, DC327
—— *Canadian diaries and autobiographies,* BE726, DB185
Matthews, William R. *Guide to doctoral dissertations in Victorian literature, 1886–1958,* BE751
Matthias Lexers Mittelhochdeutsches Taschenwörterbuch, Lexer, Matthias von, AC405
Mattill, Andrew J. *Classified bibliography of literature on the Acts of the Apostles,* BC122
Mattill, Mary B. *Classified bibliography of literature on the Acts of the Apostles,* BC122
Mattingly, David. *An atlas of Roman Britain,* DC313
Mattson, Mark T. *Atlas of the 1990 census,* CG109, CL303
—— *The historical and cultural atlas of African Americans,* CC339
Matulic, Rusko. *Bibliography of sources on Yugoslavia,* DC609
Mature woman in America, Dolan, Eleanor F., CC61
—— Gropp, Dorothy M., CC61
Matz, David. *Greek and Roman sport,* BK26
Matzerath, Horst. *Modern urban history research in Europe, USA, and Japan,* CC299
Mauer, Mare. *Eesti kirjandus vōōrkeeltes,* BE1124
Maunier, René. *Bibliographie économique, juridique et sociale de l'Égypte moderne, (1798–1916),* DD149
—— *Manuel bibliographique des sciences sociales et économiques,* CA14
Maurel, Jean-François. *Sources bibliographiques de l'Afrique de l'Ouest et de l'Afrique equatoriale d'expression française,* DD40
Maurepas, Arnaud de. *Les grands hommes d'état de l'histoire de France,* AH199
Maurer, Barbara. *Hochschulschriften zu Schwarz-Afrika,* DD30

Maurer, David J. *U.S. politics and elections,* CJ105
Maurer, David W. *The American language,* BD107
—— *Language of the underworld,* AC129
Maurer, Margarete. *Leben und Arbeit von Frauen, Frauenforschung und Frauenbewegung in Afrika,* DD7
Maurice, E. Grace. *Union list of manuscripts in Canadian repositories,* DB195
Mauricio, Rufino. *Pacific Basin and Oceania,* DF3
Maurists. *Histoire littéraire de la France,* BE1171
Mauritania
atlases, CL339
bibliography, DD178
current surveys, DD62
encyclopedias, DD48
government publications
  bibliography, AF230
statistics, CG344
Mauritania, Calderini, Simonetta, DD18
—— Gerteiny, A. G., DD48
—— Handloff, Robert E., DD62
Mauritius, CG345
bibliography, DD18, DD121, DD179
encyclopedias, DD48
government publications, AF234
  bibliography, AF222
Mauritius. Archives Dept. *Bibliography of Mauritius, (1502–1954),* DD179
Mauritius. Central Statistical Office. *Annual digest of statistics,* CG345
Mauritius, Bennett, Pramila Ramgulam, DD18
—— Bowman, Larry W., DD179
—— Selvon, Sydney, DD48
Mauser, Wolfram. *Literaturpsychologie, 1945–1987,* BE26
Mavituna, Ferda. *Biochemical engineering and biotechnology handbook,* EK43
Mawer, A. *Chief elements used in English place-names,* CL201
Mawson, Christopher Orlando Sylvester. *Dictionary of foreign terms,* AC187
—— *The Harper dictionary of foreign terms,* AC187
Max-Planck-Institut fü Ausländisces Öffentliches Recht und Völkerrecht. *Encyclopedia of public international law,* CK100
Maxwell, Margaret. *Handbook for AACR2 1988 revision,* AK194
Maxwell, Shirley. *Historic American Buildings Survey/Historic American Engineering Record,* BF219
Maxwell-Hyslop, A. R. *The dictionary of classical mythology,* CF27
May, Charles E. *Twentieth century European short story,* BE986
May, Donald Curtis. *Handbook of probability and statistics, with tables,* EB63, EB83
May, George S. *Automobile industry, 1896–1920,* CH383
—— *Automobile industry, 1920–1980,* CH383
May, Herbert G. *Oxford annotated Bible, with the Apocrypha,* BC94
—— *Oxford Bible atlas,* BC200
May, James D. *Avant-garde choral music,* BJ292
May, Kenneth Ownsworth. *Bibliography and research manual of the history of mathematics,* EB8, EB14
Mayall, David. *The autobiography of the working class,* CH679
Mayer, Enrique. *International auction records,* BF109
Mayer, Fanny Hagin. *The Yanagita Kunio guide to the Japanese folk tale,* CF98
Mayer, Hans Eberhard. *Bibliographie zur Geschichte der Kreuzzüge,* DA168
—— *Crusades,* DA168
—— *Geschichte der Kreuzzüge,* DA168
Mayer, Leo Ary. *Bibliography of Jewish art,* BF194
—— *Bibliography of Jewish numismatics,* BF194, BG174
—— *Bibliography of Moslem numismatics, India excepted,* BG174
Mayer, Ralph. *Art terms and techniques,* BF91

—— *Artist's handbook of materials and techniques*, BF127, BF304

—— *HarperCollins dictionary of art terms and techniques*, BF91

Mayer, Sydney L. *European manuscript sources of the American Revolution*, DB90

—— *Rand McNally encyclopedia of World War II*, DA206

—— *The two World Wars*, DA191

Mayer-Serra, Otto. *Música y músicos de Latinoamérica*, BJ121

Mayerchak, Patrick M. *Scholars' guide to Washington, D.C. for Southeast Asian studies*, DE101, DE120

Maygill's survey of cinema, BH240

Mayhew, Anthony Lawson. *Glossary of Tudor and Stuart words, especially from the dramatists*, AC101

Mayhew, Susan. *The concise Oxford dictionary of geography*, CL48

Maylender, Michele. *Storia delle accademie d'Italia*, AL69

Maynadies, Michel. *Bibliographie algérienne*, DD125

Maynard, Donald N. *Knott's handbook for vegetable growers*, EJ248

Maynard, John T. *Understanding chemical patents*, EA263

Maynard's industrial engineering handbook, EK233

Mayne, Alan J. *Resources for the future*, CA15

Mayo, Robert Donald. *English novel in the magazines, 1740–1815*, BE669

Mayotte, DD121

Mayr, Helmut. *A guide to fossils*, EF248

Mayrhofer, Manfred. *Etymologisches Wörterbuch des Altindoarischen*, AC707

—— *Kurzgefasstes etymologisches Wörterbuch des Altindischen*, AC707, AC708

Mays, James Luther. *Harper's Bible commentary*, BC172

Mays, Terry M. *Historical dictionary of international organizations in sub-Saharan Africa*, DD6

Mazda, F. F. *Electronics engineer's reference book*, EK137

Maze-Sencier, Geneviève. *Dictionnaire des maréchaux de France*, AH195

Mazingira Institute. *Women & development*, DD168

Mazza, Karen A. *Integrating women's studies into the curriculum*, CC492

Mazzeno, Laurence W. *Victorian novel*, BE668

Mazzoni, Guido. *Avviamento allo studio critico delle lettere italiane*, BE1289

M'baye, Saliou. *Guide des archives de l'Afrique occidentale française*, DD106

—— *Sources de l'histoire démographique des pays du Sahel conservées dans les archives*, CG307, DD102

Mbilinyi, Marjorie J. *Women in Tanzania*, DD235

McAfee, Michael J. *Military uniforms in America*, CJ634

McAinsh, T. F. *Physics in medicine & biology encyclopedia*, EH89

McAleer, Beth D. *The directory of North American fisheries and aquatic scientists*, EG48

McAleese, Ray. *The encyclopaedia of educational media communications and technology*, CB170

McAlester, Lee. *Field guide to American houses*, BF252

McAlester, Virginia. *Field guide to American houses*, BF252

McAlister, Micheal J. *The language of visual effects*, BH259

McAlpin Collection of British History and Theology. *Catalogue of the McAlpin collection of British history and theology*, BC227, DC321

McAninch, Sandra. *Sun power*, EK212

McArthur, Feri. *The Oxford companion to the English language*, BD94

McArthur, Tom. *The Oxford companion to the English language*, BD94

McBrearty, James C. *American labor history and comparative labor movements*, CH633

McBride, Elizabeth A. *British command papers*, AF195, AF206

McBride, William G. *High interest easy reading*, CB191

McBurney, William Harlin. *Check list of English prose fiction, 1700–1739*, BE669, BE678, BE681

McCabe, James Patrick. *Critical guide to Catholic reference books*, BC12, BC13, BC391, BC437

McCaffery, Larry. *Postmodern fiction*, BE247

McCaffree, Mary Jane. *Protocol*, AL155

McCagg, William O. *Atlas of Russian and East European history*, DC56

—— *Historical atlas of East Central Europe*, DC56

McCallum, Heather. *Directory of Canadian theatre archives*, BH54

—— *Theatre resources in Canadian collections*, BH54

McCalpin, Deborah J. *Health media review index*, EH43

McCann, Mary Ann. *AMA handbook of poisonous and injurious plants*, EG152

McCardle, Ellen Steele. *Social networks and mental health*, CC29

McCarthy, J. Thomas. *McCarthy's desk encyclopedia of intellectual property*, CK134

McCarthy, John R. *Higher education finance*, CB222

McCarthy, Justin. *The Arab world, Turkey, and the Balkans, (1878–1914)*, CG373

McCarthy's desk encyclopedia of intellectual property, McCarthy, J. Thomas, CK134

McCarty, Clifford. *Published screenplays*, BH168

McCarty, J. W. *Australians 1888*, DF37

McCarus, Ernest Nasseph. *A Kurdish-English dictionary*, AC567

McCauley, Martin. *Directory of Russian MPs*, CJ385

McClean, Andrew. *Security, arms control, and conflict reduction in East Asia and the Pacific*, CJ674

McClellan, Elisabeth. *Historic dress in America 1607–1800*, BG111

—— *Historic dress in America 1800–1870*, BG111

—— *History of American costume, 1607–1870*, BG111

McClintock, Marsha Hamilton. *The Middle East and North Africa on film*, DD71, DE34

McConnell, Fraiser. *Papua New Guinea*, DF49

McCorkle, Barbara B. *Recent literature in discovery history*, CL11

McCormick, Donald. *Spy fiction*, BE272

McCormick, E. H. *New Zealand literature*, BE863

McCormick, John O. *A syllabus of comparative literature*, BE21

McCormick, Mairi. *A dictionary of words about alcohol*, CC129

McCoy, Garnett. *Archives of American art*, BF58

McCoy, Judy. *Rap music in the 1980s*, BJ340

McCrank, Lawrence J. *Bibliographical foundations of French historical studies*, DC162

McCrea, Barbara P. *The European political dictionary*, CJ322

—— *The Soviet and East European political dictionary*, CJ396

McCready, Warren T. *Bibliografía temática de estudios sobre el teatro español antiguo*, BE1466

McCreery, James L. *American glass*, BG76

McCrum, Blanche P. *Guide to the study of the United States of America*, DB13

McCulloch, Alan. *Encyclopedia of Australian art*, BF76, BF140

McCulloch, Walter Fraser. *Woods words*, EJ181

McCullough, Kathleen. *Concrete poetry*, BE313

McCullough, Rita I. *Sources*, CC502

McCurdy, Howard E. *Public administration*, CJ469, CJ470

McCusker, John J. *Money and exchange in Europe and America, 1600–1775*, CH284

McDaniel, George. *IBM dictionary of computing*, EK181

McDavid, Raven I. *The American language*, BD107

McDermott, James A. *Recommended law books*, CK128

McDermott, John. *Punctuation for now*, AC111

McDermott, Robert A. *Focus on Buddhism*, BC472

—— *Focus on Hinduism*, BC481

McDonagh, Don. *The complete guide to modern dance*, BH152

McDonald, Archie P. *Encyclopedia USA*, DB47

McDonald, Colin S. *Dictionary of Canadian artists*, BF314

McDonald, David Roark. *Masters' theses in anthropology*, CE27

McDonald, Elvin. *The American Horticultural Society encyclopedia of gardening*, EJ232

McDonald, Gordon C. *Area handbook for the Democratic Republic of the Congo (Congo Kinshasa)*, DD62

—— *Area handbook for the People's Republic of the Congo (Congo Brazzaville)*, DD62

McDonald, James. *A dictionary of obscenity, taboo & euphemism*, AC130

McDonald, James R. *The broadcaster's dictionary*, BH318

McDonald, Jan. *Australian artists' index*, BF140

McDonald, Peter. *The literature of soil science*, EJ4

McDormand, Thomas Bruce. *Judson concordance to hymns*, BC319

McDowell, Colin. *McDowell's directory of twentieth century fashion*, BG115

McDowell's directory of twentieth century fashion, McDowell, Colin, BG115

McEvedy, Colin. *Atlas of world population history*, CG44

McFarland, D. M. *Ghana*, DD48

—— *Upper Volta*, DD48

McFarland, David. *The Oxford companion to animal behaviour*, CD120

McFarland, George Bradley. *Thai-English dictionary*, AC778

McFarland, Keith D. *The Korean War*, DE213

McFeely, Mary Drake. *Women's work in Britain and America from the nineties to World War I*, CC503

McGarry, Daniel D. *World historical fiction guide*, BE250

McGee, Harold. *The curious cook*, EJ218

—— *On food and cooking*, EJ219

McGee, Leo. *Education of the black adult in the United States*, CB38

McGee, M.D. *African newspapers on microfilm*, AE79

McGehee, A. Harvey. *Two centuries of American medicine, 1776–1976*, EH211

McGill University. *An introduction to the literature of vertebrate zoology*, EG215

McGill University. Faculty of Medicine. *Bibliotheca Osleriana*, EH206

McGillivray, Alice V. *America at the polls 2*, CJ240

—— *America votes*, CJ241

—— *Congressional and gubernatorial primaries*, CJ254

—— *Presidential primaries and caucuses, 1992*, CJ254

McGillivray's theatre guide, BH87

McGilvray, J. W. *Irish economic statistics*, CG254

McGinnies, William G. *Deserts of the world*, CL58, EF17

McGlynn, Eileen A. *Middle American anthropology*, CE90

McGonagle, John J. *The Arthur Andersen European Community sourcebook*, AF22

McGrath, Alister E. *The Blackwell encyclopedia of modern Christian thought*, BC229

McGrath, D. F. *Bookman's price index*, AA262

McGraw-Hill dictionary of art, BF75, BF77

McGraw-Hill dictionary of chemistry, EE43

McGraw-Hill dictionary of earth sciences, EF15

The McGraw-Hill dictionary of international trade and finance, Gipson, Carolyn Renee, CH123

McGraw-Hill dictionary of modern economics, CH70

McGraw-Hill dictionary of physics, ED22

McGraw-Hill dictionary of scientific and technical terms, EA84, EA93, ED22, EF15

McGraw-Hill encyclopedia of astronomy, EA81

McGraw-Hill encyclopedia of chemistry, EA81

The McGraw-Hill encyclopedia of economics, CH51

McGraw-Hill encyclopedia of engineering, EA81

McGraw-Hill encyclopedia of environment science & engineering, EA81

McGraw-Hill encyclopedia of food, agriculture & nutrition, EJ23

McGraw-Hill encyclopedia of physics, EA81

McGraw-Hill encyclopedia of science & technology, EA79, EA81, EA167, EA179, EE43, EF69, EJ23

McGraw-Hill encyclopedia of the geological sciences, EF69

McGraw-Hill encyclopedia of world drama, BE230, BH72

The McGraw-Hill handbook of essential engineering information and data, EK17

McGraw-Hill modern men of science, EA179

McGraw-Hill modern scientists and engineers, EA179

McGraw-Hill personal computer programming encyclopedia, EK207

The McGraw-Hill real estate handbook, CH542

McGraw-Hill world futures and options directory, CH439

McGraw-Hill yearbook of science and technology, EA81, EA167, EE43

McGregor, Ronald Stuart. *The Oxford Hindi-English dictionary,* AC485

McGrew, Margaret P. *Encyclopedia of medical history,* EH195

McGrew, Roderick E. *Encyclopedia of medical history,* EH195

McGuiness, Ignatius. *A lexicon of St. Thomas Aquinas based on the Summa theologica and selected passages of his other works,* BB63

McGuinness, Brian. *Wittgenstein,* BB80

McGuire, Martin. *Introduction to classical scholarship,* BE997, DA93

McGuire, Martin Rawson Patrick. *Introduction to medieval Latin studies,* BD145

McGuire, Paula. *American political leaders,* CJ158

McGuire, William. *American social leaders,* CA64

McHale, Vincent E. *Political parties of Europe,* CJ320

McHenry, Renée E. *Directory of transportation libraries and information centers in North America,* CH449

———— *Intercity bus lines,* CH444

McHenry, Robert. *Famous American women,* CC576

———— *Liberty's women,* CC576

———— *Webster's American biographies,* AH60

———— *Webster's American military biographies,* CJ641, CJ648

McHugh, Roger. *Short history of Anglo-Irish literature from its origins to the present day,* BE803

McIlwaine, J. H. St. J. *Theses on Africa, 1963–1975,* DD33

McIlwaine, John. *Africa,* DD86

McInnis, Raymond G. *Research guide for psychology,* CD4

McIntosh, Margaret E. *Educating the gifted,* CB185

McIntyre, Sylvia. *Bibliography of British and Irish municipal history,* DC348

McKay, George Leslie. *American book auction catalogues, 1713–1934,* AA265

McKay, John C. *A guide to Germanic reference grammars,* BD114

———— *A guide to romance reference grammars,* BD151

McKay, William Angus. *The Macmillan dictionary of Canadian biography,* AH94

McKearin, George S. *American glass,* BG76

McKearin, Helen. *American glass,* BG76

McKee, Cynthia Ruiz. *Cash for college,* CB384

McKee, Phillip C. *Cash for college,* CB384

McKee, Thomas Hudson. *National conventions and platforms of all political parties, 1789–1905,* CJ264

McKendry, Blake. *Dictionary of folk artists in Canada from the 17th century to the present,* BF314, BG33

———— *Folk art,* BG33

McKenna, Brian. *Irish literature, 1800–1875,* BE806

———— *Irish official publications,* AF211

McKenzie, Roderick. *A Greek-English lexicon,* AC444

McKernan, Michael. *Australians : a historical dictionary,* DF37

———— *Australians : events and places,* DF37

McKerns, Joseph P. *Biographical dictionary of American journalism,* AE150

McKerrow, R. B. *Dictionary of printers and booksellers in England, Scotland and Ireland and of foreign printers of English books, 1557–1640,* AA306

———— *Introduction to bibliography for literary students,* AA3

———— *Printers' & publishers' devices in England & Scotland, 1485–1640,* AA250

McKinney, Mary Jane. *Handbook of financial markets and institutions,* CH234

McKinney's consolidated laws of New York annotated, New York (State). [Laws, etc.], CK179

McKinstry, E. Richard. *The Edward Deming Andrews Memorial Shaker Collection,* BC381

McKirahan, Richard D. *Plato and Socrates,* BB55, BB56

McKittrick agency list, CH573

McKnight, Scot. *Dictionary of Jesus and the Gospels,* BC128

McKusick, Victor A. *Mendelian inheritance in man,* EG342, EH189

McLachlan, Keith Stanley. *A bibliography of Afghanistan,* DE112

———— *A bibliography of the Iran-Iraq borderland,* DE35

McLane, Charles B. *Soviet-African relations,* DC599, DD107, DD112

———— *Soviet-Asian relations,* DC599

———— *Soviet-Middle East relations,* DC599

McLaren, James. *A new concise Xhosa-English dictionary,* AC810

McLaughlin, Thomas. *Critical terms for literary study,* BE61

McLean, George F. *A bibliography of Christian philosophy and contemporary issues,* BC218

McLean, Janice W. *Consultants and consulting organizations directory,* CH617

McLean, Martin. *International handbook of education systems,* CB125

McLean, Mervyn. *An annotated bibliography of Oceanic music and dance,* BJ322

McLeary, Ailsa. *Australians 1888,* DF37

McLeish, Kenneth. *Longman guide to Shakespeare's characters,* BE788

McLendon, Carmen C. *Dissertations in Hispanic languages and literatures,* BE1446

McLeod, W. H. *Textual sources for the study of Sikhism,* BC576

McLintock, Alexander H. *Descriptive atlas of New Zealand,* CL365

———— *Encyclopaedia of New Zealand,* DF43

McLintock, D. R. *A handbook on Old High German literature,* BE1256

McManaway, James Gilmer. *A check list of English plays, 1641–1700,* BE657

McManis, Douglas R. *Historical geography of the United States,* CL106, CL107

McMann, Evelyn de R. *Canadian who's who index, 1898–1984,* AH98

McManners, John. *The Oxford illustrated history of Christianity,* BC279

McMichael, Jeffrey. *Atlas of American sport,* BK22

McMillan, James B. *Annotated bibliography of Southern American English,* BD106

McMillen, Marilyn Miles. *Private schools in the United States,* CB136

McMorrin, Ian. *World atlas of mountaineering,* BK119

McMullan, Randall. *Dictionary of building,* EK109

McMullen, Haynes. *Libraries in American periodicals before 1876,* AK9

McMullin, Ruth. *Oral history collections,* DB33, DB36

McMullin, Thomas A. *Biographical directory of American territorial governors,* CJ287

McMurtrie, Douglas Crawford. *Locating the printed source materials for United States history,* AA442

McNamara, Martha J. *The IQ debate,* CB8, CC361

McNamee, Lawrence F. *Dissertations in English and American literature,* BE424

McNaughton, Howard Douglas. *New Zealand drama,* BE862

McNeil, Alex. *Total television,* BH299

McNeil, Barbara. *Artist biographies master index,* BF136

———— *Author biographies master index,* BE196

———— *Biography and genealogy master index,* AH9

———— *Business biography master index,* CH94

———— *Performing arts biography master index,* BH28

McNeil, R. A. *Latin American studies,* DB252

McNeill, D. B. *A dictionary of scientific units,* ED19

McNeill, Peter. *An historical atlas of Scotland, c.400–c.1600,* DC367

McNerney, Kathleen. *Women writers of Spain,* BE1444

McNutt, Dan J. *The eighteenth-century Gothic novel,* BE292

McPheron, William. *The bibliography of contemporary American fiction, 1945–1988,* BE476

———— *The bibliography of contemporary American poetry, 1945–1985,* BE495

McPherson, James M. *American political leaders,* CJ158

McPherson, Marion White. *Dictionary of concepts in general psychology,* CD26

McQuaid, James. *Index to American photographic collections,* BF344

McQuarrie, Jane. *Canadian literary periodicals index,* BE822

———— *Index to Canadian poetry in English,* BE827

McQuilton, John. *Australians : a historical atlas,* DF37

McRae, Madelyn A. *Films in the sciences,* EA34

MdR, Schwarz, Max, CJ333

MDR's sales manager's guide to the U.S. school market, CB96

MDR's school directory, CB96

Mead, Frank Spencer. *Handbook of denominations in the United States,* BC65

Meagher, Paul Kevin. *Encyclopedic dictionary of religion,* BC60

Meak, Linda. *Glossary of geographical names in six languages,* CL91

Means, Spencer. *Literary criticism index,* BE56

Means estimating handbook, EK110

Measures for psychological assessment, Chun, Ki-Taek, CD67

Measures of personality and social psychological attitudes, CD98

Measures of social psychological attitudes, Robinson, John P., CD98

———— Shaver, Phillip R., CD98

Mechanical components handbook, EK241

Mechanical design and systems handbook, EK242

Mechanical engineering
   biography, EK250
   dictionaries, EK237
   handbooks, EK238, EK240, EK241, EK242, EK243, EK244, EK245, EK246, EK247

Mechanical engineers' handbook, EK243

———— Kent, William, EK238, EK243

Mechanical engineers in America born prior to 1861, American Society of Mechanical Engineers, EK250

Mechanical engineer's pocket-book, EK238

Mechanical engineer's reference book, EK244

Meckler, Alan M. *Oral history collections,* DB33, DB36

Medcalf, Margaret. *Directory of special collections in Australiana,* DF31

Media-concerned women, CC549

Media equipment, Dosky, J. S., AK43

———— Rosenberg, Kenyon C., AK43

Media guide international, AE9

Media index, AA386

Media Network. *Guide to films on apartheid and the southern African region*, DD43
Media review, AA386
Media review digest, AA387
Media Scandinavia, AD80
Mediae latinitatis lexicon minus, Niermeyer, Jan Frederik, AC592
The mediaeval stage, Chambers, Edmund Kerchever, BE664
Medical & dental materials, EH176
Medical and dental materials, EH176
Medical and health care books and serials in print, EA37, EH23
Medical and health information directory, EH162
Medical and pharmaceutical dictionary, Bunjes, Werner Ernst, EH136
Medical anthropology, CE12, EH185
Medical bibliography (Garrison and Morton), Garrison, Fielding Hudson, EH205
—— Morton, Leslie Thomas, EH205
Medical books and serials in print, EH23
Medical books, libraries, and collectors, Thornton, John Leonard, EH28
Medical diagnosis, EH83
Medical dictionary, Gould, George M., EH93
The medical directory, EH168
Medical education, EH389
  bibliography, EH13
  directories, EH152, EH160
Medical education in the United States, Cordasco, Francesco, EH13
Medical ethics, EH239
  bibliography, EH237, EH242
  dictionaries, EH240
  encyclopedias, EH241
Medical illustration, EA220, EH51, EH236
Medical information, Strickland-Hodge, Barry, EH8
Medical instruments and apparatus, EH86
Medical internship and residency, EH160
Medical jurisprudence, EH268, EH269
  bibliography, EH271
  dictionaries, EH267, EH270
Medical landmarks USA, Lipp, Martin R., EH161
Medical legal dictionary, Bander, Edward J., EH267
Medical libraries, EH4, EH28
  directories, AK52
  guidebooks, EH161
Medical libraries (by country or region)
  Great Britain
    directories, EH167
Medical Library Association. *Handbook of medical library practice*, EH4
—— *MLA directory*, AK52
—— *NLM current catalog proof sheets*, EH49
Medical Library Association. Periodicals and Serial Publications Committee. *Vital notes on medical periodicals*, EH39
Medical Library Association directory, AK52
Medical Library Center of New York. *Vital notes on medical periodicals*, EH39
Medical Literature, inc. *Psychopharmacology abstracts*, EH323
Medical meanings, Haubrich, William S., EH116
Medical phrase index, Lorenzini, Jean A., EH101
The medical practitioners in medieval England, Talbot, Charles H., EH226
Medical reference works, 1679–1966, Blake, John Ballard, EH2
Medical register, EH169
Medical research centres, EH149, EH150
Medical risks, EH233
Medical school admission requirements, United States and Canada, EH163
Medical schools, EH163
  directories, EH151
Medical schools (by country or region)
  Great Britain
    directories, EH168
Medical sciences international who's who, EH149, EH150
Medical sociology, Bruhn, John G., CC6, EH11
Medical statistics report, CG440
Medical style and format, Huth, Edward J., EH194

Medical subject headings, CC254, EH65, EH66, EH143
Medical subject headings. Supplementary chemical records, EH144
Medical subject headings. Tree structures, EH145
Medical technology, EH109
Medical tests, EH174, EH180, EH192
The medical word book, Sloane, Sheila B., EH104
Medical word finder, Willeford, George, EH107
Medicinal herbs, EH342
Medicine
  abbreviations, EA96, EH130, EH131, EH132, EH133, EH134, EH135
  abstract journals, EA72, EF118, EH59
  acronyms, EH130, EH132
  audiovisual materials, EH43, EH44, EH45
    databases, EH42
  bibliography, EH8, EH15, EH16, EH17, EH22, EH23, EH24, EH25, EH27, EH64, EH202
    current, EA32
  bibliography of bibliography, EH9, EH10, EH14
  biobibliography, EH203, EH222
  biography, AL169, EH16, EH150, EH216, EH220, EH221, EH224
    bibliography, EH219
    international, EH226
  classification
    schedules, AK203
  congresses and meetings, AL26, EA203, EA206, EA209
    indexes, EA202, EA207
  databases, EA37, EA69, EA70, EA75, EH58, EH67
  dictionaries, EA84, EG38, EH92, EH93, EH94, EH95, EH96, EH97, EH98, EH99, EH100, EH101, EH102, EH103, EH104, EH105, EH106, EH107, EH112, EH123
    bilingual
      English-German, EH136
      French-English, EH141
      German-English, EH137, EH138, EH140
      Spanish-English, EH142
    etymology, EH116
    multilingual, EH139
  directories, EH149, EH150, EH155, EH162
    bibliography, EA140, EH148
  encyclopedias, EH80, EH84, EH88, EH89, EH176
  government publications, EH41
  guidebooks, EH161
  guides, EH2, EH3, EH5, EH6, EH7, EH8, EH15
  handbooks, EH171, EH172, EH177, EH190
  incunabula, EH33
  indexes, BE31, EA21, EA69, EA70, EA75, EC17, ED6, EE15, EG98, EG213, EH60, EH61, EH62, EH63, EH65, EH66, EH68
  library catalogs, EA17, EH47, EH48, EH49, EH50, EH51, EH52, EH53
    databases, EH46
  museums, EH161
  nomenclature, EH147
  periodicals, EH34, EH35, EH39, EH40
    databases, EH37
    union lists, EA45
  portraits, EH52
  prizes and awards, AL173, AL176, AL177, EH225
  reference books, EA10, EH2
  reviews of research, EH64
  statistics, CG60
    bibliography, EH235
  style manuals, EA162, EH193, EH194
  tables, EA154
  terminology, EH104
  thesauruses, EH143, EH144, EH145, EH146
Medicine (by country or region)
  Canada
    biography, EH228, EH229
    directories, EH166
  Great Britain
    directories, EH168, EH169
  India, EH84

  Japan
    periodicals, EA48
  United States, EH196
    biography, EH228, EH229
    directories, EH159, EH164
    history, EH215
Medicine (by subject)
  history, EH213, EH214, EH215
    17th-18th centuries, EH223
    17th-18th century, EH202
    18th-19th centuries, EH196
    bibliography, EA235, EH10, EH12, EH13, EH28, EH199, EH201, EH204, EH205, EH206, EH209, EH210, EH218
      bibliography, DB110
    biography, EH221
    encyclopedias, EH195
    Great Britain, EH226
      bibliography, EH208
    guides, EA224
    library catalogs, EH54, EH210
    United States, EH211
  social aspects, EA15
  see also **Consumer health; Health care; Tropical medicine**
Medicine, Besterman, Theodore, EH9
Medicine in Great Britain from the Restoration to the nineteenth century, 1660–1800, Rogal, Samuel J., EH208
Medicine, literature & eponyms, Rodin, Alvin E., EH123
Medieval Academy of America. *A guide to the study of medieval history*, DA134
Medieval and Renaissance studies, Hall, Louise McG, DA128
—— University of North Carolina at Chapel Hill. Library. Humanities Division, DA128
Medieval art, BF171
Medieval Celtic literature, Bromwich, R., DA138
The medieval Charlemagne legend, Farrier, Susan E., BE983
Medieval Christian literary imagery, Kaske, Robert Earl, BE5, DA138
Medieval drama, BE28
  indexes, BE662
Medieval English drama, Berger, Sidney E., BE635
Medieval heresies, Berkhout, Carl T., BC210
Medieval Hungarian historians, Halász de Beky, I. L., DC380
Medieval Ireland c.1170–1495, Asplin, P. W. A., DC392
Medieval Latin liturgy, Pfaff, Richard W., BC269, DA138
Medieval Latin palaeography, Boyle, L., DA138
Medieval Latin word-list from British and Irish sources, Baxter, James Houston, AC589
—— Johnson, Charles, AC589
Medieval literature
  bibliography, BE5, BE28, BE983, BE984, BE1201
  criticism, BE46
  guides, BE5
  translations, BE45
Medieval literature (by subject)
  symbols and symbolism, BE5
  themes, motives, BE5
  see also **Medieval drama; Romances**
The medieval literature of Western Europe, Fisher, John Hurt, BE984
Medieval manuscripts in British libraries, Ker, Neil Ripley, AA199
Medieval monasticism, Constable, G., DA138
Medieval music, Hughes, Andrew, DA138
Medieval narrative sources, Bak, János M., DA135
—— Hollingsworth, Paul, DA135
—— Quirin, Heinz, DA135
Medieval philosophers, BB67
Medieval religious houses, England and Wales, Knowles, David, BC441
Medieval religious houses, Ireland, Gwynn, Aubrey Osborn, BC441

Medieval religious houses, Scotland, Cowan, Ian Borthwick, BC441
———— Easson, David E., BC441
Medieval rhetoric, Murphy, James Jerome, BE359, DA138
Medieval Scandinavia, DC76
Medieval sculpture, Salvini, Roberta, BF393
Medieval studies, DA129
———— Crosby, Everett U., DA131
Medina, José Toribio. *Bibliografía de la imprenta en Santiago de Chile desde sus orígenes hasta febrero de 1817,* AA516
———— *Bibliografía española de las Islas Filipinas (1523–1810),* AA927
———— *Biblioteca hispano-americana (1493–1810),* AA470
———— *Biblioteca hispano-chilena (1523–1817),* AA516
———— *Diccionario biográfico colonial de Chile,* AH131
———— *Diccionario de anónimos y seudónimos hispanoamericanos,* AA153
———— *Historia y bibliografía de la imprenta en el antiguo vireinato del Río de la Plata,* AA470
———— *Imprenta en Arequipa, el Cuzco, Trujillo y otros pueblos del Perú durante las campañas de la independencia (1820–1825),* AA540
———— *La imprenta en Bogotá (1739–1821),* AA525
———— *Imprenta en Cartagena de las Indias (1809–1820),* AA525
———— *Imprenta en Guadalajara de México (1793–1821),* AA463
———— *Imprenta en Guatemala, 1660–1821,* AA481
———— *La imprenta en la Habana (1707–1810),* AA561
———— *Imprenta en la Puebla de Los Angeles (1640–1821),* AA463
———— *La imprenta en Lima (1584–1824),* AA540
———— *Imprenta en Manila,* AA928
———— *Imprenta en Manila desde sus orígenes hasta 1810,* AA927
———— *Imprenta en Mérida de Yucatán (1813–21),* AA463
———— *La imprenta en México (1539–1821),* AA463
———— *La imprenta en México, 1594–1820,* AA461
———— *Imprenta en Oaxaca (1720–1820),* AA463
———— *La imprenta en Quito (1760–1818),* AA531
———— *Imprenta en Veracruz (1794–1821),* AA463
———— *Notas bibliográficas referentes á las primeras producciones de la imprenta en algunas ciudades de la América Española,* AA470
Medina, Rubens. *Nomenclature and hierarchy—basic Latin American legal sources,* CK198
Medina-Quiroga, Cecilia. *Nomenclature and hierarchy—basic Latin American legal sources,* CK198
Medioevo latino, DA144
Medium companies of Europe, CH362
•*MEDLARS,* EH251
MEDLARS indexing manual, Charen, Thelma, EA162
Medley, D. J. *The eighteenth century, 1714–1789,* DC317
•*MEDLINE,* EH36, EH65, EH67, EH72, EH73, EH75, EH144
Mednikova, È. M. *Bol'shoĭ anglo-russkiĭ slovar',* AC675
Meeker, David. *Jazz in the movies,* BJ362
Meer, Frederik van der. *Atlas of the early Christian world,* BC290
Meer, Willemina van der. *Biografisch archief van de Benelux,* AH270
———— *Gesamtverzeichnis des deutschsprachigen Schrifttums ausserhalb des Buchhandels (GVB), 1966–1980,* AA648
Meerhaeghe, Marcel Alfons Gilbert van. *International economic institutions,* CH80
———— *Internationale economische betrekkingen en instellingen,* CH80
Meeus, Jean. *Astronomical algorithms,* EC55
———— *Astronomical formulae for calculators,* EC55
Mega anglo-hellēnikon lexikon, AC465

Mega lexikon tēs Hellēnikēs glōssēs, Dēmētrakos, Dēmētrios B., AC460
Megalē hellēnikē enkyklopaideia, AB54
Megalē Kypriakē enkyklopaideia, DC121
Meggett, Joan M. *Music periodical literature,* BJ103
Meghdessian, Samira Rafidi. *The status of the Arab woman,* CC610
Mehr, Linda Harris. *Motion pictures, television and radio,* BH180
Mehr nicht erschienen, Krieg, Michael O., AA93
Mehra, Parshotam. *A dictionary of modern Indian history, 1707–1947,* DE168
Meier, August. *Black leaders of the nineteenth century,* CC395
Meier, Clothilde. *Familiennamenbuch der Schweiz,* AJ142
Meier, Emil. *Familiennamenbuch der Schweiz,* AJ142
Meier, Heinz K. *Switzerland,* DC526
Meier, Lauren. *Historic landscape directory,* BF293
———— *Preserving historic landscapes,* BF287, BF293
Měier, M. S. *Novaĭa istoriĭa,* DA174
Meier, Matt S. *Bibliography of Mexican American history,* CC448
———— *Dictionary of Mexican American history,* CC468
———— *Mexican American biographies,* CC469
Meier, Regula A. *Liechtenstein,* DC438
———— *Switzerland,* DC526
Meier, Wilma. *Bibliography of African languages,* BD214
Meĭera, M. S. *Istoriĭa srednikh vekov,* DA133
Meijer, Reinder P. *Literature of the Low Countries,* BE1334
Meiji zenki shomoku shūsei, AA914
Meillet, Antoine. *Dictionnaire étymologique de la langue latine,* AC579
———— *Langues du monde,* BD12
Meine, Karl-Heinz. *Kartographie 1943–1954,* CL227, CL232
Meinecke, Michael. *A bibliography of the architecture, arts, and crafts of Islam to 1st Jan. 1960,* BF17
Meisel, Max. *Bibliography of American natural history,* EG71
Meissner, Bruno. *Akkadisches Handwörterbuch,* AC203
———— *Reallexikon der Assyriologie, unter Mitwirkung zahlreicher Fachgelehrter,* DA80
Meissner, Günter. *Allgemeines Künstlerlexikon,* BF135
Meissner, William W. *Annotated bibliography in religion and psychology,* BC9
Meites, Louis, ed. *Handbook of analytical chemistry,* EE82
Melanesia, AA77
Melby, Edward C. *CRC handbook of laboratory animal sciences,* EG235
Melcher, Florian. *Disciunari rumantsch grischen,* AC664
Meldrum, Marcia. *Nobel laureates in medicine or physiology,* AL169, EH216
Melich, János. *Magyar etymologiai szótár,* AC498
Melina, Lois Ruskai. *Adoption,* CC215
Mell, Clayton. *Timbers of tropical America,* EJ188
Mell, Donald C. *English poetry, 1660–1800,* BE711
Mellinkoff, David. *Mellinkoff's dictionary of American legal usage,* CK39
Mellinkoff's dictionary of American legal usage, Mellinkoff, David, CK39
Mellman, Martin. *Accountants' handbook,* CH257
Mello, Maria Chaves de. *Dicionário jurídico português-inglês, inglês-português,* CK54
Mellon, Melvin Guy. *Chemical publications,* EE5, EE115
Melloni, Biagio John. *Melloni's illustrated medical dictionary,* EH98
Melloni's illustrated medical dictionary, Dox, Ida, EH98
Mellor, Joseph William. *A comprehensive treatise on inorganic and theoretical chemistry,* EE111

Mellown, Elgin W. *A descriptive catalogue of the bibliographies of 20th century British poets, novelists, and dramatists,* BE763
Mel'nikov, O. A. *Anglo-russkiĭ astronomicheskiĭ slovar',* EC38
Melón, Esther M. *Biografías puertorriqueñas,* AH161
Melone, Albert P. *Bridges to knowledge in political science,* CJ3
Melsted, T. J. *Islandsk bogfortegnelse,* AA718
Melting point tables of organic compounds, Utermark, Walther, EE147
Melting pot, Newman, Jacqueline M., EJ205
Melton, J. Gordon. *Directory of religious organizations in the United States,* BC80
———— *Encyclopedia of African American religions,* BC56
———— *Encyclopedia of American religions,* BC65, BC66
———— *Islam in North America,* BC491
———— *Religious bodies in the United States,* BC66
———— *Religious information sources,* BC13
———— *Religious leaders of America,* BC83
Melville, Annette. *Special collections in the Library of Congress,* AK110
Melville J. Herskovits Library of African Studies. *The Africana conference paper index,* DD8
———— *Catalog of the Melville J. Herskovits Library of African Studies, Northwestern University Library and Africana in selected libraries, Evanston, Ill,* DD34
———— *Joint acquisitions list of Africana,* DD24
———— *South African political materials,* CJ413
Melzer, Annabelle. *Shakespeare on screen,* BE791
Melzi, Gaetano. *Dizionario di opere anonime e pseudonime di scrittori italiani,* AA177
Melzwig, Brigitte. *Deutsche sozialistische Literatur, 1918–1945,* BE1229, BE1249
Members of Congress : a checklist of their papers in the Manuscript Division, Library of Congress, AJ24, DB37
Members of Congress since 1789, CJ230
Members of Parliament … , Great Britain. Parliament. House of Commons, CJ354
Members of Parliament, Scotland, Foster, Joseph, CJ354
Membership directory, American Association for Artificial Intelligence, EK198
Membership directory and guide to the field, American Folklore Society, CF55
Membership register, American Psychological Association, CD35
Mémoires de la Révolution, DC180
Memorabilia mathematica, Moritz, Robert Edouard, EB55
Memorable film characters, Lieberman, Susan, BH276
Memorials, Geological Society of America, EF107
Memory, CD110
Memphis State University. Center for Research on Women. *Women of color and Southern women,* CC623
Men (by country or region)
 United States
  attitudes, CC40
Men of the reign, Ward, Thomas Humphry, AH230
Menaul, Stewart. *The illustrated encyclopedia of the strategy, tactics and weapons of Russian military power,* CJ656
Mencken, Henry Louis. *The American language,* BD107
———— *A new dictionary of quotations on historical principles from ancient and modern sources,* BE109
A Mende-English dictionary, Innes, Gordon, AC611
Mende language, AC611
Mendelian inheritance in man, McKusick, Victor A., EG342, EH189
Mendelsohn, Henry N. *An author's guide to social work journals,* CC41
Mendelson, Susan. *Social networks and mental health,* CC29

Mendelssohn, Sidney. *South African bibliography to the year 1925*, AA876

Mendenhall, Doris A. *The index of paintings sold in the British Isles during the nineteenth century*, BF302

Mendès, Catulle. *Le mouvement poétique français de 1867 à 1900*, BE1196

Mendes, Evelyse Maria Freire. *Bibliografia do pensamento político republicano (1879/1980)*, DB341

Méndez-Domínguez, Alfredo. *Mesoamerica*, CE79

Mendiburu, Manuel de. *Diccionario histórico-biográfico del Perú*, AH141

Menditte, Arnaud de. *Répertoire des archives du Maroc*, DD69

Mendonça, Melanie. *Beazley addenda*, BF324

Mendoza-López, Margarita. *Catálogo de publicaciones periódicas mexicanas*, AD62

—— *Teatro mexicano del siglo XX, 1900–1986*, BE913

Mene, Mene, Tekel, Ehrlich, Eugene H., BC155

Menendez, Albert J. *The Catholic novel*, BE258

—— *Civil War novels*, BE477, DB107

—— *School prayer and other religious issues in American public education*, CB39

—— *The subject is murder*, BE273

Menéndez y Pelayo, Marcelino. *Bibliografía hispano-latina clásica*, BE1043

Menezes, Raimundo de. *Dicionário literário brasileiro*, BE934

Meng, Werner. *International economic law*, CK112

Menges, Robert J. *Key resources on teaching, learning, curriculum, and faculty development*, CB224

Menke, Frank Grant. *The encyclopedia of sports*, BK17

Menninger, Karl. *A guide to psychiatric books in English*, EH373

Menninger Clinic (Topeka, Kansas). *Catalog of the professional library of the Menninger Foundation*, EH376

Menninger Clinic (Topeka, Kansas). Library. *Catalog of the Menninger Clinic Library, the Menninger Foundation ...* , EH376

Mennonite bibliography, 1631–1961, Springer, Nelson P., BC362

The Mennonite encyclopedia, BC361

Mennonites, BC361, BC362
  bibliography, BC360

Menos, Dennis. *Arms control fact book*, CJ697

Men's studies, August, Eugene R., CC267

Mental health
  bibliography, CC31, EH372
  careers, CC53
  dictionaries, EH384
  statistics, EH401

Mental health and social work career directory, CC53

Mental health libraries, EH388

Mental health, United States, EH401

Mental illness
  classification, EH377, EH393
  directories, CC163, CC165
  encyclopedias, EH101
  handbooks, EH391
  statistics, EH401
  therapy, EH381

The mental measurements yearbook, CD69, CD70, CD71, CD73, CD75, CD69

Mental retardation
  dictionaries, CC190
  handbooks, CC199

Menual, Stewart. *Soviet war machine*, CJ656

Menyesch, Dieter. *France-Allemagne, relations internationes et interdépendances bilatérales*, DC201

Menzel, Donald Howard. *Fundamental formulas of physics*, ED47

Menzies, Allan. *Ante-Nicene Fathers*, BC293

Merand, Patrick. *Guide de littérature africaine (de langue francaise)*, BE1516

Mercadal, Dennis. *Dictionary of artificial intelligence*, EK184

Mercatante, Anthony S. *The Facts on File encyclopedia of world mythology and legend*, CF5

Mercer, Anne. *Index to Canadian poetry in English*, BE827

Mercer dictionary of the Bible, BC146

The merchant explorer, DB4

The Merck index, EE83, EH345

•*Merck index online*, EE83, EH345

Merck manual of diagnosis and therapy, EH190

The Merck manual of geriatrics, EH191

The Merck veterinary manual, EJ125

Měřička, Václav. *The book of orders and decorations*, AL184

—— *Orders and decorations*, AL184

The Meridian handbook of classical literature, Feder, Lillian, BE1015

Meringolo, Joseph. *A research guide to Congress*, CJ196

Merit students encyclopedia, AB19

Meritt, Herbert D. *Concise Anglo-Saxon dictionary*, AC173

Merker, Paul. *Reallexikon der deutschen Literaturgeschichte*, BE1251

Merle Johnson's American first editions, Blanck, Jacob Nathaniel, BE405

—— Johnson, Merle DeVore, AA242, BE405

Merlin, Pierre. *Bibliographie internationale, retrospective (1950–1983) et partiellement commentée sur la planification des transports urbains*, BF272

—— *Bibliographie sur les villes nouvelles françaises et étrangères*, **BF273**

—— *Bibliography on French and foreign new towns*, BF273

—— *Dictionnaire de l'urbanisme et de l'aménagement*, BF273

Merola, Giovanna. *Periodici italiani, 1968–1981*, AD128

Merory, Joseph. *Food flavoring*, EJ217

Merriam, Alan P. *A bibliography of jazz*, BJ305

Merriam, Sharan B. *Handbook of adult and continuing education*, CB362

Merriam-Webster, Inc. *Webster's intermediate dictionary*, AC26

—— *Webster's new geographical dictionary*, CL97

—— *Webster's third new international dictionary of the English language, unabridged*, AC14

Merriam-Webster's collegiate dictionary, AC17

Merriam-Webster's collegiate thesaurus, AC142

Merriam-Webster's dictionary, AB26

Merriam-Webster's secretarial handbook, CH88

Merrill, Elmer Drew. *A bibliography of eastern Asiatic botany*, EG106

Merrill, George Perkins. *Contributions to the history of American geology*, EF102

—— *First 100 years of American geology*, EF102

Merrill, John Calhoun. *The foreign press*, AE141

—— *Handbook of the foreign press*, AE141

—— *The world's great dailies*, AE133

Merrill-Oldham, Jan. *Managing a library binding program*, AK238

—— *Preservation planning program*, AK238

Merriman, Arthur Douglas. *Concise encyclopaedia of metallurgy*, EK266

—— *Dictionary of metallurgy*, EK266

Merriman, Brenda Dougall. *Genealogy in Ontario*, AJ72

Merritt, Anna J. *Politics, economics, and society in the two Germanies, 1945–75*, DC238

Merritt, Frederick S. *Building design and construction handbook*, EK103

—— *Standard handbook for civil engineers*, EK61

—— *Structural steel designers' handbook*, EK111

Merritt, Richard L. *Nationalism and national development*, CJ9

—— *Politics, economics, and society in the two Germanies, 1945–75*, DC238

Merryweather, Linda. *Companion thesaurus to food science and technology abstracts*, EJ150, EJ159

Mersch, Jules. *Biographie nationale du pays de Luxembourg depuis ses origines jusqu'à nos jours*, AH268

Mershon Center for Education in National Security. *American defense annual*, CJ636

Mersky, Roy M. *Fundamentals of legal research*, CK118

—— *Index to periodical articles related to law*, CK27

—— *Legal research illustrated*, CK118

Merton, Robert King. *International encyclopedia of the social sciences*, CA36, CA44

Merwe, I. W. van der. *Tweetalige woordeboek*, AC197

Merwe, J. H. van der. *National atlas of South West Africa (Namibia)*, CL343

Mesa, Rosa Quintero. *Latin American serial documents*, AF158

Meserole, Harrison T. *A guide to English and American literature*, BE580

Meserve, Mollie Anne. *A chronological outline of world theatre*, BH94

Meserve, Walter J. *American drama*, BE467, BE667

—— *American drama to 1900*, BE462

—— *A chronological outline of world theatre*, BH94

—— *An emerging entertainment*, BE466

—— *Heralds of promise*, BE466

MeSH, CC254, EH143

MeSH tree annotations, EH145

Mesoamerica, CE79

Mesopotamia
  atlases, DA86, DE67

Mesquita de Figueiredo, Antonio. *Subsidios para a bibliografia da história local portuguesa*, DC483

Messenger, Charles. *World War Two*, DA211

Messick, Frederic M. *Primary sources in European diplomacy, 1914–1945*, CJ316, DC10

Messier, Jean-Jacques. *Bibliographie relative à la Nouvelle-France*, DB215

Messina, Angelina, R. *Catalogue of Ostracoda*, EF239

Messina, Angelina R. *Catalogue of Foraminifera*, EF238

—— *Catalogue of index Foraminifera*, EF238

Messina, James A. *The Harvard independent insider's guide to prep schools*, CB108

Messinger, Heinz. *Langenscheidt's condensed Muret-Sanders German dictionary*, AC417

Messner, Stephen D. *Minority groups and housing*, CH529

Měšťan, Antonin. *Česká literatura 1785–1985*, BE1106

—— *Geschichte der tschechischen Literatur im 19. und 20. Jahrhundert*, BE1106

Mestler, Gordon E. *Disease and destiny*, EH16

Mestre Ghigliazza, Manuel. *Efemérides biográficas (defunciones-nacimientos)*, AH101

•*METADEX*, EK260

•*METADEX collection*, EK258, EK260

Metal arts, BG148

The metal trades, CH635

Metallic materials specification handbook, Ross, Robert Ballantyne, EK280

Metallurgical abstracts, EK257, EK260

Metallurgical abstracts (general and non-ferrous), EK259

Metallurgical engineering see **Mining and metallurgical engineering**

Metallurgy
  handbooks, EK270, EK280, EK281, EK282

Metals
  abstract journals, EK257, EK259, EK260
  dictionaries, EK263
  handbooks, EK269, EK270, EK278, EK280, EK281

Metals abstracts, EK257, EK260

Metals abstracts index, EK260

Metals handbook, EK264, EK269, EK270, EK274, EK278

Metals reference book, EK281

Metaphor, BD47

Metaphor, Noppen, J. P. van, BD47

Metaphor II, Hols, Edith, BD47

—— Noppen, J. P. van, BD47

Metcalf, C. L. *Destructive and useful insects*, EG84, EG335

Metcalf, Keyes DeWitt. *Planning academic and research library buildings*, AK175

Metcalf, Robert A. *Destructive and useful insects*, EG84, EG335

Metcalf, Robert Lee. *Destructive and useful insects*, EG84, EG335

Metcalfe, W. M. *Jamieson's dictionary of the Scottish language*, AC165

Metelka, Charles J. *Dictionary of hospitality, travel, and tourism*, CL382

———— *Dictionary of tourism*, CL382

Meteorites, EF207
 bibliography, EF206
 catalogs, EF208

Meteorological abstracts and bibliography, EF143

Meteorological and geoastrophysical abstracts, EF143

Meteorological glossary, Great Britain. Meteorological Office, EF147

Meteorology
 abstract journals, EF143
 bibliography, EF142, EF162
 compendiums, EF163
 dictionaries, EF146, EF147
  bilingual
   French-English, EF149
   Spanish-English, EF150
  multilingual, EF148
 encyclopedias, EF144, EF145
 handbooks, EF152, EF153, EF154, EF155
 statistics, EF168
 tables, EF165
Meteorology (by subject)
 history
  bibliography, EF97
 study and teaching, EF151

Metford, J. C. J. *Dictionary of Christian lore and legend*, BC238

Metherell, David. *Scandinavian biographical archive*, AH164

Methoden der organischen Chemie (Houben-Weyl), EE138

Methodist reviews index 1818–1885, BC41

Methodist union catalog, Rowe, Kenneth E., BC364

Methodists, BC363, BC364, BC365, BC366, BC367

Methods of educational and social science research, Krathwohl, David R., CC28

Metra Consulting. *Handbook of national development plans*, CH142

Metress, Seamus P. *The Irish-American experience*, CC327

Metropolitan areas, CL73

Metropolitan Life Insurance Company. *Statistical bulletin*, CH528

Metropolitan Museum of Art (New York, N.Y.). *A handbook of Chinese ceramics*, BG79

Metropolitan Museum of Art (New York, N.Y.). Library. *Library catalog of the Metropolitan Museum of Art*, BF54

Metropolitan Museum of Art (New York, N.Y.). Robert Goldwater Library. *Catalog of the Robert Goldwater Library, the Metropolitan Museum of Art*, BF54

Metropolitan opera annals, Seltsam, William, BJ254

The Metropolitan Opera encyclopedia, BJ250

Metropolitan Opera Guild. *Annals of the Metropolitan Opera Guild*, BJ254

———— *The Metropolitan Opera encyclopedia*, BJ250

Mets, Lisa A. *Key resources on higher education governance, management, and leadership*, CB224

Mette, Hans Joachim. *Lexikon des frühgriechischen Epos*, AC447

Mettig, Volker. *Bibliographie zur Geschichte der deutschen Arbeiterbewegung, sozialistischen und kommunistischen Bewegung von den Anfängen bis 1863*, CH627

Metuzāle-Kangere, Baiba. *A derivational dictionary of Latvian*, AC598

Metzeltin, Michael. *Lexikon der Romanistischen Linguistik*, BD148

Metzger, Bruce Manning. *Index of articles on the New Testament and the early church published in festschriften*, BC121

———— *Index to periodical literature on Christ and the Gospels*, BC122

———— *Oxford annotated Bible, with the Apocrypha*, BC94

———— *The Oxford companion to the Bible*, BC189

———— *Oxford concise concordance to the Revised Standard Version of the Holy Bible*, BC158

Metzger, Isobel M. *Oxford concise concordance to the Revised Standard Version of the Holy Bible*, BC158

Metzger, M. D. *Serial bibliographies for medieval studies*, DA137

Metzger, Mendel. *Jewish life in the Middle Ages*, BG113

Metzger, Thérèse. *Jewish life in the Middle Ages*, BG113

Metzger, Wolfgang. *Bibliographie deutschsprachiger Sowjetunion-Reiseberichte, -Reportagen und -Bildbände, 1917–1990*, DC588

Metzner, Günter. *Heine in der Musik*, BJ75

Meulen, Jacob ter. *Bibliography of the peace movement before 1899*, CJ675

———— *From Erasmus to Tolstoy*, CJ675

Meulen, R. van der. *Brinkman's titel-catalogus*, AA754

Meuli, Judith. *Feminist chronicles, 1953–1993*, CC572

Meurs, Jos van. *Jungian literary criticism, 1920–1980*, BE24

Mével, Jean-Pierre. *Dictionnaire de l'argot*, AC355

Mēxa, Balērios G. *Hellēnikē bibliographia, 1800–1863*, AA701

Mexican American biographies, Meier, Matt S., CC469

Mexican American history, CC448, CC468

Mexican American proverbs, CC459

The Mexican-American war, Tutorow, Norman E., DB236

Mexican Americans *see* **Latinas; Latinos**

Mexican Americans, CC453

———— Pino, Frank, CC449

Mexican Americans in urban society, Camarillo, Albert, CC445

Mexican and Mexican-American agricultural labor in the United States, Sable, Martin Howard, CC451

Mexican autobiography, Woods, Richard Donovon, AH105

Mexican fiction
 biobibliography, BE916

Mexican government publications, Ker, A. M., AF157

The Mexican legal system, Avalos, Francisco, CK196

Mexican literature, BE913
 bibliography, BE910, BE912, BE914
 biobibliography, BE907, BE908, BE915
 encyclopedias, BE908
 indexes, BE909
 library catalogs, BE494
Mexican literature (by subject)
 history, BE911, BE1456

Mexican literature, Foster, David William, BE910

Mexican natives, AH100

Mexican political biographies, 1884–1935, Camp, Roderic Ai, AH106, CJ305

The Mexican Revolution, Raat, W. Dirk, DB232

Mexican theatre of the twentieth century, Lamb, Ruth S., BE914

Mexicanos distinguidos, AH103

Mexicans (by country or region)
 United States, BD176
  bibliography, CC445, CC451
  biography, CC469
  directories, CC462
  handbooks, CC466
  indexes, CC457

Mexico
 archives
  guides to records, DB238

 atlases, CL310
 bibliography, AA457, AA458, AA460, AA461, AA462, AA463, AA464, DB231
  current, AA465, AA466, AA467
 bibliography of bibliography, AA23
 biography, AA459, AH99, AH100, AH101, AH102, AH103, AH104, AH105, AH106, CJ305
  bibliography, AH109
  contemporary, AH107
  dictionaries., AH108
 directories, CE79
 encyclopedias, DB243, DB244, DB245, DB246, DB248
 government publications, AF157
 handbooks, DB248
 library resources, AK129
 periodicals, AD61, AD62, AD63
 statistics, CG117, CG118, CG119
Mexico (by subject)
 anthropology and ethnology, CE75, CE79, CE90
 economic conditions
  bibliography, DB219, DB229
 ethnic groups
  bibliography, DB223
 folklore and popular culture, CF61
 foreign relations
  bibliography, DB222
  United States, DB220, DB250
 geography, CL311
 history, CL311, DB232, DB233
  archives, DB239, DB240
  bibliography, CC452, CE75, DB164, DB167, DB217, DB221, DB224, DB225, DB226, DB228, DB229, DB234, DB236, DB237, DB249, DB271
  encyclopedias, DB242
  guides to records, DB276
  library catalogs, DB163, DB235
  statistics, CG118
 law, CK196, CK197
 military history, DB236
  bibliography, DB230
 native languages
  bibliography, BD241
 politics and government, AH106, CJ305
 religion, BC59
 social conditions, DB227
  bibliography, DB229
 women
  bibliography, DB218

México. Comisión de Estudios Militares. Biblioteca del Ejército. *Apuntes para una bibliografía militar de México, 1536–1936*, DB230

México. Dirección General de Estadística. *Anuario estadístico de los Estados Unidos Mexicanos*, CG117

México, Archivo General de la Nación, DB238

———— Philip, George D.E, DB231

Mexico (City). Universidad Nacional. Instituto de Historia. *Diccionario biográfico de historia antigua de Méjico*, AH100

México—Estados Unidos, Bustamante, Jorge A., DB220

México, la cultura, el arte y la vida cotidiana, Flores Villela, Carlos Arturo, DB224

Mexico since independence, DB291

Meyen, Fritz. *The North European nations as presented in German university publications, 1885–1957*, DC73

Meyer, A. de. *Dictionnaire d'histoire et de géographie ecclésiastiques*, BC412

Meyer, George H., Jr. *Folk artists biographical index*, BG30

Meyer, George H. *Folk artists biographical index*, BG30

Meyer, Jack Allen. *An annotated bibliography of the Napoleonic era*, DC193

Meyer, Jimmy Elaine Wilkinson. *U.S. aging policy interest groups*, CC91

Meyer, Kathi. *Katalog der Musikbibliothek Paul Hirsch, Frankfurt am Main*, BJ87

Meyer, Klaus. *Bibliographie zur osteuropäischen Geschichte*, DC37

Meyer, Kuno. *Contributions to Irish lexicography*, AC519

Meyer, Mary Keysor. *Meyer's directory of genealogical societies in the U.S.A. and Canada*, AJ55

—— *Passenger and immigration lists index*, AJ44

—— *Who's who in genealogy & heraldry*, AJ56

Meyer, Michael. *The Little, Brown guide to writing research papers*, AG4

Meyer, Michael C. *Research in Mexican history*, DB240

Meyer, Otto. *Clavis mediaevalis*, DA151

Meyer, R. J. *Gmelins Handbuch der anorganischen Chemie*, EE110

Meyer, Reinhart. *Bibliographia dramatica et dramaticorum*, BE1266

Meyer, Robert G. *The clinician's handbook*, CD106

Meyer, Robert S. *Peace organizations, past and present*, CJ692

Meyer, Ronald. *Nineteenth-century Russian literature in English*, BE1400

Meyer, William Stevenson. *Imperial gazetteer of India*, CL164

Meyers, Robert A. *Encyclopedia of astronomy and astrophysics*, EC26

—— *Encyclopedia of modern physics*, ED15

—— *Encyclopedia of physical science and technology*, EA79

Meyers, Thomas A. *The encyclopedia of technical market indicators*, CH300

Meyer's directory of genealogical societies in the U.S.A. and Canada, Meyer, Mary Keysor, AJ55

Meyers enzyklopädisches Lexikon, AB52, CL283

Meyers grosser Weltatlas, CL283

Meyers Handbuch über die Literatur, BE187

Meyers Konversations-Lexikon, AB52

Meyers neues Lexikon, AB52

Meynen, Emil. *Bibliography of mono- and multilingual dictionaries and glossaries of technical terms used in geography, as well as in related natural and social sciences*, CL53

—— *Bibliography on the colonial Germans of North America*, CC330

—— *Gazetteers and glossaries of geographical names of the member-countries of the United Nations and the agencies in relationship with the United Nations*, CL100

Meze'r, Avgusta Vladimirovna. *Slovarnyĭ ukazatel' po knigovedeniĭu*, AA8

Mezhdunarodnye otnoseniĭa, Egorov, V. N., DC586

Mezhdunarodnye vspomogatel'nye iazyki, Dulichenko, A. D., BD48

Mezhenko, ĬU. A. *Russkaĭa tekhnicheskaĭa periodika 1800–1916*, EA52

Mezhov, Vladimir Izmailovich. *Russkaĭa istoricheskaĭa bibliografiĭa, 1800–54*, DC580

—— *Russkaĭa istoricheskaĭa bibliografiĭa, 1865–76*, DC580

Mezquita y Compañía, Garrido. *Diccionario biográfico de Venezuela*, AH146

Miall's dictionary of chemistry, EE44

Michael, Marion C. *Southern literary culture*, BE569

Michael, W. H. *Official congressional directory*, CJ221

Michael J. Hindelang Criminal Justice Research Center. *Sourcebook of criminal justice statistics*, CK269

Michaelides, Solon. *The music of ancient Greece*, BJ139

Michaelis, Arnd. *Glossary of genetics*, EG343

Michaelis, Henritte. *Novo Michaelis*, AC648

Michalchi, D. E. *Slavĭanskoe ĭazykoznanie*, BD183

Michaud, Joseph François. *Biographie universelle (Michaud) ancienne et moderne*, AH22, AH31

Michaud, Louis Gabriel. *Biographie universelle (Michaud) ancienne et moderne*, AH22, AH31

Micheels-Cyrus, Madge. *Seeds of peace*, CJ689

Michel, Albert. *Tables générales*, BC398

Michel, François. *Encyclopédie de la musique*, BJ117

Michel, Jean-Pierre. *Dictionary of earth sciences*, EF84

Michel, Paul-Henri. *Répertoire des ouvrages imprimés en langue italienne au XVIIe siècle conservés dans les bibliothèques de France*, AA733

Michel, Suzanne P. *Répertoire des ouvrages imprimés en langue italienne au XVIIe siècle conservés dans les bibliothèques de France*, AA733

Michelsen, Hans. *Stedregister til Dansk Tidsskrift-Index*, AD309

Michelsen, Kari. *Sohlmans Musiklexikon*, BJ126

Michie Company. *Code of Alabama, 1975*, CK179

Michigan. [Laws, etc.]. *Michigan compiled laws annotated*, CK179

Michigan compiled laws annotated, Michigan. [Laws, etc.], CK179

Michigan early modern English materials, AC29

Michigan State University. Latin American Studies Center. *Mexican Americans*, CC449

Michigan State University. Office of Women in International Development. *Women factory workers in less developed countries*, CC605

Mickienė, Aldona. *Tarybinių lietuvių rašytojų*, BE1325

Mickolus, Edward F. *International terrorism in the 1980s*, CJ553

—— *The literature of terrorism*, CJ552

—— *Terrorism, 1980–1987*, CJ552

—— *Transnational terrorism*, CJ553

Mickwitz, Ann-Mari. *The A. E. Nordenskiöld collection in the Helsinki University Library*, CL238

Micro computer index, EK167

Microbes and minie balls, Freemon, Frank R., DB110

Microbiology
classification, EG31
dictionaries, EG27, EG39
encyclopedias, EG22, EG27
handbooks, EG54, EG56

Microbiology abstracts : algology, mycology and protozoology, EG14

Microbiology abstracts : industrial and applied microbiology, EG14

Microcomputer abstracts, EK167

Microcomputer index, EK167

Microcomputers
databases, EK167
dictionaries, EK180, EK185
encyclopedias, EK173
handbooks, EK206
indexes, EK167

Microfiche concordance to Old English, AC172

A microfilm corpus of the indexes to printed catalogues of Latin manuscripts before 1600 A.D, AA208

A microfilm corpus of unpublished inventories of Latin manuscripts through 1600 A.D, AA209

Microform market place, AA283

Microform research collections, Dodson, Suzanne Cates, AA130

Microform research collections at the British Library Lending Division, British Library. Lending Division, AA129

Microform review, AA137

Microforms and reproductions, AK251
bibliography, AA128, AA130, AA131, AA133, AA134, AA135, DA10
collections
bibliography, AA129
indexes, AA132
directories, AA283
periodicals, AA137
reviews, AA137
union lists, AA136

Microforms for historians, Munro, D. J., DA10

Micrographics, AK246

Micrographics, Saffady, William, AK250

Micrographics, 1900–1977, Gabriel, Michael, AK245

•*MICROLOG education collection*, CB52

Micronesia, 1944–1974, Marshall, Mac, CE114, DF5

Micronesia, 1975–1987, Goetzfridt, Nicholas J., CE114, DF5

—— Wuerch, William L., CE114, DF5

Micronesian languages, BD235

Microscopic anatomy of invertebrates, EG236

Microscopy, EG19, EG23

•*Microsoft bookshelf '94*, AB7, AB27, AB110, AC9, AC144, BE97, DA39

•*Microsoft encarta*, AB24

Microsoft Press computer dictionary, EK185

Middelnederlandsch handwoordenboek, Verdam, Jacob, AC294

Middelnederlandsch woordenboek, Verwijs, Eelco, AC295

The Middle Ages, DA152

Middle Ages to the early Georgians, Davies, Adriana, BF66

Middle American anthropology, McGlynn, Eileen A., CE90

Middle East *see* **Asia, West**

Middle East, DE21, DE52, DE60

—— Ziring, Lawrence, CJ420, DE57

The Middle East, 1914–1979, DE65

Middle East and Islam, DE22

Middle East and North Africa, CJ94

The Middle East and North Africa in world politics, Hurewitz, Jacob Coleman, DE64

The Middle East and North Africa on film, McClintock, Marsha Hamilton, DD71, DE34

Middle East bibliography, Silverburg, Sanford R., DE39

Middle East contemporary survey, DB294, DE61

The Middle East in conflict, DE36

The Middle East, its oil, economics and investment policies, Nicholas, David, CH192

The Middle East journal, DE24

Middle East legal systems, Amin, S. H., CK227

Middle East Libraries Committee. *Arab Islamic bibliography*, BC492

—— *Bibliographic guide to Iran*, DE181

—— *Middle East and Islam*, DE22

—— *Middle East materials in United Kingdom and Irish libraries*, DE51

—— *Union catalogue of Persian serials & newspapers in British libraries*, AD199

Middle East materials in United Kingdom and Irish libraries, Netton, Ian Richard, DE51

Middle East political dictionary, Ziring, Lawrence, CJ420, DE55, DE57

Middle East review, CH191, DD61

A Middle East studies handbook, Bacharach, Jere L., DE58

Middle Eastern studies, DE41

Middle English dictionary, AC30, AC172, AC175

—— Kurath, Hans, AC176

—— Stratmann, Franz Heinrich, AC176

Middle English prose, BE735

Middle English romance, Rice, Joanne A., BE734, BE736

Middle market directory, CH363

Middle schools, CB10

Middle Scots poets, Looney, Anna, BE810

—— Scheps, Walter, BE810

Middleton, Alex L. A. *The encyclopedia of birds*, EG260

Middleton, Haydn. *Atlas of modern world history*, DA189

Middleton, Robert Gordon. *Television service manual*, EK147

Middlewestern states, DB160, DB161, DB169, DB173
bibliography, BE567

Mideast file, DE53

Midlife and Older Women Book Project. *Ourselves, growing older*, CC95, CC564

Mieder, Wolfgang. *A dictionary of American proverbs*, BE154

—— *International proverb scholarship*, BE156, BE158

—— *Investigations of proverbs, proverbial expressions, quotations and cliches*, BE156

—— *The Prentice-Hall encyclopedia of world proverbs*, BE157

—— *Proverbs in literature,* BE156

Miekkavaara, Leena. *The A. E. Nordenskiöld collection in the Helsinki University Library,* CL238

Miethe, Terry L. *Augustinian bibliography, 1970–1980,* BB65

—— *Thomistic bibliography, 1940–1978,* BB68

Miewald, Robert D. *The bureaucratic state,* CJ76

Migdall, Susan. *Inventory of longitudinal studies of middle and old age,* CA60

Migne, Jacques Paul. *Encyclopédie théologique,* BC400

—— *Lexicon manuale ad scriptores mediae et infimae latinitatis,* AC590

—— *Patrologiae cursus completus,* DA163

Las migraciones en America Latina, Centro Paraguayo de Documentación Social, CC315

Migration
atlases, CC359, DA188
bibliography, CG12, CG18, CG67
indexes, CG18, CG67

Migration (by country or region)
Botswana, DD131
see also **Emigration; Immigration**

Migueis, Maria Amelia Porto. *Guia preliminar de fontes para a história do Brasil,* DB350

Mihailovich, Vasa D. *A comprehensive bibliography of Yugoslav literature in English, 1593–1980,* BE1499

—— *Modern Slavic literatures,* BE1076

—— *Yugoslav linguistics in English, 1900–1980,* BD190

Mihalic, Francis. *The Jacaranda dictionary and grammar of Melanesian Pidgin,* AC628

Mikail, E. H. *English drama 1900–1950,* BE638

Mikhov, Nikola V. *Bibliografskii iztochnitsi za istoriīa na Turtsiīa i Bulgariīa,* DC537

—— *Bibliographie des articles de périodiques allemands, anglais, français et italiens sur la Turquie et la Bulgarie,* DC538

—— *Neselenieto na Turtsiīa na Bulgariīa priez XVIII i XIX vekovete,* DC538

Mikotowicz, Thomas J. *Theatrical designers,* BH120

Mikrozensus, Österreichisches Statistisches Zentralamt, CG196

Miladinova, Elisaveta Khristova. *Obzor na arkhivnite fondove, kolektsii i edinichni postŭpleniīa, sŭkhraīavani v Bŭlgarski istoricheski arkhiv,* DC117

Milano, Attilio. *Bibliotheca historica italo-judaica,* BC530

Milburn, G. *A critical dictionary of educational concepts,* CB72

Mildren, K. W. *Use of engineering literature,* EK2

Miles, William. *The image makers,* CJ106

Miles, Wyndham D. *American chemists and chemical engineers,* EE99

Milestones in science and technology, Mount, Ellis, EA253

Miletich, John J. *Airline safety,* CH475

—— *States of awareness,* CD108

—— *Treatment of cocaine abuse,* CC115

—— *Work and alcohol abuse,* CC116

Milford, Robert Theodore. *A catalogue of English newspapers and periodicals in the Bodleian Library, 1622–1800,* AD104

Milgate, Murray. *The new Palgrave,* CH52

—— *The new Palgrave dictionary of money & finance,* CH268

Miliavskaīa, S. L. *Bibliografiīa stran Afriki i Arabskogo Vostoka,* DD9

—— *Izuchenie kul'tury i īazykov narodov Afriki v Sovetskom Soīuze,* DD10

Milic, Louis. *Style and stylistics,* BE374

ha-Milion he-hadash, Lazar, Yisrael, AC483

Milisavac, Zivan. *Jugoslovenski književni leksikon,* BE1498

Military and strategic policy, Beede, Benjamin R., CJ98

The military balance, CJ596, CJ599, CJ601

Military bases, CJ626

Military bases (by country or region)
United States
directories, CJ623, CJ624

Military bibliography of the Civil War, Dornbusch, Charles Emil, DB109

Military history, CJ593
atlases, DA50
bibliography, CJ562, CJ563, DB258
chronologies, DA20
encyclopedias, CJ576, CJ580, DA20, DA21, DA24, DA25, DA100
handbooks, CJ568
statistics, CJ568

Military history (by country or region)
Argentina, DB325
Australia, DF35
Balkans, DC60
Brazil, DB355
Bulgaria, DC116
Denmark, DC130
France, DC145, DC146, DC192
Germany, DC214, DC240
Great Britain, CJ653, DC271, DC277
Italy, DC418
Norway, DC464
Union of Soviet Socialist Republics, CJ659, CJ660
United States, BF390
bibliography, CJ605, DB16
guides to records, AJ18
see also **Armed forces**

The military in imperial history, Heggoy, Alf Andrew, DC145

Military intelligence, 1870–1991, House, Jonathan M., CJ608

Military leaders, AH26

Military-naval encyclopedia of religions in Russia and the Soviet Union, Jones, David R., DC566

The military-naval encyclopedia of Russia and the Soviet Union, CJ657

Military periodicals, Unsworth, Michael, CJ567

Military science
acronyms, CJ617
bibliography, CJ561, CJ565
dictionaries, CJ578, CJ582, CJ583, CJ584, CJ585, CJ586, CJ589, CJ622
education, CB361
encyclopedias, CJ571, CJ572, CJ573
guides, CJ559
quotations, CJ590, CJ591

Military science (by country or region)
Canada, CJ650
Russia and the U.S.S.R.
encyclopedias, CJ657
United States
bibliography, CJ611

Military uniforms, CJ595, CJ634

Military uniforms in America, CJ634

Militia and the national guard in America since colonial times, Cooper, Jerry, CJ608

Milivojević, Dragan Dennis. *Yugoslav linguistics in English, 1900–1980,* BD190

Milkau, Fritz. *Handbuch der Bibliothekswissenschaft,* AK38

Milkias, Paulos. *Ethiopia,* DD158

Milla Batres, Carlos. *Diccionario histórico y biográfico del Perú, siglos XV–XX,* AH140, DB387

Millares Carlo, Agustín. *Bibliografía mexicana del siglo XVI,* AA460

—— *Ensayo de una bibliografía de bibliografías mexicanas,* AA23

—— *Estudio bibliográfico de los archivos venzolanos y extranjeros de interés para la historia de Venezuela,* DB398

Miller, A. Carolyn. *Refereed and nonrefereed economic journals,* CH30

Miller, Ann E. *Checklist of nineteenth century Australian colonial statistical sources,* CG437

Miller, Barbara Stoler. *Masterworks of Asian literature in comparative perspective,* CA53

Miller, Benjamin Frank. *Encyclopedia and dictionary of medicine, nursing, and allied health,* EH279

Miller, Clara G. *Bibliography of Ontario history, 1867–1976,* DB212

Miller, Connie. *Feminist research methods,* CC504

Miller, Cynthia Pease. *A guide to research collections of former members of the United States House of Representatives, 1789–1987,* CJ201

Miller, David. *The Blackwell encyclopaedia of political thought,* CJ22

Miller, Delbert Charles. *Handbook of research design and social measurement,* CA57

Miller, E. Willard. *Environmental hazards,* EK86

Miller, Edmund Morris. *Australian literature,* BE853

Miller, Elizabeth W. *The Negro in America,* CC368

Miller, Ellen Kay. *Index to USDA Agricultural information bulletins no. 1–649,* EJ92

—— *Index to USDA Miscellaneous publications no. 1–1479,* EJ92

—— *Index to USDA Technical bulletins no. 1–1802,* EJ92

—— *USDA Agricultural handbooks no. 1–690,* EJ92

Miller, Eugene G. *Writers and philosophers,* BE191

Miller, Frederic M. *Arranging and describing archives and manuscripts,* AK188

Miller, Genevieve. *Bibliography of the history of medicine of the United States and Canada, 1939–1960,* EH204

Miller, George. *A catalogue of American watermarks, 1690–1835,* AA257

Miller, Gerald. *Handbook of public administration,* CJ482

Miller, Herbert A. *Retirement benefit plans,* CH503

Miller, J. C. P. *Table of binomial coefficients,* EB94

—— *Tables of indices and primitive roots,* EB94

—— *Tables of the Riemann Zeta function,* EB94

Miller, Jeanne. *Bibliography of the Summer Institute of Linguistics, Philippines, 1953–1984,* BD233

Miller, Joanne. *Professional Secretaries International complete office handbook,* CH87

Miller, Jordan Yale. *American drama between the wars,* BE466

Miller, Joseph. *Sears list of subject headings,* AK222

Miller, Joseph Calder. *Slavery and slaving in world history,* CC328, DD5

Miller, Judith. *Miller's international antiques price guide,* BG48

Miller, Kenneth E. *Denmark,* DC133

—— *Greenland,* DC377

Miller, Lynn. *Bibliography of women & literature,* BE401

Miller, Mamie Ruth Tanquist. *An author, title, and subject check list of Smithsonian Institution publications relating to anthropology,* CE16

Miller, Martin. *Miller's international antiques price guide,* BG48

Miller, Melanie Ann. *Birds,* EG268

Miller, P. McC. *A dictionary of social science methods,* CA39

Miller, R. H. *Handbook of literary research,* BE2

Miller, Randall M. *Dictionary of Afro-American slavery,* CC386

—— *Ethnic and racial images in American film and television,* CC334

Miller, Rex. *Television service manual,* EK147

Miller, Roger LeRoy. *Economics sourcebook of government statistics,* CH171

Miller, Ruby M. *Environmental hazards,* EK86

Miller, Sally M. *The ethnic press in the United States,* AD32, AE34

Miller, Stephen T. *Mystery, detective, and espionage fiction,* BE269

Miller, Steven I. *Second steps in sociology,* CC24

Miller, Tice L. *Cambridge guide to American theatre,* BH65

Miller, Timothy. *American communes, 1860–1960,* DB138

Miller, W. C. *Comprehensive bibliography for the study of American minorities,* BE546

Miller, Warren E. *American national election studies data sourcebook, 1952–1986,* CJ255

Miller, William G. *Subject collections*, AK100, AK119

Miller Freeman Inc. *Directory of the wood products industry*, EJ184

Miller's international antiques price guide, Miller, Judith, BG48

Milligan, George. *Vocabulary of the Greek Testament*, AC458

Million dollar directory, CH356, CH363

A million random digits, Rand Corporation, EB93

Millman, Linda Josephson. *Legal issues and older adults*, CC99

Millodot, Michel. *Dictionary of optometry*, EH121

Millroy, Wendy L. *The handbook of qualitative research in education*, CB113

Mills, A. D. *A dictionary of English place names*, CL198

Mills, J. J. *Guide to current national bibliographies in the Third World*, AA392

Mills, Jane. *Womanwords*, CC540

Mills, Mary. *State labor proceedings*, CH630

Mills, Victoria A. *Women in LC's terms*, CC542

Mills, Watson E. *A bibliography of the periodical literature on the Acts of the Apostles, 1962–1984*, BC114

—— *Mercer dictionary of the Bible*, BC146

—— *Speaking in tongues*, BC18

Milne, Alexander Taylor. *Writings on British history*, DC281

Milne, Isabel A. *A source book of Scottish history*, DC366

Milne, Tom. *The Time out film guide*, BH201

Milner, Anita Cheek. *Newspaper indexes*, AE101, AE102

Milner, Anthony Crothers. *South-East Asia*, BD229, BD236, BE1550

Milner, George Bertram. *Samoan dictionary*, AC700, AC701

Milner, Richard. *The encyclopedia of evolution*, EG26

Milner, S. *Stratigraphic atlas of North America and Central America*, EF113

Milner-Gulland, R. R. *Atlas of Russia and the Soviet Union*, DC572

—— *Cultural atlas of Russia and the Soviet Union*, DC572

Milon angli-ivri, Kaufman, Judah, AC480

Milon angli-'ivri shalem, Alcalay, Reuben, AC473

Milon ha-lashon ha-ivrit, Ben Yehuda, Eliezer, AC470

Milon 'ivri-angli shalem, AC473

Milon 'ivri shimushi, AC474

Miłosz, Czesław. *The history of Polish literature*, BE1356

Miltimore, Louise S. *Accountants' index*, CH245

MIMP, magazine industry market place, AD53

Min, Chae-sik. *The new World comprehensive English-Korean dictionary*, AC566

Mináč, Vladimír. *Slovenský biografický slovník*, AH285

Minahan, Anne. *Encyclopedia of social work*, CC46

Minary, Ruth. *Arthurian dictionary*, BE344

MInd, the meetings index, EA202

Minde-Pouet, Georg. *Grundriss zur Geschichte der deutschen Dichtung aus den Quellen*, BE1218

Miner, Brad. *The National review college guide*, CB279

Miner, Earl Roy. *History of Japanese literature*, BE1582

—— *The Princeton companion to classical Japanese literature*, BE1588

Miner, Lynn E. *Proposal planning and writing*, AL138

Mineral index, EF193

Mineral reference manual, Nickel, Ernest H., EF201

Mineralogical abstracts, CL30, EF51, EF177

Mineralogical Society (Great Britain). *Mineralogical abstracts*, EF177

Mineralogical Society of America. *Mineralogical abstracts*, EF177

Mineralogy, EF194
  abstract journals, EF58, EF177, EF178
  bibliography, EF59, EF174, EF175

  biography, EF189
  dictionaries, EF181, EF188, EF189
    bilingual
      Chinese-English, EF182
    multilingual, EF183
  encyclopedias, EF179, EF186
  field guides, EF192, EF197, EF201, EF202, EF204
  guides, EF171, EF172
  handbooks, EF191, EF195, EF198, EF201, EF202, EF203
  nomenclature, EF184, EF193
  yearbooks, EF200

Minerals, rocks, and gemstones, Börner, Rudolf, EF192

Minerals yearbook, EF200

Minerva-Handbücher, AK137

Minerva mikrofilm a/s, Copenhagen. *Topografisk, kronologisk fortegnelse over danske, færøske og grønlandske aviser 1648–1975*, AE48

Mines and mineral resources
  atlases, EF110
  guides, EF171
  handbooks, EF196
  yearbooks, EF200

Mines and mineral resources (by country or region)
  Asia, EF205
  Australia, EF205
  Canada
    bibliography, EF28
  Russia, EF205

Mingotaud, Anne-Françoise. *Handbook of monolayers*, EE150

Mingotaud, Christophe. *Handbook of monolayers*, EE150

Miniature painters, BF303, BF310, BF311

Miniatures, Foskett, Daphne, BF303

Mining and metallurgical engineering
  abstract journals, EK253, EK259, EK260
  databases, EK253
  dictionaries, EF76, EF188, EK263, EK266
    multilingual, EF183
  handbooks, EK254, EK269

Mining engineering handbook, EK254

Ministers of the Crown, Pickrill, D. A., CJ345

Minnesota. [Laws, etc.]. *Minnesota statutes annotated*, CK179

Minnesota Family Study Center. *Inventory of marriage and family literature*, CC221

Minnesota statutes annotated, Minnesota. [Laws, etc.], CK179

Minnick, Roy. *The surveying handbook*, EK62

Minnick, Wendell L. *Spies and provocateurs*, CJ536, CJ540

Minor, Mark. *Literary-critical approaches to the Bible*, BC115

Minor eastern hardwoods, Little, Elbert Luther, EJ191

The minor law books, BC92

Minor parties at British parliamentary elections, 1885–1974, Craig, Fred W. S., CJ366

Minor western hardwoods, Little, Elbert Luther, EJ191

Minorities *see* **Ethnic groups**

Minorities of Southwest China, Dessaint, Alain Y., CE107

Minority business enterprises, CH372

Minority groups and housing, Boyce, Byrl N., CH529

Minority languages in Europe, Pogarell, Reiner, BD85

•*Minority on-line information service*, CB308

Minority organizations, CC344

Minority-owned business firms, CH364

Minority Rights Group. *World directory of minorities*, CC345

Minrath, William R. *Handbook of applied mathematics*, EB64

Minter, Sue. *The complete handbook of garden plants*, EJ249

Minter-Dowd, Christine. *Finders' guide to decorative arts in the Smithsonian Institution*, BG28

Mintz, Lawrence E. *Humor in America*, CF79

Minutes, Presbyterian Church (U.S.A.). General Assembly, BC378

Minutes of the Executive Council of the American Federation of Labor, 1893–1955, CH624

Miquel, Pierre. *Atlas historique de la France*, DC166

Mir, Mustansir. *Dictionary of Qur'ānic terms and concepts*, BC205

Mir y Noguera, Juan. *Diccionario de frases de los autores clásicos españoles*, BE150

Mirador, AB79

Miraeo, Auberto. *Bibliotheca belgica*, AA580

Miraval, Paule. *Répertoire des travaux universitaires inédits sur la période révolutionnaire*, DC181

A mirror for the nation, Hanna, Archibald, BE475

Mirskii, D. S. *Contemporary Russian literature, 1881–1925*, BE1420

—— *A history of Russian literature from the earliest times to the death of Dostoevsky (1881)*, BE1420

Miscellanea musicae bio-bibliographica, Springer, Hermann, BJ57

Miscellaneous publications [Index], United States. Department of Agriculture, EJ92

Mischke, Charles R. *Standard handbook of machine design*, EK247

Misengo, M. *Women in development in Southern Africa*, DD122, DD171

Mish, Charles Carroll. *English prose fiction, 1600–1700*, BE679, BE680

Mish, John L. *English-Arabic and Arabic-English dictionary*, AC223

Mishler, Clifford. *Standard catalog of world coins*, BG188

Misianik, Jan. *Bibliografía slovenského písomníctva do knock XIX*, AA598

Misiones americanas en los archivos europeos, DB277

Miska, John P. *Canadian studies on Hungarians, 1886–1986*, DC384

—— *Ethnic and native Canadian literature*, BE828

Miss Manners' guide to excruciatingly correct behavior, Martin, Judith, AL154

Missale Romanum, BC424

Missalia ritus latini impressa, BC429

Missing persons, Nicholls, C. S., AH226

Mission handbook, BC308

Missionary Research Library (New York, N.Y.). *Dictionary catalog of the Missionary Research Library, New York*, BC309

Missions
  bibliography, BC303, BC304
  encyclopedias, BC310
  handbooks, BC308
  history, BC306
  library resources, BC305, BC309

Missions (by country or region)
  Africa, DD87
  Africa, Southern
    bibliography, DD115
  Japan, BC307
  Oceania, BC370

Missions Advanced Research and Communications Center. *Mission handbook*, BC308

Mississippi. [Laws, etc.]. *Mississippi code 1972*, CK179

Mississippi code 1972, Mississippi. [Laws, etc.], CK179

Mississippi quarterly, BE574

Missouri. [Laws, etc.]. *Vernon's annotated Missouri statutes*, CK179

Místopisný slovník Československé republiky, Chromec, Břetislav, CL131

The MIT dictionary of modern economics, CH59

MIT Science Fiction Society's index to the s-f magazines, 1951–1965, Strauss, Erwin S., BE294

Mitcham, Carl. *Bibliography of the philosophy of technology*, EA18

Mitchell, Arthur. *A contribution to the bibliography of Scottish topography*, DC360

Mitchell, Brian. *A guide to Irish parish registers*, AJ136

—— *New genealogical atlas of Ireland*, AJ136, AJ137

Mitchell, Brian R. *Abstract of British historical statistics*, CG234, CG235

—— *British historical statistics*, CG234, CG235

—— *International historical statistics*, CG70, DB7, DB290

—— *International historical statistics, Africa and Asia*, CG309, CG375

—— *International historical statistics, Europe, 1750–1988*, CG189, DC24

—— *Second abstract of British historical statistics*, CG234, CG235

Mitchell, Charity. *Speech index*, BE366

Mitchell, Chip. *The St. James encyclopedia of mortgage & real estate finance*, CH534

Mitchell, Christopher. *International relations theory*, CJ10

Mitchell, David F. *Directory of unpublished experimental mental measures*, CD75

Mitchell, Diana. . *African nationalist leaders in Rhodesia who's who*, AH327

—— *Who's who, 1981–82*, AH327

Mitchell, H.C. *Definitions of terms used in geodetic and other surveys*, EF123

Mitchell, James. *Random House encyclopedia*, AB13

Mitchell, James V. *The mental measurements yearbook*, CD69

—— *Tests in print III*, CD73

Mitchell, Jonathan. *The Cambridge atlas of the Middle East and North Africa*, DE68

Mitchell, Phillip Marshall. *A bibliographical guide to Danish literature*, BE1120

—— *A bibliography of 17th century German imprints in Denmark and the duchies of Schleswig-Holstein*, AA602

—— *Bibliography of modern Icelandic literature in translation*, BE1287

—— *Bibliography of old Norse-Icelandic romances*, BE1090

—— *History of Danish literature*, BE1118

Mitchell, Ralph. *Congressional Quarterly's guide to the U. S. Constitution*, CK173

Mitchell, Richard Scott. *Dictionary of rocks*, EF257

Mitchell, Robert. *The multicultural student's guide to colleges*, CB309

Mitchell, Robert Cameron. *Black Africa*, DD95

—— *Comprehensive bibliography of modern African religious movements*, BC19

Mitchell, Sally. *Dictionary of British equestrian artists*, BF323

—— *Victorian Britain*, BE758, DC337

Mitchell, Solomon. *Pictorial guide to identifying Australian architecture*, BF208

Mitchell-Hatton, Sarah Lu. *The Davis book of medical abbreviations*, EH133

The Mitchell Library index to periodicals, AD346

Mitchell Library, Sydney. *Index to periodicals*, AD346

Mitchenson, Joe. *Theatres of London*, BH99

Mitler, Louis. *Contemporary Turkish writers*, BE1491

—— *Ottoman Turkish writers*, BE1491

Mittelhaus, Karl. *Paulys Real-Encyclopädie der classischen Altertumswissenschaft*, DA104

Mittelhochdeutsches Handwörterbuch, Lexer, Matthias von, AC405

Mittelhochdeutsches Wörterbuch, Müller, Wilhelm, AC406

Mittellateinisches Wörterbuch bis zum ausgehenden 13. [i.e. dreizehnten] Jahrhundert, AC591

Mittelniederdeutsches Handwörterbuch, Lübben, August, AC408

Mittelniederdeutsches Wörterbuch, Schiller, K., AC408

Mitterand, Henri. *Nouveau dictionnaire étymologique et historique*, AC348

Mittleman, Milton. *UNDEX series C cumulative edition*, AF49

Mitton, Jacqueline. *A concise dictionary of astronomy*, EC35

Mitton, Simon. *The Cambridge encyclopaedia of astronomy*, EC25

Mix, Morton E. *German literature in British magazines, 1750–1860*, BE1240

Miyakawa, Takayasu. *Japan, sources of economic and business information*, CH204

MLA American bibliography, BD26, BE39

MLA annual bibliography, BD26, BE39

MLA bibliography, BD26, BE39

MLA directory, Medical Library Association, AK52

MLA directory of periodicals, BE173

—— Modern Language Association of America, BE42

MLA directory of scholarly presses in language and literature, BE173

MLA handbook for writers of research papers, AA317

—— Gibaldi, Joseph, AG2

—— Modern Language Association of America, AG1

MLA international bibliography of books and articles on the modern languages and literatures, Modern Language Association of America, BD26, BD90, BE39, BE42, BE401, BE468, BE513, BE585, BE588, BE694, BE1343, CF42

The MLA style manual, Achtert, Walter S., AA317

Mladenov, Stefan. *Bŭlgarski tulkoven rechnik, s ogled kŭm narodnite govori*, AC241

MLR, monthly labor review, United States. Bureau of Labor Statistics, CH685, CH688

Moatassime, Ahmed. *Langues, cultures et éducation au Maghreb*, DD72

Mochedlover, Helene G. *Ottemiller's index to plays in collections*, BE231

Mock, David B. *A dictionary of obituaries of modern British radicals*, AH219

Modern American literature, Curley, Dorothy Nyren, BE427, BE598, BE600, BE1069

—— Kramer, Elaine Fialka, BE1069

—— Kramer, Maurice, BE1069

Modern American usage, Follett, Wilson, AC71

Modern American women writers, BE444, BE448

The modern Arab woman, Raccagni, Michelle, CC613

Modern Arabic drama in Egypt, Badawī, Muhammad M., BE1546

Modern Arabic literature, BE1548

—— Altoma, Salih J., BE1545

—— Badawī, Muhammad M., BE1546

Modern architure, Frampton, Kenneth, BF257

Modern archives administration and records management, AK187

Modern art, Hunter, Sam, BF131

Modern art from post-impressionism to the present, BF131

Modern Australian poetry, 1920–1970, Jaffa, Herbert C., BE846

Modern Australian prose, 1901–1975, Day, Arthur Grove, BE846

Modern black writers, BE51

Modern British and American private presses, 1850–1965, British Library, AA238

Modern British drama, Carpenter, Charles A., BE638

Modern British literature, Temple, Ruth Zabriskie, BE598, BE600, BE1069

—— Tucker, Martin, BE598, BE1069

Modern Chinese authors, Shu, Austin C. W., AA190

Modern Chinese fiction, Li, Peter, BE1562

—— Mao, Nathan K., BE1562

—— Yang, Winston L. Y., BE1562

Modern Chinese society, DE130

Modern citatenboek, Ley, Gerd de, BE126

Modern Commonwealth literature, BE815

Modern concordance to the New Testament, BC157, BC161

Modern dictionary of electronics, EK133

A modern dictionary of geography, Small, Ronald John, CL51

Modern dictionary of international legal terms, CK45

Modern dictionary of Yoruba usage, Delano, Isaac O., AC818

Modern dog encyclopedia, Davis, Henry P., EJ145

Modern drama, BE638

—— Adelman, Irving, BE219

—— Dworkin, Rita, BE219

Modern drama in America and England, 1950–1970, Harris, Richard Hough, BE460, BE638

Modern drama scholarship and criticism, 1966–1980, Carpenter, Charles A., BE220, BE638

Modern encyclopedia of religions in Russia and the Soviet Union, Steeves, Paul D., DC566

The modern encyclopedia of Russian and Soviet history, DC566

The modern encyclopedia of Russian and Soviet literature, BE1415

The modern encyclopedia of Russian, Soviet and Eurasian history, DC566

Modern encyclopedia of tennis, BK101

Modern England, 1901–1984, Havighurst, Alfred F., DC303, DC331

Modern English biography, Boase, Frederic, AH222, AH230

Modern English-Canadian poetry, Stevens, Peter, BE830

Modern English-Canadian prose, Hoy, Helen, BE830

Modern English-Greek and Greeek-English desk dictionary, AC463

Modern English-Gujarati dictionary, Deśapāṇḍe, Bhāratī, AC468

—— Deśapāṇḍe, Pāṇḍuraṅga Ganeśa, AC468

Modern English-Yiddish, Yiddish-English dictionary, Weinreich, Uriel, AC816

Modern European imperialism, Halstead, John P., DC8

Modern French literature, BE1147

Modern French literature and language, Griffin, Lloyd W., BD158, BE1134

Modern geography, CL39

Modern German dialects, Noble, C. A. M., BD126

Modern German literature, BE887

—— Domandi, Agnes Körner, BE1058

Modern Greek Studies Association. *Census of modern Greek literature*, BE1274

Modern Greek studies in the West, Swanson, Donald Carl Eugene, BD141

Modern guide to synonyms and related words, AC139

Modern Hebrew-English dictionary, Zilkha, Avraham, AC484

Modern history of Ethiopia and the horn of Africa, Marcus, Harold G., DD158

Modern history of Kenya, 1895–1980, Ochieng', William R., DD166

Modern history of Somalia, Lewis, I. M., DD207

Modern Humanities Research Association. *Anglo-Norman dictionary*, AC168

—— *Annual bibliography of English language and literature*, BD90, BE588

Modern Iberian language and literature, Golden, Herbert Hershel, BD166, BE1436

Modern Ireland, Shannon, Michael Owen, DC355, DC398

Modern Irish literature, Lane, Denis, BE805

Modern Irish literature and culture, Cahalan, James M., BE801

Modern Italian history, Coppa, Frank J., DC420, DC431

—— Roberts, William, DC431

Modern Italian language and literature, Golden, Herbert Hershel, BD160, BE1293

Modern Japanese literature in translation, Kokusai Bunka Kaikan (Tokyo, Japan). Toshoshitsu, BE1584

Modern Japanese literature in western translations, BE1584

Modern Japanese novelists, Lewell, John, BE1585

Modern jazz, Bruyninckx, Walter, BJ307

Modern Language Association of America. *British newspapers and periodicals, 1641–1700*, AD107

—— *The medieval literature of Western Europe*, BE984

—— *MLA directory of periodicals,* BE42
—— *MLA directory of scholarly presses in language and literature,* BE173
—— *MLA handbook for writers of research papers,* AG1, AG2
—— *MLA international bibliography of books and articles on the modern languages and literatures,* BD26, BD90, BE39, BE42, BE401, BE468, BE513, BE585, BE588, BE694, BE1343, CF42
—— *The MLA style manual,* AA317
—— *Reproductions of manuscripts and rare printed books. Short title list,* AA134
—— *Restoration and early eighteenth-century English literature, 1660–1740,* BE746
—— *Short-title catalogue of books printed in England, Scotland, Ireland, Wales, and British America, and of English books printed in other countries, 1641–1700,* AA412, AA683
—— *Tentative dictionary of medieval Spanish,* AC749
—— *The Transcendentalists,* BE416
—— *Victorian periodicals,* AD113
—— *Victorian prose,* BE755
Modern Language Association of America. American Literature Section. *American literary manuscripts,* BE430
—— *Eight American authors,* BE403
Modern Language Association of America. Comparative Literature Section. *Yearbook of comparative and general literature,* BE41
Modern Language Association of America. Division on Literature and Science. *The relations of literature and science,* BE30
Modern Language Association of America. French III. *Bibliography of French seventeenth century studies,* BE1138
Modern Language Association of America. Germanic Section. *Bibliographie der germanistischen Zeitschriften,* AD99
Modern Language Association of America. Middle English Group. *A manual of the writings in Middle English, 1050–1500,* BE734
Modern Language Association of America. Old English Division. *A bibliography of publications on Old English literature to the end of 1972,* BE728
—— *Old English newsletter,* BE729
Modern Language Association of America. Old English Group. *Old English newsletter,* BE729
Modern Language Association of America. Victorian Division. *Victorian bibliography,* BE756
Modern language quarterly, BE339
Modern Latin American art, Findlay, James A., BF22
Modern Latin American literature, Foster, David William, BE887
Modern legal systems cyclopedia, CK31
A modern Mongolian-English dictionary, Hangin, John G., AC614
Modern mystery, fantasy, and science fiction writers, BE293
Modern nutrition in health and disease, EH310
Modern parliamentary procedure, Keesey, Ray E., CJ455
The modern Persian dictionary (Persian-Urdu-English), Razi, F. D., AC317
Modern philology, BE753
Modern plastics catalog, EK288
Modern plastics encyclopedia, EK288
Modern poetry, Alteri, Charles F., BE490
Modern proverbs and proverbial sayings, Whiting, Bartlett Jere, BE165
The modern researcher, Barzun, Jacques, DA3
Modern review, CA28
Modern revolutions and revolutionists, CJ75
Modern Romance literatures, Curley, Dorothy Nyren, BE1069
The modern Russian dictionary for English speakers, Wilson, Elizabeth A. M., AC684
Modern sculpture, Hammacher, A. M., BF393
Modern Slavic literatures, BE1076
Modern Spanish and Portuguese literatures, BE1449

Modern Swedish-English and English-Swedish dictionary, AC767
Modern urban history research in Europe, USA, and Japan, CC299
Modern veterinary practice, reference and data library, EJ106, EJ107
Modern world drama, Matlaw, Myron, BE230
Moderna svenska författare, Runnquist, Åke, BE1486
Modernism (literature), BE872
  bibliography, BE35, BE761
Modisakeng, Tiny. *A guide to periodical articles about Botswana, 1965–80,* DD130
Modlin, Marilyn J. *Direct-line distances—international edition,* CL59
—— *Direct-line distances—United States edition,* CL60
Modoc Press, Inc. *Guide to schools and departments of religion and seminaries in the United States and Canada,* BC79
Moen, Bjørn. *National population bibliography of Norway, 1945–1977,* CG269
Moffat, Donald W. *Economics dictionary,* CH60
Moffatt Bible, BC94
Mohan, Raj P. *Handbook of contemporary developments in world sociology,* CC26
Mohlenbrock, Robert H. *The field guide to U.S. national forests,* EJ186
Mohome, Paulus. *A bibliography on Bechuanaland,* DD132
—— *Bibliography on Lesotho,* DD169
—— *Bibliography on Swaziland,* DD232
Mohr, Merilyn Simonds. *The games treasury,* BK18
Mohr, Wolfgang. *Reallexikon der deutschen Literaturgeschichte,* BE1251
Mohraz, Jane E. *Peace and war,* CJ680
Möhren, Frankwalt. *Dictionnaire étymologique de l'ancien français,* AC346
Mohrmann, Christine. *Atlas of the early Christian world,* BC290
Moid, A. *A guide to periodical publications and newspapers of Pakistan,* AD207
Moir, Lindsay. *Bibliography of the Blackfoot,* CC420
Moir, Martin. *General guide to the India Office Records,* DE12, DE83
Moisan, André. *Répertoire des noms propres de personnes et de lieux cités dans les chansons de geste françaises et les oeuvres étrangères dérivées,* BE1164
Moiseev, M. A. *Sovetskaia voennaia entsiklopediia,* CJ659
Moisés, Massaud. *Bibliografia da literatura portuguêsa,* BE1367
—— *Pequeno dicionário de literatura brasileira,* BE935
Moissard, Boris. *Dictionnaire des illustrateurs,* BF384
Mojares, Resil B. *Philippine literature in English,* BE1599
Mojzes, Paul. *Church and state in postwar eastern Europe,* BC213, DC31
Mokeba, H. Mbella. *Cameroon,* DD48
Mokotoff, Gary. *Where once we walked,* CL127, CL128
Mokuau, Noreen. *Handbook of social services for Asian and Pacific islanders,* CC404
Molapo, Mathetha. *Women in Lesotho,* DD122, DD171
Molas, Joaquim. *Diccionari de la literatura catalana,* BE1450
Moldavia
  manuscripts and archives, AK153, DC561
Molde, Bertil. *Illustrerad svensk ordbok,* AC761
Molecular biology, EG324
Molecular structure
  bibliography, EE139
  databases, EE139
  indexes, EE139
Molecular structures and dimensions, EE139
Molen Van Ee, Patricia. *Maps and charts of North America and the West Indies, 1750–1789,* CL233

Molette, Charles. *Guide des sources de l'histoire des congrégations féminines françaises de vie active,* BC442
Molhuysen, Philip Christiaan. *Nieuw Nederlandsch biografisch woordenboek,* AH272
Molin, Paulette Fairbanks. *The encyclopedia of Native American religions,* BC567
Molina Navarro, Gabriel. *Índice para facilitar el manejo y consulta de los catálogos de Salvá y Heredia,* AA802, AA805, AA807
Molinaro, Julius A. *American studies and translations of contemporary Italian poetry, 1945–1965,* BE1317
—— *A bibliography of comedias sueltas in the University of Toronto library,* BE1471
—— *A bibliography of sixteenth-century Italian verse collections in the University of Toronto Library,* BE1318
Moliner, María. *Diccionario de uso del español,* AC746
Molinier, A. *Les sources de l'histoire de France depuis les origines jusqu'en 1815,* DC147
•*MOLIS,* CB308
Moll, Francesc de B. *Diccionari català-valencià-balear,* AC247
Moll, Josep. *Diccionari català-valencià-balear,* AC247
Moll, Otto E. *Sprichworter-Bibliographie,* BE156, BE158
Moll, Richard. *The public ivys,* CB278
Moll, Verna P. *Virgin Islands,* DB459
Mollema, M. P. *Books on the Netherlands in foreign languages, 1940–57,* AA138, DC450
Möller, A. P. *Almindeligt Forfatter-Lexicon for kongeriget Danmark med tilhørende bilande, fra 1814 til 1840,* BE1117
Mollett, John William. *An illustrated dictionary of art and archaeology,* BF87
Mollo, Andrew. *Army uniforms of World War I,* CJ595
Molnar, John Edgar. *Author-title index to Joseph Sabin's Dictionary of books relating to America,* AA409
Molony, Kathleen. *Korean and Japanese women,* CC609
MOMA. *Catalog of the Library,* BF55
Momeni, Jamshid A. *Homelessness in the United States,* CC203
Momigliano, Attilio. *Problemi ed orientamenti critici di lingua e di letteratura italiana,* BE1307
Mommsen, Wolfgang A. *Nachlässe in den deutschen Archiven,* DC248
Mon-Khmer languages, BD230
Monaco, James. *The encyclopedia of film,* BH283
Monaco
  atlases, DC165
  bibliography, DC449
Monaco, Hudson, Grace L., DC449
Monatliches Verzeichnis der reichsdeutschen amtlichen Druckschriften, Deutsche Bücherei, AF174
Monatliches Verzeichnis von Aufsätzen aus deutschen Zeitungen in sachlich-alphabetischer Anordnung, AE122
Moncure, James A. *Research guide to European historical biography, 1450–present,* AH162
Mondadori, Alberto. *Dizionario universale della letteratura contemporanea,* BE64
Le mondain égyptien, AH330
Mondale, Clarence C. *Region and regionalism in the United States,* DB146
Le Monde, AE120, AE121, DC208
Le Monde. Index analytique, AE120
Monell, G. E. *French consuls in the United States,* DB31
Monet, Ronald L. *Gubernatorial and presidential transitions,* CJ99
Monetary Research International. *MRI bankers' guide to foreign currency,* CH285
Money, CH290
  bibliography, BG170
  handbooks, CH284, CH285, CH286, CH287, CH288

statistics, CH293
Money and exchange in Europe and America, 1600–1775, McCusker, John J., CH284
Money and finance, CH268
The money encyclopedia, CH266
Money for artists, Green, Laura R., AL120, BF105
Money for film & video artists, Niemeyer, Suzanne, AL120, BF105
Money for performing artists, Niemeyer, Suzanne, AL120, BF105
Money for visual artists, AL120, BF105
Money Market Directories, Inc. *Directory of registered investment advisors,* CH305
Money to work II, BF106
Monfrin, Jacques. *Manuel bibliographique de la littérature française du Moyen Âge,* BE1198
Monglond, André. *France révolutionnaire et impériale,* DC176
Mongolia, DE232
  bibliography, DE233
Mongolia, Nordby, Judith, DE233
Mongolian-English dictionary, Boberg, Folke, AC612
—— Lessing, Ferdinand D., AC615
Mongolian language
  dictionaries
    bilingual
      English-Mongolian, AC613
      Mongolian-English, AC612, AC614, AC615
Mongolian literature, BE1597
Mongomery-Massingberd, Hugh. *Burke's presidential families of the United States of America,* AJ59
Mongrédien, Georges. *Dictionnaire biographique des comédiens français du XVIIᵉ siècle,* BH115
Monier-Williams, Monier. *Dictionary, English and Sanskrit,* AC706
—— *A Sanskrit-English dictionary,* AC706
Moniteur des dates, Oettinger, Eduard Maria, AH35
Moniteur universel, journal officiel, AF170
Monk, Jennifer. *The Cambridge illustrated dictionary of British heritage,* DC290
Monkhouse, Francis John. *A dictionary of geography,* CL49, CL50
—— *A dictionary of the natural environment,* CL50
Monnier, Raymonde. *Répertoire des travaux universitaires inédits sur la période révolutionnaire,* DC181
Monod, Lucien. *Aide-mémoire de l'amateur et du professional,* BF382
Monogram-Lexikon, Goldstein, Franz, BF160
Monogramme, BF385
Die Monogrammisten und diejenigen bekannten und unbekannten Künstler aller Schulen, Nagler, Georg Kasper, BF160
Monograms *see* **Artists' marks**
Monograph abstracts, AG16
Monograph series on dental materials and therapeutics, EH262, EH263
Monographic series, AA111
—— Library of Congress, AA109
Monro, Isabel Stevenson. *Costume index,* BG94, BH51
—— *Index to reproductions of American paintings,* BF61, BF63
—— *Index to reproductions of European paintings,* BF61
—— *Short story index,* BE260, BE262
Monro, Kate M. *Costume index,* BG94
—— *Index to reproductions of American paintings,* BF61, BF63
—— *Index to reproductions of European paintings,* BF61
—— *The secretary's handbook,* CH90
Monroe, Burt L. *Distribution and taxonomy of birds of the world,* EG275
—— *A world checklist of birds,* EG269
Monroe, Paul. *A cyclopedia of education,* CB71
Monroy, Guadelupe. *Fuentes de la historia contemporánea de México,* DB226
Montagné, Prosper. *Larousse gastronomique,* EJ211

Montagne, Victor Alexander de la. *Vlaamsche pseudoniemen,* AA163
Montague-Smith, Patrick W. *Debrett's correct form,* AL159
Montana. [Laws, etc.]. *Montana code annotated,* CK179
Montana Alliance for Progressive Policy. *Public opinion polling,* CJ491
Montana code annotated, Montana. [Laws, etc.], CK179
Montandon, Raoul. *Bibliographie générale des travaux palethnologiques et archéologiques (époques préhistorique, protohistorique et gallo-romaine). France ... ,* DC171
Montazem, Mir Ali Asghar. *The new English-Persian dictionary,* AC315
Montchamp, Joseph. *A dictionary of contemporary France,* DC208
Monteiro, John M. *América Latina colonial,* DB259
Montenegro, Valerie J. *AAAS science book list, 1978–1986,* EA27
—— *Best science books & A-V materials for children,* EA34
Montenegro, AD167
Monterde, Francisco. *Bibliografía del teatro en México,* BE914
—— *Diccionario Porrúa de la lengua española,* AC755
—— *Historia de la literatura mexicana,* BE1456
—— *History of Spanish literature,* BE1456
Montes de Oca N., Elvia. *Bibliografía histórica del Estado de México,* DB217
Montessus de Ballore, Fernand, Comte de. *Bibliografía general de temblores y terremotos,* EF261
Montgomery, Charles F. *History of American pewter,* BG151
Montgomery, Florence M. *Textiles in America, 1650–1870,* BG156
Montgomery, John H. *Agrochemicals desk reference,* EJ56
Montgomery, Michael. *Annotated bibliography of Southern American English,* BD106
Montgomery-Massingberd, Hugh. *Burke's Irish family records,* AJ131
The month-by-month atlas of World War II, DA211
Monthly bibliography of medical reviews, EH64
Monthly bulletin of statistics, United Nations. Statistical Office, CG57, CH243
Monthly catalog of United States government publications, United States. Superintendent of Documents, AF87, AF88, AF91, AF103, AF111, AF114, AF132
Monthly catalog of United States government publications. Periodicals supplement, United States. Superintendent of Documents, AF111, AF112
Monthly catalog of United States government publications. United States congressional serial set supplement, AF88, AF89, AF91
Monthly checklist of state publications, Library of Congress. Exchange and Gift Division, AF142
Monthly index of Russian accessions, Library of Congress. Processing Department, AA793
Monthly labor review, CH688
Monthly list of Australian government publications, AA944, AF261, DF23
The monthly list of Chinese books, AA938
Monthly list of Russian accessions, AA793
Monthly list of state publications, AF142
Monthly murders, Cook, Michael L., BE269
Monthly product announcement, CG86
Montoliu, Manuel de. *Diccionari Aguiló,* AC246
Montreal. Public Library. *Essai de bibliographie canadienne,* DB182
Montserrat, Berleant-Schiller, Riva, DB447
Montt, Luis. *Bibliografía chilena,* AA517
Monumenta Germaniae Historica. *Deutsches Archiv für Erforschung des Mittelalters,* DA142
—— *Hochschulschriften zur Geschichte und Kultur des Mittelalters 1939 bis 1972/74,* DA145
Monumenta germaniae historica, AC591
Monuments, BF390

Moody, David. *Scottish local history,* AJ123
Moody, Marilyn K. *Using government information sources,* AF62
—— *Using government publications,* AF62
Moody, Richard. *American drama,* BE467, BE667
Moody, Suzanna. *The Immigration History Research Center,* CC356
Moody, T. W. *Irish historiography, 1936–70,* DC414
—— *A new history of Ireland,* DC413
Moody's bank and finance manual, CB101, CH309
•*Moody's company data,* CH309
Moody's complete corporate index, CH309
•*Moody's corporate profiles,* CH309
Moody's handbook of common stocks, CH309
Moody's handbook of NASDAQ stocks, CH309
Moody's industrial manual, CH309
Moody's international manual, CH309
Moody's Investors Service. *[Moody's manuals],* CH309
[Moody's manuals], Moody's Investors Service, CH309
Moody's municipal & government manual, CH309
Moody's OTC industrial manual, CH309
Moody's OTC unlisted manual, CH309
Moody's public utility manual, CH309
Moody's transportation manual, CH309
Moon, Brenda Elizabeth. *Periodicals for South-East Asian studies,* AD216
Moon
  atlases, EC66, EC68, EC69
Mooney, James E. *National index of American imprints through 1800,* AA410
Mooney, James L. *Dictionary of American naval fighting ships,* CJ649
Moore, Alick. *A complete checklist of the birds of the world,* EG263
Moore, Burness E. *Glossary of psychoanalytic terms and concepts,* CD30
—— *Psychoanalytic terms and concepts,* CD30
Moore, D. M. *Flora of the British Isles,* EG168
Moore, David J. *Best resumes for scientists and engineers,* EA151
Moore, Dianne F. *HarperCollins dictionary of astronomy and space science,* EC35
Moore, Ernest. *Bibliografía de novelistas de la revolución Mexicana,* BE916
Moore, Geoffrey Hoyt. *International economic indicators,* CH109
Moore, Gloria. *Margaret Sanger and the birth control movement,* CC255
Moore, Melita H. *International economic indicators,* CH109
Moore, Patrick. *A–Z of astronomy,* EC36
—— *Amateur astronomer's glossary,* EC36
—— *Atlas of the universe,* EC67
—— *Concise atlas of the universe,* EC67
—— *The international encyclopedia of astronomy,* EC30
—— *New atlas of the universe,* EC65, EC67
—— *Patrick Moore's A–Z of astronomy,* EC36
Moore, R. I. *Atlas of world history,* DA49
Moore, Rachelle. *Women authors of modern Hispanic South America,* BE896
Moore, Raymond C. *Treatise on invertebrate paleontology,* EF243
Moore, Robert J. *A bibliography of medical and biomedical biography,* EH219
Moore, Ronald. *Margaret Sanger and the birth control movement,* CC255
Moorland, Jesse Edward. *Dictionary catalog of the Jesse E. Moorland Collection of Negro Life and History, Howard University Library, Washington, D.C,* CC379
Moorland-Spingarn Research Center. *Dictionary catalog of the Jesse E. Moorland Collection of Negro Life and History, Howard University Library, Washington, D.C.,* CC379
Moorman, Charles. *Arthurian dictionary,* BE344
Moorsom, Richard. *Namibia,* DD187
—— *Namibia in transition,* DD187
—— *The political economy of Namibia,* DD185
Mora, Enrique Ayala. *Guía de la documentación diplomática británica sobre Ecuador,* DB373

Morachevskiĭ, N. ÎA. *Russkie sovetskie pisateli-prozaiki*, BE1393

Morachevskogo, N. ÎA. *Bibliografiia periodicheskikh izdaniĭ Rossii 1901–1916*, AD142

Moraes, Rubens Borba de. *Bibliografia brasileira do período colonial*, AA508

—— *Bibliographia brasiliana*, DB346

Moraes Silva, António de. *Grande dicionário da língua portuguesa*, AC644

Morais, Armando de. *Dicionário inglês-português*, AC646

Moral education, CB15

Morales-Macedo, Fernando. *Multilingual law dictionary : English-Français-Español-Deutsch*, CK46

Moran, John B. *Creating a legend*, CJ607

Moran, Michael G. *Research in composition and rhetoric*, BE364

Moran, Robert E. *Library management consultants list*, AK176

Morant, Alfred. *General armory two*, AJ149

Morby, John E. *Dynasties of the world*, CJ78

Morcellet, Françoise. *Collins-Robert French-English, English-French dictionary*, AC335

More black American playwrights, BE513

More burs under the saddle, Adams, Ramon Frederick, DB162

More Confederate imprints, Harwell, Richard Barksdale, DB112

More Irish families, MacLysaght, Edward, AJ135

More junior authors, Fuller, Muriel, BE384

More theatre, Marill, Alvin H., BH20

More words of Wall Street, CH212

Moreau, Brigitte. *Inventaire chronologique des éditions parisiennes du XVIᵉ siècle ... d'après les manuscrits de Philippe Renouard*, AA618

Moreau, Jacqueline. *Bibliographie du Tchad*, DD140

Morehead, Alfred H. *Hoyle's rules of games*, BK128

—— *The new complete Hoyle*, BK128

Morehead, Joe. *Introduction to United States government information sources*, AF73, AF120, CJ200

—— *Introduction to United States public documents*, AF73

Morel, P. M. *Translations of Dutch literature, 1900–1957*, AA138, DC150

Moreland, George B. *Publications of the government of Pakistan, 1947–1957*, AF254

Moreno, Gabriel René. *Biblioteca peruana*, AA539

Moreno Toscano, Alejandra. *Atlas histórico de México*, DB248

Morgan, Ann Lee. *Contemporary architects*, BF260

—— *International contemporary arts directory*, BF102

Morgan, Annie Mary. *British government publications*, AF193

Morgan, Bayard Quincy. *A critical bibliography of German literature in English translation, 1481–1927*, BE1239

—— *German literature in British magazines, 1750–1860*, BE1240

Morgan, Brad. *The Olympics factbook*, BK92

Morgan, Bradley J. *Mental health and social work career directory*, CC53

—— *Sports fan's connection*, BK37

Morgan, Bryan. *Keyguide to information sources in agricultural engineering*, EJ5

Morgan, Chloe Siner. *Bibliography of British history (1700–1715) with special reference to the reign of Queen Anne*, DC316

Morgan, Dale L. *Guide to the manuscript collections of the Bancroft Library*, DB163

Morgan, Frank. *State profiles of public elementary and secondary education, 1987–88*, CB142

Morgan, Henry James. *Bibliotheca canadensis*, AA450

—— *Canadian men and women of the time*, AH98

Morgan, Jean. *Consumer sourcebook*, CH559

Morgan, Karen J. *Nutrients in foods*, EH308

Morgan, Philip D. *Books about early America*, DB78

Morgan, Robin. *Sisterhood is global*, CC568

Morgan, William. *The Navajo language*, AC616

Morgan, William Thomas. *Bibliography of British history (1700–1715) with special reference to the reign of Queen Anne*, DC316

Morgenstern, Sam. *A dictionary of musical themes*, BJ228, BJ229

—— *A dictionary of opera and song themes*, BJ229

Morice, Adrien Gabriel. *Dictionnaire historique des Canadiens et des Métis français de l'Ouest*, AH95

Morier, Henri. *Dictionnaire de poétique et de rhétorique*, BE327

Morin, Claude. *Canada's relations with Latin America and the Caribbean, 1970–1990*, DB261

Morin, Marie-Renée. *Catalogue de l'histoire de France*, DC143

Morisset, Micheline. *Canadian feature film index, 1913–1985*, BH192

Moritz, A. F. *The Oxford illustrated literary guide to Canada*, BE829

Moritz, Robert Edouard. *Memorabilia mathematica*, EB55

—— *On mathematics and mathematicians*, EB55

Moritz, Theresa Anne. *The Oxford illustrated literary guide to Canada*, BE829

Moritz, Walter. *Umfassende Bibliographie der Völker namibiens (Südwestafrikas) und Südwestangolas*, CE104

Morlet, Marie-Thérèse. *Dictionnaire étymologique des noms de famille et prénoms de France*, AJ189

Morley, Frank. *Literary Britain*, BE628

Morley, Sheridan. *The great stage stars*, BH116

Morley, W. F. E. *Atlantic provinces*, DB213

—— *Bibliography of Canadiana published in Great Britain, 1519–1763*, DB188

—— *Canadian local histories to 1950*, DB213

—— *Ontario and the Canadian North*, DB213

A Mormon bibliography, 1830–1930, Flake, Chad J., BC372

Mormon diaries & autobiographies, BC368

Mormons, BC368, BC369, BC370, BC371, BC372, BC373

Mormons and their neighbors, Wiggins, Marvin E., BC370

Mormons in the Pacific, Clement, Russell T., BC370

Mörner, M. *Fuentes para la historia de Ibero-América : Escandinavia*, DB275

Morningstar closed-end fund sourcebook, CH326

Morningstar mutual fund sourcebook, CH326

•*Morningstar mutual funds ondisc*, CH326

Morningstar variable annuity/life sourcebook, CH326

Moroccan literature, BE1515

  bibliography, BE1529

Morocco

  atlases, CG347

  bibliography, AA867, BC501, DD18, DD73, DD180

  current surveys, DD62

  encyclopedias, DD48, DD181

  government publications

    bibliography, AF227

  statistics, CG283, CG346, CG347, CG348

Morocco (by subject)

  history

    bibliography, DD69

Morocco. al-Maslahah al-Markazīyah lil-Iḥṣa'iyat. *Annuaire statistique du Maroc*, CG346

Morocco, Findlay, Anne M., DD18

—— Lawless, Richard I., DD18

—— Nelson, Harold D., DD62

—— Spencer, W., DD48

Morot-Sir, Edouard. *Littérature française*, BE1167

Morozov, P.O. *Alfavitnyi ukazatel' imen*, AA790

Morpeth, Robert S. *A dictionary of Scottish history*, DC364

Morphology (linguistics), BD43

Morreale, Don. *Buddhist America*, BC455

Morrell, Robert E. *Guide to Japanese poetry*, BE1593

—— *The Princeton companion to classical Japanese literature*, BE1588

Morrill, Chester. *Computers and data processing*, EK151

Morris, Adah V. *Nineteenth century readers' guide to periodical literature, 1890–1899*, AD280

Morris, Christopher G. *Academic Press dictionary of science and technology*, EA84

Morris, Colin. *Papal monarchy*, BC278

Morris, Dan. *Who was who in American politics*, CJ157

Morris, Derrick. *Concise encyclopedia of software engineering*, EK169

Morris, Desmond. *The mammals*, EG300

Morris, Dwight. *Handbook of campaign spending*, CJ247

Morris, Edward Ellis. *Austral English*, AC180

—— *A dictionary of Austral English*, AC179

Morris, Gwen. *Laying down the law*, CK235

Morris, Inez. *Who was who in American politics*, CJ157

Morris, James Oliver. *Bibliography of industrial relations in the railroad industry*, CH460

Morris, Leslie R. *Interlibrary loan policies directory*, AK227

Morris, Mary. *Dictionary of word and phrase origins*, AC57

—— *Harper dictionary of contemporary usage*, AC78

—— *Morris dictionary of word and phrase origins*, AC57

Morris, Peter. *Biographical dictionary of French political leaders since 1870*, CJ328

—— *Dictionary of film makers*, BH285

—— *Dictionary of films*, BH200

Morris, R. J. *Atlas of industrializing Britain 1780–1914*, DC300

Morris, Richard B. *Encyclopedia of American history*, DB44

—— *A guide to the principal sources for early American history (1600–1800) in the city of New York*, DB79

—— *Harper encyclopedia of the modern world*, DA180

Morris, Sandra Chass. *Interlibrary loan policies directory*, AK227

Morris, William. *Dictionary of word and phrase origins*, AC57

—— *Harper dictionary of contemporary usage*, AC78

—— *Morris dictionary of word and phrase origins*, AC57

Morris dictionary of word and phrase origins, Morris, William, AC57

Morris-Nygren, Mona. *Prisma's Swedish-English and English-Swedish dictionary*, AC767

Morrison, Donald George. *Black Africa*, DD95

Morrison, Ian. *The Hamlyn encyclopedia of golf*, BK84

Morrison, Joel L. *Goode's world atlas*, CL278

Morrison, John J. *Short-title catalogue of books printed in England, Scotland, Ireland, Wales, and British America, and of English books printed in other countries, 1641–1700*, AA412, AA683

Morrow, Baker H. *A dictionary of landscape architecture*, BF292

Morrow, Carolyn Clark. *Conservation treatment procedures*, AK242

—— *The preservation challenge*, AK242

Morsberger, Robert Eustis. *American screenwriters*, BH280

Morse, Grant W. *Guide to the incomparable New York times index*, AE110

Morse, John D. *Old master paintings in North America*, BF305

Morse, Joseph Laffan. *Funk & Wagnalls new encyclopedia*, AB10

Mortality, EH233

Mortality and demographic data, CG440

Morton, Andrew. *Union list of Chinese local histories in British libraries*, DE131

Morton, Bayard Quincy. *German literature in British magazines, 1750–1810*, BE1238

Morton, Brian. *Contemporary composers*, BJ209

Morton, Fred. *Birth of Botswana*, DD132

—— *Botswana*, DD48

Morton, Leslie Thomas. *A bibliography of medical and biomedical biography*, EH219
────── *Information sources in the medical sciences*, EH5
────── *Medical bibliography (Garrison and Morton)*, EH205
────── *Morton's medical bibliography*, EH205
Morton, W. L. *The Canadian centenary series*, DB203
Morton's medical bibliography, Morton, Leslie Thomas, EH205
Morykan, Dana G. *Warman's country antiques & collectibles*, BG49
Mosad Byalik. *Encyclopaedia biblica*, BC129
Mosby's medical and nursing dictionary, EH102
Mosby's medical, nursing, and allied health dictionary, EH102
Moscoso, Francisco. *América Latina colonial*, DB259
Moscow (Russia). Publichnaiâ biblioteka. Otdel spravochnobibliograficheskoĭ informatsionnoĭ raboty. *Bibliografiiâ bibliografiĭ po iâzykoznaniiu*, BD6
Moseley, Charles J. *The official World Wildlife Fund guide to endangered species of North America*, EG237
────── *Research guide to biography and criticism*, BE7
Moseley, Chris. *Atlas of the world's languages*, BD20
Moseley, William W. *Spanish literature, 1500–1700*, BE1437
Moser, Charles A. *The Cambridge history of Russian literature*, BE1419
Moser, Dietz-Rüdiger. *Neues Handbuch der deutschen Gegenwartsliteratur seit 1945*, BE1250
Moser, Gerald M. *A new bibliography of the lusophone literatures of Africa*, BE1519
Mosher, Frederic J. *The bibliographical history of anonyma and pseudonyma*, AA145
────── *A guide to Danish bibliography*, AA40
Mosher, R. B. *Executive register of the United States, 1789–1902*, CJ140
Moshoeshoe, M. M. *Women in Lesotho*, DD122, DD171
Moskin, J. Robert. *The executive's book of quotations*, CH74
Moskovskiĭ gosudarstvennyĭ universitet im. M.V. Lomonosova. TSentr po izucheniiu problem narodonaseleniiâ. *Demograficheskiĭ èntsiklopedicheskiĭ slovar'*, CG292
Moskva, AL56
Moss, Cyril. *Catalogue of Syriac printed books and related literature in the British Museum*, BD205
Moss, Martha. *Photography books index*, BF339
────── *Photography books index II*, BF339
Moss, Stephen John. *CRC handbook of bimolecular and termolecular gas reactions*, EE69
Mosses, EG193
Mosses with a hand-lens, Grout, Abel Joel, EG193
Mossman, Jennifer. *Eponyms dictionaries index*, AC53
────── *Pseudonyms and nicknames dictionary*, AA146
Mostovych, Anna. *Nonconformity and dissent in the Ukrainian SSR, 1955–1975*, CJ389
Mostyn, Trevor. *The Cambridge encyclopedia of the Middle East and North Africa*, DE54
────── *Major political events in Iran, Iraq, and the Arabian Peninsula, 1945–1990*, CJ423, DE62
Le mot juste, AC187
Mothers and mothering, CC208
Mothers and mothering, Dixon, Penelope, CC208
Motif-index of folk-literature, Thompson, Stith, CF48, CF49
The motion picture almanac, BH266
Motion picture and television almanac, BH266
Motion picture credits, BH203
Motion picture directors, Schuster, Mel, BH291
The motion picture guide, Nash, Jay Robert, BH199
The motion picture guide annual, BH199
Motion picture performers, Schuster, Mel, BH291

Motion picture series and sequels, Drew, Bernard A., BH222
Motion pictures *see* **Film**
Motion pictures 1894–1912 identified from the records of the United States Copyright Office, Walls, Howard Lamarr, BH193
Motion pictures and filmstrips, AA107
Motion pictures from the Library of Congress paper print collection, 1894–1912, Niver, Kemp R., BH190
Motion pictures, television and radio, Mehr, Linda Harris, BH180
Motive der Weltliteratur, Frenzel, Elisabeth, BE80
Motor Vehicle Manufacturers Association of the United States. *World motor vehicle data*, CH457
Motor vehicles
statistics, CH457
Mott, Frank Luther. *American journalism*, AE145
────── *History of American magazines*, AD30, AD40
Mott-Smith, Geoffrey. *The new complete Hoyle*, BK128
Motta, Giuseppe. *Dizionario commerciale*, CH127
Motteley, Paul Fleury. *Bibliographical history of electricity and magnetism, chronologically arranged*, EK126
Mottoes, BE94
────── Robbins, Ceila Dame, BE94
────── Urdang, Laurence, BE94
Mottu, Susan. *Encyclopedia of physical sciences and engineering information sources*, EA14
Motyer, J. A. *The new Bible commentary, revised*, BC171
Mouaziz, Hafida. *Langues, cultures et éducation au Maghreb*, DD72
Moule, H. F. *Historical catalogue of the printed editions of Holy Scripture in the library of the British and Foreign Bible Society*, BC95, BC99, BC100
Moulton, Charles Wells. *Library of literary criticism of English and American authors*, BE427, BE597, BE598, BE599, BE600
────── *Library of literary criticism of English and American authors through the beginning of the twentieth century*, BE598
Moulton, James Hope. *Vocabulary of the Greek Testament*, AC458
Moulton, Joy Wade. *Genealogical resources in English repositories*, AJ104
Mount, Ellis. *Milestones in science and technology*, EA253
Mountaineering, BK118, BK119, BK120
Mountains, BK118, CL62, EF9
Mountfort, Guy. *Rare birds of the world*, EG270
Moure, Nancy Dustin Wall. *Index to reproductions of American paintings appearing in more than 400 books, mostly published since 1960*, BF61, BF63
Moureaux, J. M. *Manuel bibliographique des études littéraires*, BE1128
Mourier, Athénaïs. *Notice sur le doctorat ès lettres suivie du Catalogue et de l'analyse des thèses françaises et latines admises par les facultés des lettres depuis 1810*, AG29
Moutoussamy-Ashe, Jeanne. *Viewfinders : black women photographers*, BF357
Le mouvement canadien des femmes, 1960–1990, CC525
Mouvement de la population, CG48
Mouvement de la population en Suisse, CG289
Le mouvement poétique français de 1867 à 1900, Mendès, Catulle, BE1196
Mouvements ouvriers et socialistes, CH634
Movie and video guide, BH198
Movie characters of leading performers of the sound era, Nowlan, Robert A., BH277
The movie list book, Armstrong, Richard B., BH220
Movie musicals on record, Lynch, Richard Chigley, BJ361
The movie quote book, BH262
Movie theaters *see* **Film theaters**
Movies made for television, Marill, Alvin H., BH303
Movies on TV and videocassette, Scheuer, Steven, BH198

Il movimento operaio italiano, AH262
Movimiento natural de la población española, CG284
Movimientos sociales en México (1968–1987), Köppen, Elke, DB227
Moving and relocation sourcebook, CL73
Moving pictures *see* **Film**
Moving pictures, Sheahan, Eileen, BH159
Mowrey, Peter C. *Award winning films*, BH274
Moyer, Elgin Sylvester. *Who was who in church history*, BC254
────── *Wycliffe biographical dictionary of the church*, BC254
Moyer, Ronald L. *American actors, 1861–1910*, BH126
Moyles, R. G. *English-Canadian literature to 1900*, BE830
Moys, Elizabeth M. *Manual of law librarianship*, CK2
Mozambique
bibliography, DD18, DD114, DD183, DD184
encyclopedias, DD48
government publications
bibliography, AF220
place-names, CL215
population
bibliography, DD182
Mozambique, Azevedo, Mario, DD48
────── Darch, Colin, DD18
────── Isaacman, Allen F., DD184
────── Isaacman, Barbara, DD184
────── Nelson, Harold D., DD62
Mozhaeva, Inessa Evgen'evna. *IUzhnoslaviânskie iâzyki*, BD191
Mozley and Whiteley's law dictionary, Ivamy, E. R. Hardy, CK34
MRI bankers' guide to foreign currency, CH285
Mrozek, Donald J. *Guide to the sources of United States military history*, DB16
MSDS reference for crop protection chemicals, EJ57
Msiska, Augustine W.C. *Malawi*, DD176
Muccigrosso, Robert. *Research guide to American historical biography*, AH69
Muchena, Olivia N. *Women and development in Zimbabwe*, DD253
Mudabbiri, Maḥmūd. *Farhang-i kitābhā-yi Fārsī*, AA907
Muddlman, Joseph George. *Tercentenary handlist of English & Welsh newspapers, magazines & reviews*, AE59
Muehsam, Gerd. *Guide to basic information sources in the visual arts*, BF6
Mueller, Ivan Istvan. *Gravimetric and celestial geodesy*, EF123
Mueller, James R. *The New Testament apocrypha and pseudepigrapha*, BC107
Mueller, John E. *Trends in public opinion*, CJ492
Muestras de errores y defectos de "Diccionario biográfico colonial de Chile por José Toribio Medina", Prieto del Rio, Luis Francisco, AH131
Muether, John R. *Reference works for theological research*, BC12, BC13
Muffs, Judith Herschlag. *Holocaust in books and films*, DA216
al-Mughni al-akbar, Karmī, Ḥasan Sa'īd, AC217
Mugridge, Donald H. *Guide to the study of the United States of America*, DB13
Mugridge, Ian. *United States foreign relations under Washington and Adams*, DB15
Mugwaneza, Annie. *Recueil des études et ouvrages ayant trait à la femme rwandaise*, DD199
Mühle, Peter. *Fachwörterbuch : Landwirtschaft, Fortwirtschaft, Gartenbau*, EJ28
Muir, Kenneth. *New companion to Shakespeare studies*, BE784
────── *The sources of Shakespeare's plays*, BE787
Muirden, James. *Astronomy data book*, EC56
Muir's historical atlas, Fullard, Harold, DA57
────── Treharne, R. F., DA57
Muise, D. A. *A reader's guide to Canadian history*, DB187

Mu'jam al-asmā' al-musta 'ārah wa-aṣḥābihā lā siyyama fī al-adab al-'Arabī al-ḥadīth, Dāghir, Yūsuf As'ad, AA189

Mu'jam al-lughah al-'Arabīyah al-Miṣrīyah, AC216

Mu'jam al-muṣṭalaḥāt al-fannīyah, EA104

Mu'jam al-mustalaḥat al-maktabīyah, AK49

Mukařovský, Jan. *Dějiny, české literatury*, BE1106

Muksian, Robert. *Financial mathematics handbook*, CH220

Muldoon, Maureen. *The abortion debate in the United States and Canada*, CC256

Muldrow, George M. *Dictionary of literary-rhetorical conventions of the English Renaissance*, BE351

Mulhall, Michael George. *Dictionary of statistics*, CG53

Mulher brasileira, Fundação Carlos Chagas, DB343

Mullan, Anthony Páez. *Africana serials in microform in the Library of Congress*, DD27

Mullaney, Janet Palmer. *Belles lettres*, CC534

Mullaney, Marie Marmo. *American governors and gubernatorial elections, 1979–1987*, CJ286, CJ291

—— *Biographical directory of the governors of the United States*, CJ288

Mullay, Marilyn. *Walford's guide to reference material*, AA363, EA10

Müller, Bodo. *Diccionario del español medieval*, AC750

Muller, C. F. J. *South African history and historians*, DD223

Müller, Christian. *Art and antiques dictionary*, BG43

—— *Das grosse Fachwörterbuch für Kunst und Antiquitäten*, BG43

Müller, Dieter. *Dictionary of microprocessor systems*, EK193

Müller, Eugen. *Methoden der organischen Chemie (Houben-Weyl)*, EE138

Müller, F. Max. *Sacred books of the East*, BC92, BC457

Muller, Frederik. *Bibliotheek van Nederlandsche pamfletten*, AA752

Müller, Friedrich. *Müllers Grosses deutsches Ortsbuch, Bundesrepublik Deutschland*, CL134

Müller, G. H. *[Omega]—bibliography of mathematical logic*, EB15

Müller, Georg P. *Comparative world data*, CG40

Müller, Gerhard. *Theologische Realenzyklopädie*, BC69

Müller, Hildegard. *Neue Forschungen zum Ersten Weltkrieg*, DA195

Müller, I. P. E. *Handbuch der Altertumswissenschaft*, DA81

Muller, Jacob Wijbrand. *Lijst der aardrijkskundige namen van Nederland*, CL147

Muller, Jean. *Dictionnaire abrégé des imprimeurs/éditeurs français du seizième siècle*, AA309

Müller, Joachim. *Müllers Grosses deutsches Ortsbuch, Bundesrepublik Deutschland*, CL134

Muller, Johannes. *Die wissenschaftlichen Vereine und Gesellschaften Deutschlands im neunzehnten Jahrhundert*, AL63

Müller, Kurt. *Leibniz-Bibliographie*, BB75

Müller, Meike. *China nach Mao*, DE132

Muller, Robert H. *From radical left to extreme right*, AD45

Müller, Vladimir Karlovich. *English-Russian dictionary*, AC679

Müller, Wilhelm. *Mittelhochdeutsches Wörterbuch*, AC406

Müller, Wolfgang. *Dictionary of the graphic arts industry*, AC273

Müller-Brettel, Marianne. *Bibliography on peace research and peaceful international relations*, CJ676

Müller-Karpe, Hermann. *Handbuch der Vorgeschichte*, DA82

Müllers Grosses deutsches Ortsbuch, Bundesrepublik Deutschland, Müller, Friedrich, CL134

Mulligan, Allison Smith. *Historic preservation periodicals*, BF218

Mulligan, William H. *A historical dictionary of American industrial language*, CH339

Mullin, Donald C. *Victorian plays*, BH103

Mullin, Michael. *Theatre at Stratford-upon-Avon*, BH104

Mulliner, K. *Historical dictionary of Singapore*, DE256

—— *Malaysian studies*, DE231

Mullins, Edward Lindsay Carson. *Guide to the historical and archaeological publications of societies in England and Wales, 1903–1933*, DC275, DC279, DC281

—— *Texts and calendars*, DC280, DC361

Mullis, Ina V. S. *Trends in academic progress*, CB140

Müllner, Klaus. *Bibliographie zur Transformationsgrammatik*, BD45

Mulon, Marianne. *L'onomastique française*, CL188

Multhauf, Robert P. *The history of chemical technology*, EE97

The multi-language bibliography of Jewish law, Rakover, Nahum, CK240

Multi media reviews index, 1970–72, AA387

Multicultural education abstracts, CB59

The multicultural student's guide to colleges, Mitchell, Robert, CB309

Multiculturalism in the United States, CC353

Multilateral treaties, Bowman, M. J., CK84

Multilateral treaties deposited with the Secretary-General, CK87

Multilingual demographic dictionary, CG31

Multilingual demographic dictionary. English section, CG26

A multilingual dictionary of artificial intelligence, Vollnhals, Otto, EK195

Multilingual dictionary of geodesy, EF124

Multilingual dictionary of publishing, printing and bookselling, AA275

Multilingual dictionary of technical terms in cartography, CL262

Multilingual international thesaurus of public administration, CJ479

Multilingual law dictionary : English-Français-Español-Deutsch, Egbert, Lawrence Deems, CK46

—— Morales-Macedo, Fernando, CK46

Multilingual lexicon of linguistics and philology, Nash, Rose, BD42

Multilingual thesaurus of geosciences, EF79

•*Multimedia encyclopedia of mammalian biology*, EG293

Multinational corporations, CH347, CH352, CH374

see also **International business enterprises**

Multinational enterprise, CH341

Mulvaney, D. J. *Australians to 1788*, DF37

Mumford, Laura Stempel. *Women's issues*, CC505

Mummendey, Richard. *Language and literature of the Anglo-Saxon nations as presented in German doctoral dissertations, 1885–1950*, BD155, BE594, BE1071

Munasinghe, V. R. N. *Carbohydrates*, EE116

Munch-Petersen, Erland. *A guide to Danish bibliography*, AA40

—— *Guide to Nordic bibliography*, DC71

Munda, Jôze. *Osebno kazalo*, AH309

Munden, Kenneth White. *Guide to federal archives relating to the Civil War*, DB116

Mundo Lo, Sara de. *Falkland/Malvinas Islands*, DB376

—— *Index to Spanish American collective biography*, AH112

Mundt, Hermann. *Bio-bibliographisches Verzeichnis von Universitäts- u. Hochschuldrucken (Dissertationen) vom Ausgang des 16. bis Ende des 19. Jahrhunderts*, AG32

Mundt, Robert J. *Ivory Coast*, DD48

Munford, William Arthur. *Who was who in British librarianship, 1800–1985*, AK91

Municipal/county executive directory annual, CJ273, CJ274

Municipal executive directory, CJ274

The municipal year book, CJ279

Municipal year book and public services directory, CJ370

Municipal yellow book, CH350, CJ273

Munk, William. *The roll of the Royal College of Physicians of London*, EH231

Munk Olsen, B. *L'étude des auteurs classiques latins aux XIe et XIIe siècles*, BE1045

Munk's roll, EH231

Munn, Glenn G. *Encyclopedia of banking & finance*, CH267

Munns, Edward Norfolk. *A selected bibliography of North American forestry*, EJ173

Muñoz de Linares, Elba. *Bibliografía de tesis peruanos sobre indigenismo y ciencias sociales*, DB384

Muñoz y Romero, Tomás. *Diccionario bibliográfica-histórico de los antiguos reinos, provincais, ciudades, villas, iglesias y santuarios de España*, DC512

Munro, D. J. *Microforms for historians*, DA10

Munro, David. *Chambers world gazetteer*, CL84

—— *A world record of major conflict areas*, CJ57

Munro, K. M. *Feminist legal literature*, CK10

Munro, R. W. *Johnston's gazetteer of Scotland*, CL140

Munsell's genealogical index, AJ41

Munsterberg, Hugo. *Dictionary of Chinese and Japanese art*, BF88

Munter, Robert LaVerne. *A hand-list of Irish newspapers, 1685–1750*, AE63

—— *History of the Irish newspaper, 1685–1760*, AE63

Munthe, Preben. *Aschehoug og Gyldendals store norske leksikon*, AB73

Munz, Lucile Thompson. *Index to illustrations of living things outside North America*, EA220, EG72

Munzinger, Werner. *Lexicon linguae Aethiopicae cum indice Latino*, AC310

Murata, Alice K. *Bibliography of Pacific/Asian American materials in the Library of Congress*, CC411

Muratova, K. D. *Istoriiā russkoĭ literatury XIX veka*, BE1388

Murder, CC567
bibliography, CK246

Murder ... by category, Mackler, Tasha, BE273

Murdock, Cunthia R. *Lexicon of new formal geologic names of the United States, 1981–1985*, EF77

Murdock, George Peter. *Atlas of world cultures*, CE71, CE72

—— *Ethnographic atlas*, CE62, CE71

—— *Ethnographic bibliography of North America*, CC412, CC419

—— *Outline of cultural materials*, CE2, CE59, CE61, CE94, CE107

—— *Outline of world cultures*, BJ322, BJ328, CE2, CE59

Murdock, Jean M. *International terrorism in the 1980s*, CJ553

Muret-Sanders encyclopedic dictionary of the English and German languages, AC418

Muret-Sanders German dictionary, AC417

Murfin, Marjorie E. *Reference service*, AK234

Murguia, Edward. *Ethnicity and aging*, CC68

Muriello, Karen Morris. *Theatre at Stratford-upon-Avon*, BH104

Murin, William F. *Delivering government services*, CJ471

Murison, David. *Scottish national dictionary*, AC166

Murith, Jean. *Dictionnaire des abréviations et acronymes scientifiques, techniques, médicaux, économiques, juridiques*, EA96

Murphy, Dennis D. *Directory of conservative and libertarian serials, publishers, and freelance markets*, AD54

Murphy, Henry T. *Comparative & veterinary medicine*, EJ97

Murphy, James J. *The debater's guide*, BE370

Murphy, James Jerome. *Medieval rhetoric*, BE359, DA138

—— *Renaissance rhetoric*, BE360

Murphy, John P. *Index to the supplements and suppl. volumes of Pauly-Wissowa's R.E*, DA104

Murphy, Larry. *Encyclopedia of African American religions*, BC56

Murphy, Roland Edmund. *The new Jerome biblical commentary,* BC178
Murray, Andrew. *Botswana,* DD48
Murray, David. *Museums, their history and their use,* AL89
Murray, Jacqueline. *International directory of Renaissance and Reformation associations and institutes,* DA153
Murray, James Augustus Henry. *Evolution of English lexicography,* AC5
—— *New English dictionary on historical principles,* AC30, AC31, AC33, AC175
—— *The Oxford English dictionary,* AC32
—— *The shorter Oxford English dictionary on historical principles,* AC31
Murray, Linda. *Dictionary of art and artists,* BF78
Murray, Margaret Ransome. *A bibliography of the research in tissue culture,* EG7
Murray, Peter. *Dictionary of art and artists,* BF78
Murray, Sterling E. *Anthologies of music,* BJ116
Murray's dictionary, AC30
Murrie, Eleanore Boswell. *English song-books, 1651–1702,* BJ275
Murry, Velma McBride. *Black adolescence,* CC143
Mursec, Ljudmila T. *A catalogue of rare books, pamphlets, and journals on business and economics in the Krannert Library special collection, 1500–1870,* CH19
Musacchio, Humberto. *Diccionario enciclopédico de México,* DB246
Musāḥib, Ghulām Ḥusayn. *Dāyirat al-maʿārif-i Fārsī,* AB38
Musch, Donald J. *Sources and documents of United States constitutions, second series,* CK172
•*MUSE,* BJ108
Musée royal de l'Afrique centrale. *African governmental systems in static and changing conditions,* CE103
The museum : a reference guide, BF8
Museum media, BF48
Museum of Afro-American History (Boston, Mass.). *Black writers in New England,* BE516
Museum of American Folk Art. *Bibliography of American folk art for the year,* BG10
—— *Folk artists biographical index,* BG30
—— *The quilt encyclopedia illustrated,* BG163
Museum of American Folk Art encyclopedia of twentieth-century American folk art and artists, Rosenak, Chuck, BG35
Museum of Fine Arts, Budapest, Szépművészeti Múzeum (Hungary), BF321
Museum of Mankind. Library. *Anthropological index to current periodicals in the Museum of Mankind Library,* CE35
The Museum of Modern Art artists scrapbooks, BF55
Museum of Modern Art (New York, N.Y.). *Annual bibliography of modern art,* BF55
—— *The film catalog,* BH191
—— *The film index,* BH172
Museum of Modern Art (New York, N.Y.). Library. *Catalog of the Library,* BF55
The Museum of Science and Industry basic list of children's science books, 1973–1984, Richter, Bernice, EA30
Museum of Science and Industry (Chicago, Ill.). *The Museum of Science and Industry basic list of children's science books, 1973–1984,* EA30
Museum of the American Indian, Heye Foundation. *The American Indian in graduate studies,* CC425
Museum publications, Clapp, Jane, AL86, EF24, EF25
Museum studies library shelf list, BF8
Museums, AL89
  bibliography, BF48
  directories, AL88, BF100, BF114, CE88, DB52
  Europe
    Directories., BF98
  financial aids, BF104
  guides, BF8
  publications, AL86, EF24
Museums (by country or region)
  Africa
    directories, AL87

Canada
  bibliography, BF48
  directories, AL90, BF116, CC406, EA217
Germany, BF68
Great Britain, BF66
  bibliography, BF48
  directories, BF101
Hungary, BF321
international
  directories, AL13
United States
  bibliography, BF48
  directories, AL90, BF103, BF116, CC406, EA217
Museums (by subject)
  pharmacy, EH367
  see also **Art museums; Exhibitions; Science museums**
Museums directory of the United States and Canada, AL90, BF116, EA217
Museums in Africa, Seidenspinner, Gundolf, AL87
Museums in New York, AL90, BF116, EA217
Museums of the world, BF100
Museums, sites, and collections of Germanic culture in North America, Hobbie, Margaret, CC352
Museums, their history and their use, Murray, David, AL89
Musgrave, William. *Obituary prior to 1800,* AH237
Musgrove, John. *Sir Banister Fletcher's A history of architecture,* BF255
The mushroom hunter's field guide, Smith, Alexander Hanchett, EG191
Music
  abstract journals, BJ108
  annuals, BJ192
  atlases, BJ198
  bibliography, BJ4, BJ7, BJ76, BJ84, BJ90, BJ107, BJ124, BJ178, BJ211, BJ212, BJ269
    books, BJ8, BJ9, BJ10, BJ11, BJ12, BJ14, BJ16, BJ17, BJ18, BJ22, BJ24, BJ26, BJ28, BJ29, BJ30, BJ32, BJ34, BJ38, BJ42, BJ44, BJ45, BJ48, BJ77, BJ87, BJ88, BJ89
      current, BJ47, BJ50
    current, BJ49
    music, manuscript and printed, BJ89, BJ91, BJ92, BJ93, BJ94, BJ96, BJ97, BJ98
    scores, BJ25, BJ32, BJ48, BJ51, BJ52, BJ53, BJ54, BJ55, BJ56, BJ57, BJ58, BJ60, BJ62, BJ63, BJ64, BJ65, BJ66, BJ67, BJ69, BJ72, BJ73, BJ77, BJ78, BJ82
      current, BJ53, BJ80, BJ81, BJ83
  bibliography of bibliography, BJ2, BJ23
  biobibliography, BJ209
  biography, AH213, BC314, BJ57, BJ65, BJ124, BJ130, BJ131, BJ201, BJ203, BJ204, BJ207, BJ212, BJ213, BJ215, BJ217, BJ218, BJ222
    bibliography, BJ12, BJ219, BJ221
    indexes, BJ224, BJ225, BJ226
  catalogs, BJ27
  chronologies, BJ175, BJ186, BJ187, BJ188
  compendiums, BJ176
  congresses and meetings
    indexes, BJ20
  criticism
    bibliography, BJ113
  databases, BJ53, BJ108, BJ111
  dictionaries, BJ130, BJ131, BJ146, BJ148, BJ149, BJ152, BJ156, BJ157, BJ158, BJ160
    bibliography, BJ12
    bilingual
      German-English, BJ147
      Russian-English, BJ150
    multilingual, BJ159, BJ161
  directories, BH18, BJ169, BJ170, BJ171, BJ172, BJ192
  dissertations, BJ164, BJ165, BJ166
  education, BJ26
  encyclopedias, BJ117, BJ119, BJ120, BJ122, BJ123, BJ125, BJ127, BJ128, BJ129, BJ130, BJ131, BJ132, BJ133, BJ135, BJ136, BJ137, BJ138, BJ139, BJ140, BJ141, BJ142, BJ143, BJ145, BJ153, BJ252

festschriften
  bibliography, BJ13
  guidebooks, BJ190, BJ194
  guides, BJ1, BJ3, BJ4, BJ5, BJ7
  handbooks, BJ173, BJ174, BJ175
  indexes, BJ106, BJ110, BJ111, BJ112, BJ114, BJ115, BJ116
    bibliography, BJ23
  library catalogs, BJ25, BJ34, BJ61, BJ62, BJ72, BJ82, BJ84, BJ87, BJ88, BJ89, BJ90, BJ94, BJ96, BJ97, BJ98
  library resources, BJ17, BJ170
  periodicals, BJ99, BJ100, BJ101, BJ102, BJ103, BJ104, BJ105, BJ114
  quotations, BJ162, BJ163
  style manuals, BJ189
  thematic catalogs, BJ232
    bibliography, BJ233
  union lists, BJ62
Music (by country or region)
  Africa, BF38, BJ217, BJ317, BJ330
  Arab states, BJ38
  Australia, BJ28
  Brazil, BJ132
    bibliography, BJ22
  Canada
    bibliography, BJ41
    encyclopedias, BJ134
  China, BJ18
  Croatia, BJ151
  Cuba
    dictionaries, BJ154
  Europe
    guidebooks, BJ193
  France
    bibliography, BJ76
  Germany
    biography
      bibliography, AH205
  Great Britain
    bibliography, BJ79
    guidebooks, BJ194
    library catalogs, BJ79
  Greece, ancient
    encyclopedias, BJ139
  Index, BJ156
  Ireland
    guidebooks, BJ194
  Israel, BJ65
  Japan, BJ44, BJ74
  Latin America
    bibliography, BJ11
    encyclopedias, BJ121
  New Zealand, BJ35
  Poland, BJ42
  Puerto Rico
    bibliography, BJ43
  Scandinavia
    encyclopedias, BJ126
  Serbia, BJ151
  South Africa, BJ144
  Spain
    biobibliography, BJ216
  United States, BJ140, BJ291
    bibliography, BJ36, BJ202
    biography, BJ206, BJ210
    current surveys, BA1, BF44
    directories, BJ191
    guides, BJ36
  Yugoslavia, BJ151
Music (by period)
  18th century, BJ187
  19th–20th centuries, BJ113
  19th century, BJ184, BJ291
    periodicals, BJ101
  20th century, BJ135
    biobibliography, BJ209
Music (by subject)
  history, BJ197, BJ200
  indexes, BJ109
  see also **Chamber music; Electronic music; Instrumental music; Orchestral music; Piano music; Religious music; Rock music**

Music, Brockman, William S., BJ1
Music analyses, Diamond, Harold J., BJ106
Music and dance in Puerto Rico from the age of Columbus to modern times, Thompson, Donald, BJ43
Music and dance periodicals, Robinson, Doris, BJ104
Music and opera guide, BJ192
Music article guide, BJ110
Music business, BJ179, BJ180, BJ183, BJ185
  biography, BJ201
  directories, BJ182, BJ184
Music business (by country or region)
  France, BJ76
  Great Britain, BJ184
Music business handbook & career guide, Baskerville, David, BJ179
The music catalog, AA111, BJ62, BJ82
Music criticism, Diamond, Harold J., BJ107
Music education, CB116
  directories, BJ168, BJ172
  guides, BJ6
Music Educators National Conference. *Doctoral dissertations in musicology*, BJ164
—— *Handbook of research on music teaching and learning*, CB116
Music festivals, BJ193, BJ195, BJ196
Music festivals in America, Rabin, Carol Price, BJ195
Music festivals in Europe and Britain, Rabin, Carol Price, BJ196
The music guide to Austria and Germany, Brody, Elaine, BJ190
Music guide to Belgium, Luxembourg, Holland and Switzerland, Brody, Elaine, BJ190
—— Brook, Claire, BJ190
Music guide to Great Britain, Brody, Elaine, BJ190
—— Brook, Claire, BJ190
Music guide to Italy, Brody, Elaine, BJ190
—— Brook, Claire, BJ190
Music in American higher education, Brookhart, Edward, BJ26
Music in art, BJ199
Music in early America, Hixon, Donald L., BJ59
Music in films, BJ359, BJ361, BJ362, BJ363, BJ364, BJ365
  bibliography, BJ360
  encyclopedias, BJ358
Music in Harvard libraries, Wood, David A., BJ90
Music in print annual supplement, BJ83
Music-in-print series, BJ83
Music in television, BJ359, BJ364
Music in the Hirsch Library, British Museum. Department of Printed Books. Hirsch Library, BJ85, BJ87, BJ94
Music index, BJ111
•*Music index on CD-ROM*, BJ111
Music industry directory, BJ182
Music, Jewish *see* **Jewish music**
Music lexicography, Coover, James B., BJ12
Music libraries, BJ169
•*Music library*, BJ380
Music Library Association. *Checklist of thematic catalogues*, BJ230
—— *Literature for voices in combination with electronic and tape music*, BJ276
Music Library Association. Committee on Basic Music Collection. *A basic music library*, BJ24
Music Library Association catalog of cards for printed music, 1953–1972, Olmsted, Elizabeth H., BJ63
Music literature international, BJ108
Music lover's Europe, Bernstein, Kenneth, BJ193
The music lover's guide to Europe, BJ193
Music manuscripts at Harvard, Mahrenholz Wolff, Barbara, BJ90
Music monographs in series, Blum, Fred, BJ9, BJ10, BJ45
The music of ancient Greece, Michaelides, Solon, BJ139
Music periodical literature, Meggett, Joan M., BJ103

Music, printed and manuscript, in the James Weldon Johnson Memorial Collection of Negro Arts and Letters, Brown, Rae Linda, BJ95
Music printing, BJ40
Music printing and publishing, BJ183
Music publishers
  bibliography, BJ40
  biography, BJ201
Music publishers (by country or region)
  Great Britain, BJ181
Music publishing in the British Isles from the beginning until the middle of the nineteenth century, Humphries, Charles, BJ181, BJ184
—— Smith, William C., BJ184
Music reference and research materials, Duckles, Vincent Harris, BJ4, BJ5
—— Keller, Michael A., BJ5
Music since 1900, Slonimsky, Nicolas, BJ188
Music theory from Zarlino to Schenker, Damschroder, David, BJ29
Music titles in translation, Hodgson, Julian, BJ174
La musica, BJ130, BJ131
Música y músicos de Latinoamérica, Mayer-Serra, Otto, BJ121
The musical, Wildbihler, Hubert, BJ268
A musical gazetteer of Great Britain & Ireland, Norris, Gerald, BJ194
Musical instrument collections, Coover, James, BJ367
Musical instruments, BJ310, BJ370, BJ371, BJ372
  collections, BJ367, BJ368
  dictionaries, BJ369
  encyclopedias, BJ366
Musical instruments (by subject)
  history, BJ373
Musical instruments, Marcuse, Sibyl, BJ370
Musical morphology, Levarie, Siegmund, BJ152
Musical notation, BJ21
Musical settings of American poetry, Hovland, Michael A., BJ272
Musical settings of early and mid-Victorian literature, Gooch, Bryan N. S., BJ278, BJ279
—— Thatcher, D. S., BJ279
Musical settings of late Victorian and modern British literature, Gooch, Bryan N. S., BJ279
Musical terms, symbols, and theory, Thomsett, Michael C., BJ160
Musical theater, BJ241, BJ258, BJ259, BJ261, BJ262, BJ263, BJ264, BJ265, BJ267, BJ359
  bibliography, BH40, BJ268
  encyclopedias, BJ252, BJ349
  plot summaries
    indexes, BJ245
Musical theater (by country or region)
  Spain
    bibliography, BJ266
Musical themes, BJ229, BJ230, BJ231, BJ288
The musical woman, BJ177
Musicians
  biography, BJ129, BJ213
The musician's guide, BJ182
Musicologica, Kunst, Jaap, BJ319
Musicos españoles de todos los tiempos, BJ216
Die Musik in Geschichte und Gegenwart, BJ122
Musik-lexikon, Riemann, Hugo, BJ128
Musikalisch-literarischer Monatsbericht, BJ80
Musiker, Naomi. *South African history*, DD223
Musiker, Reuben. *Guide to South African reference books*, AA353
—— *Select bibliography of South African history*, DD223
—— *South Africa*, AA72, AA353, AA354, DD18
—— *South African bibliography*, AA72, AA354
—— *South African reference books and bibliographies of 1979–1980*, AA354
Musique, BJ78
Musique dans les congrès internationaux, 1835–1939, Briquet, Marie, BJ20
Muslim economic thinking, Siddiqi, Muhammad Nejatullah, CH190
Muslim peoples, CE43
Muss-Arnolt, William. *The Book of Common Prayer among the nations of the world*, BC339

—— *The Book of Common Prayer and books connected with its origin and growth*, BC338
Mussen, Paul H. *Handbook of child psychology*, CD85
Musser, Donald W. *A new handbook of Christian theology*, BC252
Musso Ambrosi, Luis Alberto. *Bibliografía de bibliografías uruguayas*, AA31
—— *Bibliografía del Poder Legislativo desde sus comienzos hasta el ano 1965*, AF162
Mustakhlaṣāt rasāil al-duktūrāh al-Sàudīyah, AG57
Musto, Frederick W. *State legislatures*, CJ268
Musto, Ronald G. *Catholic peace tradition*, CJ677
—— *Liberation theologies*, BC219
—— *The peace tradition in the Catholic Church*, CJ677
Muthiah, S. *An atlas of India*, CL356
Mutibwa, Olivia M. N. *Women in Uganda*, DD241
Mutual fund profiles, CH314
Mutual funds
  databases, CH326
  directories, CH305, CH308, CH314
  statistics, CH326
Mutual funds panorama, CH308
Muzicka enciklopedija, Kovačević, Krešimir, BJ151
Muzykal'naia entsiklopediia, BJ123
Muzzy, Adrienne Florence. *List of clandestine periodicals of World War II*, AD18
Mwalo, Margaret. *Women in Zimbabwe*, DD253
Mwanyimi-Mbonba, Mandjumba. *Chronologie générale de l'histoire du Zaïre*, DD15, DD245
Mwanza, Ilse. *Bibliography of Zambiana theses and dissertations, 1930s–1989*, AG50, DD247
—— *Subject guide to Zambiana theses*, AG50, DD247
Mworoha, Emile. *Histoire du Burundi*, DD135
Myanmar *see* **Burma**
Myers, Allen C. *The Eerdmans Bible dictionary*, BC136
Myers, Bernard Samuel. *Encyclopedia of world art*, BF73
—— *McGraw-Hill dictionary of art*, BF77
—— *World art in our time*, BF73
Myers, Carol Fairbanks. *Black American writers*, BE532
Myers, Hector F. *Black child development in America, 1927–1977*, CC369
Myers, Jack Elliott. *The Longman dictionary of poetic terms*, BE328
Myers, Kurtz. *Index to record reviews*, BJ391
Myers, Robert A. *Amerindians of the Lesser Antilles*, CE80
—— *Dominica*, DB432
—— *Ghana*, DD18
—— *Nigeria*, DD18
—— *Resource guide to Dominica 1493–1986*, DB432
Myers, Robin. *Dictionary of literature in the English language from 1940–1970*, BE584
—— *A dictionary of literature in the English language, from Chaucer to 1940*, BE584
Myerson, Joel. *American Renaissance in New England*, BE577
—— *The Transcendentalists*, BE416
Mylne, Vivienne G. *Bibliographie du genre romanesque français, 1751–1800*, BE1191
Myśliński, Jerzy. *Bibliografia prasy polskiej, 1944–1948*, AD137
Mystery, detective, and espionage fiction, Cook, Michael L., BE269
Mystery, detective, and espionage magazines, Cook, Michael L., BE270
Mystery fiction *see* **Detective and mystery fiction**
Mysticism, BC8, BC520, BC550
  encyclopedias, BC61
Myth, legend & romance, Ó hÓgáin, Dáithí, CF89
Mythical and fabulous creatures, CF6
Mythologie générale, Guirand, Félix, CF8
Mythologies, CF7
Mythology, CF1
  dictionaries, AH36, CF2, CF10, CF11, CF12, CF13, CF14, CF15

encyclopedias, BC62, BC64, CF5, CF7, CF8, CF9, CF10, CF51
Mythology (by country or region)
  China, BF179
  Germanic countries
    dictionaries, CF35
  Greek and Roman, BF7, BF189, CF19, CF22, CF24
    bibliography, CF20
    dictionaries, CF26, CF27, CF28, CF29
    encyclopedias, BF188, CF21, CF23
    handbooks, CF25
  Irish, CF30, CF31
  Oceania, CF32
  Polynesian, CF32
  Scandinavian, CF33
  Slavic, CF34
Mythology (by ethnic group)
  Celts, CF17, CF18
  Native Americans, CF16
Mythology, Hamilton, Edith, CF1
Mythology in literature, CF3
  bibliography, BE29

N. W. Ayer and Son's directory of newspapers and periodicals, AD51, AE23
Naaman, Antoine. *Guide bibliographique des thèses littéraires canadiennes de 1921 à 1976,* BE831
—— *Répertoire des thèses littéraires canadiennes de 1921 à 1976,* BE44
Naamregister van de bekendste en meest in gebruik zynde Nederduitsche boeken, Abkoude, Johannes van, AA748
Naas, Bernard G. *American labor union periodicals,* CH635
—— *American labor unions' constitutions and proceedings,* CH636
Naas, Josef. *Mathematisches Wörterbuch mit Einbeziehung der theoretischen Physik,* EB44
Nachlässe in den Bibliotheken der Bundesrepublik Deutschland, Brandis, Tilo, DC248
—— Denecke, Ludwig, DC248
Nachlässe in den deutschen Archiven, Mommsen, Wolfgang A., DC248
Nachod, Oskar. *Bibliographie von Japan, 1906–[1943],* DE204
Nachowitz, Todd. *An alternative directory of nongovernmental organizations in South Asia,* AL15
Nadel, Ira Bruce. *Jewish writers of North America,* BE566
Nadell, Pamela S. *Conservative Judaism in America,* BC559
Naden, Corinne J. *Best books for children,* AA337
Nadurille, Ramon. *Catálogo colectivo de publicaciones periódicas existentes en bibliotecas de la República Mexicana,* AD229
Næss, Harald S. *A history of Norwegian literature,* BE1342
Naess, Harold S. *Norsk litteraturhistorisk bibliografi, 1900–1945,* BE1343
—— *Norwegian literary biography, 1956–1970,* BE1343
Naft, Stephen. *International conversion tables,* AL199
Naftalin, Mortimer L. *Historic books and manuscripts concerning general agriculture in the collection of the National Agricultural Library,* EJ69
—— *Historic books and manuscripts concerning horticulture and forestry in the collection of the National Agricultural Library,* EJ70
Nagar, Murari Lal. *TULIP,* AD192
Nagar, Sarla Devi. *TULIP,* AD192
Nagel, Gwen L. *Facts on File bibliography of American fiction, 1866–1918,* BE472
Nagel, James. *Facts on File bibliography of American fiction, 1866–1918,* BE472
Nagel, Kathleen Carter. *Textbooks in school and society,* CB19
Nagel, Stuart S. *Basic literature in policy studies,* CJ12
—— *Encyclopedia of policy studies,* CA34

Nagelkerke, Gerard A. *Netherlands Antilles,* DB449
—— *Suriname,* DB393
Nagler, Georg Kasper. *Die Monogrammisten und diejenigen bekannten und unbekannten Künstler aller Schulen,* BF160
Nagy, Ernő. *Angol-magyar műszaki szótár,* EA115
—— *English-Hungarian technical dictionary,* EA115
—— *Hungarian-English technical dictionary,* EA115
—— *Magyar-angol műszaki szótár,* EA115
Nagy, Gregory. *Greek,* BD137
Naha, Ed. *Lillian Roxon's rock encyclopedia,* BJ357
Nahm, Andrew C. *Historical dictionary of the Republic of Korea,* DE216
Naifeh, Steven W. *The best lawyers in America,* CK141
Nairn, Bede. *Australian dictionary of biography,* AH371, DF40
Nairn, John Arbuthnot. *Classical hand-list,* BE1004
—— *Hand-list of books relating to the classics and classical antiquity,* BE1004
Najnowsza twórczość literacka, 1935–37, Czachowski, Kasimierz, BE1349
Nakai, Seijiro. *Reaction index of organic syntheses,* EE145
Nakajima, Fumio. *Iwanami Ei-Wa daijiten,* AC555
Nakamura, Joyce. *Children's authors and illustrators,* BE387
The name dictionary, AJ171
Name into word, Partridge, Eric, AC59
The name is familiar, Nowlan, Robert A., BH278
Name this child, Partridge, Eric, AJ176
Namen und Daten wichtiger Personen der DDR, Buch, Günther, AH217
Namenschlüssel die Verweisungen der Berliner Titeldrucke zu Pseudonymen, Doppelnamen und Namensabwandlungen, Preussische Staatsbibliothek, AA172
Namenschlüssel zu Pseudonymen, Doppelnamen und Namensabwandlungen, AA172
Names
  personal, AJ167, AJ168, AJ169, AJ170, AJ173, AJ175, AJ176, AJ177, AJ179
    African-American, AJ174
    bibliography, AJ166
    British and American, AJ183
    dictionaries, EJ32
      multilingual, BE87
    English, AJ171, AJ172
    French, AJ190, BE1164, CL188
      dictionaries, BE1163
      indexes, BE1165
    German, AJ192, CL189
    handbooks, BE190
    Hebrew, AJ171, AJ172
    Japanese, AC556
    Jewish, AJ183, AJ201
    Mexican-American, AJ178
    Portuguese, AJ202
    pronunciation, AH36
    Russian, AJ203
  pronunciation, AC109
  surnames
    African, AJ188
    American, AJ182, AJ186
    British, AJ182, AJ184, AJ185
    French, AJ189, AJ191
    German, AJ193, AJ194, AJ195, AJ196
    Irish, AJ197
    Italian, AJ198, AJ199
    Jewish, AJ200
    Portuguese, AJ202
    Russian, AJ203, AJ204
    Scottish, AJ205
    Spanish, AJ187
    Spanish-American, AJ187
    Swiss, AJ142
  see also **Nicknames**
Names & nicknames of places & things, CL172
Names and numbers, AA282, BE172
Names from Africa, Chuks-orji, Ogonna, AJ168

Names, geographical *see* **Geographical names and terms**
The names in Roman verse, Swanson, Donald Carl Eugene, BE1046
The names of towns and cities in Britain, Gelling, Margaret, CL197
Namibia, DD190
  atlases, CL343
  bibliography, AA868, DD18, DD185, DD186, DD187
  biography, DD189
  biography (by subject)
    artists, BF142
Namibia (by subject)
  anthropology and ethnology, CE104
  history, DD188
Namibia, DD188
  —— Moorsom, Richard, DD187
  —— Schoeman, Elna, DD18
  —— Schoeman, Stanley, DD18
Namibia bibliographies, Scheven, Yvette, DD190
Namibia handbook and political who's who, Pütz, Joe, DD189
Namibia in transition, Moorsom, Richard, DD187
Namibian issue 1920–1980, Schoeman, Elna, DD185
Namibian national bibliography, AA868
Namier, Lewis Bernstein. *The House of Commons, 1715–1754,* CJ360
—— *House of Commons, 1754–1790,* CJ354
Nance, Robert Morton. *An English-Cornish dictionary,* AC274
—— *New Cornish-English dictionary,* AC274
Nancollas, George H. *Compendium of analytical nomenclature,* EE35
Nandakumar, Prema. *Indian writing in English,* BE1569
Nangle, Benjamin Christie. *Gentleman's magazine biographical and obituary notices, 1781–1819,* AH241
Nania, Georges. *Complete multilingual dictionary of computer terminology,* EK194
Nanori jiten, Ryōzō, Araki, AC556
NAPCA abstracts bulletin, United States. National Air Pollution Control Administration, EK85
Napier, John M. *The Air Force officer's guide,* CJ627
Napier, John Russell. *A handbook of living primates,* EG301
Napier, Prue H. *A handbook of living primates,* EG301
Napoleon, DC195, DC196, DC197
Napoleonic era, DC191, DC193, DC194
Napoleonic military history, Howard, Donald D., DC192
The Napoleonic source book, Haythornthwaite, Philip J., DC196
Napoleon's Europe, DC22
Nappo, Tommaso. *Archivio biografico italiano,* AH258
Nares, Robert. *Glossary of words, phrases, names, and allusions in the works of English authors, particularly of Shakespeare and his contemporaries,* AC99
Narkiss, Bezalel. *Index of Jewish art,* BF193
Narkyid, Ngawangthondup. *English-Tibetan dictionary of modern Tibetan,* AC784
Narodna biblioteka "Kiril i Metodiĭ". *Bibliografiia na bŭlgarskata bibliografiia, 1852–1944,* AA38
—— *Bibliografiia na bŭlgarskata bibliografiia, 1944–1969,* AA39
—— *Bŭlgarska vŭzrozhdenska knizhnina,* AA584
—— *Bŭlgarski knigi, 1878–1944,* AA585
—— *Istoriiata na Bŭlgariia v memoarnata literatura,* DC115
—— *Letopis na statiite ot bŭlgarskite spisaniia i sbornitsi,* AD305
Národní bibliografie České republiky. Knihy, AA600
Národní knihovna v Praze. *Bibliografický katalog ČSFR,* AG25
Narodnoe khoziaistvo SSSR, CG296
Narodnoe khoziaistvo SSSR za 70 let, CG296
Naroll, Raoul. *A handbook of method in cultural anthropology,* CE60

Narrative and dramatic sources of Shakespeare, Bullough, Geoffrey, BE786

NASA Scientific and Technical Information Facility. *Aerospace medicine and biology,* EH70

Nasatir, A. P. *French consuls in the United States,* DB31

NASB interlinear Greek-English New Testament, Marshall, Alfred, BC94

Nascentes, Antenor. *Dicionário de sinónimos,* AC653

Nascentes, Olavo Anibal. *Dicionário de sinónimos,* AC653

NASDAQ fact book & company directory, CH310

NASDAQ yellow book, CH350

NASDTEC information system, CB163

The NASDTEC manual, CB163

Naselenie SSSR za 50 let, 1941–1990, Gel'fand, V. S., CG295

Nash, Ernest. *Pictorial dictionary of ancient Rome,* DA102, DA106

Nash, Jay Robert. *Encyclopedia of world crime,* CK254

——— *The motion picture guide,* BH199

Nash, Rose. *Multilingual lexicon of linguistics and philology,* BD42

al-Nashrah al-Miṣrīyah lil-ma tbūāt, AA853

Nashrat al-idā', AA853

Nashrat al-idā al-sharīyah, AA853

Nason, James D. *Micronesia, 1944–1974,* CE114, DF5

Nasrallah, Wahib. *United States corporation histories,* CH397

Nasri, William Z. *Encyclopedia of library and information science,* AK36

Nassau guardian, DB416

Nast, Thomas. *Dictionary of American foreign affairs,* CJ119

Nataf, Georges. *Encyclopédie de la mystique juive,* BC550

Nathanail, Paul. *NTC's new college Greek and English dictionary,* AC466

Nationaal biografisch woordenboek, AH174

National Academic Recognition Information Centre (Great Britain). *International guide to qualifications in education,* CB324

National Academy of Sciences. *An assessment of research doctorate programs in the United States,* CB347, CB348

——— *Biographical memoirs,* EA188, EH219

——— *Geology and earth sciences sourcebook for elementary and secondary schools,* EF94

——— *Guide to tables in mathematical statistics,* EB73

National accounts statistics, CH243

National Agricultural Library catalog, EJ13

——— National Agricultural Library (U.S.), EJ9, EJ17

National Agricultural Library (U.S.). *AGRICOLA,* EJ14

——— *Dictionary catalog of the National Agricultural Library, 1862–1965,* EJ13

——— *Historic books and manuscripts concerning general agriculture in the collection of the National Agricultural Library,* EJ69

——— *Historic books and manuscripts concerning horticulture and forestry in the collection of the National Agricultural Library,* EJ70

——— *National Agricultural Library catalog,* EJ9, EJ17

——— *Plant science catalog,* EG107

——— *Serials currently received by the National Agricultural Library, 1975,* EJ12

National and regional atlases, CL239

National Anthropological Archives. *Catalog to manuscripts at the National Anthropological Archives, Department of Anthropology, National Museum of Natural History, Smithsonian Institution, Washington, D.C,* CE31

——— *Guide to the National Anthropological Archives, Smithsonian Institution,* CE32

National Archives and Records Service. *Guide to genealogical research in the National Archives,* AJ15

National Archives of Canada. *Government Archives Division,* DB192

——— *Manuscripts and government records in the United Kingdom and Ireland relating to Canada,* DB196

——— *National inventory of documentary sources in Canada,* DB193

National Archives of Malawi. *List of publications deposited in the Library of the National Archives, 1965–66,* AA866

——— *Malawi national bibliography,* AA866

National Archives of Pakistan. *Holdings of the newspapers and periodicals,* AE97

National Archives of Rhodesia. *List of publications deposited in the library,* AA887

National Art Library (Great Britain). *First proofs of the Universal catalogue of books on art,* BF56

National Association of Basketball Coaches of the United States. *Basketball resource guide,* BK64

National Association of Broadcasters. *Broadcast research definitions,* CH485

National Association of Credit Management. *Credit manual of commercial laws for ...,* CK165

——— *Digest of commercial laws of the world,* CK68

National Association of Independent Schools. Ad Hoc Library Committee. *Books for secondary school libraries,* AA342

National Association of School Psychologists. *A bibliographic guide to the literature of professional school psychology (1890–1985),* CD89

National Association of Schools of Public Affairs and Administration. *The Facts on File dictionary of public administration,* CJ478

——— *Public administration in American society,* CJ475

National Association of Securities Dealers. *NASDAQ fact book & company directory,* CH310

National Association of Social Workers. *Encyclopedia of social work,* CC46

——— *Professional writing for the human services,* CC54

——— *The social work dictionary,* CC47

National Association of State Directors of Teacher Education and Certification. *The NASDTEC manual,* CB163

The national atlas of Canada, Canada. Energy, Mines and Resources Canada, CL307, CL308

National atlas of China, Chang, Ch'i-yün, CL352

National atlas of Ethiopia, Ya'Ityo p̄yä kärtä šerä derejet, CL340

National atlas of Kenya, Survey of Kenya, CL341

National atlas of South West Africa (Namibia), CL343

The national atlas of Sri Lanka, Sri Lanka. Minindōru Depārtamēntuva, CL363

National atlas of Sweden, CL335

National atlas of the Democratic Republic of Afghanistan, CL350

The national atlas of the United States of America, Geological Survey (U.S.), CL298

National Audiovisual Center. *A reference list of audiovisual materials produced by the United States government, 1978,* AA382

National Audubon Society. *Audubon wildlife report,* EG87

——— *A field guide to hawks,* EG256

National basic intelligence factbook, CL68

National Basketball Association. *The Sporting news official NBA guide,* BK66

National bibliographic indexes of the socialist countries, AA396

The national bibliography of Barbados, AA557

The national bibliography of Botswana, AA851

National bibliography of Indian literature, 1901–1953, AA897

National bibliography of Nigeria, AA869

National bibliography of PSRA : Articles of the Albanian press, AD301

National bibliography of the Gambia, AA858

The national bibliography of Zambia, AA885

National black media directory, AE15

National Book Centre of Pakistan. *Books from Pakistan published during the decade of reforms, 1958–1968,* AA924

National Bureau of Standards. *Publications of the National Bureau of Standards,* EA274

——— *Standards activities of organizations in the United States,* EA276

National Bureau of Standards (U.S.). *Applied mathematics series,* EB78, EB88

——— *Computer literature bibliography,* EK158

——— *Handbook of mathematical functions with formulas, graphs, and mathematical tables,* EB76

——— *[Mathematical tables],* EB88

——— *The NBS tables of chemical thermodynamic properties,* EE94

——— *Units of weight and measure,* AL196

National Cancer Institute. *Cancer sourcebook,* EH173

National Catholic almanac, BC415

National cemeteries, BF390, CJ632

National censuses and vital statistics in Europe, 1918–1939, Library of Congress. Census Library Project, CG188

National Center for Education Statistics. *120 years of American education,* CB135

——— *The condition of education,* CB138

——— *Digest of education statistics,* CB139

——— *Directory of postsecondary institutions,* CB268

——— *Directory of public elementary and secondary education agencies,* CB97

——— *Private schools in the United States,* CB136

——— *Projections of educational statistics to […],* CB144

——— *State higher education profiles,* CB343

——— *Survey report,* CB142

——— *Trends in academic progress,* CB140

National Center for Health Statistics (U.S.). *Health, United States,* EH232

——— *Where to write for vital records,* AJ57, CK157

National Center for Prevention Services. *Health information for international travel,* EH415

National Center for State Courts. *State court caseload statistics,* CK168

National Center on Child Abuse and Neglect. *Child abuse and neglect and family violence,* CC156

——— *Child abuse and neglect and family violence thesaurus,* CC161

——— *Interdisciplinary glossary on child abuse and neglect,* CC160

National Clearinghouse for Bilingual Education. *NCBE bibliographic database,* CB40

——— *NCBE resources database,* CB41

National Clearinghouse for Mental Health Information. *Psychopharmacology abstracts,* EH323

National Climatic Center (U.S.). *Climatological data,* EF160

National college databank, CB287

National Conference of Catholic Bishops. *Lectionary for Mass,* BC422

——— *The sacramentary,* BC424

National Conference of State Historic Preservation Officers. *National register of historic places, 1966–1991,* BF250

National Conference of State Legislatures. *Election results directory,* CJ271

——— *Mason's manual of legislative procedure,* CJ456

——— *State legislative staff directory,* CJ276

National conventions and platforms of all political parties, 1789–1905, McKee, Thomas Hudson, CJ264

National costumes from East Europe, Africa and Asia, Tilke, Max, BG114

National Council for Accreditation of Teacher Education. *Teacher education program evaluation,* CB158

National Council for Research on Women (U.S.). *International centers for research on women,* CC551

——— *A women's thesaurus,* CC543

National Council for the Social Studies. *Handbook of research on social studies teaching and learning,* CB116

National Council of Nurses of the United Kingdom. *A bibliography of nursing literature,* EH273

National Council of Public History (U.S.). *The craft of public history,* DB12

National Council of Teachers of English. *Good reading,* AA326

—— *Handbook of research on teaching the English language arts,* CB118

National Council of Teachers of English. Committee to Revise High Interest-Easy Reading. *High interest easy reading,* CB191

National Council of Teachers of English. Comparative Literature Committee. *Yearbook of comparative and general literature,* BE41

National Council of Teachers of Mathematics. *Handbook of research on mathematics teaching and learning,* CB116

National Council of the Churches of Christ in the U.S.A. *Yearbook of American and Canadian churches,* BC324

National Council of the Churches of Christ in the U.S.A. Bureau of Research and Survey. *Churches and church membership in the United States,* BC85, BC88

National Council on Crime and Delinquency. *Criminal justice abstracts,* CK248

National Council on Family Relations. *History of the family and kinship,* CC213

—— *Inventory of marriage and family literature,* CC221

National Council on Measurement in Education. *Educational measurement,* CB150

—— *Standards for educational and psychological testing,* CD76

National Council on the Aging. *Abstracts in social gerontology,* CC78

National cyclopaedia of American biography, AH62, AH65, AH68

National Dance Association. *Dance directory,* BH148

National data book of foundations, AL119

National Defense Education Act of 1958, BD76

National Diet Library catalog of foreign serials, AE94

National Diet Library catalog of Japanese periodicals, AE94

National directory for the performing arts and civic centers, BH13

National directory for the performing arts/ educational, BH13

The national directory of arts & education support by business corporations, BA10

—— Fandel, Nancy A., AL121

—— Washington International Arts Letter, AL121

National directory of arts support by private foundations, BA10

National directory of children & youth services, CC48

National directory of children, youth & families services, CC48

National directory of corporate giving, AL105, AL121

National directory of corporate public affairs, CH566

National directory of courts of law, Yannone, Mark J. A., CK156

National directory of drug abuse and alcoholism treatment and prevention programs, EH411

National directory of education libraries and collections, Christo, Doris H., CB94

National directory of educational programs in gerontology and geriatrics, CC86

National directory of grants and aid to individuals in the arts, international, BA10

The national directory of internships, AL6, CB385

National directory of Latin Americanists, DB287

National directory of law enforcement administrators, correctional institutions, and related governmental agencies, CK264

The national directory of magazines, AD55

National directory of minority and women-owned business firms, CH364

National directory of minority-owned business firms, CH364

National directory of newsletters and reporting services, AE36

National directory of nonprofit organizations, CH365

The national directory of prosecuting attorneys, CK152

National directory of women-owned business firms, CH364

National District Attorneys Association. *The national directory of prosecuting attorneys,* CK152

National drug code directory, EH359

•*National economic, social and environmental data bank,* CB139

National Education Association. Research Division. *Rankings of the states,* CB149

National Education Association of the United States. *The NEA almanac of higher education,* CB329

National Education Association of the United States. Research Division. *Status of the American public-school teacher,* CB167

National Education Association–Research. *Status of the American public-school teacher,* CB167

National Endowment for the Humanities. *A century of doctorates,* CB342

—— *English-Tibetan dictionary of modern Tibetan,* AC784

National Engineering Laboratory. *Heat bibliography,* EK226

National faculty directory, CB331

The national faith of Japan, Holtom, Daniel Clarence, BC569

National Film Theatre (Great Britain). *A guide to world cinema,* BH195

National Fire Protection Association. *Fire protection handbook,* EK104

National Football League. *Official National Football League record & fact book,* BK77

National Foreign Assessment Center. *Directory of officials of the Socialist Republic of Romania,* CJ325

—— *Handbook of international economic statistics,* CH154

National Foreign Assessment Center (U.S.). *Chiefs of state and cabinet members of foreign governments,* CJ83

—— *Polar regions atlas,* DG10

National Forest Products Association. *Wood structural design data,* EK115

The national formulary, EH360, EH363

The national gazetteer of the United States of America, CL108, CL109

National Genealogical Society. *Index of Revolutionary War pension applications in the National Archives,* AJ38

National Geodetic Survey. *Geodetic glossary,* EF122

National Geographic atlas of the world, National Geographic Society, CL284

National geographic index, 1888–1988, CL33

National Geographic Society. *Historical atlas of the United States,* DB74

—— *Insignia and decorations of the United States armed forces,* AL185

—— *National Geographic atlas of the world,* CL284

—— *National geographic index, 1888–1988,* CL33

National Gerontology Resource Center (American Association of Retired Persons). *AgeLine,* CC79

—— *Thesaurus of aging terminology,* CC84

The national guide to educational credit for training programs, CB325

National guide to foundation funding in higher education, CB365

National guide to funding for libraries and information services, AK64

National health directory, EH412

National health systems of the world, Roemer, Milton Irwin, EH416

National Historical Publications and Records Commission. *Directory of archives and manuscript repositories in the United States,* DB30

National Hockey League. *The National Hockey League official guide & record book,* BK88

The National Hockey League official guide & record book, BK88

National income, CH243

National income and product accounts of the United States, CH425

National index of American imprints through 1800, Shipton, Clifford Kenyon, AA410

National index of parish registers, Steel, D. J., AJ107

National Indian Law Library. *Catalogue,* CK127

National Industrial Conference Board. *The economic almanac for … ,* CH106

National Information Center for Educational Media. *A-V online,* CB28

—— *NICEM media indexes,* AA383

—— *Training media database,* CB355

National Information Services Corporation. *Arctic & antarctic regions,* DG2

—— *GeoArchive,* EF50

—— *Water resources abstracts,* EF131

National Institute of Education. *The American freshman, national norms,* CB333

—— *Resources in education,* AK35, CB61

National Institute of Justice. *Directory of criminal justice information sources,* CK262

National Institute of Mental Health. *Changing directions in the treatment of women,* EH375

—— *Mental health, United States,* EH401

—— *Psychopharmacology abstracts,* EH323

National Institute of Standards and Technology. *Directory of international and regional organizations conducting standards-related activities,* EA271

—— *JANAF thermochemical tables,* EE93

—— *Publications of the National Institute of Standards and Technology … catalog,* EA274

—— *Standards activities of organizations in the United States,* EA276

National Institute on Aging. *Resource directory for older people,* CC89

National Institute on Alcohol Abuse and Alcoholism. *National directory of drug abuse and alcoholism treatment and prevention programs,* EH411

National Institute on Disability and Rehabilitation Research. *Digest of data on persons with disabilities,* CB206, CC198

—— *Directory of national information sources on disabilities,* CC195

National Institute on Drug Abuse. *National directory of drug abuse and alcoholism treatment and prevention programs,* EH411

National Institutes of Health. *Cancer sourcebook,* EH173

—— *Recommended dietary allowances,* EH312

National Institutes of Health. Division of Research Resources. *Guide for the care and use of laboratory animals,* EG295

National Intelligence Study Center. *Scholar's guide to intelligence literature,* CJ538

National inventory of documentary sources in Canada, National Archives of Canada, DB193

National inventory of documentary sources in the United States, AK112

National jail and adult detention directory, CK265

The national job bank, CH700

National League for Nursing. *Directory of educational software for nursing,* EH272

—— *International nursing index,* EH276

National League of Cities. *State municipal league directory,* CJ277

—— *Urban affairs abstracts,* CC304

National League of Nursing Education (U.S.). *Facts about nursing,* EH289

National Legal Aid & Defender Association. *Directory of legal aid and defender offices in the United States,* CK144

National legal bibliography, CK19, CK120
National Lending Library for Science and Technology (Great Britain). *NLL translations bulletin*, EA59, EA61
National libraries of the world, Esdaile, Arundell James Kennedy, AK118
National Library (India). *A bibliography of Indology*, CE109
National Library of Australia. *Annual catalogue of Australian publications*, AA941
—— *APAIS, Australian public affairs information service*, CA23, DF22
—— *Australian government publications*, AF261
—— *Australian national bibliography, 1901– 1950*, AA942
—— *Guide to collections of manuscripts relating to Australia*, DF32
—— *Manuscripts in the British Isles relating to Australia, New Zealand, and the Pacific*, DF15
National Library of Canada. *Canadian directories, 1790–1987*, DB200
—— *Canadian theses*, AG17
—— *Canadian translations*, AA140
—— *Canadiana*, AA456
—— *Canadiana, 1867–1900*, AA446
—— *Checklist of indexes to Canadian newspapers*, AE117
—— *Education in Canada*, CB42
—— *Interlibrary loan policies in Canada*, AK226
—— *Literary manuscripts at the National Library of Canada*, BE832
—— *Periodicals in the social sciences and humanities currently received by Canadian libraries*, AD228
—— *Provincial royal commissions and commissions of inquiry, 1867–1982*, AF154, CJ303
—— *Research collections in Canadian libraries*, AK128, DB199
National Library of Canada. Newspaper Section. *Union list of Canadian newspapers held by Canadian libraries*, AE38
National Library of Ireland. *Bibliography of Irish history*, DC397
—— *Bibliography of Irish philology and of printed Irish literature*, BD178
—— *List of publications deposited under the terms of the Industrial and Commercial Property (Protection) Act, 1927*, AA122
—— *Manuscript sources for the history of Irish civilisation*, DC403
National Library of Jamaica. *Jamaican national bibliography*, AA568
National Library of Medicine (U.S.) catalogs, EH24
National Library of Medicine audiovisuals catalog, National Library of Medicine (U.S.), EH42, EH43, EH44
National Library of Medicine catalog, EH49
National Library of Medicine classification, National Library of Medicine (U.S.), AK203
National Library of Medicine current catalog, National Library of Medicine (U.S.), EH2, EH46, EH49
National Library of Medicine literature search, EH22
National Library of Medicine recommended formats for bibliographic citation, Patrias, Karen, EA162
National Library of Medicine (U.S.). *AIDS Bibliography*, EH72
—— *Bibliography of bioethics*, EH237
—— *Bibliography of medical reviews*, EH64
—— *Bibliography of the history of medicine*, EH199
—— *Catalog*, EH48
—— *A catalogue of seventeenth century printed books in the National Library of Medicine*, EH24
—— *Current bibliographies in medicine*, EH14
—— *Early American medical imprints*, EH25
—— *Index-catalogue of the library of the Surgeon General's Office, United States Army (Army Medical Library), authors and subjects*, EH10, EH16, EH47

—— *Index medicus*, EH65
—— *Index to dental literature*, EH251
—— *International nursing index*, EH276
—— *List of journals indexed in Index medicus*, EH35
—— *Literature search*, EH14, EH71
—— *Medical subject headings*, EH143
—— *Medical subject headings. Supplementary chemical records*, EH144
—— *National Library of Medicine audiovisuals catalog*, EH42, EH43, EH44
—— *National Library of Medicine classification*, AK203
—— *National Library of Medicine current catalog*, EH2, EH46, EH49
—— *NLM current catalog proof sheets*, EH49
—— *Permuted medical subject headings*, EH146
—— *SERLINE*, EH37
National Library of Medicine (U.S.). Index Section. *Eponymous syndromes*, EH118
National Library of Medicine (U.S.). Medical Subject Headings Section. *Medical subject headings*, EH143
—— *Medical subject headings. Supplementary chemical records*, EH144
—— *Medical subject headings. Tree structures*, EH145
—— *Permuted medical subject headings*, EH146
National Library of Medicine (U.S.). Office of Health Services Research Information. *Health services*, EH402
National Library of Medicine (U.S.). Reference Section. *AIDS bibliography*, EH71
National Library of New Zealand. *Index to New Zealand periodicals*, AD347
—— *Union list of serials in New Zealand libraries*, AD247
National Library of Nigeria. *Index to Nigeriana in selected periodicals*, AD334
—— *Serials in print in Nigeria*, AD174
National Library of Wales. *Bibliography of Wales*, AA698, AD290, DC370
—— *Bibliotheca celtica*, AA698, AD290
—— *Cofrestri plwyf Cymru = Parish registers of Wales*, AJ130
—— *Llbrl Walllae*, AA699
—— *Subject index to Welsh periodicals*, AD290
National Library (Philippines). *Checklist of exchange materials*, AF257
National Library (Philippines). Filipiniana and Asia Division. *Checklist of rare Filipiniana serials (1811–1944)*, AD209
National list of scientific plant names, EG136
National Medical Audiovisual Center. *National Medical Audiovisual Center catalog*, EH45
National Medical Audiovisual Center catalog, National Medical Audiovisual Center, EH45
National Meteorological Center. *Daily weather maps*, EF169
National Micrographics Association. *Glossary of micrographics*, AK246
National minority business directory, CH372
National Museum of African Art. *Catalog of the Library of the National Museum of African Art branch of the Smithsonian Institution Libraries*, BG4
National Museum of American Art (U.S.). *The National Museum of American Art's index to American art exhibition catalogues*, BF120
The National Museum of American Art's index to American art exhibition catalogues, Yarnall, James L., BF120
National Museum of Canada. *Bulletin*, EF31
National norms for entering college freshmen, CB333
National norms for HERI faculty survey, CB335
National Opinion Research Center. *An American profile*, CJ484
—— *General social survey*, CC40
National Organization for Public Health Nursing (U.S.). *Facts about nursing*, EH289
National Organization on Legal Problems of Education. *The yearbook of education law*, CB157

National Park Foundation. *The complete guide to America's national parks*, BK124
National parks *see* **Parks and protected areas**
The national parks fishing guide, Gartner, Robert, BK116
National party conventions, 1831–1988, CJ265
National party platforms, Johnson, Donald Bruce, CJ257
National party platforms of 1980, CJ257
National Photographic Record. *Directory of British photographic collections*, BF344
National Planning Association. *Focus Japan II*, AL43, DE210
National Police Chiefs and Sheriffs Information Bureau. *National directory of law enforcement administrators, correctional institutions, and related governmental agencies*, CK264
National population bibliography of Czechoslovakia, 1945–1977, CG207
National population bibliography of Finland, CG211
National population bibliography of Flanders, 1945–1983, CG200
National population bibliography of Norway, 1945– 1977, CG269
National population censuses, 1945–1976, Goyer, Doreen S., CG7
National preservation news, Library of Congress. National Preservation Program Office, AE5
National preservation report, AE5
National prison directory, CK266
National Reference Institute (U.S.). *Who's who among human services professionals*, CC50
—— *Who's who in American education*, CB134
National Referral Center (U.S.). *Information resources in the arts*, BF107
National register of archives and manuscripts in New Zealand, AK163
National register of historic places, 1966–1991, BF250
National register of microform masters, AA135
National Research Council. *Annotated bibliography of economic geology*, EF21
—— *Guide to tables in mathematical statistics*, EB73
—— *Guide to tables in the theory of numbers*, EB75
—— *Handbook of physical constants*, EF96
—— *International critical tables of numerical data, physics, chemistry and technology*, EA136
—— *List of the serial publications of foreign governments, 1815–1931*, AF13
National Research Council. Board on Human-Resource Data and Analysis. *A century of doctorates*, CB342
National Research Council. Building Research Board. *An international directory of building research organizations*, BF283
National Research Council. Committee on Diet and Health. *Diet and health*, EH311
National Research Council. Committee on Dietary Allowances. *Recommended dietary allowances*, EH312
National Research Council. Committee on Specifications and Criteria for Biochemical Compounds. *Specifications and criteria for biochemical compounds*, EG323
National Research Council. Pacific Science Board. *Island bibliographies*, EG108
National Research Council. Subcommittee on Feed Composition. *Atlas of nutritional data on United States and Canadian feeds*, EJ126
—— *United States-Canadian tables of feed composition*, EJ130
National Research Council. Subcommittee on the Tenth Edition of the RDAs. *Recommended dietary allowances*, EH312
National Research Council Conference on Glossary of Terms in Nuclear Science and Technology. *Glossary of terms in nuclear science and engineering*, EK295
National Research Council of Canada. Library. *Union list of scientific serials in Canadian libraries*, EA45

The National review college guide, CB279
National roster of black elected officials, CJ132
National School Boards Association. *Survey of public education in the nation's urban school districts*, CB143
National Science Foundation. *AAAS science film catalog*, EA25
—— *CASPAR*, CB257
—— *A century of doctorates*, CB342
National Science Library (Canada). *Union list of scientific serials in Canadian libraries*, EA45
National security
  bibliography, CJ98
  directories, CJ145
National Security Council (U.S.). *Index to The Tower Commission report*, CJ114
National Society for Internships and Experiential Education (U.S.). *The national directory of internships*, AL6, CB385
National survey of state laws, CK180
National Technical Institute for the Deaf. *A deafness collection*, CC187
National Textbook Co. *French and English business dictionary*, AC343, CH61
—— *NTC's new college Greek and English dictionary*, AC466
National trade and professional associations of the United States, AL45, AL47, CH670
•*The national trade data bank*, CH497, CL68
National transit summaries and trends for the … section 15 report year, CH452
National Translations Center (U.S.). *Consolidated index of translations into English*, EA60
—— *Translations register-index*, EA62
The National Trust atlas, BF249
National Trust for Historic Preservation. *The historic preservation yearbook*, BF264
—— *Index to historic preservation periodicals*, BF218
—— *Landmark yellow pages*, BF265
National Trust for Scotland. *The National Trust guide*, BF249
National Trust (Great Britain). *The National Trust guide*, BF249
The National Trust guide, Greeves, Lydia, BF249
National Trust handbook for members and visitors, BF249
National tune index, Camus, Raoul F., BJ288
National tune index microfiche, Rabson, Carolyn, BJ288
National Underwriter Company. *Who writes what in life and health insurance*, CH516
National union catalog, AA106, AA107, AA109, AA110, AA111, AA112, AA113, AA150, AA421, BC16, BC102
The national union catalog, 1952–1955 imprints, AA111
National union catalog, 1956 through 1967, AA111, AA112
National union catalog. Audiovisual materials, AA111, AA381
National union catalog. Cartographic materials, AA111, CL252
National union catalog. Motion pictures and filmstrips, AA107
National union catalog. Music, books on music, and sound recordings, BJ62
National union catalog of manuscript collections, AK102, BE510, CJ176, DB34, EA192
—— Library of Congress. Manuscripts Section, DB30
National union catalog, pre-1956 imprints, AA113, BC102, BC400, BE456
National union catalog. Register of additional locations, AA111, AA114
National union catalog. U.S. books, AA111
National union catalogue. Music, books on music, and sound recordings, BJ82
National University Continuing Education Association. *Independent study catalog*, CB358
—— *Peterson's guide to certificate programs at American colleges and universities*, CB285

National University of Singapore. Library. *Index to periodical articles relating to Singapore, Malaysia, Brunei, ASEAN*, AD336
National Urban League. *The state of black America*, CC394
National Wildlife Federation. *Conservation directory*, EG79
—— *A field guide to hawks*, EG256
Nationalencyklopedin, AB98
Nationalism, CJ8, CJ34
  bibliography, CC367, CJ9
Nationalism (by country or region)
  Asia, East, CJ422
  Austria, DC88
  Balkans, DC64
  Canada, CJ301
  Germany, DC88, DC231
  Scotland, CJ375
Nationalism and national development, Deutsch, Karl Wolfgang, CJ9
Nationalism in East Asia, CJ422
Nationalism in the Balkans, DC64
Nations within a nation, Stuart, Paul, CC443
Native American art, BF318
  bibliography, BG9, CC422
Native American artists directory, Heard Museum. Library, BF318
Native American astronomy, EC60
Native American basketry, Porter, Frank W., BG159
Native American bibliography series, CC420
Native American folklore, 1879–1979, Clements, William M., CF62
The Native American in American literature, Rock, Roger O., BE552
Native American languages
  bibliography, BD239, BD240, BD241, BD242, BD243
  handbooks, BD238
  library catalogs, BD237
Native American literature, BE554
  bibliography, BD242, BE511, BE548, BE550, BE551, BE552, BE553
  collections, BE555
Native American literature, Wiget, Andrew, BE554
Native American periodicals and newspapers, 1828–1982, AE16
Native American Rights Fund. *Catalogue*, CK127
Native American studies, CC316
Native American women, Green, Rayna, CC602
Native American youth and alcohol, Lobb, Michael L., CC114
Native Americans
  archives, CC426, CC427
  atlases, CC438, CC439, CC440, CC441
  bibliography, BE552, CC413, CC414, CC415, CC416, CC417, CC418, CC419, CC420, CC421, CC423, CC434, CC602, DB214
  biography, AH63, CC434, CC437
    bibliography, BE549
    indexes, CC436
  book reviews, CC316
  databases, CC412
  directories, CC430, CC434
  dissertations, CC425
  encyclopedias, CC428, CC433, CC434
  guidebooks, CC429
  guides, CC413
  guides to research, CC588
  handbooks, CC432, CC441
  indexes, CC416
  library catalogs, CC436, DB6
  library resources, CC426
  manuscripts and archives, CE31
  newspapers, AE16, CC424
  periodicals, AE16, CC424
  portraits, BF67, CC435
  statistics, CC442, CC443, CG85
Native Americans (by country or region)
  Central America, BF28
  South America, CE91, CF69, CF74, DB383, DB384

Native Americans (by subject)
  alcohol and drug abuse
    bibliography, CC114
  archaeology and ancient history
    encyclopedias, DB49
  art, BF70
    bibliography, BG9, CC422
  arts and crafts, BG159
  astronomy, EC7, EC60
  festivals, CC429
  film portrayals, CC334
  folklore and popular culture, CF62, CF67, CF69
  history
    atlases, CC438
  law, CK127
  material culture, BG9, CC422
  religion, BC567
  reservations, CC429
    directories, CC431
  women, CC614
  see also names of specific groups, e.g., Aleuts
Native Americans, Hoxie, Frederick E., CC415
Native Americans in literature
  bibliography, BE552
Native Canadians
  bibliography, CC415, CC419, CC472
  biography, CC437
  databases, CC412
  statistics, CC442, CG85
Native languages of the Americas, BD238
The Native North American almanac, CC434
Natkiel, Richard. *Atlas of American history*, DB71
—— *Atlas of maritime history*, DA56
Natoli, Joseph P. *Psychocriticism*, BE25
Natsionalna bibliografiia na NR Bulgariia, AA37, AA583, AA589, AD86, AD305, AE46
Natsionalna bibliografiia na Republika Bŭlgariia, AA589
Natsuev, N. I. *Khudozhestvennaia literatura, russkaia i perevodnaia*, BE1398
The natural environment, Anglemyer, Mary, EK64
Natural foods, EH319
Natural history
  annuals, EG87
  bibliography, EG67, EG68, EG69, EG70, EG71
  dictionaries, EG76, EG77, EG78
  directories, EG79, EG80
  encyclopedias, EG74, EG75
  handbooks, EG81, EG82, EG83, EG85, EG86
  indexes, EG72, EG73
  library catalogs, EA12
  periodicals, EA40
Natural language processing in the 1980s, BD64
Natural resource commodities—a century of statistics, Manthy, Robert S., CH441
Natural resources, CH441
The natural sciences and American scientists in the revolutionary era, Harkanyi, Katalin, EA230
Naturalist's color guide, Smithe, Frank B., ED62
The naturalists' directory and almanac (international), EG80
Naturalized birds of the world, Lever, Christopher, EG267
Naturalized mammals of the world, Lever, Christopher, EG297
Nature and its applications, Ellis, Jessie Croft, BF60
The nature of biography, Garraty, John Arthur, BE214
The nature of woman, Warren, Mary Anne, CC536
Natürliche Bevölkerungsbewegung, CG194
Nauchaia biblioteka im. A. M. Gorkogo. Istoriia srednikh vekov, DA133
Nauchnye s'ezdy, konferentsii i soveshchaniia v SSSR, Fundamental'naia biblioteka obshchestvennykh nauk (Akademiia nauk SSSR), EA199
Nault, Clifford A. *Annals of American literature, 1602–1983*, BE436
Nauman, Ann Keith. *A biographical handbook of education*, CB132
—— *A handbook of Latin American & Caribbean national archives*, AK130, DB278

Naumann, Jens. *The United Nations system, international bibliography*, AF35
Nauta, Paul. *International guide to library and information science education*, AK54
Nautical almanac, EC78
Nautical almanacs, EC78, EC79
　databases, EC78
Navabpour, Reza. *Iran*, DE185
Navajo language, AC616
The Navajo language, Young, Robert W., AC616
Naval ceremonies, customs, and traditions, Mack, William P., CJ633
Naval Historical Center (U.S.). *Dictionary of American naval fighting ships*, CJ649
Naval history (by country or region)
　Denmark, DC130
The Naval Institute guide to combat fleets of the world, CJ594
The Naval Institute guide to the ships and aircraft of the U.S. fleet, CJ649
The Naval Institute guide to the Soviet navy, Polmar, Norman, CJ658
The Naval Institute guide to world naval weapons systems, CJ594
The naval officer's guide, CJ635
Naval officers of the American Revolution, Claghorn, Charles E., CJ639
Naval Photographic Interpretation Center. *Antarctic bibliography*, DG1
Naval science
　abbreviations, CJ621
　dictionaries, EC81, EC82
　handbooks, EC77
Naval terms dictionary, Noel, John Vavasour, CJ618
Naval warfare, CJ592, CJ600
Navalani, K. *Current Indian periodicals in English*, AD191, AD193
—— *A guide to reference materials on India*, DE156
Navaretta, Cynthia. *Guide to women's art organizations*, BF102
Navarro Viola, Alberto. *Anuario bibliográfico de la República Argentina*, AA494
Navarro Viola, Enrique. *Anuario bibliográfico de la República Argentina*, AA494
Navia, Luis E. *Socrates*, BB56
Navies
　handbooks, CJ594
Navies (by country or region)
　United States, DB60
Navies in the American Revolution, Smith, Myron J., CJ609
Navigation, EC80
　dictionaries, EC82
　handbooks, EC77
　tables, CH471, CH472
Navigation dictionary, United States. Naval Oceanographic Office, EC82
Navy League of the United States. *Almanac of seapower*, CJ649
Nawabi, Y. M. *A bibliography of Iran*, BD195, DE186
Nayler, G. H. F. *Dictionary of mechanical engineering*, EK237
Naylor, Bernard. *Directory of libraries and special collections on Latin America and the West Indies*, AK111
Naylor, Colin. *Contemporary architects*, BF260
—— *Contemporary artists*, BF138
—— *Contemporary designers*, BG29
—— *Contemporary masterworks*, BF69
—— *Contemporary photographers*, BF355
—— *International contemporary arts directory*, BF102
Naylor, Gillian. *The encyclopedia of arts and crafts*, BG19
Naylor, Lynne. *Television directors guide*, BH305
Naylor, Thomas H. *Northern New Spain*, DB249
The Nazi era, 1919–1945, Kehr, Helen, DC236
La nazione operante, Savino, Edoardo, AH263
NBA register, BK66

NBC handbook of pronunciation, Ehrlich, Eugene H., AC103, AC108
—— Hand, Raymond, AC108
The NBS tables of chemical thermodynamic properties, EE94
●*NCBE bibliographic database*, CB40
●*NCBE resources database*, CB41
NCBEL, BE585
The NEA almanac of higher education, CB329
Neagles, James C. *Confederate research sources*, AJ16
—— *The Library of Congress*, AJ17, DB143
—— *U.S. military records*, AJ18
Neagles, Mark C. *The Library of Congress*, AJ17, DB143
Neal, Jack A. *Reference guide for travellers*, CL391
Neal, Michael. *Dictionary of chemical names and synonyms*, EE42
The Neal-Schuman index to card games, Markey, Kay, BK127
Neale, Michael John. *Bearings*, EK239
—— *Lubrication*, EK239
Near-death experiences, Basford, Terry K., CC177
Near East *see* **Asia, West**
The Near East national union list, AA123
Near East studies handbook, Bacharach, Jere L., DE58
Neave, Guy R. *The encyclopedia of higher education*, CB236
Neave, Sheffield Airey. *Nomenclator zoologicus*, EG243
Nebenzahl, Kenneth. *Atlas of the American Revolution*, DB97
Nebraska. [Laws, etc.]. *Revised statutes of Nebraska*, CK179
Nechina, Militsa Vasil'evna. *Dvizhenie dekabristov*, DC577
—— *Istoriia istoricheskoĭ nauki v SSSR*, DC570
Neck-Yoder, Hilda van. *Caribbean women novelists*, BE971
Neckel, Gustav. *Edda*, BE1286
Necker, Claire. *Four centuries of cut books*, EJ140
NFD, AC30
NEDA statistical yearbook of the Philippines, CG419
Nederlands Geologisch Mijnbouwkundig Genootschap. *Geological nomenclature*, EF80
Nederlands Instituut voor het Nabije Oosten. *Late reviews AEB 1947–1984*, DA121
Nederlandsche bibliographie van 1500 tot 1540, Nijhoff, Wouter, AA746
Nederlandsche Kamer van Koophandel voor België en Luxemburg. *Catalogus van Belgische en Luxemburgse periodieken*, AD83, AD131
Nederlandsche overheidsuitgaven, AF212
Nederlandse bibliografie 1801–1832, AA755
Nederlandse bibliografie, B-lijst, AA753
Nederlandse boek in vertaling, AA138, DC450
Nederlandse boek in vertaling, 1958–1967, Raan, E. van, AA138, DC450
Nedvídková, Marie. *Bibliografický katalog ČSFR*, AG25
Needham, Richard. *Ski magazine's encyclopedia of skiing*, BK97
Neel, Ann. *Theories of psychology*, CD61
Neeson, J. M. *A bibliography of the literature on British and Irish labour law*, CH677
Neformalniye, AL57
Neft, David S. *Sports encyclopedia*, BK48, BK58, BK65
Negev, Avraham. *Archaeological encyclopedia of the Holy Land*, BC192
Neglia, Giuseppe Erminio. *Repertorio selecto del teatro hispanoamericano contemporaneo*, BE900
The Negro almanac, CC390
The Negro in America, Miller, Elizabeth W., CC368
The Negro in print, CC370
The Negro in the United States, Porter, Dorothy Burnett, CC374
Negro newspapers on microfilm, Library of Congress, AE15
—— Pride, Armistead Scott, AE15
Negroes *see* **African Americans**

Negwer, Martin. *Organic-chemical drugs and their synonyms*, EH330
Nehring, Karl. *Historische Bücherkunde Südosteuropa*, DC58
Neil, William. *Harper's Bible commentary*, BC172
Neill, Stephen Charles. *Concise dictionary of the Christian world mission*, BC310
—— *A history of the ecumenical movement*, BC276
Neilson, William Allan. *Webster's new international dictionary of the English language*, AC13
Neirynck, F. *The Gospel of Mark*, BC111
Nelli, Humbert O. *A bibliography of insurance history*, CH504
Nelson, Archibald. *Dictionary of applied geology*, EF76
Nelson, Axel Herman. *Akademiska avhandlingar vid Sveriges universitet och högskolor läsåren 1890/91–1909/10*, AG42
Nelson, Barbara J. *American women and politics*, CC506
Nelson, Bonnie R. *A guide to published library catalogs*, AA98
Nelson, Carol. *Women's market handbook*, CC563
Nelson, Carolyn. *British newspapers and periodicals, 1641–1700*, AA412, AA683, AD107
—— *Short-title catalogue of books printed in England, Scotland, Ireland, Wales, and British America, and of English books printed in other countries, 1641–1700*, AA412, AA683
Nelson, Donna E. *Developing individualized family support plans*, CC235
Nelson, Emmanuel S. *Contemporary gay American novelists*, BE402, BE469
Nelson, Garrison. *Committees in the U.S. Congress, 1947–1992*, CJ217
Nelson, Glenn C. *Ceramics*, BG65
Nelson, Harold D. *Algeria*, DD62
—— *Area handbook for Senegal*, DD62
—— *Area handbook for the United Republic of Cameroon*, DD62
—— *Ethiopia*, DD62
—— *Liberia*, DD62
—— *Libya*, DD62
—— *Malawi*, DD62
—— *Morocco*, DD62
—— *Mozambique*, DD62
—— *South Africa*, DD62
—— *Tunisia*, DD62
—— *Zimbabwe*, DD62
Nelson, John B. *Catalog of significant earthquakes, 2000 B.C.–1979, including quantitative casualties and damage*, EF260
Nelson, Kenneth Davies. *Dictionary of applied geology*, EF76
Nelson, Lester. *Digest of commercial laws of the world*, CK68
Nelson, Michael. *Congressional Quarterly's guide to the presidency*, CJ164
—— *Historic documents on the presidency, 1776–1989*, CJ187
—— *The presidency A to Z*, CJ179
Nelson, R. J. *New revised Velázquez Spanish and English dictionary*, AC740
Nelson, Randy F. *The martial arts*, BK91
Nelson's complete concordance of the New American Bible, BC162
Nelson's complete concordance of the Revised Standard Version Bible, Ellison, John William, BC158
Nelson's directory of investment managers, CH311
Nelson's directory of investment research, CH312
Nemanic, Gerald. *A bibliographical guide to Midwestern literature*, BE567
Nematological abstracts, EJ19
Nemec, B. *Ottův slovník naučný nové doby*, AB32
Nemeskurty, Istvan. *History of Hungarian literature*, BE1276
Neo-Marxism, CJ532
Neoellēnika philologika pseudonyma, Ntelopoulos, Kyriakos, AA174
Neōteron enkyklopaidikon lexikon, AB55
Nepal, DE234, DE235

atlases, CL359
bibliography
  current, AA922
biography, AH364
languages
  bibliography, BD227
statistics, CG414
Nepal (by subject)
  art, BF27
  history
    bibliography, DE236
    encyclopedias, DE90
Nepal. Central Bureau of Statistics. *Statistical pocket book, Nepal,* CG414
Nepal. Kendrīya Tathyānka Vibhāga. *Statistical pocket book, Nepal,* CG414
Nepal, Whelpton, John, DE236
Nepal Research Centre. *Nepalese national bibliography,* AA922
Nepalese national bibliography, AA922
Nerhood, Harry W. *To Russia and return,* DC551
Nersesova, E. A. *Istoriīa srednikh vekov,* DA133
Nersessian, Vrej. *Armenia,* DC85
—— *An index of articles on Armenian studies in Western journals,* DC86
Nesbitt, Bruce. *Australian literary pseudonyms,* AA193
Neselenieto na Turtsiīa na Bulgariīa priez XVIII i XIX vekovete, Mikhov, Nikola V., DC538
The N.E.S.F.A. index to short science fiction, BE294
The N.E.S.F.A index to the science fiction magazines and original anthologies, BE294
Nesheim, Asdjørn. *Lappisk (samisk) ordbok,* AC570
•*NetEc,* CH41
Netherlandic language research, Haeringen, Coenraad Bernardus van, BD128
Netherlands
  atlases, DC462
  bibliography, DC456
    17th–18th centuries, AA748, AA749
    17th–18th centuries, AA750
    19th–20th centuries, AA753, AA754, AA755
    current, AA756
    early, AA745, AA746, AA747
  bibliography of bibliography, AA56
  biography, AH269, AH270, AH271, AH272, AH273
  dissertations, AG38
  gazetteers, CL146
  government publications, AF212
  newspapers, AD132, AE65
  pamphlets
    bibliography, AA751, AA752
  periodicals, AD132, AE65
    indexes, AD320
  place-names, CL147, CL210
  statistics, CG266, CG267, CG394
  translations, AA138, DC450
Netherlands (by subject)
  elections, CJ383
  history, DC452, DC458, DC459, DC460
    archives, AK133, DC13
    bibliography, DC100, DC451, DC454, DC455, DC457
    regional and local, DC453
  overseas territories, DC452
  politics and government, DC455
    directories, CJ384
    registers, CJ384
Netherlands. Centraal Bureau voor de Statistiek. *Jaarcijfers voor Nederlanden,* CG266
The Netherlands, King, Peter, DC454
—— Krewson, Margrit B., DC456
The Netherlands and Northern Belgium, Krewson, Margrit B., DC456
Netherlands Antilles, DB448, DB449
  bibliography, DB390
Netherlands Antilles, Nagelkerke, Gerard A., DB449
Netherlands East Indies *see* **Indonesia**
Nettie Lee Benson Latin American Collection. *Bibliographic guide to Latin American studies,* DB265

—— *Catalog of the Latin American collection,* DB270
—— *Handbook of Latin American studies,* BE874, DB266
Nettl, Bruno. *Reference materials in ethnomusicology,* BJ323
Netto, Modestino Martins. *Vocabulário de intercâmbio comercial,* CH128
Netton, Ian Richard. *Middle East materials in United Kingdom and Irish libraries,* DE51
A network of knowledge, CK262
Neu, John. *Chemical, medical, and pharmaceutical books printed before 1800, in the collections of the University of Wisconsin Libraries,* EE17
—— *French political pamphlets, 1547–1648,* DC169
—— *Isis cumulative bibliography, 1966–1975,* EA233
—— *Isis cumulative bibliography, 1975–1985,* EA233
Der neue Brockhaus, AB49
Neue deutsche Biographie, AH210
Neue Folge bis zur Mitte des 20. Jahrhunderts, Gorzny, Willi, AH206
Neue Forschungen zum Ersten Weltkrieg, DA195
Neue österreichische Biographie, AH168
Neue österreichische Biographie ab 1815, AH168, AH169
Neue Wörter, Heberth, Alfred, AC436
Neuer Bildniskatalog, BF68
Neuere ausländische Austraiaca, AA574
Neuerscheinungen ausserhalb des Buchhandels, AA654
Neuerscheinungen des Buchhandels, AA654
Neues allgemeines deutsches Adels-Lexicon im Vereine mit mehreren Historikern, Kneschke, Ernst Heinrich, AJ94
Neues Handbuch der deutschen Gegenwartsliteratur seit 1945, BE1250
Neues Jahrbuch für Mineralogie, Geologie und Paläontologie, EF55, EF58, EF178
Neues Wörterbuch der Völkerkunder, CE47
Neufeld, Maurice F. *American working class history,* CH637
—— *Representative bibliography of American labor history,* CH637
Neufeldt, Harvey G. *Education of the black adult in the United States,* CB38
Neufeldt, Victoria. *Webster's new World children's dictionary,* AC27
—— *Webster's new World dictionary of American English,* AC20
Die neuiranischen Sprachen der Sowjetunion, Oranskiĭ, I. M., BD196
Neumann, Erich Peter. *The Germans,* CJ493
Neumüller, Otto-Albrecht. *Römpps Chemie-Lexikon,* EE32
Neural computers, EK157
  bibliography, EK155
NeuralSource, Wasserman, Philip D., EK157
Neurochemistry, EH184
Neurolinguistics, BD78, CD117
Neurology
  dictionaries, EH119
  encyclopedias, CD23, EH87, EH379
  handbooks, CD122, EH183
Neuropsychology, CD102
Neuroscience year, Adelman, George, EH87
—— Smith, Barry, EH87
Neurosciences abstracts, EG14
Neuva epanortosis al Diccvionario de anónimos y seudónimos de J.T. Medina, Victoria, Ricard, AA153
Neuwirth, Paul D. *Cashin's handbook for auditors,* CH259
Nevada. [Laws, etc.]. *Nevada revised statutes, annotated,* CK179
Nevada revised statutes, annotated, Nevada. [Laws, etc.], CK179
Neville, E. H. *Farey series of order 1025,* EB94
—— *Rectangular-polar conversion tables,* EB94
Nevins, Allan. *Civil War books,* DB111

New, William H. *Critical writings on Commonwealth literatures,* BE816
—— *Literary history of Canada,* BE826
The new A to Z of women's health, Ammer, Christine, EH81
The new A to Zax, Evans, Barbara Jean, AJ50
New acronyms, initialisms & abbreviations, AC42
New African yearbook, DD63
New American Bible, BC94, BC421
The new American family, CC244
New American Foundation. *Unity in diversity,* CJ111
The New American guide to athletics, sports, & recreation, Norback, Craig T., BK19
The new American immigration, Cordasco, Francesco, CC319
New American standard Bible, BC94
New American standard exhaustive concordance of the Bible, BC163
New American world, DB63
New and comprehensive gazetteer of England and Wales, Bell, James, AJ113
New and emerging foundations, AL112
New and improved college book, CB254
The new Appleton dictionary of the English and Portuguese languages, Houaiss, Antônio, AC647
The new Arthurian encyclopedia, BE343
New atlas of African history, Freeman-Grenville, Greville Stewart Parker, DD65
New atlas of the universe, Moore, Patrick, EC65, EC67
The new Bible commentary, revised, Guthrie, Donald, BC171
New Bible dictionary, BC147
New bibliographic series, EH22
New bibliography of the literatures of Spain and Spanish America, Grismer, Raymond Leonard, BE873
A new bibliography of the lusophone literatures of Africa, Moser, Gerald M., BE1519
New bibliography of writings on varieties of English, Glauser, Beat, BD108
—— Görlach, Manfred, BD108
—— Schneider, Edgar W., BD108
New book of forms, Turco, Lewis, BE326
The new book of knowledge, AB20
New book of knowledge annual, AB20
The new book of world rankings, Kurian, George Thomas, CG51
New books on women and feminism, CC520
The new Britton and Brown illustrated flora of the northeastern United States and adjacent Canada, Gleason, Henry Allan, EG173
New Brown, Driver, Briggs, Gesenius Hebrew and English lexicon, Briggs, Charles Augustus, BC133
—— Brown, Francis, AC476, BC133
—— Driver, S. R., BC133
New Caledonia
  bibliography, DF41
  biography, AH382
The new Cambridge bibliography of English literature, BE585, BE586, BE715
The new Cambridge history of India, DE169
New Canadian quotations, Colombo, John Robert, BE102
New Cassell's French dictionary, AC342
New Cassell's German dictionary, Betteridge, Harold T., AC414
A new Catholic commentary on Holy Scripture, BC177
New Catholic encyclopedia, BC60, BC397, BC401
The new cavalcade, BE541
The new Century classical handbook, CL104
New Century cyclopedia of names, AH29, BE209
New Century dictionary of the English language, AC11
The new Century handbook of classical geography, CL104
The new child protection team handbook, CC172
New college Greek and English dictionary, AC466
The new Columbia encyclopedia, CL47
New Commonwealth government books from AGPS, AF266

New companion to Shakespeare studies, Muir, Kenneth, BE784

—— Schoenbaum, Samuel, BE784

New complete book of etiquette, AL158

New complete book of the American musical theater, Ewen, David, BJ261

The new complete Hoyle, BK128

New complete walker, Fletcher, Colin, BK113

The new comprehensive American rhyming dictionary, Young, Sue, AC117

A new concise Xhosa-English dictionary, McLaren, James, AC810

New consultants, CH617

New Cornish-English dictionary, Nance, Robert Morton, AC274

The new cosmopolitan world atlas, Rand McNally and Company, CL288

New cyclopedia of practical quotations, BE105

New day/New Deal, Kyvig, David E., DB128

New Deal, DB124, DB131
  bibliography, DB128

New dictionary, Bedrossian, Matthias, AC226

New dictionary of American family names, Smith, Elsdon Coles, AJ186

New dictionary of American politics, CJ128

New dictionary of American slang, Chapman, Robert L., AC120

New dictionary of British history, Steinberg, Sigfrid H., DC293

The new dictionary of Catholic spirituality, BC402

A new dictionary of chemistry, EE44

A new dictionary of liturgy & worship, BC268

New dictionary of modern sculpture, Maillard, Robert, BF397

A new dictionary of political analysis, CJ40

A new dictionary of quotations on historical principles from ancient and modern sources, Mencken, Henry Louis, BE109

The new dictionary of sacramental worship, BC427

A new dictionary of scientific and technical terms, Khaṭīb, Ahmad Shafiq, EA103

New dictionary of statistics, Webb, Augustus Duncan, CG53

New dictionary of the liturgy, Podhradsky, Gerhard, BC428

New dictionary of theology, BC239, BC407

New discoveries and perspectives in the world of art, Argan, Giulio Carlo, BF73

The new dog encyclopedia, EJ145

The new Encyclopaedia Britannica, AB8, AB12

The new encyclopedia of archaeological excavations in the Holy Land, BC194

New encyclopedia of furniture, Aronson, Joseph, BG121

The new encyclopedia of motorcars, 1885 to the present, EK39

New encyclopedia of science fiction, Gunn, James, BE286

The new encyclopedia of the opera, Ewen, David, BJ489

New England diaries, 1602–1800, Forbes, Harriette M., BE507, DB66

New England Historic Genealogical Society. *Genealogist's handbook for Atlantic Canada research,* AJ70

New England Round Table of Children's Librarians. *Appraisal,* EA26

New England Science Fiction Association index to short science fiction, BE294

New England states, DB153
  registers, AJ65

New England states (by subject)
  history
      bibliography, DB152
  literature, BE577

New England verse, BE492

New English Bible, BC94

New English-Croatian and Croatian-English dictionary, Bogadek, Francis Aloysius, AC711

New English dictionary on historical principles, AC173

—— Murray, James Augustus Henry, AC30, AC31, AC33, AC175

New English-Hindustani dictionary, Bate, John Drew, AC489

—— Fallon, S. W., AC489

The new English-Persian dictionary, Montazem, Mir Ali Asghar, AC315

New English-Russian dictionary, AC675

The new enlarged Schöffler-Weis German and English dictionary, Schöffler, Herbert, AC422

New era and the New Deal, 1920–1940, Burke, Robert E., DB128

—— Lowitt, Richard, DB128

The new Eurasia, DC600

New Eusebius, Stevenson, James, BC285

New exhaustive concordance of the Bible, BC165

New feminist scholarship, Williamson, Jane, CC516

The new field book of reptiles and amphibians, Cochran, Doris Mabel, EG245

A new Fijian dictionary, Capell, Arthur, AC319

The new film index, MacCann, Richard Dyer, BH235

The new financial instruments, Walmsley, Julian, CH322

New functional Hebrew-English, English-Hebrew dictionary, Goldberg, Nathan, AC478

The new Funk & Wagnalls encyclopedia, AB10

New genealogical atlas of Ireland, Mitchell, Brian, AJ136, AJ137

New geographical dictionary, CL97

New geographical literature and maps, Royal Geographical Society (London), CL19

New gold in your attic, Bradley, Van Allen, AA237

New governmental advisory organizations, CJ134

New Greek-English interlinear New Testament, Brown, Robert K., BC94

—— Comfort, Philip W., BC94

•*New Grolier multimedia encyclopedia,* AB25

The new Grove dictionary of American music, BJ140, BJ225

The new Grove dictionary of jazz, BJ306

The new Grove dictionary of music and musicians, BJ140, BJ141, BJ143, BJ183, BJ219, BJ251, BJ371

The New Grove dictionary of musical instruments, BJ371

The new Grove dictionary of opera, BJ251

New guide to government publications, Newsome, Walter L., AF77

The new guide to the diplomatic archives of Western Europe, Thomas, Daniel H., DC18

New Guinea *see* **Papua New Guinea**

A New Guinea bibliography, Butler, Alan, DF48

New Guinea periodical index, AD348

New Hampshire. [Laws, etc.]. *New Hampshire revised statutes annotated, 1955,* CK179

New Hampshire revised statutes annotated, 1955, New Hampshire. [Laws, etc.], CK179

A new handbook of Christian theology, BC252

The new Harvard dictionary of music, BJ153, BJ225

New Hebrides *see* **Vanuatu**

New Hindustani-English dictionary, Fallon, S. W., AC489

A new history of French literature, BE1174

A new history of Ireland, DC399, DC413

A new history of Ireland. Ancillary publications, DC411

The new Hollstein Dutch & Flemish etchings, BF382

New Iberian world, DB292

The new IEEE standard dictionary of electrical and electronics terms, Institute of Electrical and Electronics Engineers, EK131

The new illustrated encyclopedia of world history, Langer, William Leonard, DA35

The new intellectuals, Logan, Terence P., BE650

The new international atlas, Rand McNally and Company, CL289

New international dictionary of acronyms in library and information science and related fields, Sawoniak, Henryk, AK45

The new international dictionary of biblical archaeology, BC195

The new international dictionary of New Testament theology, BC148

New international dictionary of the Christian church, Douglas, James Dixon, BC148, BC236

New international version [Bible], BC94

The new interpreter's Bible, BC174

A new introduction to bibliography, Gaskell, Philip, AA3, EE11

The new Jerome biblical commentary, BC178

New Jersey. [Laws, etc.]. *New Jersey statutes annotated,* CK179

New Jersey statutes annotated, New Jersey. [Laws, etc.], CK179

New keramic gallery, Chaffers, William, BG77

New King James Version exhaustive concordance, BC164

New language of politics, Safire, William L., CJ127

The new Larousse encyclopedia of animal life, EG302

New Larousse encyclopedia of mythology, CF8

The new layman's Bible commentary in one volume, BC179

New Malaysian who's who, AH361

The new members of congress almanac, Trammell, Jeffrey B., CJ220

New Mexico. [Laws, etc.]. *New Mexico statutes, 1978 annotated,* CK179

New Mexico statutes, 1978 annotated, New Mexico. [Laws, etc.], CK179

New model English-Thai dictionary, So Sethaputra, AC780

The new Moulton's library of literary criticism, BE427, BE596, BE598, BE599

—— Bloom, Harold, BE600

New murderers' who's who, Gaute, J. H. H., CK254

—— Odell, Robin, CK254

New Orleans times-picayune [index], AE104

New our bodies, ourselves, CC95, CC564

The new Oxford atlas, Oxford University Press, CL286

The new Oxford book of English verse, 1250–1950, Gardner, Helen Louise, BE720

New Oxford companion to music, BJ138, BJ142

New Oxford history of music, BJ197, BJ200

New paintings, Kultermann, Udo, BF307

The new Palgrave, CH52

The new Palgrave dictionary of money & finance, CH268

The new Pelican guide to English literature, BE616

The new Penguin dictionary of geography, CL43

The new Penguin dictionary of quotations, BE110

New periodical title abbreviations, AD23

The new periodicals index, AD279

New Persian-English dictionary, Hayyīm, Sulaymān, AC314

A new photographic atlas of the moon, Kopal, Zdeněk, EC66

New political parties of Eastern Europe and the Soviet Union, CJ317

The new practical navigator, EC77

The new Princeton encyclopedia of poetry and poetics, BE329

—— Brogan, Terry V. F., BE696

—— Preminger, Alex, BE696

New pronouncing dictionary of the Spanish and English languages, AC740

The new quotable woman, BE111

A new reader's guide to African literature, Zell, Hans M., BE1508

New Redhouse Turkish-English dictionary, AC792

The new religions of Japan, Earhart, H. Byron, BC36

New religious movements in the United States and Canada, Choquette, Diane, BC28

New research centers, AL82, EA147

New revised Velázquez Spanish and English dictionary, Velázquez de la Cadena, Mariano, AC740

New rhyming dictionary and poets' handbook, Johnson, Burges, AC114

New Robert's rules of order, De Vries, Mary Ann, CJ457

The new royal dictionary, Craven, Thomas, AC488

The new Royal Horticultural Society dictionary of gardening, EG125, EJ242

The new Sabin, Thompson, Lawrence Sidney, AA411

New Schaff-Herzog encyclopedia of religious knowledge, BC67

New serial titles, AA111, AD225, AD226

New special libraries, AK123

The new standard Jewish encyclopedia, BC552

The new state of the world atlas, Kidron, Michael, CL280

The new Steinerbooks dictionary of the paranormal, Riland, George, CD136

The new Strong's exhaustive concordance of the Bible, Strong, James, BC165

New technical books, New York Public Library, EA33

New Testament abstracts, BC118, BC123

New Testament Apocrypha, Schneemelcher, Wilhelm, BC94

New Testament Apocrypha and pseudepigrapha, Charlesworth, James H., BC94, BC107

A New Testament commentary, BC179

New Testament in modern English, BC94

—— Philips, J. B., BC94

New Testament octapla, Weigle, Luther A., BC94

New-town planning, Golany, Gideon, BF273

New trade names, CH348

New training organizations, CH718

The new unabridged English-Persian dictionary, Āryānpūr Kāshānī, 'Abbās, AC313

New Welsh dictionary, AC805

The new Westminster dictionary of liturgy and worship, BC268

The new Westminster dictionary of the Bible, Gehman, Henry Snyder, BC138

The new Wildhagen German dictionary, Wildhagen, Karl, AC424

The new World comprehensive English-Korean dictionary, AC566

New York Academy of Medicine. Library. *Author catalog*, EH50

—— *Catalog of biographies*, EH224

—— *Dental bibliography*, EH245

—— *Illustration catalog*, EH51

—— *Portrait catalog*, EH52

New York Botanical Garden. *A bibliography of eastern Asiatic botany*, EG106

—— *The New York Botanical Garden illustrated encyclopedia of horticulture*, EJ233

—— *Wild flowers of the United States*, EG180

The New York Botanical Garden illustrated encyclopedia of horticulture, Everett, Thomas H., EJ233

New York daily tribune index, AE109

New York Graphic Society. *Fine art reproductions of old & modern masters*, BF196

New York Historical Society. *The New-York Historical Society dictionary of artists in America, 1564–1860*, BF155

The New-York Historical Society dictionary of artists in America, 1564–1860, Groce, George C., BF155

New York Public Library. *The artists file*, BF141

—— *Blacks in film and television*, BH165

—— *Bulletin*, AA265, AL149, BF110, EK23

—— *A check list of cumulative indexes to individual periodicals in the New York Public Library*, AD252

—— *Dictionary catalog*, CC381

—— *Dictionary catalog of the Map Division*, CL248

—— *Guide to research collections of the New York Public Library*, AK115

—— *History of aeronautics*, EK23

—— *New technical books*, EA33

—— *The New York Public Library book of chronologies*, DA40

—— *The New York Public Library book of twentieth-century American quotations*, BE112

—— *Provençal literature and language including the local history of southern France*, BE1373

—— *The Slavic literatures*, BE1075

New York Public Library, AK115

New York Public Library. Art and Architecture Division. *Bibliographic guide to art and architecture*, BF45

—— *Dictionary catalog*, BF45, BF57

New York Public Library. Dance collection. *Bibliographic guide to dance*, BH135

—— *Dictionary catalog of the Dance Collection*, BH33, BH135

—— *Index to dance periodicals*, BH137

New York Public Library. Early Childhood Resource and Information Center. *Resources for early childhood*, CC149

New York Public Library. East European Newspaper Collection. *The East European Newspaper Collection of the Slavic and Baltic Division, the New York Public Library*, AE42

New York Public Library. Local History and Genealogy Division. *Dictionary catalog of the Local History and Genealogy Division*, DB25, DB179

New York Public Library. Map Division. *Dictionary catalog of the Map Division*, CL255

New York Public Library. Music Division. *Bibliographic guide to music*, BJ50, BJ88

New York Public Library. Prints Division. *Dictionary catalog of the Prints Division*, BF366

—— *Print file*, BF366

New York Public Library. Rare Book Division. *Checklist of additions to Evans' American bibliography in the Rare Book Division of the New York Public Library*, AA408

New York Public Library. Reference Department. *Dictionary catalog of the history of the Americas*, DB5, DB25, DB179

—— *Dictionary catalog of the Jewish collection*, BC540

—— *Dictionary catalog of the Music Collection*, BJ88

—— *Dictionary catalog of the Research Libraries of the New York Public Library, 1911–1971*, DB5

—— *Subject catalog of the World War I collection*, DA196

New York Public Library. Research Libraries. *Bibliographic guide to government publications—foreign*, AF83, AF148

—— *Bibliographic guide to government publications—U.S*, AF83

—— *Bibliographic guide to microform publications*, AA128

—— *Bibliographic guide to psychology*, CD7

—— *Bibliographic guide to Soviet and East European studies*, DC45

—— *Bibliographic guide to technology*, EK4, EK5

—— *Bibliographic guide to theatre arts*, BH33

—— *Catalog of government publications*, AF83

—— *Catalog of government publications in the Research Libraries*, AF10

—— *Catalog of the theatre and drama collections*, BH33

—— *Dictionary catalog of the music collection*, BJ50, BJ88

—— *Dictionary catalog of the Research Libraries*, AF83

—— *Dictionary catalog of the Research Libraries of the New York Public Library*, BC540, DC45

—— *Dictionary catalog of the Research Libraries of the New York Public Library, 1911–1971*, AA116

—— *Dictionary catalog of the Teachers College Library*, CB6

—— *Guide to festschriften*, AA126

—— *Hebrew-character title catalog of the Jewish collection*, BC540

—— *Photographica*, BF338

—— *Subject catalog of the World War II collection*, DA196

New York Public Library. Slavonic Division. *Dictionary catalog of the Slavonic collection*, DC45

The New York Public Library book of chronologies, Wetterau, Bruce, DA40

The New York Public Library book of twentieth-century American quotations, BE112

The New York Public Library desk reference, AB107

New York (State). [Laws, etc.]. *McKinney's consolidated laws of New York annotated*, CK179

New York State Library School Association. *New York State library school register, 1887–1926*, AK92

New York State library school register, 1887–1926, New York State Library School Association, AK92

New York State School of Industrial and Labor Relations. *American labor union periodicals*, CH635

—— *Library catalog*, CH640

New York theatre critics' reviews, BH58

The New York theatrical sourcebook, BH86

New York times, AH10

The New York times atlas of the world, CL285

New York times biographical edition, AH48

New York times biographical service, AH48

The New York times encyclopedia of television, BH313

The New York times film reviews, BH241

New York times index, AE106, AE108, AE109, AE110, AE112, CH35

The New York times obituaries index, 1858–1968, AH17

The New York times obituaries index, 1969–1978, AH18

The New York times theater reviews, BH59

New York University. Institute of Fine Arts. Conservation Center. *Library catalog of the Conservation Center, New York University, Institute of Fine Arts*, BF200

New Zealand

atlases, CL365, CL366

bibliography, AA946, AA947, DF8, DF42

current, AA948, AA949

bibliography of bibliography, AA87

biography, AH373, AH377, AH378, AH379, AH380, DF46, DF47

contemporary, AH381

dissertations, AG60

encyclopedias, DF43

gazetteers, CL169

government publications, AA86, AF267, AF268

library resources, AK104, DF11

manuscripts and archives, AK163, DF15

newspapers, AE100

periodicals, AD213

indexes, AD347

place-names, CL219

statistics, CG439, CG440, CG441

New Zealand (by subject)

foreign relations, DF44

history, DF45

music, BJ35

politics and government sourcebooks, CJ451

religion, BC42

New Zealand. Advisory Committee on the Teaching of the Maori Language. *A dictionary of the Maori language*, AC610

New Zealand. Department of Internal Affairs. *The dictionary of New Zealand biography*, AH378, AH380, DF47

New Zealand. Dept. of Health. *Mortality and demographic data*, CG440

New Zealand. Dept. of Statistics. *New Zealand official year-book*, CG441

New Zealand. General Assembly. Library. *Copyright publications*, AA947

New Zealand. Government Printing Office. *Guide to government information*, AF267

New Zealand. Parliament. Library. *Union catalogue of New Zealand newspapers preserved in public libraries, newspaper offices, etc.*, AE100

New Zealand, Bloomfield, Gerald T., CG439

New Zealand atlas, CL365

New Zealand books in print, AA948

New Zealand Council for Educational Research. *A directory of philanthropic trusts in New Zealand*, AL128

New Zealand drama, McNaughton, Howard Douglas, BE862

New Zealand fiction, Jones, Johanna, BE861

—— Jones, Joseph, BE861

New Zealand Film Archive. *Maori and Pacific films from New Zealand 1901–1984*, DF4
The New Zealand foreign affairs handbook, Hoadley, Steve, DF44
New Zealand guide, CL169
New Zealand in maps, CL366
New Zealand information sources, AA86, AF268
New Zealand Institute of International Affairs. *The New Zealand foreign affairs handbook*, DF44
——— *The South Pacific foreign affairs handbook*, DF18
New Zealand law register, CK233
New Zealand Library Association. *A bibliography of New Zealand bibliographies*, AA87
——— *DILSI, NZ*, AK63
New Zealand literature, BE861, BE862, BE864
indexes, BE849
New Zealand literature (by subject)
history, BE863
New Zealand literature, McCormick, E. H., BE863
New Zealand literature to 1977, Thomson, John E., BE864
New Zealand national bibliography, AA947, AA949
New Zealand national bibliography to the year 1960, Bagnall, Austin Graham, AA946, DF42
New Zealand novel, 1860–1965, Stevens, Joan, BE861
New Zealand novels and novelists, 1861–1979, Burns, James, BE861
New Zealand official year-book, CG441
The New Zealand politics source book, CJ451
New Zealand who's who, Aotearoa, AH379
New Zealand women, AH377, DF46
Newald, Richard. *Geschichte der deutschen Literatur von den Anfängen bis zur Gegenwart*, BE1255
Newberry Library. *Atlas of Great Lakes Indian history*, CC438
——— *Bibliographical inventory of the early music in the Newberry Library, Chicago, Illinois*, BJ96
——— *A catalog of the Greenlee collection*, DC489
——— *A check list of courtesy books in the Newberry Library*, AL151
——— *Checklist of French political pamphlets 1560–1653 in the Newberry Library*, DC169
——— *Dictionary catalog of the Edward E. Ayer collection of Americana and American Indians in the Newberry Library*, DB6
——— *Historical atlas and chronology of county boundaries, 1788–1980*, CL300
——— *The Newberry Library catalog of early American printed sheet music*, BJ97
——— *U.S.iana, 1650–1950*, AA241
Newberry Library. Center for the History of the American Indian. *A bibliographical guide to the history of Indian-white relations in the United States*, CC423
——— *Native American women*, CC602
——— *The Newberry Library Center for the History of the American Indian bibliographical series*, CC421
Newberry Library. Edward E. Ayer Collection. *A bibliographical check list of North and Middle American Indian linguistics in the Edward E. Ayer Collection*, BD237
——— *Dictionary catalog of the Edward E. Ayer collection of Americana and American Indians in the Newberry Library*, DB6
The Newberry Library catalog of early American printed sheet music, Newberry Library, BJ97
The Newberry Library Center for the History of the American Indian bibliographical series, Newberry Library. Center for the History of the American Indian, CC421
Newbery and Caldecott Medal and Honor books, Peterson, Linda Kauffman, AA343
Newby, James Edward. *Black authors*, BE527
Newcomb, Lawrence. *Newcomb's wildflower guide*, EG177
Newcomb's wildflower guide, Newcomb, Lawrence, EG177
Newell, Christopher. *Dictionary of Victorian painters*, BF323

Newell, James E. *The St. James encyclopedia of mortgage & real estate finance*, CH534
Newhall, Beaumont. *A catalogue of the Epstean collection on the history and science of photography and its applications especially to the graphic arts*, BF336
Newitt, M. D. D. *The Comoro Islands*, DD142
The newly independent states of Eurasia, Batalden, Stephen K., DC598
Newman, Edgar Leon. *Historical dictionary of France from the 1815 restoration to the Second Empire*, DC204
Newman, Eric P. *Early paper money of America*, BG194
Newman, H. Morton. *Verbis non factis*, CJ242
Newman, Harold. *An illustrated dictionary of ceramics*, BG67
——— *An illustrated dictionary of glass*, BG66
——— *An illustrated dictionary of jewelry*, BG83, BG146
——— *An illustrated dictionary of silverware*, BG146
Newman, Jacqueline M. *Melting pot*, EJ205
Newman, John. *Vietnam literature*, BE417, DE278
Newman, L. M. *German language and literature*, BD123
Newman, Michele M. *Films in the sciences*, EA34
Newman, Oksana. *European market share reporter*, CH596
Newman, P. R. *Companion to Irish history, 1603–1921*, DC408
Newman, Peter. *Atlas of the English civil war*, DC324
Newman, Peter K. *The new Palgrave*, CH52
——— *The new Palgrave dictionary of money & finance*, CH268
Newman, Richard. *Black access*, CC371
——— *Black index*, CC384
Newman, Roxana Ma. *An English-Hausa dictionary*, AC811
Newman, William M. *Atlas of religious change in America, 1952–1971*, BC85
——— *Atlas of religious change in America, 1971–1980*, BC85
Newnes dictionary of dates, Collison, Robert Lewis, AL143
Newnes engineer's reference book, EK244
Newnham, Jeffrey. *The dictionary of world politics*, CJ26
News bureau contacts, AE128
News bureaus in the U.S, AE128
News media yellow book of Washington and New York, CH350
NewsBank. Film and television, BH236
NewsBank, inc. *Film and television*, BH236
NewsBank index, AE111
NewsBank index to periodicals, AE111
NewsBank names in the news, AE111
NewsBank performing arts, BH9
•*NewsBank reference service plus*, AE111, BH9, BH236
NewsBank review of the arts, AE111
NewsBank urban affairs library, AE111
The newsletter yearbook/directory, AE35
Newsletters, AD52, AE35, AE36, AE37
Newsletters (by subject)
finance, CH297
law, CK123
Newsletters directory, AE36
Newsletters in print, AE36
Newsom, Carol A. *The women's Bible commentary*, BC180
Newsome, Walter L. *New guide to government publications*, AF77
•*Newspaper abstracts ondisc*, AE112
Newspaper advertising sources, CH601
Newspaper and gazette report, AE5
•*Newspaper and periodical abstracts*, AE112
Newspaper columnists, AE129
Newspaper indexes, Milner, Anita Cheek, AE101, AE102
Newspaper indexes in the Newspaper and Current Periodical Room, Pluge, John, AE102

Newspaper libraries, AE30
Newspaper libraries, Wall, Celia Jo, AE30
Newspaper libraries in the U.S. and Canada, Special Libraries Association. Newspaper Division, AE30
Newspaper press directory, AD1, AE2
The newspaper press in Britain, Linton, David, AE58
Newspapers
bibliography, AE3, AE6, AE9, AE146
Jewish, AD7
bibliography and union lists
international, AE10, AE11
bibliography of bibliography, AE29
databases, AE111
bibliography, AD271
directories, AE113
directories, AE9
indexes, AE111, AE112, AE115, AE125
bibliography, AE101, AE102
databases, AE112
indexes (by country or region)
international, AE103
Russia and the U.S.S.R., AE103
newsletters, AE5
statistics, AE21
union lists, AE12, AE13, AE14
Newspapers (by country or region)
Afghanistan
bibliography, AE90
Africa, AE4
bibliography, AE79, DD26
Arab states
bibliography, AE85
Asia, AE4
Asia, Southeast, AE82
Asia, West, AE84
bibliography, AE85
Australia
union lists, AE99
Austria, AD81, AE44
Baltic States, AE75
Belarus
union lists, AE71
Belgium, AD82, AE45
Bulgaria
bibliography, AE46
Canada
bibliography, AE39
directories, AD51, AE23
indexes, AE117, AE118, CH38
union lists, AE38, AE117
Caribbean, AE41
China, AE87
bibliography, AE86
Commonwealth, AE7
Czechoslovakia, AE47
Denmark
bibliography, AE48
catalogs, AE48
Europe, AE4
bibliography, AE8
directories, AD1, AE2
Europe, Eastern, AE43
library catalogs, AE42
Finland, AE49
former Soviet republics
translations, AE68
France
dictionaries, DC208
history, AE52
indexes, AE120, AE121
Germany
history, AE54
indexes, AE122, AE123
union lists, AE53
Great Britain, AE56, AE57, AE58
bibliography, AE59
directories, AD1, AE2
indexes, AE124, AE125
regional and local, AE55
Hungary, AD123
India, AD190, AE88
Indonesia, AD195, AE89

international, AE3, AE4, AE14
directories, AD1, AD118, AE2
union lists, AE12
Iran
bibliography, AE90
Iraq
bibliography, AE91
Ireland, AD124
bibliography, AE63
Ireland, Northern, AE61
Israel, AE92
Italy
history, AE64
Japan
bibliography, AD202, AE94
catalogs, AE94
directories, AE93, AE95
union lists, AE96
Latin America, AE4
bibliography, AE1
union lists, AE1, AE40
Montenegro
bibliography, AD167
Netherlands
directories, AD132, AE65
New Zealand
union lists, AE100
Nigeria, AD174, AD175
North America
bibliography, AE1
union lists, AE1, AE16
Oceania, AE4
Pakistan, AD206, AD207
union lists, AE97
Philippines, AE98
bibliography, AD209
Poland
bibliography, AE67
library catalogs, AE66
Romania, AD140
Russia and the U.S.S.R.
bibliography, AE69, AE70, AE72, AE73
Scandinavia
directories, AD80
Scotland, AE62
bibliography, AD119
Serbia
bibliography, AD167
South Africa, AD177, AE80
bibliography, AE81
union lists, AE81
Spain
bibliography, AE76
indexes, AE126
Switzerland, AE77
Turkey
bibliography, AE78
union lists, AE78
Ukraine
bibliography, AE72
union lists, AE71
United States
bibliography, AE1, AE15, AE18, AE19, AE20, AE34
chronologies, AE26
databases, AE106
directories, AD51, AD52, AD57, AD58, AE22, AE23
history, AE28
indexes, AE106, AE108, AE109, AE110, AE114
Roman Catholic, AE33
statistics, AE22, AE28
union lists, AE1, AE18, AE19, AE26, AE27, AE32
U.S.S.R
bibliography, AE74, AE75
translations, AE68
union lists, AE71
Vietnam, AD212
bibliography, AD211
Newspapers (by language)
Arabic, AE84
Germanic
union lists, AE8
Newspapers (by subject)
features, AE127
history, AE133, AE146
news bureaus, AE128
see also **Ethnic press**
Newspapers, a reference guide, Schwarzlose, Richard Allen, AE29, AE146
Newspapers and periodicals appearing in Israel, Israel. Lishkat ha-'itonut ha-memshaltit, AE92
Newspapers and periodicals from Romania, AD139
Newspapers and periodicals in the American Native Press Archives, AE16
Newspapers in Australian libraries, AE99
Newspapers in microform, AE13, AE27
Newspapers of east central and southeastern Europe in the Library of Congress, Library of Congress. Slavic and Central European Division, AE43
Newspapers of the Soviet Union in the Library of Congress, Library of Congress, AE43, AE75
Newspapers on microfilm, AA136
Newspapers online, AE113
Newspapers published in Great Britain and Ireland, 1801–1900, AE56
—— British Museum, AD114
Newspapers received currently in the Library of Congress, Library of Congress. Serial and Government Publications Division, AE11, AE75
Newspeak, Green, Jonathon, AC123
Newton, Alfred. *Dictionary of birds,* EG257
Newton, Francis P. *American bibliography,* AA417
Newton, Judy Ann. *The Ku Klux Klan,* DB50
—— *Racial & religious violence in America,* CC357
Newton, Michael. *The Ku Klux Klan,* DB50
—— *Mass murder,* CK246
—— *Racial & religious violence in America,* CC357
Newton, Velma. *Commonwealth Caribbean legal literature,* CK200
—— *Legal literature and conditions affecting legal publishing in the Commonwealth Caribbean,* CK200
Ngā Tāngata taumata rau, AH378, DF47
Ngcobo, Zipho G. *An annotated bibliography on women,* DD229
Ngoga, Alphonse. *Bibliographie annotée sur la population du Rwanda,* CG352, DD197
Ng'ombe, Roger M. Stephen. *A selected bibliography of the Federation of Rhodesia and Nyasaland,* DD119, DD176, DD248
Ngugi wa Thiong'o, the making of a rebel, Sicherman, Carol, DD166
Ngụyên, Dình-Hòa. *Essential English-Vietnamese dictionary,* AC803
—— *Vietnamese-English student dictionary,* AC804
Nguyên, Dình Thâm. *Studies on Vietnamese language and literature,* BD231, BE1601
Nguyen, Patricia Thi My-Huong. *Essential English-Vietnamese dictionary,* AC803
Nicaragua
bibliography, AA490, AA491
biography, DB313
government publications, AF159
registers, CJ325
statistics, CG132
Nicaragua (by subject)
foreign relations, CJ114
politics and government, DB315
Nicaragua. Dirección General de Estadística. *Anuario estadístico de la República de Nicaragua,* CG132
Nicaragua, Woodward, Ralph Lee, DB316
Nicaraguan literature, BE917
Nicaraguan national bibliography, 1800–1978, AA491
"Nice guys finish seventh", Keyes, Ralph, BE106
NICEM. *A-V online,* CB28
—— *Training media database,* CB355
NICEM media indexes, National Information Center for Educational Media, AA383
Nichiporuk, Walter. *A bibliography on meteorites,* EF206
Nicholas, David. *Commodities futures trading,* CH435
—— *Immunology,* EG4
—— *The Middle East, its oil, economics and investment policies,* CH192
—— *Virology,* EG346
Nicholas, Larraine. *International dictionary of ballet,* BH142
Nicholas, Robin. *Immunology,* EG4
—— *Virology,* EG346
Nicholi, Armand M. *The Harvard guide to modern psychiatry,* EH394
Nicholls, Ann. *Cambridge guide to the museums of Britain and Ireland,* BF98
—— *The Cambridge guide to the museums of Europe,* BF98
—— *The directory of museums & living displays,* AL88
Nicholls, C. S. *Missing persons,* AH226
Nicholls, Peter. *The encyclopedia of science fiction,* BE286
—— *Science fiction encyclopedia,* BE286
Nicholls, Robert P. *Guide to historic and significant gardens of America,* BF296
—— *The traveler's guide to American gardens,* BF296
Nichols, Madaline W. *Bibliographical guide to materials on American Spanish,* BD175
—— *Revistas hispanoamericanas,* AD299
Nichols, Monte C. *Mineral reference manual,* EF201
Nichols, Stephen W. *The Torre-Bueno glossary of entomology,* EG338
Nicholson, Frances. *Political and economic encyclopaedia of Western Europe,* CJ319
Nicholson, Margaret. *Dictionary of American-English usage,* AC71
Nicholson, Norman Leon. *The maps of Canada,* CL309
Nicholson, Reynold A. *Literary history of the Arabs,* BE1546
Nickel, Ernest H. *Mineral reference manual,* EF201
Nickel, Jacqueline M. *National directory of Latin Americanists,* DB287
Nickles, John Milton. *Geologic literature on North America, 1785–1918,* EF36
Nicknames, AJ180, AJ181, BE190
Nicknames and sobriquets of U.S. cities, states and counties, Alexander, Gerard L., CL173
—— Kane, Joseph Nathan, CL173, CL179
Nickson, R. Andrew. *Paraguay,* DB380
Nicodème, Jacques. *Répertoire des inventaires des archives conservées en Belgique, parus avant le 1ier Janvier 1969,* DC106
Nicol, Donald MacGillivray. *A biographical dictionary of the Byzantine Empire,* DA165
Nicolai, Martha. *German literature in British magazines, 1750–1860,* BE1240
Nicolaisen, Wilhelm Fritz Hermann. *The names of towns and cities in Britain,* CL197
—— *Scottish place-names,* CL205
Nicolas, Maurice. *Bibliographie de la Martinique,* DB445
Nicolay, H. H. *Rocks and minerals,* EF202
Nicoll, Allardyce. *British drama,* BE666
—— *English drama, 1900–1930,* BE666
—— *History of English drama, 1660–1900,* BE453, BE636, BE666
—— *Short-title alphabetical catalogue of plays produced or printed in England from 1660–1900,* BE453, BE636
Nicolle, David. *Arms and armour of the crusading era, 1050–1350,* CJ575
Nicolosi, Lucille. *Terminology of communication disorders,* EH122
Nicolson, Ranald. *An historical atlas of Scotland, c.400–c.1600,* DC367
Nicot, Jean. *Inventaire des archives de la Tunisie,* DD69
—— *Répertoire des archives du Maroc,* DD69
Nida, Eugene Albert. *Greek-English lexicon of the New Testament,* AC455

NIDS, AK112

Niebuhr, Gary Warren. *A reader's guide to the private eye novel*, BE274

Niederdeutsche bibliographie, Borchling, Conrad, AA637

Niedermann, Max. *Wörterbuch der litauischen Schriftsprache, litauisch-deutsch*, AC602

Niederösterreichischer Amtskalender, CJ327

Niedersächsische Staats– und Universitätsbibliothek Göttingen. *A catalogue of English books printed before 1801 held by the University Library at Göttingen*, AA682

Nield, Jonathan. *Guide to the best historical novels and tales*, BE250

Nielsen, Frederik. *Danske Digtere i det 20. arhundrede*, BE1115

Nielsen, Konrad. *Lappisk (samisk) ordbok*, AC570

Nielsen, Lauritz Martin. *Dansk Bibliografi, 1482– 1550, 1551–1600*, AA603

Nielsen, Mark C. *Atlas of religious change in America, 1952–1971*, BC85

Nielsen, Niels. *Atlas over Danmark*, CL324
———— *Danmark*, CL132

Niemeyer, Suzanne. *Money for film & video artists*, AL120, BF105
———— *Money for performing artists*, AL120, BF105
———— *Money for visual artists*, AL120, BF105
———— *Research guide to American historical biography*, AH69

Niemi, Richard G. *Trends in public opinion*, CJ484, CJ492
———— *Vital statistics on American politics*, CJ163

Nienaber, Grabriel Stefanus. *Hottentot (Khoekhoen) place names*, CL216

Nienaber, Petrus Johannes. *Bibliografie van Afrikaanse boeke*, AA875
———— *Bronnegids by die studie van die Afrikaanse taal en letterkunde*, BD132

Nienhauser, William H. *The Indiana companion to traditional Chinese literature*, BE1554

Nienholdt, Eva. *Katalog der Lipperheideschen Kostümbibliothek*, BG93

Nierenberg, William Aaron. *Encyclopedia of earth system science*, EF6

Niermeyer, Jan Frederik. *Mediae latinitatis lexicon minus*, AC592

Nieswender, Rosemary. *Russia, the USSR, and Eastern Europe*, DC32

Nieto López, J. de Jesús. *Diccionario histórico del México contemporáneo, 1900–1982*, DB247

Nietzsche, Friedrich Wilhelm, BB78

Nieuw Nederlandsch biografisch woordenboek, AH271
———— Molhuysen, Philip Christiaan, AH272

Nigarishī jāmi bar jahān-i kitābshināsī hā-yi Īrān, Tasbīḥī, Ghulām Ḥusayn, AA80

Niger
   atlases, CL339
   government publications
      bibliography, AF230
   statistics, CG349

Niger. Ministère du Développement et de la Coopération. *Annuaire statistique*, CG349

Niger, Decalo, S., DD48

Nigeria, DD193
   atlases, CL342
   bibliography, AA869, AA870, DD18, DD192, DD194
   biography, AH322, AH323, DD196
   current surveys, DD62
   dissertations, AG47, AG48
   encyclopedias, DD48
   government publications, AF235, AF236
   newspapers, AD174, AD175
   periodicals, AD174, AD175
      indexes, AD334
   statistics, CG350
Nigeria (by subject)
   history
      bibliography, CC598, DD191, DD195
      law, CK226
      press, AD173

Nigeria. Federal Office of Statistics. *Annual abstract of statistics - Federation of Nigeria, Federal Office of Statistics*, CG350

Nigeria, Chapin Metz, Helen, DD62
———— DeLancey, Mark W., DD192
———— Eitner, Kurt, DD193
———— Library of Congress. African Section, AF235, AF236
———— Lockwood, Sharon Burdge, AF236
———— Myers, Robert A., DD18
———— Oyewole, Anthony, DD48

Le Nigeria contemporain, DD194

Nigeria in maps, Barbour, K. Michael, CL342

Nigerian artists, Kelly, Bernice M., BF142

Nigerian government publications, 1966–1973, Stanley, Janet L., AF236

Nigerian legal bibliography, Jegede, Oluremi, CK226

Nigerian legal periodicals, CK226

Nigerian literature, BE1530, BE1531

Nigerian literature, Baldwin, Claudia, BE1530

Nigerian official publications, 1869–1959, Conover, Helen F., AF235

Nigerian periodicals and newspapers, 1950–1970, University of Ibadan. Library, AD175

Nigerian periodicals and newspapers, 1950–70, AA870

Nigerian periodicals index, DD44

Nigerian publications, AA869

Nigerian publications, 1950–1970, University of Ibadan. Library, AA870

Nigerian universities dissertation abstracts, AG47

Nigerian women in development, Coles, Catherine M., CC598, DD191

Nihon Bōeki Shinkōkai. *Directory of Japanese-affiliated companies in the USA & Canada*, CH353
———— *Japan trade directory*, CH408

Nihon bungakushi, Kindai, gendai hen, Keene, Donald, BE1582

Nihon bungei shi, Konishi, Jin'ichi, BE1582

Nihon Bungeika Kyōkai hen. *Bungei nenkan*, BE1583

Nihon hakushi gakuiroku, AG54

Nihon hakushiroku, AG54, AH357

Nihon jinmei chimei jiten, AC556

Nihon Kindai Bungakkan hen. *Nihon kindai bungaku meicho jiten*, BE1590

Nihon kindai bungaku daijiten, BE1589

Nihon kindai bungaku meicho jiten, BE1590

Nihon Kindai Bungakukan (Tokyo). *Nihon kindai bungaku daijiten*, BE1589

Nihon koten bungaku daijiten, BE1591

Nihon mukashibanashi meii, CF98

Nihon no sankō tosho, AA355

Nihon no Sankō Tosho Henshū Iinkai. *Guide to Japanese reference books*, AA355

Nihon PEN Kurabu. *Modern Japanese literature in translation*, BE1584

Nihon shimbun nenkan, AD202

Nihon Shinbun Kyōkai. *Nihon shinbun nenkan*, AE95

Nihon shinbun nenkan, AE95

Nihon shoseki sōmokuroku, AA917

Nihon shoshi no shoshi, Amano, Keitaro, AA81

Nihon shuppan nenkan, AA918

Nihon tōkei nenkan, CG402

Nihon zasshi sōran, AD201, AD202

Nihon zenkoku shoshi, AA916

Nihon zenkoku shoshi shomei choshamei sakuin, AA916

Nijhoff, Wouter. *Nederlandsche bibliographie van 1500 tot 1540*, AA746

Nijhoffs geschiedenislexicon Nederland en België, Volmuller, H. W. J., DC459

Nijhoff's Index op de Nederlandse en Vlaamse periodieken, AD320

Nikolaeva, P. A. *Russkie pisateli*, BE1423

Niles, Ann. *An index to microform collections*, AA132

Niles, Doris. *A bibliography of the dance collection of Doris Niles and Serge Leslie*, BH133

Niles, Susan A. *South American Indian narrative, theoretical and analytical approaches*, CF69, CF74

Nilon, Charles H. *Bibliography of bibliographies in American literature*, BE410

Nilsen, Don Lee Fred. *Humor in American literature*, BE411

NIN, CB163

Nine thousand words, AC92

Nineteenth and twentieth century drama, Thompson, Lawrence Sidney, BE655

Nineteenth-century American choral music, DeVenney, David P., BJ291

Nineteenth-century American drama, Hennessee, Don A., BE640
———— Hixon, Donald L., BE464, BE640

Nineteenth century American poetry, Jason, Philip K., BE493

Nineteenth century art, Rosenblum, Robert, BF131

Nineteenth century Australian periodicals, Stuart, Lurline, BE857

Nineteenth-century autograph music manuscripts in the Pierpoint Morgan Library, Pierpont Morgan Library, BJ89
———— Turner, J. Rigbie, BJ89

Nineteenth-century fiction, Wolff, Robert Lee, BE683, BE687

Nineteenth-century literature criticism, BE54

Nineteenth-century musical chronicle, A, Hall, Charles J., BJ187

Nineteenth century painters and painting, Norman, Geraldine, BF319

The nineteenth-century periodical press in Britain, Madden, Lionel, AD110

The nineteenth-century photographic press, Sennett, Robert S., BF335

Nineteenth-century photography, Johnson, William S., BF331

Nineteenth century postage stamps of the United States, BG204

Nineteenth century readers' guide to periodical literature, 1890–1899, AD280

Nineteenth-century rhetoric, Houlette, Forrest, BE355

Nineteenth-century Russian literature in English, Proffer, Carl R., BE1400

Nineteenth century short title catalogue, AA687, BE687

Nineteenth century theatre, BE639

Nineteenth-century theatrical memoirs, Johnson, Claudia D., BH125

Niobey, Georges. *Grand Larousse de la langue française*, AC329

Nirk, E. *Eesti kirjanduse biograafiline leksikon*, BE1123

Nirk, Endel. *Estonian literature*, BE1125

Nish, C. *French régime*, DB205

Nishiura, Elizabeth. *American battle monuments*, BF390, CJ632

Nissen, Claus. *Die botanische Buchillustration*, EG92
———— *Die zoologische Buchillustration*, EG212

•*NIST JANAF thermochemical tables*, EE93

•*NIST structures & properties database and estimation program*, EE93

al-Nitāj al-fikrī al-'Irāqi li-ám, AA908

Nite, Norm N. *Rock on*, BJ356
———— *Rock on almanac*, BJ332

Nitecki, Joseph Z. *Directory of library reprographic services*, AK244

Nitkina, N. V. *Ukazateli soderzhaniiā russkikh zhurnalov i prodolzhaiushchikhsiā izdaniī 1755– 1970 gg*, AD326

Nitsch, Kazimierz. *Słownik staropolski*, AC629

The NIV complete concordance, BC159

The NIV exhaustive concordance, Goodrick, Edward W., BC159

NIV interlinear Hebrew-English New Testament, Kohlenberger, John R., BC94

NIV triglot Old Testament, BC94

Niver, Kemp R. *Early motion pictures*, BH190
———— *Motion pictures from the Library of Congress paper print collection, 1894–1912*, BH190

Nixon, Judith M. *American directory of organized labor,* CH660
—— *Industry and company information,* CH330
—— *Organization charts,* CH603
Nixon, Marion. *The Oxford book of vertebrates,* EG238
Nkabinde, Thokozile. *Swaziana,* DD231
—— *Women in Lesotho,* DD122, DD171
NKJV exhaustive concordance, BC164
NLL translations bulletin, EA61
—— *National Lending Library for Science and Technology (Great Britain),* EA59
NLM audiovisuals catalog, EH44
NLM current catalog proof sheets, Medical Library Association, EH49
—— *National Library of Medicine (U.S.),* EH49
NNB, Strohmeyer, Eckhard, AA868
Nobel laureates in chemistry, 1901–1992, AL166, EE103
Nobel laureates in economic sciences, AL167, CH102
Nobel laureates in literature, AL168, BE210
Nobel laureates in medicine or physiology, AL169, EH216
The Nobel Peace Prize and the laureates, Abrams, Irwin, AL164
Nobel prize winners, AH30, AL170, AL173, EH225
The Nobel Prize winners : chemistry, AL171, AL172, ED55, EE104
—— Magill, Frank Northen, AL166, EE103
Nobel prize winners in chemistry, 1901–1961, Faber, Edward, AL171, EE104
—— Farber, Eduard, AL165, EE102
Nobel prize winners in medicine and physiology, 1901–1965, Sourkes, Theodore L., AL177
The Nobel Prize winners : physics, AL172, ED55
Nobel prizes, AH30, AL164, AL168, AL169, AL170, AL173, AL174, AL175, AL176, AL177, BE210, ED56, EE105, EH216, EH225
Nobel prizes (by subject)
chemistry, AL165, AL166, AL171, EE102, EE103, EE104
economics
biography, AL167, CH102
physics, AL172, ED55
Nobelstiftelsen. *Chemistry,* AL171, AL174, EE104, EE105
—— *Physics,* AL172, AL175, ED55, ED56
—— *Physiology or medicine,* AL176
Noble, C. A. M. *Modern German dialects,* BD126
Nocq, Henry. *Le poinçon de Paris,* BG141
Nodrum, Charles. *Encyclopedia of Australian art,* BF76
Noel, John Vavasour. *Naval terms dictionary,* CJ618
Noël Hume, Ivor. *Guide to artifacts of colonial America,* DB54
—— *Historical archaeology,* DB54
Noelle-Neumann, Elisabeth. *The Germans,* CJ493
Noether, Dorit. *Encyclopedic dictionary of chemical technology,* EK54
Noether, Herman. *Encyclopedic dictionary of chemical technology,* EK54
Noeẃ, Henri. *Bibliographie de l'histoire de Belgique,* DC100
Nof, Shimon Y. *Handbook of industrial robotics,* EK230
—— *International encyclopedia of robotics,* EK232
Noffsinger, James Philip. *World War I aviation books in English,* DA193
Nofsinger, Mary M. *Children and adjustment to divorce,* CC216
Nōhon shūhō, AA916
Nöhring, Jürgen. *Dictionary of medicine,* EH137, EH138
Noise, EK87, EK116
Nokes, David. *Annotated critical bibliography of Augustan poetry,* BE711
Nolan, Joseph R. *Black's law dictionary,* CK33
Nöldeke, Theodor. *Wörterbuch der klassischen arabischen Sprache,* AC225
Nolte, William. *Managing archival and manuscript repositories,* AK188

Nomenclátor de Aguascalientes, CL114
Nomenclátor de Baja California, CL114
Nomenclátor de Colima, CL114
Nomenclátor de estado de Coahuila, CL114
Nomenclátor de estado de Mexico, CL114
Nomenclátor de estado de Michoacan, CL114
Nomenclátor de estado de Puebla, CL114
Nomenclátor de estado de Queretaro, CL114
Nomenclátor de estado de Tabasco, CL114
Nomenclátor de estado de Veracruz, CL114
Nomenclátor de Guanajuato, CL114
Nomenclátor de Jalisco, CL114
Nomenclátor de Morelos, CL114
Nomenclátor de Nayarit, CL114
Nomenclátor de Nuevo Leon, CL114
Nomenclátor de San Luis Potosi, CL114
Nomenclátor de Tamaulipas, CL114
Nomenclátor de Tlaxcala, CL114
Nomenclátor de Zacatecas, CL114
Nomenclator litterarius, Ruttkowski, W. V., BE88
Nomenclator zoologicus, EG244
—— Neave, Sheffield Airey, EG243
Nomenclature and hierarchy—basic Latin American legal sources, Medina, Rubens, CK198
Nomenclature of inorganic chemistry, EE112
Nomenclature of organic chemistry, International Union of Pure and Applied Chemistry. Commission on the Nomenclature of Organic Chemistry, EE136
Nomina anatomica avium, World Association of Veterinary Anatomists, EG279
Nomina geographica, Egli, Johann Jacob, CL170
Noms et prénoms de France, AJ189
Non-national bibliography of French demographers, Lunazzi, Marie-Claude, CG218
Nonconformity and dissent in the Ukrainian SSR, 1955–1975, Liber, George, CJ389
Nonformal education in Latin America, Poston, Susan L., CB43
Nonprescription drugs, EH352
Nonprofit almanac, AL139
Nonprofit organization management, AL10, CH615
Nonsexist research methods, Eichler, Margrit, CC560
The nonsexist word finder, AC77
Nonverbal communication, CD116
Noonan, Barry Christopher. *Women's periodicals and newspapers from the 18th century to 1981,* AE25
Noory, Samuel. *Dictionary of pronunciation,* AC108
Noppen, J. P. van. *Metaphor,* BD47
—— *Metaphor II,* BD47
Norback, Craig T. *Dow Jones-Irwin guide to franchises,* CH359
—— *The New American guide to athletics, sports, & recreation,* BK19
Norback, Peter G. *Dow Jones-Irwin guide to franchises,* CH359
—— *The New American guide to athletics, sports, & recreation,* BK19
Nordby, Judith. *Mongolia,* DE233
Nordens litteratur, BE1091
Nordic archaeological abstracts, DA72
Nordic Council. *Yearbook of Nordic statistics,* CG190
Nordic Council of Ministers. *Yearbook of Nordic statistics,* CG190
Nordic Statistical Secretariat. *Yearbook of Nordic statistics,* CG190
Nordling, Carl. *Physics handbook,* ED38
Nordmann, Almut. *Who's who in African literature,* BE1512
Nordquist, Joan. *Current Central American–U.S. relations,* DB300
—— *Domestic violence,* CC217
—— *The elderly in America,* CC72
—— *The feminist movement,* CC507
—— *The feminization of poverty,* CC263
—— *The homeless in America,* CC204
—— *Substance abuse I : drug abuse,* CC117
—— *Substance abuse II : alcohol abuse,* CC118
Norgaard, Ole. *Kenya in the social sciences,* DD165
Norges litteratur, Dahl, Willy, BE1337

Norges litteratur historie, Beyer, Edvard, BE1337
Norges offisielle statistikk, CG271
Norman, Buford. *The wordworthy computer,* BE3
Norman, F. *Theses in Germanic studies,* BE1237
Norman, Geraldine. *Nineteenth century painters and painting,* BF319
Norman, Jeremy M. *Morton's medical bibliography,* EH205
Normandy, Elizabeth L. *Nigeria,* DD192
Normandy campaign, 1944, Baxter, Colin F., DA170
Norrgard, Lee E. *Final choices,* CC184
Norris, Gerald. *A musical gazetteer of Great Britain & Ireland,* BJ194
Norris, Herbert. *Church vestments,* BC312
—— *Costume and fashion,* BC312
Norse, Old *see* **Icelandic language**
Norse sagas translated into English, Fry, Donald K., BE1088
Norsk allkunnebok, AB75
Norsk anonym– og pseudonym-lexikon, Pettersen, Hjalmar Marius, AA179
Norsk bibliografisk bibliotek, AD321, AD322, AH274, BE1343
Norsk biografisk leksikon, AH275
Norsk biografisk oppslagsliteratur, Andresen, Harald, AH277
Norsk bokfortegnelse, AA759, AA761
Norsk bokfortegnelse = Norwegian national bibliography, AA759
Norsk-engelsk teknisk ordbok, Ansteinsson, John, EA121
Norsk forfatter-lexikon, 1814–1880, Halvorsen, Jens Braage, BE1087, BE1341
Norsk kvinnelitteraturhistorie, BE1344
Norsk literaturhistorie, Bull, Francis, BE1339
Norsk litteraturhistorisk bibliografi, 1900–1945, Øksnevad, Reidar, BE1343
Norsk littertur historie, Beyer, Harald, BE1338
Norsk lokalhistorisk litteratur, 1946–1970, Universitetsbiblioteket i Oslo, DC469
Norsk militarhistorisk bibliografi, Johnsen, Arne Odd, DC464
Norsk riksmålsordbok, Knudsen, Trygve, AC617
Norsk sitatleksikon, BE146
Norsk slektshistorisk forening. *Norsk biografisk oppslagsliteratur,* AH277
Norsk tidsskriftindex, AD321, AD322, AH274
Norske arkivkatalogar, Nysæter, Egil, DC465
North, Eric McCoy. *The book of a thousand tongues,* BC103
North, John S. *Waterloo directory of Irish newspapers and periodicals, 1800–1900,* AD114, AD124
—— *Waterloo directory of Scottish newspapers and periodicals, 1800–1900,* AD114, AD119, AE62
—— *The Waterloo directory of Victorian periodicals, 1824–1900,* AD114
North, Maurice. *Cassell's colloquial German,* AC437
North, Simon Newton Dexter. *History and present condition of the newspaper and periodical press of the United States,* AE21, AE28
North America
maps
library catalogs, CL233
statistics, CG38
bibliography, CG71, CG72
North America (by subject)
anthropology and ethnology, CE78
censuses
handbooks, CG38
discovery and exploration, DB5
library catalogs, DB2, DB4
folklore and popular culture, CF64, CF67
history
bibliography, DB5, DB25, DB179
encyclopedias, DB83
guides to records, DB61
library catalogs, DB2
native languages, BD237, BD239
bibliography, BD240, BD242
overseas territories, DB83

politics and government
  handbooks, CJ87
North American Conference on British Studies. *Modern England, 1901–1984,* DC331
North American fighting uniforms, Bowers, Michael, CJ634
North American forest and conservation history, Fahl, Ronald J., EJ172, EJ174
North American forest history, Davis, Richard C., EJ172, EJ174
North American horticulture, EG155
North American Indian language materials, 1890–1965, Evans, G. Edward, BD240
North American negro poets, Porter, Dorothy Burnett, BE536
North American Society for Sport History. *Sport on film and video,* BK36
North American trees, Preston, Richard Joseph, EG199
North Carolina. [Laws, etc.]. *General statutes of North Carolina,* CK179
North Carolina Central University. School of Library Science. African-American Materials Project. *Black American writers, 1773–1949,* BE526
North Dakota. [Laws, etc.]. *North Dakota century code,* CK179
North Dakota century code, North Dakota. [Laws, etc.], CK179
The North European nations as presented in German university publications, 1885–1957, Meyen, Fritz, DC73
North frontier of New Spain, Gerhard, Peter, DB225
North Korea *see* **Korea, North**
North Korea, An, Tai Sung, CJ441, DE219
North Nigerian publications, AA870
Northcutt, Wayne. *Historical dictionary of the French Fourth and Fifth Republics, 1946–1991,* DC205
Northern Ireland. Dept. of Finance and Personnel. *Northern Ireland annual abstract of statistics,* CG240
Northern Ireland. General Register Office. *Annual report of the Registrar General,* CG233, CG239
  —— *Ulster year book,* CG241
Northern Ireland, Shannon, Michael Owen, DC355
Northern Ireland : a political directory, 1966–88, Flackes, William D., CJ374
Northern Ireland annual abstract of statistics, CG240
Northern Ireland Information Service. *Ulster year book,* CG241
Northern Ireland newspapers, 1737–1987, AE61
Northern Ireland Working Party on Resources for Local Studies. *Northern Ireland newspapers, 1737–1987,* AE61
Northern New Spain, Barnes, Thomas Charles, DB249
Northwest Passage, DB181
Northwestern University. Library. *Catalog of the African collection,* DD34
Northwestern University. Library. African Department. *Joint acquisitions list of Africana,* DD24
Northwestern University. Transportation Center. Library. *Catalog of the Transportation Center Library, Northwestern University ... ,* CH443
Norton, Arthur P. *Norton's 2000.0,* EC71
Norton, Augustus R. *International terrorism,* CJ550
Norton, F. J. *A dictionary of British folktales in the English language,* CF88
Norton, Jane Elizabeth. *Guide to the national and provincial directories of England and Wales, excluding London, published before 1856,* AL1, AL7, CH366, CH381
Norton, Mary Beth. *Guide to historical literature,* DA1
Norton, Philip. *Dissension in the House of Commons,* CJ359
The Norton anthology of American literature, BE332, BE442, BE506
The Norton anthology of English literature, BE332, BE506, BE618, BE619

Norton anthology of literature by women, Gilbert, Sandra M., BE619
  —— Gubar, Susan, BE619
The Norton anthology of modern poetry, BE332, BE506
Norton anthology of poetry, Allison, Alexander W., BE720
The Norton/Grove concise encyclopedia of music, BJ143
Norton's 2000.0, Norton, Arthur P., EC71
Norway
  archives
    catalogs, DC465
  bibliography, AA759, DC469
    19th–20th centuries, AA760
    19th–20th century, AA758
    current, AA761
    early, AA757
  biography, AD321, AH164, AH274, AH275
    bibliography, AH277
    contemporary, AH276
  government publications, AF213
  periodicals
    indexes, AD321, AD322, AH274
  statistics, CG268, CG269, CG270, CG271
Norway (by subject)
  foreign relations, DC466
  history, DC72, DC463
    bibliography, DC467, DC468
    regional and local, DC469
  military history, DC464
  population, CG269
  travelers' accounts, DC468
Norway. Forsvarsdepartementet. Krigshistoriske avdeling. *Norsk militarhistorisk bibliografi,* DC464
Norway. Statistisk sentralbyrå. *Befolkningsstatistikk,* CG268
  —— *Historiske tabeller over folkemengde, giftermål og dødsfall 1911–1976,* CG270
  —— *National population bibliography of Norway, 1945–1977,* CG269
Norway, Sather, Leland B., DC467
Norwegian English dictionary, AC621
Norwegian-English technical dictionary, EA121
Norwegian foreign policy, Ørvik, Nils, DC466
Norwegian language
  bibliography, BD129, BE1083
  dictionaries, AC617
    bilingual, AC619
      English-Norwegian, AC618
      Norwegian-English, AC620, AC621
  etymology, AC290
  dictionaries, AC622
Norwegian literary biography, 1956–1970, Haukaas, Kaare, BE1343
  —— Næss, Harold S., BE1343
Norwegian literature
  bibliography, BD129, BE1083, BE1090, BE1341, BE1343
  biobibliography, BE1340
  biography, BE1341
  translations, BE1088
  women authors, BE1344
Norwegian literature (by subject)
  history, BE1337, BE1338, BE1339, BE1342
  bibliography, BE1343
Norwegian local history, Hill, Dennis Auburn, DC469
  —— University of Wisconsin-Madison, DC469
The Norwegian national bibliography, AA761
Norwegian scholarly books, 1825–1967, Universitetsforlaget, AA760
Norwegisch-dänisches etymologisches Wörterbuch, Falk, Hjalmar Sejersted, AC290
Norwich, John Julius. *Great architecture of the world,* BF253
Nos ancêtres au XVIIᵉ siècle, Godbout, Archange, AJ71
Nosovský, Karel. *Soupis československé literatury za léta 1901–1925,* AA599
The nostalgia entertainment sourcebook, BH15

Nostrand, Howard Lee. *Research on language teaching,* BD75
Nostrand, Richard L. *Borderlands sourcebook,* DB164
Notable American women, AH66, BE443
Notable black American women, AH67
Notable Hispanic American women, AH78
Notable names in American history, AH68
Notable names in medicine and surgery, Bailey, Hamilton, EH220
  —— Bishop, W. J., EH220
Notable names in the American theatre, BH117
Notable women in the American theatre, BH118
Notas bibliográficas referentes á las primeras produciones de la imprenta en algunas ciudades de la América Española, Medina, José Toribio, AA470
Note al Thesaurus linguae latinae, Ferrua, Antonio, AC571, BE1047
Note annuelle de statistique, Cameroon. Dept. of Statistics and National Accounts, CG321
Notes and queries, BE169
Nöth, Winfried. *Handbook of semiotics,* BD54
Notice sur le doctorat ès lettres suivie du Catalogue et de l'analyse des thèses françaises et latines admises par les facultés des lettres depuis 1810, Mourier, Athénaïs, AG29
Notice to mariners, EC80
Notices généalogiques. 1–8. sér, Woelmont, Henri de, AJ89
Notizie, BC409
Noto, Paolo. *Archivio biografico italiano,* AH258
Nõukogude Eesti raamat, 1940–1954, Friedrich Reinhold Kreutzwaldi nimeline Eeste NSV Riiklik Raamatukogu (Tallinn), AA608
Nõukogude Eesti raamat, 1955–1965, Kuldkepp, E., AA608
  —— Topovere, P., AA608
Nõukogude Eesti raamat, 1966–1970, AA608
Nourie, Alan. *American mass-market magazines,* AD29
Nourie, Barbara. *American mass-market magazines,* AD29
Nouveau dictionnaire breton, Hermon, Roparz, AC237
Nouveau dictionnaire de géographie universelle, Vivien de Saint Martin, Louis, CL96
Nouveau dictionnaire de la sculpture moderne, Maillard, Robert, BF397
Nouveau dictionnaire des difficultés du français, AC365
Nouveau dictionnaire des difficultés du français moderne, Hanse, Joseph, AC370
Nouveau dictionnaire des synonymes, AC362
Nouveau dictionnaire étymologique et historique, Dauzat, Albert, AC348
Nouveau guide de généalogie, Aublet, Robert, AJ83
Nouveau Larousse gastronomique, EJ211
Nouveau Larousse illustré, AB43
Nouveau petit Larousse, AC333
Nouvelle bibliographie critique des mémoires sur l'époque napoléonienne, écrits ou traduits en français, Tulard, Jean, DC194
Nouvelle biographie générale depuis les temps plus reculés jusqu'à nos jours, AH31
Nouvelle biographie nationale, AH175
Nouvelle biographie universelle, AH31
Nouvelle biographie universelle ancienne et moderne, Hoefer, Jean Chrétien Ferdinand, AH22
Nouvelles tables d'intégrales définies, Haan, David Bierens de, EB86
Nouvo vocabolario illustrato della lingua italiana, Devoto, Giacomo, AC525
Nova bibliotheca anglo-judaica, Goldschmidt-Lehmann, Ruth P., BC517
Novaîa istoriîa, DA174
Novaîa otechestvennaîa i inostrannaîa literatura po obshchestvennym naukam. Slaviîanovedenie i balkanistika, DC43
Novaîa Otechestvennaîa literatura po obshchestvennym naukam, BD27

Novaia sovetskaia i inostrannaia literatura po obshchestvennym naukam. Problemy slavianovedeniia i balkanistiki, DC43

Novaia sovetskaia literatura po iazykoznaniiu, BD27

Novaia sovetskaia literatura po obshchestvennym nauckam, DA71

Novaia sovetskaia literatura po obshchestvennym naukam, BD27

Novak, Arne. *Czech literature,* BE1106

—— *Stručné dejiny literatury české,* BE1106

Novak, Barbara. *American painting of the nineteenth century,* BF309

Novakovic, Stojan. *Srpska biblijografija za noviju književnost,* AA844

Novedades editoriales españolas, AA826

Novel: a guide to the novel from its origins to the present day, Roberts, Andrew Michael, BE611

La novela española, 1700–1850, Brown, Reginald F., BE1473

Novels in English by women, 1891–1920, Daims, Diva, BE480, BE750

—— Grimes, Janet, BE474, BE480, BE750

Novels of the Mexican Revolution, BE916

Novissimo dizionario della lingua italiana, Palazzi, Fernando, AC526

Novo dicionário Aurélio, AC642

Novo dicionário Aurélio da língua portuguesa, AC642

Novo dicionário da língua portuguesa, Ferreira, Aurélio Buarque de Holanda, AC642

Novo dicionário de termos técnicos inglês-português, Fürstenau, Eugênio, EA123

Novo Michaelis, Michaelis, Henritte, AC648

Novum auctarium bibliotheca hagiographica graeca, Halkin, François Halkin, BC259

Novum glossarium mediae latinitatis, AC593

Novyĭ entsiklopedicheskiĭ slovar', AB89

NOW Legal Defense & Education Fund, CK162

Now read on, Hicken, Mandy, BE254

Nowak, Ronald M. *Walker's mammals of the world,* EG303

Nowlan, Gwendolyn Wright. *Cinema sequels and remakes,* BH222

—— *Movie characters of leading performers of the sound era,* BH277

—— *The name is familiar,* BH278

Nowlan, Robert A. *Cinema sequels and remakes,* BH222

—— *Movie characters of leading performers of the sound era,* BH277

—— *The name is familiar,* BH278

Noyce, John L. *The directory of British alternative periodicals, 1965–1974,* AD111

Noyce, Wilfrid. *World atlas of mountaineering,* BK119

Noyes, Gertrude Elizabeth. *The English dictionary from Cawdrey to Johnson, 1604–1755,* AC8

Noyes Data Corporation. *Chemical guide to the United States,* EE60

NST, AD225

NTC's dictionary of advertising, Wiechmann, Jack G., CH571

NTC's dictionary of faux amis, Kirk-Greene, C. W. E., AC340

NTC's dictionary of trade name origins, Room, Adrian, CH343

NTC's French and English business dictionary, AC343, CH61

NTC's new college Greek and English dictionary, Nathanail, Paul, AC466

•*NTDB,* CH497

Ntelopoulos, Kyriakos. *Neoellēnika philologika pseudonyma,* AA174

•*NTIS bibliographic database,* EA64

Ntumy, Michael A. *South Pacific islands legal systems,* CK236

Nubian language, AC623

NUC. Audiovisual materials, AA107, AA381

NUC : books, AA111, AA892

NUC. Cartographic materials, CL252

NUC register of additional locations, AA114

NUCEA. *Peterson's guide to certificate programs at American colleges and universities,* CB285

The nuclear arms race, Gay, William, CJ670

Nuclear data sheets, ED42

Nuclear engineering
  abstract journals, EK293, EK294
  databases, EK293, EK294
  dictionaries, EK295
  directories, EK222, EK296

Nuclear magnetic resonance spectroscopy, EE113
  tables, EE142

Nuclear medicine, EH188

Nuclear physics
  abstract journals, EK294
  databases, EK294
  dictionaries, EK295
    bilingual
      Russian-English, ED28
  tables, ED49

Nuclear power plants, EK297

Nuclear power plants worldwide, EK297

The nuclear present, Burns, Grant, CJ666

Nuclear science abstracts, EK293, EK294

Nuclear warfare, CJ670
  bibliography, CJ665, CJ666
  encyclopedias, CJ682

Nuclear weapons, CJ597, CJ654, CJ670
  bibliography, CJ665, CJ666

The nuclear weapons world, CJ597

NUCMC, DB34

NUDA, AG47

Nudansk ordbog, AC286

Nuessel, Frank H. *The image of older adults in the media,* CC73

—— *Theoretical studies in Hispanic linguistics (1960–),* BD168

Nuestro progreso en cifras, CG134

Nueva revista de filología hispánica, BE1432

Nuevo diccionario biografico argentino (1750–1930), AH117

Nuevo repertorio bibliográfico venezolano, Villasana, Angel Raúl, AA551

Number theory, EB75

Numen, BC11

A numerical finding list of British command papers published 1833–1961/62, Di Roma, Edward, AF195, AF201, AF206

—— Rosenthal, Joseph A., AF201, AF206

Numerical integration, EB71

Numerical list of current publications of the U.S. Dept. of Agriculture, Zimmerman, Fred Lyon, EJ88

Numerical lists and schedule of volumes of the reports and documents of the … Congress, … session, AF88, AF91

Numismatic bibliography, Clain-Stefanelli, Elvira Eliza, BG170

Numismatic bibliography of the Far East, Bowker, Howard F., BG171

Numismatic literature, BG175

Numismatics, Grierson, Philip, BG172

Nuñez, Benjamin. *Dictionary of Afro-Latin American civilization,* CC387

Nungezer, Edwin. *Dictionary of actors and of other persons associated with the public representation of plays in England before 1642,* BH119

Nunn, Godfrey Raymond. *Asia,* DE1

—— *Asia and Oceania,* DE11, DF13

—— *East Asia,* DE1

—— *Indonesian newspapers,* AE89

—— *Japanese periodicals and newspapers in Western languages,* AD217

—— *South and Southeast Asia,* DE1

—— *Southeast Asian periodicals,* AD186, AD216

Nuñnez Segura, José. *Literatura colombiana,* BE947

La nuova Italia, CL144, CL145

Il nuovo dizionario Hazon Garzanti, AC532

Nurm, E. *Õigekeelsuse sõnaraamat,* AC305

Nursai, Ata M. *Bibliographie zur Afghanistan-Literatur 1960–1987,* DE113

Nursery rhymes, BE721

Nursey-Bray, Paul F. *Anarchist thinkers and thought,* CJ506

Nursing
  bibliography, EH23, EH273, EH278

  biography, EH283, EH287, EH288
  databases, EH67, EH275
  dictionaries, EH102, EH279
  directories, EH283
  faculty
    directories, EH281
  handbooks, EH284
  indexes, EH274, EH276, EH277, EH278
  periodicals
    databases, EH37
  statistics, EH289
  thesauruses, EH280

Nursing (by subject)
  history, EH286
    bibliography, EH285

Nursing, Bullough, Bonnie, EH285

•*Nursing & allied health (CINAHL),* EH275

Nursing & allied health (CINAHL) … subject heading list, EH280

•*Nursing & allied health database,* EH280

Nursing and allied health (CINAHL) subject headings, EH275

Nursing citation index, Institute for Scientific Information, EH276

Nursing education, EH272

Nursing education (by country or region)
  Canada
    directories, EH282
  United States
    directories, EH282

Nursing homes
  directories, EH156

Nursing studies index, EH278

Nutrition, EH311
  abstract journals, EH295, EJ104
  bibliography, EH17, EH290, EH291, EH293, EJ214
  dictionaries, EH301
  encyclopedias, EH296, EH297, EH298, EH299, EH300, EJ23, EJ210
  guides, EH290, EJ214
  handbooks, EH290, EH302, EH303, EH304, EH306, EH307, EH309, EH310, EH312, EH313, EJ148, EJ156, EJ214, EJ216
  ibliography, EH294, EJ223
  tables, EH308

Nutrition abstracts and reviews, EH295, EJ19, EJ104

Nutrition abstracts and reviews. Series A. Human and experimental, EH295

Nutrition abstracts and reviews. Series B. Livestock feeds and feeding, EH295

The nutrition and health encyclopedia, Tver, David F., EH300

The nutrition desk reference, Garrison, Robert H., EH299

Nutritive value of American foods in common units, Adams, Catherine F., EH302

Nutting, M. Adelaide. *History of nursing,* EH286

Nutting, Wallace. *Furniture treasury (mostly of American origin),* BG119

Nuwe praktiese woordeboek, Engels-Afrikaans, Afrikaans-Engels, Terblanche, Hendrik Josephus, AC199

Nuyts, Jan. *A comprehensive bibliography of pragmatics,* BD65

Ny illustrerad svensk litteraturhistoria, BE1485

Nyasaland
  bibliography, DD119
  government publications, AF226

Nybakken, Elizabeth I. *American families,* CC234

Nybakken, Oscar Edward. *Greek and Latin in scientific terminology,* EA94

Nyberg, Cheryl Rae. *Subject compilations of state laws*, CK181

Nyeko, Balam. *Swaziland*, DD18

Nykysuomen sanakirja, Suomalaisen Kirjallisuuden Seura, AC320

Nynorsk etymologisk ordbog, Torp, Alf, AC622

Nyrop, Richard. *Rwanda*, DD62

Nysæter, Egil. *Norske arkivkatalogar*, DC465

Nytt norsk forfatterleksikon, Dahl, Willy, BE1340

Nyvall, Robert F. *Field crop diseases handbook*, EJ58

O conto brasileiro e sua crítica, Gomes, Celuta Moreira, BE931

Ó Cuív, Brian. *A literary history of Ireland from earliest times to the present day*, BE803

O. Henry awards, BE483

Ó hÓgáin, Dáithí. *Myth, legend & romance*, CF89

Ó Maoláin, Ciarán. *Latin American political movements*, CJ97

—— *The radical right*, CJ79, CJ80

OAG business travel planner, CL394

OAG travel planner, hotel & motel red book, CL394

Oak Ridge Associated Universities. *Industrial energy use data book*, EK221

Oakes, Elizabeth H. *Guide to social science resources in women's studies*, CA5

Oakley, Stewart P. *Scandinavian history, 1520–1970*, DC74

Oakman, Robert L. *Computer methods for literary research*, BE6

Oaks, Robert. *A research guide to Congress*, CJ196

O'Bannon, Loran S. *Dictionary of ceramic science and engineering*, EK265

Obdeijn, Herman. *The political role of Catholic and Protestant missions in the colonial partition of Black Africa*, DD87

Ober, Kenneth H. *Bibliography of modern Icelandic literature in translation*, BE1287

Oberg, Erik. *Machinery's handbook*, EK245

Oberlin College. Library. *Spanish drama collection in the Oberlin College Library*, BE1467

Oberman, Cerise. *Theories of bibliographic education*, AK229

Obermeyer-Marnach, Eva. *Österreichisches biographisches Lexikon 1815–1950*, AH169

Oberösterreichischen Landesarchiv. *Bibliographie zur oberösterreichischen Geschichte, 1891–1926*, DC92

Oberschelp, Reinhard. *Gesamtverzeichnis des deutschsprachigen Schrifttums (GV); 1911–1965*, AA647

Obituaries, Jarboe, Betty, AH5

Obituaries from the Times 1951–1960, AH32

Obituaries from the Times 1961–1970, AH33

Obituaries from the Times 1971–1975, AH34

Obituaries index II, AH18

Obituary notices of Fellows of the Royal Society, Royal Society (Great Britain), EA182, EA189, EH219

Obituary prior to 1800, Musgrave, William, AH237

Obituary record of graduates, Yale University, AH61

Objartel, Georg. *Deutsches Wörterbuch*, AC407

Obojski, Robert. *Catalogue of the world's most popular coins*, BG191

—— *Illustrated encyclopedia of world coins*, BG178

Obolensky, Dimitri. *An introduction to Russian language and literature*, BD186, BE1382

Obras de referencia de América Latina, Geoghegan, Abel Rodolfo, AA349

Obraz współczesnej literatury polskiej, 1884–[1934], Czachowski, Kasimierz, BE1349

Obreen, Henri. *Bibliographie de l'histoire de Belgique*, DC100

O'Brien, Betty A. *Religion index two*, BC14

O'Brien, Catherine. *Subject index to Current population reports*, CG97

O'Brien, Elmer J. *Religion index two*, BC14

—— *Theology in transition*, BC220

O'Brien, Jacqueline Wasserman. *The lively arts information directory*, BH14

—— *Statistics sources*, CG68

O'Brien, James G. *Elder neglect and abuse*, CC71

O'Brien, Nancy P. *Core list of books and journals in education*, CB16

—— *Test construction*, CD70

O'Brien, R. L. *Welding handbook*, EK249

O'Brien, Robert. *The encyclopedia of alcoholism*, CC125

—— *The encyclopedia of drug abuse*, CC124

—— *The encyclopedia of New England*, DB153

O'Brien, Robert Alfred. *Spanish plays in English translation*, BE1468

O'Brien, Steven. *American political leaders*, CJ158

O'Brien, Thomas C. *Corpus dictionary of Western churches*, BC234

—— *Encyclopedic dictionary of religion*, BC60

O'Brien, Tim. *The amusement park guide*, BK126

Observatoire de Strasbourg. *Acronyms & abbreviations in astronomy, space sciences, & related fields*, EC33

—— *Astronomy, space sciences and related organizations of the world*, EC44

Observatories, EC47

The observer's handbook, Royal Astronomical Society of Canada, EC57

Obshchee i prikladnoe i͡azykoznanie, BD7

Obshchee iazikoznanie, BD7

Obshchie bibliografi russkikh knig grazhdanskoĭ pechati, 1708–1955, Gosudarstvennai͡a publichnai͡a biblioteka imeni M.E. Saltykova-Shchedrina, AA63, AA796, AD143

Obshchie bibliografii russkikh periodicheskikh izdaniĭ, 1703–1954, i materialy po statistike russkoĭ periodicheskoĭ pechati, Gosudarstvennai͡a publichnai͡a biblioteka imeni M.E. Saltykova-Shchedrina, AD143

L'obsolète, Duchesne, Alain, AC377

Obst, Fritz Jürgen. *The completely illustrated atlas of reptiles and amphibians for the terrarium*, EG252

Obudho, Constance E. *Black-white racial attitudes*, CC372

Obudho, Robert A. *Afro-American demography and urban issues*, CC373

—— *Demography, urbanization, and spatial planning in Kenya*, DD166

Obzor na arkhivnite fondove, kolekt͡sii i edinichni postŭpleniĭa, sŭkhraiàvani v Bŭlgarski istoricheski arkhiv, Bŭlgarski istoricheski arkhiv, DC117

O'Callaghan, T. C. *Bibliography of theses in geology, 1965–66*, EF44

Ocampo, Aurora M. *Diccionario de escritores mexicanos*, BE915

—— *Diccionario de escritores mexicanos, siglo XX*, BE907

Ocampo López, Javier. *Historiografía y bibliografía de la emancipación del Nuevo Reino de Granada*, DB367

O'Carroll, Michael. *Theotokos*, BC403

Occasional paper, International Monetary Fund, CH163

—— Tropical Science Center (San José, Costa Rica), DB302

The occult in the western world, Kies, Cosette N., CD130

Occultism, AL73, CD137

bibliography, CD130

encyclopedias, CD134

Occupation and health, EH409

Occupational costume in England …, Cunnington, Cecil Willett, BG99

Occupational education, CB209, CB368, CH697

bibliography, CB351

dictionaries, CB172

Occupational education, CB258, CB297

Occupational health, BF127, EH409, EH426

Occupational outlook handbook. Vocational careers sourcebook, CB214

Occupational outlook handbook, CH704

—— United States. Bureau of Labor Statistics, CB208, CH707

Occupational outlook quarterly, CH704

Occupational safety and health, Pease, Elizabeth Sue, EH403

Occupations, CB211, CH692, CH693, CH696, CH699, CH700, CH701, CH703, CH704, CH705, CH708, CJ109

bibliography, CB208, CH707

databases, CB210, CB213

directories, CH694

fiction, BE1269

handbooks, CB214, CD129, CH702, CH706

Ocean world encyclopedia, Groves, Donald G., EF218

Oceania

atlases, CL367, CL368

bibliography, AA950, CE114, CE115, DF1, DF2, DF3, DF5, DF6, DF7, DF8, DF10, DF12

bibliography of bibliography, AA77

biography, AH382, AH383, AH384, AH385

filmography, DF4

guides, DF12

handbooks, DF19

library catalogs, CE115, DF10

manuscripts and archives, DF14, DF15

newspapers, AE4

periodicals, AD213, DF2

statistics, CG38, CG45, CG370, CG434

bibliography, CG376

Oceania (by subject)

anthropology and ethnology, CE114, DF5

art, BG12

bibliography, BG8

censuses

handbooks, CG38

economic conditions

bibliography, CH202

foreign relations, DF18

history, DF9, DF16, DF17

law, CK234, CK236

music, BJ322

politics and government, CJ414, CJ446

religion, BC370

Oceania, Oliver, Douglas L., CE116

Oceania, a regional study, DF19

Oceanic abstracts, EF214

Oceanic abstracts with indexes, EF214

Oceanic citation journal with abstracts, EF214

Oceanic index, EF214

Oceanic languages, BD232

Oceanic Research Institute. *Oceanic abstracts*, EF214

Oceanographic abstracts, EF215

Oceanographic abstracts and bibliography, EF215

Oceanographic abstracts and oceanographic bibliography section, EF215

Oceanographic bibliography, EF215

Oceanographic index, Sears, Mary, EF210, EF211, EF212

Oceanographic literature review, EF215

Oceanography

abstract journals, EF214

atlases, CL290, CL296, EF224, EF226

bibliography, EF213

biography, EF218, EF221

databases, EF214

dictionaries, EF220

directories, EF222

encyclopedias, EF216, EF218, EF219

handbooks, EF223

indexes, EF210, EF211, EF212

library catalogs, EF209, EF213

Oceanography (by subject)

study and teaching, EF151

Oceans, CL63, DA8, EF10

atlases, CL290, CL296, EF224, EF225, EF226

encyclopedias, EF217

handbooks, CH466

nomenclature, CL171

Oceans Institute of Canada. *Maritime affairs—a world handbook*, CH466

Ocelli nominum, Fitzgerald, Wilma, AA197

Ochieng', William R. *Modern history of Kenya, 1895–1980*, DD166

—— *Themes in Kenyan history*, DD166

Ochoa, George. *A cast of thousands*, BH205

Ochsenbein, François. *Sky catalogue 2000.0*, EC72

Ockeloen, G. *Catalogus dari buku-buku jang diterbitkan di Indonesia*, AA901
Ockerman, Herbert W. *Food science sourcebook*, EJ171
Ockert, Roy A. *History and theories of working-class movements*, CH631
O'Clair, Robert. *The Norton anthology of modern poetry*, BE332, BE506
OCLC. *United States Newspaper Program national union list*, AE32
•*OCLC education library*, CB17
O'Clery, Conor. *The dictionary of political quotations on Ireland, 1886–1987*, CJ377, DC409
O'Connell, Agnes N. *Women in psychology*, CD52
O'Connell, J. B. *The Roman martyrology*, BC426
O'Connell, Matthew J. *Dictionary of proper names and places in the Bible*, BC149
O'Connell, Merrilyn Rogers. *A bibliography on historical organization practices*, BF117
O'Connell, Susan M. *AAAS science book list, 1978–1986*, EA27
—— *Best science books & A-V materials for children*, EA34
O'Connor, Ann. *Congress A to Z*, CJ204
O'Connor, Anthony M. *Urbanization in tropical Africa*, CC300
O'Connor, Karen. *Public interest law groups*, CK153
O'Connor, Susan J. *Detailed statistics on the urban and rural population of Cuba, 1950 to 2010*, CG170
Ocran, Emanuel Benjamin. *Ocran's acronyms*, EA97
Ocran's acronyms, Ocran, Emanuel Benjamin, EA97
Odada, J. E. O. *Socio-economic profiles*, DD166
Odagiri, Hiroko. *The Princeton companion to classical Japanese literature*, BE1588
Odagiri, Susumu. *Nihon kindai bungaku daijiten*, BE1589
O'Danachair, Caoimhin. *A bibliography of Irish ethnology and folk tradition*, CF81
O'Day, Alan. *Irish historical documents since 1800*, DC415
Odd, Gilbert E. *Encyclopedia of boxing*, BK70
O'Dea, Geraldine. *A source book of Irish government*, CJ378
Odelain, O. *Dictionary of proper names and places in the Bible*, BC149
Odell, George Clinton Densmore. *Annals of the New York stage*, BH105
Odell, Robin. *New murderers' who's who*, CK254
O'Dell, Sterg. *Chronological list of prose fiction in English printed in England and other countries, 1475–1640*, BE679, BE680
Odishaw, Hugh. *Handbook of physics*, ED33
O'Donnol, Shirley Miles. *American costume, 1915–1970*, BH90
O'Donoghue, David James. *The poets of Ireland*, BE807
O'Donoghue, Michael. *The literature of mineralogy*, EF172
O'Dowd, Mary. *Sources for early modern Irish history, 1534–1641*, DC410
O'Dwyer's directory of corporate communications, CH555
O'Dwyer's directory of public relations firms, CH567
OED, AC30
OERI directory of computer tapes, United States. Office of Educational Research and Improvement, CB147
Oerke, Bess Viola. *An illustrated history of those frills and furbelows of fashion which have come to be known as: accessories of dress*, BG110
Oesterley, Hermann. *Historisch-geographisches Wörterbuch des deutschen Mittelalters*, CL191
Oesterreichische Bibliographie, AA574
Oesterreichische Bibliographie. Reihe A, AA575
Oettinger, Eduard Maria. *Moniteur des dates*, AH35
Oetzel, Roberta M. *NeuralSource*, EK157
Ofcansky, Thomas P. *British East Africa, 1856–1963*, DD108
Ofeigsson, Jón. *Íslandsk-dansk ordbog*, AC506

Office for Official Publications of the European Communities. *Directory of community legislation in force and other acts of the community institutions*, CK203
Office-holders in modern Britain, CJ344
Office of Educational Research and Improvement *directory of computer tapes*, CB147
Office practice handbooks, CH86, CH87, CH88, CH90
Officer's guide, CJ629
Officers of the army and navy (regular) who served in the Civil War, Powell, William Henry, CJ647
Officers of the army and navy (volunteer) who served in the Civil War, CJ647
The official ABMS directory of board certified medical specialists, EH164
The official atlas of the Civil War, United States. War Dept, DB123
Official baseball guide, BK61
Official Catholic directory, BC411
Official code of Georgia annotated, Georgia. [Laws, etc.], CK179
Official congressional directory, United States. Congress, CJ134, CJ215, CJ217, CJ221
The official encyclopedia of bridge, BK130
Official export guide, CH146
Official gazette of the United States Patent and Trademark Office. Patents, EA259, EA264
Official gazette of the United States Patent and Trademark Office. Trademarks, EA265
Official gazettes, AF6, AF170
The official GRE/CGS directory of graduate programs, CB301
The official guide to MBA programs, admissions, & careers, CH81
The official guide to U.S. law schools, CK154
The official hotel red book and directory, CJ394
Official methods of analysis of the Association of Official Analytical Chemists, EE84, EJ59
Official military atlas of the Civil War, United States. War Dept, DB106
The official museum directory, AL90, BF116, EA217
Official National Football League record & fact book, National Football League, BK77
Official NBA guide, BK66
Official place names in the Republic of South Africa and in South-west Africa, CL156
Official publication, Association of American Feed Control Officials, EJ110
Official publications in Britain, Butcher, David, AF176
Official publications of British East Africa, Conover, Helen F., DD108
—— Library of Congress. African Section, AF223, DD108
—— Walker, Audrey A., DD108
Official publications of French Equatorial Africa, Library of Congress. African Section, AF224
Official publications of French West Africa, Conover, Helen F., AF230
Official publications of Sierra Leone and Gambia, Library of Congress. African Section, AF225
Official publications of Somaliland, 1941–1959, Conover, Helen F., DD207
—— Library of Congress. General Reference and Bibliography Division, AF237
Official publications of the Soviet Union and Eastern Europe, 1945–1980, AF165
Official publications of Western Europe, AF164
Official publishing, Cherns, J. J., AF3
Official record, United States. Department of Agriculture. Division of Publications, EJ92
Official records of the American civil war, DB106
Official records of the Union and Confederate Navies in the War of Rebellion, DB106
Official red book of United States coins, BG195
Official register of the United States, CJ140
Official rules of sports & games, BK45
The official United States golf course directory and guide, BK85
The official United States Tennis Association yearbook and tennis guide with the official rules, United States Tennis Association, BK104

The official Washington post index, AE116
Official who's who among students in American universities and colleges, CB332
The official World Wildlife Fund guide to endangered species of North America, EG237
Official year book - Malaysia, CG413
The official year book of the Church of England, BC333
Official year book of the Commonwealth of Australia, CG436
Official year book of the Union and of Basutoland, Bechuanaland Protectorate and Swaziland, CG357
Official yearbook of Australia, CG436
Officieel jaarboek van de belgische pers, AD82
Offord, M. H. *Using French synonyms*, AC360
Oficina Literária Afrânio Coutinho. *Enciclopédia de literatura brasileira*, BE929
Ofori, Patrick E. *Black African traditional religions and philosophy*, BC34, BC497
—— *Christianity in tropical Africa*, BC221, BC497
—— *Islam in Africa south of the Sahara*, BC497
—— *Retrospective index to Nigerian doctoral dissertations and masters theses, 1895–1980*, AG48
Ogareff, Val. *Leaders of the Soviet Republics, 1955–1972*, CJ392
Ogawa, Dennis M. *The Japanese in Hawaii*, CC408
Ogbondah, Chris W. *The press in Nigeria*, AD173
Ogden, Tom. *Two hundred years of the American circus*, BH11
Ogilvie, Grania. *The dictionary of South African painters and sculptors, including Namibia*, BF142
Ogilvie, Marilyn Bailey. *Women in science*, EA180
Ogot, B. A. *Kenya*, DD48
Ogsberg, Sally R. *Environmental protection directory*, EK73
Ogston, R. *Concise illustrated dental dictionary*, EH255
Ohadedara, Aditya. *A bibliography of Indology*, CE109
O'Hara, Frederic J. *A guide to publications of the Executive branch*, AF131
O'Hara, Frederick M. *Handbook of United States economic and financial indicators*, CH236
O'Hara, Georgina. *Encyclopedia of fashion*, BG98
O'Higgins, Paul. *A bibliography of the literature on British and Irish labour law*, CH677
Ohio. [Laws, etc.]. *Page's Ohio revised code annotated*, CK179
Ohio State University. *Current digest of the post-Soviet press*, AE68
Ohio State University. Center for Medieval and Renaissance Studies. *Old English newsletter*, BE729
Ohles, John F. *Biographical dictionary of American educators*, CB130
—— *Private colleges and universities*, CB280, CB281
—— *Public colleges and universities*, CB281
Ohles, Shirley M. *Private colleges and universities*, CB280, CB281
—— *Public colleges and universities*, CB281
Ohly, Rajmund. *Primary technical dictionary English-Swahili*, AC757
Ohta, Thaddeus Y. *Japanese national government publications in the Library of Congress*, AF252
Õigekeelsuse sõnaraamat, Nurm, E., AC305
Oil and gas international yearbook, EK307
Oil and petroleum yearbook, EK307
Oizon, René. *Atlas départemental*, CL328
Ok, Necdet. *1928–1965 [i.e., Bin dokuz yüz yirmi sekiz, bin dokuz yüz altmışbeş] yılları arasında Türkiyede basılmış bibliyografyaların bibliyografyası*, AA68
Okie, Howard Pitcher. *Old silver and old Sheffield plate*, BG147
Okinshevich, Leo. *Latin America in Soviet writings*, DB260
Oklahoma. [Laws, etc.]. *Oklahoma statutes annotated*, CK179

Oklahoma statutes annotated, Oklahoma. [Laws, etc.], CK179

Ökonomisches Wörterbuch Aussenwirtschaft, CH126

Okpaku, Joseph. *Arts and civilization of black and African peoples*, DD58

Øksnevad, Reidar. *Norsk litteraturhistorisk bibliografi, 1900–1945*, BE1343

Okuka, Miloš. *A bibliography of recent literature on Macedonian, Serbo-Croatian, and Slovene languages*, BD189

OLAC (Organization). *Enciclopédia de literatura brasileira*, BE929

Ólafur Þ. Kristjánsson. *Íslenzkar æviskrár frá lannámstímum til ársloka 1965*, AH254

Ólason, Páll Eggert. *Íslenzkar æviskrár frá landnámstímum til ársloka 1940*, AH254

Olbrich, Harald. *Lexikon der Kunst*, BF74

Olbrich, Wilhelm. *Der Romanführer*, BE195

Olby, Robert C. *Companion to the history of modern science*, EA255

Olcott, Nicholas. *State constitutional conventions, commissions & amendments, 1959–1978*, CK174

Old age pensions, CH503

Old and Middle English language studies, Tajima, Matsuji, BD102

Old and Middle English poetry to 1500, Beale, Walter H., BE695

Old English and Middle English poetry, Pearsall, Derek Albert, BE718

Old English bibliography, BE729

Old English language, Robinson, Fred C., DA138

Old English newsletter, BE728, BE729

Old English word studies, Cameron, Angus, BD99

Old handmade lace, Jackson, Emily, BG160

Old Javanese-English dictionary, Zoetmulder, P. J., AC560

Old master paintings in North America, Morse, John D., BF305

Old master print references, Mason, Lauris, BF363

Old Norse-Icelandic studies, Bekker-Nielsen, Hans, BD129, BE1083, DA138

Old Norse language *see* **Icelandic language**

Old Norse literature *see* **Icelandic literature; Sagas; Scalds and scaldic poetry**

Old pewter, Cotterell, Howard Herschel, BG150

Old silver and old Sheffield plate, Okie, Howard Pitcher, BG147

The old South, Green, Fletcher M., DB156

Old Testament abstracts, BC123, DC124

Old Testament pseudepigrapha, Charlesworth, James H., BC94

Older Americans information directory, CC87

The older volunteer, Bull, C. Neil, CC63

Older women in 20th-century America, Borenstein, Audrey, CC61

Older workers, Rix, Sara E., CC101

Oldfield, J. E. *Feeds & nutrition*, EJ122

Oldham, Keith B. *An atlas of functions*, EB68

Olea, Ricardo A. *Geostatistical glossary and multilingual dictionary*, EF78

O'Leary, Stella. *Classical scholarship*, BE997, DA93

O'Leary, Timothy J. *Circum-Mediterranean peasantry*, CE97

—— *Ethnographic bibliography of North America*, CC412, CC419

—— *Ethnographic bibliography of South America*, CE81

—— *Lapps ethnographic bibliography*, CE94

O'Leary, William M. *Practical handbook of microbiology*, EG54, EG56

Oleksiw, Susan. *Reader's guide to the classic British mystery*, BE266

Olevnik, Peter P. *American higher education*, CB215

—— *The financing of American higher education*, CB226

Oli, Gian Carlo. *Nouvo vocabolario illustrato della lingua italiana*, AC525

—— *Vocabolario illustrato della lingua italiana*, AC525

Olitzky, Kerry M. *Reform Judaism in America*, BC559

Oliver, Derek. *The international encyclopedia of hard rock & heavy metal*, BJ355

Oliver, Donna L. *The anti-cult movement in America*, BC32

Oliver, Douglas L. *Oceania*, CE116

Oliver, Elizabeth. *Researcher's guide to British film & television collections*, BH181

Oliver, John E. *The encyclopedia of climatology*, EF144

Oliver, Roland Anthony. *The Cambridge encyclopedia of Africa*, DD50

—— *The Cambridge history of Africa*, DD57

Oliver, W. H. *The Oxford history of New Zealand*, DF45

Ollard, Sidney Leslie. *Dictionary of English church history*, BC332

Ollis, W. David. *Comprehensive organic chemistry*, EE118

Ollivier, Louis. *Dictionary of animal production terminology*, EJ114

Olmsted, Elizabeth H. *Music Library Association catalog of cards for printed music, 1953–1972*, BJ63

Olmsted, Hugh M. *Translations and translating*, BD89

Olney, P. J. S. *International zoo yearbook*, EG233

-ologies & -isms, AC79

Oloruntimehin, Benjamin. *Arts and civilization of black and African peoples*, DD58

Olsen, Wallace C. *Agricultural economics and rural sociology*, EJ6

—— *The literature of agricultural engineering*, EJ3

—— *The literature of animal science and health*, EJ98

Olson, Ann. *Women in the world*, CC582

Olson, James Stuart. *Dictionary of the Vietnam War*, DE279

—— *Historical dictionary of the 1920s*, DB133

—— *Historical dictionary of the New Deal*, DB131

—— *Historical dictionary of the Spanish Empire, 1402–1975*, DC515

—— *The history of cancer*, EH26

Olson, Kent C. *Finding the law*, CK115

—— *How to find the law*, CK115

—— *Legal research in a nutshell*, CK115

Olson, May E. *The German language press of the Americas*, AE1

Olson, Nancy. *Cataloging service bulletin index*, AK195

Olson, Stan. *National guide to foundation funding in higher education*, CB365

—— *National guide to funding for libraries and information services*, AK64

Olson, William J. *Britain's elusive empire in the Middle East, 1900–1921*, DE37

Olsson, Bernt. *Litteraturens historia i Sverige*, BE1484

Olsson, Nils William. *Swedish passenger arrivals in New York, 1820–1850*, AJ43

—— *Swedish passenger arrivals in U.S. ports, 1820–1850 (except New York)*, AJ43

—— *Tracing your Swedish ancestry*, AJ43

Olton, Roy. *The international relations dictionary*, CJ30

Olver, F. W. J. *Bessel functions*, EB94

Olympic Games, BK92, BK93, BK94, BK95

bibliography, BK6

The Olympics, Mallon, Bill, BK6

The Olympics factbook, BK92

O'Malley, John W. *Catholicism in early modern history*, BC413, DC28

O'Malley, William T. *Anglo-Irish literature*, BE797

Oman, Mary. *Anthropological and cross-cultural themes in mental health*, EH372

Oman, DE238

Oman, Clements, Frank A., DE237

Oman and southeastern Arabia, Shannon, Michael Owen, DE238

Omara-Otunnu, Amii. *Politics and the military in Uganda, 1890–1985*, DD239

Ombudsman, CJ55

O'Meara, Dan. *The struggle for South Africa*, DD208

[Omega]—bibliography of mathematical logic, EB15

Omni gazetteer of the United States of America, CL109

On account of sex, Heim, Kathleen M., AK14, AK73

—— Phenix, Katharine, AK73

On Canadian literature, 1806–1960, Bell, Inglis Freeman, BE826

—— Watters, Reginald Eyre, BE826

On cassette, AA385

On food and cooking, McGee, Harold, EJ219

On Internet, CH495

On mathematics and mathematicians, Moritz, Robert Edouard, EB55

On the screen, Fisher, Kim N., BH160

On the trail of the UCC, BC384

Oncogenes and growth factors abstracts, EG14

Ondrasik, Allison. *DataMap*, CG16

The one hundred best colleges for African-American students, CB310

One hundred books famous in science, Horblit, Harrison D., EA232

One hundred families of flowering plants, EG176

One hundred libraries statistical survey 1985–86, AK95

One hundred noteworthy firsts in juvenile literature, AA245

One hundred twenty years of American education, CB135

One hundred years of economic statistics, Liesner, Thelma, CH158

One-parent children, the growing minority, Gouke, Mary Noel, CC145

O'Neill, Hugh B. *Companion to Chinese history*, DE143

O'Neill, Patrick. *German literature in English translation*, BE1241

O'Neill, Patrick Geoffrey. *Dictionary of Japanese Buddhist terms*, BC478

—— *Japanese names*, AC556

O'Neill, Robert Keating. *English-language dictionaries, 1604–1900*, AC6

Congressional Quarterly's guide to the presidency, CJ178

Onions, C. T. *Oxford dictionary of English etymology*, AC58

—— *A Shakespeare glossary*, BE772, BE773

—— *The shorter Oxford English dictionary on historical principles*, AC31

Online public access catalog directory, AK209

Online searching, AK193, CA43

bibliography, AK189

Online searching (by subject)

chemistry, EE9

Only the best, CB176

Onofrei, Neonila. *Bibliografia românească modernă, 1831–1918*, AA781

—— *Bibliografia românească veche, 1508–1830*, AA780

Onomástica geral da geografia brasileira, CL183

Onomasticon, Ferrari, Luigi, BE1312

Onomasticon goedelicum locorum et tribuum Hiberniae et Scotiae, Hogan, Edmund, CL202, CL208

L'onomastique française, Mulon, Marianne, CL188

Ontario and the Canadian North, Morley, W. F. E., DB213

Ontario Historical Society. *Bibliography of Ontario history, 1867–1976*, DB212

Ontario royal commissions and commissions of inquiry, 1867–1978, Tampold, Ana, AF155

—— Waintman, Susan, AF155

Ontario since 1867, Bishop, Olga B., DB212

ONTERIS, CB57

Ontiveros, Suzanne R. *Global terrorism*, CJ549

—— *Women in the Third World*, CC595

De ontwikkelingsgang der Nederlandsche letterkunde, Winkel, Jan te, BE1336

Ooteghem, Jules van. *Bibliotheca graeca et latina à l'usage des professeurs des humanités gréco-latines*, BE1005

OPAC directory, AK209

O'Pecko, Michael T. *The twentieth-century German novel*, BE1268

Opelík, Jiří. *Slovník českých spisovatelů*, BE1105

Open secrets, Makinson, Larry, CJ248

Opera, BJ234, BJ235, BJ236, BJ237, BJ238, BJ239, BJ240, BJ243, BJ244, BJ246, BJ249, BJ251, BJ254, BJ255, BJ256, BJ257
  bibliography, BJ242
  biography
    bibliography, BJ219
  discography, BJ381
  encyclopedias, BJ247, BJ248, BJ250, BJ252, BJ253
  librettos, BE464
  plot summaries
    indexes, BJ245

Opera, Marco, Guy A., BJ242

Opera and concert singers, Farkas, Andres, BJ219

Opera handbook, Lazarus, John, BJ247

Opera plot index, Studwell, William E., BJ246

Opera production, Eaton, Quaintance, BJ235

Operations research
  indexes, EB21, EK160

Operettas, BJ252

Operti, Piero. *Dizionario storico della letteratura italiana*, BE1302

Opfell, Olga S. *Queens, empresses, grand duchesses, and regents*, CJ318
  —— *Women prime ministers and presidents*, CJ67

Ophthalmic drug facts, EH346

Ophthalmic eponyms, Thornton, Spencer P., EH126

Ophthalmology, EH346
  dictionaries, EH110, EH113
  eponyms, EH126

Opie, Iona Archibald. *A dictionary of superstitions*, CF53
  —— *Oxford dictionary of nursery rhymes*, BE721

Opie, Peter. *Oxford dictionary of nursery rhymes*, BE721

Opinion Research Service (U.S.). *American public opinion index*, CJ485

Opis na starite pechatani bulgarski knigi, 1802–1877 g, Pogorelov, Valerii Aleksandrovich, AA587

Opisanie izdaniĭ, napechatannykh pri Petre Pervom, Gosudarstvennaia publichnaia biblioteka imeni M.E. Saltykova-Shchedrina, AA789, AA791

Opitz, Glenn B. *Dictionary of American painters, sculptors & engravers*, BF154
  —— *Dictionary of American sculptors*, BF398
  —— *Mantle Fielding's dictionary of American painters, sculptors & engravers*, BF154

Opitz, Helmut. *World guide to libraries*, AK121

Oppelt, Norman T. *Guide to prehistoric ruins of the Southwest*, BG54
  —— *Southwestern pottery*, BG54

Oppenheim, Micha Falk. *Judaica reference sources*, BC513

Opschoor, Johannes. *Botswana's environment*, DD130

Optical Society of America. *Handbook of optics*, ED37

Optics, ED37

Options for replacing and reformatting deteriorated materials, Banks, Jennifer, AK238

Optometry
  dictionaries, EH121

Opubor, Alfred. *Arts and civilization of black and African peoples*, DD58

Opus, BJ388

Opyt rossiĭskoi bibliografiĭ, Sopikov, Vasiliĭ Stephanovich, AA790

Oraham, Alexander Joseph. *Oraham's dictionary of the stabilized and enriched Assyrian language and English*, AC772

Oraham's dictionary of the stabilized and enriched Assyrian language and English, Oraham, Alexander Joseph, AC772

Oral history, DB33, DB36, DD11
  bibliography, DC332
  directories, AK85

Oral history (by country or region)
  United States, BF59

Oral history (by subject)
  art, BF59

Oral history, Perks, Robert, DC332

Oral history collections, McMullin, Ruth, DB36
  —— Meckler, Alan M., DB33, DB36

Oral history index, Wasserman, Ellen A., DB33

Oral interpretation of literature, Doll, Howard D., BE14

Oran, Daniel. *Law dictionary for nonlawyers*, CK40
  —— *Oran's dictionary of the law*, CK40

Oran's dictionary of the law, Oran, Daniel, CK40

Oranskiĭ, I. M. *Die neuiranischen Sprachen der Sowjetunion*, BD196

Orators, BE346, BE358, CC530

Orbase, Lily O. *Bibliography of Philippine bibliographies, 1962–1985*, AA82

Orbell, John. *A guide to tracing the history of a business*, CH398

Orbis, CJ94

Orbis geographicus, CL56

Orbis Latinus, Grässe, Johann Georg Theodor, CL103

Orchard, Bernard. *Catholic commentary*, BC177

Orchestral catalogue, BJ92

Orchestral music, BJ293, BJ295

Orchin, Milton. *The vocabulary of organic chemistry*, EE146

Ordaz, Luis. *Repertorio selecto del teatro hispanoamericano contemporaneo*, BE900

Ordbog over det danske sprog, Danske sprog- og litteraturselskab, AC285

Ordbog over det gamle norsk sprog, Fritzner, Johan, AC504

Ordbok öfver svenska medeltids-språket, Söderwall, Knut Fredrik, AC763

Ordbok öfver svenska språket, Svenska akademien, AC764

Order statistics, EB9

Orders and decorations, AL179, AL181, AL182, AL184, AL188, AL189
  military, AL183, AL185

Orders and decorations, Měřička, Václav, AL184

Orders and decorations of all nations, Werlich, Robert, AL188

Orders and families of recent mammals of the world, EG304

Orders, decorations and insignia, military and civil, Wyllie, Robert E., AL189

Orders, medals and decorations of Britain and Europe in colour, Hieronymussen, Poul Ohm, AL181

Ordnance Survey. *The Ordnance Survey gazetteer of Great Britain*, CL139

The Ordnance Survey gazetteer of Great Britain, CL139

Ordway, Frederick I. *Annotated bibliography of space science and technology, with an astronomical supplement*, EK24

Oreggioni, Alfredo F. *Diccionario de literatura uruguaya*, BE958

Oregon. [Laws, etc.]. *Oregon revised statutes annotated*, CK179

Oregon revised statutes annotated, Oregon. [Laws, etc.], CK179

O'Reilly, Patrick. *Bibliographie de Tahiti et de la Polynésie française*, DF51
  —— *Bibliographie méthodique, analytique et critique de la Nouvelle-Calédonie*, DF41
  —— *Bibliographie méthodique, analytique et critique des Nouvelles-Hébrides*, DF52
  —— *Calédoniens*, AH382
  —— *Hébridais*, AH383, DF52
  —— *Tahitiens*, AH384

Orenstein, Ruth M. *Fulltext sources online*, AD271

Ores, EF203
  bibliography, EF175

Orgambide, Pedro G. *Enciclopedia de la literatura argentina*, BE920

Organ, Troy Wilson. *An index to Aristotle in English translation*, BB57

Organic-chemical drugs and their synonyms, Negwer, Martin, EH330

Organic chemical process encyclopedia, Sittig, Marshall, EE144

Organic compounds
  handbooks, EE148
  melting points, EE147

Organic gardening, EJ21

Organic name reactions, Krauch, Helmut, EE137

Organic plant protection, EJ21

Organic syntheses, EE145

Organisation for Economic Co-operation and Development. *Directory of development research and training institutes in Europe*, AL79
  —— *Directory of non-governmental environment and development organisations in OECD member countries*, CH114
  —— *A study of the Soviet economy*, CH186

Organisch-chemische Arzneimittel und ihre Synonyma, EH330

Organizaciones no gubernamentales de Uruguay, Barreiro, Fernando, AL53

Organization behavior in American public administration, Payad, Aurora T., CJ472

Organization charts, CH603

Organization for Economic Cooperation and Development. Directorate for Scientific Affairs. *Directory of water pollution research laboratories*, EK94

Organization of African Unity. Scientific, Technical, and Research Commission. *West African international atlas*, CL338

Organization of American States. *Anuario interamericano de derechos humanos*, CK108
  —— *Boletin estadístico de la OEA*, CG121
  —— *Latin American prose in English translation*, BE885
  —— *Pan American book shelf*, AA471

Organization of American States. Columbus Memorial Library. *Creative literature of Trinidad and Tobago*, BE981

Organization of American States. General Secretariat. *Inter-American treaties and conventions*, CK88

Organization of the government of Canada, CJ304

Organizational behavior, CD128
  handbooks, CH602

Organizations, management, and control, Stout, Russell, CH609

Organizations master index, AL20

Organizing artists, BF102

Organizing your photographs, Robl, Ernest H., BF347

Organometallic compounds, EE120, EE128

Organophosphorus compounds, EE129

Orgelbrand, Samuel. *S. Orgelbranda Encyklopedja pow-szechna z ilustracjami i mapami*, AB77

Orgill, Andrew. *The Falklands War*, DB375

Oriental art, BF126
  —— Auboyer, Jeannine, BF35

Oriental bibliography, DE7

Oriental carpets, Erdmann, Kurt, BG166
  —— Thompson, Jon, BG165

Oriental dictionaries, Wajid, Mohammad, AC194

Oriental literatures *see* **Asian literatures**

Oriental rugs, Eiland, Murray L., BG165

Orientalische Bibliographie, DE7

Orientalische Kostüme, Tilke, Max, BG114

Origin and history of Irish names of places, Joyce, Patrick W., CL209

Origin and meaning of place names in Canada, Armstrong, George Henry, CL181

The origin of English surnames, Reaney, Percy Hide, AJ185

The original British theatre directory, BH87

Original index to art periodicals, Frick Art Reference Library, BF19

The original lists of persons of quality, emigrants, religious exiles, political rebels ... and others who went from Great Britain to the American plantations, Hotten, John Camden, AJ63

Originals, Amos, William, BE251, BE688

Origini e dottrina del fascismo, Evola, Niccoló Domenico, DC422

Origins, BC437

—— Partridge, Eric, AC58, AC60

Origins, evolution, and nature of the Cold War, Black, J. L., CJ7

Origins of chemical names, Flood, Walter Edgar, EE29

Origins of photography, Gernsheim, Alison, BF328

—— Gernsheim, Helmut, BF328

Orimoloye, S. A. *Biographia Nigeriana*, AH322

Oriol, William E. *Federal public policy on aging since 1960*, CC74

Orjuela, Héctor H. *Bibliografía de la poesía colombiana*, BE944, BE948

—— *Bibliografía del teatro colombiano*, BE945, BE948

—— *Fuentes generales para el studio de la literatura colombiana*, BE946

Ormis, Ján Vladimir. *Slovník slovenských pseudonymov*, AA165

Ormond, Richard. *Dictionary of British portraiture*, BF66

Ornamental plants, EG158

Orne, Jerrold. *The language of the foreign book trade*, AA276

Ornithology
  encyclopedias, EG254

Orovio, Helio. *Diccionario de la música cubana*, BJ154

Orozco Tenorio, José. *Las publicaciones periódicas mexicanas*, AD63

Orr, Leonard. *Catalogue checklist of English prose fiction, 1750–1800*, BE681

—— *A dictionary of critical theory*, BE85

—— *Research in critical theory since 1965*, BE52

Orr, Oliver H. *Guide to the study of the United States of America*, DB13

Orrick, Sarah. *Environmental profiles*, EK75

ORSTOM. *Sources d'information sur l'Afrique noire francophone et Madagascar*, DD40

Országh, László. *Angol-magyar keziszotar*, AC496

—— *A concise English-Hungarian dictionary*, AC496

—— *A concise Hungarian-English dictionary*, AC495

—— *Magyar-angol kéziszótár*, AC495

—— *A magyar nyelv értelmező szótára*, AC493

Országos Széchényi Könyvtár. *A magyar hírlapirodalom első századia, 1705–1805*, AD121

Orta Doğu Teknik Üniversitesi (Ankara, Turkey). *Graduate theses*, AG44

Ortamo, Anna-Maija. *Suomen aikakauslehdistön bibliografia 1782–1955*, AD89

Ortega, José. *Diccionario de la literatura boliviana*, BE922

Ortega Torres, José Joaquín. *Historia de la literatura colombiana*, BE947

Ortelius, Abraham. *Mapmakers of the sixteenth century and their maps*, CL273

Orth, Donald J. *Geographic names & the federal government*, CL99

Orthodontics, Weinberger, Bernhard Wolf, EH266

Orthodox church in Byzantine Empire, Hussey, Joan Mervyn, BC278

Orthodox Eastern Church. *Service book of the Holy Orthodox-Catholic Apostolic church*, BC450

Orthodox Eastern churches *see* **Eastern churches**

Ortiz, Patricia. *Amazonía ecuatoriana*, DB322

Ørvik, Nils. *Norwegian foreign policy*, DC466

O'Ryan, Jan Enrique. *Bibliografía guatemalteca de los siglos XVII y XVIII*, AA481

Osanka, Franklin Mark. *Sourcebook on pornography*, CC290

Osborn, Herbert. *A brief history of entomology*, EG336

Osborn, M. Livia. *A reference companion to the history of abnormal psychology*, CD101

Osborne, Arthur Leslie. *Dictionary of English domestic architecture*, BF241

Osborne, Harold. *The Oxford companion to art*, BF78

—— *The Oxford companion to the decorative arts*, BG20

—— *The Oxford companion to twentieth-century art*, BF89

—— *The Oxford dictionary of art*, BF90

Osborne, Richard H. *Centers for training in physical anthropology*, CE88

Osborne, Robert A. *60 years of the Oscar*, BH275

Osborn's concise law dictionary, Bone, Sheila, CK34

—— Rutherford, Leslie, CK34

Osburn, Charles B. *The present state of French studies*, BE1139

—— *Research and reference guide to French studies*, BE1129

Osburn, Margaret. *Population/family planning thesaurus*, CC254

Oscar movies, Pickard, Roy, BH275

Osebno kazalo, Munda, Jože, AH309

Osen, L. M. *Women in mathematics*, EB104

Oshana, Maryann. *Women of color*, CC611

Osier, Donald V. *A century of serial publications in psychology, 1850–1950*, CD12

Osifchin, Gary P. *The new members of congress almanac*, CJ220

Osiobe, Stephen A. *Nigerian universities dissertation abstracts*, AG47

Osipow, Samuel H. *Handbook of vocational psychology*, CD129

Osler, William. *Bibliotheca Osleriana*, EH206

Osler Library. *Bibliotheca Osleriana*, EH206

Osman, Madina M. *Somali-English dictionary*, AC725

Osmanische Bibliographie mit Besonderer Berücksichtigung der Türkei in Europa, Kornrumpf, Hans-Jürgen, DC61, DC536

Osmańczyk, Edmund Jan. *The encyclopedia of the United Nations and international agreements*, AF41

Osmond, Jonathan. *German reunification*, CJ332

Osofsky, Joy D. *Handbook of infant development*, CD87

Osol, Arthur. *Blakiston's Gould medical dictionary*, EH93

Ospina, Joaquín. *Diccionario biográfico y bibliográfico de Colombia*, AH133

Ośrodek Informacji Naukowej (Polska Akademia Nauk). *Biogramy uczonych polskich*, AH278

Ośrodek Przetwarzania Informacji. *Katalog rozpraw doktorskich i habilitacyjnych*, AG39

Oss, J. F. van. *Chemical technology*, EK50

Osselton, N. E. *Engels woordenboek*, AC296

L'Osservatore romano, weekly edition in English, BC437

Osso, Nyaknno. *Who's who in Nigeria*, AH323, DD196

Ossorguine-Bakounine, Tatiana. *L'emigration russe*, AD300

—— *L'émigration russe en Europe*, AD218

Ost, Leopold. *Karl Georgs Schlagwort-katalog*, AA642

Osteopathy, EH154

Oster, Daniel. *Dictionnaire de littérature française contemporaine*, BE1151

Oster Soussouev, Pierre. *Dictionnaire des citations françaises*, BE133

Östergren, Olof. *Nusvensk ordbok*, AC762

Osterlind, Steven J. *Evaluation resource handbook*, CD65

Österman, Jonny. *Physics handbook*, ED38

Österreich-Lexikon, DC96

Österreichische Bibliographie, AA649

Österreichische historische Bibliographie, DC94

Österreichische Nationalbibliothek. *200 Jahre Tageszeitung in Österreich, 1783–1983*, AE44

—— *Oesterreichische Bibliographie*, AA574

—— *Oesterreichische Bibliographie. Reihe A*, AA575

Österreichischen Statistisches Zentralamt. *Statistisches Jahrbuch für die Republik Österreich*, CG198

Österreichischer Amtskalender, CJ327

Österreichisches biographisches Lexikon 1815–1950, AH169

Österreichisches Personen Lexikon, Ackerl, Isabella, AH166

Österreichisches statistisches Handbuch, CG198

Österreichisches Statistisches Zentralamt. *Demographisches Jahrbuch Österreichs*, CG194

—— *Mikrozensus*, CG196

—— *Sozialstatistische Daten*, CG197

—— *Statistik in Österreich, 1918–1938*, CG195

Österreichs Presse, Werbung, Graphik Handbuch, AD81

Osterwalder, Marcus. *Dictionnaire des illustrateurs*, BF384

Osteuropäische Volkstrachten, Tilke, Max, BG114

Ostler, Rosemarie. *Theoretical syntax 1980–1990*, BD44

Ostracoda, EF239

Ostrander, W. L. *The centennial of the United States Military Academy at West Point, New York, 1802–1902*, CJ611

Ostroff, Harriet. *Index to personal names in the National union catalog of manuscript collections, 1959–1984*, DB34

Ostrow, Rona. *The dictionary of marketing*, CH581

Ostvold, Harold. *Literature of agricultural research*, EJ1

O'Súilleabháin, Seán. *Handbook of Irish folklore*, CF81

Oswald, Arthur. *English mediaeval architects*, BF261

Otchere, Freda E. *African studies thesaurus*, DD51

Othmer, Donald F. *Encyclopedia of chemical technology*, EK51, EK52

Otieno, James O. *Socio-economic profiles*, DD166

Otis Guernsey Burns Mantle theater yearbook, BE454

O'Toole, G. J. A. *The encyclopedia of American intelligence and espionage*, CJ541

O'Toole, James M. *Understanding archives and manuscripts*, AK188

O'Toole, Thomas E. *Guinea (Republic of Guinea/Conakry)*, DD48

Otruby, Mojmfra. *Čeští spisovatelé 19. a počátku 20. století*, BE1105

Ōtsuki, Fumihiko. *Dai-genkai*, AC549

Ott, J. Steven. *The Facts on File dictionary of nonprofit organization management*, AL10, CH615

Ottemiller, John H. *Ottemiller's index to plays in collections*, BE231

Ottemiller's index to plays in collections, Ottemiller, John H., BE231

Ottinger, Cecilia A. *Community college fact book*, CB337

Ottino, Giuseppe. *Bibliotheca bibliographica italica*, AA51, AA54

Ottley, George. *A bibliography of British railway history*, CH461

Otto, Eberhard. *Lexikon der Ägyptologie*, DA125

Otto, Johannes. *Bibliographie deutschsprachiger bevölkerungswissenschaftlicher Literatur, 1978–1984*, CG3, CG221

Otto, Mary L. *Administering grants, contracts, and funds*, AL129

Otto, Walter. *Handbuch der Archäologie*, DA81

Ottoman Turkish writers, Mitler, Louis, BE1491

Ottův slovník naučný, AB32

Ottův slovník naučný nové doby, Nemec, B., AB32

Ouellet, R. *Bas-Canada*, DB203

Oughton, Marguerita. *Geographers*, CL82

Oukada, Larbi. *Louisiana French*, BD159

An ounce of prevention, AK243

Our bodies, ourselves, CC95, CC564

Our Italian surnames, Fucilla, Joseph Guerin, AJ199

Our Sunday Visitor's Catholic encyclopedia, BC404

Ours, Robert M. *College football encyclopedia*, BK78

Ourselves, growing older, Boston Women's Health Book Collective, CC564

—— Doress-Worters, Paula Brown, CC95, CC564

—— Midlife and Older Women Book Project, CC564

—— Siegal, Diana Laskin, CC564

Ousby, Ian. *The Cambridge guide to literature in English,* BE608
Outdoor recreation, BK14, BK19, BK107, BK108
Outhwaite, William. *The Blackwell dictionary of twentieth-century social thought,* CA30
Outline and bibliographies of Oriental art, BF35
Outline of cultural materials, CE61
———— Murdock, George Peter, CE2, CE59, CE94, CE107
An outline of European architecture, Pevsner, Nikolaus, BF257
Outline of world cultures, Murdock, George Peter, BJ322, BJ328, CE2, CE59
Outlines of Chinese symbolism and art motives, BF179
Outre-mer, CG214
Outsider art, BG27
Outstanding women athletes, Woolum, Janet, BK41
Outward signs, West, Edward N., BC208
Ouvrages généraux de l'histoire de France, 1870–1959, DC143
Overesch, Manfred. *Chronik deutscher Zeitgeschichte,* DC260
Overzichten van de archieven en verzamelingen in de openbare archiefbewaarplaatsen in Nederland, DC458
Owen, Bill. *Big broadcast, 1920–1950,* BH311
Owen, Bobbi. *Costume design on Broadway,* BH120
———— *Lighting design on Broadway,* BH120
———— *Scenic design on Broadway,* BH120
Owen, Dolores B. *Abstracts and indexes in science and technology,* EA76
Owen, Gareth. *Atlas of world political flashpoints,* CJ72
Owen, H.G. *Atlas of continental displacement,* EF112
Owen, Nancy R. *Authors,* BE206
———— *Authors: critical & biographical references,* BE197
Owen, Wyn F. *Guide to graduate study in economics, agricultural economics, public administration, and doctoral programs in business administration in the United States and Canada,* CH79
Owens, Louis. *American Indian novelists,* BE550
Owens, Peter L. *Radical geography,* CL18
The Oxbridge directory of ethnic periodicals, CC336
Oxbridge directory of newsletters, AE37, BE43
Oxenhorn, Douglas. *Money for visual artists,* AL120, BF105
Oxenvad, Erik. *Nudansk ordbog,* AC286
Oxford. University. Committee for Advanced Studies. *Abstracts of dissertations for the degree of doctor of philosophy,* AG34
Oxford advanced learner's dictionary of current English, AC683
Oxford American dictionary, AC18
Oxford American prayer book commentary, Shepherd, Massey Hamilton, BC349
The Oxford annotated Apocrypha, BC94
Oxford annotated Bible, BC94
Oxford annotated Bible, with the Apocrypha, May, Herbert G., BC94
———— Metzger, Bruce Manning, BC94
The Oxford anthology of English literature, BE332, BE506
———— Kermode, Frank, BE618
The Oxford atlas, CL286
Oxford Bible atlas, BC200
Oxford Bibliographical Society. *Proceedings and papers,* AD104
Oxford book of ballads, Kinsley, James, BE632
Oxford book of English verse, Quiller-Couch, Arthur, BE720
Oxford book of military anecdotes, Hastings, Max, CJ591
The Oxford book of prayer, BC207
The Oxford book of vertebrates, Whiteley, Derek, EG238
Oxford books, Madan, Falconer, AA678
Oxford Cartographers Ltd. *Peters atlas of the world,* CL287
Oxford children's encyclopedia, AB21

Oxford classical dictionary, BE1014, DA103
Oxford companion to American literature, Hart, James David, BE431, BE435
The Oxford companion to American theatre, Bordman, Gerald Martin, BH64, BH65
The Oxford companion to animal behaviour, CD120
The Oxford companion to art, BF78, BF89, BF90
The Oxford companion to Australian folklore, CF99
The Oxford companion to Australian literature, Wilde, William H., BE860
The Oxford companion to Australian sport, BK27
Oxford companion to Canadian history and literature, Story, Norah, BE833
The Oxford companion to Canadian literature, BE833
The Oxford companion to Canadian theatre, BH73
———— Benson, Eugene, BE833
———— Conolly, Leonard W., BE833
The Oxford companion to chess, Hooper, David, BK133
The Oxford companion to children's literature, Carpenter, Humphrey, BE377
The Oxford companion to classical literature, Howatson, M. C., BE1014
Oxford companion to English literature, BE739
———— Drabble, Margaret, BE610
The Oxford companion to film, BH253
The Oxford companion to French literature, Harvey, Paul, BE1158
The Oxford companion to gardens, BF290
The Oxford companion to German literature, Garland, Henry B., BE1244
The Oxford companion to law, Walker, David M., CK32
The Oxford companion to medicine, EH88
Oxford companion to music, Scholes, Percy A., BJ142
The Oxford companion to politics of the world, CJ29
The Oxford companion to popular music, Gammond, Peter, BJ346
Oxford companion to ships and the sea, BK121
The Oxford companion to Spanish literature, BE1452
The Oxford companion to the Bible, BC189
Oxford companion to the decorative arts, BF90, BG20
The Oxford companion to the English language, BD94
The Oxford companion to the literature of Wales, BE814
The Oxford companion to the mind, CD25
The Oxford companion to the politics of the world, CJ33
The Oxford companion to the Supreme Court of the United States, CK187
The Oxford companion to the theatre, BH74
The Oxford companion to twentieth-century art, BF89, BF90
The Oxford companion to world sports and games, BK20
Oxford concise concordance to the Revised Standard Version of the Holy Bible, Metzger, Bruce Manning, BC158
———— Metzger, Isobel M., BC158
Oxford dictionary, AC30
The Oxford dictionary for scientific writers and editors, EA161
The Oxford dictionary for writers and editors, AA277, EA161
The Oxford dictionary of abbreviations, AC44
The Oxford dictionary of American legal quotations, CK57
The Oxford dictionary of art, BF90
Oxford dictionary of ballet, BH143
The Oxford dictionary of Byzantium, DA166
Oxford dictionary of current idiomatic English, AC80
The Oxford dictionary of English Christian names, Withycombe, Elizabeth Gidley, AJ177
The Oxford dictionary of English etymology, AC51, AC52, AC56, AC58
Oxford dictionary of English place-names, CL193
Oxford dictionary of English proverbs, BE159

Oxford dictionary of geography, CL48
The Oxford dictionary of modern Greek, Pring, Julian Talbot, AC467
Oxford dictionary of modern quotations, Augarde, Tony, BE113
The Oxford dictionary of modern slang, AC131
The Oxford dictionary of music, Kennedy, Michael, BJ138
The Oxford dictionary of natural history, EF14, EG75, EG78, EG124, EG227
The Oxford dictionary of new words, AC96
Oxford dictionary of nursery rhymes, Opie, Iona Archibald, BE721
The Oxford dictionary of Popes, Kelly, J. N. D., BC431
The Oxford dictionary of quotations, BE113
The Oxford dictionary of saints, Farmer, David Hugh, BC265
The Oxford dictionary of the Christian church, BC240, BC337
The Oxford-Duden German dictionary, AC419
The Oxford-Duden pictorial French-English dictionary, AC344
The Oxford-Duden pictorial German-English dictionary, AC344, AC420
The Oxford-Duden pictorial Portuguese-English dictionary, AC649
The Oxford-Duden pictorial Serbo-Croat & English dictionary, AC714
The Oxford-Duden pictorial Spanish-English dictionary, AC736
The Oxford encyclopaedia of European Community law, Toth, A. G., CK205
Oxford encyclopedia of trees of the world, EG198
The Oxford encyclopedic English dictionary, AC40
Oxford English, Dear, Ian, BD96
The Oxford English-Arabic dictionary of current usage, AC219
Oxford English dictionary, AC30, AC31, AC32, AC33, AC34, AC38, AC82, AC172, AC173, AC179
•*Oxford English dictionary on compact disc,* AC33
Oxford English-Russian dictionary, Falla, P. S., AC683
The Oxford English-Turkish dictionary, AC791
Oxford Greek-English learner's dictionary, Stavropoulos, D. N., AC465
Oxford guide to British women writers, Shattock, Joanne, BE623
The Oxford guide to card games, Parlett, David Sidney, BK129
The Oxford guide to classical mythology in the arts, 1300–1990s, Reid, Jane Davidson, BF189, CF24
The Oxford guide to English usage, Weiner, E. S. C., AC88
The Oxford-Harrap standard German-English dictionary, AC421
The Oxford Hindi-English dictionary, AC485
The Oxford history of Australia, DF39
The Oxford history of Australian literature, BE854
Oxford history of England, DC296
The Oxford history of English literature, BE617, BE664
The Oxford history of Hungarian literature from the earliest times to the present, Czigány, Lóránt, BE1276
The Oxford history of music, BJ197, BJ200
The Oxford history of New Zealand, DF45
The Oxford history of New Zealand literature in English, BE863
Oxford history of South Africa, Thompson, Leonard Montheath, DD211
———— Wilson, Monica, DD211
Oxford history of the Christian church, BC278
Oxford illustrated dictionary, AC41
Oxford illustrated encyclopedia of peoples and cultures, CE44
The Oxford illustrated history of Christianity, BC279
The Oxford illustrated literary guide to Canada, Moritz, A. F., BE829
The Oxford illustrated literary guide to Great Britain and Ireland, Eagle, Dorothy, BE614

The Oxford illustrated literary guide to the United States, Ehrlich, Eugene H., BE438
Oxford junior encyclopedia, AB21
Oxford Latin dictionary, AC577
The Oxford literary guide to Australia, BE855
Oxford literary guide to Great Britain and Ireland, Eagle, Dorothy, BE614
—— Stephens, Meic, BE614
Oxford literary guide to the British Isles, Carnell, Hilary, BE614
—— Eagle, Dorothy, BE614
The Oxford miniguide to English usage, AC88
Oxford Movement, BC214
The Oxford Movement and its leaders, Crumb, Lawrence N., BC214
Oxford paperback dictionary, AC18
Oxford Russian-English dictionary, Wheeler, Marcus, AC677, AC678, AC683, EA127
Oxford Shakespeare concordances, BE776
The Oxford thesaurus, Urdang, Laurence, AC146
The Oxford Turkish dictionary, İz, Fahir, AC791
The Oxford Turkish-English dictionary, AC791
Oxford universal dictionary, AC31
Oxford University Press. *The new Oxford atlas*, CL286
Oxford University Press. Dictionary Dept. *The Oxford-Duden pictorial Serbo-Croat & English dictionary*, AC714
Oxford University Press. Dictionary Dept. German Section. *The Oxford-Duden pictorial German-English dictionary*, AC420
The Oxford writers' dictionary, AA277
Oxtoby, Willard Gurdon. *Ancient Iran and Zoroastrianism in festschriften*, BC575
Oyewole, Anthony. *Nigeria*, DD48
Ozar ha-sepharim, Benjacob, Isaac, BC509
Özgüven, Necdet. *Langenscheidt's standard Turkish dictionary*, AC789
Ozhegov, Sergei Ivanovich. *Slovar' russkogo iazyka*, AC672
Ozment, Steven. *Reformation Europe*, DC28
Ozols, Selma Aleksandra. *Latvia*, DC437
Ozouf, Mona. *A critical dictionary of the French Revolution*, DC183

Paasche, Fredrik. *Norsk litteraturhistorie*, BE1339
Pabanel, Jean-Pierre. *Femmes et enfants au Burundi*, DD134
Pacific/Asian American Mental Health Research Center. *Bibliography of Pacific/Asian American materials in the Library of Congress*, CC411
—— *Pacific/Asian American research*, CC403
Pacific/Asian American research, Doi, Mary L., CC403
Pacific Basin and Oceania, Fry, Gerald, DF3
A Pacific bibliography, Taylor, Clyde Romer Hughes, DF8
Pacific Collection accession list, AA950
Pacific Collection legal deposit accessions, AA950
Pacific Island studies, DF6
Pacific Islands *see* **Oceania**
Pacific Islands yearbook, AH385
Pacific law bibliography, Elliott, Jacqueline D., CK234
Pacific region, DE17
    handbooks, DE16
Pacific research centres, EA146
Pacific Rim countries (by subject)
    economic conditions, CH200
    economic development
        bibliography, CH201
    politics and government
        biography, CJ415, DE20, DF20
Paciorek, Michael J. *Sports and recreation for the disabled*, BK40
Pack, Nancy C. *How libraries must comply with the Americans with Disabilities Act (ADA)*, AK66
Packard, Francis Randolph. *History of medicine in the United States*, EH215
Packard, Robert T. *Encyclopedia of architecture*, BF234
Packard, William. *The Facts on File dictionary of the theatre*, BH69

—— *The poet's dictionary*, BE330
Packer, James I. *The Bible almanac*, BC185
—— *New dictionary of theology*, BC239
Packer, Sybil P. *McGraw-Hill dictionary of chemistry*, EE43
Packman, James. *Guide to the best fiction, English and American*, BE240
Pactor, Howard S. *Colonial British Caribbean newspapers*, AE41
Paczkowski, Andrzej. *Polska prasa konspiracyjna (1939–1945) i powstania warszawskiego w zbiorach Biblioteki Narodowej*, AE66
Paden, John N. *Black Africa*, DD95
Paden fen Fryslan, Wumkes, G. A., BE1068
Padfield, Timothy. *Tracing your ancestors in the Public Record Office*, AJ97
Padilha, Sylvia F. *Processo de modernização do Brasil, 1850–1930*, DB348
Padwick, E. W. *A bibliography of cricket*, BK71
Paenson, Isaac. *English-French-Spanish-Russian manual of the terminology of public international law (law of peace) and international organizations*, CK103
—— *English-French-Spanish-Russian manual of the terminology of the law of armed conflicts and of international humanitarian organizations*, CK104
—— *English-French-Spanish-Russian systematic glossary of the terminology of statistical methods*, CG27
Paes, José Paulo. *Pequeno dicionário de literatura brasileira*, BE935
Paetow, Louis John. *A guide to the study of medieval history*, DA134, DA135
Paetzel, Hans W. *Complete multilingual dictionary of advertising, marketing and communications*, CH552
Page, Donald M. *Bibliography of works on Canadian foreign relations, 1945–1970*, DB186
—— *Bibliography of works on Canadian foreign relations, 1971–1975*, DB186
Page, G. Terry. *International dictionary of education*, CB77
—— *International dictionary of management*, CH614
Page, James A. *Black Olympian medalists*, BK93
—— *Selected black American, African, and Caribbean authors*, BE544
Page, Penny Booth. *Alcohol use and alcoholism*, CC119
—— *Children of alcoholics*, CC120
Pagel, Julius Leopold. *Biographisches Lexikon*, EH222
Pagell, Ruth A. *International business information*, CH5
Page's Ohio revised code annotated, Ohio. [Laws, etc.], CK179
Pagliaini, Attilio. *Catalogo generale della libreria italiana, 1847–99*, AA727, AA730, AA734
Pahlavi texts, BC92
Paine, Fred K. *Magazines*, AD41
Paine, Janice T. *Social casework. Cumulative index, 1920–1989*, CC44
Paine, Nancy E. *Magazines*, AD41
Painter's dictionary of materials and methods, Taubes, Frederic, BF304
Painting
    biography, BF299, BF301, BF310, BF311, BF312, BF315, BF320, BF324
    catalogs, BF321
    dictionaries, BF300
    directories, BF305, BF306
    encyclopedias, BF299
    handbooks, BF301, BF304
    indexes, BF298, BF302
    sales, BF302
Painting (by country or region)
    Canada, BF314
    China, BF313
    Europe, BF308
        indexes, BF61
    Great Britain, BF323
    Greece, BF324

    Hungary, BF321
    Italy, BF183
        collections, BF325
    United States, BF309
        guides, BF297
        indexes, BF61, BF63
Painting (by period)
    19th century, BF319
    20th century, BF307
    Renaissance, BF308
Painting (by subject)
    history, BF308
    symbols and symbolism, BF165
    see also **Portraits**
Painting and bronze price guide, Jacobsen, A., BF111
Painting in America, from 1502 to the present, Richardson, Edgar Preston, BF309
Painting in Canada, Harper, J. Russell, BF314
Painting in the twentieth century, Haftmann, Werner, BF307
PAIS, CA24
El país. Indice, AE126
•*PAIS international*, CA25
PAIS international in print, CA25
•*PAIS on CD-ROM*, CA25
PAIS subject headings, Picon, Alice, CA25
—— Sloan, Gwen, CA25
Pakan, William A. *Graphic arts encyclopedia*, BF369
Pakistan. *Catalogue of the government of Pakistan publications*, AF254, AF255
Pakistan
    archives, DE239
    bibliography, AA924, AA925, CJ443, DE32, DE240, DE241
        current, AA923
    biography, AH334, AH365, AH366
    government publications, AF254, AF255, AF256
    maps, CL360
    newspapers, AD206, AD207, AE97
    periodicals, AD206, AD207
    statistics, CG417
Pakistan (by subject)
    history
        bibliography, DE242
        encyclopedias, DE90
    population, CG416
    statistics, CG415
    see also **Bangladesh**
Pakistan. Federal Bureau of Statistics. *Pakistan demographic survey*, CG416
Pakistan. Statistics Division. *Pakistan statistical yearbook*, CG417
Pakistan, Taylor, David D., DE242
Pakistan : a comprehensive bibliography, CJ443, DE241
Pakistan Bibliographical Working Group. *Pakistan national bibliography, 1947–1961*, AA925
Pakistan demographic survey, CG416
Pakistan government publications, Siddiqui, Akhtar H., AF256
The Pakistan national bibliography, AA925
Pakistan national bibliography, 1947–1961, Pakistan Bibliographical Working Group, AA925
Pakistan statistical yearbook, CG417
Pakistani serials, Mahmud ul-Hassan, AD206
Paladin dictionary of battles, Harbottle, Thomas Benfield, DA22
Palaeontologi, Lambrecht, Kalman, EF252
Palaeontologisches Zentralblatt, EF55
Paläozoologie, EF246
Palau y Dulcet, Antonio. *Manual del librero hispano-americano*, AA806
Palazzi, Fernando. *Il libro dei mille savi*, BE140
—— *Novissimo dizionario della lingua italiana*, AC526
Palder, Edward L. *The catalog of catalogs III*, CH556
Palen, Roberta. *Guide to the publications of interstate agencies and authorities*, AF141
Paleography, AA216, BE1018

Paleontological Society. *Handbook of paleontological techniques,* EF247
Paleontology, EF243, EF246, EF249
  abstract journals, EF55, EF58, EF60
  bibliography, CE14, EA16, EB10, EC15, ED5, EE13, EF47, EF57, EF141, EF173, EF227, EF231, EF232, EF237, EG6, EG105, EG211, EG312
  biobibliography, EF252
  biography, EF245
  classification, EF240
  directories, EF245
  encyclopedias, EF235
  fossil indexes, EF236
  handbooks, EF247, EF248
  indexes, EF234
  nomenclature, EF236
Paleontology (by country or region)
  North America, EF242
    bibliography, EF49, EF230
Paleontology (by subject)
  history, EF105
Palestine
  atlases, CL358
  bibliography, DE244
Palestine (by subject)
  foreign relations (by country or region)
    Great Britain, DE243
  see also **Israel**
The Palestine question, Perry, Glenn E., DE244
Palfrey, Thomas Rossman. *A bibliographical guide to the Romance languages and literatures,* BD152, BE1073
Palgrave's dictionary of political economy, CH52
Pali-English dictionary, Pali Text Society, AC625
Pali language
  dictionaries, AC626
    bilingual
      Pali-English, AC624, AC625
Pali Text Society. *Pali-English dictionary,* AC625
  —— *Sacred books of the Buddhists,* BC457
Palic, Vladimir M. *Government publications,* AF11
Pallay, Steven G. *Cross index title guide to classical music,* BJ178
  —— *Cross index title guide to opera and operetta,* BJ178
Palliser, Bury. *History of lace,* BG160
Pallmann, Reinhold. *Erklärung der Abkürzungen auf Münzen der neueren Zeit, des Mittelalters und des Altertums, sowie auf Denkmünzen und münzartigen Zeichen,* BG184
Pallot, James. *The encyclopedia of film,* BH283
Pallotta, Gino. *Dizionario della politica italiana,* CJ382
  —— *Dizionario politicio e parlamentare italiano,* CJ382
Palm, Charles G. *Guide to the Hoover Institution archives,* DA172
Palm, Johann Friedrich. *Handwörterbuch der griechischen Sprache,* AC445
Palm, Julius Philip de. *Encyclopedie van de Nederlandse Antillen,* DB448
Palm, Mary Egdahl. *A literature guide for the identification of plant pathogenic fungi,* EG189
Palmatier, Robert A. *Sports talk,* BK28
Palmberg, R. *Select bibliography of error analysis and interlanguage studies,* BD80
Palmegiano, Eugenia M. *The British Empire in the Victorian press, 1832–1867,* DC343
Palmer, Alan. *An encyclopaedia of Napoleon's Europe,* DC22
  —— *Encyclopedia of Napoleon's Europe,* DC197
Palmer, Alan Warwick. *Who's who in Shakespeare's England,* BE788
Palmer, Edward H. *A concise dictionary of the Persian language,* AC316
Palmer, Eileen C. *Index to children's plays in collections, 1975–1984,* BE390
Palmer, Frederick. *Encyclopaedia of oil painting,* BF304
Palmer, Helen H. *American drama criticism,* BE457
  —— *English novel explication,* BE671, BE675
  —— *European drama criticism, 1900–1975,* BE232

Palmer, Henrietta. *List of English editions and translations of Greek and Latin classics printed before 1641,* BE1028
Palmer, James C. *Dictionary of educational acronyms, abbreviations, and initialisms,* CB78
  —— *Key resources on community colleges,* CB224
Palmer, Pete. *The encyclopedia of sports,* BK17
  —— *Total baseball,* BK62
Palmer, Ralph S. *Handbook of North American birds,* EG271
Palmer, Scott. *British film actors' credits, 1895–1987,* BH211
  —— *Who's who of British film actors,* BH211
Palmer, Stanley H. *Economic arithmetic,* CH188
•*Palmer's index to the Times 1790–1905 on CD-ROM,* AE125
Palmer's index to the Times newspaper, 1790–June 1941, AE125
Palmisano, Joseph M. *Mental health and social work career directory,* CC53
Palmore, Erdman Ballagh. *Developments and research on aging,* CC94
Palmquist, Peter E. *Photographers,* BF345
Paloposki, Toivo J. *Quellenkunde zur Geschichte Finnlands,* DC138
Palperi, Maija. *Suomen aikakauslehti-indeksi,* AD311
Palumbo, Pier Fausto. *Bibliografia storico internazionale, 1940–1947,* DA12
Pamphlets in American history, DB20
  —— Barnard, Henry, CH641
Pamphlets on American writers, University of Minnesota, BE444
Pan African Congress on Prehistory and Quarternary Studies. *African archaeology,* DD13
Pan-Africanism, Williams, Michael W., DD16
Pan American book shelf, AA471
Pan American Institute of Geography and History. *Bibliografía selectiva de las culturas indígenas de América,* CE78
  —— *Boletín bibliográfico de antropología americana,* CE76
  —— *Directorio de antropólogos latinoamericanos, México,* CE86
  —— *Historiografía de Cuba,* DB425
  —— *Misiones americanas en los archivos europeos,* DB277
  —— *Research guide to Costa Rica,* DB304
Pan American Institute of Geography and History. Comisíon de Historia. Committee on Folklore. *Bibliografía del folklore peruano,* CF70
Pan American Union. *Repertorio de publicaciones periódicas actuales latinoamericanas,* AD67
Pan American Union. Division of Music and Visual Arts. *A guide to the music of Latin America,* BJ11
Pan American Union. Division of Philosophy and Letters. *Diccionario de la literatura latinoamericana,* BE892
  —— *Latin American prose in English translation,* BE885
Panagiotou, Nikos. *Kypriakē vivliographia,* AA590
Panama, DB317
  bibliography, AA492, AA493, DB320
  government publications, AF159
  library catalogs, DB318
  manuscripts and archives, DB319
  statistics, CG133, CG134
Panama (by subject)
  historiography, DB319
  history, DB319, DB320
    bibliography, DB298
Panama. Direccíon de Estadística y Censo. *Estadística panamena,* CG133
Panama. Dirección de Estadística y Censos. *Panama en cifras,* CG134
Panama. Universidad. Biblioteca. *Bibliografía de libros y folletos, 1958–1960,* AA493
Panama, Langstaff, Eleanor De Selms, DB320
Panama Canal, DB318
Panama en cifras, CG134
Panamanian historical sources, Ward, Christopher, DB319

Pandit, Harshida. *Women of India,* CC612
Pandya, Jayendra Farsuram. *Government publications of India,* AF248
Pane, Remigio Ugo. *English translations from the Spanish, 1484–1943,* BE1447
Paneth, Donald. *The encyclopedia of American journalism,* AE138
Pānini to Postal, Salus, Peter H., BD69
The Panjābi dictionary, Singh, Maya, AC627
Panjabi language, AC627
Pankhurst, Richard Keir Pethick. *The dictionary of Ethiopian biography,* AH318
Pannekoek, Antonie. *A history of astronomy,* EC61
Panorama de la literatura argentina contemporanea, Pinto, Juan, BE920
Panorama de la literatura nicaragüense, Arellano, Jorge Eduardo, BE917
Panorama of EC industry, CH184
Panoramic maps of Anglo-American cities, Library of Congress. Geography and Map Division, CL234
Panoramic maps of cities in the United States and Canada, Library of Congress. Geography and Map Division, CL234
Pantoflíček, Jaroslav. *Atlas Republiky Československé,* CL322
Pantzer, Katharine F. *A short-title catalogue of books printed in England, Scotland, & Ireland and of English books printed abroad, 1475–1640,* AA671
Panzer, Georg Wolfgang Franz. *Annalen der ältern deutschen Litteratur,* AA639
  —— *Annales typographici ab artis inventae origine ad annum MD,* AA226
Papachristou, Judith. *Bibliography in the history of women in the progressive era,* CC508
Papadakis, Nikos. *International law of the sea,* CK79
Papadopoulos, Thōmas I. *Hellēnikē vivliographia,* AA704
The papal encyclicals, Catholic Church. Pope, BC434
Papal monarchy, Morris, Colin, BC278
Papal pronouncements, Carlen, Claudia, BC433
Papenbroeck, Daniel Van. *Acta sanctorum quotquot toto orbe coluntur,* BC257
Paper, Jordan D. *Guide to Chinese prose,* BE1558
Paper money of the United States, Friedberg, Robert, BG194
Paperbacks in print, AA685
Paperbound books in print, AA434
Papers, American Association of Architectural Bibliographers, BF205
Papers of geographical periodicals and serials, CL8
Papiers du Consulat de France á Alger, Centre des archives diplomatiques de Nantes (France), DD125
  —— Even, Pascal, DD125
Pappas, George S. *United States Army unit histories,* CJ628
Paprikoff, George I. *Works of Bulgarian emigrants,* AA586
Papua New Guinea
  bibliography, AA951, DF48, DF49
  bibliography of bibliography, AA77
  government publications, AF269
  periodicals
    indexes, AD348
Papua New Guinea, McConnell, Fraiser, DF49
Papua New Guinea national bibliography, AA951
Paquet, Léonce. *Les présocratiques,* BB58
Para un estudío sobre la violencia en Columbia, Cardona Grisález, Guillermo, DB364
Paraguay
  bibliography, AA469, AA534, AA535, AA536, AA537, DB379, DB380
  biography, AH138, AH139
  government publications, AF159
  statistics, CG156
Paraguay (by subject)
  history, DB380
Paraguay, Jones, David Lewis, DB379
  —— Nickson, R. Andrew, DB380
Paraguay … años de bibliografía, AA537

The Paraguayan bibliography, Fernández-Caballero, Carlos F. S., AA536

Paraguayan literature, BE953

Paralipomena, BF324

Parapsychology, BC64, CD137
  abstract journals, CD132
  bibliography, CD131
  dictionaries, CD135, CD136
  encyclopedias, CD133, CD134
  handbooks, CD138
  see also **Occultism**

Parapsychology, White, Rhea A., CD131

Parapsychology abstracts international, CD132

Paravisini-Gebert, Lizabeth. *Caribbean women novelists*, BE971

Parc, Françoise. *Vocabulaire de technologie éducative et de formation*, CB172

Parch, Grace D. *Directory of newspaper libraries in the U.S. and Canada*, AE30

Pareles, Jon. *The Rolling Stone encyclopedia of rock & roll*, BJ350

Parent-child attachment, Watkins, Kathleen Pullan, CC155

Parent compound handbook, EE86

Parenti, Marino. *Dizionario dei luoghi di stampa falsi, inventati o supposti in opere di autori e traduttori italiani*, AA195

Parents
  bibliography, CC145, CC155

The parent's desk reference, Franck, Irene M., CC238

Parezo, Nancy J. *Southwest Native American arts and material culture*, BG9, CC422

Parfitt, George A. E. *A biographical dictionary of English women writers, 1580–1720*, BE620

Pargellis, Stanley. *The eighteenth century, 1714–1789*, DC317

Parham, Iris A. *Gerontological social work*, CC43

Páricsy, Pál. *Bibliography of creative African writing*, BE1505

Parini, Jay. *The Columbia history of American poetry*, BE503

Parins, James W. *American Indian and Alaska native newspapers and periodicals*, CC424
  —— *A biobibliography of native American writers, 1772–1924*, BE551, CC420

The Paris commune, 1871, University of Sussex. Library, DC202

The Paris Opéra, Pitou, Spire, BJ257

Parise, Frank. *The book of calendars*, EC84

Parish, David W. *A bibliography of state bibliographies, 1970–1982*, AF143
  —— *State government reference publications*, AF144

Parish, James Robert. *The complete actors' television credits, 1948–1988*, BH312
  —— *Gays and lesbians in mainstream cinema*, BH229

The parish churches and nonconformist chapels of Wales, Rawlins, Bert J., AJ127

Parish registers of Wales, AJ127

The Parisian stage, Wicks, Charles Beaumont, BE1186

Park, Helen. *List of architectural books available in America before the Revolution*, BF223

Park, Hong-Kyu. *Studies on Korea*, DE214

Park, Karin R. *Publication grants for writers & publishers*, BA11

Parke, Nathan Grier. *Guide to the literature of mathematics and physics including related works on engineering science*, EB3, ED2

Parker, Betty June. *American dissertations on foreign education*, CB24
  —— *Education in England and Wales*, CB44
  —— *Education in the People's Republic of China, past and present*, CB47
  —— *U.S. higher education*, CB225

Parker, C. C. *Information sources in science and technology*, EA6

Parker, David L. *Guide to dance in film*, BH149

Parker, Earl Randall. *Materials data book for engineers and scientists*, EK279

Parker, Franklin. *American dissertations on foreign education*, CB24
  —— *Education in England and Wales*, CB44
  —— *Education in the People's Republic of China, past and present*, CB47
  —— *U.S. higher education*, CB225

Parker, Geoffrey. *The Times atlas of world history*, DA58

Parker, Harold M. *Bibliography of published articles on American Presbyterianism, 1901–1980*, BC377

Parker, Henry H. *Dictionary of the Hawaiian language*, AC469

Parker, J. Carlyle. *Library service for genealogists*, AJ19

Parker, J. H. *A bibliography of comedias sueltas in the University of Toronto library*, BE1471

Parker, James. *A glossary of terms used in heraldry*, AJ164

Parker, John. *Who's who in the theatre*, BH122

Parker, Patricia L. *Charles Brockden Brown*, BE478
  —— *Early American fiction*, BE478

Parker, R. H. *A dictionary of business quotations*, CH72

Parker, Richard A. *Designing and conducting survey research*, CA58

Parker, Sybil P. *McGraw-Hill dictionary of earth sciences*, EF15
  —— *McGraw-Hill dictionary of scientific and technical terms*, EA93
  —— *McGraw-Hill encyclopedia of the geological sciences*, EF69
  —— *Synopsis and classification of living organisms*, EG28

Parker School of Foreign and Comparative Law. *A bibliography on foreign and comparative law*, CK8
  —— *Guide to foreign legal materials*, CK208

Parkinson, Claire L. *Breakthroughs*, EA254

Parkinson, John A. *Victorian music publishers*, BJ184

Parkinson, Roger. *The encyclopedia of modern war*, CJ576

Parks, Edna D. *Early English hymns*, BC320

Parks, George B. *The Greek and Latin literatures*, BE1010
  —— *The Romance literatures*, BE1074

Parks, Roger N. *Bibliographies of New England history*, DB152

Parks and protected areas, BK116, BK124, BK125
  directories, BF250

Parlagi, Imre. *Das geistige Ungarn*, AH248

Parlementaires français, Bonét-Maury, Géo, AH200, CJ329
  —— Samuel, René Claude Louis, AH200, CJ329

Parlett, David Sidney. *The Oxford guide to card games*, BK129

The Parliament of Great Britain, Goehlert, Robert, CJ351

Parliamentary companion, CJ357

Parliamentary debates, Great Britain. Parliament, AF208

Parliamentary election results in Ireland, 1801–1922, Walker, Brian Mercer, CJ379

Parliamentary guide and work of general reference for Canada, the provinces, Northwest Territories and Newfoundland, CJ295

Parliamentary handbook of the Commonwealth of Australia, CJ449, CJ450

Parliamentary history of England from the earliest period to the year 1803, Cobbett, William, AF208

Parliamentary procedure, CJ224, CJ225, CJ226, CJ227, CJ228, CJ453, CJ454, CJ455, CJ456, CJ457, CJ458
  handbooks, CJ452

Parliaments of the world, CJ90

Parmeggiani, Luigi. *Encyclopaedia of occupational health and safety*, EH409

Parmley, Robert O. *Mechanical components handbook*, EK241

Parodies, BE722, BE723

Parodies, Macdonald, Dwight, BE723

Parodies of the works of English and American authors, Hamilton, Walter, BE722

Parole, CK267

Parra, Manuel Germán. *Bibliografía indigenista de México y Centroamérica (1850–1950)*, CE82

Parrinder, Edward Geoffrey. *Dictionary of non-Christian religions*, BC75

Parris, Judith H. *Convention decisions and voting records*, CJ263

Parrish, Michael. *Soviet security and intelligence organizations, 1917–1990*, CJ542
  —— *U.S.S.R. in World War II*, DA200

Parrish, T. Michael. *Confederate imprints*, DB112

Parrish, Thomas. *The Simon and Schuster encyclopedia of World War II*, DA208

Parry, Clive. *The consolidated treaty series*, CK85
  —— *An index of British treaties, 1101–1968*, CK98
  —— *Parry and Grant encyclopaedic dictionary of international law*, CK105

Parry, Donald W. *A bibliography on temples of the ancient Near East and Mediterranean world*, BF220

Parry, John H. *New Iberian world*, DB292

Parry, John J. *Bibliography of critical Arthurian literature for the years 1922–1929*, BE339
  —— *Bibliography of critical Arthurian literature for the years 1930–1935*, BE339

Parry, Pamela Jeffcott. *Contemporary art and artists*, BF62
  —— *Photography index*, BF62, BF339, BF367
  —— *Print index*, BF62, BF367

Parry, Robert B. *Information sources in cartography*, CL220
  —— *World mapping today*, CL269

Parry and Grant encyclopaedic dictionary of international law, Parry, Clive, CK105

Parsifal-Charles, Nancy. *The dream*, CD109

Parsiism, BC92

Parsons, Henry S. *A check list of American 18th century newspapers in the Library of Congress*, AE20
  —— *Dramatic compositions copyrighted in the United States*, BE461

Parsons, Henry Spaulding. *A check list of foreign newspapers in the Library of Congress*, AE10

Parsons, Karen Toombs. *United States congressional districts*, CJ239

Parsons, Neil Quentin. *High Commission territories, 1909–1964*, DD170

Parsons, Quentin Neil. *The High Commission territories, 1909–1964*, DD117, DD232

Parsons, Stanley B. *United States congressional districts*, CJ239

Parsons, Wilfrid. *Early Catholic Americana*, BC392

Partial autobiographies, BE563

Particle Data Group. *Review of particle properties*, ED49

Particles (physics), ED49

Partington, Angela. *The Oxford dictionary of quotations*, BE113

Partington, James Riddick. *A history of chemistry*, EE98

Partington, Paul G. *Who's who on the postage stamps of Eastern Europe*, BG205

Partnow, Elaine. *Macmillan biographical encyclopedia of photographic artists & innovators*, BF354
  —— *Quotable woman, 1800–1981*, BE111
  —— *Quotable woman from Eve to 1799*, BE111

Partridge, Eric. *Concise dictionary of slang and unconventional English*, AC132
  —— *Dictionary of Forces' slang*, AC132
  —— *A dictionary of slang and unconventional English*, AC132
  —— *Dictionary of the underworld, British and American*, AC132
  —— *Name into word*, AC59
  —— *Name this child*, AJ176
  —— *Origins*, AC58, AC60
  —— *Shakespeare's bawdy*, BE772
  —— *Slang, today and yesterday*, AC132

Partridge-Brown, Mary. *In-vitro fertilization clinics*, CC229

Party and government officials of the Soviet Union, 1917–1967, Institut zur Erforschung der UdSSR, CJ393
Party organisations, CJ58
Party organizations, CJ58
Paruch, Józef. *Słownik skrótów,* AC637
Paryl, Władysław. *Językoznawstwo polonistyczne,* BD193
PASCAL, AD254, BB24, BE38, CE23, EA72, EF118, EA72, EF118
PASCAL. v. 4, Sciences de la terre, EF59
Paschek, Carl. *Personalbibliographie zur deutschen Literaturgeschichte,* BE1221
Pasierbsky, Fritz. *Deutsche Sprache im Reformationszeitalter,* BD122
Pask, Judith M. *User education for online systems in libraries,* AK189
Paskoff, Paul F. *Iron and steel in the nineteenth century,* CH383
Pasqualaggi, Gilles. *Dictionnaire des sciences économiques,* CH66
Pass, Christopher. *Harper dictionary of economics,* CH62
Passano, Giambattista. *Dizionario di opere anonime e pseudonime di scrittori italiani,* AA177
Passé de l'Afrique par l'oralité, DD11
Passek, Jean Loup. *Dictionnaire du cinéma,* BH247
Passenger and immigration lists bibliography, 1538–1900, Filby, P. William, AJ29
Passenger and immigration lists index, AJ44
Passenger lists, AJ25, AJ37, AJ40, AJ43, AJ44, AJ61, AJ62, AJ64, AJ68, AJ93
 bibliography, AJ29
Passmore, Gloria C. *Catalogue of the parliamentary papers of Southern Rhodesia, 1899–1953,* AF242, DD176
Passmore, J. Robert. *Bibliography on world conflict and peace,* CJ664
Passow, Franz. *Handwörterbuch der griechischen Sprache,* AC445
A past renewed, Epstein, Catherine, DA47
Past worlds, DA88
Pastor, Ludwig. *Geschichte der Päpiste,* BC432
——— *History of the popes,* BC432
Paszek, Lawrence J. *United States Air Force history,* CJ613
Pásztor, L. *Guide delle fonti per storia dell'America Latina negli archivi della Santa Sede e negli archivi ecclesiastici d'Italia,* DB275
Patai, Raphael. *Encyclopedia of Zionism and Israel,* BC548
Patell, Cyrus R. K. *Cambridge history of American literature,* BE439
Patent and trademark tactics and practice, Burge, David A., EA257
Patents, EA257, EA258, EA262, EA263, EA266, EA267
 digests and collections, CK68
 encyclopedias, CK134
 guides, EA261
 translations, EA60
 indexes, EA63
Patents (by country or region)
 United States, EA264
 indexes, EA259
 see also **Trademarks**
Pathak, Ram Chandra. *Bhargava's standard illustrated dictionary of the English language (Anglo-Hindi ed.),* AC486
Pathological psychology, CD101
Pathology, EH207
Patnode, Darwin. *Robert's rules of order,* CJ457
Patrias, Karen. *National Library of Medicine recommended formats for bibliographic citation,* EA162
Patrick Moore's A–Z of astronomy, Moore, Patrick, EC36
Patrinacos, Nicon D. *A dictionary of Greek Orthodoxy,* BC451
A patristic Greek lexicon, Lampe, Geoffrey William Hugo, AC457
Patrologia, BC301

Patrologiae cursus completus, Migne, Jacques Paul, DA163
Patrologie, Altaner, Berthold, BC300
Patrology, BC293, BC300, BC301
 bibliography, BC116, BC220, BC295, BC297, BC298
 handbooks, BC296
 indexes, BC299
 texts, BC294
Patrology, Graef, Hilda C., BC300
——— Quasten, Johannes, BC301
Pattanayak, Debi Prasanna. *Classified bibliography of linguistic dissertations on Indian languages,* BD225
Patterns of global terrorism, CJ185
Patterns of poetry, Williams, Miller, BE326
Patterson, Austin McDowell. *French-English dictionary for chemists,* EE48
——— *A guide to the literature of chemistry,* EE2
——— *Patterson's German-English dictionary for chemists,* EE51
Patterson, Charles D. *ARBA guide to library science literature, 1970–1983,* AK8
Patterson, Charlotte A. *Plays in periodicals,* BE233
Patterson, Larry K. *Handbook of monolayers,* EE150
Patterson, Margaret C. *Author newsletters and journals,* BE43
——— *Literary research guide,* BE396
Patterson, Marvin W. *Key resources on higher education governance, management, and leadership,* CB224
Patterson, Maureen L. P. *South Asian civilisations,* DE80
——— *South Asian library resources in North America,* DE87
Patterson's American education, CB104, CB105, CB282
Patterson's elementary education, CB105
Patterson's German-English dictionary for chemists, Patterson, Austin McDowell, EE51
Patterson's schools classified, CB104, CB282
Pauer, Gyula. *The historical atlas of political parties in the United States Congress, 1789–1989,* CJ258, DB73
——— *The historical atlas of the Congresses of the Confederate States of America, 1861–1865,* CJ292
Paul, Barbara Dotts. *The Germans after World War II,* DC239
Paul, Ellen. *Adoption choices,* CC230
——— *The adoption directory,* CC228
Paul, Hermann. *Deutsches Wörterbuch,* AC407
——— *Grundriss der germanischen Philologie unter Mitwirkung zahlreicher Fachgelehrter,* AJ192, CL189
Paul, Morris Rea. *Dictionary of color,* ED61
Paul, Shalom M. *Illustrated dictionary & concordance of the Bible,* BC142
Paul, T. Otis. *Encyclopedia of blindness and vision impairment,* CC189, EH90
Paulhart, Herbert. *Österreichische historische Bibliographie,* DC94
Paulhart, Hermine. *Österreichische historische Bibliographie,* DC94
Paulidēs, Antros. *Megalē Kypriakē enkyklopaideia,* DC121
Pauling, Linus. *World encyclopedia of peace,* CJ686
Paullin, Charles Oscar. *Atlas of the historical geography of the United States,* DB69, DB75
Paulos Milkias. . *Ethiopia,* DD158
Paulsen, Thomas D. *The naval officer's guide,* CJ635
Paulus, Rolf. *Bibliographie zur deutschen Lyrik nach 1945,* BE1272
Pauly, August Friedrich von. *Paulys Real-Encyclopädie der classischen Altertumswissenschaft,* BB54, DA104
——— *Real-Encyclopädie der classischen Altertumswissenschaft,* DA101
Pauly-Wissowa, DA104
Pauly's Real-Encyclopädie der classischen Altertumswissenschaft, DA101
——— Pauly, August Friedrich von, BB54, DA104
——— Wissowa, Georg, BB54

Paulys Realencyclopadie der classischen Altertumswissenschaft : Register der Nachträge und Supplemente, Gartner, Hans, DA104
——— Wunsch, Albert, DA104
Pausch, Lois M. *A guide to library service in mathematics,* EB1
Pavière, Sidney H. *Dictionary of British sporting painters,* BF323
Pavone, Claudio. *Guida generale degli archivi di Stato italiani,* AK150, DC429
Pawlik, Kurt. *International directory of psychologists, exclusive of the U.S.A,* CD48
Paxton, John. *Calendar of creative man,* DA36
——— *Commonwealth political facts,* CJ373
——— *Companion to Russian history,* DC567
——— *Companion to the French Revolution,* DC187
——— *Encyclopedia of Russian history,* DC567
——— *European Communities,* AF24
——— *European political facts, 1648–1789,* CJ314
——— *Everyman's dictionary of abbreviations,* AC45
——— *Historical tables, 58 BC–AD 1990,* DA38
——— *The statesman's year-book world gazetteer,* CL92
Payad, Aurora T. *Organization behavior in American public administration,* CJ472
PAYE. *Performing arts yearbook for Europe,* BH16
Paying less for college, CB386, CB388, CB390
Paylore, Patricia. *Deserts of the world,* CL58, EF17
Payne, Blanche. *The history of costume,* BG112
Payne, Chris. *Virology,* EG345
Payne, Christopher. *Sotheby's concise encyclopedia of furniture,* BG129
Payne, Peter A. *Concise encyclopedia of biological & biomedical measurement systems,* EH82
Payne, Ronald. *Dictionary of espionage,* CJ540
——— *Who's who in espionage,* CJ540
Payne Smith, J. *Compendious Syriac dictionary,* AC773
Payne Smith, Robert. *Compendious Syriac dictionary,* AC773
——— *Thesaurus syriacus,* AC773
Paz, Julín. *Catálogo de manuscritos de América existentes en la Biblioteca Nacional,* DB268, DE245
PDR family guide to prescription drugs, EH347
PDR guide to drug infractions, side effects, indications, EH347
•*PDR library on CD-ROM,* EH347
Peabody Museum of Archaeology and Ethnology. Library. *Author and subject catalogues of the Tozzer Library,* CE30
Peace *see* **Arms control and peace research**
Peace and international conflict resolution, CJ688
The peace and nuclear war dictionary, Ali, Sheikh Rustum, CJ682, CJ683
Peace and war, Carroll, Berenice A., CJ680
Peace archives, Green, Marguerite, CJ671
Peace Corps, CJ678, CJ702
The Peace Corps, Ridinger, Robert B. Marks, CJ678
Peace movements of the world, CJ693
Peace organizations, past and present, Meyer, Robert S., CJ692
Peace Palace (Hague, Netherlands). *From Erasmus to Tolstoy,* CJ675
Peace research abstracts journal, CJ681
Peace resource book, CJ694
The peace tradition in the Catholic Church, Musto, Ronald G., CJ677
Peacetime army, 1900–1941, Fletcher, Marvin, CJ608
Peacock, Philip R. *Dictionnaire français-anglais, anglais-français des termes médicaux et biologiques,* EH141
Peake, Arthur Samuel. *Commentary on the Bible,* BC168
Peake, Dorothy M. *Play index,* BE234
Peake, Hayden B. *The reader's guide to intelligence periodicals,* CJ543
Peake, Louis A. *The United States in the Vietnam War, 1954–1975,* DE275
Peake's commentary on the Bible, Black, Matthew, BC168

Pearce, David W. *The MIT dictionary of modern economics,* CH59

Pearce, E. A. *The Times Books world weather guide,* EF163

Pearce, Jill. *Gardner's chemical synonyms and trade names,* EE39

Pearce, Roy Harvey. *The continuity of American poetry,* BE504

The pearl of great price, BC371

Pearlstein, Toby. *General transportation,* CH444

Pearsall, Derek Albert. *Old English and Middle English poetry,* BE718

Pearson, Barbara C. *Guide to the petroleum reference literature,* EK298

Pearson, Carl E., ed. *Handbook of applied mathematics,* EB67

Pearson, Egon Sharpe. *Biometrika tables for statisticians,* EB90

Pearson, J. D. *Arab Islamic bibliography,* BC492

—— *A bibliography of pre-Islamic Persia,* DE187

—— *A bibliography of the architecture, arts, and crafts of Islam to 1st Jan. 1960,* BF17

—— *Guide to manuscripts and documents in the British Isles relating to Africa,* DC345, DD38, DD39

—— *A guide to manuscripts and documents in the British Isles relating to South and South-East Asia,* DE12

—— *Guide to manuscripts and documents in the British Isles relating to the Middle East and North Africa,* DD38, DE50

—— *Guide to the manuscripts and documents in the British Isles relating to Africa,* DD105

—— *Index Islamicus, 1906–1955,* BC502

—— *International African bibliography, 1973–1978,* DD23

—— *South Asian bibliography,* DE81

—— *A world bibliography of African bibliographies,* AA70

—— *A world bibliography of Oriental bibliographies,* AA73

Pearson, Karl. *Tables for statisticians and biometricians,* EB90

Pearson, Kenneth H. *Encyclopedia Canadiana,* DB198

Pearson, Michael. *The nuclear arms race,* CJ670

Pearson, P. David. *Handbook of reading research,* CB114

Pearson, Roger. *Anthropological glossary,* CE50

Pease, Elizabeth Sue. *Occupational safety and health,* EH403

Pease, Mina. *UNDEX series C cumulative edition,* AF49

Peaslee, Amos Jenkins. *Constitutions of nations,* CK73

—— *International governmental organizations,* AF18

Peatross, C. Ford. *Historic America,* BF219

Peavy, Charles D. *Afro-American literature and culture since World War II,* BE528

Péchoin, Daniel. *Thésaurus Larousse,* AC363

Pechota, Vratislav. *A bibliography on foreign and comparative law,* CK8

Peck, David R. *American ethnic literatures,* BE511, BE546

Peckham, Robert S. *A bibliography on Kenya,* DD167

Peddie, Robert Alexander. *Subject index of books published before 1880,* AA94, AA104

Pedraza Jiménez, Felipe B. *Manual de literatura española,* BE867, BE1429

—— *Manual de literature hispanoamericana,* BE867, BE1429

Pedreira, Antonio Salvador. *Bibliografía puertorriqueña (1492–1930),* DB453

Peebles, Patrick. *Sri Lanka,* CG424

Peel, Albert. *The Congregational two hundred, 1530–1948,* BC385

Peel, Bruce Braden. *Bibliography of the Prairie Provinces to 1953,* DB213, DB216

Peeters-Fontainas, Jean F. *Bibliographie des impressions espagnoles des Pays-Bas Méridionaux,* AA747

Pegler, Martin. *The dictionary of interior design,* BG127

Pehnt, Wolfgang. *Knaurs Lexikon der modernen Architektur,* BF233

Pei, Mario Andrew. *Dictionary of foreign terms,* AC188

Peintre graveur, Bartsch, Adam von, BF381, BF382

Peintre-graveur français, Robert-Dumesnil, A. P. F., BF377

Peintre-graveur français continué, Baudicour, Prosper de, BF377

Peintre-graveur illustré, Delteil, Löys, BF377

—— Wechsler, Herman J., BF377

Peintres naïfs, Jakovsky, Anatole, BF315

Peiris, H. A. *Political parties in Sri Lanka since independence,* CJ444

Pekelis, Carla. *A dictionary of colorful Italian idioms,* AC544

The Pelican guide to English literature, BE616

Pelican history of art, BF133

Pélissier, René. *Africana,* DD12, DD118

—— *Du Sahara à Timor,* DD12, DD118

Pellechet, Marie Léontine Catherine. *Catalogue général des incunables des bibliothèques publiques de France,* AA234

Pelletier, Paul A. *Prominent scientists,* EA196

Pelliccia, Guerrino. *Dizionario degli istituti di perfezione,* BC439

Pellicer, J. A. *Bibliotheca hispana,* AA811

Pemberton, John E. *The bibliographic control of official publications,* AF2

—— *How to find out in mathematics,* EB4

Pemsel, Helmut. *Atlas of naval warfare,* CJ600

—— *A history of war at sea,* CJ600

—— *Von Salamis bis Okinawa,* CJ600

The pen is ours, Yellin, Jean Fagan, BE534

Pena, Joaquín. *Diccionario de la música Labor,* BJ124

Pence, Richard A. *Computer genealogy,* AJ5

Penco, Wilfredo. *Diccionario de literatura uruguaya,* BE958

Penfold, Merimeri. *The book of New Zealand women,* AH377, DF46

The Penguin atlas of the diasporas, DA188

Penguin dictionary of architecture, BG21

—— Fleming, John, BF244

The Penguin dictionary of art and artists, BF78

Penguin dictionary of astronomy, EC35

The Penguin dictionary of biology, Abercrombie, M., EG29

The Penguin dictionary of British natural history, Fitter, Richard Sidney Richmond, EG77

The Penguin dictionary of decorative arts, Fleming, John, BG21

Penguin dictionary of design and designers, BG22

Penguin dictionary of economics, Bannock, G., CH54

—— Baxter, R. E., CH54

—— Rees, R., CH54

Penguin dictionary of English, Garmonsway, George Norman, AC461

—— Simpson, Jacqueline, AC461

The Penguin dictionary of English and European history, DC23

The Penguin dictionary of foreign terms and phrases, AC187

Penguin dictionary of quotations, Cohen, J. M., BE110

—— Cohen, M. J., BE110

The Penguin dictionary of religions, BC73

The Penguin dictionary of surnames, Cottle, Basil, AJ182

Penguin dictionary of the theatre, Taylor, John Russell, BH75

The Penguin dictionary of twentieth-century quotations, BE110

The Penguin encyclopedia of modern warfare, Macksey, Kenneth, CJ574

Penguin guide to compact discs, Greenfield, Edward, BJ379

The Penguin guide to compact discs and cassettes, March, Ivan, BJ379

Penguin guide to compact discs and cassettes yearbook, Greenfield, Edward, BJ379

Penguin-Hellenews anglo-hellēnikon lexikon, AC461

Penguin history of New Zealand literature, Evans, Patrick, BE863

Penguin new literary history of Australia, Hergenham, Laurie, BE854

Penn, Peter. *Gazetteer of China,* CL161

Pennak, Robert William. *Collegiate dictionary of zoology,* EG230

—— *Fresh-water invertebrates of the United States,* EG241

Pennell, E. N. *Dictionary of fictional characters,* BE189

Penney, Clara Louisa. *List of books printed 1601–1700, in the Library,* AA818

—— *List of books printed before 1601 in the Library of the Hispanic Society of America,* AA818

—— *Printed books, 1468–1700, in the Hispanic Society of America,* AA818

Penney, Edmund F. *The Facts on File dictionary of film and broadcast terms,* BH260

Penninger, Frieda Elaine. *English drama to 1660 excluding Shakespeare,* BE652

Pennington, Jean A. Thompson. *Bowes and Church's food values of portions commonly used,* EH303, EJ216

Pennington, Lee. *Complete index for the six volumes of Wild flowers of the United States,* EG180

Pennsylvania. [Laws, etc.]. *Purdon's Pennsylvania statutes, annotated,* CK179

Penny, Anne. *The concise Oxford dictionary of geography,* CL48

Pension funds, Gunderson, Nels L., CH500

The Pentateuch and Haftorahs, BC183

Pentecostal movement, BC374, BC375

Penzler, Otto. *Detectionary,* BE267

—— *Encyclopedia of mystery and detection,* BE267

People & events of the American Revolution, Dupuy, Trevor Nevitt, DB94

People in history, AH19, AH54

People in world history, AH19, AH54

The people speak, CJ250

The people's almanac, AB108

People's chronology, Trager, James, AB27, DA39

The Peoples Republic of Benin, Allen, Christopher, DD129

The People's Republic of China, Pinard, Jeanette I., CK228

The People's Republic of China, 1949–1979, DE149

People's Republic of China—atlas, United States. Central Intelligence Agency, CL355

People's Republic of the Congo, Adloff, R., DD48

—— Thompson, V. McLean, DD48

Pepper, George Wharton. *An analytical index to the Book of Common Prayer and a brief account of its evolution,* BC348

Peptides, EE114

Pequena bibliografía crítica da literatura brasileira, Carpeaux, Otto Maria, BE925

Pequeno dicionário brasileiro da língua portuguêsa, Lima, Hildebrando de, AC643

Pequeno dicionário de literatura brasileira, BE935

Peradotto, John Joseph. *Classical mythology,* CF20

Peral, Miguel Angel. *Diccionario biográfico mexicano,* AH102

Peraza Sarausa, Fermín. *Anuario bibliográfico cubano,* AA559

—— *Bibliografía colombiana,* AA523

—— *Diccionario biográfico cubano,* AH150, AH151

—— *Directorio de revistas y periódicos de Cuba,* AD74

—— *Personalidades cubanas,* AH152

—— *Revolutionary Cuba,* AA562

Perception, CD114

handbooks, CD113

Perception, Emmett, Kathleen, CD107

Percy, William A. *Encyclopedia of homosexuality,* CC277

Pereira, Janet Aileen. *A check list of selected material on Samoa,* DF54
Pereira Salas, Eugenio. *Guía bibliográfica para el estudio del folklore chileno,* CF71
The perennial dictionary of world religions, BC70
Pérez, Angel. *Adiciones y continuación de "La imprenta en Manila" de d. J. T. Medina,* AA928
Pérez, Janet. *Dictionary of the literature of the Iberian peninsula,* BE1070
Pérez, Louis A. *Cuba,* DB426
—— *The Cuban revolutionary war, 1953–1958,* DB430
—— *A guide to Cuban collections in the United States,* DB427
—— *Historiography in the Revolution,* DB429
Pérez, Paola. *10 años de investigaciones sobre la mujer en Nicaragua 1976–1986,* DB314
Pérez Cabrera, José Manuel. *Historiografía de Cuba,* DB425
Pérez Marchant, Braulio. *Diccionario biográfico del Ecuador,* AH135
Pérez Ortiz, Rubén. *Bibliografía de bibliografías colombianas,* AA29
—— *Seudónimos colombianos,* AA158
Pérez Pimentel, Rodolfo. *Diccionario biográfico del Ecuador,* AH136
Performing arts
  bibliography, BH3
  biography, BH22, BH23, BH24, BH25, BH26, BH27
    indexes, BH28, BH29
  chronologies, DA36
  dictionaries, BH12
  directories, BF107, BH13, BH14, BH15, BH16, BH17, BH18
  encyclopedias, BH10
  guides, BH1
  handbooks, BH20, BH21
  indexes, BH8
  library catalogs, BH33
  library resources, BH15
  library resources, BH5, BH6, BH7, BH17
  manuscripts, BH7
  prizes and awards, BH19
  reviews, BH9
Performing arts (by country or region)
  United States
    current surveys, BA1, BF44
  U.S.S.R.
    handbooks, BE1410
  see also **Dance; Radio; Television; Theater**
Performing arts, BH9
Performing arts biography master index, McNeil, Barbara, BH28
Performing arts books, 1876–1981, BH3
Performing arts directory, BH18
Performing arts libraries and museums of the world, BH5
Performing arts research, Whalon, Marion K., BH1
Performing arts resources, BH6
Performing arts yearbook for Europe, BH16
Périodex, AD294
Periodic and special reports on population, United States. Bureau of the Census, CG90
Periodica chemica, EE19
Periodica musicalia (1789–1830), Fellinger, Imogen, BJ114
Periodical articles on religion, 1890–1899, Richardson, Ernest Cushing, BC47
Periodical classes, Harvard University. Library, AD10
Periodical directories and bibliographies, AD42
Periodical literature on American music, 1620–1920, Warner, Thomas E., BJ46
Periodical literature on United States cities, Shearer, Barbara Smith, DB145
Periodical source index, AJ45
Periodical title abbreviations, AD23
Periodicals
  abbreviations, AD9, AD22, AD23, AD24, BC25, EA38, EA47

  bibliography, AA103, AA661, AD2, AD3, AD4, AD5, AD6, AD8, AD10, AD11, AD12, AD13, AD14, AD15, AD16, AD17, AD18, AD19, AD20, AD21, AD42
    current, AD66, CA18
    Finland, AD89
    Jewish, AD7
    Senegal, AD176, DD104
  databases, AD6, AD15, AD18, AD19
    bibliography, AD271
    directories, AD2
  directories, AD42
  guides for authors, AD26, AD27
  indexes, AD253, AD254, AD259, AD260, AD262, AD269, AD270, AD279, AD280, AD283, AD286, AD288, BA2, BB24, BE38, CE23
    bibliography, AD248, AD249, AD250, AD251, AD252
    Canada, AD293, AD294
    United States, AD258, AD274
  library catalogs, AD116
  reviews, AA378
  selection, AA374, AA375, AA378
    for children, AA376
    public libraries, AA377
    school libraries, AA377
  translations, AD25
  union lists, AD186, AD218, AD226, AD227, AD236, AD237
    bibliography, AD219
  union lists (by location)
    Africa, AD238, DD28
    Belgium, AD230
    Canada, AD220, AD228
    France, AD231, AD232, AD233
    Germany, AD234, AD235
    Great Britain, AD215, AD216
    Italy, AD239
    Luxembourg, AD230
    Mexico, AD229
    Netherlands, AD240
    New Zealand, AD247
    Philippines, AD209, AD244, AD245
    South Africa, AD243
    Spain, AD241
    Switzerland, AD242
    United States, AD220, AD222, AD223
Periodicals (by country or region)
  Africa, AD169, DD27
    abstract journals, DD45
    indexes, DD22
    union lists, AD238, DD28
  Africa, East
    indexes, DD92
  Africa, Southern
    indexes, DD92
  Albania
    indexes, AD301
  Arab states
    bibliography, AD182, AD183, AD184
    union lists, AD184
  Asia, South
    union lists, AD215
  Asia, Southeast
    bibliography, AD185
    indexes, AD336
    union lists, AD186, AD216
  Asia, West
    bibliography, AD182, AD183, AD184
    union lists, AD184
  Australia, AD213, AD214, BE857
    indexes, AD346
  Austria, AD81
  Basque region
    bibliography, AD158
  Belgium, AD82, AD83, AD84, AD85, AD131
    indexes, AD302, AD303, BE1066
  Brazil, AD72
  British Empire and Commonwealth, DC343
  Brunei
    indexes, AD336
  Bulgaria
    indexes, AD304, AD305

  Cambodia, AD212
  Canada
    directories, AD51, AE23
    indexes, AD293, AD294, AD312
  Czechoslovakia
    indexes, AD307
  Denmark
    indexes, AD308, AD309, AD310, AE119
  Europe
    directories, AD1, AE2
    Russian-language, AD300
  Finland
    indexes, AD311
  France
    bibliography, AE51, BE1143
    history, AE52
    indexes, AD312
  Germany
    indexes, AD313, AD314, AD315, AD316
  Great Britain
    bibliography, AD111, AD112
    directories, AD1, AE2
    indexes, AD261, AD264, AD281, AD282, AD287, AD289, AD292, BA6
    union lists, AD222
  Hungary, AD120, AD122, AD123
    indexes, AD317
  India, AD190, AD191, AD192, AD193
    indexes, AD337, AD338, AD339
  Indonesia, AD194, AD195, AD196, AD197
  international
    directories, AD1, AD118, AE2
  Iran
    bibliography, AD198
  Iraq
    bibliography, AE91
  Ireland, AD124, DC394
  Israel, AD200
    indexes, AD340
  Italy, AD125, AD126, AD128
    bibliography, AD129, CH657
      current, AD130
    indexes, AD318, AD319
  Japan
    bibliography, AD201, AD202
    indexes, AD342
    union lists, AD217, AD223
  Kenya
    bibliography, AD172
  Laos, AD212
  Latin America, AD64, AF158
    bibliography, AD65, AD67, AD68
    indexes, AD295, AD296, AD297, AD298, AD299
      bibliography, AD248
  Lithuania
    union lists, AD220
  Luxembourg, AD83, AD131
  Malaysia
    bibliography, AD203, AD204, AD205
    indexes, AD336
    union lists, AD205
  Mexico
    bibliography, AD61, AD62, AD63
    indexes, BE909
  Montenegro
    bibliography, AD167
  Netherlands
    directories, AD132, AE65
    indexes, AD320
  New Zealand, AD213
    indexes, AD347
  Nigeria, AD174, AD175
    indexes, AD334
  Norway
    indexes, AD321, AD322, AH274
  Oceania, AD213
  Pakistan, AD206, AD207
  Papua New Guinea
    indexes, AD348
  Philippines, AD208
    bibliography, AD209, AD245, BE1600
    indexes, AD344

Poland, AD133
  bibliography, AD135, AD137
  library catalogs, AD134
Portugal
  bibliography, AD138
Romania, AD140
  bibliography, AD139
  indexes, AD323, AD324
Russia
  bibliography, AD142, AD144, AD145,
  AD146, AF214
Russia and the U.S.S.R.
  bibliography, AD143, AD149
    current, AD150
  indexes, AD325
    bibliography, AD326
  union lists, AD234
Scandinavia
  directories, AD80
Scotland
  bibliography, AD119
Serbia
  bibliography, AD167
Singapore
  indexes, AD336, AD345
South Africa, AD177
  bibliography, AD178
  indexes, AD335
South America
  bibliography, AD69
Spain
  bibliography, AD151, AD152, AD153,
  AD154, AD155, AD156
    current, AD159
  indexes, AD327, AD328, AD329
Sweden
  bibliography, AD160, AD161
Switzerland
  bibliography, AD162, AD163, AD164
    current, AD165
  indexes, AD330
Taiwan
  bibliography, AD210
Thailand
  union lists, AD246
Tunisia
  bibliography, AD179, AD180, AD181
Turkey
  indexes, AD331
Ukraine, AD166
United States
  abstract journals, AD284
  bibliography, AD29, AD30, AD31, AD32,
  AD33, AD34, AD35, AD36, AD38, AD39,
  AD40, AD41, AD43, AD46, BE420, BE422,
  CH29
  databases, AD272, AD273, AD278, AD285
  directories, AD51, AD53, AD54, AD56,
  AD57, AD58, AE23
  guides, BE421
  history, AD29, AD30, AD31, AD32, AD33,
  AD35, AD36, AD38, AD39, AD40, AD41,
  AD43, AD48
  indexes, AD256, AD258, AD261, AD272,
  AD273, AD274, AD277, AD278, AD281,
  AD282, AD285, AD287
  periodicals
    abstract journals, AD284
  Southern states
    bibliography, AD44
    history, AD44
  union lists, AD225
U.S.S.R.
  bibliography, AD141, AD146, AD147, AD148
  library catalogs, AD141
Venezuela
  indexes, BE963
Vietnam, AD212
  bibliography, AD211
Wales
  indexes, AD290
Yugoslavia
  bibliography, AD168, BE1500

indexes, AD306, AD332, AD333
Periodicals (by language)
  Farsi, AD199
  French, AD79
  German, AD76, AD77
  Polish
    bibliography, AD136
  Russian, AD78
  Slavic
    union lists, AD232
  Spanish
    bibliography, AD157
Periodicals (by subject)
  architecture, BF225, BF226
  armed forces, CJ567
  art, BF46, BF49
  classical literature, BE1008
  Commonwealth literature, BE818
  education, CB22
  history, DA15
  history and area studies, DA13, DA14
  humanities, AD64, AD68
  literature, BE170
    directories, BE174
  political science, CJ101
  psychology, CB22, CD13
  religion, BC23, BC25
  social and behavioral sciences, AD68, CD14
  women, CC523
  see also Ethnic press; Little magazines
Periodicals, annuals and government serials held in
  the Architectural Association Library,
  Architectural Association (Great Britain). Library,
  BF225
—— Underwood, Elizabeth, BF225
Periodicals directory, AD18
Periodicals for school media programs, AA377
Periodicals for South-East Asian studies, Moon,
  Brenda Elizabeth, AD216
Periodicals from Africa, Travis, Carole, AD238,
  DD28
Periodicals in print, AD202
Periodicals in South African libraries, AD243
Periodicals in the social sciences and humanities
  currently received by Canadian libraries, National
  Library of Canada, AD228
Periodicals supplement, AF112
Periodicheskaia pechat' SSSR 1917–1949,
  Vsesoiuznaia Knizhnaia Palata, AD118
Periodici italiani, 1886–1957, AD128
Periodici italiani 1914–1919, Cavallo, Maria Lucia,
  DC426
—— Tanzarello, Ettore, DC426
Periodici italiani, 1968–1981, Barachino, Maria,
  AD128
—— Merola, Giovanna, AD128
—— Stocco, Carla, AD128
Periodici italiani scientifici, tecnici e di cultura
  generale, Consiglio nazionale delle ricerche
  (Italy), AD126
Periódicos brasileiros de ciência e technologia,
  AD72
Periódicos brasileiros de cultura, Rio de Janeiro.
  Instituto Brasileiro de Bibliografia e
  Documentação, AD72
Periódicos y revistas españolas e
  hispanoamericanas, AD157
Périodiques d'architecture, BF225
Périodiques slaves en caracatères cyrilliques,
  Bibliothèque Nationale (France). Département des
  Périodiques, AD231
Périodiques slaves en caractères cyrilliques,
  Bibliothèque Nationale (France). Département des
  Périodiques, AD232
Periodychni vydannîa URSR, 1917–1960,
  Knyzhkova palata Ukraïns'koi RSR, AE72
Periodychni vydannîa URSU, 1918–1950,
  Knyzhkova Palata Ukraïns'koi RSR, AD166
Peripatetics, CC479
Perkins, Agnes. Dictionary of American children's
  fiction, 1859–1959, BE382
—— Dictionary of British children's fiction,
  BE383

—— The Phoenix Award of the Children's
  Literature Association, 1985–1989, BE388
Perkins, Barbara. Benét's reader's encyclopedia of
  American literature, BE431
Perkins, C. R. Information sources in cartography,
  CL220
—— World mapping today, CL269
Perkins, Charles C. Cyclopedia of painters and
  paintings, BF299, BF312
Perkins, David. A history of modern poetry, BE719
Perkins, George. Harper handbook to literature,
  BE84
Perkins, George B. Benét's reader's encyclopedia of
  American literature, BE431
Perkins, Kenneth J. Tunisia, DD48
Perks, Robert. Oral history, DC332
Perl, T. Math equals, EB104
Perleberg, Max. Who's who in modern China,
  AH341
Perlmutter, Barry F. Handbook of family
  measurement techniques, CC239
The permanence and care of color photographs,
  Wilhelm, Henry Gilmer, BF351
Permanent Committee on Geographical Names for
  British Official Use. A gazetteer of Albania,
  CL129
—— A gazetteer of Greece, CL142
—— Glossaries, CL267
Permanent Consultative Committee on Official
  Statistics (Great Britain). Guide to current official
  statistics, CG238
Permanent Inter-State Committee for Drought
  Control in the Sahel. Sources de l'histoire
  démographique des pays du Sahel conservées dans
  les archives, CG307, DD102
Permanent International Committee of Linguists.
  Linguistic bibliography for the year [...] and
  supplement for the years [...], BD25, BD149
Permanent International Committee of Linguists.
  Committee for Terminology. A glossary of
  American technical linguistic usage, 1925–1950,
  BD39
•Permanent inventory of agricultural research
  projects, EJ74
Permuted and subject index to Computing reviews,
  EK166
Permuted (KWIC) index to Computing reviews,
  EK166
Permuted medical subject headings, EH146
Pernot, Hubert. Bibliographie hellénique du dix-
  huitième siècle, AA703
—— Bibliographie ionienne, AA703
Péron, Yves. Atlas de la Haute-Volta, CL339
Peronism and the three Perons, Horvath, Laszlo,
  DB327
Perpustakaan Nasional (Indonesia). Katalog majalah
  terbitan Indonesia, AD194
—— Katalog surat kabar, AE89
Perpustakaan Negara Malaysia. Terbitan bersiri kini
  Malaysia (bukan kerajaan), AD204
Perren, Richard. Japanese studies from pre-history to
  1990, DE202
Perrett, Bryan. Encyclopaedia of the Second World
  War, DA206
Perretta, Don. Encyclopedia of rock, BJ345
Perrin, D. D. Purification of laboratory chemicals,
  EE85
Perrins, Christopher M. The encyclopedia of birds,
  EG260
—— Handbook of the birds of Europe, the Middle
  East and North Africa, EG262
—— The illustrated encyclopedia of birds, EG264
Perrot, Claude Hélène. Passé de l'Afrique par
  l'oralité, DD11
—— République du Congo-Brazzaville, DD144
Perrot, Paul N. The history and art of glass, BG53
Perry, David W. Hymns and tunes indexed by first
  lines, tune names, and metres, compiled from
  current English hymnbooks, BC321
Perry, Edward S. The new film index, BH235
Perry, Gerald J. AIDS information sourcebook,
  EH170
Perry, Glenn E. The Palestine question, DE244

Perry, James L. *Handbook of public administration*, CJ481, CJ482

Perry, Jeb H. *Variety obits*, BH29

Perry, John H. *Perry's chemical engineers' handbook*, EK57

Perry, Margaret. *The Harlem Renaissance*, BE529

Perry, Robert H. *Perry's chemical engineers' handbook*, EK57

Perry, Ruth M. *Southwest Native American arts and material culture*, BG9, CC422

Perryman, Wayne R. *International subscription agents*, AK170

Perry's chemical engineers' handbook, EK57

Persecution and resistance under the Nazis, Wiener Library, London, DC244

PERSI, AJ45

Persian and Afghan newspapers in the Library of Congress, 1871–1978, Pourhadi, Ibrahim Vaqfi, AE90

Persian literature, Storey, Charles Ambrose, BE1574

Persian serials and newspapers in British libraries, AD199

Person, James E. *Statistical forecasts of the United States*, CG105, CH110

Personal computer programming encyclopedia, EK207

Personal finance, CH213

Personal name index to "The New York times index," 1851–1974, Falk, Byron A., AE108

Personal names, Smith, Elsdon Coles, AJ166

Personal writings by women to 1900, BE489

—— Davis, Gwenn, BE508

Personalbibliographie zur deutschen Literaturgeschichte, Hansel, Johannes, BE1221

Personalbibliographien österreichischer Dichter und Schriftsteller, Stock, Karl F., BE1096

Personalidades cubanas, Peraza Sarausa, Fermín, AH152

Personalidades dominicanas, AH155

Personalities Caribbean, AH149

Personalities in the Caribbean, AH149

Personality, CD95, CD96, CD98

Personality tests and reviews, Buros, Oscar Krisen, CD69

Personnalités chinoises d'aujourd'hui, Goldfiem, Jacques de, AH345

Personnel administration in libraries, Creth, Sheila D., AK178

—— Duda, Frederick, AK178

Personnel executives contactbook, CH715

Personnel literature, CH709

Personnel management, AK178, CH713

  abstract journals, CH710

  bibliography, CH720

  congress and meetings, AL32

  dictionaries, CH711, CH714

  directories, CH715, CH720

  handbooks, CH712, CH717, CH719

  indexes, CH709

  thesauruses, CH652

Personnel management abstracts, CH710

Persons, Stow. *Socialism and American life*, CJ527

Persons who shape our destiny, AH366

Personu un prieksmetu alfabetiskais rādītājs, DC436

Perspectives, Knevitt, Charles, BF95

Perthes, Justus. *Almanach de Gotha*, AJ75

Peru

  bibliography, AA538, AA539, AA540, AA541, AA542, DB381, DB383, DB384

    current, AA543, AA544

  bibliography of bibliography, AA30

  biography, AH140, AH141, AH142, DB387

  encyclopedias, DB388

  gazetteers, CL125

  government publications, AF159

  statistics, CG157, CG158, DB389

Peru (by subject)

  archaeology and ancient history

    bibliography, DB385

  ethnic groups, CE74

  folklore and popular culture, CF70

  foreign relations, DB336

  history, DB279

    bibliography, DB271, DB382

    encyclopedias, AH140, DB387

    guides to records, DB276

    manuscripts and archives, DB386

    statistics, CG158

Peru. Archivo General de la Nación. *Guía del archivo histórico*, DB386

Perú. Dirección Nacional de Estadística y Censos. *Anuario estadístico del Perú*, CG157

Peru, Fisher, John Robert, DB382

Perú, las provincias en cifras, 1876–1981, CG158

Perú : series estadísticas 1970–92, DB389

Perú y su literatura, Rodríguez Rea, Miguel Angel, BE955

Peruvian literature, BE956

  bibliography, BE955

  biobibliography, BE954

  handbooks, BE957

Peruvian literature, Foster, David William, BE955

Pervin, Lawrence A. *Handbook of personality*, CD96

Pesante, Alessandra. *Bibliografia di bibliografie*, AA50

Pešata, Zdeňka. *Čeští spisovatelé 19. a počátku 20. století*, BE1105

Pescow, Jerome K. *Encyclopedia of accounting systems*, CH251

Peskett, Pamela. *Record offices*, AJ100

Peskinoi, B. A. *Russkie pisateli vtoroi poloviny XIX nachala XX vv. (do 1917 goda)*, BE1392

Pesonen, Maritta. *Englanti-suomi suursanakirja*, AC322

Pessin, Allan H. *The complete words of Wall Street*, CH212

—— *The illustrated encyclopedia of the securities industry*, CH211

Pestana, Harold R. *Bibliography of congressional geology*, EF37

Pesticide fact handbook, EJ60

The pesticide manual, EJ61

Pesticides, EJ49

  abstract journals, EH420

  directories, EJ45

  handbooks, EJ46, EJ48, EJ52, EJ60, EJ61

Pesticides abstracts, EH420, EH421

•*Pesticides disc*, EJ46

Petchenik, Barbara Bartz. *Atlas of early American history*, DB96

Peteraitis, Vilius. *Lietuviškai angliškas žodynas*, AC603

Peters, Arno. *Peters atlas of the world*, CL287

Peters, Francis Edwards. *Greek philosophical terms*, BB42

Peters, Franz. *Gmelins Handbuch der anorganischen Chemie*, EE110

Peters, Gary L. *Biographical dictionary of geography*, CL83

—— *Dictionary of concepts in human geography*, CL38

—— *Dictionary of concepts in physical geography*, CL37

Peters, Howard M. *Understanding chemical patents*, EA263

Peters, Jean. *The bookman's glossary*, AA271

Peters, Susanne. *Directory of museums in Africa*, AL87

Peters atlas of the world, Peters, Arno, CL287

Petersen, Anne C. *Encyclopedia of adolescence*, CC159, CD83

Petersen, Carl Sophus. *Illustreret dansk Litteraturhistorie*, BE1121

Petersen, Neal H. *American intelligence, 1775–1990*, CJ544

Petersen, Paul D. *Eastern Christianity*, BC446

—— *Politics and religion*, BC15

Petersen, Renee. *Dictionary of demography : biographies*, CG43

—— *Dictionary of demography : multilingual glossary*, CG28

—— *Dictionary of demography : terms, concepts, and institutions*, CG29

Petersen, Svend. *A statistical history of the American presidential elections*, CJ256

Petersen, Toni. *Art & architecture thesaurus*, BF94

—— *Guide to indexing and cataloging with the Art & architecture thesaurus*, BF94

Petersen, William. *Dictionary of demography : biographies*, CG43

—— *Dictionary of demography : multilingual glossary*, CG28

—— *Dictionary of demography : terms, concepts, and institutions*, CG29

Peterson, Bernard L. *Century of musicals in black and white*, BE531

—— *Contemporary black American playwrights and their plays*, BE521, BE530

—— *Early black American playwrights and dramatic writers*, BE531

Peterson, Clarence S. *Consolidated bibliography of county histories in fifty states in 1961*, DB139

Peterson, John. *Historical dictionary of Saudi Arabia*, DE253

Peterson, Linda Kauffman. *Newbery and Caldecott Medal and Honor books*, AA343

Peterson, Martin S. *Encyclopedia of food science*, EJ152

—— *Encyclopedia of food technology*, EJ155

Peterson, Roger Tory. *A field guide to the birds*, EG272

—— *The Peterson field guide series*, EG85

The Peterson field guide series, Peterson, Roger Tory, EG85

Peterson's annual guide to independent secondary schools, CB109

Peterson's annual guide to undergraduate study, CB286, CB298

Peterson's annual guides to graduate study, CB302

•*Peterson's career options*, CB213

•*Peterson's career planning service*, CB213

Peterson's caring for kids with special needs, CC163

Peterson's college database, CB286, CB213, CB283, CB298, CB387

Peterson's college money handbook, CB386

•*Peterson's college selection service*, CB283, CB298

Peterson's competitive colleges, CB284

•*Peterson's financial aid service*, CB386, CB387, CB388, CB390

•*Peterson's freshman financial aid database*, CB386, CB387, CB388

•*Peterson's gradline*, CB302

Peterson's grants for graduate students, CB389

Peterson's grants for graduate study, CB389

Peterson's guide to certificate programs at American colleges and universities, CB285

Peterson's guide to colleges with programs for learning-disabled students, CB315

Peterson's guide to four-year colleges, CB283, CB286, CB298

Peterson's guide to private secondary schools, CB109

Peterson's guide to two-year colleges, CB283, CB286, CB298

Peterson's national college databank, CB287

•*Peterson's noninstitutional aid database*, CB386, CB387, CB390

Peterson's paying less for college, CB386

Peterson's public schools USA, CB148

Peterson's register of higher education, CB288

Peterson's sports scholarships and college athletic programs, CB391

Peterson's two-year colleges, CB298

•*Peterson's undergraduate database*, CB283

Petit, Louis. *Bibliographie hellénique du dix-huitième siècle*, AA703

Petit, Louis David. *Bibliographie der Middelnederlandsche taal– en letterkunde*, BE1335

Petit, Patrick J. *Encyclopedia of legal information sources*, CK124

Petit de Julleville, Louis. *Histoire de la langue et de la littérature française des origines à 1900*, BE1175

Petit dictionnaire de l'ancien français, Vandaele, Hilaire, AC384

Petit dictionnaire provençal-français, Levy, Emil, AC655

Petit Larousse illustré, 1990, AC333

Le petit Robert, AJ191

Le petit Robert 2, AJ191

Petit supplément au Dictionnaire de Du Cange, Schmidt, Charles, AC587

Les petites revues littéraires, 1914–1939, Admussen, Richard L., BE1143

Petkova, Zornitsa Malcheva. *Bibliografiia na bŭlgarskata bibliografiia, 1944–1969*, AA38, AA39

Petras, Kathryn. *Jobs '93*, CH705

Petras, Ross. *Jobs '93*, CH705

Petrik, Géza. *Magyar könyvészet, 1712/1860–1911/20*, AA709

Petro, Julius. *A descriptive atlas of the Pacific islands*, CL368

The petroleum dictionary, Boone, Lalia Phipps, EK304

———— Tver, David F., EK306

Petroleum dictionary for office, field and factory, Porter, Hollis Paine, EK305

Petroleum engineering
  bibliography, EK302
  dictionaries, EK303, EK304, EK305, EK306
    bilingual
      English-Russian, EF88
  guides, EK298
  handbooks, EK308

Petroleum engineering handbook, EK308

Petroleum industry
  bibliography, EK299, EK301, EK302
  dictionaries, EK303, EK306
  directories, EF91, EK307
  statistics, EK301

Petroleum industry (by subject)
  history
    bibliography, EK300

Petroleum production handbook, EK308

Petroleum Research Corp. *Bibliography of theses written for advanced degrees in geology and related sciences at universities and colleges in the United States and Canada through 1957*, EF43

Petrology, EF256
  abstract journals, EF178
  classification, EF255
  dictionaries, EF257, EF259
    bilingual
      Russian-English, EF258
  encyclopedias, EF253
  handbooks, EF254

Petronio, Guiseppe. *Dizionario enciclopedico della letteratura italiana*, BE1300

Petrov, Julia A. *Foreign language, area, and other international studies*, BD76

Petrov, S. O. *Knigi grazhdanskoi pechati XVIII veka*, AA788

———— *Knigi pervoi chetverti XIX veka*, AA842

Petrova, Ivanka Apostolova. *Istoriiata na Bŭlgariia v memoarnata literatura*, DC115

Petrović, Milomir. *Srpska bibliografija*, AA797

Petrovich, Michael B. *Yugoslavia*, DC609

Petrunoff, Vance T. *Directory of foreign trade organizations in Eastern Europe*, CH131

Pets, EJ134

Pettersen, Hjalmar Marius. *Bibliotheca norvegica*, AA757

———— *Norsk anonym– og pseudonym-lexikon*, AA179

Petteys, Chris. *Dictionary of women artists*, BF143, BF152

Petti, Kerstin. *English-Swedish Swedish-English dictionary*, AC766

Petti, Vincent. *English-Swedish Swedish-English dictionary*, AC766

Pettman, Charles. *Africanderisms*, AC183

Pevsner, Nikolaus. *Academies of art past and present*, BF257

———— *History of building types*, BF257

———— *An outline of European architecture*, BF257

———— *The Penguin dictionary of architecture*, BF244

Pewter, BG149, BG150, BG151

Pewter down the ages, Cotterell, Howard Herschel, BG150

Pewter in America, Laughlin, Ledlie Irwin, BG151

Pezo, Vladimir. *Hrvatski biografski leksikon*, AH307

Pfaff, Richard W. *Medieval Latin liturgy*, BC269, DA138

Pfannkuch, Hans-Olaf. *Elsevier's dictionary of environmental hydrogeology*, EF132

Pfannl, Beth Kempler. *Tinker guide to Latin American and Caribbean policy and scholarly resources in metropolitan New York*, DB288

Pfannmüller, Gustav. *Handbuch der Islam-Literatur*, BC498

Pfannschmidt, Ernst Erik. *Twentieth-century lace*, BG161

Pfatteicher, Philip H. *Commentary of the Lutheran book of worship*, BC358

———— *Dictionary of liturgical terms*, BC268

Pfeifer, Wolfgang. *Etymologisches Wörterbuch des Deutschen*, AC427

Pfeiffer, Charles F. *The Biblical world*, BC196

Pfeiffer, Joachim. *Literaturpsychologie, 1945–1987*, BE26

Pfeiffer, Robert H. *Apocrypha according to the Authorized Version*, BC94

Pfeiffer, Rudolf. *History of classical scholarship from 1300 to 1850*, BE1021, DA107

———— *History of classical scholarship from the beginnings to the end of the Hellenistic age*, BE1021, BE1024, DA107, DA113

Pfister, Max. *Lessico etimologico italiano*, AC538

Pflücke, Maximilian. *Periodica chemica*, EE19

Pflug, Günther. *Lexikon des gesamten Buchwesens*, AA270

Phaidon guide to pewter, Brett, Vanessa, BG149

Pham, Henry Thuoc V. *A bibliography of Vietnamese magazines, newspapers and newsletters published in the United States and other countries*, AD211

Phan Thiên Châu. *Vietnamese communism*, CJ445

The pharmaceutical codex, Pharmaceutical Society of Great Britain. Dept. of Pharmaceutical Sciences, EH361

Pharmaceutical Society of Great Britain. Dept. of Pharmaceutical Sciences. *The pharmaceutical codex*, EH361

Pharmacological and chemical synonyms, Marler, E. E. J., EH329

Pharmacology
  abstract journals, EH323
  bibliography, EH317, EH318
  databases, EH58, EH357
  dictionaries, EH327, EH329
    multilingual, EH328, EH331
  dispensatories and pharmacopoeias, EH353, EH354, EH357, EH358, EH360, EH361, EH362, EH363, EH364
    Great Britain, EH356
  guides, EH316
  handbooks, EE83, EH337, EH345
  periodicals, EH34

Pharmacology (by subject)
  history, EH366
  see also **Drugs**

Pharmacopoeia internationalis, EH358

The pharmacopoeia of the United States of America, EH362, EH363

Pharmacy, EH326, EH368
  abstract journals, EH322
  bibliography, EH317, EH318
  dictionaries, EH327
    bilingual
      English-German, EH136
    multilingual, EH328, EH331
  guides, EH316
  see also **Drugs**

Pharmacy museums, Griffenhagen, George B., EH367

Pharmacy museums and historical collections in the United States and Canada, Griffenhagen, George B., EH367

Pharmacy museums and historical collections on public view in the United States and Canada, Hamarneh, Sami Khalaf, EH367

———— Stieb, Ernst Walter, EH367

Pharmacy museums and historical collections on public view, U.S.A, Hamarneh, Sami Khalaf, EH367

Ph.D. Saudi dissertation abstracts, Alī, Kamāl Muḥammad, AG57

Pheby, John. *The Oxford-Duden pictorial Serbo-Croat & English dictionary*, AC714

Phelps, Edith M. *Debate index*, BE368

Phelps, Erin. *Inventory of longitudinal studies in the social sciences*, CA60

Phelps, Roger P. *A guide to research in music education*, BJ6

Phenix, Katharine. *On account of sex*, AK14, AK73

Phi Delta Kappa. *Dictionary of education*, CB75

———— *The Phi Delta Kappa Gallup polls of attitudes toward education, 1969–1988*, CB137

The Phi Delta Kappa Gallup polls of attitudes toward education, 1969–1988, Bugher, Wilmer, CB137

Philadelphia Bibliographical Center and Union Library Catalogue. *Union list of microfilms*, AA136

Philadelphia Free Library. *The Edwin A. Fleischer Collection of Orchestral Music*, BJ98

Philanthropic studies index, AL95

Philanthropic trusts in Australia, AL127

Philanthropists, AL118

Philately *see* **Postage stamps**

Philately, Collectors Club (New York, N.Y.). Library, BG200

Philip, George D.E. *Mexico*, DB231

Philipp, Hans-Jürgen. *Saudi Arabia*, DE254

Philipp, Werner. *Gesamtverzeichnis russischer und sowjetischer Periodika und Serienwerke*, AD234

Philippides, Dia Mary L. *Census of modern Greek literature*, BE1274

Philippine-American relations, DB21, DE249

Philippine atlas, Fund for Assistance to Private Education, CL361

Philippine bibliography, AA930

Philippine drama, BE1598

Philippine ethnography, Saito, Shiro, CF111

Philippine government publications, AF257

The Philippine Islands, 1493–1898, Blair, Emma Helen, DE246

Philippine languages, BD233, BD234
  see also **Pilipino language**

Philippine literature, BE1599, BE1600

Philippine literature in English, BE1599

———— Tonogbanua, Francisco G., BE1600

Philippine literature in English, 1898–1957, Yabes, Leopoldo Y., BE1600

Philippine national bibliography, AA931, AG55

Philippine newspapers, Saito, Shiro, AE98

Philippine newspapers in selected American libraries, Saito, Shiro, AE98

Philippine retrospective national bibliography, 1523–1699, Bernardo, Gabriel Adriano, AA926

Philippine social sciences and humanities review, BE1600

Philippine statistical yearbook, CG419

Philippine union catalog, AA930

Philippines
  atlases, CL361, CL362
  bibliography, AA926, AA927, AA928, AA929, BE876, DB268, DE245, DE246, DE248, DE250
    current, AA930, AA931, AG55
  bibliography of bibliography, AA82
  biography, AH367
  dissertations, AA931, AG55, AG56
  gazetteers, CL168
  government publications, AD208, AF257, AF258, AF259
  newspapers
    union lists, AE98
  periodicals, AD208
    indexes, AD344
  statistics, CG419, CG420

Philippines (by subject)
anthropology and ethnology, CE111
education, CL361
folklore and popular culture, CF94
foreign relations, DB21, DE249
history
bibliography, DE99, DE247
sourcebooks, DE247
migration, CC409
population
statistics, CG418
Philippines. National Economic and Development Authority. *Philippine statistical yearbook,* CG419
Philippines. National Science Development Board. *Compilation of graduate theses prepared in the Philippines,* AG56
Philippines. National Statistics Office. *Vital statistics report,* CG420
Philippines, Richardson, Jim, DE250
Philips, Billy U. *Medical sociology,* CC6, EH11
Philips, C. H. *Historical writing on the peoples of Asia,* DE18
Philips, J. B. *New Testament in modern English,* BC94
Philip's atlas of world history, DA49
Philler, Theresa Ammannito. *An annotated bibliography on technical writing, editing, graphics, and publishing, 1950–1965,* EA164
The Phillimore atlas and index of parish registers, AJ113
Phillips, Casey R. *Historical journals,* DA15
Phillips, Claude S. *The African political dictionary,* CJ403
Phillips, Dennis J. *Teaching, coaching, and learning tennis,* BK103
Phillips, Gillian. *Canada's relations with Latin America and the Caribbean, 1970–1990,* DB261
Phillips, John B. *Directory of patent depository libraries,* EA266
Phillips, Lawrence Barnett. *Dictionary of biographical reference,* AH20
Phillips, Philip Lee. *List of maps of America in the Library ... preceded by a list of works relating to cartography,* CL236
Phillips, Phoebe. *The collectors' encyclopedia of antiques,* BG38
——— *The encyclopedia of glass,* BG59
Phillips, Walter Alison. *History of the Church of Ireland,* BC340
Philological quarterly, BE36, BE40, BE743
Philology *see* **Languages; Linguistics**
Philosopher's guide to sources, research tools, professional life and related fields, De George, Richard T., BB1, BB2
The philosopher's index, BB7, BB8, BB25
Philosophical studies of home economics in the United States, Brown, Marjorie M., EJ199
Philosophische Dissertationen deutscher Universitäten 1660–1750, Marti, Hanspeter, BB16
Philosophy
abstract journals, BB25
bibliography, BB5, BB6, BB7, BB8, BB9, BB10, BB17, BB22, BB26, BC31, CD11
current, BB12, BB13
bibliography of bibliographies, BB11
biography, BB37, BB48, BB54
congresses and meetings, BB17
databases, BB25
dictionaries, BB37, BB38, BB40, BB41, BB42, BB43, BC74
directories, BB44, BB45
dissertations, BB15, BB16
encyclopedias, BB26, BB29, BB30, BB34, BB35
guides, BB1, BB2, BB3
indexes, AD254, BB24, BB25, BE38, CE23
periodicals, BB14
women philosophers, BB4, BB47
Philosophy (by country or region)
China, BB19
India
bibliography, BB18, BB21
dictionaries, BB39
encyclopedias, BB33

Philosophy (by period)
19th century, BB78, BB79
20th century, BB81
ancient, BB51, BB52, BB53, BB55, BB56, BB57, BB59
bibliography, BB58
biography, BB54
dictionaries, BB42
medieval, BB60, BB61, BB62, BB63, BB64, BB65, BB68
bibliography, BB66
biography, BB67
modern, BB73, BB75, BB76
Renaissance, BB69
bibliography, BB70
Philosophy (by subject)
history, BB46, BB50, BB81
bibliography, BB22, BB49
see also **Aesthetics**
Philosophy, Bynagle, Hans E., BB1
Philosophy and literature, BE191
Philosophy and psychology, Harvard University. Library, BB6, CD11
Philosophy and religion
bibliography, BB23, BC21
dictionaries, BC74
Philosophy journals and serials, Ruben, Douglas H., BB14
Philosophy of religion, Wainwright, William J., BB23, BC21
Philosophy of the grammarians, Coward, Harold G., BB33
——— Raja, K. Kunjunni, BB33
Philosophy, policies and programs for early adolescent education, Blyth, Dale A., CB10
Phinney, John F. S. *The history of anthropology,* CE15
Phipps, Frances. *The collector's complete dictionary of American antiques,* BG39
Phobias, CD100, EH378
The Phoenix Award of the Children's Literature Association, 1985–1989, BE388
Phonetic symbol guide, Ladusaw, William A., BD10
——— Pullum, Geoffrey K., BD10, BD15
Phonetics, BD15
dictionaries, BD36
Photogrammetric engineering, EF18
The photograph collector's guide, Witkin, Lee D., BF352
The photograph collectors' resource directory, BF352
Photographers, BF345
Photographers encyclopaedia international, BF353
Photographers encyclopaedia international 1839 to the present, BF353
Photographer's market, BF346
Photographic abstracts, BF332
Photographic atlas of the moon, Kopal, Zdeněk, EC66
Photographic literature, Boni, Albert, BF326
Photographica, New York Public Library. Research Libraries, BF338
Photographs, Blodgett, Richard E., BF352
Photographs at auction, 1952–1984, BF348
Photography
abstract journals, BF332
auction records, BF348, BF356
audiovisual materials, BF327
bibliography, BF326, BF327, BF333, BF336, BF357
biography, BF353, BF354, BF357
contemporary, BF355
biography (by period)
19th century, BF356
catalogs, BF365
collections, BF349, BF352
directories, BF344, BF347
dictionaries, BF342, BF343
directories, BF345, BF346
encyclopedias, BF340, BF341
indexes, BF339, BF356
library catalogs, BF336, BF337, BF338

periodicals
indexes, BF330
research
handbooks, BF350
Photography (by country or region)
Germany, BF329
Great Britain, BF328
Photography (by period)
19th century, BF335
bibliography, BF328, BF331
Photography (by subject)
history, BF345
bibliography, BF334
preservation, BF351, BF352
Photography and literature, BF333
Photography and photographers to 1900, Sennett, Robert S., BF335
Photography books index, Moss, Martha, BF339
Photography books index II, Moss, Martha, BF339
Photography index, Parry, Pamela Jeffcott, BF62, BF339, BF367
Photohistorica, European Society for the History of Photography, BF332
Phousaras, G. I. *Bibliographia tōn Hellēnikōn bibliographiōn, 1791–1947,* AA47
Phrases make history here, CJ377, DC409
•*PHYS,* ED10
Physical anthropology, CE64
Physical disability, CC186
Physical education
bibliography, BK3
encyclopedias, BK15
indexes, BK10
Physical education index, BK10
Physicians, AL169, EH216, EH220
biography, EA172, EA183, EA190, EH217, EH227
directories, EH150, EH164
library catalogs, EH224
Physicians (by country or region)
Canada, EH228
biography, EH229
directories, EH166
Great Britain, EH226
biography, EH230, EH231
directories, EH168, EH169
United States, EH228
biography, EH229
directories, EH157
Physicians' current procedural terminology, EH147
Physicians' desk reference, EH347, EH348
Physicians' desk reference for nonprescription drugs, EH347, EH348
Physicians' desk reference for opthalmology, EH347
•*Physicians' desk reference (PDR),* EH347
Physicians' genRx, EH349
Physicists, ED30, ED54
directories, EC45, ED31
A physicist's desk reference, ED48
Physics
abstract journals, ED10, ED11
bibliography, BE31, CE14, EA16, EA21, EA22, EB10, EB16, EC15, EC17, ED4, ED5, ED6, ED7, EE13, EE15, EF57, EF141, EF173, EF232, EG6, EG98, EG105, EG211, EG213, EG312, EH68
biography, AL172, ED54, ED55
databases, ED9, ED10, ED11
dictionaries, EA90, ED18, ED19, ED20, ED21, ED23, ED24
bilingual
German-English, ED25, ED26
Russian-English, ED27
directories, EC45, ED22, ED29, ED30, ED31
dissertations, ED8
encyclopedias, EC29, ED12, ED13, ED14, ED15, ED16, ED17, ED20
eponyms, EA85
guides, EB3, ED1, ED2, ED3
handbooks, EC54, ED32, ED33, ED36, ED38, ED39, ED40, ED45, EE70
indexes, ED4
prizes and awards, AL172, AL175, ED55, ED56
style manuals, ED51

tables, EA155, EA156, ED38, ED41, ED42, ED43, ED44, ED46, ED47, ED48, ED50

Physics (by subject)
history
bibliography, ED52, ED53

Physics, Nobelstiftelsen, AL172, AL175, ED55, ED56

Physics abstracts, ED9, ED10, ED11, EK128

Physics briefs, ED10

•*Physics briefs online,* EC23, ED10

Physics handbook, Nordling, Carl, ED38

Physics in medicine & biology encyclopedia, EH89

Physics literature, Whitford, Robert Henry, ED3

Physics vade mecum, ED48

Physikalische Berichte, ED10

Physiology
biography, AL169, EH216
encyclopedias, CD99
prizes and awards, AL173, EH225

Physiology or medicine, Nobelstiftelsen, AL176

Phytochemical dictionary, EG161

Pianarosa, Albertina. *Le bilinguisme chez l'enfant et l'apprentissage d'une langue seconde,* BD60

—— *Child bilingualism and second language learning,* BD60

Pianigiani, Ottorino. *Vocabolario etimologico della lingua italiana,* AC539

Piano and organ catalogue, BJ92

Piaseckyj, Oksana. *Bibliography of Ukrainian literature in English and French,* BE1494

Picard, Paul R. *Churches & church membership in the United States,* BC87

Picaresque literature, BE1475, BE1476

Piccialuti Caprioli, Maura. *Bibliografia dell'Archivio centrale dello Stato, 1953–1978,* DC427

Piccirelli, Annette. *Inventing and patenting sourcebook,* EA262

Pichanick, J. *Rhodesian literature in English,* BE1541

Pichois, Claude. *Littérature française,* BE1176

Pick, Albert. *Standard catalog of world paper money,* BG189

Pick, Bernhard. *Ante-Nicene Fathers,* BC293

Pick, Franz. *All the monies of the world,* BG182, CH286

Pickard, Roy. *Award movies,* BH274
—— *Oscar movies,* BH275
—— *Who played who in the movies,* BH276
—— *Who played who on the screen,* BH276

Pickaxe and pencil, Bloxom, Margucrite D., DB124

Picken, Mary (Brooks). *The fashion dictionary,* BG100
—— *Language of fashion,* BG100

Pickering, David. *The Facts on File dictionary of the theatre,* BH69

Pickering, W. R. *Information sources in the medical sciences,* EH317

Pickett, Calder M. *An annotated journalism bibliography, 1958–1968,* AE134

Pickford, Cedric Edward. *Arthurian bibliography,* BE338, BE339

Pickford, Ian. *Jackson's silver & gold marks of England, Scotland & Ireland,* BG138

Pickles, J. D. *The new Cambridge bibliography of English literature,* BE585

Pickrill, D. A. *Ministers of the Crown,* CJ345

Pick's currency yearbook, CH288

Pickup, Laurie. *Urban transport and planning,* BF269, CH451, EK121

Picoche, Jacqueline. *Dictionnaire étymologique du français,* AC351

Picon, Alice. *PAIS subject headings,* CA25

Picot, Paul. *Atlas of ore minerals,* EF203

Pictorial dictionary of ancient Athens, Traulos, Ioannes N., DA102, DA106

Pictorial dictionary of ancient Rome, Nash, Ernest, DA102, DA106

Pictorial dictionary of British 18th century furntiture design, BG120

Pictorial dictionary of British 19th century furniture design, BG120

Pictorial guide to identifying Australian architecture, Apperley, Richard, BF208
—— Irving, Robert, BF208
—— Mitchell, Solomon, BF208
—— Reynolds, Peter, BF208

A pictorial history of boxing, Fleischer, Nat, BK69

A pictorial history of the American theatre, 1860–1985, Blum, Daniel C., BH96

Picture books for children, Cianciolo, Patricia Jean, AA340

Picture collections, Mexico, BF349

Picture research, Schultz, John, BF350

Picture researcher's handbook, BF349

Picture sources 4, Robl, Ernest H., BF347

Picture sources UK, Eakins, Rosemary, BF349
—— Loving, Elizabeth, BF349

Pictured-key nature series, Jaques, Harry Edwin, EG83

Pictures
collections, BF349
indexes, BF60, BF61, BF62, BF63, BF367
research
handbooks, BF350
see also **Book illustration**

Picturesque expressions, AC81

Pidduck, William. *Left in Britain during 1973 and 1974,* CJ509
—— *The radical right and patriotic movements in Britain,* CJ338

Pidgeon, Alice. *Law books in print,* CK21

Pidgin languages, BD55
dictionaries
bilingual
Pidgin-English, AC628

Piecos gados, Ancitis, Valdemars, BE1320

Piedracueva, Haydée. *Bibliography of Latin American bibliographies, 1975–1979,* AA24

Pieges et difficultées de la langue française, Girodet, Jean, AC369

Piekarski, Vicki. *The frontier experience,* DB165

Piekarz, M. *Jewish publications in the Soviet Union, 1917–1960,* BC535

Pieper, M. *Study and research guide in computer science,* EK202

Piepkorn, Arthur Carl. *Profiles in belief,* BC65, BC270

Pierce, Peter. *The Oxford literary guide to Australia,* BE855

Pierce, Phyllis S. *The Dow Jones averages, 1885–1990,* CH325

Pierce, William L. *The encyclopedia of adoption,* CC223

Piercy, William C. *Dictionary of Christian biography and literature to the end of the sixth century A.D.,* BC249

Pierpont Morgan Library. *The Mary Flagler Cary music collection,* BJ89
—— *Nineteenth-century autograph music manuscripts in the Pierpoint Morgan Library,* BJ89

Pierreuse, Bernard. *Catalogue général de l'édition musicale en France,* BJ76
—— *General catalog of music publishing in France,* BJ76

Pierson, William Harvey. *Arts of the United States,* BF197

Piesarkas, B. *Anglų-lietuvių kalbų žodynas,* AC604

Piesarskas, Bronius. *Lietuvių-anglų kalbų žodynas,* AC604

Pietzschke, Fritz. *Novo Michaelis,* AC648

Pig news and information, EJ19

Piggott, Michael. *A guide to commonwealth government information sources,* AF263

Pigler, Andor. *Barockthemen,* BF172

Pike, Douglas. *Australian dictionary of biography,* AH371, DF40

Piland, Sherry. *Women artists,* BF16

Pile, John F. *Dictionary of 20th-century design,* BG130

Pilecky-Dekajlo, Adriana. *Foreign newspapers held by the Center for Research Libraries,* AE3

Pilger, Mary Anne. *Crafts index for young people,* BK139

Pilgrimage in the Middle Ages, Davidson, Linda Kay, DA132

Pilipenko, Hélène. *Récapitulation des périodiques officiels parus en Tunisie de 1881 à 1955,* AF239

Pilipino language, BD234

Pilkington, Walter. *American notes and queries,* BE168

Pillet, Alfred. *Bibliographie der Troubadours,* BE1374

Pilling, J. C. *Bibliographies of the languages of the North American Indians,* BD240

Pillsbury, Richard. *Atlas of American sport,* BK22

A pilot bibliography of South African English literature (from the beginnings to 1971), University of South Africa. Library. Subject Reference Dept, BE1538

Pinard, Jeanette L. *The People's Republic of China,* CK228

Pinaud, Pierre-François. *Guide du chercheur pour la période 1789–1815,* DC153

Pinchemel, Phillipe. *Geographers,* CL82

Pinches, Rosemary. *Burke's family index,* AJ150

Pincoe, Ruth. *Directory of Canadian theatre archives,* BH54

Pinder, John. *European political parties,* CJ320

Pine, E. G. *Author's and writer's who's who,* BE211

Pine, L. G. *Dictionary of mottos,* BE94

Pine-Coffin, R. S. *Bibliography of British and American travel in Italy to 1860,* DC424

Piñero García, Juan. *Musicos españoles de todos los tiempos,* BJ216

Pinfold, John R. *African population census reports,* CG313
—— *Tibet,* DE269

Pingaud, Bernard. *Écrivains d'aujourd'hui, 1940–1960,* BE1150

Pinkus, B. *Russian publications on Jews and Judaism in the Soviet Union, 1917–1967,* BC535

Pino, Frank. *Mexican Americans,* CC449

Pinsker, Sanford. *Jewish-American history and culture,* BC551

Pinson, Koppel. *Bibliographical introduction to nationalism,* CJ9

Pintér, Jenő. *Magyar irodalomtörténete,* BE1281

Pinther, Miklos. *Atlas of Great Lakes Indian history,* CC438

Pinto, Juan. *Panorama de la literatura argentina contemporanea,* BE920

The pinyin Chinese-English dictionary, AC267

Pipelines, Tilson, Marie, CH444

Piper, Alan J. *Medieval manuscripts in British libraries,* AA199

Pipers Enzyklopädie des Musiktheaters, BJ252

Pipics, Zoltán. *Dictionarium bibliothecarii practicum,* AK48
—— *Könyvtáros gyakorlati szótára,* AK48
—— *Librarian's practical dictionary in twenty-two languages,* AK48

Pippidi, D.M. *Dictionar de istorie veche a Românie,* DC498

Pipping, Fredrik Wilhelm. *Luettelo suomeksi präntätyistä kirjoista, kuin myös muutamista muista teoksista, joissa löytyy joku kirjoitus suomen, kielellä, tahi joku johdatus sitä tuntemaan,* AA609, AA610

Pirenne, Henri. *Bibliographie de l'histoire de Belgique,* DC100, DC451

Pirenne, L. P. L. *De Rijksarchieven in Nederland,* DC458

Pirot, Louis. *Dictionnaire de la Bible,* BC152

Pirsoul, Léon. *Dictionnaire bio-bibliographique des littérateurs d'expression wallonne, 1622 à 1950,* BE1098

PISAL, AD243

Pisaneschi, Janet I. *Learning AIDS,* EH21

Pisateli Moskvy, Ionov, E. P., BE1422

Pisateli Sovetskő Litvy, BE1325

Pisier, George. *Bibliographie méthodique, analytique et critique de la Nouvelle-Calédonie, 1955–1982,* DF41

Pitkin, R. E. *Theological dictionary of the New Testament*, AC456, BC143

Pitman, Patricia. *Encyclopedia of murder*, CK254

Pitman, Paul. *Short guide to the archives of the Quai d'Orsay*, DC155

Pitou, Spire. *The Paris Opéra*, BJ257

Pitschmann, Louis A. *Scholar's guide to Washington, D.C. for northwest European studies*, DC16

Pitt, Barrie. *The chronological atlas of World War II*, DA211

Pitt, Frances. *The chronological atlas of World War II*, DA211

Pittàno, Giuseppe. *Sinonimi e contrari*, AC543

Pitts, Michael R. *Radio soundtracks*, BH309

Piveteau, Jean, ed. *Traité de paléontologie*, EF249

Pla Brugat, Dolores. *Extranjeros en México, 1821–1990*, DB223

Place, Jean-Michel. *Bibliographie des revues et journaux littéraires des XIXe et XXe siècles*, AD96, BE1144

Place, Joseph. *Bibliographie des auteurs modernes de langue française (1801–1975)*, BE1208

Place guide, CL110

Place-name changes 1900–1991, Room, Adrian, CL93

Place-names *see* **Geographical names and terms**

Place-names in classical mythology, Bell, Robert E., CF21

Place names of Africa, 1935–1986, Kirchherr, Eugene C., CL155

Place-names of Great Britain and Ireland, Field, John, CL196, CL209

The place-names of Roman Britain, Rivet, Albert Lionel Frederick, CL199

The place-names of Scotland, Johnston, James B., CL203

Places rated almanac, Boyer, Rick, CL75
—— Savageau, David, CL74, CL75

Placzek, Adolf K. *Macmillan encyclopedia of architects*, BF262
—— *Who's who in architecture*, BF262

The plains & the Rockies, Wagner, Henry R., DB168

Plamenatz, Ilija P. *Yugoslav abbreviations*, AC715

Planat, Paul Amédée. *Encyclopédie de l'architecture et de la construction*, BF237

Planché, J. R. *Cyclopaedia of costume*, BG96

Planetaria, EC47

Planetary astronomy from the Renaissance to the rise of astrophysics, Taton, René, EC59
—— Wilson, Curtis, EC59

Planets, EC64

Plang Phloyphrom. *Pru's standard Thai-English dictionary*, AC779

Plank, Lois R. *Encyclopedia of accounting systems*, CH251

Plank, Tom M. *Accounting desk book*, CH262
—— *Encyclopedia of accounting systems*, CH251

Planning academic and research library buildings, Leighton, Philip D., AK175

Planning, equipping, and staffing a document reprographic service, Keene, James A., AK249

Planning library facilities, Stephenson, Mary Sue, AK180

Plano, Jack C. *American political dictionary*, CJ122, CJ126
—— *Dictionary of political analysis*, CJ40, CJ41
—— *The international relations dictionary*, CJ30
—— *Latin America*, CJ309, CJ311, CJ312
—— *Latin American political dictionary*, CJ309
—— *The public administration dictionary*, CJ477, CJ478
—— *The Soviet and East European political dictionary*, CJ396

Plant, Richard. *Bibliography of theatre history in Canada*, BH39

Plant, animal & anatomical illustration in art & science, Bridson, Gavin D. R., EA220

The plant-book, Mabberley, D. J., EG117

Plant breeding abstracts, EJ19

Plant diseases of international importance, EJ62

Plant engineering and maintenance, EK251, EK252

Plant science catalog, National Agricultural Library (U.S.), EG107

Planta, Robert de. *Disciunari rumantsch grischen*, AC664

Plantagenet chronicles, Hallam, Elizabeth M., DC310

The Plantagenet encyclopedia, DC310

•*PLANTGENCD*, EJ18

Plants
  diseases, EG189
    dictionaries, EJ30
    handbooks, EJ58, EJ62
  illustrations, EG73

Plants in danger, EG162

Plants of the world, Wit, H. C. D. de, EG183

Plarr, Victor Gustave. *Plarr's lives of the fellows of the Royal College of Surgeons of England*, EH230

Plarr's lives of the fellows of the Royal College of Surgeons of England, Plarr, Victor Gustave, EH230

Plastics, EK286
  catalogs, EK288
  dictionaries, EK291
    bilingual
      German-English, EK292
  encyclopedias, EK285
  guides, EK287
  handbooks, EK289, EK290

Plastics catalog, EK288

Plastics engineering handbook, EK290

Plastics technical dictionary, Wittfoht, Annemarie, EK292

Plate tectonics, EF66

Platnauer, Maurice. *Fifty years of classifical scholarship*, BE994

Plato, BB52, BB55, BB59

Plato, Cherniss, H. F., BB55

Plato and Socrates, McKirahan, Richard D., BB55, BB56

The Plato manuscripts, Yale University. Library, BB59

Platt, Elizabeth T. *Aids to geographical research*, CL4, CL12

Platt, Heidi. *Longman dictionary of language teaching and applied linguistics*, BD77

Platt, John. *Longman dictionary of language teaching and applied linguistics*, BD77

Platt, Lyman De. *Genealogical historical guide to Latin America*, AJ74
—— *Guía genealógico-histórica de Latinamérica*, AJ74

Platt, Suzy. *Respectfully quoted*, BE116

Platts, John Thompson. *Dictionary of Urdū, classical Hindī and English*, AC485, AC801

Plaut, W. Gunther. *The Torah*, BC184

Play index, BE234

Playfair, George M. H. *The cities and towns of China*, CL160

Playhouse America!, BH88

Plays in periodicals, Patterson, Charlotte A., BE233

The playwright's companion, BH85

Playwriting, BH85

Płaza, Stanisław. *Źródła rękopiśmienne do dziejów wsi w Polsce feudalnej*, DC479

Plechl, Helmut. *Orbis Latinus*, CL103

Plechl, Sophie-Charlotte. *Orbis Latinus*, CL103

Plevin, Arlene. *The bicyclist's sourcebook*, BK72

Plischke, Elmer. *U.S. foreign relations*, CJ107

Ploetz, Karl Julius. *Manual of universal history*, DA35

Plomer, H. R. *Dictionary of the printers and booksellers who were at work in England, Scotland and Ireland from 1726 to 1775; those in England*, AA306
—— *Dictionary of the printers who were at work in England, Scotland and Ireland, from 1641 to 1667*, AA306

Plot locator, BE194

Plots and characters in classic French fiction, Hicks, Benjamin E., BE1152

Pluge, John. *African newspapers in the Library of Congress*, DD26
—— *A bibliography of U.S. newspaper bibliographies*, AE29
—— *Indexes in the Newspaper and Current Periodicals Room*, AE101
—— *Newspaper indexes in the Newspaper and Current Periodical Room*, AE102

Plumb, Trevor W. *Australians : a historical atlas*, DF37

Plummer, Alfred. *The international critical commentary on the Holy Scriptures of the Old and New Testaments*, BC173

Plunkett, E. R. *Handbook of industrial toxicology*, EH426

Plunkett, Michael. *Afro-American sources in Virginia*, CC382

PMLA, BD26, BE39

Poblaciones de las parroquias, Ecuador, 1950–1982, CG153

Pocari, Serafino. *Modern European imperialism*, DC8

Pochmann, Henry August. *Bibliography of German culture in America to 1940*, CC329, CC330

Pocket book of British ceramic marks, Cushion, John Patrick, BG70

Pocket Oxford guide to sailing terms, BK121

Podell, Janet. *Facts about the states*, CG104
—— *Speeches of the American presidents*, CJ188

Podhradsky, Gerhard. *Lexikon der Liturgie*, BC428
—— *New dictionary of the liturgy*, BC428

Podvez'ko, M. L. *Ukraïns'ko-anglïĭskyĭ slovnyk*, AC797

Podzimek, Jaroslav. *National population bibliography of Czechoslovakia, 1945–1977*, CG207

•*Poem finder on disc*, BE319, BE320

La poésie lyrique des troubadours, Jeanroy, Alfred, BE1372

Poetics
  dictionaries, BE326, BE327, BE329, BE330, BE351
  see also **Versification**

Poetry
  anthologies, BE315
  bibliography, BE313, BE315
  biobibliography, BE325
  collections, BE332, BE506
  criticism
    collections, BE325
  databases, BE315, BE319, BE320
  dictionaries, BE328, BE329
  discography, BE323, BE324
  indexes, BE315, BE316, BE317, BE319, BE320, BE321, BE322, BE323, BE376, BJ289
  publications
    directories, BE331
  themes, motives
    indexes, BE318
  translations
    indexes, BE316
  women poets
    indexes, BE314

Poetry by American women, 1900–1975, Reardon, Joan, BE496

Poetry by American women, 1975–1989, Reardon, Joan, BE496

Poetry by women to 1900, Davis, Gwenn, BE489

Poetry criticism, BE325

Poetry explication, Kuntz, Joseph M., BE491, BE710, BE1192
—— Martinez, Nancy C., BE491, BE710, BE1192

Poetry handbook, Deutsch, Babette, BE326

Poetry index annual, BE319, BE321

Poetry of the Romantic period, Jackson, James Robert de Jager, BE718

Poetry of the Scots, Glen, Duncan, BE810

Poetry themes, Marcan, Peter, BE318

The poet's dictionary, Packard, William, BE330

Poet's market, BE331

Poèts nègres des États-Unis, Wagner, Jean, BE533

The poets of Ireland, O'Donoghue, David James, BE807

Poff, Cathryn. *The map catalog*, CL266

Pogarell, Reiner. *Minority languages in Europe*, BD85

Poggendorff, Johann Christian. *Biographisch-literarisches Handwörterbuch zur Geschichte der exakten Wissenschaften*, EA181

Pogonowski, Iwo. *Poland : a historical atlas*, DC482

Pogorelov, Valerii Aleksandrovich. *Opis na starite pechatani bulgarski knigi, 1802–1877 g*, AA587

Pohler, Johann. *Bibliotheca historico-militaris*, CJ562

Le poinçon de Paris, Nocq, Henry, BG141

Le Point, DC208

Point de repère, AD294

Point of order, Cann, Marjorie Mitchell, CJ452

Pointon, G. E. *BBC pronouncing dictionary of British names*, AC102

Poirier, Claude. *Dictionnaire du français québécois*, AC385

Poirier, Lucien. *Répertoire bibliographique de textes de présentation générale et d'analyse d'oeuvres musicales canadiennes (1900–1980)*, BJ41

Poisoning *see* **Toxicology**

Poisonous and venomous marine animals of the world, Halstead, Bruce W., EG239

Poisonous plants of the United States and Canada, Kingsbury, John Merriam, EG150

Poitevin, Néstor E. *Catálogo analítico de las publicaciones de la Academia Nacional de la Historia, 1903–1986*, DB323

Pók, Attila. *A selected bibliography of modern historiography*, DA44

Pokornowski, Illa M. *African dress II*, BG90

Pokorny, Julius. *Indogermanisches etymologisches Wörterbuch*, AC515

—— *Vergleichendes Wörterbuch der indogermanischen Sprachen*, AC515

Polain, Louis. *Catalogue des livres imprimés au quinzième siècle des bibliothèques de Belgique*, AA235

—— *Catalogue général des incunables des bibliothèques publiques de France*, AA234

—— *Marques des imprimeurs et libraires en France au XV siècle*, AA251

Poland, Jean M. *A guide to the literature of electrical and electronics engineering*, EK124

Poland
  associations
    directories, AL71
  bibliography, AA762, AA763, AA764, BE1354, DC470, DC474, DC475, DC476, DC478
    20th century, AA765, AA766, AA767, AA768
    current, AA769
  bibliography of bibliography, AA57, AA58, AA59, AA60
  biography, AH278, AH279, AH280, AH281, AH282
  dissertations, AG39
  encyclopedias, DC480, DC481
  gazetteers, CL148
  government publications, AF165
  newspapers, AE66, AE67
  periodicals, AD133, AD135, AD137
    library catalogs, AD134
  place-names, CL211
  registers, CJ325
  statistics, CG275, CG276
    bibliography, CG274
Poland (by subject)
  history, DC477
    atlases, DC482
    bibliography, DC35, DC471, DC472, DC473
    manuscripts and archives, DC479
  music, BJ42
  population, CG272, CG273, CG276

Poland. Główny Urząd Statystyczny. *Bibliografia wydawnictw Głownego Urzędu Statystycznego*, CG274

—— *Rocznik statystyczny*, CG275

—— *Roczniki statystyczne*, CG276

Poland. Ministerstwo Oświaty i Szkolnictwa Wyższego. *Katalog rozpraw doktorskich i habilitacyjnych*, AG39

Poland, Kanka, August Gerald, DC470

—— Sanford, George, DC475

Poland : a historical atlas, Pogonowski, Iwo, DC482

•*Polar pac*, DG5

Polar record, Scott Polar Research Institute, DG9

Polar regions
  atlases, DG10
  bibliography, DG5
  databases, DG5
  library catalogs, DG5
  see also **Antarctic; Arctic**

Polar regions atlas, National Foreign Assessment Center (U.S.), DG10

Poldauf, Ivan. *Česko-anglický slovník*, AC280

Pole, J. R. *The Blackwell encyclopedia of the American Revolution*, DB93

Poles (by country or region)
  United States
    bibliography, CC335

Police
  abstract journals, CK250
  dictionaries, CK259
  directories, CK264
  encyclopedias, CK252, CK255

Police (by country or region)
  United States
    directories, CK150

The police dictionary and encyclopedia, Fay, John, CK259

Police science abstracts, CK250

Policies of publishers, Kim, David U., AK165

Policy analysis and management, Goehlert, Robert, CA11

Policy sciences, CA11, CA34

Policy studies, CA34

Policy studies journal, CJ12

•*POLIS*, AF203

Polish abbreviations, Library of Congress. Slavic and Central European Division, AC636

Polish American history and culture, Zurawski, Joseph W., CC335

Polish drama, BE1361

Polish encyclopaedia, DC480

Polish-English dictionary of science and technology, EA122

Polish Jewish history, Hundert, Gershon David, DC34

Polish language
  abbreviations, AC636, AC637
  bibliography, BD193
  dictionaries, AC629, AC630, AC631, AC632
    bilingual, AC634
      Polish-English, AC633, AC635
    etymology, AC638, AC639
  encyclopedias, BD192
  pronunciation, AC640

Polish Library (London, England). *Bibliography of books in Polish or relating to Poland published outside Poland since Sept. 1st, 1939*, AA767

—— *Catalogue of periodicals in Polish or relating to Poland and other Slavonic countries, published outside Poland since September 1st, 1939*, AD136

Polish literature
  bibliography, BE1346, BE1349, BE1351, BE1354, BE1357, BE1360
  biobibliography, BE1345, BE1346, BE1350, BE1351, BE1357, BE1360
  dictionaries, BE1359
  encyclopedias, BE1353
  translations, BE1347, BE1348, BE1354, BE1358
    bibliography, BE1355

Polish literature (by subject)
  history, BE1352, BE1356

Polish literature in English translation, Coleman, Marion Moore, BE1348

Polish music, Smialek, William, BJ42

Polish National Committee of America. *Polish encyclopaedia*, DC480

Polish plays in English translations, Taborski, Boleslaw, BE1361

Polish plays in translation, Gerould, Daniel, BE1361

Polish research guide. *Informator nauki polskiej*, AL70

The Polish short story in English, Maciuszko, Jerzy J., BE1355

Polish statistical yearbook, CG275

Polish University College (London, England). *Bibliography of books in Polish or relating to Poland published outside Poland since Sept. 1st, 1939*, AA767

Politēs, Nikolaos G. *Hellēnikē bibliographia*, AA705

Political action committees, CJ147

Political Africa, Segal, Ronald, AH316, CJ409

Political and economic encyclopaedia of South America and the Caribbean, DB283

Political and economic encyclopaedia of the Soviet Union and Eastern Europe, DC52

—— White, Stephen, CJ391

Political and economic encyclopaedia of Western Europe, CJ319

Political and social science journals, CJ16

Political Australia, Macintyre, Clement, CJ448, DF36

Political campaign communication, Kaid, Lynda Lee, CJ103

Political cartoons *see* **Cartoons**

Political consultants, CJ141

Political conventions, CJ265

Political conventions (by country or region)
  United States
    handbooks, CJ263, CJ264
  see also **Political parties**

Political corruption, Johansen, Elaine, CJ102

Political dictionary of the Arab world, Shimoni, Yaacov, CJ424, CJ439, DE55, DE70

Political dictionary of the Middle East in the twentieth century, Levine, Evyatar, CJ424, CJ439

—— Shimoni, Yaacov, CJ424, CJ439

Political dictionary of the state of Israel, CJ439

—— Rolef, Susan Hattis, CJ424, DE55, DE70

Political dissent, Degenhardt, Henry W., CJ61

The political economy of Namibia, Eriksen, Tore Linné, DD185

Political economy of race and class in South Africa, Magubane, Bernard, DD211

Political ethics, CJ6, CJ60, CJ462
  bibliography, CJ102

Political facts of the United States since 1789, Austin, Erik W., CJ148, DB53

Political handbook of the world, CJ77, CJ88, CJ95

Political leaders in Black Africa, Wiseman, John A., AH316, CJ404, CJ406, CJ409

Political leaders in Weimar Germany, Stachura, Peter D., DC262

Political leaders of contemporary Africa south of the Sahara, CJ404

—— Glickman, Harvey, AH316, CJ406, CJ409

Political leaders of the contemporary Middle East and North Africa, CJ417

—— Reich, Bernard, CJ404

The political left in the American theatre of the 1930's, Duffy, Susan, BH41

Political oratory, CJ188

The political participation of women in the United States, Stanwick, Kathy, CC512

Political parties
  directories, CJ79
  encyclopedias, CJ77
  handbooks, CJ58

Political parties (by country or region)
  Africa, North, CJ405, CJ418
  Asia, CJ414, CJ446
  Asia, West, CJ405, CJ418
  Canada, CJ97, CJ297
  Europe, CJ320
  Europe, Eastern, CJ317
  Europe, Western, CJ323
  Great Britain, CJ350
  Latin America, CJ97
  Oceania, CJ414
  United States, CJ257, CJ265
    bibliography, CJ105, CJ259, CJ260
    encyclopedias, CJ261, CJ262
    handbooks, CJ263, CJ264, CJ266
    history, CJ242
      atlases, CJ258, DB73

West Indies, CJ97
see also **Political conventions**
Political parties & elections in the United States,
CJ262
Political parties and civic action groups,
Schapsmeier, Edward L., CJ97, CJ266
—— Schapsmeier, Frederick H., CJ97
Political parties and elections, CJ262
Political parties in Sri Lanka since independence,
Peiris, H. A., CJ444
Political parties in the European Community, Henig,
Stanley, CJ320
Political parties of Africa and the Middle East,
CJ405, CJ418
Political parties of Asia and the Pacific, CJ414,
CJ446
Political parties of Europe, CJ320
Political parties of the Americas, AH110, CJ97,
CJ306
Political parties of the Americas, 1980s to 1990s,
Ameringer, Charles D., CJ97
Political parties of the Americas and the Caribbean,
Coggins, John, CJ97
—— Lewis, D. S., CJ97
Political parties of the world, Day, Alan J., CJ77
Political profiles, CJ159
Political quotations, CJ44, CJ45
—— Thomsett, Jean F., CJ45
—— Thomsett, Michael C., CJ45
Political quotations on Ireland, 1886–1987, CJ377,
DC409
Political register, Poore, Benjamin Perley, CJ140
Political resource directory, CJ141
Political risk assessment, Jodice, David A., CJ11
Political risk yearbook, CJ59
The political role of Catholic and Protestant
missions in the colonial partition of Black Africa,
Obdeijn, Herman, DD87
Political scandals and causes célèbres since 1945,
CJ60
Political science
abstract journals, CJ19, CJ20
atlases, CJ72, CJ73
bibliography, CJ6, CJ11, CJ12, CJ13, CJ15
bibliography of bibliography, CJ14
biography, CJ65, CJ69, CJ158
chronologies, CJ63, CJ91
compendiums, CJ86
databases, CJ20
dictionaries, CA40, CJ36, CJ39, CJ40, CJ41,
CJ42, CJ127
directories, CJ46, CJ48, CJ49, CJ81, CJ82, CJ83
encyclopedias, CJ21, CJ22, CJ25, CJ26, CJ27,
CJ28, CJ29, CJ30, CJ31, CJ32, CJ33, CJ35, CJ38,
CJ52, CJ77, CJ155
guides, CJ1, CJ3, CJ4, CJ5
handbooks, CJ51, CJ53, CJ54, CJ59, CJ61, CJ89,
CJ90, CJ91, CJ92, CJ93, CJ462, CL68
indexes, CJ17, CJ18
periodicals
guides for authors, CJ16
quotations, CJ44, CJ45
research methods, CJ4, CJ56
reviews of research, CA26
style manuals, CJ4
terminology, CJ36, CJ43
yearbooks, CJ59, CJ64, CJ94, CJ95
Political science (by subject)
education, CJ47
history, CJ23
Political science, Harmon, Robert B., CJ1
—— Lowery, Roger C., CJ4
—— York, Henry E., CJ1, CJ5
Political science abstracts, CJ13
Political science bibliographies, Harmon, Robert B.,
CJ14
Political science, government and public policy
series, Universal Reference System, CJ13
Political science journal information, Martin, Fenton
S., CJ16
Political science research methods, Johnson, Janet
Buttolph, CJ56
Political science thesaurus II, CJ20

Political scientists, CJ154, CJ155
Political slogans, CJ242
Political systems, CJ51
Political terrorism, Schmid, Alex Peter, CJ554
Political violence in the United States, 1875–1974,
Manheim, Jarol B., CJ104
Political who's who of Namibia, Pütz, Joe, DD189
Politics and class formation in Uganda, Mamdani,
Mahmood, DD239
Politics and religion, BC15
Politics and the military in Uganda, 1890–1985,
Omara-Otunnu, Amii, DD239
Politics, economics, and society in the two
Germanies, 1945–75, Merritt, Anna J., DC238
Politics in America, CJ207, CJ214
The politics of African and Middle Eastern states,
Drabek, Anne Gordon, CJ400
Polk bank directory, CH277
Polk financial institutions directory, CH277
Polk world bank directory, CH277
•*POLL,* CJ494
Pollack, Frances M. *Index of twentieth century*
artists, BF156
Pollack, Sandra. *Contemporary lesbian writers of the*
United States, BE402, BE469
Pollak, Oliver B. *Theses and dissertations on*
Southern Africa, DD32
Pollak, Roman. *Bibliografia literatury polskiej*
okresu odrodzenia, BE1357
Pollard, Alfred W. *Catalogue of books printed in the*
XVth century now in the British Museum, AA219
—— *Short-title catalogue of books printed in*
England, Scotland, & Ireland and of English
books printed abroad, 1475–1640, AA412,
AA665, AA671, AA672, AA674, AA678, AA683,
AD107, BE680
Pollay, Richard W. *Information sources in*
advertising history, CH547
Pollen, John Hungerford. *First proofs of the*
Universal catalogue of books on art, BF56
•*Polling the nation,* CJ485
Pollner, Clausdirk. *Auswahlbibliographie zum*
Studium der anglistischen Sprachwissenschaft,
BD91
Pollock, Bruce. *Popular music, 1920–1979,* BJ333
Pollock, Sean R. *Statistical forecasts of the United*
States, CG105, CH110
•*POLLSTART,* CJ491
Pollution abstracts, EK71
Pollution research index, EK76
•*Pollution/toxicology CD-ROM,* EF214, EH421
Polmar, Norman. *The Naval Institute guide to the*
Soviet navy, CJ658
—— *World War II,* DA207
Polner, Murray. *American Jewish biographies,* AH79
La Pologne au XIIIᵉ Congrès International des
Sciences Historiques à Moscou, DC472
La Pologne en France, Lorentowicz, Jan, BE1354
Polomé, Edgar C. *Research guide on language*
change, BD68
Polsby, Nelson W. *Handbook of political science,*
CJ53
Polscy pisarze współczesni, Bartelski, Lesław M.,
BE1345
Polska Akademia Nauk. *Słownik staropolski,* AC629
Polska Akademia Nauk. Instytut Badań Literackich.
Bibliografia literatury polskiej okresu odrodzenia,
BE1357
Polska Akademia Nauk. Instytut Historii.
Bibliografia historii Polski, DC473
Polska Akademia Nauk. Instytut Historii, Zakład
Informacji Naukowej. *Bibliografia historii polskiej*
... , DC477
Polska Akademia Nauk. Instytut Jezyka Polskiego.
Bibliografia onomastyki polskiej, CL211
Polska Akademia Nauk. Komitet Historii Nauki.
Bibliografia kopernikowska, EC5
Polska Akademia Nauk. Komitet Nauk
Historycznych. *La Pologne au XIIIᵉ Congrès*
International des Sciences Historiques à Moscou,
DC472
Polska Akademia Nauk. Komitet Słowianoznawstwa.
Słownik starożytności słowiańskich, DC53

Polska Akademia Nauk. Pracownia Historii
Czasopiśmiennictwa Polskiego XIX–XX Wieku.
Bibliografia prasy polskiej, 1944–1948, AE66
—— *Bibliografia prasy polskiej, 1944–1948,*
AD137
Polska bibliografia bibliogiczna, AA57
Polska literatura w przekładac, Ryll, Ludomira,
BE1358
Polska prasa konspiracyjna (1939–1945) i powstania
warszawskiego w zbiorach Biblioteki Narodowej,
Biblioteka Narodowa (Poland), AE66
Polski Akademja Umiejętności. *Polski słownik*
biograficzny, AH279
Polski słownik biograficzny, AH279
Polskie wydawnictwa informacyjne, 1945–1981,
Barteczko, Ewa, AA347
Polskiej Akademii Nauk. *Członkowie Polskiej*
Akademii Nauk, AH280
Polunin, Oleg. *Flowers of Europe,* EG178
Polyglot dictionary of musical terms, BJ159
Polymer handbook, EK289
Polymers, EK284
encyclopedias, EK285
guides, EK287
handbooks, EK283, EK289
Polynesia *see* **Oceania**
Polzer, Charles W. *Northern New Spain,* DB249
Pomerans. *Plants of the world,* EG183
Pomeranz, William E. *Scholars' guide to*
Washington, D.C. for Russian, Central Eurasian,
and Baltic studies, DC556
Pomeroy, Robert W. *The craft of public history,*
DB12
Pompe, S. *Indonesian law 1949–1989,* CK230
Ponce, Andrea C. *List of Philippine government*
publications, 1945–1958, AF259
Ponchie, Jean-Pierre. *French periodical index,*
AD312
Pond, Grace. *The complete cat encyclopedia,* EJ141
Ponko, Vincent. *Britain in the Middle East, 1921–*
1956, DE38
Pons Wörterbuch der deutschen Umgangssprache,
Küpper, Heinz, AC430
Pontifical Institute of Mediaeval Studies. *Dictionary*
of Old English, AC172
Pontificia Biblioteca missionaria. *Bibliografia*
missionaria, BC303
Pontificia Università lateranense. Istituto Giovanni
XXIII. *Bibliotheca sanctorum,* BC260
Pontificia Universitas Urbaniana. *Bibliografia*
missionaria, BC303
Pontificio Istituto biblico. *Elenchus of Biblica,*
BC119
Pontius, Frederick W. *Water quality and treatment,*
EK98
Poole, Mary Elizabeth. *United States government*
publications, AF100
Poole, Trevor B. *UFAW handbook on the care and*
management of laboratory animals, EG295, EJ129
Poole, William Frederick. *Poole's index to*
periodical literature, 1802–81, AD282
Poole's index : date and volume key, AD281
Poole's index to periodical literature, 1802–81,
AD261, AD282, AD286, BE239, BE409, BE420
Poore, Benjamin Perley. *A descriptive catalogue of*
the government publications of the United States,
Sept. 5, 1774–March 4, 1881, AF97, AF98
—— *Political register,* CJ140
Poor's manual of railroads, CH313
Poortinga, Y. *Friesch woordenboek,* AC391
Poovendran, P. *An atlas of India,* CL356
Pop, Sever. *La dialectologie,* BD57
Pope, Barbara H. *Historical periodicals directory,*
DA14
Pope, Rex. *Atlas of British social and economic*
history since c. 1700, DC299
Pope-Hennessy, John. *History of Western sculpture,*
BF393
The Pope speaks, BC437
Popes and European revolution, Chadwick, Owen,
BC278
Popes, cardinals, bishops, BC430, BC431, BC432,
BC434

•*POPINFORM*, CC257, CG17, EH78

Popkin, Debra. *Modern French literature*, BE1147

Popkin, Michael. *Modern black writers*, BE51
—— *Modern French literature*, BE1147

•*POPLINE*, CC248, CC257, CG17, EH36, EH78

Popova, L. P. *The modern Russian dictionary for English speakers*, AC684

Popplestone, John A. *Dictionary of concepts in general psychology*, CD26

Populaire prozaschrijvers van 1600 tot 1815, Buisman, M., BE1327

Popular American composers from revolutionary times to the present, Ewen, David, BJ271

Popular chemical dictionary, EE31

Popular culture *see* **Folklore and popular culture**

A popular dictionary of Buddhism, Humphreys, Christmas, BC477

A popular dictionary of Sikhism, Cole, W. Owen, BC572

Popular encyclopedia of plants, EG179

Popular entertainment
   biography, BH27
   directories, BH15
   guides, BH1, BH2
   handbooks, CF56

Popular entertainment research, Pruett, Barbara J., BH1

Popular Hinduism and Hindu mythology, Holland, Barron, BC482

Popular literature
   bibliography, BE434
   Handbooks, manuals, etc., BE254

Popular literature (by country or region)
   United States, BE434

Popular music, BJ333
   bibliography, BJ231, BJ335, BJ336, BJ339, BJ341
   biography, BJ326, BJ348, BJ351
   chronologies, BJ331, BJ334
   discography, BJ343, BJ344
   encyclopedias, BJ326, BJ346, BJ347, BJ349
   guides, BJ335, BJ339
   indexes, BJ316
   see also **Folk music; Music in film**

Popular music, Gray, Michael H., BJ383
   Iwaschkin, Roman, BJ339
—— Shapiro, Nat, BJ333
   Tudor, Dean, BJ344

Popular music, 1900–1919, Cohen-Stratyner, Barbara N., BJ333

Popular music, 1920–1979, Pollock, Bruce, BJ333
—— Shapiro, Nat, BJ333

Popular music periodicals index, BJ110

Popular music since 1955, Taylor, Paul, BJ341

Popular names of U.S. government reports, AF132
—— Bernier, Bernard A., AF101

Popular periodical index, AD283

The popular school, Logan, Terence P., BE649

Popular song index, Havlice, Patricia Pate, BJ285

Popular titles and subtitles of musical compositions, Berkowitz, Freda Pastor, BJ173

Popular U.S. government publications, AF77

Population
   atlases, CG44
   bibliography, CG1, CG5, CG6, CG7, CG9, CG11, CG12, CG13, CG18, CG67
   compendiums, CG63
   databases, CC257, CG17, EH78
   encyclopedias, CG19
   handbooks, CG39
   indexes, CG18, CG67
   statistics, CC296, CG49, CG50, CG54, CG62, CG64

Population (by subject)
   history
      atlases, CG44

Population, CG213

Population abstract of the United States, CG76

Population and the population explosion, Goode, Stephen H., CG5

Population and vital statistics, CG250

Population and vital statistics report, CG54, CG181

Population and vital statistics report. Special supplement, CG54

Population Association of America. *Population index*, CG18, CG67

The population atlas of China, CG385

Population bibliography, CC246

Population by age and marital status, CG268

Population censuses and other official demographic statistics of Africa (not including British Africa), Library of Congress. Census Library Project, CG312

Population censuses and other official demographic statistics of British Africa, Dubester, Henry J., CG312
—— Library of Congress. Census Library Project, CG312

La population de la région du Sahel, CG308

Population/family planning thesaurus, Lucas, Caroline, CC254

Population forecasting, CG50, CG59, CG64, CG65

Population forecasting (by country or region)
   United States
      handbooks, CG103

Population forecasts, CG435

Population index, CG18, CG67

Population index bibliography, CG18, CG67

Population information in nineteenth century census volumes, Schulze, Suzanne, CG98

Population information in twentieth century census volumes, 1950–1980, Schulze, Suzanne, CG98

Population Information Network for Africa. *Annotated bibliography on the population of Ethiopia*, CG329
—— *Bibliographie annotée sur la population du Rwanda*, CG352, DD197
—— *Kenya population*, CG337
—— *La population de la région du Sahel*, CG308
—— *Population of Ghana*, CG333

•*Population information online*, CC257, CG17, EH78

Population literature, CG18, CG67

Population of Ghana, CG333

The population of Indonesia, Heilig, Gerhard, CG392

The population of Japan, Taeuber, Irene B., CG404

The population of the United States, Bogue, Donald J., CG73

Population planning, CC255
   bibliography, CC246, CC251
   biography, CC238
   statistics, CC250
   terminology, CC254

Population Reference Bureau. *The Population Reference Bureau's population handbook*, CG39

The Population Reference Bureau's population handbook, Haupt, Arthur, CG39

Population statistics, CG268
—— Benjamin, Bernard, CG236

Population trends, Great Britain. Office of Population Censuses and Surveys, CG232

Porcelain *see* **Ceramics and glass**

Porgès, Laurence. *Bibliographie des régions du Sénégal*, DD202
—— *Sources d'information sur l'Afrique noire francophone et Madagascar*, DD40

Pornography, CC290
   bibliography, CC276
   see also **Erotic art; Erotic poetry**

Porras Collantes, Ernesto. *Bibliografía de la novela en Colombia*, BE948

Portales, Carlos. *Bibliografía sobre relaciones internacionales y política exterior de Chile, 1964–1980*, DB359

Porte, Jacques. *Encyclopédie des musiques sacrées*, BJ118

Porter, A.N. *Atlas of British overseas expansion*, DC346

Porter, David L. *Biographical dictionary of American sports*, BK13
—— *Biographical dictionary of American sports : baseball*, BK52
—— *Biographical dictionary of American sports : basketball and other indoor sports*, BK63
—— *Biographical dictionary of American sports : football*, BK74
—— *Biographical dictionary of American sports : outdoor sports*, BK14
—— *A cumulative index to the Biographical dictionary of American sports*, BK21

Porter, Dorothy Burnett. *Afro-Braziliana*, CC475, DB347
—— *Dictionary catalog of the Jesse E. Moorland Collection of Negro Life and History, Howard University Library, Washington, D.C*, CC379
—— *The Negro in the United States*, CC374
—— *North American negro poets*, BE536
—— *Working bibliography on the Negro*, CC374
—— *A working bibliography on the Negro in the United States*, CC375

Porter, Frank W. *In pursuit of the past*, CC420
—— *Native American basketry*, BG159

Porter, Gareth. *Vietnam*, DE277

Porter, Glenn. *Encyclopedia of American economic history*, CH49, DB42

Porter, Harvey. *English-Arabic and Arabic-English dictionary*, AC223
—— *Wortabet's Arabic-English dictionary*, AC224

Porter, Hollis Paine. *Petroleum dictionary for office, field and factory*, EK305

Porter, Kenneth I. *British union-catalogue of periodicals*, AD237

Porter, Kirk H. *National party platforms*, CJ257

Porter, Malcolm. *The world atlas of revolutions*, CJ74

Porter, Marsha. *Video movie guide*, BH202

Porter, Roy. *Dictionary of the history of science*, EA246
—— *The earth sciences*, EF103

Porter Sargent, CB107

Portilla, Miguel León. *Diccionario Porrúa de historia, biografía y geografía de México*, DB243

Pôrto, Angela. *Processo de modernização do Brasil, 1850–1930*, DB348

Portocarrero S., Felipe. *Compendio estadístico del Perú, 1900–1990*, CG157, DB389

Portoghesi, Paolo. *Dizionario enciclopedico di architettura e urbanistica*, BF276

Portrait catalog, New York Academy of Medicine. Library, EH52

The portrait in Britain and America, Simon, Robin, BI320

Portrait index of North American Indians in published collections, Frazier, Patrick, BF67, CC435

Portrait register, Lee, Cuthbert, BF65

Portraits
   bibliography, BF23
   indexes, BF65, BF66, BF67, BF68, BF320, CC435

Portraits of linguists, Sebeok, Thomas Albert, BD70

Portraits of pioneers in psychology, CD50

Ports of the world, CH464

Portsmouth Polytechnic. Cartographic Unit. *World mapping today*, CL269

Portugal
   atlases, CL331, CL332, CL333
   bibliography, AA468, AA770, AA800, DC484, DC490
      15th–19th centuries, AA816, AA817
      current, AA771, AA778, AA779
      early, AA772, AA773, AA774, AA775, AA776, AA777
   biography, AH287
   dissertations, DC491
   library catalogs, DC489
   periodicals, AD138
   statistics, CG277, CG278

Portugal (by subject)
   foreign relations
      India, DE161
   history, DC483, DC486, DC487
      bibliography, DC485, DC488
      dissertations, DB267, DC510

overseas territories
  government publications
    bibliography, AF220
Portugal, Unwin, P. T. H., DC490
Portuguese, DE5
Portuguese Africa, Gibson, Mary Jane, AF220, DD114, DD184
A Portuguese-English dictionary, Taylor, James Lumpkin, AC650
Portuguese-English, English-Portuguese law dictionary, CK54
The Portuguese in Asia, De Silva, Daya, DE5
Portuguese language
  bibliography, BD163, BD164, BE926, BE1362
  dictionaries, AC641, AC642, AC643, AC644, AC648
    bilingual
      English-Portuguese, AC645, AC646
      Portuguese-English, AC647, AC650
    pictorial, AC649
  etymology, AC651
  festschriften, BD166, BE1436
  synonyms, AC652, AC653
Portuguese language and Luso-Brazilian literature, Chamberlain, Bobby J., BD163, BE926, BE1362
Portuguese literature
  bibliography, BD163, BE926, BE1362, BE1363, BE1448
  biobibliography, BE888, BE1364, BE1367
  criticism
    collections, BE1449
  encyclopedias, BE1366
  festschriften, BD166, BE1436
  regional and dialect
    Africa, BD163, BE926, BE1362
  translations, BE1448
Portuguese literature (by subject)
  history, BE1365, BE1368
Portuguese-speaking Africa 1900–1979, Gowan, Susan Jean, DD114, DD184
Pos, H. J. *Eerste Nederlandse systematisch ingerichte encyclopaedie*, AB36
Posada, Eduardo. *Bibliografía bogotana*, AA526
Posener, Georges. *Dictionary of Egyptian civilization*, DA123
Posner, Arlene. *China*, DE133
Posner, Julia L. *CWLA's guide to adoption agencies*, CC231
Post, Chandler Rathfon. *History of European and American sculpture from the early Christian period to the present day*, BF393
Post, Elizabeth L. *Emily Post's etiquette*, AL156
Post, Emily. *Emily Post's etiquette*, AL156
Post, Jeremiah B. *Travel in the United States*, CL377
Post, Joyce A. *Gerontology and geriatrics libraries and collections in the United States and Canada*, CC88
——— *Travel in the United States*, CL377
Post magazine almanac, CH514
Post report, United States. Department of State, CL57
Post-Soviet archives, Karasik, Theodore, DC557
Postage stamps
  bibliography, BG201
  catalogs, BG206
  handbooks, BG203
  library catalogs, BG200, BG201
  periodicals, BG199
Postage stamps (by country or region)
  Europe, Eastern, BG205
  United States, BG198, BG204
    dictionaries, BG202
Postharvest news and information, EJ19
Postlethwaite, T. Neville. *Encyclopedia of comparative education and national systems of education*, CB70
——— *The international encyclopedia of education*, CB70
Postmodern fiction, BE247
Poston, Susan L. *Nonformal education in Latin America*, CB43
Poston, Thurman R. *Eshbach's handbook of engineering fundamentals*, EK16

Postwar foreign newspapers, Library of Congress. Serial Division, AE12
Postwar Japanese women writers, Schierbeck, Sachiko Shibata, BE1595
Potchefstroom University for Christian Higher Education. *Index to literature on race relations in South Africa, 1910–1975*, DD220
Poteet, G. Howard. *Published radio, television, and film scripts*, BH168
Potemra, Michal. *Bibliografía inorečových novín a časopisov na Slovensku do roku 1918*, AE47
——— *Bibliografía slovenských novín a časopisov do roku 1918*, AE47
Potenza, R. *Multilingual thesaurus of geosciences*, EF79
Potgieter, Pieter Jacobus Johannes Stephanus. *Index to literature on race relations in South Africa, 1910–1975*, DD220
Potparič, O. *A dictionary of medical and surgical syndromes*, EH114
Potter, Clare. *Lesbian periodicals index*, CC271, CC286
Potter, Frans de. *Vlaamsche bibliographie*, AA581
Potter, Karl H. *Advaita Vedānta up to Samkara and his pupils*, BB33
——— *Encyclopedia of Indian philosophies*, BB18, BB33
——— *Guide to Indian philosophy*, BB21
——— *Indian metaphysics and epistemology*, BB33
Potter, Neal. *Trends in natural resource commodities*, CH441
Potter, Robert B. *Barbados*, DB421
——— *St. Vincent and the Grenadines*, DB457
The potter's dictionary of materials and techniques, Hamer, Frank, BG65
Pottery *see* **Ceramics and glass**
Pottery analysis, Rice, Prudence M., BG72
Pottery and ceramics, Campbell, James Edward, BG51
Potthast, August. *Bibliotheca historica medii aevi*, DA136
Pottier, Bernard. *Bibliographie américaniste, linguistique amérindienne*, BD239
Potts, Deborah. *Zimbabwe*, DD18
Potvin, Gilles. *Encyclopedia of music in Canada*, BJ134
Poucet, Jacques. *Introduction aux études classiques*, DA91
Pouchert, Charles J. *The Aldrich library of ^{13}C and ^{1}H FT NMR spectra*, EE113
——— *Aldrich library of FT-IR spectra*, ED43, EE140
——— *The Aldrich library of infrared spectra*, EE141
——— *Aldrich library of NMR spectra*, ED43, EE142
Pough, Frederick H. *A field guide to rocks and minerals*, EF204
Poultney, David. *Dictionary of Western church music*, BC322, BJ155
Poulton, Helen. *Historian's handbook*, DA2
Pourcelet, François. *Guide des papiers des ministres et secrétaires d'État de 1871 à 1974*, DC152
Pourhadi, Ibrahim Vaqfi. *Persian and Afghan newspapers in the Library of Congress, 1871–1978*, AE90
Poverty
  bibliography, CC260, CC261, CC263, CC264
  handbooks, CC51
Poverty (by country or region)
  Southern states, CC262
Poverty in developing countries, CC264
Powell, Antoinette Paris. *Bibliography of landscape architecture, environmental design, and planning*, BF288
Powell, C. E. *Authors of plant names*, EG119
Powell, David. *The wisdom of the novel*, BE114
Powell, James M. *Medieval studies*, DA129
Powell, James R. *Core list of books and journals in science and technology*, EA19
Powell, Ken. *English historical facts, 1485–1603*, DC323

Powell, Margaret S. *Bibliography of place-name literature*, CL177
Powell, Marjorie. *Teacher attitudes*, CB159
——— *Teacher effectiveness*, CB160
Powell, Mark Allan. *The Bible and modern literary criticism*, BC115
Powell, Ronald R. *Basic research methods for librarians*, AK7
——— *Qualitative research in information management*, AK7
Powell, Russell H. *Core list of books and journals in science and technology*, EA19
——— *Handbooks and tables in science and technology*, EA152
Powell, Warren H. *Inorganic chemical nomenclature*, EE107
Powell, William Henry. *List of officers of the army of the United States from 1779–1900*, CJ646
——— *List of officers of the army of the United States from 1779 to 1900*, CJ644
——— *Officers of the army and navy (regular) who served in the Civil War*, CJ647
Power, D'Arcy. *Lives of the fellows of the Royal College of Surgeons of England, 1930–1951*, EH230
——— *Plarr's lives of the fellows of the Royal College of Surgeons of England*, EH230
Power, Patrick C. *Literary history of Ireland*, BE803
Powers, John. *The Yogācāra school of Buddhism*, BC471
Powicke, Frederick Maurice. *Handbook of British chronology*, BE612, DC295
Powis Smith, J. M. *Complete Bible*, BC94
Pownall, David E. *Articles on twentieth century literature*, BE27, BE761
Powys, Marian. *Lace and lace-making*, BG161
Pozin, Mikhail A. *Russian-English/English-Russian dictionary of free market era economics*, CH71
Poznan, DC476
The practical book of Oriental rugs, Lewis, George Griffin, BG168
Practical dictionary for adults, Kouyoumdjian, Mesrob G., AC227
A practical English-Chinese pronouncing dictionary, Chen, Janey, AC257
Practical guide to Canadian legal research, Castel, Jacqueline R., CK195
——— Latchman, Omeela K., CK195
A practical guide to graduate research, Stock, Molly, AG5
A practical guide to impractical pets, Dolensek, Emil P., EJ134
Practical guide to planned giving, AL140
A practical guide to the "misteaks" made in census indexes, AJ20
Practical handbook of microbiology, EG56
——— O'Leary, William M., EG54
Practical medical dictionary, Stedman, Thomas Lathrop, EH105
Practical modern English-Malay dictionary, Winstedt, Richard Olof, AC607
Practical picture research, Evans, Hilary, BF350
The practical Sanskrit-English dictionary, Apte, Vaman Shivaram, AC702
The practice of pharmacy, EH326
Prado Velázquez, Ernesto. *Diccionario de escritores mexicanos*, BE915
Praechter, Karl. *Grundriss der Geschichte der Philosophie*, BB50
Praeger encyclopedia of art, BF77
Praesent, Hans. *Bibliographie von Japan, 1906–[1943]*, DE204
Prager, Leonard. *Yiddish literary and linguistic periodicals and miscellanies*, BE1081
Pragmatics, BD65
Prang, M. E. *Confederation to 1949*, DB205
"Prasa," Robotnicza Spółdzielnia Wydawnicza, Warsaw. Zakład Badań Prasoznawczych. *Materiały do bibliografii dziennikarstwa i prasy w Polsce, w latach 1944–1954*, AE67
Prather-Moses, Alice Irma. *The international dictionary of women workers in the decorative arts*, BG34

Pratt, David. *Systematic dictionary of mammals of the world*, EG290

Pratt, Frantz. *Haiti*, DB439

Pratt, Stanley E. *Pratt's guide to venture capital sources*, CH230

Pratt, T. K. *Dictionary of Prince Edward Island English*, AC160

Pratt's guide to venture capital sources, CH230

Prause, Marianne. *Bibliographie zur Kunstgeschichte des 19. Jahrhunderts*, BF32

Pravda, Alex. *Who's who in Russia and the new states*, AH180

Pravda [index], AE68

Prawer, Siegbert S. *Theses in Germanic studies*, BE1237

Prayer book concordance, Bushey, Galen, BC347

Prayer in the public schools, CB39

Prayers, BC207

Pražák, Vilém. *Soupis československé literatury za léta 1901–1925*, AA599

Pre-cinema history, Hecht, Hermann, BH166

Pre-Columbian contact with the Americas across the oceans, Sorenson, John L., DB22

Pre-Columbian Middle America, BF28

Pre-confederation, Waite, P. B., DB205

Pre-Socratic philosophers, BB58

Prebish, Charles S. *Historical dictionary of Buddhism*, BC456

Precious stones *see* **Gems**

The predecessors of Shakespeare, Logan, Terence P., BE648

Predicasts F&S index Europe, CH337

Predicasts F&S index international, CH337

Predicasts F&S index United States, CH337

Predicasts forecasts, CH423, CH426

Predicasts overview of markets and technology, CH337

Pregnancy, CC225, EH341
    see also **Abortion; Teenage pregnancy**

A prehistoric bibliography, Bonser, Wilfrid, DC305

Prein, Wolfgang. *Handbuch der Monogramme in der europäischen Graphik vom 15. bis zum 18. Jahrhundert*, BF385

Preisigke, Friedrich. *Wörterbuch der griechischen Papyrusurkunden*, AC446

Preissle, Judith. *The handbook of qualitative research in education*, CB113

Prejudice : racist-religious-nationalist, Kehr, Helen, BC541

A preliminary annotated bibliography of Pilipino linguistics (1604–1976), Makarenko, Vladimir A., BD234

A preliminary bibliography of early man in eastern North America, 1839–1973, Storck, Peter L., CE84

Preliminary checklist of Russian, Ukrainian, and Belorussian newspapers since January 1, 1917, AE71

Prelinger, Richard. *Footage 89*, BH178

—— *Footage 91*, BH178

Preminger, Alex. *The new Princeton encyclopedia of poetry and poetics*, BE329, BE696

—— *Princeton handbook of poetic terms*, BE329

Prendergast, Terrence. *Dictionary of the New Testament*, BC145

Prentice, H. T. *International directory of botanical gardens*, EG146

Prentice-Hall dictionary of business, finance and law, Rice, Michael Downey, CH342

The Prentice-Hall encyclopedia of world proverbs, Mieder, Wolfgang, BE157

Prentice Hall guide to English literature, BE611

The Prentice Hall real estate investor's encyclopedia, Blankenship, Frank J., CH532

Presbyterian bibliography, Prince, Harold B., BC376, BC379

Presbyterian Church (U.S.A.). General Assembly. *Minutes*, BC378

Presbyterian Historical Society. *Guide to the manuscript collections of the Presbyterian Church, U.S.*, BC376

Presbyterians, BC376, BC377, BC378, BC379

Presencia española en los Estados Unidos, CC464

The present state of French studies, Osburn, Charles B., BE1139

The present state of scholarship in historical and contemporary rhetoric, BE361

The present state of scholarship in sixteenth-century literature, BE987

La presenza delle Romania in Italia nel secolo XX, Buonincontro, Pasquale, DC495

The preservation challenge, Morrow, Carolyn Clark, AK242

Preservation planning program, Darling, Pamela W., AK238

Preservation work in libraries, AK237, AK238, AK239, AK240, AK241, AK242, AK243

Preserving archives and manuscripts, Ritzenthaler, Mary Lynn, AK188

Preserving historic landscapes, Chittenden, Betsy, BF293

—— Meier, Lauren, BF287, BF293

Preserving your American heritage, Wright, Norman Edgar, AJ27

The presidency, Goehlert, Robert, CJ165

The presidency A to Z, CJ179, CJ204

—— Congressional Quarterly, Inc, CJ178

President Idi Amin Dada of Uganda, a bibliography, Afolabi, M. O., DD240

Presidential advisory commissions, AF132, CJ186

Presidential advisory commissions, 1973–1984, CJ186

Presidential also-rans and running mates, 1788–1980, Southwick, Leslie H., CJ192

Presidential ballots, 1836–1892, Burnham, Walter Dean, CJ243

The presidential-congressional political dictionary, Elliot, Jeffrey M., CJ115

Presidential elections since 1789, CJ250

Presidential executive orders and proclamations, AF128

Presidential families of the United States of America, AJ59

Presidential libraries, AK102, CJ174, CJ175, CJ176

Presidential libraries and collections, Veit, Fritz, AJ24, CJ175, DB37

Presidential primaries and caucuses, 1992, McGillivray, Alice V., CJ254

Presidential vetoes, 1789–1988, United States. Congress. Senate. Library, AF133

Presidential vote, 1896–1932, Robinson, Edgar Eugene, CJ243

Presidents
    archives, CJ174
    bibliography, CJ99, CJ165, CJ167, CJ168, CJ171, CJ172, CJ173
    biography, AJ59, CJ189, CJ190, CJ191
    elections
        statistics, CJ243
    encyclopedias, CJ179
    guides, CJ164, CJ165, CJ166
    handbooks, CJ184
    library resources
        manuscripts and archives, AK102, CJ176
    manuscripts and archives, CJ175
    public papers, AF135
        indexes, AF130
    quotations, CJ180
    sourcebooks, CJ187
    speeches, CJ188
Presidents (by country or region)
    United States
        biography
            bibliography, CJ106
            encyclopedias, CJ115, CJ178
Presidents (by subject)
    elections, CJ192, CJ251
        statistics, CJ250
    history, CJ191, CJ242
The presidents, CJ191
President's office files, CH624
Presner, Lewis A. *The international business dictionary and reference*, CH63
Les présocratiques, Paquet, Léonce, BB58

Press
    encyclopedias, AE142
    surveys, AE141, AE142
Press (by country or region)
    international
        directories, AE143
    Italy
        history, AE64
    Nigeria, AD173
    Switzerland, AE77
The press in Africa, AE4
Press in India, AE88
The press in Nigeria, Ogbondah, Chris W., AD173
Press, radio & TV guide, AD213
Press, radio & TV guide : Australia, New Zealand and the Pacific Islands, AE99
Pressat, Roland. *The dictionary of demography*, CG30

—— *Dictionnaire de démographie*, CG30

La presse d'information, Bertelson, Lionel, AE45

Presse Handbuch, AD81

Die Presse in Afrika, Feuereisen, Fritz, AE4

Presse in Asien und Ozeanien, Feuereisen, Fritz, AE4

—— Schmacke, Ernst, AE4

Presse in Europa, Feuereisen, Fritz, AE4

Presse in Lateinamerika, Feuereisen, Fritz, AE4

—— Schmacke, Ernst, AE4

Presse periodique madrilène entre 1871–1885, Cazottes, Gisèle, AE76

Presse quotidienne française, Derieux, Emmanuel, AE52

—— Texier, Jean C., AE52

Presse- und Medienhandbuch, AD103

Pressley, Robert J. *CRC handbook of lasers*, EC49, ED34

Pressure groups, CJ218, CJ223
    directories, CC91, CJ131, CJ142, CJ144, EJ44
Pressure groups (by country or region)
    United States, CJ248, CJ249
        handbooks, CJ266
    see also **Lobbyists**
Pressure on Pretoria, Kalley, Jacqueline Audrey, DD215

Preston, Antony. *Atlas of maritime history*, DA56

Preston, Percy. *Dictionary of pictorial subjects from classical literature*, BF189, CF24

Preston, Richard Joseph. *North American trees*, EG199

Pretoria. State Library. *A list of South African newspapers, 1800–1982, with library holdings*, AE81

Pretz, Bernhard. *Dictionary of military and technological abbreviations and acronyms*, CJ588

Pretzel, Ulrich. *Matthias Lexers Mittelhochdeutsches Taschenwörterbuch*, AC405

Preuss, Arthur. *Dictionary of secret and other societies*, AL75, AL76

Preuss, Emil. *Bibliotheca scriptorum classicorum*, BE992

Preuss, Gisela. *Meyers Handbuch über die Literatur*, BE187

Preussische Akademie der Wissenschaften. *Altfranzösisches Wörterbuch*, AC383

—— *Jahrbuch über die Fortschritte der Mathematik*, EB26

Preussische Staatsbibliothek. *Berliner Titeldrucke*, AA121

—— *Namenschlüssel die Verweisungen der Berliner Titeldrucke zu Pseudonymen, Doppelnamen und Namensabwandlungen*, AA172

Prevention education, Derivan, William J., CC112

Previté-Orton, Charles William. *Shorter Cambridge medieval history*, DA157

Prévost, Michel. *Dictionnaire de biographie française*, AH194

Prezzolini, Giuseppe. *Repertoria bibliografico della storia e della critica della letteratura italiana dal 1933 al 1942*, BE1295

—— *Repertorio bibliografico della storia e della critica della letteratura italiana dal 1902 al 1932*, BE1295

Prial, Frank. *The companion to wine*, EJ225

Pribić, Rado. *Nobel laureates in literature*, AL168, BE210

Pribylovskiĭ, Vladimir. *Dictionary of political parties and organizations in Russia*, CJ386

Price, Anne. *Children's catalog*, AA338

Price, Arnold Hereward. *Federal Republic of Germany*, DC232

Price, David H. *Atlas of world cultures*, CE72

Price, Edward T. *A geographical bibliography for American college libraries*, CL17

Price, Glanville. *Romance linguistics and the romance languages*, BD149

Price, Helen C. *Theses on Africa, 1976–1988*, DD33

Price, Joseph L. *A new handbook of Christian theology*, BC252

Price, Martin J. *Coins*, BG185

Price, Warren C. *An annotated journalism bibliography, 1958–1968*, AE134

――― *The literature of journalism*, AE135, AE136

Price index of art auctions, BF111

Price list, AF113

The price of admission, Makinson, Larry, CJ249

Price Waterhouse information guide, CH145

Prichard, Mari. *The Oxford companion to children's literature*, BE377

Prichard, Susan Perez. *Film costume*, BH169

Prickett, Robert L. *Publication sources in educational leadership*, CB178

Pride, Armistead Scott. *Negro newspapers on microfilm*, AE15

Priebe, Richard. *Ghanaian literatures*, BE1528

Pries, Nancy. *American diaries*, BE507, BE509, DB66

Priestley, Brian. *Jazz*, BJ299

Prieto, Antonio. *Historia de la literatura española*, BE1457

Prieto del Río, Luis Francisco. *Muestras de errores y defectos colonial de "Diccionario biográfico colonial de Chile por José Toribio Medina"*, AH131

Primack, Alice Lefler. *Finding answers in science and technology*, EA7

Primary commodity markets and models, Labys, Walter C., CH434

Primary sources for Victorian studies, Storey, Richard, BE606

Primary sources in European diplomacy, 1914–1945, Messick, Frederic M., CJ316, DC10

Primary technical dictionary English-Swahili, AC757

A primer on organizational behavior, Bowditch, James L., CH602

Los primeros pasos, Castro Arroyo, María de los Angeles, DB450

Primo catalogo collettivo delle biblioteche italiane, Rome. Centro Nazionale per il Catalogo Unico delle Biblioteche Italiane e per le Informazioni Bibliografiche, AA124, AA731

Prince, Harold B. *Presbyterian bibliography*, BC376, BC379

Prince, Mary Miles. *Bieber's dictionary of legal abbreviations*, CK42

――― *World dictionary of legal abbreviations*, CK41, CK42

Princes Risborough Laboratory. *Handbook of hardwoods*, EJ187

The Princeton companion to classical Japanese literature, Miner, Earl Roy, BE1588

The Princeton encyclopedia of classical sites, DA105

Princeton encyclopedia of poetry and poetics, BE329

Princeton handbook of poetic terms, Hardison, O. B., BE329

――― Preminger, Alex, BE329

――― Warnke, Frank J., BE329

Princeton Review (Firm). *The student access guide to the best ... colleges*, CB293

The Princeton review student access guide to the best ... colleges, CB293

Princeton University. Office of Population Research. *Population index*, CG18, CG67

Principal international businesses, CH406

Principal officers of the Department of State and United States chiefs of mission, 1778–1990, United States. Department of State. Office of the Historian, CJ183

The Principality of Liechtenstein, DC439

Principles of bibliographical description, Bowers, Fredson Thayer, AA1

The principles of classification and a classification of mammals, Simpson, George Gaylord, EG305

Pring, Julian Talbot. *The Oxford dictionary of modern Greek*, AC467

Pringle, David. *Imaginary people*, BE188

The Print Council index to oeuvre-catalogues of prints by European and American artists, Riggs, Timothy A., BF364

Print Council of America. *The Print Council index to oeuvre-catalogues of prints by European and American artists*, BF364

Print file, New York Public Library. Prints Division, BF366

Print index, Parry, Pamela Jeffcott, BF62, BF367

Print media production source, CH601

Print price index, Falk, Peter Hastings, BF371

Print prices current, BF371

Print reference sources, BF363

Printed books, 1468–1700, in the Hispanic Society of America, Hispanic Society of America, AA818

The printed Hebrew books in Jerusalem during the first half century (1841–1891), AA909

Printed in Tanzania, AA880, AA881

Printed maps in the atlases of Great Britain and Ireland, Chubb, Thomas, CL228

Printers' & publishers' devices in England & Scotland, 1485–1640, McKerrow, R. B., AA250, AA254

Printers' marks, AA250, AA251, AA252, AA253, AA254

Printers' marks, Roberts, William, AA253

Printing and publishing, AK165

bibliography, AA266, AA267

current, AA268, AK17

biography, AA306, AA307, AA310

catalogs, AA435, AA436

copy preparation, AA323

databases, AA282, AK33, BE172

dictionaries, AA270, AA271, AA272, AA274, AA277

multilingual, AA273, AA275, AA276

directories, AA278, AA279, AA281, AA282, AA283, AA284, AA292, AD17, BE172, BE173, BE174, BE175, BE176

bibliography, AA280

encyclopedias, BF369

handbooks, AA295, AA296

library catalogs, AA299

periodicals, AA269

Printing and publishing (by country or region)

Commonwealth

directories, AA290

Europe

directories, AA287

France

bibliography, AA308

biography, AA309, AA311

directories, AA288

German-speaking countries

directories, AA289

Germany

directories, AA286

India

directories, AA294

Italy

biography, AA305

directories, AA291

history, AA301

Latin America

directories, AA285

United Kingdom

directories, AA290

United States

history, AA302, AA304

Printing and publishing (by subject)

education, CB20

history, AA297, AA298, AA299, AA300, AA303

women, CC518

Printing for Parliament, 1641–1700, AF188

The printing of mathematics, Chaundy, Theodore W., EB97

The printing trades, CH635

Printmaking & picture printing, Bridson, Gavin D. R., BF359

Prints and engravings

bibliography, BF358, BF361, BF362, BF363, BF364

biography, BF382, BF386

catalogs, BF364, BF381

exhibitions, BF368

handbooks, BF373, BF375

indexes, BF367, BF368

library catalogs, BF365

Prints and engravings (by country or region)

Europe, BF381

France, BF380

Great Britain

bibliography, BF359

Prints and engravings (by subject)

history, BF376, BF377, BF378, BF379, BF381, BF382

Prints and printmaking, Lister, Raymond, BF359

Prints and the print market, Donson, Theodore B., BF375

Prints and their creators, Zigrosser, Carl, BF379

Prints of the twentieth century, Castleman, Riva, BF376

Printworld directory of contemporary prints and prices, BF371

Prinz, Otto. *Mittellateinisches Wörterbuch bis zum ausgehenden 13. [i.e. dreizehnten] Jahrhundert*, AC591

――― *Tusculum-Lexicon*, BE1026

Prior, M. E. *Census of British newspapers and periodicals, 1620–1800*, AD106

Prioul, Christian. *Atlas du Rwanda*, CL344

Příruční slovník jazyka českého, AC277

――― Česká Akademie Věd a Umění. Třída 3, AC276

Prisma's Swedish-English and English-Swedish dictionary, AC767

Prisons and prisoners

directories, CK261, CK263, CK264, CK265, CK266

Příspěvky ke knihopisu, Voit, Petr, AA596

Pritchard, Alan. *Alchemy*, EE14

――― *A guide to computer literature*, EK152

Pritchard, Jacki. *The abuse of elderly people*, CC100

Pritchard, James Bennett. *The Harper atlas of the Bible*, BC199

――― *Harper concise atlas of the Bible*, BC199

Pritzel, Georg August. *Index londinensis to illustrations of flowering plants, ferns and fern allies*, EG104

――― *Thesaurus literaturae botanicae*, EG97

Private colleges and universities, Ohles, John F., CB280, CB281

――― Ohles, Shirley M., CB281

Private independent schools, CB110

Private Libraries Association. *Private press books*, AA243

Private libraries of musicians and musicologists, Folter, Siegrun H., BJ34

Private press books, AA238, AA243

Private press books, AA243

Private school education in the U.S, Songe, Alice H., CB34

Private schools, CB107, CB110

bibliography, CB34

directories, CB91, CB108, CB109

statistics, CB136

see also **Public schools**

Private schools in the United States, Benson, Peter L., CB136

Private secondary schools, CB109

Private security services, CK253

Prize stories, BE483

Prizes and awards, AL161, AL162, AL163, BE180

Prizes and awards (by subject)

children's literature, AA343, BE388

education, CB86
film, BH273, BH274, BH275
history, DA28
librarianship, BE178
literature, AL162, BE177, BE178, BE179, BE180
performing arts, BH19
science
Canada, EA197
United States, EA197
theater, BH93
see also Fellowships and scholarships
Prizewinning literature, Strachan, Anne, BE179
Pro-choice/pro-life, Fitzsimmons, Richard, CC251
Pro file, BF251
Pro football guide, BK79
Pro Football Hall of Fame. *Professional football*, BK80
The Pro Football Hall of Fame, Harrington, Denis J., BK76
PRO microfilm catalogue, DC286
Probability, EB30
Probability and statistics, Handbook of, EB63
Probation, CK267
Probation and parole directory, CK267
Problem words and expressions, AC84
Problemi ed orientamenti critici di lingua e di letteratura italiana, Momigliano, Attilio, BE1307
Problems of early childhood, Hirsch, Elisabeth S., CC146
Probyn, Clive. *English fiction of the eighteenth century, 1700–1789*, BE691
Procedure in the U.S. House of Representatives, CJ224
Proceedings, American Antiquarian Society, AA248, AE19, BE501
Proceedings and papers, Oxford Bibliographical Society, AD104
Proceedings in print, EA211
Proceedings of the Royal Society of London, Royal Society (Great Britain), EA182
Process and chemical engineering, EK49
Processo de modernização do Brasil, 1850–1930, Pôrto, Angela, DB348
Prochaska, Alice. *Irish history from 1700*, DC404
Procházka, Jindřich. *Slovník anglicko-český a česko-anglický*, AC281
Proché, Peter. *Bibliographie zur Aussenpolitik der Republik Österreich seit 1945*, DC87
Prochner, Lawrence. *International handbook of early childhood education*, CB119
Prochnow, Herbert V., Jr. *Toastmaster's treasure chest*, BE362
Prochnow, Herbert V. *Speaker's & toastmaster's handbook*, BE362
——— *Toastmaster's treasure chest*, BE362
Proctor, Robert. *Index to the early printed books in the British Museum*, AA219, AA227
Product evaluations, AD278
Production engineering, EK248
Production handbook, CH623
Production yearbook, EJ80
Products (mathematics), EB87
Proeve eener Ned, Chijs, Jacobus Anne van der, DE174
Professional and occupational licensing directory, CH706
Professional careers sourcebook, CB208, CH702, CH707
Professional ethics, CB220, CC233, CH85, CH317, CK64, CK160, EH175
bibliography, AL9, CH565
Professional football, Smith, Myron J., BK80
The professional geographer, CL26, CL27
Professional Lobbying and Consulting Center. *The lobbying handbook*, CJ149
Professional Secretaries International. *Professional Secretaries International complete office handbook*, CH87
Professional Secretaries International complete office handbook, Jaderstrom, Susan, CH87
Professional women and minorities, CH686
Professional writing for the human services, CC54

Professional's guide to public relations services, Weiner, Richard, CH569
Proffer, Carl R. *Nineteenth-century Russian literature in English*, BE1400
ProFile, BF251
Profile of education doctorates, Hill, Susan, CB341
Profile of teachers in the U.S.—1990, Feistritzer, C. Emily, CB166
Profiles in belief, Piepkorn, Arthur Carl, BC65, BC270
Profiles in Canadian literature, Heath, Jeffrey, BE819
Profiles of American colleges, CB250
Profiles of Singapore, AH362, AH369
Program evaluation, Dynes, Patrick S., CJ464
Program for Art on Film (New York, N.Y.). *Architecture on screen*, BF247
——— *Art on screen*, BF96
——— *Films and videos on photography*, BF327
Programa nacional de estadísticas de salud, CG136
The progress of Afro-American women, Sims, Janet L., CC376
Progress of medieval and Renaissance studies in the United States and Canada, BE28
Progressive jazz, Bruyninckx, Walter, BJ307
Progressive reform, Buenker, John D., DB125
Progressivism and muckraking, Filler, Louise, DB125
"Proias" lexikon tēs neas Hellēnikēs glōssēs, AC462
Proizvedeniia sovetskikh pisatelei v perevodakh na inostrannye iazyki, BE1401
Project for Historical Biobibliography. *Biobibliography of British mathematics and its applications*, EB19
•*Project Hermes*, CK190
Project on Asian Philosophies and Religions. *Guide to Buddhist religion*, BC472
Projections of educational statistics to [...], CB144
Projek Perpustakaan Nasional. *Bibliografi nasional Indonesia*, AA902
Prokhorov, A. M. *Bol'shaia sovetskaia entsiklopediia*, AB82
Prologue : journal of the National Archives, AK114, DB38
Prominent families in America with British ancestry, AI58
Prominent Hungarians, Fekete, Márton, AI252
Prominent personalities in the USSR, Institute for the Study of the USSR, AI304
Prominent scientists, Pelletier, Paul A., EA196
Promodata, AD177
PROMPT, CH337
Promptbooks, BH42
Pronay, Nicholas. *British official films in the Second World War*, DA204
Pronko, Leonard Cabell. *Guide to Japanese drama*, BE1592
A pronouncing and etymological dictionary of the Gaelic language, Maclennan, Malcolm, AC394
A pronouncing dictionary of American English, Kenyon, John Samuel, AC106
Pronouncing dictionary of proper names, AC109
A pronouncing dictionary of the Spanish and English languages, AC740
Pronouncing Gaelic dictionary, MacAlpine, Neil, AC394
Pronouncing gazetteer and geographical dictionary of the Philippine Islands, United States. Bureau of Insular Affairs, CL168
•*Properties of organic compounds*, EE149
Properties of the National Trust, BF249
The Prophets, BC94
Proposal planning and writing, Miner, Lynn E., AL138
Proposal writing, AL92, AL138, EA160
Proposals that work, Locke, Lawrence F., EA160
Propyläen Kunstgeschichte, BF133
Prosecuting attorneys, The national directory of, CK152
Prosocial development in children, Honig, Alice S., CC147
•*Prospector's choice*, AL122

Pross, Catherine A. *Guide to the identification and acquisition of Canadian government publications*, AF155
Prostitution, CC291
Prostitution, CC291
Proteins, EG160
Protest & crime in China, Teng, Ssu-Yü, DE136
Protestant denominations
yearbooks, BC323
Protestant denominations (by country or region)
France, BC323
Protestant denominations (by subject)
missions, BC308
Protestant Episcopal Church see Episcopal Church
Protestant Episcopal Church in the U.S.A. *The Book of Common Prayer and administration of the sacraments and other rites and ceremonies of the church*, BC347, BC349
Protestantism
directories, BC324
encyclopedias, BC67
yearbooks, BC324
Protocol, McCaffree, Mary Jane, AL155
Proulx, Gerard-J. *Standard dictionary of meteorological sciences*, EF149
Proum, Im. *English-Khmer dictionary*, AC563
Prouty, Chris. *Ethiopia and Eritrea*, DD48
Prouty, Howard H. *Variety television reviews, 1923–1988*, BH298
Provan, Jill. *Health media review index*, EH43
Provençal language
bibliography, BD177
dictionaries
bilingual
Provençal-French, AC655
Provençal-French, AC654
Provençal literature
bibliography, BE1370, BE1371, BE1373, BE1374, BE1375
library catalogs, BE1373
manuscripts, BE1369
Provençal literature (by subject)
history, BE1372
Provençal literature and language including the local history of southern France, New York Public Library, BE1373
Provence (France), DC165
The proverb, Taylor, Archer, BE164
Proverb literature, Stephens, Thomas Arthur, BE162
Proverbs, BE151, BE153, BE155, BE157, BE159, BE163, BE164, BE165, BE166
bibliography, BE156, BE158, BE162, CF92
collections, CC459
Proverbs (by country or region)
Asia, East, BE167
Asia, Southeast, BE167
Canada, BE154
China, BE160
United States, BE154
Proverbs (by language)
Arabic, BE124
Chinese, BE167
Italian, BE161
Japanese, BE152, BE167
Spanish, BE149
see also Quotations
Proverbs, Gluski, Jerzy, BE155
Proverbs in literature, Mieder, Wolfgang, BE156
Proverbs, sentences, and proverbial phrases, Whiting, Bartlett Jere, BE166
Providing reference services for archives and manuscripts, Pugh, Mary Jo, AK188
Provinces and provincial capitals of the world, Fisher, Morris, CL86
Provincial royal commissions and commissions of inquiry, 1867–1982, Maillet, Lise, AF154, CJ303
Provinciale Bibliotheek van Friesland. *Catalogus der Friesche taal- en letterkunde en overige Friesche geschriften*, BE1067
A provisional checklist of species for flora North America (revised), EG137

Provisional survey of materials for the study of neglected languages, Blass, Birgit A., BD71
—— Gage, William W., BD71
—— Johnson, Dora E., BD71
Provorse, Carl. *The encyclopedia of the Central West,* DB173
Prozorov, P. *Sistematicheskiĭ ukazatel' knig i stateĭ po grecheskoĭ filologii, napechatannykh v Rossii s XVII stoletiia po 1892 god na russkom i inostrannykh iazykakh,* BD138
Prpič, George J. *Croatia and the Croatians,* DC608
Prucha, Francis Paul. *Atlas of American Indian affairs,* CC440
—— *A bibliographical guide to the history of Indian-white relations in the United States,* CC423
—— *Handbook for research in American history,* DB8
—— *Indian-white relations in the United States,* CC423
Prudnikov, Anatoliĭ Platonovich. *Integrals and series,* EB91
Pruett, Barbara J. *Popular entertainment research,* BH1
Pruett, James W. *Research guide to musicology,* BJ7
Prunes, Lourenço Mario. *Atlas do Brasil Globo,* CL316
Pru's standard Thai-English dictionary, Plang Phloyphrom, AC779
The Prussian instructions, BC40
Pruuden, Salme. *Catalogue of books and periodicals on Estonia in the British Library Reference Division,* DC135
Pruys, Karl H. *Wörterbuch zur Publizistik,* AE140
Pryor, Judith. *Delivering government services,* CJ471
Prytherch, Raymond John. *Harrod's librarians glossary,* AK42
—— *Librarianship and information work worldwide,* AK79
—— *Now read on,* BE254
—— *Sources of information in librarianship and information science,* AK1
—— *Walford's guide to reference material,* AA363
Przebienda, Edward. *Monthly catalog of United States government publications,* AF111
—— *Words and phrases index,* AC155
Przewodnik bibliograficzny, AA765, AA769
Przewodnik bibljograficzny, AA768
Przewodnik po jezykoznawstwie polskim, Handke, Kwiryna, BD193
—— Rzetelska-Feleszko, Ewa, BD193
Przewodnik polonisty, Czachowska, Jadwiga, AA58
Psacharopoulos, George. *Economics of education,* CB70
Pschyrembel, Willibald. *Klinisches Wörterbuch,* EH112
Pschyrembel Wörterbuch Gynäkologie und Geburtshilfe, EH112
Pseudonyme, Weigand, Jörg, AA173
Pseudonymregister, Andersson, Per, AA186
Pseudonyms *see* **Anonyms and pseudonyms**
Pseudonyms, Clarke, Joseph F., AA148
Pseudonyms and nicknames dictionary, AA146
PSI, AL95
PsycBOOKS, CD16, CD17
Psychiatric dictionary, Campbell, Robert Jean, EH382
A psychiatric glossary, EH385
Psychiatry
  bibliography, EH370, EH371, EH373, EH374
  biography, EH387
  dictionaries, EH382, EH383, EH384, EH385, EH390
  directories, EH387
  encyclopedias, CD23, CD24, EH379
  guides, CD3, EH369
  handbooks, EH391, EH394
  library catalogs, EH376
  nomenclature, EH393
  treatises, EH400
Psychiatry (by subject)
  education, EH389
  history, EH396, EH397, EH398

  sourcebooks, EH399
Psychiatry and psychology in the visual arts and aesthetics, Kiell, Norman, BF29
Psychoanalysis
  bibliography, CD9
  encyclopedias, CD23, CD24, EH379
Psychoanalysis and literature
  bibliography, BE24, BE26
Psychoanalysis and religion, Beit-Hallahmi, Benjamin, BC5
Psychoanalysis, psychology, and literature, Kiell, Norman, BE19, BE25, BE26, BF29
Psychoanalytic terms and concepts, CD30
Psychocriticism, Natoli, Joseph P., BE25
Psychohistorian's handbook, Lawton, Henry, DA5, DA43
Psychohistorical inquiry, Gilmore, William J., DA5, DA43
Psychohistory, DA5, DA43
Psycholinguistics, BD78, BD79, CD117
Psychological abstracts, CD1, CD16, CD17, CD18, CD34
Psychological and medical aspects of induced abortion, Winter, Eugenia B., CC259, EH31
Psychological and medical effects of concentration camps and religious persecution on survivors of the Holocaust, Eitinger, Leo, DA215
—— Krell, Robert, DA215
Psychological bulletin [indexes], CD15
The psychological foundations of education, Baatz, Olga K., CD88
Psychological index 1894–1935, CD18
Psychological review [indexes], CD15
Psychologists, CD46
The psychologists, Krawiec, T. S., CD49
The psychologist's companion, Sternberg, Robert J., CD43
Psychology
  abstract journals, CD17
  bibliography, BB6, CA10, CD6, CD7, CD8, CD10, CD11, CD12, CD44
  biography, CD47, CD48, CD49, CD50, CD51, CD52, CD55, CD62
  databases, CD16, CD17
  dictionaries, CD27, CD28, CD29, CD30, CD31, CD32, CD33
  directories, CD35, CD37, CD38, CD39, CD46, CD48
  encyclopedias, CD19, CD20, CD21, CD22, CD23, CD24, CD25, CD26, EH379
  financial aids, CD36
  guides, CD1, CD2, CD3, CD4, CD5
  handbooks, CD41, CD61, CD122
  indexes, CD15, CD16, CD18
  periodicals, CB22, CD13, CD14
  research methods, CD63, CD64, CD65, CD66
  reviews of research, CD44, CD45
  statistics, CD64, CD66
  style manuals, CD42, CD43
  tests and measurements
    bibliography, CB151, CD67, CD68, CD69, CD70, CD72, CD73
    databases, CB151, CD68, CD69
    directories, CD74, CD75
    reviews of research, CD71
    standards, CD76
  thesauruses, CD34
Psychology (by subject)
  computer applications, CD40
  history, CD53, CD54, CD55, CD62
    bibliography, CD58, CD60
    guides, CD56, CD57
    manuscripts and archives, CD58
  see also **Developmental psychology; Educational psychology; Industrial and organizational psychology; Pathological psychology; Social psychology**
Psychology, Baxter, Pam M., CD1
The psychology almanac, Wilkening, H., CD66
Psychology and art
  bibliography, BF29
Psychology and literature
  bibliography, BE19, BE24, BE25, BE26

Psychology and religion, BC20, CD59
  bibliography, BC5, BC9
Psychology and theology in Western thought, 1672–1965, Vande Kemp, Hendrika, BC20, CD59
Psychology of religion, Capps, Donald, BC9
Psychopathology, EH392
Psychopharmacology abstracts, EH323
Psychotherapy
  bibliography, CC210, EH375
  dictionaries, CC227, EH386
Psychotropic drugs, EH351
Psychware, Krug, Samuel E., CD40
Psychware sourcebook, Krug, Samuel E., CD40
•*PsycINFO,* CD17
•*PsycLIT,* CD16, CD17
PTLA, AA436
•*PTS F&S index,* CH337
•*PTS international forecasts,* CH426
•*PTS marketing and advertising reference service,* CH548
PTS newsletter database, AK206
•*PTS PROMPT,* CH337
•*PTS U.S. forecasts,* CH423
Pubblicazioni edite dallo stato o col suo concorso, Italy. Provveditorato Generale dello Stato, AD319
Public administration
  abstract journals, CJ476
  bibliography, CJ464, CJ466, CJ467, CJ469, CJ470, CJ471, CJ472, CJ473, CJ474, CK15
  dictionaries, CJ479
  encyclopedias, CJ477, CJ478
  guides, CJ459, CJ460, CJ461, CJ469, CJ470
  handbooks, CJ480, CJ481, CJ482
Public administration (by country or region)
  Arab states
    bibliography, CJ468
  Canada
    bibliography, CJ465
  developing countries
    handbooks, CJ483
  United States
    bibliography, CJ463, CJ475
  see also **Management**
Public administration, CJ473
—— British Council, CJ473
—— McCurdy, Howard E., CJ469, CJ470
Public administration desk book, CJ459
—— Coleman, James R., CJ460
The public administration dictionary, Chandler, Ralph C., CJ477, CJ478
—— Plano, Jack C., CJ478
Public administration in American society, Rouse, John Edward, CJ475
Public administration in the Third World, CJ483
Public administration research guide, Cherry, Virginia R., CJ459, CJ460
—— Holzer, Marc, CJ460
Public administration series, CJ474
Public Affairs Information Service. *PAIS international in print,* CA25
Public Affairs Information Service bulletin, CA25
Public Affairs Information Service foreign language index, CA25
Public affairs information sources, CA1
Public Archives Canada. *Catalogue of pamphlets in the Public Archives of Canada, with index,* AA451
—— *Guide to the reports of the Public Archives of Canada, 1872–1972,* DB193
Public Archives of Canada. *General inventory,* DB194
—— *Union list of manuscripts in Canadian repositories,* DB195
Public colleges and universities, Ohles, John F., CB281
Public defenders, CK144
Public documents of the first fourteen Congresses, 1789–1817, Greely, Adolphus Washington, AF92
Public finance, CH219
  statistics, CH241, CH242, CH243, CH244
Public finance, Marshall, Marion B., CH219
Public general acts, CK214
Public health
  abstract journals, EH408

bibliography, EH405, EH407
directories, EH162, EH412
government publications, EH41
guides, EH403
handbooks, CC51
statistics, EH232
Public health (by country)
United States
handbooks, EH413
Public health (by subject)
history, EH417
legal aspects, EH413
Public health law manual, Grad, Frank P., EH413
Public interest law, CK9
Public interest law, Epstein, Lee, CK9
—— George, Tracey E., CK9
—— Kobylika, Joseph F., CK9
Public interest law groups, O'Connor, Karen, CK153
Public interest profiles, CJ142
Public international law, CK82
—— Beyerly, Elizabeth, CK76
Public international law and international organization, Kleckner, Simone-Marie, CK78
The public ivys, Moll, Richard, CB278
Public libraries
statistics, AK99
Public Library Association. *Books for public libraries*, AA325
—— *Statistical report ... Public Library Data Service*, AK99
Public library catalog, AA328
—— Entin, Paula B., BE245
—— Yaakov, Juliette, BE245
Public Library Data Service statistical report, AK99
Public Management Institute. *The complete grants sourcebook for higher education*, CB372
Public opinion
databases, CJ485, CJ491, CJ494
indexes, CJ485
polls, CJ484, CJ485, CJ486, CJ487, CJ488, CJ490, CJ491, CJ492, CJ493, CJ494, CJ496
bibliography, CJ495
indexes, CJ489
Public opinion (by subject)
education, CB137
•*Public opinion location library*, CJ494
Public opinion polling, Lake, Celinda C., CJ491
Public opinion polls and survey research, Walden, Graham R., CJ495
Public papers of the presidents of the United States, United States. President, AF130, AF135, AF136
The public policy dictionary, Kruschke, Earl R., CJ38
The public record, Ireland. Public Record Office, DC401
Public Record Office film catalogue, DC286
Public Record Office handbooks, DC286
Public relations *see* **Advertising and public relations**
Public relations & ethics, Ferré, John P., CH565
Public Relations Society of America. *Codes of professional standards*, CH565
Public schooling in America, Van Scotter, Richard D., CB123
Public schools
directories, CB97
handbooks, CB123
ratings, CB148
statistics, CB148, CB167
see also **Private schools**
Public schools USA, Harrison, Charles Hampton, CB148
Public sector productivity, Holzer, Marc, CJ466
Public Works Historical Society. *Public works history in the United States*, DB19
Public works history in the United States, Hoy, Suellen M., DB19
Publicaciones oficiales de Chile, 1973–1983, AF161
Las publicaciones oficiales de México, Fernández de Zamora, Rosa María, AF157
Publicaciones periódicas argentinas, AD71
Publicaciones periódicas argentinas, 1781–1969, Ferreira Sobral, Eduardo F., AD70

Publicaciones periódicas existentes en la Biblioteca Nacional, Biblioteca Nacional (Spain), AD152
Las publicaciones periódicas mexicanas, Orozco Tenorio, José, AD63
Publicacões de Arquivo Nacional 1886–1990, DB350
Publication grants for writers & publishers, Park, Karin R., BA11
Publication manual of the American Psychological Association, AG1, CD42
Publication sources in educational leadership, Richardson, Michael D., CB178
Les publications en série éditées au Sénégal, 1856–1982, Bibliothèque Nationale (France), AD176, DD104
Publications list and comprehensive indexes (1967–1982), United Nations Centre Against Apartheid, DD224
Publications of societies, Bowker, Richard Rogers, AL38
Publications of the Geological Survey, 1879–1961, United States. Geological Survey, EF39
Publications of the Geological Survey of Canada, 1917–1952, Leafloor, Lorne B., EF33
Publications of the government of British Columbia, 1871–1947, Holmes, Marjorie C., AF155
Publications of the government of Ontario, 1867–1900, Bishop, Olga B., AF155
Publications of the government of Ontario, 1901–1955, MacTaggart, Hazel I., AF155
Publications of the government of Ontario, 1956–1971, MacTaggart, Hazel I., AF155
Publications of the government of Pakistan, 1947–1957, Moreland, George B., AF254
Publications of the government of the Province of Canada, 1841–1867, Bishop, Olga B., AF155
Publications of the governments of Nova Scotia, Prince Edward Island, New Brunswick, 1758–1952, Bishop, Olga B., AF155
Publications of the governments of the Northwest Territories, 1876–1905 and of the Province of Saskatchewan, 1905–1952, MacDonald, Christine, AF155
Publications of the National Bureau of Standards, National Bureau of Standards, EA274
Publications of the National Institute of Standards and Technology ... catalog, National Institute of Standards and Technology, EA274
Publications of the World Health Organization, World Health Organization, EH407
Publications officielles, AF168
Les publications officielles des pouvoirs publics, Dampierre, Jacques de, AF169
Publicațiunile periodice românești (ziare, gazete, reviste), AD140
The published diaries and letters of American women, Goodfriend, Joyce D., BE509
Published radio, television, and film scripts, Poteet, G. Howard, BH168
Published screenplays, McCarty, Clifford, BH168
Publishers and publishing *see* **Printing and publishing**
Publishers' Association. *Directory of publishing. United Kingdom, Commonwealth and overseas*, AA290
Publishers' catalogs annual, AA435
Publishers' circular and bookseller, AA686
Publishers directory, AA284
Publishers, distributors, and wholesalers of the United States, AK33
Publishers' international ISBN directory, AA279
Publisher's trade list annual, AA425, AA436, AA438
Publishers' trade list annual index, Abbott, Anthony, AA436
Publishers' weekly, AA437, AA898
Publishers' weekly interim index, AA432
Publishing opportunities in business and economics, CH27
Puckett, Newbell Niles. *Black names in America*, AJ174
Puerto Rican authors, Hill, Marnesba D., BE980
—— Schleifer, Harold B., BE980

Puerto Rican literature
bibliography, BE978, BE979, DB453
biobibliography, BE980
encyclopedias, BE980
Puerto Rican literature, Foster, David William, BE978
Puerto Rican Research and Resources Center. *The Puerto Ricans*, CC450
Puerto Ricans
bibliography, CC450
Puerto Ricans (by country or region)
United States
directories, CC462
handbooks, CC466
Puerto Ricans (by subject)
language, BD176
The Puerto Ricans, Puerto Rican Research and Resources Center, CC450
Puerto Ricans and other minority groups in the continental United States, Herrera, Diane, CC446
Puerto Ricans in the United States, Herrera, Diane, CC446
Puerto Rico
bibliography, AA35, DB452, DB453
current, AA569
biography, AH159, AH160, AH161
encyclopedias, DB454, DB455
gazetteers, CL126
guides, DB450
Puerto Rico (by subject)
history, DB451, DB456
music
bibliography, BJ43
Puerto Rico. [Laws, etc.]. *Laws of Puerto Rico annotated*, CK179
Puerto Rico. Oficina del Indice Histórico. *Tesauro de datos históricos*, DB456
Puerto Rico, Cevallos, Elena E., DB451
Pugh, Geoff. *Sources in European political history*, DC17
Pugh, Mary Jo. *Providing reference services for archives and manuscripts*, AK188
Puhvel, Jaan. *Hittite etymological dictionary*, AC490
Pukui, Mary Kawena. *Hawaiian dictionary*, AC469
Pulis, Jane F. *Index to festschriften in librarianship, 1967–1975*, AK13
Pulleyblank, E. G. *Historical writing on the peoples of Asia*, DE18
Pullum, Geoffrey K. *A bibliography of contemporary linguistic research*, BD4
—— *Phonetic symbol guide*, BD10, BD15
Pulsiano, Phillip. *An annotated bibliography of North American doctoral dissertations on Old English language and literature*, BD101, BE728, BE730
—— *Medieval Scandinavia*, DC76
Pult, Chasper. *Disciunari rumantsch grischen*, AC664
Punch, Terrence M. *Genealogist's handbook for Atlantic Canada research*, AJ70
Punctuate it right!, Shaw, Harry, AC112
Punctuation for now, McDermott, John, AC111
Pundeff, Marin V. *Bulgaria*, DC112
Pundt, Helen Marie. *AHEA*, EJ202
Punley, Randolph J. *The American Indian index*, CC430
Punsalan, Victoria J. *Refereed and nonrefereed economic journals*, CH30
Puppo, Mario. *Manuale critico-bibliografico per lo studio della letteratura italiana*, BE1290
Purcell, Gary R. *Developing collections of U.S. government publications*, AF72
—— *Reference sources in library and information services*, AK2
Purchasing, CH590
Purdon, M. E. *Dictionary of the dance*, BH147
Purdon's Pennsylvania statutes, annotated, Pennsylvania. [Laws, etc.], CK179
Purdy, Virginia Cardwell. *American women and the U.S. armed forces*, CJ612
Pure & applied science books, 1876–1982, EA20
Pürer, Heinz. *200 Jahre Tageszeitung in Österreich, 1783–1983*, AE44

INDEX

Purification of laboratory chemicals, Perrin, D. D., EE85

Purnell, C. J. *Catalogue,* AA120

Purnell, Louis R. *Catalog of the type specimens of invertebrate fossils,* EF241

Purser, Philip. *Halliwell's television companion,* BH314

The pursuit of the White House, Thomas, G. Scott, CJ252

Purvey, P. Frank. *Coins of England and the United Kingdom,* BG190

Pusan perimeter, Korea, 1950, Edwards, Paul M., DA170

Püschner, Manfred. *Antifaschistischer Widerstand und Klassenkampf,* DC233

Pushkarev, Sergei Germanovich. *Dictionary of Russian historical terms from the eleventh century to 1917,* DC584

Pussey, Gérard. *Dictionnaire des illustrateurs,* BF384

Putevoditel' po bibliografii, biobibliografii, istoriografii, khronologii i entsiklopedii literatury, Fomin, Aleksandr Grigor'evich, BE1389

Pütz, Joe. *Namibia handbook and political who's who,* DD189

——— *Political who's who of Namibia,* DD189

Putzel, Henry. *United States reports,* CK190

Puxty, Anthony G. *Multinational enterprise,* CH341

Puzininy, Jadwigi. *Indeks a tergo do Słownika języka polskiego,* AC632

Pyke, E. J. *Biographical dictionary of wax modellers,* BF396

Pyle, Robert M. *The IUCN invertebrate red data book,* EG234

Pynsent, Robert B. *Česko-anglický slovník,* AC280

——— *Reader's encyclopedia of Eastern European literature,* BE988

Qā'imat al-intāj al-fikrī al-Qaṭarī li-'ām, AA932

al-Qāmūs al-dimūghrāfī al-thulāthī, CG31

Qāmūs al-siḥāfah al-Lubnānīyah, 1858–1974 : wa-huwa mujam yua/a1 rrif wa-yu rrikh lil-ṣuḥuf wa-al-dawrīyāt al-latī aṣdarahā al-Lubnāniyūn fī Lubnān wa-al-khārij, Dāghir, Yūsuf Asád, AE91

Qatar
  bibliography
    current, AA932
Qatar (by subject)
  history
    bibliography, DE251
Qatar, Unwin, P. T. H., DE251

QER, CH112

Quadrilingual economics dictionary, Jong, Frits J. de, CH69

Quah, Jon S. T. *Singapore,* DE257

Quah, Stella R. *Singapore,* DE257

Quakers *see* **Friends, Society of**

Qualifications in education, CB324

Qualitative research in information management, Glazier, Jack D., AK7

——— Powell, Ronald R., AK7

Quan-guo xinshumu, AA893

Quantum Research Corporations. *CASPAR,* CB257

Quarterly bibliography of computers and data processing, EK164, EK168

Quarterly bulletin of Chinese bibliography, AA895

Quarterly bulletin of statistics for Asia and the Pacific, CG370, CG434

Quarterly cumulative index medicus, EH16, EH60, EH61, EH62

Quarterly cumulative index to current medical literature, EH61

Quarterly economic review, CH112

The quarterly Index Islamicus, BC499, BC502

Quarterly index to periodical literature, Eastern and Southern Africa, DD92

Quarterly list ... of official publications, AF190

Quarterly strategic bibliography, CJ566

Quasten, Johannes. *Patrology,* BC301

Quatremère, Étienne Marc. *Thesaurus syriacus,* AC773

Quay, Richard H. *The financing of American higher education,* CB226

——— *Research in higher education,* CB216

Quebec (by subject)
  history
    bibliography, DB178, DB215
Quebec, Beaulieu, André, DB213

Québec (Province). Commission de toponymie. *Répertoire toponymique du Québec,* CL113

Queens, empresses, grand duchesses, and regents, Opfell, Olga S., CJ318

Queen's University of Belfast. Institute of Irish Studies. *Parliamentary election results in Ireland, 1801–1922,* CJ379

The queens' vernacular, Rodgers, Bruce, CC284

Quelle, Fred. *Profile of teachers in the U.S.—1990,* CB166

Quellenkunde zur Geschichte Finnlands, Paloposki, Toivo J., DC138

Quellet, Henri. *Bibliographia indicum, lexicorum et concordantiarum auctorum Latinorum,* BE1044

Quem é quem no Brasil, AH125

Quemada, Bernard. *Trésor de la langue française,* AC331

Quemner, Th. A. *Dictionnaire juridique,* CK48

Quenstedt, A. *Palaeontologi,* EF252

Quenstedt, Werner. *Palaeontologi,* EF252

Quérard, Joseph Marie. *La France littéraire,* AA624, AA631

——— *La littérature française contemporaine, 1827–49,* AA631

——— *Les supercheries littéraires dévoilées,* AA169, AA624

The questions of King Milinda, BC92

Qui est qui en Belgique francophone, AH177

Qui êtes-vois?, AH201

Quick, Anne. *Chaucer, a bibliographical introduction,* DA138

Quick, John. *Artists' and illustrators' encyclopedia,* BF91

Quick reference to veterinary medicine, EJ128

Quién es quién en América del Sur, AH120

Quién es quién en Bolivia, AH123

Quién es quién en Colombia, 1978, AH134

Quién es quién en el Paraguay?, AH139

Quién es quién en el Peru, Requejo, Juan Vicente, AH142

Quién es quién en el Uruguay, AH145

Quién es quién en la Argentina, AH121

Quién es quién en las letras españolas, Instituto Nacional del Libro Español, BE1458

Quién es quién en Venezuela, AH147

Quienes son los escritores argentinos, BE921

Quigley, Ellen. *Canadian writers and their works: fiction series,* BE819

——— *Canadian writers and their works: poetry series,* BE819

Quiller-Couch, Arthur. *Oxford book of English verse,* BE720

The quilt encyclopedia illustrated, Houck, Carter, BG163

Quilting, 1915–1983, Makowski, Colleen Lahan, BG164

Quilts, BG164
  encyclopedias, BG163

Quinlan, David. *British sound films,* BH186

——— *Illustrated encyclopedia of film character actors,* BH284

——— *Illustrated guide to film directors,* BH290

——— *Quinlan's illustrated directory of film comedy actors,* BH284

——— *Quinlan's illustrated directory of film stars,* BH284

——— *Quinlan's illustrated registry of film stars,* BH284

Quinlan's illustrated directory of film comedy actors, Quinlan, David, BH284

Quinlan's illustrated directory of film stars, Quinlan, David, BH284

Quinlan's illustrated registry of film stars, Quinlan, David, BH284

Quinn, Arthur Hobson. *American fiction : an historical and critical survey,* BE485

——— *History of the American drama from the beginnings to the Civil War,* BE466

——— *History of the American drama from the Civil War to the present day,* BE466

Quinn, Bernard. *Churches & church membership in the United States,* BC87

Quinn, David B. *New American world,* DB63

Quinn, Edward. *The reader's encyclopedia of world drama,* BH70

Quinn, Karen Jane. *A manual of Old English prose,* BE731

Quinn, Kenneth P. *A manual of Old English prose,* BE731

Quinn, Mary Louise. *Water publications of state agencies,* EK89

Quirin, Heinz. *Einführung in das Studium der mittelalterlichen Geschichte,* DA135

——— *Medieval narrative sources,* DA135

Quotable lawyer, Frost, Elizabeth, CK57

——— Shrager, David S., CK57

The quotable Shakespeare, DeLoach, Charles, BE774

Quotable woman, 1800–1981, Partnow, Elaine, BE111

Quotable woman from Eve to 1799, Partnow, Elaine, BE111

Quotations, BE90, BE92, BE93, BE95, BE97, BE98, BE99, BE100, BE101, BE102, BE103, BE105, BE106, BE107, BE108, BE109, BE110, BE111, BE112, BE113, BE114, BE115, BE116, BE118, BE119, BE120, BE122, BE123, BE362
  bibliography, BE16, BE117
  handbooks, BE117
Quotations (by country or region)
  Canada, BE104
  Ireland, CJ377, DC409
Quotations (by ethnic group)
  Jewish, BE121
Quotations (by language)
  Arabic, BE124
  Dutch, BE125, BE126
  Farsi, BE124
  French, BE92, BE127, BE128, BE129, BE130, BE131, BE132, BE133
  German, BE134, BE135, BE136, BE137
  Greek, BE138, BE144
  Italian, BE132, BE139, BE140, BE141, BE142
  Latin, BE142, BE143, BE144, BE145
  multilingual, BE91
  Norwegian, BE146
  Spanish, BE96, BE147, BE148, BE150
Quotations (by subject)
  architecture, BF95
  arms control and peace research, CJ689
  art, BF95, BF145
  baseball, BK50
  business, CH72, CH73, CH74
  economics, CH73
  education, CB84, CB85
  film, BH262
  geography, CL54
  law, CK57
  libraries, AK51
  music, BJ162, BJ163
  political science, CJ45
  politics and government, CJ180
  presidents, CJ180
  religion, BC89, BC90, BC155, BC156
  Shakespeare, BE774, BE775
  sociology, CC22
  sports and games, BK31
  travel and tourism, CL383
  see also **Proverbs**
Quotations in black, BE115

Quote it!, Gerhart, Eugene C., CK57

Quote it II, Gerhart, Eugene C., CK57

The quote sleuth, Shipps, Anthony W., BE117

Quraishi, Salim. *The bibliography of South Asian periodicals,* AD215

The Qurân, BC92, BC206

•*R & TA on CD-ROM,* BC46

RAA, BF33, BF43

Raabe, Paul. *Die Autoren und Bücher des literarischen Expressionismus,* BE1230

—— *Index Expressionismus*, BE1223

Raan, E. van. *Bibliografie van vertalingen van Noord- en Zuidnederlandse werken*, AA138, DC450

—— *Nederlandse boek in vertaling, 1958–1967*, AA138, DC450

Raat, W. Dirk. *The Mexican Revolution*, DB232

Rabchuk, Gordon. *An annotated bibliography of works on daily newspapers in Canada, 1914–1983*, AE39

Rabie, P. S. *Hottentot (Khoekhoen) place names*, CL216

Rabin, Carol Price. *Music festivals in America*, BJ195

—— *Music festivals in Europe and Britain*, BJ196

Rabin, Jack. *Handbook of public administration*, CJ482

Rabkin, Jacob. *Current legal forms, with tax analysis*, CK164

Rabson, Carolyn. *National tune index microfiche*, BJ288

Raccagni, Michelle. *The modern Arab woman*, CC613

Race and ethnic relations *see* **Ethnic groups**

Race relations abstracts, CC340

Race relations survey, DD209, DD220

Races of Europe, Ripley, William Zebina, CE95

Rachel Carson Council. *A search for environmental ethics*, EK65

Rachlin, Harvey. *The money encyclopedia*, CH266

Rachow, Louis. *Guide to the performing arts*, BH8

Racial & religious violence in America, Newton, Michael, CC357

Racial and religious violence in America, CC357

Racial proverbs, Champion, Selwyn Gurney, BE153

Racinet, A. *Costume historique*, BG96

—— *The historical encyclopedia of costumes*, BG96

Racism, CC314

bibliography, CC30, CC333

Rackham, Thomas W. *Atlas of the moon*, EC68

Radar, EK145

handbooks, EK141

RADAR, AD294

Radar handbook, EK141

Råde, Lennart. *Beta mathematics handbook*, EB92

Radials bulletin, AK29

Radical geography, Owens, Peter L., CL18

Radical periodicals in America, 1890–1950, Goldwater, Walter, AD33

The radical right, Ó Maoláin, Ciarán, CJ79, CJ80

The radical right and patriotic movements in Britain, Pidduck, William, CJ338

Radicalism

biography, AH219, AH221, CJ156

periodicals, AD33, AD45

Radicalism (by country or region)

United States

periodicals, AD33

see also **Conservatism; Liberalism**

Radin, P. *Catalogue of Mexican pamphlets in the Sutro collection (1623–[1888])*, DB235

Radio

bibliography, CC398

dictionaries, BH318, CH484

directories, AD51, AE23, CH489, CH494

dissertations, BH295, BH296

handbooks, EK142

library resources, BH180

operators' manuals, EK144

periodicals, BH175

Radio (by country or region)

Europe

directories, AD1, AE2

Great Britain

directories, AD1, AE2

international

directories, AD1, AE2

see also **Television**

Radio advertising source, CH601

Radio amateur's handbook, EK144

Radio Liberty research bulletin, CJ394

Radio local markets source, CH601

Radio programs

catalogs, BH308, BH309, BH310, BH311

Radio scripts, BH168

Radio soundtracks, Pitts, Michael R., BH309

Radio's golden years, Terrace, Vincent, BH311

Radler, Rudolf. *Kindlers neues Literatur Lexikon*, BE69

Radley, Arthur Farrand. *Austria*, DC91

Radovich, Milan M. *Serbs in the United States and Canada*, CC321, CC473

Radstone, Susannah. *Women in film*, BH255

Radu, Michael. *Latin American revolutionaries*, CJ308

Radvansky, Susan. *Image of a continent*, DF25

Rae, Kenneth. *An international vocabulary of technical theatre terms in eight languages*, BH81

The RAE table of earth satellites, 1957–1989, EK34

Rafail, Patrice A. *A guide to manuscript collections in the history of psychology and related areas*, CD58

Rafailovich, Miriam H. *Women in chemistry and physics*, EA187, ED57, EE106

Raffé, Walter George. *Dictionary of the dance*, BH147

Raffin, Elisabeth. *Bibliographie zur Grammatik der deutschen Dialekte*, BD127

Ragatz, Lowell Joseph. *A guide for the study of British Caribbean history, 1763–1834*, DB407

Ragazzini, Giuseppe. *The Follett Zanichelli Italian dictionary*, AC533

Rageau, Jean-Pierre. *Atlas des diasporas*, DA188

—— *A strategic atlas*, CJ73

Raghu Vira. *A comprehensive English-Hindi dictionary of governmental and educational words and phrases*, AC487

Raglin, Lorraine. *Black women in television*, BH294

Ragsdale, Bruce A. *Biographical directory of the United States Congress, 1774–1989*, CJ232

—— *Black Americans in Congress, 1870–1989*, CJ231

Rahim, Enayetur. *Scholars' guide to Washington, D.C. for South Asian studies*, DE85

Rahman, H. U. *A chronology of Islamic history, 570–1000 CE*, DE63

Rahmato, Dessalegn. *Short guide to the study of Ethiopia*, DD156

Rahner, Karl. *Dictionary of theology*, BC408

—— *Encyclopedia of theology*, BC231

—— *Sacramentum mundi*, BC405

Rai, Priya Muhar. *Sikhism and the Sikhs*, BC573

Raict, E. *Õigekeelsuse sõnaraamat*, AC305

Railroad facts, CH462

Railroad gazette international, CH463

Railroads

annuals, CH459

bibliography, CH460

directories, CH463

library catalogs, CH458

statistics, CH462

yearbooks, CH462

Railroads (by country or region)

Great Britain

bibliography, CH461

Railroads, Koeneman, Joyce, CH444

—— Martinello, Gilda, CH444

Railroads in the age of regulation, 1900–1980, Bryant, Keith L., CH383

Railroads in the nineteenth century, Frey, Robert L., CH383

Railway directory, CH463

Railway directory & yearbook, CH463

Railway economics, Bureau of Railway Economics, CH458

Railway gazette yearbook, CH463

Raimo, John W. *Biographical directory of American colonial and Revolutionary governors, 1607–1789*, CJ288

—— *Biographical directory of the governors of the United States*, CJ288

—— *A guide to manuscripts relating to America in Great Britain and Ireland*, DB32

Raimond, Jean. *Handbook to English romanticism*, BE759

Rainbow, Edward L. *Research in music education*, BJ6

Rainey, Anson F. *The Macmillan Bible atlas*, BC197

Rainwater, Dorothy T. *American jewelry manufacturers*, BG89

—— *Encyclopedia of American silver manufacturers*, BG148

Rainwater, Robert. *Guide to the literature of art history*, BF1

Raish, Martin H. *Pre-Columbian contact with the Americas across the oceans*, DB22

Raising the curtain, AL58

Raistrick, Donald. *Index to legal citations and abbreviations*, CK42, CK43

—— *Lawyers' law books*, CK220

Raja, K. Kunjunni. *Philosophy of the grammarians*, BB33

Rajannan, Busnagi. *Dravidian languages and literatures*, BD226

Rake, Alan. *Who's who in Africa*, AH316, CJ404, CJ406, CJ409

Rakel, Robert E. *Conn's current therapy*, EH177

Rakipov, N. G. *Elsevier's dictionary of agriculture and food production*, EJ31

—— *English-Russian dictionary of agriculture*, EJ27

Rakover, Naḥum. *The multi-language bibliography of Jewish law*, CK240

Ralston, Anthony. *Encyclopedia of computer science*, EK171

Ralston, Valerie Hunter. *Water resources*, EK90

Raluy Poudevida, Antonio. *Diccionario Porrúa de la lengua española*, AC755

Rama Reddy, E. *Social science information*, CA6

Ramachandra Rao, Saligrama Krishna. *Encyclopaedia of Indian medicine*, EH84

Ramachandran, V. S. *Encyclopedia of human behavior*, CD20

Ramage, Craufurd Tait. *Beautiful thoughts from Greek authors*, BE138

—— *Beautiful thoughts from Latin authors*, BE145

—— *Familiar quotations from Greek authors*, BE138

—— *Familiar quotations from Latin authors*, BE145

Ramage, David. *Finding-list of English books to 1640 in libraries in the British Isles (excluding the national libraries and the libraries of Oxford and Cambridge)*, AA671, AA672

Rambaldo, Hartmut. *Grundriss zur Geschichte der deutschen Dichtung aus den Quellen*, BE1218

Rambo, Lewis. *Psychology of religion*, BC9

Ramirez S., Jésus. *Bibliografía indígena andina peruana (1900–1968)*, DB383

Ramondino, Salvatore. *Dictionary of foreign terms*, AC188

Ramore, L. *Women in development in Southern Africa*, DD122, DD171

Ramos, Roberto. *Bibliografía de la revolución mexicana*, DB232, DB233

Ramos, Teresita V. *Tagalog dictionary*, AC774

Ramos Guédez, José Marcial. *Bibliografía Afrovenezolana*, CC476

RAMP (Program). *Modern archives administration and records management*, AK187

—— *Planning, equipping, and staffing a document reprographic service*, AK249

Rampaging herd, Adams, Ramon Frederick, DB162

Ramsaran, Susan. *Everyman's English pronouncing dictionary*, AC105

Ramsay, Jeff. *Birth of Botswana*, DD132

—— *Botswana*, DD48

Ramsey, Jackson Eugene. *Handbook for professional managers*, CH622

Ramsey, L. G. G. *The complete color encyclopedia of antiques*, BG37

Ramson, W. S. *The Australian national dictionary*, AC178

Rana, Mahendra Singh. *Indian government and politics*, CJ434

Rana, Phyllis G. *Black child development in America, 1927–1977*, CC369

Ranade, Ashok D. *Keywords and concepts*, BJ156

Rancoeur, René. *Bibliographie de la littérature française du Moyen Âge à nos jours*, BE1140

Rand, Benjamin. *Bibliography of philosophy*, BB26

The Rand chronology of international terrorism, CJ552

Rand Corporation. *A million random digits*, EB93

—— *Selected Rand abstracts*, CA26

Rand Corporation, CA26

Rand McNally and Company. *Atlas of mankind*, CE70

—— *Atlas of the American Revolution*, DB97

—— *The new cosmopolitan world atlas*, CL288

—— *The new international atlas*, CL289

—— *Rand McNally commercial atlas and marketing guide*, CL304

—— *Standard highway mileage guide*, CL305

—— *The World book atlas*, CL295

Rand McNally atlas of the oceans, CL290, EF224

Rand McNally atlas of world history, DA49

The Rand McNally bankers directory, CH278

Rand McNally commercial atlas and marketing guide, Rand McNally and Company, CL304

Rand McNally cosmopolitan world atlas, CL288

The Rand McNally credit union directory, CH279

The Rand McNally encyclopedia of military aircraft, 1914–1980, CJ577

Rand McNally encyclopedia of World War II, Keegan, John, DA206

—— Mayer, Sydney L., DA206

Rand McNally illustrated atlas of China, CL355

Randall, Phyllis R. *Women speaking*, BD84, CC495

Randel, Don Michael. *The new Harvard dictionary of music*, BJ153

Randle, Patricio H. *Atlas del desarrollo territorial de la Argentina*, CL314

Randolph, Ruth Elizabeth. *Harlem Renaissance and beyond*, BE545

The Random House collector's encyclopedia, BG40

The Random House college dictionary, AC19

The Random House dictionary of the English language, AC12, AC19

The Random House encyclopedia, AB13, DA37

—— Mitchell, James, AB13

—— Stein, Jess M., AB13

Random House encyclopedia of antiques, BG40

Random House (Firm). *Shōgakukan Randamu Hausu Ei-Wa daijiten*, AC557

The Random House international encyclopedia of golf, Campbell, Malcolm, BK81

The Random House thesaurus, AC143

The Random House thesaurus of slang, AC127

The Random House timetables of history, DA37

Random House Webster's college dictionary, AC19

Random House word menu, Glazier, Stephen, AC74

Ranke, Kurt. *Enzyklopädie des Märchens*, CF50

Ranken, Michael D. *Food industries manual*, EJ166

Rankings of the states, National Education Association. Research Division, CB149

Rankova, Mariiíà. *Bŭlgarski-angliĭsko rechnik*, AC239

Ransohoff, Paul. *Psychology of religion*, BC9

Ransom, Jay Ellis. *Fossils in America*, EF250

—— *Harper & Row's complete field guide to North American wildlife*, EG86

Rao, S. Balu. *Who's who of Indian writers, 1983*, BE1570

Rao, Vijaya. *World guide to social work education*, CC49

Raoult, Jean François. *Dictionnaire de géologie*, EF83

Rap, Philip George. *Lijst der aardrijkskundige namen van Nederland*, CL147

Rap music in the 1980s, McCoy, Judy, BJ340

Rape

bibliography, CC217

directories, CC36

Raper, P. E. *Bronnegids vir toponimie en topologie*, CL217

—— *Hottentot (Khoekhoen) place names*, CL216

Raper, Richard. *Consolidated indexes*, DC296

Raphael, Maxwell I. *Tentative bibliography of Brazilian belles-lettres*, BE937

Rapp, George Robert. *Encyclopedia of minerals*, EF186

Rappaport, Barry. *Uranometria 2000.0*, EC75

Rappoport, Zvi. *CRC handbook of tables for organic compound identification*, EE151

Rapport sur la paléobotanique dans le monde, Boureau, Édouard, EG101

Rara arithmetica, Smith, David Eugene, EB18

Rare Bibles, Rumball-Petre, Edwin A. R., BC104

Rare birds of the world, Mountfort, Guy, EG270

Rare books *see* **Early and rare books**

Rare plants of the world, Belousova, L. S., EG156

Rasmussen, Carl. *Zondervan NIV atlas of the Bible*, BC201

Rasmussen, R. Kent. *Dictionary of African historical biography*, AH310

—— *Zimbabwe*, DD48

Rasor, Eugene L. *Battle of Jutland*, DA170

—— *British naval history since 1815*, DC333

—— *Falklands/Malvinas campaign*, DA170, DB375

—— *General Douglas MacArthur, 1880–1964*, DA170

—— *Spanish Armada of 1588*, DA170, DC505

Rassam, Ghassan N. *Multilingual thesaurus of geosciences*, EF79

La Rassegna della letteratura italiana, BE1296

Ratcliffe, Dorothy Una. *Catalogue of the Romany collection*, CC479

Rath, Frederick L. *A bibliography on historical organization practices*, BF117

Rath, Vimal. *Index of Indian economic journals, 1916–1965*, CH195

Rather, John Carson. *Library of Congress filing rules*, AK211

Rather, L. J. *A commentary on the medical writings of Rudolf Virchow*, EH207

The rating guide to franchises, Foster, Dennis L., CH403

The rating guide to life in America's small cities, Thomas, G. Scott, CL75

Rating of graduate programs, Andersen, Charles J., CB347

—— Roose, Kenneth D., CB347, CB348

Ratner, Lorman. *Multiculturalism in the United States*, CC353

Rau, William E. *A bibliography of pre-independence Zambia*, DD248, DD249

Raugel, Félix. *Larousse de la musique*, BJ120

Raup, David. *Handbook of paleontological techniques*, EF247

Rausch, Wilhelm. *Bibliographie zur Geschichte der Städte Österreichs*, DC90

Rautenberg, Ursula. *Die Rezeption mittelalterlicher deutscher Dichtung*, BE1271

Rave, Paul Ortwin. *Kunstgeschichte in Festschriften*, BF50, BF51

Raven, James. *British fiction, 1750–1770*, BE681

Ravenhall, Mary. *Annotated bibliography and index covering CPL bibliographies*, BF271

Ravier, Emile. *Bibliographie des oeuvres de Leibniz*, BB75

Ravines, Rogger. *Introducción a una bibliografía general de la arqueología del Perú, 1860–1988*, DB385

Rawlins, Bert J. *The parish churches and nonconformist chapels of Wales*, AJ127

Rawson, Hugh. *Wicked words*, AC133

Ray, Donald Iain. *Dictionary of the African left*, CJ407

Ray, Harold Lloyd. *Sports talk*, BK28

Ray, Martyn S. *Chemical engineering*, EK47, EK48

Ray, Mary Helen. *Guide to historic and significant gardens of America*, BF296

—— *The traveler's guide to American gardens*, BF296

Ray, Nisith Ranjan. *Dictionary of national biography*, AH351

Ray, Shyamal Kumar. *Bibliography of anthropology of India*, CE110

Ray, Sunanda. *Women and HIV/AIDS*, CC570

Raynaud, Gaston. *Bibliographie des chansonniers français*, BE1200

Rayner, P. Alan. *English silver coinage from 1649*, BG190

Razi, F. D. *The modern Persian dictionary (Persian-Urdu-English)*, AC317

•*RCSD*, AL80

Rea, Louis M. *Designing and conducting survey research*, CA58

Rea, Mark S. *Lighting handbook*, EK140

Reaction index of organic syntheses, Sugasawa, Shigehiko, EE145

Read, Campbell B. *Encyclopedia of statistical sciences*, EB34

Read, Conyers. *Bibliography of British history, Tudor period, 1485–1603*, DC318

Read, Danny L. *The literature of jazz*, BJ304

Read, Gardner. *Thesaurus of orchestral devices*, BJ372

Read, Herbert Edward. *Concise history of modern painting*, BF307

Read, Peter G. *Dictionary of gemmology*, EF185

Read, Phyllis J. *The book of women's firsts*, CC579

Read, Phyllis Rogers. *Numerical list of current publications of the U.S. Dept. of Agriculture*, EJ88

Read this first, AK231

The reader's adviser, AA329

Reader's Digest Association South Africa. *Reader's digest atlas of Southern Africa*, CL345

Reader's digest atlas of Southern Africa, Reader's Digest Association South Africa, CL345

Reader's digest family legal guide, CK135

Reader's digest family word finder, AC143

Reader's digest illustrated encyclopedic dictionary, AC16

Reader's digest of books, Keller, Helen Rex, BE193

Reader's encyclopedia, Benét, William Rose, BE58

Reader's encyclopedia of American literature, BE431

Reader's encyclopedia of Eastern European literature, BE988

Reader's encyclopedia of Shakespeare, Campbell, James Oscar, BE783

The reader's encyclopedia of the American West, DB174

The reader's encyclopedia of world drama, Gassner, John, BH70

Readers' guide abstracts, AD284, AD285, AD284

A reader's guide to Canadian history, DB187

A reader's guide to contemporary literary theory, Selden, Raman, BE53

The reader's guide to intelligence periodicals, Peake, Hayden B., CJ543

A reader's guide to Japanese literature, Rimer, J. Thomas, BE1594

Reader's guide to literary terms, Beckson, Karl E., BE76

—— Ganz, Arthur F., BE76

Readers' guide to periodical literature, AD256, AD284, AD285, AD288, AD289, BA6, BE260, BE262, BE409, BE499, AD285

Reader's guide to the classic British mystery, Oleksiw, Susan, BE266

A reader's guide to the great religions, Adams, Charles J., BC1

A reader's guide to the private eye novel, Niebuhr, Gary Warren, BE274

Reader's guide to twentieth-century science fiction, BE295

Reader's handbook of famous names in fiction, allusions, references, proverbs, plots, stories, and poems, Brewer, Ebenezer Cobham, BE181

A reader's Hebrew-English lexicon of the Old Testament, Armstrong, Terry A., BC133

Readett, Alan G. *Dictionary of commercial, financial and legal terms*, CK44

Readex Corporation. *Early American imprints, 1639–1800*, BJ59

Reading, CB60, CB120

bibliography, CB48, CB49, CB190

dictionaries, CB74

handbooks, CB114

see also **Literacy**

Reading abstracts, CB60

Reading and writing in the arts, Goldman, Bernard, BF124

Reading research, CB114

Reading the literatures of Asian America, Lim, Shirley, BE547

—— Ling, Amy, BE547

Readings in historic preservation, Massey, James C., BF219

Reagent chemicals, American Chemical Society, EE61

Reagents for organic synthesis, EE131

Real Academia Española. *Diccionario de la lengua española,* AC727

—— *Diccionario histórico de la lengua española,* AC726, AC728

Real-Encyclopädie der classischen Altertumswissenschaft, DA104

—— Pauly, August Friedrich von, DA101

Real estate
    bibliography, CH531
    dictionaries, CH532, CH533, CH535, CH536, CH537
    directories, CH222, CH388, CH524, CH538, CH539, CH540, CH541
    encyclopedias, CH534
    handbooks, CH530, CH542, CH543
    statistics, CH222, CH388, CH524, CH539, CH544, CH545
    see also **Housing**

Real estate appraisal bibliography, 1973–1980, CH531

Real estate dictionary, Thomsett, Michael C., CH537

The real estate directory of major investors, developers and brokers, CH540

Real estate handbook, CH542, CH543

The real estate industry, Harris, Laura A., CH530

Real estate investor's encyclopedia, CH532

The real estate sourcebook, CH540

Realencyklopädie für protestantische Theologie und Kirche, Hauck, Albert, BC67, BC69

—— Herzog, Johann Jakob, BC67, BC69

Realidad y perspectiva, DB314

Realism in European theatre and drama, 1870–1920, Boyer, Robert D., BE218

Reallexikon der Assyriologie, DA125

Reallexikon der Assyriologie, unter Mitwirkung zahlreicher Fachgelehrter, DA80

Reallexikon der deutschen Literaturgeschichte, BE1251

Reallexikon der germanischen Altertumskundes, DC230

Reallexikon der Vorgeschichte, Ebert, Max, DA82

Reallexikon für Antike und Christentum, BC248

Reallexikon zur byzantinischen Kunst, Wessel, Klaus, BF80

Reallexikon zur deutschen Kunstgeschichte, BF79

Reams, Bernard D. *Constitution of the United States,* CK172

—— *Constitutions of the states,* CK175

Reaney, Percy Hide. *A dictionary of British surnames,* AJ184, AJ185

—— *The origin of English surnames,* AJ185

Reardon, Joan. *Poetry by American women, 1900–1975,* BE496

—— *Poetry by American women, 1975–1989,* BE496

Reasearch [sic] trends in Sanskrit, Lakshminarasimha Moorty, C., BD197

Réau, Louis. *Dictionnaire polyglotte des termes d'art et d'archéologie,* BF92

—— *Iconographie de l'art chrétien,* BF185

Rebach, Howard M. *Handbook of clinical sociology,* CC25

—— *Substance abuse among ethnic minorities in America,* CC122

Rebadavia, Consolacion B. *Checklist of Philippine government publications, 1917–1949,* AF258

Rebellion records, DB106

Rébora, Piero. *Cassell's Italian-English, English-Italian dictionary,* AC528

Récapitulation des périodiques officiels parus en Tunisie de 1881 à 1955, Dār al-Kutub al-Qawmīyah (Tunisia), AF239

Recent American opera, Kornick, Rebecca Hodell, BJ238

Recent geographical literature, maps, and photographs, CL19

Recent literature in discovery history, McCorkle, Barbara B., CL11

Recent literature of the Renaissance, BE985

Recent publications in the social and behavioral sciences, CA9

Recent research on Anglo-Irish writers, Finneran, Richard J., BE798

Recent research on women in Brazil, Hahner, June Edith, DB343

Recent Soviet archival literature, DC562

Recent studies in myths and literature, 1970–1990, BE29

The recent study of Hebrew, Waldman, Nahum M., BD207

Receuil Mourier-Deltour, AG29

Rechcígl, Miloslan. *Czechoslovak contribution to world culture,* BE1106

Rechenbach, Charles William. *Swahili-English dictionary,* AC758

La recherche documentaire en droit, Tanguy, Yann, CK209

Rechnik na bŭlgarskiia ezik, AC242

Rechnik na bŭlgarskite psevdonimi, Bogdanov, Ivan, AA164

Rechnik na suvremennais bulgarski ezik, Bŭlgarskata Akademiía na Naukite, AC242

Recipes *see* **Cookbooks; Formulas and recipes**

Reckendorf, Hermann. *Wörterbuch der klassischen arabischen Sprache,* AC225

Recommended dietary allowances, National Research Council. Committee on Dietary Allowances, EH312

—— National Research Council. Subcommittee on the Tenth Edition of the RDAs, EH312

Recommended law books, CK128

Recommended reference books for small and medium-sized libraries and media centers, AA356

Record, Samuel James. *Timbers of the New World,* EJ188

—— *Timbers of tropical America,* EJ188

The record interpreter, Martin, Charles Trice, AA215

Record offices, Gibson, Jeremy Sumner Wycherley, AJ100

Record repositories in Great Britain, DC288

Record sources for local history, Riden, Philip, DC350

Recorded classical music, Cohn, Arthur, BJ377

Recorded music
    bibliography, BJ384
    catalogs, BJ374, BJ385, BJ386, BJ388, BJ389
    catalogs and discographies, BJ48, BJ375, BJ377, BJ379, BJ382, BJ383
    databases, BJ380
    dictionaries, BJ392, BJ393
    discography, BJ374
    indexes, BJ227
    library catalogs, BJ61, BJ62
    reviews, BJ390
        indexes, BJ391

Recorded plays, Hoffman, Herbert H., BH56

Records management, DB140

Records of early English drama, Johnson, Alexandra F., BE662

The records of German history in German and certain other record offices, Haase, Carl, DC247

Records of the presidency, Schick, Frank Leopold, AJ24, CJ174, DB37

Recreation, BK108, BK109
    bibliography, BK8

Recreation and outdoor life directory, BK108

Rectangular-polar conversion tables, Neville, E. H., EB94

Recueil de statistiques libanaises, CG410

Recueil de theses africanistes, droit et science politique 1967–1984, Lafond, Mireille, DD29

Recueil des études et ouvrages ayant trait à la femme rwandaise, Mugwaneza, Annie, DD199

Recueils bibliographiques concernant la Mauritanie, Robert, Dieter, DD178

Recueils collectifs de poésies libres et satiriques publiés depuis 1600 ... , Lachèvre, Frédéric, BE1194

The red book, AK220

Red data book, International Union for Conservation of Nature and Natural Resources, EG149, EG234, EG250, EG278, EG296

Redden, Kenneth Robert. *Modern legal systems cyclopedia,* CK31

Reddig, Jill Swanson. *Guide to ecology information and organizations,* EG62

Redding, J. Saunders. *The new cavalcade,* BE541

Reddy, Marlita A. *Statistical record of Hispanic Americans,* CC471, CG84

—— *Statistical record of Native North Americans,* CC442, CG85

Redfern, Bernice. *Women of color in the United States,* CC614

Redfern, James. *A glossary of Spanish literary composition,* BE1453

Redgrave, G. R. *Short-title catalogue of books printed in England, Scotland, & Ireland and of English books printed abroad, 1475–1640,* AA412, AA665, AA671, AA672, AA674, AA678, AA683, AD107, BE680

Redhouse, James William. *Redhouse yeni Türkçe-İngilizce sözlük,* AC792

—— *Turkish and English lexicon,* AC793

Rediscovery of creation, Sheldon, Joseph Kenneth, BC223, EG66

Redman, Barbara Klug. *Guide to programs in nursing in four-year colleges and universities,* EH282

Reed, A. W. *Aboriginal place names and their meanings,* CL218

—— *Concise Māori dictionary,* AC609

—— *A dictionary of Maori place names,* CL219

Reed, Clyde F. *Selected weeds of the United States,* EG181

Reed, Dale. *Guide to the Hoover Institution archives,* DA172

Reed, Jeffrey G. *Library use,* CD5

Reed, Marcia. *American diaries,* BE507, BE509, DB66

Reed, Maxine K. *The encyclopedia of television, cable, and video,* BH315

Reed, Monica. *Directory of anthropological resources in New York City libraries,* CE88

Reed, Robert M. *The encyclopedia of television, cable, and video,* BH315

REED, BE662

Reed-Scott, Jutta. *Preservation planning program,* AK238

Reeder, DeeAnn M. *Mammal species of the world,* EG299

Reel guide to Herstory, AE25

Reel women, Acker, Ally, BH279

Reep, Diana C. *Business and technical writing,* CH428

Rees, Alan M. *The consumer health information source book,* EH27

—— *Encyclopedia of health information sources,* EH15

Rees, Charles W. *Comprehensive heterocyclic chemistry,* EE117

Rees, Eiluned. *Libri Walliae,* AA699

Rees, Nigel. *Bloomsbury dictionary of phrase & allusion,* BE86

—— *Dictionary of popular phrases,* BE86

—— *Why do we say— ?,* AC61

Rees, Philip. *Biographical dictionary of the extreme right since 1890,* CJ68

—— *Fascism and pre-fascism in Europe, 1890–1945,* CJ321

—— *Fascism in Britain,* CJ339

Rees, R. *Penguin dictionary of economics,* CH54

Rees, Robert A. *Fifteen American authors before 1900,* BE404

Reese, Rosemary S. *A bibliography on historical organization practices,* BF117

Reeves, Diane Lindsey. *Child care crisis*, CC173
Refaussé, Raymond. *Directory of Irish archives*, AJ133
Referativnyĭ zhurnal, EA73
Refereed and nonrefereed economic journals, Miller, A. Carolyn, CH30
Reference aid, AD212
Reference and information services, AK235
Reference and online services handbook, AK236
Reference bibliography for liturgics, BC267
Reference book for world traders, Croner, U. H. E., CH138
Reference book of corporate managements, CH385
Reference books
 bibliography, AA349, AA351, AA352, AA353, AA354, AA355, AA356, AA358, AA363, AK233
 book reviews, AA330, AA346, AA348, AA359, EA10
 library catalogs, AA350
 reviews, AA357
Reference books (by subject)
 medicine, EH2
Reference books bulletin, AA330, AA357
Reference books for small and medium sized libraries, AA358
Reference books for the historian of science, Jayawardene, S. A., EA234
The reference catalogue of current literature, AA691
A reference companion to the history of abnormal psychology, Howells, John G., CD101
Reference data for engineers, EK142
Reference data for radio engineers, EK142
Reference encyclopedia of American psychology and psychiatry, Klein, Barry T., CD3
Reference encyclopedia of the American Indian, Klein, Barry T., CC428
Reference guide for English studies, Marcuse, Michael J., BE393, BE396, BE398
Reference guide for travellers, Neal, Jack A., CL391
Reference guide to American literature, BE449
Reference guide to English, Maclin, Alice, BD111
Reference guide to English literature, BE626
Reference guide to historical fiction for children and young adults, Adamson, Lynda G., BE256
Reference guide to science fiction, fantasy, and horror, Burgess, Michael, BE281, BE291
A reference guide to the literature of travel, Cox, Edward Godfrey, CL7
Reference guide to the United States Supreme Court, Elliot, Stephen P., CK192
A reference guide to United States Department of State special files, Haines, Gerald K., CJ177
Reference guide to United States military history, DB51
Reference guides to state history and research, DB144
Reference handbook of research and statistical methods in psychology, CD64
A reference index to twelve thousand Spanish American authors, Grismer, Raymond Leonard, BE873
A reference list of audiovisual materials produced by the United States government, 1978, National Audiovisual Center, AA382
Reference list of current periodicals, CE35
Reference manual for telecommunications engineering, Freeman, Roger L., EK146
The reference manual of woody plant propagation, Dirr, Michael A., EJ247
Reference materials in ethnomusicology, Nettl, Bruno, BJ323
Reference materials on Mexican Americans, Woods, Richard D., CC453
Reference service, Murfin, Marjorie E., AK234
Reference service for publications of intergovernmental organizations, AF5
Reference services review, AA359
The reference shelf, BE363, BE368, BE373
Reference sources for small and medium-sized libraries, AA358
Reference sources in history, Fritze, Ronald H., DA2
Reference sources in library and information services, Purcell, Gary R., AK2

Reference sources in science, engineering, medicine, and agriculture, Malinowsky, H. Robert, EA5
Reference sources in urban and regional planning, Weintraub, Irwin, BF268
Reference work, AK233, AK234, AK235
 handbooks, AK236
Reference works for theological research, Kepple, Robert J., BC12, BC13
—— Muether, John R., BC13
Reference works in British and American literature, Bracken, James K., BE393, BE396, BE398, BE763
Reflecting apartheid, Dubbeld, Catherine E., BE1534
Reflections on childhood, CC162
Reform Judaism in America, BC559
Reformation, BC287, DC26, DC28
 bibliography, DC25, DC27, DC226
 directories, DA153
Reformation (by country or region)
 Germany, DC227
 Spain, DC504
Reformation Europe, DC28
Reformed Church in America, BC380
Refranero general, ideológico español, Martínez Kleiser, Luis, BE149
Refrigeration *see* **Heating and refrigeration**
Refugee abstracts, CK83
Refugee and immigrant resource directory, Schorr, Alan Edward, CC34
Refugee resettlement in the United States, Haines, David W., CC322
Refugees
 abstract journals, CK83
 bibliography, CC319
 directories, CC34
 handbooks, CC350
Refugees (by country or region)
 United States
  bibliography, CC322
Refugees in the United States, CC354
Refussé, Raymond. *Directory of Irish archives*, DC400
Regents of nations, Truhart, Peter, CJ91
Reggentin-Scheidt, Christa. *Jazz index*, BJ303
Régi magyar könyvtár, Szabó, Károly, AA713, AA714, DC378
Régi magyarországi nyomtatványok, 1473–1600, Magyar Tudományos Akadémia, Budapest, AA713
Regimental histories of the Civil War, DB109
Regimental publications and personal narratives of the Civil War, DB109
Reginald, Robert. *Arms control, disarmament and military security dictionary*, CJ682, CJ683
—— *Science fiction and fantasy literature*, BE296
—— *Science fiction and fantasy literature, 1975–1991*, BE296
Region and regionalism in the United States, Steiner, Michael, DB146
Regional Center for Book Promotion in Latin America and the Caribbean. *Boletín bibliográfico*, AA473
—— *Editoriales, distribuidoras y librerías*, AA285
Regional differences in America, CG77, DB150
Regional Institute for Population Studies. *Population of Ghana*, CG333
Regional interest magazines of the United States, AD43
Regional planning, CC302, CC303
 dictionaries, BF277
 directories, BF279, BF282
Regional, state, and local organizations, AL42
Regional statistics, Balachandran, M., CG91
Regional theatre directory, BH88
Regionalism in literature, BE677
Register der Schlagwöter 1896–1974, Zeller, Otto, AD255
Register of additional locations, AA112, AA114
Register of corporations, directors and executives, CH313, CH367
Register of debates in Congress, AF127

Register of development research projects in Africa, DD54
Register of indexers, AK214
Register of Middle English religious and didactic verse, Brown, Carleton Fairchild, BE697, BE698
Register of post-graduate dissertations in progress in history and related subjects, DA16, DB191
Register of ships, CH465
Register of Swiss surnames, AJ142
Register til en del norske tidsskrifter, Deichmanske Bibliotek, Oslo, AD321, AH274
Register til norske tidsskrifter, AD321, AH274
Register und Auswertung zur 22. Auflage des etymologischen Wörterbuch von Friedrich Kluge, Seebold, Elmar, AC428
Register zu den Nachträgen in Wurzbachs 'Biographischen Lexikon d. Kaiserthums Österreich', AH170
Registers of births, etc., AJ57, CK157
The Registrar-General's annual report, CG239
The Registrar General's statistical review of England and Wales, Great Britain. Office of Population Censuses and Surveys, CG233
Registro civil do Brasil, Centro Brasileiro de Estudos Demograficos, CG142
Registro de lexicografía hispánica, Romera-Navarro, Miguel, AC753
Regueiro, José M. *Spanish drama of the Golden Age*, BE1465, BE1470, BE1478
Rehder, Alfred. *Bibliography of cultivated trees and shrubs hardy in the cooler temperate regions of the Northern Hemisphere*, EG204
—— *Manual of cultivated trees and shrubs hardy in North America*, EG200
Rehrauer, George. *Cinema booklist*, BH170
—— *The Macmillan film bibliography*, BH170
Rehrig, William H. *The heritage encyclopedia of band music*, BJ294
Reich, Bernard. *Historical dictionary of Israel*, DE192
—— *Political leaders of the contemporary Middle East and North Africa*, CJ404, CJ417
—— *United States foreign policy and the Middle East/North Africa*, DE3, DE40
Reich, Dorothy. *A history of German literature*, BE1259
Reich, Warren T. *Encyclopedia of bioethics*, EH241
Reichardt, Dieter. *Lateinamerikanische Autoren*, BE893
Reichardt, H. *The VNR concise encyclopedia of mathematics*, EB69
Reichenberger, Arnold Gottfried. *Spanish drama of the Golden Age*, BE1465, BE1478
Reichenberger, Kurt. *Das spanische Drama im Goldenen Zeitalter*, BE1469
Reichenberger, Roswitha. *Das spanische Drama im Goldenen Zeitalter*, BE1469
Reichert, Herbert William. *International Nietzsche bibliography*, BB78
Reichler, Joseph L. *The great all-time baseball record book*, BK59
Reichling, Dietrich. *Appendices ad Hainii-Copingeri Repertorivm bibliographicvm*, AA228
Reichmann, Oskar. *Frühneuhochdeutsches Wörterbuch*, AC401
—— *Sprachgeschichte*, BD125
Rcid, Anthony. *Indonesian serials, 1942–1950, in Yogyakarta libraries*, AD195
Reid, Daniel G. *Dictionary of Christianity in America*, BC235
Reid, Elspeth. *Sub-doctoral theses on Canada accepted by universities in the United Kingdom & Ireland 1899–1986*, DB190
Reid, Francis. *ABC of stage lighting*, BH76
Reid, Jane Davidson. *The Oxford guide to classical mythology in the arts, 1300–1990s*, BF189, CF24
Reid, Joyce M. H. *Atlas of the Bible*, BC198
—— *Concise Oxford dictionary of French literature*, BE1158
Reid, Richard. *Book of buildings*, BF253
Reid, W. Malcolm. *Smith's guide to the literature of the life sciences*, EG5

Reiersen, Olav. *English-Norwegian technical dictionary*, EA121
—— *Norsk-engelsk teknisk ordbok*, EA121
Reifenberg, Benno. *Die grossen Deutschen*, AH208
Reilly, Catherine W. *English poetry of the First World War*, BE712
—— *English poetry of the Second World War*, BE712
Reilly, Edwin D. *Encyclopedia of computer science*, EK171
Reilly, Elizabeth Carroll. *A dictionary of colonial American printers' ornaments and illustrations*, AA252
Reilly, John M. *Twentieth-century crime and mystery writers*, BE212
Reilly, John W. *The language of real estate*, CH536
Reiman, Donald H. *English romantic poetry, 1800–1835*, BE713
—— *Romantics reviewed*, BE757
Reinecke, John E. *A bibliography of pidgin and creole languages*, BD55
Reinehr, Robert C. *Handbook of old-time radio*, BH310
Reinfeld, Fred. *Catalogue of the world's most popular coins*, BG191
Reinhart, Theodore J. *Engineered materials handbook*, EK274
Reisner, Robert George. *Fakes and forgeries in the fine arts*, BF30
Reiss, Edmund. *Arthurian legend and literature*, BE340
Reiss, Louise Horner. *Arthurian legend and literature*, BE340
Reisser, Marsha J. *Black music and musicians in The new Grove dictionary of American music and The new Harvard dictionary of music*, BJ225
—— *Black music biography*, BJ220
—— *Black music in the United States*, BJ33
Reithmaier, Lawrence W. *Aviation/space dictionary*, EK29
Reitman, Édouard. *Bibliographie de Tahiti et de la Polynésie française*, DF51
Reitz, Karl. *A bibliography of Shinto in Western languages*, BC570
Rela, Walter. *A bibliographical guide to Spanish American literature*, BE868
—— *Brazilian literature*, BE930
—— *Diccionario de autores teatrales uruguayos & breve historia del teatro uruguayo*, BE959
—— *Diccionario de escritores uruguayos*, BE959
—— *Fuentes para el estudio de la literatura uruguaya*, BE959
—— *Fuentes para el estudio de la nueva literatura brasileña, de las vanguardias a hoy*, BE936
—— *Guía bibliográfica de la literatura hispano-americana desde siglo XIX hasta 1970*, BE868
—— *Literatura uruguaya*, BE958, BE959
—— *Spanish American literature*, BE868
Las relaciones de Bolivia, Chile y Perú, Cajías, Lupe, DB336
Relaciones literarias entre España e Italia, Siracusa, Joseph, BE1442
Relaciones México–Estados Unidos, DB220
The relations of literature and science, BE30
—— Schatzberg, Walter, BE30
Religion
  associations, BC80
  bibliography, BB23, BC7, BC8, BC13, BC14, BC16, BC19, BC20, BC21, BC28, BC30, BC31, BC32, BC36, BC37, BC38, CD59
    current, BC22
  bibliography of bibliography, BC4
  biography, BC84
  book reviews, BC51, BC52, BC53
  databases, BC41, BC46
  dictionaries, BC71, BC72, BC73, BC74, BC76
  dissertations, BC26
  encyclopedias, BC55, BC58, BC59, BC60, BC61, BC63, BC64, BC65, BC67, BC68, BC70
  guides, BC1, BC2, BC3
  indexes and abstract journals, BC42, BC43, BC44, BC45, BC46, BC47, BC48, BC49
    bibliography, BC50

library catalogs, BC40
manuscripts and archives, BC228
periodicals, BC23, BC24, BC25
quotations, BC89, BC90
reviews of research, BC51
Religion (by country or region)
  Africa, BC33, BC221
  Africa, South of the Sahara, BC34, BC35, DD90
  Australia, BC42
  Canada
    encyclopedias, BC66
  China, BC37, BC38
  Europe, BC6
  Japan, BC36, BC464
  New Zealand, BC42
  Russia and the U.S.S.R., DC566
  South Africa, BC49
  Spain, DC504
  Union of Soviet Socialist Republics, BC39, BC81
  United States, BC28, BC30, BC31, BC32, BC65
    atlases, BC85
    bibliography, BC27
    encyclopedias, BC66
    Southern states, BC29
    statistics, BC85, BC86, BC87, BC88, BC291
Religion (by subject)
  Christian religion
    manuscripts and archives, BC228
  courses of study, BC79
  foundations and philanthropic organizations, BC78
  history, BC222
    bibliography, BC11
  mysticism, BC8
  non-Christian religions, BC75, BC76, BC92
  psychology and religion, BC5, BC9
  sacred books, BC92, BC95, BC98, BC99, BC105, BC106, BC107, BC108, BC118, BC122
    bibliography, BC100, BC101, BC109, BC110, BC112, BC114
    see also **Christian religion; Theology**
Religion and education
  bibliography, CB37, CB39, CB223
Religion and politics *see* **Politics and religion**
Religion and psychology *see* **Psychology and religion**
Religion and society in North America, BC30
—— Brunkow, Robert deV, DB10
Religion and sociology, BC7
Religion and the American experience, 1620–1900, Holley, E. Jens, DB10
—— Young, Arthur P., DB10
Religion in American life, Burr, Nelson Rollin, BC27
—— Jamison, A. Leland, BC27
—— Smith, James Ward, BC27
Religion in England, 1688–1791, Rupp, Ernest Gordon, DC278
Die Religion in Geschichte und Gegenwart, BC68
Religion in the Soviet republics, BC81
Religion in the Soviet Union, Korsch, Boris, BC39
Religion index one, BC44, BC53
Religion index one : periodicals, BC41, BC45
Religion index two, BC44, BC45
—— O'Brien, Betty A., BC14
Religion index two : multi-author works, BC41
•*Religion indexes : RIO/RIT/IBRR*, BC41
Religion journals and serials, Fieg, Eugene C., BC23
Religion, learning, and science in the Abbasid period, Young, M. J. L., BE1546
Religion on the American frontier, Sweet, William Warren, BC286
Religious & inspirational books & serials in print, BC22
Religious and inspirational books and serials in print, BC22
Religious and theological abstracts, BC46
Religious bibliographies in serial literature, Walsh, Michael J., BC50
Religious bodies, United States. Bureau of the Census, BC291
Religious bodies in the United States, Melton, J. Gordon, BC66

Religious books, 1876–1982, BC16
Religious books and serials in print, BC22
Religious colleges and universities in America, Hunt, Thomas C., CB223
Religious education, CB36
  bibliography, CB37, CB39
  directories, BC77, BC79, CB305
Religious houses, BC438, BC441
Religious houses of medieval England, Knowles, David, BC441
Religious information sources, Melton, J. Gordon, BC13
Religious leaders of America, BC83
Religious music
  bibliography
    scores, BJ68
  encyclopedias, BJ118
Religious orders, BC228, BC440, BC442
Religious periodicals directory, Cornish, Graham P., BC23
Religious periodicals of the United States, Lippy, Charles H., BC24
Religious schools in America, Hunt, Thomas C., CB37
Religious studies review, Council of Societies for the Study of Religion, BC26
Relouzat, Claude. *Bibliographie de la Martinique*, DB445
Remedial education, CB191
  bibliography, CB190
Remington, Joseph P. *Remington's pharmaceutical sciences*, EH326
Remington, Robin Alison. *The international relations of Eastern Europe*, DC36
Remington's pharmaceutical sciences, EH326
Remington's practice of pharmacy, EH326
Remley, Mary L. *Women in sport*, BK7
Remos y Rubio, Juan Nepomuceno José. *Historia de la literatura cubana*, BE977
Remote sensing, EF18
Renaissance, BF171, DC430
  atlases, DA158
  bibliography, BE20, BF37, DA140
  dictionaries, BF83
  directories, DA153
  encyclopedias, DA146
  library catalogs, BF52
Renaissance (by subject)
  art, BF391
Renaissance art, Earls, Irene, BF83
Renaissance artists & antique sculpture, Bober, Phyllis Pray, BF391
Renaissance dictionaries, Starnes, DeWitt Talmage, AC595
Renaissance humanism, 1300–1550, Kohl, Benjamin G., BE20
Renaissance linguistics archive, 1350–1700, BD67
Renaissance philosophy, BB69
Renaissance rhetoric, Murphy, James Jerome, BE360
Renda, Umberto. *Dizionario storico della letteratura italiana*, BE1302
Rendell-Dunn, A. J. *Spanish-English horticultural dictionary*, EJ239
Rendle, Bernard John. *World timbers*, EJ189
René-Moreno, Gabriel. *Biblioteca boliviana*, AA500, AA505
—— *Catálogo de la bibliografía boliviana*, AA503
Renetsky, Alvin. *Directory of internships, work experience programs, and on-the-job training opportunities*, CB364, CH695
Rengger, Nicholas J. *Treaties and alliances of the world*, CK107
Reno, Edward A. *League of Nations documents, 1919–1946*, AF29
Renou, Louis. *Bibliographie védique*, BC484
Renouard, Philippe. *Imprimeurs & libraires parisiens du XVIe siècle*, AA310
—— *Répertoire des imprimeurs parisiens, libraires, fondeurs de caractères et correcteurs d'imprimerie*, AA311
Renstrom, Peter G. *The American law dictionary*, CK136

—— *The constitutional law dictionary*, CK129

—— *The electoral politics dictionary*, CJ121, CJ124

Renwick, Roger de V. *The British traditional ballad in North America*, BE630

Renzetti Marra, S. *Bibliografia dell'Italia antica*, DC417

•*REPÉRE*, AD294

Répertoire alphabétique des thèses de doctorat ès lettres des universités françaises, 1810–1900, Maire, Albert, AG28

Répertoire archéologique de la France, DC172

Répertoire bibliographique de la philosophie, BB13

Répertoire bibliographique de la traduction, BD88

Répertoire bibliographique de textes de présentation générale et d'analyse d'oeuvres musicales canadiennes (1900–1980), BJ41

Répertoire bibliographique des livres imprimés en France au seizième siècle, AA619, AA620, AA623

Répertoire bibliographique des livres imprimés en France au XVIIe siècle, AA620, AA623

Répertoire bibliographique des livres imprimés en France au XVIIIe siècle, Desgraves, Louis, AA620, AA623

Répertoire bibliographique des thèses françaises (1885–1975) concernant la littérature française des origines à nos jours, Gabel, Gernot U., BE1145

Répertoire bibliographique des traductions et adaptations françaises du théâtre étranger du XVᵉ siècle à nos jours, Horn-Monval, Madeleine, BE1178

Répertoire canadien sur l'éducation, CB52

Répertoire chronologique des littératures modernes, International Federation for Modern Languages and Literature, BE17

Répertoire collectif des quotidiens et hebdomadaires, Bibliothèque Nationale (France). Département des Périodiques, AE51

Répertoire d'art et d'archéologie, AD254, BB24, BE38, BF33, BF34, BF43, BF55, CE23, BF33

Répertoire de bibliographie française, AA614

Répertoire de généalogies françaises imprimées, Arnaud, Etienne, AJ82

Répertoire de la presse du Congo Belge (1884–1958) et du Ruanda-Urundi (1920–1958) … , Berlage, Jean, AD171

Répertoire de la presse et des publications périodiques françaises, 1977/1978, AD97

Répertoire de la presse et des publications périodiques tunisiennes, Abdeljaoued, Mohamed, AD179

Répertoire de l'histoire de la Révolution française, Walter, Gérard, DC176

Répertoire de manuscrits mediévaux contenant des notations musicales, Corbin, Solange, BJ55

Répertoire des archives du Maroc, Menditte, Arnaud de, DD69

—— Nicot, Jean, DD69

Répertoire des articles relatifs à l'histoire et à la littérature juives, parus dans les périodiques, de 1665 à 1900, Schwab, Moïse, DC545

Répertoire des associations de bibliothécaires membres de la Fédération internationale, International Federation of Library Associations, AK53

Répertoire des bibliothèques et des catalogues de manuscrits grecs, Richard, Marcel, AA210

Répertoire des catalogues de ventes de livres imprimés, Blogie, Jeanne, AA259

Répertoire des catalogues de ventes publiques, Lugt, Frits, BF112, BF302

Répertoire des historiens français pour la période moderne et contemporaine, Faugères, Arlette, DC163

—— Ferré, Régine, DC163

Répertoire des imprimeurs parisiens, libraires, fondeurs de caractères et correcteurs d'imprimerie, Renouard, Philippe, AA311

Répertoire des index et lexiques d'auteurs latins, Faider, Paul, BE1031, BE1044

Répertoire des inventaires des archives conservées en Belgique, parus avant le 1ⁱᵉʳ Janvier 1969, Nicodème, Jacques, DC106

Répertoire des lexiques du vieux français, Levy, Raphael, AC389

Répertoire des livres au format de poche, AA635

Répertoire des mémoires de licence et des thèses de doctorat présentés dans les départements d'histoire contemporaine des universités belges, Hendrickx, Jean-Pierre, DC105

Répertoire des noms de famille suisses, AJ142

Répertoire des noms propres de personnes et de lieux cités dans les chansons de geste françaises et les oeuvres étrangères dérivées, Moisan, André, BE1164

Répertoire des organisations de travailleurs au Canada, Canada. Labour Data Branch, CH662

Répertoire des ouvrages imprimés en langue italienne au XVIIe siècle conservés dans les bibliothèques de France, Michel, Suzanne P., AA733

Répertoire des périodiques de langue française, philosophiques, historiques, philologiques et juridiques, AL61

—— Caron, Pierre, AD94

Répertoire des périodiques paraissant en Belgique, Hove, Julien van, AD84

Répertoire des périodiques publiés par les organisations internationales, AD21

Répertoire des plus anciens textes en prose française, Woledge, Brian, BE1202

Répertoire des publications en série de lministration française (périodiques et collections), AF171

Répertoire des publications gouvernementales du Québec de 1867 à 1964, Beaulieu, André, AF155

—— Bonenfant, Jean-Charles, AF155

—— Hamelin, Jean, AF155

Répertoire des publications officielles (séries et périodiques), AF171

Répertoire des publications périodiques et de serie de l'administration française, AF171

Répertoire des publications sériées canadiennes, AD60

Répertoire des sociétés françaises de sciences philosophiques, historiques, philologiques et juridiques, Caron, Pierre, AL61

Répertoire des sources historiques du Moyen Âge, Chevalier, Cyr Ulysse Joseph, AH11, DA130

Répertoire des thèses africanistes françaises, DD31

Répertoire des thèses concernant les études slaves, Seydoux, Marianne, DC555

Répertoire des thèses de doctorat européennes, AG21

Répertoire des thèses en cours portant sur des sujets d'histoire et autres sujets connexes, DB191

Répertoire des thèses littéraires canadiennes de 1921 à 1976, Naaman, Antoine, BE44

Répertoire des travaux universitaires inédits sur la période révolutionnaire, Miraval, Paule, DC181

Répertoire du livre suisse, AA835

Répertoire du théâtre camerounais, Zimmer, Wolfgang, BE1526

Répertoire international de la littérature de l'art, BF33, BF34, BF43

Répertoire international de la presse musicale, BJ112

Répertoire international des études canadiennes, DB201

Répertoire international des médiévistes, DA154

Répertoire international des musiques électroacoustiques, Davies, Hugh, BJ311

Répertoire international des sources musicales, BJ57, BJ77

Répertoire international des éditeurs et diffuseurs de langue française, AA288

Répertoire méthodique de l'histoire moderne et contemporaine de la France pour les années 1898–1913, DC198

Répertoire mondial des institutions de formation et de recherche en droit international, CK106

Répertoire mondial des institutions de sciences sociales, CA48

Répertoire national des annuaires français, 1958– 1968, Bibliothèque Nationale (France). Département des Périodiques, AD93

Répertoire pratique des périodiques [belges] édités en langue française, Marechal, Yvon, AD85

Répertoire topo-bibliographique des abbayes et prieurés, Cottineau, L. H., BC438

Répertoire toponymique du Québec, CL113

Repertoria bibliografico della storia e della critica della letteratura italiana dal 1933 al 1942, Prezzolini, Giuseppe, BE1295

Repertorim bibliographicum, Hain, Ludwig Friedrich Theodor, AA222, AA227, AA230, AA231, AA233

Repertorio analitico della stampa italiana, AD129, AE64

Repertorio bibliográfico de las relaciones entre la península Ibérica y el Norte de África, siglos XV– XVI, García-Arenal, Mercedes, DD70

Repertorio bibliografico della letteratura italiana, Bosco, Umberto, BE1295

Repertorio bibliografico della storia e della critica della letteratura italiana dal 1902 al 1932, Prezzolini, Giuseppe, BE1295

Repertorio bibliográfico hondureño, Durón, Jorge Fidel, AA488

Repertorio de publicaciones periódicas actuales latinoamericanas, Pan American Union, AD67

Repertorio del teatro chileno, Durán Cerda, Julio, BE939

Repertorio selecto del teatro hispanoamericano contemporaneo, Neglia, Giuseppe Erminio, BE900

—— Ordaz, Luis, BE900

Repertorium Biblicum Medii Aevi, BC116

Repertorium bibliographicum, Hain, Ludwig Friedrich Theodor, AA223, AA228

Repertorium commentationum a societatibus litterariis editarum, Reuss, Jeremias David, BE31, DA9, EA21, EC17, ED6, EE15, EG98, EG213, EH68

Repertorium der diplomatischen Vertreter aller Länder seit dem Westfälischen Frieden (1648), CJ81

Repertorium der mineralogischen und krystallographischen Literatur, 1876–[1902], EF174

Repertorium der Musikwissenschaft, Kahl, Willi, BJ17

Repertorium der technischen Journal-Literatur, 1823–1908, EA74

Repertorium der technischen literatur, EA74

Repertorium der verhandelingen en bijdragen betreffende de geschiedenis des vaderlands, in tijdschriften en mengelwerken, DC457

Repertorium fontium historiae medii aevi, DA136

Repertorium lexicographicum graecum, Riesenfeld, Blenda, BE1044

—— Riesenfeld, Harald, BE1031, BE1044

Repertorium op de koloniale litteratuur, Hooykaas, J. C., DE175

Repertorium op de literatuur betreffende de Nederlandsche koloniën, Hartman, A., DE175

Repertorium typographicum, Weller, Emil Ottokar, AA639

Repertorium über die in Zeit- und Sammelschriften der Jahre 1812–1890 enthaltenen Aufsätze und Mitteilungen schweizergeschichtlichen Inhaltes, Brandstetter, Josef Leopold, AH298, AH300, DC522, DC523

Repertorium über die vom Jahre 1800 bis zum Jahre 1850 in Akademischen Abhandlungen, Gesellschaftsschriften und wissenschaftlichen Journalen auf dem Gebiete der Geschichte und ihrer Hülfswissenschaften erschienenen Aufsätze, Koner, Wilhelm, DA9

Repertorium van boeken en tijdschriftartikelen betreffende de geschiedenis van Nederland, DC457

Repertorium van de België verschijnende tijd-schriften, AD84

Repertorium van de Vlaamse gouwen en gemeenten, Wachter, Leo de, DC103

Repertorium van geschiedschrijvers in Nederland, 1500–1800, Haitsma Mulier, E. O. G., DC461
Repertory of disarmament research, CJ695
Report of the congressional committees investigating the Iran-Contra Affair, United States. Congress. Senate. Select Committee to Investigate Covert Arms Transactions with Iran, CJ114
Report of the President's Special Review Board, United States. President's Special Review Board, CJ114
Report of the Registrar General on vital statistics, 1981, Sri Lanka, CG425
Report on registration of births and deaths, CG422
Report on the registration of births and deaths and marriages, CG422
Report on vital statistics, Ireland. Central Statistics Office, CG251
Report series codes dictionary, EA65
Report writing
  bibliography, CH428
  manuals, AG1, AG2, AG4, AG5, AG6
Reports of the Bureau of Applied Social Research on microfiche, CA12
Representations of primes by quadratic forms, Gupta, H., EB94
Representative American speeches, BE363
Representative bibliography of American labor history, Neufeld, Maurice F., CH637
Reprints
  bibliography, AA393, AA398, AA399
Reproductions of manuscripts and rare printed books. Short title list, Modern Language Association of America, AA134
Reproductively active chemicals, Lewis, Richard J., EE80
Reprography and micrographics, AK249, AK250
  bibliography, AK245
  directories, AK244, AK247
  handbooks, AK248
Reptile book, EG246
Reptiles *see* **Amphibians and reptiles**
Reptiles and amphibians of North America, Leviton, Alan E., EG251
The reptiles of North America, Ditmars, Raymond Lee, EG246
Republic of China yearbook, CG429, DE265
Republic of Guinea-Bissau, Forrest, J., DD48
—— Lobban, Richard A., DD48
The Republic of Turkey, Witherell, Julian W., DC540
Republica de Colombia. Biblioteca nacional. *Catálogo de todos los periódicos que existen desde su fundación hasta el año de 1935, inclusive,* AD73
República Dominicana en cifras, CG173
Republika e Shqipërisë. Ministria e Ekonomise. Drejtoria e Statistikës. *Vjetari statistikor i Shqipërisë,* CG192
La République Démocratique du Soudan, El-Singaby, Talaat, DD225
République du Congo-Brazzaville, Perrot, Claude Hélène, DD144
République du Sénégal. Ministère du Plan et du Développement. *Bibliographie des régions du Sénégal,* DD202
Requejo, Juan Vicente. *Quién es quién en el Peru,* AH142
Requirements for certification of teachers, counselors, librarians, administrators for elementary and secondary schools, CB164
Research abstracts, AG16
Research and Information Centre on Eritrea. *Bibliography on Eritrea,* DD153
Research and reference guide to French studies, Osburn, Charles B., BE1129
Research catalog of the Library of the American Museum of Natural History, American Museum of Natural History. Library, EG67
Research catalogue of the American Geographical Society, American Geographical Society of New York, CL28
Research centers, AL81
  directories, CA56, CB88, EH149

Research centers (by country or region)
  China, EA148
  Europe
    directories, AL79, EA141
  Netherlands, CA51
  Pacific Rim, EA146
  United Kingdom
    directories, EA143
  United States, AL83, CJ280
    directories, AL80, AL82, AL84, EA147
  U.S.S.R., AL85
    directories, AL79
•*Research centers and services database,* AL80
Research centers directory, AL81, AL82, EA147
Research Centre for Communication and Development (Kathmandu, Nepal). *SAARC women,* AH363
Research Clearinghouse and Curriculum Integration Project on Women of Color and Southern Women. *Women of color and Southern women,* CC623
Research collections in Canadian libraries, DC46
—— National Library of Canada, AK128, DB199
Research collections in labor studies, CH624
Research design and social measurement, CA57
Research Foundation for Jewish Immigration. *Biographisches Handbuch der deutschsprachigen Emigration nach 1933,* AH203
—— *Jewish immigrants of the Nazi period in the USA,* DA218, DB126
Research guide for psychology, McInnis, Raymond G., CD4
Research guide for studies in infancy and childhood, Haag, Enid E., CC139, CD77, CD80
A research guide for undergraduate students, Baker, Nancy L., BE2, BE396
Research guide for undergraduates in political science, Anderson, Peter J., CJ3
—— Kalvelage, Carl, CJ3
—— Segal, Morley, CJ3
Research guide in political science, Kalvelage, Carl, CJ3
—— Segal, Morley, CJ3
Research guide on language change, BD68
Research guide to American historical biography, AH69, AH162
Research guide to Andean history, DB279
Research guide to Argentine literature, Foster, David William, BE919
—— Foster, Virginia Ramos, BE919
Research guide to biography and criticism, BE7
Research guide to Central America and the Caribbean, DB301, DB414
A research guide to central party and government meetings in China, 1949–1986, Lieberthal, Kenneth, DE147
A research guide to China-coast newspapers, 1822–1911, King, Frank H. H., AE86
A research guide to Congress, Manion, Judith, CJ196
Research guide to Costa Rica, Elizondo, Carlos L., DB304
Research guide to current military and strategic affairs, Arkin, William M., CJ559
Research guide to English translation of Chinese verse, Dang, Shu-leung, BE1552
—— Ho, Pung, BE1552
—— Wong, Kai-chee, BE1552
Research guide to European historical biography, 1450–present, AH162
Research guide to libraries and archives in the Low Countries, Brogan, Martha L., AK133, DC13
Research guide to musicology, Pruett, James W., BJ7
Research guide to philosophy, Tice, Terrence N., BB3
Research guide to religious studies, Wilson, John Frederick, BC3
Research guide to science fiction studies, Currey, L. W., BE281
—— Justus, Douglas R., BE281
—— Schlobin, Roger C., BE281
—— Tymn, Marshall B., BE281
Research guide to the arid lands of the world, Hopkins, Stephen T., EF1

A research guide to the health sciences, Haselbauer, Kathleen J., EH17
Research guide to the history of Western art, Kleinbauer, W. Eugene, BF5
Research guide to the Russian and Soviet censuses, CG302
Research guides in military studies, CJ608
Research in archives, Brooks, Phillip Coolidge, DB27
Research in British universities, polytechnics and colleges, BA8, CA46, EA138, EG47
Research in composition and rhetoric, BE364
—— Lunsford, Ronald F., BE364
—— Moran, Michael G., BE364
Research in critical theory since 1965, Orr, Leonard, BE52
Research in dance, Bopp, Mary S., BH130
Research in education, AK35, CB61
Research in higher education, Quay, Richard H., CB216
Research in Mexican history, Greenleaf, Richard E., DB240
Research in ministry, BC41, BC446
Research in music education, Froehlich, Hildegard C., BJ6
—— Rainbow, Edward L., BJ6
Research in progress in German studies, BE1237
Research in social anthropology, 1975–1980, Webber, Jonathan, CE28
Research Institute for the Study of Man. *The complete Caribbeana, 1900–1975,* DB405
Research institutions and learned societies, AL83, AL116
Research into higher education abstracts, CB235
Research libraries
  guides, AK4
  statistics, AK96
Research Libraries Group. *Bibliography of American imprints to 1901,* AA402
Research Libraries Group. Art and Architecture Program. *SCIPIO,* BF113
Research Library on African Affairs (Accra, Ghana). *Ghana national bibliography bi-monthly,* AA860
Research material for Hong Kong studies, DE150
Research methodology in social science in India, CA59
Research methods in cultural anthropology, Bernard, H. Russell, CE56
Research methods in plant science, Klein, Richard M., EG151
Research on language teaching, Nostrand, Howard Lee, BD75
Research on men who batter, Gondolf, Edward W., CC211
Research on Zambian women in retrospect and prospect, Bardouille, Raj, DD246
Research opportunities in Renaissance drama, BE635
Research Publications, inc. *American fiction, 1774–1850,* BE482
—— *Bibliography and reel index,* CG93
—— *Dictionary catalog of the Harris collection of American poetry and plays, Brown University Library, Providence, Rhode Island,* BE494
—— *Early English newspapers,* AE57
—— *Guide to the microfilm edition of International population census publication, 1945–1967,* CG9
—— *A guide to the microfilm edition of International population census publications, 1945–1967,* CG11
—— *League of Nations documents, 1919–1946,* AF29
—— *United States decennial census publications, 1790–1970,* CG9
Research services directory, AL81, AL84
Research Society for Victorian Periodicals. *The Waterloo directory of Victorian periodicals, 1824–1900,* AD114
Research studies in education, CB25
Research tips in international law, CK74
Research trends in Sanskrit, BD197

The researcher's guide to American genealogy, Greenwood, Val D., AJ11

Researcher's guide to archives and regional history sources, DB35

Researcher's guide to British film & television collections, BH181

A researcher's guide to sources on Soviet social history in the 1930s, DC592

Researcher's guide to Washington experts, Washington Researchers, CJ146

Réseau d'information en économie générale (France). *Ecodoc*, CH39

Réseau sahélien d'information et de documentation scientifiques et techniques. *RESINDEX*, DD103

Reshimat ma'arim be-mada'e ha-yahadut, BC544

Residential treatment facilities for emotionally disturbed children, CC165

RESINDEX, DD103

Resistance, war and liberation, DD123

Resnick, Rosa Perla. *World guide to social work education*, CC49

Resort to arms, Small, Melvin, CJ598

The resource book of Jewish music, Heskes, Irene, BJ37

Resource directory for older people, CC89

Resource directory for the disabled, Shrout, R. N., CC197

Resource guide to Dominica 1493–1986, Myers, Robert A., DB432

Resource guide to special education, Davis, William Edmund, CB203

A resource guide to themes in contemporary American song lyrics, 1950–1985, Cooper, B. Lee, BJ316

Resourceful woman, Brennan, Shawn, CC558

Resources for Australian and New Zealand studies, Bloomfield, Valerie, DF11

Resources for Brazilian studies at the Bibliothèque nationale, Jackson, William Vernon, DB351

Resources for early childhood, Scheffler, Hannah Nuba, CC149

Resources for educational equity, CB18

Resources for middle childhood, Sheiman, Deborah Lovitky, CC150, CD79

Resources for Soviet, East European and Slavonic studies in British libraries, Walker, Gregory, DC51

Resources for the future, Mayne, Alan J., CA15

Resources for the Future (organization). *Natural resource commodities—a century of statistics*, CH441

Resources for the history of computing, Bruemmer, Bruce, EK208

Resources in education, AK28, AK35, BE348, CB1, CB54, CB56, CB61, CB83, CB158, CB194, CD90, CD91, CD92

Resources of American music history, BJ170

Respectfully quoted, BE116

Respiration and circulation, Altman, Philip L., EG53

Restle, Marcell. *Reallexikon zur byzantinischen Kunst*, BF80

Restoration
   abstract journals, BF198
   bibliography, BF117
   see also **Conservation; Art—restoration and conservation**

Restoration and conservation
   handbooks, BF351

Restoration and early eighteenth-century English literature, 1660–1740, Lund, Roger D., BE746

Restoration and eighteenth-century poetry, 1660–1780, Rothstein, Eric, BE718

Restoration and eighteenth century theatre, Stratman, Carl Joseph, BE647

Restoration and eighteenth century theatre research, Stratman, Carl Joseph, BH47

Restoration drama, Taylor, Thomas J., BE647

Restoration England, 1660–1689, Sachse, William Lewis, DC303, DC319

Restoration manual, Bullock, Orin M., BF265

Restrup, Ole. *Danske Digtere i det 20. arhundrede*, BE1115

Resumen estadístico, CG140

Resúmenes sobre población en América Latina, CG123

Résumés, EA151

Retana y Gamboa, Wenceslao Emilio. *Aparato bibliográfico de la historia general de Filipinas*, AA929

——— *La imprenta en Filipinas*, AA929

——— *Tablas cronológica y alfabética de imprentas e impresores de Filipinas*, AA929

Retirement benefit plans, Miller, Herbert A., CH503

A retrospective bibliography of American demographic history from colonial times to 1983, Gerhan, David R., CG92, DB14

Retrospective index to film periodicals, 1930–1971, Batty, Linda, BH231

Retrospective index to Nigerian doctoral dissertations and masters theses, 1895–1980, Ofori, Patrick E., AG48

Retrospective index to theses of Great Britain and Ireland, 1716–1950, AG35

Retrospective national bibliographies, AA395

Retrospective South African national bibliography for the period, 1926–1958, AA876

Retrospektivnaia gosudarstvennaia bibliografiia SSSR, Semenovker, B. A., AA786

Réunion
   atlases, CL276
   bibliography, DD121, DD142, DD175

Reuss, Jeremias David. *Repertorium commentationum a societatibus litterariis editarum*, BE31, DA9, EA21, EC17, ED6, EE15, EG98, EG213, EH68

Révai nagy lexikona, AB60

The Revels history of drama in English, BE467, BE664, BE667

Reverdy, Georges. *Atlas historique des routes de France*, DC167

Reverse acronyms, initialisms & abbreviations dictionary, AC42

Reverse dictionary, AC136

Review of agricultural entomology, EG337, EJ19

Review of applied entomology, EG337, EJ19

Review of Australia's demographic trends, CG435

Review of inter-American bibliography, AA476

Review of medical and veterinary entomology, EG337, EJ19

Review of medical and veterinary mycology, EJ19

Review of particle properties, ED49

Review of plant pathology, EJ19

Review of religion, BC26

Review of research in education, CB121

Review of reviews, AD286

Review of Russian émigré books, DC30

Review of the arts, BH9, BH236

Reviewing Shakespeare, BE780

Reviews in anthropology, CE37

Reviews of modern physics, ED46

Reviews of research, AD113

The revised English Bible with the Apocrypha, BC94

A revised guide to the law and legal literature of Mexico, Clagett, Helen Lord, CK197

Revised medieval Latin word-list from British and Irish sources, Latham, Ronald Edward, AC589

Revised new general catalogue of nonstellar astronomical objects, Sulentic, Jack W., EC75

——— Tifft, William G., EC75

Revised New Testament, BC94

Revised statutes of Canada, 1985, Canada, CK193

Revised statutes of Nebraska, Nebraska. [Laws, etc.], CK179

Revista de bibliografía chilena, AA518, AA519

Revista de bibliografía chilena y extranjera, AA520

Revista de filología española, AC753, BE1432

Revista interamericana de bibliografía, AA471, AA476

Revistas españolas, 1973–1978, Instituto Bibliográfico Hispánico, AD155

Revistas hispanoamericanas, Leavitt, Sturgis Elleno, AD299

Las revistas literarias de Hispano-américa, Carter, Boyd George, BE882

Revolution and structural change in Latin America, Chilcote, Ronald H., DB254

La Révolution française, Manceron, Claude, DC186

Revolutionary America, 1763–1789, Gephart, Ronald M., DB88

Revolutionary and dissident movements, CJ61

Revolutionary Cuba, AA562

Revolutions, CJ74

Revolutions and revolutionists, Blackey, Robert, CJ75

Revue belge de philologie et d'histoire, DC104

Revue bibliographique de Sinologie, DE134

Revue de l'art, BF46

Revue de l'institut, international de statistique, International Statistical Institute, EB13

Revue de Qumran, BC112

Revue des bibliothèques, AA308

Revue des revues, BE32

Revue d'histoire ecclésiastique, BC271

Revue d'histoire littéraire de la France, BE1140

Revue d'histoire littéraire du Québec et du Canada français, BE838

Revue philosophique de Louvain, BB13

Revue semestrielle des publication mathématiques, EB26

Revues d'architecture et de construction en France au XIX siècle, Lemoine, Bertrand, BF46

——— Lipstadt, Helene, BF46

Les revues littéraires éphémères paraissant à Paris entre 1900 et 1914, Arbour, Roméo, AD90

Rey, Alain. *Dictionnaire alphabétique et analogique de la langue française*, AC334

——— *Dictionnaire des expressions et locutions*, AC371

——— *Dictionnaire des littératures de langue française*, BE1149

——— *Dictionnaire du français non conventionnel*, AC354

——— *Dictionnaire historique de la langue française*, AC349

——— *Dictionnaire universel des noms propres, alphabétique et analogique*, AJ191

——— *Le petit Robert 2*, AJ191

Rey-Debove, Josette. *Dictionnaire universel des noms propres, alphabétique et analogique*, AJ191

Reyes Monroy, José Luis. *Bibliografía de la imprenta en Guatemala*, AA481

Reynal, Vicente. *Diccionario de hombres y mujeres ilustres de Puerto Rico y de hechos históricos*, AH160

Reynards, Keith W. *Aslib directory of information sources in the United Kingdom*, AK141

Reynolds, Barbara. *Cambridge Italian dictionary*, AC529, AC534

——— *Concise Cambridge Italian dictionary*, AC529, AC535

Reynolds, Cecil R. *Concise encyclopedia of special education*, CB195

——— *Encyclopedia of special education*, CB195, CB196

——— *Handbook of psychological and educational assessment of children*, CD93

——— *The handbook of school psychology*, CD94

Reynolds, Frank E. *Guide to Buddhist religion*, BB20, BC470, BC472

Reynolds, Hugh. *The executive branch of the U.S. government*, CJ170

Reynolds, Jacqueline A. *The scientific traveler*, EA218

Reynolds, James E. F. *The extra pharmacopoeia*, EH357

Reynolds, Lloyd George. *Trade union publications*, CH658

Reynolds, Maynard Clinton. *Handbook of special education*, CB204

Reynolds, Michael M. *Guide to theses and dissertations*, AG7

Reynolds, Moira Davison. *Women advocates of reproductive rights*, CC258

Reynolds, Peter. *Pictorial guide to identifying Australian architecture*, BF208

Reynolds, Thomas H. *Foreign law*, CK3

Reza, S. Mohammad. *Persons who shape our destiny*, AH366

Rezak, Ira. *Nobel laureates in medicine or physiology*, AL169, EH216

Rézeau, Pierre. *Dictionnaire du français parlé*, AC353

Die Rezeption mittelalterlicher deutscher Dichtung, Grosse, Siegfried, BE1271

RGG, BC68

Rheims, Maurice. *19th century sculpture*, BF393
—— *Dictionnaire des mots sauvages (écrivains des XIXe et XXe siècles)*, AC358

Rhetoric, CA55
  bibliography, BE348, BE349, BE352, BE354, BE355, BE359, BE360, BE361, BE364
  dictionaries, BE78, BE327, BE351, BE356

Rhetoric and public address, Cleary, James W., BE349
—— Haberman, Frederick W., BE349

Rhetorik, Topik, Argumentation, Dyck, Joachim, BE372
—— Jamison, Robert, BE372

Rhoads, James Berton. *A guide to manuscripts in the presidential libraries*, AK102, CJ176

Rhode Island. [Laws, etc.]. *General laws of Rhode Island, 1956*, CK179

Rhodes, Carolyn H. *First person female American*, BE508

Rhodes, Dennis E. *Dictionary of anonymous and pseudonymous English literature*, AA150

Rhodes-Livingstone Institute. *A selected bibliography of the Federation of Rhodesia and Nyasaland*, DD119, DD176, DD248

Rhodesia national bibliography, AA887, AA888

Rhodesia national bibliography, 1890 to 1930, Hartridge, Anne, AA886

Rhodesia, Northern, DD119
  see also **Zambia**

Rhodesia, Southern *see* **Zimbabwe**

Rhodesia/Zimbabwe, Doro, Marion E., DD251

Rhodesian literature in English, Pichanick, J., BE1541

The Rhodesias and Nyasaland, Library of Congress. African Section, AF226
—— Walker, Audrey A., DD176

Rhymers' lexicon, Lathrop, Lorin Andrews, AC115

Rhyne, Charles S. *Law and judicial systems of nations*, CK65

Rial Roade, Juan. *Estadísticas históricas de Uruguay, 1850–1930*, CG160

RIBA annual review of periodical articles, BF222

RIBA drawings collection, BF230

RIBA library bulletin, BF222

Ribbe, Wolfgang. *Taschenbuch für Familiengeschichtsforschung*, AJ95

Ribelles Comín, José. *Bibliografía de la lengua valenciana. ...*, AA819

Ribera, Almerico. *Enciclopedia biografica e bibliografica "Italiana"*, AH261

Ricapito, J. V. *Bibliografía razonada y anotada de las obras maestras de la picaresca española*, BE1476

Ricci, Franco Maria. *Top symbols and trademarks of the world*, CH370

Ricci, Julio. *Elsevier's banking dictionary in seven languages*, CH271

Ricci, Patricia. *Standards*, EA275

Ricci, Robert. *The language of twentieth century music*, BJ149

Ricci, Seymour de. *The book collector's guide*, AA244
—— *Census of medieval and Renaissance manuscripts in the United States and Canada*, AA212

Rice, Edward. *Eastern definitions*, BC76

Rice, Geoffrey M. *The Oxford history of New Zealand*, DF45

Rice, Joanne A. *Middle English romance*, BE734, BE736

Rice, Michael Downey. *Prentice-Hall dictionary of business, finance and law*, CH342

Rice, Mitchell F. *Black American health*, EH405
—— *Health of black Americans from post reconstruction to integration, 1871–1960*, EH405

Rice, Prudence M. *Pottery analysis*, BG72

Rice, Thomas Jackson. *English fiction, 1900–1950*, BE682

Richard, Alfred Charles. *Censorship and Hollywood's Hispanic image*, BH230
—— *The Hispanic image on the silver screen*, BH230

Richard, François. *Guide de la littérature québécoise*, BE844

Richard, Marcel. *Répertoire des bibliothèques et des catalogues de manuscrits grecs*, AA210

Richard, Stephen. *British government publications*, AF193
—— *Directory of British official publications*, AF178

Richards, Berry G. *Magazines for libraries*, AA375

Richards, Horace Gardiner. *Annotated bibliography of quaternary shorelines, 1945–1964*, EF38

Richards, J. F. *The new Cambridge history of India*, DE169

Richards, J. M. *Who's who in architecture*, BF262

Richards, Jack C. *Longman dictionary of language teaching and applied linguistics*, BD77

Richards, Melville. *The names of towns and cities in Britain*, CL197
—— *Welsh administrative and territorial units, medieval and modern*, AJ128

Richardson, Alan. *Dictionary of Christian theology*, BC243
—— *A theological word book of the Bible*, BC150
—— *The Westminster dictionary of Christian theology*, BC243

Richardson, Donna L. *Youth information resources*, CC141

Richardson, Edgar Preston. *Painting in America, from 1502 to the present*, BF309

Richardson, Ernest Cushing. *An alphabetical subject index and index encyclopaedia to periodical articles on religion, 1890–1899*, BC47
—— *Ante-Nicene Fathers*, BC293
—— *Periodical articles on religion, 1890–1899*, BC47

Richardson, Gary A. *American drama from the Colonial period through World War I*, BE466

Richardson, Jeanne M. *Science and engineering literature*, EA4, EA5

Richardson, Jim. *Philippines*, DE250

Richardson, John. *The local historian's encyclopedia*, AJ105

Richardson, Larry L. *Introduction to library research in German studies*, BE1212

Richardson, Michael D. *Publication sources in educational leadership*, CB178

Richardson, R. Alan. *Science and technology in Canadian history*, EA236

Richardson, R. C. *Bibliography of British economic and social history*, DC1, DC272
—— *Study of history*, DA44

Richardson, Selma K. *Magazines for children*, AA376, AA377
—— *Magazines for young adults*, AA377

Richel, Veronica C. *German stage, 1767–1890*, BE1261

Riches, Phyllis M. *Analytical bibliography of universal collected biography*, AH21

Richett, Diana. *Anarchisme*, CJ506

Richmond, Gail Levin. *Federal tax research*, CK119

Richmond, Joy S. *Medical reference works, 1679–1966*, EH2

Richmond, Mary L. Hurt. *Shaker literature*, BC382

Richmond, W. Edson. *Ballad scholarship*, BE633

Richter, Alan. *Dictionary of sexual slang*, CC283

Richter, Bernice. *The Museum of Science and Industry basic list of children's science books, 1973–1984*, EA30

Richter, Gerhild. *Bibliography on peace research and peaceful international relations*, CJ676

Richter, Heinz A. *Greece and Cyprus since 1920*, DC374

Richter, Klaus. *The completely illustrated atlas of reptiles and amphibians for the terrarium*, EG252

Richter, Max Moritz. *Lexikon der Kohlenstoff-Verbindungen*, EE122, EE143

Rickert, Blandine M. *Major modern dramatists*, BE229

Rickert, Friedhelm. *Major modern dramatists*, BE229

Rickert, Jon E. *A guide to North American bird clubs*, EG273

Rickett, Harold William. *Wild flowers of the United States*, EG180

Rickman, John. *Index psychoanalyticus 1893–1926*, CD9

Ricks, Stephen David. *A bibliography on temples of the ancient Near East and Mediterranean world*, BF220

Rico, Francisco. *Historia y crítica de la literatura española*, BE894

Riddick, Floyd M. *Riddick's Senate procedure*, CJ227

Riddick, John F. *Glimpses of India*, DE159

Riddick's Senate procedure, United States. Congress. Senate, CJ227

Riddles, CF92

Ride, W. D. L. *International code of zoological nomenclature*, EG228

Riden, Philip. *Record sources for local history*, DC350

Rider, Fremont. *American genealogical-biographical index to American genealogical, biographical and local history materials*, AJ35
—— *American genealogical index*, AJ35

The Rider encyclopedia of Eastern philosophy and religion, BB31, BC57

Ridge, John Drew. *Annotated bibliographies of mineral deposits in Africa, Asia (exclusive of the USSR) and Australasia*, EF175
—— *Annotated bibliographies of mineral deposits in Europe*, EF175
—— *Annotated bibliographies of mineral deposits in the Western hemisphere*, EF175
—— *Selected bibliographies of hydrothermal and magmatic mineral deposits*, EF175

Ridgway, Robert. *Color standards and color nomenclature*, ED62

Ridinger, Robert B. Marks. *African archaeology*, DD13
—— *Anthropological fieldwork*, CE11
—— *The homosexual and society*, CC274
—— *The Peace Corps*, CJ678

Ridpath, Ian. *Norton's 2000.0*, EC71

RIE, AK35, CB56, CB61, CD91

Rieber, Hans. *Handbook of paleozoology*, EF246

Riedl, John Orth. *Catalogue of Renaissance philosophers (1350–1650)*, BB70

Riegel, Emil Raymond. *Riegel's handbook of industrial chemistry*, EK58

Riegel's handbook of industrial chemistry, Riegel, Emil Raymond, EK58

Rieger, Rigomar. *Glossary of genetics*, EG343
—— *Glossary of genetics and cytogenetics*, EG343

Riemann, Hugo. *Musik-lexikon*, BJ128
—— *Riemann musik Lexikon*, BJ125

Riemann, Nana. *Bibliografi over moderne dansk rigssprog, 1850–1978*, BD131

Riemann musik Lexikon, Riemann, Hugo, BJ125

Riemens, Leo. *Grosses Sängerlexikon*, BJ214

Riesenfeld, Blenda. *Repertorium lexicographicum graecum*, BE1031, BE1044

Riesenfeld, Harald. *Repertorium lexicographicum graecum*, BE1031, BE1044

Rietstap, Johannes Baptist. *Armorial général*, AJ160, AJ161

Riff, M. A. *Dictionary of modern political ideologies*, CJ25

Rifkind, Carole. *Field guide to American architecture*, BF252

Rigaudy, J. *Nomenclature of organic chemistry*, EE136

Rigdon, Walter. *Biographical encyclopaedia and who's who of the American theatre*, BH117

Rigg, A. G. *History of Anglo-Latin literature*, BE1049

Rigg, J. A. *Zambia*, DD18

Riggar, T. F. *Staff training*, CH713

———— *Stress burnout,* CD124

Riggs, Robert E. *Dictionary of political analysis,* CJ40, CJ41

Riggs, Timothy A. *The Print Council index to oeuvre-catalogues of prints by European and American artists,* BF364

Righetti, Marina. *Enciclopedia dell'arte medievale,* BF72

Right and left (Political science), CJ68, CJ139, CJ152, CJ509

   bibliography, BH41, CC487, CJ111, CJ112, DB342

   biography, CJ156

   directories, CJ79, CJ80, CJ338, CJ512

   encyclopedias, DB129

Right and left (Political science) (by country or region)

   Canada, CJ515

   Latin America, DB254

   see also **Conservatism; Fascism; Radicalism**

The right college, CB289

The right guide, CJ80

Right minds, Wolfe, Gregory, CJ152

The right wing collection of the University of Iowa Libraries, 1918–1977, University of Iowa. Libraries, CJ112

The rights of women, CC565

Rigollot, L. M. *Acta sanctorum quotquot toto orbe coluntur,* BC257

Het Rijksarchief in de provinciën, DC107

De Rijksarchieven in Nederland, DC458

Rijksuniversiteit te Leiden. *Criminology, penology, and police science abstracts,* CK250

Rijksuniversiteit te Leiden. Afrika-Studiecentrum. *State formation, religion, and land tenure in Cameroon,* DD138

Rijksuniversiteit te Utrecht. Bibliotheek. *Catalogus van academische geschriften in Nederland verschenen,* AG38

RILA, BF33, BF34, BF43, BF50

Riland, George. *The new Steinerbooks dictionary of the paranormal,* CD136

Riley, Eileen. *Major political events in South Africa, 1948–1990,* CJ411, DD210

———— *World elections on file,* CJ88, CJ92

Riley, Mary F. *Dissertations in philosophy accepted at American universities, 1861–1975,* BB15

Riley, Raymond Charles. *Belgium,* DC101

Riley, Robert. *United States & Canada,* BG157

Riley, Sam G. *American magazine journalists, 1741–1850,* AE148

———— *Corporate magazines of the United States,* CH28

———— *Magazines of the American South,* AD44

———— *Regional interest magazines of the United States,* AD43

Riley, Victor J. *Theses in Germanic studies,* BE1237

Riley-Smith, Jonathan Simon Christopher. *The atlas of the Crusades,* DA160

•*RILM abstracts 1970–1987,* BJ108

RILM abstracts of music literature, BJ164

———— International Repertory of Music Literature, BJ108

Rimal, Nirmal. *Who's who—Nepal, 1992,* AH364

Rimer, J. Thomas. *Guide to Japanese poetry,* BE1593

———— *A reader's guide to Japanese literature,* BE1594

Rimmer, Brenda M. *International guide to official industrial property publications,* EA267

Rinderknecht, Carol. *A checklist of American imprints,* AA414

Rinfret, Édouard G. *Le théâtre canadien d'expression française,* BE843

The ring index, EE86

Ring systems handbook, EE22, EE86, EE132

Ringe, Sharon H. *The women's Bible commentary,* BC180

Ringelheim, Joan Miriam. *A catalogue of audio and video collections of Holocaust testamony,* DA220

Ringgren, Helmer. *Theologisches Wörterbuch zum Alten Testament,* AC475, BC134

Ringler, Susan J. *Bibliography and index of English verse in manuscript, 1501–1558,* BE714

Ringler, William A. *Bibliography and index of English verse in manuscript, 1501–1558,* BE714

———— *Bibliography and index of English verse printed 1476–1558,* BE714

Rink, Evald. *Technical Americana,* EA237, EK3

Rinker, Harry L. *Warman's Americana & collectibles,* BG49

———— *Warman's country antiques & collectibles,* BG49

Rinn, Roger C. *Author's guide to journals in psychology, psychiatry and social work,* CD14

Rinzler, Carol Ann. *The dictionary of medical folklore,* CF52

Rio de Janeiro. Instituto Brasileiro de Bibliografia e Documentação. *Periódicos brasileiros de cultura,* AD72

Rio de Janeiro. Instituto Nacional do Livro. *Bibliografia brasileira,* AA507

Riou, Yves-François. *Les manuscrits classiques latins des bibliothèques publiques de France,* AA211

Ripley, Gordon. *Canadian literary periodicals index,* BE822

———— *Canadian serials directory,* AD60

———— *Index to Canadian poetry in English,* BE827

Ripley, William Zebina. *Races of Europe,* CE95

———— *Selected bibliography of the anthropology and ethnology of Europe,* CE95

RIPM, BJ112

Rips, Rae Elizabeth. *United States government publications,* AF70

The rise and fall of the Soviet Union, DC589

Rise of photography, Gernsheim, Helmut, BF328

Rise of the American novel, Cowie, Alexander, BE485

Rishworth, Susan Knoke. *Spanish-speaking Africa,* AF227

RISM, BJ69, BJ77, BJ169

Rister, Herbert. *Bibliographie der ehemaligen preussischen Ostprovinzen,* DC474

———— *Schrifttum über das Posener Land 1961–1970,* DC476

———— *Schrifttum über Polen (ohne Posener Land),* DC476

Ristow, Walter William. *Guide to the history of cartography,* CL240

Rita-Ferreira, A. *Bibliografia etnologica de Mocambique (das origens a 1954),* DD184

Ritchie, John. *Australian dictionary of biography,* AH371, DF40

Ritchie, Maureen. *Women's studies,* CC480, CC509

The rites of Eastern Christendom, King, Archdale Arthur, BC448

The rites of the Catholic Church, Catholic Church. Liturgy and Ritual, BC425

Ritt, J. F. *Nouvelles tables d'intégrales définies,* EB80

Ritter, Audrey L. *A deafness collection,* CC187

Ritter, Charles F. *American legislative leaders, 1850–1910,* CJ289

Ritter, Gerhard A. *Bibliographie zur Geschichte der deutschen Arbeiterschaft und Arbeiterbewegung 1863 bis 1914,* CH626, CH627

Ritter, Harry. *Dictionary of concepts in history,* DA45

Ritter, Joachim. *Historisches Wörterbuch der Philosophie,* BB40

Ritzenthaler, Mary Lynn. *Preserving archives and manuscripts,* AK188

Ritzler, Remigius. *Hierarchia catholica medii aevi,* BC430

Riva Agüero, José de la. *Diccionario histórico-biográfico del Perú,* AH141

Rivas Dugarte, Rafael Angel. *Bibliografía sobre el español del Caribe hispánico,* BD174

Rivera, Feliciano. *Dictionary of Mexican American history,* CC468

Rivera de Alvarez, Josefina. *Diccionario de literatura puertorriqueña,* BE980

Rivera-Worley, Carmen. *Social and behavioral aspects of female alcoholism,* CC111

Rivers, CL61, EF8

   bibliography, EK101

Riverside Shakespeare, Evans, G. Blakemore, BE772, BE774, BE777, BE778

Rivet, Albert Lionel Frederick. *The place-names of Roman Britain,* CL199

Rix, Helmut. *Dictionnaire étymologique de la langue grecque,* AC449

Rix, L. B. *Rhodesian literature in English,* BE1541

Rix, Sara E. *Older workers,* CC101

Rizner, L'udovít Vladimir. *Bibliografia písomníctva slovenského na sposob slovníka od najstarších čias do konca r. 1900,* AA598

Rizzoli Ricordi. *Enciclopedia della musica,* BJ133

Rječnik hrvatskoga ili srpskoga jezika, Jugoslavenska akademija znanosti i umjetnosti, AC709

RMA annual statement studies, CH421, CH424

Roach, Helen Pauline. *Spoken records,* BE323

Road abstracts, EK118

Road map of Finland, Finland. Maanmittaushallitus, CL325

Roads

   abstract journals, EK118

   handbooks, EK120

   statistics, EK122, EK123

Roatta, Camilla. *The Follett Zanichelli Italian dictionary,* AC533

Robb, D. M. *Art and architecture in the Western world,* BF129

Robbins, Ceila Dame. *Mottoes,* BE94

Robbins, Chandler S. *Birds of North America,* EG274

Robbins, John Albert. *American literary manuscripts,* BE430

Robbins, Keith. *The Blackwell biographical dictionary of British political life in the twentieth century,* CJ348, DC340

Robbins, Naomi C. *Mexico,* DB231

Robbins, Rossell Hope. *The index of Middle English verse,* BE697, BE714

Roberge, Paul T. *Germanic and its dialects,* BD113

Robert, Adolphe. *Dictionnaire des parlementaires français,* AH200, CJ329, DC211

Robert, Dieter. *Recueils bibliographiques concernant la Mauritanie,* DD178

Robert, Henry Martyn. *Robert's rules of order,* CJ457

———— *The Scott, Foresman Robert's rules of order newly revised,* CJ457

Robert, Hervé. *Les grands hommes d'état de l'histoire de France,* AH199

Robert, Paul. *Dictionnaire alphabétique et analogique de la langue française,* AC329, AC334

———— *Le petit Robert 2,* AJ191

Robert, Sarah Corbin. *Robert's rules of order,* CJ457

Robert, Willem Carel Hendrik. *Contributions to a bibliography of Australia and the South Sea Islands,* DF1

Le Robert & Collins dictionnaire français-anglais, anglais-français, senior, AC336

Robert-Dumesnil, A. P. F. *Peintre-graveur français,* BF377

Robert Goldwater Library. *Catalog of the Robert Goldwater Library, the Metropolitan Museum of Art,* BF54

Robert Morris Associates. Annual statement studies. *RMA annual statement studies,* CH424

Robert-Tornow, Walter Heinrich. *Geflügelte Worte,* BE135

Roberts, A. D. *Dictionary of antibiotics and related substances,* EE125, EH335

Roberts, Alexander. *Ante-Nicene Fathers,* BC293

Roberts, Andrew Michael. *Novel: a guide to the novel from its origins to the present day,* BE611

Roberts, Brian. *Chronological list,* DG9

Roberts, D. Hywel E. *Wales,* DC369

Roberts, Elfed Vaughan. *Historical dictionary of Hong Kong & Macau,* DE151

Roberts, Frank C. *Obituaries from the Times 1951–1960,* AH32

Roberts, G. D. *Standard dictionary of Canadian biography,* AH96

Roberts, Harold Selig. *Roberts' dictionary of industrial relations*, CH654

Roberts, Helene E. *Iconographic index to New Testament subjects represented in photographs and slides of paintings in the visual collections, Fine Arts Library, Harvard University*, BF175, BF298

—— *Iconographic index to Old Testament subjects*, BF175, BF298

Roberts, John E. *A guide to official gazettes and their contents*, AF6

Roberts, John Morris. *French Revolution documents*, DC189

Roberts, Kate Louise. *Hoyt's new cyclopedia of practical quotations*, BE105

Roberts, Laurance P. *A dictionary of Japanese artists*, BF144

—— *Japanese museums*, BF144

—— *Roberts' guide to Japanese museums*, BF144

Roberts, Nancy L. *American peace writers, editors, and periodicals*, CJ701

Roberts, Vera Mowry. *Notable women in the American theatre*, BH118

Roberts, Willard Lincoln. *Encyclopedia of minerals*, EF186

Roberts, William. *Modern Italian history*, DC420, DC431

—— *Printers' marks*, AA253

Roberts' dictionary of industrial relations, Roberts, Harold Selig, CH654

Roberts' guide to Japanese museums, Roberts, Laurance P., BF144

Robert's rules of order, Patnode, Darwin, CJ457

—— Robert, Henry Martyn, CJ457

—— Robert, Sarah Corbin, CJ457

Robertson, Allen. *The dance handbook*, BH153

Robertson, Colin L. *Short title catalogue of books printed before 1701 in the Foreign Office Library*, DC274

Robertson, David. *A dictionary of modern politics*, CJ31

—— *The Facts on File dictionary of military science*, CJ589

—— *Guide to modern defense and strategy*, CJ578

Robertson, Jack. *Twentieth-century artists on art*, BF145

Robertson, James Alexander. *The Philippine Islands, 1493–1898*, DE246

Robertson, James I. *Civil War books*, DB111

Robertson, John George. *A history of German literature*, BE1259

Robertson, M. J. M. *Directory of world futures and options*, CH436

Robertson, William O. *Handbook of poisoning*, EH423

Robey, John S. *Analysis of public policy*, CA11

Robijns, J. *Algemene muziek encyclopedie*, BJ127

Robin, Helenan S. *Dictionary of political analysis*, CJ40, CJ41

Robinet, J. F. E. *Dictionnaire historique et biographique de la Révolution et de l'Empire*, DC185

Robinson, Alice M. *Notable women in the American theatre*, BH118

Robinson, Anthony Meredith Lewin. *Catalogue of theses and dissertations accepted for degrees by the South African universities*, AG49

Robinson, Arthur Howard. *Cartographical innovations*, CL262

Robinson, Doris. *Fine arts periodicals*, BF47

—— *Music and dance periodicals*, BJ104

Robinson, Edgar Eugene. *Presidential vote, 1896–1932*, CJ243

—— *They voted for Roosevelt*, CJ243

Robinson, Elizabeth. *British catalogue of music, 1957–1985*, BJ25

Robinson, F. J. G. *A bibliography of eighteenth century legal literature*, CK4

—— *Book subscription lists*, AA298

Robinson, Francis. *Atlas of the Islamic world since 1500*, DE71

—— *The Cambridge encyclopedia of India, Pakistan, Bangladesh, Sri Lanka, Nepal, Bhutan, and the Maldives*, DE90

Robinson, Fred C. *A bibliography of publications on Old English literature to the end of 1972*, BE728

—— *Old English language*, DA138

Robinson, J. Hedley. *Astronomy data book*, EC56

Robinson, John P. *Measures of personality and social psychological attitudes*, CD98

—— *Measures of social psychological attitudes*, CD98

Robinson, John William. *English theatrical literature, 1559–1900*, BH38, BH40

Robinson, Judith Schiek. *A guide to U.S. government scientific and technical resources*, EA1

—— *Subject guide to U.S. government reference sources*, AF74

—— *Tapping the government grapevine*, AF75

Robinson, Kerry A. *Foundation guide for religious grant seekers*, BC78

Robinson, Mairi. *The concise Scots dictionary*, AC163

Robinson, Maurice Arthur. *Indexes to all editions of Brown-Driver-Briggs Hebrew lexicon*, AC476

Robinson, Michael C. *Public works history in the United States*, DB19

Robinson, R. H. O. B. *Lives of the fellows of the Royal College of Surgeons of England, 1952–1964*, EH230

Robinson, R. K. *Encyclopaedia of food science, food technology, and nutrition*, EH297

Robinson, Richard. *Business history of the world*, CH399

—— *United States business history, 1602–1988*, CH399

Robinson, Ruth. *The UFAW handbook on the care and management of laboratory animals*, EJ129

Robinson, Thomas A. *The early church*, BC222

Robl, Ernest H. *Organizing your photographs*, BF347

—— *Picture sources 4*, BF347

Robles, Philip K. *United States military medals and ribbons*, AL186

Robotics, EK186, EK230, EK232, EK234, EK235 see also **Artificial intelligence**

Robotics sourcebook and dictionary, Tver, David R., EK234

Robson, S. O. *Old Javanese English dictionary*, AC560

Rocca, Giancarlo. *Dizionario degli istituti di perfezione*, BC439

Rocca, Raymond G. *Bibliography on Soviet intelligence and security services*, CJ545

Rocco, Emmanuele. *Dizionario di opere anonime e pseudonime di scrittori italiani*, AA177

Roche, Elizabeth. *A dictionary of early music*, BJ157

Roche, Jerome. *A dictionary of early music*, BJ157

Rochester Institute of Technology. Graphic Arts Research Center. *Abstracts of photographic science and engineering literature*, BF332

Rock, Mary G. *Handbook of information sources and research strategies in public administration*, CJ459

Rock, Roger O. *The Native American in American literature*, BE552

Rock encyclopedia, BJ357

Rock films, BJ363

Rock-forming minerals, Deer, William Alexander, EF195

Rock music, BJ363

bibliography, BJ336, BJ338

biography, BJ342, BJ350, BJ351, BJ355, BJ356, BJ357

discography, BJ342, BJ356, BJ378

encyclopedias, BJ345, BJ350, BJ352, BJ357

handbooks, BJ332

Rock on, Nite, Norm N., BJ356

Rock on almanac, Nite, Norm N., BJ332

The rock who's who, Helander, Brock, BJ342

Rockabilly, Cooper, B. Lee, BJ336

Rockets and missiles, CJ570

The rockhound's manual, Fay, Gordon S., EF197

Rockie, John D. *Gravimetric and celestial geodesy*, EF123

Rockin' the classics and classicizin' the rock, Duxbury, Janell R., BJ378

Rocks, EF253, EF255, EF256, EF257

handbooks, EF254

Rocks and minerals, Nicolay, H. H., EF202

Rockwood, D. Stephen. *American third parties since the Civil War*, CJ259

Rocky Mountain states, DB173

Rocq, Margaret M. *U.S. sources of petroleum and natural gas statistics*, EK301

Rocznik demograficzny, CG276

Rocznik statystyczny, CG275

Roczniki statystyczne, CG276

Rodale, Jerome I. *Synonym finder*, AC140

—— *Word finder*, AC140

Rodale's illustrated encyclopedia of herbs, EJ234

Roddy, Kevin P. *Renaissance rhetoric*, BE360

Rodegem, F. M. *Documentation bibliographique sur le Burundi*, DD135

Roden, Robert F. *Later American plays, 1831–1900*, BE464

Röder, Werner. *Biographisches Handbuch der deutschsprachigen Emigration nach 1933*, AH203

Rodger, Richard. *Bibliography of European economic and social history*, DC1, DC272

Rodgers, Bruce. *The queens' vernacular*, CC284

Rodgers, Frank. *A guide to British government publications*, AF179

—— *Serial publications in the British parliamentary papers, 1900–1968*, AF207

Rodin, Alvin E. *Medicine, literature & eponyms*, EH123

Rodionoff, Nicholas R. *Soviet geography*, CL151

Rodionova, Z. V. *Russko-angliĭskiĭ slovar' obshchestvenno-politicheskoĭ leksiki*, CA40

Rodrigues, José Honório. *A pesquisa histórica do Brasil*, DB340

—— *História da história do Brasil*, DB357

Rodrigues, Louis J. *Harrap's diccionario de expresiones idiomáticas*, AC745

Rodrigues, Rita de Cássia. *Bibliografia da música brasileira*, BJ22

Rodríguez, Andrés. *Literatura Chicana*, BE558

Rodríguez Câeres, Milagros. *Manual de literatura española*, BE867, BE1429

Rodríguez Castelo, Hernán. *Literatura ecuatoriana, 1830–1980*, BE953

Rodriguez de Areia. *Angola*, DD128

Rodriguez Demorizi, Emilio. *Seudónimos dominicanos*, AA159

Rodriguez Moñino, Antonio R. *Catálogo de los manuscritos poéticos castellanos existentes en la Biblioteca de The Hispanic Society of America (siglos XV, XVI y XVII)*, BE1465, BE1478

—— *Manual bibliográfico de cancioneros y romanceros*, BE1478

Rodríguez Rea, Miguel Angel. *Perú y su literatura*, BE955

Roe, Keith E. *Dictionary of theoretical concepts in biology*, EG44

Roeckle, Heidi. *Liechtensteinische Bibliographie 1960–1973*, DC440

Roemans, Robert. *Bibliografie van de Vlaamse tijdschriften*, AD303, BE1065, BE1066

—— *Bibliographie van de moderne Vlaamsche literatuur, 1893–1930*, AD303, BE1066

Roemer, Milton Irwin. *National health systems of the world*, EH416

Roeming, Robert F. *Catalog of little magazines*, AD46

Roepke, Kurt. *Schriften zur Geschichte der Juden*, BC529

Roesch, Roberta. *The encyclopedia of depression*, EH380

Roessingh, M. P. H. *Guides to the sources in the Netherlands for the history of Latin America*, DB275

Roff, William R. *Bibliography of Malay and Arabic periodicals published in the Straits Settlements and peninsular Malay states 1876–1941*, AD205

—— *Guide to Malay periodicals*, AD205

Rogal, Samuel J. *Calendar of literary facts*, BE192, BE437
—— *A chronological outline of American literature*, BE437
—— *A chronological outline of British literature*, BE613
—— *Medicine in Great Britain from the Restoration to the nineteenth century, 1660–1800*, EH208
Rogaly, Gail Lynda. *South Africa's foreign relations, 1961–1979*, DD221
Rogers, Alisdair. *The student's companion to geography*, CL3
Rogers, Chester B. *The electoral politics dictionary*, CJ121
Rogers, Colin Darlington. *Tracing your English ancestors*, AJ106
Rogers, D. M. *Catalogue of Catholic books in English printed abroad or secretly in England, 1558–1640*, BC388
—— *The contemporary printed literature of the English Counter-Reformation between 1558 and 1640*, BC388
Rogers, Frank. *Archives New Zealand*, AK163
Rogers, Julia Ellen. *The shell book*, EG307
Rogers, Malcolm. *Dictionary of British portraiture*, BF66
Rogers, Paul Patrick. *Diccionario de seudónimos literarios españoles, con algunas iniciales*, AA185
—— *Spanish drama collection in the Oberlin College Library*, BE1467
Rogers, Rosemarie. *Handbook of major Soviet nationalities*, CC349
Roget, Peter Mark. *Thesaurus of English words and phrases*, AC145
Roget's 21st century thesaurus, AB26
Roget's international thesaurus, AB27, AC144
Roget's thesaurus in dictionary form, AC138
Roget's thesaurus of English words and phrases, AC144, AC145, AC435, BC157
Roget's thesaurus of the Bible, Day, A. Colin, BC157
Rogoshin, V.N. *Ukazatel'*, AA790
Rogozhin, N. P. *Literaturno-khudozhestvennye al'manakhi i sborniki*, BE1406
Roh, Jae Min. *Selected black American, African, and Caribbean authors*, BE544
Rohm, Kenneth G. *Refereed and nonrefereed economic journals*, CH30
Rohn, Peter H. *World treaty index*, CK89
Rohwer, Jürgen. *Neue Forschungen zum Ersten Weltkrieg*, DA195
Roitt, Ivan M. *Encyclopedia of immunology*, EG21, EH85
Rojas Uzcátegui, José de la Cruz. *Bibliografía del teatro venezolano*, BE966
Rojnič, Matko. *A guide to Yugoslav libraries and archives*, DC611
Rokiski Lázaro, Gloria. *Bibliografía de la poesía española del siglo XIX (1801–1850)*, BE1479
Roland, Charles G. *Sir William Osler*, EH209
Roland-Cabaton, M. A. *Bibliotheca indosinica*, DE96
Roldán Oliarte, Esteban. *Cuba en la mano*, DB424
The role of women in librarianship, 1876–1976, AK14, AK73
Rolef, Susan Hattis. *Political dictionary of the State of Israel*, CJ424, CJ439, DE55, DE70
Rolfes, Irene. *Suriname*, DB393
—— *Women in the Caribbean*, DB404
The roll of the Royal College of Physicians of London, Royal College of Physicians of London, EH231
Rolland, H. *Armorial général*, AJ161
—— *General illustrated armorial*, AJ160
Rolland, V. *Armorial général*, AJ161
—— *General illustrated armorial*, AJ160
Roller, David C. *The encyclopedia of Southern history*, DB159
Rolli, Madeline. *Bibliographie de la littérature française, 1930–1939 … complément à Bibliographie de H. P. Thieme*, BE1209
Rollin, Jack. *The World Cup, 1930–1990*, BK99

The Rolling Stone encyclopedia of rock & roll, BJ350
Rollins, Alden M. *Rome in the fourth century* A.D. , DA94
Rollins, Arline McClarty. *One-parent children, the growing minority*, CC145
Rollins, Hyder E. *An analytical index to the ballad-entries (1557–1709) in the Registers of the Company of Stationers of London*, BE634
Rollyson, Carl E. *Biography*, BE215
Roloff, Walter. *German literature in British magazines, 1750–1860*, BE1240
Rolston, Bill. *A social science bibliography of Northern Ireland, 1945–1983*, DC356
Rom see **Peripatetics**
Romain, Alfred. *Dictionary of legal and commercial terms*, CK49
—— *Wörterbuch der Rechts- und Wirtschaftssprache*, CK49
Romaine, Lawrence B. *A guide to American trade catalogs, 1744–1900*, CH400
Roman, Susan. *Sequences*, BE246
Roman, Viorel S. *Albanien*, DC80
Roman Britain, CL199
Roman Catholic Church
  atlases, BC289, BC420
  bibliography, BC388, BC389, BC391, BC392, BC393
  biography, AH75, AH225, AH228, BC416, BC417, BC418, BC419
  dictionaries, BC406, BC407, BC408
  directories, BC409, BC410, BC411
  encyclopedias, BC396, BC397, BC398, BC399, BC400, BC401, BC402, BC403, BC404, BC405, BC412
  handbooks, BC396
  newspapers, AE33
  papal and anciliar documents, BC433
  papal and conciliar documents, BC281, BC285, BC434, BC435, BC436, BC437
  periodicals
    indexes, AD265, AD266, BC394, BC395
    union lists, AD227
  yearbooks, BC415
Roman Catholic Church (by country or region)
  England, BC410
  Great Britain, BC388
  Latin America, DB255
  United States, CB36, CB305
  Wales, BC410
Roman Catholic Church (by subject)
  authors, BE446
  education, CB36, CB305
  history, BC412, BC413, BC414, DC28
    bibliography, BC389
  liturgy and ritual, BC421, BC422, BC423, BC424, BC425, BC426, BC427, BC428, BC429
  missions, BC304
    bibliography, BC303
  peace research, CJ677
  popes, cardinals, bishops, BC430, BC431, BC432
  religious orders, BC438, BC439, BC440, BC441, BC442
  saints, BC403
  Vatican, DC605
  see also **Patrology**
Roman emperors, Grant, Michael, DA115
Roman law, CK52
Roman literature, BE201
The Roman martyrology, Catholic Church. Martyrology, BC426
The Roman missal, BC422
Romance bibliography, BD153
Romance languages
  bibliography, BD150, BD152, BD153, BD154, BE1073
  bibliography of bibliography, BD149
  dissertations, BD155, BE1071
  grammar
    bibliography, BD151
  guides, BD152, BE1073
  handbooks, BD148

Romance languages and literatures as presented in German doctoral dissertations, 1885–1950, Flasche, Hans, BD155, BE1071
Romance linguistics and the romance languages, Bach, Kathryn F., BD149
Romance literatures
  bibliography, BD152, BD153, BE1072, BE1073
  criticism
    collections, BE1069
    dissertations, BD155, BE1071
  guides, BD152, BE1073
  translations
    bibliography, BE1074
The Romance literatures, Parks, George B., BE1074
Romances
  bibliography, BE335, BE336, BE337, BE736, BE983, BE1201
  biography, BE344
  dictionaries, BE344, BE1163
  indexes, BE1165
  manuscripts
    catalogs, BE335
Romances (by country or region)
  Latin America
    bibliography, BE878
  see also **Arthurian romances**
Der Romanführer, BE195
Romania
  bibliography, AA780, AA781, AA782, DC495
    current, AA783
  dissertations, AG40
  encyclopedias, DC498
  government publications, AF165
  newspapers, AD140
  periodicals, AD139, AD140
    indexes, AD323, AD324
  registers, CJ325
  statistics, CG279
Romania (by subject)
  ethnic attitudes, DC493
  historiography
    biobibliography, DC497
  history, DC494
    bibliography, DC496
Romania, Deletant, Andrea, DC496
Romania in the First World War, Torrey, Glenn E., DC496
Romanian language
  dictionaries, AC656, AC657, AC658, AC659, AC660, AC661
    bilingual, AC662
      Romanian-English, AC663
Romanian literature
  bibliography, BE1376, BE1377, BE1378
  biobibliography, BE1378
  encyclopedias, BE1380
Romanian literature (by subject)
  history, BE1379, BE1381
Romanian statistical yearbook, CG279
Romanini, Angiola Maria. *Enciclopedia dell'arte medievale*, BF72
Romanische Bibliographie, BD153
Romanization tables, BD10
Romano, Giorgio. *Bibliografia italo-ebraica (1848–1977)*, BC530
Romano, Ruggiero. *Enciclopedia*, AB63
Romano-British bibliography, 55 B.C.–A.D. 449, Bonser, Wilfrid, DC305
Romanowski, Patty. *The Rolling Stone encyclopedia of rock & roll*, BJ350
Romansh language
  dictionaries, AC664
    multilingual, AC665
Romantic movement
  bibliography, BE40, BE702, BE713, BE754
  book reviews, BE757
  encyclopedias, BE759
The Romantic movement, BE40, BE702
The Romantic movement bibliography, 1936–1970, BE40
—— Elkins, Aubrey Christian, BE754
—— Forstner, Lorne J., BE754

Romantic poetry by women, Jackson, James Robert de Jager, BE708
Romantics reviewed, Reiman, Donald H., BE757
Romany catalogue, CC479
Rome
 atlases, DA119
 bibliography, DA94
 biography, DA115
 handbooks, DA102, DA108
Rome. Centro Nazionale per il Catalogo Unico delle Biblioteche Italiane e per le Informazioni Bibliografiche. *Primo catalogo collettivo delle biblioteche italiane,* AA124, AA731
Rome in the fourth century A.D. , Rollins, Alden M., DA94
Romem. J. M. *Eerste Nederlandse systematisch ingerichte encyclopaedie,* AB36
Romer, Alfred Sherwood. *Bibliography of fossil vertebrates exclusive of North America, 1509–1927,* EF233
Romera-Navarro, Miguel. *Registro de lexicografía hispánica,* AC753
Romero de Valle, Emilia. *Diccionario manual de literatura peruana y materias afines,* BE957
Romero Pinillos, María Elena. *Compendio estadístico del Perú, 1900–1990,* CG157, DB389
Romeuf, Jean. *Dictionnaire des sciences économiques,* CH66
Romig, Walter. *The guide to Catholic literature,* BC390
Römische Geschichte, eine Bibliographie, Christ, Karl, DA94
Römpps Chemie-Lexikon, EE32
Ronart, Nandy. *Concise encyclopaedia of Arabic civilization,* DD76
Ronart, Stephan. *Concise encyclopaedia of Arabic civilization,* DD76
Ronconi, Enzo. *Dizionario generale degli autori italiani contemporanei,* BE1301
Rondeau, G. *Bibliographie sélective, terminologie et disciplines connexes,* BD58
Ronsard et ses amis, Jurgens, Madeleine, DC151
Rony, A. Kohar. *Southeast Asia,* AD185
Rood, Karen L. *American literary almanac,* BE437
Roof, Michael K. *Detailed statistics on the population of Israel by ethnic and religious group and urban and rural residence, 1950 to 2010,* CG399
——— *Detailed statistics on the urban and rural population of Turkey, 1950 to 2000,* CG291
Room, Adrian. *Classical dictionary,* CF29
——— *A concise dictionary of modern place-names in Great Britain and Ireland,* CL200, CL209
——— *Corporate eponymy,* CH386
——— *Dictionary of astronomical names,* EC37
——— *Dictionary of changes in meaning,* AC82
——— *Dictionary of coin names,* BG180
——— *Dictionary of trade name origins,* CH343
——— *Dictionary of translated names and titles,* BE87
——— *NTC's dictionary of trade name origins,* CH343
——— *Place-name changes 1900–1991,* CL93
——— *Room's classical dictionary,* CF29
Room's classical dictionary, Room, Adrian, CF29
Rooney, John F. *Atlas of American sport,* BK22
——— *This remarkable continent,* DB76
Roorbach, Orville Augustus. *Bibliotheca americana,* AA416, AA418
Roos, Charles. *Medical reference works, 1679–1966,* EH2
Roos, Frank John. *Bibliography of early American architecture,* BF204, BF221
——— *Writings on early American architecture,* BF221
Roose, Kenneth D. *Rating of graduate programs,* CB347, CB348
Roosens, Laurent. *History of photography,* BF334
The roots of English, Claiborne, Robert, AC51
Roots of international style architecture, Wodehouse, Lawrence, BF204
Roper, Brent S. *Social and behavioral aspects of female alcoholism,* CC111

Roper, Fred W. *Introduction to reference sources in the health sciences,* EH6
Roper, Michael. *Planning, equipping, and staffing a document reprographic service,* AK249
Roper Center for Public Opinion Research. *Public opinion location library,* CJ494
Rosa Martínez, Luis de la. *Lexicón histórico-documental de Puerto Rico (1912–1899),* DB455
Rosa-Nieves, Cesáreo. *Biografías puertorriqueñas,* AH161
Rosaler, Robert C. *Standard handbook of plant engineering,* EK252
Rosasco de Chacón, Carlota. *Introducción a los estudios bolivianos contemporáneos, 1960–1984,* DB334
Rösch-Sondermann, Hermann. *Bibliographie der lokalen Alternativpresse,* AD102
Rose, Brian Geoffrey. *TV genres,* BH293
Rose, Herbert Jennings. *A handbook of Greek literature,* BE1032
——— *A handbook of Latin literature,* BE1048
Rose, Jonathan. *British literary publishing houses, 1820–1880,* AA297
——— *British literary publishing houses, 1881–1965,* AA297
Rose, Richard. *The international almanac of electoral history,* CJ89
Rose, Robert F. *Business serials of the U.S. government,* CH26
Rose, Rose K. *Women in chemistry and physics,* EA187, ED57, EE106
Rosen, Fred S. *Dictionary of immunology,* EH124
Rosen, George. *A history of public health,* EH417
Rosen, Sumner M. *Face of the nation, 1987,* CC46
Rosenak, Chuck. *Museum of American Folk Art encyclopedia of twentieth-century American folk art and artists,* BG35
Rosenak, Jan. *Museum of American Folk Art encyclopedia of twentieth-century American folk art and artists,* BG35
Rosenbach, Abraham Simon Wolf. *Early American children's books,* AA247
Rosenbaum, Barbara. *Index of English literary manuscripts,* BE603
Rosenbaum, Karol. *Encyklopédia slovenských spisovateľov,* BE1425
Rosenberg, Betty. *Genreflecting,* BE248
Rosenberg, Jerry Martin. *Dictionary of artificial intelligence and robotics,* EK186
——— *Dictionary of banking,* CH273
——— *Dictionary of business and management,* CH344
——— *Dictionary of international trade,* CH124
——— *Dictionary of investing,* CH302
——— *Investor's dictionary,* CH302
Rosenberg, Judith K. *Watergate,* CJ108
Rosenberg, Kenyon C. *A basic classical and operatic recordings collection for libraries,* BJ381
——— *Basic classical and operatic recordings collection on compact discs for libraries,* BJ381
——— *Dictionary of library and educational technology,* AK43
——— *Media equipment,* AK43
——— *Watergate,* CJ108
Rosenberg, Marc. *Der goldschmiede Merkzeichen,* BG142
Rosenberg, Sheldon. *Handbook of applied psycholinguistics,* BD79
Rosenberg-Dishman, Marie Barovic. *Women and society,* CC510
Rosenblum, Morris. *A dictionary of dermatologic terms,* EH111
Rosenblum, Robert. *19th century art,* BF131
——— *Cubism and twentieth-century art,* BF307
——— *Nineteenth century art,* BF131
Rosenfield, Eugene. *Ethiopia and Eritrea,* DD48
Rosenne, Shabtai. *Documents on the International Court of Justice,* CK110
Rosenof, Theodore. *Second World War and the atomic age, 1940–1973,* DA170
Rosenstiel, Annette. *Education and anthropology,* CE17

Rosenthal, Eric. *Southern African dictionary of national biography,* AH311
Rosenthal, Harold D. *The concise Oxford dictionary of opera,* BJ253
Rosenthal, Joseph A. *A numerical finding list of British command papers published 1833–1961/62,* AF195, AF201, AF206
Rosero, Rocío. *Bibliografía sobre la mujer en el Ecuador,* DB371
Roses, Lorraine Elena. *Harlem Renaissance and beyond,* BE529, BE545
Rosichan, Richard H. *Stamps and coins,* BG203
Ross, Charlotte T. *Bibliography of Southern Appalachia,* DB157
Ross, Harris. *Film as literature, literature as film,* BH177
Ross, Ian Campbell. *Index to statistics and probability,* EB30
Ross, James Patterson. *Lives of the fellows of the Royal College of Surgeons of England, 1965–1973,* EH230
Ross, John A. *Family planning and child survival programs as assessed in 1991,* CC250
——— *International encyclopedia of population,* CG19
Ross, John M. *Trials in collections,* CK247
Ross, Joseph A. *The complete words of Wall Street,* CH212
Ross, Lynn C. *Career advancement for women in the federal service,* CJ109
Ross, Martha. *Rulers and governments of the world,* CJ91
Ross, Robert Ballantyne. *Metallic materials specification handbook,* EK280
Ross, Robert L. *Australian literary criticism, 1945–1988,* BE856
Ross, Stanley Ralph. *The motion picture guide,* BH199
Ross, Stanley Robert. *Fuentes de la historia contemporánea de México,* DB234
Ross, Steven T. *French military history, 1661–1799,* DC146
Rossel, Sven Hakon. *A history of Danish literature,* BE1118
——— *A history of Scandinavian literature, 1870–1980,* BE1092
——— *Skandinavische Literatur, 1870–1970,* BE1092
Rossi, Ernest E. *The European political dictionary,* CJ322
——— *Latin America,* CJ309, CJ311, CJ312
——— *Latin American political dictionary,* CJ309
Rossi, Peter Henry. *Handbook of survey research,* CD63
Rossi, Peter N. *Articles on the Middle East, 1947–1971,* DE24
Rossiĭskaia Akademiia nauk. *Social sciences and humanities in Russia,* CA16
Rossiĭskaia knizhnaia palata. *Letopis' avtoreferatov dissertatsiĭ,* AG46
Rossiĭskaia Akademiia Nauk. Biblioteka. *Bibliografiia izdaniĭ Akademii nauk,* AL55
Rössler, Hellmuth. *Biographisches Wörterbuch zur deutschen Geschichte,* AH215, DC222
——— *Sachwörterbuch zur deutschen Geschichte,* DC222
Rossman, Amy Y. *A literature guide for the identification of plant pathogenic fungi,* EG189
Rossol, Monona. *The artist's complete health and safety guide,* BF127, BF304
Rost, Valentin Christian Friedrich. *Handwörterbuch der griechischen Sprache,* AC445
Rostaing, Charles. *Dictionnaire étymologique des noms de lieux en France,* CL185
——— *Dictionnaire étymologique des noms de rivières et de montagnes en France,* CL186
Rosten, Leo. *Leo Rosten's treasury of Jewish quotations,* BE121
Roster, Peter. *Bibliografía del teatro hispanoamericano contemporaneo (1900–1980),* BE900

Roteiro sumrio dos arquivos portugueses de interesse para o pesquisador da história do Brasil, Boschi, Caio César, DB350

Roth, Catharine. *Articles on American literature, 1950–1967,* BE408

Roth, Cecil. *Magna bibliotheca anglo-judaica,* BC517

Roth, Rudolph. *Sanskrit-Wörterbuch,* AC703

Roth Publishing, Inc. *Master index to poetry,* BE319

Rothaus, Barry. *Historical dictionary of the French Revolution, 1789–1799,* DC185

Rothbart, Harold A. *Mechanical design and systems handbook,* EK242

Rothbart, Linda S. *Trucking,* CH444

Rothbart, Margarete Johanna. *Bibliographie internationale des travaux historiques publiés dans les volumes de "Mélanges",* DA6

Rothberg School for Overseas Students. *2000 books and more,* BC515

Rothe, Eva. *Grundriss zur Geschichte der deutschen Dichtung aus den Quellen,* BE1218

Rothenberg, Marc. *The history of science and technology in the United States,* EA238

Rothman, Barbara Katz. *Encyclopedia of childbearing,* CC225

Roth's American poetry annual, BE499, BE502

Roth's essay index, BE319

Roth's index to short stories, BE319

Rothstein, Eric. *Restoration and eighteenth-century poetry, 1660–1780,* BE718

Rothwell, Kenneth Sprague. *Shakespeare on screen,* BE791

Rothwell, William. *Anglo-Norman dictionary,* AC168

Rotoli, Nicholas John. *Black American playwrights, 1800 to the present,* BE513

Rottenberg, Dan. *Finding our fathers,* AJ21

Rotuma, DF7

Rouch, Alain. *Littératures nationales d'écriture française,* BE1517

Roud, Richard. *Cinema,* BH246

Rounds, Dorothy. *Articles on antiquity in festschriften,* DA67

Rouse, John Edward. *Public administration in American society,* CJ475

Rouse, Richard H. *Serial bibliographies for medieval studies,* DA137

Rouse, Ruth. *A history of the ecumenical movement,* BC276

Rousseaux, Colin G. *Handbook of toxicologic pathology,* EH425

Roussel, M. *Les présocratiques,* BB58

Rousselet, Louis. *Nouveau dictionnaire de géographie universelle,* CL96

Rousset de Pina, Jean. *Récapitulation des périodiques officiels parus en Tunisie de 1881 à 1955,* AF239

Routh, C. N. R. *Who's who in Tudor England,* DC298

The Routledge dictionary of quotations, BE98

The Routledge dictionary of twentieth-century political thinkers, CJ69

Routledge history of English poetry, Foakes, R. A., BE718

Roux, Edward. *Time longer than rope,* DD211

Roux-Fouillet, Paul. *Catalogue des périodiques clandestins diffusés en France de 1939 à 1945,* AD91

Roux-Fouillet, Renée. *Catalogue des périodiques clandestins diffusés en France de 1939 à 1945,* AD91

Rowan, Bonnie G. *Scholars' guide to Washington, D.C. : film and video collections,* BH182

Rowe, Helen. *A guide to the records of Bermuda,* DB422

Rowe, John W. *Handbook of the biology of aging,* CC97

Rowe, Kenneth E. *Methodist union catalog,* BC364
—— *United Methodist studies,* BC366

Rowe, Patricia M. *Detailed statistics on the urban and rural population of Cuba, 1950 to 2010,* CG170

—— *Detailed statistics on the urban and rural population of Mexico, 1950 to 2010,* CG119

Rowe, Robert Seaman. *Bibliography of rivers and harbors and related fields in hydraulic engineering,* EK101

Rowell's American newspaper directory, AD51, AE23

Rowland, A. Westley. *Key resources on institutional advancement,* CB224, CB227

Rowland, Benjamin. *The Harvard outline and reading lists for Oriental art,* BF35

Rowland, Ian. *Timor,* DE177

Rowland, J. F. B. *Information sources in chemistry,* EE3

Rowlands, William. *Cambrian bibliography,* AA700

Rowles, Ruth Anderson. *The historical atlas of political parties in the United States Congress, 1789–1989,* CJ258, DB73

Rowley, H. H. *Atlas of the Bible,* BC198
—— *Atlas of the early Christian world,* BC290
—— *Dictionary of the Bible,* BC141
—— *Eleven years of Bible bibliography,* BC117
—— *Peake's commentary on the Bible,* BC168

Rowley, Jennifer E. *Abstracting and indexing,* AK215

Rowntree, Derek. *A dictionary of education,* CB79

Rowse, Tim. *Australians from 1939,* DF37

Roxon, Lillian. *Lillian Roxon's rock encyclopedia,* BJ357

Roy, A. *India and the Soviet Union,* DC599

Roy, Frederick Hampton. *The encyclopedia of aging and the elderly,* CC81

Roy, Mary L. *Inland water transportation,* CH444

Roy, Prannot. *Compendium of Indian elections,* CJ431

Roy, Prannoy. *India decides,* CJ431

Roy Burman, B. K. *Bibliography of census publications in India,* CG391

Royal Aerospace Establishment. *The RAE table of earth satellites, 1957–1989,* EK34

Royal Anthropological Institute of Great Britain and Ireland. *Index to current periodicals received in the Library of the Royal Anthropological Institute,* CE35

Royal Anthropological Institute of Great Britain and Ireland. Library. *London bibliography of the social sciences,* CA13

Royal Astronomical Society of Canada. *The observer's handbook,* EC57

Royal College of Nursing. *A bibliography of nursing literature,* EH273

Royal College of Physicians of London. *The roll of the Royal College of Physicians of London,* EH231

Royal College of Science and Technology (Glasgow, Scotland). Andersonian Library. *Bibliotheca chemica,* EE16

Royal College of Surgeons. *Plarr's lives of the fellows of the Royal College of Surgeons of England,* EH230

Royal Commonwealth Society. Library. *Biography catalogue of the Library of the Royal Commonwealth Society,* AH238
—— *Subject catalogue of the Library of the Royal Empire Society, formerly Royal Colonial Institute,* DC344

Royal families of the world, AJ76

Royal Geographical Society (London). *A gazetteer of Albania,* CL129
—— *A gazetteer of Greece,* CL142
—— *New geographical literature and maps,* CL19

Royal Geological and Mining Society of the Netherlands. *Geological nomenclature,* EF80

Royal Historical Society (Great Britain). *Annual bibliography of British and Irish history,* DC282
—— *Bibliography of British history,* DC270
—— *Bibliography of British history, 1851–1914,* DC330
—— *Bibliography of British history, Stuart period, 1603–1714,* DC315
—— *The eighteenth century, 1714–1789,* DC317
—— *Guide to the historical publications of the societies of England and Wales,* DC275
—— *Writings on British history,* DC281

Royal Horticultural Society dictionary of gardening, EG125

Royal Horticultural Society (Great Britain). *The American Horticultural Society encyclopedia of garden plants,* EG116, EJ231
—— *Dictionary of gardening,* EG125
—— *The European garden flora,* EG169

Royal Horticultural Society of London at the Royal Botanic Gardens, Kew. *Index londinensis to illustrations of flowering plants, ferns and fern allies,* EG104

Royal Institute of British Architects. *The Royal Institute of British Architects comprehensive index to architectural periodicals, 1956–1970,* BF222

Royal Institute of British Architects. Library. *Architectural periodicals index,* BF207
—— *Catalogue of the Royal Institute of British Architects Library,* BF230

The Royal Institute of British Architects comprehensive index to architectural periodicals, 1956–1970, BF207
—— Royal Institute of British Architects, BF222

Royal Institute of International Affairs. *Chronology and index of the Second World War 1938–1945,* DA209

Royal Institute of International Affairs Library. *Index to periodical articles,* DA171

Royal Institute of Linguistics and Anthropology. *Netherlands Antilles,* DB449

Royal Irish Academy (Dublin). *Contributions to a dictionary of the Irish language,* AC519
—— *Dictionary of the Irish language,* AC519
—— *Medieval Ireland c.1170–1495,* DC392
—— *A new history of Ireland,* DC413
—— *Parliamentary election results in Ireland, 1801–1922,* CJ379

Royal Navy in World War Two, Law, Derek G., DA200

Royal Netherlands Academy. *Shorter encyclopaedia of Islam,* BC505

Royal Pharmaceutical Society of Great Britain. Dept. of Pharmaceutical Sciences. *The extra pharmacopoeia,* EH357

Royal Photographic Society of Great Britain. *Imaging abstracts,* BF332
—— *Photographic abstracts,* BF332

Royal School of Church Music. *Hymns and tunes indexed by first lines, tune names, and metres, compiled from current English hymnbooks,* BC321

Royal Society (Great Britain). *Biographical memoirs of fellows of the Royal Society,* EA182, EA189, EH219
—— *Catalogue of scientific papers, 1800–1900,* CE14, EA16, EA22, EB10, EB16, EC15, ED5, ED7, EE13, EF57, EF141, EF173, EF232, EG6, EG105, EG211, EG312
—— *International catalogue of scientific literature,* CE14, EA16, EB10, EC15, ED5, EE13, EF57, EF141, EF173, EF232, EG6, EG105, EG211, EG312
—— *Obituary notices of Fellows of the Royal Society,* EA182, EA189, EH219
—— *Proceedings of the Royal Society of London,* EA182
—— *Royal Society mathematical tables,* EB94

Royal Society (Great Britain). Library. *Book catalogue of the Library of the Royal Society,* EA23
—— *Catalogue of scientific papers,* BE31, EA21, EC17, ED6, EE15, EG98, EG213, EH68

Royal Society mathematical tables, EB82
—— Royal Society (Great Britain), EB94

Royal Society of Canada. *Inventaire chronologique …,* AA447

Royal Society of Chemistry (Great Britain). *The agrochemicals handbook,* EJ46
—— *Analytical abstracts,* EE20
—— *Chemical engineering and biotechnology abstracts,* EK49
—— *Hazards in the chemical laboratory,* EE75
—— *Index of reviews in organic chemistry,* EE134

Royal Statistical Society (Great Britain). *London bibliography of the social sciences,* CA13

Royle, Trevor. *Companion to Scottish literature,* BE811
—— *Dictionary of military quotations,* CJ591
Roysdon, Christine. *American engineers of the nineteenth century,* EK21
Rozhnova, L. A. *Sovetskaia bolgaristika,* DC113
RQ, AA21
R.R. Bowker Company. *Educational film & video locator of the Consortium of College and University Media Centers and R. R. Bowker,* AA380, CB31
—— *Health science books, 1876–1982,* EH19
—— *Pure & applied science books, 1876–1982,* EA20
RSANB, 1926–1958, AA876
RSR, AA359
Rúam ráichou wárasán nai Prathét Thai, AD246
Rübel Asiatic Research Collection. *Catalog of the Rübel Asiatic Research Collection,* BF53
Ruben, Douglas H. *Drug abuse and the elderly,* CC121
—— *Handbook for assessing and treating addictive disorders,* CC135
—— *Philosophy journals and serials,* BB14
Rubens, Alfred. *A history of Jewish costume,* BG113
—— *Jewish iconography,* BG113
Rubenstein, Charlotte Streifer. *American women sculptors,* BF400
Rubert, Steven C. *Zimbabwe,* DD48
Rubin, Don. *Canada's playwrights,* BE821
Rubin, Harvey W. *Dictionary of insurance terms,* CH509
Rubin, Louis Decimus. *A bibliographical guide to the study of Southern literature,* BE574
—— *The history of Southern literature,* BE575
—— *Southern writers,* BE578
Rubin, Melvin L. *Dictionary of eye terminology,* EH110
Rubin, Richard. *Human resource management in libraries,* AK178
—— *Incest, the last taboo,* CC218
Rubincam, Milton. *Genealogical research,* AJ10
Rubinstein, Danny. *The West Bank handbook,* CJ436
Rubinstein, Ruth. *Renaissance artists & antique sculpture,* BF391
Rubinton, Phyllis. *Core readings in psychiatry,* EH371
Ruble, Blair A. *Soviet research institutes project,* AL85
Ruby, Douglas A. *Guide to graduate study in economics, agricultural economics, public administration, and doctoral programs in business administration in the United States and Canada,* CH79
Ruch, Theodore Cedric. *Bibliographia primatologica,* EG214
Ruck, Elaine H. *Index of themes and motifs in twelfth-century French Arthurian poetry,* BE1165
Rudall, Brian H. *Computers and literature,* BE8
Rudder, Robert S. *The literature of Spain in English translation,* BE1448
Rudick, Michael. *Bibliography and index of English verse in manuscript, 1501–1558,* BE714
Rudisill, Richard. *Directories of photographers,* BF345
—— *Photographers,* BF345
Rudloff, Willy. *World-climates,* EF164
Ruecker, Norbert. *Jazz index,* BJ303
Ruetz, Eva. *The new Wildhagen German dictionary,* AC424
Ruf, Wolfgang. *Lexikon Musikinstrumente,* BJ369
Ruffner, Frederick G. *Allusions—cultural, literary, biblical, and historical,* AC65, BE74
Ruffner, James A. *Climates of the states,* EF158
—— *Eponyms dictionaries index,* AC53
Rug and textile arts, Arthur D. Jenkins Library, BG153
Rugg, Evelyn. *A bibliography of comedias sueltas in the University of Toronto library,* BE1471
Rugg, Frederick E. *Rugg's recommendations on the colleges,* CB349
Rugg's recommendations on the colleges, Rugg, Frederick E., CB349

Rugs
 handbooks, BG169
 indexes, BG153
 library catalogs, BG153
Rugs (by country or region)
 Asia, West
  handbooks, BG165, BG168
  history, BG166
Rugs (by subject)
 history, BG167
Ruh, Kurt. *Die deutsche Literatur des Mittelalters,* BE1253
Ruhe, Ernstpeter. *Algerien-Bibliographie,* DD126
Ruhl, Klaus-Jörg. *Der spanische Bürgerkrieg,* DC518
Ruhlen, Merritt. *Guide to the languages of the world,* BD16
—— *A guide to the world's languages,* BD16
Ruiz Castañeda, María del Carmen. *Catálogo de seudónimos, anagramas, iniciales y otros alias usados por escritores mexicanos y extranjeros que han publicado en México,* AA152
Ruiz de Gauna, Adolfo. *Catálogo de publicaciones periódicas vascas de los siglos XIX y XX,* AD158
Ruiz-Fornells, Enrique. *Dissertations in Hispanic languages and literatures,* BE1446
Ruiz Naufal, Victor M. *El territorio mexicano,* CL311
Ruiz Torres, Francisco. *Diccionario de términos médicos, inglés-español, español-inglés,* EH142
Rükl, Antonín. *Atlas of the moon,* EC68
Rula, Dragan. *Titova reč u publikacijama JNA 1941–1980,* DC610
The rule book, BK46
Rumania, Fischer-Galati, Stephen A., DC496
Rumball-Petre, Edwin A. R. *Rare Bibles,* BC104
Rummel, Kathleen Kelly. *Politics, economics, and society in the two Germanies, 1945–75,* DC238
Runchock, Rita. *Super LCCS,* AK202
Runcorn, S. K. *International dictionary of geophysics,* EF11
Runge, Gretchen E. *Correlation index,* EA66
Runic literature, AA717, BE1082, BE1284
Runkel, Margaret. *A guide to usage for writers and students in the social sciences,* CA55
Runkel, Philip Julian. *A guide to usage for writers and students in the social sciences,* CA55
Runnquist, Åke. *Moderna svenska författare,* BE1486
Ruoff, A. LaVonne Brown. *American Indian literatures,* BE553
Ruoff, James E. *Crowell's handbook of Elizabethan & Stuart literature,* BE739
Ruokonen, Kyllikki. *Finland—sources of information,* DC139
—— *India information sources, economics and business,* CH196
—— *Japan, sources of economic and business information,* CH204
Rupesinghe, Kumar. *Ethnic conflict and human rights in Sri Lanka,* DE260
Rupp, Ernest Gordon. *Religion in England, 1688–1791,* BC278
Rupp, Heinz. *Deutsches Literatur-Lexikon,* BE1246
Ruppert, Edward E. *Microscopic anatomy of invertebrates,* EG236
Ruppert, James. *Guide to American poetry explication,* BE491
Rupprecht, Hans-Albert. *Wörterbuch der griechischen Papyrusurkunden,* AC446
Rural development abstracts, EJ19
Rural development in Tanzania, Serkkola, Ari, DD236
Rural sociology, CH46
Rural sociology, Berndt, Judy, CC4
Rusch, Frederik L. *Psychocriticism,* BE25
Rush, George E. *Dictionary of criminal justice,* CK257

Rush, Theressa Gunnels. *Black American writers,* BE532
Rusinek, Michał. *Polska literatura w przekładac,* BE1358
Russell, Candice S. *Family therapy glossary,* CC226
Russell, Charles H. *The encyclopedia of aging and the elderly,* CC81
Russell, James. *Marx-Engels dictionary,* CJ523
Russell, Jeffrey B. *Medieval heresies,* BC210
Russell, Norma Jean. *Blackfoot dictionary of stems, roots, and affixes,* AC717
Russell, Percy. *The nutrition and health encyclopedia,* EH300
Russell's official national motor coach guide, CL395
Russia
 associations, AL56
 bibliography, AA796
  16th and 17th centuries, AA787
  18th century, AA788, AA789, AA790, AA791
  current, AA795
 bibliography of bibliography, AA61, AA64, AA66
 biography, AH180, AH283, AH284, AH305
 dissertations, AG45, AG46
 government publications, AD144, AF214
 newspapers, AE69, AE70, AE73, AE74
 periodicals, AD142, AD145, AD146, AD149, AD150
  indexes, AD325
   bibliography, AD326
 statistics, CG293
Russia (by subject)
 economic conditions
  bibliography of bibliography, CH22
 folklore and popular culture, CF83
 history
  atlases, DC571
  encyclopedias, DC583
  library resources, DC556
 humanities
  bibliography, CA16
 law, CK223
 music, BJ204
 population
  statistics, CG293
 social and behavioral sciences
  bibliography, CA16
Russia & Eurasia facts and figures annual, CG297
Russia and the commonwealth A to Z, Wilson, Andrew, DC597
Russia and the Soviet Union, Horecky, Paul Louis, DC550
Russia and the United States, Bolkhovitinov, N. N., DC559
Russia and the U.S.S.R.
 abstract journals, DC38
 atlases, DC572
 bibliography, AA794, DC32, DC550, DC552, DC558, DC603
  dissertations, DC553
  general, AA784, AA785
 bibliography of bibliography, AA63
 biography, DC54, DC55, DC578, DC594
 dissertations, DC554
 guides, DC29
 library catalogs, DC45, DC49
 manuscripts and archives, AK106, DC560, DC566
 statistics, CG297
Russia and the U.S.S.R. (by subject)
 anthropology and ethnology, CE20
 armed forces
  encyclopedias, CJ657
 censuses, CG302
 education
  bibliography, CB45
 foreign relations (by country or region)
  Africa, DD107
  United States, DC568
 geography, CL13
 government officials, CJ385
 historiography, DC570, DC573
  dictionaries, DC584

history, DC578
  bibliography, DC42, DC548, DC574, DC575, DC576, DC577, DC579, DC580, DC581, DC582
  encyclopedias, DC567
  manuscripts and archives, DC564
history (by period)
  Revolution, 1917–1921, DC594, DC596, DC601
place-names, CL93
political parties, CJ386
politics and government, CJ386
  directories, CJ387
  encyclopedias, DC597
religion, DC566
social conditions
  bibliography, DC581
statistics and demography, CG302
travelers' accounts, DC551
  see also **Former Soviet republics; Ukraine**
Russia in the twentieth century, Bakhmeteff Archive of Russian and East European History and Culture, DC558
Russia, the Soviet Union, and Eastern Europe, Hoover Institution on War, Revolution, and Peace, DC49
Russia, the USSR, and Eastern Europe, Horak, Stephan M., DC32
Russia/U.S.S.R., Thompson, Anthony, DC552
Russian and Soviet education, 1731–1989, Brickman, William W., CB45
Russian and Soviet perspectives on South Africa, Knox-Davies, Laetitia, DD219
Russian autocrats from Ivan the Great to the fall of the Romanov dynasty, Egan, David R., DC578
Russian bibliography, libraries and archives, Simmons, John S. G., AB86
Russian dictionaries, Aav, Yrjö, AC696
  —— Aissing, Alena, AC697
Russian drama, BE1410
The Russian emigration, AD300
Russian emigré journals, 1855–1917, AD218
Russian émigré literature, BE1390
The Russian Empire and the Soviet Union, Grant, Steven A., AK106, DC560
Russian-English biological dictionary, Dumbleton, C. W., EG35
Russian-English chemical and polytechnical dictionary, Callaham, Ludmilla Ignatiev, EE53
Russian-English dictionary, AC680
  —— Smirnitskiĭ, Aleksandr Ivanovich, AC678, AC681
Russian-English dictionary of earth sciences, Burgunker, Mark E., EF87
Russian-English dictionary of mathematics, Efimov, Oleg P., EB52
Russian-English dictionary of musical terms, Katayen, Lelia, BJ150
Russian-English dictionary of social sciences, Smith, R. E. F., CA41
Russian-English dictionary of socio-political terms, CA40
Russian-English dictionary of the mathematical sciences, EB53
Russian-English/English-Russian dictionary of free market era economics, Pozin, Mikhail A., CH71
Russian-English forestry and wood dictionary, Linnard, William, EJ180
Russian-English-German-French dictionary of computer science, EK192
Russian-English-German-French hydrological dictionary, Singer, Lothar, EF135
Russian-English nuclear dictionary, ED28
Russian-English petrographic dictionary, Telberg, Vladimir George, EF258
Russian-English physics dictionary, Emin, Irving, ED27
Russian-English scientific and technical dictionary, Alford, Mark Hugh Tankerville, EA124
A Russian-English social science dictionary, Smith, R. E. F., CA41
Russian-English translators dictionary, Zimmerman, Mikhail G., EA130

Russian-Georgian dictionary, Chubinashvili, D., AC397
Russian government today, CJ387
Russian historical sources, AH284
Russian history atlas, Gilbert, Martin, DC571
Russian history since 1917, Harvard University. Library, DC585
Russian imperial government serials on microfilm in the Library of Congress, Library of Congress, AD144, AF214
Russian language
  abbreviations, AC685, AC686, AC687, AC688, AC690
  bibliography, BD185, BD187, BD188
  dictionaries, AC666, AC667, AC668, AC670, AC671, AC672, AC674
    abbreviations, AC689
    abridged, AC682, EA128
    bibliography, AC696, AC697, AC698, AC699
    bilingual, AC677, EA127, EB53
      English-Russian, AC675, AC679, AC682, AC684, AC695, EA128
      Russian-English, AC669, AC676, AC678, AC680, AC681, AC683, CA40, CA41
    idioms and usage, AC695
  dictionaries (by subject)
    historiography, DC584
    etymology
      dictionaries, AC691
  guides, BD186, BE1382
  idioms and usage, AC694
  obsolete and provincial words, AC673
  synonyms, AC692, AC693
Russian literature
  bibliography, BE1383, BE1384, BE1385, BE1386, BE1388, BE1389, BE1392, BE1394, BE1395, BE1397, BE1399, BE1400, BE1404, BE1406, BE1407, DC579
    current, BE1398
  bibliography of bibliography, BE1396
  biobibliography, BE1393, BE1402, BE1407, BE1422
  biography, BE1424
  dictionaries, BE1416
  directories, BE1422
  dissertations, BE1408
  encyclopedias, BE1411, BE1412, BE1413, BE1414, BE1415
  guides, BD186, BE1382
  library catalogs, BE1394, BE1395
  translations, BE1385, BE1391, BE1400, BE1401, BE1403, BE1405, BE1409
Russian literature (by subject)
  history, BE1417, BE1418, BE1419, BE1420, BE1421
  influence studies, BE1403
Russian literature in the Hispanic world, Schanzer, George O., BE1403
Russian literature, theatre, and art, Ettlinger, Amrei, BE1409
  —— Gladstone, Joan M., BE1409
Russian literature under Lenin and Stalin, 1917–1953, Struve, Gleb, BE1421
Russian military power, CJ656
Russian publications on Jews and Judaism in the Soviet Union, 1917–1967, Altshuler, Mordechai, BC535
  —— Greenbaum, Alfred Abraham, BC535
  —— Pinkus, B., BC535
Russian surnames, Unbegaun, Boris Ottokar, AJ204
Russian, Ukrainian, and Belorussian newspapers, 1917–1953, Horecky, Paul Louis, AE71, AE75
  —— Library of Congress. Slavic and Central European Division, AE75
Russian writings on Tanganyika, Zanzibar, and Tanzania, Darch, Colin, DD107
Russika und Sowjetika unter den deutschsprachigen Hochschulschriften, 1961–1973, Bruhn, Peter, DC553
Russische Abkürzungen, Scheitz, Edgar, AC689
Die russischen Verben, AC669
Russisches etymologisches Wörterbuch, Vasmer, Max, AC691

Russisches geographisches Namenbuch, CL152
Russkaîa émigratsiîa, AD300
Russkaîa istoricheskaîa bibliografiîa, 1800–54, Mezhov, Vladimir Izmailovich, DC580
Russkaîa istoricheskaîa bibliografiîa 1855–64, Lambin, Petr Petrovich, DC580
Russkaîa istoricheskaîa bibliografiîa, 1865–76, Mezhov, Vladimir Izmailovich, DC580
Russkaîa khudozhestvennaîa literatura i literaturovedenie, Kandel', Boris L'vovich, BE1396
Russkaîa obshchestvennaîa biblioteka imeni I.S. Turgeneva (Paris, France). *L'emigration russe,* AD300
Russkaîa periodicheskaîa pechat', AD146
Russkaîa periodicheskaîa pechat' 1703–1900 gg, Lisovskiĭ, Nikolai Mikhailovich, AD145
Russkaîa tekhnicheskaîa periodika 1800–1916, Mezhenko, ÎU. A., EA52
Russkie anonimnye i podpisannye psevdonimami proizvedenniîa pechati, Gosudarstvennaîa publichnaîa biblioteka imeni M.E. Saltykova-Shchedrina, AA183
Russkie biograficheskie i biobibliograficheskie slovari, Kaufman, Isaak Mikhailovich, AH305
Russkie entsiklopediĭ, Kaufman, Isaak Mikhailovich, AB86, AB90
Russkie literaturnye al'manakhi i sborniki XVIII-XIX vv, BE1406
  —— Smirnov-Sokol'skiĭ, Nikolai Pavlovich, BE1404
Russkie pisateli, BE1423
Russkie pisateli pervoi poloviny XIX veka, BE1392
Russkie pisateli vtoroi poloviny XIX nachala XX vv. (do 1917 goda), Gosudarstvennaîa biblioteka SSSR imeni V.I. Lenina, BE1392
Russkie pisateli XVIII veka, BE1392
Russkie sovetskie pisateli—poéty, BE1402
Russkie sovetskie pisateli-prozaiki, Gosudarstvennaîa publichnaîa biblioteka imeni M.E. Saltykova-Shchedrina, BE1393
Russkiĭ biograficheskiĭ slovar' ..., AH284
Russkiĭ fol'klor, CF83
Russko-angliiskii iadernyi slovar', Voskoboinik, David I., ED28
Russko-angliiskii slovar', AC680, AC681
Russko-angliĭskiĭ slovar' obshchestvenno-politicheskoĭ leksiki, Rodionova, Z. V., CA40
Russko-angliĭskiĭ slovar' obshchestvennykh nauk, CA41
Russko-anglo-nemetsko-frantsuzskiĭ slovar' po vychislitel'noĭ tekhnike, Maslovskiĭ, E. K., EK192
Russkoe istoricheskoe obshchestvo (Leningrad). *Russkiĭ biograficheskiĭ slovar' ...,* AH284
Russo, Nancy Felipe. *Women in psychology,* CD52
Rust, Brian A. L. *Brian Rust's guide to discography,* BJ382
  —— *The complete entertainment discography, from 1897 to 1942,* BJ343
  —— *Jazz records, 1897–1942,* BJ309
Rust, Werner. *Verzeichnis von unklaren Titelkürzungen deutscher und ausländischer Zeitschriften,* AD24
Ruszkiewicz, John. *Scott, Foresman handbook for writers,* BD96
Rüterwörden, Udo. *Hebräisches und aramäisches Handwörterbuch über das Alte Testament ... ,* AC477
Rutgers Center of Alcohol Studies. *A dictionary of words about alcohol,* CC129
Rutgers University. Center for Urban Policy Research. *America's elderly,* CC93
  —— *The city,* CC297
  —— *The environmental impact handbook,* EK80
Rutgers University. Graduate School. *A syllabus of comparative literature,* BE21
Rutherford, Donald. *Dictionary of economics,* CH64
Rutherford, John. *An annotated bibliography of the novels of the Mexican Revolution of 1910–1917,* BE916
Rutherford, Leslie. *Osborn's concise law dictionary,* CK34

Rutinel Domínguez, Ulises. *Diccionario histórico dominicano*, DB436

Rutkow, Ira M. *The history of surgery in the United States, 1775–1900*, EH196

Ruttkowski, W. V. *Nomenclator litterarius*, BE88

Ruvigny and Raineval, Melville Amadeus Henry Douglas Heddle de la Caillemotte de Massue de Ruvigny, *9th Marquis of*. *Titled nobility of Europe*, AJ81

Ruyssen, Geneviève. *Fonds parisiens d'archives de l'architecture*, BF225

Rwanda
  atlases, CL344
  bibliography, AA871, DD18, DD111, DD198, DD244
  current surveys, DD62
  government publications
    bibliography, AF229
  periodicals, AD171
  statistics, CG351
Rwanda (by subject)
  population, CG352, DD197
  women, DD199

Rwanda. Direction Générale de la Statistique. *Bulletin de statistique. Supplément annuel*, CG351

Rwanda. Ministère du plan. Centre de documentation. *Documentation sur le Rwanda*, DD198

Rwanda, Fegley, Randall, DD18
  ———— Nyrop, Richard, DD62

Ryan, Bryan. *Hispanic writers*, BE890

Ryan, Halford R. *American orators before 1900*, BE346
  ———— *American orators of the twentieth century*, BE346

Ryan, James G. *Irish records*, AJ138

Ryan, Joe. *First stop*, AB16

Ryan, Joseph M. *The educator's desk reference (EDR)*, CB4

Ryan, Victoria. *Historical directory of trade unions*, CH668

Ryans, Cynthia C. *Small business*, CH332

Ryder, A. F. C. *Guides to materials for West African history in European archives*, DD105

Ryder, Dorothy E. *Canadian reference sources*, AA456

Rydings, H. Anthony. *Hong Kong union catalogue*, DE150

Rydon, Joan. *A biographical register of the Commonwealth Parliament, 1901–1972*, CJ450

Ryle, Anne. *-ologies & -isms*, AC79

Rylko, Henry M. *Artificial intelligence*, EK153

Ryll, Ludomira. *Polska literatura w przekładac*, BE1358

Ryōzō, Araki. *Nanori jiten*, AC556

Ryskamp, George R. *Tracing your Hispanic heritage*, AJ141

Ryukyu Islands, King, Norman D., DE203

Ryzhik, Iosif Moisevich. *Table of integrals, series, and products*, EB85

Rzetelska-Feleszko, Ewa. *Przewodnik po jezykoznawstwie polskim*, BD193

S & L quarterly, CH291

S & P statistical service, CH223

S. A. Katalogus, AA877

S. Orgelbranda Encyklopedja pow-szechna z ilustracjami i mapami, Orgelbrand, Samuel, AB77

S.A. catalogue, AA877

Saagpakk, Paul Friidrih. *Eesti-inglise sõnaraamat*, AC307

Saal, Friedrich Wilhelm. *Chronik deutscher Zeitgeschichte*, DC260

SAARC women, Aryal, Deepak Kumar, AH363

Saareste, Andrus Kustas. *Eesti keele môisteline sônaraamat*, AC306

Saarestem, Albert. *Eesti-saksa sõnaraamat kolmas muutmatu trük teisest, dr. Jakob Hurt'i poolt redigeeritud väljaandest*, AC309

Saban, R. *Bibliographie de la Guyane Française*, DB377

Sabatier, Robert. *Histoire de la poésie française*, BE1197

Sabin, Joseph. *Bibliotheca americana*, AA409
  ———— *Dictionary of books relating to America, from its discovery to the present time*, AA404, AA409, AA411

Sabin, Robert. *The international cyclopedia of music and musicians*, BJ137

Sabine, Peter Aubrey. *Chambers earth sciences dictionary*, EF13

Sable, Martin Howard. *Communism in Latin America*, CJ513
  ———— *Guide to the writings of pioneer Latinoamericanists of the United States*, DB296
  ———— *Holocaust studies*, DA216
  ———— *Latin American Jewry*, BC526
  ———— *Latin American studies in the non-Western world and Eastern Europe*, DB260
  ———— *Mexican and Mexican-American agricultural labor in the United States*, CC451

Sabor, Josefa Emilia. *Manual de fuentes de información*, AA349

Sabosik, Patricia E. *Choice ethnic studies reviews*, CC316

Sabourin, Conrad. *La francité canadienne*, BD162

SABREB, AA889

Sacca, Elizabeth J. *Visual arts reference and research guide*, BF29

Sachar, Brian. *Atlas of European architecture*, BF253

Sachdev, Paul. *International handbook on abortion*, CC253

Sachet, Marie-Hélène. *Island bibliographies*, EG108

Sachs, Curt. *The history of musical instruments*, BJ373

Sachs, Lothar. *A guide to statistical methods and to the pertinent literature*, EB17

Sachs, Michael. *World guide to scientific associations and learned societies*, AL24, EA201

Sachse, William Lewis. *Restoration England, 1660–1689*, DC303, DC319

Sächsische Akademie der Wissenschaften zu Leipzig. *Althochdeutsches Wörterbuch*, AC399

Sachwörterbuch der Geschichte Deutschlands und der deutschen Arbeiterbewegung, DC257

Sachwörterbuch zur deutschen Geschichte, Rössler, Hellmuth, DC222

Sack, Sallyann Amdur. *A guide to Jewish genealogical research in Israel*, AJ143
  ———— *Where once we walked*, CL127, CL128

Sackett, Susan. *The Hollywood reporter book of box office hits*, BH272

Sacks, Michael. *Core readings in psychiatry*, EH371

The sacramentary, Catholic Church, BC424

Sacramento Blake, Augusto Victorino Alves do. *Diccionario bibliographico brasileiro*, AA509

Sacramentum mundi, BC231, BC405

Sacramentum verbi, BC130

Sacred books
  bibliography, AA113, BC102
  collections, BC91, BC92
  quotations, BC89, BC90
Sacred books (by subject)
  Buddhism, BC468
  Hinduism, BC484, BC489
  Islam, BC204
  Koran, BC204
  Vedas, BC484, BC489

The sacred books of China, BC92

Sacred books of the Buddhists, BC457

Sacred books of the East, BC92, BE1555
  ———— Müller, F. Max, BC457

The sacred laws of the Âryas, BC92

Sacred music *see* **Religious music**

Sacris, Carolina Nemenzo. *A preliminary annotated bibliography of Pilipino linguistics (1604–1976)*, BD234

SADCC literature and literature on SADCC, Löfgren, Ake, DD116

The Saddharma-pundarika, BC92

Sadeniemi, Matti. *Nykysuomen sanakirja*, AC320

Sader, Luke. *Leonard Maltin's movie and video guide*, BH198

Sader, Marion. *Comprehensive index to English-language little magazines, 1890–1970*, AD263, AD287, BE420, BE500

Sadie, Stanley. *Music printing and publishing*, BJ183
  ———— *The new Grove dictionary of American music*, BJ140
  ———— *The new Grove dictionary of music and musicians*, BJ141
  ———— *The New Grove dictionary of musical instruments*, BJ371
  ———— *The new Grove dictionary of opera*, BJ251
  ———— *The Norton/Grove concise encyclopedia of music*, BJ143

Sadleir, Michael. *XIX century fiction*, BE683, BE687

Sadler, Geoff. *Twentieth-century western writers*, BE212, BE579

Sadler, Judith DeBoard. *Families in transition*, CC219

Sadler, M. J. *Encyclopaedia of food science, food technology, and nutrition*, EH297

Sadock, Benjamin J. *Comprehensive glossary of psychiatry and psychology*, EH383
  ———— *Comprehensive textbook of psychiatry/V*, EH400

Sadoul, Georges. *Dictionary of film makers*, BH285
  ———— *Dictionary of films*, BH200

Sadowska, Genowefa. *Catalogue of periodicals in Polish or relating to Poland and other Slavonic countries, published outside Poland since September 1st, 1939*, AD136

SAE glossary of automotive terms, EK40

SAE handbook, EK40, EK41

Saenger, Erwin. *British union-catalogue of periodicals*, AD236

Sáenz, Gerardo. *Diccionario de seudónimos y escritores Iberoamericanos*, AA154

Safadi, Yasin H. *Union catalogue of Arabic serials and newspapers in British libraries*, AE84

Safety, environmental protection, and analysis, EK49

Saffady, William. *Micrographics*, AK250

Saffroy, Gaston. *Bibliographie généalogique, héraldique et nobiliaire de la France*, AJ87

Saffroy, Genevieve. *Bibliographie généalogique, héraldique et nobiliaire de la France*, AJ87

Safire, William L. *New language of politics*, CJ127
  ———— *Safire's new political dictionary*, CJ127

Safire's new political dictionary, Safire, William L., CJ127

Safla, Roucaya. *Catalogue du fonds "Iles de l'océan Indien"*, DD203
  ———— *Iles du sud-ouest de l'océan Indien*, DD121, DD142, DD175
  ———— *Iles du sud-ouest de l'océn Indien*, DD179

Safrai, Ze'ev. *The Macmillan Bible atlas*, BC197

Sagar, Anand. *Directory of publishers and booksellers in India*, AA294

Sagar, D. J. *Major political events in Indo-China, 1945–1990*, CJ421
  ———— *Political parties of Asia and the Pacific*, CJ414, CJ446

Sagar, H. L. *Who's who, Indian personages*, AH354

Sagas
  bibliography, BE1090
  translations, BE1088

Sage, William W. *Laos*, DE222, DE223

Sage family studies abstracts, CC222

Sage public administration abstracts, CJ476

Sage race relations abstracts, CC340

Sage urban studies abstracts, CC301

Saggio di bibliografia araldica italiana, Azzi Vitalleschi, Giustiniano degli, AJ139
  ———— Spreti, Vittorio, AJ139

Saggio di bibliografia sui problemi storici, teorici e pratici della traduzione, Briamonte, Nino, BD86

Saggistica letteraria italiana, Fucilla, Joseph Guerin, BE1292

Saglio, Edmond. *Dictionnaire des antiquités grecques et romaines d'après les textes et les monuments*, DA99

Saha, Santosh C. *Indo-U.S. relations, 1947–1988*, DE160

Sahara, DD48

Sahel
  bibliography, DD103
  statistics, CG307, DD102
Sahel (by subject)
  history, CG307, DD102
  population, CG308
Sahel, a guide to the microfiche collection, DD103
Sahel Institute. *Sources de l'histoire démographique des pays du Sahel conservées dans les archives,* CG307, DD102
Sahitya Akademi. *Who's who of Indian writers, 1983,* BE1570
Sahli, Nancy Ann. *Women and sexuality in America,* CC275
Sailing and water sports, BK121, BK122, BK123
  dictionaries, EC81
The sailing dictionary, Schult, Joachim, BK123
Sainsbury, Diana. *Dictionary of microbiology and molecular biology,* EG27
St. Augustine's Abbey (Ramsgate, England). *The book of saints,* BC261
Saint-Andre-Utudjian, Eliane. *A bibliography of West African life and literature,* BE1507
St. Andrew Bible missal, BC421
—— Catholic Church, BC421
St. Anthony's almanac, BC415
The St. James encyclopedia of mortgage & real estate finance, Newell, James E., CH534
St. James guide to biography, AH7, BE216
St. James guide to English literature, Vinson, James, BE626
St. James world futures and options directory, CH439
St. John, Ronald Bruce. *Libya,* DD18, DD48
St. John's Gospel, 1920–1965, Malatesta, Edward, BC105
St. Louis post-dispatch [index], AE104
Saint Lucia, CG178
St. Martin's anthologies of English literature, Alexander, Michael, BE618
—— Jeffares, Norman, BE618
Saint Simon, François de. *Dictionnaire de la noblesse française,* AJ88
Saint Vincent and the Grenadines, CG179, DB457
St. Vincent and the Grenadines, Potter, Robert B., DB457
Saints, BC257, BC258, BC261, BC262, BC263, BC264, BC265, BC266, BC426, BF180, BF181, BF183, BF184, BF185
  bibliography, BC259
  biography, BC259, BC260
The saints, BC266
Saints and their emblems, Drake, Maurice, BF181
Saints in Italian art, Kaftal, George, BF183
Saintsbury, George. *Rhymers' lexicon,* AC115
Sainty, John Christopher. *Office-holders in modern Britain,* CJ344
Sáinz de Robles, Federico Carlos. *Diccionario de sabiduría,* BE147
—— *Ensayo de un diccionario de la literatura,* BE70
Saishin kenchiku ei-wa jiten, BF242
Saito, Shiro. *Filipinos overseas,* CC409
—— *Philippine-American relations,* DB21, DE249
—— *Philippine ethnography,* CE111
—— *Philippine newspapers,* AE98
—— *Philippine newspapers in selected American libraries,* AE98
Saito, Toshio. *Concordance to Middle English metrical romances,* BE736
Sakala, Carol. *Women of South Asia,* CC615
Sakharov, G. V. *Slovar' sokrashcheniĭ russkogo ĭazyka,* AC685
Sakr, Carmelita S. *American labor union periodicals,* CH635
Sakthivel, S. *A bibliography of Dravidian linguistics,* BD226
Sakuntala Sharma, J. *Classified bibliography of linguistic dissertations on Indian languages,* BD225
Salad, Mohamed Khalief. *Somalia,* DD207
SALALM. *A bibliography of Latin American bibliographies,* AA24

—— *Indexed journals,* AD248
SALALM bibliography, Seminar on the Acquisition of Latin American Library Materials, AA536
Salaman, R. A. *Dictionary of tools used in the woodworking and allied trades, c. 1700–1970,* BG128
Salaries of municipal officials, CJ279
Salazar, Blanca Cecilia. *Bibliografía selectiva sobre desarrollo rural en el Ecuador,* DB372
Salazar, Daniel. *Teatro mexicano del siglo XX, 1900–1986,* BE913
Salda, Anne C. M. *The International Monetary Fund,* AF57
Saldana, Richard H. *A practical guide to the "misteaks" made in census indexes,* AJ20
The sale catalogues of British government publications, 1836–1921, Great Britain. Stationery Office, AF191
Salem, Dorothy C. *African American women,* AH55
Salem, James M. *Drury's guide to best plays,* BE225
—— *A guide to critical reviews,* BH61
The Salem College guide to sources on commercial aviation, CH476
Sales & marketing management magazine, CH592
Sales catalog index project input on-line, BF113
Saletore, Rajaram Narayan. *Encyclopaedia of Indian culture,* DE170
Saliba, M. *Arab Gulf states,* DE43
Ṣāliḥ, Jahānshāh. *The new unabridged English-Persian dictionary,* AC313
Salinger, Peter Shmuel. *Anglo-Jewish bibliography, 1971–1990,* BC517
Salisbury, J. Kenneth. *Mechanical engineer's handbook,* EK238
Salmon, Amédée. *Lexique de l'ancien français,* AC378
Salmonsen Leksikon tidsskrift, AB35
Salmonsens Konversationsleksikon, AB35
Salmonsens Store illustrerede Konversationsleksikon, AB35
Sālnāmah-i āmāri-i … kishvar, CG396
Salomon, Brownell. *Critical analyses in English renaissance drama,* BE653
Salt, Denys. *Austria,* DC91
Salt deposits, EF199
Salter, Charles A. *Knight's foodservice dictionary,* EJ157
Salter, Christopher L. *Atlas of China,* CL353
Salter, Frank K. *The bibliography of human behavior,* CA10, CD8
Salton, Mark W. *Glossary of numismatic terms in English, French, German, Italian, Swedish,* BG179
Saltykova-Shchedrina, M. E. *Russkie sovetskie pisateli—poéty,* BE1402
Salu, Luc. *History of photography,* BF334
—— *Photography and literature,* BF333
Salus, Peter H. *Pānini to Postal,* BD69
Salvá y Pérez, Vicente. *Catálogo de la biblioteca de Salvá,* AA805, AA807
Salvador, El *see* **El Salvador**
Salvat, Juan. *Salvat universal diccionario enciclopédico,* AB96
Salvat universal diccionario enciclopédico, AB96
Salvendy, Gavriel. *Handbook of human factors,* EK228
—— *Handbook of industrial engineering,* EK229
Salvini, Roberta. *Medieval sculpture,* BF393
Salys, Anton. *Wörterbuch der litauischen Schriftsprache, litauisch-deutsch,* AC602
Salzman, Jack. *Cambridge handbook of American literature,* BE431
Salzman, Paul. *English prose fiction, 1558–1700,* BE679, BE680, BE692
Samaraweera, Vijaya. *Sri Lanka,* DE261
Samardžić, Radovan. *Srpska bibliografija,* AA797
Śamasujjāmāna, Ābula Phajala. *Who's who in Bangladesh art, culture, literature, 1901–1991,* AH335
Samatar, Said S. *Somalia,* DD207
Sambhi, Piara Singh. *A popular dictionary of Sikhism,* BC572

Sambrano Urdaneta, Oscar. *Contribución a una bibliografía general de la poesía venezolana en el siglo XX,* BE967
Sambraus, Hans Hinrich. *A colour atlas of livestock breeds,* EJ137
Sambrook, John J. *English architecture,* BF241
Samelson, Ken. *The great all-time baseball record book,* BK59
Sāmkhya, Bhattacharya, Ram Shankar, BB33
—— Larson, Gerald James, BB33
Samlaren, BE1487
Sammons, Vivian O. *Blacks in science and medicine,* EA183, EH217
Samoa
  bibliography, DF53, DF54
Samoan dictionary, Milner, George Bertram, AC700, AC701
Samoan Islands bibliography, Holmes, Lowell Don, DF53
Samoan language, AC700, AC701
Samoot satidt rai, Bpra tet Thai, CG433
SAMP catalog, Center for Research Libraries, DE77
Samples, Gordon. *Drama scholars' index to plays and filmscripts,* BH168
Sampson, George. *Concise Cambridge history of English literature,* BE617
Sampson, Henry T. *Ghost walks,* BH109
Samsons, Vilis. *Latvijas PSR mazā enciklopēdija,* DC436
Samuel, Alan Edouard. *Greek and Roman chronology,* DA112
Samuel, René Claude Louis. *Parlementaires français,* AH200, CJ329
Samuelson, Elliot D. *Unmarried couples,* CC243
Samura, Hachiro. *Kokusho kaidai,* AA915
Samzelius, Jonas. *Svensk litteraturhistorisk bibliografi,* BE1487
San Cristóval, Evaristo. *Diccionario histórico-biográfico del Perú,* AH141
San Francisco chronicle [index], AE104
San Francisco Public Library. *The Chinese in California,* CC405
San Francisco Public Library. Friends. *Blacks and their contributions to the American West,* CC360
San Francisco Theological Seminary, San Anselmo, Calif. Department of New Testament Literature. Graduate Seminar in New Testament. *Bibliography of New Testament literature, 1900–1950,* BC118
San Vicente Tello, Victoria. *México,* DB238
The Sanatsugâtîya, BC92
SANB, AA876
SANB : South African national bibliography, AA878
Sanborn, Paul J. *The American Revolution, 1775–1783,* DB92
Sanborn Map Company. *Fire insurance maps in the Library of Congress,* CL235
Sanchez, Denise. *Feminist periodicals, 1855–1984,* CC521
Sánchez, Edith. *Cross-border links,* AL34
Sanchez, James. *Index to The Tower Commission report,* CJ114
Sánchez, T. A. *Bibliotheca hispana,* AA811
Sánchez Alonso, Benito. *Fuentes de la historia española e hispanoamericana,* DC506
—— *Historia de la historiografía española,* DC506
Sánchez Chinchilla, Luis Angel. *Atlas estadístico de Costa Rica, no. 2,* CL313
Sánchez López, Luis María. *Diccionario de escritores colombianos,* BE949
Sánchez Reyes, Enrique. *Bibliografía hispano-latina clásica,* BE1043
Sancti Thomae Aquinatis Opera omnia, Busa, Roberto, BB64
Sandahl, Linda J. *Encyclopedia of rock music on film,* BJ363
Sandberg, Graham. *A Tibetan-English dictionary with Sanskrit synonyms,* AC783
Sandberg, Larry. *The folk music sourcebook,* BJ324
Sandbergs Bokhandel, Stockholm. *A catalogue of the works of Linnaeus issued in commemoration of the 250th anniversary of the birthday of Carolus Linnaeus, 1707–1778,* EG109

Sandeen, Ernest Robert. *American religion and philosophy*, BC31

Sander, Daryl. *Focus on teens in trouble*, CC174

Sanders, Christopher. *Íslensk-ensk orðabók*, AC508

Sanders, Gabriel. *Bibliographie signalétique du latin des chrétiens*, BD146

Sanders, Irwin Taylor. *East European peasantries*, CE96

Sanders, Keith R. *Political campaign communication*, CJ103

Sanderson, Michael W. B. *Sea battles*, DA21

Sandinista Nicaragua, DB315

Sandler, Gerald. *Disease data book*, EH178

Sandler, Todd. *International terrorism in the 1980s*, CJ553

Sándor, Bortnyik. *Magyar életrajzi lexikon*, AH249

•*SANDRA*, EE115

Sands, Kathleen M. *American Indian women*, CC588

Sandvik, Harald. *Norsk militarhistorisk bibliografi*, DC464

Sandys, John Edwin. *Companion to Latin studies*, DA108, DA109

—— *A history of classical scholarship*, BE1022, BE1024, DA113

Sanford, George. *Poland*, DC475

Sanger, Margaret, CC255

Sanguin, André Louis. *Géographie politique*, CL20

Sanilevici, Renée. *Bibliography of Israeli law in European languages*, CK231

A Sanskrit-English dictionary, Monier-Williams, Monier, AC706

Sanskrit language
  bibliography, BD198
  dictionaries, AC705, AC707
    bilingual, AC703, AC704, AC708
      Sanskrit-English, AC702, AC706
    etymology, AC708
    German, AC703, AC704
  dissertations, BD197
Sanskrit literature
  bibliography, BD198
  dissertations, BD197

Sanskrit-Wörterbuch, Böhtlingk, Otto von, AC703

Sanskrit-Wörterbuch in kürzerer Fassung, Böhtlingk, Otto von, AC704

Santagata, Marco. *IUPI*, BE1316

Santamaria, Catherine. *Directory of special collections in Australiana*, DF31

Santesson, Rudolf. *Comprehensive English-Swedish dictionary*, AC769

—— *Stora engelsk-svenska ordboken*, AC768, AC769

—— *Svensk-engelsk ordbok*, AC769

Santi, Albert. *The St. James encyclopedia of mortgage & real estate finance*, CH534

Santifaller, Leo. *Österreichisches biographisches Lexikon 1815–1950*, AH169

Santoro, Carla Masotti. *A world directory of criminological institutes*, CK268

Santos Gómez, Susana. *Bibliografía de viajeros a la Argentina*, DB329

Santoso, Wartini. *Katalog majalah terbitan Indonesia*, AD194

—— *Katalog surat kabar*, AE89

Santschy, Jean-Louis. *Manuel analytique et critique de bibliographie générale de l'histoire suisse*, DC527

Sanz, Carlos. *Bibliotheca americana vetustissima : últimas adiciones*, DB3

—— *Gran secreto de la carta de Colón*, DB3

—— *Henry Harrissee*, DB3

Sanz, María Teresa. *Publicaciones oficiales de Chile, 1973–1983*, AF161

São Tomé e Principe
  bibliography, DD114
  government publications
    bibliography, AF220

Sapegno, Natalino. *Storia della letteratura italiana*, BE1303

Sapra, P. *Directory of periodicals published in India, 1991*, AD193

Saprykina, ĨU. M. *Istoriĩa srednikh vekov*, DA133

Saraiva, António José. *História da literatura portuguêsa*, BE1368

Sardegna, Jill. *Encyclopedia of blindness and vision impairment*, CC189, EH90

Sarel, Baruch. *A comprehensive etymological dictionary of the Hebrew language for readers of English*, AC471

Saretsky, Gary D. *Index to ETS research report series, 1948–1991*, CB153

Sarg, Michael. *The cancer dictionary*, EH108

Sargent, Charles Sprague. *The silva of North America*, EG201

Sargent, Helen Child. *English and Scottish popular ballads*, BE632

Sargent, Lyman Tower. *British and American utopian literature, 1516–1985*, BE684

Sarjeant, William A. S. *Geologists and the history of geology*, EF108

Sarkesian, Sam C. *U.S. national security policy and strategy*, CJ98

Särkkä, Heikki. *Englantilais-suomalais-englantilainen yleiskielen käyttösanakirja*, AC323

Sarrazin, Gregor Ignatz. *Shakespeare-lexicon*, BE773

Sarton, George. *Critical bibliography of the history of science and its cultural influences*, EA241

—— *A guide to the history of science*, EA239, EG8

—— *Introduction to the history of science*, EA256

Sartori, Claudio. *Enciclopedia della musica*, BJ133

—— *I libretti italiani a stampa dalle origini al 1800*, BJ243

Sartori, Eva. *French women writers*, BE1157

—— *Women's studies in Western Europe*, CC626

Sartwell, Crispin. *A companion to aesthetics*, BB27

Sarvāṅgī Aṅgrejī-Gujarātī kośa, AC468

Sass, Hans-Martin. *Martin Heidegger*, BB82

The Satapathabrâhmana, BC92

Satar, Abdul. *National atlas of the Democratic Republic of Afghanistan*, CL350

Satchidanandan, K. *Who's who of Indian writers, 1983*, BE1570

Satellite environment handbook, Johnson, Francis S., EK33

Satellites
  chronologies, EK34
  handbooks, EK33, EK34

Sater, Ana Lya. *Latin American Jewish studies*, DC526

Sather, Leland B. *Norway*, DC467

—— *Sweden*, DC520

Satué, Angel. *Diccionari etimològic i complementari de la llengua catalana*, AC248

Satyaprakash. *A bibliography of Sanskrit language and literature*, BD198

—— *Buddhism*, BC473

—— *Bangla Desh*, DE116

Sauber, S. Richard. *Family therapy*, CC227

Saudi Arabia, DE253
  biography, AH368
  chronologies, CJ423, DE62
  dissertations, AG57
  government publications, AF260
  statistics, CG421
Saudi Arabia (by subject)
  history
    bibliography, DE252, DE254

Saudi Arabia. Maṣlaḥat al-Iḥṣā'at al-'Āmah. *al-Kitāb al-iḥṣā'ī al-sanawī*, CG421

—— *Statistical yearbook*, CG421

Saudi Arabia, Clements, Frank A., DE252

—— Philipp, Hans-Jürgen, DE254

Saul, C. Daphne. *South African periodical publications, 1800–1875*, AD178

Saul, Nigel. *The Batsford companion to medieval England*, DC311

Saulnier, Eugène. *Bibliographie des travaux publiés de 1866 à 1897 sur l'histoire de la France de 1500 à 1789*, DC173

Saulnier, V. L. *Bibliographie de la littérature française du seizième siècle*, BE1204

Saunders, C. C. *South Africa*, DD48

Saunders, D. Gail. *Guide to the records of the Bahamas*, DB418

Saunders, John L. *Directory of unpublished experimental mental measures*, CD75

Saunders dictionary & encyclopedia of laboratory medicine and technology, Bennington, James L., EH109

Sauneron, Serge. *Dictionary of Egyptian civilization*, DA123

Sauvage, Pierre. *American directors*, BH290

Sauvaget, Jean. *Introduction to the history of the Muslim East*, BC500

Sauvalle, Hélène. *République du Congo-Brazzaville*, DD144

Savadjian, Léon. *Bibliographie balkanique 1920–1938*, DC59

Savage, George. *Concise history of bronzes*, BF396

—— *Dictionary of 19th century antiques and later objets d'art*, BG44

—— *Dictionary of antiques*, BG44

—— *An illustrated dictionary of ceramics*, BG67

Savage, James. *A genealogical dictionary of the first settlers of New England*, AJ65

Savage, Nicholas. *British architectural books and writers, 1556–1785*, BF216

Savageau, David. *Places rated almanac*, CL74, CL75

Savez društava bibliotekara FNRJ. *Bibliografija jugoslovenskih bibliografija, 1945–55*, AA69

Savez književnika Jugoslavije. *Adresar pisaca Jugoslavije*, BE1496

Savidge, Charlotte. *The Facts on File dictionary of the theatre*, BH69

Saville, John. *Dictionary of labour biography*, AH220

Savings institution directory, CH280

Savino, Edoardo. *La nazione operante*, AH263

Savitt, Todd Lee. *Dictionary of American medical biography*, EH228

Savola, Kristen L. *Inventory of longitudinal studies in the social sciences*, CA60

Sawers, Robin. *Harrap's concise German and English dictionary*, AC416

Sawicki, David S. *Urban planning*, BF268

Sawoniak, Henryk. *Bibliografia bibliografii polskich, 1951–1960*, AA60

—— *Bibliografia bibliografij polskich do 1950 roku*, AA59

—— *New international dictionary of acronyms in library and information science and related fields*, AK45

Sawyer, Malcolm C. *A biographical dictionary of dissenting economists*, CH92

Sax, N. Irving. *Dangerous properties of industrial materials*, EE79, EE80

Sax's dangerous properties of industrial materials, Lewis, Richard J., EE79, EE80

Sayre, John R. *The United States Congress*, CJ198

SB, CH528

Sbornik, AH284

Sbrega, John J. *The war against Japan, 1941–1945*, DA202

•*SCAD+ CD*, AF25

Scalds and scaldic poetry, BE1089

Scales, Sara Matthews. *Dissertations in Hispanic languages and literatures*, BE1446

—— *Western European dissertations on the Hispanic and Luso-Brazilian languages and literatures*, BE1446

Scalisi, Philip. *Classic mineral localities of the world*, EF205

Scammon, Richard M. *America at the polls*, CJ240

—— *America votes*, CJ241

Scandals, CJ60

Scandinavia
  bibliography, DC71
    dissertations, DC73
  biography, AH164, AH165
  newspapers, AD80
  periodicals, AD80
  statistics, CG190
Scandinavia (by subject)
  history, DC75, DC76

bibliography, DC74, DC77
regional and local, DC72
see also **names of individual countries**
Scandinavian biographical archive, AH164
Scandinavian history, 1520–1970, Oakley, Stewart P., DC74
Scandinavian languages
bibliography, BD130
dictionaries
bibliography, AC190
Scandinavian literature
bibliography, BE1082, BE1085
biography, BE1086, BE1087
encyclopedias, BE1086
Scandinavian literature (by subject)
history, BE1084, BE1091, BE1092
Scandinavian mythology, Lindow, John, CF33
Scanlan, Jean M. *Business online*, CH6
Scanlon, George T. *A bibliography of the architecture, arts, and crafts of Islam to 1st Jan. 1960*, BF17
Scannell, T. B. *A Catholic dictionary*, BC396
Scano, Carmen. *Dizionario delle scrittrici italiane contemporanee (arte, lettere, scienze)*, BE1313
Scarano, Filippo. *Chi à?*, AH259
Scarborough, William. *Collection of Chinese proverbs*, BE160
Scarre, Christopher. *Smithsonian timelines of the ancient world*, DA84
Scarrow, Howard A. *Canada votes*, CJ298
Scenic design on Broadway, Owen, Bobbi, BH120
Schaal, Richard. *Verzeichnis deutschsprachiger musikwissenschaftlicher Dissertationen 1861–1960*, BJ165
———— *Verzeichnis deutschsprachiger musikwissenschaftlicher Dissertationen 1961–1970*, BJ165
Schacht, John H. *Bibliography for the study of magazines*, AD41
Schaefer, Barbara Kirsch. *Using the mathematical literature*, EB5
Schaefer, D. C. *Handbuch zur Geschichte der Naturwissenschaften und der Technik … ,* EA251
Schaeffer, Ronald. *United States in World War I*, DA197
Schaf, Frank L. *Intelligence, espionage, counterespionage, and covert operations*, CJ535
Schäfer, Jürgen. *Early modern English lexicography*, AC7
Schaff, Philip. *Bibliotheca symbolica ecclesiae universalis*, BC311
———— *History of the Christian church*, BC280
———— *Select library of Nicene and post-Nicene Fathers of the Christian church*, BC294
Schaff-Herzog encyclopedia of religious knowledge, BC67
Schaie, K. Warner. *Handbook of the psychology of aging*, CC97
Schaller, Helmut Wilhelm. *Bibliographie der Bibliographien zur slavischen Sprachwissenschaft*, BD182
———— *Bibliographie zur Balkanphilologie*, BD202
———— *Bibliographie zur russischen Sprache*, BD187
Schamel, Charles E. *Guide to the records of the United States House of Representatives at the National Archives, 1789–1989*, CJ203
Schanz, Martin. *Geschichte der römischen Literatur bis zum Gesetzgebungswerk des Kaisers Justinian*, BE1052
Schanzer, George O. *Russian literature in the Hispanic world*, BE1403
Schapsmeier, Edward L. *Encyclopedia of American agricultural history*, EJ71
———— *Political parties and civic action groups*, CJ97, CJ266
Schapsmeier, Frederick H. *Encyclopedia of American agricultural history*, EJ71
———— *Political parties and civic action groups*, CJ97, CJ266
Scharff, Robert. *Encyclopedia of sailing*, BK122
———— *Formulas, methods, tips, and data for home and workshop*, EA279

Schatoff, Michael. *Half a century of Russian serials, 1917–1968*, AD78
Schatz, Natalie. *Federal information sources in health and medicine*, EH41
Schatzberg, Walter. *Relations of literature and science*, BE30
Der Schauspielführer, Gregor, Joseph, BE1263
Scheer, Matthias K. *Japanese law in Western languages*, CK232
———— *Japanisches Recht in westlichen Sprachen*, CK232
Scheer, Wilbert E. *The Dartnell personnel administration handbook*, CH712
Scheffler, Hannah Nuba. *Infancy*, CC148, CD78
———— *Resources for early childhood*, CC149
Scheick, William J. *Seventeenth-century American poetry*, BE497
Scheiding, Ursula. *Index litteraturae entomologicae*, EG328
Scheines, Elizabeth. *Art on screen*, BF96
Scheitz, Edgar. *Dictionary of Russian abbreviations*, AC689
———— *Russische Abkürzungen*, AC689
Schellinger, Paul E. *St. James guide to biography*, AH7, BE216
———— *Twentieth-century science-fiction writers*, BE212
Schenk, Trudy. *The Wuerttemberg emigration index*, AJ46
Schenk, Werner. *A dictionary of Russian verbs*, AC669
Schenkel, Martin. *Deutsche Bibliothekskataloge im 19. Jahrhundert*, AA118
Schenkling, Sigmund. *Index litteraturae entomologicae*, EG331
Scheps, Walter. *Middle Scots poets*, BE810
Scherer, Anton. *Südosteuropa-Dissertationen, 1918–1960*, DC67
Scherer, John L. *Terrorism*, CJ552
Scherer, Wilhelm. *Geschichte der deutschen Literatur*, BE1227
Scheub, Harold. *African oral narratives, proverbs, riddles, poetry, and song*, CF92
Scheuer, Steven. *Movies on TV and videocassette*, BH198
Scheurweghs, Gustave. *Analytical bibliography of writings on modern English morphology and syntax, 1877–1960*, BD92
Scheven, Yvette. *Bibliographies for African studies, 1970–1986*, DD88, DD190
———— *Namibia bibliographies*, DD190
Schiavone, Giuseppe. *International organizations*, AL21
Schick, Frank Leopold. *Records of the presidency*, AJ24, CJ174, DB37
———— *Statistical handbook on aging Americans*, CC104, CG106
———— *Statistical handbook on U.S. Hispanics*, CC471, CG84
Schick, I. T. *Battledress*, CJ595
Schick, Renee. *Records of the presidency*, CJ174
———— *Statistical handbook on aging Americans*, CC104, CG106
———— *Statistical handbook on U.S. Hispanics*, CC471, CG84
Schicke, Walter. *Melting point tables of organic compounds*, EE147
Schieferdecker, A. A. G. *Geological nomenclature*, EF80
Schier, Peter. *China's new party leadership*, CJ426
Schierbeck, Sachiko Shibata. *Postwar Japanese women writers*, BE1595
Schiffer, Wilhelm. *A bibliography of Shinto in Western languages*, BC570
Schild, Ulla. *Who's who in African literature*, BE1512
Schilder, Kees. *State formation, religion, and land tenure in Cameroon*, DD138
Schiller, Gertrud. *Ikonographie der christlichen Kunst*, BF186
Schiller, K. *Mittelniederdeutsches Wörterbuch*, AC408

Schimmelman, Janice Gayle. *American imprints on art through 1865*, BF36
———— *Architectural treatises and building handbooks available in American libraries and bookstores through 1800*, BF223
Schindler, Stanley. *Combined retrospective index to book reviews in humanities journals, 1802–1974*, BA7
Schindlmayr, A. *Keysers Lexikon der Pflanzen*, EG133
Schiötz, Eiler H. *Utlendingers reiser i Norge*, DC468
Schipper, Martin. *American Federation of Labor records*, CH624
The Schirmer guide to schools of music and conservatories throughout the world, Uscher, Nancy, BJ172
Schizophrenia, EH374
Schlachter, Gail Ann. *Directory of financial aids for minorities*, CB377
———— *Directory of financial aids for women*, CB378, CC546
———— *Financial aid for research and creative activities abroad*, CB366
———— *Financial aid for study and training abroad*, CB366
———— *Library science dissertations, 1925–1972*, AK26
———— *Library science dissertations, 1973–1981*, AK26
———— *Reference sources in library and information services*, AK2
Schlachter, Wolfgang. *Bibliographie der uralischen Sprachwissenschaft 1830–1970*, BD208
Schlager, Paul. *Grundriss zur Geschichte der deutschen Dichtung aus den Quellen*, BE1218
Schlagwort-katalog, AA642
Schlarwort-Verzeichnis, AA660
Schlauch, Margaret A. *Bibliography of critical Arthurian literature for the years 1930–1935*, BE339
Schlebecker, John T. *Bibliography of books and pamphlets on the history of agriculture in the United States, 1607–1967*, EJ72
———— *The many names of country people*, EJ32
Schlechta, Karl. *International Nietzsche bibliography*, BB78
Schleifer, Harold B. *Puerto Rican authors*, BE980
Schleifer, Rudolf. *Stieler's atlas of modern geography*, CL291
Schleiffer, Hedwig. *Index to economic history essays in festschriften, 1900–1950*, CH20
Schlereth, Thomas J. *Material culture*, BG3
Schlesinger, Arthur M. *The almanac of American history*, DB56
———— *The dynamics of world power*, DB136
Schlesinger, Benjamin. *Abuse of the elderly*, CC55
Schlesinger, Rachel. *Abuse of the elderly*, CC55
Schlessing, Anton. *Deutscher Wortschatz*, AC435
Schlessinger, Bernard S. *The basic business library*, CH8
———— *Who's who of Nobel Prize winners, 1901–1990*, AH30, AL170
Schlessinger, June H. *Who's who of Nobel Prize winners, 1901–1990*, AH30, AL170
Schlicke, Priscilla. *Walford's guide to reference material*, AA363, EA10
Schlickeysen, F. W. A. *Erklärung der Abkürzungen auf Münzen der neueren Zeit, des Mittelalters und des Altertums, sowie auf Denkmünzen und münzartigen Zeichen*, BG184
Schlobin, Roger C. *The literature of fantasy*, BE297
———— *Research guide to science fiction studies*, BE281
———— *Year's scholarship in science fiction and fantasy*, BE299, BE310
Schlomann, Alfred. *Technologisches Wörterbuch*, EA102
Schlosser, Julius, Ritter von. *La letteratura artistica*, BF37
Schlueter, June. *Encyclopedia of British women writers*, BE621, BE623
———— *The English novel*, BE674
———— *Modern American literature*, BE427

Schlueter, Paul. *Encyclopedia of British women writers*, BE621, BE623
—— *The English novel*, BE674
—— *Modern American literature*, BE427
Die Schlüsselliteratur, Schneider, Georg, BE71
Schmacke, Ernst. *Die Presse in Afrika*, AE4
—— *Presse in Asien und Ozeanien*, AE4
—— *Presse in Lateinamerika*, AE4
Schmale, Franz-Josef. *Deutschlands Geschichtsquellen im Mittelalter vom Tode Kaiser Heinrichs V. bis zum Ende des Interregnum*, DC228
Schmale-Ott, Irene. *Deutschlands Geschichtsquellen im Mittelalter vom Tode Kaiser Heinrichs V. bis zum Ende des Interregnum*, DC228
Schmalzriedt, Egidius. *Wörterbuch der Mythologie*, CF10
Schmeckebier, Laurence Frederick. *Government publications and their use*, AF76
Schmid, Alex Peter. *Political terrorism*, CJ554
Schmid, Bona. *I segreti dell'inglese*, AC530
Schmid, Hermann Ludwig. *Mathematisches Wörterbuch mit Einbeziehung der theoretischen Physik*, EB44
Schmid, Joseph. *Kirchenlateinisches Wörterbuch*, AC582
Schmid, Wilhelm. *Geschichte der griechischen Literatur*, BE1035
Schmidgall Tellings, A. Ed. *Contemporary Indonesian-English dictionary*, AC518
Schmidt, Alexander. *Shakespeare-lexicon*, BE773
Schmidt, Alvin J. *Fraternal organizations*, AL36
Schmidt, Charles. *Petit supplément au Dictionnaire de Du Cange*, AC587
Schmidt, Christian D. *Bibliographie zur osteuropäischen Geschichte*, DC37
Schmidt, Christoph. *Ausgewählte Bibliographien und Bibliothekskatalog zur russischen Sozialgesichte (1861–1917)*, DC581
Schmidt, Hans Joachim. *Index der zahnärztlichen Zeitschriften der Welt*, EH247
Schmidt, Karen A. *Understanding the business of library acquisitions*, AK168
Schmidt, Klaus. *Index deutschsprachiger Zeitschriften, 1750–1815*, AD316
—— *Zeitschriften-Index*, AE122
Schmidt, Nancy J. *Children's books on Africa and their authors*, DD14
—— *Sub-Saharan African films and filmmakers*, BH171
—— *Sub-Saharan African films and filmmakers, 1987–1992*, DD43
Schmidt, Peter. *Index zu deutschen Zeitschriften der Jahre 1773–1830*, AD315
Schmidt, Richard. *Sanskrit-Wörterbuch in kürzerer Fassung*, AC704
Schmidt-Dumont, Marianne. *Zeitschriftenverzeichnis Moderner Orient*, AD184
Schmidt-Künsemüller, Friedrich Adolf. *Lexikon des gesamten Buchwesens*, AA270
Schmit, J. Alexandre. *Catalogue de l'histoire de France*, DC143
Schmitt, Barton D. *Child protection team handbook*, CC172
Schmitt, Charles B. *The Cambridge history of Renaissance philosophy*, BB69
Schmitt, Christian. *Lexikon der Romanistischen Linguistik*, BD148
Schmitt, Franz Anselm. *Beruf und Arbeit in deutscher Erzählung*, BE1269
—— *Stoff- und Motivgeschichte der deutschen Literatur*, BE1231
Schmitt, Fritz. *Abriss der deutschen Literaturgeschichte in Tabellen*, BE1252
—— *Deutsche Literaturgeschichte in Tabellen*, BE1252
Schmitt, Otto. *Reallexikon zur deutschen Kunstgeschichte*, BF79
Schmittroth, Linda. *Statistical record of women worldwide*, CC583
Schmuck, Hilmar. *Gesamtverzeichnis des deutschsprachigen Schrifttums ausserhalb des Buchhandels (GVB), 1966–1980*, AA648

—— *Gesamtverzeichnis des deutschsprachigen Schrifttums (GV), 1700–1910*, AA643
Schnabel, Thomas. *Bibliographie zum Nationalismus*, CJ9
Schnapper, Edith B. *British union-catalogue of early music printed before the year 1801*, BJ54
Schneemelcher, Wilhelm. *New Testament Apocrypha*, BC94
Schneider, Alfons Maria. *Byzanz*, DA161
Schneider, Ben Ross. *Index to the London stage, 1660–1800*, BH101
Schneider, Carl J. *The ABC-CLIO companion to women in the workplace*, CC566, CH650
Schneider, Dorothy. *The ABC-CLIO companion to women in the workplace*, CC566, CH650
Schneider, Edgar W. *A bibliography of writings on varieties of English, 1965–1983*, BD108
—— *New bibliography of writings on varieties of English*, BD108
Schneider, Edward L. *Handbook of the biology of aging*, CC97
Schneider, Gail T. *Encyclopedia of school administration & supervision*, CB180
Schneider, Georg. *Handbuch der Bibliographie*, AA9
—— *Die Schlüsselliteratur*, BE71
—— *Theory and history of bibliography*, AA9
Schneider, Gerhard. *Exegetical dictionary of the New Testament*, BC137
Schneider, Joanne. *Women in Western European history*, DC5
Schneider, Johannes. *Mittellateinisches Wörterbuch bis zum ausgehenden 13. [i.e. dreizehnten] Jahrhundert*, AC591
Schneider, Marshall J. *Modern Spanish and Portuguese literatures*, BE1449
Schneider, Max. *Deutsches Titelbuch*, BE1273
Schnell, Ralf. *Geschichte der deutschsprachigen Literatur seit 1945*, BE1260
Schneller, Anne. *American doctoral dissertations on Africa 1886–1972*, DD32
Schobinger, Jean-Pierre. *Grundriss der Geschichte der Philosophie*, BB50
The Schocken guide to Jewish books, BC518
Schoder, Raymond V. *Wings over Hellas*, DA116
Schoeffler, O. E. *Esquire's encyclopedia of 20th century men's fashions*, BG97, BG115
Schoeman, Elna. *Economic interdependence in southern Africa, 1961–1989*, DD116
—— *Namibia*, DD18
—— *Namibian issue 1920–1980*, DD185
—— *South Africa and the United Nations*, DD224
—— *South African sanctions directory, 1946–1988*, DD215
—— *Southern African Development Coordination Conference (SADCC)*, DD116
Schoeman, Stanley. *Namibia*, DD18
Schoenbaum, Samuel. *Annals of English drama, 975–1700*, BE660
—— *New companion to Shakespeare studies*, BE784
Schoenberg, Arnold. *Fundamentals of musical composition*, BJ29
Schoenburg, Nancy. *Lithuanian Jewish communities*, CC355
Schoenburg, Stuart. *Lithuanian Jewish communities*, CC355
Schoenebaum, Eleanora W. *Political profiles*, CJ159
Schoenhals, Kai P. *Dominican Republic*, DB433
—— *Grenada*, DB437
Schöffer, Ivo. *Biografisch woordenboek van Nederland*, AH271
Schöffler, Herbert. *The new enlarged Schöffler-Weis German and English dictionary*, AC422
Schofield, Richard N. *A bibliography of the Iran-Iraq borderland*, DE35
Scholars, AH76
A scholars' guide to humanities and social sciences in the Soviet successor states, AL59, DC593
A scholars' guide to humanities and social sciences in the Soviet Union, AL59, DC593
Scholar's guide to intelligence literature, Georgetown University. Library, CJ538

Scholars' guide to Washington, D.C. : film and video collections, Rowan, Bonnie G., BH182
Scholars' guide to Washington, D.C. for cartography and remote sensing imagery, Ehrenberg, Ralph E., CL257
Scholars' guide to Washington, D.C. for Central and East European studies, Dillon, Kenneth J., DC14
Scholars' guide to Washington, D.C. for East Asian studies, Kim, Hong N., DE103
Scholars' guide to Washington, D.C. for Latin American and Caribbean studies, Grow, Michael, DB273
Scholars' guide to Washington, D.C. for Middle Eastern studies, Dorr, Steven R., DE49
Scholar's guide to Washington, D.C. for northwest European studies, Pitschmann, Louis A., DC16
Scholars' guide to Washington, D.C. for Russian, Central Eurasian, and Baltic studies, Grant, Steven A., DC556
Scholars' guide to Washington, D.C. for South Asian studies, Rahim, Enayetur, DE85
Scholars' guide to Washington, D.C. for Southeast Asian studies, Mayerchak, Patrick M., DE101, DE120
Scholars' guide to Washington, D.C. for southwest European studies, Higbee, Joan Florence, DC15
Scholarship book, Cassidy, Daniel J., CB374
Scholarships *see* Fellowships and scholarships
Scholarships, fellowships & grants for programs abroad, CB369
Scholarships, fellowships, and loans, CB392
Scholarships, fellowships, grants, and loans, CB258, CB393
Scholberg, Henry. *Bibliography of Goa and the Portuguese in India*, DE161
Scholderer, V. *Short-title catalogue of books printed in the Netherlands and Belgium and of Dutch and Flemish books printed in other countries from 1470 to 1600, now in the British Museum*, AA745
Scholefield, Guy Hardy. *A dictionary of New Zealand biography*, AH380
Scholes, Percy A. *Concise Oxford dictionary of music*, BJ138
—— *Oxford companion to music*, BJ142
Scholze, Werner. *The Oxford-Duden German dictionary*, AC419
Schomburg Center for Research in Black Culture. *Bibliographic guide to black studies*, CC380, CC381
—— *Freedom's lawmakers*, DB102
—— *The Kaiser index to black resources, 1948–1986*, CC383
Schomburg Collection of Negro Literature and History. *Dictionary catalog*, CC381
Schonbert, David. *Jewish law*, CK240
Schöne, Albrecht. *Emblemata*, BF168
School administration and supervision, CB180
School desegregation, CB32
School directory, CB96
School law, CB154, CB155, CB157
School management and organization
　abstract journals, CB179
　dictionaries, CB181
　encyclopedias, CB180
School of American Research. *An author, title, and subject check list of Smithsonian Institution publications relating to anthropology*, CE16
School prayer and other religious issues in American public education, Menendez, Albert J., CB39
School psychologists
　handbooks, CB212
School universe data book, CB96
Schools abroad of interest to Americans, CB92
SchoolTechNews, CB176
Schoonees, Pieter Cornelis. *Groot woordeboek*, AC198
Schor, Joel. *A list of references for the history of black Americans in agriculture, 1619–1974*, EJ73
Schorr, Alan Edward. *Hispanic resource directory*, CC463
—— *Refugee and immigrant resource directory*, CC34

Schorta, Andrea. *Disciunari rumantsch grischen,* AC664

Schotel, Gilles Dionysius Jacobus. *Biographisch woordenboek der Nederlanden,* AH269

Schotten, Shalom. *Archaeological atlas of the world,* DA89

Schottenloher, Karl. *Bibliographie zur deutschen Geschichte im Zeitalter der Glaubensspaltung 1517–1585,* DC226, DC227

Schöttgen, Christian. *Bibliotheca latina, mediae et infimae aetatis,* BE993

Schraeder, Peter J. *Cameroon,* DD18, DD138
——— *Djibouti,* DD18

Schrag, Calvin O. *Women philosophers,* BB48

Schramm, Hugo. *Moniteur des dates,* AH35

Schramm, Laurier Lincoln. *The language of colloid and interface science,* EE45

Schreiner, Rupert. *Ikonographie der christlichen Kunst,* BF186

Schrenk, Josef. *Handbibliographie zur neueren Linguistik in Osteuropa,* BD5

Schriften über Münzkunde, Leitzmann, Johan Jakob, BG173

Schriften zur Geschichte der Juden, Kisch, Guido, BC529
——— Roepke, Kurt, BC529

Schriftsteller der DDR, Albrecht, Günter, BE1061

Schriftstellerinnen und Schriftsteller der Gegenwart: Schweiz, Boulanger, Grégoire, BE1490

Schrifttum über das Posener Land 1961–1970, Rister, Herbert, DC476

Schrifttum über Polen mit besonderer Berücksichtigung des posener Landes, DC476

Schrifttum über Polen (ohne Posener Land), DC476

Schröder, Brigitte. *Bibliographie zur deutschen historischen Städteforschung,* BF274, DC266

Schroeder, Carol L. *Bibliography of Danish literature in translation, 1950–1980,* BE1112

Schroeder, Eileen E. *State education documents,* CB106

Schroeder, Susan. *Cuba,* CG171, DB428

Schröer, Helmut. *Handbuch der Geschichte der Philosophie,* BB49

Schrötter, Friedrich. *Wörterbuch der Münzkunde,* BG181

Schubert, Joachim. *Dictionary of effects and phenomena in physics,* ED23

Schuck, Henrik. *Illustrerad svensk litteraturhistoria,* BE1485

Schuder, Werner. *Kürschner Nekrolog, 1936–1970,* BE1059

Schuessler, Axel. *A dictionary of early Zhou Chinese,* AC268

Schuh, Dwight R. *Bowhunter's encyclopedia,* BK117

Schuh, Randall T. *The Torre-Bueno glossary of entomology,* EG338

Schuhmacher, Stephan. *The encyclopedia of Eastern philosophy and religion,* BB31, BC57

Schullian, Dorothy. *Catalogue of incunabula and manuscripts in the Army Medical Library,* EH24

Schult, Joachim. *The sailing dictionary,* BK123

Schulte, Janet E. *The female experience in eighteenth- and nineteenth-century America,* CC488

Schultz, Arthur R. *Bibliography of German culture in America to 1940,* CC329
——— *German-American relations and German culture in America,* CC330

Schultz, Barbara. *Picture research,* BF350

Schultz, John. *Picture research,* BF350

Schultz, Jon S. *Statutes compared,* CK181

Schultz, Leonard P. *Handbook of tropical aquarium fishes,* EG285

Schultz, Marilyn Spigel. *Encyclopedia of community planning and environmental management,* CC302

Schulz, Ann. *International and regional politics in the Middle East and North Africa,* CJ419

Schulz, Friedrich Ernst. *Dramenlexikon,* BE1261

Schulz, Hans. *Deutsches Fremdwörterbuch,* AC409

Schulz, Hedda. *From CA to CAS ONLINE,* EE6

Schulz, Heinrich E. *Party and government officials of the Soviet Union, 1917–1967,* CJ393
——— *Who was who in the USSR,* AH304

Schulz, René. *Dictionary of microprocessor systems,* EK193

Schulze, Suzanne. *Population information in nineteenth century census volumes,* CG98
——— *Population information in twentieth century census volumes, 1950–1980,* CG98

Schulze, Ursula. *Wörterbuch der mittelhochdeutschen Urkundensprache,* AC413

Schumacher, John N. *Philippine retrospective national bibliography, 1523–1699,* AA926

Schumann, Andreas. *Bibliographie der deutschsprachigen Lyrikanthologien, 1840–1914,* BE1272

Schuon, Karl. *U.S. Marine Corps biographical dictionary,* CJ642
——— *U.S. Navy biographical dictionary,* CJ642

Schuppe, Wolfgang. *Technical dictionary of data processing,* EK190

Schur, Norman W. *British English, A to Zed,* AC83
——— *British self-taught,* AC83
——— *English English,* AC83

Schuster, Marilyn R. *Selected bibliography for integrating research on women's experience in the liberal arts curriculum,* CC482

Schuster, Mel. *Motion picture directors,* BH291
——— *Motion picture performers,* BH291

Schutte, G. J. *A critical survey of studies on Dutch colonial history,* DC452

Schützeichel, Rudolf. *Deutsche Namenkunde,* AJ195

Schuursma, Ann Briegleb. *Ethnomusicology research,* BJ325

Schwab, Moïse. *Index of articles relative to Jewish history and literature published in periodicals, from 1665 to 1900,* BC545
——— *Répertoire des articles relatifs à l'histoire et à la littérature juives, parus dans les périodiques, de 1665 à 1900,* BC545

Schwabe, Ludwig. *History of Roman literature,* BE1053

Schwade, Arcadio. *Shintō-bibliography in western languages,* BC571

Schwalbe, J. *Virchow-Bibliographie, 1843–1901,* EH207

Schwamenthal, Riccardo. *Dizionario dei proverbi italiani,* BE161

Schwanbeck, Gisela. *Bibliographie der deutschsprachigen Hochschulschriften zur Theaterwissenschaft von 1885 bis 1952,* BE235

Schwändt, Ernst. *Index of microfilmed records of the German Foreign Ministry and the Reich's Chancellery covering the Weimar period, deposited at the National Archives,* DC252

Schwann opus, BJ385, BJ388

Schwann spectrum, BJ389

Schwartz, Elliott Shelling. *Electronic music,* BJ312

Schwartz, Laurens R. *The computer artist's handbook,* BF374

Schwartz, Lillian. *The computer artist's handbook,* BF374

Schwartz, Maurice L. *The encyclopedia of beaches and coastal environments,* EF4

Schwartz, Nancy B. *Historic American Buildings Survey/Historic American Engineering Record,* BF219

Schwartz, Narda Lacey. *Articles on women writers,* BE412

Schwartz, Philip. *Biographical directory of national librarians,* AK84

Schwartzberg, Joseph E. *A historical atlas of South Asia,* DE91

Schwarz, C. M. *Chambers English dictionary,* AC36

Schwarz, Hans. *Bibliographisches Handbuch zur Sprachinhaltsforschung,* BD22

Schwarz, Klaus. *Hochschulschriften zu Schwarz-Afrika,* DD30

Schwarz, Max. *MdR,* CJ333

Schwarz-Mackensen, Gesine. *Deutsches Wörterbuch,* AC439

Schwarzkopf, LeRoy C. *Government reference serials,* AF79, AF84
——— *Guide to popular U.S. government publications,* AF77

Schwarzlose, Richard Allen. *Newspapers, a reference guide,* AE29, AE146

Schweiger, Anneliese. *Bibliographie zur Geschichte der Städte Österreichs,* DC90

Schweikart, Larry E. *Banking and finance, 1913–1989,* CH265, CH383
——— *Banking and finance to 1913,* CH265, CH383

Schweitzer, Marjorie M. *Anthropology of aging,* CC59, CE3

Schweizer, J. *Dictionary of the Asante and Fante language, called Tshi (Twi),* AC794

Das schweizer Buch, AA649, AA835, AA838, AA839, AH301

Schweizer Bücherverzeichnis, AA835, AA838, AA839, AH301

Schweizer Buchhandel, Adressbuch, AA289

Schweizer Lexikon, AB100, DC530

Schweizer Lexikon 91, AB100, DC530

Schweizer Ortsnamen, Studer, Julius, CL214

Schweizer Zeitschriftenverzeichnis, AD162

Schweizerische Bibliographie für Statistik und Volkswirtschaft, CG287

Das schweizerische Buch, AA836

Schweizerische Bundesversamlung, 1920–1968, Gruner, Erich, CJ388

Die schweizerische Bundesversammlung, 1848–1920, Gruner, Erich, CJ388

Schweizerische Gesellschaft für Familienforschung. *Familiennamenbuch der Schweiz,* AJ142

Schweizerische Gesellschaft für Statistik und Volkswirtschaft. *Schweizerische Bibliographie für Statistik und Volkswirtschaft,* CG287

Schweizerische Landesbibliothek. *Bibliographie der Schweizergeschichte,* AH299, DC528
——— *Bibliographie der schweizerischen Amtsdruckschriften,* AF217
——— *Catalogue de la Bibliothèque Nationale Suisse á Berne,* AA837
——— *Katalog der Schweizerische Landesbibliothek Bern,* AA838, AH301
——— *Das schweizer Buch,* AA839
——— *Systematisches Verzeichnis,* AA835
——— *Verzeichnis der laufenden schweizerischen Zeitschriften = Catalogue des périodiques suisses, revues, journaux, annuaires, almanachs, collections, etc,* AD163

Schweizerische Nationalbibliographie, AD162

Schweizerischer Zeitschriften- und Zeitungskatalog, AD164

Schwennicke, Detlev. *Europäische Stammtafeln,* AJ77

Schwertner, Siegfried M. *IATG,* BC25
——— *Theologische Realenzyklopädie,* BC69

Schwerzel, Marleen. *Directory of social research organisations in the United Kingdom,* AL66, CA56

Schwiebert, John E. *Writing across the curriculum,* CB218

Schyns, Joseph. *1500 modern Chinese novels and plays,* BE1559

SCI JCR, EA136

Sciattara, Diane. *Serials for libraries,* AA374

Science
   abbreviations, EA96, EA97, EA98, EA99
   abstract journals, EA72, EF118
      bibliography, EA76
   audiovisual materials, EA25
   bibliography, CE14, EA13, EA14, EA16, EA19, EA20, EA22, EA34, EA53, EB10, EB16, EC15, ED5, ED7, EE13, EF57, EF141, EF173, EF232, EG6, EG105, EG211, EG312
      current, EA32, EA33, EA35, EA36
   biobibliography, EA181
   biography, EA175
      indexes, EA195, EA196
   book reviews, EA34, EA53
      indexes, EA54
   chronologies, EA249, EA252, EA254
   congresses and meetings, AL26, EA203, EA204, EA205, EA206, EA209
      indexes, EA202, EA207
   copy preparation, EA161
   databases, EA36, EA37, EA69, EA70, EA75

dictionaries, EA84, EA86, EA88, EA89, EA90, EA91, EA93
  bibliography, AC192, EA95
  bilingual
    English-Arabic, EA103, EA104
    French-English, EA107, EA108, EA110
    German-English, EA111, EA113
    Italian-English, EA117
    Japanese-English, EA120
    Polish-English, EA122
    Russian-English, EA124, EA130
    Spanish-English, EA133
  multilingual, EA87, EA100, EA101, EA129
directories, EA137, EA145
  bibliography, EA140, EH148
dissertations, EA55, EA56, EA57, EA58
encyclopedias, CA31, EA79, EA81, EA83
filmography, EA34
guides, EA1, EA2, EA3, EA4, EA5, EA6, EA7
handbooks, EA150, EA153
  bibliography, EA152
indexes, CE14, EA16, EA69, EA70, EA71, EA73, EA75, EB10, EC15, ED5, EE13, EF57, EF141, EF173, EF232, EG6, EG105, EG211, EG312
  bibliography, EA76
juvenile works
  bibliography, EA26, EA27, EA28, EA29, EA30, EA34
library catalogs, EA12, EA17
manuscripts
  catalogs, EA244
periodicals, EA19, EA38, EA39, EA40, EA42, EA43, EA44, EA136
  abbreviations, EA47
  bibliography, EA41, EE18
  early works to 1800, EA243
  indexes, EA22, EB16, ED7
  union lists, EA45
prizes and awards, EA197
reference books, EA10
research methods, EA8
reviews of research, EA138
  indexes, EA71
style manuals, EA38, EA157, EA158, EA161, EA221
tables, EA150, EA154, EA156
translations, AD25, EA59, EA60, EA61
  indexes, EA63
yearbooks, EA165, EA166, EA167, EA168, EA169
Science (by country or region)
  Canada
    biography, CA61, EA170
  Europe, EA218
    directories, EA142
  Great Britain
    directories, EA138
    library catalogs, EA23
  Hungary, DC389
  Japan
    bibliography, EA9
    facilities in the U.S., EA139
    periodicals, EA48, EA49, EA50
  United States
    bibliography, EA230
    biography, CA61, EA170
  U.S.S.R.
    periodicals, EA51, EA52
Science (by period)
  to 1800
    bibliography, BE31, EA21, EA227, EC17, ED6, EE15, EG98, EG213, EH68
    periodicals
      indexes, BE31, EA21, EC17, ED6, EE15, EG98, EG213, EH68
Science (by subject)
  history, EA218, EA245, EA251, EA255
    bibliography, EA229, EA232, EA233, EA234, EA235, EA239, EA240
      current, EA241, EA242
    biobibliography, EA181, EA247
    biography, EA171, EA178, EA184, EA188
      indexes, EA193

Canada
  bibliography, EA236
chronologies, EA253
databases, EA241, EA242
dictionaries, EA246
directories, EA248
encyclopedias, EA78, EA247
Great Britain, EA244
guides, EA224, EA248
library catalogs, EA225, EA235, EH54
manuscripts
  library catalogs, EA226
periodicals, EA42
treatises, EA256
United States, EA230
  bibliography, EA238
philosophy
  bibliography, EA11
  encyclopedias, EA78
science in non-Western cultures, EA24
social aspects, EA15
see also **Engineering; Technology**
Science & computer literacy audiovisuals, CB28
Science & technology in fact and fiction, Kennedy, DayAnn M., EA28
Science abstracts, ED9, ED11, EK128, EK162
Science across cultures, Selin, Helaine, EA24
Science and engineering literature, Malinowsky, H. Robert, EA4, EA5
——— Richardson, Jeanne M., EA4
Science and religion, BC215
Science and technology, Grogan, Denis Joseph, EA3
Science and technology annual reference review, EA53
Science and technology desk reference, EA153
Science and technology in Canadian history, Richardson, R. Alan, EA236
Science and technology in fact and fiction, EA28
Science books & films, EA25, EA34
Science books : a quarterly review, EA34
Science citation index, BA3, EA71, EA75, EA136, EA75
•*Science citation index compact disc edition with abstracts,* EA75
Science citation index journal citation reports, EA136
Science fair project index, 1960–1972, EA31
Science fiction, Hardy, Phil, BH224
Science fiction & fantasy book review annual, BE298
Science fiction and fantasy authors, Currey, L. W., BE285
Science fiction and fantasy book review index, BE290
Science fiction and fantasy book review index, 1980–1984, Hall, Halbert W., BE290
Science fiction and fantasy literature, Reginald, Robert, BE296
Science fiction and fantasy literature, 1975–1991, Reginald, Robert, BE296
Science fiction and fantasy reference index, 1878–1985, BE299
——— Hall, Halbert W., BE290
Science fiction and fantasy reference index, 1985–1991, Hall, Halbert W., BE299
Science fiction and fantasy research index, Hall, Halbert W., BE299
Science fiction and fantasy series and sequels, Cottrill, Tim, BE284
Science fiction book review index, BE290
——— Hall, Halbert W., BE290, BE299
Science fiction book review index, 1974–1979, Hall, Halbert W., BE290
Science fiction criticism, Clareson, Thomas D., BE301, BE310
Science fiction encyclopedia, Clute, John, BE286
——— Nicholls, Peter, BE286
Science fiction, fantasy & horror, BE283, BE300
Science fiction, fantasy, and Gothic literature
  bibliography, BE276, BE277, BE279, BE281, BE282, BE284, BE285, BE287, BE288, BE291, BE296, BE297, BE299, BE300, BE301, BE302, BE310, BE684
  biobibliography, BE295, BE296, BE306

  biography, BE303
  book reviews, BE290, BE298
  criticism, BE292, BE293, BE299, BE304, BE305, BE310
    bibliography, BE289
  dictionaries, BE309
  dissertations, BE281
  encyclopedias, BE286, BE308
  guides, BE276, BE277, BE281
  indexes, BE280, BE283, BE294
  periodicals, BE307
  see also **Horror fiction**
Science fiction, fantasy, and horror reference, Justice, Keith L., BE291
Science fiction, fantasy, and weird fiction magazines, Tymn, Marshall B., BE307
Science fiction in America, 1870s–1930s, BE301
Science fiction in print, BE300
Science fiction magazines, Hall, Halbert W., BE307
Science fiction reference guide, Tymn, Marshall B., BE278
Science-fiction, the early years, Bleiler, Everett Franklin, BE280
Science fiction writers, Bleiler, Everett Franklin, BE303
Science film catalog, EA25
La science historique bulgare, DC111
La science historique polonaise dans l'historiographie mondiale, DC472
Science [indexes], CD15
Science Management Corporation. *Digest of data on persons with disabilities,* CB206, CC198
Science museums, AL90, BF116, EA216, EA217
Science of religion, BC11, BC48
Science of religion bulletin, BC48
Science Reference Library (British Library). *Japanese journals in English,* EA50
Science tracer bullets, EA35
Science year, EA168
Sciences au Rwanda, Walraet, Marcel, AA871
Scientific and technical abbreviations, signs and symbols, Zimmerman, Oswald Theodore, EA99
Scientific and technical aerospace reports, EK27
——— United States. National Aeronautics and Space Administration, EK26, EK28
Scientific and technical books and serials in print, EA36
Scientific and technical information sources, Chen, Ching-chih, EA2
Scientific and technical organizations and agencies directory, EA200
Scientific and technical periodicals of the seventeenth and eighteenth centuries, Kronick, David A., EA243
Scientific and technical serial publications of the Soviet Union, 1945–1960, Library of Congress. Science and Technology Division, EA51
Scientific books, libraries and collectors, Thornton, John Leonard, EA240
Scientific DataLink index to artificial intelligence research, EK154
Scientific discoveries, EA252, EA254
Scientific expeditions, EA219
Scientific expeditions, Terek, Eugenie, EA219
Scientific illustration, EA220, EA221, EA222, EA223, EG58, EG73
  see also **Medical illustration**
Scientific libraries, EA144
Scientific Manpower Commission. *Professional women and minorities,* CH686
Scientific meetings, EA203
Scientific societies in the United States, Bates, Ralph Samuel, EA198
Scientific terminology, EA94
The scientific traveler, Tanford, Charles, EA218
Scientific units, A dictionary of, ED19
Scientists
  biography, EA171, EA172, EA173, EA174, EA175, EA176, EA179, EA183, EA187, EA190, ED57, EE106, EH217
    indexes, EA193, EA195, EA196
  databases, EA37
  directories, EA137

Scientists (by country or region)
  Canada
    biography, EA185
  Europe
    directories, EA191
  Great Britain
    biography, EA182, EA186, EA189
  Russia and the U.S.S.R.
    biography, EA178
  United States
    biography, EA177, EA184, EA185, EA188
    indexes, EA192
Ščipák, Josef. *Atlas ČSSR*, CL323
•*SCIPIO*, BF113
•*SCISEARCH*, EA75
•*SciTech reference plus*, CA61, CH349, EA36, EA37, EA170, EA213
Sclater, Neil. *Encyclopedia of electronics*, EK129
The SCOLMA directory of libraries and special collections on Africa in the United Kingdom and Western Europe, DD41
Scoor-oot, Stevenson, James A. C., AC167
Scotland
  atlases, DC367
  bibliography, AA695, AA697, DC357, DC360, DC361
    current, AA696
  biography, AH242, AH243, AH244
  encyclopedias, DC363, DC364
  gazetteers, CL140, CL141
  genealogy, AH242
  government publications, DC359
  guides to records, DC358
  newspapers, AE62
  periodicals, AD119
    bibliography, AD105
Scotland (by subject)
  history, AJ123, DC359, DC362, DC365, DC366
    atlases, DC367
    bibliography, DC361
  place-names, CL203, CL204, CL205
  politics and government, CJ375
    directories, CJ354
  religion, BC341, BC342
Scotland. General Registry Office of Births, Deaths and Marriages. *Guide to the public records of Scotland deposited in H. M. General Register House, Edinburgh*, DC358
Scotland, Bold, Alan Norman, BE809
  —— Grant, Eric G., DC357
Scotland in literature, BE809
Scotland in the nineteenth century, Haythornthwaite, J. A., DC359
Scots (by country or region)
  United States
    registers, AJ62, AJ69
Scots heraldry, Innes, Thomas, AJ157
Scott, David H. *Mene, Mene, Tekel*, BC155
Scott, David Logan. *Wall Street words*, CH227
Scott, Gillian. *Complete annotated catalogue PMB manuscript series microfilms PMB 1–1030*, DF14
Scott, Gregory E. J. *Almanac of modern terrorism*, CJ555
Scott, Hew. *Fasti ecclesiae Scoticanae*, BC342
Scott, Ian. *Hong Kong*, DE152
Scott, Jeannine B. *Afro-American demography and urban issues*, CC373
Scott, Kathleen. *The travellers, Canada to 1900*, DB189
Scott, Mark W. *Shakespearean criticism*, BE769
Scott, Mary Augusta. *Elizabethan translations from the Italian*, BE1297
Scott, Mona L. *Conversion tables*, AK204
Scott, Pamela. *Buildings of the District of Columbia*, BF254
Scott, Randall W. *Comic books and strips*, CF72
Scott, Robert. *A Greek-English lexicon*, AC444, AC445, AC450, AC457
Scott, Ronald Bodley. *The Oxford companion to medicine*, EH88
Scott, Samuel F. *Historical dictionary of the French Revolution, 1789–1799*, DC185

Scott, Thomas. *Concise encyclopedia biochemistry*, EG315
  —— *Concise encyclopedia of biochemistry*, EG316
Scott, Foresman advanced dictionary, AC23, AC507
Scott, Foresman beginning dictionary, AC24
Scott, Foresman handbook for writers, Hairston, Maxine, BD96
  —— Ruszkiewicz, John, BD96
Scott, Foresman intermediate dictionary, AC25
The Scott, Foresman Robert's rules of order newly revised, Robert, Henry Martyn, CJ457
Scott-Kilvert, Ian. *British writers*, BE201, BE622
Scott Polar Research Institute. *Polar record*, DG9
Scott standard postage stamp catalogue, BG206
Scottish biographical dictionary, AH243
Scottish Episcopal Church, BC334
Scottish family histories, Ferguson, Joan P. S., AJ121
Scottish Gaelic union catalogue, Ferguson, Mary, AA697
Scottish historical clubs, 1908–1927, DC362
Scottish History Society. *A contribution to the bibliography of Scottish topography*, DC360
Scottish language
  dictionaries, AC164, AC165
Scottish literary journal, BE808
Scottish literature, BE809, BE811
  bibliography, BE808
  poetry, BE810
Scottish literature in English and Scots, Aitken, William Russell, BE808
Scottish local history, Moody, David, AJ123
The Scottish nation, Anderson, William, AH242
Scottish national dictionary, AC30, AC163, AC166
Scottish nationalism and cultural identity in the twentieth century, Bryan, Gordon, CJ375
Scottish place-names, Mackenzie, William Cook, CL204
  —— Nicolaisen, Wilhelm Fritz Hermann, CL205
Scottish texts and calendars, Stevenson, David, DC361
Scottish Working Group on Official Publications. *Directory of official publications in Scotland*, AF12
Screen, J. E. O. *Finland*, DC140
  —— *A guide to foreign language courses and dictionaries*, AC195
Screen achievement records bulletin, BH203
Screen international, BH267
Screen world, BH268
Screenwriters
  biography, BH280
  filmography, BH207, BH210
Scripta mathematica, EB11
Scriptorium, AA200
Scripture index to The new international dictionary of New Testament theology, Townsley, David, BC148
Scrittori e idee : dizionario critico della letteratura italiana, Fusco, Enrico M., BE1302
Scrivener, David. *Bibliography of arms control verification*, CJ679
Scruton, Roger. *A dictionary of political thought*, CJ32
Scullard, H. H. *Oxford classical dictionary*, DA103
Scullard, Howard Hayes. *Atlas of the classical world*, DA120
  —— *Shorter atlas of the classical world*, DA120
Sculptors
  biography, BF396
Sculpture
  biography, BF389, BF394, BF395, BF397, BF398, BF399, BF400
  catalogs, BF391, BF399
  dictionaries, BF389
  guides, BF387
  history, BF392, BF393
  indexes, BF388
Sculpture, Keutner, Herbert, BF393
Sculpture, 19th & 20th centuries, Licht, Fred, BF393
Sculpture index, Clapp, Jane, BF367, BF388
SDI, CJ620
Sea battles, Sanderson, Michael W. B., DA21

Seaby, Herbert Allen. *English silver coinage from 1649*, BG190
Seager, Joni. *Women in the world*, CC582
Seagraves, Eleanor R. *The natural environment*, EK64
  —— *A search for environmental ethics*, EK65
Seal, Graham. *The Oxford companion to Australian folklore*, CF99
Seal, Robert A. *Bibliography of astronomy, 1970–1979*, EC2, EC18
  —— *A guide to the literature of astronomy*, EC4
Sealock, Margaret M. *Bibliography of place-name literature*, CL177
Sealock, Richard B. *Bibliography of place-name literature*, CL177
Seals of Chinese painters and collectors of the Ming and Ch'ing periods, Contag, Victoria, BF313
  —— Wang, Chi-chien, BF162, BF313
Seaman, Donald. *Encyclopedia of modern murder*, CK254
Seaman, Gary. *Chinese religion*, BC37
Search, BF209
A search for environmental ethics, Anglemyer, Mary, EK65
Search for security, CJ50
  —— Allen, Anne, AL121
Search for the Northwest Passage, Day, Alan Edwin, DB181
Searching America : history and life, Falk, Joyce Duncan, DB24
  —— Kinnell, Susan K., DB24
Searching for your ancestors, Doane, Gilbert Harry, AJ7
Searching the law, the states, Doyle, Francis R., CK121
Searfoss, D. Gerald. *Handbook of accounting and auditing*, CH260
Searing, Susan E. *The history of women and science, health, and technology*, EA231
  —— *Introduction to library research in women's studies*, CC483
  —— *Women, race, and ethnicity*, CC625
  —— *Women's studies*, CC501
Sears, Jean L. *Using government information sources*, AF62
  —— *Using government publications*, AF62
Sears, Mary. *Oceanographic index*, EF210, EF211, EF212
Sears, Minnie Earl. *Essay and general literature index*, AH12, BA4, BE37
  —— *Sears list of subject headings*, AK222
  —— *Song index*, BJ283, BJ284, BJ287, BJ289
Sears list of subject headings, Sears, Minnie Earl, AK222
Seaton, Douglass. *The art song*, BJ273
Sebba, Gregor. *Bibliographia Cartesiana*, BB72, BB76
  —— *Descartes and his philosophy*, BB76
Sebeok, Thomas Albert. *Current trends in linguistics*, BD137, BD238
  —— *Encyclopedic dictionary of semiotics*, BD52
  —— *Native languages of the Americas*, BD238
  —— *Portraits of linguists*, BD70
Sebert, L. M. *The maps of Canada*, CL309
Secchia, Pietro. *Enciclopedia dell'antifascismo e della Resistenza ...*, DC432
Seccombe, Ian J. *Jordan*, DE212
  —— *Syria*, DE262
Seccombe, Matthew. *British newspapers and periodicals, 1641–1700*, AA412, AA683, AD107
Seche, Luiza. *Dicţionarul explicativ al limbii române*, AC659
Seche, Mircea. *Dicţionarul explicativ al limbii române*, AC659
Seckinger, Ron L. *Guide to selected diplomatic archives of South America*, AK130, DB278
Second abstract of British historical statistics, Jones, H. G., CG234, CG235
  —— Mitchell, Brian R., CG234, CG235
Second Barnhart dictionary of new English, AC95
Second bibliography and catalogue of fossil vertebrata of North America, Hay, Oliver Perry, EF230

Second handbook of research on teaching, CB117

Second language instruction/acquisition abstracts, CB62

Second steps in sociology, Fredericks, Marcel A., CC24

The Second World War, Cantwell, John D., DA204, DC286

—— Funk, Arthur Layton, DA201

Second World War and the atomic age, 1940–1973, Cronon, Edmund David, DA170

—— Rosenof, Theodore, DA170

Il secondo dopoguerra in Italia, 1945–1960, D'Andrea, Anna, DC421

Secret societies, AL73, AL74, AL75, AL78, CB398

encyclopedias, AL76

Secret societies (by country or region)

Canada, AL36

United States, AL36

encyclopedias, AL77

The secret societies of all ages and countries … , Heckethorn, Charles William, AL74

The secret wars, Smith, Myron J., CJ546

The secretary's handbook, Taintor, Sarah Augusta, CH90

Secretary's handbooks *see* **Office practice**

Secular music in America, 1801–1825, Wolfe, Richard J., BJ66

Securities

dictionaries, CH303

ratings, CH321

statistics, CH310

Security, arms control, and conflict reduction in East Asia and the Pacific, McClean, Andrew, CJ674

Security dealers of North America, CH231

Sedge, Douglas. *Annotated critical bibliography of Jacobean and Caroline comedy*, BE646

Sedgwick, Romney. *House of Commons, 1715–1754*, CJ354, CJ360

Sédillot, René. *All the monies of the world*, BG182, CH286

—— *Toutes les monnaies du monde*, CH286

Sedimentology, EF64

abstract journals, EF178

bibliography, EF126, EF127

Sedlak, Michael W. *American educational history*, CD33

Seebold, Elmar. *Etymologisches Wörterbuch der deutschen Sprache*, AC428

—— *Register und Auswertung zur 22. Auflage des etymologischen Wörterbuch von Friedrich Kluge*, AC428

Seed identification manual, Martin, Alexander Campbell, EG154

Seeds of peace, Larson, Jeanne, CJ689

Seekings, Jeremy. *South Africa's townships 1980–1991*, DD222

Seeley, Charlotte Palmer. *American women and the U.S. armed forces*, CJ612

Seeley, Robert A. *The handbook of non-violence*, CJ685

Seely, Bruce E. *Iron and steel industry in the 20th century*, CH383

Seely, P. A. *Bibliography of place-name literature*, CL177

Séenz de la Calzada, Carlos. *Diccionario biográfico de Venezuela*, AH146

Seewann, Gerhard. *Bestandskatalog der Bibliothek des Südost-Instituts München*, DC65

Sefamí, Jacobo. *Contemporary Spanish American poets*, BE904

Ha-Sefarim ha-ivriyim she-nidpesu bi-Yerushalayim … 1841–1891, Halevy, Shoshana Dyamont, AA909

Sefrin, Pirmin. *Hierarchia catholica medii aevi*, BC430

Segadas Machado-Guimarães, Argeu de. *Diccionario bio-bibliographico brasileiro*, AH126

Segal, Aaron. *An atlas of international migration*, CC359

Segal, Morley. *Bridges to knowledge in political science*, CJ3

—— *Research guide for undergraduates in political science*, CJ3

—— *Research guide in political science*, CJ3

Segal, Morris Hirsch. *Milon ha-lashon ha-ivrit*, AC470

Segal, Ronald. *The new state of the world atlas*, CL280

—— *Political Africa*, AH316, CJ409

Segen, J. C. *The dictionary of modern medicine*, EH103

Segrais, René le Juge de. *Vocabulaire-atlas héraldique en six langues*, AJ165

Segrave, Kerry. *Women serial and mass murderers*, CC567

I segreti dell'inglese, Hofmann Cortesi, Livio, AC530

Séguineau, R. *Dictionary of proper names and places in the Bible*, BC149

Segundo catalog de tesis sobre historia de México, Greaves, Cecilia, DB237

Sehimi, Mustapha. *La grande encyclopédie du Maroc*, DD181

Sehlinger, Peter J. *A select guide to Chilean libraries and archives*, DB361

Seidel, Alison P. *Literary criticism and authors' biographies*, BE206

Seidell, Atherton. *Solubilities of inorganic and organic substances*, EE81

Seidelmann, P. Kenneth. *Explanatory supplement to the Astronomical almanac*, EC79

Seidenspinner, Gundolf. *Museums in Africa*, AL87

Seidman, Joel Isaac. *Communism in the United States*, CJ507

Seidman, Paula. *ERIC directory of education-related information centers*, CB99

Seigneuret, Jean-Charles. *Dictionary of literary themes and motifs*, BE183

Seiichi, Iwao. *Dictionnaire historique du Japon*, DE208

Seismicity of the United States, 1568–1989 (revised), Stover, Carl W., EF262

Seismology, EF261

see also **Earthquakes**

Sekai dai-hyakka jiten, AB70

Selbie, John A. *Encyclopaedia of religion and ethics*, BC55

Selden, Raman. *A reader's guide to contemporary literary theory*, BE53

Seldin, Maury. *The real estate handbook*, CH543

A select bibliography of chemistry, 1492–1892, Bolton, Henry Carrington, EE10, EE11

A select bibliography of Danish works on the history of towns published 1960–1976, Jansen, Henrik M., DC132

Select bibliography of error analysis and interlanguage studies, Palmberg, R., BD80

Select bibliography of medical biography, Thornton, John Leonard, EH219, EH227

Select bibliography of South African history, Musiker, Reuben, DD223

Select bibliography of the French Second Empire, DC199

Select bibliography of works in English on Russian history, 1801–1917, Shapiro, David, DC575

Select bibliography on international organization, AF21

Select biographical sources, Hepworth, Philip, AH235

A select guide to Chilean libraries and archives, Sehlinger, Peter J., DB361

Select library of Nicene and post-Nicene Fathers of the Christian church, BC294

Select list of British parliamentary papers, 1833–1899, Ford, Percy, AF196

Select list of British parliamentary papers, 1955–1964, Ford, Percy, AF196

—— Marshallsay, Diana, AF196

A select list of reports of inquiries of the Irish Dáil and Senate, 1922–72, Ford, Percy, CJ376

Select numismatic bibliography, Clain-Stefanelli, Elvira Eliza, BG170

A selected and annotated bibliography of economic literature on the Arabic speaking countries of the Middle East, CH193

Selected bibliographies of hydrothermal and magmatic mineral deposits, Ridge, John Drew, EF175

Selected bibliography for integrating research on women's experience in the liberal arts curriculum, Schuster, Marilyn R., CC482

Selected bibliography of books on the Second World War … , Funk, Arthur L., DA201

Selected bibliography of German literature in English translation, 1956–1960, Smith, Murray F., BE1239

A selected bibliography of modern historiography, Pók, Attila, DA44

A selected bibliography of North American forestry, Munns, Edward Norfolk, EJ173

A selected bibliography of Slavic linguistics, Stankiewicz, Edward, BD184

Selected bibliography of the anthropology and ethnology of Europe, Ripley, William Zebina, CE95

Selected bibliography of the Dominican Republic, Hitt, Deborah S., DB434

—— Wilson, Larman C., DB434

Selected bibliography of the Federation of Rhodesia and Nyasaland, Ng'ombe, Roger M. Stephen, DD176, DD248

—— Rhodes-Livingstone Institute, DD119, DD176, DD248

A selected bibliography on Native American astronomy, Collea, Beth A., EC7

Selected black American, African, and Caribbean authors, Page, James A., BE544

A selected discography of solo song, Stahl, Dorothy, BJ281

Selected highlights of crime and delinquency literature, CK248

Selected musical terms of non-Western cultures, Kaufmann, Walter, BJ318

Selected Rand abstracts, Rand Corporation, CA26

Selected statistical series, 1951–1990, CG361

Selected tables in mathematical statistics, EB95

Selected translations in mathematical statistics and probability, EB20

Selected values of chemical thermodynamic properties, EE94

Selected water resources abstracts, EF129, EK68, EF131

Selected weeds of the United States, United States. Agricultural Research Service, EG181

Selecting and appraising archives and manuscripts, Ham, F. Gerald, AK188

Selecting and organizing state government publications, Lane, Margaret T., AF138

Sélection du Reader's Digest. S.A.R.L. Grand atlas de la France, CL329

A selective bibliography on the conservation of research library materials, Banks, Paul Noble, AK237

A selective guide to Chinese literature, 1900–1949, BE1560

Selective guide to climatic data sources, Hatch, Warren L., EF162

Selective guide to colleges, CB270

Selective guide to published climatic data sources, EF162

Selective inventory of information services, CA49

Selective inventory of social science information and documentation services, CA49

Selesnick, Sheldon T. *The history of psychiatry*, EH396

Self, James. *Japanese art signatures*, BF144, BF161

Self, Phyllis C. *Physical disability*, CC186

Seligman, Edwin Robert Anderson. *Encyclopaedia of the social sciences*, CA33

Seligman, Janet. *Iconography of Christian art*, BF186

Selim, George Dimitri. *Arab-world newspapers in the Library of Congress*, AE85

—— *Arabic-English and English-Arabic dictionaries in the Library of Congress*, AC220

Selin, Helaine. *Science across cultures*, EA24

Sell, Violet. *Subject index to poetry for children and young people*, BE322

Sellen, Betty-Carol. *20th century American folk, self-taught, and outsider art,* BG27
—— *Feminists, pornography & the law,* CC276
Sellers, John R. *Civil War manuscripts,* DB115
—— *Manuscript sources in the Library of Congress for research on the American Revolution,* DB91
—— *Maps and charts of North America and the West Indies, 1750–1789,* CL233
Seller's guide to government purchasing, CH590
Sellier, André. *Atlas des peuples d'Europe centrale,* DC57
Selnow, Gary W. *Regional interest magazines of the United States,* AD43
Selth, Jefferson P. *Alternative lifestyles,* CC2
Seltsam, William. *Metropolitan opera annals,* BJ254
Seltz-Petrash, Ann. *AAAS science film catalog,* EA25
Seltzer, Leon E. *Columbia Lippincott gazetteer of the world,* CL85
Selvaggio, Marc S. *American guide series,* CL387
Selvon, Sydney. *Mauritius,* DD48
Semantics
  bibliography, BD22, BD51
Semantics, Gordon, W. Terrence, BD51
Semendîaev, K. A. *Handbook of mathematics,* EB62
Semenovker, B. A. *Retrospektivnaîa gosudarstvennaîa bibliografîîa SSSR,* AA786
Le semestriel des arts, BF109
Seminar on the Acquisition of Latin American Library Materials. *Annual report on Latin American and Caribbean bibliographic activities,* AA24
—— *Cuban exile periodicals at the University of Miami Library,* AD47, CC458
—— *SALALM bibliography,* AA536
Seminars directory, CH716
Semiotics
  bibliography, BD53
  dictionaries, BD38, BD52
  handbooks, BD54
Semiotics and language, Courtés J., BD52
—— Greimas, Algirdas Julien, BD52
Semiotik-Bibliographie I, Eschbach, Achim, BD53
Semitic languages, BD203
Semper ex Africa, Hess, Robert L., DD84
Sen, Siba Pada. *Dictionary of national biography,* AH350, AH351
Sen, Sukumar. *An etymological dictionary of Bengali, c.1000–1800 A.D,* AC233
Senalp. Leman. *Atatürk kaynakçasi,* DC533
Senarai penerbitan-penerbitan lengkap, Malaysia. Jabatan Cetak Kerajaan (Sabah), AF253
Senate executive documents and reports, AF117
Senate manual, CJ227
—— United States. Congress. Senate, CJ228
Senate procedure, CJ227
Sendrey, Alfred. *Bibliography of Jewish music,* BJ19
Senecal, Michael D. *Almanac of American presidents,* CJ184
Senegal, AD176, DD104
  atlases, CL339
  bibliography, DD201, DD202
    current, AA872
  biography, DD200
  current surveys, DD62
  encyclopedias, DD48
  government publications
    bibliography, AF230
  statistics, CG353
Senegal (by subject)
  economic conditions
    statistics, CG353
Sénégal. Direction de la Statistique. *Situation économique du Sénégal,* CG353
Senegal, Colvin, L. G., DD48
—— Hue, Pascal, DD201
Le Sénégal en chiffre, CG353
Senegalese literature, BE1532
Senegalese literature, Blair, Dorothy S., BE1532
Senekal, Jan. *Bronne by die studie van Afrikaanse prosawerke,* BE1536
Sengo Nihon joryū sakka no rireki, BE1595
Sengo Nihon no kokusai seijigaku, DE201

Senior citizen services, CC90
Senior citizens information sources, CC96
Senior high school library catalog, AA344
The senior movement, Wallace, Steven P., CC102
Senn, Alfred. *Wörterbuch der litauischen Schriftsprache, litauisch-deutsch,* AC602
Sennett, Robert S. *The nineteenth-century photographic press,* BF335
—— *Photography and photographers to 1900,* BF335
Sentman, Catherine. *The music lover's guide to Europe,* BJ193
Sentner, Janet P. *Feminism and women's issues,* CC514
Sequels, Hicken, Marilyn E., BE246, BE255
—— Husband, Janet, BE255
Sequences, Roman, Susan, BE246
Serban, William. *Stained glass,* BG51
Serbia
  bibliography, AA797
  periodicals, AD167
The Serbian bibliography, AA797
Serbo-Croatian language
  abbreviations, AC715
  bibliography, BD189, BD190, BD191
  dictionaries, AC709
    bilingual, AC714
      Serbo-Croatian-English, AC710, AC711, AC712, AC713
SerboCroatian-English dictionary, Benson, Morton, AC710
—— Šljivić-Šimšić, Biljana, AC710
Serbs in the United States and Canada, Gakovich, Robert P., CC321, CC473
Sereville, Etienne de. *Dictionnaire de la noblesse française,* AJ88
Serial bibliographies and abstracts in history, Henige, David P., DA13
Serial bibliographies for medieval studies, Rouse, Richard H., DA137
Serial publications in anthropology, CE25
Serial publications in the British Museum (Natural History) Library, British Museum (Natural History). Library, EA40
Serial publications in the British parliamentary papers, 1900–1968, Rodgers, Frank, AF207
Serial publications of the Soviet Union, 1939–1957, Library of Congress. Cyrillic Bibliographic Project, AD147
Serial set index, AF87
Serial sources for the BIOSIS data base, EG18
Serialized fiction, BE690
Serials currently received by the National Agricultural Library, 1975, National Agricultural Library (U.S.), EJ12
The serials directory, AD15
•*Serials directory [database],* AD15
Serials directory update, AD15
Serials for libraries, Ganly, John, AA374
Serials guide to ethnoart, BG12
—— Burt, Eugene C., BG13
Serials holdings in the Linda Hall Library [as of April 30] 1989, Linda Hall Library, EA44
Serials in print in Nigeria, AD174
Serials in the British Library, AD116, AD237
The serials librarian, AD200
Serials review, AA378
Serie archivos estatales y municipales de México, DB238
Serie estadística, Instituto Nacional de Estadística y Censos (Ecuador), CG155
Serie guías, Universidad Nacional Autónoma de México. Instituto de Investigaciones Bibliográficas, DB241
Series (mathematics), EB87, EB91
  tables, EB85
Series episcoporum ecclesiae catholicae, Engels, Odilo, BC430
—— Fachgelehrten, Stefan, BC430
Serís, Homero. *Bibliografía de la lingüística española,* BD169, BE1438
—— *Manual de bibliografía de la literatura española,* BE1438

—— *Manuel de bibliografía de la literatura española,* BD169
Serkin, Stuart D. *The new members of congress almanac,* CJ220
Serkkola, Ari. *Rural development in Tanzania,* DD236
Serle, Geoffrey. *Australian dictionary of biography,* AH371, DF40
•*SERLINE,* EH37
Serow, William J. *Handbook on international migration,* CC350
Serrano y Sanz, Manuel. *Apuntes para una biblioteca de escritoras españolas,* BE1441
Service book of the Holy Orthodox-Catholic Apostolic church, Orthodox Eastern Church, BC450
Service companies, CH356
Service etiquette, Swartz, Oretha D., AL157
Service industries, CH356, CH416
Service industries USA, CH416
Les services bibliographiques dans le monde, AA16
Services for blind and visually impaired persons in the United States and Canada, CC191
Servicio bibliográfico chileno, Zamorano y Caperan, AA512
Servotte, Jozef V. *Dictionnaire commercial et financier,* CH129
Šešplaukis, Alfonsas. *Lituanica collections in European research libraries,* DC445
Set designers, BH208
Seth, Ronald. *Encyclopedia of espionage,* CJ540
Sethī, Ātmarāma. *Indian library directory,* AK158
Setterwall, Kristian. *Svensk historisk bibliografi 1771–1874,* DC521
Seudónimos colombianos, Pérez Ortiz, Rubén, AA158
Seudónimos dominicanos, Rodriguez Demorizi, Emilio, AA159
Seuphor, Michel. *Dictionary of abstract painting,* BF300
Ševčenko, Ihor. *Literature in various Byzantine disciplines, 1892–1977,* DA163
Seven hundred years of oriental carpets, Erdmann, Kurt, BG166
Seven-language thesaurus of European animals, Gozmany, László, EG225
Seventeenth-century American poetry, Scheick, William J., BE497
Seventh Day Adventist Medical Center. *Cumulative index to nursing & allied health literature,* EH274
Sex and age distributions of population, CG65
Sex and gender issues, Beere, Carole A., CC557
Sex and sexual behavior, CC142, CC168, CC275, CC281
  bibliography, CC185, CC248, CC269, CC557
  dictionaries, CC279, CC280, CC282, CC283, CC284
  encyclopedia, CC278
  handbooks, CC289
  tests and measurements, CC292
Sex and sexual behavior (by subject)
  aging, CC77
Sex differences and learning, Grambs, Jean Dresden, CB7
Sex differences in education, CB7
Sex role stereotyping in the mass media, Friedman, Leslie, CC270
Sex roles, CC267, CC270
  terminology, CC540
Sexism, CC560
Sexism in language, CC540
  bibliography, BD82
Sexsmith, Ann. *The left in Britain,* CJ509
—— *The underground and alternative press in Britain,* AD112
Sexual abuse, CC167, CC211
Sexual assault and child sexual abuse, Webster, Linda, CC36
Sexual harassment, Eisaguirre, Lynne, CC561
Sexual harassment in the workplace, Aaron, Titus E., CC555
Sexuality and aging, Wharton, George F., CC77
Sexuality-related measures, CC292

Sexwale, Bunie. *Women in Lesotho,* DD122, DD171
Seychelles
   bibliography, DD18, DD121, DD203
   government publications
      bibliography, AF222
Seychelles, Bennett, George, DD18
────── Franda, Marcus F., DD203
Seydel, Dietrich. *Informationshandbuch internationale Beziehungen und Länderkunde,* DA173
Seydoux, Marianne. *Répertoire des thèses concernant les études slaves,* DC555
Seyfert, Carl K. *The encyclopedia of structural geology and plate tectonics,* EF66
Seymore, Bruce. *International affairs directory of organizations,* CJ690
Seymour, E. L. D. *The Wise garden encyclopedia,* EJ235
Seymour, Nancy N. *An index-dictionary of Chinese artists, collectors, and connoisseurs with character identification by modified stroke count,* BF146
Seymour, Richard K. *A bibliography of word formations in the Germanic languages,* BD115
Seymour-Smith, Charlotte. *Dictionary of anthropology,* CE48
Seymour-Smith, Martin. *Dictionary of fictional characters,* BE188, BE189
Seyn, Eugène de. *Dictionnaire biographique des sciences, des lettres et des arts en Belgique,* AH176
────── *Dictionnaire des attributs, allégories, emblèmes et symboles,* BF173
────── *Dictionnaire des écrivains belges,* AH176
────── *Dictionnaire des écrivains belges, bio-bibliographie,* BE1102
────── *Dictionnaire historique et géographique des communes belges,* CL130
Sezgin, Fuat. *Geschichte des arabischen Schrifttums,* BE1549
SFBRI, BE290
SFFBRI, BE290
Sgard, Jean. *Bibliographie de la presse classique, 1600–1789,* AD79
Shaaber, Matthias Adam. *Check-list of works of British authors printed abroad in languages other than English, to 1641,* AA673
Shabat, M. TS. *Obshchee i prikladnoe iazykoznaniye,* BD7
Shackelford, Jean A. *Urban and regional economics,* CH21
Shackelford & Associates Systems Design. *Biographical directory,* AK81
Shadily, Hassan. *English-Indonesian dictionary,* AC517
────── *An Indonesian-English dictionary,* AC517
Shafer, Neil. *Standard catalog of world paper money,* BG189
Shafritz, Jay M. *Almanac of modern terrorism,* CJ555
────── *The dictionary of 20th-century world politics,* CJ33
────── *Dorsey dictionary of American government and politics,* CJ122
────── *The Facts on File dictionary of education,* CB80
────── *The Facts on File dictionary of military science,* CJ589
────── *The Facts on File dictionary of nonprofit organization management,* AL10, CH615
────── *The Facts on File dictionary of personnel management and labor relations,* CH711
────── *The Facts on File dictionary of public administration,* CJ478
────── *The HarperCollins dictionary of American government and politics,* CJ122, CJ205
────── *Words on war,* CJ591
Shafritz, Todd J. A. *The Facts on File dictionary of military science,* CJ589
Shain, Michael. *Van Nostrand Reinhold dictionary of information technology,* EK183
Shaker literature, Richmond, Mary L. Hurt, BC382
Shakers, BC381, BC382

library catalogs, BG16
Shakespeare, William, BE796
   bibliography, BE766, BE767, BE768, BE780, BE795
   characters, BE788, BE789
   concordances, BE776, BE777, BE778
   criticism
      collections, BE769
   dictionaries, AC99, BE772, BE773, BE789
   editions, BE765
   encyclopedias, BE785
   film and video adaptations, BE791
   handbooks, BE783, BE784
   influence, BE785
   library catalogs, BE737, BE770, BE771
   musical settings, BE790
   periodicals, BE779, BE780, BE781, BE782
   place-names, BE794
   promptbooks, BE793
   quotations, BE774, BE775
   reviews of research, BE768, BE782
   sources, BE786, BE787
   stage history, BE792
Shakespeare, BE768
Shakespeare A to Z, Boyce, Charles, BE783
Shakespeare and the classical tradition, Velz, John W., BE795
Shakespeare and the musical stage, Hotaling, Edward R., BE790
Shakespeare around the globe, BE792
Shakespeare Association of America. *Shakespeare quarterly,* BE780
A Shakespeare bibliography, Birmingham Shakespeare Library, BE770
Shakespeare companion, Halliday, Ernest, BE783
A Shakespeare glossary, Onions, C. T., BE772, BE773
Shakespeare in production, 1935–1978, Babula, William, BE792
Shakespeare Jahrbuch, BE779
Shakespeare-lexicon, Schmidt, Alexander, BE773
A Shakespeare music catalogue, Gooch, Bryan N. S., BJ71
Shakespeare on screen, Rothwell, Kenneth Sprague, BE791
The Shakespeare promptbooks, Shattuck, Charles Harlen, BE793
Shakespeare quarterly, BE780
Shakespeare studies, BE781
Shakespeare survey, BE782
Shakespearean criticism, BE769
Shakespearean criticism yearbook, BE769
Shakespeare's bawdy, Partridge, Eric, BE772
Shale, M. *Situation of women in Lesotho,* DD122, DD171
Shale, Richard. *Academy awards,* BH275
────── *The Academy Awards index,* BH275
The Shambhala dictionary of Buddhism and Zen, BC479
Shamos, Michael Ian. *The illustrated encyclopedia of billiards,* BK68
Shamurina, E. I. *Teoriia i praktika bibliografii,* AA7
Shandanova, Liliana. *Gürtsiia i bŭlgaro-grŭtskite otnosheniia v bŭlgarskata nauchna knizhnina, 1878–1980,* DC110
Shanker, S. G. *A Wittgenstein bibliography,* BB83
Shanker, V. A. *A Wittgenstein bibliography,* BB83
Shankle, George Earlie. *American nicknames,* BE190
────── *State names, flags, seals, songs, birds, flowers and other symbols,* AL191
Shankman, Arnold M. *American Indian archival material,* CC427
Shanks, Thomas G. *The American atlas,* CL66
────── *The international atlas,* CL65
Shannon, Edgar Finley. *An atlas of English literature,* BE627
Shannon, James P. *The corporate contributions handbook,* AL134
Shannon, Michael Owen. *Irish Republic,* DC398
────── *Modern Ireland,* DC355, DC398
────── *Northern Ireland,* DC355
────── *Oman and southeastern Arabia,* DE238
Shapiro, Cecile. *Fine prints,* BF375

Shapiro, David. *Select bibliography of works in English on Russian history, 1801–1917,* DC575
Shapiro, Elliott. *Handbook of early American sheet music, 1768–1889,* BJ56
Shapiro, Fred R. *The Oxford dictionary of American legal quotations,* CK57
Shapiro, James S. *The Columbia history of British poetry,* BE717
Shapiro, Mitchell E. *Television network daytime and late-night programming, 1959–1989,* BH304
────── *Television network prime-time programming, 1948–1988,* BH304
────── *Television network weekend programming, 1959–1990,* BH304
Shapiro, Nat. *An encyclopedia of quotations about music,* BJ163
────── *Popular music,* BJ333
────── *Popular music, 1920–1979,* BJ333
Shapiro, Stuart Charles. *Encyclopedia of artificial intelligence,* EK170
Shapley, Harlow. *A source book in astronomy,* EC62
Sharada, B. A. *Dissertations in Indian linguistics and on Indian languages,* BD225
Sharma, B. R. *Rare plants of the world,* EG156
Sharma, H. D. *Indian reference sources,* AA360
Sharma, Jagdish Saran. *India since the advent of the British,* DE171
────── *Indian socialism,* CJ508
Sharma, Ram Sharan. *Survey of research in economic and social history of India,* CH197
Sharma, Suresh K. *Social sciences in modern India,* CA28
Sharp, D. W. A. *Dictionary of chemistry,* EE44
────── *Miall's dictionary of chemistry,* EE44
Sharp, Dennis. *Illustrated encyclopedia of architects and architecture,* BF224
────── *Sources of modern architecture,* BF224
Sharp, Harold S. *Advertising slogans of America,* CH570
────── *Handbook of geographical nicknames,* CL173
────── *Index to characters in the performing arts,* BH21
Sharp, J. Michael. *The directory of congressional voting scores and interest group ratings,* CJ218
Sharp, Marjorie Z. *Index to characters in the performing arts,* BH21
Sharpe, Richard. *A bibliography of Celtic-Latin literature, 400–1200,* BE1042
Shaskolsky, D. L. *Basutoland bibliography,* DD169
Shattock, Joanne. *Oxford guide to British women writers,* BE623
Shattuck, Charles Harlen. *The Shakespeare promptbooks,* BE793
Shatzkin, Mike. *The ballplayers,* BK48
Shatzman, Israel. *Illustrated encyclopaedia of the classical world,* DA100
Shaver, James P. *Handbook of research on social studies teaching and learning,* CB116
Shaver, Phillip R. *Measures of personality and social psychological attitudes,* CD98
────── *Measures of social psychological attitudes,* CD98
Shavit, David. *United States in Africa,* DB284, DC568, DD96, DE15, DE56
────── *United States in Asia,* DB284, DC568, DE15, DE56
────── *The United States in Latin America,* DB284
────── *United States in the Middle East,* DB284, DC568, DE15, DE56
────── *United States relations with Russia and the Soviet Union,* DC568
Shaw, Bradley A. *Latin American literature in English translation,* BE886
Shaw, Brent D. *The early church,* BC222
Shaw, Caroline S. *Cape Verde,* DD18
Shaw, Daphne. *Catalogue of British scientific and technical books,* EA13
Shaw, Dennis F. *Information sources in physics,* ED1
Shaw, Gareth. *British directories,* AL1, AL7, CH366, CH381

Shaw, Graham. *The bibliography of South Asian periodicals*, AD215
—— *The South Asia and Burma retrospective bibliography (SABREB)*, AA889
Shaw, Harry. *Dictionary of problem words and expressions*, AC84
—— *Punctuate it right!*, AC112
Shaw, Marian. *Essay and general literature index*, AH12, BA4, BE37
Shaw, R. B. *A bibliography for the study of African politics*, CJ397
Shaw, Ralph R. *American bibliography*, AA417, AA418, CL243
—— *Theory and history of bibliography*, AA9
Shaw, Warren. *Dictionary of the Third Reich*, DC259
—— *The Third Reich almanac*, DC259
Shayne, Mette. *African newspapers currently received by American libraries*, AE79, DD26
She said / he said, Henley, Nancy, BD82
—— Wood, Elizabeth J., CC40
Sheahan, Eileen. *Moving pictures*, BH159
Sheard, Kevin. *Academic heraldry in America*, CB395
Shearer, Barbara S. *State names, seals, flags, and symbols*, AL192, DB151
Shearer, Barbara Smith. *Finding the source of medical information*, EH3
—— *Periodical literature on United States cities*, DB145
Shearer, Benjamin F. *Periodical literature on United States cities*, DB145
—— *State names, seals, flags, and symbols*, AL192, DB151
Sheehan, Michael. *Bibliography of arms control verification*, CJ679
Sheehan, Michael M. *Domestic society in medieval Europe*, DC11
Sheehan, Steven. *The artist's handbook of materials and techniques*, BF304
Sheehy, Eugene P. *Bibliography of American folk art for the year*, BG10
Sheffield, Philip. *British education thesaurus*, CB81
Sheiman, Deborah Lovitky. *Infancy*, CC148, CD78
—— *Resources for middle childhood*, CC150, CD79
Sheldon, Joseph Kenneth. *Rediscovery of creation*, BC223, EG66
Sheldon, Kathleen E. *Guide to social science resources in women's studies*, CA5
The shell book, Rogers, Julia Ellen, EG307
Shell Oil Company. Exploration Department. *Stratigraphic atlas of North America and Central America*, EF113
Shelley, Bruce L. *Dictionary of Christianity in America*, BC235
Shells, EG306, EG307
Shemanski, Frances. *A guide to fairs and festivals in the United States*, AL148
Shemel, Sidney. *This business of music*, BJ185
Shepard, Leslie. *Encyclopedia of occultism & parapsychology*, CD134
Shepherd, Massey Hamilton. *Oxford American prayer book commentary*, BC349
Shepherd, Simon. *A biographical dictionary of English women writers, 1580–1720*, BE620
Shepherd, Walter. *Shepherd's glossary of graphic signs and symbols*, BF177
Shepherd, William Robert. *Historical atlas*, DA57
Shepherd's glossary of graphic signs and symbols, Shepherd, Walter, BF177
Shepherd's historical atlas, DA57
Sheppard, Jocelyn. *The bibliography of contemporary American fiction, 1945–1988*, BE476
Sheppard, Julia. *British archives*, AJ98, AK145
Sheppard, Lancelot. *New dictionary of the liturgy*, BC428
Sheppard's international directory of print and map sellers, CL260
Shera, Jesse Hauk. *Dictionary of American library biography*, AK86
Sheridan, Maurice. *EC legal systems*, CK204
—— *EFTA legal systems*, CK204

Sheriff, Abdul. *Zanzibar under colonial rule*, DD250
Sherman, Barbara Smiley. *Directory of residential treatment facilities for emotionally handicapped children and youth*, CC165
Sherman, Joan R. *Invisible poets*, BE533
Sherman, John. *The Arab-Israeli conflict 1945–1971*, DE72
Sherman, Marc I. *Human rights*, CK77
Shermis, Michael. *Jewish-Christian relations*, BC17
Sherratt, Andrew. *The Cambridge encyclopedia of archaeology*, DA74
Sherrill, Jan-Mitchell. *The gay, lesbian, and bisexual students' guide to colleges, universities, and graduate schools*, CB290
Shertzer, Margaret D. *The secretary's handbook*, CH90
Sherwood, P. A. *A concise Hungarian-English dictionary*, AC495
Shetler, Stanwyn G. *A provisional checklist of species for flora North America (revised)*, EG137
Shewan, Don. *Atlas of world political flashpoints*, CJ72
Shiel, Suzanne. *Annotated bibliography of Canadian demography*, CG116
Shield of republic, sword of empire, Fredriksen, John C., CJ605
Shields, Dorothy. *The dictionary of Canadian quotations and phrases*, BE104
Shields, Graham J. *Gibraltar*, DC269
—— *Spain*, DC507
Shields, Nancy Catchings. *Italian translations in America*, BE1297
Shields-West, Eileen. *The World almanac of presidential campaigns*, CJ251
Shier, Louise A. *A Coptic bibliography*, BC454, BE1521
Shiers, George. *Bibliography of the history of electronics*, EK127
Shigley, Joseph Edward. *Standard handbook of machine design*, EK247
Shih, Tian-Chu. *Health-related cookbooks*, EH294, EJ223
Shike, Moshe. *Modern nutrition in health and disease*, EH310
Shilling, Alison Watt. *Dictionary of Bahamian English*, AC161
Shils, Maurice E. *Modern nutrition in health and disease*, EH310
Shim, Jae K. *Accounting handbook*, CH263
—— *Dictionary of accounting terms*, CH254
—— *Dictionary of personal finance*, CH213
—— *Encyclopedic dictionary of accounting and finance*, CH253
—— *Source*, CH320
Shimer, Hervey Woodburn. *Index fossils of North America*, EF242
Shimoni, Yaacov. *The biographical dictionary of the Middle East*, DE66
—— *Political dictionary of the Arab world*, CJ424, CJ439, DE55, DE70
—— *Political dictionary of the Middle East in the twentieth century*, CJ424, CJ439
Shimose, Pedro. *Diccionario de autores iberoamericanos*, BE888
Shinar, Pessah. *Essai de bibliographie sélective et annotée sur l'Islam maghrébin contemporain*, BC501, DD73
Shinmura, Izuru. *Kōjien*, AC550
Shinoda, Gretchen W. *Focus Japan II*, AL43, DE210
Shintei genkai, AC549
Shintō, BC568, BC569, BC570, BC571
Shintō-bibliography in western languages, Schwade, Arcadio, BC571
Shipley, Joseph Twadell. *The Crown guide to the world's great plays, from ancient Greece to modern times*, BE236
—— *Dictionary of early English*, AC100
—— *Guide to great plays*, BE236
Shipley, Lloyd W. *Information resources in the arts*, BF107
Shipley, Robert Morrill. *Dictionary of gems and gemology*, EF187
Shipman, David. *The great movie stars*, BH286

Shippen, Edward. *Officers of the army and navy (regular) who served in the Civil War*, CJ647
Shipping, Billy, George J., CH444
Shipping world year book, CH464
Shipps, Anthony W. *The quote sleuth*, BE117
Ships and shipping, AJ93
   annuals, CH464
   dictionaries, CH468
   directories, CH464, CH467
   handbooks, CH466, CH469
   registers, CH465
   statistics, CH470
   tables of distances, CH471, CH472
   see also **Warships**
Shipton, Clifford Kenyon. *American bibliography*, AA405
—— *National index of American imprints through 1800*, AA410
—— *Sibley's Harvard graduates*, AH70
Shiri, Keith. *Directory of African film-makers and films*, BH212
Shirley, Rodney W. *The mapping of the world*, CL241
Shirley, Virginia S. *Table of isotopes*, ED42, ED46
—— *Table of radioactive isotopes*, ED42
Shivangulula, D. H. *A descriptive list of United Nations reference documents on Namibia (1946–1978)*, DD186
Shmelev, D. N. *Slovar' russkogo iazyka XI-XVII vv*, AC673
Shmeruk, Kh. *Jewish publications in the Soviet Union, 1917–1960*, BC535
Shnitnikov, Boris Nikolayevich. *Kazakh-English dictionary*, AC561
Shock and vibration handbook, EK246
Shockley, Ann Allen. *Afro-American women writers, 1746–1933*, BE519
Shoebridge, Michele. *Information sources in sport and leisure*, BK8
Shoemaker, Richard H. *American bibliography*, AA417, AA418, CL243
—— *Checklist of American imprints for 1820–1829*, AA418
Shōgakukan Randamu Hausu Ei-Wa daijiten, AC557
Shōjun, Bandō. *A bibliography on Japanese Buddhism*, BC464
Shona language, AC716
Shook, E. W. *Anthropological bibliography of aboriginal Panama*, DB302
Shore, Rima. *The international dictionary of 20th-century biography*, AH49
Shore, Steven N. *Encyclopedia of astronomy and astrophysics*, EC26
—— *Encyclopedia of modern physics*, ED15
Shorelines, EF38
Short, Charles. *Harper's Latin dictionary*, AC574
Short, Craig R. *Directory of music faculties in colleges and universities, U.S. and Canada*, BJ168
Short, David. *Czechoslovakia*, DC126
Short biographical dictionary of English literature, Cousin, John W., BE625
A short dictionary of Anglo-Saxon poetry in a normalized early West-Saxon orthography, Bessinger, Jess Balsor, AC169
Short dictionary of architecture, Beatty, Betty, BF244
—— Ware, Dora, BF244
Short dictionary of furniture, Gloag, John, BG126
Short glossaries, Great Britain. War Office. General Staff. Geographical Section, CL267
Short guide to the archives of the Quai d'Orsay, Pitman, Paul, DC155
Short guide to the study of Ethiopia, Dessalegn Rahmato, DD156
—— Hidaru, Alula, DD156
—— Rahmato, Dessalegn, DD156
Short guide to writing about art, Barnet, Sylvan, BF124
Short history of Anglo-Irish literature from its origins to the present day, Harmon, Maurice, BE803
—— McHugh, Roger, BE803

Short history of Irish literature, Deane, Seamus, BE803

Short history of modern Arabic literature, Badawī, Muhammad M., BE1546

Short history of nursing, Dock, Lavinia L., EH286

—— Stewart, Isabel Maitland, EH286

A short history of Syriac literature, Wright, William, BE1551

Short stories, BE486
  adaptations, BH218
  African-American authors, BE538
  bibliography, BE479, BE986
  biobibliography, BE261
  criticism
    collections, BE263
  indexes, BE260, BE262, BE264, BE483, BE538

Short stories (by country or region)
  Brazil, BE931
  Canada, BE835
  Latin America
    bibliography, BE903
  Mexico
    bibliography, BE912
  Poland
    bibliography, BE1355

Short stories on film and video, Emmens, Carol A., BH218

Short story criticism, BE263, BE325

Short story index, BE262

—— Cook, Dorothy Elizabeth, BE260, BE262

—— Monro, Isabel Stevenson, BE262

—— Yaakov, Juliette, BE260

Short-title alphabetical catalogue of plays produced or printed in England from 1660–1900, Nicoll, Allardyce, BE453, BE636

Short-title catalog of books printed in Italy and of books in Italian printed abroad, 1501–1600, held in selected North American libraries, AA735

A short-title catalogue arranged geographically of books printed and distributed by printers, publishers and booksellers in the English provincial towns and in Scotland and Ireland up to and including the year 1700, Clough, Eric A., AA678

Short-title catalogue of book printed in the Netherlands and Belgium, AA750

Short title catalogue of books printed before 1701 in the Foreign Office Library, Robertson, Colin L., DC271

Short title catalogue of books printed in England …, Wing, Donald Goddard, AA665, AA678, AA679, AD107, BE740

Short-title catalogue of books printed in England, Scotland, & Ireland and of English books printed abroad, 1475–1640, Pollard, Alfred W., AA412, AA665, AA671, AA672, AA674, AA678, AA683, AD107, BE680

—— Redgrave, G. R., AA412, AA665, AA672, AA674, AA678, AA683, AD107, BE680

Short-title catalogue of books printed in England, Scotland, Ireland, Wales, and British America, and of English books printed in other countries, 1641–1700, Wing, Donald Goddard, AA412, AA683

Short-title catalogue of books printed in France and of French books printed in other countries from 1470 to 1600, now in the British Museum, British Museum. Department of Printed Books, AA615

Short-title catalogue of books printed in Italy and of Italian books printed in other countries from 1465 to 1600, now in the British Museum, British Museum. Department of Printed Books, AA728, AA729, AA735

Short-title catalogue of books printed in Spain and of Spanish books printed elsewhere in Europe before 1601, now in the British Museum, British Museum. Department of Printed Books, AA813, AA816

Short-title catalogue of books printed in the German-speaking countries and German books printed in other countries from 1455 to 1600, now in the British Museum, British Museum. Department of Printed Books, AA638

Short-title catalogue of books printed in the Netherlands and Belgium and of Dutch and Flemish books printed in other countries from 1470 to 1600, now in the British Museum, British Museum. Department of Printed Books, AA745

Short title catalogue of eighteenth century printed books in the National Library of Medicine, Blake, John Ballard, EH24

Short title catalogue of French books, 1601–1700, British Museum. Department of Printed Books, AA615

—— Goldsmith, Valentine Fernande, AA615

Short-title catalogue of Portuguese books printed before 1601, now in the British Museum, British Museum. Department of Printed Books, AA468, AA775

A short title catalogue of serials printed in England, Scotland, Ireland, and British America, AD107

A short title catalogue of Spanish and Portuguese books, 1601–1700, in the Library of the British Museum (The British Library—Reference Division), Goldsmith, Valentine Fernande, AA816

Short-title catalogues of Portuguese books and of Spanish-American books printed before 1601, British Museum, AA775

Short-title catalogues of Portuguese books and of Spanish-American books printed before 1601, now in the British Museum, British Museum. Department of Printed Books, AA468

Short-title catalogues of Spanish, Spanish-American and Portuguese books printed before 1601 in the British Museum, British Museum. Department of Printed Books, AA468

The short-title Evans, AA410

Short vocabulary of Old Russian, Lunt, Horace Gray, AC671

Shorter atlas of the classical world, Heyden, A. A. M. van der, DA120

—— Scullard, Howard Hayes, DA120

Shorter Cambridge medieval history, Previté-Orton, Charles William, DA157

Shorter dictionary of English furniture, Edwards, Ralph, BG123

Shorter encyclopaedia of Islam, BC505

Shorter lexicon of the Greek New Testament, Gingrich, Felix Wilbur, AC453

The shorter new Cambridge bibliography of English literature, BE586

The shorter Oxford English dictionary on historical principles, Murray, James Augustus Henry, AC31

Shorter Persian-English dictionary, Ḥayyim, Sulaymān, AC314

Shorto, H. L. *Bibliographies of Mon-Khmer and Tai linguistics*, BD230

Shortridge, Barbara G. *Atlas of American women*, DB74

Showalter, Dennis E. *German military history, 1648–1982*, DC240

Showalter, Elaine. *Modern American women writers*, BE448

Showers, Victor. *World facts and figures*, CG55

Shōzaburo, Kanazawa. *Jirin*, AC548

Shrader, Charles R. *U.S. military logistics, 1607–1991*, CJ608

Shrader, Charles Reginald. *Reference guide to United States military history*, DB51

Shrager, David S. *Quotable lawyer*, CK57

Shreir, Sally. *Women's movements of the world*, CC554

Shrimpton, Leanda. *Contemporary masterworks*, BF69

—— *International dictionary of opera*, BJ249

Shrock, Robert R. *Index fossils of North America*, EF242

Shrout, R. N. *Resource directory for the disabled*, CC197

Shteĭnpress, B. S. *Entsiklopedicheskiĭ muzykal'nyĭ slovar'*, BJ119

Shtetl finder, Cohen, Chester G., CL127

Shu, Austin C. W. *Modern Chinese authors*, AA190

Shugar, Gershon J. *Chemical technician's ready reference handbook*, EE87

—— *Chemist's ready reference handbook*, EE87

Shukman, Harold. *The Blackwell encyclopedia of the Russian Revolution*, DC594

Shulman, Frank Joseph. *Burma*, DE120

—— *East Asian resources in American libraries*, DE106

—— *Japan*, DE205

Shult, Linda. *Women, race, and ethnicity*, CC625

Shunami, Shlomo. *Bibliography of Jewish bibliographies*, BC519

Shundov, V. I. *Slavianskoe iazykoznanie*, BD183

Shupe, Anson D. *The anti-cult movement in America*, BC32

Shuppan nenkan, AA918

Shuteriqi, Dhimitër S. *Historia e letërsisë shqiptare*, BE1094

Siam *see* **Thailand**

Siamese language *see* **Thai language**

Siberia, DC604

Siberia and the Soviet Far East, Collins, David Norman, DC603

Sibirskaia sovetskaia entsiklopediia, DC604

—— Azadovskiĭ, M.K, DC604

Sibley, Charles Gald. *Distribution and taxonomy of birds of the world*, EG275

—— *A world checklist of birds*, EG269

Sibley, Francis M. *Dictionary of quotations in geography*, CL54

Sibley, John Langdon. *Biographical sketches of those who attended Harvard College with bibliographical and other notes*, AH70

Sibley's Harvard graduates, AH70

Sichel, Beatrice. *Economics journals and serials*, CH31

Sichel, Werner. *Economics journals and serials*, CH31

Sicherman, Barbara. *Notable American women*, AH66

Sicherman, Carol. *Ngugi wa Thiong'o, the making of a rebel*, DD166

Sicignano, Robert. *Handbook of United States economic and financial indicators*, CH236

Siddiqi, Muhammad Nejatullah. *Muslim economic thinking*, CH190

Siddiqui, Akhtar H. *A guide to periodical publications and newspapers of Pakistan*, AD207

—— *Pakistan government publications*, AF256

—— *Publications of the government of Pakistan, 1947–1957*, AF254

Sidelnikov, S. I. *Istoriki-slavisty SSSR*, DC54

Sieben, H. J. *Bibliographia patristica. Supplementum*, BC295

Siebenhundert Jahre Orientteppich, Erdmann, Kurt, BG166

Le siècle des lumières, Conlon, Pierre M., AA622

Sieg, Herbert. *Uniforms of the world*, CJ595

Siegal, Diana Laskin. *Ourselves, growing older*, CC95, CC564

Siegel, Eric R. *A bibliography for the study of African politics*, CJ397

Siegel, Esther. *Guide to dance in film*, BH149

Siegel, Joel G. *Accounting handbook*, CH263

—— *Dictionary of accounting terms*, CH254

—— *Dictionary of personal finance*, CH213

—— *Encyclopedic dictionary of accounting and finance*, CH253

—— *Source*, CH320

Siegel, Jonathan P. *The Macmillan dictionary of political quotations*, CJ44, CJ45

Siegel, P. B. *Dictionary of farm animal behaviour*, EJ116

Sienkewicz, Thomas J. *The classical epic*, BE1006

Sienkiewicz, Witold. *Mały słownik historii Polski*, DC481

Sierra Club. *World directory of environmental organizations*, EK77

Sierra Club's world directory of environmental organizations, EK77

Sierra Leone
  atlases, CL342
  bibliography, DD18, DD205
    current, AA873
  biography, AH324
  current surveys, DD62

encyclopedias, DD48
government publications
bibliography, AF225
library catalogs, DD204
statistics, CG354
Sierra Leone. Central Statistics Office. *Annual statistical digest,* CG354
Sierra Leone. Library Board. *Sierra Leone publications,* AA873
Sierra Leone, Binns, Margaret, DD18
—— Binns, Tony, DD18
—— Foray, C. P., DD48
Sierra Leone in maps, Clarke, John I., CL342
Sierra Leone publications, Sierra Leone. Library Board, AA873
Sieveking, Paul. *British biographical archive,* AH224
Siewert, John A. *Mission handbook,* BC308
Sifakis, Carl. *The dictionary of historic nicknames,* AJ180
—— *Encyclopedia of American crime,* CK254
—— *Encyclopedia of assassinations,* CJ556
—— *Encyclopedia of gambling,* BK137
—— *Mafia encyclopedia,* CK254
Sifakis, Stewart. *Who was who in the Civil War,* DB121
•*SIFT (Summary of Information on Film and Television),* BH185
SIGCAT CD-ROM compendium, AF107
Sigelverzeichnis für die Bibliotheken der Bundesrepublik Deutschland, Voigt, Wolfgang, AD235
Sigfús Blöndal. *Íslandsk-dansk ordbog,* AC506
Sigles nationaux & internationaux, AC345
Sign language, BD49
Signals and signalling, EC80
Signs & symbols in Christian art, Ferguson, George Wells, BF182
Sijthoff's Adresboek voor Boekhandel, Uitgeverij, grafische Industrie, Gids voor Dagbladen en Tijdschriften, AA292
Sikhism, BC572, BC573, BC576
dictionaries, BC76
Sikhism and the Sikhs, Rai, Priya Muhar, BC573
Sikhs (by country or region)
United States, CC331
Sikhs in North America, Tatla, Darshan Singh, CC331
Sikkim, DE86
Sikorskii, N. M. *Dopolneniia, razyskivaemye izdaniia utocheneniia,* AA791
Siksika language, AC717
Sikula, John P. *Handbook of research on teacher education,* CB162
Silbey, Joel H. *Encyclopedia of the American legislative system,* CJ116
Silcock, Howard L. *Solabilities of inorganic and organic compounds,* EE91
Siles Guevara, Juan. *Bibliografía de bibliografías bolivianas,* AA27
Silet, Charles L. P. *Images of American Indians on film,* CC334
Silkenat, James R. *Guide to foreign law firms,* CK58
Sill, Gertrude Grace. *Handbook of symbols in Christian art,* BF182
Sill, Michael. *The atlas of Nepal in the modern world,* CL359
Sills, David L. *International encyclopedia of the social sciences,* CA36, CA44
Silva, Innocencio Francisco da. *Diciondrio bibliografico portuguêz,* AA777
Silva Castro, Raúl. *Historia bibliográfica de la novela chilena,* BE938
The silva of North America, Sargent, Charles Sprague, EG201
Silver, Alain. *Film noir,* BH224
Silver, Andrew M. *ERIC directory of education-related information centers,* CB99
Silver, Helene. *A new reader's guide to African literature,* BE1508
Silver and gold of Great Britain and North America, BG136

Silver collectors' glossary and a list of early American silversmiths and their marks, French, Hollis, BG63, BG144
Silver plate *see* **Gold and silver plate**
Silverburg, Sanford R. *Middle East bibliography,* DE39
—— *United States foreign policy and the Middle East/North Africa,* DE3, DE40
Silverman, Stephen J. *Proposals that work,* EA160
Silverstein, Natalie Anne. *Prevention education,* CC112
Silverwork
dictionaries, BG136, BG146
directories, BG143, BG147
Silverwork (by country or region)
Great Britain, BG138
United States, BG145, BG148
biography, BG144
Silvester, Robert. *United States theatre,* BH44
Silvestre, Louis Catherine. *Marques typographiques,* AA251, AA254
Silvet, J. *Eesti-inglise sõnaraamat,* AC308
—— *Inglise-Eesti sonaraamat,* AC308
Silvics of forest trees of the United States, EG202
Sim, Janet. *Black artists in the United States,* BF24
Sim, Richard. *Guerrilla and terrorist organisations,* CJ61
Simbabwe, Geschichte, Politik, Wirtschaft, Gesellschaft, Baumhögger, Goswin, DD251
Simchera, V. M. *Statisticheskie publikatsii v SSSR,* CG301
Simches, Seymour O. *Modern French literature and language,* BD158, BE1134
—— *Modern Iberian language and literature,* BD166, BE1436
—— *Modern Italian language and literature,* BD160, BE1293
Simek, Rudolf. *Dictionary of northern mythology,* CF35
Similes dictionary, BE89
Simko, Ján. *Anglicko-slovenský slovník,* AC719
Simmonds, Eva. *Guide to Restoration and Augustan literature,* BE611
Simmons, Donita Vasiti. *Women in the South Pacific,* CC616
Simmons, John S. G. *A bibliographical guide to the Russian language,* BD188
—— *Guide to Russian reference books,* AA351
—— *Russian bibliography, libraries and archives,* AB86
Simmons, Merle Edwin. *A bibliography of the romance and related forms in Spanish America,* BE878
Simmons, Pamela. *Bibliography on the society, culture, and political economy of post-independence Botswana,* DD131
Simmons Market Research Bureau. *Simmons study of media and markets,* CH599
Simmons study of media and markets, CC244, CH599
Simms, Michael. *The Longman dictionary of poetic terms,* BE328
Simon, Alfred. *Encyclopedia of theater music,* BJ267
—— *Songs of the American theater,* BJ267
—— *Songs of the theater,* BJ267
Simon, André Louis. *Bibliotheca gastronomica,* EJ206
—— *Dictionary of gastronomy,* EJ213
Simon, James E. *Herbs,* EG110
Simon, K. R. *Istoriia srednix vekov,* DA133
—— *Istoriia SSSR,* DC548
Simon, Robin. *The portrait in Britain and America,* BF320
The Simon and Schuster encyclopedia of World War II, DA208
Simon and Schuster's international dictionary, AC737
Simón Díaz, José. *Bibliografía de la literatura hispánica,* BE1439
—— *Bibliografía regional y local de España,* DC508
—— *Impresos del siglo XVII,* AA808

—— *Impresos localizados (siglos XV–XVII),* DC508
—— *Manual de bibliografía de la literatura española,* BE1440
Simón Palmer, María del Carmen. *Escritoras españolas del siglo XIX,* BE1441
Simonds, E. H. S. *Bibliographies of Mon-Khmer and Tai linguistics,* BD230
Simone, Franco. *Dizionario critico della letteratura francese,* BE1154
Simoneau, Karin. *Folk literature of South American Indians,* CF74
Simonescu, Dan. *Bibliografia românească veche, 1508–1830,* AA780
Simoni, Anna. *Catalogue of books from the Low Countries 1601–1621 in the British Library,* AA750
Simoni, Anna E. C. *Dictionary of anonymous and pseudonymous English literature,* AA150
Simonic, Franc. *Slovenska bibliografija,* AA798
Simons, M. L. *Cyclopaedia of American literature,* BE433
Simonson, Donald G. *Dictionary of banking terms,* CH272
Simony, Maggy. *The traveler's reading guide,* CL379
Simonyi, Zsigmond. *Magyar-nyelvtörténeti szótár a legrégibb nyelvemlékektöl a nyelvújjtásig,* AC494
A simplified dictionary of modern Samoan, Allardice, R. W., AC700
Simpson, Anthony E. *Guide to library research in public administration,* CJ459
Simpson, Donald H. *Biography catalogue of the Library of the Royal Commonwealth Society,* AH238, DC344
—— *Manuscript catalogue of the Library of the Royal Commonwealth Society,* DC344
Simpson, Donald Penistan. *Cassell's Latin dictionary,* AC575
Simpson, George Gaylord. *The principles of classification and a classification of mammals,* EG305
Simpson, J. A. *Concise Oxford dictionary of proverbs,* BE159
—— *The Oxford dictionary of modern slang,* AC131
—— *The Oxford English dictionary,* AC33
Simpson, J. M. Y. *The encyclopedia of language and linguistics,* BD34
Simpson, Jacqueline. *Penguin dictionary of English,* AC461
Simpson, James Beasley. *Contemporary quotations,* BE118
—— *Simpson's contemporary quotations,* BE118
Simpson, Michael A. *Dying, death, and grief,* CC180
Simpson, Robert Lawrence. *Historical dictionary of France from the 1815 restoration to the Second Empire,* DC204
Simpson's contemporary quotations, Simpson, James Beasley, BE118
Sims, Janet L. *The progress of Afro-American women,* CC376
Sims, Michael. *American & Canadian doctoral dissertations & master's theses on Africa, 1886–1974,* DD32
Sims, Nicholas A. *British writing on disarmament from 1914–1978,* CJ673
Sims, R. W. *Animal identification,* EG205
Sims-Williams, Ursula. *Union catalogue of Persian serials & newspapers in British libraries,* AD199
Sinclair, Alison. *Madrid newspapers, 1661–1870,* AE76
Sinclair, Cecil. *Tracing your Scottish ancestors,* AJ124
Sinclair, Janet. *A dictionary of ballet terms,* BH146
Sinclair, John. *BBC English dictionary,* AC35
Sinclair, Stéphane. *Atlas de géographie historique de la France et de la Gaule,* DC166
Sinclair, Wayne A. *Diseases of trees and shrubs,* EG203
Singapore
bibliography, AA933, DE229, DE255
biography, AH362, AH369

periodicals
  indexes, AD345
  statistics, CG422, CG423
Singapore (by subject)
  history, DE256
    bibliography, DE99, DE257
Singapore. Dept. of Statistics. *Yearbook of statistics: Singapore,* CG423
Singapore. Registry of Births and Deaths. *Report on registration of births and deaths,* CG422
Singapore, Quah, Stella R., DE257
Singapore national bibliography, AA933
Singapore periodicals index, AD345
Singer, Hans Wolfgang. *Allgemeiner Bildniskatalog,* BF68
Singer, Isidore. *Jewish encyclopedia,* BC546
Singer, Joel David. *Resort to arms,* CJ598
Singer, Loren R. *Visual arts reference and research guide,* BF29
Singer, Lothar. *Russian-English-German-French hydrological dictionary,* EF135
Singer, Richard B. *Medical risks,* EH233
Singerman, Robert. *Antisemitic propaganda,* BC508
—— *Jewish and Hebrew onomastics,* AJ201
—— *Jewish serials of the world,* AD16
—— *Jews in Spain and Portugal,* BC531
—— *Judaica Americana,* BC525
—— *Spanish and Portuguese Jewry,* BC531
Singers
  bibliography, BJ219
  biography, BJ214
Singh, A. *Afro-American poetry and drama, 1760–1975,* BE512
Singh, Amar Kaur Jasbir. *A guide to source materials in the India Office Library and Records for the history of Tibet, Sikkim and Bhutan 1765–1950,* DE86
Singh, Amritjit. *Indian literature in English, 1827–1979,* BE1542, BE1567
Singh, B. N. *Dictionary of Indian philosophical concepts,* BB39
Singh, Bhupal. *Survey of Anglo-Indian fiction,* BE1568
Singh, Maya. *The Panjábí dictionary,* AC627
Singh, Mohinder. *Government of India publications,* AF247
—— *Government publications of India,* AF248
—— *State government publications in India, 1947–1982,* AF249
Singh, Sunita. *Women's studies in India,* CC618
Singh, Uma S. *Plant diseases of international importance,* EJ62
Singh, V. B. *Elections in India,* CJ435
—— *State elections in India,* CJ435
Single parents, CC145
Singleton, Paul. *Dictionary of microbiology and molecular biology,* EG27
Singleton, Ralph S. *Filmmakers dictionary,* BH261
Sinkankas, John. *A collector's guide to minerals and gemstones,* EF191
—— *Gemology,* EF176
Sinn, Elizabeth. *Research material for Hong Kong studies,* DE150
Sinnott, Roger W. *Sky catalogue 2000.0,* EC72
Sinonimi e contrari, Pittàno, Giuseppe, AC543
Sintesis bibliografica de filologia griega, Cirac Estopañan, Sebastian, BD136
Síntesis estadística del Ecuador, Dirección General de Estadística y Censos (Ecuador), CG154
Sipe, Lynn F. *Western Sahara,* DD242
SIPRI yearbook of world armaments and disarmament, CJ602
Sir Banister Fletcher Library. *Architectural periodicals index,* BF207
Sir Banister Fletcher's A history of architecture, Fletcher, Banister, BF255
Sir Thomas Malory and the Morte Darthur, Life, Page West, BE340
Sir William Osler, EH209
Siracusa, Joseph. *Relaciones literarias entre España e Italia,* BE1442
Sirén, Osvald. *Chinese painting,* BF313
Sirven, Pierre. *Atlas du Rwanda,* CL344

•*SIS,* EJ74
Sistematicheskiĭ ukazatel' knig i stateĭ po grecheskoĭ filologii, napechatannykh v Rossii s XVII stolĕtiĭa po 1892 god na russkom i inostrannykh ĭazykakh, Prozorov, P., BD138
Sisterhood is global, CC568
Sittig, Marshall. *Handbook of toxic and hazardous chemicals and carcinogens,* EH427
—— *Organic chemical process encyclopedia,* EE144
La situation démographique, CG219
Situation économique du Sénégal, Sénégal. Direction de la Statistique, CG353
Situation of women in Lesotho, Shale, M., DD122, DD171
Sitzman, Glenn L. *African libraries,* AK155
Sivanandan, Ambalavaner. *Coloured minorities in Britain,* CC326
Sive, Mary Robinson. *China,* DE133
Sivolgin, Vladimir Epifanovich. *Ekonomika SSSR,* CH22
Six-guns and saddle leather, Adams, Ramon Frederick, DB162
Six thousand words, AC92
Sixteen modern American authors, BE399, BE404, BE413
Sixth book of junior authors & illustrators, Holtze, Sally Holmes, BE384
Sixth report, 1890–1932, United States Geographic Board, CL175
[Sixty years of recorded jazz], Bruyninckx, Walter, BJ307
Sixty years of the Oscar, BH275
Sjöberg, Åke W. *The Sumerian dictionary of the University Museum of the University of Pennsylvania,* AC204
Skachkov, V. M. *Periodychni vydannĩa URSR, 1917–1960,* AE72
Skachkov, Vasyl' Mykytovych. *Periodychni vydannĩa URSU, 1918–1950,* AD166
Skalak, Richard. *Handbook of bioengineering,* EH181
Skandinavische Literatur, 1870–1970, Rossel, Sven Hakon, BE1092
Skandinavischen Seminar der Wissenschaften der Universität Göttingen. *Bibliographie der Runeninschriften nach Fundorten,* BE1082
Skapa, Barbara A. *A bibliography on Kenya,* DD167
Skapura, Robert. *The cover story index, 1960–1991,* AD269
Skautrup, Peter. *Danmark,* CL132
Skeat, T. C. *The catalogues of the manuscript collections,* AA205
Skeat, Walter William. *Concise etymological dictionary of the English language,* AC62
—— *Etymological dictionary of the English language,* AC58, AC62
—— *Glossary of Tudor and Stuart words, especially from the dramatists,* AC101
Skells, J. W. *Printed maps in the atlases of Great Britain and Ireland,* CL228
Škerlj, Ružena. *Anglesko-slovenski slovar,* AC723
—— *Veliki angleško-slovenski slovar,* AC721
Ski magazine's encyclopedia of skiing, BK97
Skidmore, Gail. *From radical left to extreme right,* AD45
Skidmore, Thomas E. *The Cambridge encyclopedia of Latin America and the Caribbean,* DB281
Skiing, BK96, BK97
Skill, Thomas. *Television,* BH292
Skillin, Marjorie E. *Words into type,* AA322
Skinner, Chris. *Handbook for research students in the social sciences,* CA2
Skinner, G. W. *Modern Chinese society,* DE130
Skinner, Quentin. *The Cambridge history of Renaissance philosophy,* BB69
Skinner's oil and gas international yearbook, EK307
Skirball, Sheba F. *Films of the Holocaust,* DA221
Sklar, R. L. *A bibliography for the study of African politics,* CJ397
Skog, Lawrence E. *A provisional checklist of species for flora North America (revised),* EG137

Skolnik, Herman. *The literature matrix of chemistry,* EE7
Skolnik, Merrill Ivan. *Radar handbook,* EK141
Skønlitteratur i danske Tidsskrifter, 1913-1942, Elkjaer, Kjeld, BE1116
Skønlitteratur i danske Tidsskrifter 1943–1962, Eisenberg, Alex, BE1116
—— Torfing, Grethe, BE1116
Skorokhod, N. S. *Russko-anglo-nemetsko-frantsuzskiĭ slovar' po vychislitel'noĭ tekhnike,* EK192
Skorupka, Stanisław. *Maly słownik języka polskiego,* AC630
Skowronski, JoAnn. *Women in American music,* BJ223
Skretvedt, Randy. *The nostalgia entertainment sourcebook,* BH15
Skrifter utg. av Svenska historiska föreningen, DC521
Skrifter utgivna av Svenska litteratursällskapet, BE1487
Skrzyńska, Maria. *Słownik naukowo-techniczny angielsko-polski,* EA122
—— *Słownik naukowo-techniczny polsko-angielski,* EA122
Skupien, Janet. *Body movement and nonverbal communication,* CD116
Sky and telescope, EC43
Sky and telescope cumulative index, Bausch, Judith Lola, EC43
Sky atlas 2000.0, Tirion, Wil, EC72, EC76
Sky catalogue 2000.0, EC72, EC76
SLA biennial salary survey, AK179
S.L.A. list of translations, EA62
SLA triennial salary survey, AK179
Slack, Robert C. *Bibliographies of studies in Victorian literature for the thirteen years 1932–1944,* BE753
Slade, Carole. *Form and style,* AG1
Slang and euphemism, Spears, Richard A., AC134
Slang and its analogues, past and present, Farmer, John Stephen, AC122
Slang, today and yesterday, Partridge, Eric, AC132
Slater, Thomas J. *Handbook of Soviet and East European films and filmmakers,* BH271
Slauson, Nedra G. *Index to illustrations of living things outside North America,* EA220, EG72
—— *Index to illustrations of the natural world,* EA220, EG73
Slaven, Anthony. *Dictionary of Scottish business biography, 1860–1960,* CH97
Slavens, Thomas P. *Research guide to musicology,* BJ7
—— *Research guide to philosophy,* BB3
—— *Research guide to religious studies,* BC3
—— *Research guide to the history of Western art,* BF5
Slavery
  bibliography, CC328, CC377, DA68, DD5
Slavery (by country or region)
  Caribbean, DB407
  United States
    encyclopedias, CC386
  West Indies, DB407
Slavery and slaving in world history, Miller, Joseph Calder, CC328, DD5
Slavianovedenie v dorevoliutsionnoi Rossii, DC55
Slavianovedenie v SSSR, Bromlei, ĬU. V., DC54
—— D'iakov, V. A., DC54
Slavĩanskoe ĩazykoznanie, BD183
Slavic and East European resources in Canadian academic and research libraries, Budurowycz, Bohdan, DC46
Slavic Cyrillic union catalog of pre-1956 imprints, Library of Congress. Catalog Publication Division, AA784, AA785
Slavic ethnic libraries, museums and archives in the United States, Wynar, Lubomyr Roman, AK116
Slavic languages
  bibliography, BD5, BD180, BD183, BD184
  bibliography of bibliography, BD182
  dictionaries
    bibliography, AC193

dissertations, BE1408
grammar, BD181
Slavic linguistics, BD183
Slavic literatures, BE1076, BE1077, BE1078
  translations
    bibliography, BE1075
The Slavic literatures, Lewanski, Richard Casimir, BE1075
Slavic review, DC554
Slavic studies
  bibliography, DC41
  biography, DC54, DC55
  periodicals
    guides for authors, AD26
Slavic studies, DC29
Slavica-Auswahl-Katalog der Universitätsbibliothek Jena, Universitätsbibliothek Jena, BE1077
Slavs, DC53
Sławiński, Janusz. *Słownik terminów literackich,* BE1359
Sławski, Franciszek. *Słownik etymologiczny języka polskiego,* AC639
Sledge, William H. *Core readings in psychiatry,* EH371
Slee, Debora A. *Health care terms,* EH125
Slee, Vergil N. *Health care terms,* EH125
Sleep, CD111
Sleumer, Albert. *Kirchenlateinisches Wörterbuch,* AC582
——— *Liturgischen Lexikons,* AC582
Slick, Sam L. *Historical dictionary of the Spanish Empire, 1402–1975,* DC515
Slide, Anthony. *The American film industry,* BH254, BH316, CH483
——— *International film industry,* BH254
——— *International film, radio, and television journals,* BH175
——— *Sourcebook for the performing arts,* BH17
——— *The television industry,* BH316, CH483
Slide buyers' guide, Cashman, Norine D., BF195
Slingerland, Jean Harris. *The Wellesley index to Victorian periodicals, 1824–1900,* AD292
Sliosberg, A. *Elsevier's dictionary of pharmaceutical science and techniques in five languages,* EH328
Šljivić-Šimšić, Biljana. *SerboCroatian-English dictionary,* AC710
——— *Srpskohrvatski-engleski rečnik,* AC710
Sloan, Dauphine. *Dictionary of political parties and organizations in Russia,* CJ386
Sloan, Gwen. *PAIS subject headings,* CA25
Sloan, W. David. *American journalism history,* AE147
Sloane, David E. E. *American humor magazines and comic periodicals,* AD28
Sloane, Richard. *The Sloane-Dorland annotated medical-legal dictionary,* EH269
Sloane, Sheila B. *The medical word book,* EH104
Sloane, Thomas O'Conor. *Henley's twentieth century book of formulas, processes and trade secrets,* EA278
The Sloane-Dorland annotated medical-legal dictionary, Sloane, Richard, EH269
Slocum, Robert B. *Biographical dictionaries and related works,* AH4, AH6
Slodnjak, Anton. *Geschichte der slowenischen Literatur,* BE1497
Słomczewska, J. *555 książek wydanych w okresie powojennym,* AA766
Slonim, Maureen. *Children, culture, and ethnicity,* CC151
——— *Resources for middle childhood,* CC150, CD79
Slonimsky, Nicolas. *Baker's biographical dictionary of musicians,* BJ203
——— *The international cyclopedia of music and musicians,* BJ137
——— *Lectionary of music,* BJ158
——— *Music since 1900,* BJ188
Slöör, Anna. *Englantilais-suomalainen sanakirja,* AC324
Slovak-English phraseological dictionary, Konuš, Joseph James, AC718

Slovak language
  abbreviations, AC282
  dictionaries
    bilingual
      Slovak-English, AC718, AC719
Slovak literature, BE1425
Slovakia
  biography, AH285
Slovaks, CC323
Slovar' geograficheskikh nazvaniĭ SSSR, CL153
Slovar' literaturovedcheskikh terminov, Timofeev, Leonid Ivanovich, BE1416
Slovar' pseudonimov russkikh pisateleĭ, uchenykh i obshchestvennykh deĭateleĭ, Masanov, Ivan Filippovich, AA183, AA184
Slovar' russkikh narodnykh govorov, Institut russkogo ĭAzyka (Akademiĭa nauk SSSR). Slovarnyĭ sektor, AC670
Slovar' russkogo ĭazyka, Akademiĭa Nauk SSSR. Institut ĭAzykoznaniĭa, AC666, AC674
——— Ozhegov, Sergei Ivanovich, AC672
Slovar' russkogo ĭazyka XI-XVII vv, AC673
Slovar' russkoĭ transkriptsii geograficheskikh nazvaniĭ, Volostnova, M. B., CL154
Slovar' sinonimov russkogo ĭazyka, AC693
——— Aleksandrova, Zinaida Evgen'evna, AC692
Slovar slovenskega knjižnega jezika, Inštitut za slovenski jezik (Slovenska akademija znanosti in umetnosti), AC720
Slovar' sokrashcheniĭ russkogo ĭazyka, Alekseev, Dmitriĭ Ivanovich, AC685
Slovar' sovremennogo russkogo literaturnogo ĭazyka, AC666
Slovar' sovremennogo russkogo literaturnogo ĭazyka, Akademiĭa Nauk SSSR. Institut Russkogo ĭAzyka, AC667
Slovari, izdannye v SSSR, Akademiĭa Nauk SSSR. Institut Russkogo ĭAzyka, AC698
Slovarnyĭ ukazatel' po knigovedeniĭu, Meze'r, Avgusta Vladimirovna, AA8
Slovene-English dictionary, Kotnik, Janko, AC722
Slovenes in the United States and Canada, Dwyer, Joseph D., CC321, CC473
Slovenia, DC129
  bibliography, AA798
  biography, AH309
Slovenian language
  bibliography, BD189, BD190, BD191
  dictionaries, AC720
    bilingual, AC723
      English-Slovenian, AC721
      Slovenian-English, AC721, AC722
Slovenska bibliografija, Simonic, Franc, AA798
Slovenski biografski leksikon, AH309
Slovensko-angleški slovar, Kotnik, Janko, AC722
Slovensko-anglický frazeologický slovník, AC718
Slovenský bibliografia, AA591
Slovenský biografický slovník, AH285
Slovenský štatistický úrad v Bratislave. *Statistická ročenka České a Slovenské federativní republiky,* CG208
Slovník anglicko-česky, Jung, Václav, AC279
Slovník anglicko-český a česko-anglický, Procházka, Jindřich, AC281
Slovník české literatury 1970–1981, Forst, Vladimír, BE1105
Slovník českých spisovatelů, BE1111
——— Havel, Rudolf, BE1105
——— Opelík, Jiří, BE1105
Slovník českých spisovatelů beletristů, 1945–1956, Kunc, Jaroslav, BE1110
Slovník jazyka českého, Trávníček, František, AC278
Slovník slovenských pseudonymov, Ormis, Ján Vladimir, AA165
Slovník slovenských pseudonymov 1919–1944, Kormúth, Dezider, AA160
Slovník soudobých českých spisovatelů, Kunc, Jaroslav, BE1110
Slovník spisovného jazyka českého, Československá Akademie Věd. Ústav pro Jazyk Český, AC277
Slovnyk ukraïns'koi movy, AC798
Slovnyk ukraïns'kykh psevdonimiv ta kriptonimiv (XVI–XX st.), Dei, Oleksii Ivanovych, AA188

Słownik etymologiczny języka polskiego, Brückner, Alexander, AC638
——— Sławski, Franciszek, AC639
Słownik geograficzny Królestwa polskiego i innych krajów słowiańskich, CL148
Słownik języka polskiego, AC631, AC632
Słownik naukowo-techniczny angielsko-polski, Skrzyńska, Maria, EA122
Słownik naukowo-techniczny polsko-angielski, EA122
Słownik polskich towarzystw naukowych, AL71
Słownik pseudonimów i kryptonimów pisarzy polskich oraz Polski dotyczących, Bar, Adam, AA180
Słownik skrótów, Paruch, Józef, AC637
Słownik staropolski, Polska Akademia Nauk, AC629
Słownik starożytności słowiańskich, Polska Akademia Nauk. Komitet Słowianoznawstwa, DC53
Słownik terminów literackich, BE1359
Słownik współczesnych pisarzy polskich, Korzeniewska, Ewa, BE1350, BE1351
Słownik wymowy polskiej PWN, AC640
Sluglett, Peter. *Theses on Islam, the Middle East and North-West Africa, 1880–1978, accepted by universities in the United Kingdom and Ireland,* DD74, DE44
——— *Tuttle guide to the Middle East,* DE23
Small, Melvin. *Resort to arms,* CJ598
Small, Ronald John. *A dictionary of the natural environment,* CL50
——— *A modern dictionary of geography,* CL51
Small business, CH332, CH333, CH377
  directories, CH368
  handbooks, CH140
Small business, Ryans, Cynthia C., CH332
Small business sourcebook, CH333
Small business start-up index, CH333
A smaller Latin-English dictionary, AC578
Smallwood, Carol. *Current issues resource builder,* CA50
——— *Free resource builder for librarians and teachers,* CA50
SME mining engineering handbook, EK254
Smelser, Neil J. *Handbook of sociology,* CC27
Smet, Joseph de. *Woordenboek der toponymie van Westelijk Vlaanderen, Vlaamsch Artesië, het Land van den Hoek,* CL210
Smethurst, J. M. *The eighteenth century short title catalogue 1990,* AA681
Smets, Kristine. *Foreign newspapers held by the Center for Research Libraries,* AE3
Smetschka, Barbara. *Leben und Arbeit von Frauen, Frauenforschung und Frauenbewegung in Afrika,* DD7
Smialek, William. *Polish music,* BJ42
Smirnitskiĭ, Aleksandr Ivanovich. *Russian-English dictionary,* AC678, AC681
Smirnov-Sokol'skiĭ, Nikolai Pavlovich. *Russkie literaturnye al'manakhi i sborniki XVIII–XIX vv,* BE1404
Smit, E. M. *Bibliografie der geschiedenis van Nederland,* DC451
Smit, Pieter. *History of the life sciences,* EG8
Smith, Alan. *The Country life international dictionary of clocks,* BG87
Smith, Albert Hugh. *English place-name elements,* CL201
Smith, Alexander Hanchett. *A field guide to western mushrooms,* EG190
——— *The mushroom hunter's field guide,* EG191
Smith, Allen. *Directory of oral history collections,* DB36
Smith, Ann G. *A biographical register, 1788–1939,* AH372
Smith, Anna Piszczan-Czaja. *Encyclopedia of German-American genealogical research,* AJ22, AJ90
Smith, Bardwell. *Guide to Buddhist religion,* BC472
Smith, Barry. *Neuroscience year,* EH87
Smith, Betty. *Japanese journals in English,* EA50
Smith, C. G. *The Times Books world weather guide,* EF163

Smith, Carleton Sprague. *American hymns old and new*, BC317

Smith, Chester M. *American philatelic periodicals*, BG199

Smith, Christine M. *Historical bibliography of art museum serials from the United States and Canada*, BF49

Smith, Clifford Neal. *Encyclopedia of German-American genealogical research*, AJ22, AJ90

Smith, Colin. *Collins Spanish-English, English-Spanish dictionary*, AC731, AC738

——— *The place-names of Roman Britain*, CL199

Smith, Curtis C. *Twentieth-century science-fiction writers*, BE306

Smith, Dan. *The war atlas*, CJ603

Smith, David A. *The college student's guide to transferring schools*, CB294

Smith, David Eugene. *Rara arithmetica*, EB18

Smith, David G. *The Cambridge encyclopedia of earth sciences*, EF3

Smith, David M. *Dictionary of human geography*, CL44

Smith, Dennis. *Scottish family histories*, AJ121

Smith, Denzell S. *The later Jacobean and Caroline dramatists*, BE651

——— *The new intellectuals*, BE650

——— *The popular school*, BE649

——— *The predecessors of Shakespeare*, BE648

——— *Studies in Jacobean drama, 1973–1984*, BE646

Smith, Diane H. *Complete guide to citing government documents*, AF69

——— *The complete guide to citing government information resources*, AF69

——— *Management of government information resources in libraries*, AF61

Smith, Dorothy B. Frizzell. *Subject index to poetry for children and young people*, BE322

Smith, Dwight L. *American and Canadian West*, DB165

——— *History of Canada*, DB187

Smith, Dwight La Vern. *The War of 1812*, DB100

Smith, Edward Conrad. *Dictionary of American politics*, CJ128

Smith, Edward H. *Mechanical engineer's reference book*, EK244

Smith, Elsdon Coles. *American surnames*, AJ186

——— *New dictionary of American family names*, AJ186

——— *Personal names*, AJ166

Smith, Eric. *A dictionary of classical reference in English poetry*, BE716

Smith, F. Seymour. *The classics in translation*, BE1011

Smith, Frank. *A genealogical gazetteer of England*, AJ112

——— *Genealogical research in England and Wales*, AJ99

Smith, Frank A. *Transportation in America*, CH453

Smith, Frederick. *The great song thesaurus*, BJ286

Smith, George Adam. *Atlas of the historical geography of the Holy Land*, BC202

Smith, Gerald Rex. *The Yemens*, DE280

Smith, Gerald Stanton. *Eighteenth century Russian literature, culture and thought*, BE1385

Smith, Graeme Kinross. *Australia's writers*, BE848

Smith, Gregory White. *The best lawyers in America*, CK141

Smith, H. Daniel. *Focus on Hinduism*, BC481

Smith, Harold. *The British labour movement to 1970*, CH638

Smith, Harold Eugene. *Historical and cultural dictionary of Thailand*, DE266

Smith, Helmer. *A critical Pali dictionary*, AC626

Smith, Hilda L. *Women and the literature of the seventeenth century*, BE740

Smith, Hugh. *Academic dress and insignia of the world*, CB396

Smith, Inese A. *The Baltic states*, DC70

Smith, Irene. *History of the Newbery and Caldecott medals*, AA343

Smith, J. H. *Ford list of British parliamentary papers, 1965–1974*, AF196

Smith, James Ward. *Religion in American life*, BC27

Smith, Jessie Carney. *Ethnic genealogy*, AJ8

——— *Notable black American women*, AH67

——— *Statistical record of black America*, CC400, CG83

Smith, John David. *Black slavery in the Americas*, CC377

——— *Dictionary of Afro-American slavery*, CC386

Smith, John F. *Critical bibliography of building conservation*, BF206

Smith, John William. *The urban politics dictionary*, CJ42

Smith, Joseph. *Bibliotheca anti-Quakeriana*, BC352

——— *Bibliotheca Quakeristica*, BC352

——— *Descriptive catalogue of Friends' books*, BC353

Smith, K. W. *Bibliography of South African history*, DD223

Smith, Linda C. *Reference and information services*, AK235

Smith, Lyn Wall. *Index to reproductions of American paintings appearing in more than 400 books, mostly published since 1960*, BF61, BF63

Smith, Margaret M. *Index of English literary manuscripts*, BE603

Smith, Margo L. *Anthropological bibliographies*, CE19

Smith, Martin A. *Encyclopedia of physical sciences and engineering information sources*, EA14

Smith, Murray F. *Selected bibliography of German literature in English translation, 1956–1960*, BE1239

Smith, Myron J. *The airline bibliography*, CH476

——— *American Civil War navies*, CJ609

——— *American naval bibliography*, CJ609, CJ610

——— *American Navy, 1798–1860*, CJ609

——— *American Navy, 1865–1918*, CJ609

——— *American Navy, 1918–1941*, CJ609

——— *American warplanes 1908–1988*, DA170

——— *Baseball*, BK60

——— *Battle of Pearl Harbor*, DA170

——— *Battles of Coral Sea and Midway, May–June 1942*, DA170

——— *Cloak and dagger fiction*, BE271

——— *The college football bibliography*, BK75

——— *Navies in the American Revolution*, CJ609

——— *Professional football*, BK80

——— *The secret wars*, CJ546

——— *The Soviet navy, 1941–1978*, CJ633

——— *United States Navy and Coast Guard, 1946–1983*, CJ609, CJ610

——— *Watergate*, CJ110

——— *World War I in the air*, DA193

——— *World War II*, DA200

——— *World War II at sea*, DA200

Smith, Paul. *Contemporary legend*, CF37

Smith, Peter R. *Dictionary of architectural and building technology*, BF240

Smith, R. E. F. *Russian-English dictionary of social sciences*, CA41

——— *A Russian-English social science dictionary*, CA41

Smith, Richard. *Concise Coptic-English lexicon*, AC273

Smith, Robert A. *Late Georgian and Regency England, 1760–1837*, DC303, DC320

Smith, Robert C. *Avondale to Zimbabwe*, CL157

Smith, Robert Chester. *Guide to the art of Latin America*, BF22

Smith, Robert McCaughan. *The independent learners' sourcebook*, CB350

Smith, Robert V. *Graduate research*, EA8

Smith, Roger C. *Smith's guide to the literature of the life sciences*, EG5

Smith, Roger P. *Clinical toxicology of commercial products*, EH424

Smith, Ronald L. *Who's who in comedy*, BH24

Smith, Stephen L. J. *Dictionary of concepts in recreation and leisure studies*, BK109

Smith, Sweetman R. *The dictionary of marketing*, CH581

Smith, Tom W. *Trends in public opinion*, CJ492

Smith, Valerie. *African American writers*, BE542

Smith, Virginia Carlson. *The women's movement in the seventies*, CC498

Smith, W. A. *Dictionary of anonymous and pseudonymous English literature*, AA150

Smith, Whitney. *Flags and arms across the world*, AL193

——— *Flags through the ages and across the world*, AL193, AL194

Smith, William. *Chambers/Murray Latin-English dictionary*, AC578

——— *Dictionary of Christian antiquities*, BC246, BC249

——— *Dictionary of Christian biography*, BC249

——— *A dictionary of Greek and Roman geography*, CL105

Smith, William C. *Music publishing in the British Isles from the beginning until the middle of the nineteenth century*, BJ181, BJ184

Smith-Morris, Miles. *World development directory*, CH134

Smithe, Frank B. *Naturalist's color guide*, ED62

Smithells, Colin J. *Smithells metals reference book*, EK281

Smithells metals reference book, Smithells, Colin J., EK281

Smith's guide to the literature of the life sciences, Smith, Roger C., EG5

Smithsonian Astrophysical Observatory. *Smithsonian Astrophysical Observatory star atlas of reference stars and nonstellar objects*, EC73, EC74

——— *Star catalog*, EC74

Smithsonian Astrophysical Observatory star atlas of reference stars and nonstellar objects, Smithsonian Astrophysical Observatory, EC73, EC74

Smithsonian Institution. *A bibliography of eastern Asiatic botany*, EG106

——— *Finders' guide to decorative arts in the Smithsonian Institution*, BG28

——— *Handbook of North American Indians*, CC419, CC432

——— *Smithsonian physical tables*, ED50

——— *Smithsonian timelines of the ancient world*, DA84

Smithsonian Institution. Bureau of American Ethnology. *An author, title, and subject check list of Smithsonian Institution publications relating to anthropology*, CE16

——— *Catalog to manuscripts at the National Anthropological Archives, Department of Anthropology, National Museum of Natural History, Smithsonian Institution, Washington, D.C*, CE31

——— *Index to Bulletins 1–100 of the Bureau of American Ethnology*, CE83

Smithsonian Institution. Conservation Analytical Laboratory. *International index of conservation research*, BF199

Smithsonian Institution. Libraries. *Catalog of the Cooper-Hewitt Museum of Design Library of the Smithsonian Institution Libraries*, BG15

Smithsonian physical tables, Smithsonian Institution, ED50

Smithsonian timelines of the ancient world, DA84

Smits, Rudolf. *Half a century of Soviet serials, 1917–1968*, AD147

Smitten, Jeffrey R. *English novel explication*, BE675

Smock, Raymond. *A guide to manuscripts in the presidential libraries*, AK102, CJ176

Smolyarova, N. A. *Elsevier's dictionary of glaciology in four languages*, EF125

Smyers, Virginia L. *Bibliography of American literature*, BE400

Smyth, Daragh. *Guide to Irish mythology*, CF30, CF31

Snarr, Neil. *Sandinista Nicaragua*, DB315

Snead, Rodman E. *World atlas of geomorphic features*, EF114

Sneath, Peter. *Bergey's manual of systematic bacteriology*, EG309

Snell, Bruno. *Lexikon des frühgriechischen Epos*, AC447

Snell, Foster Dee. *Encyclopedia of industrial chemical analysis*, EE27

Snell, Walter Henry. *A glossary of mycology*, EG138

—— *Three thousand mycological terms*, EG138

Snellaert, F. A. *Vlaamsche bibliographie*, AA581

Snelling, John. *The Buddhist handbook*, BC458

Sniderman, Florence M. *Dramatic criticism index*, BE219

Snow, Bonnie. *Drug information*, EH318

Snow, Philip A. *A bibliography of Fiji, Tonga, and Rotuma*, DF7

Snoxall, R. A. *A concise English-Swahili dictionary*, AC759

—— *Luganda-English dictionary*, AC396

Snyder, Louis L. *Louis L. Snyder's historical guide to World War II*, DA208

Snyder, Louis Leo. *Encyclopedia of nationalism*, CJ34

—— *Encyclopedia of the Third Reich*, DC258, DC259

—— *The Third Reich, 1933–1945*, DC241

Snyder, Paula. *The European women's almanac*, CC569

Snyder, Thomas D. *120 years of American education*, CB135

So Sethaputra. *New model English-Thai dictionary*, AC780

Sobel, Robert. *Biographical directory of the Council of Economic Advisers*, CH95

—— *Biographical directory of the governors of the United States*, CJ288

—— *Biographical directory of the United States executive branch, 1774–1989*, CJ189

Sobin, Julian M. *Encyclopedia of China today*, DE141

Soboul, Albert. *Dictionnaire historique de la Révolution française*, DC184

Sobsey, Richard. *Disability, sexuality, and abuse*, CC185

Soccer, BK98, BK99

Social action
  directories, AL48

Social action (by country or region)
  Ireland, AL67

Social and behavioral aspects of female alcoholism, Chalfant, H. Paul, CC111

Social and behavioral science research, Krathwohl, David R., CC28

Social and behavioral sciences
  abstract journals, AD254, BB24, BE38, CA24, CE23
  bibliography, CA1, CA4, CA7, CA8, CA9, CA11, CA12, CJ13
    current, CA13, CA27, EA32
  bibliography of bibliographies, CA14
  biography, CA36, CA37, CA44, CA61, CA62, CA63, CC50, EA170
  congresses and meetings, AL32
    bibliography, AL27
    indexes, AL29
  databases, CA3, CA25, CA27
  dictionaries, CA38, CA39, CA40, CA42, CA43
    bilingual
      Russian-English, CA41
  directories, CA48, CA49
    Great Britain, CA46
  dissertations, AG53, CA20, CA21
  encyclopedias, CA30, CA31, CA32, CA33, CA35, CA36, CA37, CA44
  financial aids, CA52
  guides, CA1, CA4, CA5, CA6, CA7, CA8
  guides for authors, CC54
  handbooks, CA57, CA62
  indexes, AD254, AD288, BB24, BE38, CA23, CA24, CA25, CA27, CA29, CE23, DF22
  library resources, CA13
  periodicals, AD66, CA18, CD14
    bibliography, CA19
    guides, AD117
  quotations, CA36, CA44
  research, CB113
  research centers
    directories, CA56

research methods, CA2, CA57, CA58, CA59, CC28, CC560
reviews of research, CA3, CA26, CA46, CA47, CA51, CA60
sourcebooks, CA50
statistics, CA54
style manuals, CA55
synonyms and antonyms, CA43
thesauruses, CA43

Social and behavioral sciences (by country or region)
  Asia, CA53
  Australia
    indexes, CA23, DF22
  Hungary, DC389
  India, CA6, CA59
    periodicals
      indexes, CA28
    reviews of research, CA45
  Russia
    bibliography, CA16
  Sri Lanka, DE258

Social and behavioral sciences (by subject)
  history
    bibliography, CD60, EA235
  history (by period)
    20th century, CA30
  philosophy, CA30

A social and economic atlas of India, TT. Maps & Publications Private Ltd, CH198

A social and religious history of the Jews, Baron, Salo Wittmayer, BC561

Social casework. Cumulative index, 1920–1989, Kendall, Katherine A., CC44

Social classes, CC9

Social conditions and social welfare, CC29
  associations, AL23
  bibliography, CA15, CC31, CC32
  biography, CC39
  directories, CA15
  encyclopedias, CA35
  guides for authors, CC41

Social conditions and social welfare (by country or region)
  United States
    directories, CC461

The social history of art, Hauser, Arnold, BF130

Social indicators III, CG78

Social indicators of development, CG41, CH159

Social networks and mental health, Biegel, David E., CC29

Social protest from the left in Canada, 1870–1970, Weinrich, Peter, CJ515

Social psychology, CD96
  encyclopedias, CD95
  handbooks, CD97
  tests and measurements, CD98

Social reformers, CC38
  biography, CA64

Social science abstracts, CG18, CG67

A social science bibliography of Northern Ireland, 1945–1983, DC356

The social science encyclopedia, CA37

Social Science Federation of Canada. *Historical statistics of Canada*, CG113, DB209

Social science information, Rama Reddy, E., CA6

Social science quotations, CA36, CA44

Social science reference sources, Li, Tze-chung, CA4

Social Science Research Council. *East Central Europe*, DC33

—— *Southeastern Europe*, DC59

Social science research index, CA21

The social sciences, CA7

—— Herron, Nancy L., CA4

—— Wepsiec, Jan, CA19

Social sciences and humanities in Russia, Rossiĭskaĭa Akademiĭa nauk, CA16

Social sciences and humanities index, AD288, BA5, CA29

Social sciences citation index, BA3, CA27

Social sciences in modern India, CA28

Social sciences in the USSR, CA16

Social sciences index, AD288, CA24, CA29

Social security, CH519
  bibliography, CH498, CH499
  handbooks, CH520
  statistics, CH526

Social security abstracts, CH498

Social security bulletin, CH526

Social security handbook, CH519

Social security programs throughout the world, CH520

Social stratification, Kinloch, Graham Charles, CC9

Social stratification in the Middle East and North Africa, Banuazizi, Ali, DE26

Social studies teaching and learning, CB116

Social support and health, CC31

Social support networks, Biegel, David E., CC29

Social surveys, CD63, CD65, CJ488
  bibliography, CJ495
  handbooks, CA58, CJ491
  polls, CJ492

Social welfare in America, CC32

Social work
  abstract journals, CC45
  bibliography, CC43
  biography, CC39, CC50
  careers, CC53
  dictionaries, CC47
  directories, CC48, CC50
  encyclopedias, CC46
  guides for authors, CC54
  handbooks, CC52, CC235
  periodicals, CC41
  statistics, CC52

•*Social work abstracts*, CC45

Social work almanac, Ginsberg, Leon H., CC52

The social work dictionary, Barker, Robert L., CC47

Social work education, CC42, CC49

Social work education, Li, Hong-Chan, CC42

Social work research & abstracts, CC45

Social work year book, CC46

Socialism *see* **Communism and socialism**

Socialism and American life, Egbert, Donald Drew, CJ527

Socialism in literature, BE1229, BE1249

Socialist states *see* **Communist states**

Sociedad Española de Estudios Clásicos. *Bibliografía de los estudios clásicos en España*, DA95

Sociedad Mexicana de Inteligencia Artificial. *The AI directory*, EK198

Società Retorumantscha. *Disciunari rumantsch grischen*, AC664

Societatea de Ştiinţe Filologice din Republica Socialistă România. *Bibliografia românească modernă, 1831–1918*, AA781

Société, culture et histoire du Rwanda, Hertefelt, Marcel d', DD198

Société des américanistes. *Bibliographie américaniste, linguistique amérindienne*, BD239

Société des Libraires et Éditeurs de la Suisse Romande. *Catalogue des éditions de la Suisse romande*, AA836

—— *Catalogue des ouvrages de langue francaise publiés en Suisse*, AA836

Société d'Études Historiques de la Nouvelle-Calédonie. *Bibliographie méthodique, analytique et critique de la Nouvelle-Calédonie*, DF41

Société d'histoire et d'épistémologie des sciences du langage. *Renaissance linguistics archive, 1350–1700*, BD67

Société française d'études et de réalisations cartographiques. *Atlas départemental*, CL328

Société internationale arthurienne. *Bulletin bibliographique de la Société internationale arthurienne*, BE338

Société Rencesvals. *Bulletin bibliographique de la Société Rencesvals*, BE1201

Societies *see* **Associations, societies, and academies**

Society for Analytical Chemistry. *Analytical abstracts*, EE20

Society for French Studies (Great Britain). *Current research in French studies at universities & polytechnics in the United Kingdom & Ireland,* BE1142

Society for Historians of American Foreign Relations. *Guide to American foreign relations since 1700,* DB15

Society for Industrial and Applied Mathematics. *Combined membership list of the American Mathematical Society, the Mathematical Association of America, and the Society for Industrial and Applied Mathematics,* EB56

Society for Old Testament Study. *Book list,* BC117

Society for Research in Child Development. *Child development abstracts and bibliography,* CC157, CD81

Society for Research into Higher Education. *Research into higher education abstracts,* CB235

Society for the Advancement of Scandinavian Study (U.S.). *Directory of Scandinavian studies in North America,* DC77

Society for the History of Technology. *Current bibliography in the history of technology,* EA242

Society for the North American Cultural Survey. *This remarkable continent,* DB76

Society for the Study of Labour History. *Labour and social history theses,* CH295, DC283

Society for the Study of Southern Literature. *Southern writers,* BE578

Society for the Study of Southern Literature. Committee on Bibliography. *Southern literature, 1968–1975,* BE574

Society for Theatre Research. *Directory of theatre resources,* BH53

Society of Actuaries. *Year book,* CH515

Society of Actuaries yearbook, CH515

Society of American Archivists. *A glossary for archivists, manuscript curators, and records managers,* AK184
—— *Guidelines for college and university archives,* AK186
—— *Understanding archives and manuscripts,* AK188

Society of American Foresters. *Forestry handbook,* EJ185

Society of Architectural Historians. *Bibliography of doctoral dissertations relating to American architectural history, 1897–1991,* BF227
—— *Buildings of the United States,* BF254

Society of Automotive Engineers. *Lubrication,* EK239
—— *SAE handbook,* EK41

Society of Biblical Literature. *Harper's Bible commentary,* BC172
—— *Harper's Bible dictionary,* BC139
—— *Harper's Bible pronunciation guide,* BC140
—— *Index of articles on the New Testament and the early church published in festschriften,* BC121

Society of Dyers and Colourists. *Colour index,* ED63

Society of Economic Geologists. *Annotated bibliography of economic geology,* EF21

Society of Genealogists. *The dictionary of genealogy,* AJ111

Society of Genealogists (Great Britain). *Cofrestri plwyf Cymru = Parish registers of Wales,* AJ130

Society of Indexers. *Indexing and abstracting,* AK217

Society of Manufacturing Engineers. *Tool and manufacturing engineers handbook,* EK248

Society of Mining Engineers mining engineering handbook, EK254

Society of Nursing Professionals. *Who's who in American nursing,* EH283

Society of Photographic Scientists and Engineers. *Abstracts of photographic science and engineering literature,* BF332

Society of Technical Writers and Publishers. *An annotated bibliography on technical writing, editing, graphics, and publishing, 1950–1965,* EA164

Socio-economic development bibliography, Swaziland. Economic Planning Office, DD230

Socio-economic profiles, DD166

Sociolinguistics, BD80, BD81, BD83, BD85
Sociolinguistics (by language)
 Slavic languages
  bibliography, BD180
Sociological abstracts, CC13, CC20, CC13
Sociological Abstracts, Inc. *Linguistics and language behavior abstracts,* BD31
—— *Second language instruction/acquisition abstracts,* CB62
—— *Thesaurus of sociological indexing terms,* CC20
Sociology, CC24
 abstract journals, CC13
 bibliography, CC4, CC5, CC6, CC7, CC8, CC9, CC10, CE4, EH11
  current, CC13
 biography, CA63, CC39
 dictionaries, CC17, CC18, CC19
 encyclopedias, CC14, CC15, CC16
 guides, CC1, CC23, EJ6
 guides to research, CC24
 handbooks, CC25, CC26, CC27
 indexes, CC12
 periodicals, CC11
 quotations, CC22
 terminology, CC20, CC21
 see also **Clinical sociology; Educational sociology**
Sociology, Aby, Stephen H., CC1
—— Wepsiec, Jan, CC10
Sociology of aging, Harris, Diana K., CC70
The sociology of contemporary Quebec nationalism, Lambert, Ronald D., CJ301
Sociology of education abstracts, CB63
Sociology of leisure and sport abstracts, BK11
Sociology of medicine and health care, Litman, Theodor J., CC6, EH11
Sociology of poverty in the United States, Chalfant, H. Paul, CC260
The sociology of religion, Blasi, Anthony J., BC7
The sociology of work, Ghorayshi, Parvin, CC7
Socrates, BB55, BB56
Socrates, Navia, Luis E., BB56
Soden, Wolfram von. *Akkadisches Handwörterbuch,* AC203
—— *Reallexikon der Assyriologie, unter Mitwirkung zahlreicher Fachgelehrter,* DA80
Soderburg, Paul. *The big book of halls of fame in the United States and Canada,* BK32
Söderwall, Knut Fredrik. *Ordbok öfver svenska medeltids-språket,* AC763
Sofiano, T. A. *Anglo-russkiĭ geologicheskiĭ slovar',* EF89
Softball, BK56
Software, EK169
The software encyclopedia, EK201
Sögel, E. *Eesti kirjanduse biograafiline leksikon,* BE1123
Sögel, Endel. *Eesti kirjanduse ajalugu,* BE1125
Sogô, Masaki. *Jisho kaidai jiten,* AB72
Sohlmans Musiklexikon, BJ126
Soil science
 bibliography, EJ4
 dictionaries
  multilingual, EJ26
 encyclopedias, EJ22
 guides, EJ4
 handbooks, EJ53, EJ54, EJ63
Soil taxonomy, EJ54, EJ63
•*SOILCD,* EJ18
Soils and fertilizers abstracts, EJ19
Soiuz sovetskikh sotsialisticheskikh respublik, AB84
Sokal, Michael M. *A guide to manuscript collections in the history of psychology and related areas,* CD58
Sokoloff, Michael. *A dictionary of Jewish Palestinian Aramaic of the Byzantine period,* AC472
Sokrashcheniia v sovetskikh izdaniiakh, Kramer, Alex A., AC687
Sokurova, M. V. *Obshchie bibliografi russkikh knig grazhdanskoĭ pechati, 1708–1955,* AA63

Solano Santos, Sagrario. *Diccionario de términos literarios,* BE75
Solar energy, EK212
Solé, Carlos A. *Bibliografía sobre el español de América, 1920–1986,* BD175
—— *Latin American writers,* BE891
Soleinne, Martineau de. *Bibliothèque dramatique de Monsieur de Soleinne,* BE1184
Solicitors' and barristers' directory and diary, CK221
Soliday, Gerald L. *History of the family and kinship,* CC213
Solís, Gerardo. *West's Spanish-English/English-Spanish law dictionary,* CK55
Sollitto, Sharmon. *Bibliography of society, ethics, and the life sciences,* EH237
Soloman, Alan C. *A bibliography for the study of African politics,* CJ397
Solomon, Sheila. *Dictionary of eye terminology,* EH110
Solomon Gebre Christos. *A decade of Ethiopian languages publications, 1959–1969,* AA857
Solomon Islands, DF50
 statistics, CG442
Solomon Islands bibliography to 1980, Edridge, Sally, DF50
Solon, Louis Marc Emmanuel. *Ceramic literature,* BG55
Solórzano, Lucia. *Barron's 300 best buys in college education,* CB291
Solov'ev, L. P. *Bibliograficheskiĭ ukazatel' geodezicheskoĭ literatury za 40 let 1917–1956,* EF23
Solow, Linda. *A checklist of music bibliographies and indexes in progress and unpublished,* BJ23
Solow, Linda I. *The Boston composers project,* BJ67
Solt, Marilyn Leathers. *Newbery and Caldecott Medal and Honor books,* AA343
Soltani, Poori. *A directory of Iranian periodicals,* AD198
Soltow, Martha Jane. *American women and the labor movement, 1825–1974,* CC503, CC511
—— *Worker benefits, industrial welfare in America, 1900–1935,* CH505
Solubilities, inorganic and metal organic compounds, Linke, William F., EE81
Solubilities of inorganic and organic compounds, Vsesoiuznyĭ Institut Nauchnoĭ i Tekhnicheskoĭ Informatsii (Russia), EE91
Solubilities of inorganic and organic substances, Seidell, Atherton, EE81
Solubility, EE81
 handbooks, EE91
Solurova, M. V. *Obshchie bibliografii russkikh periodicheskikh izdaniĭ, 1703–1954, i materialy po statistike russkoĭ periodicheskoĭ pechati,* AD143
Solvents, EK56
Somali-English dictionary, Abraham, Roy Clive, AC724
—— Zorc, R. David Paul, AC725
Somali language
 dictionaries
  bilingual
   English-Somali, AC724
   Somali-English, AC724, AC725
Somalia
 bibliography, DD18, DD107, DD109, DD206, DD207
 current surveys, DD62
 encyclopedias, DD48
 government publications
  bibliography, AF237
 statistics, CG355
Somalia, Castagno, Margaret, DD48
—— Chapin Metz, Helen, DD62
—— DeLancey, Mark W., DD18
—— Laitin, David D., DD207
—— Salad, Mohamed Khalief, DD207
—— Samatar, Said S., DD207
Somalia statistical abstract, CG355
Somer, Elizabeth. *The nutrition desk reference,* EH299

Somer, John L. *American and British literature, 1945–1975*, BE414, BE761

Somerville, Keith. *Angola*, DD128

Something about the author, BE389

Sommaire des périodiques, AD302

Sommario di statistiche storiche, 1926–1985, CG256

Sommario storico di statistiche sulla popolazione, CG257

Sommer, Elyse. *Similes dictionary*, BE89

Sommer, Francis E. *Catalogue of incunabula and manuscripts in the Army Medical Library*, EH24

Sommer, Mike. *Similes dictionary*, BE89

Sommer, P. *Bibliographie cartographique internationale*, CL226

Sommerfelt, Alf. *Norsk riksmålsordbok*, AC617

Sommers, Richard. *The era of the Civil War—1820–1876*, DB113

Somoshegyi-Szokol, Gaston. *Contemporary Chilean literature in the University Library at Berkeley*, BE942

Sonderegger, Stefan. *Sprachgeschichte*, BD125

Søndergaard, Jens. *Dansk juridisk bibliografi*, CK207

Song index, Sears, Minnie Earl, BJ283, BJ284, BJ287, BJ289

Songe, Alice H. *American universities and colleges*, CB292

——— *Private school education in the U.S*, CB34

——— *World guide to library, archive, and information science associations*, AK55

Songs, BJ271, BJ272, BJ273, BJ274
  bibliography, BJ267, BJ275, BJ278, BJ279, BJ280, BJ284
  discography, BJ281
  indexes, BJ258, BJ267, BJ277, BJ282, BJ283, BJ284, BJ285, BJ286, BJ287, BJ289, BJ315, BJ316
  library catalogs, BJ327

Songs (by country or region)
  Provence, BE1371
  Spain
    bibliography, BE1477
    manuscripts, BE1478

Songs from Hollywood musical comedies, 1927 to the present, Woll, Allen L., BJ365

Songs in collections, DeCharms, Désirée, BJ284

Songs of the American theater, Lewine, Richard, BJ267

——— Simon, Alfred, BJ267

Songs of the theater, Lewine, Richard, BJ267

Sonneck, Oscar George Theodore. *Bibliography of early secular American music (18th century)*, BJ64, BJ68

——— *Catalogue of opera librettos printed before 1800*, BJ239

——— *Dramatic music (class M 1500, 1510, 1520)*, BJ240

The sonnet in England and America, Donow, Herbert S., BE700

Sonnino, Lee A. *Handbook to sixteenth-century rhetoric*, BE351

Sontheimer, Walther. *Der kleine Pauly*, DA101

Sontz, Ann H. L. *The American college president, 1636–1989*, CB228

Soothill, William Edward. *A dictionary of Chinese Buddhist terms*, BC480

Soper, Elizabeth W. *The Facts on File dictionary of education*, CB80

Sophocles, Evangelinus Apostolides. *Greek lexicon of the Roman and Byzantine periods*, AC459

Sopikov, Vasiliĭ Stephanovich. *Opyt rossiiskoi bibliografiĭ*, AA790

Soraas, Haakon. *English-Norwegian dictionary*, AC618

Sorbelli, Albano. *Dizionario bio-bibliografico dei bibliotecari e bibliofili italiani dal sec. XIV al XIX*, AK90

Sören Sörensen. *Ensk-Íslensk orðabók*, AC507

Sorensen, Toben. *Stedregister til Dansk Tidsskrift-Index*, AD309

Sorenson, John L. *Pre-Columbian contact with the Americas across the oceans*, DB22

Sörensen, Sören. *Ensk-Íslensk orðabók*, AC507

Soria, Regina. *Dictionary of nineteenth-century American artists in Italy, 1760–1914*, BF319

Sororities see **Secret societies**

Sors, Andrew I. *Pollution research index*, EK76

Sosa, Ernest. *A companion to epistemology*, BB28

Sosa, Francisco. *Biografías de Mexicanos distinguidos*, AH103

Sosa de Newton, Lily. *Diccionario biográfico de mujeres argentinas*, AH118

Sötér, Istvan. *Magyar irodalom története*, BE1281

Sotheby's concise encyclopedia of furniture, BG129

Sotheby's concise encyclopedia of glass, BG61

Sotheby's concise encyclopedia of porcelain, BG62

Sotheby's concise encyclopedia of silver, Truman, Charles, BG143

The Sotheby's directory of silver, 1600–1940, Brett, Vanessa, BG143

Sotiron, Minko. *An annotated bibliography of works on daily newspapers in Canada, 1914–1983*, AE39

Souchal, François. *French sculptors of the 17th and 18th centuries*, BF399

Soukup, Paul A. *Christian communication*, BC224

Soul music A–Z, Gregory, Hugh, BJ353

Soul music who's who, Tee, Ralph, BJ353

Soule, James. *Glossary for horticultural crops*, EJ243

Soulen, Richard N. *Handbook of biblical criticism*, BC190

Sound recordings
  catalogs, AA385, BJ387

Soupis bibliografi novín a casopisu vydanvanych na uzemi Ceskoslovenske republiky, AE47

Soupis bibliografí novin a časopisů, vydávaných na území Československé republiky, Malec, Karel, AD88

Soupis československé literatury za léta 1901–1925, AA599

Soupis periodik geologických věd, Lomský, Josef, EF41

The source, AJ23, CH607

——— Shim, Jae K., CH320

Source book for African anthropology, Hambly, Wilfrid Dyson, CE102

A source book for ancient church history, Ayer, Joseph Cullen, BC281

Source book for food scientists, EJ171

A source book in astronomy, Shapley, Harlow, EC62

Source book in astronomy and astrophysics, 1900–1975, Gingerich, Owen, EC62

——— Lang, Kenneth R., EC62

A source-book of biological names and terms, Jaeger, Edmund Carroll, EG41

Source book of flavors, Heath, Henry B., EJ217

Source book of health insurance data, CH527

Source book of health insurance data. Update, CH527

A source book of Irish government, CJ378

A source book of Scottish history, Dickinson, William Crofts, DC366

Source book profiles, AL111

Source guide for toponymy and topology, CL217

Source index, EA41, EE18

Sourcebook for bibliographic instruction, AK231

A sourcebook for Hispanic literature and language, Bleznick, Donald W., BD172, BE1426

A sourcebook for research in law and medicine, Fiscina, Salvatore F., EH268

Sourcebook for research in music, Crabtree, Phillip, BJ2

Sourcebook for the performing arts, Slide, Anthony, BH17

Sourcebook of contemporary North American architecture from postwar to postmodern, Wright, Sylvia Hart, BF260

Sourcebook of county demographics, CH600

Sourcebook of criminal justice statistics, CK269

Sourcebook of demographics and buying power for every county in the USA, CH600

Sourcebook of geopolitical crisis, CJ72

Sourcebook of global statistics, Kurian, George Thomas, CG10

The sourcebook of library technology, AK177

The sourcebook of medical illustration, EH236

The sourcebook of zip code demographics, CH600

Sourcebook on Canadian women, Hauck, Philomena, CC603

A sourcebook on child sexual abuse, Finkelhor, David, CC167

Sourcebook on food and nutrition, EH313

Sourcebook on pornography, Osanka, Franklin Mark, CC290

Sourcefinder, CH720

Sources, McCullough, Rita I., CC502

Sources and documents of United States constitutions, Swindler, William F., CK175

Sources and documents of United States constitutions, second series, CK172

Sources and literature of English history from the earliest times to about 1485, Gross, Charles, DC304

The sources and literature of Scottish church history, Macgregor, Malcolm B., BC341

Sources and methods, CH691

Sources bibliographiques de l'Afrique de l'Ouest et de l'Afrique equatoriale d'expression française, Brasseur, Paule Marion, DD40

——— Maurel, Jean-François, DD40

Sources bibliographiques des états de l'ancien domaine colonial belge d'Afrique centrale, Hategekimana, Grégoire, DD111

Les sources de l'histoire de France depuis les origines jusqu'en 1815, DC147

Sources de l'histoire démographique des pays du Sahel conservées dans les archives, M'baye, Saliou, CG307, DD102

Les sources de l'histoire littéraire aux Archives Nationales, Gallet-Guerne, Danielle, BE1148

Sources d'information sur l'Afrique noire francophone et Madagascar, Porgès, Laurence, DD40

Sources du travail bibliographique, Malclès, Louise-Noëlle, AA6, AA12, AA352

Sources for early modern Irish history, 1534–1641, Edwards, R. Dudley, DC410

Sources for English local history, Stephens, W. B., DB147, DC350, DC351

Sources for social, economic and market research (North, Central & South America), CG71

Sources for the early history of Ireland, Kenney, James Francis, DC395

Sources for the history of houses, Harvey, John Hooper, BF206

Sources for the history of Irish civilisation, Hayes, Richard J., DC394

Sources for U.S. history, Stephens, W. B., DB147

Sources for West Indian studies, Ingram, Kenneth E., DB413

Sources in British political history, 1900–1951, Cook, Chris, DC17, DC335

Sources in European political history, Cook, Chris, DC17

Sources of African and Middle-Eastern economic information, Blauvelt, Euan, CH189

Sources of Anglo-Saxon literary culture, Biggs, Frederick M., BE731

——— Hill, Thomas D., BE731

——— Szarmach, Paul E., BE731

Sources of Asian/Pacific economic information, Blauvelt, Euan, CH202

Sources of European economic and business information, CH185

Sources of European economic information, Blauvelt, Euan, CH185

——— Durlacher, Jennifer, CH185

Sources of information in librarianship and information science, Prytherch, Raymond John, AK1

Sources of information in the social sciences, CA8

——— Webb, William H., CA4, CA7

Sources of information in transportation, CH444

Sources of information in water resources, Giefer, Gerald J., EK88

Sources of Jamaican history, 1655–1838, Ingram, Kenneth E., DB443

Sources of library statistics, 1972–1982, Lynch, Mary Jo, AK98

Sources of modern architecture, Sharp, Dennis, BF224
Sources of serials, AD17
The sources of Shakespeare's plays, Muir, Kenneth, BE787
Sources of world financial and banking information, CH221
Sources on the history of women's magazines, 1792–1960, Zuckerman, Mary Ellen, CC523
Sourkes, Theodore L. *Nobel prize winners in medicine and physiology, 1901–1965,* AL177
Sousa, J. Galante de. *Enciclopédia de literatura brasileira,* BE929
Sousa-Farinha, B. J. de. *Summario da Bibliotheca lusitana,* AA774
Souter, Alexander. *Glossary of later Latin to 600 A.D.,* AC583
South, Aloha. *Guide to federal archives relating to Africa,* DD36, DD38, DD42
────── *Guide to non-federal archives and manuscripts in the United States relating to Africa,* DD36, DD42
South, Malcolm. *Mythical and fabulous creatures,* CF6
South Africa
 atlases, CL346
 bibliography, AA874, AA875, AA876, AA877, CJ410, DD18, DD213, DD214, DD217, DD224
  current, AA878
  bibliography of bibliography, AA72
 biography, AH311, AH313, AH315, AH325
  contemporary, CJ412, DD212
 biography (by subject)
  artists, BF142
 chronologies, CJ411, DD209, DD210
 current surveys, DD62
 dissertations, AG49
 encyclopedias, DD48
 newspapers, AE80
  bibliography, AE81
  union lists, AE81
 periodicals, AD178, DD211
  databases, AD335
  indexes, AD335
 reference books
  bibliography, AA353, AA354
 statistics, CG356, CG357, CG358, CG359
South Africa (by subject)
 economic sanctions, DD215
 ethnic groups
  bibliography, DD220
 ethnic relations, DD209
 foreign relations
  bibliography, DD218, DD219, DD221
 history
  bibliography, DD216, DD223
 music, BJ144
 place-names, CL156, CL216, CL217
 politics and government, CJ410, CJ411, CJ412, CJ413, DD208, DD210, DD212, DD213, DD222
 religion, BC49
 social conditions, DD222
 see also **Apartheid**
South Africa. Bureau of Statistics. *Statistical yearbook,* CG359
South Africa. Directorate of Surveys and Mapping. *Reader's digest atlas of Southern Africa,* CL345
South Africa. Office of Census and Statistics. *Official year book of the Union and of Basutoland, Bechuanaland Protectorate and Swaziland,* CG357
────── *Uniestatistieke oor vyftig jaar jubileumuitgawe,* CG358
South Africa. Place Names Committee. *Amptelike plekname in die Republiek van Suid-Afrika en in Suidwes-Afrika, goedgekeur tot 1 April 1977,* CL156
South Africa, Musiker, Reuben, AA72, AA353, AA354, DD18
────── Nelson, Harold D., DD62
────── Saunders, C. C., DD48
────── Stultz, Newell M., DD216

South Africa and the United Nations, Schoeman, Elna, DD224
South Africa under apartheid, Kalley, Jacqueline Audrey, DD216
South African bibliography, Musiker, Reuben, AA72, AA354
South African bibliography to the year 1925, Mendelssohn, Sidney, AA876
South African catalogue of books, AA877
South African history, Musiker, Naomi, DD223
South African history and historians, DD223
South African Institute of Race Relations. *Race relations survey,* DD209
South African Library Association. *Index to South African periodicals,* AD335
South African literature
 encyclopedias, BE1533
 guides, BE1535
 works in English
  bibliography, BE1534, BE1538
  indexes, BE1537
South African music encyclopedia, BJ144
South African national bibliography, AA876, AA878
South African newspapers on microfilm, Coetzee, J. C., AE80
The South African novel in English since 1950, Gorman, G. E., BE1535
South African periodical publications, 1800–1875, Saul, C. Daphne, AD178
South African political materials, Wynne, Susan G., CJ413
South African reference books and bibliographies of 1979–1980, Musiker, Reuben, AA354
South African review, DD211
South African sanctions directory, 1946–1988, Schoeman, Elna, DD215
South African theological bibliography, BC49
South Africa's foreign relations, 1961–1979, Rogaly, Gail Lynda, DD221
South Africa's foreign relations, 1980–1984, Kalley, Jacqueline Audrey, DD221
South Africa's road to change, 1987–1990, Kalley, Jacqueline Audrey, DD216
South Africa's townships 1980–1991, Seekings, Jeremy, DD222
South America
 bibliography, AA472, CL11
 periodicals, AD69
South America (by subject)
 anthropology and ethnology, CE81
 discovery and exploration, DB5
  library catalogs, DB2, DB4
 economic conditions
  bibliography, CH179
 folklore and popular culture, CF74
 history
  bibliography, DB5
  library catalogs, DB2
 native languages, BD237, BD239
  bibliography, BD243
 politics and government, CJ312
South America, Central America, and the Caribbean, CJ94, DB295
South American Indian narrative, theoretical and analytical approaches, Niles, Susan A., CF69, CF74
South and Southeast Asia, Nunn, Godfrey Raymond, DE1
South Asia, DE91
────── Sukhwal, B. L., CL21
The South Asia and Burma retrospective bibliography (SABREB), Shaw, Graham, AA889
South Asia Library Group. *Directory of South Asian library resources in the UK and the Republic of Ireland,* DE82
────── *South Asian bibliography,* DE81
South Asia Microform Project. *SAMP catalog,* DE77
South Asian Association for Regional Cooperation. *SAARC women,* AH363
South Asian bibliography, DE81
South Asian civilisations, Patterson, Maureen L. P., DE80

South Asian history, 1750–1950, Case, Margaret H., DE76
South Asian languages, BD224
South Asian library resources in North America, DE87
South Asian studies, DE88
South Carolina. [Laws, etc.]. *Code of laws of South Carolina, 1976,* CK179
South China Morning Post Ltd. *Who's who in Hong Kong,* AH348
South Dakota. [Laws, etc.]. *South Dakota codified laws,* CK179
South Dakota codified laws, South Dakota. [Laws, etc.], CK179
South-East Asia, BD229, BD236, BE1550
South in American literature, 1607–1900, Hubbell, Jay B., BE575
South Pacific bibliography, AA950
The South Pacific foreign affairs handbook, Hoadley, Steve, DF18
South Pacific islands legal systems, CK236
South Pacific periodicals index, University of the South Pacific. Pacific Information Centre, DF2
South Slavic languages, BD191
Southan, Joyce E. *A survey of classical periodicals,* BE1008
Southard, Samuel. *Death and dying,* CC181
Southeast Asia, Library of Congress, AD185
Southeast Asia Microforms Project. *Southeast Asia microforms project resources,* AE83
Southeast Asia microforms project resources, The-Mulliner, Lian, AE83
Southeast Asian languages
 bibliography, BD228
 guides, BD229, BD236, BE1550
Southeast Asian literature
 guides, BD229, BD236, BE1550
Southeast Asian literatures in translation, Jenner, Philip N., BE1542
Southeast Asian periodicals, Nunn, Godfrey Raymond, AD186, AD216
Southeast frontier of New Spain, Gerhard, Peter, DB225
Southeastern Europe, Horecky, Paul Louis, DC33, DC59
Southern, Eileen. *Biographical dictionary of Afro-American and African musicians,* BJ217
Southern, Richard. *An international vocabulary of technical theatre terms in eight languages,* BH81
Southern African Development Coordination Conference. *SADCC literature and literature on SADCC,* DD116
Southern African Development Coordination Conference (SADCC), Schoeman, Elna, DD116
Southern African dictionary of national biography, Rosenthal, Eric, AH311
Southern African history before 1900, Elphick, Richard, DD223
────── Jarrick, Inez, DD223
────── Thompson, Leonard Monteath, DD120, DD223
Southern African material in anthologies of English literature in the Strange Library of Africana, Strange Library of Africana, BE1537
Southern African Research Service. *South African review,* DD211
Southern African update, DD124, DD214
Southern American English, BD106
Southern Asia accessions list, Library of Congress. Orientalia Division, DE79
Southern Baptist Convention. *Annual,* BC329
Southern black creative writers, 1829–1953, Foster, Mamie Marie Booth, BE518
Southern elections, Bartley, Numan V., CJ290
Southern literary culture, Emerson, O. B., BE569
Southern literary culture, 1969–1975, Andrews, William L., BE569
────── Wages, Jack D., BE569
Southern literature, 1968–1975, Society for the Study of Southern Literature. Committee on Bibliography, BE574
────── Williams, Jerry T., BE574
Southern poor whites, Flynt, J. Wayne, CC262

Southern primaries and elections, 1920–1949, Heard, Alexander, CJ290
———— Strong, Donald S., CJ290
Southern states, DB154
  bibliography, BE574, DB112, DB156
  dissertations, BE569
  encyclopedias, DB158, DB159
  library resources, DB157
  periodicals, AD44
Southern states (by subject)
  elections, CJ290
  literature, BE568, BE571, BE575
  poverty, CC262
  religion
    bibliography, BC29
  travelers' accounts, DB108, DB155
Southern Sudan, Wawa, Yosa H., DD228
Southern writers, BE578
Southgate, Robert L. *Black plots & black characters,* BE539
Southon, I. W. *Dictionary of alkaloids,* EE123, EH334
Southwest Native American arts and material culture, Parezo, Nancy J., BG9, CC422
The Southwest Pacific, Thompson, Anne-Gabrielle, DF12
Southwestern American literature, Anderson, John Q., BE570
Southwestern pottery, Oppelt, Norman T., BG54
Southwestern states (by subject)
  ceramics and glass, BG54
Southwick, Leslie H. *Presidential also-rans and running mates, 1788–1980,* CJ192
Souza, Bernardino José de. *Dicionário da terra e da gente do Brasil,* CL183
Sovetskaia antarkticheskaia ekspeditsiia. Atlas Antarktiki, CL370
Sovetskaia arkheologicheskaia literatura, DA71
Sovetskaia bolgaristika, Diabina, N. I., DC113
Sovetskaia istoricheskaia entsiklopediia, DC569
Sovetskaia khudozhestvennaia literatura i kritika, BE1397
Sovetskaia khudozhestvennaia literatura i kritika, 1938/48, 1949/51–1964/65, BE1398
Sovetskaia strana v period grazhdanskoi voiny (1918–1922 gg.), DC590
Sovetskaia strana v period vosstanovleniia narodnogo khoziaistva, 1921–1925 gg, DC590
Sovetskaia voennaia entsiklopediia, CJ659, CJ660
Sovetskiĭ roman, ego teoriia i istoriia, Akademiia Nauk SSSR. Biblioteka, BE1383
Sovetskoe literaturovedenie i kritika, Akademiia Nauk SSSR. Fundamental'naia Biblioteka Obshchestvennykh Nauk, BE1384
Sovetskoe slavianovedenie, Kaloeva, I. A., DC42
Soviet-African relations, McLane, Charles B., DC599, DD107, DD112
Soviet African studies, 1918–59, Holdsworth, Mary, DD112
The Soviet air and strategic rocket forces, 1939–1980, CJ655
Soviet and communist quotations, CJ524
Soviet and East European abstract series, DC38
Soviet and East European foreign policy, DC36
The Soviet and East European political dictionary, McCrea, Barbara P., CJ396
Soviet and Russian newspapers at the Hoover Institution, Hoover Institution on War, Revolution, and Peace, AE70
Soviet armed forces review annual, CJ661
The Soviet army, 1939–1980, CJ655
Soviet Asia, bibliographies, Allworth, Edward, CC308
Soviet-Asian relations, McLane, Charles B., DC599
Soviet Central Asia, CC308
Soviet dissertations for advanced degrees in Russian literature and Slavic linguistics, 1934–1962, Magner, Thomas F., BE1408
Soviet dissident literature, Woll, Josephine, BE1407
Soviet, East European & Slavonic studies in Britain, DC41
Soviet economic facts, 1917–81, Clarke, Roger A., CH181

Soviet education, Yoo, Yushin, CB45
Soviet foreign policy, 1918–1945, Johnston, Robert H., DC586
Soviet foreign relations and world communism, Hammond, Thomas Taylor, CJ501
Soviet geography, American Geographical Society of New York, CL275
———— Library of Congress. Reference Department, CL151
Soviet historians on Latin America, Bartley, Russell H., DB260
Soviet intelligence and security services, CJ545
Soviet Jewish history, 1917–1991, Luckert, Yelena, BC536, DC587
Soviet law in English, Kavass, Igor I., CK223
A Soviet lexicon, Laird, Roy D., CJ395
Soviet-Middle East relations, McLane, Charles B., DC599
Soviet military encyclopedia, CJ660
The Soviet navy, 1941–1978, Smith, Myron J., CJ655
Soviet nuclear weapons policy, Green, William C., CJ654
Soviet perception of Canada, 1917–1987, Black, J. L., DB180
Soviet perception of Canada, 1945–1987, Black, J. L., DB180
Soviet publications on Judaism, Zionism, and the State of Israel, 1984–1989, Korsch, Boris, BC536, DC587
Soviet research institutes project, Ruble, Blair A., AL85
Soviet Russian literature, Struve, Gleb, BE1421
Soviet Russian literature in English, Gibian, George, BE1391
Soviet Russian literature since Stalin, Brown, Deming, BE1421
Soviet security and intelligence organizations, 1917–1990, Parrish, Michael, CJ542
Soviet serials currently received at the Center for Research Libraries, Center for Research Libraries, AD141
Soviet studies guide, DC591
Soviet successor states *see* **Former Soviet republics**
Soviet Union. Glavnoe arkhivnoe upravlenie. *Lichnye arkhivnye fondy v gosudarstvennykh kranilishchakh SSSR,* DC565
Soviet Union and Eastern Europe, Horak, Stephan M., DC32
Soviet Union and the NATO powers, CJ596
Soviet urban and regional planning, White, Paul M., CC306
A Soviet view of Africa, Darch, Colin, DD107, DD147, DD207
Soviet view of Arica, Darch, Colin, DD158
Soviet war machine, Menual, Stewart, CJ656
Sovietico-Turcica, BD210
Sowerwine-Mareschal, Marie-Aude. *Anarchisme,* CJ506
Sowjetische Forschungen zur Geschichte der deutsch-russischen Beziehungen von den Anfängen bis 1949, Borck, Karin, DC237
Sozialstatistische Daten, Österreichisches Statistisches Zentralamt, CG197
•*SPAAR information system,* EJ74
Space astronomy and astrophysics, EC58
Space engineering *see* **Aeronautical and space engineering**
Space sciences
  bibliography, EH70
  dictionaries
    abbreviations, EC33
    multilingual, EC41
  directories, EC44
  encyclopedias, EC31
  indexes, EH70
  see also **Aeronautical and space engineering**
Space sciences dictionary, Kleczek, Josip, EC41
Spagnol, Elena. *Dizionario di citazioni,* BE141
———— *Il libro delle citazioni,* BE141
Spahn, Janet M. *From radical left to extreme right,* AD45
Spahn, Mark. *Kan-Ei jukugo ribasu jiten,* AC558

Spahn, Theodore Jurgen. *From radical left to extreme right,* AD45
Spain
  atlases, CL331, CL333, CL334
  bibliography, AA67, AA800, AA801, AA802, AA803, AA804, AA806, AA807, AA809, AA821, AH290, BE1435, DC503
    15th–19th centuries, AA808, AA810, AA811, AA812, AA813, AA816, AA817, AA818, AA820
    16th-19th centuries, AA814, AA815
    20th century, AA822, AA823, AA824
    current, AA825, AA826, AA827
    early, AA819
    works in Catalan, AA799
  biography, AH287, AH288, AH289
    bibliography, AA67, AA801, AH290, BE1435
    contemporary, AH291
  dissertations, AG41
  gazetteers, CL149
  newspapers, AE76
    indexes, AE126
  periodicals, AD151, AD153, AD154, AD155, AD156
    current, AD159
    indexes, AD327, AD328, AD329
  statistics, CG280, CG281, CG282, CG284
Spain (by subject)
  foreign relations
    bibliography, DC502
  foreign relations (by country or region)
    North America, DB61
  historiography and historical methods, DC506, DC506
  history, DC4, DC515, DC516, DC517
    bibliography, DC499, DC501, DC507, DC509
    dissertations, DB267, DC510
    encyclopedias, DC512, DC513, DC514
    manuscripts and archives, DC511
    state and local government, DC508
  overseas territories, DC515
    government publications
      bibliography, AF227
    statistics, CG283, CG348
  religion, DC504
Spain. Dirección General de Archivos y Bibliotecas. *Catálogo colectivo de publicaciones periódicas en bibliotecas españolas,* AD241
Spain. Inspección Tecnica de Archivos. *Guía de los archivos estatales españoles,* DC511
Spain. Subdirección General de Archivos. *Guía de los archivos estatales españoles,* DC511
Spain, Shields, Graham J., DC507
Spain and Spanish America in the libraries of the University of California, University of California, Berkeley. Library, AA809
Spalding, Keith. *An historical dictionary of German figurative usage,* AC423
Spalding, W. F. *Tate's modern cambist,* CH287
———— *Tate's money manual,* CH287
Spangler, Stella S. *Science & technology in fact and fiction,* EA28
Spanier, Jerome. *An atlas of functions,* EB68
Der spanische Bürgerkrieg, Ruhl, Klaus-Jörg, DC518
Das spanische Drama im Goldenen Zeitalter, Reichenberger, Kurt, BE1469
Spanish & Mexican records of the American Southwest, Beers, Henry Putney, DB26, DB171
Spanish America after independence, c.1820–c.1870, DB291
Spanish-American art, BF20
Spanish American authors, Flores, Angel, BE889
Spanish-American drama
  bibliography, BE897, BE900, BE1470
  biobibliography, BE1464
  library catalogs, BE1470
Spanish-American languages
  bibliography, BD175
Spanish-American literature
  bibliography, BD171, BE868, BE871, BE872, BE877, BE878, BE879, BE880, BE1430, BE1432
  biobibliography., BE888, BE890

biography, BE891
dissertations, BE1446
encyclopedias, BE70
guides, BD172, BE867, BE1426, BE1427, BE1429
indexes, BE873
library catalogs, BE880
periodicals, BE882
women authors
bibliography, BE896
Spanish-American literature (by subject)
history, BE865, BE867, BE894, BE1429, BE1457
Spanish-American literature, Anderson Imbert, Enrique, BE865
—— Rela, Walter, BE868
Spanish American literature in the Yale University Library, Yale University. Library, BE880
Spanish American modernism, Anderson, Robert Roland, BE872
Spanish-American poetry
biobibliography, BE904
Spanish American theatre, Allen, Richard F., BE897
The Spanish-American War, Venzon, Anne Cipriano, DB101
Spanish American women writers, BE896
—— Cortina, Lynn Ellen Rice, BE896
—— Marting, Diane E., BE896
Spanish and English of United States Hispanos, Teschner, Richard V., BD176
Spanish and Portuguese Jewry, Singerman, Robert, BC531
Spanish and Spanish American literature, Woodbridge, Hensley Charles, BD171, BE1430
Spanish Armada of 1588, Rasor, Eugene L., DA170, DC505
Spanish artists from the fourth to the twentieth century, BF147
Spanish books in print, AA827
Spanish, Catalan, and Galician literary authors of the twentieth century, Zubatsky, David S., BE881, BE1445
Spanish Civil War, DC516, DC517, DC518
Spanish drama
bibliography, BE1459, BE1460, BE1461, BE1462, BE1463, BE1466, BE1467, BE1469, BE1470, BE1471, BE1472
biobibliography, BE1464
library catalogs, BE1459, BE1460, BE1461, BE1467, BE1470, BE1471, BE1472
manuscripts
catalogs, BE1465
translations, BE1468
Spanish drama collection in the Oberlin College Library, Oberlin College. Library, BE1467
Spanish drama of the Golden Age, Hispanic Society of America. Library, BE1465
—— Regueiro, José M., BE1470, BE1478
—— Reichenberger, Arnold Gottfried, BE1478
—— University of Pennsylvania. Libraries, BE1470
Spanish Empire, 1402–1975, DC515
Spanish-English, English-Spanish dictionary, AC735
Spanish-English/English-Spanish law dictionary, CK55
Spanish-English horticultural dictionary, Bourke, D. O'D, EJ239
Spanish etymological dictionary, AC744
Spanish fiction
bibliography, BE1473, BE1474, BE1475, BE1476
Spanish language
bibliography, BD168, BD169, BD170, BD171, BE1430
dictionaries, AC726, AC727, AC728
bibliography, AC751, AC752
bilingual, AC731
Spanish-English, AC729, AC730, AC732, AC733, AC734, AC735, AC736, AC737, AC738, AC739, AC740, AC744
etymology, AC742, AC743, AC744
idioms and usage, AC745, AC746
indexes, AC753
medieval–18th century, AC749, AC750

regional and dialect, AC754, AC755
visual, AC736
festschriften, BD166, BE1436
idioms and usage, AC745, AC746
old Spanish
bibliography, BD165
regional and dialect
Americas, BD172, BE1426
bibliography, BD173
Caribbean, BD174
United States, BD176
synonyms
dictionaries, AC747
synonyms and antonyms, AC748
Spanish-language reference books, AA361
Spanish literature
bibliography, BD169, BD171, BE1430, BE1431, BE1432, BE1434, BE1438, BE1439, BE1440, BE1442, BE1448
bibliography of bibliography, BE1445
biobibliography, BE888, BE890, BE1458
criticism
collections, BE1449
dictionaries, BE75
dissertations, BE1446
encyclopedias, BE70, BE1451
festschriften, BD166, BE1436
guides, BD172, BE867, BE1426, BE1427, BE1428, BE1429
handbooks, BE1452
translations, BE1448
bibliography, BE1447
women authors
biobibliography, BE1441, BE1444
Spanish literature (by period)
16th–17th centuries
bibliography, BE1437
medieval
bibliography, BE1433
biobibliography, BE1443
Spanish literature (by subject)
history, BE867, BE894, BE1429, BE1454, BE1455, BE1456, BE1457
Spanish literature, 1500–1700, Moseley, William W., BE1437
Spanish personal names, Gosnell, Charles Francis, AJ206
Spanish plays in English translation, O'Brien, Robert Alfred, BE1468
Spanish poetry
bibliography, BE1477, BE1479
library catalogs, BE1478
manuscripts, BE1477, BE1478
Spanish Protestants and reformers in the sixteenth century, Kinder, A. Gordon, DC504
Spanish proverbs, Iscla Rovira, Luis, BE149
Spanish-speaking Africa, Rishworth, Susan Knoke, AF227
Spanish-speaking Americans *see* **Latinas; Latinos**
Spanish surnames in the Southwestern United States, Woods, Richard D., AJ187
Spann, Gustav. *Bibliographie zur österreichischen Zeitgeschichte, 1918–1985,* DC89
Sparke, Archibald. *A bibliography of unfinished books in the English language, with annotations,* AA662
Sparkes, Ivan George. *Dictionary of collective nouns and group terms,* AC85
Sparks, H. F. D. *Apocryphal Old Testament,* BC94
Sparks, Kenneth R. *A bibliography of doctoral dissertations in television and radio,* BH296
Sparks, Linda. *American college regalia,* CB397
—— *College admissions,* CB230
—— *Institutions of higher education,* CB229
Spasova, Mariia Vladimorova. *Bŭlgarski periodichen pechat, 1944–1969,* AD87
Spaventa Filippi, Silvio. *Il libro dei mille savi,* BE140
Speake, Jennifer. *Biblical quotations,* BC154
—— *Concise Oxford dictionary of proverbs,* BE159
—— *Encyclopedia of the Renaissance,* DA146
—— *Treasury of Biblical quotations,* BC154

Speaker's & toastmaster's handbook, Prochnow, Herbert V., BE362
The speakers of the U.S. House of Representatives, Kennon, Donald R., CJ199
Speaking in tongues, BC18
Spear, Dorothea N. *Bibliography of American directories through 1860,* AL8, CH401
Spearman, Horace Ralph. *The British Burma gazetteer,* CL159
Spearritt, Peter. *Australians,* DF37
—— *Australians 1938,* DF37
Spears, Richard A. *Slang and euphemism,* AC134
Special bibliographic series, African Bibliographic Center, DD21
Special collections in children's literature, AK113
Special collections in college and university libraries, AK125
Special collections in the Library of Congress, Library of Congress, AK110
Special collections in Western Europe, AK131
Special edition, Einstein, Daniel, BH300
Special education
abstract journals, CB194, CD92
bibliography, CB190, CB192, CB193
databases, CB194, CD92
dictionaries, CB197, CB199
multilingual, CB198
directories, CB188, CB201, CB202
encyclopedias, CB195, CB196
handbooks, CB203, CB204, CB205
statistics, CB207
tests and measurements, CB189
Special education (by subject)
law, CB156
see also **Gifted children**
Special education, Sternlicht, Manny, CB192
Special Education Programs (U.S.). Division of Innovation and Development. *To assure the free appropriate public education of all children with disabilities,* CB207
Special education : research and practice, CB204
Special effects and stunts guide, BH207
Special Interest Group on CD-ROM Applications and Technology. *SIGCAT CD-ROM compendium,* AF107
Special issues and indexes of periodicals, AD34, CH29
Special libraries, AK181
directories, AK61, AK123, AK126
Special libraries, Ahrensfeld, Janet, AK181
—— Christianson, Elin, AK181
—— King, David, AK181
Special Libraries Association. *Consolidated index of translations into English,* EA60
—— *Dictionary of report series codes,* EA65
—— *Directory of members,* AK61
—— *Directory of transportation libraries and information centers in North America,* CH449
—— *Faking it,* BF30
—— *Insurance and employee benefits literature,* CH501
—— *Map collections in the United States and Canada,* CL259
—— *SLA biennial salary survey,* AK179
—— *Technical book review index,* EA54
—— *Translations register-index,* EA62
—— *Union list of astronomy serials,* EC21
Special Libraries Association. Newspaper Division. *Newspaper libraries in the U.S. and Canada,* AE30
Special Libraries Association. Petroleum Section. Committee on U.S. Sources of Petroleum and Natural Gas Statistics. *U.S. sources of petroleum and natural gas statistics,* EK301
Special Libraries Association. Science-Technology Division. *Handbook of scientific and technical awards in the United States and Canada, 1900–1952,* EA197
Special Libraries Council of Philadelphia and Vicinity. *Correlation index,* EA66
Special operations and elite units 1939–1988, Beaumont, Roger A., CJ608

Specialized books on space flight and related disciplines, EK24

Specialized catalogue of United States stamps, BG206

Specialized legal research, CK119

Specialized study options U.S.A, Howard, Edrice, CB317

Specifications and criteria for biochemical compounds, National Research Council. Committee on Specifications and Criteria for Biochemical Compounds, EG323

Specifications for the quality control of pharmaceutical preparations, EH358

Spectator insurance year book, CH521

Spector, Robert Donald. *Backgrounds to Restoration and eighteenth-century English literature,* BE747
—— *English Gothic,* BE292

Spector, Sheila. *Jewish mysticism,* BC520

Spectrum, AL46, BJ389

Speech, BE357, CA55
bibliography, BE349
collections, BE347, BE362, BE363, BE365, BE367
dissertations, BE345, BE350, BE353
indexes, BE358, BE366, CC530

Speech (by country or region)
United States
bibliography, BE346
see also **Debating; Political oratory; Rhetoric**

Speech Association of America. *A history and criticism of American public address,* BE365

Speech index, Sutton, Roberta Briggs, BE366

Speeches of the American presidents, CJ188

Speeckaert, Georges Patrick. *Bibliographie sélective sur l'organisation internationale, 1885–1964,* AF21
—— *International institutions and international organization,* AF21

Speigelberg, Friedrich. *The Bible of the world,* BC91

Spell, Jefferson Rea. *Revistas hispanoamericanas,* AD299

Spence, Lewis. *A dictionary of medieval romance and romance writers,* BE344
—— *Encyclopedia of occultism,* CD134

Spencer, David G. *Restoration and eighteenth century theatre research,* BH47

Spencer, Donald D. *Computer dictionary,* EK187
—— *Illustrated computer graphics dictionary,* EK188

Spencer, Dorothy Mary. *Indian fiction in English,* BE1567

Spencer, Douglas Arthur. *Focal dictionary of photographic technologies,* BF340

Spencer, Robert F. *Atlas for anthropology,* CE73

Spencer, W. *Morocco,* DD48

Sperber, Hans. *American political terms,* CJ129

Sperling, Louise. *A general bibliography of the Gambia, up to 31 December 1977,* DD160

Sperling, Walter. *Landeskunde DDR,* DC267

Sperner, E. *Encyklopädie der mathematischen Wissenschaften mit Einschluss ihrer Anwendungen,* EB36

Sperry, Kip. *Index to genealogical periodical literature,* AJ47
—— *A survey of American genealogical periodicals and periodical indexes,* AJ33

Spevack, Marvin. *Complete and systematic concordance to the works of Shakespeare,* BE776, BE777, BE778
—— *Harvard concordance to Shakespeare,* BE776, BE778

Spezialwörterbuch für Handel und Wirtschaft, Eichborn, Reinhart von, CH67

SPI plastics engineering handbook of the Society of the Plastics Industry, Inc, EK290

Spiceland, J. David. *International guide to accounting journals,* CH249

Spiegel, Ruth W. *Arts in America,* BF12

Spielman, Linda June. *A literature guide for the identification of plant pathogenic fungi,* EG189

Spiers, John. *The left in Britain,* CJ509
—— *The underground and alternative press in Britain,* AD112

Spies, S. B. *Bibliography of South African history,* DD223

Spies and provocateurs, Minnick, Wendell L., CJ536, CJ540

Spiller, Robert E. *Literary history of the United States,* BE439, BE440

Spiller, Roger J. *Dictionary of American military biography,* CJ641, CJ648

Spillner, Paul. *Internationales Wörterbuch der Abkürzungen von Organisationen,* AL11
—— *Ullstein-Abkürzenglexikon,* AL11

Spinelli, Donald C. *French language and literature,* BD156, BE1130

Spinks, Cary W. *A bibliography of modern Irish and Anglo-Irish literature,* BE804

Spirduso, Waneen Wyrick. *Proposals that work,* EA160

Spirituality, BC54, BC402
dictionaries, BC242

Spiro, Socrates. *Arabic-English dictionary of the modern Arabic of Egypt,* AC221
—— *English Arabic vocabulary of the modern and colloquial Arabic of Egypt,* AC221

Spisok periodicheskikh izdaniĭ RSFSR, AD150

Spitler, James F. *Detailed statistics on the urban and rural population of Pakistan, 1950 to 2010,* CG415
—— *Detailed statistics on the urban and rural population of Turkey, 1950 to 2000,* CG291

Spiwak, H. J. *International glossary of technical terms used in housing and town planning,* BF278

Spoken records, Roach, Helen Pauline, BE323

Spomer, Cynthia Russell. *American directory of organized labor,* CH660

•*SPORT,* BK11

Sport & leisure, BK11

Sport bibliography, BK11

Sport bibliography update, BK11

•*Sport discus,* BK11

Sport in Britain, Cox, Richard William, BK1

Sport on film and video, BK36

Sport thesaurus, BK11

Sporting news. *The Sporting news official NBA guide,* BK66

Sporting news, BK9

The Sporting news baseball guide, BK61

The Sporting news official NBA guide, BK66

Sports and games
abstract journals, BK11
annuals, BK43
atlases, BK22
bibliography, BK2, BK3, BK5, BK8
biography, BK14, BK63
databases, BK11, BK44
dictionaries, BK24, BK25, BK27, BK28
  multilingual, BK29
directories, BK32, BK33, BK37, BK38
encyclopedias, BK13, BK15, BK16, BK17, BK19, BK20, BK23
  indexes, BK21
filmography, BK36
handbooks, BK40
indexes, BK9, BK10, BK11
museums, BK35
quotations, BK30, BK31
records, BK42
rules, BK18, BK45, BK46, BK47
statistics, BK43, BK44

Sports and games (by country or region)
Australia, BK27
Great Britain, BK1
Greece, ancient, BK26
Rome, ancient, BK26

Sports and games (by subject)
ethics, BK4
fellowships and scholarships, CB391
history, BK16

Sports and physical education, Gratch, Bonnie, BK3

Sports and recreation for the disabled, Paciorek, Michael J., BK40

Sports encyclopedia, Cohen, Richard M., BK48
—— Neft, David S., BK48, BK58, BK65

Sports encyclopedia North America, BK23

Sports ethics in America, Jones, Donald G., BK4

Sports fan's connection, BK37

Sports halls of fame, Gelbert, Doug, BK35

•*Sports Illustrated CD-ROM sports almanac,* BK44

The Sports Illustrated sports almanac, BK44

Sports market place, BK38

Sports market place register, BK38

Sports medicine, EH127

Sports quotations, Maikovich, Andrew J., BK31

Sports rules encyclopedia, BK47

Sports scholarships and college athletic programs, CB391

Sports talk, Palmatier, Robert A., BK28

Sportsguide, BK38

Sposato, Kenneth A. *The dictionary of American clock & watch makers,* BG89

Spot TV & cable source, CH601

Spottswood, Richard K. *Ethnic music on records,* BJ329

Spouse abuse, Engeldinger, Eugene A., CC209

Der Sprach-Brockhaus, AC410

Die Sprache, BD201

Sprachen der Welt, Klose, A., BD13

Die Sprachen und Literaturen der Romanen im Spiegel der deutschen Universitätsschriften, 1885–1950, Flasche, Hans, BD155, BE1071

Sprachgeschichte, BD125

Sprachwissenschaftliches Wörterbuch, Knobloch, Johann, BD41

Spradling, Mary Mace. *In black and white,* AH41

Sprague, William Buell. *Annals of the American pulpit,* BC255

Spravochnik po istorii dorevoliutsionnoi Rossii, DC582

Spravochnik po matematike, EB62

Spravochnik po rastrorimosti, EE91

Spreti, Vittorio. *Enciclopedia storico-nobiliare italiana,* AJ139
—— *Saggio di bibliografia araldica italiana,* AJ139

Sprichworter-Bibliographie, Moll, Otto E., BE156, BE158

Springer, Hermann. *Miscellanea musicae bio-bibliographica,* BJ57

Springer, Nelson P. *Mennonite bibliography, 1631–1961,* BC362

Springer, Otto. *Langenscheidt's new Muret-Sanders encyclopedic dictionary of the English and German languages,* AC418

Sprug, Joseph W. *Index to fairy tales, myths and legends,* BE243

Sprung, Barbara. *Resources for educational equity,* CB18

Spurrell, William. *Geiriadur saesneg a chymraeg,* AC807

Spurrell's English-Welsh dictionary, AC807

Spurrell's Welsh-English dictionary, AC807

Spy/counterspy, Buranelli, Nan, CJ540
—— Buranelli, Vincent, CJ536, CJ540

Spy fiction, McCormick, Donald, BE272

Spyclopaedia, Deacon, Richard, CJ540

Squarotti, Giorgio Bárberi. *Grande dizionario della lingua italiana,* AC524

Squire, Larry R. *Encyclopedia of learning and memory,* CD110

Squire, W. Barclay. *Catalogue of printed music published between 1487 and 1800 now in the British Museum,* BJ54

Squitier, Karl A. *Thesaurus Linguae Graecae canon of Greek authors and works,* AC443, BE1036

SRDS direct marketing list source, CH601

SRDS newspaper circulation analysis, AE21
—— Standard Rate & Data Service, AE21

Sri Lanka
atlases, CL363
bibliography, AA934, AA935
manuscripts, DE163
statistics, CG424, CG425, CG426, CG427

Sri Lanka (by subject)
history
  bibliography, DE258, DE259, DE260, DE261
  encyclopedias, DE90
politics and government, CJ444

Sri Lanka. Minindōru Depārtamēntuva. *The national atlas of Sri Lanka*, CL363
Sri Lanka, Peebles, Patrick, CG424
——— Samaraweera, Vijaya, DE261
Sri Lanka (Ceylon) since independence (1948–1974), De Silva, Daya, DE258
Sri Lanka jatika grantha namavaliya. Ilankait teciya nurpattiyal, AA934, AA935
Sri Lanka national bibliography, AA934, AA935
Srī Laṅkā saṅkhyāta nibandhaya, CG426
Sri Lanka since independence, De Silva, Daya, DE258
SRI microfiche library, CG99
Srinivasa Iyengar, K. R. *Indian writing in English*, BE1569
Śródka, Andrzej. *Biogramy uczonych polskich*, AH278
Srpska biblijografija za noviju književnost, Novakovic, Stojan, AA844
Srpska bibliografija, AA797
Srpska književna periodika 1768–1941, BE1500
Srpskohrvatski-engleski rečnik, Benson, Morton, AC710
——— Šljivić-Šimšić, Biljana, AC710
SShA/SSSR fakty i tsifry, CG42
SSSR v tsifrankh, CG296
Staatliche Archivverwaltung of the German Democratic Republic. *Übersicht über die Quellen zur Geschichte Lateinamerikas in Archiven der D.D.R*, DB275
Staatliches Institut für Musikforschung Preussischer Kulturbesitz. *Periodica musicalia (1789–1830)*, BJ114
Staatsalmanak voor het Koninkrijk der Nederlanden, CJ384
Staatsbibliothek Preussischer Kulturbesitz. *Bibliographia cartographica*, CL247
Staatslexikon, CJ334
Stachura, Peter D. *Political leaders in Weimar Germany*, DC262
——— *The Weimar era and Hitler, 1917–1933*, DC242
Stade, George. *British writers*, BE622
——— *European writers*, BE201
Stadler, Wolfgang. *Lexikon der Kunst*, BF75
Stadshistoriska institut (Sweden) *International bibliography of urban history*, DC72
Stadt- und Universitätsbibliothek Frankfurt am Main. *Current contents Africa*, DD22
Stadtbibliothek Frankfurt am Main. *Katalog der Judaica und Hebraica*, BC532
Stadte, Stadtplane, Platze, Strassen, Brucken, BF278
Städtebibliographie Deutschlands, DC265
•*Staff directories on CD-ROM*, CJ137, CJ215, CK149
Staff training, Crimando, William, CH713
Staff training and user awareness in preservation management, Boomgaarden, Wesley L., AK238
Stafford, Beth. *Directory of women's studies programs & library resources*, CC548
Stafford, Maureen. *An illustrated dictionary of ornament*, BG24
Stafleu, F. A. *Index herbariorum*, EG153
Stafleu, Frans A. *Index nominum genericorum (plantarum)*, EG129
Stafleu, Frans Anthonie. *Taxonomic literature*, EG93
Stage deaths, BH127
Stage lighting, BH80, BH120
   bibliography, BH50, BH52
   dictionaries, BH76
Stage lives, BH128
Stage props, BH86, BH92
Stage scenery, BH80, BH90, BH114, BH120
   bibliography, BH50, BH52
   handbooks, BH89
Stage scenery, machinery, and lighting, Stoddard, Richard, BH52
Stagg, Eduardo. *West's Spanish-English/English-Spanish law dictionary*, CK55
Stahl, Dorothy. *A selected discography of solo song*, BJ281
Stählin, Otto. *Geschichte der griechischen Literatur*, BE1035

Stained glass, Brady, Darlene, BG51
——— Serban, William, BG51
Stained glass before 1540, Caviness, Madeline Harrison, BG52
Stained glass before 1700 in American collections, Caviness, Madeline Harrison, BG52
Staley, James T. *Bergey's manual of systematic bacteriology*, EG309
Stalins, Gaston Ferdinand Laurent. *Vocabulaire-atlas héraldique en six langues*, AJ165
Stambler, Irwin. *The encyclopedia of folk, country, & western music*, BJ326
——— *Encyclopedia of pop, rock & soul*, BJ351
Stamm, Alice. *Historic America*, BF219
Stamm Leitfaden durch Presse und Werbung, AD103
Stamm-Leitfaden für presse und Werbung, AD103
Stammhammer, Josef. *Bibliographie des Socialismus und Communismus*, CJ510
Stammler, Wolfgang. *Die deutsche Literatur des Mittelalters*, BE1253
——— *Reallexikon der deutschen Literaturgeschichte*, BE1251
Stamp, L. Dudley. *Chisholm's handbook of commercial geography*, CL43, CL67
——— *A glossary of geographical terms*, CL42
La stampa periodica romana dell' Ottocento, Majolo Molinari, Olga, AD127
Stamper, Eugene. *Handbook of air conditioning, heating, and ventilating*, EK225
Stamps and coins, Rosichan, Richard H., BG203
Stams, W. *National and regional atlases*, CL239
Standaard modern citatenboek, Ley, Gerd de, BE126
•*Standard & Poor's corporate descriptions*, CH313, CH367
Standard & Poor's Corporation. *Standard corporation descriptions*, CH313
——— *Standard corporation records*, CH313
Standard & Poor's corporation descriptions, CH313
Standard & Poor's corporation records, CH313
Standard & Poor's industry surveys, CH417
Standard & Poor's Lipper mutual fund profiles, CH314
Standard & Poor's ratings handbook, CH321
•*Standard & Poor's register—biographical*, CH387
Standard & Poor's register of corporations, directors and executives, CH313, CH367, CH387
Standard & Poor's security dealers of North America, CH231
Standard & Poor's security price index record, statistical service, CH223
Standard & Poor's statistical service, CH223
Standard & Poor's stock market encyclopedia, CH404
Standard catalog for high school libraries, AA344
Standard catalog of U.S. paper money, Krause, Chester L., BG197
Standard catalog of world coins, Krause, Chester L., BG188
Standard catalog of world gold coins, BG188
Standard catalog of world paper money, Pick, Albert, BG189
Standard code of parliamentary procedure, Sturgis, Alice, CJ458
Standard corporation descriptions, Standard & Poor's Corporation, CH313
Standard corporation records, Standard & Poor's Corporation, CH313
Standard cyclopedia of horticulture, Bailey, Liberty Hyde, EJ233
The standard Danish-English, English-Danish dictionary, AC289
Standard definitions of broadcast research terms, CH485
Standard dictionary, AC10
Standard dictionary of Canadian biography, AH96
Standard dictionary of meteorological sciences, Proulx, Gerard-J, EF149
Standard dictionary of the social sciences, Koschnick, Wolfgang J., CA38
Standard directory of advertisers, CH572, CH573, CH574
Standard directory of advertising agencies, CH572, CH573, CH574

Standard directory of international advertisers & advertising agencies, CH574
Standard directory of international advertisers & agencies, CH572, CH573, CH574
Standard directory of newsletters, AE37
Standard directory of worldwide marketing, CH574
Standard education almanac, CB122
Standard encyclopedia of the world's mountains, Huxley, Anthony Julian, CL61, CL62, CL63, EF8, EF9, EF10
Standard encyclopedia of the world's oceans and islands, Huxley, Anthony Julian, CL61, CL62, CL63, EF8, EF9, EF10
Standard encyclopedia of the world's rivers and lakes, Gresswell, R. Kay, CL61, CL62, CL63, EF8, EF9, EF10
——— Huxley, Anthony Julian, CL62, CL63, EF9, EF10
Standard English-Spanish and Spanish-English dictionary, AC735
A standard English-Swahili dictionary, Inter-territorial Language (Swahili) Committee to the East African Dependencies, AC756
The standard Finnish-English English-Finnish dictionary, Wuolle, Aino, AC325
Standard handbook for civil engineers, EK61
Standard handbook for electrical engineers, EK143
Standard handbook for mechanical engineers, EK240
Standard handbook of engineering calculations, EK18
Standard handbook of environmental engineering, EK82
Standard handbook of machine design, EK247
Standard handbook of plant engineering, EK252
Standard handbook of stamp collecting, Cabeen, Richard McP., BG203
Standard highway mileage guide, Rand McNally and Company, CL305
Standard illustrated dictionary of the English language, AC486
Standard illustrated dictionary of the Hindi language, AC486
Standard index of short stories, 1900–1914, Hannigan, Francis J., BE262
Standard industrial classification manual, CH379
The standard Jewish encyclopedia, BC552
Standard mathematical tables and formulae, EB84
Standard medical almanac, EH234
Standard methods for the examination of water and wastewater, American Public Health Association, EE62
The standard periodical directory, AD56
Standard Rate & Data Service. *SRDS newspaper circulation analysis*, AE21
Standard rate and data service, CH601
Standard Shona dictionary, Hannan, M., AC716
A standard Swahili-English dictionary, AC758
——— Inter-territorial Language (Swahili) Committee to the East African Dependencies, AC756
Standardized plant names, American Joint Committee on Horticultural Nomenclature, EG118
Standards, EA268, EA269, EA270, EA271, EA272, EA273, EA274, EA275, EA276
Standards, Ricci, Patricia, EA275
Standards activities of organizations in the United States, EA276
Standards for educational and psychological testing, American Psychological Association, CD76
Standards of practice handbook, Association for Investment Management and Research, CH317
——— Financial Analysts Federation, CH317
Standing Conference of National and University Libraries. *A finding-list of English books to 1640 in libraries in the British Isles (excluding the national libraries and the libraries of Oxford and Cambridge)*, AA672
——— *A guide to Latin American and Caribbean census material*, CG122
Standing Conference on Library Materials on Africa. *Periodicals from Africa*, AD238, DD28

———— *Theses on Africa accepted by universities in the United Kingdom and Ireland,* DD33

The Stanford companion to Victorian fiction, Sutherland, John, BE689

Stanford University. *Computer science technical reports,* EK156

Stanford University. Libraries. *Peronism and the three Perons,* DB327

Stanisławski, Jan. *Wiedza Powszechna compact Polish and English dictionary,* AC633

———— *Wielki słownik angielsko-polski,* AC635

———— *Wielki słownik polsko-angielski,* AC635

Staniveciene, Eugenijus. *Tarybinis lietuvių literatūros mokslas ir kritika apie literatūrini palikima, 1944–1958,* BE1321

———— *Tarybinis lietuviu literaturos mokslas ir kritika apie literaturini palikima, 1959–1970,* BE1321

Stankiewicz, Edward. *A selected bibliography of Slavic linguistics,* BD184

Stanley, Harold W. *Vital statistics on American politics,* CJ163

Stanley, Janet L. *African art,* BF25

———— *Nigerian government publications, 1966–1973,* AF236

Stansfield, Geoffrey. *Keyguide to information sources in museum studies,* BF8

Stansfield, William D. *A dictionary of genetics,* EG339, EG341

Stansifer, Charles L. *Costa Rica,* DB305

Stanton, B. F. *Agricultural economics and rural sociology,* EJ6

Stanton, Michael N. *English literary journals, 1900–1950,* BE591

Stanton, Robert J. *A bibliography of modern British novelists,* BE685

Stanton Library (North Sydney, N.S.W.). *Australian architectural periodicals index,* BF208

Stanwick, Kathy. *The political participation of women in the United States,* CC512

Stapf, O. *Index londinensis to illustrations of flowering plants, ferns and fern allies,* EG104

Stapf, Paul. *Handbuch der deutschen Literaturgeschichte,* BE1219

Staples, Amy J. *Historical dictionary of the Third French Republic, 1870–1940,* DC207

Stapleton, Michael. *Cambridge guide to English literature,* BE608

STAR, EK26, EK28

Star atlas and reference handbook, EC71

Star atlas of reference stars and nonstellar objects, EC73

Star catalog, EC73

———— Smithsonian Astrophysical Observatory, EC74

Star Wars *see* **Strategic Defense Intitiative**

Stark, Lewis M. *Checklist of additions to Evans' American bibliography in the Rare Book Division of the New York Public Library,* AA408

Starnawski, Jerzy. *Warsztat bibliograficzny historyka literatury polskiej (na tle dyscyplin pokrewnych),* BE1360

Starnes, DeWitt Talmage. *The English dictionary from Cawdrey to Johnson, 1604–1755,* AC8

———— *Renaissance dictionaries,* AC595

Starr, Edward Caryl. *A Baptist bibliography,* BC326

STARR, EA53

Stars, EC70

  atlases, EC67, EC71, EC73, EC75, EC76

  catalogs, EC72, EC74

    bibliography, EC8

Startsev, Ivan Ivanovich. *Khudozhestvennaia literatura narodov SSSR v perevodakh na russkii iazyk,* BE1405

Stasiuleviciute, E. *Anglų-lietuvių kalbų žodynas,* AC604

State administrative officials classified by functions, CJ278

State and federal courts, judges, and clerks, CK156

State and local government
  bibliography, CJ267, CJ268, CJ471
  biography, CJ285, CJ286, CJ287, CJ288, CJ289, CJ291

  directories, CB98, CJ138, CJ271, CJ272, CJ273, CJ274, CJ275, CJ276, CJ277, CJ282
  encyclopedias, CJ269
  handbooks, CG104, CJ270, CJ278, CJ279, CJ280, CJ281, CJ282, CJ283
  manuscripts and archives, DB141
  sourcebooks, CJ284
  statistics, CJ283

State and local government (by subject)
  elections, CJ291

The state and local government political dictionary, Elliot, Jeffrey M., CJ269

State and local statistics sources, CG94

State and metropolitan area data book, CG79

State and national voting in federal elections, 1910–1970, Cox, Edward Franklin, CJ253

State and provincial government publications, AF138, AF145

  bibliography, AF140, AF141, AF143, AF144
  directories, CB106
  guides, AF146
  handbooks, AF137, AF139
  reference books, AF146

State and regional associations of the United States, AL45, AL47, CH670

State blue books, legislative manuals, and reference publications, AF146

The state-by-state guide to women's legal rights, CK162

State censuses, Dubester, Henry J., CG90

State censuses microfiche collection, CG90

State constitutional conventions, commissions & amendments, 1959–1978, Olcott, Nicholas, CK174

———— Vonderhaar, Mark, CK174

State constitutional conventions, commissions & amendments, 1979–1988, CK174

State constitutional conventions from independence to the completion of the present Union, 1776–1959, Browne, Cynthia E., CK174

State court caseload statistics, CK168

State court clerks & county courthouses, CK156

State document checklists, Dow, Susan L., AF140

State education agencies, CB98

State education documents, CB106

State education journal index, CB64

State elections in India, Bose, Shankar, CJ435

———— Singh, V. B., CJ435

State elective officials and the legislatures, CJ278

State executive directory annual, CJ271, CJ275

State finances, CG80

State formation, religion, and land tenure in Cameroon, Schilder, Kees, DD138

State government finances, CG80

State government publications in India, 1947–1982, Singh, Mohinder, AF249

State government reference publications, Parish, David W., AF144

State government research checklist, AF145

State government research directory, AL81, CJ280

State higher education profiles, CB343

State Historical Society of Wisconsin. *American Federation of Labor records,* CH624

———— *Native American periodicals and newspapers, 1828–1982,* AE16

———— *Women's periodicals and newspapers from the 18th century to 1981,* AD48, AE25

State Historical Society of Wisconsin. Library. *Hispanic Americans in the United States,* AE31

———— *Subject catalog of the library of the State Historical Society of Wisconsin, Madison, Wisconsin,* CH641

State information book, CJ282

State labor proceedings, Fink, Gary M., CH630

State legislative and administrative materials, CJ267

State Legislative Leaders Foundation (U.S.). *Inside the legislature,* CJ272

State legislative leadership, committees, and staff, CJ272, CJ278

State legislative manuals on microfiche, CJ284

State legislative sourcebook, CJ281

State legislative staff directory, CJ276

State legislatures, Goehlert, Robert, CJ268

State Library (South Africa). *RSANB, 1926–1958,* AA876

———— *South African newspapers on microfilm,* AE80

———— *Swaziland official publications, 1880–1972,* AF238

State maps on file, Martin Greenwald Associates, CL302

State municipal league directory, CJ277

State names, flags, seals, songs, birds, flowers and other symbols, Shankle, George Earlie, AL191

State names, seals, flags, and symbols, Shearer, Benjamin F., AL192, DB151

The state of black America, National Urban League, CC394

The state of food and agriculture, EJ83

The state of the states in developmental disabilities, CC199

The state of the world atlas, CL280

The state of the world's children, CC176

State policy data book, CJ283

State Policy Research, Inc. *States in profile,* CJ283

State profiles of public elementary and secondary education, 1987–88, Morgan, Frank, CB142

State publications, Lane, Margaret T., AF137

State publications and depository libraries, Lane, Margaret T., AF139

State reference publications, AF146

———— Hellebust, Lynn, CJ284

State University of New York at Albany. Film and Television Documentation Center. *Film literature index,* BH232

State University of New York at Binghamton. Center for Medieval and Early Renaissance Studies. *A bibliography of publications on Old English literature to the end of 1972,* BE728

———— *Old English newsletter,* BE729

State University of New York at Binghamton. Center for Social Analysis. *Political handbook of the world,* CJ95

State yellow book, CH350, CJ271, CJ282

Statelova, Elena Boianova. *Istoriiata na Bŭlgariia v memoarnata literatura,* DC115

Statement of treaties and international agreements, CK87

The states and small business, CH368

States in profile, CJ283

States of awareness, Miletich, John J., CD108

Statesman's year-book, CJ62, CL92

The statesman's year-book world gazetteer, Paxton, John, CL92

Statesmen who changed the world, CJ70

Stationers' Company (London). *An analytical index to the ballad-entries (1557–1709) in the Registers of the Company of Stationers of London,* BE634

———— *A transcript of the registers of the Company of Stationers of London, 1554–1640,* AA674, BE680

Statistical abstract, CG166, CG176, CG317, CG355, CG362

———— Bahrain. Maktab al-Iḥṣā, CG377

———— Cyprus. Financial Secretary's Office. Statistics Section, CG203

———— Kenya. Central Bureau of Statistics, CG336

———— Uganda. Office of the President. Statistics Division, CG366

———— Western Samoa. Department of Statistics, CG443

Statistical abstract for British India, CG389

Statistical abstract for the Netherlands East Indies, CG394

Statistical abstract for the United Kingdom, Great Britain. Board of Trade, CG231

Statistical abstract, India, CG389

Statistical abstract of Botswana, CG317

Statistical abstract of Ceylon, CG426

Statistical abstract of Iceland, CG249

Statistical abstract of Ireland, CG252

Statistical abstract of Israel, Israel. ha-Lishkah ha-Merkazit li-Statistiskah, CG398

Statistical abstract of Latin America, CG124

Statistical abstract of Sri Lanka, CG426

Statistical abstract of Syria, CG428

Statistical abstract of the Democratic Socialist Republic of Sri Lanka, CG426

Statistical abstract of the Indian Union, CG389

Statistical abstract of the Maltese Islands, CG264

Statistical abstract of the United States, CG75, CG79, CG81, EJ84

Statistical abstract of Western Samoa, CG443

Statistical bibliography, CG432

Statistical bulletin, CG318, CH528

Statistical bulletin for Latin America, CG120

Statistical bulletin of Liberia, CG339

Statistical bulletin of the OAS, CG121

Statistical Committee of the Commonwealth of Independent States. *Demographic yearbook*, CG202

Statistical dictionary, CG21

Statistical digest of Bangladesh, CG378

Statistical digest of East Pakistan, CG378

Statistical digest of Pakistan, CG417

Statistical forecasts of the United States, CG105, CH110

Statistical hand book of the Republic of Ghana, Ghana. Central Bureau of Statistics, CG332

Statistical handbook, Arab Republic of Egypt, CG328

Statistical handbook of Japan, CG403

Statistical handbook on aging Americans, CC104, CG106

Statistical handbook on the American family, CG107

Statistical handbook on U.S. Hispanics, Schick, Frank Leopold, CC471, CG84

—— Schick, Renee, CC471, CG84

Statistical handbook on women in America, CG108

—— Taeuber, Cynthia Murray, CC583

A statistical history of the American presidential elections, Petersen, Svend, CJ256

Statistical information on the financial services industry, CH237

Statistical Institute of Jamaica. *Demographic statistics*, CG175

—— *Statistical abstract*, CG176

Statistical masterfile, CG96, CG69

Statistical Office of the European Communities. *ACP basic statistics*, CG45

—— *Basic statistics of the community*, CG182

—— *Befolkningsstatistik*, CG183

—— *Europe in figures*, CG184

Statistical pocket book, Nepal, Nepal. Kendrīya Tathyāṅka Vibhāga, CG414

Statistical pocket book of Bangladesh, CG378

Statistical pocket book of Ethiopia, CG330

Statistical pocketbook of Indonesia, CG393

A statistical portrait of higher education, Harris, Seymour Edwin, CB340

Statistical record of Asian Americans, CC410, CG82

Statistical record of black America, CC400, CG83

Statistical record of Hispanic Americans, CC471, CG84

Statistical record of Native North Americans, CC442, CG85

Statistical record of older Americans, CC105

Statistical record of the environment, EK84

Statistical record of women worldwide, CC583

Statistical reference index, CG69, CG99

Statistical report … Public Library Data Service, AK99

Statistical review of England and Wales, Great Britain. Office of Population Censuses and Surveys, CG233

Statistical service, CH223

Statistical services directory, CG37

Statistical services of the United States government, CG89

Statistical Society of Canada. *Directory of members*, CG35, EB57

Statistical Society of Canada
    directories, CG35, EB57

Statistical tables for biological, agricultural and medical research, Fisher, Ronald A., EG61

Statistical theory and method, EB29

Statistical theory and method abstracts, EB12, EB29

Statistical vocabulary, Inter-American Statistical Institute, CG22

Statistical year book, CG334, CG442

Statistical year book of Maldives, CG411

Statistical year-book of the League of Nations, CG52, CG57

Statistical yearbook, CB145, CG52, CG164, CG201, CG204, CG334

—— Jordan. Dā'irat al-Iḥṣā'at al-'Ammah, CG405

—— Lutheran Church—Missouri Synod, BC357

—— Saudi Arabia. Maṣlaḥat al-Iḥṣā'at al-Āmah, CG421

—— South Africa. Bureau of Statistics, CG359

—— Turkish Federated State of Cyprus, CG204

—— United Nations. Economic Commission for Africa, CG306

—— United Nations. Statistical Office, CG57, CG430

Statistical yearbook (Amman, Jordan), CG405

Statistical yearbook, Arab Republic of Egypt, CG328

Statistical yearbook — Central Statistical Office, Zambia. Central Statistical Office, CG367

Statistical yearbook for Arab countries, CG372

Statistical yearbook for Asia and the Far East, CG370, CG434

Statistical yearbook for Asia and the Pacific, CG370, CG434

Statistical yearbook for Latin America and the Caribbean, CG120

Statistical yearbook of Albania, CG192

Statistical yearbook of Bangladesh, CG378

Statistical yearbook of Bhutan, CG379

Statistical yearbook of China, CG384

Statistical yearbook of community, technical, and junior colleges, CB338

Statistical yearbook of Finland, CG212

Statistical yearbook of Greece, CG243

Statistical yearbook of Indonesia, CG393

Statistical yearbook of Iran, CG396

Statistical yearbook of Jamaica, CG177

Statistical yearbook of Norway, CG271

Statistical yearbook of Sweden, CG286

Statistical yearbook of the Netherlands, CG266, CG267

Statistical yearbook of the People's Republic of Poland, CG275

Statistical yearbook of the Republic of China, CG430

Statistical yearbook of the Socialist Federal Republic of Yugoslavia, CG304

Statistical yearbook of Turkey, CG290

Statistical yearbook of Zimbabwe, CG368

Statistical yearbook, Thailand, CG433

Statistical yearbook (Unesco), CB145

Statistiche demografiche, CG258

Statisticheski godishnik, CG201

Statisticheskie publikatsii v SSSR, Mashikhin, Evgeniĭ Aleksandrovich, CG301

Statisticians, EB13
    directories, CG35, EB57

Statistická ročenka České a Slovenské federativní republiky, CG208

Statistická ročenka Československé Socialistické Republiky, CG208

Statistički godišnjak Jugoslavije, CG304

Statistički godišnjak, Yugoslavia. Direkcija državne statistike, CG305

Statistics Africa, Harvey, Joan M., CG311

Statistics America, Harvey, Joan M., CG71

Statistics and demography
    atlases, CG44
    bibliography, CG1, CG2, CG3, CG4, CG6, CG7, CG8, CG9, CG10, CG11, CG12, CG13, CG14, CG16, CG18, CG67, CG68, CG92, CG116, CG217, CG218, CG221, CG287, DB14, EB9, EB12
    biography, CG43
    compendiums, CG46, CG47, CG50, CG51, CG53, CG55, CG56, CG58, CG59, CG60, CG63, CH600
    dictionaries, CG21, CG22, CG24, CG25, CG26, CG29, CG30, CG32, CG33, EB43, EB45
        bilingual
            Chinese-English, CG34
        multilingual, CG27, CG28
        polyglot, CG31
        Russian, CG292

    directories, CG35, CG37, EB57
    encyclopedias, CG19, CG20, EB37
    handbooks, CG39, CG40, CG41, CH89, CH159, EB65
    indexes, CG15, CG16, CG18, CG67, EB21, EB22, EK160
    surveys
        directories, CG36
    yearbooks, CG57
Statistics and demography (by country or region)
    international, CB145, CG57
        compendiums, CG48, CG61, CG66
        yearbooks, CG52
    see also **Industrial statistics; Mathematical statistics**

Statistics Asia & Australasia, Harvey, Joan M., CG376

Statistics Canada. *Canada year book*, CG110

—— *Guide to Statistics Canada data on women*, CG114

—— *Historical statistics of Canada*, CG113, DB209

—— *Market research handbook*, CH595

Statistics Canada. Library Services Division. *Statistics Canada catalogue*, CG114, CG115

Statistics Canada catalogue, Statistics Canada. Library Services Division, CG114, CG115

The statistics cumindex, Dolby, J. L., EB24

Statistics Europe, Harvey, Joan M., CG187

Statistics of education in the United States, CB146

Statistics of Iceland, CG250

Statistics of national income and expenditure, CH243

Statistics on marriages, CG422

Statistics on marriages and divorces, CG422

Statistics sources, CG68

Statistik in Österreich, 1918–1938, Gehart, Alois, CG195

Statistik Indonesia, CG393

Statistika rechi, 1957–1985, Alekseev, P. M., BD64

—— Bektaev, K. B., BD64

—— Chizhakovskiĭ, V. A., BD64

Statistikē en Helludi, Kladas, S., CG242

Statistikē epeteris tes Hellados, CG243

Statistikē tes physikes kineseos tou plethysmou tes Hellados, CG244

Statistikē vivliographia peri Hellados, 1821–1971, Chouliarakes, Michael G., CG242

Statistique générale de la Tunisie, CG365

Statistique internationale des grandes villes, CG47, CG56

Statistiques du mouvement de la population, Luxembourg. Service central de la statistique et des études économiques, CG262

Statistiques historiques, CG263

Statistisch jaaroverzicht van Nederlandsch-Indie, CG266, CG394

Statistischer Wochendienst, CG223

Statistisches Handbuch für die Republik Österreich, CG198

Statistisches Handbuch von Deutschland, 1928-1944, Germany (Territory under Allied Occupation, 1945–1955 : U.S. Zone), CG222

Statistisches Jahrbuch, Liechtenstein. Amt für Volkswirtschaft, CG259

Statistisches Jahrbuch der Deutschen Demokratischen Republik, CG224, CG225, CG226

Statistisches Jahrbuch der Schweiz, CG288

Statistisches Jahrbuch für das Deutsche Reich, CG222

Statistisches Jahrbuch für das vereinte Deutschland, CG224, CG225, CG226

Statistisches Jahrbuch für die Bundesrepublik Deutschland, CG224, CG225, CG226

Statistisches Jahrbuch für die Republik Österreich, CG198

Statistisches Wörterverzeichnis, CG21

Statistisk årbog, CG210

Statistisk årbok, CG271

Statistisk årbok for Kongeriket Norge, CG271

Statistisk årbok for Norge, CG271

Statistisk årsbok för Sverige, CG286

Statistiske meddelelser, CG209

Statististical sources and methods, CH691
Statisztikai adatforrások, Fóti, Istvánné, CG246
Statisztikai évkönyv, CG247
Statisztikai szótár, Hungary. Központi Statisztikai Hivatal, CG21
Statliga publikationer, årsbibliografi, AF215, AF216
Staton, Frances M. *A bibliography of Canadiana,* DB188
Statsky, William P. *West's legal theasurus/dictionary,* CK56
Statt, David A. *The concise dictionary of management,* CH616
Status of the American public-school teacher, CB167
The status of the Arab woman, Meghdessian, Samira Rafidi, CC610
Statutes (by country or region)
  United States, CK177, CK178
    states, CK180, CK181
Statutes at large, CK94, CK95, CK177
The statutes at large of the United States of America ..., United States. [Laws, etc.], CK176
Statutes compared, Schultz, Jon S., CK181
Statutes in force, CK214
Statutes of Canada, CK193
Stauber, Ronald. *A Zuni atlas,* CC439
Staudinger, Evelyn Ruth. *Stained glass before 1540,* BG52
Stauffer, David McNeely. *American engravers upon copper and steel,* BF386
Stauffer, Donald Alfred. *The art of biography in 18th century England,* AH239
——— *English biography before 1700,* AH239
Stavropoulos, D. N. *Oxford Greek-English learner's dictionary,* AC465
STC, AA671
Steadman, Susan M. *Dramatic re-visions,* BH34
Stearn, William T. *Botanical Latin,* EG143
Stebbins, Chantal. *Dictionary of legal quotations,* CK57
Stebbins, Christine Depp. *Commodity trading manual,* CH440
Stede, William. *Pali-English dictionary,* AC625
Stedman, Preston. *The symphony,* BJ295
Stedman, Thomas Lathrop. *Illustrated Stedman's medical dictionary,* EH270
——— *Practical medical dictionary,* EH105
——— *Stedman's medical dictionary,* EH105
Stedman's abbrev. , EH134
Stedman's abbreviations, acronyms & symbols, EH134
Stedman's ICTV virus words, EG347
Stedman's medical dictionary, Stedman, Thomas Lathrop, EH105
Stedregister til Dansk Tidsskrift-Index, Michelsen, Hans, AD309
——— Sorensen, Toben, AD309
Stedregister til Dansk Tidsskrift Index 1915–1970, AD309
Steel, A. E. F. *National index of parish registers,* AJ107
Steel, D. J. *National index of parish registers,* AJ107
Steel, EK107, EK108
Steel construction, EK107
Steel engravings in nineteenth century British topographical books, Holloway, Merlyn, BF359
Steele, Colin. *Directory of libraries and special collections on Latin America and the West Indies,* AK111
——— *Major libraries of the world,* AK120
Steels alert, EK260
Steels supplement to Metals abstracts, EK260
Steen, Edwin Benzel. *Baillière's abbreviations in medicine,* EH135
——— *Dictionary of biology,* EG45
Steensel van der Aa, E. van. *Bibliographie zum deutschen Liberalismus,* DC235
Steere, Edward. *A standard English-Swahili dictionary,* AC756
Steere, Norman V. *CRC handbook of laboratory safety,* EE88
Steere, William C. *Wild flowers of the United States,* EG180

Steeves, Paul D. *Modern encyclopedia of religions in Russia and the Soviet Union,* DC566
Stefănescu, Stefan. *Enciclopedia istoriografiei românești,* DC497
Stefanllari, Ilo. *Fjalor anglisht-shqip,* AC206
Steffens, Joan. *Lapps ethnographic bibliography,* CE94
Stegemeyer, Anne. *Who's who in fashion,* BG116
Stegmüller, Friedrich. *Repertorium Biblicum Medii Aevi,* BC116
Stegun, Irene A. *Handbook of mathematical functions with formulas. graphs, and mathematical tables,* EB76
Stehle, Dorothy. *The Near East national union list,* AA123
Stein, Alice P. *American nursing,* EH287
Stein, Barbara. *Kunstgeschichte in Festschriften,* BF51
Stein, Henri. *Manuel de bibliographie générale,* AA10
Stein, J. Stewart. *Construction glossary,* EK112
Stein, Jess M. *American college dictionary,* AC15
——— *Random House encyclopedia,* AB13
——— *The Random House thesaurus,* AC143
Stein, Morris Isaac. *Gifted, talented, and creative young people,* CB187
Stein, Regina. *The timetables of Jewish history,* DA31
Stein, Rita. *Literary tour guide to the United States : South and Southwest,* BE438
——— *Literary tour guide to the United States : West and Midwest,* BE438
——— *Major modern dramatists,* BE229
——— *Modern British literature,* BE600
Stein, Stanley J. *Latin America,* CH180
Stein, Werner. *Kulturfahrplan,* DA32
Steinbeck, George. *The futures markets dictionary,* CH437
Steinberg, Sigfrid H. *Cassell's encyclopaedia of literature,* BE59
——— *Historical tables, 58 BC–AD 1990,* DA38
——— *New dictionary of British history,* DC293
——— *Steinberg's dictionary of British history,* DC293
Steinberg's dictionary of British history, Steinberg, Sigfrid H., DC293
Steinbichler, Eveline. *Lexikon für die Apothekenpraxis in sieben Sprachen,* EH331
Steinbrunner, Chris. *Detectionary,* BE267
——— *Encyclopedia of mystery and detection,* BE267
Steiner, Dale R. *Historical journals,* DA15
Steiner, Lisa A. *Dictionary of immunology,* EH124
Steiner, Michael. *Region and regionalism in the United States,* DB146
Steiner, Urban J. *Contemporary theology,* BC220
Steinerbooks dictionary of the paranormal, CD136
Steinfirst, Susan. *Folklore and folklife,* CF40
Steinhauer, Kurt. *Hegel bibliography,* BB79
Steinitz, Wolfgang. *Wörterbuch der deutschen Gegenwartssprache,* AC412
Steinmetz, E. F. *Vocabularium botanicum,* EG144
Steinmetz, Sol. *The American heritage dictionary of science,* EA86
——— *The Barnhart dictionary of etymology,* AC48
——— *The Barnhart dictionary of new English since 1963,* AC95
Steinmetz, Suzanne K. *Handbook of marriage and the family,* CC241
Steinmetz archive data catalogue and guide, Steinmetzarchief, CA51
Steinmetzarchief. *Steinmetz archive data catalogue and guide,* CA51
Steinmeyer, Elias von. *Althochdeutsches Wörterbuch,* AC399
Steinmueller, John E. *Catholic biblical encyclopedia,* BC126
Steinschneider, Moritz. *Ozar ha-sepharim,* BC509
Steirlin, Henri. *Encyclopedia of world architecture,* BF253
Steitz, Lothar. *Bibliographie zur Aussprache des Latein,* BD144

Stella, Gian Carlo. *Africa orientale (Eritrea, Abissinia, Somalia) e colonialismo italiano,* DD109
Stelter, Gilbert A. *Canada's urban past,* DB210
Stelzner, Robert. *Literatur Register der organischen Chemie,* EE122
Stember, Sol. *The bicentennial guide to the American Revolution,* DB95
Stenesh, J. *Dictionary of biochemistry,* EG324
——— *Dictionary of biochemistry and molecular biology,* EG324
Stengel, Edmund. *Chronologisches Verzeichnis französischer Grammatiken,* BD157
Stenkvist, Jan. *Svensk litteratur 1870–1970,* BE1481
Stennik, ĬU. V. *Istoriĭa russkoĭ literatury XVIII veka,* BE1386, BE1387
Stenton, Michael. *Who's who of British members of Parliament,* CJ354, CJ362
Stepanov, V. P. *Istoriĭa russkoĭ literatury XVIII veka,* BE1386, BE1387
Stepanova, A. G. *Bibliografiĭa bibliografiĭ po ĭazykoznaniĭu,* BD6
Stepfamilies, Gruber, Ellen J., CC212
Stephen, Henry. *Solubilities of inorganic and organic compounds,* EE91
Stephen, Leslie. *Dictionary of national biography,* AH226
Stephen T. *Solubilities of inorganic and organic compounds,* EE91
Stephens, Lester D. *Historiography,* DA44
Stephens, Meic. *A dictionary of literary quotations,* BE119
——— *The Oxford companion to the literature of Wales,* BE814
——— *The Oxford illustrated literary guide to Great Britain and Ireland,* BE614
——— *Oxford literary guide to Great Britain and Ireland,* BE614
Stephens, Norris L. *Collected editions, historical sets, and monuments of music,* BJ58
Stephens, Thomas Arthur. *Proverb literature,* BE162
Stephens, Thomas M. *Dictionary of Latin American racial and ethnic terminology,* CC460
Stephens, W. B. *Sources for English local history,* DB147, DC350, DC351
——— *Sources for U.S. history,* DB147
Stephenson, Mary Sue. *Planning library facilities,* AK180
Stephenson, Richard W. *Civil War maps,* CL301, DB122
——— *Map collections in the United States and Canada,* CL259
Sterba, Gunther. *The aquarium encyclopedia,* EG282
Sterling, Christopher H. *The mass media,* CH496
Stern, Ailene L. *Legal looseleafs in print,* CK122
Stern, Arthur C. *Air pollution,* EK78
Stern, Ephraim. *Illustrated dictionary & concordance of the Bible,* BC142
——— *The new encyclopedia of archaeological excavations in the Holy Land,* BC194
Stern, Geoffrey. *Atlas of communism,* CJ525
Stern, Gerry. *Stern's sourcefinder,* CH720
Stern, Irwin. *Dictionary of Brazilian literature,* BE928
——— *Modern Spanish and Portuguese literatures,* BE1449
Stern, Malcolm H. *Americans of Jewish descent,* AJ66
——— *First American Jewish families,* AJ66
——— *Reform Judaism in America,* BC559
Stern, Stephen. *American and Canadian immigrant and ethnic folklore,* CF66
Stern, Yvette Borcia. *Stern's sourcefinder,* CH720
Sternberg, Robert J. *Handbook of human intelligence,* CD112
——— *The psychologist's companion,* CD43
——— *Writing the psychology paper,* CD43
Sternfeld, Wilhelm. *Deutsche Exil-Literatur, 1933–1945,* BE1232
Sternlicht, Manny. *Special education,* CB192
Stern's performing arts directory, BH18
Stern's sourcefinder, CH720

Sternstein, Jerome L. *Encyclopedia of American biography,* AH60

Steroids, EE130

Steuart, Robert D. *Library management,* AK174

Steuler, Ursula. *Bibliographie zur deutschen Lyrik nach 1945,* BE1272

Steunou, Jacqueline. *Bibliografia de los cancioneros castellanos del siglo XV y repertorio de sus generos poeticos,* BE1477

Stevanovic, Bosiljka. *Free voices in Russian literature, 1950s–1980s,* BE1407

Steven Spielberg Jewish Film Archive. *Films of the Holocaust,* DA221

Stevens, Alan M. *Contemporary Indonesian-English dictionary,* AC518

Stevens, Albert Clark. *The cyclopaedia of fraternities,* AL77

Stevens, Bonnie Klomp. *A guide to literary criticism and research,* BE9

Stevens, David. *English Renaissance theatre history,* BH45

Stevens, Gwendolyn. *The women of psychology,* CD51, CD52

Stevens, Henry. *Catalogue of the American books in the library of the British Museum at Christmas MDCCCLVI,* AA419

Stevens, Joan. *New Zealand novel, 1860–1965,* BE861

Stevens, Matthew. *Jewish film directory,* BH225

Stevens, Paul Douglas. *A reader's guide to Canadian history,* DB187

Stevens, Peter. *Modern English-Canadian poetry,* BE830

Stevens, S. S. *Handbook of experimental psychology,* CD114

Stevens, Vance. *Bibliography of computer-aided language learning,* BD73

Stevens' handbook of experimental psychology, CD114

Stevenson, Allan. *Les filigranes,* AA256

Stevenson, Burton Egbert. *The home book of Bible quotations,* BC156

———— *The home book of proverbs, maxims and familiar phrases,* BE163

———— *Home book of quotations, classical and modern,* BE95, BE120, BE163

———— *Home book of Shakespeare quotations,* BE775

———— *Macmillan book of proverbs, maxims and famous phrases,* BE163

Stevenson, C. F. *List of named glaciological features in Canada,* CL112

Stevenson, David. *Scottish texts and calendars,* DC361

Stevenson, George A. *Graphic arts encyclopedia,* BF369

Stevenson, Isabelle. *The Tony Award,* BH93

Stevenson, James. *New Eusebius,* BC285

Stevenson, James A. C. *Scoor-oot,* AC167

Stevenson, Joan C. *Dictionary of concepts in physical anthropology,* CE45

Stevenson, John. *British historical facts,* DC323

———— *Columbia dictionary of European political history since 1914,* DC20

———— *Irish historical documents since 1800,* DC415

———— *Longman handbook of modern British history, 1714–1987,* DC21, DC294

———— *The Longman handbook of modern European history, 1763–1985,* DC21

Stevenson, Lionel. *English novel, a panorama,* BE691

———— *The history of the English novel,* BE691

———— *Victorian fiction,* BE668, BE686, BE703, BE755

Stevenson, Robert C. *The Judson Burmese-English dictionary,* AC244

Stevenson, Rosemary M. *Index to Afro-American reference resources,* CC378

Stevenson, W. B. *Analytical concordance to the Bible,* BC167

Stevenson, Wendy B. *Scottish texts and calendars,* DC361

Steward, Julian Haynes. *Handbook of South American Indians,* CE91

Stewardson, Jerry L. *A bibliography of bibliographies on patristics,* BC298

Stewart, Dave N. *Tax research techniques,* CK119

Stewart, George Rippey. *American given names,* AJ175

———— *American place-names,* CL180

Stewart, Isabel Maitland. *A history of nursing, from ancient to modern times,* EH286

———— *Short history of nursing,* EH286

Stewart, James D. *British union-catalogue of periodicals,* AD236

Stewart, John. *Antarctica,* DG8

Stewart, John Alexander. *A Burmese-English dictionary,* AC245

Stewart, Ken. *The Oxford literary guide to Australia,* BE855

Stewart, Larry L. *A guide to literary criticism and research,* BE9

Stewart, Powell. *British newspapers and periodicals, 1632–1800,* AE56

Stewart, Robert. *Dictionary of political quotations,* CJ45

Stewart, Walter J. *Guide to the records of the United States House of Representatives at the National Archives, 1789–1989,* CJ203

Stickney, Patricia J. *World guide to social work education,* CC49

Stieb, Ernst Walter. *Pharmacy museums and historical collections on public view in the United States and Canada,* EH367

Stieler, Adolf. *Stieler's atlas of modern geography,* CL291

Stieler's atlas of modern geography, Stieler, Adolf, CL291

Stier, Hans-Erich. *Grosser Atlas zur Weltgeschichte,* DA51

Stievater, Susan M. *Biographies of creative artists,* BF138

Stikords-katalog over norsk litteratur, 1883–1907, Hauff, Nils Selmer, AA758

Stikordsregister til den danske Skønlitteratur. 1841/1908–1909/40, Ehrencron-Müller, Holger, AA607

Stiles, Charles Wardell. *Index-catalogue of medical and veterinary zoology—authors,* EH101

Stiles, W. S. *Color science,* ED64

Still more words of Wall Street, CH212

Stiller, Johanna. *Schrifttum über Polen (ohne Posener Land),* DC476

Stillwell, Margaret Bingham. *Incunabula and Americana, 1450–1800,* AA218

Stillwell, Richard. *The Princeton encyclopedia of classical sites,* DA105

Stimmel, Barry. *The facts about drug use,* CC136

Stineman, Esther. *American political women,* CJ160

———— *Women's studies,* CC501

Stitt, Iain P. A. *The Arthur Andersen European Community sourcebook,* AF22

Stocco, Carla. *Periodici italiani, 1968–1981,* AD128

Stock, Karl F. *Bibliographie österreichischer Bibliographien, Sammelbiographien und Nachschlagewerke,* AA36

———— *Personalbibliographien österreichischer Dichter und Schriftsteller,* BE1096

Stock, Marylène. *Bibliographie österreichischer Bibliographien, Sammelbiographien und Nachschlagewerke,* AA36

———— *Personalbibliographien österreichischer Dichter und Schriftsteller,* BE1096

Stock, Molly. *A practical guide to graduate research,* AG5

The stock exchange official intelligence, CH327

Stock exchange official yearbook, CH327

Stock exchanges, CH210, CH307
  directories, CH215, CH216, CH310, CH436
Stock exchanges (by country or region)
  Great Britain, CH327

Stock guide, CH313

Stock market encyclopedia, CH404

Stock photo deskbook, BF347

Stock reports, CH313

Stockbridge, John Calvin. *Anthony memorial,* BE494

Stockholm International Peace Research Institute. *World armaments and disarmament,* CJ602

The stockman's handbook, Ensminger, M. Eugene, EJ135

Stocks, CH231, CH318, CH323, CH325
  abbreviations, CH210, CH315
  price indexes, CH232
  prices, CH300
  statistics, CH419
Stocks (by country or region)
  United States, CH404

Stockwell, John. *In search of enemies,* DD128

Stoddard, Charles Hatch. *Essentials of forestry practice,* EJ190

Stoddard, Ellwyn R. *Borderlands sourcebook,* DB164

Stoddard, Glenn M. *Essentials of forestry practice,* EJ190

Stoddard, Richard. *Stage scenery, machinery, and lighting,* BH52

———— *Theatre and cinema architecture,* BH35

Stoddard, Roger E. *Catalogue of books and pamphlets unrecorded in Oscar Wegelin's Early American poetry, 1650–1820,* BE498

Stoddart, Linda. *Conditions of work and quality of working life,* CH661

Stoff- und Motivgeschichte der deutschen Literatur, Schmitt, Franz Anselm, BE1231

Stoffer, Janet Y. *Science fair project index, 1960–1972,* EA31

Stogdill, Ralph Melvin. *Bass & Stogdill's handbook of leadership,* CD126

———— *Handbook of leadership,* CD126, CH608

———— *Leadership abstracts and bibliography, 1904 to 1974,* CH608

———— *Stogdill's handbook of leadership,* CD126

Stogdill's handbook of leadership, Stogdill, Ralph Melvin, CD126

Stohl, Michael. *Political terrorism,* CJ554

Stoîanov, Manò Manev. *Bŭlgarska vŭzrozhdenska knizhnina,* AA584

Stojan, Petro E. *Bibliografio de internacia lingvo,* BD50

Stoke, Sybil. *Comparative public administration,* CJ467

Stokes, Francis Griffin. *A dictionary of the characters and proper names in the works of Shakespeare,* BE789

Stokes, Gale. *Nationalism in the Balkans,* DB64

Stokes, Roy Bishop. *A bibliographical companion,* AA11

———— *Esdaile's manual of bibliography,* AA2

Stoll, Béla. *A Magyar irodalomtörténet bibliográfiája,* BE1279

Stoll, Christoph. *Bibliographie der Personalbibliographien zur deutschen Gegenwartsliteratur,* BE1221

Stone, A. V. *Rocks and minerals,* EF202

Stone, Calvin Perry. *Annual review of psychology,* CD44

Stone, Evelyn M. *American psychiatric glossary,* EH385

Stone, F. Gordon A. *Comprehensive organometallic chemistry,* EE120

Stone, Louise W. *Anglo-Norman dictionary,* AC168

Stone, Martha. *A bibliography of Canadian demography,* CG116

Stoner, K. Lynn. *Latinas of the Americas,* CC617, DB262

Stoob, Heinz. *Bibliographie zur deutschen historischen Städteforschung,* BF274, DC266

Stopford, John M. *Directory of multinationals,* CH354

———— *Multinational enterprise,* CH341

Stoppelli, Pasquale. *Dizionario Garzanti dei sinonimi e dei contrari,* AC541

Stora, Benjamin. *Dictionnaire biographique de militants nationalistes algériens,* DD127

Stora engelsk-svenska ordboken, AC768

———— Santesson, Rudolf, AC769

Storck, Peter L. *A preliminary bibliography of early man in eastern North America, 1839–1973,* CE84

Stordeur, Danielle. *Bibliographie du Tchad,* DD140

Storey, Charles Ambrose. *Persian literature,* BE1574

Storey, Jill. *AAAS science book list supplement,* EA27

Storey, R. L. *Chronology of the medieval world, 800 to 1491,* DA156, DA184

Storey, Richard. *Primary sources for Victorian studies,* BE606

Storia della letteratura italiana, Cecchi, Emilio, BE1303

—— De Sanctis, Francesco, BE1304

—— Dotti, Ugo, BE1305

—— Flora, Francesco, BE1306

Storia della stampa italiana, AE64

Storia delle accademie d'Italia, Maylender, Michele, AL69

Storia mondiale dell'arte, BF134

Storm, Colton. *Catalogue of the Everett D. Graff Collection of Western Americana,* DB6

Storm data for the United States, 1970–1974, EF165

Storm data for the United States, 1975–1979, EF165

Storms, EF165

Storrs, Thomas I. *The bankers' handbook,* CH282

Story, G. M. *Dictionary of Newfoundland English,* AC159

Story, Norah. *Oxford companion to Canadian history and literature,* BE833

Storzer, Gerald H. *Dictionary of modern French idioms,* AC368

Stott, D. I. *Dictionary of immunology,* EG33

Stout, Chris E. *Handbook for assessing and treating addictive disorders,* CC135

Stout, Harry S. *Dictionary of Christianity in America,* BC235

Stout, Russell. *Organizations, management, and control,* CH609

Stovall, Floyd. *Eight American authors,* BE403

Stover, Carl W. *Seismicity of the United States, 1568–1989 (revised),* EF262

Stover, Catherine. *Inventory of the records of the National Arts Club, 1898–1960,* BF58

Stowe's clerical directory, BC344

Strachan, Anne. *Prizewinning literature,* BE179

Strache, Neil E. *Hispanic Americans in the United States,* AE31

—— *Women's periodicals and newspapers from the 18th century to 1981,* AE25

Straje, Mihail. *Dictionar de pseudonime, alonime [sic], anagrame, asteronime, criptonime ale scriitorilor si publicistilor români,* AA182

Straka, Georges. *Dictionnaire étymologique de l'ancien français,* AC346

Strange, Heather. *Aging & cultural diversity,* CC75

Strange Library of Africana. *Southern African material in anthologies of English literature in the Strange Library of Africana,* BE1537

Straniero, Michele L. *Dizionario dei proverbi italiani,* BE161

Strasser, Wolfgang. *Bibliographie zur Aussenpolitik der Republik Österreich seit 1945,* DC87

Strassmayr, Eduard. *Bibliographie zur oberösterreichischen Geschichte, 1891–1926,* DC92

Straszewska, Sophie. *Dictionary of animal production terminology,* EJ114

A strategic atlas, Chaliand, Gérard, CJ73

Strategic Defense Initiative, CJ606, CJ620

Strategic Defense Initiative, Lawrence, Robert M., CJ606

Strategic survey, CJ601

The strategy handbook, Hay, Michael, CH613

Stratford, Jean Slemmons. *Guide to statistical materials produced by governments and associations in the United States,* CG95

Stratford, Juri. *Guide to statistical materials produced by governments and associations in the United States,* CG95

Strathclyde University. Department of Marketing. *Dictionary of marketing and advertising,* CH549

Stratigraphic atlas of North America and Central America, Shell Oil Company. Exploration Department, EF113

Stratman, Carl Joseph. *American theatrical periodicals, 1789–1967,* BH36

—— *Bibliography of English printed tragedy, 1565–1900,* BE654

—— *Bibliography of medieval drama,* BE237, BE635

—— *Bibliography of the American theatre, excluding New York City,* BH43, BH46

—— *Britain's theatrical periodicals, 1920–1967,* BH36

—— *Restoration and eighteenth century theatre,* BE647

—— *Restoration and eighteenth century theatre research,* BH47

Stratmann, Franz Heinrich. *A Middle-English dictionary,* AC176

Stratton, George Burder. *World list of scientific periodicals published in the years 1900–1960,* EA46

Stratton, Peter. *A student's dictionary of psychology,* CD31, CD32

Strauch, Katina. *Theories of bibliographic education,* AK229

Straukaitė, Danutė. *Tarybų Lietuvos rašytojai : biobibliografinis,* BE1325

Straumanis, Alfreds. *Baltic drama,* BE989

Straus, Murray Arnold. *Handbook of family measurement techniques,* CC239

Strauss, Diane Wheeler. *Handbook of business information,* CH334

Strauss, Erwin S. *MIT Science Fiction Society's index to the s-f magazines, 1951–1965,* BE294

Strauss, Gerhard. *Lexikon der Kunst,* BF74

Strauss, Herbert Arthur. *Biographisches Handbuch der deutschsprachigen Emigration nach 1933,* AH203

—— *Jewish immigrants of the Nazi period in the USA,* DA218, DB126

Stravinskas, Peter M. J. *Our Sunday Visitor's Catholic encyclopedia,* BC404

Strayer, Joseph Reese. *Dictionary of the Middle Ages,* DA148

Streeter, Victor Lyle. *Handbook of fluid dynamics,* ED39

Streit, Robert. *Bibliotheca missionum,* BC304

Ştrempel, Gabriel. *Bibliografia românească modernă, 1831–1918,* AA781

Stress burnout, Riggar, T. F., CD124

Strichart, Stephen S. *Peterson's guide to colleges with programs for learning-disabled students,* CB315

Stricker, George. *Handbook of developmental psychology,* CD86

Strickland, J. T. *Directory of archives, libraries and schools of librarianship in Africa,* AK154

Strickland-Hodge, Barry. *Medical information,* EH8

Strijp, Ruud. *Cultural anthropology of the Middle East,* CE112

Strikes and agreements file, 1893–1953, CH624

Stringer, Jenny. *Concise Oxford companion to English literature,* BE610

Stroebel, Leslie D. *Dictionary of contemporary photography,* BF343

—— *Focal encyclopedia of photography,* BF340

Strohmeyer, Eckhard. *NNB,* AA868

—— *Umfassende Bibliographie der Völker namibiens (Südwestafrikas) und Südwestangolas,* CE104

Strong, Donald S. *Southern primaries and elections, 1920–1949,* CJ290

Strong, James. *Exhaustive concordance of the Bible,* BC151, BC159, BC165

—— *The new Strong's exhaustive concordance of the Bible,* BC165

Strong, John. *Guide to Buddhist religion,* BC472

Strong, Reuben Myron. *A bibliography of birds,* EG276

Strong, Susan R. *History of American ceramics,* BG54, BG56

Strong, William S. *The copyright book,* AA316

Stroobant, P. *Bibliography of astronomy, 1881–1898, on microfilm,* EC14

Strosetzki, Christoph. *Bibliographie der Hispanistik in der Bundesrepublik Deutschland, Österreich und der deutschsprachigen Schweiz,* BD167

Stroud, John. *World encyclopedia of civil aircraft,* CJ577

Stroynowski, Juliusz. *Who's who in the socialist countries,* AH47

—— *Who's who in the socialist countries of Europe,* AH163

Strubbe, Egied I. *De chronologie van de middeleeuwen en de moderne tijden in de Nederlanden,* DC460

Stručné dejiny literatury české, Novak, Arne, BE1106

Stručny etymologický slovník jazyka českého se zvláštním zřetelem k slovům kulturním a cizím, Holub, Josef, AC283

Structural engineering, EK107, EK108, EK115

dictionaries, EK112

handbooks, EK103, EK105, EK106, EK111, EK113

Structural engineering handbook, EK113

Structural steel designers' handbook, Merritt, Frederick S., EK111

Structure reports, EE89

•*Structures & properties database and estimation program,* EE93

Struggle for empire, Lydon, James G., DB80

The struggle for South Africa, Davies, Robert H., DD208

Strukturnoe i prokladnoe iazykoznanie, BD7

Strunk, William. *Elements of style,* CA55

Struve, Gleb. *Russian literature under Lenin and Stalin, 1917–1953,* BE1421

—— *Soviet Russian literature,* BE1421

Stuart, Lurline. *Nineteenth century Australian periodicals,* BE857

Stuart, Merrill M. *A bibliography of master's theses in geography,* CL27

Stuart, Paul. *Nations within a nation,* CC443

Stuart, S. N. *Threatened birds of Africa and related islands,* EG278

Stuart-Fox, David J. *Bibliography of Bali,* DE178

Stuart-Fox, Martin. *Historical dictionary of Laos,* DE224

Stubbs, Michael. *Malawi in maps,* CL342

Stubbs, Walter. *Congressional committees, 1789–1982,* CJ219

The student access guide to the best ... colleges, CB293

Student aid, CB376, CB382, CB392

databases, CB388, CB390

Student expenses at postsecondary institutions, CB259, CB375

Student movements, CB326

Student political activism, CB326

Student politics and higher education in the United States, Altbach, Philip G., CB217

The student sociologist's handbook, Bart, Pauline, CC23

The student's companion to geography, CL3

Student's dictionary of psychology, Hayes, Nicky, CD32

—— Stratton, Peter, CD31, CD32

Students' favourite dictionary, English-to-Bengali & English, Dev, Ashu Tosh, AC232

Students, foreign *see* **Foreign students**

The students' guide to graduate studies in the UK, CB321

Student's manual of bibliography, Esdaile, Arundell James Kennedy, AA2

Studer, Julius. *Schweizer Ortsnamen,* CL214

Studer, Maja. *Analytische Bibliographie der Gesamtregister schweizerischer Zeitschriften,* AD330

Studi medievali, DA144

Studies in conservation, BF198

Studies in economics and political science, CA13

Studies in enterprise, Baker Library, CH389, CH390

—— Daniells, Lorna M., CH390

Studies in human sexuality, Frayser, Suzanne G., CC269

Studies in Jacobean drama, 1973–1984, Lidman, Mark J., BE646, BE648
Studies in Japanese literature and language, Yoshizaki, Yasuhiro, BD222, BE1596
Studies in Mycenaean inscriptions and dialect, 1953–1964, BD139
Studies in Mycenaean inscriptions and dialect, 1965–1978, Baumbach, Lydia, BD139
Studies in public policy, CJ342
Studies in short fiction, BE264
Studies of British newspapers and periodicals from their beginning to 1800, AE58
—— Weed, Katherine Kirtley, AD109, AE60
Studies of Chinese religion, Thompson, Laurence G., BC37
Studies on Korea, DE214
Studies on Vietnamese language and literature, Nguyên, Dình Thâm, BD231, BE1601
Studies on women abstracts, CC531
Studio dictionary of design and decoration, BG25
The studio handbook of minerals, EF191
Studwell, William E. *Ballet plot index*, BH138
—— *Christmas carols*, BJ274
—— *Opera plot index*, BJ246
Study abroad, CB370
—— Judkins, David, CB243
Study and research guide in computer science, Tölle, Wolfgang, EK202
Study of history, Richardson, R. C., DA44
The study of Judaism, BC521
The study of liturgy, BC269
Study of media and markets, CH599
A study of modern Chinese government publications, 1912–1949, Tsai, David W., AF243
Study of Russian history from British archival sources, Hartley, Janet M., DC563
A study of the Soviet economy, CH186
Studying the presidency, CJ166
Stuiber, Alfred. *Patrologie*, BC300
Stuiveling, Garmt. *Guide littéraire de la Belgique, de la Hollande, et du Luxembourg*, BE982
Stultz, Newell M. *South Africa*, DD216
Stupkiewicz, Stanisław. *Bibliografia literatury polskiej okresu odrodzenia*, BE1357
Sturges, Claire. *Who's who in British economics*, CH103
Sturges, R. P. *Who's who in British economics*, CH103
Sturgis, Alice. *Standard code of parliamentary procedure*, CJ458
Sturgis, Russell. *Dictionary of architecture and building*, BF238
Sturgis' illustrated dictionary of architecture and building, BF238
Sturgis standard code of parliamentary procedure, CJ458
Sturm, Heribert. *Biographisches Lexikon zur Geschichte der böhmischen Länder*, AH181
Sturm, Rudolf. *Czechoslovakia*, DC126
Sturm, Terry. *The Oxford history of New Zealand literature in English*, BE863
Sturtevant, William C. *Handbook of North American Indians*, CC419, CC432
Stuteley, Richard. *Economist guide to business numeracy*, CH89
Stutley, James. *Dictionary of Hinduism*, BC488
—— *Harper's dictionary of Hinduism*, BC488
Stutley, Margaret. *Dictionary of Hinduism*, BC488
—— *Harper's dictionary of Hinduism*, BC488
—— *An illustrated dictionary of Hindu iconography*, BF192
Style and stylistics, Milic, Louis, BE374
Style manual, United States. Government Printing Office, AA323
Style manual for political science, American Political Science Association, CJ4
Style manuals, AA317, AA319, AA322, AA323, AA324, AG6, CA55, EA159
Style manuals (by subject)
   law, CK66
   medicine, EA162, EH193, EH194
   physics, ED51
   psychology, CD42, CD43

   science, EA158
   see also **Copy preparation**
Stylebook, EH193
Stylistics
   bibliography, BE374, BE1072, BE1363
   dictionaries, BE375
Suárez, Victor M. *Imprenta en Mérida de Yucatán (1813–21)*, AA463
Suavet, Thomas. *Dictionnaire économique et social*, CH55
Sub-doctoral theses on Canada accepted by universities in the United Kingdom & Ireland 1899–1986, Reid, Elspeth, DB190
Sub-Saharan African films and filmmakers, Schmidt, Nancy J., BH171
Sub-Saharan African films and filmmakers, 1987–1992, Schmidt, Nancy J., DD43
Subarctic Athabascans, Hippler, Arthur E., CC414
—— Wood, John R., CC414
Subculture
   directories, AL44
Subculture (by country or region)
   Ireland, AL67
[Subject bibliographies], United States. Superintendent of Documents, AF113
A subject bibliography of the First World War, Enser, A. G. S., DA193
Subject bibliography of the Second World War, Enser, A. G. S., DA193, DA200
Subject catalog, Library of Congress, AA111
Subject catalog of the Department library, United States. Department of Health, Education, and Welfare. Library, CB35
Subject catalog of the library of the State Historical Society of Wisconsin, Madison, Wisconsin, State Historical Society of Wisconsin. Library, CH641
Subject catalog of the special Panama Collection of the Canal Zone Library-Museum, Canal Zone. Library-Museum, Balboa Heights, DB318
Subject catalog of the World War I collection, New York Public Library. Reference Department, DA196
Subject catalog of the World War II collection, New York Public Library. Research Libraries, DA196
Subject cataloging manual, Library of Congress. Office for Subject Cataloging Policy, AK221
—— Library of Congress. Subject Cataloging Division, AK219, AK220
Subject catalogue of paintings in public collections, BF321
Subject catalogue of the history of medicine and related sciences, Wellcome Institute for the History of Medicine, EH54
Subject catalogue of the House of Commons Parliamentary papers, 1801–1900, Cockton, Peter, AF194
Subject catalogue of the Library of the German Archaeological Institute at Rome, Deutsches Archäologisches Institut. Römische Abteilung. Bibliothek, DA63
Subject catalogue of the Library of the Royal Empire Society, formerly Royal Colonial Institute, Royal Commonwealth Society. Library, DC344
Subject collections, Ash, Lee, AK100, AK119
—— Miller, William G., AK119
Subject collections in children's literature, Field, Carolyn W., AK113
Subject collections in European libraries, Lewanski, Richard Casimir, AK119
Subject compilations of state laws, CK181
Subject directory of special libraries and information centers, AK126
Subject guide to Books in print, AA425, AA426, AA436, AA438
Subject guide to Canadian books in print, AA455
Subject guide to children's books in print, AA428
Subject guide to classical instrumental music, Goodenberger, Jennifer, BJ293
Subject guide to forthcoming books, AA432
Subject guide to German book in print, AA660
Subject guide to government reference books, Wynkoop, Sally, AF74

Subject guide to major United States government publications, Williams, Wiley J., AF63
Subject guide to major United States publications, Jackson, Ellen, AF63
Subject guide to microforms in print, AA131
Subject guide to periodical indexes and review indexes, Kujoth, Jean Spealman, AD250
Subject guide to U.S. government reference sources, Robinson, Judith Schiek, AF74
Subject guide to Zambiana theses, Mwanza, Ilse, AG50, DD247
Subject headings, AK219, AK221
   databases, AK220
   schedules, AK220, AK222
Subject headings (by subject)
   Africa, DD51
   education, CB82
   medicine, EH143
   political science, CJ43
   sociology, CC21
Subject headings and classification on peace and international conflict resolution, CJ688
Subject index of books published before 1880, Peddie, Robert Alexander, AA94, AA104
Subject index of modern books acquired, 1961–1970, British Library. Department of Printed Books, AA104
Subject index of the modern works added to the library, 1881–1900, British Museum. Department of Printed Books, AA94, AA104
Subject index to children's magazines, AD268
Subject index to Current population reports, O'Brien, Catherine, CG97
Subject index to periodicals, AD289, BA6
Subject index to poetry for children and young people, BE322
—— Andrews, Eva L., BE322
—— Smith, Dorothy B. Frizzell, BE322
Subject index to Welsh periodicals, AA698, AD290
The subject is murder, Menendez, Albert J., BE273
Subramaniam, Venkateswarier. *Public administration in the Third World*, CJ483
Subscription books bulletin, AA357
Subscription books bulletin reviews, AA330
Subsidia hagiographica, BC259
Subsidios para a bibliografia da história local portuguêsa, Biblioteca Nacional de Lisboa, DC483
Subsidios para um diccionario de pseudonymos, iniciaes e obras anonymas de escriptores portuguezes, contribuiçao para o estudo da litteratura portugueza, Fonseca, Martinho Augusto Ferreira da, AA181
Substance abuse & kids, CC131
Substance abuse among ethnic minorities in America, CC122
Substance abuse I : drug abuse, Nordquist, Joan, CC117
Substance abuse II : alcohol abuse, Nordquist, Joan, CC118
Substance abuse residential treatment centers for teens, CC132
Suburbia, Zikmund, Joseph, CC307
Suburbs, CL77
Successful candidates for the degrees of D.Phil., M.Litt., M.Sc., and Diploma in Law with the titles of their theses, University of Oxford, AG34
Successful dissertations and theses, Madsen, David, AG3
Suchan, Elke. *Bibliographie unselbständiger Literatur-Linguistik*, BD1
Suchlicki, Jaime. *The Cuban revolution*, DB431
Suchodolski, Bogdan. *Wielka encyklopedia powszechna PWN*, AB78
Sudan, DD226
   bibliography, DD18, DD148, DD225, DD228
   biography, AH326
   current surveys, DD62
   encyclopedias, DD48
   library catalogs, DD227
Sudan (by subject)
   foreign relations
      bibliography, DD228

religion, BC452
Sudan, Chapin Metz, Helen, DD62
——— Daly, M. W., DD18
——— Fluehr-Lobban, Carolyn, DD48
——— Lobban, Richard A., DD48
——— Voll, John Obert, DD48
Suddarth, Doris Smith. *The Lippincott manual of nursing practice,* EH284
Sudman, A. *Norsk allkunnebok,* AB75
Südost-Institut München. Bibliothek. *Bestandskatalog der Bibliothek des Südost-Instituts München,* DC65
Südosteuropa-Dissertationen, 1918–1960, Scherer, Anton, DC67
Südosteuropa-Handbuch, DC68
Sued Badillo, Jalil. *Bibliografía antropológica para el estudio de los pueblos indígenas en el Caribe,* CE85
Suetens, Ivo. *Bibliographie numismatique: supplément : ordres et decorations,* BG172
Sufism, BC76, BC491
Sugasawa, Shigehiko. *Reaction index of organic syntheses,* EE145
Sugden, Edward Holdsworth. *Topographical dictionary to the works of Shakespeare and his fellow dramatists,* BE794
Sugnet, Christopher L. *Vietnam War bibliography,* DE276
Suh, Dae-Sook. *Korean Communism, 1945–1980,* CJ442
Suicide, CC183
Suid-Afrikaans katalogus von boeke, AA877
Suid-Afrikaanse statistieke, CG359
Suid-Afrikaanse teologiese bibliografie, BC49
Suit your spirit, CL392
Sukhachev, N. L. *Lingvisticheskie atlasy,* BD21
Sukhwal, B. L. *South Asia,* CL21
Sulentic, Jack W. *Revised new general catalogue of nonstellar astronomical objects,* EC75
Sulimierski, Filip. *Słownik geograficzny Królestwa polskiego i innych krajów słowiańskich,* CL148
Sullivan, Alvin. *British literary magazines,* BE590
Sullivan, Eric. *The marine encyclopaedic dictionary,* CH468
Sullivan, Eugene J. *The adult learner's guide to alternative and external degree programs,* CB359
Sullivan, Howard A. *French language and literature,* BD156, BE1130
——— *The Wayne State University collection of comedias sueltas,* BE1472
Sullivan, Irene F. *Dictionary of Native American mythology,* CF16
Sullivan, Kathryn. *Catholic biblical encyclopedia,* BC126
Sullivan, Kaye. *Films for, by, and about women,* CC513
Sullivan, William M. *Dissertations and theses on Venezuelan topics, 1900–1985,* DB400
Sulṭānī, Pūrī. *A directory of Iranian periodicals,* AD198
Sulzer, Jack. *Guide to the publications of interstate agencies and authorities,* AF141
The Sumerian dictionary of the University Museum of the University of Pennsylvania, AC204
Sumerian language
  dictionaries
    bilingual
      Sumerian-English, AC204
      Sumerian-German, AC202
Šumerisches Lexikon, Deimel, Anton, AC202
Sumerkin, Alexander. *Free voices in Russian literature, 1950s–1980s,* BE1407
Summario da Bibliotheca lusitana, Sousa-Farinha, B. J. de, AA774
Summary guide to Corpus vasorum antiquorum, Carpenter, Thomas H., BG78
Summary guide to the archive and manuscript collections relevant to the former British colonial territories in the United Kingdom for the Joint Copyists Standing Committee of the Commonwealth Archivists' Association, Burdett, Anita L. P., DC345
Summary statistics, CB334

Summer Institute of Linguistics. *Bibliography of the Summer Institute of Linguistics,* BD9
Summer Institute of Linguistics—Philippines. *Bibliography of the Summer Institute of Linguistics, Philippines, 1953–1984,* BD233
Summer schools, CB244
Summers, Della. *Longman dictionary of contemporary English,* AC39
Summers, Harry G. *Korean War almanac,* DE218
Summers, Montague. *A Gothic bibliography,* BE302
Summers, Wilford I. *American electricians' handbook,* EK134
Sun power, McAninch, Sandra, EK212
Sunal, Dennis W. *Astronomy education materials resource guide,* EC19
A Sung bibliography, DE135
Sunnucks, Anne. *The encyclopaedia of chess,* BK135
Sunset, Lancaster, Henry Carrington, BE1182
Suomalais-englantilainen sanakirja, Wuolle, Aino, AC325
Suomalais-englantilainen suursanakirja, Alanne, Vieno Severi, AC321
Suomalaisen Kirjallisuuden Seura. *Nykysuomen sanakirja,* AC320
Suomalaisen Kirjallisuuden Seuran toimituksia, AA612
Suomalaisia aikakauslehtiartikkeleita, uutuusindeksi, AD311
Suomen aikakauslehdistön bibliografia 1782–1955, Kurikka, Jussi, AD89
Suomen aikakauslehti-indeksi, AD311
Suomen Akatemia. *Bibliographia studiorum uralicorum, 1917–1987,* DC602
Suomen elämäkerrasto, Heikinheimo, Ilmari, AH187
Suomen historiallinen bibliografia, DC141
Suomen kartasto, Geografiska Sällskapet i Finland, Helsingfors, CL326
Suomen kirjailijat 1917–1944, BE1127
Suomen kirjailijat, 1945–1970, Launonen, Hannu, BE1127
Suomen kirjailijat, 1945–1980, Hirvonen, Maija, BE1127
Suomen kirjallisuus, AA612
Suomen sanomalehdistön bibliografia, 1771–1963, Kaarna, Väinö, AE49
Suomen tieteellisten Kirjastojen opas, Liinamaa, Matti, AK134
Suomen tilastollinen vuosikirja, CG212
Suomessa ilmestyneen kirjallisuuden luettelo, AA611
Super LCCS, Droste, Kathleen, AK202
——— Runchock, Rita, AK202
Les supercheries littéraires dévoilées, Quérard, Joseph Marie, AA169, AA624
Supernatural fiction writers, BE303
Superstition
  dictionaries, CF53
Supplément au Lexicon linguae Aethiopicae … (1865) et édition du lexique de Juste d'Urbin (1850–1855), Grébaut, Sylvain, AC311
Supplement to a guide to source materials for the study of Barbados history, 1627–1834, Handler, Jerome S., DB420
Supplement to Charles Evans' American bibliography, Bristol, Roger Pattrell, AA403
Supplement to employment and earnings, CH682
Supplement to Hain's Repertorium bibliographicum, Copinger, Walter Arthur, AA222, AA223, AA228
Supplement to the dictionary of American library biography, Wiegand, Wayne A., AK86
Supplement to the Oxford companion to Canadian history and literature, Toye, William, BE833
A supplement to the Oxford English dictionary, AC34
Supplement zu Hain und Panzer, Burger, Konrad, AA220, AA223
Supplement zu Heinsius', Hinrichs' und Kaysers Bücher-Lexikon … , Thelert, Gustav, AA646
Supplementary English glossary, Davies, Thomas Lewis Owen, AC97
Supplementary index to Giles' "Chinese biographical dictionary", Gillis, Irvin Van Gorder, AH339
——— Yü, Ping-yüeh, AH339

A supplementary Russian-English dictionary, Marder, Stephen, AC678
Suppléments au Peintre-graveur de Adam Bartsch, Weigel, Rudolph, BF382
The Supreme Court A to Z, CJ179, CJ204, CK188
Supreme Court Historical Society. *The Supreme Court justices,* CK189
——— *Supreme Court of the United States, 1789–1980,* CK183
The Supreme Court justices, CK189
Supreme Court of the United States, 1789–1980, Blandford, Linda A., CK183
Supreme Court reports, lawyers' edition, CK190
Suratteau, Jean-René. *Dictionnaire historique de la Révolution française,* DC184
Surface chemistry, EE45
Surgeons (by country or region)
  Canada
    biography, EH229
  United States
    biography, EH229
Surgery, EH196
  biography, EH220
Surgery (by country or region)
  Great Britain
    biography, EH230
Suriname, DB391, DB392
  bibliography, DB390, DB393
Suriname, Derkx, Jo, DB393
——— Hoefte, Rosemarijn, DB392
——— Nagelkerke, Gerard A., DB393
——— Rolfes, Irene, DB393
Suriname and the Netherlands Antilles, Brown, Enid, DB390
Surkov, A. A. *Kratkaia literaturnaia entsiklopediia,* BE1413
The surnames, families, literature, honours and biographical history of the people of Scotland, AH242
Surnames of Ireland, MacLysaght, Edward, AJ197
The surnames of Scotland, Black, George Fraser, AJ205
A survey of American genealogical periodicals and periodical indexes, Sperry, Kip, AJ33
Survey of Anglo-Indian fiction, Singh, Bhupal, BE1568
Survey of black newspapers in America, La Brie, Henry, AE15
The survey of buying power data service, CH592
A survey of classical periodicals, Southan, Joyce E., BE1008
Survey of current business, CH420, CH425
A survey of English dictionaries, Mathews, Mitford McLeod, AC4
[Survey of English place-names], English Place-Name Society, CL195
Survey of historic costume, Tortora, Phyllis G., BG108
Survey of Japanese collections in the United States, Fukuda, Naomi, DE206
Survey of Kenya. *National atlas of Kenya,* CL341
A survey of materials for the study of the uncommonly taught languages, Center for Applied Linguistics, BD71
Survey of materials for the study of uncommonly taught languages, Hatfield, Debora, BD71
Survey of members, including classification listings, American Economic Association, CH91
Survey of modern fantasy literature, BE304
Survey of Pakistan. *Atlas of Pakistan,* CL360
Survey of Polish literature and culture, Kridl, Manfred, BE1352
Survey of public education in the nation's urban school districts, National School Boards Association, CB143
Survey of race relations in South Africa, DD209
A survey of recent Chilean historiography, 1965–1976, DB358
Survey of research in economic and social history of India, CH197
Survey of science, EG25
Survey of science fiction literature, BE305
Survey of social science, CH53

Survey report, National Center for Education Statistics, CB142

Survey Research Consultants International. *Index to international public opinion,* CJ489

Surveying, EK62

The surveying handbook, EK62

Susheel Kaur. *Directory of periodicals published in India, 1991,* AD193

Sussex, Roland. *Bibliography of computer-aided language learning,* BD73

Sussman, Allen E. *The encyclopedia of deafness and hearing disorders,* CC189

Sussman, Lance Jonathan. *Reform Judaism in America,* BC559

Sussman, Marvin B. *Handbook of marriage and the family,* CC241

Susumu, Ono. *Iwanami kogo jiten,* AC547

Sutcliffe, Anthony. *History of urban and regional planning,* BF270, CC303

Sutherland, Donald Martell. *A catalogue of English newspapers and periodicals in the Bodleian Library, 1622–1800,* AD104

Sutherland, John. *Longman companion to Victorian fiction,* BE689

——— *The Stanford companion to Victorian fiction,* BE689

Sutherland, L. P. *The federal legal directory,* CK146

Sutherland, N. S. *The international dictionary of psychology,* CD32

Sutherland, Neil. *Contemporary Canadian childhood and youth,* CC152

——— *History of Canadian childhood and youth,* CC153

Sutker, Patricia B. *Comprehensive handbook of psychopathology,* EH392

Sutlive, Vinson H. *Ethnohistory,* CE57

Sutro Library. *Catalogue of Mexican pamphlets in the Sutro collection (1623–[1888]),* DB235

The Sutta-nipâta, BC92

Sutter's international red series, AH171, AH212, AH291

Sutton, Roberta Briggs. *Speech index,* BE366

Sužiedelis, Simas. *Encyclopedia Lituanica,* DC441

Suzuki, Peter T. *French, German, and Swiss university dissertations on twentieth century Turkey,* DC541

SvB, AA833

Svecevičius, B. *Lietuvių-anglų kalbų žodynas,* AC601

Svecevicius, Bronius. *Lithuanian-English dictionary,* AC604

Svendsen, P. *Norsk literaturhistorie,* BE1339

Svenkerud, Herbert. *Cappelens store engelsk-norsk ordbok,* AC619

Svensk biografisk handbok, AH294

Svensk biografisk uppslagslitteratur, Ågren, Sven, AH295

Svensk bok-katalog, AA830, AA831, AA832

Svensk bokförteckning, AA831, AA832, AA833, AD161

Svensk bokhandel, AA832, AA833

Svensk dramatisk litteratur under åren 1840–1913, Wingren, G., BE1484

Svensk-engelsk ordbok, AC769

Svensk-engelsk teknisk ordbok, Engström, Einar, EA135

Svensk etymologisk ordbok, Hellquist, Elof, AC770

Svensk festskriftsbibliografi, åren 1891–1925, Taube, Gurli Elisa (Westgren), AA127

Svensk festskriftsbibliografi, åren 1936–1960, Malmström, Rosa, AA127

Svensk historisk bibliografi, DC521

Svensk historisk bibliografi 1771–1874, Setterwall, Kristian, DC521

Svensk historiska föreningen. *Svensk historisk bibliografi,* DC521

Svensk litteratur 1870–1970, Brandell, Gunnar, BE1481

Svensk litteraturhistorisk bibliografi, BE1483, BE1487

Svensk litteraturhistorisk bibliografi intill år 1900, Hagström, Tore, BE1483

Svensk slangordbok, Gibson, Haldo, AC760

Svensk tidskriftsförteckning, AD161

Svensk uppslagsbok, AB99

Svenska akademien. *Ordbok öfver svenska språket,* AC764

Svenska arkeologiska samfundet. *Swedish archaeological bibliography,* DA72

Svenska bibliotekariesamfundets skriftserie, AH295

Svenska litteratursällskapet (Uppsala, Sweden). *Svensk litteraturhistorisk bibliografi,* BE1487

Svenska män och kvinnor, AH292

Svenska Sällskapet för Antropologi och Geografi. *Atlas över Sverige,* CL335

Svenska Stadshistoriska Institut. *International bibliography of urban history,* DC132

Svenskt anonym– och pseudonym-lexikon, Bygdén, Anders Leonard, AA187

Svenskt biografiskt lexikon, AH292, AH293

Svenskt boklexikon, 1830–65, Linnström, Hjalmar, AA830, AA831

Svenskt författarlexikon, 1900–1940, Åhlén, Bengt, BE1480

Svenskt litteraturlexikon, BE1488

Sverchevskaîa, A. K. *Bibliografiîa Türtsii, 1713–1917,* DC532

Sveriges bibliografi, 1481–1600, Anderson, Aksel, AA828

——— Klemming, G. E., AA828

Sveriges bibliografi, 1600-talet, Collijn, Isak, AA828

Sveriges bibliografi intill år 1600, AA828

Sveriges, dramatiska litteratur till och med 1875, Klemming, G. E., BE1484

Sveriges officiella statistik i sammadrag, CG286

Sveriges periodiska litteratur, Lundstedt, Bernhard Wilhelm, AD160

Sveriges statliga publikationer, bibliografi, AF215, AF216

Sverrir Hólmarsson. *Íslensk-ensk orðabók,* AC508

Svod etnograficheskikh poniatiî i terminov, CE47

Svodnyi katalog knig na inostrannykh iazikakh, izdannykh v Rossii v XVII veke, 1701–1800, Filov, V. A., AA791

Svodnyi katalog russkoî knigi grazhdanskoi pechati XVIII veka, 1725–1800, AA791

Svodnyi ukazatel' bibliograficheskikh spiskov i karkotek, sostavlennykh bibliotekami Sovetskogo Soîuza. Obshchestvennye nauki. *Khudozhestvennaîa literatura,* Gosudarstvennaîa biblioteka SSSR imeni V.I. Lenina, AA62

Svodnyi ukazatel' bibliograficheskikh spiskov i kartotek, AA64

SWA, DE33

Swahili bibliography of the East African coast, Wilding, Richard, DD110

Swahili-English dictionary, Madan, Arthur Cornwallis, AC756

——— Rechenbach, Charles William, AC758

Swahili language
dictionaries
bilingual
English-Swahili, AC757, AC759
Swahili-English, AC756, AC758

Swanekamp, Joan. *English ayres,* BJ275

Swannack-Nunn, Susan. *Directory of scientific research institutes in the People's Republic of China,* EA148

Swanson, Alan. *Sweden,* DC520

Swanson, Donald Carl Eugene. *Modern Greek studies in the West,* BD141

——— *The names in Roman verse,* BE1046

Swanson, Dorothy. *American working class history,* CH637

Swanson, Edward Benjamin. *A century of oil and gas in books,* EK302

Swanson, Ellen. *Mathematics into type,* EB99

Swanson, Kathryn. *Affirmative action and preferential admissions in higher education,* CB231

——— *Affirmative action in higher education,* CB231

SWAPO. Dept. of Information and Publicity. *To be born a nation,* DD185

Swartley, Willard M. *Annotated bibliography of Mennonite writings on war and peace, 1930–1980,* BC360

Swartz, Jon David. *Handbook of old-time radio,* BH310

Swartz, Oretha D. *Service etiquette,* AL157

Swaziana, University College of Swaziland. Library, DD231

Swaziland
bibliography, AA879, DD18, DD117, DD231, DD232
encyclopedias, DD48
government publications, AF238
bibliography, AF218
statistics, CG360

Swaziland (by subject)
economic conditions
bibliography, DD230
social conditions
bibliography, DD230
women, DD229

Swaziland. Central Statistical Office. *Annual statistical bulletin,* CG360

Swaziland. Economic Planning Office. *Socio-economic development bibliography,* DD230

Swaziland, Arnheim, Johanna, DD232

——— Booth, Alan R., DD231

——— Grotpeter, John J., DD48

——— Nyeko, Balam, DD18

——— Wallace, Charles Stewart, DD232

Swaziland national bibliography, AA879

Swaziland official publications, 1880–1972, AA879, AF238, DD231

Sweden
atlases, CL335
bibliography, DC520
19th-20th centuries, AA830
current, AA831, AA832, AA833
early, AA828, AA829
biography, AH164, AH292, AH293, AH294
bibliography, AH295
dissertations, AG42
festschriften
bibliography, AA127
government publications, AF215, AF216
periodicals, AD160, AD161
statistics, CG285, CG286

Sweden (by subject)
history, DC72, DC519
bibliography, DC521
travelers' accounts, DC519

Sweden. Riksdagsbibliotek. *Årsbibliografi över Sveriges offentliga publikationer,* AF215

Sweden, Sather, Leland B., DC520

Swedes (by country or region)
United States, AJ43
manuscripts; archives, CC338

Swedish-American Historical Society. *Guide to Swedish-American archival and manuscript sources in the United States,* CC338

Swedish archaeological bibliography, DA72

Swedish archaeology, DA72

Swedish drama, BE1484

Swedish-English technical dictionary, Engström, Einar, EA135

Swedish government publications, annual bibliography, AF216

Swedish imprints, 1731–1833, AA829

Swedish language
dictionaries, AC761, AC762, AC763, AC764
bilingual, AC766, AC768
Swedish-English, AC765, AC767, AC769
etymology
dictionaries, AC770
slang, AC760

Swedish literature
bibliography, BE1483, BE1487
biobibliography, BE1480
biography, BE1480, BE1481, BE1486, BE1488
dictionaries, BE1488

Swedish literature (by subject)
history, BE1481, BE1482, BE1485
bibliography, BE1483, BE1487

The Swedish national bibliography, AA830, AA831, AA832

Swedish passenger arrivals in New York, 1820–1850, Olsson, Nils William, AJ43

Swedish passenger arrivals in U.S. ports, 1820–1850 (except New York), Olsson, Nils William, AJ43

Sweeney, Jerry K. *A handbook of American diplomacy*, CJ150

Sweeney, Patricia E. *Biographies of British women*, AH240

Sweet, Jeffrey. *The best plays of [...]*, BE454

Sweet, Louise Elizabeth. *Circum-Mediterranean peasantry*, CE97

Sweet, William Warren. *Religion on the American frontier*, BC286

Sweet & Maxwell's complete law book catalogue, CK14

Sweetio, Francisco. *Bibliotheca belgica*, AA580

Sweetland, Richard C. *Test critiques*, CD71

—— *Tests*, CD72

Sweetman, Jack. *American naval history*, DB60

Swezey, Kenneth M. *Formulas, methods, tips, and data for home and workshop*, EA279

Swiatek, Anthony. *Encyclopedia of United States silver & gold commemorative coins, 1892–1954*, BG193

Swidwinska-Krzyżanowska, Zofia. *A history of Polish literature*, BE1352

Swierenga, Robert P. *Dutch emigrants to the United States, South Africa, South America, and Southeast Asia, 1835–1880*, AJ67

—— *Dutch immigrants in U.S. ship passenger manifests, 1820–1880*, AJ68

Swift, Catherine G. *Union list of higher degree theses of the universities of New Zealand*, AG60

Swift, Lloyd H. *Botanical bibliographies*, EG94

Swiggers, Pierre. *Bibliographie sélective de linguistique romane et française*, BD150

SWIM, AA829

Swimming, BK100

Swinbank, Jean C. M. *Buttress's world guide to abbreviations of organizations*, AL14

Swindler, William F. *Bibliography of law and journalism*, AE135

—— *Sources and documents of United States constitutions*, CK175

—— *Sources and documents of United States constitutions, second series*, CK172

Swiss literature, BE1490
   bibliography, BE1055
   biobibliography, BE1057, BE1059, BE1060
   periodicals
      bibliography, BE1489
   women authors
      biobibliography, BE1062
Switzerland
   bibliography, AA834, AA835, AA836, AA837, AA839, AH300, DC523, DC525
   biography, AH296, AH297, DC529
      bibliography, AA838, AH298, AH299, AH300, AH301, DC522, DC523, DC528
      contemporary, AH213
   dissertations, AG43
   encyclopedias, AB100, DC530
   gazetteers, CL150
   government publications, AF217
   newspapers, AE77
   periodicals, AD163
      bibliography, AD162, AD164
      indexes, AD330
   statistics, CG288, CG289
Switzerland (by subject)
   archaeology and ancient history, DC175
   cities, DC524
   history, AB100, AH296, DC526, DC527, DC529, DC530
      bibliography, AH298, AH299, DC522, DC528
   law, CK224
   place-names, CL212, CL213, CL214
   politics and government, CJ388
      encyclopedias, CJ334
Switzerland. Eidgenössisches Statistisches Amt. *Bevölkerungsbewegung in der Schweiz*, CG289

—— *Schweizerische Bibliographie für Statistik und Volkswirtschaft*, CG287

Switzerland, Meier, Heinz K., DC526

Sworakowski, Witold S. *Communist International and its front organizations*, CJ503, CJ511

—— *World communism*, CJ529

Sydler, Jean-Pierre. *Vocabulaire international des termes d'urbanisme et d'architecture*, BF278

Sydow, P. *Thesaurus litteraturae mycologicae et lichenologicae ratione habita praecipue omnium quae adhuc scripta sunt de mycologia applicata quem congesserunt*, EG188

Sydsaeter, Knut. *Economists' mathematical manual*, CH84

Sykes, Charles J. *The National review college guide*, CB279

Sykes, Egerton. *Everyman's dictionary of nonclassical mythology*, CF13

—— *Who's who in non-classical mythology*, CF14

Sykes, J. B. *Concise Oxford dictionary of current English*, AC177

—— *Guide to the bibliography of astronomy, 1881–1989, on microfilm*, EC14

—— *The Oxford-Duden German dictionary*, AC419

Sykes, Wendy. *Directory of social research organisations in the United Kingdom*, AL66, CA56

A syllabic dictionary of the Chinese language, Williams, Samuel Wells, AC256

A syllabus of comparative literature, Livingston College, BE21

Sylvestre, Guy. *Canadian writers*, BE834

Symbol guide, CH315

Symbol sourcebook, Dreyfuss, Henry, BF166

Symboler, Liungman, Carl G., BF170

Symbolism for designers, Whittick, Arnold, BF177

Symbolism in art
   indexes, BF193, BG113

Symbols and sacred objects, The woman's dictionary of, CF15

Symbols and symbolism, AL73, BC208, BF171, BF189, CF24
   classification, BF175
   dictionaries, BF164, BF170, CF11, CF15, EA92
   encyclopedias, BF188, CF23
Symbols and symbolism (by subject)
   art, BF163, BF165, BF166, BF167, BF168, BF169, BF172, BF173, BF174, BF176, BF177, BF178, BF179, BF180, BF181, BF182, BF184, BF185, BF187, BF190, BF191, BF298
   religion, BF178, BF182, BF185, BF187, BF190, BF191, BF192, BF298
Symbols, signs and signets, Lehner, Ernst, BF169

Symbols, signs and their meaning and uses in design, Whittick, Arnold, BF177

Symonds, Craig L. *Battlefield atlas of the Civil War*, DB123

The symphony, Stedman, Preston, BJ295

Symphony orchestras, BJ296

Symphony orchestras of the United States, BJ296

Symphony orchestras of the world, Craven, Robert R., BJ296

Syndicat national des annuaires et supports divers de publicité. *Répertoire national des annuaires français, 1958–1968*, AD93

Syndicate directory, AE129

Syndicated columnist contacts, AE129

Syndicated columnists, Weiner, Richard, AE129

Syndicated television, Erickson, Hal, BH301

Syndromes, EH114
   dictionaries, EH118, EH120

Synge, Hugh. *The IUCN plant red data book*, EG149

Synge, Patrick M. *The color dictionary of flowers and plants for home and garden*, EG175

Synonym finder, La Roche, Nancy, AC140

—— Rodale, Jerome I., AC140

—— Urdang, Laurence, AC140

A synonymized checklist of the vascular flora of the United States, Canada, and Greenland, Kartesz, John T., EG132

Synonymwörterbuch, Görner, Herbert, AC434

Synopsis and classification of living organisms, EG28

Synoptical index of the reports of the statistician, 1863 to 1894, Thompson, George Fayette, EJ93

Syntax (linguistics), BD44

Syria
   bibliography
      current, AA936, AA937
   statistics, CG428
Syria (by subject)
   history
      bibliography, DE262
Syria. Wizārat al-Takhtīt al-Qawmī. Mudīrīyat al-Ihsā. *al-Majmū al-ihsāīya*, CG428

Syria, Seccombe, Ian J., DE262

Syriac language
   dictionaries, AC773
      bilingual, AC771, AC772
      Latin, AC771
Syriac literature, BD205, BE1551

The Syrian national bibliography, AA936, AA937

System der organischen Verbindungen, Deutsche Chemische Gesellschaft, EE115

The system of mineralogy of James Dwight Dana and Edward Salisbury Dana, Yale University, 1837–1892, Dana, James Dwight, EF194

Systematic dictionary of mammals of the world, Burton, Maurice, EG290

Systematisches Verzeichnis, Schweizerische Landesbibliothek, AA835

Systematisches Verzeichnis der schweizerischen oder die Schweiz betreffenden Veröffentlichungen, AA838, AH301

Système Communautaire d'Accès á la Documentation, AF25

Syväoja, Olli. *Englanti-suomi suursanakirja*, AC322

Sz. Debreczeni, Kornélia. *Magyar írói álnév lexikon*, AA176

Szabó, Károly. *Régi magyar könyvtár*, AA713, AA714, DC378

Szajkowski, Bogdan. *Marxist governments*, CJ528

—— *New political parties of Eastern Europe and the Soviet Union*, CJ317

Szajkowski, Zosa. *Franco-Judaica*, BC533

—— *Index of articles relative to Jewish history and literature published in periodicals, from 1665 to 1900*, BC545

Szarmach, Paul E. *Sources of Anglo-Saxon literary culture*, BE731

Szarvas, Gábor. *Magyar-nyelvtörténeti szótár a legrégibb nyelvemlékektöl a nyelvújításig*, AC494

Szasz, Paul C. *International environmental law*, CK91

Szczawiński, Paweł. *Biogramy uczonych polskich*, AH278

Szelle, Béla. *Akadémiai kislexikon*, AB58

Szentirmay, Paul. *DILSI, NZ*, AK63

Szentirmay, Thiam Ch'ng. *DILSI, NZ*, AK63

Szeplaki, Joseph. *Hungarians in the United States and Canada*, CC321, CC473

Szépművészeti Múzeum (Hungary). *Museum of Fine Arts, Budapest*, BF321

Szilard, Paula. *Food and nutrition information guide*, EH291

Szilvássy, Zoltánne. *Magyarországi irodalom idegen nyelven*, BE1280

Szinnyei, József. *Magyar írók*, AH247, AH250, BE1282

Szladits, Charles. *A bibliography on foreign and comparative law*, CK8

—— *Guide to foreign legal materials*, CK208, CK210

—— *Guide to foreign legal materials : French*, CK202

Szladits' bibliography on foreign and comparative law, CK8

Szmuk, Szilvia E. *A catalogue of comedias sueltas in The New York Public Library*, BE1459

Szmulewicz, Efraín. *Diccionario de la literatura chilena*, BE941

Szonyi, David M. *The Holocaust*, DA216

Sztripszky, Hiador. *Adalekok Szabó Károly Régi magyar köyvtaar c. munkájának I–II kötetéhez*, AA714

Szucs, Loretto Dennis. *The archives*, AJ24, DB37

Szwed, John F. *Afro-American folk culture*, CF58

Szy, Tibor. *Hungarians in America*, AH251

Szymanek, Bogdan. *Bibliography of morphology, 1960–1985*, BD43

Szymanski, Herman A. *Infrared band handbook*, EE90

Szymczak, Mieczysław. *Słownik języka polskiego*, AC631

The T. L. Yüan bibliography of Western writings on Chinese art and archaeology, Yüan, T'ung-li, BF40

Tabellen zur angewandten Physik, Ardenne, Manfred, ED41

Taber's cyclopedic medical dictionary, EH106

Tablas cronológica y alfabética de imprentas e impresores de Filipinas, Retana y Gamboa, Wenceslao Emilio, AA929

Table des noms propres avec toutes leurs variantes, Flutre, Fernand, BE1163

Table des noms propres de toute nature compris dans les chansons de geste imprimées, Langlois, Ernest, BE1164

Table des pièces de théâtre décrites dans le catalogue de la bibliothèque de M. de Soleinne, Burnet, Charles, BE1184

Table générale des noms réels, Brunet, Gustave, AA169

Table of binomial coefficients, Miller, J. C. P., EB94

Table of definite and indefinite integrals, Apelblat, Alexander, EB77

Table of distances between ports, CH471

Table of integrals, series, and products, Gradshtein, Izrail Solomonovich, EB85

Table of isotopes, ED46
—— Lederer, Charles Michael, ED42, ED46
—— Shirley, Virginia S., ED42

Table of radioactive isotopes, Browne, Edgardo, ED42

A table of series and products, Hansen, Eldon R., EB87

Tableaux démographiques, Croze, Marcel, CG215

Tables annuelles de constantes, EA156

Tables du journal Le temps, AE121

Tables for identification of organic compounds, Frankel, Max, EE151

Tables for statisticians and biometricians, Pearson, Karl, EB90

Tables générales, Loth, Bernard, BC398
—— Michel, Albert, BC398

Tables in mathematical statistics, EB73

Tables of and annotated index to the Congressional series of United States public documents, AF99
—— United States. Superintendent of Documents, AF90

Tables of higher functions, Lösch, Friedrich, EB76

Tables of indices and primitive roots, Miller, J. C. P., EB94
—— Western, A. E., EB94

Tables of integral transforms, Bateman Manuscript Project, EB80

Tables of natural and common logarithms to 110 decimals, Mansell, W. E., EB94

Tables of physical and chemical constants and some mathematical functions, Kaye, G. W. C., ED44

Tables of the Riemann Zeta function, Haselgrove, C. B., EB94
—— Miller, J. C. P., EB94

Taborski, Boleslaw. *Polish plays in English translations*, BE1361

Tactile map collections, CL258

Taddey, Gerhard. *Lexikon der deutschen Geschichte*, DC221

Taehan Min'guk ch'ulp'anmul ch'ongmongnok, AA920

Taeuber, Cynthia Murray. *Statistical handbook on women in America*, CC583, CG108

Taeuber, Irene B. *General censuses and vital statistics in the Americas*, CG72

—— *The population of Japan*, CG404

Tafeln höherer Funktionen, Emde, Fritz, EB76
—— Jahnke, Eugen, EB76

Taft, William H. *Encyclopedia of twentieth-century journalists*, AE152

Taft corporate directory, AL105

Taft corporate giving directory, AL105

Taft Foundation reporter, AL115

Taft Group. *America's new foundations*, AL99
—— *Corporate and foundation grants*, AL103
—— *Corporate giving yellow pages*, AL106
—— *The directory of corporate and foundation givers*, AL107
—— *National directory of nonprofit organizations*, CH365

Taft guide to corporate giving contacts, AL106

Tagalog dictionary, Ramos, Teresita V., AC774

Tagalog drama, BE1598

Tagalog language, BD234
  dictionaries
    bilingual
      Tagalog and English, AC774

Tahiti
  bibliography, DF51
  biography, AH384

Tahitiens, O'Reilly, Patrick, AH384

Tai languages, BD230

Taintor, Sarah Augusta. *The secretary's handbook*, CH90

Tairas, J. N. B. *Indonesia*, AA79

Taiwan
  atlases, CL352
  bibliography
    current, AA938
  current surveys, CG429, DE265
  dissertations, AG58
  periodicals, AD210
  statistics, CG384, CG429, CG430, CG431, DE265

Taiwan (by subject)
  history, DE263
    bibliography, DE264
    general histories, DE148
  women, CC619
  see also **China**

Taiwan, Lee, Wei-chin, DE264

Taiwan statistical data book, CG431

Tajik language, BD196

Tajima, Matsuji. *Old and Middle English language studies*, BD102

Takhtadzhïàn, A. L. *Floristic regions of the world*, EG163

Takkala, Marketta. *Suomen aikakauslehdistön bibliografia 1782–1955*, AD89

Talbert, Richard J. A. *Atlas of classical history*, DA117

Talbot, A. M. *Atlas of the Union of South Africa*, CL346

Talbot, Charles H. *The medical practitioners in medieval England*, EH226

Talbot, Dawn E. *Japan's high technology*, EA9

Talbot, William John. *Atlas of the Union of South Africa*, CL346

Tale of the future, Clarke, Ignatius Frederick, BE282

Tale type- and motif-indexes, Azzolina, David S., CF47

Tallman, Johanna E. *Handbook of scientific and technical awards in the United States and Canada, 1900–1952*, EA197

Talmud, BC181, BC549, CK239

Talocci, Mauro. *Guida alle bandiere di tutto il mondo*, AL195
—— *Guide to the flags of the world*, AL195

Talvart, Hector. *Bibliographie des auteurs modernes de langue française (1801–1975)*, BE1208

Tamar, Tal. *Littérature annotée littérature orale d'Afrique noire*, CF91

Tamarkin, Stan. *The Yiddish dictionary sourcebook*, AC631

Tambs, Lewis A. *Academic writer's guide to periodicals*, AD26

Tamil language
  dictionaries, AC776

bilingual
  English-Tamil, AC775

Tamil lexicon, AC776

Tamiment Library. *Catalog of the Tamiment Institute Library of New York University*, CH642

Tamkoç, Metin. *A bibliography on the foreign relations of the Republic of Turkey, 1919–1967, and brief biographies of Turkish statesmen*, DC539

Tamm, B. G. *Concise encyclopedia of software engineering*, EK169

Tampold, Ana. *Ontario royal commissions and commissions of inquiry, 1867–1978*, AF155

Tanaka, Hideo. *Ei-Beihō jiten*, CK51

Tanakh, BC94

Tanford, Charles. *The scientific traveler*, EA218

Tanganyika African National Union, Howell, John Bruce, DD233

Tanghe, Raymond. *Bibliography of Canadian bibliographies*, AA22

Tanguay, Cyprien. *Dictionnaire généalogique des familles canadiennes*, AJ71, AJ73

Tanguy, Yann. *La recherche documentaire en droit*, CK209

Tannenbaum, Dorothy R. *Elizabethan bibliographies [concise bibliographies]*, BE741

Tannenbaum, Samuel A. *Elizabethan bibliographies [concise bibliographies]*, BE741

Tanner, Helen Hornbeck. *Atlas of Great Lakes Indian history*, CC438

Tanner, John. *Encyclopaedic dictionary of heraldry*, AJ162, AJ163

Tanner, Norman P. *Decrees of the ecumenical councils*, BC436

Tanselle, George Thomas. *Guide to the study of United States imprints*, AA400

Tansey, Richard G. *Gardner's art through the ages*, BF129

Tanur, Judith M. *International encyclopedia of statistics*, CG20, EB37

Tanzania
  atlases, CL342
  bibliography, AA880, AA881, DD18, DD233, DD235, DD236
  current surveys, DD62
  encyclopedias, DD48
  government publications, AF221, AF223
  statistics, CG361, CG362

Tanzania (by subject)
  history, DD234

Tanzania, Darch, Colin, DD18
—— Herrick, A. B, DD62
—— Kurtz, L. S., DD48

Tanzania in maps, Berry, L., CL342

Tanzania national bibliography, AA880, AA881

Tanzarello, Ettore. *Periodici italiani 1914–1919*, DC426

Tanzi, Héctor José. *Historiografía argentina contemporánea*, DB333

Taoism, BB31, BC57
  collections, BC92
  dictionaries, BC76
  encyclopedias, BB31, BC57

Tapley, Bryon D. *Eshbach's handbook of engineering fundamentals*, EK16

Tapping the government grapevine, Robinson, Judith Schiek, AF75

Taragano, Martin. *Basketball biographies*, BK67

Taras, Raymond C. *Handbook of political science research on the USSR and Eastern Europe*, CJ390

Tarassuk, Leonid. *The complete encyclopedia of arms & weapons*, CJ569

Tarbert, Gary C. *Book review index*, AA366
—— *Children's book review index*, AA368
—— *Periodical directories and bibliographies*, AD42

Tariff
  handbooks, CH146
  periodicals, CH156

Tariff (by country or region)
  United States, CH155

Tarling, Nicholas. *The Cambridge history of Southeast Asia*, DE92

Tarrab, Elca. *La francité canadienne*, BD162
The tartans of the clans and families of Scotland, Innes, Thomas, AJ126
Tarybinė lietuvių literatūra ir kritika, Lietuvos TSR Mokslų Akademija. Lietuvių Kalbos ir Literatūros Institutas, BE1324
Tarybinis lietuvių literatūros mokslas ir kritika apie literatūrini palikimą, 1944–1958, Lietuvių kalbos ir literatūros institutas (Lietuvos TSR Mokslų akademija), BE1321
Tarybinis lietuviu literaturos mokslas ir kritika apie literaturini palikima, 1959–1970, Staniveciene, Eugenijus, BE1321
—— Vosylius, Jonas, BE1321
Tarybinių lietuvių rašytojų, BE1325
Tarybų Lietuvos rašytojai, Baltūsis, Juozas, BE1325
—— Lankutis, Jonas, BE1325
—— Maldonis, Alfonsas, BE1325
Tarybų Lietuvos rašytojai : biobibliografinis, Dagytė, Emilija, BE1325
—— Straukaitė, Danutė, BE1325
Tasbīḥī, Ghulām Ḥusayn. *Nigarishī jāmiʿ bar jahān-i kitābshināsi hā-yi Īrān*, AA80
Taschenberg, O. *Bibliotheca zoologica*, EG209
Taschenbuch der Mathematik, EB62
Taschenbuch der Zeitrechnung des deutschen mittelalters und der Neuzeit, Asch, Jürgen, DC223
—— Grotefend, Hermann, DC223
Taschenbuch für das Wissenschaftliche Leben, AL64
Taschenbuch für Familiengeschichtsforschung, AJ95
Taszycki, Witold. *Bibliografia onomastyki polskiej*, CL211
Tata Institute of Fundamental Research. *World directory of mathematicians*, EB60
Tate, Michael L. *Indians of Texas*, CC420
—— *Upstream people*, CC420
Tate, William. *Tate's modern cambist*, CH287
—— *Tate's money manual*, CH287
Tatem, Moira. *A dictionary of superstitions*, CF53
Tate's modern cambist, Tate, William, CH287
Tate's money manual, Spalding, W. F., CH287
—— Tate, William, CH287
Tatla, Darshan Singh. *Immigrants, minorities and race relations*, CC337
—— *Sikhs in North America*, CC331
Taton, René. *Planetary astronomy from the Renaissance to the rise of astrophysics*, EC59
Tattersall, Ian. *Encyclopedia of human evolution and prehistory*, CE40
Tatum, Charles M. *Chicano literature*, BE560
—— *Handbook of Latin American popular culture*, DB289
Taube, A. M. *Russko-angliiskii slovar'*, AC680
Taube, Gurli Elisa (Westgren). *Svensk festskriftsbibliografi, åren 1891–1925*, AA127
Taubes, Frederic. *Painter's dictionary of materials and methods*, BF304
Taufmann, Jürgen. *Atlas zur deutschen Zeitgeschichte, 1918–1968*, DC264
Tauro, Alberto. *Enciclopedia ilustrada del Perú*, DB388
•*TAURUSondisc U.S. government organization manual*, CJ151
Tavaglione, David. *Acronyms and abbreviations of computer technology and telecommunications*, EK189
Tavoni, Mirko. *Renaissance linguistics archive, 1350–1700*, BD67
Tax, Sol. *Serial publications in anthropology*, CE25
Tax Foundation. *Facts and figures on government finance*, CH244
Tax research techniques, Gardner, Robert L., CK119
—— Stewart, Dave N., CK119
Taxonomic literature, Stafleu, Frans Anthonie, EG93
Taxonomic terminology of the higher plants, Featherly, Henry Ira, EG126
Taylor, Archer. *The bibliographical history of anonyma and pseudonyma*, AA145
—— *Dictionary of American proverbs and proverbial phrases, 1820–1880*, BE165
—— *Index to The proverb*, BE164
—— *The proverb*, BE164
Taylor, Barry. *Andorra*, DC82

—— *European economic and social history, 1450–1789*, DC1
Taylor, Beverly. *Arthurian legend and literature*, BE340
Taylor, Clyde Romer Hughes. *Bibliography of publications on the New Zealand Maori and the Moriori of the Chatham Islands*, DF8
—— *A Pacific bibliography*, DF8
Taylor, David D. *Pakistan*, DE242
Taylor, E. A. *Library resources in London and South East England*, AK148
Taylor, Eva Germaine Rimington. *The mathematical practitioners of Hanoverian England, 1714–1840*, EB102
—— *Mathematical practitioners of Tudor and Stuart England*, EB102, EB103
Taylor, Fredric. *The Cambridge photographic atlas of the planets*, EC64
Taylor, Gary. *William Shakespeare, a textual companion*, BE796
Taylor, James. *Dictionary of the Third Reich*, DC259
—— *The Third Reich almanac*, DC259
Taylor, James Lumpkin. *A Portuguese-English dictionary*, AC650
Taylor, John Russell. *Penguin dictionary of the theatre*, BH75
Taylor, Joshua Charles. *Learning to look*, BF124
Taylor, L. J. *FLA theses*, AK24
—— *Library resources in London and South East England*, AK148
Taylor, Michael John Haddrick. *Encyclopedia of the world's air forces*, CJ579
Taylor, Paul. *Popular music since 1955*, BJ341
Taylor, Paul F. *The ABC-CLIO companion to the American labor movement*, CH651
Taylor, Peter J. *Library and information studies in the United Kingdom and Ireland, 1950–1974*, AK23
—— *World government*, CJ93
Taylor, Robert Allen. *La littérature occitane du Moyen Age*, BE1375, DA138
Taylor, Robert H. *Asia and the Pacific*, DE16
Taylor, Thomas J. *American theatre history*, BH48
—— *Restoration drama*, BE647
Taylor, Wendell Hertig. *A catalogue of crime*, BE266
Taylor's encyclopedia of government officials, federal and state, Clements, John, CJ133
Tazawa, Yutaka. *Biographical dictionary of Japanese art*, BF144
TCG theatre directory, BH88
Tchad relance économique en chiffres, CG323
Tchemerzine, Avenir. *Bibliographie d'éditions originales et rares d'auteurs français des XVᵉ, XVIᵉ, XVIIᵉ et XVIIIᵉ siècles contenant environ 6000 facsimilés de titres et de gravures*, AA621
TCI, BH86
Te Ying Han tsung ho kò chi ta tzù tien, EA101
Teacher attitudes, Powell, Marjorie, CB159
Teacher education program evaluation, Ayers, Jerry B., CB158
Teacher effectiveness, Powell, Marjorie, CB160
Teachers and teacher education, CB163
  dictionaries, CB161, CB269
  encyclopedias, CB70
  handbooks, CB117, CB162
  statistics, CB167
Teachers and teacher education (by country or region)
  United States
    statistics, CB166
Teachers and teaching
  bibliography, CB158, CB159, CB160
  handbooks, CB116, CB164
  statistics, CB165
  surveys, CB335
A teacher's treasury of quotations, CB85
Teaching aids, CA50, CB14, CB267
  directories, CB86
  handbooks, CB186
Teaching aids (by subject)
  China, DE133
Teaching, coaching, and learning tennis, Phillips, Dennis J., BK103

Teaching English as a second language, Goldstein, Wallace L., BD110
Teaching technologies in libraries, AK193
Teague, Cynthia M. *Cartographic citations*, CL263
Teague, Edward H. *Index to Italian architecture*, BF231
—— *World architecture index*, BF231
Teatro español, Cotarelo y Mori, Emilio, BE1463
Teatro hispanoamericano, Allen, Richard F., BE897
El teatro lírico español, Iglesias de Souza, Luis, BJ266
Teatro mexicano del siglo XX, 1900–1986, Mendoza-López, Margarita, BE913
Tebbel, John William. *A history of book publishing in the United States*, AA304
Technical Americana, Rink, Evald, EA237, EK3
Technical book review index, EA54
Technical bulletins [Index], United States. Department of Agriculture, EJ92
Technical dictionary English-Italian, Italian-English, EA116, EA118
Technical dictionary of chemistry and technical chemistry, EE50
Technical dictionary of data processing, Bürger, Erich, EK190
The technical editor's and secretary's desk guide, Freedman, George, EA159
Technical libraries, EA144
Technical manual and dictionary of classical ballet, Grant, Gail, BH145
Technical meetings index, EA204
Technical publications announcements, EK28
Technical reports
  abbreviations, EA65
  bibliography, EK156
  databases, EA64
  indexes, EA64, EA66, EA77
Technical reports in computer science, EB28
Technical services in libraries, AK228
  see also **Acquisitions and collection development in libraries; Cataloging**
Technical standards, Crawford, Walt, AK65
Technical studies in the field of fine arts, BF198
Technical translations, EA62
Technical writing, EA158, EA159, EA161, EA163
  bibliography, CH428, EA164
Technik und Wirtschaft in fremden Sprachen, AC192, EA95
Technologisches Wörterbuch, EA102
Technology
  abbreviations, EA96, EA97, EA98, EA99
  abstract journals, EA72, EF118
    bibliography, EA76
  bibliography, EA13, EA19, EA20, EA53
    current, EA32, EA33, EA35, EA36
  book reviews, EA53
    indexes, EA54
  congresses and meetings, AL26, EA203, EA204, EA205, EA206, EA209
    indexes, EA202
  databases, EA36, EA37, EA67
  dictionaries, EA88, EA93
    bibliography, AC192, EA95
    bilingual
      Czech-English, EA106
      English-Arabic, EA103, EA104
      English-Portuguese, EA123
      English-Russian, EA126
      English-Spanish, EA134
      French-English, EA107, EA108, EA109, EK9
      German-English, EA112, EA113, EA114, EK10
      Hungarian-English, EA115
      Italian-English, EA116, EA117, EA118
      Japanese-English, EA119, EA120
      Norwegian-English, EA121
      Polish-English, EA122
      Russian-English, EA124, EA125
      Spanish-English, EA131, EA132, EA133
      Swedish-English, EA135
      Bulgarian., EA105
    multilingual, EA100, EA101, EA102, EA129

directories, EA145
encyclopedias, CA31, EA79, EA81, EA82
guides, EA1, EA2, EA3, EA4, EA6, EA7
handbooks, EA153
    bibliography, EA152
indexes, EA67, EA73, EA74
    bibliography, EA76
juvenile works
    bibliography, EA28, EA29
library catalogs, EA17
periodicals, EA19, EA39, EA43, EA44
    union lists, EA45
prizes and awards, EA197
reference books, EA10
reviews of research, EA138
tables, EA156
translations, EA59, EA60
    indexes, EA63
yearbooks, EA165, EA167, EA169
Technology (by country or region)
Europe
    directories, EA142
Great Britain
    directories, EA138
Hungary, DC389
Japan
    bibliography, EA9
    facilities in the U.S., EA139
    periodicals, EA48, EA49, EA50
    translations, EA139
U.S.S.R.
    periodicals, EA51, EA52
Technology (by subject)
history
    bibliography, EA228
        current, EA242
    Canada
        bibliography, EA236
        chronologies, EA250
        early works to 1800, EA237, EK3
    United States
        bibliography, EA238
philosophy
    bibliography, EA18
social aspects, EA15
see also Engineering; Science
Technology and culture, EA242
Technology and culture. Current bibliography in the history of technology, EA228
Technology book guide, EK4
Tee, Ralph. Soul music who's who, BJ353
Teed, Peter. A dictionary of twentieth century history, DA181
Teenage parents, CC220
Teenage pregnancy, CC220
Teeter, Mark H. Soviet research institutes project, AL85
Tehran Book Processing Centre. A directory of Iranian periodicals, AD198
Teichert, Curt. Treatise on invertebrate paleontology, EF243
Teissier, Raoul. Tahitiens, AH384
Teitelbaum, Michele. Aging & cultural diversity, CC75
Teixidor, Felipe. Anuario bibliográfico mexicano, AA458
Telberg, Val. Russian-English dictionary of musical terms, BJ150
Telberg, Vladimir George. Russian-English petrographic dictionary, EF258
Telecommunication
abbreviations, EK189
acronyms, EK189
dictionaries, AK43, CH487, EK149
directories, CH492
encyclopedias, CH481
handbooks, EK142, EK146
history
    bibliography, EK127
Telecommunications and networking glossary, Machovec, George S., CH487
Telecommunications directory, CH492

Telecommunications systems and services directory, CH492
Telefax international, CH490
Telek, J. History of Hungary and the Hungarians, 1848–1971, DC385
Telephone directory of members, American Economic Association, CH91
The telescope handbook and star atlas, Howard, Neale E., EC51
Television
adaptations, BH20
    bibliography, BH165, BH294, CC398
biography, BH22, BH319, BH320
databases, BH297
dictionaries, BH260, BH317, BH318, CH484
directories, AD51, AE23, BH263, BH265, BH267, BH319, CH489, CH493, CH494
dissertations, BH295, BH296
encyclopedias, BH313, BH314, BH315, BH316, CH483
guides, BH292, BH293
handbooks, BH270, EK148
indexes, BH232, BH297
library resources, BH178, BH179, BH180, BH181, BH182
periodicals, BH175
program credits, BH305, BH312
reviews, BH298
reviews and criticism, BH236
Television (by country or region)
Europe
    directories, AD1, AE2
Great Britain
    directories, AD1, AE2, BH264
international
    directories, AD1, AE2
Television (by subject)
repairing, EK147
treatment of minorities, CC334
Television, Cassata, Mary B., BH292
Television & cable factbook, CH493
Television directors guide, BH305
Television drama series programming, Gianakos, Larry James, BH302
Television engineering handbook, EK148
Television factbook, CH493
The television industry, Slide, Anthony, BH316, CH483
Television network daytime and late-night programming, 1959–1989, Shapiro, Mitchell E., BH304
Television network prime-time programming, 1948–1988, Shapiro, Mitchell E., BH304
Television network weekend programming, 1959–1990, Shapiro, Mitchell E., BH304
Television programs
catalogs, BH299, BH300, BH301, BH302, BH303, BH304, BH306, BH307
encyclopedias, BH314
Television scripts
bibliography, BH168
Television service manual, Middleton, Robert Gordon, EK147
Television writers guide, BH305
Telex-Verlag Jaeger + Waldmann. J+W telefax international, CH490
Telgen, Diane. Notable Hispanic American women, AH78
Temperance biography, CC138
Temple, Ruth Zabriskie. The Greek and Latin literatures, BE1010
——— Modern British literature, BE598, BE600, BE1069
——— The Romance literatures, BE1074
Templeman, William Darby. Bibliographies of studies in Victorian literature for the thirteen years 1932–1944, BE753
Temples of the ancient Near East and Mediterranean world, BF220
Le temps, AE121
Temu, A. J. History of Tanzania, DD235
Ten eventful years, DA209

Ten Middle English Arthurian romances, Jost, Jean E., BE736
Ten-year index of AMA publications, American Management Association, CH604
Ten years of socio-economic development in the Lao People's Democratic Republic, CG409
Tenfelde, Klaus. Bibliographie zur Geschichte der deutschen Arbeiterschaft und Arbeiterbewegung 1863 bis 1914, CH626, CH627
Teng, Ssu-yü. An annotated bibliography of selected Chinese reference works, AA362, DE123
——— Protest & crime in China, DE136
Tennessee. [Laws, etc.]. Tennessee code annotated, CK179
Tennessee code annotated, Tennessee. [Laws, etc.], CK179
Tenney, Merrill C. The Bible almanac, BC185
Tennis, BK101, BK102, BK103, BK104
Tennyson, Robert D. Evaluation and educational technology, CB168
Tentative bibliography of Brazilian belles-lettres, Ford, Jeremiah D. M., BE937
——— Raphael, Maxwell I., BE937
——— Whittem, Arthur, BE937
Tentative dictionary of medieval Spanish, Boggs, Ralph Steele, AC749
Tenu'ah tiv'it shel ha-ukhlosiyah, CG400
Teodorov-Balan, Aleksandŭr. Bŭlgarski knigopis za sto godini, 1806–1905, AA588
Teoriiā i praktika bibliografii, Masanov, I͡Uriĭ Ivanovich, AA7
TePaske, John J. Research guide to Andean history, DB279
Tepper, Michael. American passenger arrival records, AJ25
Terbitan bersiri kini Malaysia (bukan kerajaan), Perpustakaan Negara Malaysia, AD204
Terblanche, Hendrik Josephus. Nuwe praktiese woordeboek, Engels-Afrikaans, Afrikaans-Engels, AC199
Tercentenary handlist of English & Welsh newspapers, magazines & reviews, AE59
Tercentenary handlist of English and Welsh newspapers, magazines and reviews, Times, London, AD114
Terek, Eugenie. Scientific expeditions, EA219
Term catalogues, 1668–1709 A.D. with a number for Easter term, 1711 A.D, Arber, Edward, AA675, AA676
Term papers see Theses and term paprs
Terminologicheskie slovari, Kaufman, Isaak Mikhailovich, AC699
Terminologie de l'education spéciale, CB198
Terminology, BD58
Terminology of communication disorders, Nicolosi, Lucille, EH122
Terminology of forest science, technology, practice, and products, EJ183
Terminology of special education, CB198
Terminology of the law of armed conflicts, CK104
Terminology : special education, CB198
Terminorum musicae index septem lingus redactus, BJ159
Terpenes, EE121
Terrace, Vincent. The complete actors' television credits, 1948–1988, BH312
——— Encyclopedia of television, BH306
——— Fifty years of television, BH299
——— Radio's golden years, BH311
Terras, Victor. Handbook of Russian literature, BE1411
Terrell, Peter. Collins German-English, English-German dictionary, AC415
Terres, John K. The Audubon Society encyclopedia of North American birds, EG277
El territorio mexicano, CL311
Terrorism, CJ61, CJ548, CJ549, CJ551, CJ554, CJ555, CJ556, CJ558
bibliography, CJ546, CJ550, CJ552
chronologies, CJ553
indexes, CJ557

Terrorism, CJ557
—— Atkins, Stephen E., CJ548
—— Bhan, Susheela, CJ550
—— Scherer, John L., CJ552
Terrorism, 1980–1987, Flemming, Peter A., CJ552
—— Mickolus, Edward F., CJ552
Terrorism 1980–1990, Lakos, Amos, CJ550
Terry, Charles Sanford. *Catalogue of the publications of Scottish historical and kindred clubs and societies and of the volumes relative to Scottish history issued by His Majesty's Stationery Office, 1780–1908, with a subject-index,* DC275
—— *Catalogue of the publications of Scottish historical and kindred clubs and societies and of the volumes relative to Scottish history issued by His Majesty's Stationery Office, 1780–1908, with a subject-index,* DC281
—— *Catalogue of the publications of Scottish historical and kindred clubs and societies and of the volumes relative to Scottish history issued by His Majesty's Stationery Office, 1780–1908, with a subject-index,* DC361
—— *Catalogue of the publications of Scottish historical and kindred clubs and societies and of the volumes relative to Scottish history issued by His Majesty's Stationery Office, 1780–1908, with a subject-index,* DC362
—— *Index to the papers relating to Scotland,* DC362
Terry, Garth M. *Yugoslav history,* DC609
Terry, John V. *Dictionary for business & finance,* CH274
Terry, Walter. *Ballet,* BH154
—— *Ballet guide,* BH154
Tervarent, Guy de. *Attributs et symboles dans l'art profane, 1450–1600,* BF171
Tesauro de datos históricos, DB456
Teschner, Richard V. *El diccionario del español chicano,* AC754
—— *Spanish and English of United States Hispanos,* BD176
Teses, pesquisas, antropólogos, CE88
Tesfayesus Mahary. *Annotated bibliography on the population of Ethiopia,* CG329
Tesis doctorales, AG41
Tesis presentadas a la Universidad de Buenos Aires, Universidad de Buenos Aires. Instituto Bibliotecológico, AG18
Tesler, Mario. *Diccionario argentino de seudónimos,* AA156
Test construction, O'Brien, Nancy P., CD70
Test critiques, CD71
Tests, CD72
Tests and measurements
  bibliography, CB189
  handbooks, CD93
Tests and measurements (by subject)
  education, CB70, CB150, CB151, CB152, CD68, CD74
  marriage and the family, CC239
  psychology, CB151, CD67, CD68, CD69, CD70, CD71, CD72, CD73, CD74, CD75, CD76
  sex and sexual behavior, CC292
  social psychology, CD98
Tests in microfiche, Educational Testing Service, CB151, CD68
Tests in print III, CD73
Teuffel, Wilhelm Sigismund. *Geschichte der römischen Literatur,* BE1053
—— *History of Roman literature,* BE1052, BE1053
Tew, Eyvind S. *Bibliography of reports arising out of meetings held by international organizations,* AL33
Texas. [Laws, etc.]. *Vernon's annotated Texas statutes and codes,* CK179
The Texas collection of comedias sueltas, Boyer, Mildred Vinson, BE1460
Texier, Jean C. *Presse quotidienne française,* AE52
Textbooks, CB19
Textbooks in print, AA431
Textbooks in school and society, Woodward, Arthur, CB19

Textile arts index, 1950–1987, Jackson, R. D., BG153
—— Wilson, S. T., BG153
Textiles
  dictionaries
    multilingual, BG154
  encyclopedias, BG155
  indexes, BG153
  library catalogs, BG153
Textiles (by country or region)
  North America, BG157
  United States
    dictionaries, BG156
Textiles (by subject)
  history, BG152
Textiles in America, 1650–1870, Montgomery, Florence M., BG156
Textor, Robert B. *A cross-cultural summary,* CE62
Texts and calendars, Mullins, Edward Lindsay Carson, DC280, DC361
The texts of Confucianism, BC92
The texts of Tâosim, BC92
Textual sources for the study of Sikhism, McLeod, W. H., BC576
Textual sources for the study of Zoroastrianism, BC576
Teze de doctorat, AG40
Tezla, Albert. *Hungarian authors,* BE1283
—— *Introductory bibliography to the study of Hungarian literature,* BE1278, BE1283
Thacker, Eric. *The essential jazz records,* BJ308
Thackeray, Frank W. *Statesmen who changed the world,* CJ70
Thackrah, John Richard. *Encyclopedia of terrorism and political violence,* CJ558
—— *Malta,* DC448
Thai-English dictionary, McFarland, George Bradley, AC778
Thai-English student's dictionary, Haas, Mary Rosamond, AC777
Thai language, BD230
  dictionaries
    bilingual
      English-Thai, AC780
      Thai-English, AC777, AC778, AC779
Thai national bibliography, AA939
Thailand
  bibliography, AA939, DE267
  bibliography of bibliography, AA83
  encyclopedias, DE266
  statistics, CG433
    bibliography, CG432
Thailand (by subject)
  history
    bibliography, DE99
Thailand. National Statistical Office. *Annotated statistical bibliography,* CG432
Thailand, Hart, Don Vorhis, AA83
—— Watts, Michael, DE267
The Thames and Hudson dictionary of art and artists, BF78
The Thames and Hudson dictionary of art terms, Lucie-Smith, Edward, BF86
The Thames and Hudson encyclopaedia of 20th-century music, Griffiths, Paul, BJ135
Thames and Hudson encyclopaedia of graphic design and designers, Livingston, Alan, BF369
—— Livingston, Isabella, BF369
The Thames and Hudson encyclopedia of 20th-century architecture, BF233
Thames and Hudson manual of pottery and ceramics, Hamilton, David, BG65
Thar she went, Langdon, Robert, DF9
Thatcher, D. S. *Musical settings of early and mid-Victorian literature,* BJ279
—— *Musical settings of late Victorian and modern British literature,* BJ279
Thatcher, David S. *Musical settings of early and mid-Victorian literature,* BJ278
—— *A Shakespeare music catalogue,* BJ71
Thatcher, Mary. *Cambridge South Asian archive,* DE89

Thawley, J. D. *Guide to the availability of theses,* AK224
Thawley, John. *Bibliographies on the Australian aborigine,* DF28
Thayer, J. H. *Greek lexicon of the Roman and Byzantine periods,* AC459
The-Mulliner, Lian. *Historical dictionary of Singapore,* DE256
—— *Southeast Asia microforms project resources,* AE83
Theater
  adaptations, BH20
  annuals, BH107, BH111
  bibliography, BH31, BH32, BH34, BH38, BH40, BH43, BH45, BH46, BH47, BH49, BH52, BH57
    dissertations, BH37
  biography, BH22, BH63, BH112, BH113, BH114, BH115, BH116, BH117, BH118, BH120, BH121, BH124
    bibliography, BH125
    indexes, BH122, BH123, BH126, BH127, BH128, BH129
  chronologies, BH94, BH97, BH102
  courses of study
    directories, BH84
  dictionaries, BE913, BH76, BH77, BH78, BH79, BH80, BH81, BH82, BH91
  directories, BH83, BH85, BH86, BH88
  encyclopedias, BH62, BH63, BH64, BH67, BH68, BH69, BH70, BH71, BH72, BH73, BH74, BH75, BH98, BH113
  guides, BH30
  handbooks, BH89, BH90, BH109
  indexes, BH55, BH57
  library catalogs, BH33
  library resources, BH53
  periodicals, BH36
  reviews, BH58, BH59
    indexes, BH61
Theater (by country or region)
  Asia, BH31
    encyclopedias, BH66
  Cameroon, BE1526
  Canada, BH73
    archives, BH54
    bibliography, BH39
    library resources, BH54
  Europe, BG107
  France
    bibliography, BE1186
  Germany, BE1262
    encyclopedias, BE1263
  Great Britain, BE664, BE665, BH38, BH40, BH47, BH103
    bibliography, BE639, BE647
    biography, BH119
    directories, BH87
    history, BE663, BH99, BH101, BH104, BH107
    reviews, BH60
  Mexico, BE913
  New York
    history, BH105
  United States, BE466, BE573
    annuals, BE454
    bibliography, BH48
    encyclopedias, BH65
    guides, BH49
    history, BH95, BH96, BH98, BH100, BH105, BH110
      bibliography, BH41, BH44
    indexes, BE463
    regional and local, BH43, BH46
Theater (by subject)
  history, BH97, BH102, BH106
    19th century, BH103
    bibliography, BH38, BH39, BH42, BH43, BH46, BH47, BH48, BH49
    Great Britain, BH108
    Renaissance, BH45
  history (by period)
    Restoration and 18th century, BH47
  prizes and awards, BH93
  see also **Drama; Musical theater**

Theater yearbook, BE454
Theaters
  bibliography, BH35
  directories, BH13, BH88, BH99, BH106
Theaters (by country or region)
  Great Britain, BE467, BE667
  United States
    directories, BH110
    history, BH110
Theaters (by subject)
  architecture
    bibliography, BH35
Theatre, Leonard, William Torbert, BH20
Theatre and cinema architecture, Stoddard, Richard, BH35
Theatre at Stratford-upon-Avon, Mullin, Michael, BH104
Theatre backstage from A to Z, Boulanger, Norman, BH76
—— Lounsbury, Warren C., BH76, BH80
Le théâtre canadien d'expression française, Rinfret, Édouard G., BE843
Theatre Communications Group. *Theatre profiles*, BH88
Theatre companies of the world, BH106
Theatre crafts international, BH86
Theatre, film, and television biographies master index, La Beau, Dennis, BH28
Theatre index, BH60
Theatre language, Bowman, Walter Parker, BH77
Theatre lighting from A to Z, Boulanger, Norman, BH76
Théâtre noir, Waters, Harold A., BE1518
Theatre profiles, BH88
Theatre record, BH60
Theatre resources in Canadian collections, McCallum, Heather, BH54
Theatre world, BH111, BH156
Theatre world annual (London), BH107
Theatres of London, Mander, Raymond, BH99
—— Mitchenson, Joe, BH99
Theatrical costume, Kesler, Jackson, BH51
Theatrical designers, BH114, BH120
Theatrical directors, BH121
Thelert, Gustav. *Supplement zu Heinsius', Hinrichs' und Kaysers Bücher-Lexikon ...*, AA646
Thematic catalogues in music, Brook, Barry S., BJ230
Thematic list of descriptors—anthropology, CE52
Thematic list of descriptors—economics, CE52, CH43
Thematic list of descriptors—political science, CE52, CJ43
Thematic list of descriptors—sociology, CC21, CE52
Thematische Sammelverzeichnisse der Musik, Wettstein, Hermann, BJ233
Themes & motifs in western literature, Daemmrich, Horst S., BE182
Themes and settings in fiction, Hartman, Donald K., BE253
Themes in cultural psychiatry, Faheem, Ahmed D., EH372
—— Favazza, Armando R., EH372
Themes in Kenyan history, Ochieng', William R., DD166
Theodoratus, Robert J. *Europe*, CE98

Theologische Realenzyklopädie, BC25, BC69
Theologischer Jahresbericht, BC226
Theologisches Begriffslexikon zum Neuen Testament, BC148
Theologisches Taschenlexikon, BC231
Theologisches Wörterbuch zum Alten Testament, Botterweck, G. Johannes, AC475, BC134
Theologisches Wörterbuch zum Neuen Testament, AC456, BC143
Theology
  bibliography, BC12, BC219, BC220
  dictionaries, BC243, BC407, BC408
  dictionaries (by language)
    German, BC153
  encyclopedias, BC69, BC130, BC231, BC239, BC405
  guides, BC209
  handbooks, BC252
Theology (by country or region)
  Great Britain
    library catalogs, BC227, DC321
Theology in transition, O'Brien, Elmer J., BC220
Theoretical chemical engineering, EK49
Theoretical chemical engineering abstracts, EK49
Theoretical studies in Hispanic linguistics (1960–), Nuessel, Frank H., BD168
Theoretical syntax 1980–1990, Ostler, Rosemarie, BD44
Theories, Dictionary of, CA31
Theories of bibliographic education, Oberman, Cerise, AK229
—— Strauch, Katina, AK229
Theories of psychology, Neel, Ann, CD61
Theory and history of bibliography, Schneider, Georg, AA9
—— Shaw, Ralph R., AA9
Theotokos, O'Carroll, Michael, BC403
Therapeutics, EH190
  current surveys, EH83
  handbooks, EH177
Thermochemical data of pure substances, Barin, Ihsan, EE63
Thermochemical tables, EE93
Thermochemistry, EE63
  databases, EE93
  tables, EE93, EE93
Thermodynamics, EE94
Thernstrom, Stephan. *Harvard encyclopedia of American ethnic groups*, CC342
•*Thesauri*, AK216
Thesauros tēs hellēnikēs glōssēs, Estienne, Henri, AC442
Thesaurus and dictionary of the English language, AC141
Thesaurus BIT, CH652
Thesaurus construction, Aitchison, Jean, AK218
Thesaurus des institutions de l'ancienne Russie, Eeckaute, Denise, DC584
A thesaurus dictionary of the English language, AC141
Thesaurus graecae linguae, AC442
Thesaurus guide, AK216
Thésaurus Larousse, AC363
Thesaurus linguae graecae, AC447, AC443, BE1036
Thesaurus Linguae Graecae canon of Greek authors and works, Berkowitz, Luci, AC443, BE1036
—— Johnson, William A., AC443, BE1036
—— Squitier, Karl A., AC443, BE1036
Thesaurus linguae latinae, AC571, AC572, AC573, AC591, BE1047
Thesaurus literaturae botanicae, Pritzel, Georg August, EG97
Thesaurus litteraturae mycologicae et lichenologicae ratione habita praecipue omnium quae adhuc scripta sunt de mycologia applicata quem congesserunt, Lindau, Gustav, EG188
Thésaurus multilingue international en administration publique, CJ479
A thesaurus of African languages, Mann, Michael, BD217
Thesaurus of aging terminology, CC79, CC84
Thesaurus of agricultural organisms, pests, weeds, and diseases, EJ33

Thesaurus of book digests, Haydn, Hiram, BE193
Thesaurus of book digests, 1950–1980, Weiss, Anne, BE193
—— Weiss, Irving, BE193
A thesaurus of British archaeology, Adkins, Lesley, DC309
Thesaurus of English words and phrases, Roget, Peter Mark, AC145
Thesaurus of ERIC descriptors, CB56, CB83, CD91
Thesaurus of orchestral devices, Read, Gardner, BJ372
Thesaurus of psychological index terms, CD17, CD34
The thesaurus of slang, Lewin, Esther, AC127
Thesaurus of sociological indexing terms, Booth, Barbara, CC20
Thesaurus pseudonymorum quae in litteratura hebraica et judaeo-germanica inveniuntur, Chajes, Saul, AA161
Thesaurus syriacus, Payne Smith, Robert, AC773
Thesaurus totius Hebraitatis et veteris et recentioris, AC470
Thesauruses, AK218
  bibliography, AK216
Thesauruses (by subject)
  law, CK56
These are the names, AJ171
Theses and dissertations on Southern Africa, Pollak, Oliver B., DD32
Theses and term papers
  guides, AG5
  manuals, AG1, AG2, AG3, AG4, AG6
  see also **Dissertations**
Thèses de doctorat en langue française relatives à la musique, BJ166
Theses in American literature, 1896–1971, Howard, Patsy C., BE425
Theses in English literature, 1894–1970, Howard, Patsy C., BE593
Theses in Germanic studies, Prawer, Siegbert S., BE1237
—— Riley, Victor J., BE1237
—— University of London. Institute of Germanic Studies, BE1237, DC219
Theses in progress at British universities and other institutions of higher education, BE1237
Theses on Africa, 1963–1975, McIlwaine, J. H. St. J., DD33
Theses on Africa, 1976–1988, Hewson, Colin, DD33
—— Price, Helen C., DD33
Theses on Africa accepted by universities in the United Kingdom and Ireland, Standing Conference on Library Materials on Africa, DD33
Theses on Asia accepted by universities in the United Kingdom and Ireland, 1877–1964, Bloomfield, Barry Cambray, DE9
Theses on Caribbean topics, 1778–1968, Baa, Enid M., DB411
Theses on Germany accepted for higher degrees by the universities of Great Britain and Ireland, 1900–1975, Gabel, Gernot U., DC219
Theses on Islam, the Middle East and North-West Africa, 1880–1978, accepted by universities in the United Kingdom and Ireland, Sluglett, Peter, DD74, DE44
Thesing, William B. *English prose and criticism, 1900–1950*, BE760
Thewlis, James. *Concise dictionary of physics and related subjects*, ED24
—— *Encyclopaedic dictionary of physics*, ED13
They never said it, Boller, Paul F., BE90
They voted for Roosevelt, Robinson, Edgar Eugene, CJ243
Thibault, Pierre. *Les grands hommes d'état de l'histoire de France*, AH199
Thieme, Frank. *Bibliographie bevölkerungswissenschaftlicher Aufsätze und Kurzartikel im damaligen Deutschen Reich erschienener sozialwissenschaftlicher und erbbiologischer Fachzeitschriften zwischen 1900 und ca. 1945*, CG229
Thieme, Hugo Paul. *Bibliographie de la littérature française de 1800 à 1930*, BE1137, BE1209

Thieme, Ulrich. *Allgemeines Lexikon der bildenden Künstler*, BF135, BF147, BF148, BF149

Thienen, Gerard van. *Incunabula in Dutch libraries*, AA232

Thiery, Herman. *Dictionnaire filmographique de la littérature mondiale*, BH216

Thinès, Georges. *Dictionnaire général des sciences humaines*, CA42

Third Barnhart dictionary of new English, AC95

Third book of junior authors, De Montreville, Doris, BE384

———— Hill, Donna, BE384

Third French Republic, 1870–1940, DC207

Third Reich, DC255, DC258, DC259, DC263

The Third Reich 1933–1939, DC241

The Third Reich, 1933–1945, Snyder, Louis Leo, DC241

The Third Reich almanac, Taylor, James, DC259

The Third Reich at war, DC241

Third World *see* **Developing countries**

Third World in film and video, Cyr, Helen W., BH221

Third World resource directory, Fenton, Thomas P., DD93, DE17, DE21

———— Heffron, Mary J., DD93, DE17, DE21

Third World resource directory, 1994–1995, DA11

Third World struggle for peace with justice, Fenton, Thomas P., CJ669

This business of music, Shemel, Sidney, BJ185

This day in American history, Gross, Ernie, DB59

This remarkable continent, DB76

Tholen, E. *Iconclass*, BF175

Thomann, Arthur E. *Elsevier's dictionary of technology*, EA134

Thomas, Antoine. *Dictionnaire général de la langue française*, AC330

Thomas, Carol H. *Directory of college facilities and services for people with disabilities*, CB311

Thomas, Clayton L. *Taber's cyclopedic medical dictionary*, EH106

Thomas, Daniel H. *The new guide to the diplomatic archives of Western Europe*, DC18

Thomas, Edmund J. *Writers and philosophers*, BE191

Thomas, Evangeline. *Women religious history sources*, BC228

Thomas, G. Scott. *The pursuit of the White House*, CJ252

———— *The rating guide to life in America's small cities*, CL75

Thomas, Henry. *Short-title catalogue of Portuguese books printed before 1601, now in the British Museum*, AA775

———— *Short-title catalogues of Portuguese books and of Spanish-American books printed before 1601, now in the British Museum*, AA468

Thomas, J. E. *International biography of adult education*, CB363

Thomas, Jack Ray. *Biographical dictionary of Latin American historians and historiography*, DB296

Thomas, James L. *Directory of college facilities and services for people with disabilities*, CB311

Thomas, James P. *Handbook of perception and human performance*, CD113

Thomas, John Bernard. *International dictionary of education*, CB77

Thomas, Joseph. *History of philosophy*, BB46

———— *Universal pronouncing dictionary of biography and mythology*, AH36

Thomas, L. L. *Kościuszko Foundation dictionary*, AC634

Thomas, Nicholas. *International dictionary of films and filmmakers*, BH250

Thomas, Philip A. *How to use a law library*, CK218

Thomas, R. J. *Geiriadur Prifysgol Cymru*, AC806

Thomas, Robert L. *New American standard exhaustive concordance of the Bible*, BC163

Thomas, Stephen B. *The yearbook of education law*, CB157

Thomas, W. O. *Y geiriadur mawr*, AC805

Thomas Aquinas, Saint, BB61, BB62, BB63, BB64, BB68

bibliography, BB66

Thomas food industry register, EJ163

•*Thomas register [database]*, CH369

Thomas' register of American manufacturers and Thomas' register catalog file, CH369

•*Thomas register on CD-ROM*, CH369

Thomason, George. *Catalogue of the pamphlets, books, newspapers, and manuscripts relating to the Civil War, the Commonwealth, and Restoration collected by George Thomason, 1640–1661*, AA677

Thomason tracts, AA677

Thomassery, Marguerite. *Catalogue des périodiques d'Afrique noire francophone (1858–1962) conservés à l'IFAN*, AD170

Thomison, Dennis. *The black artist in America*, BF64

———— *Library science dissertations, 1925–1972*, AK26

———— *Library science dissertations, 1973–1981*, AK26

Thomistic bibliography, 1920–1940, Bourke, Vernon J., BB61, BB66, BB68

Thomistic bibliography, 1940–1978, Miethe, Terry L., BB68

Thompson, Alexander John. *Logarithmetica Britannica*, EB96

Thompson, Alice M. C. *A bibliography of nursing literature*, EH273

Thompson, Andrew. *The dictionary of contemporary politics of Central America and the Caribbean*, CJ311

———— *The dictionary of contemporary politics of South America*, CJ312

Thompson, Ann. *Which Shakespeare?*, BE765

Thompson, Anne-Gabrielle. *The Southwest Pacific*, DF12

Thompson, Annie F. *Music and dance in Puerto Rico from the age of Columbus to modern times*, BJ43

Thompson, Anthony. *Russia/U.S.S.R*, DC552

———— *Vocabularium bibliothecarii*, AK49

Thompson, Arthur W. *Guide to the principal sources for American civilization, 1800–1900, in the city of New York*, DB79, DB98

Thompson, Donald. *Music and dance in Puerto Rico from the age of Columbus to modern times*, BJ43

Thompson, Edward Maunde. *Handbook of Greek and Latin palaeography*, AA216, BE1018

———— *An introduction to Greek and Latin palaeography*, AA216, BE1018

Thompson, Elizabeth H. *A.L.A. glossary of library terms*, AK40

Thompson, Esther Katherine. *History of agriculture in the southern United States to 1860*, EJ68

Thompson, George A. *Key sources in comparative and world literature*, BE33

Thompson, George Fayette. *Index to authors with titles of their publications appearing in the documents of the U.S. Dept. of Agriculture, 1841–1897*, EJ90

———— *Index to literature relating to animal industry in the publications of the Department of Agriculture, 1837–1898*, EJ91

———— *Synoptical index of the reports of the statistician, 1863 to 1894*, EJ93

Thompson, Ida. *The Audubon Society field guide to North American fossils*, EF251

Thompson, John W. *Index to illustrations of the natural world*, EA220, EG72, EG73

Thompson, Jon. *Oriental carpets*, BG165

Thompson, Laurence G. *Chinese religion*, BC37

———— *Chinese religion in Western languages*, BC37

———— *Guide to Chinese religion*, BC38

———— *Studies of Chinese religion*, BC37

Thompson, Lawrence Sidney. *A bibliography of American doctoral dissertations in classical studies and related fields*, BE1009, DA97

———— *Bibliography of dissertations in classical studies*, BE1009, DA97

———— *A bibliography of French plays on microcards*, BE1185

———— *A bibliography of Spanish plays on microcards*, BE1470

———— *The new Sabin*, AA411

———— *Nineteenth and twentieth century drama*, BE655

Thompson, Leonard Monteath. *History of South Africa*, DD211

———— *Southern African history before 1900*, DD120, DD223

Thompson, Leonard Montheath. *Oxford history of South Africa*, DD211

Thompson, Morris Mordecai. *Maps for America*, CL268

Thompson, Oscar. *The international cyclopedia of music and musicians*, BJ137

Thompson, Ralph. *American literary annuals & gift books, 1825–1865*, BE415

Thompson, Stith. *Motif-index of folk-literature*, CF48, CF49

———— *The types of the folktale*, CF45, CF88

Thompson, Susan J. *A chronology of geological thinking from antiquity to 1899*, EF104

Thompson, V. McLean. *People's Republic of the Congo*, DD48

Thomsen, Svend. *Danske blandede Tidsskrifter, 1855–1912*, AD310

Thomsett, Jean F. *Political quotations*, CJ45

Thomsett, Michael C. *Insurance dictionary*, CH510

———— *Investment and securities dictionary*, CH303

———— *Musical terms, symbols, and theory*, BJ160

———— *Political quotations*, CJ45

———— *Real estate dictionary*, CH537

———— *Treasury of business quotations*, CH72

———— *Webster's new World investment and securities dictionary*, CH303

Thomson, David. *A biographical dictionary of film*, BH287

———— *Biographical dictionary of the cinema*, BH287

Thomson, Derick S. *Companion to Gaelic Scotland*, DC363

Thomson, Ellen Mazur. *American graphic design*, BF369

Thomson, Francis J. *Elsevier's dictionary of financial terms in English, German, Spanish, French, Italian, and Dutch*, CH214

Thomson, Ian. *The documentation of the European Communities*, AF26

Thomson, John E. *New Zealand literature to 1977*, BE864

Thomson, Ruth Gibbons. *Index to full length plays, 1895 to 1925*, BE238

———— *Index to full length plays, 1926 to 1944*, BE238

Thomson, S. K. *Interlibrary loan procedures*, AK225

Thomson, Theodore Radford. *A catalogue of British family histories*, AJ110

Thomson bank directory, CH278

Thomson credit union directory, CH279

Thomson savings directory, CH280

Thorin, Suzanne E. *International directory of braille music collections*, BJ171

Thorn, John. *Total baseball*, BK62

Thorn, Philip. *Who owns what in world banking*, CH281

Thornback, Jane. *The IUCN mammal red data book*, EG296

Thornberry, Patrick. *World directory of minorities*, CC345

Thorndale, William. *Map guide to the U.S. federal censuses, 1790–1920*, AJ26, CL306

Thorndike, David. *The Thorndike encyclopedia of banking and financial tables*, CH269

Thorndike, Edward L. *Scott, Foresman advanced dictionary*, AC23

———— *Scott, Foresman beginning dictionary*, AC24

———— *Scott, Foresman intermediate dictionary*, AC25

The Thorndike encyclopedia of banking and financial tables, Thorndike, David, CH269

Thorne, Barrie. *Language and sex*, BD82

———— *Language, gender, and society*, BD82, BD84, CC495

———— *She said / he said*, BD82

Thornton, John Leonard. *Medical books, libraries, and collectors,* EH28
—— *Scientific books, libraries and collectors,* EA240
—— *Select bibliography of medical biography,* EH219, EH227
—— *Thornton's medical books, libraries, and collectors,* EH28
Thornton, Peter. *Authentic decor,* BG133
Thornton, Richard H. *An American glossary,* AC153
Thornton, Spencer P. *Ophthalmic eponyms,* EH126
Thornton's medical books, libraries, and collectors, Thornton, John Leonard, EH28
Thorpe, Alana I. *A.J. Lohwater's Russian-English dictionary of the mathematical sciences,* EB53
Thorpe, Frances. *British official films in the Second World War,* DA204
—— *International directory of film and TV documentation centres,* BH179
Thorpe, James. *The use of manuscripts in literary research,* BE10
Thorpe, Jocelyn Field. *Thorpe's dictionary of applied chemistry,* EE46
Thorpe's dictionary of applied chemistry, Thorpe, Jocelyn Field, EE46
Thorsen, Kristine A. *Poetry by American women, 1900–1975,* BE496
Thorson, James L. *Reader's guide to twentieth-century science fiction,* BE295
Thorson's guide to campus-free college degrees, CB256
Those who were there, DE100
Thoumin, Jean-Adrien. *Bibliographie rétrospective des périodiques français de littérature musicale, 1870–1954,* BJ105
Thrall, William Flint. *A handbook to literature,* BE84
Thrapp, Dan L. *Encyclopedia of frontier biography,* DB175
Threatened birds of Africa and related islands, Collar, N. J., EG278
—— Stuart, S. N., EG278
Threatened birds of the Americas, EG278
Threatened mammalian taxa of the Americas and the Australasian zoogeographic region, EG296
Three centuries of drama, Wells, Henry Willis, DE453, BE636
Three centuries of English and American plays, Wells, Henry Willis, BE453, BE636
Three centuries of English and American plays, a checklist, Bergquist, G. William, BE453, BE636
Three hundred best buys in college education, CB291
Three hundred most selective colleges, CB245
Three hundred years of psychiatry, 1535–1860, Hunter, Richard Alfred, EH399
Three-month economic review, CH112
Three thousand mycological terms, Snell, Walter Henry, EG138
Three thousand years of urban growth, Chandler, Tertius, CC296
—— Fox, Gerald, CC296
Through a woman's I, Addis, Patricia K., BE508, CC485
Through the pale door, Frank, Frederick S., BE288
Thrush, Paul W. *A dictionary of mining, mineral, and related terms,* EF188
Thư mục quốc gia, AA940
Thung, Yvonne. *A checklist of Indonesian serials in the Cornell University Library (1945–1970),* AD196
Thuraisingham, Ajita. *ASEAN,* DE94
Thürauf, Ulrich. *Bibliographie zur deutschen Geschichte im Zeitalter der Glaubensspaltung 1517–1585,* DC227
Thurston, Herbert. *Lives of the saints,* BC263
•*TIARA CD-ROM,* CK92
Tibet
    bibliography, DE75, DE268, DE269
Tibet (by subject)
    history
        bibliography, DE269
        library resources, DE86
Tibet, Pinfold, John R., DE269

Tibetan-English dictionary, Buck, Stuart H., AC782
—— Jäschke, Heinrich August, AC786
Tibetan-English dictionary of modern Tibetan, Goldstein, Melvyn C., AC785
A Tibetan-English dictionary with Sanskrit synonyms, Das, Sarat Chandra, AC783
Tibetan language
    dictionaries
        bilingual
            English-Tibetan, AC781, AC784
            Tibetan-English, AC782, AC783, AC785, AC786
Tice, Terrence N. *Research guide to philosophy,* BB3
Tichauer, Werner Guttentag. *Bibliografía boliviana,* AA501
—— *Bio-bibliografía boliviana,* AA502
Tiedemann, Eva. *Deutsche Exil-Literatur, 1933–1945,* BE1232
Tiefer, Charles. *Congressional practice and procedure,* CJ225
Tiele, P. A. *Bibliotheek van Nederlandsche pamfletten,* AA752
Tien, H. C. *Gazetteer of China,* CL161
Tiepolo, Maurizio. *Congo Brazzaville,* DD143
Tierney, Helen. *Women's studies encyclopedia,* CC537
Tietjen, Gary L. *A topical dictionary of statistics,* CG32, EB45
Tietz, Norbert W. *Clinical guide to laboratory tests,* EH174
Tietze, Wolf. *Westermann Lexikon der Geographie,* CL40
Tifft, William G. *Revised new general catalogue of nonstellar astronomical objects,* EC75
Tigerstedt, E. N. *Ny illustrerad svensk litteraturhistoria,* BE1485
Tigré language, AC310
Tilden, Anita S. *Biographical and historical index of American Indians and persons involved in Indian affairs,* CC436
Tilke, Max. *Folk costumes from East Europe, Africa, and Asia,* BG114
—— *National costumes from East Europe, Africa and Asia,* BG114
—— *Orientalische Kostüme,* BG114
—— *Osteuropäische Volkstrachten,* BG114
—— *Trachten und Kostüme aus Europa, Afrika und Asien in Form, Schnitt und Farbe,* BG114
Tillema, Herbert K. *International armed conflict since 1945,* CJ563
Tilley, Morris Palmer. *Dictionary of the proverbs in England in the sixteenth and seventeenth centuries,* BE159, BE166
Tillman, Barry. *Human factors design handbook,* EK236
Tillman, Peggy. *Human factors design handbook,* EK236
Tilson, Marie. *Pipelines,* CH444
Tilton, James R. *Annotated bibliography on childhood schizophrenia, 1955–1964,* EH374
Timberlake, Andrea. *Women of color and Southern women,* CC623
Timbers of the New World, Record, Samuel James, EJ188
Timbers of tropical America, Mell, Clayton, EJ188
—— Record, Samuel James, EJ188
Timbra, Edgars. *Latviešu pirmspadomju literatūra,* BE1320
Time
    conversion tables, EC86
Time lines on file, CL282, DA55
Time longer than rope, Roux, Edward, DD211
The Time out film guide, BH201
Time series of historical statistics 1867–1992, CG248
Timelines, Dickson, Paul, DB134
The Times atlas and encyclopedia of the sea, EF225
The Times atlas of China, CL354
The Times atlas of the Bible, BC199
The Times atlas of the moon, EC69
The Times atlas of the Second World War, DA212
Times atlas of the world, CL94, CL292, CL293

The Times atlas of world history, DA58, DA88
The Times Books world weather guide, Pearce, E. A., EF163
Times guide to the House of Commons, CJ358
The Times index, Times (London), AE125
Times, London. *Index-gazetteer of the world,* CL94
—— *Tercentenary handlist of English and Welsh newspapers, magazines and reviews,* AD114
—— *The Times index,* AE125
Times of India, BC473, DE116
Timetables of history, DA37
—— Grun, Bernard, DA32
The timetables of Jewish history, Gribetz, Judah, DA31
Timetables of science, Bunch, Bryan H., EA254
—— Hellemans, Alexander, EA252, EA254
The timetables of technology, Bunch, Bryan H., EA250
Timmons, Christine. *Britannica book of English usage,* AC66
Timofeev, Leonid Ivanovich. *Slovar' literaturovedcheskikh terminov,* BE1416
Timofeev, Petr Petrovich. *Anglo-russkiĭ geologicheskiĭ slovar',* EF89
Timor, Rowland, Ian, DE177
Tingley, Donald F. *Women and feminism in American history,* CC484
Tingley, Elizabeth. *Women and feminism in American history,* CC484
Tinker, Lynne. *Annotated bibliography of library automation,* AK190
Tinker guide to Latin American and Caribbean policy and scholarly resources in metropolitan New York, DB288
Tinkham, Sandra Shaffer. *The consolidated catalog to the Index of American design,* BG17
Tinling, Marion. *Women remembered,* CC574
Tinsley, Elizabeth J. *Worldwide directory of national earth-science agencies and related international organizations,* EF92
La tipografia cinquecentina italiana, Ascarelli, Fernanda, AA305
Tipper, Allison. *British directories,* AL1, AL7, CH366, CH381
Tips for travelers series, CJ185
Tirion, Wil. *Sky atlas 2000.0,* EC72, EC76
—— *Uranometria 2000.0,* EC75
Tirol, Marcel. *Bibliographie critique du roman canadien-français, 1837–1900,* BE842
TISAL, AD243
Tischler, Alice. *A descriptive bibliography of art music by Israeli composers,* BJ65
Tischler, Gerhard. *Internationale Musical-Bibliographie,* BJ268
Tishler, William H. *American landscape architecture,* BF294
Tismaneanu, Vladimir. *Latin American revolutionaries,* CJ308
A title guide to the talkies, Dimmitt, Richard Bertrand, BH217
Title guide to the talkies, 1964 through 1974, Aros, Andrew A., BH217
Title guide to the talkies, 1975 through 1984, Aros, Andrew A., BH217
Titled nobility of Europe, Ruvigny and Raineval, Melville Amadeus Henry Douglas Heddle de la Caillemotte de Massue de Ruvigny, 9th Marquis of, AJ81
Titles and forms of address, AL160
Titles in series, Baer, Eleanora A., AA95
Titles of completed theses in home economics and related fields in colleges and universities of the United States, United States. Agricultural Research Service, EJ196
Titles of dissertations and theses completed in home economics, American Home Economics Association, EJ194, EJ196
Titles of dissertations approved for the Ph.D., M.Sc., and M.Litt. degrees in the University of Cambridge, AG36
Titles of dissertations in progress, DA16
Titles of English books (and of foreign books printed in England), Allison, Antony Francis, AA665

Titmus, Colin J. *Lifelong education for adults,* CB70
Tito, Josip (Broz), DC610
Titova, Z. D. *Ukazateli soderzhaniȋa russkikh zhurnalov i prodolzhaȋushchikhsȋa izdaniĭ 1755–1970 gg,* AD326
Titova, Zoia Dmitrievna. *Etnografiȋa,* CE20
Titova reč u publikacijama JNA 1941–1980, DC610
Titus, Edna Brown. *Union list of serials in libraries of the United States and Canada,* AD226
•*TMD,* CB355
To assure the free appropriate public education of all children with disabilities, CB207
To be born a nation, SWAPO. Dept. of Information and Publicity, DD185
To Russia and return, Nerhood, Harry W., DC551
Toase, Charles A. *Bibliography of British newspapers,* AE55
Toase, Mary. *Current British journals,* AD115
Toastmaster's treasure chest, Prochnow, Herbert V., Jr, BE362
———— Prochnow, Herbert V., BE362
Toba, Sueyoshi. *A bibliography of Nepalese languages and linguistics,* BD227
Tobey, Jeremy L. *The history of ideas,* BB22
Tobias, Barbara. *American autobiography, 1945–1980,* AH89, DB67
Tobias, Norman. *The international military encyclopedia,* CJ572
Tobias, Richard C. *Bibliographies of studies in Victorian literature for the thirteen years 1932–1944,* BE753
———— *Guide to the year's work in Victorian poetry and prose,* BE755
Tobin, James Edward. *Dictionary of Catholic biography,* BC419
Tobler, Adolf. *Altfranzösisches Wörterbuch,* AC383
Tod, Dorothea D. *A check list of Canadian imprints, 1900–1925,* AA452
Todd, David Keith. *The water encyclopedia,* EF140, EK96
———— *Water publications of state agencies,* EK89
Todd, Hollis N. *Dictionary of contemporary photography,* BF343
Todd, Janet M. *British women writers,* BE621
———— *A dictionary of British and American women writers, 1660–1800,* BE447, BE621
———— *Dictionary of British women writers,* BE621
Todd, Loreto. *International English usage,* AC86
Todd, M. Catherine. *A bibliography on Bechuanaland,* DD132
Todoriev, Simeon Todorov. *Kratŭk bŭlgarsko-angliĭski politekhnicheski rechnik,* EA105
Todorov, Tzvetan. *Encyclopedic dictionary of the sciences of language,* BD38
Toffler, Betsy-Ann. *Dictionary of advertising and direct mail terms,* CH550
Togo
  atlases, CL339
  bibliography, CG364, DD237
  encyclopedias, DD48
  government publications
    bibliography, AF224, AF230
  statistics, CG363
Togo. Direction de la statistique. *Annuaire statistique,* CG363
Togo, Decalo, S., DD48
Tölfræðihandbók, CG249
Tolkovyi slovar' russkogo ȋazyka, AC674
Tolkovyi slovar' zhivogo velikorusskago ȋazyka, Dal', Vladimir Ivanovich, AC668
Tölle, Manfred. *Bibliographie deutschsprachiger bevölkerungswissenschaftlicher Literatur, 1978–1984,* CG3, CG221
Tölle, Wolfgang. *Study and research guide in computer science,* EK202
Tollefson, Alan M. *A bibliography of presidential commissions, committees, councils, panels, and task forces, 1961–1972,* AF132
Toller, T. Northcote. *Anglo-Saxon dictionary,* AC171
Tolnai, Márton. *Guide to research and scholarship in Hungary,* DC389
Tolstikov, E. I. *Atlas Antarktiki,* CL370

Tomašević, Nebojša. *World encyclopedia of naive art,* BF315
Tomita, Shigeaki. *Modern Chinese society,* DE130
Tomkeieff, S.I. *Dictionary of petrology,* EF259
Tomlinson, Amanda. *The companion thesaurus to food science and technology abstracts,* EJ159
Tomlyn, Bo. *Electronic music dictionary,* BJ313
Tommaseo, Nicholò. *Dizionario della lingua italiana,* AC524
Tommila, Päivi. *Suomen aikakauslehdistön bibliografia 1782–1955,* AD89
Tonga, DF7
Tongren, Hale N. *Beacham's marketing reference,* CH579
Tønnesen, Helge. *Topografisk, kronologisk fortegnelse over danske, færøske og grønlandske aviser 1648–1975,* AE48
Tonogbanua, Francisco G. *Philippine literature in English,* BE1600
The Tony Award, Stevenson, Isabelle, BH93
Tool and manufacturing engineers handbook, EK248
Tool engineers handbook, EK248
Toole-Stott, Raymond. *Circus and allied arts,* BH4
Tooley, Ronald Vere. *Tooley's dictionary of mapmakers,* CL274
Tooley's dictionary of mapmakers, Tooley, Ronald Vere, CL274
•*Toolworks reference library,* AB107
Toomey, Alice F. *World bibliography of bibliographies, 1964–1974,* AA14, AA20
Tootill, Elizabeth. *The Facts on File dictionary of biology,* EG36
Top symbols and trademarks of the world, CH370
Top trademarks annual, CH370
Topete, José Manuel. *A working bibliography of Brazilian literature,* BE937
Topical bibliography, Association for Anthropology and Gerontology, CC59, CE3
A topical dictionary of statistics, Tietjen, Gary L., CG32, EB45
Topical index of population census reports, 1900–1930, United States. Bureau of the Census, CG90
Topics in gerontology, CC76
Topics in the philosophy of language, BB36
Topografisk, kronologisk fortegnelse over danske, færøske og grønlandske aviser 1648–1975, Minerva mikrofilm a/s, Copenhagen, AE48
Topographical dictionary of England, Lewis, Samuel, CL137
Topographical dictionary of Ireland, Lewis, Samuel, CL143
Topographical dictionary of Scotland, Lewis, Samuel, CL141
Topographical dictionary of Wales, Lewis, Samuel, CL206
Topographical dictionary to the works of Shakespeare and his fellow dramatists, Sugden, Edward Holdsworth, BE794
Topographical works in the library of the British Museum relating to Great Britain and Ireland, DC347
Toponimia de la República Argentina, CL119
Topovere, P. *Nõukogude Eesti raamat, 1955–1965,* AA608
The Torah, BC94
———— Plaut, W. Gunther, BC184
Torbet, Laura. *The encyclopedia of crafts,* BK138
Torfing, Grethe. *Skønlitteratur i danske Tidsskrifter 1943–1962,* BE1116
Torgeson, Kathryn W. *The Garland recipe index,* EJ208
Torke, Hans-Joachim. *Lexikon der Geschichte Russlands,* DC583
Toro, Fernando de. *Bibliografía del teatro hispanoamericano contemporaneo (1900–1980),* BE900
Toro, Josefina de. *A bibliography of the collective biography of Spanish America,* AH113
Toro y Gisbert, Miguel de. *Dictionnaire des synonymes de la langue française,* AC359
Toronto Area Archivists Group. Education Foundation. *An ounce of prevention,* AK243
Toronto globe and mail, AE118, CH38

Toronto medieval bibliographies, DA138
Toronto Public Libraries. *A bibliography of Canadiana,* DB188
Toronto Public Library. *Canadian catalogue of books published in Canada, about Canada,* AA445
Torp, Alf. *Norwegisch-dänisches etymologisches Wörterbuch,* AC290
———— *Nynorsk etymologisk ordbog,* AC622
Torre, Stephen. *The Australian short story, 1940–1980,* BE858
Torre-Bueno, José Rollin de la. *The Torre-Bueno glossary of entomology,* EG338
The Torre-Bueno glossary of entomology, Torre-Bueno, José Rollin de la, EG338
Torre-Bueno's glossary of entomology, Tulloch, George S., EG338
Torre Revello, José. *Bibliografía de las Islas Malvinas,* DB376
Torres-Seda, Olga. *Caribbean women novelists,* BE971
Torrey, Glenn E. *Romania in the First World War,* DC496
Torrey Botanical Club. *Index to American botanical literature,* EG115
Tortajada, A. *Materiales de investigación,* AD329
Történeti statisztikai idösorok, 1867–1992, CG248
Tortora, Phyllis G. *Survey of historic costume,* BG108
Tosi, Francesca Ferratini. *Catalogo della stampa periodica della Biblioteche dell' Istituto Nazionale per la Storia del Movimento di Liberazione in Italia e degli Istituti associati, 1900/1975,* DC426
Tosti, Mark. *Oran's dictionary of the law,* CK40
Total baseball, BK48, BK62
Total quality management, CH607
Total television, McNeil, Alex, BH299
Toth, A. G. *The Oxford encyclopaedia of European Community law,* CK205
Toth, Robert B. *Standards activities of organizations in the United States,* EA276
Tóth, Zoltán. *Magyar történeti bibliográfia, 1825–1867,* DC383
Totok, Wilhelm. *Bibliographischer Wegweiser der philosophischen Literatur,* BB9
———— *Handbuch der bibliographischen Nachschlagewerke,* AA12
———— *Handbuch der Geschichte der Philosophie,* BB49
Totten, Samuel. *Cooperative learning,* CB11
Tottle, Charles Ronald. *An encyclopaedia of metallurgy and materials,* EK266
Touchton, Judith G. *Fact book on women in higher education,* CB344
Tougas, Gérard. *A checklist of printed materials relating to French-Canadian literature, 1763–1968,* BE844
———— *Histoire de la littérature canadienne-française,* BE840
———— *History of French-Canadian literature,* BE840
Touliatos, John. *Handbook of family measurement techniques,* CC239
Toulmin, John. *EC legal systems,* CK204
Toupet, Charles. *Atlas de la République Islamique du Mauritanie,* CL339
Touring Club Italiano. *Atlante internazionale del Touring Club Italiano,* CL294
Touring guide to Revolutionary War sites, DB95
Tourism see **Travel and tourism**
Tourism's top twenty, CL386
Tourtier-Bonazzi, Chantal de. *Guide des papiers des ministres et secrétaires d'État de 1871 à 1974,* DC152
Tous les livres au format de poche, AA635
Toussaint, A. *Bibliography of Mauritius, (1502–1954),* DD179
Toute l'histoire par les dates et les documents, Jouette, André, DC161
Toutes les monnaies du monde, Sédillot, René, CH286

Tov, Emanuel. *A classified bibliography of lexical and grammatical studies on the language of the Septuagint*, BD140

Tovar, Antonio. *Catálogo de las lenguas de América del Sur*, BD243

Toward a feminist tradition, Daims, Diva, BE474
—— Grimes, Janet, BE474

Towe, Roger. *Designers international index*, BG32

Tower Commission report, CJ114

Towers, Deirdre. *Dance film and video guide*, BH149

Town planning glossary, Venturi, Marco, BF278

Town records, West, John, DC353

Townley, John M. *The trail west*, DB166

Townshend, A. *Dictionary of analytical reagents*, EE124

Township atlas of the United States, Andriot, John L., CG76, CL297

Townsley, David. *Scripture index to The new international dictionary of New Testament theology*, BC148

Toxic and hazardous materials, EH419

Toxic substances, BF127, EE75

Toxicity bibliography, EH421

Toxicology
  abstract journals, EH420
  bibliography, EH418, EH419
  databases, EH421
  encyclopedias, EH422
  guides, EH418
  handbooks, EH423, EH424, EH425, EH426, EII427, EII428

Toxics A to Z, EH428

•*TOXLINE*, EH421

Toye, William. *Supplement to the Oxford companion to Canadian history and literature*, BE833

Tozzer Library. *Author and subject catalogues of the Tozzer Library*, CE22, CE30, CE36
—— *Tozzer Library index to anthropological subject headings*, CE53

Tozzer Library index to anthropological subject headings, CE29, CE30, CL29
—— Tozzer Library, CE53

TQM *see* **Total quality management**

TR news, EK119

Tracey, Esther M. *Illustration index*, BF60

Tracey, William R. *The human resources glossary*, CH714

Trachten und Kostüme aus Europa, Afrika und Asien in Form, Schnitt und Farbe, Tilke, Max, BG114

Trachtenberg, Stanley. *American humorists, 1800–1950*, BE411

Tracing family history in New Zealand, Bromell, Anne, AJ145

Tracing your ancestors in the Public Record Office, Cox, Jane, AJ97

Tracing your English ancestors, Rogers, Colin Darlington, AJ106

Tracing your family history in Australia, Vine Hall, Nick, AJ144

Tracing your Hispanic heritage, Ryskamp, George R., AJ141

Tracing your Irish ancestors, Grenham, John, AJ132

Tracing your Scottish ancestors, Sinclair, Cecil, AJ124

Tracing your Swedish ancestry, Olsson, Nils William, AJ43

•*Trade and industry ASAP*, CH338

•*Trade and industry index*, CH35, CH338

•*Trade and industry index ASAP*, CH35

Trade associations and professional bodies of the United Kingdom, CH82

Trade catalogs, CH400

Trade directories of the world, CH83

•*Trade names database*, CH348

Trade names dictionary. Company index, CH348

Trade shows and professional exhibits directory, CH557

Trade shows worldwide, CH557

Trade union handbook, Marsh, Arthur Ivor, CH669

Trade union publications, Reynolds, Lloyd George, CH658

Trade unions
  bibliography, CH634

directories, AL45, CH670, CH671
encyclopedias, CH648, CH651
indexes, CH643
periodicals, CH656
  indexes, CH645
  union lists, CH635
publications
  bibliography, CH658
Trade unions (by country or region)
Canada, CH662
Europe
  dictionaries, CH665
Great Britain
  bibliography, CH625, CH638
  directories, CH668, CH669
  handbooks, CH669
Great Britian
  periodicals, CH655
Italy, DC428
Latin America
  directories, CH667
United States
  biography, CH678
  collections, CH624, CH630, CH636
  directories, CH660, CH663
  history, CH675

Trade unions of the world, CH671

Trade yearbook, CH151, EJ81

Trademarks, CH370, CH371, EA257
  databases, CH348
  dictionaries, CH343
  digests and collections, CK68
  directories, CH348
  encyclopedias, CK134
Trademarks (by country or region)
United States, EA265
  indexes, EA260
Trademarks (by subject)
  chemistry, EE39
  history, CH564
  see also **Patents**

•*Trademarkscan—federal*, CII371

Trademarkscan—state, CH371

Traditional jazz, Bruyninckx, Walter, BJ307

Traditional medicine, Harrison, Ira E., CE12, EH185

Traditional tunes of the Child ballads, Bronson, Bertrand Harris, BF632, BJ314

Trafzer, Clifford. *Yakima, Palouse, Cayuse, Umatilla, Walla Walla, and Wanapum Indians*, CC420

Tragedy, CH654

Trager, James. *People's chronology*, AB27, DA39

Trager, Oliver. *Abortion*, CC245

The trail west, Townley, John M., DB166

T.R.A.I.N, CB357

The trainer's resource, CH717

Training and development organizations directory, CH718

•*Training media database*, CB355

Traister, John E. *Encyclopedic dictionary of electronic terms*, EK130

Traister, Robert J. *Encyclopedic dictionary of electronic terms*, EK130

Traité de paléontologie, Piveteau, Jean, ed, EF249

Traité de zoologie, EG242

Trammell, Jeffrey B. *The new members of congress almanac*, CJ220

Tranfaglia, Nicola. *Storia della stampa italiana*, AE64

The trans-Mississippi West, DB169

Transcendentalism, BE416

The Transcendentalists, BE416

Transcript of the registers of the Company of Stationers of London, 1554–1640, Arber, Edward, AA670, BE634, BE680
—— Stationers' Company (London), AA674, BE680

Transcription and transliteration, Wellisch, Hans H., BD10

Transdex, AF102, AF108

Transdex index, AF108, AF109

Transfer and interference in language, Dechert, Hans W., BD80

Transfer of power in Africa, Gifford, Prosser, DD4
—— Louis, W. R., DD4

Transfer students, CB262, CB294

Transfer vectors for Poole's Index to periodical literature, Dearing, Vinton A., AD281

Transformational grammar
  bibliography, BD45
  dictionaries, BD46

Transit fact book, CH454

Translated contents lists of Russian periodicals, Great Britain. Department of Scientific and Industrial Research, EA59

Translated names and titles, Dictionary of, BE87

Translation
  bibliography, BD86, BD88, BD89
  directories, BD87
  handbooks, BD87

Translation & translators, Congrat-Butlar, Stefan, BD87

Translation monthly, EA62

Translations
  bibliography, AA140, AA141, AA142, AA143, AA144
  indexes, AA141, AA144

Translations (by country or region)
Germany
  bibliography, AA139
Netherlands, AA138, DC450

Translations (by language)
Polish
  bibliography, BE1347

Translations (by subject)
  literature (by country or region)
    Philippines, BE1599, BE1600
  mathematics, EB20
  periodicals, AD25
  science, EA61

Translations and translating, Olmsted, Hugh M., BD89

Translations journals, International Translations Centre, AD25

Translations of Dutch literature, 1900–1957, Morel, P. M., AA138, DC450

Translations register-index, EA60, EA62, EA63

Transliterated dictionary of the Russian language, AC682, EA128

Transliterated English-Yiddish dictionary, Harduf, David Mendel, AC814

Transliterated Yiddish-English dictionary = Transliterirter Yidish-Englisher verterbukh, Harduf, David Mendel, AC814

Transliteration, BD10

Transnational business information, CH117

Transnational corporations and labor, Fenton, Thomas P., CH666

Transnational corporations in South Africa and Namibia, DD185
—— United Nations Centre on Transnational Corporations, DD215

Transnational terrorism, Mickolus, Edward F., CJ553

Transportation
  abstract journals, EK119
  bibliography, BF269, BF272, CH442, CH444
    current, CH443
  dictionaries, CH447, CH448
    multilingual, CH446
  directories, CH451, EK121
  library catalogs, CH443
  library resources
    directories, CH449
  statistics, CH452, CH454, EK122, EK123
  yearbooks, CH451, EK121
Transportation (by country or region)
United States
  statistics, CH453
  see also **Aviation; Railroads; Ships and shipping**

Transportation and distribution dictionary, CH447

Transportation engineering
  abstract journals, EK118, EK119
  handbooks, EK120

Transportation in America, Smith, Frank A., CH453

Transportation-logistics dictionary, CH448
Transportation research abstracts, EK119
Transportation research news, EK119
Traoré, Mamadou. *Atlas du Mali,* CL339
Trap, Jens Peter. *Danmark,* CL132
Trapani, Margi. *Learning AIDS,* EH21
Trapido, Joel. *An international dictionary of theatre language,* BH79
Trask, David F. *The craft of public history,* DB12
Trattner, Walter I. *Biographical dictionary of social welfare in America,* CC39
———— *Social welfare in America,* CC32
Traub, Thomas. *Resources for the history of computing,* EK208
Traugott, Santa. *American national election studies data sourcebook, 1952–1986,* CJ255
Traulos, Ioannes N. *Pictorial dictionary of ancient Athens,* DA102, DA106
Travaux et publications parus en français sur la Russie et l'URSS, DC41
Travel accounts and descriptions of Latin America and the Caribbean, 1800–1920, Welch, Thomas L., DB263, DB409
The travel agent's dictionary, CL381
Travel and tourism, CL371
bibliography, BK5, CL374, CL379
dictionaries, CL381, CL382
directories, CL385
encyclopedias, CL380
guidebooks
bibliography, CL389, CL390, CL391
handbooks, CH621, CL386
indexes, CL378
quotations, CL383
Travel and tourism (by country or region)
Asia, South, CL376
United States, CL377
Travel and tourism (by subject)
college students, CB93
health aspects, EH415
see also **Guidebooks**
The travel and tourism index, CL378
The travel catalogue, Cure, Karen, CL371
The travel dictionary, Dervaes, Claudine, CL381
Travel for the disabled, Hecker, Helen, CL384
Travel guidebooks in review, CL392
Travel in Asia, Edgar, Neal L., CL373
Travel in Canada, Corley, Nora Teresa, CL372
Travel in the United States, Post, Joyce A., CL377
Travel research bibliography, CL374
Travel through pictures, Ellis, Jessie Croft, BF60
Travelers' accounts
bibliography, CL7
Travelers' accounts (by country or region)
Argentina, DB329
Asia, West, DE27, DE47, DE48
Canada, DB189
Caribbean, DB263, DB409
Colombia, DB366
Greece, DE47
Italy, DC424
Latin America, DB263, DB292, DB409
Mexico, DB221
Norway, DC468
Russia and the U.S.S.R., DC551
South America, CL11
Sweden, DC519
United States, DB11, DB107, DB108, DB155, DB161, DB166
Travelers' guide to African customs & manners, Devine, Elizabeth, CL388
The traveler's guide to American gardens, BF296
Travelers' guide to Asian customs & manners, Chambers, Kevin, CL388
Travelers' guide to Latin American customs and manners, Devine, Elizabeth, CL388
Travelers' guide to Middle Eastern and North African customs and manners, Devine, Elizabeth, CL388
The traveler's reading guide, CL379
The travellers, Canada to 1900, Waterston, Elizabeth, DB189
The travellers' dictionary of quotations, CL383

Travels in America from the voyages of discovery to the present, Cole, Garold, DB11
Travels in South Asia, Kaul, H. K., CL376
Travels in the Confederate states, Coulter, Ellis Merton, DB108, DB155
Travels in the new South, Clark, Thomas Dionysius, DB108, DB155
Travels in the old South, Clark, Thomas Dionysius, DB108, DB155
Travis, Carole. *A guide to Latin American and Caribbean census material,* CG122
———— *Libraries and special collections on Latin America and the Caribbean,* AK111
———— *Periodicals from Africa,* AD238, DD28
Trávníček, František. *Slovník jazyka českého,* AC278
Treasure, Geoffrey. *Who's who in British history,* DC298
———— *Who's who in early Hanoverian Britain,* DC298
Treasure house of the living religions, Hume, Robert Ernest, BC90
Treasury bulletin, CH244
Treasury of American design, Hornung, Clarence Pearson, BG18
Treasury of Biblical quotations, Speake, Jennifer, BC154
Treasury of business quotations, Thomsett, Michael C., CH72
A treasury of Jewish quotations, BE121
A treasury of names, AJ176
Treaties
collections, AF17, CK85, CK86, CK90, CK114
databases, CK92
indexes, CK84, CK87, CK88, CK89
surveys, CK107
Treaties (by country or region)
Canada, CK97
Great Britain, CK98
United States
collections, CK92, CK93, CK94, CK95
Treaties and alliances of the world, CK107
Treaties and other international acts, CK92, CK95
Treaties and other international agreements of the United States of America, 1776–1949, United States. Treaties, CK94
Treaties in force, United States. Department of State, CK93
Treaties in force for Canada, Canada. Department of External Affairs. Treaty Section, CK97
Treatise on invertebrate paleontology, EF243
———— Teichert, Curt, EF243
Treatment of cocaine abuse, Miletich, John J., CC115
Treatments of psychiatric disorders, EH381
Treaty series, CK98
———— League of Nations, CK85, CK86, CK89, CK90
———— United Nations, CK86, CK87, CK89, CK90
•*TREECD,* EJ18
Trees, EG194, EG195, EG196, EG197, EG198, EG199, EG200, EG201, EG202, EG203
bibliography, EG204
Treese, Joel D. *Black Americans in Congress, 1870–1989,* CJ231
Trefny, Beverly Robin. *Index to children's plays in collections, 1975–1984,* BE390
Trefousse, Hans Louis. *Historical dictionary of Reconstruction,* DB105
Trehane, Piers. *Index hortensis,* EG139
Treharne, R. F. *Muir's historical atlas,* DA57
Treichler, Paula A. *A feminist dictionary,* CC539
Treitel, Corinna. *Feminist research methods,* CC504
Trelles y Govín, Carlos Manuel. *Bibliografía cubana del siglo XIX,* AA563
———— *Bibliografía cubana del siglo XX,* AA563, AA564
———— *Biblioteca científica cubana,* AA563
———— *Biblioteca geográfica cubana,* AA563
———— *Biblioteca histórica cubana,* AA563
———— *Ensayo de bibliografía cubana de los siglos XVII y XVIII,* AA563
Tremaine, Marie. *Arctic bibliography,* DG4

———— *A bibliography of Canadian imprints, 1751–1800,* AA453
———— *A bibliography of Canadiana,* DB188
Tremblay, Florent A. *Bibliotheca lexicologiae Medii Aevi,* BD147
Treml, Vladimir G. *Soviet dissident literature,* BE1407
Trenckner, Vilhelm. *A critical Pali dictionary,* AC626
Trends in academic progress, Educational Testing Service, CB140
Trends in natural resource commodities, Christy, Francis Jr, CH441
———— Potter, Neal, CH441
Trends in public opinion, Niemi, Richard G., CJ484, CJ492
Trenkov, Khristo. *Bibliografiıa na bŭlgarskata bibliografiıa, 1852–1944,* AA38
Trent, William Peterfield. *Cambridge history of American literature,* BE439
Trepp, Leo. *The complete book of Jewish observance,* BC560
Trëshnikov, A. F. *Geograficheskiĭ entsiklopedicheskiĭ slovar',* CL88
Trésor de chronologie d'histoire et de géographie pour l'étude et l'emploi des documents du moyen âge, Mas-Latrie, Louis, Comte de, DA155
Trésor de la langue française, Imbs, Paul, AC331
Trésor de la langue française au Québec, AC385
Trésor de livres rares et précieux, Grässe, Johann Georg Theodor, AA88
Trevelyan, Joanna E. *Alternative medicine,* EH30
Treves, Marco. *Artists on art,* BF145
Trewin, J. C. *British drama,* BE666
Trials in collections, Ross, John M., CK247
Tribal arts review, BG12
Tribhuvan University. Central Library. *Nepalese national bibliography,* AA922
Tribology handbook, EK239
The tribune, DB416
Triennial report—Council of Urban Boards of Education, CB143
Triffin, Nicholas. *Law books in print,* CK21
Trigg, George L. *Encyclopedia of applied physics,* ED14
———— *Encyclopedia of physics,* ED16
Trilingual demographic dictionary, CG31
Trimmer, Joseph. *Guide to MLA documentation,* AG2
Trinder, Barrie Stuart. *The Blackwell encyclopedia of industrial archaeology,* CH47, DA178
———— *Companion to the Industrial Revolution,* DC336
Trinick, Michael. *The National Trust guide,* BF249
Trinidad and Tobago, DB458
bibliography, AA570, BE981
statistics, CG180, CG181
Trinidad and Tobago, Chambers, Frances, DB458
Trinidad and Tobago national bibliography, AA570
Tripp, Edward. *Crowell's handbook of classical mythology,* CF25
Tripp, Rhoda Thomas. *The international thesaurus of quotations,* BE95
Trisco, Robert. *A guide to American Catholic history,* BC389
Trittschuh, Travis. *American political terms,* CJ129
Trivette, Carol M. *Enabling and empowering families,* CC235
Troĭanovskiĭ, Igor Aleksandrovich. *Religion in the Soviet republics,* BC81
Troike, Rudolph C. *Bibliography of bibliographies of the languages of the world,* BD3, BD8
Trois mois de nouveautés, AA636
Troise, Fred L. *The water encyclopedia,* EF140, EK96
Tron, Joan R. *Natural resource commodities—a century of statistics,* CH441
Tronik, Ruth. *Israeli periodicals & serials in English & other European languages,* AD200
Tropical abstracts, DD136
Tropical diseases bulletin, EH79
Tropical medicine, EH79

Tropical Science Center (San José, Costa Rica). *Occasional paper*, DB302

Tropical veterinary bulletin, EJ105

Trost, Barry M. *Comprehensive organic synthesis*, EE119

Trotsky, Leon, CJ505

Trotsky bibliography, Lubitz, Wolfgang, CJ505

Trotskyist serials bibliography 1927–1991, Lubitz, Wolfgang, CJ517

Troubadors *see* **Provençal literature**

Trouble is their business, Conquest, John, BE267

Trousson, Raymond. *Lettres françaises de Belgique*, BE1100

Troy, June. *A prehistoric bibliography*, DC305

Troy, Leo. *Almanac of business and industrial financial ratios*, CH418

Trubacheva, O. N. *Etimologicheskiĭ slovar' russkogo ĭazyka*, AC691

Trucking, CH445

Trucking, Rothbart, Linda S., CH444

Trucksource, CH445

Trudel, Marcel. *Atlas de la Nouvelle-France*, DB208

——— *Histoire de la Nouvelle-France*, DB203

True characters, Bold, Alan Norman, BE251

——— Giddings, Robert, BE251

Truhart, Peter. *Regents of nations*, CJ91

Truitt, Evelyn Mack. *Who was who on screen*, BH213

Trujillo, Roberto G. *Literatura Chicana*, BE558

Truman, Charles. *Sotheby's concise encyclopedia of silver*, BG143

Try us, CH372

Tryneski, John. *Requirements for certification of teachers, counselors, librarians, administrators for elementary and secondary schools*, CB164

Tryon, Alice F. *Ferns and allied plants*, EG166

Tryon, Rolla M. *Ferns and allied plants*, EG166

Trzyna, Thaddeus C. *Environmental protection directory*, EK73

Tsai, David W. *A study of modern Chinese government publications, 1912–1949*, AF243

Tsai, Meishi. *Contemporary Chinese novels and short stories, 1949–1974*, BE1561

Tsaveas, Th. N. *Mega anglo-hellēnikon lexikon*, AC465

Tschakert, Lydia. *Bücherkunde für Germanisten*, BE1211

Tschižewskij, Dmitrij. *Istoriīa ukraïns'koï literatury vid pochatkiv do doby realizmu*, BE1193

Tsien, Tsuen-Hsuin. *China*, AA74

Tsimmerman, Mikhail G. *Anglo-russkiĭ ĭadernyĭ slovar'*, ED28

——— *Russian-English translators dictionary*, EA130

Tsouras, Peter. *The United States Army*, CJ619

——— *Warrior's words*, CJ591

Tsuge, Gen'ichi. *Japanese music*, BJ44

TT. Maps & Publications Private Ltd. *A social and economic atlas of India*, CH198

Tuarascáil ar staidreamh beatha, Ireland. Central Statistics Office, CG251

Tubesing, Richard L. *Architectural preservation and urban renovation*, BF267

——— *Architectural preservation in the United States, 1941–1975*, BF267

Tuck, Donald H. *Encyclopedia of science fiction and fantasy through 1968*, BE286

Tucker, John. *Íslensk-ensk orðabók*, AC508

Tucker, John Mark. *American library history*, AK71

Tucker, Martin. *The critical temper*, BE597

——— *Library of literary criticism of English and American authors through the beginning of the twentieth century*, BE598

——— *Literary exile in the twentieth century*, BE207

——— *Modern British literature*, BE598, BE600, BE1069

——— *Modern Commonwealth literature*, BE815

Tudor, Dean. *Popular music*, BJ344

Tudor England, DC322

Tudor England, 1485–1603, Levine, Mortimer, DC303

Tudor period, 1485–1603, DC318

Tuffrau, Paul. *Histoire de la littérature française*, BE1172

——— *Manual illustré de la litterature française*, BE1172

Tuft, Eleanor. *American women artists, past and present*, BF16

Tufts, Susan E. *State government research directory*, CJ280

Tuğlaci, Pars. *Çağdaş Türkiye*, DC531

Tuin, J. D. van der. *Elsevier's dictionary of hydrology and water quality management*, EF136

Tukey, John Wilder. *Index to statistics and probability*, EB30

——— *The statistics cumindex*, EB24

The Tukey index, EB28

Tulane University. Latin American Library. *Catalog of the Latin American Library of the Tulane University Library, New Orleans*, DB269

Tulard, Jean. *Dictionnaire du cinéma*, BH288

——— *Dictionnaire Napoléon*, DC195

——— *Histoire et dictionnaire de la Révolution française*, DC188

——— *Nouvelle bibliographie critique des mémoires sur l'époque napoléonienne, écrits ou traduits en français*, DC194

TULIP, Nagar, Murari Lal, AD192

Tulloch, George S. *The Torre-Bueno glossary of entomology*, EG338

——— *Torre-Bueno's glossary of entomology*, EG338

Tulloch, Sara. *The Oxford dictionary of new words*, AC96

Tully, R. I. J. *Scientific books, libraries and collectors*, EA240

Tuma, Jan J. *Engineering mathematics handbook*, EK19

——— *Handbook of physical calculations*, ED40

Tuman, Walter Vladimir. *Bibliography of computer-aided language learning*, BD73

Tune in yesterday, Dunning, John, BH308

Tuneld, John. *Akademiska avhandlingar vid Sveriges universitet och högskolor läsåren 1910/11 1939/40*, AG42

Tung, Julia. *Bibliography of Chinese academic serials, pre-1949*, AD189

Tung, Louise Watanabe. *Japanese/English English/Japanese glossary of scientific and technical terms*, EA120

Tunisia
atlases, CL339
bibliography, AA882, BC501, DD18, DD73
current surveys, DD62
encyclopedias, DD48
history
   bibliography, DD238
periodicals, AD179, AD180, AD181
statistics, CG365

Tunisia (by subject)
history
   bibliography, DD69

Tunisia. Maktabah al-Qawmīyah. *Bibliographie historique sur la Tunisie, 1881–1955*, DD238

Tunisia, Findlay, Allan M., DD18

——— Lawless, Richard I., DD18

——— Nelson, Harold D., DD62

——— Perkins, Kenneth J., DD48

Tunisian literature, BE1515, BE1539

Tunnell, Arthur L. *Standard dictionary of Canadian biography*, AH96

Tuomikoski, Aune. *Englantilais-suomalainen sanakirja*, AC324

Tur-Sinai, Naphtali Hertz. *Milon ha-lashon ha-ivrit*, AC470

Turabian, Kate L. *A manual for writers of term papers, theses, and dissertations*, AG6

Turaev, S. V. *Slovar' literaturovedcheskikh terminov*, BE1416

Turaiev, S. *Diccionario de autores hondureños*, BE906

——— *Glosario de términos literarios*, BE906

Turco, Lewis. *New book of forms*, BE326

Türk ansiklopedisi, AB101

Türk arkeologi dergisi makaleler bibliografyasi, Işik, M. Asif, DC531

Türkçe sözlük, Eren, Hasan, AC787

Turkey
bibliography, AA840, DC61, DC532, DC534, DC536, DC540
   current, AA841
bibliography of bibliography, AA68
biography, AH302
dissertations, AG44, DC541
encyclopedias, DC542
periodicals
   indexes, AD331
statistics, CG290, CG291, CG373, DC538

Turkey (by subject)
archaeology and ancient history, DC531
foreign relations, DC539
history, DC537, DC538
   bibliography, DC535
   statistics, CG373
politics and government, DC533

Turkey, Güçlü, Meral, DC534

Turkey—politics and government, Bodurgil, Abraham, DC533

Turkic languages, BD209, BD210, BD211, DE31

The Turkic languages and literatures of Central Asia, Loewenthal, Rudolf, BD209

Turkina, Eiženija. *Latviešu-anglu vārdnīca*, AC599

Turkington, Carol. *The encyclopedia of deafness and hearing disorders*, CC189

Turkish and English lexicon, Redhouse, James William, AC793

Turkish-English dictionary, Hony, H. C., AC790

Turkish Federated State of Cyprus. *Statistical yearbook*, CG204

Turkish language
bibliography, BD212
dictionaries, AC787
   bilingual
      Turkish-English, AC789, AC790, AC791, AC792, AC793
   multilingual, AC788
   regional and dialect, AC788
handbooks, BD212

Turkish literature, BE1491

Turkish Republic of Northern Cyprus. *Statistical yearbook*, CG204

Türkiye bibliyografyasi, AA840

Türkiye istatistik yilligi, Devlet Istatistik Enstitüsü (Turkey), CG290

Türkiye makaleler bibliyoğrafyasi, AD331

Türkiye tarih yayinlari bibliyoğrafyasi, Koray, Enver, DC535

Turks and Caicos Islands, Boultbee, Paul G., DB417

Turley, Raymond Victor. *Information sources in science and technology*, EA6

Turnbull, Deborah A. *Keyguide to information sources in aquaculture*, EJ7

Turner, Ann. *Historical dictionary of Papua New Guinea*, DF49

Turner, Carann. *Population/family planning thesaurus*, CC254

Turner, Carlton E. *Cocaine*, EH320

Turner, Carol A. *Directory of foreign document collections*, AF149

Turner, D. John. *Canadian feature film index, 1913–1985*, BH192

Turner, Dorothy Rivers. *A comparative dictionary of Indo-Aryan languages*, AC516

Turner, Eugene J. *We the people*, CC358, DB74

Turner, Frederick J. *Guide to the study and reading of American history*, DB13

Turner, George W. *The Australian concise Oxford dictionary of current English*, AC177

Turner, Harold W. *Bibliography of new religious movements in primal societies*, BC19

——— *Comprehensive bibliography of modern African religious movements*, BC19

Turner, J. Rigbie. *Nineteenth-century autograph music manuscripts in the Pierpoint Morgan Library*, BJ89

Turner, Nicholas. *Handbook for biblical studies*, BC190

Turner, Ralph Lilley. *A comparative dictionary of Indo-Aryan languages,* AC516

Turner, Roland. *Great engineers and pioneers in technology,* EK20

Turoff, Sidney. *Minority groups and housing,* CH529

Turri, Vittorio. *Dizionario storico della letteratura italiana,* BE1302

Turtles of the world, Ernst, Carl H., EG247

TUSAS, BE468

Tusculum-Lexicon, BE1026

Tuska, Jon. *Frontier experience,* BE570, DB165

Tutin, Thomas Gaskell. *Flora Europaea,* EG170

—— *Flora of the British Isles,* EG168

Tutorow, Norman E. *The Mexican-American war,* DB236

—— *War crimes, war criminals, and war crimes trials,* CK80, DA203

Tuttle, Lisa. *Encyclopedia of feminism,* CC535

Tuttle guide to the Middle East, DE23

TV directors guide, BH305

TV directory, CH493

TV genres, BH293

TV movies and video guide, BH198

Tver, David F. *Encyclopedic dictionary of sports medicine,* EH127

—— *Industrial medicine desk reference,* EH128

—— *The nutrition and health encyclopedia,* EH300

—— *The petroleum dictionary,* EK306

Tver, David R. *Robotics sourcebook and dictionary,* EK234

Tveterås, Egil. *Aschehoug og Gyldendals store norske leksikon,* AB73

Tweetalige woordeboek, Bosman, Daniël Brink, AC197

Twelve thousand words, AC92

Twentieth century : a guide to literature from 1900 to the present day, Williams, Linda R., BE611

Twentieth-century American dramatists, MacNicholas, John, BE452

Twentieth-century American folk, self-taught, and outsider art, BG27

Twentieth-century American historians, Wilson, Clyde W., DB65

Twentieth-century American Jewish fiction writers, BE566

Twentieth-century American literature, BE428

Twentieth century American nicknames, AJ181

Twentieth-century artists on art, Robertson, Jack, BF145

The twentieth century atlas of the Christian world, Freitag, Anton, BC289

Twentieth century authors, BE203

—— Kunitz, Stanley Jasspon, BE205

Twentieth century book of formulas, EA278

Twentieth-century British literature, BE601

Twentieth-century children's writers, BE391

—— Kirkpatrick, D. L., BE212

Twentieth-century crime and mystery writers, BE275

—— Reilly, John M., BE212

Twentieth century encyclopedia of religious knowledge, Loetscher, Lefferts Augustine, BC67

The twentieth-century English novel, Cassis, A. F., BE672

Twentieth century European short story, May, Charles E., BE986

Twentieth-century evangelicalism, Blumhofer, Edith Waldvogel, BC212

The twentieth-century German novel, O'Pecko, Michael T., BE1268

Twentieth century : historical figures born before 1900, Davies, Adriana, BF66

Twentieth-century lace, Pfannschmidt, Ernst Erik, BG161

Twentieth-century literary criticism, BE54

Twentieth-century literary movements index, BE55

Twentieth century literature, BE27

Twentieth-century music, Burbank, Richard, BJ186

Twentieth-century musical chronicle, A, Hall, Charles J., BJ187

Twentieth century parody, American and British, Lowrey, Burling, BE723

Twentieth-century presidential bibliography series, CJ167

Twentieth-century romance and historical writers, BE249

—— Henderson, Lesley, BE212

Twentieth century Russian literature, Harvard University. Library, BE1395

Twentieth-century science-fiction writers, BE306

—— Schellinger, Paul E., BE212

—— Watson, Noelle, BE212

Twentieth-century short story explication, Walker, Warren S., BE264, BE479

Twentieth century western writers, BE579

—— Sadler, Geoff, BE212

Twenty-five T'ang poets, BE1552

Twenty-five years of Descartes scholarship, 1960–1984, Chappell, V. C., BB72

Twenty modern British playwrights, King, Kimball, BE645

Twenty years of silents, 1908–1928, Weaver, John T., BH214

Twi language, AC794

Twining, David Thomas. *Guide to the republics of the former Soviet Union,* DC600

Twintigduizend citaten, aphorismen en spreekwoorden, Margadant, Steven Willem Floris, BE126

Twitchett, Denis Crispin. *The Cambridge encyclopedia of China,* DE140

—— *Cambridge history of China,* DE146

—— *The Times atlas of China,* CL354

Two centuries of American medicine, 1776–1976, Bordley, James, EH211

Two hundred years of the American circus, Ogden, Tom, BH11

Two thousand books and more, BC515

The two World Wars, Mayer, Sydney L., DA191

Twomey, Michael W. *Medieval Christian literary imagery,* BE5

Twyman, Robert W. *The encyclopedia of Southern history,* DB159

Tyagi, R. P. *Annotated and classified bibliography of Indian demography,* CG387

Tyler, Don. *Hit parade,* BJ334

Tyler, Gary R. *Drama criticism,* BE221

Tymn, Marshall B. *Research guide to science fiction studies,* BE281

—— *Science fiction, fantasy, and weird fiction magazines,* BE307

—— *Science fiction reference guide,* BE278

—— *Survey of science fiction literature,* BE305

—— *Year's scholarship in science fiction and fantasy,* BE299, BE310

—— *Year's scholarship in science fiction, fantasy and horror literature,* BE310

Tynan, Daniel J. *Biographical dictionary of contemporary Catholic American writing,* BE446

Type and motif-index of the folktales of England and North America, Baughman, Ernest Warren, CF48

The types of the folktale, Aarne, Antti Amatus, CF45, CF88

—— Thompson, Stith, CF88

Typographia Scoto-Gadelica, Maclean, Donald, AA697

Tyrrell, John. *A guide to international music congress reports in musicology, 1900–1975,* BJ20

Tyske arkivalier om Danmark 1848–1945, DC130

Den tyske marines arkiv 1848–1945, DC130

Tyson, George F. *A guide to manuscript sources in United States and West Indian depositories relating to the British West Indies during the era of the American Revolution,* DB415

Tz'u hai, AC254

Übersicht über die Quellen zur Geschichte Lateinamerikas in Archiven der D.D.R, Staatliche Archivverwaltung of the German Democratic Republic, DB275

UCLA Latin American Center Publications (Firm). *Statistical abstract of Latin America,* CG124

Ucrainica at the University of Toronto Library, University of Toronto. Library, DC546

Udaondo, Enrique. *Diccionario biográfico colonial argentino,* AH119

Uden, Grant. *A dictionary of British ships and seamen,* CJ653

Udinsky, B. Flavian. *Evaluation resource handbook,* CD65

UdSSR : Enzyklopädie der Union der Sozialistischen Sowjetrepubliken, Becker, H., AB83

—— Fickenscher, W., AB83

Ueberweg, Friedrich. *Grundriss der Geschichte der Philosophie,* BB50

The UFAW handbook on the care and management of laboratory animals, EJ129

—— Poole, Trevor B., EG295

Uffelman, Larry K. *The nineteenth-century periodical press in Britain,* AD110

Uganda
 bibliography, DD18
  current, AA883
 current surveys, DD62
 government publications, AF221, AF223, AF240
 statistics, CG366

Uganda (by subject)
 history
  bibliography, DD239, DD240
 women, DD241

Uganda. Office of the President. Statistics Division. *Statistical abstract,* CG366

Uganda, Byrnes, Rita M., DD62

—— Collison, Robert L., DD18

—— Gray, Beverly Ann, AF240, DD240

—— Jorgensen, Jan Jelmert, DD239

Uganda, an annotated bibliography of source materials, Gertzel, Cherry J., DD239

Uganda national bibliography, AA883

Uglow, Jennifer S. *The Continuum dictionary of women's biography,* AH25

Uhlan, Miriam. *Guide to special issues and indexes of periodicals,* AD34, CH29

Ühlein, Erhard. *Römpps Chemie-Lexikon,* EE32

Uhlendorf, B. A. *A biographical directory of librarians in the United States and Canada,* AK83

Uhlirz, Karl. *Handbuch der Geschichte Österreichs und seiner Nachbarländer Böhmen und Ungarn,* DC93

Uhlirz, Mathilde. *Handbuch der Geschichte Österreichs und seiner Nachbarländer Böhmen und Ungarn,* DC93

Uj magyar lexikon, AB61

U.K. Serials Group. *Current British journals,* AD115

UK Christian handbook, BC251

Ukazatel', Rogoshin, V.N, AA790

Ukazateli soderzhaniia russkikh zhurnalov i prodolzhaiushchikhsia izdanii 1755–1970 gg, Masanov, Iuriĭ Ivanovich, AD326

UKOP, AF182

Ukraine
 atlases, DC544
 bibliography, AA842, DC547
 encyclopedias, DC543, DC545
 library catalogs, DC546
 manuscripts and archives, AK153, DC561
 newspapers, AE72
 periodicals, AD166

Ukraine (by subject)
 history, DC546, DC547
  bibliography, DC35
 politics and government, CJ389

Ukraine, Wynar, Bohdan S., DC547

Ukraine, a historical atlas, Magocsi, Paul R., DC544

Ukrainian-English dictionary, AC797

Ukrainian language
 bibliography, BD185
 dictionaries, AC798
  bilingual
   Ukrainian-English, AC796, AC797
   Ukrainian-Russian, AC795

Ukrainian literature
 bibliography of bibliography, BE1492
 biobibliography, BE1495
 translations, BE1494

Ukrainian literature (by subject)
 history, BE1493

Ukrains'ka radians'ka literaturna bibliohrafiia, Hol'denberh, Lev Izraïlevych, BE1492
Ukrainskaia Sovetskaia Sotsialisticheskaia Respublika, DC545
Ukrains'ki pys'mennyky, BE1495
Ukraïns'ko-angliĭskyĭ slovnyk, Podvez'ko, M. L., AC797
Ukraïns'ko-anhliis'kyi slovnyk, Andrusyshen, C. H., AC796
Ukrainsko-russkii slovar', Akademiia Nauk URSR, Kiev. Instytut movoznavstva, AC795
ULCN : union list of Canadian newspapers, AE38
ULI market profiles, CH544
Ulibarri, George S. *Guide to materials on Latin America in the National Archives of the United States,* DB280
Ulický, Ladislav. *Comprehensive dictionary of physical chemistry,* EE25
Ullmann, Fritz. *Ullmann's encyclopedia of industrial chemistry,* EK53
Ullmann, Manfred. *Wörterbuch der klassischen arabischen Sprache,* AC225
Ullmann's encyclopedia of industrial chemistry, Ullmann, Fritz, EK53
Ullmann's Enzyklopädie der technischen Chemie, EK53
Ullstein-Abkürzengslexikon, Spillner, Paul, AL11
Ulmer, Anne C. *A history of Scandinavian literature, 1870–1980,* BE1092
Ulpis, A. *Knygos lietuvių kalba,* AA741
Ulrich, Carolyn F. *Books and printing,* AA269
—— *The little magazine,* AD35
Ulrich, Horst. *DDR Handbuch,* CJ330
Ulrich's international peridicals directory, AD17
Ulrich's international periodicals directory, AD13, AD15, AD18, AD19, BB14, EA36, EA37, EA73, EH23
Ulrichs' periodicals directory, AD18
Ulrich's plus, AD19, AD18
Ulrich's quarterly, AD13, AD17, AD19
Ulrich's update, AD18, AD19
Ulster year book, CG241
The ultimate language of real estate, CH536
Umfassende Bibliographie der Völker namibiens (Südwestafrikas) und Südwestangolas, Strohmeyer, Eckhard, CE104
UMI article clearinghouse, AD20
UMI article clearinghouse catalog, AD20
An unabridged Malay-English dictionary, Winstedt, Richard Olof, AC607
Unanue, Emil R. *Dictionary of immunology,* EH124
Unbegaun, Boris Ottokar. *A bibliographical guide to the Russian language,* BD188
—— *Russian surnames,* AJ204
Uncertain judgement, Lewis, John Rodney, CK80, DA203
UNCTAD commodity yearbook, CH438
Und wie funktioniert dies?, EA82
The underground and alternative press in Britain, Spiers, John, AD112
The underground dictionary, Landy, Eugene E., AC126
Underground literature (by country or region)
France, AD91
U.S.S.R.
bibliography, BE1407
biobibliography, BE1407
Underground press, AD102
bibliography, BE1329
Underground press (by country or region)
Great Britain, AD111, AD112
Poland, AE66
see also **Alternative press**
Undergrounds, Danky, James Philip, AD221
Understanding archives and manuscripts, O'Toole, James M., AK188
Understanding body movement, Davis, Martha, CD116
Understanding chemical patents, Maynard, John T., EA263
Understanding the business of library acquisitions, AK168

Understanding United States foreign trade data, Bailey, Victory B., CH155
—— Bowden, Sara R., CH155
Underwood, Elizabeth. *Periodicals, annuals and government serials held in the Architectural Association Library,* BF225
Underwriters' registry for iron vessels, CH465
UNDEX. *United Nations documents index,* AF50
UNDEX, AF48
—— United Nations, AF49
UNDEX series C cumulative edition, Mittleman, Milton, AD199
—— Pease, Mina, AF49
UNDOC, AF48, DD224
•*UNESBIB,* AF59
Unesco. *Bibliographic guide to studies on the status of women,* CC589
—— *Bibliographic services throughout the world,* AA16
—— *Bibliographie cartographique internationale,* CL226
—— *Copyright laws and treaties of the world,* AA313, CK67
—— *Current sociology,* CC11
—— *Directory of meteorite collections and meteorite research,* EF208
—— *Index translationum,* AA144
—— *International bibliography of social and cultural anthropology,* CE24
—— *International bibliography of sociology,* CC8
—— *International directory of marine scientists,* EF221
—— *International glossary of hydrology,* EF133
—— *International yearbook of education,* CB128
—— *Statistical yearbook,* CB145
—— *Study abroad,* CB370
—— *Terminology of special education,* CB198
—— *World guide to higher education,* CB328
—— *World survey of education,* CB124
Unesco
bibliography, AF58
databases, AF59
guides, AF58
publications
indexes, AF60
Unesco. General Information Programme. *Bibliographic services throughout the world,* AA16
Unesco. International Scientific Committee for the Drafting of a General History of Africa. *General history of Africa,* DD58
Unesco. Social and Human Sciences Documentation Centre. *Liste mondiale des périodiques spécialisés dans les sciences sociales,* AD66, CA18
—— *Selective inventory of social science information and documentation services,* CA49
—— *World directory of peace research and training institutions,* CJ696
•*UNESCO databases,* AF59
Unesco-ICOM Documentation Centre. *Directory of museums in Africa,* AL87
Unesco list of documents and publications, United Nations Educational, Scientific and Cultural Organization, AF60
Unesco statistical yearbook, CB145
Unesco studies on peace and conflict, CJ698
Unesco yearbook on peace and conflict studies, CJ698
•*UNESDATA,* AF59
•*UNESIS,* AF59
Unger, Leonard. *American writers,* BE201, BE444
Ungherini, Aglauro. *Manuel de bibliographie biographique et d'iconographie des femmes célèbres,* AH37
UNICEF. *The state of the world's children,* CC176
UNIDIR repertory of disarmament research, CJ695
Uniestatistieke oor vyftig jaar jubileumuitgawe, South Africa. Office of Census and Statistics, CG358
Uniform crime reports for the United States, CK270
Uniform system of citation, CK66
Uniforms of the world, Knötel, Herbert, CJ634
—— Knötel, Richard, CJ595, CJ634

The Union, DB116
Union académique internationale. *Novum glossarium mediae latinitatis,* AC593
Union army, 1861–1865, Welcher, Frank Johnson, DB119
Union catalogue of Arabic serials and newspapers in British libraries, Auchterlonie, Paul, AE84
Union catalogue of New Zealand newspapers preserved in public libraries, newspaper offices, etc., New Zealand. Parliament. Library, AE100
Union catalogue of Persian serials & newspapers in British libraries, AD199, AE90
Union catalogue of printed books of 15th, 16th and 17th centuries in European astronomical observatories, Grassi, Giovanna, EC12
Union catalogue of printed books of the XV and XVI centuries in astronomical European observatories, EC12
Union catalogue of scientific libraries in the University of Cambridge, EA212
Union catalogue of the periodical publications in the university libraries of the British Isles, AD236
Union catalogue of the serial publications of the Indian government, 1858–1947, held in libraries in Britain, Macdonald, Teresa, AF246
Union catalogue of theses and dissertations of the South African universities, 1942–1958, Malan, Stephanus I., AG49
Union checklist of Filipiniana serials, University of the Philippines. Library, AD245
Unión de Universidades de América Latina. Hemeroteca Universitaria Latinoamericana. *Guía de publicaciones periódicas de universidades latinoamericanas,* AD65
Union list of astronomy serials, Lola, Judith A., EC21
Union list of Canadian newspapers, AE38
Union list of Canadian newspapers held by Canadian libraries, National Library of Canada. Newspaper Section, AE38
Union list of Chinese local histories in British libraries, Morton, Andrew, DE131
Union list of Commonwealth newspapers in London, Oxford and Cambridge, Hewitt, Arthur Reginald, AE7
Union list of film periodicals, Brady, Anna, BH174
Union list of geographical serials, Fellmann, Jerome D., CL25
—— Harris, Chauncy Dennison, CL25
Union list of geologic field trip guidebooks of North America, EF93
Union list of higher degree theses in Australian university libraries, AG59
Union list of higher degree theses of the universities of New Zealand, Swift, Catherine G., AG60
Union list of higher degree theses of the unversities of New Zealand, Cochrane, John, AG60
Union list of Latin American newspapers in libraries in the United States, Gropp, Arthur Eric, AE40
Union list of little magazines, Indiana University. Libraries, AD224
Union list of manuscripts in Canadian repositories, DB195
Union list of microfilms, Philadelphia Bibliographical Center and Union Library Catalogue, AA136
Union list of Middle East periodicals, AD184
Union list of New Zealand newspapers before 1940, Harvey, D. R., AE100
Union list of newspapers in Australian libraries, AE99
Union list of newspapers on microfilm in Japan, AE96
A union list of non-Canadian newspapers held by Canadian libraries, AE38
Union list of of architectural records in Canadian public collections, Leggat, Portia, BF210
Union list of periodicals in Thailand, AD246
A union list of printed Indic texts and translations in American libraries, Emeneau, Murray Barnson, BE1564
Union list of scientific serials in Canadian libraries, EA45
Union list of serials, AF13

Union list of serials in libraries of the United States and Canada, AD114, AD219, AD225, AD226, AD236

Union list of serials in New Zealand libraries, National Library of New Zealand, AD247

Union list of serials of government agency libraries of the Philippines, University of the Philippines. Inter-Departmental Reference Service, AD244

Union list of southeast Asian newspapers in Australian libraries, AE82

Union list of theses of the University of New Zealand, 1910–1954, Jenkins, David Lloyd, AG60

Union list of Victorian serials, Fulton, Richard D., AD222

Union lists of serials, Library of Congress. General Reference and Bibliography Division, AD219

Union of International Associations. *The 1,978 international organizations founded since the Congress of Vienna,* AL22

—— *Les congrès internationaux de 1681 à 1899,* AL31

—— *Directory of periodicals published by international organizations,* AD21

—— *Who's who in international organizations,* AH50

—— *Yearbook of international congress proceedings,* AL33

Union of Soviet Socialist Republics
  abstract journals, DC30
  archives, AK109, DC50
  associations, AL57
  atlases, CL336
  bibliography, AA786, AA792, AA793, AA796, DC41, DC555, DC590, DC591
  bibliography of bibliography, AA61, AA62, AA64, AA65, AA66, AA396
  biography, AH179, AH303, AH304, AH305, AH306, DC595
  dissertations, AG45
  encyclopedias, DC569
  gazetteers, CL152, CL153
  government publications, AF165
  handbooks, CC346
  manuscripts and archives, AK153, DC559, DC561, DC562, DC563, DC565
  newspapers, AE69, AE70, AE71, AE72, AE73, AE74, AE75
    translations, AE68
  periodicals, AD141, AD146, AD147, AD148, AD149, AD150
    indexes, AD325
      bibliography, AD326
  registers, CJ325
  statistics, CG42, CG295, CG296, CG297, CG300, CH181
    bibliography, CG299, CG301
Union of Soviet Socialist Republics (by subject)
  armed forces, CJ661
    bibliography, CJ655
    encyclopedias, CJ656, CJ658, CJ660
  economic conditions, CH181, CH186
    bibliography of bibliography, CH22
    encyclopedias, DC52
  ethnic attitudes, BC536, DC587
  ethnic groups, CC346
    handbooks, CC349
  folklore and popular culture, CF83
  foreign relations, DB180
    bibliography, CJ501, DD112, DD219
    library resources, DC586
    manuscripts and archives, DC586
    sourcebooks, DB64
  foreign relations (by country or region)
    Africa, DC599
    Asia, DC599
    Asia, West, DC599
    India, DC599
    United States, DC559, DC568
  government officials, CJ392
  historiography, DB260
  history
    atlases, DC571
    bibliography, DC549, DC588, DC589

  encyclopedias, DC52, DC583
  library resources, DC556, DC592
  manuscripts and archives, DC559
  Revolution, DC595
    bibliography, BE1399
  intelligence service, CJ542
  military history, CJ659
  music, BJ204
  nuclear weapons, CJ654
  place-names, CL153, CL154
  politics and government, CJ390
    dictionaries, CJ395
    directories, CJ393, CJ394
    encyclopedias, CJ396, DC52
    registers, CJ392
  religion, BC39, BC81, BC535, BC536, DC587
  see also **Former Soviet republics; Ukraine**
Union Research Institute (Kowloon, Hong Kong). *Who's who in Communist China,* AH343
Union statistics for fifty years, CG358
Union Theological Seminary (New York, N.Y.). Library. *Alphabetical arrangement of main entries from the shelf list,* BC40

—— *Catalogue of the McAlpin collection of British history and theology,* BC227, DC321
Unione missionaria del clero in Italia. *Bibliografia missionaria,* BC303
UNISIST (Program). *Bibliographic services throughout the world,* AA16

—— *Modern archives administration and records management,* AK187

—— *Planning, equipping, and staffing a document reprographic service,* AK249
Unit histories of the United States Air Forces, Dornbusch, Charles Emil, CJ628
Unit histories of World War II, United States. Office of Military History, CJ628
United Arab Emirates, DE270
United Arab Emirates, Clements, Frank A., DE270
United Church of Christ. *Year book,* BC386
United Church of Christ, BC383, BC384, BC385, BC387
  yearbooks, BC386
United Methodist Church. Commission on Archives and History. *The encyclopedia of world Methodism,* BC363
United Methodist Church (U.S.). *General minutes of the annual conferences of the United Methodist Church,* BC365
United Methodist studies, BC366
United Nations. *ACCIS guide to United Nations information sources on food and agriculture,* EJ8

—— *ACCIS guide to United Nations information sources on the environment,* EK69

—— *Treaty series,* CK86, CK87, CK89, CK90

—— *UNDEX,* AF49

—— *United Nations juridical yearbook,* CK111

—— *The world's women, 1970–1990,* CC585

—— *Yearbook of the United Nations,* AF56

—— *Yearbook on human rights,* CK109
United Nations
  annuals, CK111
  bibliography, AF35
  biography, AF42
  chronologies, AF32
  databases
    bibliography, AF43
  directories, AF42
  encyclopedias, AF41
  guides, AF32, AF41
  handbooks, AF44
  periodicals, AF47, AF55
  publications, AF9, AF30, AF31, AF53, AF55, AF56, EJ8
    bibliography, AF46
    databases, AF40
    guides, AF3, AF34, AF45
    index, AF48
    indexes, AF36, AF37, AF38, AF39, AF40, AF49, AF50, AF51, AF54
  yearbooks, AF56, CG57

United Nations. Advisory Committee for the Co-ordination of Information Systems. *ACCIS guide to United Nations information sources on food and agriculture,* EJ8

—— *ACCIS guide to United Nations information sources on the environment,* EK69

—— *Books in print of the United Nations system,* AF46

—— *Directory of United Nations databases and information systems,* AF43

—— *Directory of United Nations serial publications,* AF47
United Nations. Centre for Development Planning, Projections, and Policies. *World economic survey,* CH164
United Nations. Dag Hammarskjöld Library. *Checklist of United Nations documents, 1946–49,* AF52

—— *List of United Nations document series symbols,* AF53

—— *United Nations documents index,* AF50, AF54
United Nations. Department of Economic and Social Affairs. *Analytical bibliography of international migration statistics,* CG12

—— *Demographic yearbook,* CG49
United Nations. Department of International Economic and Social Affairs. *World demographic estimates and projections, 1950-2025,* CG59

—— *World economic survey,* CH164

—— *World population prospects,* CG65

—— *World survey on the role of women in development,* CC627
United Nations. Department of International Economic and Social Affairs. Population Division. *Adolescent reproductive behaviour,* CC248
United Nations. Department of Technical Cooperation for Development. *World cartography,* CL271
United Nations. Economic and Social Commission for Asia and the Pacific. *Annotated bibliography on women in development in Asia and the Pacific,* CC586

—— *Statistical yearbook for Asia and the Pacific,* CG370, CG434
United Nations. Economic and Social Commissions for Western Asia. *al-Qāmūs al-dīmūghrāfi al-thulāthī,* CG31
United Nations. Economic and Social Council. *Index to proceedings of the Economic and Social Council,* AF36
United Nations. Economic Commission for Africa. *Statistical yearbook,* CG306
United Nations. Economic Commission for Africa. Library. *Africa index,* DD25
United Nations. Economic Commission for Europe. *Directory of bodies concerned with urban and regional research,* BF279
United Nations. Economic Commission for Latin American and the Caribbean. *Anuario estadístico de América Latina y el Caribe,* CG120
United Nations. Economic Commission for Western Asia. *Bibliography of population literature in the Arab world,* CG371
United Nations. General Assembly. *Index to proceedings of the General Assembly,* AF37
United Nations. Office for Ocean Affairs and the Law of the Sea. *The law of the sea,* CK79
United Nations. Secretary-General. *Multilateral treaties deposited with the Secretary-General,* CK87
United Nations. Security Council. *Index to proceedings of the Security Council,* AF38
United Nations. Statistical Office. *Growth of world industry,* CH427

—— *International trade statistics yearbook,* CH157

—— *Monthly bulletin of statistics,* CG57, CH243

—— *Population and vital statistics report,* CG54

—— *Statistical yearbook,* CG57, CG430

—— *World trade annual,* CH165
United Nations. Trusteeship Council. *Index to proceedings of the Trusteeship Council,* AF39

United Nations Centre Against Apartheid. *Publications list and comprehensive indexes (1967–1982),* DD224
United Nations Centre for Disarmament. *United Nations disarmament yearbook,* CJ699
United Nations Centre for Human Rights. *Human rights,* CK113
—— *Human rights bibliography,* CK77
United Nations Centre for Human Settlements. *Directory of human settlements management and development training institutions in developing countries,* BF279
United Nations Centre on Transnational Corporations. *Transnational corporations in South Africa and Namibia,* DD215
United Nations Conference on Trade and Development. *Handbook of international trade and development statistics,* CH160
—— *UNCTAD commodity yearbook,* CH438
United Nations Decade for Women. *Women and development,* CC606, CH115
United Nations disarmament yearbook, CJ699
United Nations document index, AF48
United Nations document series symbols, 1946–1977, AF53
United Nations document series symbols, 1978–1984, AF53
United Nations document symbols, AF53
United Nations documents index, AF50, AF51, AF52
—— United Nations. Dag Hammarskjöld Library, AF50, AF54
United Nations Educational, Scientific and Cultural Organization. *Bibliography of publications issued by Unesco or under its auspices,* AF60
—— *Handbook on the international exchange of publications,* AK169
—— *Unesco list of documents and publications,* AF60
United Nations Industrial Development Organization. *Industry and development,* CH384
United Nations Institute for Disarmament Research. *UNIDIR repertory of disarmament research,* CJ695
United Nations Institute for Namibia. *A descriptive list of United Nations reference documents on Namibia (1946–1978),* DD186
United Nations Institute for Namibia, Luska, Zambia. Seminar on Namibian Bibliography and Documentation. *Namibia bibliographies,* DD190
United Nations Institute for Training and Research. *Directory on European training institutions in the fields of bilateral and multilateral diplomacy, public administration and management, economic and social development,* CJ47
United Nations Interregional Crime and Justice Research Institute. *A world directory of criminological institutes,* CK268
United Nations juridical yearbook, United Nations, CK111
United Nations Library (Geneva). *Human rights bibliography,* CK77
—— *League of Nations & United Nations monthly list of selected articles,* CH23
United Nations Population Fund. *Women in Ghana,* DD163
The United Nations system, international bibliography, Hüfner, Klaus, AF35
United Presbyterian Church in the U.S.A. *Minutes,* BC378
United States
  archives
    guides to records, AK114, DB38
  atlases, CG109, CL66, CL237, CL243, CL244, CL298, CL300, CL303, CL304, CL305, DB72
    handbooks, CL268
    regional and local, CL297, CL300, CL302
  atlases (by subject)
    religion, BC85
  bibliography, AA21, AA400, AA435
    19th century, AA413, AA414, AA415, AA416, AA417, AA418, AA419
    20th century, AA420, AA421, AA422, AA423, AA430

current, AA422, AA424, AA427, AA428, AA430, AA431, AA432, AA433, AA434, AA436, AA437, AA438, AA440
    databases, AA426
  early, AA401, AA403, AA404, AA405, AA406, AA407, AA408, AA409, AA410
  pamphlets, AA439
  regional, AA441, AA442, AA443
bibliography (by period)
  early, AA402
biography, AH43, AH56, AH58, AH60, AH62, AH65, AH66, AH68, AH69, AH71, AH72, CC396
  bibliography, AH89, DB67
  college graduates, AH61, AH70
  contemporary, AH75, AH76, AH79, AH82, AH83, AH84, AH85, AH86, AH87, AH88, BC416
  indexes, AH54
encyclopedias, DB47
gazetteers, CL108, CL109
government libraries, AK124
government periodicals
  bibliography of bibliography, AF85
government publications, CK244
  bibliography, AF77, AF78, AF79, AF80, AF81, AF82, AF84, CG95, DE114
  catalogs and indexes, AF90, AF92, AF93, AF94, AF95, AF96, AF97, AF98, AF99, AF100, AF101, AF102, AF103, AF107, AF108, AF109, AF110, AF111, AF113, AF114, AF116
  congressional committee hearings, AF118, AF121, AF122, AF123, AF126
    databases, AF119
  congressional committee prints, AF124
  databases, AF105, AF106, AF107
    directories, AF65, AF104
  executive branch, AF128, AF129, AF130, AF131, AF132, AF133, AF134, AF135, AF136
  guides, AF11, AF62, AF63, AF70, AF71, AF72, AF73, AF74, AF75, AF76
  indexes, AD277, AD291, AF115
  legislative branch, AF117
  legislative debates, AF127
  library resources, AF86
  maps, CL229
  municipal publications, AF147
  periodicals, AF68, AF112
  serial set, AF87, AF88, AF89, AF91, AF118, CC417
  state publications, AF137, AF140, AF141, AF143, AF144
    bibliography, AF142
  style manuals, AF69
government publications (by subject)
  medicine, EH41
handbooks, DB55
library resources, AK124, AK126
library resources (by subject)
  Asia, East, AK108, DE104
manuscripts and archives, DB29
  guides, DB27
newsletters
  directories, AD52
newspapers, AE28
  bibliography, AE18, AE19, AE20
  chronologies, AE26
  directories, AD52, AD57, AD58
  indexes, AE109, AE110
  union lists, AE18, AE19, AE26, AE27
periodicals
  bibliography, AD43, AD45, AD47, CC458
  directories, AD49, AD50, AD52, AD53, AD54, AD55, AD56, AD57, AD58
  indexes, AD258, AD287
  union lists, AD225
statistics, CG42, CG75, CG76, CG81, CG103, CJ234, EJ84
  bibliography, CG71, CG72, CG86, CG90, CG92, CG93, CG94, CG95, DB14
  compendiums, CG77, CG79, DB150
  databases, CG101, CG102
  guides, CG89
  historical, CG87

  indexes, CG96, CG98, CG99
  periodicals, CG88
statistics (by subject)
  ethnic groups, CC400, CC410, CC442, CG82, CG83, CG85
  Latinos, CC471, CG84
United States (by subject)
  antiques, BG49
  archaeology and ancient history, CE84
  armed forces, CJ223, CJ625
    bibliography, AJ30, CJ606, CJ608, CJ609, CJ610
    biography, AL180, CJ637, CJ638, CJ639, CJ640, CJ641, CJ642, CJ643, CJ644, CJ646, CJ647, CJ648
    decorations and insignia, AL180, AL183, AL185, AL186, AL187
    dictionaries, CJ584, CJ615, CJ616, CJ618, CJ619
    directories, CJ623, CJ624
    etiquette, AL157
    handbooks, CJ628, CJ630, CJ631
    history, AL186
    officers, CJ637
    registers, CJ645
    women, CJ612
    yearbooks, CJ636
  art, BF12, BF82
    archives, BF58
    directories, BF103
  cartography, CL244
  censuses
    atlases, AJ26, CG109, CL303, CL306
  ceramics and glass, BG56, BG57, BG76
  civil rights, CC392
  climate, EF156, EF158, EF159, EF160
    atlases, EF170
    maps, EF169
  coins, medals, currency, BG193
  costume and fashion, BG111
  decorative arts, BG117
  diplomacy, CJ150
  economic conditions, CH107, CH167, CH168, CH169, CH171, CH173, CH174, CH236
    atlases, CL304
    bibliography, CH172
    handbooks, CG103, CH170
  economic history
    encyclopedias, CH49, DB42
  education, higher, CB344
    directories, CB304
    foreign students, CB316
  elections, CJ192, CJ251
    bibliography, CJ106
    statistics, CJ241, CJ246, CJ256
  emigrants
    registers, AJ60
  ethnic groups, CC353, CC614
    bibliography, CC30, CC68, CC313
    databases, AE107, CC339
    dissertations, CF44
    encyclopedias, CC342
    Europeans, CC69
    film portrayals, CC334
    Irish, DC402
    Latinas, AH78
  executive branch
    encyclopedias, CJ179
  folklore and popular culture, CF66, CF73, CF75
  foreign relations, DE160
    archives, CJ177
    bibliography, CJ107, CJ169, CJ566, DB15, DB127, DD218
    chronologies, DB57
    databases, CJ185
    directories, DD52
    encyclopedias, CJ118, CJ119, DB43
    handbooks, CJ150
    sourcebooks, DB64, DB136
  foreign relations (by country or region)
    Africa, North, DE3, DE40
    Africa, South of the Sahara, DD96
    Asia, DE15

Asia, West, DE3, DE40, DE56
  Central America, DB300
  Iran, CJ114
  Latin America, DB284
  Mexico, DB220, DB250
  Nicaragua, CJ114
  Philippines, DB21, DE249
  Russia and the U.S.S.R., DC568
  Turkey, DC540
  Union of Soviet Socialist Republics, DC559
furniture, BG119
geography, CL71, CL76
  bibliography, CL107
government officials, CJ153
  biography, CJ143
  directories, CJ140
history
  archives
    guides to records, AK114, DB38
  atlases, DB69, DB71, DB74, DB75, DB76
  bibliography, CL106, DB10, DB12, DB13,
    DB17, DB19, DB20, DB23, DB24, DB25,
    DB179
  bibliography of bibliography, DB9
  biography, DB102, DB104
  chronologies, DB58, DB59, DB135
  encyclopedias, DB40, DB44, DB47
  fiction, BE470
  guides, DB8
  guides to records, DB29, DB34, DB61
  Latinos, CC448, CC468
  library catalogs, CH641, DB1
  library resources, DB52
  manuscripts and archives, DB17, DB26,
    DB29, DB31, DB34, DB52, DB81
    guides, AJ24, DB30, DB32, DB35, DB37
  politics and government, DB132
  regional and local, AJ17, AL192, CC464,
    CL178, DB26, DB139, DB143, DB144, DB145,
    DB146, DB147, DB151
    bibliography, CL107, DB142
    guides, DB140
    Middle West, DB160, DB161, DB169,
      DB173
    New England, DB152, DB153
    Rocky Mountain states, DB173
    South, DB50, DB108, DB117, DB154,
      DB155, DB156, DB157, DB158, DB159
    Southwest, DB249
    West, CC360, CC452, DB26, DB68, DB162,
      DB163, DB164, DB165, DB166, DB167,
      DB168, DB169, DB170, DB171, DB172,
      DB174, DB175, DB176
  religion, BC286
  social conditions, DB46
  sourcebooks, DB63, DB137
  sources, DB18
  statistics, CG92, DB14
  women, CC484
history (by period)
  17th and 18th centuries, DB78, DB80, DB82
    bibliography, DB79
    manuscripts and archives, DB81
  19th century, DB99, DB104, DB105, DB147
    bibliography, DB79, DB98, DB100, DB101
    Civil War, AH71, AJ16, CJ292, CJ647,
      CL299, CL301, DB77, DB106, DB107,
      DB109, DB110, DB111, DB112, DB113,
      DB114, DB115, DB116, DB117, DB118,
      DB119, DB120, DB121, DB122, DB123
    encyclopedias, DB103
  20th century, DA197, DA207, DA218, DB124,
    DB125, DB126, DB127, DB128, DB135
    chronologies, DB134
    dictionaries, DB130
    encyclopedias, DB131, DB133
    Vietnam War, BE417, DE275, DE278,
      DE279
  American Revolution, BE709, DB82, DB84,
    DB85, DB86, DB87, DB88, DB89, DB90,
    DB92, DB93
    atlases, DB96, DB97
    handbooks, DB94, DB95

  manuscripts, DB91
    manuscripts and archives, DB61
immigration, DB41
  atlases, CC358
  bibliography, CC311, CC319
  manuscripts and archives, CC356
industrial design, BG26
industry
  history, CH395
journalism, AE144, AE150, AE152
languages
  bibliography, BD106
law
  guides, CK115, CK118
  statutes
    states, CK179
legislative branch
  directories, CJ135
metalwork, BG148, BG151
military history, DB51
  atlases, DB77
  bibliography, CJ605, DB16
  guides to records, AJ18, CJ612, CJ613
music, BJ140, BJ291
naval history, DB60
overseas territories, CJ287
place-names, CL110, CL176, CL177, CL178,
  CL179, CL180, CL182
political parties, CJ264
  handbooks, CJ263
  third parties, CJ259, CJ261
politics and government, CJ207, CJ209, DB132
  acronyms, CJ125
  bibliography, CJ98, CJ99, CJ100, CJ102,
    CJ103, CJ104, CJ105, CJ106, CJ107, CJ108,
    CJ110, CJ111, CJ112, DB125
  biography, CJ153, CJ156, CJ158, CJ159,
    CJ160, CJ161, CJ162, DB102
  compendiums, CJ148, DB53
  dictionaries, CJ122, CJ127, CJ128, CJ129,
    CJ205, CJ206
  directories, AL80, CJ131, CJ132, CJ134,
    CJ136, CJ138, CJ141, CJ142, CJ144, CJ145,
    CJ146, CJ151
    databases, CJ137, CJ214
  encyclopedias, CJ115, CJ117, CJ118, CJ119,
    CJ120, CJ121, CJ122, CJ123, CJ124, CJ126,
    DB45, DB129
  executive branch, CJ114
    archives, CJ174, CJ177
    bibliography, AF128, CJ165, CJ167, CJ168,
      CJ169, CJ170, CJ171, CJ172, CJ173
    biography, CJ189, CJ190, CJ191
    directories, CJ135, CJ137, CJ146, CJ181,
      CJ182
    guides, CJ164, CJ165, CJ166
    guides and bibliography, AF131
    handbooks, CJ184, CJ186
    history, CJ187, CJ191
    library resources, CJ174, CJ175
    manuscripts, AK102, CJ176
    publications, AF132
    quotations, CJ180
    registers, CJ183
    sourcebooks, CJ187, CJ188
  handbooks, CJ149, CJ151
  history, DB45
  indexes, CJ113
  officials and employees
    directories, CJ181, CJ182
  periodicals, CJ101, CJ208
  sourcebooks, DB137
  statistics, CJ163
population, CG73, CG76
  statistics, CG79
population forecasting, CG73
postage stamps, BG204
public administration
  bibliography, CJ463
refugees
  bibliography, CC322
religion, BC27, BC30, BC32, BC59, BC65,
  BC235, BC270

  atlases, BC85
  directories, BC324
  statistics, BC85, BC86, BC87, BC88, BC291
  yearbooks, BC324
social conditions
  guides to records, CC526, DB39
  history, DB46
  statistics, CA54, CG78
state and local government
  bibliography, CJ267, CJ268
  biography, CJ285, CJ286, CJ287, CJ288,
    CJ289, CJ291
  directories, CJ133, CJ138, CJ271, CJ272,
    CJ273, CJ274, CJ275, CJ277, CJ282
  elections, CJ290, CJ291
  encyclopedias, CJ269
  handbooks, CG104, CJ270, CJ278, CJ279,
    CJ280, CJ281, CJ282, CJ283
  manuscripts and archives, DB141
  statistics, CG80, CJ283
statistics
  bibliography, CG68
statistics and demography
  atlases, CL304
textiles, BG157
travelers' accounts, DB11
vital statistics, CG100, EH406
  indexes, CG97
women in education, CB344
United States. Adjutant General's Office. *American
  decorations,* AL187
United States. Administrative Office of the United
  States Courts. *Annual report of the Director for
  the twelve month period ending [...],* CK169
——— *United States court directory,* CK149
United States. Agricultural Research Service.
  Selected weeds of the United States, EG181
——— *Titles of completed theses in home economics
  and related fields in colleges and universities of
  the United States,* EJ196
United States. Agricultural Research Service. Animal
  Disease and Parasite Research Division. *Index-
  catalogue of medical and veterinary zoology,*
  EJ101
United States. Air Force. *The United States Air
  Force dictionary,* CJ615
United States. Air Force
  dictionaries, CJ619
  handbooks, CJ627
  history, CJ614
United States. Air Force. Aeronautical Chart and
  Information Center. *The Times atlas of the moon,*
  EC69
United States. Air Force. Geophysics Laboratory.
  Handbook of geophysics and space environments,
  EF155
United States. Arms Control and Disarmament
  Agency. *World military expenditures and arms
  transfers,* CJ596
United States. Army, CJ608
  biography, CJ644, CJ646
  dictionaries, CJ619, CJ622
  handbooks, CJ629
United States. Army (by subject)
  history, CJ628
United States. Army. Military History Institute. *The
  era of the Civil War—1820–1876,* DB113
United States. Army. Signal Corps. *Bibliography of
  meteorology,* EF142
United States. Atomic Energy Commission. *Nuclear
  science abstracts,* EK294
United States. Bureau of American Ethnology.
  Handbook of South American Indians, CE91
——— *Index to Bulletins 1–100 of the Bureau of
  American Ethnology,* CE83
United States. Bureau of Animal Industry.
  Zoological Division. *Index-catalogue of medical
  and veterinary zoology,* EJ101
United States. Bureau of Economic Analysis. *Long
  term economic growth,* CH173
——— *Survey of current business,* CH425
United States. Bureau of Foreign and Domestic
  Commerce. *Foreign commerce yearbook,* CH152

United States. Bureau of Indian Affairs. Library. *Biographical and historical index of American Indians and persons involved in Indian affairs,* CC436

United States. Bureau of Industrial Economics. *Franchise opportunities handbook,* CH359

United States. Bureau of Insular Affairs. *Pronouncing gazetteer and geographical dictionary of the Philippine Islands,* CL168

United States. Bureau of Justice Statistics. *Sourcebook of criminal justice statistics,* CK269

United States. Bureau of Labor. *History and growth of the United States census,* CG90
—— *Index of all reports issued by bureaus of labor statistics in the United States prior to March 1902,* CH644

United States. Bureau of Labor Statistics. *BLS publications, 1886–1971,* CH639
—— *Directory of national unions and employee associations,* CH663
—— *Employment, hours and earnings, states and areas,* CH681
—— *Employment, hours and earnings, United States,* CH682
—— *Handbook of labor statistics,* CH687
—— *Labor force statistics derived from the Current population survey,* CH685
—— *MLR, monthly labor review,* CH685, CH688
—— *Occupational outlook handbook,* CB208, CH704, CH707

United States. Bureau of Statistics. *History of wages in the United States from colonial times to 1928,* CH689

United States. Bureau of the Census. *1990 census of population and housing,* CH692
—— *Bibliography and reel index,* CG93
—— *Census catalog and guide,* CG86
—— *Census of agriculture,* EJ78
—— *Census of housing,* CH545
—— *Century of population growth,* CG90
—— *City government finances,* CG74
—— *Congressional district atlas,* CJ238
—— *County and city data book,* CG75
—— *General censuses and vital statistics in the Americas,* CG72
—— *Historical statistics of the United States,* CG87
—— *History and present condition of the newspaper and periodical press of the United States,* AE28
—— *Housing construction statistics, 1889 to 1964,* CH545
—— *Periodic and special reports on population,* CG90
—— *Religious bodies,* BC291
—— *Social indicators III,* CG78
—— *State and metropolitan area data book,* CG79
—— *State government finances,* CG80
—— *Statistical abstract of the United States,* CG81, EJ84
—— *Subject index to Current population reports,* CG97
—— *Survey of current business,* CH425
—— *Topical index of population census reports, 1900–1930,* CG90
—— *USA/USSR facts and figures,* CG42
—— *Vital statistics of the United States,* CG88
—— *World population 1983,* CG62
—— *World population profile,* CG63

United States. Central Intelligence Agency. *Chiefs of state and cabinet members of foreign governments,* CJ83
—— *Council of Ministers of the Socialist Republic of Vietnam,* CJ325
—— *Directory of Chinese officials and organizations,* CJ427, CJ428
—— *Directory of officials of the German Democratic Republic,* CJ325
—— *Directory of officials of the People's Socialist Republic of Albania,* CJ325
—— *Directory of officials of the Socialist Federal Republic of Yugoslavia,* CJ325
—— *Directory of Soviet officials,* CJ325

—— *Handbook of international economic statistics,* CH154
—— *People's Republic of China—atlas,* CL355

United States. Central Intelligence Agency. Directorate of Intelligence. *Directory of Iranian officials,* CJ325

United States. Central Intelligence Agency. National Foreign Assessment Center. *Directory of officials of Czechoslavak Socialist Republic,* CJ325
—— *Directory of officials of the Hungarian People's Republic,* CJ325
—— *Directory of officials of the Republic of Cuba,* CJ325
—— *Directory of officials of the Socialist Republic of Vietnam,* CJ325

United States. Civil Service Commission. Library. *Personnel literature,* CH709

United States. Civil War Centennial Commission. *Civil War books,* DB111

United States. Coast Guard, CJ610

United States. Congress. *Biographical directory of the United States Congress, 1774–1989,* CJ232
—— *Congressional Quarterly's guide to Congress,* CJ193
—— *Congressional record,* AF64, AF127, CJ217
—— *A descriptive catalogue of the government publications of the United States, Sept. 5, 1774–March 4, 1881,* AF97
—— *Official congressional directory,* CJ134, CJ215, CJ217, CJ221
—— *The United States congressional directories, 1789–1840,* CJ222

United States. Congress
atlases, CJ236
bibliography, AF120, CJ198, CJ199, CJ200, CJ225
biography, CJ199, CJ210, CJ212, CJ214, CJ221, CJ230, CJ232
committee hearings, AF121, AF125, AF126
  databases, AF118, AF119
  indexes, AF118
committee prints, AF124
committees, CJ215, CJ216, CJ217, CJ219, CJ221, CJ222
congressional districts, CJ210, CJ214, CJ221, CJ234, CJ235, CJ236, CJ237, CJ238, CJ239
databases, CJ209, CJ215
dictionaries, CJ205, CJ206
directories, CJ210, CJ211, CJ214, CJ216, CJ217, CJ218, CJ219, CJ220, CJ221, CJ222
elections, CJ234, CJ249
encyclopedias, CJ115, CJ116
guides, CJ193, CJ194, CJ195, CJ196
handbooks, CJ204, CJ223, CJ224, CJ225, CJ227, CJ228, CJ229
periodicals, CJ207, CJ208, CJ209
registers, CJ222
rules and practice, CJ224, CJ225
staff members, CJ215
statistics, CJ229
voting records, CJ210, CJ213, CJ214, CJ218, CJ223

United States. Congress. House. *Comprehensive index to the publications of the United States government, 1881–1893,* AF98
—— *Constitution, Jefferson's manual and rules of the House of Representatives of the United States,* CJ226
—— *Deschler's rules of order,* CJ454
—— *Historical statistics of the United States,* CG87

United States. Congress. House
archives, CJ201
handbooks, CJ226
rules and practice, CJ226

United States. Congress. House. Commission on the Bicentenary. *Women in Congress, 1917–1990,* CJ233

United States. Congress. House. Office of the Historian. *Black Americans in Congress, 1870–1989,* CJ231
—— *Women in Congress, 1917–1990,* CJ233

United States. Congress. House. Office of the Law Revision Counsel. *United States code,* CK177

United States. Congress. House. Speaker, CJ199

United States. Congress. Joint Committee on Printing. *Official congressional directory,* CJ221

United States. Congress. Joint Economic Committee. *Economic indicators,* CH168

United States. Congress. Senate. *Guide to the records of the United States House of Representatives at the National Archives, 1789–1989,* CJ203
—— *Public documents of the first fourteen Congresses, 1789–1817,* AF92
—— *Riddick's Senate procedure,* CJ227
—— *Senate manual,* CJ228

United States. Congress. Senate
archives, CJ202
history
  bibliography, CJ197
rules and practice, CJ227, CJ228

United States. Congress. Senate. Historical Office, CJ197

United States. Congress. Senate. Library. *Presidential vetoes, 1789–1988,* AF133

United States. Congress. Senate. Select Committee to Investigate Covert Arms Transactions with Iran. *Report of the congressional committees investigating the Iran-Contra Affair,* CJ114

United States. Constitution. *The Constitution of the United States of America,* CK173

United States. Constitution, CK170, CK171
  encyclopedias, CK129, CK130, CK187
  sourcebooks, CK172

United States. Defense Mapping Agency. *Distances between ports,* CH471
—— *Gazetteer,* CL95
—— *Gazetteer of the People's Republic of China,* CL162
—— *International code of signals,* EC80

United States. Defense Mapping Agency. Hydrographic Center. *World port index,* CH469

United States. Defense Mapping Agency. Topographic Center. *Glossary of mapping, charting, and geodetic terms,* CL52

United States. Department of Agriculture. *Agricultural handbooks [Index],* EJ92
—— *Agricultural information bulletins [Index],* EJ92
—— *Agricultural statistics,* EJ77
—— *Annual reports [Index],* EJ92
—— *Chronological landmarks in American agriculture,* EJ67
—— *Department bulletins [Index],* EJ92
—— *Experiment station record,* EJ95
—— *Farmers' bulletins [Index],* EJ92
—— *Home economics research report,* EJ193
—— *List of available publications of the United States Department of Agriculture,* EJ86
—— *Miscellaneous publications [Index],* EJ92
—— *Technical bulletins [Index],* EJ92

United States. Department of Agriculture
publications, EJ85, EJ86, EJ87, EJ88, EJ92, EJ93, EJ94
  indexes, EJ89, EJ90, EJ91

United States. Department of Agriculture. Agricultural History Program Area. *A list of references for the history of black Americans in agriculture, 1619–1974,* EJ73

United States. Department of Agriculture. Division of Publications. *Index to publications of the United States Department of Agriculture, 1901–40,* EJ92
—— *Official record,* EJ92

United States. Department of Agriculture. Human Nutrition Information Service. *Composition of foods,* EH314, EJ220

United States. Department of Agriculture. Nutrition Monitoring Division. *Composition of foods,* EH314, EJ220

United States. Department of Commerce. *Directory of federal statistical data files,* CG101
—— *U.S. industrial outlook,* CH380

United States. Department of Commerce. Office of Business Analysis. *The national trade data bank,* CH497

United States. Department of Commerce. Office of Commercial Information Management Systems. *Foreign traders index,* CH118

United States. Department of Commerce. Office of Technical Services. *Correlation index of technical reports (AD-PB reports),* EA77

United States. Department of Defense, CJ630

United States. Department of Education. Division of International Education. *English-Tibetan dictionary of modern Tibetan,* AC784

United States. Department of Education. Office of Postsecondary Education. *Foreign language, area, and other international studies,* BD76

United States. Department of Energy. *Energy research abstracts,* EK215

United States. Department of Health and Human Services. Division of Black American Affairs. *Historically black colleges and universities fact book,* CB307

United States. Department of Health, Education, and Welfare. Library. *Author-title catalog of the Department Library,* CB35

—— *Subject catalog of the Department library,* CB35

United States. Department of Housing and Urban Development. *Directory of information resources in housing and urban development,* BF280

United States. Department of Justice directories, CK146, CK149

United States. Department of State. *The biographic register,* CJ143

—— *Countries of the world and their leaders yearbook,* CJ64

—— *Country reports on human rights practices,* CK109

—— *Dictionary of international relations terms,* CJ37

—— *Post report,* CL57

—— *Treaties in force,* CK93

—— *U.S. foreign affairs on CD-ROM,* CJ185

United States. Department of State archives, CJ177
bibliography, CJ169
registers, CJ183

United States. Department of State. Historical Office. *A catalog of files and microfilms of the German Foreign Ministry archives, 1920–1945,* DC253

United States. Department of State. Office of the Historian. *Principal officers of the Department of State and United States chiefs of mission, 1778–1990,* CJ183

United States. Department of the Army. *Ryukyu Islands,* DE203

United States. Department of the Interior. *Contributions to North American ethnology,* CE83

United States. Department of the Interior. Division of Documents. *Comprehensive index to the publications of the United States government, 1881–1893,* AF98

United States. Department of the Interior. Library. *Biographical and historical index of American Indians and persons involved in Indian affairs,* CC436

United States. Department of Transportation. Urban Mass Transportation Administration. *A directory of urban public transportation service,* CH450

United States. Environmental Data Service. *Climatological data,* EF159

United States. Environmental Protection Agency. *Air pollution abstracts,* EK85
—— *Pesticide fact handbook,* EJ60

United States. Environmental Science Services Administration. *ESSA libraries holdings in oceanography and marine meteorology, 1710–1967,* EF213

United States. Federal Highway Administration. *Highway statistics,* EK122, EK123

United States. Federal Reserve Board. *Federal reserve bulletin,* CH241

United States. Federal Transit Administration. *National transit summaries and trends for the ... section 15 report year,* CH452

United States. Food and Drug Administration. *National drug code directory,* EH359

United States. Foreign Broadcast Information Service. *Index to the Foreign Broadcast Information Service (FBIS) daily reports,* AF106
—— *Reference aid,* AD212

United States. Forest Service. *Atlas of United States trees,* EJ191

United States. Forest Service. Timber Management Research. *Silvics of forest trees of the United States,* EG202

United States. General Accounting Office. Office of Special Investigations. *Investigators' guide to sources of information,* CH206

United States. General Services Administration. *Catalog of federal domestic assistance,* CH167

United States. Geological Survey. *Lexicon of geologic names of the United States,* EF77
—— *Maps for America,* CL268
—— *Publications of the Geological Survey, 1879–1961,* EF39

United States. Geological Survey publications, EF39

United States. Geological Survey. Library. *Catalog of the United States Geological Survey Library,* EF46

United States. Government Printing Office. *Style manual,* AA323
—— *Word division,* AA323

United States. Health Care Financing Administration. *The International classification of diseases, 9th revision, clinical modification,* EH55

United States. Human Resources Research Institute. *Guide to captured German documents,* DC249

United States. Hydrographic Office. *Gazetteer of the Japanese Empire,* CL167

United States. Interdepartmental Committee on Culture and Scientific Cooperation. *Handbook of South American Indians,* CE91

United States. International Communication Agency. Office of Research. *Soviet research institutes project,* AL85

United States. Joint Chiefs of Staff. *Department of Defense dictionary of military and associated terms,* CJ584

United States. Joint Publications Research Service. *Bibliography-index to current U.S. JPRS translations,* AF102
—— *Reference aid,* AD212
—— *Transdex,* AF108
—— *Transdex index,* AF109

United States. [Laws, etc.]. *The statutes at large of the United States of America ...,* CK176
—— *United States code,* CK177
—— *United States code annotated,* CK178

United States. Marine Corps. *List of officers of the Navy of the United States and of the Marine Corps from 1775 to 1900,* CJ638

United States. Marine Corps, CJ607, CJ626, CJ631
handbooks, CJ633

United States. Minority Business Development Agency. *Franchise opportunities handbook,* CH359

United States. National Aeronautics and Space Administration. *Scientific and technical aerospace reports,* EK26, EK28

United States. National Aeronautics and Space Administration. Scientific and Technical Information Program. *Aerospace medicine and biology,* EH70

United States. National Air Pollution Control Administration. *NAPCA abstracts bulletin,* EK85

United States. National Archives and Records Administration. *American women and the U.S. armed forces,* CJ612
—— *The archives,* AJ24, DB37
—— *A guide to pre-federal records in the National Archives,* DB81
—— *Guide to the archives of the government of the Confederate States of America,* DB114

—— *Guide to the National Archives of the United States,* AK114, DB38
—— *Guide to the records of the United States House of Representatives at the National Archives, 1789–1989,* CJ203, CJ212
—— *Guide to the records of the United States Senate at the National Archives,* CJ203
—— *Guide to the records of the United States Senate at the National Archives, 1789–1989,* CJ212

United States. National Archives and Records Service. *A catalogue of files and microfilms of the German Foreign Ministry archives, 1867–1920,* DC250
—— *Guide to cartographic records in the National Archives,* CL242
—— *Guide to federal archives relating to Africa,* DD42
—— *Guide to materials on Latin America in the National Archives of the United States,* DB280
—— *Guides to German records microfilmed at Alexandria, Va,* DC254
—— *Index of microfilmed records of the German Foreign Ministry and the Reich's Chancellery covering the Weimar period, deposited at the National Archives,* DC252
—— *A list of archival references and data of documents from the archives of the German Foreign Ministry, 1867–1920,* DC251

United States. National Climatic Center. *Climatological data,* EF159

United States. National Criminal Justice Information and Statistics Service. *Sourcebook of criminal justice statistics,* CK269
—— *State court caseload statistics,* CK168

United States. National Historical Publications and Records Commission. *Historical documentary editions,* DB18

United States. National Historical Publications Commission. *Guide to archives and manuscripts in the United States,* CC332, DB30

United States. National Ocean Service. *Geodetic glossary,* EF122

United States. National Oceanic and Atmospheric Administration. *Climates of the states,* EF158

United States. National Office of Vital Statistics. *Vital statistics of the United States,* CG88

United States. National Park Service. *Black writers in New England,* BE516
—— *Catalog of national historic landmarks,* BF248
—— *Historic landscape directory,* BF293
—— *National register of historic places, 1966–1991,* BF250
—— *Preserving historic landscapes,* BF287

United States. National Technical Information Service. *Directory of federal laboratory & technology resources,* EA214
—— *Directory of federal statistical data files,* CG101
—— *Directory of Japanese technical resources in the United States,* EA139
—— *Federally sponsored training materials,* CB351
—— *Government reports announcements & index,* EA64

United States. Naval History Division. *Civil War naval chronology, 1861–1865,* DB120
—— *Dictionary of American naval fighting ships,* CJ649
—— *United States naval chronology,* DA210

United States. Naval Oceanographic Office. *Glossary of oceanographic terms,* EF220
—— *Navigation dictionary,* EC82
—— *World port index,* CH469

United States. Navy. *List of officers of the Navy of the United States and of the Marine Corps from 1775 to 1900,* CJ638

United States. Navy, CJ610, CJ626, CJ649
bibliography, CJ609
biography, CJ639
dictionaries, CJ619
abbreviations, CJ621

handbooks, CJ633, CJ635
United States. Office for the Bicentennial of the House of Representatives. *A guide to research collections of former members of the United States House of Representatives, 1789–1987,* CJ201
United States. Office of Business Economics. *Business statistics,* CH420
United States. Office of Consumer Affairs. *Consumer's resource handbook,* CH561
United States. Office of Economic Opportunity. *Catalog of federal domestic assistance,* CH167
United States. Office of Education. *Biennial survey of education,* CB146
—— *A century of doctorates,* CB342
—— *Education literature, 1907–1932,* CB12
United States. Office of Educational Research and Improvement. *Directory of public elementary and secondary education agencies,* CB97
—— *Higher education,* CB221
—— *OERI directory of computer tapes,* CB147
—— *Resources in education,* AK35, CB61
—— *State higher education profiles,* CB343
—— *State profiles of public elementary and secondary education, 1987–88,* CB142
United States. Office of Educational Research and Improvement. Center for Education Statistics. *Digest of education statistics,* CB139
—— *Directory of postsecondary institutions,* CB268
—— *Profile of education doctorates,* CB341
United States. Office of Experiment Stations. *Experiment station record,* EJ95
United States. Office of Federal Statistical Policy and Standards. *Directory of federal statistical data files,* CG101
United States. Office of Management and Budget. *Catalog of federal domestic assistance,* CH167
United States. Office of Military History. *Unit histories of World War II,* CJ628
United States. Office of Personnel Management. *Federal career directory,* CH696
United States. Office of Personnel Management. Library. *Personnel literature,* CH709
United States. Office of Postsecondary Education. *Higher education opportunities for minorities and women annotated selections,* CB381
United States. Office of Refugee Resettlement. *Refugee resettlement in the United States,* CC322
United States. Office of the Federal Register. *Code of federal regulations,* CK182
—— *Codification of presidential proclamations and executive orders,* AF134
—— *Public papers of the presidents of the United States,* AF136
—— *The United States government manual,* CJ151
United States. Office of the Special Assistant for Consumer Affairs. *Consumer's resource handbook,* CH561
United States. Office of Water Research and Technology. *Selected water resources abstracts,* EF129, EK68
United States. Patent and Trademark Office. *Directory of patent depository libraries,* EA266
—— *Index of patents issued from the United States Patent and Trademark Office,* EA259
—— *Index of trademarks issued from the United States Patent and Trademark Office,* EA260
—— *Official gazette of the United States Patent and Trademark Office. Patents,* EA264
—— *Official gazette of the United States Patent and Trademark Office. Trademarks,* EA265
United States. President. *Codification of presidential proclamations and executive orders,* AF134
—— *A compilation of the messages and papers of the Presidents,* AF135
—— *Economic report of the President transmitted to the Congress,* CH174
—— *Public papers of the presidents of the United States,* AF130, AF135, AF136
United States. President elections, CJ252

United States. President's Special Review Board. *Report of the President's Special Review Board,* CJ114
United States. Public Health Service. *Bibliography of the history of medicine,* EH199
—— *Film catalog,* EH45
—— *Public health law manual,* EH413
United States. Securities and Exchange Commission. *Directory of registered investment advisors,* CH305
United States. Securities and Exchange Commission bibliography, CH296
United States. Select Commission on Immigration and Refugee Policy. *U.S. immigration policy and the national interest,* CC319
United States. Small Business Administration. *Handbook of small business data,* CH377
United States. Small Business Administration. Office of Advocacy. *The states and small business,* CH368
United States. Small Business Administration. Office of International Trade. *Exporter's guide to federal resources for small business,* CH140
United States. Social Security Administration. *Four decades of international social security research,* CH499
—— *Social security bulletin,* CH526
—— *Social security handbook,* CH519
—— *Social security programs throughout the world,* CH520
United States. Soil Conservation Service. *Soil taxonomy,* EJ63
United States. Soil Management Support Services. *Keys to soil taxonomy,* EJ54
United States. Superintendent of Documents. *Catalog of the public documents of Congress and of other departments of the government of the United States for the period March 4, 1893–Dec. 31, 1940,* AF87, AF88, AF98, AF103, AF110
—— *Checklist of United States public documents, 1789–1909,* AF99
—— *List of publications of the Agricultural Department, 1862–1902, with analytical index,* EJ87
—— *Monthly catalog of United States government publications,* AF87, AF88, AF91, AF103, AF111, AF114, AF132
—— *Monthly catalog of United States government publications. Periodicals supplement,* AF111, AF112
—— *Monthly catalog of United States government publications. United States congressional serial set supplement,* AF89, AF91
—— *Numerical lists and schedule of volumes of the reports and documents of the … Congress, … session,* AF88
—— *[Subject bibliographies],* AF113
—— *Tables of and annotated index to the congressional series of United States public documents,* AF90
—— *United States congressional serial set catalog,* AF91
—— *U.S. government subscriptions,* AF116
United States. Superintendent of Documents. Library. *Checklist of United States public documents, 1789–1976,* AF95
United States. Supreme Court. *The Constitution of the United States of America,* CK173
—— *United States reports,* CK190
—— *United States Supreme Court decisions,* CK184
United States. Supreme Court, CK191
bibliography, CK125, CK184, CK186, CK189
encyclopedias, CK129, CK130, CK133, CK185, CK187, CK188
handbooks, CK192
indexes, CK183
United States. Treaties. *Treaties and other international agreements of the United States of America, 1776–1949,* CK94
—— *United States treaties and other international agreements,* CK95, CK176

United States. War Dept. *The official atlas of the Civil War,* DB123
—— *Official military atlas of the Civil War,* DB106
—— *War of the Rebellion,* DB106
United States. Weather Bureau. *Climatological data,* EF159
United States. Work Projects Administration. *Bibliography of research projects reports,* AA443
—— *Catalogue of Mexican pamphlets in the Sutro collection (1623–[1888]),* DB235
—— *[Mathematical tables],* EB88
—— *Pickaxe and pencil,* DB124
The United States, DB55
United States & Canada, BG157
United States Air Force, Watson, Bruce W., CJ619
—— Watson, Susan M., CJ619
The United States Air Force dictionary, Air University. Aerospace Studies Institute, CJ615
United States Air Force history, Paszek, Lawrence J., CJ613
The United States and Africa, Witherell, Julian W., DD17
United States and Canada, BG157
The United States and Russia, DB64
United States and sub-Saharan Africa, Witherell, Julian W., DD17
The United States Army, CJ619
United States army list, CJ646
United States Army unit histories, Controvich, James T., CJ628
—— Pappas, George S., CJ628
United States atlases, Library of Congress. Map Division, CL237
United States Board on Geographic Names. *Decisions on geographic names in the United States,* CL174, CL175
—— *Foreign gazetteers [of the] U.S. Board on Geographic Names,* CL87
—— *Gazetteer,* CL87, CL95
—— *Gazetteer of the People's Republic of China,* CL162
—— *The national gazetteer of the United States of America,* CL108
United States business history, 1602–1988, Robinson, Richard, CH399
United States-Canadian tables of feed composition, EJ130
United States catalog, AA422, AA423, AA430
United States chiefs of mission, CJ183
United States Civil Service Commission. *Official register of the United States,* CJ140
United States Coast and Geodetic Survey. *Earthquake history of the United States,* EF262
United States code, AF67, CK178
—— United States. [Laws, etc.], CK177
United States code annotated, United States. [Laws, etc.], CK178
United States code service, CK178
United States Conference of Mayors. *Urban affairs abstracts,* CC304
The United States Congress, Goehlert, Robert, CJ198
The United States congressional directories, 1789–1840, United States. Congress, CJ222
United States congressional districts, CJ239
United States congressional serial set catalog, AF88, AF89, AF91
United States congressional serial set supplement, AF88, AF89
United States corporation histories, Nasrallah, Wahib, CH397
United States court directory, United States. Administrative Office of the United States Courts, CK149
United States decennial census publications, CG9
United States decennial census publications, 1790–1970, Research Publications, inc, CG9
United States earthquakes, EF263
United States employment opportunities, CH701
United States Employment Service. *Dictionary of occupational titles,* CH693
The United States energy atlas, Cuff, David J., EK223

United States food laws, regulations, and standards, Hui, Y. H., EJ162
United States foreign policy and the Middle East/ North Africa, Reich, Bernard, DE3
—— Silverburg, Sanford R., DE3, DE40
United States foreign relations under Washington and Adams, Mugridge, Ian, DB15
United States Geographic Board. *Sixth report, 1890–1932,* CL175
United States golf course directory and guide, BK85
United States government depository publications, AF114
United States government documents on women, 1800–1990, Huls, Mary Ellen, AF66, CC494
United States government information sources, AF73
The United States government manual, CJ134, CJ151, CJ215, CL242
United States government organization manual, CJ151
United States government periodicals index, AD291, AF115
United States government publications, AA113, AF100, BC102
—— Boyd, Anne Morris, AF70
—— Hickcox, J. H., AF93
United States government publications catalogs, Zink, Steven D., AF85
United States government publications (non-depository), AF114
United States Historical Documents Institute. *Checklist of United States public documents, 1789–1976,* AF95
—— *Cumulative title index to United States public documents, 1789–1976,* AF96
United States in Africa, Shavit, David, DB284, DC568, DD96, DE15, DE56
United States in Asia, Shavit, David, DB284, DC568, DE15, DE56
The United States in Latin America, Shavit, David, DB284
United States in the Middle East, Shavit, David, DB284, DC568, DE15, DE56
The United States in the Vietnam War, 1954–1975, Peake, Louis A., DE275
United States in World War I, Schaeffer, Ronald, DA197
United States Institute of Peace. *Guides to Library of Congress subject headings and classification on peace and international conflict resolution,* CJ688
United States intelligence, CJ547
United States International Trade Commission. *Harmonized tariff schedule of the United States,* CH155
United States law week, CK190, CK191
United States lawyers reference directory, CK155
United States local histories in the Library of Congress, Library of Congress, DB142
United States–Mexico border, Jamail, Milton H., DB250
United States–Mexico borderlands, CC452, DB167
United States/Middle East diplomatic relations, 1784–1978, Bryson, Thomas A., DE3
United States Military Academy. *Biographical register of the officers and graduates of the U.S. Military Academy at West Point, N.Y.,* CJ640
—— *The centennial of the United States Military Academy at West Point, New York, 1802–1902,* CJ611
United States Military Academy. Dept. of Military Art and Engineering. *The West Point atlas of American wars,* DB77
—— *West Point atlas of the Civil War,* DB77
United States military medals and ribbons, Robles, Philip K., AL186
United States military records, AJ18
United States naval chronology, United States. Naval History Division, DA210
United States Naval Institute. *The Naval Institute guide to the Soviet navy,* CJ658
United States Naval Observatory. Nautical Almanac Office. *Explanatory supplement to the Astronomical almanac,* EC79

United States Navy, Watson, Bruce W., CJ619
—— Watson, Susan M., CJ619
United States Navy and Coast Guard, 1946–1983, Smith, Myron J., CJ609, CJ610
United States Navy and Marine Corps bases, domestic, CJ626
United States Navy and Marine Corps bases, overseas, CJ626
United States Newspaper Program. *United States Newspaper Program national union list,* AE32
United States Newspaper Program national union list, AE32
United States Newspaper Program planning guide and resource notebook, AE32
United States of America national bibliographical services and related activities in 1965–1967, Jones, Helen Gertrude (Dudenbostel), AA21
United States of America Standards Institute. *USA standard glossary of terms in nuclear science and technology,* EK295
United States official hotel directory, CL394
United States official hotel directory and railroad indicator, CL394
The United States pharmacopeia, EH363
United States Pharmacopeial Convention. *USAN and the USP dictionary of drug names,* EH332
The United States pharmacopoeia, EH360, EH362
United States pharmacopoeia dispensing information, EH364
United States political science documents, CJ20
The United States postage stamps of the 19th century, Brookman, Lester G., BG204
United States relations with Russia and the Soviet Union, Shavit, David, DC568
United States reports, United States. Supreme Court, CK190
The United States Senate, Baker, Richard A., CJ197
United States Supreme Court bulletin, CK191
United States Supreme Court decisions, Guenther, Nancy Anderman, CK184
United States Tennis Association. *The official United States Tennis Association yearbook and tennis guide with the official rules,* BK104
United States theatre, Silvester, Robert, BH44
United States Travel Data Center. *Tourism's top twenty,* CL386
United States treaties, CK92
United States treaties and other international agreements, United States. Treaties, CK95, CK176
United States treaty index, CK96
Units of weight and measure, Chisholm, L. J., AL196
Unity in diversity, CJ111
Universal author repertoire of Italian essay literature, Fucilla, Joseph Guerin, BE1292
Universal catalogue of books on art, BF56
A universal color language, ED60
Universal decimal classification, AK205
Universal encyclopedia of mathematics, EB46
Universal English-Gujarati dictionary, Deśapāṇḍe, Pāṇḍuraṅga Ganeśa, AC468
Universal life supplement, CH517
The universal list of Indian periodicals, AD192
Universal pronouncing dictionary of biography and mythology, Thomas, Joseph, AH36
Universal Reference System. *Political science, government and public policy series,* CJ13
Universalia, AB40
Universidad de Buenos Aires. *Argentine bibliography,* AA497
—— *Bibliografía argentina,* AA497, DB324
Universidad de Buenos Aires. Instituto Bibliotecológico. *Tesis presentadas a la Universidad de Buenos Aires,* AG18
Universidad de Guanajuato. Departamento de Investigaciones Bibliotecológicas. *Directorio de publicaciones periódicas mexicanas,* AD61
Universidad de Madrid. *Catálogo de las tesis doctorales manuscritas en la Universidad de Madrid,* AG41
Universidad de San Marcos (Lima). Biblioteca. *Boletin bibliográfico,* AA541

Universidad Nacional Autónoma de México. Centro de Investigaciones Interdisciplinarias en Humanidades. *Movimientos sociales en México (1968–1987),* DB227
Universidad Nacional Autónoma de México. Instituto de Historia. *Historia y bibliografía de los congresos internacionales de ciencias antropológicas, 1865–1954,* CE6
Universidad Nacional Autónoma de México. Instituto de Investigaciones Bibliográficas. *Serie guías,* DB241
Universidad Nacional de Córdoba. *Cordoba Durchmusterung (CoD),* EC75
Universidad Nacional de La Plata. Biblioteca. *Catálogo de periódicos sudamericanos existentes en la Biblioteca Pública de la Universidad (1791–1861),* AD69
Universität Bayreuth. Forschungsinstitut für Musiktheater. *Pipers Enzyklopädie des Musiktheaters,* BJ252
Universität Frankfurt am Main. Institut für Jugendbuchforschung. *Lexikon der Kinder- und Jugendliteratur,* BE385
Universität Göttingen. Skandinavisches Seminar. *Bibliographie der Runenkunde,* BE1082
Universität Kiel. Bibliothek. *Islandkatalog der Universitäts-bibliothek Kiel und der Universitäts- und Stadtbibliothek Köln,* AA719
Universität Wien. Philosophische Fakultät. *Verzeichnis über die seit dem Jahre 1872 an der Philosophischen Fakultät der Universität in Wien eingereichten und approbierten Dissertationen,* AG23
Universitäts-Sternwarte zu Bonn. *Bonner Durchmusterung (BD),* EC75
Universitätsbibliothek Jena. *Slavica-Auswahl-Katalog der Universitätsbibliothek Jena,* BE1077
Université de la Réunion. *Catalogue du fonds "Iles de l'ocean Indien",* DD203
Université de la Réunion. Service commun de la documentation. *Iles du sud-ouest de l'océan Indien,* DD121, DD142, DD175, DD179
Université de Louvain. Institut Orientaliste. *Dictionnaire étymologique du proto-indo-européen,* AC513
Université de Poitiers. Centre d'études supérieures de civilisation médiévale. *Cahiers de civilisation médiévale,* DA141
Universiteit van Amsterdam. Oost-Europa Instituut. *Biographical dictionary of dissidents in the Soviet Union, 1956–1975,* AH303
Universitetsbiblioteket i Oslo. *Bibliografi til Norges historie,* DC463
—— *Norsk lokalhistorisk litteratur, 1946–1970,* DC469
Universitetsforlaget. *Norwegian scholarly books, 1825–1967,* AA760
Universities and colleges
 bibliography, CB219, CB224, CB229
 classification, CB322
 courses of study, CB275
  dance, BH148
  film, BH263
  television, BH263
  theater, BH84
 curricula, CB273
 databases, CB260
 departments
  African-American studies, CC364
  astronomy, EC45, ED31
  chemistry, EE57
  history, DA27
  physics, EC45, ED31
  political science, CJ49
  psychology, CD37, CD38
  religion, BC77
 directories, CB249, CB250, CB251, CB260, CB261, CB265, CB270, CB271, CB272, CB275, CB276, CB279, CB293, CB301, CB309, CB310, CB311, CB312, CB332, CB346, CB347, CB348, CB349
 faculty
  directories, CB330

fellowships and scholarships, CB383
financial aid, CB383, CB390
　databases, CB388
　handbooks, CB397
　names, CB292
　ratings, CB249, CB251, CB279, CB349
　statistics, CB336, CB343, CB347, CB348
Universities and colleges (by country or region)
　British Commonwealth
　　directories, CB319
　Canada
　　directories, CB274, CB286, CB302
　Europe
　　directories, CB318
　Great Britain
　　directories, CB321
　Great Britain (by subject)
　　admission, CB324
　international
　　directories, AL13, CB241
　Latin America
　　bibliography, AD65
　United States, CB306
　　associations, CB266
　　bibliography, CB223
　　directories, AL82, CB245, CB248, CB252,
　　　CB253, CB254, CB255, CB262, CB264,
　　　CB266, CB268, CB271, CB273, CB274,
　　　CB278, CB280, CB281, CB284, CB286,
　　　CB287, CB288, CB289, CB291, CB299,
　　　CB300, CB302, CB304, CB314, CB315,
　　　CB330, CB358, CB359, CH76, EA147
　　entrance requirements, CB316
　　foreign students, CB316
　　rankings, CB345
　　statistics, CB334, CB345
　United States (by subject)
　　admission, CB230
　international
　　directories, CB240
Universities and colleges (by subject)
　administration, CB228
　admission, CB231, CD38
　curricula, CB285
　faculty, CB220
　　directories, CB331
　fellowships and scholarships, CB259, CB371,
　　CB375
　finance, CB222, CB227
　Greek-letter societies, CB398
　insignia, CB395, CB396
　performing arts
　　directories, BH13
　sports and games, CB391
　teachers and teaching
　　surveys, CB335
Universities Federation for Animal Welfare. The
　UFAW handbook on the care and management of
　laboratory animals, EJ129
University and college libraries, AK125
　statistics, AK95, AK96
University College of Swaziland. Swaziland national
　bibliography, AA879
University College of Swaziland. Library. Swaziana,
　DD231
University Film and Video Association. A
　bibliography of theses and dissertations on the
　subject of film, 1916–1979, BH176
University Microfilms International. Black
　newspapers index, AE105
—— Books on demand, AA398
—— Research abstracts, AG16
—— Terrorism, CJ557
—— UMI article clearinghouse catalog, AD20
—— The Washington post index, AE116
University of Alaska. Institute of Social, Economic,
　and Government Research. The Alaska Eskimos,
　CC414
　　An Aleut bibliography, CC418
University of Alberta. Sexual Abuse and Disabilities
　Project. Disability, sexuality, and abuse, CC185

University of Arizona. Office of Arid Lands
　Research. Inventory of geographical research on
　desert environments, CL58, EF17
University of Arizona. Office of Arid Lands Studies.
　Deserts of the world, CL58, EF17
University of Birmingham. European bibliography of
　Soviet, East European and Slavonic studies, DC41
University of Bradford. School of Peace Studies. The
　international peace directory, CJ691
University of British Columbia. Library. A checklist
　of printed materials relating to French-Canadian
　literature, 1763–1968, BE844
University of California, Berkeley. Chicano Studies
　Library Publications Unit. Chicano anthology
　index, CC457
—— Chicano database, CC455
University of California, Berkeley. Institute of
　International Studies. Western European censuses,
　1960, CG186
University of California, Berkeley. Library.
　Contemporary Chilean literature in the University
　Library at Berkeley, BE942
—— Spain and Spanish America in the libraries of
　the University of California, AA809
University of California, Davis. Agricultural History
　Center. A list of references for the history of black
　Americans in agriculture, 1619–1974, EJ73
University of California, Los Angeles. Center for the
　Study of Comparative Folklore and Mythology. An
　annotated bibliography of Chicano folklore from
　the Southwestern United States, CF68
University of California, Los Angeles. Chicano
　Research Center. Chicano database, CC455
University of California, Los Angeles. Committee on
　Latin American Studies. Statistical abstract of
　Latin America, CG124
University of California, Los Angeles. Laboratory
　for Research in Higher Education. The American
　freshman, national norms, CB333
University of California, Los Angeles. Latin
　American Center. Latin America, CH180
University of California, Los Angeles. Library.
　Middle American anthropology, CE90
University of California, Los Angeles. Women's
　Studies Program. Guide to social science
　resources in women's studies, CA5
University of California, Santa Barbara. Library.
　Reference Dept. French literature, BE1136
University of California, Santa Cruz. University
　Library. Catalog of the South Pacific collection,
　CE115, DF10
University of Cambridge. Abstracts of dissertations
　approved for the Ph.D., M.Sc., and M.Litt.
　degrees in the University of Cambridge during the
　academical year, AG36
University of Cambridge. Centre for South Asian
　Studies. Cambridge South Asian archive, DE89
University of Canterbury. Library. New Zealand
　drama, BE862
University of Chicago. The University of Chicago
　Spanish dictionary, AC739
University of Chicago. Far Eastern Library. Chinese
　local histories, DE131
University of Chicago. Oriental Institute. Assyrian
　dictionary, AC200, AC204
—— The Hittite dictionary of the Oriental Institute
　of the University of Chicago, AC491
University of Chicago Press. Chicago guide to
　preparing electronic manuscripts, AA324
—— Manual of style, AA319
The University of Chicago Spanish dictionary,
　AC739
University of Cincinnati. Shakespeare studies,
　BE781
University of Cincinnati. Center for the Study of the
　Practice of Architecture. Pro file, BF251
University of Cincinnati. Dept. of Chemistry.
　Organic Division. The vocabulary of organic
　chemistry, EE146
University of Cincinnati. Library. Catalog of the
　Modern Greek collection, DC375
University of Colorado, Boulder. Business Research
　Division. Tourism's top twenty, CL386

University of Colorado (Boulder Campus). Progress
　of medieval and Renaissance studies in the United
　States and Canada, BE28
University of Connecticut. Consortium for Research
　on Black Adolescence. Black adolescence, CC143
University of Connecticut. Roper Center for Public
　Opinion. Guide to the Bureau of Applied Social
　Research, CA12
University of Exeter. Centre for Arab Gulf Studies.
　Middle East materials in United Kingdom and
　Irish libraries, DE51
University of Florida. Libraries. Catalog of the
　Latin-American collection, DB269
—— Latin American serial documents, AF158
University of Florida. Libraries. Catalog Dept.
　Caribbean acquisitions, AA556
University of Hawaii at Manoa. Center for Korean
　Studies. Studies on Korea, DE214
University of Hawaii at Manoa. Industrial Relations
　Center. Roberts' dictionary of industrial relations,
　CH654
University of Hawaii at Manoa. Pacific Islands
　Studies Program. A guide to films about the
　Pacific Islands, DF4
University of Ibadan. Library. Africana catalogue of
　the Ibadan University Library, Ibadan, Nigeria,
　DD195
—— Nigerian periodicals and newspapers, 1950–
　1970, AD175
—— Nigerian publications, 1950–1970, AA870
University of Illinois at Urbana-Champaign.
　Musicological Archives for Renaissance
　Manuscript Studies. Census-catalogue of
　manuscript sources of polyphonic music, 1400–
　1550, BJ69
University of Illinois at Urbana-Champaign.
　Women's Studies Program. Women scholars in
　women's studies, CC552
University of Illinois Film Center. Film and video
　resources about Africa, DD43
University of Iowa. Libraries. The right wing
　collection of the University of Iowa Libraries,
　1918–1977, CJ112
University of Kansas. Libraries. Descriptive catalog
　of the history of economics collection, (1850–
　1930), CH24
University of Leeds. Department of Theology and
　Religious Studies. Science of religion, BC48
University of Leeds. Library. Catalogue of the
　Icelandic collection, AA717, BE1284
University of London. Institute of Classical Studies.
　Studies in Mycenaean inscriptions and dialect,
　1965–1978, BD139
—— A survey of classical periodicals, BE1008
University of London. Institute of Commonwealth
　Studies. Commonwealth elections, 1945–1970,
　CJ371
—— A Gibraltar bibliography, DC268
—— Union list of Commonwealth newspapers in
　London, Oxford and Cambridge, AE7
University of London. Institute of Education. The
　world year book of education, CB129
University of London. Institute of Germanic Studies.
　German language and literature, BD123
—— Germanistik in Festschriften von den
　Anfängen (1877) bis 1973, BD112
—— Theses in Germanic studies, BE1237, DC219
University of London. Institute of Historical
　Research. Bibliography of historical works issued
　in the United Kingdom, DA12
—— Bibliography of the registers (printed) of the
　universities, inns of court, colleges and schools of
　Great Britain and Ireland, AH234
—— Fasti ecclesiae Anglicanae, BC331
—— A guide to the historical and archaeological
　publications of societies in England and Wales,
　1903–1933, DC279
—— Guide to the historical publications of the
　societies of England and Wales, DC275
—— Historical research for university degrees in
　the United Kingdom, DA17, DC284
—— Microforms for historians, DA10
—— Office-holders in modern Britain, CJ344

—— Writings on British history, DC281

University of London. Institute of Latin American Studies. *Doctoral dissertations in history and the social sciences on Latin America and the Caribbean accepted by universities in the United Kingdom, 1920–1972,* CA22

—— *A guide to Latin American and Caribbean census material,* CG122

University of London. School of Oriental and African Studies. *A bibliography of the Iran-Iraq borderland,* DE35

—— *Historical writing on the peoples of Asia,* DE18

—— *International African bibliography,* DD23

University of London. School of Oriental and African Studies. Library. *Index Islamicus, 1906–1955,* BC502

—— *Library catalogue,* DD35

—— *Western books on China published up to 1850 in the Library of the School of Oriental and African Studies, University of London,* DE137

University of London. Warburg Institute. *Census of Antique Works of Art Known to Renaissance Artists at the Warburg Institute of the University of London,* BF391

University of Madras. *Tamil lexicon,* AC776

University of Maryland, College Park. *Focus Japan II,* AL43, DE210

University of Maryland, College Park. Center for Studies in Nineteenth-Century Music. *Répertoire international de la presse musicale,* BJ112

University of Maryland, College Park. National Trust for Historic Preservation Library. *Index to historic preservation periodicals,* BF218

University of Massachusetts at Amherst. *Guide to the study of United States history outside the U.S., 1945–1980,* DB17

—— *Peterson's grants for graduate study,* CB389

University of Miami. Cuban and Caribbean Library. *Catalog of the Cuban and Caribbean Library, University of Miami, Coral Gables, Florida,* DB408

University of Miami. Library. *Cuban exile periodicals at the University of Miami Library,* AD47, CC458

University of Michigan. Center for Afroamerican and African Studies. *Black immigration and ethnicity in the United States,* CC311

University of Michigan. Center for Japanese Studies. *Survey of Japanese collections in the United States,* DE206

University of Michigan. Institute of Public Administration. *Comparative public administration,* CJ467

The University of Michigan index to labor union periodicals, CH645

University of Minnesota. *Pamphlets on American writers,* BE444

University of Minnesota. Dept. of Family Social Science. *Inventory of marriage and family literature,* CC221

University of Minnesota. Immigration History Research Center. *The Immigration History Research Center,* CC356

University of Minnesota. Social Welfare History Archives. *Women's history sources,* CC526, DB39

University of Minnesota catalog of the James Ford Bell Library, DB4

University of Mississippi. John Davis Williams Library. *Plot locator,* BE194

University of Mississippi. Research Institute of Pharmaceutical Sciences. *Cocaine,* EH320

University of Natal. Durban Women's Bibliography Group. *Women in Southern Africa,* DD123

University of Newcastle upon Tyne. *Biobibliography of British mathematics and its applications,* EB19

University of North Carolina at Chapel Hill. Library. Humanities Division. *Medieval and Renaissance studies,* DA128

University of Notre Dame. Library. *Directory of Roman Catholic newspapers on microfilm,* AE33

University of Nottingham. Department of Adult Education. *International biography of adult education,* CB363

University of Oklahoma. Western History Collections. *American Indian resource materials in the Western History Collections, University of Oklahoma,* CC426

University of Oxford. *Successful candidates for the degrees of D.Phil., M.Litt., M.Sc., and Diploma in Law with the titles of their theses,* AG34

University of Papua New Guinea. Michael Somare Library. *A New Guinea bibliography,* DF48

University of Pennsylvania. Libraries. *Spanish drama of the Golden Age,* BE1470

University of Pennsylvania. University Museum. *The Sumerian dictionary of the University Museum of the University of Pennsylvania,* AC204

University of Pennsylvania law review, CK66

University of Pittsburgh. Center for International Studies. *Economics working papers bibliography,* CH41

University of Pittsburgh. Dept. of Economics. *Economic books,* CH14

University of Pittsburgh. University Center for International Studies. *United States political science documents,* CJ20

University of Pittsburgh. University Libraries. *Cuban periodicals in the University of Pittsburgh libraries,* AD75

—— *Economic books,* CH14

University of Prince Edward Island. *Canadian review of studies in nationalism,* CJ8

University of Puerto Rico ((Río Piedras Campus). *A bibliography of the collective biography of Spanish America,* AH113

University of Puerto Rico (Rio Piedras Campus). Library. *Anuario bibliográfico puertorriqueño,* AA569

University of Reading. Library. *The Cole Library of early medicine and zoology,* EH53

University of Regina. Canadian Plains Research Center. *Canadian studies on Hungarians, 1886–1986,* DC384

University of Rhodesia. Library. *Catalogue of the C. M. Doke collection on African languages in the Library of the University of Rhodesia,* BD216

University of South Africa. Institute for Theological Research. *History of the church in southern Africa,* DD115

University of South Africa. Library. Subject Reference Dept. *A pilot bibliography of South African English literature (from the beginnings to 1971),* BE1538

University of Strathclyde. Centre for the Study of Public Policy. *International register of research on British politics,* CJ342

University of Sussex. Library. *The Paris commune, 1871,* DC202

University of Texas at Austin. Bureau of Business Research. *Atlas of Central America,* CL312

—— *Atlas of Mexico,* CL310

University of Texas at Austin. Center for Intercultural Studies on Folklore and Oral History. *Guía bibliográfica para el estudio del folklore chileno,* CF71

University of Texas at Austin. Library. Latin American Collection. *Catalog of the Latin American Collection,* DB265, DB270

—— *Latin American serials list,* DB270

University of Texas at Austin. Population Research Center. *International population census bibliography,* CG6, CG9, CG11, CG13

University of the Orange Free State. Institute for Contemporary History. *Bibliographies on South African political history,* CJ410, DD213

University of the Philippines. Institute of Public Administration. Library. *List of Philippine government publications, 1945–1958,* AF259

University of the Philippines. Inter-Departmental Reference Service. *Union list of serials of government agency libraries of the Philippines,* AD244

University of the Philippines. Library. *Philippine bibliography,* AA930

—— *Union checklist of Filipiniana serials,* AD245

University of the South Pacific. Extension Centre, Western Samoa. Samoan History Writing Project. *A check list of selected material on Samoa,* DF54

University of the South Pacific. Pacific Information Centre. *South Pacific bibliography,* AA950

—— *South Pacific periodicals index,* DF2

University of the State of New York. Foreign Area Materials Center. *East Asian resources in American libraries,* DE106

University of the Witwatersrand. Library. *Southern African update,* DD124

University of Toronto. Centre for Medieval Studies. *Old English word studies,* BD99

University of Toronto. Centre for Medieval Studies. Dictionary of Old English Project. *Dictionary of Old English,* AC172

University of Toronto. Library. *A bibliography of comedias sueltas in the University of Toronto library,* BE1471

—— *A bibliography of sixteenth-century Italian verse collections in the University of Toronto Library,* BE1318

—— *Catalogue of Italian plays, 1500–1700, in the library of the University of Toronto,* BE1314

—— *Ucrainica at the University of Toronto Library,* DC546

University of Utah. Libraries. *Holdings of the University of Utah on Utah and the Church of Jesus Christ of Latter-Day Saints,* BC373

University of Wales. Board of Celtic Studies. *Geiriadur Prifysgol Cymru,* AC806

University of Wales. Board of Celtic Studies. History and Law Committee. *A bibliography of the history of Wales,* DC370

University of Warwick. Library. *Economics working papers bibliography,* CH41

University of Washington. East Asia Library. *Zen Buddhism,* BC474

University of Washington. School of International Studies. *Ethnicity and nationality,* CC310

University of Western Ontario. Population Studies Centre. *A bibliography of Canadian demography,* CG116

University of Wisconsin. African Studies Program. *African oral narratives, proverbs, riddles, poetry, and song,* CF92

University of Wisconsin-Madison. *Norwegian local history,* DC469

University of Wisconsin-Madison. African Studies Program. *A guide to original sources for precolonial western Africa published in European languages,* DD99

University of Wisconsin-Madison. Dept. of Scandinavian Studies. *Icelandic libraries and archives,* DC390

University of Wisconsin-Madison. Libraries. *Catalog of little magazines,* AD46

—— *Chemical, medical, and pharmaceutical books printed before 1800, in the collections of the University of Wisconsin Libraries,* EE17

—— *Hispanic Americans in the United States,* AE31

University of Wisconsin System. Women's Studies Librarian. *Feminist collections,* CC519

—— *New books on women and feminism,* CC520

—— *Women, race, and ethnicity,* CC625

University of Zambia. Institute for African Studies. *Bibliography of Zambiana theses and dissertations, 1930s–1989,* AG50, DD247

Unlisted drugs, EH365

Unmarried couples, Samuelson, Elliot D., CC243

Unpublished U.S. Senate committee hearings on microfiche, AF122

Unpuzzling your past, Croom, Emily Anne, AJ6

Unsere Vornamen im Wandel der Jahrhunderte, Bahlow, Hans, AJ167

Unsworth, Michael. *Military periodicals,* CJ567

Unsworth, Walter. *Encyclopedia of mountaineering,* BK120

Unterberger, Amy L. *Business biography master index,* CH94
—— *Who's who in technology,* EK15
Unterman, Alan. *Dictionary of Jewish lore and legend,* BC555, CF54
Unwin, Derick. *The encyclopaedia of educational media communications and technology,* CB170
Unwin, P. T. H. *Bahrain,* DE115
—— *Portugal,* DC490
—— *Qatar,* DE251
The Upanishads, BC92
Upham, Martin. *Employers' organizations of the world,* CH664
Uphof, Johannes Cornelis Theodorus. *Dictionary of economic plants,* EG164
Upjohn, Everard Miller. *History of world art,* BF134
Upjohn, Richard. *Channels,* AL60
Upper Volta *see* **Burkina Faso**
Upper Volta, McFarland, D. M., DD48
Uppsala. Universitet. Litteraturvetenskapliga institutionen. Avdelningen för dramaforskning. *Dramatik trykt på svenska 1914–1962,* BE1484
Uppvall, Axel Johan. *The history of the Scandinavian literatures,* BE1084
Upstream people, Tate, Michael L., CC420
Upton, William Treat. *Bibliography of early secular American music (18th century),* BJ64
Uralic languages, BD208
Uralic peoples, DC602
Uralistiikan tutkimuksen bibliografia, DC602
Uranometria 2000.0, Tirion, Wil, EC75
Urbain-Gabriel, Br. *Pru's standard Thai-English dictionary,* AC779
Urban, Bernd. *Literaturpsychologie, 1945–1987,* BE26
Urban, Paul K. *Who was who in the USSR,* AH304
Urban affairs abstracts, CC304
Urban America examined, Casper, Dale E., CC295
Urban and regional economics, Shackelford, Jean A., CH21
Urban documents microfiche collection, AF147
Urban Documents Program. *Contemporary subject headings for urban affairs,* BF277
Urban economics, CH21
Urban Institute. *America's homeless,* CC200
Urban Land Institute. *ULI market profiles,* CH544
Urban planning, Alexander, Ernest R., BF268
—— Berger, Marilyn, BF268
The urban politics dictionary, Smith, John William, CJ42
The urban South, Brown, Catherine L., DB154
Urban studies
bibliography, CC294, CC373
Urban studies (by country or region)
Scandinavia, DC72
Urban transport and planning, Banister, David, BF269, CH451, EK121
—— Pickup, Laurie, CH451, EK121
Urban transport systems, CH451, EK121
Urban transportation, CH450
statistics, CH452, CH454
see also **Mass transportation**
Urban transportation, Cortelyou, Catherine, CH444
Urbańczyk, Stanisław. *Encyklopedia języka polskiego,* BD192
Urbanization, CC293, CC302, CC303, CC307, CJ42
abstract journals, CC301, CC304
bibliography, CC295
directories, BF279, BF280
encyclopedias, BF276
guides, BF268, CC298
handbooks, CC299
library resources, BF281
quotations, CC297
reviews of research, CC299
Urbanization (by country or region)
Africa, CC300
Canada, DB210
see also **Cities; City planning**
Urbanization in tropical Africa, O'Connor, Anthony M., CC300

Urbin, Juste d'. *Supplément au Lexicon linguae Aethiopicae … (1865) et édition du lexique de Juste d'Urbin (1850–1855),* AC311
Urch, George E. F. *Education in Sub-Saharan Africa,* CB46
Urdang, Laurence. *Allusions—cultural, literary, biblical, and historical,* AC65, BE74
—— *Dictionary of advertising terms,* CH571
—— *Dictionary of borrowed words,* AC186
—— *Idioms and phrases index,* AC91
—— *Loanwords dictionary,* AC186
—— *Mottoes,* BE94
—— *Names & nicknames of places & things,* CL172
—— *-ologies & -isms,* AC79
—— *The Oxford thesaurus,* AC146
—— *Picturesque expressions,* AC81
—— *Synonym finder,* AC140
—— *Twentieth century American nicknames,* AJ181
Urdu-English dictionary, AC800
Urdu language
bibliography, BD200
dictionaries
bilingual
English-Urdu, AC799
Urdu-English, AC800
multilingual, AC801
Urdu language and literature, Mahmud, Shabana, BD200
Urdu literature
bibliography, BD200
Urech, Édouard. *A dictionary of life in Bible times,* BC193
Uribe, Maruja. *Bibliografía selectiva sobre desarrollo rural en Bolivia,* DB338
—— *Bibliografía selectiva sobre desarrollo rural en el Ecuador,* DB372
Uribe, Susana. *Fuentes de la historia contemporánea de México,* DB226
Urioste, Donaldo. *Chicano perspectives in literature,* BE558
Urquhart, Fred. *Dictionary of fictional characters,* BE188, BE189
Urrutia Montoya, Miguel. *Compendio de estadísticas históricas de Colombia,* CG151
Uruguay
bibliography, AA469, AA545, DB396
current, AA511, AA546, AA547
bibliography of bibliography, AA31
biography, AH143, AH144, AH145, DB395
government publications, AF159, AF162
statistics, CG159, CG161
Uruguay (by subject)
history, DB394, DB396
statistics, CG160
social conditions, DB397
Uruguay. Biblioteca Nacional. *Anuario bibliográfico uruguayo,* AA546
Uruguay. Dirección General de Estadística y Censos. *Anuario estadístico, Uruguay,* CG159
—— *Estadísticas vitales,* CG161
Uruguay, Finch, M. H. J., DB396
Uruguayan literature
bibliography, BE959, BE960
biobibliography, BE958, BE959
chronologies, BE958
encyclopedias, BE958
Urzędowy wykaz druków, 1928–39, AA769
U.S. Fish and Wildlife Service. *Wildlife abstracts,* EG217
—— *Wildlife review,* EG218
U.S. Immigration and Naturalization Service. *Chinese-American calendar for the 102 Chinese years commencing Jan. 24, 1849, and ending Feb. 5, 1951,* EC88
U.S. aging policy interest groups, CC91
U.S. agricultural groups, EJ44
U.S. Air Force biographical dictionary, DuPre, Flint O., CJ642
U.S. and Canadian businesses, 1955 to 1987, Geahigan, Priscilla Cheng, CH389, CH390
•*U.S. code of federal regulations,* CK182

U.S. college-sponsored programs abroad, CB242
U.S. congressional committee prints on microfiche, AF124
U.S. congressional serial set catalog : numerical lists and schedule of volumes, AF88
U.S. custom house guide, CH146
U.S. defense and military fact book, Borklund, Carl W., CJ630
U.S. directory of marine scientists, EF222
U.S. employment opportunities, CH701
U.S. exports, CH155
•*U.S. exports and imports of merchandise on CD-ROM,* CH155
•*U.S. foreign affairs on CD-ROM,* CJ185
U.S. foreign relations, Plischke, Elmer, CJ107
U.S. government organization manual, CJ134
U.S. government periodicals index, AD291, AF115
U.S. government research and development reports, EA64
U.S. government research reports, EA64
U.S. government statistics, CG89
U.S. government subscriptions, AF116
U.S. higher education, Parker, Franklin, CB225
US ICOMOS Historic Landscapes Committee. *Historic landscape directory,* BF293
U.S. immigration policy and the national interest, United States. Select Commission on Immigration and Refugee Policy, CC319
U.S. imprints on Sub-Saharan Africa, DD89
U.S. industrial outlook, CH380, CH497
U.S. Latino literature, Zimmerman, Marc, BE559
U.S. manufacturers directory, CH345
U.S. Marine Corps biographical dictionary, Schuon, Karl, CJ642
U.S. military logistics, 1607–1991, Shrader, Charles R., CJ608
U.S. military records, Neagles, James C., AJ18
U.S. national security policy and strategy, Sarkesian, Sam C., CJ98
—— Vitas, Robert A., CJ98
U.S. national security policy groups, Watson, Cynthia Ann, CJ145
U.S. Navy biographical dictionary, Schuon, Karl, CJ642
U.S. observatories, Kirby-Smith, H. T., EC47
U.S. ocean scientists & engineers: 1987 directory, EF222
U.S. politics and elections, Maurer, David J., CJ105
U.S. real estate register, CH541
U.S. relations with South Africa, Lulat, Y. G.-M, DD218
The U.S. savings and loan directory, CH280
The U.S. savings institutions directory, CH280
The U.S. Securities and Exchange Commission, Graham, John W., CH296
U.S. sources of petroleum and natural gas statistics, Special Libraries Association. Petroleum Section. Committee on U.S. Sources of Petroleum and Natural Gas Statistics, EK301
The U.S. Supreme Court, Martin, Fenton S., CK186
The USA and Canada, CJ94
USA standard glossary of terms in nuclear science and technology, United States of America Standards Institute, EK295
USA today, AE114
USA today [index], AE104, AE112, AE114
USA/USSR facts and figures, CG42
USAN and the USP dictionary of drug names, EH332
Uscher, Nancy. *The Schirmer guide to schools of music and conservatories throughout the world,* BJ172
USDA Agricultural handbooks no. 1–690, Miller, Ellen Kay, EJ92
Use of biological literature, Bottle, R. T., EG2
—— Wyatt, H. V., EG2
The use of chemical literature, EE3
Use of earth sciences literature, 1973, Wood, David Norris, EF2
The use of economics literature, CH3
Use of engineering literature, Mildren, K. W., EK2
The use of manuscripts in literary research, Thorpe, James, BE10
Use of mathematical literature, EB6

Use of medical literature, EH5

Use of physics literature, Coblans, Herbert, ED1

User education for online systems in libraries, Pask, Judith M., AK189

A user's guide to POPLINE keywords, CC257, CG17, EH78

A user's guide to the official records of the American Civil War, Aimone, Alan Conrad, DB106

USGPI, AD291, AF115

Ushakova, D. N. *Tolkovyi slovar' russkogo iazyka,* AC674

Usher, George. *A dictionary of botany,* EG140

U.S.iana, 1650–1950, Howes, Wright, AA241

Using a law library, Clinch, Peter, CK218

Using French synonyms, Batchelor, R. E., AC360

Using government information sources, Sears, Jean L., AF62

Using government publications, Moody, Marilyn K., AF62

—— Sears, Jean L., AF62

Using the biological literature, Davis, Elisabeth B., EG1

Using the mathematical literature, Schaefer, Barbara Kirsch, EB5

USP, EH362, EH363

USP DI, EH364

USP DI update, EH364

USP dictionary of drug names, EH332

USSR, CG297

The USSR and the Soviet bloc, Andor, L. E., DD112, DD219

The USSR in figures, CG296

The U.S.S.R. in maps, Dewdney, John C., CL336

U.S.S.R. in World War II, Parrish, Michael, DA200

Utah, BC373
   bibliography, BC369

Utah. [Laws, etc.]. *Utah code annotated 1953,* CK179

Utah code annotated 1953, Utah. [Laws, etc.], CK179

Utah State University. International Feedstuffs Institute. *International feed descriptions, international feed names, and country feed names,* EJ123

Utermark, Walther. *Melting point tables of organic compounds,* EE147

Utlendingers reiser i Norge, Schiötz, Eiler H., DC468

Utopian societies, DB149

Utopias, BE308, DB138
   bibliography, BE684

Utter, Glenn H. *American political scientists,* CJ155

Uusi tietosanakirja, AB39

Uyehara, Cecil H. *Leftwing social movements in Japan,* CJ512

Uzbay, Ekrem. *Langenscheidt's standard Turkish dictionary,* AC789

Uzbek-English dictionary, Waterson, Natalie, AC802

Uzbek language, AC802

V. & H. Rolland's illustrations to the Armorial générale, AJ160

Vacant, Alfred. *Dictionnaire de théologie catholique,* BC398

Vacation study abroad, CB244, CB370

Vacations abroad, CB370

Vademecum deutscher Forschungsstätten, AL64

Vademecum deutscher Lehr- und Forschungsstätten, AL64

Väestö, CG213

Vaganay, Hugues. *Bibliographie hispanique extra-péninsulaire,* AA810

Vaillancourt, Pauline M. *Cancer journals and serials,* EH38

Vaisse, Emilio. *Bibliografía general de Chile,* AA514

Vaisto, Erkki. *Finland—sources of information,* DC139

Valbuena Briones, Angel. *Literatura hispanoamericana,* BE1457

Valbuena Prat, Angel. *Historia de la literatura española,* BE1457

Valderama, David M. *A revised guide to the law and legal literature of Mexico,* CK197

Valdman, Albert. *Bibliographie des études créoles languages et littétures,* BD55

Valenstein, Suzanne G. *A handbook of Chinese ceramics,* BG79

Valenteĭ, D. I. *Bibliografiia po problemam narodonaseleniia,* CG298

—— *Demograficheskiĭ ėntsiklopedicheskiĭ slovar',* CG292

—— *Literatura o narodonaselenii,* CG298, CG299

Valentine, Alan Chester. *The British establishment, 1760–1784,* AH229

Valentine, Stuart P. *International dictionary of the securities industry,* CH304

Valenzuela, Gilberto. *Apéndice a la Bibliografía guatemalteca,* AA482

—— *Bibliografía guatemalteca,* AA481

Valenzuela Reyna, Gilberto. *Bibliografía guatemalteca,* AA481

Valk, Barbara G. *BorderLine,* CC452, DB167

—— *Latin American studies,* DB252

Valkanikē vivliographia, Dēmadēs, K. A., DC66

Vallasi, George A. *The Columbia encyclopedia,* AB6

Vallée, François. *Grand dictionnaire français-breton,* AC238

Valles, Roberto. *Bibliografía mexicana del siglo XVIII,* AA462

Valley, Shea L. *Handbook of geophysics and space environments,* EF155

Vallillo, Stephen M. *Theatrical directors,* BH121

Vallinkoski, J. *Suomen historiallinen bibliografia,* DC141

Valsing, Ruth. *Dictionary of the American West,* AC149

Valtion virallisjulkaisut, AF167

Valtón, Emilio. *Impresos mexicanos del siglo XVI (incunables americanos) en la Biblioteca Nacional de México, el Museo Nacional y el Archivo General de la Nación,* AA464

The Value Line investment survey, CH316

The value of a dollar, CH111

Valverde Tellez, Emeterio. *Bio-bibliografía eclesiástica mexicana (1821–1943),* AH104

Valynseele, Joseph. *Dictionnaire des maréchaux de France,* AH195

—— *Intermédiaire des chercheurs et curieux,* BE185

Vamplew, Wray. *Australians : historical statistics,* DF37

—— *The Oxford companion to Australian sport,* BK27

Van Amerongen, C. *The way things work,* EA82

Van Balen, John. *Geography and earth sciences publications,* CL34

Van Cleve, John V. *Gallaudet encyclopedia of deaf people and deafness,* CC188

Van Couvering, John A. *Encyclopedia of human evolution and prehistory,* CE40

Van Dale groot woordenboek der Nederlandse taal, AC292

van de Kieft, C. *Mediae latinitatis lexicon minus,* AC592

Van den Bark, Melvin. *American thesaurus of slang,* AC119

Van den Dungen, Peter. *From Erasmus to Tolstoy,* CJ675

Van der Bent, A. J. *Handbook, member churches,* BC250

Van der Leeden, Frits. *Geraghty & Miller's groundwater bibliography,* EF130

—— *The water encyclopedia,* EF140, EK96

—— *Water resources of the world,* EK99

Van der Walt, Hester. *South African newspapers on microfilm,* AE80

Van Derhoof, Jack Warner. *Bibliography of novels related to American frontier and colonial history,* BE470

Van Doren, Charles. *Webster's American biographies,* AH60

Van Dulken, Stephen. *International guide to official industrial property publications,* EA267

Van Dyne, Susan R. *Selected bibliography for integrating research on women's experience in the liberal arts curriculum,* CC482

Van Goor's aardrijkskundig woordenboek van Nederland, Laan, Kornelis ter, CL146

Van Hasselt, Vincent B. *Handbook of adolescent psychology,* CD84

—— *Handbook of family violence,* CC240

Van Hoosen, Andrea M. *African language materials in the collection of Boston University's African Studies Library,* BD215

Van Keuren, Frances Dodds. *Guide to research in classical art and mythology,* BF7, CF19

Van Minden, Jack J. R. *Dictionary of marketing research,* CH582

Van Nostrand Reinhold Company. *The VNR concise encyclopedia of mathematics,* EB69

Van Nostrand Reinhold dictionary of information technology, Longley, Dennis, EK183

Van Nostrand Reinhold encyclopedia of chemistry, EE33

Van Nostrand's scientific encyclopedia, EA83

Van Orman, Richard A. *A classified bibliography of the periodical literature of the trans-Mississippi West (1811-1957),* DB169

Van Scotter, Richard D. *Public schooling in America,* CB123

Van Tassel, David D. *U.S. aging policy interest groups,* CC91

Van Tieghem, Paul. *Répertoire chronologique des littératures modernes,* BE17

Van Uytfanghe, Marc. *Bibliographie signalétique du latin des chrétiens,* BD146

Van Vynckt, Randall. *International dictionary of architects and architecture,* BF236

Van Willigen, John. *Anthropology in use,* CE18

—— *The Indian city,* CC305

Van Zandt, Franklin K. *Boundaries of the United States and the several states,* CL76

VanArsdel, Rosemary T. *Victorian periodicals,* AD113

Vance, Harold. *Bibliography on the petroleum industry,* EK299

Vance, John T. *Guide to the law and legal literature of Mexico,* CK197

Vance, Lucile E. *Illustration index,* BF60

Vandaele, Hilaire. *Petit dictionnaire de l'ancien français,* AC384

Vande Kemp, Hendrika. *Psychology and theology in Western thought, 1672–1965,* BC20, CD59

Vanden, Harry E. *Latin American Marxism,* CJ513

VandenBerge, Peter N. *Historical directory of the Reformed Church in America, 1628–1992,* BC380

Vanderbilt, Amy. *The Amy Vanderbilt complete book of etiquette,* AL158

Vanderhoof, V. L. *Bibliography of fossil vertebrates,* EF228, EF230

Vanderlinden, Jacques. *African law bibliography,* CK225

—— *Bibliographies internationales de la doctrine juridique africaine,* CK225

Vanderstappen, D. *National population bibliography of Flanders, 1945–1983,* CG200

Vanderstappen, Harrie A. *The T. L. Yüan bibliography of Western writings on Chinese art and archaeology,* BF40

Vanderwerf, Mary Ann. *Science & technology in fact and fiction,* EA28

Vangelova, Ivanka. *Istoriiata na Bŭlgariia v memoarnata literatura,* DC115

VanGrasstek, Craig. *Scholars' guide to Washington, D.C. for Latin American and Caribbean studies,* DB273

Vanguardism in Latin American literature, Forster, Merlin H., BE872

—— Foster, Merlin H., BE936

—— Jackson, K. David, BE936

Vann, J. Don. *Victorian novels in serial,* BE690

—— *Victorian periodicals,* AD113

Vannes, René. *Essai de terminologie musicale,* BJ161

Vanuatu
   bibliography, DF52

biography, AH383
Vanwijngaerden, Frans. *Handbook on the international exchange of publications*, AK169
Vardiabasis, Demos. *Survey of social science*, CH53
Vargas Ugarte, Rubén. *Impresos peruanos*, AA542
Vargha, Kálmán. *A Magyar irodalomtörténet bibliográfiája*, BE1279
Variety and Daily variety television reviews, BH298
Variety entertainment and outdoor amusements, Wilmeth, Don B., BH2
Variety film reviews, BH242
Variety international film guide, BH269
Variety music cavalcade, 1620–1969, Mattfeld, Julius, BJ331
Variety obits, Perry, Jeb H., BH29
Variety obituaries, BH25, BH29
Variety television reviews, 1923–1988, BH298
Variety's directory of major U.S. show business awards, Kaplan, Mike, BH19
Variety's film reviews, BH242
Variety's who's who in show business, BH26
Varona, Esperanza Bravo de. *Cuban exile periodicals at the University of Miami Library*, AD47, CC458
Vas-Zoltán, Péter. *Guide to research and scholarship in Hungary*, DC389
Vása, Pavel. *Slovník jazyka českého*, AC278
Vasan, R. S. *Latin words & phrases for lawyers*, CK53
Vases, BG78
Vasev, V. M. *Afrika*, DD49
Vasmer, Max. *Etimologicheskiĭ slovar' russkogo ĭazyka*, AC691
———— *Russisches etymologisches Wörterbuch*, AC691
———— *Russisches geographisches Namenbuch*, CL152
Vasseur, André. *Bibliographie des revues et journaux littéraires des XIXᵉ et XXᵉ siècles*, AD96, BE1144
Vassilian, Hamo B. *Armenian American almanac*, CC348
———— *Ethnic cookbooks and food marketplace*, EJ224
Vatican City State, Walsh, Michael J., DC605
Vatican Council (2nd : 1962–1965). *Documents of Vatican II*, BC437
Vatican II, BC435
Vaughan, David. *The encyclopedia of dance & ballet*, BH141
Vaughan, Paul. *Community languages*, BD83
Vaughan, William. *Handbook of optics*, ED37
Vaughan, William Edward. *Irish historical statistics*, CG253
The Vaughan Williams Memorial Library catalogue of the English Folk Dance and Song Society, Vaughan Williams Memorial Library, London, CF85
Vaughan Williams Memorial Library, London. *The Vaughan Williams Memorial Library catalogue of the English Folk Dance and Song Society*, CF85
Vaughn, Jack A. *Drama A to Z*, BH82
VAZ, AD5
Vázquez de Parga, Margarita. *International bibliography of directories and guides to archival repositories*, DA175
Vázquez Machicado, José. *Catálogo descriptivo del material del Archivo de Indias referente a la historia de Bolivia*, DB338
Vázquez-Presedo, Vicente. *Estadísticas históricas argentinas (comparadas)*, CG137, DB331
Veach, Robert M. *Bibliography of society, ethics, and the life sciences*, EH237
Veaner, Allen B. *Microform review*, AA137
Vecchi Galli, Paula. *IUPI*, BE1316
The Vedânta sûtras, BC92
Vedas, BC484, BC489
Vedeneeva, Klavdiĩa. *Russian-English translators dictionary*, EA130
Vedic bibliography, Dandekar, Ramchandra Narayan, BC484
A Vedic concordance, Bloomfield, Maurice, BC489
Vedic hymns, BC92

Vedic index of names and subjects, Macdonnell, Arthur Anthony, BC490
Vega, Vicente. *Diccionario ilustrado de frases célebres y citas literarias*, BE96
Veigl, Hans. *Das grosse Buch der Österreicher*, AH167
Veilleux, Raymond F. *Tool and manufacturing engineers handbook*, EK248
Veillitte, Claire C. *A Canadian Indian bibliography, 1960–1970*, CC472
Veinstein, André. *Bibliothèques et musées des arts du spectacle dans le monde*, BH5
Veit, Fritz. *Presidential libraries and collections*, AJ24, CJ175, DB37
Vekene, Emil van der. *Bibliotheca bibliographica historiae sanctae inquisitionis*, BC272
Velásquez Gallardo, Pablo. *Catálogo colectivo de publicaciones periódicas existentes en bibliotecas de la República Mexicana*, AD229
Velázquez de la Cadena, Mariano. *New revised Velázquez Spanish and English dictionary*, AC740
Velázquez Spanish and English dictionary, AC740
Velie, Alan R. *American Indian literature*, BE555
Velikaĩa oktiabr'skaĩa sotsialisticheskaĩa revoliutsiĩa, DC590, DC601
Velikaĩa Oktiabr'skaĩa sotsialisticheskaĩa revoliutsiĩa v proizvedeniĩakh sovetskikh pisateleĭ, Gosudarstvennaĩa biblioteka SSSR imeni V.I. Lenina, BE1399
Veliki anglešsko-slovenski slovar, Grad, Anton, AC721
Velký anglicko-český slovník, Hais, Karel, AC279
Velleman, Antoine. *Dicziunari scurznieu da la lingua ladina*, AC665
Vellut, Jean Luc. *Guide de l'étudiant en histoire du Zaire*, DD15, DD245
Velz, John W. *Shakespeare and the classical tradition*, BE795
Vem är det?, AH294
Vem och vad?, AH190
Vendryes, Joseph. *Lexique étymologique de l'irlandais ancien*, AC522
Venezky, Richard L. *Dictionary of Old English*, AC172
Venezuela
 atlases, CL318
 bibliography, AA548, AA549, AA550, AA551, DB401
  current, AA552, AA553
 bibliography of bibliography, AA32
 biography, AH146, AH147
 dissertations, DB400
 government publications, AF159, AF163
 guides, DB398
 statistics, CG162
Venezuela (by subject)
 ethnic groups, CC476
 history, DB398
  bibliography, DB401
  chronologies, DB403
  encyclopedias, DB402
  guides, DB399
Venezuela. Dirección de Cartografía Nacional. *Atlas de Venezuela*, CL318
Venezuela, Waddell, D. A. G., DB401
Venezuelan history, Lombardi, John V., DB399
Venezuelan literature
 bibliography, BE961, BE963, BE964, BE965, BE966, BE967
 biobibliography, BE962
Vengerov, Semen Afanas'evich. *Istochniki slovaria russkikh pisatelei*, BE1424
Venkova-Ilieva, Liliĩana. *Voenna istoriĩa na Bŭlgariĩa, 681–1945*, DC116
Vennetier, Pierre. *Atlas de la Côte d'Ivoire*, CL339
Venomous snakes of the world, Harding, Keith A., EG249
Venture capital sources, CH230
Venturi, Marco. *Town planning glossary*, BF278
Venzon, Anne Cipriano. *The Spanish-American War*, DB101
Ver Nooy, Winifred. *An index to one-act plays*, BE228

Vera, Eduardo S. *Encyclopedia of applied physics*, ED14
Vera, Francisco. *La cultura española medieval*, BE1443
Verband der Deutschen Akademien. *Deutsches biographisches Jahrbuch*, AH207
Verband Österreichischer Zeitungsherausgeber und Zeitungsverleger. *200 Jahre Tageszeitung in Österreich, 1783–1983*, AE44
———— *Presse Handbuch*, AD81
Verbis non factis, Blake, Fay M., CJ242
Verbo, AB81
Vercelloni, Virgilio. *European gardens*, BF295
Verdades que levantan roncha, Victoria, Ricardo, AA153
Verdam, Jacob. *Middelnederlandsch handwoordenboek*, AC294
———— *Middelnederlandsch woordenboek*, AC295
Verdenius, W. J. *A concise bibliography of ancient Greek literature*, BE1030
———— *Concise bibliography of Greek language and literature*, BE1030
Verdonik, Frederick. *Inventory of longitudinal research on childhood and adolescence*, CA60
Vereinigung Schweizerischer Bibliotheke. *Verzeichnis ausländischer Zeitschriften und Serien in schweizerischen Bibliotheken*, AD242
Veress, Endre. *Bibliografia româna-ungara*, AA782
Verfasser-register zu den jahrgägen 1897/98–1992/23, AG43
Verfasser- und Stichwortregister zu Deutsche Bibliographie, AA649, AA839
Vergason, Glenn A. *Dictionary of special education and rehabilitation*, CB199
Verger, Fernand. *Dictionnaire de la géographie*, CL45
Vergleichendes Wörterbuch der gotischen Sprache, Feist, Sigmund,, AC440
Vergleichendes Wörterbuch der indogermanischen Sprachen, Pokorny, Julius, AC515
———— Walde, Alois, AC515
Verhaar, H. L. *Biographical dictionary of dissidents in the Soviet Union, 1956–1975*, AH303
Verkova, P. N. *Bibliografiĩa v pomoshch' nauchnoĭ rabote*, AA65
Verma, Rajiva. *Indian literature in English, 1827–1979*, BE1542, BE1567
Vermeule, Cornelius Clarkson. *A bibliography of applied numismatics in the fields of Greek and Roman archaeology and the fine arts*, BG176
Vermomde en naamlooze schrijvers, Doorninck, Jan Izaak van, AA178
Vermomde Nederlandsche en Vlaamsche schrijvers, Kempenaer, A. de, AA178
Vermont. [Laws, etc.]. *Vermont statutes annotated*, CK179
Vermont statutes annotated, Vermont. [Laws, etc.], CK179
Vernacular architecture *see* **Folk architecture**
Vernacular architecture in America, Cuthbert, John A., BF213
Vernadsky, George. *Dictionary of Russian historical terms from the eleventh century to 1917*, DC584
Vernet, André. *Histoire des bibliothèques françaises*, AK107
Vernoff, Edward. *The international dictionary of 20th-century biography*, AH49
Vernon Law Book Company. *Code of Alabama, 1975*, CK179
Vernon's annotated Missouri statutes, Missouri. [Laws, etc.], CK179
Vernon's annotated Texas statutes and codes, Texas. [Laws, etc.], CK179
Veröffentlichungsverzeichnis, Germany (West). Statistisches Bundesamt, CG223
Versailles and after, Killen, Linda, DB127
Verschueren, Jef. *A comprehensive bibliography of pragmatics*, BD65
Verschueren, Karel. *Handbook of environmental data on organic chemicals*, EK83
Verseform, Brogan, Terry V. F., BE311
Versification, BE330
 bibliography, BE311

dictionaries, BE326
see also **Poetics**
Versins, Pierre. *Encyclopédie de l'utopie, des voyages extraordinaires, et de la science fiction,* BE308
Verstappen, Berth. *Ethnic conflict and human rights in Sri Lanka,* DE260
Vertebrates (fossil), EF227, EF233, EF237
bibliography, EF228, EF230
Vertical file index, AA439
Vertical file service catalog, AA439
Vervaeck, Solange. *Bibliographie de l'histoire de Belgique,* DC99
——— *Instruments biographiques pour l'histoire contemporaine de la Belgique,* AH178
Verwijs, Eelco. *Middelnederlandsch woordenboek,* AC295
Verzeichnis ausgewählter wissenschaftlicher Zeitschriften des Auslandes, Deutsche Forschungsgemeinschaft, AD5
Verzeichnis ausländischer Zeitschriften und Serien in schweizerischen Bibliotheken, Vereinigung Schweizerischer Bibliothekare, AD242
Verzeichnis der an der Universität Wien approbierten Dissertationen, Alker, H., AG23
——— Alker, Lisl, AG23
Verzeichnis der bildenden Künstler von 1880 bis heute, BF139
Verzeichnis der Fest- und Denkschriften von Unternehmungen und Organisationen der Wirtschaft im Hamburgisches Welt-Wirtschafts-Archiv, Hamburgisches Welt-Wirtschafts-Archiv, CH392
Verzeichnis der im deutschen Sprachbereich erschienenen Drucke des XVI. Jahrhunderts, AA640
Verzeichnis der im Jahre … erschienen Musikalien, BJ16
Verzeichnis der laufenden schweizerischen Zeitschriften = Catalogue des périodiques suisses, revues, journaux, annuaires, almanachs, collections, etc, Schweizerische Landesbibliothek, AD163
Verzeichnis der Märchentypen, CF45
Verzeichnis der Musikzeitschriften des 19. Jahrhunderts, Fellinger, Imogen, BJ101, BJ114
Verzeichnis der Österreichischen Hochschulschriften, AA574
Verzeichnis der Österreichischen Neuerschienungen, AA574
Verzeichnis der schriftlichen Nachlässe im deutschen Archiven und Bibliotheken, DC248
Verzeichnis der Veröffentlichungen des Statistischen Bundesamtes, CG223
Verzeichnis der Zeitschriften in der Bibliothek der Römisch-Germanischen Kommission, Beck, Diemut, BE1008
Verzeichnis des Buchhandels anderer Länder, AA289
Verzeichnis deutschsprachiger musikwissenschaftlicher Dissertationen 1861–1960, Schaal, Richard, BJ165
Verzeichnis deutschsprachiger musikwissenschaftlicher Dissertationen 1961–1970, Schaal, Richard, BJ165
Verzeichnis lieferbarer Bücher, AA660
Verzeichnis über die seit dem Jahre 1872 an der Philosophischen Fakultät der Universität in Wien eingereichten und approbierten Dissertationen, Universität Wien. Philosophische Fakultät, AG23
Verzeichnis von unklaren Titelkürzungen deutscher und ausländischer Zeitschriften, Rust, Werner, AD24
Verzeichnis vor- und frühgeschichtlicher Bibliographien, Gerlach, Gudrun, DC6
Verzosa, Natividad P. *Bibliography of Philippine bibliographies, 1593–1961,* AA82
——— *Philippine retrospective national bibliography, 1523–1699,* AA926
Veselitskiĭ, V. V. *Slovari, izdannye v SSSR,* AC698
Vessie, Patricia Armstrong. *Zen Buddhism,* BC474
•*VETCD,* EJ18
Veterinarians, EJ118

biography, EJ40
Veterinary bulletin, EJ18, EJ19, EJ103, EJ105, EJ117
Veterinary encyclopedia, EJ109
Veterinary medicine, EH23
Veterinary medicine, EJ96
Veterinary pharmaceuticals & biologicals, EJ131
Veterinary reference service, EJ106, EJ107
Veterinary reviews, EJ105
Veterinary subject headings, Mack, Roy, EJ117
Veterinary update, EJ106, EJ107
Vetter, Betty M. *Professional women and minorities,* CH686
Vevers, H. Gwynne. *Nomenclator zoologicus,* EG244
Viajes relativos a Chile, Feliú Cruz, Guillermo, DB358
Vianu, Tudor. *Bibliografia literarii romîne, 1948–1960,* BE1376
Viard, Georges. *Lexique historique de la France d'ancien régime,* DC174
Viaux, Jacqueline. *Bibliographie du meuble (mobilier civil français),* BG118
Vibration, EK87, EK246
Vicaire, Georges. *Bibliographie gastronomique,* EJ207
——— *Manuel de l'amateur de livres du XIXe siècle, 1801–1893,* AA632
Vice presidents, CJ189
Victoria, Ricard. *Neuva epanortosis al Diccvionario de anónimos y seudónimos de J.T. Medina,* AA153
Victoria, Ricardo. *Errores y omisiones del Diccionario de anónimos y seudónimos hispaoanoamericanos de José Toribio de Medina,* AA153
——— *Verdades que levantan roncha,* AA153
Victoria history of the counties of England, DC352
Victoria University (Toronto, Ont.). Centre for Reformation and Renaissance Studies. *International directory of Renaissance and Reformation associations and institutes,* DA153
Victorian bibliography, BE753, BE756
Victorian Britain, DC337
——— Mitchell, Sally, BE758
Victorian England, 1837–1901, Altholz, Josef Lewis, DC303, DC325
Victorian fiction, BE668, BE689
——— Ford, George H., BE686, BE984
——— Stevenson, Lionel, BE668, BE686, BE703, BE755
Victorian music publishers, Parkinson, John A., BJ184
Victorian novel, Mazzeno, Laurence W., BE668
Victorian novels in serial, Vann, J. Don, BE690
Victorian periodicals, AD113
Victorian periodicals review, AD110
Victorian plays, Mullin, Donald C., BH103
Victorian poetry, BE755
Victorian poets, Faverty, Frederic Everett, BE686, BE703, BE706, BE755, BE984
Victorian prose, De Laura, David J., BE984
——— DeLaura, David J., BE686, BE703, BE755
Victorian science and religion, Eisen, Sydney, BC215
Victorian serials, AD222
Victorian studies, BE752, BE753, BE756
Victorians : historical figures born between 1800 and 1860, Kilmurray, Elaine, BF66
Vidal, Dominique. *An A to Z of the Middle East,* DE55
Vidal-Naquet, Pierre. *The Harper atlas of world history,* DA54
Vidal Sassoon International Center for the Study of Antisemitism (Universiṭah ha-'Ivrit bi-Yerushalayim). *Antisemitism,* BC508
Video
catalogs, AA384
guides, BH202
indexes, AA380, CB31
Video (by subject)
architecture, BF247
Video movie guide, Martin, Mick, BH202
——— Porter, Marsha, BH202

The video source book, AA384
VideoHound's golden movie retriever, BH202
Vidyarthi, Lalita Prasad. *Research methodology in social science in India,* CA59
Vielhaber, Christian. *Bibliographie zur Bevölkerungsforschung in Österreich, 1945–1978,* CG193
Vielliard, Françoise. *Manuel bibliographique de la littérature française du Moyen Âge,* BE1198
Vienna Institute for Comparative Economic Studies. *COMECON data,* CH182
Vienticuatrod diarios, Madrid, 1830–1900, AE126
Vierck, Elizabeth. *Fact book on aging,* CC106
Viereck, Leslie A. *Alaska trees and common shrubs,* EJ191
Viereck, Wolfgang. *A bibliography of writings on varieties of English, 1965–1983,* BD108
Vierordt, Hermann. *Biographisches Lexikon der hervorragenden Ärzte aller Zeiten und Völker,* EH222
Vietnam
bibliography, AA940, DE272, DE276
biography, AH370
encyclopedias, DE273
guides, DE271
library resources, DE272
registers, CJ325
sourcebooks, DE277
Vietnam (by subject)
history
bibliography, BE417, DE275, DE278
encyclopedias, DE279
politics and government, CJ445
Vietnam, DE277
——— Cotter, Michael, DE271
——— Marr, David G., DE274
Vietnam conflict, Burns, Richard Dean, DE95
——— Leitenberg, Milton, DE95
Vietnam literature, Newman, John, BE417, DE278
Vietnam War
bibliography, BE417, DE95, DE100, DE275, DE276, DE278
dictionaries, AC121
encyclopedias, DE279
sourcebooks, DE277
Vietnam War bibliography, Sugnet, Christopher L., DE276
Vietnam War in literature, Jason, Philip K., BE417, DE278
Vietnamese communism, Phan Thiên Châu, CJ445
Vietnamese-English student dictionary, Nguyên, Dình-Hòa, AC804
Vietnamese language
bibliography, BD231, BE1601
dictionaries
bilingual
English-Vietnamese, AC803
Vietnamese-English, AC804
Vietnamese literature, BD231, BE1601
bibliography, BE417, DE278
Viewfinders : black women photographers, Moutoussamy-Ashe, Jeanne, BF357
Vigfússon, Gudbranur. *An Icelandic-English dictionary,* AC503
Vigor, Peter Hast. *Books on communism and the communist countries,* CJ514
Vigouroux, Fulcran Grégoire. *Dictionnaire de la Bible,* BC152
The Viking opera guide, BJ244
Vikor, Desider L. *Encyclopedia of public affairs information sources,* CA1
Viles, Heather A. *The student's companion to geography,* CL3
Vilhauer, Jerry. *Introduction to micrographics,* AK251
Vilks, A. *Enciklopēdiskā vārdnica,* DC435
Villacorta Calderon, José Antonio. *Bibliografía guatemalteca,* AA485
Village records, West, John, DC353
Villalón Galdames, Alberto. *Bibliografía jurídica de América Latina, 1810–1965,* CK199
Villasana, Angel Raúl. *Ensayo de un repertorio bibliográfico venezolano,* AA551

—— *Nuevo repertorio bibliográfico venezolano*, AA551

Villeneuve, Frédéric. *Essai de bibliographie canadienne*, DB182

Viller, Marcel. *Dictionnaire de spiritualité*, BC54

Villiers, Hugues. *Guide de recherches sur le Vietnam*, DE272

Vinayā texts, BC92

Viñaza, Cipriano Muñoz y Manzano. *Biblioteca histórica de la filología castellana*, BD170

Vinberg, N. A. *Sovetskaia arkheologicheskaia literatura*, DA71

Vince, Ronald W. *A companion to the medieval theatre*, BE222

Vincent, Benjamin. *Dictionary of dates and universal information relating to all ages and nations*, DA33

Vincent, David. *The autobiography of the working class*, CH679

Vincent, Jack. *Aves*, EG278

—— *Endangered birds of the world*, EG278

Vindel, Francisco. *Manual gráfico-descriptivo del bibliófilo hispano-americano (1475–1850)*, AA820

Vine Hall, Nick. *Tracing your family history in Australia*, AJ144

Viney, Wayne. *History of psychology*, CD57

Vingt ans de recherche historique en Belgique, 1969–1988, DC102

Vinken, P. J. *Handbook of clinical neurology*, EH183

Vinogradov, V. A. *Bibliographia studiorum uralicorum, 1917–1987*, DC602

Vinogradov, V. V. *Bibliograficheskiĭ ukazatel' literatury po russkomu iazykoznaniiu s 1825 po 1880 god*, BD185

Vinokur, G. O. *Tolkovyi slovar' russkogo iazyka*, AC674

Vinson, James. *American writers since 1900*, BE449

—— *American writers to 1900*, BE449

—— *Contemporary dramatists*, BE223

—— *International dictionary of films and filmmakers*, BH250

—— *St. James guide to English literature*, BE626

Vinterverg, Hermann. *Dansk-engelsk Ordbog*, AC287

Vinton, John. *Dictionary of contemporary music*, BJ145

—— *Dictionary of twentieth-centry music*, BJ145

Viographiko lexiko prosopikoteton, AH246

Viola, Lynne. *A researcher's guide to sources on Soviet social history in the 1930s*, DC592

Violence, CC33, CC357, CJ104

Violence against women, Wilson, Carolyn F., CC517

Violence in the family, Kemmer, Elizabeth Jane, CC214

Viollet-le-Duc, Eugène Emmanuel. *Dictionnaire raisonné de l'architecture françcaise du XIe au XVIe siècle*, BF237

—— *Dictionnaire raisonné du mobilier français de l'époque carlovingienne à la Renaissance*, BG124

—— *Foundations of architecture*, BF237

Virchow, Rudolf Ludwig Karl. *A commentary on the medical writings of Rudolf Virchow*, EH207

Virchow-Bibliographie, 1843–1901, Schwalbe, J., EH207

Virendra Kumar. *Dictionary of pseudonmys [sic] in Indian literature*, AA192

Virgin Islands
  bibliography, DB459

Virgin Islands, Moll, Verna P., DB459

Virgin Islands code, annotated, Virgin Islands of the United States. [Laws, etc.], CK179

Virgin Islands of the United States. [Laws, etc.]. *Virgin Islands code, annotated*, CK179

Virginia. [Laws, etc.]. *Code of Virginia, 1950*, CK179

Virology, EG89, EG344, EG345, EG346, EG347

Virology, Hull, Roger, EG345

—— Nicholas, Robin, EG346

Virology and AIDS abstracts, EG14

The viruses, Fraenkel-Conrat, Heinz, EG344

Vischer, Lukas. *Documentary history of the faith and order movement 1927–1963*, BC282

Visher, Stephen Sargent. *Climatic atlas of the United States*, EF170

The Visigoths in Gaul and Spain, A.D. 418–711, Ferreiro, Alberto, DC4

Vision and vision disorders, EH90

Visser, A. D. *Elsevier's dictionary of soil mechanics in four languages*, EJ26

Visser, W. A. *Geological nomenclature*, EF80

Visual arts, Fleming, John, BF132

—— Honour, Hugh, BF132

Visual arts reference and research guide, Sacca, Elizabeth J., BF29

—— Singer, Loren R., BF29

Visual dictionary of art, Hill, Ann, BF78

Visual index of artists' signatures and monograms, Jackson, Radway, BF158

Visual Resources Association. *Slide buyers' guide*, BF195

Vital and health statistics series, Walsh, Jim, CG100, EH406

Vital notes on medical periodicals, EH39

Vital speeches of the day, BE367

Vital statistics, CG54
  bibliography, EH235

Vital statistics (by country or region)
  United States, CG100, EH406
    directories, AJ57, CK157

Vital statistics, CG209, CG400

Vital statistics, 1967–1980, Sri Lanka, CG427

Vital statistics of India, India. Office of the Registrar, CG388

Vital statistics of the United States, CG88

Vital statistics on American politics, Stanley, Harold W., CJ163

Vital statistics on Congress, CJ229

Vital statistics report, Bahamas. Department of Statistics, CG165

—— Philippines. National Statistics Office, CG420

Vitale, Philip H. *Bibliography, historical and bibliothecal*, AA13

Vitamins, EH309

Vitas, Robert A. *U.S. national security policy and strategy*, CJ98

Vitek, John D. *This remarkable continent*, DB76

Vitorović, Nada. *Veliki anglešco-slovenski slovar*, AC721

Vitošević, Dragiša. *Srpska književna periodika 1768–1941*, BE1500

Vitullo-Martin, Julia. *The executive's book of quotations*, CH74

Viudas Camarasa, Antonio. *Dialectología hispánica y geografía lingüística en los estudios locales (1920–1984)*, BD173

Vivian, Kim. *Concise history of German literature to 1900*, BE1259

Viviano, Benedict. *Illustrated dictionary & concordance of the Bible*, BC142

Vivien de Saint Martin, Louis. *Nouveau dictionnaire de géographie universelle*, CL96

Vivliographikē Hetaireia Kyprou. *Kypriakē vivliographia*, AA590

Vivliographikē Hetaireia tēs Hellados. *Hellēnikē vivliographia*, AA708

Vivó, Paquita. *The Puerto Ricans*, CC450

Vjetari statistikor i Shqipërisë, CG192

Vlaamsche bibliographie, AA581

—— Snellaert, F. A., AA581

Vlaamsche pseudoniemen, Montagne, Victor Alexander de la, AA163

De Vlaamse schrijvers in het Engels vertaald, 1481–1949, Arents, Prosper, BE1064

VLB, AA660

The VNR concise encyclopedia of mathematics, EB69

VNR index of chemical and physical data, James, A. M., ED43

Vocabolario degli Accademici della Crusca, Accademia della Crusca (Florence), AC523

Vocabolario della lingua italiana, AC527

—— Accademia d'Italia, AC523

Vocabolario etimologico della lingua italiana, Pianigiani, Ottorino, AC539

Vocabolario illustrato della lingua italiana, Devoto, Giacomo, AC525

—— Oli, Gian Carlo, AC525

Vocabolario vasco, Griera y Gaja, Antonio, AC228

Vocabula amatoria, Farmer, John Stephen, AC122

Vocabulaire-atlas héraldique en six langues, Stalins, Gaston Ferdinand Laurent, AJ165

Vocabulaire d'astronomie, EC42

Vocabulaire de technologie éducative et de formation, Brisebois, Madeleine, CB172

Vocabulaire de théologie biblique, BC144

Vocabulaire international des termes d'urbanisme et d'architecture, BF278

Vocabulaire technique et critique de la philosophie, Lalande, André, BB41

Vocabulário de intercâmbio comercial, Netto, Modestino Martins, CH128

Vocabularium bibliothecarii, Thompson, Anthony, AK49

Vocabularium bibliothecarii : supplementum hungaricum, Zoltán, Pipics, AK49

Vocabularium botanicum, Steinmetz, E. F., EG144

Vocabulary of animal husbandry terms, EJ114

Vocabulary of communism, De Koster, Lester, CJ522

Vocabulary of educational technology and training, CB172

The vocabulary of organic chemistry, University of Cincinnati. Dept. of Chemistry. Organic Division, EE146

Vocabulary of technical terms, Centre International d'Étude des Textiles Anciens, BG154

The vocabulary of the church, White, Richard Clark, BC245

Vocabulary of the Greek Testament, Moulton, James Hope, AC458

Vocal music, BJ276

Vocational & technical audiovisuals, CB28

Vocational careers sourcebook, CB208, CB214, CH707

Vocational education, CB297, CB368, CH697
  directories, AL6, CB295, CB296, CB385

Vocational guidance, CB209, CB211, CH701, CH705
  bibliography, CB208, CH707
  databases, CB210, CB213
  directories, CH698
  handbooks, CB214, CD129, CH702

Vocelli, Virginia S. *The basic business library*, CH8

Voclno, Michael C. *Labor and industrial relations journals and serials*, CH659

Voegelin, Charles. *Classification and index of the world's languages*, BD16

Voegelin, Florence. *Classification and index of the world's languages*, BD16

Voenna istoriia na Bŭlgariia, 681–1945, DC116

Voennyi ėnotsiklopedicheskiui slovar', CJ659

Voet, Leon. *De chronologie van de middeleeuwen en de moderne tijden in de Nederlanden*, DC460

Vogelsang, Thilo. *Bibliographie zur Zeitgeschichte, 1953–1989*, DA169

Vogt, Joseph. *Bibliographie zur antiken Sklaverei*, DA68

Vogt, W. Paul. *Dictionary of statistics and methodology*, CG33

Vohra-Sahu, Indu. *Pacific/Asian American research*, CC403

Voigt, Wolfgang. *Sigelverzeichnis für die Bibliotheken der Bundesrepublik Deutschland*, AD235

Voit, Petr. *Příspěvky ke knihopisu*, AA596

Volcanoes of the world, EF265

Volcanology, EF264, EF265
  bibliography, EF261

Völklein, Sonja. *The musical*, BJ268

Volkoff, Marie Anne. *L'émigration russe en Europe*, AD218

Volkskundliche Bibliographie, CF42

Voll, John Obert. *The contemporary Islamic revival*, BC496

—— *Sudan*, DD48

Vollmar, Edward R. *The Catholic church in America*, BC393

Vollmer, Hans. *Allgemeines Lexikon der bildenden Künstler*, BF148
—— *Allgemeines Lexikon der bildenden Künstler des XX. Jahrhunderts*, BF135, BF148, BF149

Vollnhals, Otto. *A multilingual dictionary of artificial intelligence*, EK195

Vollst andiges Bücher-Lexikon, Kayser, Christian Gottlob, AA646

Vollständiges Bücher-Lexikon, Kayser, Christian Gottlob, AA655

Vollständiges Bücher-Lexikon, 1750–1910, Kayser, Christian Gottlob, AA645

Vollständiges Wörterbuch zu den Liedern der Edda, Gering, Hugo, BE1286

Volmuller, H. W. J. *Nijhoffs geschiedenislexicon Nederland en België*, DC459

Volnaía russkaía pechat', Gosudarstvennaía publichnaía biblioteka imeni M.E. Saltykova-Shchedrina. Gazetnyĭ otdel', AE69

Volostnova, M. B. *Dictionary of Russian geographical names*, CL154
—— *Slovar' russkoĭ transkriptsii geograficheskikh nazvaniĭ*, CL154

Volunteer workers, CC63, CC98

Volunteerism, AL123, CC35

Volunteerism and older adults, Kouri, Mary K., CC98

Volz, Ingrid. *Antifaschistischer Widerstand und Klassenkampf*, DC233

Von CA bis CAS ONLINE, EE6

Von Egidy, Heidi. *Namibia handbook and political who's who*, DD189

von Krücken, Oskar. *Das geistige Ungarn*, AH248

Von Ostermann, Georg Frederick. *Manual of foreign languages for the use of librarians, bibliographers, research workers, editors, translators, and printers*, AK46, AK50, BD11, BD17

Von Salamis bis Okinawa, Pemsel, Helmut, CJ600

von Scholz, Wilhelm. *Die grossen Deutschen*, AH208

Von wem ist das Gedicht?, Dühmert, Anneliese, BE1270

Vonderhaar, Mark. *State constitutional conventions, commissions & amendments, 1959–1978*, CK174

Voorhoeve, J. *Encyclopedie van Suriname*, DB391

Voort van der Kleij, J. J. van der. *Middelnederlandsch handwoordenboek*, AC294

Vorderwinkler, William. *Encyclopedia of tropical fishes*, EG284

Vorgrimler, Herbert. *Dictionary of theology*, BC408

Vorlat, Emma. *Analytical bibliography, 1961–1970*, BD92

Vorster, W. S. *South African theological bibliography*, BC49

Vorzeit und Karolinger, Levison, Wilhelm, DC228
—— Löe, Heinz, DC228

Vosburgh, Marion E. *A bibliography of librarianship*, AK11

Voskoboinik, David I. *Anglo-russkiĭ ĭadernyĭ slovar'*, ED28
—— *Russko-angliiskii iadernyi slovar'*, ED28

Voss, Fridtjof. *Norsk sitatleksikon*, BE146

Vosylius, Jonas. *Tarybinis lietuviu literaturos mokslas ir kritika apie literaturini palikima, 1959–1970*, BE1321

Vox diccionario manual de sinónimos y antónimos, AC748

Vox Graeca, Allen, William Sidney, AC452

Vox latina, Allen, William Sidney, AC452, AC594

Vox: new college Spanish and English dictionary, AC741

Voyages and travels *see* **Travellers' accounts**

Voyages and travels in Greece, the Near East and adjacent regions made previous to the year 1801, Weber, Shirley Howard, DE47, DE48

Voyages and travels in the Near East made during the XIX century, Weber, Shirley Howard, DE47, DE48

Voyageurs francophones en Amérique hispanique au cours du XIXᵉ siècles, Kirchheimer, Jean-Georges, DB263, DB409

Vrana, Stan A. *Interviews and conversations with 20th-century authors writing in English*, BE450

Vries, Ad de. *Dictionary of symbols and imagery*, BF174

Vries, Jan de. *Altnordisches etymologisches Wörterbuch*, AC511

Het vrije boek in onvrije tijd, Jong, Dirk de, BE1329

Vrije Universiteit te Amsterdam. Instituut voor Godsdienstwetenschap. *Science of religion*, BC48

Vronskaya, Jeanne. *A biographical dictionary of the former Soviet Union*, AH179
—— *Biographical dictionary of the Soviet Union, 1917–1988*, AH163, AH179

Vsesoíuznaía knizhnaía palata. *Letopis' periodicheskikh i prodolzhaíushchikhsía izdaniĭ. Biulleteni*, AE74
—— *Literaturno-khudozhestvennye al'manakhi i sborniki*, BE1406
—— *Periodicheskaía pechat' SSSR 1917–1949*, AD148

Vsesoíuznoe obshchestvo politicheskikh kator-zhan i ssyl'no-poselentsev. Deíateli revolíutsionnogo dvizheniía v Rossii, AH283

Vsesoíuznyĭ Institut Nauchnoĭ i Tekhnicheskoĭ informatsii (Russia). Solubilities of inorganic and organic compounds, EE91

Vsesoíznaía knizhnaía palata. *Letopis' gazetnykh stateĭ*, AE103

Vseviov, L. M. *Sovetskaía arkheologicheskaía literatura*, DA71

Vŭzvŭzova Karateodorova, Kirila. *Obzor na arkhivnite fondove, kolektsii i edinichni postŭpleniía, sŭkhraíavani v Bŭlgarski istoricheski arkhiv*, DC117

Vvedenskiĭ, B. A. *Malaía sovetskaía entsiklopediía*, AB88

Vyas, Anju. *Women's studies in India*, CC618

Vyhnanek, Louis Andrew. *Reference sources in history*, DA2

Wa-Ei Ei-Wa kagaku kōgaku yōgo jiten, EA120

Waal, H. van de. *Iconclass*, BF175

Wabeke, Bertus H. *A guide to Dutch bibliographies*, AA56

WAC stats, CC584

Wace, Henry. *Dictionary of Christian biography*, BC249
—— *Dictionary of Christian biography and literature to the end of the sixth century A.D*, BC249

Wachter, Leo de. *Repertorium van de Vlaamse gouwen en gemeenten*, DC103

Waddell, D. A. G. *Venezuela*, DB401

Wadsworth, Anne Johnston. *Political campaign communication*, CJ103

Waetzoldt, Stephan. *Bibliographie zur Architektur im 19 Jahrhundert*, BF211

Wagenaar, P. G. J. M. *De Rijksarchieven in Nederland*, DC458

Wages, Jack D. *Southern literary culture, 1969–1975*, BE569

Waggoner, Diana. *Hills of faraway*, BE304

Waggoner, Hyatt H. *American poets, from the Puritans to the present*, BE504

Wagman, Donald D. *The NBS tables of chemical thermodynamic properties*, EE94

Wagner, Anton. *The Brock bibliography of published Canadian plays in English, 1766–1978*, BE820

Wagner, Francis S. *Hungarian Revolution in perspective*, DC380

Wagner, Frank D. *United States reports*, CK190

Wagner, Günter. *Exegetical bibliography of the New Testament*, BC114, BC118

Wagner, Henry R. *The plains & the Rockies*, DB168

Wagner, Jane. *Bernstein's reverse dictionary*, AC136

Wagner, Jean. *Black poets of the United States*, BE533
—— *Poèts nègres des États-Unis*, BE533

Wagner, M. L. *Dizionario etimologico sardo*, AC538

Wagner-Neumann, Gretel. *Katalog der Lipperheideschen Kostümbibliothek*, BG93

Wagonheim, Sylvia Stoler. *Annals of English drama, 975–1700*, BE660

Wahby, Taufiq. *A Kurdish-English dictionary*, AC568

Wahlhandbuch für die Bundesrepublik Deutschland, CJ335

Wahlstatistik in Deutschland, CJ336

Wahrig, Gerhard. *Brockhaus Wahrig*, AC400
—— *Deutsches Wörterbuch*, AC411
—— *Grosse deutsche Wörterbuch*, AC411

Wai, Lokky. *Annotated bibliography of Canadian demography*, CG116

Waintman, Susan. *Ontario royal commissions and commissions of inquiry, 1867–1978*, AF155

Wainwright, M. D. *Government archives in South Asia*, DE84
—— *Guide to Western manuscripts and documents in the British Isles relating to South and South East Asia*, DE12, DE13

Wainwright, M. Doreen. *Guide to manuscripts and documents in the British Isles relating to Africa*, DC345, DD38, DD39
—— *A guide to manuscripts and documents in the British Isles relating to the Far East*, DE105
—— *Guide to manuscripts and documents in the British Isles relating to the Middle East and North Africa*, DD38, DE50

Wainwright, William J. *Philosophy of religion*, BB23, BC21

Waiser, W. A. *Documenting Canada*, AF156, DB206

Waite, Ellen J. *Women in LC's terms*, CC542

Waite, P. B. *Pre-confederation*, DB205

Waite, Ronald A. *The relations of literature and science*, BE30

Waithe, Mary Ellen. *A history of women philosophers*, BB47

Waitz, Georg. *Dahlmann-Waitz Quellenkunde der deutschen Geschichte*, DC215, DC226

Wajid, Mohammad. *Oriental dictionaries*, AC194

Wakefield, Gordon S. *The Westminster dictionary of Christian spirituality*, BC242

Wakelyn, Jon L. *American legislative leaders, 1850–1910*, CJ289
—— *Biographical dictionary of the Confederacy*, AH71

Wakeman, Geoffrey. *Printmaking & picture printing*, BF359

Wakeman, John. *World authors, 1950–1970*, BE205
—— *World authors, 1970–1975*, BE205
—— *World film directors*, BH290

Walberg, Herbert J. *Handbook of special education*, CB204
—— *International encyclopedia of education*, CB70

Walch, Margaret. *The color compendium*, BF125, ED59

Walch, Timothy. *American educational history*, CB33

Walde, Alois. *Lateinisches etymologisches Wörterbuch*, AC584
—— *Vergleichendes Wörterbuch der indogermanischen Sprachen*, AC515

Walden, Graham R. *Public opinion polls and survey research*, CJ495

Waldman, Carl. *Atlas of the North American Indian*, CC441
—— *Who was who in Native American history*, CC437

Waldman, Harry. *Dictionary of robotics*, EK235
—— *The dictionary of SDI*, CJ620

Waldman, Nahum M. *The recent study of Hebrew*, BD207

Waldon, Freda Farrell. *Bibliography of Canadiana published in Great Britain, 1519–1763*, DB188

Waldron, Zoe. *National guide to funding for libraries and information services*, AK64

Wales, Katie. *A dictionary of stylistics*, BE375

Wales
atlases, CL137
bibliography, AA698, AA699, AA700, DC369, DC370

current, AA698
biography, AH245
gazetteers, CL137, CL206
periodicals
indexes, AD290
statistics, CG233
Wales (by subject)
education, CB44
history, AJ128, DC368
place-names, CL136
Wales, Huws, Gwilym, DC369
Walewski, Władysław. *Słownik geograficzny Królestwa polskiego i innych krajów słowiańskich,* CL148
Walford, A. J. *Walford's guide to reference material,* EA10
Walford, Albert John. *A guide to foreign language courses and dictionaries,* AC195
—— *Walford's guide to current British periodicals in the humanities and social sciences,* AD117
—— *Walford's guide to reference material,* AA363
Walford's guide to current British periodicals in the humanities and social sciences, AD117
Walford's guide to reference material, AA363, EA10
Walker, Alvin. *Thesaurus of psychological index terms,* CD34
Walker, Audrey A. *Official publications of British East Africa,* AF223, DD108
—— *Official publications of Sierra Leone and Gambia,* AF225
—— *The Rhodesias and Nyasaland,* AF226, DD176
Walker, Barbara G. *The woman's dictionary of symbols and sacred objects,* CF15
—— *The woman's encyclopedia of myths and secrets,* CF9
Walker, Barbara K. *Twentieth-century short story explication,* BE264
Walker, Betty K. *Guide to the manuscript collections of the Presbyterian Church, U.S.,* BC376
Walker, Brian Mercer. *Parliamentary election results in Ireland, 1801–1922,* CJ379
Walker, C. Eugene. *The handbook of clinical psychology,* CD104
Walker, Charls E. *The bankers' handbook,* CH282
Walker, David. *Biographical directory of American territorial governors,* CJ287
Walker, David M. *The Oxford companion to law,* CK32
Walker, Egbert H. *A bibliography of eastern Asiatic botany,* EG106
Walker, Ernest P. *Walker's mammals of the world,* EG303
Walker, Gay. *The preservation challenge,* AK242
Walker, George Benjamin. *Hindu world,* BC485
Walker, Gregory. *Library resources in Britain for the study of Eastern Europe and the former U.S.S.R,* DC51
—— *Official publications of the Soviet Union and Eastern Europe, 1945–1980,* AF165
—— *Resources for Soviet, East European and Slavonic studies in British libraries,* DC51
Walker, John. *Halliwell's film guide,* BH196
—— *Halliwell's filmgoer's and video viewer's companion,* BH249
Walker, John Albert. *Glossary of art, architecture & design since 1945,* BF93
Walker, John M. *Language of biotechnology,* EK45, EK46
Walker, Mary. *Jane's defence glossary,* CJ587
Walker, Michael. *Lexicon of economic thought,* CH48
Walker, Peter M. B. *Cambridge air and space dictionary,* EK30
—— *Cambridge dictionary of science and technology,* EA88
—— *Chambers biology dictionary,* EG30
—— *Chambers earth sciences dictionary,* EF13
—— *Chambers science and technology dictionary,* EF13

Walker, Philip. *Dictionary of woodworking tools c. 1700–1970, and tools of allied trades,* BG128
Walker, Warren S. *Twentieth-century short story explication,* BE264, BE479
Walker, William O. *Harper's Bible pronunciation guide,* BC140
Walker's mammals of the world, Nowak, Ronald M., EG303
—— Walker, Ernest P., EG303
Walkowicz, Chris. *Atlas of dog breeds of the world,* EJ146
Wall, C. Edward. *Abbreviations,* AC46
—— *Periodical title abbreviations,* AD23
—— *Words and phrases index,* AC155
Wall, Celia Jo. *Newspaper libraries,* AE30
Wall, Edward. *Cumulative author index for Poole's index to periodical literature, 1802–1906,* AD282
Wall, John. *Directory of British photographic collections,* BF344
Wall, Richard. *Union list of film periodicals,* BH174
Wall Street journal. Index, AE115
Wall Street journal, CH45
Wall Street journal [index], AE104, AE112, CH35, CH45
The Wall Street review of books, CH13
Wall Street words, Scott, David Logan, CH227
Wallace, Charles Stewart. *Swaziland,* DD232
Wallace, David H. *The New-York Historical Society dictionary of artists in America, 1564–1860,* BF155
Wallace, Ian. *East Germany,* DC243
Wallace, Irving. *The people's almanac,* AB108
Wallace, Melanie. *Political violence in the United States, 1875–1974,* CJ104
Wallace, Raymond J. *History and theories of working-class movements,* CH631
Wallace, Steven P. *The senior movement,* CC102
Wallace, W. Stewart. *The Macmillan dictionary of Canadian biography,* AH94
Wallace-Hadrill, John Michael. *Frankish church,* BC278
Wallach, Jacques B. *Interpretation of diagnostic tests,* EH192
Wallach, Jeffrey J. *Medical legal dictionary,* EH267
Wallechinsky, David. *The complete book of the Olympics,* BK94
—— *The complete book of the Winter Olympics,* BK95
—— *The people's almanac,* AB108
Wallen, Denise. *Funding for anthropological research,* CE55
—— *Funding for museums, archives, and special collections,* BF104
Waller, A.R. *Cambridge history of English literature,* BE617
Waller, Robert. *Almanac of British politics,* CJ349, CJ361
—— *The atlas of British politics,* CJ349
Wallis, Helen. *Cartographical innovations,* CL262
Wallis, Peter John. *Biobibliography of British mathematics and its applications,* EB19
—— *Book subscription lists,* AA298
Wallis, R. V. *Biobibliography of British mathematics and its applications,* EB19
Walloon literature, BE1098
Walls, David. *The activist's almanac,* AL48
Walls, Howard Lamarr. *Motion pictures 1894–1912 identified from the records of the United States Copyright Office,* BH193
Walls, Jerry G. *The completely illustrated atlas of reptiles and amphibians for the terrarium,* EG252
Walmsley, Julian. *The new financial instruments,* CH322
Walne, Peter. *Dictionary of archival terminology,* AK183
—— *Guide to manuscript sources for the history of Latin America and the Caribbean in the British Isles,* DB274
—— *Guide to the manuscript sources for the history of Latin America and the Caribbean in the British Isles,* DB275
—— *Modern archives administration and records management,* AK187

Walraet, Marcel. *Bibliographie du Katanga,* DD15, DD245
—— *Sciences au Rwanda,* AA871
Walrond-Skinner, Sue. *A dictionary of psychotherapy,* EH386
Walsh, Clifford. *Jowitt's dictionary of English law,* CK38
Walsh, Frances. *A bibliography of nursing literature,* EH273
Walsh, Gretchen. *African language materials in the Boston University Libraries,* BD215
Walsh, James Edward. *A catalogue of the fifteenth-century printed books in the Harvard University Library,* AA224
Walsh, Jim. *Maps contained in the publications of the American bibliography, 1639–1819,* CL243
—— *Vital and health statistics series,* CG100, EH406
Walsh, Michael J. *Butler's lives of the saints,* BC263
—— *Religious bibliographies in serial literature,* BC50
—— *Vatican City State,* DC605
Walsh, Ruth M. *Job satisfaction and motivation,* CD125
Walsh, S. Padraig. *Anglo-American general encyclopedias,* AB15
—— *General world atlases in print, 1972–1973,* CL223
Walsh, Stephen. *The Viking opera guide,* BJ244
Walsh, W. Bruce. *Handbook of vocational psychology,* CD129
Walsh, William. *Commonwealth literature,* BE817
—— *Indian literature in English,* BE1569
Walter, Gérard. *Catalogue de l'histoire de la révolution française,* DC177
—— *Répertoire de l'histoire de la Révolution française,* DC176
Walter, William G. *Dictionary of microbiology,* EG39
Walter Breen's complete encyclopedia of U.S. and colonial coins, Breen, Walter H., BG193
Walters, LeRoy. *Bibliography of bioethics,* EH237
—— *Bioethics,* EH242
Walters, S. M. *The European garden flora,* EG169
Walther, Hermann. *Bibliographie der Musikbuchreihen 1886–1990,* BJ9, BJ45
Walton, E.K. *Dictionary of petrology,* EF259
Walton, John Nicholas. *The Oxford companion to medicine,* EH88
Walzel, Oskar. *Geschichte der deutschen Literatur,* BE1227
Walzer, Pierre-Olivier. *Lexikon der Schweizer Literaturen,* BE1490
Wamberg, Kjeld. *Veterinary encyclopedia,* EJ109
Wang, Alvin Yafu. *Author's guide to journals in the behavioral sciences,* CD14
Wang, Chi-chien. *Seals of Chinese painters and collectors of the Ming and Ch'ing periods,* BF162, BF313
Wang, En-kuang. *Chung-kuo tu shu kuan ming lu,* AK156
Wang, Margaret C. *Handbook of special education,* CB204
Wantrup, Jonathan. *Australian rare books, 1788–1900,* DF29
Want's federal-state court directory, CK156
War, CJ57, CJ573, CJ576
atlases, CJ600, DA50, DB77
bibliography, BC360, CE9, CE10, CJ563, CJ680
encyclopedias, CJ574, DA20, DA24, DA25
handbooks, CJ568
quotations, CJ591
statistics, CJ568, CJ598
The war against Japan, 1941–1945, Sbrega, John J., DA202
The war atlas, Kidron, Michael, CJ603
War crimes, CK80, DA203
War crimes, war criminals, and war crimes trials, Tutorow, Norman E., CK80, DA203
The War of 1812, Smith, Dwight La Vern, DB100
The War of the American Revolution, Blanco, Richard L., DB86

War of the Rebellion, United States. War Dept, DB106

War words, Greet, William Cabell, AC104

Warburg, Karl. *Illustrerad svensk litteraturhistoria*, BE1485

Warburton, Elizabeth Anne. *A bibliography on South American economic affairs*, CH179

Ward, A. C. *Longman companion to twentieth century literature*, BE764

Ward, A. W. *Cambridge history of English literature*, BE617

Ward, Barry. *Vernacular architecture in America*, BF213

Ward, Carlton. *Directory of historic American theatres*, BH110

Ward, Christopher. *Panamanian historical sources*, DB319

Ward, Dederick C. *Bibliography of theses in geology, 1964*, EF44

—— *Geologic reference sources*, EF20

Ward, Elizabeth. *Film noir*, BH224

Ward, Gary L. *Encyclopedia of African American religions*, BC56

Ward, Geoff. *Guide to romantic literature, 1780–1830*, BE611

Ward, Gerald W. R. *Decorative arts and household furnishings in America, 1650–1920*, BG117

Ward, H. L. D. *Catalogue of romances in the Department of Manuscripts in the British Museum*, BE335

Ward, Harold R. *Handbook of radar measurement*, EK145

Ward, Philip. *Diccionario Oxford de literatura española e hispanoamericana*, BE1452

—— *The Oxford companion to Spanish literature*, BE1452

Ward, Thomas Humphry. *Men of the reign*, AH230

Ward, William Smith. *British periodicals & newspapers, 1789–1832*, AD108

—— *Index and finding list of serials published in the British Isles, 1789–1832*, AD108

—— *Literary reviews in British periodicals, 1789–1797*, BE748

—— *Literary reviews in British periodicals, 1798–1820*, BE757

—— *Literary reviews in British periodicals, 1821–1826*, BE757

Wards, Ian. *New Zealand atlas*, CL365

Ward's business directory of U.S. private and public companies, CH373, CH422, CH373

Ward's directory of largest U.S. corporations, CH373

Wardwell, Walter I. *Chiropractic*, EH197

Ware, Dora. *An illustrated dictionary of ornament*, BG24

—— *Short dictionary of architecture*, BF244

Ware, Martin. *World medical periodicals*, EH40

Wares, Alan Campbell. *Bibliography of the Summer Institute of Linguistics*, BD9

—— *Bibliography of the Wycliffe Bible Translators*, BD9

Warfare and armed conflicts, Clodfelter, Micheal, CJ568

Warfare in primitive societies, Divale, William Tulio, CE9, CE10

Warfare in the classical world, Warry, John, CJ580

—— Warry, John Gibson, DA100

Warfield, Gerald. *The investor's guide to stock quotations and other financial listings*, CH323

—— *Writings on contemporary music notation*, BJ21

Warman's Americana & collectibles, BG49

Warman's antiques and their prices, BG49

Warman's country antiques & collectibles, Morykan, Dana G., BG49

—— Rinker, Harry L., BG49

Warmelo, N. J. van. *Anthropology of southern Africa in periodicals to 1950*, CE100

Warner, Carolyn. *The last word*, CC544

Warner, Ezra J. *Biographical register of the Confederate Congress*, DB121

—— *Generals in blue*, DB121

—— *Generals in gray*, DB121

Warner, Thomas E. *Periodical literature on American music, 1620–1920*, BJ46

Warnke, Frank J. *Princeton handbook of poetic terms*, BE329

Warp & weft, Burnham, Dorothy K., BG154

Warr, George C. W. *History of Roman literature*, BE1053

Warrack, John Hamilton. *The concise Oxford dictionary of opera*, BJ253

Warren, J. W. *The Facts on File dictionary of physics*, ED18

Warren, Mary Anne. *The nature of woman*, CC536

Warrior's words, Tsouras, Peter, CJ591

Warry, John. *Warfare in the classical world*, CJ580

Warry, John Gibson. *Warfare in the classical world*, DA100

The wars in Vietnam, Cambodia and Laos, 1945–1982, Burns, Richard Dean, DE95

Wars of the Roses, Hallam, Elizabeth M., DC310

Warships, CJ594, CJ649, DB60

Warsztat bibliograficzny historyka literatury polskiej (na tle dyscyplin pokrewnych), Starnawski, Jerzy, BE1360

Wartburg, Walther von. *Bibliographie des dictionnaires patois galloromans (1550–1967)*, AC390

—— *Dictionnaire étymologique de la langue française*, AC347

—— *Französisches etymologisches Wörterbuch*, AC346, AC350, AC352, AC387, AC538

Warwick, Ronald. *Commonwealth literature periodicals*, BE818

The Warwick guide to British labour periodicals, 1790–1970, Harrison, Royden John, CH655

Wasberg, Gunnar C. *Norsk militarhistorisk bibliografi*, DC464

Washburn, Edward W. *International critical tables of numerical data, physics, chemistry and technology*, EA156

Washington, Helen. *The big book of halls of fame in the United States and Canada*, BK32

Washington, Valora. *Black children and American institutions*, CC140

Washington (D.C.)
  directories, AL49
  library resources, DB273, DC556, DE49, DE85, DE101, DE103

Washington, AL49

Washington alert, AF64

Washington information directory, AL49

Washington International Arts Letter. *National directory of arts & education support by business corporations*, AL121, BA10

Washington monitor's Federal yellow book, CJ182

Washington post [index], AE104, AE112, AE116

Washington representatives, CJ130, CJ131, CJ144

Washington Researchers. *European markets*, CH375

—— *How to find information about companies*, CH331

—— *Researcher's guide to Washington experts*, CJ146

Washington (State). [Laws, etc.]. *West's revised code of Washington annotated*, CK179

Washington times [index], AE104

Wasmuth, Günther. *Wasmuths Lexikon der Baukunst*, BF239

Wasmuths Lexikon der Baukunst, BF239

Wass, Hannelore. *Death education*, CC179

Wasserman, Ellen A. *Oral history index*, DB33

Wasserman, Paul. *Awards, honors, and prizes*, AL161

—— *Catalog of museum publications & media*, BF48

—— *Commodity prices*, CH432

—— *Consultants and consulting organizations directory*, CH617

—— *Consumer sourcebook*, CH559

—— *Encyclopedia of business information sources*, CH329

—— *Encyclopedia of health information sources*, EH15

—— *Encyclopedia of public affairs information sources*, CA1

—— *Encyclopedia of senior citizens information sources*, CC96

—— *Statistics sources*, CG68

Wasserman, Philip D. *NeuralSource*, EK157

Wasserman, Steven R. *Encyclopedia of physical sciences and engineering information sources*, EA14

—— *The lively arts information directory*, BH14

—— *Moving and relocation sourcebook*, CL73

—— *Recreation and outdoor life directory*, BK108

Wasson, Tyler. *Nobel prize winners*, AH30, AL170

Wasznik, Jan Hendrik. *Reallexikon für Antike und Christentum*, BC248

Watanabe Hisako. *Japanese/English English/Japanese glossary of scientific and technical terms*, EA120

Watches *see* **Clocks and watches**

Watchmakers and clockmakers of the world, Baillie, Granville Hugh, BG88

Water
  analysis, EE62
  bibliography, EF126

Water and wastewater control engineering, EK92

Water and water pollution handbook, EK97

The water encyclopedia, Van der Leeden, Frits, EF140, EK96

Water Environment Federation. *Standard methods for the examination of water and wastewater*, EE62

Water pollution, EE62
  bibliography, EK91
  dictionaries, EK92
  handbooks, EF140, EK96, EK97
  research centers directories, EK94

Water publications of state agencies, Giefer, Gerald J., EK89

Water quality and treatment, EK98

Water resources
  bibliography, EF128, EF129, EK68, EK88, EK89, EK90, EK91, EK100
  databases, EF131
  dictionaries, EK92
  government publications, EK89
  handbooks, EF140, EK95, EK96, EK97, EK98
  research centers directories, EK93
  statistics, EK99

Water resources, Ralston, Valerie Hunter, EK90

•*Water resources abstracts*, EF129, EF131, EK68

Water Resources Center Archives (Calif.). *Dictionary catalog of the Water Resources Center Archives, University of California, Berkeley*, EK91

Water resources of the world, Van der Leeden, Frits, EK99

Water Resources Scientific Information Center. *Water resources abstracts*, EF131

Water sports *see* **Sailing and water sports**

Watergate, Rosenberg, Kenyon C., CJ108

—— Smith, Myron J., CJ110

The Watergate investigation index, Garza, Hedda, CJ113

Waterhouse, Ellis. *Dictionary of 16th and 17th century British painters*, BF323

Waterloo Computing in the Humanities (Group). *The Waterloo directory of Victorian periodicals, 1824–1900*, AD114

Waterloo directory of Irish newspapers and periodicals, 1800–1900, North, John S., AD114, AD124

Waterloo directory of Scottish newspapers and periodicals, 1800–1900, North, John S., AD114, AD119, AE62

The Waterloo directory of Victorian periodicals, 1824–1900, Wolff, Michael, AD114, AD124

Waterlow's solicitors' and barristers' diary, CK221

Waterlow's solicitors' and barristers' directory, CK221

Watermarks, AA255, AA256, AA257

Waters, Clara (Erskine) Clement. *Handbook of Christian symbols and stories of the saints as illustrated in art*, BF176

—— *Handbook of legendary and mythological art*, BF176

Waters, Grant M. *Dictionary of British artists, working 1900–1950*, BF316

Waters, Harold A. *Théâtre noir*, BE1518

Waters, S. A. *Cruden's complete concordance of the Old and New Testaments*, BC165

Waters, Willard O. *American imprints, 1648–1797, in the Huntington Library, supplementing Evans' American bibliography*, AA407

Waterson, Natalie. *Uzbek-English dictionary*, AC802

Waterston, Elizabeth. *The travellers, Canada to 1900*, DB189

Wathern, Peter. *Environmental impact assessment*, EK66

Watkins, Calvert. *The American heritage dictionary of Indo-European roots*, AC47

Watkins, Kathleen Pullan. *Day care*, CC154

—— *Infancy*, CC148, CD78

—— *Parent-child attachment*, CC155

Watkins, Mel. *Canada*, DB202

Watling, Ann Elizabeth. *A literature guide for identifying mushrooms*, EG192

Watling, Roy. *A literature guide for identifying mushrooms*, EG192

Watson, Andrew G. *Catalogue of dated and datable manuscripts, c.700–1600 in the Department of Manuscripts, the British Library*, AA203

Watson, Bruce W. *United States Air Force*, CJ619

—— *The United States Army*, CJ619

—— *United States intelligence*, CJ547

—— *United States Navy*, CJ619

Watson, Cynthia Ann. *U.S. national security policy groups*, CJ145

Watson, David G. *Molecular structures and dimensions*, EE139

Watson, G. Llewellyn. *Feminism and women's issues*, CC514

Watson, George. *Concise Cambridge bibliography of English literature, 600–1950*, BE603

—— *The new Cambridge bibliography of English literature*, BE585

—— *The shorter new Cambridge bibliography of English literature*, BE586

Watson, J. R. *Handbook to English romanticism*, BE759

Watson, Noelle. *Contemporary novelists*, BE252

—— *Twentieth-century science-fiction writers*, BE212

Watson, Robert Irving. *The great psychologists*, CD62

—— *The history of psychology and the behavioral sciences*, CD60

Watson, Susan M. *United States Air Force*, CJ619

—— *The United States Army*, CJ619

—— *United States intelligence*, CJ547

—— *United States Navy*, CJ619

Watson-Jones, Virginia. *Contemporary American women sculptors*, BF152, BF400

Watstein, Sarah. *AIDS and women*, EH29

—— *On account of sex*, AK14

Watt, Arthur Dwight. *Index of generic names of fossil plants, 1974–1978*, EF236

Watt, Bernice K. *Composition of foods*, EH314, EJ220

Watt, Robert. *Bibliotheca britannica*, AA664, BE581

Wattenbach, Wilhelm. *Deutschlands Geschichtsquellen im Mittelalter bis zur mitte des dreizehnten Jahrhunderts*, DC228

Watters, Carolyn. *Dictionary of information science and technology*, AK44

Watters, Reginald Eyre. *Checklist of Canadian literature and background materials, 1628–1960*, BE826

—— *On Canadian literature, 1806–1960*, BE826

Watts, Michael. *Thailand*, DE267

Watts, Thomas D. *Black alcohol abuse and alcoholism*, CC123

—— *Native American youth and alcohol*, CC114

Watts-Williams, J. *Cofrestri plwyf Cymru = Parish registers of Wales*, AJ130

Watznauer, Adolf. *Wörterbuch Geowissenschaften*, EF85

Wauchope, Robert. *Handbook of Middle American Indians*, CE89

Waugh, Charles. *Science fiction and fantasy series and sequels*, BE284

Wauters, Alphonse Jules. *Bibliographie du Congo, 1880–1895*, DD15, DD245

Wawa, Yosa H. *Bibliography on Sudan international relations*, DD228

—— *Southern Sudan*, DD228

Wawilor, S. I. *Enzyklopädie der Union der Sozialistischen Sowjetrepubliken*, AB84

Wawrzyszko, Aleksandra K. *A bibliographical guide to the study of Chinese language and linguistics*, BD218

Wax, Imy F. *The K & W guide to colleges for the learning disabled*, CB313

Waxman, Meyer. *A history of Jewish literature*, BE1577

Way, Peter O. *Detailed statistics on the urban and rural population of Indonesia, 1950 to 2010*, CG395, CG415

The way things work, Van Amerongen, C., EA82

The way to play, BK46

Wayne, Stephen J. *Studying the presidency*, CJ166

Wayne State University. *The Wayne State University collection of comedias sueltas*, BE1472

The Wayne State University collection of comedias sueltas, Wayne State University, BE1472

We shall be heard, Manning, Beverley, BE358, CC530

We the people, Allen, James Paul, CC358, DB74

—— Turner, Eugene J., DB74

Weale, William Henry James. *Bibliographia liturgica*, BC429

Weapons, CJ569, CJ575

Weapons, CJ581

—— Diagram Group, CJ569

Weapons systems, CJ570, CJ604

Wearing, J. P. *American and British theatrical biography*, BH129

—— *English drama and theatre, 1800–1900*, BE639

—— *The London stage, 1890–1899*, BH108

Weast, Robert C. *CRC handbook of chemistry and physics*, EE70

—— *CRC handbook of data on organic compounds*, EE149

—— *Handbook of data on organic compounds*, EE149

Weather *see* **Climatology**

The weather almanac, Bair, Frank E., EF156

Weather Bureau (U.S.). *Climatological data*, EF160

The weather handbook, EF166

Weaver, Jack W. *Immigrants from Great Britain and Ireland*, CC332, DC402

Weaver, John T. *Forty years of screen credits, 1929–1969*, BH214

—— *Twenty years of silents, 1908–1928*, BH214

Weaver, Sally M. *A Canadian Indian bibliography, 1960–1970*, CC472

Weaving, BG158

Weaving arts of the North American Indian, Dockstader, Frederick J., BG156

Webb, Alfred John. *Compendium of Irish biography*, AH255

Webb, Augustus Duncan. *New dictionary of statistics*, CG53

Webb, Barbara. *The sailing dictionary*, BK123

Webb, Edwin C. *Enzyme nomenclature 1984*, EG321

Webb, William H. *Sources of information in the social sciences*, CA4, CA7, CA8

Webber, Elizabeth. *Grand allusions*, BE81

Webber, Frederick Roth. *Church symbolism*, BF187

Webber, Jonathan. *Research in social anthropology, 1975–1980*, CE28

Webber, Rosemary. *World list of national newspapers*, AE14

Weber, David C. *Planning academic and research library buildings*, AK175

Weber, Harry B. *The modern encyclopedia of Russian and Soviet literature*, BE1415

Weber, Lynn. *Women of color and Southern women*, CC623

Weber, Marvin J. *CRC handbook of laser science and technology*, EC49, ED34

Weber, Nancy Smith. *The mushroom hunter's field guide*, EG191

Weber, R. David. *Energy information guide*, EK213, EK214

—— *Energy update*, EK214

—— *Financial aid for research and creative activities abroad*, CB366

—— *Financial aid for study and training abroad*, CB366

Weber, Shirley Howard. *Voyages and travels in Greece, the Near East and adjacent regions made previous to the year 1801*, DE47, DE48

—— *Voyages and travels in the Near East made during the XIX century*, DE47, DE48

Weber, Wolfgang. *Biographisches Lexikon zur Geschichtswissenschaft in Deutschland, Österreich und der Schweiz*, DC225

Weberman, Ben. *Dictionary of banking terms*, CH272

Webster, A. B. *Dictionary of farm animal behaviour*, EJ116

Webster, Duane. *Preservation planning program*, AK238

Webster, James K. *Toxic and hazardous materials*, EH419

Webster, John B. *A bibliography of Malawi*, DD176

—— *A bibliography on Bechuanaland*, DD132

—— *Bibliography on Kenya*, DD108, DD165, DD167

—— *Bibliography on Lesotho*, DD169

—— *Bibliography on Swaziland*, DD232

Webster, John G. *Encyclopedia of medical devices and instrumentation*, EI186

Webster, Linda. *Sexual assault and child sexual abuse*, CC36

Webster, Robert. *Gems, their sources, descriptions, and identification*, EF180

Webster's American biographies, McHenry, Robert, AH60

—— Van Doren, Charles, AH60

Webster's American military biographies, CJ648

—— McHenry, Robert, CJ641

Webster's biographical dictionary, AH38

Webster's collegiate thesaurus, AC142

Webster's compact dictionary of quotations, AB26

Webster's dictionary of English usage, AB26, AC87

Webster's dictionary of synonyms, AC147

Webster's geographical dictionary, CL97

Webster's intermediate dictionary, AC26

Webster's new biographical dictionary, AB26, AH38

Webster's new dictionary of synonyms, AC142, AC147

Webster's new geographical dictionary, CL97

Webster's new international dictionary of the English language, AC13

Webster's new World children's dictionary, AC27

Webster's new World dictionary, AC27

Webster's new World dictionary of American English, AC20, AC147

Webster's new World dictionary of mathematics, Karush, William, EB42

Webster's new World dictionary of media and communications, Weiner, Richard, CH488

Webster's new World dictionary of quotable definitions, BE122

Webster's new World dictionary of synonyms, Kent, Ruth Kimball, AC147

Webster's new World dictionary of the American language, AC20

Webster's new World encyclopedia, AB14

Webster's new World Hebrew dictionary, Baltsan, Hayim, AC474

Webster's new World investment and securities dictionary, Thomsett, Michael C., CH303

Webster's new World medical word finder, Willeford, George, EH107

Webster's ninth new collegiate dictionary, AC17

Webster's secretarial handbook, CH88

Webster's third new international dictionary of the English language, unabridged, AC14, AC17, AC63, AC92

Webster's word histories, AC63

Wechsler, Herman J. *Peintre-graveur illustré*, BF377

Weck, Johannes. *Dictionary of forestry in five languages*, EJ182

Wecken, Friedrich. *Taschenbuch für Familiengeschichtsforschung*, AJ95

Wedborn, Helena. *Women in the First and Second World Wars*, DA192

Wedepohl, Karl Hans. *Handbook of geochemistry*, EF19

Wedertz, Bill. *Dictionary of naval abbreviations*, CJ618, CJ621

Wedgeworth, Robert. *World encyclopedia of library and information services*, AK39

Wedgwood, Josiah Clement. *History of Parliament, 1439–1509*, AH231, CJ354, CJ355

Wee, Yeow Chin. *An illustrated dictionary of Chinese medicinal herbs*, EH350

Weed, Katherine Kirtley. *Studies of British newspapers and periodicals from their beginning to 1800*, AD109, AE60

Weed abstracts, EJ19

Weeds
   dictionaries, EJ33
     multilingual, EJ34
   handbooks, EJ55, EJ64

Weeds of the United States and their control, Lorenzi, Harri, EJ55

Weekes, Richard V. *Muslim peoples*, CE43

Weekley, Ernest. *Etymological dictionary of modern English*, AC64

Weekly business statistics, CH425

Weekly compilation of presidential documents, AF136

Weekly record, AA437, AA440

Weeks, Albert Loren. *Brassey's Soviet and communist quotations*, CJ524

Weeks, Gerald R. *Family therapy*, CC227

Weeks, John M. *Introduction to library research in anthropology*, CE2

Weeks, Kent R. *An historical bibliography of Egyptian prehistory*, DA122

Wefelmeyer, Thomas. *Bibliographie zur alteuropäischen Religionsgeschichte*, BC6

Wegelin, Oscar. *Early American plays, 1714–1830*, BE453, BE636

———— *Early American poetry*, BE498

Wegner, Judith Romney. *Bibliography of Israel law in English and other European languages*, CK231

Wegner, Karl F. *Forestry handbook*, EJ185

Wegweiser für Forschungen nach Vorfahren aus den osterdeutschen und sudetendeutschen Gebieten, AJ78

Wehmann, Howard H. *A guide to pre-federal records in the National Archives*, DB81

Wehr, Hans. *A dictionary of modern written Arabic*, AC222

Wehrle, Hugo. *Deutscher Wortschatz*, AC435

Wei, Karen T. *Library and information science in China*, AK16

———— *Women in China*, CC619

Weibel, Kathleen. *The role of women in librarianship, 1876–1976*, AK73

The Weidenfeld atlas of maritime history, DA56

Weidner, Ernst. *Reallexikon der Assyriologie, unter Mitwirkung zahlreicher Fachgelehrter*, DA80

Weidner, Ruth Irwin. *American ceramics before 1930*, BG57

Weigall, David. *Britain & the world, 1815–1986*, DC338

Weigand, Jörg. *Pseudonyme*, AA173

Weigel, Rudolph. *Suppléments au Peintre-graveur de Adam Bartsch*, BF382

Weights and measures, AL196, AL197, AL198, AL199, AL200, AL201, AL202, EA150, ED19

Weigle, Luther A. *The Bible word book*, BC135

———— *New Testament octapla*, BC94

Weihrauch, John L. *Composition of foods*, EH314, EJ220

Weik, Martin H. *Communications standard dictionary*, EK149

Weil, Stephen E. *Art law*, BF122

Weilant, Edward. *Chronology of world events, 1972–1989*, CJ484

The Weimar era and Hitler, 1917–1933, Stachura, Peter D., DC242

The Weimar Republic, DC242

Weinberg, Gerhard L. *Guide to captured German documents*, DC249

Weinberg, Meyer. *World racism and related inhumanities*, CC333

Weinberg, Robert E. *Biographical dictionary of science fiction and fantasy artists*, BE303, BF372

Weinberger, Bernhard Wolf. *Dental bibliography*, EH245

———— *An introduction to the history of dentistry*, EH266

———— *Orthodontics*, EH266

Weindling, Paul. *Information sources in the history of science and medicine*, EA224

Weiner, Alan R. *The insurance industry*, CH522

———— *Literary criticism index*, BE56

Weiner, Carolynn Newitt. *Union list of film periodicals*, BH174

Weiner, E. S. C. *The Oxford English dictionary*, AC33

———— *The Oxford guide to English usage*, AC88

Weiner, Richard. *Professional's guide to public relations services*, CH569

———— *Syndicated columnists*, AE129

———— *Webster's new World dictionary of media and communications*, CH488

Weinreich, Beatrice. *Yiddish language and folklore*, BD134

Weinreich, Uriel. *Modern English-Yiddish, Yiddish-English dictionary*, AC816

———— *Yiddish language and folklore*, BD134

Weinrich, Peter. *Social protest from the left in Canada, 1870–1970*, CJ515

Weinshank, Donald J. *A concordance to Darwin's Origin of species, first edition*, EG68

Weinstein, Sylvia J. *The Garland recipe index*, EJ208

Weinstein, Warren. *Burundi*, DD48

Weintraub, Irwin. *Reference sources in urban and regional planning*, BF268

Weis, Frederick Lewis. *Colonial clergy and the colonial churches of New England*, BC255

———— *Colonial clergy of Maryland, Delaware and Georgia*, BC255

———— *Colonial clergy of the Middle Colonies*, BC255

———— *Colonial clergy of Virginia, North Carolina, and South Carolina*, BC255

Weisbard, Phyllis Holman. *The history of women and science, health, and technology*, EA231

———— *Jewish law*, CK240

Weise, Frieda O. *Health statistics*, EH235

Weisman, Herman M. *Basic technical writing*, EA163

Weisner, Herbert. *Lexikon der deutschsprachigen Gegenwartsliteratur*, BE1248, BE1250

Weiss, Allan Barry. *A comprehensive bibliography of English-Canadian short stories, 1950–1983*, BE835

Weiss, Anne. *American authors and books, 1640 to the present day*, BE432

———— *Reflections on childhood*, CC162

———— *Thesaurus of book digests, 1950–1980*, BE193

Weiss, Christine. *Die französische Afrikapolitik*, DD2

Weiss, Edith Brown. *International environmental law*, CK91

Weiss, Irving. *American authors and books, 1640 to the present day*, BE432

———— *Reflections on childhood*, CC162

———— *Thesaurus of book digests, 1950–1980*, BE193

Weissbach, Oskar. *Beilstein guide*, EE115

Weissensteiner, Friedrich. *Österreichisches Personen Lexikon*, AH166

Weissman, Dick. *The folk music sourcebook*, BJ324

Weitenkampf, Frank. *Dictionary of biographical reference*, AH20

Weitz, Margaret Collins. *Femmes*, CC620

Weitzel, Rolf. *Handbuch der bibliographischen Nachschlagewerke*, AA12

Weixlmann, Joseph. *American short fiction criticism and scholarship, 1959–1977*, BE479, BE548

Welbourn, R. B. *Dictionary of medical ethics*, EH240

Welch, D'Alté Aldridge. *A bibliography of American children's books printed prior to 1821*, AA248

Welch, Jeffrey Egan. *Literature and film*, BH177

Welch, John W. *A biblical law bibliography*, CK241

———— *A bibliography on temples of the ancient Near East and Mediterranean world*, BF220

Welch, Kenneth R. G. *Venomous snakes of the world*, EG249

Welch, Thomas L. *The Aztecs*, CC477

———— *Bibliografía de la literatura ecuatoriana*, BE950

———— *Bibliografía de la literatura paraguaya*, BE953

———— *Bibliografía de la literatura uruguaya*, BE960

———— *The Incas*, CC478, DB385

———— *Travel accounts and descriptions of Latin America and the Caribbean, 1800–1920*, DB263, DB409

Welch, Windon Chandler. *Chinese-American calendar for the 102 Chinese years commencing Jan. 24, 1849, and ending Feb. 5, 1951*, EC88

Welcher, Frank Johnson. *Chemical solutions*, EE92

———— *Union army, 1861–1865*, DB119

Welcher Stein ist das?, Börner, Rudolf, EF192

Welding, EK249

Welding handbook, EK249

Welland, Dennis. *A guide to manuscripts relating to America in Great Britain and Ireland*, DB32

Wellburn, Peter. *Scottish family histories*, AJ121

Wellcome Historical Medical Library. *A catalogue of printed books in the Wellcome Historical Medical Library*, EH210

———— *Current work in the history of medicine*, EH54, EH218

———— *The medical practitioners in medieval England*, EH226

Wellcome Institute for the History of Medicine. *Subject catalogue of the history of medicine and related sciences*, EH54

Wellek, René. *A history of modern criticism*, BE57, BE426, BE595

Weller, Carol. *Educators' desk reference for special learning problems*, CB205

Weller, Emil Ottokar. *Die falschen und fingirten Druckorte*, AA196

———— *Repertorium typographicum*, AA639

Wellesley College. Center for Research on Women. *The women's review of books*, CC534

The Wellesley index to Victorian periodicals, 1824–1900, AD280, AD292

Wellheiser, Johanna G. *An ounce of prevention*, AK243

Welling, William. *Collectors' guide to nineteenth-century photographs*, BF352

Wellington, Jean Susorney. *Dictionary of bibliographic abbreviations found in the scholarship of classical studies and related disciplines*, BE1019

Wellisch, Hans H. *Indexing and abstracting*, AK217

———— *Norway*, DC467

———— *Sweden*, DC520

———— *Transcription and transliteration*, BD10

Wellness media, CB28

Wells, Daniel A. *Literary index to American magazines, 1815–1865*, BE420

Wells, Evelyn. *What to name the baby*, AJ176

Wells, Henry Willis. *Three centuries of drama*, BE453, BE636

———— *Three centuries of English and American plays*, BE453, BE636

Wells, John Edwin. *Manual of the writings in Middle English, 1050–1400*, BE734, BE736

Wells, Robert V. *A retrospective bibliography of American demographic history from colonial times to 1983*, CG92, DB14

Wells, Rulon. *The Plato manuscripts*, BB59
Wells, Stanley W. *The Cambridge companion to Shakespeare studies*, BE784
—— *English drama, excluding Shakespeare*, BE641
—— *Shakespeare*, BE768
—— *William Shakespeare, a textual companion*, BE796
Wells, Susan M. *The IUCN invertebrate red data book*, EG234
Welmers, Beatrice F. *Igbo*, AC501
Welmers, William E. *Igbo*, AC501
Welsch, Erwin K. *Archives and libraries in a new Germany*, AK133, AK139, DC13, DC247, DC390
—— *Archives and libraries in France*, AK133, AK136, DC13, DC158, DC390
—— *Libraries and archives in France*, AK136, DC158
—— *Libraries and archives in Germany*, AK139
Welsh, Brian W. W. *Dictionary of development*, CH120
Welsh, Doris Varner. *Catalog of the William B. Greenlee collection*, DC489
—— *Checklist of French political pamphlets 1560–1653 in the Newberry Library*, DC169
Welsh (by country or region)
United States, DC368
Welsh Academy. *The Oxford companion to the literature of Wales*, BE814
Welsh administrative and territorial units, medieval and modern, Richards, Melville, AJ128
Welsh County Archivists' Group. *Cofrestri plwyf Cymru = Parish registers of Wales*, AJ130
Welsh-English, English-Welsh dictionary, AC805
Welsh family history, AJ129
Welsh language
dictionaries, AC806
bilingual
English-Welsh, AC807
Welsh-English, AC805, AC807
Welsh literature, BE814
bibliography, BE813
biography, BE812
Welsh women, Holt, Constance Wall, DC368
Weltgeschichte in einem Griff, Jung, Kurt Michael, DC224
Weltgeschichte in Stichworten, Jung, Kurt Michael, DC224
Die Weltliteratur, BE72
Wemyss, Stanley. *The languages of the world, ancient and modern*, BD18
Wenckstern, Friedrich von. *Bibliography of the Japanese Empire*, DE204
Wenger, Leopold. *Reallexikon für Antike und Christentum*, BC248
Wenk, Arthur B. *Analyses of nineteenth- and twentieth-century music, 1940–1985*, BJ113
Wenner-Gren Foundation for Anthropological Research, New York. *Inventory of ethnological collections in museums of the United States and Canada*, CE88
Wennrich, Peter. *Anglo-amerikanische und deutsche Abkurzungen in Wissenschaft und Technik*, EA98
—— *International dictionary of abbreviations and acronyms of electronics, electrical engineering, computer technology, and information processing*, EK196
—— *International encyclopedia of abbreviations and acronyms of organizations*, AL11
Wentworth, Harold. *American dialect dictionary*, AC154
—— *Dictionary of American slang*, AC120, AC135
Wenzel, Duane. *The Museum of Science and Industry basic list of children's science books, 1973–1984*, EA30
Wepsiec, Jan. *Social sciences*, CA19
—— *Sociology*, CC10
Wer ist wer?, AH211
Wer war wer, DDR, AH216
Werblowsky, R. J. Zwi. *Encyclopedia of the Jewish religion*, BC547

Werlich, Robert. *Orders and decorations of all nations*, AL188
Wernich, Albrecht Ludwig Agathon. *Biographisches Lexikon der hervorragenden Ärzte aller Zeiten und Völker*, EH222
Wertheimer, Marilyn Lou. *History of psychology*, CD57
Wertheimer, Michael. *History of psychology*, CD57
—— *Portraits of pioneers in psychology*, CD50
Wertheimer, Stephen. *The complete guide to corporate fund raising*, AL133
Wertsman, Vladimir. *Free voices in Russian literature, 1950s–1980s*, BE1407
WerWasWo?, AA660
Wery, Mary K. *American women and the labor movement, 1825–1974*, CC503, CC511
Wescott, Steven D. *A comprehensive bibliography of music for film and television*, BJ364
Wessel, Klaus. *Reallexikon zur byzantinischen Kunst*, BF80
West, Clarence J. *International critical tables of numerical data, physics, chemistry and technology*, EA156
West, Dorothy Herbert. *Essay and general literature index*, AH12, BA4, BE37
—— *Play index*, BE234
West, Edward N. *Outward signs*, BC208
West, G. D. *Index of proper names in French Arthurian prose romances*, BE1165
—— *An index of proper names in French Arthurian verse romances, 1150–1300*, BE1165
West, Geoffrey P. *Black's veterinary dictionary*, EJ111
West, John. *Town records*, DC353
—— *Village records*, DC353
West, Jonathan P. *Borderlands sourcebook*, DB164
West, Ruth. *The alternative health guide*, EH186
—— *Alternative medicine*, EH30
West African international atlas, CL338
West Bank data project, Benvenisti, Meron, CJ436
The West Bank handbook, Benvenisti, Meron, CJ436
West German cinema, 1985–1990, Helt, Marie E., BH187
—— Helt, Richard C., BH187
West German cinema since 1945, Helt, Richard C., BH187
West Germany
guides to records, DB239
West Germany, Detwiler, Donald S., DC232
West India Reference Library (Jamaica). *Jamaican national bibliography*, AA568
West Indian literature, Allis, Jeannette B., BE968
West Indies
bibliography, DB407
manuscripts and archives, DB413, DB415
West Indies (by subject)
anthropology and ethnology, CE80
West Indies and Caribbean year book, CG163
The West Point atlas of American wars, United States Military Academy. Dept. of Military Art and Engineering, DB77
West Point atlas of the Civil War, Esposito, Vincent J., DB77
—— United States Military Academy. Dept. of Military Art and Engineering, DB77
West Publishing Company. *Code of Alabama, 1975*, CK179
—— *West's law and commercial dictionary in five languages*, CK46
West Virginia. [Laws, etc.]. *West Virginia code, annotated*, CK179
West Virginia code, annotated, West Virginia. [Laws, etc.], CK179
Westbrook, Perry D. *A literary history of New England*, BE577
Westcott, W. Wynn. *The extra pharmacopoeia*, EH357
Westendorf, Wolfhart. *Bermerkungen und Korrekturen zum Lexikon der Ägyptologie*, DA125
—— *Lexikon der Ägyptologie*, DA125
Westergren, Bertil. *Beta mathematics handbook*, EB92
Westerman, Cheryl I. *The writer's advisor*, BE11

Westermann Lexikon der Geographie, CL40
Western, A. E. *Tables of indices and primitive roots*, EB94
Western, Dominique Coulet. *A bibliography of the arts of Africa*, BF38, BG4
The Western, Hardy, Phil, BH224
Western American literature, BE570, BE572
Western books on China published up to 1850 in the Library of the School of Oriental and African Studies, University of London, University of London. School of Oriental and African Studies. Library, DE137
Western Canada since 1870, Artibise, Alan F. J., DB211
Western Europe, CJ94
Western European censuses, 1960, Blake, Judith, CG186
Western European costume, 13th to 17th century, and its relation to the theatre, Brooke, Iris, BG107
—— Landes, William-Alan, BG107
Western European costume and its relation to the theatre, Brooke, Iris, BG107
Western European dissertations on the Hispanic and Luso-Brazilian languages and literatures, Chatham, James R., BE1446
—— Scales, Sara Matthews, BE1446
Western European painting of the Renaissance, Mather, Frank Jewett, BF308
Western European political parties, CJ323
Western histories of linguistic thought, Koerner, E. F. K., BD59
Western Literature Association (U.S.). *A literary history of the American West*, BE576
Western manuscripts from classical antiquity to the Renaissance, Braswell, Laurel Nichols, AA198
Western mysticism, Bowman, Mary Ann, BC8
Western Sahara, DD242
government publications
bibliography, AF227
Western Sahara, Hodges, T., DD48
—— Sipe, Lynn F., DD242
Western Samoa, CG443
Western Samoa. Department of Statistics. *Statistical abstract*, CG443
Western states, DB162, DB165, DB169, DB174, DB176
bibliography, BE570, BE572, CC360, DB166
dictionaries, AC148, AC149
guides to records, DB26, DB171
library catalogs, DB170
manuscripts and archives, DB26, DB171
Western states (by subject)
literature, BE570, BE572, BE576, BE579
see also **Rocky Mountain states**
Western words, Adams, Ramon Frederick, AC148
Western Writers of America. *Dictionary of the American West*, AC149
Western writings on Chinese art and archaeology, BF40
Westfall, Gloria. *Bibliography of official statistical yearbooks and bulletins*, CG14
—— *French colonial Africa*, AF228
—— *French official publications*, AF170, AF172
—— *Guide to official publications of foreign countries*, AF8
•*WESTLAW*, CK33, CK179
The Westminster dictionary of Christian ethics, BC241
The Westminster dictionary of Christian spirituality, BC242
The Westminster dictionary of Christian theology, BC243
Westminster dictionary of church history, BC244
Westminster dictionary of the Bible, Davis, John D., BC138
The Westminster dictionary of worship, BC268
West's annotated California codes, California. [Laws, etc.], CK179
West's Colorado revised statutes annotated, Colorado. [Laws, etc.], CK179
West's federal forms, CK164
West's Florida statutes annotated, Florida. [Laws, etc.], CK179

West's law and commercial dictionary in five languages, CK46

West's legal desk reference, CK161

West's legal forms, CK164

West's legal theasurus/dictionary, Statsky, William P., CK56

West's Louisiana statutes annotated, Louisiana. [Laws, etc.], CK179

West's revised code of Washington annotated, Washington (State). [Laws, etc.], CK179

West's Smith-Hurd Illinois compiled statutes annotated, Illinois. [Laws, etc.], CK179

West's Spanish-English/English-Spanish law dictionary, Solís, Gerardo, CK55

West's Wisconsin statutes annotated, Wisconsin. [Laws, etc.], CK179

Wetta, Frank Joseph. *Celluloid wars,* CJ608

Wetterau, Bruce. *Macmillan concise dictionary of world history,* DA26

———— *The New York Public Library book of chronologies,* DA40

Wettstein, Hermann. *Bibliographie musikalischer thematischer Werkverzeichnisse,* BJ232

———— *Thematische Sammelverzeichnisse der Musik,* BJ233

Wexler, Paul. *Judeo-Romance linguistics,* BD154

Wexler, Philip. *Information resources in toxicology,* EH418

Weyl, Theodor. *Methoden der organischen Chemie (Houben-Weyl),* EE138

Whalen, William Joseph. *Handbook of secret organizations,* AL78

Whaling ships, DF9

Whalon, Marion K. *Performing arts research,* BH1

Wharton, George F. *Sexuality and aging,* CC77

Wharton-Lake, Beverly D. *Creative literature of Trinidad and Tobago,* BE981

What a bunch of characters!, Caden, Tom Scott, BH277

What do I read next?, BE259

What they said, BE123

What to name the baby, Wells, Evelyn, AJ176

The what, where, when of theater props, James, Thurston, BH92

What you need to know about psychiatric drugs, Yudofsky, Stuart C., EH351

Wheat, Carl Irving. *Mapping the Transmississippi West, 1540–1861,* CL244

Wheat, James Clements. *Maps and charts published in America before 1800,* CL245

Wheatcroft, Andrew. *The world atlas of revolutions,* CJ74

Wheaton, Bruce R. *Inventory of published letters to and from physicists, 1900–1950,* ED53

———— *Literature on the history of physics in the 20th century,* ED52, ED53

Wheeler, Alwyne C. *Fishes of the world,* EG288

Wheeler, Brian K. *A field guide to hawks,* EG256

Wheeler, Daniel. *History of modern art,* BF131

Wheeler, Douglas L. *Historical dictionary of Portugal,* DC492

Wheeler, Helen Rippier. *The bibliographic instruction-course handbook,* AK232

Wheeler, James O. *A bibliography of geographic thought,* CL5

———— *Bibliography on geographic thought, 1950– 1982,* CL5

———— *Dictionary of quotations in geography,* CL54

Wheeler, Leslie. *American social leaders,* CA64

Wheeler, Marcus. *Oxford Russian-English dictionary,* AC677, AC678, AC683, EA127

Wheeler, Marjorie W. *Geologic reference sources,* EF20

Whelpton, John. *Nepal,* DE236

Where once we walked, Mokotoff, Gary, CL127, CL128

———— Sack, Sallyann Amdur, CL127

Where the whalers went, DF9

Where to write for vital records, AJ57, CK157

Wheye, Darryl. *The birder's handbook,* EG258

———— *Birds in jeopardy,* EG259

Whibley, Leonard. *Companion to Greek studies,* DA108, DA109

Which dictionary?, Loughridge, Brendan, AC3

Which Shakespeare?, Thompson, Ann, BE765

Whiffen, Marcus. *American architecture since 1780,* BF252

Whisenhunt, Donald W. *Encyclopedia USA,* DB47

Whisker, James B. *An American political dictionary,* CJ123

———— *Dictionary of concepts on American politics,* CJ123

———— *Glossary of U.S. government vocabulary,* CJ123

Whistling's Handbuch, BJ60

Whitaker, Allan. *The language of biotechnology,* EK46

Whitaker, Cathy Seitz. *Alternative publications,* AA280

Whitaker, Jerry C. *Television engineering handbook,* EK148

Whitaker, Katherine C. *The martial arts,* BK91

Whitaker, Richard E. *The Eerdmans analytical concordance to the Revised Standard Version of the Bible,* BC166

———— *Graphic concordance to the Dead Sea scrolls,* BC556

Whitaker, Roger. *East European peasantries,* CE96

Whitaker's almanack, AB109

Whitaker's book list, AA688, AA690

Whitaker's books in print, AA685, AA691

Whitaker's books of the month and books to come, AA684, AA688

Whitaker's cumulative book list, AA684, AA690

Whitaker's five-year cumulative book list, AA690, AA692

Whitby, Thomas J. *Studies in human sexuality,* CC269

Whitby, Thomas Joseph. *Introduction to Soviet national bibliography,* AA792, AA794, AD150

White, Barbara Anne. *American women's fiction, 1790–1870,* BE480

White, Beatrice. *Index ... to The Elizabethan stage...,* BE665

White, Carl Milton. *Sources of information in the social sciences,* CA8

White, Charlotte. *Portraits of pioneers in psychology,* CD50

White, Cynthia Leslie. *Women's magazines, 1693– 1968,* AD48

White, D. Jerry. *Early English drama, Everyman to 1580,* BE656

White, David Allen. *Shakespeare A to Z,* BE783

White, E. B. *Elements of style,* CA55

White, Glenn D. *The audio dictionary,* BJ393

White, Herbert S. *Managing the special library,* AK181

White, J. Peter. *Australians to 1788,* DF37

White, J. Todd. *Fighters for independence,* DB89

White, James J. *Plant, animal & anatomical illustration in art & science,* EA220

White, James P. *Materials and strategies for the education of trainable mentally retarded learners,* CB193

White, Jane N. *Higher education literature,* CB232

White, Jess R. *Sports rules encyclopedia,* BK47

White, John A. *Production handbook,* CH623

White, Katherine P. *Folk artists biographical index,* BG30

White, Linda. *English-Basque dictionary,* AC231

White, Pamela. *Index of English literary manuscripts,* BE603

White, Paul M. *Soviet urban and regional planning,* CC306

White, Ray Lewis. *Index to Best American short stories and O. Henry prize stories,* BE483

White, Rhea A. *Exceptional human experience,* CD132

———— *Parapsychology,* CD131

White, Richard Clark. *The vocabulary of the church,* BC245

White, Robert B. *The English literary journal to 1900,* BE592

White, Sarah Harriman. *World historical fiction guide,* BE250

White, Stephen. *Handbook of reconstruction in Eastern Europe and the Soviet Union,* CJ391

———— *Political and economic encyclopaedia of the Soviet Union and Eastern Europe,* CJ391, DC52

White, Virgil D. *Genealogical abstracts of Revolutionary War pension files,* AJ38

———— *Index to old wars pension files, 1815–1926,* AJ48

———— *Index to War of 1812 pension files,* AJ48

White, Wayne E. *Articles on the Middle East, 1947– 1971,* DE24

White, William. *The Bible almanac,* BC185

Whiteford, Andrew Hunter. *United States & Canada,* BG157

The Whitehall companion, CJ343

Whitehouse, David. *Archaeological atlas of the world,* DA89

Whitehouse, Ruth D. *Archaeological atlas of the world,* DA89

———— *The Facts on File dictionary of archaeology,* DA79

Whiteley, Derek. *The Oxford book of vertebrates,* EG238

Whiteley, Martha Annie. *Thorpe's dictionary of applied chemistry,* EE46

Whitelock, Dorothy. *English historical documents,* DC297

Whitener, Summer D. *Profile of education doctorates,* CB341

White's conspectus of American biography, AH68

Whiteside, Lowell S. *Catalog of significant earthquakes,* EF260

Whitfield, Francis. *Kościuszko Foundation dictionary,* AC634

Whitfield, Francis J. *A history of Russian literature from the earliest times to the death of Dostoevsky (1881),* BE1420

Whitfield, Philip. *Macmillan illustrated animal encyclopedia,* EG298

Whitford, Robert Henry. *Physics literature,* ED3

Whiting, Bartlett Jere. *Dictionary of American proverbs and proverbial phrases, 1820–1880,* BE165

———— *Early American proverbs and proverbial phrases,* BE165

———— *Modern proverbs and proverbial sayings,* BE165

———— *Proverbs, sentences, and proverbial phrases,* BE166

Whiting, Gertrude. *Lace guide for makers and collectors,* BG162

Whitley, William Thomas. *A Baptist bibliography,* BC327

Whitman, Alden. *American reformers,* CC38

Whitmore, John Beach. *Genealogical guide,* AJ109

Whitnah, Donald R. *Government agencies,* CJ120

Whitrow, Magda. *Isis cumulative bibliography,* EA233

Whittaker, William. *A bibliography of Afghanistan,* DE112

Whittem, Arthur. *Tentative bibliography of Brazilian belles-lettres,* BE937

Whitten, Bessie E. *Manufacturing,* CH396

Whitten, David O. *Manufacturing,* CH396

Whitten, Phillip. *Encyclopedia of anthropology,* CE39

Whittick, Arnold. *Symbolism for designers,* BF177

———— *Symbols, signs and their meaning and uses in design,* BF177

Whittingham, Nik-ki. *Arts management in the '90s,* BF39

Whittington, Jennifer. *Literary recordings,* BE324

Whittington, Lloyd R. *Whittington's dictionary of plastics,* EK291

Whittington's dictionary of plastics, EK291

Whitworth, Judith A. *Dictionary of medical eponyms,* EH99

Who audits America, CH256

WHO chronicle, EH315

Who done it?, Hagen, Ordean, BE271

WHO drug information, EH315

Who gets grants/who gives grants, AL124

Who is publishing in science, EA137

Who is where in world banking, CH281
Who is who, AH286
Who is who [in] government, politics, banking and industry in Latin America, AH111, CJ310
Who is who in Kenya, AH320, DD166
Who is who in service to the earth, AL23, EK75
Who knows, a guide to Washington experts, CJ146
Who owns what in world banking, CH281
Who owns whom, CH374
Who owns whom. Australasia and Far East, CH374
Who owns whom. Continental Europe, CH374
Who owns whom. North America, CH374
Who owns whom. United Kingdom and Republic of Ireland, CH374
Who played who in the movies, Pickard, Roy, BH276
Who played who on the screen, Pickard, Roy, BH276
WHO/Unesco Panel on Terminology. *International glossary of hydrology*, EF133
Who was really who in fiction, Bold, Alan Norman, BE251
Who was who, AH232, AH233
Who was who, 1900–1980, AH350
Who was who among English and European authors, 1931–1949, BE211
Who was who in America, AH72, AH82
Who was who in American art, Falk, Peter H., BF153
Who was who in American history—science and technology, EA184
Who was who in American politics, Morris, Dan, CJ157
Who was who in British librarianship, 1800–1985, Munford, William Arthur, AK91
Who was who in church history, Moyer, Elgin Sylvester, BC254
Who was who in Fiji, AH376
Who was who in journalism, 1925–1928, AE153
Who was who in Native American history, Waldman, Carl, CC437
Who was who in the Civil War, Sifakis, Stewart, DB121
Who was who in the Greek world, 776 BC–30 BC, DA114
—— Bowder, Diana, DA115
Who was who in the Roman world, 753 BC–AD 476, DA115, DA114
Who was who in the theatre, DH122
Who was who in the theatre, 1912–1976, BH122
Who was who in the USSR, Institut zur Erforschung der UdSSR, AH304
Who was who on screen, Truitt, Evelyn Mack, BH213
Who writes what, CH516
Who writes what in life and health insurance, CH516
Who wrote the movie and what else did he write?, Academy of Motion Pictures Arts and Sciences, BH210
—— Writers Guild of America, BH210
The whole library handbook 2, Eberhardt, George M., AK69
Whole world handbook, CB93
Wholesale trade, CH346
Who's doing what?, AL50
Who's doing what in development education?, AL50
Who's inventing what?, EA264
Who's new wave in music, BJ352
Who's notable in Mexico, AH108
Who's wealthy in America, AH80
Who's who, AH233
—— India. Parliament. Lok Sabha, CJ432
—— India. Parliament. Rajya Sabha, CJ432
Who's who, 1981–82, Mitchell, Diana, AH327
Who's who among black Americans, AH73, CC397
Who's who among Hispanic Americans, AH81, CC470
Who's who among human services professionals, CC50
Who's who among living authors of older nations, Lawrence, Alberta, BE211
Who's who among students in American universities and colleges, CB332
Who's who and why in Jamaica, AH158
Who's who de la dictature de Guinée équatoriale, DD152

Who's who in advertising, CH575
Who's who in Africa, Rake, Alan, AH316, CJ404, CJ406, CJ409
Who's who in African literature, Jahn, Janheinz, BE1512
Who's who in America, AH65, AH72, AH82, AH97, BC367, CK158
Who's who in America : indices and necrology, AH82
Who's who in American art, BF102, BF157
Who's who in American education, CB133, CB134
Who's who in American education, 1928–68, CB134
Who's who in American history, AH72, EA184
Who's who in American Jewry, AH83
Who's who in American law, CK158
Who's who in American music, BJ218
Who's who in American nursing, EH283
Who's who in American politics, CJ161
Who's who in architecture, Placzek, Adolf K., BF262
—— Richards, J. M., BF262
Who's who in art, BF150
Who's who in Asian and Australasian politics, CJ415, DE20, DF20
Who's who in Australia, AH375
Who's who in Australian libraries, AK82
Who's who in Austria, AH171
Who's who in Bangladesh, AH334
Who's who in Bangladesh art, culture, literature, 1901–1991, AH335
Who's who in Brazil, AH127
Who's who in British economics, CH103
Who's who in British history, DC298
Who's who in Canada, AH97
Who's who in Canadian literature, BE836
Who's who in children's books, Fisher, Margery Turner, BE381
Who's who in China, AH342, CJ426
Who's who in China. Current leaders, AH346
Who's who in colored America, AH73
Who's who in comedy, Smith, Ronald L., BH24
Who's who in commerce and industry, CH105
Who's who in Communist China, AH343
Who's who in Congress, including committees and key staff, CJ216
Who's who in Costa Rica, AH115
Who's who in early Hanoverian Britain, Treasure, Geoffrey, DC298
Who's who in economics, CH104
Who's who in educational administration, American Association of School Administrators, CB183
Who's who in Egypt and the Middle East, AH330
Who's who in Egypt and the Near East, AH330
Who's who in engineering, EK13, EK14
Who's who in entertainment, BH27
Who's who in espionage, Dobson, Christopher, CJ540
—— Payne, Ronald, CJ540
Who's who in Europe, AH53
Who's who in European institutions and enterprises, CJ65
Who's who in European politics, CJ324
Who's who in fashion, Stegemeyer, Anne, BG116
Who's who in Fiji, Berwick, Sam, AH376
Who's who in finance and industry, CH105
Who's who in Finland, AH189
Who's who in France, AH201
Who's who in France: Paris, AH201
Who's who in frontier science and technology, EA185
Who's who in frontiers of science and technology, EA185
Who's who in genealogy & heraldry, Meyer, Mary Keysor, AJ56
Who's who in Germany, AH212
Who's who in government, CJ162
Who's who in graphic art, BF383
Who's who in Hakushi in great Japan, AH357
Who's who in history, DC298
Who's who in Hollywood, BH289
Who's who in Hong Kong, AH348
Who's who in India, Burma and Ceylon, AH352
Who's who in insurance, CH513, CH523

Who's who in international affairs, CJ65
Who's who in international banking, CH289
Who's who in international organizations, AH50
Who's who in Ireland, Cairnduff, Maureen, AH257
Who's who in Israel and Jewish personalities from all over the world, AH356
Who's who in Italy, AH265
Who's who in Japan, AH359
Who's who in Japanese government, CJ440
Who's who in journalism, AE153
Who's who in late medieval England, Hicks, Michael A., DC298
Who's who in Latin America, AH110, AH111, CJ306, CJ310
Who's who in Lebanon, AH360
Who's who in library and information services, AK83, AK93
Who's who in library service, AK83, AK93
Who's who in literature, AH213
Who's who in Malaysia & Singapore, AH362, AH369
Who's who in Methodism, BC367
Who's who in Mexico today, Camp, Roderic Ai, AH107
Who's who in modern China, Perleberg, Max, AH341
Who's who in modern Japanese prints, Blakemore, Frances, BF358
Who's who in music and musicians' international directory, BJ213
Who's who in New Zealand, AH381
Who's who in New Zealand library and information service, AK94
Who's who in Nigeria, AH323, DD196
Who's who in non-classical mythology, Sykes, Egerton, CF14
Who's who in Oceania, 1980–1981, AH385
Who's who in Poland, AH282
Who's who in religion, BC84
Who's who in Roman Britain and Anglo-Saxon England, Fletcher, Richard A., DC298
Who's who in Russia and the new states, AH180
Who's who in Saudi Arabia, AH368
Who's who in Scandinavia, AH165
Who's who in science and engineering, EA190
Who's who in science and technology in Nigeria, Akinyoto, Adetunji, AH323, DD196
Who's who in science in Europe, EA191
Who's who in Scotland, AH244
Who's who in Shakespeare's England, Palmer, Alan Warwick, BE788
Who's who in show business, BH26
Who's who in Sierra Leone, AH324
Who's who in Singapore, AH362, AH369
Who's who in South African politics, CJ412, DD212
Who's who in Spain, AH291
Who's who in special libraries, AK61
Who's who in spy fiction, BE272
Who's who in Stuart England, Hill, C. P., DC298
Who's who in Switzerland, including the Principality of Liechtenstein, AH297
Who's who in technology, EK15
Who's who in technology today, EK15
Who's who in the Arab world, AH329
Who's who in the arts, AH213
Who's who in the arts and literature, AH213
Who's who in the East, AH84
Who's who in the leading city and county governments and local authorities, CJ273
Who's who in the Methodist church, BC367
Who's who in the Midwest, AH85
Who's who in the Peace Corps, CJ702
Who's who in the People's Republic of China, CJ426
—— Bartke, Wolfgang, AH344, CJ426, CJ428
Who's who in the socialist countries, Lewytzkyj, Borys, AH47, AH306
Who's who in the socialist countries of Europe, AH163
Who's who in the South and Southwest, AH86
Who's who in the Soviet Union, AH306
Who's who in the theatre, BH22, BH122
Who's who in the United Nations and related agencies, AF42

Who's who in the West, AH87
Who's who in the world, AH45, AH51
Who's who in Tudor England, Holmes, Peter, DC298
—— Routh, C. N. R., DC298
Who's who in Turkey, AH302
Who's who in U.A.R. and the Near East, AH330
Who's who in Vietnam, AH370
Who's who in world agriculture, EJ40
Who's who in world Jewry, AH52
Who's who in writers, editors & poets, United States & Canada, BE451
Who's who, Indian personages, AH354
Who's who, Jamaica, British West Indies, AH158
Who's who—Nepal, 1992, AH364
Who's who of Afghanistan, AH332, AH333
Who's who of American women, AH88, CB101
Who's who of Australian women, Lofthouse, Andrea, AH374
Who's who of Australian writers, BE859
Who's who of British film actors, Palmer, Scott, BH211
Who's who of British Members of Parliament, CJ362
—— Stenton, Michael, CJ354
Who's who of British scientists, 1980/81, EA186
The who's who of children's literature, Doyle, Brian, BE379
Who's who of Indian writers, 1983, BE1570
Who's who of Nobel Prize winners, 1901–1990, Schlessinger, Bernard S., AH30, AL170
—— Schlessinger, June H., AH30, AL170
Who's who of southern Africa, AH315
Who's who of women in world politics, CJ71
Who's who on the postage stamps of Eastern Europe, Partington, Paul G., BG205
Why do we say— ?, Rees, Nigel, AC61
Whyld, Kenneth. *The Oxford companion to chess*, BK133
Whyte, Donald. *A dictionary of Scottish emigrants to the U.S.A*, AJ69
Wiarda, Howard J. *Materials for the study of politics and government in the Dominican Republic, 1930–1966*, DB434
Wick, Charles. *Tool and manufacturing engineers handbook*, EK248
Wick, Vivian. *Architecture on screen*, BF247
Wicked words, Rawson, Hugh, AC133
Wicker, Gerald L. *Gifted & talented information resources*, CB188
Wickersheimer, Ernest. *Dictionnaire biographique des dédecines en France au Moyen Âge*, EH226
Wickham, Glynne William Gladstone. *Early English stages, 1300–1600*, BE664
Wickremasinghe, W. *Scholarships, fellowships & grants for programs abroad*, CB369
Wickremasinghe, Walter. *Handbook of world education*, CB327
Wicks, Charles Beaumont. *The Parisian stage*, BE1186
Widdowson, J. D. A. *Dictionary of Newfoundland English*, AC159
Widdowson, Peter. *A reader's guide to contemporary literary theory*, BE53
Widener Library shelflist, DB270
—— Harvard University. Library, AA115
Widmann, Hans. *Bibliographien zum deutschen Schrifttum der Jahre 1939–1950*, AA46
Wie funktioniert das?, EA82
Wie is dat?, AH273
Wie is wie in Vlaanderen, 1989–1993, Decan, Rik, AH177
Wiechmann, Jack G. *NTC's dictionary of advertising*, CH571
Wieczynski, Joseph L. *The modern encyclopedia of Russian and Soviet history*, DC566
Wiedemann, F. J. *Eesti-saksa sõnaraamat kolmas muutmatu trük teisest, dr. Jakob Hurt'i poolt redigeeritud väljaandest*, AC309
Wiedemann, Ferdinand Johann. *Eesti-saksa sõnaraamat kolmas muutmatu trük teisest, dr. Jakob Hurt'i poolt redigeeritud väljaandest*, AC306
Wiederrecht, Ann E. *The women's movement in the seventies*, CC498

Wiedman, Dennis William. *Ethnohistory*, CE57
Wiedza Powszechna compact Polish and English dictionary, Jáslan, Janina, AC633
Wiegand, Herbert Ernst. *Lexikon der Germanistischen Linguistik*, BD124
Wiegand, Wayne A. *Encyclopedia of library history*, AK72
—— *Supplement to the dictionary of American library biography*, AK86
Wieger, Leon. *Chinese characters*, AC255
Wiehe, Holger. *Íslandsk-dansk ordbog*, AC506
Wielewinski, Bernard. *Doctoral dissertations and masters theses regarding Polish subjects, 1900–1985*, DC478
Wielka encyklopedia powszechna PWN, AB76, AB78
Wielki słownik angielsko-polski, Stanisławski, Jan, AC635
Wielki słownik polsko-angielski, Jassem, Wiktor, AC635
—— Stanisławski, Jan, AC635
Wiener, Philip P. *Dictionary of the history of ideas*, BB29
Wiener Library, London. *After Hitler Germany, 1945–1963*, DC244
—— *From Weimar to Hitler*, DC244
—— *German Jewry*, BC541
—— *Persecution and resistance under the Nazis*, DC244
Wiener Musikaleinhandel von 1700 bis 1778, Gericke, Hannelore, BJ181
Wiener Sprachgesellschaft. *Indogermanische Chronik*, BD201
Wierzbowski, Teodor. *Bibliographia polonica XV ac XVI ss*, AA764
Wieschhoff, Heinrich Albert. *Anthropological bibliography of Negro Africa*, CE105
Wieselgren, Oscar. *Svenska män och kvinnor*, AH292
Wiesinger, Peter. *Bibliographie zur Grammatik der deutschen Dialekte*, BD126, BD127
Wiesner, Herbert. *Bibliographie der Personalbibliographien zur deutschen Gegenwartsliteratur*, BE1221
Wiezell, Richard. *The new Wildhagen German dictionary*, AC424
Wiget, Andrew. *Native American literature*, BE554
Wiggins, Gary. *Chemical information sources*, EE8
Wiggins, Marvin E. *Mormons and their neighbors*, BC370
Wigoder, Geoffrey. *A dictionary of the Jewish-Christian dialogue*, BC554
—— *The encyclopedia of Judaism*, BC547
—— *Encyclopedia of the Jewish religion*, BC547
—— *Illustrated dictionary & concordance of the Bible*, BC142
—— *The new standard Jewish encyclopedia*, BC552
Wijk, Dr. N. van. *Franck's Etymologisch woordenboek der Nederlandsche taal*, AC299
Wiktor, Christian L. *Canadian treaty calendar*, CK97
—— *Marine affairs bibliography*, CK81
Wilamowitz-Moellendorff, Ulrich von. *Geschichte der Philologie*, BE1021, DA107
—— *History of classical scholarship*, BE1021, DA107
Wilbert, Johannes. *Folk literature of South American Indians*, CF74
Wilbur, Leslie C. *Handbook of energy systems engineering*, EK218
Wilcha, Jennifer. *The college student's guide to transferring schools*, CB294
Wilcocks, Julie. *Countries and islands of the world*, CL98
Wilcox, Bonnie. *Atlas of dog breeds of the world*, EJ146
Wilcox, Laird M. *Guide to the American left*, CJ139
—— *Guide to the American occult*, CD137
—— *Guide to the American right*, CJ80
Wilcox, Ruth Turner. *The dictionary of costume*, BG101

—— *Folk and festival costume of the world*, BG101
Wilczynski, Jozef. *An encyclopedic dictionary of Marxism, socialism and communism*, CJ522
Wild flowers of the United States, Rickett, Harold William, EG180
Wildavsky, Aaron. *American political scientists*, CJ155
Wildbihler, Hubert. *Internationale Musical-Bibliographie*, BJ268
—— *The musical*, BJ268
Wilde, William H. *Australian literature to 1900*, BE846
—— *The Oxford companion to Australian literature*, BE860
Wildenstein, Daniel. *Documents inedits sur les artistes français du dix-huitième siècle*, DC151
Wilder, Elizabeth. *Guide to the art of Latin America*, BF22
Wilder, George Durand. *The five thousand dictionary*, AC262
Wildflower guide, EG177
Wildhaber, Robert. *Internationale Volkskundliche Bibliographie*, CF42
Wildhagen, Karl. *The new Wildhagen German dictionary*, AC424
Wilding, Norman W. *Catalog of the parliamentary papers of southern Rhodesia and Rhodesia, 1954–1970*, AF242
—— *Catalogue of the parliamentary papers of Southern Rhodesia and Rhodesia, 1954–1970, and the Federation of Rhodesia and Nyasaland, 1954–1963*, AF241, DD176
—— *An encyclopaedia of Parliament*, CJ353
Wilding, Richard. *Swahili bibliography of the East African coast*, DD110
Wildlife abstracts, EG217, EG218
Wildlife refuges *see* **Parks and protected areas**
Wildlife review, EG217, EG218
•*Wildlife worldwide*, EG218
Wildová Tosi, Alena. *Bibliografia degli studi italiani sulla Cecoslovacchia (1918–1978)*, DC127
Wile, Annadel N. *The combined retrospective index set to journals in political science, 1886–1974*, CJ18
—— *C.R.I.S*, CC12, DA4
Wiley, Bell I. *Civil War books*, DB111
—— *Compendium of the war of the rebellion*, DB119
Wiley, David S. *Africa on film and videotape, 1960–1981*, DD43
Wiley, Paul L. *British novel*, BE682
Wilgat, Janina. *Bibliografia polska 1901–1939*, AA765
—— *Polska literatura w przekładac*, BE1358
Wilgus, Alva Curtis. *Latin America in the nineteenth century*, DB263, DB409
Wilhelm, Henry Gilmer. *The permanence and care of color photographs*, BF351
Wilhoit, Frances Goins. *Mass media bibliography*, AE131
Wilkas, Lenore. *International subscription agents*, AK170
Wilkening, Gregory. *The psychology almanac*, CD66
Wilkening, H. *The psychology almanac*, CD66
Wilkening, Peter. *The psychology almanac*, CD66
Wilkes, G. A. *A dictionary of Australian colloquialisms*, AC180
Wilkes, Joseph A. *Encyclopedia of architecture*, BF234
Wilkins, Ernest Hatch. *A history of Italian literature*, BE1308
Wilkinson, Allen P. *Everybody's guide to the law*, CK159
Wilkinson, Audine. *Economic literature on the Commonwealth Caribbean*, DB410
Wilkinson, Bertie. *High Middle Ages in England, 1154–1377*, DC303, DC308
Wilkinson, Carroll Wetzel. *Women working in nontraditional fields*, CC515
Wilkinson, Endymion. *The history of imperial China*, DE124

Wilkinson, Geoffrey. *Comprehensive coordination chemistry,* EE68

────── *Comprehensive organometallic chemistry,* EE120

Wilkinson, P. C. *Dictionary of immunology,* EG33

Wilkinson, Richard James. *Malay-English dictionary (romanised),* AC606

Will, Samuel F. *A bibliography of American studies on the French Renaissance, (1500–1600),* BE1207

Willard, Frances Elizabeth. *A woman of the century,* AH74

Willeford, George. *Medical word finder,* EH107

────── *Webster's new World medical word finder,* EH107

Willemsen, Carl Arnold. *Bibliographie zur Geschichte Kaiser Friedrichs II. und der letzten Staufer,* DC229

Willenberg, Gabi. *Bibliography of semiotics, 1975–1985,* BD53

Willet, Shelagh M. *Lesotho,* DD18, DD170

Willetts, Pamela Jean. *Handlist of music manuscripts acquired 1908–67,* BJ93

Willging, Eugene Paul. *Catholic serials of the nineteenth century in the United States,* AD227

William Green papers, 1934–1955, CH624

William S. Hein & Company. *World law school directory,* CK63

William Shakespeare, BE785

────── Chambers, Edmund Kerchever, BE664, BE665

William Shakespeare, a textual companion, Wells, Stanley W., BE796

Williams, B. R. *The Oxford history of New Zealand,* DF45

Williams, Bridget. *The book of New Zealand women,* AH377, DF46

Williams, C. J. *Cofrestri plwyf Cymru = Parish registers of Wales,* AJ130

────── *The parish churches and nonconformist chapels of Wales,* AJ127

Williams, Charles Alfred Speed. *Encyclopedia of Chinese symbolism and art motives,* BF179

Williams, David F. *Concise encyclopedia of medical & dental materials,* EH176

Williams, David Russell. *Music theory from Zarlino to Schenker,* BJ29

Williams, E. Neville. *The Facts on File dictionary of European history, 1485–1789,* DC23

Williams, Ethel L. *Biographical directory of Negro ministers,* BC256

────── *The Howard University bibliography of African and Afro-American religious studies,* BC33

Williams, Forrest. *The martial arts,* BK91

Williams, Gareth. *Interdisciplinary dictionary of weed science,* EJ34

Williams, Geoffrey J. *A bibliography of Sierra Leone, 1925–1967,* DD205

────── *Independent Zambia,* DD249

Williams, Gwyneth. *The dictionary of contemporary politics of southern Africa,* CJ408

Williams, Harry Franklin. *An index of mediaeval studies published in festschriften, 1865–1946,* DA139

Williams, Herbert William. *A dictionary of the Maori language,* AC610

Williams, James G. *Encyclopedia of microcomputers,* EK173

Williams, Jerry T. *Southern literature, 1968–1975,* BE574

Williams, John T. *Anthropology journals and serials,* CE26

Williams, Lee H. *The Allende years,* DB360

Williams, Leslie R. *Encyclopedia of early childhood education,* CB66

Williams, Linda R. *Twentieth century : a guide to literature from 1900 to the present day,* BE611

Williams, M. Jane. *Big gifts,* AL141

Williams, Marty. *An annotated index of medieval women,* CC575, DA149

Williams, Michael W. *The African American encyclopedia,* CC385

────── *Pan-Africanism,* DD16

Williams, Miller. *Patterns of poetry,* BE326

Williams, Moelwyn I. *A directory of rare book and special collections in the United Kingdom and the Republic of Ireland,* AK143

Williams, Neville. *Chronology of the expanding world, 1492–1762,* DA184

────── *Chronology of the medieval world, 800 to 1491,* DA156

────── *Chronology of the modern world, 1793–1965,* DA184

Williams, Peter W. *Encyclopedia of American social history,* DB46

────── *Encyclopedia of the American religious experience,* BC59

Williams, Phil. *The dictionary of 20th-century world politics,* CJ33

Williams, Phillip. *A glossary of special education,* CB197

Williams, R. C. *Bibliography of the seventeenth-century novel in France,* BE1190

Williams, Robert. *Lexicon Cornu-Britannicum,* AC275

Williams, Robyn. *Anarchist thinkers and thought,* CJ506

Williams, Roger John. *The encyclopedia of biochemistry,* EG325

Williams, Sam P. *Guide to research collections of the New York Public Library,* AK115

Williams, Samuel Wells. *A syllabic dictionary of the Chinese language,* AC256

Williams, Stanley T. *Bergey's manual of systematic bacteriology,* EG309

Williams, Stephen J. *Y geiriadur mawr,* AC805

Williams, Stephen N. *The dictionary of British and American homophones,* AC89

Williams, T. Harry. *Dictionary of American military biography,* CJ641, CJ648

Williams, Tim Guyse. *BBC world service glossary of current affairs,* CJ36

Williams, Trevor Illtyd. *A biographical dictionary of scientists,* EA172

Williams, Wiley J. *Subject guide to major United States government publications,* AF63

Williams, William. *Dictionary of the New Zealand language,* AC610

Williamson, George C. *Bryan's dictionary of painters and engravers,* BF312

Williamson, Jane. *Feminist resources for schools and colleges,* CC481

────── *New feminist scholarship,* CC516

Williamson, John B. *The senior movement,* CC102

Williamson, Mary F. *Art and architecture in Canada,* BF31

Williamson, Michael M. *Writing across the curriculum,* CB218

Williamson, Peter. *The strategy handbook,* CH613

Willihnganz, Shirley C. *Public relations & ethics,* CH565

Willingham, Robert Marion. *Confederate imprints,* DB112

Willing's press guide, AD118

Willins, Michael. *Photographer's market,* BF346

Willis, Alan. *American suburbs rating guide and fact book,* CL77

Willis, John. *Dance world,* BH156

────── *A pictorial history of the American theatre, 1860–1985,* BH96

────── *Screen world,* BH268

Willis, John Christopher. *Dictionary of the flowering plants and ferns,* EG117, EG182

Willis, John T. *Theologisches Wörterbuch zum Alten Testament,* AC475, BC134

Willis, Stephen. *Walford's guide to reference material,* AA363

Willis-Thomas, Deborah. *Black photographers, 1840–1940,* BF357

────── *An illustrated bio-bibliography of black photographers, 1940–1988,* BF357

Willison, I. R. *The new Cambridge bibliography of English literature,* BE585

Wills, Elizabeth Carter. *Federal copyright records, 1790–1800,* AA406

Wills, Geoffrey. *A concise encyclopedia of antiques,* BG41

Wilson, Francis Michael Glenn. *Catalogue of the parliamentary papers of Southern Rhodesia, 1899–1953,* AF242, DD176

Wilmarth, Mary Grace. *Lexicon of geologic names of the United States,* EF77

Wilmes, Douglas R. *American writers before 1800,* BE445

Wilmeth, Don B. *American and English popular entertainment,* BH2

────── *The American stage to World War I,* BH49

────── *Cambridge guide to American theatre,* BH65

────── *The language of American popular entertainment,* BH12

────── *Variety entertainment and outdoor amusements,* BH2

Wilpert, Gero von. *Erstausgaben deutscher Dichtung,* BE1233

────── *Lexikon der Weltliteratur,* BE72

Wilson, A. J. C. *International tables for crystallography,* EF117

Wilson, Andrew. *Russia and the commonwealth A to Z,* DC597

Wilson, Arnold. *Dictionary of British marine painters,* BF323

────── *Dictionary of British military painters,* BF323

Wilson, Bernard E. *The Newberry Library catalog of early American printed sheet music,* BJ97

Wilson, Beverly. *Human rights organizations and periodicals directory,* CK147

Wilson, Bruce. *Manuscripts and government records in the United Kingdom and Ireland relating to Canada,* DB196

Wilson, Carol R. *The World Bank Group,* CH208

Wilson, Carolyn F. *Violence against women,* CC517

Wilson, Charles Reagan. *Encyclopedia of Southern culture,* DB158

Wilson, Christopher. *The dictionary of demography,* CG30

Wilson, Clyde W. *American historians 1607–1865,* DB65

────── *American historians, 1866–1912,* DB65

────── *Twentieth-century American historians,* DB65

Wilson, Colin. *Encyclopedia of modern murder,* CK254

────── *Encyclopedia of murder,* CK254

Wilson, Craig A. *Policies of publishers,* AK165

Wilson, Curtis. *Planetary astronomy from the Renaissance to the rise of astrophysics,* EC59

Wilson, Don E. *Mammal species of the world,* EG299

Wilson, Druid. *Geologic names of North America,* EF77

Wilson, Edwin Graves. *Keats, Shelley, Bryon, Hunt, and their circles,* BE754

Wilson, Elizabeth A. M. *The modern Russian dictionary for English speakers,* AC684

Wilson, Erlene B. *The 100 best colleges for African-American students,* CB310

Wilson, Eunice. *Dangerous sky,* DA170

Wilson, Frank Percy. *Oxford dictionary of English proverbs,* BE159

────── *The Oxford history of English literature,* BE617

Wilson, George Buckley. *A dictionary of ballet,* BH144

Wilson, Harris W. *English prose and criticism in the nineteenth century,* BE755

Wilson, J. G. *Appleton's cyclopaedia of American biography,* AH58

Wilson, J. L. *Dictionary of the Grebo language,* AC441

Wilson, John Frederick. *Church and state in America,* DB10

────── *Research guide to religious studies,* BC3

Wilson, Larman C. *Selected bibliography of the Dominican Republic,* DB434

Wilson, Lofton. *Guide to Latin American pamphlets from the Yale University Library,* DB271

Wilson, M. J. *A dictionary of social science methods,* CA39

Wilson, Monica. *Oxford history of South Africa,* DD211

Wilson, N. C. *Scotland in the nineteenth century,* DC359

Wilson, R. M. *A dictionary of British surnames,* AJ184

Wilson, R. McL. *The future of Coptic studies,* BC453, BE1520

Wilson, Raymond L. *Index of American print exhibitions, 1785–1940,* BF120

—— *Index of American print exhibitions, 1882–1940,* BF368

Wilson, S. T. *Textile arts index, 1950–1987,* BG153

Wilson, Terry P. *Bibliography of the Osage,* CC420

Wilson, W. J. *Census of medieval and Renaissance manuscripts in the United States and Canada,* AA212

•*Wilson business abstracts,* CH37

•*Wilsondisc book review digest,* AA365

•*Wilsondisc cumulative book index,* AA422, AA430

Wilsted, Thomas. *Managing archival and manuscript repositories,* AK188

Winakor, Geitel. *The history of costume,* BG112

Winans, Robert B. *A descriptive checklist of book catalogues separately printed in America, 1693–1800,* AA99, BF223

Winderbaum, Larry. *Martial arts encyclopedia,* BK90

Windhausen, John D. *Sports encyclopedia North America,* BK23

Windisch, Éva V. *A Magyar irodalomtörténet bibliográfiája,* BE1279

Windward Islands, DB460

Wines, EJ225, EJ226, EJ227

Winey, Michael. *The era of the Civil War—1820–1876,* DB113

Wing, Donald Goddard. *Short title catalogue of books printed in England ...,* AA665, AA678, AA679, AD107, BE740

—— *Short-title catalogue of books printed in England, Scotland, Ireland, Wales, and British America, and of English books printed in other countries, 1641–1700,* AA412, AA683

Wingate, I.B. *Fairchild's dictionary of textiles,* BG98

Winge, Mette. *Danske Digtere i det 20. arhundrede,* BE1115

Wingert, Paul Stover. *History of world art,* BF134

Wingren, G. *Svensk dramatisk litteratur under ären 1840–1913,* BE1484

Wings over Hellas, Schoder, Raymond V., DA116

Winick, Charles. *Dictionary of anthropology,* CE50, CE51

Winick, Myron. *The Columbia encyclopedia of nutrition,* EH296

Wininger, Salomon. *Grosse jüdische National-Biographie,* BC566

Winkel, Jan te. *De ontwikkelingsgang der Nederlandsche letterkunde,* BE1336

Winklepleck, Julie. *Resourceful woman,* CC558

Winkler, Heinrich. *Bibliographie zum Nationalismus,* CJ9

Winkler, Johan. *Friesch woordenboek,* AC391

Winkler, Paul W. *Anglo-American cataloguing rules,* AK194

Winkler Prins' Algemeene encyclopaedie, AB37

Winkler Prins encyclopedie, AB37

Winkler Prins encyclopedie van Vlaanderen, DC109

Winnovich, Karen. *War crimes, war criminals, and war crimes trials,* CK80, DA203

Winship, Michael. *Bibliography of American literature,* BE400

Winslow, Donald J. *Life-writing,* BE217

Winsnes, A. H. *Norsk literaturhistorie,* BE1339

Winstedt, Richard Olof. *Practical modern English-Malay dictionary,* AC607

—— *An unabridged Malay-English dictionary,* AC607

Winston, Michael R. *Dictionary of American Negro biography,* AH64

Winter, Eugenia B. *Psychological and medical aspects of induced abortion,* CC259, EH31

Winter, Georgie. *Black adolescence,* CC143

Winter, Kaarina. *Suomen sanomalehdistön bibliografia, 1771–1963,* AE49

Winternitz, Moriz. *Concise dictionary of Eastern religion,* BC92

—— *General index to the names and subject matter of the Sacred books of the East,* BC92

—— *Geschichte der indischen Litteratur,* BE1571

—— *A history of Indian literature,* BE1571

Winters, Christopher. *International dictionary of anthropologists,* CE67

Winters, Harold A. *Basic geographical library,* CL17

—— *A geographical bibliography for American college libraries,* CL17

The Winterthur Museum Libraries collection of printed books and periodicals, Henry Francis du Pont Winterthur Museum. Libraries, BG16

Winther, Oscar Osburn. *A classified bibliography of the periodical literature of the trans-Mississippi West (1811-1957),* DB169

Winthrop, Robert H. *Dictionary of concepts in cultural anthropology,* CE46

Wintle, Justin. *The dictionary of biographical quotation of British and American subjects,* BE103

—— *Dictionary of war quotations,* CJ591

—— *The dragon's almanac,* BE167

Wintle, Michael J. *The Netherlands,* DC454

Wirtschaft und Statistik, CG223

Wisconsin, CH641

Wisconsin. [Laws, etc.]. *West's Wisconsin statutes annotated,* CK179

The wisdom of the novel, Powell, David, BE114

Wise, Edith C. *Bibliography of American folk art for the year,* BG10

Wise, Rosemary. *A guide to international music congress reports in musicology, 1900–1975,* BJ20

Wise, Terence. *Armies of the Crusades,* CJ595

The Wise garden encyclopedia, Seymour, E. L. D., EJ235

Wiseman, John A. *Botswana,* DD18

—— *Political leaders in Black Africa,* AH316, CJ404, CJ406, CJ409

Wises New Zealand guide, CL169

Wissenschaftliche Kommission Deutsch-Französisches Wörterbuch zur Kunst. *Glossarium artis,* BF84

Die wissenschaftlichen Vereine und Gesellschaften Deutschlands im neunzehnten Jahrhundert, Müller, Johannes, AL63

Wissenschaftlicher Jahresbericht über die morgenländischen Studien, DE7

Wissowa, Georg. *Der kleine Pauly,* DA101

—— *Paulys Real-Encyclopädie der classischen Altertumswissenschaft,* BB54, DA104

Wit, H. C. D. de. *Plants of the world,* EG183

Wit and humor, BE411
   see also **American wit and humor**

Wit and wisdom of politics, Henning, Charles, CJ45

Witherell, Julian W. *Afghanistan,* DE114

—— *Bibliographie du Burundi,* DD135

—— *French-speaking central Africa,* AF229

—— *French-speaking West Africa,* AF230

—— *Ghana,* AF231

—— *Libya, 1969–1989, an American perspective,* DD114

—— *Madagascar and adjacent islands,* AF222, DD175

—— *Official publications of French Equatorial Africa,* AF224

—— *The Republic of Turkey,* DC540

—— *The United States and Africa,* DD17

—— *United States and sub-Saharan Africa,* DD17

Witherick, M. E. *A modern dictionary of geography,* CL51

Withers, Sonia. *A biographical dictionary of scientists,* EA172

Withey, Elsie Rathburn. *Biographical dictionary of American architects (deceased),* BF263

Withey, Henry F. *Biographical dictionary of American architects (deceased),* BF263

Withycombe, Elizabeth Gidley. *Annals of English literature, 1475–1950,* BE612

—— *The Oxford dictionary of English Christian names,* AJ177

Witkin, Lee D. *The photograph collector's guide,* BF352

Witlieb, Bernard. *The book of women's firsts,* CC579

Witt, Elder. *Congressional Quarterly's guide to the U.S. Supreme Court,* CK192

—— *The Supreme Court A to Z,* CK188

Witt, Maria. *New international dictionary of acronyms in library and information science and related fields,* AK45

Witt Library. *A checklist of painters, c.1200–1976, represented in the Witt Library, Courtauld Institute of Art, London,* BF322

Witte, Edith. *German-English mathematical vocabulary,* EB51

Wittfoht, Annemarie. *Kunststofftechnisches Wörterbuch,* EK292

—— *Plastics technical dictionary,* EK292

Wittgenstein, Ludwig, BB80, BB83

Wittgenstein, Frongia, Guido, BB80

A Wittgenstein bibliography, Shanker, V. A., BB83

Wittgenstein papers, Wright, G. H., BB83

Wittman, Sandra M. *Writing about Vietnam,* BE417, DE278

Wittmann, Alfred. *Dictionary of data processing,* EK197

Wittmer, Donna Sasse. *Prosocial development in children,* CC147

Wittrock, M. C. *Handbook of research on teaching,* CB117

WLN (Organization). *Polar pac,* DG5

Wöchentliches Verzeichnis, AA654

Woddis, Carole. *The Back Stage theater guide,* BH62

Wodehouse, Lawrence. *American architects from the Civil War to the First World War,* BF204

—— *American architects from the First World War to the present,* BF204

—— *British architects, 1840–1976,* BF204, BF259

—— *Indigenous architecture worldwide,* BF204

—— *Roots of international style architecture,* BF204

Woel, Cai Mogens. *Dansk forfatterleksikon,* BE1122

Woelfel, Charles J. *Encyclopedia of banking & finance,* CH267

Woelmont, Henri de. *Notices généalogiques. 1–8. sér,* AJ89

Woerner, Gert. *The encyclopedia of Eastern philosophy and religion,* BB31, BC57

Wöffen, Angela. *Lexikon deutschsprachiger Schriftstellerinnen, 1800–1945,* BE1056

Wogan, Daniel S. *A literatura hispano-americana no Brasil, 1877–1944,* BE879

Wohlauer, Gabriele E. M. *German chemical abbreviations,* EE52

Wojcicka, Janina. *Polish abbreviations,* AC636

Woldman's engineering alloys, EK282

Woledge, Brian. *Bibliographie des romans et nouvelles en prose française antérieurs à 1500,* BE1202

—— *Répertoire des plus anciens textes en prose française,* BE1202

Wolf, Kirsten. *Medieval Scandinavia,* DC76

Wolf, Lucien. *Bibliotheca anglo-judaica,* BC517

Wolf, Siegmund A. *Wörterbuch des Rotwelschen,* AC431

Wolf, Ulrike. *Bibliography of Western European-Latin American relations,* DB264

Wolf, Walter. *Index to reviews, symposia volumes and monographs in organic chemistry,* EE135

Wolfe, Gary K. *Critical terms for science fiction and fantasy,* BE309

Wolfe, Gregory. *Right minds,* CJ152

Wolfe, Richard J. *Secular music in America, 1801–1825,* BJ66

Wolfenstine, Manfred R. *The manual of brands and marks,* EJ132

Wolfert, Marion. *German immigrants,* AJ49

Wolff, Ernest. *Chinese studies,* DE125

Wolff, Ilse R. *German Jewry,* BC541

—— *Persecution and resi...ance under the Nazis,* DC244

Wolff, John U. *An Indonesian-English dictionary,* AC517

Wolff, Kathryn. *AAAS science book list, 1978–1986,* EA27

—— *AAAS science book list supplement,* EA27

—— *AAAS science film catalog,* EA25

—— *Best books for children,* EA34

—— *Best science books & A-V materials for children,* EA34

—— *Best science films, filmstrips, and videocassettes for children,* EA34

Wolff, Michael. *The Waterloo directory of Victorian periodicals, 1824–1900,* AD114, AD124

Wolff, Philippe. *Bibliographie d'histoire des villes de France,* DC212, DC265

—— *Europe,* DC2

Wolff, Robert Lee. *Nineteenth-century fiction,* BE683, BE687

Woll, Allen L. *Dictionary of the black theatre,* BH109

—— *Ethnic and racial images in American film and television,* CC334

—— *Songs from Hollywood musical comedies, 1927 to the present,* BJ365

Woll, Josephine. *Soviet dissident literature,* BE1407

Wollaston, Arthur Naylor. *A complete English-Persian dictionary,* AC318

Wollheim, William. *Book of Jewish books,* BC518

Wolman, Benjamin B. *Dictionary of behavioral science,* CD29

—— *Handbook of clinical psychology,* EH395

—— *Handbook of developmental psychology,* CD86

—— *Handbook of general psychology,* CD41

—— *Handbook of parapsychology,* CD138

—— *International directory of psychology,* CD39, CD45

—— *International encyclopedia of psychiatry, psychology, psychoanalysis, and neurology,* CD23, EH379

Wolman, Yecheskel. *Chemical information,* EE9

Wolseley, Isabel. *The journalist's bookshelf,* AE136

Wolseley, Roland Edgar. *The journalist's bookshelf,* AE136

A woman of the century, Willard, Frances Elizabeth, AH74

The woman's dictionary of symbols and sacred objects, Walker, Barbara G., CF15

The woman's encyclopedia of myths and secrets, Walker, Barbara G., CF9

Womanwords, Mills, Jane, CC540

Women
  abstract journals, CC531
  associations
    bibliography, CC486
    directories, AL18
  atlases, CC581, CC582
  autobiographies, CC485
  bibliography, CC376, CC489, CC491, CC500, CC501, CC505, CC514, CC536, CC556, CC557, CC597, CC623, CC625
    current, CC519, CC520
    women in specific countries or regions
      United States, BE509
  biography, AH25, AH37, AH46, AH55, AH66, AH88, AH118, AH218, AH227, AH240, AH363, CC576, CC578, CC580
    bibliography, BE725
  book reviews, CC534
  chronologies, CC573
  diaries and letters
    bibliography, BE725
  dictionaries, CC538, CC539
  directories, CC545, CC551, CC552, CC553, CC554
  encyclopedias, CC535, CC536, CC537
  filmography, CC513, CC611
  government publications, AF66, CC494
  grants-in-aid, CB381
  guides, CC480, CC483
  guides to records, CC524

handbooks, CC558, CC561, CC562, CC622
indexes, AH15, CC529
manuscripts and archives, CC526, DB39
newspapers, AE25
periodicals, AE25, CC523
  indexes, AD37, CC521, CC522
periodicals (by country or region)
  Great Britain
    history, AD48
  United States
    history, AD48
quotations, BE111, CC544
statistics, CC583, CC584, CC585
  bibliography, CG114
terminology, CC540
thesauruses, CC542, CC543
Women (by country or region)
  Africa, CC592, CC593, CC594
    bibliography, DD7
  Africa, East, DD165
  Africa, Southern, DD122, DD123, DD171
  Americas, CC617, DB262
  Arab states, CC610, CC613
  Argentina, AH118
  Asia, CC586
  Asia, South, CC615
  Asia, Southeast, CC599
  Australia, AH374
  Bolivia, DB335
  Botswana, DD122, DD171
  Brazil, DB343
  Burundi, DD134
  Canada, CC603
    archives, CC525
    biography, CC580
    indexes, CC527
    thesauruses, CC541
  Caribbean, DB404
  China, CC619
  developing countries, CB27, CC621
  Ecuador, DB371
  England, CC624
  Europe, CC569, DC5
    biography, CC575, DA149
  France, CC620
  Ghana, DD163
  Great Britain, CC524, CC587, DA194
    bibliography, CC607
  India, CC618
    bibliography, CC612
  Ireland
    bibliography, CC591, DC393
  Islamic states
    bibliography, CC590
  Italy
    biography, AH264
  Jamaica
    biography, AH156
  Japan, CC604, CC609
  Kenya, DD165, DD168
  Korea, CC609
  Latin America, CC608
  Lesotho, DD122, DD171
  Malawi, DD122, DD171
  Mexico
    bibliography, DB218
  New Zealand, AH377, DF46
  Nicaragua
    bibliography, DB314
  Nigeria, CC598, DD191
  Oceania, CC586, CC616
  Rwanda
    bibliography, DD199
  Swaziland
    bibliography, DD229
  Taiwan, CC619
  Tanzania, DD235
  Uganda
    bibliography, DD241
  United States, CC493
    atlases, DB74
    attitudes, CC40
    bibliography, CC601, CC614

    biography, AH57, AH67, AH74, AH78, AH90, CC579, CC580
    Chicanas, CC444, CC596
    chronologies, CC572
    manuscripts and archives, DB172
    Native Americans, CC602
    statistics
      handbooks, CG108
  Uruguay, AH143, DB395
  Wales, DC368
  Zambia, DD122, DD171
    bibliography, DD246
    directories, DD246
  Zimbabwe, DD253
Women (by occupation or profession)
  anthropologists, CE69
  architects, BF214
  armed forces personnel, CJ612
  artists, BF16, BF102, BF140, BF143, BF152, BF400, BG34
  authors, BE399, BE401, BE402, BE412, BE443, BE444, BE447, BE448, BE474, BE480, BE508, BE519, BE534, BE545, BE607, BE620, BE621, BE623, BE740, BE750, BE845, BE883, BE896, BE1056, BE1062, BE1157, BE1243, BE1313, BE1344, BE1441, BE1444, BE1502, BE1586, BE1595, DF21
  biologists, EA231
  chemists, EA187, ED57, EE106
  education, higher, CB344
  engineers, EA194
  executives, AH77, CH101, CH606
  filmmakers, BH255
  government, CJ233
  health professionals, EA231
  home economists, EA231
  librarians, AK14, AK73
  managers, AH77, CH101, CH606
  mathematicians, EB104
  musicians, BC314, BJ177, BJ207, BJ215, BJ222
    bibliography, BJ223
    biography, BJ208
    discography, BJ376
  philosophers, BB4, BB47, BB48
  physicians, EH32
  physicists, EA187, ED57, EE106
  poets, BE314, BE489, BE496, BE536
  politicians, CJ67, CJ71, CJ233
    biography, CJ160
  psychologists, CD51, CD52
  scientists, EA180, EA231
    indexes, EA194
  screenwriters, BH215
  technologists, EA231
  theater personnel, BH34, BH118
Women (by subject)
  abortion
    bibliography, CC259, EH31
  aging, CC61, CC95, CC489
  alcohol and drug abuse, CC111, CC133
  careers, CC503, CC511, CC515, CC566, CH629, CH650, CJ109
  communication, BD84, CC495
  consumerism, CC563
  crime, CC37
  diseases, CC550, CC570
    bibliography, EH29
  economic conditions, CC263, CC589, CC606, CH115
    atlases, CC581, CC582
    bibliography, AF66, CC494
  education, CB27, CB126, CC492
    directories, CB247
  fellowships and scholarships, CB378, CC546
  health care, CC95, CC564, EH81, EH198
    directories, CC133
  historic sites, CC574
  history, BE358, CC484, CC488, CC496, CC508, CC529, CC530, CC624, DC5
    bibliography, DB48
    guides to records, CC526, DB39
  history (by period)
    medieval, CC575, DA149

labor and industrial relations, CC503, CC511
language, BD84, CC495
legal rights, CC565, CK162
mass media
directories, CC549
mental health
bibliography, EH375
murder, CC567
mythology, CF9, CF22
Native Americans, CC588
political activity, CC487, CC499, CC506, CC512, CC577
poverty, CC261, CC263
public speaking
indexes, BE358, CC530
sex and sexual behavior, CC275, CC282
sexual abuse, CC517
social conditions, CC298, CC490, CC510, CC589
atlases, CC581, CC582
bibliography, AF66, CC494, CC502
speech and rhetoric, BE358, CC530
symbols and symbolism, CF15
World Wars
bibliography, DA192
see also Feminism
Women & development, DD168
Women, 1870–1928, Barrow, Margaret, CC524
Women advocates of reproductive rights, Reynolds, Moira Davison, CC258
Women and aging, Coyle, Jean M., CC489
Women and American politics, Center for the American Women and Politics (Eagleton Institute of Politics), CC512
Women and development, CC621
—— Joint Bank-Fund Library, CC606, CH115
Women and development in Zambia, Antkiewicz, Susan, DD246
Women and development in Zimbabwe, Muchena, Olivia N., DD253
Women and deviance, Davis, Nanette J., CC490
Women and employment, CC515, CC566, CH650, CJ109, EA231
bibliography, CH629
directories, CH364
statistics, CH686
Women and feminism in American history, Tingley, Elizabeth, CC484
Women and geography, Lee, David R., CL16
Women and HIV/AIDS, CC570
Women and Law in Southern Africa Project. An annotated bibliography on women, DD229
Women and literature, BE401
Women and mass communications, Lent, John A., CC500
Women and medicine, EH198
Women and politics, CJ67, CJ160, CJ233
Women and religion, BC180, BC228
bibliography, BC10
Women and religion, Finson, Shelley Davis, BC10
Women and sexuality in America, Sahli, Nancy Ann, CC275
Women and society, Rosenberg-Dishman, Marie Barovic, CC510
Women and the American left, Buhle, Mari Jo, CC487
Women and the British empire, Bailey, Susan F., CC587
Women and the First World War in England, Markmann, Sigrid, DA194
Women and the law
bibliography, CK10
Women and the literature of the seventeenth century, Smith, Hilda L., BE740
Women and the military, CJ612
Women and urban society, Diner, Hasia R., CC298
Women and women's issues, Beere, Carole A., CC556, CC557
Women and work, paid and unpaid, Ferber, Marianne A., CH629
Women anthropologists, CE69
Women artists, Piland, Sherry, BF16
Women artists in America, BF152

Women artists in the United States, Chiarmonte, Paula L., BF16, BF152
Women athletes, BK7, BK41
Women authors, BE401
African-American authors
bibliography, BE524
bibliography, BE412, BE474, BE480, BE519, BE536, BE740, BE1502
biobibliography, BE607, BE845, DF21
biography, BE402, BE447
diaries and letters, BE508, BE509
Women authors (by country or region)
Africa, BE1502
Caribbean, BE971
Commonwealth, BE750
English-speaking countries
bibliography, BE708
France, BE1157
German-speaking countries, BE1062
Germany, BE1056, BE1243
Great Britain, BE620, BE621, BE623, BE750
Italy, BE1313
Japan, BE1586, BE1595, CC604
Latin America
bibliography, BE896
translations, BE883
Norway, BE1344
Spain, BE1441, BE1444
Women authors of modern Hispanic South America, Cypress, Sandra Messinger, BE896
—— Kohut, David R., BE896
—— Moore, Rachelle, BE896
Women composers, Frasier, Jane, BJ376
Women composers & hymnists, Claghorn, Charles Eugene, BC314, BJ207
Women composers, conductors, and musicians of the twentieth century, LePage, Jane Weiner, BC314, BJ207, BJ215
Women dramatists (by country or region)
Great Britain, BE456
United States, BE455, BE456, BE459
Women factory workers in less developed countries, Joel, Susan, CC605
Women, health, and medicine in America, EH198
Women in administration and management, Leavitt, Judith A., CH606
Women in America, Haber, Barbara, CC493
Women in American labor history, CC511
Women in American music, Skowronski, JoAnn, BJ223
Women in Botswana, Henderson, Francine I., DD122, DD171
Women in business, AH77, CH101, CH364
bibliography, CH606
biography, CH94
Women in chemistry and physics, EA187, ED57, EE106
Women in China, Wei, Karen T., CC619
Women in Congress, 1870–1989, CJ212
Women in Congress, 1917–1990, CJ233
Women in developing countries, CC595, CC600, CC622, CC627
bibliography, CC605, DD246
handbooks, CC618
publications, CC547
Women in development, CC622
Women in development in Southern Africa, DD122, DD131, DD171, DD246
Women in education
statistics, CB344
Women in English social history, 1800–1914, Kanner, Barbara, CC607
Women in espionage, Mahoney, M. H., CJ539
Women in film, BH279
Women in film, BH255
Women in Ghana, Ardayfio-Schandorf, Elizabeth, DD163
Women in Ireland, Brady, Anna, CC591, DC393
Women in Japanese society, Huber, Kristina R., CC604
Women in LC's terms, Dickstein, Ruth, CC542

Women in Lesotho, Lewis, Shelby, DD122, DD171
—— Mapetia, E. R. M., DD122, DD171
—— Molapo, Mathetha, DD122, DD171
—— Moshoeshoe, M. M., DD122, DD171
—— Nkabinde, Thokozile, DD122, DD171
—— Sexwale, Bunie, DD122, DD171
Women in literature, BE401, BE740
Women in management, Leavitt, Judith A., CH606
Women in mathematics, Osen, L. M., EB104
Women in medicine, EH32
Women in music, Hixon, Donald L., BJ222
Women in North America, CC580
Women in particular, Herman, Kali, AH90
Women in psychology, CD52
Women in rural development in Kenya, Tanzania and Zimbabwe, DD168
—— Bell, Simon, DD165, DD235, DD253
Women in science, Ogilvie, Marilyn Bailey, EA180
Women in Southeast Asia, Fan, Kok-sim, CC599
Women in Southern Africa, DD123
Women in Spanish America, Knaster, Meri, CC608, CC617, DB262
Women in sport, Remley, Mary L., BK7
Women in Tanzania, Mascarenhas, Ophelia, DD235
Women in the Caribbean, Cohen Stuart, Bertie A., DB404
Women in the fine arts, Anderson, Janet A., BF16
Women in the First and Second World Wars, Wedborn, Helena, DA192
Women in the Muslim world, Bodman, Herbert L., CC590
Women in the South Pacific, Simmons, Donita Vasiti, CC616
Women in the theater, BH34
Women in the Third World, Byrne, Pamela R., CC595
—— Fenton, Thomas P., CC600
Women in the West, DB172
Women in the workplace, CC566, CH650
Women in the world, Seager, Joni, CC582
Women in Uganda, Mutibwa, Olivia M. N., DD241
Women in Western European history, Frey, Linda, DC5
Women in Zambia, Chitambo, A. M., DD246
Women in Zimbabwe, Macnamara, Eve, DD253
—— Mwalo, Margaret, DD253
—— Zatezat, Elinor, DD253
Women of classical mythology, Bell, Robert E., CF22
Women of color, Burnham, Linda, CC545
—— Oshana, Maryann, CC611
Women of color and Southern women, CC623
Women of color in the United States, Redfern, Bernice, CC614
Women of Color Resource Center. Women of color, CC545
Women of distinction in Jamaica, Guy, Henry A., AH156
Women of eastern and southern Africa, Bullwinkle, Davis, CC593
The women of England from Anglo-Saxon times to the present, CC624
Women of India, Pandit, Harshida, CC612
Women of mathematics, EB104
Women of northern, western, and central Africa, Bullwinkle, Davis, CC594
Women of psychology, Gardner, Sheldon, CD52
—— Stevens, Gwendolyn, CD51, CD52
Women of South Asia, Sakala, Carol, CC615
Women online, CC571
Women-owned business firms, CH364
Women philosophers, Barth, Else M., BB4
—— Kersey, Ethel M., BB48
Women prime ministers and presidents, Opfell, Olga S., CJ67
Women, race, and ethnicity, CC625
Women religious history sources, BC228
Women remembered, Tinling, Marion, CC574
Women rulers of Europe, CJ318
Women scholars in women's studies, CC552
Women scientists
biography, EA187, ED57, EE106
Women scientists from antiquity to the present, Herzenberg, Caroline L., EA194

Women serial and mass murderers, Segrave, Kerry, CC567

Women speaking, Jarrard, Mary E. W., BD84, CC495

Women studies abstracts, CC532

Women who ruled, Jackson, Guida, CC578

Women working in nontraditional fields, Wilkinson, Carroll Wetzel, CC515

Women writers, from page to screen, Fenton, Jill Rubinson, BH215

Women writers of Germany, Austria, and Switzerland, BE1062

Women writers of Spain, BE1444

Women writers of Spanish America, Marting, Diane E., BE896

Women's Action Coalition (New York, N.Y.). *WAC stats,* CC584

Women's associations worldwide, AL18

The women's atlas of the United States, Gibson, Anne, CC581

The women's Bible commentary, BC180

Women's colleges, Adler, Joe anne, CB247

The women's companion to international film, BH255

The women's desk reference, Franck, Irene M., CC562

Women's diaries, journals, and letters, Cline, Cheryl, BE508, BE725

Women's education in the Third World, Kelly, David H., CB27

Women's history sources, CC526, DB39
—— Hinding, Andrea, BC228, DB172

Women's information directory, AE25, CC553

Women's Institute for Freedom of the Press. *DWM : a directory of women's media,* CC549

Women's issues, Mumford, Laura Stempel, CC505

Women's magazines, 1693–1968, White, Cynthia Leslie, AD48

Women's market handbook, Nelson, Carol, CC563

The women's movement in the seventies, Krichmar, Albert, CC498

Women's movements of the world, CC554

Women's periodicals and newspapers from the 18th century to 1981, Danky, James Philip, AD48
—— Hady, Maureen E., AD48, AE25
—— State Historical Society of Wisconsin, AD48

Women's poetry index, Guy, Patricia A., BE314

Women's recovery programs, CC133

The women's review of books, CC534

Women's rights
handbooks, CC568

The women's rights movement in the United States, 1848–1970, Krichmar, Albert, CC499

Women's sexuality, CC282

Women's studies, CC492, CC509, CC548, CC618
abstract journals, CC531, CC532
bibliography, CC505, CC625
databases, CC571
directories, CC551, CC552, CC554
guides, CA5, CC480, CC481, CC482, CC483
guides for authors, CC559
indexes, CC454, CC528, CC532, CC533
periodicals, CC518
research methods, CC504
Women's studies (by country or region)
Europe, Western, CC626

Women's studies, Carter, Sarah, CC480
—— Loeb, Catherine, CC501
—— Ritchie, Maureen, CC509

Women's studies encyclopedia, CC537

Women's studies in India, Vyas, Anju, CC618

Women's studies in Western Europe, CC626

Women's studies index, CC533

A women's thesaurus, CC543
—— Capek, Mary Ellen S., CC542, CC623

Women's work in Britain and America from the nineties to World War I, McFeely, Mary Drake, CC503

Wong, Kai-chee. *Research guide to English translation of Chinese verse,* BE1552

Wood, Casey Albert. *An introduction to the literature of vertebrate zoology,* EG215

Wood, Christopher. *Dictionary of Victorian painters,* BF323

Wood, Clement. *The complete rhyming dictionary and poet's craft book,* AC116
—— *Wood's unabridged rhyming dictionary,* AC116

Wood, David A. *History of music,* BJ90
—— *Music in Harvard libraries,* BJ90

Wood, David Norris. *Information sources in the earth sciences,* EF2
—— *Use of earth sciences literature, 1973,* EF2

Wood, Donna. *Brands and their companies,* CH348
—— *Companies and their brands,* CH348
—— *International brands and their companies,* CH348
—— *International companies and their brands,* CH348

Wood, Elizabeth J. *She said, he said,* CC40

Wood, Floris W. *American profile,* CC40, CJ484
—— *She said, he said,* CC40

Wood, Frederick Thomas. *English prepositional idioms,* AC90

Wood, Herbert. *Guide to the records deposited in the Public Record Office of Ireland,* DC401

Wood, John R. *The Alaska Eskimos,* CC414
—— *Aleut bibliography,* CC414, CC418
—— *Subarctic Athabascans,* CC414

Wood, Karen A. *Popular names of U.S. government reports,* AF101

Wood, M. Sandra. *How to find information about AIDS,* EH20

Wood, Patrick W. *Checklist of bibliographies appearing in the Bulletin of bibliography 1897–1987,* AA90

Wood, EJ178, EJ187, EJ188, EJ189, EK114, EK115
dictionaries, EJ177
bilingual
Russian-English, EJ180

Wood dictionary, EJ178

Wood engineering handbook, EK114

Wood handbook, EK114

Wood products industry, EJ184

Wood structural design data, EK115

Woodall's campground directory, BK111

Woodall's trailering parks and campgrounds, BK111

Woodbridge, Hensley Charles. *Guide to reference works for the study of the Spanish language and literature and Spanish American literature,* BD171, BE1430
—— *Spanish and Spanish-American literature,* BD171, BE1430

Woodbury, Marda. *Childhood information resources,* CC139, CC141, CD77, CD80
—— *A guide to sources of educational information,* CB5
—— *Youth information resources,* CC141, CD80

Woodbury, Walter E. *Encyclopaedic dictionary of photography,* BF340

Woodcock, John. *Archaeological atlas of the world,* DA89

Woodford, Susan. *Renaissance artists & antique sculpture,* BF391

Woodhead, D. R. *A dictionary of Iraqi Arabic,* AC214

Woodhead, James A. *Magill's survey of science. Earth science series,* EF12

Woodhead, Peter. *Keyguide to information sources in archaeology,* BF8, DA61
—— *Keyguide to information sources in museum studies,* BF8

Woodhouse, Sidney Chawner. *English-Greek dictionary,* AC448

Woodhouse, Tom. *The international peace directory,* CJ691

Woodhouse, William. *The Penguin encyclopedia of modern warfare,* CJ574

Woodill, Gary. *International handbook of early childhood education,* CB119

Woodress, James. *Eight American authors,* BE403

Woodress, James Leslie. *American fiction, 1900–1950,* BE481

—— *Dissertations in American literature, 1891–1966,* BE425

Woodring, Carl. *The Columbia history of British poetry,* BE717

Woodrow Wilson International Center for Scholars. *Scholars' guide to Washington, D.C. : film and video collections,* BH182
—— *Scholars' guide to Washington, D.C. for cartography and remote sensing imagery,* CL257
—— *Scholars' guide to Washington, D.C. for Central and East European studies,* DC14
—— *Scholars' guide to Washington, D.C. for East Asian studies,* DE103
—— *Scholars' guide to Washington, D.C. for Latin American and Caribbean studies,* DB273
—— *Scholars' guide to Washington, D.C. for Middle Eastern studies,* DE49
—— *Scholar's guide to Washington, D.C. for northwest European studies,* DC16
—— *Scholars' guide to Washington, D.C. for Russian, Central Eurasian, and Baltic studies,* DC556
—— *Scholars' guide to Washington, D.C. for South Asian studies,* DE85
—— *Scholars' guide to Washington, D.C. for Southeast Asian studies,* DE101
—— *Scholars' guide to Washington, D.C. for southwest European studies,* DC15

Woods, Geraldine. *Drug abuse in society,* CC137

Woods, Richard D. *Hispanic first names,* AJ178
—— *Reference materials on Mexican Americans,* CC453
—— *Spanish surnames in the Southwestern United States,* AJ187

Woods, Richard Donovon. *Mexican autobiography,* AH105

Woods, Robert S. *An English-classical dictionary for the use of taxonomists,* EG46
—— *Glossary of succulent plant terms,* EG135

Woods & Poole Economics. *The complete economic and demographic data source,* CG103

Woods Hole Oceanographic Institution. *Oceanographic index,* EF212

Wood's unabridged rhyming dictionary, Wood, Clement, AC116

Woods words, McCulloch, Walter Fraser, EJ181

Woodson, Wesley F. *Human factors design handbook,* EK236

Woodward, Arthur. *Textbooks in school and society,* CB19

Woodward, Bernard Barham. *Catalogue of the books, manuscripts, maps and drawings in the British Museum (Natural History),* EA12

Woodward, David R. *America and World War I,* DA197

Woodward, Gertrude Loop. *A check list of English plays, 1641–1700,* BE657

Woodward, Ralph Lee. *Belize,* DB303
—— *El Salvador,* DB307
—— *Guatemala,* DB309
—— *Nicaragua,* DB316

Woodworking tools, BG128

Woodworth, David. *Current British journals,* AD115

Woody landscape plants, EJ246

Woodyard, George W. *A bibliography of Latin American theater criticism, 1940–1974,* BE899

Woolery, George W. *Animated TV specials,* BH307
—— *Children's television,* BH307

Woolum, Janet. *Outstanding women athletes,* BK41

Woolven, G. B. *Bibliography of British industrial relations,* CH625

Woolven, Gillian B. *Bibliography of British industrial relations,* CH638
—— *The Warwick guide to British labour periodicals, 1790–1970,* CH655

Woordenboek der nederlandsche taal, AC293

Woordenboek der toponymie van Westelijk Vlaanderen, Vlaamsch Artesië, het Land van den Hoek, Flou, Karel de, CL210

Wootton, A. C. *Chronicles of pharmacy,* EH368

Word division, United States. Government Printing Office, AA323

Word finder, Rodale, Jerome I., AC140

Word menu, AC74

Word of God, Bailey, Lloyd R., BC94

Word perfect, Clark, John Owen Edward, AC68

Wordell, Charles B. *Language of the underworld*, AC129

Words and phrases index, AC91
—— Wall, C. Edward, AC155

Words into type, Skillin, Marjorie E., AA322

Words of the Vietnam War, Clark, Gregory R., AC121, DE279

Words of Wall Street, CH212

Words on cassette, AA385

Words on tape, AA385

Words on war, Shafritz, Jay M., CJ591

Words to rhyme with, Espy, Willard R., AC113

Words to the wise, Clardy, Andrea, CC559

Wordwatcher's guide to good writing & grammar, Freeman, Morton S., AC73

The wordworthy computer, Feldman, Paula R., BE3

Work, Monroe Nathan. *Bibliography of the Negro in Africa and America*, CC368

Work
bibliography, CC7, CC116

Work and alcohol abuse, Miletich, John J., CC116

Work related abstracts, CH646

Work, study, travel abroad, CB93

Worker benefits, industrial welfare in America, 1900–1935, Soltow, Martha Jane, CH505

Workers abroad, CB370

A working bibliography of Brazilian literature, Topete, José Manuel, BE937

Working bibliography on the Negro, Porter, Dorothy Burnett, CC374

A working bibliography on the Negro in the United States, Porter, Dorothy Burnett, CC375

Working class (by country or region)
Great Britain
bibliography, CH631
biography, CH679
periodicals, CH655
United States
bibliography, CH631, CH637

Working environment, CH661

Working press of New York City, AD57

Working press of the nation, AD57

Works in African history, Henige, David P., DD47

Works of Bulgarian emigrants, Paprikoff, George I., AA586

The works of Charles Darwin, Freeman, Richard Broke, EG70

The works of John Locke, Attig, John C., BB71

Workshops, EA279

World agricultural economics and rural sociology abstracts, CH46, EJ19

World air transport statistics, CH477

World almanac and book of facts, AB26, AB27, AB110

World Almanac, Inc. *Geo-data*, CL90

The World almanac of presidential campaigns, Shields-West, Eileen, CJ251

World architecture index, Teague, Edward H., BF231

World armaments and disarmament, CJ602

World armies, CJ599

World art in our time, Myers, Bernard Samuel, BF73

World artists, 1950–1980, Marks, Claude, BF138

World artists, 1980–1990, Marks, Claude, BF138

World Association of Veterinary Anatomists. *Nomina anatomica avium*, EG279

World atlas of agriculture, EJ75

The world atlas of archaeology, DA88, DA90

The world atlas of architecture, BF253

World atlas of geology and mineral deposits, Derry, Duncan R., EF110

World atlas of geomorphic features, Snead, Rodman E., EF114

A world atlas of military history, Banks, Arthur, DA50

World atlas of mountaineering, Noyce, Wilfrid, BK119

The world atlas of revolutions, Wheatcroft, Andrew, CJ74

World atlas of the child, International Bank for Reconstruction and Development, CC175

The world atlas of wine, Johnson, Hugh, EJ226

World authors, BH290

World authors, 1950–1970, BE203
—— Wakeman, John, BE205

World authors, 1970–1975, BE203, BE205

World authors, 1975–1980, BE203
—— Colby, Vineta, BE205

World authors, 1980–1985, BE203, BE205

World automotive market report, CH456

World aviation directory, CH478, EK32

World ballet and dance, BH157

World Bank. *Women and development*, CC606, CH115
—— *World debt tables*, CH161
—— *World development report*, CH162
—— *World tables*, CG66

The World Bank Group, Wilson, Carol R., CH208

World bibliographical series, DD18

A world bibliography of African bibliographies, Besterman, Theodore, AA70

World bibliography of armed land conflict from Waterloo to World War I, Floyd, Dale E., DA170

A world bibliography of bibliographies, Besterman, Theodore, AA14, AA15, AA70, AA73, EH9

World bibliography of bibliographies, 1964–1974, Toomey, Alice F., AA14, AA20

World bibliography of international documentation, Dimitrov, Théodore Delchev, AF7

A world bibliography of national bibliographies, AA391

A world bibliography of Oriental bibliographies, Besterman, Theodore, AA73

World bibliography of social security, CH498

The World book atlas, CL295

World book dictionary, AB28, AC28

World book encyclopedia, AB22, AB28, AC28, CL295

The World book encyclopedia of people and places, CL41

•*World book information finder*, AB22, AB28, AC28

World book science annual, EA168

World book year book, AB22

World cartography, CL271

World chamber of commerce directory, CH133

A world checklist of birds, Monroe, Burt L., EG269

World Christian encyclopedia, BC233, BC292

World-climates, Rudloff, Willy, EF164

World coin encyclopedia, Junge, Ewald, BG178

World collectors annuary, BF109

World communism, Sworakowski, Witold S., CJ529

World comparisons, CG58

World Council of Churches. *Handbook, member churches*, BC250

World Council of Churches, BC250

World Council of Churches. Commission on Faith and Order. *Documentary history of faith and order, 1963–1993*, BC282

World Council of Churches. Library. *Classified catalog of the ecumenical movement*, BC273

The World Cup, 1930–1990, Rollin, Jack, BK99

World currency yearbook, CH288

World debt tables, CH161

World declaration on the survival, protection, and development of children, CC176

World demographic estimates and projections, 1950–2025, CG59

World development directory, CH134

•*World development indicators*, CG41, CH159, CH162

World development report, CH162

World dictionary of awards and prizes, AL162, BE180

World dictionary of legal abbreviations, Kavass, Igor I., CK41, CK42
—— Prince, Mary Miles, CK42

A world dictionary of livestock breeds, types and varieties, Mason, I. L., EJ136

A world directory of criminological institutes, CK268

World directory of crystallographers and of other scientists employing crystallographic methods, EF119

The world directory of diplomatic representation, CJ81

World directory of environmental organizations, EK75, EK77

World directory of geography, CL56

World directory of human rights research and training institutions, CK106

World directory of human rights teaching and research institutions, CA48

World directory of map collections, CL261

World directory of mathematicians, EB60

World directory of medical schools, EH151

World directory of mineralogists, International Mineralogical Association, EF189

World directory of minorities, CC345

World directory of multinational enterprises, CH354

World directory of peace research and training institutions, CA48, CJ696

World directory of peace research institutions, CJ696

World directory of pesticide control organisations, EJ45

World directory of social science institutions, CA48

World directory of teaching and research institutions in international law, CK106

World economic outlook, CH163

World economic report, CH164

World economic survey, CH164

World education encyclopedia, CB127

World elections on file, CJ92
—— Arms, Thomas S., CJ88
—— Riley, Eileen, CJ88

World Employment Programme. *Poverty in developing countries*, CC264

World encyclopedia of 20th century murder, CK254

World encyclopedia of cartoons, BF383

World encyclopedia of cities, Kurian, George Thomas, CL64

World encyclopedia of civil aircraft, Angelucci, Enzo, CJ577
—— Stroud, John, CJ577

The world encyclopedia of food, Coyle, L. Patrick, EJ209

World encyclopedia of library and information services, AK39

World encyclopedia of naive art, Bihalji-Merin, Oto, BF315
—— Tomašević, Nebojša, BF315

World encyclopedia of organized crime, CK254

World encyclopedia of peace, CJ686

World encyclopedia of police forces and penal systems, Kurian, George Thomas, CK255

World encyclopedia of political systems & parties, CJ77

The world encyclopedia of soccer, LaBlanc, Michael L., BK98

World energy and nuclear directory, EK222, EK296

World energy directory, EK222, EK296

The world factbook, CL68

•*World factbook plus navigator*, CL68

World facts and figures, Showers, Victor, CG55

World film directors, BH290

The world financial system, Fraser, Robert, CH226

World futures and options directory, CH439

World government, CJ93

World guide to abbreviations of organizations, AL14

World guide to higher education, CB328

World guide to libraries, AK121, EA144

World guide to library, archive, and information science associations, AK55

The world guide to mountains and mountaineering, Cleare, John, BK118

World guide to scientific associations and learned societies, AL24, EA201

World guide to scientific organizations, AL24, EA201

World guide to social work education, Rao, Vijaya, CC49
—— Resnick, Rosa Perla, CC49
—— Stickney, Patricia J., CC49

World handbook of educational organization and statistics, CB124
World Health Organization. *ICD-10*, EH377
—— *International digest of health legislation*, CK69
—— *The international pharmacopoeia*, EH358
—— *International statistical classification of diseases and related health problems*, EH56
—— *Lexicon of psychiatric and mental health terms*, EH384
—— *Publications of the World Health Organization*, EH407
—— *WHO drug information*, EH315
—— *World health statistics annual*, CG60
World health statistics annual, CG60
World historical fiction guide, McGarry, Daniel D., BE250
—— White, Sarah Harriman, BE250
World history of art, Fleming, John, BF132
—— Honour, Hugh, BF132
World history of psychiatry, Howells, John G., EH398
World human rights guide, Humana, Charles, CK109
World in figures, CG55, CG61
A world in turmoil, Edelheit, Hershel, DA222
World index of economic forecasts, CH122
World index of Polish periodicals published outside of Poland since September 1939, AD135
World index of scientific translations, EA63
World Jewish Congress. *The Jewish press of the world*, AE6
World labour report, CH690
World law school directory, CK63
World list of abbreviations of scientific, technological and commerical organizations, AL14
World list of national newspapers, Webber, Rosemary, AE14
World list of scientific periodicals published in the years 1900–1960, AD237, EA46, EH40
World list of social science periodicals, AD66, CA18
World list of universities, CB241
World livestock disease report, EJ133
World mapping today, CL269
The world measurement guide, AL200
World Medical Association. *World medical periodicals*, EH40
World medical periodicals, EH40
World meetings, AL32
World Meetings Information Center. *World meetings*, AL32
World meetings outside U.S.A. and Canada, EA205
World meetings: United States and Canada, EA204, EA205
World Meteorological Organization. *Guide to meteorological instruments and methods of observation*, EF153
—— *International glossary of hydrology*, EF133
—— *International meteorological vocabulary*, EF148
World Meterological Organization. *Guide to hydrological practices*, EF138
World Methodist Council. *The encyclopedia of world Methodism*, BC363
World military expenditures and arms transfers, United States. Arms Control and Disarmament Agency, CJ596
World motor vehicle data, CH457
World museum publications 1982, BF48
World nuclear directory, EK222, EK296
World ocean atlas, CL296, EF226
World of Information (Firm). *Africa review*, DD61
World of learning, AL13, CJ94
The world of musical comedy, Green, Stanley, BJ265
World of winners, AL161, AL163
World palaeontological collections, Cleevely, R. J., EF244
World paper money, BG189
World Peace Through Law Center. *Law and judicial systems of nations*, CK65
World philosophy, BB10
World photography sources, Bradshaw, David N., BF347

World political flashpoints, CJ72
World population 1983, CG62
World population : an analysis of vital data, CG50
World population growth and aging, Keyfitz, Nathan, CG50
World population policy, Driver, Edwin D., CG1
World population profile, CG62, CG63
World population projections, CG64
World population prospects, CG65
World port index, CH469
World press encyclopedia, AE142
World racism and related inhumanities, Weinberg, Meyer, CC333
World radio TV handbook, CH494
A world record of major conflict areas, Munro, David, CJ57
World report on palaeobotany, EG101
World retail directory and sourcebook, CH116
World service glossary of current affairs, CJ36
World Shakespeare bibliography, BE780
World shipping statistics, CH470
World social science information directory, CJ696
World space directory, CH478, EK32
World sports and games, BK20
World survey of climatology, EF167
World survey of education, CB124
World survey on the role of women in development, CC627
World tables, CG66
World tables update, CG66
World timbers, Rendle, Bernard John, EJ189
World trade annual, CH165
World trade resources guide, CH135
World transindex, EA63
World translations index, AD25, EA62, EA63
World treaty index, Rohn, Peter H., CK89
World veterinary directory, EJ120
World War I aviation books in English, Noffsinger, James Philip, DA193
World War I in the air, Smith, Myron J., DA193
World War II, Polmar, Norman, DA207
—— Smith, Myron J., DA200
World War II almanac, 1931–1945, Goralski, Robert, DA210
World War II at sea, Smith, Myron J., DA200
World War II books in English 1945–1965, Ziegler, Janet, DA201
The World War II databook, Ellis, John, DA205
World War Two, Messenger, Charles, DA211
World Wars, DA218, DB126
  archives, DA204
  atlases, DA211, DA212
  bibliography, DA192, DA193, DA195, DA196, DA197, DA200, DA201, DA202, DC200, DC233
  biography, DA199
  chronologies, DA198, DA209, DA210, DA222
  encyclopedias, DA199, DA206, DA207, DA208, DC255, DC432
  guides to records, DA204
  handbooks, DA205
  manuscripts and archives, DA191
  poetry
    bibliography, BE712
  underground press
    bibliography, BE1329
World wars (by country or region)
  France, DC200
  Great Britain
    bibliography, DA194
  Italy, DC426
World weather guide, EF163
World weather records, Clayton, Henry Helms, EF168
World weather records, 1971–80, EF168
World who's who in commerce and industry, CH105
World who's who in finance and industry, CH105
World Wildlife Fund. *The official World Wildlife Fund guide to endangered species of North America*, EG237
World Without War Council. *Peace archives*, CJ671
World words, Greet, William Cabell, AC104
The world year book of education, CB129

World Zionist Organization. *2000 books and more*, BC515
Worldcasts. Product, CH426
Worldcasts. Regional, CH426
Worldmark encyclopedia of the nations, CJ28, CJ35, CJ270
Worldmark encyclopedia of the states, CJ270
World's best drama index, BE319
World's best orations, Brewer, David Josiah, BE347
The world's encyclopaedia of recorded music, Clough, Francis F., BJ375
The world's great dailies, Merrill, John Calhoun, AE133
The world's major languages, BD19
The world's master paintings, Wright, Christopher, BF306
The world's news media, AE143
The world's women, 1970–1990, CC585
The world's worst weeds, EJ64
The Worldwide bibliography of art exhibition catalogues, 1963–1987, BF119
Worldwide directory of national earth-science agencies and related international organizations, Tinsley, Elizabeth J., EF92
Worldwide family history, Currer-Briggs, Noel, AJ2
Worldwide franchise directory, CH407
Worldwide government directory, with international organizations, CJ82
•*Worldwide standards service*, EA272
Worldwide travel information contact book, CL385
Worrall, Mary. *Oxford children's encyclopedia*, AB21
Worsdell, W. C. *Index londinensis to illustrations of flowering plants, ferns and fern allies*, EG104
Worshipful Company of Clockmakers (London). *The clockmakers' library*, BG81
—— *Clocks and watches*, BG81
Wortabet, John. *English-Arabic and Arabic-English dictionary*, AC223
—— *Wortabet's Arabic-English dictionary*, AC224
Wortabet, William Thomson. *Wortabet's Arabic-English dictionary*, AC224
Wortabet's Arabic-English dictionary, Wortabet, William Thomson, AC224
Wörterbuch Chemie und chemische Technik, EE50
Wörterbuch der aegyptischen Sprache, Erman, Adolf, AC303
Wörterbuch der deutschen Gegenwartssprache, AC403, AC412
Wörterbuch der deutschen Umgangssprache, AC429
Wörterbuch der Ethnologie, CE47
Wörterbuch der griechischen Papyrusurkunden, Preisigke, Friedrich, AC446
Wörterbuch der klassischen arabischen Sprache, AC225
Wörterbuch der Landwirtschaft, EJ29
Wörterbuch der litauischen Schriftsprache, litauisch-deutsch, Niedermann, Max, AC602
Wörterbuch der mittelhochdeutschen Urkundensprache, AC413
Wörterbuch der Münzkunde, Schrötter, Friedrich, BG181
Wörterbuch der Mythologie, CF10
Wörterbuch der Philosophie, BB38
Wörterbuch der philosophischen Begriffe, BB43
—— Eisler, Rudolf, BB40
Wörterbuch der Rechts- und Wirtschaftssprache, Romain, Alfred, CK49
Wörterbuch der Sportwissenschaft, BK29
Wörterbuch der Verhaltensforschung, Immelmann, Klaus, CD121
Wörterbuch der Volkswirtschaft, Elster, Ludwig, CH68
Wörterbuch des Rotwelschen, Wolf, Siegmund A., AC431
Wörterbuch für Recht, Wirtschaft und Politik, Dietl, Clara-Erika, CK49
Wörterbuch Geowissenschaften, Watznauer, Adolf, EF85
Wörterbuch Kristallografie, Backhaus, Karl-Otto, EF116
Wörterbuch Musik, BJ147

Wörterbuch zur Publizistik, Koszyk, Kurt, AE140

Worth, Dean S. *A selected bibliography of Slavic linguistics*, BD184

The Worth book of softball, Dickson, Paul, BK56

Worthing, Charles R. *The pesticide manual*, EJ61

Wortman, William A. *A guide to serial bibliographies for modern literatures*, BE34

Wozniak, Robert H. *A century of serial publications in psychology, 1850–1950*, CD12

Wrestling, BK105, BK106

Wright, Andrew. *Court-hand restored*, AA215

Wright, Austin. *Bibliographies of studies in Victorian literature for the thirteen years 1932–1944*, BE753

Wright, Carroll D. *Index of all reports issued by bureaus of labor statistics in the United States prior to March 1902*, CH644

Wright, Christopher. *The world's master paintings*, BF306

Wright, David F. *New dictionary of theology*, BC239

Wright, Derek J. *Directory of medical and health care libraries in the United Kingdom and Republic of Ireland*, EH167

Wright, G. H. *Wittgenstein papers*, BB83

Wright, Glenn T. *Historical records of the government of Canada*, DB192

Wright, H. Stephen. *Keeping score*, BJ360

Wright, J. F. *Index to reports of Geological Survey of Canada from 1927–50*, EF31

Wright, James D. *Handbook of survey research*, CD63

Wright, Joan. *Going places*, CL390

Wright, John Kirtland. *Aids to geographical research*, CL4, CL12

——— *Atlas of the historical geography of the United States*, DB75

Wright, Joseph. *English dialect dictionary*, AC156

Wright, Lissie. *The IUCN amphibia-reptilia red data book*, EG250

Wright, Lyle Henry. *American fiction, 1774–1850*, BE482

——— *American fiction, 1851–1875*, BE482

——— *American fiction, 1876–1900*, BE482

Wright, Martin. *World development directory*, CH134

Wright, Michael. *The complete handbook of garden plants*, EJ249

Wright, Norman Edgar. *Preserving your American heritage*, AJ27

Wright, Roosevelt. *Black alcohol abuse and alcoholism*, CC123

Wright, Stephen G. *Ethiopian incunabula*, AA856

Wright, Sylvia Hart. *Sourcebook of contemporary North American architecture from postwar to postmodern*, BF260

Wright, Thomas. *Glossary of words, phrases, names, and allusions in the works of English authors, particularly of Shakespeare and his contemporaries*, AC99

Wright, William. *A short history of Syriac literature*, BE1551

Wrightsman, Lawrence S. *Measures of personality and social psychological attitudes*, CD98

The writer, BE175

The writer's advisor, BE11

Writers' and artists' year book, BE174

Writers and philosophers, Thomas, Edmund J., BE191

Writers and their work, BE622

Writers conferences, BE171

Writer's digest, BE176

The writers directory, BE212, BE451

Writers for children, BE392

A writer's guide to book publishing, Balkin, Richard, AA295

Writers Guild of America. *Who wrote the movie and what else did he write?*, BH210

Writer's handbook, BE175

Writers in Finland, 1917–1944, BE1127

The writer's market, BE176, BF346

Writers of the Caribbean and Central America, Fenwick, M. J., BE870

Writers on the American screen, Langman, Larry, BH215

Writers' Program (New York, N.Y.). *The film index*, BH172

Writing about music, BJ189

——— Basart, Ann Phillips, BJ99

Writing about Vietnam, Wittman, Sandra M., BE417, DE278

Writing across the curriculum, Anson, Christopher M., CB218

Writing the psychology paper, Sternberg, Robert J., CD43

The Writings, BC94

Writings on American history, DB23

——— Dougherty, James J., DB23

Writings on American history, 1962–1973, Dougherty, James J., DB23

——— Masterson, James R., DB23

Writings on British history, DC279, DC281

Writings on Canadian English, 1792–1987, Avis, Walter S., BD105

Writings on Canadian English, 1976–1987, Lougheed, W. C., BD105

Writings on contemporary music notation, Warfield, Gerald, BJ21

Writings on early American architecture, Roos, Frank John, BF221

Writings on Irish history, DC399

Written languages of the world, BD13

Wroughton, John. *English historical facts, 1485–1603*, DC323

WTI, EA63

Wu, Eugene. *Contemporary China*, AA362, DE123

——— *Leaders of twentieth-century China*, AH347

Wu, Jen-yung. *Chung-kuo tù shu kuan ming lu*, AK156

Wubben, C. H. Ebbinge. *Middelnederlandsch handwoordenboek*, AC294

Wucher King, J. *Egypt*, DD48

Wuerch, William L. *Micronesia, 1975–1987*, CE114, DF5

The Wuerttemberg emigration index, Schenk, Trudy, AJ46

Wulf, B. *Bibliographie analytique de l'archéologie de l'Iran ancien*, DE180

Wulff, Hans Jürgen. *Bibliographie der Filmbibliographien = Bibliography of film bibliographies*, BH173

Wumkes, G. A. *Bodders yn de Fryske striid*, BE1068

——— *Paden fen Fryslan*, BE1068

Wunder, John R. *Historians of the American frontier*, DB68

Wunsch, Albert. *Paulys Realencyclopadie der classischen Altertumswissenschaft : Register der Nachträge und Supplemente*, DA104

Wunschheim, Johannes. *Bibliographie zur oberösterreichischen Geschichte, 1891–1926*, DC92

Wuolle, Aino. *Englantilais-suomalainen koulusanakirja*, AC325

——— *The standard Finnish-English English-Finnish dictionary*, AC325

——— *Suomalais-englantilainen sanakirja*, AC325

Wurl, Joel. *The Immigration History Research Center*, CC356

Wurzbach, Constantin. *Biographisches Lexikon des Kaiserthums Oesterreich*, AH169, AH170, AH247

●*WWAP*, CJ161

Wyatt, Antony. *Challinor's dictionary of geology*, EF71

Wyatt, H. V. *Information sources in the life sciences*, EG2

——— *Use of biological literature*, EG2

Wyckoff, Ralph W. G. *Crystal structures*, EF120

Wycliffe biographical dictionary of the church, Moyer, Elgin Sylvester, BC254

Wyczynski, Paul. *Dictionnaire des auteurs de langue française en Amérique du Nord*, BE841

Wydawnictwo Interpress. *Who's who in Poland*, AH282

Wyle, Dorothea Ensko. *American silversmiths and their marks IV*, BG144

Wylie, Enid. *Union list of higher degree theses in Australian university libraries*, AG59

Wyllie, Robert E. *Orders, decorations and insignia, military and civil*, AL189

Wyman, Charles William Henry. *A bibliography of printing, with notes and illustrations*, AA266

Wyman, Donald. *Wyman's gardening encyclopedia*, EJ236

Wyman's gardening encyclopedia, Wyman, Donald, EJ236

Wynar, Anna T. *Encyclopedic directory of ethnic newspapers and periodicals in the United States*, AE34

Wynar, Bohdan S. *American reference books annual*, AA346

——— *ARBA guide to biographical dictionaries*, AH1, AH4

——— *Best reference books, 1986–1990*, AA348

——— *Dictionary of American library biography*, AK86

——— *Ukraine*, DC547

Wynar, Lubomyr Roman. *American political parties*, CJ260

——— *Encyclopedic directory of ethnic newspapers and periodicals in the United States*, AE34

——— *Guide to reference materials in political science*, CJ1

——— *Guide to the American ethnic press*, AD58

——— *Reference service*, AK234

——— *Slavic ethnic libraries, museums and archives in the United States*, AK116

Wynbrandt, James. *The encyclopedia of genetic disorders and birth defects*, EH91

Wynkoop, Sally. *Subject guide to government reference books*, AF74

Wynne, Owen E. *Biographical key—names of birds of the world—to authors and those commemorated*, EG280

Wynne, Susan G. *South African political materials*, CJ413

Wynne-Davies, Marion. *Bloomsbury guide to English literature*, BE611

——— *Guide to English Renaissance literature, 1500–1600*, BE611

——— *Prentice Hall guide to English literature*, BE611

Wyoming. [Laws, etc.]. *Wyoming statutes, annotated*, CK179

Wyoming statutes, annotated, Wyoming. [Laws, etc.], CK179

Wyszecki, Günter. *Color science*, ED64

Wytrzens, Günther. *Bibliographie der literarwissenschaftlichen Slawistik*, BE1078

——— *Bibliographie der russischen Autoren und anonymen Werke*, BE1078

——— *Bibliographische Einführung in das Studium der slavischen Literaturen*, BE1078

Wyzga, Marilyn C. *A selected bibliography on Native American astronomy*, EC7

Xhosa language dictionaries, AC808, AC809, AC810, AC811

XIX century fiction, Sadleir, Michael, BE683, BE687

Xûan-Tuón. *A bibliography of Vietnamese magazines, newspapers and newsletters published in the United States and other countries*, AD211

Xydis, Dorothy Peaslee. *Constitutions of nations*, CK73

——— *International governmental organizations*, AF18

Yaakov, Juliette. *Children's catalog*, AA338

——— *Fiction catalog*, BE245

——— *Junior high school library catalog*, AA345

——— *Play index*, BE234

——— *Public library catalog*, AA328, BE245

——— *Short story index*, BE260

Yabes, Leopoldo Y. *Philippine literature in English, 1898–1957*, BE1600

Yad Vashem Martyrs' and Heroes Memorial Authority, Jerusalem. *Joint documentary projects*, DA219

Yahni, Roberto. *Enciclopedia de la literatura argentina*, BE920

Ya'Ityo p̄yā kārtā śerā derejet. *National atlas of Ethiopia*, CL340

Yakima, Palouse, Cayuse, Umatilla, Walla Walla, and Wanapum Indians, Trafzer, Clifford, CC420

Yale daily news, CB274

Yale law journal, CK66

Yale University. *Biographical notices of graduates of Yale College*, AH61

—— *Obituary record of graduates*, AH61

Yale University. Dept. of Anthropology. *Folk classification*, CE7

Yale University. Institute of Far Eastern Languages. *Dictionary of spoken Chinese*, AC261

Yale University. Library. *Catalog of the Yale collection of Western Americana*, DB170

—— *Guide to Latin American pamphlets from the Yale University Library*, DB271

—— *The Plato manuscripts*, BB59

—— *Spanish American literature in the Yale University Library*, BE880

Yale University. Library. Yale Collection of German Literature. *German Baroque literature*, BE1234

Yale University. Library. Yale Collection of Western Americana. *Catalog of the Yale collection of Western Americana*, DB170

Yale University. School of Nursing. *Nursing studies index*, EH278

Yale University Holocaust video testimonies, DA220

Yamasaki, Shigehisa. *Chronological table of Japanese art*, BF88

The Yanagita Kunio guide to the Japanese folk tale, CF98

Yancy, Preston M. *The Afro-American short story*, BE538

Yang, Paul Fu-mien. *Chinese dialectology*, BD219, BD220, BD221

—— *Chinese lexicology and lexicography*, BD220

—— *Chinese linguistics*, BD219, BD220, BD221

Yang, Teresa S. *Asian resources in American libraries*, DE106

—— *Bibliography of the Chinese language*, BD221

—— *East Asian resources in American libraries*, DE106

Yang, Winston L. Y. *Asian resources in American libraries*, DE106

—— *Bibliography of the Chinese language*, BD221

—— *Classical Chinese fiction*, BE1562
Modern Chinese fiction, BE1562

Yannone, Mark J. A. *National directory of courts of law*, CK156

Yantis, Netti Schreiner. *Genealogical and local history books in print*, AJ34

Yapp, Peter. *The travellers' dictionary of quotations*, CL383

Yar-Shater, Ehsan. *Encyclopædia Iranica*, DE188

Yarber, William L. *Sexuality-related measures*, CC292

Yaremko, R. M. *Reference handbook of research and statistical methods in psychology*, CD64

Yarnall, James L. *The National Museum of American Art's index to American art exhibition catalogues*, BF120

Yarwood, Doreen. *Chronology of western architecture*, BF253

—— *Costume of the western world*, BG102

—— *Encyclopaedia of world costume*, BG102

—— *Fashion in the western world, 1500–1900*, BG102

—— *International dictionary of architects and architecture*, BF236

Yasner, J. *Study and research guide in computer science*, EK202

Yassif, Eli. *Jewish folklore*, CF84

Yatco, Jacinta C. *List of Philippine government publications, 1945–1958*, AF259

Yates, Buck. *Biographical register of the Confederate Congress*, DB121

Yates, Frank. *Statistical tables for biological, agricultural and medical research*, EG61

Ybarra-Frausto, Tomás. *Arte Chicano*, BF20, CC455

Yeager, Gertrude Matyoka. *Bolivia*, DB338

Year book, Society of Actuaries, CH515

—— United Church of Christ, BC386

Year book, Australia, CG436

The year book of education, CB129

Year book of labour statistics, CH691

Year book of the churches, BC324

A year book of the Commonwealth, CJ372

Year book of the Evangelical and Reformed Church, Evangelical and Reformed Church, BC386

Yearbook, American Baptist Churches in the U.S.A, BC328

—— Evangelical Lutheran Church in America, BC356

—— Greek Orthodox Archdiocese of North and South America, BC447

—— International Court of Justice, CK110

Yearbook and directory of osteopathic physicians, American Osteopathic Association, EH154

Yearbook / IWGIA, CE63

Yearbook of American and Canadian churches, BC291, BC324

Yearbook of American churches, BC324

Yearbook of comparative and general literature, BE12, BE41

The yearbook of education law, CB157

Yearbook of food and agricultural statistics, CH151, EJ80, EJ81

Yearbook of forest products, EJ192

Yearbook of forest products statistics, EJ192

Yearbook of industrial statistics, CH427

Yearbook of international commodity statistics, CH438

Yearbook of international congress proceedings, AL33

Yearbook of international organizations, AF16, AH50

Yearbook of international trade statistics, CH157

Yearbook of national accounts statistics, CH243

Yearbook of Nordic statistics, CG190

Yearbook of physical anthropology, CE64

Yearbook of railroad facts, CH462

Yearbook of school law, CB157

Yearbook of science and the future, EA169

Yearbook of statistics Malaysia, CG412

Yearbook of statistics: Singapore, CG423

Yearbook of the American short story, BE486

Yearbook of the European convention on human rights, CK108

Yearbook of the United Nations, United Nations, AF56

Yearbook on human rights, United Nations, CK109

Yearbook on international communist affairs, CJ529, CJ530

Year's art, BF101

The year's scholarship in science fiction and fantasy, BE310

—— Schlobin, Roger C., BE299

—— Tymn, Marshall B., BE299

Year's scholarship in science fiction, fantasy and horror literature, Tymn, Marshall B., BE310

The year's work in classical studies, BE1007

The year's work in English studies, BE418, BE589, BE641, BE647, BE673, BE755

Year's work in librarianship, AK78

The year's work in modern language studies, BD28, BE1343

The year's work in Old English studies, BE729

The year's work in Scottish literary and linguistic studies, BE808

Yedidia, A. *Catalogue of Mexican pamphlets in the Sutro collection (1623–[1888])*, DB235

Yee, Sin Joan. *Women in the South Pacific*, CC616

Yeh, Hsiu-shu. *Jen k'ou hsüeh Ying Han Han Ying fen lei tz'u hui*, CG34

Yellin, Jean Fagan. *The pen is ours*, BE534

Yemen, DE280

The Yemens, Smith, Gerald Rex, DE280

Yeni Türk ansiklopedisi, AB102

Yeni yayinlar, AA841

Yeoman, Richard S. *A catalog of modern world coins, 1850–1964*, BG192

—— *A guide book of United States coins*, BG195

Yepsen, Roger B. *The encyclopedia of natural insect & disease control*, EJ21

Yerushalmi, Yosef. *Mafteaḥ le-khitve-èt be-' Ivrit*, AD340

The Yiddish dictionary sourcebook, Galvin, Herman, AC813

Yiddish-English dictionary, Harkavy, Alexander, AC815

Yiddish language
  bibliography, BD134
  dictionaries, AC812
    bilingual, AC816
      English-Yiddish, AC813
      Yiddish-English, AC814, AC815

Yiddish language and folklore, Weinreich, Beatrice, BD134

—— Weinreich, Uriel, BD134

Yiddish linguistics, Bratkowsky, Joan Gloria, BD134

Yiddish literary and linguistic periodicals and miscellanies, Prager, Leonard, BE1081

Yiddish literature, BE1080, BE1081
  translations, BE1079

Yiddish literature (by country or region)
  United States
    handbooks, BE565
  see also **Hebrew literature**

Yiddish literature in English translation, Abramowicz, Dina, BE1079

Yim, Seong-sook. *Linguistique coréenne*, BD223

Yivo Institute for Jewish Research, N.Y. *Joint documentary projects*, DA219

Yoak, Stuart D. *Constitution of the United States*, CK172

—— *Constitutions of the states*, CK175

Yoga, BC487

The Yogācāra school of Buddhism, Powers, John, BC471

Yogi, Stan. *Asian American literature*, BE546

Yolton, Jean S. *John Locke, a reference guide*, BB77

Yolton, John W. *The Blackwell companion to the Enlightenment*, BE749, DC19

—— *John Locke, a reference guide*, BB77

Yon, André. *Dictionnaire des critiques littéraires*, BE1159

Yonge, Charlotte Mary. *History of Christian names*, AJ179

Yonge, Ena L. *A catalogue of early globes made prior to 1850 and conserved in the United States*, CL246

Yoo, Yushin. *Books on Buddhism*, BC475

—— *Buddhism*, BC459

—— *Soviet education*, CB45

York, Henry E. *Political science*, CJ1, CJ5

York dictionary of English-French-German-Spanish literary terms and their origin, Elkhadem, Saad, BE88

Yorke, Amanda. *The Cambridge handbook of contemporary China*, DE148

Yoruba language
  dictionaries, AC818
    bilingual
      Yoruba-English, AC817

Yoshizaki, Yasuhiro. *Studies in Japanese literature and language*, BD222, BE1596

You and the law, CK163

Youden, W. W. *Computer literature bibliography*, EK158

Young, A. *Bessel functions*, EB94

Young, Arthur P. *American library history*, AK27

—— *Cities and towns in American history*, DB148

—— *Higher education in American life, 1636–1986*, CB26, CB233

—— *Religion and the American experience, 1620–1900*, DB10

Young, Charles James. *American orders & societies and their decorations*, AL178

Young, Copeland H. *Inventory of longitudinal studies in the social sciences*, CA60

Young, Heartsill. *The ALA glossary of library and information science*, AK40

Young, James S. *The United States congressional directories, 1789–1840*, CJ222

Young, Jordan R. *The nostalgia entertainment sourcebook*, BH15

Young, Josiah U. *African theology*, BC35, DD90

Young, M. J. L. *Religion, learning, and science in the Abbasid period*, BE1546

Young, Margaret Labash. *Life sciences organizations and agencies directory*, EG49

Young, Michael L. *American dictionary of campaigns and elections*, CJ121, CJ124

—— *Dictionary of polling*, CJ496

Young, Patricia A. *Feminists, pornography & the law*, CC276

Young, Robert. *Analytical concordance to the Bible*, BC167

Young, Robert J. *French foreign policy, 1918–1945*, DC203

Young, Robert W. *The health care data source book*, EH179

—— *The Navajo language*, AC616

Young, Sue. *The new comprehensive American rhyming dictionary*, AC117

Young, Vernon R. *Modern nutrition in health and disease*, EH310

Young, William C. *American theatrical arts*, BH6, BH7

—— *Famous actors and actresses on the American stage*, BH123

—— *Famous American playhouses*, BH110, BH123

—— *Theatre companies of the world*, BH106

Young, William J. *The United States energy atlas*, EK223

Young adults *see* **Children and youth**

Youngs, J. William T. *The Congregationalists*, BC387

Youth information resources, Woodbury, Marda, CC141, CD80

Yoyotte, Jean. *Dictionary of Egyptian civilization*, DA123

Yu, Chŏng-nyŏl. *World encyclopedia of peace*, CJ686

Yu, David C. *Guide to Chinese religion*, BC38

Yu, Elena S. H. *Bibliography of Pacific/Asian American materials in the Library of Congress*, CC411

Yu, Ping-Kuen. *Chung-kuo shih hsüeh lun wên yin tê*, DE139

Yü, Ping-yüeh. *Supplementary index to Giles' "Chinese biographical dictionary"*, AH339

Yu lien yen chiu so (Kowloon, Hong Kong). *Who's who in Communist China*, AH343

Yüan, T'ung-li. *China in Western literature*, BF40, DE127, DE129, DE138

—— *The T. L. Yüan bibliography of Western writings on Chinese art and archaeology*, BF40

Yucatan, DB245

Yudofsky, Stuart C. *What you need to know about psychiatric drugs*, EH351

Yugoslav abbreviations, Plamenatz, Ilija P., AC715

Yugoslav history, Terry, Garth M., DC609

Yugoslav linguistics in English, 1900–1980, Milivojevič, Dragan Dennis, BD190

Yugoslav literature in English, BE1499

Yugoslav periodicals, AD168

Yugoslavia
  archives
    directories, DC611
  bibliography, AA843, AA844, AA846, DC609
    current, AA845
  bibliography of bibliography, AA69, AA396
  biography, AH307, AH308, AH309
  encyclopedias, DC612
  government publications, AF165
  periodicals, AD168, BE1500
    indexes, AD306, AD332, AD333
  registers, CJ325
  statistics, CG303, CG304, CG305
Yugoslavia (by subject)
  history, DC610
    bibliography, DC607, DC609

Yugoslavia. Direkcija državne statistike. *Statistički godiúsnjak*, CG305

Yugoslavia, Friedman, Francine, DC606

—— Horton, John J., DC607

—— Petrovich, Michael B., DC609

Yugoslavian language *see* **Serbo-Croatian language**

Yugoslavian literature, BE1497, BE1498, BE1499, BE1500
  biobibliography, BE1496

Yule, Henry. *Hobson-Jobson*, AC162

Yurkiw, Peter. *Union list of manuscripts in Canadian repositories*, DB195

Yurt ansiklopedisi, DC542

Yust, Walter. *10 eventful years*, DA209

Yvert, Benoît. *Dictionnaire des ministres de 1789 à 1989*, CJ328, DC211

YWES, BE589

Zabielska, Janina. *Bibliography of books in Polish or relating to Poland published outside Poland since Sept. 1st, 1939*, AA767

Zabik, Mary Ellen. *Nutrients in foods*, EH308

Zadneprovskaĩa, T. N. *Sovetskaĩa arkheologicheskaĩa literatura*, DA71

Zaehner, Robert Charles. *The dawn and twilight of Zoroastrianism*, BC577

Zafarullah, Habib Mohammad. *Government and politics in Bangladesh*, DE117

Zafren, Herbert Cecil. *Jewish newspapers and periodicals on microfilm available at the American Jewish Periodical Center*, AD11

Zahlenwerte und Funktionen aus Physik, Chemie, Astronomie, Geophysik und Technik, Landolt, Hans Heinrich, EA155

Zaĩchik, B. I. *Russko-anglo-nemetsko-frantsuzskiĩ slovar' po vychislitel'noĩ tekhnike*, EK192

Zaide, Gregorio F. *Documentary sources of Philippine history*, DE247

Zaide, Sonia M. *Documentary sources of Philippine history*, DE247

Zaimont, Judith Lang. *The musical woman*, BJ177

Zaĩonchkovskiĩ, Petr Andreevich. *Istoriĩa dorevoliutsionnoĩ Rossii v dnevnikakh i vospominaniĩakh*, DC579

—— *Spravochnik po istorii dorevoliutsionnoi Rossii*, DC582

Zaïre
  atlases, CL339
  bibliography, AA884, DD111, DD143, DD243, DD244
  current surveys, DD62, DD62
  encyclopedias, DD48
  periodicals, DD243
Zaïre (by subject)
  history
    bibliography, DD15, DD245
  see also **Congo**

Zaire, Bobb, F. Scott, DD48

—— Chapin Metz, Helen, DD62

Zaïrian literature, BE1540

Zak, Louise Allen. *English drama of the nineteenth century*, BE640

Zakia, Richard. *Focal encyclopedia of photography*, BF340

Zalacain, Victoria. *Atlas de España y Portugal*, CL331, CL333

Zaleha Tamby. *Cambodia*, DE122

Zalucky, Henry K. *Compressed Russian*, AC690

—— *Dictionary of Russian technical and scientific abbreviations*, EA129

Zamarriego, Tomás. *Enciclopedia de orientación bibliográfica*, AA91

Zambia
  atlases, CL342
  bibliography, AA885, DD18, DD119, DD248, DD249
  current surveys, DD62
  dissertations, AG50, DD247
  government publications, AF226
  statistics, CG367
Zambia (by subject)
  status of women, DD122, DD171, DD246

Zambia. Central Statistical Office. *Statistical yearbook — Central Statistical Office*, CG367

Zambia, Bliss, Anne M., DD18

—— Grotpeter, John J., DD48

—— Kaplan, Irving, DD62

—— Rigg, J. A., DD18

Zambia in maps, Davies, D. Hywel, CL342

Zamora, Stephen. *Basic documents of international economic law*, CK112

Zamorano y Caperan. *Servicio bibliográfico chileno*, AA512

Zanchelli Italian dictionary, AC533

Zandvoort, R. W. *Engels woordenboek*, AC296

Zangwill, O. L. *The Oxford companion to the mind*, CD25

Zanutto, Silvio. *Bibliografia etiopica in continuazione alla "Bibliografia etiopica" di G. Fumagalli*, DD156

Zanzibar, DD250
  see also **Tanzania**

Zanzibar under colonial rule, Ferguson, Ed, DD250

—— Sheriff, Abdul, DD250

Zapadov, M. S. *Russkaĩa periodicheskaĩa pechat'*, AD146

Zappella, Giuseppina. *Iconografia rinascimentale italiana*, BF72

—— *IRIDE*, BF72

Zarb, Frank G. *Handbook of financial markets*, CH218

Zarzuela, BJ260

Zasshi kiji sakuin, AD342

Zasshi shimbun sōkatarogu, AD202

Zatezat, Elinor. *Women in Zimbabwe*, DD253

Zaunmüller, Wolfram. *Bibliographisches Handbuch der Sprachwörterbücher*, AC196

Zayas, Gabriela. *Diccionario Oxford de literatura española e hispanoamericana*, BE1452

Zayas de Lima, Perla. *Diccionario de autores teatrales argentinos, 1950–1990*, BE921

Zdobnov, Nikolai Vasilevich. *Istoriĩa russkoĩ bibliografii nachala XX veka*, AA66

Zeichen, Text, Bedeutung, Eschbach, Achim, BD53

Das Zeitalter der Glaubensspaltung (1500–1618), Dotzauer, Winfried, DC226

Zeitrechnung des deutschen Mittelalters und der Neuzeit, Grotefend, Hermann, DC223

Zeitschrift für Kristallographie, Mineralogie und Petrographie, EE89

Zeitschrift für Krystallographie und Mineralogie, EF174

Zeitschrift für romanische Philologie, BD153

Zeitschrift für schweizerische Geschichte, AH299, DC528

Zeitschrift für schweizerisches Recht, CK224

Zeitschriften der Berliner Spätaufklärung, AD315

Zeitschriften-Index, Schmidt, Klaus, AE122

Zeitschriftenverzeichnis Moderner Orient, Bloss, Ingeborg, AD184

Zeitungs-Index, AE123

Zeitungskatalog der Schweiz, AD165

Zeleznik, Karen. *Science fair project index, 1960–1972*, EA31

Zelinsky, Wilbur. *This remarkable continent*, DB76

Zell, Hans M. *The African book world and press*, AA293, AK62

—— *African books in print*, AA848

—— *The African studies companion*, DD55

—— *Bibliography of non-periodical literature on Sierra Leone, 1925–1966*, DD205

—— *A new reader's guide to African literature*, BE1508

Zeller, Otto. *IBN*, AH16

—— *Internationale Bibliographie der Zeitschriftenliteratur aus allen Gebieten des Wissens*, AD255

—— *Internationale Jahresbibliographie Südwestasien*, DE33

—— *Register der Schlagwöter 1896–1974*, AD255

Zeller, Wolfram. *IBN*, AH16

—— *Internationale Bibliographie der Zeitschriftenliteratur aus allen Gebieten des Wissens*, AD255

—— *Internationale Jahresbibliographie Südwestasien*, DE33

Zeman, Jarold K. *The Hussite movement and the reformation in Bohemia, Moravia and Slovakia (1350–1650)*, DC128
Zeman, Otakar. *Anglicko-český geologický slovník*, EF82
Zen Buddhism, BC462, BC467, BC474, BC478
— **encyclopedias,** BB31, BC57
Zen Buddhism, Gardner, James L., BC467
—— Vessie, Patricia Armstrong, BC474
Zen nihon shuppanbutsu so-mokuroku, Kokuritsu Kokkai Toshokan (Japan), AA916
The Zend-Avesta, BC92
Zenker, Julius Theodor. *Bibliotheca orientalis*, DE7
Zenkoku maikuro shinbun shozō ichiran, AE96
Zenkovsky, Serge A. *Guide to the bibliographies of Russian literature*, BE1396
Zentner, Christian. *The encyclopedia of the Third Reich*, DC255
—— *Grosse Lexikon des Dritten Reiches*, DC255
Zentralblatt für Bakteriologie, EG313
Zentralblatt für Bakteriologie, Parasitenkunde, Infektions-Krankheiten und Hygiene, EG313
Zentralblatt für Geologie und Paläontologie, EF58, EF60
Zentralblatt für Mathematik und ihre Grenzgebiete, EB15, EB31
Zentralblatt für Mineralogie, EF58, EF178
Zentralblatt für Mineralogie, Geologie und Paläontologie, EF58, EF60
Zentralblatt für Zoologie, EG219
Zepper, John T. *Russian and Soviet education, 1731–1989*, CB45
Zeri, Federico. *Census of pre-nineteenth-century Italian paintings in North American public collections*, BF325
Zernova, Antonina S. *Knigi kirillovskoĭ pechati, izdannye v Moskve v XVI-XVII vekakh*, AA787
Zeugómlēs, Geōrgios. *"Proïas" lexikon tēs neas Hellēnikēs glōssēs*, AC462
Zeuschner, Raymond Bud. *The debater's guide*, BE370
Zevin, Shlomo Josef. *Encyclopedia Talmudica*, BC549, CK239
Zewde, Bahru. *History of modern Ethiopia*, DD154
Zgraon, Florentina. *Dicţionarul limbii române literare vechi, 1640–1780*, AC658
Zhechev, Nikolaĭ. *Istoriĭata na Bŭlgariĭa v memoarnata literatura*, DC115
Zhukov, E. M. *Sovetskaĭa istoricheskaĭa entsiklopediĭa*, DC569
Zhurnal'naĭa letopis', AD325
Zidouemba, Dominique. *Directory of documentation, libraries and archives services in Africa*, AK154
Ziefle, Helmut W. *Dictionary of modern theological German*, BC153
Ziegelmueller, George. *Argumentation*, BE371
Ziegenfuss, James T. *Law, medicine & health care*, EH271
Ziegler, Janet. *World War II books in English 1945–1965*, DA201
Ziegler, Konrat. *Der kleine Pauly*, DA101
Ziegler, Peter A. *Geological atlas of Western and Central Europe*, EF115
Zigrosser, Carl. *Guide to the collecting and care of original prints*, BF379
—— *Prints and their creators*, BF379
Zijlstra, Gea. *Index nominum genericorum (plantarum)*, EG129
Zijlstra, Miep. *Algemene muziek encyclopedie*, BJ127
Zikeev, Nikolay T. *Scientific and technical serial publications of the Soviet Union, 1945–1960*, EA51
Zikmund, Joseph. *Suburbia*, CC307
Zilkha, Avraham. *Modern Hebrew-English dictionary*, AC484
Zim, Herbert S. *Birds of North America*, EG274
Zimbabwe
bibliography, AA886, AA887, AA888, DD18, DD251, DD252, DD253
biography, AH327
current surveys, DD62
encyclopedias, DD48

gazetteers, CL157
government publications, AF226, AF241, AF242
statistics, CG368
Zimbabwe. Central Statistical Office. *Statistical yearbook of Zimbabwe*, CG368
Zimbabwe, Nelson, Harold D., DD62
—— Potts, Deborah, DD18
—— Rasmussen, R. Kent, DD48
—— Rubert, Steven C., DD48
Zimbabwe, history, politics, economics, society, Baumhögger, Goswin, DD251
Zimbabwe national bibliography, AA887, AA888
Zimbabwean literature, BE1541
Zimbabwean political material published in exile, 1959–1980, Johnstone, I. J., DD252
Zimmer, Wolfgang. *Répertoire du théâtre camerounais*, BE1526
Zimmerman, David R. *Zimmerman's complete guide to nonprescription drugs*, EH352
Zimmerman, Dorothy Wynne. *French women writers*, BE1157
Zimmerman, Fred Lyon. *Numerical list of current publications of the U.S. Dept. of Agriculture*, EJ88
Zimmerman, Gary J. *German immigrants*, AJ40, AJ49
Zimmerman, Irene. *Current national bibliographies of Latin America*, AA472
—— *A guide to current Latin American periodicals*, AD68
Zimmerman, Marc. *U.S. Latino literature*, BE559
Zimmerman, Mikhail G. *Anglo-russkiĭ ĭadernyĭ slovar'*, ED28
—— *Russian-English translators dictionary*, EA130
Zimmerman, Oswald Theodore. *Scientific and technical abbreviations, signs and symbols*, EA99
Zimmermann, Harald. *Brockhaus Wahrig*, AC400
Zimmermann, Hartmut. *DDR Handbuch*, CJ330
Zimmerman's complete guide to nonprescription drugs, Zimmerman, David R., EH352
Zinberg, Israel. *Geshikhte fun der literatur bay Yidn*, BE1578
—— *A history of Jewish literature*, BE1578
Zink, Christoph. *Dictionary of obstetrics and gynecology*, EH112
Zink, Steven D. *Guide to the Presidential advisory commissions, 1973–1984*, AF132, CJ186
—— *United States government publications catalogs*, AF85
Zinkus, Jonas. *Lietuviškoji tarybinė enciklopedija*, DC443
—— *Lithuania*, DC444
Zinner, Ernst. *Geschichte und Bibliographie der astronomischen Literatur in Deutschland zur Zeit der Renaissance*, EC20
Zionism
encyclopedias, BC548, DE192
Zipin, Amnon. *Bibliography of modern Hebrew literature in translation*, BE1576
Zipparro, Vincent J. *Davis' handbook of applied hydraulics*, EK102
Ziring, Lawrence. *The Asian political dictionary*, CJ416
—— *The Middle East*, CJ420, DE57
—— *Middle East political dictionary*, CJ420, DE55, DE57
Zitatenlexikon, BE137
Zito, Dorothea R. *A guide to research in gerontology*, CC103
Zito, George V. *A guide to research in gerontology*, CC103
Zittel, Karl Alfred von. *Geschichte der Geologie und Paläontologie bis Ende des 19. Jahrhunderts*, EF105
—— *History of geology and palaeontology to the end of the nineteenth century*, EF105
Zivilstandsstatistik, Liechtenstein. Amt für Volkswirtschaft, CG260
Zivný, Ladislas J. *Bibliografický katalog*, AA592
Živsa, Irena. *Bibliographie der Personalbibliographien zur deutschen Gegenwartsliteratur*, BE1221

Zoëga, Geir Tómasson. *A concise dictionary of old Icelandic*, AC509
Zoetmulder, P. J. *Old Javanese-English dictionary*, AC560
Zoghby, Samir M. *Islam in sub-Saharan Africa*, BC497
Zollar, Ann Creighton. *Adolescent pregnancy and parenthood*, CC220
Zolli, Paolo. *Dizionario etimologico della lingua italiana*, AC537
Zoltán, Flavy. *A magyar sajtó bibliográfiája, 1945–1954*, AD120
Zoltán, Pipics. *Vocabularium bibliothecarii : supplementum hungaricum*, AK49
Zoltán, Tóth. *Magyar történeti bibliográfia, 1825–1867*, DC383
Zombeck, Martin V. *Handbook of space astronomy and astrophysics*, EC58
Zona de protectorado y de los territorios de soberanía de España en el norte de Africa, Instituto Nacional de Estadística (Spain), CG283, CG348
Zondervan NIV atlas of the Bible, Rasmussen, Carl, BC201
Zonhoven, L. M. J. *Late reviews AEB, 1947–1984*, DA121
The zoological record, EG220, EG223, EG331
•*Zoological record online*, EG221
Die zoologische Buchillustration, Nissen, Claus, EG212
Zoologischer Bericht im Auftrage der Deutschen Zoologischen Gesellschaft, EG222
Zoologischer Jahresbericht, EG223
Zoology
abstract journals, EG217, EG219, EG220, EG221
bibliography, BE31, CE14, EA16, EA21, EB10, EC15, EC17, ED5, ED6, EE13, EE15, EF57, EF141, EF173, EF232, EG6, EG98, EG105, EG205, EG206, EG207, EG208, EG209, EG210, EG211, EG212, EG213, EG214, EG215, EG312, EH68
dictionaries, EG227, EG228, EG229, EG230
multilingual, EG225
encyclopedias, EG224, EG226
generic indexes, EG243, EG244
handbooks, EG232, EG233, EG234, EG235, EG238
indexes, EG216, EG218, EG222, EG223
library catalogs, EH53
treatises, EG239, EG240, EG241, EG242
Zoos
directories, AL88
handbooks, EG233
Zophy, Angela Marie Howard. *Handbook of American women's history*, DB48
Zophy, Jonathan W. *An annotated bibliography of the Holy Roman Empire*, DC12
—— *Holy Roman Empire*, DC12
Zorack, John L. *The lobbying handbook*, CJ149
Zorc, R. David Paul. *Somali-English dictionary*, AC725
Zoroastrianism, BC574, BC575, BC576, BC577
dictionaries, BC76
Zoroastrians, Boyce, Mary, BC574, BC576
Żródła rękopiśmienne do dziejów wsi w Polsce feudalnej, Płaza, Stanisław, DC479
Zubatsky, David S. *Doctoral dissertations in history and the social sciences on Latin America and the Caribbean accepted by universities in the United Kingdom, 1920–1972*, CA22
—— *Jewish autobiographies and biographies*, AH39
—— *Jewish genealogy*, AJ146
—— *Latin American literary authors*, BE881, BE1445
—— *Spanish, Catalan, and Galician literary authors of the twentieth century*, BE881, BE1445
Zuck, Virpi. *Dictionary of Scandinavian literature*, BE1086
Zuckerman, Ed. *Almanac of federal PACs*, CJ147
Zuckerman, Mary Ellen. *Sources on the history of women's magazines, 1792–1960*, CC523

Zufferey, François. *Bibliographie des poètes provençaux des XIV* et XV* siècles*, BE1374

Zukerman, Elyse. *Changing directions in the treatment of women*, EH375

Zulkarjono, Maesarah. *Daftar majalah Indonesia yang telah mempunyai ISSN*, AD197

Züllig, Monika. *Kommentierte Bibliographie zur slavischen Soziolinguistik*, BD180

Zulu-English dictionary, AC819

Zulu language dictionaries, AC819

Zuni, CC439

A Zuni atlas, Ferguson, T. J., CC439

Zupko, Ronald Edward. *A dictionary of weights and measures for the British Isles*, AL201

—— *French weights and measures before the Revolution*, AL202

Zurawski, Joseph W. *Polish American history and culture*, CC335

Zurcher, Arnold John. *Dictionary of American politics*, CJ128

Zürcher, Josef. *Lexicon academicum*, BB52

Zurick, Timothy. *Army dictionary and desk reference*, CJ622

Zusne, Leonard. *Eponyms in psychology*, CD33

Zussman, J. *Rock-forming minerals*, EF195

Zwanzig Jähre Vereinte Nationen ... 1945–1965, Hüfner, Klaus, AF35

Zwanziger, Ronald. *Bibliographie der Namenforschung in Österreich*, CL184

Zweep, W. van der. *Interdisciplinary dictionary of weed science*, EJ34

Zweifel, Frances W. *A handbook of biological illustration*, EA223, EG58

Zweihundert Jahre Tageszeitung in Österreich, 1783–1983, AE44

Zweite Vatikanische Konzil, BC435

Zwemer, Diane K. *Key resources on community colleges*, CB224

Zwemer, Thomas J. *Boucher's current clinical dental terminology*, EH252

Zwillinger, Daniel. *Handbook of differential equations*, EB70, EB71

—— *Handbook of integration*, EB71

Zwirn, Jerrold. *Congressional publications and proceedings*, AF120, CJ200

Zydlo, Stanley M. *The American Medical Association handbook of first aid & emergency care*, EH172

Zylka, Romauld. *Geological dictionary*, EF81